Air-Britain

ERH 2005

European Registers Handbook 2005

Edited by David Partington

Published by: Air-Britain (Historians) Ltd

Sales Department: 41 Penshurst Road, Leigh, Tonbridge, Kent TN11 8HL, England

Membership Enquiries: 1 Rose Cottages, 179 Penn Road, Hazlemere, Buckinghamshire HP15 7NE, England

Further information is available on our website: http://www.air-britain.co.uk

ISBN O-85130-361-7 ISSN 0950-7477

Cover Photo : Antonov An-2P HA-ANI against a dramatic storm backdrop at the Schaffen-Diest Fly In on 14.8.04. (Dave Partington)

Rear Cover -

Top : Piper Super Cruiser PH-NDA is the second of the type to carry these marks and is seen at Rotterdam 6.04 after being repainted in the original's colour scheme. (Henk Wadman)

Centre : CASA-built Jungmann LX-ZAZ did not make it to the Air-Britain Fly In but made a colourful impact on the French RSA Rally at Chambley on 17.7.04. (Dave Partington)

Lower : SE-CGM is a Norseman IV floatplane which can be chartered for fishing and hunting trips in Northern Sweden., seen here at Vilhelmina on 21.4.04. (Jonny Andersson)

Printed by Bell & Bain Ltd, Glasgow G46 7UQ

Air-Britain supports the fight against terrorism and the efforts of the Police and other Authorities in protecting airports and airfields from criminal activity.
If you see anything suspicious do not hesitate to call the
Anti-Terrorist Hotline 0800 789321
or alert a Police Officer.

EUROPEAN REGISTERS HANDBOOK 2005

CONTENTS:

EUROPEAN REGISTERS HANDBOOK 2005

INTRODUCTION

Welcome to the 20th annual edition of European Registers Handbook, inevitably containing more entries than ever! The information within is that received up to May 1st 2005 and includes everything published in the "Overseas Registers" section of **Air-Britain News** up to the May issue together with some later additions already available from various reliable sources and contributors.

As for the last three years, we are now established in A4 size to reduce the actual number of pages and make for greater printing economy. As last year we now include all countries of continental Europe up to the Russian border, a total of 42 states in all. Further attempts to standardise or correct aircraft designations have been made although we hope that the major manufacturers are now well sorted - however the explanation repeated in the notes opposite may still be found useful in this respect. Some more corrections to glider designations have also been made and important notes on these are to be found on page 6.

It is worth mentioning that this is the only book with Europe-wide coverage which includes ALL the previous identities of each aircraft, adds details of aircraft known to be reserved or on permits which often do not appear in official lists, includes all gliders and balloons, and also makes an effort to identify and list all known microlights - especially in countries where their registers are not published. As in earlier years we have problems with the inaccessibility of data in several countries but it is interesting to see that, in the light of September 11th, some countries are now calling for complete transparency and the availability of all civil registers on-line. Meanwhile following welcome official updates to the Spanish register, and more Portuguese data, only Germany among the larger countries maintains stringent data protection legislation. Such problems rarely affect airliner and business jet entries where manufacturers' data and delivery information is generally more widely available. However, as the biggest growth sector in civil aviation is currently the microlight/ultralight area, we are clearly in need of more official data, particularly from Germany. Welcome observations and reports have again helped the swell the French and Italian ULM sections so please keep these coming in future.

As ever, we are most grateful for the support of some very co-operative manufacturers of aircraft, gliders and balloons; and of course to the many enthusiasts in Britain and Europe who regularly send reports and observations. Why not join their number? Please send reports either to Ian Burnett as Editor of "Overseas Registers" (post to Langstone, Riseley, Swallowfield, Reading, Berks RG7 1QL or e-mail **Ian.Burnett@air-britain.co.uk**) or to the ERH Editor at the address below - or preferably to both! It is useful to quote details such as names, c/ns or call-signs *actually seen* on the aircraft rather than quoting what is in this book - these things can change and we would like to know if they do. Reports including microlight registrations,call-signs and glider tail codes would also be particularly useful as these *do* often change. If you are unable to identify a new type or registration why not take a photo if possible and send it with your report - every little helps!

As usual this Editor's main task has been to work with material provided for use in "Overseas Registers", which is of course pre-processed with a massive input from the incomparable Ian Burnett, I can only really repeat here our joint thanks for the continued support of many contributors whether regular or infrequent, without whom both our efforts would be so much poorer. This year these include, in alphabetical order, Joe Anderson, Trevor Ansell, Ray Barber, Denis Birch, Nigel Burch, Phil Butler, Mike Cain, Russell Carter, Richard Cawsey, Chris Chatfield, Jacques Chillon, Paul Compton/Nordic Research, Don Crump, Antoin Daltun, Richard Dayman, Ray Deerness, Martin Degg, Doug Fitton, Alan Gray, Kay Hagby, Anton Heumann, Paul Hewins, Peter Hillman, Nigel Hitchman, Mike Hollick, Mike Hooks, Balazs Horvath, Vlado Hrabec, Vojislav Jereb, Nick Johns, Geoff Jones, Lawrence Jones, Bob Kent/Aviation Research UK, Paul Kiddell, Hans Kofoed, Erik Kristensen, Vaclav Kudela, Loet Kuipers, Frederic Lagerquist, Arno Landewers, Lionel Laporte, Joachim Lippl, Pete Longley, Kenneth Magnusson, Andy Marden, Alan Mawman, Andras Meszaros, Adrian Morgan, Tony Morris, Tavs As Mortensen, Justin Palmer, Simon Palmer, Gordon Perry, John Porter, Hans Radier, Michael Riede, Bob Rongé, Dominique Roosens, Claude Schmit, Don Schofield, John Scotford, Stephen Simms, Graham Slack, Colin Smith, Terry Smith, Tony Smith, David Sparrow, Paulo Stanchina, Jos Stevens, Robert Swan, Marc Tanz, Luis Tavares, Robert Taylor, Barrie Towey, Jim Tyerman, José Ramon Valero, Kristof Vandermoere, Henk Wadman, Dave Walker, Peter Watson, Rod Webb, Pete Webber, Dave Wise, Luc Wittemanns, Andy Wood and the Air-Britain Travel participants. Grateful acknowledgement must also be made to Aerodata Quantum +, Aeromedia, Airnieuws, AMCAR, Aviation Society of Antwerp, Avion Revue, Scramble, numerous websites both official and unofficial, the many AB-IX correspondents and to other Air-Britain annual and periodical publications. This year a team of 'updaters' has worked hard behind the scenes to keep the editor's files up to date while he busies himself with other tasks; their names too are included in the list above. To anyone else not named here but who has provided data during the year, our thanks and apologies for the omission!

As many readers will know, additions to all of the Registers in this volume are published regularly in the "Overseas Registers" section of the monthly **"Air-Britain News"**. Further details of Air-Britain membership and publications may be found at the back of this book, alternatively anyone who is not already a member is invited to write to Barry Collman at 1,Rose Cottages, 179 Penn Road, Hazlemere, Bucks HP15 7NE for additional information.

Any further comments, additions or amendments to this European Registers Handbook will as always be gratefully received by the Editor at the address below or by e-mail to: **Dave.Partington@air-britain.co.uk**

David Partington,
"The Haven",
Nympsfield Road,
Nailsworth,
Gloucestershire GL6 0EA
United Kingdom

May 2005

IMPORTANT NOTE

The publication of these Registers should not be taken to imply that access to Civil Airfields is always permissable, or that photography of civil aircraft is authorised. Visitors should check these points beforehand as many states do not allow open access to civil airfields and an interest in aviation may not always be tolerated or understood.

USER'S GUIDE TO THE EUROPEAN REGISTERS HANDBOOK

The aim of this book is to identify the civil aircraft of Western Europe (except for the UK and Eire, published in a separate volume) including gliders, balloons and microlights. Four information 'fields' are available for each entry as follows:

REGISTRATION

The basic form of aircraft identification, usually painted on the aircraft itself (but not always as in the case of some microlights), which consists of the nationality prefix followed by the individual alphabetical or numerical identifier. Types such as gliders, balloons, ulms may be allocated separate blocks in some countries, in others they may be combined in the same sequence. In some countries the registration marks are allocated in strict alphabetical order, eg Spain, while others use blocks representing different classes, eg Germany, Switzerland, Austria, by weight, number of engines, etc, Sweden has separate blocks for jets, helicopters, etc, the former Czechoslovakia used the first letter to identify year of manufacture, Finland uses blocks for different manufacturers, while France has separate sections for vintage, homebuilt and overseas-based aircraft but registers microlights using only the number of the Département in which they are based. Other countries use completely unsequenced allocations, as in Italy, Belgium, Iceland, but may include blocks for particular operators. A brief study of any country's entries should quickly reveal the system adopted.

Where possible, if a registration has been used more than once, multiple use is indicated by a figure in brackets in the registration column, eg D-ABOM(2), LN-ORH(4). We must emphasise that these suffix marks are not carried on the aircraft themselves but are to assist in identifying different aircraft over a period of time. Austria now has a system which allows for multiple use of the same marks simultaneously for balloons registered to the same owner. These are distinguished by letters (a), (b) and (c) etc in the listing although true identification may be difficult in reality unless a c/n can be found!. In many countries gliders use a one, two or even three-letter code/competition number which may not necessarilly be a part of the registration. Where known, these are added in the registration column thus: F-CFAN-J43, PH-754-YX, OO-ZSG-V. In a small number of cases lack of space results in the code being given in the second column after the type.

Registrations known to have been reserved but not yet officially taken up or certificated (depending on national practice) are indicated as such in the second column following the type, the same location being used to identify aircraft known to be flying only on Permits.

AIRCRAFT TYPE

The manufacturer or designer and actual model are quoted here, as far as possible using the official FAA designation. If the manufacturer has changed during the production run of a particular type this may be shown in cases where the date or unit of change can be clearly identified. In other cases we tend to adopt the original manufacturer's designation and only change this when a new model or type designation results. Thus de Havilland Tiger Moths will never be BAe Tiger Moths but the Learjet models produced entirely by Bombardier (the 45 and 60) are listed as such. There are bound to be some anomalies in this system but the overall aim is to be both informative and accurate, even if these aims sometimes conflict.

Sometimes models may have changed names during a production run but retained the same designation (usually for ease of certification) which is the only part of the data to be published. Robin DR.400 production for example has the 400/120 Petit Prince replaced by the Dauphin 2+2 but during the transition period only by observing the name on the actual aircraft can the correct model be positively identified. We have now taken a cut-off date of the 1988 model to change the names listed for the DR.400/120 and DR.400/160 series, and 1991 for the DR.400/140. As this is fairly arbitrary any reports of actual names carried would still be most welcome! Also in France, the Rallye 100T appears to be a marketing exercise since all the aircraft are actually registered as the pre-existing MS.880B Rallye Club.

In some countries the builder of a kit or home-built aircraft may be shown in front of the normal type or designer name, usually separated by an oblique. Any notable modifications to model or to engine, or other significant information about a particular aircraft may also be added in brackets in this column.

CONSTRUCTOR'S NUMBER (C/n)

The constructor's number (also known as the manufacturer's serial number) is the only reliable permanent identification of each single airframe allocated at the time of building and remaining with the aircraft throughout any changes of owner or nationality. Specific changes may occur in the case of modification, rebuild, or the use of 'spare' fuselages. Such known cases are usually noted in column two. Users of this book may often find the fuselage or frame number (f/n) quoted in significant cases in order to clarify a particular identity - in the case of Piper Cubs and Super Cubs for example this number differs from the actual c/n but is often mistakenly quoted for it as the identification plate is in an accessible location! C/ns officially quoted, but known to be incorrect, are written between quotation marks and may merit further comment. A few aircraft may legitimately carry more than one c/n, as in the case of Cessna models built as 'knock-down' units in the US for assembly by Reims Aviation in France. Many aircraft carry the c/n on an external plate or have it painted on the rear fuselage or rudder.

PREVIOUS IDENTITY

Every time that an aircraft changes its country of registration a new identity will be allocated by the relevant authority. In Spain an internal change of owner is now sufficient to trigger a new identity! The immediate previous identity is given next to the aircraft c/n and if several identities are quoted the oldest is at the bottom of the list. A basic history of each aircraft's past can thus be read from the listing. Registrations which have been allocated, but not taken up, are shown in brackets. Those which have been incorrectly applied or which are unofficial or unauthorised are shown in quotation marks. A question mark indicates that a particular identity in unconfirmed or incomplete.

ABBREVIATIONS

It is intended to produce a more detailed guide to previous identity information in a future edition of ERH but in the meantime some assistance may be found in the following list of abbreviations. Volunteers to extend this will not be turned away!

AAF	Austrian Air Force
ALAT	Aviation Légère de l'Armée de Terre (French Army Aviation)
BelAF	Belarus Air Force
BFAF	Burkina Faso Air Force
BGA	British Gliding Association
BulAF	Bulgarian Air Force
CAF	Canadian Armed Forces
CamAF	Cambodian Air Force
CEV	Centre d'Essais en Vol (French Flight Test Centre)
CofA	Certificate of Airworthiness
CPLAF	Chinese People's Liberation Air Force
CzAF	Czech Republic Air Force
DOSAAF	Dobrovol'noe Obshchestvo Sodeistviya Armii, Aviasii i Flotu (Voluntary Society for Cooperation with the Army, Air Force and Navy - the Soviet youth and reserve training organisation)
EAF	Egyptian Air Force
FAP	Forca Aérea Portuguesa (Portuguese Air Force)
FLARF	Federatsiya Lyubitelei Aviatsii Rossiskoi Federatsii (Federation of Aviation Enthusiasts of the Russian Federation)
Fr.AF	French Air Force (the Armée de l'Air)
Fr.Navy	French Navy (Aéronavale)
Fr.Mil	One or more of the French forces
Fv	Flygvapnet (Royal Swedish AF serial)
HAF	Hellenic Air Force (Greece) , also Hungarian Air Force
HAFB	Hot Air Free Balloon
IAC	Irish Air Corps
IAF	Iraqi Air Force
IDFAF	Israeli Defence Force/Air Force
JRV	Jugoslovensko Ratno Vazduhoplovstvo (Yugoslav Air Force)
KLu	Koninklijke Nederlandse Luchtmacht (Royal Netherlands Air Force)
LAAF	Libyan Arab Air Force
LSK	Luftstreitkrafte (The former East German Air Force)
MLD	Royal Netherlands Naval Air Service
MM	Matricola Militare (Italian Air Force serial)
NEJSGSA	Near East Joint Services Gliding & Soaring Association (UK)
ntu	Not taken up
OGMA	Oficinas Gerais de Material Aeronautico (Portuguese aircraft manufacturer)
PLAAF0C	People's Liberation Army Air Force of China
PLW	Polskie Lotnictwo Wosjkowe (Polish Air Force)
RAFGGA	Royal Air Force Germany Gliding Association (UK)
RAFGSA	Royal Air Force Gliding & Soaring Association (UK)
RCAF	Royal Canadian Air Force - now CAF: Canadian Armed Forces
RDAF	Royal Danish Air Force
RHAF	Royal Hellenic (Greek) Air Force - now HAF
RJAF	Royal Jordanian Air Force
RNoAF	Royal Norwegian Air Force
RSrp	Republika Srpska (Serbian Republic military forces)
RusAF	Russian Air Force
SAAF	South African Air Force
SLN-	'Serial' for aircraft at RCAF Solingen, Germany, Flying Club
Sov.mil	Soviet military forces
SpAF	Spanish Air Force
SwAF	Swiss Air Force
TAF	Turkish Air Force
UAE	United Arab Emirates
UkrAF	Ukraine Air Force
Wfu	Withdrawn from use
W/o	Written off
. . + . . .	(in serial) German military serial with unit and identity

GLIDER MANUFACTURERS

Thanks to Richard Cawsey we have taken the first steps towards standardising some of the names of glider manufacturers and types. The list below may help to understand some of the data included in this edition and the changes that may appear to have been made.

Fournier: Construction of the RF-3 by Alpavia and the RF-4D, RF-5 and RF-5B by Sportavia is now recognised in the type designation.

Glaser-Dirks: Became DG Flugzeugbau in 1996. We have attempted to determine the cut-off points for each model that was in production when the change occurred. Models built in Slovenia by Elan are identifiable by type and by the E in the c/n. Elan itself changed title to AMS-FLIGHT on 1.9.99 but this does not seem to have resulted in any change of designation.

Glasflügel: The model 304B is built by Jastreb, and the 304C by HpH.

Rolladen-Schneider: The company suffered acute financial problems and was taken over by DG Flugzeugbau in 2003. Only the LS8 has remained in production and retains the same model designation. However we have now revised and corrected all the designations of the original manufacturer's models.

Scheibe: Batches of the SF-25B and SF-25C were built by Sportavia and these are now identified in the type designation.

Schempp-Hirth: The prolific Standard Cirrus design was built by several manufacturers. A single c/n sequence was shared by Schempp-Hirth and Grob, but the Grob-built examples can be identified by a G suffix on the c/n. Other builders with separate c/n sequences are Lanaverre in France and by VTC and Jastreb in the former Yugoslavia. The Discus CS is a model b built by Orlican in the Czech Republic - now a division of Schempp-Hirth.

Schleicher: Various c/n suffixes can be found which identify other builders. SH is used for K8Bs built by Schempp-Hirth; Si or Sie for the Ka6CR built by Siebert; Bi for the same model built by Bitz; Gö for K8B production in Switzerland by Götz. A or AB can indicate amateur-built examples although at batch of ASK13s c/ns 13618AB to 13693AB was factory-built by JUBI.

SZD: The c/n prefix letter indicates the build location: B at Bielsko, F at Krosno, P at Jezow, S at WSK-Swidnik, W at Wroclaw. X is used for prototypes.

As time goes by we will no doubt attempt further clarification of other models, not only of gliders but also delving into the mysteries of the rapidly multiplying ULM sector. Further comments will of course be most welcome.

CS - PORTUGAL

Although an updated Portuguese Register was published in 2004 the official listing still suffers from many entries with CofAs which expired at least ten years ago or which are known to have been written-off and these have been removed below. Others with expiry or cancellation dates since 1990 but reported to be extant, together with some earlier expiries which may be candidates for rebuild or restoration, are indicated with an asterisk (*).

Regn.	Type	C/n	Prev.Id.
CS-AAP(*)	Piper J-3C-85 Cub (Under restoration)	21984	G-AKBT
	(c/n suspect - 21984 was not built)		
CS-AAQ	Piper J-3C-65 Cub	22021	G-AKBU
	(c/n refers to spare frame built from spares 1947 -		
	the real 22021 was current as N77531 until 1977)		
CS-ABA(*)	Piper PA-12 Super Cruiser (Exp .72,for rebuild)	12-65	
CS-ABK	Piper J-3C-65 Cub	17674	
CS-ABO	Piper PA-25 Pawnee	25-646	N10F
CS-ABW	Piper J-3C-65 Cub	17242	
CS-ABY(*)	Piper J-3C-65 Cub (Stored, Beja)	17243	
CS-ACE(*)	Piper PA-18 Super Cub 95 (Exp 11.71)	18-661	N10F
CS-ACF	Piper PA-18A-150 Super Cub	18-5414	(HK-939P)
			N10F
CS-ACH	Piper PA-18 Super Cub 95	18-6863	N10F
CS-ACY	Culver V	348	
CS-ADF	Cessna 150A	15059232	N7132X
CS-ADU(*)	Piper PA-18A-150 Super Cub (Exp 7.62)	18-6715	N10F
CS-AEL(*)	OGMA/de Havilland DH.82 Tiger Moth	P-65	FAP1 . .
	(Under restoration, Alverca)		
CS-AFF(*)	OGMA/ de Havilland DH.82 Tiger Moth	DHTM.18A	FAP1 . .
	(To Museo do Ar)		
CS-AFG	Beech A23-24 Musketeer Super III	MA-350	
CS-AFI	Piper PA-28-180 Cherokee D	28-5463	N2110R
CS-AFP	SEEMS MS.892A Rallye Commodore 150	10503	F-BMVR
CS-AFQ(*)	Piper PA-28-180 Cherokee E (Stored)	28-5613	N11C
CS-AFR(*)	CEA Jodel DR.1050 Ambassadeur (Stored)	39	F-BJQP
CS-AFU	Piper PA-28R-200 Cherokee Arrow	28R-35786	N5044S
CS-AGA	Rockwell S.2R-600 Thrush Commander	1484R	N8884Q
CS-AGB(*)	American AA-1 Yankee (W/o 1988?)	AA1-0377	N6177L
CS-AGI	SOCATA MS.893A Rallye Commodore 180	11782	
CS-AGK(*)	SOCATA MS.894A Minerva 220 (Stored)	11833	
CS-AGP	Rockwell Commander 112A	0192	N1192J
CS-AGQ(*)	Rockwell Commander 112A (Exp 1.82)	0172	N1172J
CS-AGW	Piper PA-23-250 Turbo Aztec E	27-4665	N14054
CS-AGZ	SOCATA MS.894A Minerva 220	11940	
CS-AHE	Reims/Cessna F337F Skymaster	F33700037	
	(Reims-assembled 337F with US c/n 33701374)		
CS-AHG(*)	Grumman G.44 Widgeon (To Museu do Ar)	1242	FAP120
CS-AHI	Reims/Cessna F150L	F15000759	
CS-AHN	Reims FR172H Rocket	FR17200293	
CS-AHO	Rockwell S.2R Thrush Commander	1610R	CR-LNO
			CS-AHO
			N5510X
CS-AHQ	Reims FR172H Rocket	FR17200318	
CS-AHS(*)	Cessna A188B Agwagon C	18800873	N4473Q
	(Wreck, Coimbra)		
CS-AHU	Wassmer WA.52 Europa	43	
CS-AHV	Reims FR172H Rocket	FR1720 0333	
CS-AHW	Cessna 414	414-0280	N1565T
CS-AHX	Reims FR172H Rocket	FR17200332	
CS-AIA	Piper PA-18 Super Cub 125	18-1295	CR-AKA
			FAP3206
			N10F
CS-AIB(*)	Beagle A.109 Airedale	B-527	G-ASCB
	(Stored Ota, for Museu do Ar)		
CS-AIC	Piper PA-28-180 Cherokee C	28-4230	N4874L
CS-AID	SOCATA MS.893A Rallye Commodore 180	10920	
CS-AIG	Alon A-2 Aircoupe	B-280	N5480F
CS-AII	Piper PA-28-180 Cherokee D	28-4436	N5151L
CS-AIJ	SOCATA MS.893A Rallye Commodore 180	11000	F-BNGV
CS-AIP	Piper PA-22-160 Tri-Pacer	22-7615	CR-LEM
			G-ARGF
			N10F
CS-AIQ	SOCATA MS.893A Rallye Commodore 180	11446	
CS-AIS(*)	Beech A23-24 Musketeer Super III	MA-106	HB-ENU
	(Exp 9.93)		
CS-AIT	SOCATA MS.880B Rallye Club	1538	
CS-AIW	SOCATA MS.880B Rallye Club	1348	
CS-AIY(*)	SOCATA MS.893A Rallye Commodore 180	11455	
	(W/o 1988?)		
CS-AJA	Wassmer Jodel D.120A Paris-Nice	338	
CS-AJB	SOCATA MS.893A Rallye Commodore 180	12034	
CS-AJC	Bellanca 7ECA Citabria	661	
CS-AJD	Cessna 421B Golden Eagle	421B0270	N3395Q
CS-AJE	Helio H-295 Courier	1404	
CS-AJG	Reims FR172J Rocket	FR17200380	
CS-AJI (*)	Cessna A188B Agtruck (Exp 5.89, dism)	18801069T	N21840
CS-AJJ	Cessna 182P Skylane	18261398	N21078
CS-AJN(*)	Slingsby T.66 Nipper Mk.III (For rebuild)	1620/S.114	
CS-AJS	Rockwell S.2R Thrush Commander	1504R	CR-LNN
			CS-AJS
			N8804Q
CS-AJW	Reims FR172J Rocket	FR17200364	
CS-AKB	Cessna F172H	F172-0465	
CS-AKE	Cessna F172H	F172-0575	N14622
CS-AKF	Cessna 172C	17249439	N1839Y
CS-AKH	Cessna F172F	F172-0153	OE-DLB
CS-AKI	Cessna F172H	F172-0504	
CS-AKJ	Cessna P206A Super Skylane	P206-0183	N2683X
CS-AKM	Cessna 182N Skylane	18260359	N92796
CS-AKN(*)	Reims/Cessna F172H (W/o 5.96)	F17200655	N10655
CS-AKS	Cessna 150B	15059582	N1182Y
CS-AKV	Cessna F172G	F172-0303	
CS-AKX	Cessna 182M Skylane	18259880	N91710
CS-AKY	Cessna U206E Stationair	U20601678	N9478G
CS-AKZ	Reims FR172G Rocket	FR17200168	D-ECFM
CS-ALA	Piper PA-22-108 Colt	22-9749	N10F
CS-ALB	Paulistinha 56-C1	1162	PP-HME
CS-ALD(*)	Tipsy T.66 Nipper Mk.II (Exp 2.80)	41	(OY-ACR)
CS-ALE(*)	Helio H-250 Courier (Exp 8.78)	2502	(ET-ABN)
CS-ALF	Piper PA-32-260 Cherokee Six	32-631	N3718W
CS-ALI	Alpavia/ Fournier RF-3	72	
CS-ALM	Piper PA-23-160 Apache	23-1252	N3302P
	(Exp 1.94. For rebuild?)		
CS-ALO	Piper PA-28-180 Cherokee B	28-1542	N7592W
CS-ALP	Piper PA-22-108 Colt	22-9368	N10F
CS-ALS	Mooney M.20E Super 21	554	
CS-ALT	Piper PA-24-180 Comanche	24-3404	N8197P
			N10F
CS-ALV(*)	Beagle A.109 Airedale (W/o 1996)	B-529	
CS-ALX	Piper PA-32-300 Cherokee Six	32-40154	N4157W
CS-ALZ(*)	Piper PA-32-260 Cherokee Six	32-716	N3758W
	(Exp 12.74, stored .98)		
CS-AMB(*)	Auster D4/108 (Exp 5.66)	3603	
CS-AMG(*)	OGMA/Auster D5/160 (Exp 5.73)	10	
CS-AMJ(*)	OGMA/Auster D4/108 (Exp 10.73)	36	
CS-AMX(*)	OGMA/Auster D5/160 (Preserved, Alverca)	81	
CS-AMZ	OGMA/Auster D5/160	99	
CS-ANB(*)	OGMA/Auster D5/160	101	
	(Exp 10.82, displayed Faro)		
CS-AND(*)	OGMA/Auster D5/160 (Exp 12.81)	108	
CS-ANF	OGMA/Auster D5/160	131	
CS-ANK(*)	OGMA/Auster D5/160 (Exp 10.73)	119	
CS-ANP(*)	OGMA/Auster D5/160 (Exp 3.72)	124	
CS-ANT(*)	OGMA/Auster D5/160 (Exp 12.81. Stored)	128	
CS-ANV(*)	OGMA/Auster D5/160 (Exp 2.74)	130	
CS-AOA(*)	Piper PA-34-200 Seneca (W/o 9.10.94)	34-7350126	N15998
CS-AOB(*)	Reims FR172J Rocket (W/o .93)	FR17200367	
CS-AOD	Cessna 210L Centurion	21059722	N22217
CS-AOE	Reims/Cessna F150L	F15000915	
CS-AOJ	Piper PA-32-300 Cherokee Six	32-7340136	N55779
CS-AOO	Piper PA-28-180 Cherokee Challenger	28-7305192	N11C
CS-AOT	Reims/Cessna F150L	F15000976	F-BRGV
			(CN-TBD)
CS-APA	Reims/Cessna F150L	F15001068	F-BSGQ
			(F-BVBD)
CS-APC	Piper PA-34-200 Seneca	34-7450080	N56539
CS-APG(*)	Cessna 182P Skylane (W/o 30.5.95)	18262625	N52461
CS-APN	Reims/Cessna F172M	F17201158	F-BRGR
CS-APQ(*)	Rockwell S.2R Thrush Commander	1823R	N5623X
	(Intended for rebuild?)		
CS-APT	Piper PA-28-180 Cherokee Archer	28-7405105	EC-YYT
			N9532N
CS-APU(*)	Piper PA-28-180 Cherokee Archer	28-7405109	EC-YYU
	(Impounded in Morocco)		N9542N
CS-APW	Grumman G.164A Agcat	1247	N9735
CS-APY	Grumman G.164A Agcat	1238	N9757
CS-AQD	Rockwell S.2R Thrush Commander	1865R	CR-AQJ
			N5665X
CS-AQE	Rockwell S.2RThrush Commander	1831R	CR-AQI
			N5631X
CS-AQH(*)	Dornier Do.27A-3 (W/o 1996)	384	FAP3462
			LC+161
			GA+381
CS-AQI (*)	Dornier Do.27A-3 (To Museu do Ar)	350	FAP3339
			QW+703
			PL+427
CS-AQM(*)	OGMA/DHC-1 Chipmunk T.20 (Stored)	OGMA-4	FAP1314
CS-AQN	Piper PA-18-150 Super Cub	18-7723	FAP ?
			61-2929
CS-AQQ(*)	Piper PA-18-135 Super Cub (Exp 7.85)	18-2561	FAP ?
			52-6243
CS-AQU(*)	Cessna A188B Agtruck	18803313T	N1978J
	(Reims-assembled with "c/n" 0029)		
CS-AQX	Reims/Cessna F172N	F17201903	
CS-AQY(*)	Piper PA-38-112 Tomahawk (W/o 1991)	38-79A0875	N9676N
CS-ARA(*)	Aero Commander 100 (Exp 7.90)	084	
CS-ARB	Piper PA-28RT-201T Turbo Arrow IV	28R-8031171	N9602N
			N82593
CS-ARC	Reims/Cessna F152 (W/o 11.1.98)	F15201790	F-WZIM
CS-ARD	Piper PA-31-325 Navajo C/R	31-7912102	N35379
CS-ARF(*)	Cessna A188B Agtruck	18803512T	N2779J
	(Exp 12.92, dismantled)		
CS-ARG	Cessna A188B Agtruck	18803531T	N2837J
CS-ARH(*)	Reims/Cessna F152 (W/o 6.96)	F15201837	F-WZIY
CS-ARI	Robin HR.100/210 Safari	159	F-BUHV
CS-ARJ (*)	Cessna 402B Utiliner (Exp 12.93)	402B0119	PJ-SAA
			HP-717
			C9-ANL
			CR-ANL
			N7869Q
CS-ARK	SOCATA MS.893A Rallye Commodore 180	11432	CS-AIL

CS-ARL	Cessna 402B Utiliner	402B0318	PJ-SAB
			HP-693
			C9-AOT
			CR-AOT
			ZS-IUO
			N1559T
CS-ARM(*)	Piper PA-34-220T Seneca III (W/o 24.7.91)	34-8133112	N83934
CS-ARN(*)	Cessna 402B Utiliner	402B0443	PJ-SAC
	(Exp 7.83. Stored for spares)		HP-718
			C9-AON
			CR-AON
			ZS-IVV
			N69333
CS-ARO(*)	Rockwell Commander 680FLP	1651-32	I-ZANU
	(Exp 11.85, stored Alverca)		N4598E
CS-ARP	Cessna R182 Skylane RG	R18201652	N6226S
CS-ARQ(*)	Piper PA-36-375 Brave (W/o .92)	36-8102023	N6191A
CS-ARW(*)	Piper PA-36-375 Brave (W/o .91)	36-8002001	N3773E
CS-ARY	Piaggio FWP.149D	038	D-ENTL
			90+26
			BF+403
			BF+703
CS-ARZ(*)	Cessna A.152 Aerobat (W/o 7.92)	A1521032	N758ZH
CS-ASB(*)	Grumman G.164B Agcat (W/o 7.97)	795B	
CS-ASF	Cessna A188B Agtruck	18801920T	G-BETS
			SE-GGV
			N70431
CS-ASG	Rockwell Commander 690B	11452	N115SB
			N210EC
			N119SA
			(N81734)
CS-ASH	Mooney M.20J Model 201	24-0998	N3974H
CS-ASI	Piper PA-36-375 Brave	36-8002031	N2456V
CS-ASJ	Hoffmann H-36 Dimona	36269	
CS-ASK	Piper PA-36-285 Pawnee Brave	36-7660050	N57732
CS-ASM	Grumman G.164B Agcat	811B	
CS-ASN	Grumman G.164B Agcat	812B	
CS-ASO	Cessna 152	15282784	OY-CPN
			N89553
CS-ASP	Cessna 152	15282438	N69019
CS-ASQ	Cessna 152	15281019	N48874
CS-ASR	Cessna 152	15282999	N46113
CS-AST	Cessna 172N	17272060	N6753E
CS-ASU	Cessna 172N	17272821	N6470D
CS-ASW	Piper PA-36-285 Pawnee Brave	36-7660003	N57604
CS-ASX	Reims/Cessna F150M	F15001371	PH-BAR
CS-ASZ	Mooney M.20J Model 201	24-0958	G-BHRV
			N3839H
CS-AUA	Piper PA-36-285 Pawnee Brave	36-7360027	N56070
CS-AUC	Piper PA-36-375 Brave	36-8202001	N2321X
CS-AUD	Reims/Cessna F172M	F17200983	D-EGJL
CS-AUE	Piper PA-34-200T Seneca II	34-7870101	N2936M
CS-AUF	Cessna TU206G Turbo Stationair II	U20603577	D-EHLK(2)
			N7240N
CS-AUG	Cessna 150L	15074780	N10084
CS-AUH	Cessna 150L	15072396	EC-ECY(2)
			N6896G
CS-AUI	Cessna 152	15283688	N4876B
CS-AUJ	Cessna 152	15282656	N89162
CS-AUK	Cessna 152	15280376	N24783
CS-AUM	Beech F33A Bonanza	CE-763	N24162
CS-AUN	Cessna 152 (W/o)	15280040	N757VP
CS-AUO	Cessna A185F Skywagon	18502324	N53028
CS-AUP	Cessna 172C	17248845	N8345X
CS-AUR	Cessna 152	15283659	N4826B
CS-AUS	Cessna 152	15280296	N24507
CS-AUT	Reims/Cessna F172H	F17200664	G-AXVX
CS-AUW	Cessna T210L Turbo Centurion	21060642	N1606X
CS-AVA	Cessna 152	15283295	G-BOBI
			(G-BHJD)
			N48172
CS-AVB	Cessna 152	15279539	N714YN
CS-AVC	Cessna 152	15279621	N757BY
CS-AVD	Cessna 152	15279997	N757TS
CS-AVG	Maule MX7-180 Star Rocket	11055C	N61254
CS-AVH	Piper PA-28RT-201 Arrow IV	28R-7918069	G-BORU
			N1015S
			N9614N
CS-AVI	Reims/Cessna F150L	F15000824	G-PAGE
			PH-CEU
CS-AVJ (*)	Cessna 172N (W/o .95)	17269875	N738CQ
CS-AVK	Mooney M.20J Model 201	24-1384	N5648U
CS-AVL	Beech 76 Duchess	ME-332	N6718D
CS-AVM	Piper PA-31-350 Navajo Chieftain	31-7752159	N503SC
			G-BFDB
			N27339
CS-AVS	Cessna 182J Skylane	18257261	N3161F
CS-AVT	Cessna 172M	17261830	N12132
CS-AVV	Piper PA-38-112 Tomahawk	38-79A0588	N2358K
CS-AXA(*)	Jodel D.9 Bébé (To Museu do Ar, Alverca)	436	
CS-AXB(*)	Jurca MJ.2BTempête (To Museu do Ar, Sintra)	9	
CS-AYA	Cessna F150J	F150-0401	D-EABB
CS-AYC	Cessna R.172K Hawk XP	3056	N758FG
CS-AYG	Reims/Cessna F152	F15201573	G-BGHK
CS-AYH	Reims/Cessna F152	F15201612	G-BGOF
CS-AYI	Cessna Turbo 310R	310R1408	N4943A
CS-AYJ	Reims/Cessna F150L	F15000916	D-ECWL

CS-AYK	Cessna 152	15282482	G-BPBH
			N69102
CS-AYL	Piper PA-28-140 Cherokee B	28-26315	N5585U
CS-AYM	Cessna A.152 Aerobat	A1520995	N761XR
CS-AYN	Cessna A.152 Aerobat	A1520990	N761VU
CS-AYR	Cessna 152	15281575	G-PACK
			N65477
CS-AYT	Dornier 228-200	8084	VP-FBK
			G-MAFS
			D-ILAB
			(D-CLAB)
CS-AYU	Cessna 152	15282355	N68749
CS-AYV	Cessna 172N	17273832	N5747J
CS-AYW	Cessna R.172K Hawk XP	3060	N758FL
CS-AYX	Cessna 152	15284658	N6296M
CS-AYY	Cessna 501 Citation I/SP	501-0183	ZS-KPA
			N6777V
CS-AYZ	Cessna R.172K Hawk XP	3001	N758CZ
CS-AZA	Cessna 152	15282210	N68249
CS-AZB	Cessna 152	15281900	G-SACA
			G-HOSE
			N67538
CS-AZD	Cessna 172RG Cutlass RG	172RG0979	G-RGII
			N9702B
CS-AZF	SOCATA TB-9 Tampico	1454	F-OHDC
			F-WNGY
CS-AZG	SOCATA TB-9 Tampico	1455	F-OHDD
CS-AZI	Beech F33A Bonanza	CE-312	N9777S
CS-AZJ	Cessna 172N	17271535	N3410E
CS-AZK	Mooney M.20J Model 201	24-1525	N57881
CS-AZL	Douglas C-47B	14799/26244	9Q-CGW
			(9Q-CGC)
			ZS-DJZ
			VP-YSO
			ZS-DJZ
			G-AMSR
			KJ952
			43-48983
CS-AZQ	OGMA/DHC-1 Chipmunk T.20	OGMA-13	FAP-1323
CS-AZU	Piper PA-36-375 Brave	36-8302015	VH-HSR
			N82678
CS-AZV	Piper PA-32R-301 Saratoga	32R-8013038	G-BHNN
			N3578C
CS-AZW	Cessna 402B	402B1231	N4185G
CS-AZX	OGMA/DHC-1 Chipmunk T.20	OGMA-24	FAP-1334
CS-AZY	OGMA/DHC-1 Chipmunk T.20	OGMA-40	FAP-1350
	(UK based from 6.00)		
CS-DAA	SOCATA TB-9 Tampico	1553	F-OHDJ
CS-DAB	SOCATA TB-9 Tampico	1554	F-OHDK
CS-DAC	OGMA/DHC-1 Chipmunk T.20 (To UK)	OGMA-43	FAP-1353
CS-DAG	Cessna 172RG Cutlass RG	172RG0009	G-BHEP
	(Reims-assembled with c/n 0003)		N4668R
CS-DAH(*)	Cessna TP.206A Turbo Skywagon	0241	G-AYJU
	(W/o 28.5.96)		N176WM
			(N4641F)
CS-DAI	OGMA/DHC-1 Chipmunk T.20	OGMA-30	FAP-1340
CS-DAJ	OGMA/DHC-1 Chipmunk T.20	OGMA-32	FAP-1342
CS-DAK	Cessna 152	15284563	N5363M
CS-DAL	Cessna R.172K Hawk XP	3296	N758RH
			V3-HEI
			N758RH
CS-DAR(*)	OGMA/DHC-1 Chipmunk T.20	OGMA-66	FAP-1376
	(Preserved, OGMA Alverca)		
CS-DAS	Cessna 152	15281047	N48916
CS-DAT	Cessna 152	15283914	N6258B
CS-DAU	Cessna 172P	17273917	N7572J
CS-DAV	Cessna 182M Skylane	18259745	N71764
CS-DAY	Aviat Pitts S-2B	5282	
CS-DAZ	Cessna 152	15283262	N47883
CS-DBA	Mooney M.20J Model 201	24-3100	G-MASL
			N1012U
CS-DBB	Mooney M.20K Model 252 TSE	25-1150	N252AB
			G-BREO
			N252BX
CS-DBC	Cessna 172N	17271143	N205JA
			N2072E
CS-DBD	Reims/Cessna FTB337G Super Skymaster	0032	FAP-3731
			CS-ABR
CS-DBE	SOCATA MS.893A Rallye Commodore 180	10663	F-BODH
CS-DBF	Cessna 172M	17261139	N20263
CS-DBG	Piper PA-28-140 Cherokee F	28-7325436	N55580
	(Fuselage stored, Portimao)		
CS-DBH	Commander Aircraft 114B	14591	N6015K
CS-DBI	HOAC DV-20 Katana	20016	OE-COM
CS-DBK	Piper PA-28R-200 Cherokee Arrow II	28R-7235205	G-BAAP
			(G-AZYO)
			N11C
CS-DBN	Cessna 172N	17270051	N738LA
CS-DBO	Britten-Norman BN-2A-20 Islander	352	LN-FSK
			F-OGNV
			N352BN
			C-GCXB
			N24JA
			G-BBJC
CS-DBR	Piper PA-23-250 Aztec D	27-4021	G-BCPF
			N6748Y
			N10F

CS-DBU	Piper PA-36-375 Brave	36-8302017	N90905
CS-DBW	Beech C24R Sierra	MC-660	N6042V
CS-DBX	Piper PA-36-375 Brave	36-7802033	N3881E
CS-DBZ	Grumman G.164A Agcat	797	EC-ECP G-WOLL G-AYTM N6555
CS-DCB	Cessna 421B Golden Eagle	421B0548	G-OLDE G-BBSV (N69917)
CS-DCC	Grumman G.164A Agcat	1103	C-FJSH N4832
CS-DCD	SOCATA TB-9 Tampico	1127	F-GKUC
CS-DCF	Piper PA-31-350 Chieftain	31-8052174	PH-ECO N4501Y
CS-DCH	SOCATATB-10 Tobago	20	F-GBHJ
CS-DCJ	Piper PA-36-285 Pawnee Brave	36-7560076	N9965P
CS-DCK	Dassault Falcon 20E	297	N297AG PK-TIR N121EU (N370EU) N4443F F-WMKF
CS-DCL	Reims FR172F Rocket	FR17200133	D-ECOR(2) F-WLIT
CS-DCN	Robin DR.400/180R Remo 180	1235	OE-DIN
CS-DCO	Cessna 152	15284611	N5548M (N272SP) N5548M
CS-DCP	Beech A90-1 King Air (U-21)	LM-22	N7034K 66-18021
CS-DCQ	Piper PA-28-140 Cherokee E	28-7225536	C-FBLD CF-BLD
CS-DCR	Cessna T210N Turbo Centurion II	21063671	N4914C
CS-DCS	Beech 76 Duchess	ME-404	LX-TWN F-GKDH N771AW EI-BKW ST-AKB EI-BKW N3834Z
CS-DCT	Cessna 750 Citation X	750-0134	N51780
CS-DCU	Cessna 172N	17267812	N75563
CS-DCV	Cessna 180H	18052109	D2-EKM CR-LKM G-AXWW N9009M
CS-DCW	Piper PA-34-200T Seneca II	34-8170017	F-GFEM N82772
CS-DCX	SOCATA MS.893A Rallye Commodore 180	11669	D-EGGD
CS-DCY	Piper PA-18-150 Super Cub	18-8479	SE-FAK N4299Y
CS-DCZ	Cessna T210N Turbo Centurion II	21063239	N7581N
CS-DDC	Piper PA-38-112 Tomahawk	38-79A0987	N8211P OE-CPB N9713N
CS-DDD	SOCATA TB-10 Tobago	350	D-ESLX LX-EUR
CS-DDF	Beech B200 Super King Air/Catpass 250	BB-1129	N66404
CS-DDG	Rockwell Commander 112	294	F-GMCC N1294J
CS-DDH	SOCATA TB-10 Tobago	280	F-GDBH
CS-DDI	Dassault Falcon 900	143	VP-BZB ZS-ZBB F-GNMR F-WWFH
CS-DDJ	Cessna 152	15283947	D-EPTL N65478
CS-DDK	SOCATA TB-20 Trinidad	1900	F-OIUM
CS-DDL	Piper PA-36-285 Pawnee Brave	36-7460017	N43706
CS-DDM	Cessna 182S	18280437	F-GUFA N4219M
CS-DDO	Cessna A152 Aerobat	A1520804	CS-DDN C-GVNC N738SL
CS-DDP	Cessna 152	15285620	C-FFIP N94198
CS-DDQ	Reims/Cessna F172N	F17201702	D-EFER(2)
CS-DDR	Cessna 172S	172S8760	N854SP
CS-DDS	Reims FR172J Rocket	FR17200409	F-BUMH
CS-DDT	SOCATA TB-10 Tobago	32	F-GBHR
CS-DDU	Beech 200 Super King Air	BB-640	N47CF N581
CS-DDV	Cessna S550 Citation S/II	S550-0147	OO-OSA (OO-SAL) N1296N
CS-DDW	Cessna 152	15279470	N714VQ
CS-DDX	Robin ATL L	11	F-GFNK
CS-DDY	Cessna 152	15285474	N93370
CS-DDZ	Gates Learjet 31	31-034	N349SA N45PK N604LH 9V-ATB N5015U
CS-DEA	SOCATA TB-200 Tobago XLS	2017	F-OJBA F-WWRF

CS-DEB	SOCATA TB-200 Tobago XLS	2046	F-OJBB
CS-DEC	SOCATA TB-200 Tobago XLS	2047	F-OJBC
CS-DED	SOCATA TB-200 Tobago XLS	2055	F-OJBD
CS-DEE	SOCATA TB-20 Trinidad	2080	F-OIUA
CS-DEF	SOCATA TB-200 Tobago XLS	2066	F-OJBE
CS-DEG	SOCATA TB-200 Tobago XLS	2067	F-OJBF
CS-DEH	SOCATA TB-200 Tobago XLS	2068	F-OJBS
CS-DEI	SOCATA TB-200 Tobago XLS	2069	F-OJBT
CS-DEJ	SOCATA TB-200 Tobago XLS	2070	F-OJBU
CS-DEK	SOCATA TB-200 Tobago XLS	2071	F-OJBV
CS-DEL	SOCATA TB-200 Tobago XLS	2072	F-OJBX
CS-DEM	SOCATA TB-200 Tobago XLS	2073	F-OJBY
CS-DEN	SOCATA TB-200 Tobago XLS	2079	F-OJBZ
CS-DEO	SOCATA TB-20 Trinidad	2085	F-OIUB
CS-DEP	SOCATA TB-20 Trinidad	2086	F-OIUC
CS-DEQ	Piper PA-34-220T Seneca V	3449233	N5341L
CS-DER	Piper PA-34-220T Seneca V	3449236	N5342Z
CS-DFB	Dassault Falcon 900	94	N94WA A7-AAE F-WWFC
CS-DFC	Dassault Falcon 2000	148	F-WWVC
CS-DFD	Dassault Falcon 2000	174	F-WWMA
CS-DFE	Dassault Falcon 2000	205	F-WWVS
CS-DFF	Dassault Falcon 2000EX	41	F-WWGW
CS-DFG	Dassault Falcon 2000EX	44	F-WWGA
CS-DFH	Dassault Falcon 900	91	N991EJ CS-DFA N91WF A7-AAD F-WWFH
CS-DFK	Dassault Falcon 50 (Reservation .04)	62	N562EJ N50FH N292BC N77FJ F-WZHE
CS-DFM	Cessna 560XL Citation Excel	560-5257	N5196U
CS-DFN	Cessna 560XL Citation Excel	560-5283	N5097H
CS-DFO	Cessna 560XL Citation Excel	560-5314	N5000R
CS-DFP	Cessna 560XL Citation Excel	560-5315	N5095N
CS-DFQ	Cessna 560XL Citation Excel	560-5334	N5093L
CS-DFR	Cessna 560XL Citation Excel	560-5355	N5200Z
CS-DFS	Cessna 560XL Citation Excel	560-5372	N5091J
CS-DFT	Cessna 560XL Citation XLS	560-5512	N52433
CS-DFU	Cessna 560XL Citation XLS	560-5520	N5269A
CS-DFW	Hawker 800XP	258664	N664XP
CS-DFX	Hawker 800XP	258656	N656XP
CS-DFY	Hawker 800XP	258663	N663XP
CS-DFZ	Hawker 800XP	258673	N673XP
CS-DGA(*)	Douglas C-47A (Exp 6.79. Preserved as "CS-TDA" at Lisbon)	19503	4X-AOC EI-ACK 43-15037
CS-DGE	OGMA/Auster D5/180	132	
CS-DGF	OGMA/Auster D5/180	133	
CS-DGG(*)	OGMA/Auster D5/180 (Exp 11.79)	110	
CS-DGH	Beech D55 Baron	TE-684	
CS-DGK	Rockwell Commander 114	14302	
CS-DGL	Beech P35 Bonanza	D-7230	N8605M
CS-DHA	Cessna 550 Citation Bravo	550-1005	N5247U
CS-DHB	Cessna 550 Citation Bravo	550-1009	N5155G
CS-DHC	Cessna 550 Citation Bravo	550-1013	N5166U
CS-DHD	Cessna 550 Citation Bravo	550-1017	N51666
CS-DHE	Cessna 550 Citation Bravo	550-1022	N5168Y
CS-DHF	Cessna 550 Citation Bravo	550-1025	N5172M
CS-DHG	Cessna 550 Citation Bravo	550-1034	N52086
CS-DHH	Cessna 550 Citation Bravo	550-1043	N52235
CS-DHI	Cessna 550 Citation Bravo	550-1048	N5353S
CS-DHJ	Cessna 550 Citation Bravo	550-1082	N5180C
CS-DHK	Cessna 550 Citation Bravo	550-1090	N51038
CS-DHL	Cessna 550 Citation Bravo	550-1092	N52645
CS-DHM	Cessna 550 Citation Bravo	550-1093	N5263D
CS-DHN	Cessna 550 Citation Bravo	550-1098	N5132T
CS-DHO	Cessna 550 Citation Bravo	550-1099	N5180C
CS-DHP	Cessna 550 Citation Bravo (Reservn)	550-1104	N52144
CS-DIA	Cessna 152	15284274	N5159L
CS-DIB	Cessna 152	15282845	G-BOIW N89731
CS-DIC	PZL M-18B Dromader	1Z023-10	SP-FBT
CS-DID	Piper PA-34-220T Seneca V	3449229	SE-ITX N9518N
CS-DIE	Piper J-3C-65 Cub	13950	N2075N 45-55184
CS-DIF	Cessna 152	15281979	G-BPTF N67715
CS-DIG	Cessna 560 Citation Ultra	560-0637	N5073G
CS-DIH	Cessna 172R	17280412	N972RA
CS-DKA	Gulfstream IVSP	1480	N482QS N480GA
CS-DKB	Gulfstream V (Res 6.04)	642	N510QS CS-DKB N510QS N562GA
CS-DMA	Beechjet 400	RK-401	N36701
CS-DMB	Beechjet 400	RK-403	N36803

CS-DMC	Beechjet 400	RK-404	N37204
CS-DNE	Cessna 650 Citation VII	650-7093	N793QS
CS-DNF	Cessna 650 Citation VII	650-7080	N780QS
CS-DNG	Cessna 650 Citation VII	650-7081	N781QS
CS-DNJ	Hawker 800XP	258399	N899QS
CS-DNK	Hawker 800XP	258430	N31590
CS-DNL	Hawker 800XP (Damaged 9.3.05)	258439	N31596
CS-DNM	Hawker 800XP	258422	N822QS
CS-DNN	Hawker 800XP	258435	N835QS
CS-DNO	Hawker 800XP	258457	N41984
CS-DNP	Dassault Falcon 2000	109	N2218
			F-WWVD
			CS-DNP
			F-WWVD
CS-DNQ	Dassault Falcon 2000	115	F-WWVK
CS-DNR	Dassault Falcon 2000	120	F-WWVP
CS-DNS	Dassault Falcon 2000	139	F-WWVR
CS-DNT	Hawker 800XP	258468	N43436
CS-DNU	Hawker 800XP	258479	N44779
CS-DNV	Hawker 800XP	258499	N51099
CS-DNW	Cessna 560XL Citation Excel	560-5221	N5094D
CS-DNX	Hawker 800XP	258511	N5011J
CS-DNY	Cessna 560XL Citation Excel	560-5216	N5103J
CS-DNZ	Cessna 560XL Citation Excel	560-5235	N5086W
CS-DRA	Hawker 800XP	258686	N61746
CS-DRB	Hawker 800XP	258690	N36690

Aircraft sold/delivered to Portugal for which no CS- marks are at present known:

CS- . . .	Air Tractor AT-400	400-0516	SE-IOE
			SU-JAF
			SE-IOE
CS- . . .	Cessna 172	unkn	HH-GLA
CS- . . .	Cessna 172M	17263470	N5256R
CS- . . .	Reims/Cessna F172N	F17201879	N47PT
			F-WBQT
			F-GBQT
CS- . . .	Dornier Do.27H-2	2013	D-EFQK(2)
			HB-HAC
			V-606
CS- . . .	Grumman GA-7 Cougar	0057	LN-ALY
			OY-GAV
			N770GA
CS- . . .	Piper PA-28-180 Cherokee D	28-5171	G-AWAR
CS- . . .	Piper PA-36-285 Pawnee Brave	36-7460022	N44118
CS- . . .	Piper PA-28-140 Cherokee	28-23991	OY-BCP
			N9872W
CS- . . .	Piper PA-36-285 Pawnee Brave	36-7460017	N43706
CS- . . .	Piper PA-38-112 Tomahawk	38-78A0141	G-BTAP
			N9603T

CS-GAA(*)	Beagle-Wallis WA.116 Series 1 (Exp 7.93)	B.202	G-ARZA
			XR942
			G-ARZA
CS-HAA(*)	SNCASO SO.1221-S Djinn (Exp 9.67)	1013/FR46	F-BHOU
			F-WHOU
CS-HAC(*)	SNCASO SO.1221-S Djinn (Exp 6.67)	1044/FR94	F-BJON
CS-HAJ(*)	Bell 47G-2 (H-13E conversion) (Exp 11.92)	738	N6398X
			CF-NXP
			N6398X
			51-13973
CS-HAM(*)	Bell 47D-1 (Barnes Conversion) (Exp 7.81)	SA2	N74090
CS-HAQ(*)	Bell 47G-2 (Exp 6.82)	2218	N6725D
CS-HAV	Hughes 269C	89-0826	G-HUSH
CS-HAZ	Hughes 269C	1084	SE-HMI
CS-HBT	Bell UH-1E (204)	6167	N5010J
			BuA154945
CS-HBU(*)	Bell UH-1E (204) (Exp 6.93)	6203	N48SS
			BuA155348
CS-HBV	Bell TH-1L (204)	6426	N540GH
			N540AH
			N434RR
			BuA157831
CS-HCH	Robinson R-22 Beta	2038	
CS-HCM(*)	Robinson R-22 Beta (Exp 9.93)	2156	
CS-HCO	Agusta-Bell 206B Jet Ranger II	8678	I-BDPL
CS-HCP	Aérospatiale AS.350BA Ecureuil	2551	F-WYMX
CS-HCQ	Robinson R-22M Mariner	2281M	
CS-HCR	Robinson R-22 Beta	2209	N23466
CS-HCY	Aérospatiale AS.350B Ecureuil	1730	G-DSAM
			D-HHGG
CS-HDB	Robinson R-44 Astro	0023	
CS-HDD	Hughes 269B	16-0235	G-OHSD
			N9457F
CS-HDJ	Aérospatiale AS.355F1 Ecureuil 2	5092	I-ELDI
			G-BRUY
			N330E
			N330P
			N5788U
CS-HDK	Aérospatiale AS.350BA Ecureuil	1871	D-HHFZ
CS-HDM	Robinson R-44 Astro	0183	
CS-HDO	Agusta-Bell 206B Jet Ranger II	8559	3A-MMM
			I-ELSI
CS-HDQ	Westland-Bell 47G-3B-1	WA/443	XT554
CS-HDS	Bell 222	47028	G-META
			N5733H
CS-HDT	Bell 222	47050	G-METC
			G-JAMC
CS-HDU	Bell 222	47055	G-METB
CS-HDV	Agusta-Bell 206B Jet Ranger II	8591	G-BWZB
			F-GCFS
CS-HDX	Bell 222	47071	N307CK
			N8114X
CS-HEC	Aérospatiale AS.350BA Ecureuil (Wreck noted 5.00)	2245	EC-FGD
CS-HED	Aérospatiale AS.350B2 Ecureuil	2669	D-HJOE
			HB-XZY
			D-HWPL
CS-HEE	Aérospatiale AS.355F1 Ecureuil 2	5006	F-W . . .
CS-HEK	Bell 206B Jet Ranger II	2914	N6280J
			(C- . . . .)
			N1078Q
CS-HEL	Aérospatiale AS.350B2 Ecureuil	2594	D-HEPB
			VH-HRK
			ZK-HLZ
CS-HEM	Agusta A.109E Power	11041	
CS-HEN	Aérospatiale AS.350BA Ecureuil	1845	LN-OPC
			OE-KXF
			D-HHZZ
CS-HEO	Aérospatiale AS.350B2 Ecureuil	1222	RP-C8880
			F-WQDS
			C-GSBO
			N144BH
			N3609D
CS-HEP	Bell 206B Jet Ranger II	2800	N27785
CS-HER	Agusta A.109E Power	11083	
CS-HES	Aérospatiale AS350B1 Ecureuil	2224	F-GKAS
CS-HEU	Robinson R-44 Raven	0831	
CS-HEV	Robinson R-44 Raven	0779	
CS-HEW	Schweizer 269C-1	0119	
CS-HEX	Eurocopter EC.120B Colibri	1183	
CS-HEY	Aérospatiale AS.350B2 Ecureuil	9027	D-HXST
CS-HEZ	Bell 212	30557	EC-GHP
			EC-256
			EC-FYB
			N83079
			VH-HVX
			ZK-HBK
			LN-OQY
			(G-BHAG)
			LN-OQY
			N83072
CS-HFA	PZL W-3AM Sokol	370705	SP-SYI
CS-HFB	Bell 206B Jet Ranger II	3640	D-HSBA
			G-IMLH
			N18096
CS-HFC	Bell 206L3 Long Ranger III	51358	D-HHTB
			HB-XVS
			N7133D
			C-FIFV
CS-HFD	Schweizer 269C-1	0058	I-EAHS
			HB-XJU
CS-HFF	Robinson R-22B2 Beta	3431	
CS-HFH	Aérospatiale AS.365N Dauphin 2	6128	HL9230
			D-HMKE
			F-WYMP

CS-TEB	Lockheed 1011 Tristar 500	1240	V2-LEO
			CS-TEB
CS-TEH	Airbus A310-304	483	F-WWCS
CS-TEI	Airbus A310-304	495	F-WWCO
CS-TEJ	Airbus A310-304	494	F-WWCM
CS-TEW	Airbus A310-304	541	F-WWCR
CS-TEX	Airbus A310-304	565	F-WWCC
CS-TEZ	Airbus A310-304	472	VP-BAF
			N472GE
			EC-GIL
			EC-396
			D-APON
			A6-KUC
			C-GIWD
			F-WWCB
CS-TFC	Beech 58 Baron	TH-524	N8130R
CS-TGF(*)	Dornier 228-202 (Exp 11.93. Stored)	8159	D-COBE(2)
			D-CBDN(2)
CS-TGG	Dornier 228-202	8160	D-CORA(4)
			D-CBDQ(2)
CS-TGH(*)	Dornier 228-202 (Exp 11.93. Stored)	8152	D-CAOT(3)
			D-CBDO(3)
			TC-FBX
			D-CBDC(2)
CS-TGL	BAe. ATP	2019	G-BRTG
			G-11-19
CS-TGN	BAe. ATP	2031	G-11-31
CS-TGO	Dornier 228-202	8119	D-CMUC
			D-CIMC(2)
CS-TGP	Boeing 737-3Q8 (Reserved as OO-TNF, 2.05)	24131	OO-LTX
			EC-FFC
			EC-592
			EC-EII
			EC-159

CS-TGU	Airbus A310-304	571	F-GJKQ
			TU-TAC
			F-WWYM
			F-GHYM
CS-TGV	Airbus A310-304	651	TU-TAD
			F-WWCC
CS-TGX	BAe. ATP	2025	G-BRLY
			TC-THP
			G-BRLY
CS-TGY	BAe. ATP	2049	G-BTZJ
			PK-MTY
			(PK-MAE)
			G-BTZJ
CS-TGZ	Boeing 737-43Q	28491	N120AF
			OO-CTG
			F-GLTG
			OO-CTG
			TC-IAG
			B-18673
CS-TJE	Airbus A321-211	1307	D-AVZM
CS-TJF	Airbus A321-211	1399	D-AVZI
CS-TJG	Airbus A321-211	1713	D-AVZS
CS-TKI	Airbus A310-304	448	C-GRYA
			D-APOM
			A6-KUB
			C-GDWD
			F-WWCO
CS-TKJ	Airbus A320-232	795	C-FTDA
			F-WWDX
CS-TKK	Airbus A320-214	2390	F-WWII
CS-TKL	Airbus A320-214	2425	F-WWBH
CS-TLJ	Short SD.3-60 Variant 300	SH.3692	OY-MUD
			N693PC
			G-BMNH
			G-14-3662
CS-TLK	SAAB 2000	014	SE-014
			F-GTSB
			D-ADSB
			SE-014
CS-TLL	Boeing 737-3K9	24213	PR-BRE
			CS-TIG
CS-TLM	Boeing 767-33AER	25535	N535AW
			VH-NOE
			V5-NMB
			VH-NOE
			OO-VAS
			F-GKAU
			VH-NOE
			N768TA
			N6018N
CS-TLN	SAAB 2000	016	SE-016
			F-GNEH
			EI-CPW
			F-GTSC
			D-ADSC
			SE-016
CS-TLO	Boeing 767-383ER	24318	N318SR
			LN-RCH
			SE-DKO
CS-TLP	Dassault Falcon 2000EX/EASy	39	F-WWGU
CS-TMH	Short SD.3-60 Variant 100	SH.3694	G-BMNJ
			N694PC
			G-BMNJ
			G-14-3694
CS-TMK	Dassault Falcon 900	66	F-GJPM
			F-WWFE
CS-TMN	Short SD.3-60 Variant 100	SH.3638	G-ISLE
			G-BLEG
CS-TMP	Lockheed 1011-500 Tristar	1248	SE-DVI
			(9Y-BWC)
			V2-LEK
			CS-TEG
			JY-AGJ
			N64959
CS-TMQ	Dassault Falcon 900	175	F-WWFN
CS-TMR	Lockheed 1011-500 Tristar	1241	SE-DVF
			CS-TEC
CS-TMT	Airbus A330-322	096	OO-SFX
			9M-MKZ
			F-WWKP
CS-TMU	Beech 1900D	UE-335	N23269
			EC-GZL
			N23269
CS-TMV	Beech 1900D	UE-341	N23309
			EC-HBG
			N23309
CS-TMW	Airbus A320-214	1667	F-WWII
CS-TMX	Lockheed 1011-385-3 Tristar	1206	N765DA
			C-GAGG
CS-TMY	Short SD.3-60	SH.3632	G-BLCP
			OY-MMA
			(SE-KSU)
			OY-MMA
			EI-BYU
			OY-MMA
			G-BLCP
CS-TNA	Airbus A320-211	185	F-WWDB

CS-TNB	Airbus A320-211	191	F-WWDH
CS-TNE	Airbus A320-211	395	F-WWBJ
CS-TNF	Airbus A320-211	407	F-WWDH
CS-TNG	Airbus A320-214	945	F-WWIX
CS-TNH	Airbus A320-214	960	F-WWBH
CS-TNI	Airbus A320-214	982	F-WWDF
CS-TNJ	Airbus A320-214	1181	F-WWDS
CS-TNK	Airbus A320-214	1206	F-WWIL
CS-TNL	Airbus A320-214	1231	F-WWIJ
CS-TNM	Airbus A320-214	1799	F-WWIF
CS-TNN	Airbus A320-214	1816	F-WWID
CS-TOA	Airbus A340-312	041	F-WWJB
CS-TOB	Airbus A340-312	044	F-WWJN
CS-TOC	Airbus A340-312	079	F-WWJS
CS-TOD	Airbus A340-312	091	F-WWJA
CS-TPA	Fokker F.28-0100	11257	(N208BN)
			PH-LMF
			PH-EZA
CS-TPB	Fokker F.28-0100	11262	PH-EZE
CS-TPC	Fokker F.28-0100	11287	PH-LML
CS-TPD	Fokker F.28-0100	11317	PH-LNA
			PH-EZU
CS-TPE	Fokker F.28-0100	11342	PH-LNJ
CS-TPF	Fokker F.28-0100	11258	PH-FZD
			TR-LCR
			PH-EZD
CS-TPG	Embraer EMB-145EU	145014	PT-SYK
CS-TPH	Embraer EMB-145EU	145017	PT-SYN
CS-TPI	Embraer EMB-145EU	145031	PT-SYZ
CS-TPJ	Embraer EMB-145EU	145037	PT-SZD
CS-TPK	Embraer EMB-145EU	145041	PT-SZG
CS-TPL	Embraer EMB-145EU	145051	PT-SZQ
CS-TPM	Embraer EMB-145ER	145095	PT-SBR
CS-TPN	Embraer EMB-145ER	145099	PT-SBV
CS-TQA	Airbus A320-214	1439	EI-CWU
	(Res as OK-GEA for 2005)		OO-SNI
			F-WWBM
CS-TQB	Airbus A320-214	1450	EI-CWV
	(Res as OK-GEB for 2005)		OO-SNJ
			F-WWBX
CS-TQD	Airbus A320-214	870	HB-IJT
			F-WWBX
CS-TQF	Airbus A330-322	087	C-FRAP
			D-AERH
			F-WWKF
CS-TQG	Airbus A320-211	0022	N220AN
			VH-HYA
			F-WWDR
CS-TQH	Airbus A320-211	0023	N230AN
			VH-HYB
			F-WWDS
CS-TTA	Airbus A319-111	750	D-AVYO
CS-TTB	Airbus A319-111	755	D-AVYJ
CS-TTC	Airbus A319-111	763	D-AVYS
CS-TTD	Airbus A319-111	790	D-AVYC
CS-TTE	Airbus A319-111	821	D-AVYN
CS-TTF	Airbus A319-111	837	D-AVYL
CS-TTG	Airbus A319-111	906	D-AVYN
CS-TTH	Airbus A319-111	917	D-AVYJ
CS-TTI	Airbus A319-111	933	D-AVYP
CS-TTJ	Airbus A319-111	979	D-AVYM
CS-TTK	Airbus A319-111	1034	D-AVYL
CS-TTL	Airbus A319-111	1100	D-AVYX
CS-TTM	Airbus A319-111	1106	D-AVWR
CS-TTN	Airbus A319-111	1120	D-AVYI
CS-TTO	Airbus A319-111	1127	D-AVYH
CS-TTP	Airbus A319-111	1165	D-AVWV
CS-XAA(*)	Evans VP-1 Volksplane (Exp 4.87)	V-1766	
CS-XAB	Taylor JT.1 Monoplane	ASVP/JT1/1/P	
CS-XAC	Aero Designs Pulsar XP	292	
CS-XAD	Ultravia Pelican PL	503	
CS-XAF	Rans S-10 Sakota	0194169	
CS-XAG	Zenair CH-601HDS Zodiac	6-3238	
CS-XAI	JWGrega GN-1 Aircamper	2432	
CS-XAJ	Rans S-6ESCoyote II	0893533	
CS-XAK	Jabiru SK	P-138	
CS-XAL	Arnet Pereyra Aventura II	AP-2A0053	
CS-XAM	Velocity XLRGElite	3RX055	
	(Reported crashed & Dbf)		
CS-XAN	Ultravia Pelican VS	0621	
CS-XAO	Van's RV-6	25362	
CS-XAP	Alpi Aviation Pioneer 300S	28	
CS-XAQ	Van's RV-9A	90067	
CS-XAR	Dyn'Aero MCR-01	22	F-PMOR
			F-WQUH
CS-XHA	Rotorway Exec 162F	6102	N14897
CS-XHB	Rotorway Exec 162F	6103	
CS-XHC	Rotorway Exec 162F	6156	
CS-XHE	Rotorway Exec 162F	6273	
CS-X . .	Rand-Robinson KR-2	PFA/129-11068	G-BSKR

BALLOONS

CS-BAB(*)	Cameron O-105 HAFB (Exp 3.90)	1963	
CS-BAC(*)	Cameron N-65 HAFB (Exp 5.92)	1284	LX-HII
CS-BAE	Colt 90A HAFB	2355	
CS-BAF	Colt 90A HAFB	2522	
CS-BAG	Ultramagic M-77 HAFB	77/108	
CS-BAH	Cameron N-77 HAFB	1491	LX-ISP
CS-BAI	Cameron N-65 HAFB	3225	
CS-BAJ	Cameron C-80 HAFB	3834	
CS-BAK	Cameron N-77 HAFB	3841	
CS-BAL	Ultramagic M-105 HAFB	105/38	
CS-BAM	Cameron V-90 HAFB	3345	
CS-BAN	Cameron C-80 HAFB	3966	
CS-BAP	Sky Propane Cylinder SS HAFB	64	
CS-BAQ	Sky 65 HAFB	63	
CS-BAS	Cameron N-90 HAFB	4144	
CS-BAT	Sky 65 HAFB	095	
CS-BAU	Sky 65 HAFB	106	
CS-BAV	Sky 65 HAFB	108	
CS-BAW	Cameron C-80 Concept HAFB	4414	
CS-BAX	Ultramagic M-160 HAFB	160/19	
CS-BAY	Cameron N-77 HAFB	4356	
CS-BAZ	Cameron N-105 HAFB	4524	
CS-BBA	Cameron N-105 HAFB	4549	
CS-BBB	Ultramagic M-90 HAFB	90/31	
CS-BBC	Ultramagic M-65C HAFB	65/92	
CS-BBD	Cameron C-80 Concept HAFB	4897	
CS-BBE	Cameron C-80 Concept HAFB	10123	
CS-BBF	Ultramagic M-77 HAFB	77/206	
CS-BBG	Ultramagic M-77 HAFB	77/213	
CS-BBH	Ultramagic F-21 Gas Cylinder SS HAFB	F21/02	
CS-BBI	Ultramagic F-25 HAFB	F25/..	
CS-BBK	Ultramagic M-90 HAFB	90/..	
CS-B . .	Lindstrand LBL-210A HAFB	068	G-BVXZ

GLIDERS AND MOTOR-GLIDERS

CS-PAE(*)	Grunau Baby IIb (To Museu do Ar, Alverca)	3567	
CS-PAM(*)	EoN Baby 1 (Exp 3.79, stored)	EON/B/035	
CS-PAO(*)	EoN Baby 1 (Stored)	EON/B/034	
CS-PAP(*)	Grunau Baby III (Exp 9.81)	31-53	
CS-PAQ	Schleicher Rhönlerche II	381	
CS-PAR(*)	Schleicher Rhönlerche II (Exp 4.82)	382	
CS-PAS(*)	Schleicher Rhönlerche II (Stored)	802	
CS-PAV(*)	Schleicher Rhönlerche II (Exp 9.80)	820	
CS-PAZ	SZD-22C Mucha Standard	F-770	
CS-PBA	Schleicher Rhönlerche II	3087	
CS-PBB(*)	Scheibe Bergfalke II (Exp 12.86)	341	
CS-PBC(*)	Schleicher Rhönlerche II (Exp 5.89)	3084/Br	
CS-PBD	LET L-13 Blanik	173350	
CS-PBE	Siebert SIE-3	3010	
CS-PBG	Scheibe SF-27M-A	6327	CS-AXC D-KHOE
CS-PBH	Grob G.103A Twin II Acro	3733-K-48	D-6188
CS-PBJ	Centrair ASW-20FL	20154	F-CFLO
CS-PBK-C1	LAK-12 Lietuva	6226	
CS-PBL-C2	LAK-12 Lietuva	6231	
CS-PBM	LET L-13 Blanik	827421	OK-2730
CS-PBN-C3	PZL PW-5 Smyk (Crashed 24.4.03)	17.09.021	
CS-PBP	Grob G.103A Twin II Acro	3708-K-44	D-3789
CS-PBQ	LET L-13 Blanik	027325	DOSAAF
CS-PBR-C4	PZL PW-5 Smyk	17.11.020	
CS-PBS-C5	PZL PW-5 Smyk	17.12.004	SP-3640
CS-PBT-C6	PZL PW-5 Smyk	17.12.009	(SP-3645)?
CS-PBU	Grob G.102 Astir CS Jeans	2155	D-4894
CS-PBV-ZE	LAK-17A	109	
CS-PBW-C17	LAK-17A	110	
CS-PBX	PZL PW-6UGapa	78.02.08	
CS-PBY	LET L-13 Blanik (Wreck noted 5.00)	173220	
CS-PBZ	Schleicher ASK 21	21395	FAP:10102/1002
CS-PCB	PZL PW-5 Smyk	17.03.014	EC-GLQ
CS-PCC	Schleicher ASK 21	21410	FAP:10104/1004
CS-PCD-K17	Glaser-Dirks DG-300 Elan	3E-36	F-CFVK
CS-PCE-TW	Glaser-Dirks DG-300 Elan	3E-416	OE-5510
CS-PRP	LET L-13 Blanik	174222	DOSAAF

MICROLIGHTS

CS-UAA	Quicksilver MX-II HP	1265	
CS-UAB	Quicksilver MX-II HP	1266	
CS-UAC	Cosmos Bidulm 53	B0032	
CS-UAD	Quicksilver MXL-II	1267	
CS-UAE	Quicksilver MX Sprint II	131	
CS-UAF	Quicksilver MXL-II	1291	
CS-UAH	Quicksilver MXL-II	1349	
CS-UAI	Quicksilver GT-400	1343	
CS-UAJ	Quicksilver MXL-II Sport	1697	
CS-UAK	Whittaker MW-5K Sorcerer	5K-0010-02	
CS-UAL	Whittaker MW-5K Sorcerer	5K-0013-02	
CS-UAO	Ferrari Tucano	0065	
CS-UAP	Quicksilver GTS-400	1287	
CS-UAQ	Allferrari Cormorano	1197	
CS-UAT	Quicksilver MXL-II	1157	
CS-UAU	Quicksilver MXL-II Sport	165	
CS-UAW	Quicksilver MXL-II	1517	
CS-UAX	Quicksilver MXL-II	1452	
CS-UAY	Whittaker MW-5	5K-0016-02	
CS-UAZ	Cosmos Hermes 15	B432	
CS-UBA	Quicksilver MXL-II	191	
CS-UBB	Type unknown	unkn	
CS-UBF	Denney Kitfox	unkn	
CS-UBG	Ultralair Weedhopper JC-31 Premier AX3	0112856	
CS-UBH	Ultralair Weedhopper JC-31 Premier AX3	0112855	
CS-UBI	Cobra AJS-2000	R644988	
CS-UBJ	Quicksilver MX Sprint II	041	
CS-UBK	Quicksilver GTS-500	0030	
CS-UBL	Quicksilver MXL-II	189	
CS-UBU	Quicksilver MXL-II Sport	190	
CS-UBV	Quicksilver GT-500	0094	
CS-UBW	Poari I	1	
CS-UBX	Quicksilver GTS-400	1242	
CS-UBY	Cosmos Turbo 6	675	
CS-UBZ	Quicksilver MXL-II	2335	
CS-UCA	Ultralair Weedhopper AX3-503D (See CS-UDA, same c/n quoted)	B1112965	
CS-UCB	Ultralair Weedhopper AX-2	B1102953	
CS-UCC	Ultralair Weedhopper JC-24S	1101149	
CS-UCD	Air Création Safari GT BI/SX16	91-252	
CS-UCE	Air Création Safari GT BI/SX16	unkn	
CS-UCF	Air Création Safari GT BI 503	8-91-282	
CS-UCG	Air Création Safari GT BI 503	8-91-288	
CS-UCI	Quicksilver MXL-II Sport	82	
CS-UCJ	Quicksilver MXL-II Sport	255	
CS-UCK	Quicksilver MXL-II Sport	165	
CS-UCL	Quicksilver MXL-II Sport	867	
CS-UCM	Air Création Safari GT BI 503/1	10-91-325	
CS-UCN	Air Création Safari GT BI 503/1	91-285	
CS-UCO	Air Création Safari GT BI 503/1	8-91-328	
CS-UCQ	Quicksilver GT-500	unkn	
CS-UCR	Cosmos Chronos	B-650	
CS-UCS	Cosmos Bidulm 53	unkn	
CS-UCT	Cosmos Bidulm 53	unkn	
CS-UCV	Cosmos Turbo 163	B-522	
CS-UCX	Ultralair Weedhopper Europa II	302	
CS-UCY	Tango II GT Turbo 163	39142	
CS-UCZ	Ferrari Tucano	0055	
CS-UDA	Ultralair Weedhopper Premier AX3 (See CS-UCA, same c/n quoted)	B1112965	
CS-UDB	Ultralair Weedhopper AX2-503	B1112962	
CS-UDC	Ultralair Weedhopper AX2-503	B1112963	
CS-UDD	Ultralair Weedhopper AX2	B1112964	
CS-UDE	Cosmos Chronos 14	B-731	
CS-UDF	Cosmos Chronos	B-730	
CS-UDG	Cosmos Chronos 16	B-725	
CS-UDJ	Kolb Twin Star Mk.II	TS-III	
CS-UDK	Ultralair Weedhopper AX-3	B2043007	
CS-UDL	Ultralair Weedhopper AX-3	B2033000	
CS-UDM	Ultralair Weedhopper JC-31 Premier AX3	B2032999	
CS-UDN	Rans S-4 Coyote 1	91162	
CS-UDO	Ferrari Tucano	199	
CS-UDR	Cosmos Chronos 14	B-784	
CS-UDS	Cosmos Chronos	7794	
CS-UDT	Cosmos Chronos	780	
CS-UDU	Cosmos Chronos 16	781	
CS-UDV	Cosmos Chronos 16	774	
CS-UDW	Epervier UL-582	6	
CS-UDX	Quicksilver MXL-II	unkn	
CS-UDY	Ultralair Weedhopper AX-3	B2083054	
CS-UDZ	Daxiwings Falcon XP B2	01	
CS-UEB	Ultralair Weedhopper AX-2	B3013091	
CS-UEC	Ultralair Weedhopper AX-3	B3023092	
CS-UED	Air Création GT BI Q18	04-92-105	
CS-UEE	Air Création GT BI Q18	03-02-95	
CS-UEG	Air Création Safari GT-BI/SX-16	10 92-264	
CS-UEH	Quicksilver MXL-II Sport	342	
CS-UEJ	Comco Ikarus Fox-C22	9211-3479	
CS-UEK	Daxiwings Falcon XP B2	600238	
CS-UEL	Volero Volero	V4924	
CS-UEM	Quicksilver GT-500	207	
CS-UEN	Falcon B1	SMO 16	
CS-UEO	Quicksilver GT-500	200	
CS-UEP	Dynali Chickinox Kot Kot	2992-P4	
CS-UEQ	Dynali Chickinox Kot Kot	2992-P5	
CS-UES	Quicksilver MXL-II Sport	340	
CS-UET	Comco Ikarus Fox-C22	4100-5177	
CS-UEV	Quicksilver MXL-II Sport	384	
CS-UEW	Cosmos Hermes 16	B-670	
CS-UEX	TLUltralight TL-32 Typhoon	93A001	
CS-UEZ	Quicksilver MXL-II Sport	303	
CS-UFA	Quicksilver MXL-II Sport	297	
CS-UFB	Quad City Challenger II	CH2-1092-894	
CS-UFC	Comco Ikarus Fox-C22	9306-3524	
CS-UFD	Comco Ikarus Fox-C22	4170-9983	
CS-UFE	Sunrise II	1	D-MXCL
CS-UFF	Synairgie Pelican 21	000125D	
CS-UFG	Cosmos Chronos	B-769	
CS-UFH	Tango II GT	7861	
CS-UFI	Synairgie Pelican 21	01	

CS-UFJ	Jose Figueira Probe I 43	CA-001E
CS-UFK	Quicksilver MXL-II Sport	488
CS-UFL	Quicksilver MXL-II Sport (Cr 27.11.04)	489
CS-UFM	Ferrari Tucano	0242
CS-UFN	A.L.A. JF 91	35
CS-UFO	Falcon DXW	3
CS-UFP	Comco Ikarus Fox-C22	9311-3553
CS-UFQ	Comco Ikarus Fox-C22	9311-3554
CS-UFR	Quicksilver GT-500	232
CS-UFS	Quicksilver GT-500	231
CS-UFT	Ferrari ATAS-21	258
CS-UFU	Rans S-6ES Coyote II	0792330
CS-UFV	Cosmos Chronos 16	21012
CS-UFW	Cosmos Chronos 16	unkn
CS-UFX	Cosmos Chronos 16	865
CS-UFY	Cosmos Chronos 16	21020
CS-UFZ	Rans S-6ES Coyote II	0792331
CS-UGA	Rans S-6ES Coyote II	0293448
CS-UGB	Rans S-6ES Coyote II	0593501
CS-UGC	Rans S-6ES Coyote II	0493479
CS-UGD	Ultralair Weedhopper AX-3	C3113178
CS-UGE	Quicksilver MXL-II	527
CS-UGF	Rans S-6ES Coyote II	0493478
CS-UGG	Tecnam P.92 Echo	2
CS-UGH	Albatros AE-209	54
CS-UGI	Chickinox Kot-Kot	4091-P3
CS-UGJ	Chickinox Kot-Kot	4692-P10
CS-UGK	Chickinox Kot-Kot	4692-P15
CS-UGL	Ultralair Weedhopper AX-3	12595
CS-UGM	Rans S-6ES Coyote II	0593506
CS-UGN	Murphy Maverick	072M
CS-UGO	Comco Ikarus Fox-C22	9408-3618
CS-UGP	Skycraft AJS-2000	9040
CS-UGQ	Chickinox Kot-Kot	4692-P12
CS-UGR	Rans S-6ES Coyote II	0494608
CS-UGS	Ferrari Tucano	P305
CS-UGT	Rans S-6ES Coyote II	0195722
CS-UGU	Quicksilver MXL-II	1351
CS-UGV	Rans S-6ES Coyote II	0493476
CS-UGW	SMAN Pétrel	11
CS-UGY	Tecnam P.92 Echo	98
CS-UGZ	Rans S-6XL Coyote II	0195727
CS-UHA	Air Création GT-BI/SX	3984635
CS-UHB	Tecnam P.92 Echo	134
CS-UHC	Tecnam P.92 Echo	135
CS-UHD	Ferrari Tucano	P-306
CS-UHE	Tecnam P.92 Echo	146
CS-UHF	Ultralair Weedhopper AX-3-16	E-4103227
CS-UHG	Quicksilver MX-IISprint	273
CS-UHH	Air Création Safari GT-BI	192026
CS-UHI	Rans S-6ES Coyote II	0495800
CS-UHJ	Ferrari Tucano	P-307
CS-UHK	Quicksilver MX-IISprint	165
CS-UHL	Quicksilver GT-400	1240
CS-UHM	Campana AN-400	21
CS-UHN	Rans S-6S Coyote II	1193558
CS-UHO	Rans S-12XL Airaile	01960683
CS-UHP	Rans S-6XL Coyote II	0495788
CS-UHQ	Ultralair Weedhopper AX-3-16	E-4083220
CS-UHR	Jabiru SK	0102
CS-UHS	Comco Ikarus Fox-C22	9610-3719
CS-UHT	Comco Ikarus Fox-C22 floatplane	9610-3718
CS-UHU	Jabiru SK	P0103
CS-UHV	Jabiru SK	P0104
CS-UHW	Rans S-12XL Airaile	01960678
CS-UHX	Comco Ikarus Fox-C22	9405-3604
CS-UHY	Rans S-12XL Airaile	01960673
CS-UHZ	Ultralair Weedhopper AX-3-16	E-4103219
CS-UIA	Rans S-6ES Coyote II	1191236
CS-UIB	Best Off Sky Ranger	0195
CS-UIC	Ultravia Pelican VS	635
CS-UID	Tecnam P.96 Golf	007
CS-UIE	Jabiru SK	P-135
CS-UIF	Jabiru SK	P-136
CS-UIG	Jabiru SK	P-137
CS-UIH	Quicksilver MXL-II	443
CS-UII	Rans S-12XL Airaile	11960756
CS-UIJ	Tecnam P.92 Echo	268
CS-UIK	Best Off Sky Ranger	SK 0115497
CS-UIL	Jabiru SK	P-149
CS-UIM	Jabiru SK	P-152
CS-UIN	Jabiru SK	P-153
CS-UIO	Rans S-6ES Coyote IIXL	"11869061"
	(C/n incorrect. Possibly 11961061 ex N7214W)	
CS-UIP	Quicksilver MXL-IISport	773
CS-UIQ	Jabiru SK	P-180
CS-UIR	Raj Hamsa X'Air 502 TPE	363
CS-UIS	Tecnam P.96 Golf	028
CS-UIT	Tecnam P.96 Golf	029
CS-UIU	Aviakit Hermes	"1-800-8"
CS-UIW	Tecnam P.96 Light	040
CS-UIX	Aviatika MAI-890	0051
CS-UIY	Tecnam P.96 Light	030
CS-UIZ	Raj Hamsa X'Air	349
CS-UJA	Aviasud AE209 Albatros	11
CS-UJB	Jabiru SK	P-179
CS-UJC	Jabiru SK	P-181

CS-UJD	Jabiru SK	P-180
CS-UJE	Quicksilver MXL-IISport	772
CS-UJF	Rans S-6ES Coyote IIXL	12961080
CS-UJG	Rans S-6ES Coyote IIXL	10971083
CS-UJH	Quicksilver GT-400	1436
CS-UJI	Tecnam P.96 Light	074
CS-UJJ	Tecnam P.96 Light	073
CS-UJK	Quicksilver MXL-IISport	775
CS-UJL	Raj Hamsa X'Air	398
CS-UJM	Quicksilver "N/PT"	1290
CS-UJN	Raj Hamsa X'Air 502 TPE	370
CS-UJO	Raj Hamsa X'Air 502 TPE	376
CS-UJP	Raj Hamsa X'Air 502 TPE	384
CS-UJQ	SG.2 Storm 300P	0012P
CS-UJR	Tecnam P.96 Light	085
CS-UJS	DEA Yuma	11298 KS
CS-UJT	Nando Groppo Groppino	058
CS-UJU	Jabiru SK	P-182
CS-UJV	Tecnam P.92 Echo	415
CS-UJW	Tecnam P.96 Golf	084
CS-UJX	Tecnam P.92 Echo	416
CS-UJY	Tecnam P.92 Echo	457
CS-UJZ	TL Ultralight TL-96 Star	99S38
CS-UKA	Best Off Sky Ranger	SKR 00.01.02
CS-UKB	Microleve Corsario Mk.IV	203
CS-UKC	Jabiru SK	P-261
CS-UKD	Jabiru SK	P-271
CS-UKE	Jabiru SK	P-276
CS-UKF	TL Ultralight TL-96 Star	048
CS-UKG	TL Ultralight TL-96 Star	058
CS-UKH	Best Off Sky Ranger	SKR 00.06.049
CS-UKI	Daxiwings Falcon XP B2	FW/82/04/00/001
CS-UKJ	Air Création GT-BI/16SX	03-1991
CS-UKK	Air Création GT-BI/XP15	123-9312
CS-UKL	Best Off Sky Ranger	59
CS-UKM	Quicksilver GT-500	500-0242
CS-UKN	Best Off Sky Ranger	00.1060
CS-UKO	Quicksilver MXL-IISport	779
CS-UKP	Raj Hamsa X'Air 602 TPE	593
CS-UKQ	Air Création GT-BI/XP15	0293038
CS-UKR	Tecnam P.92RG	009
CS-UKS	Tecnam P.92 Echo	538
CS-UKT	Tecnam P.96 Light	4426806
CS-UKU	ATEC Zephyr 2000	2230600
CS-UKV	Vol Mediterrani JLEsqual VM-1P	056
CS-UKW	Best Off Sky Ranger	0104084
CS-UKX	Tecnam P.96 Light	174
CS-UKY	Quicksilver MXL-IISport	827
CS-UKZ	Vol Mediterrani JLEsqual VM-1P	057
CS-ULA	Loehle Sport Parasol	SP 0973263 LE
CS-ULB	Best Off Sky Ranger	SKR 12081
CS-ULC	Tecnam P.92 Echo	593
CS-ULD	Raj Hamsa X'Air 602	591
CS-ULE	Raj Hamsa X'Air 602	620
CS-ULF	Tecnam P.92 Echo	592
CS-ULG	Tecnam P.92 Echo	375
CS-ULH	Quicksilver MXL-IISport	780
CS-ULI	Moyes Dragonfly	551
CS-ULJ	Best Off Sky Ranger	SKR 0109138
CS-ULK	Best Off Sky Ranger	SKR 0204189
CS-ULL	Vol Mediterrani Esqual VM-1P	P-004
CS-ULM	Kappa 77 KP-2 Sova	5966G
CS-ULN	Best Off Sky Ranger	SKR 0205200
CS-ULO	Best Off Sky Ranger	SKR 0205219
CS-ULP	Rans S-6XL Coyote	0495790
CS-ULQ	Vol Mediterrani Esqual VM-1P	P-061
CS-ULR	Quicksilver MXL-II Sport	801
CS-ULS	Jabiru SK	P475
CS-ULT	ATEC Zephyr 2000	7641002A
CS-ULU	Zenair CH-601UL Zodiac	6-3656
CS-ULV	Road Air Flamingo	044
CS-ULW	Quicksilver MXL-II Sport	529
CS-ULX	Tecnam P.92 Echo	698
CS-ULY	Best Off Sky Ranger	SKR 0209230
CS-ULZ	Aerospool WT-9 Dynamic	DY 021/2002
CS-UMA	Fantasy Air Allegro 2000P	02-606
CS-UMB	Fantasy Air Allegro 2000P	02-607
CS-UMC	Tecnam P.92 Echo	730
CS-UMD	Aerospool WT-9 Dynamic	DY 024/2003
CS-UME	Road Air Flamingo	035
CS-UMF	DTA Voyager II	A506224
CS-UMG	Quicksilver MXL-II Sport	869
CS-UMH	Best Off Sky Ranger	SKR 0204175
CS-UMI	Aerospool WT-9 Dynamic	DY 031/2003
CS-UMJ	Evektor EV.97 Eurostar	2003-1605
CS-UMK	Aerospool WT-9 Dynamic	DY 030/2003
CS-UML	Quicksilver MXL-II Sport	0861
CS-UMM	Kappa 77 Sova	79931
CS-UMN	Quicksilver MXL-II Sport	879
CS-UMO	Quicksilver MXL-II Sport	880
CS-UMP	Alpha Bravo Funk FK-9	AB 09-101
CS-UMQ	Raj Hamsa X'Air 602TPE	334
CS-UMR	ATEC Zephyr 2000	Z 210500A
CS-UMS	Moragón M-1	M1-03-001P
CS-UMT	Evektor EV.97 Eurostar	2003-1615
CS-UMU	Evektor EV.97 Eurostar	2003-1803
CS-UMV	Moragón M-1	M1-03-002P

CS-UMW	TL-2000 Sting	03ST52	
CS-UMX	ATEC Zephyr 2000	Z 8400903A	
CS-UMY	Tecnam P.92 Echo	65	
CS-UMZ	Pelicano Sea Max P22	004	PU-PEL
CS-UNA	EET Sky Ranger	SKR 0209239	
CS-UNB	Alpha Bravo Funk FK-9	AB 09-102	
CS-UNC	SG Aviation Storm RG-P	100122-P-01	
CS-UND	Tecnam P.2002 Sierra	unkn	
CS-UNE	SG Aviation Rally 105	unkn	
CS-UNG	ATEC Zephyr 2000	unkn	
CS-UNH	ATEC Zephyr 2000	unkn	
CS-UNN	Pelicano Sea Max P22	009	
CS-UNQ	Pelicano Sea Max P22	unkn	
CS-U . .	Dragon Fly	unkn	I-2692
CS-U . .	Light Aero Avid Flyer	329	G-BRNS
CS-U . .	Light Aero Avid Flyer	908/PFA/189-12023	G-BTMS
CS-U . .	Melvin/ Denney Kitfox II	615	N90EV
CS-U . .	Solar Wings Pegasus XL-R	SW-WA-1551	G-MYCH

D - GERMANY

CLASS A : Aircraft of over 20 metric tonnes (20,000 kgs)

Regn.	Type	C/n	Prev.Id.
D-AAAC	Fokker F.27 Friendship 500	10448	HB-ITY D-AAAC HB-ITY PH-JLN F-BSUN (PH-FPY)
D-ABAA(2)	Boeing 737-76Q	30271	N271CH PR-SAH N314ML N1786B
D-ABAB(3)	Boeing 737-76Q	30277	N277CH PR-SAA
D-ABAC(3)	Boeing 737-86J	30501	
D-ABAD(3)	Boeing 737-86J	30876	
D-ABAE(2)	Boeing 737-86J	30877	N1786B
D-ABAF(4)	Boeing 737-86J	30878	N1787B
D-ABAG(3)	Boeing 737-86J	30879	
D-ABAH(2)	Boeing 737-46J	27826	
D-ABAI	Boeing 737-46J	28038	
D-ABAK(3)	Boeing 737-46J	28271	
D-ABAL	Boeing 737-46J	28334	
D-ABAM(3)	Boeing 737-46J	28867	
D-ABAN(3)	Boeing 737-86J	28068	N35153
D-ABAO	Boeing 737-86J	28069	N5573B
D-ABAP(2)	Boeing 737-86J	28070	
D-ABAQ(2)	Boeing 737-86J	28071	
D-ABAR(2)	Boeing 737-86J	28072	N1786B
D-ABAS(4)	Boeing 737-86J	28073	N1795B
D-ABAT(2)	Boeing 737-46J	29120	N1786B
D-ABAU	Boeing 737-46J	29121	N1786B
D-ABAV(2)	Boeing 737-86J	30498	N1787B
D-ABAW(2)	Boeing 737-86J	30062	N1786B
D-ABAX(2)	Boeing 737-86J	30063	
D-ABAY(2)	Boeing 737-86J	30499	
D-ABAZ(2)	Boeing 737-86J	30500	
D-ABBA	Boeing 737-86J	30570	
D-ABBB	Boeing 737-86J	32624	
D-ABBC	Boeing 737-86J	32625	
D-ABBD	Boeing 737-86J	30880	
D-ABBE(2)	Boeing 737-86J	30881	
D-ABBF	Boeing 737-86J	32917	
D-ABBG	Boeing 737-86J	32918	
D-ABBH	Boeing 737-86J	32919	
D-ABBI(2)	Boeing 737-86J	32920	
D-ABBJ	Boeing 737-86Q	30286	N1787B
D-ABBK	Boeing 737-8BK	33013	
D-ABBL	Boeing 737-85F	28821	F-GRNC N1786B
D-ABBM	Boeing 737-85F	28823	F-GRNA N1795B N1784B
D-ABBN	Boeing 737-76Q	30293	
D-ABBO	Boeing 737-86J	30827	
D-ABBP	Boeing 737-86J	29641	
D-ABBQ	Boeing 737-86N	28608	EC-HHG N1786B
D-ABBR	Boeing 737-85F (Reservation .05)	28825	SE-DVU N501GX N1784B N1787B
D-ABCD	Canadair CL.600-2B16 Challenger IV	5565	N604KB C-GLKS
D-ABEA(2)	Boeing 737-330	24565	
D-ABEB(3)	Boeing 737-330	25148	
D-ABEC(2)	Boeing 737-330	25149	
D-ABED(2)	Boeing 737-330	25215	
D-ABEE	Boeing 737-330	25216	
D-ABEF(3)	Boeing 737-330	25217	
D-ABEH(2)	Boeing 737-330	25242	
D-ABEI (2)	Boeing 737-330	25359	(D-ABJK)
D-ABEK(2)	Boeing 737-330	25414	(D-ABJL)
D-ABEL(3)	Boeing 737-330	25415	(D-ABJM)
D-ABEM(2)	Boeing 737-330	25416	(D-ABJN)
D-ABEN(2)	Boeing 737-330	26428	(D-ABJP)
D-ABEO(2)	Boeing 737-330	26429	(D-ABJR)
D-ABEP(2)	Boeing 737-330	26430	(D-ABJS)
D-ABER(2)	Boeing 737-330	26431	TC-SUK D-ABER(2) (D-ABJT)
D-ABES(2)	Boeing 737-330	26432	(D-ABJU)
D-ABET(2)	Boeing 737-330	27903	(D-ABKM)
D-ABEU(2)	Boeing 737-330	27904	(D-ABKN)
D-ABEW(2)	Boeing 737-330	27905	(D-ABKP)
D-ABIA(2)	Boeing 737-530 (Reservation 1.05)	24815	OK-SWY D-ABIA(2) N3521N
D-ABIB(2)	Boeing 737-530	24816	OK-SWZ D-ABIB(2)
D-ABIC(2)	Boeing 737-530	24817	
D-ABID(2)	Boeing 737-530	24818	
D-ABIE(2)	Boeing 737-530	24819	
D-ABIF(2)	Boeing 737-530	24820	
D-ABIH(2)	Boeing 737-530	24821	
D-ABII (2)	Boeing 737-530	24822	
D-ABIK(2)	Boeing 737-530	24823	
D-ABIL(2)	Boeing 737-530	24824	
D-ABIM(2)	Boeing 737-530	24937	
D-ABIN(2)	Boeing 737-530	24938	
D-ABIO(2)	Boeing 737-530	24939	
D-ABIR(3)	Boeing 737-530	24941	
D-ABIS(2)	Boeing 737-530	24942	
D-ABIT(2)	Boeing 737-530	24943	
D-ABIU(2)	Boeing 737-530	24944	
D-ABIW(2)	Boeing 737-530	24945	
D-ABIX(2)	Boeing 737-530	24946	
D-ABIY(2)	Boeing 737-530	25243	
D-ABIZ(2)	Boeing 737-530	25244	
D-ABJA	Boeing 737-530	25270	
D-ABJB	Boeing 737-530	25271	
D-ABJC	Boeing 737-530	25272	
D-ABJD	Boeing 737-530	25309	
D-ABJE	Boeing 737-530	25310	
D-ABJF	Boeing 737-530	25311	
D-ABJH	Boeing 737-530	25357	
D-ABJI	Boeing 737-530	25358	
D-ABLC	Airbus A321-211	1012	F-WQRS G-CBOI OO-SUC D-AVZH
D-ABNF	Boeing 757-230	25140	
D-ABOA	Boeing 757-330	29016	N757X
D-ABOB(2)	Boeing 757-330	29017	N6067B
D-ABOC(2)	Boeing 757-330	29015	N6069B
D-ABOE	Boeing 757-330	29012	N1012N
D-ABOF(2)	Boeing 757-330	29013	
D-ABOG(2)	Boeing 757-330	29014	N1786B
D-ABOH(2)	Boeing 757-330	30030	N1787B
D-ABOI	Boeing 757-330	29018	N1002R
D-ABOJ	Boeing 757-330	29019	
D-ABOK(2)	Boeing 757-330	29020	N1795B
D-ABOL(2)	Boeing 757-330	29021	
D-ABOM(2)	Boeing 757-330	29022	
D-ABON(2)	Boeing 757-300	29023	
D-ABTA	Boeing 747-430	24285	
D-ABTB	Boeing 747-430	24286	
D-ABTC	Boeing 747-430	24287	
D-ABTD	Boeing 747-430	24715	
D-ABTE	Boeing 747-430	24966	N6046P
D-ABTF	Boeing 747-430	24967	
D-ABTH	Boeing 747-430	25047	
D-ABTK	Boeing 747-430	29871	(D-ABVI (2))
D-ABTL	Boeing 747-430	29872	(D-ABVG)
D-ABTM	Boeing 747-430 (On order)	33430	
D-ABTN	Boeing 747-430 (On order)	33431	
D-ABTO	Boeing 747-430 (On order)	33432	
D-ABTP	Boeing 747-430 (On order)	33433	
D-ABUA(2)	Boeing 767-330ER	26991	
D-ABUB(2)	Boeing 767-330ER	26987	
D-ABUC(2)	Boeing 767-330ER	26992	
D-ABUD(2)	Boeing 767-330ER	26983	
D-ABUE(2)	Boeing 767-330ER	26984	N1788B
D-ABUF(2)	Boeing 767-330ER	26985	
D-ABUH(2)	Boeing 767-330ER	26986	
D-ABUI (2)	Boeing 767-330ER	26988	
D-ABUZ	Boeing 767-330ER	25209	N634TW D-ABUZ
D-ABVA	Boeing 747-430	23816	N6055X
D-ABVB	Boeing 747-430	23817	N5573S
D-ABVC	Boeing 747-430	24288	

D-ABVD	Boeing 747-430	24740	N60668
D-ABVF	Boeing 747-430	24761	N6018N
D-ABVH	Boeing 747-430	25045	
D-ABVK	Boeing 747-430	25046	N6009F
D-ABVL	Boeing 747-430	26425	N60659
D-ABVM(2)	Boeing 747-430	29101	(V8-AC2)
D-ABVN	Boeing 747-430	26427	
D-ABVP	Boeing 747-430	28284	
D-ABVR	Boeing 747-430	28285	
D-ABVS	Boeing 747-430	28286	
D-ABVT	Boeing 747-430	28287	
D-ABVU	Boeing 747-430	29492	
D-ABVW	Boeing 747-430	29493	
D-ABVX	Boeing 747-430	29868	
D-ABVY	Boeing 747-430	29869	
D-ABVZ	Boeing 747-430	29870	
D-ABWH	Boeing 737-330	24284	
D-ABXI	Boeing 737-330 (Res as PR-GLF .04)	23529	LZ-BOG
			D-ABXI
D-ABXK	Boeing 737-330 (Res as PR-GLJ .04)	23530	LZ-BOH
			D-ABXK
D-ABXL	Boeing 737-330	23531	
D-ABXM	Boeing 737-330	23871	
D-ABXN	Boeing 737-330	23872	
D-ABXO	Boeing 737-330	23873	
D-ABXP	Boeing 737-330	23874	
D-ABXR	Boeing 737-330	23875	
D-ABXS	Boeing 737-330	24280	
D-ABXT	Boeing 737-330	24281	
D-ABXU	Boeing 737-330	24282	
D-ABXW	Boeing 737-330	24561	
D-ABXX	Boeing 737-330	24562	
D-ABXY	Boeing 737-330	24563	
D-ABXZ	Boeing 737-330	24564	
D-ABYX	Boeing 747-230B Combi	22670	
D-ABZA	Boeing 747-230B Combi	23287	N6038E
D-ABZD	Boeing 747-230B Combi (Reservation 2.03)	23407	N6005C
D-ACCC	Aérospatiale/Alenia ATR-72-212	379	ZK-JSY
	(Reservation 3.05)		D-ACCC
			N69901
			F-WWLD
D-ACFA	BAe.146 Series 200	E-2200	G-BTVT
			G-6-200
			(I-FLRZ)
D-ACHA	Canadair CL.600-2B19 Regional Jet	7378	C-FMLF
D-ACHB	Canadair CL.600-2B19 Regional Jet	7391	C-GGKF
			C-FVAZ
D-ACHC	Canadair CL.600-2B19 Regional Jet	7394	C-GGKD
			C-FMLU
D-ACHD	Canadair CL.600-2B19 Regional Jet	7403	C-FMNB
D-ACHE	Canadair CL.600-2B19 Regional Jet	7407	C-FMLB
D-ACHF	Canadair CL.600-2B19 Regional Jet	7431	C-FMLI
D-ACHG	Canadair CL.600-2B19 Regional Jet	7439	C-FMMX
D-ACHH	Canadair CL.600-2B19 Regional Jet	7449	C-FMOS
D-ACHI	Canadair CL.600-2B19 Regional Jet	7464	C-FMKV
D-ACHK	Canadair CL.600-2B19 Regional Jet	7499	C-FMLI
D-ACIR(2)	Embraer EMB.145	145230	PT-SHT
D-ACJA	Canadair CL.600-2B19 Regional Jet	7122	C-FMKT
D-ACJB	Canadair CL.600-2B19 Regional Jet	7128	C-FMMQ(3)
D-ACJC	Canadair CL.600-2B19 Regional Jet	7130	C-FMMW(3)
D-ACJD	Canadair CL.600-2B19 Regional Jet	7135	C-FMNH(3)
D-ACJE	Canadair CL.600-2B19 Regional Jet	7165	C-FMNH(4)
D-ACJF	Canadair CL.600-2B19 Regional Jet	7200	
D-ACJG	Canadair CL.600-2B19 Regional Jet	7220	C-FMMW(4)
D-ACJH	Canadair CL.600-2B19 Regional Jet	7266	
D-ACJI	Canadair CL.600-2B19 Regional Jet	7282	C-FNMY
D-ACJJ	Canadair CL.600-2B19 Regional Jet	7298	
D-ACLA	Canadair CL.600-2B19 Regional Jet	7004	C-GRJJ
			(D-ARJA)
D-ACLB	Canadair CL.600-2B19 Regional Jet	7005	C-GRJN
			(D-ARJB)
D-ACLC	Canadair CL.600-2B19 Regional Jet	7006	C-GRJO
			(D-ARJC)
D-ACLD(2)	Canadair CL.600-2B19 Regional Jet	7009	C-FMKW
			C-GRJQ
D-ACLE(2)	Canadair CL.600-2B19 Regional Jet	7010	C-GRJW
D-ACLF	Canadair CL.600-2B19 Regional Jet	7015	C-FMLQ
			(D-ARJF)
D-ACLG(2)	Canadair CL.600-2B19 Regional Jet	7016	C-FMLS
D-ACLH(2)	Canadair CL.600-2B19 Regional Jet	7007	C-FMKV
D-ACLI (2)	Canadair CL.600-2B19 Regional Jet	7019	C-FMLV
D-ACLJ(2)	Canadair CL.600-2B19 Regional Jet	7021	C-FMML
D-ACLK(2)	Canadair CL.600-2B19 Regional Jet	7023	C-FMMQ
			(D-ACLG)
			(D-ARJG)
D-ACLL(2)	Canadair CL.600-2B19 Regional Jet	7024	C-FMMT
			(D-ACLH)
			(D-ARJH)
D-ACLM(2)	Canadair CL.600-2B19 Regional Jet	7025	C-FMMW
			(D-ACLI)
			(D-ARJI)
D-ACLP	Canadair CL.600-2B19 Regional Jet	7064	C-FMNX
D-ACLQ	Canadair CL.600-2B19 Regional Jet	7073	C-FMLF
D-ACLR	Canadair CL.600-2B19 Regional Jet	7086	C-FMLU
D-ACLS	Canadair CL.600-2B19 Regional Jet	7090	(N412SW)
D-ACLT	Canadair CL.600-2B19 Regional Jet	7093	(N413SW)
D-ACLU	Canadair CL.600-2B19 Regional Jet	7104	C-FXPI

D-ACLV	Canadair CL.600-2B19 Regional Jet	7113	C-FMMQ
D-ACLW	Canadair CL.600-2B19 Regional Jet	7114	C-FMMT
D-ACLY	Canadair CL.600-2B19 Regional Jet	7119	C-FMND
D-ACLZ	Canadair CL.600-2B19 Regional Jet	7121	C-FMNQ
D-ACPA	Canadair CL.600-2C10 Regional Jet 700	10012	C-GHZV
D-ACPB	Canadair CL.600-2C10 Regional Jet 700	10013	C-GHZY
D-ACPC	Canadair CL.600-2C10 Regional Jet 700	10014	C-GISW
D-ACPD	Canadair CL.600-2C10 Regional Jet 700	10015	C-GISZ
D-ACPE	Canadair CL.600-2C10 Regional Jet 700	10027	C-GIAZ
D-ACPF	Canadair CL.600-2C10 Regional Jet 700	10030	C-GIBI
D-ACPG	Canadair CL.600-2C10 Regional Jet 700	10034	C-GIBO
D-ACPH	Canadair CL.600-2C10 Regional Jet 700	10043	C-GHZY
D-ACPI	Canadair CL.600-2C10 Regional Jet 700	10046	C-GIAE
D-ACPJ	Canadair CL.600-2C10 Regional Jet 700	10040	C-GKCO
			C-GICN
D-ACPK	Canadair CL.600-2C10 Regional Jet 700	10063	C-GIBN
D-ACPL	Canadair CL.600-2C10 Regional Jet 700	10076	C-GIAE
D-ACPM	Canadair CL.600-2C10 Regional Jet 700	10080	C-FZRA
			C-GIAO
D-ACPN	Canadair CL.600-2C10 Regional Jet 700	10083	C-GIAU
D-ACPO	Canadair CL.600-2C10 Regional Jet 700	10085	C-FZYS
D-ACPP	Canadair CL.600-2C10 Regional Jet 700	10086	C-GIGJ
D-ACPQ	Canadair CL.600-2C10 Regional Jet 700	10091	C-GZJA
			C-GIBL
D-ACPR	Canadair CL.600-2C10 Regional Jet 700	10098	C- . . . .
D-ACPS	Canadair CL.600-2C10 Regional Jet 700	10100	C- . . . .
D-ACPT	Canadair CL.600-2C10 Regional Jet 700	10103	C-GJLZ
D-ACRA	Canadair CL.600-2B19 Regional Jet	7567	C-FMNX
D-ACRB	Canadair CL.600-2B19 Regional Jet	7570	C-FMOW
D-ACRC	Canadair CL.600-2B19 Regional Jet	7573	C-FMNQ
D-ACRD	Canadair CL.600-2B19 Regional Jet	7583	C-FMNB
D-ACRE	Canadair CL.600-2B19 Regional Jet	7607	C-FMML
D-ACRF	Canadair CL.600-2B19 Regional Jet	7619	C-FMLI
D-ACRG	Canadair CL.600-2B19 Regional Jet	7630	C-FMOW
D-ACRH	Canadair CL.600-2B19 Regional Jet	7738	C-FMLF
D-ACRI	Canadair CL.600-2B19 Regional Jet	7862	C-GZPA
			C-FMLT
D-ACRJ	Canadair CL.600-2B19 Regional Jet	7864	C-GZOZ
			C-FMMT
D-ACRK	Canadair CL.600-2B19 Regional Jet	7901	C-FVAZ
D-ACRL	Canadair CL.600-2B19 Regional Jet	7902	C-FMND
D-ACRM	Canadair CL.600-2B19 Regional Jet	7478	I-ADJA
	(Reservation 3.05)		C-GIDJ
			C-FMNY
D-ACRN	Canadair CL.600-2B19 Regional Jet	7486	I-ADJB
	(Reservation 3.05)		C-GIGH
			C-FMMB
D-ACRO	Canadair CL.600-2B19 Regional Jet	7494	I-ADJC
	(Reservation 3.05)		C-GIHG
			C-FMKV
D-ACRP	Canadair CL.600-2B19 Regional Jet	7625	I-ADJD
	(Reservation 3.05)		C-GJYW
D-ACRQ	Canadair CL.600-2B19 Regional Jet	7629	I-ADJE
	(Reservation 3.05)		C-GJYX
D-ADAM(4)	VFW-614 (ATTAS Test Airframe)	G-017	D-BABP
D-ADBN	Boeing 737-31S	29058	
D-ADBS	Boeing 737-31S	29116	
D-ADEP	Fokker F.27 Friendship 600	10318	OY-CCK
			G-BLMM
			P2-ANS
			VH-FNS
			PH-FKN
D-ADHA	Bombardier DHC-8Q-402	4028	C-GFBW
D-ADHB	Bombardier DHC-8Q-402	4029	C-GFCA
D-ADHC	Bombardier DHC-8Q-402	4045	C-GDIW
D-ADHD	Bombardier DHC-8Q-402	4056	C-GFYI
D-ADHE	Bombardier DHC-8Q-402	4066	C-GEOA
D-ADIA(2)	Boeing 737-36Q	30333	N1786B
D-ADIB(3)	Boeing 737-36Q	30334	N1786B
D-ADIC(2)	Boeing 737-36Q	30335	N1786B
D-ADIF	Boeing 737-3L9	25125	G-BZZB
			D-ADBG
			OY-MMW
			PP-SOR
			OY-MMW
D-ADIG	Boeing 737-3L9	26441	G-BZZA
			D-ADBA
			OY-MAL
D-ADIH	Boeing 737-3Y0	23921	N921NB
			F-GNFT
			PH-OZB
			9H-ADR
			PH-OZB
			5B-CIO
			F-GLTT
			EI-BTT
D-ADII	Boeing 737-329	23775	N775AA
			OO-SBZ
			(TF-ELR)
			OO-SBZ
D-ADIJ	Boeing 737-3M8	25041	TF-ELC
			OO-LTL
			EI-TVP
			OO-LTL
D-ADIK	Boeing 737-382 (Reservation 2004)	24365	9H-ADM
			CS-TIB
D-ADLH	Dornier 728-100 (Reservation 8.1.02)	7002	

D-ADLR	Gulfstream 550 (Reservation 3.05)	unkn	
D-ADNA	Airbus A319-133	1053	D-AVYN
D-ADNB	Bombardier CL.700-1A10 Global Express	9071	C-GHDQ
D-ADND	Canadair CL.600-2B16 Challenger	5403	N604DC C-GLWV
D-ADNE	Canadair CL.600-2B16 Challenger	5422	N605DC C-GLXU
D-ADOP	Fokker F.27 Friendship 600	10316	OY-BVF PH-SFG A40-FN HL5262 A40-FN G-AVDN PH-FKL
D-ADUP	Fokker F.27 Friendship 500	10686	OE-IPN N51OAW PH-EXF
D-AELE	Fokker F.27 Friendship 600	10477	OY-SLE S2-ABO PH-FRB PH-EXC PH-EXB
D-AELG	Fokker F.27 Friendship 600	10338	VR-BLZ PH-XPS LX-LGD PH-FLI
D-AELH	Fokker F.27 Friendship 600	10340	VR-BLX PH-SFJ A2-AEC F-BYAA OO-SBP PH-FLL
D-AELJ	Fokker F.27 Friendship 600	10342	F-BYAB OO-HLN PH-FLN OY-DNF PH-FLN
D-AELK	Fokker F.27 Friendship 600	10361	F-GCJV EC-BOE PH-FMH
D-AELL	Fokker F.27 Friendship 200	10414	PH-FON VT-ETE PH-FON TF-FLO HL5209 PH-FON
D-AELM	Fokker F.27 Friendship 600	10450	OY-CCL D-AARS OY-CCL EC-DSH 9M-MCY PH-FTR I-ALML PH-FTR TU-TIA TU-VAJ
D-AERF	Airbus A330-322	082	F-WWKD
D-AERK	Airbus A330-322	120	F-WWKN
D-AERQ	Airbus A330-322	127	F-WWKO
D-AERS	Airbus A330-322	171	C-FRAV F-GJSV C-FRAV D-AERS F-WWKM
D-AETV	Canadair CL.600-2B16 Challenger	5417	N605MP C-GLYA
D-AEVA	Dornier 728-100 (Reservation 8.1.02)	7001	
D-AEWA	BAe.146 Series 300	E-3163	G-BTJG HB-IXY G-BTJG G-3-163 G-BTJG EC-FIU EC-876 G-BTJG G-6-163 N885DV G-6-163
D-AEWB	BAe.146 Series 300	E-3183	G-BUHB G-6-183 G-BSYS G-6-183
D-AEWD	BAe.146 Series 200A	E-2069	OO-DJC G-UKLN OO-DJC (OO-DJY) G-BNKJ N407XV G-5-069 G-BNKJ G-5-069

D-AEWE	BAe.146 Series 200A	E-2077	OO-DJD G-UKRH OO-DJD (OO-DJZ) G-BRNG N408XV G-5-077
D-AEWG	Aérospatiale/Alenia ATR-72-212	347	F-WWEC
D-AEWH	Aérospatiale/Alenia ATR-72-212	359	F-WWEV
D-AEWI	Aérospatiale/Alenia ATR-72-212	404	F-WWLO
D-AEWK	Aérospatiale/Alenia ATR-72-212	446	F-WWEA
D-AEWL	BAe.146 Series 300 (Reservation 2.05)	E-3123	EI-DEV G-UKHP G-5-123
D-AEWM	BAe.146 Series 300	E-3125	G-UKSC G-5-125
D-AEWN	BAe.146 Series 300 (Reservation 2.05)	E-3158	G-UKRC G-6-158 G-BSMR G-6-158
D-AEWO	BAe.146 Series 300 (Reservation 2.05)	E-3162	G-UKAG G-6-162
D-AEWP	BAe.146 Series 300	E-3165	G-BSNR EC-FGT EC-807 G-6-165 G-BSNR N886DV G-BSNR (N886DV) G-6-165
D-AEWQ	BAe.146 Series 300	E-3203	G-BTTP G-6-203
D-AFFI	Fokker F.27-050	20272	PH-LXL
D-AGEA(2)	Boeing 737-322 (Permit 3.05)	23951	N319UA
D-AGEB(2)	Boeing 737-322 (Reservation .05)	24320	N352UA
D-AGEG	Boeing 737-35B	24237	UR-GAF D-AGEG G-EURP (D-AGED)
D-AGEJ	Boeing 737-35B	24221	OO-SEJ D-AGEJ PT-TEW D-AGEJ (OO-SLR) D-AGEJ OY-MMR G-CMMR OY-MMR N1786B
D-AGEK	Boeing 737-3M8	25015	SX-BLB D-AGEK PT-TET D-AGEK N799BB I-TEAI OO-LTF
D-AGEL	Boeing 737-75B	28110	N1791B
D-AGEN	Boeing 737-75B	28100	N1786B
D-AGEP	Boeing 737-75B	28102	N5573B
D-AGEQ	Boeing 737-75B	28103	
D-AGER	Boeing 737-75B	28107	N1002R
D-AGES	Boeing 737-75B	28108	
D-AGET	Boeing 737-75B	28109	
D-AGEU	Boeing 737-75B	28104	
D-AGMR	Boeing 737-430	27007	TC-SUS D-ABKL(2)
D-AGPA	Fokker F.28-0100	11276	PH-CXA N850US PH-ZCI PH-EZF
D-AGPB	Fokker F.28-0100	11278	PH-CXB N851US PH-EZG
D-AGPC	Fokker F.28-0100	11280	PH-CXC N852US PH-EZH
D-AGPD	Fokker F.28-0100	11281	PH-CXD N853US PH-EZI
D-AGPE	Fokker F.28-0100	11300	PH-CXE N862US PH-EZC
D-AGPF	Fokker F.28-0100	11303	PH-CXF N863US PH-EZD
D-AGPG	Fokker F.28-0100	11306	PH-CXG N864US PH-EZF
D-AGPH	Fokker F.28-0100	11308	PH-CXH N856US PH-EZI
D-AGPI	Fokker F.28-0100	11310	PH-CXI N866US PH-EZJ
D-AGPJ	Fokker F.28-0100	11312	PH-CXJ N867US PH-EZU

D-AGPK	Fokker F.28-0100	11313	PH-CXK
			N868US
			PH-EZR
D-AGPL	Fokker F.28-0100	11314	PH-CXL
			N869US
			PH-EZH
D-AGPM	Fokker F.28-0100	11331	PH-CXM
			N880US
			PH-EZT
D-AGPN	Fokker F.28-0100	11333	PH-CXN
			N881US
			PH-EZW
D-AGPO	Fokker F.28-0100	11334	PH-CXO
			N882US
			PH-EZD
D-AGPP	Fokker F.28-0100	11337	PH-CXP
			N883US
			PH-EZO
D-AGPQ	Fokker F.28-0100	11338	PH-CXQ
			N884US
			PH-EZS
D-AGPR	Fokker F.28-0100	11391	PH-CXR
			N896US
			PH-EZB
D-AGPS	Fokker F.28-0100	11399	PH-CXS
			N899US
			PH-EZL
D-AHEI	Canadair CL.600-2B16 Challenger	5463	N463AG
			C-GLYC
D-AHFA	Boeing 737-8K5	27981	N737BX
D-AHFB	Boeing 737-8K5	27982	N35030
D-AHFC	Boeing 737-8K5	27977	N5573P
D-AHFD	Boeing 737-8K5	27978	N35161
D-AHFE	Boeing 737-8K5	27979	N3502P
D-AHFF	Boeing 737-8K5	27980	N3509J
D-AHFG	Boeing 737-8K5	27989	
D-AHFH	Boeing 737-8K5	27983	N1786B
D-AHFI	Boeing 737-8K5	27984	N1787B
D-AHFJ	Boeing 737-8K5	27990	
D-AHFL	Boeing 737-8K5	27985	N1786B
D-AHFM	Boeing 737-8K5	27986	
D-AHFN	Boeing 737-8K5	28228	N1786B
D-AHFO	Boeing 737-8K5	27987	
D-AHFP	Boeing 737-8K5	27988	
D-AHFQ	Boeing 737-8K5	27992	N1786B
D-AHFR	Boeing 737-8K5	30593	N1787B
D-AHFS	Boeing 737-8K5	28623	
D-AHFT	Boeing 737-8K5	30413	N1015B
D-AHFU	Boeing 737-8K5	30414	
D-AHFV	Boeing 737-8K5	30415	
D-AHFW	Boeing 737-8K5	30882	N1786B
D-AHFX	Boeing 737-8K5	30416	N1786B
D-AHFY	Boeing 737-8K5	30417	N1787B
D-AHFZ	Boeing 737-8K5	30883	
D-AHIA	Boeing 737-73S	29082	D-ASKH
			N1787B
D-AHIB	Boeing 737-73S	29083	D-AWOH
D-AHIC	Boeing 737-7BK	30617	N1878B
D-AHID	Boeing 737-73S	29080	EI-CRQ
			N1782B
			N1786B
D-AHIE	Boeing 737-73S	29081	TC-SUF
			PH-AAQ
			4X-ABR
			N1786B
D-AHIF	Boeing 737-73S	29079	TC-SUE
			PH-AAP
			4X-ABJ
			N1786B
D-AHLA(3)	Airbus A310-304	520	F-WWCI
D-AHLD(4)	Boeing 737-5K5	24926	HA-LER
			D-AHLD(4)
D-AHLE(4)	Canadair CL.600-2B16 Challenger	5462	N462PG
			C-GLYO
D-AHLF(3)	Boeing 737-5K5	24927	
D-AHLG(6)	Boeing 737-5K5	24776	HA-LEP
			D-AHLE(3)
D-AHLH(2)	Boeing 737-8K5	30783	N1796B
D-AHLI (2)	Boeing 737-5K5	25037	
D-AHLN(2)	Boeing 737-5K5	25062	SX-BFP
			D-AHLN(2)
D-AHLO(2)	Boeing 737-4K5	24128	
D-AHLP(2)	Boeing 737-8K5	32905	N6065Y
D-AHLQ(2)	Boeing 737-8K5	32906	N1786B
D-AHLR(3)	Boeing 737-8K5	32907	
D-AHLV(2)	Airbus A310-204	430	F-WWBL
D-AHLW	Airbus A310-204	427	F-WWBK
D-AHLX	Airbus A310-204	487	F-WWBO
D-AHLZ(2)	Airbus A310-204	468	F-WWBMD-
AHOI (2)	BAe.146 Series 300A	E-3187	G-BSYT
			EC-FKF
			EC-899,
			G-BSYT
			G-6-187
D-AIAH	Airbus A300B4-603	380	F-WWAA
D-AIAI	Airbus A300B4-603	391	F-WWAL
D-AIAK	Airbus A300B4-603	401	F-WWAO

D-AIAL	Airbus A300B4-603	405	F-WWAP
D-AIAM	Airbus A300B4-603	408	F-WWAQ
D-AIAN	Airbus A300B4-603	411	F-WWAR
D-AIAP	Airbus A300B4-603	414	F-WWAS
D-AIAR	Airbus A300B4-603	546	F-WWAP
D-AIAS	Airbus A300B4-603	553	F-WWAX
D-AIAT	Airbus A300B4-603	618	F-WWAM
D-AIAU	Airbus A300B4-603	623	F-WWAT
D-AIAX	Airbus A300B4-605R	773	F-WWAO
D-AIAY	Airbus A300B4-605R	608	A6-EKF
			F-WWAD
D-AIAZ	Airbus A300B4-605R	701	A6-EKM
			F-WWAN
D-AICA(2)	Airbus A320-212	774	F-WWDN
D-AICB(2)	Airbus A320-212	793	F-WWDU
D-AICC(2)	Airbus A320-212	809	F-WWIE
D-AICD(2)	Airbus A320-212	884	F-WWDE
D-AICE	Airbus A320-212	894	F-WWDI
D-AICF(2)	Airbus A320-212	905	F-WWDP
D-AICG	Airbus A320-212	957	F-WWBE
D-AICH(2)	Airbus A320-212	971	F-WWBY
D-AICI	Airbus A320-212	1381	F-WWIP
D-AICJ	Airbus A320-212	1402	F-WWDB
D-AICK(2)	Airbus A320-212	1416	F-WWDZ
D-AICL	Airbus A320-212	1437	F-WWBG
D-AICM	Airbus A320-214	1929	OO-TCH
			F-WWID
D-AIDC	Airbus A310-304	485	F-OITP
			5Y-KQL
			D-AIDC
			5Y-KQL
			F-WWCJ
D-AIDD	Airbus A310-304	488	F-WWCE
D-AIDF	Airbus A310-304 (Permit 1.05)	524	F-WWCA
D-AIFA	Airbus A340-313X	352	F-WWJU
D-AIFB	Airbus A340-313X	355	F-WWJX
D-AIFC	Airbus A340-313X	379	F-WWJJ
D-AIFD	Airbus A340-313X	390	F-WWJE
D-AIFE	Airbus A340-313X	434	F-WWJT
D-AIFF	Airbus A340-313X	447	F-WWJB
D-AIGA	Airbus A340-311	020	F-WWJK
D-AIGB	Airbus A340-311	024	F-WWJO
D-AIGC	Airbus A340-311	027	F-WWJR
D-AIGD	Airbus A340-311	028	F-WWJS
D-AIGF(2)	Airbus A340-311	035	F-WWJV
D-AIGH(2)	Airbus A340-311	052	F-WWJO
D-AIGI (2)	Airbus A340-311	053	F-WWJJ
D-AIGK(2)	Airbus A340-311	056	F-WWJK
D-AIGL	Airbus A340-313X	135	F-WWJS
D-AIGM	Airbus A340-313X	158	F-WWJN
D-AIGN	Airbus A340-313X	213	F-WWJM
D-AIGO	Airbus A340-313X	233	F-WWJJ
D-AIGP	Airbus A340-313X	252	F-WWJM
D-AIGR	Airbus A340-313X	274	F-WWJI
D-AIGS	Airbus A340-313X	297	F-WWJK
D-AIGT	Airbus A340-313X	304	F-WWJY
D-AIGU	Airbus A340-313X	321	F-WWJM
D-AIGV	Airbus A340-313X	325	F-WWJN
D-AIGW	Airbus A340-313X	327	F-WWJO
D-AIGX	Airbus A340-313X	354	F-WWJV
D-AIGY	Airbus A340-313X	335	F-WWJS
D-AIGZ	Airbus A340-313X	347	F-WWJT
D-AIHA	Airbus A340-642	482	F-WWCS
D-AIHB	Airbus A340-642	517	F-WWCR
D-AIHC	Airbus A340-642	523	F-WWCV
D-AIHD	Airbus A340-642	537	F-WWCZ
D-AIHE	Airbus A340-642	540	F-WWCF
D-AIHF	Airbus A340-642	543	F-WWCE
D-AIHH	Airbus A340-642	566	F-WWCJ
D-AIHI	Airbus A340-642	569	F-WWCB
D-AIHK	Airbus A340-642	580	F-WWCN
D-AIHL	Airbus A340-642	583	F-WWCQ
D-AIJO(3)	Airbus A319-133X	2192	D-AVYB
	(Permit 12.04, intended for Ukraine)		F-WWBN
			D-AVYB
D-AIKA(2)	Airbus A330-343X	570	F-WWYV
D-AIKB	Airbus A330-343X	576	F-WWKN
D-AIKC	Airbus A330-343X	579	F-WWKG
D-AIKD	Airbus A330-343X	629	F-WWYF
D-AIKE	Airbus A330-343X	636	F-WWYL
D-AIKF	Airbus A330-343X	642	F-WWKV
D-AIKG	Airbus A330-343X	645	F-WWKE
D-AIKH	Airbus A330-343X	648	F-WWKG
D-AIKI	Airbus A330-343X (Reservation .04)	687	
D-AIKJ	Airbus A330-343X (Reservation .04)	701	
D-AILA	Airbus A319-114	609	D-AVYF
D-AILB	Airbus A319-114	610	D-AVYG
D-AILC	Airbus A319-114	616	D-AVYI
D-AILD	Airbus A319-114	623	D-AVYL
D-AILE	Airbus A319-114	627	D-AVYO
D-AILF	Airbus A319-114	636	D-AVYS
D-AILH	Airbus A319-114	641	D-AVYV
D-AILI	Airbus A319-114	651	D-AVYY
D-AILK	Airbus A319-114	679	D-AVYG(2)
D-AILL	Airbus A319-114	689	D-AVYL(2)
D-AILM	Airbus A319-114	694	D-AVYR(2)
D-AILN	Airbus A319-114	700	D-AVYU(2)

D-AILP	Airbus A319-114	717	D-AVYA
D-AILR	Airbus A319-114	723	D-AVYD(3)
D-AILS	Airbus A319-114	729	D-AVYF(3)
D-AILT	Airbus A319-114	738	D-AVYN(3)
D-AILU	Airbus A319-114	744	D-AVYI (3)
D-AILW	Airbus A319-114	853	D-AVYO(4)
D-AILX	Airbus A319-114	860	D-AVYS(4)
D-AILY(2)	Airbus A319-114	875	D-AVYC(5)
D-AIMD	Airbus A330-223	322	F-WIHM OO-SFT F-WWYT
D-AIME	Airbus A330-223	324	OO-SFU F-WWYU
D-AIMF	Airbus A340-311	047	F-WQRH OO-SCY F-GNID (OO-SLI)
D-AIMG	Airbus A340-311	051	F-WQRI OO-SCZ F-GNIE (OO-SLJ)
D-AIPA	Airbus A320-211	069	F-WWII
D-AIPB	Airbus A320-211	070	F-WWIJ
D-AIPC	Airbus A320-211	071	F-WWIO
D-AIPD	Airbus A320-211	072	F-WWIP
D-AIPE	Airbus A320-211	078	F-WWIU
D-AIPF	Airbus A320-211	083	F-WWDE
D-AIPH	Airbus A320-211	086	F-WWDJ
D-AIPK	Airbus A320-211	093	F-WWDQ
D-AIPL	Airbus A320-211	094	7T-VKO D-AIPL F-WWDR
D-AIPM	Airbus A320-211	104	F-WWIG
D-AIPP	Airbus A320-211	110	F-WWID
D-AIPR	Airbus A320-211	111	F-WWIE
D-AIPS	Airbus A320-211	116	F-WWIK
D-AIPT	Airbus A320-211	117	F-WWIL
D-AIPU	Airbus A320-211	135	F-WWDB
D-AIPW	Airbus A320-211	137	F-WWDD
D-AIPX	Airbus A320-211	147	F-WWDN
D-AIPY	Airbus A320-211	161	F-WWIA
D-AIPZ	Airbus A320-211	162	F-WWDS
D-AIQA	Airbus A320-211	172	F-WWIK
D-AIQB	Airbus A320-211	200	F-WWDJ
D-AIQC	Airbus A320-211	201	F-WWDL
D-AIQD	Airbus A320-211	202	F-WWDM
D-AIQE	Airbus A320-211	209	F-WWDY
D-AIQF	Airbus A320-211	216	F-WWDR
D-AIQH	Airbus A320-211	217	F-WWDS
D-AIQK	Airbus A320-211	218	F-WWDX
D-AIQL	Airbus A320-211	267	F-WWDY
D-AIQM	Airbus A320-211	268	F-WWIB
D-AIQN	Airbus A320-211	269	F-WWIC
D-AIQP	Airbus A320-211	346	F-WWDX
D-AIQR	Airbus A320-211	382	F-WWIZ
D-AIQS	Airbus A320-211	401	F-WWBD
D-AIQT	Airbus A320-211	1337	F-WWDO
D-AIQU	Airbus A320-211	1365	F-WWIG
D-AIQW	Airbus A320-211	1367	F-WWIH
D-AIRA	Airbus A321-131	458	F-WWIQ
D-AIRB	Airbus A321-131	468	F-WWIS
D-AIRC	Airbus A321-131	473	D-AVZC
D-AIRD	Airbus A321-131	474	D-AVZD
D-AIRE	Airbus A321-131	484	D-AVZF
D-AIRF	Airbus A321-131	493	D-AVZH
D-AIRH	Airbus A321-131	412	D-AVZA F-WWIC
D-AIRK	Airbus A321-131	502	D-AVZL
D-AIRL	Airbus A321-131	505	D-AVZM
D-AIRM	Airbus A321-131	518	D-AVZT
D-AIRN	Airbus A321-131	560	D-AVZK(2)
D-AIRO	Airbus A321-131	563	D-AVZN(2)
D-AIRP	Airbus A321-131	564	D-AVZL(2)
D-AIRR	Airbus A321-131	567	D-AVZM(2)
D-AIRS	Airbus A321-131	595	D-AVZX(2)
D-AIRT	Airbus A321-131	652	D-AVZI (3)
D-AIRU	Airbus A321-131	692	D-AVZT(3)
D-AIRW	Airbus A321-131	699	D-AVZY(3)
D-AIRX	Airbus A321-131	887	D-AVZI (5)
D-AIRY	Airbus A321-131	901	D-AVZK(5)
D-AISB	Airbus A321-231	1080	D-AVZP
D-AISC	Airbus A321-231	1161	D-AVZG
D-AISD	Airbus A321-231	1188	D-AVZJ
D-AISE	Airbus A321-231	1214	D-AVZS
D-AISF	Airbus A321-231	1260	D-AVZI
D-AISG	Airbus A321-231	1273	D-AVZU
D-AISY(2)	Fokker F.27 Friendship 600	10391	OY-CCR G-BNTB 9Q-CLK PH-FNO
D-AJAD	Dassault Falcon 900EX	64	N900VM
D-AJAG	Canadair CL.600-2B16 Challenger	5528	N528DT C-GLYO
D-AJET	BAe.146 Series 200	E-2201	G-6-201
D-AJGK	Gulfstream IVSP	1459	(D-AJJJ) N399GA
D-AKNF	Airbus A319-112	0646	D-AVYB
D-AKNG	Airbus A319-112	0654	D-AVYX
D-AKNH	Airbus A319-112	0794	D-AVYD
D-AKNI	Airbus A319-112	1016	D-AVYK
D-AKNJ	Airbus A319-112	1172	D-AVWF
D-AKNK	Airbus A319-112 (Reservation 3.05)	1077	N718UW D-AVWI
D-AKNL	Airbus A319-112 (Reservation 3.05)	1084	N719US D-AVWK
D-AKNM	Airbus A319-112 (Reservation 3.05)	1089	N720US D-AVYC
D-AKNN	Airbus A319-112 (Reservation 3.05)	1136	N726US D-AVYM
D-AKNO	Airbus A319-112 (Reservation 3.05)	1147	N727UW D-AVWI
D-AKNP	Airbus A319-112 (Reservation 3.05)	1155	N728UW D-AVYS
D-AKNQ	Airbus A319-112 (Reservation 3.05)	1170	N729US D-AVWQ
D-AKNR	Airbus A319-112 (Reservation 3.05)	1209	N736US D-AVYI
D-AKNS	Airbus A319-112 (Reservation 3.05)	1277	N743UW D-AVWJ
D-AKNX	Airbus A320-212	0525	N601LF PH-VAD C-GTDB F-GJVV
D-AKNY	Airbus A320-212	0579	N811LF PH-VAE C-GJUM C-GVXD F-WWDU
D-AKNZ	Airbus A320-212	0645	N711LF PH-VAC C-GJUP C-GVXE F-WWDL
D-AKUE	Canadair CL.600-2B16 Challenger	5173	N181JC C-GLXY
D-ALAB	Airbus A320-232	575	F-WWDO
D-ALCA	McDonnell-Douglas MD-11F	48781	N9020Q
D-ALCB	McDonnell-Douglas MD-11F	48782	N9166N
D-ALCC	McDonnell-Douglas MD-11F	48783	
D-ALCD	McDonnell-Douglas MD-11F	48784	
D-ALCE	McDonnell-Douglas MD-11F	48785	
D-ALCF	McDonnell-Douglas MD-11F	48798	
D-ALCG	McDonnell-Douglas MD-11F	48799	
D-ALCH	McDonnell-Douglas MD-11F	48801	
D-ALCI	McDonnell-Douglas MD-11F	48800	
D-ALCJ	McDonnell-Douglas MD-11F	48802	N9166N
D-ALCK	McDonnell-Douglas MD-11F	48803	
D-ALCL	McDonnell-Douglas MD-11F	48804	
D-ALCM	McDonnell-Douglas MD-11F	48805	N6069R
D-ALCN	McDonnell-Douglas MD-11F	48806	
D-ALCO	McDonnell-Douglas MD-11F (Res 24.3.04)	48413	PP-VQL
D-ALCP	McDonnell-Douglas MD-11F (Res 24.3.04)	48414	PP-VQM
D-ALCQ	McDonnell-Douglas MD-11F	48431	N431LT I-DUPB
D-ALCR	McDonnell-Douglas MD-11F	48581	N581LT I-DUPC
D-ALCS	McDonnell-Douglas MD-11F	48630	N630LT I-DUPD
D-ALIE	Embraer EMB-170-100LR	17000059	PT-SVI
D-ALPA	Airbus A330-223	403	F-WWKO
D-ALPB	Airbus A330-223	432	F-WWYG
D-ALPC	Airbus A330-223	444	F-WWKD
D-ALPD	Airbus A330-223	454	F-WWKG
D-ALPE	Airbus A330-223	469	F-WWKO
D-ALPF	Airbus A330-223	476	F-WWKT
D-ALPG	Airbus A330-223	493	F-WWKI
D-ALSA	Airbus A321-211	1629	D-AVZC
D-ALSB	Airbus A321-211	1994	D-AVZR
D-ALSC	Airbus A321-211	2005	D-AVXI
D-ALSD	Airbus A321-211	1607	I-PEKN D-AVZN
D-ALTB	Airbus A320-214	1385	F-WWIT
D-ALTC	Airbus A320-214	1441	F-WWBQ
D-ALTD	Airbus A320-214	1493	F-WWDY
D-ALTF	Airbus A320-214	1553	F-WWEP
D-ALTG	Airbus A320-214	1762	F-WWBR
D-ALTH	Airbus A320-214	1797	F-WWDV
D-ALTI	Airbus A320-214	1806	F-WWIJ
D-ALTJ	Airbus A320-214	1838	F-WWBM
D-ALTK	Airbus A320-214	1931	F-WWIH
D-ALTL	Airbus A320-214	2009	F-WWBOD-
AMGL	BAe.146-Series 200	E-2055	G-CBFL SE-DRF N697AA N145AC G-5-055 N145AC G-5-055
D-AMIM	Canadair CL.600-2B16 Challenger	5317	C-FYXC
D-AMTH	Airbus A321-211 (Reservation 3.03)	761	F-GTAF D-AVZJ
D-ANFA	Aérospatiale/Alenia ATR-72-202	224	F-WWEQ
D-ANFB	Aérospatiale/Alenia ATR-72-202	229	F-WWEX
D-ANFC	Aérospatiale/Alenia ATR-72-202	237	F-WWEG

D-ANFD	Aérospatiale/Alenia ATR-72-202	256	F-WWEE
D-ANFE	Aérospatiale/Alenia ATR-72-202	294	F-WWLS
D-ANFF	Aérospatiale/Alenia ATR-72-202	292	F-WWLT
D-ANFG	Aérospatiale/Alenia ATR-72-212A	658	F-WWEL
D-ANFH	Aérospatiale/Alenia ATR-72-212A	660	F-WWEM
D-ANFI	Aérospatiale/Alenia ATR-72-212A	662	F-WWEN
D-ANFJ	Aérospatiale/Alenia ATR-72-212A	664	F-WWEO
D-ANFK	Aérospatiale/Alenia ATR-72-212A	666	F-WWEP
D-ANFL	Aérospatiale/Alenia ATR-72-212A	668	F-WWEQ
D-ANJA	Airbus A321-211	0519	HB-IOB D-AVZU
D-ANKE	Canadair CL.600-2B16 Challenger	5494	N494JC C-GLXH
D-ANNA	Airbus A320-233	0916	N972PG EI-TAI N459TA F-WWDX
D-ANNI	Airbus A320-233 (Reservation 22.3.04)	0902	N457TA F-WWDN
D-AOLA	SAAB 2000	008	SE-008 D-ADIB(2) SE-008
D-AOLB	SAAB 2000	005	SE-005 HB-IZB SE-005
D-AOLT	SAAB 2000	037	HB-IZU SE-037
D-APAA	Airbus A319-132LR	1947	D-AVWI
D-APAB	Airbus A319-132LR	1955	D-AVWD
D-APAC	Airbus A319-132LR	1727	D-AVWQ
D-APAD	Airbus A319-133X	1880	D-AVYM F-WWBF
D-AQUA	BAe.146 Series 300	E-3118	G-OAJF HB-IXZ G-6-118 G-OAJF
'D-AQUI'	*See D-CDLH*		
D-ARFA	Airbus A321-231	1218	D-ALAN(2) D-AVZA
D-ARFB	Airbus A321-231	1199	D-ALAM(2) D-AVZM
D-ARFC	Airbus A320-232	0580	D-ALAC F-WWDV
D-ARFD	Airbus A320-232	2108	(F-OKRM) F-WWDM F-WWFI
D-ARFE	Airbus A320-232	0575	D-ALAB F-WWDO
D-ARFF	Airbus A320-214	2128	F-WWDT (F-OKRN) F-WWDT
D-ARND	Airbus A330-223	312	D-AIMC HB-IQN F-WWYO
D-ARNO	Airbus A330-223	308	D-AIMB HB-IQM F-WWYK
D-ARTN	Canadair CL.600-2B16 Challenger (Res .04)	5585	C-GLXO

D-ASAA to D-ASAZ Test registrations for Airbus A300 and A310 freighter conversions

D-ASAX	VFW-Fokker VFW-614 (Preserved at Bremen) (Advanced Technology Demonstrator)	G-015	F-GATI D-BABN
D-ASDB	VFW-Fokker VFW-614 (Permit 4.03)	G-019	OY-RRW D-ASDB 17+03
D-ASFB	Airbus A340-213X (Permit 1.03)	204	V8-AC3 V8-HB3 (V8-HM8) F-WWJB
D-ASIE	Canadair CL.600-2B16 Challenger	5475	N475AD C-GLXO
D-ASKY	Fokker F.27 Friendship 200 (Reservation)	10674	VT-SSB LN-AKC (SE-KXY) LN-AKC PH-EXG
D-ASTS(2)	Canadair CL.600-2B16 Challenger	5378	C-GDBZ
D-ATUA	Boeing 737-804 (Reservation .05)	30465	SE-DZL PH-AAV G-BYNC N1786B (SE-DZK)
D-ATUB	Boeing 737-804 (Reservation .05)	30466	SE-DZM PH-ABE G-BYNB N1786B
D-ATUI	Boeing 737-86Q	30287	

D-AUAA to D-AUAZ Reserved for Airbus A318 Test Registrations

D-AUKE	Canadair CL.600-2B16 Challenger	5389	N604JE C-GLXM
D-AVRA	Avro 146-RJ85	E-2256	G-6-256
D-AVRB	Avro 146-RJ85	E-2253	G-BVWD G-6-253
D-AVRC	Avro 146-RJ85	E-2251	G-6-251
D-AVRD	Avro 146-RJ85	E-2257	G-6-257
D-AVRE	Avro 146-RJ85	E-2261	G-6-261
D-AVRF	Avro 146-RJ85	E-2269	G-JAYV
D-AVRG	Avro 146-RJ85	E-2266	G-6-266
D-AVRH	Avro 146-RJ85	E-2268	G-OCLH G-6-268
D-AVRI	Avro 146-RJ85	E-2270	G-CLHX G-6-270
D-AVRJ	Avro 146-RJ85	E-2277	G-BWKY G-6-277
D-AVRK	Avro 146-RJ85	E-2278	G-6-278
D-AVRL	Avro 146-RJ85	E-2285	G-6-285
D-AVRM	Avro 146-RJ85	E-2288	G-6-288
D-AVRN	Avro 146-RJ85	E-2293	G-6-293
D-AVRO	Avro 146-RJ85	E-2246	G-6-246
D-AVRP	Avro 146-RJ85	E-2303	G-6-303
D-AVRQ	Avro 146-RJ85	E-2304	G-6-304
D-AVRR	Avro 146-RJ85	E-2317	G-6-317

D-AVWA to D-AVWZ Reserved for Airbus A319 Test Registrations

D-AVXA to D-AVXZ Reserved for Airbus A321 Test Registrations

D-AVYA to D-AVYZ Reserved for Airbus A319 Test Registrations

D-AVZA to D-AVZZ Reserved for Airbus A321 Test Registrations

D-AWBA	BAe.146 Series 300A	E-3134	ZK-NZF G-5-134 G-11-134
D-AWDL	BAe.146 Series 100	E-1011	G-UKJF C-GNVY N803RW (N103RW) G-5-513 PT-LEQ
D-AWUE	BAe.146 Series 200	E-2050	PK-PJP G-5-517 G-5-004
D-AXEL	Airbus A330-223	305	D-AIMA HB-IQL F-WWYI

D-AYXA to D-AYXC Reserved for Testzwecke TFTS

D-AZEM	Dassault Falcon 900EX EASy	133	F-WQBK F-WWFK

CLASS B : Aircraft of between 14 and 20 Metric Tonnes

D-BACH	DHC-8 Dash Eight 314	365	VH-TQA D-BACH C-FWBB
D-BADA	Dornier 328-310	3224	D-BDXB
D-BADC	Dornier 328-310	3216	N328NP D-BIUU D-BDXD(5)
D-BAKB	Fokker F.27 Friendship 600	10261	F-GHRC PH-FGC ST-ALF PH-FGC TG-TOA P2-ANF P2-BNF (F-BVTU) JA8636 PH-FGC
D-BAKC	Fokker F.27 Friendship 600	10195	F-GFJS PT-ODM PH-FDK PK-PFR JA8605 PH-FDKD-
BAKD	Fokker F.27 Friendship 600	10179	SP-FNF D-BAKD F-GKJC PH-FCT ST-ALG PH-FCT TG-AEA P2-ANE P2-MNE JA8603 (JA8303) PH-FCT
D-BAKE(3)	Fokker F.27 Friendship 200	10263	PH-FGE TF-FLM TF-FIM JA8638 PH-FGE
D-BAKF	Fokker F.27 Friendship 200	10249	PH-KFG I-ATIM PH-FFP

D-BAKG	Fokker F.27 Friendship 200	10240	PH-FFF
			TF-FLP
			OH-LKB
			TF-FLT
			HL5202
			PH-FFF
D-BAKH	Fokker F.27 Friendship 200	10233	PH-FEY
			TT-WAD
			PH-FEY
			TF-FLS
			G-BDVT
			S2-ABL
			PH-FEY
			9V-BAR
			9M-AMN
			PH-FEY
D-BAKJ	Fokker F.27 Friendship 200	10321	PH-FKR
			ST-AWB
			PH-FKR
			(PH-FJA)
			PT-BFZ
			(PH-LMP)
			PH-FKR
			LN-RNX
			I-ATIF
			PH-FKR
D-BAKK	Fokker F.27 Friendship 200	10229	G-BHMW
			F-BSIF
			F-OGIF
			F-BUTA
			JA8618
			PH-FEU
D-BCRO	Aérospatiale/Alenia ATR-42-300	122	F-WWES
D-BCRP	Aérospatiale/Alenia ATR-42-300	158	F-WWEE
D-BCRQ	Aérospatiale/Alenia ATR-42-300	233	F-WWEO
D-BCRR	Aérospatiale/Alenia ATR-42-300	255	F-WWEC
D-BCRS	Aérospatiale/Alenia ATR-42-300	287	F-WWLL
D-BCRT	Aérospatiale/Alenia ATR-42-300	289	F-WWLN
D-BDNL	Dassault Falcon 2000	119	F-WQBN
			F-GXDP
			F-WWVO
D-BDTM	DHC-8 Series 314	545	C-FCSG

D-BDXA to D-BDXZ Test Registrations for Dornier 328-300 production

D-BEBA	DHC-8 Series 314	543	
D-BEJR	Dornier 328-300 (Permit)	3102	
D-BERT(3)	Dassault Falcon 2000EX	30	F-WWGG
D-BEST	Dassault Falcon 2000	50	F-WWME
D-BGAB	Dornier 328-300	3134	D-BDXP(1)
D-BGAE	Dornier 328-300	3146	D-BDXC(2)
D-BGAG	Dornier 328-300	3133	D-BDXO(1)
D-BGAL	Dornier 328-300	3131	D-BDXN(1)
D-BGAQ	Dornier 328-300	3130	D-BDXM(1)
D-BGAR	Dornier 328-300	3152	D-BDXO(2)
D-BGAS	Dornier 328-300	3139	D-BDXZ(1)
D-BHAM	DHC-8 Series 311	313	OE-LEC
			(D-BSEE)
			OE-LEC
			C-GFOD
D-BHAS	DHC-8 Series 311	503	C-GDLD
D-BHAT	DHC-8 Series 311	505	C-GDFT
D-BHHH	Aérospatiale/Alenia ATR-42-300	173	F-WWED
D-BHOQ	DHC-8 Series 314	544	C-GHRI
D-BIER	DHC-8 Series 102	310	OE-LEA
			C-GFCF
D-BILL	Dassault Falcon 2000EX EASy	33	F-WWGL
D-BIRD(3)	Dassault Falcon 2000EX	7	F-WWGF
D-BJET	Dornier 328JET (Prototype) (Permit)	3002	D-CATI (3)
D-BJJJ	Aérospatiale/Alenia ATR-42-300	278	F-WWEC
D-BKIM	DHC-8 Series 311A	356	C-GFOD
D-BKKK	Aérospatiale/Alenia ATR-42-512	532	F-WWLP
D-BKLI	Cessna 750 Citation X (Permit 12.03)	750-0219	N5192E
D-BLDI	Cessna 750 Citation X	750-0218	N5223X
D-BLEJ	DHC-8 Series 314	521	C-FDHU
D-BLLL	Aérospatiale/Alenia ATR-42-512	549	F-WWLB
D-BLUE	Cessna 750 Citation X	750-0140	N5112K
D-BMMM	Aérospatiale/Alenia ATR-42-512	546	F-WWLE
D-BMUC	DHC-8 Series 314	350	C-GUAY
D-BMVV	Dassault Falcon 2000EX	42	F-GUTC
			F-WWGX
D-BNNN	Aérospatiale/Alenia ATR-42-512	551	F-WWLL
D-BOBL	DHC-8 Series 102	225	C-GFQL
			D-BOBL
			C-GFQL
D-BOBO(2)	DHC-8 Series 102	153	C-GFOD
D-BOBU	DHC-8 Series 301A	252	C-GFCF
D-BOBY(4)	DHC-8 Series 102	177	C-GFQL
D-BOOK	Dassault Falcon 50	215	XA-SIM
			N297FJ
			F-WWHT
D-BOOO	Aérospatiale/Alenia ATR-42-512	559	F-WWLM
D-BPAD	DHC-8 Series 314	523	C-FDHW
D-BPPP	Aérospatiale/Alenia ATR-42-512	581	F-WWLE
D-BQQQ	Aérospatiale/Alenia ATR-42-512	584	F-WWEP
D-BRRR	Aérospatiale/Alenia ATR-42-512	601	F-WWEC
D-BSIK	Dassault Falcon 2000 (Reservn 2.05)	27	F-GJSK
			G-JCBI
			F-WWMM
D-BSNA	Canadair CL.600-1A11 Challenger	1066	N51TJ
			N701GA
			N701QS
			N721SW
			N67B
			C-GLXD
D-BSSS	Aérospatiale/Alenia ATR-42-512	602	F-WW..
D-BTEN	Cessna 750 Citation X	750-0085	N985QS
D-BTTT	Aérospatiale/Alenia ATR-42-512	603	F-WW..
D-BUSY	Canadair CL.600-1A11 Challenger	1070	N670CL
			N24JK
			N70DJ
			HZ-MF1
			N3237S
			C-GLXO
D-BVIP	Aérospatiale/Alenia ATR-42-320	333	F-WQNO
			VP-BOG
D-BWAL	Dornier 328-300 (Permit)	3099	

CLASS C : Aircraft of between 5.7 and 14 Metric Tonnes

D-CAAA(3)	Cessna 560XL Citation XLS (Res. 05)	560-5555	(D-CLDI)
D-CAAM	Dornier 228-212	8205	D-CBDH(4)
D-CACB	Beech 200T Super King Air	BT-27	N7244N
			AE-576
			N2854B
D-CADN	Beech B300 Super King Air	FL-101	N82311
D-CAHR	SAAB-Scania SF.340A (Reservation 10.03)	074	SE-E74
			N406BH
			SE-E74
D-CAKE(2)	Cessna 650 Citation VI	650-0240	PH-MFX
			N51143
D-CALL(3)	Cessna 550 Citation II	550-0834	N834CB
D-CALM(2)	Dornier 228-101	7051	
D-CAMM	Beech 350 Super King Air	FL-64	
D-CAMS	Cessna 560 Citation V	560-0243	N39N
			N12890
D-CAPA(2)	Beech 1900C	UB-72	N504RH
			OY-JRS
			D-CAPA(2)
			OK-SEB
			D-CAPA(2)
			N3076N
D-CAPO(2)	Gates Learjet 35A	35A-159	N93CK
			N93C
D-CARA(2)	Beech 1900C	UB-59	N72391
D-CARE(4)	Cessna 650 Citation III	650-0134	N1239L
			N123SL
			N27SD
			N75RN
			N75RD
			(N1323Y)
D-CARL	Gates Learjet 35A	35A-387	
D-CASA(3)	Cessna 560 Citation Encore	560-0544	N701DK
			N901DK
D-CASB	SAAB-Scania SF.340B	223	SE-KSI
			VH-EKK
			SE-KSI
			SE-G23
D-CASC	SAAB-Scania SF.340B	229	SE-KSK
			VH-KDR
			SE-KSK
			SE-G29
D-CASD	SAAB-Scania SF.340B	221	F-GPKM
			HB-AKM
			SE-G21
D-CATL	Gates Learjet 55	55-051	N55KD
			N55KS
			N22GH
			N22G
			N734
D-CAUW	Cessna 560 Citation V	560-0578	(D-CSUN)
			N5264N
D-CAVE	Gates Learjet 35A	35A-423	(N335GA)
			N200TC
			N369XL
D-CAWI	Dornier 228-101	7014	D-IAWI
			(D-ICIO)
			(N1339U)
D-CAWU	Cessna 560 Citation V	560-0042	N42CV
			(N26648)
D-CBBB(3)	Cessna 560XL Citation XLS (Res. 05)	560-5567	(D-CKLI)
D-CBCB(2)	Beech 1900D	UE-296	F-GRMD
			(F-GRPM)
			N21572

D-CBDA to D-CBDZ Test Registrations for Dornier 228 production

D-CBDQ(7)	Dornier 228-202	8157	G-BVTZ
			D-CTCB
			D-CBDV(4)
			TC-FBM
			D-CIRC
			(TC-FBM)
			D-CBDF(2)

D-CBEN	Cessna 560 Citation Ultra (Permit 6.04)	560-0282	N51055
D-CBIG(2)	Beech 1900D	UE-288	N11320 TC-CNK N11320
D-CBIN	Fairchild Swearingen SA.227AT Merlin IVC	AT-440B	I-FSAD N36JP N56TA
D-CBMW(2)	Hawker 800XP	258345	D-CBMV N1135A
D-CBPL	Cessna 650 Citation III	650-0149	(CS-DNE) N139N N139M N649CC N1236B
D-CBSF	Beech 1900D	UE-8	N55778
D-CCAA	Gates Learjet 35A	35A-315	N662AA N927GL
D-CCAB	Cessna 550 Citation II	550-0827	
D-CCAS	Short SD.3-60 Variant 300	SH.3737	G-OLBA G-BOFG
D-CCBW	Beech B300 Super King Air (Permit 6.04)	FL-46	N81623
D-CCCA	Gates Learjet 35A	35A-160	
D-CCCB	Gates Learjet 35A	35A-663	N91480
D-CCCC(2)	Fairchild Swearingen SA.227AT Merlin IVC	AT-511	N600N N600L N3108F
D-CCCF	Cessna 550 Citation II	500-0189	HB-VGP D-CAAT N98601
D-CCEU	Cessna 650 Citation III	650-0190	N260VP N350CD N190JJ N142B (N2621U)
D-CCGG	Bombardier Learjet 60	60-256	OY-LJK N5013K
D-CCGN	Gates Learjet 55	55-017	N760AQ
D-CCHB	Gates Learjet 35A	35A-089	N3547F
D-CCIR	Dornier 328-130	3100	D-CDXA(4)
D-CCWD	Cessna 550 Citation Bravo (Res .04)	550-0864	OE-GTZ N864CB
D-CDAU	SAAB-Scania SF.340B (Reservation 4.05)	340B-185	F-GPKG HB-AKG SE-F85
D-CDEN(2)	Bombardier Learjet 45	45-148	N8084R
D-CDLH	Junkers Ju 52/3mg8e (Painted as D-AQUI which was c/n 5489, later LN-DAH and Luftwaffe - regd LN-KAF in 5.46 this was rebuilt with fuselage of c/n 130714 (LN-KAL ntu) in 1947)	130714	N52JU N130LW HC-ABS LN-KAF (LN-KAL) Luftwaffe
D-CDLR	Grob G.850 Strato 2C	30001	
D-CDNX	Bombardier Learjet 60	60-231	N3015M
D-CDNY	Bombardier Learjet 60	60-160	
D-CDNZ	Bombardier Learjet 60	60-161	
D-CDSF	Gates Learjet 35A	35A-421	I-VULC N413JP N3AH (N88AH) N85QA N85CA N44MJ
D-CDOL	Dornier 328-100	3003	
D-CDXA to D-CDXZ	Test Registrations for Dornier 328-100 production		
D-CEBM	Cessna 560 Citation V (Reservation .05)	560-0558	(N558GG) N558CG N558V N560RV N5174WD-
CEFM	Cessna 550 Citation Bravo (Res 9.04)	550-1018	SU-HEC N5259Y
D-CEIS	Beech 400A Beechjet	RK-10	(D-CLSG) N2842B
D-CEMG	Cessna 560 Citation V	560-0463	N48LQ N48LC N58KJ N56K N50612
D-CEMM(2)	Bombardier Learjet 45	45-144	N5011L
D-CESH	Bombardier Learjet 45	45-017	N417LJ (D-CWER)
D-CETV	Bombardier Learjet 60	60-148	N80701
D-CEWR(3)	Bombardier Learjet 45	45-213	N50126
D-CFAI (5)	Gates Learjet 35A	35A-365	G-GJET G-CJET G-SEBE G-ZIPS (N4564S) G-ZONE
D-CFAN(2)	BAe.125 Series 800B	258094	G-5-576
D-CFAX	Gates Learjet 35A	35A-135	N135GJ I-ZOOM N11AK N719US D-CDAX N22MJ (OO-LFX)

D-CFCF(2)	Gates Learjet 35A	35A-413	N27KG N413MA F-GHAE N2637Z HB-VHE
D-CFFB	Bombardier Learjet 60	60-107	N107LJ
D-CFFU	Dornier 228-212	8180	
D-CFLY	Cessna 560 Citation V	560-0145	N57ML N57MK (N6877L)
D-CFMA	Beech B300 Super King Air	FL-76	N8274U
D-CFMB	Beech B300 Super King Air	FL-97	N8297L
D-CFTG	Gates Learjet 35A	35A-204	(N277AM) N7PE N99ME N87MJ D-COSY N1466B
D-CFUX	Gates Learjet 55	55-061	N132L N222MC N117EL
D-CFXH	Short SD.3-60 Variant 300	SH.3742	N742CC (G-BOWF) G-14-3742
D-CGBR	Gates Learjet 55	55-122	OE-GRO C-FHJB N99KV N99KW N18ZD N8568P N10870
D-CGFA	Gates Learjet 35A	35A-179	N801PF C-FHLO N718SW (N696SC) N718SW D-CAPD (D-CCAR) N39412
D-CGFB	Gates Learjet 35A	35A-268	N2U N510SG (N286CP) N3857N YV-286CP N10870
D-CGFC	Gates Learjet 35A	35A-331	N435JW N700NW I-EJIB HB-VGU N1087D
D-CGFD	Gates Learjet 35A	35A-139	N15SC
D-CGFE	Gates Learjet 36A	36A-062	N4291N
D-CGFF	Gates Learjet 36A	36A-063	N1048X N6340T
D-CGFG	Gates Learjet 35A	35A-222	N789KW HB-VFZ N90AL I-EJID HB-VFZ N1468B
D-CGFH	Gates Learjet 35A	35A-607	N68MJ PT-LIJ N72614 N39399D-CGFI
	Gates Learjet 35A	35A-612	N36BP N551HM N551TW N501TW N2FU N8568D N3812G
D-CGFJ	Gates Learjet 35A	35A-643	N643MJ G-LJET (N35NK) G-LJET N39418
D-CGGG(2)	Gates Learjet 31A	31A-227	N40073 N30054
D-CGRC	Gates Learjet 35A	35A-223	N215JW
D-CHAN	Cessna 550 Citation Bravo	550-0874	N5194B
D-CHEF(6)	Hawker 800XP	258514	N4021Z
D-CHEP	Cessna 550 Citation II	550-0697	HB-VMP N697EA ZS-NFL N6851C
D-CHER	Bombardier Learjet 60	60-051	OY-LJH N63BL N5051X
D-CHFB(2)	MBB HFB-320 Hansa Jet (Reservation .04)	1043	TC-LEY 16+03 D-CIRI (1)
D-CHGS	Beech B300 Super King Air	FL-322	N3222K (D-CVVV) N3222K
D-CHLE	Bombardier Learjet 60	60-211	N5012Z
D-CHSW	Beech 400A Beechjet	RK-84	N8138M

D-CIAA	Dornier 328-110 (Permit 11.04)	3104	G-BYTY
			D-CDXB
			5N-BRI
			D-CDXJ
D-CIAB	Dornier 328-110 (Permit 11.04)	3053	G-BZIF
			F-GNBS
			D-CDXU
D-CIAC	Dornier 328-110 (Permit 11.04)	3083	5N-SPC
			D-CDXO
D-CIAO(2)	Beech B300 Super King Air	FL-279	9H-ADV
			N3179Q
D-CICE	Dornier 228-101	7073	
D-CIFA(3)	Cessna 550 Citation II	550-0378	OH-CAT
			N3999H
			YV-299CP
			N27468
D-CIMM(2)	Bombardier Learjet 60	60-214	N5016Z
D-CIRB(2)	Dornier 328-110	3017	HB-AEF
			D-CDHB
			(D-CERL)
D-CIRC(2)	Dornier 328-110	3041	HB-AEI
			D-CDXH(1)
D-CIRD	Dornier 328-110 (Permit 12.03)	3011	HB-AEG
			D-CDOG
D-CITA(3)	Bombardier Learjet 60	60-069	N60CE
			N50324
D-CITI	Dornier 328-100	3004	
D-CITY(2)	Gates Learjet 35A	35A-177	N174CP
			N77CQ
			N77CP
			N1461B
D-CJET(3)	Hawker 800XP	258358	N240B
D-CJPG	Gates Learjet 35A	35A-108	N86PC
			(N86PQ)
			N86PC
			F-GCLE
			D-COCO(2)
D-CJRA	BAe Jetstream 3103 (Permit 10.02)	603	N603JS
			V2-LEZ
			OY-EDA
			SE-KHB
			D-CONE(2)
			G-31-42
			D-CONE (2)
			G-31-42
D-CKKK	Bombardier Learjet 60	60-144	N60144
D-CLBA	Beech 400A Beechjet	RK-25	N81918
			(VR-CDA)
			N81918
D-CLBB	Dassault Falcon 20E -5	315/517	F-GSXF
			F-SEBI
			F-GDLO
			OO-VPQ
			F-BVPQ
			F-WRQP
D-CLBC	BAe. 125-800B (Permit 2.05)	258050	G-OURA
			G-ICFR
			N9LR
			G-5-503
			I-OSLO
			G-5-503
			G-BUCR
			HZ-OFC
			G-5-503D-
CLBD	Hawker 800XP (Reservation .05)	258405	N866RB
			N866RR
			N405XP
D-CLBE	Dassault Falcon 20E	279/502	N854GA
			F-GROC
			N279AL
			F-GHFQ
			I-FKET
			F-WMKJ
D-CLBR	Dassault Falcon 20C	52	N825TC
			N85DB
			N72ET
			N881F
			F-WNGN
D-CLED	LET L-410-UVP-E20C Turbolet	912533	OY-TCL
			OK-WDL
			(PT- . . .)
			OK-WDP
			CCCP67673
D-CLEO	Cessna 560 Citation V	560-0159	N68MA
			(N68854)
D-CLET	LET L-410-UVP-E20C Turbolet	912603	LV-WYV
			OK-WDP
			J2-KBF
			OK-WDL
D-CLOG(2)	Beech B300 Super King Air	FL-276	N3176T
D-CLUB(6)	Bombardier Learjet 60	60-249	N4004Q
			N50422
D-CLUE	Cessna 650 Citation III	650-0174	N674CC
			(N1782E)
D-CMAD	Gates Learjet 55C	55C-143	N10871
D-CMEI	Cessna 560 Citation V (Permit 12.04)	560-0117	N6804F
D-CMET	Dassault Falcon 20E	329/523	F-WRQV
D-CMMM	Gates Learjet 24D	24D-328	D-IMMM
D-CMPI	Cessna 650 Citation VII	650-7055	N817MZ
			N317MZ
			N317M
			N755CM
			N5185V
D-CMRM	Gates Learjet 31A	31A-213	N5009V
D-CMSC	Bombardier Learjet 45	45-097	N5017J
D-CMTM(4)	Dornier 328-110	3094	
D-CNAC	Fairchild SA.227DC Metro 23	DC-895B	N30384
D-CNAF	Fairchild Swearingen SA.227AC Metro III	AC-505B	TF-BBG
			F-GHVC
			HB-LND
			EC-DXS
			HB-LND
			N31014
D-CNAG	Fairchild SA.227EDC Metro 23	DC-893B	N3032A
D-CNAY	Fairchild Swearingen SA.227AT Merlin IVC	AT-493	PH-RAX
			F-GGLG
			N121FA
			OY-CHC
			N3075A
			CP-2109
			N3075A
D-CNCJ	Cessna 650 Citation VII	650-7102	
D-CNIK	Bombardier Learjet 40	45-2006	N50111
D-CNRY	BAe Jetstream 3103	610	SE-KHC
			OY-EDB
			SE-KHC
			D-CONI (2)
			G-31-50
D-COCA(3)	Beech 1900D	UE-224	N224YV
D-CODE	Dornier 228-101	7083	(D-CEVA)
D-COEB	Beech B300 Super King Air	FL-255	N3205M
D-COKE	Gates Learjet 35A	35A-447	N300FN
			N127K
D-COLA	Beech B300 Super King Air	FL-75	HB-GJB
			N8097Y
D-COLB	Fairchild Swearingen SA.227AC Metro III	AC-754B	N54NE
			N2746Z
D-COLD	Fairchild Swearingen SA.227AC Metro III	AC-421B	SE-LI M
			Fv.88003
			N5498M
D-COLE(2)	SAAB-Scania SF.340A	144	LV-WTF
			LV-PMG
			ZK-NSM
			SE-KRT
			D-CHBB
			SE-F44
D-COLT(2)	Fairchild Swearingen SA.227AC Metro III	AC-690	N715C
			N690NE
			N2706B
D-COMM(4)	Dornier 328-110	3117	D-CDXL(5)
	(Res as 9H-AET 12.04, not yet taken up)		(D-CGAC)
			D-CDXH(4)
D-COOL(2)	Gates Learjet 55	55-052	N551DB
			N55GF
			YV-292CP
D-COSA(2)	Dornier 328-110	3085	D-CDXR(2)
D-COTT(2)	Dornier 228-212 (Permit 6.04)	8241	(Thailand)
			D-COTT(2)
			(NAF-036)
			D-CBDM(7)
D-COXB	LET L-410-UVP Turbolet	820924	DDR-SXB
D-COXC	LET L-410-UVP Turbolet	820925	DDR-SXC
D-CPPP	Cessna 550 Citation Bravo	550-0865	N505X
D-CPRP	Dornier 328-110	3066	D-CDXL(2)
D-CPRV	Dornier 328-110	3093	D-CDXD(3)
D-CPRW	Dornier 328-100	3097	D-CDXY(3)
D-CPRY	Dornier 328-110	3106	D-CDXC(4)
D-CPWF	Dornier 328-110	3112	D-CFWF
			D-CGAN
			D-CDXE(4)
D-CRAN(2)	Bombardier Learjet 60 (Permit 3.05)	60-019	HB-VKI
			N40366
			N50153
D-CREW(2)	Dornier 328-110	3113	D-CGAO
			D-CDXF(4)
D-CRIS	IAI-1125 Astra SPX	107	N997GA
D-CROB	Bombardier Learjet 60 (Permit 6.03)	60-261	
D-CRRR(2)	Cessna 650 Citation III	650-0187	LN-AAA
			N39VP
			D-CAYK
			(N78PT)
			N70PT
			(N55PC)
			N500RP
			N187CM
			N2617K
D-CSAG(2)	Beech 1900D	UE-353	N23527
D-CSAL	Fairchild Swearingen SA.227AC Metro III	AC-601	I-FSAH
			N90AG
			OY-BPJ,
			N3117K
D-CSAP	Gates Learjet 31A	31A-057	N9147Q
D-CSFD	Cessna S550 Citation S/II	S550-0148	N170RD
			ZS-IDC
			N1296Z

D-CSIE	Gates Learjet 31A	31A-207	N50126
D-CSIM	Bombardier Learjet 60 (Reservation .04)	60-274	N4003K
D-CSIX	Bombardier Learjet 60	60-120	N120LJ
D-CSUN	Cessna 560 Citation V	560-0078	OY-CKT
			SE-DLI
			N2846B
D-CSWF	Fairchild Swearingen SA.227DC Metro 23	DC-896B	N3042E
D-CTLX	Cessna 560XL Citation XLS (Resrvn .05)	560-5569	
D-CUNO	Beech B300 Super King Air	FL-311	N5011K
D-CURT	Gates Learjet 31A	31A-042	D-CGGG(1)
D-CUTT	Dornier 228-212	8200	D-CBDC(4)
D-CVHI	Cessna 560XL Citation Excel	560-5195	N51143
D-CVIP(2)	Gates Learjet 55	55-109	N348HM
D-CVVV	Beech B300 Super King Air (Reservn 7.03)	FL-322	N3222K
D-CWAY	Gates Learjet 55	55-107	N304AT
			N155JT
			N760G
			N1466G
D-CWDL	Gates Learjet 55	55-084	I-FLYJ
			N740AC
			N85643
			N39413
D-CWER	Bombardier Learjet 45	45-010	
D-CWHS	Bombardier Learjet 60	60-246	N5035F
D-CWKM	Beech B300 Super King Air	FL-410	N61740
D-CWWW	Cessna 560XL Citation Excel	560-5316	N5096S
D-CXXX	Douglas C-47B-15DK	16124/32872	G-AMPZ
			EI-BDT
			G-AMPZ
			TF-AIV
			G-41-3-66
			PH-RIC
			G-AMPZ
			OD-AEQ
			G-AMPZ
			KN442
			44-76540
D-CZAR	Cessna 560 Citation V	560-0114	OE-GPS
			N6803T

CLASS E : Single-Engined Aircraft under 2 Metric Tonnes

D-EAAA	Bölkow BO.209 Monsun 150FF	161	
D-EAAB(3)	Piper PA-46-310P Malibu	46-8608054	N719LR
			N9539N
			N9094Z
D-EAAC	Bölkow BO.209 Monsun 160RV	163	
D-EAAD(4)	Cessna 152	15281564	N65459
D-EAAE(2)	Mooney M.20F Executive	22-1345	N6983V
D-EAAF(3)	Diamond DA 20-A1 Katana	10197	N155SE
D-EAAG	Bölkow B0.209 Monsun 160RV	167	
D-EAAH	Bölkow B0.209 Monsun 160RV	168	
D-EAAI	Bölkow B0.209 Monsun 160RV	169	
D-EAAJ(2)	Eingartner/Brditschka HB-207 Alfa (Permit 6.00)	207-006	
D-EAAK	Bölkow B0.209 Monsun 150FF	171	
D-EAAL(2)	Reims/Cessna F182Q Skylane	F18200059	
D-EAAM	Bölkow B0.209 Monsun 160RV	173	
D-EAAN	Bölkow B0.209 Monsun 160RV	174	
D-EAAO(2)	Reims/Cessna F182Q Skylane	F18200063	(D-EAAD)
D-EAAP	Bölkow B0.209 Monsun 160RV	176	
D-EAAQ(3)	Schillen BMS.80 Comet-Sappho (Permit 7.99)	001-90	
D-EAAR(2)	Mooney M.20J Model 201	24-0964	(N3860H)
D-EAAT	Bölkow BO.209 Monsun 150FF	179	
D-EAAU	Bölkow BO.209 Monsun 160FV	180	
D-EAAV	SOCATA MS.892A Rallye Commodore 150	11816	F-BSMT
D-EAAW	Bölkow BO.209 Monsun 160RV	181	
D-EAAX	Mooney M.20J Model 201	24-0675	N2135D
			D-ELLL(1)
D-EAAY(3)	Cessna 172N	17273474	N4927G
D-EAAZ(2)	Reims/Cessna F172N	F17201660	
D-EABB(2)	Piper PA-12 Super Cruiser	12-3115	N4219M
			NC4219M
D-EABC(2)	Mooney M.20F Executive	690058	
D-EABD	Cessna 172B	17248613	N8113X
D-EABF(3)	SOCATA TB-9 Tampico	1066	
D-EABG(2	Reims FR172F Rocket	FR17200084	
D-EABH	Bölkow BO.208C Junior	694	
D-EABK	Bölkow BO.208C Junior	697	
D-EABL(2)	Piper PA-28R-200 Cherokee Arrow	28R-35131	N9419N
D-EABM(2)	SOCATA TB-10 Tobago	1043	
D-EABP(2)	Reims/Cessna F152 II	F15201575	
D-EABQ(2)	SIAI-Marchetti S.205/20R	4-242	
D-EABS(3)	Cessna 172P	17276179	N97325
D-EABT(2)	CEA Jodel DR.1050 Ambassadeur	209	F-BJUI
D-EABU(3)	Wassmer Jodel D.120A Paris-Nice	205	F-BKCU
D-EABV(2)	Cessna 150H	15068826	N23251
D-EABW(2)	Cessna 152	15282703	N89289
D-EABZ(3)	Cessna 152	15279736	N757GU
D-EACA(2)	Fuji FA-200-160 Aero Subaru	89	
D-EACB(2)	Bölkow BO.209 Monsun	105A	HB-UEN
			D-EBOJ(1)
D-EACC	SOCATA MS.880B Rallye Club	1334	
D-EACD(2)	Fuji FA-200-180 Aero Subaru	133	
D-EACE	Fuji FA-200-160 Aero Subaru	131	
D-EACF(2)	Robin DR.300/180R Remorqueur	625	
D-EACG	CEA DR.360 Chevalier	626	
D-EACH	Piper PA-28-151 Cherokee Warrior	28-7415065	N9610N
D-EACI	SAN Jodel D.117A Grand Tourisme	830	OE-ABI
D-EACJ	Reims FR172G Rocket	FR17200183	(D-EFHL)
D-EACL(2)	CEA Jodel DR.1050 Ambassadeur	20	D-EOAB
			F-BJLN
D-EACM	Piper PA-24-260 Comanche C	24-4968	HB-OIW
			D-EACM
			N9460P
D-EACN	Piper PA-28-180 Cherokee F	28-7105041	N5187S
D-EACO(2)	Reims/Cessna FRA150M Aerobat	FRA1500330	PH-BER
			N72567
			F-WZDC
			N81956
D-EACP	Wassmer WA.41 Baladou	155	F-BOYQ
D-EACS(6)	Cessna 172R	17280159	N401ER
D-EACT	CEA DR.253B Régent	192	
D-EACU	CEA DR.253B Régent	193	
D-EACV	Robin DR.300/125	633	
D-EACW	SOCATA MS.883 Rallye 115	1511	F-BRYR
D-EACX	SOCATA TB-20 Trinidad	697	
D-EACZ	Champion 7GCBC Citabria	677-74	OE-AOA
D-EADA(2)	Diamond DA 20-A1 Katana	10265	
D-EADB(2)	Cessna P210N Pressurized Centurion II	P21000610	N2738C
			N734QE
D-EADC(2)	Piper PA-46-310P Malibu	46-8508005	N4376B
D-EADF(2)	Piper PA-28-235 Cherokee Pathfinder	28-7510048	N33580
D-EADH	Beech N35 Bonanza	D-6620	5Y-ADM
			3D-AAU
			5Y-ADM
			N9439Y
D-EADI	Robin DR.400/180R Remorqueur	791	
D-EADJ	Cessna 150M	15078101	N9150U
D-EADL(2)	HOACDV-20 Katana	20105	C-FVQB
			N105DV
D-EADM	Cessna 182K Skylane	18257960	N2760Q
D-EADN	Piper PA-28-140 Cherokee Cruiser	28-7325358	N11C
D-EADO	Cessna F172H	F172-0445	
D-EADP(2)	Piaggio FWP.149D (Cld but under repair .03)	009	90+04
			BB+391
D-EADR	Cessna 210L Centurion	21060579	OO-ADR
			N94276
D-EADU(2)	Cessna 152	15283229	N47477
D-EADW	Piper PA-28-180 Cherokee D	28-5308	N7861N
D-EADY	Cessna 172N	17271568	N3491E
D-EAEA	Piper PA-28-151 Cherokee Warrior	28-7415319	N9568N
D-EAEB	Piper PA-18 Super Cub 95	18-3085	OL-L11
			L-11
			53-4685
D-EAEC	Robin DR.300/180R Remorqueur	554	
D-EAED	Fuji FA-200-160 Aero Subaru	77	
D-EAEE	Fuji FA-200-180 Aero Subaru	91	
D-EAEF(3)	Cessna 152	15285296	N67394
D-EAEG(2)	Cessna 152	15283792	N5176B
D-EAEH(2)	Cessna 152	15285703	N94514
D-EAEI (2)	Cessna 172N	17273171	N6232F
D-EAEJ	Cessna 182K Skylane	18257849	(D-EMAF)
			HB-CSN
			N2649Q
D-EAEK(2)	Reims/Cessna FR182 Skylane RG	FR18200012	PH-ABK
D-EAEL(3)	Reims/Cessna F152	F15201495	HB-CXX
D-EAEM	CEA DR.253B Régent	180	
D-EAEO(2)	Cessna 172P	17276044	N90ER
			(N96223)
D-EAEP(2)	Robin DR.400/180S	1904	
D-EAER	Piper PA-18 Super Cub 95	18-1521	ALAT
			51-15521
D-EAES(2)	Cessna 172N	17269365	N62LA
			N337ER
D-EAET	Piper PA-18 Super Cub 95	18-1571	ALAT
			51-15571
D-EAEU	Piper PA-18 Super Cub 95	18-1652	ALAT
			51-15652
D-EAEV	Robin DR.300/108	556	
D-EAEW(2)	Extra EA.300	V-1	
D-EAEX	Reims/Cessna F172N	F17202027	HB-CFD
			(D-EIZT)
D-EAEZ	SOCATA MS.893A Rallye Commodore 180	11630	F-BSDY
D-EAFB(3)	Cessna 172S	172S8771	N390SP
D-EAFC	SAN Jodel DR.1050 Ambassadeur	111	PH-ONE
			(PH-ONO)
D-EAFE(2)	Mooney M.20K Model 231	25-0854	N5791R
D-EAFF(2)	Piper PA-28-140 Cherokee C	28-26920	N5287S
D-EAFG	Macchi AL.60B-2	6255/75	
D-EAFH	SEEMS MS.892A Rallye Commodore 150	10480	F-BLSU
D-EAFI	Fuji FA-200-160 Aero Subaru	111	
D-EAFJ(2)	SOCATA TB-10 Tobago	894	
D-EAFK	Piper PA-28-180 Cherokee C	28-2509	N8329W
D-EAFM(2)	Piper PA-28-180 Cherokee F	28-7105168	D-EAPD
			N2148T
D-EAFN	Robin DR.300/180R Remorqueur	578	
D-EAFO(2)	Cessna 182Q Skylane	18267187	N97772
D-EAFP	CEA DR.253B Régent	183	
D-EAFQ	CEA DR.253B Régent	186	
D-EAFR	Gyroflug SC-01 Speed Canard	S-21	
D-EAFS(2)	SOCATA TB-20 Trinidad	918	

D-EAFT	Reims/Cessna FRA150L Aerobat	FRA1500187	HB-CEW D-ECWN
D-EAFU(2)	Cessna T.207A Turbo Stationair 8 (STOL)	20700613	N73673
D-EAFW(2)	Piper PA-28RT-201T Turbo Arrow IV	28R-8331002	N8272B
D-EAFX(2)	Mooney M.20K Model 231 (Damaged 18.10.03)	25-0865	N5807X
D-EAFY	Beech C33A Debonair 285	CE-176	OH-BDC
D-EAFZ	SOCATA TB-20 Trinidad	924	
D-EAGA	Gardan GY-80 Horizon 180	245	
D-EAGB(2)	Reims/Cessna F172N	F17202007	PH-RAM PH-AYJ(3)
D-EAGC	Cessna F172H	F172-0637	(D-EBEB)
D-EAGD	Cessna 172D	17250108	OE-DCB N2508U
D-EAGF(3)	Cessna 150F	15063628	N7028F
D-EAGI	SOCATA MS.893A Rallye Commodore 180	11410	
D-EAGJ(2)	Diamond DA 20-A1 Katana	10115	N542SS
D-EAGK	Cessna F150J	F150-0508	
D-EAGL(2)	Cessna P210N Pressurized Centurion II (Written-off in Uganda 23.10.00)	P21000587	N732MS
D-EAGM(2)	Cessna 172N	17273791	N5430J
D-EAGN	SOCATA MS.883 Rallye 115	1383	
D-EAGO	SOCATA MS.893A Rallye Commodore 180	11004	
D-EAGQ(2)	Diamond DA 20-A1 Katana	10130	N559SS
D-EAGR	SOCATA MS.893A Rallye Commodore 180	11412	
D-EAGS(2)	Piper PA-28-181 Archer II	2890005	N9105V
D-EAGT(4)	American AG-5B Tiger	10131	OY-CKZ (SE-KVA) N502IT
D-EAGU(2)	SOCATA MS.880B Rallye Club	1611	F-BSFO
D-EAGV	Rockwell 114 Commander	14410	(D-EKCG)
D-EAGY	SOCATA MS.883 Rallye 115	1365	
D-EAGZ	Robin DR.400/180 Régent	1414	I-SAGA
D-EAHA(2)	SOCATA MS.880B Rallye Club	1689	(D-EFHL)
D-EAHB	SOCATA MS.880B Rallye Club	1690	
D-EAHC(2)	Castermans/ Sequoia F.8LFalco	1728	
D-EAHD	SOCATA MS.880B Rallye Club	1787	
D-EAHF	SOCATA MS.893A Rallye Commodore 180	11708	
D-EAHG(2)	Grumman AA-5B Tiger	AA5B-0469	N6148A
D-EAHI (2)	Piper PA-28RT-201 Arrow IV	28R-7918222	N62TJ N2925L
D-EAHJ(2)	Cessna 152	15284471	OH-CVN C-GRTC N4269M
D-EAHK(2)	Robin DR.400/180R Remorqueur	1314	
D-EAHL(2)	SOCATA MS.894A Minerva 220	11836	(G-AYVW)
D-EAHM	Fuji FA-200-180 Aero Subaru	106	
D-EAHN(2)	Cessna 172N	17269925	N738ES
D-EAHO(2)	Cessna 172P	17274783	N53590
D-EAHR	SAN Jodel DR.1050 Ambassadeur	372	
D-EAHS	SOCATA MS.893E Rallye 180GT Gaillard	12311	F-BUVC
D-EAHT	Cessna TU206F Turbo Stationair	U20602201	HB-CDT N7431Q
D-EAHU(2)	Piper PA-28-181 Archer II	28-8190075	N82855
D-EAHW(2)	Robin DR.400/180 Régent	1373	
D-EAHX	Piper PA-18 Super Cub 95	18-3432	D-EAWK(1) 96+12 NL+109 AC+520 AA+520 AS+520 54-732
D-EAHZ	Piper PA-38-112 Tomahawk II	38-81A0002	HB-PFN
D-EAIB	Bölkow BO.209 Monsun 160FV	186	
D-EAIC(2)	Mooney M.20J Model 201	24-0399	
D-EAID(2)	Piper PA-28-181 Archer II	2890009	N9107J
D-EAIF(3)	Cessna 152	15282287	N684Q N68412
D-EAIG	Bölkow BO.209 Monsun 160RV	191	
D-EAIH(2)	Reims/Cessna F182P Skylane	F18200017	D-EATH
D-EAII (2)	Cessna 182P Skylane	18263683	N4682K
D-EAIJ(3)	American AG-5B Tiger	10133	N1197J
D-EAIK(2)	SOCATA MS.880B Rallye Club	1904	F-BSZZ
D-EAIL(2)	Cessna 177 Cardinal	17700868	N29408
D-EAIM(2)	Fuji FA-200-160 Aero Subaru	173	
D-EAIN(3)	Aquila AT-01	115	
D-EAIO	Robin DR.300/180R Remorqueur	549	
D-EAIP	Fuji FA-200-180 Aero Subaru	92	
D-EAIQ	Fuji FA-200-180 Aero Subaru	100	
D-EAIR(2)	Bölkow BO.209 Monsun 160RV	199	
D-EAIS(2)	Beech F33A Bonanza	CE-1243	N3083K
D-EAIT	Mooney M.20K Model 231	25-0771	
D-EAIU	Cessna 150B	15059663	OE-AIU N1263Y
D-EAIV	Piper PA-28RT-201T Turbo Arrow IV	28R-7931062	N3072N
D-EAIZ	Aquila AT-01 (Model A210)	105	
D-EAJA	Gardan GY-80 Horizon 180	210	
D-EAJB(3)	SOCATA Rallye 100T	3042	OY-AJB F-ODIH
D-EAJC	Dornier Do.27B-1	292	56+24 SE+534 SC+712
D-EAJD(3)	Blair/ Denney Kitfox V Speedster (Permit 3.00)	S 95100156	
D-EAJG	Robin DR.300/180R Remorqueur	712	
D-EAJH	Robin DR.300/180R Remorqueur	726	
D-EAJI	Robin DR.300/180R Remorqueur	722	

D-EAJJ	SOCATA MS.893A Rallye Commodore 180	10531	OO-SPD F-BNBC
D-EAJK	Mooney M.20M Model 257 TLS	27-0148	
D-EAJM	Cessna R182 Skylane RG	R18200243	N3152C
D-EAJP(2)	Cessna TU206G Turbo Stationair 6-II	U20604465	N756YP
D-EAJR	Robin DR.400/180R Remorqueur	815	
D-EAJS	Extra EA.400	11	
D-EAJU	Bek Ju 87 replica (Permit 5.00)	1959	
D-EAJW	SOCATA TB-10 Tobago	147	
D-EAKA	Reims/Cessna F150M	F15001157	
D-EAKB	Reims/Cessna F150M	F15001158	
D-EAKC(2)	SOCATA TB-10 Tobago	1160	
D-EAKD(2)	SOCATA TB-10 Tobago	1161	
D-EAKE	Reims/Cessna F177RG Cardinal RG	F177RG0124	
D-EAKF(2)	SOCATA MS.893A Rallye Commodore 180	10813	F-BPQC
D-EAKG(2)	Piper PA-28-236 Dakota	28-7911115	N3066T
D-EAKH	Reims FR172J Rocket	FR17200526	
D-EAKI (2)	Cessna 172R	17280117	N9859F
D-EAKJ	SOCATA TB-10 Tobago	1162	
D-EAKK	Piper PA-28-181 Archer II	28-7990417	N2125G
D-EAKL(2)	Robin DR.400/180R Remo 180	2228	
D-EAKM	SAN Jodel DR.1050 Ambassadeur	139	OE-AKM
D-EAKN(2)	Dornier Do.27H-2	2011	HB-HAA V-604
D-EAKO(3)	Piper PA-28RT-201T Turbo Arrow IV	28R-8131146	N8401A
D-EAKP(2)	Piper PA-28-181 Archer II	28-8590048	N69093
D-EAKQ	OMF-100-160 Symphony	0005	
D-EAKR(2)	OMF-100-160 Symphony	0006	
D-EAKT	Robin DR.400/180R Remorqueur	900	
D-EAKU(2)	Piper PA-28-181 Archer II	28-8590082	N2531X
D-EAKV	SOCATA TB-10 Tobago	1164	
D-EAKW(2)	Wohltmann (Hinz) BL2 Ara	1751	
D-EAKX	OMF-100-160 Symphony	0008	
D-EAKY(2)	Reims/Cessna F177RG Cardinal RG (Reims-assembled 177RG c/n 177RG0198)	F177RG0035	OE-DEE
D-EAKZ(2)	SOCATA TB-10 Tobago	1163	
D-EALA	Reims/Cessna F152	F15201468	
D-EALB	Beech A23-24 Musketeer Super III	MA-61	SE-EUW
D-EALC	Piper PA-28-180 Cherokee G	28-7205311	N11C
D-EALD	SOCATA ST-10 Diplomate	128	
D-EALE	Cessna F172F	F172-0178	
D-EALF	Robin DR.400/180 Régent	976	(D-EOKC)
D-EALG	Lake LA-4-200 Buccaneer	558	N9972F D-EALG OY-DVN N39794
D-EALH	Piper PA-28-181 Archer II	28-8090276	N8175N
D-EALI	Mooney M.20F Executive 21	680123	N3800N
D-EALK	Reims/Cessna F152	F15201705	
D-EALN	SOCATA MS.880B Rallye Club	2355	I-RALH
D-EALO(3)	Lohmann/ Etrich Taube 7 (Reservn .04)	T301-04-005	
D-EALP	Reims/Cessna FRA150M Aerobat	FRA1500298	(G-BEOE) (5Y-AZY)
D-EALR	Reims FR172J Rocket	FR17200564	
D-EALS	Reims FR172J Rocket	FR17200577	
D-EALU	Piper PA-38-112 Tomahawk	38-79A0921	N9699N
D-EALW	SOCATA MS.894A Minerva 220	12002	F-BTPT
D-EALX(2)	Reims/Cessna F150L	F15000766	OE-ALX
D-EALY(2)	Commander Aircraft 114B	14585	
D-EALZ	Cessna P206D Super Skylane	P206-0603	N5703J
D-EAMA	Fuji FA-200-160 Aero Subaru	73	
D-EAMB(2)	Bölkow BO.208C Junior	597	OE-AMB D-ECGE(1)
D-EAMC(4)	Sopport/ Dallach D4/E-BK/S Fascination	EB022	
D-EAMD(2)	Piper PA-28RT-201T Turbo Arrow IV	28R-8331042	N4308Z
D-EAME	Cessna 182J Skylane	18257363	N3363F
D-EAMF	Fuji FA-200-180 Aero Subaru	81	
D-EAMG(2)	Reims/Cessna F182Q Skylane	F18200038	(D-EAMT) OE-DIP
D-EAMH(3)	SOCATA TB-10 Tobago	153	OE-DUZ
D-EAMI	Fuji FA-200-160 Aero Subaru	151	
D-EAMK	Cessna T210F Turbo-System Centurion	T210-0059	N6159R
D-EAML(2)	Cessna T206H Turbo Stationair	T20608348	N5146F
D-EAMM	Wassmer WA.52 Europa	88	
D-EAMN(2)	Piper PA-28-181 Cherokee Archer II	28-7890515	N36428
D-EAMO	Fuji FA-200-180 Aero Subaru	148	
D-EAMR(2)	Cessna 182J Skylane	18257493	N4786J D-EHKN N3493F
D-EAMS(2)	Piper PA-28-181 Archer II	28-8690046	N9085N N9512N
D-EAMT(4)	Mooney M.20J Model 205	24-3084	9H-ACJ(2) SE-KYB N5272N
D-EAMV	Fuji FA-200-160 Aero Subaru	177	
D-EAMW	Fuji FA-200-180 Aero Subaru	178	
D-EAMX(2)	Diamond DA 40DStar	D4.078	
D-EAMY	Piper PA-28-140 Cherokee Cruiser	28-7325212	N11C
D-EAMZ	Fuji FA-200-160 Aero Subaru	165	
D-EANA(2)	SOCATA TB-20 Trinidad	1308	N5555T
D-EANC(3)	Piper PA-18 Super Cub 95	18-2013	I-BDUE I-EIPU/ EI-83 MM52-2413 52-2413
D-EANE	Piper PA-28-151 Cherokee Warrior	28-7415155	N9515N
D-EANF	Reims/Cessna F172N	F17201684	

D-EANH(2)	SOCATA TB-10 Tobago	1626	
D-EANJ(2)	Reims/Cessna F172P	F17202110	D-EANH(1)
			(D-ECQY)
D-EANK(2)	Grob G.115A	8012	
D-EANM	PZL-110 Koliber 150	038936	SP-ARY
D-EANO	Piper PA-28-181 Cherokee Archer II	28-7890433	N9648C
D-EANP(2)	Diamond DA 20-A1 Katana	10140	N859DF
D-EANQ	Wassmer WA.51A Pacific	28	F-BSNQ
D-EANS	Mooney M.20G Statesman	680008	N586MA
D-EANT	Reims FR172G Rocket	FR17200194	
D-EAOA	Piper PA-28-181 Archer II	2890052	N9133X
D-EAOB	Piper PA-28-181 Archer II	2890082	N9147X
D-EAOD	Reims/Cessna F152	F15201910	
D-EAOE	Cessna 172RG Cutlass RG	172RG0380	N4795V
D-EAOF(3)	Mooney M.20S Eagle	30-0024	N2137V
D-EAOJ	SOCATA TB-10 Tobago	995	
D EAOK	Piper PA-28-160 Cherokee B	28-681	OY-AOK
			N5577W
D-EAOL(2)	Zlin 381 Bestmann	16	OE-ACE
			OK-ZFQ
D-EAON	Piper PA-28R-200 Cherokee Arrow II	28R-7535273	N1408X
D-EAOO	Cessna T210N Turbo Centurion II	21063856	N6289C
D-EAOP	Beech K35 Bonanza	D-6028	D-ENOC
D-EAOR	Reims FR172F Rocket	FR17200071	
D-EAOT(2)	SANJodel DR.1050 Ambassadeur	147	OE-AOT
D-EAOU	SOCATA TB-20 Trinidad	999	
D-EAOV	Robin DR.400/180R Remorqueur	1959	
D-EAOY	SOCATA TB-20 Trinidad	998	
D-EAOZ	SOCATA TB-21 Trinidad TC	632	
D-EAPA	Grumman AA-5 Traveler	AA5-0752	(N1352R)
D-EAPB	Robin DR.400/180R Remorqueur	1629	
D-EAPD(2)	Mooney M.20J Model 201	24-0520	HB-DFE
D-EAPF	Robin DR.400/180R Remorqueur	1630	
D-EAPG	Mooney M.20K Model 252 TSE	25-1147	
D-EAPH	Zlin Z.526AFS Akrobat	1230	
D-EAPJ(2)	Reims/Cessna F150M	F15001262	
D-EAPK	Cessna 182P Skylane	18263975	N9915E
	(Reims-assembled with "c/n" 0026)		
D-EAPL(2)	Robin DR.400/180 Régent	1783	
D-EAPM(2)	Feichtinger/ Piel CP.301E Emeraude	065	OE-APR
D-EAPO	Piper PA-28RT-201 Arrow IV	28R-8018033	N8149D
D-EAPP	Piper PA-28-140 Cherokee Cruiser	28-7325261	N11C
D-EAPR	SOCATA TB-10 Tobago	739	
D-EAPS	Cessna 172L	17259327	N7627G
D-EAPT(2)	Beech C23 Sundowner	M-2357	N6334X
D-EAPU	Cessna 172N	17272551	SE-IYM
			N5376D
D-EAPW(3)	Piper PA-28-181 Archer II	28-8090298	N82018
D-EAPX	Piper PA-46-310P Malibu	4608051	N9092W
D-EAPY(2)	Piper PA-28RT-201T Turbo Arrow IV	28R-8431024	N43596
D-EAPZ	Cessna 172R	17280269	N427ES
D-EAQA	Test registration for Aquila AT-01 production		
D-EAQH	Piper PA-28-161 Cadet	2841116	N91716
			N9647N
D-EAQK	Piper PA-28-140 Cherokee Cruiser	28-7625065	N9639N
D-EAQM	Maule MX7-180 Star Rocket	11044C	N6116Q
D-EARB(2)	Mooney M.20F Executive	22-1259	HB-DWG
D-EARC	Rockwell Commander 112A	468	OY-PRD
			(SE-FLX)
			(N1468J)
D-EARE	Reims/Cessna F150L	F15000792	
D-EARF	Robin DR.400/180R Remorqueur	1718	
D-EARH(3)	Diamond DA 40D Star	D4.130	
D-EARK(2)	SIAT 223A-1 Flamingo	013	HB-EVH
			D-ENBJ(1)
D-EARL(2)	Cessna T210M Turbo Centurion	21061747	N8719J
			N732SW
D-EARM	Beech F35 Bonanza	D-4256	OO-JAO
			OO-JAC
D-EARN(2)	Piper PA-28-161 Cadet	2841113	N9645N
D-EARO	Cessna 182N Skylane	18260106	N92237
D-EARP	SOCATA MS.880B Rallye Club	2054	F-BTRE
D-EARR	Beech C23 Sundowner 180	M-2275	
D-EARS(2)	Lake LA-4-200 Buccaneer	1106	N8543J
D-EART	Mooney M.20K Model 231	25-0376	
D-EARU(2)	Reims/Cessna F172N	F17201817	(D-EOVV)
D-EARV	Grob G.115C	82039/C	
D-EARW	Piper PA-46-350P Malibu Mirage	4622068	N91811
D-EARY(3)	Piaggio FWP.149D	057	(D-EIJR)
			HB-EVU
			90+43
			SB+212
			SC+402
			AS+484
D-EARZ	Piper PA-28-180 Cherokee D	28-5345	OY-BKT
D-EASA	SOCATA MS.893A Rallye Commodore 180	10942	
D-EASB(3)	Cessna 172N	17272535	N5347D
D-EASC(2)	Piper PA-28-181 Archer II	28-8090212	N81418
D-EASD	Fuji FA-200-160 Aero Subaru	87	
D-EASF	Piper PA-28R-201 Cherokee Arrow III	28R-7737090	N38359
D-EASG(5)	Robin DR.400/180R Remorqueur	1529	HB-EQL
			F-GCUX
D-EASH	Piper PA-28-180 Cherokee Archer	28-7505038	N9608N
D-EASI (2)	Piper PA-28-140 Cherokee Cruiser	28-7725095	N9542N
D-EASJ	Bölkow BO.208C Junior	695	OE-ASR
			D-EABI (1)
D-EASK	Sportavia-Pützer RF-6	6002	
D-EASL	Piper PA-28-180 Cherokee Archer	28-7505160	N9614N
D-EASM	Cessna 182M Skylane	18259654	(N71534)
D-EASN	Mooney M.20J Model 201	24-1244	N1154Y
D-EASO	SOCATA MS.893A Rallye Commodore 180	10989	
D-EASP	SOCATA MS.880B Rallye Club	1609	F-BSDU
D-EASR(3)	Grob G.115D2 (Reservn .04)	82011	G-BVHF
			D-EARV(1)
D-EAST(3)	HOAC DV-20 Katana	20027	OE-CDD(2)
			N27DV
D-EASW	SAN Jodel DR.1050 Ambassadeur	131	F-BJJP
D-EASY	Reims FR172F Rocket	FR17200064	
D-EATB	SOCATA MS.892A Rallye Commodore 150	10953	OY-TRU
			SE-CIX
D-EATC	Cessna 150C	15059805	N2005Z
D-EATE(2)	Cessna 172D	17249983	N5099C
			N711RN
			N2383U
D-EATH(2)	Piper PA-28R-201T Turbo Arrow III	28R-7803346	
D-EATJ	RFB Fantrainer 600	D1	98+30
D-EATK	SOCATA TB-10 Tobago	1114	
D-EATM	Piper PA-28R-200 Cherokee Arrow II	28R-7335100	N15883
D-EATN	SAN Jodel DR.1050 Ambassadeur	451	
D-EATO	Wassmer CE.43 Guepard	438	
D-EATP(2)	RFB Fantrainer 400	011	98+77
			D-EATP(2)
D-EATQ	Bellanca 7GCBC Citabria	835-75	OE-AOO
D-EATR	RFB Fantrainer 600	001	98+75
			D-EATR
D-EATS(3)	Piper PA-18-135 Super Cub	18-3351	N4282V
			EI-129
			I-EIHD
			53-7751
D-EATT	Piper PA-28R-200 Cherokee Arrow B	28R-7135095	N5095S
D-EATV(2)	Piper PA-28R-201T Turbo Cherokee Arrow III	28R-7703303	N40435
D-EATW(2)	Diamond DA 20-A1 Katana	10141	
D-EATX(2)	Gyroflug SC-01B-160 Speed Canard	S-48	
D-EATY(2)	Piper PA-18 Super Cub 95	18-1511	OO-HBS
	(C/n officially quoted as 18-3080)		OO-SPK
			ALAT
			551-15511
D-EAUA	SOCATA TB-10 Tobago	1097	
D-EAUB(4)	Cessna 172N	17270150	N172TA
			N738QG
D-EAUC	Grumman American AA-5A Cheetah	AA5A-0349	D-EOGN
			HB-UCI
D-EAUF	SOCATA MS.893E Rallye 180GT Gaillard	12267	F-BUJE
D-EAUG	Bücker Bü.131/APM-150 Jungmann	75	HB-UUG
			A-62
			HB-USG
			A-62
D-EAUK	Bücker Bü.131/APM-150 Jungmann	27	HB-UUK
			A-18
D-EAUO	Robin DR.400/180R Remo 180	2371	
D-EAUR	SOCATA TB-10 Tobago	1099	
D-EAUS(2)	Gyroflug SC-01B-160 Speed Canard	S-10	
D-EAUT(3)	Piper PA-18-150 Super Cub	18-7909190	N9754N
D-EAUU(2)	Bücker Bü.133C Jungmeister	10	OE-AUU
			D-EEEY(2)
			U-63
D-EAUW	Werner Rieseler R.III.22/K	1853	
D-EAUX(2)	Piper PA-28-180 Cherokee D	28-5423	N7996N
D-EAVA	Cessna 182M Skylane	18259806	N91525
D-EAVB	Beech F33A Bonanza	CE-1127	
D-EAVC	Reims/Cessna F172N	F17201728	N9900A
D-EAVE(2)	SOCATA TB-10 Tobago	930	
D-EAVG	Reims/Cessna F172M	F17201362	(D-EDRO)
D-EAVI (3)	Nachson/ Velocity J-II	01	
D-EAVJ	Piper PA-28R-201 Arrow III	28-7837282	OE-DEP
			N36512
D-EAVL	SAN Jodel DR.1050 Ambassadeur	360	
D-EAVM	AIAA/ Stampe SV-4C	1134	F-BALM
			Fr.Mil
D-EAVS	Robin DR.300/180R Remorqueur	706	
D-EAVV	Bücker Bü.131B Jungmann	12	HB-UUB
			A-5
D-EAWA	Gardan GY-80 Horizon 180	256	
D-EAWC	Mooney M.20E Chaparral	690036	N9172V
D-EAWD(2)	Fieseler Fi.156C-3 Storch	5440	D-EBGY(1)
	(C/n quoted as "2072-9")		Fv5825
			PP+QA
D-EAWF(2)	Cessna P210N Pressurized Centurion	P21000618	N734XN
D-EAWG	Cessna 182P Skylane	18264392	N1606M
	(Reims-assembled with "c/n" 0055)		
D-EAWH	Robin DR.400/180R Remorqueur	1440	
D-EAWI (2)	Wegner/ Brändli BX-2 Cherry	AB-01	
D-EAWK(2)	Beech A36 Bonanza	E-2174	N184SB
D-EAWL(2)	Zlin Z.42M	0060	DDR-WNR
			DM-WNR
D-EAWN	Zlin Z.50LA	0026	HA-SIA
D-EAWP(3)	Mooney M.20K Model 231	25-0605	N1149E
D-EAWS(3)	Cessna T210R Turbo Centurion II	21064989	(N8518U)
D-EAWT	Robin HR.200/100 Club	18	
D-EAWU(2)	Cessna 172S	172S8148	N7267Q
D-EAWW(2)	Piper PA-28R-201 Arrow III	28R-7837199	N9469C
D-EAWZ	Reims/Cessna F172M	F17201169	

D-EAXA	Grumman AA-5 Traveler	AA5-0497	(N7197L)
D-EAXB	Grumman AA-5 Traveler	AA5-0518	(N9518L)
D-EAXC	Grumman AA-5 Traveler	AA5-0544	N9544L
D-EAXD	Grumman AA-5 Traveler	AA5-0545	(N9545L)
D-EAXE	Grumman AA-5 Traveler	AA5-0553	(N9553L)
D-EAXG	Grumman AA-1B Trainer	AA1B-0352	(N8852L)
D-EAXH	Grumman AA-1B Trainer	AA1B-0356	(N8856L)
D-EAXI (2)	Denney Kitfox IV	C9909-0251	
D-EAXL	CASA I-131E Jungmann	2154	(D-EGXT) F-AZGH E3B-538
D-EAXP	Korte/ Aero Designs Pulsar XP	1809	
D-EAXT(2)	Piaggio FWP.149D	150	91+28 AC+464 AC+402 AS+084 KB+127
D-EAXU	SOCATA MS.893A Rallye Commodore 180	10935	F-BPAO
D-EAXZ	Cessna 175C Skylark	17557032	OE-DCH N8332T
D-EAYA	Cessna 150B	15059377	OE-AYA N7277X
D-EAYB	Piper PA-28R-201 Cherokee Arrow III	28R-7737112	N38732
D-EAYO(2)	Beech A36AT Bonanza	E-2651	
D-EAYP	Beech A36AT Bonanza	E-2656	
D-EAYQ	Beech A36AT Bonanza	E-2661	
D-EAYR	Piper PA-28R-200 Cherokee Arrow II	28R-7335191	N55187
D-EAYS	Cessna 172N	17271029	N241FR N241ER N1509E
D-EAYX	Piper PA-32R-301T Saratoga II TC	3257024	D-ESUV(2) N9295X
D-EAYZ(2)	Cessna 150E	15061491	OE-AYZ N4091U
D-EAZE	Focke-Wulf FW.44J Stieglitz	2779	OH-SZI SZ-20 RNoAF 9 D-EXWP
D-EAZG(2)	Extra EA.200	02	
D-EAZO	Bücker Bü.131 Jungmann	52	HB-UTK A-41
D-EAZT	SOCATA TB-10 Tobago	1113	
D-EAZW	Zech/ Neico Lancair 320	1700	
D-EBAA(2)	Reims/Cessna F182Q Skylane	F18200110	
D-EBAB(2)	Piper PA-28-151 Cherokee Warrior	28-7415059	N9607N
D-EBAC(2)	Dornier Do.27A-4	381	56+76 PA+323 KD+. . . PG+102
D-EBAE	CEA DR.253B Régent	147	(G-AXDG)
D-EBAF	Piper J-3C-65 Cub	13197	SL-AAR F-BDTF 45-4457
D-EBAG(2)	Reims/Cessna F172N	F17201655	
D-EBAH(3)	Echtle/ Brditschka HB-207A Alpha	207-007	
D-EBAI	CEA DR.253B Régent	144	F-BRFZ
D-EBAJ(3)	Robin R.3000/140	102	D-EHIA(1)
D-EBAK(4)	Diamond DA 20-A1 Katana	10330	N330DA
D-EBAL(2)	Piper PA-18-150 Super Cub	18-5364	N5884 ALAT N10F
D-EBAM(2)	Cessna 210L Centurion II	21061120	N210GV N210GM
D-EBAN(2)	SOCATA MS.883 Rallye 115	1586	
D-EBAO	CEA DR.253B Régent	151	
D-EBAP(2)	SOCATA TB-10 Tobago	1069	
D-EBAR(3)	SOCATA TB-9 Tampico	933	
D-EBAS(3)	Piper PA-28RT-201T Turbo Arrow IV	28R-8231024	N8062L
D-EBAV(2)	Wassmer WA.52 Europa	19	F-WSQG
D-EBAW(3)	Piper PA-18-150 Super Cub	18-5389	ALAT N10F
D-EBAX(3)	Grumman AA-5 Traveler	AA5-0751	(N1351R)
D-EBAY	Robin DR.300/180R Remorqueur	595	
D-EBAZ(6)	Baaz/ Neico Lancair 320	489/1697	
D-EBBA(3)	Lang/ Aero Designs Pulsar XP	EB 432	
D-EBBB	Piper PA-18 Super Cub 95	18-3425	96+07 PZ+901 QZ+010 AC+514 AA+514 AS+514 54-725
D-EBBC(2)	SOCATA TB-9 Tampico	1420	I-IAGU
D-EBBD	Reims FR172F Rocket	FR17200066	
D-EBBE(3)	SAN Jodel D.140C Mousquetaire III	119	F-BMBA
D-EBBF	Cessna 182M Skylane	18259573	N71314
D-EBBG	Cessna 207 Skywagon 207	20700108	(N91186)
D-EBBI (5)	WDFL Dallach D4 Fascination VLA (Permit 5.04)	1003	
D-EBBJ	Reims FR172F Rocket	FR17200119	
D-EBBK(2)	SOCATA TB-10 Tobago	399	F-OGKG
D-EBBM(3)	Cessna 172N	17268151	N733AU
D-EBBN	Navion Rangemaster H	NAV-4-2530	(N2530T)
D-EBBR(2)	Piper PA-18-95 Super Cub (Reservation 1.99)	18-1586	(D-EHBR) D-ELTQ ALAT 51-15586
D-EBBS(3)	Beech B36TC Bonanza	EA-457	N2749N
D-EBBT	Dornier Do.27A-1	185	55+53 AC+911 AS+911
D-EBBU	Cessna 182H Skylane	18256627	N8527S
D-EBBV	Robin HR.100/285 Tiara	524	G-BGWD F-BXRF
D-EBBW(2)	PZL-104 Wilga 35A	62167	DDR-WBW DM-WBW
D-EBBX	Piper PA-28RT-201T Turbo Arrow IV	28R-8531015	N9147Y
D-EBBY(2)	Reims/Cessna F172M	F17201337	
D-EBBZ	Beagle 121 Pup 150	142	G-AXSE G-35-142
D-EBCA(2)	Cessna F172H	F172-0628	
D-EBCB(2)	Cessna R172K Hawk XP (Res .05)	R1722399	N736BP
D-EBCC	SAN Jodel DR.1050M Excellence	488	
D-EBCD	Piper PA-28-161 Cherokee Warrior II	28-7816268	N9515N
D-EBCE(2)	Piper PA-28RT-201T Turbo Arrow IV	28R-8031093	N8190R
D-EBCH	Piper PA-28-180 Cherokee G	28-7205261	N11C
D-EBCI (2)	Piper PA-28-181 Cherokee Archer II	28-7690247	(D-EEEL) N9556N
D-EBCK	Procaer F15B Picchio	35	OE-DGE
D-EBCL	Reims/Cessna F150M	F15001405	
D-EBCN	SNCAN/ Stampe SV.4C	543	F-BDCN (OO-CDN) F-BDCN
D-EBCP	Beech C23 Sundowner 180	M-1948	
D-EBCR(2)	Cessna 180H	18051589	5N-ADL N1789X
D-EBCS(3)	Robin DR.500/200i Président	0005	
D-EBCT(2)	Cessna 152	15280950	N48746
D-EBCU(2)	Cessna F172H	F172-0642	
D-EBCV	HOAC DV-20 Katana	20018	N18DV
D-EBCW	Cessna R172K Hawk XP	R1722565	N736JN
D-EBDB	Piper PA-28-140 Cherokee B	28-26026	OY-BDD
D-EBDD(2)	Reims/Cessna F182Q Skylane	F18200100	
D-EBDE	Piaggio FWP.149D	131	(91+10) D-EBDE KB+108
D-EBDI (2)	Cessna 152	15281119	N49045
D-EBDL	Piper PA-46-310P Malibu	46-8608018	N9226M
D-EBDM	Cessna 172P	17276375	N98897
D-EBDO(4)	Oberbach/ Van's RV-4	01	
D-EBDR(2)	Dornier Do.27A-1	272	56+05 YA+014 ? LC+158
D-EBDT(2)	Mudry CAP.231	10	F-GGYH F-WZCJ
D-EBDU(2)	Mooney M.20J Model 201	24-0880	(N4790H)
D-EBDW	HOAC DV-20 Katana	20050	
D-EBDX	Aerodiffusion Jodel D.1190-S Compostela	E-95	OE-CFW D-EBDX EC-BDX
D-EBDY(3)	Cessna 172RG Cutlass RG II	172RG0745	N6518V
D-EBEA	Mudry CAP.10B	84	
D-EBEC(3)	Diamond DA 20-A1 Katana	10331	N731DA
D-EBED	SAAB S.91B Safir	91291	
D-EBEE	Reims/Cessna F150K	F15000610	OO-HBE (OO-WIE)
D-EBEF(2)	Beech C23 Sundowner 180	M-2195	
D-EBEG(2)	Piper PA-28R-201T Turbo Cherokee Arrow III	28R-7703064	N2401Q
D-EBEH(2)	Cessna 172C Skyhawk	17249296	N1596Y
D-EBEI (2)	Messerschmitt Me.108D-1	2246	N108HP N54208 Luftwaffe
D-EBEK(2)	Piper PA-28R-200 Cherokee Arrow II	28R-7335205	N55264
D-EBEL(4)	Grob G.115	8063	F-GGON D-EIAU
D-EBEM(2)	Piper PA-28R-200 Cherokee Arrow II	28R-7335235	N55453
D-EBEN(2)	Mooney M.20L PFM	26-0013	
D-EBEO	Reims/Cessna F182Q Skylane	F18200129	
D-EBEP(4)	Piper PA-28RT-201T Turbo Arrow IV	28R-7931150	N2195Y
D-EBER(4)	HK Wega Ex	006	
D-EBES(2)	Piper PA-28R-201T Turbo Cherokee Arrow III	28R-7703063	N2295Q
D-EBET	SNCAN/ Stampe SV.4C	567	F-BDDM
D-EBEV(2)	Reims/Cessna F172N	F17202023	(PH-AYE)
D-EBEW(6)	Piper PA-18 Super Cub 95 (Spare frame no.18-5019 fitted earlier)	18-1005	D-EKAV(2) RHAF 51-15308
D-EBEX	Cessna 140	10300	N73084
D-EBEY	Piper PA-28-161 Warrior II	28-7916441	N2815S
D-EBEZ(2)	Piper PA-28RT-201 Arrow IV	28R-7918208	N2895Y
D-EBFA(2)	Piper PA-28-236 Dakota	28-7911253	N2940N
D-EBFB	Piper PA-18 Super Cub 95	18-3217	OL-L43 L-143 53-4817
D-EBFC	Piper PA-18 Super Cub 95	18-3161	OL-L83 L-83 53-4761
D-EBFD	Piper PA-18 Super Cub 95	18-3197	OL-L02 L-123 53-4797
D-EBFE	SAN Jodel DR.1050 Ambassadeur	276	
D-EBFG	SOCATA TB-10 Tobago	905	
D-EBFH(2)	Robin DR.400/180 Régent	2570	

D-EBFI(2)	Wassmer Jodel D.120 Paris-Nice	82	F-BIKN
D-EBFK(2)	Robin DR.400/180R Remorqueur	1960	
D-EBFL	RFB Fanliner FL-1	01	
D-EBFM	Maier/ Van's RV-4	AB-01	
D-EBFN	Cessna 172N	17271227	N2306E
D-EBFO	Cessna 172A	47746	N6846X
D-EBFR	Cessna 172M	17263520	N5321R
D-EBFS	Robin DR.300/180R Remorqueur	667	
D-EBFT	Grob G.115B	8102	VH-AYB D-ERFI F-GGOR (HB- . . .)
D-EBFU	Piper PA-18 Super Cub 95	18-3126	L-52 53-4726
D-EBFW(2)	Messerschmitt Me.108B Taifun	1561	OY-AIH F-BBRH Luftwaffe D-IBHS
D-EBFY	Pützer Elster C	022	
D-EBGB(2)	Piper PA-28-160 Cherokee	28-82	OO-RPC D-EBRO N11C (N5073W)
D-EBGC(2)	Piper PA-18-135 Super Cub	18-2549	PH-NYL ALAT 52-6231
D-EBGD(2)	Cessna F150J	F150-0511	(HB-CTY)
D-EBGE(2)	Piper PA-38-112 Tomahawk	38-79A0986	N9710N
D-EBGF(7)	Grob G.120A (Permit 3.02)	85006	VH-AYB
D-EBGG(2)	Reims FR172G Rocket	FR17200151	
D-EBGH	Cessna F150J	F150-0528	HB-CUA F-BRBU
D-EBGK	SOCATA MS.887 Rallye 125	2117	F-BTVL
D-EBGL	Great Lakes 2T-1A-1	0504	N504GL
D-EBGM(2)	Robin DR.400/180R Remo 180	2477	
D-EBGN	Piper PA-28R-201T Turbo Cherokee Arrow III	28R-7703232	N38504
D-EBGO(2)	Cessna 182J Skylane	18257497	N3497F
D-EBGR	Rösinger/ Murphy Renegade Spirit RG90	001	
D-EBGS	Robin DR.400/180R Remorqueur	1438	
D-EBGT	Cessna F150J	F150-0462	
D-EBGW(3)	Cessna 172RG Cutlass RG	172RG0935	N9637B
D-EBGZ	Robin DR.400/180R Remorqueur	803	
D-EBHA(2)	Robin DR.400/RP Remorqueur	1784	
D-EBHB(3)	Robin DR.400/180 Régent	1311	
D-EBHC(2)	Dornier Do.27A-4	512	HB-HAI D-EFMG(2) 57+58 MB+904 JC+904 JC+390 LB+163
D-EBHD(2)	Reims/Cessna F172P	F17202198	
D-EBHF	Cessna 152	15280844	N25902
D-EBHG	Bölkow BO.209 Monsun 160RV	160	(D-EBJT)
D-EBHI (2)	Piper PA-28-161 Warrior II	28-7916284	N9601N
D-EBHJ(2)	SNCAN/ Stampe SV.4C	165	F-BBPH
D-EBHK	Piper PA-28R-200 Cherokee Arrow II	28R-7235230	N5375T
D-EBHL(3)	SNCAN/ Stampe SV.4C	216	Fr.AF (F-BNGC) Fr.Navy Fr.AF
D-EBHM	Cessna 172M	17261888	N12216
D-EBHN(2)	Mooney M.20K Model 231	25-0316	OE-KPS N231MX
D-EBHO(3)	Bellanca 7GCBC Citabria	759-74	OE-AOM
D-EBHP	Piper PA-22-150 Tri-Pacer	22-3141	HB-OPB
D-EBHR	AIAA/ Stampe SV.4A	1120	F-BAHE Fr.AF
D-EBHS	Mooney M.20J Model 201	24-0019	
D-EBHU	Cessna 175B Skylark	17556978	N8278T
D-EBHV	Piper PA-18 Super Cub 95	18-2058	PH-JKB R-73 52-2458
D-EBHW	Cessna 182M Skylane	18259877	N91704
D-EBHY(2)	Piper PA-18 Super Cub 95	18-2099	D-EBHL(1) ALAT 52-2499
D-EBHZ	Beech A36AT Bonanza	E-2717	
D-EBIA	Binder CP.301S Smaragd	100	
D-EBIB(2)	SAN Jodel DR.1050 Ambassadeur	184	
D-EBIC(2)	Cessna 175C Skylark	17557119	N8519X
D-EBID	Piper PA-18 Super Cub 95	18-5660	N10F
D-EBIE(2)	Mooney M.20K Model 231	25-0665	N11620
D-EBIF(2)	Piper PA-28R-200 Cherokee Arrow B	28R-7135194	N1973T
D-EBIG(3)	Diamond DA 20-A1 Katana	10033	N608F
D-EBIH(2)	Robin HR.100/210D Safari	199	
D-EBII	Robin HR.100/210D Safari	200	
D-EBIJ	Robin DR.400/180 Régent	969	
D-EBIL(2)	Piper PA-28-140 Cherokee Cruiser	28-7625104	N9507N
D-EBIN(3)	Diamond DA 40 Star	40023	
D-EBIO	Reims/Cessna F177RG Cardinal RG	F177RG0048	
D-EBIP(2)	Cessna F150F	F150-0048/15063375	(N6775F)
D-EBIQ(2)	Cessna 175B	17556814	OE-DCF N8114T
D-EBIS(2)	Piper J-3C-65 Cub	12513	(D-EDUS) (Norway) 44-80217

D-EBIT	Piper PA-24-250 Comanche	24-393	N10F
D-EBIV(4)	Piper PA-28-161 Warrior II	28-7916175	N9558N
D-EBIW(2)	Cessna U206G Stationair II (Soloy) (Operates on skis/wheels or floats) (Permit 7.04)	U20603896	C-GBIW N7358C
D-EBIX(3)	Mudry CAP.10B	220	OO-OFD
D-EBIY	Piper PA-28RT-201T Turbo Arrow IV	28R-7931229	N2858D
D-EBIZ(3)	Diamond DA 40 Star	40052	
D-EBJA(3)	Cessna 172N	17270249	N738UN
D-EBJB(2)	Piper PA-18-135 Super Cub	18-3922	N4282R EI-226 I-EIJW 54-2522
D-EBJH(2)	Reims/Cessna F172N Skyhawk II	F17201567	
D-EBJL(2)	Cessna P210N Pressurized Centurion II	P21000042	N116RS G-IAIN N3623P
D-EBJN	Bölkow BO.209 Monsun 150FF	154	
D-EBJO	Bölkow BO.209 Monsun 150FF	155	
D-EBJP	Bölkow BO.209 Monsun 160RV	156	
D-EBJQ	Bölkow BO.209 Monsun 150FF	157	
D-EBJR(2)	Cessna 182T Skylane	18281313	N21002
D-EBJS(2)	Dornier Do.27A-1	604	57+65 BD+398
D-EBJW	Dallach D4 Fascination	WD-003	
D-EBKA	Piper PA-22-108 Colt	22-8296	N10F
D-EBKB	Mooney M.20J Model 201	24-0500	N201XP
D-EBKD	Morane-Saulnier MS.880B Rallye Club	115	F-BKKH (D-EMPY)
D-EBKI (3)	Cessna 182S	18280493	N7269V
D-EBKK(2)	Piper PA-46-310P Malibu	4608120	N183WW N133WW N9136J
D-EBKL	Dornier Do.27B-1	363	56+68 LC+160 AS+942
D-EBKO(2)	Cessna 172B	17248348	PH-KKO N7848X
D-EBKP(2)	Reims/Cessna FR172K Hawk XP	FR17200661	N988PK HB-CNU
D-EBKR	Gyroflug SC-01B-1601 Speed Canard	S-13	
D-EBKS	SOCATA MS.893A Rallye Commodore 180	11454	F-BSCQ
D-EBKT	de Havilland DH.82A Tiger Moth	85223/ E-13	(D-EAPN) OY-DYJ D-EDOM(1) DE153
D-EBKU(2)	Piper PA-28-181 Archer II	28-7990543	N2903E
D-EBKW	Weiler/ Pottier P.180 S	155	
D-EBKY	Bölkow BO.207	234	
D-EBKZ	Robin DR.400/180 Régent	1055	
D-EBLA(2)	Mooney M.20K Model 231	25-0457	N4044H
D-EBLB	Cessna F150J	F150-0496	
D-EBLC	Cessna F150J	F150-0495	
D-EBLD(2)	Cessna F172G	F172-0189	OE-DLD
D-EBLE(2)	Beech 77 Skipper	WA-150	
D-EBLG	Cessna F150J	F150-0488	
D-EBLI	Bölkow BO.207	223	
D-EBLJ	Reims FR172G Rocket	FR17200148	
D-EBLK	Reims/Cessna F150K	F15000542	
D-EBLL	Reims/Cessna F172H	F17200663	
D-EBLR	Reims/Cessna F150K	F15000576	
D-EBLS	Reims FR172G Rocket	FR17200207	
D-EBLT	Cessna 172B Skyhawk	17248473	N7973X
D-EBLV	Reims/Cessna F172H	F17200660	
D-EBLW(2)	Piper PA-28RT-201 Arrow IV	28R-8118056	PH-SDE OO-HKS N83364
D-EBLX	SEEMS MS.892A Rallye Commodore 150	10449	F-BLSX
D-EBLY(2)	Bölkow BO.207	288	D-EUXY HB-UXY D-ENWE(1)
D-EBMA	Bölkow BO.207	235	
D-EBMC	Cessna F172H	F172-0633	
D-EBMD	Cessna F172H	F172-0645	
D-EBME(2)	Reims/Cessna F177RG Cardinal RG	F177RG0116	PH-OOG
D-EBMF	Cessna F172H	F172-0641	
D-EBMG	Reims FR172F Rocket	FR17200063	
D-EBMH	Reims FR172F Rocket	FR17200069	
D-EBMI	SAN Jodel DR.1050 Ambassadeur	353	
D-EBMK(2)	Beech B36TC Bonanza	EA-422	N6844L N37PM N6844L
D-EBMM(3)	HOAC DV-20 Katana	20137	
D-EBMN	Piper PA-38-112 Tomahawk	38-78A0397	(D-EOMN) N9705N
D-EBMP	Cessna F150J	F150-0513	
D-EBMR	Reims FR172F Rocket	FR17200123	(G-AXDA)
D-EBMS(2)	Maule MX7-235 Star Rocket	10067C	N6115Y
D-EBMT	Reims FR172F Rocket	FR17200112	
D-EBMU(2)	Beech C23 Sundowner	M-1467	OE-DMU D-ENNQ
D-EBMV	Gardan GY-80 Horizon 160	117	
D-EBMW(4)	Cessna 207 Skywagon 207	20700088	OE-DEV (N91138)
D-EBMZ	Reims FR172F Rocket	FR17200122	
D-EBNC	SOCATA MS.893E Rallye 180GT Gaillard	12632	F-BXDU
D-EBNE	Cessna 182E Skylane	18253770	N9370X
D-EBNI	Cessna 182E Skylane	18254109	N3109Y

D-EBNK	Beech B24R Sierra 200	MC-222	
D-EBNL	Beech B24R Sierra 200	MC-233	
D-EBNN	Beech B24R Sierra 200	MC-260	
D-EBNO(2)	Beech F33A Bonanza	CE-484	
D-EBNQ	Beech V35B Bonanza	D-9602	
D-EBNS	Piper PA-18A-150 Super Cub	18-6117	G-JELY PH-MAV N8182D
D-EBNT	Berndt/ Jurca MJ-5 Sirocco	023	(D-EBTK(2))
D-EBNY	Cessna 150D	15060497	N4497U
D-EBOA(2)	Haubensack/ Europa Avn Europa	161	
D-EBOB(2)	Piper PA-18-150 Super Cub	18-7501	N10F
D-EBOC(4)	Piper PA-28-181 Archer II	2890029	N9123N
D-EBOD(3)	Reims/Cessna F152	F15201618	
D-EBOE	Bölkow BO.209 Monsun 160RV	102	
D-EBOF(3)	Piaggio FWP.149D	109	90+89 AC+448 JC+390 AS+445
D-EBOG	Nitzsche/ Jodel D.9 Bébé (Reservation 2.01)	AB13	
D-EBOI	Bölkow BO.209 Monsun 150FF	104	
D-EBOJ(2)	Bölkow BO.209 Monsun 160FV (Built 1974 by R.Ficht using a new airframe and retaining the documents and c/n of HB-UEN/ D-EBOJ(1). The latter was rebuilt as D-EACB with c/n 105A)	"105"	
D-EBOK(2)	Mooney M.20K Model 231	25-0256	N231HD
D-EBOL(5)	Piper PA-38-112 Tomahawk	38-78A0267	N9669N
D-EBOM(2)	Beech F33A Bonanza	CE-1147	
D-EBON(2)	Cessna 172P	17275093	PH-SCV N54961
D-EBOP(3)	Reims/Cessna F172N	F17201865	
D-EBOQ(2)	Bölkow BO.209 Monsun 150FV	109	
D-EBOR(3)	Cessna F172G	F172-0197	
D-EBOS	Bölkow BO.209 Monsun 150FV	110	
D-EBOU(2)	SNCAN/ Stampe SV.4C	326	OO-AKC F-BCVS Fr.AF
D-EBOV(2)	Cessna 172B	17248526	D-ELIM N8026X
D-EBOW(2)	Bölkow BO.209 Monsun 160RV	112	
D-EBOX	Cessna 150	17179	N5679E
D-EBOZ(2)	SNCAN/ Stampe SV.4C	297	F-BCGY
D-EBPA(4)	Piper PA-28-181 Archer III	2843596	N3093L
D-EBPD	Bölkow BO.209 Monsun 150RV	115	
D-EBPE	Cessna 175C Skylark (Franklin engine)	17557085	N8385T
D-EBPH	Bölkow BO.209 Monsun 150FF	118	
D-EBPI	Bölkow BO.207	237	
D-EBPJ	Bölkow BO.209S Monsun 130FF	119	
D-EBPK(2)	Sportavia-Pützer RS-180 Sportsman	6009	
D-EBPM	Sportavia-Pützer RS-180 Sportsman	6011	
D-EBPO(2)	Sportavia-Pützer RS-180 Sportsman	6013	
D-EBPP	CASA I-131E Jungmann	2091	E3B-489
D-EBPR	Robiv HR.200/120B	302	S5-DGR D-EBPR
D-EBPT	Bücker Bü.131 Jungmann (Marked "A-50")	62	A-50
D-EBPY	Wassmer Jodel D.120 Paris-Nice	242	
D-EBQU	SEEMS MS.885 Super Rallye	5423	
D-EBRA	Erco 415CD Ercoupe	4833	OO-JDN NC94722
D-EBRB(2)	SOCATAMS.880BRallye Club	2951	OE-DRB
D-EBRC	Piper PA-28-181 Archer II	28-8190243	N83913
D-EBRD	SOCATA TB-20 Trinidad	467	
D-EBRE(2)	Piper PA-28-181 Archer II	28-8090017	N2972V
D-EBRF	Piper PA-28R-200 Cherokee Arrow	28R-35658	N3034R
D-EBRH	Cessna P210N Pressurized Centurion II	P21000396	N6330K
D-EBRI (2)	Piper PA-28-181 Cherokee Archer II	28-7790055	N4680F
D-EBRK(2)	Tecnam P.92J Echo-VLA	005	
D-EBRM(2)	Cessna 172M	17267348	4X-CGL N73291
D-EBRO(4)	Cessna 172S	172S8175	N7256X
D-EBRP	Wassmer WA.81 Piranha	816	F-GAIR
D-EBRS	Mooney M.20J Model 201 (*C/n corrected*)	24-1639	N5763H
D-EBRT	Reims/Cessna FR172K Hawk XP	FR17200610	G-BFRT (LN-ALQ)
D-EBRU	Cessna 140	12604	OE-ABH(1) HB-CAE
D-EBRV	Servatius/ Van's RV-8 (Permit 3.04)	80303	
D-EBRY	Cessna F172E	F172-0052	
D-EBSA(2)	Piper PA-28-180 Cherokee D	28-5329	N7918N
D-EBSB	Piper PA-28-140 Cherokee C	28-26566	N5901U
D-EBSC	Robin DR.400/180R Remorqueur	1310	
D-EBSD(2)	Cessna T.207A Turbo Stationair 8	20700644	N207PP N75798
D-EBSE(2)	Cessna T.207ATurbo Skywagon	20700370	OE-DFV N1770U
D-EBSF	Robin DR.400/180R Remorqueur	1041	
D-EBSG	SOCATA MS.894A Minerva 220	11828	F-BSMU
D-EBSH(2)	SNCAN/Stampe SV.4A	634	F-BUDY F-BDMD
D-EBSI	Cessna 172B	17248089	N7589X
D-EBSJ	SOCATA Rallye 150ST-D	2614	F-BXDH
D-EBSK	Robin DR.400/180R Remorqueur	991	
D-EBSL	CEA DR.250/160 Capitaine	10	F-BMZI
D-EBSM	SOCATA MS.892A Rallye Commodore 150	11750	F-BSMF
D-EBSN(2)	Piper PA-28-181 Archer II	28-8190159	N8332K
D-EBSO	SOCATA MS.880B Rallye Club	1376	
D-EBSP	Cessna 182P Skylane	18263620	N6061J
D-EBSQ	Robin DR.400/180R Remorqueur	1802	

D-EBSS(3)	Aero-Jodel D.11AClub	604	OE-ASS
D-EBST	Robin DR.400/180R Remorqueur	876	
D-EBSU	Cessna 175B	17556862	N8162T
D-EBSV	Uetz Jodel D.11A Club	1021	HB-SVD
D-EBSW	Cessna 182J Skylane	18256859	N2759F
D-EBSX	Reims/Cessna F150M	F15001402	
D-EBSY(2)	Reims/Cessna F172N	F17201598	
D-EBSZ	Robin DR.400/180R Remorqueur	1854	
D-EBTA	Bölkow BO.207	239	
D-EBTC	Piper PA-28-140 Cherokee B	28-25392	N8194N
D-EBTD	Piper PA-28R-200 Cherokee Arrow	28R-35065	N9358N
D-EBTM	Robin DR.400/180 Régent	1038	
D-EBTT	Reims/Cessna F172N	F17201877	
D-EBTU(3)	Grob G.115A	8028	D-EKVG
D-EBTV	Reims FR172F Rocket	FR17200144	
D-EBTW	Cessna 210L Centurion II	21061264	N2388S
D-EBTY	Cessna 150D	15060459	N4459U
D-EBUA(3)	Cessna 182P Skylane (Reims-assembled with "c/n" 0004)	18263790	(9A-D . .) D-EBUA(3) N6650M
D-EBUB	Cessna 170B	26934	HB-COX N2991D
D-EBUC(4)	Bücker Bü.181B-1 Bestmann (Reservation 4.04, on rebuild)	331396/FR.11	N9269Z F-BBMI VN174 Luftwaffe
D-EBUE	Cessna F150J	F150-0473	
D-EBUF(3)	Piper PA-28-161 Warrior II	28-7916570	OO-SUF N2942G
D-EBUG	Piper J-3C-90 Cub	12324	HB-OSB 44-80028
D-EBUH(2)	Dornier Do.27Q-5	2063	
D-EBUL(2)	SOCATA MS.883 Rallye 115	1588	F-BTHL
D-EBUN(2)	Cessna T210N Turbo Centurion II (Reims-assembled with c/n 0018)	21063136	N6660N
D-EBUR(2)	Piper J-3C-65 Cub	12408	HB-OEK 44-80112
D-EBUS(2)	Piper PA-12 Super Cruiser	12-2857	N3973M NC3973M
D-EBUT(4)	SNCAN/ Stampe SV.4C	304	F-BCLD
D-EBUU	SOCATA MS.893A Rallye Commodore 180	10981	F-BRJI
D-EBUX(2)	Cessna 172RG Cutlass RG	172RG0803	N9355B
D-EBUZ	Piper PA-18-150 Super Cub	18-6769	N3299P
D-EBVA(2)	Cessna F172H	F172-0419	(D-EDGE)
D-EBVG	SIAT 223A-1 Flamingo	012	HB-EVG D-EJDU(1)
D-EBVH	SOCATA MS.880B Rallye Club	1355	
D-EBVI	Cessna F172E	F172-0054	
D-EBVJ	Cessna 150F	15063532	N6932F
D-EBVM(2)	Piper PA-28-161 Cadet	2841143	N9184Q
D-EBVO(2)	Reims/Cessna F152	F15201767	
D-EBVP	SOCATA MS.894A Minerva 220	1056	
D-EBVR	Piper PA-28-161 Cadet	2841172	N9185N
D-EBVS(3)	Cessna A185F Skywagon	18503782	N102PM N9636Q
D-EBVU	Cessna F172F	F172-0112	
D-EBVY	Luscombe 8F Silvaire	6211	N1584B
D-EBVZ	Beech F33A Bonanza	CE-1078	
D-EBWA	Piper PA-28-140 Cherokee	28-20209	N6185W
D-EBWB	Piper PA-28-235 Cherokee	28-10611	N9037W
D-EBWF	Piper PA-28-140 Cherokee E	28-7225454	N11C
D-EBWG	SOCATA MS.893ED Rallye 180GT Gaillard	12683	F-ODDM
D-EBWI	Beech 35-C33 Debonair	CD-851	
D-EBWJ	SOCATA Rallye 150T-D	2660	F-ODDB
D-EBWL	SOCATA MS.894A Minerva 220	12094	F-BUVI
D-EBWM	SOCATA Rallye 235E-D Gabier	12707	F-ODDC
D-EBWO(2)	Robin DR.400/180R Remorqueur	1508	
D-EBWP	Piper PA-28R-200 Cherokee Arrow II	28R-7335224	N1776P
D-EBWQ	SOCATA MS.893E Rallye 180GT Gaillard	12723	F-ODDQ
D-EBWR	SOCATA Rallye 100S-D Sport	2298	F-BULP
D-EBWS(2)	Cessna T210N Turbo Centurion II	21064341	N6339Y
D-EBWT	SOCATA Rallye 100ST-D	2758	
D-EBWU	Piper PA-28-140 Cherokee	28-20377	N6321W
D-EBWV	SOCATA MS.893ED Rallye 180GT Gaillard	12700	F-ODDT
D-EBWW	Piper PA-28-180 Cherokee D	28-4499	(D-EFWQ) N5208L
D-EBWX	SOCATA Rallye 235E-D Gabier	12771	
D-EBWY	Zlin Z.226T Trenér 6 (Third prototype, converted from Z.126)	870	F-BKRX OO-AJT OK-JED OK-JEB
D-EBWZ(3)	SOCATA Rallye 235E-D Gabier	12765	F-BNGU
D-EBXA	Reims FR172E Rocket	FR17200056	
D-EBXF	Piper PA-18 Super Cub 95	18-3456	96+32 NL+110 AC+528 AS+528 54-756
D-EBXG	Wallerkowski Hornisse	01	
D-EBXH	Reims/Cessna F150M	F15001370	PH-AXK
D-EBXI	Reims FR172E Rocket	FR17200053	
D-EBXM	Reims/Cessna F172N	F17201525	
D-EBXN	Reims/Cessna F172N	F17201548	
D-EBXO(2)	Wallerkowski HW04 Tourist	01	
D-EBXP	Reims/Cessna F182Q Skylane	F18200050	
D-EBXQ	Reims/Cessna F172N	F17201759	
D-EBXR	Reims/Cessna FR172K Hawk XP	FR17200597	HB-CXO

D-EBXS	Reims/Cessna F172N	F17201521	
D-EBXT	Cessna 210K Centurion	21059455	OE-DSP N8155G
D-EBXU	Reims FR172E Rocket	FR17200050	
D-EBXW	Reims/Cessna F150M	F15001407	
D-EBYB	Piper PA-18 Super Cub 95 (F/n 18-7841 fitted)	18-4648	N10F
D-EBYC(2)	Beech V35B Bonanza	D-10033	
D-EBYE	Mooney M.20F Executive	670383	G-AYBF N3290F
D-EBYF(2)	Simon/ Piel CP.301E Emeraude	AB.416	
D-EBYG(3)	Cessna 182K Skylane	18257946	OO-SIV (D-ENCY) N2746Q
D-EBYK	Diamond DA 40 Star	40349	
D-EBYP(3)	Maule M6-235 Super Rocket	7402C	OH-MEN N5652V
D-EBYQ(3)	Cessna 182P Skylane (Reims-assembled with "c/n" 0009)	18263886	OO-ADI D-EEMK (SE-GKI) N6903M
D-EBYS(2)	Reims/Cessna F172N	F17201579	
D-EBYT(2)	Reims/Cessna F152	F15201487	
D-EBYU	Grumman AA-1 Yankee	AA1-0312	N2NZ D-ELXD N6112L
D-EBYV(2)	Piper PA-38-112 Tomahawk	38-78A0560	N9691N
D-EBYX(3)	Piper PA-18 Super Cub 95	18-3450	96+26 NL+103 AC+535 AS+535 54-750
D-EBYZ	Scheibe SF.23A Sperling	2017	
D-EBZA(2)	Piper PA-28RT-201T Turbo Arrow IV	28R-8131160	N8406J
D-EBZH	SOCATA TB-10 Tobago	213	
D-EBZI	Cessna F150G	F150-0172	
D-EBZK	Reims/Cessna F172M	F17201458	
D-EBZL	SOCATA TB-10 Tobago	214	
D-EBZM	Cessna T210L Turbo Centurion	21061425	N732DC
D-EBZP	Robin DR.400/180R Remorqueur	1418	
D-EBZQ	SOCATA MS.893A Rallye Commodore 180	11771	F-BSZQ
D-EBZT	Mooney M.20J Model 201	24-0811	(N4700H)
D-EBZU	Cessna F150G (W5/33 engine)	F150-0186	
D-EBZV	Cirrus SR20	1245	N898CD
D-EBZW(2)	Mooney M.20K Model 231	25-0385	OE-DVU N3981H
D-ECAA	Reims/Cessna FA150K Aerobat	FA1500053	
D-ECAB(2)	Klemm Kl.107C	154	
D-ECAD(4)	SOCATA MS.893A Rallye Commodore 180	12066	F-BTPZ
D-ECAE	Reims/Cessna FA150K Aerobat	FA1500057	
D-ECAF(3)	Piper PA-18-135 Super Cub	18-3862	PH-KNO (PH-KNR) R-172 54-2462
D-ECAG(3)	SOCATA TB-20 Trinidad	725	
D-ECAH	Klemm Kl.107B	126	
D-ECAI	Piper PA-18 Super Cub 95	18-1550	ALAT 51-15550
D-ECAJ	Diamond DA 20-A1 Katana	10018	N605F
D-ECAK(3)	Cessna R.172K Hawk XP	2868	N736XK
D-ECAL(3)	Boeing Stearman A75-N1 (Painted as '450')	75-1696	N54426 41-8137
D-ECAM(2)	Piper PA-28-140 Cherokee Cruiser	28-7325421	N11C
D-ECAN(5)	Diamond DA 20-A1 Katana	10146	
D-ECAO(3)	Cessna 172R	17280049	N9796F
D-ECAP(2)	Piper PA-28-180 Cherokee Challenger	28-7305172	N11C
D-ECAQ(2)	Bücker Bü.131 Jungmann	28	OE-AKW HB-URC A-19
D-ECAS(2)	Piper J-3C-65 Cub (c/n officially quoted as 12809 in error)	12989	HB-OGR HB-ODF 44-80693
D-ECAT(3)	Piper PA-28-161 Cadet	2841112	N9646N N9175Q
D-ECAU	Reims/Cessna FA150K Aerobat	FA1500080	(D-EHBL)
D-ECAV(3)	Diamond DA 40D Star (Res .05)	D4.114	
D-ECAW(3)	Gyroflug SC-01 Speed Canard	S-5	
D-ECAX(2)	Scheibe SF.23A-1 Sperling	2011	
D-ECAY(3)	Cessna 172R	17280126	N9861F
D-ECAZ(4)	Cessna 182 (Reservation? Probably F.182P c/n F18200001 ex D-EKMO)		
D-ECBA(2)	Piper PA-28R-200 Cherokee Arrow II	28R-7635398	N4294F
D-ECBB(2)	Mooney M.20K Model 252 TSE	25-1002	N252AX
D-ECBC(2)	Beech F33A Bonanza	CE-1240	
D-ECBD(2)	Bede BD-5B (Reservation 12.99)	01	
D-ECBE(4)	Piper PA-46-500TP Malibu Meridian	4697063	N253MM
D-ECBF(2)	Reims/Cessna F172N	F17201922	(F-GCHP)
D-ECBH(2)	SOCATA MS.893E Rallye 180GT Gaillard	13231	F-GBSE
D-ECBJ (2)	Gyroflug SC-01B Speed Canard	S-11	
D-ECBK	Reims/Cessna F172H	F17200685	
D-ECBL(2)	Beech A36 Bonanza	E-1541	OY-CBI
D-ECBM	Reims/Cessna F150K	F15000564	
D-ECBN	Reims/Cessna F172H	F17200699	
D-ECBO	Bölkow BO.207	228	
D-ECBP	Reims/Cessna F150K	F15000609	
D-ECBR	Cessna 210F Centurion	21058747	HB-CBR N1847F
D-ECBS	Reims/Cessna F150K	F15000608	
D-ECBT	Reims/Cessna F150K	F15000605	
D-ECBV	Reims FR172G Rocket	FR17200175	
D-ECBW(2)	Piaggio P.149D	316	92+19 AC+467 AS+467
D-ECBX(4)	Reims/Cessna F150L	F15000685	
D-ECBY(2)	Reims/Cessna F172H	F17200717	
D-ECBZ	Reims/Cessna F172H	F17200684	
D-ECCA(3)	Sondermann/ Christen Eagle II	0471	
D-ECCB	Reims/Cessna F172H	F17200669	
D-ECCC(2)	CASA I-131E Jungmann (Officially ex.E3B-619 but this is c/n 2219 / N72480)	2230	E3B-630
D-ECCF(4)	Männich/ Rans S-7M Courier (Res. .04)	01	
D-ECCG(2)	SOCATA MS.893A Rallye Commodore 180	11664	
D-ECCI	Klemm Kl.35D	1904	SE-BHX Fv5069
D-ECCK(2)	Reims/Cessna FR172K Hawk XP	FR17200668	
D-ECCL	SOCATA MS.880B Rallye Club (Wfu, stored)	1561	
D-ECCM	SOCATA MS.880B Rallye Club	1581	
D-ECCN(3)	Piper PA-28-161 Warrior II	2816093	N9183X
D-ECCO	Piper PA-28-140 Cherokee	28-20535	N6462W
D-ECCP	SOCATA MS.880B Rallye Club	1601	
D-ECCQ	SOCATA MS.893A Rallye Commodore 180	11456	
D-ECCS	SOCATA MS.893A Rallye Commodore 180	11466	F-BNGU
D-ECCT	SOCATA MS.893A Rallye Commodore 180	11469	
D-ECCU(3)	Heliopolis Gomhouria Mk.6	174	SU-337
D-ECCV	SOCATA MS.893A Rallye Commodore 180	11489	
D-ECCW(2)	Piper PA-18-150 Super Cub	18-7880	OE-ANE N10F
D-ECCY	Cessna F172F	F172-0136	
D-ECCZ	SOCATA MS.893A Rallye Commodore 180	11498	
D-ECDA(3)	HOACDV-20 Katana	20150	OE-ADA
D-ECDB	Reims/Cessna F150K	F15000623	
D-ECDC(3)	Claren Ente Ki 1 (Permit 5.99)	001	
D-ECDD	Reims FR172G Rocket	FR17200199	
D-ECDE(2)	Cessna 152	15284281	N5245L
D-ECDH	SOCATA MS.880B Rallye Club (Stored)	1607	
D-ECDI (2)	Robin DR.400/135TDI (Thielert diesel)	2531	
D-ECDJ	Cessna 207 Skywagon 207	20700176	N1576U
D-ECDL	Navion Rangemaster H	NAV-4-2522	N2520T
D-ECDM	Reims/Cessna FA150K Aerobat	FA1500021	
D-ECDN	SEEMS MS.885 Super Rallye	5359	OE-CDN (D-EHDE)
D-ECDP	Reims/Cessna FA150K Aerobat	FA1500023	
D-ECDQ(2)	Reims/Cessna F172N	F17201646	
D-ECDT(2)	Piper PA-28R-201T Turbo Arrow III	28R-7803150	N2856M
D-ECDU(2)	Piper PA-38-112 Tomahawk	38-80A0036	N25140
D-ECDV	Reims/Cessna F150K	F15000599	
D-ECDW	Aero Commander 200D	368	N5565M
D-ECEA	CEA Jodel DR.1050 Ambassadeur	620	
D-ECEB(2)	SAN Jodel DR.1050 Ambassadeur	174	
D-ECED(2)	Mooney M.20F Executive	670121	N9544M
D-ECEE	Reims/Cessna F150L	F15000729	
D-ECEF(2)	Reims/Cessna F172N	F17201544	
D-ECEH	Klemm Kl.107C	127	
D-ECEI (2)	Reims/Cessna F150L	F15000733	
D-ECEJ	Reims/Cessna F172H	F17200693	
D-ECEL(2)	Cessna 182R Skylane	18268466	N9892E
D-ECEM(3)	Mooney M.20F Executive	22-1262	
D-ECEN	HOACDV-20 Katana	20039	N39DV
D-ECEO(3)	Piper PA-22-108 Colt	22-9144	OY-EAV N10F
D-ECER(3)	Robin DR.400/180 Régent	1294	
D-ECES(2)	Piper PA-16 Clipper (Reservation)	16-500	D-EIOG HB-OOG
D-ECEV(2)	Reims/Cessna F150K	F15000585	
D-ECEW(2)	Reims/Cessna F150K	F15000587	
D-ECEY(2)	Reims/Cessna F150L	F15000666	
D-ECFA(2)	Cessna T210K Turbo Centurion	21059212	N8212M
D-ECFB	Reims/Cessna F172H	F17200725	
D-ECFC(2)	Piper PA-28-181 Cherokee Archer II	28-7690103	N8124C
D-ECFD	Reims/Cessna F150L	F15000737	
D-ECFE	Oberlerchner JOB 15-150	058	OE-CAO
D-ECFF	Reims/Cessna F172L	F17200806	
D-ECFG	Piper PA-22-108 Colt	22-9591	OE-CFG N5781Z
D-ECFI	Oberlerchner JOB 15-150	060	OE-CAR
D-ECFK	Morane-Saulnier MS.880B Rallye Club	301	HB-EDS
D-ECFM(3)	Pützer Elster B	005	97+03 D-EJIH
D-ECFP	Reims/Cessna F150K	F15000588	
D-ECFR	Reims/Cessna F150K	F15000596	
D-ECFT	Reims FR172G Rocket	FR17200198	
D-ECFU	Bölkow BO.208C Junior	569	
D-ECFW	Reims/Cessna F172H	F17200740	(G-AXUV)
D-ECFY	Cessna 182H Skylane	18255948	N1848X
D-ECFZ	Reims/Cessna F172K	F17200801	
D-ECGA(2)	Beech B36TC Bonanza	EA-392	N6749P
D-ECGC(2)	Piper PA-12 Super Cruiser (Res .05)	12-3395	D-ELGD N4443M NC4443M
D-ECGD	Reims FR172H Rocket	FR17200247	
D-ECGH(2)	Piper PA-18 Super Cub 95	18-3449	96+25 NL+115 AC+534 (D-EMDY) AC+534 AA+534 AS+534 54-749

D-ECGI	Bölkow BO.208C Junior	598	
D-ECGK	Cessna 182N Skylane	18260407	N92876
D-ECGL	Reims/Cessna F150L	F15000680	
D-ECGM	Reims FR172H Rocket	FR17200239	
D-ECGN	Reims/Cessna FA150L Aerobat	FA1500116	
D-ECGR	Reims/Cessna F177RG Cardinal RG	F177RG0004	(N8090G)
	(Reims-assembled 177RG with c/n 177RG0090)		
D-ECGS	Reims/Cessna F177RG Cardinal RG	F177RG0005	(N8094G)
	(Reims-assembled 177RG with c/n 177RG0094)		
D-ECGT(2)	Reims/Cessna FRA150M Aerobat	FRA1500262	
D-ECGU(2)	Reims/Cessna FA150K Aerobat	FA1500068	
D-ECGW	Cessna 182N Skylane	18260460	N8920G
D-ECGX	Reims/Cessna F150L	F15000678	
D-ECGZ	Reims FR172H Rocket	FR17200238	
D-ECHA(3)	Christen A-1 Husky	1058	N29732
D-ECHB	Reims/Cessna F150K	F15000572	
D-ECHD	Reims FR172G Rocket	FR17200173	
D-ECHE(2)	Reims/Cessna F172H	F17200733	
D-ECHF	Reims FR172H Rocket	FR17200252	
D-ECHH	Reims/Cessna F150L	F15000664	
D-ECHI	Cessna 172A	47057	N7457T
D-ECHL(3)	Robin DR.400/180 Régent	497	
D-ECHM	Reims FR172G Rocket	FR17200164	
D-ECHO	Cessna 172A	47343	N7743T
D-ECHP	Reims/Cessna F150L	F15000662	
D-ECHQ	Piper PA-28-181 Cherokee Archer II	28-7890505	N36321
D-ECHR	Reims/Cessna F177RG Cardinal RG	F177RG0008	(N8206G)
	(Reims-assembled 177RG with c/n 177RG0106)		
D-ECHS	Reims/Cessna F172K	F17200770	
D-ECHT(2)	Reims FR172H Rocket	FR17200251	
D-ECHU(2)	Reims/Cessna F150L	F15000681	
D-ECHW	Reims/Cessna F150L	F15000699	
D-ECHY(3)	Piper PA-28R-201T Turbo-Arrow III	28R-7803070	N9853K
D-ECHZ(2)	Piper PA-38-112 Tomahawk	38-78A0554	N9690N
D-ECIA(3)	Robin DR.400/180S Régent	1995	
D-ECIB(2)	Wassmer Jodel D.120 Paris-Nice	186	
D-ECIC	Klemm Kl.35D-160	2013	SE-BHU
			Fv5064
D-ECIE	Reims/Cessna F172K	F17200795	
D-ECIF(2)	SOCATA Rallye 180T-D Galérien	2974	
D-ECIG(3)	Diamond DA 20-A1 Katana	10184	C-GAHQ
			N284DA
D-ECIH	Klemm Kl.107C	128	
D-ECII (3)	Cessna L-19A Bird Dog (305A)	21510	OE-CCB
	(Permit 8.99)		AAF: 3A-CB
			51-4625
D-ECIJ	Reims/Cessna F172H	F17200708	(YU-BHJ)
D-ECIK(2)	Reims FR172H Rocket	FR17200240	
D-ECIL	Auster Mk.5	1575	G-ANIL
			TJ527
D-ECIM(4)	Piper PA-28-140 Cherokee	28-7225596	C-FFQR
			CF-FQR
			N11C
D-ECIO	Reims/Cessna F177RG Cardinal RG	F177RG0013	(N8225G)
	(Reims-assembled 177RG with c/n 177RG0125)		
D-ECIP(3)	Robin R.3000/160	152	
D-ECIQ(2)	Piper J-3C-65 Cub	18167	N98024
			NC98024
D-ECIS(3)	Cessna 150B	59433	OE-AIS
			N7333X
D-ECIV	Piper J-3C-85 Cub	11364	SL-AAK
			ALAT
			43-30073
D-ECIY	Reims/Cessna F150L	F15000731	
D-ECJA(2)	Diamond DA 40D Star	D4.123	OE-VPY
D-ECJB(3)	Robin DR.400/180 Régent	2291	
D-ECJC	Reims/Cessna F172H	F17200734	
D-ECJE	Reims/Cessna F172H	F17200737	
D-ECJF	Reims/Cessna F177RG Cardinal RG	F177RG0015	(N8230G)
	(Reims-assembled 177RG with c/n 177RG0130)		
D-ECJG	Cessna 182N Skylane	18260517	N8977G
D-ECJK	Reims FR172G Rocket	FR17200212	
D-ECJL	Reims/Cessna F172H	F17200742	
D-ECJM(2)	Reims/Cessna F172P	F17202091	
D-ECJN	Reims/Cessna F172H	F17200744	
D-ECJP(2)	SOCATA TB-20 Trinidad	292	
D-ECJR	Reims/Cessna F177RG Cardinal RG	F177RG0029	(N8286G)
	(Reims-assembled 177RG with c/n 177RG0186)		
D-ECJS	Reims FR172G Rocket	FR17200176	
D-ECJT	Reims/Cessna F172H	F17200736	
D-ECJU	Reims/Cessna F172K	F17200804	
D-ECJV	Reims FR172H Rocket	FR17200269	
D-ECJX(2)	Reims FR172H Rocket	FR17200272	
D-ECJY(2)	Reims/Cessna F150L	F15000727	
D-ECKA	Beech P35 Bonanza	D-7194	
D-ECKB(2)	Beech F33A Bonanza	CE-1614	N8240X
			(F-GIFM)
D-ECKD	Reims FR172H Rocket	FR17200243	
D-ECKE(2)	Piper PA-28-160 Cherokee	28-372	N5316W
D-ECKF	Reims/Cessna F177RG Cardinal RG	F177RG0021	"PH-LTU"
	(Reims-assembled 177RG with c/n 177RG0154)		(PH-LTT)
			D-ECKF
			(N8254G)
D-ECKH(2)	Holtz/ Neico Lancair 235 (Permit 5.99)	362B	
D-ECKI (3)	Rockwell Commander 112A	298	N1298J
D-ECKK	Reims FR172H Rocket	FR17200259	
D-ECKL(2)	Robin DR.400/180R Remorqueur	1589	

D-ECKM	Reims/Cessna F172K	F17200789	
D-ECKN	Reims/Cessna F172K	F17200787	
D-ECKO(2)	Grumman AA-5 Traveler	AA5-0667	
D-ECKP	Reims/Cessna F172K	F17200768	
D-ECKR	Reims FR172H Rocket	FR17200249	
D-ECKS	Reims/Cessna F172H	F17200750	
D-ECKT	Reims FR172G Rocket	FR17200177	
D-ECKV	Reims FR172G Rocket	FR17200166	
D-ECKW	Cessna 182N Skylane	18260439	N92948
D-ECKY(3)	SOCATA MS.893E Rallye 180GT Gaillard	13010	
D-ECLC(2)	Mooney M.20K Model 252 TSE	25-1182	
D-ECLD	Beech 35-C33 Debonair	CD-1012	
D-ECLE(2)	Reims/Cessna F172N	F17201563	
D-ECLF	Beech 35-C33 Debonair	CD-1014	
D-ECLG(2)	Cessna 172RG Cutlass RG	172RG0767	N6544V
D-ECLH	Beech 35-C33 Debonair	CD-1016	
D-ECLI	Beech 35-C33 Debonair	CD-1017	
D-ECLK(2)	Piper PA-18-135 Super Cub	18-3321	EI-104
			I-EIKD
			53-7721
D-ECLM(2)	Piper PA-28RT-201T Turbo Arrow IV	28R-8331046	N4322N
			N9534N
			N4312V
D-ECLO(3)	Reims/Cessna F182Q Skylane	F18200169	F-ODNO
D-ECLP(2)	Piper PA-28-180 Cherokee D	28-4404	N5121L
D-ECLR(2)	Piper PA-28-140 Cherokee	28-24130	N1718J
D-ECLT(2)	Cessna 182P Skylane	18264355	N1504M
	(Reims-assembled with "c/n" 0048)		
D-ECLW(2)	Reims FR172E Rocket	FR17200052	
D-ECLX(2)	Reims FR172E Rocket	FR17200054	
D-ECMA(2)	Cessna 172M	17266437	N80195
D-ECMB	Cessna 207 Skywagon 207	20700195	(N1595U)
D-ECMC	Reims/Cessna F172K	F17200780	(G-AYTI)
D-ECMD	Reims FR172H Rocket	FR17200261	
D-ECMF(2)	Mooney M.20J Model 201	24-1011	(N4005H)
D-ECMG	Reims/Cessna F177RG Cardinal RG	F177RG0009	(N8210G)
	(Reims-assembled 177RG with c/n 177RG0110)		
D-ECMH(3)	Piper PA-28-181 Archer II	2890068	N9138Z
D-ECMI (2)	Robin DR.400/180R Remo 180	2160	
D-ECMJ	Reims/Cessna F177RG Cardinal RG	F177RG0022	(N8256G)
	(Reims-assembled 177RG with c/n 177RG0156)		
D-ECMK(2)	Kritzinger/ Sequoia F.8L Falco	1730	
D-ECML	Reims/Cessna F150L	F15000717	
D-ECMM	SAN Jodel D.150 Rapid	17	
D-ECMN	Reims/Cessna F172K	F17200784	
D-ECMP(2)	Cessna 172N	17273915	N256FR
			N256ER
			N7557J
D-ECMQ	Reims FR172H Rocket	FR17200232	
D-ECMR	Reims FR172H Rocket	FR17200230	
D-ECMS	Reims/Cessna F172K	F17200778	
D-ECMT	Reims FR172H Rocket	FR17200237	
D-ECMW	Reims/Cessna F150L	F15000697	
D-ECMX(3)	Reims/Cessna F150L	F15001412	OE-CMX
D-ECMY	Beech 35-C33A Debonair	CE-59	
D-ECMZ(2)	Piper PA-28-151 Cherokee Warrior	28-7415283	HB-OMZ
			N9533N
D-ECNA(2)	Cessna 172K Skyhawk	17257639	N78493
D-ECNB(2)	Mooney M.20J Model 201	24-0059	
D-ECNC	Piper PA-28-180 Cherokee D	28-5029	N6575J
D-ECND	Bölkow B0.209 Monsun 160FV	128	(D-EFJF)
D-ECNE	Cessna F172G	F172-0234	HB-CBP
D-ECNG	Reims/Cessna F177RG Cardinal RG	F177RG0027	(N8282G)
	(Reims-assembled 177RG with c/n 177RG0182)		
D-ECNI	Cessna 150G	15066209	N8309J
D-ECNJ	Reims FR172H Rocket	FR17200226	
D-ECNK	Cessna 182N Skylane	18260469	N8929G
D-ECNL	Cessna 150J Commuter	15069649	N50927
D-ECNN	Reims/Cessna F177RG Cardinal RG	F177RG0012	(N8223G)
	(Reims-assembled 177RG with c/n 177RG0123)		
D-ECNO	Cessna 150G	15066927	N3027S
D-ECNP(2)	Cessna T210K Turbo Centurion	21059456	N8156G
D-ECNQ	Reims/Cessna F150L	F15000659	
D-ECNS(2)	Piper PA-32-300 Cherokee Six	32-7840153	N31908
D-ECNT	Reims/Cessna F150L	F15000723	
D-ECNV	Reims/Cessna F150L	F15000718	
D-ECNW(2)	SOCATA MS.893ED Rallye 180GT Gaillard	13009	
D-ECNX	Reims/Cessna F177RG Cardinal RG	F177RG0038	(N1802Q)
	(Reims-assembled 177RG with c/n 177RG0202)		
D-ECNY(2)	Reims/Cessna FR182 Skylane RG	FR18200030	OE-DNY
			PH-AYG
D-ECNZ	SIAI-Marchetti S.205-20/R	377	OO-JDC
D-ECOA(2)	Christen A-1 Husky	1142	
D-ECOB(2)	Reims/Cessna F172K	F17200765	
D-ECOC(2)	Reims/Cessna F172K	F17200766	
D-ECOE	Reims/Cessna F172K	F17200769	
D-ECOG(2)	Piper PA-28R-200 Cherokee Arrow II	28R-7635266	N75116
D-ECOH(2)	Mooney M.20J Model 205	24-3011	OE-KEC
			N205ME
D-ECOJ	Reims/Cessna F150L	F15000714	F-WLIM
D-ECOK	Kreutzer/ Jodel D.9 Bébé	AB-10	
D-ECOL(3)	SOCATA TB-20 Trinidad	1749	
D-ECON(2)	Diamond DA 40D Star	D4.018	
D-ECOO(2)	Cessna 172RG Cutlass RG	172RG0060	N5464R
	(Reims-assembled with c/n 0001)		
D-ECOP(2)	Reims/Cessna F172K	F17200791	
D-ECOR(3)	Pegasus	001	

D-ECOS(3)	Piper PA-38-112 Tomahawk	38-79A1086	N24119
D-ECOT(3)	Beech F33A Bonanza	CE-1716	N8146T
D-ECOU	Reims/Cessna F172K	F17200797	
D-ECOV	Schwindt/ Jodel D.112 Club	278	SL-AAO
D-ECOW(2)	Reims/Cessna F177RG Cardinal RG	F177RG0028	(N8284G)
	(Reims-assembled 177RG with c/n 177RG0184)		
D-ECOX	Dornier Do.27Q-1	2018	
D-ECOY	Piaggio FWP.149D	020	90+11
			AC+443
			DB+394
D-ECOZ(4)	Reims FR172H Rocket	FR17200274	
D-ECPA(2)	Piper PA-28-181 Archer III	2843357	N4140L
D-ECPB(2)	Christen A-1 Husky	1107	
D-ECPC	Reims/Cessna FA150L Aerobat	FA1500097	
D-ECPD(2)	Piper PA-28R-200 Cherokee Arrow II	28R-7535180	N33697
D-ECPE	Aeromere F8L Falco III	235	
D-ECPF	Reims/Cessna F150L	F15000663	
D-ECPG(2)	SIAT 223A-1 Flamingo	017	HB-EVN
			D-ENBN(1)
D-ECPH(2)	Mooney M.20J Model 201	24-0966	N3865H
D-ECPI (3)	Sonntag/ Sequoia F.8L Falco	1649	
D-ECPJ	Reims/Cessna F150L	F15000702	(D-ECMW)
D-ECPM(2)	Cessna P210N Pressurized Centurion	P21000087	LN-HOT
			(LN-BEE)
			N4716P
D-ECPO	Reims/Cessna FA150L Aerobat	FA1500113	F-WLIP
D-ECPP	Reims/Cessna FA150L Aerobat	FA1500114	(OY-BYL)
			D-ECPP
			(G-AYUZ)
D-ECPQ	Reims/Cessna FA150L Aerobat	FA1500115	
D-ECPS(2)	SOCATA Rallye 180T-D Galérien	2975	
D-ECPT	Reims FR172H Rocket	FR17200284	
D-ECPV	Reims FR172H Rocket	FR17200288	
D-ECPW(2)	Robin DR.400/180 Régent	1664	(D-EEWP)
D-ECPX	Reims/Cessna F172L	F17200820	
D-ECPY(2)	Orlican L-40 Meta-Sokol	150909	
D-ECPZ	Reims FR172H Rocket	FR17200282	
D-ECQA	Piper PA-18 Super Cub 95	18-3182	R-84
			L-108
			53-4782
D-ECQC	Reims/Cessna FRA150L Aerobat	FRA1500124	
D-ECQD	Reims FR172H Rocket	FR17200286	
D-ECQE	Reims FR172E Rocket	FR17200002	N20002
D-ECQG	Reims/Cessna F172L	F17200816	
D-ECQH	Reims FR172H Rocket	FR17200283	
D-ECQI	Reims FR172H Rocket	FR17200285	
D-ECQL	Reims/Cessna F150L	F15000764	
D-ECQO	Cessna F172H	F172-0347	
D-ECQP(2)	Grumman AA-5A Cheetah	AA5A-0187	
D-ECQQ	Reims/Cessna F150L	F15000768	
D-ECQV	Reims/Cessna F172L	F17200824	
D-ECQW	Reims/Cessna F172L	F17200826	
D-ECQX	Reims/Cessna F172L	F17200827	
D-ECRA	Reims FR172H Rocket	FR17200295	
D-ECRB(2)	Piper PA-46-500TP Malibu Meridian	4697061	N633RB
D-ECRD	Beech V35B Bonanza	D-9181	
D-ECRE	Reims/Cessna F150L	F15000770	
D-ECRF(2)	Beech B36TC Bonanza	EA-299	N24RF
			N6450A
D-ECRH	Reims/Cessna F150M	F15001233	N67266
D-ECRI	Mooney M.20C Mark 21	2176	N6429U
D-ECRK(2)	Robin DR.400/180 Régent	2387	
D-ECRL	Reims/Cessna F172L	F17200832	
D-ECRM	Reims FR172H Rocket	FR17200296	
D-ECRO	SIAT 223 V-1 Flamingo	001	"D-EDON"
D-ECRQ	Reims FR172H Rocket	FR17200299	
D-ECRR(2)	Riechers/ Aero Designs Pulsar XP (Permit 2.00)	421 SB	
D-ECRS(2)	Cessna 182S Skylane	18280021	N97SD
D-ECRV	Reims/Cessna F150L	F15000758	
D-ECRW	Reims FR172H Rocket	FR17200306	
D-ECRX	Reims/Cessna F172L	F17200855	
D-ECRZ	Reims/Cessna F172L	F17200854	
D-ECSA(2)	Mooney M.20J Model 201	24-0086	
D-ECSB(2)	Piper PA-28-140 Cherokee B	28-25086	N7233F
D-ECSD	Reims/Cessna FA150L Aerobat	FA1500120	PH-LUE
			(LN-BEK)
D-ECSE(2)	Reims FR172H Rocket	FR17200292	
D-ECSF	Piper PA-28-140 Cherokee	28-21121	HB-OYG
			(N6941W)
D-ECSG	Reims/Cessna F172L	F17200813	
D-ECSI	Piper PA-28-180 Cherokee C	28-2325	N8197W
D-ECSJ	Reims/Cessna F150L	F15000780	
D-ECSL	Reims/Cessna F172L	F17200837	
D-ECSM(2)	Robin DR.400/180 Régent	1957	
D-ECSO(2)	Boeing Stearman A75-N1	75-1391	OO-STM
			N59257
			(OO-JKT)
			N59257
			BuA.03614
D-ECSQ(2)	Sportavia-Pützer RS-180 Sportsman	6003	
D-ECSR	Reims/Cessna FRA150L Aerobat	FRA1500140	
D-ECSS	Reims/Cessna F172L	F17200844	
D-ECST	Gardan GY-80 Horizon 180	131	
D-ECSU	Piper PA-28-140 Cherokee	28-20516	N11C
			N6444W
D-ECSW	Reims/Cessna F172L	F17200846	
D-ECSY(2)	Cessna 210N Centurion	21063434	N5432A

D-ECSZ	Reims/Cessna F172L	F17200848	
D-ECTA	Reims FR172H Rocket	FR17200313	
D-ECTC(2)	Reims/Cessna F172P	F17202105	
D-ECTE	Cessna F150H	F150-0275	
D-ECTG(2)	Reims FR172E Rocket	FR17200038	D-ENBS
			(HB-CTI)
D-ECTH	Piper PA-28-140 Cherokee C	28-26676	N5845U
D-ECTK	American AA-1 Yankee	AA1-0327	N6127L
D-ECTL	Reims FR172H Rocket	FR17200315	
D-ECTN	CEA DR.340 Major	439	
D-ECTO(2)	Reims/Cessna F150L	F15000746	
D-ECTQ	Cessna 182P Skylane	18261034	(D-EIWI)
			(D-EECD)
			N7394Q
D-ECTR	Reims/Cessna F150L	F15000742	
D-ECTS(2)	Beech F33A Bonanza	CE-1186	N3113T
D-ECTT	Reims/Cessna F150L	F15000884	
D-ECTV	Piper PA-22-108 Colt	22-8861	HB-OTV
			N10F
D-ECTW(2)	Zlin Z.143L	0024	
D-ECTZ	Reims/Cessna F150L	F15000897	
D-ECUA(2)	Piper PA-28-151 Cherokee Warrior	28-7415228	HB-PMX
			D-EHRH(1)
			N9537N
D-ECUB(2)	Reims/Cessna F172N	F17201823	
D-ECUC(2)	Aeronca 7DC Champion (7AC convn)	7AC-3889	OO-SPA
D-ECUE	Reims/Cessna F150L	F15000901	
D-ECUJ	Reims/Cessna FRA150L Aerobat	FRA1500184	
D-ECUK	Jodel D.9 Bébé	AB-07	
D-ECUL(2)	Piper PA-28-161 Warrior II	28-8316010	N8292R
D-ECUM	Piper PA-12 Super Cruiser	12-276	N98924
			NC98924
D-ECUN(2)	Ambrosini F.7 Rondone II	010	
D-ECUO	Reims/Cessna F172M	F17200921	
D-ECUP(2)	Alpavia Jodel D.117A Grand Tourisme	1061/05	
D-ECUQ(2)	Reims/Cessna F172M	F17200925	
D-ECUS(4)	Piper PA-28R-200 Cherokee Arrow II	28R-7435118	N40742
D-ECUU	Reims/Cessna F172M	F17200932	
D-ECUV(2)	Reims/Cessna F172M	F17200934	
D-ECUW	Wassmer Jodel D.120R Paris-Nice	157	
D-ECUZ	Auster Mk.5 Alpha	3414	G-APUL
D-ECVA	GEMS MS.892A Rallye Commodore 150	10529	
D-ECVB	Reims/Cessna F172M	F17200937	
D-ECVC	Reims FR172J Rocket	FR17200361	
D-ECVE	GEMS MS.892A Rallye Commodore 150	10536	
D-ECVF	Reims FR172J Rocket	FR17200378	
D-ECVH	Reims FR172J Rocket	FR17200381	
D-ECVI	GEMS MS.892A Rallye Commodore 150	10537	
D-ECVJ	Reims FR172J Rocket	FR17200382	
D-ECVK(2)	Reims/Cessna F172M	F17201397	
D-ECVL	Cessna 182P Skylane	18261603	(N21389)
D-ECVN(2)	SNCAN/Stampe SV.4C	434	F-BCVN
D-ECVO	GEMS MS.892A Rallye Commodore 150	10543	
D-ECVS	Reims/Cessna F150L	F15000902	
D-ECVT	Reims/Cessna F150L	F15000904	
D-ECVU	Cessna F172G	F172-0182	
D-ECVX	Reims/Cessna F150L	F15000910	
D-ECVY	Champion 7GCB Challenger	152	N9948Y
D-ECVZ(2)	Reims/Cessna F177RG Cardinal RG	F177RG074	
D-ECWA	Piper PA-24-260 Comanche	24-4104	N8698P
			N10F
D-ECWB	Reims/Cessna F172M	F17200940	
D-ECWC(2)	SOCATA MS.893E Rallye 180GT Gaillard	12639	F-BVNY
D-ECWF	Reims/Cessna F172M	F17200943	
D-ECWJ	Reims FR172J Rocket	FR17200387	
D-ECWK	Reims/Cessna F150L	F15000912	
D-ECWM	Reims/Cessna F150L	F15000917	
D-ECWN(2)	Robin DR.400/180 Régent	2145	
D-ECWP	Reims/Cessna F172M	F17200948	
D-ECWQ	Reims/Cessna F172M	F17200950	
D-ECWR	Reims/Cessna F172M	F17200951	
D-ECWT	SOCATA MS.893E Rallye 180GT Gaillard	12641	F-BXMJ
D-ECWV	Cessna 182P Skylane	18261627	N21418
D-ECWX	Cessna 182P Skylane	18261823	N79461
D-ECWY	Beech V35 Bonanza	D-8079	
D-ECXB	Cessna 182PSkylane	18261668	N21492
D-ECXC	Cessna 182P Skylane	18261618	N21407
D-ECXD	Cessna 182P Skylane	18261583	N21356
D-ECXF	Reims FR172J Rocket	FR17200397	(OE-DTG)
D-ECXG	Reims FR172J Rocket	FR17200399	
D-ECXI (2)	Reims/Cessna F150M	F15001249	HB-CXI
			N31056
D-ECXJ	Reims/Cessna F172M	F17200974	
D-ECXK	Reims/Cessna F172M	F17200975	
D-ECXM	Reims FR172J Rocket	FR17200407	
D-ECXN	Reims FR172J Rocket	FR17200410	
D-ECXR	Reims/Cessna F177RG Cardinal RG	F177RG0076	
D-ECXS	Cessna 182P Skylane	18261750	N78101
D-ECXT	Cessna 182P Skylane	18261848	N79935
D-ECXU	Piper PA-18 Super Cub 95	18-1484	ALAT
			51-15484
D-ECYC(2)	Cessna 182P Skylane (W/o 31.8.04)	18261833	(N79555)
D-ECYF(2)	Cessna T210L Turbo Centurion	21059915	N30370
D-ECYG(2)	Reims/Cessna F150L	F15000918	
D-ECYM(3)	Cessna 182P Skylane	18262593	N52417
D-ECYO	Reims/Cessna F150L	F15000934	
D-ECYS(2)	Scheibe SF-23C Sperling	3500	

D-ECYY	Wassmer WA.54 Atlantic	143	
D-ECZA	Procaer F.15B Picchio	24	
D-ECZB	Reims FR172F Rocket	FR17200107	
D-ECZC	CEA Jodel DR.1050 Ambassadeur	28	F-BJOY
D-ECZD	Piper PA-18-100 Super Cub	18-3196	OL-L22
	(PA-18 Super Cub 95 re-engined)		L-122
			53-4796
D-ECZH	Reims/Cessna FR172K Hawk XP	FR17200672	I-ECZH
			D-ECZH
D-ECZI	Piper J-3C-85 Cub (J-3C-65 convtd .99)	20488	N7224H
			NC7224H
D-ECZJ	Reims/Cessna F172M	F17200967	
D-ECZK	Reims/Cessna F172M	F17200968	
D-ECZL(3)	Mooney M.20J Model 205	24-3333	
D-ECZN	Reims FR172J Rocket	FR17200388	
D-ECZO(2)	Reims FR172J Rocket	FR17200389	
D-ECZR	Reims FR172J Rocket	FR17200391	
D-ECZS	Reims FR172J Rocket	FR17200394	
D-ECZU	GEMS MS.892A Rallye Commodore 150	10504	
D-ECZV	Reims/Cessna F172M	F17201410	
D-EDAA(2)	Diamond DA 40DStar	D4.085	
D-EDAB(2)	Piper PA-28R-180 Cherokee Arrow	28R-30279	N3937T
D-EDAC(5)	Diamond DA 20-A1 Katana	10320	
D-EDAD(3)	Piper PA-28-180 Cherokee Archer	28-7405196	N43520
			N9638N
D-EDAE(2)	Reims/Cessna F150L	F15000908	D-EDEA(1)
D-EDAF(2)	Piper PA-22-160 Tri-Pacer	22-6869	OY-AEY
D-EDAG(2)	Piper PA-38-112 Tomahawk	38-80A0034	N25137
D-EDAH(4)	Beech 35-C33 Debonair	CD-918	N19J
			N462KK
			D-EMYU
D-EDAI	Cessna 182N Skylane	18260236	N92504
D-EDAJ	Cessna 172M	17261886	N12214
D-EDAK(3)	Cessna 172N	17268783	N734DW
D-EDAL(2)	Reims FR172J Rocket	FR17200366	
D-EDAM(3)	Diamond DA 40DStar (Res as OM-HLL)	D4.087	OE-VPU
D-EDAN(2)	Cessna 150J	15070110	N60156
D-EDAO	Cessna 172N	17268025	N75900
D-EDAP(2)	Cessna 150L	15075118	N10898
D-EDAQ(2)	Bellanca 17-31ATC Turbo Viking	74-31100	N44313
			D-EDAQ
			N1HE
D-EDAR(3)	Cessna 150J	15071060	N5560G
D-EDAS(4)	Diamond DA 20-A1 Katana	10239	
D-EDAT(5)	Cessna 172S Skyhawk SP	172S8132	N871SP
D-EDAU	Piper PA-28-181 Cherokee Archer II	28-7890363	N6342C
D-EDAV(3)	Robin DR.400/180R Remorqueur	1743	F-GEKR
D-EDAW(4)	Wördemann/ Pottier P.230S Panda	465	
D-EDAX(3)	Cessna 172M	17265372	N5199H
D-EDAY(2)	Cessna T210N Turbo Centurion II	21064305	N6240Y
D-EDAZ(4)	Diamond DA 40D Star	D4.088	OE-VPY
D-EDBB(2)	Robin HR.100/210D Safari	213	
D-EDBC(2)	Reims/Cessna F182Q Skylane	F18200149	HB-CIK
			D-EFPV
			(D-EFQF)
D-EDBD	SOCATA MS.880B Rallye Club	2372	F-BUXF
D-EDBE(4)	Cessna 182P Skylane	18264362	N1520M
	(Reims-assembled with "c/n" 0053)		
D-EDBF(3)	Robin DR.400/180RP Remorqueur	1857	
D-EDBG(3)	Piper PA-28-181 Archer II	2890150	N92104
D-EDBH(2)	Reims/Cessna FR182 Skylane RG	FR18200007	
D-EDBI (2)	CASA I-131E Jungmann	2085	E3B-374
D-EDBJ(2)	Diamond DA 40D Star	D4.128	OE-VPW
D-EDBK	Reims/Cessna F182Q Skylane	F18200085	
D-EDBL(2)	Reims/Cessna FR182 Skylane RG	FR18200006	
D-EDBM(2)	PZL-104 Wilga 35	61118	DDR-WBM
			DM-WBM(2)
D-EDBO(2)	Piper PA-32RT-300T Turbo Lance II	32R-7987061	N3057D
	(Permit .02)		
D-EDBP(2)	Robin DR.400/180R Remo 180	2178	
D-EDBQ	Reims/Cessna F172N	F17201569	PH-AXL
			F-WZDD
D-EDBR	Reims/Cessna F172P	F17202082	
D-EDBS(2)	Beech F33A Bonanza	CE-1615	
D-EDBT(2)	CASA I-131E Jungmann	2083	E3B-479
D-EDBU(3)	Piper PA-46-310P Malibu	4608013	SE-IUM
			N9084N
D-EDBV(2)	Piper PA-28-236 Dakota	28-8011131	N8247T
D-EDBW(3)	Piaggio FWP.149D	107	90+88
			AC+438,
			CA+012
			AS+426
D-EDBX	Cessna 182P Skylane	18263175	OY-RPN
			D-EOQQ
			N7392N
D-EDBY	Linzenkirchner/ Piel CP.301A Emeraude	AB.423	
D-EDBZ	Reims/Cessna F182Q Skylane	F18200090	
D-EDCA(2)	Beech V35B Bonanza	D-9131	N4262A
D-EDCB(2)	Piper PA-22-108 Colt	22-8719	D-EDCA
			N10F
D-EDCC(5)	Piper PA-32-300 Cherokee Six	32-7840193	N22408
D-EDCD(3)	Cessna 182P Skylane	18262697	OY-BFF
			(N52596)
D-EDCE	Piper PA-22-108 Colt	22-8665	
D-EDCF	Wassmer WA.41 Baladou	157	F-BPTZ
	(Wfu. Dismantled by 6.00)		

D-EDCG	Dornier Do.27B-1	245	55+87
			PA+316
			PA+109
			PG+107
D-EDCI	Piper PA-18 Super Cub 95	18-1976	L-5
			52-2376
D-EDCK(2)	SNCAN/ Stampe SV.4C	540	F-BDCK
D-EDCL	SIAT 223 A-1 Flamingo	052	EC-52A
D-EDCM(3)	Piper PA-28RT-201 Arrow IV	28R-8018103	N8259X
D-EDCN	Cessna TR182 Turbo Skylane RG	R18200742	N736MU
D-EDCO	Cessna 175B Skylark	17556812	OE-DCE
			N8112T
D-EDCP	Reims/Cessna F152	F15201507	
D-EDCQ	Reims/Cessna F172N Skyhawk II	F17201736	
D-EDCR(2)	Cessna TR182 Turbo Skylane RG	R18201099	(N756KY)
D-EDCS	Dornier Do.27A-1	268	56+01
			SA+115
			SA+723
			D-ELMU
			GB+ . . .
D-EDCU	Cessna 182G Skylane	18255342	(N2142R)
D-EDCV	Dornier Do.27A-4	390	56+82
			PE+220
			PP+104
			PL+424
D-EDCW	Reims/Cessna F172N	F17201776	
	(Thielert Centurion Diesel engine installed .03)		
D-EDCZ	Piaggio FWP.149D	019	90+10
			AC+442
			ND+107
			DB+393
D-EDDA	Piper PA-18-150 Super Cub	18-7583	
D-EDDB(2)	Cessna 172P	17274499	N52352
D-EDDC(2)	Piper PA-28R-200 Cherokee Arrow II	28R-7535186	N33749
D-EDDD	CASA I-131E Jungmann	2223	E3B-604
D-EDDE	Wassmer Jodel D.120R Paris-Nice	20	F-BHTT
D-EDDF(2)	Diamond DA 20-A1 Katana	10145	OE-CKA(2)
D-EDDI (2)	CASA I-131E Jungmann	2172	E3B-552
D-EDDK	Piper PA-28R-200 Cherokee Arrow II	28R-7535189	N33760
D-EDDL(3)	Cessna R182 Skylane RG	R18201887	N5534T
D-EDDM(2)	PZL-104 Wilga 35A	118413	
D-EDDN	Mooney M.20C Mark 21	2595	(N6891U)
D-EDDO(2)	Grumman AA-5B Tiger	AA5B-0005	N6144A
D-EDDP	Cessna 182L Skylane	18258765	(N3465R)
D-EDDT	Mooney M.20C Ranger	680103	N6802N
D-EDDU(5)	Piper PA-28R-201T Turbo Arrow III	28R-7803065	OY-BTK
D-EDDV(3)	Cessna 172S	172S8165	N7256C
D-EDDW	Piper PA-22-108 Colt	22-8879	D-EDDI
			N10F
D-EDDY	Dornier Do.27Q-5	2096	
D-EDDZ	PZL-104 Wilga 35A	129453	
D-EDEB(5)	Cessna 172S	172S8558	N299ME
D-EDED(3)	Mooney M.20J Model 201	24-1149	N1138Z
D-EDEF	Bücker Bü.131 Lerche R-180	63	HB-ESA
			A-87
			HB-ESA
D-EDEG(4)	Beech B36TC Bonanza	EA-447	N7243E
D-EDEH(3)	Robin DR.400/180R Remorqueur	1429	
D-EDEK(3)	Piper PA-28-236 Dakota	28-8011082	N8143H
D-EDEL(3)	Piper PA-32-300 Cherokee Six D	32-7140009	N8617N
D-EDEM(4)	de Havilland DH.82A Tiger Moth	86403	PH-III
			D-EDEM(1)
			NL971
D-EDEO	Reims/Cessna F150L	F15000925	
D-EDEQ(2)	Beech B24R Sierra 200	MC-239	
D-EDER(3)	Beech B24R Sierra 200	MC-250	
D-EDEU	Reims/Cessna F172M	F17200958	
D-EDEW(4)	Cessna 172R (Permit .05)	17281237	N66101
D-EDEX	Klemm Kl.35D Special	1916	SE-BPI
			Fv5027
D-EDEY	Reims/Cessna F172M	F17200973	F-WLIL
D-EDFA(2)	Robin DR.400/RP Remorqueur	1803	
D-EDFB(3)	Piper PA-28-181 Archer II	28-8190131	N8318S
D-EDFC	Cessna F150H	F150-0246	
D-EDFD(2)	Piper PA-28-181 Archer II	2890145	N649CT
			N9203D
D-EDFE(2)	Cessna 172R	17280109	N9869F
D-EDFF	Cessna F172H	F172-0463	
D-EDFG	Cessna F172H	F172-0481	
D-EDFH(3)	Zlin Z.142	0217	HA-SFH
D-EDFI (2)	Diamond DA 40D Star	D4.105	
D-EDFJ(2)	Cessna 150G	15066503	N8603J
D-EDFK	SOCATA MS.893A Rallye Commodore 180	11775	F-BSXX
D-EDFL	Dornier Do.27B-3	392	56+84
			YA+913
			D-EDFL
			D-EBIV
D-EDFM	Robin DR.400/180 Régent	1326	
D-EDFN(4)	Diamond DA 40D Star	D4.109	
D-EDFO(3)	Reims/Cessna F172N	F17201558	
D-EDFP	SIAI-Marchetti S.205-22/R	4-127	D-EDPF
			OO-RAS
D-EDFR	Robin DR.400/180R Remorqueur	1334	
D-EDFS	Dornier Do.27H-2	2006	
D-EDFT	Piper PA-18 Super Cub 95	18-3452	96+28
			NL+119
			AC+527
			AS+527
			54-752

D-EDFU	Piper PA-22-108 Colt	22-8904	N10F
D-EDFW(2)	Mooney M.20K Model 231	25-0532	G-BPCR
			N98433
D-EDFY	Cessna 182H Skylane	18256023	N1923X
D-EDFZ	Piper PA-18 Super Cub 95	18-3427	96+09
			NL+1 . .
			AC+516
			AA+516
			AS+516
			54-727
D-EDGA(4)	Piper PA-28-161 Warrior II	28-8516024	N9512N
D-EDGD	Piper PA-18 Super Cub 95	18-1387	ALAT
			51-15387
D-EDGE(6)	Extra EA.300/L	1175	
D-EDGF	SIAI-Marchetti SF.260	2-38	OH-SRB
			(OO-HEW)
D-EDGG	Reims/Cessna F152	F15201932	
D-EDGH	Gyroflug SC-01 Speed Canard	S-17	
D-EDGI (2)	Mooney M.20K Model 231	25-0193	N231CE
D-EDGK	Cessna TR182 Turbo Skylane RG	R18200941	PH-AYM
			N738MD
D-EDGL	Reims/Cessna F150M	F15001235	
D-EDGM	Robin DR.400/180 Major	2384	
D-EDGN(2)	Piper PA-18 Super Cub 95	18-3419	D-EDSN(1)
			96+01
			AC+510
			AS+510
			54-719
D-EDGS	Aquila AT-01 (Model A210)	102	
D-EDGU	Cessna F150H	F150-0232	
D-EDGV	Rockwell Commander 114A	14531	
D-EDGW	SOCATA MS.880B Rallye Club	2509	F-BVLS
D-EDGY	Cessna F172H	F172-0451	
D-EDGZ	Horstmann/ Jurca MJ.5-D2 Sirocco	025D	
D-EDHB(3)	Piper PA-28-181 Archer II	28-8690038	N9091B
			(N173AV)
			N9500N
D-EDHC	Beech 23 Musketeer	M-454	OE-DRK
			SE-EEP
			D-ENXI
D-EDHD	Cessna F172H	F172-0321	N17012
D-EDHE	Pützer Elster C	041	
D-EDHF(2)	Mooney M.20J Model 201	24-0199	
D-EDHG	Robin DR.400/180 Régent	873	
D-EDHH	Piper PA-28R-200 Cherokee Arrow B	28R-7135063	N2118T
D-EDHI	Piper PA-28-180 Cherokee C	28-3149	N9107J
D-EDHK(2)	Beech F33A Bonanza	CE-1319	
D-EDHM	Robin DR.400/180 Régent	1574	
D-EDHN(2)	Cessna 172R	17280183	
D-EDHO	Piper PA-28-180 Cherokee C	28-3324	N9249J
D-EDHP	Beech V35 Bonanza	D-8568	HB-EHC
			N6207V
D-EDHQ	SOCATA MS.893A Rallye Commodore 180	11928	F-BTIY
D-EDHR	Gardan GY-80 Horizon 180	197	
D-EDHS(2)	SOCATA TB-20 Trinidad	1456	F-GLFT
D-EDHT	Winter/ Druine D.31 Turbulent KWSA	D31-01	ZS-UHT
D-EDHU	Cessna F150H	F150-0236	
D-EDHV	Piper PA-18 Super Cub 95	18-1514	(D-EEMV)
			ALAT
			51-15514
D-EDHW	Beech A36 Bonanza	E-1044	
D-EDHZ(2)	Piper PA-18 Super Cub 95	18-3129	(OO-HBV)
			D-EHTR
			OL-L55
			L-55
			53-4729
D-EDIA	Piper PA-28R-200 Cherokee Arrow II	28R-7535228	N1058X
D-EDIB(2)	Reims/Cessna F172P	F17202131	
D-EDIC(2)	Reims/Cessna F150L	F15001264	
D-EDIE(2)	Cessna 172RG Cutlass RG	172RG1058	N9856B
D-EDIF(3)	Robin DR.400/180 Régent	925	
D-EDIG(2)	SOCATA MS.893A Rallye Commodore 180	11971	F-BTJC
D-EDII (2)	Aviat Pitts S-2B	5209	
D-EDIJ	Reims/Cessna F172P	F17202174	
D-EDIK(2)	Piper PA-28R-200 Cherokee Arrow B	28R-7135202	N1974T
D-EDIL(2)	Reims/Cessna F172M	F17201418	
D-EDIM(3)	Robin DR.400/160 Chevalier	1009	
D-EDIN(2)	Reims/Cessna F150M	F15001267	
D-EDIO	SOCATA TB-10 Tobago	229	
D-EDIQ(2)	Pützer Elster C	038	D-EDWU
	(C/n 009 rebuilt 1997 with fuselage & c/n of D-EDWU)		
D-EDIS(3)	Piper PA-28RT-201T Turbo Arrow IV	28R-8031102	N8211C
D-EDIT	Piper J-3C-90 Cub (J-3C-65 convtd .99)	12722	44-80426
	(Officially quoted with the fuselage number 12552 as c/n)		
D-EDIU	Bölkow BO.208C Junior	701	
D-EDIW(3)	Mooney M.20K Model 252 TSE	25-1173	
D-EDIX(2)	Cessna 175 Skylark	55114	N9314B
D-EDIZ(2)	Cessna F172G	F172-0219	
D-EDJA	Reims/Cessna F150L	F15001100	
D-EDJC	Reims/Cessna F172M	F17201178	
D-EDJE	Reims/Cessna F177RG Cardinal RG	F177RG0108	
D-EDJF(2)	Mooney M.20K Model 231	25-0442	D-EKDW
			(N3666H)
D-EDJG	Reims/Cessna F150L	F15001112	
D-EDJH	Reims/Cessna FRA150L Aerobat	FRA1500241	
D-EDJI	Reims/Cessna FRA150L Aerobat	FRA1500242	
D-EDJJ (2)	Cessna 172N	17273723	N5786J

D-EDJK	Reims/Cessna F172M Skyhawk II	F17201161	
D-EDJL	Reims/Cessna F172M	F17201162	
D-EDJN(2)	Piper PA-28R-200 Cherokee Arrow II	28R-7635264	HB-PAS
			N75086
D-EDJP(2)	SOCATA Rallye 235E Gabier	13339	
D-EDJR	Reims/Cessna F172M	F17201176	
D-EDJW	Cessna 182P Skylane	18263107	N7323N
D-EDJY	Reims FR172J Rocket	FR17200503	
D-EDKA(2)	Cessna F172G	F172-0270	
D-EDKB	Piper PA-28-235 Cherokee C	28-11230	N9490W
D-EDKC	SOCATA MS.892A Rallye Commodore 150	10609	OY-DKB
D-EDKD	SOCATA TB-10 Tobago	230	
D-EDKE(2)	SOCATA TB-9 Tampico	231	
D-EDKH	Morane-Saulnier MS.880B Rallye Club	21	F-BKDJ
D-EDKI	Cessna 182F Skylane	18254573	N3173U
D-EDKK	SOCATA MS.893A Rallye Commodore 180	10934	F-BPYY
D-EDKL(2)	Robin DR.400/235 Remorqueur	1845	
	(Originally Porsche-powered DR.400/RP, converted 5.02)		
D-EDKM	Piper PA-18-135 Super Cub	18-4027	EI-283
			MM542627
			I-EIVJ
			54-2627
D-EDKN	Beech A36 Bonanza	E-1697	
D-EDKO	Cessna 172D	17249967	N2367U
D-EDKR(2)	Piaggio FWP.149D	093	90+75
			BF+406
			AS+412
D-EDKS(2)	Mooney M.20K Model 252 TSE	25-1223	
D-EDKT(2)	Cessna U206G Stationair 6	U20604816	PH-ALH
	(Reims-assembled with "c/n" 0012)		PH-AYI
			N734AJ
D-EDKU(2)	Piper PA-28-180 Cherokee Challenger	28-7305115	N11C
D-EDKV	Piper PA-28R-200 Cherokee Arrow	28R-35709	N4969S
D-EDKX	SOCATA TB-10 Tobago	215	
D-EDLB(2)	Cessna 172S	172S9339	N53300
D-EDLC(2)	Cessna P210N Pressurized Centurion II	P21000608	N734NX
D-EDLE(3)	Piper PA-28RT-201T Turbo Arrow IV	28R-8131027	N8298H
D-EDLF(3)	Robin DR.400/180 Régent	2115	
D-EDLI (2)	Robin DR.400/180R Remorqueur	1991	
D-EDLK	Reims FR172E Rocket	FR17200007	
D-EDLL(2)	Boeing Stearman A75N1	75-2764	C-FUCB
			CF-UCB
			N49948
			41-25275
D-EDLM(2)	Gyroflug SC-01B-160 Speed Canard	S-36	F-GGCA
D-EDLN(2)	Cessna 152	15280618	N25367
D-EDLO(3)	Robin DR.400/180 Régent	2308	
D-EDLP	Reims FR172E Rocket	FR17200018	(G-AVYI)
D-EDLS	Cessna F150H	F150-0324	
D-EDLT(2)	Piper PA-28R-201 Arrow III	28R-7837093	N2574M
D-EDLV	Reims FR172E Rocket	FR17200009	
D-EDLW(2)	Brditschka HB-207R Alfa	207059	
D-EDLX	SOCATA Rallye 180T-D Galérien	3088	OE-DHL
D-EDMA(4)	Dornier Do.27A-4	396	56+88
			PS+716
			QW+720
			PL+426
D-EDMB(2)	SOCATA MS.880B Rallye Club	2510	F-BVLT
D-EDMC(2)	Schmidl/ Light Aero Avid Flyer Magnum	1815	
D-EDMD	SOCATA TB-9 Tampico	232	
D-EDME	Bölkow BO.208C Junior	571	
D-EDMF(2)	Piper PA-18-150 Super Cub	18-8780	OO-LAP
			D-ECOL(2)
			N4444Z
			N9659N
D-EDMG(2)	Cessna 152	15285279	N64830
D-EDMH(3)	SOCATA TB-20 Trinidad	2168	
D-EDMI (3)	Commander Aircraft 114B	14645	
D-EDMJ	General Avia F.22BV Pinguino	013	
D-EDMK(2)	Oberlerchner JOB 15-150	052	OE-CAM
D-EDML	SOCATA MS.893E Rallye 180GT Gaillard	12183	F-BUCS
D-EDMM	Robin DR.400/180R Remorqueur	707	
D-EDMN	Piper PA-28R-200 Cherokee Arrow II	28R-7235240	N1218T
D-EDMO	Cessna 182H	18256158	N2058X
D-EDMP(4)	Reims/Cessna F152	F15201885	HB-CFX
D-EDMR(2)	SOCATA TB 21 Trinidad TC	793	I-GLMC
			F-ODSD
D-EDMS(2)	Diamond DA 40D Star	D4.024	
D-EDMT	Reims/Cessna F172N	F17201570	
D-EDMU	Piper J-3C-85 Cub	5082	N30744
			NC30744
D-EDMV	SOCATA TB-10 Tobago	328	
D-EDMW	Piper PA-18 Super Cub 95	18-3426	96+08
			SA+120
			AC+515
			AS+515
			54-726
D-EDMZ	SOCATA TB-10 Tobago	787	
D-EDNA	Bölkow BO.208C Junior	578	
D-EDNC	Wassmer WA.51 Pacific	08	
D-EDNE	Bölkow BO.208C Junior	579	
D-EDNF	CEA Jodel DR.1050 Ambassadeur	34	F-BJYC
D-EDNG	SOCATA TB-9 Tampico	238	
D-EDNL(2)	Piper PA-28R-200 Cherokee Arrow II	28R-7435240	OE-DRI
			N42850
D-EDNM	Reims/Cessna F150M	F15001166	
D-EDNP	Zlin Z.43	0059	

D-EDNR	SOCATA TB-9 Tampico	211	
D-EDNS	Mooney M.20E Chaparral	700041	N9482V
D-EDNT	Beech G35 Bonanza	D-4481	N174B
D-EDNU	Dornier Do.27B-3	401	56+92 MC+901 JB+901 AC+959
D-EDNW(2)	Dornier Do.27B-1	176	55+46 AS+902 AC+906 AS+906
D-EDNY(2)	Grumman AA-5B Tiger	AA5B-1096	EC-DGF N4527C
D-EDOA	Piper PA-28R-201 Arrow III	28R-7837298	N39474
D-EDOB(2)	SOCATA TB-10 Tobago	242	
D-EDOC(3)	Cessna T210M Turbo Centurion (Reims-assembled with "c/n" 0005)	21061910	PH-DOC (PH-MDA) G-DAWN (N732ZS)
D-EDOD(2)	SOCATA TB-9 Tampico	239	
D-EDOE(2)	Schmidt/ Denney Kitfox IV	1691	
D-EDOF(3)	Robin DR.400/180R Remorqueur	965	
D-EDOG(3)	Impulse 120TD	TD-8	
D-EDOH	Piper J-3C-65 Cub (C/n unknown - officially registered as "43-79321")	unkn	SL-AAZ F-BGQV 43-.....
D-EDOK(2)	Robin DR.400/180 Régent	1898	F-GGXL
D-EDOL(2)	Wassmer Jodel D.120A Paris-Nice	179	
D-EDOM(2)	Robin HR.200/120B Super Club	61	(D-EHKW)
D-EDON(3)	Beech A36 Bonanza	E-2071	
D-EDOR(2)	Cessna 182P Skylane (Reims-assembled with "c/n" 0025)	18263993	N9933E
D-EDOS(2)	Reims/Cessna F172P	F17202223	
D-EDOT(2)	Piper J-3C-65 Cub (Officially regd.with f/n 11671 as c/n)	11843	(D-EBOR(1)) 44-79547
D-EDOV(2)	Cessna F172G	F172-0227	
D-EDOW(2)	Schlör / Stern ST-87 Europlane 1	1830	
D-EDPB(2)	Bunte/ Van's RV-4	1632	
D-EDPD	Piper PA-28R-200 Cherokee Arrow II	28R-7235056	N4456T
D-EDPE	Piper PA-18-150 Super Cub	18-7736	N10F
D-EDPF(2)	Piper PA-18 Super Cub 95	18-3423	96+05 NL+111 AC+503 AS+502 54-723
D-EDPG	SOCATA TB-10 Tobago	243	
D-EDPI	Morane-Saulnier MS.885 Super Rallye	133	OY-AFY
D-EDPK	Robin DR.400/180R Remorqueur	994	
D-EDPL	Robin DR.400/180R Remorqueur	1004	
D-EDPM(2)	Robin DR.400/200R Remo 200	2209	HB-KDQ
D-EDPO(2)	Piaggio FWP.149D	168	91+46 JD+393 JE+393
D-EDPR	Dornier Do.27B-3	398	56+90 PX+221 PP+106 PC+224
D-EDPS(2)	Cessna 172RG Cutlass RG	172RG0114	N6204R
D-EDPU	Aeromere F.8L Falco America	234	(D-ENSO)
D-EDPV	Cessna 172RG Cutlass RG	172RG0557	(F-GCQJ) N5531V
D-EDPW(4)	Cessna 170B	25509	OO-GYM D-EMIT N4565C
D-EDPX	Reims/Cessna F152	F15201933	
D-EDPY	Weihermuller/ Binder CP.301S Smaragd	AB.701	
D-EDPZ	Dornier Do.27A-3	367	56+69 YA+908 AC+957
D-EDQC	Reims/Cessna F182Q Skylane	F18200026	
D-EDQE(2)	Robin DR.400/180R Remo 180	2193	
D-EDQF(2)	Robin DR.400/180R Remorqueur	1670	
D-EDQI	Cessna F172H	F172-0520	
D-EDQK	Reims/Cessna F172M Skyhawk II	F17201338	
D-EDQL	Reims FR172J Rocket	FR17200555	
D-EDQQ	Cessna 182P Skylane (Reims-assembled with "c/n" 0013)	18263892	N6929M
D-EDQR	Robin DR.400/180R Remorqueur	1047	
D-EDQU	Reims FR172E Rocket	FR17200060	
D-EDQV	CEA DR.315 Petit Prince	477	
D-EDQW	Cessna 210D Centurion	21058342	HB-CMX (D-ECMX) HB-CMX N3842Y
D-EDRA	CEA DR.250/160 Capitaine	50	
D-EDRB(3)	Cessna 177B Cardinal	17701422	N30720
D-EDRD	SOCATA MS.893ED Rallye 180GT Gaillard	12701	
D-EDRF(2)	Reims/Cessna F172P	F17202183	
D-EDRG	SOCATA Rallye 235E-D Gabier	12714	
D-EDRH	Piper PA-28-151 Cherokee Warrior	28-7415359	N9580N
D-EDRI (5)	Piper PA-28R-201T Turbo Cherokee Arrow III	28R-7703247	N38592
D-EDRJ	Cessna 182S	18280514	N7282D
D-EDRK(3)	Dieth/ Stephens Acro Sport II	1654	
D-EDRL(2)	Robin DR.400/180RRemorqueur	1391	OE-DRP
D-EDRM	Cessna P210N Pressurized Centurion II	P21000448	OE-DUK N731EV

D-EDRN	Reims/Cessna F172M	F17201249	
D-EDRO(4)	Piper PA-28RT-201 Arrow IV	28R-8118021	N8287U
D-EDRP(2)	Reims/Cessna F172P	F17202179	
D-EDRQ	SOCATA Rallye 100ST-D	2910	
D-EDRR	Cessna 210B	21057992	OE-DKM N9692X
D-EDRS	Dornier Do.27B-1	306	56+31 PF+220 PF+110 PL+413
D-EDRT	SOCATA MS.893ED Rallye 180GT Gaillard	12755	
D-EDRV(2)	Robin DR.400/180R Remorqueur	1446	D-EEKL(2) OE-DRV
D-EDRW	Cessna 182P (Reims-assembled with "c/n" 0032)	18264059	N6002F
D-EDRX	SOCATA Rallye 100ST-D	2911	
D-EDRY	Piper PA-18 Super Cub 95	18-7194	N3196Z
D-EDSA	Cessna 180F Skywagon	18051308	N4608U
D-EDSB(2)	Seger/ Pottier P.50P	01	
D-EDSC	Reims/Cessna F172H	F17200688	
D-EDSD	Robin DR.400/180R Remorqueur	1299	
D-EDSE	Cessna 205	205-0399	N8399Z
D-EDSF	Piaggio P.149D	276	OE-DSF 91+91 AC+427 AS+427
D-EDSG(2)	Reims/Cessna FR172K Hawk XP	FR17200665	
D-EDSH	Cessna 210A	21057733	OE-DSH N9433X
D-EDSJ	Reims/Cessna F152	F15201493	
D-EDSK	Reims/Cessna F172M	F17201269	
D-EDSL	Piper PA-18 Super Cub 95	18-3438	96+17 AC+506 AS+505 54-738
D-EDSM	Dornier Do.27A-1	279	56+11 DB+901 GD+159 LB+159 CC+. . .
D-EDSN(2)	HOAC DV-20 Katana	20146	
D-EDSP	Dornier Do.27A-3	465	57+36 MB+902 JC+902 AA+934 ?
D-EDSR(2)	Cessna 172P	17275353	N62896
D-EDSS	CEA DR.315 Petit Prince	407	
D-EDST	Mooney M.20F Executive	22-1296	
D-EDSU	Cessna 182F	18254714	N3314U
D-EDSW(2)	Walker/ Stoddard-Hamilton Glasair IIS-RG (Permit 8.02)	2179	
D-EDSZ	Reims/Cessna F152	F15201518	
D-EDTA	Piper PA-28-180 Cherokee C	28-3631	N9510J
D-EDTB	Cessna F172H	F172-0415	
D-EDTC(2)	Reims/Cessna F172M	F17201323	(SE-GKG)
D-EDTE	Piper PA-18-150 Super Cub	18-7662	N10F
D-EDTG(2)	Piper PA-28-180 Cherokee D	28-4842	TF-VON N6424J
D-EDTH(2)	HOAC DV-20 Katana	20052	
D-EDTI	Morane-Saulnier MS.885 Super Rallye	257	HB-EDW
D-EDTJ	Cessna F172H	F172-0474	
D-EDTK	SAN Jodel D.117 Grand Tourisme	420	F-BHNE
D-EDTL(2)	Cessna A.152 Aerobat	A1521033	N758ZJ
D-EDTO	Cessna 150D	15060482	N4482U
D-EDTP	Zlin Z.526 Trenér Master	1048	
D-EDTQ(2)	Extra EA.300	048	N104EX Chile 028 D-ETXG(2)
D-EDTR	Cessna T210L Turbo Centurion	21060162	N59211
D-EDTS	Piper PA-28-181 Archer II	28-8090010	N8229E N9611N
D-EDTT(2)	Cessna P210N Pressurized Centurion II	P21000462	OE-DUD (N73IHM)
D-EDTU(2)	Cessna 172N	17274459	N52249
D-EDTW	Gyroflug SC-01B-160 Speed Canard	S-6	
D-EDTY(3)	Cessna 172S	172S9084	N5193C
D-EDUC(3)	Piper PA-28-181 Archer II	2890170	N92327
D-EDUD(2)	Piper PA-28-181 Archer II	28-8090148	N81219
D-EDUE	CEA DR.253 Régent	174	
D-EDUF(3)	Cessna 172N	17272224	N9320E
D-EDUG(2)	SAN Jodel DR.1050 Ambassadeur	186	
D-EDUH(2)	Pützer Elster B	020	97+13 D-EDYM
D-EDUK(2)	Reims/Cessna F172M	F17201214	
D-EDUM(2)	Piper PA-28-181 Archer II	2890055	N9134R
D-EDUN(3)	Piper PA-18 Super Cub 95 (Has f/n 18-1515 ex.51-15540 changed when in ALAT service)	18-1602	(D-ENCG) ALAT 51-15602
D-EDUO	CEA DR.315 Petit Prince	481	
D-EDUP(2)	Piper PA-28-181 Archer II	28-8190081	N8289Y
D-EDUQ(2)	Piper PA-32-260 Cherokee Six	32-637	N11C
D-EDUR(2)	SIAI-Marchetti SF-260	1-10	OO-RUR F-BRUR OO-HAP
D-EDUS(3)	Cessna 172N	17270580	N739JM
D-EDUT	Piper J-3C-90 Cub	8962	HB-ODM 42-38393

D-EDUU(2)	Piper PA-28-181 Archer II	2890100	N9158D
D-EDUV(2)	SAN Jodel DR.1050 Ambassadeur	187	
D-EDUW(2)	Piper PA-28-140 Cherokee	28-23243	N9759W
			(G-AVKV)
			N9759W
D-EDUX(3)	Pitts S-1S Special	AB-K-025 (502)	
D-EDUY	Robin DR.300/180R Remorqueur	490	F-BSBU
D-EDUZ(2)	Reims FR172E Rocket	FR17200035	
D-EDVA(2)	SOCATA MS.880B Rallye-Club	2335	OO-LVA
			F-BUVM
D-EDVB	Reims/Cessna F172M	F17201439	
D-EDVC	Reims/Cessna F172M	F17201442	
D-EDVD	Reims/Cessna F172M	F17201452	
D-EDVE(3)	Robin DR.400/200R Remorqueur	1826	
	(Re-engined & type change 12.03)		
D-EDVG	Reims/Cessna F172N	F17201604	
D-EDVH(2)	Christen A-1 Husky	1106	
D-EDVI (2)	Reims/Cessna F172N	F17201594	
D-EDVJ	Piper PA-28-140 Cherokee E	28-7225453	N11C
D-EDVK	Piper PA-28-180 Cherokee G	28-7205304	N11C
D-EDVM	SOCATA MS.893E Rallye 180GT Gaillard	12788	
D-EDVN	SOCATA MS.893E Rallye 180GT Gaillard	12789	
D-EDVP	SOCATA Rallye 150T-D	2776	
D-EDVR	Reims/Cessna F150M	F15001363	
D-EDVS	Mooney M.20F Executive	670359	HB-DVS
D-EDVT(2)	Mooney M.20E Chaparral	690038	HB-DVT
D-EDVX	Mooney M.20E Chaparral	21-0017	HB-DVX
D-EDVZ	Reims/Cessna F150L	F15001003	F-BUMR
D-EDWA	Pützer Elster C	034	
D-EDWB(2)	Cessna P210N Pressurized Centurion II	P21000571	N732AC
D-EDWC(2)	Cessna 170B (Permit .05)	25732	N3088A
D-EDWD	CASA I-131E Jungmann	2146	E3B-546
D-EDWF	Robin HR.100/210D Safari	196	
D-EDWH(2)	Piper PA-28R-201T Turbo Cherokee Arrow III		
		28R-7703266	N38722
D-EDWI	Pützer Elster C	036	
D-EDWJ (2)	CASA I-131E Jungmann	2136	E3B-453
D-EDWK	CASA I-131E Jungmann	2080	E3B-470
D-EDWN(2)	Robin DR.400/180R Remorqueur	1927	
D-EDWO(3)	Cessna 182S (Permit 3.00)	18280687	N24311
D-EDWP	Beech F33A Bonanza	CE-654	
D-EDWQ	Cessna 172R	17280536	N9552W
D-EDWR(2)	SIAI-Marchetti SF.260C	725	
D-EDWS(2)	Reims/Cessna F182Q Skylane	F18200034	
D-EDWW(2)	Piper PA-28R-200 Cherokee Arrow II	28R-7335436	N56438
D-EDWZ	CASA I-131E Jungmann	2015	E3B-411
D-EDXA	Reims/Cessna FA150K Aerobat	FA1500032	
D-EDXB	Reims/Cessna F172H	F17200712	
D-EDXD	Reims FR172G Rocket	FR17200211	
D-EDXE	Reims/Cessna F172H	F17200726	
D EDXF	Reims FR172G Rocket	FR17200169	
D-EDXG(3)	Drescher/ Skystar Kitfox V (Permit 11.99)	S 9508-0142	
D-EDXL	Reims/Cessna F172M	F17201098	
D-EDXM	Reims/Cessna F172M	F17201100	
D-EDXP	Reims/Cessna F172M	F17201106	
D-EDXR	Reims/Cessna F172M	F17201034	F-BUMA
D-EDXT	Grumman AA-5A Cheetah	AA5A-0085	OY-GAK
D-EDXW	SOCATA TB-10 Tobago	462	
D-EDXX	SOCATA TB-10 Tobago	461	
D-EDYA	Bölkow BO.207	286	HB-UYA
			D-ENVY
D-EDYC(2)	Piper PA-28RT-201T Turbo Arrow IV	28R-7931165	N2174Z
D-EDYH	Piper PA-12 Super Cruiser	12-3480	SL-ABE
			F-BEGP
			NC4052H
D-EDYL(2)	Pützer Elster B	019	97+12
			D-EDYL
D-EDYQ(2)	Piper PA-32-260 Cherokee Six	32-415	(N3529W)
			N11C
D-EDYS(2)	Cessna 150F	15063806	YN-BBH
			AN-BBH
			N7706F
D-EDYT	Piper J-3C-65 Cub	11771	HB-OEG
			43-30480
D-EDYV	Focke-Wulf FW.44J Stieglitz	2549	Fv667
	(Identity as officially quoted from evidence on aircraft - but also believed ex Fv5771 therefore c/n 2814)		
D-EDZE	Cessna 210	57160	N7460E
D-EDZI	Cessna F172E	F172-0023/17250578	OE-DEO
			(N2978U)
D-EDZL	Cessna 182P	18263772	N6598M
	(Reims-assembled with "c/n" 0001)		
D-EDZM	Cessna 182P	18263788	N6644M
	(Reims-assembled with "c/n" 0002)		
D-EDZN	Reims/Cessna F150M	F15001168	
D-EDZO(2)	Cessna 182P Skylane	18263549	N5811J
D-EDZQ	Piper PA-28R-180 Cherokee Arrow	28R-31120	N3172R
D-EDZU	Cessna 182H Skylane	18256163	N2063X
D-EDZW	Piper PA-38-112 Tomahawk II	38-81A0103	N26022
D-EEAA	Reims/Cessna FR172K Hawk XP	FR17200639	
D-EEAB	Bölkow BO.208C Junior	681	
D-EEAC	Bölkow BO.208C Junior	682	
D-EEAD	Stark/ Piel CP.301A Emeraude	101-052	OY-EAD
D-EEAE(3)	Beech B36TC Bonanza	EA-666	N432A
D-EEAF(3)	Dornier Do.27B-1	274	HB-HAF
			D-EATA(1)
			56+07
			AC+926
			AS+926

D-EEAG(2)	Oberlerchner JOB 15-150	053	OE-CAG
D-EEAH	Bölkow BO.208C Junior	658	(D-EJMH)
D-EEAI	Bölkow BO.208C Junior	686	
D-EEAK(3)	Cessna 172R	17280246	N97GG
			N422ES
D-EEAL(2)	Piper PA-28-180 Cherokee D	28-4734	N6326J
D-EEAM(2)	Cessna 170B	25080	HB-COM
			N8228A
D-EEAN(2)	Piper PA-28-181 Archer II	28-8390025	N8322X
D-EEAO(2)	Cessna P210R Pressurized Centurion II	P21000846	N5289A
D-EEAP	Reims FR172F Rocket	FR17200067	
D-EEAR	SAN Jodel D.140C Mousquetaire III	143	
D-EEAS(3)	Cessna P210N Pressurized Centurion II	P21000328	N4809K
D-EEAT	Reims FR172F Rocket	FR17200062	(G-AXBT)
D-EEAU(3)	Robin HR.200/120B	274	
D-EEAV(2)	SOCATA TB-21 Trinidad TC	2124	
D-EEAW(2)	Diamond DA 40DStar	D4.042	
D-EEAX(3)	Cessna 172S Skyhawk SP	172S8218	N218SP
D-EEAY	Ruschmeyer R90-230RG	017	
D-EEAZ	Piaggio P.149D	323	92+25
			AS+403
			AS+473
D-EEBA(3)	Diamons DA.20-A1 Katana	10026	C-FUIU
D-EEBB	Cessna F150J	F150-0507	
D-EEBC(2)	Reims/Cessna F150M	F15001270	
D-EEBD	Cessna F172H	F172-0640	
D-EEBE(2)	Piper PA-38-112 Tomahawk	38-80A0112	N24817
D-EEBF(2)	Maule M-6-235 Super Rocket	7490C	N5671T
D-EEBG	Reims/Cessna F152	F15201437	
D-EEBH(2)	Zlin Z.526 Trenér Master (Reservation .04)	1068	LZ-713
			LZ-012
D-EEBK	Piper PA-28R-200 Cherokee Arrow II	28R-7435014	N56574
D-EEBL	Piper PA-28RT-201T Turbo Arrow IV	28R-8031065	N8158B
D-EEBM	Robin DR.400/180 Régent	929	
D-EEBN(2)	Beech F33A Bonanza	CE-1280	N3217M
D-EEBO(2)	Reims/Cessna F150M	F15001273	
D-EEBP	Reims/Cessna F182Q Skylane	F18200041	
D-EEBS(2)	Zlin Z.526F Trenér Master	1151	(D-EJLL)
			SP-CDM
D-EEBT(2)	Beech F33A Bonanza	CE-1479	N44LR
D-EEBU	Piper PA-28-235 Cherokee B	28-10848	N9190W
D-EEBV	Ruschmeyer R90-230RG	011	
D-EEBW	Mooney M.20J Model 201	24-0424	
D-EEBX(2)	Zlin Z.526M Trenér Master (Reservation .04)	1060	LZ-710
			LZ-10
D-EEBY(4)	Zlin Z.526 Trenér Master (Reservation .04)	1087	LZ-720
			LZ-020
D-EEBZ	SOCATA TB-10 Tobago	983	
D-EECA	Beech V35B Bonanza	D-9120	
D-EECB	Reims FR172J Rocket	FR17200487	
D-EECC(3)	Cessna 172R (Thielert diesel)	17281213	N2121F
D-EECD(3)	Diamond DA 40 Star	40018	
D-EECE	Reims FR172J Rocket	FR17200495	
D-EECF	Cessna 182P Skylane	18262784	N52706
D-EECH	Cessna 182P Skylane	18262850	N52794
D-EECI (2)	Piper PA-46-350P Malibu	4622123	N312CC
			JA4194
			N111K
			JA4194
			N9208Z
			(N444JM)
			N9208Z
D-EECK(2)	OMF-100-160 Symphony	0042	(D-EFEM(4))
			(N420MF)
D-EECL(3)	Rockwell Commander 112TC	13039	N112FH
D-EECM(2)	Reims/Cessna F172M	F17201444	
D-EECO	Beech V35B Bonanza	D-9229	
D-EECP(2)	Piper PA-28-161 Warrior II	28-8116242	N9543N
D-EECQ	Reims/Cessna F172M	F17201280	
D-EECR(4)	Ruschmeyer R90-230FG (Reservn .04)	030	(D-EEFX)
D-EECT(3)	Ruschmeyer R90-230RG (Reservn .04)	028	N127AB
			D-EE CT(3)
			D-EEDQ(2)
D-EECU(2)	Robin DR.400/180R Remorqueur	1215	
D-EECV	Reims/Cessna F172N	F17201634	(SU- . . .)
D-EECW(2)	Heliopolis Gomhourla Mk.6	186	SU-345
			EAF-345
D-EEDA(4)	Diamond DA 40D Star	D4.001	
D-EEDD(2)	Diamond DA 20-A1 Katana	10315	N315DA
D-EEDE	SOCATA MS.883 Rallye 115	1573	F-BTHJ
D-EEDF(2)	Cessna 172N	17269683	N737UJ
D-EEDG	Reims/Cessna F172M	F17200906	
D-EEDH	Reims/Cessna F172M	F17200913	
D-EEDI (2)	Sebald/ Monnett Sonerai IVS	VS-1	
D-EEDJ	Reims FR172J Rocket	FR17200355	
D-EEDK(2)	Reims/Cessna F150L	F15000941	(D-EGKD)
D-EEDL	Reims FR172J Rocket	FR17200359	
D-EEDP	Reims/Cessna F150L	F15000878	
D-EEDS(2)	Beech A36AT Bonanza	E-2714	
D-EEDT	Reims/Cessna F172M	F17200919	
D-EEDU	Cessna 182P Skylane	18261537	N21284
D-EEDV	Cessna 182P Skylane	18261524	N21262
D-EEDW(2)	SNCAN/ Stampe SV.4C	245	F-BCKD
D-EEDX	Cessna 182P Skylane	18261530	N21272
D-EEEA	SOCATA TB-10 Tobago	116	
D-EEEB(2)	Reims/Cessna F182Q Skylane	F18200112	OY-CBR
			PH-AYD(2)

D-EEEC	SOCATA TB-10 Tobago	118	
D-EEED(2)	Zlin Z.526M Trenér Master	1033	HB-TCI
			D-EJAB(5)
			OO-YGO
			(OO-UGO)
			YU-DIK
			JRV41108
			OK-XRC
D-EEEE(2)	SOCATA TB-20 Trinidad	300	
D-EEEF	Robin DR.400/160 Chevalier	883	
D-EEEG(2)	Gyroflug SC-01 Speed Canard	S-15	
D-EEEH	SOCATA Rallye 180TS Galérien	3322	
D-EEEI	SOCATA Rallye 180TS Galérien	3321	
D-EEEK	CASA I-131E Jungmann	2056	E3B-455
D-EEEL(2)	Piper PA-28RT-201 Arrow IV	28R-8018055	N8178A
D-EEEM	SOCATA Rallye 235E-D Gabier	13155	
D-EEEN	Mooney M.20J Model 201	24-0975	N3882H
D-EEEP	SOCATA TB-9 Tampico	140	
D-EEEQ(3)	SOCATA TB-200 Tobago XL	1760	
D-EEER	SOCATA TB-10 Tobago	137	
D-EEET	SOCATA TB-10 Tobago	136	
D-EEEU	Morane-Saulnier MS.885 Super Rallye	136	F-BKLL
D-EEEW	Gyroflug SC-01B Speed Canard	A-3	
D-EEEX	Gyroflug SC-01B Speed Canard	A1-80	
D-EEEY(3)	Piper PA-46-350P Malibu Mirage	4622005	N9148V
D-EEEZ	Krauss/ Rutan VariEze VW-VP	A-0329	
D-EEFA	Piper PA-28-140 Cherokee C	28-26658	N5827U
D-EEFC	Piper PA-24-260 Comanche C	24-4932	N9425P
D-EEFE	Reims/Cessna F172P	F17202168	
D-EEFF	Ficht/ Bölkow BO.209 Monsun 160RV (from parts)	301	
D-EEFG(3)	Beech F33A Bonanza	CE-1626	N82689
D-EEFH	Piper PA-28-140 Cherokee C	28-26736	N5885U
D-EEFJ	Piper PA-28R-200 Cherokee Arrow	28R-35660	N3036R
D-EEFK(2)	Mooney M.20K Model 252 TSE	25-1175	
D-EEFL(2)	Beech F33A Bonanza	CE-1752	
D-EEFM	Piper PA-28R-200 Cherokee Arrow	28R-35674	N4902S
D-EEFN(2)	Mooney M.20J Model 205	24-3215	
D-EEFO	Piper PA-28R-200 Cherokee Arrow	28R-35679	N4907S
D-EEFP	Reims/Cessna F172M	F17201238	
D-EEFQ(2)	Cessna 172R	17280342	N9496F
D-EEFR	Reims/Cessna F172M	F17201246	
D-EEFU(2)	Rallye 235ED Gabier	13329	
D-EEFV	Piper PA-28-180 Cherokee E	28-5757	N3655R
D-EEFW	SOCATA MS.893A Rallye Commodore 180	11461	F-BSAU
D-EEFY(2)	Reims/Cessna F172P	F17202229	
D-EEFZ	Cessna 172R	17280341	N9491Z
D-EEGB	Beech B24R Sierra 200	MC-262	
D-EEGC	Robin DR.400/180R Remorqueur	1357	
D-EEGD	Piaggio P.149D	315	92+18
			CA+478
			AC+466
			AS+466
D-EEGE(2)	Cessna T210N Turbo Centurion II	21063674	N4920C
D-EEGF	Robin DR.400/180 Régent	1013	
D-EEGG(2)	Mooney M.20J Model 205 (Permit 7.04)	24-3015	
D-EEGH(2)	Commander Aircraft 114B	14632	
D-EEGI	Piper PA-28-181 Cherokee Archer II	28-7790403	N2539Q
D-EEGJ	Piper PA-28-181 Archer II	2890066	N9137X
D-EEGK(2)	Cessna 182J Skylane	18256742	N2642F
D-EEGL	Reims/Cessna F172M	F17201335	
D-EEGM	Cessna T210M Turbo Centurion	21062433	PH-ADK
	(Reims-assembled with c/n 0010)		D-EGSD
	(Accident 8.8.00)		PH-LTM
			(PH-AYM)
			N761QL
D-EEGN(2)	CASA I-131E Jungmann	2095	E3B-351
D-EEGO	Piper PA-28-140 Cherokee Cruiser	28-7725210	N9632N
D-EEGP	Reims/Cessna F172N	F17201981	
D-EEGT	Robin DR.400/180 Régent	1061	
D-EEGW(3)	Cessna TR182 Turbo Skylane RG	R18200667	OY-SFK
			N9194R
D-EEGZ	Reims/Cessna F177RG Cardinal RG	F177RG0121	
D-EEHA	American AA-5 Traveler	AA5-0031	(N5831L)
D-EEHB	American AA-5 Traveler	AA5-0032	(N5832L)
D-EEHC	American AA-5 Traveler	AA5-0117	(N6017L)
D-EEHD	American AA-5 Traveler	AA5-0118	(N6018L)
D-EEHE(3)	Piper PA-32RT-300 Lance II	32R-7885004	N2204M
	(Permit .05)		C-GJVE
			N2204M
D-EEHF	American AA-5 Traveler	AA5-0136	(N6036L)
D-EEHG(2)	Cessna 182Q Skylane	18267235	N97871
D-EEHH(2)	Ruschmeyer R90-230RG	007	
D-EEHK	American AA-5 Traveler	AA5-0288	(N7288L)
D-EEHL(2)	Mooney M.20J Model 201	24-1612	
D-EEHM	American AA-5 Traveler	AA5-0318	(N5418L)
D-EEHN	American AA-5 Traveler	AA5-0345	(N5445L)
D-EEHO	Piper PA-28-140 Cherokee	28-20779	CF-RWL
D-EEHP(2)	Reims/Cessna F182Q Skylane	F18200165	OE-DOV
D-EEHR	Cessna 182P Skylane	18261008	N7368Q
D-EEHS	American AA-5 Traveler	AA5-0411	
D-EEHT	American AA-5 Traveler	AA5-0412	
D-EEHU	PZL-104 Wilga 35A	86269	DDR-WHU
			DM-WHU
D-EEHW	Cessna P210N Pressurized Centurion II	P21000455	N731FX
	(Soloy conversion, 2.00)		
D-EEHX	Ruschmeyer R90-230RG	008	
D-EEHY(2)	Ruschmeyer R90-230RG	029	(D-EEDZ(2))

D-EEHZ(2)	Ruschmeyer R90-230RG	009	
D-EEIA(3)	Robin DR.400/180R Remorqueur	1692	
D-EEID	Reims FR172J Rocket	FR17200512	
D-EEIE	Reims/Cessna F177RG Cardinal RG	F177RG0117	
D-EEII (3)	Diamond DA 40DStar	D4.080	D-ETHF
	(Built as DA 40 c/n 40080, convtd to DA 40D)		OE-VTA
D-EEIJ	Cessna T182T Turbo Skylane	T18208130	N5171X
D-EEIL(3)	Piper PA-18-150 Super Cub	18-7909091	N82295
D-EEIM	Robin DR.400/180R Remorqueur	849	
D-EEIN (3)	Robin DR.400/180R Remorqueur	1938	
D-EEIP(2)	Bölkow BO.209 Monsun 160RV	152	HB-UEP
			D-EBJL
D-EEIS(2)	Cessna 150L	15075235	N11165
D-EEIT	SOCATA TB-200 Tobago XL	1625	
D-EEIU	Cessna F172H	F172-0512	PH-AAC
D-EEIV	Reims/Cessna F172M	F17201372	
D-EEIW	Reims/Cessna F172M	F17201371	
D-EEJA(2)	Yakovlev Yak-50	80-1705	DDR-WQO
D-EEJB	Robin DR.400/180R Remorqueur	968	
D-EEJC	Robin HR.200/100 Club	40	
D-EEJD	Robin HR.200/100 Club	42	
D-EEJE	Robin DR.400/180S	1894	
D-EEJF	Piper PA-46-310P Malibu	4608135	OE-KEF
			N67JB
D-EEJG	Cessna 172N	17272269	N9455E
D-EEJH	Mooney M.20J Model 201	24-0586	
D-EEJJ(3)	Cessna 172R (Res .05)	17280813	N24056
D-EEJL	Reims/Cessna F152	F15201545	
D-EEJM(2)	Cessna 172N	17270216	N7381C
D-EEJO	Robin HR.100/210D Safari	202	
D-EEJP(2)	Cessna F150G	F150-0175	OE-CMU
			D-EFMU
			(D-EHER)
D-EEJQ	Cessna 152	15283155	N46978
D-EEJR(2)	Ruschmeyer R90-230RG	020	
D-EEJT(2)	Timmermann/ Denney Kitfox II	01/248	
D-EEKA	Zlin Z.226T Trenér 6	195	OE-CKA
			OK-MGW
D-EEKC	Wassmer CE.43 Guepard	469	
D-EEKD	Piper PA-28-180 Cherokee C	28-1999	N7952W
			6Y-JGM
			N7952W
D-EEKE	Beech F33A Bonanza	CE-1145	N500TK
			N500TL
D-EEKF	Reims/Cessna F172M	F17201260	
D-EEKG	Reims/Cessna F150M	F15001230	
D-EEKH	Gardan GY-80 Horizon 160	16	D-EGZB
			HB-DVA
D-EEKI	Wassmer WA.54 Atlantic	123	
D-EEKK	Jodel D.119OS Compostela	E.99	EC-BAC
D-EEKN	Cessna 172S	172S8308	N2431X
D-EEKO	Cessna 150F	15062773	N8673G
D-EEKP	SOCATA TB-20 Trinidad	324	
D-EEKR	Robin DR.400/180R Remorqueur	746	F-BTZA
D-EEKW	Mraz M.1C Sokol	211	HB-TAD
D-EELA	Grumman AA-5 Traveler	AA5-0724	N5140A
			(N1324R)
D-EELB	Robin DR.300/180R Remorqueur	534	LX-FIZ
			F-BSLI
D-EELC(3)	Beech F33A Bonanza	CE-1589	N33PN
			F-GIFJ
D-EELD	Droge/ Jurca MJ.5-D2 Sirocco	030	
D-EELE	CASA I-131E Jungmann	2195	E3B-589
D-EELF	Gardan GY-80 Horizon 180	149	
D-EELH(2)	Cessna 172N	17271463	N3192E
D-EELI	CEA DR.250/160 Capitaine	69	F-BNVG
D-EELL(2)	Diamond DA 40D Star	D4.118	
D-EELM	Grumman AA-5B Tiger	AA5B-0151	
D-EELN	SOCATA Rallye 180TS Galérien	3359	
D-EELO	Robin DR.400/180R Remorqueur	951	
D-EELQ	Robin DR.400/180R Remorqueur	944	
D-EELR	Robin DR.400/180R Remorqueur	950	
D-EELT	Cessna 172C Skyhawk	17248963	N8463X
D-EELU(2)	Mooney M.20E Chaparral	700002	N9332V
D-EELV	Cessna 172N	17273031	N1941F
D-EELW(2)	Beech F33A Bonanza	CE-1180	N3121A
D-EELY	Piper PA-28-161 Warrior II	28-8216121	N9636N
D-EELZ(2)	Gyroflug SC01B-160 Speed Canard	S-4	(D-EBDA)
D-EEMA	SOCATA MS.892A Rallye Commodore 150	11440	F-BRYH
D-EEMC	Cessna 172M	17266840	N109IU
D-EEMD	Cessna T210L Turbo Centurion	21060911	N5331V
D-EEME	Cessna T210N Turbo Centurion II	21064262	N6135Y
D-EEMG	Cessna 210C	21058150	HB-CMG
			N3650Y
D-EEMH(2)	Cessna 172RG Cutlass RG	172RG1053	N9843B
D-EEMI	Piper PA-28-151 Cherokee Warrior	28-7415223	N9535N
D-EEMK(3)	Grumman-American AA-5B Tiger	AA5B-1014	OY-GAU
D-EEML	Robin HR.200/100 Club	101	
D-EEMM(2)	Sondermann/ Christen Eagle II	S-0470	
D-EEMN	Cessna FR.182 Skylane RG	0040	PH-AXB
D-EEMO	SOCATA MS.892E Rallye 150GT	12377	F-BVNO
D-EEMP	Reims/Cessna F150M	F15001247	
D-EEMR	Reims/Cessna F172M	F17201356	(F-BXZV)
			(D-EJTA)
D-EEMS	Piper PA-18 Super Cub 95	18-3229	OL-L52
			L-155
			53-4829

D-EEMT(3)	Extra EA.200	1032	
D-EEMU	Robin DR.400/180 Régent	1036	
D-EEMV(2)	Cessna 172N	17270839	N739VK
D-EEMW	Beech A36TC Bonanza	EA-190	
D-EEMY	Piper PA-32R-300 Lance	32R-7780248	N2489Q
D-EENA(2)	SOCATA TB-21 Trinidad TC	1378	HB-KDU D-ERHP
D-EENB	Cessna 182P Skylane	18262476	N52239
D-EENC	Cessna 182P Skylane	18262616	N52449
D-EEND	Cessna 182P Skylane	18262622	N52457
D-EENE	Reims/Cessna F150L	F15001073	
D-EENF	Reims/Cessna F150L	F15001075	
D-EENG	Reims/Cessna F150L	F15001076	
D-EENI	Reims/Cessna F150L	F15001086	
D-EENK	Reims/Cessna F172M	F17201119	
D-EENL	Reims/Cessna F172M	F17201121	
D-EENO(2)	Cessna T210N Turbo Centurion II	21064162	N5321Y
D-EENP	Reims FR172J Rocket	FR17200482	
D-EENQ	Reims FR172J Rocket	FR17200484	
D-EENR	Reims/Cessna F172M Skyhawk	F17201152	
D-EENT	Reims FR172J Rocket	FR17200473	
D-EENU	Reims FR172J Rocket	FR17200474	
D-EENW	Reims/Cessna F150L	F15001089	
D-EENX	Reims/Cessna F150L	F15001059	
D-EEOB(2)	Aviamilano F.8L Falco Srs II (Permit .05)	114	G-OCDS G-VEGL OO-MEN I-VEGL
D-EEOC	Cessna 182P Skylane (Reims-assembled with "c/n" 0024)	18263948	N9887E
D-EEOE(2)	Beech F33A Bonanza	CE-1647	N82627
D-EEOF	Robin DR.400/180 Régent	1435	
D-EEOH(2)	Diamond DA 40 Star	40014	
D-EEOI	Reims/Cessna F150M	F15001279	
D-EEOK	Reims/Cessna F172M	F17201286	
D-EEOL	Beech V35B Bonanza	D-10294	N66696
D-EEOM	Reims/Cessna F172M	F17201295	
D-EEOO	Cessna 210M Centurion II (Reims-assembled with c/n 0013)	21062648	F-WZJE N761ZL
D-EEOP	Robin DR.400/180R Remorqueur	1434	
D-EEOR(2)	Reims/Cessna FR172K Hawk XP	FR17200624	PH-JET
D-EEOS	Reims/Cessna F172P Skyhawk II	F17202078	
D-EEOV	Robin DR.400/180 Régent	1427	F-GCAP
D-EEOW	SOCATA MS.894A Minerva 220	11024	F-BRDD
D-EEPA(2)	Piper PA-28-181 Archer II	28-8690045	N9288Y
D-EEPB	Wassmer WA.40A Super IV	78	PH-TAK SE-CWI
D-EEPE	Robin DR.400/180R Remorqueur	1222	
D-EEPF(2)	Robin DR.400/180S	1958	
D-EEPG(2)	Robin R.2160D	160	HB-EQH F-ODIK
D-EEPH	Reims/Cessna F172M	F17201216	(D-EOFY)
D-EEPI	Wassmer WA.54 Atlantic	151	
D-EEPJ	Dornier Do.27A-1	173	55+43 AC+923 AS+923
D-EEPK(2)	CASA I-131E Jungmann	2101	E3B-303
D-EEPL	Reims/Cessna F172N	F17201539	
D-EEPM	Piper PA-28R-200 Cherokee Arrow II	28R-7435283	N43613
D-EEPN	Dornier Do.27A-4 (Permit 7.04)	395	56+87 QA+101 QW+709 PL+435 D-EJIG
D-EEPO	Cessna 182P Skylane	18263418	N9652G
D-EEPP	Beech B24R Sierra 200 (Damaged 20.6.04)	MC-378	OE-DFP
D-EEPQ	Robin DR.400/180 Régent	1234	
D-EEPR	Piper PA-38-112 Tomahawk	38-78A0292	N9676N
D-EEPU	Reims/Cessna F150M	F15001286	
D-EEPW	Reims/Cessna F182P Skylane	F18200003	
D-EEPY	Cessna TR182 Turbo Skylane RG	R18201431	N4796S
D-EEQA(2)	Reims/Cessna F172N	F17201697	
D-EEQH(2)	Reims/Cessna F182Q Skylane	F18200078	
D-EEQI (2)	Piper PA-38-112 Tomahawk	38-79A0747	N9679N
D-EEQP	CASA I-131E Jungmann	2100	E3B-493
D-EEQS	Reims/Cessna F172N	F17201909	(LN-HOJ)
D-EEQT	Reims/Cessna F172N	F17201920	
D-EEQW	Piper PA-18 Super Cub 95	18-3421	96+03 NL+106 AC+512 AA+512 AS+512 54-721
D-EERA	Wassmer CE.43 Guepard	467	
D-EERB(2)	Piper PA-28-181 Archer II	28-8090366	N82408
D-EERC	Wassmer WA.54 Atlantic	154	
D-EERD	Piper PA-28-181 Cherokee Archer II	28-7790240	N9564N
D-EERF(2)	Wassmer WA.54 Atlantic	135	
D-EERG(2)	Beech F33A Bonanza	CE-1266	
D-EERH(3)	Diamond DA 40D Star	D4.124	OE-VPU
D-EERI (3)	Piper PA-28R-201T Turbo Arrow III	28R-7803273	N9691C
D-EERJ(2)	Fläming Air FA-02 Smaragd VLA (Permit .04)	104	
D-EERK(2)	Reims/Cessna FR182 Skylane RG	FR18200063	
D-EERL	Wassmer CE.43 Guepard	470	
D-EERM	Piper PA-28-180 Cherokee Archer	28-7405206	N9512N
D-EERN(2)	SOCATA TB-20 Trinidad	643	F-GENX
D-EERP	Piaggio P.149D	259	91+77 AC+410 AS+410
D-EERQ	Wassmer WA.81 Piranha	818	
D-EERS(2)	SOCATA TB-20 Trinidad	334	
D-EERT(2)	Reims/Cessna F172M	F17201416	
D-EERU	Reims/Cessna F152	F15201662	N1659C
D-EERV	Wassmer WA.81 Piranha	823	
D-EERZ	Piper PA-24-260 Comanche C	24-4920	N9415P
D-EESA	Reims/Cessna F172M	F17201244	
D-EESB(2)	Cessna 172P	17275461	N63648
D-EESC	Reims/Cessna F172M	F17201289	
D-EESF	Scheibe SF-41 Merlin (Permit .05)	unkn	
D-EESG(2)	Reims/Cessna F172M	F17201315	
D-EESH	Reims/Cessna F172M	F17201318	
D-EESI	Reims/Cessna F172M	F17201322	
D-EESJ	Reims/Cessna F172M	F17201325	
D-EESL	Reims FR172J Rocket	FR17200549	
D-EESM	Reims/Cessna F172N	F17201547	
D-EESO	Piper PA-28R-200 Cherokee Arrow II	28R-7435189	N41478
D-EESR	Piper PA-38-112 Tomahawk	38-79A0751	N9680N
D-EESS	Cessna P210N Pressurized Centurion II (Robertson STOL version)	P21000648	N5169W
D-EEST(2)	Piper PA-28R-200 Cherokee Arrow B	28R-35749	N5017S
D-EESY	Brand/ Rutan VariEze	1523/01E	
D-EETB(3)	Hackel/ Fläming Air Zlin Trener Baby (Res. 04)	104	
D-EETC	Cessna F172H	F172-0625	
D-EETD	Cessna F150J	F150-0456	
D-EETE	Piper PA-28R-200 Cherokee Arrow	28R-35179	N9463N
D-EETF(2)	Reims/Cessna F177RG Cardinal RG	F177RG0137	OE-DRD D-EHRD
D-EETI	SOCATA MS.893A Rallye Commodore 180	11417	
D-EETL(3)	Diamond DA 20-A1 Katana	10321	
D-EETM(2)	Robin DR.400/180R Remorqueur	1230	
D-EETN(2)	Robin DR.400/180R Remorqueur	1293	
D-EETO	Cessna F172H	F172-0646	
D-EETP	Cessna F150J	F150-0433	
D-EETQ	Cessna F150J	F150-0435	
D-EETR	Piper PA-28-140 Cherokee B	28-25767	N5598F
D-EETS(2)	Cessna 172P	17275904	N65836
D-EETT(2)	Piper PA-18-150 Super Cub	18-850	R-201 51-15685
D-EETU(3)	Haubold/ Aero Designs Pulsar XP	1810	
D-EETW(2)	Diamond DA 20-A1 Katana	10253	
D-EETX	Cessna 182K Skylane	18258070	OE-DEB N3070Q
D-EEUA	SOCATA MS.893ED Rallye 180GT Gaillard	13110	
D-EEUB	SOCATA MS.893ED Rallye 180GT Gaillard	13111	
D-EEUD(2)	SOCATA TB-20 Trinidad	275	
D-EEUE	SOCATA Rallye 180TS Galérien	3193	
D-EEUF	SOCATA Rallye 180T-D Galérien	3194	
D-EEUH	SOCATA Rallye 180T-D Galérien	3195	
D-EEUI	SOCATA Rallye 180T-D Galérien	3196	
D-EEUJ	SOCATA Rallye 180TS Galérien (Permit .05)	3197	
D-EEUK(2)	SOCATA Rallye 150T-D	2971	F-GBCC
D-EEUM(2)	SOCATA TB-10 Tobago	270	
D-EEUO	SOCATA Rallye 180TS Galérien	3245	
D-EEUP	SOCATA Rallye 180TS Galérien	3246	
D-EEUQ	SOCATA Rallye 180TS Galérien	3247	
D-EEUR	SOCATA Rallye 180TS Galérien	3248	
D-EEUS	SOCATA Rallye 180TS Galérien (Stored .02)	3249	
D-EEUT	Piper PA-18-150 Super Cub	18-8726	N4395Z
D-EEUU(2)	Cessna 172P	17274551	N52538
D-EEUV	SOCATA Rallye 180TS Galérien	3251	
D-EEUW	SOCATA Rallye 180TS Galérien	3252	
D-EEUX	Huss/ Denney Kitfox 4-1200	1758	
D-EEVA(3)	Robin DR.400/160D Major 80	1576	
D-EEVB	Reims/Cessna F172M	F17201209	
D-EEVD	Reims/Cessna F172M	F17201202	
D-EEVH	Reims/Cessna F150M	F15001190	
D-EEVI (3)	Mooney M.20J Model 201	24-1648	
D-EEVJ	Reims/Cessna F172M	F17201270	
D-EEVK(2)	SIAT 223A-1 Flamingo	014	HB-EVK D-ENBK(1)
D-EEVM	Reims/Cessna F172M	F17201291	
D-EEVN	Reims/Cessna F172M	F17201293	
D-EEVO(2)	Mooney M.20J Model 201	24-0829	N4735H
D-EEVQ(2)	Reims/Cessna F152	F15201655	N1662Q
D-EEVV	CASA I-131E Jungmann	2218	E3B-618
D-EEVX	American AG-5B Tiger	10144	
D-EEVY	Cessna 170A	19537	D-ELYC N5503C
D-EEVZ	SOCATA TB-9 Tampico	895	
D-EEWA(3)	Beech F33A Bonanza	CE-1226	OE-KBE N23EL
D-EEWB	Reims/Cessna F172L	F17200880	
D-EEWC	Cessna P210N Pressurized Centurion II	P21000542	N2108J (N731SA)
D-EEWD	Beech F33A Bonanza	CE-905	
D-EEWE(2)	Robin DR.400/180R Remorqueur	1973	
D-EEWF(3)	Cessna 172P	17275316	N62632
D-EEWG(2)	Cessna 172P	17274944	(D-EEAS) N54282
D-EEWH	Cessna F172H	F172-0603	D-EETM
D-EEWI	Beech F33A Bonanza	CE-509	
D-EEWK	Robin HR.100/210D Safari	195	

D-EEWL	Piper PA-18 Super Cub 95	18-3448	96+24
			NL+114
			AC+533
			AS+533
			54-748
D-EEWM	SOCATA MS.893ED Rallye 180GT Gaillard	13181	
D-EEWN	Beech A36 Bonanza	E-1823	
D-EEWO	Piper PA-18-150 Super Cub	18-554	R-202
	(Dismantled, 9.99, f/n 18-486)		51-15668
			N7183K
D-EEWP(3)	Ruschmeyer R90-230G	013	D-EEBY
D-EEWS	SOCATA MS.880B Rallye Club	2112	F-BTVT
D-EEWX	Beech F33A Bonanza	CE-947	HB-EWX
D-EEWY	Reims/Cessna F172M	F17200956	
D-EEXA	Reims/Cessna F177RG Cardinal RG	F177RG0061	
D-EEXE(2)	Heliopolis Gomhouria Mk.6	148	SU-325
			EAF-325
D-EEXG	Cessna T210L Turbo Centurion	21059508	N4608Q
D-EEXH	Reims/Cessna F150L	F15000795	
D-EEXI (2)	Bleriot XI Replica	001	
	(Possibly ex D-EFTV(4))		
D-EEXJ	Reims/Cessna F150L	F15000797	
D-EEXK	Reims/Cessna F150L	F15000803	
D-EEXL(2)	Piper PA-28-161 Warrior II	28-8116115	F-GFIG
			N8316D
D-EEXM	Reims/Cessna F172L	F17200851	
D-EEXN	Reims/Cessna F172L	F17200858	
D-EEXS	Reims/Cessna F172L	F17200840	
D-EEXX	Reims/Cessna F177RG Cardinal RG	F177RG0044	
D-EEXY(2)	Impulse 180TD (Reservation)	TD-5	
D-EEXZ	Cessna 182P Skylane	18261174	(N20745)
D-EEYC	Reims/Cessna F150L	F15000773	
D-EEYD	Reims/Cessna F150L	F15000799	
D-EEYE	Reims/Cessna F150L (Permit .05)	F15000805	
D-EEYG	Reims/Cessna F172L	F17200869	
D-EEYI	Reims/Cessna F172L	F17200872	
D-EEYJ	Reims FR172H Rocket	FR17200322	
D-EEYM	Reims FR172H Rocket (Res as SP-KUW)	FR17200328	
D-EEYN	Reims FR172H Rocket	FR17200329	
D-EEYO	Reims/Cessna F150L	F15000808	
D-EEYP	Reims/Cessna F150L	F15000811	
D-EEYQ	Reims/Cessna F150L	F15000812	
D-EEYS(2)	Stegner/ Pitts S-1-11B (Res .05)	479	
D-EEYY	Reims/Cessna F172L	F17200876	
D-EEYZ	Reims/Cessna F177RG Cardinal RG	F177RG0045	N4939
D-EEZA	Reims/Cessna F177RG Cardinal RG	F177RG0062	
D-EEZB	Reims/Cessna F177RG Cardinal RG	F177RG0060	
D-EEZC	Reims/Cessna FRA150L Aerobat	FRA1500149	
D-EEZD	Reims/Cessna FRA150L Aerobat	FRA1500159	
D-EEZE	Reims/Cessna F172L	F17200875	
D-EEZF	Cessna 182P Skylane	18261171	(N20742)
D-EEZH	Reims/Cessna F172L	F17200871	
D-EEZJ	Cessna 182P Skylane	18261450	(N21154)
D-EEZL	Cessna 182P Skylane	18261713	(N21555)
D-EEZM	Reims/Cessna F150L	F15000804	(G-AZKY)
D-EEZP(2)	Zuckschwerdt/ Rutan VariEze	1005	
D-EEZQ	Reims/Cessna F150L	F15000865	
D-EEZR	Reims/Cessna F150L	F15000868	
D-EEZT	Reims/Cessna F172L	F17200867	
D-EEZU	Reims FR172H Rocket	FR17200310	
D-EEZV	Reims FR172H Rocket	FR17200338	
D-EEZW	Reims/Cessna F172L	F17200884	
D-EEZX	Reims FR172H Rocket	FR17200339	
D-EEZY	Reims FR172H Rocket	FR17200340	
D-EEZZ(2)	Kämmerer/ Impulse 180TD (Reservn .04)	TD-4	
D-EFAC(4)	Robin DR.400/180R Remo 180	2333	
D-EFAD(3)	Mooney M.20K Model 252 TSE	25-1157	N252BW
D-EFAE	Robin DR.400/180R Remorqueur	798	
D-EFAF	Stark Turbulent D-1	111	
D-EFAG(3)	Piper PA-18 Super Cub 95	18-1543	D-EFTG(1)
			ALAT
			51-15543
D-EFAI	Zlin Z.326 Trenér Master	876	SE-CWK
			D-EFAI
			(D-ENQE)
D-EFAJ	Dornier Do.27B-1	104	55+01
			AC+901
			AS+901
D-EFAL(3)	Grob G.115A	8013	
D-EFAM(5)	Cessna 182S	18280442	N7269H
D-EFAN(5)	Piper PA-28-161 Cherokee Warrior II	28-7716163	N9647N
D-EFAO	Piper PA-18-150 Super Cub	18-5362	ALAT
			N10F
D-EFAP(2)	Cessna P210N Pressurized Centurion II	P21000680	N5382W
D-EFAQ	Scintex CP.301C Emeraude	540	
D-EFAR(5)	Fürstenwalde Farman III (1910) replica (Reservn)	01	
D-EFAS	Cessna 140	10463	N76069
D-EFAT(3)	SOCATA MS.883 Rallye 115	1566	F-BTHI
D-EFAU(2)	Reims/Cessna F172M	1313	PH-JAK
			G-BCUI
D-EFAW(2)	Mooney M.20K Model 252 TSE	25-1184	
D-EFAX(3)	Reims/Cessna F182Q Skylane	F18200137	PH-AXO
D-EFAY	Piper PA-28-161 Warrior II	28-8516070	N2495X
D-EFBA(2)	Reims/Cessna F152	F15201845	PH-MJE
			PH-AXH
D-EFBB	Beech 23 Musketeer	M-106	HB-ENB
D-EFBC	Robin DR.400/140 Major	884	

D-EFBE	Piper PA-18 Super Cub 95	18-6278	N8674D
D-EFBF	Sportavia RS-180 Sportsman	6014	
D-EFBH	Sportavia RS-180 Sportsman	6015	
D-EFBI (2)	Sportavia RS-180 Sportsman	6016	
D-EFBJ(2)	SOCATA TB-9 Tampico	1041	
D-EFBK(2)	Robin DR.400/180R Remorqueur	1535	
D-EFBL	Piper PA-28-180 Cherokee G	28-7205282	N11C
D-EFBM	Sportavia RS-180 Sportsman	6019	
D-EFBN	Sportavia RS-180 Sportsman	6020	
D-EFBO(2)	Dornier Do.27A-1	338	56+52
			BD+399
			AB+399
D-EFBQ	Sportavia RS-180 Sportsman	6021	
D-EFBR	Piper PA-18 Super Cub 95	18-3457	96+33
			NL+112
			AC+539
			AS+539
			54-757
D-EFBT(2)	Reims/Cessna F172N	F17201751	(D-EILW)
			PH-AXI
			(D-EMSP)
D-EFBW	Robin R.2160D Acrobin	117	F-OCSK
D-EFBZ	SOCATA TB-200 Tobago XL	1530	
D-EFCA	Cessna 172C	17249056	N1356Y
D-EFCB(2)	CASA I-131E Jungmann	2225	E3B-606
D-EFCC	Reims FR172F Rocket	FR17200089	
D-EFCE	Cessna 172C Skyhawk	17249065	N1365Y
D-EFCH(2)	Piper PA-46-310P Malibu	46-8608037	N9082E
D-EFCI (2)	Gulfstream American AA-5B Tiger	AA5B-1170	
D-EFCJ	Piper PA-28-180 Cherokee F	28-7105040	N5186S
D-EFCK	Piper PA-18 Super Cub 95	18-3436	96+15
			NL+101
			AC+504
			AS+503
			54-736
D-EFCL(2)	Robin DR.400/180R Remorqueur	751	F-BTZD
D-EFCM(3)	Cessna 182Q Skylane II	18267597	N5248N
D-EFCN	Piper PA-18 Super Cub 95	18-3439	96+18
			NL+117
			AC+524
			AS+524
			54-739
D-EFCO(2)	Wassmer WA.54 Atlantic	147	HB-DCO
D-EFCP	Piper PA-28-140 Cherokee F	28-7325302	N11C
D-EFCR(2)	Piper PA-28-181 Archer II	2890013	N9108Q
D-EFCU	SOCATA MS.893E Rallye 180GT Gaillard	12604	TL-HCU
D-EFCV	Piper PA-28RT-201 Arrow IV	28R-8018048	N81677
D-EFDA	Piper PA-24-250 Comanche	24-2977	N7850P
			N10F
D-EFDB	Piper PA-18-135 Super Cub	18-3923	EI-227
			I-EIJX
			54-2523
D-EFDC(2)	SOCATA MS.893A Rallye Commodore 180	11776	F-BSMJ
D-EFDD	SAN Jodel DR.1050 Sicile	486	
D-EFDE(2)	Cessna 177A Cardinal	17701273	N30466
D-EFDH	SOCATA TB-10 Tobago	716	
D-EFDI (3)	Piper PA-28-181 Archer II	28-8290111	N8180U
D-EFDK	Grumman AA-5 Traveler	AA5-0646	
D-EFDL	Grumman AA-5 Traveler	AA5-0645	
D-EFDN	Reims/Cessna F152 II	F15201721	
D-EFDP	Dornier Do.27A-4	463	57+34
			PZ+222
			PG+105
			QM+019
			KD+113
			(D-ENLC)
D-EFDQ	Reims/Cessna F172M	F17201298	
D-EFDR(2)	Piper PA-46-310P Malibu	4608061	N9124B
D-EFDS	Reims/Cessna F172M	F17201312	
D-EFDT(2)	Cessna 172N	17270544	N739GZ
D-EFDU(2)	Reims/Cessna F152	F15201738	
D-EFEA(3)	Piper PA-28-181 Archer II	28-8290163	HB-PHF
			(HB-PHC)
D-EFEB(2)	Reims/Cessna F172N	F17201737	
D-EFEC(2)	Cessna 140	14812	HB-CAM
			N3540V
D-EFED(2)	Robin DR.400/180 Régent	1203	
D-EFEE(2)	Cessna 172M	17260996	G-BSAY
			N20086
D-EFEF	Stark Turbulent D	112	
D-EFEG(2)	Reims/Cessna F172N	F17201734	
D-EFEJ	Piper PA-28-181 Cherokee Archer II	28-7790329	HB-PBL
			N167OH
D-EFEK(2)	Reims/Cessna F152	F15201522	
D-EFEL	Aeronca 65CA	C1868	HB-URU
D-EFEM(5)	OMF-100-160 Symphony (Reservn .04)	0060	
D-EFEN(2)	Reims/Cessna F152	F15201526	
D-EFEO(2)	Christen A-1 Husky	1130	
D-EFEP(2)	Cessna 172	36481	N8781B
D-EFES(2)	Piper PA-28-161 Warrior II	28-8316037	N9627N
D-EFEU	Aero-Jodel D.11A Club	AB.6	
D-EFEV(3)	Reims/Cessna F172P	F17202176	
D-EFEX	Piper PA-22-150 Tri-Pacer	22-4892	N10F
D-EFEY	Piper PA-28R-200 Cherokee Arrow	28R-35718	N4993S
D-EFEZ	Klemm Kl.107B	111	
D-EFFA(4)	Ruschmeyer R.90-230RG	018	D-ELVY(2)
			(D-EEBY(2))

D-EFFC	Jodel DR.250/160 Capitaine	49	
D-EFFD	Robin DR.400/125 Petit Prince	716	
D-EFFE(2)	Reims/Cessna F172M Skyhawk II	F17201394	
D-EFFF	Robin DR.400/180 Régent	721	
D-EFFG	CEA DR.253B Régent	171	
D-EFFH	Cessna T210L Turbo Centurion	21060616	N8128L
D-EFFI (3)	Hankers/ Van's RV-4	1588/V-1	
D-EFFK	Piper PA-28R-200 Cherokee Arrow II	28R-7235273	N1384T
D-EFFL(3)	Piper PA-28R-201 Arrow	2837034	N9187X
D-EFFM	SAN Jodel D.150 Rapid	59	
D-EFFN	Piper PA-28-180 Cherokee G	28-7205309	N1497T
D-EFFO(2)	Reims/Cessna F150M	F15001319	
D-EFFP	Piper PA-32-300 Cherokee Six	32-7440042	N57317
D-EFFQ(2)	SOCATA TB-20 Trinidad GT	2051	
D-EFFS	Mooney M.20F Executive	680149	N3902N
D-EFFT	Reims/Cessna F150M	F15001251	
D-EFFU	Berger/ Piel CP.301A Emeraude	AB-420	
D-EFFV	Piper PA-28-181 Cherokee Archer II	28-7790327	N9597N
D-EFFW	Gardan GY-80 Horizon 160	43	OO-JON
D-EFFX(2)	Grob G.115A	8048	
D-EFFY(4)	Grob G.115A	8041	
D-EFGB	Cessna F150H	F150-0248	
D-EFGD	Mooney M.20C Mark 21	3393	HB-DWE
			N3410X
D-EFGF(2)	Cessna 150M	15078657	N704JW
D-EFGG(2)	Robin HR.200/120B	276	
D-EFGH(2)	Robin DR.400/200R Remo 200	2433	
D-EFGJ	HOACDV-20 Katana	20013	C-FSLY
			OE-CDD
D-EFGK(2)	Piper PA-28RT-201T Turbo Arrow IV	28R-8231035	N8144R
D-EFGL(2)	Reims/Cessna FR182 Skylane RG	FR18200032	
D-EFGM	Reims/Cessna F172P	F17202102	PH-AXJ
D-EFGO	Cessna 150	17640	N7840E
D-EFGS(2)	Göbel / Brändli BX-2 Cherry	21	
D-EFGV	Robin DR.400/140 Major	816	
D-EFGX	Reims/Cessna F172N	F17201793	
D-EFGY(2)	Cessna F172E	F172-0069	
D-EFHA	Piper PA-28-160 Cherokee B	28-1293	N5724W
D-EFHC	Cessna F172H	F172-0596	
D-EFHE(2)	Cessna F150G	F150-0093	
D-EFHF	Morane-Saulnier MS.885 Super Rallye	59	F-BKER
D-EFHG(2)	Robin HR.200/120B	264	
D-EFHJ	Piper J-3C-65 Cub	18970	N98739
			NC98739
D-EFHK(2)	SOCATA MS.893A Rallye Commodore 180	11668	
D-EFHL(3)	Piper PA-28R-200 Cherokee Arrow II	28R-7435246	N43084
D-EFHM(2)	SOCATA TB-200 Tobago XL	1748	
D-EFHN(2)	Robin DR.400/180 Régent	1512	
D-EFHO(3)	Reims/Cessna F172N	F17201907	OE-DHO
			LN-HOI
D-EFHP	Piper PA-28-151 Cherokee Warrior	28-7615428	N9634N
D-EFHQ	Robin DR.400/180R Remorqueur	1513	
D-EFHR	Piper PA-28-180 Cherokee D	28-4509	N5216L
D-EFHS	Beech F33A Bonanza	CE-812	OE-DUB
D-EFHT	Reims/Cessna F172M	F17201411	(D-EOVO)
D-EFHV	Robin DR.400/180R Remorqueur	1452	
D-EFHW	Rockwell Commander 112A	402	N1402J
D-EFIA	Reims/Cessna F152	F15201755	
D-EFIC	Cessna 182J Skylane	18257150	N3050F
D-EFID(2)	Cessna F172H	F172-0537	
D-EFIE	Koller/ Aero-Jodel D11A Club	"Liz.639"	OE-ACX
D-EFIG	Cessna 182J Skylane	18257180	N3080F
D-EFIH(2)	SOCATA TB-10 Tobago	470	
D-EFII	Piper PA-28-140 Cherokee E	28-7225106	N11C
D-EFIK	CEA Jodel DR.1050 Ambassadeur	553	F-BLZU
D-EFIL(2)	Piper PA-38-112 Tomahawk	38-80A0100	D-EEIL(2)
			N9702N
D-EFIM(2)	Cessna 172M	17263568	N1423V
D-EFIO	Grumman AA-5B Tiger	AA5B-0108	
D-EFIP(3)	SOCATA ST-10 Diplomate	129	LX-VIP
			D-EHAX(2)
D-EFIQ	Cessna F172G	F172-0271	
D-EFIS(2)	Reims FR172F Rocket	FR17200108	
D-EFIV(2)	Reims/Cessna F152	F15201769	
D-EFIX(2)	CASA I-131E Jungmann	2063	E3B-471
D-EFIY	SNCAN/ Stampe SV.4C	136	F-BBIY
			F-BBHY
D-EFJA(2)	Reims/Cessna F152	F15201778	
D-EFJB(2)	Böhm Starlite SL-1/B	001/1678	
D-EFJC	Bölkow BO.209 Monsun 160RV	125	
D-EFJD	Bölkow BO.209 Monsun 160FV	126	
D-EFJG	Bölkow BO.209 Monsun 160RV	129	
D-EFJH	Bölkow BO.209 Monsun 160RV	130	
D-EFJI	Bölkow BO.209 Monsun 160RV	131	(D-ELIE)
D-EFJJ	Bölkow BO.209 Monsun 160FV	132	
D-EFJK	Bölkow BO.209 Monsun 160RV	133	(D-EDAK(2))
D-EFJL	Bölkow BO.209 Monsun 160RV	134	
D-EFJM	Bölkow BO.209 Monsun 160FV	135	
D-EFJN	Bölkow BO.209 Monsun 150FF	136	I-SUDB
			D-EFJN
D-EFJP	Bölkow BO.209 Monsun 150FF	138	(D-EFSG)
D-EFJQ(2)	Reims/Cessna F172N	F17201919	
D-EFJR(2)	CASA I-131E Jungmann	2072	E3B-465
D-EFJS(2)	Reims/Cessna F182Q Skylane	F18200116	
D-EFJV	Reims/Cessna F172N	F17201937	
D-EFJX	Reims/Cessna F172N	F17201962	
D-EFJZ	Reims/Cessna F172N	F17201967	

D-EFKA(3)	Piper PA-28R-201T Turbo Arrow III	28R-7803337	N36726
D-EFKB	Piper PA-18-180 Super Cub	18-5390	ALAT
			N10F
D-EFKD	Reims/Cessna F172N	F17202000	
D-EFKF	Robin DR.400/180R Remorqueur	1550	
D-EFKG	Beech V35B Bonanza	D-9759	
D-EFKK	Mooney M.20F Executive	22-1202	
D-EFKM	Reims/Cessna F172N	F17202004	
D-EFKN	Reims/Cessna F152	F15201713	
D-EFKO(2)	Piper PA-28-140 Cherokee	24-24639	N7288J
D-EFKP(2)	Piper PA-28-181 Cherokee Archer II	28-7890477	N31733
D-EFKR	Reims/Cessna FR172K Hawk XP II	FR17200635	PH-AXT
D-EFKS(2)	Mooney M.20K Model 252 TSE	25-1164	N252MM
			D-EFKS(2)
D-EFKT(2)	Cessna 177RG Cardinal RG	177RG1341	N53081
D-EFKV	Robin DR.400/180 Régent	1549	
D-EFKW(2)	Reims/Cessna F172P	F17202151	
D-EFKZ	Robin HR.200/120B	260	
D-EFLA(2)	SOCATA TB-10 Tobago	679	
D-EFLB	Cessna 172N	17271629	N4555E
D-EFLC	Piper PA-18 Super Cub 95	18-3422	96+04
			NL+105
			AC+513
			AA+513
			AS+513
			54-722
D-EFLD	Piper PA-28-181 Archer II	28-7990106	N2125A
D-EFLE(2)	Piper PA-28-180 Cherokee Challenger	28-7305370	N55326
D-EFLF	Cessna 172N	17272217	N9303E
D-EFLH	Cessna 172RG Cutlass RG	172RG0351	N4660V
D-EFLI (3)	Piper PA-28-181 Archer II	28-8190082	N82891
D-EFLJ	Cessna F172F	F172-0139	
D-EFLK	Cessna 152 II	15284190	N4601L
D-EFLL	Cessna 172P	17275489	N63841
D-EFLM	Piaggio FWP.149D	082	90+64
			GA+402
			AS+491
D-EFLO(2)	SOCATA TB-10 Tobago	633	
D-EFLP	Piper PA-28-151 Cherokee Warrior	28-7415195	N9520N
D-EFLQ	Piper PA-28-140 Cherokee D	28-7125370	N8589N
D-EFLR	Reims/Cessna F177RG Cardinal RG	F177RG0055	
D-EFLS(2)	Piper PA-28RT-201T Turbo Arrow IV	28R-7931022	N2129K
D-EFLT(2)	SOCATA TB-10 Tobago	678	
D-EFLU(2)	Robin DR.300/180R Remoqueur	525	
D-EFLV	Piper PA-28-140 Cherokee D	28-7125248	N5082S
D-EFLX	Lauxen/ Denney Kitfox V Speedster	S 94030004B	
D-EFLY(2)	Robin DR.300/108 2+2	519	
D-EFLZ	SOCATA TB-10 Tobago	1067	
D-EFMA(2)	Maule MX.7-235 Star Rocket	10070C	N61245
D-EFMB	Bölkow BO.208C Junior	632	
D-EFMC	Bölkow BO.208C Junior	633	
D-EFMD(2)	Robin DR.400/180 Régent	1477	
D-EFME	Bölkow BO.208C Junior	635	
D-EFMH(2)	CASA I.131E Jungmann (Lycoming)	2066	E3B-473
D-EFMI (2)	Gyroflug SC-01B-160 Speed Canard	S-28	(D-EAMT)
D-EFMJ(2)	Piper PA-28-140 Cherokee C	28-26832	N5933U
D-EFMK	CEA DR.253B Régent	123	
D-EFML	Fairchild F.24R-46A Argus III	947	HB-EIR
			HB709
			43-14983
D-EFMN(2)	Robin DR.400/180R Remorqueur	1460	
D-EFMO(2)	Cessna 152	15281868	N67498
D-EFMP	Reims/Cessna F172N	F17202018	
D-EFMR	Reims/Cessna F172M	F17201378	
D-EFMS(3)	Maule MX-7-235 Star Rocket	4058C	N6119V
			(D-EJSO)
D-EFMU(2)	Cessna 152	15283254	N47809
D-EFMV(3)	HOACDV-20 Katana	20103	C-GFQW
			N203DV
D-EFMY	Piper PA-28-140 Cherokee	28-20703	N6609W
D-EFMZ	Aviat A-1 Husky	1280	
D-EFNA	Oberlerchner JOB 15-180/2 (Built as -150)	063	OE-CAX
D-EFNB	SOCATA TB-10 Tobago	820	
D-EFNC	Cessna 172RG Cutlass RG	172RG0310	N5263U
D-EFNE(2)	Aerotek Pitts S-2B	5024	N20NE
			(N5316C)
D-EFNH	Reims/Cessna FR182 Skylane RG	FR18200058	
D-EFNI (2)	Oberlerchner JOB 15-150/2	067	OE-CAT
D-EFNK(3)	Cessna 172N	17271263	N2392E
D-EFNL	Robin DR.400/180R Remorqueur	1551	
D-EFNN	Mooney M.20E Chaparral	21-1178	N6844V
D-EFNP(2)	Piper PA-28RT-201 Arrow IV	28R-7918018	N2125K
D-EFNS(2)	Piper PA-28-181 Archer II	28-8090282	N44WK
			N8187Z
D-EFNT	Cessna TR182 Turbo Skylane RG	R18200772	OE-DNT
			N736UQ
D-EFNW	Reims/Cessna FR182 Skylane RG	FR18200015	(D-EDBV)
D-EFNX	Reims/Cessna F152	F15201563	
D-EFNY	Bölkow BO.208C Junior	606	
D-EFOB(2)	Dornier Do.27A-4	389	56+81
			QW+111
			QW+715
			QM+615
			PL+423
D-EFOC(2)	Piper PA-18-150 Super Cub (Quoted c/n is incorrect - this was D-ECBE. Thought to be c/n 18-3127 ex.L-53 /53-4727)	18-3084	
D-EFOD(2)	Piper PA-28-140 Cherokee	28-7325043	OY-DLZ
			N15341

D-EFOF(2)	SOCATA TB-9 Tampico	108	
D-EFOH	Klemm Kl.107C	139	
D-EFOJ	Robin DR.400/120D Petit Prince	1565	
D-EFOK(2)	Piper PA-28-140 Cherokee F	28-7325289	N11C
D-EFOL(2)	Piper PA-28-140 Cherokee F	28-7325316	N11C
D-EFOM	DHC-1 Chipmunk 22 (Franklin)	C1/0248	G-AOJN
			WD306
D-EFOO	Cessna T210N Turbo Centurion II	21064296	N6208Y
D-EFOP(2)	Cessna F172E	F172-0025/17250580	OE-DCO
			(N2980U)
D-EFOQ	Scintex CP.301C Emeraude	542	
D-EFOR(2)	Binder CP.301S Smaragd	107	
D-EFOS(2)	Mooney M.20K Model 252 TSE	25-1090	N252YV
D-EFOW(2)	Cessna T210L Turbo Centurion	21061148	PH-PLX
			OO-ADI
			D-EATX
			N2187S
D-EFOX(4)	Piaggio FWP.149D	126	91+05
			BF+414
			AS+013
			KB+103
D-EFPA(3)	Piper PA-28-181 Archer II	2890077	N9143X
D-EFPB(3)	Cessna 172R	17280365	
D-EFPC	Mooney M.20J Model 201	24-0131	
D-EFPD	Piper PA-28-180 Cherokee Challenger	28-7305121	(N15696)
			N11C
D-EFPE(2)	Reims/Cessna F172P	F17202119	
D-EFPF(2)	Cessna 172RG Cutlass RG	172RG0484	N5248V
D-EFPH(2)	Philips/ Denney Kitfox IV Speedster	LCS152	
D-EFPJ	SOCATA TB-9 Tampico	107	
D-EFPK	SOCATA TB-10 Tobago	104	
D-EFPM	Cessna 182G Skylane	18255416	HB-CMP
			N2316R
D-EFPN	Piper PA-28RT-201 Arrow IV	28R-7918143	N29699
D-EFPO	Bölkow BO.207	262	
D-EFPP	Cessna TR182 Turbo Skylane RG	R18201436	N4846S
D-EFPQ	Robin DR.400/180 Régent	1322	
D-EFPR	Pützer Elster C	042	97+19
			D-ELBC
D-EFPS	SNCAN/ Stampe SV-4C	415	F-BCQY
D-EFQA	Bölkow BO.207	265	
D-EFQB	Robin DR.400/180R Remorqueur	1367	
D-EFQE	Bölkow BO.207	266	
D-EFQF(2)	Grob G.115A	8053	F-GGOF
			F-WGOF
			(PH-SBD)
D-EFQG	Grob G.115A	8017	F-GGOA
			F-WGOA
D-EFQH	Grob G.115A	8080	F-GGOG
D-EFQI	Piper PA-22-108 Colt	22-9365	
D-EFQN(2)	Robin DR.400/180 Régent (Permit 5.03)	1744	(F-GNBJ)
			D-EFQN(2)
			F-GEKS
D-EFQO(2)	Grob G.115A	8018	F-GGOO
			D-EANP
D-EFQP	CASA I-131E Jungmann	2046	E3B-442
D-EFQR	Robin DR.400/180 Régent	1369	
D-EFQT	Dornier Do.27A-3	437	57+11
			BF+950
			KD+101
D-EFQV	Dornier Do.27B-1	175	55+45
			CC+053
			AC+925 ?
			AS+925 ?
D-EFRA	Cessna F172D	F172-0005/17250071	(N2471U)
D-EFRC	Cessna F172H	F172-0651	
D-EFRD	Cessna F172H	F172-0654	
D-EFRF	Reims FR172F Rocket	FR17200088	
D-EFRG	Cessna 172RG Cutlass RG	172RG0554	N5527V
D-EFRH(4)	Cessna P210N Pressurized Centurion II	P21000621	N80FJ
			HB-CQD
			PH-DZI
			HB-CQD
			N74DD
			N4595W
D-EFRI(4)	Hüfner/ Votec 322 (Reservn .04)	488	
D-EFRK	Mooney M.20J Model 201	24-0730	(N4433H)
D-EFRL	Mooney M.20K Model 231	25-0153	
D-EFRN	SOCATA Rallye 180TS Galérien	3335	
D-EFRP	Cessna 172P	17274657	N53001
D-EFRQ	SOCATA Rallye 110ST Galopin	3332	
D-EFRR(2)	American AG-5B Tiger	10161	N1198N
D-EFRS	Robin DR.400/120D Petit Prince	1714	
D-EFRV	Reims/Cessna F172P	F17202096	
D-EFRW	Reims/Cessna F172P	F17202090	
D-EFRX	SOCATA Rallye 110ST Galopin	3333	
D-EFSA(3)	Diamond DA 40D Star	D4.096	
D-EFSB(3)	Aquila AT-01	114	
D-EFSC(4)	Dornier Do.27A-4	2109	MAAW-16
			D-EGVQ
			D-12/OT-AMK
			OL-D12
			D-12
D-EFSE(3)	Cessna P210N Pressurized Centurion II	P21000814	N4680A
D-EFSF(2)	Reims/Cessna FR172K Hawk XP	FR17200658	PH-PWH
			PH-AXT(3)
D-EFSG(2)	Cessna 180J Skywagon	18052662	D-EFJO
			N9967N

D-EFSH(2)	Piper PA-28RT-201T Turbo Arrow IV	28R-8031127	N9910D
			N9569N
D-EFSI	Bölkow BO.207	213	HB-UXM
			D-EFSI
D-EFSK(2)	Cessna 182T	18281232	N2128T
D-EFSL	Cessna 182Q Skylane (Cr 24.7.04)	18265374	N735EV
D-EFSM(2)	Cessna 150L	15072950	N1650Q
D-EFSN	Cessna 172RG Cutlass RG	172RG1026	N9772B
D-EFSO(2)	Piper PA-28-140 Cherokee F	28-7325365	N11C
D-EFSR	Piper PA-28-181 Archer II	28-8190003	N8247E
D-EFSS(2)	Mooney M.20M Model 257 TLS	27-0129	N888JS
			N230M
D-EFST(4)	Reims/Cessna FR172K Hawk XP	FR17200594	OE-DIX
D-EFSU(3)	Beech F33A Bonanza	CE-1519	
D-EFSV(2)	Cessna 182Q Skylane	18267470	N4945N
D-EFSW(2)	Piper PA-18 Super Cub 100	18-3437	96+16
	(Built as PA-18-95)		PX+901
			QZ+030
			AC+505
			AS+504
			54-737
D-EFSY	Bölkow BO.207	216	
D-EFSZ	Mooney M.20K Model 231	25-0467	N277TA
			N4090H
D-EFTB(2)	Piper PA-18 Super Cub 95	18-3455	96+31
			NL+. . .
			AC+537
			AS+537
			54-755
D-EFTC	Bölkow BO.209 Monsun 150FF	172	G-AZTC
			D-EAAL
D-EFTD(2)	Cessna F172H	F172-0611	CS-DAN
			D-EADA(1)
			LX-IPH
D-EFTE(3)	Klemm L 25-1A	152	G-AAHW
			D-ELFK
			G-AAHW
D-EFTG(3)	Diamond DA 20-A1 Katana	10178	OK-BLC
			C-GRUV
D-EFTH(2)	Cessna 195B	16087	N195MB
			N2102C
D-EFTI	Bölkow BO.207	219	
D-EFTJ	Koch Fokker DR.1 replica	003	G-BWRJ
			D-EFTN(1)
D-EFTK	Reims/Cessna F172M	F17201265	
D-EFTL	Reims/Cessna F172M	F17201273	
D-EFTN(2)	de Havilland DH.82A Tiger Moth	"84764"	G-ANIX
	(Composite rebuild using identity of c/n		D-EFTF(2)
	84764, ex T6390, D-ELOM, dbf 12.63)		
D-EFTO(3)	Reims/Cessna F152	F15201958	
D-EFTP	Reims FR172H Rocket	FR17200276	
D-EFTQ	Robin DR.400/180R Remorqueur	1472	
D-EFTR(2)	SOCATA TB-10 Tobago	206	
D-EFTS	SAN Jodel DR.1050 Ambassadeur	397	
D-EFTT(3)	Aquila AT01	AT01-123	
D-EFTU(2)	Piaggio FWP.149D	091	90+73
			AS+404
D-EFTW(2)	Robin DR.400/180 Régent	1274	
D-EFTX	Boeing Stearman A75N1 Kaydet	75-3475	G-BHUW
	(Wears code '475')		N474
			N64639
			BuA30038
D-EFTY(3)	Klemm Kl.35D	1462	G-BWRD
	(Painted as Luftwaffe '7')		D-EFTG(2)
			D-EHUX(2)
			SE-AIP
			Fv5081
			SE-AIP
D-EFTZ	Cessna 172RG Cutlass RG	172RG0814	N9403B
D-EFUB	Klemm Kl.35D	1810	HB-UXC
			SE-BGH
			Fv5011
D-EFUE	Reims/Cessna F152	F15201533	
D-EFUF	Stark Turbulent D-1M	115	
D-EFUG(3)	Reims/Cessna F152	F15201554	
D-EFUI	Reims/Cessna F152	F15201550	
D-EFUK(2)	Reims/Cessna F172N	F17201841	
D-EFUL	Piper J-3C-65 Cub	11313	HB-OAI
			43-30022
D-EFUM(2)	Piper PA-28-140 Cherokee Cruiser	28-7725080	N9530N
D-EFUN(3)	Reims FR172E Rocket	FR17200043	
D-EFUO	Reims/Cessna F172N	F17201840	(D-EJCU)
D-EFUP	Fischer RW3-P75 Multoplan	005	
D-EFUS(2)	SOCATA MS.880B Rallye Club	2149	F-BUCA
D-EFUV(2)	Cessna 140	10385	N81091
D-EFUX(2)	Beech F33A Bonanza	CE-1150	
D-EFVA	FVA-18/3 Krähe V-1	01	
D-EFVB	Reims/Cessna FR172K Hawk	FR17200636	
D-EFVD	Cessna T210M Turbo Centurion	21062650	N761ZN
	(Reims-assembled with c/n 0012) (Permit 4.02)		
D-EFVF	Robin DR.400/180 Régent	1343	
D-EFVH(2)	Beech F33A Bonanza	CE-1770	N15229
			N1529L
			(D-EEJJ)
D-EFVI	Piaggio P.149D	254	(91+72)
			D-EFVI
			AC+405
			AS+405

D-EFVL	Cessna F150F	F150-0057/15063485	(G-ATOF)
			(N6885F)
D-EFVM(2)	Ludwig/ Stark Turbulent D	AB-501	D-EGSU
D-EFVQ	Reims/Cessna F172P	F17202085	
D-EFVS	Wassmer WA.52 Europa	22	
D-EFVU	Cessna 182H Skylane	18256080	N1980X
D-EFVZ	Zendler Hina BL2-ARA	1777	
D-EFWA(2)	SOCATA Rallye 100ST-D	3043	OY-ARG
			F-ODII
D-EFWB	Reims/Cessna F150M	F15001151	
D-EFWC(2)	Piper PA-24-250 Comanche	24-3294	OE-DST
			N8139P
			N10F
			(N8049P)
D-EFWD	Beech V35B Bonanza	D-10347	
D-EFWE	Piper PA-28-140 Cherokee	28-20715	N6682W
D-EFWF	Piper PA-28R-200 Cherokee Arrow II	28R-7535170	(D-ILAX)
			N33651
D-EFWJ	Wassmer WA.54 Atlantic	109	(D-EAIJ)
D-EFWL	Wassmer WA.54 Atlantic	107	
D-EFWM	Piper PA-28-181 Cherokee Archer II	28-7790419	N2917Q
D-EFWO(2)	Robin DR.400/180R Remorqueur	1546	
D-EFWP(2)	Piaggio FWP.149D	118	90+98
			D-EKLI
			AS+459
D-EFWR	Piper PA-28R-201T Turbo Cherokee Arrow III		
		28R-7703140	N5655V
D-EFWS(2)	Cessna 172R	17280615	N95520
D-EFWT	SOCATA TB-10 Tobago	291	
D-EFWU	Bölkow BO.208 Junior	573	
D-EFWW	Piper PA-28-180 Cherokee Archer	28-7405075	N9648N
D-EFWX	Folz / WAR FW190	001-EB	
	(Painted as Luftwaffe "14")		
D-EFWZ	Piper PA-28-235 Cherokee	28-10207	N8676W
D-EFXA	SOCATA MS.880B Rallye Club	1220	
D-EFXC(2)	Piper PA-28-161 Cadet	2841051	N9632N
			N9163K
D-EFXD(2)	Piper PA-28-161 Cadet	2841070	N91642
D-EFXE(2)	Piper PA-28-161 Cadet	2841069	N9164Z
D-EFXF(2)	Piper PA-28-161 Cadet	2841082	N9504N
			N9167H
D-EFXG	Piper PA-28-161 Cadet	2841087	N9170H
D-EFXI (2)	Piper PA-28-161 Cadet	2841118	N9649N
D-EFXL	Piper PA-28-161 Cadet	2841126	N9181G
D-EFXM	Piper PA-28-161 Cadet	2841128	N9181J
D-EFXO	Robin DR.300/108 2+2	496	
D-EFXP(2)	Piper PA-28-161 Cadet	2841163	N9514N
D-EFXQ	Piper PA-28-161 Cadet	2841168	N9515N
D-EFXR	Piper PA-28-161 Cadet	2841201	N9189W
D-EFXS	Piper PA-28-161 Cadet	2841243	N9192P
D-EFXT	Piper PA-28-161 Cadet	2841244	N9192X
D-EFXU	Robin DR.300/180R Remorqueur	497	
D-EFXY	Piper PA-18-150 Super Cub	nil	(RBAF)
	(Built from spare fuselage no.18-4963)		
D-EFXZ	Piper PA-28-161 Cadet	2841286	N92032
D-EFYA	Reims/Cessna F182Q Skylane	F18200142	PH-AXZ
D-EFYB(2)	Piper PA-32-300 Cherokee Six	32-7340188	OY-DLK
			CS-AOU
			N56526
D-EFYC	Cessna F172G	F172-0223	
D-EFYD	Cessna 170B	20628	N2476D
D-EFYF(2)	Piper PA-28RT-201 Arrow IV	28R-8118063	N83691
D-EFYH(2)	Cessna 152	15283107	N46802
D-EFYK(2)	Piper PA-18 Super Cub 95	18-3424	96+06
			SE+540
			CA+511
			D-9503
			(D-EMEV)
			CA+511
			AC+511
			AS+511
			54-724
D-EFYL(2)	Pützer Elster B	014	97+07
			D-EFYL
D-EFYN(3)	Reims/Cessna F172P	F17202089	
D-EFYP	Pützer Elster C	002	
D-EFYQ	Cessna F172G	F172-0259	
D-EFYS(3)	Mudry CAP.231	16	F-GGYS
D-EFYX(2)	Ryan Navion A	NAV-4-1385	N4385K
D-EFYZ(2)	Piaggio FWP.149D	101	90+82
			ND+103
			D-EHUW
			AS+403
D-EFZB(2)	Piper PA-28-161 Warrior II	28-8016233	N9608N
D-EFZC	SIAI-Marchetti S.208	2-18	
D-EFZF	Cessna 172N	17271249	N2360E
D-EFZG	Cessna 172RG Cutlass RG	172RG0559	N5533V
D-EFZH	Cessna 172N	17268307	N733HM
D-EFZI	Piper PA-18 Super Cub 95	18-6109	OE-AEE
			N10F
D-EFZJ	Cessna 172RG Cutlass RG	172RG0046	N5204R
D-EFZK	Cessna R172K Hawk XP	R1722496	N736FR
D-EFZM	Dornier Do.27A-4	483	57+48
			GA+376
			KD+141 ?
D-EFZO	Cessna F172F	F172-0156	
D-EFZR	Cessna 172N	17272920	N7398D

D-EFZS	Cessna 172P	17275531	N64189
D-EFZT	Cessna 182K Skylane	18258476	N2876R
D-EFZV	CEA DR.253B Régent	106	6V-ABU
			F-OCKM
D-EFZW(2)	HOAC DV-20 Katana	20061	
D-EGAA(2)	Cessna F150H	F150-0359	
D-EGAB(2)	Cessna 182J Skylane	18256709	N2609F
D-EGAC(3)	Piper PA-46-350P Malibu Mirage	4636305	OY-LAC
D-EGAD(2)	Fuji FA-200-160 Aero Subaru	121	
D-EGAE	Fuji FA-200-180 Aero Subaru	114	
D-EGAF	Piper J-3C-65 Cub	12943	HB-ONI
			44-80647
D-EGAG(3)	SOCATA TB-20 Trinidad	1675	
D-EGAH(2)	Cessna 182P	18263909	OO-GAI
	(Reims-assembled with "c/n" 0015)		OO-CKC
			HB-CKC
			OO-GAI
			N6988M
D-EGAJ	Fuji FA-200-160 Aero Subaru	123	
D-EGAK(3)	Piper PA-28R-200 Cherokee Arrow II	28R-7635091	N7035C
D-EGAL(3)	Bölkow BO.208C Junior	641	
D-EGAM(3)	Fuji FA-200-180 Aero Subaru (Marked FH20/180)	117	
D-EGAN(2)	Piper PA-28-181 Archer II	28-8590023	N9514N
D-EGAO	Dornier Do.27B-3	2200	(D-EFKP)
D-EGAP(3)	Dornier Do.27Q-5	2045	D-EKYC
D-EGAQ(2)	Piper PA-18-150 Super Cub	18-8344	N4163Z
D-EGAS(4)	Mooney M.20J Model 205	24-3164	
D-EGAT(2)	Piper PA-28-151 Cherokee Warrior	28-7415083	N9623N
D-EGAU	Piper PA-28-181 Archer II	28-8090215	N8145Y
D-EGAV	Wassmer Jodel D.120	141	
D-EGAW(2)	Robin HR.100/200B (Permit .05)	117	
D-EGAX(3)	Piper PA-28RT-201T Turbo Arrow IV	28R-7931187	N28529
D-EGAY(2)	Christen A-1 Husky	1113	
D-EGAZ(4)	Cessna 172RG Cutlass RG	172RG0531	OY-BNN
			(D-EBNM),
			OY-BNN, N5435V
D-EGBA(2)	Heliopolis Gomhouria Mk.6	184	SU-346
			EAF-346
D-EGBB(2)	Robin HR.200/120B	268	
D-EGBD	Reims/Cessna F150L	F15000947	
D-EGBE(2)	Reims/Cessna F172M	F17200977	
D-EGBG	Reims/Cessna F172M	F17200979	
D-EGBH(2)	Robin DR.400/180R Remorqueur	1742	
D-EGBI (2)	PZL-104 Wilga 35	61113	DDR-WBH
			DM-WBH(2)
D-EGBJ	Reims/Cessna F172M	F17200980	
D-EGBK	Reims/Cessna F172M	F17200981	
D-EGBL(2)	Piper PA-28-161 Warrior II	28-8016345	PH-WLS
			N8226X
D-EGBM(3)	CASA I-131E Jungmann	"2062"	E3B-415
	(Same c/n quoted as HB-UVU. Previous identity confirmed correct)		
D-EGBN	Reims/Cessna FRA150L Aerobat	FRA1500192	(OO-FCF)
D-EGBO	SAN Jodel DR.1050 Ambassadeur	367	(D-EDRO)
D-EGBP	Reims FR172J Rocket	FR17200417	
D-EGBQ	Reims FR172J Rocket	FR17200419	
D-EGBR(2)	Focke-Wulf FW.44J Stieglitz	2906	OH-SZK
	(Used parts of SZ-5 and SZ-21 in rebuild		SZ-9
	in Finland 1977-81)		D-EXWS(2)
D-EGBV	Reims/Cessna F172M (on rebuild)	F17200986	
D-EGBW	Reims/Cessna F172M	F17200987	
D-EGBX(2)	Cessna 182P Skylane	18262656	N52523
D-EGBY	Bölkow BO.208 Junior	533	D-EGQA(1)
D-EGCA	Cessna F172H	F172-0425	
D-EGCB	Reims/Cessna F150L	F15000965	
D-EGCC	CEA DR.253B Régent	178	
D-EGCD	Cessna 172N	17268311	N733HR
D-EGCF	Piper PA-18-150 Super Cub	18-8547	SE-GCE
			Fv51238
D-EGCG	Robin DR.400/180R Remorqueur	1413	
D-EGCH	Bellanca 7GCBC Citabria	733-74	OE-AOH
D-EGCI (2)	Grob G.115A	8015	(D-EGRN(2))
D-EGCJ	Reims/Cessna F150L	F15000968	
D-EGCK(2)	Grob G.115C1	82066	N115LR
D-EGCN	Reims/Cessna FRA150L Aerobat	FRA1500211	
	(Reservation .01)		
D-EGCP	Reims/Cessna F172M	F17200989	
D-EGCQ	Reims/Cessna F172M	F17200993	
D-EGCS	Reims/Cessna F172M	F17201001	
D-EGCT(2)	Reims/Cessna F152	F15201692	
D-EGCU	Cessna F172H	F172-0401	
D-EGCW(2)	Reims/Cessna F152	F15201691	
D-EGDA(2)	Robin DR.400/180 Régent	2293	
D-EGDB(2)	Grumman AA-5A Cheetah	AA5A-0551	
D-EGDC	Grumman AA-5B Tiger	AA5B-0728	
D-EGDD	Grumman AA-5B Tiger	AA5B-0827	
D-EGDE	Cessna F150G	F150-0114	
D-EGDF	Grumman AA-5B Tiger	AA5B-0776	
D-EGDG	Grumman AA-5A Cheetah	AA5A-0656	
D-EGDH	Grumman AA-5B Tiger	AA5B-0932	
D-EGDI	SOCATA MS.892A Rallye Commodore 150	10550	
D-EGDK	SOCATA MS.893E Rallye 180GT Gaillard	12209	F-BUXL
D-EGDL	Grumman AA-5B Tiger	AA5B-0779	
D-EGDM(2)	Cessna 150M	15077827	N7730U
D-EGDN	Grumman AA-5B Tiger	AA5B-0750	
D-EGDO(2)	Cessna F172H	F172-0334	
D-EGDR	Grumman AA-5B Tiger	AA5B-1132	(N4527C)
D-EGDV(2)	Robin DR.400/180R Remorqueur	1578	

D-EGDX	Robin DR.400/180R Remorqueur	1588	
D-EGDY	Cessna F150G	F150-0086	
D-EGEB(2)	Cessna 172M	17263918	N21262
D-EGEC(2)	Piaggio FWP.149D	153	91+31
			ND+104
			KB+130
D-EGEE	SIAI-Marchetti S.205-22/R	4-130	
D-EGEF(2)	SOCATA MS.893ED Rallye 180GT Gaillard	13301	
D-EGEG(2)	Cessna 172B	17248683	N8183X
D-EGEH(3)	SOCATA TB-10 Tobago	105	
D-EGEI	Piaggio FWP.149D	121	91+01
			D-ELHU
			AS+410
D-EGEL(4)	SOCATA Rallye 180TS Galérien	3239	PH-AFE
D-EGEM(3)	Blume Bl 502 V-2 (Permit 2.05)	03	D-EGEM(1)
D-EGEN(2)	Maier/ Piel CP.301A Emeraude	AB.402	
D-EGEP(2)	Wassmer CE.43 Guepard	435	
D-EGER(2)	Piper PA-28-235 Cherokee E	28-7110002	N8582N
D-EGET(2)	SOCATA MS.893ED Rallye 180GT Gaillard	13300	
D-EGEV(2)	Fuji FA-200-180 Aero Subaru	204	
D-EGEW(3)	Extra EA.300	016	
D-EGEX(2)	Robin DR.400/RP Remorqueur	1847	
D-EGFA(3)	Reims/Cessna F150M	F15001228	
D-EGFD	Reims/Cessna F152	F15201630	OE-CFD
D-EGFE(2)	SOCATA MS.880B Rallye Club	867	F-BONS
D-EGFG	Piper PA-18 Super Cub 95	18-3420	96+02
			NL+107
			AC+501
			AS+509
			54-720
D-EGFH	Pützer Elster B	043	97+20
			D-ELBD
D-EGFI	Bölkow BO.208C Junior	638	
D-EGFK	Cessna 182M Skylane	18259666	(N71566)
D-EGFM	Reims FR172H Rocket	FR17200277	
D-EGFN	Robin DR.400/180R Remorqueur	1586	
D-EGFO	Bölkow BO.208C Junior	639	
D-EGFR	Dornier Do.27A-1	160	55+36
			BD+9 . .
			SE+521
			SC+718
			QM+606
			PC+113
D-EGFS	Piper PA-18-150 Super Cub	18-7709056	HB-PBM
			N83524
D-EGFT	Piper PA-28-181 Archer II	28-7990296	N2223P
D-EGFU	Bölkow BO.208C Junior	640	
D-EGFV	Robin R.3000/120D	116	
D-EGFW	Piper PA-38-112 Tomahawk	38-81A0005	N25460
D-EGGC	Cessna 172P	17274492	N52303
D-EGGE(2)	Zlin Z.526F Trenér Master	1062	HA-SAH
D-EGGF	Cessna 172RG Cutlass RG	172RG0301	N107JB
			N5250U
D-EGGG(2)	Beech C24R Sierra 200	MC-626	N60137
D-EGGH	SOCATA MS.893A Rallye Commodore 180	11633	F-BSFV
D-EGGI (2)	Piper PA-28-235 Cherokee Pathfinder	28-7610074	N8361C
D-EGGJ	Cessna 172P	17274402	N52053
D-EGGK	Cessna 172N	17269306	N737CC
D-EGGL	Cessna 172M	17261484	N20677
D-EGGM	Piper PA-18-150 Super Cub	18-5401	ALAT
			N10F
D-EGGN	Gardan GY-80 Horizon 150	1	F-BLIB
D-EGGO(3)	Cessna T210J Turbo-System Centurion	T210-0404	N4207P
			D-EBSS(1)
			N2254R
D-EGGR	Beech F33A Bonanza	CE-393	
D-EGGS	Bölkow BO.209 Monsun 160RV	175	HB-UEO
			D-EAAO(1)
D-EGGU	Cessna F172H	F172-0459	
D-EGGV	Cessna 182P Skylane	18262176	N58615
D-EGGW(2)	SOCATA TB-9 Tampico	261	
D-EGGX	Cessna 172RG Cutlass RG	172RG0307	N5260U
D-EGGY	Cessna F150H	F150-0237	
D-EGGZ	Cessna R182 Skylane RG	R18200175	N2390C
D-EGHA(3)	Piper PA-28R-201T Turbo Arrow III	28R-7803264	N9540C
D-EGHB	SAN Jodel D.140C Mousquetaire III	136	F-BMBU
D-EGHE	Piper PA-24-260 Comanche B	24-4473	N9012P
D-EGHF	Cessna 172RG Cutlass RG	172RG0177	OE-KHF
			F-GHXU
			N6394R
D-EGHG(2)	Grässer/ Neico Lancair 235	002	
D-EGHH(2)	Piper PA-28RT-201T Turbo Arrow IV	28R-8131003	N8271N
D-EGHI	CEA DR.253B Régent	154	
D-EGHJ	CEA DR.315 Petit Prince	419	
D-EGHL	Cessna 182J Skylane	18256806	N2706F
D-EGHM	Cessna F150J	F150-0480	F-BRBT
D-EGHN	Cessna F172H	F172-0629	
D-EGHO(2)	Cessna 182P Skylane	18263484	N5667J
D-EGHP	Cessna 172RG Cutlass RG	172RG1155	N9423D
D-EGHQ	Robin DR.400/180R Remorqueur	1570	
D-EGHR	Rohn Doppelraab IV	EB.1	D-5412
D-EGHS	Robin DR.400/180R Remorqueur	893	
D-EGHT(2)	Beech F33A Bonanza	CE-1732	N80617
D-EGHV	Piper PA-28-181 Archer II	28-8090278	N8182D
D-EGHW(2)	Bölkow BO.209 Monsun 150FV	170	HB-UER
			D-EAAJ
D-EGHY	Piper PA-28-180 Cherokee D	28-5473	N2158R

D-EGHZ	Beech V35B Bonanza	D-10024	
D-EGIB(2)	Piper PA-28-181 Archer II	28-8190017	N8257E
D-EGIC(2)	Bölkow BO.208C Junior	642	
D-EGID(2)	Wassmer WA.52 Europa	64	
D-EGIE	Piper PA-46-350P Malibu Mirage	4622128	I-EXPA
			D-EXPA
			N9217Z
			N339W
D-EGIF(3)	Friedrich/ Brditschka HB-207VRG Alfa (Permit 9.01)	207018	
D-EGIG	Luscombe 8A Silvaire	4252	OO-GMA
			N1525K
D-EGII	Huschle/ Stephens Acro Sport II	388	
D-EGIK(2)	Piper PA-28-140 Cherokee	28-21605	N11C
D-EGIL(2)	Piper PA-28R-200 Cherokee Arrow II	28R-7535218	N1018X
D-EGIM(2)	Piper PA-28R-200 Cherokee Arrow II	28R-7235304	N11C
D-EGIN	Piper PA-18 Super Cub 95	18-5652	N10F
D-EGIP(3)	Cessna P210R Pressurized Centurion II	P21000849	N5361A
D-EGIR(2)	Reims/Cessna F172M	F17201360	
D-EGIS(2)	Piper PA-38-112 Tomahawk	38-78A0264	N9725N
D-EGIT(2)	Piaggio P.149D	260	91+78
			AC+411
			AS+411
D-EGIV(2)	Piper PA-28-181 Archer II	28-7990568	N2936A
D-EGIW(2)	Wassmer WA.52 Europa	63	
D-EGIZ(2)	Robin DR.400/180R Remorqueur	1039	
D-EGJA	Reims/Cessna F172M	F17201003	
D-EGJC	Reims/Cessna F172M	F17201006	
D-EGJD	Reims FR172J Rocket	FR17200420	
D-EGJE	Reims FR172J Rocket	FR17200421	
D-EGJF	Reims FR172J Rocket	FR17200422	
D-EGJH(2)	Reims/Cessna F172N	F17201930	
D-EGJJ	Reims/Cessna F177RG Cardinal RG	F177RG0086	
D-EGJK	Cessna 182P Skylane	18262660	N52535
D-EGJM(2)	Robin DR.400/180 Régent	2296	
D-EGJN	Piper PA-18-150 Super Cub	18-564	R-210
			51-15678
			N7193K
D-EGJO	Cirrus SR20	1440	N497CD
D-EGJP	Cessna U206F Stationair	U20601972	N51014
D-EGJS	Reims/Cessna F150L	F15001046	
D-EGJT(2)	Robin HR.200/120B Club	306	
D-EGJU	Cessna 182P Skylane	18262275	N58752
D-EGJX	Reims/Cessna F150L	F15000974	
D-EGKA	Cessna 182H Skylane	18256265	N2365X
D-EGKB	Reims FR172E Rocket	FR17200008	
D-EGKC	Reims/Cessna F150L	F15000978	
D-EGKD(2)	Reims/Cessna F150L (Rotax 912S conv.)	F15000980	
D-EGKE(2)	SOCATA Rallye 180TS Galérien	3325	
D-EGKF(2)	SOCATA TB-10 Tobago	166	
D-EGKH(3)	SOCATA TB-10 Tobago	168	
D-EGKJ(2)	SOCATA TB-10 Tobago	170	
D-EGKK	Piper PA-28R-200 Cherokee Arrow II	28R-7335442	N56472
D-EGKL	Cessna 182J Skylane	18257059	N2959F
D-EGKN	SOCATA TB-10 Tobago	189	
D-EGKP	SOCATA TB-9 Tampico	195	
D-EGKQ	SOCATA TB-9 Tampico	196	
D-EGKR(2)	Cessna T210M Turbo Centurion (Reims-assembled with "c/n" 0006)	21061914	OO-BVC
			D-EBVC
			HB-CXR
			(N732ZW)
D-EGKT	Reims/Cessna F172P	F17202058	
D-EGKU	Bölkow BO.207	252	
D-EGKV	Piper PA-38-112 Tomahawk	38-78A0123	N9519T
D-EGKW(2)	Klinke K1	001	
D-EGKY(2)	Reims/Cessna F150L	F15001051	
D-EGLB	Reims/Cessna F172N	F17201810	
D-EGLE	Bölkow BO.207	254	
D-EGLF	Reims/Cessna FR182 Skylane RG	FR18200034	
D-EGLG(2)	Reims/Cessna F152	F15201600	
D-EGLI	Bölkow BO.207 (Reservation)	255	
D-EGLJ	Cessna 172P	17276144	N97005
D-EGLK(2)	Schwämmle HS-3 Motorlerche	844	
D-EGLL(3)	Cessna 172R	17280332	N95216
D-EGLM	Cessna 172N	17271780	N5224E
D-EGLN	Cessna 172P	17276274	N98291
D-EGLO	Bölkow BO.207	256	(G-ASCW)
			D-EGLO
D-EGLP	Reims/Cessna FRA150M Aerobat	FRA1500319	
D-EGLQ	Robin DR.400/140 Major	858	
D-EGLR	Robin DR.400/180 Régent	857	
D-EGLT(2)	Cessna 172M	17262963	N13716
D-EGLU	Bölkow BO.207	257	G-ASAY
			D-EGLU
D-EGLV	Piper PA-18-150 Super Cub	18-8009036	N6102A
			N9760N
D-EGLW(2)	Cessna 172S	172S8731	N814SP
D-EGLX	Cessna 172N	17271099	LZ-. . .
			D-EGLX
			N1697E
D-EGMA(2)	Beech F33A Bonanza	CE-903	N6746L
D-EGMB	Reims/Cessna F172P	F17202121	
D-EGMC	CEA DR.253B Régent (Permit)	155	
D-EGMD	CEA DR.315 Petit Prince	422	
D-EGME(3)	Piaggio FWP.149D	183	91+61
			BF+420
			AS+022
			KB+145

D-EGMF	Reims/Cessna FR172K Hawk XP	FR17200592	
D-EGMG	Piper J-3C-65 Cub	12005	G-CVIL
			OO-VIL
			OO-VVV
			44-79709
D-EGMH	SOCATA MS.893E Rallye 180GT Gaillard	12318	F-BUZF
D-EGMK	Piper PA-28R-200 Cherokee Arrow II	28R-7335424	N56370
D-EGMM	SOCATA MS.894A Minerva 220	11831	F-BSMM
D-EGMO(3)	Piper PA-18 Super Cub 95	18-3195	OL-L21
			L-121
			53-4795
D-EGMR	SIAI-Marchetti SF.260	2-55	OY-BEA
D-EGMS	Robin DR.400/180 Régent	1836	
D-EGMT	Reims/Cessna F182Q (Porsche engine)	F18200057	
D-EGMV	Reims/Cessna F152	F15201762	
D-EGMW	Reims/Cessna F177RG Cardinal RG	F177RG0133	(D-EGWM)
D-EGMX	Reims/Cessna F152	F15201601	PH-AYL
D-EGMY(2)	Bölkow BO.208C Junior	644	
D-EGNA(2)	Wassmer WA.54 Atlantic	128	
D-EGNB	SOCATA Rallye 150TD	2805	
D-EGNC	SOCATA MS.893ED Rallye 180GT Gaillard	12847	
D-EGND	SOCATA Rallye 150TD	2804	
D-EGNE	Bölkow BO.208 Junior	526	
D-EGNF	SOCATA Rallye 150TD	2968	
D-EGNG	SOCATA MS.893ED Rallye 180GT Gaillard	12825	
D-EGNH	SOCATA MS.893ED Rallye 180GT Gaillard	12826	
D-EGNI (2)	Piper PA-28-140 Cherokee C	28-26712	N5936U
D-EGNJ	SOCATA Rallye 150TD	2806	
D-EGNK	SOCATA MS.893ED Rallye 180GT Gaillard	12827	
D-EGNM(2)	Piper PA-28-181 Archer II	28-8290010	N8438L
D-EGNN	SOCATA Rallye 150TD	2807	
D-EGNO(2)	Cessna 172P	17275546	N64331
D-EGNP(2)	Diamond DA 40-180 Star	40015	
D-EGNR	Reims/Cessna F172P	F17202116	
D-EGNS	SOCATA MS.893ED Rallye 180GT Gaillard	12866	
D-EGNU(3)	Cessna F172H	F172-0379	
D-EGNY	Bölkow BO.208 Junior	530	
D-EGOA	Piper PA-28-181 Archer II	28-8190020	N8257V
D-EGOB(2)	Robin DR.300/125 Petit Prince	662	
D-EGOC(2)	Bölkow BO.208C Junior	646	
D-EGOD(2)	Robin HR.100/210D Safari	160	F-BUPY
D-EGOE	Robin HR.100/210D Safari	166	F-BUPV
D-EGOF(3)	Piper PA-28-161 Warrior II	28-8216122	N9637N
D-EGOG(3)	Grözinger/ Viking Dragonfly	293	
D-EGOJ	Reims/Cessna F152	F15201647	
D-EGOK(3)	Piper PA-28-140 Cherokee	28-21724	N11C
D-EGOL(3)	Piper PA-28RT-201T Turbo Arrow IV	28R-7931197	N29322
D-EGOM(2)	Cessna 182P Skylane	18262263	CS-AOQ
			N58733
D-EGON	Fieseler Fi.156C-3 Trop Storch	5987	PH-NEL
			(PH-NDF)
			(PH-PBD)
			VN266
			Luftwaffe
D-EGOO(2)	Cessna P210N Pressurized Centurion II	P21000147	N6156P
D-EGOS	Piaggio FWP.149D	061	90+47
			AC+406
			DA+389
D-EGOT(2)	Grumman AA-5A Cheetah	AA5A-0032	PH-GOL
			OO-HAH
D-EGOV(2)	Beech F33A Bonanza	CE-1576	N81863
D-EGOW(2)	Cessna T210M Turbo Centurion	21062673	PH-AXP
	(Reims-assembled with "c/n" 0014)		N6065B
D-EGOZ(2)	Beech F33A Bonanza	CE-959	OE-KEK
			N1814D
D-EGPA(2)	Piper PA-28-181 Cherokee Archer II	28-7690189	N9529N
D-EGPC	Champion 7GCBC Citabria	0156	
D-EGPD(2)	Piper PA-28-181 Cherokee Archer II	28-7790477	N4575Q
D-EGPE(3)	CASA I-131E Jungmann	2092	D-EGRF
			E3B-441
D-EGPF(2)	Reims/Cessna FA150L Aerobat	FA1500094	D-ECHQ
D-EGPG(2)	Robin DR.400/120D Petit Prince	1544	
D-EGPH	Bellanca 7GCBC Citabria	798-75	N8586V
D-EGPI (3)	Cessna F150G	F150-0169	
D-EGPK	Cessna TR182 Turbo Skylane RG	R18200804	N123CC
			(N736ZM)
D-EGPL(2)	Piper PA-28-236 Dakota	28-8011103	N8197L
D-EGPM	Piper PA-28-140 Cherokee E	28-7225452	N11C
D-EGPP	Mooney M.20J Model 201	24-1644	
D-EGPR(2)	Piper PA-28-181 Archer II	28-8190292	N84196
D-EGPW	Great Lakes 2T-1A-1	0505	N505GL
D-EGQA(2)	Bölkow BO.208C Junior	647	
D-EGQC	Reims/Cessna F172N	F17201618	
D-EGQF	Reims/Cessna F172N	F17201593	
D-EGRA(4)	SOCATA MS.894A Minerva 220	11835	F-BSMV
D-EGRC	SOCATA TB-10 Tobago	15	F-ODKD
D-EGRD	SOCATA TB-10 Tobago	46	F-ODMD
D-EGRE(4)	SOCATA TB-10 Tobago	119	
D-EGRF(4)	Diamond DA 40D Star	D4.107	
D-EGRG	Reims FR172F Rocket	FR17200120	
D-EGRK	Piper PA-28R-200 Cherokee Arrow II	28R-7235299	N11C
D-EGRM	CASA I-131E Jungmann	2143	E3B-543
D-EGRO(3)	Grobholz G-2000 Symphonie	EB-01	
D-EGRP(3)	Piper PA-28-161 Cadet	2841207	N158ER
D-EGRS	SOCATA TB-10 Tobago	43	F-ODME
D-EGRT(2)	Beech C23 Sundowner	M-2358	N18355
D-EGRU	Oberlerchner JOB 15-180/2	055	OE-CAI

D-EGRV(3)	Piper PA-28-235 Cherokee C	28-11217	ZS-JWT
			ZS-HSC
			ZS-FVZ
			N11C
D-EGRW	Piper PA-28-235 Cherokee C	28-11251	N8508N
D-EGRX	SOCATA TB-10 Tobago	47	F-ODMF
D-EGRY(2)	Robin DR.400/180R Remorqueur	1206	SE-GRY
D-EGRZ	SOCATA TB-10 Tobago	65	
D-EGSA(2)	SOCATA TB-20 Trinidad	2148	
D-EGSC	Reims/Cessna F172N	F17201898	(PH-AXD)
D-EGSD(3)	Mooney M.20R Ovation	29-0073	
D-EGSE(2)	Piper PA-28R-200 Cherokee Arrow II	28R-7635272	N75170
D-EGSF	Reims/Cessna F172N	F17201711	
D-EGSH	Grumman AA-5A Cheetah	AA5A-0563	N26399
D-EGSI (2)	Cessna T210L Turbo Centurion II	21060057	N59058
D-EGSJ	CEA DR.253B Régent	199	
D-EGSK	Robin DR.300/180R Remorqueur	653	
D-EGSL(3)	Cessna R182 Skylane RG II	R18201364	N4641S
D-EGSM(2)	Piper PA-28-180 Cherokee Challenger	28-7305506	D-EBFH
			N55944
D-EGSO	SOCATA MS.893A Rallye Commodore 180	10818	F-BPSA
D-EGSP(2)	Piper PA-28R-200 Cherokee Arrow II	28R-7535299	N1493X
D-EGSR	Reims/Cessna F172N	F17201857	
D-EGSS	Seyboth/ Impulse 120TD (Permit 9.04)	TD-10	
D-EGST	Cessna F172F	F172-0141	
D-EGSU(2)	CEA Jodel DR.1050M Ambassadeur	21	F-BJLQ
D-EGSW	Cessna 180J Skywagon	18052645	N9990N
D-EGSX	SOCATA TB-9 Tampico	929	
D-EGSY(2)	SOCATA TB-10 Tobago	1078	
D-EGTA(2)	Grob G.115TA	8501	
D-EGTB(2)	Bek Me.109R3	1727	
D-EGTD	Reims/Cessna FR182 Skylane RG	FR18200003	
D-EGTE(2)	Robin DR.400/180 Régent	1953	F-GJQD
D-EGTG	Reims/Cessna FR182 Skylane RG	FR18200005	
D-EGTH	Reims/Cessna F172N	F17201516	F-WLIP
D-EGTJ	Cessna TR182 Turbo Skylane RG	R18201437	N4847S
D-EGTL	Grumman AA-5 Traveler	AA5-0602	
D-EGTM	Reims/Cessna F172N	F17201698	
D-EGTN(3)	Cessna 152	15280509	N25036
D-EGTP	Robin DR.400/180 Régent	1261	
D-EGTQ	Robin DR.400/180R Remorqueur	1264	
D-EGTR(2)	SOCATA TB-20 Trinidad	706	
D-EGTS(2)	Piper PA-38-112 Tomahawk	38-79A1059	N23871
D-EGTT	SOCATA MS.893E Rallye 180GT Gaillard	13084	SE-GTT
D-EGTU(2)	SOCATA MS.880B Rallye Club	1164	F-BPGE
D-EGTV	Piper PA-38-112 Tomahawk	38-78A0545	N9716N
D-EGTW(2)	Robin DR.400/180R Remorqueur	1260	
D-EGTY(2)	Morane-Saulnier MS.505 Criquet (Permit)	73	G-BWRF
			D-EFTY(2)
			F-BAUV
			Fr.AF
D-EGTZ	Cessna 172N	17270995	N1428E
D-EGUG	Cessna 170B	26213	N2569C
D-EGUH(2)	Reims/Cessna F152	F15201590	
D-EGUJ	Cessna 172N Skyhawk II	17271599	N3591E
D-EGUK(2)	Cessna 172N	17269403	N737GH
D-EGUL(2)	Cessna T210N Turbo Centurion II	21063924	OE-DUL
			(N6588C)
D-EGUM	Piper J-3C-65 Cub	12859	HB-OAF
			44-80563
D-EGUN(3)	Robin DR.400/180RRemorqueur	2472	
D-EGUP(2)	Reims/Cessna F172N	F17201946	(PH-AXU)
D-EGUQ(2)	Piper PA-28-140 Cherokee	28-21577	N11C
D-EGUS(2)	SOCATA TB-10 Tobago	714	
D-EGUT(3)	Cessna TR182 Turbo Skylane RG	R18200668	N9204R
D-EGUV(2)	Piper PA-28-140 Cherokee	28-21619	N11C
D-EGUW(2)	Beech V35B Bonanza	D-9505	
D-EGUY	Gyroflug SC-01B-160i Speed Canard	S-7	
D-EGVA(2)	Piper PA-28R-200 Cherokee Arrow II	28R-7635229	N9255K
D-EGVC	Dornier Do.27A-4	2059	OL-D03/
			OT-AMC
			D-3/D-9506
D-EGVE	Bölkow BO.208C Junior	661	
D-EGVF(2)	Reims/Cessna F172N	F17201924	(PH-AXJ)
D-EGVG(2)	Reims/Cessna F172N	F17201933	(PH-AXK)
D-EGVH(2)	Robin R.2160D Acrobin	199	
D-EGVI	Bölkow BO.208C Junior	662	
D-EGVK	Wassmer WA.54 Atlantic	127	
D-EGVL	Wassmer WA.54 Atlantic	129	
D-EGVM	SNCAN/ Stampe SV.4C	218	F-BCNZ
			Fr.AF
D-EGVN	Dornier Do.27A-4	2106	HC-. . .
			G-BNVX
			7P-AAX
			D-EGVN
			D-O9/OT-AMH
			OL-DO9
			D-9
D-EGVS	Piper J-3L Cub	12769	D-EGYS
			HB-OAA
			44-80473
D-EGVT	Beech C24R Sierra 200	MC-605	N2012Z
D-EGVV	Test registration for Grob G.115 production		
D-EGVW	Cessna F172G	F172-0209	D-EDOF
D-EGVX	Test registration for Grob G.115 production		
D-EGVZ	Robin DR.400/180R Remorqueur	1593	
D-EGWA(2)	Gardan GY-80 Horizon 180	203	OY-DTJ

D-EGWB	SOCATA MS.893E Rallye 180GT Gaillard	12330	F-BUXO
D-EGWC	Piper J-3C-65 Cub	6679	D-ECWC
			N37900
			NC37900
D-EGWD	Pützer Elster B	030	97+18
			D-ELBY
D-EGWE	Piper PA-28-180 Cherokee C	28-2043	
D-EGWF(2)	Reims/Cessna F182Q Skylane	F18200140	PH-AXX
D-EGWG(2)	Robin DR.400/180R Remorqueur	1214	
D-EGWH	Piper J-3C-90/SGAC Marabout	EN.1	F-BGKF
D-EGWK	Piaggio FWP.149D	174	91+52
			SC+336
			AS+415
			KB+139
D-EGWL(2)	SOCATA Rallye 235E-D Gabier	12797	F-GALE
D-EGWM(2)	Beth/ Pitts S-1S Special	AB-K-098	
D-EGWN	Fuji FA-200-160 Aero Subaru	227	
D-EGWO	Beech A-23 Musketeer II	M-771	
D-EGWP(2)	Mraz M.1DSokol	304	G-BWRG
			D-EGWP(2)
			(D-EFTB)
			HB-TBG
			OK-DIX
D-EGWR	Piper PA-28-161 Cherokee Warrior II	28-7816670	N9630N
D-EGWS(2)	Mooney M.20J Model 201	24-0240	(N201HU)
D-EGWT	Robin R.2160D Acrobin	174	
D-EGWY	Bölkow BO.208C Junior	666	
D-EGWZ(3)	Gyroflug SC.01B-160 Speed Canard	S-38	
D-EGXA	Bölkow BO.208C Junior	667	
D-EGXE	Cessna 182J Skylane	18256983	N2883F
D-EGXI (2)	Grob G.115A	8029	
D-EGXO	Bölkow BO.208C Junior	669	
D-EGXP	Mannebeck/ Aero Designs Pulsar XP	XP-002	
D-EGXY(2)	SNCAN/ Stampe SV.4C	651	F-BDMU
D-EGYA	Beech C23 Sundowner 180	M-1923	
D-EGYC(2)	Cessna F172H	F172-0328	
D-EGYD(2)	Beech C24R Sierra 200	MC-479	
D-EGYF(2)	SOCATA TB-10 Tobago	433	
D-EGYH(2)	SOCATA MS.893ED Rallye 180GT Gaillard	12990	
D-EGYI	SOCATA Rallye 100ST-D	2956	
D-EGYJ	SOCATA MS.893ED Rallye 180GT Gaillard	12992	
D-EGYK(2)	SOCATA MS.893ED Rallye 180GT Gaillard	12991	
D-EGYM(2)	Reims/Cessna F172M	F17201344	
D-EGYN(2)	Reims/Cessna F172M	F17201241	
D-EGYP(2)	SOCATA MS.893ED Rallye 180GT Gaillard	13012	
D-EGYQ	Cessna 182C Skylane	52862	N8962T
D-EGYS(2)	SOCATA Rallye 180TD Galérien	3023	
D-EGYU	SOCATA Rallye 180TD Galérien	3024	
D-EGYW(2)	SOCATA Rallye 180TD Galérien	3026	
D-EGYX(4)	SOCATA MS.893A Rallye Commodore 180	10625	
D-EGYZ	SOCATA MS.893A Rallye Commodore 180	10615	
D-EGZA	Piper J-3C-90 Cub	10086	OE-AEW
			NC60443
			43-1225
D-EGZB(3)	Cessna 172M	17265568	N444DA
			N6754H
D-EGZC(3)	Cessna 172P	17274803	N53701
D-EGZE	Cessna F172F	F172-0120	
D-EGZH	Bölkow BO.208C Junior	675	
D-EGZJ(3)	Cessna F172H	F172-0553	
D-EGZL	Bölkow BO.208C Junior	678	
D-EGZM	Bölkow BO.208C Junior	679	
D-EGZN(2)	SEEMS MS.885 Super Rallye	270	F-BKUX
D-EGZO	Bölkow BO.208C Junior	575	
D-EGZP	Bayer Leverkusen/ Binder CP.301S Smaragd	AB.708	
D-EGZR	Heliopolis Gomhouria Mk.6	185	SU-347
D-EGZT	Reims/Cessna F172N	F17201891	(PH-AXG)
D-EGZU(2)	Cessna 210B	21057970	OE-DED(1)
			N9670X
D-EGZW	Piper PA-38-112 Tomahawk	38-81A0104	N26024
D-EGZY	Cessna 182H Skylane	18256276	N2376X
D-EHAA	Robin DR.400/180R Remorqueur	1541	
D-EHAB(2)	Piper PA-28-181 Cherokee Archer II	28-7790293	N9587N
D-EHAC(2)	Bölkow BO.208C Junior	709	(D-ENVD)
D-EHAD	Cessna 172	29059	N6959A
D-EHAE(2)	Robin DR.400/180R Remorqueur (W/o 10.6.02)	1211	
D-EHAG(2)	Cessna 182G Skylane	18255275	N2075R
D-EHAH(4)	Piper PA-32R-301T Saratoga IITC	3257103	OY-JAH
			N9527N
D-EHAI (2)	Robin DR.400/180R Remorqueur	1547	
D-EHAJ	Fuji FA-200-160 Aero Subaru	88	
D-EHAK(2)	Piper PA-32R-300 Cherokee Lance	32R-7680154	(D-EFAN)
	(Permit 5.04)		N8616E
D-EHAL(3)	Piper PA-28RT-201 Arrow IV	28R-8118006	N8275Y
D-EHAM(2)	Cessna 172B	17248415	N7915X
D-EHAN(3)	Mooney M.20C Mark 21	3314	N200EK
			D-EHAH
D-EHAO(2)	Piper PA-28-151 Cherokee Warrior	28-7515278	OY-CBE
			N32942
D-EHAP(3)	Piper PA-18 Super Cub 95	18-1530	D-EOCF
			ALAT
			51-15530
D-EHAR(4)	Heier/ Neico Lancair 235	229	
D-EHAS	Piper PA-22-150 Tri-Pacer	22-5510	
D-EHAU(2)	Hauser/ Neico Lancair 235	1645	
D-EHAV(2)	Aviat Pitts S-2B	5302	N98AV
D-EHAW(2)	Fuji FA-200-160 Aero Subaru (Marked FH20/160)	120	

D-EHAY	CEA DR.253B Régent	190	
D-EHAZ(4)	Hötzel / Brändli BX-2 Cherry	1694	
D-EHBA(2)	Cessna F172G	F172-0319	
D-EHBB	SOCATA MS.893A Rallye Commodore 180	11777	F-BSXY
D-EHBC(2)	SIAI-Marchetti SF.260	2-59	OO-HOC
D-EHBD(3)	Rockwell Commander 114B	14522	OE-KBD
			D-EIKU
			N5905N
D-EHBE(2)	Cessna F150G	F150-0116	
D-EHBI (3)	Reims/Cessna F152	F15201534	
D-EHBK	Reims/Cessna FA150K Aerobat	FA1500075	
D-EHBL(2)	Cessna F172G	F172-0194	OO-HBF
			OO-WIF
			OO-SIF
D-EHBM(3)	Cessna 172R	17281211	N2117X
D-EHBN	Reims/Cessna F172N	F17201755	
D-EHBS(3)	Cessna F150H	F150-0125	D-EMIF(2)
D-EHBT(2)	Tennant/ Europa Avn Europa	SB193, formerly 1796	
D-EHBU	Wassmer Jodel D.112 Club	1114	F-BKCX
D-EHBY	SAN Jodel D.140 Mousquetaire	32	F-BIZQ
D-EHCA	Cessna 210J Centurion	21059179	N3379S
D-EHCB	Piper PA-18 Super Cub 95	18-3219	OL-L45
	(Restoration, reserved .02)		L-145
			53-4819
D-EHCC(3)	Grob G.115A	8056	
D-EHCD	Piper PA-18 Super Cub 95	18-3137	OL-L63
			L-63
			53-4737
D-EHCE(2)	Christen A-1 Husky	1148	
D-EHCF	Piper PA-18 Super Cub 95	18-3190	OL-L16
			L-116
			53-4790
D-EHCH(2)	Mooney M.20M Model 257 TLS	27-0077	
D-EHCK	Piper PA-18 Super Cub 95	18-1491	ALAT
			51-15491
D-EHCL	Piper PA-18 Super Cub 95	18-1436	ALAT
			51-15436
D-EHCM(2)	SOCATA MS.893A Rallye Commodore 180	11501	F-BSCR
D-EHCN(3)	Piper PA-28-161 Cadet	2841202	N91891
D-EHCO	Piper PA-18 Super Cub 95	18-1529	ALAT
			51-15529
D-EHCP(2)	Reims/Cessna F172N	F17201760	
D-EHCQ	Mooney M.20M Model 257 TLS	27-0205	D-ELVY(3)
	(Reservation .05)		G-BWIS
D-EHCR	Reims/Cessna F172N	F17201762	
D-EHCS	Robin DR.400/180 Régent	1628	
D-EHCU	Piper PA-18 Super Cub 95	18-1447	N1156R
			ALAT
			51-15447
D-EHCW(2)	Beech B36TC Bonanza	EA-412	N72319
			N6866W
D-EHDA(3)	Müller/ Sequoia F.8L Falco	406	D-EHDA(2)
	(Built with parts of Laverda F.8L c/n 406 and Sequoia plans following w/o of c/n 406, 15.3.80. Sequoia c/n unknown)		
D-EHDD(2)	Piper PA-28-151 Cherokee Warrior	28-7415293	OE-DMV
			N9560N
D-EHDE(3)	Commander Aircraft 114B	14545	N132A
D-EHDF	Piaggio FWP.149D	170	91+48
			EB+389
			DA+387
			KB+146
D-EHDG(2)	Robin HR.100/210D Safari	175	F-OCTY
D-EHDJ	Wassmer WA.52 Europa	68	
D-EHDL(2)	Piper PA-32R-301T Turbo Saratoga	32R-8229035	N8147H
D-EHDM(3)	Piper PA-28-181 Archer II	28-8490072	N4359U
D-EHDO(3)	AIAA/ Stampe SV.4A	1080	F-BCDO
			Fr.Navy
D-EHDQ(2)	Robin DR.400/180 Régent	1647	
D-EHDR(2)	Robin DR.400/180R Remorqueur	1646	
D-EHDS(3)	SIAT 223K-1 Flamingo	018	HB-EVB
			D-ENBP(1)
D-EHDT(2)	CASA I-131E Jungmann 180	2181	E3B-564
D-EHDU	Cessna 172C	17249360	D-EHPI
			N1660Y
D-EHDW(3)	Hawickhorst/ Pitts S-1S Special	AB-K-O99	
D-EHDZ(2)	Piper PA-28RT-201T Turbo Arrow IV	28R-7931142	N2081Y
D-EHEB(4)	Berger/ Jodel D.92 Bébé	AB18	D-EKYH(1)
D-EHEC(4)	Lancair LC40-550FG Colombia 300	40006	PH-HLW
			N500HL
D-EHED(3)	Piper PA-18-150 Super Cub	18-5993	OE-AED
			(XB-ZUU)
			N7789D
D-EHEE	Mooney M.20F Executive	680180	
D-EHEF(2)	Cessna F150G	F150-0154	
D-EHEG(2)	Robin DR.400/180RRemorqueur	1078	
D-EHEI	Piper PA-28R-200 Cherokee Arrow II	28R-7235040	N4415T
D-EHEL(3)	Piper PA-28-180 Cherokee Challenger	28-7305160	N11C
D-EHEM(5)	HOAC DV-20 Katana	20065	
D-EHEN(2)	Aerotek Pitts S-2A	2088	G-BCXD
			N80044
D-EHEO	Robin DR.400/180 Régent	747	
D-EHEQ	Focke-Wulf FW.44J Stieglitz	unkn	SE-BZI
			Fv664
D-EHER(5)	Piper PA-28-181 Archer II	28-8390008	N8293L
D-EHES(2)	Robin DR.400/180R Remorqueur	1049	
D-EHET(6)	SOCATA MS.893A Rallye Commodore 180	11491	OO-ACM
D-EHEU(3)	Cessna 182S	18280155	

D-EHEV(2)	Robin DR.400/180R Remorqueur	1079	
D-EHEX(2)	Cessna 150M	15078724	N704MR
D-EHEY	Beech C23 Sundowner 180	M-2078	
D-EHEZ(2)	Robin DR.400/180 Régent	1080	
D-EHFA(2)	Piper PA-28-181 Cherokee Archer II	28-7790485	N5616V
D-EHFC(2)	Piper PA-28-140 Cherokee Cruiser	28-7725172	N9609N
D-EHFE(2)	Piper PA-28-180 Cherokee E	28-5658	(D-EKSY)
			N3322R
D-EHFF	Piper PA-28R-200 Cherokee Arrow II	28R-7335084	(D-EEPD)
			N11C
D-EHFG(2)	Beech F33A Bonanza	CE-730	
D-EHFH(2)	Robin DR.400/180R Remorqueur	1886	
D-EHFI	Cessna F172G	F172-0220	
D-EHFK	Piper PA-28-140 Cherokee B	28-26086	N98174
D-EHFL	Piper PA-28R-200 Cherokee Arrow	28R-35245	N2674R
D-EHFM	Piper PA-28-180 Cherokee E	28-5610	N3687R
D-EHFN(3)	Robin DR.400/180R Remorqueur	1936	
D-EHFO	Piper PA-28-140 Cherokee E	28-7225136	N11C
D-EHFP	Piper PA-28-140 Cherokee B	28-25596	N98007
D-EHFR(2)	Cessna 172M	17265729	N9645Q
D-EHFS(2)	Reims/Cessna F172N	F17201944	D-EDXC(2)
			OE-DSV
D-EHFU	Cessna F172F	F172-0164	
D-EHFW	Piper PA-28R-180 Cherokee Arrow	28R-30405	N4544J
D-EHFZ	Piper PA-28R-200 Cherokee Arrow II	28R-7235279	N1405T
D-EHGA(2)	Grumman AA-5B Tiger	AA5B-0009	N1509R
D-EHGD	Robin DR.400/180 Régent	2159	
D-EHGE(2)	Rockwell Commander 114	14385	
D-EHGG(2)	Gross/ Dallach D4/E Fascination (Permit 8.00)	EB018	
D-EHGH	Beech F33A Bonanza	CE-1438	N5516K
D-EHGI (2)	Piper PA-28RT-201T Turbo Arrow IV	28R-8031056	N8152Q
D-EHGK	Piper PA-28-180 Cherokee Challenger	28-7305428	N15689
D-EHGM(3)	Piper PA-28-161 Cadet	2841084	N9169E
D-EHGO(2)	Rockwell Commander 114	14389	
D-EHGQ	Robin R.2160D	270	
D-EHGR	Piper PA-28RT-201T Turbo Arrow IV	28R-8231015	N80039
D-EHGS	Reims/Cessna F150L	F15000735	PH-TGS
D-EHGT	Beech F33A Bonanza	CE-1148	
D-EHGV	Robin DR.400/180 Régent	2248	
D-EHGW(2)	Piper PA-28-161 Cherokee Warrior II	28-7816073	N47430
D-EHGX	Cessna 182R Skylane	18268476	N9972E
D-EHGZ	Horstmann/ Jodel D.18	115	
D-EHHB(2)	Cessna 172S	172S8813	N3506Z
D-EHHC	Fuji FA-200-160 Aero Subaru	112	
D-EHHE	Aeromere F.8L Falco III America	227	HB-UOI
			D-EHHE
D-EHHF(3)	Piper PA-28RT-201 Arrow IV	28R-7918064	N3004T
D-EHHG(2)	Robin DR.400/180R Remorqueur	1972	
D-EHHH(2)	Steen Skybolt (Reservation)	1729	
D-EHHI (2)	Christen A-1 Husky	1080	N9594F
D-EHHJ	Beech E33 Bonanza	CD-1165	N8384N
D-EHHK	CEA Jodel DR.1050 Ambassadeur	47	HB-EBP
D-EHHL	Mooney M.20F Executive	670325	N2931L
			(D-ECTJ)
			N2931L
D-EHHM	Cessna F172H	F172-0352	
D-EHHN	Wassmer Jodel D.112 Club	886	D-EJCS(1)
			F-PJCS
D-EHHO	Piper PA-24-250 Comanche	24-3211	N7974P
D-EHHP	Robin R.1180TD Aiglon	231	
D-EHHS	Cessna 177A Cardinal	17701294	N30509
D-EHHT(2)	de Havilland DH.82A Tiger Moth	85478/E-3	D-EDAM(2)
	(Identity officially quoted as T6746 which was		D-EDAN
	D-EDAM(1) c/n 85033 cr 4.58 and combined		DE482
	with D-EDAN to build D-EDAM(2) in 1972)		
D-EHHU	Cessna F172F	F172-0129	
D-EHHV	Piper PA-28-181 Archer II	28-8490064	N9580N
D-EHHW(2)	Piper PA-28-160 Cherokee	28-546	TJ-ADK
			TU-TDG
			D-EMBA
			N11C
			N5465W
D-EHHX	Cessna P210N Pressurized Centurion II	P21000679	N5379W
D-EHHY	CEA DR.220A 2+2	103	F-BPKA
D-EHHZ	Piaggio FWP.149D	063	90+49
			DB+389
D-EHIA(2)	Robin R.3000/160	172	
D-EHIE	CEA Jodel DR.1050 Ambassadeur	291	
D-EHIF(2)	Cessna F172G	F172-0299	
D-EHIG(3)	Piper PA-28RT-201T Turbo Arrow IV	28R-7931114	N2153V
D-EHIK(3)	Piper PA-28RT-201T Turbo Arrow IV	28R-8531013	N91082
D-EHIL(3)	Christen Pitts S-2B	5203	N317JK
D-EHIM	Beech 35 Bonanza	D-499	OO-NDH
			D-EHIM
			OO-ECI
			HB-ECI
			NC90580
D-EHIN(2)	Cessna F172H	F172-0342	
D-EHIO	Robin DR.400/RP Remorqueur	1765	
D-EHIP(2)	Robin R.3000/160	138	
D-EHIR	Erco 415C Ercoupe	2650	N2027H
D-EHIS	Stark Turbulent D (V-4)	104	
D-EHIX(2)	Cessna 182J Skylane	18257185	N3085F
D-EHIY	Robin DR.400/180 Régent	1221	EC-EQS
			D-EEIY
D-EHIZ	Bücker Bü.181B-1 Bestmann	FR.20	SL-ABI
			F-BBLX
			Luftwaffe

D-EHJA(2)	Cessna P210N Pressurized Centurion II	P21000016	3D-PJM
			N210FW
			N7581P
D-EHJB(2)	Cessna 172N	17273633	N9682G
D-EHJC	Piper PA-18-150 Super Cub	18-5334	(D-EDBH)
			N5883
			ALAT
			N10F
D-EHJD	Piper PA-28-180 Cherokee F	28-7105090	N3986R
D-EHJG(2)	SOCATA TB-9 Tampico	751	
D-EHJH	SOCATA TB-9 Tampico	756	
D-EHJI	SOCATA TB-9 Tampico	757	
D-EHJJ	SOCATA TB-10 Tobago	768	
D-EHJK	Piaggio FWP.149D	031	90+21
			AC+421
D-EHJL	Piaggio FWP.149D	045	90+31
			AC+441
			AS+441
			GA+394
			D-EGEW
			GA+394
D-EHJM	Mooney M.20J Model 201	24-0190	N201RM
D-EHJN	Piper PA-28-235 Cherokee Pathfinder	28-7410011	N56575
D-EHJO	SOCATA TB-10 Tobago	767	
D-EHJP(2)	Robin DR.400/180 Régent	2181	
D-EHJS	SAN Jodel DR.1050 Ambassadeur	358	
D-EHJT	SOCATA MS.880B Rallye Club	1178	F-BPGD
D-EHJV	Wassmer WA.51A Pacific	74	
D-EHKA	SAN Jodel DR.1050 Ambassadeur	476	
D-EHKB	Robin R.1180TD Aiglon	262	
D-EHKC(2)	Piper PA-28R-201T Turbo Cherokee Arrow III		
		28R-7703408	N47607
D-EHKD	Cessna 182K Skylane	18258418	PH-WIT
			D-EGGO
			N2818R
D-EHKE(2)	Robin DR.400/180 Régent	2285	
D-EHKF(2)	Heigl / Denney Kitfox III	908	
D-EHKG	Piper PA-28R-200 Cherokee Arrow II	28R-7235267	N1353T
D-EHKH	Piper PA-28R-200 Cherokee Arrow	28R-35119	D-EHGM
			N9407N
D-EHKK(3)	Reims/Cessna FR172K Hawk XP	FR17200630	PH-RAS
			(PH-RAF)
D-EHKL	Robin DR.400/180R Remorqueur	1209	
D-EHKM	Piper PA-32R-300 Lance	32R-7780071	N7648F
D-EHKN(2)	Cessna U206GStationair II	U20603690	OE-DKN
			N7585N
D-EHKO(2)	Klemm Kl.35D	1854	D-EBIB
			SE-BHR
			Fv5020
D-EHKP	Piper PA-28-151 Cherokee Warrior	28-7715088	N9508N
D-EHKR	CEA DR.340 Major	425	F-BRVF
D-EHKS	Piper PA-32-300 Cherokee Six E	32-7240038	N8691N
D-EHKT	Mooney M.20J Model 201	24-1550	N5808Y
D-EHKU(2)	Beech F33A Bonanza	CE-1474	OY-GEE
D-EHKY	Bölkow BO.207	272	
D-EHLA	Bölkow BO.207	273	
D-EHLB	Cessna 182L Skylane	18258691	N3391R
D-EHLC	Cessna 182L Skylane	18258771	N3471R
D-EHLD(3)	Piper PA-28-161 Cadet	2841050	N9631N
			N9162Z
D-EHLE(4)	Piper PA-28-161 Cadet	2841081	N91663
D-EHLF	Cessna F172H	F172-0515	
D-EHLG(3)	Cessna 150L	15073550	N16217
D-EHLH	Cessna 182K Skylane	18258475	N2875R
D-EHLI (2)	Piper PA-28R-200 Cherokee Arrow II	28R-7435260	N43310
D-EHLJ	Piper PA-18 Super Cub 95	18-3440	QZ+020
			AC+531
			AS+531
			54-740
D-EHLL	Reims FR172E Rocket	FR17200023	
D-EHLM(2)	Diamond DA 20-A1 Katana	10229	
D-EHLN	Morane-Saulnier MS.885 Super Rallye	236	F-BKUE
D-EHLO(3)	Diamond DA 20-A1 Katana	10233	
D-EHLP	Darter Commander 100	10A-085	N5554M
D-EHLR	Robin DR.400/180R Remorqueur	1162	
D-EHLS	Piper PA-28R-200 Cherokee Arrow II	28R-7235052	N4451T
D-EHLT	Cessna 172N	17270921	N739YV
D-EHLU	Bölkow BO.207	277	
D-EHLY(2)	Piper PA-28-181 Cherokee Archer II	28-7790224	N9557N
D-EHMA(2)	Dornier Do.27A-4	388	56+80
			QW+110
			QW+701
			QM+614
			PL+422
D-EHMB(2)	Reims/Cessna F172P	F17202237	LN-AFD
			OY-BHD
			(G-BLZO)
D-EHMC	Cessna F150J	F150-0529	
D-EHME(2)	Robin DR.400/140 Major	879	
D-EHMH	Piper PA-28-180 Cherokee F	28-7105180	N5143S
D-EHMI	Piper PA-18-150 Super Cub	18-6242	N8584D
D-EHMK	Piper PA-28-160 Cherokee	28-560	D-EMMJ
			N11C
D-EHMM(2)	Great Lakes 2T-1A-2	0762	N3767F
D-EHMN	Piper PA-28RT-201T Turbo Arrow IV	28R-7931158	N2128Z
D-EHMO(2)	Mönke Hummel	1623/002	

D-EHMQ	Cessna 172N (Permit 11.01)	17273091	N4863F
	(Thielert TAE-125 diesel engine fitted 12.01)		
D-EHMS(3)	Zlin Z.143L	0023	
D-EHMU	Beech 35-33 Debonair	CD-82	N662V
D-EHMV	Piper PA-28-151 Cherokee Warrior	28-7415190	N9512N
D-EHMW(2)	Mooney M.20J Model 201	24-1394	
D-EHMZ	SAN Jodel DR.1050 Ambassadeur	485	
D-EHNA	Piper PA-22-108 Colt	22-9112	SE-CZX
D-EHNB	Piper PA-28-140 Cherokee	28-22717	N4341J
D-EHND	Reims/Cessna F152	F15201576	
D-EHNE	Cessna 150D	15060367	N4367U
D-EHNF	Reims/Cessna F152	F15201584	
D-EHNG	Reims/Cessna F152	F15201585	
D-EHNJ	Mooney M.20E Super 21	1151	OY-DDR
			N3475X
D-EHNL(2)	Christen A-1 Husky	1178	
D-EHNM	SOCATA Rallye 235E-D Gabier	13324	LN-BIE
D-EHNN(2)	Reims/Cessna F152	F15201602	D-EGLH
D-EHNQ	SOCATA MS.893E Rallye 180GT Gaillard	12524	F-BVNQ
D-EHNS	SOCATA TB-21 Trinidad TC	554	
D-EHNW	Cessna T210L Turbo Centurion	21060771	N1750X
D-EHOA	Rockwell Commander 114A	14537	
D-EHOB(2)	Piper PA-28-180 Cherokee C	28-2941	N8931J
D-EHOD(3)	Beech V35B Bonanza	D-10149	
D-EHOF(4)	Reims/Cessna F172P	F17202250	
D-EHOG(2)	Commander Aircraft 114B	14592	N60132
D-EHOH(3)	HOACDV-20 Katana	20044	N44DV
			C-FSIQ
D-EHOI	Cessna 152	15279589	N757AQ
D-EHOJ(3)	Diamond DA 40DStar	D4.056	
D-EHOK(2)	Piper PA-28-180 Cherokee C	28-2997	N8974J
D-EHOL(3)	Reims/Cessna F172M	F17201328	PH-JDB
			D-EDZJ
D-EHOM(2)	Robin DR.400/180R Remorqueur	1204	
D-EHON(2)	Robin DR.400/180R Remorqueur	1205	
D-EHOP(2)	Bölkow BO.207	206	
D-EHOR(2)	Piper PA-28-180 Cherokee C	28-2965	N8947J
D-EHOS	Beech F33A Bonanza	CE-847	
D-EHOT	Cessna 172	28683	N6083A
D-EHOU	SOCATA MS.880B Rallye Club	1852	F-BSMY
D-EHOW(2)	Rockwell Commander 114A	14536	
D-EHOZ(2)	Reims/Cessna F152	F15201636	
D-EHPA(2)	Piper PA-46-350P Malibu	4622057	N9167H
D-EHPB	Piper PA-28RT-201T Turbo Arrow IV	28R-8131001	N8268T
D-EHPC	Reims/Cessna F182Q Skylane	F18200067	N70846
D-EHPD	Piper PA-28-180 Cherokee G	28-7205318	N11C
D-EHPE	S.A.I. KZ-III	69	OY-DSY
D-EHPF	Cessna 150M	15076751	N45140
D-EHPG	Cessna T210L Turbo Centurion II	21061020	N2053S
D-EHPH	Bellanca 7GCBC Citabria	734-74	OE-AOI
D-EHPI (2)	Piper PA-28-140 Cherokee B	28-25752	N8887N
D-EHPK	Mooney M.20J Model 201	24-0137	HB-DWK
D-EHPL(2)	Robin HR.100/210D Safari	194	
D-EHPM	Haubs/ Polliwagen (Res. for restoration .02)	001	
D-EHPN	Cessna 172N	17272748	N6362D
D-EHPO	Cessna 172C	17249362	N1662Y
D-EHPP(2)	Timmermann/ Christen Eagle II	229	
D-EHPR	Piper PA-32R-301T Turbo Saratoga SP	32R-8129073	N959CJ
			N326SP
			N4446M
			XB-CTR
			N8393T
D-EHPS	Piper PA-28-180 Cherokee Challenger	28-7305424	N55609
D-EHPW(4)	Diamond DA 20-C1 Katana	C0122	N970CT
D-EHPY(2)	Reims/Cessna F172N	F17201799	
D-EHPZ	Piper PA-32R-301 Saratoga SP	32R-8013078	N81751
			N9535N
D-EHQI	SIAT 223 V-3 Flamingo	003	
D-EHQT(2)	Reims/Cessna FR182 Skylane RG	FR18200011	HB-CHH
			OE-DNG
D-EHRB(3)	Piper PA-46-350P Malibu Mirage	4622043	OY-JEJ
			N9175P
D-EHRC	Reims/Cessna F177RG Cardinal RG	F177RG0135	
D-EHRD(2)	SOCATA TB-21 Trinidad TC	698	
D-EHRE	Piper PA-22-160 Tri-Pacer	22-7011	N3056Z
D-EHRF(2)	Cessna 172N	17272487	N5272D
D-EHRG	Doppelraab RE2 (Stored)	516	D-1824
			D-KOBA
			D-1824
D-EHRH(2)	Hoffmann/ Aero Designs Pulsar XP	333/1805	
D-EHRI	Cessna 172A	47693	N9893T
D-EHRK	SIAI-Marchetti SF.260	2-51	
D-EHRL(2)	Kotschi/ Pitts S-1S Special	AB-K-024 (501)	
D-EHRM	Mooney M.20F Executive	700044	N9476V
D-EHRN(2)	Cessna 210L Centurion	21060326	(F-BVVT)
			N93264
D-EHRO(2)	Piper PA-28-181 Cherokee Archer II	28-7790546	N38378
D-EHRP	SOCATA MS.893A Rallye Commodore 180	11778	F-BSXZ
D-EHRS(2)	Reims/Cessna FR172K Hawk XP	FR17200622	N70788
D-EHRT	Reims FR172H Rocket	FR17200270	(D-ECJX)
D-EHRU	Cessna 175 Skylark	55620	N7320M
D-EHRV	Cessna 172RG Cutlass RG	172RG1048	N98238
D-EHRW	Piper PA-28-181 Archer II	28-8590060	N6917C
D-EHSA	Cessna 182F Skylane	18254655	N3255U
D-EHSC	Cessna 140	14442	N2211V
D-EHSE(3)	Robin DR.400/180 Régent	2579	
D-EHSF(2)	Wassmer WA.40 Super IV	25	F-BKAY
D-EHSG(2)	Piper PA-28R-200 Cherokee Arrow II	28R-7535346	N1595X

D-EHSH	SOCATA MS.893A Rallye Commodore 180	10811	
D-EHSI (2)	Piper PA-28R-200 Cherokee Arrow II	28R-7235092	N4564T
D-EHSJ	Cessna F150H	F150-0267	
D-EHSL	SOCATA MS.880B Rallye Club	1207	
D-EHSM	Maule M-4-210C Rocket	1045C	
D-EHSN	SOCATA MS.880B Rallye Club	1256	
D-EHSO(2)	Piper PA-28-140 Cherokee Cruiser	28-7625189	N9562N
D-EHSP	SOCATA MS.893A Rallye Commodore 180	10915	
D-EHSQ	SOCATA MS.893A Rallye Commodore 180	10828	
D-EHSR	SOCATA MS.893A Rallye Commodore 180	10823	
D-EHSS(2)	Reims/Cessna F172H (Reservation)	F17200702	D-ECEZ(2)
D-EHST(2)	Cessna 210L Centurion	21061066	N2100S
D-EHSW	SOCATA MS.880B Rallye Club	1240	
D-EHSX	SOCATA MS.893A Rallye Commodore 180	10829	
D-EHSY	Cessna F172E	F172-0078	
D-EHSZ	Cessna 182P Skylane	18263106	PH-IFL
			N7322N
D-EHTB	CEA DR.360 Major	517	
D-EHTC	Robin R.2100A Club	139	
D-EHTE	Piper PA-28-160 Cherokee	28-617	N5526W
D-EHTG	Aquila A310	102	
D-EHTL(2)	Langer/ Rutan Cozy BL	001	
D-EHTM(2)	Cessna U206G Stationair 6	U20605848	D-ELPZ(2)
			OE-KDA
			C-GIIW
			(N6265X)
D-EHTN(2)	Cessna 172N	17272699	N6293D
D-EHTP	Robin DR.400/180R Remorqueur	1342	
D-EHTS(2)	Robin DR.400/180R Remorqueur	1631	
D-EHTU	Piper J-3C-65 Cub	12602	OE-ADV
			Czech.AF
			44-80306
D-EHTW(4)	Zlin Z.526A Akrobat	1055	HA-SAF
			N1189X
			HA-SAF
D-EHUA	Cessna 182P Skylane	18264046	N9986E
	(Reims-assembled with "c/n" 0031)		
D-EHUB(2)	Commander Aircraft 114B	14556	N6007S
D-EHUC	Hainz/ Aero-Jodel D.11A Club	V-2	
D-EHUD(2)	Reims/Cessna FR172K Hawk XP	FR17200642	N1019Z
D-EHUE(2)	Cessna 152	15282964	N45966
D-EHUF(2)	Cessna 175A Skylark	56285	(D-EHUQ)
			N6785E
D-EHUG(4)	Hirsch/ Aero Designs Pulsar XP	1840	
D-EHUH(3)	SOCATA MS.892A Rallye Commodore 150	11426	SE-ERX
D-EHUI	Cessna 182P	18264041	N9981E
	(Reims-assembled with "c/n" 0030)		
D-EHUL(3)	Piper PA-28-181 Archer II	28-8290007	N84363
D-EHUM(4)	Reims/Cessna F152	F15201502	
D-EHUN(2)	Auster J/1 Autocrat	2119	OY-DPE
D-EHUP(2)	Reims/Cessna F152	F15201645	
D-EHUQ(2)	Bölkow BO.207	207	
D-EHUR(2)	Robin DR.300/108 2+2	529	
D-EHUS(2)	Reims FR172F Rocket	FR17200138	F-WLIT
D-EHUT(2)	Piper PA-28-181 Archer III	2890226	N9253X
D-EHUU	Robin DR.400/160 Chevalier	705	
D-EHUV(2)	Robin DR.400/180 Régent	1596	
D-EHUW(3)	Staub/ Binder CP.301S Smaragd	AB.703	
D-EHUX(3)	SOCATA TB-20 Trinidad	453	
D-EHUY	Piper PA-28-140 Cherokee Cruiser	28-7725073	N9527N
D-EHUZ(2)	Reims/Cessna F172N	F17201881	"D-EOSJ"
D-EHVA	Piper PA-22-108 Colt	22-9622	N10F
D-EHVC	Beech V35B Bonanza	D-10241	
D-EHVD(2)	SIAT 223K-1 Flamingo	20	HB-EVD
			D-ENBR(1)
D-EHVG	Robin DR.400/180R Remorqueur	1633	
D-EHVH	Piaggio P.149D	345	92+27
			AC+451
			AS+451
D-EHVI	Piper PA-22-108 Colt	22-9510	
D-EHVL	Cessna 172C	17249517	N2017Y
D-EHVM(2)	Beech B36TC Bonanza	EA-315	N724T
			N6511X
D-EHVO(2)	Piaggio FWP.149D	081	90+63
			JA+391
			AS+490
D-EHVR	Piaggio FWP.149D	054	90+40
			SC+331
			AS+481
D-EHVS	Reims/Cessna F172N	F17201693	
D-EHVT	Reims/Cessna F172N	F17201706	
D-EHVY	Mooney M.20D Master	165	N6739U
D-EHWA	Cessna 182G Skylane	18255467	N2367R
D-EHWB(2)	Beech C23 Sundowner 180	M-2233	
D-EHWC(2)	Wolfrum/ Stoddard-Hamilton Glasair IIRG	1039	
D-EHWD	Beech F33A Bonanza	CE-440	
D-EHWE(3)	Ehringhaus/ Denney Kitfox II	472	
D-EHWF	Robin DR.400RP Remo 212	1800	
D-EHWG(2)	Robin DR.400/180S Régent	2026	
D-EHWH(2)	Zlin Z.50LS	0040/03	OK-PRH
D-EHWI (2)	Mooney M.20K Model 231	25-0221	N231FL
D-EHWJ	Beech C23 Sundowner 180	M-1479	
D-EHWK	Cessna 182G Skylane	18255475	N2375R
D-EHWL(3)	Dallach D4 Fascination VLA (Permit 9.04)	1002	
D-EHWM	Beech B24R Sierra 200	MC-175	
D-EHWN(3)	Piper PA-28-181 Archer II	28-8590008	N144AV
D-EHWP(2)	Cessna 140	13721	N4250N
			NC4250N

D-EHWR	Reims/Cessna FR182 Skylane RG	FR18200020	(G-BGAR)
D-EHWS(2)	Robin DR.400/180 Régent	1985	
D-EHWT	Gardan GY-80 Horizon 180	223	
D-EHWY	Beech A23 Musketeer Custom	M-678	
D-EHWZ(2)	Reims/Cessna FR182 Skylane RG	FR18200022	(PH-ADM)
			PH-AXW
D-EHXG	Rockwell Commander 112	53	N1053J
D-EHXI	Rockwell Commander 112	119	N1175J
			(N1119J)
D-EHXK	Rockwell Commander 112	121	N1005J
			(N1121J)
D-EHXL	Rockwell Commander 112A	129	N1176J
			(N1129J)
D-EHXM	Rockwell Commander 112A	191	N1149J
			(N1191J)
D-EHXN	Rockwell Commander 112A	209	N1209J
D-EHXO	Rockwell Commander 112A	214	N1214J
D-EHXR	Rockwell Commander 112A	324	N1324J
D-EHXS	Rockwell Commander 112A	357	N1357J
D-EHXU	Rockwell Commander 112A	467	N1467J
D-EHXW	Rockwell Commander 112A	475	(N1475J)
D-EHXX	Rockwell Commander 112A	279	N1279J
D-EHXY	Rockwell Commander 112A	489	(N1489J)
D-EHXZ	Bölkow BO.207	289	HB-UXZ
			(D-ENWI)
D-EHYD	Aeronca 7AC Champion	3957	N85224
D-EHYF	Erco Ercoupe 415E de luxe	4907	N94794
D-EHYG	Piper J-4A Cub Coupé	4-880	N26758
			NC26758
D-EHYH	Ranz/ Jodel D.9 Bébé	AB.14 (Liz.225)	
D-EHYL(3)	Diamond DA 40D Star	D4.057	
D-EHYM	Piper J-3C-85 Cub	10776	D-EDIF
			PH-NFI
			PH-NAE
			43-29485
D-EHZK	Beech C24R Sierra 200	MC-648	N60181
D-EHZW	Piper PA-28RT-201T Turbo Arrow IV	28R-8231043	N81852
D-EIAA	Reims/Cessna F152	F15201537	
D-EIAB(2)	Aerotek Pitts S-2A	2240	N31496
D-EIAE	CEA DR.220 2+2	42	F-BOKM
D-EIAG(3)	Piper PA-28-181 Cherokee Archer II	28-7890545	D-EDYP(2)
			N39625
D-EIAH(2)	Piper PA-46-310P Malibu	46-8508060	N4391V
D-EIAI	Piper PA-28-181 Archer II	28-8090365	N8240T
D-EIAJ	Neico Lancair 360 (Permit .02)	1894	
D-EIAK(2)	Reims/Cessna FA152 Aerobat	FA1520424	
D-EIAL	Piper PA-28-161 Warrior II	28-8116076	N8291D
D-EIAM	Piper PA-28-180 Cherokee F	28-7105141	N1687T
D-EIAN	Grob G.115A	8062	
D-EIAO	SOCATA MS.893E Rallye 180GT Gaillard	12310	F-BUVB
D-EIAP	SAN Jodel DR.1050 Ambassadeur	356	
D-EIAR	CEA DR.250/160 Capitaine	98	
D-EIAS	Cessna TU206F Turbo Stationair	U20603187	N8326Q
D-EIAT	Piper PA-28R-200 Cherokee Arrow B	28R-7135210	N1975T
D-EIAV	Robin DR.400/180R Remorqueur	1658	
D-EIAW(3)	Beech V35B Bonanza	D-10289	N66648
D-EIAX	Cessna TR182 Turbo Skylane RG	R18201462	N4923S
D-EIAY	Grob G.115A	8050	
D-EIAZ	Rockwell Commander 112A	314	N1314J
D EIBA	Piper PA-28-181 Cherokee Archer II	28-7690150	N9518N
D-EIBB	SOCATA MS.892A Rallye Commodore 150	10801	F-BPHQ
D-EIBD	Rockwell Commander 114B	14400	
D-EIBE	Dornier Do.27A-1	310	56+34
			GD+154
			LB+154
			CC+ . . .
			CB+002
D-EIBF	Reims/Cessna F152	F15201566	
D-EIBG	Reims/Cessna F152	F15201574	
D-EIBI	Reims/Cessna F182Q Skylane	F18200062	
D-EIBJ	Diamond DA 20-A1 Katana	10270	
D-EIBK	Piper PA-28-161 Warrior II	28-8116197	N83658
D-EIBL	Piper PA-18A-150 Super Cub	18-8009024	N63928
D-EIBO(2)	Cessna P210N Pressurized Centurion II	P21000714	N6100W
D-EIBR	Piper PA-38-112 Tomahawk	38-81A0117	N23137
D-EIBW	Piper PA-28RT-201T Turbo Arrow IV	28R-8131162	N8406V
D-EIBY	Robin HR.100/200B	126	F-BTBY
D-EICA	Mooney M.20F Executive	700035	N9446V
D-EICB	Cessna 172RG Cutlass RG	172RG0543	N5479V
D-EICC	Robin DR.300/180R Remorqueur	727	
D-EICD	Piaggio FWP.149D	182	91+60
			BF+419
			AS+021
			KB+144
D-EICE	Piper PA-28R-201T Turbo Arrow III	28R-7803330	N36620
D-EICF	Cherdron/ Christen Eagle II	0162	
D-EICG	Piper PA-28R-200 Cherokee Arrow II	28R-7535128	N33162
D-EICH(4)	Beech F33A Bonanza	CE-1162	N3144W
D-EICI (2)	Aviat A-1 Husky	1296	
D-EICK	Piper PA-28R-200 Cherokee Arrow	28R-35601	N3046R
D-EICN(2)	Piper PA-28R-201T Turbo Arrow IV	28R-8431025	N4356X
D-EICO(4)	Piper PA-46-500TP Malibu Meridian	4697125	N5361C
D-EICR	Piper PA-28-181 Archer II	28-8490075	N4359T
			(D-EFZN)
D-EICS	Cessna U206F Stationair II	U20603118	N8257Q
D-EICT	Piper PA-28RT-201T Turbo Arrow IV	28R-8231055	N8216J
D-EICY	Reims/Cessna F177RG Cardinal RG	F177RG0167	(D-EIMP)

D-EIDA	Fuji FA-200-160 Aero Subaru	164	
D-EIDC	Fuji FA-200-180 Aero Subaru	223	
D-EIDE	Fuji FA-200-180 Aero Subaru	214	
D-EIDG	Fuji FA-200-180AO Aero Subaru	270	
D-EIDH(2)	Fuji FA-200-180 Aero Subaru	279	
D-EIDI (2)	Cessna 182F Skylane	18254782	D-ENMI
			N3382U
D-EIDJ	Fuji FA-200-160 Aero Subaru	267	
D-EIDK	Fuji FA-200-160 Aero Subaru	203	
D-EIDL	Fuji FA-200-180 Aero Subaru	206	
D-EIDM	Fuji FA-200-160 Aero Subaru	221	
D-EIDO	Fuji FA-200-180AO Aero Subaru	248	
D-EIDP(2)	Beech F33A Bonanza	CE-1482	
D-EIDR	Fuji FA-200-160 Aero Subaru	180	
D-EIDS	Fuji FA-200-180 Aero Subaru	273	
D-EIDU	Fuji FA-200-180AO Aero Subaru	274	
D-EIDV	Fuji FA-200-160 Aero Subaru	162	N73542
D-EIDW	Fuji FA-200-180 Aero Subaru	208	
D-EIDX	Fuji FA-200-180AO Aero Subaru	264	
D-EIDY	Fuji FA-200-180AO Aero Subaru	275	
D-EIDZ	Fuji FA-200-180AO Aero Subaru	276	
D-EIEA	Reims/Cessna F152	F15201598	
D-EIEB	Reims/Cessna F152	F15201613	
D-EIED	Reims/Cessna F172N	F17201852	
D-EIEE	Reims/Cessna F172N Skyhawk II	F17201875	
D-EIEH	Robin DR.400/180R Remorqueur	1405	
D-EIEI (2)	Piper PA-18 Super Cub 95	18-1374	(D-EKQJ)
	(See D-EKRG)		ALAT
			51-15374
D-EIEK	Piper PA-28-180 Cherokee C	28-2821	N8852J
D-EIEL	Zlin Z.526 Trenér Master	1011	D-EIFL
			OK-VRF
D-EIEM	SOCATA TB-20 Trinidad	311	
D-EIEN	SOCATA TB-9 Tampico	313	
D-EIEO	SOCATA TB-10 Tobago	314	
D-EIEP(2)	Grob G.115A	8031	
D-EIER(2)	Robin DR.400/180R Remorqueur	1198	
D-EIET	Robin DR.400/180R Remo 180	2114	
D-EIEW	Extra Pitts S-1E Special	8-9043	
D-EIFA(2)	Piper PA-46-350P Malibu Mirage	4622099	OY-FFA
			SE-KMC
D-EIFB(2)	SOCATA TB-21 Trinidad TC	717	
D-EIFC	Reims/Cessna FR182 Skylane RG	FR18200002	
D-EIFE	Piaggio FWP.149D	129	91+08
			BF+417
			AS+016
			KB+106
D-EIFG	Piper PA-28R-200 Cherokee Arrow II	28R-7635161	N8442C
D-EIFH	Piper PA-38-112 Tomahawk	38-78A0414	N9679N
D-EIFI (2)	Cessna 210E Centurion	21058615	OE-DEI
			N4915U
D-EIFJ	Mooney M.20K Model 231	25-0118	N231JJ
D-EIFK	Fuji FA-200-180 Aero Subaru	185	
D-EIFL(4)	Bölkow BO.209 Monsun 160FV	151	HB-UEC
			D-EBJK(1)
D-EIFM	Reims/Cessna F152 II	F15201709	
D-EIFN	Piper PA-28-181 Archer III	2890229	N9255F
D-EIFO	Piper PA-28-181 Cherokee Archer II	28-7890548	N39645
D-EIFP(2)	Reims/Cessna F152	F15201961	SE-IPF
D-EIFS	Andres/ Binder CP.301S Passat	AB.01	
D-EIFT	Robin DR.400/180R Remorqueur	1014	
D-EIFV	Cessna 172R	17280898	N2150K
D-EIFW(2)	Heuer FW190 (Half-scale)	333AB	
D-EIGA	Reims/Cessna F172N	F17201846	(D-ELFS)
D-EIGB	Mooney M.20E Chapparral	700031	N30PK
			D-EIGB
			N9443V
D-EIGC	Piper PA-28-236 Dakota	2811033	N92139
D-EIGD	Gardan GY-80-160D Horizon	247	
D-EIGE	Reims/Cessna F172N	F17201808	
D-EIGF	Gardan GY-80 Horizon 160D	248	
D-EIGH(2)	Piper PA-28-181 Archer II	2890127	N9185K
D-EIGI	Piper PA-28-181 Archer II	28-8090279	
D-EIGK	Mudry CAP.10B	74	F-BXHM
D-EIGL	Piper PA-28-181 Archer II	28-8690009	N2608Y
D-EIGO(2)	Beech F33A Bonanza	CE-1720	OE-KSB
D-EIGP	Piper PA-28-180 Cherokee Challenger	28-7305460	N55647
D-EIGW	Piper PA-28-181 Archer III	2843375	OY-LAD
			N9526N
D-EIGZ	SOCATA TB-21 Trinidad TC	1478	
D-EIHA	Piper PA-28-161 Warrior II	28-7916296	N9609N
D-EIHD	Stampe & Renard/ Stampe SV.4B	1169	G-AZUL
			V-27
D-EIHG(2)	Reims/Cessna FA150K Aerobat	FA1500064	D-ECAN(2)
D-EIHH(3)	Mudry CAP.231	07	F-GSHH
D-EIHI	Reims/Cessna F152	F15201591	
D-EIHK(2)	Piper PA-28-161 Warrior II	2816002	N9089K
D-EIHL(2)	Piper PA-28-140 Cherokee F	28-7325400	D-EHWW(1)
			N11C
D-EIHM	Piper PA-28-181 Archer II	28-8290052	N8358F
D-EIHN	SOCATA MS.883 Rallye 115	1645	F-BTHN
D-EIHO	Piper PA-38-112 Tomahawk	38-79A0256	(SX-ALW)
			D-EIHO
			N9710N
D-EIHP	CessnaTR.182 Turbo Skylane RG	R18201982	N6326T
D-EIHQ	HOAC DV-20 Katana	20084	
D-EIHS	SOCATA MS.880B Rallye Club	2044	F-BTPO

D-EIHW	Cessna TU206G Turbo Stationair 6-II	U20606114	(N5443Z)
D-EIHY	Piper PA-28RT-201 Arrow IV	28R-8018068	
D-EIIA(3)	Robin R.3000/160	164	
D-EIIB	Piper PA-28RT-201T Turbo Arrow IV	28R-7931275	N2957D
D-EIIC(3)	Klemm Kl.35D (Permit)	3171	(D-EHDY(3))
			D-EBBW
			OE-ABW
D-EIID	Piper PA-28-181 Archer II	28-8090361	N8237Z
D-EIIE	Piper PA-28-235 Cherokee	28-10224	N8691W
D-EIIF(3)	Christen Pitts S-2A	5139	N15F
D-EIIG	Reims/Cessna F182Q Skylane	F18200069	
D-EIIH(3)	Reims/Cessna F172M	F17201248	D-EGYR(2)
D-EIII (3)	Bücker Bü.133D Jungmeister	1069	SpAF:E1- . . .
D-EIIJ	Mooney M.20K Model 231	25-0830	N5764N
D-EIIK	Robin HR.200/100 Club	31	
D-EIIL	Robin HR.200/100 Club	34	
D-EIIM	Robin DR.400/180R Remorqueur	956	
D-EIIN	Robin DR.400/180 Régent	946	
D-EIIO(2)	Robin DR.400/180 Régent	2441	
D-EIIP	Reims/Cessna F182Q Skylane	F18200091	
D-EIIR(3)	Aeronca 11BC Chief	11AC-1048	N9411E
			NC9411E
D-EIIS(2)	Bücker Bü.133C Jungmeister	1013	SpAF:ES1-7
			35-7
D-EIIT(2)	Piper PA-28-161 Warrior II	2816011	N9118X
D-EIIX	Aviat Pitts S-2A	5210	
D-EIIY	Mooney M.20J Model 201	24-1152	N1139L
D-EIJA	SOCATA MS.880B Rallye Club	2516	F-BVNN
D-EIJB	Robin DR.400/180 Régent	2232	
D-EIJF	Coopavia Piel CP.301A Emeraude	206	F-BIJF
D-EIJH	Piper PA-28-181 Archer II	28-7990552	N2914N
D-EIJI	Robin DR.400/180 Régent	1029	
D-EIJJ	Cessna 152	15285216	N6273Q
D-EIJK(2)	Kurz Rieseler Ma.III	N01/1848	
D-EIJL	CASA I-131E Jungmann	2088	E3B-392
D-EIJN	Piper PA-28-181 Archer II	28-8190019	N8257H
D-EIKA(2)	Mooney M.20J Model 201	24-1645	
D-EIKB	Morane-Saulnier MS.885 Super Rallye	51	F-BKEX
D-EIKC(2)	Cessna P210N Pressurized Centurion II	P21000554	N731XF
D-EIKD	Reims/Cessna F172P	F17202107	
D-EIKE(2)	Mooney M.20J Model 205	24-3209	
D-EIKF	Reims/Cessna FR172K Hawk XP	FR17200675	
D-EIKH(2)	Grob G.115A	8077	
D-EIKI	SOCATA MS.893E Rallye 180GT Gaillard	12182	F-BUCR
D-EIKL	CEA DR.220 2+2	22	F-BOCP
D-EIKM	Beech V35B Bonanza	D-9919	N4KM
D-EIKN(2)	Cessna 172S	172S8126	N866SP
D-EIKO	Robin DR.400/180R Remorqueur	1130	(F-GABH)
D-EIKP(2)	Cessna 172RG Cutlass RG	172RG0645	N6382V
D-EIKR(2)	Robin DR.400/180 Régent	1839	F-ODSI
D-EIKS(2)	Reims/Cessna F182Q Skylane	F18200075	
D-EIKT	Reims/Cessna F172N	F17202012	
D-EIKV(2)	Reims/Cessna FR172K Hawk XP	FR17200667	
D-EIKW(2)	Piper PA-28-236 Dakota	28-8211013	G-BOJE
			N84600
D-EIKY	Bücker Bü.133D-1 Jungmeister	2005	OE-AKE
D-EILA(2)	Cessna T210L Turbo Centurion	21061046	OE-DFT
			D-ECCC
			N2079S
D-EILB	PZL-104 Wilga 35A	62177	(D-EWBO)
			DDR-WBO
			DM-WBO
D-EILD(2)	Rockwell Commander 112A (Permit .05)	183	EC-CMQ
			N1066J
D-EILE(3)	Commander Aircraft 114B	14549	D-EJKE(2)
			LX-BUG
			D-ERPA(1)
			N172A
D-EILF(2)	Piper PA-28-160 Cherokee	28-368	C-GBBE
			SLN- . .
			D-EJPI (1)
			N11C
D-EILG	Piper PA-28-181 Archer II	28-7990495	N2852N
D-EILH(2)	Robin DR.400/RP Remorqueur	1837	OE-KLH
			D-ELSR
D-EILI (2)	Cessna 182R Skylane	18268449	N9810E
D-EILJ	SOCATA TB-9 Tampico	920	
D-EILK	Piper PA-28-181 Archer III	2843144	N4123Q
D-EILM	SOCATA MS.887 Rallye 125	2178	F-BVLN
D-EILO(2)	Piper PA-28-181 Archer II	28-7990379	N2163Y
D-EILP	Reims/Cessna F152	F15201922	
D-EILQ	Reims/Cessna F152	F15201893	N90740
D-EILR	Reims/Cessna F172P	F17202165	
D-EILS	Piper PA-28RT-201 Arrow IV	28R-7918126	N28409
D-EILT(2)	Mooney M.20F Executive	22-1343	
D-EILU	Piper PA-38-112 Tomahawk	38-79A0673	N9659N
D-EILW(2)	Beech 77 Skipper	WA-95	
D-EILX	Cessna 172RG Cutlass RG	172RG0817	D-EOCD
			(N9417B)
D-EILY	Wassmer WA.52 Europa	49	
D-EIMB	Beech C24R Sierra 200	MC-603	
D-EIMC	Reims/Cessna F172N	F17201859	
D-EIMD	Reims/Cessna F172P	F17202054	
D-EIMF	Beech V35B Bonanza	D-9245	N9245Q
D-EIMG	Piper PA-28-181 Archer II	28-8090040	N4513L
D-EIMH	Reims/Cessna F172P	F17202147	
D-EIMI	Reims/Cessna F172N	F17201906	

D-EIMK	Krause/ Super Acro Sport	1	
D-EIML(2)	Reims/Cessna F172P	F17202252	
D-EIMM(2)	Cessna P210N Pressurized Centurion	P21000225	HB-CJT
			N9FV
			(N4588K)
D-EIMN	Reims/Cessna F172P Skyhawk II	F17202171	F-WZDT
			(D-EGLK)
D-EIMO	Cessna T210G Turbo-System Centurion	T210-0276	N6876R
D-EIMP(2)	Cessna 182R Skylane	18267947	PH-AXP
			N9434H
D-EIMR	Reims/Cessna F172P	F17202136	(D-EODZ)
D-EIMT	Reims/Cessna F152	F15201941	
D-EIMU	Bellanca 7ECA Citabria	956-73	
D-EIMV	Reims/Cessna F172P	F17202143	
D-EIMW	Reims/Cessna F150K	F15000531	PH-ALF
D-EIMY	Reims/Cessna F172N	F17201908	
D-EIMZ	Reims/Cessna F172P	F17202226	F-WZIB
D-EINB	Navion Rangemaster H	NAV-4-2543	(N2543T)
D-EINC(2)	Cessna 172R	17280001	N172KS
D-EINE(2)	CASA I-131E Jungmann	2202	E3B-582
D-EINF	Navion Rangemaster H	NAV-4-2546	(N2546T)
D-EING	Navion Rangemaster H	NAV-4-2547	(N2547T)
D-EINH(2)	Robin DR.300/108 2+2	530	
D-EINK(2)	Piper PA-28RT-201T Turbo Arrow IV	28R-8331034	N4301K
D-EINL	Navion Rangemaster H	NAV-4-2544	D-EINC
			(N2544T)
D-EINS(2)	Maule MXT-7-180 Starcraft	14111C	
D-EINU	Stark Turbulent D	132	HB-SVF
			D-EKEV
D-EINY	Wassmer WA.54 Atlantic	111	
D-EINZ	Piper PA-18-150 Super Cub	18-8310	N7443Z
D-EIOF	Hoffmann H-40	40001	
D-EIOI	Mooney M.20K Model 231	25-0315	SE-IEI
			N231MV
D-EIOO	CASA I-131E Jungmann	2215	D-EDNN(1)
			E3B-615
D-EIOR	Mooney M.20J Model 201	24-0622	N102CK
			N4106H
D-EIOS(2)	Reims/Cessna F152	F15201934	
D-EIOU(2)	Piper PA-28RT-201T Turbo Arrow IV	28R-7931270	N2510U
			N9597N
D-EIPA	Piper PA-28RT-201T Turbo Arrow IV	28R-7931242	N2874W
D-EIPC	Beech C23 Sundowner 180	M-1835	
D-EIPE	Reims/Cessna FR172K Hawk XP	FR17200613	
D-EIPF	Reims/Cessna F177RG Cardinal RG	F177RG0176	
D-EIPG	Mooney M.20E Chaparral	690017	N9089V
D-EIPH	Beech A23A Musketeer Custom	M-967	
D-EIPK	Mooney M.20F Executive	700036	N9451V
D-EIPL	Piaggio P.149D	279	OE-DKK
			91+93
			AC+430
			AS+430
D-EIPM	Reims/Cessna F152	F15201515	
D-EIPO	Reims/Cessna F152	F15201500	
D-EIPP	Christen A-1 Husky	1081	N9594P
D-EIPS(2)	Aerotek Pitts S-2A	2027	N27PS
D-EIPT	Reims/Cessna F172N	F17201721	
D-EIPU	Robin DR.400/180R Remorqueur	1622	
D-EIPV	SOCATA TB-20 Trinidad	443	
D-EIQC	Reims/Cessna F150L	F15001064	
D-EIQD	Reims/Cessna FRA150L Aerobat	FRA1500216	
D-EIQI	Reims/Cessna F150L	F15001067	
D-EIQK	Reims/Cessna F172M	F17201052	
D-EIQO	Reims FR172J Rocket	FR17200447	
D-EIQP	Reims FR172J Rocket	FR17200455	
D-EIQQ	Reims FR172J Rocket	FR17200462	
D-EIQS	Reims/Cessna F177RG Cardinal RG	F177RG0093	
D-EIQU	Reims/Cessna F172M	F17201081	
D-EIQV	Reims/Cessna F150L	F15001054	
D-EIRA	Piper PA-28-180 Cherokee Archer	28-7505174	N9623N
D-EIRB	Reims/Cessna FR182 Skylane RG	FR18200023	PH-AXX
D-EIRC(2)	American AG-5B Tiger	10006	N1190N
D-EIRD	Reims/Cessna F172N	F17201935	
D-EIRE	Beech V35B Bonanza	D-9201	
D-EIRF(4)	SOCATA TB-20 Trinidad	583	F-GLPG
			N102U
D-EIRH	Reims/Cessna F172N	F17202022	
D-EIRK(2)	SOCATA TB-20 Trinidad	386	D-EKTN
D-EIRL(2)	Robin DR.400/180 Régent	2191	
D-EIRM	Reims/Cessna F172N	F17201571	
D-EIRN	Reims/Cessna F172P	F17202038	
D-EIRS	Cessna 180K Skywagon	18053164	
D-EIRT(2)	Robin DR.400/180 Régent	2412	
D-EIRV(2)	Aerotek Pitts S-1S (Reservation .04)	1-0045	PH-PUP
			N3KZ
			N9TH
D-EIRW(2)	Piper PA-32-300 Cherokee Six	32-40074	HB-OMC
			N4052W
D-EIRX	Reims/Cessna F172P	F17202109	
D-EIRZ	Reims/Cessna F152	F15201844	
D-EISA	SAN Jodel D.140B Mousquetaire II	67	OE-DOP
D-EISC	Gyroflug SC-01B-160 Speed Canard	S-14	
D-EISD	Robin DR.400/180R Remorqueur	1903	
D-EISF	Robin DR.400/180R Remorqueur	1115	
D-EISG	Robin DR.400/180R Remorqueur	1116	
D-EISH	Robin DR.400/180R Remorqueur	1117	
D-EISI	Robin DR.400/180R Remorqueur	1129	

D-EISJ	SOCATA MS.893A Rallye Commodore 180 (Originally built as MS.894A Minerva 220)	11869	D-EOBJ
D-EISK(2)	Cessna 172R	17280165	
D-EISL	PiperPA-28-181 Archer II	28-8190116	PH-SDC N8312H
D-EISM	Cessna 182Q Skylane	18265651	N735SQ
D-EISO(2)	Piper PA-18-150 Super Cub	18-9000	I-CGAG N9700N
D-EISP	Reims/Cessna FR172K Hawk XP	FR17200633	
D-EISQ	Cessna TU206F Turbo Stationair	U20602990	N2715Q (D-ECBS(2)) N2715Q
D-EISR	Robin DR.400/180R Remorqueur	1650	
D-EISS	Piper PA-28R-200 Cherokee Arrow B	28R-7135079	N5077S
D-EIST	Piper PA-28-181 Archer II	28-8090041	N2317U
D-EISU	Piper PA-28-161 Warrior II	28-7916540	N2916Y
D-EISY	Piper PA-22-150 Tri-Pacer	22-3369	D-EFIT N10F
D-EITA(2)	Piper PA-28RT-201T Turbo Arrow IV	28R-8031086	N81837
D-EITC	Reims/Cessna F152	F15201819	
D-EITD	Reims/Cessna F152	F15201759	
D-EITE(2)	Reims/Cessna F172P	F17202245	
D-EITG	Reims/Cessna F172N	F17202002	
D-EITH(2)	Piper PA-28RT-201T Turbo Arrow IV	28R-7931038	N2222L
D-EITI (2)	Piper PA-28-181 Archer II	28-7990554	N2917X
D-EITK	Reims/Cessna F152	F15201896	
D-EITL	Piper PA-28R-200 Cherokee Arrow II	28R-7335018	N15085
D-EITM	Reims/Cessna FR172K Hawk XP	FR17200662	
D-EITN	Cessna 172E	17251442	D-EFGY N5542T
D-EITO	SOCATA MS.893E Rallye 180GT Gaillard	12128	F-BTVV
D-EITP(2)	Reims/Cessna F172P	F17202249	
D-EITR	Robin DR.400/180R Remorqueur	1651	
D-EITT(2)	Fuji FA-200-180 Aero Subaru	189	
D-EITY	Piper PA-28RT-201T Turbo Arrow IV	28R-8031063	N8156U
D-EIUA	SOCATA MS.893E Rallye 180GT Gaillard	12496	F-BVNL
D-EIUB	SOCATA MS.880B Rallye Club	2541	F-BVZE
D-EIUH	Piper PA-18 Super Cub 95	18-3125	D-EETU OL-L51 L-51 53-4725
D-EIUL	Piper PA-28R-201 Arrow III	28R-7837250	PH-SRV OO-HCO N31755
D-EIUW	Reims/Cessna FA152 Aerobat	0421	
D-EIVA	Piper PA-28RT-201T Turbo Arrow IV	28R-7931301	N8083N
D-EIVB	PZL-110 Koliber 150	03920049	
D-EIVC	Reims/Cessna F182Q Skylane	F18200162	
D-EIVD	PZL-110 Koliber 150	03920050	
D-EIVE	Dornier Do.27A-1	328	56+46 LC+161 JA+382
D-EIVF	PZL-110 Koliber 150	03930051	
D-EIVH	PZL-110 Koliber 150	03930053	
D-EIVI (3)	Cessna 172N	17271061	N1601E
D-EIVJ	PZL-110 Koliber 150	03940054	
D-EIVK	PZL-110 Koliber 150	03940055	
D-EIVL	SOCATA MS.894A Minerva 220	11881	F-BTHE
D-EIVM	Reims/Cessna F150M	F15001404	
D-EIVN	Reims/Cessna F150M	F15001392	
D-EIVO	Reims/Cessna F172M	F17201482	
D-EIVQ	Reims/Cessna F172M	F17201504	
D-EIVR(3)	PZL-110 Koliber 150	03900043	
D-EIVS	PZL-110 Koliber 150	03900044	
D-EIVT(2)	PZL-150 Koliber 150	04950079	
D-EIVU(2)	PZL-110 Koliber 150	03920046	
D-EIVV	PZL-110 Koliber 150	03920047	
D-EIWA	Reims/Cessna F150M	F15001173	
D-EIWB(2)	Piper PA-28-181 Archer II	2890119	N9179Z
D-EIWE(2)	Zlin Z.143L	0007	
D-EIWF	Beech K35 Bonanza	D-5969	HB-EGX
D-EIWG(2)	SOCATA TB-10 Tobago	148	D-EEEJ
D-EIWJ	Yakovlev Yak-50	80-1704	DDR-WQN
D-EIWK(2)	Piper PA-28-236 Dakota	28-8011100	N81879
D-EIWM(2)	Piper PA-46-350PMalibu	4636202	N41346
D-EIWN	Robin DR.400/200R Remo 200	2268	
D-EIWO	Piper PA-28R-180 Cherokee Arrow	28R-30424	N4562J
D-EIWP(2)	Robin DR.400/180RP Remo 212	1806	
D-EIWR	Robin R.2160D	177	
D-EIWW(2)	CASA I-131E Jungmann	2028	D-ENHD E3B-432
D-EIWZ	RFB Fantrainer 600 (Permit)	005	98+76 D-EIWZ
D-EIXB	Rockwell Commander 114	14102	N4709W
D-EIXE	Rockwell Commander 114B	14200	(N4870W)
D-EIXI	Rockwell Commander 114B	14277	(N4957W)
D-EIXK	Rockwell Commander 112TC	13030	N1841J
D-EIXL(2)	Reims/Cessna F172M	F17200998	OE-DTE
D-EIXR	Rockwell Commander 114B	14299	(N4979W)
D-EIXS	Rockwell Commander 114B	14248	
D-EIXT	Rockwell Commander 114B	14261	(N4939W)
D-EIXX	Aviat A-1 Husky	1295	
D-EIYA	Reims/Cessna F172N	F17201792	
D-EIYB	Reims/Cessna F152	F15201592	
D-EIYC	Reims/Cessna F172N Skyhawk II	F17201831	
D-EIYD	Reims/Cessna F152	F15201562	
D-EIYF	Reims/Cessna F152	F15201594	

D-EIYJ	Reims/Cessna F172N	F17201869	
D-EIYL(2)	Cessna 172RG Cutlass RG	172RG0886	N9567B
D-EIYN	Reims/Cessna F172N	F17201855	
D-EIYR	Reims/Cessna F172N	F17201838	
D-EIYS	Reims/Cessna F182Q Skylane	F18200123	
D-EIYT	Reims/Cessna F172N	F17201926	
D-EIYV	Reims/Cessna F152	F15201726	
D-EIYW	Reims/Cessna F172N	F17201943	
D-EIYY	Reims/Cessna F172N	F17201961	
D-EIZB	Reims/Cessna F172P	F17202079	
D-EIZC(2)	Reims/Cessna F172P	F17202154	
D-EIZD(2)	Beech F33A Bonanza	CE-1359	OY-GEY
D-EIZE	Beech F33A Bonanza	CE-774	
D-EIZF	Beech F33A Bonanza	CE-775	
D-EIZG	Beech F33A Bonanza	CE-779	
D-EIZH	Beech F33A Bonanza	CE-784	
D-EIZJ	Beech F33A Bonanza	CE-788	
D-EIZK	Beech F33A Bonanza	CE-789	
D-EIZL	Beech F33A Bonanza	CE-791	
D-EIZM	Reims/Cessna F182Q Skylane	F18200138	
D-EIZN	Reims/Cessna FR182 Skylane RG II	FR18200055	
D-EIZP(2)	Reims/Cessna F152	F15201811	
D-EIZQ(2)	Beech F33A Bonanza	CE-1093	
D-EIZR(2)	Beech F33A Bonanza	CE-1094	
D-EIZS	Reims/Cessna F172N	F17202011	
D-EIZT(2)	Beech F33A Bonanza	CE-1095	
D-EIZV	Cessna TR182 Turbo Skylane RG	R18201480	N4941S
D-EIZW	Reims/Cessna F152	F15201814	
D-EIZY	Cessna 172RG Cutlass RG	172RG0562	N5537V
D-EJAD(2)	Reims/Cessna F182Q Skylane	F18200163	
D-EJAE(3)	Wassmer WA.40 Super IV	30	D-EJAE(1)
D-EJAG(3)	Manhart/ Brditschka HB-207V RG Alpha	207024	
D-EJAH(2)	SOCATA TB-10 Tobago	600	
D-EJAI (2)	Piaggio FWP.149D	094	90+76 BF+407 AS+421
D-EJAK(2)	Piper PA-28-236 Dakota	28-7911242	N2909W
D-EJAL(2)	Cessna F150F	F150-0045/15063307	(N6707F)
D-EJAM(2)	Reims/Cessna F172M	F17201497	
D-EJAN(3)	SOCATA TB-10 Tobago	580	
D-EJAO	Piper J-3C-65 Cub	12162	G-AJAO OO-RAM ALAT 44-79866
D-EJAP	Cessna 172	28916	N6816A
D-EJAR(3)	Diamond DA 20-A1 Katana	10133	N563SS
D-EJAS(4)	Robin DR.400/180R Remorqueur	1266	
D-EJAT	Piper PA-22-150 Tri-Pacer	22-1067	N1269C
D-EJAY(2)	SOCATA TB-20 Trinidad	1611	
D-EJBA(2)	Robin DR.300/180R Remorqueur	589	
D-EJBB	Robin DR.300/180R Remorqueur	590	
D-EJBC	Robin DR.300/180R Remorqueur	594	
D-EJBD	CEA DR.253B Régent	187	
D-EJBF	CEA DR.360 Major	598	
D-EJBG	Robin DR.300/108 2+2	592	
D-EJBH	Robin DR.300/108 2+2	593	
D-EJBI	Bölkow BO.207 (Permit 6.04)	242	G-EJBI D-EJBI
D-EJBK	Cessna 172N	17270466	N739DS
D-EJBL(2)	Diamond DA 20C-1 Katana (Permit .05)	C0190	N909DC
D-EJBM	Mooney M.20F Aerostar 220	700051	HB-DFV D-EHOF(3) N9497V
D-EJBR	Mooney M.20J Model 201	24-1660	
D-EJBS	Cessna 150F	15064510	N3110X
D-EJBW(2)	Piper PA-28R-201T TurboCherokee Arrow III	28R-7703407	OE-KBW D-EMOC(2) N47606
D-EJBY	Bölkow BO.207	245	
D-EJCA(3)	Commander Aircraft 114B	14544	N6007S
D-EJCC	Piper PA-46-310P Malibu	46-8508055	OE-KKM (N530DR) N530DP N4391H
D-EJCD	Cessna 182P (Reims-assembled with "c/n" 0063)	18264442	OE-DIF N1782M
D-EJCF	Reims/Cessna F182P Skylane II	F18200011	
D-EJCH(2)	Macchi MB.308	71/5844	D-EJUP(1) I-NCOM
D-EJCI (2)	Reims/Cessna F182P Skylane	F18200019	
D-EJCK	Reims/Cessna F182P Skylane	F18200015	
D-EJCM	Cessna T210L Turbo Centurion	21061215	N2272S
D-EJCO(2)	Cessna 177B Cardinal	17702193	N35079
D-EJCP	Reims/Cessna F152	F15201632	
D-EJCS(2)	SIAT 223A-1 Flamingo	016	HB-EVM
D-EJDC	Gyroflug SC-01B-160 Speed Canard	S-47	
D-EJDE(2)	Gyroflug SC-01B-160 Speed Canard	S-51	
D-EJDF	Drees Star-Lite SL-1	001	
D-EJDI	Cessna 150F	15061588	N6288R
D-EJDK	Cessna P210N Pressurized Centurion II	P21000808	N4598A
D-EJDZ	FFT Eurotrainer 2000A	A-1	
D-EJEB(2)	Mooney M.20A	1676	OE-DOM N6080X
D-EJEC(2)	Piper PA-28-181 Archer II	28-8090369	N8241F
D-EJED(2)	Robin DR.400/180R Remorqueur	1317	
D-EJEE	SAN Jodel DR.1050M Excellence	487	

D-EJEF(4)	Feldmann/ Denney Kitfox IV	01/1745	
D-EJEG(2)	Beech F33A Bonanza	CE-723	
D-EJEK(2)	Robin DR.400/180R Remo 180	1141	F-GABX
D-EJEL(3)	Cessna 182P Skylane	18262613	HB-CEB N52444
D-EJEM(2)	Cessna F172G	F172-0261	
D-EJEN(2)	Piper PA-18 Super Cub 95	18-5644	OE-AEN 2A-AS N10F
D-EJER	Aeronca 11AC Chief	1609	OO-KER OO-LUC
D-EJET(2)	Piper PA-28R-200 Cherokee Arrow II	28R-7535325	N1559X
D-EJEV(2)	Cessna F150G	F150-0190	
D-EJEX	Dornier Do.27Q-1	2021	
D-EJFA(2)	Piper J-5A Cub Cruiser	5-529	N35021 NC35021
D-EJFD	Gyroflug SC-01B-160 Speed Canard	S-19	
D-EJFF	Piper PA-28R-200 Cherokee Arrow II	28R-7435285	N43642
D-EJFK	Piper PA-28-181 Archer II	2890140	N9196Z
D-EJFL(2)	Beech V35B Bonanza	D-9717	(D-EANG(2)) ZS-JFI N9377S
D-EJFN	Neumayer/ Stoddard-Hamilton Glasair II-FT	1057AB	
D-EJFO	Bölkow BO.207	248	
D-EJFR	CEA Jodel DR.1050 Ambassadeur	406	F-BLAG
D-EJFU(3)	Mooney M.20J Model 201	24-1617	
D-EJFW	Schöneseifen/ Jurca FW.190-A5 (Permit 4.99)	E-01/293	
D-EJGA	Cessna 172C	17249395	N1695Y
D-EJGB	Mooney M.20K Model 231	25-0711	(N1172G)
D-EJGD	Mooney M.20K Model 231	25-0703	(D-EJGO(3)) N231AV (N1170X)
D-EJGF	Yakovlev Yak-18A	0527	DM-WGI LSK-. . .
D-EJGI	Piper J-3C-65 Cub	13204	(D-EIJG) D-EJGI OE-ABD HB-OVO 45-4464
D-EJGO(4)	Goldbrunner/ Marco J-5	001	
D-EJGR	Piper PA-18 Super Cub 95	18-3454	96+30 NL+116 AC+536 AS+536 54-754
D-EJGS	Yakovlev Yak-50	791505	DDR-WQP DM-WQP
D-EJGZ	Cessna 172N	17268340	N733JX
D-EJHA(2)	Me.109B-1 Scale Replica (Permit 9.04)	881	
D-EJHB(2)	Beech A36 Bonanza	E-2286	N7205C
D-EJHD	Dinkl / Jurca MJ.5 Sirocco	D-29	
D-EJHE	Mooney M.20F Executive	670388	N3295F
D-EJHF(2)	Piper PA-46-310P Malibu	4608081	OE-KEG D-EIIA N9119N
D-EJHG	Gold/ Aero Designs Pulsar XP	P 001	
D-EJHH	SAN Jodel D.150 Mascaret	54	
D-EJHK	Wassmer WA.51 Pacific	05	
D-EJHL	Cessna 172N	17273730	N5204J
D-EJHM	Rockwell 114B Commander	14366	PH-CGY (PH-CHI) OO-TRL N5788N
D-EJHO	Oberlerchner JOB 15-150/2	062	OE-CAY
D-EJHP	Cessna 172M	17264376	N9574V
D-EJHS	Beech F33A Bonanza	CE-1661	N8051H
D-EJHW(2)	Robin DR.400/200R Remo 200	2389	
D-EJIA	Robin R.3000/160	157	
D-EJIB(2)	Piper PA-46-310P Malibu	4608095	N9122D
D-EJIC	SAN Jodel DR.1050 Ambassadeur	199	
D-EJII	Cessna P210N Pressurized Centurion II	P21000823	N4801A (D-EVAL) N4801A C-GEWN N480IA (N828VG) N4801A
D-EJIM(3)	Piper PA-18 Super Cub 95	18-1531	OO-BLV OO-HNC ALAT 51-15531
D-EJIP(2)	Iser/ Kelly Hatz CB-1	273	
D-EJIR(2)	Reims/Cessna F150M	F15001260	
D-EJIS(2)	SOCATA TB-20 Trinidad	2112	
D-EJIV	Orlican L-40 Meta-Sokol	150405	OK-NMK
D-EJIW	Orlican L-40 Meta-Sokol	150408	
D-EJJG	Gralfs/ Europa Avn Europa	1781	
D-EJJJ	Dornier Do.27B-1	192	55+59 PF+219 PF+106 PD+107
D-EJJM	Robin DR.400/180R Remo 180	2346	
D-EJJO	SAN Jodel DR.1050 Ambassadeur	123	F-BJJO
D-EJKA(2)	SNCAN/ Stampe SV.4A (Permit 7.99) (Flies in green camouflage Fr.AF c/s)	396	G-BWRE D-EJKA(2) F-BDOT Fr.AF

D-EJKB	Bäuerle/ Neico Lancair IVB (Permit 7.04)	IV-00-20	
D-EJKC	SOCATATB-9 Tampico	1374	I-IAFZ
D-EJKF	Sautter/ Denney Kitfox III	1641	
D-EJKG	Seufert Sisler Cygnet SF-2A	001	
D-EJKH	Erco Ercoupe 415D (W/o 2.5.03)	2249	N99626
D-EJKL	Cessna 172N	17270102	N738NF
D-EJKM	Piper PA-28-140 Cherokee E	28-7225449	N11C
D-EJKO	Cessna F172G	F172-0268	
D-EJKR	Rehmann RE-3/ Steen Skybolt	001	
D-EJKS(3)	Extra EA.300/S	010	
D-EJKT	Zlin Z.526F Trenér Master	1109	DDR-WKT DM-WKT
D-EJKW	Piper PA-28RT-201 Arrow IV	28R-7918049	N2187P
D-EJLA	Bölkow BO.208C Junior	581	
D-EJLE	Bölkow BO.208C Junior	582	
D-EJLF	Cessna 150M	15078648	N704JM
D-EJLG(2)	Robin DR.400/180 Régent	2391	
D-EJLH	Piper PA-28RT-201 Arrow IV	28R-7918146	N29566
D-EJLI	Bölkow BO.208C Junior	583	
D-EJLK	Piper PA-38-112 Tomahawk	38-78A0651	PH-SRS N9703N
D-EJLL(2)	Zlin Z.526F Trenér Master	1113	SP-CDK
D-EJLM	Piper PA-28-235 Cherokee Charger	28-7310117	N55141
D-EJLR	Robin DR.400/180 Régent	1762	
D-EJLT	Rockwell Commander 114B	14195	PH-VON N4865W
D-EJLU	Bölkow BO.208 Junior	550	
D-EJLW	Beech F33A Bonanza	CE-1497	
D-EJLY	Cessna 182K Skylane	18257879	N2679Q
D-EJMA	Bölkow BO.208C Junior	651	
D-EJMB	Bölkow BO.208C Junior	652	
D-EJMC(2)	Donnerhack Master Crow	1	
D-EJME(2)	Cessna 182K Skylane	18258194	N3194Q
D-EJMF	Bölkow BO.208C Junior	656	
D-EJMM	Zlin Z.526F Trenér Master	1280	SP-EMM
D-EJMO(3)	American AG-5B Tiger	10149	N1197Y
D-EJMP(2)	Cessna 182Q Skylane	18266213	N759SB
D-EJMR	Reims/Cessna F172N Skyhawk II	F17201749	PH-JMR PH-AYN
D-EJMS(2)	Strauber/ Neico Lancair 360 (C/n 1804 given earlier)	396	
D-EJMT(2)	Cessna 172N	17273182	N6290F
D-EJMU	Bölkow BO.208C Junior	585	
D-EJMV	Piper PA-46-310P Malibu	4608085	N69074
D-EJNA	Bölkow BO.208C Junior	587	
D-EJNB	Cessna U206G Stationair 6 (Soloy conversion .00)	U20606560	PH-JNB OY-SUV (SE-. . .) OY-SUV N9597Z
D-EJNC	Extra EA.230	002	
D-EJNG	Cessna R182 Skylane RG	R18200337	N4182C
D-EJNI	Bölkow BO.208C Junior	589	
D-EJNO	SEEMS MS.880B Rallye Club	304	OE-CGW(1)
D-EJNW	Diamond DA 20-A1 Katana	10149	C-FXTY
D-EJNY	Cessna F172H	F172-0558	
D-EJNZ	SAN Jodel DR.1050 Ambassadeur	169	F-BJNZ
D-EJOA	Bücker Bü.133C Jungmeister	48	HB-MIK U-49
D-EJOB(2)	Oberlerchner JOB 15-150/2	070	OE-DOB (D-EKEM)
D-EJOD(3)	Pützer Elster B	V-1	D-EJOB(1)
D-EJOE	Piper PA-28-161 Warrior II	28-7916468	N2845N
D-EJOF(4)	Piper PA-28RT-201T Turbo Arrow IV	28R-7931257	N2920F
D-EJOG	Orlican L-40 Meta-Sokol	150402	OK-NMB
D-EJOH(4)	SOCATA TB-20 Trinidad	1627	
D-EJOI	Focke-Wulf FW.44J Stieglitz	2929	(D-EHDW) OH-SZA SZ-26
D-EJON(4)	Commander Aircraft 114B	14547	
D-EJOO	Piper PA-28-181 Archer II	2890072	HB-PLS
D-EJOP(2)	Reims/Cessna F182Q Skylane	F18200164	
D-EJOR	Erco 415CD Ercoupe	4737	N9963F HB-ERD OO-EXE (NC94630)
D-EJOS(2)	Cessna T210N Turbo Centurion II	21063980	N4675Y
D-EJOY	Piper PA-28R-200 Cherokee Arrow	28R-35616	N3054R
D-EJPA(3)	Reims FR172J Rocket	FR17200429	HB-CFE D-EGJT(1)
D-EJPB	Piper PA-28-235 Cherokee Charger	28-7310007	N11C
D-EJPC	Cessna 182P Skylane (Reims-assembled with "c/n" 0037)	18264106	N6091F
D-EJPD(2)	Commander Aircraft 114B	14599	
D-EJPE(2)	Reims/Cessna F152	F15201577	(F-GBQC)
D-EJPF(2)	Cessna 152	15279420	C-GTVJ N714TM
D-EJPG	SOCATA TB-10 Tobago	394	
D-EJPH	SOCATA TB-10 Tobago	396	
D-EJPI (3)	Cessna 172N	17269682	C-GZLA (N737UH)
D-EJPJ	SOCATA TB-10 Tobago	398	
D-EJPK	SOCATA TB-10 Tobago	407	
D-EJPL	SOCATA TB-20 Trinidad	408	
D-EJPM	Marschall / Denney Kitfox II	512	
D-EJPO	Piper PA-22-108 Colt	22-9330	N10F
D-EJPP	Jentsch/ Prescott Pusher (Permit 17.9.03)	055	
D-EJPQ	SOCATA TB-10 Tobago	430	

D-EJPR	SOCATA TB-20 Trinidad	424	
D-EJPS	Cessna 172N	17272803	C-GSRF
			N6443D
D-EJPT	Grumman AA-5B Tiger	AA5B-0416	
D-EJPU	Beech 35-B33 Debonair	CD-499	SE-CPP
			D-EJPU
D-EJQF	Robin DR.400/180R Remorqueur	1617	
D-EJQO(2)	Piper PA-18 Super Cub 95	18-3206	OL-L32
			L-132
			53-4806
D-EJRC	SOCATA TB-10 Tobago	362	HB-KAA
D-EJRD	Robin DR.400/180R Remorqueur	1660	F-WZZU
D-EJRE(2)	Reims/Cessna F172M	F17201334	D-EFCM(2)
			HB-CWW
			(OE-DTU)
D-EJRK	Piper PA-38-112 Tomahawk	38-79A0894	N9672N
D-EJRL(2)	Limbacher/ Rand-Robinson KR-2 (W/o 9.02)	01/1688	
D-EJRP	Bellanca 17-30A Viking	76-30818	C-GBDT
D-EJRR	Piper PA-18 Super Cub 95	18-3429	96+10
			SB+220
			AC+518
			AS+518
			54-729
D-EJRU	Cessna F150G	F150-0166	
D-EJRV	SOCATA TB-9 Tampico	921	
D-EJRW	Cessna 172R	17280198	
D-EJSA(2)	Mooney M.20JModel 205	24-3348	ZS-NPF
D-EJSB	Piper PA-28-180 Cherokee G	28-7205086	N11C
D-EJSC	Robin R.3000/160	171	
D-EJSD	Robin DR.400/180R Remo 180	2011	
D-EJSF(2)	SOCATA MS.983A Rallye Commodore 180	11000	CS-AIJ
	(Reservation .05)		F-BNGV
D-EJSG	Cessna 182Q Skylane	18265989	N759GT
D-EJSH	Robin DR.400/180R Remo 180	2348	
D-EJSM(3)	Piper PA-28RT-201T Turbo Arrow IV	28R-8031050	N8167B
			N9618N
D-EJSP(2)	Mooney M.20M Model 257 TLS	27-0055	
D-EJSR(2)	Robin DR.400/180S Régent	2085	
D-EJST	Piper PA-28R-201 Arrow III	28R-7837243	N31675
D-EJSU	Cessna F172H	F172-0449	
D-EJSW	Champion 7GCBC Citabria	110	N1845G
D-EJSY	Piper PA-28R-201T Turbo Cherokee Arrow III		
		28R-7703099	N106WC
			N9643N
D-EJTA(2)	Robin DR.400/180 Régent	2184	
D-EJTC	Cessna 182P Skylane	18263630	N6090J
D-EJTD	Reims/Cessna 182P Skylane	0003/63779	N6615M
D-EJTF	Piper PA-32R-301 Saratoga SP	3213034	N9195X
D-EJTG	Piper PA-28-161 Cadet	2841306	N9263N
			N9207Z
D-EJTH	Thümmler/ Brändli BX-2 Cherry	1607	
D-EJTI	Piper PA-28-161 Cadet	2841308	N9265N
			N9208X
D-EJTJ	Piper PA-46-310P Malibu	4608105	N68FB
			D-ENFB(2)
			N9132B
D-EJTL	Piper PA-28-161 Cadet	2841313	N9270N
			N9210N
D-EJTN	Piper PA-28-161 Cadet	2841312	N9269N
			N9210F
D-EJTR	Bücker Bü.131 Jungmann	49	HB-UTR
			A-38
D-EJTU	Beech F33A Bonanza	CE-1381	N133EK
			N5579Z
D-EJUD(2)	Judd/ Steen Skybolt (Reservn 5.99)	M212/M202/98	
D-EJUF(2)	Beech F33A Bonanza	CE-1247	
D-EJUG(2)	Däumer/ Van's RV-4	3394	
D-EJUI	Aeronca 65CA	C13661	N33798
			NC33798
D-EJUK	Klemm Kl.107B	124	
D-EJUM(3)	Piper J-3C-65 Cub	1165	(D-EDIX)
			G-AFFJ
D-EJUR(2)	Robin R.1180TD Aiglon	267	OE-DRX
D-EJUT(3)	Piper PA-28-180 Cherokee B	28-904	HB-OVV
			N7174W
D-EJUW	Orlican L-40 Meta-Sokol	150409	
D-EJVC	Christen Pitts S-2B	5141	SE-KOD
			N6052U
D-EJVL	Mooney M.20E Super 21	670018	HB-DVL
			N3225F
D-EJVR(2)	Maule MXT-7-180 Starcraft	14115C	
D-EJVU	Beech A23-24 Musketeer Super III	MA-355	
D-EJVY	Beech A23-24 Musketeer Super III	MA-354	
D-EJWB(2)	Piper PA-28-161 Cadet	2841083	N9169B
D-EJWD	Döring/ Europa Aviation Europa (Permit)	1854AB	
D-EJWE	Piper PA-28-235 Cherokee B	28-10896	N9228W
D-EJWF	Piper PA-28-181 Archer II	2890148	SE-KMV
D-EJWG	Mooney M.20K Model 231	25-0400	(N4047H)
D-EJWK	Robin DR.400/180 Régent	744	
D-EJWM	Reims/Cessna F172N	F17201874	
D-EJWO	Cessna F172H	F172-0411	
D-EJWP	SOCATA TB-20 Trinidad	1100	N2805V
D-EJWR	Cessna 172N	17273829	N5733J
D-EJWS(3)	Grumman AA-5 Traveler	AA5-0355	N5455L
D-EJWU	Cessna F172H	F172-0417	
D-EJWV	Piper PA-28R-201T Turbo Arrow III	28R-7803224	N6387C
D-EJWY	CEA Jodel DR.1050 Ambassadeur	208	F-BJZE

D-EJXC	Reims/Cessna F172M	F17201007	
D-EJXD	Reims/Cessna F172M	F17201017	
D-EJXH	Reims/Cessna F150L	F15000985	
D-EJXM	Reims/Cessna F172M	F17201012	
D-EJXN	Reims/Cessna F172M	F17201013	
D-EJXO(2)	Reims/Cessna F172M	F17201174	
D-EJXP	Reims/Cessna F150L	F15001014	
D-EJXQ	Reims/Cessna F172M	F17201020	
D-EJXR	Reims/Cessna F150L	F15001018	
D-EJXS	Reims/Cessna F172M	F17201022	
D-EJXT	Reims/Cessna F172M	F17201023	
D-EJXW(2)	Reims/Cessna F172M	F17201157	
D-EJXY(2)	Reims/Cessna F150L	F15001091	
D-EJYC(2)	SIAI-Marchetti S.205-18/R	219	
D-EJYD	Piper J-3C-65 Cub	11658	G-AJDS
			43-30367
D-EJYF	Aero-Jodel D.11A Club	AB.5 (Liz.228/625)	
D-EJYR(3)	SOCATA MS.880B Rallye Club	1105	
D-EJYT(2)	SAN Jodel DR.1050 Ambassadeur	200	(D-ELFI)
D-EJYW	RFB RW3-P75	022	
D-EJYX(2)	Bölkow BO.207	292	
D-EJYZ	Cessna 175A Skylark	56267	N6767E
D-EKAA	Reims/Cessna FR172K Hawk XP	FR17200631	
D-EKAB(2)	Piper PA-18A-135 Super Cub	18-2810	HB-OOW
			N10F
D-EKAC	Cessna 150	17835	N6435T
D-EKAD(4)	Cessna P210N Pressurized Centurion II	P21000644	N27AM
			N5139W
D-EKAE	Piper PA-28R-201 Arrow III	28R-7837253	N31882
D-EKAH(2)	Beech F33A Bonanza	CE-757	N23791
D-EKAI (2)	Robin DR.400/180 Régent	1127	
D-EKAJ(2)	Cessna 182P Skylane	18264327	N1429M
	(Reims-assembled with "c/n" 0050)		
D-EKAK(2)	Beagle B.121 Pup 150	135	G-AXSB
			G-35-135
D-EKAL(2)	Piper PA-28R-200 Cherokee Arrow II	28R-7635198	N8726E
D-EKAM(2)	Piper PA-28-181 Archer II	2890129	N9187Q
D-EKAN(2)	Piper PA-28R-200 Cherokee Arrow B	28R-35672	N3062R
D-EKAO	Piper PA-28R-201 Arrow III	28R-7837212	N9632C
D-EKAP(3)	Piper PA-28R-200 Cherokee Arrow II	28R-7435178	N41403
D-EKAS(2)	Schneider TC-1 Dragonfly	X-01	
D-EKAT(3)	Piper PA-28RT-201T Turbo Arrow IV	28R-7931185	N28518
D-EKAU(2)	Piper PA-46-350P Malibu Mirage	4622100	N558RS
			N9193V
D-EKAV(3)	American AA-1A Trainer	AA1A-0448	OY-AYH
			(N6248L)
D-EKAW	Beech 35-33 Debonair	CD-27	
D-EKAY	Piper PA-18 Super Cub 95	18-1340	D-ENLG
			ALAT
			51-15340
D-EKAZ(2)	Piper PA-28-181 Archer III	2843141	N9293N
D-EKBA(2)	SOCATA TB-200 Tobago XL	1798	
D-EKBB(3)	Fuji FA-200-180 Aero Subaru	99	OY-FRI
			LX-JFY
			LX-MDM
			D-EMYY
D-EKBC	Reims FR172G Rocket	FR17200205	
D-EKBD	Reims FR172G Rocket	FR17200174	
D-EKBE(2)	Jodel D.9 Bébé	Liz.301	(D-EGBM(2))
D-EKBF(2)	Piper PA-28R-200 Cherokee Arrow II	28R-7235310	N1517T
D-EKBG	Reims/Cessna FA150K Aerobat	FA1500052	
D-EKBI (2)	SOCATA TB-20 Trinidad	355	HB-EZY
D-EKBJ	Robin R.3000/120D	129	HB-KBT
D-EKBK	Cessna P210N Pressurized Centurion II	P21000661	N5244W
	(STOL conversion)		
D-EKBL(2)	SOCATA TB-10 Tobago	732	
D-EKBO(2)	Piper PA-18 Super Cub 95	18-3453	96+29
			NL+120
			AC+509
			AS+508
			54-753
D-EKBR	Piper PA-28R-201T Turbo Cherokee Arrow III		
		28R-7703241	N38753
D-EKBT	Beech B36TC Bonanza	EA-514	
D-EKBW	Mooney M.20F Executive	670340	N2981L
D-EKBY	Cessna FP172D Skyhawk Powermatic		
		FP172-0002/P17257166	(N8566X)
D-EKCA	Gardan GY-80 Horizon 160	96	
D-EKCB	Reims/Cessna F172N	F17201739	
D-EKCD	SOCATA MS.893A Rallye Commodore 180	11434	F-BSAT
D-EKCE(2)	Cessna 172M	17263000	N13762
D-EKCG(2)	Commander Aircraft 114B	14548	N162A
D-EKCH	Christen A-1 Husky	1087	N9596G
D-EKCI	Oberlerchner JOB 15-180/2	065	OE-CAV
D-EKCL	Reims/Cessna F172N	F17201676	
D-EKCM(2)	Driessen/ Pottier P.220S Koala	1835	
D-EKCP	Reims/Cessna F150M	F15001395	
D-EKCR	Beech 35 Bonanza	D-686	HB-ECR
			NC90573
D-EKCT	Robin DR.400/180R Remorqueur	1331	
D-EKCW	Piper PA-28-181 Archer II	28-8190018	N8257G
D-EKDB	Mooney M.20K Model 231	25-0565	N231BW
D-EKDE(3)	Piper PA-28-235 Cherokee B	28-10961	N9285W
D-EKDF(2)	Akaflieg München Mü.30 Schlacro (Permit 12.99)	001	
D-EKDG	Robin DR.400/180R Remorqueur	1638	
D-EKDH	Robin DR.400/120D Petit Prince	1644	
D-EKDI	Bölkow BO.208C Junior	593	

D-EKDL	Piper PA-28-161 Warrior II	28-7916562	N2941F
D-EKDN	Beech A36 Bonanza	E-2353	N7241Y
D-EKDR	Zlin Z.226T Trenér 6	156	OE-CMW
			OK-MFL
D-EKDS	Rockwell Commander 114	14206	N4876W
D-EKDT	Bähr/ Aero Designs Pulsar XP (Permit 11.99)	EB 00	
D-EKDU	Bölkow BO.208C Junior	595	(HB-UXW)
D-EKDV	HOAC DV-20 Katana	20075	
D-EKDY(2)	Reims/Cessna F172N	F17201939	
D-EKEA	Hinz BL1-KEA	1	
D-EKEB(3)	Mooney M.20J Model 205	24-3364	
D-EKEC(2)	Reims/Cessna F172N Skyhawk II	F17201960	
D-EKEG(3)	Reims/Cessna FR172K Hawk XP	FR17200666	N8495B
D-EKEH(2)	Piper PA-28-181 Archer II	2890080	SE-KEH
D-EKEI	Piper PA-38-112 Tomahawk	38-80A0096	N9700N
D-EKEK	Klemm Kl.107C	132	
D-EKEL(3)	SOCATA MS.893E Rallye 180GT Gaillard	12633	
D-EKEM(3)	Piper PA-38-112 Tomahawk	38-80A0097	N9701N
D-EKEN(2)	Reims/Cessna F172N	F17201991	
D-EKEP(3)	Cessna F150J	F150-0424	
D-EKET(3)	Cessna F150J	F150-0395	
D-EKEW(5)	Extra EA.500 (Permit 15.9.03)	01	
	(Originally built as Extra EA.400T, converted .03)		
D-EKEZ	Aeromere F.8L Falco	210	
D-EKFA	Champion 7GCB Challenger	7GCB-159	
D-EKFB(2)	Piper PA-28RT-201T Turbo Arrow IV	28R-8131062	N83245
D-EKFC	Mooney M.20J Model 205	24-3083	
D-EKFD(3)	Piper PA-46-350P Malibu Mirage	4622008	OE-KFD
			D-ENII (2)
			N9151X
D-EKFF	Piper PA-28RT-201T Turbo Arrow IV	28R-8131022	N8296P
D-EKFG	Dornier Do.27A-4	471	57+40
			XB+901
			GA+374
			KD+129
D-EKFH	Robin R.2160D Acrobin	122	
D-EKFI	Piper PA-12 Super Cruiser	12-1528	D-EMCO
			N2413M
			NC2413M
D-EKFK	Gyroflug SC-01B-160 Speed Canard	S-22	
D-EKFL	Piper PA-28-181 Archer II	28-8190110	N8309H
D-EKFM(2)	SOCATATB-10 Tobago	760	OE-KFM
D-EKFN	CEA DR.250/160 Capitaine	36	PH-REN
D-EKFR	Cessna 172N	17271154	N2093E
D-EKFS(2)	Stuttgart FS-28 Avispa	V-1/1832	D-EAFS(1)
D-EKFT	Mooney M.20J Model 201	24-0834	(N4748H)
D-EKFV	Cessna T206H Turbo Stationair	T20608262	N4193N
D-EKFW	Piper PA-28-181 Cherokee Archer II	28-7690339	N6108J
			N9582N
D-EKFY	Piper PA-18-150 Super Cub	18-8123	N4113Z
D-EKGA(2)	Cessna 152	15279906	N757PX
D-EKGB(2)	Diamond DA 40D Star	D4.069	
D-EKGC	Zlin Z.43	0017	LSK-22
D-EKGE	SIAI-Marchetti S.205-18/R	358	
D-EKGH(4)	Fürstenwalde Albatros B1 replica	01	
D-EKGI	SIAI-Marchetti S.205-18/R	365	
D-EKGK	Kitplane, type unknown (Reservation 11.99)	262	
D-EKGL	Mooney M.20J Model 205	24-3232	N91ZL
D-EKGM	Piper PA-18-100 Super Cub	18-1527	F-BOMR
	(Built as PA-18 Super Cub 95)		ALAT
			51-15527
D-EKGN	Zlin Z.43	0022	LSK-16
D-EKGO	SIAI-Marchetti S.205-20/R	4-110	
D-EKGR(4)	Extra EA.400	28	
D-EKGS	Robin DR.400/180R Remorqueur	1092	
D-EKGT	HOAC DV-20 Katana	20104	C-FVPV
			N104DV
D-EKGW	Cirrus SR20	1194	N265CD
D-EKHA(4)	Aero Designs Pulsar XP (Reservation)	1930	
D-EKHB(2)	Mooney M.20E Super 21	1202	HB-DWA
			N9255M
D-EKHD(2)	Focke-Wulf FW.44J Stieglitz	"648"	LX-OOI
			HB-EBO
			D-EBOB(1)
			SE-AYY
			Fv648
D-EKHE(2)	SOCATA MS.880B Rallye Club	2288	F-BULE
D-EKHF(2)	Fahr/ Jurca MJ.2 Tempête	AB-01	
D-EKHG(2)	SOCATA MS.887 Rallye 125	2161	(D-EAPW)
			F-BUCF
D-EKHI (2)	SOCATA MS.887 Rallye 125	2177	F-BVLO
D-EKHJ	Cessna 210K Centurion	21059285	N8285M
D-EKHK	SOCATA MS.894E Minerva 220GT	12204	F-BULC
D-EKHL(2)	SOCATA MS.893E Rallye 180GT Gaillard	12207	F-BUXJ
D-EKHM(2)	SOCATA MS.893E Rallye 180GT Gaillard	12525	F-BVNS
D-EKHN(2)	SOCATA MS.893E Rallye 180GT Gaillard	12526	F-BVNT
D-EKHO(2)	Piper PA-18 Super Cub 95	18-1009	RHAF115312
			51-15312
D-EKHQ	SOCATA MS.894E Minerva 220GT	12147	F-BUVE
D-EKHR	Cessna F172F	F172-0094	
D-EKHS(2)	Piper PA-32RT-300T Turbo Lance II	32R-7887160	N39755
D-EKHT	SOCATA MS.894E Minerva 220GT	12146	F-BUNY
D-EKHU	Laverda F.8L Falco IV	405	
D-EKHV	SOCATA MS.894E Minerva 220GT	12203	F-BULB
D-EKHW(2)	Piper PA-28RT-201T Turbo Arrow IV	28R-8031094	
D-EKHY(2)	SOCATA MS.893A Rallye Commodore 180	10723	
D-EKHZ	Cessna 182Q	18266466	OE-KHZ
			N94628
D-EKIA	Robin DR.400/180S Régent	1893	
D-EKIB(2)	Piper PA-18-150 Super Cub	18-8321	N5736Y
D-EKIC	Nord 1203 Norécrin II	309	HB-DAK
D-EKIE	Dornier Do.27A-1	172	55+42
			AC+922
			AS+922
D-EKIF	de Havilland DH.82A Tiger Moth	83091	G-AOED
	(Damaged 19.10.02)		R5216
D-EKIG	SAN Jodel DR.1050 Ambassadeur	108	
D-EKIH(3)	SOCATA MS.893A Rallye Commodore 180	12078	OE-KTH
	(Built as MS.894A Minerva 220, mod 7.99)		HB-ETH
			SE-FSX
D-EKIL(2)	SOCATA MS.893A Rallye Commodore 180	10724	
D-EKIM(2)	Piper PA-28RT-201T Turbo Arrow IV	28R-7931243	N2888Y
D-EKIN(3)	Piper PA-28-181 Archer II	2890141	SE-KIZ
D-EKIO	Piper PA-28-161 Cadet	2841171	SE-KIO
D-EKIP	Piper J-3C-65 Cub	9086	N42033
			NC42033
D-EKIQ	Cessna F150F	F150-0024/15062944	(N8844G)
D-EKIR	Piper PA-18-150 Super Cub	18-3698	HB-OOY
D-EKIS(2)	Piper J-3C-65 Cub Special	20791	D-ECIS(1)
			N2024M
			NC2024M
D-EKIT(2)	Reims/Cessna F172N	F17201994	
D-EKIW	Beech 35-33 Debonair	CD-180	
D-EKIZ(2)	Bellanca 8GCBC Scout 180	92-74	OE-AOG
D-EKJA	SOCATA MS.893E Rallye 180GT Gaillard	12379	F-BVAG
D-EKJB	Robin DR.400/180R Remorqueur	1001	
D-EKJD	Reims FR172J Rocket	FR17200582	
D-EKJH(2)	Beech F33A Bonanza	CE-1125	N517RM
D-EKJL(2)	Cessna R182 Skylane RG	R18200529	N1712R
D-EKJM	Montjoje/ Denney Kitfox II	1625/528	
D-EKKA	Piper J-3C-65 Cub	6298	HB-OXB
			N35331
			NC35331
D-EKKB	Reims/Cessna F150K	F15000545	
D-EKKC	Reims FR172F Rocket	FR17200130	
D-EKKD	Reims/Cessna F172H	F17200665	(D-EKKR)
D-EKKE	Piper PA-24-250 Comanche	24-469	N5415P
D-EKKF(3)	Piper PA-18 Super Cub 95	18-1418	ALAT
			51-15418
D-EKKG	Reims/Cessna F150K	F15000616	
D-EKKH(3)	Diamond DA 20-A1 Katana	10019	N606F
			(N474F)
			N606F
D-EKKI	Cessna 182F Skylane	18254908	N3508U
D-EKKJ(2)	Piper PA-28-140 Cherokee C	28-26874	N98386
D-EKKK(3)	Diamond DA 20-A1 Katana	10219	N697DA
D-EKKL(3)	Diamond DA 40 Star	40072	
D-EKKM	Reims FR172G Rocket	FR17200158	
D-EKKN	Reims FR172G Rocket	FR17200149	
D-EKKP	Robin DR.500/200i Président	0018	
D-EKKR(2)	Aeronca 65C	C.1738	D-EKON(1)
			HB-UPI
D-EKKS(3)	Cessna 172N	17272162	N8275E
D-EKKT	Cessna 210J Centurion	21059153	N3353S
D-EKKU(2)	CEA DR.253B Régent	159	
D-EKKV(2)	Piper PA-28RT-201T Turbo Arrow IV	28R-8031042	N600KR
			N9585N
D-EKKW(2)	SOCATA MS.892E Rallye 150GT	12238	(D-EARU)
			F-BULY
D-EKKY(2)	Hankers/ Stephens Laser	1962	
D-EKKZ	Piper PA-28-180 Cherokee Challenger	28-7305446	N55690
D-EKLA(2)	Wassmer WA.51 Pacific	96	F-BUKH
D-EKLB(2)	Beech A36 Bonanza	E-2444	D-EKFJ
D-EKLC	Extra EA400 (Reservation)	04	
D-EKLE(2)	Grob G.115A	8069	
D-EKLF(2)	Reims/Cessna F152	F15201812	HB-CFU
D-EKLG(3)	Robin DR.400/180 Régent (Reserved for rebuild)	2281	
D-EKLH	Piper PA-28-161 Cadet	2841125	N9511N
			N9181D
D-EKLL	Piper PA-38-112 Tomahawk	38-79A0512	N2391G
D-EKLM	Cessna T210M Turbo Centurion	21061592	(N732LG)
D-EKLS	Cessna 150F	15062405	PH-ALS
			N8305G
D-EKLT	Piper PA-28-181 Archer II	28-7990427	N28901
D-EKLW	Beech V35B Bonanza	D-9714	N7258R
D-EKLX	Morane-Saulnier MS.885 Super Rallye	160	F-BKLY
D-EKLY	Piaggio FWP.149D	119	(90+99)
			D-EKLY
			AS+461
D-EKMB(5)	SOCATA TB-10 Tobago	1133	OE-KMB
D-EKMC	Cessna TP.206E Turbo Super Skylane	00611	N5711J
D-EKMD(2)	SOCATA TB-9 Tampico	212	OE-KMD
			D-EBZD
D-EKME(2)	SOCATA TB-200 Tobago XL	1446	
D-EKMF	Mooney M.20J Model 201	24-0429	
D-EKMG	Cessna 172N Skyhawk	17270868	N739WQ
D-EKMJ	Zlin Z.43	0027	LSK-21
D-EKMK	Aeromere F.8L Falco	232	
D-EKMM(3)	Aerotek Pitts S-2A	2106	N2CQ
D-EKMN	Zlin Z.43	0018	LSK-23
D-EKMO(3)	Zlin Z.43	0012	LSK-25
D-EKMP(2)	Zlin Z.43	0024	LSK-18
D-EKMQ	Zlin Z.43	0026	LSK-20

D-EKMR(2)	SOCATA TB-20 Trinidad	617	F-GENV
D-EKMS(2)	Cessna TR182 Turbo Skylane RG	R18200623	N4903R
D-EKMU(2)	Reims/Cessna FR182 Skylane RG	FR18200028	
D-EKMV	SOCATA TB-20 Trinidad	724	
D-EKMW(3)	Mair/ Neico Lancair IV-PT (Reservation .04)	1	
D-EKMX	Zlin Z.43	0025	LSK-19
D-EKMY	Bölkow BO.208C Junior	514	G-ASAS D-ENCY(1)
D-EKMZ	Zlin Z.43	0021	LSK-27
D-EKNA	Mooney M.20F Executive	670297	N9737M
D-EKNB	Cessna F172H	F172-0541	
D-EKNE(3)	Cessna TR182 Turbo Skylane RG	R18200854	N737MR
D-EKNI	SOCATA MS.892A Rallye Commodore 150	10551	
D-EKNK	Cessna 172RG Cutlass RG	172RG0568	N5550V
D-EKNM	Cessna R182 Skylane RG	R18200568	N1809R
D-EKNO(2)	Mooney M.20J Model 201	24-0045	
D-EKNR	Piper PA-28RT-201 Arrow IV	28R-7918187	I-NALD N2873D
D-EKNS(2)	Cessna 177RG Cardinal RG	177RG1103	N45313
D-EKNW	Piper PA-32-260 Cherokee Six	32-714	N3789W
D-EKOA	Piper PA-28RT-201T Turbo Arrow IV	28R-8131112	N8364Z
D-EKOB(2)	Piper PA-28R-201 Cherokee Arrow III	28R-7737170	N47499
D-EKOC(3)	Mooney M.20J Model 205	24-3064	N5684D (N205BG) N5684D
D-EKOE(2)	Kögler/ Dallach D4/E-BK/S Fascination	EB024	
D-EKOF	S.A.I. KZ-VII Laerke	192	(F-AZGK) D-EKOF HB-EPV
D-EKOG(2)	Reims/Cessna F172N	F17201975	(D-EOOX)
D-EKOH(2)	Piper PA-18-150 Super Cub	18-3224	OL-L50 L-150 53-4824
D-EKOL	Piper PA-18-150 Super Cub	18-5612	N10F
D-EKOM(3)	Piper PA-28RT-201T Turbo Arrow IV	28R-8031034	N3563X
D-EKOO	HOAC DV-20 Katana	20015	
D-EKOQ	Cessna 172A	47504	N9704T
D-EKOR(3)	Cessna 172R	17281199	N21596
D-EKOT(2)	Cessna F172G	F172-0274	
D-EKOX(2)	Reims/Cessna F172N	F17201685	
D-EKOY	Extra EA.400	17	
D-EKPA	Cessna F172E	F172-0084	
D-EKPC(2)	Mooney M.20J Model 201	24-1625	
D-EKPD	Beech B36TC Bonanza	EA-492	N15519
D-EKPE(3)	Reims/Cessna F152	F15201956	
D-EKPG	Cessna 172S	172S8469	N309ME
D-EKPH(2)	Pietsch/ Aero Designs Pulsar XP (Permit 7.00) (Originally reserved as c/n 1836)	403SB	
D-EKPI	Piper PA-28-160 Cherokee B	28-1138	N5704W
D-EKPL(2)	Cessna 172N	17273995	N5163K
D-EKPM	Reims/Cessna F172M	F17201480	
D-EKPO(2)	Cessna 182J Skylane	18257303	N3303F
D-EKPP	Mooney M.20J Model 201	24-0268	
D-EKPR	Piper PA-28-181 Archer II	28-8190114	N8311A
D-EKPU	Cessna F172F	F172-0088	
D-EKPY	Cessna F172F	F172-0169	
D-EKQC	Piper PA-18 Super Cub 95	18-1461	ALAT 51-15461
D-EKQD	Piper PA-18 Super Cub 95	18-1508	ALAT 51-15508
D-EKQF	Piper PA-18 Super Cub 95	18-1621	ALAT 51-15621
D-EKQI (2)	Reims/Cessna F150K	F15000600	
D-EKQM	Robin DR.400/180R Remorqueur	1482	OE-KAM D-EKFM(1)
D-EKQO	Cessna 182N Skylane	18260102	N92228
D-EKRA	Cessna F172G	F172-0286	
D-EKRC	Cessna F172F	F172-0174	
D-EKRD	Piper PA-38-112 Tomahawk	38-79A0920	N9697N
D-EKRE(2)	Bücker Bü.133C Jungmeister	5	HB-MKF U-58
D-EKRF	Robin HR.100/250TR Safari	551	
D-EKRK	Korff Impulse 130 (Permit .03)	01	
D-EKRM(2)	Cessna 172P	17274481	SE-KRM N52285
D-EKRS	Cessna T210L Turbo Centurion	21059569	N4669Q
D-EKRT	Diamond DA 40 Star	40050	
D-EKRU	Beech E33C Bonanza	CJ-25	
D-EKSA(2)	Piper PA-28RT-201T Turbo Arrow IV	28R-8031096	N81981
D-EKSB	Beech 35-B33 Debonair	CD-702	HB-EKL
D-EKSC	Gyroflug SC-01B-160 Speed Canard	S-20	
D-EKSD	Cessna 152	15283480	N49604
D-EKSE(2)	Robin DR.400/180R Remorqueur	1396	OE-KSE D-EISE(2)
D-EKSF	Cessna P210N Pressurized Centurion II	P21000503	N731NF
D-EKSG(2)	Piper PA-28-181 Archer II	28-8290075	N8020K
D-EKSI (2)	Robin DR.400/180R Remorqueur	1380	
D-EKSL	Cessna T210N Turbo Centurion II	21064855	(N5254U)
D-EKSO(2)	Robin DR.400/180R Remorqueur	1708	OE-KBF D-EEWF(2)
D-EKSP	Cessna 182H Skylane	18256425	N8325S
D-EKSR	Robin DR.400/180S Régent	2035	
D-EKSS	Mooney M.20J Model 205	24-3278	
D-EKST	Cessna F172G	F172-0267	OO-RPA PH-RPA
D-EKSU	Cessna 150D	15060091	N7991Z
D-EKSV	Diamond DA 20-A1 Katana	10122	N549SS
D-EKSW	Robin DR.400/180R Remorqueur	844	
D-EKSY(2)	Piper PA-28-180 Cherokee C	28-3535	F-OCJU N9424J
D-EKTB	SOCATA TB-10 Tobago	371	
D-EKTC	Piper PA-28R-201T Turbo Arrow III	28R-7803364	N21431
D-EKTD	SOCATA TB-10 Tobago	374	
D-EKTF	SOCATA TB-10 Tobago	375	
D-EKTG	SOCATA TB-10 Tobago	376	
D-EKTH	SOCATA TB-9 Tampico	387	
D-EKTI (2)	Beech A-36 Bonanza	E-1646	
D-EKTJ	SOCATA Rallye 180TS Galérien	3374	
D-EKTK	SOCATA TB-10 Tobago	366	
D-EKTM	SOCATA TB-10 Tobago	367	
D-EKTO	Cessna F172G	F172-0180	
D-EKTY(2)	Dornier Do.27A-1	322	56+41 D-9500
D-EKUC(2)	Piper PA-28-180 Cherokee Challenger	28-7305470	N55791
D-EKUF	Beech G35 Bonanza	D-4713	N12B
D-EKUG	Cessna 150	17818	N6418T
D-EKUH(2)	Luscombe 8F Silvaire	6295	HB-DUC NC1868B
D-EKUI	Dornier Do.27A-4	230	D-EKUT(2) D-EBAJ 55+83 YA+907 D-EHYL
D-EKUL(2)	Piper PA-28-181 Archer II	28-8090042	N2322U
D-EKUM	Rhein RW-3-V2 Multoplan (Permit .03)	2	
D-EKUN(3)	SOCATA MS.893E Rallye 180GT Gaillard	12180	F-BUCN
D-EKUO	Morane-Saulnier MS.885 Super Rallye	245	F-BKUO
D-EKUP(2)	Cessna 182E Skylane	18253847	HB-CBB OE-DDB (N2847Y)
D-EKUQ	Piper PA-18-100 Super Cub (Converted from PA-19 Super Cub 95)	18-6413	N8974D
D-EKUR(2)	Mooney M.20K Model 231	25-0437	(N3655H)
D-EKUT(3)	Dornier Do.27Q-4	2024	HB-FAA
D-EKUW(2)	Piper PA-28RT-201T Turbo Arrow IV	28R-8031167	N82557
D-EKVA(2)	Beech A36 Bonanza	E-2328	N2644M
D-EKVB	Cessna 150L	15073720	N18002
D-EKVF	Robin DR.400/180 Régent	1697	G-BLYS
D-EKVH	Piper PA-46-310P Malibu (Reserved as F-GTFM)	46-8408041	HB-PKB (D-EIDN(2)) HB-PKB D-ERAS HB-PKB (D-ERAS) HB-PKB D-ELBU(3) N43467
D-EKVL	Robin DR.400/180R Remorqueur	1196	
D-EKVM(2)	Cessna U206G Stationair 6-II	U20605474	HB-CLK N6394U
D-EKVW	Cessna P210N Pressurized Centurion (Robertson STOL conversion)	P21000579	N732GV
D-EKWA(4)	Cessna 182P Skylane (Reims-assembled with "c/n" 0041)	18264136	N6234F
D-EKWF	Piper PA-28-140 Cherokee E	28-7225456	N11C
D-EKWG(2)	Mooney M.20K Model 252 TSE	25-1091	N252YW
D-EKWH(2)	Piper PA-38-112 Tomahawk	38-78A0173	N9718N
D-EKWM	Cessna 182E Skylane	18254307	OE-DDE N3307Y
D-EKWR(2)	Robin DR.400/180 Régent	2327	
D-EKWS(2)	Robin DR.400/180RP Remorqueur	1790	
D-EKWT	Piper PA-24-260 Turbo Comanche C	24-4937	N9429P
D-EKWW	Piper PA-38-112 Tomahawk	38-78A0420	N9727N
D-EKXA	Beech F33C Bonanza	CJ-29	
D-EKXB	CEA DR.253B Régent	162	
D-EKXC	CEA DR.253B Régent	164	
D-EKXD	CEA DR.253B Régent	166	
D-EKXE	Beech F33A Bonanza	CE-298	
D-EKXO	Beech A23-24 Musketeer Super III	MA-363	
D-EKYL	Piper PA-18 Super Cub 95 (Crashed 2.8.03)	18-4462	N2872P
D-EKYM(2)	Scheibe SF.23A Sperling	2019	
D-EKYP	Scheibe SF.23A Sperling	2008	
D-EKYS(2)	Mooney M.20J Model 201	24-1095	
D-EKYT(3)	Piper PA-28-140 Cherokee C	28-26868	N5967U
D-EKYV(2)	Piper PA-28R-200 Cherokee Arrow	28R-35750	N5018S
D-EKYW(2)	Robin DR.400/180 Régent	1702	
D-EKYX	Scintex CP.301C Emeraude	523	
D-EKZI	Piper PA-28-140 Cherokee	28-21427	N11C
D-EKZK	SEEMS MS.880B Rallye Club	371	F-BKZK
D-EKZO	Piper PA-28-140 Cherokee	28-21443	N11C
D-EKZY	Piper PA-28-140 Cherokee	28-21419	N11C
D-ELAB(2)	Cessna 152	15280850	N25908
D-ELAC(2)	Bölkow BO.208C Junior	626	
D-ELAD(2)	Reims/Cessna F172P	F17202232	
D-ELAG(2)	Cessna TU206G Turbo Stationair II	U20603740	N9964N
D-ELAH(2)	Gardan GY-80 Horizon 180	141	
D-ELAI	Bellanca 17-31 ATC Viking 260	73-31059	
D-ELAJ	Piper PA-28-140 Cherokee E	28-7225471	N11C
D-ELAK(2)	Piper PA-28-140 Cherokee E	28-7225094	N4210T
D-ELAL(5)	American AG-5B Tiger	10143	PH-MLD
D-ELAM(2)	Piper PA-28RT-201 Arrow IV	28R-7918175	N2853L
D-ELAN(2)	Bramsche/ Piel CP.301 Emeraude	AB.419	
D-ELAO(2)	Piper PA-46-310P Malibu	46-8608019	HB-POA I-GHIO G-BMMT N9230T

D-ELAQ(2)	Piper PA-28-181 Cherokee Archer II	28-7890432	N9567N
D-ELAR(3)	Robin DR.400/RP Remorqueur	1793	
D-ELAS(2)	Zlin Z.126 Trenér 2 (Dismantled and stored)	865	OE-AES
			2A-AN
D-ELAU	Piper PA-28-140 Cherokee Cruiser	28-7325296	N11C
D-ELAV(3)	Piper PA-28-181 Archer II	28-8190151	N8326B
D-ELAX	Cessna 172 (W/o 2.4.00)	29817	N8017B
D-ELAY	Bellanca 17-31 ATC Turbo-Viking	72-31034	
D-ELAZ(2)	Robin DR.300/108 2+2	542	
D-ELBA(3)	Diamond DA 20-A1 Katana	10276	C-GAHT
D-ELBB	SAN Jodel D.150 Mascaret	30	
D-ELBC(2)	Robin R.2160D Acrobin	121	(F-ODHO)
D-ELBD(3)	Piper PA-28-181 Archer III	2843079	N9273N
D-ELBE(4)	Cessna 182R Skylane	18268208	(N2499E)
D-ELBH(2)	SOCATA MS.880B Rallye Club	1372	F-BRRB
D-ELBL(2)	Piper PA-18-135 Super Cub	18-3944	(D-EBKP)
	(Reservation .02)		EI-245
			I-EIQS
			54-2544
D-ELBO(2)	Piper PA-28-235 Cherokee D	28-11375	N8573N
D-ELBS(2)	Piper PA-28-181 Cherokee Archer II	28-7890317	OY-CBS
			(N3614M)
			(D-EIIW)
			OY-CBS
			N3614M
D-ELBT(2)	Robin DR.400/RP Remorqueur	1798	
D-ELBW	Reims/Cessna F172N Skyhawk II	F17201557	
D-ELBY(4)	SOCATA Rallye 235A	13331	F-GDRB
D-ELCA	Göbel/ Binder CP.301S Smaragd	AB.434	
D-ELCB	Fuji FA-200-180 Aero Subaru	272	
D-ELCC	Piper PA-38-112 Tomahawk	38-79A0672	N9697N
D-ELCD	Piper PA-38-112 Tomahawk	38-80A0095	N9689N
D-ELCE(2)	Piper PA-28-181 Cherokee Archer II	28-7790043	N4550F
D-ELCG	Reims/Cessna F172N Skyhawk II	F17201947	
D-ELCH(3)	Commander Aircraft 114B	14566	
D-ELCI (2)	Piper PA-28-181 Cherokee Archer II	28-7690293	N75097
D-ELCL	Piper PA-28RT-201T Turbo Arrow IV	2831016	N9135Z
D-ELCM	Piper PA-28-181 Archer II	28-8690043	N565DH
			N9202C
			N9274Y
D-ELCO(4)	Diamond DA 40 Star	40256	C-GDMQ
D-ELCP	Mooney M.20G Statesman	680070	N3969N
D-ELCQ	Piper PA-28-140 Cherokee	28-24206	N1783J
D-ELCR	SNCAN/ Stampe SV-4C	20	F-BLCO
			Fr.AF
D-ELCS(2)	Cessna 182Q Skylane	18267140	N97586
			D-ELCS
			N97586
D-ELCT	Piper PA-28-181 Archer II	2890049	N9130X
D-ELCU	Piper PA-18 Super Cub 95	18-3114	L-40
			53-4714
D-ELCV	Piper PA-28-161 Warrior II	28-8216045	N9591N
D-ELCW	Piper PA-28R-201T Turbo Arrow	2803010	N9185X
D-ELCY	CEA DR.250/160 Capitaine	93	
D-ELDA	Wassmer WA.52 Europa	61	"D-EFDA"
D-ELDB	Piper PA-28RT-201 Arrow IV	28R-8018067	N8198Z
D-ELDC(2)	Piper PA-28-181 Archer III	2890208	SE-KXF
D-ELDD	Beech F33A Bonanza	CE-869	
D-ELDI (2)	Piper PA-28-236 Dakota	28-7911065	N2151J
D-ELDK(2)	Mooney M.20M Model 257 TLS	27-0027	
D-ELDM(2)	SOCATA TB-20 Trinidad	860	OY-CDM
D-ELDO(3)	Piper PA-28-161 Cadet	2841340	N9215Q
			N128ND
			(OH-PFI)
			(OH-PFA)
D-ELDP	Robin DR.400/180R Remorqueur	1461	
D-ELDW	Piper PA-28RT-201T Turbo Arrow IV	28R-8031164	N8253C
			N9595N
D-ELEA	Cessna F172H	F172-0394	
D-ELEB(2)	CASA I-131E Jungmann	2145	E3B-528
D-ELEC	Piper PA-22-160 Tri-Pacer	22-6321	N9310D
D-ELED(2)	HOAC DV-20 Katana	20026	
D-ELEF(3)	Robin DR.400/RP Remorqueur	1818	
D-ELEG(3)	Diamond DA 20-A1 Katana	10017	N126MF
			N517WA
D-ELEK(3)	SOCATA TB-10 Tobago	143	F-GCOH
D-ELEN(2)	Piper PA-28-140 Cherokee D	28-7125103	N1788T
D-ELEO	Reims FR172H Rocket	FR17200228	N9448
D-ELEP	Diemer/ Piel CP.301A Emeraude	AB.404	
D-ELEQ	Klemm Kl.107C	148	
D-ELES(2)	Beech C24R Sierra 200	MC-669	
D-ELET(4)	Piper PA-32R-301T Saratoga II TC	3257056	N41257
D-ELEV(2)	Piaggio FWP.149D	144	91+22
			GA+405
			AS+079
			(KB+121)
D-ELEX(3)	Piper PA-46-350P Malibu Mirage	4636105	N92832
D-ELEY(2)	Mooney M.20J Model 201	24-0231	PH-IHD
			N201HD
D-ELFC	Piper PA-28R-180 Cherokee Arrow	28R-30398	N4539J
D-ELFD	Diamond DA 20-C1 Katana	C0100	N811CT
			C-GFLR
D-ELFE(3)	Grob G.115A	8060	I-GROF
D-ELFF(2)	Piper PA-28-181 Archer II	28-8090068	N8077M
D-ELFG	Piper PA-28R-200 Cherokee Arrow II	28R-7335196	N55221
D-ELFH	Cessna 172E	17250984	C-GLHE
			D-EDTH
			N3784S

D-ELFI (3)	Piper PA-28-140 Cherokee E	28-7225112	N11C
D-ELFK(2)	Robin DR.400/180R Remo 180	2513	
D-ELFN	Reims/Cessna F172M	F17201499	
D-ELFP	Cessna 182N Skylane	18260301	N92663
D-ELFR	Robin DR.400/180 Régent	1341	
D-ELFS(2)	Robin DR.400/180R Remorqueur	1875	
D-ELFT(2)	Piper PA-28-161 Cadet	2841287	N9526N
			N92043
D-ELFU(2)	LFU 205	V-1	
D-ELFW(2)	Focke-Wulf FW.44J Stieglitz	2924	N212S
			OH-SZM
			SZ-21
D-ELFY(2)	SOCATA MS.894A Minerva 220	11626	
D-ELGA(2)	PZL-104 Wilga 35A	21930951	
D-ELGB(2)	Piaggio FWP.149D	112	90+92
			MB+383
			JC+393
			AS+422
D-ELGC	Piper PA-18 Super Cub 95	18-6456	N9084D
D-ELGE(2)	Piper PA-38-112 Tomahawk	38-79A0447	N9729N
D-ELGH(2)	Piper PA-28R-200 Cherokee Arrow II	28R-7535150	N33426
D-ELGI (2)	Piper PA-28-151 Cherokee Warrior	28-7415150	N9513N
D-ELGK	Piper PA-12 Super Cruiser	12-2345	N3501M
			NC3501M
D-ELGL(2)	Cessna 172N	17271825	N5297E
D-ELGM	Piper PA-24-250 Comanche	24-782	N5708P
D-ELGN	Cessna F172F	F172-0107	
D-ELGO(2)	Piper PA-38-112 Tomahawk	38-78A0142	N9666N
D-ELGR(2)	Cessna 172N	17271094	N1687E
D-ELGT(2)	Cessna 182R Skylane	18268360	N6349E
D-ELGV	CEA DR.315 Petit Prince	448	
D-ELGW	CEA DR.253B Régent	160	
D-ELHA(3)	Piper PA-28-151 Cherokee Warrior	28-7615220	OE-DHA
			N99560N
D-ELHE(2)	SOCATA MS.894A Minerva 220	11996	F-BTPU
D-ELHF(2)	Mooney M.20J Model 201	24-1610	N5752E
D-ELHG(3)	Robin DR.400/180 Régent	1600	
D-ELHI (2)	Robin DR.400/180 Régent	1208	
D-ELHK	Beech V35B Bonanza	D-10020	
D-ELHL(2)	Piper PA-32R-301T Turbo Saratoga SP	32R-8429013	N4360H
D-ELHM	Piper PA-18 Super Cub 95	18-1336	ALAT
			51-15336
D-ELHN	Reims/Cessna F172M	F17201141	HB-CEG
D-ELHP	Piper PA-18-150 Super Cub	nil	(RBAF)
	(Built from spare fuselage no.18-4908)		
D-ELHQ	CEA DR.300/180R (Convtd.from DR.315)	479	
D-ELHS	Fuji FA-200-180 Aero Subaru	80	
D-ELHT	Piper PA-18 Super Cub 95	18-1015	ALAT
			51-15318
D-ELHV	Fuji FA-200-180 Aero Subaru	82	
D-ELHW	Mooney M.20J Model 201	24-0421	N201AX
D-ELHY(2)	Grumman AA-5B Tiger	AA5B-0975	G-BLHP
			OO-RTH
			(OO-HRR)
D-ELIA	SAN Jodel D.150 Mascaret	57	
D-ELIB(2)	Reims/Cessna F150M	F15001419	
D-ELIC(2)	Piper PA-28-140 Cherokee	28-20515	N6443W
D-ELIF(3)	Cessna 172S Skyhawk SP	172S9075	N5191G
D-ELIG(3)	Piper PA-28-140 Cherokee Cruiser	28-7325309	N11C
D-ELII	Piper PA-28-140 Cherokee C	28-26664	N5833U
D-ELIK	Klemm Kl.107B	104	
D-ELIL(4)	Piper PA-28-181 Archer II	28-7990114	N3020A
D-ELIM(2)	Wassmer WA.54 Atlantic	119	
D-ELIN(2)	Piper PA-28-181 Cherokee Archer II	28-7890345	N6446C
			N9540N
D-ELIO	CEA DR.253B Régent	172	
D-ELIP(3)	Lipp/ Denney Kitfox III (Permit)	1036	
D-ELIS(3)	SIAI-Marchetti SM.1019A (Reservation .04)	045	EI-445/
			MM57238
D-ELIT(2)	Piper PA-28R-201T Turbo Arrow III	28R-7803363	N21349
D-ELIX	Erco Ercoupe 415C	1079	N93757
D-ELIZ(2)	SOCATA ST-10 Diplomate	120	
D-ELJA(2)	Gruber/ Neico Lancair 235	1705	
D-ELJH	Hirt Starlite SL-1	1	
D-ELJI	Robin R.1180TD Aiglon	242	HB-EQI
D-ELJK(2)	Diamond DA 40D Star	D4.108	
D-ELJR	SAN Jodel DR.1050M-1 Excellence	468	(D-EHPL)
			F-BLJR
D-ELJS	Bücker Bü.131 Jungmann (Lycoming)	70	(D-EEJS)
			A-57
D-ELKA(3)	Piper PA-28R-201T Turbo Cherokee Arrow III		
		28R-7703174	N5982V
D-ELKC	Piper PA-28-181 Archer III	2843246	N4135Z
D-ELKE(2)	Piper PA-28-161 Warrior II	2816062	N9138N
D-ELKH	Morane-Saulnier MS.500 Criquet	699	F-BEJE
			Fr.AF
D-ELKI (2)	Reims/Cessna F172N	F17201918	
D-ELKK	Krause/ Steen Skybolt	3	
D-ELKN	Cessna 172R	17281208	N2109J
D-ELKR(2)	Leverkusen/ Rand-Robinson KR-2/B	1808/002	
D-ELKU(2)	Reims/Cessna FR172K Hawk XP	FR17200656	
D-ELKW	Wirth/ Rutan Long-Ez (W/o 8.7.02)	1083	
D-ELKY	Pützer Elster B	032	
D-ELLA(2)	SOCATA MS.894E Minerva 220GT	12198	F-BVZB
D-ELLB(2)	Piper PA-28-236 Dakota	2811024	N91637
D-ELLC	Piper PA-28-161 Warrior II	28-8116178	(N83514)
D-ELLD	Piper PA-28RT-201T Turbo Arrow IV	28R-7931303	N8090P

D-ELLE(2)	Reims/Cessna F182P Skylane	F18200002	
D-ELLG	Beech A36 Bonanza	E-2423	
D-ELLH	Piper PA-28-181 Archer II	2890134	N9190V
D-ELLI	Cessna 210	57339	N9539T
D-ELLK	Piper PA-28-161 Cadet	2841288	N9527N
			N92067
D-ELLL(2)	Robin HR.200/120B	44	HB-EXK
D-ELLM(2)	Nord 1002 Pingouin (Reservation .04)	88	N108U
			F-BBBZ
			Fr.AF
D-ELLN	Piper PA-28-161 Warrior II	2816058	N9132Z
D-ELLO(3)	Piper PA-18-150 Super Cub	18-7409041	I-MIGO
			N9735N
D-ELLP	SOCATA MS.893A Rallye Commodore 180	11823	
D-ELLS	SOCATA MS.883 Rallye 115	1587	F-BTHK
D-ELLU(2)	Piper PA-28-181 Archer II	28-8190271	N8408T
D-ELLV(2)	Rockwell Commander 112A	416	SE-FLV
			(N1416J)
D-ELLX	Piper PA-28-181 Archer II	2890101	N9158Z
D-ELLY(3)	DHC-1 Chipmunk 22 (Permit 3.05)	C1/0584	G-JAKE
			G-BBMY
			WK565
D-ELLZ	Cessna 182R Skylane	18267974	(PH-AXO)
			N9650H
D-ELMA(2)	Piper PA-28-235 Cherokee Pathfinder	28-7510110	N1589X
			N9584N
D-ELMC(2)	Mooney M.20K Model 252 TSE	25-1116	
D-ELMG	Reims/Cessna F150M	F15001299	LX-AVD
			LX-AIO
			(F-GAAA)
D-ELMH	Grumman AA-5B Tiger	AA5B-0107	
D-ELMI (3)	Cessna 182J Skylane	18257426	N3426F
D-ELMK	Beech A36 Bonanza	E-1544	
D-ELMM(2)	Robin DR.400/180R Remo 180	2006	
D-ELMN	CEA Jodel DR.1050 Sicile (Res as F-GSMN)	437	F-BLMN
D-ELMO	CEA Jodel DR.1050 Ambassadeur	210	
D-ELMR	Bareiss/ Brändli BX-2 Cherry	Eb 001/83	
D-ELMS(2)	Piper PA-28RT-201T Turbo Arrow IV	28R-8031133	N82377
D-ELMU(2)	Bölkow BO.208C Junior	705	(D-ENYO)
D-ELMY(3)	Aviat A-1 Husky	1325	
D-ELMZ	Piper PA-28-180 Cherokee D	28-5156	LN-LMZ
D-ELNA(2)	Cessna F172G	F172-0238	
D-ELNB	Cessna F172H	F172-0530	
D-ELNC	Cessna F150H	F150-0357	
D-ELNF	Cessna F172H	F172-0540	
D-ELNI (2)	Piper PA-18 Super Cub 95	18-456	Greek AF
			50-1800
D-ELNN(2)	SOCATA Rallye 110ST Galopin	3383	F-GENN
			F-OGMB
D-ELNP	Cessna F150H	F150-0355	
D-ELNQ	Cessna F172H	F172-0547	
D-ELNY(2)	Beech F33A Bonanza	CE-787	
D-ELOA	Piper PA-28-161 Warrior II	28-8016239	N9613N
D-ELOB(3)	Reims/Cessna F172M	F17201103	
D-ELOC	Piper PA-18-150 Super Cub	18-6635	OO-CIP
			N10F
			N9370D
D-ELOD(2)	Cessna F172G	F172-0203	
D-ELOF	Piper PA-18-135 Super Cub	18-2490	HB-OEC
			N10F
D-ELOG(2)	Cessna F150G	F150-0096	
D-ELOK(2)	Piper PA-18-150 Super Cub	18-8797	N4450Z
D-ELOL(3)	Cessna F172G	F172-0207	
D-ELOO	Cessna F172G	F172-0290	
D-ELOS(3)	Diamond DA 20-A1 Katana	10216	N691DA
D-ELOT(3)	Reims/Cessna F152	F15201637	OY-BNC
D-ELOU	Beech A23A Musketeer	M-937	N2338W
D-ELOV(3)	Piper PA-32RT-300T Turbo Lance II	32R-7887155	N39728
D-ELOW	Piper PA-18-150 Super Cub	18-7095	
D-ELOX	Klemm Kl.35D	1959	LN-TAI
			Fv5040
D-ELOY	Reims/Cessna F182Q Skylane	F18200073	
D-ELOZ(2)	Robin DR.300/108 2+2	526	
D-ELPA(3)	Piper PA-28-181 Archer III	2843590	N3043N
D-ELPC	Piper PA-28-181 Cherokee Archer II	28-7790292	N9586N
D-ELPD	Reims/Cessna F172N	F17201825	
D-ELPF	SIAI-Marchetti SF.260C	715/ 47-004	I-ALPF
D-ELPI(3)	Cessna 172S	172S9784	N6612D
D-ELPK	Mooney M.20C Ranger	20-1255	
D-ELPL	Cessna P210N Pressurized Centurion II	P21000535	N46932
			D-ELPL
			(N731QW)
D-ELPM(2)	Piper PA-28-161 Warrior II	28-8116298	N8427H
D-ELPN	HOAC DV-20 Katana	20023	
D-ELPP(2)	HOAC DV-20 Katana	20094	N194DV
D-ELPR	Hohenstein/ Europa Avn Europa	190SB	
	(Converted to tri-gear) (Permit 12.97)		
D-ELPS(2)	Styrsky/ Neico Lancair 235 Pegasos	001/475	
D-ELPT	Fuji FA-200-180AO Aero Subaru	261	
D-ELPU(2)	Reims/Cessna F172P	F17202149	
D-ELPY(2)	SOCATA MS.893E Rallye 180GT Gaillard	12315	F-GFVX
			HB-ETG
			F-BUZC
D-ELQC	Piper PA-28-181 Archer III	2843558	N53654
D-ELQE	SEEMS MS.885 Super Rallye	5412	
D-ELQI	Cessna 172E	17251424	N5524T
D-ELQU	Mooney M.20A	1597	N6009X

D-ELQY	Piper PA-18 Super Cub 95	18-3083	L-9
			53-4683
D-ELRA	Cessna T206H Turbo Stationair	T20608316	N3549Z
D-ELRB	Reims FR172F Rocket	FR17200096	
D-ELRC	Reims FR172F Rocket	FR17200092	
D-ELRD	Reims FR172F Rocket	FR17200095	
D-ELRE(2)	Reims/Cessna F152 II	F15201763	
D-ELRF(2)	Piper PA-28-140 Cherokee C	28-26670	N5839U
D-ELRI (3)	Hartz/ Piel CP.301E Emeraude	AB.405	D-ECAG(2)
D-ELRK	Cessna F150J	F150-0493	
D-ELRN	Extra EA.400	20	
D-ELRO(2)	Beech B36TC Bonanza	EA-377	N67269
D-ELRP	Reims/Cessna F182Q Skylane	F18200056	
D-ELRS	Robin DR.400/180R Remorqueur	1231	
D-ELRT	Robin DR.400/180R Remorqueur	1236	
D-ELRY	Gardan GY-80 Horizon 160	64	
D-ELSA(3)	Piper PA-28R-200 Cherokee Arrow II	28R-7535039	N9614N
D-ELSB	Robin DR.400/180R Remorqueur	1145	
D-ELSC(2)	Robin DR.400/180R Remorqueur	1108	LN-SAT
			SE-GRH
D-ELSD	Cessna 152	15281427	N49987
D-ELSE	Cessna 182G Skylane	18255547	N2447R
D-ELSF	Dornier Do.27B-1	273	56+06
			AS+901
D-ELSI (2)	Piper PA-28-181 Cherokee Archer II	28-7790206	N9547N
D-ELSM	SAN Jodel D.117A Grand Tourisme	839	F-BITL
D-ELSN	Cessna 172R	17280158	
D-ELSO	SAN Jodel DR.1050 Ambassadeur	396	
D-ELSP	Grob G.115A	8016	
D-ELSR(2)	Robin DR.400/180R Remo 180	2012	
D-ELST(2)	Cessna 172N	17273727	(D-EGPB(2))
			N5196J
D-ELSU(3)	Piper PA-32RT-301 Saratoga SP	32R-8013088	N8188M
D-ELSV(2)	Reims/Cessna F172P	F17202242	
D-ELSW	Cessna 180K Skywagon	18052975	N2533K
D-ELTA	Beech K35 Bonanza	D-5968	
D-ELTB(2)	Reims/Cessna F182Q Skylane II	F18200082	
D-ELTC(2)	Reims/Cessna F182Q Skylane	F18200139	
D-ELTD	Piper PA-18-150 Super Cub	18-1460	ALAT
			51-15460
D-ELTE(2)	Piper PA-12 Super Cruiser	12-1874	N3204M
			NC3204M
D-ELTG(2)	HOAC DV-20 Katana	20022	
D-ELTI (3)	Piper PA-12 Super Cruiser	12-3462	D-ELQB
			D-ELOB
			N4036H
			NC4036H
D-ELTM	Mooney M.20F Executive	680147	
D-ELTO(2)	Schoon/TEAM Minimax 1600R (C/n now MK118?)	1883	
D-ELTP	Piper PA-18 Super Cub 95	18-1567	ALAT
			51-15567
D-ELTT	Dornier Do.27B-3	430	57+04
			CB+003
			LC+156 ?
D-ELTU(2)	SOCATA MS.893E Rallye 180GT Gaillard	12326	F-BUVH
D-ELTW	Diamond DA 20-A1 Katana	10324	
D-ELTY(2)	Pützer Elster B	008	97+06
			D-EDEQ
D-ELTZ	Cessna T210N Turbo Centurion II	21064486	ZS-LTU
			N9364Y
D-ELUC(2)	Piper PA-28R-201T Turbo Cherokee Arrow III		
	(Permit 22.10.03 after rebuild)	28R-7703370	N47401
D-ELUD	Zlin Z.126 Trenér 2	841	
D-ELUE(2)	Piper PA-28-161 Warrior II	28-7916484	N2856Y
D-ELUF(2)	Piper PA-18-180 Super Cub	18-2046	PH-LUF
	(Originally built as Super Cub 95 / L-18C)		PH-JWK
			R-50
			52-2446
D-ELUH(2)	Piper PA-28R-201T Turbo Cherokee Arrow III		
		28R-7703324	N43986
D-ELUI	Reims/Cessna F172N	F17201719	
D-ELUK(2)	Piper PA-18-150 Super Cub	18-7446	N6813P
D-ELUM	Piper J-3C-65 Cub	11005	HB-OFG
	(C/n officially listed as 13249 which was originally		43-29714
	HB-OFG, now HB-OCK. D-ELUM has f/n 10830 = c/n 11005)		
D-ELUP(3)	Reims/Cessna F172N	F17201528	PH-SRO
			OO-LWC
			PH-SRO
D-ELUV(2)	Cessna 170B	20471	D-ELIL
			OO-SPA
			N2319D
D-ELUW(2)	Aeromere F.8L Falco III	226	
D-ELUX(2)	Huber/ Monnett Moni H1	1	
D-ELVA	Cessna F172E	F172-0067	
D-ELVB(2)	Hoffmann H-40-02	002	D-EABY(3)
D-ELVC(2)	Piper PA-28-181 Archer III	2943324	N41770
			N9514N
D-ELVD	Reims FR172F Rocket	FR17200085	
D-ELVE(2)	Piper PA-28R-200 Cherokee Arrow II	28R-7635327	N6255J
D-ELVF	Reims FR172F Rocket	FR17200070	
D-ELVG(2)	Robin DR.400/180R Remo 180	2383	
D-ELVH	Reims FR172F Rocket	FR17200117	
D-ELVI	Piper PA-28-180 Cherokee B	28-720	N7037W
D-ELVJ	Reims FR172F Rocket	FR17200118	
D-ELVK	Dornier Do.27A-1	329	56+47
			GC+377
			AS+943

D-ELVO(2)	Cessna F172H	F172-0325	(D-EGDO)
D-ELVP	Gardan GY-80 Horizon 160	75	F-BLVP
D-ELVS	PZL-104 Wilga 35	19880863	SP-FWA
D-ELWA(2)	SIAI-Marchetti SF.260	2-44	HB-EMK
D-ELWC(3)	Piper PA-28-181 Archer III	2943345	OY-PAW
			N9513N
D-ELWD	Robin R.3000/160	145	
D-ELWE(2)	Cessna 172RG Cutlass RG	172RG0133	OE-DVR
			N6271R
D-ELWF	Grob G.115A	8049	
D-ELWG	Reims/Cessna F150M	F15001308	
D-ELWH	Mooney M.20K Model 231	25-0123	N3702H
			N231BW
D-ELWI	Cessna 170B	26722	N4378B
D-ELWK(2)	Mooney M.20K Model 231	25-0378	N231RN
D-ELWM(2)	Robin DR.400/180 Régent	2515	
D-ELWN	HOAC DV-20 Katana	20156	
D-ELWO	Piper PA-28-180 Cherokee B	28-1706	N7748W
D-ELWP	Hirt/ Denney Kitfox IV-1200 (Permit)	1733	
	(C/n now quoted as DCU-025)		
D-ELWR	Cessna 172RG Cutlass RG	172RG0133	OE-DVR
			N6271R
D-ELWS	Air Products F-1A Aircoupe	5752	G-AROR
			N25B
D-ELWT	Grob G.115C	82040C	D-EXER
D-ELWU	Cessna 150	17833	OE-ADW
			N6433T
D-ELWW	Piper PA-28-140 Cherokee Cruiser	28-7525259	N9640N
D-ELXI	Cessna F172H	F172-0431	
D-ELXP	Cessna 172N	17271831	N5305E
D-ELYA	Maule MX.7-180 Star Rocket	11042C	N6116E
D-ELYC(2)	Piper PA-28-181 Archer III	2943329	OY-JAT
			N9519N
D-ELYD	Auster Mk.5	1790	G-ANKI
			TW446
D-ELYH	Piper PA-18 Super Cub 95	18-7069	
D-ELYK	Cessna TU206G Turbo Stationair 6-II	U20606285	N6466Z
D-ELYN(3)	Aerotek Pitts S-2A	2005	N52SH
	(Permit 2.04)		N919F
			N80000
D-ELYP(2)	Robin R.2160D (Converted fron R.2100A .89)	138	
D-ELYQ	Klemm Kl.107C	152	
D-ELYS	Cessna 172	29353	N7253A
D-ELYW	Piper PA-18A-125 Super Cub	18-7096	
	(Built as PA-18-150)		
D-ELZC	Piper PA-28-181 Archer III	2843548	N53662
D-ELZH	Grob G.115C	82020	
D-ELZI (2)	Piper PA-28-161 Cadet	2841242	N9192J
D-ELZU	Cessna F172E	F172-0051	
D-EMAA	Piper PA-28-180 Cherokee Archer	28-7405073	N9645N
D-EMAB(2)	Reims/Cessna F172P	F17202236	
D-EMAC(4)	Piper PA-28R-200 Cherokee Arrow	28R-35155	N318MC
			HB-OZP
			N9441N
D-EMAD(2)	Piper PA-18-100 Super Cub	18-2030	R-33
	(Built as PA-18 Super Cub 95)		52-2430
D-EMAE(2)	Mooney M.20F Executive	22-1211	
D-EMAF(3)	SOCATA MS.893A Rallye Commodore 180	10721	F-BPBU
D-EMAG(2)	Cessna 170B	27036	OE-DBO
			HB-CPC
			N3493D
D-EMAH	Orlican L-40 Meta-Sokol	150503	OK-NMF
D-EMAI	Piper PA-18-135 Super Cub	18-7180	N3185Z
	(Built as PA-18-150)		
D-EMAJ	Piper PA-28-181 Archer II	28-8190165	N83353
D-EMAK(3)	Beech F33A Bonanza	CE-1506	
D-EMAL(3)	Piper PA-18-150 Super Cub	1809023	OY-JEH
D-EMAM(2)	Piper PA-18 Super Cub 95	18-2037	R-39
			52-2437
D-EMAN(2)	CEA Jodel DR.1050 Ambassadeur	44	F-BJUC
D-EMAO(2)	Piper PA-28RT-201T Turbo Arrow IV	28R-8031085	N8182R
D-EMAP(2)	Piper PA-28-181 Cherokee Archer II	28-7790453	N3345Q
D-EMAR(2)	Piper PA-28R-200 Cherokee Arrow II	28R-7635372	N6990J
D-EMAT(2)	Timmermann/ Christen Eagle II	02/1602-348	
D-EMAV(2)	Mraz K-65 Cap	741	D-EKUS
	(Officially regd.as a Fieseler Fi.156 Storch)		HB-IKA
			OK-DF .
D-EMAW	Scheibe SF.23A-1 Sperling	2500	
D-EMAX(3)	Focke-Wulf FW.44J Stieglitz	83	(D-EMIQ(2))
			D-EMIL(3)
			D-EFUD
			SE-AWT
			Fv.631
D-EMAZ(4)	Mooney M.20M Model 257 TLS	27-0273	N91706
D-EMBA(3)	Piaggio FWP.149D	055	90+41
			ND+206
			AS+482
D-EMBB	Dornier Do.27B-1	307	56+32
			PA+319
			PF+111
			PL+414
D-EMBC	Cessna F150J	F150-0501	
D-EMBD(2)	Piper PA-28-180 Cherokee G	28-7205314	N11C
D-EMBF	Fuji FA-200-160 Aero Subaru	152	
D-EMBG	Fuji FA-200-180 Aero Subaru	157	
D-EMBI (2)	Beech A36AT Bonanza	E-2710	N55764
D-EMBL	Piper PA-28-180 Cherokee D	28-5315	N7950N
D-EMBM	Piper PA-28RT-201 Arrow IV	28R-7918173	N2845G
D-EMBO(2)	Gardan GY-80 Horizon 180	157	
D-EMBR	Cessna TU206F Turbo Stationair	U20601761	(N9561G)
D-EMBS	Reims FR172H Rocket	FR17200275	
D-EMBU(2)	Piper PA-28RT-201T Turbo Arrow IV	28R-7931252	N2909N
D-EMBV	Fuji FA-200-180 Aero Subaru	242	
D-EMBW	Piper PA-28R-201T Turbo Cherokee Arrow III		
		28R-7703394	N47533
D-EMCB	Piper PA-28-140 Cherokee D	28-7125520	N1849T
D-EMCC	Piper PA-28R-200 Cherokee Arrow II	28R-7235219	N5294T
D-EMCD	Piper PA-28R-200 Cherokee Arrow II	28R-7235150	N2872T
D-EMCG(2)	Reims/Cessna F172P	F17202206	
D-EMCH	Piper PA-28-180 Cherokee Challenger	28-7305375	N55404
D-EMCI	Piper PA-18A-150 Super Cub	18-5549	N6968D
D-EMCL	Piper PA-28-151 Cherokee Warrior	28-7415086	N9626N
D-EMCN	Piper PA-38-112 Tomahawk	38-78A0324	N9693N
D-EMCO(2)	Piper PA-28-235 Cherokee	28-10365	N8817W
D-EMCP	Reims/Cessna F172N	F17201678	
D-EMCR	Cessna TR182 Turbo Skylane RG	R18200794	OO-ADM
			PH-ADM
			"PH-NEL"
			PH-ADM
			PH-AYC
			N736YX
D-EMCS	Piper PA-28-151 Cherokee Warrior	28-7415298	N9561N
D-EMCT	Cessna 182M Skylane	18259492	N71089
D-EMCU	Piper PA-28-235 Cherokee	28-10366	N8818W
D-EMCV	Cessna 182P Skylane	18263396	I-AMCW
			N9471G
D-EMDA	Cessna 172E Skyhawk	17250594	N2994U
D-EMDD	Reims/Cessna F150K	F15000603	
D-EMDE	Cessna 172E	17250596	N2996U
D-EMDF	Reims/Cessna F172H	F17200715	
D-EMDG	Reims FR172G Rocket	FR17200201	
D-EMDH	Reims/Cessna F150K	F15000617	
D-EMDI	Cessna F172E	F172-0022/17250577	(N2977U)
D-EMDK	Reims/Cessna F172H	F17200713	
D-EMDL	Reims FR172G Rocket	FR17200200	
D-EMDM	Piper PA-28R-200 Cherokee Arrow II	28R-7335225	N55384
D-EMDN(2)	SOCATA TB-9 Tampico	907	
D-EMDS	Reims FR172H Rocket	FR17200290	
D-EMDW	Wassmer WA.52 Europa	26	
D-EMDY(2)	Cessna 172B	17248053	D-ELGB
			N7553X
D-EMED(4)	Piper PA-28RT-201T Turbo Arrow IV	28R-8131138	N83890
			(N21MH)
			N83890
D-EMEE(2)	Cessna 172N	17271788	N5236E
D-EMEI	Zlin Z.526L Trenér Master	1155	OE-AGA
D-EMEJ	Dornier Do.27A-3	429	57+03
			GB+901
			LC+155
D-EMEK(2)	Piper PA-18 Super Cub 95	18-3433	96+13
			SC+340
			AC+521
			AA+521
			AS+521
			54-733
D-EMEL(3)	Pützer Elster B	016	97+09
			D-EDIF
D-EMEM(3)	Piper PA-28-181 Archer II	28-8290157	N82469
			N9530N
D-EMEP(3)	Piper PA-38-112 Tomahawk	38-78A0620	N4469E
D-EMER	Piper J-3C-85 Cub	13210	HB-OCB
			45-4470
D-EMES(2)	Piper PA-28R-201T Turbo Arrow III	28R-7803214	N6258C
D-EMEV(2)	Gardan GY-80 Horizon 160D	221	F-BRLS
D-EMEX(2)	SOCATA MS.880B Rallye-Club	1921	F-BTIJ
D-EMEY	Piper PA-28-161 Cherokee Warrior II	28-7716186	N5612V
D-EMFA	Morane-Saulnier MS.885 Super Rallye	5135	
D-EMFC(4)	Diamond DA 20-A1 Katana	10129	N558ND
			N558SS
D-EMFE	Beech V35B Bonanza	D-10263	
D-EMFF	SOCATA MS.893E Rallye 180GT Gaillard	12739	F-GAFL
D-EMFG(3)	Cessna P210N Pressurized Centurion II	P21000458	N731GW
D-EMFH(2)	Diamond DA 20-A1 Katana	10305	N605DA
D-EMFJ	Piper PA-28-236 Dakota	28-8011027	N81170
D-EMFM(2)	Cessna 152	15279655	N757DK
D-EMFN	Diamond DA 20-A1 Katana	10165	
D-EMFP	Piper PA-28RT-201 Arrow IV	28R-8118058	N8354A
D-EMFR	Cessna 172P Skyhawk II	17274651	N52980
D-EMFS	Cessna F150G	F150-0174	(OH-CER)
D-EMFU	Bölkow BO.208C Junior	574	
D-EMFW(2)	Mang FW.190 Replica (Reservation .04)	1	
D-EMFX	SOCATA TB-9 Tampico Club	932	
D-EMFY(2)	Reims/Cessna F172N Skyhawk	F17201606	
D-EMGA	SAN Jodel D.140C Mousquetaire III	114	F-BKSZ
D-EMGC	Mooney M.20K Model 231	25-0409	
D-EMGG	Piper PA-28-181 Archer II	28-7990387	N2245Y
D-EMGH	SAN Jodel DR.1050 Sicile	480	
D-EMGI(2)	Mooney M.20M Model 257 TLS	27-0256	N2156F
D-EMGK	HOAC DV-20 Katana	20140	
D-EMGM	Wassmer WA.52 Europa	32	
D-EMGO	Cessna F172H	F172-0440	
D-EMGS	Piper PA-28R-200 Cherokee Arrow II	28R-7335421	N56365
D-EMGW	Reims/Cessna FR182 Skylane RG	FR18200024	

D-EMHA(2)	Cessna 182Q Skylane (SMA diesel engine fitted 10.04)	18267287	(D-ESAH) YV-180P N4665N
D-EMHB	Cessna F172F	F172-0152	N5054T D-EMHB
D-EMHC	Piper PA-18 Super Cub 95	18-3430	96+11 AC+519 AA+519 AS+519 54-730
D-EMHD	Bücker Bü.131 Jungmann	23	N131BJ HB-USL A-14
D-EMHE	Mooney M.20E Super 21	719	
D-EMHF	Mooney M.20E Super 21	670004	
D-EMHG	Grässer/ Viking Dragonfly	001	
D-EMHH(2)	Cessna 172RG Cutlass RG	172RG0198	G-OIFR G-BHJG N6529R
D-EMHI (2)	Piper PA-18-180 Super Cub	18-8245	N5995Z
D-EMHL	Rockwell Commander 114B	14151	N4821W
D-EMHM	Cessna T210M Turbo Centurion	21062746	N6331B
D-EMHN	Klemm Kl.35D	1842	SE-BPL Fv5065
D-EMHO(2)	Mooney M.20J Model 201	24-1002	(N3991H)
D-EMHP	Robin R.1180TD Aiglon	238	
D-EMHS(3)	Cessna 177B Cardinal	17701687	N34169
D-EMHW(2)	Piper PA-28-161 Warrior III	2842176	(D-EASS(3)) N53642
D-EMIA	Morane-Saulnier MS.885 Super Rallye	53	F-BKEV
D-EMIB(2)	Beech A36 Bonanza	E-1578	
D-EMIC(3)	OMF-100-160 Symphony	0003	
D-EMIE(2)	Piper PA-46-310P Malibu	46-8508057	N4391S
D-EMIG	Focke-Wulf FW.44J Stieglitz	2293	SE-BXO Fv625
D-EMIH	Dornier Do.27Q-5	2027	
D-EMIK(2)	Robin DR.400/140B Major	1107	
D-EMIL(4)	Focke-Wulf FW.44J Stieglitz	unkn	D-EMIL(2) (D-EKNE) (D-EKXG) SE-BXG Fv662
D-EMIM(2)	Extra EA.300	03	G-OHIM D-EBTS G-OHIM D-EBTS
D-EMIO(3)	Champion 7FC Tri-Traveler	455	D-EMIO(1) N9923Y
D-EMIP(2)	Robin DR.400/180R Remorqueur	1375	
D-EMIS(2)	Cessna F172H	F172-0335	
D-EMIT(2)	Cessna 182P Skylane	18262063	N58439
D-EMIW	Piper PA-24-250 Comanche	24-1917	N6892P N10F
D-EMIY	Ströhle/ Aero Designs Pulsar XP (C/n formerly quoted as 1839)	AB431	
D-EMIZ(3)	Aerotek Pitts S-1S	1-0028	YV-24P YV-TAPA
D-EMJA(2)	Arau/ Dallach D4 E-BK 914F Fascination	EB023	
D-EMJB(2)	Cessna 172N	17269627	N737RY
D-EMJH(2)	Robin DR.400/180 Régent	2324	
D-EMJI	SOCATA MS.893A Rallye Commodore 180	12061	
D-EMJK	SOCATA MS.893A Rallye Commodore 180	12071	F-BUGB (D-ENME(2))
D-EMJN(2)	HOAC DV-20 Katana	20155	
D-EMJP	Piper PA-18 Super Cub 95	18-3199	D-EABS(2) OL-L03 L-125 53-4799
D-EMJR	Great Lakes 2T-1A-2	0786	N3818F
D-EMJT	SOCATA TB-20 Trinidad	711	
D-EMKA(3)	Dornier Do.27B-1	152	55+32 PG+216 PF+108 PD+103
D-EMKB	Hirth Hi-27 Akrostar Mk.II	4001	
D-EMKC	Piper PA-28R-201T Turbo Cherokee Arrow III	28R-7703427	N47696
D-EMKE(3)	Reims/Cessna F182Q Skylane	F18200115	PH-AYN
D-EMKG	SOCATA TB-20 Trinidad	705	
D-EMKH(2)	Beech F33A Bonanza	CE-1341	
D-EMKI (2)	Beech 77 Skipper	WA-94	
D-EMKJ	Mooney M.20C Mark 21	2550	HB-DEC N6845U
D-EMKL	Robin DR.400/180R Remo 180	2187	F-WZZX
D-EMKO(4)	SOCATA TB-9 Tampico	1110	I-TNAC F-OGSA
D-EMKP(2)	Krause/ Light Aero Avid Flyer	682-AB	
D-EMKR	Wassmer WA.52 Europa	59	
D-EMKS	Reims/Cessna F182Q Skylane II	F18200054	
D-EMKU	Binder CP.301S Smaragd	103	
D-EMKV	Reims/Cessna F172N	F17201559	
D-EMKY	Binder CP.301S Smaragd	104	
D-EMLA	Kibler/ Piel CP.301E Emeraude	AB.425	
D-EMLB	Reims/Cessna F172N	F17201580	
D-EMLD	Robin DR.400/180R Remorqueur	1494	
D-EMLE(2)	Piper PA-18-150 Super Cub (Built from spare fuselage no.18-4912)	nil	(RBAF)

D-EMLG	Cessna F172H	F172-0565	D-EBCG OY-AGJ
D-EMLH	Piper PA-28-181 Archer II	28-8090015	N2971Q
D-EMLI	Cessna 182S	18280645	
D-EMLL	Mooney M.20K Model 231	25-0699	N1169D
D-EMLR	Pilatus P.2-05	25	U-105 A-105
D-EMLS	Cessna T210L Turbo Centurion	21060094	(G-BCJJ) N59107
D-EMLT	Cessna R172K Hawk XP	R1722495	N736FQ
D-EMLW	Beech A24R Sierra	MC-81	OY-AJD N9729Q
D-EMLY	Piper PA-18 Super Cub 95	18-7235	N3295Z
D-EMLZ	Zeddies/ Skystar Kitfox V	S9502-0105	(D-ESLZ(3))
D-EMMA	Piper PA-18-150 Super Cub	18-6466	N10F
D-EMMB(2)	Piper PA-28-181 Archer II	2890051	N9133N
D-EMMC	SOCATA MS.880B Rallye Club	1254	
D-EMMD	SOCATA MS.893A Rallye Commodore 180	10930	
D-EMME	Piper PA-18-150 Super Cub	18-5107	N6985B
D-EMMF(3)	Piper PA-46-350P Malibu Mirage	4622103	OY-JEU N9197F
D-EMMG	SAN Jodel DR.1050 Ambassadeur	371	
D-EMMH	Cessna F172H	F172-0528	
D-EMMI (3)	Focke-Wulf FW.44J Stieglitz	unkn	D-ECAN SE-BWN Fv667
D-EMMJ(2)	Piper PA-28R-180 Cherokee Arrow	28R-30580	D-ELRF N4680J
D-EMMK(2)	Mooney M.20J Model 201	24-1260	N1157S
D-EMML(3)	Mooney M.20K Model 252 TSE	25-1153	HB-DHC
D-EMMM	Fuji FA-200-160 Aero Subaru	154	
D-EMMO(3)	Cessna 182R Skylane	18267964	N9565H
D-EMMP	Morane-Saulnier MS.880B Rallye Club	72	F-BKDZ
D-EMMQ	Laverda F.8L Falco IV	415	
D-EMMR	Laverda F.8L Falco IV	420	
D-EMMS	Cessna 185 Skywagon	185-0163	TJ-ADG TR-LKK F-OBVB N9963X
D-EMMT	Cessna F172F	F172-0148	
D-EMMU(2)	Piper PA-28-180 Cherokee F	28-7105056	N5196S
D-EMMV	Piper J-3C-90 Cub	12837	D-EHAC HB-OGU 44-80541
D-EMMW	Piper PA-32-300 Cherokee Six C	32-40922	N5225S
D-EMMX(2)	Maule MX.7-235 Star Rocket	10057C	N5GF
D-EMMY	Piper PA-18-150 Super Cub	18-7403	N10F
D-EMMZ(2)	Mooney M.20J Model 205	24-3367	
D-EMNA(2)	Heier/ Rutan Long-Ez	448	D-EFAR(3)
D-EMNC	Tecnam P.92J Echo-VLA	004	
D-EMNH	Piper PA-38-112 Tomahawk	38-78A0355	N6249A
D-EMNL	SIAI-Marchetti SF.260	2-37	OO-ADF OO-HAQ I-SJAQ
D-EMNQ	Dornier Do.27B-1	305	56+30 EA+384 QM+613 PL+412
D-EMNU	Beech A23-24 Musketeer Super III	MA-36	
D-EMOA	Mooney M.20J Model 201	24-1652	
D-EMOB(2)	Cessna 172RG Cutlass RG	172RG0523	HB-CNW (N5406V)
D-EMOC(3)	Mooney M.20J Model 205	24-3071	N205YY
D-EMOD(3)	Rockwell Commander 114	14421	(N5876N)
D-EMOE	Reims/Cessna F172N	F17201984	
D-EMOF	Focke-Wulf FW.44J Stieglitz	ASJA-82	SE-CBE Fv630
D-EMOH(3)	Mooney M.20J Model 201	24-1599	
D-EMOI	Robin DR.400/180R Remorqueur	1392	
D-EMOJ	Mooney M.20J Model 205	24-3042	
D-EMOK	Höxter/ Aero-Jodel D.11A Club	AB.14	
D-EMOL(3)	Reims FR172F Rocket	FR17200079	
D-EMOM(2)	Mooney M.20J Model 201	24-0990	(N3947H)
D-EMON(6)	HOAC DV-20 Katana	20012	C-FSRX N15DV OE-CDV
D-EMOO(3)	Dallach/ Stevens Akro Diabolo 2	EB-002	
D-EMOP	Piper PA-22 Tri-Pacer 125	22-329	D-EMOL N1416A
D-EMOR(3)	Mooney M.20J Model 205	24-3058	
D-EMOU(2)	Mooney M.20J Model 205	24-3172	
D-EMOV(2)	Reims/Cessna FR172K Hawk XP	FR17200660	
D-EMOW	Piper PA-18 Super Cub 105 (Built as PA-18 Super Cub 95)	18-7353	N10F
D-EMOX(2)	Beech F33A Bonanza	CE-875	
D-EMOY	Piper PA-28-161 Warrior II	28-8016365	N8240G
D-EMOZ(2)	Niederdellmann/ Binder CP.301S Smaragd	AB.22	
D-EMPB	Robin DR.400/180R Remorqueur	825	
D-EMPC	Reims/Cessna F152	F15201466	
D-EMPD	Rockwell Commander 114B	14431	
D-EMPE(3)	Mooney M.20J Model 205	24-3186	N9118X
D-EMPF(2)	Cessna 177RG Cardinal RG	177RG1344	OO-RAD N53096
D-EMPG	Reims/Cessna F172N	F17201692	
D-EMPH	Cessna 180K Skywagon	18052979	N2537K
D-EMPI	Morane-Saulnier MS.885 Super Rallye	85	
D-EMPK(3)	Piper PA-28-181 Archer III	2843588	N30884

D-EMPL(3)	HOAC DV-20 Katana	20041	
D-EMPM	SNCAN/ Stampe SV.4C	159	F-BMKM
			CEV
			F-BFLH
			CEV
			F-BDKY
D-EMPN	Piper PA-28RT-201T Turbo Arrow IV	28R-7931254	N2915A
D-EMPO	Morane-Saulnier MS.885 Super Rallye	5143	(D-EMTO)
D-EMPR	Piper PA-28-181 Archer II	28-7990579	N2952N
D-EMPT	Reims/Cessna FR172K Hawk XP	FR17200629	
D-EMPU(3)	OMF-100-160 Symphony (Permit .03)	0021	
D-EMQA	Cessna F172E	F172-0037/17250707	(N3507S)
D-EMQE	Cessna F172E	F172-0056	
D-EMRA(2)	Mooney M.20J Model 205	24-3195	
D-EMRD	Beech V35B Bonanza	D-10138	
D-EMRE	Piper PA-18-150 Super Cub (Dam.3.6.04)	18-6237	N8579D
D-EMRF	Robin DR.400/180R Remo 180	2071	
D-EMRH	SOCATA TB-10 Tobago	14	HB-EYU
			F-ODKC
D-EMRI	Cessna 172A	47638	N9838T
D-EMRO	Scintex Piel CP.301C Emeraude	518	
D-EMRP	Cessna 177B Cardinal	17702363	N11736
D-EMRS	Reims/Cessna F152	F15201511	
D-EMRT	SOCATA TB-20 Trinidad	452	
D-EMRU	Cessna 172	29004	OE-DBF
			N6904A
D-EMRW	Piper PA-28R-200 Cherokee Arrow II	28R-7235213	N5275T
D-EMRY(2)	Piper PA-28R-201 Cherokee Arrow III	28R-7737066	N5617V
D-EMRZ	Robin DR.400/180 Régent	718	
D-EMSA	Morane-Saulnier MS.880B Rallye Club	79	
D-EMSB	Cessna 152	15281418	N49969
D-EMSC	Cessna 152	15281440	N64829
D-EMSD	Reims/Cessna FR182 Skylane RG	FR18200053	(PH-AXP)
D-EMSE(2)	Cessna 172P	17276280	N98346
D-EMSF	Zlin Z.142	0001	OK-078
D-EMSG(2)	Reims/Cessna F152	F15201795	PH-CBE
D-EMSH(2)	Reims/Cessna F152	F15201935	
D-EMSI	Morane-Saulnier MS.885 Super Rallye	129	
D-EMSJ	Reims/Cessna F152	F15201787	PH-CBC
D-EMSK	Reims/Cessna F172M	F17201340	(SE-GKH)
D-EMSL	Robin DR.300/180R Remorqueur	464	F-BRZR
D-EMSM	Cessna 150M	15077389	N63551
D-EMSN	Cessna 150M	15077564	N6164K
D-EMSO	Morane-Saulnier MS.885 Super Rallye	5127	
D-EMSP(2)	Reims/Cessna F172N	F17201743	
D-EMSQ	Reims/Cessna F152	F15201808	PH-CBH
D-EMST	Piper PA-28-140 Cherokee D	28-7125141	N5587U
D-EMSW	Mooney M.20F Aerostar 220	22-0010	(D-EHTW)
			N9619V
D-EMSX	Cessna 172P	17274630	N52893
D-EMSY	Morane-Saulnier MS.885 Super Rallye	165	(D-EMTU)
D-EMSZ	Cessna 172P	17275049	N54759
D-EMTA(2)	Grob G.115A	8057	
D-EMTB	Cessna F150H (Rotax engine)	F150-0329	
D-EMTD(2)	Mooney M.20J Model 205	24-3279	
D-EMTH	Piper PA-18 Super Cub 95	18-1569	ALAT
	(W/o 23.3.00; reserved for rebuild)		51-15569
D-EMTI (2)	SOCATA TB-10 Tobago	1608	
D-EMTK(2)	Piper PA-28RT-201T Turbo Arrow IV	28R-8131039	SE-KGI
			N8305D
D-EMTN	Reims FR172G Rocket	FR17200147	
D-EMTO(2)	Piper PA-28-181 Cherokee Archer II	28-7890547	N39635
D-EMTP	Robin DR.400/180R Remorqueur	1328	F-GBII
D-EMTT	Fuji FA-200-180 Aero Subaru	190	(D-EITT(1))
D-EMTU	Morane-Saulnier MS.885 Super Rallye	168	
D-EMTW	Piper PA-38-112 Tomahawk	38-78A0583	ZS-KHS
			N4381E
D-EMTY	Morane-Saulnier MS.885 Super Rallye	5169	
D-EMUA	CEA Jodel DR.1050M-1 Sicile Record	630	
D-EMUE	SAN Jodel DR.1050 Ambassadeur	359	
D-EMUF	Eichelsdörfer/ Piel CP.301A Emeraude	AB.412	
D-EMUG(2)	Gardan GY-80 Horizon 160	91	F-BMUG
D-EMUH	Bölkow BO.208C Junior	623	
D-EMUK(2)	Beech V35B Bonanza	D-9986	
D-EMUL(2)	Cessna 120	11226	N76794
			NC76794
D-EMUM(2)	Piper PA-18-150 Super Cub	18-7709158	N82464
D-EMUN	Cessna 175 Skylark	55239	N9439B
D-EMUP(2)	Piper PA-28-140 Cherokee D	28-7125047	N1731T
D-EMUR(2)	Sportavia-Pützer RS-180 Sportsman	6008	
D-EMUT(4)	Cessna 172R	17280524	N9574D
D-EMUX(3)	Maule MXT-7-180A Starcraft	21021C	N1033Y
D-EMVA(3)	SOCATA TB-21 Trinidad TC	2015	
D-EMVB	Pützer Elster B	029	97+17
			D-ELBU
D-EMVE	Morane-Saulnier MS.880B Rallye Club	5219	
D-EMVG	Mroczeck/ Neico Lancair 320 II (Permit 11.99)	1852	
D-EMVI	SEEMS MS.880B Rallye Club	5312	
D-EMVP	OMF-100-135D Symphony (Permit 11.03)	0001	
D-EMVR	Cessna 182Q Skylane	18267132	N97560
D-EMVT	Arado Ar.79B	0047	D-ECUV(1)
			SL-AAP
			VA+HP
D-EMVZ	SOCATA TB-9 Tampico	1793	
D-EMWA(2)	Mooney M.20M Model 257 TLS	27-0167	
D-EMWB(2)	Cessna 182P Skylane	18264338	N1463M
	(Reims-assembled with "c/n" 0047)		

D-EMWC	Piper PA-28R-180 Cherokee Arrow	28R-30532	N4642J
D-EMWD	Piper PA-28R-180 Cherokee Arrow	28R-30648	N28WD
			D-EMWD
			N4927J
D-EMWE(2)	Cessna 172M	17266864	N1135U
D-EMWF(2)	Reims/Cessna F172N (Permit .04)	F17201587	
D-EMWH	Piper PA-28R-200 Cherokee Arrow	28R-35355	N3018R
D-EMWI	Cessna F172E	F172-0033/17250643	(N3043U)
D-EMWJ(3)	Cessna 172R	17280986	N7261S
D-EMWK(2)	Cessna TR182 Skylane RG	R18200703	N9407R
D-EMWL	Piper PA-28R-200 Cherokee Arrow	28R-35706	N4986S
D-EMWM(2)	Mooney M.20J Model 201	24-0993	N3960H
D-EMWO	Oberlerchner JOB 15-150	056	OE-CAA(1)
D-EMWP	Piper PA-28-140 Cherokee C	28-26820	N11C
D-EMWQ	Piper PA-28-140 Cherokee C	28-26819	N5992U
D-EMWR(2)	Beech F33A Bonanza	CE-1554	N8105X
D-EMWS	Piper PA-28-140 Cherokee D	28-7125170	N11C
D-EMWT(2)	Beech F33A Bonanza	CE-1529	
D-EMWU	Cessna F172E	F172-0043	
D-EMWW	Piper PA-28R-200 Cherokee Arrow B	28R-7135166	N2203T
D-EMWX	Piper PA-28-140 Cherokee D	28-7125389	N8590N
D-EMWY	Cessna F172E	F172-0038/17250739	(N3539S)
D-EMWZ	Piper PA-28-235 Cherokee D	28-11377	N8574N
D-EMXB	Cessna F172H	F172-0623	
D-EMXD	CEA DR.253B Régent	158	
D-EMXE	Cessna 177 Cardinal	17701149	N30249
D-EMXG	Cessna F172H	F172-0630	
D-EMXI	SIAT 223A-1 Flamingo	015	HB-EVL
			D-ENBL
D-EMYC	Brillinger/ Jodel D.9 Bébé	AB.1	
D-EMYE	Beech 35-C33 Debonair	CD-913	
D-EMYH	Mraz M.1D Sokol	350	OK-BXW
D-EMYJ	Fuji FA-200-160 Aero Subaru	72	
D-EMYL	Piper J-3C-65 Cub	11740	HB-OSR
			43-30449
D-EMYN(2)	SOCATA MS.893A Rallye Commodore 180	10619	
D-EMYP(2)	SOCATA MS.893A Rallye Commodore 180	10620	
D-EMYR(2)	Mooney M.20J Model 201	24-0527	
D-EMYS(3)	Mylius My.102 Tornado	V-1	
D-EMYX(2)	SOCATA MS.893A Rallye Commodore 180	10624	
D-EMYZ(2)	SAN Jodel DR.1050M Excellence	191	F-BJNX
D-EMZB	Cessna F172H	F172-0618	
D-EMZC	Reims FR172G Rocket	FR17200154	
D-EMZD	Reims FR172G Rocket	FR17200157	
D-EMZE(2)	Piper PA-28-161 Archer III	2842206	N3092J
D-EMZF	Reims/Cessna F172H	F17200667	
D-EMZG	Reims/Cessna F150K	F15000537	
D-EMZH	Reims/Cessna F150K	F15000579	
D-EMZI	Cessna F172F	F172-0166	
D-EMZO	SOCATA MS.893A Rallye Commodore 180	10569	
D-EMZY(2)	Piper PA-28-161 Cherokee Warrior II	28-7816011	N40069
D-ENAB(2)	SOCATA MS.893A Rallye Commodore 180	11460	F-BSZE
			OY-DJW
			F-BNGV
D-ENAC(2)	SOCATA MS.880B Rallye Club	1699	OE-DHC
			D-EOVK
			F-BSVK
D-ENAD	Wassmer Jodel D.120 Paris-Nice	138	
D-ENAF(2)	Piper PA-32R-300 Lance	32R-7780304	N3314Q
D-ENAI	Reims/Cessna F152	F15201737	
D-ENAK(2)	Piper PA-28RT-201T Turbo Arrow IV	28R-7931097	N385A
			N9615N
D-ENAL(2)	Reims/Cessna F152	F15201768	
D-ENAM(2)	Rockwell Commander 114	14008	N1908J
D-ENAN(2)	Piper PA-18 Super Cub 95	18-2072	R-61
			52-2472
D-ENAP	Mraz M.1D Sokol	274	OK-DHO
D-ENAQ	Piper PA-18 Super Cub 95	18-7397	N10F
D-ENAR(2)	Cessna TR182 Turbo Skylane RG	R18201433	C-GTSN
			N4825S
D-ENAS(4)	Cessna 172S Skyhawk SP	172S8631	OE-DAL(2)
			N650SP
D-ENAT(5)	Reims/Cessna F152	F15201753	
D-ENAV(2)	Piper PA-28-161 Cherokee Warrior II	28-7716106	(OO-FVP)
			D-ENAV(2)
			N9625N
D-ENAW(3)	Piper PA-28R-201 Arrow III	28R-7837143	N3947M
D-ENAY	Focke-Wulf FW.44J Stieglitz	unkn	D-EGAM
			SE-BWH
			Fv663
D-ENAZ	Stark Turbulent D-1	125	
D-ENBA	Cessna 205	205-0075	N1875Z
D-ENBB(3)	Piper PA-38-112 Tomahawk	38-82A0035	N91461
D-ENBC	Cessna F172H	F172-0373	
D-ENBF	Cessna F172H	F172-0524	
D-ENBH	Piper PA-28R-180 Cherokee Arrow	28R-30556	N4660J
D-ENBJ(2)	Piper PA-28R-180 Cherokee Arrow	28R-30675	N4939J
D-ENBL(2)	Piper PA-28R-200 Cherokee Arrow II	28R-7235235	N5494T
D-ENBM(2)	Piper PA-28R-180 Cherokee Arrow	28R-30678	N4941J
D-ENBO(2)	Piper PA-28RT-201T Turbo Arrow IV	28R-8031048	N3579K
D-ENBP(2)	Reims FR172F Rocket	FR17200068	
D-ENBR(3)	Ruschmeyer R.90-230RG	021	
D-ENBU(2)	Piper PA-28-181 Archer II	28-8390034	N9630N
D-ENBW	Robin DR.400/180R Remorqueur	1715	
D-ENBY(2)	Champion 7GCB Challenger	7GCB-100	OE-ADN
D-ENBZ	Cessna F150J	F150-0429	
D-ENCA(3)	Beech V35B Bonanza	D-10134	

D-ENCB(3)	Reims/Cessna F172N Skyhawk II	F17201797	
D-ENCC(2)	Piper PA-18-150 Super Cub	18-1483	ALAT 51-15483
D-ENCD(3)	Reims/Cessna F172N Skyhawk II	F17201795	
D-ENCG(3)	Reims/Cessna FR172K Hawk XP	FR17200637	
D-ENCI	Bölkow BO.208 Junior	511	(CS-ALX)
D-ENCL	Reims/Cessna F172P	F17202227	
D-ENCO(2)	Piper PA-28-140 Cherokee D	28-7125097	N1782T
D-ENCT	Mooney M.20M Model 257 TLS	27-0313	N1020G
D-ENCU(2)	Cessna F172G	F172-0307	
D-ENCW	Piper PA-28-140 Cherokee E	28-7225455	N11C
D-ENCY(4)	Cessna 177RG Cardinal RG	177RG0069	N8069G
D-ENDA(2)	Ruschmeyer MF-85-NDAE	V001	D-EEHE(2) (D-EJHR)
D-ENDC	Langer/ Brändli BX-2 Cherry	Eb 001	
D-ENDE(3)	Reims/Cessna F182Q Skylane	F18200146	
D-ENDI (3)	de Havilland DH.82A Tiger Moth	82335	G-ANDI N40DH G-ANDI (G-ANDM) N9240
D-ENDK	Robin DR.400/180 Régent	1318	
D-ENDO(2)	Cessna F172G	F172-0289	
D-ENDR	Cessna 172N	17268804	N734EU
D-ENDT	Reims/Cessna F150M	F15001171	
D-ENDY	Bölkow BO.208C Junior	520	
D-ENEA(2)	Cessna 182P Skylane	18260895	N9355G
D-ENEB	Aeromere F.8L Falco III	201	
D-ENEC(2)	Piper PA-32R-301T Turbo Saratoga SP	32R-8129056	N8360A
D-ENED	Wassmer Jodel D.120R Paris-Nice	139	
D-ENEE(2)	Piper PA-28-181 Archer II	2890070	N4311Z
D-ENEF	Piper J-3C-90 Cub	6347	N35441 NC35441
D-ENEG	Cessna 180 Skywagon	31463	N4564B
D-ENEH(5)	SOCATA TB-10 Tobago	1136	
D-ENEJ	SOCATA MS.880B Rallye Club (Permit .04)	1660	
D-ENEL(2)	Cessna T210N Turbo Centurion II	21064002	N4755Y
D-ENEN(2)	Robin R.3000/160	148	
D-ENEP(2)	Bölkow BO.208C Junior	619	
D-ENER(4)	Piper PA-28-160 Cherokee C	28-2392	VH-NER D-EMGU N5877W
D-ENET(3)	Beech B36TC Bonanza	EA-584	N44RN
D-ENEU(2)	Piper PA-28-161 Cadet	2841114	N9175Q N9646N
D-ENEW(2)	Cessna 182P Skylane	18262589	N52412
D-ENEY	SAN Jodel DR.1050 Ambassadeur	145	F-BJNH
D-ENEZ(3)	Piper PA-28-161 Warrior II	28-8116207	N3998P D-ENEZ(3) N8378B
D-ENFA(3)	Cessna F172H (Res as F-GUCT)	F172-0489	
D-ENFC	Piper PA-18-135 Super Cub	18-3830	R-140 54-2430
D-ENFD	Reims/Cessna F172N	F17201819	PH-AYE
D-ENFE	SAN Jodel DR.1050 Ambassadeur	381	
D-ENFF	Piper PA-28-161 Warrior II	28-8116075	N8291B
D-ENFH	SOCATA MS.893E Rallye 180GT Gaillard	12988	
D-ENFL	Grumman AA-5B Tiger	AA5B-0310	
D-ENFP	Piper PA-28-181 Archer II	28-8190173	N8342U
D-ENFR	Cessna 172P	17275499	N6286A (N694) N63937
D-ENFS	Cessna 172M	17266396	N30MX N30MP (N80136)
D-ENFU	Piper PA-18-150 Super Cub	18-6588	N9282D
D-ENFY	Cessna F172D	F172-0018/17250303	(N2703U)
D-ENGA(3)	Cessna 172RG Cutlass RG	172RG0432	N4964V
D-ENGB	Robin DR.400/180R Remorqueur	1735	
D-ENGD	Grob G.115D Acro	82018	
D-ENGE(2)	Fläming Air FA-01 Super Saphir (Res .05)	104	
D-ENGI (2)	Reims/Cessna F150M	F15001314	
D-ENGK	Kälberer/ Viking Dragonfly Mk.II (Not completed)	01	
D-ENGM	Piper PA-28R-201T Turbo Arrow III	28R-7803327	N36515
D-ENGO(2)	SOCATA TB-10 Tobago	934	
D-ENGS(2)	Auster 5 Alpha	3406	D-ECUR
D-ENGW	SOCATA MS.880B Rallye Club	1127	F-BPBI
D-ENGY(2)	Piper PA-28-181 Cherokee Archer II	28-7690338	N6107J N9581N
D-ENHB	Robin HR.100/210D Safari	212	
D-ENHF(2)	Mooney M.20J Model 205 (Res as F-GPHF)	24-3290	
D-ENHG	Robin DR.400/180 Régent	2004	
D-ENHK(2)	Piper PA-28-181 Archer II	28-8290135	N8209B
D-ENHL	Reims/Cessna F150M	F15001258	
D-ENHM(2)	Cessna 182T Skylane	18281092	N5176D
D-ENHR	Robin HR.200/100 Club	98	
D-ENHS(2)	Piper PA-28-181 Archer II	28-8490032	N4332D
D-ENHU	Cessna 182G Skylane	18255099	N3699U
D-ENHV	Robin DR.400/180 Régent	2200	
D-ENIA	Cessna 150	17844	OE-AIP N6444T
D-ENIB	Aeromere F.8L Falco III	203	
D-ENID	Champion 7FC Tri-Traveller	105	HB-UAG
D-ENIE	Cessna 172N	17271889	N5557E
D-ENIF(3)	Diamond DA 20A-1 Katana	10050	N108CM C-GKAC

D-ENIH(3)	Stinson 108-1 Voyager (Reservation 4.99)	108-1-1341	LV-NJH NC8341K
D-ENIK	Piper PA-12 Super Cruiser	12-1221	N2728M NC2728M
D-ENIM(2)	Robin DR.400/RP Remorqueur	1827	
D-ENIN	Stark Turbulent D	122	
D-ENIP	Mraz M.1C Sokol	267	OK-DHH
D-ENIS	Auster Mk.5	1812	TW473
D-ENIX(3)	Piper PA-28-140 Cherokee C	28-26640	N5811U
D-ENIY	Piper PA-28-161 Warrior II	28-8616026	N9095V (N162AV) N9640N
D-ENJA	Piaggio FWP.149D	024	90+14 AC+434 DD+394
D-ENJB	Wassmer WA.52 Europa	45	
D-ENJC	Wassmer WA.52 Europa	44	
D-ENJD	Robin HR.100/200B	128	
D-ENJH	Piaggio FWP.149D	077	90+59 MC+381 JB+392
D-ENJK	CEA DR.360 Major	641	
D-ENJL	Wassmer WA.52 Europa	46	
D-ENJM	SOCATA MS.892A Rallye Commodore 150	11877	F-BTJB
D-ENJN	Robin DR.300/180R Remorqueur	708	
D-ENJQ	Piaggio FWP.149D	042	90+29 EA+391 GA+391
D-ENJR	Piper PA-18A-135 Super Cub (Quoted officially with f/n 18-3300 as c/n)	18-3345	EI-125 I-EIKX MM537745 53-7745
D-ENJU	SOCATA MS.893A Rallye Commodore 180	11970	F-BTJE
D-ENJW	Piaggio FWP.149D	069	90+52 JA+389
D-ENKA	GEMS MS.892A Rallye Commodore 150	10465	
D-ENKC(2)	Cessna 152	15283246	N47770
D-ENKF	Robin DR.400/180 Régent	693	D-EFEE(1)
D-ENKM	Heliopolis Gomhouria Mk.6	177	SU-341
D-ENKO	Cessna 150E	15061021	OE-AYU N2521J
D-ENKS	Cessna 172R	17280136	
D-ENKT	Reims/Cessna F150M Commuter	F15001357	PH-ENK D-EFAX PH-AYF
D-ENKU	Aero Commander 100	10A-128	
D-ENKW	Piper PA-28R-201 Cherokee Arrow III (Reserved as OH-JTM 1.05)	28R-7737074	SE-GPV
D-ENKY(2)	Sportavia-Pützer RS-180 Sportsman	6007	
D-ENLA	Reims/Cessna F150K	F15000575	
D-ENLB(3)	Piper PA-28R-200 Cherokee Arrow II	28R-7235261	N300LB
D-ENLC(2)	Piper PA-18 Super Cub 95	18-2033	R-36 52-2433
D-ENLD	Reims/Cessna F172H	F17200686	
D-ENLE	Reims FR172G Rocket	FR17200152	
D-ENLF	Piper PA-18 Super Cub 95	18-1337	(G-BERU) D-ENLF ALAT 51-15337
D-ENLH	Piper PA-18 Super Cub 95	18-1394	ALAT 51-15394
D-ENLK(2)	Piper PA-18 Super Cub 95	18-1556	ALAT 51-15556
D-ENLL	Piper PA-18 Super Cub 95	18-1578	ALAT 51-15578
D-ENLM	Piper PA-18 Super Cub 95	18-1592	ALAT 51-15592
D-ENLS	Robin DR.400/180 Régent	724	
D-ENLT	Robin DR.400/180R Remorqueur	725	
D-ENLU	Cessna F150H	F150-0220	N20220
D-ENLW	Cessna U206G Stationair 6-II	U20606858	N9418R
D-ENLY	Piper PA-28R-201 Arrow III	28R-7837211	N9608C
D-ENMC(2)	Mooney M.20K Model 252 TSE	25-1195	
D-ENMD(3)	Diamond DA 20-A1 Katana	10062	C-FWNJ
D-ENMK(2)	Kempf / Denney Kitfox IV-1200	1788	
D-ENMM(2)	Zlin Z.50LA	0027	HA-SIB
D-ENMO(2)	Grob G.115C (Originally built as G.115, wfu 4.90, converted .02, listed as model "NMO-01")	8007	D-EGFB
D-ENMR	SOCATA MS.893A Rallye Commodore 180	12072	F-BUGC (D-ENMF)
D-ENMS(2)	HOACDV-20 Katana	20145	OE-AGY D-EDSV
D-ENMT	Cessna 172P	17275060	N54831
D-ENMW	Cessna 150C	15059943	N150EK D-ENMO N78437
D-ENMY(3)	Mylius My 200	0104	
D-ENNA(3)	Cessna F172G	F172-0305	
D-ENNE(3)	SOCATA TB-9 Tampico Club	1132	
D-ENNF	SOCATA TB-9 Tampico Club	1134	
D-ENNO(2)	Piper PA-28R-201 Arrow III	28R-7837056	N6188H
D-ENNP	Piper PA-28-180 Cherokee Challenger	28-7305483	N55851
D-ENNR	Beech F33A Bonanza	CE-428	
D-ENNU(2)	Piper PA-28-161 Cadet	2841085	N9505N N9169Z
D-ENNY(2)	Piper PA-28-161 Warrior II	28-7716179	N9503N
D-ENOB	Aeromere F.8L Falco	206	

D-ENOC(2)	Reims/Cessna F172N	F17201872	
D-ENOD	Cessna 172	36382	N8682B
D-ENOE	Diamond DA 40 Star	40359	
D-ENOH(3)	SNCAN/Stampe SV-4C (Res .05)	383	N383DK N48002 F-BCQI
D-ENOL(3)	Diamond DA 20-A1 Katana	10238	
D-ENOM	Aero-Jodel D.11A Club	AB.13	
D-ENOP(3)	Mooney M.20K Turbo 231	25-0017	N4563H
D-ENOR	Cessna 140	11087	N76647
D-ENOS(2)	Piper PA-18 Super Cub 95	18-3156	OL-L78 L-78 53-4756
D-ENOT(3)	SOCATA MS.883 Rallye 115	1390	F-BRYC
D-ENOU	Quist/ Neico Lancair 320	369	
D-ENOV(2)	Cessna 150M	15078295	N9346U
D-ENOX(2)	Piper PA-28R-201T Turbo Cherokee Arrow III	28R-7703141	N5656V
D-ENPA(2)	Piper PA-28-161 Warrior II	2816005	N9107R
D-ENPB	Cessna F172H	F172-0598	
D-ENPC	Cessna F172H	F172-0600	
D-ENPE(2)	Robin DR.400/180 Régent	1590	(D-EFDX)
D-ENPF	Piper PA-28-181 Archer II	28-8290049	N8454E
D-ENPH	Pfeiffer/ Neico Lancair 320	1711	
D-ENPK	SOCATA MS.886 Rallye 160	1683	F-BTHQ
D-ENPL(2)	Rockwell Commander 114A (Built from Commander 114B airframe c/n 14441 ex N5896N)	14509	
D-ENPM	Cessna 172S	172S9316	N5325J
D-ENPR	Piper PA-28-181 Archer II	28-8090016	N2972G
D-ENPS	Piper PA-28-151 Cherokee Warrior	28-7415324	N9571N
D-ENPW	Piper PA-28R-201T Turbo Arrow	2803008	N91832
D-ENPY	Piper PA-28-180 Cherokee B	28-1088	N11C N7257W
D-ENQA	Cessna F172D	F172-0014/17250227	(N2627U)
D-ENQE	Cessna F172F	F172-0109	
D-ENQO	Piper PA-18-150 Super Cub	18-8202	N4135Z
D-ENQY	Piper PA-28R-180 Cherokee Arrow	28R-30677	N4940J
D-ENRA	Cessna 170B	26989	OE-DBB HB-COY N3446D
D-ENRB	Beech A36TC Bonanza	EA-74	
D-ENRC(2)	Cessna T182T Turbo Skylane	T18208194	N53374
D-ENRD	SOCATA TB-20 Trinidad	1253	
D-ENRE(2)	Piper PA-46-310P Malibu	46-8608004	N9104P N9103M
D-ENRG	Piper PA-32R-301T Turbo Saratoga SP	32R-8129088	N8416T
D-ENRH	Aermacchi AL.60B-2	6243/63	
D-ENRI	Schriek/ Piel CP.301A Emeraude	AB.410	
D-ENRK	Piper PA-28-161 Warrior II	28-8016234	N9609N
D-ENRO(3)	Röllinghoff/ Dallach D4-ERI Fascination (Permit)	D4-001	
D-ENRP	Cessna 172R	17280076	N9850F
D-ENRW	Cessna TU206G Turbo Stationair II	U20604072	N756GD
D-ENSA(2)	Mooney M.20M Model 257 TLS	27-0010	
D-ENSC	Gyroflug SC-01B Speed Canard	S-26	
D-ENSO(2)	Cessna F172G	F172-0312	
D-ENSR	Mayer/ Stoddard-Hamilton Glasair II-SRG	2317	
D-ENST	Piper PA-28-140 Cherokee Cruiser	28-7725164	N9603N
D-ENSW	Piper PA-32R-301T Turbo Saratoga SP	32R-8129045	N8341A
D-ENSX	Piper PA-28-181 Archer III	2890220	N9250J
D-ENSY(2)	Piper PA-28-181 Cherokee Archer II	28-7790450	N3335Q
D-ENTB(2)	Piper PA-28R-201T Turbo Arrow III	28R-7803188	N3707M
D-ENTD(2)	Mooney M.20J Model 205	24-3048	
D-ENTE(6)	Dornier Do.27A-4 (Reservation 1.04)	472	D-ENTF(2) P2-UIE D-EAEI (1) 57+41 AC+912 LA+155 GA+375 KD+130
D-ENTI (2)	Pallaske/ Denney Kitfox 4-1200 Speedster	KCS-142/1029	
D-ENTO(2)	American AG-5B Tiger	10166	N1198T
D-ENTP	Piaggio FWP.149D	027	90+17 AC+403 DE+393
D-ENUA	Piper PA-18 Super Cub 95	18-1478	ALAT 51-15478
D-ENUB(2)	Reims/Cessna F172M	F17201379	
D-ENUC(2)	Ercoupe 415D	4718	OO-PTE OO-FIL OO-LXG PH-NCG NC94617
D-ENUF(2)	Cessna 172R	17280002	N172SE
D-ENUI	Piper PA-18 Super Cub 95	18-2084	ALAT 52-2484
D-ENUK	Cessna 172	28294	HB-CPF N5694A
D-ENUQ	Piper PA-18 Super Cub 95	18-7376	N10F
D-ENUR(2)	Mattleuer PUL 10	1793	
D-ENUS(3)	Reims/Cessna F172P	F17202160	
D-ENUT	Piper PA-18 Super Cub 95	18-7260	N3379Z
D-ENVA(2)	Zlin Z.43 (Reservation)	0023	D-ENDB(2) LSK-17
D-ENVF(2)	Cessna 182Q	18266288	N759VF
D-ENVI	Bölkow BO.207	283	
D-ENVM	CEA DR.250/160 Capitaine	73	F-BNVM

D-ENVO	Bölkow BO.207	284	
D-ENVP(2)	OMF-100-160 Symphony	0013	(N130MF) (D-EPIO)
D-ENVR	CEA DR.250/160 Capitaine	77	F-BNVR
D-ENVU	Bölkow BO.207	285	
D-ENWA	Bölkow BO.207	287	
D-ENWB	Piper PA-24-260 Comanche C	24-4926	N9420P
D-ENWE(2)	Cessna 182J Skylane	18257197	N3097F
D-ENWH	Cessna U206F Stationair	U20602788	N35898
D-ENWM(2)	Cirrus SR20	1040	N146CD
D-ENWP	Robin DR.400/180 Régent	2339	
D-ENWQ	Diamond DA 40 Star	40039	
D-ENWS	Airconcept Vowi 10	76001 (002)	
D-ENWU(2)	Mooney M.20J Model 205	24-3099	
D-ENWW	SAN Jodel DR.1050 Ambassadeur	491	
D-ENXB	Piper PA-28-161 Cherokee Warrior II	28-7716035	N1658H
D-ENXF	Piper PA-28-161 Cadet	2841299	N9205Z
D-ENXI (2)	Piper PA-28-161 Cadet	2841013	N9153X
D-ENXM	Piper PA-28-161 Cadet	2841295	N9204X
D-ENYE	Bölkow BO.208C Junior	703	
D-ENYP(3)	SOCATA MS.880B Rallye Club	1121	
D-ENYR(2)	Cessna 172C	17249253	SE-EAB N1553Y
D-ENYS	Aeronca 11BC Chief	1608	OO-TWM
D-ENYZ(2)	Gardan GY-80 Horizon 160D	151	F-BNQH
D-ENZA	Cessna 150C	15059757	N1957Z
D-ENZE	Scheibe SF.23C Sperling	3501	
D-ENZL	Piper PA-28-140 Cherokee Cruiser	28-7625216	N9577N
D-ENZM	Grob G.115B (Reserved as F-GNBI)	8010	
D-ENZO(2)	SOCATA TB-10 Tobago	1060	
D-ENZU	Piper PA-22-108 Colt	22-9524	
D-ENZY(2)	SOCATA TB-20 Trinidad	1184	
D-EOAC	Dornier Do.27A-4	452	57+24 PG+218 PG+108 QM+008 KD+ . . . ?
D-EOAD	Dornier Do.27A-4	459	57+30 PK+222 PL+105 QM+015 KD+ . . . ?
D-EOAE(2)	Oberlerchner Job 15-150	051	OE-CAL OE-VAL
D-EOAG	Robin DR.300/180R Remorqueur	669	
D-EOAH	SOCATA MS.880B Rallye Club	1518	F-BRYI
D-EOAJ	Piaggio FWP.149D	028	90+18 AC+409 DE+394
D-EOAK(2)	Dornier Do.27A-4	481	57+47 BF+951 GB+374 KD+139
D-EOAL(2)	Beech B36TC Bonanza	EA-301	N117FM N6454L
D-EOAO	Piaggio FWP.149D (Built from Piaggio c/n 327)	003	90+03 AC+426 DC+393 BA+393 AS+478
D-EOAP	SOCATA ST-10 Diplomate	146	F-BTIQ
D-EOAR(2)	Piper PA-18A-150 Super Cub (officially quoted with f/n 18-3892 as c/n)	18-3875	PH-WAR R-185 54-2475
D-EOAT	Dornier Do.27A-1	319	56+39 YA+903 YA+003
D-EOBA	SOCATA MS.893A Rallye Commodore 180	10817	F-BPHV
D-EOBB(2)	Robin DR.400/RP Remorqueur	1810	
D-EOBC(3)	Reims/Cessna F172N	F17201828	OY-BNJ
D-EOBD	Fuji FA-200-180 Aero Subaru	119	
D-EOBE	SOCATA MS.880B Rallye Club	1865	
D-EOBF	SOCATA MS.880B Rallye Club	1866	
D-EOBH	SOCATA MS.893A Rallye Commodore 180	11820	
D-EOBK	Reims/Cessna F177RG Cardinal RG (Reims-assembled 177RG with US c/n 177RG0200)	F177RG0036	(N . . . . .)
D-EOBL(2)	Cessna 172N	17273840	N5809J
D-EOBM(2)	Robin HR.100/210D Safari	146	OE-DRE
D-EOBN	Fuji FA-200-180 Aero Subaru	125	
D-EOBO(2)	Reims/Cessna F182Q Skylane	F18200092	OY-CBO PH-AXF
D-EOBP	Fuji FA-200-160 Aero Subaru	128	
D-EOBR	Robin DR.300/108 2+2	602	
D-EOBS	Robin DR.300/180R Remorqueur	606	
D-EOBU	Piaggio FWP.149D	138	91+17 BB+395 KB+115
D-EOBV(2)	Piper PA-46-310P Malibu	46-8508095	OE-KTA (D-ELUZ) N9127Y (SE-IOP)
D-EOBW	Piaggio FWP.149D	158	91+36 AS+402 AS+090 KB+135
D-EOCA	Piper PA-18 Super Cub 95	18-1481	D-EHCN ALAT 51-15481

D-EOCB(2)	Cessna 152	15284798	N4673P
D-EOCC(2)	Cessna 172N	17270077	N738MD
D-EOCD(4)	Cessna 172S	172S9675	N61216
D-EOCG(2)	Reims/Cessna F172P	F17202205	
D-EOCH	Fuji FA-200-180 Aero Subaru	140	
D-EOCK	Fuji FA-200-160 Aero Subaru	142	
D-EOCL	Fuji FA-200-160 Aero Subaru	149	
D-EOCM(2)	Piper PA-28-181 Archer II	2890118	N9176P
D-EOCN(2)	Beech C24R Sierra	MC-770	N6188A
D-EOCO	SOCATA MS.893A Rallye Commodore 180	11843	F-BSZV
D-EOCR(2)	Cessna 172RG Cutlass RG	172RG0115	N6207R
D-EOCS	Aero Z.131 (C-104)	213	HB-USY
D-EOCT(3)	Cessna 177RG Cardinal RG	177RG1339	N53078
D-EOCU	American AA-5 Traveler	AA5-0018	(N5818L)
D-EOCW	Robin DR.300/180R Remorqueur	639	
D-EOCX	Robin DR.300/180R Remorqueur	643	
D-EOCZ	CEA DR.253B Régent	194	
D-EODA(2)	SOCATA TB-20 Trinidad	2033	
D-EODB	SOCATA MS.892A Rallye Commodore 150	11845	F-BSZY
D-EODC	SOCATA MS.892A Rallye Commodore 150	10714	F-BOVF
D-EODE	SOCATA MS.883 Rallye 115	1565	F-BTHH
D-EODG	SIAI-Marchetti SF.260	111	OO-HID
			OY-DND
D-EODH	SOCATA MS.880B Rallye Club	1920	
D-EODI	SOCATA MS.880B Rallye Club	1910	
D-EODK	SOCATA MS.893A Rallye Commodore 180	11889	
D-EODM(2)	Robin DR.300/180R Remorqueur	547	
D-EODN	SNCAN/ Stampe SV.4C	113	F-BCFY
D-EODO	Robin DR.300/180R Remorqueur	645	
D-EODR	CEA DR.360 Chevalier	652	
D-EODS	Wassmer WA.52 Europa	35	
D-EODT	CEA DR.253B Régent	198	
D-EODU	Robin DR.300/108 2+2	650	
D-EODV(2)	Reims/Cessna FR182 Skylane RG	FR18200069	
D-EODW(2)	Reims/Cessna FR182 Skylane RG II	FR18200070	
D-EODY	Reims FR172H Rocket	FR17200308	
D-EOEC	Bölkow BO.209 Monsun 150FV	201	
D-EOEG	Piper PA-28-235 Cherokee	28-10411	HB-OLG
			N8857W
D-EOEI	HOAC DV-20 Katana	20102	C-FVOQ
			N202DV
D-EOEM	Reims/Cessna F172N	F17201581	SE-GZL
D-EOEN	CEA Jodel DR.1050M-1 Sicile Record	623	PH-PEN
D-EOEO	Piper PA-28R-201 Arrow III	28R-7837079	N2281M
D-EOER	Reims/Cessna F172N	F17201986	
D-EOES	SOCATA MS.894A Minerva 220	11873	F-BSXF
D-EOEU	Cessna 172R	17280200	N9949F
D-EOEW	Robin DR.400/180R Remorqueur	1465	
D-EOFA	Reims/Cessna F150L	F15001005	F-BURC
D-EOFC	Piper PA-28-180 Cherokee Challenger	28-7305332	N11C
D-EOFF(2)	Piper PA-28-161 Warrior III	2843238	G-BYFP
			N4137N
			N41270
D-EOFG	Cessna 210D Centurion	21058225	OE-DFG
			N3725Y
D-EOFH	Reims/Cessna F172P	F17202071	
D-EOFK	Reims/Cessna F172N	F17201993	(D-EDFJ)
D-EOFO	Reims/Cessna F150M	F15001210	
D-EOFP	Reims/Cessna F172P	F17202095	
D-EOFS(2)	Grob G.115A	8039	
D-EOFU(2)	Reims/Cessna F172N	F17201575	
D-EOFW	Piper PA-28-181 Archer II	2890096	N9154R
D-EOFY	Reims/Cessna F172M	F17201051	
D-EOGA	Reims/Cessna F172M	F17201317	
D-EOGB(2)	Piper PA-46-310P Malibu	4608070	N9131B
			N9593N
D-EOGE(2)	Piaggio FWP.149D	125	91+04
			BF+413
			AS+012
			KB+102
D-EOGI	Dornier Do.27A-4	473	57+42
			EA+385
			KD+131 ?
D-EOGK	Cessna 172N	17271511	N3338E
D-EOGP	Cessna 172RG Cutlass RG	172RG0545	N5481V
D-EOGS	Robin DR.400/RP Remorqueur	1808	
D-EOGU	Reims/Cessna F172M	F17201346	
D-EOHA	Reims/Cessna F172M	F17201420	
D-EOHC	Reims/Cessna F150M	F15001292	
D-EOHD	Piper PA-28-181 Archer II	2890116	N9152Q
D-EOHF	Robin DR.400/180 Régent	1397	
D-EOHH	Reims/Cessna F172N	F17201804	
D-EOHK	Mooney M.20C Ranger	20-1230	
D-EOHM	Cessna 172N	17270905	N739YD
D-EOHP	SAN Jodel DR.1050 Ambassadeur	297	F-BKHB
D-EOHR	Cessna 152 Commuter	15281123	N49051
D-EOHT	SOCATAST-10 Diplomate (Permit 3.00)	145	OE-DHT
			F-BTIP
D-EOHU	Reims/Cessna F172N	F17201614	
D-EOIA(2)	Robin DR.400/180R Remo 180	2061	
D-EOIC(3)	Piper PA-28-181Archer III	2843049	N9272N
D-EOII (2)	Piper J-3C-65 Cub	13113	HB-OII
			F-BFBC
			44-80817
D-EOIT	Piper PA-28-180 Cherokee E	28-5647	N2556R
D-EOJA	Reims/Cessna F172N	F17201534	
D-EOJC	Cessna 172P	17274457	SE-IPO
			N52247

D-EOJE	Reims/Cessna F172N	F17201537	(F-GASO)
D-EOJH	Beech C23 Sundowner	M-2216	HB-EJH
D-EOJI	Reims/Cessna F172N	F17201628	
D-EOJM	Piper J-3C-90 Cub Special	22633	N4494M
			NC4494M
			NC3400N
D-EOJN	Piper PA-38-112 Tomahawk	38-79A0528	SE-ICD
D-EOJO	Reims/Cessna F172N	F17201551	
D-EOJT	Cessna 150L	15075013	N10759
D-EOJU	Reims/Cessna F172N	F17201635	
D-EOJX	Reims/Cessna F150L	F15000738	
D-EOKA	Robin HR.200/100 Club	49	
D-EOKB(2)	Mooney M.20R Ovation	29-0122	
D-EOKC(2)	Cessna P210N Pressurized Centurion II	P21000134	N6005P
D-EOKG	Mooney M.20K Model 252 TSE	25-1213	OE-KMO(1)
			D-EOWK
D-EOKI	Reims FR172F Rocket	FR17200131	
D-EOKK	Cessna 152	15281132	N49068
D-EOKL	Gardan GY-80 Horizon 180	246	
D-EOKO(3)	Reims/Cessna F172N	F17201895	
D-EOKS	Christen A-1 Husky	1103	
D-EOKT(2)	Cessna 177RG Cardinal RG	177RG1325	N53022
D-EOLA	CEA DR.315 Petit Prince	317	F-BPRD
D-EOLB	Cessna 172N	17270813	N739UH
D-EOLC	Cessna 172RG Cutlass RG	172RG0208	N6606R
D-EOLD(3)	Taylorcraft BC-12D	10218	OE-AFV
			D-EMAF(1)
			N44418
			NC44418
D-EOLE	Cessna 182P Skylane	18263838	(F-BOFU)
	(Reims-assembled with "c/n" 0008)		N6790M
D-EOLG	Cessna 182L Skylane	18258630	N3330R
D-EOLH	Cessna 210N Centurion II	21064220	N5479Y
D-EOLI (2)	Reims/Cessna F182Q Skylane	F18200081	
D-EOLK	Robin DR.400/180 Régent	2434	
D-EOLL(2)	Cessna 177RG Cardinal RG	177RG1318	(D-EOKT)
			N52948
D-EOLM(3)	Cessna 172R	17280125	
D-EOLP	Reims/Cessna F182Q Skylane	F18200160	(OY-BNT)
D-EOLS	Robin DR.300/180R Remorqueur	555	
D-EOLT(2)	Beech B36TC Bonanza	EA-470	N2844B
D-EOLU	Reims/Cessna F182Q Skylane	F18200086	
D-EOLV	Cessna 172RG Cutlass RG	172RG0691	N6430V
D-EOLY(2)	Reims/Cessna F182Q Skylane	F18200079	
D-EOLZ	Cessna 172RG Cutlass RG	172RG0552	N5524V
D-EOMA(2)	Diamond DA 20-A1 Katana	10314	N644DA
D-EOMB	Reims/Cessna F172P	F17202222	
D-EOMC	Reims/Cessna F172L	F17200900	F-BTUX
D-EOME(2)	Reims/Cessna F172N	F17201679	
D-EOMF(3)	Cessna 172N	17268877	N734HY
D-EOMG(2)	Cessna 172N	17270151	N738QH
D-EOMI	Navion Rangemaster G	NAV-4-2479	HB-ESN
			(D-EBMY)
			N2479T
D-EOMK	Robin DR.400/180 Régent	1267	
D-EOMM	CASA I-131E Jungmann	2001	E3B-404
D-EOMN(2)	Cessna 172P	17276594	N9638L
D-EOMP	Piper PA-28-181 Cherokee Archer II	28-7890124	N47721
D-EOMQ	Piaggio FWP.149D	051	90+37
			SB+211
			SC+401
			AS+478
D-EOMR	Reims/Cessna F172P	F17202241	
D-EOMS(2)	SOCATAMS.894AMinerva 220	11078	OO-CYF
			F-BSCP
D-EOMT	Cessna 152	15283960	N6617B
D-EOMW	Cessna 172N	17268110	N76064
D-EOMX	Cessna 172P	17275304	N62587
D-EOMZ	Cessna 172RG Cutlass RG	172RG1074	N9905B
D-EONA(2)	Piaggio P.149D	312	92+16
			AC+463
			AS+463
D-EONC	Piper PA-28-181 Archer II	2890122	SE-KIS
D-EONE(2)	Beech F33A Bonanza (Res .05)	CE-1106	N3021U
D-EONH	Stinson L-5C Sentinel	76-3615 ?	(G-BNUM)
	(C/n unconfirmed, serial quoted as c/n)		N8035H
			N63485
			44-17328
D-EONI	Cessna F172H	F172-0590	
D-EONN	Reims/Cessna F172N	F17201805	
D-EONT(2)	Cessna 152	15281309	N49493
D-EONU	Cessna F172H	F172-0583	
D-EONW	Reims/Cessna F182Q Skylane	F18200051	
D-EONX	Cessna U206G Stationair 6-II	U20605584	N5150X
	(Soloy conversion)		
D-EOOB	Reims/Cessna F172N	F17201956	
D-EOOC	Reims/Cessna F172N	F17201957	
D-EOOD	Reims/Cessna F172N	F17201958	
D-EOOE	CEA DR.250/160 Capitaine	84	F-BOCE
D-EOOF(2)	Piper PA-18 Super Cub 95	18-1500	D-EOCE
			ALAT
			51-15500
D-EOOG	Reims/Cessna F172N Skyhawk II	F17201952	
D-EOOI	Springer/ Neico Lancair 235	007	D-ESAR
D-EOOL(2)	Piper PA-28-236 Dakota	28-8311004	N8290Z
D-EOOM(2)	Cessna 172D (Permit 9.99)	17249978	OO-MET
			N2378U

D-EOOO(2)	Cessna P210N Pressurized Centurion (Soloy conversion)	P21000439	N731CM
D-EOOP	Reims/Cessna F152	F15201588	D-EOOO(1)
D-EOOR	Reims/Cessna F172N	F17201973	
D-EOOS	SNCAN/ Stampe SV.4A	336	F-BCGC
D-EOOW	Reims/Cessna F172N	F17201971	
D-EOOY(2)	HOAC DV-20 Katana	20064	
D-EOPA	Piper PA-18 Super Cub 95	18-1523	N8944 D-ECEI ALAT 51-15523
D-EOPC	Reims/Cessna F182Q Skylane	F18200159	
D-EOPD	Reims/Cessna F172N	F17201955	
D-EOPE	SOCATA ST-10 Diplomate	107	F-OCPE
D-EOPF	Piper PA-32R-300 Lance	32R-7780098	N8443F
D-EOPG(2)	Piper PA-46-350P Malibu Mirage	4622064	N255SW N350KM N350PM N91782
D-EOPH	Cessna 172RG Cutlass RG	172RG0652	N6389V
D-EOPI	Erco 415D Ercoupe	541	(D-EBUY) D-EBUP N87368
D-EOPK	Reims/Cessna F182Q Skylane	F18200044	OY-BUW
D-EOPM	Piper PA-28-181 Cherokee Archer II	28-7790104	N5944F N9516N
D-EOPR(2)	Cessna 182Q Skylane (Porsche engine)	18266605	N95709
D-EOPS	Reims/Cessna F152	F15201670	
D-EOPW(2)	Piper PA-46-350P Malibu Mirage	4622192	N369Z (N695MA)
D-EOPY	Reims/Cessna F150M (W/o 23.3.82)	F15001424	
D-EOPZ	Laubenthal/ Murphy Renegade (Permit 8.02)	1926	N630WR
D-EOQA	Reims/Cessna F150L	F15001124	
D-EOQE	Reims/Cessna F172M	F17201188	
D-EOQG	Reims/Cessna F172M	F17201191	
D-EOQK	Reims/Cessna F172M	F17201199	
D-EOQL	Reims/Cessna F172M	F17201203	
D-EOQM	Reims/Cessna F172M	F17201211	
D-EOQP	Cessna 182P Skylane	18263114	N7330N
D-EOQY	SNCAN/ Stampe SV.4A	468	F-GCCY EC-AYL F-BDBE
D-EORA	Reims/Cessna F172M	F17201374	
D-EORC(2)	Piper PA-28-181 Archer II	2890132	SE-KIY "SE-KIS"
D-EORD	Reims/Cessna F172N	F17201959	(D-EOOF)
D-EORE(2)	Reims/Cessna F177RG Cardinal RG	F177RG0174	
D-EORF	Reims/Cessna F172N	F17201954	"D-EOCY"
D-EORH	Morane-Saulnier MS.885 Super Rallye	47	D-EBRR(2) D-EMPU(2) (D-EMPI)
D-EORI	Cessna 210L Centurion	21061343	(N2625S)
D-EORK(2)	Piper PA-28RT-201T Turbo Arrow IV	28R-8131017	N8284H
D-EORM	Beech A24R Musketeer Super	MC-65	HB-EWK
D-EORO	Piper PA-28R-200 Cherokee Arrow II	28R-7335306	N55894
D-EORR	Reims/Cessna F172N	F17201814	
D-EORT	Cessna 172N	17270994	N1426E
D-EORZ	CEA DR.250/160 Capitaine (W/o 6.8.00)	100	
D-EOSA	Piper PA-28-181 Cherokee Archer II	28-7790189	N9535N
D-EOSB(2)	Grob G.115A	8037	HB-UGF (D-EGVV)
D-EOSC(2)	Kurz/ Udet U12K Flamingo Replica	01	
D-EOSD	Mooney M.20J Model 201	24-0598	N7201K
D-EOSG	Cessna 172R	17281200	N21379
D-EOSI	Wassmer WA.40A Super IV (Reservation .04)	27	HA-VEV D-EOSI HB-DCH F-BKCC
D-EOSM	Seiss/ Udet U12a Flamingo (Permit 12.04) (Painted as "D-1202")	1785	
D-EOSO	Reims/Cessna F182Q Skylane	F18200064	
D-EOSR	Robin DR.400/180R Remorqueur	1575	
D-EOST	SOCATA MS.893A Rallye Commodore 180	12070	F-BUGA (D-ENMD)
D-EOSU	Cessna TU206F Turbo Stationair	U20603298	N8439Q
D-EOSY	Cessna 182P Skylane	18263184	OY-BIT SE-GGD N7403N
D-EOTA(2)	Grob G.115A	8047	
D-EOTB	Robin DR.400/180 Régent	1607	
D-EOTC	SOCATA TB-10 Tobago	1115	
D-EOTE	Reims/Cessna F172N	F17201627	
D-EOTI	Reims/Cessna F172N	F17201538	
D-EOTK	Piper PA-22-150 Tri-Pacer	22-2752	HB-OTK D-EFYV N2341P
D-EOTO	Reims/Cessna F172N	F17201629	
D-EOTT	Reims/Cessna F172N	F17201816	
D-EOTU	Reims/Cessna F150M	F15001383	
D-EOTW	Reims/Cessna F172P	F17202088	
D-EOTY	Reims/Cessna F182Q	F18200052	CS-DBS D-EOTY
D-EOUC	Cessna 172R	17280197	
D-EOUH	Cessna 182M Skylane	18259392	OE-DUH OE-BUM N70848
D-EOUI	LET Z-37A-2 Cmelák	20-02	DDR-SWI DM-SWI

D-EOUK	Cessna 207 Skywagon 207	20700008	HB-CUK N91009
D-EOUV	Becker/ Binder CP.301S Mistral	AB.01	
D-EOVA	Reims/Cessna F172N	F17201625	
D-EOVC	Cessna 182Q Skylane	18266760	OH-CVC N96564
D-EOVE	Reims/Cessna F172N	F17201636	
D-EOVI	Reims/Cessna F172N	F17201701	
D-EOVL	SOCATA MS.893A Rallye Commodore 180	10717	F-BOVL
D-EOVU	Reims/Cessna F172N	F17201624	
D-EOVX	Reims/Cessna FR172KHawk XP	FR17200620	OE-DVX
D-EOVY	Reims/Cessna F172N	F17201520	
D-EOWA	Reims/Cessna F172N	F17201724	
D-EOWB	Reims/Cessna F172P	F17202164	
D-EOWC	Piper PA-28RT-201T Turbo Arrow IV	28R-8231008	N8454T
D-EOWE	Reims/Cessna F172N	F17201729	
D-EOWG(2)	HOACDV-20 Katana	20019	N19DV
D-EOWH	Piper PA-22-108 Colt	22-9426	(D-EHWH) HB-OWH D-ENSY N5643Z
D-EOWI (2)	Reims/Cessna F172N	F17201733	
D-EOWJ	SOCATA Rallye 180TD Galerien	3135	F-GBCO
D-EOWM(2)	Maule MX.7-180 Star Rocket	11047C	N6121Q
D-EOWN	Cessna 172RG Cutlass RG	172RG0704	D-EIKP N6443V
D-EOWO	Reims/Cessna F172M	F17201218	(SE-GKM)
D-EOWP	Piper PA-38-112 Tomahawk	38-79A0336	OY-BRR
D-EOWR	Cessna 210N Centurion II	21064234	N5516Y
D-EOWS(2)	Mooney M.20J Model 201	24-1227	N1151L
D-EOWV	Cessna 172RG Cutlass RG	172RG0675	N6413V
D-EOWW(2)	Aquilla AT-01	110	
D-EOWY	Reims/Cessna F172N	F17201696	
D-EOXA	Reims/Cessna F172N	F17201705	
D-EOXC(2)	Piper PA-28-181 Archer III	2843149	PH-AEF N9291S
D-EOXE(2)	LET Z-37A-2 Cmelák	16-01	DDR-SRE DM-SRE
D-EOXG	Dätwyler/Piper J-3C-100-D1 Cub	MDC-1036	HB-OXG
D-EOXI	Reims/Cessna F172M	F17201419	
D-EOXO	Reims/Cessna F172N	F17201708	
D-EOXQ	PZL-104 Wilga 35	107336	DDR-WRK DM-WRK
D-EOXR	PZL-104 Wilga 35	96324	DDR-WRA DM-WRA
D-EOXS	PZL-104 Wilga 35	96330	DDR-WRG DM-WRG
D-EOXT	Bölkow BO.208C Junior	570	HB-UXT D-EDMA(1)
D-EOXU	Reims/Cessna F172N	F17201714	
D-EOXY(2)	LET Z-37A-2 Cmelák	19-03	DDR-SRY DM-SRY
D-EOYE	Reims/Cessna F172N	F17201752	
D-EOYH	SOCATA TB-9 Tampico	272	OE-DYH
D-EOYO	Reims/Cessna F182Q Skylane	F18200087	
D-EOYS	Cessna 172N	17269857	N214FR N214ER N738BV
D-EOYU	Reims/Cessna F172N	F17201803	
D-EOYW	LET Z-37A-2 Cmelák	19-01	DDR-SRW DM-SRW
D-EOYX	LET Z-37A-2 Cmelák (Damaged 9.4.00)	19-04	DDR-SRZ DM-SRZ
D-EOYZ	LET Z-37-2 Cmelák	06-29	DDR-SNZ DM-SNZ
D-EOZA	SEEMS MS.880B Rallye Club	326	F-BKZA
D-EOZC	SOCATA TB-21 Trinidad TC	806	SE-KBB
D-EOZD	SOCATA MS.893E Rallye 180GT Gaillard	12529	F-BVZD
D-EOZE	Reims/Cessna F172N	F17201716	
D-EOZH	Piper PA-28R-180 Cherokee Arrow	28R-30695	HB-OZH N4948J
D-EOZI	Reims/Cessna FRA150M Aerobat	FRA1500335	
D-EOZK(2)	Winkler/ EEL ULF-2	032	
D-EOZL	LET Z-37A-2 Cmelák	12-21	DDR-SLL DM-SLL(2)
D-EOZN	Piper PA-28-140 Cherokee B	28-25146	HB-OZN N7234F
D-EOZW	Aermacchi AL.60B-2	6267/87	
D-EOZX	LET Z-37A-2 Cmelák	19-02	DDR-SRX DM-SRX
D-EOZY	Dornier Do.27B-1	224	55+77 PD+334 PD+109 PF+106
D-EOZZ	Binder CP.301S Smaragd	AB.25	
D-EPAA	Piper PA-28-181 Archer II	28-8490074	PH-JVT N43573
D-EPAB	Reiss/ Brändli BX-2 Cherry	002	
D-EPAC(2)	Piper PA-20 Pacer 135	20-674	G-BFAO ZS-CMH ZS-CAH
D-EPAD	Cessna 172N	17269018	N734PY
D-EPAG	SOCATA TB-20 Trinidad	2118	N200DB
D-EPAI	Piper PA-46-350P Malibu Mirage	4622122	N50MP (N48CK) N9227R
D-EPAK	DHC-1 Chipmunk 22	C1/0328	G-BDIC WD388

D-EPAL	Piper PA-28-181 Cherokee Archer II	28-7890054	N47335
D-EPAN	Cessna 172N (Permit 8.02)	17273933	(YU- . . .)
			N9847J
D-EPAO	Piper PA-28-151 Cherokee Warrior	28-7615121	SE-GLX
D-EPAP	Piper PA-28RT-201T Turbo Arrow IV	28R-8231004	N214CD
			N8448E
D-EPAS(2)	Piper PA-28-181 Archer III	2843080	N92854
D-EPAT	Piper PA-28-161 Warrior III (Diesel engine)	2842084	N41815
D-EPAW	Zlin Z.42M	0065	DDR-WNW
			DM-WNW
D-EPBB	Cessna 150K	15071458	N5958G
D-EPBC	HOAC DV-20 Katana	20005	OE-CDI
D-EPBM	Miny/ Aero Designs Pulsar XP (Permit 3.00)	420AB	
D-EPBW(2)	Piper PA-28-160 Cherokee	28-337	N202W
			D-EFRO
			N11C
D-EPCA(2)	Cessna 172S	172S9070	N2172W
D-EPCG	Güthoff/ Brditschka HB-207 VRG Alfa (Permit .00)	207013	
D-EPCH	Schneider/ Zenith CH-601 HD Zodiac	6-1724	
D-EPCL	DHC-1 Chipmunk 22	C1/0137	OO-NCL
			G-AOUN
			WB689
D-EPCM	Piper PA-28-161 Cadet	2841335	N92043
			(N125ND)
D-EPCN	Piper PA-28-161 Warrior II	2816102	N9196X
			(HB-PNN)
D-EPCO	CessnaR.172K Hawk XP	R1722439	N736DF
D-EPDA	Diamond DA 20-A1 Katana	10255	
D-EPDB	Diamond DA 20-A1 Katana	10166	
D-EPDH	Grob G.115A	8022	LV-RTA
			LV-DML
D-EPDR	HOAC DV-20 Katana	20091	
D-EPEB	Beech A36 Bonanza	E-2731	TC-SMS
			N80287
D-EPEG	Engmann/Slepcev Storch SS-4 (Permit 9.99)	SS4-051	
D-EPEP	Piper PA-28-181 Archer III	2890217	N92263
D-EPET(2)	Extra EA330/L (Permit)	02	
D-EPEW	Mooney M.20K Model 231	25-0170	N231DN
D-EPFM	Robin DR.400/RP Remorqueur	1841	OE-KMP
			D-EGMP(2)
D-EPFW	Cessna F150G	F150-0151	D-ENYQ(2)
D-EPGC	Cessna TR182 Turbo Skylane RG	R18202018	OE-KEE
			D-EFIB(3)
			N6423T
D-EPGS	Robin DR.400/180R Remo 180	2167	
D-EPHA	Piper PA-28RT-201T Turbo Arrow IV	28R-8031151	N8245S
D-EPHB	Cessna TR182 Turbo Skylane RG	R18200858	(D-EVAS)
			N737NC
D-EPHC	Beech A36 Bonanza	E-1773	PH-ASB
			C-FGYI
			N979P
			YV-1979P
D-EPHD	Pitts S-2A Special	K-0009	
D-EPHL	Piper PA-28RT-201T Turbo Arrow IV	28R-8631004	N9129Z
D-EPHM(3)	Pitzer/ Stoddard-Hamilton Glastar GS-1	5563	
D-EPHN	Robin DR.500/200i Président	007	
D-EPHP	Robin DR.400/180 Régent	2244	
D-EPHW	Piper PA-28RT-201 Arrow IV	28R-7918005	N3066K
D-EPIA	Cessna 152	15280580	N25299
D-EPIC	Cessna 172N	17267785	N75530
D-EPIE	Piper PA-28RT-201T Turbo Arrow IV	28R-7931119	N2102V
D-EPIH	Bölkow BO.208C Junior	674	F-BPIH
			D-EGZG(1)
D-EPIK	Piper PA-32R-300 Cherokee Lance	32R-7680107	N8352C
D-EPIL	Pilatus P.2-06	75	HB-RAP
			U-155
D-EPIM	SOCATA TB-20 Trinidad	1116	N200DB
			D-EALJ
D-EPIO	OMF-100-160 Symphony (Reservation 4.01)	0013	
D-EPIP	Cessna 177RG Cardinal RG	177RG0362	N1962Q
D-EPIT(2)	Cessna 172B	17248088	D-EBSE
			N7588X
D-EPIZ	Christen Pitts S-2B	5159	OH-TOM
			N5342K
D-EPJD	III Sky Arrow 650TC	C006	N271SA
D-EPJH	Holland/ Aero Designs Pulsar XP (Permit 11.99)	1799	
D-EPJK	Kurz/ Siebel 202/K replica (Permit 8.02)	1	
D-EPJM	Cessna 172R	17280336	D-EPRP
			N9525
D-EPJS	Beech A36 Bonanza Soloy	E-2997	N1067Z
D-EPKA	Afflerbach/ Bede BD-5B (Reservn .04)	01BD	
D-EPKD	Piper PA-46-500TP Malibu Meridian	4697019	PY-GPT
			N519MM
			(OY-NEW)
D-EPKF	Hohnholz/ Denney Kitfox IV	1768/FCU 055	
D-EPKH	Gieffers/ Murphy Renegade Spirit 912	1636	(D-ERGB)
D-EPKN	SOCATA Rallye 235ED Gabier	13019	EL-WHS
			EL-AHS
			EL-SPC
			F-ODMB
D-EPKO	Piper PA-46-310P Malibu	4608017	N9101Z
D-EPLA	Wassmer WA.52 Europa	62	OE-KLA
			HB-DCG
			(D-EGRJ(1))
D-EPLH	Cessna R182 Skylane RG	R18200063	N7572W
			N84W
			N7572W
D-EPLK	Piper PA-46-310P Malibu	46-8608030	N68JT
			N62JT
			N9515N
			N9294A
D-EPLZ	Cessna 182S	18280344	N2624L
D-EPMA	Mooney M.20M Model 257 TLS	27-0147	N133PR
D-EPMB	Piper PA-18-150 Super Cub	18-1591	D-EKQY
			(D-EKQI)
			ALAT
			51-15591
D-EPMC	Pitzer/ Aero Designs Pulsar XP	1768/FCU055	(D-EPMY)
D-EPMI	Robin HR.200/120B	262	
D-EPMK	Cessna TU206G Turbo Stationair 6-II	U20605119	N4827U
D-EPMM	Piper PA-24-260 Comanche B	24-4456	N8995P
D-EPMO	Zlin Z.526F Trenér Master	1282	SP-EMO
D-EPMS	Cessna TU206F Turbo Stationair	U20602695	N33254
D-EPNR	SOCATA Rallye 235ED Gabier	12906	HB-EYR
			(YV-1444P)
D-EPNU	Piper PA-28-236 Dakota	28-7911324	CS-AUY
			N80904
D-EPOE	Piper PA-46-350P Malibu Mirage	4622180	N92581
			D-EPOE
			N9251R
D-EPOI	Extra EA.300	024	LN-ACN
			D-EDCM
D-EPOP	Diamond DA 40 Star	40071	
D-EPOT	Piper PA-28-236 Dakota	28-7911108	(SE-LDT)
			OH-POT
			N70WH
			N2089R
D-EPPA	Robin DR.400/180 Régent	2282	
D-EPPE	Piper PA-32-300 Cherokee Six	32-7640116	HB-PPE
			OE-DIT
			N4487F
D-EPPL	Piper PA-28-181 Archer III	2843044	N9268L
D-EPPM	Schulze/ Denney Kitfox Speedster	1686	
D-EPPN	Neumann/ Denney Kitfox IV-1200	KBS-081	
D-EPPP	Mooney M.20J Model 205	24-3292	
D-EPPR	Beech C23 Sundowner	M-2075	N2074K
D-EPPW	Mooney M.20K Model 231	25-0624	N1150Z
D-EPRA	Piper PA-36-310PMalibu (Permit 10.99)	4608055	N777PG
			N9580N
			N9119N
D-EPRE	Cessna P210N Pressurized Centurion II	P21000570	N731ZT
D-EPRI	Robin R.2160D	131	HB-EXZ
D-EPRK	Kehl/ Aero Designs Pulsar XP	01	
D-EPRL	Leveringhaus/ Capella XLS-TR	1746	
D-EPRO	Cessna 150M	15076080	(D-ERLE)
			N66493
D-EPRS	Cessna T206H Stationair TC	T20608172	N2443V
D-EPRW	Beech B36TC Bonanza	EA-521	
D-EPSG	HOAC DV-20 Katana	20055	C-FSRZ
D-EPSM	Bölkow BO.207 (Reservation, on rebuild)	258	D-EGLY
D-EPSR	Cessna R182 Skylane RG	R18201281	(D-EWGA)
			F-GHAO
			N2008S
D-EPST(2)	Cessna 172R	17280154	N715GT
D-EPSW	Cessna F150H	F150-0223	HB-CSW
D-EPTA	Röckeisen/ Avid Flyer Speedwing Mk.IV	313/1721	
D-EPTB	Maule MX-7-235 Star Rocket	10004C	N39TB
D-EPTC	Piper PA-46-350P Malibu Mirage	4636012	N92575
D-EPTD	Boeing Stearman E-75	75-5322	N131TP
			N5272N
			42-17159
D-EPTH	Morane-Saulnier MS.885 Super Rallye	253	OE-DFO
			D-EDFO(2)
			F-BKUG
D-EPTI	Brändli BX-2 Cherry (Permit 8.04)	173SB	
D-EPTP	American AG-5B Tiger	10173	N11986
D-EPTU	Cessna 150M	15076423	N3214V
D-EPUD	Bölkow BO.209 Monsun 160FV	196	HB-UED
			D-EAIL(1)
D-EPUB	Piper PA-28-181 Archer III	2843114	N41211
D-EPUL	Robin DR.300/180R Remorqueur	513	F-BSJO
D-EPUM	Brditschka HB-207VRG Alfa (Res .04)	01/207023	
D-EPUP	HOACDV-20 Katana	20154	OE-CDA
D-EPUR	Mudry CAP.10B	96	HB-SAY
			F-BXHZ
D-EPUT	Cessna 172M	17262514	N13124
D-EPVA	Piper PA-28-180 Cherokee Challenger	28-7305352	N222MM
			N35286
D-EPVR	Cessna 182L	18258851	F-GKGK
			TR-LCV
			TN-ABD
			TR-LNO
			N42095
D-EPWB	Binder/Europa Aviation Europa	1/149	
D-EPWC	Piper PA-28R-201T Turbo Cherokee Arrow III	28R-7703323	N43975
D-EPWE	Cessna 172N	17272533	N5345D
D-EPWF	Cessna TU206G Turbo Stationair II	U20603901	I- IPAE
			N7363C
D-EPWL	Beech F33A Bonanza	CE-1587	N8187Z
D-EPWM	Beech F33A Bonanza	CE-1712	
D-EPWP	Beech F33A Bonanza	CE-1654	
D-EPXP	Baumgartner/ Aero Designs Pulsar XP	1776	
D-EPZL	PZL-104 Wilga 35A	21960957	

D-EPZY	SOCATA TB-20 Trinidad	2139	TC-MRB F-OIUU
D-EQAI	Diamond DA 40D Star	D4.023	
D-EQAP	Cessna TR182 Turbo Skylane RG	R18201179	SE-IXZ N756WL
D-EQAS	Beech V35 Bonanza	D-8390	N3750Q
D-EQAX(2)	Focke-Wulf FW.44J Stieglitz	1899	ZS-WRI D-EFUR Fv617
D-EQBB	Diamond DA 20-C1 Katana	C0126	N626DC
D-EQCA	Commander Aircraft 114B	14565	
D-EQCO(2)	Diamond DA 40D Star	D4.094	
D-EQCT	Schneider/ Denney Kitfox Vixen 1200	FCV 008	
D-EQFA	Robin DR.400/180R Remorqueur	1470	HB-EQF
D-EQIA	Robin DR.500/200i Président	0003	
D-EQMF	Cessna 182Q Skylane	18267051	HB-CCX N97302
D-EQMI	Robin HR.200/120B Super Club	273	
D-EQMS	Homebuilt, type unknown (Reservation)	007	
D-EQOA	Bücker Bü.133CJungmeister	53	D-EIIH(2) SpanishAF
D-EQQQ(2)	Diamond DA 40D Star	D4.115	
D-EQTT	SOCATA ST-10 Diplomate	116	HB-EQT D-ELEZ(2)
D-EQUI	Aquila AT-01 (A201)	100, formerly A210-100	
D-EQUS	Luscombe 8E Silvaire	5651	G-BSHJ N2924K NC2924K
D-EQWM	Maier FW.190 (Half-scale replica) (Permit .02)	S-001	
D-ERAB	Piper PA-28RT-201T Turbo Arrow IV	28R-7931277	N2963A
D-ERAD	Robin DR.400/180 Régent (W/o 6.3.05)	2217	
D-ERAE	Cessna 172S Skyhawk SP	172S8015	S5-DGT N23338
D-ERAF(2)	Grob G.115E (Development a/c, Permit 1.99)	82085	
D-ERAG	Kriwanek/ Dallach D4/E Fascination	EB010	
D-ERAL	Cessna 172N	17271122	N2024E
D-ERAM	Mooney M.20M Model 257 TLS	27-0097	N712D
D-ERAN	Zlin Z.143L	0014	
D-ERAP(3)	Peter/ Dallach D4/E-BK/S Fascination	EB020	
D-ERAS(2)	Piper PA-28-151 Cherokee Warrior	28-7415284	N41584
D-ERAT	SIAI-Marchetti S.208	2-25	I- LARS
D-ERAW	Mooney M.20M Model 257 TLS	27-0092	
D-ERAZ	Cessna 172N	17272506	N5306D
D-ERBB	CASA I-131E Jungmann	unkn	E3B-347
D-ERBC	Kleitz/ Druine D.5 Turbi (Rotax 912) (Permit 2.04)	85	
D-ERBE	Cessna P210N Pressurized Centurion II	P21000769	N6408W
D-ERBF	Reims/Cessna F172N	F17201904	G-MOGG G-BHDY (LN-HOH)
D-ERBG(2)	Maule MXT-7-180A Star Rocket	21082C	N4247U
D-ERBM	Jodel D.117 (Built as D.11A)	615	OE-ABM
D-ERBT	Mudry CAP.10B	15	Fr.AF: F-TFVI F-TESM
D-ERBW	Piper PA-28-180 Cherokee D	28-4761	N6351J
D-ERBY	Robin DR.400/180S Régent	2067	
D-ERCA	Rockwell Commander 114A	14500	N114BK N5884N
D-ERCB	Diamond DA 40D Star	D4.027	OE-VPU
D-ERCF	SOCATATB-20 Trinidad	1924	
D-ERCI	Zlin Z.526F Trenér Master (Permit 2.05)	1249	SP-CPI
D-ERCL	Steen Skybolt (Reservation 6.99)	unkn	
D-ERCM	Diamond DA 20-A1 Katana	10243	
D-ERCS	Maule MXT-7-180 Starcraft	14114C	
D-ERDA	SNCAN/ Stampe SV.4C	599	D-EOWS(1) F-BDET
D-ERDB	Piper PA-28-180 Cherokee Challenger	28-7305284	N16563
D-ERDE	American AG-5B Tiger	10158	(PH-MLE) N1198E
D-ERDG	HOAC DV-20 Katana	20020	OE-V . .
D-ERDJ	Piper PA-18-150 Super Cub	18-2546	EC-DLM D-EMMX(1) (D-ELKF) ALAT 52-6228
D-ERDP	Diamond DA 20-A1 Katana	10031	N331CH
D-ERDZ	American AG-5B Tiger	10159	N1198G
D-ERED	SOCATA TB-9 Tampico Club	1609	
D-EREE	Cessna 172P	17274041	N5281K
D-EREI	Reichart/ Brditschka HB-207VRG Alfa	207-028	
D-EREK(2)	SAAB S.91B Safir	91343	SE-ITF (LN-HAI) RNoAF 57343
D-EREN	Cessna TR182 Turbo Skylane RG	R18201019	N182RH N739ZJ
D-ERER	Remmers/ Stephens Acro Sport II	1506	
D-ERES	Dallach D5/E-BK/914 Evolution (Permit .05)	D5/004	
D-EREV	HOAC DV-20 Katana	20144	
D-EREW	Cessna P210N Pressurized Centurion II (Soloy conversion)	P21000669	HB-CQG N5284W
D-ERFA(2)	Diamond DA 40 Star	40020	
D-ERFB	Piper PA-28-181 Archer II	28-8490001	N4317M
D-ERFC	Piper PA-46-350P Malibu Mirage	4636091	G-PALL G-RMST
D-ERFD	Beech G35 Bonanza	D-4776	HB-EFD F-DAFB
D-ERFI (2)	Diamond DA 40D Star	D4.127	

D-ERFL	Mooney M.20J Model 205	24-3206	N91VR N12WA (D-EKJH(1)) N12WA
D-ERFM	Diamond DA 40DStar	D4.044	
D-ERFS	Mooney M.20J Model 201	24-1176	N1142U
D-ERFU	Mooney M.20M Model 257 TLS	27-0089	
D-ERFW	FW.190A-1 Scale Replica (Reservn .04)	209	OO-90
D-ERGC	Piper PA-46-350P Malibu Mirage	4622200	N100VC (N800RG) N100VC N9258D
D-ERGI	Piper PA-46-350P Malibu Mirage	4636094	N9278V
D-ERGO	Robin DR.400/160D Major	2024	
D-ERGR	CASA I-131E Jungmann	2010	E3B-406
D-ERGS	Beech F33A Bonanza	CE-1758	N80639
D-ERGT	Reims FR172H Rocket	FR17200229	N229FL D-ECOA(1)
D-ERHA	Mooney M.20R Ovation	29-0054	
D-ERHB(2)	Mooney M.20E Super 21	344	HB-DEE (N6984U)
D-ERHE	SOCATA TB-20 Trinidad	432	F-GDQK F-ODQK
D-ERHG	Beech F33A Bonanza	CE-1507	N67HG D-EARY(2)
D-ERHH	Piper J-3F-50 Cub	1997	OY-AIS (SE-AIS)
D-ERHK	Beech F33A Bonanza	CE-1608	N8235W
D-ERHM	SOCATA TB-10 Tobago	1747	
D-ERHN	Piper PA-28RT-201 Arrow IV	28R-8218007	N84571
D-ERHS	SOCATA TB-20 Trinidad	584	F-GJAL N103J
D-ERHV	Hassler/ Denney Kitfox III	758	
D-ERIA	Robin DR.400/200R Remo 200	2205	
D-ERIC	Piper PA-28-140 Cherokee	28-21907	C-GEXM N7193R
D-ERIF	Piper PA-28RT-201T Turbo Arrow IV	28R-8131163	N8411Y
D-ERII	Reims/Cessna F150L (To Italy 3.03?)	F15000740	OE-CVY HB-CVY
D-ERIK	Jodel D.119	1243	OE-ACZ
D-ERIM	Mooney M.20M Model 257 TLS	27-0198	
D-ERIN	Piper PA-28R-201 Arrow	2844016	N4132U SP-FEL N4132U (SP-FEL) N9529N
D-ERIR	Renger/ Impulse 160TD (Diesel)	TD-7	
D-ERIZ	SOCATA MS.893E Rallye 180GT Gaillard	13050	OE-DIZ
D-ERJA	Beech C23 Sundowner	M-2136	N6015W
D-ERJC	SOCATA TB-200 Tobago XL	1630	
D-ERJM	SOCATA TB-10 Tobago	1731	
D-ERKA	Reims/Cessna F172N	F17201870	N5189D D-EFOS(1)
D-ERKB	Piper PA-28-181 Archer II	28-8190293	OH-PDN SE-ILC
D-ERKF	Dudeck/ Denney Kitfox 4-1200	1757	
D-ERKH	Heumann/ Aero Designs Pulsar XP	001	
D-ERKK	Barland/ Murphy Rebel	1	
D-ERKM	Zlin Z.142	0526	OK-VNG
D-ERKP	Cessna F150G	F150-0140	OE-AVO
D-ERKR	Roth/ Van's RV-4	3614	
D-ERKW	Westermeier/ Aero Designs Pulsar XP (P 10.99)	1907	
D-ERKY	Piper PA-28RT-201T Turbo Arrow IV	28R-8031068	LX-SKY N81623
D-ERLA	SNCAN/ Stampe SV.4C	101	D-EBHL(2) F-BBVA
D-ERLB	Cessna T182 Turbo Skylane	18267773	(D-EGRR) SE-IHU N5531N
D-ERLE(2)	Diamond DA 20-A1 Katana	10231	
D-ERLH	Grob G.115C2	82058/C2	(D-EPST)
D-ERLI	Cessna 182T	18281307	N2096Q
D-ERLO	Oberbach/ Van's RV-6 (C/n formerly quoted as 1871)	002	
D-ERLP	Funke/ Denney Kitfox III	1028	
D-ERLR	Beech F33A Bonanza	CE-1565	N8233X
D-ERMA(2)	Piper PA-18-135 Super Cub	18-3982	I-BUNO I-EIUJ/ E!-260 MM54-2582 54-2582
D-ERMB	Beech F33A Bonanza	CE-1500	N150RM
D-ERMH	Zlin Z.42MU	0019	DDR-WMH DM-WMH
D-ERMI	Piper PA-28R-201T Turbo Arrow III	28R-7803247	N9264C
D-ERMK	Oberbach/ Van's RV-7 (Permit .04)	003	
D-ERMM	Aquila AT-01	108	
D-ERMO	Diamond DA 20-A1 Katana	10099	C-FDVK
D-ERMP	Grob G.115C	82036/C	N115SR
D-ERMR	Cessna 172P	17274404	N52066
D-ERNA	SOCATA TB-200 Tobago XL	1612	
D-ERNB	Cessna T206H Turbo Stationair	20608346	N51431
D-ERNI (2)	SOCATA TB-9 Tampico Club	1647	
D-EROB	SNCAN/ Stampe SV.4C	151	D-ECDI (2) F-BNDI Fr.AF/CEV
D-EROC	HOAC DV-20 Katana	20090	

D-EROE	Diamond DA 40D Star (Res .05)	D4.010	OY-TDI
D-EROG	American AG-5B Tiger	10115	N1196Z
D-EROH	Cessna 182R Skylane	18268155	OH-CTR
			G-BOPF
			N9984H
D-EROK	Diamond DA 20-A1 Katana	10155	
D-EROL	Zlin Z.143L	0026	
D-ERON	SOCATA TB-20 Trinidad	1441	F-GLFN
D-EROP	Amann/ Europa Avn Europa	240.0	
D-EROS	Piper PA-28-161 Warrior II	28-8116181	N8352P
D-EROW	Cessna 172R	17280328	
D-EROY	Mooney M.20M Model 257 TLS	27-0154	
D-ERPA(2)	Beech F33A Bonanza	CE-1452	HB-KCU
D-ERPC	Cessna 152	15280733	N25565
D-ERPE	Reims/Cessna F172N	F17201979	D-EIYZ
D-ERPH	Cessna 172N	17271171	N2159E
D-ERPI	Cessna U206G Stationair II (Reservation)	U20603596	SE-GUF
			N7272N
D-ERPL	Cessna 172P Skyhawk II	17274722	N53328
D-ERPM	Diamond DA 40 Star	40062	G-CBFC
D-ERPS	Poth/ Pottier P.220S Koala	1849	
D-ERPW	Cessna 182Q Skylane	18267212	N61PG
			N97827
D-ERRE	Rengers/ Aero Designs Pulsar XP (Permit 10.99)	402	
D-ERRK	Beech A36 Bonanza	E-2913	N1565F
D-ERRN	Ripplinger/ Aero Designs Pulsar XP (Permit 12.99)	432/007	
D-ERRO	Piper PA-28R-201 Arrow	2844005	N92698
D-ERRP(2)	Diamond DA 40D Star	D4.098	
D-ERRR	Cessna P210N Pressurized Centurion II	P21000227	N4590K
D-ERRS	Bretzke/ Neico Lancair 360	3118	
D-ERRV	Van's (Reservation - Type unconfirmed)	2293	
D-ERRY	Piaggio FWP.149D (Reservn 2.00)	160	D-EFWP(1)
			91+38
			JD+394
			AS+096
			KB+137
D-ERSB	Piper PA-28-161 Warrior II	28-8016122	N8115V
D-ERSE	Cessna 172P	17275559	OH-COB
			N64422
D-ERSH	Diamond DA 20-A1 Katana	10004	OE-V . .
			N848DF
			C-FTJG
D-ERSL	Mooney M.20J Model 201	24-1049	D-EEGH(1)
			N4070H
D-ERSM	Europa Avn Europa XS TG (Permit 7.04)	542	
D-ERSO	Mooney M.20J Model 201	24-1672	N224DM
D-ERSS	Piper PA-28-181 Archer II	2890076	OH-PSS
D-ERST	SOCATA TB-9 Tampico Club	1295	
D-ERTA	Griener/Messerschmitt M17 replica (Permit 3.04)	1994/1	
D-ERTB	Cessna 177RG Cardinal RG	177RG0962	N303RN
D-ERTD	Cessna 172S (Diesel engine, 4.03)	172S9292	N5278N
D-ERTH	Laverda F.8L Falco Srs.IV (Res .05)	417	(D-EHNI(3))
			D-EFEV(2)
D-ERTI	Cessna 182Q Skylane	18266337	N759XH
D-ERTY(2)	DHC-1 Chipmunk 22	C1/0718	G-BDCB
			(D-E . . .)
			G-BDCB
			WP835
D-ERUG	PZL-150 Koliber 150	3900042	SE-KUG
			(SE-KUO)
			(G- . . . .)
			PH-BIJ
D-ERUT	Diamond DA 20A-1 Katana	10181	N854DF
D-ERUV	Focke-Wulf FW.44JStieglitz (Reservation 9.99) (Swedish serial quoted as c/n, true c/n unknown)	"666"	Fv666
D-ERVB	Zlin Z.143L	0012	
D-ERWA	Piper PA-28-181 Archer II	28-8590078	N2491Y
D-ERWB	Piper PA-46-350P Malibu Mirage	4622125	N192PM
			N9223R
D-ERWE	Mooney M.20R Ovation	29-0011	
D-ERWF	Commander Aircraft 114B	14580	
D-ERWH	Rall/ Europa Avn Europa (Permit .00)	1889	
D-ERWK	HOAC DV-20 Katana	20051	
D-ERWM	Cessna 172M	17264449	N9669V
D-ERWP	Aquila AT-01	112	
D-ERWT	Zlin Z.43	0082	OM-KOR
			OK-KOR
D-ERWW	Mooney M.20K Model 231	25-0676	N1164A
D-ERXP	Aero Designs Pulsar XP	425	
D-ERYS	Cessna 170B	25390	D-EMEE(1)
			N3148B
D-ERYW	Mooney M.20L PFM	26-0035	P4-ING
			G-RAAD
			N160MP
D-ESAA	Cessna 172S	172S8791	N2477B
D-ESAB	Lake LA-4-200 Buccaneer	975	EI-BSR
			N3076P
D-ESAC	Cessna 177RG Cardinal RG	177RG0066	N8066G
D-ESAD	Cessna 172R	17280149	
D-ESAE	Cessna 172SP Skyhawk SP	172S08118	
D-ESAH(2)	Piper PA-28-181 Archer II	2890120	OH-PBM
			OY-JEG
D-ESAL	Cessna 172N Skyhawk II	17272082	N7307E
D-ESAM(2)	Robin DR.400/180R Remo 180	2471	
D-ESAN(2)	Piper PA-28-181 Archer III	2843028	N9181J
D-ESAP	Cessna 182Q Skylane	18267138	N97582

D-ESAT	Commander Aircraft 114B	14551	N6000Z
D-ESAY	Cessna P210N Pressurized Centurion II	P21000629	HB-CQX
			D-EMAZ(3)
			N4896
D-ESBB(2)	Diamond DA 40DStar	D4.025	
D-ESBG(2)	Reims/Cessna F172P	F17202126	OO-LVD
			D-EILV
			(D-EDDL)
D-ESBH	Messerschmitt Bf.108B	3701-14	HB-ESM
			G-AFZO
			AW167
			D-IJHW
D-ESBK	Piper PA-12 Super Cruiser	12-1612	N2367M
			NC2367M
D-ESBM	Cessna 172R	17280327	
D-ESBO	Reims/Cessna F172P	F17202254	LN-RAW
D-ESBR	Robin R.2160D	275	
D-ESBW	Piper PA-28RT-201T Turbo Arrow IV	28R-7931251	OE-KBT
			OY-PEE
			N2904G
D-ESCE	Scheidl/ Impulse 120TD (Permit 3.04)	TD-6	
D-ESCG	Reims/Cessna F172M	F17201426	HB-CXD
D-ESCH	Piper PA-28RT-201 Arrow IV	28R-7918093	N2147X
D-ESCN	Beech F33A Bonanza	CE-1466	N33VW
			G-TERI
			N5664X
D-ESCO	Cessna 172N	17273735	N5214J
D-ESCP	Diamond DA 20-A1 Katana	10107	N533SS
D-ESDA	Cessna 152	15280868	N25937
D-ESDB	American AG-5B Tiger	10147	N1198A
D-ESDF	Piper PA-28R-201 Arrow III	28R-7837182	OE-DRT
			N9237C
D-ESDJ	SOCATA TB-20 Trinidad GT	2029	
D-ESDT	Diamond DA 40DStar	D4.061	
D-ESEC	SOCATA TB-20 Trinidad	1112	D-EANG(3)
D-ESEF	Aquila AT-01	113	
D-ESEL	Piper PA-28RT-201T Turbo Arrow IV	28R-8131010	G-BSZR
			N8281B
D-ESEO(2)	Stoddard-Hamilton Glasair III (Res .05)	3095SB	
D-ESER(2)	SIAI-Marchetti SM.1019A	043	EI-443/
			MM57236
D-ESES	Cessna TR182 Turbo Skylane RG	R18201379	N4686S
D-ESEX(2)	SAN Jodel D.117A Grand Tourisme	837	OE-ATI
D-ESFA	Cirrus SR20 (Reservation .05)	1153	N789CD
D-ESFC	Robin DR.400/180 Régent	2305	
D-ESFD	Reims/Cessna F152	F15201467	OO-CPP
D-ESFG	HOACDV-20 Katana	20088	N200DV
D-ESFH	Diamond DA 40 Star	40055	
D-ESFL	Christen A-1 Husky	1351	
D-ESFR	Beech F33A Bonanza	CE-1535	N81562
			N4341J
			(SE-KTL)
			N81562
D-ESFS	Cessna 172N	17268127	N76108
D-ESFW	HOAC DV-20 Katana	20056	
D-ESGB	Bauernfeind/ S-H GlaStar GS-1 (Permit .01)	5448	
D-ESGC	Piper PA-28-180 Cherokee Archer	28-7405005	PH-SWD
			OE-DML
			N9558N
D-ESGI	Cessna 172N	17273033	N1943F
D-ESGJ	Cessna 172N	17271222	N2289E
D-ESGK	HOAC DV-20 Katana	20079	
D-ESGR	Gyroflug SC-01B Speed Canard	S-23	D-ECEX(2)
D-ESGT	SOCATA TB-9 Tampico	1419	I-IAGT
D-ESGW	Cessna 172N	17273058	N1969F
D-ESHA	Schmaderer/ Aero Designs Pulsar XP	EB-001	
D-ESHB	Commander Aircraft 114B	14572	
D-ESHD	Drache/ Piel CP.301A Emeraude	AB-407	HB-SPC
			D-ENUR
D-ESHH(2)	Cessna R182 Skylane RG	R18201624	N6144S
			(D-ESTE)
			N6144S
D-ESHK	Robin R.3000/160	162	
D-ESHM(2)	Diamond DA 20-A1 Katana	10191	N668DA
D-ESHO	Robin DR.400/180R Remo 180	2245	
D-ESHP	Aeromere F.8L Falco III	205	LX-AIW
			D-ENUB(1)
D-ESHW	Commander Aircraft 114B	14558	
D-ESIA	Robin DR.400/200R Remo 200	2246	
D-ESIL	Cessna 150L	15075403	N11415
D-ESIR(3)	Diamond DA 20-A1 Katana	10106	N532SS
D-ESIS	Cessna 182S	18280486	
D-ESIX	Dornier Do.27B-1 (Permit 16.9.03)	357	56+63
			AC+936
			AS+936
D-ESJD	Drumm/ Van's RV-6A	1689	
D-ESJG(2)	Cessna 172R	17281215	N21765
D-ESJO	Piper J-3C-65 Cub	13260	D-EKQE
			PH-UCX
			45-4520
D-ESJP	SOCATA TB-20 Trinidad	870	D-EAFA(3)
D-ESKA	Diamond DA 20-A1 Katana	10093	N195DA
			C-GKAC
D-ESKF	Cessna 172P	17275390	N63097
D-ESKG	Cessna 172P	17275228	SE-KKH
			N62202
D-ESKH	SOCATA Rallye 180T-D Galérien	3213	OE-DKH

D-ESKI	Cessna TU206G Turbo Stationair 6-II	U20604873	HB-CKN
	(Soloy conversion)		(D-EMRK(2))
			N28SC
			N734TZ
D-ESKK	SIAI-Marchetti S.205-20/R	221	PH-RYK
			(PH-NOW)
D-ESKL	Cessna 172D	17250189	N2589U
D-ESKM	Beech F33A Bonanza	CE-1736	N80990
D-ESKR	Roth/ Van's RV-4RG	4317	
D-ESKS	Piper PA-18 Super Cub 95	18-1427	OY-EFO
			D-EECY
			ALAT
			51-15427
D-ESKT	Diamond DA 40 Star	40351	
D-ESKW(2)	Cessna 172N	17270079	N738MF
D-ESKY	Cessna R182 Skylane RG	R18200477	SE-KRY
			N9874C
D-ESLB(2)	Cessna 182P	18263591	CS-DCG
			HB-CWV
			N5967J
D-ESLF	Ruschmeyer R90-230G	05	(D-EEHQ)
D-ESLG	SIAI-Marchetti SM.1019A	017	EI-417/
			MM57210
D-ESLL	Cessna 177RG Cardinal RG	177RG0020	N8020G
D-ESLZ(3)	Zeddies/ Denney Kitfox V	S 9502-0105	
	(Reserved as D-EMLZ, 3.99)		
D-ESMA	Bölkow BO.207	259	D-EGMA(1)
D-ESMF	Diamond DA 40 Star	40077	
D-ESMG	Gess/ Van's RV-6	1692	
D-ESMH	Piper PA-28RT-201T Turbo Arrow IV	28R-8131006	N8277S
D-ESMI	Robin DR.400/180R Remo 180	2080	
D-ESMM	Piper PA-28-181 Cherokee Archer II	28-7790091	N5336F
D-ESMN	Cessna 172N	17267781	N888TJ
			N75526
D-ESMP	Reims/Cessna F172N	F17201633	G-BFKA
D-ESMR	Robin R.1180TD Aiglon	281	PH-RBA
D-ESMS	Cessna TR182 Turbo Skylane RG	R18201407	N4739S
D-ESNB	Mooney M.20J Model 201	24-0426	OE-KFC
			HB-DFC
D-ESND	Kitplane, type unknown (Reservation 10.99)	1	
D-ESNQ	Zlin Z.142	0234	OM-LNQ
			OK-LNQ
D-ESOC	SOCATA TB-10 Tobago	1794	
D-ESOF	Extra EA.300/L	1177	
D-ESOK	Mraz M.1D Sokol	281	D-ENEV
			OK-DHU
D-ESON	Piper PA-28-236 Dakota	28-8611002	HB-POT
			N9203M
D-ESOR	Piper PA-28R-201T Turbo Cherokee Arrow III		
		28R-7703254	N38637
D-ESPA	Piper PA-28-181 Archer II	28-8490041	N4334Z
D-ESPE	Piper PA-46-350P Malibu Mirage	4622063	N186DM
			N9179P
D-ESPH	Greuner/ Van's RV-6 (Permit 11.99)	1937	
D-ESPM	Impulse Aircraft Impulse 180TD (Res .05)	TD3	
D-ESPR	Piper PA-28-151 Cherokee Warrior	28-7715284	OE-DKA
			N9574N
D-ESPS	de Havilland DH.82ATiger Moth	83683	HB-UCX
	(C/n quoted officially as "T7218" which was the		D-EHAL(2)
	serial of c/n 83688, crashed as G-AHUO .53)		(D-EAKP)
			D-EKAL(1)
			G-ANGD
			T7213
D-ESPW	Cessna R172K Hawk XP	R1722690	N736YH
D-ESPX	Great Lakes 2T-1A-2	1006	N933EB
			N5762N
D-ESPY	Cirrus SR20	1345	LX-TIM
			N8124W
D-ESQE	LET Z-37 Cmelák	08-29	DDR-SQE
			DM-SQE
D-ESRA	SOCATA TB-10 Tobago	1369	
D-ESRE	Ehmann RE-4 Grasmücke	01	
D-ESRG(2)	Cessna 150M	15077275	N63385
			(D-ECDR)
			N63385
D-ESRK(2)	Aquila AT-01	117	
D-ESRL(2)	Mooney M.20R Ovation	29-0064	
D-ESRP(2)	Cessna 172R	17280360	N443ES
D-ESRR	Cessna 172R	17280212	
D-ESRT	Cessna 182P	18260834	N26561
			D-ECRG
			N9294G
D-ESRV(2)	Van's RV-6	1	
D-ESRW	Weihermüller/ Zenai CH-601DZodiac	6-8503	
D-ESSB(2)	Cessna 172R	17280133	
D-ESSC(3)	Cessna 172S	172S9538	N118FS
	(Reserved as D-ESJG ?)		(D-ESSC(2))
D-ESSH	LET Z-37A Cmelák	20-14	D-ESVK
			DDR-SVK
			DM-SVK
D-ESSJ	Mooney M.20K Model 231	25-0465	OE-KHS
			N4088H
D-ESSK	Piper PA-28-151 Cherokee Warrior	28-7515397	N1174X
D-ESSM	Mooney M.20C Mark 21 (Permit 2.00)	2810	N7847V
D-ESSN	LET Z-37A Cmelák	18-02	DDR-SSN
			DM-SSN
D-ESSO(2)	Mooney M.20M Model 257 TLS	27-0204	

D-ESSS(3)	Piper PA-46-500TPMalibu Meridian	4697070	D-FOXI
			N53322
D-ESST	Cessna 172N	17271634	N4769E
D-ESSV(2)	Beech A36 Bonanza	E-2587	N58JM
			N8094K
D-ESTA	SOCATA TB-20 Trinidad	1362	
D-ESTB	Piper PA-28-161 Cadet	2841333	N9216N
D-ESTE	Stemme S-15	15-001	
D-ESTF(2)	Tremmel/ Aerostyle Breezer (Permit 11.04)	008	D-MAJH ?
D-ESTI	Piper PA-28-161 Cadet	2841350	N9233N
D-ESTL	Markett/ Neico Lancair 320 (Permit .02)	FB145AB	
D-ESTN	Piper PA-28-161 Warrior II	2816101	N92333
D-ESTO	Piper PA-28-161 Cadet	2841304	N9261N
			N9196X
D-ESTR	HOAC DV-20 Katana	20029	
D-ESUB	Schreiber/ Neico Legacy 2000 (Res. 04)	L2K-183	
D-ESUN	Zlin Z.226T	357	DM-WIE
D-ESUR	Ressel/ Neico Lancair 360	1761	(D-EIRR(2))?
D-ESUX	LET Z-37A Cmelák	19-21	DDR-SUX
			DM-SUX
D-ESVC	Cirrus SR20	1485	N54138
D-ESVH	LET Z-37A Cmelák	20-11	DDR-SVH
			DM-SVH
D-ESVL	LET Z-37A Cmelák	20-15	DDR-SVL
			DM-SVL
D-ESVO	LET Z-37A Cmelák	20-18	DDR-SVO
			DM-SVO
D-ESVU	LET Z-37A Cmelák	20-24	DDR-SVU
			DM-SVU
D-ESVW	LET Z-37A Cmelák	20-26	DDR-SVW
			DM-SVW
D-ESWA(2)	SOCATA MS.893A Rallye Commodore 180	11712	F-BSVC
D-ESWE	LET Z-37A Cmelák	21-04	DDR-SWE
			DM-SWE
D-ESWH	LET Z-37A Cmelák	21-07	DDR-SWH
			DM-SWH
D-ESWK	Kunert Buddy Baby	001	
D-ESWM	LET Z-37A Cmelák	22-04	DDR-SWM
			DM-SWM
D-ESWO	LET Z-37A Cmelák	17-05	DDR-SWO
			DM-SWO
			SP-GDA
D-ESWP	Piper PA-20-135 Pacer	20-1053	N10339
			N791
D-ESWS	Wegscheider/ Neico Lancair 320	1586	
D-ESSX	Cessna P210N Pressurized Centurion II	P21000657	D-EKWO
			N5227W
D-ESYL	Gyroflug SC-01B-160 Speed Canard	S-53	
D-ESZN	Bitz/ Bücker Bü.133D-1 Jungmeister	2002	G-BSZN
			N8103
			D-ECAY(1)
D-ETAA	Piper PA-38-112 Tomahawk	38-79A0582	N2341K
D-ETAB	Piper PA-38-112 Tomahawk	38-78A0243	N9913T
D-ETAC	Piper PA-38-112 Tomahawk	38-79A0298	N2408D
D-ETAD	Piper PA-38-112 Tomahawk	38-79A0220	N2534C
D-ETAE	Cessna 172N	17267614	N73701
D-ETAF(3)	Extra EA.400	09	
D-ETAG	Cessna 182R Skylane	18267994	N9749H
			(N182PW)
			N9749H
D-ETAI	Piper PA-28RT-201T Turbo.Arrow IV	28R-8131147	N8402H
D-ETAJ	Piper PA-28-181 Archer II	2890161	N9117Q
			(F-GJOD)
D-ETAK	Piper PA-28-181 Archer II	2890162	N9212N
			(SE-KME)
D-ETAL	Ohlrogge/ Rand-Robinson KR-2 (Tri-gear convn.)	1	
D-ETAN(2)	HOAC DV-20 Katana	20122	
D-ETAP(2)	Piper PA-28-181 Archer III	2843254	N41330
D-ETAR	Cessna 182Q Skylane	18266456	N94597
D-ETAS(3)	Piper PA-28-161 Warrior III	2842153	N5351F
D-ETAT(3)	Diamond DA 20-A1 Katana	10180	N671DA
D-ETAX	Mooney M.20J Model 201	24-1006	HB-DGA
			N3997H
D-ETBA	Mooney M.20M Model 257 TLS	27-0006	N1036M
D-ETBB	Cessna 172M	17261629	N92818
D-ETBD	SOCATA TB-20 Trinidad	989	HB-KCP
D-ETBE	Cessna U206G Stationair II (Soloy)	U20603989	N16737
			HB-CKX
			N250ST
			N638HM
			(N756CS)
D-ETBH	SOCATA TB-10 Tobago	029	OH-TBA
			F-GBHQ
			(F-ODKM)
D-ETBK	Cessna 152	15282677	G-BTBK
			N89218
D-ETBL	Piper PA-46-310P Malibu	4608001	N181CA
			OY-CEL
D-ETBR	Bek Me 109R4	002	
D-ETBT	Piper PA-38-112 Tomahawk	38-79A0299	N2409D
D-ETBW	Wams/ Aero Designs Pulsar XP	413	
D-ETBX	Beck/ Aero Designs Pulsar XP	1814	
D-ETCB	Piper PA-28-181 Archer II	2890179	N9145B
D-ETCC	Piper PA-28-181 Archer II	2890180	N9145H
D-ETCH	Piper PA-28-181 Archer II	2890016	N9111F
D-ETCI	Cessna 172N	17270556	N739HM
D-ETCL	Piper PA-28-181 Archer II	2890188	N9180W

D-ETCM	Piper PA-28-181 Archer II	2890184	N9177J
D-ETCN	Piper PA-28-181 Archer II	2890186	N9178B
D-ETCP	Piper PA-28-181 Archer II	2890193	N9226Z
D-ETCR	Cessna 152	15279929	N757QW
D-ETCX	Piper PA-28-181 Archer II	2890195	N9234D
D-ETDA	Schroeder/ Jodel D.18	375	
D-ETDB	Bartling/ Cozy BL (Permit 4.99)	01, formerly 1608	(D-EEDB)
D-ETDF	Evers/Brditschka HB-207VRG Alpha (Permit 2.04)	207-004	(PH-STP)
D-ETDI	Robin R.3000/160	159	
D-ETDP	Piper PA-28-181 Cherokee Archer II	28-7890043	G-BIDP N44956
D-ETEA(2)	Diamond DA 40D Star	D4.004	
D-ETEC(3)	SOCATA MS.880B Rallye-Club (Rebuild using parts of D-EODF/D-ETEC(2) c/n 849)	1521	OY-DJL
D-ETED	Robin DR.400/180R	2347	
D-ETEE	Marthiens/ Stoddard-Hamilton Glasair IIRG-S	V-1/2038	
D-ETEG	Beech F33A Bonanza	CE-1440	N5541L
D-ETEL(2)	Diamond DA 20-A1 Katana	10241	
D-ETEN	SOCATA TB-21 Trinidad TC	1377	
D-ETES	SOCATA TB-10 Tobago	1667	
D-ETET	Cessna 150L	15073183	N5283Q
D-ETEW(2)	Extra EA.300/L	084	
D-ETEX	Diamond DA 20-A1 Katana	10242	
D-ETFA	Piper PA-32RT-300 Lance II	32R-7985033	N2218D
D-ETFB(2)	SOCATA TB-10 Tobago	451	OE-KMF
D-ETFD	Beech F33A Bonanza	CE-1492	N15482
D-ETFL	Piper PA-28-181 Cherokee Archer II	28-7690058	N7145C
D-ETFS	Reims/Cessna F150L	F15000821	D-EEWA
D-ETFW	HOAC DV-20 Katana	20059	
D-ETGE	Cessna 180H	18052249	ZP-TGE ZP-PGE N9749G
D-ETGJ	Thiel / Denney Kitfox III	982	
D-ETHA	Mooney M.20M Model 257 TLS	27-0082	N23WA D-EEWA(2)
D-ETHB	Bücker/ Brändli BX-2 Cherry	101	
D-ETHC	de Havilland DH.82ATiger Moth	82018	PH-CRO G-AISY VT-CZV G-AISY N6740
D-ETHE	Aviat Pitts S-2B (Permit .04)	5164	N5KE
D-ETHG	Aquila AT-01 (Model A210)	101	(D-ECCX(2))
D-ETHH	Meier/ Rutan Long-Ez	1082	
D-ETHL	Mooney M.20M Model 257 TLS	27-0133	
D-ETHM	Beech A36 Bonanza	E-3023	N3267Q
D-ETHN	Pilatus P.2-05 (Permit 10.99)	27	HB-RAT U-107 A-107
D-ETHP	Pfeiffer/ Denney Kitfox IV-1200	JCU 113	
D-ETHS	Mooney M.20K Model 252 TSE	25-1123	HB-DGU
D-ETHW	Cessna TU206G Turbo Stationair II (Soloy conversion)	U20603923	N103CS C-GDCF N7596C
D-ETIB	Mooney M.20K Model 231	25-0397	N4042H
D-ETIF	Piper PA-28RT-201T Turbo Arrow IV	28R-8131021	N8290K
D-ETIG	American AG-5B Tiger	10139	N1197T
D-ETIH	Mooney M.20K Model 231	25-0741	HB-DGH
D-ETII	Lake LA-4-200 Buccaneer	921	N2820P
D-ETIK	Piper PA-28-161 Warrior III	2816116	N9254N
D-ETIM(2)	Piper PA-18 Super Cub 95	18-1500	D-EOOF(2) D-EOCE ALAT 51-15500
D-ETIN	HOAC DV-20 Katana	20110	
D-ETIS	Piper PA-28-181 Archer III	2843133	N41237
D-ETIT	Tittl / Denney Kitfox	1684	
D-ETIV	Piper PA-28-181 Archer III	2843326	N4179R N9518N
D-ETIX	Piper PA-28-161 Warrior III	2842001	N9217N
D-ETIZ	Mooney M.20K Model 231	25-0479	N9404P
D-ETJA	Piper PA-28-181 Archer II	28-8690044	N9178Y
D-ETJG	Piper PA-46-350P Malibu Mirage	4622121	N91947 (N555PS) N9215Q
D-ETJK	Cessna 140	8216	G-BSYE D-ESYE (D-ETDS) G-BSYE N89196 NC89196
D-ETJR	Kit Aircraft (Type unknown)	2	
D-ETKA	Piper PA-28RT-201T Turbo Arrow IV	28R-8031173	OO-JJA N82623
D-ETKB	Cessna 172N	17270174	N738RG
D-ETKC	Cessna 172N	17272983	N1279F
D-ETKD	Cessna 152	15285609	N94150
D-ETKE	Cessna 172N	17273452	N4905G
D-ETKG	Cessna F172H (Permit 7.99)	F172-0429	N5002X D-ELXY
D-ETKH	Aviat A-1 Husky	1281	
D-ETKK	Cessna T210MTurbo Centurion (Permit .02)	21062669	SP-FMK D-ETKK N887MM N888MM (N6045B)

D-ETKM	Cessna 172N Skyhawk II	17272198	N8425E
D-ETKP	Cessna 150L	15073727	(OY- . . .) G-BPWO N18010
D-ETKR	Cessna 150M	15078318	(OY- . . .) G-BPUZ N9369U
D-ETKS	Cessna TR182 Turbo Skylane RG	R18200937	G-GARY N738KV
D-ETLA	Piper PA-28-181 Archer III	2843015	N9260J
D-ETLB	Cessna 172R	17281183	N2155A
D-ETLF	Robin DR.500/200i Président	0028	
D-ETLH	Aquila AT01	106	
D-ETLI	Hoffmann/ Denney Kitfox IV Speedster	1749/KBS-077	
D-ETLK(2)	Diamond DA 20-A1 Katana	10293	N293DA
D-ETLL	Cessna 150M	15077050	N123WT N63032
D-ETLO	HOAC DV-20 Katana (Permit 3.00)	20028	N29DV
D-ETLS(2)	Mooney M.20MModel 257 TLS	27-0211	N281FH
D-ETLT	Aquila AT-01	116	
D-ETLU	Diamond DA 20-A1 Katana	10292	C-GSMR
D-ETLX	Piper PA-28-181 Archer III	2890212	N92509
D-ETMA	SOCATA TB-9 Tampico	128	HB-EZO (D-ETMC) HB-EZO
D-ETMB	Stark Turbulent D-1	135	HB-SVG D-EKUV
D-ETMH	Cessna 172M	17266298	N9661H
D-ETMI	Robin DR.400/180R Remo 180	2144	
D-ETMJ	Mylius My 104 (Reservation)	unkn	
D-ETMM	Cessna P210N Pressurized Centurion II	P21000780	N6443W
D-ETMN	Cessna 172R	17281138	N52803
D-ETMS	Stehr/ Denney Kitfox	681/1690	
D-ETMT	Beech F33A Bonanza	CE-1669	N8061P
D-ETMV	Cessna 152	15283134	N46890
D-ETMY	Mylius My-103 Mistral (Permit)	V-1	
D-ETNA	SOCATA TB-200 Tobago XL	1656	
D-ETNT	Cessna TR182 Turbo Skylane RG	R18201812	N4979T
D-ETOI	SAN Jodel DR.1050 Ambassadeur	483	D-EARL(1)
D-ETOL	Cessna 182Q Skylane	18267591	N5237N
D-ETOM	Cessna 152	15284787	N4629P
D-ETON	SOCATA TB-10 Tobago	1190	N55391
D-ETOP(2)	SOCATA TB-20 Trinidad	2102	
D-ETOR	Beech F33A Bonanza	CE-1050	N7214Z
D-ETOW(2)	Diamond DA 40 Star	40268	
D-ETOY	CASA I-131E Jungmann	2151	(D-EDWV) E3B-535
D-ETPA(3)	Piper PA-28-181 Archer III	2843553	N53596
D-ETPE	Piper PA-28-181 Archer III	2843003	N9256N
D-ETPG	Grob G.140 (Permit 12.02)	86000	(D-ETBG)
D-ETPH	Piper PA-18 Super Cub 95	18-2006	SE-I MG OY-DVV EI-79/ MM522406/ I-EIFI 52-2406
D-ETPL	Piper PA-28-161 Cadet	2841362	N92494 (N628FT) (N9234Q)
D-ETPM	Piper PA-28-161 Cadet	2841363	N9234Q (N629FT) (N9235D)
D-ETPS	Piper PA-28-161 Cadet	2841364	N9237Q (N630FT) (N9236J)
D-ETPW	Piper PA-46-310P Malibu	46-8608002	D-ENHP N9094T (N193M) N9094T
D-ETPY	Piper PA-28-161 Cadet	2841365	N9250G (N631FT) (N9228J)
D-ETRA	Beech C24R Sierra	MC-547	N22PZ N22PS
D-ETRB	Cessna 182Q Skylane	18267479	SP-FNT D-ETRB N6664X YV-1883P (N4955N)
D-ETRG	Cessna 152	15285109	N5410Q
D-ETRI	Fürstenwalde Etrich Taube D2 Replica (Permit 3.00)	1913	
D-ETRS	Robin DR.400/180S Régent	2095	
D-ETRV	Cessna 175C Skylark	17557046	HB-CRV (N8346T)
D-ETRY	Diamond DA 20-A1 Katana	10323	
D-ETSA	Bölkow BO.209 Monsun	197	HB-UEI D-EAIM(1)
D-ETSB	Beyer/ Denney Kitfox III	810	
D-ETSE	Beech K35 Bonanza	D-6113	N805R
D-ETSI	Piper PA-46-310P Malibu	46-8508012	HB-PKY D-EKLG(1) N4379M
D-ETSM	Piper PA-28RT-201T Turbo Arrow IV	28R-7931200	N29580
D-ETSR	Robin DR.400/200R Remo 200	2243	
D-ETSW	Piper PA-32R-301 Saratoga IIHP	3213077	N9238Q
D-ETSY	Aviat A-1 Husky	1377	

D-ETTB	Borgwardt/ Neico Lancair 320	1644	
D-ETTC(2)	Diamond DA 20-A1 Katana	10161	C-GCVV
			N851DF
D-ETTD	Cessna 172R	17281218	N2168Z
D-ETTG	Piper PA-46-310P Malibu	46-8508079	N6915P
			(N88PL)
			N6915P
D-ETTH	Extra EA.400	21	
D-ETTI	Piaggio FWP.149D	025	I-ATTI
			D-EHUG(2)
			90+15
			AC+401
			DE+391
D-ETTK	Cessna 172R	17281219	N2169M
D-ETTL	Cessna 172R	17281217	N21714
D-ETTO	Extra EA.300/L	1174	
D-ETTR	Cessna 172R	17281221	N21703
D-ETTS	Cessna 172R	17281220	N2170D
D-ETTT(2)	Cessna 172R Skyhawk	17280331	N9511W
D-ETUA	Cessna TU206G Turbo Stationair 6	U20606048	HB-CJP
			N4914Z
D-ETUI	Aeronca 65CA Super Chief	17951	N36894
			NC36894
D-ETUS	Robin DR.400/180R Remo 180	2188	
D-ETUV	Cessna 182Q Skylane	18266403	N94108
D-ETVH	Robin DR.400/180R Remo 180	2157	F-GLVH
D-ETWA	Piper PA-46-310P Malibu	46-8408014	N4320E
D-ETWB	Cessna 172M	17264568	N9950V
D-ETWF	Frank/ Denney Kitfox II	597	
D-ETWH	Mooney M.20M Model 257 TLS	27-0140	
D-ETWK	Küster/ Denney Kitfox III	809/1765	
D-ETWM(2)	Piper PA-28-181 Archer III	2843325	N41885
D-ETWO	Warrings/Dallach D4/E Fascination (Permit)	E-006	
D-ETWR	Diamond DA 20-A1 Katana	10128	OE-AMF
			N557SS
D-ETWW	Cessna 172N	17270981	N1383E
D-ETZE	Extra EA.300/L	024	
D-EUAP	Piper PA-28RT-201T Turbo Arrow IV	28R-8131166	N8412H
D-EUBA	SIAI-Marchetti S.205-18/F	352	D-EKGA(1)
D-EUCA	Commander Aircraft 114B	14571	
D-EUCB(2)	Buchhold Rieseler R.III.22/K (Permit .01)	1856	
D-EUCE(2)	Cessna 172RG Cutlass RG	172RG0475	I-TYPE
			N5219V
D-EUCH	HOAC DV-20 Katana	20083	
D-EUCO	Cessna 172N	17273373	N4825G
D-EUDA	Diamond DA 20-A1 Katana	10268	
D-EUDO	Piper PA-28-236 Dakota	28-7911111	N333WE
			N3022R
D-EUDR	Piper PA-46-310P Malibu	4608040	N54FM
			N9111Z
D-EUEU	Piper PA-32-301 Saratoga	32-8106068	I-CONT
			N8392W
D-EUFC	Cessna U206G Stationair 6	U20604101	HB-CJO
			C-GJKD
			N206DG
			C-GBBV
			N756HJ
D-EUFD(2)	SOCATA TB-20 Trinidad	2019	
D-EUFM	Weltin UFM-13 Lambada S (Exhibited .00)	unkn	
D-EUFR	Beech A36 Bonanza	E-3021	
D-EUGC	Grob G.115A	8021	HB-UGC
			(D-EGVV)
D-EUGS	HOAC DV-20 Katana	20034	
D-EUGW	Cessna 172N	17273946	N9877J
D-EUHF	Mooney M.20J Model 205	24-3360	
D-EUHP	Cessna T.207A Turbo Stationair 7 /Soloy	00553	N70549
D-EUHS	Reims/Cessna F172P	F17202197	SE-IHS
D-EUHU	SOCATA TB-20 Trinidad	1521	
D-EUHW	Beech A36 Bonanza	E-2990	N3218G
D-EUIB	Cessna P210N Pressurized Centurion II	P21000162	N6292P
D-EUJF	Heimes/ Aero Designs Pulsar XP (Permit)	1874	
D-EUJL	Lenhard/ Stoddard-Hamilton Glasair III	"00"	
D-EUKA	Swoboda/ Europa Aviation Europa	1782	
D-EUKD	Grob G.115C	82071/C1	
D-EUKI	Kienle/ Brditschka HB-207VRG Alfa	207056	
D-EULE(2)	Diamond DA 20-A1 Katana	10193	C-GFTO
			N693DA
D-EULF	Cessna 150L	15074244	N19216
D-EULI	Bronner / Rutan Long-Ez	1044	
D-EUMI	Robin R.2160D Acrobin	304	
D-EUML	Löffler/ Murphy Rebel	1798	
D-EUMM	Diamond DA 20-A1 Katana	10250	
D-EUMT	Yakovlev Yak-52 (Permit 12.01)	9011004	
D-EUOS	Cessna P210N Pressurized Centurion II	P21000368	N4918K
D-EUPA	Hoffmann/ Europa Avn Europa	271/1843	
D-EURA	Jodel D.92 Bébé	216	D-ENIC
			SL-AAM
D-EURE	SOCATA TB-9 Tampico Club	1319	
D-EURO	SOCATA TB-9 Tampico Club	1399	
D-EURR	Hinz BL2-ARA (Reservation)	1909	
D-EURS	Piper PA-46-310P Malibu	4608093	N9121N
D-EURU	Rupprecht/ Europa Aviation Europa (Permit 29.8.03)	1954	
D-EUSA	Cessna 150H	15068758	N23154
D-EUTC	Cessna 172S	172S8810	N2726X
D-EUTE	American AG-5B Tiger	10080	N1194L
D-EUTT	Diamond DA 20-A1 Katana	10246	
D-EUTZ	Mooney M.20K Model 252 TSE	25-1056	N252DW

D-EUUH	Cessna 150M (Res .05)	15079342	PH-TXD
			(PH-USB)
			N714QC
D-EUUU	Champion 7EC Traveler	7FC-404	D-EBMQ
	(Converted from 7FC Tri-Traveler)		N9829Y
D-EUUZ	Bücker Bü.131APMJungmann	15	HB-UUZ
			A-8
D-EUVM	Piper PA-28-161 Warrior II	28-7916119	N21619
D-EUVT	Kitplane (Reservation - Type unknown)	XS 01	
D-EUWE	Hinz BL 2-2ARA	1716	
D-EUWH	Extra EA.300/L	01	
D-EUWM	Beech F33A Bonanza	CE-1635	N82689
D-EUWN	Stoddard-Hamilton Glastar GS-1	5468	
D-EUWW	Robin DR.400/180 Régent	2249	
D-EVAB	HOAC DV-20 Katana	20025	
D-EVAC	Robin DR.400/180 Régent	2418	
D-EVAD(2)	Reims FR172J Rocket (Res .05)	FR17200357	I-CCAD
D-EVAF	Cessna 150L	15073798	N18118
D-EVAG	Piper PA-28RT-201T Turbo Arrow IV	28R-8131187	N82001
			N9569N
			N84209
D-EVAH	Piper PA-28RT-201T Turbo Arrow IV	28R-8031016	N8116B
D-EVAJ	Van's RV-8 (Permit 7.04)	01/451	
D-EVAL(2)	Grob G.115D2	82044/D2	
D-EVAM(2)	Cessna 172R	17280083	N382ES
D-EVAN	Cessna 152	15284234	N4826L
D-EVAO	Cessna 172R	17280395	
D-EVAR	Beech F33A Bonanza	CE-1651	N55389
D-EVAS(2)	Cessna 152	15284799	N4680P
D-EVAT	Piper PA-28-181 Archer II	28-8590057	N6915R
D-EVAU	SOCATA TB-20 Trinidad	1569	
D-EVBA	Beech F33A Bonanza	CE-908	N36641
D-EVBE	Cessna U206G Stationair 6-II (Soloy)	U20606381	N7595Z
D-EVBH	HOACDV-20 Katana	20138	OE-AHO
D-EVBI	Beech F33A Bonanza	CE-909	N36667
D-EVBO	HOAC DV-20 Katana	20060	OE-ADI (2)
			D-ENMH
			OE-UDV
D-EVCB	HOAC DV-20 Katana	20040	OE-AIB
			N41DV
D-EVCM	Cessna R172K Hawk XP	R1722972	I-AMCV
			N58ER
			(N758BU)
D-EVCO	Cessna 152	15281216	N49275
D-EVCR	Diamond DA 40 Star	40056	
D-EVDC	Piper PA-28R-200 Cherokee Arrow B	28R-7135126	VH-SLH
			N8595N
D-EVDI	Reims/Cessna F172M	F17201320	OE-DTU
D-EVEB	Beech F33A Bonanza	CE-1380	N725MA
			N1569F
D-EVEE	Beech F33A Bonanza	CE-1354	N5583R
D-EVEI	Beech A36 Bonanza	E-2722	TC-ARZ
			TC-ARI
			N80225
D-EVEL	Cessna 172N	17273253	N333WB
			N7364F
D-EVEM	Robin DR.400/140B Major	1398	PH-SRW
D-EVEN	SOCATA TB-9 Tampico Club	1320	
D-EVER(2)	Piper PA-46-500TP Malibu Meridian	4697105	N429MM
D-EVET	Resch/ Stephens Acro Sport II	1652	
D-EVEW	Beech C24R Sierra	MC-651	N6014Y
D-EVEZ	Resch/ Jodel D.18	104	
D-EVFG	Beech S35 Bonanza	D-7675	HB-EKN
			I-FARE
			HB-EKN
D-EVFH	Cessna 172N	17268918	N734KR
D-EVFM	Piper PA-28-181 Archer II	28-8290063	N8466W
D-EVFR	Cessna 150J	15070974	N61337
D-EVGH	Piper PA-28RT-201T Turbo Arrow IV	28R-7931002	N44DY
			N2079B
D-EVGM	Robin DR.400/180R Remo 180	2143	
D-EVGR	Beech F33A Bonanza	CE-1494	N334MW
D-EVHB	Piper PA-38-112 Tomahawk	38-80A0012	N24849
D-EVHH	Robin DR.400/180R Remo 180	2449	
D-EVHM(3)	SOCATA TB-20 Trinidad	2144	D-EVHV(1)
D-EVHP	Piper PA-28-181 Archer II	28-8290131	N8208Q
			HB-PMR
D-EVHS	Piper PA-28-181 Archer II	28-8390061	HB-PHS
D-EVIA	Robin R.2160D Acrobin	289	
D-EVIB(2)	Piper PA-28-181 Archer III	2843043	N9274L
D-EVIC	Piper PA-28-181 Archer III	2843071	N9285N
D-EVID	Piper PA-28RT-201T Turbo Arrow IV	28R-8331045	N43081
D-EVII (2)	Aviat A-1 Husky	1241	
D-EVIJ	SOCATA TB-9 Tampico	1840	F-GTQA
			(5N-. . .)
			F-OIDJ
D-EVIK	Beech A36 Bonanza	E-2347	N900TT
			N2611L
D-EVIL	Cessna 172N	17270159	N781MB
D-EVIM	HOAC DV-20 Katana	20033	
D-EVIN	SOCATA TB-10 Tobago	1476	
D-EVIO(2)	Piper PA-32RT-300 Lance II	32R-7885144	G-WOZA
			G-BYBB
			N31957
D-EVIP(2)	Cessna 172N	17272002	N6283E
D-EVIS	SOCATA TB-200 Tobago XL	1474	
D-EVIT	Cessna TU206F Turbo Stationair	U20602246	N1538U

D-EVIY	Christen A-1 Husky (Permit .05)	1156	HB-KIV D-EHNP(3)
D-EVJO	Cessna 172P	17274591	N52715
D-EVKB	Piper PA-28-181 Archer II	28-8390054	N4300Z
D-EVKG	Piper PA-46-310P Malibu	4608022	N9094Z N9103Q
D-EVKV	Diamond DA 40 Star	40350	
D-EVLA(2)	WDFL Dallach D4 Fascination VLA	1001	
D-EVLB	Reims/Cessna FR172K Hawk XP	FR17200659	OE-DSX
D-EVLF	HOAC DV-20 Katana	20117	
D-EVLS	Diamond DA 20-A1	10244	
D-EVMC	Cessna 182P Skylane	18264653	N9034M
D-EVMH	SOCATA TB-200 Tobago XL	1629	
D-EVMI	Piper PA-28R-200 Cherokee Arrow II	28R-7535099	I- KIMI N32914
D-EVMK	HOAC DV-20 Katana	20048	N48DV
D-EVMO	Reims/Cessna F152	F15201517	D-EEJI
D-EVNM	SOCATA TB-200 Tobago XL	1439	D-EVHM F-OHDA
D-EVOB	Cessna 172N	17273543	N5094G
D-EVOC	Cessna 172N	17271387	N2961E
D-EVOG	Robin DR.500/200i Président	0019	
D-EVOI	HOAC DV-20 Katana	20130	
D-EVOM	Cessna 150M	15079122	N714EP
D-EVON	SOCATA TB-200 Tobago XL	1475	F-WNGZ
D-EVOO	HOAC DV-20 Katana	20042	
D-EVOP(2)	SIAT 223A-1 Flamingo	002	HB-EVO D-EHQE HB-EVO D-EHQE
D-EVOR	HOAC DV-20 Katana	20017	
D-EVOS	Cessna 182Q Skylane	18266835	N96740
D-EVOT	Krieger/ Zenith CH-601 HD/S Zodiac	6-3102	
D-EVOX	HOAC DV-20 Katana	20038	
D-EVPA	Piper PA-46-350P Malibu Mirage	4622138	N9210P (N9234Z)
D-EVPI	Cessna 172N	17268881	N734JC
D-EVPM	Cessna 172S	172S08418	N690SA
D-EVPW	Diamond DA 20-A1 Katana	10144	
D-EVRA	Robin DR.400/180R Remo 180	2207	
D-EVRF	Falkenstrein/ Van's RV-7 (Permit 6.04)	70151	
D-EVRK	Piper PA-28RT-201T Turbo Arrow IV	28R-8131207	N36008 N8469C
D-EVRS	Ruttkay/ WT9 Dynamic (Permit 5.04)	448/DB-01/02	
D-EVSA	Grob G.115D2 Bavarian	82002/D2	
D-EVSC	Cessna 172P	17276141	N96997 C-GSIU
D-EVSM	Piper PA-46-350P Malibu Mirage	4622072	HB-PMO
D-EVSR	Robin DR.400/180 Régent (Permit .05)	2066	
D-EVST	Robin DR.500/200i Président	0017	
D-EVTA	Piper PA-28-181 Archer II	2843033	N92703
D-EVTE	Robin R.3000/160	168	
D-EVTO	Piper PA-28-161 Warrior II	28-8016271	N81615
D-EVTZ	SOCATA TB-20 Trinidad	1767	
D-EVUG	Grünig/ Neico Lancair 360 (Permit)	1762	
D-EVUJ	Piper PA-28RT-201T Turbo Arrow IV	28R-7931134	N2124N N2152X
D-EVVA	Mooney M.20M Model 257 TLS	27-0002	N1002K
D-EVVV	Extra EA.300/S	006	
D-EVWM	Beech A36 Bonanza	E-3012	N10575
D-EWAA(2)	Cessna 172R	17280406	N9518Z
D-EWAC(2)	Zlin Z.126 Trenér 2	791	D-EJEW OK-IGG
D-EWAD	Reims/Cessna F150L	F15000919	D-EGBC
D-EWAE	Cessna 172R	17280045	N352ES
D-EWAF	Cessna 182Q Skylane	18265548	LN-VIM N735NE
D-EWAG	Diamond DA 20-A1 Katana	10163	
D-EWAH	SOCATA MS.883 Rallye 115	1366	OO-CBL F-BRMQ
D-EWAI	Diamond DA 20-A1 Katana	10162	
D-EWAK	Kirchhof / Denney Kitfox IV-1200	1687/1744	
D-EWAL (2)	Diamond DA 40DStar	D4.064	
D-EWAN	Grob G.115C	82041C	PH-SPX D-EWAN
D-EWAO	HOAC DV-20 Katana	20085	(D-EWRD)
D-EWAP	Extra EA.300	034	D-EKFD(1)
D-EWAQ	Diamond DA 40DStar	D4.048	
D-EWAR	Piper PA-28-161 Warrior II	28-8616053	N9082X
D-EWAS	Schulze/ Denney Kitfox III	1160	
D-EWAT	Commander Aircraft 114B	14564	
D-EWAU	Cessna 172R	17280329	N9502R (D-ESKW)
D-EWAV	Diamond DA 20-A1 Katana	10164	
D-EWAW	Cessna 172P	17275329	N62709
D-EWAX	HOAC DV-20 Katana	20068	
D-EWAY	HOAC DV-20 Katana	20069	
D-EWAZ	SOCATA TB-200 Tobago XL	1628	
D-EWBB	PZL-104 Wilga 35A	61107	DDR-WBB DM-WBB(2)
D-EWBC	Cessna R182 Skylane RG	R18200442	N9199C
D-EWBE	Cessna 172N Skyhawk II	17268608	N733WN
D-EWBG	PZL-104 Wilga 35A	61112	DDR-WBG DM-WBG(2)
D-EWBJ	PZL-104 Wilga 35A	61115	DDR-WBJ DM-WBJ(2)
D-EWBM	Mooney M.20M Model 257 TLS	27-0225	
D-EWBN	PZL-104 Wilga 35A	62175	DDR-WBN DM-WBN(2)
D-EWBQ	PZL-104 Wilga 35A	62179	DDR-WBQ DM-WBQ(2)
D-EWBS	PZL-104 Wilga 35A	62181	DDR-WBS DM-WBS(2)
D-EWBT	PZL-104 Wilga 35A	62182	DDR-WBT DM-WBT (2)
D-EWBU	PZL-104 Wilga 35A	62183	DDR-WBU DM-WBU(2)
D-EWBV	PZL-104 Wilga 35A	62166	DDR-WBV DM-WBV(2)
D-EWBX	PZL-104 Wilga 35A	62162	DDR-WBX DM-WBX(2)
D-EWBY	PZL-104 Wilga 35A	62163	DDR-WBY DM-WBY(2)
D-EWBZ	PZL-104 Wilga 35A	140537	DDR-WBZ DM-WBZ(2)
D-EWCB	Cessna 182Q Skylane	18265707	N735UZ
D-EWCE	Cessna 210D Centurion	21058403	D-EMWJ N3903Y
D-EWCN	Orlican L-40 Meta-Sokol	150511	DM-WCN
D-EWCR	Maule M-6-235 Super Rocket	7443C	N600AB
D-EWCT	Diamond DA 40 Star	40024	
D-EWDA	Diamond DA 20-A1 Katana	10271	
D-EWDC	Diamond DA 20-A1 Katana	10316	N646DA
D-EWDM	Aerotek Pitts S-2A	2046	OO-WDM OO-XDM D-EILH(1) YV-38P YV-TAEF
D-EWDZ	Cessna 210N Centurion II (Reservation)	21060761	D-EDMI (1) N1740X
D-EWEB	Cessna P210N Pressurized Centurion II	P21000597	N732XW
D-EWEF	Diamond DA 20-A1 Katana	10295	N44UV N595DA
D-EWEI	Mooney M.20M TLS Model 257	27-0323	
D-EWEJ	Zlin Z.226T Trenér 6	243	DM-WEJ
D-EWEK	Piper PA-22-108 Colt (Permit)	22-9654	D-EKCE N5830Z
D-EWEL	Ebel/ Zenair CH-601HDS Super Zodiac (Permit 10.04)	6-8418	
D-EWES	SOCATA TB-21 Trinidad TC	963	HB-KDJ D-EPRD OE-KHG
D-EWET	Robin DR.400/180R Remo 180	2448	
D-EWEW	SOCATA TB-20 Trinidad	2012	(D-EUFD)
D-EWFA	Zlin Z.43	0038	DDR-WFA DM-WFA(3)
D-EWFB	Zlin Z.43	0039/01	DDR-WFB DM-WFB(2)
D-EWFC	Zlin Z.43	0040/01	DDR-WFC DM-WFC(2)
D-EWFD	Zlin Z.43	0041/02	DDR-WFD DM-WFD(2)
D-EWFE	Zlin Z.43	0042/02	DDR-WFE DM-WFE(2)
D-EWFG	Zlin Z.43	0043/02	DDR-WFG DM-WFG(2)
D-EWFH	Zlin Z.43	0044/02	DDR-WFH DM-WFH(2)
D-EWFI	Zlin Z.43	0074	DDR-WFI DM-WFI (2)
D-EWGB	Piper PA-18-150 Super Cub	18-7442	D-EMFI (1) N4346P
D-EWGO	Goldbrunner G8UL (Permit 6.01)	1847	
D-EWGS	Diamond DA 20-A1 Katana	10171	C-FYVM
D-EWHA	PZL-104 Wilga 35A	74213	DDR-WHA DM-WHA(2)
D-EWHB	Cessna 172P	17275482	N63775
D-EWHC	PZL-104 Wilga 35A	74215	DDR-WHC DM-WHC(2)
D-EWHD	PZL-104 Wilga 35A	74216	DDR-WHD DM-WHD(2)
D-EWHE	PZL-104 Wilga 35A	86226	DDR-WHE DM-WHE(2)
D-EWHF	PZL-104 Wilga 35A	86227	DDR-WHF DM-WHF(2)
D-EWHI	PZL-104 Wilga 35A	86229	DDR-WHI DM-WHI (2)
D-EWHJ	Zlin Z.526 Trenér Master	1006	SE-XFE D-EGED(2) OK-V . .
D-EWHK	PZL-104 Wilga 35A	86230	DDR-WHK DM-WHK
D-EWHL	PZL-104 Wilga 35A	86231	DDR-WHL DM-WHL
D-EWHM	PZL-104 Wilga 35A	86232	DDR-WHM DM-WHM
D-EWHN	PZL-104 Wilga 35A	86233	DDR-WHN DM-WHN
D-EWHO	Beech A36AT Bonanza	E-2707	
D-EWHP	PZL-104 Wilga 35A	86264	DDR-WHP DM-WHP
D-EWHR	PZL-104 Wilga 35A	86266	DDR-WHR DM-WHR

D-EWHS	PZL-104 Wilga 35A	86267	DDR-WHS DM-WHS
D-EWHT	PZL-104 Wilga 35A	86268	DDR-WHT DM-WHT
D-EWHV	PZL-104 Wilga 35A	96319	DDR-WHV DM-WHV
D-EWHW	PZL-104 Wilga 35A	96320	DDR-WHW DM-WHW
D-EWHY	PZL-104 Wilga 35A	96322	DDR-WHY DM-WHY
D-EWHZ	PZL-104 Wilga 35A	96323	DDR-WHZ DM-WHZ
D-EWIA	Zlin Z.226T Trenér 6	353	DDR-WIA DM-WIA
D-EWIG	American AG-5B Tiger	10096	N196AH D-EWIG N1195P
D-EWIH	Rockwell Commander 114B	14153	N4823W
D-EWIK	Cessna 177B Cardinal	17702091	OE-DTS (N34922)
D-EWIL	Zlin Z.526F Trenér Master	1260	YR-ZAG
D-EWIM	Beech F33A Bonanza	CE-1388	N5584N
D-EWIN	Grob G.115C	82053C	N115AH
D-EWJW	Wilkenloh/ Neico Lancair 360	382SB	
D-EWKA	Cessna 152	15281131	N47064
D-EWKE	Keiper/ Denney Kitfox III	1074	
D-EWKH	Buchs/ Neico Lancair 320	1737	
D-EWKI	Zlin Z.143L	0025	
D-EWKK	Cessna 152	15280245	N129SC (N24380)
D-EWKL	Extra EA.300/L	064	
D-EWKU	Kuche/ Stoddard-Hamilton Glasair II-SRG	2101	
D-EWLA	Robin DR.400/180R Remo 180	2447	
D-EWLU	Diamond DA 40DStar	D4.005	OE-VPW
D-EWMA	Zlin Z.42MU	0012	DDR-WMA DM-WMA
D-EWMB	Diamond DA 20-A1 Katana	10248	
D-EWMC	Zlin Z.42MU	0014	DDR-WMC DM-WMC
D-EWMD	Zlin Z.42MU	0015	DDR-WMD DM-WMD
D-EWME	Zlin Z.42MU	0069	DDR-WME DM-WME
D-EWMF	Zlin Z.42MU	0017	DDR-WMF DM-WMF
D-EWMG	WDFL Dallach D4/E Fascination (Permit) (C/n formerly quoted as 1905)	EB011	
D-EWMH	Cessna 182S	18280293	N2385N
D-EWMI	Aviat A-1 Husky	1376	
D-EWMK	Zlin Z.42MU	0021	DDR-WMK DM-WMK
D-EWML	Zlin Z.42MU	0022	DDR-WML DM-WML
D-EWMM	Zlin Z.42MU	0023	DDR-WMM DM-WMM
D-EWMN	Zlin Z.42MU	0024	DDR-WMN DM-WMN
D-EWMO	Zlin Z.42MU	0025	DDR-WMO DM-WMO
D-EWMP	Zlin Z.42MU	0026	DDR-WMP DM-WMP
D-EWMQ	Zlin Z.42MU	0028	DDR-WMQ DM-WMQ
D-EWMR	Zlin Z.42MU	0029	DDR-WMR DM-WMR
D-EWMS	Zlin Z.42MU	0030	DDR-WMS DM-WMS
D-EWMT	Zlin Z.42MU	0031	DDR-WMT DM-WMT
D-EWMU	Zlin Z.42MU	0032	DDR-WMU DM-WMU
D-EWMV	Zlin Z.42MU	0033	DDR-WMV DM-WMV
D-EWMW	Zlin Z.42MU	0034	DDR-WMW DM-WMW
D-EWMX	Zlin Z.42MU	0035	DDR-WMX DM-WMX
D-EWMY	Zlin Z.42MU	0036	DDR-WMY DM-WMY
D-EWMZ	Zlin Z.42MU	0037	DDR-WMZ DM-WMZ
D-EWNA	Zlin Z.42MU	0038	DDR-WNA DM-WNA
D-EWNC	Zlin Z.42MU	0040	DDR-WNC DM-WNC
D-EWND	Zlin Z.42MU	0041	DDR-WND DM-WND
D-EWNE	Zlin Z.42MU	0042	DDR-WNE DM-WNE
D-EWNG	Zlin Z.526F Trenér Master	1076	N3459
D-EWNK	Zlin Z.42MU	0047	DDR-WNK DM-WNK
D-EWNL	Zlin Z.42MU	0049	DDR-WNL DM-WNL
D-EWNO	Zlin Z.42MU	0051/02	DDR-WNO DM-WNO

D-EWNQ	Zlin Z.42MU	0053/02	DDR-WNQ DM-WNQ
D-EWNT	Zlin Z.42M	0062	DDR-WNT DM-WNT
D-EWNU	Zlin Z.42M	0063	DDR-WNU DM-WNU
D-EWNX	Zlin Z.42M	0066	DDR-WNX DM-WNX
D-EWNY	Zlin Z.42M	0067	DDR-WNY DM-WNY
D-EWOB	Zlin Z.42M	0084	DDR-WOB DM-WOB
D-EWOC	Zlin Z.42M	0085	DDR-WOC DM-WOC
D-EWOD	Zlin Z.42M	0086	DDR-WOD DM-WOD
D-EWOE	Zlin Z.42M	0087	DDR-WOE DM-WOE
D-EWOF	Zlin Z.42M	0111	DDR-WOF DM-WOF
D-EWOG	Zlin Z.42M	0112/04	DDR-WOG DM-WOG
D-EWOH	Zlin Z.42M	0113	DDR-WOH DM-WOH
D-EWOI	Zlin Z.42M	0114/04	DDR-WOI DM-WOI
D-EWOK	Zlin Z.42M	0115	DDR-WOK DM-WOK
D-EWOL	Zlin Z.42M	0130/05	DDR-WOL DM-WOL
D-EWOM	Zlin Z.42M	0131	DDR-WOM DM-WOM
D-EWON	Zlin Z.42M	0132	DDR-WON DM-WON
D-EWOP	Zlin Z.42M	0133/05	DDR-WOP DM-WOP
D-EWOQ	Zlin Z.42MU	0157	DDR-WOQ DM-WOQ
D-EWOR(2)	Röhl / Brändli BX-2 Cherry (Permit)	313/38	
D-EWOW	Kitplane, type unknown (Reservation 4.99)	1548	
D-EWPA	PZL-104 Wilga 35A	118411	DDR-WPA DM-WPA
D-EWPB	Zlin Z.50LS	0064	
D-EWPD	Cirrus SR20	1351	N1334C
D-EWPE	Beech F33A Bonanza	CE-1391	N5586M
D-EWPG	Robin R.3000/160	166	
D-EWPH	Held/ Brditschka HB-207VRG Alfa	207020	
D-EWPM	Beech F33A Bonanza	CE-1774	N1551N
D-EWPR	Cessna 172N	17272032	N6539E
D-EWPW	Beech A36AT Bonanza	E-2950	(N820V) N10PW
D-EWPZ	Champion 8KCAB Super Decathlon	975-2004	
D-EWQA	Zlin Z.526AFS Akrobat	1205	DDR-WQA DM-WQA
D-EWQC	Zlin Z.526AFS Akrobat	1207	DDR-WQC DM-WQC
D-EWQH	Zlin Z.526AFS Akrobat	1212	DDR-WQH DM-WQH
D-EWQL	Zlin Z.526AFS Akrobat	1217	DDR-WQL DM-WQL
D-EWRA	Joerges Wright Flyer Model A Replica	1770	
D-EWRC	PZL-104 Wilga 35A	96326	DDR-WRC DM-WRC
D-EWRE	PZL-104 Wilga 35A	96328	DDR-WRE DM-WRE
D-EWRF	PZL-104 Wilga 35A	96329	DDR-WRF DM-WRF
D-EWRG	Dornier Do.27B-1	276	HB-HAG D-EMAE(1) 56+09 BD+928 AC+928 AS+928
D-EWRH	PZL-104 Wilga 35A	96331	DDR-WRH DM-WRH
D-EWRI	PZL-104 Wilga 35A	107337	DDR-WRI DM-WRI
D-EWRJ	PZL-104 Wil ga 35A	107338	DDR-WRJ DM-WRJ
D-EWRK (2)	Zlin Z.50LS	0066	OK-WRL
D-EWRL	PZL-104 Wil ga 35A	118391	DDR-WRL DM-WRL
D-EWRM	PZL-104 Wilga 35A	118392	DDR-WRM DM-WRM
D-EWRN	PZL-104 Wilga 35A	118393	DDR-WRN DM-WRN
D-EWRO	PZL-104 Wilga 35A	118394	DDR-WRO DM-WRO
D-EWRP	PZL-104 Wilga 35A	118395	DDR-WRP DM-WRP
D-EWRR	Wittek/ Pottier P.220S Koala	313	
D-EWRU	PZL-104 Wilga 35A	118399	DDR-WRU DM-WRU
D-EWRV	PZL-104 Wilga 35A	118400	DDR-WRV DM-WRV
D-EWRX	PZL-104 Wilga 35A	118408	DDR-WRX DM-WRX

D-EWRY	PZL-104 Wilga 35A	118409	DDR-WRY DM-WRY
D-EWRZ	PZL-104 Wilga 35A	118410	DDR-WRZ DM-WRZ
D-EWSH	Huber/ Colomban MC-100 Banbi	02	
D-EWSM	HOAC DV-20 Katana	20043	
D-EWSP	Diamond DA 40D Star	D4.043	
D-EWSR	Robin DR.400/180 Régent	2196	
D-EWSS	Robin DR.400/180 Régent	2079	
D-EWST	Cessna TR182 Turbo Skylane RG (Stored)	R18201091	N756KE
D-EWTC	Commander 114TC	20010	
D-EWTE	Cessna 182Q Skylane	18267125	N97536
D-EWTM	Van's RV-6 (Reservation)	1845	
D-EWTR	Zlin Z.326A Akrobat (Permit 5.99)	555	DM-WKA
D-EWUW	Cessna 140	8880	N89831 NC89831
D-EWVZ	SOCATA TB-20 Trinidad	1711	
D-EWWA	Diamond DA 20-A1 Katana	10120	N547SS
D-EWWB	Boeing Stearman A75-N1 (PT-13D)	75-5659	(D-EQHB) SE-AMT G-BAVN 4X-AMT 42-17496
D-EWWE (2)	Diamond DA 40D Star	D4.030	
D-EWWF	HOAC DV-20 Katana	20057	
D-EWWG	Diamond DA 40 Star	40027	
D-EWWH	Hohmann/ Neico Lancair 320	001	
D-EWWM	Piper PA-28-181 Archer III	2890223	N9227R
D-EWWW(2)	Cessna 182Q	18266579	PH-MMA (PH-GAC) (PH-MAD) (PH-ZAP) N95613 N684WB N95613
D-EXAB	Cessna 205 (Permit 7.03)	205-0294	OY-DPF HB-CMW N8294Z
D-EXAC(2)	Extra EA.400	18	
D-EXAI	Piper PA-18 Super Cub 95	18-3184	OE-ADM D-EDVO R-86 (OL-L110) 53-4784
D-EXAM	Mooney M.20R Ovation	29-0042	
D-EXAS	Piper PA-38-112 Tomahawk	38-80A0071	HB-PFI N9698N
D-EXBA	Zlin Z.526F Trenér Master	1124	N29RW N840C
D-EXBC	Cessna 182S	18280113	HB-CIZ N446ES
D-EXCA	Commander Aircraft 114B	14557	
D-EXDA	Diamond DA 20-A1 Katana	10275	
D-EXDB	Dörnemann/ Aero Designs Pulsar XP	410	
D-EXDD	Grob G.115A	8009	VH-YYX D-EMFT (D-EIEP)
D-EXED	Piper PA-46-350P Malibu Mirage	4636282	OY-FIA
D-EXES	Diamond DA 40DStar	D4.062	
D-EXEW	Extra EA.300/L	05	
D-EXEX	Bölkow BO.209 Monsun 160FV	103	HB-UEA D-EBOF(2)
D-EXFD	Extra EA.300/L	1180	
D-EXFT	Extra EA.200	025	
D-EXFX	Diamond DA 40 Star	40054	
D-EXGC	Extra EA.200	027	
D-EXGH	Extra EA.300/L	143	
D-EXGM	Gmachel/ Impulse 130NG (Permit 3.04)	NG2	
D-EXGV	Robin HR.100/250TR Président	547	F-BXGV
D-EXGW	Welz/ Stoddard-Hamilton Glasair III	3256	
D-EXHB	Cessna 182P Skylane	18262472	N8505Z N1279M D-EENA N52233
D-EXHG	Extra EA.300/L	03	
D-EXIA	Robin DR.500/200i Président	0024	
D-EXIK	Extra EA.400	13	
D-EXIL	SOCATA TB-20 Trinidad	1298	
D-EXIR	Extra EA.300/L	1185	
D-EXIT	SOCATA TB-20 Trinidad	1299	
D-EXJM	SOCATA TB-20 Trinidad	1297	
D-EXKA	Piper PA-28-161 Cherokee Warrior II	28-7816601	N31967
D-EXKB	Aviat A-1 Husky	1244	
D-EXKG	Extra EA.400	26	
D-EXKJ	Jautz/ Dallach D4/E Fascination (Res 10.99)	D4	
D-EXLH	Extra EA.400	06	
D-EXMB	Mooney M.20K Model 231	25-0813	N5744N
D-EXME	Maule MX-7-180 Star Rocket	11037C	N5671N
D-EXMI	Robin DR.400/180R Remo 180	2078	
D-EXMM	de Havilland DH.82A Tiger Moth	82814	G-ERTY D-EFYZ(1) LX-JON G-ANDC R4897

D-EXOB	Cessna 140 (Reservation .05)	12502	N418R C-FJTN CF-JTN N2173N NC2173N
D-EXOT	Piper PA-46-310P Malibu	46-8508010	N4378T (N55BT) N4378T
D-EXPC	Champion 8KCAB Super Decathlon	956-2004	
D-EXPD	Piper PA-46-350P Malibu Mirage	4636100	OY-JAM
D-EXPH	Aerotek Pitts S-2A	2015	N80007 (D-EPIT) N80007
D-EXPK	Kroker/ Van's RV-6A	1301	
D-EXPO	Piper PA-28-181 Archer III	2843083	N92876
D-EXPS	Extra EA.300/L	090	
D-EXRB	Extra EA.230 (Reservation 2.99)	001	N230X D-EKEW(2)
D-EXRR	Extra EA.200	018	G-XTRR D-EVNO
D-EXRV	Hühn/ Van's RV-4	2849	
D-EXSL	Extra EA.300/L	08	
D-EXSR	Aquila AT-01	AT01-128	D-EWPX
D-EXTA	Piper PA-46-350P Malibu Mirage	4636026	N9264Q
D-EXTC	Fürle/ Denney Kitfox IV-1200 (Permit)	003	
D-EXTL	Lukasczyk /Van's RV-4 (Permit 6.04)	495	
D-EXTR/S/T	Test Registrations for Extra EA.200/300 production		
D-EXTX/Y/Z	Test Registrations for Extra EA.400 production		
D-EXUG	Extra EA.300/L	152	
D-EXVR	Aviat Pitts S-2B	5272	
D-EXWL	Focke-Wulf FW.44J Stieglitz	2776	D-EXEK OH-XEK FinAF:SZ-14 RNorAF:3 D-EXWL
D-EXWM	Aviat A-1 Husky	1350	
D-EXWP	American Champion 8KCAB Decathlon	930-2003	
D-EXWS	Aerotek Pitts S-2A	2269	OE-AHH D-ELUP(2) N255CA
D-EXXA	Piper PA-28R-201 Arrow	2837033	N9185Z
D-EXXB	Piper PA-28R-201 Arrow	2837036	N91871
D-EXXC	Piper PA-28R-201 Arrow	2837037	N91886
D-EXXD	Piper PA-28R-201 Arrow	2837054	N9235F
D-EXXE	SOCATA TB-200 Tobago XL	1447	
D-EXXI	SOCATA TB-20 Trinidad	1481	
D-EXXP	Müller/ Aero Designs Pulsar XP	1887	
D-EXXX	Mudry CAP.10B	259	
D-EXYY	HOAC DV-20 Katana	20037	
D-EXYX	Alpavia Jodel D.117A Grand Tourisme	1038	D-ENTI (1)
D-EXYZ	Christen A-1 Husky	1059	HB-KIR D-ECHX(2) N2974C
D-EXZY	Kitplane, type unknown (Reservation 6.99)	122	
D-EYAA	Robin DR.400/180R Remorqueur	1386	HB-EYA
D-EYAE	Diamond DA 20-A1 Katana	10082	N522SS
D-EYAK	Nanchang CJ-6 (Carries serial "1")	132007	PLAAFoC
D-EYAL	Cessna T182T Turbo Skylane	T18208095	N35520
D-EYAM	Reims/Cessna F172K	F17200774	D-ECGV
D-EYAS	Siebenritt/ Jodel DR.1050M	AB 834-M	
D-EYAT	Cirrus SR20	1053	N154CD
D-EYCG	Yakovlev Yak-50	781310	
D-EYCM	Cessna 152	15280506	N25029
D-EYDI (2)	Cessna 182L Skylane (Reservation) [Rebuild using parts of c/n 18256346 ex (D-EYDI (1)), D-EFZE, N2446X]	18258917	D-ECLS(2) N42235
D-EYDT	Piper PA-38-112 Tomahawk (Permit 8.98)	38-82A0108	N9158A
D-EYES	Diamond DA 20-A1 Katana	10137	
D-EYEY	Piper PA-28RT-201T Turbo Arrow IV	28R-8031007	N8105Z
D-EYGA	Gabbe/ Europa Avn Europa	1784	
D-EYGL	Zlin Z.126	796	OK-IGL
D-EYHB	Breit/ Brditschka HB-207 Alfa (Permit 8.99)	207-025	
D-EYII	SIAI-Marchetti SM.1019A	068	EI-465/ MM57258
D-EYKL	Deyerling/ Dallach D4-ES Fascination	EB 016	
D-EYLE	PZL-104 Wilga 35A	20890888	SP-FWI
D-EYMH	Grob G.115B	8109	VH-AYE(3) D-ELCF(2)
D-EYML	Mooney M.20J Model 205	24-3249	SE-KUM
D-EYOA/B	Test registrations for OMF-100-160 Symphony		
D-EYPA	Piper PA-28-181 Archer III	2843035	N9268B
D-EYPC	Cessna R182 Skylane RG	R18201822	N4407F (C-GPGH) (N5138T)
D-EYPS	Extra EA.300/L	1190	
D-EYRM	Maule M-6-235 Super Rocket	7472C	N5665K
D-EYSA	SOCATA TB-20 Trinidad	654	D-ESTU F-GFQR (N20GN)
D-EYSY	Cessna 172R	17281214	
D-EYTG	Yakovlev Yak-18A	unkn	G-BVVX SovAF 307

D-EYTT	Zlin Z.226 Trenér 6	171-15	HB-TRT D-EHSE(1) OK-MFZ
D-EYYY	Piper PA-28RT-201 Arrow IV (Permit .01)	28R-8018104	N8262V
D-EZAG	Piper PA-28RT-201T Turbo Arrow IV	28R-8131058	N8320J
D-EZAI	HOAC DV-20 Katana	20121	
D-EZAK	Morane-Saulnier MS.505 Criquet	700	F-BDQT
D-EZAP	Cessna 152	15283078	N46598
D-EZAR	Aviat A-1 Husky	1235	
D-EZAS(2)	Piper PA-28-181 Archer III	2843253	N4127N
D-EZBA	Reims/Cessna F152	F15201884	N3953A
D-EZBC	Clemens/ Aero Designs Pulsar XP	1861	
D-EZDA	Diamond DA 20-A1 Katana	10266	
D-EZDB	Diamond DA 20-A1 Katana	10267	D-EQDA
D-EZDC	Diamond DA 40 Star	40019	
D-EZDS	Zlin Z.526 Trenér Master	886	F-GNQN F-BMQN
D-EZEA	SOCATA TB-21 Trinidad TC	2149	
D-EZEB	Piper PA-28-181 Archer III	2843007	N9255N
D-EZEE	Fehrling/ Rutan VariEze	1	
D-EZEI (2)	Piper PA-28-181 Archer III	2843091	N92885 (N971PA)
D-EZEL	Robin DR.400/180R Remo 180	2345	
D-EZEN	Piper PA-28-151 Cherokee Warrior	28-7615093	OO-DFM N8336C
D-EZEW	Piper PA-28-181 Archer III	2890228	N9251R
D-EZFF	Robin DR.400/180R Remo 180	2113	
D-EZFS	HOAC DV-20 Katana	20045	N45DV C-FSIU
D-EZFV	Piper PA-28-161 Warrior III	2842212	D-EXPA N30970
D-EZFW	Hanusa/ Jurca MJ.8/FW.190A Replica	1656	
D-EZGA	Cessna 152	15285178	N6164Q
D-EZHB	Robin DR.400/180 Régent	1450	F-GCID
D-EZHL	Robin DR.400/180RRemorqueur	1303	OE-KHL D-EHWN(1)
D-EZIA	Robin DR.500/200i Président	0016	
D-EZIC	Diamond DA 20-A1 Katana	10054	N228P
D-EZII	Erco 415DErcoupe (Reservation 12.99)	1769	N99146 NC99146
D-EZIP	Piper PA-28-181 Archer III	2843013	N92580 D-ESAN(1)
D-EZIS	Piper PA-28-181 Archer III (Damaged 30.5.01)	2843056	N9278N
D-EZKK	Mooney M.20K Model 231	25-0128	N231KK
D-EZLS	HOACDV-20 Katana	20092	N192DV
D-EZMA	Aviat A-1 Husky	1245	HB-KDZ D-EXKL
D-EZMB	Reims FR172GRocket (W/o 1.7.01)	FR17200172	OE-KSW D-EBLM
D-EZMC	Beech C24R Sierra	MC-477	N24013
D-EZMH	Heeren/ Denney Kitfox Vixen 1200	JCV 021	
D-EZMS	Fuji FA-200-160 Aero Subaru	86	HB-ESR
D-EZMY	Kitplane (Reservn 1.00, type unknown)	S 004	
D-EZOE	Cessna R182 Skylane RG	R18200540	N1734R (D-EASG) N1734R
D-EZOF	Piper PA-28-181 Archer II	28-7990236	N2121K
D-EZOZ	Extra EA.300/L (W/o 6.3.99)	029	D-ETZJ
D-EZPA	Piper PA-46-350P Malibu Mirage	4622184	N9251K
D-EZRL	Laudenbach/ Zenair CH-601 Zodiac (Res 6.99)	6-3666	
D-EZRS	Robin DR.400/180 Régent	2309	
D-EZSB	Reims/Cessna F172N	F17201607	N289YY D-EOHI
D-EZTT	Zlin Z.526AFS Akrobat	1211	DDR-WQG DM-WQG
D-EZUG	Christen Pitts S-2B	5129	N6032R
D-EZUM(2)	Aquila AT-01 (Model A210)	107	
D-EZUP	HOAC DV-20 Katana	20008	
D-EZWF	Robin R.3000/160 (W/o 23.4.05)	132	F-GGJZ
D-EZWM	CASA I-131E Jungmann (Permit 8.99)	unkn	E3B-568
D-EZWO	Siek/ Funk FK-12 Comet (Reservn .04)	493	
D-EZWZ	Morane-Saulnier MS.885 Super Rallye	82	HB-EDL
D-EZXL	Scheck/ Zenair CH-601XL Zodiac (Res.04)	00	
D-EZYA	Diamond DA 40 Star	40081	
D-EZYB	Diamond DA 40 Star	40082	OE-VPW
D-EZYC	Diamond DA 40 Star	40083	
D-EZZA	Diamond DA 20-A1 Katana	10020	C-FZYU N321FT
D-EZZB	Diamond DA 20-A1 Katana	10084	N524SS
D-EZZC	Diamond DA 20-A1 Katana	10095	N529SS
D-EZZD	Diamond DA 20-A1 Katana	10103	N173AA
D-EZZM	HOAC DV-20 Katana	20058	PH-ZZM
D-EZZZ	Fieseler Fi.156C-3 Storch (Wfu)	4370	D-EBGY(2) (D-EAXY) Fv3805 CK+KI

CLASS F :
Single-Engined Aircraft of between 2 and 5.7 Metric Tonnes

D-FABE	CCF/North American Harvard IV	CCF4-499	AA+624 52-8578
D-FAIR	Antonov An-2	17205	(54+02) LSK-450
D-FALB	Cessna 208B Grand Caravan	208B0744	
D-FALF	SOCATA TBM-700	157	
D-FALK	Cessna 208 Caravan I	20800023	N9354F
D-FAME(2)	CCF/North American Harvard IV	CCF4-77	G-BKCK N13631 G-BKCK N13631 RCAF20286
D-FAMT	Pilatus PC-9/B (Permit .04)	164	HB-HQK(2)
D-FANS	Pilatus PC-12/45	108	ZS-ONR N667JJ (ZS-BBO) N667JJ
D-FAPC	Pilatus PC-12/45	579	
D-FASS	North American AT-6D Harvard III	88-13483	SAAF7429 EX847
D-FAST(2)	Cessna 208 Caravan I	20800207	N208MC N208MT
D-FAXI	Pilatus PC-6/B2-H4 Turbo Porter	862	(F-GPGA) G-ITPS
D-FBAW	Antonov An-2T	1G160-01	(54+13) LSK-804
D-FBJU	Antonov An-2	1G63-29	DOSAAF-04
D-FBMT	Pilatus PC-9/B	165	HB-HQL(2)
D-FBOY	SOCATA TBM-700	171	F-WWRP
D-FBPS	Cessna 208B Grand Caravan	208B0494	LV-YJC N208BA N1219G
D-FCJA	Pilatus PC-12	177	HB-FSM
D-FCLG	Pilatus PC-6/B2-H2 Turbo-Porter	636	F-BOSZ
D-FCMT	Pilatus PC-9/B (Permit 11.04)	166	
D-FCOM	Cessna 208B Grand Caravan	208B0933	N5265N
D-FDFF	Pilatus PC-6/B2-H2 Turbo Porter	629	HB-FDF 5Y-AHR HB-FDF
D-FDHM	Pilatus PC-6/C1-H2 Turbo Porter	688	HB-FEG
D-FDLR	Cessna 208B Grand Caravan	208B0708	
D-FDME	Messerschmitt Bf.109G-10 (Permit .00)	151591	ZK-CIX D-FEHD(2) Luftwaffe
D-FDMT	Pilatus PC-9/B (Permit 6.04)	167	HB-HPI
D-FEAR	Pilatus PC-6/B2-H4 Turbo Porter	748	HB-FIE A4O-AL
D-FEJE	Pilatus PC-6/B2-H4 Turbo Porter	941	HB-FMK
D-FELI	Pilatus PC-6/B2-H4 Turbo Porter	845	JA8223 HB-FAB
D-FEMT	Pilatus PC-9/B	168	
D-FFBZ(2)	Pilatus PC-6/B2-H4 Turbo Porter	869	
D-FFMT	Pilatus PC-9/B (Permit 6.04)	169	
D-FGAK	Cessna 208B Grand Caravan (Reservation)	208B0893	N208GC N52609
D-FGEE	Grob G.500 Egrett	10002	
D-FGGG	Antonov An-2T	113901	(54+09) LSK-469 DM-WCX
D-FGMT	Pilatus PC-9/B	170	
D-FGRO	Grob G.500 Egrett Strato I	10005	
D-FGYY(2)	SOCATA TBM-700 (Permit 2.00)	162	
D-FHEW	Cessna 208B Grand Caravan	208B0401	N401MC N1214Z
D-FHGK	Noorduyn/North American AT-16 Harvard IIb	14-324	G-AXCR U-322 FE590 42-787
D-FHGL	North American SNJ-5 Texan (Regd with "c/n" 51-819, see USN serial)	88-14713	N2965S (D-FIII) C.6-162/793-15 N7804B BuA51819
D-FHMT	Pilatus PC-9/B (Permit 7.04)	171	HB-HQD
D-FICA	Pilatus PC-6/B2-H4 Turbo Porter	919	N919MA HB-FLM 7T-WLA HB-FLM
D-FIJL	Antonov An-2T	1G157-04	DDR-WJL DM-WJL
D-FINA	Cessna 208B Grand Caravan	208B0475	N1202D 9M-PMT N1220D N5094D
D-FIPS	Pilatus PC-6/B2-H4 Turbo Porter	874	HB-FKO V5-ODH HB-FKO
D-FIRE	SOCATA TBM-700A	137	
D-FISH	Cessna 208 Caravan amphibian (Permit 3.05)	20800363	N41145 N5124F
D-FIVE	SOCATA TBM-700	186	
D-FJAK	Yakovlev Yak-3M	0470107	N551BH
D-FJJF	Antonov An-2T	1G108-70	DDR-WJF DM-WJF
D-FJKA	Antonov An-2T	19318	DDR-WJP LSK-839
D-FJMO	Pilatus PC-6/B1-H2 Turbo Porter	561	F-GOMO N1421Z
D-FJMT	Pilatus PC-9/B	173	
D-FKAI	SOCATA TBM-700	288	
D-FKMA	Antonov An-2T	117411	(54+01) LSK-440

D-FKMB	Antonov An-2T	17308	(54+03)
	(Permit .04)		LSK-451
D-FKMC	Antonov An-2T	17612	(54+05)
			LSK-454
D-FKMD	Antonov An-2T	17812	(54+07)
	(Permit .04) (Painted as "D-FONE")		LSK-456
D-FKME	Antonov An-2T	17805	(54+08)
			LSK-457
D-FKMG	Antonov An-2T	12801	LSK-801
D-FKMI	Antonov An-2T	17207	(54+16)
			LSK-845
			DM-SKA
D-FKMT	Pilatus PC-9/B (Permit 7.04)	176	HB-HPE
			D-FLFA
			HB-HPE
D-FLAK	Yakovlev Yak-3U (Reservation .04)	0470202	
D-FLAX	Cessna 208B Grand Caravan (Ntu ?)	208B0604	N64BP
D-FLIP	Cessna 208B Grand Caravan	208B0331	N3331
			9M-PMO
			N1036C
D-FLIZ(2)	Cessna 208 Caravan 1	20800241	OO-NKA
			N241KA
			Peru EP857
			N241KA
			N1130K
D-FLOH	Cessna 208B Grand Caravan	208B0576	N1041F
D-FMBB(2)	Messerschmitt Me.109G-6	156	C4K- . . .
	(Constructed from a Hispano HA.1112-MIL airframe and parts from D-FMBB(1))		
D-FMDM	North American AT-6A Harvard	88-15778	F-BJBH
	(Reservation 11.8.03, F-BJBH still reported current)		H-16
			EZ214
			SAAF7578
			EZ214
			41-34087
D-FMOR	SOCATA TBM-700 (Reservation 1.99)	148	
D-FNRE	SOCATA TBM-700A	142	
D-FNVA	Antonov An-2T	19320	(D-FORK)
			(54+15)
			LSK-817
D-FOAA	PZL-106A Kruk (Reservation 11.98, believed	48039	DDR-TAA
	still at Finow Museum. Permit issued 11.99)		DM-TAA
D-FOAB	PZL-106A Kruk (2-seat conversion)	48040	DDR-TAB
			DM-TAB
D-FODS	PZL-106BRKruk (Reservation 8.99)	09870206	DDR-TDS
D-FODW	PZL-106BRKruk (Reservation 8.99)	09870198	DDR-TDW
			SP-WBF
D-FODZ	PZL-106BRKruk (Reservation 8.99)	09870208	DDR-TDZ
D-FOEB	PZL-106BRKruk (Reservation 8.99)	10880210	DDR-TEB
D-FOEG	PZL-106BRKruk (Reservation 8.99)	10880215	DDR-TEG
D-FOEH	PZL-106BRKruk (Reservation 8.99)	10880216	DDR-TEH
D-FOEL	PZL-106BRKruk (Reservation 8.99)	10880225	DDR-TEL
D-FOEM	PZL-106BRKruk (Reservation 8.99)	10880226	N117RA
			D-FOEM
			DDR-TEM
D-FOEN	PZL-106BRKruk (Reservation 8.99)	10880227	DDR-TEN
D-FOEQ	PZL-106BRKruk (Reservation 8.99)	10890235	DDR-TEQ
D-FOFM	Antonov An-2T	12802	(54+11)
			LSK-802
D-FOJB	Antonov An-2T	1G86-42	DDR-WJB
			DM-WJB
D-FOJN	Antonov An-2T	1G166-39	DDR-WJN
			DM-WJN
D-FOKK	Antonov An-2T	19504	DDR-SKK
			DM-SKK
D-FOKY	Antonov An-2T	1G86-49	DDR-SKY
			DM-SKY
D-FOLE(2)	Cessna 208B Grand Caravan	208B0523	
D-FOME	PZL M-18A Dromader	1Z021-11	EC-HKY
			D-FOME
			DDR-TME
D-FOMG	PZL M-18A Dromader (Accident 7.10.02)	1Z021-13	DDR-TMG
D-FOMH	PZL M-18A Dromader	1Z021-14	DDR-TMH
D-FOMI	PZL M-18A Dromader (Accident 7.10.02)	1Z021-15	DDR-TMI
D-FOMK	PZL M-18A Dromader	1Z021-17	EC-HKZ
			D-FOMK
			DDR-TME
D-FONC	Antonov An-2TD (Wfu, stored)	1G180-42	DDR-SKC(2)
			LSK-800
D-FOND	Antonov An-2P	19508	DDR-SKD(2)
			LSK-815
D-FONF	Antonov An-2P	117419	DDR-SKF(2)
			LSK-811
D-FONJ	Antonov An-2T	19317	DDR-SKJ(2)
			LSK-866
D-FONL	Antonov An-2T	17802	DDR-SKL(2)
			LSK-888
D-FOOT	EKW C-3605 (Permit .05)	274	HB-RDB
			C-494
D-FOTO(2)	Cessna 208 Caravan I	20800192	N9773F
D-FPET	Antonov An-2R (Reservation, damaged 7.97)	1G186-23	OK-JII
D-FREE	Pilatus PC-6/B1-H2 Turbo-Porter	731	HB-F . .
			C-GZCZ
			VH-ZCZ
			A14-705
			A14-731
			HB-FFS
D-FROG(3)	Cessna 208 Caravan I	20800112	SE-LER
			D-FILM
			N9649F
D-FROH	Pilatus PC-6/B2-H4 Turbo-Porter	654	HB-FDT
			F-BSTF
			HB-FDT
D-FSCB	Pilatus PC-6/B1-H2 Turbo-Porter	634	C-FPZB
			ZK-FZB
			VH-FZB
			LN-BIJ
			HB-FCU
D-FSJP	SOCATA TBM-700	130	N38KJ
			C-GSMO
			N700AP
			F-WWRM
D-FSKY	Pilatus PC-6/B2-H4 Turbo-Porter	878	
D-FSTN	Grob G.520 Egrett II	10003	D-FEGR
			N27ES
			D-FGEO
D-FTAN	SOCATA TBM-700	24	PH-AJS
			F-GLBD
D-FTBG	Grob G.160A (Permit 3.04)	87001	
D-FTBM	SOCATA TBM-700 (Reservation .03)	258	OH-KJJ
D-FUKK	CCF/North American Harvard IV	CCF4-46	N305GS
			RCAF20255
D-FUKM	Antonov An-2T	17710	(D-FKMF)
			(54+06)
			LSK-455
D-FUMP	Cessna 208B Grand Caravan	208B0743	
D-FURY	North American AT-6D-NT Texan	88-18109	N7420C
			42-86328
D-FVIP	DHC-2 Beaver Mk 1 Floatplane	1512	N6246X
			ZK-CCY
			VH-XIX
			ZK-CCY
D-FWAC	North American AT-6D-NT Texan	121-42032	Sp.AF:C6-125
	(Reservation .05)		Sp.AF:421-43
			BuA91036
			44-81310
D-FWCK	Flug Werke FW.190A-8/N	990002	
D-FWJA	Antonov An-2T	1G86-41	(D-FAJA)
			DDR-WJA
			DM-WJA
D-FWJC	Antonov An-2T	1G86-50	DDR-WJC
			DM-WJC
D-FWJD	Antonov An-2T	1G98-51	(D-FCJD)
			DDR-WJD
			DM-WJD
D-FWJE	Antonov An-2T	1G108-69	(D-FCJE)
			DDR-WJE
			DM-WJE
D-FWJG	Antonov An-2T	1G142-32	(D-FCJG)
			DDR-WJG
			DM-WJG
D-FWJK	Antonov An-2T	1G142-34	(D-FCJK)
			DDR-WJK
			DM-WJK
D-FWJM	Antonov An-2T	1G166-38	DDR-WJM
			DM-WJM
D-FWJO	Antonov An-2T	1G174-26	DDR-WJO
			DM-WJO
D-FWME	Hispano HA.1112-ML	139	N3109G
	(Converted to Bf 109G-4 standard .04)		G-AWHG
			C4K-75
D-FWUB	Bronner MJ80 (Reservation)	1876	
	(Focke-Wulf FW 190A-4 full-size replica)		
D-FWWC	Colling Focke-Wulf FW 190A-8 Replica	990001	
D-FYAK	LET/Yakovlev Yak-11	170103	G-DYAK
			G-BWFU
			OK- . . .
D-F . . .	Yakovlev Yak-3UM	0470109	N234BJ
D-F . . .	Yakovlev Yak-11	171314	F-AZSF
			EAF: . . .

CLASS G : Twin-Engined Aircraft of below 2 Metric Tonnes

D-GAAA	Diamond DA 42 Twin Star (Res 4.05)	42.013	OE-VPY
D-GAAB	Piper PA-34-200T Seneca II	34-7670050	N139RJ
			N4463X
D-GABE(2)	Piper PA-34-220T Seneca III	34-8133181	N2913A
D-GABO	LET Aero 145	19-020	OK-NHL?
D-GABS	Partenavia P.68C-TC	399-47-TC	
D-GABT	Piper PA-34-220T Seneca III	34-8333098	N8210L
			N9511N
D-GABY(2)	Piper PA-30 Twin Comanche B	30-1405	OE-FPG
			N8397Y
			N10F
D-GACR	Piper PA-34-220T Seneca III	34-8133215	N8429L
D-GACW	Piper PA-34-220T Seneca III	3433152	N91678
D-GADA	LET Aero 145	15-018	OK-NHC
D-GADE	Cessna 336 Skymaster	336-0058	N1758Z
D-GADN	Piper PA-34-200 Seneca	34-7250161	OK-CKK
			D-GADN
			N4545T

D-GADS	Piper PA-39 Twin Comanche C/R	39-67	PH-GAD G-AYFI N8922Y N9705N
D-GADY	Cessna 336 Skymaster (Wfu)	336-0158	N3858U
D-GAFC	Piper PA-44-180 Seminole	44-7995048	N21399
D-GAFI (2)	Piper PA-30 Twin Comanche B	30-1194	N10240 D-GAFI (2) TJ-ADY F-OCHU N8080Y
D-GAGE	Piper PA-30 Twin Comanche	30-804	N7715Y
D-GAHB(2)	Piper PA-34-220T Seneca III	34-8233005	N84556
D-GAHS	Piper PA-30 Turbo Twin Comanche C	30-1929	PH-ATV N8773Y
D-GAIR	Piper PA-34-200T Seneca II	34-8070003	N81008
D-GAKK	Piper PA-34-200T Seneca II	34-7770097	D-IKKD OE-FDZ D-IHNI N9008F
D-GALE	LET L-200A Morava	170712	DDR-WLB DM-WLB OE-FTU OK-PHA
D-GALF	Piper PA-30 Turbo Twin Comanche C	30-1966	HB-LFH N8809Y
D-GALX	Piper PA-30 Twin Comanche B	30-1957	N30DB C-FOVG CF-OVG N8494Y
D-GAMA	Piper PA-44-180T Turbo Seminole	44-8207017	N8246S
D-GAMB	Piper PA-34-200T Seneca II	34-8070110	C-FSHC N81404 N32DD N81404
D-GAME	Piper PA-34-200 Seneca	34-7350289	OE-FKA N56144
D-GAMU	Piper PA-44-180T Turbo Seminole	44-8107034	N8153H ZP-PTV
D-GAMW	Piper PA-34-200T Seneca II	34-7870468	OY-PEO N30699
D-GANA	Partenavia P.68B	117	
D-GANS(2)	Piper PA-44-180 Seminole	44-7995207	G-BOFV N2198K
D-GAPP	Piper PA-44-180 Seminole	4496001	N9256R
D-GARE(2)	Piper PA-34-200T Seneca II	34-7870205	SE-GVN
D-GASA(2)	LET Aero 145	19-014	G-AROE (D-GONE) G-AROE OK-NHF
D-GASM	Piper PA-34-200T Seneca II	34-7970163	D-IASM N3067U
D-GAST	Piper PA-30 Twin Comanche	30-379	N7362Y N10F
D-GATA	Partenavia P.68B	82	
D-GATB(2)	Piper PA-34-200T Seneca II (Reservation .05)	34-7870236	N678CW D-GOSK D-IEBH N5979N
D-GATE(2)	Piper PA-34-220T Seneca V	3449007	N9285D
D-GAVA(2)	Piper PA-34-200T Seneca II	34-7870112	N3426M
D-GAWO	Piper PA-34-220T Seneca III	3433038	N9121K
D-GAZE	Piper PA-30 Twin Comanche	30-681	N7646Y N10F
D-GBAV	Piper PA-44-180T Turbo Seminole	44-8107051	N83709
D-GBCW	Piper PA-34-220T Seneca III	34-8233044	N8472E
D-GBGK	Partenavia P.68C-TC	267-18-TC	N2958W
D-GBIG	Piper PA-34-200T Seneca II	34-8070018	N8110J
D-GBMW	Piper PA-34-200T Seneca II	34-7570011	OY-PET N32174
D-GBNI	Piper PA-30 Twin Comanche B	30-1462	EC-BNI N8394Y
D-GBPN	Piper PA-34-200T Seneca II	34-7770167	D-ILAC N1066Q
D-GBRD	Partenavia P.68B	14	OY-DZR
D-GBRS	Partenavia P.68B	34	HB-LHN
D-GBSK	Piper PA-44-180T Turbo Seminole	44-8107050	N8363D
D-GBSL	Beech E95 Travel Air	TD-715	OY-BSL D-GECA
D-GBWA	Piper PA-34-200T Seneca II	34-7670245	D-IAWA N75375
D-GCAD	Diamond DA 42 Twin Star (Reservation 4.05)	42.011	(G-CDGZ) OE-VPI
D-GCAT	Piper PA-34-220T Seneca V	3449167	N4169Z
D-GCCC	Piper PA-34-220T Seneca III	34-8233108	N8161C
D-GCCF	Piper PA-34-200T Seneca II	34-8070001	N45123
D-GCMH	Piper PA-44-180 Seminole	44-7995306	N2916N
D-GCPA(2)	Scheele/Colomban MC-15 Cri-Cri (Reservn 12.99)	473-001 CS.PA	
D-GCRI	Grünenthal/ Colomban MC-12 Cri-Cri (Written off 29.8.99)	1537	
D-GDCO	Piper PA-23-160 Apache	23-1800	SE-EDG D-GABA N4369P
D-GDDC	Piper PA-34-200T Seneca II	34-7770016	D-IMGU N5401F

D-GDEC	Piper PA-34-200T Seneca II	34-7870272	D-IDEC PH-KAM N31890
D-GDEF	Klein/ Rutan Defiant KII	161-AB	
D-GDMF	Piper PA-34-220T Seneca III	34-8133113	N122RM N8396L
D-GDTP	Piper PA-34-200T Seneca II	34-7970122	SE-IAZ
D-GDWL	Piper PA-34-220T Seneca III	3448025	N9121G
D-GDWR	Piper PA-34-200T Seneca II	34-7970448	OY-CBJ N2499U
D-GEAB	Piper PA-30 Twin Comanche B	30-1373	N8247Y
D-GEAS	Piper PA-34-200T Seneca II	34-8070186	LN-MTS SE-IDH
D-GEBA	Piper PA-34-200T Seneca II	34-7670179	N21AG D-GEBA D-IEBA N8761E
D-GEBD	Piper PA-44-180T Turbo Seminole	44-8207018	N92PA N9588N
D-GEDM	Piper PA-44-180 Seminole	44-7995232	N3042N
D-GEDU	Piper PA-34-220T Seneca III	34-8133176	N8417G D-GERN N8417G
D-GEHB	Piper PA-30 Twin Comanche B	30-1417	N8283Y
D-GEIS	Piper PA-34-200T Seneca II	34-7870302	D-INIS N36203
D-GEJJ	Piper PA-34-220T Seneca III	3433123	N9143Z
D-GEJL	Piper PA-34-200T Seneca II	34-7870265	N31744
D-GEKW	Piper PA-34-220T Seneca III	34-8133140	D-IILY N8403L
D-GELA	Partenavia P.68B	137	
D-GELB	PZL M-20-03 Mewa	1AH003-07	
D-GELD(2)	Piper PA-34-200T Seneca II	34-7670323	OE-FLH N3899F
D-GELI	Partenavia P.68B	108	
D-GELX	Piper PA-34-220T Seneca V	3449059	N41184
D-GELY	Piper PA-44-180 Seminole	44-7995036	N20957
D-GEMA(2)	Partenavia P.68B	175	(YV-1834P)
D-GEMB	Partenavia P.68B	188	
D-GEMC	Partenavia P.68B	200	
D-GEMF	Partenavia P.68C-TC	237-03-TC	
D-GEMI	Partenavia P.68C-TC	247-09-TC	
"D-GENI"(3)	Diamond DA-42 Twin Star (Unofficial regn)	unkn	
D-GEPA	Piper PA-34-220T Seneca III	3433041	N9120D
D-GERB	Partenavia P.68 Observer	173	
D-GERS	Piper PA-34-220T Seneca V	3449083	N61RC
D-GERT	Partenavia P.68B	47	
D-GERY	Partenavia P.68B (Permit 10.04)	49	
D-GEST	Grumman GA-7 Cougar	0102	
D-GETT	Piper PA-34-200T Seneca II	34-7770376	D-IETT N44924
D-GEVA	Piper PA-34-200 Seneca	34-7250165	N4894T
D-GEWU	Beech 76 Duchess	ME-398	
D-GFCM	Piper PA-44-180 Seminole	44-7995027	N39705
D-GFEY	Piper PA-34-200T Seneca II	34-7870343	D-IFEY N36599
D-GFGH	Piper PA-34-220T Seneca III	3447018	N9271L
D-GFKH	Piper PA-34-220T Seneca III	3448028	N9155H
D-GFPE	Piper PA-30 Turbo Twin Comanche C	30-1962	OE-FPE N8846Y N9694N
D-GFPG	Partenavia P.68B	170	
D-GFPI	Partenavia P.68B	158	N146BK (N2084J) D-GFPI
D-GFTL	Piper PA-39 Twin Comanche C/R	39-124	N228MF N9659N
D-GGAB	Piper PA-34-220T Seneca IV	3447020	N9275C
D-GGDH	Heuer/ Colomban MC-15 Cri-Cri	164	
D-GGFB	Bulmahn/ Colomban MC-15 Cri-Cri	365	
D-GGGA	Piper PA-34-220T Seneca III	34-8533034	N2477Y N9547N
D-GGGG	Piper PA-23-160 Apache	23-1579	D-GIBA N10F
D-GGOH	Piper PA-34-200T Seneca V	3449074	N41238
D-GGOW	Piper PA-34-200 Seneca	34-7350225	N55521
D-GGRO	Piper PA-34-200T Seneca II	34-7570322	N4354X N9600N
D-GGRT	Piper PA-34-220T Seneca III	34-8333003	N8230S
D-GGRZ	Piper PA-34-200T Seneca II	34-7770373	N7714M C-GRHW N7714M N9599N
D-GGTT	Piper PA-34-220T Seneca III	34-8333115	N43129 N9535N N43129 N9522N
D-GHAN	Vulcanair P.68C	416	
D-GHBN	Aero 45	51159	OK-HGD
D-GHBW	Piper PA-34-200T Seneca II (Reservation .04)	34-7970355	I-MEPI N2184K
D-GHCH	PZL M20-03 Mewa	1AH002-17	
D-GHEB	Piper PA-34-200T Seneca II	34-7870168	N9367C N9550N
D-GHFW(2)	Piper PA-30 Twin Comanche B	30-1326	N8228Y N10F
D-GHGM	Piper PA-34-200 Seneca	34-7250157	N4502T

D-GHHZ	Zeiler/ Colomban MC-15 Cri-Cri	Z-01	
D-GHIK	Piper PA-39 Twin Comanche C/R	39-130	D-GHSH G-AZNM N8967Y
D-GHPA	Piper PA-34-220T Seneca III	3433131	D-IHPA(2) D-GHPA N9150Z
D-GHSB	Piper PA-34-220T Seneca V	3449182	N41825
D-GHWB	Huber/ Colomban MC-15 Cri-Cri	H/EB-01/149	
D-GHWW	Piper PA-23-160 Apache (Reservn 6.99)	23-1816	N4315P
D-GICE	Piper PA-44-180 Seminole	44-96136	N5352H
D-GIES	Piper PA-34-220T Seneca III	34-8333020	F-GIES D-GABU(2) N83010
D-GIFK	Piper PA-34-220T Seneca III (Formerly c/n 34-8233170)	34-8333028	N8291D N9540N N823IA
D-GIGI (3)	Piper PA-34-220T Seneca III	34-8233117	HB-LNF
D-GIGY	Beech 76 Duchess	ME-80	
D-GIHZ	Beech 76 Duchess	ME-4	HB-GGT N18876
D-GILA	Partenavia P.68B	52	
D-GILD	Piper PA-34-200T Seneca II	34-7570164	N33805
D-GINA(2)	Partenavia P.68B	59	
D-GIOW	Piper PA-34-200T Seneca II	34-7570270	D-IKOW N1520X
D-GIPA(2)	Piper PA-34-220T Seneca IV	3449048	D-IOSK(2)
D-GIPC	Piper PA-34-220T Seneca IV	3448057	N92485
D-GIRL(2)	Piper PA-30 Twin Comanche	30-63	HB-LAG N7052Y
D-GISE	Piper PA-34-200T Seneca II	34-7870193	D-IHSE N9508C
D-GITA	Partenavia P.68B	92	
D-GITY(2)	Partenavia P.68C-TC	360-41-TC	HB-LRK D-GAHI N360TC
D-GIWL	Piper PA-34-200T Seneca II	34-7570307	D-IFWL N3903X
D-GIWO	Piper PA-34-200T Seneca II	34-7670076	OE-FRS N4579X
D-GJBA	Piper PA-34-200T Seneca II	34-8070116	N8149H
D-GJET	Piper PA-44-180T Turbo Seminole	44-8107003	N8196U
D-GJFN	Piper PA-34-220T Seneca III	34-8133061	SE-IYR OY-CGI N8371J
D-GJPA	Piper PA-44-180 Seminole	4496184	N3090K
D-GJTL	Piper PA-34-220T Seneca III	34-8233147	N8207J
D-GJVM	Piper PA-34-200T Seneca II	34-7970225	(D-GFOX) OE-FOX N28598
D-GKFE	Cessna 337A Super Skymaster	33700358	N958TM N6358F
D-GKHF	Piper PA-34-200T Seneca II	34-7970255	D-IKHF N29545
D-GKIM	Piper PA-34-200T Seneca II	34-7970228	N28710
D-GKKD(2)	Piper PA-44-180T Turbo Seminole	44-8207016	N94PA N81419 N9550N N82525
D-GKMI	Piper PA-34-200T Seneca II	34-8070290	I-ARMT N8252D N963PG
D-GKMP	Knittel/ Colomban MC-15 Cri-Cri	1569	
D-GLAD	Piper PA-34-200T Seneca II	34-7970427	LX-YES N2967X
D-GLBR	Piper PA-34-200T Seneca II	34-7570025	D-GAWF(2) D-IAWF N32485
D-GLIN(2)	Linkohr/ Colomban MC-15 Cri-Cri	312	
D-GLIV	Piper PA-34-200T Seneca II	34-7870203	PH-FEJ OO-FEJ PH-FEJ N9620C
D-GLLW	Piper PA-34-200T Seneca II	34-8070170	HB-LLW N8176T
D-GLOC	Piper PA-34-200T Seneca II	34-7870093	OE-FTM N2786M
D-GLUT	Piper PA-44-180T Turbo Seminole	44-8107019	N82556
D-GLUX	Diamond DA 42 Twin Star (Res 4.05)	42.015	
D-GLUZ	Luz/ Colomban MC-15 Cri-Cri (Permit 11.04)	1646-01	
D-GMAB	Piper PA-34-220T Seneca III	3433168	N9220J N9180W
D-GMAI	Piper PA-39 Twin Comanche C/R	39-50	N8892Y
D-GMBE	Piper PA-34-200T Seneca II	34-7870209	D-IMBE N9679C
D-GMBK	Piper PA-34-220T Seneca III	34-8233035	OE-FEK N8467Z
D-GMCW	Piper PA-34-200T Seneca II	34-7770163	N999LF
D-GMFB	Piper PA-34-220T Seneca III	34-8433036	EC-FNE LN-KLV N4348P
D-GMOF	Piper PA-34-200T Seneca II	34-7870301	D-IMOF N36184
D-GMOH	Piper PA-34-200T Seneca II	34-7870281	D-IMOH
D-GMUT	Piper PA-34-220T Seneca III	3433091	N9136P
D-GMST	Piper PA-34-220T Seneca III	34-8433055	(HA-. . .) D-ILHW(3) D-GISY N4365G
D-GMWA	Piper PA-30 Twin Comanche B	30-1178	N8064Y
D-GMWF	Piper PA-34-200 Seneca	34-7250105	N4471T
D-GMYU	Beech 76 Duchess	ME-330	OE-FEW D-GBTE
D-GMZE	Piper PA-34-200T Seneca II	34-7870452	OO-CFA N21901
D-GNAT	Piper PA-34-220T Seneca III	34-8133223	N8434P
D-GNIT	Partenavia P.68B (Reservation.05)	23	G-UNIT G-BCNT
D-GNNN	Piper PA-34-220T Seneca III	3447017	N9272L
D-GNOM	Piper PA-34-220T Seneca III	34-8233022	N8460K
D-GNSL	Meinhardt/ Colomban MC-15 Cri-Cri (Reservation 5.99)	256AB	(D-GERM)
D-GOBB	Piper PA-34-200 Seneca	34-7350253	N55871
D-GOFW	Piper PA-44-180 Seminole	44-7995123	N3011C
D-GOGO(2)	Partenavia P.68C-TC	343-31-TC	
D-GOJR	Piper PA-34-220T Seneca III	34-8233036	N84671
D-GOKI	Piper PA-44-180T Turbo Seminole	44-8107005	N8226A
D-GOLD(2)	Piper PA-34-220T Seneca V	3449054	N9293W
D-GOLF	Piper PA-23-160 Apache	23-1361	N3398P (D-GEKL) N3398P
D-GOMM	Piper PA-34-220T Seneca III	34-8433020	SE-KOT N4324K
D-GONG	Piper PA-34-200T Seneca II	34-7570047	D-IJSK N44007
D-GOOO	Piper PA-34-200T Seneca II	34-7970360	OE-FBP N19499 N9591N
D-GOPR	Piper PA-34-200T Seneca II	34-7970332	N274L HB-LLI
D-GOPS	Piper PA-34-200T Seneca II	34-7970028	D-GOBC N2169D
D-GORC	Piper PA-34-200T Seneca II	34-8170068	N8310H
D-GOSR	Piper PA-34-220T Seneca III	34-8133017	N8340S
D-GOVA	Piper PA-34-200T Seneca II	34-8070209	PH-SYC N81922
D-GPCS	Piper PA-34-200T Seneca II	34-8070261	N8231H
D-GPEZ	Piper PA-30 Twin Comanche C	30-1871	N8798Y N9703N
D-GPJB	Piper PA-34-220T Seneca III	34-8133173	N84131
D-GPTT	Piper PA-34-220T Seneca IV	3448043	N9245J
D-GRCP	Piper PA-34-220T Seneca III	34-8433001	N4323M N9501N N9542N
D-GRHZ	Hermle/ Colomban MC-15 Cri-Cri	469	
D-GRRR	Piper PA-44-180T Turbo Seminole	44-8107038	N8332A
D-GRUS	Piper PA-34-220T Seneca V	3449161	N4174P
D-GSKY	Piper PA-34-220T Seneca V	3449102	N41225
D-GSMH	Hagensieker/ Colomban MC-15 Cri-Cri	2175	
D-GTDI	Diamond DA 42D Twin Star (Reservn .04)	42.004	OE-VDB
D-GUFI	Piper PA-34-220T Seneca V	3449225	OY-LAZ N9528N
D-GULL	LET L.200D Morava	171407	OK-UHA
D-GUTE	Piper PA-34-200T Seneca II	34-7770382	N44989
D-GVPA	Piper PA-34-220T Seneca V	3449291	N5362T
D-GVST	Piper PA-34-200T Seneca II	34-7870263	N31725
D-GWFA	Kuhlmann/ Colomban MC-15 Cri-Cri	71	
D-GWIT	Piper PA-34-220T Seneca V	3449132	N41488 (D-GWIT) N9530N
D-GWPL	Piper PA-34-220T Seneca III	34-8433005	N4323Y N9509N
D-GWWW	Piper PA-34-220T Seneca V	3449021	N92882
D-GXPA	Piper PA-34-220T Seneca V	3449243	N53492
D-GXXX	Piper PA-34-220T Seneca V	3449110	G-VDAC N818JM N9513N
D-GYRO	Vulcanair P.68C-TC Observer	415-05-OTC	
D-GZXA	Piper PA-44-180 Seminole	4496136	N5352H
D-GZXB	Piper PA-44-180 Seminole	4496165	N53590
D-G . . .	Piper PA-30 Twin Comanche B	30-1657	N30DB C-FOVG CF-OVG N8494Y
D-G . . .	Piper PA34-220T Seneca III	34-7670179	N21AG D-GEBA D-IEBA N8761E

CLASS H : All Rotary-winged Aircraft without Weight Limit

D-HAAA(3)	Westland-Bell 47G-3B1 /Soloy	WA/386	G-BHKB XT227
D-HAAD(2)	Agusta A.109A	7122	VR-CCO ZK-HBC(2) N91969 XC-CAL

D-HAAE	Hiller UH-12E Soloy	2039	C-GMTF
			N9060F
			CF-OKC
			CF-MHI
D-HAAG	Agusta A.109A-II	7274	I-DACC
D-HAAH(2)	Aérospatiale SA.360C Dauphin	1005	N47287
D-HAAK(2)	Aérospatiale SA.365C3 Dauphin 2	5039	YR-DFD
D-HAAL	Aérospatiale SA.360C Dauphin	1030	
D-HAAM	Aérospatiale AS.350B Ecureuil	1910	
D-HAAN	Helibras HB.350B Esquilo	HB1038/1580	PT-HMB
D-HAAP	Agusta A.109C (To Ukraine 12.8.03)	7617	JA9989
D-HAAR(2)	Enstrom 280C Shark	1189	(D-HAAH)
			D-HGBX
			SE-HKX
D-HAAZ	Agusta A.109A	7230	SX-HCA
			D-HORN(2)
			N24PT
			N12FU
			I-VDMC
D-HABB	Bell 206L Long Ranger	45783	N102RD
D-HABM	Agusta A.109E Power	11080	
D-HABN	Hughes 269A (TH-55A)	105-0394	N62468
			64-18082
D-HABY(2)	Westland-Bell 47G-3B1/Soloy	WA/610	G-BHKD
			XT848
D-HACC(3)	Bell 407	53322	N322RT
D-HACK	Agusta-Bell 47J-2A	2071	5B-CAF
			CR-1
D-HADG	Westland-Bell 47G-3B1	WA/508	OE-CXA
			D-HHRW
			XT801
D-HADK	Robinson R-22B2 Beta	3138	
D-HAEK	Hughes 269C	114-0377	JA7574
D-HAEW	Enstrom F-28A-D	095	
D-HAFA(4)	Bell 206B Jet Ranger II	124	G-HELO
			G-BAZN
			9J-RIN
			ZS-HCJ
D-HAFB(2)	Westland-Bell 47G-3B1	WA/426	D-HAFW
			(D-HAFN)
			XT514
D-HAFC(2)	Agusta-Bell 206B Jet Ranger II	8323	OE-BXR(1)
D-HAFD(5)	Agusta-Bell 206B Jet Ranger II	8534	G-BMCH
			SE-HGR
D-HAFE(3)	Bell 206L3 Long Ranger III	51112	OE-BXF(2)
D-HAFF(3)	Westland-Bell 47G-3B1	WA/705	G-BEGA
			XW185
D-HAFG(4)	Agusta-Bell 212 (Res .05)	5632	
D-HAFH(2)	Bell 205A-1	30291	SE-HVT
			LN-OPS
			N5019N
D-HAFI (2)	Agusta-Bell 206B Jet Ranger II	8492	OE-BXT(1)
D-HAFJ	Westland-Bell 47G-3B1	WA/701	XW181
D-HAFK	Westland-Bell 47G-3B1	WA/331	XT172
D-HAFL(2)	Bell 205A-1	30056	LN-ORY
			SE-HLU
			AMDB-102
D-HAFO(2)	Bell 205A-1	30256	SE-HMS
			N16750
D-HAFR(2)	Bell 205A-1	30318	N8227H
			LN-OLM
			C-GFHN
D-HAFS(3)	Agusta-Bell 412 (Res .05)	25514	Uganda AF:
			406
D-HAFT	Aérospatiale AS.350B Ecureuil (W/o 7.3.01)	1457	
D-HAFU(3)	Aérospatiale AS.350B Ecureuil	1788	
D-HAFV(3)	Agusta-Bell 412	25509	Uganda AF:
			401
D-HAFW	Bell 205A-1	30290	EC-GPP
			EC-GCG
			EC-857
			LN-OPA
			OE-EXZ
			N2670N
			C-GUMJ
			OE-EXZ
D-HAFY(2)	Agusta-Bell 206B Jet Ranger III	8654	
D-HAFZ	Westland-Bell 47G-3B1	WA/702	XW182
D-HAGA	Sud Avn SA.318C Alouette Astazou	1933	
D-HAGI	Sud Avn SA.318C Alouette Astazou	1944	
D-HAGR	Hiller UH-12E (Soloy)	5184	N4033J
D-HAHN(4)	Aérospatiale AS.350B2 Ecureuil	9003	
D-HAIR(2)	Robinson R-22B2 Beta	3359	
D-HAIT	Eurocopter EC.135P1	0112	
D-HAJO(2)	Bell 212	30573	
D-HAKG	Hughes 269C	59-0798	
D-HAKN	Agusta-Bell 47G-2	268	74+26
			AS+380
			LA+110
			AS+068
D-HAKW	Küffner KH92/ Rotorway Exec 90	92001	
	(Permit expired, to Sinsheim Museum)		
D-HAKY(2)	Bell 206B Jet Ranger II	2687	OE-DXU
			D-HAKY(2)
			N2755C
D-HALB(2)	Schweizer 269C	S-1465	

D-HALD	Robinson R-44 Raven	1376	
D-HALF(3)	Robinson R-44 Raven	1353	
D-HALJ	Robinson R-44 Astro	0544	
D-HALK(2)	Eurocopter EC.120B Colibri	1278	
D-HALL(3)	Robinson R-44 Astro	0578	
D-HALM(3)	Robinson R-44 Raven	1354	
D-HALN(2)	Robinson R-44 Raven II	10588	
D-HALO(2)	Robinson R-44 Raven	1314	
D-HALP	Robinson R-44 Astro	0614	
D-HALQ	Robinson R-44 Raven II	10370	
D-HALS	Bell 212	30575	
D-HALT(3)	Bell 206L-3 Long Ranger III (Dbr 6.8.03)	51578	C-FNLC
D-HALU(3)	Robinson R-44 Raven	1310	
D-HALV(2)	Robinson R-44 Raven	1461	
D-HALW	Robinson R-22B2 Beta	3316	
D-HALY(2)	Robibson R-44 Raven	1460	
D-HALZ(2)	Robinson R-44 Raven	1424	
D-HAMA	Sud Avn SA.318C Alouette Astazou	1984	
D-HAMB	MBB Bö.105	S-205	HB-XFN
			D-HDFT(2)
D-HAMF	Agusta A.109A	7217	N77HG
			C-GDDA
			N9046U
D-HAMR	Robinson R-22 Beta	1168	N8051M
D-HAMS(3)	Agusta-Bell 47G-4A (Reservation 10.99)	2530	G-BYCI
			EC-BSC
D-HAMY(2)	MBB Bö.105	S-426	D-HDMY
D-HAND	Bell 212	30568	
D-HANK	Schweizer 269C	S-1811	
D-HANT	MBB Bö.105S	S-776	N8776
	(Reservation 12.04)		N829MB
			D-HDYL
D-HAOD	Schweizer 269C	S-1544	JA7872
D-HAPE(2)	Bader/Canadian Home Rotors Safari (Res .05)	2118	
D-HAPI (2)	Aérospatiale AS.350B Ecureuil	1184	F-WZF .
D-HAPP	Bell 47G-4A (W/o 4.6.01)	7736	C-GUKW
D-HAQE	Bell UH-1D (205)	8057	(70+27)
D-HARD(2)	Bell 206A Jet Ranger	486	N2288W
D-HARI (4)	Agusta A.109E Power	11014	G-POWR
			G-BXUD
D-HARK(2)	MBB Bö.105S	S-775	N8775
	(Reservation 12.04)		N828MB
			D-HDYK
D-HARO(2)	MBB Bö.105S	S-831	OE-XFS
			HB-XXK
			D-HFCO
D-HARS	Schönherr GMS-3	001	
D-HARZ	Bell 212	30598	
D-HASA(4)	Bell 206L-3 Long Ranger III	51278	G-SEAN
			N7061H
D-HASB	Bell 47G-2	1466	N2816B
D-HASC	Bell 47G-5	7843	N1393X
D-HASW	Westland-Bell 47G-3B-1	WA/521	XT814
D-HATI	Bell UH-1D (205)	8064	(70+34)
D-HATO	Bell UH-1D (205)	8065	(70+35)
D-HATS(2)	Westland-Bell 47G3B1 /Soloy	WA/709	HB-XMM
			XW189
D-HATU	Bell UH-1D (205) (To museum 7.00)	8066	(70+36)
D-HAUA(2)	Aérospatiale AS.350BA Ecureuil	2056	D-HAUN
D-HAUC(2)	Agusta-Bell 47G-3B-1	1585	XT121
D-HAUD(2)	Aérospatiale AS.355N Ecureuil 2	5538	F-WYMA
			F-WZKL
D-HAUE(2)	Bell 206B Jet Ranger II	4195	
D-HAUF(3)	Aérospatiale AS.350B2 Ecureuil	2361	D-HECS
			F-GGPY
D-HAUG	Sikorsky S-58C	58-836	R.Belg.AF
			B-15/OT-ZKP
			OO-SHP
			N869
D-HAUH	Westland-Bell 47G-3B1	WA/441	(D-HOBZ)
			XT552
D-HAUI	Westland-Bell 47G-3B1	WA/368	XT209
D-HAUK	Aérospatiale AS.350BA Ecureuil	1750	D-HFFG
D-HAUL	Aérospatiale SA.360C Dauphin	1009	F-GCMG
D-HAUM(2)	Aérospatiale AS.350B1 Ecureuil	1939	D-HAUX
	(Rebuild using parts of D-HAUM(1) c/n 1359		D-HAHG
	and identity of D-HAUX)		
D-HAUO(2)	Aérospatiale AS.350B3 Ecureuil	3342	F-WQDN
D-HAUQ	Aérospatiale AS.350B Ecureuil (Reservation)	1850	F-GFBC
D-HAUR	Aérospatiale AS.350B2 Ecureuil	2394	HB-XUY
D-HAUS(3)	Aérospatiale SA.360C Dauphin	1022	JA9277
D-HAUT(2)	Robinson R-44 Astro	0504	
D-HAUU	Aérospatiale AS.350B1 Ecureuil	2072	D-HAUZ
			HB-XUK
			I-ORTA
D-HAUV	Eurocopter EC.120B Colibri	1010	
D-HAUW	Aérospatiale AS.350B3 Ecureuil	3170	
D-HAVI	Agusta-Bell 206A Jet Ranger II	8234	
D-HAVM	Robinson R-22 Beta	1592	
D-HAWA(2)	Enstrom F-28A-D	255	
D-HAWB	Hemberger Skorpion	unkn	
D-HAWI(2)	MBB Bö.105S	S-853	D-HMB .
			N4302G
			D-HFHK
D-HAWK(2)	MBB-Kawasaki BK.117B-2	7225	D-HFDP
D-HAWY	MBB Bö.105	S-594	(D-HDQQ)
D-HAXA	Aérospatiale SA.330J Puma	1201	

D-HAXC	Aérospatiale SA.330J Puma	1241	
D-HAXD	Aérospatiale SA.330J Puma	1285	
D-HAXE	Aérospatiale SA.330J Puma	1289	
D-HAXG	Aérospatiale SA.330J Puma	1332	
D-HAXH	Aérospatiale SA.330J Puma	1410	
D-HAXI	Aérospatiale SA.330J Puma	1429	
D-HAXJ	Aérospatiale SA.330J Puma	1434	
D-HAXK	Aérospatiale SA.330J Puma	1442	
D-HAXL	Aérospatiale SA.330J Puma	1454	
D-HAXM	Aérospatiale SA.330J Puma	1496	F-WZCE
D-HAXN	Aérospatiale SA.330J Puma	1499	
D-HAXO	Aérospatiale SA.330J Puma	1537	
D-HAXP	Aérospatiale SA.330J Puma	1545	
D-HAXQ	Aérospatiale SA.330J Puma	1549	
D-HAXR	Aérospatiale SA.330J Puma	1553	
D-HAXS	Aérospatiale SA.330J Puma	1573	
D-HAXT	Aérospatiale SA.330J Puma	1577	
D-HAXU	Aérospatiale SA.330J Puma	1596	
D-HAXV	Aérospatiale SA.330J Puma	1592	
D-HAXW	Aérospatiale SA.330J Puma	1594	
D-HAYA	MBB Bö.105C	S-126	D-HDDS
D-HAYE	MBB Bö.105C	S-140	(D-HDEH)
D-HAYI	MBB Bo.105	S-368	(D-HDLD)
D-HAZY(2)	MBB Bö.105	S-832	D-HAIY(2)
			D-HFCP
D-HBAD(4)	Bell 206B Jet Ranger II	3819	N3203Z
D-HBAG	Sikorsky S-76C	760426	N101MY
			N101MM
D-HBAS	Aérospatiale AS.350B1 Ecureuil	2204	F-GHFL
	(Reserved as F-GMBZ & F-GUPF .99, ntu)		N607S
D-HBAT(2)	Schneider Sch-2	AB 1	
D-HBAY(3)	MBB-Kawasaki BK.117B-2	7205	LN-OSY
			D-HIMV
D-HBBA	Hughes 369HS	34-0574S	N5197Y
			G-NUNK
			G-BMSP
			C-GOEA
D-HBBB(2)	MBB-Kawasaki BK.117B-2	7220	LN-OSV
			D-HFDK
D-HBBH	Blunck Invader Gyrocopter	BB1-3509	
D-HBBY	Eurocopter EC.135P2	0262	D-HECJ
D-HBBZ(4)	Eurocopter EC.135P2	0269	
D-HBDD	Robinson R-22B2 Beta	3710	
D-HBEE	Schweizer 269C	S-1597	N41S
D-HBEL(2)	Bell 407	53236	(N6375S)
D-HBEN(2)	Bell 407	53153	
D-HBER(2)	Schweizer 269C	S-1522	N69A
D-HBFJ	Hughes 269C	100-0980	N1112P
D-HBGF	Elisport CH-7 Angel (Reservation 11.99)	136	
D-HBGR	Sikorsky S-76B	760320	
D-HBGS	MBB Bö.105C	S-11	(D-HBAY)
D-HBHF(2)	Robinson R-44 Raven	1184	OE-XHU
D-HBIN	Schweizer 269C	S-1639	N86G
D-HBIO	Eurocopter EC.120B Colibri	1201	
D-HBJA	Sud Avn SA.318C Alouette Astazou	2017	77+28
D-HBJE	Sud Avn SA.318C Alouette Astazou	2046	77+34
D-HBJF	Sud Avn SA.318C Alouette Astazou	2047	77+35
D-HBJG	Sud Avn SA.318C Alouette Astazou	2107	77+57
D-HBJH	Sud Avn SA.318C Alouette Astazou	2108	77+58
D-HBJJ	Sud Avn SA.318C Alouette Astazou	2116	77+62
D-HBJK	Sud Avn SA.318C Alouette Astazou	2248	77+78
D-HBJL	Sud Avn SA.318C Alouette Astazou	2086	77+48
D-HBJM	Sud Avn SA.318C Alouette Astazou	2091	77+49
D-HBJN	Sud Avn SA.318C Alouette Astazou	2100	77+53
D-HBJO	Sud Avn SA.318C Alouette Astazou	2101	77+54
D-HBJP	Sud Avn SA.318C Alouette Astazou	2105	77+55
D-HBJR	Sud Avn SA.318C Alouette Astazou	2130	77+71
D-HBJS	Sud Avn SA.318C Alouette Astazou	2131	77+72
D-HBJT	Sud Avn SA.318C Alouette Astazou	2132	77+73
D-HBJU	Sud Avn SA.318C Alouette Astazou	2134	77+74
D-HBJV	Sud Avn SA.318C Alouette Astazou	2016	77+27
D-HBJW	Sud Avn SA.318C Alouette Astazou	2092	77+50
D-HBJY	Sud Avn SA.318C Alouette Astazou	2061	77+39
D-HBJZ	Sud Avn SA.318C Alouette Astazou	2032	77+31
D-HBKA(2)	MBB-Kawasaki BK.117C-1 (W/o 27.7.00)	7530	
D-HBKK	MBB-Kawasaki BK.117B-2	7009	
D-HBLE	Westland-Bell 47G-3B1/Soloy	WA/450	HB-XLE
			XT561
D-HBLN	Eurocopter EC-135P-1	0192	
D-HBLU	Bell 407	53299	HB-XQY
			N8226X
D-HBMB(2)	Robinson R-44 Raven II	10394	
D-HBND	MBB-Kawasaki BK.117B-2	7056	OO-XCY
			D-HBND
			OO-VCY
			OO-XCY
			(OO-VCY)
			(N156BK)
			D-HBND
D-HBOC	MBB Bö.105C	S-325	(D-HDJC)
D-HBOO	Booms/ Rotorway Exec 90 (Reservation .04)	3031	
D-HBRB(2)	MBB-Kawasaki BK.117B-2	7250	D-HBWG
			(D-HFIO)
D-HBRE	MBB-Kawasaki BK.117B-2	7184	G-HMBB
			D-HIMA
			(N5405K)
D-HBRO(2)	Robinson R-22B2 Beta	unkn	

D-HBSI	MBB Bö.105C	S-9	(D-HMTU)
D-HBWA	Aérospatiale AS.365N4 / Eurocopter EC.155B Dauphin	6581	
D-HBWB(2)	Aérospatiale AS.365N4 / Eurocopter EC.155B Dauphin	6586	
D-HBWC	McDonnell-Douglas MD-900 Explorer	00093	N7003M
D-HBWD	McDonnell-Douglas MD-900 Explorer	00096	N7054D
D-HBWE	McDonnell-Douglas MD-900 Explorer	00097	N70078
D-HBWF(3)	McDonnell-Douglas MD-900 Explorer	00098	N70349
D-HBWG(2)	McDonnell-Douglas MD-900 Explorer	00099	N70389
D-HBWH	MBB Bö.105S (Permit 12.04)	S-929	D-HBOA(2)
D-HBWP	Bell 212	30645	N59586
D-HBXL	Robinson R-22 Beta	2185	N2342N
D-HBYA	Eurocopter EC.135P2	0057	
D-HBYB	Eurocopter EC.135P2	0059	D-HECR
			D-HBYB
D-HBYC	Eurocopter EC.135P2	0060	
D-HBYD	Eurocopter EC.135P2	0061	D-HEC.
			D-HBYD
D-HBYE	Eurocopter EC.135P2	0075	D-HECG
			D-HBYE
D-HBYF	Eurocopter EC.135P2	0078	
D-HBYG(2)	Eurocopter EC.135P1	0080	
D-HBYH(2)	Eurocopter EC.135P2	0100	
D-HBYI (2)	Eurocopter EC.135P2	0096	
D-HBZS	Bell 212	30879	
D-HBZT	Bell 212	30943	
D-HCAM	Aérospatiale AS.355F2 Ecureuil 2 (Reservn 3.00)	unkn	
D-HCAP	Hughes 269B	116-0290	D-HDUR
			LN-ORL
D-HCAT(2)	Robinson R-44 Astro	0180	
D-HCCS	Schweizer 269C	S-1741	
D-HCFE	Robinson R-44 Astro	0233	
D-HCHS(2)	Hughes 369E	0230E	OE-XXL
			N1602N
D-HCKV	Agusta A.109A-II	7345	N109HC
			N2GN
D-HCLA	Aérospatiale AS.350B3 Ecureuil	3400	
D-HCOL	Aérospatiale AS.350B2 Ecureuil	2814	F-WYMI
D-HCOR	Aérospatiale AS.350B Ecureuil	1601	
D-HCRS	Aérospatiale AS.350B2 Ecureuil	9034	F-GTRF
D-HCWB	Schweizer 269C	S-1772	N69A
D-HDAC(2)	MBB-Kawasaki BK.117B-2	7005	D-HBKG
D-HDAN(4)	Aérospatiale AS.350B3 Ecureuil	3124	
D-HDDP	MBB Bö.105C	S-123	
D-HDEC(2)	Eurocopter EC.135P2	0321	
D-HDFU(2)	MBB Bö.105	S-206	
D-HDHD(4)	Hughes 269C	98-0730	SpAF HE.20-08/
			"78-37"
D-HDHL	Hughes 269C	.8-0...	SpAF HE.20-/
			"78- "
D-HDIM(2)	Robinson R-22B2 Beta	3609	N73221
D-HDIX(3)	Agusta-Bell 206B Jet Ranger II	8364	D-HDCS(3)
			HB-XPA
			D-HHRT
D-HDKW	Agusta-Bell 47G-2	238	74+07
			AS+397
D-HDMA(3)	Eurocopter EC.135P2	0239	
D-HDML(2)	MBB Bö.105	S-438	
D-HDNM	MBB Bö.105LS	S-459	
D-HDNO(3)	MBB-Kawasaki BK.117C-1	7548	
D-HDOL	Eurocopter EC.135T2	0327	
D-HDPS(3)	MBB-Kawasaki BK.117B-2	7074	EC-EVT
			D-HBNV
D-HDRB(3)	Eurocopter EC.135P2	0233	
D-HDRC(3)	Eurocopter EC.135P2	0234	
D-HDRD(3)	Eurocopter EC.135P2	0369	
D-HDRE(3)	Eurocopter EC.135P2	0373	
D-HDRF(4)	MBB-Kawasaki BK.117B-2	7094	D-HMB .
			PT-HKF
			N114AE
			N214AE
			N522MB
			D-HBPO
D-HDRH(3)	MBB-Kawasaki BK.117B-2	7199	I-BKBO
			D-HIMP(1)
			N54114
			D-HIMP(1)
D-HDRR(2)	MBB-Kawasaki BK.117C-2	9038	
D-HDSR(2)	MBB-Kawasaki BK.117C-1	7545	
D-HDWM	Hughes 369HS (Stored, 6.00)	73-0498S	F-GBGR
			D-HDWM
D-HEAA	MBB Bö.105	S-904	
D-HEAS(3)	Bell 206B Jet Ranger II	4163	LN-OBE
			C-FKDT
D-HEAT	Aérospatiale AS.350BA Ecureuil	2881	OE-XLB
			F-WQDV
D-HEBA(2)	Bell 47G-3B1 Soloy	3575	N51SP
			66-8075
D-HEBE	Brantly B-2	40	N4998C
D-HEBI (2)	Bell 206B Jet Ranger II	3662	G-BSBJ
			N3171P
			N678LD
D-HEBM	Bell 206B Jet Ranger II	3533	I-MIBA
			N2300H
D-HEBS	Bell 47J-2 Ranger	2855	N73291

D-HECA to HECZ Test registrations for Eurocopter Deutschland for EC.135 production

D-HECI (2)	Westland-Bell 47G-3B-1	WA/591	XT829
D-HECY(3)	Eurocopter EC-135D-1	S-02	
D-HECZ	Eurocopter EC-135B-1	S-03	
D-HEDB	Bell 206B3 Jet Ranger III	4197	N206KV
			N908CA
			C-GLZA
D-HEDI (2)	Sud Avn SA.318C Alouette Astazou	2026	
D-HEDY	Eurocopter EC-135T-1	0087	CC- CFG
D-HEEC	Aérospatiale AS.350B Ecureuil (Cld, under rebuild)	1934	
D-HEEE(2)	MBB Bö.105S	S-713	LX-HAR
			D-HEEE(2)
			(N713XY)
			D-HDRA
D-HEER(2)	Enstrom 280F	1501	N966D
			N9660
			N8617Z
D-HEFE(2)	Bell 206B Jet Ranger II	2631	(D-HXXH)
			(N4380A)
			I-GRAO
			N5016V
D-HEGA(2)	Aérospatiale AS.332L1 Super Puma	2234	
D-HEGB	Aérospatiale AS.332L1 Super Puma	2265	F-WYML
D-HEGC	Aérospatiale AS.332L1 Super Puma	2268	
D-HEGO	Aérospatiale AS.332L1 Super Puma (Reservation 4.04)	2050	G-TIGL
D-HEHA	Eurocopter EC.120B Colibri	1292	
D-HEHB	Bell 206L Long Ranger	45011	
D-HEHC	Aérospatiale AS.350B2 Ecureuil	3129	F-GPRP
D-HEHD	Schweizer 269C	S-1464	PH-WRA
			OO-TZZ
			(OO-GBZ)
			G-BSLR
			N69A
D-HEHR	Ehringhaus Revolution Mini-500 (Permit)	100	
D-HEIA(2)	Bell 47G3B1 /Soloy	3433	N54SP
			64-17867
D-HEJA	Robinson R-44 Raven II	10446	
D-HEKW	Bell 206B Jet Ranger II	2101	
D-HELB	Bell 222B	47154	JA9691
			N32064
D-HELC	Popp HP-1 Gyrocopter	01	
D-HELD(3)	Enstrom 480 Turbine	5008	OO-VLW
			G-BWHE
D-HELF(2)	Bell 206L Long Ranger	45029	N9954K
D-HELG	Eurocopter EC.120B Colibri (Permit .04)	1170	D-HOLB
			F-WQDP
D-HELI (2)	Aérospatiale AS.350BA Ecureuil	1241	F-WZFL
D-HELK(2)	Hughes 269C	40-0912	N1094A
D-HELL(3)	Robinson R-44 Raven II	10358	
D-HELM(2)	MBB Bö.105	S-851	(D-HFHS)
D-HELO(2)	Agusta-Bell 47G-2	228	D-HAUS(1)
			74+04
			AS+395
D-HELP(4)	Aérospatiale AS.350B Ecureuil	1009	F-GLYR
			G-BWNA
			G-BFNC
			F-WXFN
D-HELT	Agusta-Bell 47J	1058	G-APTH
			5N-ACP
			G-APTH
D-HEMB	Hemberger TH-II	TH-II-01	
D-HEMD(4)	Schweizer 269C-1	0060	
D-HEMM	Robinson R-22 Beta	2248	
D-HEMS(2)	MBB-Kawasaki BK.117B-2	7203	D-HIMT
D-HENA	Aérospatiale AS.350B Ecureuil	1781	OE-KXC
			D-HENA
D-HENG	Hughes 369D	27-0088D	CS-H . .
			D-HLUD
			LY-H . .
			D-HLUD
			CS-HCS
			D-HLUD
			C-GYTZ
D-HENN	Aérospatiale AS.350B2 Ecureuil	2371	D-HFSB
			(CS-HFS)
			D-HFSB
D-HEOP	Robinson R-44 Astro	0008	N2361V
D-HEOY	Eurocopter EC.135T1	0035	I-HEMS
			D-HEC .
D-HEPE	MBB-Kawasaki BK.117B-2	7247	D-HBWF(2)
			(D-HFIL)
D-HEPP	Bell 212	30650	
D-HEPT	Aérospatiale AS.350BA Ecureuil	1237	F-WYMG
			N36062
D-HERA	Bell 47G-4A	3368	ZS-HDH
			5R-MDM
			N1194W
D-HERI (2)	Aérospatiale AS.350B2 Ecureuil	2827	N60972
D-HERO	Agusta-Bell 47G-4A	2543	
D-HERR(2)	Bell 47G-4A	6685	F-GEDY
			C-FXFX
			CF-XFX
D-HERZ	Bell 47G-2	1992	74+36
			AS+395
			YA+031
			PA+120

D-HESA	Agusta-Bell 206B Jet Ranger II	8373	
D-HESK	Robinson R-22B2 Beta	2844	
D-HEST	Schweizer 269C-1	0031	
D-HEUR(2)	Eurocopter EC.135T1	0042	
D-HEVA	Enstrom F-28F	784	D-HVHM
			JA7858
D-HEWR	Aérospatiale AS.350B Ecureuil	1789	(F-GJPS)
			D-HEWR
D-HEXE(5)	MBB Bö.105C	S-125	D-HBOA(1)
			D-HDDU
			(D-HDDR)
D-HFAB	Schweizer 269C	S-1516	N6042K
D-HFAI (2)	Aérospatiale AS.355F1 Ecureuil 2	5009	N5774M
			HC-BFC
			N5774M
D-HFAX(2)	Aérospatiale AS.350B2 Ecureuil	2585	HB-XZJ
			F-WYMG
D-HFAY	Bell 206B Jet Ranger II	2776	N250TV
			N2766L
D-HFCA(3)	Robinson R-44 Astro	0260	SE-JFF
D-HFCB(2)	Robinson R-44 Astro	0135	
D-HFCC(2)	Robinson R-44 Raven II	10022	
D-HFCD(2)	Robinson R-22B2 Beta	3634	
D-HFCE(2)	Aérospatiale AS.350BA Ecureuil	1669	F-GEJB
			(JA9342)
D-HFCF(2)	Robinson R-44 Astro	0021	OK-YIK
D-HFEH	Westland-Bell 47G-4A (Reservn .03)	WA/719	(D-HWAL(1))
			G-AXKN
			EC-EDF
			G-AXKN
			G-17-4
D-HFEM	Aérospatiale AS.350BEcureuil	1322	TF-SYR
			TR-GRO
			D-HKHL
D-HFER	Robinson R-22 Beta	2250	N2349X
D-HFFF(2)	MBB Bö.105	S-811	D-HDZU
D-HFGD	Aérospatiale AS.350B Ecureuil	1846	
D-HFGH	Robinson R-22 Beta	2448	N83117
D-HFHF(2)	Robinson R-22B2 Beta	3027	
D-HFHL	MBB Bö.105	S-854	
D-HFHS(2)	Eurocopter EC.135T1 (Permit 11.02)	0028	D-HECA
D-HFIN	MBB-Kawasaki BK.117B	7249	
D-HFIX	Aérospatiale AS.350B2 Ecureuil	9010	
D-HFJS	Aérospatiale AS.350B Ecureuil	2014	CS-HBF
D-HFLI	Hughes 269C	110-0988	N1108W
D-HFLO(3)	Robinson R-22B2 Beta	2661	D-HFRH
D-HFLY(2)	Robinson R-22B2 Beta	3417	N75071
D-HFMW(2)	Agusta A.109A-II	7307	G-JLCY
			N109AB
D-HFNH	Robinson R-22B2 Beta	2800	
D-HFNU	MBB Bö.105	S-889	
D-HFOX	Hughes 369D	38-0289D	OK- . . .
			D-HFOX
			ZK-HLP
D-HFRD(2)	Enstrom F-28F	707	N86201
D-HFSF(2)	Aérospatiale AS.350B Ecureuil	1690	D-HALL(2)
D-HFSJ	Sud Avn SA.316B Alouette III	2244	OE-OXW
			N224E
			TG-TEJ
D-HFSO	Robinson R-22B2 Beta	2882	OE-XPK
			N7118Z
D-HFUN	Hughes 269C (HKP 5B)	81-1075	D-HROM
			Swed.Army :
			05229
			SE-HMF
D-HFUX	Robinson R-22 Beta	1058	N8045X
D-HFWO(2)	Agusta-Bell 47G-2 (Reservation)	"636"	
D-HGAB(2)	MBB Bö.105	S-848	D-HFHF
D-HGAS	Robinson R-44 Astro	0864	
D-HGBW	Huschle/ Canadian Home Rotors Safari (Res .02)	001	
D-HGGE	Hughes 269C	126-0567	D-HAES
			JA7607
D-HGGG	Westland-Bell 47G-3B-1	WA/364	XT205
D-HGIG	Hiller UH-12B	733	N8505
			0-5
			54-2939
D-HGMS	Bell 206B Jet Ranger II	4373	
D-HGPP	Bell 212	30807	
D-HGSA	MBB Bö.105C	S-12	(D-HMDI)
D-HGSB	MBB Bö.105C	S-13	
D-HGSC	MBB Bö.105C	S-14	
D-HGSD	MBB Bö.105C	S-15	
D-HGSE	MBB Bö.105	S-908	
D-HGSF	MBB Bö.105	S-913	
D-HGSG	MBB Bö.105	S-914	
D-HGSH	MBB Bö.105	S-915	
D-HGSI	MBB Bö.105	S-916	
D-HGSJ	MBB Bö.105	S-917	
D-HGSK	MBB Bö.105	S-918	
D-HGSL	MBB Bö.105	S-919	
D-HGSM	MBB Bö.105	S-920	
D-HGSN	MBB Bö.105	S-921	
D-HGSO	MBB Bö.105	S-922	
D-HGSP	MBB Bö.105	S-923	
D-HGSQ	MBB Bö.105	S-924	
D-HGSR	MBB Bö.105	S-925	
D-HGSS	MBB Bö.105	S-926	

D-HGST	MBB Bö.105	S-927	
D-HGSU	MBB Bö.105	S-928	
D-HGSV	MBB Bö.105CBS-4	S-761	SE-JDJ XA-NAN N728MB D-HDXW
D-HGUN	Schweizer 269C	S-1563	F-GLRT N41S
D-HGYN(2)	Eurocopter EC.135P2	0303	
D-HGYR	Schuffenhauer Gyrocopter	SG-3	
D-HHAS	Schweizer 269C	S-1800	OE-XLL(2) D-HSPL N41S
D-HHBB(4)	Bell 407 (Permit 1.99)	53311	N82317
D-HHBG	MBB Bö.105	S-625	D-HDSU VH-PHO VH-NSL D-HDSU 9V-BNP (N4572M) D-HDSU
D-HHBI (2)	Bell 206B Jet Ranger II	4210	
D-HHBP	Aérospatiale AS.350B1 Ecureuil	1973	
D-HHBW	MBB Bö.105	S-346	N6170K XC-CAR N46981 D-HDJX
D-HHCC(2)	Bell 412	36066	N6227S
D-HHCW(3)	Bell 407	53058	
D-HHDM	Bell 412EP	36355	N7008Q
D-HHEA	MBB-Kawasaki BK.117C-2	9004	D-HDMG(3) D-HMBJ
D-HHED	Robinson R-44 Astro	0803	N214BC
D-HHEM	Robinson R-22B2 Beta	3602	N7529H
D-HHEX	Schweizer 269C	S-1596	OO-FEE D-HHEX N41S
D-HHFB	Hughes 269C	90-0971	OE-CXD D-HLUX N1104U
D-HHFW	Bell 206B Jet Ranger II	4257	
D-HHGB	Aérospatiale AS.350B Ecureuil	1708	
D-HHGH	Schweizer 269C-1	0022	PH-GUN OO-GUN N41S
D-HHHH	Westland-Bell 47G-3B-1	WA/417	XT505
D-HHHL(2)	Robinson R-22B2 Beta	3215	
D-HHHS(2)	Bell 206L-3 Long Ranger III	51454	SE-HVG OY-HVG SE-HVG C-FJYL
D-HHIT(2)	Eurocopter EC.135P2	0380	
D-HHJR	Rotorway Exec 90	3519	
D-HHKW	Bell 206B Jet Ranger II	3651	(N206AJ) N202WW N2289T
D-HHLA	Robinson R-44 Astro	0079	
D-HHMB	Robinson R-44 Raven	1432	
D-HHMM(2)	Bell 206L-3 Long Ranger III	51247	C-FBYX
D-HHMP(2)	Bell 206B Jet Ranger II	3823	
D-HHMV	Aérospatiale AS.350BA Ecureuil	9029	
D-HHOL	Schweizer 269C	S-1452	
D-HHOT	Schweizer 269C	S-1450	
D-HHPO	Schweizer 269C	S-1594	N86G
D-HHPP	Bell 212	30801	
D-HHRB	Becher/ Elisport CH-7 Angel	CH 008	
D-HHRF	Robinson R-22 Beta	2355	N8008Q
D-HHRR(2)	Robinson R-22 Beta	1081	HB-XUG (D-HRUS) HB-XUG
D-HHRW(2)	Bell 206L Long Ranger	45082	N17EA N16762
D-HHSB(3)	Enstrom F-28C Turbo	431	OE-XAM G-SHDD G-BNBS SE-HIL
D-HHSM(3)	Bell 222B	47139	N91GC N878TX
D-HHSN	Eurocopter EC.120B Colibri	1229	
D-HHSP	Enstrom F-28A-D	087	
D-HHST(3)	Bell 206B Jet Ranger II	3567	N3181P N22976
D-HHTA(2)	Aérospatiale AS.350B2 Ecureuil	9054	
D-HHTF	HTM FJ-Sky-Trac	14	
D-HHTP	Agusta-Bell 206B Jet Ranger II	8549	SE-HGK
D-HHTS	Eurocopter EC.135P2	0381	
D-HHTW	McDonnell-Douglas MD-900 Explorer	00032	HL9225 N9132N
D-HHUB	Aérospatiale AS.350B2 Ecureuil	2406	HB-XVD
D-HHUD	Bell 206B Jet Ranger II	2327	N65CW N700WD
D-HHUU	Bell 412	36057	N6162A
D-HHVV(2)	Bell 412	36059	N6173A
D-HHWE	Ewig/ Elisport CH-7 Angel	035/3514	
D-HHWF	Bell 206B Jet Ranger II	2530	N5008Z
D-HHWS	Hughes 269C	80-0028	
D-HHWW	Aérospatiale AS.350B2 Ecureuil	2437	

D-HIAR	Robinson R-44 Astro	0432	
D-HIBC	McDonnell-Douglas MD-900 Explorer	00052	N9224U
D-HIBY(3)	MBB Bö.105D	S-75	HB-XLV G-BCRG D-HDBZ
D-HICA(3)	Bell 47G-4A	7637	N14SP
D-HICE(2)	Westland-Bell 47G-3B-1	WA/327	XT168
D-HIEV	Bell 206B Jet Ranger II	2967	N2JC N5734M
D-HIFR(2)	MBB-Kawasaki BK.117B-2	7001	D-HMBF(4) D-HBKC
D-HIGH(2)	Robinson R-22 Beta	2171	N23399
D-HIIH	Robinson R-22 Mariner	0661M	VH-HII N661FR
D-HIII (2)	MBB Bö.105	S-874	N3203L D-HMBN(3) (D-HFNF)
D-HIIX	Aérospatiale AS.350B2 Ecureuil	9005	
D-HIKE	Hughes 369E	0148E	VH-JBE N5229J
D-HIKO(2)	Hughes 269C	26-0469	JA7585
D-HIKS(2)	Robinson R-22 Beta	2219	
D-HILE	Robinson R-22 Beta	1355	
D-HILF(5)	MBB-Kawasaki BK.117B-2	7096	D-HMB. PT-HJM N118MB D-HBPQ
D-HILL(2)	Robinson R-44 Astro	0018	N2363A
D-HILV(2)	Hughes 369E	0323E	HB-XVF N16030
D-HIMB	MBB-Kawasaki BK.117B-2	7185	JY-ACC D-HIMB (N5406V) D-HIMB
D-HIMP(2)	Robinson R-44 Astro	0335	
D-HIMU	MBB-Kawasaki BK.117B-2	7204	
D-HINA(2)	Schweizer 269C	S-1383	N41S
D-HIND(2)	Elisport CH-7 Angel (W/o 24.10.02)	A063	
			N8604F
D-HIOU	Bell 47G-4	3347	N1217W CF-SCF
D-HIPO(2)	Bell 47G-4A	7661	G-OIBC G-FORE N1415W
D-HIPP(2)	Bell 212	30661	
D-HIPT	Eurocopter EC.135P1	0109	
D-HIPY(2)	Bell 206B Jet Ranger II	4186	
D-HIRK	Aérospatiale AS.355F2 Ecureuil 2	5155	D-HEUH F-WQDB G-BPRK N361E
D-HIRL	Agusta A.109E Power (Permit 12.04)	11158	N32GH D-HOME(3)
D-HIRO	Robinson R-22 Beta	2336	
D-HIRR(2)	Robinson R-44 Astro	0459	
D-HISA	Schweizer 269C	S-1425	F-GKJM
D-HISF	Bell 407	53039	C-FZIY N97PM N1164Z
D-HISW	Hughes 269C	31-0105	
D-HITA(2)	Hughes 369E	0281E	I-HENO HB-XTH
D-HITE	Eurocopter EC.120B Colibri	1276	F-WQDB
D-HITH	McDonnell-Douglas MD-900 Explorer	00029	N9125N
D-HIZZ	Robinson R-44 Astro	0109	
D-HJAN	Henseleit/ Elisport CH-7 Angel	"3521", " 007"	
D-HJAR	Eurocopter EC.135T1	0044	
D-HJER	McDonnell-Douglas MD-600N (W/o 4.6.04)	RN-054	D-HIER N654S N3218G
D-HJET(2)	Bell 206B Jet Ranger II	3777	HB-XSB N3181G
D-HJHE	Robinson R-22 Beta	1772	D-HFLO(2)
D-HJJJ	MBB Bö.105S	S-741	(D-HDXC)
D-HJMB	Eurocopter EC.120B Colibri	1301	
D-HJOE(2)	Aérospatiale AS.350BA Ecureuil	9013	
D-HJOH	Schweizer 269C	S-1500	F-GFEK(2)
D-HJPH	Robinson R-44 Astro	0196	
D-HJPW	Schweizer 269C	S-1394	HB-XUQ
D-HJSP	Bell 407	53500	
D-HJUS	Hughes 369HS	109-0207S	N4259K JA9040
D-HJUX(3)	Hughes 269C	61-1055	HA-MSV PH-HHD OY-HSF D-HDEA(3) N5017V
D-HKAI (2)	Hughes 269C	39-0781	F-GRCR D-HESP PH-WPL
D-HKBD	Eurocopter EC.135T2 (Reservation 7.02)	0243	
D-HKEL	Schweizer 269C	S-1679	N86G
D-HKEM(2)	Bell 47G-4A /Soloy	7635	N605
D-HKIT	Hughes 269C	77-0615	OY-HDR D-HKIT SE-HHK
D-HKKK	Westland-Bell 47G-3B-1	WA/708	XW188

D-HKLE	Eurocopter EC.120B Colibri	1107	F-GSLH
			HB-ZCK
			F-WQDR
D-HKMC	Aérospatiale AS.350B3 Ecureuil	3222	
D-HKMG	Aérospatiale AS.350BA Ecureuil	2650	
D-HKMM	Eurocopter EC.120B Colibri	1217	
D-HKMW	Robinson R-44 Astro	0121	
D-HKUG	Eurocopter EC.135P1	0090	
D-HLDM	Eurocopter EC.135P2 (Permit 4.05)	0392	
D-HLEU	Eurocopter EC-135TI	0007	
D-HLFM	Schweizer 269C	S-1748	
D-HLHL	Robinson R-22 Beta (W/o 11.12.01)	2301	N80074
D-HLIX	Aérospatiale AS.350BA Ecureuil	1525	F-GBMR
D-HLKB	Bell 206B Jet Ranger II	4209	
D-HLLL(2)	MBB Bö.105	S-875	N4345F
			D-HMBM(2)
			(D-HSNG)
D-HLPY	Bell 206L-4 Long Ranger IV	52185	
D-HLRG(2)	MBB-Kawasaki BK.117C-2	9029	
D-HLRZ	Aérospatiale AS.365N4 / Eurocopter EC.155B Dauphin	6545	
D-HLSZ	MBB Bö.105S	S-683	N911HM
			N4573L
			D-HDUY
D-HLTA	Aérospatiale AS.365N4 / Eurocopter EC.155B Dauphin	6546	
D-HLTB	MBB-Kawasaki BK.117B-2	7224	(N8196H)
			D-HFDO
D-HLTC	Aérospatiale AS.365N4 / Eurocopter EC.155B Dauphin	6547	
D-HLTD(2)	Aérospatiale AS.365N4 / Eurocopter EC.155B Dauphin	6558	
D-HLTE	Aérospatiale AS.365N4 / Eurocopter EC.155B Dauphin	6557	
D-HLTF	Aérospatiale AS.365N4 / Eurocopter EC.155B Dauphin	6559	
D-HLTG	Aérospatiale AS.365N4 / Eurocopter EC.155B Dauphin	6569	
D-HLTH(2)	Aérospatiale AS.365N4 / Eurocopter EC.155B Dauphin	6562	
D-HLTI (2)	Aérospatiale AS.365N4 / Eurocopter EC.155B Dauphin	6576	
D-HLTJ(2)	Aérospatiale AS.365N4 / Eurocopter EC.155B Dauphin	6577	
D-HLTK(2)	Aérospatiale AS.365N4 / Eurocopter EC.155B Dauphin	6595	F-WQDT
D-HLTL	Aérospatiale AS.365N4 / Eurocopter EC.155B Dauphin	6599	
D-HLTM	Aérospatiale AS.365N4 / Eurocopter EC.155B Dauphin	6601	
D-HLTN	Eurocopter EC-155B1 Dauphin (Permit 4.04)	6659	
D-HLUC	Hughes 269C	129-0859	OE-CXR
			D-HAKO(3)
D-HLUX(3)	Hughes 369D	29-0450D	CS-H . .
			D-HDOR
			LY-HAS
			D-HDOR
			CS-H . .
			D-HDOR
			C-GRYV
D-HMAS	Bell 206B Jet Ranger II	4351	
D-HMAX(3)	Kaman K-1200 K-Max	A94-0021	OE-XKM
			N21MX

D-HMBA to HMBZ Test registrations for Eurocopter Deutschland for BK-117 production

D-HMCB	Bell 206B Jet Ranger II	4120	
D-HMDX(2)	McDonnell-Douglas MD-900 Explorer	00036	N9198Y
D-HMEC(2)	MBB-Kawasaki BK.117C-1	7538	D-HMB .
D-HMEI	Bell 206B Jet Ranger II	2550	
D-HMIC	Hughes 369E	0362E	OE-XKK
			D-HMIC
D-HMIK	Hughes 369D	127-0251D	CS-HCX
			D-HMIK
			C-GSZV
D-HMIM	Schweizer 269C	S-1637	N86G
D-HMIN	Schweizer 269C (HKP 5B) (W/o 10.6.02)	S-1191	Swed.Army:
			05236
D-HMIT	Agusta-Bell 206A Jet Ranger II	8256	F-GBRE
			3A-MCC
			F-BSEG
D-HMIX(2)	Hughes 269C	98-0729	SpAF HE.20-07/
			"78-36"
D-HMKI	Eurocopter EC.120B Colibri	1190	
D-HMMD	Bell 206B Jet Ranger II	4158	N254SH
D-HMMM(2)	MBB-Kawasaki BK.117B-2	7228	SE-JBC
			D-HMBN(7)
			(D-HFDS)
D-HMMW	Aérospatiale AS.350B2 Ecureuil	2727	F-WYMT
D-HMOE	Hughes 369D	91-1077D	OM-MDD
			D-HMAU
			N9114Y
			C-GZXX
			N5284C
D-HMON(2)	Bell 407	53001	N407BT
			C-FWQY
D-HMOT(2)	Bell 206B Jet Ranger II	3947	
D-HMRG	Hughes 369HS	70-0241S	
D-HMSB	Eurocopter EC.120B Colibri	1359	
D-HMUF	MBB-Kawasaki BK.117A-4	7105	D-HBPZ
D-HMUG	MBB Bö.105C	S-121	D-HDDM
			(D-HDDN)
D-HMUM(2)	MBB-Kawasaki BK.117A-4	7080	(D-HBPA)
D-HMUS	MBB-Kawasaki BK.117B-2	7031	(D-HBMF)
D-HMUZ(4)	MBB-Kawasaki BK.117B-2	7100	D-HBPU
D-HMVA	Eurocopter EC.135P1	0046	
D-HMVP	Eurocopter EC.135P1	0030	D-HECM
			F-WQEX
			D-HETZ
			D-HEC .
D-HMWP	Robinson R-22B Beta	0686	
D-HMXB	Hughes 269B	116-0281	SE-HCT
			OY-HAS
			SE-HCT
D-HNAH(2)	Robinson R-44 Astro	0244	
D-HNAS	Robinson R-44 Raven	1028	
D-HNEU(2)	Schweizer 269C	S-1530	OY-HDP
			D-HBAL
D-HNFC(3)	Fröhlich/ Elisport CH-7 Angel Kompress	0029	
D-HNFO	Molderings/ Elisport CH-7 Angel	094	D-HWMO
D-HNIC	Bell 222B	47142	N811CE
			N31904
D-HNIN	Schweizer 269C	S-1381	
D-HNNN(2)	MBB Bö.105	S-662	D-HDUD
D-HNOF	Fröhlich/ Elisport CH-7 Angel	A068	
D-HNSL	Elisport CH-7 Angel (Reservation)	022	
D-HNTB	Schweizer 269C	S-1257	Swed.Army:
			05239
D-HNWA	MBB Bö.105	S-398	D-HDLN
D-HNWD	MBB Bö.105	S-431	D-HDME
D-HNWE	MBB Bö.105	S-456	D-HDNJ
D-HNWF	MBB Bo.105	S-626	(D-HDSV)
D-HNWG	MBB Bö.105	S-684	D-HDUZ
			(N4573S)
D-HNWH	MBB Bo.105	S-714	(N714XY)
			D-HDRB
D-HNWJ	MBB Bö.105	S-777	D-HDYM
D-HNWK	MBB-Kawasaki BK.117B-2	7200	(D-HIMQ)
D-HNWL	MBB-Kawasaki BK.117B-2	7212	(D-HFDC)
D-HNWM(2)	Aérospatiale AS.365N4 / Eurocopter EC.155B Dauphin	6613	F-WQDN
D-HNWN	Aérospatiale AS.365N4 / Eurocopter EC.155B Dauphin (Permit 12.04)	6643	F-WQDY
D-HNWO	MBB-Kawasaki BK.117C-1	7552	
D-HNWP	MBB-Kawasaki BK.117C-1	7553	
D-HNWQ	MBB-Kawasaki BK.117C-1	7554	
D-HOBB(3)	Bell 206B Jet Ranger II (Reservation)	"007"	
D-HOBO(3)	Schweizer 269C	S-1401	HB-XVK
D-HOBS(3)	Hughes 269C	128-0755	SpAF HE.20-16/
			"78-45"
D-HOBV	Agusta A.109E Power	11146	
D-HOBY(2)	Hughes 369D	107-0215D	VH-HRJ
			N8689F
D-HOED	Agusta-Bell 47G-2	259	74+17
			AS+059
D-HOEM	Eurocopter EC.135P2	0238	
D-HOER	Eurocopter EC.120B Colibri	1203	
D-HOFF(2)	Eurocopter EC.135P2	0260	
D-HOFY	Sud Avn SA.318C Alouette Astazou	1883	
D-HOHL	Hughes 269C	88-0706	SpAF HE.20-09/
			"78-38"
D-HOHO(2)	McDonnell-Douglas 369E	0240E	N1603L
D-HOLA	Enstrom F-28A-D	184	
D-HOLD	Enstrom F-28A-D	185	
D-HOLF	Hughes 269C	76-0519	SE-HHC
D-HOLL	Schweizer 269C	S-1203	N41S
D-HOLM(2)	Hughes 269C	98-0726	SpAF HE.20-04/
			"78-33"
D-HOLY(2)	Bell 206L-4 Long Ranger IV	52039	N206RT
D-HOLZ(2)	Hughes 369E	0146E	SE-HNT
			LN-OTU
			SE-HNT
			LN-OMY
			SE-HNT
D-HOMA	Robinson R-22 Beta	1073	N8038Q
D-HONE(2)	Eurocopter EC.135P2	0338	
D-HONI	Robinson R-22 Beta	1405	
D-HONY(2)	Bell 206B Jet Ranger II	2433	N5002U
D-HOOK(3)	Bell 205A-1	30206	N205AH
			N49641
D-HOON	Agusta-Bell 206B Jet Ranger II	8597	
D-HOOO	Enstrom F-28A-D	256	
D-HOPA(2)	Hughes 269B	19-0410	
D-HOPE	Aérospatiale SA.365C2 Dauphin 2	5009	F-WXFD
D-HOPI(2)	Eurocopter EC.135P2	0323	
D-HOPN	Aérospatiale SA.342J Gazelle	1601	
D-HOPO	Aérospatiale SA.342J Gazelle	1708	
D-HOPP(2)	Aérospatiale SA.342J Gazelle	1695	
D-HOPQ	Aérospatiale SA.365C2 Dauphin 2	5062	
D-HOPS(2)	Agusta-Bell 47G-2	282	HB-XCH
			TR-LLY
			F-OBVK
D-HOPY(2)	Bell 206L-3 Long Ranger III	51287	

D-HORG	Agusta-Bell 206B Jet Ranger II	8375	G-BBXN HP-634 G-BBXN
D-HORN(3)	Hughes 269C	88-0704	SpAF HE.20-01/ "78- . ."
D-HOSB(2	Sikorsky S-76A	760191	
D-HOSE(4)	Schweizer 269C-1	0047	
D-HOSF	Sikorsky S-76B	760413	N5006B
D-HOSI (2)	SNCASE SE.3160 Alouette III	1524	ZK-HYM JA9030
D-HOST(2)	Schweizer 269C	S-1531	N41S
D-HOTO(2)	Robinson R-22 Beta	2251	
D-HOTT(2)	Bell 206L-3 Long Ranger III	51587	C-FNOQ
D-HOUV	Huschle/ Elisport CH-7 Angel	3511	
D-HOWA	Mil Mi-8T	10535	94+02 LSK-906
D-HOWB	Mil Mi-8T	10536	94+03 LSK-907
D-HOXC	Mil Mi-8T	10583	DDR-SPC DM-SPC
D-HOXP	Mil Mi-8T	105102	DDR-SPP
D-HOXQ	Mil Mi-8T	105103	DDR-SJA
D-HOYG	Hughes 269C	48-0678	
D-HOZI	Mil Mi-8T	0826	94+15 D-HOZI DDR-VHL LSK-397
D-HOZJ	Mil Mi-8T	10520	94+16 D-HOZJ DDR-VHM LSK-971
D-HPEP	Robinson R-22 Beta	2327	
D-HPET	Hughes 369D	37-0095D	OE-KXL D-HMOL(1) C-GYUA
D-HPFA	Robinson R-44 Astro	0096	
D-HPHP	Robinson R-44 Raven II	10318	
D-HPIP	Robinson R-22 Beta	2352	
D-HPIX	Aérospatiale AS.350B3 Ecureuil	3789	
D-HPMM	Eurocopter EC.135P2	0242	D-HECA
D-HPNA	McDonnell-Douglas MD-900 Explorer	00059	N9223K
D-HPNB	McDonnell-Douglas MD-900 Explorer	00061	N92139
D-HPNC	McDonnell-Douglas MD-900 Explorer	00062	N3064K
D-HPOL	Aérospatiale AS.350B2 Ecureuil (Permit expired 18.03.97)	2637	HB-XYS
D-HPOL(2)	MBB Bö.105	S-782	N5366Y D-HDYR
D-HPPP	MBB Bö.105	S-734	C-GJDA N734MB D-HDRV
D-HPRO	Bell 407	53196	
D-HPWR	Agusta A.109E Power	11208	
D-HQIX	Aérospatiale AS.350B3 Ecureuil	3479	
D-HQQQ(2)	MBB-Kawasaki BK.117B-2	7071	PT-YMD D-HECC SE-JBG D-HMBG(1) N117VB N117VU N953MB D-HBNS
D-HRAM	Aérospatiale AS.350B Ecureuil	2591	
D-HRAV	Robinson R-44 Astro	0741	N7187H
D-HRBW	Robinson R-22 Beta	1826	N4064S
D-HRED	Elisport CH-7 Angel (Permit 9.04)	0052	
D-HRET	Eurocopter EC.135T1	0045	
D-HRFA	Agusta-Bell 206B Jet Ranger II	8693	F-GHDR
D-HRGB	Eurocopter EC.120B Colibri	1320	SE-JGM
D-HRHM	Eurocopter EC.135T1	0027	
D-HRIC(2)	Schweizer 269C	S-1802	N41S
D-HRIK	Eurocopter EC.120B Colibri	1038	HB- . . . D-HMHR
D-HRIM	Schweizer 269C	S-1801	
D-HRIT	Schweizer 269C (Accident 26.8.02)	S-1799	N41S
D-HRMM	Bell 206B Jet Ranger II	4339	
D-HROM	Schweizer 269C	S-1317	N58SA G-BXUP SE-HTB N69A
D-HROY	Robinson R-44 Astro	0487	
D-HRPA	Eurocopter EC.135P2	0230	
D-HRPB	Eurocopter EC.135P2	0318	
D-HRPS	Robinson R-22 Beta	2200	N2345W
D-HRRR	Robinson R-22 Beta	0754	G-MUSI
D-HRUT	Schweizer 269C	S-1533	N69A
D-HRWI	Warnholz/ Elisport CH-7 Angel	CH-042	
D-HRWK	Schweizer 269C (HKP 5B)	S-1268	(D-HMEN(2)) Swed.Army: 05244
D-HRWW	Wittman/ Elisport CH-7 Angel	A-141	
D-HSAB	MBB MBB Bö.105S	S-873	(D-HFNE)
D-HSAN(2)	Eurocopter EC.135P2	0276	
D-HSAS	MBB-Kawasaki BK.117B-2	7241	N3176Q D-HMBO(2) D-HFIF
D-HSAT	MBB-Kawasaki BK.117B-2	7233	(D-HFDX)

D-HSAV	Agusta-Bell 206B Jet Ranger II	8733	TC-HKJ D-HSAV I-GPFP I-PIEF
D-HSDA	Bell 206L-4 Long Ranger IV	52057	C-GLZW
D-HSDD	McDonnell-Douglas MD-900 Explorer	00026	N9094T (D-HMDX) (D-HMCD)
D-HSEA	Schweizer 269C	S-1681	N69A
D-HSEP	Schweizer 269C (Accident 22.5.02)	S-1451	F-GKAI D-HLEX N41S
D-HSFB	MBB-Kawasaki BK.117B-2	7240	D-HFIE
D-HSGD	Bell 206B Jet Ranger II	3119	N5754J
D-HSKY	Bell 407	53109	
D-HSLA(2)	Sikorsky S-76A	760205	N63GH FAG-002 RJAG-737
D-HSML	MBB-Kawasaki BK.117C-1	7514	N40027 D-HMB .
D-HSNA	PZL W-3A Sokol	370503	
D-HSNB	PZL W-3A Sokol	370708	SP-SYM
D-HSNC(2)	Eurocopter EC.135T1	0092	
D-HSND	PZL W-3A Sokol (Reservation)	unkn	
D-HSNE	PZL W-3A Sokol (Reservation)	unkn	
D-HSNF	PZL W-3A Sokol (Reservation)	unkn	
D-HSNG	PZL W-3A Sokol (Reservation)	unkn	
D-HSOS	Eurocopter EC.135P1	0071	
D-HSPA	Schweizer 269C (HKP 5B)	S-1189	Swed.Army : 05234
D-HSPB	Hughes 269C (HKP 5B)	20-0903	Swed.Army : 05223 SE-HKY (ZK-HOI)
D-HSPE	Hughes 269C (HKP 5B)	31-1040	Swed.Army 05230 SE-HKZ N1099D
D-HSPF	Schweizer 269C (HKP 5B)	S-1190	Swed.Army : 05235
D-HSPG	Hughes 269C (HKP 5B)	71-1067	Swed.Army : 05228 SE-HMA N5020K
D-HSPI	Hughes 269C (HKP 5B)	41-1052	Swed.Army : 05225 SE-HLN
D-HSPJ	Schweizer 269C (HKP 5B)	S-1256	Swed.Army : 05239
D-HSPK	Schweizer 269C (HKP 5B)	S-1167	Swed.Army : 05231
D-HSPM	Hughes 269C (HKP 5B)	61-1053	Swed.Army : 05226 SE-HLO
D-HSPN	Schweizer 269C (HKP 5B)	S-1168	Swed.Army : 05232
D-HSPO	McDonnell-Douglas 369E	0207E	HA-MSF
D-HSPP	Schweizer 269C (HKP 5B)	S-1259	Swed.Army : 05242
D-HSPS	Hughes 269C (HKP 5B)	71-1069	Swed.Army : 05227
D-HSPU	Schweizer 269C (HKP 5B)	S-1188	Swed.Army : 05233
D-HSPV	Schweizer 269C (HKP 5B)	S-1267	Swed.Army : 05242
D-HSPW	Hughes 269C (HKP 5B)	20-0898	Swed.Army : 05222 SE-HKT
D-HSSS	MBB-Kawasaki BK.117B-2	7245	D-HFIJ
D-HSUN(2)	Eurocopter EC.120B Colibri	1272	
D-HSUS	Robinson R-44 Astro	0105	
D-HSYG	Gebel / Rotorway Exec 90 (Permit)	3508	
D-HTAC(2)	Robinson R-44 Astro	0405	
D-HTCH	Robinson R-22 Beta	2328	(D-HKAI) N2361K
D-HTEC	Eurocopter EC.120B Colibri	1121	
D-HTEP	Eurocopter EC.120B Colibri	1187	F-WQDC
D-HTHA	MBB Bö.105S	S-858	(D-HFHP)
D-HTHB	MBB Bö.105S	S-866	N3202Y D-HMBK(1) (D-HFHX)
D-HTIB(2)	MBB-Kawasaki BK.117b-2	7022	EC-EZT N117UV N39281 D-HBKX
D-HTIK	Robinson R-22 Beta	2135	
D-HTIM(2)	Bell 222B	47153	JA9668
D-HTLL	Eurocopter EC.120B Colibri	1100	F-WQDP
D-HTME	McDonnell-Douglas 369E	0479E	
D-HTOM	Bell 206B Jet Ranger II	2434	N4811E PT-HPJ N5002K
D-HTOR	Hughes 269C	98-0727	SpAF HE.20-05/ "78- . ."
D-HTRI (2)	Bell 206B Jet Ranger II	4331	
D-HTSB	MBB Bö.105C	S-1	D-HMBN D-HABV

D-HTTT	MBB-Kawasaki BK.117B-2	7246	D-HFIK
D-HTWO	Eurocopter EC.135P2	0343	
D-HUAB	MBB Bö.105C (Reservation)	S-203	D-HDFH(2)
D-HUAC	MBB Bö.105C (Reservation)	S-204	D-HDFS(2)
D-HUAE	Eurocopter EC.120B Colibri	1144	F-WQDC
D-HUAF	Aérospatiale SA.315B Lama	2486	(D-HUAD)
			N315LG
			D-HURA
			F-GEHK
			I-MADO
D-HUAH	Robinson R-44 Astro	0279	
D-HUAK	Eurocopter EC.120B Colibri	1299	
D-HUAX	McDonnell-Douglas MD-900 Explorer	00047	N92067
	(Permit 12.04)		
D-HUBE	MBB Bö.105S	S-883	D-HMBT(2)
			D-HFNO
D-HUBI	Robinson R-22 Beta	1877	
D-HUBU	Revolution Mini-500 (Permit .01)	340	
D-HUBY(2)	Robinson R-44 Raven	0988	
D-HUBZ	Robinson R-22B2 Beta	3327	OE-XPE
D-HUGH	Schweizer 269C	S-1432	N433MS
D-HUGI	Robinson R-22 Beta	1878	
D-HUGO	Bell 206B3 Jet Ranger III (Reservation .04)	4290	9A-HMF
			N289CA
D-HUHN	MBB Bö.105	S-867	N32022
			D-HMBL(2)
			(D-HFHY)
D-HUHU	Robinson R-22 Beta	2237	N2351X
D-HUKI	Robinson R-22 Beta (Reservation)	2183	N2342W
D-HULF	Hughes 369E (Damaged)	0150E	G-BMFW
D-HULI	Robinson R-22 Beta	1879	
D-HUND	Robinson R-44 Astro	0126	
D-HUPE	MBB Bö.105	S-871	N4346G
			D-HMBL(3)
			(D-HFNC)
D-HUPS	Robinson R22B2 Beta	3195	G-JNET
D-HUSA	Schweizer 269C-1	0046	
D-HUTA	Bell 407	53158	
D-HUTE(2)	McDonnell-Douglas 369E	0203E	HA-MSB
D-HUUU	MBB-Kawasaki BK.117B-2	7242	(D-HFIG)
			N3202U
			D-HMBN
D-HUWE(2)	Schweizer 269C	S-1737	D-HEXI (4)
			D-HCDK
D-HVBA	Eurocopter EC.135T1	0145	
D-HVBB	Eurocopter EC.135T1	0146	D-HEC .
D-HVBC	Eurocopter EC.135T1	0148	
D-HVBD	Eurocopter EC.135T1	0150	D-HECW
D-HVBE	Eurocopter EC.135T1	0152	D-HEC .
D-HVBF	Eurocopter EC.135T1	0171	
D-HVBG	Eurocopter EC.135T1	0176	
D-HVBH	Eurocopter EC.135T1	0121	
D-HVBI	Eurocopter EC.135T1	0177	
D-HVBJ	Eurocopter EC.135T1	0211	
D-HVBK	Eurocopter EC.135T1	0217	
D-HVBL	Eurocopter EC.135T2	0256	
D-HVBM	Eurocopter EC.135T2	0258	
D-HVBN	Eurocopter EC.135T2	0261	
D-HVBO	Eurocopter EC.135T2	0263	
D-HVBP	Eurocopter EC.135T2	0264	
D-HVBQ	Eurocopter EC.135T2	0266	
D-HVBR	Eurocopter EC.135T2	0286	
D-HVBS	Eurocopter EC.135T2	0295	
D-HVBT	Eurocopter EC.135T2	0299	
D-HVBU	Eurocopter EC.135T2	0301	
D-HVBV	Eurocopter EC.135T2	0304	
D-HVBW	Eurocopter EC.135T2	0342	
D-HVBX	Eurocopter EC.135T2	0349	D-HECP
D-HVBY	Eurocopter EC.135T2	0353	
D-HVHM(2)	Enstrom F-28F (Reservation .05)	817	
D-HVIP(3)	Aérospatiale AS.350B2 Ecureuil	9030	
D-HVST	McDonnell-Douglas MD.520N	LN-076	N52319
D-HVVV	Bell 47G-4A /Soloy	7608	HB-XKY
			N52OPA
D-HVWF	Horstmann/ Rotorway Exec 162F	6160	
D-HWAL(3)	Agusta-Bell 47G-4A	WA/719	G-BYCH
	(Used parts of c/n WA/719 G-AXKN in rebuild)		EC-BMB
			MM80504
D-HWEG	Aérospatiale AS.350B2 Ecureuil	9035	N130WE
D-HWES	Robinson R-44 Raven II	10417	
D-HWFH	Eurocopter EC.135P2	0277	
D-HWFW	Bell 206B Jet Ranger II	4159	HB-XYF
D-HWIN	Hughes 269C	96-0542	F-GMIK
			D-HGIS
			SE-HNX
			LN-OTX
			SE-HNX
			PH-HGH
			N5083U
			C-GGAN
			N7426F
D-HWIT	Robinson R-44 Astro	0147	
D-HWJW	Wilkenloh/ Rotorway Exec 162F (Wfu)	96-01/16214	
D-HWKW	McDonnell-Douglas 369E	0537E	N9237X
D-HWLL	Bell 206B Jet Ranger II	2359	N119AJ
D-HWOL	Wollscheid KW-1/ Rotorway Exec 90	6024	(D-HEES)
	(W/o 9.9.04)		
D-HWPP	Bell 206L-3 Long Ranger III	51480	C-FKKE
D-HWPY	Bell 206L-3 Long Ranger III	51491	N600TH
			N4309M
D-HWUE	Enstrom F-28F	814	
D-HWVS	MBB-Kawasaki BK.117C-2	9027	
D-HWWG	Robinson R-44 Astro	0075	N5484X
			(D-HWAL)
			N5484X
D-HWWW	MBB-Kawasaki BK.117B-2	7248	D-HFIM
D-HWVS	MBB-Kawasaki BK.117C-1 (Reservation 5.02)	9027	
D-HXGA	Hughes 369HE	59-0102E	HB-XGA
			D-HCAB
			G-AYNK
			EI-AUA
			N9012F
D-HXXL(2)	MBB-Kawasaki BK.117 (Permit .00)	7007	D-HMB .
			F-WMBB
			D-HBKI
D-HXXL(3)	Bell 206B Jet Ranger III	4024	TC-HCC
			C-FCYG
D-HXXX	McDonnell-Douglas 369E	0322E	G-TUBE
D-HXYZ(2)	Hughes 269C	14-0272	G-LEMJ
			G-BMYW
			N8999F
D-HYES	Robinson R-22 Beta	2167	
D-HYNO	Robinson R-22 Beta	1707	N1707R
			(D-H . . .)
			OY-HFH
D-HYYY	Eurocopter EC.135TI	0006	(D-HSML)
D-HZAK	Robinson R-22B2 Beta	2862	
D-HZIK	Robinson R-22B2 Beta	2853	
D-HZPJ	Mil Mi-2	568838104	DDR-VGE
			LSK-312
D-HZPO	Mil Mi-2	543048083	DDR-VGK
			LSK-500
D-HZXA	MBB Bö.105M (Permit .02)	5016	80+16
D-HZXB	MBB Bö.105M (Permit .02)	5074	80+74
D-HZXD	MBB Bö.105M (Permit .02)	5025	80+25
D-HZXE	MBB Bö.105M (Permit .02)	5062	80+62
D-HZXF	MBB Bö.105M (Permit .02)	5057	80+57
D-HZXG	MBB Bö.105M (Permit .03)	5002	80+02
D-HZXH	MBB Bö.105M (Permit .03)	5003	80+03
D-HZXI	MBB Bö.105M (Permit .03)	5014	80+14
D-HZYA(2)	MBB Bö.105M (Permit 7.04)	5071	80+71
D-HZYB(2)	MBB Bö.105M (Permit 7.04)	5115	81+15
D-HZYC(2)	MBB Bö.105M (Permit 7.04)	5051	80+51
D-HZYD(2)	MBB Bö.105M (Permit 7.04)	5005	80+05
D-HZYE(2)	MBB Bö.105M (Permit 7.04)	5054	80+54
D-HZYF(2)	MBB Bö.105M (Permit 7.04)	5079	80+79
D-HZYG(2)	MBB Bö.105M (Permit 7.04)	5091	80+91
D-HZYH(2)	MBB Bö.105M (Permit 7.04)	5088	80+88
D-HZYI(2)	MBB Bö.105M (Permit 7.04)	5090	80+90
D-HZYJ(2)	MBB Bö.105M (Permit 7.04)	5007	80+07
D-HZYL	MBB Bö.105M (Permit 9.02)	5006	80+06
D-HZYN	MBB Bö.105M (Permit .02)	5080	80+80
D-HZYO	MBB Bö.105M (Permit .02)	5030	80+30
D-HZYP	MBB Bö.105M (Permit .02)	5041	80+41
D-HZYQ	MBB Bö.105M (Permit .02)	5096	80+96
D-HZYR	MBB Bö.105M (Permit .02)	5100	81+00
D-HZYS	MBB Bö.105M (Permit .02)	5056	80+56
D-HZYT	MBB Bö.105M (Permit .02)	5060	80+60
D-HZYU	MBB Bö.105M (Permit .02)	5037	80+37
D-HZYV	MBB Bö.105M (Permit .02)	5095	80+95
D-HZYW	MBB Bö.105M (Permit .02)	5053	80+53
D-HZYX	MBB Bö.105M (Permit .02)	5011	80+11
D-HZYZ	MBB Bö.105M (Permit .02)	5072	80+72
D-HZZZ	Robinson R-22 Beta	2040	N2322B
D-H...	Aérospatiale AS.332L1 Super Puma	2018	G-PUMG
			F-ODOS
D-H . . .	Aérospatiale AS.332L Super Puma	2115	G-TIGZ
			C-GQKK
			G-TIGZ
D-H . . .	Cole/ Canadian Home Rotors Safari	BB2082	N557XS
D-H . . .	Enstrom 280C Turbo Shark	1114	N51687
D-H . . .	Robinson R-22 Beta	3664	N74317
D-H . . .	Rotorway Exec 162F	6285	N728BG
D-H . . .	Schweizer 269C	S-1448	F-GGVJ
			D-HGUS

CLASS I : Twin-Engined Aircraft of 2 to 5.7 Metric Tonnes

D-IAAA(2)	Piper Aerostar 601P	62P-0924-8165048	N6896X
D-IAAC	Cessna 441 Conquest II	441-0073	N88834
D-IAAG(3)	Cessna 340	340-0325	N69482
D-IAAH(2)	Beech C90A King Air	LJ-1247	N5651J
D-IAAM	Reims/Cessna FT337GP Super Skymaster	FP33700020	D-GAAM
	(Reims-assembled P337G Pressurized Skymaster		F-WZDY
	US c/n P3370231)		(N1ZN) ?
D-IAAP	Cessna Turbo 310R	310R1348	(N3999A)
D-IAAT	Cessna 421C Golden Eagle	421C0496	N8482N
D-IAAZ	Cessna 404 Titan (Wfu)	404-0416	N8805K
D-IABB(4)	Aero Commander 680FL	1633-119	(D-IGCP)
			HB-GCP

D-IABC(4)	Aero Commander 680V	1684-65	EC-HDE
			N10TG
			N1UT
			N1BA
			N81D
D-IACC	Beech 95-B55 Baron	TC-1737	OE-FME(1)
D-IACL	Cessna 340A II	340A0459	(N6275N)
D-IADE	Cessna 340A	340A0607	OE-FSK(2)
			D-IFAW
			N8661K
D-IADM(2)	Dassault/Dornier Alpha Jet (Permit 3.02)	A-111	41+11
D-IADR(2)	Cessna 340A / RAMVI	340A0441	(N555HL)
			N6245X
D-IAEB	Britten-Norman BN-2A-8 Islander	218	OH-BNB
			G-51-218
D-IAFC(3)	Cessna T303 Crusader	T30300244	N9959C
D-IAFF(2)	Beech C90A King Air	LJ-1229	N422TW
			N422RJ
			N5547Y
D-IAFM	Cessna 414	414-0354	N1574T
D-IAFS	Beech 95-B55 Baron	TC-1796	N8773R
D-IAGC	Cessna 340/RAM	340-0109	N222BQ
			N222BG
			N222BC
			N500TM
			(N4559L)
D-IAGG	Raytheon 390 Premier	RB-35	N435K
D-IAGL	Cessna 421B Golden Eagle	421B0006	N8006Q
D-IAHB	Cessna 414	414-0547	N1990G
D-IAHT(3)	Mitsubishi MU-2B-26A	352SA	N41AD
			N41WB
			N978MA
			N234BC
			N737MA
D-IAHW	Cessna 340A	340A0355	N6LR
			N37337
D-IAIN	Cessna 340A	340A0921	N2741N
			(N200MR)
			N2741N
D-IAJJ	Cessna 500 Citation	500-0245	N245BC
			(N245MG)
			9M-FAZ
			XC-BUR
			TI-AHH
			(TI-AHE)
			N5245J
D-IAJK(2)	Beech B200 Super King Air	BB-1565	D-IMGI
			N23FH
			N1094Y
D-IAKK	Beech B200 Super King Air	BB-1265	N550TF
			N550TP
			N29979
D-IALL(2)	Cessna 525 CitationJet	525-0143	D-IOMP
D-IAMA	Piper PA-23-250 Aztec E	27-7305204	N40485
D-IAMO(2)	Cessna 525A CitationJet CJ2	525A-0166	N5218R
D-IANA(3)	Beech B200 Super King Air	BB-1517	N3217V
D-IANI	Cessna 340A	340A0101	N3929S
			C-GFWZ
			(N1545G)
D-IAPA	Piper PA-31T1 Cheyenne I	31T-8104032	(N5SS)
			N5SL
			N821CM
			N2496X
D-IAPD(3)	Cessna 404 Titan	404-0679	N679R
			N6762R
			(N3336K)
			N6762R
D-IAPS(2)	Beech A55 Baron	TC-499	(D-ILFW)
			D-ILFY
D-IARC	Cessna 404 Titan	404-0020	OO-GIS
			SE-GZA
			Fv87002/872
			N3985C
D-IARP	Cessna 340	340-0326	N69484
D-IARZ	Cessna 421A Golden Eagle	421A0136	(N4046L)
D-IAST	Beech E55 Baron	TE-905	OE-FPD
			(D-INAD)
D-IATM	Beech B200 Super King Air	BB-1595	N713FP
D-IATT	Raytheon 390 Premier	RB-48	N51480
D-IAVA(2)	Piper PA-23-250 Aztec E	27-7405378	G-HFTG
	(Reservation 3.05)		G-BSOB
			G-BCJR
			N54040
D-IAWD(2)	Piper PA-42-720 Cheyenne IIIA	42-5501051	B-3621
	(Reservation .05)		N9240Q
			(D-IOSF)
D-IAWE	Piper PA-42-720 Cheyenne IIIA	42-5501052	B-3622
	(Reservation .05)		N92402
			(D-IOSG)
D-IBAB(6)	Beech 300LW Super King Air	FA-225	N82396
D-IBAD(4)	Beech B200 Super King Air	BB-1229	
D-IBAG(3)	Rockwell Commander 690A	11211	
D-IBAM(2)	Cessna 340A	340A0091	(N1392G)
D-IBAR(4)	Beech B200 Super King Air	BB-1280	
D-IBAU	Cessna 401A	401A0101	(N6175Q)
D-IBAZ	Piper PA-23-250 Aztec B	27-2221	N5193Y
			N10F

D-IBBA(2)	Cessna 525 CitationJet	525-0025	D-IOBO(1)
			N9LR
			(N1330D)
D-IBBB(7)	Raytheon 390 Premier	RB-82	N61882
D-IBBH(3)	Cessna 414A Chancellor	414A0238	(N8846K)
D-IBBK	Cessna 340A	340A0338	LX-RST
			F-GEJL
			D-ILAK
			N37310
D-IBBP	Beech C90A King Air	LJ-1716	N61716
D-IBCB	Beech B200 Super King Air	BB-1729	5B-CKJ
	(Permit 11.04)		N728AM
			N207TS
			N44724
D-IBDH	Beech C90B King Air	LJ-1307	N8053U
D-IBDM	Dassault/Dornier Alpha Jet (Permit 3.02)	A-130	41+30
D-IBEL(2)	Cessna 340A	340A1814	G-ENAM
			N1232G
D-IBER(4)	Beech 300LW Super King Air	FA-184	
D-IBFE	Beech B200 Super King Air	BB-1716	N3216G
D-IBFS	Beech B200 Super King Air	BB-1349	N200KG
			N200KA
D-IBFT	Beech B200 Super King Air	BB-1535	N1135Z
D-IBHE	Cessna 310R	310R0066	N3370Q
D-IBHM	Cessna 414	414-0487	N7855Q
D-IBHS	Cessna T337C Turbo Super Skymaster	33700820	N2520S
D-IBIE	Cessna 340A	340A0715	(PH-AXG)
			N98954
D-IBIJ	Cessna 402B	402B0327	YU-BIJ
			N3189K
D-IBIN(2)	Swearingen SA.226TC Metro II	TC-252	PH-RAZ
			OY-AZW
			D-IBCF
			OY-AZW
			N5456M
D-IBIT(2)	Cessna 525 CitationJet CJ	525-0393	
D-IBIW(2)	Piper PA-31T1 Cheyenne I	31T-8004011	N76TG
			(N803AW)
			N76TG
			N707CM
			N208SW
			N2418W
D-IBJH	Cessna T303 Crusader	T30300297	N5433V
D-IBJJ	Cessna 525A CitationJet CJ2	525A-0125	N525CG
			N525CC
			N125CE
			N52038
D-IBMC(2)	Beech C90 King Air	LJ-931	HB-GIE
			I-FIRS
			N931KA
			HB-GHB
D-IBMM	Cessna 310Q	310Q0905	N69638
D-IBMP(2)	Beech B200 Super King Air	BB-1284	N6321V
			ZS-LWE
			N72410
D-IBMS(3)	Cessna 525 CitationJet	525-0309	
D-IBNK	Beech 300LW Super King Air	FA-204	N5662T
D-IBON(3)	Cessna 340A	340A0603	N8612K
D-IBOS(5)	Cessna 404 Titan	404-0809	SE-IRB
			D-IBUB(2)
			N67659
D-IBPN	Beech 58P Baron	TJ-424	N6526S
D-IBPW	Cessna 340A	340A0924	N39983
			XB-BHW
			(N2742A)
D-IBRH	Piper PA-23-250 Aztec E	27-7305137	N40374
D-IBRO(2)	Cessna T303 Crusader	T30300215	HB-LRP
			N9824C
D-IBSA	Piper PA-31T Cheyenne II	31T-8120033	N42TW
			N2589Z
D-IBSF	Beech B60 Duke (Reservation .05)	P-536	N80WE
D-IBUF(3)	Dornier Do.28D-6 Turbo Skyservant (Model 128-6)	4302	
D-IBUR(4)	Cessna T303 Crusader	T30300079	N2255C
D-IBWA	Cessna 340A	340A1510	N6870T
D-IBWF	Cessna 402B	402B0221	(N7893Q)
D-ICAC(3)	Cessna 551 Citation II/SP	551-0010	N55AL
			(N31DA)
			YV-137CP
			N3291M
D-ICBB	Cessna 340A	340A0541	SE-KCA
			D-ICBB
			N1MT
			(N4403A)
D-ICDE	Cessna T303 Crusader	T30300057	N1297C
D-ICDM	Dassault/Dornier Alpha Jet	A-35	40+35
D-ICDO	Dornier Do.228-200 (Permit)	4359	
D-ICDS(2)	Claudius Dornier CD-2 Seastar	1001	
D-ICDY	Dornier Do.28D-2 Skyservant	4164	58+89
D-ICEE(2)	Cessna 525 CitationJet	525-0096	N5153X
D-ICEL(3)	Piper Aerostar 601P	61P-0577-7963252	N8091J
			C-FDNJ
			N8091J
D-ICEN(2)	Cessna 340A	340A0555	OE-FUA
	(Written-off 21.8.00)		N340GT
			N340HB
			N4584N
D-ICEY	Cessna 525 CitationJet	525-0286	N51666

D-ICFG	Cessna 340A	340A0537	N4345C
D-ICGA	Piper PA-31T2 Cheyenne IIXL	31T-8166056	N550TL
			N550T
			N9165Y
			(N715CA)
D-ICGB	Piper PA-42-720 Cheyenne IIIA	42-5501007	N834CM
			N142TW
			N142PC
D-ICHG	Beech B200 Super King Air	BB-1400	N8085D
D-ICHO	Cessna T337GP Pressurized Skymaster	P3370288	N2QR
D-ICHS(2)	Cessna 425 Conquest I	425-0233	N80938
			N1262H
D-ICIA	Cessna 500 Citation	0086	LX-YKH
			C-FMAN
			N503GP
			N586CC
D-ICIM	Beech 58TC Baron	TK-48	
D-ICJL	Cessna T303 Crusader	T30300109	N7SX
			N3681C
D-ICKC	Cessna 414	414-0472	OE-FKH(1)
			N1679T
D-ICKM	Beech B200 Super King Air	BB-1005	OE-FKW
			D-ICOH
D-ICKS(2)	Claudius Dornier CD-2 Seastar	1002	
D-ICKY	Beech B-60 Duke	P-342	
D-ICLY	Cessna T303 Crusader	T30300159	N6588C
D-ICMS(2)	Cessna 525A CitationJet CJ2	525A-0108	N5136J
D-ICOL(2)	Cessna 525 CitationJet	525-0353	N5211Q
D-ICRF	Cessna 404 Titan Courier	404-0406	N8776K
D-ICRK	Swearingen SA.226TC Metro II	TC-333	4X-CSD
			N1007A
D-ICSB	Reims/Cessna FT337GP Super Skymaster (Reims-assembled P337G Pressurized Skymaster with US c/n P3370047)	FP33700003	G-BAGP
D-ICSS	Cessna 525 CitationJet	525-0121	TC-EMA
			N5264S
D-ICTA	Cessna 551 Citation II /SP	551-0051	(D-IHAT)
			N6863C
D-ICUS	Cessna 340A	340A1012	N4350C
D-ICVA	Beech 58P Baron	TJ-422	N6587M
D-ICVW(3)	Cessna 421C Golden Eagle	421C0260	N6146G
D-ICVY	Beech 95-58P Baron	TJ-46	N1546L
D-ICWB	Cessna 525 CitationJet	525-0349	
D-ICWD	Beech B200C Super King Air	BL-49	D-ICWM
			N51CV
			Z-TAM
			N17KK
			(EI-BME)
			N3836E
			(XA- . . .)
D-ICWS	Reims/Cessna FT337GP Super Skymaster (Reims-assembled P337G Pressurized Skymaster with US c/n P3370195)	FP33700014	
D-IDAC(2)	Cessna 421C Golden Eagle II	421C0024	N421TF
			N421WT
			N98409
D-IDAG(2)	Cessna 525 CitationJet	525-0144	
D-IDAK(4)	Beech C90 King Air	LJ-647	LX-DAK
			N9075S
D-IDAS(3)	Cessna 525 CitationJet CJ	525-0389	N389CJ
			N5156D
D-IDAX(2)	Cessna 425 Conquest I	425-0209	D-IMPC(1)
			N13EB
			N13FH
			N1224K
D-IDBB(2)	Dornier Do.28D-2 Skyservant	4080	58+05
			D-9571
D-IDBH(2)	Dornier Do.28D-2 Skyservant	4167	58+92
D-IDBU	Piper PA-42-720 Cheyenne IIIA	42-5501029	N700CC
			(N800DG)
			N41OLD
			G-BLSA
D-IDCA(2)	Beech 95-B55 Baron	TC-1942	
D-IDCV	Beech C90B King Air	LJ-1622	D-ICDV
			N4172Q
D-IDEA(3)	Swearingen SA.226T Merlin III	T-322	N312AC
			N70312
			D-IOKG
			OO-HSA
			N1006K
D-IDEE(3)	Piper PA-60-602P Aerostar	60-8365012	I-TOLA
			N64716
D-IDEK(2)	Beech B60 Duke	P-306	N5403U
			(N38EW)
			N5403U
			YV-35CP
			YV-TAKJ
D-IDES(2)	Dornier Do.28D-2 Skyservant	4187	59+12
D-IDEY	Beech 65-88 Queen Air	LP-5	N881E
D-IDHB(2)	DHC-6 Twin Otter 200 (Permit 1.00)	132	RP-C1776
			N501BA
			CF-WZH
D-IDIA	Piper PA-42-720 Cheyenne IIIA (Permit 11.99)	42-5501055	N955TA
			(OY- . . .)
			JA8724
			N9198F
			D-IOSG(2)
D-IDIT(2)	Cessna 414 (RAM Srs VI)	414-0953	N9KJ
			(N11FX)
			N9KJ
			N9KT
			(N5401G)
D-IDIX(3)	Beech C90A King Air	LJ-1571	N90KA
D-IDMH	Cessna 525A CitationJet CJ2	525A-0174	N5076K
D-IDOS(2)	Cessna 404 Titan	404-0665	N5375C
D-IDOZ	Dornier Do.28D-2 Skyservant (Permit)	4200	59+25
D-IDPA	Reims/Cessna FT337GP Super Skymaster (Reims-assembled P337G Pressurized Skymaster with US c/n P3370231)	FP33700017	
D-IDPW(2)	Cessna 421C Golden Eagle	421C1201	N26517
D-IDRB(2)	Cessna 421C Golden Eagle	unkn	
D-IDRH	Dornier Do.28D-2 Skyservant	4127	58+52
D-IDRM	Piper PA-23-250 Aztec E	27-7305183	N40466
D-IDRR	Dornier Do.28D-2 Skyservant	4129	58+54
D-IDSF(3)	Piper PA-42-720 Cheyenne IIIA	42-8001009	(D-IASB(2))
			N849AM
			OB-1649
			N151PC
			(N401MD)
			N151PC
			N825NW
			C-GNRD
D-IDTH	Cessna 421C Golden Eagle III	421C1062	N6865D
D-IDVL	Beech 65 Queen Air	LC-148	
D-IEAA	Cessna 414A Chancellor	414A0635	
D-IEAH	Beech 65-C90A King Air	LJ-1216	D-IHAH
			N1562Z
D-IEBE(2)	Beech C90A King Air	LJ-1267	A6-FAE
			HB-GIM
D-IEBM	Beech 300LW Super King Air	FA-217	N911RB
			N8115M
D-IECS	Cessna 414	414-0023	OE-FMB
			N8123Q
D-IEDI (3)	Beech B200 Super King Air	BB-1633	N2345M
D-IEEE(4)	Cessna 421BGolden Eagle	421B0523	PH-WES
			HB-LHG
			OE-FST
			HB-LHG
			N69886
D-IEFB	Beech B200 Super King Air	BB-897	N200TM
			N1837S
D-IEFD	Cessna 525A CitationJet CJ2	525A-0049	N51575
D-IEHB(2)	Beech 95-B55 Baron	TC-1961	OE-FMF
D-IEHP	Cessna 340A	340A0242	HB-LIO
			N3953G
D-IEJB	Reims/Cessna F337F Super Skymaster (Reims-assembled 337F with US c/n 33701383)	F33700043	(N1783M)
D-IERS	Cessna T303 Crusader	T30300134	N5409C
D-IESE	Piper PA-31 Navajo C	31-7812102	N27712
D-IESG	Beech B60 Duke	P-341	
D-IESK	Cessna 340	340-0231	SE-GOC
			G-BBAA
			N7852Q
D-IESS	Swearingen SA.226TC Metro II	TC-338	N90141
			H4-SIA
			N1008K
D-IETL	Beech 95-A55 Baron	TC-259	OH-ABD
D-IETZ	Cessna 525A CitationJet CJ2 (Reservation .04)	525A-0033	HB-VNO
			N163PB
D-IEVE	Aero Commander 680FP	1431-150	N600EJ
			N600BR
			(OO-TCA)
			N600BR
			N357CK
			KAF-301
			N6350U
D-IEWR	Piper PA-23-250 Aztec D	27-4451	N13806
D-IEWS	Cessna 525 CitationJet	525-0217	N5202D
D-IEXB	Beech 99	U-70	G-NUIT
			C-GESP
			N8013R
			N1191C
D-IEXE	Beech 99	U-46	N99LM
			D-IEXE
			LN-SAX
			SE-FOR
			N855SA
D-IEXF	Beech 99	U-62	LN-SAZ
			OO-WAZ
			F-BSUJ
			N1178C
D-IFAO	Cessna 340A	340-0021	(D-IFFL)
			OE-FFL
			N3KP
			N98531
D-IFAR(2)	Piper PA-23-250 Aztec D	27-4431	N13779
D-IFBN	Pilatus Britten-Norman BN-2B-26 Islander	2185	G-BLNF
D-IFBU	Piper PA-31 Navajo C	31-8012050	N3557W
D-IFCC	Fouga CM.170R Magister	079	93+02
			SB+202
			SC+603
			(AA+179)
D-IFDH	Cessna 525 CitationJet CJ	525-0517	N52626

D-IFDK	Cessna 421C Golden Eagle	421C0445	SE-IHO
			LN-VIL
			N6708C
D-IFFB	Beech 300LW Super King Air	FA-224	N56449
D-IFFM	Cessna 414	414-0801	N1221G
			(N15CT)
			N1221G
D-IFGW	Cessna 414	414-0608	OE-FGO
			N1980G
D-IFHI	Beech C90 King Air	LJ-977	N1813P
D-IFHS(2)	Cessna 411	411-0138	N4938T
D-IFHZ	Piper PA-31T1 Cheyenne IA	31T-1104016	N91201
D-IFIG	Ted Smith Aerostar 601P	61P-0183-012	OE-FIG
			N246HG
			N7467S
D-IFIK	Cessna 421C Golden Eagle	421C1115	N2652Y
D-IFIS	Cessna 525 CitationJet CJ	525-0442	N5187Z
D-IFJM	Cessna 421C Golden Eagle	421C1244	N2734N
D-IFKU	Pilatus Britten-Norman BN-2B-20 Islander	2290	G-BVXY
D-IFLC	Cessna 421A Golden Eagle	421A0033	N2933Q
D-IFMC	Raytheon 390 Premier	RB-27	N3216P
			D-IFMC
			N3216P
D-IFMG	Raytheon 390 Premier	RB-109	N50078
D-IFMI	Beech C90A King Air	LJ-1101	N17EL
			N17FL
			N72206
D-IFOX	Pilatus Britten-Norman BN-2B-26 Islander	2186	G-BLNG
D-IFPS	Cessna 340A	340A0540	OE-FCF
			(N4374A)
D-IFSA	de Havilland DH.104 Dove 7XC	04531	
D-IFSB(2)	Cessna 421B Golden Eagle	421B0561	N421SB
			N8216Q
D-IFSH(2)	Piper PA-42-720 Cheyenne IIIA	42-5501014	D-IDSF(2)
			N45SL
			C-FSOZ
			N900MP
			N916CM
			N4115F
D-IFTI	Pilatus Britten-Norman BN-2B-20 Islander	2299	G-BWYY
D-IFUN(2)	Beech 200 Super King Air	BB-575	D-ISJP
			VT-SLS
			OY-PAL
			N307P
			N580
			N6656W
D-IFUP	Cessna 525 CitationJet	525-0172	VP-CTA
			N350GM
			D-IAVB
			N172CJ
			N5156B
D-IFUT	Pilatus Britten-Norman BN-2B-20 Islander	2300	G-OBNG
	(Reservation 5.04)		G-BWYZ
D-IFWA	Cessna 340A	340A0094	PH-AIC
			D-IFDF
			(N1395G)
D-IGAS(4)	Cessna 525 CitationJet	525-0223	
D-IGBB	Beech 58P Baron	TJ-193	N6030Q
D-IGBH	Beech 58P Baron	TJ-188	N770JC
			N80AJ
			N96487
			G-BIYS
			G-UBKP
D-IGCA	Piper PA-23-250 Aztec C	27-2924	N696JA
			N5794Y
D-IGCW	Cessna T303 Crusader	T30300177	N9457C
D-IGGO	Cessna 421B Golden Eagle	421B0221	TC-GPS
			N5978M
D-IGKN	Beech C90A King Air	LJ-1077	N4B
			N4CH
			N69297
D-IGME(2)	Cessna 525 CitationJet	525-0279	
D-IGOB	Piaggio P.180 Avanti	1016	I-PJAT
D-IGPP	Cessna 421	421-0109	TC-DVK
	(Permit expired)		YU-BEJ
			N3128K
D-IGPS	Cessna T303 Crusader	T30300308	N303PK
			N303ER
			N6332V
D-IGRO	Cessna 525A CitationJet CJ2	525A-0230	
	(Reservation 9.04)		
D-IHAH(2)	Beech C90B King Air	LJ-1370	N1570C
D-IHAK(2)	Cessna 421C Golden Eagle	421C0128	N3876C
			G-FIHL
			N3876C
D-IHAP(2)	Cessna 525A CitationJet CJ2	525A-0026	D-IMYA
			N126CJ
			(N5203S)
D-IHBB(2)	Cessna 340A	340A0217	I-CCTT
			N3880G
D-IHBL	Fairchild Swearingen SA.227TT Fairchild 300	TT-512A	N123GM
			N927DC
			N13JV
			N3108G
D-IHCC	Beech 95-B55 Baron	TC-2215	
D-IHDE	Beech C90 King Air	LJ-725	
D-IHDS	Cessna Turbo 310R	310R0658	N98242

D-IHEB(4)	Cessna 525 CitationJet	525-0064	
D-IHEF	Cessna 414	414-0456	N1663T
D-IHFW(2)	Piper PA-23-250 Turbo Aztec D	27-4189	N6845Y
D-IHGB(2)	Piper PA-23-250 Aztec D	27-4281	LX-KRL
			D-IHGF
			N6925Y
D-IHHE	Beech C90A King Air	LJ-1327	N8227P
D-IHHH(3)	Piper PA-42-1000 Cheyenne 400	42-5527038	HK-3459P
			HK-3459
			HK-3459X
			(N518B)
			N9127N
D-IHHN	Cessna 525A CitationJet CJ2	525A-0041	N43ND
D-IHJK	Piper PA-31T1 Cheyenne I	31T-8104057	N62BW
			N134CC
			(N169KD)
			N134CC
D-IHJL	Piper PA-31T-1A Cheyenne IA	31T-1104015	S5-CEJ
			D-IIAH
			N9168T
D-IHKL	Cessna T303 Crusader	T30300135	N5423C
D-IHKM	Beech C90A King Air	LJ-1158	N38H
			N793PA
D-IHLA(2)	Piper PA-42-720 Cheyenne IIIA	42-8301001	N842PC
			JA8869
			N842PC
D-IHLB(3)	Cessna 402B	402B1340	N6377X
D-IHLK	Cessna 421B Golden Eagle	421B0451	(N41101)
D-IHML	Cessna 421C Golden Eagle	421C1080	N25M
			N68661
D-IHMV	Beech C90A King Air	LJ-1325	N8135M
D-IHSI	Rockwell Commander 695	95039	N9790S
D-IHSW	Beech C90B King Air	LJ-1315	N8103E
D-IHUC(2)	Gulfstream Commander 695	95069	(D-IHUK)
			N695EC
			HB-LQA
			VR-CBP
			N14CX
			N14CN
			N9821S
D-IHVA(2)	Piper PA-42-720 Cheyenne IIIA	42-5501025	N4118N
	(Permit 8.04)		
D-IHYL(2)	Piper PA-31T1 Cheyenne I	31T-8104033	N94EG
	(Reservation .04)		N881SW
			N23TC
			N881SW
D-IIAH(2)	Beech B200 Super King Air	BB-1741	N2341K
D-IIAS	Cessna 421C Golden Eagle	421C1055	HB-LQH
			N67979
D-IICE	Beech 200 Super King Air	BB-269	N269D
			N180SN
			N100SM
			N18269
D-IIGI	Rockwell 690A Commander	11172	N60B
			TF-ERR(3)
			C-GERR
			TF-ERR(3)
			N9164N
D-IIGP	Piper PA-34-220T Seneca V	3449235	D-GIGP
	(Permit .04)		I-....
			N53486
			(G-EZHW)
			N9526N
D-IIHA	Beech C90 King Air	LJ-562	N137B
			(N333FJ)
			N137B
D-IIHS	Beech 58P Baron	TJ-345	N3839B
D-IIKB(2)	Cessna 340A	340A0906	TC-OTK
			N2701X
			VH-JLT
			ZK-JLT
			N2701X
D-IIKM	Beech C90A King Air	LJ-1120	N7237K
D-IIPW	Beech 58P Baron	TJ-97	5N-ASG
D-IITR	Cessna 421B Golden Eagle	421B0234	D-IHJF
			OE-FGH
			N5991M
D-IITS	Cessna 340	340-0068	HB-LGR
			(I-MELE)
			N5916M
			(I-ALBB)
D-IIVK	Cessna T303 Crusader	T30300287	N5096V
D-IIWA	Piper Aerostar 602P	62P-0903-8165032	N666BC
	(Permit 10.04)		N68936
D-IIWB(2)	Beech C90A King Air	LJ-1340	N10799
			LV-WCW
			LV-PGL
D-IIWE	Aero Commander 500B	1301-116	OE-FAL
D-IIXX	Piper PA-31T1 Cheyenne I	31T-8104066	D-IHMM
			N82LC
			N32LC
			N600DR
			N2590Y
			(N259PC)
			N2590Y
D-IIYY	Cessna 421C Golden Eagle	421C0621	LX-SKY
			D-ISAL
			N88636

D-IJET(4)	Piaggio P.180 Avanti	1056	
D-IJGW	Cessna 425 Conquest I	425-0193	N1221X
D-IJHW	Piper PA-34-220T Seneca V	3433161	D-IJHP D-GAJP N9182D
D-IJOA	Cessna 525A CitationJet CJ2	525A-0034	N5211F
D-IKAI	Piaggio P.180 Avanti	1014	I-ACTC
D-IKAL(2)	Cessna 525A CitationJet CJ2	525A-0193	N5183U
D-IKBA	Dornier 228-201	8066	D-CBDR(5) D-CANA(3) HB-LPC D-IAHG D-CECK
D-IKEO	Cessna 340 III	340-0527	N41045
D-IKES	Beech C90 King Air	LJ-942	
D-IKET	Piper PA-31T Cheyenne II	31T-8020017	N154CA (N802SW) I-APIT N802SW (N100ES) N802SW N2359W
D-IKEW	Piper PA-31T Cheyenne II	31T-7820066	N6108A
D-IKHS	Piper Aerostar 601P	61P-0542-231	N8059J
D-IKIM	Beech C90A King Air	LJ-1324	N82430
D-IKIW	Beech C90A King Air	LJ-641	N7128H G-BMEF N7338R (N27CG) N7338R
D-IKJH	Cessna T303 Crusader	T30300209	N9741C
D-IKJS	Cessna 525A CitationJet CJ2	525A-0029	N92CJ N5132T
D-IKKY	Mitsubishi MU-2B-40 Solitaire	420SA	I-SOLT N5KD N154MA
D-IKLN	Beech B200 Super King Air	BB-1369	(N5670M) D-IVHM N778HP N5649V
D-IKMS	Beech C90B King Air	LJ-1441	F-GSDM N995TA ZS-NUE N3271S
D-IKOB(2)	Beech B200 Super King Air	BB-921	N244JB N76MP
D-IKOP	Cessna 525 CitationJet	525-0016	N216CJ (N1328M)
D-IKRP	Cessna 421C Golden Eagle II	421C0214	TC-DBH (D-ICKK) N42ITS N5467G YV-175CP N5467G
D-IKST(2)	Cessna 421C Golden Eagle II	421C1024	N432SW ZK-FYY NZ7941 (NZ7924) N6793X
D-IKSW	Cessna T337GP Pressurized Skymaster	P3370124	N60E N6CE
D-IKUB	Beech 95-55 Baron	TC-145	N55AW D-IKUB
D-IKUR	de Havilland DH.104 Dove 2B	04296	HB-LAR G-AMEI
D-ILAM	Cessna 525A CitationJet CJ2	525A-0070	N5157E
D-ILAS(4)	Cessna T303 Crusader	T30300087	N2282C
D-ILAT(2)	Cessna 525 CitationJet	525-0209	
D-ILAY(2)	Cessna 414	414-0360	N1580T
D-ILCA(3)	Piper PA-31 Navajo C	31-7912035	N27897
D-ILCB	Cessna 525 CitationJet	525-0193	N193CJ
D-ILCC(3)	Cessna 551 Citation II /SP (Formerly c/n 550-0298)	551-0335	N431DS N74KV N68873
D-ILCE(2)	Piper PA-31T1 Cheyenne 1	31T-8004053	N2372V N2335X
D-ILCY	Beech A60 Duke	P-150	(OH-BDE)
D-ILDK	Cessna 340A	340A0972	HB-LMZ OE-FCH (N5703C)
D-ILDL	Cessna 525A CitationJet CJ2	525A-0167	N51806
D-ILEO	Cessna T303 Crusader	T30300052	N114TM D-ILEO N9894T
D-ILFA(2)	Pilatus Britten-Norman BN-2B-26 Islander	2243	G-BSWO
D-ILFB	Pilatus Britten-Norman BN-2B-26 Islander	2271	G-BUBO
D-ILFH(2)	Pilatus Britten-Norman BN-2B-26 Islander	2212	G-BPXS
D-ILFW	Beech 95-A55 Baron (Reservation 2.00)	TC-499	D-ILFY
D-ILGA(4)	Piper PA-31T1 Cheyenne 1A	31T-1104014	N9382T
D-ILGI (2)	Beech C90A King Air	LJ-1090	N7210H
D-ILHW(3)	Piper PA-34-220T Seneca III	34-8433055	G-GISY N4356G
D-ILIN	Beech 200 Super King Air	BB-545	OY-CBY
D-ILIT	deHavilland DH.89ADragon Rapide (Permit 12.99)	6879	G-AMAI D-ILIT "G-RCYR" EC-AGP G-AMAI NR803
D-ILKA(2)	Dornier 228-100	7005	LN-HTB D-IDOM(2)
D-ILKC	Beech 65-A90 King Air	LJ-211	N9OJR N76CV N76CB N553Z N550Z N867K
D-ILKY	Beech 95-B55 Baron	TC-1048	
D-ILLF	Beech B200 Super King Air	BB-1568	N1067V
D-ILLI (2)	Beech B60 Duke	P-537	(D-ILAH)
D-ILLL(4)	Cessna 525 CitationJet CJ	525-0518	
D-ILMC	Cessna 414	414-0906	N4635G D-ILMC N4635G
D-ILME(2)	Cessna 525 CitationJet CJ	525-0421	
D-ILPB	Dornier Do.28A-1	3015	TF-DOV (OO-MAI) D-ILPB 15+01 ND+108 CA+041 D-IBAK
D-ILPC(3)	Cessna 425 Corsair	425-0131	OE-FAM(2) OE-FIB N385MA N977MP (N489BC) N54BC N6883L
D-ILSA(2)	Piper PA-23-250 Aztec E	27-7305215	N40490
D-ILUB	Cessna 340	340-0076	N4090L
D-ILVW(4)	Cessna 404 Titan	404-0427	N89DS C-GNWF N80DS (N26771) N8832K
D-ILWA	Cessna 340A (Robertson STOL)	340A0502	N6333X
D-ILWB	Dornier 228-201	8035	D-CDIZ D-IASX (D-IDBF)
D-ILWD	Dornier 228-200	8069	D-CHOF
D-ILWS	Dornier 228-200	8002	D-CBDU(6) OY-CHJ 9M-AXB D-IDCO 9M-AXB D-IDCO
D-ILYS	Cessna 441 Conquest II	441-0355	N355VB AP-BCW N1213S
D-IMAC(2)	Cessna 525 CitationJet CJ	525-0396	N51575
D-IMAX(5)	Cessna 525A CitationJet CJ2	525A-0195	N51942
D-IMCB	Rockwell Commander 700	70007	N700GA
D-IMCM	Reims/Cessna F337F Super Skymaster (Reims-assembled 337F with US c/n 33701401)	F33700047	(D-GMCC) OO-GCM N5443
D-IMEL	Beech E55 Baron	TE-855	N9443Q
D-IMHH	Piper PA-60-602P Aerostar	60-8365010	N6901D
D-IMHW(2)	Cessna 340A	340A1518	N6871C
D-IMIC	Cessna 340A	340A1223	HB-LNW N68279
D-IMIK(2)	Dornier 228-200	8058	D-CMIC VH-NSX D-IHKB G-SJAD VH-NSC D-IERA (D-CERA)
D-IMIM (2)	Piper PA-42-720 Cheyenne III	42-8001048	N830CM
D-IMKL	Cessna 340A	340A1279	N68692
D-IMKU	Piper PA-23-250 Aztec B	27-2095	N5077Y
D-IMMA	Cessna 340A (W/o 3.3.05)	340A1205	I-AFSA N6825C
D-IMMD	Cessna 525 CitationJet	525-0211	
D-IMME(3)	Cessna 551 Citation II /SP	551-0400	N280JS N95CT N550WR (N67983)
D-IMMF(2)	Cessna 551 Citation II /SP	551-0560	N560AJ ZS-LNP N1298J
D-IMMI (3)	Cessna 525 CitationJet	525-0303	N51612
D-IMMM(3)	Cessna 525 CitationJet CJ (Dam. 12.3.04)	525-0460	N5185V
D-IMMO(3)	Piper PA-60-700P Aerostar	60-8423002	N700ET N700AH N9564N
D-IMMP	Cessna 525 CitationJet	525-0354	N821P N5225K
D-IMON(2)	Beech 200 Super King Air	BB-276	TF-ELT(5) N198SC EC-FQQ N130LP N205X
D-IMPC(2)	Cessna 525 CitationJet	525-0126	D-IHGW VP-CFP D-IFUP(1) N14TV N1264V N5090Y

D-IMPL(2)	Cessna Turbo 310R	310R1375	OE-FCD N4155A
D-IMRT	Cessna T303 Crusader	T30300097	N2679C
D-IMRX	Cessna 501 Citation I /SP	501-0688	
D-IMTT(2)	Messerschmitt Me.262 (Wearing "red 13" marks)	501244	US Navy Luftwaffe
D-IMUB	Cessna 414A Chancellor	414A0233	(N8834K)
D-IMWK(2)	Fairchild Swearingen SA.227TT Merlin IIIC	TT-529A	N3109S
D-IMWM	Cessna 340	340-0095	N4507Q
D-IMWW	Beech E55 Baron	TE-930	(OH-BBW)
D-INAC(2)	DHC-6-300 Twin Otter (Permit 4.04)	663	D4-CAY CR-CAY
D-INAG	Beech 95-B55 Baron	TC-1550	
D-INAS(3)	Beech C90A King Air	LJ-1551	XA-GPA N3111K
D-INAZ	Beech B60 Duke	P-532	N6738Z
D-INBK	Beech B60 Duke	P-478	N555BK D-ILMS(2)
D-INCS	Cessna 525 CitationJet (Permit 3.05)	525-0466	N119CS (D-ILLL(3)) N119CS
D-INDI (2)	Cessna 421B Golden Eagle	421B0317	D-IJCZ I-CLAA N5945M
D-INEC	Beech B60 Duke	P-549	N614EC N610PG N742RH N570U
D-INEW	Ted Smith Aerostar 601P	61P-0167-006	N7535S
D-INGA(3)	Cessna 425 Corsair	425-0003	N98751
D-INGE(3)	Cessna 340A	340A1258	N8841N (N777TG) N8841N
D-INGI	Cessna 340A	340A0037	N98569
D-INGO(2)	Cessna 340A	340A1025	N340MM N4756A
D-INGU	Piper Aerostar 601P	61P-0613-7963276	N8211J
D-INKA(8)	de Havilland DH.104 Dove 5 (Reservation .04)	04266	G-BLRN WB531
D-INNN	Piper PA-31T Cheyenne II	31T-8120102	N822SW
D-INOB	Cessna 525A CitationJet CJ2	525A-0196	N5166T
D-INOC	Cessna 525 CitationJet CJ	525-0477	N5216A
D-INRR	Cessna 414A Chancellor	414A0097	PH-LTO N4828A
D-INSP	Beech B60 Duke	P-554	N120SP N99VT N3699R
D-INTA	Cessna 421B Golden Eagle	421B0246	HB-LHP D-IJUM N300RX N300PX (N3362Q)
D-INWG(2)	Beech B60 Duke	P-446	N7860X
D-INWK	Swearingen SA.226T Merlin IIIA	T-255	N5349M
D-IOBO(2)	Cessna 525A CitationJet CJ2	525A-0032	D-IOBU N5250E
D-IOFA	Cessna T303 Crusader	T30300038	N9690T
D-IOHL	Cessna 441 Conquest II	441-0357	PH-BMP N1214B
D-IOLA(2)	Pilatus Britten-Norman BN-2B-26 Islander	2187	G-BLNH
D-IOLB	Cessna 404 Titan	404-0691	SE-IVG VH-PVG N67632
D-IOLT(2)	Cessna T303 Crusader	T30300294	N5357V
D-IONE	Piper PA-42-720 Cheyenne IIIA	42-8001002	C-GIDC N61QR N610R N21PL
D-IORE	Cessna 404 Titan	404-0604	I-NARA OY-BNZ N2683F
D-IORF	Britten-Norman BN-2A-26 Islander	2020	N100DA N60PA G-BEXJ N412JA G-51-2020 G-BEXJ
D-IOSA	Piper PA-42-720 Cheyenne IIIA	42-5501041	N9578N
D-IOSB	Piper PA-42-720 Cheyenne IIIA	42-5501042	
D-IOSC	Piper PA-42-720 Cheyenne IIIA	42-5501043	D-IOKP D-IOSC
D-IOSD	Piper PA-42-720 Cheyenne IIIA	42-5501044	
D-IOSJ	Piper PA-34-220T Seneca V	3449047	
D-IOSL	Piper PA-34-220T Seneca V	3449150	
D-IOTA	Beech 58P Baron	TJ-312	N3693L
D-IOTT(2)	Piper PA-31T Cheyenne II	31T-7920010	N6196A
D-IOVB	Cessna 421C Golden Eagle II	421C1061	N6798X
D-IPCS	Cessna 525 CitationJet	525-0264	EC-HBC VP-CHV (D-IKHV)
D-IPMG	Cessna T303 Crusader	T30300222	N121JH N9858C
D-IPMI	Cessna 525 CitationJet CJ	525-0533	(D-IPMM)
D-IPOS	Cessna 425 Corsair	425-0120	N425R N68817
D-IPRC	Cessna 340A	340A1248	TC- . . . N87453 - ? - (N87453)

D-IPSY	Beech B200 Super King Air	BB-1591	N1819H
D-IPVD	Cessna 525A CitationJet CJ2	525A-0218	
D-IPWA	Cessna 421B Golden Eagle	421B0632	N4939M D-ILYR (N1536G)
D-IQAS	Piper PA-42-1000 Cheyenne 400LS	42-5527022	(N322KW) N551AC N41187
D-IRAS	Cessna T303 Crusader	T30300143	PH-JAF OY-BHC SE-IHZ (N5524C)
D-IRES	Dornier Do.28D-2 Skyservant (To museum)	4186	59+11
D-IRIS	Beech F90 King Air	LA-229	N7209Z
D-IRKE	Cessna 525 CitationJet	525-0123	
D-IRMA	Cessna 525 CitationJet CJ	525-0366	N5223Y
D-IROL	Dornier Do.228-100	7003	D-CBD . SE-KHL LN-HPA D-IDNI
D-IROM	Beech E18S	BA-328	HB-GJG N328N N621AA N729KB N561FD N5619D
D-IRON	Cessna 525 CitationJet	525-0168	
D-IRTY	Cessna 340A	340A0707	N8603G F-GFYP N8603G
D-IRVA(2)	Cessna T303 Crusader	T30300050	N2181W D-INAA (N9883T)
D-IRWP	Beech B60 Duke	P-581	D-IUTE N39JT N37JT N850YR
D-IRWR	Cessna 525 CitationJet	525-0118	N118AZ (N61TF) N52178
D-ISAZ	Beech B200 Super King Air	BB-983	(N983AJ) D-ISAZ N983EB D-ILTO N87FE N6JE (D-IKFC) N6JE N6JL
D-ISCA	Cessna T303 Crusader	T30300175	N9382C
D-ISCH(2)	Cessna 525A CitationJet CJ2	525A-0052	
D-ISGW	Cessna 525 CitationJet	525-0070	N70HW
D-ISHW	Cessna 525 CitationJet	525-0289	
D-ISHY	Reims/Cessna F406 Caravan II	F406-0027	PH-FWH F-WZDX
D-ISIG	Piper PA-31T1 Cheyenne I	31T 8104055	N123AT N48TW (N880WW) N48TW N2491Y
D-ISIX	Beech C90A King Air	LJ-1355	N995PA D-ISIX N8105D
D-ISJP	Cessna 525A CitationJet CJ2	525A-0030	N302DM N5223Y
D-ISLA(2)	Cessna T303 Crusader	T30300226	F-GFTP N510TF N9868C
D-ISSS(2)	Cessna 500 Citation I	500-0392	I-FLYB N26461
D-ISTA	Cessna 340	340-0323	OY-BYG D-IKEB
D-ISTB	Beech F90 King Air	LA-227	N330VP N7206Z
D-ISTC	Mitsubishi MU-2B-40 Solitaire	436SA	N62CP (N928VF) N62CP N670CA N214MA
D-ISUN(2)	Cessna 525A CitationJet CJ2	525A-0143	
D-ISWA	Cessna 525 CitationJet	525-0236	
D-ISXT	Raytheon 390 Premier	RB-50	N390NS N344W
D-ITAN	Cessna 525 CitationJet CJ	525-0399	(VP-CTN) N5135A
D-ITLL	Beech F90 King Air	LA 192	N17TS N6331Q
D-ITMS	Beech E50 Twin Bonanza	EH-56	N211EL A-711 HB-HOU
D-ITOL	Cessna T303 Crusader	T30300048	G-BTDJ I-BELT N377CB (N377GS) N377CB N9839T
D-ITOP	Beech C90A King Air	LJ-1606	N4206U

D-ITPV	Piaggio P.180 Avanti	1012	N180TE
D-ITSV	Cessna 525 CitationJet	525-0084	
D-ITTT(2)	Cessna 421C Golden Eagle	421C0803	HB-LQD N4266P N805WW N26561
D-IUAC	Cessna 525A CitationJet CJ2	525A-0106	N5148B
D-IUDE	Beech C90A King Air	LJ-1323	N90KA
D-IURS	Cessna 525 CitationJet	525-0343	N5244F
D-IUSA	Beech B60 Duke	P-565	N3828L
D-IUTA(2)	Rockwell 690C Jetprop 840	11639	HB-LOL N63RB (N5891K)
D-IUTE(2)	Beech B60 Duke	P-593	N593HP XB-EJZ N821BE
D-IUTI	Beech B60 Duke	P-582	N518D
D-IVAN	Beech B200 Super King Air	BB-1662	S5-CEC N3262P
D-IVER	DHC-6-300 Twin Otter	411	SE-IYP LN-FKG CS-TFF LN-FKC C-FHBR HK-2950X C-FHBR
D-IVIP	Beech B200 Super King Air	BB-1672	
D-IWAN(2)	Cessna 525A CitationJet CJ2	525A-0223	N5166T
D-IWHL	Cessna 525 CitationJet	525-0029	N13308
D-IWID	Beech C90A King Air	LJ-1450	N3265K
D-IWIL	Cessna 525 CitationJet	525-0221	
D-IWIR	Cessna 525A CitationJet CJ2	525A-0102	N888KL
D-IWMS	Hispano HA.200 Saeta (Permit)	20/73	EC-FVU EC-648 A10B-67 C10B-67 E14B-67
D-IWSH	Beech B200 Super King Air	BB-1462	N82425
D-IWUT	Cessna 421B Golden Eagle	421B0832	G-BDCS N1931G
D-IWWW(2)	Raytheon 390 Premier	RB-89	N61589
D-IXEB	Cessna 340A	340A0097	N1530G
D-IXIE	Beech F90 King Air	LA-96	N96NA D-IXIE N932G N37390 N3739C
D-IXKJ	Piper PA-60 Aerostar 601P	61P-0607-7963272	D-IASS(2) N606AC G-SILK N8207J
D-IXTT	High Performance Aircraft TT62 Alekto (Permit 2.05)	PT1	
D-IXXX(3)	Piper PA-31T2 Cheyenne IIXL	31T 1166003	D-ICDU N2604R (N68TW) N2604R
D-IZAC	Beech B100 King Air	BE-29	D-IERI N7729B N333NB N888RK N18429
D-IZZI	Cessna 421C Golden Eagle II	421C1256	N398EP (N398EB) N1200K
D-IZZY(2)	Piaggio P.180 Avanti	1034	N680JP I-RAIH
D-I . . .	Beech B300 Super King Air	FL-410	N61740
D-I . . .	Beech B300 Super King Air	FL-322	N3222K
D-I . . .	Beech B60 Duke	P-536	N80WE
D-I . . .	Piper PA-23-250 Aztec E	27-7405378	G-HFTG G-BSOB G-BCJR N54040
D-I . . .	Swearingen SA.226TC Merlin III	TC-252	PH-RAZ OY-AZW D-IBCF OY-AZW N5456M

CLASS K :
Self-Launching and Winch-Launched Powered Gliders

D-KAAA	Sportavia/ Scheibe SF 25B Falke	4851	
D-KAAB	Sportavia/ Scheibe SF 25B Falke	4852	
D-KAAC	Sportavia/ Scheibe SF 25B Falke	4853	
D-KAAE	Sportavia/ Scheibe SF 25B Falke	4855	
D-KAAF	Sportavia/ Scheibe SF 25B Falke	4856	
D-KAAG	Sportavia/ Scheibe SF 25B Falke	4857	
D-KAAH(2)	Glaser-Dirks DG-600M	6-72M23	
D-KAAJ	Sportavia/ Scheibe SF 25B Falke	4860	
D-KAAK	Scheibe SF-25C Falke	4402	
D-KAAL(4)	Sportavia-Pützer RF-5B Sperber	51075	PH-741 D-KAIT
D-KAAO(3)	Sportavia/ Fournier RF-4D	4040	OE-9055 D-KIRO
D-KAAS(2)	Scheibe SF-25C Falke 2000 (Coded 'LBS')	44454	
D-KAAT(3)	Scheibe SF-25B Falke	46257	
D-KAAV	Scheibe SF-25B Falke	46220	
D-KAAW	Scheibe SF-25C Falke	4406	
D-KAAY(2)	Scheibe SF-25C Falke	4408	
D-KAAZ(2)	Scheibe SF-25C Falke	44249	
D-KABA(3)	Scheibe SF-25C Falke 2000	44311	
D-KABB(2)	Grob G.102 Astir CS/TOP	1024	D-5873
D-KABE	Scheibe SF-24A/KM29	4002	
D-KABF(2)	HOAC HK-36R Super Dimona	36321	OE-9371
D-KABG(2)	Sportavia/ Fournier RF-5	5072	
D-KABH	Sportavia/ Fournier RF-4D	4152	
D-KABI (2)	Sportavia/ Fournier RF-5	5083	HB-2012
D-KABK(2)	Glaser-Dirks DG-400	4-254	
D-KABL(3)	Scheibe SF-25C Falke 2000	44505	
D-KABM	Scheibe SFS-31 Milan	6603	
D-KABO(2)	Schempp-Hirth Janus CM	10	
D-KABR(2)	Scheibe SF-25C Falke 2000	44444	
D-KABS(3)	Schleicher ASW 28-18E (Permit 7.04)	28714	
D-KABU(2)	Scheibe SF-25C Falke	44128	(D-KLDE)
D-KABW	Scheibe SF-25B Falke	46123	
D-KABX	Scheibe SF-25D Falke	46124D	
D-KABY(2)	Schleicher ASW 22BLE	22044	
D-KACB(2)	Schempp-Hirth Duo Discus T	87/401	D-KLSA
D-KACC	Scheibe SF-25B Falke	4660	
D-KACD	Scheibe SF-25B Falke	4662	
D-KACE(2)	Schempp-Hirth Ventus 2cM	113	
D-KACF	Scheibe SF-25B Falke	4663	
D-KACH(4)	Scheibe SF-25C Falke	44213	OE-9137 D-KDFU(1)
D-KACI	Blessing Raab Krähe III V-6 (Quoted c/n is that of the builder - Raab c/n is 8)	5	
D-KACJ(3)	Scheibe SF-25C Rotax-Falke	44604	
D-KACK(2)	Scheibe SF-25C Rotax-Falke	44664	
D-KACL(2)	HOAC HK-36TTS Super Dimona (Res 3.00)	36514	OE-9454
D-KACN(2)	Glaser-Dirks DG-500M	5E126M53	
D-KACO(3)	AVO 68v Samburo	008	OE-9118
D-KACP(3)	Nitsche AVO 68-R115 Samburo	006	
D-KACS(2)	Scheibe SF-28A Tandem-Falke	5766	
D-KACW(2)	Aerotechnik L-13SL Vivat	930506	
D-KADA(2)	Hoffmann H-36 Dimona	36231	
D-KADC	Scheibe SF-25B Falke	46127	
D-KADF	Scheibe SF-25D Falke	46129D	
D-KADG(6)	Glaser-Dirks DG-800	8-2A2	
D-KADH	Scheibe SF-25B Falke	46131	
D-KADI (4)	Glaser-Dirks DG-400	4-28	(F-WFVA)
D-KADK	Scheibe SF-25B Falke	46133	
D-KADL	Scheibe SF-25B Falke	46134	
D-KADM(2)	Schempp-Hirth Ventus-2cT (Permit 5.04)	123	
D-KADO(4)	Schempp-Hirth Ventus 2cM	36/64	
D-KADP	Schempp-Hirth Ventus-2cM (Permit 5.04)	143	
D-KADR(2)	Schempp-Hirth Duo Discus T	53/338	
D-KADS	Schempp-Hirth Nimbus 3T	11/68	HB-2144 D-KHIH
D-KADT	Technoflug Piccolo	007	
D-KADU(2)	Scheibe SF-25C Falke	44193	
D-KADW	HOAC HK-36TTC Super Dimona	36537	
D-KADY(3)	Technoflug Piccolo B	083	
D-KAEB(2)	Schempp-Hirth Discus bT	153/547	
D-KAEC(2)	Schleicher ASH 26E	26177	
D-KAED	Sportavia/ Scheibe SF 25B Falke	4865	
D-KAEE	Sportavia/ Scheibe SF 25D Falke	4866D	(D-KAOA)
D-KAEI	Doppelraab VII M (ACOG 1)	1	(D-KAMG) D-1577
D-KAEJ(2)	Glaser-Dirks DG-400	4-171	
D-KAEK	Scheibe SFS-31 Milan	6610	
D-KAEL(2)	LET L-13M Blanik	026055	D-3720
D-KAER	Scheibe SF-25C Falke	46229C	
D-KAES	Scheibe SF-25C Falke	4410	
D-KAET	Scheibe SF-25C Falke	4411	
D-KAEX	Scheibe SF-25C Falke	46231C	
D-KAEZ	Scheibe SF-25C Falke 2000 (Permit 7.04)	46233C	
D-KAFB(2)	Scheibe SF 25C Falke	44698	
D-KAFF	Technoflug Piccolo B	111	
D-KAFG-PV	Schempp-Hirth Standard Cirrus B/TOP	681	D-2285
D-KAFI (3)	Brditschka AVO-68R Samburo	018	D-KEGN OE-9152
D-KAFL(2)	Schempp-Hirth Discus-2T	38	
D-KAFM	Hoffmann H-36 Dimona	3693	
D-KAFO(2)	Sportavia/ Fournier RF-5	5090	
D-KAFR	Glaser-Dirks DG-400	4-105	(ZK-GPL)
D-KAFU(2)	Sportavia/ Fournier RF-5	5091	
D-KAFV	Grob G.102 Astir CS77/TOP	1656	D-4824
D-KAFW	Hoffmann H-36 Dimona	3632	
D-KAFZ	Schleicher ASH 26E	26080	
D-KAGA(2)	Scheibe SF-25C Rotax-Falke	44632	
D-KAGB(3)	Scheibe SF 25C Falke	44700	
D-KAGC	Scheibe SF-25C Rotax-Falke	44646	
D-KAGD	Schleicher ASH 26E	26100	
D-KAGE	Scheibe SF-25A Motorfalke	4508	(D-KAME)
D-KAGF	Scheibe SF-25C Rotax-Falke	44658	
D-KAGG	Scheibe SF-25C Falke	44670	
D-KAGH	Grob G.102 Astir CS Jeans/TOP	2213	D-3827

D-KAGI	Scheibe SF-25A Motorfalke	4509	
D-KAGJ(2)	Scheibe SF-25C Falke	44678	
D-KAGK(2)	Scheibe SF 25C Falke	44689	
D-KAGL(2)	Hoffmann HK-36R Super Dimona	36332	
D-KAGM(3)	Schleicher ASH 26E	26219	
D-KAGO(4)	Hoffmann H-36 Dimona	3617	
D-KAGQ	Scheibe SF-25B Falke	46183	
D-KAGR	Scheibe SF-25C Falke	46184	
D-KAGS(2)	Schleicher ASH 26E	26089	
D-KAGU(2)	Schempp-Hirth Discus 2T	25/163	
D-KAGV	Schempp-Hirth Ventus cM	29/462	
D-KAGW	Schleicher ASW 20L/TOP	20242	D-3182
D-KAGY(2)	Schleicher ASH 25E (Code: GY)	25112	
D-KAHB(2)	Grob G.109B	6378	
D-KAHC	Sportavia/ Fournier RF-5	5018	
D-KAHD	Sportavia/ Fournier RF-5	5020	
D-KAHF(2)	Schempp-Hirth Discus bM	4/447	
D-KAHG(3)	Schempp-Hirth Nimbus 4DM	17/26	
D-KAHN	Sportavia/ Scheibe SF 25B Falke	4807	
D-KAHQ	Sportavia/ Scheibe SF 25B Falke	4809	
D-KAHR	Sportavia/ Scheibe SF 25B Falke	4810	
D-KAHS	Schleicher ASW 20/TOP	20247	D-3376
D-KAHT	Technoflug Piccolo B	092	
D-KAHW	Schempp-Hirth Ventus cM	34/466	
D-KAIA(2)	Technoflug Piccolo	011	5H-MTF D-KAIA(2)
D-KAID(2)	Hoffmann H-36 Dimona	3687	
D-KAIG	Sportavia/ Fournier RF-4D	4157	(PT-DVX)
D-KAIH	Sportavia/ Scheibe SF-25C Falke	4206	
D-KAII	Sportavia/ Scheibe SF-25C Falke	4207	
D-KAIN(2)	Scheibe SF-25C Falke	44270	
D-KAIR	Glaser-Dirks DG-400	4-60	G-BLAB
D-KAIT(2)	Hoffmann H-36 Dimona	3648	OE-9211
D-KAIX(3)	Schempp-Hirth Nimbus-4DM	8/16	N142AB D-KHIA
D-KAIZ	Glaser-Dirks DG-400	4-44	
D-KAJA(3)	Schleicher ASH 26E	26134	
D-KAJB(2)	Glaser-Dirks DG-400 (Reservation)	4-35	
D-KAJC	Sportavia/ Scheibe SF-25C Falke	4241	
D-KAJE(2)	Sportavia/ Scheibe SF-25C Falke	4243	
D-KAJH(2)	Glaser-Dirks DG-400	4-232	
D-KAJK(2)	Glaser-Dirks DG-400	4-158	
D-KAJM(2)	Lange E1 Antares (Permit 12.04)	08	
D-KAJO(2)	Glaser-Dirks DG-400	4-241	I-CAJO
D-KAJP	Valentin Taifun 17E-II	1135	
D-KAJR	Schempp-Hirth Ventus cT	113/384	
D-KAJS-S6	Schleicher ASH 25E	25068	
D-KAJU(2)	Grob G.109B	6261	
D-KAJW	Schempp-Hirth Discus bT	116/470	
D-KAKE	Scheibe SF-25A Motorfalke	4525	
D-KAKG	Schleicher ASW 24E	24856	
D-KAKI	Scheibe SF-25A Motorfalke	4533	
D-KAKK	Grob G.109B	6327	
D-KAKO(4)	Schleicher ASH 25M	25166	D-2715
D-KAKU	Scheibe SF-25A Motorfalke	4536	
D-KALA(2)	Scheibe SF-25B Falke	46209	OE-9201 OE-9156 D-KFVN (D-KASE)
D-KALB(2)	Sportavia/ Fournier RF-4D	4146	
D-KALC	Sportavia/ Fournier RF-4D	4102	
D-KALD(2)	Hoffmann HK-36R Super Dimona	36311	
D-KALE(3)	Schempp-Hirth Ventus 2cM	108/223	
D-KALF(2)	LF-820E (Permit 10.99)	1	
D-KALG	Sportavia/ Fournier RF-4D	4108	
D-KALH(2)	Schleicher ASH 26E	26047	OO-LAU
D-KALI(2)	Schempp-Hirth Ventus-2cM	140	
D-KALJ(2)	Scheibe SF-25B Falke	4632	
D-KALL(2)	Scheibe SF-25B Falke	4634	
D-KALM(2)	Scheibe SF-25B Falke	4644	
D-KALN	Scheibe SF-25B Falke	4637	
D-KALO(2)	AVO 68v Samburo	029	
D-KALP	Doppelraab IV/V-M	1021/542	D-4688
D-KALR	Ruppert Rhönlerche II (Constructed from Rhönlerche II c/n 3026 ex.D-5301)	01	
D-KALT-LT	Schempp-Hirth Nimbus 3DT	22	
D-KALZ	Schempp-Hirth Ventus 2cM	10/27	
D-KAMA	Scheibe SF-25A Motorfalke	4527	
D-KAMB(2)	Grob G.109/2400	6010	
D-KAMF	Schleicher ASW 28-18E (Permit 9.04)	28720	
D-KAMG(2)	Scheibe SF-27M-A	6319	OE-9034 D-KECJ(2)
D-KAMI (2)	Hoffmann H-36 Dimona II	36259	OE-9300
D-KAMK	Sportavia-Pützer RF-5B Sperber	51056	N55JH D-KEAK
D-KAML(2)	Glaser-Dirks DG-400	4-186	
D-KAMM	Scheibe SF-25C Falke	44205	(D-KDFI)
D-KAMN	Scheibe SF-25C Rotax-Falke	44519	
D-KAMO(2)	Scheibe SF-25C Rotax-Falke	44621	
D-KAMR	Schempp-Hirth Discus bT	42/355	
D-KAMS(2)	Technoflug Carat	CA004	
D-KAMT	Aeromot AMT-200 Super Ximango	200-060	
D-KAMU(2)	Grob G.109/2400	6138	
D-KAMV	Grob G.103C Twin IIISL	35026	
D-KAMW	Glaser-Dirks DG-500M	5E15M9	
D-KAMX	Grob G.103C Twin IIISL	35034	
D-KAMY(3)	Scheibe SF-25C Rotax-Falke	44547	

D-KANA(3)	Eiriavion PIK-20E	20204	OY-XJN (OH-554)
D-KANC(3)	Grob G.109	6039	
D-KAND(2)	DG Flugzeugbau DG-800LA	8-25A22	
D-KANE	Scheibe SF-27M-B	6330	
D-KANF(2)	Technoflug Piccolo	014	
D-KANI	Scheibe SF-25A Motorfalke	4543	
D-KANN	Scheibe SF-27M-A (Reservation 6.99)	6306	G-AWSX D-KIMK
D-KANO(4)	Hoffmann H-36 Dimona	3622	
D-KANT(2)	Sportavia/ Fournier RF-4D	4086	F-BOXO
D-KANU(2)	Schleicher ASK 16	16023	
D-KAOC	Sportavia/ Scheibe SF 25B Falke	4868	
D-KAOD(2)	Sportavia/ Scheibe SF-25C Falke	4229	
D-KAOE(2)	Sportavia/ Scheibe SF-25C Falke	4230	
D-KAOH	Sportavia/ Scheibe SF-25C Falke 2000	4203	
D-KAOL(2)	Schempp-Hirth Nimbus-4M	17/41	
D-KAOO	Scheibe SF-25C Falke	4419	
D-KAOR	Scheibe SF-25B Falke	AB.46306	
D-KAOS	Scheibe SF-28A Tandem-Falke	5703	
D-KAOT(2)	Alpavia/ Fournier RF-3	22	OE-9155 D-KEHL F-BMDC
D-KAOU	Sportavia/ Scheibe SF-25C Falke	4234	
D-KAOX	Sportavia/ Scheibe SF-25C Falke	4239	
D-KAPA(2)	Sportavia/ Fournier RF-4D	4052	C-FAZO CF-AZO N2187 D-KAQE
D-KAPC	Scheibe SF-25B Falke	4667	
D-KAPG(2)	Hoffmann HK-36R Super Dimona	36389	
D-KAPI (2)	Grob G.109/2400	6072	(VH- . . .)
D-KAPL	Schleicher ASH 26E	26205	
D-KAPM	Schempp-Hirth Ventus cT	164/535	
D-KAPP	Sportavia/ Scheibe SF-25C Falke	4252	
D-KAPR	Glaser-Dirks DG-400	4-228	
D-KAPS(2)	DG Flugzeugbau DG-800LA	8-62A37	
D-KAPT	Sportavia/ Fournier RF-4D	4083	PH-DYL OO-WAD
D-KAPV	Schempp-Hirth Ventus 2cM	72/148	
D-KAPW	Lange E1 Antares	12	
D-KAQA	Sportavia/ Fournier RF-4D	4038	
D-KAQI	Sportavia/ Fournier RF-4D	4053	
D-KAQY(2)	Schleicher ASK 14	14022	HB-2002
D-KARA(4)	Scheibe SF-25C Rotax-Falke	44607	
D-KARE	Scheibe SF-25A Motorfalke	4556	
D-KARF	Scheibe SF-25C Falke 2000	44268	
D-KARG	Hoffmann H-36 Dimona	36104	
D-KARH	Schempp-Hirth Ventus bT	13/148	D-KADR
D-KARJ	AVO-68S Samburo	012	HB-2039 OE-9140 OE-9117
D-KARK	Grob G.109B	6243	LN-GMS
D-KARL(2)	Sportavia/ Fournier RF-4D	4155	
D-KARP	Grob G.109	6146	OY-XMP
D-KARR(2)	Schempp-Hirth Discus bT	91/429	
D-KARS	ICA/Brasov I S.28M2/G	69	
D-KART	Scheibe SF-25A Motorfalke (Rotax engine conversion)	4523	OE-9019 (D-KAJU)
D-KARU	Scheibe SF-25D Falke	4608D	
D-KARW	Glaser-Dirks DG-400	4-53	
D-KARZ	Glaser-Dirks DG-400	4-26	
D-KASA	Scheibe SF-25B Falke	46186	
D-KASC(3)	Schempp-Hirth Ventus 2cM	155/. . .	
D-KASD(3)	Hoffmann HK-36R Super Dimona	36387	
D-KASE(4)	Schempp-Hirth Ventus cT	90/337	
D-KASH(2)	Scheibe SF-25C Falke 2000	44411	
D-KASI	Scheibe SF-25B Falke	46194	
D-KASK	Scheibe SF-25B Falke	46196	
D-KASL	Scheibe SF-25B Falke	46197	
D-KASM	Scheibe SF-25B Falke	46198	
D-KASO	Scheibe SF-25B Falke	46200	
D-KASP(2)	Scheibe SF-25C Rotax-Falke	44539	
D-KASR	Scheibe SF-25C Falke 2000	46203C	
D-KAST(2)	Scheibe SF-25C Falke	46213C	
D-KASU(2)	Scheibe SF-25B Falke	46224	
D-KASV	Scheibe SF-25D Falke	46215D	
D-KASW(2)	Schleicher ASH 26E	26172	
D-KASX(2)	Schempp-Hirth Standard Cirrus B/TOP	685	D-6602
D-KASY(2)	Scheibe SF-25B Falke	46230	
D-KASZ	Scheibe SF-25C Falke	44395	
D-KATC	Scheibe SF-25B Falke	4674	
D-KATD(2)	Technoflug Piccolo	009	
D-KATE(2)	Technoflug Piccolo B	091	
D-KATF	Sportavia/ Fournier RF-5	5050	
D-KATG	Glaser-Dirks DG-500M	5E90M38	(D-KCGM)
D-KATH	Technoflug Piccolo	017	
D-KATI (2)	Sportavia/ Fournier RF-5	5016	
D-KATL(2)	Grob G.103C Twin IIISL	35005	
D-KATM(2)	Sportavia-Pützer RF-5B Sperber	51077	(VH-. . .)
D-KATO	Sportavia/ Fournier RF-5	5093	
D-KATP	Schleicher ASH 26E	26032	
D-KATS	Glaser-Dirks DG-400	4-22	
D-KATT	Technoflug Piccolo	006	
D-KATW	Grob G.109B	6313	G-BLMY
D-KATX	Diamond HK 36 TTC Super Dimona (Permit 3.04)	36533	N533TT C-GHUV OE-9433

D-KATY(2)	Scheibe SF-25C Falke 2000	4446	OE-9084 D-KDAF
D-KATZ(2)	Sportavia/ Fournier RF-5	5122	
D-KAUB(2)	AVO 68s Samburo 2000	010	OE-9119
D-KAUC	Hoffmann H-36 Dimona	36256	
D-KAUF(2)	Grob G.109B	6287	
D-KAUH	Schempp-Hirth Ventus cT	155/502	
D-KAUP	Sportavia/ Fournier RF-5	5118	
D-KAUW	Glaser-Dirks DG-600/18M	6-70M17	
D-KAUZ	Scheibe SF-25C Falke	4455	(D-KOAB)
D-KAVA	Scheibe SF-25B Falke	46241	
D-KAVC	Scheibe SF-25C Falke	46243C	
D-KAVF(2)	DG Flugzeugbau DG-800B	8-107B41	
D-KAVH	Scheibe SF-25B Falke	46248	
D-KAVI (2)	Böcker Doppelraab V (Bömora)	AB-03	
D-KAVL	Scheibe SF-25C Falke	4422	
D-KAVO(2)	Schleicher ASH 26E	26203	
D-KAVR	Schleicher ASK 16	16009	
D-KAVS	Schleicher ASK 16	16010	
D-KAVT	Schleicher ASK 16	16011	
D-KAVU	Schleicher ASK 16	16003	
D-KAVV	Lo 170-2M	V-1	D-0117
D-KAWA(2)	Scheibe SF-25C Falke	44650	
D-KAWB(2)	Schleicher ASH 26E	26003	D-6161
D-KAWC(2)	Scheibe SF-25E Super-Falke (Reservation 12.99)	4307	OE-9163 D-KMTF (D-KDDB)
D-KAWD	Sportavia/ Scheibe SF-25C Falke	4215	
D-KAWE(2)	Schempp-Hirth Ventus bT	8/133	
D-KAWG	Hoffmann H-36 Dimona	3520	
D-KAWI	Grob G.109B	6343	
D-KAWJ-8F	Glaser-Dirks DG-800	8-21A18	
D-KAWL	Scheibe SF-25B Falke	AB.46304	
D-KAWN	Schleicher ASW 20L/TOP	20258	D-7647
D-KAWO	Hoffmann H-36 Dimona	3698	
D-KAWR	Technoflug Piccolo B	079	
D-KAWS	Hoffmann HK-36R Super Dimona	36336	
D-KAWT	Grob G.109B	6254	
D-KAWW	Schempp-Hirth Nimbus 4T	19	
D-KAXA	Schleicher ASK 16	16032	
D-KAXC	Schleicher ASK 16	16041	
D-KAXD(2)	Schleicher ASW 24/TOP	24822	
D-KAXE	Schleicher ASK 16	16044	
D-KAXG(2)	Scheibe SF-25C Rotax-Falke	44550	
D-KAXI	Schleicher ASW 24E	24823	
D-KAXK	Schleicher ASW 24E	24817	
D-KAXL-M4	Schleicher ASH 25E	25109	
D-KAXN	Schleicher ASW 22BE	22052	D-4942
D-KAXP	Schleicher ASW 24E	24842	
D-KAXQ	Schleicher ASW 24/TOP	24847	
D-KAXR	Schleicher ASW 24E	24849	
D-KAXU	Schleicher ASH 25E	25142	
D-KAXV	Schleicher ASW 24E	24855	
D-KAXW	Schleicher ASW 22BE	22066	
D-KAXX	Schleicher ASW 24E	24829	
D-KAXY(2)	Schleicher ASW 22BLE	22062	
D-KAYC	Technoflug Piccolo B	121	
D-KAYV	Schempp-Hirth Ventus bT	16/154	
D-KAYX	HOAC HK-36TTC Super Dimona	36692	
D-KAYY(2)	Schempp-Hirth Ventus 2cM	21/39	
D-KAZE(3)	HOAC HK-36TTC Super Dimona	36695	
D-KAZF	SZD-41AT Jantar Standard Turbo	B-749	D-4200
D-KAZT	Stemme S-10VT	11-040	
D-KAZW	Aerotechnik L-13SL Vivat	930514	
D-KAZX-ZX	Glaser-Dirks DG-400	4-9	D-KAML
D-KBAA	Schempp-Hirth Nimbus 4M	6/22	
D-KBAB	Scheibe SF-25B Falke	4676	
D-KBAC(2)	Sportavia-Pützer RF-5B Sperber	51009	OO-PLB PL-70 D-KAUA
D-KBAF	Scheibe SF-25B Falke	4680	
D-KBAI	Scheibe SF-25B Falke	4683	
D-KBAJ(2)	Schleicher ASH 26E	26152	
D-KBAK(2)	Hoffmann H-36 Dimona	3501	OE-9199
D-KBAM	Sportavia/ Fournier RF-5	5063	
D-KBAN	Sportavia/ Fournier RF-5	5064	
D-KBAP	Sportavia/ Scheibe SF 25B Falke	4802	
D-KBAR	Scheibe SF-25D Falke	4804D	
D-KBAS(2)	Glaser-Dirks DG-400	4-62	PH-1227 D-KBWB
D-KBAU(2)	Schleicher ASH 26E	26130	
D-KBAZ	Scheibe SF-25D Falke	4818D	
D-KBBA	Schleicher ASH 25E	25077	
D-KBBB	Grob G.109B	6301	
D-KBBF(2)	Stemme S 10-VT	11-085	
D-KBBO	Schleicher ASW 22M	22041M	OY-XOI D-KBBO OY-XOI D-KBBO
D-KBBS	Hoffmann HK-36R Super Dimona	36306	
D-KBBT	Schempp-Hirth Ventus bT	1/96	
D-KBBU	HOAC HK-36TTC Super Dimona	36534	OE-9434
D-KBBW	Grob G.109B	6337	
D-KBBY-CM	Schleicher ASW 22M	22023M	
D-KBCA	Scheibe SF-25C Falke 2000	44410	
D-KBCB	Scheibe SF-25C Falke 2000	44579	
D-KBCC	Schempp-Hirth Ventus cT	105/367	

D-KBCD(2)	Scheibe SF 25C Falke	44702	
D-KBCE	Technoflug Piccolo	034	
D-KBCF	Scheibe SF-25C Falke 2000	44556	
D-KBCG	Scheibe SF-25C Falke 2000	44524	
D-KBCH	Schempp-Hirth Ventus cM	26/459	
D-KBCK	Scheibe SF-25C Falke	44686	
D-KBCM	Scheibe SF-25C Falke 2000	44603	
D-KBCN	Scheibe SF-25C Falke 2000	44633	
D-KBCP	Valentin Taifun 17E II	1109	
D-KBCR	Valentin Taifun 17E	1021	
D-KBCS	Schempp-Hirth Ventus 2cM	76/159	
D-KBCW	Glaser-Dirks DG-600/18M	6-73M21	
D-KBDA	Sportavia/ Fournier RF-4D	4158	
D-KBDB-KR	Glaser-Dirks DG-600/18M	6-87M33	
D-KBDC	Glaser-Dirks DG-600/18M	6-62M13	
D-KBDF	Hoffmann HK-36R Super Dimona	36397	
D-KBDP	Schleicher ASH 26E	26147	
D-KBDS	Technoflug Piccolo B	071	
D-KBDV	Schempp-Hirth Ventus cM	110/611	
D-KBEB(3)	Schleicher ASH 26E	26208	
D-KBEE	Schleicher ASW 22M	22028M	
D-KBEJ	Schleicher ASH 26E	26126	
D-KBEK(2)	HOAC HK-36TTC Super Dimona	36696	
D-KBEL	Technoflug Piccolo B	087	
D-KBEM	Glaser-Dirks DG-400	4-175	
D-KBER	Grob G.109	6058	
D-KBEW	Schempp-Hirth Discus bT	107/454	
D-KBFD-FD	Schleicher ASH 25Mi	25173	D-1724
D-KBFF	HOAC HK-36TS Super Dimona	36416	OE-9416
D-KBFG	Schempp-Hirth Nimbus 3DT	43	
D-KBFH	Schleicher ASH 25E	25059	
D-KBFO	Schempp-Hirth Nimbus 4T	15	
D-KBFR	Grob G.109B	6334	
D-KBFU-FU	Schleicher ASH 25E	25168	
D-KBFW	AVO 68v Samburo 2000	007	OE-9120
D-KBFX	Schempp-Hirth Ventus cT	94/345	RAFGSA16
D-KBGG	Schempp-Hirth Nimbus 3DM	21/49	OY-XTU
D-KBGM	Valentin Taifun 17E	1023	
D-KBGN	Grob G.109B	6209	
D-KBGR	Scheibe SF-25C Falke 2000	44363	
D-KBGV	Schempp-Hirth Discus bT	47/363	
D-KBHD	Schleicher ASW 22BLE	22058	
D-KBHE	Schleicher ASH 26E	26112	
D-KBHF	Schleicher ASH 26E	26029	
D-KBHG	Schempp-Hirth Ventus cM	13/437	
D-KBHH-S	Schempp-Hirth Ventus cT	115/386	D-5888
D-KBHI	Aerotechnik L-13SEH Vivat	940516	D-KOLB
D-KBHJ	Valentin Taifun 17E	1062	
D-KBHK(2)	Schempp-Hirth Discus bT	21/311	
D-KBHL	Glaser-Dirks DG-400	4-182	
D-KBHR	Schempp-Hirth Ventus cM	51/495	PH-1044 D-KBFL(1)
D-KBHS	Schleicher ASW 22BE	22061	
D-KBHW	Schleicher ASW 20/TOP	20006	D-7552
D-KBIA	Scheibe SF-25B Falke	46156	
D-KBIC	Scheibe SF-25B Falke	46158	
D-KBIE	Scheibe SF-25D Falke	46160D	
D-KBIG	Scheibe SF-25D Falke	46162D	
D-KBIH	Scheibe SF-25B Falke	46163	
D-KBII (2)	Schempp-Hirth Ventus cM	3/403	
D-KBIK	Scheibe SF-25C Falke	4401	
D-KBIL	Scheibe SF-25B Falke	46166	
D-KBIM	Scheibe SF-25B Falke	46167	
D-KBIO(2)	Glaser-Dirks DG-500M	5E51M23	OY-XTW
D-KBIP	Scheibe SF-25B Falke	46170	
D-KBIQ	Scheibe SF-25B Falke	46171	
D-KBIT(2)	Sportavia/ Fournier RF-5	5046	
D-KBIU	Scheibe SF-25D Falke	46174D	
D-KBIV(2)	Schempp-Hirth Duo Discus T	107/43	
D-KBIX(2)	Schempp-Hirth Ventus cM	88/571	
D-KBJF	Schempp-Hirth Ventus cT	178/583	
D-KBJL	Schleicher ASW 22BLE	22065	
D-KBJM	Schleicher ASW 28-18E (Permit 7.04)	28716	
D-KBJP	Schempp-Hirth Ventus-2cxT	132	
D-KBKA	Schempp-Hirth Discus bT	49/366	
D-KBKB	Hoffmann HK-36R Super Dimona	36323	
D-KBKD	Schempp-Hirth Discus bT	162/570	
D-KBKJ	Schleicher ASH 26E	26067	
D-KBKL-NX	Schleicher ASH 25EB	25190	
D-KBKM	Schleicher ASH 26E	26087	
D-KBLA	Schleicher ASK 16	16031	
D-KBLB	Valentin Taifun 17E	1104	
D-KBLF-LF	Lange E1 Antares (Reservation .05)	unkn	
D-KBLI	Schempp-Hirth Ventus cT	85/330	
D-KBLL	Glaser-Dirks DG-600/18M	6-105M47	HB-2216
D-KBLN	HOAC HK-36TTC Super Dimona	36601	
D-KBLO	Grob G.109B	6572	
D-KBLS	HOAC HK-36TTC Super Dimona	36553	
D-KBLW	Glaser-Dirks DG-600/18M	6-53M7	D-5807
D-KBMC	DG Flugzeugbau DG-505MB	5E241MB18	
D-KBMH	Hoffmann H-36 Dimona	36232	OE-9276
D-KBML	Schleicher ASH 26E	26013	D-0962 (D-KWML(1)) D-0962
D-KBMR	Schleicher ASH 25Mi (Permit 3.01)	25224	
D-KBMS	DG Flugzeugbau DG-800B	8-267B175	
D-KBNA	Grob G.109B	6441	

D-KBNG	Schleicher ASH 25M	25098M	OE-9347
D-KBNO	Glaser-Dirks DG-500M	5E68M29	
D-KBNT	Schempp-Hirth Ventus cT	122/396	
D-KBOB	Hoffmann H-36 Dimona	3620	
D-KBOE	Hoffmann H-36 Dimona	3628	
D-KBON	HOAC HK-36TC Super Dimona	36521	
D-KBOV	Schleicher ASW 24E	24825	
D-KBOX	IAR IS-28M2/GR	79	D-KUNT
			YR-2511
D-KBOY	Technoflug Piccolo B	066	
D-KBPB	Glaser-Dirks DG-400	4-265	
D-KBPC	Schleicher ASH 25M	25200	(OO-WZW)
D-KBPK	Hoffmann HK-36R Super Dimona	36391	
D-KBPM(2)	Schleicher ASW 28-18E (Permit 5.04)	28711	
D-KBPP	Schempp-Hirth Ventus-2cM (Permit 3.04)	141	
D-KBPT	Schleicher ASH 25M	25184	
D-KBPV	Eiriavion PIK-20E	20209	
D-KBRD	Schempp-Hirth Discus bT	103/445	
D-KBRE	Stemme S-10	10-3	
D-KBRU	Grob G.109B	6575	
D-KBSA	DG Flugzeugbau DG-800B (Permit 4.01)	8-205B127	
D-KBSD	DG Flugzeugbau DG-800LA	8-16A13	
D-KBSH	HOAC HK-36TS Super Dimona	36651	
D-KBSL	Schempp-Hirth Ventus-2cM	103/215	OY-SXL
D-KBSM	Scheibe SF-25B Falke	46105	D-KECS
D-KBSR	Schleicher ASH 26E	26114	
D-KBSX	Schempp-Hirth Ventus cM	108/607	
D-KBTB	Schempp-Hirth Nimbus 4DM	26/37	
D-KBTL	Schempp-Hirth Ventus 2cM	120/258	
D-KBTR	Glaser-Dirks DG-500M	5E6M4	F-CHJA
			D-KGBE
D-KBTS	Schempp-Hirth Discus bM	5/456	
D-KBTT	Hoffmann HK-36R Super Dimona	36357	OE-9375
D-KBTW	Schempp-Hirth Ventus-2cM (Permit 7.04)	146	
D-KBUA	Scheibe SF-25C Falke 2000	44478	
D-KBUB	Scheibe SF-25C Falke 2000	44462	
D-KBUC	Scheibe SF-25C Falke 2000	44476	
D-KBUD	Scheibe SF-25C Falke 2000	44517	
D-KBUE	Scheibe SF-25C Rotax-Falke	44545	
D-KBUF	Scheibe SF-25C Rotax-Falke	44557	
	(Tricycle u/c modification)		
D-KBUG	Scheibe SF-25C Falke 2000	44420	
D-KBUH	Scheibe SF-25C Rotax-Falke	44640	
D-KBUI	Scheibe SF-25C Falke 2000	44490	
D-KBUK	Scheibe SF-25C Rotax-Falke	44587	
D-KBUL	Scheibe SF-25C Rotax-Falke	44611	
D-KBUM	Scheibe SF-25C Rotax-Falke	44558	
D-KBUN	Scheibe SF-25C Rotax-Falke	44657	
D-KBUO	Scheibe SF-25C Rotax-Falke	44642	
D-KBUP	Scheibe SF-25C Rotax-Falke	44586	
D-KBUQ	Scheibe SF-25C Rotax-Falke	44625	
D-KBUR	Scheibe SF-25C Rotax-Falke	44631	
D-KBUS(2)	Scheibe SF-25C Rotax-Falke	44622	
D-KBUT	Scheibe SF-25C Rotax-Falke	44565	
D-KBUU	Scheibe SF-25C Rotax-Falke	44651	
D-KBUV	Scheibe SF-25C Rotax-Falke	44623	
D-KBUW	Scheibe SF-25C Rotax-Falke	44627	
D-KBUX	Scheibe SF-25C Rotax-Falke	44626	
D-KBUY	Scheibe SF-25C Rotax-Falke	44669	
D-KBUZ	Scheibe SF-25C Falke 2000	44616	
D-KBVB	Schempp-Hirth Ventus 2cM	39/69	
D-KBVF-VF	DG Flugzeugbau DG-800B	8-191B113	
D-KBVH-VH	Schempp-Hirth Discus bT	125/483	
D-KBWB(2)	DG Flugzeugbau DG-800LA	8-1A1	D-KADG(5)
D-KBWC	Scheibe SF 25C Falke	44704	
D-KBWF	Schleicher ASH 26E (Reservation .05)	26017	D-KRMA
D-KBWG	Schempp-Hirth Ventus cM	35/471	
D-KBWH	Schleicher ASH 25E	25106	
D-KBWK	Schleicher ASH 26E	26075	
D-KBWL	Schempp-Hirth Nimbus 4DM	3/9	
D-KBWM	Schleicher ASW 20L/TOP	20409	OE-9368
			OE-5368
D-KBWS(2)	Schleicher ASH 26E	26051	
D-KBWW	Hoffmann HK-36R Super Dimona	36310	
D-KBXH	Schempp-Hirth Ventus cM	72/537	
D-KBYT	Grob G.109	6025	
D-KBYY	Kickert ETA (Permit 3.05)	05	
D-KCAA(2)	Scheibe SF-25C Rotax-Falke	44620	
D-KCAB	Sportavia/ Scheibe SF 25B Falke	4820	
D-KCAD(2)	Grob G.109B	6418	
D-KCAE(2)	Schempp-Hirth Standard Cirrus/TOP	381	D-9226
D-KCAG	Scheibe SF-25D Falke	46140D	
D-KCAJ(2)	Scheibe SF-25B Falke	46207	(D-KASD)
D-KCAK(2)	Schempp-Hirth Ventus 2cM	63/125	
D-KCAM(2)	Schempp-Hirth Discus bT	157/558	HB-2277
D-KCAO	Scheibe SF-25D Falke	46149D	
D-KCAQ	Scheibe SF-25D Falke	46151D	
D-KCAR(2)	HOAC HK-36R Super Dimona	36396	
D-KCAS	Schempp-Hirth Ventus 2cM	94/195	
D-KCAT(2)	Schempp-Hirth Nimbus 4DM	48/65	
D-KCAX	Sportavia-Pützer RF-5B Sperber	51023	
D-KCBB	Eiriavion PIK-20E	20268	
D-KCBC	Schempp-Hirth Ventus cM	27/460	(OE-9340)
D-KCBN	Hoffmann HK-36R Super Dimona	36339	
D-KCBO	Schleicher ASW 24E	24824	
D-KCBP	Schempp-Hirth Discus-2T	37/204	
D-KCBR	Schempp-Hirth Ventus 2cM	101/211	OO-HVD

D-KCBS-BS	DG Flugzeugbau DG-800B	8-264B172	
D-KCBT	Hoffmann H-36 Dimona	3635	
D-KCCA	Hoffmann H-36 Dimona	3606	
D-KCCB	Valentin Taifun 17E	1028	
D-KCCC	Hoffmann H-36 Dimona	36262	OE-9305
D-KCCH(2)	Schleicher ASH 26E	26060	
D-KCCN	Schleicher ASH 26E	26144	
D-KCCO	HOAC HK-36TTC Super Dimona	36563	
D-KCCP	Hoffmann H-36 Dimona	3521	
D-KCCW	HOAC HK-36TTC Super Dimona	36688	
D-KCDB	Schleicher ASW 28-18E (Permit 9.04)	28719	
D-KCEE	Schempp-Hirth Ventus cM	42/481	
D-KCEF	Glaser-Dirks DG-500M	5E40M18	LX-CPF
D-KCEH-B9	Schempp-Hirth Discus bT	36/347	
D-KCEK	Schempp-Hirth Ventus bT	24/182	
D-KCEL	Schempp-Hirth Discus bT	45/359	
D-KCFB	Technoflug Piccolo	025	
D-KCFD	Technoflug Piccolo	027	
D-KCFE(2)	Schempp-Hirth Duo Discus T	50/332	
D-KCFF	Technoflug Piccolo	029	
D-KCFI	Technoflug Piccolo	032	
D-KCFL	Schempp-Hirth Discus bT	94/433	
D-KCGA-GA	Schempp-Hirth Ventus cM	62/519	
D-KCGB	Stemme S-10	10-13	
D-KCGM(2)	Schempp-Hirth Nimbus 4DM	50/68	
D-KCHA(2)	Schempp-Hirth Nimbus-4DM	56/76	
D-KCHB	Schempp-Hirth Ventus cT	128/402	
D-KCHE	Glaser-Dirks DG-400	4-46	
D-KCHF	Eiriavion PIK-20E	20205	
D-KCHH	Glaser-Dirks DG-400	4-164	
D-KCHJ	Schempp-Hirth Nimbus 4DM	41	
D-KCHL	Schempp-Hirth Ventus cM	54/501	
D-KCHM-HM	Schleicher ASW 22BLE	22073	
D-KCHO	Technoflug Piccolo B	078	
D-KCHS(2)	Schempp-Hirth Ventus 2cT	40/131	
D-KCHT	Hoffmann HK-36R Super Dimona	36341	
D-KCHW	Schempp-Hirth Duo Discus T	99/425	
D-KCIB(2)	Sportavia/ Fournier RF-5	5105	
D-KCID(2)	Sportavia/ Fournier RF-5	5115	
D-KCIE	Sportavia/ Fournier RF-5	5103	
D-KCIF(2)	Glaser-Dirks DG-400	4-213	
D-KCII	Sportavia-Pützer RF-5B Sperber	51008	
D-KCIJ	Sportavia-Pützer RF-5B Sperber	51011	
D-KCIK	Sportavia-Pützer RF-5B Sperber	51003	
D-KCIL(2)	Technoflug Piccolo B	104	
D-KCIN	Sportavia-Pützer RF-5B Sperber	51015	
D-KCJJ	HOAC HK-36TC Super Dimona	36565	OE-9450
D-KCJT-JT	Schempp-Hirth Ventus 2cM	52/106	
D-KCLA	Schleicher ASW 28-18E (Permit 3.04)	28703	
D-KCLB(2)	Schleicher ASW 20CL/TOP	20738	D-3838
D-KCLD	Scheibe SF-28A Tandem-Falke	5774	
D-KCLI	Scheibe SF-28A Tandem-Falke	5779	
D-KCLO	Grob G.109B	6346	
D-KCLS	Technoflug Piccolo	012	
D-KCMH	Schleicher ASH 26E	26024	
D-KCMI	Schempp-Hirth Ventus-2cxM	144	
D-KCML	Lange E1 Antares (Permit 4.04)	04	
D-KCMM-MM	Schempp-Hirth Nimbus 3DM	2/14	
D-KCMO	Schempp-Hirth Ventus-2cxT	131	
D-KCOA	SZD-45A Ogar	B-661	
D-KCOC	SZD-45A Ogar	B-752	
D-KCOD	SZD-45A Ogar	B-754	
D-KCOE	HOAC H-36VT Dimona	36275	OE-9318
D-KCOK	Hoffmann H-36 Dimona	3623	
D-KCOL	AVO 68v Samburo	025R	
D-KCOR(2)	Schleicher ASH 25M	25222	D-1746
D-KCPC	Sportavia/ Fournier RF-5	5124	
D-KCPE(2)	DG Flugzeugbau DG-800B	8-128B57	
D-KCPF(2)	Glaser-Dirks DG-500M	5E32M16	
D-KCPR	Scheibe SF-25C Falke 2000	44512	
D-KCPS	Schempp-Hirth Ventus cM	52/498	
D-KCRA	Grob G.109B	6520	
D-KCRE-RE	Glaser-Dirks DG-400	4-194	
D-KCRH	Schleicher ASH 25M	25245	
D-KCRM	Schempp-Hirth Ventus 2cT	41/134	
D-KCRO	Schempp-Hirth Ventus cT	139/427	
D-KCRT	Schempp-Hirth Janus CT	14/273	
D-KCSA(2)	Aerotechnik L-13SL Vivat	930511	
D-KCSG	Schleicher ASW 24E	24835	
D-KCSW	DG Flugzeugbau DG-800B	8-226B140	
D-KCSX	Schempp-Hirth Ventus 2cM	118/253	
D-KCTA(2)	Hoffmann H-36 Dimona (Permit 2.00)	36103	OO-VIE
			D-KFLG
D-KCTB(2)	Hoffmann H 36 Dimona	36235	PH-896
			F-WGAO
D-KCTF	Technoflug TFK-2 Carat	001	
D-KCTK	Schempp-Hirth Ventus-2cT	107	
D-KCTT	Schempp-Hirth Ventus cM	53/500	
D-KCTO-TO	Glaser-Dirks DG-800B	8-59B8	
D-KCUM	Stemme S-10VT	11-042	
D-KCVH	DG Flugzeugbau DG-808B (Res.05)	8-333B232	
D-KCVV	Scheibe SF 25E Super Falke	4324	OO-CVV
			D-KEFR
D-KCWB	Glaser-Dirks DG-400	4-267	
D-KCWD	Schleicher ASH 26E	26108	
D-KCWE	Schempp-Hirth Discus bT	48/364	
D-KCWH	Schempp-Hirth Janus CM	16/196	D-4109

D-KCWJ	Schempp-Hirth Duo Discus T	102/428	
D-KCWM	Grob G.103C Twin IIISL	35029	
D-KCWS	Schempp-Hirth Discus bT	63/387	
D-KCWW	Schleicher ASH 26E	26104	
D-KCYI	Schleicher ASK 16	16030	G-BCYI
			D-KIWE(1)
D-KDAA	Scheibe SF-25C Falke	4441	(D-KATZ)
D-KDAB	Scheibe SF-25C Falke	4442	
D-KDAC(2)	Scheibe SF-25C Falke 2000	44265	(D-KDBX)
D-KDAD(2)	Scheibe SF-25C Falke	4451	
D-KDAE	Glaser-Dirks DG-400	4-202	F-CGRC
D-KDAG	Scheibe SF-25C Falke	4447	
D-KDAI	Scheibe SF-25C Falke	4449	
D-KDAJ	Scheibe SF-25C Falke	4450	
D-KDAL(3)	Schempp-Hirth Discus-2T	34/191	
D-KDAN(2)	Hoffmann HK-36R Super Dimona	36337	
D-KDAO	Scheibe SF-28A Tandem-Falke	5715	
D-KDAR(2)	Technoflug Piccolo	047	
D-KDAS(2)	Schempp-Hirth Ventus cT	159/513	
D-KDAX	Schleicher ASH 25M	25113	D-5242
D-KDBA	Scheibe SF-25C Falke	44247	
D-KDBC	Scheibe SF-25C Falke	44248	
D-KDBD	Scheibe SF-25E Super-Falke	4343	
D-KDBG(2)	Hoffmann HK-36R Super Dimona	36392	OE-9392
D-KDBI (2)	Scheibe SF-25C Falke	44258	
D-KDBJ	Scheibe SF-25C Falke	44255	
D-KDBK	Scheibe SF-25K Falke	4901	
D-KDBL(2)	Scheibe SF-25C Falke 2000 (ex 1700)	44266	
D-KDBM(2)	Scheibe SF-25C Falke	44271	
D-KDBN(2)	Scheibe SF-25C Falke	44263	
D-KDBO(2)	Scheibe SF-25C Falke	44269	
D-KDBQ(2)	Scheibe SF-25C Falke 2000	44273	
D-KDBR(2)	Scheibe SF-25C Falke	44277	
D-KDBS(2)	Scheibe SF-25E Super-Falke	4347	
D-KDBU(3)	Scheibe SF-25C Falke	44279	
D-KDBV	Scheibe SF-25C Falke	44264	
D-KDBW	Scheibe SF-25C Falke	44261	
D-KDBY(2)	Scheibe SF-25C Falke 2000	44272	
D-KDCB(2)	Rolladen-Schneider LS9 (Permit 4.00)	9007	
D-KDCC(3)	Schempp-Hirth Discus-2cT (Permit 9.04)	1	
D-KDCE(2)	Scheibe SF-25C Falke	44235	
D-KDCG	Scheibe SF-25C Falke 2000	44389	HB-2115
			D-KNIE(2)
D-KDCH	Scheibe SF-25E Super-Falke	4337	
D-KDCJ(2)	Scheibe SF-25C Falke	44239	
D-KDCK(2)	Scheibe SF-25C Falke	44243	
D-KDCN(2)	Scheibe SF-25C Falke	44242	
D-KDCO	Scheibe SF-25C Falke	44237	
D-KDCS	Scheibe SF-25C Falke	44245	
D-KDCT	Scheibe SF-25C Falke	44240	
D-KDDA(2)	Scheibe SF-25E Super-Falke	4311	
D-KDDC	Scheibe SF-25E Super-Falke	4308	
D-KDDD	Scheibe SF-25E Super-Falke	4309	
D-KDDF	Scheibe SF-25C Falke	44131	
D-KDDG	Scheibe SF-25C Falke	44132	
D-KDDK	Scheibe SF-25C Falke	44136	
D-KDDP	Scheibe Bergfalke IVM	5901	
D-KDDT	Schempp-Hirth Duo Discus T	73/375	
D-KDDW	Glaser-Dirks DG-600M	6-91M37	
D-KDEB	Scheibe SF-25C Falke	44144	
D-KDEG	Scheibe SF 25C Falke	44149	
D-KDEH(2)	HOAC HK-36TTC Super Dimona	36664	
D-KDEJ	Scheibe SF-25C Falke	44177	
D-KDEK	Scheibe SF-25C Falke	44180	
D-KDEN	Scheibe SF-25C Falke	44184	
D-KDEO	Scheibe SF-25C Falke	44185	
D-KDET	Scheibe SF-25C Falke	44190	
D-KDEU	Scheibe SF-25C Falke	44194	
D-KDEZ	Scheibe SF-25C Falke	44199	
D-KDFA	Scheibe SF-25C Falke	44200	
D-KDFB(2)	Scheibe SF-25C Falke	44214	
D-KDFC	Scheibe SF-25C Falke	44201	
D-KDFE(2)	Scheibe SF-25C Falke	44211	
D-KDFF(4)	Stemme S-10VT	11-029	
D-KDFG	Scheibe SF-25C Falke	44207	
D-KDFI (2)	Scheibe SF-25C Falke	44217	
D-KDFJ(3)	Scheibe SF-25C Falke	44222	
D-KDFK(2)	Schleicher ASH 26E	26018	
D-KDFL	Scheibe SF-25B Falke	46118	OE-9035
			(D-KABQ)
D-KDFM(2)	Scheibe SF-25C Falke	44218	
D-KDFN(4)	Scheibe SF-25E Super-Falke	4335	
D-KDFS	Scheibe SF-25C Falke	44208	
D-KDFT	Scheibe SF-25C Falke	44216	
D-KDFU(2)	Scheibe SF-25C Falke	44221	
D-KDGB	Scheibe SF-25C Falke 2000	44280	
D-KDGD	Scheibe SF-25C Falke 2000	44284	
D-KDGH(2)	Scheibe SF-25C Falke	44288	
D-KDGI (2)	Scheibe SF-25C Falke	44289	
D-KDGM	Scheibe SF-35	4701	
D-KDGN(2)	Scheibe SF-25C Falke	44293	
D-KDGP(2)	Scheibe SF-25C Falke	44295	
D-KDGT(2)	Scheibe SF-25K Falke	4904	
D-KDGU(3)	Scheibe SF-25C Falke 2000	4356C	
D-KDGW(3)	Scheibe SF-25C Falke 2000	44303	
D-KDGX	Scheibe SF-25K Falke	4906	
D-KDHF	Schempp-Hirth Discus bT	58/380	
D-KDHH-IHH	Schempp-Hirth Ventus cM	50/494	
D-KDHL	Glaser-Dirks DG-600/18M	6-99M45	OO-IVC
D-KDIE	Schempp-Hirth Ventus bT	59/271	
D-KDIM	Hoffmann H-36 Dimona	3601	
D-KDIT	Grob G.109B	6385	
D-KDJG	Schleicher ASH 26E	26138	
D-KDJK	AVO-68R Samburo	028	OE-9165
D-KDJR	Schempp-Hirth Ventus 2cM	65/133	
D-KDKD	Hoffmann HK-36R Super Dimona	36328	
D-KDKR	Diamond HK 36 TTC Super Dimona	36690	
D-KDKW	DG Flugzeugbau DG-800B	8-199B121	VH-XHG
			(D-KIWA(2))
D-KDLA	Grob G.109B (Permit 4.02)	6219	OY-XMG
D-KDLB	Schleicher ASH 26E	26118	
D-KDLS	Technoflug Piccolo B	116	
D-KDMA	Brditschka HB-23/2400SP (Permit)	23042	OE-9325
D-KDMD	DG Flugzeugbau DG-800B	8-224B138	
D-KDMJ	HOAC HK-36TTC Super Dimona	36697	
D-KDMS	Grob G.109	6059	
D-KDNM	Grob G.109B	6373	OE-9258
D-KDOM	Hoffmann HK-36R Super Dimona	36313	
D-KDON	Glaser-Dirks DG-400	4-41	
D-KDOS-OS	Schempp-Hirth Discus bT	46/362	
D-KDOT	HOAC HK-36TTC Super Dimona	36603	
D-KDOV	Schleicher ASH 25M	25143	D-7062
D-KDPB	Hoffmann HK-36R Super Dimona	36348	
D-KDPC	Grob G.102 Astir CS/TOP	1263	D-7358
D-KDPG	DG Flugzeugbau DG-800B	8-249B162	D-KSHG
D-KDPI	Glaser-Dirks DG-400	4-96	HB-2234
			(D-KMOA)
			HB-2234
			OO-DGI
D-KDPR	Hoffmann HK-36R Super Dimona	36340	
D-KDPS	Hoffmann HK-36R Super Dimona	36361	
D-KDPT	Hoffmann HK-36R Super Dimona	36362	
D-KDPV	Hoffmann HK-36R Super Dimona	36364	
D-KDPZ-PZ	Schempp-Hirth Ventus cT	156/503	
D-KDRA	Hoffmann HK-36R Super Dimona	36334	
D-KDRD	Stemme S-10VT	11-078	(D-KSMG)
D-KDSA(2)	Glaser-Dirks DG-400	4-256	
D-KDST(2)	DG Flugzeugbau DG-800B	8-175B99	
D-KDSY	Schleicher ASH 26E	26084	
D-KDTA	Grob G.109	6090	
D-KDTB	Grob G.109	6089	
D-KDTH	Grob G.109B	6415	N721DL
D-KDUG	Schleicher ASH 26E	26040	
D-KDUL	Glaser-Dirks DG-500M	5E19M11	
D-KDUO	Schempp-Hirth Duo Discus T	85/399	
D-KDUT	Schempp-Hirth Discus bT	8/271	
D-KDVS	Schempp-Hirth Ventus-2cT	122	
D-KDWD	DG Flugzeugbau DG-800B	8-126B55	N98NL
D-KDWN	Grob G.109B	6221	
D-KDWR	Glaser-Dirks DG-400	4-97	
D-KDWS	Valentin Kiwi	K-3012	
D-KEAA	Sportavia/ Fournier RF-5	5092	
D-KEAB	Hirth Doppelraab V	523/57-2/53	D-4663
D-KEAF	Sportavia/ Scheibe SF-25C Falke	4225	
D-KEAH	Sportavia/ Fournier RF-5	5110	
D-KEAL	Sportavia-Pützer RF-5B Sperber	51028	
D-KEAS(2)	Schempp-Hirth Ventus cT	165/540	
D-KEAT	Scheibe SF-25B Falke	46253	
D-KEAZ(2)	Scheibe SF-25C Rotax-Falke	44578	
D-KEBA(2)	Hoffmann H-36 Dimona	3667	
D-KEBE(2)	Grob G.109	6043	
D-KEBH(3)	HOAC HK-36TC Super Dimona	36519	
D-KEBL	Scheibe SFS-31 Milan	6602	D-KEBK
D-KEBP	Glaser-Dirks DG-400	4-19	
D-KEBR	Schempp-Hirth Discus bT	152/544	(D-KEBS)
D-KEBS	Scheibe SF 25C Falke 2000	44394	
D-KEBT(2)	Eiriavion PIK-20E	20210	
D-KEBV	Schempp-Hirth Nimbus 3DM	16/39	
D-KEBW	Glaser-Dirks DG-400	4-79	
D-KEBY	Akaflieg München Mü 23 Saurier	V-1	
D-KECA(2)	Eiriavion PIK-20E	20246	
D-KECB	Schleicher ASK 14	14014	
D-KECD(2)	Schempp-Hirth Ventus cT	111/379	
D-KECK(2)	Scheibe SF-25B Falke	4697	
D-KECM	Scheibe SF-25B Falke	46100	
D-KECN	Scheibe SF-25B Falke	46101	
D-KECO(2)	Grob G.109/2400	6042	
D-KECP(2)	Glaser-Dirks DG-400	4-10	
D-KECQ	Scheibe SF-25D Falke	46103D	
D-KECT	Scheibe SF-27M-A	6318	
D-KECU	Scheibe SF-24B Motorspatz	4030	
D-KEDA(2)	SZD-45A Ogar	B-663	
D-KEDB(2)	Scheibe SF-25B Falke	4638	
D-KEDD(3)	Schempp-Hirth Duo Discus T	108	
D-KEDE(3)	Schleicher ASK 14	14016	
D-KEDG(2)	Scheibe SF-25B Falke	4642	
D-KEDI(3)	DG Flugzeugbau DG-800B	8-181B105	
D-KEDJ(2)	Schempp-Hirth Ventus cM	43/483	
D-KEDO(2)	DG Flugzeugbau DG-808B (Permit.05)	8-324B224	
D-KEDU	Raab Krähe IV (Permit 9.99)	05	
D-KEDY	DG Flugzeugbau DG-808xB Competition (Reservation .05)	8-331B230X3	
D-KEEB	Scheibe SF-25C Rotax-Falke	44535	
D-KEEE	Sportavia/ Fournier RF-4D	4039	OE-9020

D-KEEG	Scheibe SF-25C Rotax-Falke	44592	
D-KEEH	Scheibe SF 25C Falke	44691	
D-KEEI	Schempp-Hirth Ventus 2cT	25/93	
D-KEEN	DG Flugzeugbau DG-800B	8-164B88	
D-KEEP	Scheibe SF-28A Tandem-Falke	5730	(D-KOAS)
D-KEFC	Scheibe SF-25C Falke	44153	
D-KEFG	Scheibe SF-25C Falke	44157	
D-KEFI (2)	Scheibe SF-25C Falke	44159	
D-KEFJ	Scheibe SF-25C Falke	44162	
D-KEFK	Scheibe SF-25E Super-Falke	4318	
D-KEFO	Scheibe SF-25C Falke	44163	
D-KEFS	Scheibe SF-25C Falke	44167	
D-KEFT	Scheibe SF-25C Falke	44170	
D-KEFW	Scheibe SF-25C Falke	44168	
D-KEFY(2)	Scheibe SF-25C Falke	44174	
D-KEFZ	Scheibe SF-25C Falke	44172	
D-KEGB	Scheibe SF-25C Falke 2000	44466	
D-KEGF	Schleicher ASH 26E	26046	D-8771
D-KEGL(2)	Scheibe SF-25C Rotax-Falke	44525	
D-KEGM	Schleicher ASH 25E	25047	
D-KEGO(2)	Hoffmann H-36 Dimona	36261	OE-9308
D-KEGR	Glaser-Dirks DG-400	4-261	
D-KEGS	Grob G.109	6140	N426BG
D-KEHA	Eiriavion PIK-20E	20239	
D-KEHB(2)	Schleicher ASH 25Mi	25235	
D-KEHC	Glaser-Dirks DG-400	4-34	
D-KEHE	Schleicher ASK 14	14017	
D-KEHF	Glaser-Dirks DG-400	4-163	I-KEHF D-KEHF
D-KEHG	Schleicher ASH 25E	25070	
D-KEHH-IHH	Schempp-Hirth Ventus bT	20/170	D-4110
D-KEHK(2)	Lange E1 Antares (Permit 3.04)	02	
D-KEHM	Technoflug Piccolo	004	
D-KEHO(2)	Grob G.109	6022	
D-KEHU(2)	Hoffmann HK-36R Super Dimona	36315	
D-KEHY(2)	Hoyer / Marco J-5/Ho	01	
D-KEHZ	Schempp-Hirth Nimbus 4M	15/38	
D-KEIA(2)	Scheibe SF-25C Falke	4491	
D-KEIE(2)	Scheibe SF-25C Falke	4494	
D-KEIH	Scheibe SF-25C Falke	4488	
D-KEIJ	Scheibe SF-25C Falke	4490	
D-KEIK	Schleicher ASK 16	16019	
D-KEIL	Sportavia/ Fournier RF-5 (Permit)	5066	F-BPLY
D-KEIM(2)	Hoffmann H-36 Dimona	36142	
D-KEIN(2)	Schempp-Hirth Discus bT	25/318	
D-KEIS(3)	AMS Flight Carat A	CA009	
D-KEIZ(2)	Schleicher ASW 24E	24850	
D-KEJA-JA	Schempp-Hirth Ventus cM	24/457	
D-KEJC-JC	Schempp-Hirth Janus CT	1/167	
D-KEJD	Glaser-Dirks DG-400	4-131	
D-KEJE-JE	Glaser-Dirks DG-400	4-73	
D-KEJK	Schempp-Hirth Nimbus 3DM	11/29	
D-KEKB	Schempp-Hirth Ventus cT	97/350	
D-KEKE	Stemme S-10VT	11-009	D-KSTE(9)
D-KEKF	Glaser-Dirks DG-400	4-18	
D-KEKG	DG Flugzeugbau DG-800S	8-332B231	
D-KEKH	Scheibe SF-25C Falke	44244	(D-KDCU)
D-KEKK	Hoffmann H-36 Dimona	36248	
D-KEKM	Grob G.109B	6427	
D-KEKO(3)	Grob G.109B	6252	
D-KEKS	Scheibe SF-25C Falke 2000	44391	
D-KELA(2)	Scheibe SF-25C Falke 2000	44479	
D-KELE	Schleicher ASW 24E	24834	OE-9355
D-KELF	Schleicher ASW 24E	24816	
D-KELG	Hoffmann H-36 Dimona	36257	
D-KELH-IHB	Schempp-Hirth Ventus cM	30/463	
D-KELI	Grob G.109	6013	
D-KELJ	DG Flugzeugbau DG-505MB	5E190B5	HB-2333 (D-KLOC)
D-KELL	Sportavia-Pützer RF-5B Sperber	51079	
D-KELM	Hoffmann H-36 Dimona	3633	
D-KELN	Hoffmann H-36 Dimona	3697	
D-KELO	Eiriavion PIK-20E	20243	
D-KELR	Technoflug Piccolo	042	
D-KELS	Eiriavion PIK-20E	20261	
D-KELV	HOAC HK-36TTC Super Dimona	36718	
D-KELY	Hoffmann H-36 Dimona	3625	
D-KELZ(3)	Scheibe SF-25C Falke 2000	44451	
D-KEMA(2)	Glaser-Dirks DG-400	4-170	
D-KEMB	DG Flugzeugbau DG-800B	8-179B103	
D-KEME	Schempp-Hirth Ventus bT	44/234	D-8898
D-KEMG	Glaser-Dirks DG-800B	8-47B2	D-KIPB
D-KEMH	Schempp-Hirth Nimbus 3DM	12/34	
D-KEMI	Schleicher ASK 16	16040	
D-KEMJ	Schempp-Hirth Duo Discus T	23/284	(D-7605)
D-KEMK	Schempp-Hirth Discus bT	139/515	
D-KEMO	Schleicher ASK 16B	16039	N16KS HB-2039
D-KEMP	Sportavia/ Fournier RF-5	5096	
D-KEMS	Hoffmann H-36 Dimona	3641	
D-KEMW	Schleicher ASH 26E	26050	
D-KEMY	Schleicher ASW 24E	24810	
D-KENC	Valentin Taifun 17E (Reservation 12.99)	1014	
D-KENI(2)	Schleicher ASH 25M	25237	
D-KENJ	Technoflug Piccolo B	094	
D-KENN-NN	Schleicher ASW 20L/TOP	20333	D-7544
D-KEOA	Grob G.109B	6281	

D-KEOB	Grob G.109B	6283	
D-KEOC	Grob G.109B	6288	
D-KEOD	Grob G.109B	6294	
D-KEOF	Grob G.109B	6305	
D-KEOH	Grob G.109B	6312	
D-KEOI	Grob G.109B	6309	
D-KEOJ	Grob G.109B	6324	
D-KEOK	Grob G.109B	6328	
D-KEOM	Grob G.109B	6298	
D-KEOP	Grob G.109B	6314	
D-KEOR	Scheibe SF 25C Rotax-Falke	44685	
D-KEOS	Scheibe SF 25C Falke	44692	
D-KEOT	Scheibe SF 25C Falke	44706	
D-KEPA	Schleicher ASH 25E (Permit)	25031	
D-KEPB	Grob G.109B	6347	
D-KEPC	Glaser-Dirks DG-400	4-66	
D-KEPI	Grob G.109	6023	
D-KEPO	Hoffmann H-36 Dimona	3689	
D-KEPP	Hoffmann H-36 Dimona	3618	
D-KEPS	Schempp-Hirth Discus bT	23/316	
D-KEPT	HOAC HK-36TTC Super Dimona	36544	F-CHQA OE-9444
D-KERA(2)	Glaser-Dirks DG-400	4-159	
D-KERC	Grob G.109	6102	
D-KERD	Glaser-Dirks DG-400	4-166	
D-KERF-RF	Schempp-Hirth Nimbus 3MR	1	
D-KERG(3)	DG Flugzeugbau DG-800B	8-309B209	
D-KERJ	Grob G.109B	6372	
D-KERK	Grob G.109B	6428	G-BMLY
D-KERL(2)	Sportavia/ Fournier RF-4D	4046	OY-DXW
D-KERN	Technoflug Piccolo B	080	
D-KERO(2)	DG Flugzeugbau DG-800B	8-233B147	
D-KERR	DG Flugzeugbau DG-800B	8-293B198	
D-KERW	Schleicher ASH 26E	26078	
D-KESD	HOAC HK-36TTC Super Dimona	36556	
D-KESE	Sportavia/ Fournier RF-5	5008	(D-KIGY)
D-KESJ	Schempp-Hirth Discus-2T	29/175	
D-KESP(2)	Schempp-Hirth Ventus 2cM ("ES")	71/146	
D-KESS(2)	Scheibe SF-25C Falke	44110	
D-KEST	Glaser-Dirks DG-400	4-20	
D-KESU	Schempp-Hirth Ventus 2cM	56/110	
D-KETA	Kickert ETA	1	
D-KETB	Grob G.109B	6503	
D-KETL-4H	Grob G.102 Astir CS 77/TOP	1662	D-3873
D-KETT(3)	DG Flugzeugbau DG-800B	8-203B125	
D-KETY	Sportavia/ Scheibe SF-25C Falke	4227	
D-KETZ	Grob G.109B	6361	HB-2110 (EAF-672)
D-KEUL	Akaflieg Karlsruhe AK 1	01	
D-KEUN	Valentin Taifun 17E	1063	G-OFUN D-KHVA(5)
D-KEUP	Glaser-Dirks DG-600M (W/o 28.7.00)	6-52M6	D-5808
D-KEUX	Fournier RF-9	10	
D-KEVA(2)	DG Flugzeugbau DG-800B	8-99B34	
D-KEVE	Grob G.109B	6397	G-LIVE
D-KEVI	Pfeifer C 10/85	1	
D-KEVL	Schleicher ASH 26E (Permit .05)	26207	EC-INA
D-KEWA	Hoffmann H-36 Dimona	3532	
D-KEWD	Grob G.109B	6431	
D-KEWE	Schempp-Hirth Ventus cT	109/372	
D-KEWI (3)	Schleicher ASH 26E	26044	
D-KEWL	Hoffmann H-36 Dimona	3657	
D-KEWR	Glaser-Dirks DG-800	8-49A33	
D-KEWS	Schempp-Hirth Ventus bT	2/101	
D-KEWW	Scheibe SF-25C Rotax-Falke	44608	
D-KEXI	Technoflug Piccolo	016	
D-KEXO	Hoffmann H-36 Dimona	36238	
D-KEXX-XXL	Schempp-Hirth Nimbus 3DT	2	
D-KEXY(2)	Technoflug Piccolo	048	D-KIBI (3)
D-KEYY-YY	Schempp-Hirth Ventus cM	7/423	
D-KEZA	Grob G.109B	6259	
D-KEZL	Scheibe SF-25C Falke 2000	44485	
D-KFAA	Schempp-Hirth Ventus 2cM	23/44	
D-KFAB	Schempp-Hirth Ventus 2cM	80/167	
D-KFAC(3)	Schempp-Hirth Ventus 2cM	68/140	D-KETU
D-KFAF	Schempp-Hirth Nimbus 4DM	5/12	
D-KFAG(2)	Scheibe SF-25C Rotax-Falke	44618	
D-KFAI	Valentin Taifun 17E	1055	OO-TAI D-KHVA(2)
D-KFAL	Doppelraab IV MSR	EB-2	D-6207
D-KFAN(2)	Glaser-Dirks DG-500M (Permit .04)	5E95M41	HB-2239
D-KFAR	Grob G.109B	6211	HB-2080
D-KFAS(2)	DG Flugzeugbau DG-800B	8-288B194	
D-KFAT	Scheibe SF-25C Rotax-Falke	44569	
D-KFBA	Valentin Taifun 17E	1084	
D-KFBB	Hoffmann HK-36R Super Dimona	36356	
D-KFBE	Scheibe SF-25C Falke	44210	
D-KFBG	Eiriavion PIK-20E	20223	
D-KFBK	Valentin Taifun 17E-II	1118	OE-9313 D-KHVA(36)
D-KFBM-BM	Schleicher ASW 28-18E (Permit 5.04)	28708	
D-KFBO	Schleicher ASH 26E	26137	
D-KFBW	Aeromot AMT-200 Super Ximango	200-070	
D-KFBZ	Hoffmann H-36F Dimona (Modified by Frisch Engineering to Rotax 912)	3669	
D-KFCB	DG Flugzeugbau DG-800B	8-214B131	
D-KFCD	Hoffmann HK-36R Super Dimona	36350	

D-KFCE	Scheibe SF-25C Rotax-Falke	44533	
D-KFCH	Technoflug Piccolo B	098	
D-KFCK	SZD-45A Ogar	B-649	DDR-3503
			DM-3503
D-KFCM	Hoffmann H-36 Dimona	3681	
D-KFCO	Grob G.109	6120	OE-9259
			F-WAQL
D-KFCP	Glaser-Dirks DG-400	4-263	HB-2158
D-KFCW	Grob G.109B	6249	
D-KFDG(3)	DG Flugzeugbau DG-808B (Coded 'DG')	8-219B133	
D-KFDI	Valentin Taifun 17E-II	1127	F-CGAI
			F-WGAI
			(D-KHVA)
D-KFDS	Schempp-Hirth Duo Discus T (Permit 4.01)	17/269	
D-KFEB	Grob G.109B	6430	
D-KFEC	Scheibe SF-25C Rotax-Falke	44571	
D-KFEE	Hoffmann H-36 Dimona	36273	
D-KFEL	Scheibe SF-25C Falke 2000	44495	
D-KFEM(2)	Kickert ETA	04	
D-KFEN	DG Flugzeugbau DG-808B	8-317B217	
D-KFFA(2)	Glaser-Dirks DG-400	4-220	D-KAHM(2)
D-KFFB(2)	Schempp-Hirth Discus bT	3/252	
D-KFFC	Schempp-Hirth Discus 2T	26/166	
D-KFFF	Scheibe SF-25C Falke 2000	44385	(D-KFFA)
D-KFFG	Scheibe SF-25C Falke 2000	44457	
D-KFFK	DG Flugzeugbau DG-800B	8-158B82	
D-KFFO-N1	Schempp-Hirth Duo Discus T	92/411	
D-KFFR	Glaser-Dirks DG-500M	5E18M10	
D-KFFW-FW	Schempp-Hirth Ventus 2cT	48/149	D-4539
D-KFGB	DG Flugzeugbau DG-808B	8-319B219	
D-KFGE	Eiriavion PIK-20E	20278	
D-KFGG	Schempp-Hirth Discus bT	134/508	
D-KFGH	Schempp-Hirth Janus CT	8/252	
D-KFGM	Scheibe SF-25C Falke 2000	44400	
D-KFGN	Nitschke AVO-68R Samburo	024R	OE-9166
D-KFGS	Schempp-Hirth Ventus 2cM	49/101	
D-KFGT(2)	HOAC HK-36TTC Super Dimona	36572	
D-KFGW	Schempp-Hirth Ventus 2cT	6/14	
D-KFHA(2)	Schempp-Hirth Nimbus 4DM	7/15	(D-9153)
D-KFHD	Schleicher ASH 26E	26165	
D-KFHI	Sportavia/ Fournier RF-4D	4090	SE-TGY
D-KFHW	DG Flugzeugbau DG-808S	8-330B229	
D-KFIF	Schleicher ASW 22BE	22056	
D-KFIH	Valentin Taifun 17E	1057	SE-UBA
			D-KHVA(4)
D-KFIR	Schempp-Hirth Ventus-2cM (Permit 7.04)	147	
D-KFIT	Glaser-Dirks DG-400	4-23	OO-FIT
			(OO-ZUD)
			(OO-PUD)
D-KFJD	DG Flugzeugbau DG-808S	8-326B226	
D-KFKA	Schempp-Hirth Ventus bT	4/120	D-1137
D-KFKF	Hoffmann H-36 Dimona	3511	
D-KFKL	Schempp-Hirth Duo Discus T	90/408	
D-KFKS	Eiriavion PIK-20E	20217	LN-GME
			G-LYDE
D-KFLA-HW	Glaser-Dirks DG-800B	8-48B3	
D-KFLL-LL	Schempp-Hirth Duo Discus T	42/318	
D-KFLO	Glaser-Dirks DG-400	4-138	
D-KFLY	Valentin Kiwi	3007	
D-KFMD	Schempp-Hirth Discus 2cT (Permit .05)	3/. .	
D-KFMF	Schempp-Hirth Discus bT	110/460	
D-KFMH	Schleicher ASH 26E	26035	
D-KFMN	Schempp-Hirth Ventus 2cM	121/264	
D-KFMO	Hoffmann H-36 Dimona	36227	OE-9269
D-KFND	Schempp-Hirth Duo Discus T	105/431	
D-KFNT	Schempp-Hirth Discus bT	2/250	D-5070
D-KFNW	Grob G.103C Twin IIISL	35045	
D-KFOR	Scheibe SF-25C Rotax-Falke	44563	
D-KFOW-OW	Schleicher ASH 25E	25025	
D-KFOX	Schleicher ASH 26E	26166	
D-KFPS	Aerotechnik L-13SDM Vivat	950607	
D-KFRA	Scheibe SF-25C Falke 2000	44441	
D-KFSG	Scheibe SFS-31 Milan	6612	(D-KAUT)
D-KFSK	HOAC HK-36TTC Super Dimona	36577	
D-KFSL	Grob G.102 Astir CS77/TOP	1703	D-7632
D-KFSM	Glaser-Dirks DG-400	4-245	
D-KFSN	AVO 68V Samburo 2000	019	
D-KFSO	HOAC HK-36TC Super Dimona	36505	OE-9406
D-KFSP	Brditschka HB-21	21017	OE-9168
D-KFSS	Schleicher ASH 26E	26002	
D-KFST	Sportavia/ Fournier RF-4D	4151	OO-YES
			PH-JFE
D-KFSV	Hoffmann HK-36R Super Dimona	36314	
D-KFTA	HOAC HK-36TS Super Dimona	36512	
D-KFTB	Alpavia/ Fournier RF-3	53	F-BMTB
D-KFTL	Schleicher ASH 25EB	25239	
D-KFTT	Schempp-Hirth Ventus 2cM	82/172	
D-KFUW	Scheibe SF-25C Falke 2000	44491	
D-KFVA	Sportavia/ Fournier RF-5	5099	
D-KFVS	Scheibe SF-25C Falke 2000	44515	
D-KFWC	Hoffmann H-36 Dimona	3613	
D-KFWH(2)	Schempp-Hirth Ventus 2cT	29/100	
D-KFWI	Hoffmann HK-36R Super Dimona	36344	
D-KFWJ	Scheibe SF-25C Falke 2000	44267	
D-KFWP	Schleicher ASK 16	16036	
D-KFWS	Schempp-Hirth Ventus 2cM	66/135	
D-KFZA	Technoflug Piccolo B	097	

D-KFZW	Hoffmann HK-36R Super Dimona	36395	
D-KGAA	Sportavia/ Scheibe SF-25C Falke	4217	
D-KGAB	Sportavia/ Scheibe SF-25C Falke	4218	
D-KGAC(2)	Hoffmann HK-36R Super Dimona	36319	I-NAOS
			OE-9351
D-KGAD	Sportavia/ Scheibe SF-25C Falke 2000	4220	
D-KGAE	Sportavia/ Scheibe SF-25C Falke	4221	
D-KGAF	Hoffmann H-36 Dimona	3503	
D-KGAH	Scheibe SF-25C Falke	44296	
D-KGAI	Scheibe SF-25C Falke	44460	
D-KGAJ	Scheibe SF-25C Rotax-Falke	44606	
D-KGAK	Scheibe SF-25C Falke	44346	
D-KGAL	Scheibe SF-25C Falke	44310	
D-KGAM	Scheibe SF-25C Falke	44322	
D-KGAN	Valentin Taifun 17E	1052	D-ECAN(3)
			D-KGAN
D-KGAO	Scheibe SF-25C Falke	44437	
D-KGAP	Scheibe SF-25C Falke	44326	
D-KGAQ	Scheibe SF-25C Rotax-Falke	44617	
D-KGAR	Scheibe SF-25C Falke	44340	
D-KGAS	Scheibe SF-25C Falke 2000	44367	
D-KGAT(2)	Scheibe SF-25C Falke	44483	
D-KGAU	Scheibe SF-25C Falke 2000 (ex 1700)	44527	
D-KGAV	Scheibe SF-25C Falke 2000 (ex 1700)	44567	
D-KGAW	Scheibe SF-25C Falke	44506	
D-KGAX	Scheibe SF-25C Falke	44585	
D-KGAY	Scheibe SF-25C Falke	44548	
D-KGBA	Valentin Taifun 17E-II	1108	
D-KGBB	Schempp-Hirth Ventus cT	101/360	
D-KGBI	Stemme S-10VT	11-030	
D-KGBL	ICA/Brasov I S.28M2/G	70	
D-KGBN	Scheibe SF-25C Rotax-Falke	44628	
D-KGBR	Schempp-Hirth Ventus-2cT (Permit 5.04)	126	
	(Reserved as LN-GCY 12.03)		
D-KGBT	Schempp-Hirth Discus bT	136/511	
D-KGCA	Stemme S-10V	14-019M	
D-KGCB	Stemme S-10V	14-047M	
D-KGCC	Scheibe SF-25B Falke	AB46307	
D-KGCD(5)	Stemme S-10	10-50	
D-KGCF	Stemme S-10V	14-018M	
D-KGCG-MO	Stemme S-10	10-22	
D-KGCH(3)	Stemme S-10	10-52	
D-KGCI (6)	Stemme S10V (Formerly c/n 14-003)	14-056M	OO-VCN
			D-KGCI (4)
D-KGCL(2)	Stemme S-10V	14-007	
D-KGCN	Stemme S-10	10-31	
D-KGCP	Stemme S-10	10-36	
D-KGCQ	Stemme S-10V	14-038M	(D-KSTE)
D-KGCR(2)	Stemme S-10VT	11-001	
D-KGCW	Stemme S-10	10-40	
D-KGCY(3)	Stemme S-10V (Formerly c/n 14-004)	14-057M	
D-KGCZ(3)	Stemme S-10V	14-017	
D-KGDA(3)	Stemme S-10V	14-024	
D-KGDB(3)	Stemme S-10V	14-025	
D-KGDD(3)	Stemme S-10V	14-026	
D-KGDE	Grob G 109B	6341	OE-9250
D-KGDS	Schleicher ASW 24E	24841	
D-KGED	Stemme S-10V	14-016M	(D-KDKS)
	(Originally built as S-10 c/n 10-16)		HB-2185
			D-KGCD(1)
D-KGER	DG Flugzeugbau DG-800B	8-65B9	(D-KKER)
D-KGFA	Grob G.109B	6201	
D-KGFC	Grob G.109B	6207	
D-KGFD	Grob G.109B	6212	G-BNZF
			D-KGFD
D-KGFH	Grob G.109	6080	F-WAQK
D-KGFI	Grob G.109B	6218	
D-KGFL	Sportavia/ Fournier RF-5	5038	
D-KGFM	Grob G.109B	6205	
D-KGFO(2)	Lange E1 Antares (Permit 4.04)	05	
D-KGFP	Grob G.109B	6251	
D-KGFQ	Grob G.109B	6245	
D-KGFR	Grob G.109B	6253	
D-KGFS	Grob G.109B	6226	
D-KGFT	Grob G.109B	6206	
D-KGFU	Grob G.109B	6264	
D-KGFV	Grob G.109B (Damaged 9.00, stored)	6263	
D-KGFW	Grob G.109B	6238	
D-KGFX	Grob G.109B	6247	
D-KGFY	Grob G.109B	6256	
D-KGFZ	Grob G.109B	6282	
D-KGGG	DG Flugzugbau DG-300 Club Elan GG300		
	(Solo 2350 engine) (Permit .05)	3E-313C22	D-1930
D-KGGL	Schleicher ASH 26E	26034	
D-KGGM	Schempp-Hirth Ventus-2cT	124	
D-KGGO(2)	Schleicher ASH 25M (Permit 3.00)	25216	
D-KGGX	Schempp-Hirth Duo Discus T	110/. . .	
D-KGHB	Schempp-Hirth Nimbus 4DM	40/. .	
D-KGHF	DG Flugzeugbau DG-808B	8-271B179	
D-KGHP	Schleicher ASH 25M	25203	
D-KGHS	Glaser-Dirks DG-400	4-236	OY-PVX
D-KGHW-HW	Schleicher ASH 25E	25014	
D-KGIN(2)	Glaser-Dirks DG-500M	5E92M39	
D-KGJB	AMS Flight Carat A	CA010	
D-KGKB	Schleicher ASH 26E	26148	
D-KGKG	Schleicher ASW 22BE	22060	
D-KGKS-V8	Schleicher ASH 26E	26014	D-5599

D-KGKW	DG Flugzeugbau DG-505MB	5E243MB20	
D-KGLA(2)	DG Flugzeugbau DG-800S	8-66B11	D-KUDS
D-KGLM	Grob G.109B	6237	
D-KGLT	Stemme S-10VT	11-048	
D-KGLW	HOAC HK-36TTC Super Dimona	36667	
D-KGMB	DG Flugzeugbau DG-808B	8-303B203	
D-KGMD-MD	Schleicher ASH 26E	26121	
D-KGMS	Schleicher ASW 24E	24828	G-BVUP
			D-KEWI(2)
D-KGMW	Schempp-Hirth Nimbus 4DM	18/27	
D-KGMY	Schempp-Hirth Ventus bT	3/116	
D-KGND	Stemme S-10V	14-026M	
	(Originally built as Stemme S-10 c/n 10-26)		
D-KGOD(2)	Schempp-Hirth Ventus cT	171/561	
D-KGOM	Hoffmann H-36 Dimona	3644	
D-KGOR	Schleicher ASK 16	16020	I- AGOR
			D-KGOR
D-KGOS	Valentin Taifun 17E	1024	
D-KGPA	Hoffmann HK-36R Super Dimona	36343	
D-KGPB	HOAC HK-36TS Super Dimona	36586	
D-KGPF	Scheibe SF-25D Falke	46157D	OE-9179
			D-KBIB
D-KGPG-33	Glaser-Dirks DG-500M	5E72M30	(D-KGPL)
D-KGPI (2)	Glaser-Dirks DG-800B	8-53B6	
D-KGPR	Aerotechnik L-13SEH Vivat	940522	OK-4101
D-KGRA(2)	Scheibe SF-24B Motorspatz	4035	D-KAHH
			(D-KIBU)
D-KGRB	Scheibe SF-24A Motorspatz (Reservation 12.99)	4011	D-KADA(1)
D-KGRH	Scheibe SF-25C Rotax-Falke	44654	D-KIEO
D-KGRM	Hoffmann H-36 Dimona	36193	OE-9245
D-KGRO	Test registration for Burkhardt Grob production		
D-KGRS	Sportavia/ Fournier RF-5 (Permit .01)	5068	OE-9033
D-KGRU	Sportavia/ Fournier RF-4D	4132	OY-XBA
			SE-TGU
D-KGSE-SE	Schempp-Hirth Ventus cT	107/370	D-KBEK
D-KGSF	Schempp-Hirth Duo Discus T	3/232	
D-KGSO	DG Flugzeugbau DG-800B	8-223B137	
D-KGST	Hoffmann H-36 Dimona	36100	
D-KGSW	Schempp-Hirth Ventus cM	59/514	
D-KGTA(2)	HOAC HK-36R Super Dimona	36410	
D-KGTB	HOAC HK-36R Super Dimona	36411	
D-KGTC	HOAC HK-36R Super Dimona	36414	
D-KGTD	HOAC HK-36TS Super Dimona	36508	
D-KGTE	HOAC HK-36TS Super Dimona	36510	
D-KGTF	HOAC HK-36TC Super Dimona	36605	
D-KGTG	HOAC HK-36TC Super Dimona (Permit 3.00)	36517	OE-9417
D-KGTH	HOAC HK-36TTC Super Dimona (Res 3.00)	36700	
D-KGTI	HOAC HK-36TTC Super Dimona	36689	
D-KGTJ	HOAC HK-36TTC Super Dimona	36723	
D-KGUA	Hoffmann HK-36R Super Dimona	36381	
D-KGUB	Hoffmann HK-36R Super Dimona	36382	
D-KGUI	Schleicher ASW 24E	24813	F-CGKR
			D-KAXF
D-KGUY	Schempp-Hirth Ventus-2cxM (Permit .05)	149	
D-KGVS	Schempp-Hirth Ventus cM	40/478	
D-KGVV	DG Flugzeugbau DG-808B	8-311B211	
D-KGWB	Glaser-Dirks DG-400	4-95	
D-KGWG	Sportavia/ Fournier RF-4D	4020	F-BORG
D-KGWH	Grob G.109B	6511	
D-KGWS	Schempp-Hirth Ventus 2cM	13/30	
D-KGWW	Stemme S-10	10-37	
D-KGWX	DG Flugzeugbau DG-800B	8-231B145	
D-KGZT-99	Schempp-Hirth Nimbus 3DT	5	
D-KHAA(2)	Technoflug Piccolo B	081	
D-KHAC	Hoffmann HK-36R Super Dimona	36359	
D-KHAG	Schempp-Hirth Nimbus 4DT (Permit 11.02)	12/70	
D-KHAI	Borowski AN-20K Piccolo	001	
D-KHAL	Schleicher ASK 16B	16043	OE-9132
			(D-KAXD)
D-KHAM	Schempp-Hirth Nimbus 4DM	19/28	
D-KHAN	Technoflug Piccolo	046	
D-KHAS(2)	Schleicher ASW 24E	24812	OE-9337
D-KHAU	Schleicher ASH 25E	25090	F-CHAU
			F-WHAU
D-KHBA	Grob G.109B	6370	
D-KHBB(2)	Schleicher ASH 26E	26095	
D-KHBC	Schleicher ASW 24/TOP	24804	
D-KHBD	DG Flugzeugbau DG-800B	8-266B174	(D-KTEO)
D-KHBE(2)	Glaser-Dirks DG-400	4-279	
D-KHBG	HOAC HK-36TTC Super Dimona	36668	
D-KHBS	Glaser-Dirks DG-400	4-290	
D-KHCC	Schempp-Hirth Ventus bT	34/215	
D-KHCD-LN	Schempp-Hirth Discus bT	17/303	
D-KHCE	Schempp-Hirth Ventus cM	84/563	
D-KHCF	Schempp-Hirth Ventus 2cT	78	
D-KHCM	DG Flugzeugbau DG-800B	8-276B184	(D-KHCB)
D-KHCO	Valentin Taifun 17E-II	1110	
D-KHCT	Schempp-Hirth Duo Discus T	82	
D-KHDF	Hoffmann H-36 Dimona	3656	
D-KHDG	Schleicher ASH 25E	25163	
D-KHDK	Schempp-Hirth Discus bT	30/327	
D-KHDP	DG Flugzeugbau DG-808B	8-297B202	
D-KHDU	Schleicher ASH 26E	26178	
D-KHDV	Glaser-Dirks DG-400	4-280	
D-KHEA	Sportavia/ Scheibe SF 25B Falke	4821	
D-KHEB	Sportavia/ Scheibe SF 25B Falke	4822	
D-KHEC(2)	Scheibe SF-25C Falke 2000	44494	

D-KHEF(2)	Sportavia/ Scheibe SF-25C Falke	4244	(D-KAJF)
D-KHEH(2)	Grob G.109B	6436	
D-KHEM(2)	Schempp-Hirth Ventus cT	135/415	
D-KHEN(2)	Scheibe SF-25C Rotax-Falke	44634	
D-KHEP	Sportavia/ Scheibe SF 25B Falke	4833	
D-KHEV	Sportavia/ Scheibe SF 25B Falke	4839	
D-KHEW	Sportavia/ Scheibe SF 25B Falke	4840	
D-KHEX	Sportavia/ Scheibe SF 25B Falke	4841	
D-KHEY	Sportavia/ Scheibe SF 25B Falke	4842	
D-KHEZ(2)	Valentin Taifun 17E	1072	F-WGAE
			D-KHVA
D-KHFB(2)	Hoffmann HK-36R Super Dimona	36346	
D-KHFC(2)	Schempp-Hirth Ventus 2cM	157/ . . .	
D-KHFD	Scheibe SF-25D Falke	4846D	
D-KHFE	Sportavia/ Scheibe SF 25B Falke	4847	
D-KHFF	Sportavia/ Scheibe SF 25B Falke	4848	
D-KHFG	Sportavia/ Scheibe SF 25B Falke	4849	
D-KHFL	Schleicher ASW 20/TOP	20002	D-3860
D-KHFM	Schleicher ASH 25Mi (Permit 7.01)	25225	(D-KBEN)
D-KHFN	Stemme S-10VT	11-067	
D-KHFP-JOY	Schleicher ASH 26E	26026	G-MORE
			BGA4075/HNP
D-KHFR	Franke Doppelraab 7M (Hankur 1)	001	D-5626(1)
D-KHFS	Stemme S-10	10-5	HB-2250
			D-KHFS
D-KHGA	Scheibe SF-25C Falke 2000	44358	
D-KHGB	Schempp-Hirth Standard Cirrus/TOP	477	D-3719
D-KHGG	Schleicher ASW 22BLE	22050	
D-KHGH	Scheibe SF-28A Tandem-Falke	57120	
D-KHGK	Schempp-Hirth Discus 2T	24/161	
D-KHGN	Schleicher ASW 20CL TOP	20757	HB-2178
			HB-1740
D-KHGO	Gomolzig RF-9-ABS	9021	(D-KABS)
D-KHGR	Schleicher ASH 25E	25149	D-0825
D-KHGS	Schempp-Hirth Ventus bT	27/194	
D-KHHA	Valentin Taifun 17E-II	1126	
D-KHHD	Technoflug Piccolo (Permit .01)	054	
D-KHHG(2)	Schleicher ASH 25M	25174	D-5763
D-KHHI (2)	Schleicher ASH 26E	26199	
D-KHHL	Technoflug Piccolo	050	
D-KHHO	Schleicher ASH 25M	25188	
D-KHHS	Technoflug Piccolo	039	
D-KHHT	Scheibe SF-25C Falke 2000	44354	
D-KHIG-3	Schempp-Hirth Janus CM	14/190	
D-KHIK	Schempp-Hirth Janus CM	18/202	
D-KHIM	Valentin Taifun 17E	1032	
D-KHIR	Hoffmann H-36 Dimona	3619	
D-KHIS	Valentin Kiwi	3005	
D-KHJB	Glaser-Dirks DG-500M	5E14M8	
D-KHJC	Schempp-Hirth Discus bT	146/525	
D-KHJG	Sportavia/ Fournier RF-4D	4129	F-BPLM
D-KHJM	DG Flugzeugbau DG-800B	8-125B54	
D-KHJO	Schleicher ASK 14	AB14061	(D-KICH)
D-KHJR	Eiri PIK-20E	20228	G-BHFR
D-KHJT	Technoflug Piccolo	013	
D-KHKA-KC	Schempp-Hirth Nimbus 2M V-2	02	
D-KHKG	Grob G.103C Twin IIISL	35036	
D-KHKI	Technoflug Piccolo B	089	
D-KHKK	Schempp-Hirth Discus 2T (Permit 4.01)	6/96	
D-KHKW	Glaser-Dirks DG-400	4-217	
D-KHLJ	HOAC HK-36TTC Super Dimona	36604	
D-KHLL	Grob G.103C Twin IIISL	35033	
D-KHLS	Schleicher ASH 26E	26224	
D-KHMA	Grob G.109B	6257	
D-KHMB	Schleicher ASH 26E	26007	
D-KHMC	Grob G 109B	6289	PH-1065
			SE-UAA
D-KHMG	Hoffmann HK-36R Super Dimona	36318	
D-KHMI	DG Flugzeugbau DG-808S	8-248B161	N949AB
D-KHML	Rolladen-Schneider LS9 (Permit 1.00)	9003	
D-KHMM	Scheibe SF-25C Falke 2000	44384	
D-KHMS	Glaser-Dirks DG-400	4-132	
D-KHMW	Glaser-Dirks DG-600M	6-50M5	
D-KHMY	Schleicher ASH 25M	25201	
D-KHNO	Valentin Taifun 17E	1007	(D-KEKO(2))
D-KHOA	Scheibe SF-27M-A	6323	
D-KHOB(3)	Schempp-Hirth Ventus cM ("9A")	80/553	
D-KHOC	Scheibe SF-27M-A	6325	
D-KHOE(2)	HOAC HK-36TTC Super Dimona	36575	
D-KHOI	Scheibe SF-25C Falke	4425	
D-KHOJ	Scheibe SF-25C Falke	4426	
D-KHOL(2)	Schleicher ASH 25E	25135	
D-KHOM	Scheibe SF-25C Falke	4429	
D-KHOO(2)	Rolladen-Schneider LS9 (Permit 10.99)	9006	
D-KHOP(2)	Scheibe SF-28A Tandem-Falke	5706	
D-KHOX	Hoffmann HK-36R Super Dimona	36402	
D-KHOY	Technoflug Piccolo	002	
D-KHPC	Schempp-Hirth Ventus cM	48/489	
D-KHPE	Glaser-Dirks DG-600M	6-55M9	
D-KHPG	Schempp-Hirth Ventus-2cxM	138/313	
D-KHPH	Valentin Taifun 17E	1036	
D-KHPI	Schleicher ASW 28-18E (Permit 7.04)	28717	
D-KHPS	Grob G.109B	6296	
D-KHPU	Schempp-Hirth Ventus 2cM	105/218	
D-KHRA	Hoffmann HK-36R Super Dimona	36380	
D-KHRB	Hoffmann HK-36R Super Dimona	36376	
D-KHRC	Hoffmann HK-36R Super Dimona	36377	

D-KHRL-RL	Schleicher ASH 25M (Permit 1.00)	25214	
D-KHRW	Schleicher ASW 22BE (Permit)	22051	D-4753
D-KHSC	Schempp-Hirth Nimbus 2M	06	
D-KHSF	Schempp-Hirth Ventus cT	125/399	HB-2128
D-KHSS-SS	Schempp-Hirth Nimbus 3T	24/90	
D-KHST	DG Flugzeugbau DG-808B	8-318B218	
D-KHSU	DG Flugzeugbau DG-808B	8-314B214	
D-KHSW	Valentin Mistral CM	MC-071/85	
D-KHTA	Grob G.109B	6501	
D-KHTB	Grob G.109B	6543	
D-KHTP	Schempp-Hirth Discus-2T	33	
D-KHUB	DG Flugzeugbau DG-800B	8-162B86	
D-KHUL	Hoffmann H-36 Dimona	3699	
D-KHVI	Grob G.102 Astir CS77/TOP	1797	D-7773
D-KHVL	Scheibe SF-25C Rotax-Falke	44554	
D-KHWA	Glaser-Dirks DG-400	4-229	
D-KHWC	Schempp-Hirth Nimbus 2M V-1	01	
D-KHWD	Sportavia/ Fournier RF-4D (Permit)	4060	F-BOXH
D-KHWE	Brditschka HB-23/2400SP	23029-U	OE-9304
D-KHWG	AVO 68R Samburo	009R	OE-9121
	(Converted from AVO 68v c/n 009, 6.99)		
D-KHWH	Grob G.109B	6321	G-KIAM
D-KHWK	Glaser-Dirks DG-600/18M	6-78M25	
D-KHWM	Glaser-Dirks DG-400	4-255	
D-KHWW	DG Flugzeugbau DG-800B	8-283B191	
D-KHXX(2)	Schempp-Hirth Nimbus 4M ("XX")	1/5	
D-KHXY	Schempp-Hirth Ventus cM	107/606	
D-KHYN	Schempp-Hirth Discus bT	117/473	
D-KHZZ	Grob G.103C Twin IIISL	35037	
D-KIAA(2)	Scheibe SF-25C Falke 2000	44438	
D-KIAB(2)	Scheibe SF-25C Falke 2000	44439	
D-KIAC(2)	Scheibe SF-25C Falke 2100	44440	
D-KIAD	Scheibe SF-25C Falke 2000	44443	
D-KIAE	Scheibe SF-25C Falke 2000	44455	
D-KIAF	Scheibe SF-25C Falke 2000	44445	
D-KIAG	Scheibe SF-25C Falke 2000	44442	
D-KIAH(2)	Scheibe SF-25C Falke 2000	44456	
D-KIAI (2)	Scheibe SF-25C Falke 2000	44467	
D-KIAK(2)	Scheibe SF-25C Falke 2000	44463	
D-KIAL	Scheibe SF-25C Falke 2000	44450	
D-KIAM	Scheibe SF-25C Falke 2000	44446	
D-KIAN	Scheibe SF-25C Falke 2000	44468	
D-KIAO(2)	Glaser-Dirks DG-400	4-130	I-GIOO D-KERO
D-KIAP	Scheibe SF-25C Falke 2000	44465	
D-KIAR	Scheibe SF-25C Falke 2000	44458	
D-KIAS	Scheibe SF-25C Falke 2000	44470	
D-KIAT	Scheibe SF-25C Falke 2000	44472	
D-KIAU	Scheibe SF-25C Falke 2000	44461	
D-KIAV(2)	Scheibe SF-25E Super Falke	4334	G-BFHN D-KDFW
D-KIAW	Scheibe SF-25C Falke 2000	44473	
D-KIAX	Scheibe SF-25C Falke 2000	44475	
D-KIAY(3)	Scheibe SF-25C Falke 2000	44482	
D-KIAZ	Scheibe SF-25C Falke 2000	44474	
D-KIBA(2)	Eiriavion PIK-20E	20207	
D-KIBB(2)	Schempp-Hirth Duo Discus T	114/. . .	
D-KIBC(2)	HOAC HK-36R Super Dimona	36360	
D-KIBN	Eiriavion PIK-20E	20251	OE-9255 D-KERH
D-KIBO(3)	Schempp-Hirth Janus BM	1/56	
D-KIBS	Hoffmann H-36 Dimona	36242	
D-KIBT-BT	Schempp-Hirth Discus bT	142/520	
D-KIBU(3)	Glaser-Dirks DG-400	4-204	
D-KIBY	Schempp-Hirth Janus CM	3	(D-KJMB)
D-KICA(4)	Schempp-Hirth Ventus 2cM	124/273	
D-KICB(2)	DG Flugzeugbau DG-800B	8-125B53	
D-KICC(3)	Schempp-Hirth Ventus 2cM	79/162	
D-KICD(2)	Schleicher ASK 14	14057	OO-ICD D-KICD
D-KICE(3)	Schleicher ASK 14	14058	
D-KICF(2)	Schleicher ASK 14	14059	
D-KICG(3)	Schleicher ASK 14/KM29	14055	
D-KICH(3)	Schleicher ASK 16	16002	
D-KICI (3)	Hoffmann H-36 Dimona	3604	
D-KICK(2)	Schleicher ASH 26E	26085	
D-KICM	Schempp-Hirth Ventus cM	55/504	
D-KICO(2)	Valentin Taifun 17E-II	1121	
D-KICP	Schleicher ASW 24E	24860	
D-KICR(2)	Schempp-Hirth Ventus 2cT	80/245	
D-KICS	DG Flugzeugbau DG-800B	8-151B75	
D-KICX	Schempp-Hirth Ventus-2cT	121	
D-KICY	Scheibe SF-25A Motorfalke	4534	(D-KAKO)
D-KIDA(2)	Hoffmann H-36 Dimona	3614	
D-KIDB	Eiri PIK-20E	20269	
D-KIDD(2)	Schempp-Hirth Discus bT	144/522	
D-KIDF	Schleicher ASH 26E	26153	
D-KIDH	Schleicher ASH 26E	26031	D-1349
D-KIDI (2)	FBW Valentin Kiwi	K-3011	
D-KIDK	Schempp-Hirth Discus bT	6/264	
D-KIDL	Glaser-Dirks DG-500M	5E31M15	
D-KIDM(2)	Schleicher ASH 25M	25199	
D-KIDO(2)	Schleicher ASH 26E	26107	
D-KIDS	Glaser-Dirks DG-400	4-208	
D-KIDX	Schempp-Hirth Nimbus-4DM	54/74	
D-KIEA	Scheibe SF-25C Rotax-Falke	44648	
D-KIEB-E4	Schempp-Hirth Ventus cT	112/381	
D-KIEC	Scheibe SF-25C Rotax-Falke	44647	
D-KIED	Hoffmann H-36 Dimona	3651	
D-KIEE	Scheibe SF-25C Falke	44644	
D-KIEF	Schempp-Hirth Janus CT	7/244	
D-KIEG	Glaser-Dirks DG-600M	6-84M30	
D-KIEH	Glaser-Dirks DG-600M	6-85M31	
D-KIEI (2)	Scheibe SF-25C Falke	44674	
D-KIEJ(5)	Scheibe SF-25C Rotax-Falke	44687	
D-KIEK	Scheibe SF-25C Rotax-Falke	44638	
D-KIEL(4)	Schempp-Hirth Duo Discus T	57/344	
D-KIEM	Schempp-Hirth Ventus bT	29/198	
D-KIEN	Scheibe SF-25C Rotax-Falke	44653	
D-KIEO(2)	Scheibe SF-25C Rotax-Falke	44671	
D-KIEP(2)	Scheibe SF-25C Rotax-Falke	44668	
D-KIEQ(3)	Scheibe SF-25C Rotax-Falke	44682	
D-KIER	Scheibe SF-25C Rotax-Falke	44637	
D-KIES	Glaser-Dirks DG-400	4-106	
D-KIET(2)	Scheibe SF-25C Rotax-Falke	44672	
D-KIEU	Schleicher ASW 24E	24840	
D-KIEV(2)	Scheibe SF-25C Rotax-Falke	44679	
D-KIEW	Scheibe SF-25C Rotax-Falke	44629	
D-KIEX	Scheibe SF-25C Rotax-Falke	44643	
D-KIEY	Scheibe SF-25C Rotax-Falke	44676	
D-KIEZ	Scheibe SF-25C Rotax-Falke	44639	
D-KIFA(3)	Eiriavion PIK-20E	20247	
D-KIFB(2)	Glaser-Dirks DG-400	4-205	
D-KIFF	Scheibe SFS-31 Milan	6604	
D-KIFH (2)	Schleicher ASH 26E	26163	
D-KIFI	Scheibe SF-25A Motorfalke	4505	
D-KIFO (2)	Schempp-Hirth Duo Discus T	46/324	
D-KIFP	Sportavia/ Fournier RF-5	5088	
D-KIFR	Valentin Taifun 17E	1006	
D-KIFW	Glaser-Dirks DG-400	4-76	D-KOBI (3)
D-KIFZ	Schempp-Hirth Discus bT	59/381	
D-KIGB	Technoflug Piccolo B	082	
D-KIGE(3)	Grob G.109B	6246	
D-KIGF	Schleicher ASH 26E	26180	
D-KIGH	Schleicher ASH 25M	25189	
D-KIGI	Sportavia/ Fournier RF-5	5004	
D-KIGM-GM	Schempp-Hirth Discus bT	7/269	
D-KIGP	Schleicher ASH 26E	26038	
D-KIGR-GR	Schleicher ASH 25E	25035	
D-KIGS	Grob G.102 Astir CS77/TOP	1717	D-2535
D-KIGT	Sportavia/ Fournier RF-4D	4154	OE-9029
D-KIGU	Sportavia/ Fournier RF-5	5006	
D-KIGV-GV	Schempp-Hirth Ventus bT	7/131	
D-KIGW	Grob G.109B	6573	
D-KIGY(2)	Schleicher ASH 25EB	25243	
D-KIHA	Sportavia/ Fournier RF-5	5009	
D-KIHB(2)	Schempp-Hirth Ventus cM	104/600	
D-KIHD(2)	Schempp-Hirth Ventus cM	39/477	
D-KIHE	Sportavia/ Fournier RF-5	5010	
D-KIHG	Grob G.102 Astir CS/TOP	1305	D-7347
D-KIHH	Glaser-Dirks DG-400	4-55	
D-KIHK	Glaser-Dirks DG-400	4-80	
D-KIHN	Schempp-Hirth Discus bT	4/257	
D-KIHO	Sportavia/ Fournier RF-5	5012	
D-KIHP(2)	Schempp-Hirth Ventus cT ("HP")	133/412	
D-KIHR-HR	Glaser-Dirks DG-600/18M	6-110M51	(D-KCWC)
D-KIHW(2)	Schempp-Hirth Duo Discus T	112/. . .	
D-KIIA(2)	Brditschka HB-21/2400B	21028	OE-9217
D-KIIF	Schleicher ASH 25Mi	25229	
D-KIII (2)	Schempp-Hirth Ventus cM	14/441	HB-2166 D-KCPA
D-KIIK-7K	Schempp-Hirth Ventus bT	25/189	D-1419
D-KIIL	Schempp-Hirth Discus bT	132/502	
D-KIIN	Schempp-Hirth Ventus cM	69/533	
D-KIIR	Schleicher ASH 26E	26215	
D-KIIT-1T	DG Flugzeugbau DG-1000T (Permit 1.04)	10-28T1	
D-KIIV-TB	Schempp-Hirth Ventus aM	1/48	
D-KIIX- I I	Schempp-Hirth Ventus cT	66/286	
D-KIJC	Glaser-Dirks DG-600M	6-77M24	
D-KIJD	DG Flugzeugbau DG-808B	8-295B200	
D-KIJH	Schempp-Hirth Ventus 2cM	8/25	
D-KIJO	Glaser-Dirks DG-600/18M	6-97M43	
D-KIJT	DG Flugzeugbau DG-800B	8-178B102	
D-KIKA(2)	Schleicher ASW 20L/TOP ("IKT")	20395	D-2694
D-KIKD	Hoffmann HK-36R Super Dimona	36303	
D-KIKE	Alpavia/ Fournier RF-3	42	
D-KIKI	Alpavia/ Fournier RF-3	38	
D-KIKK	Schempp-Hirth Ventus cT	146/452	
D-KIKL	Schleicher ASH 25M	25176	
D-KIKO(2)	Grob G.109	6017	
D-KIKR-KR	Schempp-Hirth Ventus cT	132/410	
D-KIKS	DG Flugzeugbau DG-800B	8-169B93	
D-KIKT	Glaser-Dirks DG-400	4-167	
D-KIKW	Schempp-Hirth Discus bT	149/539	
D-KILD	Hoffmann HK-36R Super Dimona	36329	
D-KILE(2)	Glaser-Dirks DG-600/18M	6-90M36	(PH-939)
D-KILG	Hoffmann H-36 Dimona	3636	
D-KILH	Schempp-Hirth Ventus 2cM	12/29	
D-KILI (2)	IAR IS-28M2/G	68	YR-1995
D-KILK	Schleicher ASH 25E	25072	
D-KILL(2)	HOAC HK-36R Super Dimona	36325	OE-9361
D-KILM	Glaser-Dirks DG-600M	6-57M11	
D-KILS	Rolladen-Schneider LS9 (Permit)	9000	
D-KILT	Sportavia/ Fournier RF-4D	4027	

D-KILU(2)	Akaflieg Berlin B-13 ("CD")	001	
D-KILZ(2)	Schempp-Hirth Ventus 2cM	99/209	
D-KIMA(2)	Schempp-Hirth Ventus bT	39/229	
D-KIMB	Glaser-Dirks DG-400	4-201	
D-KIMC	Grob G.109	6093	
D-KIME(2)	Technoflug Piccolo B	058	
D-KIMG(2)	Technoflug Piccolo B	056	
D-KIMH-MH	Schleicher ASW 24E	24805	
D-KIMJ(2)	Schempp-Hirth Discus bT	27/321	
D-KIMK	Schleicher ASW 24E	24845	
D-KIMM(2)	Scheibe SF-25C Falke	4456	OY-VTX
			(D-KOAC)
D-KIMO(2)	Schempp-Hirth Duo Discus T (Res 2.00)	9/254	
D-KIMP	Sportavia/ Fournier RF-5	5070	
D-KIMR(2)	Glaser-Dirks DG-400	4-231	
D-KIMS	Hoffmann H-36 Dimona	3665	
D-KIMU	Schempp-Hirth Discus bT	62/386	
D-KIMW(3)	Schempp-Hirth Ventus 2cM	70/142	
D-KINA(2)	Scheibe SF-25C Falke 2000	44464	
D-KIND	Sportavia/ Fournier RF-5	5056	
D-KINE(2)	Grob G.109B	6423	
D-KING(2)	Diamond HK-36TTC Super Dimona	36691	
D-KINI (2)	Grob G.109	6029	
D-KINK	Grob G.109B	6366	(EAF675)
D-KINN-BB	Glaser-Dirks DG-800	8-19A16	
D-KINO	Alpavia/ Fournier RF-3	75	
D-KINT	Scheibe SF-25C Falke 2000	44412	
D-KINY	Grob G.109	6060	
D-KINZ-NZ	Schempp-Hirth Discus bT	18/304	
D-KIOA(2)	Scheibe SF-25C Falke 2000	44486	
D-KIOB(2)	Scheibe SF-25C Falke 2000	44488	
D-KIOC(2)	Scheibe SF-25C Falke 2000	44489	
D-KIOD(3)	Scheibe SF-25C Falke 2000	44496	
D-KIOE(2)	Scheibe SF-25C Falke 2000	44498	
D-KIOF(2)	Scheibe SF-25C Falke 2000	44493	
D-KIOG(3)	Scheibe SF-25C Falke 2000	44504	
D-KIOH(2)	Schleicher ASW 20/TOP	20038	D-7948
D-KIOI (2)	Scheibe SF-25C Falke 2000	44516	
D-KIOK(3)	Scheibe SF-25C Falke 2000	44522	
D-KIOL	Scheibe SF-25C Falke 2000	44511	
D-KIOM	Scheibe SF-25C Falke 2100	44521	
D-KION	Scheibe SF-25C Rotax-Falke	44526	
D-KIOO	Scheibe SF-25C Falke 2000	44528	
D-KIOP	Scheibe SF-25C Falke 2000	44523	
D-KIOQ	Scheibe SF-25C Rotax-Falke	44529	
D-KIOR	Scheibe SF-25C Falke 2000	44530	
D-KIOS	Scheibe SF-25C Rotax-Falke	44538	
D-KIOT	Scheibe SF-25C Falke 2000	44514	
D-KIOU(2)	Scheibe SF-25C Rotax-Falke	44551	
D-KIOV	Scheibe SF-25C Rotax-Falke	44541	
D-KIOW	Scheibe SF-25C Rotax-Falke	44537	
D-KIOX	Scheibe SF-25C Falke 2000	44507	
D-KIOY	Scheibe SF-25C Rotax-Falke	44596	
D-KIOZ	Scheibe SF-25C Rotax-Falke	44544	
D-KIPA	Scheibe SF-25C Falke	44111	
D-KIPC	Scheibe SF-25C Falke	44113	
D-KIPD	Scheibe SF-25C Falke	44114	
D-KIPE	Scheibe SF-25C Falke	44115	
D-KIPF	Stemme S-10	10-10	
D-KIPH	Schempp-Hirth Ventus cT	116/390	
D-KIPI	Grob G.109	6068	
D-KIPL	Technoflug Piccolo	036	
D-KIPM	Scheibe SF-25C Falke	44318	HB-2060
			(D-KOOI)
D-KIPP	Schleicher ASK 16	16025	
D-KIPS	Hoffmann H-36 Dimona	36204	N89PS
			OE-9264
D-KIPW	Schleicher ASH 26E	26143	
D-KIPZ-PZ	Schempp-Hirth Ventus 2cT	20/82	
D-KIQX	Schleicher ASH 25E	25087	PH-969
			D-KIQU
D-KIRA	Fournier RF-4	02	
D-KIRC(2)	Schleicher ASW 22BLE	22072	
D-KIRE	Sportavia/ Fournier RF-4D	4011	
D-KIRF	Glaser-Dirks DG-400	4-94	
D-KIRG	Schempp-Hirth Discus bT	29/326	
D-KIRI	Akaflieg Darmstadt D-39b	40	
D-KIRK	Sportavia-Pützer RF-5B Sperber	51063	
D-KIRL(2)	Schleicher ASH 25E	25034	OH-800
D-KIRN	Scheibe SF-25B Falke	4606	(D-KODO)
D-KIRO(2)	Grob G.109B	6200	
D-KIRR	Glaser-Dirks DG-500M	5E30M14	
D-KIRW	Roth Moroe WR-II	364-58-2-89	D-4363
D-KISB	Hoffmann HK-36R Super Dimona	36345	
D-KISF	Technoflug Piccolo B	075	
D-KISG	Schleicher ASH 25E	25084	
D-KISH	Schempp-Hirth Ventus cT	70/293	
D-KISI (4)	Grob G.109B	6408	
D-KISJ	Schempp-Hirth Janus CT	16/277	
D-KISK(3)	Schempp-Hirth Ventus-2cT	125/ . . .	
D-KISL	Schleicher ASK 14	14053	
D-KISN	Schleicher ASW 22BLE	22057	D-KIWW
			F-WGKS
D-KISO(3)	Schleicher ASK 16 V-1	16001	
D-KISS	Schleicher ASK 14	14049	
D-KISV	Schempp-Hirth Duo Discus T	97/423	
D-KISW	Glaser-Dirks DG-400	4-197	

D-KISY(3)	Schleicher ASH 25E (Code -ISY)	25145	
D-KITA	Alpavia/ Fournier RF-3	58	
D-KITB	Sportavia/ Fournier RF-5	5069	
D-KITE	Alpavia/ Fournier RF-3	65	
D-KITF	Technoflug Piccolo B	119	
D-KITH	Schempp-Hirth Discus bT	44/358	
D-KITI	Alpavia/ Fournier RF-3	57	
D-KITL-TL	Schempp-Hirth Ventus cT	86/331	
D-KITT(4)	Schempp-Hirth Ventus 2cM	88/184	
D-KITY	Schleicher ASK 16	16028	
D-KIVA	Scheibe SF-25A Motorfalke	4503	
D-KIVE	Schleicher ASK 16	16013	
D-KIVI (2)	Valentin Kiwi	3002	
D-KIVO	Kaiser K 16X	002	
D-KIVP	Schempp-Hirth Ventus cM	102/595	
D-KIVU(2)	Valentin Taifun 17E	1019	
D-KIVW-VW	Schleicher ASW 24E	24803	
D-KIVY	Schleicher ASK 16	16015	
D-KIWA(2)	DG Flugzeugbau DG-800B	8-196B118	
D-KIWB	Schleicher ASW 15B/KM27	15001M	
	(Converted from ASW-15 airframe c/n 15440)		
D-KIWC	Scheibe SF-25C Rotax-Falke	44589	
D-KIWE(2)	Schempp-Hirth Nimbus 3T	27/93	
D-KIWF-GL	Schempp-Hirth Ventus cM	9/424	
D-KIWG	Glaser-Dirks DG-600/18M	6-94M40	OE-9340
D-KIWK-WK	Schleicher ASH 25E	25079	
D-KIWM	Schempp-Hirth Ventus cT	154/497	
D-KIWP	Schleicher ASK 16B	16042	
D-KIWS	Glaser-Dirks DG-400	4-65	
D-KIWY	AVO 68v Samburo	015	
D-KIXI	Sportavia/ Fournier RF-4D	4153	OE-9028
D-KIXT	Schleicher ASH 25E	25040	D-4920
D-KIYL	DG Flugzeugbau DG-800B	8-192B114	
D-KIYY	Schempp-Hirth Ventus bT	42/232	
D-KIYZ	Schleicher ASH 26E	26201	
D-KIZY-ZY	DG Flugzeugbau DG-800B	8-94B29	
D-KJAA(2)	Schleicher ASH 25M	25192	
D-KJAD	Hoffmann HK-36R Super Dimona	36358	
D-KJAK	Grob G.103C Twin IIISL	35040	
D-KJAN(2)	DG Flugzeugbau DG-800B	8-130B59	
D-KJAS	Schleicher ASH 26E	26162	
D-KJBA	Scheibe SF-25C Falke 2000	44399	
D-KJBW	Glaser-Dirks DG-600/18M	6-81M27	
D-KJCB	Schempp-Hirth Nimbus 3T	14/71	BGA3648/FZE
			D-KAHA(2)
D-KJCT	Schleicher ASH 26E	26132	
D-KJET	Grob G.109	6015	(D-KISA)
D-KJFS-CH	Schempp-Hirth Discus bT	20/307	
D-KJHE	Glaser-Dirks DG-400	4-154	HB-2112
D-KJHK	Schempp-Hirth Ventus bT	5/124	
D-KJHL-IKK	Schempp-Hirth Discus 2T (Permit 2.00)	1/64	
D-KJJI	Schempp-Hirth Ventus cM	92/580	
D-KJJP	Schleicher ASW 24E	24809	
D-KJMA-MA	Schempp-Hirth Janus CM	2	
D-KJMG-JM	Schleicher ASH 26E	26169	
D-KJMM	Schempp-Hirth Nimbus 4DM	29/43	
D-KJNN	Sportavia/ Fournier RF-4D	4135	F-BPLP
D-KJOH	Schleicher ASH 26E	26008	D-2603
D-KJOM	Stemme S 10-VT	11-087	
D-KJOS	DG Flugzeugbau DG-800B	8-165B89	
D-KJOY	Schempp-Hirth Ventus 2cM	16/34	D-0575
D-KJQA	Sportavia RF-5B Sperber	51067	
D-KJRA	Schempp-Hirth Ventus cT	185/610	
D-KJRW-RW	Schempp-Hirth Discus bT	60/382	
D-KJSM	Schempp-Hirth Discus 2T	21/157	
D-KJST	Technoflug Piccolo	005	HB-2131
			D-KAFT
D-KJSW	Schempp-Hirth Ventus-2cT	135/ . . .	
D-KJTN	Valentin Taifun 17E	1074	
D-KJUL	Grob G.109	6018	
D-KJUN-V5	Schempp-Hirth Nimbus 3T	18/81	
D-KJWD	Schempp-Hirth Janus CM	25/223	D-KCGE
D-KJWE-L4	Schleicher ASH 26E	26200	(D-KKMK(1))
D-KJWL	Eiri PIK-20E	20249	LX-CAF
D-KJWT	DG Flugzeugbau DG-800B	8-74B15	
D-KKAA	Schleicher ASH 26E	26214	
D-KKAB(2)	Schempp-Hirth Ventus-2cxT (Permit 7.03)	113	
D-KKAC	Schempp-Hirth Ventus cM	74/541	N144AB
			D-KKAB
D-KKAD	Scheibe SF-25C Falke 2000	44373	
D-KKAE	Schempp-Hirth Ventus 2cT	5/13	
D-KKAG	Schempp-Hirth Ventus 2cM	20/38	
D-KKAH(3)	Stemme S 10-VT	11-093	
D-KKAI	Grob G.102 Astir CS/TOP	1303	D-7325
D-KKAJ(2)	Schempp-Hirth Ventus-2cM	128	D-5568
D-KKAL(2)	Rolladen-Schneider LS8-t	8473	
D-KKAN	Diamond HK 36 TTC Super Dimona	36722	
D-KKAO	Schempp-Hirth Ventus-2cT	109	
D-KKAR	Schempp-Hirth Ventus 2cT	100/ . . .	
D-KKAS-25	Schleicher ASH 25E	25066	
D-KKAT	Schleicher ASW 28-18E (Permit 11.04)	28721	
D-KKBA	Glaser-Dirks DG-400	4-281	(D-KODM)
D-KKBB-4T	Schempp-Hirth Janus CT	22/300	
D-KKBL	Schleicher ASH 25M	25236	
D-KKBM	Schleicher ASW 24E	24858	
D-KKBS	Schempp-Hirth Ventus cM	10/426	
D-KKCC	HOAC HK-36TTS Super Dimona	36588	

D-KKCE-CE	Rolladen-Schneider LS8-st (Permit .05)	8507	
D-KKCH	Schempp-Hirth Ventus cM	71/536	PH-900
D-KKCO	Schleicher ASH 25E	25117	
D-KKDB -DB	Schleicher ASH 25M	25169	D-2524
D-KKDF	Lange E1 Antares (Permit 3.04)	03	
D-KKDH	DG Flugzeugbau DG-800B	8-305B205	
D-KKDS	DG Flugzeugbau DG-808S	8-329B228	
D-KKDU	Schempp-Hirth Duo Discus T	58/345	
D-KKDV-M	Schempp-Hirth Ventus cM	12/434	OE-9334
D-KKEC	Scheibe SF-25C Falke	44368	
D-KKEE	Schempp-Hirth Ventus-2cM	135	
D-KKEJ	Glaser-Dirks DG-600/18M	6-96M42	
D-KKEK	Schleicher ASH 26E	26068	
D-KKEM	Schempp-Hirth Ventus cM	76/547	
D-KKFF-SKY	Schleicher ASH 26E	26202	
D-KKFL	Sportavia RF-5B Sperber	51021	(D-KCAV)
D-KKFM(2)	DG Flugzeugbau DG-800B	8-159B83	
D-KKFS	Schempp-Hirth Duo Discus T	47/326	
D-KKFT	Schleicher ASH 26E	26212	
D-KKFW	DG Flugzeugbau DG-800B	8-127B56	
D-KKGD	Schempp-Hirth Discus bT	135/510	
D-KKGG	Valentin Taifun 17E	1008	HB-2076
			D-KIHB(1)
D-KKGH-GH	Schempp-Hirth Discus bT	80/412	
D-KKGL	Schempp-Hirth Duo Discus T	33/307	
D-KKGR	Schempp-Hirth Ventus 2cT	57/187	
D-KKGS	Schempp-Hirth Ventus cM	78/551	
D-KKGU	Schempp-Hirth Duo Discus T	115/. . .	
D-KKHB(2)	Technoflug Piccolo B	084	HB-2252
			(D-KIMZ)
D-KKHF	Grob G.103C Twin IIISL	35010	N103SL
			D-KOID(2)
D-KKHG	Schempp-Hirth Discus bT	98/440	
D-KKHR	Schleicher ASH 26E	26045	
D-KKHW	Akaflieg Darmstadt D-39HKW	01	
D-KKII	Schempp-Hirth Ventus 2cM	2/16	
D-KKIK-IK	Schempp-Hirth Ventus 2cT	1/1	
D-KKIL -GW	Schempp-Hirth Ventus cM	75/544	
D-KKIS	DG Flugzeugbau DG-800B	8-106B40	
D-KKJB	Schempp-Hirth Ventus 2cM	18/36	
D-KKJP-22	Schleicher ASW 22BE	22042	
D-KKJS	Schempp-Hirth Ventus 2cM	117/251	
D-KKKB	Schleicher ASH 26E	26065	
D-KKKK(2)	Schempp-Hirth Discus 2cT (Res .05)	4/ . .	
D-KKKL(2)	Schleicher ASW 22BLE 50R	22076	
D-KKKW	Schempp-Hirth Ventus 2cT	84/252	
D-KKLB	Schleicher ASH 26E	26093	
D-KKLD	Aerotechnik L-13SDM Vivat	970615	
D-KKLH	Schempp-Hirth Ventus cM	77/548	
D-KKLL	Grob G.109B	6271	
D-KKLS-13	Schempp-Hirth Discus bT	82/415	
D-KKLW	Schleicher ASH 25M	25206	
D-KKLY	Schleicher ASH 25M	25242	
D-KKMA	Hoffmann H-36 Dimona	36222	SE-UBR
D-KKMK(2)	Schleicher ASH 26E	26010	D-0726
D-KKMM	Schempp-Hirth Janus CM	24/220	G-LIME
D-KKOP	Stemme S 10-VT	11-086	
D-KKPA	Technoflug Piccolo	044	
D-KKPB	Lange E1 Antares (Permit 3.04)	07	
D-KKPC	Schleicher ASH 25M (Permit 9.99)	25218	
D-KKPE	Schempp-Hirth Nimbus 4DM	31/45	
D-KKPO	Schempp-Hirth Discus bT	15/300	
D-KKPP	Schempp-Hirth Ventus cM	106/603	
D-KKRM	DG Flugzeugbau DG-800LA	8-86A42	
D-KKSA	Schleicher ASW 24E	24819	
D-KKSC	Valentin Taifun 17E	1013	
D-KKSG	Rolladen-Schneider LS9 (Permit)	9002	
D-KKSK	Schleicher ASW 24E	24889	
D-KKSM	Schempp-Hirth Duo Discus T	75/378	
D-KKSX	Rolladen-Schneider LS8-t (Permit 7.03)	8416	D-4674
D-KKTB	Schempp-Hirth Ventus cM	79/552	
D-KKTE	Glaser-Dirks DG-400	4-4	
D-KKTH	Schleicher ASH 25Mi (Permit .99)	25212	
D-KKTK	Alpavia/ Fournier RF-3	68	OE-9159
			D-KITO
D-KKTT	Schleicher ASW 24E	24806	
D-KKUA	Schleicher ASW 22BLE 50R	22086	
D-KKUB	DG Flugzeugbau DG-808B	8-321B221	
D-KKUM-X33	Kickert ETA	3	
D-KKUP-KV	Schleicher ASW 22BLE	22043	
D-KKUR	Schleicher ASH 26E	26217	
D-KKVB	Schempp-Hirth Nimbus 4DM	16/25	
D-KKVF	Schempp-Hirth Ventus cM	68/532	
D-KKVS	Lange E1 Antares (Permit 2.05)	09	
D-KKWD	Schempp-Hirth Ventus 2cT	101/...	
D-KKWE	Schempp-Hirth Ventus 2cM	4/18	
D-KKWI	Schempp-Hirth Ventus 2cT	98/...	
D-KKWW	Schempp-Hirth Discus bT	137/512	
D-KKXL	Schempp-Hirth Ventus 2cM	44/83	
D-KKXX	Schempp-Hirth Ventus-2cT (Permit .05)	138/ . . .	
D-KKYB	Schleicher ASH 25E	25029	(D-KEJB)
			D-3125
D-KKYD	Schleicher ASH 25M	25197	
D-KLAB	Scheibe SF-25B Falke	46206	(D-KASC)
D-KLAC(2)	Schempp-Hirth Ventus 2cT	30/102	
D-KLAD(2)	Schempp-Hirth Nimbus 4M ("AD")	4/17	
D-KLAH-AH	Schempp-Hirth Ventus cT	106/369	

D-KLAI	HOAC HK-36TTC Super Dimona	36567	
D-KLAK(2)	Alpavia/ Fournier RF-3	12	F-BLXD
D-KLAM	Sportavia/ Fournier RF-5	5123	
D-KLAN	Glaser-Dirks DG-400	4-234	
D-KLAR	Schleicher ASK 14	14038	
D-KLAT	Hoffmann H-36 Dimona	36246	
D-KLAU	Scheibe SF-25C Falke 2000	44481	
D-KLAX	Scheibe SF-25C Falke 2000	44428	
D-KLAY	Schempp-Hirth Janus CT	15/276	D-4530
D-KLBA	Scheibe SF-25B Falke	4621	OE-9341
			D-KEGI
D-KLBB	Schleicher ASW 24E	24801	
D-KLBD	Schleicher ASH 25EB28 (Permit .05)	25249	
D-KLBE	Technoflug Piccolo B	106	
D-KLBG	Schempp-Hirth Ventus cT	158/511	
D-KLBI	Technoflug Piccolo	053	
D-KLBP	Schleicher ASH 25M	25186	
D-KLBR	Glaser-Dirks DG-600/18M	6-104M38	OH-843
D-KLBW	Grob G.109B	6368	
D-KLBY	Klotz Moka 1	1	
D-KLCA	DG Flugzeugbau DG-800B	8-200B122	
D-KLCB	DG Flugzeugbau DG-800B	8-291B196	
D-KLCC(2)	Stemme S-10VT	11-072	
D-KLCH	Schempp-Hirth Discus bT (Res .05)	84/418	V5-GAB
D-KLDA	Scheibe SF-25C Falke	44124	
D-KLDB(2)	SZD-45A Ogar	B-762	DDR-3509
			DM-3509
D-KLDD	Scheibe SF-25C Falke	44127	
D-KLDH(2)	Schempp-Hirth Discus bT ("DH")	1/245	
D-KLDT	Scheibe SF-25C Rotax-Falke	44636	
D-KLEB	Schempp-Hirth Ventus cT	177/581	
D-KLEC	Scheibe SF-25C Rotax-Falke	44546	
D-KLEE	Sportavia/ Fournier RF-5	5076	
D-KLEF	HOAC HK-36TC Super Dimona (Res 3.00)	36661	
D-KLEH(2)	Hoffmann H-36 Dimona	36213	SU-184
			OE-9316
			D-KFLB
D-KLEM(2)	HOAC HK-36TTC Super Dimona	36657	
D-KLEO(3)	Rolladen-Schneider LS8-t (Permit 5.03)	8471	
D-KLER	Sportavia/ Fournier RF-5	5051	
D-KLES	Schempp-Hirth Nimbus 3DM	13/36	F-CFUK
			D-KFUK
D-KLEU	Glaser-Dirks DG-400	4-180	
D-KLFA	Grob G.109B	6210	HB-2079
D-KLFB	Schempp-Hirth Duo Discus T	80/393	
D-KLFR	Schempp-Hirth Ventus 2cT	87/. . .	
D-KLFV	Schempp-Hirth Discus bM	9/542	
D-KLFW	Hoffmann H-36 Dimona	36249	OE-9290
D-KLGA	Schleicher ASH 26E	26058	
D-KLGB	Schempp-Hirth Discus 2T	12/123	
D-KLGH(2)	HOAC HK-36TTS Super Dimona	36621	
D-KLGR	Glaser-Dirks DG-400	4-129	G-BUXG
			D-KEHJ
D-KLGS	Schleicher ASH 26E	26077	
D-KLHA	Schempp-Hirth Discus bT	79/411	
D-KLHB	Schleicher ASH 26E	26049	
D-KLHG	Schleicher ASW 24/TOP	24821	
D-KLHH	Technoflug Piccolo	043	
D-KLHL-HL	Schleicher ASW 22BLE	22070	
D-KLHM	Schempp-Hirth Nimbus 4DM	21/31	
D-KLHS	Schleicher ASH 26E	26066	
D-KLHW	Schleicher ASH 25EB	25172	
D-KLHZ	Glaser-Dirks DG-800	8-72A40	
D-KLIA	Schleicher ASH 26E	26081	
D-KLIC	Grob G.102 Astir CS77/TOP	1648	OE-9323
			D-4823
D-KLID	Aerotechnik L-13SDM Vivat	970613	
D-KLIF	HOAC HK-36TC Super Dimona	36728	
D-KLII	Schleicher ASW 24/TOP	24807	HB-2227
			D-KCCL
D-KLIK	Sportavia/ Fournier RF-5	5125	
D-KLIL	Eiriavion PIK-20E	20224	
D-KLIM	Technoflug Piccolo	049	
D-KLIN(3)	Hoffmann H-36 Dimona	3616	HB-2066
D-KLIO	Scheibe SF-25A Motorfalke	4520	OE-9015
			D-KAJE(1)
D-KLIP	Glaser-Dirks DG-400	4-153	OO-NIN
D-KLIR	Sportavia/ Fournier RF-5	5052	
D-KLIS	Schempp-Hirth Ventus 2cT	36/124	
D-KLIX(2)	SZD-45A Ogar	B-767	DDR-3514
			DM-3514
D-KLJC	Glaser-Dirks DG-400	4-114	
D-KLJP	Schleicher ASH 25E	25082	
D-KLKA	Schempp-Hirth Ventus cT	169/556	
D-KLKG	Schleicher ASH 26E	26135	(D-KLUF)
D-KLKL	Schleicher ASH 25E	25053	
D-KLKM	Eiriavion PIK-20E	20258	HB-2050
D-KLLI (2)	Schleicher ASH 25E	25153	
D-KLLL(2)	Schempp-Hirth Ventus 2cT	68/207	
D-KLLW	Schempp-Hirth Ventus cM	58/508	
D-KLLX	Schempp-Hirth Ventus 2cM	17/35	
D-KLLZ	Rolladen-Schneider LS9 (Permit 5.01)	9009	
D-KLMB-TE	Schempp-Hirth Duo Discus T	93/413	
D-KLMC	Glaser-Dirks DG-600/18M	6-106M48	
D-KLMD	Schleicher ASH 25E	25050	HB-2171
			D-KCCH(1)
D-KLMI	Hoffmann HK-36R Super Dimona	36365	

D-KLMJ	Hoffmann HK-36R Super Dimona	36366	
D-KLMK	Hoffmann HK-36R Super Dimona	36367	
D-KLML	Hoffmann HK-36R Super Dimona	36368	
D-KLMM	Hoffmann HK-36R Super Dimona	36369	
D-KLMN	Hoffmann HK-36R Super Dimona	36370	
D-KLOA	Schleicher ASW 24E	24859	
D-KLOF	Rolladen-Schneider LS9 (Permit 11.99)	9004	
D-KLOR	Sportavia/ Fournier RF-5	5053	
D-KLOU(2)	Scheibe SF-25C Falke 2000	44508	
D-KLPC	Glaser-Dirks DG-400	4-190	
D-KLPH	Hoffmann HK-36R Super Dimona	36383	PH-1030
			D-KMDD
D-KLPN	Glaser-Dirks DG-400	4-251	
D-KLPP-PP	Glaser-Dirks DG-400	4-179	
D-KLPR	DG Flugzeugbau DG-800B	8-85B22	
D-KLPW	Schleicher ASH 26E	26113	
D-KLPY	Schleicher ASH 26E	26079	
D-KLRD	SZD-45A Ogar	B-648	DDR-3502
			DM-3502
D-KLRK	Hoffmann H-36 Dimona	3626	PH-724
D-KLRS(2)	Glaser-Dirks DG-400	4-81	
D-KLRW	Schempp-Hirth Ventus 2cM	111/	
D-KLSB	Scheibe SF-25C Falke 2000	44503	
D-KLSC	Schleicher ASK 14	AB14066	
D-KLSE	Schempp-Hirth Ventus 2cM	106/219	
D-KLSG	Scheibe SF-25C Falke 2000	44336	
D-KLSH	Schempp-Hirth Ventus 2cM	31/55	
D-KLSI	Grob G.103C Twin IIISL	35044	
D-KLSM	Schempp-Hirth Ventus-2cxM	148	
D-KLSR	HOAC HK-36TTC Super Dimona	36686	
D-KLST-8T	Rolladen-Schneider LS8-t (Permit 5.01)	8400	
D-KLSV(2)	HOAC HK-36TTC Super Dimona (Res 3.00)	36660	
D-KLSW(2)	Scheibe SF-25C Rotax-Falke	44580	
D-KLSX-SX	Schleicher ASH 26E	26097	D-6826
D-KLTB	DG Flugzeugbau DG-800B	8-306B206	
D-KLTE	Valentin Taifun 17E	1077	(D-KLET)
D-KLTF	Technoflug Carat	CA006	
D-KLTI	DG Flugzeugbau DG-800B	8-238B152	
D-KLUB(2)	Scheibe SF-25C Rotax-Falke	44543	
D-KLUW	Valentin Taifun 17E	1035	
D-KLUX(2)	Schempp-Hirth Ventus 2cM	58/114	
D-KLUZ	SZD-45A Ogar	B-659	DDR-3506
			DM-3506
			(SP-0020)
D-KLVE	HOAC HK-36TS Super Dimona	36506	
D-KLVG	AVO 68v Samburo 2000	023	
D-KLVI	Grob G.109B	6559	
D-KLVO	Schleicher ASK 14	14019	(D-KEHO)
D-KLVW	HOAC HK-36TTC Super Dimona	36662	
D-KLWA	DG Flugzeugbau DG-800B	8-96B31	
D-KLWG	HOAC HK-36TTS Super Dimona	36584	
D-KLWM	Scheibe SF-25C Rotax-Falke	44690	
D-KLWS	Schempp-Hirth Ventus cM	91/578	
D-KLWW	ICA/Brasov I S.28M2/G	71	
D-KLYY	Schempp-Hirth Ventus cM	28/461	D-2444
D-KLZM	Rolladen-Schneider LS9 (Permit)	9001	
D-KMAB	Scheibe SF-25D Falke	46107D	
D-KMAC(3)	DG Flugzeugbau DG-800B	8-262B170	
D-KMAD	Scheibe SF-25B Falke	46109	
D-KMAG	Scheibe SF-25B Falke	46112	
D-KMAH(2)	Schempp-Hirth Ventus 2cM	19/37	D-KNHC(1)
			D-3241
D-KMAI	Scheibe SF-25B Falke	46114	
D-KMAL(2)	HOAC HK-36TTS Super Dimona	36585	
D-KMAM	Stemme S-10V	14-020	F-CGYO
			(D-KGDC(2))
D-KMAN	Scheibe Bergfalke IVSM	5902	
D-KMAR	Scheibe SF-25C Falke 2000	4415	
D-KMAS	Schleicher ASH 26E	26102	
D-KMAX	Scheibe SF-25C Falke 2000	44381	
D-KMBA	Schempp-Hirth Ventus 2cM	114/	
D-KMBB	Scheibe SF-25D Falke	46182D	
D-KMBE	Schempp-Hirth Ventus 2cM	116/248	
D-KMBG(2)	Grob G.109B	6558	
D-KMBP	Schleicher ASW 22BE	22045	VH- . . .
D-KMCA	Scheibe SF-25C Rotax-Falke	44605	
D-KMCB	Stemme S-10	10-6	
D-KMCD	DG Flugzeugbau DG-800B	8-180B104	
D-KMCI	Stemme S-10VT	11-046	
D-KMCL	Technoflug Piccolo B	120	
D-KMCM-CM	Rolladen-Schneider LS8-t	8418	D-5984
D-KMCO	Glaser-Dirks DG-600M	6-54M8	F-CGRQ
			D-KBDG(2)
D-KMCW	DG Flugzeugbau DG-800B	8-149B73	
D-KMDB	Hoffmann HK-36R Super Dimona	36385	
D-KMDC	Hoffmann HK-36R Super Dimona	36384	
D-KMDG(2)	Glaser-Dirks DG-600/18M	6-38M1	
D-KMDK	Schleicher ASH 25M	25182	
D-KMDO	Stemme S-10VT	11-069	
D-KMDP	Alpavia/ Fournier RF-3	37	F-BMDP
D-KMDS	Schempp-Hirth Discus bT	72/400	
D-KMDZ	Alpavia/ Fournier RF-3	50	F-BMDZ
D-KMEA	Stemme S 10-VT	11-080	
D-KMED	Grob G.109B	6291	
D-KMEI	Technoflug Piccolo B	063	
D-KMEJ	DG Flugzeugbau DG-800B	8-134B63	
D-KMEM	Sportavia/ Fournier RF-4D	4037	G-BMEM
			CN-TZZ
D-KMER	Valentin Taifun 17E	1018	
D-KMES	Schleicher ASK 16	16034	
D-KMET	Schleicher ASK 16	16007	
D-KMEY	Scheibe SF-25C Falke 2000	44484	
D-KMFB	DG Flugzeugbau DG-808B	8-320B220	
D-KMFE	Schempp-Hirth Discus bT	26/319	
D-KMFF	Schleicher ASH 26E	26194	
D-KMFN-FN	Schempp-Hirth Ventus 2cT	33/115	
D-KMFS	Scheibe SF-25C Falke	44215	OO-VZA
			D-KDFV(1)
D-KMFW	DG Flugzeugbau DG-800B	8-54B7	D-KNMB(2)
	(Reservation, on rebuild)		
D-KMGB	Scheibe SF-28A Tandem-Falke	5752	
D-KMGE(2)	Schempp-Hirth Duo Discus T ("GE")	18/271	
D-KMGO	HOAC HK-36TTC Super Dimona	36568	
D-KMGR	Schempp-Hirth Ventus 2cT	18/76	
D-KMGS	Schleicher ASH 26E	26117	
D-KMHA	Valentin Taifun 17E	1061	HB-2113
	(Repaired using new fuselage c/n 1105)		D-KMHA
D-KMHB-HB	Valentin Kiwi	3006	
D-KMHG	Schleicher ASH 25M	25175	
D-KMHK	Technoflug Piccolo	052	
D-KMHS	Schempp-Hirth Ventus 2cM	11/28	
D-KMHW	DG Flugzeugbau DG-800LA	8-58A35	
D-KMIC	Eiri PIK-20E	20285	HB-2057
D-KMIF	Schleicher ASK 16	16033	
D-KMIG -IG	Schempp-Hirth Nimbus 3T	21/85	
D-KMII -CD	Schempp-Hirth Ventus bT	33/208	
D-KMIJ-WJ	Schempp-Hirth Ventus bT	65/280	
D-KMIL(2)	Schempp-Hirth Ventus bT	11/146	
D-KMIM-IM	Schempp-Hirth Janus CT	5/200	
D-KMIN	Schempp-Hirth Nimbus 3T	17/80	
D-KMJE	Scheibe SF-25C Falke	44105	
D-KMJF	Scheibe SF-25C Falke (W/o 27.5.00)	44106	
D-KMJH	Scheibe SF-25C Falke	44108	
D-KMJI	Scheibe SF-25C Falke	44109	
D-KMKA	Valentin Taifun 17E-II	1134	HB-2162
			D-KHVA
D-KMKH	Schempp-Hirth Ventus cTT (Permit 10.02)	290	D-2976
D-KMKM	Schleicher ASW 24E	24818	
D-KMKN-KN	Schempp-Hirth Discus bT	166/579	
D-KMKR	Hoffmann H-36 Dimona	36255	
D-KMKS	Hoffmann HK-36R Super Dimona	36409	
D-KMKW-AX	Schleicher ASH 25E	25151	D-6925
D-KMLA	DG Flugzeugbau DG-808B	8-296B201	
D-KMLH-LH	Schempp-Hirth Ventus bT	40/230	
D-KMLI	Grob G.103C Twin IIISL	35024	D-KJHF
D-KMLL	Scheibe SF-25C Falke 2100	44510	
D-KMLN	Schempp-Hirth Ventus 2cM	7/24	F-CGLU
			D-8137
D-KMLR	Glaser-Dirks DG-400	4-152	
D-KMLV	Grob G.109B	6260	
D-KMMA	Schempp-Hirth Ventus 2cM	14/31	
D-KMMC-MC	Schempp-Hirth Discus bT	118/474	
D-KMMG	Scheibe SF-36B	4105	G-BKAH
			(D-KOGF)
D-KMML(3)	HOAC HK-36TTC Super Dimona	36573	
D-KMMM	Scheibe SF-25C Falke 2000	44502	
D-KMMO	Schleicher ASH 26E	26173	
D-KMMR	Schempp-Hirth Discus bT	64/389	
D-KMMW	Schempp-Hirth Ventus cM	31/464	
D-KMNC-NC	Grob G.103C Twin IIISL	35023	
D-KMNW	Glaser-Dirks DG-400	4-249	
D-KMOB	Grob G.103C Twin IIISL	35031	
D-KMOD	Scheibe SF-25C Rotax-Falke	44610	
D-KMOE	Schempp-Hirth Ventus cT	129/406	
D-KMOR	Scheibe SF-25C Falke 2000	44532	
D-KMPA	Sportavia/ Scheibe SF-25C Falke	4248	(D-KAJK)
D-KMPB(2)	Schempp-Hirth Ventus 2cM	46/95	
D-KMPE	Sportavia/ Scheibe SF-25C Falke	4253	
D-KMPF	Sportavia-Pützer RF-5B Sperber	51071	
D-KMPK	Schempp-Hirth Ventus 2cM	34/60	
D-KMPP	Schleicher ASH 25M	25191	
D-KMPR	Schleicher ASH 26E	26056	
D-KMPS	Sportavia/ Scheibe SF-25C Falke	4255	
D-KMRA	Glaser-Dirks DG-400	4-92	HB-2085
D-KMRD	Schleicher ASH 26E	26083	
D-KMRH	Scheibe SF-25C Rotax-Falke	44540	(D-KIOU)
D-KMRL	DG Flugzeugbau DG-800B	8-261B169	
D-KMRM	Grob G.109	6076	(D-KIRC)
D-KMRV-RV	Schempp-Hirth Ventus 2cM	54/108	
D-KMSA	Technoflug Piccolo B	090	
D-KMSB	Glaser-Dirks DG-400	4-48	G-DGLM
			D-KMDH
D-KMSC	Scheibe SF-25C Rotax-Falke	44577	
D-KMSE	Reichelt Erpel	V-1	
D-KMSF-SF	Schempp-Hirth Ventus cT	100/357	
D-KMSH	Schleicher ASW 24E	24837	
D-KMSL	Hoffmann H-36 Dimona	36250	
D-KMSQ	Scheibe SF-25C Falke 2000	4435	
D-KMSR	Scheibe SF-25C Falke	4436	
D-KMSS	Scheibe SF-25C Falke	4437	
D-KMSV	Scheibe SF-25C Falke	4440	
D-KMSY	Schempp-Hirth Ventus 2cM	61/121	
D-KMTB	Glaser-Dirks DG-800LA	8-20A17	

D-KMTL(2)	Schempp-Hirth Ventus cM	5/413	D-KLAZ
D-KMTO	DG Flugzeugbau DG-800LA	8-17A14	
D-KMTT	Hoffmann H-36 Dimona	3630	
D-KMTW	DG Flugzeugbau DG-800B	8-275B183	
D-KMUE	Stemme S-10	10-12	
D-KMWA	Schempp-Hirth Ventus-2cM	95/200	N5FU
D-KMWD	Schempp-Hirth Discus bT	86/421	
D-KMWF	Schempp-Hirth Ventus 2cM	81/171	
D-KMWM	DG Flugzeugbau DG-800B	8-193B115	
D-KMWP	Schleicher ASH 26E	26115	
D-KMWS	Glaser-Dirks DG-600M	6-43M2	
D-KMWW	Glaser-Dirks DG-400	4-250	
D-KNAB	Scheibe SF-25C Falke 2000	44338	
D-KNAC	Scheibe SF-25C Falke 2000	44341	
D-KNAD	Scheibe SF-25C Falke 2000	44337	
D-KNAE(2)	Scheibe SF-25C Falke 2000	44345	
D-KNAG(2)	Scheibe SF-25C Falke 2000	44419	
D-KNAJ	Scheibe SF-25C Falke 2000	44352	
D-KNAK(5)	Alpavia/ Fournier RF-3	88	OE-9102 D-KILE(1)
D-KNAL	Scheibe SF-25C Falke 2000	44178	
D-KNAM(2)	Scheibe SF-25C Falke 2000	44356	
D-KNAO	Scheibe SF-25C Falke 2000	44361	
D-KNAP	Scheibe SF-25C Falke 2000	44353	
D-KNAQ(2)	Scheibe SF-25C Falke 2000	44366	
D-KNAR	Scheibe SF-25C Falke 2000	44359	
D-KNAS	Scheibe SF-25C Falke 2000	44365	
D-KNAT	Scheibe SF-25C Falke 2000	44364	
D-KNAU(2)	Scheibe SF-25E Super Falke	4363	
D-KNAW	Scheibe SF-25C Falke 2000	44372	
D-KNAY	Scheibe SF-25C Falke 2000	44374	
D-KNAZ	Scheibe SF-25C Falke 2000	44371	
D-KNBE	Schempp-Hirth Ventus cT	141/435	D-5092
D-KNCL	Schempp-Hirth Duo Discus T	11/257	D-2091
D-KNCM	Schempp-Hirth Ventus cM	98/589	
D-KNDS	Schempp-Hirth Discus-2T	36/201	
D-KNEB	Grob G.109B	6340	
D-KNEC	Grob G.109B	6350	
D-KNED	Grob G.109B	6354	
D-KNEE	Grob G.109B	6351	
D-KNEF	Grob G.109B	6358	
D-KNEG	Grob G.109B	6359	
D-KNEH	Grob G.109B	6380	
D-KNEI	Grob G.109B	6379	OH-747
D-KNEL	Grob G.109B	6426	
D-KNEM	Grob G.109B	6422	
D-KNEN	Grob G.109B	6438	
D-KNEO	Grob G.109B	6439	
D-KNER	Grob G.109B	6551	
D-KNES	Grob G.109B	6421	
D-KNEU	Aerotechnik L-13SL Vivat	920423	
D-KNEW	Grob G.109B	6360	(EAF-671)
D-KNEX	Grob G.109B	6402	
D-KNFA	Schempp-Hirth Discus bT	150/541	
D-KNFN	Schempp-Hirth Discus bT	88/425	
D-KNFU	Schempp-Hirth Discus bT	151/543	
D-KNGD	Schleicher ASH 25M (Permit 5.00)	25217	
D-KNGS	Schempp-Hirth Ventus cM	57/507	
D-KNHB	Schleicher ASH 26E	26048	
D-KNHC(2)	Schempp-Hirth Ventus 2cM	152/ . . .	
D-KNHD	Schempp-Hirth Ventus cT	136/418	
D-KNHW	DG Flugzeugbau DG-800B	8-240B154	
D-KNIA	Scheibe SF-25C Falke 2000	44377	
D-KNIB	Scheibe SF-25C Falke 2000	44378	
D-KNIC	Scheibe SF-25C Falke 2000	44379	
D-KNID	Scheibe SF-25C Falke 2000	44380	
D-KNIF(2)	Scheibe SF-25C Falke 2000	44390	
D-KNIG(2)	Scheibe SF-25C Falke 2000	44397	
D-KNIH(2)	Scheibe SF-25C Falke 2000	44398	
D-KNII (2)	Scheibe SF-25C Falke 2000	44402	
D-KNIJ(2)	Scheibe SF-25C Falke 2000	44404	
D-KNIK	Scheibe SF-25C Falke 2000	44405	
D-KNIL(2)	Scheibe SF-25C Falke 2000	44417	
D-KNIM(2)	Scheibe SF-25C Falke 2000	44418	
D-KNIN(2)	Scheibe SF-25C Falke 2000	44421	
D-KNIO(2)	Scheibe SF-25C Falke 2000	44423	
D-KNIP	Scheibe SF-25C Falke 2000	44416	
D-KNIQ	Scheibe SF-25C Falke 2000	44403	
D-KNIR	Scheibe SF-25C Falke 2000	44426	
D-KNIS	Scheibe SF-25C Falke 2000	44424	
D-KNIT	Scheibe SF-25C Falke 2000	44427	
D-KNIU(2)	Scheibe SF-25C Falke 2000	44429	
D-KNIV	Scheibe SF-25C Falke 2000	44432	
D-KNIW	Scheibe SF-25C Falke 2000	44409	
D-KNIX	Scheibe SF-25C Falke 2000	44196	HB-2041 (D-KDAM)
D-KNIZ	Scheibe SF-25C Falke 2000	44430	
D-KNJA	Technoflug Piccolo B	022	OE-9307 D-KCTC
D-KNKK	Glaser-Dirks DG-400	4-141	(ZS- . . .)
D-KNKN	Scheibe SF-25K Falke	4902	
D-KNLH	Schempp-Hirth Nimbus 4DM	4/10	
D-KNNN	Grob G.109B	6202	OY-XNN D-KGFB
D-KNOL	Schleicher ASK 14	14001	HB-2395 PH-1049 D-KIKY

D-KNOM	DG Flugzeugbau DG-800B	8-167B91	
D-KNOP	Scheibe SF-25C Falke 2000	44116	
D-KNOR	Scheibe SF-25C Falke	44118	
D-KNOS	Schleicher ASW 28-18E (Permit 3.04)	28704	
D-KNOW	Grob G.109B	6267	N713BR N53553
D-KNOX(2)	Valentin Taifun 17E	1010	
D-KNPF	Knechtel KN-1	V-1	
D-KNRA	Glaser-Dirks DG-400 (Permit 3.00)	4-157	F-CFVH
D-KNRV	Schempp-Hirth Duo Discus T	32/305	
D-KNSN	HOAC HK-36TC Super Dimona	36576	
D-KNTI	Schempp-Hirth Ventus 2cT	92/...	
D-KNUE	Technoflug Piccolo B	062	D-MNUE D-KNUE
D-KNUM	Valentin Taifun 17E II	1115	
D-KNUS	Schleicher ASK 16	16027	
D-KNUT(2)	Hoffmann H-36 Dimona (Permit 3.00)	3677	
D-KNWF	Hoffmann H-36 Dimona	36247	OE-9383 D-KITT(2)
D-KNWN	Schleicher Rhönlerche II-Storch	1	
D-KNWS	Schempp-Hirth Discus bT	56/377	
D-KOAB	*Test Registration for Schleicher production*		
D-KOAD	Scheibe SF-25C Falke	4457	
D-KOAG	Scheibe SF-25C Falke 2000	4460	
D-KOAH	Scheibe SF-28A Tandem-Falke	5716	
D-KOAK(2)	Schempp-Hirth Ventus cM	73/539	
D-KOAM(2)	Schempp-Hirth Ventus cM	81/555	
D-KOAS(2)	Grob G.109	6113	
D-KOAU	Scheibe SF-25C Falke	4463	
D-KOAW	Scheibe SF-25C Falke	4464	
D-KOAZ	Scheibe SF-25C Falke	4467	
D-KOBA(3)	Grob G.102 Astir CS/TOP	1025	D-5874
D-KOBB(2)	HOAC HK-36TTC Super Dimona	36560	
D-KOBC(2)	Schleicher ASH 26E	26193	
D-KOBD(2)	Glaser-Dirks DG-600M	6-48M4	
D-KOBE(3)	Glaser-Dirks DG-400	4-69	
D-KOBG(2)	Schempp-Hirth Nimbus 3DT	7	
D-KOBH(2)	Schempp-Hirth Discus bT	154/549	
D-KOBI (4)	Glaser-Dirks DG-400	4-161	
D-KOBJ	Scheibe SF-25C Falke	4468	
D-KOBK	Scheibe SF-25C Falke	4469	
D-KOBL(2)	Grob G.109B	6579	
D-KOBM	Glaser-Dirks DG-600M	6-56M10	(D-KEJB(2))
D-KOBN	Scheibe SF-25C Rotax-Falke	44609	
D-KOBO	Raab Krähe IV	102	
D-KOBR	Glaser-Dirks DG-600M	6-71M20	
D-KOBT	Schempp-Hirth Discus bT	109/458	
D-KOBY(2)	Scheibe SF-25B Falke	4616	
D-KOCA(2)	Technoflug Piccolo B	088	
D-KOCB	DG Flugzeugbau DG-800S	8-335B234	
D-KOCC	Grob G.109	6012	
D-KOCD	Scheibe SF-25C Falke 2000	44492	
D-KOCH(3)	HOAC HK-36TTC Super Dimona	36666	
D-KOCI (2)	Sportavia/ Fournier RF-5	5127	G-BJCG (D-KOCI)
D-KOCK	Scheibe SF-25C Rotax-Falke	44534	
D-KOCO(2)	Valentin Taifun 17E	1045	
D-KOCP	DG Flugzeugbau DG-800B	8-104B38	G-BXFA D-KOCP
D-KODA(2)	Scheibe SF-25C Falke 2000	44422	
D-KODC	Scheibe SF-25D Falke	4613D	
D-KODD	Scheibe SF-25B Falke	4615	
D-KODE(2)	Scheibe SF-25B Falke	4604	
D-KODG	Scheibe SF-25D Falke	4618D	
D-KODH-44	Schempp-Hirth Ventus 2cM	96/ . . .	G-OODH
D-KODI	Scheibe SF-25B Falke	4605	
D-KODO(2)	Scheibe SF-25B Falke	4614	
D-KODV-DV	Schempp-Hirth Discus 2T (Permit 8.00)	4/80	
D-KOEA	Scheibe SF-28A Tandem-Falke	5731	
D-KOEB(4)	Schempp-Hirth Ventus cT	142/439	
D-KOEF	Scheibe SF-28A Tandem-Falke	5736	
D-KOEI (2)	Scheibe SF-28A Tandem-Falke	5744	
D-KOEJ	Scheibe SF-28A Tandem-Falke	5740	
D-KOEL(2)	Valentin Taifun 17E	1020	
D-KOEN	Scheibe SF-25C Falke	4473	
D-KOEP	Scheibe SF-25C Falke	4475	
D-KOEQ	Scheibe SF-25C Falke 2000	4476	
D-KOER	Scheibe SF-25C Falke	4477	
D-KOES	Sportavia/ Fournier RF-5	5047	
D-KOET	Scheibe SF-25C Falke	4478	
D-KOEU	Scheibe SF-25C Falke 2000	4479	
D-KOEV	Scheibe SF-25C Falke	4480	
D-KOEX	Scheibe SF-28A Tandem-Falke	5746	
D-KOFB	Schempp-Hirth Ventus 2cM	125/274	
D-KOFC(2)	Glaser-Dirks DG-400	4-278	
D-KOFE(2)	Schempp-Hirth Ventus cT	184/604	OY-XUU
D-KOFI (2)	Scheibe SF-25B Falke	4625	
D-KOFN	Glaser-Dirks DG-600M	6-74M22	
D-KOFO(2)	Detmold K.8B/Lloyd	8724M	
D-KOFU	Scheibe SF-25A Motorfalke	4551	
D-KOFY(3)	Valentin Taifun 17E-II	1103	
D-KOGA	Kaiser K 12	12001M	
D-KOGB	Schleicher ASH 26E	26015	
D-KOGE(2)	SZD-45A Ogar	B-647	DDR-3501 DM-3501(2)
D-KOGM	Schempp-Hirth Nimbus 3DT	27	
D-KOGN	Scheibe SF-25C Falke 2000	44531	

D-KOGO(3)	Sportavia RF-5B Sperber	51057	D-KEAN
D-KOGR	SZD-45A Ogar	B-662	DDR-3507
			DM-3507
D-KOGS	AVO 68v Samburo	027	
D-KOGY(2)	Valentin Taifun 17E (Reservation 11.99)	1058	(D-KBHA)
			F-CGAH
			F-WGAH
			D-KBHA
D-KOHA	Sportavia/ Fournier RF-4D	4072	
D-KOHB(3)	Stemme S 10-VT	11-081	
D-KOHE	Sportavia/ Fournier RF-4D	4073	
D-KOHG	Schleicher ASK 14	14036	
D-KOHI (2)	Sportavia/ Fournier RF-4D	4081	
D-KOHK(2)	Schempp-Hirth Ventus 2cT	24/92	
D-KOHL	Schleicher ASK 14	14046	
D-KOHO	Sportavia/ Fournier RF-4D	4079	
D-KOHS	Glaser-Dirks DG-400	4-287	
D-KOHU	Sportavia/ Fournier RF-4D	4091	
D-KOHW	Stemme S-10V	14-009	OO-CSZ
	(Originally built as S-10 c/n 10-62)		D-KGDB
			D-KSTE
D-KOII	Scheibe SF 25C Falke	44697	
D-KOIL	Schleicher ASH 26E	26131	
D-KOIM	Scheibe SF-25C Falke 2000	44659	
D-KOIS	Hoffmann HK-36R Super Dimona	36333	
D-KOIW	Schempp-Hirth Discus bT	104/449	
D-KOJB	Scheibe SF-25C Rotax-Falke	44591	
D-KOJO	Schempp-Hirth Nimbus 4M	9/26	
D-KOKA(2)	Valentin Taifun 17E	1003	(D-KJMS)
D-KOKH	DG Flugzeugbau DG-800B	8-197B119	
D-KOKI (2)	Scheibe SF-25A Motorfalke	4553	D-KOGI (1)
D-KOKK	Glaser-Dirks DG-500M	5E87M37	
D-KOKO(2)	Sportavia/ Fournier RF-5	5042	
D-KOKS(2)	Hoffmann HK-36R Super Dimona	36386	OE-9400
			F-CGAZ
D-KOLA(3)	Schleicher ASH 25E	25067	
D-KOLC	Schempp-Hirth Discus bM	3/438	
D-KOLD	Sportavia-Pützer RF-5B Sperber	51061	
D-KOLE(2)	DG Flugzeugbau DG-808B	8-312B212	
D-KOLG-AR	Schleicher ASH 26E	26091	
D-KOLH	Grob G.109B	6295	
D-KOLI	AVO 68v Samburo	013	
D-KOLK	Technoflug Piccolo	038	
D-KOLL	Glaser-Dirks DG-400	4-1	G-KOLL
			D-KOLL
D-KOLN	Schempp-Hirth Nimbus 2M	05	
D-KOLT	Scheibe SF-25C Falke 2000	44449	
D-KOMA	Schleicher ASK 14	14025	
D-KOMB	Brditschka HB-23/2400SP	23039-U	OE-9324
D-KOME	Schleicher ASK 14	14027	
D-KOMH	HOAC HK-36TTC Super Dimona	36593	
D-KOMI (2)	Sportavia/ Scheibe SF-25C Falke	4254	
D-KOMM	Scheibe SF-25B Falke	4658	
D-KOMO(2)	Glaser-Dirks DG-400	4-71	LN-GMW
			G-BLCX
D-KOMS	Grob G.109	6101	
D-KOMT-MT	Schempp-Hirth Ventus 2cT	65/202	
D-KOMU	Schleicher ASK 14	14029	
D-KOMY(2)	Schempp-Hirth Ventus 2cM ("9A")	9/26	
D-KONB(2)	Schleicher ASK 14	14043	
D-KOND	Schleicher ASK 14	14042	
D-KONE	Schleicher ASK 14	14044	
D-KONF	Sportavia/ Fournier RF-5	5057	
D-KONG	Sportavia/ Fournier RF-5	5058	
D-KONH	Sportavia/ Fournier RF-5	5059	
D-KONI (2)	Schleicher ASH 25M	25179	
D-KONK(2)	Fedrau Aquila	001	
D-KONO(2)	Röhrdanz JR1 Tinetta 17R/70	01	
	(Rebuild from Taifun 17E D-KONO(1) c/n 01)		
D-KONX-NX	Schleicher ASW 22BLE	22048	
D-KONY(2)	Hoffmann H-36 Dimona	36131	OE-9234
D-KONZ	Scheibe SF-25C Falke 2000	44477	
D-KOOC(2)	Scheibe SF-25C Falke 2000	44314	
D-KOOD(2)	Scheibe SF-25C Falke 2000	44313	
D-KOOE(2)	Scheibe SF-25C Falke 2000	44315	
D-KOOF	Scheibe SF-25C Falke	44305	
D-KOOG(2)	Scheibe SF-25C Falke 2000	44316	
D-KOOH(3)	Scheibe SF-25C Falke 2000	44319	
D-KOOI (2)	Scheibe SF-36R	4103	
D-KOOJ	Scheibe SF-25C Falke 2000	AB44321	
D-KOOK	Scheibe SF-25C Falke 2000	44320	
D-KOOL	Scheibe SF-25C Falke 2000	44323	
D-KOOM	Scheibe SF-25C Falke	4484	HB-2028
			(D-KEID)
D-KOOO	Scheibe SF-36B	4106	
D-KOOP	Scheibe SF-36A	4101	
D-KOOS	Scheibe SF-25C Falke	44329	
D-KOOT	Scheibe SF-25C Falke 2000	44330	
D-KOOU	Scheibe SF-25C Falke 2000	44331	
D-KOOV(2)	Scheibe SF-25C Falke 2000	44332	VH-HDM
			D-KOOV(2)
D-KOOX	Scheibe SF-25C Falke 2000	44327	
D-KOPA	Hoffmann H-36 Dimona	36267	
D-KOPC	Glaser-Dirks DG-400	4-237	
D-KOPF(2)	Sportavia/ Fournier RF-5	5082	JA2127
			D-KIEL(1)
D-KOPP	Hoffmann H-36 Dimona	3654	

D-KOPR	Hoffmann HK-36R Super Dimona	36347	
D-KOPY	DG Flugzeugbau DG-800LA	8-40A30	HB-2267
D-KOQY	Scheibe SF-25C Falke 2000	44206	(D-KDFH)
D-KORA	Sportavia/ Fournier RF-5	5025	
D-KORC	Sportavia/ Fournier RF-5	5030	
D-KORD	Valentin Taifun 17E	1016	
D-KORE	Scheibe SFS-31 Milan (Permit 9.99)	6601	OE-9083
			D-KORO(1)
D-KORF-WG	Schempp-Hirth Nimbus 2M	07	(D-KOKI)
D-KORG	Glaser-Dirks DG-400	4-145	OY-XYW
D-KORI	Grob G.109	6099	
D-KORK(2)	Scheibe SF-25C Falke	44328	
D-KORL	Raab Krähe IV	14	D-KODL
	(Ntu, now in Deutsches Museum)		(D-KOPD)
			D-KEDI (1)
D-KORM	Sportavia/ Fournier RF-4D	4035	F-BORM
D-KORO(2)	Schempp-Hirth Ventus cT	103/364	
D-KORR	Schleicher ASH 26E	26061	
D-KORT	Kortenbach Kora I	V-2	
D-KORU	Stemme S-10	10-11	
D-KOSA	Sportavia/ Scheibe SF-25C Falke	4250	(D-KOJA)
D-KOSD	Scheibe SF-25B Falke	4690	
D-KOSG	Scheibe SF-25D Falke	4693D	
D-KOSH(2)	Schempp-Hirth Duo Discus T	44/320	
D-KOSJ-SJ	Schleicher ASW 20L/TOP	20573	D-1646
D-KOSL	Scheibe SF-27M-A	6316	(D-KHIL)
D-KOSM	Scheibe SF-27M-A	6317	
D-KOSN	Nitsche AVO 68-R100 Samburo	008	
D-KOSO(2)	Hoffmann H-36 Dimona	3647	HB-2065
D-KOSR	Schempp-Hirth Ventus bT	52/254	
D-KOSS	Scheibe SF-25C Falke	44675	
D-KOST(2)	Scheibe SF-25C Falke 2000	44286	(D-KDGN)
D-KOSY	Schempp-Hirth Ventus cT	99/354	
D-KOTT(3)	Scheibe SF-25C Rotax-Falke	44688	
D-KOTZ(2)	Schempp-Hirth Ventus-2cxM	150	
D-KOUH	Schleicher ASH 25Mi	25230	
D-KOWB-WB	Schleicher ASH 25M	25901	
D-KOWC	Scheibe SF-25C Falke	44302	HB-2054
			(D-KDGY)
D-KOWE(2)	Schempp-Hirth Nimbus 4M	2/11	
D-KOWF	Glaser-Dirks DG-400	4-70	
D-KOWI	Brditschka HB-23/2400SP	23044	
D-KOWM	Schempp-Hirth Ventus 2cM	104/217	
D-KOWO	Valentin Taifun 17E	1087	
D-KOWR	Stemme S 10-VT	11-081	
D-KOWW	Scheibe SF-36R	4102	
D-KOYY-YY	Schempp-Hirth Nimbus 4T	9	
D-KOZX(6)	Schempp-Hirth Discus-2cT (Permit 11.04)	2	
D-KOZZ	*Test Registration for Rolladen-Schneider LS9 production*		
D-KPAA	Hoffmann HK-36R Super Dimona	36378	
D-KPAB	Hoffmann HK-36R Super Dimona	36379	
D-KPAC	Schempp-Hirth Discus bT	124/482	
D-KPAF	Scheibe SF-25C Falke 2000	44513	
D-KPAK	Schempp-Hirth Ventus 2cM	50/104	
D-KPAL-VX	Schleicher ASH 26E	26176	
D-KPAN	Nitsche AVO 68-R100 Samburo	003	
D-KPAS(2)-28	Schleicher ASW 28-18E (Permit 12.03)	28701	
D-KPBG	Schempp-Hirth Duo Discus T	25/286	
D-KPCC	Diamond HK-36TTC Super Dimona	36694	
D-KPDG	DG Flugzeugbau DG-800B	8-174B98	
D-KPDJ	Schempp-Hirth Ventus 2cM	133/ . . .	
D-KPER	Schempp-Hirth Ventus-2cxT	127	
D-KPFM-BL	Schleicher ASW 22BLE (Permit 5.01)	22084	
D-KPGC	Schempp-Hirth Duo Discus T	26/288	
D-KPGS-2L	Schempp-Hirth Ventus 2cT	71/226	
D-KPHJ	Schempp-Hirth Nimbus 3DM	26/59	LX-CHJ
D-KPIB	Schempp-Hirth Ventus cM	96/587	
D-KPIF	Scheibe SF 25C Falke	44701	
D-KPII	DG Flugzeugbau DG-800B	8-250B163	
D-KPIN	Schempp-Hirth Ventus cM	65/527	F-CGLR
D-KPIR	Hoffmann H-36 Dimona	3624	OE-9210
D-KPIW	Lange E1 Antares (Permit 3.05)	11	
D-KPJS-JS	Schempp-Hirth Nimbus 4M	7/23	
D-KPLA	Schleicher ASW 24E	24815	I-KKFA
			D-KKFA(2)
D-KPLH	Schempp-Hirth Ventus 2cM	85/178	
D-KPMH	Schempp-Hirth Nimbus 3DM	7/23	G-BPMH
D-KPMM	Schempp-Hirth Duo Discus T (Permit 9.04)	37/312	
D-KPMS	Schempp-Hirth Ventus 2cT	23/88	
D-KPMW	Grob G.102 Astir CS/TOP	1008	D-6504
D-KPOL	Scheibe SF-25C Falke 2000	44536	
D-KPPP	Glaser-Dirks DG-400	4-188	OE-9273
D-KPRW-RW	Schleicher ASH 25M	25164	D-5547
D-KPSN	Scheibe SF-25C Rotax-Falke (ex Falke 2000)	44518	
D-KPSW	Schempp-Hirth Ventus 2cM	109/224	
D-KPTL	Grob G.109B	6216	OO-DPC
D-KPTZ	Schempp-Hirth Nimbus 4DM	25/35	
D-KPUA	DG Flugzeugbau DG-800LA	8-22A19	
D-KPUK	Aerotechnik L-13SL Vivat	940521	OK-4100
D-KPUR	Schleicher ASH 25M (Permit 7.99)	25213	
D-KPWD	Glaser-Dirks DG-600/18M	6-88M34	
D-KPYB	Schempp-Hirth Ventus 2cT	140/ . . .	
D-KPYY	Schempp-Hirth Ventus 2cM	107/220	
D-KPZG	Schleicher ASW 28-18E (Permit 5.04)	28705	
D-KPZZ-ZZ	Schempp-Hirth Nimbus 4DT	4/7	
D-KQAS	Schempp-Hirth Ventus-2cxT	128	
D-KRAB	HOAC HK-36TTC Super Dimona	36678	

D-KRAI	Schempp-Hirth Discus bT	74/402	
D-KRAK-AK	Schempp-Hirth Discus bM	6/463	
D-KRAM	Scheibe SF-25C Rotax-Falke	44582	
D-KRAN	Scheibe SF-25C Rotax-Falke	44652	D-KIEP
D-KRAP	Schempp-Hirth Discus bT	102/444	
D-KRAS-AS	Schleicher ASH 25M	25183	
D-KRAW	Schleicher ASH 26E	26103	
D-KRBH-BH	Schempp-Hirth Ventus 2cT	31/103	
D-KRBP	Schleicher ASH 25M	25177	
D-KRDG	DG Flugzeugbau DG-500MB	5E193MB8	
D-KREB	Schempp-Hirth Ventus cM	93/582	
D-KREH-4D	Schempp-Hirth Nimbus 4DM	1/4	
D-KREM	Schleicher ASH 25EB	25178	
D-KRES	HOAC HK-36TTC Super Dimona	36602	
D-KRGA-RG	Schempp-Hirth Nimbus 4M (Permit 2.01)	11/33	D-4295
	(Formerly Nimbus 4 c/n 12/33)		
D-KRGD	Nitsche AVO 68-R100 Samburo	007	
D-KRGO	Schleicher ASH 25EB28	25246	
D-KRGW	Schempp-Hirth Ventus cM	100/591	
D-KRHA	Grob G.109B	6406	G-BNAY
			N920BG
D-KRHB	Schempp-Hirth Ventus 2cM	153/. . .	
D-KRHG-HG	Schleicher ASH 25Mi (Permit .00)	25211	
D-KRHL	Rolladen-Schneider LS9 (Permit 12.99)	9005	
D-KRHT	Schleicher ASH 26E (Formerly ASH-26)	26071	D-9426
D-KRID	DG Flugzeugbau DG-505MB	5E246B22	
D-KRII	DG Flugzeugbau DG-800B	8-172B96	
D-KRJS	Schleicher ASH 26E	26025	D-8839
D-KRLD	Schleicher ASH 25Mi	25223	
D-KRLH	Schleicher ASH 26E	26119	
D-KRMR	Scheibe SF 27M-B (Reservation 9.03)	4553	D-KOLE(1)
D-KROG	Schempp-Hirth Discus bT	126/484	
D-KROP	Grob G.109	6124	PH-948
			N3837S
D-KRPS-MR	Schleicher ASH 26E	26151	D-KZZZ
D-KRRB	Schleicher ASH 28-18E (Res .05)	28727	
D-KRRK(2)	Valentin Taifun 17E-II/2400	1128	OE-9330
			D-KHVA
D-KRRR	DG Flugzeugbau DG-800B	8-132B61	
D-KRSA	Schleicher ASH 25M	25238	
D-KRTS-JR	Schempp-Hirth Ventus 2cT	19/81	
D-KRUG-OK	Schleicher ASH 26E	26006	
D-KRUM	Scheibe SF-25C Rotax-Falke	44566	
D-KRVG	Rolladen-Schneider LS9 (Permit 6.00)	9008	
D-KRWA	Aeromot AMT-200 Super Ximango	200-093	PP-XAD
D-KRWK	Schleicher ASH 26E	26216	
D-KRWR	Glaser-Dirks DG-600M	6-95M41	
D-KSAA	Schleicher ASH 25Mi (Permit 5.01)	25219	OO-YPA
D-KSAC	Schempp-Hirth Ventus-2cxT (Permit 9.03)	112	
D-KSAG(3)	Schleicher ASH 25EB	25247	
D-KSAK	Scheibe SF-25C Rotax-Falke	44619	
D-KSAM	Nitsche AVO 68-R115 Samburo Turbo	001	
	(Permit 6.99)		
D-KSAS-AS	Schleicher ASW 22BLE 50R	22071	D-KKUH
D-KSBC	Grob G.103C Twin IIISL	35038	
D-KSBD	HOAC HK-36TTC Super Dimona	36522	OE-9422
D-KSBH	Stemme S-10V	14-028	G-JULS
			D-KGDC(3)
D-KSBS	Schleicher ASH 26E	26145	
D-KSCF	Glaser-Dirks DG-500M	5E59M24	
D-KSCH	HOAC HK-36R Super Dimona	36327	OE-9365
D-KSDB	Grob G.103C Twin IIISL	35004	
D-KSDF(2)	Valentin Taifun 17E-II	1111	OE-9497
			D-KRRK(1)
			OE-9297
			D-KHVA
D-KSDI	Schleicher ASH 26E	26198	
D-KSDL	Aerotechnik L-13SDL Vivat	910428	OK- . . . .
D-KSDU	Schempp-Hirth Ventus 2cT	104/ . . .	
D-KSEF	Schempp-Hirth Duo Discus T	1/187	
D-KSEL	Schempp-Hirth Duo Discus T	10/256	
D-KSEM	HOAC HK-36TTS Super Dimona	36515	
D-KSEP-BS	Schempp-Hirth Ventus cT	162/526	
D-KSFC	Hoffmann HK-36R Super Dimona	36342	
D-KSFE	Stemme S-10V	14-059M	OE-9397
	(C/n also quoted as 14-006)		D-KGCZ(2)
D-KSFM	Glaser-Dirks DG-500M	5E98M44	OE-9388
D-KSFN	Schempp-Hirth Discus 2T	15/128	
D-KSFO	HOAC HK-36TTC Super Dimona	36636	OE-9436
D-KSFU	HOAC HK-36TC Super Dimona	36648	
D-KSFW	Schempp-Hirth Duo Discus T	78/390	
D-KSGS(2)	Schempp-Hirth Duo Discus T	67/360	
D-KSHA	Schempp-Hirth Nimbus 4DM	13/22	
D-KSHB	Hoffmann HK-36R Super Dimona	36403	OE-9403
			(D-KAIB(2))
D-KSHJ	Schempp-Hirth Duo Discus T	81/395	
D-KSHL	Aerotechnik L-13SL Vivat	920426	
D-KSHS	Schempp-Hirth Discus bT	130/495	
D-KSHW	Schleicher ASW 24E	24838	HB-2195
D-KSHX	Schleicher ASH 25M	25140	D-9525
			OE-5525
D-KSIE(2)	Stemme S-10V (Permit)	14-012	PH-1055
			D-KGDE(1)
D-KSIG	DG Flugzeugbau DG-800LA	8-15A12	
D-KSIO	Stemme S 10-VT	11-095	
D-KSJM-JM	Schempp-Hirth Ventus-2cM	47/97	
D-KSKA	DG Flugzeugbau DG-800B	8-260B168	

D-KSKI (2)	Schempp-Hirth Discus 2T	2/66	
D-KSKS	DG Flugzeugbau DG-800B	8-89B25	
D-KSLA	DG Flugzeugbau DG-800B	8-91B27	
D-KSLG	Grob G.103C Twin IIISL	35002	
D-KSLH	Lange E1 Antares (Permit 12.04)	06	
D-KSLQ	Schempp-Hirth Duo Discus T	36/310	
D-KSLS	Schempp-Hirth Discus bT (Reservation .01)	148/535	
D-KSMB	Schleicher ASW 28-18E (Permit 12.04)	28724	
D-KSMC	Schleicher ASH 26E	26023	
D-KSMH	Schleicher ASH 25M	25160	D-0541
D-KSOL(2)	Grob G.103C Twin IIISL	35039	
D-KSPC	Schleicher ASH 26E	26120	D-KSUT(1)
D-KSPK	Scheibe SF-25C Rotax-Falke	44635	
D-KSPL(2)	Glaser-Dirks DG-400	4-286	
D-KSPM	DG Flugzeugbau DG-800B	8-157B81	
D-KSPP	Schleicher ASH 25Mi	25231	
D-KSPR	Glaser-Dirks DG-500M	5E80M33	
D-KSPT	Schempp-Hirth Ventus bT	3/233	HB-2104
D-KSRJ	Schleicher ASH 26E	26021	D-5771
D-KSRV	Schempp-Hirth Discus bT	138/514	
D-KSRW	Schleicher ASH 26E	26101	
D-KSSB	Diamond HK-36TTC Super Dimona	36732	
D-KSSK(2)	Schleicher ASH 25EB28	25232	
D-KSSW	Schempp-Hirth Ventus cM	61/523	
D-KSTE to D-KSTI	*Test Registrations for Stemme S-10VT production*		
D-KSTS	Schleicher ASH 26E	26005	
D-KSTY	Studeny STY-1	1	
D-KSUB	Hoffmann HK-36R Super Dimona	36390	
D-KSUF	Stemme S-10VT	10-080	
D-KSUT(3)	Schleicher ASH 26E	26220	
D-KSVB	Schleicher ASW 22BLE 50R	22082	
D-KSWB	HOAC HK-36TTC Super Dimona	36558	F-CHQB
D-KSWG	SZD-45A Ogar (Permit 11.99)	B-753	D-KLHP
			DDR-3508
			DM-3508
D-KSWH	Schempp-Hirth Ventus cM	97/587	OH-861
D-KSWJ	Schleicher ASH 26E	26098	
D-KSWR	Schleicher ASW 22BLE 50R	22083	(D-KSSK(1))
D-KSWS	Technoflug Piccolo B	096	
D-KSXC	Schempp-Hirth Ventus 2cT	96/...	
D-KSXR	Schleicher ASH 26E	26154	
D-KSZX	Schleicher ASW 22BLE 50R	22080	VH-ZBB
			D-KMOL
D-KTAK(2)	Schleicher ASW 28-18E (Permit 3.04)	28710	
D-KTAL	Stemme S-10V	14-049M	G-LINA
	(Formerly Stemme S-10 c/n 10-49)		D-KFDF
D-KTAS	Schempp-Hirth Ventus 2cT	21/85	
D-KTAW	Technoflug Piccolo B	073	
D-KTBB	Glaser-Dirks DG-800B	8-67B12	
D-KTBC	Glaser-Dirks DG-400	4-67	(D-KXCB(1))
			OE-9225
D-KTBT	Schempp-Hirth Discus bT	141/516	
D-KTCB	Schleicher ASH 26E	26128	(D-5222)
D-KTCH	Technoflug Piccolo B	099	
D-KTCJ	Schempp-Hirth Duo Discus T	74/377	
D-KTCW	DG Flugzeugbau DG-800LA	8-46A32	
D-KTDD-OS	Glaser-Dirks DG-800A	8-52A34	
D-KTDH	Schempp-Hirth Duo Discus T	96/422	
D-KTDM	Schempp-Hirth Ventus 2cM	15/32	D-4486
D-KTDW	AMS Flight Carat A	CA014	
D-KTEG	Schleicher ASH 26E	26129	
D-KTEN	DG Flugzeugbau DG-800B	8-155B79	
D-KTFP	Schempp-Hirth Nimbus 3T (Permit 3.00)	4/51	HB-2147
			D-KAPE
			VH-GAA
D-KTFW	Glaser-Dirks DG-600/18M	6-89M35	(D-KGBD)
			EC-FJC
			D-1245
D-KTGE	DG Flugzeugbau DG-800B	8-232B146	
D-KTGG	Schempp-Hirth Ventus cM	99/592	HB-2244
D-KTGR	Technoflug Piccolo B	074	
D-KTGS-8T	Rolladen-Schneider LS8-t (Permit 3.03)	8466	
D-KTGT	Schleicher ASH 26E	26139	HB-2304
D-KTHA-WII	Schempp-Hirth Ventus 2cM	35/62	
D-KTHB	Schempp-Hirth Ventus 2cM	38/68	
D-KTHK	Schleicher ASH 26E	26086	
D-KTHN	Schempp-Hirth Discus bT	160/564	
D-KTHT	HOAC HK-36TTS Super Dimona	36513	
D-KTHW	DG Flugzeugbau DG-800B	8-265B173	
D-KTIA	Scheibe SF-25C Rotax-Falke	44560	
D-KTIB	Scheibe SF-25C Rotax-Falke	44572	
D-KTIC	Scheibe SF-25C Rotax-Falke	44555	
D-KTID	Scheibe SF-25C Rotax-Falke	44575	
D-KTIE	Scheibe SF-25C Rotax-Falke	44568	
D-KTIF	Scheibe SF-25C Rotax-Falke	44549	
D-KTIG	Scheibe SF-25C Rotax-Falke	44552	
D-KTIH(2)	Scheibe SF-25C Rotax-Falke	44593	
D-KTII	Scheibe SF-25C Rotax-Falke	44573	
D-KTIJ	Scheibe SF-25C Rotax-Falke	44594	
D-KTIK	Scheibe SF-25C Rotax-Falke	44588	
D-KTIL	Scheibe SF-25C Rotax-Falke	44562	
D-KTIM	Scheibe SF-25C Rotax-Falke	44564	
D-KTIO	Scheibe SF-25C Rotax-Falke	44559	
D-KTIP	Scheibe SF-36R	4107	
D-KTIQ	Scheibe SF-25C Rotax-Falke	44597	
D-KTIR	Scheibe SF-25C Rotax-Falke	44590	
D-KTIS	Scheibe SF-25C Rotax-Falke	44584	

D-KTIT(2)	Scheibe SF-25C Rotax-Falke	44599	
D-KTIU(3)	Scheibe SF-25C Falke	44225	OE-9142
			D-KDFN(3)
D-KTIV(2)	Scheibe SF-25C Rotax-Falke	44614	
D-KTIW(2)	Scheibe SF-25C Rotax-Falke	44615	
D-KTIX	Scheibe SF-25C Rotax-Falke	44624	
D-KTIY	Scheibe SF-25C Falke	44681	
D-KTIZ	Scheibe SF-25C Falke	44300	OE-9176
			D-KDGU(2)
D-KTJM	Valentin Kiwi	K3017	HB-2220
			D-KEGX(5)
D-KTKM	Glaser-Dirks DG-600/18M	6-103M46	
D-KTLL(2)	DG Flugzeugbau DG-800B	8-152B76	
D-KTMD	DG Flugzeugbau DG-800B	8-281B189	
D-KTME-ME	Schempp-Hirth Ventus 2cT	47/147	
D-KTMH	Schleicher ASH 26E	26009	D-5961
D-KTMI	Scheibe SF 28A Tandem-Falke	5764	SE-TME
			D-KACQ
D-KTMS	Schempp-Hirth Ventus 2cM	158/. . .	
D-KTMW	DG Flugzeugbau DG-800B	8-69B14	
D-KTOA, B, C	*Test registrations for DG Flugzeugbau production*		
D-KTOH	Schempp-Hirth Nimbus 4DM	47/64	
D-KTOL	HOAC HK-36TTC Super Dimona	36600	
D-KTOM-HE	Schempp-Hirth Ventus 2cM	91/190	
D-KTOY	DG Flugzeugbau DG-800B	8-263B171	
D-KTPR	Technoflug Piccolo B	072	
D-KTRB	DG Flugzeugbau DG-800B	8-119B48	
D-KTRT-XT	Schempp-Hirth Ventus-2cxT	111	
D-KTSG-SG	Schempp-Hirth Discus bT	100/442	
D-KTTI-ITI	Rolladen-Schneider LS8-t (Permit 7.03)	8434	D-3075
D-KTTT	Schempp-Hirth Nimbus 3DM (Permit 3.00)	18/42	OH-840
D-KTVI	Lange E1 Antares (Permit 2.05)	10	
D-KTVS	Schleicher ASH 26E	26069	
D-KTWI	Valentin Taifun 17E-II	T-1136	(D-KAJP)
D-KTWG	DG Flugzeugbau DG-800B	8-146B70	
D-KTWR	Glaser-Dirks DG-800LA	8-80A41	
D-KTWS	Schleicher ASH 26E	26140	
D-KUAS	Schleicher ASH 25Mi (Permit)	25204	
D-KUBA	Scheibe SF-24B Motorspatz (Reservation 2.99)	4031	OE-9007
			D-KIBE(1)
D-KUBO	Schempp-Hirth Discus bT	131/498	
D-KUCB	Schempp-Hirth Ventus-2cT	130/. . .	
D-KUDL	Hoffmann HK-36R Super Dimona	36398	
D-KUDU	DG Flugzeugbau DG-808xB Competition		
	(Reservation .05)	8-334B233X4	
D-KUEL	Schempp-Hirth Ventus 2cM	77/160	D-5048
	(Formerly Ventus 2c 53/160)		
D-KUEM	Schleicher ASW 22BLE	22068	
D-KUEP	Alpavia/ Fournier RF-3	82	F-BMTQ
D-KUFO	Scheibe SF-25C Rotax-Falke	44663	
D-KUFP	HOAC HK-36R Super Dimona	36331	F-CGAY
D-KUGK	DG Flugzeugbau DG-800B	8-257B165	
D-KUHE	DG Flugzeugbau DG-800B	8-103B37	
D-KUHL	Schempp-Hirth Ventus cM	90/575	
D-KUHN	HOAC HK-36TTC Super Dimona	36693	
D-KUHR	Schempp-Hirth Discus bM	2/423	
D-KUHU	Scheibe SF-25C Falke	44660	
D-KUKI	Glaser-Dirks DG-400 (Reservation 11.99)	4-156	I-KFAP
			D-KFAP
D-KULA-VFR	Schleicher ASH 25M (Reservation 11.99)	25180	D-KGGO(1)
D-KULE	DG Flugzeugbau DG-800LA	8-7A6	
D-KULI	Schleicher ASH 25M	25220	D-KSAG(1)
	(Crashed as D-KSAG 24.3.01, rebuilt)		
D-KULM	Technoflug Piccolo B	085	
D-KULT(3)	DG Flugzeugbau DG-808B	8-304B204	
D-KULY	Valentin Taifun 17E-II (Reservation .04)	1106	OE-9293
			D-KHVA(31)
D-KUNI	Scheibe SF-25C Falke	44667	
D-KUNK(2)	Schempp-Hirth Duo Discus T ('NK')	2/229	
D-KUPC	Schleicher ASW 28-18E (Permit 7.04)	28735	
D-KURA	Technoflug Piccolo B	060	
D-KURO	HOAC HK-36TTC Super Dimona	36715	
D-KURS	Sportavia/ Fournier RF-5	5036	N555VM
			OE-9030
D-KURT(3)	Scheibe SF 25C Rotax-Falke	44693	
D-KURZ	Scheibe SF-25C Falke	44612	
D-KUSF	Stemme S-10VT	11-035	
D-KUSS	Glaser-Dirks DG-500M	5E147M59	
D-KUSU	Scheibe SF-25C Falke	44645	
D-KUWE	Schempp-Hirth Ventus 2cM	129	
D-KUYH	Schempp-Hirth Janus CM	23/216	JA2360
D-KVAL	Schleicher ASH 26E	26191	
D-KVAS-26	Schleicher ASH 26E	26001	
D-KVCB	DG Flugzeugbau DG-800B	8-235B149	
D-KVFL	Scheibe SF-25C Rotax-Falke	44613	
D-KVIE-MK	Stemme S-10VT	11-044	
D-KVKA	Schempp-Hirth Discus bT	159/561	
D-KVMC	Grob G.109B	6352	N109KC
D-KVNV	Schleicher ASH 25E (Permit .05)	25108	D-1275
D-KVOK	HOAC HK-36TTC Super Dimona	36566	
D-KVRS	Glaser-Dirks DG-500M	5E61M26	
D-KVVJ-VJ	Schempp-Hirth Discus bT	90/427	
D-KVVR	DG Flugzeugbau DG-808B	8-315B215	
D-KVVV	Schempp-Hirth Janus CM	6	OE-9229
			D-KBOS
			OO-BPC
			(D-KIBC)

D-KVZC	Glaser-Dirks DG-800B	8-68B13	
D-KWAG	DG Flugzeugbau DG-800LA	8-5A4	
D-KWAL	Schleicher ASH 26E	26106	
D-KWAP-30	DG Flugzeugbau DG-800B	8-272B180	
D-KWAS	Schempp-Hirth Ventus 2cM	127/...	
D-KWAT	Watzlawek M76	001	(D-KFHR)
D-KWAX	HOAC HK-36TS Super Dimona	36501	
D-KWAZ	HOAC HK-36TTS Super Dimona	36509	
D-KWBE	DG Flugzeugbau DG-800B	8-247B160	
D-KWBM	Schempp-Hirth Discus bM	1/384	
D-KWDG(2)	DG Flugzeugbau DG-800B	8-148B72	
D-KWEL	Scheibe SF-25C Rotax-Falke	44666	
D-KWEN	Nitsche AVO 68-R100 Samburo	002	
D-KWER	HOAC HK-36TTC Super Dimona	36578	
D-KWES	Schleicher ASW 22BLE	22069	D-6822
D-KWFG	Scheibe SF-25C Rotax-Falke	44576	
D-KWGL	Schempp-Hirth Nimbus-4M	18/42	
D-KWHB	Schleicher ASH 26E	26030	
D-KWHF	Schleicher ASH 26E (Permit .05)	26127	HB-2306
D-KWHJ	Technoflug Piccolo B	115	
D-KWHN	Hoffmann H-36 Dimona	36229	F-CGAS
			F-WGAS
D-KWII	DG Flugzeugbau DG-800LA	8-18A15	
D-KWIK	Valentin Taifun 17E	1098	PH-816
			D-KHVA
D-KWIL	Schleicher ASH 26E	26004	
D-KWIN	Huber Windex 1200C (Permit 8.04)	AB001	
D-KWIT	Scheibe SF 25C Falke	44297	OE-9177
			(D-KDGQ)
D-KWKW	Schleicher ASH 26E	26019	D-1807
D-KWML(2)	Schleicher ASH 26E	26054	
D-KWNW	Schempp-Hirth Discus bT	71/398	
D-KWOK	Schleicher ASH 26E	26179	
D-KWPG-PG	Schempp-Hirth Discus bT	113/466	
D-KWRR	Schempp-Hirth Ventus cM	109/608	
D-KWRT	Schleicher ASH 26E	26109	
D-KWSC	Hoffmann H-36 Dimona	36233	OE-9286
D-KWSE	Glaser-Dirks DG-600/18M	6-114M54	
D-KWSF	Grob G.109B	6224	HB-2209
			D-KGFK
D-KWSJ	Aerotechnik L-13SL Vivat	930510	
D-KWSL	Grob G.103C Twin IIISL	35046	
D-KWST	Schleicher ASH 26E	26063	
D-KWTI	Gyroflug (?)	1136	
D-KWTR	Schempp-Hirth Duo Discus T (Permit 3.01)	15/263	
D-KWTT	Eiri PIK-20E	20232	LX-CWC
			D-KEHI (2)
D-KWUG	Schempp-Hirth Duo Discus T	51/335	
D-KWVE	Scheibe SF-25C Rotax-Falke	44553	
D-KWWE-2E	Schempp-Hirth Ventus 2cM	1/5	
D-KWWF	HOAC HK-36TTS Super Dimona	36622	
D-KWWJ	Schempp-Hirth Discus 2T (Permit 1.01)	5/92	
D-KWWM	Schleicher ASH 26E	26020	
D-KWWS	Grob G.109B	6363	G-BMCM
			(EAF-674)
D-KWWW	HOAC HK-36TTC Super Dimona	36569	
D-KWYS	Glaser-Dirks DG-800A	8-4A3	
D-KXAS(2)	Schempp-Hirth Ventus cT	71/295	OO-ZYU
			D-KMHN
D-KXCB(2)	Schempp-Hirth Duo Discus T	83/397	
D-KXCM	Schempp-Hirth Ventus 2cM	67/138	
D-KXCP	Glaser-Dirks DG-400	4-178	HB-2118
D-KXCZ(2)	Stemme S-10VT	11-074	(D-KLCC(1))
D-KXGS	DG Flugzeugbau DG-800B	8-307B207	
D-KXIK	Schempp-Hirth Ventus-2cT	108	BGA 5060
			D-KXIK
D-KXKX	DG Flugzeugbau DG-808XB (Resvn .04)	8-325B225X2	
D-KXLH	Schempp-Hirth Ventus 2cM	53/107	
D-KXOW	Glaser-Dirks DG-400	4-184	OY-XOW
D-KXWW	Schempp-Hirth Discus 2T	20	HB-2389
			(D-KLLS)
D-KXXB-1c	DG Flugzeugbau DG-808XB	8-316B216X1	
	(Permit 11.04)		
D-KXXH	Schleicher ASH 26E (Permit .05)	26160	N10ZQ
			N519JK
D-KXXL	Akaflieg Stuttgart Icaré (Damaged 15.7.98)	2	
D-KYAA	DG Flugzeugbau DG-800B	8-292B197	
D-KYAS	Schleicher ASH 26E	26175	
D-KYBD	Technoflug Piccolo B	077	D-MYBD
D-KYBL	Scheibe SF-25C Rotax-Falke	44413	D-KEGL(1)
D-KYCB	DG Flugzeugbau DG-800B	8-187B111	D-KERG(2)
D-KYDM-45	Schempp-Hirth Ventus 2cM	132/...	
D-KYES	DG Flugzeugbau DG-800B	8-294B199	
D-KYGI	Scheibe SF-25C Falke 2000	44408	OY-XYG
			(D-KNIN)
D-KYGL	Scheibe SF-25C Rotax-Falke	44641	
D-KYHF	Schempp-Hirth Nimbus 4M	5/20	
D-KYHN	Scheibe SF-25C Rotax-Falke	44630	
D-KYLA-9T	Schleicher ASH 26E	26211	
D-KYNG	Scheibe SF 25C Falke (Permit 4.04)	44699	
D-KYNT	Scheibe SF-25C Rotax-Falke	44583	
D-KYPS	DG Flugzeugbau DG-808B	8-310B210	
D-KYSA	DG Flugzeugbau DG-800B	8-114B43	
D-KYSI	HOAC HK-36TC Super Dimona	36730	
D-KYSS	Nitsche AVO 68-R115 Samburo Turbo	005	
D-KYTT	Schempp-Hirth Ventus 2cT	28/98	
D-KYXL	Schempp-Hirth Nimbus 4DM	24/34	D-KCGG

D-KYYK -Y9	Schempp-Hirth Discus bT	37/348	D-1817
D-KYYY	Schempp-Hirth Janus CM	27/227	OY-XYY
D-KZAR	Schleicher ASH 26E	26155	
D-KZAS	Schleicher ASK 21Mi (Permit 12.04)	21784	
D-KZGO	Schleicher ASH 25E	25132	
D-KZIG	Scheibe SF-25C Rotax-Falke	44680	
D-KZSE	Grob G.103C Twin IIISL	35047	
D-KZSF	Glaser-Dirks DG-400	4-284	
D-KZWU	Stemme S-10VT	11-068	
D-KZZZ(2)	Schleicher ASH 25M	25215	D-KLLG D-KLKW

CLASS L : Airships

D-LDFO	WDL-1 (PL4360A) Airship	101A	JA1002 D-LDFN
D-LDFQ	WDL-1B Airship (Dismantled)	106	JA1007 D-LDFQ
D-LDFR	WDL-1B Airship	107	JA1008 D-LDFR
D-LION	Zeppelin LZ N07 Airship (Reservation)	W3	
D-LJOE	Cargo-Lifter Joey B (Permit 10.99)	1	
D-LZFN	Zeppelin LZ N07-100 Airship (Permit)	001	
D-LZZF	Zeppelin LZ-N07-100 Airship	003	(D-LION)

CLASS M : Microlights

D-MAAA	Flight Team Spider D	049
D-MAAB	Fresh Breeze 110 AL2F	326
D-MAAC	NST Minimum Nimbus 62	M527
D-MAAD	Platzer Kiebitz-B	144
D-MAAF(1)	Ultra-Vector F 610	1399
D-MAAG	Behlen Power-Trike Euro III	8400100
D-MAAH	UPM Funplane	19002
D-MAAK	Ultraleichtverbund Bi 90	963
D-MAAP	Alpi Aviation Pioneer 300	66
D-MAAQ	UPM Funplane	86006
D-MAAR	Impulse 3300TD	TD-30
D-MAAS	Fresh Breeze 110 AL2F	356
D-MAAV	B&F Funk FK-14 Polaris	039
D-MABC(2)	Ultraleichtverbund Bi 90	21226
D-MABD	Aviasud Mistral BA-53	003
D-MABF	Interplane Skyboy ZK	004.03.03.TD
D-MABH	B&F Funk F-14 Polaris	unkn
D-MABK	UPM Funplane	86007
D-MABL	Fresh Breeze 110 AL4H	27
D-MABN	Albatros	109
D-MABO	Comco Fox D	8505-FD27
D-MABS	Comco Ikarus C-42	0203-6464
D-MABT	Ultra-Vector H	1758
D-MABX	Moyes Dragonfly floatplane	D02002
D-MABY	Warnke Euro III Trike	SI 030
D-MABZ	Fisher FP-202 Koala	2183
D-MACA	Aeroprakt A-22 Vision	0033-011
D-MACB	UPM Funplane Trike	86010
D-MACC	NST Minimum	46/85-1501
D-MACD	Sky-Craft AJS-2000	033
D-MACE	Behlen Power-Trike Vampir II	85013
D-MACG	NST Minimum Focus 18	M184
D-MACI	Klüver Kaiman Trike	080706
D-MACL	Comco Fox-C22	8705-3059
D-MACO	Ultraleichtverbund Bi 90	993
D-MACP	Sky-Walker II	202
D-MACQ	Platzer kiebitz II	052
D-MACR	NST Minimum Saphir 16	M307
D-MACS	Evektor EV-97 Eurostar 2000R	2004-2015
D-MACX	Comco Fox-C22	8901-3163
D-MACY	Comco Fox-C22	8904-3171
D-MACZ	Aviasud AE209 Albatros	121
D-MADC	Ultraleichtverbund Bi 90	21002
D-MADD	Fair Fax Euro III Trike	026
D-MADE	Schmidtler Ranger M	M1817
D-MADG	NST Minimum	M576
D-MADH	Sky-Walker II	211
D-MADK	Aerostyle Breezer	034
D-MADL	NST Schwarze Mimimum	462
D-MADM	Take Off Maximum Lotus 16	027020
D-MADN	Sky-Walker II	208
D-MADP	Klüver Racer SX 12	371903
D-MADR	ATEC Zephyr 2000	Z 351202TU
D-MADS	Wisch Star-Trike Hazard 15M	127.04.898
D-MADT	Sky-Walker II	218
D-MADU	Comco Ikarus Fox II Doppel	8604-3013
D-MADV	Fair Fax Trike	27
D-MADW	Fisher FP-202 Koala	001
D-MADZ	Ultraleichtverbund Bi 90	21003
D-MAEB	ASO Viper 15 Trike	15/16791
D-MAEC	Schönleber DS Enduro Trike Lotus 18	03/0489
D-MAED	Fair Fax Euro III Trike	029
D-MAEE	Ultraleichtverbund Bi 90	21043
D-MAEF	Cosmos	unkn
D-MAEG	ASO Viper 15M Trike	15/18290
D-MAEH	Mosquito IB	004
D-MAEI	Sky-Walker II	235
D-MAEJ	Fisher FP-404 Classic	Schmidt 1
D-MAEK	Comco Ikarus Fox-C22	9003-3222
D-MAEL	Comco Ikarus Fox D	014
D-MAEM	Comco Ikarus Fox-C22	9003-3224
D-MAEP(2)	Kümmerle Mini-Fly-Set	44465
D-MAER	Ultraleichtverbund Bi 90	21000
D-MAES(2)	Kümmerle Mini-Fly-Set	73085-3
D-MAET	Behlen Power-Trike	90026
D-MAEU	Sky-Walker II	246
D-MAEV	Fair Fax DR Hazard Trike	D009
D-MAEW	HFL Stratos 300K	300-019K
D-MAEX	Schmidtler Enduro Focus 18	010885
D-MAFA	Fantasy Air Allegro	02-414
D-MAFB	Sky-Walker II	248
D-MAFC(2)	Remos G.3 Mirage	0923
D-MAFD	Ultraleichtverbund Bi 90	21010
D-MAFE	UPM Cobra Raven Trike	910113
D-MAFF	Flight Design CT-2K	unkn
D-MAFH	Fisher FP-202 Koala	002 Wachter
D-MAFI	Dallach Sunrise IIA	027
D-MAFJ	Ultraleichtverbund Bi 90	3957004
D-MAFK	Sky-Walker II	253
D-MAFL	Flight Design CT-2K (W/o 22.12.04, USA)	unkn
D-MAFM	Klüver Twin Racer Quartz SX 16	834910
D-MAFN	Klüver Twin Racer Quartz SX 16	835910
D-MAFO	NST Minimum	M525
D-MAFP	Comco Ikarus Fox-C22	8911-3247
D-MAFQ	Ultraleichtverbund Bi 90	21049
D-MAFS	Pioneer Flightstar	672
D-MAFT	Aviasud Mistral 53	006
D-MAFU(1)	Sky-Walker II	250
D-MAFU(2)	UPM Funplane	unkn
D-MAFW	NST Minimum	M324
D-MAFX	Dallach Sunrise II	028
D-MAFZ	Behlen Power-Trike	90016
D-MAGA	Behlen Power-Trike Vampir II	89040
D-MAGB	Ultraleichtverbund Bi 90	21093
D-MAGC	Ultraleichtverbund Bi 90	21080
D-MAGE	Comco Ikarus Fox-C22	042
D-MAGG	Dallach Sunrise II	018
D-MAGI	UPM Cobra Trike	920119
D-MAGK(2)	Tandem Air Sunny Sport	045-93
D-MAGL	TVS 700 Tandem Air Sunny Sport	08.91
D-MAGN	Magni M-18 (?) Gyro	unkn
D-MAGY	Remos G.3 Mirage	151
D-MAHA	Behlen Power Trike Vampir II	85/029
D-MAHB	Fair Fax DR Trike	D026
D-MAHE	B&F Funk FK-9 Mk.IV	09-244
D-MAHF	Enduro DS	20KS20
D-MAHL	Fresh Breeze 110 AL4H	24
D-MAHL	ATEC Zephyr 2000	Z 550402A
D-MAHN	Comco Ikarus Fox II Doppel	8605-3016
D-MAHW	Behlen Power-Trike	92002
D-MAHZ	Solid Air Twin Diamant Trike	T-011
D-MAID	Behlen Power-Trike	830025
D-MAIE	Ultraleichtverbund Bi 90	4105552
D-MAIH	Tandem Air Sunny Sport	13.91
D-MAII	Take Off Maximum Trike	75109
D-MAIS	Tandem Air Sunny Sport	42.92
D-MAIT	Fl;ight Team Twister 912	unkn
D-MAIW	Klüver Twin Racer SX 16	542008
D-MAJA	Drachenstudio Piccolo	01/92
D-MAJB	Klüver Racer SX 12	443904
D-MAJH(2)	Aerostyle Breezer	008
D-MAJJ	FUL Graffiti Trike	022/0082
D-MAJS	Scheibe Uli 1	5208
D-MAJU	Junkers Profly JUL Trike	94/1061
D-MAKA	Tandem Air Sunny Sport	013.08.04
D-MAKE	Comco Ikarus Fox II Doppel	8607-3024
D-MAKI	Ultraleichtverbund Bi 90	unkn
D-MAKJ	Kümmerle Mini-Fly-Set	1279 91-5
D-MAKK	Albatros	165
D-MAKL	NST Minimum	M319
D-MAKM	Schmidtler Enduro Trike	02-014
D-MAKN	Tandem Air Sunny Targa	TA 009.94
D-MAKP	UPM Cobra BF 52UL Trike	940126
D-MAKW(2)	Aerostyle Breezer	031
D-MAKZ	ASO Viper	VI22048308
D-MALA	ASO Viper Hazard 15 Trike	11039208
D-MALB	Comco Ikarus Sherpa II	8407-1072
D-MALD	Fair Fax DR Hazard 15	D029
D-MALE	FUL Graffiti Trike	031/0097
D-MALF	B&F Funk FK-9 Mk.III	09-210
D-MALG	Fair Fax Trike	021
D-MALL	Fresh Breeze 110 AL 4B	107
D-MALM	Platzer Kiebitz-B8	115
D-MALN	Comco Ikarus Fox-C22	002
D-MALO	Take Off Maximum Hazard 15M	T055051
D-MALS	Light Aero Avid Flyer	618
D-MALU	NST Minimum Saphir 17	M163
D-MALV	Fair Fax AH Trike	25
D-MALW	Flight Team Spider D	D022
D-MAMC	WDFL Dallach D4 Fascination BK	130
D-MAME	Comco Ikarus Fox-C22	9103-3323
D-MAMG	Schönleber Enduro KS Speed 14	3585491

D-MAMI	Comco Ikarus Fox-C22	021
D-MAMR	Steinbach Austro-Trike	108/85
D-MAMS	Comco Ikarus C-42B	0304-6541
D-MAMV	Flight Design CT-2K	02.05.04.23
D-MAND	ASO Viper 15 Trike	15/17791
D-MANE	Fresh Breeze 110 AL 2F	57
D-MANI	ASO Viper 15 Trike	15/12291
D-MANJ	Behlen Power-Trike	86017
D-MANK	Comco Ikarus C-42B	0204-6471
D-MANN	Scheibe Ultra	3404
D-MANO	Fair Fax DR Hazard 15M	D022
D-MANR	Pago Jet M4	951102
D-MANT	ATEC Zephyr 2000	ZP 630903
D-MANY	Klüver Bison II Trike	247901
D-MANZ	Schmidtler Enduro Trike	02-005
D-MAOB	Kappa KP-2U Sova	8400 I
D-MAOC	Pago Jet M4	RB97002
D-MAOE	NST Minimum Nimbus	M295
D-MAOR(2)	Comco Ikarus Fox II Doppel	8605-3017
D-MAOS	Flight Team Twister	D-002
D-MAPA	Pioneer Flightstar	383
D-MAPB	UPM Cobra Raven Trike	900101
D-MAPC	AJS Sky-Craft	2000-37
D-MAPD	Fantasy Air Allegro 2000	02-415
D-MAPE	WDFL Dallach D4 Fascination BK	117
D-MAPG	Light Aero Avid Flyer IV	1305
D-MAPH	NST Minimum Saphir 16	M621
D-MAPI	Schmidtler Enduro	18/40
D-MAPK	Drachenstudio Royal Karat 13	01-9307
D-MAPO	NST Minimum Saphir	M86
D-MAPP	NST Minimum	M548
D-MAPT	Ultraleichtverbund Bi 90	553
D-MAQB	NST Minimum Saphir 17	128850
D-MARB	Ultralight Flight Phantom	0311-041001
D-MARD	Steinbach Austro Trike Euro III	134
D-MARF(2)	Comco Ikarus Sherpa II	8503-1093
D-MARH	Flight Team Spider Hazard 13M	D005
D-MARI	FUL Graffiti Trike	0340/0106
D-MARJ	Klüver Racer SX 12	444904
D-MARK(2)	Schmidtler Enduro	unkn
D-MARL	Sky-Walker II	322
D-MARN	Comco Ikarus Fox-C22	9004-3262
D-MARP	Fresh Breeze	unkn
D-MARR(2)	ARCO Spacer L	665
D-MARS	B&F Funk FK-12 Comet	12-055
D-MART	Fresh Breeze 110 AL 2F	36
D-MARU	Behlen Power-Trike	91025
D-MARW	Ultraleichtverbund Bi 90	21216
D-MARX	Flight Team Spider	5
D-MARY	Aerostyle Breezer	018
D-MARZ	Comco Ikarus Fox-C22	9110-3369
D-MASA	Comco Ikarus Fox D	012
D-MASC	Comco Ikarus Fox-C22	9205-3375
D-MASE	Behlen Power-Trike /Rotax 582	980014
D-MASF	Warnke Skylight Trike	031
D-MASG	Comco Ikarus C-42B	0407-6616
D-MASH(2)	Comco Ikarus C-42B	0404-6599
D-MASI	Fresh Breeze 122 AL 2F	377
D-MASJ	Flight Team Twister	D003
D-MASM	Schmidtler Ranger M	1813
D-MASR	Comco Ikarus Fox-C22	9009-3293
D-MASS	Scheibe Ultra	3401
D-MAST	Flight Team Twister	1
D-MASW	Sky-Walker II	167
D-MASX	Comco Ikarus Fox-C22	9106-3327
D-MASY	Aerostyle Breezer	022
D-MASZ	Comco Ikarus C-42B	0310-6573
D-MATB	Krampen Ikarus S	53
D-MATE	Sky-Walker II	314
D-MATF	ATEC Zephyr 2000	Z 750 403 S
D-MATK	Schönleber DS Lotus Trike	01/0190
D-MATL	ARCO Spacer L	11812
D-MATP	Klüver Racer Quartz SX 12	080303
D-MATR	Fläming Air FA-01 Smaragd	01/03
D-MATT	NST Minimum	M416
D-MATW	Albatros	116
D-MATZ	Scheibe Uli 1	5207
D-MAUI	Aériane Sirocco II	031
D-MAUM	Drachenstudio Royal Trike	03-9612
D-MAUS	Flight Team Spider	D045
D-MAVB	Comco Ikarus Fox-C22	9109-3335
D-MAVH	Löbenstein Racer SX 12	001
D-MAVI	Light Aero Avid Flyer IV	441
D-MAVK	Rans S-6 Coyote II	0792329
D-MAVS	Kümmerle Mini-Fly-Set	1270/91-5
D-MAWE	UL-F Jochum Eagle III	970502
	(Possibly re-regd, same c/n quoted for D-MKME)	
D-MAWH	ASO Viper 15/582 Trike	12033206
D-MAWI	Comco Ikarus Fox-C22	8807-3140
D-MAWL	Sky-Walker II	391
D-MAWO	Comco Ikarus Fox-C22	8907-3198
D-MAWR	Comco Ikarus C-42B	0305-6528
D-MAWS	Fresh Breeze 110 AL2F	152
D-MAWT	NST Minimum SierrAIIM	151
D-MAWW	Behlen Power-Trike /Rotax 582	9800015
D-MAXE	Ultraleichtverbund Bi 90	21313
D-MAXL	Tecnam P.92 Echo 100S	663

D-MAXS	Comco Ikarus Fox-C22	9303-3496
D-MAXT	WDFL Sunwheel R	003
D-MAXW	Behlen Power-Trike	85012
D-MAXX	Alpha Aero Tech Spotter G97	unkn
D-MAXY(2)	Flight Design CT2SW	04.03.03
D-MAYA	Kümmerle Mini-Fly-Set Saphir 17	258/86-4
D-MAYT	Junkers L582 Trike	094002/II
D-MAZA	Comco Ikarus Fox-C22	9208-3386
D-MAZD	UPM Funplane Lotus 18	003
D-MAZP	Air Création XP-15	A01010-1007
D-MAZT	Kümmerle Mini-Fly-Set	1312/91-6
D-MAZZ	Schmidtler Enduro Lotus 18	02-008
D-MBAC	Sky-Walker II	205
D-MBAD	Behlen Power-Trike	89000109
D-MBAE	Klüver Racer SX 12	834012
D-MBAG	Aquilair	unkn
D-MBAK	Bek ME 109R	001
D-MBAL	Comco Ikarus Fox-C22	9110-3384
D-MBAN	Dallach Sunrise II	010
D-MBAO	Behlen Trike Vampir II	87027
D-MBAR	Ultralight Flight Phantom	410
D-MBAS	HFL Stratos 300K	300-009K
D-MBAT	UPM Funplane	900085
D-MBAU	Büttner Crazyplane III	003
D-MBAW	Platzer Kiebitz-B	033
D-MBBA	Comco Ikarus Fox-C22	9202-3377
D-MBBC	Platzer Kiebitz-B	100
D-MBBE	LO-120	EB 001
D-MBBH	Krampen Ikarus S	65
D-MBBI	Fresh Breeze 110 AL 2F	40
D-MBBL	Take Off Merlin Karat 13	21193
D-MBBM	Platzer Kiebitz-B6	023
D-MBBN	HFL Stratos IIe	002
D-MBBO	Fresh Breeze 110 AL2F	96
D-MBBR(1)	Scheibe Uli 1	5205
D-MBBR(2)	Drachenstudio Royal	190598
D-MBBS	Comco Ikarus Fox-C22	920 .-3412
D-MBBT	FUL Graffiti Trike	036/0102
D-MBBW	Comco Ikarus Fox-C22	9201-3372
D-MBCA(2)	Schmidtler Enduro	02-015
D-MBCB	Albatros 64	166
D-MBCD(2)	Dallach Sunrise IIA	030
D-MBCH	Scheibe Ultra	3408
D-MBCN	Take Off Merlin Trike	205093
D-MBCO	Aerostyle Breezer	042
D-MBCR	Magni M-16 Tandem Trainer Gyro	unkn
D-MBCS(1)	Magni M-14 Scout Gyro	unkn
D-MBCS(2)	Zenair CH-601D Zodiac	1402195372002
D-MBCT	Behlen Power-Trike	89014
D-MBCZ	Magni M-14 Scout Gyro	114-04-2713
D-MBDB	Comco Ikarus Fox D	005
D-MBDD	Kümmerle Mini-Fly-Set	1084-1
D-MBDE	NST Minimum Saphir 17	34765
D-MBDG	Dyn'Aero MCR-01 ULC	194
D-MBDS	Rans S-6 Coyote II	0293446
D-MBEA	MKB Ranger M	0100785
D-MBEC	Light Aero Avid Flyer	808
D-MBEE	Behlen Power-Trike /Rotax 582	980022
D-MBEF	HFL Stratos 300	300-002
D-MBEG	Me 109 Scale Replica	003
D-MBEI	Schönleber DS Trike	10293
D-MBEK(2)	Behlen Power-Trike /Rotax 582	980022
D-MBEL	Ultraleichtverbund Bi 90	21298
D-MBEN	Fresh Breeze 122 AL 2F	241
D-MBEO	Platzer Kiebitz-B	048
D-MBES(1)	Fisher FP-202 Koala	1988/1/1
D-MBES(2)	Tecnam P.92 Echo 100S	662
D-MBET	Tandem Air Sunny Sport	22.91
D-MBEW	Behlen Power-Trike	877947/900/12
D-MBEX	Comco Ikarus C-42B	0206-6466
D-MBFA	UPM Cobra Raven Trike	91108
	(Correct c/n may be 910108)	
D-MBFC	Ultraleichtverbund Bi 90	21312
D-MBFF	Konsuprod Mosquito IB	016
D-MBFJ	Comco Ikarus C-42B	0404-6588
D-MBFK	Comco Ikarus Fox-C22	9208-3437
D-MBFM	Rans S-10 Sakota	0189040
D-MBFR	Light Aero Avid Flyer IV	1103
D-MBFW	Light Aero Avid Flyer IV	1102
D-MBGG	Comco Ikarus C-42B	0208-6497
D-MBGH	Behlen Power-Trike /Rotax 582	950002
D-MBGR	FUL Graffiti Trike	027/0093
D-MBHA	Remos G.3 Mirage	140
D-MBHG	Aériane Sirocco	140
D-MBHH	Pioneer Flightstar	384
D-MBHJ	Comco Ikarus Fox-C22	9309-3508
D-MBHL	Flight Design CT-2K	02.03.06.15
D-MBHM	UPM Funplane	850001
D-MBHO	Flight Team Spider Hazard 13	D016
D-MBHR	Air Création XP GT 582S	0494
D-MBHT	Fresh Breeze 110 AL 2F	158
D-MBHW	Fresh Breeze 122 AL 2F	420
D-MBIA	Comco Ikarus Fox-C22	9202-3385
D-MBIC	Fresh Breeze 110 AL 2F	151
D-MBII	Comco Ikarus C-42B	0207-6495
D-MBIL	Platzer Kiebitz-B4	082
D-MBIR	Fresh Breeze 110 AL 2F	361

D-MBJH	ASO Viper Trike	12059404
D-MBJK	Klüver Bison Trike	089706
D-MBJR	Take Off Maximum Karat 13	083121
D-MBJU	Junkers Profly JUL Trike	4339
D-MBKA	B&F Funk Fk-9 Mk.III	09-03-200
D-MBKE	Air Création GTE 582S	7954557569
D-MBKG	Ultraleichtverbund Bi 90	21090
D-MBKK	Ghostbuster	95001
D-MBKL	Fly Synthesis Storch	unkn
D-MBLC	Vogt LO-120S	006
D-MBLF	Sky-Service Pago Jet M4	95302
D-MBLG	Flight Design CTSW	04.07.02
D-MBLI	Behlen Power-Trike	94001
D-MBLN	Platzer Motte B2	32
D-MBLP	Ultraleichtverbund Bi 90	21239
D-MBLR	B&F Funk FK-9 Mk.IV	09-04-248
D-MBLS	ASO Viper Trike	VIII 22071503
D-MBLU	Tecnam P.92 Echo Super	unkn
D-MBLW	NST Minimum Zephir	M440
D-MBMA	Ultraleichtverbund Bi 90	7894016045
D-MBMB	NST Minimum	0474
D-MBME	Comco Ikarus C-42B	0306-6560
D-MBMG	Behlen Power-Trike Vampir II	89023
D-MBMH	Ultraleichtverbund Bi 90	927
D-MBMI	Rans S-12 Airaile	1092298
D-MBMW	Schmidtler Enduro Focus 18	M868086
D-MBNS	Büttner Crazyplane III	7
D-MBNY	Light Aero Avid Flyer IV	1228
D-MBOC	HFL Stratos 300	300-007
D-MBOD	NST Minimum Saphir	M159
D-MBOL	Sky-Walker II	263
D-MBOP	Schönleber DS Speed KS 14	L04/0489
D-MBOS	J-3 Kitten	8610-3
D-MBOY	UPM Cobra Raven Trike	900092
	(Same c/n also quoted for D-MULB)	
D-MBPQ	Fresh Breeze 122 AL 2F	463
D-MBPR	Behlen Power-Trike	88017
D-MBPV	MKB Enduro Focus 18M	00187
D-MBPW	Tandem Air Sunny Sport	006
D-MBRB	Ultralight Flight Phantom T-44	328
D-MBRD	Comco Ikarus C-42B	0207-6468
D-MBRE	Flight Team Spider	D041
D-MBRH	Kiggen/Heiland Air Création GTE	54173187195
D-MBRK	Rans S-6 Coyote II	0992357
D-MBRP	Fresh Breeze 110 AL4H	21
D-MBRT	Drachenstudio Royal Trike	01-9610
D-MBRZ	Aerostyle Breezer	033
D-MBSE	ARCO Spacer L	1178
D-MBSF	Behlen Power-Trike /Rotax 582	97006
D-MBSJ	UL-F Jochum Eagle III	980907
D-MBSK	Comco Ikarus Fox-C22	9105-3325
D-MBSM	Dallach Sunrise II	005
D-MBSO	NST Minimum	M551
D-MBSR	NST Minimum Zephir	421
D-MBSS	Comco Ikarus C-42B	0308-6549
D-MBST	Comco Ikarus Fox-C22	9308-3516
D-MBSU	FUL Graffiti Trike	024/0090
D-MBSV	Drachenstudio Royal Trike	150996
D-MBSW	Sky Walker II	161
D-MBSX	Albatros SX	200
D-MBTB	Drachenstudio Royal Karat 13	02-9308
D-MBTL	NST Minimum	M221
D-MBTS	Solid Air Diamant Twin	T-009
D-MBTT	Tandem Air Sunny Targa	TA 008.93
D-MBTU	Rans S-6 Coyote II	unkn
D-MBTX	Warnke Trike	SI 033
D-MBUF	Schmidtler Enduro Lotus 16	020993
D-MBUM	Bäumer Racer (Homebuilt)	01/90
D-MBUR	Flight Team Spider	D042
D-MBUT	Solid Air Diamant Sierra Trike	014
D-MBVB	Comco Ikarus Fox-C22	9108-3337
D-MBVL	Comco Ikarus C-42B	0206-6483
D-MBVO	Take Off Merlin Karat 13	22344
D-MBWB	Seiffert Mini II	10
D-MBWC	Tandem Air Sunny Sport	005.05.02SP
D-MBWG	Pago Jet M4	96701
D-MBWO	Drachenstudio Royal Trike	170/879
D-MBWP	Behlen Trike	83/1
D-MBWS	Light Aero Avid Flyer IV	939
D-MBWT	Air-Light Wild Thing	082
D-MBXX	UL-F Jochum Eagle III	970803
D-MBYE	Klüver Twin Racer SX 16	950103891
D-MBYS	Light Aero Avid Flyer	443C
D-MBYV	Light Aero Avid Flyer	1101D
D-MBYZ	Flight Team Spider Trike	D032
D-MBZZ	Tandem Air Sunny Sport	25.91
D-MCAA	UPM Cobra Trike	91107
	(Correct c/n may be 910107)	
D-MCAB(1)	Fair Fax DR Hazard 15	D015
D-MCAB(2)	Comco Ikarus C-42B	0408-6615
D-MCAC	Klüver Twin Racer SX 16	616205
D-MCAD	Fresh Breeze 110 AL2F	30
D-MCAE	Comco Ikarus Fox	004
D-MCAH	Comco Ikarus Fox-C22	9009-3272
D-MCAK	Fresh Breeze 122 AL 2F	341
D-MCAL	Ultraleichtverband Bi 90	B21152
D-MCAM	Sky Walker II	387

D-MCAN	ARCO Spacer L	689
D-MCAS	Solid Air Diamant Euro III	016
D-MCAT	Behlen Power Trike II	980020
D-MCAW	Behlen Power-Trike /Rotax 582	93003
D-MCAX	NST Minimum Saphir	M530
D-MCBB	Schönleber DS Trike	5153
D-MCBC	UL-F Jochum Eagle III	980405
D-MCBQ	Fresh Breeze 110 AL 2F	105
D-MCBS	ASO Viper Trike	V III 22071807
D-MCCE	Sky-Walker II	237
D-MCCI	Büttner Crazyplane III	86
D-MCCL	Comco Ikarus Fox-C22	9107-3368
D-MCCP	Behlen Power-Trike	95003
D-MCCR	Platzer Kiebitz B	084
D-MCCS	Ultraleichtverbund Bi 90	985
D-MCCX(2)	B&F Funk FK-14 Polaris	023
D-MCDC	UL-F Jochum Eagle III	970501
D-MCDF	Take Off Merlin Trike	23135
D-MCDH	Remos G.3 Mirage	142
D-MCDI	Sky-Service Pago Jet	95201
D-MCDK	NST Minimum	M541
D-MCDP(2)	Büttner Crazyplane III	82
D-MCDR	Kilb Air Création GTE 5	AC 004
D-MCDV	Comco Ikarus Fox-C22	9109-3356
D-MCDW	Ultraleichtverbund Bi 90	21053
D-MCDX	Schönleber Trike	TK 01/0395
D-MCEC	NST Minimum	M569
D-MCEH	Ultraleichtverbund Bi 90	21297
D-MCEK	Comco Ikarus Fox-C22	9106-3331
D-MCES(2)	HFL Stratos 300K	300-028K
D-MCET	Flight Team Spider Hazard 15	002
D-MCFA	Light Aero Avid Flyer SW	1304D
D-MCFB	Tecnam P.92 Echo 2000S	633
D-MCFI	Auto Gyro	unkn
D-MCFK	B&F Funk FK-9TG Mk.IISmart	013
D-MCFR	Light Aero Avid Flyer	418
D-MCGB	Drachenstudio Royal Trike	03-03039
D-MCGE	Ultraleichtverbund Bi 90	690
D-MCGM	Remos G3 Mirage	095
D-MCGN	Flight Design CT2SW	04.08.02
D-MCHA	Fisher FP-404 Classic	001
D-MCHB	NST Minimum	120623
D-MCHF	Rans S-10 Sakota	0491128
D-MCHG	Aeropro Eurofox	14404
D-MCHK	Dallach Sunrise IIA	032
D-MCHL	Comco Ikarus C-42B	0307-6566
D-MCHM	ASO Viper Trike	VIII 122070503
D-MCHP	Albatros 52	131
D-MCHR	NST Minimum	M577
D-MCHS	ASO Viper Trike	VII 2049309
D-MCHW	NST Minimum	M567
D-MCIB	NST Minimum Saphir 17	M297
D-MCII	Schmidtler Enduro Trike	865186
D-MCIL	UPM Cobra BF 52 UL Trike	950134
D-MCIN	Schönleber DS Trike	11290
D-MCJA	Fresh Breeze 110 AL 2F	38
D-MCJJ	Behlen Power-Trike /Rotax 582	980016
D-MCJN	Behlen Power Trike II	97010
D-MCJW	FUL Graffiti Trike	037/0103
D-MCKK	TL Ultralight TL-2000 Sting	03 ST 60
D-MCKT	Comco Ikarus Fox-C22	9207-3428
D-MCLA	Fresh Breeze 110 AL 2F	213
D-MCLU	Albatros Milan	08085
D-MCMA	NST Minimum Zephir CX	M524
D-MCMC	Tandem Air Sunny Sport	2-91
D-MCMK	FUL Graffiti Trike	001/0045
D-MCMP	Ultraleichtverbund Bi 90	21060
D-MCNO	Fresh Breeze 122 AL 2F	212
D-MCOB	Tandem Air Sunny Sport	1-91
D-MCOG	Fresh Breeze 110 AL 4H	25
D-MCOL	Kümmerle Mini-Fly-Set	73185-3
D-MCOM	Comco Ikarus C-42B	0304-6532
D-MCON	Sky-Walker II	264
D-MCOQ	Warnke Trike	S1/009
D-MCOR	Fresh Breeze 122 AL 2F	389
D-MCOW	Sky-Walker II	236
D-MCOY	Rans S-6ES Coyote II	0392280
D-MCPI	Büttner Crazyplane I	103
D-MCPK	B&F Funk FK-14B Polaris	14-036
D-MCPM(2)	Büttner Easy Plane	8
D-MCRA	TL Ultralight TL-2000 Sting	03 ST 39
D-MCRB	Ultralight Flight Phantom	402
D-MCRC	Light Aero Avid Flyer IV	870
D-MCRH	NST Schwarze Trike	MT66
D-MCRL	Kappa KP-2U Sova	unkn
D-MCRS	Rans S-10S Sakota	1191140
D-MCSA	Light Aero Avid Flyer	1154D
D-MCSB	Schmidtler Enduro Trike	01-002
D-MCSW	Sky-Walker II	162
D-MCTO	Warnke Trike	034
D-MCTR	Fresh Breeze 110 AL 2F	42
D-MCTS	Warnke Skylight Trike	2
D-MCUL	Ultraleichtverbund Bi 90	21178
D-MCUP	WDFL Dallach D4 Fascination BK	116
D-MCVW	B&F Funk FK-12 Comet	12-052
D-MCWA	Albatros 64	130
D-MCWB	Roman-Weller UW 9 Sprint	03

D-MCWE	Ultraleichtverbund Bi 90	21036	
D-MCWK	Comco Ikarus C42	0203-6457n	
D-MCWM	FUL Graffiti Trike	38/0104	
D-MCWR	Comco Ikarus C42B	0307-6559	
D-MCWT	Comco Ikarus C42B	0301-6530	
D-MCWW	Fair Fax DR Trike	1022	
D-MCYZ	Fresh Breeze 110 AL 2F	93	
D-MDAA	Klüver Twin Racer SX 16	555203	
D-MDAB	Schönleber DS Lotus 18 Trike	020490	
D-MDAL	Dallach Sunrise IIA	033	
D-MDAM	ASO Viper Trike	12059404	
D-MDAN	Sky-Walker II	232	
D-MDAS	Tandem Air Sunny Targa	TA 07.93	
D-MDAT	Take Off Merlin 1100	28368	
D-MDAV	Behlen Power Trike II	89044	
D-MDBB	Dallach Sunrise IIA	020	
D-MDBG	Fresh Breeze 110 AL2F	33	
D-MDBH	WDFL Sunwheel	008	
D-MDBI	Flight Team Spider	D038	
D-MDBK	Pago Jet M4	961201	
D-MDBL	Take Off Merlin Trike	22114	
D-MDBO	B&F Funk FK-9 Mk.III	09-03U-220	
D-MDBS	Mantel Mono-Dragster	2248410002	
D-MDBX(2)	HFL Stratos IIe	11e/005	
D-MDCA	Comco Ikarus C-42B	0207-6450	
D-MDCC	Comco Ikarus Fox-C22S	0301-3750	
D-MDCD	Zenair CH-701D STOL	7-9305	
D-MDCL	Behlen Power-Trike	88023	
D-MDCM	NST Minimum Sierra	SN 105	
D-MDCS	Schmidtler Enduro Trike	02-003	
D-MDCW	NST Minimum	M323	
D-MDDB	B&F Funk FK-9	09-022	
D-MDDD	Aviasud Mistral BRD	085	
D-MDDD(2)	Remos G.3 Mirage	unkn	
D-MDDP	Sky-Walker II	392	
D-MDDT	Behlen Power Trike II	98011	
D-MDEA	Wisch Star-Trike	12601	
D-MDEB	Behlen Power-Trike	95001	
D-MDEC(2)	Fresh Breeze 110 AL 2F	421	
D-MDED	ICP MXP-740 Savannah	083	
D-MDEE	Fresh Breeze 110 AL 2F	411	
D-MDEF	Behlen Power-Trike	94003	
D-MDEG	Magni M-14 Scout 2000 gyro	214042723	
D-MDEI	Take Off Merlin Trike	25125	
D-MDEL	Seiffert Mini-Speed Trike	unkn	
D-MDEO	Comco Ikarus Fox-C22	9104-3334	
	(Possibly ex D-MDEG, or clerical error?)		
D-MDET	NST Minimum Pamir	M523	
D-MDEW	Fresh Breeze 110 AL 2F	12	
D-MDFA	Fantasy Air Allegro	02-416	
D-MDFC	Ultraleichtverbund Bi 90	976-4105546	
D-MDFD	Fresh Breeze 110 AL2F	35	
D-MDFF	Comco Ikarus C-42B	0403-6596	
D-MDFG	NST Minimum	MT81	
D-MDFI	Ultraleichtverbund Bi 90	B21122	
D-MDFR	LO-120S	011	
D-MDFS	Remos G.3 Mirage	145	
D-MDGS	UPM Cobra Trike	900099	
D-MDHE	Comco Ikarus Fox-C22	9303-3481	
D-MDHF	Tandem Air Sunny	46.93	
D-MDHG	Behlen Power-Trike	97011	
D-MDHH	Kümmerle Mini-Fly-Set	1278/91-5	
D-MDHP	Ultralight Flight Phantom	327	
D-MDHW	Tecnam P.92 Echo Short Wing S	858	
D-MDHX	Büttner Crazyplane IV	14	
D-MDII	FUL Graffiti Trike	030/0096	
D-MDIN	Dallach Sunrise IIA	026	
D-MDIS	MKB Ranger M	01/006/85	
D-MDIW	Zenair CH-601D Zodiac	6-9299	
D-MDKE	Drachenstudio Piccolo II Trike	099306	
D-MDKH	Comco Ikarus Fox-C22	8705-3062	
D-MDKK	Remos G.3 Mirage	144	
D-MDKL	NST Minimum SierrAII	558	
D-MDKM	Behlen Power-Trike Hazard 15M	91034	
D-MDKR	Comco Ikarus Fox II Doppel	8608-3029	
D-MDKT	Comco Ikarus Fox-C22	9103-3315	PH-2G8
D-MDKU	Light Aero Avid Flyer IV	1155C	
D-MDLB	Interplane Skyboy ZK	69/2003	
D-MDLF	Tandem Air Sunny Sport	007.03.03 SP	
D-MDLT	Sky-Service Pago Jet M4	95303	
D-MDLW	Comco Ikarus Fox-C22	9111-3357	
D-MDMA	Behlen Power-Trike	86027	
D-MDMD	Comco Ikarus C-42B	0302-6506	
D-MDMC	Behlen Power-Trike	M878502	
D-MDMJ	Behlen Power-Trike Vampir II	88018	
D-MDMK	Behlen Power-Trike	7017	
D-MDMR	Behlen Power-Trike Vampir II	M876642	
D-MDMT	Comco Ikarus Fox-C22	8905-3201	
D-MDMV	Fresh Breeze 110 AL 2F	413	
D-MDMY	Comco Ikarus Fox-C22	9008-3292	
D-MDNK	Pago Jet M4	960501	
D-MDOB	Behlen Power-Trike	93002	
D-MDOC	Tandem Air Sunny	30.92	
D-MDOG(2)	B&F Funk FK-9 Mk.II	006	
D-MDOL	Junkers Profly JUL Trike	00594	
D-MDOR	Platzer Kiebitz B2	186	
D-MDOX	Steinbach Austro Trike Spot IIM	1915	
D-MDPA	Schmidtler Ranger M	18-24	
D-MDPD	Zenair CH-601D Zodiac	6-9298	
D-MDPG	Take Off Merlin Karat 13	20573	
D-MDPW	Drachenstudio Royal Trike	13-0696	
D-MDRB	Ultralight Flight Phantom T44	0293	
D-MDRF	Remos G.3 Mirage	097	
D-MDRM	Take Off Merlin Trike	25516	
D-MDRP	WDFL Sunwheel	002	
D-MDRS	Air-Light Wild Thing	083	
D-MDRT	Platzer Kiebitz-B4	099	
D-MDSB	Take Off Merlin Trike/La Mouette	26356	
D-MDSC	UPM Funplane	860016	
D-MDSF	Behlen Power-Trike Vampir II	89014	
D-MDSG	Take Off Merlin Trike	21393	
D-MDSK	Flight Team Spider Hazard 13	D013	
D-MDSL	Comco Ikarus Fox-C22B	9202-3389	
D-MDSM	Kilb Air Création GTE 5	AC 005	
D-MDSO	Ultraleichtverbund Bi 90	529	
D-MDSR	Flight Team Spider Trike	D023	
D-MDSS	HFL Stratos IIe	IIe-008	
D-MDSW	Flight Team Spider Trike	D039	
D-MDTA	FUL Graffiti Trike	002/0049	
D-MDTG	Fresh Breeze 110 AL 2A	140	
D-MDTL	Seiffert Mini II	774	
D-MDTW	Behlen Power-Trike /Rotax 582	980017	
D-MDUD	Fresh Breeze 110 AL 2F	200	
D-MDUF	Comco Ikarus C-42 Cyclone	9609-6562	
D-MDUG	Wildente	109	
D-MDUO	Comco Ikarus Fox II Doppel	001/85	
D-MDUP	Ultraleichtverbund Bi 90	623	
D-MDUS	Sky-Walker II	350	
D-MDVK	Behlen Power-Trike	91021	
D-MDWW	Comco Ikarus Fox-C22	9305-3501	
D-MDYN	Aerospool WT9 Dynamic	DY076	
D-MDZR	Fresh Breeze 122 AL 2F	170	
D-MDZZ	Sky-Service Pago Jet	95308	
D-MEAA(1)	Sky-Service Pago Jet	95301	
D-MEAA(2)	Aerostyle Breezer	027	
D-MEAB	Solid Air Diamant Trike	18	
D-MEAC	Behlen Power-Trike /Rotax 582	980023	
D-MEAF	Klüver Racer SX 12	14007	
D-MEAL	FUL Graffiti Trike	014/0074	
D-MEAS	Ultraleichtverbund Bi 90	609	
D-MEAT	Warnke Puma Sprint DS	D003	
D-MEBA	Behlen Power-Trike	86026	
D-MEBB	Comco Ikarus C-42B	0203-6470	
D-MEBE	Flight Team Spider Trike	D011	
D-MEBI	Flight Team Spider Trike	D029	
D-MEBL	Take Off Merlin Karat 13	22544	
D-MEBM	WDFL Dallach D4 Fascination BK	125	
D-MEBR	Ultraleichtverbund Bi 90	21065	
D-MEBS	Comco Ikarus Fox D	8410-FD21	
D-MEBY	Sky-Walker II	257	
D-MECA	Solid Air Diamant SierrAI	003	
D-MECC	NST Minimum Zephir	M353	
D-MECK	Evektor EV-97 Eurostar	2002-1409	
D-MECS	B&F Funk FK-9 Mk.IV	09-04-228	
D-MEDD	NST Minimum	1449	
D-MEDE	Comco Ikarus Fox-C22	9107-3365	
D-MEDI (2)	WDFL Dallach D4 Fascination BK	101	
D-MEDO	NST Minimum	M535	
D-MEDP	NST Minimum	M521	
D-MEDS	Behlen Power-Trike	002583	
D-MEDT	Kümmerle Mini-Fly-Set	1273/91-5	
D-MEDV	Comco Ikarus C-42 Cyclone	9610-6010	
D-MEEC	Ultraleichtverbund Bi 90	168308471	
D-MEEL	Comco Ikarus Fox-C22	9207-3440	
D-MEEM	Fresh Breeze 110 AL 2F	113	
D-MEEN	Eagle	unkn	
D-MEEV	Sky-Walker II	283	
D-MEFA	Schönleber DS Speed KS 14 Trike	KS01/0192	
D-MEFB	Flight Team Spider Trike	D033	
D-MEFE	Ultraleichtverbund Bi 90	6480	
D-MEFF	Aerostyle Breezer	016	
D-MEFG	Fair Fax Trike	024	
D-MEFH	Schmidtler Enduro Trike	01-003	
D-MEFI	Comco Ikarus C-42B	0303-6521	
D-MEFK	Fresh Breeze 110 AL 2F	163	
D-MEFL	Ultraleichtverbund Bi 90	552	
D-MEFM	Aerostyle Breezer	044	
D-MEFW	NST Minimum Zephir	M520/23670	
D-MEGG	Tandem Air Sunny Sport	33.92	
D-MEGI (2)	B&F Funk FK-9 Mk.II	09-005	
D-MEGW	Platzer Kiebitz-B	074	
D-MEHC	Fresh Breeze 110 AL2F	39	
D-MEHE	Behlen Power-Trike	92001	
D-MEHF	Comco Ikarus Fox-C22	8906-3197	
D-MEHG	HFL Stratos 300K	300-011K	
D-MEHK	Fresh Breeze 110 AL 2F	156	
D-MEHL (2)	Pago Jet M4	970401	
D-MEHL(3)	Zenair CH-701D STOL	7-9479	
D-MEHR	Scheibe Uli-2	3304	
D-MEHU	Fisher FP-202 Koala	2322	
D-MEHV	Behlen Power-Trike	875022	
D-MEHW	Behlen Power-Trike II Hazard 15M	910604	
D-MEIA	Flight Team Spider Hazard 13	D021	
D-MEIC	Alpi Aviation Pioneer 300	unkn	

D-MEIF	Comco Ikarus C-42	0202-6416
D-MEII	Fisher FP-202 Koala	JE 001
D-MEIN	Büttner Crazyplane I	118
D-MEIR	UPM Funplane Trike	870027
D-MEIS	Behlen Power-Trike	1000683
D-MEIT	Wisch Star-Trike Vampir II	12603895
D-MEJK	Behlen Power-Trike Vampir II	88020
D-MEJR	Comco Ikarus Fox II Doppel	8607-3027
D-MEKA	Comco Ikarus Fox I	054
D-MEKE	Flight Team Spider	D047
D-MEKI	Platzer Kiebitz-B8	031
D-MEKN	Comco Ikarus C-42B	0211-6499
D-MEKS	Aerostyle Breezer	036
D-MEKU	Platzer Motte B	047
D-MEKW	Comco Ikarus Fox D	8505-FD20
D-MELA	Magni M-16 (?) Gyro	unkn
D-MELE	Klüver Bison Trike	982704
D-MELF(2)	Schmidtler Enduro Trike	M3557747
D-MELG	Take Off Maximum Karat 13 Trike	035100
D-MELH	Remos G.3 Mirage	125
D-MELI	Comco Ikarus C-42B	0211-6512
D-MELL	LO-120S	010-A
D-MELM	Behlen Power-Trike Falcon	1718
D-MELS	Schmidtler Ranger M	14/49
D-MELW	Air-Light Wild Thing	090
D-MELX	Fresh Breeze 122 AL 2F	410
D-MELY	Light Aero Avid Flyer	936
D-MEMB	Take Off Merlin Trike	25726
D-MEME(2)	Flight Design CT2SW	04.09.04
D-MEMF	Platzer Kiebitz	255
D-MEMJ	Fresh Breeze 110 AL 2F	201
D-MEMK	ASO Viper Hazard 15 Trike	11290
D-MEMO(1)	Scheibe Ultra	3409
D-MEMO(2)	Zenair CH-701D STOL	7-9507
D-MEMR	Schmidtler Enduro Trike	02-007
D-MEND	Sky-Walker II	358
D-MENG	Sky-Walker II	234
D-MENK	Flight Design CT-2K	03.03.05.12
D-MENO	UPM Cobra BF 52UL Trike	950133
D-MENU	Behlen Power-Trike II Hazard 15	90020
D-MEPA	ASO Viper 13/582 Hazard 13 Trike	122020108
D-MEPG	Albatros AN-22	8332
D-MEPI	Fair Fax DR Trike	D012
D-MEPS	ASO Viper Trike	22038208
D-MEPU	Pioneer Flightstar	678
D-MEPW(1)	Comco Ikarus Fox-C22	8906-3204
D-MEPW(2)	Flight Design CT2SW	04.12.03
D-MERA	Kiggen/Heiland Air Création GTE 582S	9954557785
D-MERB	Ultralight Flight Phantom	0294
D-MERC	Enduro Trike (Homebuilt)	12/92
D-MERD	UPM Omega Focus 20	880032
D-MERF	Comco Ikarus Fox D	8710-FD41
D-MERG	Dallach Sunrise IIA	038
D-MERH(2)	Aerostyle Breezer	025
D-MERK	Fresh Breeze 110 AL2F	7439
D-MERL	Behlen Trike	86023
D-MERO	Scheibe UL-1 Coach IIS	003
D-MERS	Comco Ikarus Fox-C22	9204-3395
D-MERT	Albatros SX	503
D-MERZ	Scheibe Uli 1	5216
D-MESA	ASO Viper Hazard 15 Trike	11024201
D-MESB(2)	Fläming Air FA-01 Smaragd	07/04
D-MESG	Behlen Power-Trike	87028
D-MESL	Comco Ikarus Fox-C22	9203-3392
D-MESP	UPM Cobra Trike	900105
D-MESR	FUL Graffiti Trike	018/0076
D-MEST	Ultraleichtverbund Bi 90	4926438690
D-MESW	Sky-Walker II	169
D-METE	Comco Ikarus Fox-C22	9207-3417
D-METH	Platzer Kiebitz-B4	019
D-METL	Schmidtler Enduro Trike	01001
D-METT	Light Aero Avid Flyer IV	1153 D
D-METU	Aériane Sirocco II	116
D-METY	Drachenstudio Royal Trike	14-0896
D-METZ	Schmidtler Enduro Trike	02-018
D-MEUB	Junkers Profly JUL Trike	0001
D-MEUL	FUL Graffiti Trike	034/0100
D-MEUR	Flight Team Spider Hazard 15	D011
D-MEVA	HFL Stratos IIe	IIe-OO9
D-MEVC	Büttner Crazyplane III	5
D-MEVI	Light Aero Avid Flyer	972
D-MEVT	Kümmerle Mini-Fly-Set	251864
D-MEWE	Albatros 52	115
D-MEWK	ICP MXP-740V Savannah	02-07-51-152
D-MEWL	Flight Team Spider Trike	D030
D-MEWO	NST Minimum SierrAII	231
D-MEWS	WDFL Sunrise	015
D-MEWU	Klüver Kaiman Trike	701612
D-MEZE	UPM Cobra BF 52UL Trike	950132
D-MFAA	Comco Ikarus Fox-C22	8703-3036
D-MFAB	Comco Ikarus Fox II Doppel	8612-3051
D-MFAC	Comco Ikarus Fox II Doppel	8609-3033
D-MFAD	Comco Ikarus Fox II Doppel	8611-3034
D-MFAK	Fläming Air FA-01 Smaragd	unkn
D-MFAN	Comco Ikarus Fox-C22	8703-3039
D-MFAO	Comco Ikarus Fox II Doppel	8703-3037
D-MFAP	Comco Ikarus Fox II Doppel	8706-3040
D-MFAQ	Comco Ikarus Fox II Doppel	8703-3038
D-MFAS	Solid Air Twin Diamant Trike	T-010
D-MFAT	Comco Ikarus Fox II Doppel	8706-3041
D-MFAU	Comco Ikarus Fox-C22	8707-3091
D-MFAX	Comco Ikarus Fox D	8512-FD37
D-MFBA	Comco Ikarus Fox-C22	8907-3175
D-MFBB	Comco Ikarus C-42B	0307-6558
D-MFBC	Comco Ikarus Fox-C22	8907-3176
D-MFBD	Comco Ikarus Fox-C22	8905-3178
D-MFBE	Comco Ikarus Fox-C22	8907-3177
D-MFBG	Flight Design CT-2K	01.09.04.28
D-MFBH	Comco Ikarus C-42B	0310-6582
D-MFBL	MKB Enduro Focus 18	0300185
D-MFBM	Platzer Kiebitz-B8	121
D-MFBP	ASO Viper 15 Hazard Trike	15/ 2690
D-MFBW	Ultraleichtverbund Bi 90	994
D-MFBT	Fresh Breeze 110 AL2F	103
D-MFCA	Comco Ikarus Fox-C22	9308-3525
D-MFDF	WDFL Dallach D4 Fascination BK	112
D-MFDH	Behlen Power-Trike	92012
D-MFDK	Fresh Breeze 110 AL2F	72
D-MFEA	Comco Ikarus Fox-C22	8711-3098
D-MFEC	Comco Ikarus Fox-C22	8709-3093
D-MFED	Comco Ikarus Fox-C22	8709-3094
D-MFEE	Comco Ikarus Fox II Doppel	8707-3046
D-MFEH	Tandem Air Sunny Sport	29.92
D-MFEI (2)	Comco Ikarus Fox-C22	8709-3095
D-MFEL	Comco Ikarus Fox-C22	8710-3097
D-MFEM	Comco Ikarus Fox II Doppel	8604-3014
D-MFEN	Comco Ikarus Fox-C22	8711-3099
D-MFEP	Firebird M-1	59092
D-MFEQ	Comco Ikarus Fox-C22	8805-3100
D-MFER	Comco Ikarus Fox-C22	8804-3103
D-MFES	Comco Ikarus Fox-C22	8808-3102
D-MFET	Comco Ikarus Fox-C22	8807-3101
D-MFFA	Rans S-6 Coyote II	0193422
D-MFFD	Fair Fax Trike	011
D-MFFK	Fair-Fax Euro III Trike	045
D-MFFM	Fair Fax Trike	042
D-MFFN	Fair Fax DR Trike	D028
D-MFFO	B&F Funk FK-9 Mk.IV	09-04-231
D-MFFT	Comco Ikarus Fox-C22	8809-3152
D-MFFW(1)	Fair Fax DR Hazard 15M Trike	D017
D-MFFW(2)	Comco Ikarus C-42B	0303-6540
D-MFGD	Flight Design CT	02.01.05.05
D-MFGG	Albatros 52	141
D-MFGH	Albatros 64	302
D-MFGI	Fresh Breeze 110AL2F	55
D-MFGL	Fresh Breeze 110 AL 2F	343
D-MFGM	ASO Viper Trike	12044 503
D-MFGN	Flight Design CT2SW	04-02-05
D-MFGT	Albatros SX	502
D-MFHG	Comco Ikarus Fox-C22	9010-3295
D-MFHJ	NST Minimum	M540
D-MFIB	Comco Ikarus Fox-C22	8809-3161
D-MFID	Comco Ikarus Fox-C22	8811-3162
D-MFIG	Comco Ikarus Fox-C22	8903-3164
D-MFIH	Comco Ikarus Fox-C22	8903-3165
D-MFII	Comco Ikarus C-42B	0209-6500
D-MFIM	Comco Ikarus Fox-C22	8903-3167
D-MFIN	Comco Ikarus Fox-C22	8904-3168
D-MFIP	Comco Ikarus Fox II Doppel	8706-3042
D-MFIR	Comco Ikarus Fox-C22	8905-3169
D-MFIS	Comco Ikarus Fox-C22	8905-3170
D-MFIV	Comco Ikarus Fox-C22	8904-3172
D-MFIW	Comco Ikarus Fox-C22	8906-3173
D-MFIX	Dallach Sunrise IIA	004
D-MFIZ	Comco Ikarus Fox-C22	8908-3174
D-MFJS	Fair Fax DR Trike	D019
D-MFKA	Klüver Bison Trike	883806
D-MFKD	B&F Funk FK-12 Comet	12-060
D-MFKE	Comco Ikarus Fox-C22	8805-3109
D-MFKH	J-3 Kitten	01
D-MFKK	Platzer Kiebitz-B2	102
D-MFKL	Seiffert Mini II	0101/89-1
D-MFKM	B&F Funk FK-14 Polaris	14-028
D-MFKO	Sky-Walker 1+1	26122
D-MFKS	Comco Ikarus C-42B	0412-6644
D-MFKW	Comco Ikarus Fox II Doppel	8603-3012
D-MFLA	Light Aero Avid Flyer IV C	1325C
D-MFLB	ASO Viper Trike/Royal 912	15181090
D-MFLE	Comco Ikarus Fox-C22B	8809-3110
D-MFLH	Comco Ikarus Fox II Doppel	8606-3020
D-MFLI	Aviasud Mistral BRD	151
D-MFLO	Take Off Maximum Trike	109013
D-MFLS	ASO Viper Hazard 15 Trike	151 6990
D-MFLU	Albatros 64	303
D-MFLY	Behlen Power-Trike /Rotax 582	88027
D-MFMA	Comco Ikarus Fox-C22	8701-3031
D-MFMD	Comco Ikarus C-42B	0406-6600
D-MFMF	Tandem Air Sunny	15.91
D-MFMN	Fresh Breeze 110 AL 2F	10
D-MFMV	Schönleber Trike	V070198
D-MFMW	ARCO Spacer L	966
D-MFOB	Krampen Ikarus S	59
D-MFOQ	Klüver Twin Racer Quartz SX 16	236004
D-MFOS	Comco Ikarus Fox-C22	8707-3044

D-MFOX	Comco Ikarus Fox D	023
D-MFPA	Fantasy Aie Allegro 2000	unkn
D-MFPB	NST Minimum	M430
D-MFPF	FUL Graffiti Trike	028/0094
D-MFPK	Platzer Kiebitz-B2	103
D-MFPM	WDFL Dallach D4 Fascination BK	107
D-MFRA	Fresh Breeze 110 AL 2F	63
D-MFRC	FUL Maverick Trike	unkn
D-MFRD	Schönleber DS Lotus KS 16 Trike	KS01/0191
D-MFRE	NST Minimum	M231
D-MFRG	Fair Fax DR Trike	001
D-MFRI	Comco Ikarus Sherpa 1	8306-1029
D-MFRK	Light Aero Avid Flyer	809
D-MFRR	Air-Light Wild Thing	084
D-MFRW	T2	N33931534
D-MFRZ	Platzer Kiebitz-B8	135
D-MFSA	Comco Ikarus Fox-C22	8805-3108
D-MFSG(1)	ASO Viper Trike	VI 12037207
D-MFSG(2)	Platzer Kiebitz	56
D-MFSI	Fresh Breeze 110 AL2F	87
D-MFSJ	Remos G.3 Mirage	119
D-MFSL	B&F Funk FK-9 Mk.III	09-184
D-MFSS	Schmidtler Ranger M Trike	1832
D-MFST	Platzer Motte B-2	039
D-MFSW	Flight Design CT-2K	03.03.02.09
D-MFSZ	Comco Ikarus C-42B	0309-6563
D-MFTA	Comco Ikarus Fox-C22	8808-3104
D-MFTE	Comco Ikarus Fox-C22	8808-3105
D-MFTN	NST Minimum	10873
D-MFTO	Comco Ikarus Fox-C22	8808-3106
D-MFUA	ASO Viper Trike	V 15 I 14491
D-MFUE	Klüver Twin Racer SX 16	554203
D-MFUF	Klüver Twin Racer SX 16	773209
D-MFUH	Comco Ikarus C-42B	0303-6548
D-MFUI	Maverick T2	4
D-MFUL	FUL Graffiti Trike	042/0142
D-MFUN	UPM Funplane	86009
D-MFUS	Comco Ikarus Fox-C22	9211-3483
D-MFUX	Comco Ikarus Fox-C22	8705-3043
D-MFWD	Dallach Sunrise II	009
D-MFWF	Remos G.3 Mirage	135
D-MFWH	Light Aero Avid Flyer IV	1295
D-MFWO	Comco Ikarus C-42B	0412-6643
D-MFZA	B&F Funk FK-9 Mk.III	09-185
D-MFZB	Evektor EV-97 Eurostar	2005-2419
D-MGAC	Flight Design CT-2K	03.01.04.03
D-MGAD	Sky-Walker II	209
D-MGAF	Pioneer Flightstar	373
D-MGAG	Eagle	unkn
D-MGAH	Behlen Power Trike II	96007
D-MGAI	Flight Team Spider	D019
D-MGAK	Tandem Air Sunny Sport	13.91
D-MGAP	Comco Ikarus Fox-C22	9108-3355
D-MGAR	Light Aero Avid Flyer	811
D-MGAS	Zenair CH-701D STOL	7-9270
D-MGAT	Flight Team Spider Trike	D008
D-MGAY	ARCO Spacer L	361
D-MGBB	Klüver Racer SX 12	094002
D-MGBC	Büttner Crazyplane III	106
D-MGBK	Klüver Twin Racer Quartz SX	838910
D-MGBL (1)	Scheibe Ultra	3412
D-MGBN	TL Ultralight TL-2000 Sting	04 ST 87
D-MGBP	Fresh Breeze 110 AL 2F	240
D-MGBR	Aeropro Eurofox	unkn
D-MGBT	B&F Funk FK-9 Mk.III	09-03-183
D-MGBW	Flight Team Spider Hazard 13M	D007
D-MGBY	NST Minimum Saphir	1128
D-MGCB	Sky-Walker II	261
D-MGCC	Light Aero Avid Flyer IV C	942C
D-MGDP	B&F Funk FK-9 Mk.III	09-03-182
D-MGED	Comco Ikarus Fox II Doppel	8607-3030
D-MGEG	Ultraleichtverbund Bi 90	6363951644
D-MGEH	Kümmerle Mini-Fly-Set	483/86-4
D-MGEO	Warnke Skylight Trike	SI 035
D-MGER	Rans S-12 Airaile	1292339
D-MGET	Comco Ikarus Fox-C22	9205-3402
D-MGFA	Schönleber DS Lotus KS 18 Trike	KS02/0389
D-MGFC	Ultraleichtverbund Bi 90	21296
D-MGFE	Schmidtler Ranger M Trike	1821
D-MGFH	Seiffert Mini II	M-SC88646
D-MGFK	B&F Funk FK-12 Comet	12-062
D-MGFL	Light Aero Avid Flyer	683
D-MGFR	NST Minimum	M562
D-MGFU	Behlen Power-Trike	88025
D-MGFX	Swift	SA020
D-MGFY	Swift	SA034
D-MGGB	Tandem Air Sunny Sport	14.91
D-MGGF	Behlen Power Trike II	878188
D-MGGG	Platzer Kiebitz-B2	035
D-MGGK	Ultraleichtverbund Bi 90	96974171166
D-MGGM	Platzer Kiebitz-B9	021
D-MGGP	FUL Graffiti Trike	011/0072
D-MGHA	NST Minimum Zephir	2378
D-MGHB	Pioneer Flightstar	682
D-MGHD	Behlen Power-Trike	463
D-MGHE	Comco Ikarus Fox II Doppel	8606-3021
D-MGHF	Ultraleichtverbund Bi 90	21278

D-MGHH	Albatros 64	301
D-MGHI	Klüver Twin Racer SX 16	543008
D-MGHK	Büttner Crazyplane II	51
D-MGHL	Ultraleichetverbund Bi 90	635
D-MGHM	Dallach Sunrise IIA	036
D-MGHS	Light Aero Avid Flyer IV	810
D-MGHT	Take Off Merlin Trike	24565
D-MGHW	Tecnam P.96 Golf 100S	228
D-MGII	Comco Ikarus C-42B	0310-6583
D-MGIN	Ultraleichtverbund Bi 90	595
D-MGIS	Kümmerle Mini-Fly-Set	12897-8
D-MGJB	NST Minimum Santana	M503
D-MGJH	Fresh Breeze 122 AL 2F	357
D-MGJT	Klüver Bison Trike	427711
D-MGKK	Behlen Trike	90028
D-MGKL	Sky-Walker II	238
D-MGKP	Ultraleichtverbund Bi 90	21199
D-MGKU	LO-120	007 A
D-MGLH	Denney Kitfox IV	1025
D-MGLK	Ghostbuster	199651
D-MGLL	Tecnam P.96 Golf 100S	205
D-MGLM	Rans S-6 Coyote II	0293436
D-MGLR	Seiffert Mini II	100
D-MGLU	Klüver Bison Trike	645802
D-MGMB(1)	Sky-Walker II	181
D-MGMB(2)	Remos G.3 Mirage	150
D-MGMC	Schmidtler Enduro Trike	02-017
D-MGMG	Air-Light Wild Thing	073
D-MGMM	Comco Ikarus Fox-C22	9307-3528
D-MGMP	Comco Ikarus Fox-C22	9206-3404
D-MGNC	ICP MXP-740V Savannah	02-10-51-171
D-MGNI	ARCO Spacer L	877
D-MGOD	Solid Air Diamant 55db(A) Trike	023
D-MGOH	ASO Viper Trike	12022001
D-MGPC	Kiggen/Hieland Air Création GTE 582 S	4317124295
D-MGPD	Fresh Breeze 110 AL 2F	471
D-MGPG	Take Off Maximum Trike	016/0077
D-MGPP	Büttner Crazyplane II	97
D-MGPR	Solar Wings Pegasus Quasar IITC	SW-WQT-0551/SW-TQD-0111
D-MGPS	Krampen Ikarus S	62
D-MGRA	Grossklaus Silent Racer 12	06
D-MGRC	Blankert (Homebuilt)	E25
D-MGRD	Comco Ikarus Fox II Doppel	9008-3291
D-MGRE	Ultraleichtverbund Bi 90	999
D-MGRG	FUL Graffiti Trike	003/0053
D-MGRI	FUL Graffiti Trike	0055
D-MGRJ	FUL Graffiti Trike	0046
D-MGRK	FUL Graffiti Trike	010/0048
D-MGRL	FUL Graffiti Trike	019/0079
D-MGRM	Schönleber DS Lotus KS 16 Trike	KS01/1190
D-MGRO	Ultraleichtverbund Bi 90	21018
D-MGRP	NST Minimum	M539
D-MGRR	FUL Graffiti Trike	200080
D-MGRS	Ultraleichtverbund Bi 90	794
D-MGRT	Comco Ikarus Fox-C22	9211-3422
D-MGRU	ASO Viper Hazard 15 Trike	15791
D-MGRV	Comco Ikarus Fox-C22	9108-3350
D-MGRW	Sky-Walker II	278
D-MGRX	ASO Viper Trike	12052402
D-MGRY	FUL Graffiti Trike	009/0047
D-MGRZ	FUL Graffiti Trike	0050
D-MGSA	NST Schwarze Trike	M564
D-MGSC	Behlen Power-Trike	91029
D-MGSG	Comco Ikarus C-42B	0403-6591
D-MGSH	Seiffert Mini-Speed Trike	1000000
D-MGSL	NST Minimum	010205
D-MGSM	HFL Stratos IIe	IIe-011
D-MGSO	Behlen Power-Trike II	91022
D-MGSP	Büttner Crazyplane I	105
D-MGSR	Pago Jet M4	RB 98008
D-MGSS	Behlen Power-Trike	1715
D-MGST	HFL Stratos 300	300-006
D-MGSY	Schönleber Trike 4	TK01/0296
D-MGTE	UPM Cobra Trike	920114
D-MGTF	Take Off Maximum Trike	13079
D-MGTJ	Comco Ikarus Fox-C22	9106-3339
D-MGTL	Comco Ikarus Fox-C22	9106-3338
D-MGTR	Ultraleichtverbund Bi 90	3762057
D-MGTW	NST Minimum	M1454
D-MGTX	Pegasus	unkn
D-MGUD	ASO Viper Trike	VIII 22072506
D-MGUE	Albatros SX	501
D-MGUH	Air Command Elite Tandem	unkn
D-MGUI	Warnke Skylight Trike	SI 037
D-MGUL	Kiggen/Heiland Air Création GTE 5	4954433118
D-MGUS	Flight Team Spider Trike	D031
D-MGUT	Flight Team Spider Trike	D036
D-MGUZ	Klüver Twin Racer SX 16	235004
D-MGVA	Platzer Kiebitz-B8	055
D-MGVH	Konsuprod Moskito Ib	020
D-MGVL	Ultraleichtverbund Bi 90	21041
D-MGWB	Aerostyle Breezer	020
D-MGWM	Platzer Motte B-2	11
D-MGWR	Behlen Power-Trike /Rotax 582	98010
D-MGZI	Kümmerle Mini-Fly-Set	67986-4
D-MHAA	Tecnam P.92 Echo 100S	614

D-MHAC	Sky-Walker II	390
D-MHAD(2)	ASO Sonic Trike	5954173091
D-MHAF	ASO Viper Trike	10504
D-MHAG	Comco Ikarus Fox II Doppel	8603-3011
D-MHAH	Kümmerle Mini-Fly-Set Thalhofer GT	1304/91-6
D-MHAI	ASO Viper Trike	12060405
D-MHAJ	FUL Graffiti Trike	033/0099
D-MHAL	Comco Ikarus Fox-C22	9008-3280
D-MHAN	ASO Viper Trike	VIII 22064408
D-MHAO	Kiggen/Hieland Air Création GTE 582 S	5954173091
D-MHAP	Kiggen/Hieland Air Création GTE 582 S	3954317120
D-MHAQ	Kiggen/Hieland Air Création GTE 582 S	5954173195
D-MHAS	Comco Ikarus Sherpa II	8505-1098
D-MHAU	Air-Light Wild Thing	2001-06-077
D-MHAW	Air Création GTE	unkn
D-MHAZ	NST Minimum	1147
D-MHBB	Flight Design CT-2K CTSW	03.04.05.19
D-MHBE	Comco Ikarus C-42B	0210-6507
D-MHBJ	Sky-Walker II	328
D-MHBK	Comco Ikarus Fox-C22	9304-3498
D-MHBO	Ultraleichtverbund Bi 90	21123
D-MHBP	Sky-Walker II (Wfu)	272
D-MHBS(1)	Eipper Quicksilver	unkn
D-MHBS	WDFL Dallach D4 Fascination BK	109
D-MHBW	Klüver Racer Quartz SX 16	247004
D-MHCP	Büttner Crazyplane III	90
D-MHCR	Platzer Kiebitz-B9	065
D-MHDE	Skystar S34	002
D-MHDH	Solid Air Diamant Trike	017
D-MHDO	Solid Air Diamant 55dB(A) Trike	019
D-MHDS	Flight Team Spider Hazard 15	D024
D-MHDV(2)	Silent Flyer	unkn
D-MHDW	FUL Graffiti Trike	95
D-MHDZ	Pegasus Quasar II	6637
D-MHED	Comco Ikarus Fox-C22	8809-3154
D-MHEE	Comco Ikarus C-42B	0307-6557
D-MHEJ	Comco Ikarus C-42B	0411-6638
D-MHEL	Flight Team Spider Trike	D015
D-MHEM	WDFL Sunwheel	007
D-MHEN	Fresh Breeze 110 AL2F	88
D-MHET (1)	Platzer Kiebitz-B3	004
D-MHET (2)	Flight Team Spider	D052
D-MHFB	Junkers Profly JUL Trike	94/1062
D-MHFG	Ultraleichtverbund Bi 90	21052
D-MHFK	Behlen Power-Trike	90011
D-MHFL	HFL Stratos IIe	004
D-MHFM	NST Minimum Zephir	438
D-MHFW	Kümmerle Mini-Fly-Set	1284/91-5
D-MHGA	Sky-Service Pago Jet	95602
D-MHGD	Ultraleichtverbund Bi 90	21231
D-MHGE	Fresh Breeze 122 AL 2F	354
D-MHGH	Comco Ikarus C-42B	0209-6501
D-MHGK	Ultraleichtverbund Bi 90	5323804244
D-MHGP	Comco Ikarus Fox-C22	9102-3317
D-MHGR	UL-F Jochum Eagle III	980506
D-MHGS	T2	2
D-MHGT	Comco Ikarus Fox-C22	9204-3405
D-MHGW	Sky-Walker II	199
D-MHHB	Comco Ikarus Fox-C22	9305-3507
D-MHHD	Take Off Maximum Trike	095052
D-MHHG	Kümmerle Mini-Fly-Set	1275/91-5
D-MHHK	Light Aero Avid Flyer Speedwing	1229
D-MHHL	Aerospool WT9 Dynamic	DY068/2004
D-MHHO	Kiggen/Hieland Air Création GTE 582 S	7954557566
D-MHHS	MKB Ranger M Trike	1835
D-MHHT	Comco Ikarus Fox-C22	9301-3423
D-MHHZ	Schönleber Trike Speed 14	010893
D-MHIB	Kilb Air Création GTE 582 S Trike	AC 006
D-MHIE	Büttner Crazyplane II	96
D-MHII	Fisher FP-404 Classic	JE-02
D-MHIN	Take Off Merlin Trike	23955
D-MHIP	Air-Light Wild Thing	72
D-MHIT	Ultraleichtverbund Bi 90	21237
D-MHJA	Remos G.3 Mirage	131
D-MHJE	NST Minimum	031205
D-MHJF	Schönleber DS Speed KS 14 Trike	14010992
D-MHJI	Warnke Skylight Trike	026
D-MHJS	Ultraleichtverbund Bi 90	21054
D-MHJV	Fresh Breeze 110 AL2F	92
D-MHKA	Air Création GTE 582 S	5964559925
D-MHKB	Dallach Sunrise IIA	021
D-MHKE	Behlen Power-Trike	91024
D-MHKF	Rans S-6 Coyote II	1292404
D-MHKH	Sky-Walker II	216
D-MHKJ	WDFL Sunwheel	005
D-MHKK	Kümmerle Mini-Fly-Set Windfex II	9841
D-MHKL	Kiggen/Hieland Air Création GTE 5	4954433120
D-MHKM	Sky-Walker II	316
D-MHKP	Air Création GTE 582 S	3984890749
D-MHKS	Fair Fax Euro II Trike	012
D-MHKV	Schönleber DS Speed KS 14 Trike TK	02/0893
D-MHKZ	Comco Ikarus Fox-C22	0208-3749
D-MHLA	FUL Graffiti Trike	170078
D-MHLB	Fair Fax DR Trike	D014
D-MHLC	Take Off Merlin Trike	10564
D-MHLK	Fair Fax DR Trike	D027
D-MHLL	Fair Fax DR Trike	D024

D-MHLM	Behlen Trike	830037
D-MHLR	Take Off Merlin Trike	26146
D-MHLS	Behlen Power Trike II	96004
D-MHLW(2)	Pegasus Quik 912S	8112
D-MHLX	Take Off Merlin Trike	26957
D-MHMA	UPM Cobra Raven Trike	900096
D-MHMJ	Büttner Crazyplane IV	4
D-MHMM	Sky-Walker II	249
D-MHMS	Fair Fax DR Trike	D025
D-MHNE	Remos G.3 Mirage	126
D-MHNG	Comco Ikarus Fox-C22	9304-3500
D-MHNP	FUL Graffiti Trike	005/0052
D-MHNW	Seiffert Mini-Speed Trike	73
D-MHOB	Dallach Sunrise II	017
D-MHOF	WDFL Sunwheel	004
D-MHOH	Take Off Maximum Trike	039110
D-MHON	Aeropro Eurofox	12202
D-MHOR	Fresh Breeze 110 AL2F	49
D-MHOS	NST Minimum	M301
D-MHOT	Fair Fax DR Hazard 15M Trike	D020
D-MHOW	Klüver Twin Racer SX 16 Trike	541008
D-MHPA	Behlen Power-Trike	08/020
D-MHPE	WDFL Sunwheel	006
D-MHPF	Comco Ikarus Fox-C22	9104-3324
D-MHPH	B&F Funk FK-9 Mk.III	09-03U-196
D-MHRA	Solid Air Diamant Trike	006
D-MHRB	Comco Ikarus Fox-C22	8512-FD36
D-MHRF	Sky-Walker II	352
D-MHRG(1)	Fisher FP-202 Koala	St-004
D-MHRG(2)	TL Ultralight TL-232 Condor Plus	AB09
D-MHRL	Solar Wings Pegasus Quasar IITC	SW-WQT-0585/SW-TQD-0125
D-MHRM	Rans S-6 Coyote II	unkn
D-MHRS	Schönleber DS Trike	16020692
D-MHRT	Ultraleichtverbund Bi 90	21008
D-MHRW	Ultraleichtverbund Bi 90	21099
D-MHSB	ASO Viper Hazard Trike	VI 22027202
D-MHSC	J-3 Kitten	01033
D-MHSD	Behlen Trike	850026
D-MHSH	Dallach Sunrise II	002
D-MHSI	Ultraleichtverbund Bi 90	21287
D-MHSK	Take Off Maximum Trike	T079191
D-MHSM	BVL Speedy Mouse	01/ID
D-MHSO	Take Off Merlin 1100	27958
D-MHSP	FUL Graffiti Trike	012/0073
D-MHSS	Behlen Power-Trike II Hazard 15M	90025
D-MHST	Behlen Power-Trike /Rotax 582	980012
D-MHSV	Schönleber Trike Speed	14020993
D-MHTC	Kiggen/Heiland Air Création GTE 582 S	9954559387
D-MHTE	Kiggen/Heiland Air Création GTE 582 S	3964655068
D-MHTG	MKB Enduro Trike	04/003/85
D-MHTL	ASO Viper Trike	22034206
D-MHUB	Fresh Breeze 122 AL 2F	112
D-MHUE	Platzer Motte B-2	005
D-MHUG	Soarma Libre IILO-120	002A
D-MHUH	Gyrocopter, type unknown	unkn
D-MHUM	Sky-Service Pago Jet	94003
D-MHUP	Flight Design CT-2K	03.06.04.29
D-MHUS	Platzer Kiebitz-B	037
D-MHUU	Ultraleichtverbund Bi 90	21036
D-MHVK	Fresh Breeze 110 AL2F	37
D-MHVL	HFL Stratos 300	300-010K
D-MHVV	Flight Team Spider	D 18
D-MHWA	Albatros Milan	07085
D-MHWD	Flight Design CT-2K	unkn
D-MHWE	Comco Ikarus Fox-C22	9202-3374
D-MHWH	Comco Ikarus Fox-C22	9211-3448
D-MHWK	Platzer Kiebitz-B2	040
D-MHWL	Warnke Skylight Trike	027
D-MHWS	Comco Ikarus Fox	043
D-MHYF	Behlen Power-Trike	88041
D-MHZH	Solid Air Twin Diamant Trike	T005
D-MHZI	Pegasus Quasar II	6717
D-MHZT	UPM Omega Trike	88006
D-MIAA	Flight Team Spider	D 048
D-MIAB	NST Minimum	M549
D-MIAC	Comco Ikarus Fox-C22	9006-3281
D-MIAD	Platzer Kiebitz-B9 (Wears code '143')	143
D-MIAE	Firebird Tri CX	288
D-MIAG	Eagle	unkn
D-MIAL(2)	Flight Team Spider	51
D-MIAM	Light Aero Avid Flyer IV	1011
D-MIAN	Comco Ikarus Fox D	022
D-MIAR(1)	Take Off Maximum Trike	070591
D-MIAR(2)	Air-Light Wild Thing	unkn
D-MIAS	Ultra-Vector H	1424
D-MIAU	Platzer Kiebitz-B	072
D-MIAW	Krampen Ikarus S	63
D-MIBA	Kümmerle Mini-Fly-Set	127591-5
D-MIBC	Comco Ikarus Fox-C22	9009-3282
D-MIBE	Fair Fax Trike Euro III	040
D-MIBI	Fresh Breeze 110 AL 2F	153
D-MIBJ	Comco Ikarus Fox-C22	9301-3463
D-MIBL	Air Création Buggy XP	unkn
D-MIBM	Air Création Kiss	A01002-0202
D-MICA	Comco Ikarus Fox-C22	8907-3216
D-MICB	Comco Ikarus Fox-C22	8907-3217

D-MICC	Dallach Sunrise II	022
D-MICD	Comco Ikarus Fox-C22	8907-3220
D-MICE	Comco Ikarus Fox-C22	8909-3218
D-MICG	Comco Ikarus Fox-C22	9003-3221
D-MICH	Schmidtler Enduro Trike	180485
D-MICK	Comco Ikarus Sherpa I	8306-1026
D-MICL	Comco Ikarus Fox-C22	9003-3225
D-MICM	Comco Ikarus Fox-C22	9003-3226
D-MICN	Comco Ikarus Fox-C22	9004-3227
D-MIC0	Comco Ikarus Fox-C22	8908-3228
D-MICP	Comco Ikarus Fox-C22	9005-3229
D-MICQ	Comco Ikarus Fox-C22	9004-3230
D-MICR	Comco Ikarus Fox-C22	9004-3231
D-MICS	Comco Ikarus Fox-C22	9008-3232
D-MICT	Comco Ikarus Fox-C22	9004-3233
D-MICU	Comco Ikarus Fox-C22	9002-3234
D-MICW	Comco Ikarus Fox-C22	9005-3235
D-MICV	Comco Ikarus Fox D	8410-FD15
D-MICX	Comco Ikarus Fox-C22	9103-3314
D-MICZ	Comco Ikarus Fox-C22	9104-3313
D-MIDC	Comco Ikarus Fox-C22	9009-3285
D-MIDI	Alpi Aviation Pioneer 200	unkn
D-MIDN	Tecnam P.92 Echo 2000S	690
D-MIDO	Pioneer Flightstar	617
D-MIEC	Comco Ikarus Fox-C22	9008-3283
D-MIEF	Tandem Air Sunny Sport	21-91
D-MIEG	UPM Cobra Trike	900090
D-MIEH	Comco Ikarus Fox-C22	9209-3424
D-MIEK	AS0 Viper Hazard 15 Trike	041302
D-MIES	Behlen Power-Trike	90014
D-MIEZ	Scheibe Uli 1	5201
D-MIFC	Comco Ikarus Fox-C22	9009-3284
D-MIFD	Behlen Power-Trike Focus 20	89012
D-MIFI	Aerostyle Breezer	017
D-MIFK	B&F Funk FK-12 Comet	12-050
D-MIFL	Ultraleichtverbund Bi 90	B21154
D-MIFS	Ikarus Eurofox	210520044
	(Also reported as Aeropro Eurofox c/n 13703)	
D-MIFT	Comco Ikarus Fox-C22	8902-3188
D-MIFU	Schmidtler Enduro Trike	02-019
D-MIGA	Remos G.3 Mirage	134
D-MIGH	Ultraleichtverbund Bi 90	941
D-MIGS	Flight Design CT-2K	03.01.05.04
D-MIGT	Eipper Quicksilver GT	2801032
D-MIGX	Dyn'Aero MCR-01 ULC	243
D-MIHA	Comco Ikarus Fox-C22	9302-3491
D-MIHB	Comco Ikarus Fox-C22	8807-3138
D-MIHC	Comco Ikarus Fox-C22	9009-3286
D-MIHG	Behlen Power Trike II	615205
D-MIHI	Kümmerle Mini-Fly-Set	67886-4
D-MIHK	Comco Ikarus Sherpa I	8308-1038
D-MIHS	Aeropro Eurofox	13403
D-MIHV	Fresh Breeze 122 AL 2F	382
D-MIHY	Platzer Motte B-3	43
D-MIII	Comco Ikarus Fox-C22	8908-3215
D-MIIL	Platzer Motte B-3	27
D-MIIM	Ultraleichtverbund Bi 90	unkn
D-MIIW	NST Minimum	M572/92
D-MIJF	FUL Graffiti Trike	043/0149
D-MIJI	NST Minimum	M555
D-MIJR	Take Off Merlin Trike	24155
D-MIJT	NST Minimum Santana	M532
D-MIKC	Comco Ikarus Fox-C22	9010-3287
D-MIKE	Ultraleichtverbund Bi 90	21227
D-MIKG	Take Off Maximum Trike	001049
D-MIKI	Schmidtler Enduro Trike	02-013
D-MIKL	Platzer Motte B2	60
D-MIKR	Behlen Trike	84012
D-MIKS	Ultraleichtverbund Bi 90	530380431167
D-MIKY	MKB Ranger M	0100284
D-MILA(2)	Pago Jet M4	RB 97000
D-MILC	Comco Ikarus Fox-C22	9010-3288
D-MILD	Aviasud Mistral BRD	088
D-MILD	B&F Funk FK-9 Mk.IV	09-04U-233
D-MILE	Scheibe Uli 1	5226
D-MILF	Schönleber Trike	010794
D-MILG	Aerospool WT9 Dynamic	DY01802
D-MILI	Pipistrel Sinus	unkn
D-MILJ	Behlen Power-Trike II	90024
D-MILK	Remos G.3 Mirage	117
D-MILM	Comco Ikarus Fox-C22	9005-3265
D-MILO	Dallach Sunrise IIB	031
D-MILT	Seiffert Mini-Speed Trike	001
D-MILU	Ultraleichtverbund Bi 90	21151
D-MILZ	Klüver Racer SX 12 Trike	652907
D-MIMB	Comco Ikarus Fox-C22	9103-3321
D-MIMC	Comco Ikarus Fox-C22	9009-3289
D-MIMI	Comco Ikarus Fox-C22	9209-3441
D-MIML	Fisher FP-202 Koala	20290
D-MIMM	Comco Ikarus Fox-C22	9208-3416
D-MIMN	Ultraleichtverbund Bi 90	21074
D-MINE	Fresh Breeze 110 AL2A	352
D-MING	Platzer Motte-B2	013
D-MINI	Scheibe Uli 1	5209
D-MINK	NST Minimum	M447
D-MINN	Tecnam P.92 Echo	unkn
D-MINU	HFL Stratos 300	300-004

D-MINX	Tandem Air Sunny Sport	006.07.02SP	
D-MINZ	Scheibe UL-1 Coach	3202	
D-MIOA	Comco Ikarus Fox-C22	9101-3302	
D-MIOC	Comco Ikarus Fox-C22	9009-3290	
D-MIOD	Comco Ikarus Fox D	8806-FD43	
D-MIOG	Fresh Breeze 110 AL 2F	332	
D-MIOO	Light Aero Avid Flyer D	1230	
D-MIPA	Tandem Air Sunny Sport	010.01.04SP	
D-MIPC	Comco Ikarus Fox-C22	9012-3303	
D-MIPP	Aerostyle Breezer	012	
D-MIPS	Light Aero Avid Flyer C	943 C	
D-MIPV	Comco Ikarus Fox-C22	9106-3362	
D-MIPW	Schmidtler Enduro Trike	02-016	
D-MIQC	Comco Ikarus Fox-C22	9101-3304	
D-MIRA	Flight Design CT	unkn	
D-MIRB	Comco Ikarus Fox-C22	9106-3305	
D-MIRC	Albatros 52	129	
D-MIRI	Behlen Power-Trike	97003	
D-MIRJ	Comco Fox D	045	
D-MIRT	Schönleber DS Trike	030492	
D-MISA	Schmidtler Ranger M	18/37	
D-MISC	Comco Ikarus Fox-C22	9102-3306	
D-MISE	Light Aero Avid Flyer D	1231	
D-MISH	B&F Funk FK-9 Mk.III	09-03U-212	
D-MISI	Comco Ikarus Fox-C22	8612-3054	
D-MISL	Comco Ikarus Sherpa I	8305-1017	
D-MIST	Comco Ikarus Fox D	008	
D-MITB	Seiffert Mini II	4392	
D-MITC	Comco Ikarus Fox-C22	9102-3307	
D-MITE	B&F Funk FK-12 Comet	12-063	
D-MITF	Rans S-12 Airaile	0192168	
D-MITG	Comco Ikarus Fox-C22	9207-3388	
D-MITI	NST Minimum	unkn	
D-MITL	Schönleber DS Trike	020794	
D-MITT	Fresh Breeze 110 AL 2F	160	
D-MITV	Platzer Kiebitz B6-450	12	
D-MIUB	Ultraleichtverbund Bi 90	B21155	
D-MIUC	Comco Ikarus Fox-C22	9102-3308	
D-MIUS	Pioneer Flightstar	539	
D-MIVC	Comco Ikarus Fox-C22	9104-3309	
D-MIVK	Behlen Power-Trike Vampir II	85-027	
D-MIWC	Comco Ikarus Fox-C22	9105-3310	
D-MIWU	Flight Design CT-2K	unkn	
D-MIWV	Flight Team Spider	D050	
D-MIWW	Flight Team Spider	D043	
D-MIXC	Comco Ikarus Fox-C22	9102-3311	
D-MIXL	Impulse 2200TD	TD-4	
D-MIXO	Roman-Weller UW-9 Sprint	2	
D-MIZA	Pioneer Flightstar	377	
D-MIZC	Comco Ikarus Fox-C22	9102-3312	
D-MIZE	MKB Ranger M Trike	01/009/86	
D-MIZG	NST Minimum Pamir	443	
D-MIZP	Comco Ikarus Fox-C22	9009-3316	
D-MIZZ	Flight Team Spider	D044	
D-MJAB	Jabiru 450C	0538	
D-MJAE	Klüver Twin Racer Quartz SX 16	228004	
D-MJAG(2)	B&F Funk FK-9	007	
D-MJAI	Kümmerle Mni-Fly-Set	1305916	
D-MJAL	Fair Fax DR Trike	D016	
D-MJAM	Platzer Kiebitz-B6	20	
D-MJAN	Behlen Power-Trike II	90027	
D-MJAS	Ultraleichtverbund Bi 90	736	
D-MJAT	TVS 700 Tandem Air Sunny	991	
D-MJAU	Light Aero Avid Flyer	491	
D-MJBH	NST Minimum Saphir 17	976	
D-MJBL	J.Blank Trike (Homebuilt)	unkn	
D-MJBU	Comco Ikarus Fox-C22	9002-3253	
D-MJCE	Behlen Power-Trike /Rotax 582	980019	
D-MJCT	Ultraleichtverbund Bi 90	1055508906	
D-MJDO	Schmidtler Ranger M Trike	1812	
D-MJEH	Take Off Maximum Trike	T057061	
D-MJET	TVS 700 Tandem Air Sunny	006	
D-MJEW	Flight Team Spider Trike	D037	
D-MJFC	UPM Cobra BF 52UL Trike	930123	
D-MJFE	Sky Walker	240	
D-MJFK	B&F Funk FK-9 Club	unkn	
D-MJFO	Take Off Maximum Trike	107013	
D-MJGH	Comco Ikarus Fox-C22	8604-3015	
D-MJHB	Behlen Power-Trike II	90022	
D-MJHE	Remos G.3 Mirage	133	
D-MJHH	Konsuprod Moskito Ib	012	PH-2D5
D-MJHM	Take Off Maximum Trike	063071	
D-MJHS	Platzer Kiebitz-B2	068	
D-MJIY	Dallach Sunrise II	006	
D-MJJA	TVS 700 Tandem Air Sunny Sport	004	
D-MJJC	Behlen Power-Trike	960002	
D-MJJJ	Solid Air Twin Diamant	7	
D-MJJP	WDFL Dallach D4 Fascination BK	122	
D-MJJY	TVS 700 Tandem Air Sunny	003	
D-MJJZ	TVS 700 Tandem Air Sunny	002	
D-MJKB	Fair Fax AH Euro III Trike	32	
D-MJKE	Büttner Crazyplane III	2	
D-MJKG	Fresh Breeze 110 AL2F	98	
D-MJKH	Comco Ikarus Fox-C22	9006-3271	
D-MJKI	UPM Funplane	870.023	
D-MJKO	Behlen Power Trike II	89038	
D-MJKP	Behlen Power-Trike /Rotax 582	97002	

D-MJKW	Fair Fax DR Trike	D005	
D-MJLC	Solid Air Diamant 55dB(A) Trike	011	
D-MJLP	J-3 Kitten	12-8-88	
D-MJLS	Kiggen/Heiland Air Création GTE 582 S	6954556835	
D-MJMA	Skywalker 1+1	26127	
D-MJMB	Behlen Power-Trike	91027	
D-MJMJ	UPM Cobra BF 52UL Trike	940128	
D-MJMK	Fresh Breeze 110 AL 2F	332	
D-MJMM	Comco Ikarus Fox-C22	9703-3722	
D-MJMO	UPM Cobra Trike	900094	
D-MJNA	ARCO Spacer L	463	
D-MJND	Drachenstudio Piccolo II	089-94/04	
D-MJNN	Kilb Air Création GTE 5	AC 009	
D-MJOA	Behlen Power-Trike	87019	
D-MJOB	Behlen Power-Trike	92002	
D-MJOE	NST Minimum Pamir	503	
D-MJOH	Klüver Twin Racer SX 16 Trike	449007	
D-MJOY	Evektor EV-97 Eurostar	2002-1402	
D-MJPA	NST Minimum	M542	
D-MJPC	Fresh Breeze 110 AL 2F	222	
D-MJPD	Pro-Fe Banjo MH	08	
D-MJPG(2)	Rans S-12 Airaile	1091138	
D-MJPK	Light Aero Avid Flyer IV	868	
D-MJPW	Seiffert Mini-Speed Trike	7	
D-MJRB	Fresh Breeze 110 AL 2F	951105	
D-MJRN	Fresh Breeze 110 AL 2F	951103	
D-MJRR	Mantel Mono-Dragster	M508	
D-MJSF	Comco Ikarus C-42B	0307-6555	
D-MJSG	Quicksilver MX	13744	
D-MJSH	Fisher FP-202 Koala	2302	
D-MJSJ	FUL Graffiti Trike	015/0075	
D-MJSL	Air Création XP GT 582 ES	17/511994	
D-MJSN	Platzer Kiebitz-B6	034	
D-MJSS	Platzer Motte D	01	
D-MJST	Tandem Air Sunny Sport	032-92	
D-MJSW	Comco Ikarus Fox-C22	9010-3301	
D-MJTR	UPM Funplane	950050	
D-MJUA	Steinbach Austro-Trike	101	
D-MJUG	LO-120	003A	
D-MJUH	Behlen Power-Trike /Rotax 582	98009	
D-MJUK	Take Off Maximum Trike	47041	
D-MJUN	Junkers Profly JUL Trike	094/003	
D-MJUR	Comco Ikarus Fox-C22	910 .-3326	
D-MJUT	NST Minimum	M547	
D-MJUV	Junkers Profly JUL Trike	58294003	
D-MJVS	J.van Stappen (Homebuilt)	SC 89746	
D-MJWB	HFL HFL Stratos IIe	007	
D-MJWD	Ultraleichtverbund Bi 90	6118903	
D-MJWS	NST Minimum	M537	
	(Also listed, probably in error, as a UPM Funplane with this c/n)		
D-MJWW	Flight Team Spider Trike	D028	
D-MJYY	Sky Walker 1+1	26129	
D-MKAA	Ultraleichtverbund Bi 90	21064	
D-MKAB	TL Ultralight TL-96 Star	02 S 128	
D-MKAC	Air Création SX GT 582ES Quartz SX 16	AC 001	
D-MKAE(2)	Sky Walker II	193	
D-MKAF	Take Off Maximum Trike	87022	
D-MKAH	Büttner Crazyplane III	106	
D-MKAM	Flight Design CT-2K CTSW	04.03.01	
D-MKAP	Drachenstudio Royal Trike	180997	
D-MKAS	Behlen Power-Trike	91033	
D-MKAT	Tecnam P.92 Echo 2000S	655	
D-MKBA	Behlen Power-Trike /Rotax 582	980018	
D-MKBB	Platzer Kiebitz-B6	154	
D-MKBE	Comco Ikarus Sherpa I	8306-1028	
D-MKBF	Platzer Kiebitz	248	
D-MKBG	Ultraleichtverbund Bi 90	701	
D-MKBK	HFL Stratos 300	300-012K	
D-MKBL	Comco Ikarus C-42B	0206-6473	
D-MKBM	Behlen Power-Trike II	95005	
D-MKBR	NST Minimum	M531	
D-MKCH	Sky-Walker II	383	
D-MKCM	Point Avn/Albatros AN-22	01	
D-MKCT	Flight Design CT-2K	03.07.05.36	
D-MKDI	Behlen Power-Trike II	90021	
D-MKDL	NST Minimum	C2483	
D-MKDM	Behlen Power-Trike	91028	
D-MKEA	Behlen Power-Trike	89042	
D-MKEE	Comco Ikarus C-42B	0203-6459	
D-MKEH	UPM Funplane	870026	
D-MKEJ	Behlen Power-Trike	90009	
D-MKEL	Air-Light Wild Thing	071	
D-MKER	Fisher FP-202 Koala	ST-005	
D-MKES	Tandem Air Sunny Sport	26-91	
D-MKFA(1)	Ultraleichtverbund Bi 90	6613917738	
D-MKFA(2)	EEL ULF-2	003	
D-MKFF	Comco Ikarus C-42B	0301-6475	
D-MKFH	Take Off Maximum Karat 13 Trike	081111	
D-MKFS	Fresh Breeze 122 AL 2F	349	
D-MKFW	Behlen Power-Trike	94002	
D-MKGA(2)	Ultraleichtverband Bi 90	331-7740	
D-MKGB	Ultraleichtverbund Bi 90	908	
D-MKGC	Ultraleichtverbund Bi 90	3950478	
D-MKGH	Kilb Air Création GTE 5	AC 007	
D-MKGI	Comco Ikarus Fox II Doppel	8607-3025	
D-MKGR	Comco Ikarus Fox-C22	9205-3432	
D-MKHA	Flight Team Spider	D046	
D-MKHB	Behlen Power-Trike	89015	
D-MKHC	Merlin	unkn	
D-MKHE	Comco Ikarus Fox-C22	9102-3318	
D-MKHG	Behlen Power-Trike	92015	
D-MKHH	NST Minimum	M590	
D-MKHK	HFL Stratos 300	300-018K	
D-MKHL	Comco Ikarus Fox-C22	8706-3071	
D-MKHM	Sky-Walker II	329	
D-MKHP	Tandem Air Sunny	007	
D-MKHR	Behlen Power-Trike /Rotax 582	86013	
D-MKHS(2)	Rans S-6 Coyote II	0192263	
D-MKHT	Schmidtler Enduro Trike	02-012	
D-MKHW	Behlen Power-Trike	84229	
D-MKID	Ultraleichtverbund Bi 90	79282054016042	
D-MKIK	Platzer Kiebitz-B	119	
D-MKIS	Ultraleichtverbund Bi 90	9604171161	
D-MKIT	Denney Kitfox IV	1839	D-EPHS
D-MKIY	Aerospool WT9 Dynamic	DY01502	
D-MKJA	Fresh Breeze 110 AL 2F	51	
D-MKJB	Platzer Kiebitz-B	079	
D-MKJC	Fresh Breeze 110 AL 2F	66	
D-MKJD	Fresh Breeze 110 AL 2F	65	
D-MKJE	Fresh Breeze 110 AL 2F	64	
D-MKJF	Fresh Breeze 110 AL 2F	195	
D-MKJG	Fresh Breeze 110 AL 2F	56	
D-MKJH	Fresh Breeze 110 AL 2F	203	
D-MKKC	Kilb Air Création GTE 582 S Trike	AC 008	
D-MKKH	Tandem Air Sunny Sport	48.93	
D-MKKK	Remos G.3 Mirage	130	
D-MKKL	Air-Light Wild Thing	2001-06-080	
D-MKKM	Evektor EV-97 Eurostar	2004-2204	
D-MKKO	Take Off Merlin Trike	24705	
D-MKKS	AMS Flight Apis Bee 15MB	A014M06	
D-MKKW	Behlen Ladas M Trike	M041120200	
D-MKLA	Klüver Kaiman Profil 17 Trike	269916703	
D-MKLC	Klüver Bison Trike	917703	
D-MKLE	Solid Air Diamant Trike	9	
D-MKLI	ASO Viper Hazard 13 Trike	22047307	
D-MKLK	Light Aero Avid Flyer D	1271D	
D-MKLN	Comco Ikarus Fox-C22	9007-3278	
D-MKLS	Take Off Maximum Trike	093052	
D-MKLV	Ultralight Flight Phantom	312	
D-MKME	UL-F Jochum Eagle III	970502	
	(Possibly ex D-MAWE, same c/n quoted)		
D-MKMF	Comco Ikarus C-42B	0302-6476	
D-MKMG	Fresh Breeze 110 AL 2F	211	
D-MKMI	Comco Ikarus Fox D	8410-FD16	
D-MKMS	Platzer Kiebitz B	026	
D-MKNE	Kümmerle Mini-Fly-Set	1265/91-4	
D-MKNO	Flight Design CT2SW	04.08.03	
D-MKNS	Flight Design CT-2K	99.06.04.57/1	
D-MKNU	Light Aero Avid Flyer C	938 C	
D-MKOA	Fisher FP-202 Koala	001	
D-MKOB	Take Off Maximum Chronos 14	101072	
D-MKOC	Comco Ikarus Fox-C22	9304-3467	
D-MKOF	Comco Ikarus Fox-C22	9308-3477	
D-MKOG	Comco Ikarus Fox-C22	9307-3476	
D-MKOI	Comco Ikarus Fox-C22	9308-3474	
D-MKOK	Comco Ikarus Fox-C22	9307-3473	
D-MKOL	Platzer Kiebitz-B2	076	
D-MKOM	Comco Ikarus Fox-C22	8909-3240	
D-MKOO	Comco Ikarus Fox-C22	9307-3472	
D-MKOP	Comco Ikarus Fox-C22	9303-3471	
D-MKOQ	Comco Ikarus Fox-C22	9307-3470	
D-MKOS	Comco Ikarus Fox-C22	9304-3469	
D-MKOX	Air Création GTE 582 S	7974656039	
D-MKPA	Evektor EV-97 Eurostar	2002-1407	
D-MKPB	Behlen Power-Trike	85010	
D-MKPC	UPM Cobra BF 52UL Trike	950135	
D-MKPF	Eipper Quicksilver	4603	
D-MKPG	Flight Team Spider Trike	D027	
D-MKPI	Flight Team Spider Trike	D035	
D-MKPP	Comco Ikarus Fox-C22	9305-3421	
D-MKPT	Flight Team Spider Trike	D034	
D-MKPW	Backes Mini-Speed Trike (Homebuilt)	15/94	
D-MKRB(1)	Comco Ikarus Fox-C22	9305-3459	
D-MKRB(2)	Behlen Power-Trike /Rotax 582	97012	
D-MKRC	Comco Ikarus Fox-C22	9304-3458	
D-MKRD	Comco Ikarus Fox-C22	9308-3457	
D-MKRE	Comco Ikarus Fox-C22	9305-3456	
D-MKRF	Comco Ikarus Fox-C22	9305-3455	
D-MKRG	Comco Ikarus Fox-C22	9305-3454	
D-MKRH	Comco Ikarus Fox-C22	9305-3453	
D-MKRI	Comco Ikarus Fox-C22	9210-3452	
D-MKRJ	Comco Ikarus Fox-C22	9303-3451	
D-MKRK	Comco Ikarus Fox-C22	9304-3450	
D-MKRL	Comco Ikarus Fox-C22	9303-3449	
D-MKRM	Comco Ikarus Fox-C22	9303-3497	
D-MKRN	Comco Ikarus Fox-C22	9210-3447	
D-MKRP	Comco Ikarus Fox-C22	9210-3445	
D-MKRQ	Comco Ikarus Fox-C22	9210-3444	
D-MKRR	Comco Ikarus Fox-C22	9209-3443	
D-MKRS	Comco Ikarus Fox-C22	9209-3442	
D-MKRT	Ultraleichtverbund Bi 90	21204	
D-MKRU	Comco Ikarus Fox D	8810-FD44	
D-MKRW	Sky-Walker II	252	
D-MKSA	Klüver Bison	16807002	

D-MKSE	Take Off Merlin 1100	28568
D-MKSL	Comco Ikarus C-42B	0207-6474
D-MKSM	Comco Ikarus Fox-C22	9207-3426
D-MKST	ASO Viper Trike	VIII 12063408
D-MKTG	Fresh Breeze 122 AL 2F	400
D-MKTH	Zenair CH-701D STOL	7-9426
D-MKTM	Comco Ikarus Fox-C22	9107-3346
D-MKTN	Remos G.3 Mirage	096
D-MKTO	NST Minimum	M331
D-MKTS	Fresh Breeze 110 AL 2F	195
D-MKTZ	MKB Enduro Trike	08/85
D-MKUD	Comco Ikarus C-42B	0403-6590
D-MKUE	NST Minimum	M194
D-MKUK	Tandem Air Sunny Targa	TA-015
D-MKUL	Ultraleichtverbund Bi 90	601
D-MKUM	Dallach Sunrise IIA	031
D-MKUR	Schönleber Trike Speed 14	01/1293
D-MKUS	Flight Team Spider Hazard 15 Trike	D025
D-MKWB	B&F Funk FK-12 Comet	12-054
D-MKWM	FUL Graffiti Trike	024/0081
D-MKWP	Solid Air Twin Diamant	T006
D-MKWR	Flight Team Spider	D020
D-MKWS	Comco Ikarus Fox-C22	9008-3279
D-MLAA	Klüver Racer SX 12 Trike	624009
D-MLAB	Rans S-12 Airaile (Believed w/o 30.5.98)	0892256
D-MLAD	Platzer Kiebitz-B	059
D-MLAO	Comco Ikarus C-42B	0303-6525
D-MLAU	NST Minimum	M283
D-MLBB	ASO-Storch 503	11002206
D-MLBC	Rans S-6 Coyote II	0791209
D-MLBH	Comco Ikarus Fox-C22	9208-3461
D-MLBK	Comco Ikarus Fox-C22	9311-3522
D-MLBM	B&F Funk FK-9 Mk.III	09-03-213
D-MLBR	ATEC Zephyr	Z 190300S
D-MLCB	Take Off Merlin Trike	22744
D-MLCH	Sky-Walker II	395
D-MLDE	Fläming Air FA-01 Smaragd	02-03
D-MLDK	NST Minimum	M544
D-MLEA	ASO Viper Hazard 15	13451
D-MLEE	Rans S-6 Coyote II	0992351
D-MLEF	Ultraleichtverbund Bi 90	4559418
D-MLEI	Behlen Power Trike Vampir II	88018
D-MLEK	Ultraleichtverbund Bi 90	21167
D-MLES	Comco Ikarus Fox-C22	9204-3391
D-MLEV	Sky-Walker 1 + 1	26139
D-MLFE	Ultraleichtverbund Bi 90	703
D-MLFF	Comco Ikarus C-42B	0405-6604
D-MLFI	Ultraleichtverbund Bi 90	21048
D-MLFL	Dallach Sunrise IIA	039
D-MLFP	Air Energy Silent 2AE	unkn
D-MLFZ	Air-Light Wild Thing	2003-07-085
D-MLGG	Schmidtler Ranger M	18-25
D-MLHJ	Drachenstudio Royal Trike	05-9506
D-MLHM	UPM Cobra BF 52UL Raven	930121
D-MLIA	Behlen Power-Trike II	95006
D-MLII	Ultraleichtverbund Bi 90	41055519681
D-MLIM	Fresh Breeze 110 AL2F	69
D-MLIN	Tandem Air Sunny Sport	10-91
D-MLIP	Comco Ikarus Fox-C22	9105-3336
D-MLIS	Klüver Bison II Quartz SX 16	567801
D-MLIU	NST Minimum	M313
D-MLIY	Platzer Kiebitz-B	153
D-MLIZ	Comco Ikarus Fox-C22	9306-3510
D-MLJA	Klüver Bison	982704
D-MLJP	Kümmerle Mini-Fly-Set	1274/91-5
D-MLKF	Air Création Mild GT 582 ES	2
D-MLKH	Comco Ikarus Sherpa II Doppel	8501-1087
D-MLKK	Klüver Racer SX 12	442904
D-MLKS	Comco Ikarus Fox-C22	9202-3390
D-MLKW	Comco Ikarus Fox-C22	9104-3333
D-MLLA	Tandem Air Sunny Sport	035-92
D-MLLB	Take Off Maximum	027040
D-MLLC(1)	Tandem Air Sunny Sport	032-92
D-MLLC(2)	Behlen Power Trike Vampir II	M877829
D-MLLM	Büttner Crazyplane IV	2
D-MLMK	Schönleber DS Speed 14	9010891
D-MLML	Enduro Trike	1004
D-MLMM	Eipper Quicksilver GT	1250
D-MLMT	Sky-Walker 1+1	26123
D-MLNO	Rans S-9 Chaos	unkn
D-MLOE	Platzer Kiebitz-B	094
D-MLOP	UPM Funplane Trike	870019
D-MLOR	Kümmerle Mini-Fly-Set	1306/91-6
D-MLOT	Aviasud Mistral 53	011
D-MLOZ	Fresh Breeze 110 AL 2F	333
D-MLPA	WDFL Dallach D4 Fascination BK	123
D-MLPS	Rans S.12 Airaile	unkn
D-MLPW	Schönleber Trike Speed KS 14	TK 01/0395
D-MLPX	Fresh Breeze 110 AL 2F	112
D-MLRC	Dyn'Aero MCR-01	unkn
D-MLRG	Pago Jet M4	960503
D-MLRL	NST Minimum Zephir CX	M436
D-MLSC	Zenair CH-601D Zodiac	6-9271
D-MLSD	Comco Ikarus Fox-C22	9106-3340
D-MLSE	Comco Ikarus Fox-C22	9107-3343
D-MLSG	B&F Funk FK-9 Mk.III	09-181
D-MLSJ	Air Création GTE 582 S	2974656186
D-MLST	NST Minimum Zephir	M528
D-MLSV	B&F Funk FK-9 Mk.III	09-03U-204
D-MLSW(1)	UPM Cobra Raven Trike	90007
D-MLSW(2)	Remos G.3 Mirage	115
D-MLSZ	Comco Ikarus Fox-C22	9010-3294
D-MLTG	Comco Ikarus Fox-C22	9208-3387
D-MLTI	Kümmerle Mini-Fly-Set	734 85-3
D-MLTR	Comco Ikarus Fox-C22	9206-3397
D-MLTU	FUL Graffiti Trike	023/0083
D-MLUA	Platzer Kiebitz-B	049
D-MLUF	Comco Ikarus C42B	0205-6482
D-MLUI	Behlen Power-Trike	92/014
D-MLUP	Behlen Ladas M Trike	04-001-82
D-MLUW	Fresh Breeze 110 AL2F	77
D-MLUX	Comco Ikarus Fox-C22	9308-3509
D-MLVA	Fresh Breeze 122 AL 2F	242
D-MLVE	Sky-Walker II	310
D-MLVM(2)	B&F Funk FK-9	unkn
D-MLVT	Tandem Air Sunny Sport	11-91
D-MLVW	Tecnam P.92 Echo 100S	648
D-MLWB	ASO Viper Trike	3690
D-MLWC	Comco Ikarus C42B	0307-6561
D-MLWM	NST Minimum	M563
D-MLWS	Krampen Ikarus S	52
D-MLWW	WDFL Dallach D4 Fascination BK	126
D-MLZV	Solid Air Twin Diamant Trike	T004
D-MMAA	Konsuprod Moskito	005
D-MMAB	Kümmerle Mini-Fly-Set	1276/91-5
D-MMAD	Evektor EV-97 Eurostar	2004-2218
D-MMAG	Sky-Walker II	357
D-MMAI	Warnke Puma Sprint	D002
D-MMAJ	Sky-Service Pago Jet	941001
D-MMAL	Ultraleichtverbund Bi 90	21205
D-MMAN	Fresh Breeze 110 AL 2F	234
D-MMAR	Behlen Power Trike II	97005
D-MMAS	Solid-Air Diamant	013
D-MMAT	Kümmerle Mini-Fly-Set	1278/91-5
D-MMAU	Solid Air Twin Diamant Hazard	T008
D-MMAW	Kümmerle Mini-Fly-Set	1285/91-5
D-MMAX	Fresh Breeze 110 AL 2F	43
D-MMAY	Pegasus Quantum Super Sport	7444
D-MMBB	Cosmos Bi 90 Phase II/ Chronos 12	977
D-MMBJ	NST Minimum	M580
D-MMBN	Behlen Power Trike Vampir II	86017
D-MMBR	Pegasus Quantum 15	6683
D-MMBT	Behlen Power Trike II	97001
D-MMBV	ASO Viper Hazard 15	18991
D-MMBW	Seiffert Mini II	F020890
D-MMCD	Zenair CH-701D STOL	7-9383
D-MMCI	Fisher FP-202 Koala	003
D-MMCO	FUL Graffiti Trike	032/0098
D-MMDH(2)	B&F Funk FK-9	010
D-MMDR	Schmidtler Enduro Trike	02-006
D-MMDW	B&F Funk FK-9	011
D-MMEB	Comco Ikarus C-42B	0308-6556
D-MMEC	Remos G.3 Mirage	111
D-MMED	Remos G.3 Mirage	109
D-MMFA	Evektor EV-97 Eurostar 2000R	2003-1812
D-MMFK	B&F Funk FK-9	012
D-MMGB	Comco Ikarus Fox-C22	9208-3436
D-MMGD	ASO Viper Trike	4590
D-MMGH	Platzer Kiebitz-B9-450	125
D-MMGM	Take Off Maximum	17099
D-MMGR	Fresh Breeze 110 AL2F	31
D-MMGZ	NST Minimum	M464
D-MMHB	Behlen Power-Trike	87001
D-MMHE	Fresh Breeze 110 AL 2F	71
D-MMHF	Denney Kitfox IV	1841
	(C/n recorded on aircraft as 11176, 5.02)	
D-MMHH	Comco Ikarus Fox-C22	8905-3200
D-MMHI	Comco Ikarus Fox D	8410-FD17
D-MMHK	Behlen Trike	85024
D-MMHM	Schönleber Trike 40kw	TK 02/0198
D-MMHT	Fläming Air FA-01 Smaragd	05/04
D-MMHW	B&F Funk FK-9 Mk.III	09-03-190
D-MMHZ	Behlen Trike	83033
D-MMIB	NST Minimum	M545
D-MMIG	Tandem Air Sunny Sport	24.91
D-MMII	Klüver Bison	646802
D-MMIK(1)	Bobcat	146 EB
D-MMIK	Rans S-6 Coyote II	08031516-S
D-MMIL	Behlen Power Trike Vampir II	89016
D-MMIS	Behlen Power Trike Vampir II	89011
D-MMIX	Light Aero Avid Flyer IV C	1104 C
D-MMJA	ASO Viper Trike	VIII 12067501
D-MMJS	FUL Graffiti Trike	025/0091
D-MMJT	Sky-Service Pago Jet M4	94002
D-MMJV	FUL Graffiti Trike	026/0092
D-MMKB	MKB Ranger	028841
D-MMKG	MKB Ranger M	01/005/85
D-MMKL	Remos G.3 Mirage	104
D-MMKT	Flight Team Spider Trike	D040
D-MMKU	Fresh Breeze 110 AL 2F	61
D-MMKW	Comco Ikarus C-42B	0207-6489
D-MMLA	Comco Ikarus Fox-C22	9209-3430
D-MMLB	UPM Cobra BF 52 UL Trike	930122
D-MMLH	Flight Team Spider Trike	D014

D-MMLI	Behlen Power-Trike /Rotax 582	980025	
D-MMLK	Remos G.3 Mirage	127	
D-MMLL	Sky-Walker II	274	
D-MMLO	Comco Ikarus Fox-C22	9205-3403	
D-MMLU	Take Off Maximum	097062	
D-MMMB	Albatros 64	304	
D-MMMD	Ultraleichtverbund Bi 90	702	
D-MMMI	Comco Ikarus Fox-C22	9306-3506	
D-MMMM	T2	5	
	(Regn worn by a WDFL Fascination, Friedrichshafen 4.99, and by Dallach Evolution 4.01. Mock-ups?)		
D-MMMT	Behlen Power-Trike II	95008	
D-MMMW	Kiebitx-B-450	128	
D-MMND	Fresh Breeze 122 AL 2F	233	
D-MMNS	Comco Ikarus Fox-C22	8812-3184	
D-MMOC	Ultraleichtverbund Bi 90	21079	
D-MMOE	Comco Ikarus C-42B	0206-6462	
D-MMOP	B&F Funk FK-9	unkn	
D-MMPA	Fresh Breeze 110 AL 2F	951104	
D-MMPD	Flight Design CT-2K	03.02.03.07A	
D-MMPE	NST Minimum	M441	
D-MMPG	Fresh Breeze 110 AL 2F	54	
D-MMPK	ASO Viper Trike	VIII 12069502	
D-MMPL	Sky-Walker II	267	
D-MMPR	NST Schwarze-Trike	010	
D-MMPS	Solar Wings Pegasus Quantum 15	6738	D-MMTT
D-MMRA	Ultraleichtverbund Bi 90	4017031	
D-MMRB(1)	Ultralight Flight Phantom	403	
D-MMRB(2)	NST Minimum	M556	
D-MMRE	Rans S-6 Coyote II	08031514	
D-MMRH	Ultraleichtverbund Bi 90	21254	
D-MMRL	Behlen Power-Trike /Rotax 582	91026	
D-MMRM	Pegasus Quantum	7611	
D-MMRP	Kümmerle Mini-Fly-Set	67686-4	
D-MMRR	Enduro Lotus/Air Création XP	02/003	
D-MMRS	Fresh Breeze 122 AL 2F	391	
D-MMSB	Rans S-12 Airaile	1292359	
D-MMSG	Comco Ikarus Fox-C22	9110-3361	
D-MMSL	Take Off Merlin Trike	G20363	
D-MMSM(1)	Konsuprod Moskito 1b	019	
D-MMSM(2)	NST Minimum	M462	
D-MMSP	Großklaus Silent Racer	3	
D-MMSR	NST Minimum	M517	
D-MMST	Klüver Bison	0168	
D-MMSU	Platzer Kiebitz-B	111	
D-MMSW	Kümmerle Mini-Fly-Set	67786-4	
D-MMSY	ASO Viper Trike	VIII 12068501	
D-MMTC	Comco Ikarus Fox-C22	9205-3396	
D-MMTI	Fresh Breeze 110 AL2F	102	
D-MMTK	Behlen Trike Vampir II 18M	9002A785	
D-MMTW(1)	Comco Ikarus Sherpa II Doppel	8505-1099	
D-MMTW(2)	Fresh Breeze 110 AL 2F	159	
D-MMUH	Kappa KPD-2U Sova	07/98	
D-MMUM	NST Minimum	M508	
D-MMUR	Fresh Breeze 110 AL 2F	338	
D-MMUW	NST Minimum	M554	
D-MMVB	Comco Ikarus Fox-C22	8808-3149	
D-MMWA	Dallach Sunrise II	034	
D-MMWB	ASO Viper Trike	12061405	
D-MMWC	NST Minimum	M560	
D-MMWD	B&F Funk FK-9 Mk.II	009	
D-MMWE	ASO Viper Trike	12066408	
D-MMWG	UL-F Jochum Eagle III	970804	
D-MMWL	Fresh Breeze 110 AL 2F	443	
D-MMWN	Take Off Merlin Karat 13	20993	
D-MMWS	Fresh Breeze 110 AL 2F	76	
D-MMWW(1)	Platzer Kiebitz-B2	105	
D-MMWW(2)	Ultraleichtverbund Bi 90	21238	
D-MMXG	Euro-ALA Jet Fox 97	0026BIS	
D-MMYY	Schmidtler Enduro Trike	02-011	
D-MMZY	Kiggen/Heiland Air Création GTE 582 S	9954557782	
D-MMZZ	Kiggen/Heiland Air Création GTE 582 S	7954557571	
D-MNAA	Rans S-6 Coyote II	0693514	
D-MNAB	Rans S-6ES Coyote II	0391168	
D-MNAC	Rans S-6 Coyote II	0393460	
D-MNAD	Comco Ikarus Fox-C22	9309-3530	
D-MNAF	Comco Ikarus Fox-C22	9310-3532	
D-MNAG	Comco Ikarus Fox-C22	93 . .-3535	
D-MNAH	Comco Ikarus Fox-C22	93 . .-3537	
D-MNAI	Klüver Bison Profil 19	557801	
D-MNAJ (1)	Comco Ikarus Fox-C22	9101-3299/3538	
D-MNAJ (2)	Fisher FP-202 Koala	HO.001.1	
D-MNAK(2)	Rans S-6 Coyote II	0596990	
D-MNAL	Comco Ikarus C-42 Cyclone	9807-6107	
D-MNAM	Behlen Power-Trike	84009	
D-MNAO	Comco Ikarus Fox-C22	9107-3365	
D-MNAP	Light Aero Avid Flyer IV	1273D	
D-MNAQ	Rans S-6 Coyote II	0192261	OO-A52 / 59-MO
D-MNAR	Rans S-6 Coyote II	0992352	
D-MNAS(1)	Aviasud Mistral BRD	191	
D-MNAS(2)	Evektor EV-97 Eurostar	2001-1204	
D-MNAT	Air-Light Wild Thing	076	
D-MNAU	Rans S-6 Coyote II	0593493	
D-MNAV	Rans S-6 Coyote II	0393464	
D-MNAW	Platzer Kiebitz-B	148	
D-MNAX	Fisher FP-404 Classic	4169	

D-MNAY	Albatros	306	
D-MNAZ	Albatros	305	
D-MNBA(2)	Remos Gemini Ultra A	023	
D-MNBB	WDFL Sunwheel	015	
D-MNBC	B&F Funk FK-9 Mk.II	024	
D-MNBD	Klüver Bison	202708	
D-MNBE	Tandem Air Sunny Targa	TA-017	
D-MNBG	Comco Ikarus Fox-C22	9310-3541	
D-MNBH	Scheibe Uli 1	5223	
D-MNBI	Rans S-12 Airaile (Also regd 68-GH in France)	1292356	
D-MNBJ	Rans S-6 Coyote II	0693515	
D-MNBK	Rans S-6 Coyote II	0593508	
D-MNBL	Comco Ikarus Fox-C22	940 .-3546	
D-MNBM(2)	WDFL Fascination	015	
D-MNBN	Rans S-12 Airaile	1092299	
D-MNBO	Klüver Kaiman Trike	945703	
D-MNBP	Bek ME.109R Replica	003	
D-MNBQ	Tandem Air Sunny Targa	TA-003	
D-MNBR	B&F Funk FK-14 Polaris	14-019	
D-MNBT	Comco Ikarus Fox-C22	9208-3434	
D-MNBU	Comco Ikarus Fox-C22	9409-3597	
D-MNBV	Murphy Renegade	530	
D-MNBW	WDFL Sunwheel	028	
D-MNBX	Tandem Air Sunny	58.94	
D-MNBY	Light Aero Avid Flyer	499	
D-MNBZ	Platzer Kiebitz-B9	155	
D-MNCA	Comco Ikarus C-42 Cyclone	9702-6024	
D-MNCB	Tandem Air Sunny s.b.s.	11.94	
D-MNCC	Rans S-6 Coyote II	0994-676	
D-MNCD	Murphy Renegade	521	
D-MNCF	Jet Fox	D-0016	
D-MNCG	Platzer Kiebitz-B	unkn	
D-MNCH	Comco Ikarus Fox-C22	8909-3219	
D-MNCJ	Fisher Super Koala	001	
D-MNCL	Light Aero Avid Flyer	947	
D-MNCM	Eipper Quicksilver MX	1133	D-MASB
D-MNCO	Light Aero Avid Flyer	1427	
D-MNCP	ICP MXP-740V Savannah	07-98-50-091	
D-MNCU	Tecnam P.92 Echo	373	
D-MNCW	Tecnam P.92 Echo	556	
D-MNDB	B&F Funk FK-9	034	
D-MNDD	Comco Ikarus Fox-C22B	9408-3619	
D-MNDE	Comco Ikarus Fox-C22B	3686	
D-MNDF	Flight Design CT-2K	98.12.01.42	
D-MNDG	Dyn'Aero MCR-01	73	
D-MNDH	Comco Ikarus C-42	0012-6286	
D-MNDJ	Remos G.3 Mirage	079	
D-MNDK	Fantasy Air Allegro 2000	99-401	
D-MNDM	Comco Ikarus C-42 Cyclone	9803-6085	
D-MNDP	Comco Ikarus C-42 Cyclone	9809-6122	
D-MNDR	Comco Ikarus Fox-C22B	9509-3671	
D-MNDS	Rans S-12 Airaile	1292347	
D-MNDT	Comco Ikarus Fox-C22	9206-3410	
D-MNEA	Fisher FP-404 Classic	4128	
D-MNEB	Light Aero Avid Flyer IV	975	
D-MNEC	Comco Ikarus Fox-C22	9502-3653	
D-MNED	Murphy Renegade II	409	
D-MNEE	ASO-Storch	11015506	
D-MNEF	Comco Ikarus C-42 Cyclone	9806-6104	
D-MNEG	Flight Design CT-2K	02.02.04.09	
D-MNEH	Rans S-6 Coyote II	0293449	
D-MNEK	Comco Ikarus Fox-C22	9201-3360	
D-MNEL	Behlen Power-Trike	86022	
D-MNEM	EEL ULF-2	8	
D-MNEP	TEAM Airbike	002	
D-MNER	Scheibe SF-40B	3105	
D-MNES	Scout	D 012-84	
D-MNEU	Comco Ikarus C-42	0203-6428	
D-MNEV	Evektor EV.97 Eurostar	98 01 01	
D-MNEW	Schönleber DS Lotus KS 16	010790	
D-MNEZ	III Sky Arrow 450TG	058	
D-MNFA	Fantasy Air Allegro 2000	02-413	
D-MNFB	Comco Ikarus C-42 Cyclone	9901-6105	
D-MNFC	Comco Ikarus Fox-C22C	9807-3740	
D-MNFF	Rans S-6 Coyote II	0698-1241	
D-MNFH	Sky-Service Pago Jet	95603	
D-MNFJ	Comco Ikarus Fox II Doppel	8605-3019	
D-MNFK	B&F Funk FK-9	025	
D-MNFL	Fisher FP-202 Koala	Ho 001	
D-MNFM	Platzer Kiebitz-B9	003	
D-MNFN	TEAM Airbike	D-003	
D-MNFR	III Sky Arrow 450TG	047	
D-MNFT	Rans S-6 Coyote II	1092363	N7010L
D-MNFW	WDFL Sunwheel	026	
D-MNFZ	Tecnam P.92 Echo	245	
D-MNGB	Jaguar	1001	
D-MNGD	LO-120S	012A	
D-MNGE	Pioneer Flightstar	546	
D-MNGF	HFL Stratos 300	300-005	
D-MNGG	Comco Ikarus C-42 Cyclone	9901-6171	
D-MNGH	Tecnam P.92 Echo	167	
D-MNGI	B&F Funk FK-9 Mk.II	058	
D-MNGK	WDFL Fascination	020	
D-MNGM	Comco Ikarus C-42 Cyclone	9804-6125	
D-MNGS	Murphy Renegade Spirit	32004	
D-MNGT	HIF Albatros	104	
	(Also reported as Comco Ikarus Fox C22 ?)		

D-MNHA	Scheibe SF-40	3102
D-MNHB(1)	Kümmerle Mini-Fly-Set	1269/91-51 66
D-MNHB(2)?	WDFL Dallach D4 Fascination	063
D-MNHD	WDFL Dallach D4 Fascination	035
D-MNHE	Comco Ikarus C-42 Cyclone	9710-6036
D-MNHF	Rans S-12 Airaile	0691098
D-MNHG	Pioneer Flightstar	950501
D-MNHH	Rans S-6 Coyote II	1293572
D-MNHI	Kappa KPD-2U Sova	5259G
D-MNHK	LO-120S	014A
D-MNHL	B&F Funk FK-12 Comet	12-016
D-MNHO	Tandem Air Sunny s.b.s.	SuS 01.96
D-MNHR	Rans S-6 Coyote II	0594626
D-MNHS	Rans S-6TD Coyote II	0994672
D-MNHW	B&F Funk FK-12 Comet	12-026
D-MNHZ	Zenair CH-601D Zodiac	6-3413/015 0097
D-MNIC	Aviasud BA-83 Mistral	004
D-MNIE	ASO Viper Trike	15 I7990
D-MNII	Tandem Air Sunny Targa	005/92
D-MNIJ	Tandem Air Sunny s.b.s.	SuS 02.94
D-MNIK	NST Minimum	503
D-MNIL	Aerospool WT9 Dynamic	DY00601
D-MNIR	NST Minimum	081593
D-MNIS	Tandem Air Sunny s.b.s.	036/92
D-MNIT	Tecnam P.92 Echo	185
D-MNIU	B&F Funk FK-9	065
D-MNIV	Dallach Sunrise II	003
D-MNIW	Dallach Sunrise II	007
D-MNIX	Platzer Kiebitz	237
D-MNIZ	Zenair CH-601D Zodiac	6-8027/009 0397
D-MNJA	WDFL Dallach D4 Fascination BK	076
D-MNJB	Euro-ALA Jet Fox 91D	004
D-MNJC	Tecnam P.92 Echo	294
D-MNJJ	Tecnam P.92 Echo	180
D-MNJL	Aeropro Eurofox	12102
D-MNJS	WDFL Sunwheel	014
D-MNJU	Junkers Profly Ultima	JU 001 97
D-MNKA	NST Minimum	M515
D-MNKB	Comco Ikarus Fox-C22C	9704-3725
D-MNKC	Comco Ikarus C-42 Cyclone	9803-6084
D-MNKD	Comco Ikarus C-42 Cyclone	9901-6146
D-MNKE	B&F Funk FK-9TG Mk.II	091
D-MNKF	Comco Ikarus C-42 Cyclone	9709-6048
D-MNKG	Flight Design CT	97.06.01.00
D-MNKH	Tecnam P.92 Echo	126
D-MNKI	Comco Ikarus C-42 Cyclone	9804-6081
D-MNKJ	Rans S-6 Coyote II	"4172285"
	(Quoted c/n is actually Rotax engine number)	
D-MNKK	Ikarusflug Eurofox	040097
D-MNKL(2)	Flight Design CT-2K	03.01.03.03
D-MNKM	Light Aero Avid Flyer IV	1458
D-MNKP	Comco Ikarus C-42B	0206-6460
D-MNKR	Albatros SX	504
D-MNKS	Rans S-12 Airaile	1092341
D-MNKU	Ultravia Pelican Sport 450S	721
D-MNKW	Technoflug Piccolo	035
D-MNKX	Comco Ikarus C-42B	0210-6493
D-MNKY	Comco Ikarus C-42 Cyclone	9906-6190
D-MNKZ	Comco Ikarus C-42B	0210-6511
D-MNLC	Comco Ikarus Fox-C22B	9407-3606
D-MNLE	Light Aero Avid Flyer IV	1493
D-MNLF	Euro-ALA Jet Fox 91D	014
D-MNLG	B&F Funk FK-9 TG Mk.II	077
D-MNLK	Comco Ikarus Fox-C22	9108-3349
D-MNLL	Zenair CH-601D Zodiac	6-3648
D-MNLP	WDFL Dallach D4 Fascination BK	067
D-MNLR	Air-Light Wild Thing	004
D-MNLT	Rans S-6 Coyote II XL	1294712
D-MNLY	Aerostyle Breezer	003
D-MNLA	Aerospool WT9 Dynamic	DY01402
D-MNMB	WDFL Dallach D4 Fascination BK	077
D-MNMF	Tandem Air Sunny Sport	64.96
D-MNMG	Zenair CH-601D Zodiac	6-3789
D-MNMH	Fläming Air Trener Baby	02
D-MNMM	Tecnam P.96 Golf 100S	059
D-MNMP	Comco Ikarus Fox-C22	9411-3636
D-MNMS	Air-Light Wild Thing	036
D-MNNA	Albatros 64	311
D-MNNB	Albatros 64	501
D-MNNF	Air-Light Wild Thing	054
D-MNNK	Technoflug Piccolo	028
D-MNNM	Behlen Power-Trike	023
D-MNNN(1)	Comco Ikarus Fox-C22	9002-3254
D-MNNN(2)	Flight Design CT2SW	04.10.06
D-MNNO	Light Aero Avid Flyer STOL	1401C
D-MNNP	B&F Funk FK-9 Mk.II	043
D-MNNQ	B&F Funk FK-9 Mk.II	042
D-MNNZ	Comco Ikarus C-42 Cyclone	9701-6023
D-MNOA	Euro-ALA Jet Fox 97	023
D-MNOB	Comco Ikarus Fox-C22	9706-3731
D-MNOC	Comco Ikarus Fox-C22B	9602-3693
D-MNOD	Kümmerle Mini-Fly-Set	25986-4
D-MNOE	Comco Ikarus C-42 Cyclone	9804-6078
D-MNOF	Light Aero Avid Flyer IV	501
D-MNOG(2)	WDFL Dallach D4 Fascination	055
D-MNOM	B&F Funk FK-9 Mk.II	057
D-MNON	B&F Funk FK-9 Mk.II	056

D-MNOP	Konsuprod Mosquito IB	011	
D-MNOR(1)	NST Minimum	1783	
D-MNOR(2)	Flight Design CT-2K	99.10.02.72	
D-MNOX	Rans S-10 Sakota	0488010	N70301
D-MNPC	Eipper Quicksilver MXL	1148	
D-MNPE	Comco Ikarus C-42 Cyclone	9810-6144	
D-MNPF	PC Flight Pretty Flight	01	
D-MNPG	Platzer Kiebitz	218	
D-MNPL	TL Ultralight TL-96 Star	01 S 103	
D-MNPP	TL Ultralight TL-96 Star	02 S 115	
D-MNPR	Remos Gemini Ultra B	031	
D-MNPS	Tecnam P.92 Echo	321	
D-MNPU	Remos G-3 Mirage	044	
	(Same c/n quoted for D-MRIM)		
D-MNPW	ATEC Zephyr 2000	ZP 480900	
D-MNPZ	Comco Ikarus C-42 Cyclone	9708-6034	
D-MNRA	Ikarusflug Eurofox	051098	
D-MNRB	Tecnam P.92 Echo	182	
D-MNRC	Zenair CH-601D Zodiac	6-3519	
D-MNRD	Tecnam P.92 Echo	198	
D-MNRE	Comco Ikarus C-42 Cyclone	0106-6342	
D-MNRF	Ferrari Tucano A	308	
D-MNRH	Comco Ikarus Fox-C22	94 . . -3572	
D-MNRL	WDFL Sunwheel R	025	
D-MNRM	B&F Funk FK-9 Mk.II	09-02-027	
D-MNRO	B&F Funk FK-9 Mk.II	033	
D-MNRR	Ultravia Pelican Sport 450S	720	
D-MNRS	Euro-ALA Jet Fox 91D	007	
D-MNRT	Comco Ikarus C-42B	0005-6258	
D-MNRU	Comco Ikarus C-42 Cyclone	9804-6132	
D-MNRV	Tecnam P.92 Echo	338	
D-MNRW	Comco Ikarus Fox-C22B	9602-3692	
D-MNSB	Zenair CH-601D Zodiac	003	
D-MNSE	EEL ULF-2	016	
D-MNSH	Tandem Air Sunny Sport	56.93	
D-MNSI	Rans S-6 Coyote II	1294714F	
D-MNSJ	Comco Ikarus C-42 Cyclone	9807-6106	
D-MNSK	Albatros 64	308	
D-MNSL	WDFL Dallach D4 Fascination BK	097	
D-MNSM	Comco Ikarus Fox-C22B	9406-3595	
D-MNSP	Tecnam P.92S Echo 100S	473	
D-MNSR	Euro-ALA Jet Fox 91D	005	
D-MNSS	Euro-ALA Jet Fox 91D	006	
D-MNST	Euro-ALA Jet Fox 91D	008	
D-MNSU	Tecnam P.92 Echo	537	
D-MNTB	Comco Ikarus Fox-C22B	9407-3596	
D-MNTE	WDFL Dallach D4 Fascination	014	
D-MNTH	Zenair CH-601D Zodiac	6-3457	
D-MNTL	ATEC Zephyr 2000	ZP 270700	
D-MNTM	Comco Ikarus C-42 Cyclone	9710-6017	
D-MNTT	B&F Funk FK-9 Mk.II	047	
D-MNTS	Remos G-3 Mirage	051	
D-MNTT	B&F Funk FK-9	047	
D-MNTW	Tecnam P.92 Echo	187	
D-MNUI	Cosmos	unkn	
D-MNUM	Comco Ikarus Fox-C22	9207-3414	
D-MNUN	Rans S-6 Coyote II	0193420	N61832
			D-MNUN
			N61832
D-MNUR	Kappa KPD-2U Sova	050	
D-MNVB	Murphy Renegade Spirit	414	
D-MNVC	WDFL Dallach D4 Fascination BK	079	
D-MNVF	SFS Vagabund	004	
D-MNVH	ASO Storch	11017508	
D-MNVM	Light Aero Avid Flyer IV	1294D	
D-MNVV	Zenair CH-601D Zodiac	6-3652	
D-MNWB	Aeroprakt A-22 Vision	031/009	
D-MNWC	Light Aero Avid Flyer IV	1354	
D-MNWD	Comco Ikarus C-42 Cyclone	0011-6259	
D-MNWE	Tecnam P.92 Echo	324	
D-MNWH	B&F Funk FK-9 Mk.II	021	
D-MNWI	Comco Ikarus C-42 Cyclone	9609-6006	
D-MNWJ	Platzer Kiebitz-B9	060	
D-MNWL	Comco Ikarus C-42 Cyclone	9803-6089	
D-MNWN	NST Minimum	04911	
D-MNWO	Comco Ikarus C-42 Cyclone	0003-6260	
D-MNWR	EEL ULF-2	11	
D-MNWS	TL Ultralight TL-232 Condor Plus	98 C 09	
D-MNWT	Air-Light Wild Thing	028	
D-MNWW	Air-Light Wild Thing	002	
D-MNWZ	Comco Ikarus C-42 Cyclone	9804-6126	
D-MNXI	Quicksilver Sprint II	000778	
D-MNXU	Elisport CH-7 Angel	unkn	
D-MNXY	Kappa KPD-2U Sova	88103 I	
D-MNYT	Skystar S-34	012	
D-MNZB	Air-Light Wild Thing	027	
D-MNZI	Comco Ikarus C-42 Cyclone	0007-6265	
D-MNZZ	Comco Ikarus C-42 Cyclone	9806-6119	
D-MOAB	Tandem Air Sunny Sport	17.91	
D-MOAC	Technoflug Piccolo BM	109	
D-MOAE	Technoflug Piccolo BM	110	
D-MOAF	Tecnam P.92 Echo	226	
D-MOAG	WDFL Fascination	025	
D-MOAI	Tecnam P.96 Golf	10	
D-MOAJ	Zenair CH-601D Zodiac	6-3484	
D-MOAK	Rans S-6 Coyote II	1294713	
D-MOAL	Comco Ikarus C-42 Cyclone	9704-6029	

D-MOAM	Tecnam P.96 Golf	13	
D-MOAN	Platzer Kiebitz-B-450	187	
D-MOAO	Air-Light Wild Thing	040	
D-MOAP	Tandem Air Sunny Sport	38.92	
D-MOAS	Euro-ALA Jet Fox 91D	012	
D-MOAT	TEAM Airbike Tandem	AT-001	
D-MOAU	Comco Ikarus C-42 Cyclone	9909-6210	
D-MOAW	Tecnam P.92 Echo	300	
D-MOAZ	Konsuprod Moskito 1b	015	
D-MOBA	Tecnam P.96 Golf	031	
D-MOBB	Aerostyle Breezer	002	
D-MOBE	Comco Ikarus C-42 Cyclone	9908-6205	
D-MOBF	B&F Funk FK-9 Mk.II	038	
D-MOBG	Aerostyle Breezer	003	
D-MOBH	Pretty Flight	003	
D-MOBI (2)	B&F Funk FK-9 Mk.II	075	
D-MOBK	B&F Funk FK-9 TG Mk.II	046	
D-MOBL	Fisher FP-404 Classic	AB 001	
D-MOBM	Comco Ikarus C-42 Cyclone	0103-6318	
D-MOBN	Urban Air UFM-13 Lambada	1/13	
D-MOBO	B&F Funk FK-9 Mk.III	09-132	
D-MOBS(1)	UPM Cobra Raven Trike	900102	
D-MOBS(2)	B&F FunkFK-12 Comet	12-031	
D-MOBT	Light Aero Avid Flyer	617	
D-MOBY(1)	Take Off Maximum Karat 13	005059	
D-MOBY(2)	Rans S-6 Coyote II	0893532	
D-MOCA(1)	Warnke Skylight Trike	038	
D-MOCA(2)	Remos G.3 Mirage	063	
D-MOCB	WDFL Sunwheel	036	
D-MOCC	Comco Ikarus C-42 Cyclone	9707-6016	
D-MOCD	Fantasy Air Allegro	00-404	
D-MOCF	Comco Ikarus Fox-C22C	9606-3710	
D-MOCG	Evektor EV-97 Eurostar	2001-1205	
D-MOCI	Evektor EV-97 Eurostar	2001-1002	
D-MOCK	Fisher FP.202 Koala	unkn	
D-MOCO	Flight Design CT	97.08.02.06	
D-MOCS	Comco Ikarus C-42 Cyclone	9902-6165	
D-MOCT	Flight Design CT	CT 006/97	
D-MOCV	NST Minimum	1781	
D-MODC	Flight Design CT-2K	99.06.01.54	
D-MODD	Schönleber DS Trike	04/0989	
D-MODE(2)	Tandem Air Sunny	47.93	
D-MODF	MAI 890-1	142	
D-MODG	WDFL Sunwheel R	023	
D-MODI	Comco Ikarus C-42 Cyclone	9704-6018	
D-MODL	NST Minimum Zephir CX	M456	
D-MODM	Dess/ WDFL D4/B Fascination (W/o 22.3.00)	038	(D-EWSB)
D-MODS	Comco Ikarus C-42 Cyclone	0001-6223	
D-MODZ	Remos G.3 Mirage	105	
D-MOEA	Tecnam P.92 Echo 100S	372	
D-MOEC	Comco Ikarus C-42 Cyclone	9611-6030	
D-MOEE	Flight Design CT	97.12.01.16	
D-MOEG	Comco Ikarus C-42 Cyclone	0106-6343	
D-MOEH	Air-Light Wild Thing	066	
D-MOEN	Comco Ikarus Fox-C22	9403-3579	
D-MOES	Euro-ALA Jet Fox 91D	003	
D-MOET	Comco Ikarus Fox-C22	94083608	
D-MOEU	Tecnam P.92 Echo	083	
D-MOEZ	AMF Chevvron 2-32	037	
D-MOFA	ATEV Zephyr	ZP 340200	
D-MOFF	Comco Ikarus Fox-C22B	9506-3670	
D-MOFH	Euro-ALA Jet Fox 91D	022/00	
D-MOFK	B&F Funk FK-9 Mk.II	061	
D-MOFL	Comco Ikarus C-42 Cyclone	0005-6253	
D-MOFT	Platzer Kiebitz-B6	171	
D-MOFU	Rans S-10 Sakota	0697184	
D-MOGA	WDFL Sunwheel R	021	
D-MOGB	ATEC Zephyr	SF 101199	
D-MOGC	B&F Funk FK-9 Mk.IV	09-03U-215	
D-MOGH	ASO 26 Storch	160	
D-MOGK	Zenair CH-601 Zodiac	6-2008	
D-MOGL	Murphy Renegade Spirit	518	
D-MOGS	WDFL Dallach D4 Fascination	016	
D-MOHA	Rans S-12 Airaile	1292346	
D-MOHB	Remos G-3 Mirage	047	
D-MOHE	TL Ultralight TL-232 Condor Plus	98 C 08	
D-MOHF	Denney Kitfox IV	1876	
D-MOHG	Pioneer Flightstar	960701	
D-MOHI	Ikarusflug Eurofox	026096	
D-MOHK	Malchow HK-12	001	
D-MOHL	Comco Ikarus C-42	0109-6360	
D-MOHM	Comco Ikarus C-42 Cyclone	9809-6131	
D-MOHN	Scheibe Uli 1	5222	
D-MOHP	III Sky Arrow 450	086 S	
D-MOHR	Sky-Walker II	147	
D-MOHS	Weedhopper	0998	
D-MOHT	Flight Design CT-2K	unkn	
	(Also Tecnam P.92 Echo c/n 258, to EC-JBO?)		
D-MOHW	Behlen Power-Trike /Rotax 582	92028	
D-MOHY	Jet Fox 91D	00122	
D-MOIC	ASO Viper Hazard 15	11031204	
D-MOII	Comco Ikarus C-42	0103-6345	
D-MOIK	WDFL Dallach D4 Fascination	010	
D-MOIL	Comco Ikarus C-42 Cyclone	9804-6101	
D-MOIN	Warnke Skylight Trike	S2005	
D-MOIO	Me 108UL Taifun	1	
D-MOIS	Pretty Flight	02	

D-MOJA	Zenair CH-701D STOL	7-3519	
D-MOJB	Euro-ALA Jet Fox 91D	D 0013	
D-MOJE	B&F Funk FK-12 Comet	12-004	
D-MOJH	Tandem Air Sunny Targa	TA 014	
D-MOJJ	B&F Funk FK-9 Mk.III	09-170	
D-MOJO	Flightworks FW2C-80XLS Capella	061962	
D-MOJS	Comco Ikarus C-42 Cyclone	9811-6152	
D-MOJU	Comco Ikarus C-42 Cyclone	0003-6249	
D-MOKA	Scheibe Ultra	3411	
D-MOKE(1)	Racer (Homebuilt)	004/90	
D-MOKE(2)	Tecnam P.92 Echo 100S	664	
D-MOKF	B&F Funk FK-9 Mk3	098	
D-MOKG	Rans S-6ES Coyote II	0496966	
D-MOKH	Comco Ikarus C-42 Cyclone	9911-6214	
D-MOKI	Zephir CX	unkn	
D-MOKK	Comco Ikarus C-42 Cyclone	9712-6072	
D-MOKL	Rans S-6 Coyote II	10961045	
D-MOKM	Tecnam P.92 Echo	225	
D-MOKN	Platzer Kiebitz-B6	195	
D-MOKO	Konsuprod Moskito	006	
D-MOKS	Tecnam P.92 Echo	135	
D-MOKT	Tandem Air Sunny Sport	57.94	
D-MOKW	ATEC Zephyr	ZO 32	
D-MOLA(1)	Fair Fax Trike	21	
D-MOLA(2)	Solair II	unkn	
D-MOLB	Flight Team Spider Trike	DOO9	
D-MOLC	Comco Ikarus Fox-C22B	9405-3603	
D-MOLD	Konsuprod Moskito	002	
D-MOLE(1)	NST Minimum Santana	100378	
D-MOLE(2)	Comco Ikarus C-42	0101-6290	
D-MOLG	Flight Design CT	98.04.05.32	
D-MOLH	Tecnam P.92 Echo 100S	399	
D-MOLI	Pioneer Flightstar	545	
D-MOLL	Scheibe UL-1 Coach	3201	
D-MOLM	Comco Ikarus Fox-C22	9108-3352	
D-MOLO	LO-120S	021	
D-MOLR	B&F Funk FK-9 Mk.III	09-03-118	
D-MOLS	Tecnam P.92 Echo	252	
D-MOLT	ASO Viper Hazard 15	12023103	
D-MOLV	B&F Funk FK-9 Mk3	09-03-101	
D-MOLW	Platzer Kiebitz-B	066	
D-MOLY(1)	Light Aero Avid Flyer	867	
D-MOLY(2)	Tecnam P-96 Golf 100S	110	
D-MOMA	Dyn'Aero MCR-01 ULC	137	
D-MOMB	TL Ultralight TL-96 Star	02 S 120	
D-MOMC	B&F Funk FK-9 MkIII	09-03-107	
D-MOMD	Comco Ikarus C-42 Cyclone	9803-6087	
D-MOME	Me.109 Replica	005	
D-MOMF	WDFL Dallach D4 Fascination	042	
D-MOMI	ATEC Zephyr	ZP 130200	
D-MOMM	Rans S-7 Courier	0798251	
D-MOMN	Comco Ikarus C-42 Cyclone	9703-6032	
D-MOMO	Scheibe Ultra	3414	
D-MOMP	Klüver Racer Quartz SX 12	309005	
D-MOMS	Ikarusflug Eurofox	024096	
D-MONA	Ultra-Vector H	1401	
D-MONB	Comco Ikarus Fox-C22	9407-3574	
D-MONC	Rans S-6 Coyote II	0494609	
D-MOND(1)	Warnke Puma Sprint	D001	
D-MOND(2)	B&F Funk FK-12 Comet	12-024	
D-MONE	Comco Ikarus Fox D	015	
D-MONG	Albatros 64	502	
D-MONI	Power Power-Trike Euro III	84018	
D-MONJ	UPM Omega Trike	880045	
D-MONL	Comco Ikarus Fox-C22	9407-3575	
D-MONM	Platzer Kiebitz	016	
D-MONN	Impulse 100	100-3	
D-MONO	Scheibe Uli 1	5211	
D-MONT	Air-Light Wild Thing	057	
D-MONW	Comco Ikarus Fox-C22B	95 . .-3678	
D-MONY	Aeroprakt A-22 Vision	032-010	
D-MONZ	Tecnam P.96 Golf 100S	117	
D-MOOB	Kümmerle Mini Fly Set Bullet C	73285-4	
D-MOOC	Aerostyle Breezer	005	
D-MOOD	Fisher FP-404 Classic	014	
D-MOOF	Comco Ikarus Fox-C22C	9605-3708	
D-MOOG	Flight Design CT	99.08.03.63	
D-MOOH	WDFL Dallach D4 Fascination	unkn	
D-MOOI	Pretty Flight	001	
D-MOOK	Aerostyle Breezer	009	
D-MOOL	SG Aviation Storm 280	G 003	
D-MOOO	Moyes Dragonfly	D 01001	
D-MOOP	Tecnam P.92ES-100 Echo	482	
D-MOOQ	Rans S-6 Coyote II	0295739XL	
D-MOOR	Flight Design CT-2K	00.06.03.10	
D-MOOS	SG Storm 200G	508G	
D-MOOT	Tandem Air Sunny s.b.s.	SuS 03.96	
D-MOOU	SG Aviation Storm 280	G 008	
D-MOOV	Aerostyle Breezer	001	
D-MOOW	Aerostyle Breezer	006	(D-EOOV)
D-MOOY	Aerostyle Breezer	unkn	
D-MOOZ	Aerostyle Breezer	015	
D-MOPA	Fantasy Air Allegro 2000	01-411	
D-MOPC	UPM Omega Lotus 18	069/883	
D-MOPD	Remos G.3 Mirage	100	
D-MOPE	Scheibe SF-40	3101	
D-MOPF	Rans S-6 Coyote II	0895864	

D-MOPG	Comco Ikarus C-42 Cyclone	9611-6026
D-MOPH	Tecnam P.92 Echo	214
D-MOPI	B&F Funk FK-9 Mk.II	060
D-MOPL	Comco Ikarus Fox-C22	9502-3657
D-MOPM	TL Ultralight TL-96 Star	02 S 122
D-MOPO(2)	B&F Funk FK-9 Mk.III	09-142
D-MOPP	Take Off Maximum	7069
D-MOPT	Zenair CH-601D Zodiac	6-3530/013 0897
D-MOPU	Rans S-6 Coyote II	0396956
D-MOPV	B&F Funk FK-9 Mk.III	09-092
D-MOPW	Ferrari Tucano A	328
D-MOPZ	Comco Ikarus Fox-C22B	9505-3677
D-MORA	Evektor EV-97 Eurostar 2000R	2001-0908
D-MORC	B&F Funk FK-14 Polaris	14-004
D-MORD	Seiffert Mini II	296
D-MORE(1)	Warnke Skylight Trike	028
D-MORE(2)	B&F Funk FK-12 Comet	12-032
D-MORG	B&F Funk FK-9 Mk.III	09-176
D-MORJ	WDFL Sunwheel	030
D-MORK	Platzer Kiebitz-B9	129
D-MORL	Tecnam P.92 Echo	136
D-MORM	Comco Ikarus C-42 Cyclone	0003-6231
D-MORN	Platzer Kiebitz	211
D-MORO	Light Aero Avid Flyer IV	1495
D-MORR	B&F Funk FK-9 Mk.IV	09-245
D-MORS	Ultra-Vector F 610	1402
D-MORV	B&F Funk FK-14 Polaris	14-007
D-MORW	WDFL Dallach D4 Fascination	008
D-MORY	Fair Fax DR Trike	004
D-MORZ	Dallach Sunrise IIA	035
D-MOSA	Air-Light Wild Thing	033
D-MOSB	Interplane Skyboy ZK	26/97
D-MOSC	Tecnam P.92 Echo 100S	500
D-MOSD	WDFL Dallach D4 Fascination BK	062
D-MOSG(2)	Comco Ikarus C-42 Cyclone	9909-6212
D-MOSH	B&F Funk FK-9 Mk.II	078
D-MOSI	Urban Air UFM-13/15 Lambada	24/13
D-MOSK	NST Minimum Saphir 17	345
D-MOSM	Comco Ikarus Fox-C22B	940 .-3605
D-MOSP	Fantasy Air Allegro	01-701
D-MOSS	Rans S-6 Coyote II XL	1095886
D-MOST	Scheibe Ultra	3407
D-MOSW(1)	Sky-Walker 1+1	26118
D-MOSW(2)	Rans S-6 Coyote II	0803151
D-MOSY	Platzer Kiebitz	216
D-MOTA	Platzer Motte B2	04
D-MOTB	Light Aero Avid Flyer IV	1522
D-MOTC	B&F Funk FK-14 Polaris	14-003
D-MOTE	WDFL Dallach D4 Fascination BK	065
D-MOTH	Platzer Kiebitz	203
D-MOTI	Point Aviation Albatros AN-22	8327
D-MOTO	Behlen Trike	87011
D-MOTP	Tecnam P.92 Echo	319
D-MOTR	Fisher FP-404 Classic	001
D-MOTS	WDFL Dallach D4 Fascination BK	103
D-MOTT	B&F Funk FK-9 Mk.III	09-113
D-MOTU	Capella FW1 C50	691055
D-MOTV	Comco Ikarus C-42 Cyclone	9706-6070
D-MOTY	Capella FW2 BR	061941
D-MOTZ	ASO Viper Hazard 15	11026202
D-MOUG	B&F Funk FK-9 Mk.II	018
D-MOUL	Tandem Air Sunny s.b.s.	SuS-05.94
D-MOUS	Pioneer Flightstar	370
D-MOUT	B&F Funk FK-12 Comet	12-019
D-MOUZ	Platzer Motte B2/B3	48
D-MOVA	Zenair CH-601D Zodiac	6-8061/008 0297
D-MOVG	Zenair CH-601D Zodiac	6-3406/017 0097
D-MOVI	Comco Ikarus Fox-C22	9210-3429
D-MOVO	Remos Gemini Ultra	015
D-MOVW	Air-Light Wild Thing	030
D-MOVY	Rans S-12 Airaile	0794508
D-MOWA	Aerotechnik Cobra S1A	001
D-MOWB	Rans S-6 Coyote II	10971168
D-MOWE	Schmidtler Ranger M	18/22
D-MOWH	Euro-ALA Jet Fox 97	013
D-MOWI (3)	Drifter	001
D-MOWK	Comco Ikarus C-42 Cyclone	9812-6139
D-MOWL	Platzer Kiebitz B	077
D-MOWO	Comco Ikarus Fox-C22B	9604-3699
D-MOWR	Platzer Motte BR	18
D-MOWS	B&F Funk FK-9 Mk.II	085
D-MOWT	Comco Ikarus C-42 Cyclone	0004-6251
D-MOWZ	Aerotechnik Cobra S1	unkn
D-MOXE	Comco Ikarus Fox-C22	9404-3560
D-MOXI	Impulse 3300TD	15
D-MOXL	B&F Funk FK-12 Comet	12-036
D-MOXX	B&F Funk FK-9 Mk.III	09-117
D-MOYO	WDFL Sunwheel	035
D-MOYS	Platzer Kiebitz-B	053
D-MOYY	TL Ultralight TL-96 Star	01 S 109
D-MOYZ	Air-Light Wild Thing	016
D-MOZE	Moyes Dragonfly	D04003
D-MOZI	B&F Funk FK-9 Mk.II	039
D-MOZO	Comco Ikarus Fox-C22	9503-3646
D-MOZR	Comco Ikarus Fox-C22	940 .-3551
D-MOZT	Platzer Kiebitz	268
D-MOZY	Urban Air UFM-13/15 Lambada	18/13
D-MOZZ	Klüver Twin Racer Quartz SX 16	229004
D-MPAA	Remos Gemini Ultra	E11.012
D-MPAB	WDFL Dallach D4 Fascination	075
D-MPAC	Comco Ikarus Fox-C22C	9310-3542
D-MPAD	Mantel Mono-Dragster	857
D-MPAE	Bobcat	Bü-02
D-MPAG	Air-Light Wild Thing	060
D-MPAH(2)	Behlen Power Trike II	91125
D-MPAH(3)	Comco Ikarus C-42 Cyclone	0102-6314
D-MPAJ	Mantel Mono-Dragster	874225
D-MPAK	TL Ultralight TL-232 Condor Plus	AB-08/C0201
D-MPAL	TL Ultralight TL-96 Star	unkn
D-MPAM	Comco Ikarus Fox-C22B	9404-3556
D-MPAN(1)	NST Minimum Zephir CX	M467
D-MPAN(2)	Tecnam P.92 Echo 100S	488
D-MPAO	B&F Funk FK-12 Comet	012-025
D-MPAP(1)	Comco Ikarus Fox-C22	9209-3406
D-MPAP(2)	Remos G.3 Mirage	057
D-MPAQ	Comco Ikarus Fox-C22B	9407-3598
D-MPAR	Comco Ikarus Fox-C22	9403-3578
D-MPAW	Kolb Twinstar Mk.III	M3-100
D-MPAY	Aerostyle Breezer	041
D-MPBA	EEL ULF-2	002
D-MPBB	Light Aero Avid Flyer	1290
D-MPBF	B&F Funk FK-9	040
D-MPBG	Tecnam P.96 Golf 100S	097
D-MPBH	Platzer Kiebitz-B	173
D-MPBI	B&F Funk FK-14 Polaris	014-026
D-MPBK	B&F Funk FK-9 Mk.III	09-105
D-MPBL	Ultrastar	018
D-MPBM	Comco Ikarus C-42 Cyclone	9912-6227
D-MPBO	B&F Funk FK-9 Classic	066
D-MPBS	Dallach Sunrise II	012
D-MPBT	Fair Fax DR Trike	34
D-MPBV	Tecnam P.92 Echo 100S	432
D-MPBW	Air-Light Wild Thing	051
D-MPCB	Albatros	114
D-MPCC	Rans S-6 Coyote II	0495805
D-MPCF	Rans S-6 Coyote II	0396963
D-MBCH	Fisher Super Koala	B291248
D-MPCI	Remos G.3 Mirage	061
D-MPCJ	Remos G.3 Mirage	069
D-MPCL	ATEC Zephyr 2000	SF 091101
D-MPCM	B&F Funk FK-9 Mk3	094
D-MPCN	Comco Ikarus C-42 Cyclone	9704-6025
D-MPCP	Remos G.3 Mirage	059
D-MPCR	Platzer Kiebitz-B2	007
D-MPCT(3)	Flight Design CT	01.04.06.15
D-MPCW	Rans S-7 Courier	0698249
D-MPDB	EEL ULF-2	044
D-MPDD	Comco Ikarus C-42	0101-6292
D-MPDG	Platzer Kiebitz-B2	041
D-MPDH	Tandem Air Sunny Sport	31.92
D-MPDK	Air-Light Wild Thing	045
D-MPDL	Tecnam P.96 Golf 100S	047
D-MPDM	Moyes Dragonfly	D04005
D-MPDP	Remos G.3 Mirage	078
D-MPEA (1)	Schönleber DS Lotus KS 18	010490
D-MPEA(2)	ATEC Zephyr 2000	SF 040101
D-MPEB	UPM Funplane	890059
D-MPEC(1)	Homebuilt, possibly Enduro	8/90
D-MPEC(2)	Fly Synthesis Storch	160.6
D-MPED	Tecnam P.92 Echo 100S	573
D-MPEE	Comco Ikarus Fox-C22B	9501-3642
D-MPEF	Aeropro Eurofox	080099
D-MPEG	Scheibe Uli 1	5217
D-MPEI	Tecnam P.96 Golf	076
D-MPEJ	Comco Ikarus C-42 Cyclone	9807-6116
D-MPEL	Remos G.3 Mirage	unkn
D-MPEP	Comco Ikarus Fox-C22B	9603-3697
D-MPER	Scheibe Uli 1	5225
D-MPES	Euro-ALA Jet Fox 91D	010
D-MPET	Tandem Air Sunny Sport	0031001S,S
D-MPEU	Comco Ikarus Fox-C22	9 . . .-3544
D-MPEV	Evektor EV.97 Eurostar	98 03 01
D-MPEW	B&F Funk FK-9 Mk.II	064
D-MPEZ	Comco Ikarus Fox-C22	9311-3545
D-MPFA(1)	ASO Viper Trike	22035206
D-MPFA(3)	Fantasy Air Allegro	03-417
D-MPFB	ATEC Zephyr	SF 050301
D-MPFC	Comco Ikarus C-42 Cyclone	0006-6264
D-MPFF	Rans S-6 Coyote II	04981223
D-MPFI	Sky-Walker II	504
D-MPFJ	WDFL Fascination	unkn
D-MPFK	J-3 Kitten	001
D-MPFU	WDFL Dallach D4 Fascination BK	119
D-MPGA	Firebird Sierra Trike	unkn
D-MPGE	Remos G.3 Mirage	062
D-MPGG	Tecnam P.92 Echo 100S	513
D-MPGH	Tecnam P.92 Echo	243
D-MPGI	Dallach Sunrise II	011
D-MPGK	Ikarusflug Eurofox Pro	039097
D-MPGM	Flight Design CT	unkn
D-MPGN	Comco Ikarus Fox-C22	8707-3045
D-MPGS	TL Ultralight TL-96 Star	01 S 82
D-MPHA	Euro-ALA Jet Fox 97	00134
D-MPHC	Platzer Kiebitz	180

D-MPHD	Skystar S-34	013	
D-MPHE	Comco Ikarus Fox-C22B	9511-3679	
D-MPHF	Comco Ikarus C-42 Cyclone	9803-6088	
D-MPHG	Comco Ikarus C-42 Cyclone	9906-6189	
D-MPHI	Behlen Power-Trike	830002	
D-MPHK	B&F Funk FK-12 Comet	012-030	
D-MPHM	B&F Funk FK-12 Comet	012-020	
D-MPHN	Comco Ikarus C-42 Cyclone	0008-6274	
D-MPHP	Comco Ikarus C-42B	0412-6641	
D-MPHR	Capella FW2 C80	61941-1	
D-MPHS	WDFL Sunwheel R	042	
D-MPHW	WDFL Dallach D4 Fascination	023	
D-MPIC	Remos G.3 Mirage	106	
D-MPIE	Comco Ikarus Fox-C22E	9507-3669	
D-MPII	ICP MXP-740V Savannah	01-00-51-004	
D-MPIL	Comco Ikarus Fox-C22	9208-3418	
D-MPIO	Alpi Avn Pioneer 300UL	20	
D-MPIP	Tecnam P.92 Echo 100S	390	
D-MPIR	Comco Ikarus Fox-C22	9208-3427	
D-MPIT	Remos G.3 Mirage	unkn	
D-MPIW	Flight Design CT	97.11.03.15	
D-MPIX	Scheibe SF.40	3107	
D-MPJA	Remos G.3 Mirage	120	
D-MPJF	Platzer Kiebitz-B	038	
D-MPJK	Light Aero Avid Flyer	5115	
D-MPJL	Ikarusflug Eurofox	029097	
D-MPJM	Platzer Kiebitz	88	
D-MPKG	Flight Design CT	98.05.01.33	
D-MPKH	Dyn'Aero MCR-01 UL	056	
D-MPKI	LO-120S	016-A	
D-MPKK	Comco Ikarus C-42	0203-6420	
D-MPKM	B&F Funk FK-9 TG Mk.II	063	
D-MPKO	Wezel Apis 2	W001	
D-MPKP	Aviasud Mistral BRD	182/92	
D-MPKS	Comco Ikarus C-42 Cyclone	9707-6050	
D-MPKW	Comco Ikarus Fox-C22 Seaplane	9303-3344	
D-MPLA	Rans S-6S Coyote II	0196922	
D-MPLE	Take Off Maximum Hazard 15 Trike	019109	
D-MPLF	Comco Ikarus C-42 Cyclone	9906-6193	
D-MPLH	WDFL Dallach D4 Fascination	027	
D-MPLI	B&F Funk FK.12 Comet	012-001	
D-MPLK	Remos G3 Mirage RS/L	112	
D-MPLL	ASO Storch	ST 11014503	
D-MPLO	Comco Ikarus C-42 Cyclone	9801-6077	
D-MPLR	Light Aero Avid Flyer IV	1435D	
D-MPLS	Ultravia Pélican Sport 450S	714	
D-MPLT	Flight Design CT-2K	00.08.02.14	
D-MPLV	Comco Ikarus Fox-C22	9203-3401	
D-MPLW	Sky Craft 2000	2000-39	
D-MPMA	Behlen Power-Trike II	91030	
D-MPMB	Comco Ikarus C-42 Cyclone	9707-6066	
D-MPMG	Tecnam P.92 Echo 100S	443	
D-MPMK	B&F Funk FK-9 Mk.III	09-146	
D-MPMM	WDFL Dallach D5 Evolution	001	
D-MPMN	Comco Ikarus C-42 Cyclone	9803-6086	
D-MPMW	TL Ultralight TL-2000 Sting	21 ST 02	
D-MPNN	WDFLFascination D4	unkn	
D-MPNR	Tecnam P.92 Echo	325	
D-MPNT	Tecnam P.92 Echo	378	
D-MPOA	TL Ultralight TL-96 Star	00 S 71	
D-MPOE	NST Minimum	M347	
D-MPOJ	Tandem Air Sunny s.b.s.	SUS 05 96	
D-MPOL	Schmidtler Ranger M Trike	1819	
D-MPOO	Flight Design CT	unkn	
D-MPOP	Tecnam P.92 Echo	165	
D-MPOR	Comco Ikarus C-42 Cyclone	9903-6170	
D-MPOW	Remos G-3 Mirage	050	
D-MPOZ	Comco Ikarus Sherpa II	8512-1112	
D-MPPB	Air-Light Wild Thing	98-03-021	
D-MPPC	Remos G.3 Mirage	046	
D-MPPG	Flight Design CT2SW	04.10.05	
D-MPPH(1)	WDFL Sunwheel	019	
D-MPPH(2)	Aerostyle Breezer	013	
D-MPPJ	Tecnam P.96 Golf 100S	125	
D-MPPM	ATEC Zephyr 2000	ZP 511200	
D-MPPP	Murphy Renegade Spirit	506	
D-MPPR	Comco Ikarus Fox-C22	9201-3382	
D-MPPS	Comco Ikarus C-42 Cyclone	9809-6129	
D-MPPW	Klüver Twin Racer Trike	574008	
D-MPPY	TUL-2 Tandem Tulak	031	
D-MPQR	Comco Ikarus Fox-C22	9407-3581	
D-MPRA	TL Ultralight TL-96 Star	99 C 04	
D-MPRB	Tecnam P.96 Golf 100S	065	
D-MPRE	Comco Ikarus Fox-C22	9104-3345	
D-MPRG	Comco Ikarus C-42 Cyclone	9702-6068	
D-MPRH	Flight Design CT	98.02.04.24	D-MWFP
D-MPRI	Tecnam P.92 Echo 100S	554	
D-MPRK	Comco Ikarus Fox-C22	9307-3520	
D-MPRM	Comco Fox	037	
D-MPRO	Albatros	102	
D-MPRP	Comco Ikarus Fox-C22	9705-3726	
D-MPRS	Jet Fox	015	
D-MPRU	Comco Ikarus C-42 Cyclone	9704-6015	
D-MPRV	Flight Design CT	01.06.06.16	
D-MPRW	Comco Ikarus Fox-C22C	9608-3716	
D-MPSA	Air-Light Wild Thing	023	
D-MPSB	Air-Light Wild Thing (was c/n 010, 2 acft?)	047	

D-MPSC	Comco Ikarus Fox	039	
D-MPSD	B&F Funk FK-14	014-015	
D-MPSG	Zenair CH-601 Zodiac	6-3209/012 0097	
D-MPSH	Comco Ikarus C-42 Cyclone	9812-6110	
D-MPSK	Let Mont Tulak	unkn	
D-MPSN	Comco Ikarus Fox-C22	9404-3518	
D-MPSR	Light Aero Avid Flyer IV	941	
D-MPSS	Comco Ikarus C-42 Cyclone	9806-6124	
D-MPST	Air-Light Wild Thing	06 074	
D-MPSW	Comco Ikarus C-42 Cyclone	9809-6123	
D-MPSZ	Comco Ikarus C-42 Cyclone	0004-6245	
D-MPTC	Ultraleichtverbund Bi 90	942	
D-MPTH	Tecnam P.92 Echo 100S	528	
D-MPTK	Comco Ikarus C-42 Cyclone	0005-6262	
D-MPTL	Platzer Kiebitz	230	
D-MPTS	Comco Ikarus Fox-C22	9307-3515	
D-MPTU	Comco Ikarus C-42 Cyclone	9611-6019	
D-MPUC	Comco Ikarus C-42 Cyclone	0006-6256	
D-MPUD	ATEC Zephyr 2000	unkn	
D-MPUE	Urban Air UFM-11 Lambada	07/11	
D-MPUK	Comco Ikarus Fox-C22B	9503-3643	
D-MPUL(1)	Comco Ikarus Sherpa	8403-1059	
D-MPUL(2)	Impulse Aircraft Impulse 100UL	1	
D-MPUR	Comco Ikarus Fox-C22	9111-3381	
D-MPVM	Platzer Kiebitz-B6	11/2	
D-MPVP	Tecnam P.92 Echo	158	
D-MPWA	Kappa KP-2U Sova	625/98	
D-MPWE	B&F Funk FK-9 Mk.II	030	
D-MPWK	Tecnam P.92 Echo	157	
D-MPWP	Tandem Air Sunny Sport	60.95	
D-MPWR	Aeropro Eurofox	10101	
D-MPWS	Flight Design CT	98.04.04.31	
D-MPWT	Air-Light Wild Thing	047	
D-MPWZ	Flight Design CT-2K	01.02.01.04	
D-MPYA	Platzer Kiebitz-B6	008	
D-MPYT	Comco Ikarus Fox-C22	8612-3055	
D-MPYY	TL Ultralight TL-2000 Sting	04 ST 97	
D-MPYZ	B&F Funk FK-12 Comet	unkn	
D-MPZZ	Comco Ikarus C-42 Cyclone	0002-6241	
D-MQAK	Schmidtler Enduro XP-15	01-005	
D-MQAL	Alpi Avn Pioneer 300S	55	
D-MQAX	B&F Funk FK-12 Comet	012-042	
D-MQBF	B&F Funk FK-9 Mk.II	036	
D-MQBK	Light Aero Avid Flyer IV	1293	
D-MQBT	HFL Stratos 300K	300-014K	D-MJBT(1)
D-MQCC	Flight Design CT	97.08.03.07	
D-MQDM	Moyes Dragonfly	D04004	
D-MQFK	Comco Ikarus C-42 Cyclone	9708-6064	
D-MQHG(1)	Pioneer Flightstar II SL	970501	
D-MQHG(2)	Flightstar II	020401	
D-MQII	WDFL Sunwheel	46	
D-MQIK	Flight Design CT	98.06.01.34	
D-MQJB	Albatros AE 209	121	D-MACZ
D-MQKM	SFS Vagabund	07	
D-MQPG	Comco Ikarus C-42 Cyclone	0010-6229	
D-MQQQ	Rans S-12 Airaile	1292340	N7082C
D-MQRF	EEL ULF-2 Prototype	001	
D-MQRS	Tecnam P.92 Echo	096	
D-MQWT	WDFL Dallach D4 Fascination	061	
D-MQWW	Tecnam P.96 Golf 100S	140	
D-MQXZ	Tecnam P.92 Echo	127	
D-MQYJ	Platzer Kiebitz-B	010	
D-MQYV	WDFL Sunwheel R	020	
D-MRAA	Comco Ikarus C-42 Cyclone	unkn	
D-MRAB	Fisher FP-202 Koala	2183-1	
D-MRAC(3)	Platzer Kiebitz-B2	142	
D-MRAD	Comco Ikarus C-42 Cyclone	9606-6008	
D-MRAE	Remos G.3 Mirage	unkn	
D-MRAH	Platzer Kiebitz-B2	178	
D-MRAI	Denney Kitfox IV-1200	JCU-114	
D-MRAJ	SG Aviation Storm 280	D002	
D-MRAK	Comco Ikarus Fox-C22	8812-3185	
D-MRAL	Sky-Walker II	321	
D-MRAM	Light Aero Avid Flyer	1274	
D-MRAN	Rans S-6 Coyote II	1192390	
D-MRAO	Comco Ikarus Fox-C22	9 . . .-3609	
D-MRAP	Platzer Kiebitz-B9	090	
D-MRAQ	Comco Ikarus Fox-C22	9407-3549	
D-MRAS	Sky-Walker II	323	
D-MRAU	Comco Ikarus Fox-C22	8808-3139	
D-MRAW(1)	B&F Funk FK-12 Comet	012-006	
D-MRAW(2)	Ultravia Pélican Sport 450S	774	
D-MRAX	B&F Funk FK-9 Mk.III	09-102	
D-MRAY	Comco Ikarus C-42 Cyclone	9709-6035	
D-MRAZ	Light Aero Avid Flyer	"989952-199" or "9999"	
D-MRBB	Flight Design CT	97.06.02.00	
D-MRBC	Rans S-6 Coyote II	0293435	
D-MRBD	Comco Ikarus C-42 Cyclone	9801-6037	
D-MRBF	Air-Light Wild Thing	012	
D-MRBG	Flight Design CT	97.11.02.14	
D-MRBH	WDFL Dallach D4 Fascination	004	
D-MRBI	Comco Ikarus C-42 Cyclone	9609-6012	
D-MRBL	Eipper Quicksilver GT	GT-280-1193	
D-MRBO	Tecnam P.92 Echo 100S	425	
D-MRBP	Remos G-3 Mirage	049	
D-MRBZ	Flight Design CT	unkn	
D-MRCB(1)	Rans S-6 Coyote II	0295738	

D-MRCB(2)	Flight Design CT2SW	04.007.03	
D-MRCD	Comco Ikarus Fox-C22	8702-3048	
D-MRCE	Comco Ikarus C-42 Cyclone	0109-6417	
D-MRCF	Konsuprod Moskito 1b	013	
D-MRCI	Remos G-3 Mirage	unkn	
D-MRCM	Albatros 52	133	
D-MRCP	ICP MX-740V Savannah	05-96-50-042	
D-MRCT	Flight Design CT	98.01.03.20	
D-MRCU	Comco Ikarus Fox-C22B	9407-3602	
D-MRDC	Comco Ikarus Fox-C22	9502-3656	
D-MRDF	WDFL Dallach D4 Fascination	018	
D-MRDG	B&F Funk FK-9 Mk.II	037	
D-MRDK	Platzer Kiebitz-B2	132	
D-MRDL	Rans S-6 Coyote II	1193560	
D-MRDM	B&F Funk FK-12 Comet	012-008	
D-MRDW	Ultraleichtverbund Bi 90	704	
D-MRDX	Zenair CH-601D Zodiac	6-9197	
D-MREC	Comco Ikarus C-42 Cyclone	0105-6327	
D-MRED	Remos Gemini Ultra	16.17/032	
D-MREE	Rans S-6 Coyote II	594630	
D-MREG	Tecnam P.96 Golf 100S	170	
D-MREH	Comco Ikarus C-42 Cyclone	9708-6046	
D-MREI	Platzer Kiebitz-B2	039	
D-MREM	Remos Gemini Ultra	E15.16/016	
D-MREP	Comco Ikarus C-42 Cyclone	9904-6157	
D-MRER	B&F Funk FK-14 Polaris	014-006	
D-MRES	Tecnam P.96 Golf 100S	107	
D-MREU	Tandem Air Sunny	55.93	
D-MREV	Comco Ikarus C-42 Cyclone	9609-6011	
D-MREW	WDFL Dallach D4 Fascination BK	114	
D-MREX	WDFL Dallach D4 Fascination BK	078	
D-MRFB	Delda-S/A Delta Dart II	002	
D-MRFC	Ferrari Tucano-A	303	
D-MRFE	Ferrari Tucano-A	327	
D-MRFF	Comco Ikarus Fox-C22C	9705-3727	
D-MRFG	Ultra-Vector H	1383	
D-MRFH	Comco Ikarus C-42	0304-6547	
D-MRFK	B&F Funk FK-9 Mk 3	089	
D-MRFL	Comco Ikarus C-42 Cyclone	0105-6350	
D-MRFM	Comco Ikarus C-42 Cyclone	0108-6410	
D-MRFR	Comco Ikarus C-42 Cyclone	0105-"262"	
D-MRFS	Rans S-12 Airaile	1292360	
D-MRFT	Kappa KP-2U Sova	4651 G	
D-MRGA	Platzer Motte B-3	033	
D-MRGB	Murphy Renegade Spirit	387	
D-MRGD	III Sky Arrow 450TG	018	
D-MRGE(1)	Ultraleichtverbund Bi 90	935	
D-MRGE(2)	ATEC Zephyr 2000	K 001	
D-MRGH	Murphy Renegade II	458	
D-MRGL	Euro-ALA Jet Fox 91D	009	
D-MRGO	Comco Ikarus C-42 Cyclone	9805-6056	
D-MRGS	Tecnam P.96 Golf 100S	183	
D-MRGV	Comco Ikarus C-42 Cyclone	0010-6285	
D-MRGW	Sky-Walker II	221	
D-MRHA	B&F Funk FK-9 Mk.III	110	
D-MRHB	Comco Ikarus Fox-C22	940 .-3571	
D-MRHE	Flight Design CT	007/97	
D-MRHF	Behlen Power-Trike	88011	
D-MRHH	Tecnam P.92 Echo	194	
D-MRHJ	B&F Funk FK-9 Mk3	unkn	
D-MRHK	Tecnam P.92 Echo	266	
D-MRHL	Remos G.3 Mirage	041	
D-MRHM	Rans S-6ES Coyote II	0895880	
D-MRHN	Comco Ikarus Fox-C22	9208-3420	D- MIAL(1)
D-MRHO	Ultraleichtverbund Bi 90	3957005	
D-MRHP	Ultraleichtverbund Bi 90	970	
D-MRHR	Comco Ikarus Fox-C22	9309-3539	
D-MRHS	Tecnam P.92 Echo	391	
D-MRHU	B&F Funk FK-9 Mk.III	09-097	
D-MRHW(1)	Schönleber DS Speed KS 14 Trike KS	01/0391	
D-MRHW(2)	B&F Funk FK-14 Polaris	014-018	
D-MRHX	Zenair CH.601DX Zodiac	6-9067	
D-MRHZ	Zenair CH-601D Zodiac	6-3521/006 0997	
D-MRIC	Remos G-3 Mirage	unkn	
D-MRID	Comco Ikarus Fox-C22	9404-3555	
D-MRIE	Seiffert Mini II	F0111/88	
D-MRIF	Aviasud Mistral 53	010	
D-MRII	Platzer Kiebitz	168	
D-MRIK	Tecnam P.92 Echo	265	
D-MRIL	III Sky Arrow 450	066	
D-MRIM	Remos G.3 Mirage	044	
	(Same c/n quoted as D-MNPU)		
D-MRIS	Tecnam P.96 Golf	16	
D-MRIT	Aviasud Albatros	037	
D-MRIW	WDFL Dallach D4 Fascination	043	
D-MRIX	Scheibe Uli 1	5204	
D-MRIY	Scheibe Uli 1	5210	
D-MRIZ	Remos G.3 Mirage	040	
D-MRJA	Seiffert Mini II	F0209/87	
D-MRJD	B&F Funk FK-12 Comet	012-048	
D-MRJF	Comco Ikarus Fox-C22B	9510-3700	
D-MRJH	Comco Ikarus C-42 Cyclone	9710-6074	
D-MRJK	Flight Design CT	00.01.02.82	
D-MRJL	B&F Funk FK-9 Mk3	108	
D-MRJR	Flight Design CT	98.11.01.40	
D-MRJS	Rans S-10 Sakota	0490104	
D-MRJZ	Tecnam P.96 Golf	020	
D-MRKA	Konsuprod Moskito	003	
D-MRKB	Comco Ikarus Fox-C22	9308-3519	
D-MRKD	Tecnam P.96 Golf	020	
D-MRKE	Comco Ikarus C-42 Cyclone	9612-6027	
D-MRKF	Rans S-6TD Coyote II	1294703	
D-MRKG	Aeroprakt A-22 Vision	19	
D-MRKK	Flight Design CT	01.03.02.09	
D-MRKL	B&F Funk FK-12 Comet	012-009	
D-MRKM	Air-Light Wild Thing	97 02 018	
D-MRKN	Tecnam P.92 Echo 100S	507	
D-MRKO	Comco Ikarus C-42 Cyclone	9709-6055	
D-MRKP	Comco Ikarus C-42 Cyclone	9707-6069	
D-MRKR	B&F Funk FK-9 TG	053	
D-MRKS	Tecnam P.96 Golf 100S	131	
D-MRKT	Comco Ikarus C-42	0201-6405	
D-MRKW	Light Aero Avid Flyer D	1156D	
D-MRLA	Behlen Power-Trike	877353	
D-MRLB	Aerospool WT9 Dynamic	DY011 02	
D-MRLC	Dyn'Aero MCR-01 UL	104	
D-MRLD	Tecnam P.92 Echo	278	
D-MRLH	TL Ultralight TL-232 Condor Plus	AB 03	
D-MRLK	Light Aero Avid Flyer IV	1400	
D-MRLM	Sky-Walker II	393	
D-MRLS	Zenair CH-701D STOL	7-9068	
D-MRLT	Zlin Savage	45	
D-MRLW	Comco Ikarus Fox-C22B	9606-3703	
D-MRLX	Tecnam P.92 Echo 2000S	707	
D-MRMA	B&F Funk FK-9 Mk3	09-03-100	
D-MRMC	Sky-Walker II	265	
D-MRMD	B&F Funk FK-9 TG Mk.II	059	
D-MRMF	Comco Ikarus Fox-C22B	9 . . .-3681	
D-MRMG	Remos Gemini Ultra	010	
D-MRMI	Remos G.3 Mirage	038	
D-MRMK	Comco Ikarus Fox-C22	9109-3353	
D-MRMM	B&F Funk FK-9	084	
D-MRMN	Comco Ikarus Fox-C22C	9705-3715	
D-MRMP	Flight Design CT	00.11.02.23	
D-MRMR	WDFL Dallach D4 Fascination BK	111	
D-MRMS	Comco Ikarus C-42 Cyclone	9801-6075	
D-MRMU	Warnke Trike Euro III	183001	
D-MRMZ	Comco Ikarus C-42 Cyclone	9707-6045	
D-MRNG	Murphy Renegade	412	
D-MRNN	Flight Design CT	99.12.04.78	
D-MROB	Comco Ikarus C-42B	0205-6447	
D-MROC	TL Ultralight TL-232 Condor Plus	00 C 04	
D-MROD	Rans S-10 Sakota	0194170	
D-MROE	Comco Ikarus Fox-C22	9406-3573	
D-MROH	Rans S-6 Coyote II	0794652	
D-MROI	Zenair CH-701D STOL	7-9356	
D-MROK	NST Minimum	157	
D-MROM	Platzer Kiebitz-B4	109	
D-MROO	Comco Ikarus C-42B	0305-6537	
D-MROP	B&F Funk FK-9 Mk.III	09-03-158	
D-MROS	Tandem Air Sunny Sport	23.91	
D-MROT	NST Minimum	M431	
D-MROU	Comco Ikarus Fox-C22	9206-3409	
D-MROY	Comco Ikarus Fox-C22	9112-3298	
D-MRPA	Comco Ikarus C-42 Cyclone	0102-6301	
D-MRPC	TL Ultralight TL-232 Condor Plus	00 C 02	
D-MRPD	Rans S-6 Coyote II XL	08971150	
D-MRPF	B&F Funk FK-9 Mk.III Utility	09-03U-136	
D-MRPH	Fantasy Air Allegro	00-403	
D-MRPK	Comco Ikarus Fox-C22	9310-3521	
D-MRPL	Air-Light Wild Thing	2000-05-064	
D-MRPM	Sky Craft 2000	2000-31	
D-MRPR	Tecnam P.92 Echo 20000S	666	
D-MRPS	Behlen Power-Trike	unkn	
D-MRPT	B&F Funk FK-9 Mk.III	09-165	
D-MRPW	B&F Funk FK-9 Mk.II	049	
D-MRRF	WDFL Dallach D4 Fascination BK	096	
D-MRRG	WDFL Dallach D4 Fascination	049	
D-MRRH	UPM Funplane	870024	
D-MRRK	Tecnam P.92 Echo	296	
D-MRRL	Tecnam P.96 Golf	17	
D-MRRM	Sky Craft 2000	2000-38	
D-MRRP	B&F Funk FK-9	050	
D-MRRR	WDFL Sunwheel	009	
D-MRRS	Comco Ikarus Sherpa II	8310-1044	PH-1M2
D-MRRW	Comco Ikarus C-42 Cyclone	0110-6414	
D-MRRZ	Kümmerle Mini-Fly-Set	1268/91-5	
D-MRSA	WDFL Sunwheel R	032	
D-MRSB	Sky Craft AJS	2000-32	
D-MRSE	Rans S-6 Coyote II	12961078	
D-MRSG	Zenair CH-601D Zodiac UL	6-3651	
D-MRSH	Murphy Renegade Spirit	410	
D-MRSI	Zenair CH-601DX Zodiac	6-90683	
D-MRSK	Comco Ikarus C-42 Cyclone	9806-6091	
D-MRSM	Comco Ikarus Fox-C22	9406-3593	
D-MRSN	Rans S-12 Airaile	1090028	
D-MRSO	Fair Fax DR Trike	002	
D-MRSR	Tecnam P.96 Golf	002	
D-MRSS	Ultraleichtverbund Bi 90	555395	
D-MRST(1)	Schmidtler Ranger M Trike	unkn	
D-MRST(2)	Platzer Kiebitz-B6	141	
D-MRSU	NST Minimum Zephir	M497	
D-MRTA	Schmidtler Ranger M Trike	18-23	
D-MRTB	B&F Funk FK-9	026	

D-MRTE	Remos G.3 Mirage	065	
D-MRTF	Rans S-10 Sakota	0190084	
D-MRTH	Zenair CH-601D Zodiac UL	6-3485/021 0897	
D-MRTL	Comco Ikarus Fox-C22	9107-3347	
D-MRTM	Remos G-3 Mirage	066	
D-MRTN	Tecnam P.92 Echo	188	
D-MRTR	Rans S-12 Airaile	0491064	
D-MRTS	Ferrari Tucano-A	305	
D-MRTT	Comco Ikarus C-42 Cyclone	9802-6044	
D-MRTV	Comco Ikarus Fox-C22	9206-3415	
D-MRUA	TL Ultralight TL-96 Star	00 S 43	
D-MRUK	Comco Ikarus Fox-C22B	9508-3668	
D-MRUL	Rans S-12 Airaile	0291054	
	(Now quoted as 0791102, 2nd aircraft?)		
D-MRUN	Remos G-3 Mirage	073	
D-MRUT	Comco Ikarus Fox-C22	9212-3425	
D-MRUW	UW-8 Rebell	001	
D-MRVA	Zenair CH-701D STOL	7-9063	
D-MRVE	Platzer Kiebitz-B1	002	
D-MRVH	Tandem Air Sunny s.b.s.	SuS 05.95	
D-MRVK	Air-Light Wild Thing	031	
D-MRWA	Rans S-10T Sakota	1099190	
D-MRWB	Comco Ikarus Fox-C22	9211-3482	
D-MRWD	Warnke Puma Sprint Trike	D007	
D-MRWE	WDFL Dallach D4 Fascination	006	
D-MRWG	Comco Ikarus C-42 Cyclone	9803-6095	
D-MRWH	WDFL Dallach D4 Fascination	002	
D-MRWI	Fresh Breeze 110 AL2F	50	
D-MRWK	Klüver Racer Quartz SX 12 Trike	445904	
D-MRYC	WDFL Dallach D4 Fascination	060	
D-MRZJ	Comco Ikarus Fox-C22	94 . .-3590	
D-MSAC	Comco Ikarus C-42 Cyclone	9910-6221	
D-MSAD	Schönleber DS Trike	502/0991	
D-MSAE(1)	NST Minimum	M63	
D-MSAE(2)	Comco Ikarus C-42 Cyclone	0004-6252	
D-MSAF	Light Aero Avid Flyer C	869	
D-MSAG	Tandem Air Sunny Sport	62.95	
D-MSAH(1)	Ultraleichtverbund Bi 90	493	
D-MSAH(2)	B&F Funk FK-12 Comet	012-038	
D-MSAI	Tandem Air Sunny Targa	TA-013	
D-MSAK	Tandem Air Sunny Sport	39.92	
D-MSAL	Schmidtler Enduro Trike	0401086	
D-MSAN	Asso Aeri Asso V Champion V	001	
D-MSAO	Light Aero Avid Flyer	1520	
D-MSAR	Remos G.3 Mirage	146	
D-MSAS	Comco Ikarus C-42B	0304-6538	
D-MSAT	Comco Ikarus Fox-C22C	9107-3348	
D-MSAU	Tandem Air Sunny s.b.s.	SuS-10.94	
D-MSAV	Comco Ikarus Fox-C22B	9403-3577	
D-MSAW	WDFL Sunwheel R	039	
D-MSAY	B&F Funk FK-9 Mk.II	087	
D-MSBB	Comco Ikarus Fox-C22	9106-3330	
D-MSBC	WDFL Dallach D4 Fascination BK	073	
D-MSBG	Remos G-3 Mirage	054	
D-MSBH	Tecnam P.92 Echo	257	
D-MSBI	ULFlugzeugwerk SF-45SA Spirit	unkn	
D-MSBK(1)	Take Off Merlin Karat 13 Trike	21904	
D-MSBK(2)	Comco Ikarus C-42 Cyclone	9912-6225	
D-MSBM	Comco Ikarus C-42 Cyclone	9607-6002	
D-MSBN	Tandem Air Sunny s.b.s.	01-95	
D-MSBP	Comco Ikarus Fox-C22	9304-3499	
D-MSBR	Comco Ikarus C-42 Cyclone	9909-6208	
D-MSBS	Aeropro Eurofox	053098	
D-MSBT	B&F Funk FK-9TG Mk.II	062	
D-MSBV	Comco Ikarus C-42	0202-6363	
D-MSBZ	Comco Ikarus C-42 Cyclone	9902-6163	
D-MSCB	Tecnam P.92 Echo	179	
D-MSCC	Rans S-6ES Coyote II	1195900	
D-MSCE	TL Ultralight TL-96 Star	01 S 100	
D-MSCF	Comco Ikarus Fox-C22C	9706-3723	
D-MSCH	TL Ultralight TL-96 Star	00 S 75	
D-MSCL	Comco Ikarus Fox-C22	9106-3341	
D-MSCM	Comco Ikarus C-42B	0311-6478	
D-MSCN	WDFL Fascination	028	
D-MSCO	Comco Ikarus C-42 Cyclone	9906-6178	
D-MSCP	Urban UFM-11 Lambada	09/11	
D-MSCT	Flight Design CT (Cld ?)	97.09.03.09	
D-MSCT(2)	Flight Design CT	98.07.03.36	
D-MSCU	Comco Ikarus C-42 Cyclone	9711-6071	
D-MSCW	Brack/ Denney Kitfox	613	D-ERPB
D-MSCY	Urban Air Lambada UFM-13	unkn	
D-MSDB	ASO 26 Storch	160.1	
D-MSDI	Rans S-6 Coyote II	01991294	
D-MSDL	Remos G.3 Mirage	101	
D-MSDS	Kümmerle Mini-Fly-Set	1303/91-6	
D-MSDW	SDW Maximum Trike	1	
D-MSDY	Comco Ikarus C-42 Cyclone	0005-6268	
D-MSEA	WDFL Dallach D4 Fascination BK	091	
D-MSEC	Tecnam P.92 Echo	173	
D-MSED	Tecnam P.92 Echo	174	
D-MSEF	Aeropro Eurofox	076099	
D-MSEI	Behlen Power-Trike Vampir II	88012	
D-MSEJ	Rans S-6 Coyote II	0593509	
D-MSEK	Tecnam P.92SEcho 100S	536	
D-MSEL	Comco Ikarus Fox-C22	9107-3342	
D-MSEM	Light Aero Avid Flyer	619	
D-MSEN	Kümmerle Mini-Fly-Set Zephir CX	1272/91-5	
D-MSEO	Comco Ikarus C-42 Cyclone	9804-6097	
D-MSEP	Urban UFM-11 Lambada	08/11	
D-MSER	Scheibe SF-40	3106	
D-MSES	Fly Synthesis Storch	160.1	
D-MSET	Platzer Motte B2	35	
D-MSEU	Murphy Renegade Spirit	411	
D-MSEV	Evektor EV.97 Eurostar	990501	
D-MSEW	SFS Vagabund	08	
D-MSEX(1)	Behlen Trike	830014	
D-MSEX(2)	B&F Funk F-14 Polaris (noted 8.02)	unkn	
D-MSFA	Warnke Trike	M869530	
D-MSFB	Rans S-6 Coyote II	0393462	
D-MSFC	Warnke Europlane Euro III Trike	M867935	
D-MSFE	Warnke Trike	1028	
D-MSFF	Comco Ikarus C-42 Cyclone	9807-6115	
D-MSFG	Comco Ikarus C-42B	0203-6477	
D-MSFH	Evektor EV-97 Eurostar	2004-1813	
D-MSFK	B&F Funk FK-14 Polaris	014-009	
D-MSFL	Murphy Renegade Spirit	619	
D-MSFG	UPM Funplane	86011	
D-MSFO	Steinbach Austro-Trike Euro IIIM	1200	
D-MSFR	Tecnam P.96 Golf 100S	180	
D-MSFS	Comco Ikarus Fox-C22	9401-3543	
D-MSFU	Tecnam P.96 Golf	11	
D-MSFV	Comco Ikarus C-42 Cyclone	9802-6080	
D-MSFW	Comco Ikarus C-42 Cyclone	0106-6365	
D-MSGA	Konsuprod Moskito	007	
D-MSGB	TL Ultralight TL-96 Star	01 S 99	
D-MSGE	Comco Ikarus C-42 Cyclone	9902-6175	
D-MSGF	Comco Fox	unkn	
D-MSGG	Comco Ikarus C-42 Cyclone	9801-6057	
D-MSGH	Comco Ikarus C-42 Cyclone	9709-6059	
D-MSGI	Comco Ikarus C-42B	0303-6514	
D-MSGJ	Comco Ikarus C-42 Cyclone	unkn	
D-MSGK	Comco Ikarus Fox-C22	9001-3250	
D-MSGL	Behlen Power-Trike	86-015	
D-MSGM	Comco Ikarus C-42 Cyclone	9806-6120	
D-MSGO	Remos Gemini Ultra	036R	
D-MSGP	Remos G.3 Mirage	093	
D-MSGS	Tandem Air Sunny Sport	44.93	
D-MSGU	Tandem Air Sunny Targa	TA-018	
D-MSGW	Light Aero Avid Flyer	1011	
D-MSHA	Comco Ikarus C-42 Cyclone	9903-6172	
D-MSHE	Comco Ikarus Sherpa	8305-1019	
D-MSHG	Comco Ikarus Sherpa I	8304-1021	
D-MSHH	WDFL Fascination	044	
D-MSHJ	Comco Ikarus C-42 Cyclone	9807-6111	
D-MSHK	Aeropro Eurofox	083000	
D-MSHL	Tecnam P.96 Golf 100S	182	
D-MSHM	Tecnam P.92 Echo	232	
D-MSHN	Comco Ikarus Sherpa I	8307-1032	
D-MSHP	Comco Ikarus C-42 Cyclone	0001-6236	
D-MSHR	Comco Ikarus Sherpa II	8311-02	
D-MSHS	Remos G.3 Mirage	153	
D-MSIA	Comco Ikarus Sherpa II	8408-1079	
D-MSIB	Comco Ikarus Sherpa II	8410-1083	
D-MSIC	Comco Ikarus Sherpa II	8501-1088	
D-MSID	Comco Ikarus Sherpa II	850 .-1089	
D-MSIE	Comco Ikarus C-42B	0210-6491	
D-MSIF	Comco Fox D	8507-FD30	
D-MSIG(2)	TL Ultralight TL-232 Condor Plus	97 C 04	
D-MSIH	Comco Fox D	8409-FD12	
D-MSIK	WDFL Dallach D4 Fascination BK	118	
D-MSIL(1)	Comco Fox D	8507-FD31	
D-MSIL(2)	Flight Design CT2SW	04.03.02	
D-MSIM	Comco Fox D	8508-FD32	
D-MSIN	WDFL Dallach D4 Fascination	064	
D-MSIO	Rans S-10S Sakota	0989060	
D-MSIP	Comco Fox D	8503-FD24	
D-MSIR	Comco Ikarus Sherpa II	850 .-1090	
D-MSIS	Comco Fox II	8605-3018	
D-MSIT	WDFL D.4 Fascination	022	
D-MSIU	Remos G-3 Mirage	unkn	
D-MSIV	Comco Ikarus Sherpa II	8412-1075	
D-MSIW	Comco Ikarus Sherpa II	8503-1092	
D-MSIX	Comco Ikarus Sherpa II	850 .-1091	
D-MSIZ	Comco Ikarus Sherpa II	8504-1094	
D-MSJA	B&F Funk FK-9 Mk.II	073	
D-MSJL	Flight Design CT	99.12.03.77FR	
D-MSJR	NST Minimum Trike Profil 17M	206	
D-MSJS	Comco Ikarus C-42 Cyclone	9802-6054	
D-MSKA	Comco Ikarus C-42 Cyclone	9807-6121	
D-MSKB	Comco Ikarus C-42 Cyclone	9710-6062	
D-MSKC	Comco Ikarus Sherpa I	8307-1037	
D-MSKD	Comco Ikarus Sherpa II	8406-1070	
D-MSKE	Comco Ikarus Sherpa II	8402-1051	
D-MSKF	B&F Funk FK-9 Mk.II	055	
D-MSKG	Flight Design CT	99.03.01.48	
D-MSKH	III Sky Arrow 450TS	087S	
D-MSKI	Flight Design CT	97.07.02.04	
D-MSKJ	Comco Ikarus Sherpa II	8406-1068	
D-MSKK	TL Ultralight TL-96 Star	99 S 33	
D-MSKL	Comco Ikarus Sherpa II	8410-1082	
D-MSKM	Comco Ikarus Sherpa II	8409-10 . .	
D-MSKN(2)	Albatros 64	309	
D-MSKP	Comco Ikarus Fox-C22B	9403-3558	
D-MSKQ	Comco Ikarus Fox-C22	9408-3585	

D-MSKR	Comco Ikarus Sherpa II	8311-1048	
D-MSKS	Comco Ikarus Sherpa II	8403-1054	
D-MSKT	Comco Ikarus Sherpa II	8408-1077	
D-MSKV	Comco Ikarus Sherpa II	8407-1071	
D-MSKW	Comco Ikarus Sherpa II	8405-1066	
D-MSKX	Comco Ikarus Sherpa II	8407-1074	
D-MSKY	III Sky Arrow 450TS	085S	
D-MSKZ	Comco Ikarus Sherpa II	8407-1073	
D-MSLA	Comco Ikarus Sherpa II	8506-1102	
D-MSLC	Comco Ikarus Sherpa II D	8507-1104	
D-MSLD	Comco Ikarus Sherpa II D	8511-1109	
D-MSLE	Comco Ikarus Sherpa II D	8606-1122	
D-MSLG	Comco Fox	038	
D-MSLH	Comco Ikarus C-42 Cyclone	9801-6079	
D-MSLI (1)	Comco Ikarus Fox-C22	8607-3026	
D-MSLI(2)	Flight Design CT2SW	04.04.02	
D-MSLJ	Tandem Air Sunny s.b.s	SuS-08.94	
D-MSLK	B&F Funk FK-12 Comet	012-021	
D-MSLL(2)	Tecnam P.92 Echo	215	
D-MSLM	WDFL Sunwheel R	038	
D-MSLN	Mosquito lb	021	
D-MSLO	B&F Funk FK-12 Comet	012-015	
D-MSLP	B&F Funk FK-12 Comet	012-005	
D-MSLS	Zenair CH-601D Zodiac	6-3650	
D-MSLT	Rans S-7 Courier	0301302	
D-MSLU	Comco Ikarus Fox-C22B	940 .-3600	
D-MSMB	WDFL Sunwheel R	047	
D-MSMH(2)	WDFL Sunwheel (Previously c/n 017)	052	
D MSMI	Comco Ikarus Fox-C22C	9602-3682	
D-MSMK	Comco Ikarus C-42 Cyclone	0011-6296	
D-MSML(2)	Albatros 64	310	
D-MSMM (1)	Rans S-12 Airaile	1292357	
D-MSMM(2)	Flight Design CT-2K	02.07.05.30	
D-MSMR	Zenair CH-701D STOL	7-9367	
D-MSMS	Rans S-12 Airaile	0493406	
D-MSMT	Tandem Air Sunny Sport	53.93	
D-MSMV	WDFL Dallach D4 Fascination	011	
D-MSNB	Platzer Kiebitz	212	
D-MSNG	Flight Design CT-2K	01.03.03.10	
D-MSNJ	Zenair CH-601D Zodiac	6-3792	
D-MSNK	TL Ultralight TL-96 Star	00 S 56	
D-MSNR	NST Minimum Saphir 17	M471	
D-MSNU	WDFLSunwheel	unkn	
D-MSNW	Comco Ikarus Fox-C22C	9608-3711	
D-MSOB	Steinbach Austro-Trike Euro IIIM	1129	
D-MSOC	ASO Storch	11010408	
D-MSOD	Comco Ikarus Fox-C22B	9403-3547	
D-MSOE	Tandem Air Sunny s.b.s.	SuS-04.94	
D-MSOF	ASO Storch	11011408	
D-MSOG	ASO Storch	11012409	
D-MSOH	NST Minimum	218	
D-MSOI	Comco Ikarus Fox-C22B	9507-3667	
D-MSOK	Fisher Super Koala	A01	
D-MSOL(2)	Comco Ikarus C-42 Cyclone	9702-6039	
D-MSOM	Comco Ikarus C-42 Cyclone	9604-6004	
D-MSON	Comco Ikarus C-42B	0308-6553	
D-MSOO	Flight Design CT	98.02.01.21	
D-MSOP	Comco Ikarus C-42 Cyclone	9604-6005	
D-MSOQ	Zenair CH-601 Zodiac	6-3523	
D-MSOR	Comco Ikarus Fox-C22B	9208-3413	
D-MSOS	Schmidtler Ranger M Trike	M 868066	
D-MSOT	Mantel Mono-Dragster	M 873089	
D-MSOV	Comco Ikarus C-42 Cyclone	9507-0001	
D-MSOW	Solid Air Diamant 55dB(A) Trike	018	
D-MSPC	Rans S-6 Coyote II	0795856	
D-MSPE	Tandem Air Sunny s.b.s.	SuS-01.94	
D-MSPH	WDFL Dallach D4 Fascination	036	
D-MSPK	B&F Funk FK-11 (Prototype)	11912	
D-MSPL	Ultravia Pélican Sport 450S	20015/722	
D-MSPM	Dyn'Aero MCR-01 UL	091	
D-MSPO	Flight Design CT	98.03.01.25	
D-MSPP	Albatros 52	128	
D-MSPR	Ultraleichtverbund Bi 90	7373917708	
D-MSPS	NST Minimum Saphir 17	465	
D-MSPW	Schmidtler Enduro Trike	02001	
D-MSPY	Fair Fax Trike Euro III	043	
D-MSPZ	Comco Ikarus C-42 Cyclone	9903-6181	
D-MSRA	Zenair CH-701D STOL	7-9427	
D-MSRB	Zenair CH-601D Zodiac	6-3404/023 0697	
D-MSRG	WDFL Sunrise II	025	D-MLOH
D-MSRH	Zenair CH-701D STOL	001	
D-MSRJ	Tecnam P.92 Echo	233	
D-MSRL	Tecnam P.96 Golf	027	
D-MSRM	Tecnam P.92 Echo (Short wing)	unkn	
D-MSRO	Ultraleichtverbund Bi 90	674	
D-MSRP	Tecnam P.92 Echo	131	
D-MSRR	Tandem Air Sunny Targa	TA-001	
D-MSRS	Aviasud Mistral 53	008	
D-MSRT	WDFL Dallach D4 Fascination BK	095	
D-MSRU	Platzer Kiebitz-B2	087	
D-MSRV	ATEC Zephyr 2000	SF 010202	
D-MSRW	Tecnam P.96 Golf 100	025	
D-MSSA	Fly Synthesis Storch	160.4	
D-MSSB(1)	Behlen Power-Trike Vampir	87023	
D-MSSB(2)	Flight Design CT-2K	98.06.01.34	
D-MSSC	Eipper Quicksilver GT-400	GT 2801326	
D-MSSE	Tecnam P.92 Echo	233	

D-MSSG	Klüver Twin Racer SX 16 Trike	503202	
D-MSSI	Evektor EV-97 Eurostar	2004-2121	
D-MSSJ	Tecnam P.96 Golf 100S	100	
D-MSSK	Tecnam P.96 Golf	034	
D-MSSL	Comco Ikarus Fox-C22C	9606-3717	
D-MSSO	Tecnam P.92 Echo	227	
D-MSSR	Euro-ALA Jet Fox 91D	0011	
D-MSSS	B&F Funk FK-12 Comet	012-029	
D-MSST	Fantasy Air Allegro SW	unkn	
D-MSSV	B&F Funk FK-9 Mk.IV	09-04U-246	
D-MSSW	WDFL Sunwheel DZ	044	
D-MSSX	DEA Yuma 912S	1970535	
D-MSSZ	TL Ultralight TL-232 Condor II	97 C 03	
D-MSTA	TL Ultralight TL-96 Star	00 S 67	
D-MSTB	HFL Stratos 300K	300-024K	
D-MSTC	HFL Stratos 300K	300-025K	
D-MSTD	HFL Stratos 300K	300-026K	
D-MSTE(1)	Warnke Skylight Trike	1010	
D-MSTE(2)	Fantasy Air Allegro	00-701	
D-MSTG	B&F Funk FK-9 TG Mk.II	083	
D-MSTH	Comco Ikarus C-42 Cyclone	9904-6166	
D-MSTI	Comco Ikarus Fox-C22	9309-3517	
D-MSTK	Ultraleichtverbund Bi 90	B987	
D-MSTM	Flight Design CT	99.09.06.70	
D-MSTO	NST Schwarze Trike	T285	
D-MSTP	Evektor EV-97 Eurostar	2001-1208	
D-MSTR	Remos G-3 Mirage	unkn	
D-MSTS	Remos G-3 Mirage	089	
D-MSTT	NST Minimum	M250	
D-MSTU	Comco Ikarus Fox-C22	9504-3644	
D-MSTW	Fisher FP-404 Classic	C084	
D-MSTZ	Loehle Sport Parasol	002	
D-MSUB(2)	Comco Ikarus Fox-C22C	9901-3741	
D-MSUE(1)	Kümmerle Mini-Fly-Set	1309/91-6	
D-MSUE(2)	B&F Funk FK-9 Mk.III	09-03-164	
D-MSUF	B&F Funk FK-12 Comet	012-007	
D-MSUG	Comco Ikarus C-42 Cyclone	unkn	
D-MSUN	Dallach Sunrise II	016	
D-MSUR(1)	Rans S-6 Coyote II	0391171	G-MWUM
D-MSUR(2)	Comco Ikarus C-42B	0410-6631	
D-MSUW	Comco Ikarus Fox-C22C	9804-3738	
D-MSVG	Aerostyle Breezer	007	
D-MSVS(2)	Air Création GTE 582 S	7974656042	
D-MSWA	WDFL Dallach D4 Fascination	058	
D-MSWB	Tecnam P.92 Echo 100S	575	
D-MSWC	Sky-Walker II	102	
D-MSWD	Sky-Walker 1+1	26134	
D-MSWE	Sky-Walker 1+1	26135	
D-MSWF	Sky-Walker 1+1	26136	
D-MSWG	Sky-Walker 1+1	26137	
D-MSWI	Sky-Walker 1+1	26138	
D-MSWJ	Comco Fox D	8506-FD28	
D-MSWK	Tecnam P.96 Golf	026	
D-MSWL	HFL Stratos 300K	300-016K	
D-MSWN	Sky-Walker 1+1	26141	
D-MSWO	Sky-Walker 1+1	26130	
D-MSWP	Sky-Walker II	144	
D-MSWQ	Sky-Walker II	145	
D-MSWR	Sky-Walker 1+1	26146	
D-MSWS	Tecnam P.96 Golf	064	
D-MSWT	Sky-Walker II	157	
D-MSWU	Sky-Walker II	212	
D-MSWW(2)	Aerostyle Breezer	045	
D-MSWX	Sky-Walker 1+1	26124	
D-MSWY	Sky-Walker 1+1	26125	
D-MSWZ	Sky-Walker 1+1	26126	
D-MSXS	Zenair CH-701D STOL	7-9224	
D-MSYK	Platzer Kiebitz-B6	162	
D-MSYW	Sky-Walker II	185	
D-MSYY	Albatros 64	127	
D-MSYZ	Lohle Mustang 5151	001	
D-MSZT	Tandem Air Sunny Sport	012.06.04 SuS	
D-MSZW	UPM Cobra Trike	920116	
D-MTAA(2)	Comco Ikarus Fox-C22	9706-3728	
D-MTAB	Pioneer Flightstar	535	
D-MTAC(2)	WDFL Sunwheel R	043	
D-MTAD(2)	Comco Ikarus Fox-C22C	97 . . -3730	
D-MTAE	Pioneer Flightstar	538	
D-MTAF	B&F Funk FK-9 Mk.III	09-03-116	
D-MTAG	Pioneer Flightstar	540	
D-MTAH(2)	Comco Ikarus Fox-C22	9205-3398	
D-MTAJ	Tandem Air Sunny s.b.s.	03.94	
D-MTAK	Pioneer Flightstar	544	
D-MTAL	Comco Ikarus C-42 Cyclone	9706-6038	
D-MTAM	WDFL Sunwheel	049	
D-MTAN	Pioneer Flightstar	553	
D-MTAP	B&F Funk FK-12 Comet	012-045	
D-MTAQ	Pioneer Flightstar	549	
D-MTAR	Pioneer Flightstar	550	
D-MTAS	Pioneer Flightstar	551	
D-MTAU	Pioneer Flightstar	543	
D-MTAV	Tandem Air Sunny Targa	002	
D-MTAW	Comco Ikarus C-42 Cyclone	unkn	
D-MTAX	Klüver Racer SX 12 Trike	078809	
D-MTAY	Comco Ikarus Fox-C22B	9404-3576	
D-MTAZ	Klüver Twin Racer Trike	233109	
D-MTBA(2)	Comco Ikarus Fox-C22C	9705-3727	

D-MTBB	B&F Funk FK-12 Comet	012-023	
D-MTBC	Warnke Skylight Trike	043	
D-MTBD	Comco Ikarus Fox-C22	940 .-3616	
D-MTBE	Comco Ikarus Fox-C22B	9409-3617	
D-MTBF	Comco Ikarus Fox-C22C	9607-3712	
D-MTBG	LO-120S	022	
D-MTBJ	NST Minimum	M536	
D-MTBK	Comco Ikarus Fox-C22	9306-3523	
D-MTBO	Flight Design CT	unkn	
D-MTBQ	Behlen Trike	87020	
D-MTBR	Platzer Kiebitz	226	
D-MTBS	LO-120	008A	
D-MTBT	B&F Funk FK-12 Comet	012-033	
D-MTBW	Comco Ikarus C-42 Cyclone	9809-6134	
D-MTBZ	Comco Ikarus C-42 Cyclone	0002-6255	
D-MTCA	Comco Ikarus Fox-C22C	9411-3615	
D-MTCB	Flight Design CT-2K	00.02.04.86	
D-MTCC	Flight Design CT	98.04.03.30	
D-MTCF	Tecnam P.92 Echo	546	
D-MTCH	Behlen Power Trike Vampir II	0025/83	
D-MTCI	Air-Light Wild Thing	97 02 009	
D-MTCR	Remos G.3 Mirage	148	
D-MTCT	Flight Design CT	98.09.01.37	
D-MTCV	Flight Design CT	98.02.02.22	
D-MTDC	Comco Ikarus C-42 Cyclone	9801-6060	
D-MTDD	B&F Funk FK-10	001	
D-MTDL	Flight Design CT	00.09.01.17	
D-MTDN	Comco Ikarus Fox-C22B	9110-3359	
D-MTDP	Rans S-6S Coyote II	0795860	
D-MTDX	Comco Ikarus Fox-C22B	940 .-3583	
D-MTEA	Comco Ikarus Fox-C22C	9509-3680	
D-MTEB	Comco Ikarus Fox-C22B	9601-3698	
D-MTEC	Light Aero Avid Flyer D	1358	
D-MTED	Sky-Walker II	262	
D-MTEE	Platzer Kiebitz B	unkn	
D-MTEF	Ikarusflug Eurofox	048098	
D-MTEG	Comco Ikarus Fox-C22C	9804-3737	
D-MTEH	Tecnam P.92 Echo 100S	120	
D-MTEI	Rans S-6 Coyote II	895879	
D-MTEJ	Rans S-6 Coyote II	10971174 S	
D-MTEK	Comco Ikarus C-42 Cyclone	9705-6028	
D-MTES	Air-Light Wild Thing	024	
D-MTEV	Klüver Twin Racer SX 16 Trike	836910	
D-MTEZ	Comco Ikarus C-42 Cyclone	0004-6232	
D-MTFC	Comco Ikarus Fox-C22B	9403-3557	
D-MTFD	B&F Funk FK-9 Mk.II	09-126	
D-MTFF	Comco Ikarus C-42 Cyclone	9711-6092	
D-MTFH	Comco Ikarus C-42 Cyclone	0010-6291	
D-MTFJ	Warnke Skylight Trike	SI 032	
D-MTFL	Comco Ikarus Fox-C22C	9611-3720	
D-MTFT	Rans S-12 XL Airaile	06950613	
D-MTFW	Aerostyle Breezer	030	
D-MTFZ	Tecnam P.96 Golf	021	
D-MTGA	Comco Ikarus Fox-C22	9109-3354	
D-MTGB	B&F Funk FK-9TG	041	
D-MTGE	Tecnam P.92 Echo	118	
D-MTGG	Remos G.3 Mirage	077	
D-MTGH	Comco Ikarus C-42 Cyclone	99035-6168	
D-MTGM	Seiffert Mini II	FO 10189	
D-MTGS	TL Ultralight TL-232 Condor Plus	02 C 01	
D-MTHA	Platzer Kiebitz B	086	
D-MTHE	Dallach Sunrise IIa	024	
D-MTHG	Bek Me 109R	007	
D-MTHH	Albatros SX	506	
D-MTHI	Eipper Quicksilver MX	4315	
D-MTHL	Comco Ikarus C-42 Cyclone	9709-6040	
D-MTHM	Comco Ikarus C-42 Cyclone	9805-6083	
D-MTHN	Aeropro Eurofox	08900	
D-MTHR	Zenair CH-601RD Zodiac	6-8052	
D-MTHS(1)	WDFL Sunwheel R	040	
D-MTHS(2)	Mark-Flug Seahawk UL-II	unkn	
D-MTHU	Albatros SX	505	
D-MTHW	Ultraleichtverbund Bi 90	21001	
D-MTIC	WDFL Dallach D4 Fascination (Was c/n 046)	052	
D-MTIF	Aviasud Mistral	012	
D-MTIG	Tecnam P.92 Echo	216	
D-MTII	Schönleber Trike Speed 14	011093	
D-MTIL	Comco Ikarus Fox-C22B	9406-3599	
D-MTIP	Klüver Kaiman Trike	076809	
D-MTIS	Tecnam P.92 Echo	288	
D-MTIT	Platzer Kiebitz-B2	080	
D-MTIW	Fantasy Air Allegro	01-408	
D-MTIY	WDFL Sunwheel R	012	
D-MTJG	Behlen Power-Trike II Hazard 15	93001	
D-MTJW	Dyn'Aero MCR-01	96	
D-MTKB	Flight Design CT	98.03.02.26	
D-MTKD	Aerospool WT9 Dynamic	DY00401	
D-MTKE	Aeropro Eurofox	09100	
D-MTKF	Pioneer Flightstar I	980316	
D-MTKG	Flight Design CT	unkn	D-MSKG
D-MTKH	EEL ULF-2	36	
D-MTKL	ATEC Zephyr 2000	ZP 540302	
D-MTKM	WDFL Dallach D4 Fascination	033	
D-MTKN	B&F Funk FK-9 Mk.II	008	
D-MTKR	Comco Ikarus Fox-C22	9209-3431	
D-MTLD	Schönleber DS Lotus KS 16 Trike	030589	
D-MTLF	Tecnam P.92 Echo	205	
D-MTLI	HFL Stratos 300	300-029	
D-MTLM	Tandem Air Sunny	27-92	
D-MTLU	TL Ultralight TL-232 Condor	98 C 07	
D-MTLW	B&F Funk FK-12 Comet	012-27	
D-MTMA	NST Minimum	M312	
D-MTMB	Comco Ikarus C-42 Cyclone	0009-6276	
D-MTMD	Aerospool WT9 Dynamic	DY00501	
D-MTMH	Striker Silence	001	
D-MTMM(2)	Comco Ikarus C-42 Cyclone	0008-6287	
D-MTMN	Striker Silence SA.180	03	
D-MTMO	Striker Silence SA.180	002	
D-MTMR	WDFL Dallach D4 Fascination	090	
D-MTMS	ATEC Zephyr	SF 110600	
D-MTMT	Zenair CH-601D Zodiac	6-8047/004 0097	
D-MTNS	Tecnam P.92 Echo 2000S	616	
D-MTNT	Comco Ikarus Fox-C22	950 .-3645	
D-MTOE	Evektor EV-97 Eurostar	2002-1404	
D-MTOF	Take Off Maximum Hazard 15M	T033080	
D-MTOG	Tecnam P.92 Echo	117	
D-MTOH	Technoflug Piccolo BM	103	
D-MTOL	Comco Ikarus C-42 Cyclone	9904-6186	
D-MTOM	Comco Ikarus C-42 Cyclone	0007-6271	
D-MTOP	B&F Funk FK-9 Mk.II	082	
D-MTOS	Tandem Air Sunny Sport	18.91	
D-MTOY(2)	Evektor EV.97 Eurostar	99 05 07	
D-MTPA	Sky-Walker 1+1	26117	
D-MTPB	Comco Ikarus C-42B	0409-6628	
D-MTPC	Tecnam P.92 Echo	175	
D-MTPK	B&F Funk FK-9 Mk.III	09-106	
D-MTPS	Comco Ikarus Fox-C22	9501-3655	
D-MTRA	Aeropro Eurofox	09800	
D-MTRB	Comco Ikarus C-42B	0303-6518	
D-MTRD	Comco Ikarus C-42 Cyclone	0002-6228	
D-MTRH	Comco Ikarus C-42 Cyclone	9809-6128	
D-MTRI	Ikarusflug Eurofox Pro	027096	
D-MTRL	Comco Ikarus C-42 Cyclone	9607-6003	
D-MTRS	Eipper Quicksilver	3898	
D-MTRT	Comco Ikarus Fox-C22	9407-3586	
D-MTRV	Comco Ikarus C-42B	0211-6498	
D-MTRW	B&F Funk FK-9 Mk.II	014	
D-MTSA	Solid Air Twin Diamant Trike	002	
D-MTSB	B&F Funk FK-9	035	
D-MTSD	Murphy Renegade Spirit	483	
D-MTSH	Comco Ikarus C-42B	0404-6601	
D-MTSI	Comco Ikarus C-42 Cyclone	9905-6188	
D-MTSK	Fantasy Air Allegro	00-402	
D-MTSL	Remos G.3 Mirage	088	
D-MTSM	Comco Ikarus Fox-C22B	9406-3594	
D-MTSS	Rans S-6 Coyote II	0395782	
D-MTST	Behlen Power-Trike	84003	
D-MTSV	Air-Light Wild Thing	068	
D-MTTA	Pioneer Flightstar	385	
D-MTTF	Pioneer Flightstar	379	
D-MTTM	Evektor EV-97 Eurostar	2000-0610	
D-MTTP(2)	Rans S-6ES Coyote II	019811991 ES	
D-MTTR	Ultraleichtverbund Bi 90	3916759	
D-MTTS	Air-Light Wild Thing	055	
D-MTTV	Comco Ikarus Fox-C22	9208-3419	
D-MTUB	Comco Ikarus C-42 Cyclone	0003-6247	
D-MTUD	B&F Funk FK-6	002	
D-MTUH	Platzer Kiebitz	176	
D-MTUI	Tecnam P.92 Echo	261	
D-MTUS	Comco Ikarus Fox-C22B	9507-3666	
D-MTUT	Aerostyle Breezer	32	
D-MTVM	WDFL Sunwheel R	016	
D-MTVV	Comco Ikarus C-42 Cyclone	9705-6061	
D-MTVW	Comco Ikarus C-42 Cyclone	0101-6279	
D-MTWD	Ikarusflug Eurofox Pro	054098	
D-MTWE	Sky-Walker II	396	
D-MTWF	Comco Ikarus C-42 Cyclone	0109-6329	
D-MTWI	Kolb Twinstar Mk.III	M III-136	
D-MTWL	Comco Ikarus Fox-C22B	9404-3561	
D-MTWO	WDFL Sunwheel	022	
D-MTWP	Comco Ikarus C-42 Cyclone	9908-6198	
D-MTWR	Comco Ikarus C-42 Cyclone	9903-6173	
D-MTWS	Comco Ikarus C-42 Cyclone	9908-6202	
D-MTWT	Air-Light Wild Thing	001	
D-MTWZ(2)	Drachenstudio Piccolo	003	
D-MTZZ	Comco Ikarus C-42 Cyclone	0105-6352	
D-MUAB	Sky-Walker II	500	
D-MUAC	Fisher FP-404 Classic	4065	
D-MUAE	Comco Ikarus Fox-C22	8812-3183	
D-MUAG	Comco Ikarus C-42 Cyclone	9803-6138	
D-MUAK	Air-Light Wild Thing	044	
D-MUAS	Aerostyle Breezer	024	
D-MUAT	Platzer Kiebitz	219	
D-MUAZ	Behlen Power Trike II	91023	
D-MUBA	Avid Mk.IV STOL	unkn	
D-MUBB	Warnke Skylight Trike	036	
D-MUBF	Rans S-10S Sakota	1189068	
D-MUBI	Rans S-12 Airaile	01970771	
D-MUBK	Comco Ikarus Fox-C22	9403-3548	
D-MUBS	Air-Light Wild Thing	015	
D-MUBT	Comco Ikarus Fox-C22B	9404-3563	
D-MUCB	Sky-Walker II	309	
D-MUCE	Air-Light Wild Thing	022	
D-MUCH	Comco Ikarus Fox-C22	9508-3687	

D-MUCI	WDFL Sunwheel R	018	
D-MUCK	Scheibe Uli 1	5215	
D-MUCL	Aerospool WT9 Dunamic	DY053-2004	
D-MUCS	Remos G.3 Mirage	113	
D-MUCZ	Bek Me 109 R	004	
D-MUDD	Fair Fax Trike Euro III	1712	
D-MUDI	Klüver Bison Profil 19 Trike	M3485733	
D-MUDK	Comco Ikarus C-42 Cyclone	0103-6307	
D-MUDM	UPM-Trike	880051	
D-MUDO	Platzer Motte B-2	49	
D-MUDP	Comco Ikarus Fox-C22	8905-3196	
D-MUEC	Evektor EV-97 Eurostar	990403	
D-MUED(2)	B&F Funk FK-12 Comet	012-022	
D-MUEE	Comco Ikarus C-42B	0407-6613	
D-MUEF	Ikarusflug Eurofox Pro	050098	
D-MUEK	Ikarusflug Eurofox Bugrad	045098	
D-MUEN	Sky-Walker 1+1	156	
D-MUEP	ATEC Zephyr	070199A	
D-MUES	NST Minimum Santana Trike	M329	
D-MUFD	Comco Ikarus Fox-C22	9503-3631	
D-MUFE	Comco Ikarus Fox-C22	9303-3495	
D-MUFF	Comco Ikarus C-42 Cyclone	0010-6289	
D-MUFG	Comco Ikarus C-42 Cyclone	9704-6013	
D-MUFK	B&F Funk FK-9TG Mk.III	09-03-096	
D-MUFL	Light Aero Avid Flyer	1457D	
D-MUFM	Tecnam P.92 Echo	320	
D-MUFN	ATEC Zephyr	Z 500202A	
D-MUFO	Comco Ikarus Fox-C22	8709-3083	
D-MUFS	B&F Funk FK-9 Mk.III	09-03-099	
D-MUFW	Comco Ikarus C-42B	0310-6579	
D-MUGH	Comco Ikarus C-42 Cyclone	0106-6354	
D-MUGI	ATEC Zephyr 2000	SF 070301	
D-MUGK	Platzer Kiebitz-B2	117	
D-MUGL	Fantasy Air Allegro 2000	00-407	
D-MUGO	Comco Ikarus C-42	0206-6422	
D-MUGS	WDFL Sunwheel R	041	
D-MUGY	B&F Funk FK-9 Mk.III	09-03-186	
D-MUHA	Comco Ikarus C-42 Cyclone	9906-6194	
D-MUHF	Comco Ikarus Fox-C22	9403-3584	
D-MUHG	Remos G-3 Mirage	048	
D-MUHI	Ultraleichtverbund Bi 90	21000	
D-MUHK	Light Aero Avid Flyer STOL	1521D	
D-MUHL(2)	Mitchell Wing B	AB-01	
D-MUHR	Air-Light Wild Thing	003	
D-MUHS	Rans S-10S Sakota	0790109	
D-MUHU	Ultravia Pélican Sport 450S	20017	
D-MUID	Comco Ikarus C-42 Cyclone	9612-6014	
D-MUIF(2)	Ikarusflug Eurofox Basic	033097	
D-MUJF	Euro-ALA Jet Fox 97	unkn	
D-MUKA	Flight Design CT-2K	02.07.03.28	
D-MUKB	Tecnam P.92 Echo 100S	506	
D-MUKD	Comco Ikarus Fox-C22B	9702-3704	
D-MUKE	Fair Fax Trike	015	
D-MUKF	Air-Light Wild Thing	034	
D-MUKG	Comco Ikarus C-42 Cyclone	9909-6199	
D-MUKH	Comco Ikarus C-42	0204-6415	
D-MUKI	Schmidtler Ranger M Trike	18-33	
D-MUKK	Warnke Puma Sprint Trike	D006	
D-MUKL(1)	Scheibe Uli 1	5212	
D-MUKL(2)	WDFL Dallach D4 Fascination BK	071	
D-MUKM	EEL ULF-2	007	
D-MUKO	Evektor EV-97 Eurostar	2000-0811	
D-MUKS	Urban Air UFM-13 Lambada	20/13	
D-MUKU	Micro Star	01	
D-MUKW	Rans S-6 Coyote II	1294702	N8046U
D-MUKY	Moskito Ib	018	
D-MULA	Scheibe Uli I	5214	
D-MULB	UPM Cobra Trike	900092	
	(Same c/n also quoted for D-MBOY)		
D-MULE	Light Aero Avid Flyer D	1402	
D-MULG	Zenair CH-601D Zodiac	6-9225	
D-MULI (1)	Scheibe Uli 1	5203	
D-MULI (2)	Comco Ikarus C-42B	0403-6587	
D-MULJ	Platzer Kiebitz-B4	108	
D-MULK	Comco Ikarus C-42 Cyclone	9706-6043	
D-MULL	TL Ultralight TL-232 Condor Plus	01 C 01	
D-MULN	Klüver Twin Racer Trike	232109	
D-MULO	LO-120S	015A	
D-MULP	Comco Ikarus C-42 Cyclone	9708-6052	
D-MULR	Ultraleichtverbund Bi 90	940	
D-MULT	NST Minimum	359	
D-MULV	Remos G3 Mirage	072	
D-MULW	Comco Ikarus C-42 Cyclone	0001-6220	
D-MULY	Tecnam P.96 Golf	163	
D-MULZ	Comco Ikarus C-42B	0302-6524	
D-MUMA	Klüver Twin Racer SX 16 Trike	117106	
D-MUMD	Comco Ikarus C-42 Cyclone	9809-6143	
D-MUMG	Air-Light Wild Thing	065	
D-MUMI	Tecnam P.92 Echo	295	
D-MUML	Evektor EV-97 Eurostar	2001-1202	
D-MUMM	WDFL Dallach D4 Fascination	045	
D-MUMO	Lohle Mustang 5151	006	
D-MUMS	Platzer Kiebitz-B8	107	
D-MUMU	B&F Funk FK-9 Mk.II	019	
D-MUMY	Behlen Power-Trike II Focus 20	85029	
D-MUNA	Schönleber DS Speed KS 14	L01039093	
D-MUND	Platzer Motte B3	55	
D-MUNI	Bobcat	09AD91	
D-MUNK	Comco Ikarus C-42 Cyclone	9702-6031	
D-MUNO	Comco Ikarus Fox-C22B	9507-3665	
D-MUNY	Air-Light Wild Thing	053	
D-MUON	Klüver Twin Racer Quartz SX 16	504202	
D-MUPA	Tandem Air Sunny s.b.s.	SuS-V-4.95	
D-MUPF	WDFL Sunwheel R	031	
D-MUPH	Flight Design CT	unkn	
D-MUPL	Ultravia Pélican Sport 450S	20026/755	
D-MUPW	B&F Funk FK-9 Mk.II	088	
D-MUPZ	Tecnam P.96 Golf	022	
D-MUQI	Evektor EV.97 Eurostar	98 03 05	
D-MURA(1)	Warnke Skylight Trike	S 1019	
D-MURA(2)	Aeropro Eurofox	11001	
D-MURB	Mahe Scout	013	
D-MURC	B&F Funk FK-9 Mk.III	09-03-123	
D-MURD	Platzer Kiebitz-B9	160	
D-MURE	Scheibe Uli 1	5218	
D-MURG	TL Ultralight TL-96 Star	01 S 93	
D-MURI	Scheibe Uli 1	5213	
D-MURJ	Comco Ikarus C-42 Cyclone	9803-6103	
D-MURK	Comco Ikarus Fox-C22	9304-3494	
D-MURO	Comco Ikarus C-42B	0201-6317	
D-MURR	Sky-Walker 1+1	26116	
D-MURT	Comco Ikarus Fox-C22	9202-3 . . .	
D-MURX	Scheibe Uli 1	5220	
D-MUSA	Rans S-12 Airaile	0294479	
D-MUSB	Dyn'Aero MCT-01 ULC	183	
D-MUSC	Comco Ikarus Fox-C22	9006-3270	
D-MUSD	Platzer Kiebitz-B	15	
D-MUSE	Scheibe Ultra Uli 2	3303	
D-MUSH	Comco Ikarus C-42 Cyclone	0108-6411	
D-MUSI	Tecnam P.92 Echo	339	
D-MUSJ	ASO Viper Hazard 15M Trike	1102502	
D-MUSK	Fantasy Air Allegro	00-405	
D-MUSL	Comco Ikarus Fox-C22	9209-3464	
D-MUSM	Comco Ikarus Fox-C22	9502-3632	
D-MUSS	Behlen Power-Trike Vampir II	85031	
D-MUST	Behlen Power-Trike	88026	
D-MUSV	SFS Vagabund	6	
D-MUSW (1)	Schmidtler Enduro Trike	F03/86	
D-MUSW(2)	Tecnam P.92 Echo 100S	588	
D-MUTA	Platzer Kiebitz-B8	042	
D-MUTB	Remos G.3 Mirage	99	
D-MUTC	Remos G.3 Mirage	107	
D-MUTF	Tandem Air Sunny s.b.s.	SuS 04.96	
D-MUTI	Remos G.3 Mirage	94	
D-MUTJ	Dyn'Aero MCR-01 ULC	110	
D-MUTS	Schmidtler Ranger M Trike	0021	
D-MUTT	Air-Light Wild Thing	013	
D-MUTV	Platzer Kiebitz-B8	110	
D-MUUR	Air-Light Wild Thing	2000-05-070	
D-MUUU(2)	Comco Ikarus C-42 Cyclone	9810-6156	
D-MUVE	WDFL Sunwheel	051	
D-MUVI	Tecnam P.92 Echo	210	
D-MUVO	Bobcat	KA-1	
D-MUVR	Platzer Kiebitz B	137	
D-MUWE	ATEC Zephyr	ZP 390400	
D-MUWH	Comco Ikarus C-42 Cyclone	0104-6336	
D-MUWI	TL Ultralight TL-2000 Sting	04 ST 67	
D-MUWM	Comco Ikarus C-42 Cyclone	0105-6337	
D-MUWP	Urban Air UFM-13 Lambada	16/13	
D-MUWT	Air-Light Wild Thing	049	
D-MUWW	Tecnam P.92 Echo 100S	431	
D-MUXI	Remos Gemini Ultra	029	
D-MUXL	Tecnam P.96GGolf 100S	118	
D-MUXS	Comco Ikarus Fox-C22	940 .-3589	
D-MUXX	WDFL Dallach D4 Fascination	050	
D-MUXY	Tecnam P.92 Echo	562	
D-MUZE	Schmidtler Enduro Trike	02002	
D-MUZI	WDFL Dallach D4 Fascination BK	082	
D-MVAB	Comco Ikarus Fox-C22B	940 .-3601	
D-MVAC	Comco Ikarus Fox-C22	9501-3614	
D-MVAD	Platzer Kiebitz-B9	161	
D-MVAE	Tecnam P.92 Echo	234	
D-MVAG	Saurier Flug Vagabond	unkn	
D-MVAK	Comco Ikarus C-42 Cyclone	0010-6288	
D-MVAL	Rans S-6S Coyote II	1195897 S	
D-MVAM	Tecnam P.92 Echo 100S	487	
D-MVAR	Comco Ikarus C-42 Cyclone	0004-6246	
D-MVAS	Comco Ikarus C-42 Cyclone	9906-6184	
D-MVBA	WDFL Dallach D4 Fascination	048	
D-MVBB	WDFL Dallach D4 Fascination	032	
D-MVBD	ASO Viper Trike	22028202	
D-MVBF(2)	Platzer Kiebitz-B2	101	
D-MVBG	Aviasud AE-209 Albatros	940550812	
D-MVBL	Klüver Bison Trike	112706	
D-MVBM	WDFL Dallach D4 Fascination	041	
D-MVBP	Sky Walker II	384	
D-MVBR	Fläming Air FA-01 Smaragd	06/04	
D-MVBS	Scheibe SF-40	3104	
D-MVBU	Comco Ikarus Fox-C22	9407-3588	
D-MVCA	Flight Design CT	00.06.02.00	
D-MVCC	Flight Design CT	00.01.01.00	
D-MVCF	Flight Design CT	98.12.02.43	
D-MVCI	Remos G.3 Mirage	082	
D-MVCO	Urban Air UFM-10 Samba	7/10	

D-MVCT	Flight Design CT (Cancelled?)	CT 005
D-MVCY	Tandem Air Sunny Targa	TA-011.93
D-MVDC	Comco Ikarus Fox-C22	9205-3407
D-MVDH	Flight Design CT-2K	03.05.01.20
D-MVDO	B&F Funk FK-9 TG Mk.II	045
D-MVDV	TLUltralight TL-96 Star	00 S 96
D-MVEB	Comco Ikarus C-42 Cyclone	9811-6148
D-MVEC	Comco Ikarus C-42 Cyclone	0006-6237
D-MVEE	TL Ultralight TL-96 Star	00 S 60
D-MVEF	Ikarusflug Eurofox	074099
D-MVEK	Tecnam P.92 Echo 100S	483
D-MVEL	Air-Light Wild Thing	026
D-MVER	Comco Ikarus Fox-C22	9101-3300/3511
D-MVET	Comco Ikarus C-42 Cyclone	9610-6053
D-MVFB	Comco Ikarus Fox-C22	9105-3332
D-MVFC	Kappa KP-2U Sova	27/99
D-MVFF	Comco Ikarus Sherpa	8403-1053
D-MVFK	B&F Funk FK-14 Polaris	unkn
D-MVFL	Comco Ikarus Fox-C22B	9506-3664
D-MVFP	Rans S-6 Coyote II	0994675
D-MVGG	Urban Air UFM-13 Lambada	17/13
D-MVGS	Air-Light Wild Thing	029
D-MVGW	SFS Vagabund	002
D-MVHB	WDFL Dallach D4 Fascination	021
D-MVHE	WDFL Dallach D4 Fascination	026
D-MVHF	Evektor EV-97 Eurostar	2001-1010
D-MVHG	Pioneer Flightstar I	990601
D-MVHM	Dyn'Aero MCR-01 UL	109
D-MVHP	B&F Funk FK-9	090
D-MVHR	Comco Ikarus C-42 Cyclone	9804-6133
D-MVHS	Tecnam P.96 Golf 100S	060
D-MVHW	Evektor EV-97 Eurostar	2001-1212
D-MVIC	Platzer Kiebitz-B6	165
D-MVIL	Rans S-6 Coyote II	1295914
D-MVIP	Klüver Racer SX 12 Trike	641907
D-MVIR	Comco Ikarus Fox-C22B	9405-3564
D-MVIS	Comco Ikarus Fox-C22	9501-3633
D-MVJB	Comco Ikarus C-42 Cyclone	9708-6049
D-MVJL	SGAviation Storm	unkn
D-MVJR	Aeropro Eurofox	078099
D-MVKA	Comco Ikarus C-42 Cyclone	9712-6041
D-MVKB	Platzer Motte B2	58
D-MVKM	Remos G-3 Mirage	052
D-MVKO	Sky-Walker II	382
D-MVKR	Sky-Walker II	268
D-MVKV	Tecnam P.92 Echo	164
D-MVLA	Aeropro Eurofox	09500
D-MVLL	Comco Ikarus Fox-C22	950 .-3647
D-MVLO	Zenair CH-601D Zodiac	6-3790
D-MVLP	Comco Ikarus Fox-C22	9109-3351
D-MVMC	Aeropro Eurofox	11601
D-MVML	B&F Funk FK-12 Comet	012-002
D-MVMM	WDFL Dallach D4 Fascination	unkn
D-MVMS	Comco Ikarus C-42 Cyclone	0111-6344
D-MVMV	Zenair CH-601D Zodiac	6-3788
D-MVNA	SG Aviation Storm 280	004
D-MVNE	Light Aero Avid Mk.IV	1496
D-MVNO	Comco Ikarus Fox-C22C	9607-3713
D-MVOC	Zenair CH-701D STOL	7-3972
D-MVOE	WDFL Fascination	003
D-MVOG	Wisch Star-Trike Profil 17M	09870020
D-MVOI	Comco Ikarus C-42 Cyclone	9706-6033
D-MVOK	Rans S-12 Airaile	0593416
D-MVOL	Rans S-7 Courier	0597219
D-MVOM	Scheibe SF-40	3103
D-MVPG	Comco Ikarus C-42 Cyclone	0001-6239
D-MVPI	WDFL Dallach D4 Fascination BK	089
D-MVPS	Comco Ikarus C-42 Cyclone	0111-6426
D-MVRA	Comco Ikarus C-42 Cyclone	9808-6114
D-MVRH	Zenair CH-601D Zodiac	6-9193
D-MVRK	SFS Vagabund	003
D-MVRL	Aerospool WT9 Dynamic	DY01002
D-MVRR	Aeropro Eurofox	11101
D-MVRS	Tecnam P.92 Echo	155
D-MVSB	Aeropro Eurofox	096-00
D-MVSE	WDFL Dallach D4 Fascination (Cancelled)	017
D-MVSK	ASO Viper Hazard 15 Trike	15117791
D-MVSL	Comco Ikarus C-42 Cyclone	0102-6309
D-MVSP	Comco Ikarus C-42 Cyclone	0202-6432
D-MVSR	Tecnam P.92 Echo 2000RG	unkn
D-MVST	Tandem Air Sunny s.b.s.	SuS 06.96
D-MVTT	Tandem Air Sunny	0010301Sp
D-MVVA	Klüver Racer Quartz SX 12 Trike	734011
D-MVVB	AGREX	001
D-MVVH	Comco Ikarus Fox-C22B	9 . . .-3702
D-MVVR(2)	Flight Design CT	99.02.01.45
D-MVVS	Tandem Air Sunny Sport	008.07.03 S-s
D-MVVT	B&F Funk FK-14 Polaris	014-017
D-MVVV	Aviasud Mistral BRD	125
D-MVVX	Schmidtler Enduro Focus 18M Trike	040385
D-MVWR	Comco Ikarus C-42B	0204-6438
D-MVWS	Comco Ikarus C-42 Cyclone	9906-6169
D-MVXY	NST Minimum	460
D-MVYY	Ikarusflug Eurofox	022096
D-MWAA	Remos G-3 Mirage	035
D-MWAB	Comco Ikarus C-42 Cyclone	0002-6254
D-MWAC	Remos Gemini Ultra	004

D-MWAD	Behlen Power-Trike Hazard 15	92031	
D-MWAE	Platzer Kiebitz-B2	133	
D-MWAF	Take Off Maximum Trike	3059	
D-MWAG	Platzer Kiebitz-B2	030	
D-MWAH	Fisher FP-404 Classic	C087	
D-MWAI	Comco Ikarus Fox-C22C	9708-3732	
D-MWAJ	Euro-ALA Jet Fox 97	018	
D-MWAK	B&F Funk FK-9 Mk.II	052	
D-MWAL	Ultraleichtverbund Bi 90	9234016831	
D-MWAM	Comco Ikarus C-42 Cyclone	9807-6130	
D-MWAN	Rans S-12XL Airaile	08950641	
D-MWAP	Flight Design CT2SW	04.05.04	
D-MWAR	Air-Light Wild Thing WT.01	97 02 017	
D-MWAS	Flightstar II	030402	
D-MWAT	Comco Ikarus C-42 Cyclone	0007-6269	
D-MWAV	NST Minimum	M472	
D-MWAW	Comco Ikarus Fox-C22	9502-3613	
D-MWAY	Flight Design CT-2K	01.06.04.14	
D-MWBA	Weedhopper	1006	D-MDJK?
D-MWBB	Ikarusflug Eurofox	030097	
D-MWBC	Weedhopper	0999	
D-MWBE	Funbird	1005/84	
D-MWBF	WDFL Dallach D4 Fascination	046	
D-MWBH	Funbird	0143/82	
D-MWBI	Comco Ikarus C-42 Cyclone	0110-6339	
D-MWBK	Comco Fox	040	
D-MWBL	Tecnam P.92 Echo 100S	489	
D-MWBM	Comco Ikarus Fox-C22C	9710-3733	
D-MWBO	Comco Ikarus C-42	0203-6448	
D-MWBR	Murphy Renegade Spirit	607	
D-MWBS	Fläming Air FA-01 Smaragd	03/04	
D-MWBT	Tecnam P.92 Echo	374	
D-MWBV	Rans S-7 Courier	0193103	
D-MWBW	Comco Ikarus Fox-C22 (sold as CS-U . .)	9408-3612	
D-MWCA	Fair Fax DR Hazard 15M Trike	D007	
D-MWCB	Comco Ikarus Fox-C22	9408-3611	
D-MWCC	Comco Ikarus Fox-C22B	9506-3675	
D-MWCI	Remos G.3 Mirage	081	
D-MWCO	WDFL Dallach D4 Fascination	039	
D-MWCW	Evektor EV-97 Eurostar	2001-0910	
D-MWDA	WDFL Sunwheel R	001	
D-MWDB	LO-120S	025	
D-MWDE	Comco Ikarus C-42 Cyclone	0105-6303	
D-MWDG	Rans S-6 Coyote II XL	1294707	
D-MWDH	WDFL Dallach D4 Fascination	005	
D-MWDI	Platzer Kiebitz-B4	175	
D-MWDK	Remos Gemini Ultra	E12.013	
D-MWDL	Zenair CH-601D Zodiac	6-3653	
D-MWDR	Tecnam P.92 Echo	277	
D-MWDT	TL Ultralight TL-232 Condor Plus	AB 07	
D-MWEA	Rans S-6 Coyote II	0895876	
D-MWEB	Tecnam P.92 Echo 100S	561	
D-MWEC	Comco Ikarus C-42 Cyclone	9806-6098	
D-MWEF	Hummer	15184	
D-MWEG	WDFL Dallach D4 Fascination	105	
D-MWEH	Fisher Super Koala	Ei-10	
D-MWEI	Schönleber DS Trike 40kw	030389	
D-MWEL	Platzer Kiebitz	221	
D-MWEM	Comco Ikarus C-42B	0210-6505	
D-MWEP	Comco Ikarus Fox-C22B	9 . . .-3683	
D-MWER	Comco Ikarus Fox-C22	9010-3296	
D-MWES	B&F Funk FK-9 Mk.III	09-109	
D-MWET	Air-Light Wild Thing	WT01 99 04 048	
D-MWEV	Evektor EV-97 Eurostar	990509	
D-MWEW	B&F Funk FK-12 Comet	012-014	
D-MWFG	Comco Ikarus C-42 Cyclone	9805-6096	
D-MWFH	Comco Ikarus C-42 Cyclone	9903-6174	
D-MWFI	Comco Ikarus C-42	0201-6427	
D-MWFN	B&F Funk FK-9 Mk3 Club	unkn	
D-MWFR	WDFL Dallach D4 Fascination	040	
D-MWFS	Comco Ikarus C-42 Cyclone	9811-6099	
D-MWFT	Zenair CH-601D Zodiac	6-3529/014 0097	
D-MWFW	Roman-Weller UW-9 Sprint	001	
D-MWFZ	Loehle Sport Parasol	001	
D-MWGB(2)	Comco Ikarus C-42 Cyclone	9801-6063	
D-MWGE	B&F Funk FK-9 Mk.II	069	
D-MWGF	Platzer Kiebitz-B9	202	
D-MWGG	Remos G.3 Mirage	084	
D-MWGH	B&F Funk FK-9	054	
D-MWGJ	Comco Ikarus C-42 Cyclone	9810-6140	
D-MWGN	Platzer Kiebitz-B9	140	
D-MWGS	Remos Gemini Ultra (W/o 6.3.02)	009	
D-MWGT	Platzer Kiebitz-B6	182	
D-MWGW	Air-Light Wild Thing	042	
D-MWHA	Remos Gemini Ultra	030	
D-MWHB	Take Off Maximum Lotus 18	021129	
D-MWHC	Comco Ikarus C-42 Cyclone	9810-6136	
D-MWHD	UPM Cobra Trike	920117	
D-MWHE	Murphy Renegade Spirit	608	
D-MWHF	ATEC Zephyr	unkn	
D-MWHG	MKB Enduro Focus 18 Trike	030886	
D-MWHH	NST Minimum	M245	
D-MWHI	Sky-Walker II	271	
D-MWHJ	Remos Gemini Ultra	E07.08	
D-MWHK	Comco Ikarus C-42 Cyclone	9809-6145	
D-MWHL	EEL ULF-2	20	
D-MWHM	ASO 26 Storch 582	160.2	

D-MWHN	TL Ultralight TL-96 Star	00 S 52	
D-MWHO	Ultraleichtverbund Bi 90	662	
D-MWHR	Tandem Air Sunny Sport	49.93	
D-MWHS	ICP MXP-740V Savannah	10-99-50-132	
D-MWHU	Denney Kitfox IV	1860	
D-MWHV(2)	B&F Funk FK-9 Mk.III	09-03U-197	
D-MWHW	Comco Ikarus Fox-C22	9203-3373	
D-MWHY	Murphy Renegade	548	
D-MWIE	Platzer Kiebitz-B2	032	
D-MWIF	Ikarusflug Eurofox	95017	
D-MWII	WDFL Dallach D4 Fascination	024	
D-MWIK	Fair Fax Trike	016	
D-MWIL	Air-Light Wild Thing	056	
D-MWIP	Tandem Air Sunny 912	TA-020	
D-MWIR(1)	Behlen Power-Trike II	95007	
D-MWIR(2)	Comco Ikarus C-42	0203-6437	
D-MWIT	Cosmos Bi 90 Phase II/ Chronos 14	4017032	
D-MWIW	Take Off Maximum Hazard 15	037110	
D-MWJA	Zenair CH-601D Zodiac	6-3520	
D-MWJB	Remos Gemini Ultra	E13.014	
D-MWJF	Comco Ikarus Fox-C22B	9902-3742	
D-MWJH	Comco Ikarus C-42 Cyclone	9904-6179	
D-MWJN	Ultraleichtverbund Bi 90	735	
D-MWJO	WDFL Sunwheel	029	
D-MWKA	Comco Ikarus Fox-C22B	9504-3659	
D-MWKB	HFL Stratos IIe	IIe-010	D-MMDH?
D-MWKD	Platzer Kiebitz-B8	027	
D-MWKE	Comco Ikarus Fox-C22	9204-3393	
D-MWKF	Platzer Kiebitz-B8	130	
D-MWKG	Comco Ikarus Fox-C22B	9504-3660	
D-MWKH(1)	Dallach Sunrise II	019	
D-MWKH(2)	Comco Ikarus C-42B	0206-6449	
D-MWKJ(1)	WDFL Dallach D4 Fascination (Cancelled)	007	
D-MWKJ(2)	Aerospool WT9 Dynamic	DY01602	
D-MWKL	Comco Ikarus C-42 Cyclone	9804-6093	
D-MWKM	Rans S-6 Coyote II	11981281	
D-MWKN	Murphy Renegade	517	
D-MWKO	Comco Ikarus Fox-C22	9501-3610	
D-MWKP	Flight Design CT	99.12.02.76	
D-MWKS(1)	ASO Viper Hazard 15 Trike	1234	
D-MWKS(2)	Euro-ALA Jet Fox 97	027-2	
D-MWKT	Comco Ikarus Fox-C22	95013626	
D-MWKU	Comco Ikarus Fox-C22	9 . . .-3649	
D-MWKV	Platzer Kiebitz-B6	46	
D-MWKW	Platzer Kiebitz-B4	126	
D-MWLA(1)	Pioneer Flightstar	683	
D-MWLA(2)	Comco Ikarus C-42B	0410-6637	
D-MWLB	Zenair CH-601D Zodiac	6-3451/019 0097	
D-MWLC	Comco Ikarus Fox-C22	9501-3627	
D-MWLD	Comco Ikarus Fox-C22	9205-3408	
D-MWLF	Comco Ikarus Fox-C22	9505-3651	
D-MWLG	Remos G.3 Mirage	090	
D-MWLH	TL Ultralight TL-96 Star	01 S 108	
D-MWLI	Loehle Mustang 5151	009	
D-MWLL	ATEC Zephyr 2000	SF 080301	
D-MWLM	Comco Ikarus Fox-C22	9501-3628	
D-MWLR	Comco Ikarus Fox-C22	9503-3650	
D-MWLS	Comco Ikarus C-42 Cyclone	9904-6158	
D-MWLT	Klüver Bison Trike	22/708	
D-MWLU	WDFL Dallach D4 Fascination BK	094	
D-MWLV	Comco Ikarus C-42 Cyclone	9907-6197	
D-MWLZ	Comco Ikarus Fox-C22	9310-3533	
D-MWMA	Flight Design CT	97.11.03.13	
D-MWMB	Comco Ikarus C-42 Cyclone	0106-6330	
D-MWMC	Comco Ikarus C-42 Cyclone	9904-6177	
D-MWMF	Rans S-12 Airaile	1292358	
D-MWMG	Loehle Mustang 5151	008	
D-MWMH	Sky-Walker II	511	
D-MWMI	Platzer Kiebitz-B8	122	
D-MWMK	TL Ultralight TL-96 Star	99 S 31	
D-MWML	Platzer Kiebitz-B9	098	
D-MWMM	Comco Ikarus C-42 Cyclone	0004-6230	
D-MWMN	Mantel Mono-Dragster	M870226	
D-MWMS(1)	NST Minimum	M504	
D-MWMS(2)	Flight Design CT	00.04.03.93	
D-MWMW	TL Ultralight TL-2000 Sting	unkn	
D-MWMZ	Light Aero Avid Flyer IV	877	
D-MWNL	Comco Ikarus C-42 Cyclone	0009-6295	
D-MWNM	WDFL Sunwheel	027	
D-MWNN	Rans S-6ES Coyote II	1292414	
D-MWOB	Comco Ikarus Fox-C22	9 . . .-3531	
D-MWOC	Comco Ikarus Fox-C22	9 . . .-3329	
D-MWOD	Platzer Kiebitz	206	
D-MWOF	Flight Design CT2SW	04.06.04	
D-MWOK	Tecnam P.92 Echo 100S	472	
D-MWOL	WDFL Dallach D4 Fascination	001	
D-MWOP(1)	Behlen Power-Trike	87013	
D-MWOP(2)	Comco Ikarus C-42 Cyclone	0103-6315	
D-MWOR	Comco Ikarus Fox-C22	9110-3358	
D-MWOT	Comco Ikarus C-42 Cyclone	9806-6109	
D-MWOW	Comco Ikarus C-42 Cyclone	0009-6270	
D-MWPA	Remos G.3 Mirage	080	
D-MWPB	Comco Ikarus Fox II Doppel	8606-3022	
D-MWPE	TL Ultralight TL-96 Star	01 S 86	
D-MWPF	Platzer Motte	037	
D-MWPG	Comco Ikarus C-42 Cyclone	9711-6065	
D-MWPH	Comco Ikarus C-42 Cyclone	0003-6244	
D-MWPI	Comco Ikarus C-42 Cyclone (floatplane)	unkn	
D-MWPL	Murphy Renegade II	549	
D-MWPM	TL Ultralight TL-232 Condor Plus	98 C 10	
D-MWPN	Flight Design CT	98.02.02.22	
D-MWPP	Sky-Walker II	254	
D-MWPS	Flight Design CT	00.11.02.22	
D-MWPT	Malchow HK-12	02	
D-MWPW	Aviasud AE-209 Albatros	940550802	
D-MWRA	Rans S-6ES Coyote II	595817ES	
D-MWRB	Klüver Twin Racer Quartz SX 16	695010	
D-MWRC	Comco Ikarus C-42 Cyclone	9810-6142	
D-MWRD(1)	Tecnam P.92 Echo (Cancelled)	204	
D-MWRD(2)	Tecnam P.96 Golf 100S	072	
D-MWRF	Comco Ikarus C-42 Cyclone	9902-6160	
D-MWRG	Murphy Renegade Spirit	592	
D-MWRH	Evektor EV.97 Eurostar	98 02 02	
D-MWRJ	Comco Ikarus C-42 Cyclone	0003-6248	
D-MWRL	Comco Ikarus C-42 Cyclone	0001-6207	
D-MWRN	Comco Ikarus C-42 Cyclone	0102-6305	
D-MWRO	Tecnam P.92 Echo	210	
D-MWRS	Remos Gemini Ultra	007	
D-MWRT	Tecnam P.92 Echo 100S	505	
D-MWRV	ATEC Zephyr	ZF 121299	
D-MWRW	NST Minimum	unkn	
D-MWRX	Platzer Kiebitz-B2	043	
D-MWSA	ASO Viper Trike	15I1690	
D-MWSB	Sky-Walker II	269	
D-MWSC	Comco Ikarus C-42 Cyclone	0202-6456	
D-MWSD	Remos Gemini Ultra	011	
D-MWSE	Rans S-6 Coyote II	0694636	D-MNDC
D-MWSG	B&F Funk FK-14 Polaris	014-002	
D-MWSH	Platzer Kiebitz-B-450	177	
D-MWSI (1)	Dallach Sunrise II	015	
D-MWSI (2)	Schmidtler Enduro DS Trike	010987	
D-MWSK(1)	ASO Viper Trike	3101	
D-MWSK(2)	Comco Ikarus Fox-C22	9509-3688	
D-MWSM	Steinbach Austro-Trike	unkn	
D-MWSN	B&F Funk FK-9 Mk.III	09-121	
D-MWSP	Behlen Power-Trike	374	
D-MWSR	Tecnam P.92SEcho 100S	361	
D-MWSS	Comco Ikarus C-42 Cyclone	9901-6135	
D-MWST	WDFL Dallach D4 Fascination BK	074	
D-MWSV	Aerostyle Breezer	019	
D-MWSW	Take Off Maximum Trike	045021	
D-MWSY	Tandem Air Sunny Targa	010	
D-MWSZ	Zenair CH-601 Zodiac	6-3412/007 0597	
D-MWTA	Air-Light Wild Thing	058	
D-MWTB	Air-Light Wild Thing	043	
D-MWTC	Air-Light Wild Thing	007	
D-MWTD	Konsuprod Moskito	01-B	
D-MWTE	Air-Light Wild Thing	050	
D-MWTF	Air-Light Wild Thing	059	
D-MWTL	TL Ultralight TL-232 Condor Plus	96C01	
D-MWTR	Comco Ikarus C-42 Cyclone	9810-6141	
D-MWTS	Comco Ikarus Fox-C22	9405-3552	
D-MWTT (1)	Fair Fax Trike	028	
D-MWTT(2)	Remos G.3 Mirage	102	
D-MWTV	Aviasud Albatros 52	124	
D-MWTW	Comco Ikarus Fox-C22	9503-3648	
D-MWUD	Albatros 64	307	
D-MWUM	Light Aero Avid Flyer	1465	
D-MWUT	Comco Ikarus Fox-C22B	9506-3663	
D-MWVA	Klüver Bison Trike	253708	
D-MWVH	Albatros	113	65-CR
D-MWVR	Ultraleichtverbund Bi 90	3957007	
D-MWVV	Schönleber Minimum	LO 1/0288	
D-MWVY	Comco Ikarus C-42 Cyclone	0110-6421	
D-MWVZ	Schmidtler Enduro Trike	01-002	
D-MWWD	Flight Design CT	unkn	
D-MWWE	B&F Funk FK-12 Comet	unkn	
D-MWWK	Technoflug Piccolo	051	
D-MWWL	Zenair CH-701 STOL	unkn	
D-MWWM	Tecnam P.96 Golf 100	193	
D-MWWN	Tecnam P.92 Echo 100S	454	
D-MWWR(2)	Sky-Walker II	26148	
D-MWWT	Air-Light Wild Thing	032	
D-MWWW(1)	Sky-Walker 1+1	26143	
D-MWWW(2)	WDFL Dallach D4 Fascination BK	085	
D-MWXB	Comco Ikarus Fox-C22	9309-3529	
D-MWXW	Comco Ikarus Fox-C22	9501-3630	
D-MWYC	Albatros	125	
D-MWYY	B&F Funk FK-9 Mk.II	017	
D-MWZL	Comco Ikarus Fox-C22	9401-3536	
D-MXAC	Platzer Motte B Rumpf	VO 001	
D-MXAD	B&F Funk FK-12 Comet	012-046	
D-MXAF	Platzer Kiebitz A	001	
D-MXAM	B&F Funk FK-14 Polaris	014-016	
D-MXAP	WDFL Dallach D4 Fascination BK	072	
D-MXAQ	Aériane Sirocco	042	
D-MXAR	Comco Ikarus C-42 Cyclone	0103-6308	
D-MXAY	B&F Funk FK-9 TG Mk.II	068	
D-MXAZ	Götz 50	001	
D-MXBA(2)	ASO 26 Storch 503	FT460	
D-MXBC	Comco Ikarus Sherpa	8309-001	
D-MXBD	Aviasud Mistral 53	002	
D-MXBE(2)	Comco Ikarus Fox-C22B	9404-3562	
D-MXBM	Aviasud Mistral 53	001	

D-MXBV	B&F Funk FK-9 Mk.3	116	
D-MXBW	Homebuilt, type unknown	1	
D-MXBX	Rans S-12 Airaile	0594493	
D-MXBY	ASO 26 Storch	FT240	
D-MXBZ	ASO 26 Storch 503	FT234	
D-MXCC	Light Aero Avid Flyer	261	
D-MXCH	Chinook	02817	
D-MXCM	Bobcat	001	
D-MXDD	WDFL Dallach D4 Fascination	070	
D-MXDE	ASO Storch/503	11001202	
D-MXDI	Solid Air Diamant Twin Hazard 13	T003	
D-MXDL	Light Aero Avid Flyer IV	419	
D-MXEF	Aeropro Eurofox	10401	
D-MXEG	Dallach Sunrise II	014	
D-MXEN	WDFL Dallach D4 Fascination	053	
D-MXES	Aerospool WT9 Dynamic	DY00801	
D-MXET	Flight Team Spider Trike	D017	
D-MXEV	Evektor EV-97 Eurostar	2000-0611	
D-MXFK	B&F Funk FK-9 Mk.II	001	
D-MXFO	Snoopy II	001	
D-MXFT	Rans S-6 Coyote II	0889060	
D-MXFW	Aerospool WT9 Dynamic	DY00801	
D-MXGH	Comco Ikarus C-42 Cyclone	0201-6423	
D-MXGI	Comco Ikarus C-42 Cyclone	9804-6090	
D-MXHE	LO-120	001	
D-MXHL	Weedhopper	2214	
D-MXHM	Eipper Quicksilver	1100	
D-MXHT	HFL Stratos 300	300-001	
D-MXHW	Air-Light Wild Thing	014	
D-MXIL	Fly Synthesis Storch	FT 231	
D-MXIM	Bobcat	AB-RM 001	
D-MXIS	ME.13B	003	
D-MXIW	Fisher FP-202 Koala	001	
D-MXKA	NST Minimum	M249	
D-MXKD	J-3 Kitten	AF 131285L	
D-MXKF	B&F Funk FK-9 Mk.III	09-03-166	
D-MXKK	Eipper Quicksilver Sprint II	215	
D-MXKM	TL Ultralight TL-96 Star	02 S 114	
D-MXKW	S.T.A.B. Trike XP-15	unkn	
D-MXLF	B&F Funk FK-14B Polaris	014-044	
D-MXLH	WDFL Dallach D4 Fascination BK	108	
D-MXLR	Scheibe UL-1 Coach IIb	001	
D-MXMD	Light Aero Avid Flyer IV	498	
D-MXMM	Mitchell Wing	P-808	
D-MXMP	Tecnam P.92 Echo 100S	406	
D-MXMS	Air-Light Wild Thing	035	
D-MXNA	Eipper Quicksilver Sprint II	216	
D-MXNO	Bobcat	EI-01	
D-MXNP	Light Aero Avid Flyer IV	616	
D-MXNV	Eipper Quicksilver	1393	
D-MXOF	B&F Funk FK-6	003	
D-MXPA	Sky-Walker II	325	
D-MXPC	Rans S-6 Coyote II	0994677	
D-MXPE	Comco Ikarus C-42B	0210-6490	
D-MXPG(2)	Comco Ikarus C-42 Cyclone	0007-6273	
D-MXPJ	Bobcat	PAU-1	
D-MXPK	B&F Funk FK-9 Mk.II	031	
D-MXPL	Ultravia Pélican Super Sport 450S	98-001	C-IFTP
D-MXPM	Platzer Motte B2/B3	05	
D-MXPO	Comco Ikarus C-42 Cyclone	0202-6429	
D-MXPR	Comco Ikarus C-42B	0309-6567	
D-MXRA	Remos G3 Mirage	064	
D-MXRM	Reuter UL-Arco	unkn	
D-MXRS	Tecnam P.92 Echo	200	
D-MXRY	Tecnam P.96 Golf S100	unkn	
D-MXSB	Schmidtler Enduro Trike	01-002	
D-MXSP	Sky Pup	01	
D-MXSS	Tecnam P.92 Echo	197	
D-MXSX	Zenair CH-701D STOL	7-9066 / 002	
D-MXTC	Evektor EV-97 Eurostar	2003-1805	
D-MXTH	Comco Ikarus Fox-C22	9402-3550	
D-MXTN	J-3 Kitten	A001	
D-MXTO	Comco Fox II Doppel Prototype	02	
D-MXTV	J-3 Kitten	001	
D-MXUI	Solid Air Diamant	022	
D-MXUR	Light Aero Avid Flyer	262	
D-MXVL	Aeroprakt	unkn	
D-MXVO	Impulse 300	unkn	
D-MXVW	Klüver Twin Racer	423201	
D-MXWO	Eipper Quicksilver	3962	
D-MXWT	Aerospool Dynamic WT-9	unkn	
D-MXWU	Ferrari Tucano	076	
D-MXWX	Comco Ikarus Fox-C22B	9604-3701	
D-MXXI	III Sky Arrow 450	084 S	
D-MXXT	WDFL Dallach D4 Fascination BK	099	
D-MXXW(2)	Aviation Products Star Trike DS	127.08.054	
D-MXXW(3)	Bobcat	Wi 1	
D-MXXX	Fläming Air Trener Baby	03	OK-GUD 01
D-MXXZ	Tecnam P.92 Echo	253	
D-MXYZ(2)	Murphy Renegade II	584	
D-MYAA	Sky-Walker II	325	
D-MYAB	Sky-Walker II	327	
D-MYAC	Scheibe UL-1Coach IIb	002	
D-MYAF	Konsuprod Moskito Ib	014	
D-MYAK	B&F Funk FK-9 Mk.II	016	
D-MYAL	Tandem Air Sunny Sport	2-91	
D-MYAN	Rans S-6 Coyote II	1291243	

D-MYAQ	ASO Storch	11005305	
D-MYAR	Denney Kitfox IV	546	
D-MYAS	Tandem Air Sunny	010	
D-MYAU	Rans S-12 Airaile	0192170	
D-MYAV	AMF Chevvron 2-32	035	
D-MYAW	LO-120S	005A	
D-MYAX	Technoflug Piccolo BM	068	
D-MYAY	Technoflug Piccolo BM	069	
D-MYAZ	Impulse 100	2	
D-MYBA	B&F Funk FK-9 Mk.II	015	
D-MYBC	B&F Funk FK-9 Mk.II	002	
D-MYBF	ASO Storch	11006306	
D-MYBG	Fisher FP-404 Classic	01	
D-MYBI	Euro-ALA Jet Fox 91D	001	
D-MYBJ	ASO Storch	11008307	
D-MYBK	Konsuprod Moskito Ib	017	
D-MYBL	Euro-ALA Jet Fox 91D	002	
D-MYBM	Fisher FP-404 Classic	TM-01	
D-MYBN	ASO Storch	11007307	
D-MYBO	B&F Funk FK-9 Mk.II	020	
D-MYBS	Tecnam P.92 Echo 100S	581	
D-MYCC	Aeropro Eurofox	11201	
D-MYCD	ICP MXP-740V Savannah	01-09-51-097	
D-MYCT	Flight Design CT	97.10.01.10	
D-MYDM	UPM Conra Trike	910113	
D-MYDY	Platzer Kiebitz	240	
D-MYEA	Remos G3 Mirage	060	
D-MYEF	Aeropro Eurofox	10801	
D-MYEK	Tecnam P.92 Echo	244	
D-MYEN	Kappa KPD-2U Sova	6169 G	
D-MYES	Kappa KPD-2U Sova	8292 I	
D-MYET	Comco Ikarus Fox-C22	9310-3514	
D-MYEV	Evektor EV-97 Eurostar	2000-0802	
D-MYFB	Platzer Kiebitz-B2	047	
D-MYFF	Rans S-12 Airaile	01990861A	
D-MYFM	Flight Design CT2SW	04.05.02	
D-MYGG	Impulse 100	UL-4	
D-MYGH	B&F Funk FK-9 TG Mk.II	086	
D-MYGK	Comco Ikarus C-42 Cyclone (Reported as "Horus II", 5.02)	9612-6067	
D-MYGL	Comco Ikarus C-42 Cyclone	9701-6021	
D-MYGW	Platzer Kiebitz	63	
D-MYHA	ASO Storch	11009408	
D-MYHE	Light Aero Avid Flyer IV	937	
D-MYHG	Pioneer Flightstar CL	950101	
D-MYHH	WDFL Dallach D4 Fascination	034	
D-MYHK	Flight Design CT	99.06.03.56	
D-MYHL	Air-Light Wild Thing	025	
D-MYHR	ICP MXP-740V Savannah	01-01-51-051	
D-MYHS	B&F Funk FK-12 Comet	012-035	
D-MYHY	ICP MXP-740V Savannah	01-09-51-098	
D-MYIA	TL Ultralight TL-96 Star	01 S 89	
D-MYIF	Ikarusflug Eurofox	038097	
D-MYII	Comco Ikarus C-42 Cyclone	0106-6361	
D-MYIN	Aeroprakt A-22 Vision	028008	
D-MYKA	Comco Ikarus C-42 Cyclone	9710-6058	
D-MYKB	Air-Light Wild Thing	020	
D-MYKD	Comco Ikarus Fox-C22C	9 . . .-3658	
D-MYKE	Fisher Super Koala	SK 028	
D-MYKF	Zenair CH-601D Zodiac	6-3791	
D-MYKI	Comco Ikarus Fox-C22C	9605-3707	
D-MYKL	Ikarusflug Eurofox Pro	042097	
D-MYKM	Comco Ikarus C-42 Cyclone	0109-6370	
D-MYKO(1)	Comco Ikarus Fox-C22	9305-3512	
D-MYKO(2)	Remos G3 Mirage	152	
D-MYLA	TL Ultralight TL-96 Star	02 S 127	
D-MYLG	B&F Funk FK-12 Comet	012-010	
D-MYLI	Technoflug Piccolo BM	026	D-KCFC
D-MYLL	Comco Ikarus C-42 Cyclone	0201-6424	
D-MYMB	Remos G3 Mirage	075	
D-MYMI	Flight Design CT	99.09.05.69	
D-MYMM	TL Ultralight TL-232 Condor Plus	AB 02	
D-MYMS	Ultraleichtverbund Bi 90	922	
D-MYNK	Evektor EV-97 Eurostar	2002-1109	
D-MYNT	Tecnam P.92E Echo	unkn	
D-MYOB	Flight Design CT	98.04.02.29	
D-MYON	ICP MXP-740V Savannah	01-00-50-142	
D-MYOP	B&F Funk FK-9 TG Mk.III	09-03-133	
D-MYPC	Tecnam P.96 Golf 100S	171	
D-MYPE	Evektor EV-97 Eurostar	unkn	
D-MYPL	B&F Funk FK-9 Mk.II	023	
D-MYRA	B&F Funk FK-14 Polaris	014-021	
D-MYRE	Zenair CH-601D Zodiac	6-3574/002 1097	
D-MYRI	Comco Ikarus Fox-C22	9402-3567	
D-MYRS	Tandem Air Sunny	32	
D-MYRT(2)	Tecnam P.92 Echo 100S (Formerly c/n 244)	474	
D-MYSB	Flight Design CT	98.10.01.39	
D-MYSE	WDFL Dallach D4 Fascination	081	
D-MYSR	Evektor EV-97 Eurostar	2002-1214	
D-MYST	Klüver Twin Racer Quartz SX 16	419201	
D-MYSY	Comco Ikarus C-42B	0410-6629	
D-MYTH	B&F Funk FK-9 Mk.II	072	
D-MYTR	Air-Light Wild Thing	006	
D-MYTW	Flight Design CT	97.09.02.08	
D-MYUL	Rans S-6 Coyote II XL	0895877	
D-MYVO	B&F Funk FK-12 Comet	012-017	
D-MYVW	Zenair CH-601 Zodiac	6-9297	

D-MYWW	Tecnam P.96 Golf 100S	150
D-MYXA	WDFL Sunwheel R	024
D-MYXY	Tecnam P.92 Echo 100S	484
D-MYXZ	Tecnam P.92 Echo	166
D-MYYB	WDFL Dallach D4 Fascination	031
D-MYYY	Platzer Kiebitz-B4	036
D-MYYZ	Flight Design CT	97.10.02.011
D-MZAA	Fly Synthesis Storch	160.5
D-MZAB	TEAM Airbike	AB 104
D-MZAC	Remos G-3 Mirage	039
D-MZAD	WDFL Sunwheel R	045
D-MZAE	Air Energy AE-1 Silent	001
D-MZAG	J-3 Kitten	AL-1
D-MZAH	Comco Ikarus C-42 Cyclone	9805-6100
D-MZAL	Comco Ikarus C-42 Cyclone	9903-6182
D-MZAM	Comco Ikarus Fox-C22	9405-3587
D-MZAN	Comco Ikarus Fox-C22B	9507-3662
D-MZAR	Racer (Homebuilt)	02/90
D-MZAS	Comco Ikarus Fox-C22	9405-3582
D-MZAT	Comco Ikarus Fox-C22	9503-3635
D-MZAV	Comco Ikarus C-42 Cyclone	9906-6195
D-MZAY	Aviasud Mistral BA-83	009
D-MZAZ	Aeroprakt A-22 Vision	20
D-MZBA	JK-1 Elf	001
D-MZBB	Flight Design CT	99.10.03.73
D-MZBD	Impulse 100	5
D-MZBG	Comco Ikarus Fox-C22C	9511-3685
D-MZBH	WDFL Dallach D4 Fascination BK	086
D-MZBK	Tecnam P.96 Golf 100S	241
D-MZBN	Urban UFM-13 Lambada	07/13
D-MZBS	Tecnam P.92 Echo 100S	617
D-MZCH	Comco Ikarus C-42 Cyclone	9805-6127
D-MZCI	Remos G.3 Mirage	070
D-MZCU	Remos G.3 Mirage	087
D-MZCW	UPM-Trike	880057
D-MZDF(2)	Comco Fox	009
D-MZDG	B&F Funk FK-9 Mk.III	09-03-119
D-MZDY	Aerospool WT-9 Dynamic	DY00902
D-MZEB	Air-Light Wild Thing	075
D-MZEF	Comco Ikarus C-42B	0307-6565
D-MZEG	Tecnam P.92 Echo	unkn
D-MZEL	Platzer Kiebitz	198
D-MZEN	Light Aero Avid Flyer	1292
D-MZEP	ATEC Zephyr 2000	ZX 010497A
D-MZES	Flight Design CT	97.10.03.12
D-MZFF	Comco Ikarus C-42 Cyclone	9903-6159
D-MZFG	Behlen Power-Trike	89011
D-MZFT	Remos G-3 Mirage	055
D-MZGF	Ikarusflug Eurofox	unkn
D-MZGG	Urban Air Lambada UFM 13/15	7/13
D-MZGH	Loehle Mustang 5151	010
D-MZHH	WDFL Dallach D4 Fascination BK	100
D-MZHK	Comco Ikarus C-42 Cyclone	9910-6209
D-MZHS	ATEC Zephyr 2000	ZP 521200
D-MZHT	UPM-Trike	88058
D-MZHW	Dyn'Aero MCR-01 ULC	140
D-MZIH	Pioneer Flightstar CL	950302
D-MZII	Platzer Kiebitz-B8	139
D-MZIN	Comco Ikarus Fox-C22B	9404-3559
D-MZIO	Comco Ikarus Fox-C22	950 .-3634
D-MZIP	Air-Light Wild Thing	005
D-MZIS	Evektor EV.97 Eurostar	98 03 08
D-MZIW	Tandem Air Sunny Sport	61.94
D-MZJD	Flight Design CT2SW (Bt as CT-2K?)	03.05.02.21
D-MZKG	Flight Design CT-2K	01.02.03.06
D-MZKH	Air Energy AE-1 Silent	003
D-MZKL	Tecnam P.92 Echo 2000S	660
D-MZKM	TL Ultralight TL-96 Star	00 S 79
D-MZKS	Remos G-3 Mirage	053
D-MZKZ	Aerospool WT-9 Dynamic	DY003
D-MZLI	Air Energy AE-1 Silent	002
D-MZLL	Tecnam P.92 Echo 100S	455
D-MZLW	Comco Ikarus Fox-C22	9312-3534
D-MZMM	B&F Funk FK-12 Comet	012-047
D-MZMN	Comco Ikarus C-42 Cyclone	9707-6042
D-MZMS	ATEC Zephyr	Z 200400A
D-MZMZ	Comco Ikarus Fox-C22	9108-3364
D-MZNF	WDFL Sunwheel R	037
D-MZNN	Light Aero Avid Flyer	1291
D-MZNZ	Tecnam P.96 Golf 100S	108
D-MZOB	Air Energy AE-1 Silent	004
D-MZOH	Typhoon Trike (Homebuilt)	T1282667L
D-MZON	Comco Ikarus Fox-C22C	9703-3714
D-MZOO	Murphy Renegade Spirit	221
D-MZPS	Tecnam P.96 Golf 100S	202
D-MZRH	Zenair CH-601D Zodiac	001
D-MZRK	Racer (Homebuilt)	10/91
D-MZRS	Tecnam P.96 Golf	042
D-MZRX	Point Avn/Albatros AN-22M	001
D-MZRZ	Zenair CH-601D Zodiac	002
D-MZSP	Comco Ikarus C-42 Cyclone	9905-6183
D-MZSW	Ranger M	unkn
D-MZSZ	Comco Ikarus C-42 Cyclone	9910-6206
D-MZTA	Comco Ikarus Fox-C22B	3684
D-MZTF	Comco Ikarus Fox-C22C	9807-3739
D-MZTS	Remos G.3 Mirage	042
D-MZTT	Kappa KP-2U Sova	09/98
D-MZUL	B&F Funk FK-9 Mk.III Club	09-03U-175
D-MZWF	TL Ultralight TL-232 Condor Plus	99 C 05
D-MZWT	UPM-Trike	880059
D-MZWZ	Urban Air UFM-10 Samba	25/10
D-MZXX	Air-Light Wild Thing	008
D-MZYA	Kümmerle Mini-Fly-Set	1261/91-4
D-MZYS	Aeropro Eurofox	08600
D-MZYX	Dyn'Aero MCR-01 UL	98
D-MZZM	Kappa KPD-2U Sova	4448 G
D-MZZY	Remos G-3 Mirage	076
D-MZZZ	Rans S-10S Sakota	0790105

In the listings above we have retained details of duplicated registrations to help in the identification of aircraft seen before and after the last major update. Weight-shift and three-axis microlights are certified by different authorities and there are examples of registration marks apparently being used by both simultaneously.

Emphasising the difficulty of obtaining up-to-date information on any sections of the German register, reports on weight-shift microlight and paramotor registrations would be particularly welcome as many of these machines are less likely to travel outside Germany.

CLASS N : Unpowered Microlights

The D-N . . . series is used for unpowered Microlight Gliders and hang gliders. No current listing is available but reports would be welcome.

CLASS O : Balloons

Where a balloon has been replaced by an identical model, often only a replacement envelope, we have attempted to indicate this by quoting the earlier c/n in addition. Other re-used registrations are shown in the normal manner.

D-OAAA	Thunder AX8-105 SI HAFB	1984	
D-OAAE	Lindstrand LBL-120A HAFB	958	
D-OAAK	Lindstrand LBL-150A HAFB	882	
D-OAAL(2)	Schröder Fire Balloons G HAFB (Replacement for c/n 330)	1104	
D-OAAO	Cameron N-77 HAFB	793	D-Felsenkeller(1)
D-OAAR	Raven Europe S-60A HAFB	E-343	
D-OAAZ	Cameron Z-140 HAFB	10226	
D-OABB(4)	Lindstrand LBL-150A HAFB	878	G-CBXB
D-OABC(2)	Schröder Fire Balloons G HAFB	1053	
D-OABD(2)	Schröder Fire Balloons G HAFB	803	
D-OABE	Schröder Fire Balloons G HAFB	983	
D-OABF	Lindstrand LBL-150A HAFB	767	
D-OABG	Lindstrand LBL-120A HAFB	655	
D-OABH	Stuttgart K-1000/3-STU Gas Balloon	0311	D-Kabel
D-OABI	Schröder Fire Balloons G HAFB	266	
D-OABL	Colt 105A HAFB	3572	
D-OABO	Wörner NL-1000/STU Gas Balloon	1060	
D-OABP(2)	Schröder Fire Balloons G HAFB	946	
D-OABR	Cameron N-105 HAFB	3247	
D-OABT	Cameron N-105 HAFB	2146	D-Vagabund(2)
D-OACH	Cameron A-105 HAFB	505	D-OPIF D-Pfiffikus HB-BAW
D-OACT	Schröder Fire Balloons G HAFB	214	
D-OADA	Schröder Fire Balloons G HAFB	1037	
D-OADI	Schröder Fire Balloons G HAFB	753	
D-OADV	Lindstrand LBL-210A HAFB	658	
D-OAEC	Thunder AX8-90 SII HAFB	2478	
D-OAFA	Schröder Fire Balloons G HAFB (Res .04)	1088	
D-OAFB	Schröder Fire Balloons G HAFB	965	
D-OAFC	Thunder AX8-105 SII HAFB	3802	
D-OAGB	Cameron O-105 HAFB	974	D-Papage I
D-OAGF	Schröder Fire Balloons G HAFB	260	
D-OAGG	Schröder Fire Balloons G HAFB	634	
D-OAGH	Wörner NL-1000/STU Gas Balloon (W/o 1.10.01)	1069	
D-OAHG	Schröder Fire Balloons G HAFB	235	D-Fireballoon(2)
D-OAHM	Schröder Fire Balloons G HAFB	650	
D-OAHO	Thunder AX8-90 SI HAFB	2545	
D-OAHR	Thunder AX8-105 SII HAFB	2552	
D-OAHW	Thunder AX9-120 SII HAFB	2253	
D-OAIB	Thunder AX9-120 SII HAFB	4626	
D-OAIF	Schröder Fire Balloons G HAFB	184	D-Raffeisen
D-OAIG	Cameron N-77 HAFB	10219	
D-OAIR(2)	Kubicek BB- HAFB	334	OK-0334
D-OAIX	Sky 220-24 HAFB (Reservation)	096	G-BXPH
D-OAJG(2)	Schröder Fire Balloons G HAFB (Replacement for c/n 389)	1030	
D-OAKA	Thunder AX9-120 SII HAFB	4875	
D-OAKB	Lindstrand LBL-105A HAFB	462	
D-OAKE	Schröder Fire Balloons G HAFB	467	
D-OAKF	Colt 160A HAFB	1731	D-Sachsen G-BSJD
D-OAKK	Schröder Fire Balloons G HAFB	493	
D-OAKL	Schröder Fire Balloons G HAFB	655	
D-OAKO	Schröder Fire Balloons G HAFB	610	
D-OAKS	Schröder Fire Balloons G HAFB	410	
D-OAKT(2)	Cameron A-210 HAFB	4737	
D-OALA	Schröder Fire Balloons G HAFB	904	
D-OALB	Schröder Fire Balloons G HAFB	777	

D-OALF	Wörner K-1000/3-STU Gas Balloon	0277	D-Halfeneisen
D-OALI (3)	Cameron O-105 HAFB	4311	
D-OALK	Ultramagic M-145 HAFB	145/04	
D-OALP	Thunder AX8-84 SI HAFB	1037	D-Sonthofen
D-OALS(2)	Schröder Fire Balloons G HAFB	1041	
	(Replacement for c/n 529)		
D-OALZ	Schröder Fire Balloons G HAFB	546	
D-OAMB	Cameron O-90 HAFB	2225	D-Wegener
D-OAMD	Cameron N-90 HAFB	2478	
D-OAME	Cameron O-90 HAFB	2510	D-Marburg(2)
D-OAMG	Cameron N-105 HAFB	3250	
D-OAMH	Cameron A-105 HAFB	4579	
D-OAMM	Cameron N-90 HAFB	2589	D-Pinguin
D-OAMS(2)	Schröder Fire Balloons G HAFB	960	
	(Replacement for c/n 402)		
D-OAMW	Schröder Fire Balloons G HAFB	515	
D-OANA	Raven Europe S-66A HAFB	E-321	
D-OANS	Schröder Fire Balloons G HAFB	345	D-OHOT
D-OANT	Lindstrand LBL-90A	498	
D-OAOA	Schröder Fire Balloons G HAFB	263	
D-OAOB	Cameron O-120 HAFB	1670	LY-OAA D-OAOB G-BOHE
D-OAOC	Cameron A-105 HAFB	3690	
D-OAOD	Cameron A-210 HAFB	3689	
D-OAOE	Sky 180 HAFB	021	
D-OAOF	Sky 105 HAFB	026	
D-OAOG	Cameron N-160 HAFB	4592	
D-OAOH	Cameron N-145 HAFB	3554	
D-OAOI	Sky 220/24 HAFB	4871	
D-OAOK	Cameron N/Z-160 HAFB	10220	
D-OAOP	Wörner FK-5500/STU Gas Balloon	6020	
D-OAOS	Cameron A-210 HAFB	4864	
D-OAPB	Thunder AX9-120 SII HAFB	10059	
D-OAPP	Thunder AX9-120 SII HAFB	4057	
D-OAPS	Cameron N-105 HAFB	3781	
D-OARA	Thunder AX8-105 SII HAFB	2226	
D-OARC	Schröder Fire Balloons G HAFB	37	D-Arcobrau
D-OARD	Cameron A-375 HAFB	3682	
D-OARE	Augsburg K-780/2-RI Gas Balloon (Permit .04)	10147	D-Ergee VI
D-OARG	Augsburg K-1050/3-RI Gas Balloon	10120	D-Ergee V
D-OARH	Wörner K-1000/3-STU Gas Balloon	0321	
D-OARS	Thunder AX8-105 SII HAFB	2626	
D-OART	Raven-Europe S-60A HAFB (Reservation)	E-282	
D-OARW	Cameron N-120 HAFB	3153	
D-OASA	Schröder Fire Balloons G HAFB	262	
D-OASC	Schröder Fire Balloons G HAFB	861	
D-OASF	Schröder Fire Balloons G HAFB	1094	
D-OASH(2)	Wörner K-1050/S-STU Gas Balloon (Permit .04)	1053	
D-OASK	Kubicek BB-30 HAFB	237	OK-0237
D-OASS	Cameron C-80 Concept HAFB	3205	3A-MAS
D-OAST(2)	Cameron N-105 HAFB	4675	
	(Replacement for c/n 2638)		
D-OASU	Thunder AX9-120 SII HAFB	4193	
D-OASW	Schröder Fire Balloons G HAFB	369	
D-OATA	Schröder Fire Balloons G HAFB	905	
D-OATC	Schröder Fire Balloons G HAFB	600	
D-OATD	Cameron O-84 HAFB	2549	D-Bauknecht(2)
D-OATE	Lindstrand LBL-120A HAFB	958	
D-OATF	Schröder Fire Balloons G HAFB	668	
D-OATM	Schröder Fire Balloons G HAFB	212	
D-OATS	Schröder Fire Balloons G HAFB	205	
D-OAUN	Cameron A-140 HAFB	2680	D-OFUN(1) G-BTVZ
D-OAUS	Schröder Fire Balloons G HAFB	1055	
D-OAVE	GEFA-Flug AS.105GD Hot Air Airship	0030	
D-OAVW	Schröder Fire Balloons G HAFB	867	
D-OAWA	Kubicek BB-30 HAFB	318	OK-0318
D-OAWS	Sky 105 HAFB	069	
D-OAWU	Schröder Fire Balloons G HAFB	612	
D-OAWW	Schröder Fire Balloons G HAFB	665	
D-OAXL(2)	Lindstrand LBL-210A HAFB	988	
D-OAXW	Schröder Fire Balloons G HAFB	1084	
D-OBAA	Schröder Fire Balloons G HAFB	979	
D-OBAB(2)	Schröder Fire Balloons G HAFB	348	OE-ZBM
D-OBAC	Schröder Fire Balloons G HAFB	582	
D-OBAD(2)	Schröder Fire Balloons G HAFB	1034	
D-OBAF	Cameron A-120 HAFB	4452	
D-OBAH	Colt 105A HAFB	3861	
D-OBAI	Lindstrand LBL-150A HAFB	890	D-OBAY(3)
D-OBAL	Schröder Fire Balloons G HAFB	913	
D-OBAM	Lindstrand LBL-310A HAFB	190	
D-OBAR	Schröder Fire Balloons G HAFB	479	
D-OBAS	Colt 105A HAFB	3498	
D-OBAT	Cameron N-120 HAFB	10150	
D-OBAU	Thunder AX9-120 SII HAFB	2264	
D-OBAV	Cameron O-84 HAFB	2915	
D-OBAX	Aerostar S-66A HAFB	3067	
D-OBAZ	Raven Europe S-66A HAFB	E-283	D- Russberger(2)
D-OBBA	Colt 105A HAFB	2246	D-OLLA
D-OBBC	Colt 105A HAFB	4349	
D-OBBE	Schröder Fire Balloons G HAFB	270	
D-OBBF	Cameron A-340 HAFB	10390	
D-OBBI	Colt 120A HAFB (Reservation)	1732	D-Potsdam G-BSJE
D-OBBK	Schröder Fire Balloons G HAFB	1109	

D-OBBL(2)	Cameron A-120 HAFB	4774	
D-OBBM(2)	Schröder Fire Balloons G HAFB	667	
D-OBBN	Schröder Fire Balloons G HAFB	690	
D-OBBO	Thunder AX8-105 SII HAFB	4055	
D-OBBR	Schröder Fire Balloons G HAFB	349	
D-OBBS(2)	Lindstrand LBL-120AHAFB	819	
D-OBBT(2)	Cameron Brandenburger Tor SS HAFB	2742	PH-BBT
D-OBBU	Cameron N-160 HAFB	1908	OO-BBU (OO-BOY)
D-OBBY(2)	Raven S-60A HAFB	213	D-Robby
D-OBCC	Raven-Europe S-60A HAFB	E-253	
D-OBCD	Lindstrand LBL-120A HAFB	424	
D-OBCE	Schröder Fire Balloons G HAFB	578	
D-OBCF	Schröder Fire Balloons G HAFB	844	
D-OBCG	Thunder AX9-120 SII HAFB	2177	G-BUGK
D-OBCI	Schröder Fire Balloons G HAFB	509	
D-OBCS	Aerostar S-60AHAFB	S60A-3284	
D-OBCW	Wörner NL-1000/STU Gas Balloon	1059	
	(Previously listed as c/n 1051, 1996-9)		
D-OBDB	Schröder Fire Balloons GHAFB	794	
D-OBDD	Lindstrand LBL-150AHAFB	915	
D-OBDF	Cameron A-210 HAFB	4126	
D-OBDM	Schröder Fire Balloons G HAFB (Reservation)	195	D-Melitta
D-OBDS	Schröder Fire Balloons G HAFB	1120	
D-OBDW	Thunder AX8-105 SII HAFB	3530	
D-OBEC	Cameron N-133 HAFB	3926	
D-OBED(3)	Lindstrand LBL-150A HAFB	784	
	(Replacement for c/n 264)		
D-OBEE	Lindstrand LBL-105A HAFB	559	
D-OBEF	Thunder AX10-150 SII HAFB	10210	
D-OBEG	Thunder AX9-120 SII HAFB	4136	
D-OBEI (2)	Thunder AX9-120 SII HAFB	4622	
D-OBEK	Sky 120 HAFB	080	
D-OBEN	Sky 105 HAFB	100	
D-OBEO	Cameron O-120 HAFB	3126	
D-OBET	Cameron N-105 HAFB	3457	
D-OBEW	Cameron Z-120 HAFB	10183	
D-OBFB(2)	Cameron Z-105 HAFB	10595	
D-OBGH	Sky 120 HAFB	162	
D-OBGN	Schröder Fire Balloons G HAFB	165	D-Bellevue(2)
D-OBHB	Schröder Fire Balloons G HAFB	864	
D-OBHC	Ultramagic M-105 HAFB	105/34	
D-OBHG	Schröder Fire Balloons G HAFB	528	
D-OBHH	Colt 180A HAFB (Reservation)	2360	
D-OBHI	Schröder Fire Balloons G HAFB	710	D-OBHM
D-OBHR	Cameron O-105 HAFB (Reservation)	1928	D-Valerie
D-OBHS	Thunder AX8-105 SII HAFB	2551	
D-OBHT	Schröder Fire Balloons G HAFB	252	D- Brandkasse(2)
D-OBHV	Cameron Z-105 HAFB	10352	
D-OBHW	Schröder Fire Balloons G HAFB	681	
D-OBIB	Schröder Fire Balloons G HAFB	438	
D-OBID	Ultramagic M-120 HAFB	120/03	
D-OBIE	Ultramagic M-145 HAFB	145/41	
D-OBIG(3)	Cameron A-210 HAFB	4796	
	(Same c/n quoted for PH-DIA, also current)		
D-OBII	Schröder Fire Balloons G HAFB	368	D-OBIG
D-OBIL	Wörner K-1000/3-STU Gas Balloon	0285/2	D-Mobil IV
D-OBIM	Colt 300A HAFB	2416	
D-OBIN	Lindstrand LBL-105A HAFB	667	
D-OBIO	Schröder Fire Balloons G HAFB	247	D-OBIC
D-OBIP	Thunder AX8-105 SII HAFB	4225	
D-OBIS	Schröder Fire Balloons G HAFB	1036	
D-OBIT(2)	Schröder Fire Balloons G HAFB	773	
	(Replacement for c/n 116)		
D-OBIX	Schröder Fire Balloons G HAFB	387	
D-OBJJ	Lindstrand LBL-150A HAFB	682	
D-OBJW(2)	Lindstrand LBL-210A HAFB	950	
D-OBKA	Thunder AX8-105 SII HAFB	3886	
D-OBKB	Cameron A-210 HAFB	3896	
D-OBKD	Thunder AX9-140 SII HAFB	4435	
D-OBKM(2)	Kubicek BB-30Z HAFB	216	OK-0216
D-OBKS	Schröder Fire Balloons G HAFB	250	
D-OBKT	Cameron A-140 HAFB	3187	D-OSBT(1) D-OTAB(2)
D-OBKW	Cameron N-105 HAFB	10667	
D-OBLA	Cameron N-105 HAFB	3804	
D-OBLB(3)	Cameron Z-140 HAFB	10297	
D-OBLG	Aerostar S-60A HAFB	3286	
D-OBLO	Cameron N-120 HAFB	4265	D-OBLB(2)
D-OBLW	Schröder Fire Balloons G HAFB	338	
D-OBMB(2)	Kubicek BB-30Z HAFB	294	OK-0294
D-OBMG	Schröder Fire Balloons G HAFB	539	
D-OBMI	Schröder Fire Balloons G HAFB	699	
D-OBMS	Thunder AX8-105 SIIHAFB	4986	
D-OBMW(2)	Schröder Fire Balloons G HAFB	998	
D-OBNG(2)	Schröder Fire Balloons G HAFB	974	
D-OBNL	Schröder Fire Balloons G HAFB	347	
D-OBNR	Schröder Fire Balloons G HAFB	272	
D-OBNZ	Schröder Fire Balloons G HAFB	847	
D-OBOE(2)	Schröder Fire Balloons G HAFB	1086	
D-OBOL	Schröder Fire Balloons G HAFB	185	D-Bolberg(2)
D-OBOM	Lindstrand LBL-105A HAFB (Reservn)	545	
D-OBOR	Schröder Fire Balloons G HAFB	274	
D-OBOS	Schröder Fire Balloons G HAFB	884	
D-OBOX	Thunder AX8-105 SII HAFB	1749	HB-BWO D-Gemini

D-OBPP(2)	Thunder AX8-105 SII HAFB	4593	
D-OBRA	Ultramagic H-42 HAFB	42/06	
D-OBRB	Schröder Fire Balloons G HAFB	833	
D-OBRI	Schröder Fire Balloons G HAFB	541	
D-OBRM	Schröder Fire Balloons G HAFB	834	
D-OBRT(2)	Schröder Fire Balloons G HAFB	1004	
	(Replacement for c/n 309)		
D-OBRW	Cameron N-180 HAFB	3154	
D-OBSA	Colt 120A HAFB	4175	
D-OBSB	Cameron O-105 HAFB	1948	PH-BSP
D-OBSG	Lindstrand LBL-105AHAFB	627	
D-OBSH	Schröder Fire Balloons G HAFB	162	D-Luftschloss
D-OBSJ	Schröder Fire Balloons G HAFB	1000	
D-OBSK	Schröder Fire Balloons G HAFB (Reservation)	28	D-Schlossbau
D-OBSM	Cameron V-90 HAFB	2754	
D-OBSN	Cameron O-77 HAFB	894	D-Noris
D-OBSP	Schröder Fire Balloons G HAFB	84	D-Schmitt(3)
D-OBSS	Schröder Fire Balloons G HAFB	418	
D-OBST(2)	Schröder Fire Balloons G HAFB	1038	
D-OBSV	Cameron N-145 HAFB	10547	
D-OBTG(2)	Kubicek BB-37 HAFB	204	OK-0204
D-OBTH	Schröder Fire Balloons G HAFB	101	D-Alpinist
D-OBTK(2)	Cameron A-140 HAFB	4990	
D-OBTL	Cameron A-140 HAFB	3482	D-OJCA(1)
D-OBTN	Lindstrand LBL-150A HAFB	755	
D-OBTR	Thunder AX10-150 SIIHAFB	4755	
D-OBTS(2)	Schröder Fire Balloons G HAFB	798	
D-OBUL	Lindstrand LBL-150A HAFB	809	
D-OBUM	Colt 300A HAFB	2411	
D-OBUS(2)	Schröder Fire Balloons G HAFB	1010	
	(Replacement for c/n 527)		
D-OBVB	Lindstrand LBL-180A HAFB	041	
D-OBVL	Thunder AX8-105 SII HAFB	2335	
D-OBWE	Cameron A-210 HAFB	3492	
D-OBWF	Cameron A-105 HAFB (Reservation 11.99)	1540	D-Hammonia(1)
D-OBWI	Cameron A-250 HAFB	3708	
D-OBWJ	Lindstrand LBL-210AHAFB	334	
D-OBWK	Cameron A-160 HAFB	4201	
D-OBWM	Cameron A-160 HAFB	4274	
D-OBWN	Cameron N-160 HAFB	4578	
D-OBWP	Cameron A-275 HAFB	4742	
D-OBWQ	Cameron A-275 HAFB	4743	
D-OBWS	Cameron A-210 HAFB	10018	
D-OBWT	Cameron A-210 HAFB	10017	
D-OBWW(2)	GEFA-Flug AS.105GD Hot Air Airship	0007	
D-OBXX	Schröder Fire Balloons G HAFB	462	
D-OBYN	Wörner NL-1000/STU Gas Balloon	1080	
D-OBZA	Colt 105A HAFB	4412	
D-OBZR	Lindstrand LBL-310AHAFB	886	
D-OCAB	Schröder Fire Balloons G HAFB	932	
D-OCAD	Schröder Fire Balloons G HAFB	996	
D-OCAI	Schröder Fire Balloons G HAFB	342	
D-OCAL	Schröder Fire Balloons G HAFB	339	
D-OCAM	Thunder AX8-105 SII HAFB	2359	
D-OCAN	Schröder Fire Balloons G HAFB	579	
D-OCAR(2)	Cameron N-90 HAFB	10161	
D-OCAT(2)	Colt 105A HAFB	3749	
D-OCBM(2)	Ultramagic M-105 HAFB (Permit .03)	105/102	
D-OCBS	Lindstrand LBL-210A HAFB (Res 4.99)	602	
D-OCCC(2)	Cameron O-105 HAFB	4448	
D-OCCG(2)	Cameron O-105 HAFB	10221	
	(Replacement for c/n 2379)		
D-OCCM	Cameron A-140 HAFB	3545	
D-OCCO	Schröder Fire Balloons G HAFB	361	
D-OCCS	Schröder Fire Balloons G HAFB	872	
D-OCDM	Lindstrand LBL-180A HAFB	500	
D-OCDZ	Thunder AX9-120 SII HAFB	3794	
D-OCEL	Raven Europe FS-57A HAFB	E-153	D-Celle
D-OCFT	Wörner N-1000/STU Gas Balloon	1041	
D-OCGI	Thunder AX8-105SII HAFB	2356	
D-OCGN	Schröder Fire Balloons G HAFB	1114	
D-OCHA	Schröder Fire Balloons G HAFB	639	
D-OCHE	Schröder Fire Balloons G HAFB)	801	
D-OCHL	Ultramagic N-180 HAFB	180/49	
D-OCHT	Cameron A-180 HAFB	3766	
D-OCHY	Cameron A-105 HAFB	2985	
D-OCIO(3)	Schröder Fire Balloons G HAFB	925	
D-OCIX	Schröder Fire Balloons G HAFB	692	
D-OCKI	Aerostar RX-8 HAFB	3241	
D-OCKM	Wörner K-780/2-STU Gas Balloon	1040	
D-OCKY	Kubicek BB-30Z HAFB	205	OK-0205
D-OCLD	Cameron O-105 HAFB	1241	D-Nurnberg
D-OCMB	Schröder Fire Balloons G HAFB	961	
D-OCME	Schröder Fire Balloons G HAFB	469	
D-OCMF	Schröder Fire Balloons G HAFB	685	
D-OCMO	Lindstrand LBL-105A HAFB	528	D-Clauss
D-OCMS	Schröder Fire Balloons G HAFB	926	
D-OCOA	Cameron N-133 HAFB	3455	D-OOOA(1)
D-OCOC(2)	Schröder Fire Balloons G HAFB	757	
D-OCOM	Cameron A-105 HAFB	1793	D-Fuggerstadt
D-OCON	Cameron O-84 HAFB (Reservation 3.00)	2707	
D-OCOP	Schröder Fire Balloons G HAFB	903	
D-OCPC	Cameron N-145 HAFB	10111	
	(Originally allocated as A-140 c/n 4850)		
D-OCRF	Cameron N-105 HAFB	4089	
D-OCRI	Lindstrand LBL-150A HAFB	524	
D-OCRW	Cameron N-133 HAFB	10189	
D-OCST	Cameron O-120 HAFB	3090	
D-OCTA	Raven-Europe RX-7 HAFB (Permit .03)	E-202	D-Octanorm
D-OCTO	Thunder AX8-105 SII HAFB	1639	D-Jonathan
D-OCUB	Schröder Fire Balloons G HAFB	207	
D-OCVL	Schröder Fire Balloons G HAFB	617	
D-OCWH	Cameron N-105 HAFB	10015	
D-OCZL	Schröder Fire Balloons G HAFB	696	
D-ODAD	Schröder Fire Balloons G HAFB	1063	
D-ODAR	Raven-Europe RX-8 HAFB	E-199	PH-VFM
D-ODAS(2)	Kubicek BB-30 HAFB	232	OK-0232
D-ODAT	Gefa-Flug AS.105GD Hot Air Airship (Permit .04)	0009	
D-ODAU	Schröder Fire Balloons G HAFB	585	
D-ODBM	Schröder Fire Balloons G HAFB	908	
D-ODBW	Schröder Fire Balloons GHAFB (Res 2.99)	287	
D-ODDH	Wörner K-1000/3-STU Gas Balloon	0274	D-Dusseldorf
D-ODDP	Colt 120A HAFB	4188	G-BXLD
D-ODEB	Cameron A-250 HAFB (Permit .04)	4328	G-ODEB
D-ODEG	Schröder Fire Balloons G HAFB	640	
D-ODEL	Thunder AX8-90 SI HAFB	unkn	
D-ODEM	Wörner K-1260/3-STU Gas Balloon	0310	
D-ODEN	Balloon Works Firefly 8B-15 HAFB	F8B-421	N25511
D-ODER	Raven S-60A HAFB (Reservation)	337	N4397D
D-ODFB	Schröder Fire Balloons G HAFB	422	D-Treveris(2)
D-ODHB	Colt 105A HAFB	2621	
D-ODHM	Schröder Fire Balloons GHAFB	752	
D-ODIE	Schröder Fire Balloons G HAFB	535	
D-ODIN	Cameron O-84 HAFB	2652	
D-ODIT	Thunder AX8-105 SII HAFB	4063	D-Dithmarschen
D-ODKD	Colt 105A HAFB	4106	
D-ODKV(3)	Schröder Fire Balloons G HAFB	1126	
	(Replacement for c/ns 703 and 221)		
D-ODLL	Cameron A-300 HAFB	4918	
D-ODMI	Schröder Fire Balloons G HAFB	765	(D-OCAA)
D-ODMW	Schröder Fire Balloons G HAFB	290	
D-ODNI	Thunder AX8-105 SII HAFB	2236	
D-ODOC	Raven-Europe FS-57A HAFB	E-327	
D-ODON(2)	Cameron Z-105 HAFB	10516	
D-ODOR	Thunder AX10-150 SII HAFB	4554	
D-ODPM	Schröder Fire Balloons G HAFB	412	
D-ODRA	Raven-Europe FS-57A HAFB	E-292	
D-ODRH	Raven Europe S-60A HAFB	E-344	
D-ODRL	Schröder Fire Balloons G HAFB	804	
D-ODRV	Aerostar S-60A HAFB	3207	
D-ODSB	Schröder Fire Balloons G HAFB	968	
D-ODSO	Schröder Fire Balloons G HAFB	950	
D-ODST	Schröder Fire Balloons G HAFB	547	
D-ODTS	Schröder Fire Balloons G HAFB	825	
D-ODUB	Lindstrand LBL-105AHAFB	593	
D-ODUC	Schröder Fire Balloons G HAFB	746	
D-ODUD	Cameron A-180 HAFB	4163	
D-ODUE	Lindstrand LBL-120A	521	
D-ODUM	Thunder AX8-105 SII HAFB	2618	
D-ODUS	Wörner K-1000/3-STU Gas Balloon	1034	
D-ODWE	Schröder Fire Balloons G HAFB	812	
D-ODWS	Schröder Fire Balloons G HAFB	451	
D-ODYL	Cameron A-275 HAFB	4450	G-BXYL
D-ODYN(2)	Schröder Fire Balloons G HAFB	1071	
	(Replacement for c/n 613)		
D-OEAR	Raven-Europe FS-57A HAFB	E-217	D-Aerostar
D-OEAS	Schröder Fire Balloons G HAFB	626	
D-OEBH	Schröder Fire Balloons G HAFB	920	
D-OEBS	Schröder Fire Balloons G HAFB	1014	
D-OEBW	Gefa-Flug AS.105GD Hot Air Airship	0024	
D-OECO	Schröder Fire Balloons G HAFB	393	
D-OEDL	Cameron A-250 HAFB	3898	
D-OEDM(2)	Colt 105A HAFB	3940	
D-OEEE	Thunder AX8-105 SII HAFB	4569	
D-OEEH	Schröder Fire Balloons G HAFB	1134	
D-OEEJ	Schröder Fire Balloons G HAFB	460	
D-OEEU	Cameron A-400 HAFB	4508	
D-OEFC(2)	Colt 105A HAFB	4825	D-OSBC
D-OEFS	Cameron Z-105 HAFB	10618	
D-OEGP	Wörner NL-840/STU Gas Balloon	1057	
D-OEHD	Cameron A-160 HAFB	4521	
D-OEHN	Kubicek BB-30Z HAFB	221	OK-0221
D-OEIC(2	Cameron Z-150 HAFB	10523	
D-OEIF	Schröder Fire Balloons G HAFB	1121	
D-OEIM	Wörner NL-510/STU Gas Balloon	1056	
D-OEIN	Schröder Fire Balloons G HAFB	1048	
D-OEKB	Thunder AX8-105 SI HAFB	3753	
D-OEKD	Thunder AX8-105 SI HAFB (Permit .04)	3757	
D-OEKO	Aerostar S-60AHAFB	3259	
D-ODLA	Schröder Fire Balloons G HAFB	851	
D-OELD	Cameron Potts Lager Bottle 2 SS HAFB	4571	
D-OELE(3)	Schröder Fire Balloons G HAFB	750	
	(Formerly used by c/ns 79 and 234)		
D-OELG	Cameron A-160 HAFB	4253	
D-OELH	Schröder Fire Balloons G HAFB	768	
D-OELI	Schröder Fire Balloons G HAFB	842	
D-OELK	Schröder Fire Balloons G HAFB	380	
D-OELL	Schröder Fire Balloons G HAFB	1040	
D-OELM	Lindstrand LBL-120A HAFB	749	
D-OELO	Lindstrand LBL-150A HAFB	699	
D-OEMD	Schröder Fire Balloons G HAFB	658	
D-OEMS	Lindstrand LBL-150A HAFB	365	
D-OEMU	Cameron N-105 HAFB	2790	D-Rheingas(4)
D-OEMY	Lindstrand LBL-240A HAFB	846	

D-OENA	Cameron A-210 HAFB	10108	
D-OENN	Schröder Fire Balloons G HAFB	918	
D-OEON	Schröder Fire Balloons G HAFB (Reservn)	2002	
D-OEPA	Thunder AX8-105 SII HAFB	4290	
D-OEPP	Schröder Fire Balloons G HAFB	827	
D-OERD	Lindstrand LBL-150A HAFB	592	
D-OERE(2)	Schröder Fire Balloons G HAFB (Replacement for c/n 256)	858	
D-OERR	Cameron A-105 HAFB	2289	D-Dorr
D-OERT	Cameron A-210 HAFB	3322	(D-OBIG(2)) D-OERT
D-OESA	Schröder Fire Balloons G HAFB	726	
D-OESE	Cameron N-120 HAFB	4453	
D-OESI	Cameron N-120 HAFB	3809	
D-OESL	Colt 105A HAFB	3608	
D-OESM	Thunder AX8-90 SI HAFB	2501	
D-OEUE	Schröder Fire Balloons G HAFB	786	
D-OEUF	Schröder Fire Balloons G HAFB	565	
D-OEUR	Schröder Fire Balloons G HAFB	302	
D-OEUX	Thunder AX8-105 SII HAFB	2192	D-OLUX(2)
D-OEVE	Thunder AX8-90 SII HAFB	1320	D-Oeventrop
D-OEVL	Schröder Fire Balloons G HAFB	817	
D-OEVN	Lindstrand LBL-105A HAFB	145	
D-OEWA	Cameron A-140 HAFB	4444	
D-OEWB(2)	Schröder Fire Balloons G HAFB	694	
D-OEWS	Cameron O-105 HAFB	4111	
D-OEWV	Schröder Fire Balloons G HAFB	1101	
D-OEXC	Schröder Fire Balloons G HAFB	288	
D-OEZI	Cameron A-105 HAFB (Reservation .01)	4973	
D-OEZL	Cameron A-105 HAFB	2210	D-Spezi
D-OEZY	Cameron A-105 HAFB	10151	
D-OFAD	Schröder Fire Balloons Lefax SS HAFB	615	D-OFAX
D-OFAE	Lindstrand LBL-120A HAFB	975	
D-OFAJ	Schröder Fire Balloons G HAFB	870	
D-OFAR	Schröder Fire Balloons G HAFB	629	
D-OFAS	Aerostar S-60A HAFB (Permit .04)	3227	
D-OFAT(2)	Cameron A-180 HAFB	3641	
D-OFAZ	Schröder Fire Balloons G HAFB	490	
D-OFBC	Schröder Fire Balloons G HAFB	943	
D-OFBG	Raven-Europe RX-7 HAFB	E-214	D-Harxheim(2)
D-OFBH	Schröder Fire Balloons G HAFB	385	
D-OFBI	Schröder Fire Balloons G HAFB	131	
D-OFBK	Aerostar RXS-8 HAFB	3070	
D-OFBT	Schröder Fire Balloons G HAFB	646	
D-OFCS	Cameron N-105 HAFB	957	
D-OFDP	Schröder Fire Balloons G HAFB	1022	
D-OFEL	Sky 105 HAFB	145	
D-OFEM	Schröder Fire Balloons G HAFB	959	
D-OFEN	Schröder Fire Balloons G HAFB	11	D-Feuertute
D-OFER	Schröder Fire Balloons G HAFB	202	
D-OFES	Cameron N-105 HAFB (Reservation)	2697	D-Feldschlossen
D-OFEY	Schröder Fire Balloons G HAFB	1011	
D-OFFH	Cameron N-105 HAFB	4802	
D-OFFN	Lindstrand LBL-210A HAFB	483	
D-OFGR(2)	Kubicek BB-37 HAFB	199	OK-0199
D-OFHB	Schröder Fire Balloons G HAFB	1061	
D-OFHF	Schröder Fire Balloons G HAFB	621	
D-OFHH	Cameron N-105 HAFB	4803	
D-OFID	Schröder Fire Balloons G HAFB	759	
D-OFII	Schröder Fire Balloons G HAFB	760	
D-OFIL(2)	Schröder Fire Balloons G HAFB	660	
D-OFIN	Schröder Fire Balloons G HAFB	173	D-Finanzgruppe
D-OFIR	Cameron A-120 HAFB	4458	
D-OFJH	Lindstrand LBL-105A HAFB	136	
D-OFJS	Cameron N-105 HAFB	1531	D-Felsenkeller(2)
D-OFLO	Schröder Fire Balloons G HAFB	210	
D-OFLS	Cameron V-77 HAFB (Reservation 5.99)	1050	D-Otto
D-OFLX(2)	Lindstrand LBL-240AHAFB	894	
D-OFMA(2)	Thunder AX10-210 SII HAFB	4316	
D-OFMD	Schröder Fire Balloons G HAFB	868	
D-OFMG	Aerostar S-60A HAFB	3226	
D-OFMT	Schröder Fire Balloons G HAFB	873	
D-OFNY	Cameron A-105 HAFB	2409	D-Eichbaum
D-OFOA	Kubicek BB-37 HAFB	151	OK-0051
D-OFON	Cameron N-133 HAFB	10313	
D-OFOR	Schröder Fire Balloons G HAFB	589	
D-OFOS	Colt 180A HAFB	2525	
D-OFOX	Cameron Fox Head SS HAFB (Permit .03)	3270	D-Fuchs(2)
D-OFPH	Aerostar S-55A HAFB	3087	
D-OFPP	Schröder Fire Balloons G HAFB	754	
D-OFPW	Kubicek BB-30ZHAFB	240	OK-0240
D-OFRA	Schröder Fire Balloons G HAFB	294	
D-OFRB(2)	Cameron O-105 HAFB	1397	D-Zollernalb
D-OFRI	Schröder Fire Balloons G HAFB	308	
D-OFRR	Schröder Fire Balloons G HAFB	1127	
D-OFRT	Schröder Fire Balloons G HAFB	880	
D-OFSA	Schröder Fire Balloons G HAFB	468	
D-OFSD	Schröder Fire Balloons G HAFB	910	
D-OFSI	Schröder Fire Balloons G HAFB	662	D-Quattro(4)
D-OFSV	Colt 105A HAFB	4287	
D-OFTL	Schröder Fire Balloons G HAFB	691	
D-OFTM	Lindstrand LBL-105A HAFB	544	
D-OFTR	Cameron A-105 HAFB	3879	
D-OFTY	Schröder Fire Balloons G HAFB	997	
D-OFUE	Cameron V-90 HAFB	10431	

D-OFUN(2)	Cameron A-140 HAFB	3401	
D-OFUS	Schröder Fire Balloons G HAFB	483	
D-OFUX	Thunder AX8-105 SII	4301	
D-OFVA(2)	Wörner NL-1000/STU Gas Balloon	1073	
D-OFVB	Lindstrand LBL-210A HAFB	427	
D-OFVH	Lindstrand LBL-210A HAFB	849	
D-OFVV	Schröder Fire Balloons G HAFB	464	
D-OFZH	Lindstrand LBL-310A HAFB	672	
D-OGAB	Raven Europe S-60A HAFB	E-275	
D-OGAR	Aerostar S-60A HAFB	3271	
D-OGAS	Schröder Fire Balloons G HAFB	790	
D-OGAZ	Bronschofen K-780/2-Ri Gas Balloon	10413	
D-OGBA	Thunder AX9-140 SII HAFB	4044	
D-OGBB(2)	Schröder Fire Balloons G HAFB	1110	
D-OGBC	Thunder AX10-150 SII HAFB	4664	
D-OGBD	Thunder AX9-140 SII HAFB	10034	
D-OGBH	Kubicek BB-30Z HAFB	330	OK-0330
D-OGBK(2)	Cameron A-340 HAFB	10244	
D-OGBO	Colt 120A HAFB	2240	
D-OGBS	Schröder Fire Balloons G HAFB	444	
D-OGBW	Cameron A-105 HAFB	3114	
D-OGDP	Schröder Fire Balloons G HAFB	466	
D-OGEG	Cameron N-77 HAFB	4070	
D-OGEH	Lindstrand LBL-240A HAFB	685	
D-OGEN	Schröder Fire Balloons G HAFB	554	
D-OGEO	Aerostar RXS-8 HAFB	3065	
D-OGER	Raven Europe FS-57A HAFB	E-187	
D-OGET	Lindstrand LBL-310A HAFB	893	
D-OGFA	Schröder Fire Balloons G HAFB	745	
D-OGFB	Schröder Fire Balloons G HAFB	374	
D-OGGG(2)	Cameron O-105 HAFB	3392	
D-OGGO	Schröder Fire Balloons G HAFB	1093	
D-OGGY	Wörner NL-1000/STU Gas Balloon	1071	
D-OGHC	Aerostar RXS-8 HAFB	3112	
D-OGHS	Schröder Fire Balloons G HAFB	995	
D-OGIB	Schröder Fire Balloons G HAFB	333	
D-OGIE(2)	Schröder Fire Balloons G HAFB	1060	
D-OGIN	Balloon Works Firefly 9 HAFB	F9-056	N25532
D-OGIS	Schröder Fire Balloons G HAFB	568	
D-OGKW	Cameron O-84 HAFB	779	D-Bunte Kuh(1)
D-OGLA	Schröder Fire Balloons G HAFB	1099	
D-OGLI	Schröder Fire Balloons G HAFB	902	
D-OGMB	Cameron N-120 HAFB	4850	
D-OGMI	Lindstrand LBL-69A HAFB	845	
D-OGMZ(2)	Cameron Z-120 HAFB	10590	
D-OGNI	Ultramagic M-160 HAFB	160/17	
D-OGOG	Schröder Fire Balloons G HAFB	716	
D-OGOT(2)	Schröder Fire Balloons G HAFB (Replacement for c/n 194)	1047	
D-OGPK	Schröder Fire Balloons G HAFB	489	
D-OGQU	Cameron N-105 HAFB	3070	
D-OGRA	Raven Europe S-60A HAFB	E-350	
D-OGRM	Schröder Fire Balloons G HAFB	543	
D-OGRO	Cameron O-105 HAFB	2833	
D-OGRU	Cameron A-160 HAFB	3957	PH-GRU (D-OGRU)
D-OGSA	Ultramagic M-145 HAFB	145/30	
D-OGSC	Thunder AX8-105 SII HAFB	4029	
D-OGSD	Lindstrand LBL-150A HAFB	782	
D-OGSE	Schröder Fire Balloons Schwartau SS HAFB	731	
D-OGST	Colt 105A HAFB	4753	
D-OGTS	Schröder Fire Balloons G HAFB	620	
D-OGUE	Schröder Fire Balloons G HAFB	871	
D-OGUG(2)	Aerostar S-60A HAFB	3274	
D-OGVF	Schröder Fire Balloons G HAFB	149	D-Erdgas(2)
D-OGVS	Cameron O-105 HAFB (Reservation .01)	1296	D-Erdgas
D-OGVU	Colt 140A HAFB	4463	
D-OGWI	GEFA-Flug AS.105GD Hot Air Airship	0034	
D-OGWV	Ultramagic N-210 HAFB	210/22	
D-OHAB	Kubicek BB-45 HAFB	260	OK-0260
D-OHAC(2)	Schröder Fire Balloons G HAFB	797	
D-OHAD	Head AX8-88 HAFB	187	N45244
D-OHAG	Schröder Fire Balloons G HAFB	381	
D-OHAH	Thunder AX9-140SII HAFB	3795	
D-OHAI	Colt 105A HAFB	3891	
D-OHAM	Cameron N-105 HAFB (Reservation 11.99)	2683	D-Hammonia(2)
D-OHAN(2)	Ultramagic M-105 HAFB	105/76	
D-OHAP	Schröder Fire Balloons G HAFB	953	
D-OHAQ	Cameron N-105 HAFB	3373	D-OHAC(1)
D-OHAR	Cameron O-105 HAFB	10100	
D-OHAS	Schröder Fire Balloons G HAFB	641	
D-OHAW	Raven RX-7 HAFB	3187	D-Bruchhausen(1)
D-OHAX	Aerostar RX-7 HAFB	3320	
D-OHBA	Thunder AX9-140 SII HAFB (Permit .03)	2315	
D-OHBB	Thunder AX9-140 SII HAFB	2316	
D-OHBC	Thunder AX9-140 SII HAFB	2585	
D-OHBE(2)	Thunder AX10-160 SII HAFB	3784	
D-OHBF	Thunder AX9-140 SII HAFB	1726	D-Lowentor(2)
D-OHBH(2)	Thunder AX10-160 SII HAFB	10216	
D-OHBI	Thunder AX9-140 SII HAFB	3486	
D-OHBJ	Colt 210A HAFB	3610	
D-OHBK	Thunder AX10-160 SII HAFB	4589	
D-OHBL	Cameron V-90 HAFB	3229	
D-OHBM	Colt 240A HAFB	4094	
D-OHCC	Aerostar S-60A HAFB	3222	
D-OHCD	Cameron N-90 HAFB	1708	D-IBEXCO

D-OHDE	Cameron O-105 HAFB	2874	D-Wolken-hopper(2)
D-OHDG	Thunder AX8-105 SII HAFB	2336	
D-OHDH	Cameron N-120 HAFB	4049	
D-OHDI	Cameron A-105 HAFB	3162	
D-OHDM	Lindstrand LBL-105A HAFB	137	
D-OHDR	Raven Europe S-60A HAFB	E-. . .	
D-OHDV	Schröder Fire Balloons G HAFB	659	
D-OHEB	Cameron A-105 HAFB	3434	
D-OHED	Cameron O-90 HAFB	3170	
D-OHEI	Cameron O-77 HAFB	1635	D-Heilbronn(3)
D-OHEL	Cameron A-105 HAFB	2662	D-Hellenstein(2)
D-OHES	Thunder AX10-160 SII HAFB	4559	
D-OHFA	Colt 105A HAFB	1849	D-Hagdorn(1)
D-OHFF	Cameron N-105 HAFB	4804	
D-OHFJ	Ultramagic M-120 HAFB	120/08	
D-OHFQ	Schröder Fire Balloons G HAFB	1111	
D-OHFU	Cameron O-105 HAFB	3923	
D-OHGL	Schröder Fire Balloons G HAFB	470	
D-OHHH	Schröder Fire Balloons G HAFB	25	D-Super
D-OHHO	Gefa-Flug AS.105GD Hot Air Airship	0019	
D-OHIF	Cameron N-77 HAFB (Permit .04)	1352	D-Fuggerstad D-Hitachi
D-OHIO	Schröder Fire Balloons G HAFB	356	
D-OHIW(2)	Thunder AX8-105 SII HAFB	4763	
D-OHJE	Lindstrand LBL-400A HAFB	422	
D-OHJM	Schröder Fire Balloons G HAFB	204	
D-OHJO	Lindstrand LBL-400A HAFB	423	
D-OHJW	Aerostar RXS-8 HAFB	3088	
D-OHKE	Schröder Fire Balloons G HAFB	949	
D-OHKH(2)	Schröder Fire Balloons G HAFB	829	
D-OHKP	Raven-Europe S-60A HAFB	E-280	
D-OHKS	Kubicek BB-30 HAFB	248	OK-0248
D-OHLE	Thunder AX8-105 SII HAFB	2128	
D-OHLM	Schröder Fire Balloons G HAFB	730	
D-OHMA(2)	Cameron A-250 HAFB (Replacement for c/n 3580)	4940	
D-OHMB	Schröder Fire Balloons G HAFB	986	
D-OHME	Kubicek BB-30Z HAFB	285	OK-0285
D-OHMM	Raven Europe S-60A HAFB	E-338	
D-OHMW	Aerostar RX-8 HAFB	RX8-3102	N63223
D-OHOF	Raven-Euorpe FS-57A HAFB	E-281	
D-OHOH	Raven-Europe FS-57A HAFB	E-. . .	
D-OHOI	Schröder Fire Balloons G HAFB	443	
D-OHOL	Thunder AX8-105 SII HAFB (Reservation)	1896	D-Holsten
D-OHOM(2)	Schröder Fire Balloons G HAFB (Replacement for c/n 384)	859	
D-OHON	Colt Pils Bottle SS HAFB	10094	
D-OHOR	Schröder Fire Balloons G HAFB	407	
D-OHOT	Schröder Fire Balloons G HAFB	463	
D-OHOX	Thunder AX8-105 SII HAFB	10439	
D-OHPB	Schröder Fire Balloons G HAFB	962	
D-OHPH	Raven Europe S-60A HAFB	E-399	
D-OHPI	Cameron N-120 HAFB	4808	
D-OHPL	Schröder Fire Balloons G HAFB	738	
D-OHRB	Cameron V-65 HAFB (Reservation 3.00)	1985	D-Helios
D-OHRF	Schröder Fire Balloons G HAFB	434	
D-OHRM	Schröder Fire Balloons G HAFB	697	
D-OHRN	Cameron N-105 HAFB	3184	
D-OHSD	Colt 105A HAFB	4026	
D-OHSI	Thunder AX8-90 SII HAFB	3632	
D-OHSS	Schröder Fire Balloons G HAFB	672	
D-OHTB	Schröder Fire Balloons G HAFB (Permit .03)	492	
D-OHUP	Colt 140A HAFB	4053	
D-OHVB	Schröder Fire Balloons G HAFB	789	
D-OHVR(2)	Ultramagic M-145 HAFB	145/37	
D-OHVW	Cameron N-90 HAFB	1175	SE-ZBO
D-OHWK	Cameron N-105 HAFB	5881	N194DR
D-OHWM	Cameron O-84 HAFB	1749	D-Tassilo(2)
D-OHWW(2)	Cameron N-105 HAFB (Replacing c/n 2816)	10136	
D-OHXH	Raven-Europe RX-7 HAFB	E-342	
D-OHYL	Schröder Fire Balloons G HAFB	795	
D-OIAR	Raven Europe S-60A HAFB	E-386	
D-OIAT	Cameron A-120 HAFB	2817	D-OURS(1)
D-OIBB	Wörner NL-840/STU Gas Balloon	1048	
D-OIBF	Thunder AX8-105 SII HAFB	4040	
D-OIBL	Lindstrand LBL-90A HAFB	419	G-OLBL
D-OIBM	Cameron N-105 HAFB	4302	
D-OIBP(2)	Lindstrand LBL-310A HAFB	928	
D-OIDA	Balloon Works Firefly 8 HAFB (Permit .03)	F8-412	
D-OIDE	Thunder AX9-120 SII HAFB	2420	
D-OIDO	Wörner FKP-380/STU Gas Balloon	6204	
D-OIGB	Thunder AX8-90 SII HAFB	2091	
D-OIGM(2)	Schröder Fire Balloons G HAFB	783	
D-OIIC	Schröder Fire Balloons G HAFB	392	D-OEIC(1)
D-OIII	Cameron O-90 HAFB	1995	D-Drachengas(1) D-Hessen(2)
D-OIKF	Colt 180A HAFB	4447	
D-OILB	Thunder AX8-105 SIIHAFB	4618	
D-OILE	Aerostar RXS-8 HAFB	RXS8-3096	
D-OILY	Cameron O-105 HAFB	2595	G-SMAX G-MADM
D-OILZ	Cameron O-140 HAFB	2887	
D-OIMM	Schröder Fire Balloons G HAFB	500	
D-OINA	Cameron N-120SV HAFB	3875	
D-OING	Schröder Fire Balloons G HAFB	718	
D-OIOI	Cameron N-105 HAFB	2435	D-Toshiba
D-OIOO(2)	Schröder Fire Balloons G HAFB	1046	
D-OIPA	Colt 105A HAFB	4315	
D-OIRO	Schröder Fire Balloons G HAFB	739	
D-OISA	Colt 105 HAFB (Reservation)	1686	D-Schlossquell
D-OISG	Schröder Fire Balloons GHAFB	1077	
D-OISN	Schröder Fire Balloons GHAFB	1068	
D-OISO	Cameron A-105 HAFB	3276	
D-OITB	Lindstrand LBL-120A HAFB	511	
D-OIZI	Thunder AX8-105 SI HAFB	2546	
D-OJAC	Schröder Fire Balloons G HAFB	1122	
D-OJAK	Schröder Fire Balloons G HAFB	922	
D-OJAN	Schröder Fire Balloons G HAFB	813	
D-OJAT	Thunder AX10-210 SII HAFB	3932	
D-OJCA(2)	Ultramagic M-145 HAFB	145/28	
D-OJFK	Schröder Fire Balloons G HAFB	625	
D-OJFP	Thunder AX9-120 SII HAFB	10227	
D-OJFS	Lindstrand LBL-210AHAFB	940	
D-OJIL	Thunder AX10-150 SIIHAFB	4646	
D-OJJI	Thunder AX9-120 SII HAFB	2613	D-OJJJ(1)
D-OJJJ(2)	Schröder Fire Balloons G Joker SS HAFB (Permit 9.04)	1100	
D-OJLW	Schröder Fire Balloons G HAFB	373	
D-OJMC	Aerostar S-60A HAFB	3218	
D-OJMK	Thunder AX9-120 SII HAFB	4812	
D-OJMN	Thunder AX8-105 SII HAFB	2090	
D-OJOE	Colt 210A HAFB (Reservation)	2425	
D-OJOP	Lindstrand LBL-210A HAFB	714	
D-OJPI	Thunder AX8-105 SII HAFB	3797	
D-OJRW	Lindstrand LBL-150A HAFB	576	
D-OJSB	Cameron A-105 HAFB	unkn	
D-OJSM	Schröder Fire Balloons G HAFB	980	
D-OJUC(2)	Ultramagic M-105 HAFB	105/65	
D-OJUH	Colt 77A HAFB	4437	
D-OJUL	Schröder Fire Balloons G HAFB	unkn	
D-OJUP	Wörner NL-1000/STU Gas Balloon	1052	
D-OJWC(2)	Schröder Fire Balloons G HAFB (Replaced c/n 495 D-OJWC)	447	D-OLWO
D-OKAB	Cameron A-250 HAFB	4289	
D-OKAE	Lindstrand LBL-150A HAFB	494	
D-OKAF	Cameron A-105 HAFB	2974	
D-OKAI	Raven-Europe RX-7 HAFB	E-289	
D-OKAL	Schröder Fire Balloons G HAFB	399	
D-OKAM	Schröder Fire Balloons G HAFB	334	
D-OKAP	Lindstrand LBL-150A HAFB	770	
D-OKAR	Schröder Fire Balloons G HAFB	225	D-Ikarus (2)
D-OKAT	Schröder Fire Balloons G HAFB	320	
D-OKAY	Aerostar RXS-8 HAFB	3082	
D-OKBA	Thunder AX8-105 SII HAFB	4831	
D-OKBB	Schröder Fire Balloons G HAFB	249	
D-OKBC	Thunder AX8-105 SII HAFB	4488	
D-OKBE	Thunder AX8-105 SII HAFB	3650	
D-OKBF	Thunder AX8-105 SII HAFB	3511	
D-OKBG	Thunder AX8-105 SII HAFB	3651	
D-OKBH	Thunder AX8-105 SII HAFB	3887	
D-OKBI	Thunder AX8-105 SII HAFB	10007	
D-OKBJ	Thunder AX9-120 SIIHAFB	10139	
D-OKBK(2)	Thunder AX9-120 SII HAFB	4886	
D-OKBM	Thunder AX8-105 SII HAFB	4489	
D-OKBO	Thunder AX9-120 SIIHAFB	10005	
D-OKBQ	Thunder AX9-120 SIIHAFB	10006	
D-OKBR	Thunder AX9-120 SIIHAFB	4734	
D-OKBW	Thunder AX8-105 SII HAFB	4068	
D-OKBX	Thunder AX8-105 SII HAFB	4582	
D-OKBZ	Thunder AX8-105 SII HAFB	4583	
D-OKCF	Thunder AX8-90 SII HAFB	2607	
D-OKCH	Schröder Fire Balloons G HAFB	363	D-OHKH(1)
D-OKEB	Schröder Fire Balloons G HAFB	774	
D-OKEG	Lindstrand LBL-150A HAFB	889	
D-OKEH	Balloon Works Firefly F8GB-15 HAFB	F8B-464	
D-OKEM	Schröder Fire Balloons G HAFB	939	
D-OKER	Schröder Fire Balloons G HAFB	787	
D-OKEY	Schröder Fire Balloons G HAFB	636	
D-OKFR	Cameron Tiger 90 SS HAFB	4288	
D-OKGA	Schröder Fire Balloons G HAFB	896	
D-OKGB	Ultramagic N-250 HAFB	250/04	
D-OKGF	Schröder Fire Balloons G HAFB	217	
D-OKGH	Ultramagic S-105 HAFB	105/58	
D-OKHG	Schröder Fire Balloons G HAFB	32	D-Sonnenbuhl
D-OKHK	Ultramagic M-130 HAFB	130/23	
D-OKHL	Cameron N-120 HAFB	10060	
D-OKHW	Schröder Fire Balloons G HAFB	426	
D-OKIA	Colt 90A HAFB	2269	
D-OKIB(2)	Schröder Fire Balloons G HAFB	1033	
D-OKID	Colt 105A HAFB	2681	
D-OKIE	Thunder AX8-90 SII HAFB	3853	
D-OKII	Thunder AX8-105 SII HAFB	2059	D-Karriere(2)
D-OKIK	Schröder Fire Balloons G HAFB	815	
D-OKIM	Schröder Fire Balloons G HAFB	944	
D-OKIN	Schröder Fire Balloons G HAFB	957	
D-OKIT	Cameron O-84 HAFB	2172	G-BROS
D-OKIZ	Schröder Fire Balloons G HAFB	473	
D-OKLD	Cameron N-133 HAFB	4722	
D-OKLE	Cameron N-90 HAFB	3448	
D-OKLO	Schröder Fire Balloons G HAFB	772	
D-OKMF	Raven-Europe S-60A HAFB	E-245	
D-OKMO	Ultramagic M-105 HAFB	105/119	

D-OKMS	Schröder Fire Balloons G HAFB	588	
D-OKNB	Schröder Fire Balloons G HAFB	970	
D-OKOK	Thunder AX8-90 SII HAFB	2053USA	N224TC
D-OKOL	Colt 240A HAFB	2243	
D-OKOM	Colt 105A HAFB	3860	
D-OKON	Schröder Fire Balloons G HAFB	558	
D-OKPB(2)	Schröder Fire Balloons G HAFB (Replacement for c/n 532)	1106	
D-OKPC	Cameron A-180 HAFB	2562	G-BTKO
D-OKPF	GEFA-Flug AS.105GD Hot Air Airship	0015	
D-OKPG	Schröder Fire Balloons G HAFB	352	
D-OKPH	Cameron A-120 HAFB	4686	
D-OKRA	Schröder Fire Balloons G HAFB	46	D-Kranich
D-OKRE(2)	Cameron O-120 HAFB	10184	
D-OKRI	Cameron A-140 HAFB	2861	
D-OKRO(2)	Lindstrand LBL-150A HAFB	794	
D-OKRS	Cameron O-90 HAFB	3397	
D-OKRU	Aerostar S-60A HAFB	3183	D-OKRO(1)
D-OKSB	Colt 120A HAFB	2130	G-BUCD
D-OKSC	Balloon Works Firefly F9 HAFB	F9-061	
D-OKSK	Schröder Fire Balloons G HAFB	536	
D-OKSP	Aerostar S-60A HAFB	3280	
D-OKSR	Cameron 90SS Coffee Jug HAFB	3789	
D-OKSU	Kubicek BB-42Z HAFB	241	OK-0241
D-OKSW	Thunder AX8-90 SII HAFB	2358	
D-OKSY	Cameron N-120 HAFB	2864	
D-OKTO(3)	Lindstrand LBL-150A HAFB	962	
D-OKUE	Raven Europe S-60A HAFB	E-345	
D-OKUH	Cameron A-105 HAFB	2918	
D-OKUK	Kubicek BB-37	192	OK-0192
D-OKUP	Schröder Fire Balloons G HAFB	779	
D-OKUR	Schröder Fire Balloons G HAFB	138	D-Witt- gensteiner(3)
D-OKVR(2)	Schröder Fire Balloons G HAFB	952	
D-OKWB	Sky 120 HAFB	177	
D-OKWS	Schröder Fire Balloons G HAFB	824	
D-OKWW	Schröder Fire Balloons G HAFB	1119	
D-OKXC	Cameron V-77 HAFB	973	G-BKXC
D-OKZM	Lindstrand LBL-150AHAFB	795	
D-OKZO	Lindstrand LBL-150A HAFB	957	
D-OLAA	Lindstrand LBL-150AHAFB (Permit .03)	654	
D-OLAB	Thunder AX9-120 SII HAFB (Permit .03)	4462	
D-OLAC	Schröder Fire Balloons G HAFB	729	
D-OLAF	Raven Europe S-60A HAFB	E-313	
D-OLAG	Aerostar S-57A	3197	
D-OLAN	Schröder Fire Balloons G HAFB	85	D-Landshut(2)
D-OLAP	Thunder AX8-105 SII HAFB	4276	
D-OLAR	Lindstrand LBL-9OA HAFB (Permit .04)	193	
D-OLAU	Raven-Europe FS-57A HAFB	E-274	
D-OLAV	Thunder AX8-105SII HAFB	3518	
D-OLBA	Lindstrand LBL-105A HAFB	781	
D-OLBB	Schröder Fire Balloons G HAFB	455	
D-OLBC	Schröder Fire Balloons G HAFB	403	
D-OLBF	Lindstrand LBL-105A	477	
D-OLBK	Schröder Fire Balloons G HAFB	181	D-LBS(4)
D-OLBL	Lindstrand LBL-105A	254	G-LBLB
D-OLBM	Cameron N-105 HAFB	3679	
D-OLBS(3)	Cameron A-105 HAFB	4736	
D-OLBU	Cameron A-105 HAFB	1855	D-Albuch
D-OLBY	Cameron A-105 HAFB	2955	
D-OLCE	Cameron N-105 HAFB	3097	
D-OLCI(2)	Kubicek BB-37 HAFB	277	OK-0277
D-OLDD	Schröder Fire Balloons G HAFB	312	
D-OLDY(2)	Schröder Fire Balloons G HAFB	971	
D-OLEA (2)	Schröder Fire Balloons G HAFB	909	
D-OLEE	Cameron O-120 HAFB(Reservation)	3066	
D-OLEG(2)	Schröder Fire Balloons Clownkopf SS HAFB	1027	
D-OLEK	Ultramagic V-105 HAFB	105/72	
D-OLEN	Cameron N-105 HAFB (Res 3.99)	3251	
D-OLEO	Ultramagic M-120 HAFB	120/02	
D-OLES	Schröder Fire Balloons G HAFB	999	
D-OLEU(2)	Schröder Fire Balloons G HAFB	1096	
D-OLEV(2)	Schröder Fire Balloons G HAFB (Replacement for c/n 200)	728	
D-OLEW	Schröder Fire Balloons G HAFB	945	
D-OLFD	Thunder AX9-140 SII HAFB	4962	
D-OLFI (2)	Gefa-Flug AS.105GD Hot Air Airship	0023	
D-OLGA	Schröder Fire Balloons G HAFB	826	
D-OLGL	Thunder AX8-90 SI HAFB	2249	
D-OLGN	Schröder Fire Balloons G HAFB	1007	
D-OLGP	Schröder Fire Balloons G HAFB	678	
D-OLGS	Cameron Z-120 HAFB	10619	
D-OLHB	Schröder Fire Balloons G HAFB	1050	
D-OLHG	Schröder Fire Balloons G HAFB	573	
D-OLIA	Thunder AX10-160 SIIHAFB	4627	
D-OLIB	Wörner NL-1000/STU Gas Balloon	1049	
D-OLIE	Schröder Fire Balloons G HAFB	285	
D-OLIF	Schröder Fire Balloons G HAFB	40	D-Cliff
D-OLIN	Schröder Fire Balloons GHAFB	1080	
D-OLIP(2)	Schröder Fire Balloons G HAFB	531	
D-OLIV(2)	Aerostar S-60A HAFB (Formerly Raven S-60A c/n 380)	3241	
D-OLIX	Schröder Fire Balloons G HAFB	22	D-Achalm(1)
D-OLLB(2)	Thunder AX9-120 SII HAFB	4919	
D-OLLC	Thunder AX8-90 SII HAFB	1836	D-Bothfeld (1)
D-OLLD	Thunder AX8-105 SII HAFB	1987	D-Bothfeld (2)
D-OLLE(2)	Schröder Fire Balloons G HAFB	747	
D-OLLG	Thunder AX9-120 SII HAFB	4012	
D-OLLH	Thunder AX8-105 SII HAFB (Reservation)	2201	
D-OLLI	Schröder Fire Balloons G HAFB	228	
D-OLLL(2)	Cameron A-105 HAFB (Replacement for c/n 2119 ex D-Lesespass)	4744	
D-OLLP	Thunder AX9-120 SII HAFB	4916	
D-OLLY(2)	Cameron A-120 HAFB	4991	
D-OLLZ	Thunder AX10-150 SII HAFB	4514	D-OLLA(3)
D-OLMA	Raven Europe FS-57A HAFB	E-085	D-Almandin
D-OLMH	Schröder Fire Balloons G HAFB	522	
D-OLMS	Thunder AX9-120 SII HAFB	10036	
D-OLMT	Lindstrand LBL-150A HAFB	694	
D-OLMW	Gefa-Flug AS.105GD Hot Air Airship	0017	
D-OLNI	Schröder Fire Balloons G HAFB	969	
D-OLOR	Lindstrand LBL-105A HAFB	490	
D-OLOT(2)	Cameron O-105 HAFB (Replacement for c/n 2570)	10110	
D-OLOW(2)	Schröder Fire Balloons G HAFB	707	
D-OLPB	Cameron N-90 HAFB	2601	D-Light
D-OLPE	Cameron N-120 HAFB	2311	D-Dresden G-BSRE
D-OLPP(2)	Wörner NL-840/STU Gas Balloon	1044	
D-OLTB	Lindstrand LBL-120A HAFB	354	
D-OLTJ	Schröder Fire Balloons G HAFB	1008	
D-OLTM	Schröder Fire Balloons G HAFB	1018	
D-OLTS	Ultramagic N-210 HAFB	210/10	
D-OLTT	Raven Europe S-60A HAFB	E-367	
D-OLUB	Lindstrand LBL-310A HAFB	843	
D-OLUD	Schröder Fire Balloons G HAFB	549	
D-OLUG(2)	Cameron Z-120 HAFB	10349	
D-OLUS	Thunder AX8-90 SI HAFB	2488	
D-OLUX(3)	Schröder Fire Balloons G HAFB	1052	
D-OLVB(2)	Kubicek BB-70Z HAFB	299	OK-0299
D-OLVE	Wörner NL-840/STU Gas Balloon	1074	
D-OMAC(2)	Cameron N-90 HAFB (Replacement for c/n 3062)	10239	
D-OMAD	Schröder Fire Balloons G HAFB	562	
D-OMAG	Cameron V-77 HAFB	2167	D-OSEH G-BSEH
D-OMAI	Schröder Fire Balloons GHAFB	1072	
D-OMAL	Raven Europe S-60A HAFB	E-339	
D-OMAM	Schröder Fire Balloons G HAFB	400	
D-OMAR(2)	Aerostar RXS-8 HAFB	3116	
D-OMAS	Cameron N-120 HAFB	3566	
D-OMAT	Raven Europe FS-57A HAFB	E-257	HB-BXC F-GLCE
D-OMAW	Schröder Fire Balloons G HAFB	499	
D-OMAY(2)	Schröder Fire Balloons SSAuto HAFB	741	
D-OMBB	Thunder AX8-105 SI HAFB	4189	
D-OMBF	Cameron A-105 HAFB	3032	
D-OMBG	Schröder Fire Balloons G HAFB	477	
D-OMBI	Schröder Fire Balloons G HAFB	1113	
D-OMBL	Schröder Fire Balloons G HAFB	705	
D-OMBO(2)	Thunder AX9-120 SII HAFB (Permit .03)	4368	
D-OMBS	Colt 120A HAFB	3609	
D-OMBZ	Lindstrand LBL-150A HAFB	398	
D-OMCD	Cameron N-105 HAFB	3431	
D-OMCG	Schröder Fire Balloons G HAFB	48	D-Germany(2)
D-OMCR	Schröder Fire Balloons G HAFB	990	
D-OMEC(2)	Cameron N-120 HAFB	4267	
D-OMEI	Cameron A-210 HAFB(Reservation .00)	4995	
D-OMEK	Schröder Fire Balloons G HAFB	608	
D-OMEN(2)	Schröder Fire Balloons G HAFB	921	
D-OMES	Schröder Fire Balloons G HAFB	709	
D-OMET	Thunder AX7-77 SI HAFB	1572	D-Meteor D-Jever(2)
D-OMEW	Schröder Fire Balloons G HAFB	664	
D-OMEY(3)	Schröder Fire Balloons G HAFB	955	
D-OMFM	Raven Europe S-60A HAFB	E-351	
D-OMFX	Cameron N-105 HAFB	3443	PH-OMF
D-OMFY(2)	Lindstrand LBL-105A HAFB	453	D-Somfy (2)
D-OMGS	Ultranagic M-145 HAFB	145/15	
D-OMGV	Raven-Europe S-60A HAFB	E-270	
D-OMHG	Kubicek BB-37 HAFB	229	OK-0229
D-OMHM	Schröder Fire Balloons G HAFB	512	
D-OMHN	Thunder AX9-140 SII HAFB	2339	
D-OMHR	Thunder AX8-90 HAFB	3504	
D-OMHS	Schröder Fire Balloons G HAFB	445	
D-OMIC	Schröder Fire Balloons G HAFB	725	
D-OMIE	Lindstrand LBL-150A HAFB	959	
D-OMIK	Schröder Fire Balloons SS Cat HAFB	305	
D-OMIL	Cameron N-105 HAFB	3819	
D-OMIS	Lindstrand LBL-150A HAFB	540	
D-OMIX	Schröder Fire Balloons G HAFB	390	
D-OMKA	Cameron N-90 HAFB	2737	
D-OMKB	Ultramagic M-145 HAFB	145/20	
D-OMKC	Schröder Fire Balloons G HAFB	637	
D-OMKD	Ultramagic M-105 HAFB	105/84	
D-OMKE	Schröder Fire Balloons G HAFB	619	
D-OMKF	Ultramagic M-145 HAFB	145/21	
D-OMKG	Ultramagic M-145 HAFB	145/22	
D-OMKH	Ultramagic M-145 HAFB	145/23	
D-OMKI	Ultramagic M-145 HAFB	145/24	
D-OMKJ	Ultramagic M-210 HAFB	210/18	
D-OMKK	Ultramagic M-145 HAFB	145/25	
D-OMKL	Schröder Fire Balloons G HAFB	764	
D-OMKM	Ultramagic M-145 HAFB	145/26	

D-OMKN	Ultramagic M-145 HAFB	145/27	
D-OMKT	Ultramagic M-105 HAFB	105/83	
D-OMKV	Schröder Fire Balloons G HAFB	569	
D-OMKW	Schröder Fire Balloons G HAFB	811	
D-OMLE	Lindstrand LBL-150A HAFB	533	
D-OMLW	Thunder AX8-105 SII HAFB	2570	
D-OMMA(2)	Colt 105A HAFB	2639	
D-OMMB	Cameron O-120 HAFB	3965	
D-OMMC	Cameron Z-105 HAFB	10451	
D-OMMF	Schröder Fire Balloons G HAFB	609	
D-OMMG	Cameron O-105 HAFB	2806	
D-OMMH	Thunder AX8-105 SII HAFB	3528	
D-OMMI	Schröder Fire Balloons G30/24 HAFB	488	HB-BTR
D-OMML	Schröder Fire Balloons G HAFB	198	
D-OMMM(2)	Cameron O-120 HAFB	10135	
D-OMMN	Thunder AX8-105 SII HAFB	783	G-BMMN
D-OMMR	Schröder Fire Balloons G HAFB	890	
D-OMMS	Schröder Fire Balloons G HAFB	934	
D-OMMU	GEFA-Flug AS.105GD Hot Air Airship	0018	
D-OMMW	Schröder Fire Balloons G HAFB	737	
D-OMMY	Balloon Works Firefly 9 HAFB	F9-070	
D-OMNB	Thunder AX8-105 SII HAFB	3531	
D-OMNG	Schröder Fire Balloons G HAFB	606	
D-OMNK	Schröder Fire Balloons G HAFB	523	
D-OMNR	Cameron Z-120 HAFB	10233	
D-OMOG	Aerostar S-57A HAFB	3191	
D-OMOR	Raven Europe S-60A HAFB	E-302	
D-OMOS	Cameron N-105 HAFB	3008	
D-OMOZ	Aerostar S-60A HAFB	3236	
D-OMPA	Schröder Fire Balloons G HAFB	518	
D-OMPB	Ultramagic M-145 HAFB	145/32	
D-OMPD	Colt 105A HAFB	2131	
D-OMPH	Cameron N-105 HAFB	4270	
D-OMPK	Schröder Fire Balloons G HAFB	227	D-OCHR
D-OMPS	Lindstrand LBL-310A HAFB	558	
D-OMRB	Schröder Fire Balloons G HAFB	722	
D-OMRL(3)	Schröder Fire Balloons G HAFB	1005	
D-OMRV	Schröder Fire Balloons G HAFB	505	
D-OMSA	Schröder Fire Balloons G HAFB	537	
D-OMST	Colt 105A HAFB	2153	PH-IAK
D-OMTD	Cameron A-105 HAFB	4974	
D-OMTI	Schröder Fire Balloons G HAFB	647	
D-OMTW	Schröder Fire Balloons G HAFB	1067	
D-OMUB	Schröder Fire Balloons G HAFB	1029	
D-OMUC	Wörner NL-840/STU Gas Balloon	1062	
D-OMUH	Schröder Fire Balloons G HAFB	435	
D-OMUM	Cameron O-105 HAFB	4192	
D-OMUS	Schröder Fire Balloons G HAFB	1013	
D-OMUT	Raven-Europe S-60A HAFB	E-272	
D-OMUU	Schröder Fire Balloons G HAFB	458	
D-OMUV	Schröder Fire Balloons G HAFB	973	
D-OMWA	Thunder AX9-120 SII HAFB	4393	
D-OMWH	Lindstrand LBL-150A HAFB	597	
D-OMWP	Schröder Fire Balloons G HAFB	1087	
D-OMWY	Schröder Fire Balloons G HAFB	530	
D-OMZF	Thunder AX8-105 SII HAFB	4398	
D-ONAA	Stuttgart K-780/2-STU Gas Balloon	0102	D-Sony
D-ONAF	Lindstrand LBL-150A HAFB	766	
D-ONAT(2)	Schröder Fire Balloons G HAFB	882	
	(Replacement for c/n 55)		
D-ONAU	Cameron O-105 HAFB	2836	
D-ONBG(2)	Schröder Fire Balloons G HAFB	651	
D-ONBM	Colt 90A HAFB	912	G-BNBM
D-ONBY(2)	Cameron A-210 HAFB	4975	
D-ONCC	Cameron N-105 HAFB	3427	
D-ONCH	Cameron N-105 HAFB	3602	
D-ONCK	Cameron N-133 HAFB	3084	
D-ONDI	Cameron N-105 HAFB	1725	D-Mondi(1)
D-ONDO	Cameron N-105 HAFB	2851	
D-ONDY	Cameron N-105 HAFB	4630	
D-ONEE	Schröder Fire Balloons Maus SS HAFB	614	
D-ONEI	Cameron N-105 HAFB	10014	
D-ONEK	Thunder AX9-140 SII HAFB	2333	
D-ONEO	Schröder Fire Balloons G HAFB (Reservn)	2001	
D-ONES(2)	Cameron N-133 HAFB (Reservation)	4647	
D-ONET(2)	Cameron N-105 HAFB	3669	
D-ONEU	Raven Europe S-60A HAFB	E-341	
D-ONEW(2)	Schröder Fire Balloons G HAFB	963	
D-ONGA	Cameron Z-105 HAFB	10262	
D-ONGO	Cameron N-133 HAFB	3751	
D-ONHG	Thunder AX8-105 HAFB	1907	D-Wefah(2)
D-ONIB	Schröder Fire Balloons G HAFB	951	
D-ONIE(2)	Schröder Fire Balloons G HAFB	883	
D-ONIG	Cameron V-90 HAFB	3653	
D-ONIK	Schröder Fire Balloons G HAFB	295	
D-ONIL	Thunder AX8-90 SII HAFB	3534	D-ODIL
D-ONIS(2)	Schröder Fire Balloons G HAFB	1092	
	(Replacement for c/n 346)		
D-ONIX	Lindstrand LBL-120A HAFB	349	
D-ONJA	Cameron N-105 HAFB	3252	
D-ONKA	Cameron O-120 HAFB	2596	D-ONKY
			G-BTME
D-ONKE	Lindstrand LBL-105A HAFB	126	
D-ONKI (2)	Lindstrand LBL-180A HAFB	679	
D-ONKJ (2)	Lindstrand LBL-210A HAFB	818	
D-ONKO	Lindstrand LBL-105A HAFB	604	
D-ONLB	Schröder Fire Balloons G HAFB	645	

D-ONLY	Cameron A-105 HAFB	2900	
D-ONMR	Colt 105A HAFB	2120	D-ORAC
D-ONNA	Cameron A-210 HAFB	3014	
D-ONNI	Cameron N-120 HAFB	3765	
D-ONOE	Cameron O-90 HAFB	2799	D-Nordlicht(2)
D-ONOS	Kubicek BB-45 HAFB	227	OK-0227
D-ONOW	Thunder AX8-90 SI HAFB	2268	
D-ONPM	Aerostar S-60A HAFB	3223	
D-ONRA	Colt 77A HAFB	074	LN-CBC
			SE-ZVX
D-ONRJ	Lindstrand LBL-210A HAFB	555	
D-ONRW	Schröder Fire Balloons G HAFB	126	D-Sportland
D-ONSB	Colt 105A HAFB (Permit .03)	3750	
D-ONTG	Cameron O-105 HAFB	2394	D-Montgolfiere
D-ONUE	Cameron N-105 HAFB	4676	
D-ONUP	Ultramagic M-105 HAFB	105/40	
D-ONUV	Schröder Fire Balloons G HAFB	590	
D-ONWB	Stuttgart K-1000/3-STU	0312	D-Hopfenblute
D-OOAA	Schröder Fire Balloons G HAFB	848	
D-OOAC	Ultramagic M-120 HAFB	120/05	
D-OOAH	Ultramagic M-120 HAFB (Permit .03)	120/10	
D-OOAM	Schröder Fire Balloons G HAFB	542	
D-OOAS	Ultramagic S-90 HAFB	90/11	
D-OOAZ	Colt 90A HAFB	4928	
D-OOBI	Cameron A-105 HAFB	2893	
D-OOBS	Sky 105-24 HAFB	185	
D-OOBU(2)	Thunder AX9-140SII HAFB	3948	
D-OOBW(2)	Schröder Fire Balloons G HAFB	384	D-OHOM(1)
D-OOCA	Thunder AX8-105 SIIHAFB	4746	
D-OOCS	Schröder Fire Balloons GHAFB	1066	
D-OODD	Kubicek BB-30Z HAFB	225	OK-0225
D-OODI	Schröder Fire Balloons G HAFB	534	
D-OODL	Schröder Fire Balloons G HAFB	683	
D-OODM	Schröder Fire Balloons G HAFB	344	
D-OOEF	Aerostar S-60AHAFB	3256	
D-OOEH	Schröder Fire Balloons G HAFB	550	
D-OOEK	Schröder Fire Balloons GHAFB	1062	
D-OOEL(2)	Schröder Fire Balloons G HAFB	628	
D-OOEN	Raven Europe S-60A HAFB	E-197	F-GKFG
			D-Abenteuer
D-OOES	Colt 180A HAFB (Reservation)	2578	
D-OOFB	Schröder Fire Balloons G HAFB	652	
D-OOFD	Schröder Fire Balloons G HAFB	1130	
D-OOFI	Schröder Fire Balloons G HAFB	616	
D-OOFW	Schröder Fire Balloons G HAFB	756	
D-OOGB	Schröder Fire Balloons G HAFB	594	
D-OOGS	Schröder Fire Balloons G HAFB	720	
D-OOGY	Schröder Fire Balloons G HAFB	818	
D-OOHA	Cameron N/Z-133 HAFB	10185	
D-OOHB	Schröder Fire Balloons G HAFB	788	
D-OOHE	Schröder Fire Balloons G HAFB	816	
D-OOHH	GEFA-Flug AS.105GD Hot Air Airship	0029	
D-OOHK	Schröder Fire Balloons G HAFB	635	
D-OOHO	Raven Europe S-60A HAFB	E-304	
D-OOHP	Ultramagic M-65 HAFB (Reservation)	65/70	HB-QDY
D-OOHR	Schröder Fire Balloons G HAFB	611	
D-OOIL	Schröder Fire Balloons G HAFB	454	
D-OOIN	Schröder Fire Balloons G HAFB	899	
D-OOJA	Schröder Fire Balloons G HAFB	682	
D-OOKS	Schröder Fire Balloons G HAFB	948	
D-OOKW	Schröder Fire Balloons G HAFB	567	
D-OOLD	Cameron O-105 HAFB	2444	D-Goldmarie
D-OOLK	Cameron O-105 HAFB	1865	D-Wokenkratzer
D-OOLS	Schröder Fire Balloons G HAFB	351	
D-OOMA(2)	Schröder Fire Balloons G HAFB	1073	
D-OOMG	Schröder Fire Balloons G HAFB	736	
D-OOMO	Colt 120A HAFB	4628	G-BYPV
D-OOMP(2)	Kubicek BB-42Z HAFB	224	OK-0224
D-OONE(2)	Kubicek BB-30Z HAFB	233	OK-0233
D-OONN	Cameron A-210 HAFB	3284	D-ONNN
D-OOOA(2)	Cameron A-105 HAFB	2253	D-Tubingen
D-OOOD	Schröder Fire Balloons G HAFB	988	
D-OOOH(2)	Colt 140A HAFB (Reservation)	4665	
D-OOOL (2)	Kubicek BB-42Z HAFB	267	OK-0267
D-OOOR	Colt 120A HAFB	1863	G-BTLO
D-OOOS	Thunder AX8-105 SII HAFB	2132	G-BUBV
D-OOOT	Colt 120A HAFB (Reservation)	2270	
D-OOPA (2)	Colt 150A HAFB	10351	
D-OOPH	Ultramagic M-105 HAFB	105/28	
D-OOPS	Cameron V-56 HAFB	3260	
D-OOPT	Schröder Fire Balloons G HAFB	605	
D-OOPW	Schröder Fire Balloons G HAFB	513	
D-OORB	Ultramagic M-105 HAFB	105/100	
D-OORH	Schröder Fire Balloons G HAFB	140	
D-OORJ(2)	Schröder Fire Balloons G HAFB	1115	
D-OORL	Schröder Fire Balloons G HAFB	unkn	
D-OORO	Thunder AX9-140 SII HAFB	2332	
D-OORT	Cameron O-105 HAFB	2775	
D-OOSI	Ultramagic T-180 HAFB	180/31	
D-OOSK	Schröder Fire Balloons G HAFB	958	
D-OOSW	Cameron O-84 HAFB	1279	D-Enterprise
D-OOSZ	Schröder Fire Balloons G HAFB	931	
D-OOTS	Schröder Fire Balloons G HAFB	416	
D-OOTV	Cameron N-145 HAFB	10268	
D-OOTW	Schröder Fire Balloons G HAFB	744	
D-OOUM	Ultramagic H-42 HAFB	42/04	
D-OOVE	Schröder Fire Balloons G HAFB	881	

D-OOVI	Cameron Z-105 HAFB	10531	
D-OOVW	Schröder Fire Balloons G HAFB	406	
D-OOVZ	Kubicek BB-30 HAFB	191	OK-0191
D-OOWE	Wörner NL-1000/STU Gas Balloon	1055	
D-OOWS	Wörner NL-640/STU Gas Balloon	1067	
D-OOWW	Lindstrand LBL-150A	725	
D-OOZI	Thunder AX8-105 SII HAFB	2363	
D-OOZL	Wörner NL-1000/STU Gas Balloon	1079	
D-OPAC	Cameron O-120 HAFB	4474	
D-OPAD	Wörner FK-280/STU Gas Balloon	6002	
D-OPAH	Schröder Fire Balloons G HAFB	56	D-Lichtenstein
D-OPAK(2)	Schröder Fire Balloons G HAFB (Replacement for c/n 160)	898	
D-OPAL	Balloon Works Firefly 8B-15 HAFB	F8B-486	
D-OPAP(2)	Schröder Fire Balloons G HAFB	475	
D-OPAR(2)	Schröder Fire Balloons G HAFB	160	D-OPAK(1) D-Arjomari
D-OPAS	Cameron O-105 HAFB	2653	
D-OPAW	Kubicek BB-45 HAFB	324	OK-0324
D-OPAX	Augsburg K-630/I-STU Gas Balloon	0134	D-Eurpoa
D-OPBD	Wörner FKP-380/STU Gas Balloon	6201	
D-OPBL	Cameron N-105 HAFB	4203	
D-OPBP	Wörner FK-5550/STU Gas Balloon (Res.)	6004	
D-OPCI	Lindstrand LBL-150A HAFB	990	
D-OPCM	Schröder Fire Balloons G HAFB	424	
D-OPEB	Thunder AX7-77A SIII HAFB	325	
D-OPEC	Thunder AX7-77 SI HAFB	1970	
D-OPEL	Schröder Fire Balloons G HAFB	503	
D-OPEN	Schröder Fire Balloons G HAFB	273	
D-OPEP	Schröder Fire Balloons G HAFB	661	
D-OPER	Schröder Fire Balloons G HAFB	822	
D-OPET	Schröder Fire Balloons G HAFB	823	
D-OPFG	Cameron A-140 HAFB	10524	
D-OPFP	Kubicek BB-42Z HAFB	306	OK-0306
D-OPHA(2)	Lindstrand LBL-105A HAFB	955	
D-OPHC	Cameron N-105 HAFB	2871	
D-OPHS	Ultramagic N-355 HAFB	355/06	
D-OPIE	Schröder Fire Balloons Pinguin SS HAFB	341	
D-OPIH	Aerostar S-66A HAFB	3062	
D-OPIK	Schröder Fire Balloons G HAFB	895	
D-OPIT	Cameron N-133 HAFB	3992	
D-OPJA	Schröder Fire Balloons G HAFB	1097	
D-OPKW	Schröder Fire Balloons G HAFB	427	
D-OPLB	Schröder Fire Balloons GHAFB	201	D-Arolsen
D-OPLK	Schröder Fire Balloons GHAFB	791	
D-OPLR	Cameron N-90 HAFB	2351	D-Höfler
D-OPMA	Cameron O-140 HAFB	4873	
D-OPMB	Wörner NL-1000/STU Gas Balloon	1045	
D-OPMD	Thunder AX8-90 SII HAFB	2481	
D-OPMF	Schröder Fire Balloons G HAFB	430	
D-OPMI	Cameron O-120 HAFB	2686	
D-OPMK	Schröder Fire Balloons G HAFB	95	D-Feuerzahn (1)
D-OPMM	Kubicek BB-30 HAFB	190	OK-0190
D-OPMN	Colt 105A HAFB	4147	
D-OPMO	Kubicek BB- HAFB	335	OK-0335
D-OPOB	Schröder Fire Balloons GHAFB	853	
D-OPON	Schröder Fire Balloons GHAFB	314	
D-OPOW	Schröder Fire Balloons G HAFB	894	
D-OPOZ	Schröder Fire Balloons G HAFB	893	
D-OPPA	Cameron A-105 HAFB	1569	D-Lloyd(2)
D-OPPE	Lindstrand LBL-150A HAFB	364	
D-OPPI(2)	Schröder Fire Balloons G HAFB	879	
D-OPPL	Schröder Fire Balloons G HAFB	835	
D-OPPP(3)	Schröder Fire Balloons G HAFB	809	
D-OPPT	Schröder Fire Balloons G HAFB	331	
D-OPPY	Schröder Fire Balloons G HAFB	297	
D-OPRI	Schröder Fire Balloons G HAFB	359	
D-OPRO	Cameron N-90 HAFB	2906	
D-OPSD	Thunder AX8-90 SI HAFB	4625	
D-OPSI	Raven-Europe FS-57A HAFB	E-159	D-Mopsi
D-OPTA	Schröder Fire Balloons G HAFB	1056	
D-OPTJ	Thunder AX7-77 SI HAFB	800	D-Optimist
D-OPTO	Schröder Fire Balloons GHAFB	875	
D-OPUM	Cameron A-120 HAFB	3483	
D-OPUN	Cameron A-120 HAFB	3203	
D-OPUP	Schröder Fire Balloons G HAFB	564	
D-OPUS	Schröder Fire Balloons G HAFB	224	
D-OPUV	Stuttgart K-630/1-STU	0120	(D-OSIL) D-Silentium
D-OPWC	Ultramagic S-90 HAFB	90/34	
D-OPWL	Cameron Z-120 HAFB	10299	
D-OPYT	Schröder Fire Balloons G HAFB	471	
D-OQCL(2)	Lindstrand LBL-240A HAFB	588	
D-OQEL	Colt 180A HAFB	2330	
D-OQUA	Schröder Fire Balloons G HAFB	1138	
D-OQUE	Schröder Fire Balloons G HAFB	855	
D-ORAB	Lindstrand LBL-210A HAFB	815	
D-ORAC(2)	Colt 180A HAFB	3497	
D-ORAL	Schröder Fire Balloons G HAFB	907	
D-ORAM	Cameron N-105 HAFB	3294	
D-ORAR	Sky 180-24 HAFB	042	
D-ORAS	Lindstrand LBL-150A HAFB	536	
D-ORAT	Ultramagic S-105 HAFB	105/53	D-Carat
D-ORBA	Schröder Fire Balloons GHAFB	981	
D-ORCA(2)	Thunder AX8-105 SII HAFB	4438	
D-ORCC	Cameron A-140 HAFB	4485	

D-ORCI	Lindstrand LBL-150A HAFB	693	
D-ORCK	Thunder AX9-140 SII HAFB	4312	
D-ORCO	Lindstrand LBL-150A HAFB	713	
D-ORDU	Cameron A-120 HAFB (Reservation)	2902	
D-OREA(2)	Schröder Fire Balloons G HAFB	1058	
D-OREC	Schröder Fire Balloons G HAFB	663	
D-ORED(2)	Lihndstrand LBL-120A HAFB	464	
D-OREE	Cameron N-105 HAFB	4123	
D-OREG	Thunder AX8-90 SII HAFB	329	D-Regio D-Europa III
D-OREI	Cameron N-105 HAFB	3245	
D-OREK	Schröder Fire Balloons G HAFB	1081	
D-OREL(2)	Lindstrand LBL-240A HAFB	799	
D-OREM	Cameron A-250 HAFB	3224	
D-OREN	Schröder Fire Balloons G HAFB	440	
D-OREV	Cameron N-105 HAFB (Permit .03)	3109	
D-OREW	Schröder Fire Balloons G HAFB	597	
D-OREX(2)	Schröder Fire Balloons G HAFB	1095	
D-ORFA	Cameron O-105 HAFB	1209	D-OATC D-Albstadt(2) D-Bauknecht(1)
D-ORFS	Cameron Z-150 HAFB	10315	
D-ORFW	Raven Europe S-60A HAFB	E-361	
D-ORGA	Cameron N-105 HAFB	2716	
D-ORGL	Schröder Fire Balloons G HAFB	684	
D-ORGS(2)	Ultramagic M-105 HAFB	105/82	
D-ORHA	Raven Europe FS-57A HAFB	E-207	
D-ORHB	Schröder Fire Balloons G HAFB	283	D-Hessen(3)
D-ORHE	Schröder Fire Balloons G HAFB	360	
D-ORHK	Schröder Fire Balloons G HAFB	831	
D-ORHT	Lindstrand LBL-150A HAFB	561	G-BWJJ
D-ORHV	Colt 180A HAFB (Reservation 7.99)	1563	G-BRHV
D-ORHW	Schröder Fire Balloons G HAFB (Permit .03)	675	
D-ORIA	Cameron A-105 HAFB	2844	
D-ORIB	Cameron A-105 HAFB	3894	
D-ORID	Schröder Fire Balloons GHAFB	994	
D-ORIE	Schröder Fire Balloons G HAFB	307	
D-ORIF	Thunder AX8-105 SII HAFB	4528	
D-ORIS	Thunder AX8-90 SI HAFB	2406	
D-ORIT(2)	Schröder Fire Balloons G HAFB	526	
D-ORIZ	Colt 105A HAFB	4465	
D-ORJB	Schröder Fire Balloons G HAFB	544	
D-ORJL	Colt 105A HAFB	3488	
D-ORKA(2)	Wörner FK-5500/STU Gas Balloon	6016	
D-ORKE	Thunder AX8-105 SII HAFB	10215	
D-ORLC	Thunder AX8-105 SII HAFB (Permit .04)	2529	D-OBLC(1)
D-ORLI (2)	Cameron Z-105 HAFB (Replacement for A-105 c/n 2544)	10461	
D-ORMA	Schröder Fire Balloons G HAFB	425	
D-ORMD	Schröder Fire Balloons G HAFB	763	
D-ORNG	Kubicek BB-30Z HAFB	272	OK-0272
D-ORNI	Thunder AX8-105 SII HAFB	2179	
D-OROB	Schröder Fire Balloons G HAFB	843	
D-OROL	Colt 105A HAFB	3835	
D-ORON	Raven RX-7 HAFB	362	HB-BFK
D-OROP	Thunder AX8-105 SII HAFB	4352	
D-OROS	Schröder Fire Balloons G HAFB	409	
D-OROT	Colt 105A HAFB	2289	
D-OROV	Cameron N-90 HAFB	4399	D-Rheinprovinz
D-ORPP	Lindstrand LBL-120A HAFB	835	
D-ORPR	Schröder Fire Balloons G HAFB (Permit .03)	484	
D-ORRJ	Schröder Fire Balloons G HAFB	712	
D-ORRT	Cameron N-120 HAFB	3729	
D-ORRU	Schröder Fire Balloons G HAFB	570	
D-ORRZ	Schröder Fire Balloons G HAFB	478	
D-ORSB	Lindstrand LBL-150A HAFB	568	
D-ORSE	Head AX8-105 HAFB	257	
D-ORSI	Schröder Fire Balloons G HAFB	561	
D-ORSS	Cameron N-105 HAFB (Permit .04)	3193	
D-ORST(2)	Cameron A-210 HAFB (Replacement for c/n 3263)	10411	
D-ORSW	Schröder Fire Balloons G HAFB	379	
D-ORTA(2)	GEFA-Flug AS.105GD Hot Air Airship	0028	
D-ORTB	Schröder Fire Balloons G HAFB	1043	
D-ORTC	Schröder Fire Balloons G HAFB	1044	
D-ORTH	Ultramagic M-145 HAFB	145/39	
D-ORTL	Cameron A-140 HAFB	4468	
D-ORTS	Cameron A-105 HAFB	3202	
D-ORUB	Cameron N-105 HAFB	10662	
D-ORUE(2)	Cameron N-90 HAFB	1539	D-Hemden
D-ORUI (2)	Schröder Fire Balloons G HAFB (Replacement for c/n 248)	1074	
D-ORUL(3)	Kubicek BB-42Z HAFB	274	OK-0274
D-ORUM(2)	Cameron N-105 HAFB	"5001"	
D-ORUP	Schröder Fire Balloons G HAFB	648	
D-ORUT(2)	Cameron O-105 HAFB	4484	
D-ORUV	Raven Europe S-60A HAFB	E-268	
D-ORVS	Cameron O-105 HAFB	4600	
D-ORWB	Cameron C-90 HAFB	10402	
D-ORWE	Thunder AX8-105 SII HAFB	10091	
D-ORWL	Thunder AX8-105 SII HAFB (Reservation)	3825	
D-ORZG	Schröder Fire Balloons G HAFB	693	D-Erzgebirge (2)
D-OSAA	Cameron A-105 HAFB	3803	
D-OSAC	Schröder Fire Balloons GHAFB	1075	
D-OSAH	Schröder Fire Balloons G HAFB	1035	
D-OSAL	Schröder Fire Balloons G HAFB	603	
D-OSAM	Wörner FK-280/STU Gas Balloon	6001	

D-OSAN	Wörner NL-640/STU Gas Balloon	1084	
D-OSAR(2)	Schröder Fire Balloons G HAFB	836	
	(Replacement for c/n 271)		
D-OSAT	Schröder Fire Balloons G HAFB (Permit .04)	721	
D-OSAU	Wörner K-1000/3-STU Gas Balloon (Res 5.99)	0292	
	(Now shown as c/n 0229/0292)		
D-OSAV	Colt 240A HAFB	2176	
D-OSBA	Thunder AX9-120 SII HAFB	2306	
D-OSBB	Colt 105A HAFB	4046	
D-OSBJ	Thunder AX8-1065 SII HAFB	3798	
D-OSBK	Kubicek BB-30 HAFB	182	OK-0182
D-OSBM	Thunder AX9-120 SII HAFB	4556	
D-OSBS	Colt 105A HAFB	4889	
D-OSBT(2)	Cameron A-140 HAFB	4972	
D-OSBZ	Colt 69A HAFB	2334	
D-OSCA(2)	Schröder Fire Balloons G HAFB	860	
D-OSCB	Raven Europe S-60A HAFB	E-358	
D-OSCC	Lindstrand LBL-150AHAFB	584	
D-OSCT	Schröder Fire Balloons G HAFB	863	
D-OSDS	Schröder Fire Balloons G HAFB	1016	
D-OSDZ	Schröder Fire Balloons G HAFB	784	
D-OSEC	Cameron N-105 HAFB	3306	
D-OSEE(2)	Cameron A-105 HAFB	3691	
D-OSEH	Schröder Fire Balloons G HAFB	978	
D-OSEL	Schröder Fire Balloons G HAFB	830	
D-OSEN	Schröder Fire Balloons G HAFB	482	
D-OSEP	Ultramagic Z-90 HAFB	90/14	
D-OSEX	Colt 105AHAFB	2070	
D-OSFB	Schröder Fire Balloons G HAFB	465	
D-OSFD	Aerostar S-60A HAFB	3228	
D-OSFE	Thunder AX8-105 SII HAFB	2527	
D-OSFT	Kubicek BB-30 HAFB	228	OK-0228
D-OSGC	Schröder Fire Balloons G HAFB	771	
D-OSGH	Aerostar S-57A HAFB	3218	
D-OSGS	Thunder AX10-150 SII HAFB	4798	
D-OSHA	Schröder Fire Balloons G HAFB	218	
D-OSHB(2)	Schröder Fire Balloons G HAFB	1032	
D-OSHG	Ultramagic M-145 HAFB	145/06	
D-OSHI	Cameron N-105 HAFB	4303	
D-OSHR	Cameron A-210SV HAFB	3897	
D-OSHS(2)	Schröder Fire Balloons G HAFB	453	
D-OSIB	Cameron O-77 HAFB	861	D-Bamberg
D-OSIE	Schröder Fire Balloons G HAFB	807	
D-OSIG	Schröder Fire Balloons G HAFB	150	
D-OSIN	Colt 105A HAFB	2057	
D-OSIO	Schröder Fire Balloons G HAFB	912	
D-OSIS(2)	Schröder Fire Balloons G HAFB	1015	
D-OSKA(2)	Schröder Fire Balloons G HAFB	897	
D-OSKB	Schröder Fire Balloons G HAFB	687	
D-OSKF	Schröder Fire Balloons G HAFB	698	
D-OSKK	Cameron O-90 HAFB	3693	D-Kreis-Sparkasse
D-OSKR	Schröder Fire Balloons G HAFB	1103	
D-OSKU	Schröder Fire Balloons G HAFB	552	
D-OSLL	Schröder Fire Balloons G HAFB	1002	
D-OSLR	Aerostar S-60A HAFB	3275	
D-OSLS	Cameron O-84 HAFB	1551	D-Telge II
D-OSMB	Schröder Fire Balloons G HAFB	751	
D-OSMC(2)	Cameron N-105 HAFB	4721	
	(Reservation - replacement for c/n 3663)		
D-OSME	Schröder Fire Balloons G HAFB	1020	
D-OSMG	Schröder Fire Balloons GHAFB	1078	
D-OSMO	Lindstrand LBL-120A HAFB	970	
D-OSMP	Thunder AX10-160 SI HAFB (Reservation)	1419	D-OAXL D-Jupiter G-BPXP
D-OSMS	Schröder Fire Balloons G HAFB	674	
D-OSNA(2)	Thunder AX10-180 SII HAFB	3521	
D-OSOM	Raven Europe RX-7 HAFB	E-121	D-Sommer Traum
D-OSON(2)	Lindstrand LBL-150A HAFB	865	
D-OSPD	Cameron O-84 HAFB	2916	
D-OSPE	Cameron A-105 HAFB	3871	
D-OSPI	Kubicek BB-30Z HAFB	317	OK-0317
D-OSPN	Lindstrand LBL-180A HAFB	421	
D-OSPS	Balloon Works Firefly 7-15 HAFB (Res.)	F7-834-3	
D-OSPV	Lindstrand LBL-150A HAFB (Permit .03)	626	
D-OSRP	Schröder Fire Balloons G HAFB (Permit .03)	415	
D-OSSE	Lindstrand LBL-105A HAFB	796	
D-OSSH	Schröder Fire Balloons G HAFB	353	
D-OSSI	Cameron V-77 HAFB	2664	
D-OSSK	Schröder Fire Balloons G HAFB	914	
D-OSSR	Schröder Fire Balloons G HAFB	761	
D-OSSS	Schröder Fire Balloons G HAFB	793	
D-OSST	Cameron A-300 HAFB	4668	
D-OSSW	Cameron O-120 HAFB	4157	
D-OSTA(3)	Schröder Fire Balloons G HAFB	781	
D-OSTB	Schröder Fire Balloons G HAFB	633	
D-OSTC	Schröder Fire Balloons G HAFB	782	
D-OSTD	Schröder Fire Balloons G HAFB	1.96-2	
D-OSTL(2)	Schröder Fire Balloons G HAFB	852	
	(Replacement for c/n 264)		
D-OSTY	Wörner NL-840/STUGas Balloon	1063	
D-OSTZ(2)	Wörner NL-1000/STUGas Balloon	1082	
D-OSUB	Schröder Fire Balloons G HAFB	519	
D-OSUD	Schröder Fire Balloons G HAFB	607	
D-OSUL	Cameron V-90 HAFB	2807	PH-JME
D-OSUN	Schröder Fire Balloons G HAFB	571	
D-OSUS(2)	Schröder Fire Balloons G HAFB	456	
D-OSUV	Schröder Fire Balloons G HAFB (Res 8.99)	370	
D-OSVO(2)	Ultramagic M-105 HAFB	105/110	
D-OSWA	Colt 105A HAFB	2142	
D-OSWB	Cameron N-120 HAFB	3927	
D-OSWH	Cameron N-105 HAFB	3919	
D-OSWN	Lindstrand LBL-120A HAFB	541	
D-OSWR	Cameron O-90 HAFB	4284	
D-OSWT	Cameron O-120 HAFB	4285	
D-OSWU	Lindstrand LBL-120A HAFB	789	
D-OSWW	Schröder Fire Balloons G HAFB	559	
D-OSZB	Wörner K-780/2-STU Gas Balloon	1033	
D-OSZO(2)	Schröder Fire Balloons G HAFB	808	
	(Replacement for c/n 174 ex OE-SZO)		
D-OTAB(3)	Schröder Fire Balloons GHAFB	792	
D-OTAK	Aerostar RXS-8 HAFB	3077	
D-OTAM	Thunder AX8-84 SI HAFB	4516	
D-OTAN	Schröder Fire Balloons G HAFB	776	
D-OTAR	Stuttgart K-1200/3-STU Gas Balloon	0257	D-Tarkett
D-OTBA	Thunder AX7-77 SI HAFB	1902	D-Gabriele
D-OTBL	Schröder Fire Balloons G HAFB	321	
D-OTCA(2)	Schröder Fire Balloons G HAFB	1132	
D-OTDI (2)	Schröder Fire Balloons G HAFB	800	
	(Replacement for c/n 540)		
D-OTEC	Colt 120A HAFB	2391	
D-OTED	Schröder Fire Balloons G HAFB	553	
D-OTEG	Schröder Fire Balloons G HAFB	796	
D-OTEL	Cameron Telefonhäuschen Phonebox SS HAFB	1918	D-Telefon
D-OTEN	Thunder AX7-77 SI HAFB	1804	G-BTEN
D-OTGS	Cameron N-133 HAFB	3582	D-OGVG
D-OTGV	Cameron N-105 HAFB	3786	
D-OTHA	Schröder Fire Balloons G HAFB	632	
D-OTHB	Wörner FKP-380/STU Gas Balloon	6203	
D-OTHI	Ultramagic V-90 HAFB	90/24	
D-OTHL	Schröder Fire Balloons G HAFB	74	D-Reutlingen
D-OTHN	Schröder Fire Balloons G HAFB	1025	
D-OTHS	GEFA-Flug AS.105GD Hot Air Airship	0032	
D-OTHT	Schröder Fire Balloons G HAFB	631	
D-OTIL	Cameron O-84 HAFB	1321	D-Johannes
D-OTIM(2)	Schröder Fire Balloons G HAFB	799	
	(Replacement for c/n 313)		
D-OTIS	Schröder Fire Balloons G HAFB (Permit .03)	209	D-OWPG
D-OTIW	Schröder Fire Balloons G HAFB	686	
D-OTKA	Colt 105A HAFB	4227	G-BXOV
D-OTLN	Schröder Fire Balloons G HAFB	487	
D-OTMA	Raven Europe S-60A HAFB	E-193	
D-OTMF	Lindstrand LBL-120AHAFB	648	
D-OTMU	Thunder AX8-105 SII HAFB	1977	G-BTMU
D-OTOA	Colt 240A HAFB	2518	
D-OTOB(2)	Colt 180A HAFB	3468	
D-OTOC	Thunder AX9-140 SII HAFB	2293	
D-OTOE	Colt 120A HAFB	4019	
D-OTOF	Lindstrand LBL-210A HAFB	696	
D-OTOL	Cameron A-140 HAFB	10041	
D-OTOM(2)	Lindstrand LBL-210A HAFB	775	
D-OTOP	Thunder AX8-105 SII HAFB (Reservation)	2225	
D-OTOR	Colt 105A HAFB	2537	
D-OTOS	Schröder Fire Balloons G HAFB	618	
D-OTPA	Colt 105A HAFB	4128	
D-OTPU	Cameron N-105 HAFB	2591	G-BTPU
D-OTPW	Cameron N-105 HAFB	2580	D-Provital G-BTPW
D-OTRA(2)	Schröder Fire Balloons G HAFB	956	
D-OTSS	Thunder AX8-105 SII HAFB	2636	
D-OTTA	GEFA-Flug AS.105GD Hot Air Airship	0022	
D-OTTG	Lindstrand LBL-150A HAFB	997	
D-OTTI	Schröder Fire Balloons Ottifant SS HAFB	33	D-Ottifant
D-OTTP	Lindstrand LBL-210A HAFB	358	
D-OTTS	Schröder Fire Balloons G HAFB	525	
D-OTTT(2)	Cameron O-90 HAFB	4095	
D-OTTU	Cameron V-90 HAFB	2646	G-BTTU
D-OTTY(2)	Cameron C-90 Concept HAFB	10561	
D-OTUI	Cameron N-90 HAFB	4443	
D-OTUL	Schröder Fire Balloons G HAFB	577	
D-OTUM	Lindstrand LBL-150A HAFB	1012	
D-OTUT	Cameron A-210 HAFB	3557	
D-OTUV	Schröder Fire Balloons G HAFB	538	
D-OTWD	Lindstrand LBL-150AHAFB	659	
D-OTWG	Thunder AX10-160 SII HAFB	2062	G-BTWG
D-OTWO	Cameron A-120 HAFB	3271	
D-OTWR	Schröder Fire Balloons G HAFB	941	
D-OTYM	Cameron O-84 HAFB	3211	
D-OTZC	Colt 90AHAFB	1876	G-BTZC
D-OUAE(2)	Colt 105A HAFB	3536	D-OOLA
D-OUAK	Thunder AX8-105 SII HAFB	2080	G-BUAK
D-OUAM	Schröder Fire Balloons G HAFB	701	
D-OUAT	Schröder Fire Balloons GHAFB	292	D-Quatro(3)
D-OUCH	Cameron A-210 HAFB (Reservation 7.99)	3352	G-BWAX
D-OUDP	Thunder AX8-105 SII HAFB	2178	D-Reineburg(2)
D-OUDR	Thunder AX9-140 SII HAFB	4553	
D-OUDQ	Thunder AX9-120 SII HAFB	3748	
D-OUEE	Wörner K-1000/3-STU Gas Balloon	0325	D-Queen
D-OUHR	Schröder Fire Balloons G HAFB	1039	
D-OUKW	Lindstrand LBL-150AHAFB	783	
D-OULM	Cameron O-84 HAFB	1817	D-Wurttfeuer(3)
D-OULI (2)	Lindstrand LBL-310A HAFB (Res 3.00)	684	

D-OULP	Thunder AX9-120 SII HAFB (Permit .03)	2266	G-BULP
D-OUNG	Schröder Fire Balloons G HAFB	394	
D-OUOG	Colt 90A HAFB	2224	G-BUOG
D-OUPD	Schröder Fire Balloons G HAFB	622	
D-OURE	Cameron N-120 HAFB	10126	
D-OURS(3)	Cameron A-210 HAFB	4568	
D-OUSA	Raven Europe S-60A HAFB	E-311	
D-OUSS	Raven Europe S-55AHAFB	E-173	D-Russberger
D-OUTZ	Lindstrand LBL-120AHAFB	793	
D-OUUU	Cameron A-315 HAFB	3399	
D-OUWE	Cameron N-90 HAFB (Res 6.99)	2602	D-Fresh
D-OUWI	Schröder Fire Balloons G HAFB	604	
D-OUYO	Thunder AX7-77 SI HAFB	953	G-BOGL
D-OUZO(2)	Ultramagic M-130 HAFB	130/30	
D-OUZR	Thunder AX8-90 SII HAFB	4445	
D-OVAG	Cameron A-160 HAFB	4773	
D-OVAI (2)	Ultramagic M-130 HAFB	130/21	
D-OVAK	Lindstrand LBL-120AHAFB	858	
D-OVAL	Schröder Fire Balloons G HAFB	275	
D-OVAN	Ultramagic M-105 HAFB	105/95	
D-OVBA	Wörner FK-5500/STU Gas Balloon	6017	
D-OVBB	Lindstrand LBL-120AHAFB	48	
D-OVBG	Schröder Fire Balloons G HAFB	627	
D-OVBR	Schröder Fire Balloons G HAFB	325	D-OVER(1)
D-OVBW	Lindstrand LBL-120A HAFB	047	G-BVBW
D-OVDS(2)	Schröder Fire Balloons G HAFB	889	
D-OVDT	Thunder AX8-105 SII HAFB	3524	
D-OVEC	Colt 105A HAFB	3855	
D-OVEG	Cameron N-105 HAFB	2077	D-Grevenstein(2)
D-OVEL	Cameron N-105 HAFB	3951	
D-OVER(2)	Lindstrand LBL-150A HAFB	987	
D-OVES	Lindstrand LBL-120A HAFB (Permit .03)	510	
D-OVHM	Cameron A-140 HAFB	3343	
D-OVIA	Ultramagic V-105 HAFB	105/81	
D-OVID	Cameron N-105 HAFB	2687	
D-OVIT	Aerostar S-60A HAFB	3255	
D-OVKA	Kubicek BB-37 HAFB	288	OK-0288
D-OVKW	Kubicek BB-30Z HAFB	287	OK-0287
D-OVLS	Thunder AX8-90 SII HAFB	2577	G-BVLS
D-OVMH	Schröder Fire Balloons G HAFB	510	
D-OVNI	Ultramagic S-105 HAFB	105/79	
D-OVOL(3)	Lindstrand LBL-150A HAFB (Replacement for (2) c/n 256)	800	
D-OVOM	Schröder Fire Balloons G HAFB	715	
D-OVON(2)	Schröder Fire Balloons G HAFB (Replaces c/n 362)	984	
D-OVOR	Aerostar RXS-8 HAFB	3066	
D-OVRB	Schröder Fire Balloons G HAFB	987	
D-OVRR(2)	Kubicek BB-30Z HAFB	244	OK-0244
D-OVSH	Cameron O-84 HAFB	1280	D-Ostsee
D-OVSS	Thunder AX8-105 SII HAFB	3533	
D-OVUN	Schröder Fire Balloons G HAFB	887	
D-OVUS	Schröder Fire Balloons G HAFB	485	
D-OVVO	Schröder Fire Balloons G HAFB	947	
D-OVVV(2)	Lindstrand LBL-400A HAFB	396	
D-OVWB	Ultramagic VWBeetle SS HAFB	F20/01	
D-OVWW	Thunder AX7-77 SI HAFB	4338	
D-OWAA	Schröder Fire Balloons G HAFB	239	
D-OWAB	Schröder Fire Balloons G HAFB	240	
D-OWAD	Thunder AX7-65 SI HAFB	2107	
D-OWAE	Thunder AX7-65 SI HAFB	2108	
D-OWAF(3)	Thunder AX9-120 SII HAFB	4108	D-OWAY
D-OWAG(2)	Kubicek BB-42Z HAFB	320	OK-0320
D-OWAH	Thunder AX7-65 SI HAFB	2562	
D-OWAL	Schröder Fire Balloons G HAFB	186	D-Trewa
D-OWAM	Thunder AX8-84 SI HAFB	2565	
D-OWAN	Thunder AX9-140 SII HAFB	1491	D-Löwentor
D-OWAR	Thunder AX7-65 SI HAFB	2564	
D-OWAS	Colt 69A HAFB	2566	
D-OWAT	Schröder Fire Balloons G HAFB	666	
D-OWAU	Cameron N-77 HAFB	unkn	
D-OWAW	Thunder AX8-84 SI HAFB	2563	
D-OWAX	Ultramagic M65C HAFB	65/72	
D-OWAZ	Schröder Fire Balloons G HAFB	1070	
D-OWBA(2)	Wörner NL-1000/STU Gas Balloon	1070	
D-OWBB	Schröder Fire Balloons G HAFB	587	
D-OWBC	Wörner NL-840/STU Gas Balloon	1072	
D-OWBD	Ultramagic M-145 HAFB	145/38	
D-OWBE	Ultramagic M-120 HAFB	120/09	
D-OWBF	Wörner NL-1000/STU Gas Balloon	1058	
D-OWBG	Ultramagic N-250 HAFB	250/23	
D-OWBH	Ultramagic M-145 HAFB	145/. .	
D-OWBI	Wörner NL-1000/STU Gas Balloon	1081	
D-OWBJ	Ultramagic M-105 HAFB	105/. .8	
D-OWBK	Ultramagic N-300 HAFB	300/. .	
D-OWBL	Wörner NL-840/STU Gas Balloon	1078	
D-OWBS	Colt 105A HAFB	2127	
D-OWBT	Schröder Fire Balloons G HAFB	141	D-Happy
D-OWBX	Ultramagic V-65 HAFB	65/90	
D-OWBZ	Ultramagic M-65C HAFB	65/77	
D-OWCD	Cameron A-120 HAFB (Reservation)	2399	G-BWCD G-OCBC
D-OWCW(3)	Cameron N-105 HAFB	10447	
D-OWDA	Lindstrand LBL-120A HAFB	681	
D-OWDR	Schröder Fire Balloons G HAFB	583	
D-OWEB	Schröder Fire Balloons G HAFB	521	
D-OWED	Cameron N-105 HAFB	4670	
D-OWEE	Cameron A-250 HAFB	10361	
D-OWEF	Schröder Fire Balloons G HAFB	317	
D-OWEG	Schröder Fire Balloons G HAFB	289	
D-OWEI	Cameron A-105 HAFB	3846	
D-OWEK	Lindstrand LBL-120A HAFB	985	
D-OWEL(2)	Schröder Fire Balloons G HAFB	940	
D-OWEN	Lindstrand LBL-105A HAFB	711	
D-OWEY(2)	Schröder Fire Balloons G HAFB	1108	
D-OWFA	Cameron N-90 HAFB	3096	
D-OWFU	Colt 105A HAFB	1697	D-OWFO D-Schatz
D-OWGM	Schröder Fire Balloons G HAFB	711	
D-OWGU	Cameron A-105 HAFB	4050	
D-OWHC	Schröder Fire Balloons G HAFB	517	
D-OWIE	Schröder Fire Balloons G HAFB	556	
D-OWIL	Cameron O-105 HAFB	2774	
D-OWIM(2)	Schröder Fire Balloons G HAFB (Permit .04)	1017	
D-OWIS	Colt 140A HAFB	2637	G-BVTI
D-OWIY	Schröder Fire Balloons G HAFB	29	D-OWEY(1) D-Wendelstein
D-OWJK	Ultramagic M-160 HAFB	160/32	
D-OWKA	Schröder Fire Balloons G HAFB	506	
D-OWKM	Schröder Fire Balloons G HAFB	01	D-Trier(2)
D-OWKS	Schröder Fire Balloons G HAFB	876	
D-OWLN	Schröder Fire Balloons G HAFB	929	
D-OWML	Wörner NL-1000/STU Gas Balloon	1050	
D-OWMP	Schröder Fire Balloons G HAFB	574	
D-OWNT	Wörner NL-1000/STU Gas Balloon	1065	
D-OWOF	Schröder Fire Balloons G HAFB	378	
D-OWOL	Schröder Fire Balloons G HAFB	598	
D-OWOT	Cameron A-105 HAFB	1790	D- ? OE-PZM
D-OWOW	Schröder Fire Balloons G HAFB	733	
D-OWPG	Lindstrand LBL-105A HAFB	450	
D-OWPV	Ultramagic M-120 HAFB	120/06	
D-OWPM(2)	Ultramagic H-77 HAFB	77/167	
D-OWPT	Schröder Fire Balloons G HAFB	714	
D-OWPX	Ultramagic M-65C HAFB	65/125	
D-OWRM	Ultramagic M-65C HAFB	65/103	
D-OWRW	Ultramagic M-77 HAFB	77/248	
D-OWSG	Schröder Fire Balloons G HAFB	838	
D-OWSH(2)	Cameron N-105 HAFB	4584	
D-OWSI (2)	Schröder Fire Balloons G HAFB (Replacement for c/n 511)	1024	
D-OWSW(3)	Cameron N-105 HAFB (Replacement for (2) c/n 3292)	4772	
D-OWTB	Cameron O-120 HAFB	2973	
D-OWTC	Cameron N-105 HAFB	4256	
D-OWTM	Lindstrand LBL-120A HAFB	271	
D-OWUC	Ultramagic M-65C HAFB	65/104	
D-OWUE	Schröder Fire Balloons G HAFB	520	
D-OWUN	Sky 120 HAFB	051	
D-OWVD	Schröder Fire Balloons G HAFB	758	
D-OWVV	Kubicek BB-37 HAFB	183	OK-0183
D-OWWA	Schröder Fire Balloons GHAFB	1069	
D-OWWC	Ultramagic M-145 HAFB	145/42	
D-OWWE	Colt 105A HAFB	2583	D-OWWL(1)
D-OWWL(2)	Schröder Fire Balloons G HAFB	516	
D-OWXX	Ultramagic M-65C HAFB	65/102	
D-OWYZ	Cameron V-90 HAFB	2983	
D-OXAL	Schröder Fire Balloons G HAFB	1116	
D-OXAN	Schröder Fire Balloons G HAFB	975	
D-OXAV	Cameron C-80 Concept HAFB	10295	
D-OXFT	Cameron N-105 HAFB	3018	
D-OXID	Lindstrand LBL-105A HAFB	397	
D-OXIT	Lindstrand LBL-120A HAFB	871	
D-OXMO	Aerostar S-60AHAFB	3265	
D-OXOB	Raven-Europe FS-57A HAFB	E-279	D-OWOB
D-OXTT	Cameron A-120 HAFB	3267	
D-OXUS	Schröder Fire Balloons G HAFB	157	D-Limes
D-OXWH	Cameron N-120 HAFB	10358	
D-OXXA	Lindstrand LBL-105A HAFB	788	
D-OXXX	Schröder Fire Balloons G HAFB	397	
D-OXYD	Schröder Fire Balloons G HAFB	862	
D-OYCT	Cameron N-105 HAFB	3626	(D-OXTC)
D-OYEG	Specon S90 HAFB	001	
D-OYOT	Schröder Fire Balloons G HAFB	593	
D-OYPO	Wörner K-1000/3-STU Gas Balloon	1038	
D-OYPQ	Colt 180A HAFB	1569	G-HYPO
D-OYTO	Raven Europe S-60A HAFB	E-347	
D-OYYO	Schröder Fire Balloons G HAFB	821	
D-OYYY(2)	Schröder Fire Balloons G HAFB	1085	
D-OZAK	Cameron N-105 HAFB (Permit .04)	3307	(D-OBRE)
D-OZAM	Wörner NL-1000/STU Gas Balloon	1043	
D-OZAN	Lindstrand LBL-105A HAFB	395	
D-OZAO	Schröder Fire Balloons G HAFB	1125	
D-OZAR	Wörner NL-1000/STU Gas Balloon	1061	
D-OZDF	Schröder Fire Balloons G HAFB	623	
D-OZDP	Gefa-Flug AS.105GD Hot Air Airship (Permit .03)	0016	
D-OZDQ(2)	Gefa-Flug AS.105GD Hot Air Airship (Replacement for c/n 0025)	0027	
D-OZEL(2)	Schröder Fire Balloons G HAFB	1012	
D-OZEP	Schröder Fire Balloons G HAFB	441	
D-OZKA	Schröder Fire Balloons G HAFB	930	
D-OZLM	Schröder Fire Balloons G HAFB	724	
D-OZOE	Schröder Fire Balloons G HAFB	806	

D-OZOG(2)	Cameron N-105 HAFB	3142	G-BWJJ
D-OZOK	Lindstrand LBL-105A HAFB	735	G-BZOK
D-OZON	Cameron V-90 HAFB	2661	
D-OZPO	Schröder Fire Balloons G HAFB	917	
D-OZUG	Schröder Fire Balloons G HAFB	432	
D-OZZZ	Thunder AX7-77 SI HAFB	2338	

The following Balloons were identified in the former system by name only. We have now removed all those (mostly old) examples not shown on the current German register although a few others may still be active on Permits. Those remaining should have been re-registered in the D-O... sequence by 1.3.2000 and, in view of the age of most of them, are probably no longer airworthy.

GAS BALLOONS

D-Ibbenbüren	Augsburg K-1000/3-STU	0225	
D-Munte	Augsburg K-1050/3-RI	45778	
D-Rosie	Stuttgart K-780/2-STU	0305	

HOT-AIR BALLOONS

D-Albstadt (3)	Cameron O-105	1276	
D-Bones	Cameron V-77	1688	
D-Brui.........	Schröder Fire Balloons G	213	
D-Colonia	Cameron N-105	2145	
D-Daimler	Cameron N-90	2375	
D-Eimermacher	Cameron O-105	2615	G-BTUI
D-Erftkreis	Cameron O-120	2207	D-DKSK
D-Firstl	Cameron A-120	2374	
D-Goliath	Cameron N-90	2324	
D-Head	Head Balloons AX7-77B	234	
D-Magnus	Cameron V-90	2524	G-BTKM
D-Petzi (2)	Schröder Fire Balloons G	277	
D-Schmitt (4)	Schröder Fire Balloons G	265	

CLASS U : Unmanned aircraft

D-UFHA	Mistral C (Aachen University test aircraft)	unkn	
D-UISD	Universität Stuttgart Lotte (Remote-controlled airship)	unkn	

GLIDERS

D-0001	Test registration for Schleicher ASH 25, 26, ASW 28 production		
D-0002-CH	Rolladen-Schneider LS7-WL	7098	HB-3035
D-0003	LET L-13 Blanik	026639	OO-ZRL
D-0004	Scheibe Bergfalke II/55 (Permit .02)	239	
D-0005	Scheibe Zugvogel IIIA	1061	
D-0006	Schleicher Ka 6E	4132	
D-0008	Scheibe L-Spatz 55	622	
D-0009	Schleicher ASK 21	21463	
D-0010	Schleicher K 8B	AB8750	
D-0011	Schleicher ASW 19	19011	
D-0012	Marganski MDM-1 Fox	217	
D-0013	Schleicher K 8B	AB8759	
D-0014	Scheibe L-Spatz 55 (Reservation 12.99)	566	
D-0015	Test Registration for DG Flugzeugbau DG-800S production		
D-0016-IMB	Schempp-Hirth Discus CS	233CS	
D-0018	Schempp-Hirth Duo Discus	86	
D-0019	Schleicher ASK 13	13665AB	
D-0020-M1	Glasflügel H201 Standard Libelle	11	
D-0021-BA	Schempp-Hirth Nimbus 2C	224	HB-1534
D-0022-22	Akaflieg Hannover AFH 22 (Permit 6.99)	V-1	
D-0023	Glaser-Dirks DG-100G Elan	E119G88	OE-5307
D-0024	Akaflieg Hannover AFH 24 (Permit)	1	
D-0025	Glasflügel H201B Standard Libelle	467	JA2163
D-0026	Glasflügel H303 Mosquito	99	
D-0027	Schleicher ASK 13	13152	D-0227
D-0028-PD	Glaser-Dirks DG-300 Elan	3E268	
D-0029	Schempp-Hirth Standard Cirrus	496G	F-CEFY
D-0030	DG Flugzeugbau DG-1000S	10-21S21	
D-0032-KA	Rolladen-Schneider LS8-18	8291	
D-0033-MO	Glaser-Dirks DG-100 Elan	E33	HB-1535
D-0034	Schleicher K 8B	8203	
D-0035	Schleicher K 8B	8666	
D-0036	Scheibe L-Spatz 55	617	
D-0037	Göppingen Gö III Minimoa (Reservation 4.99)	AB-001M	
D-0038	Scheibe Bergfalke III	5626	D-0033
D-0039	Rolladen-Schneider LS4	4039	I-LYMA
			D-3356
D-0040	Schleicher K 8B	8850/AB	
D-0042	SG-38 Schulgleiter	1	
D-0043-TS	Glaser-Dirks DG-300 Elan	3E138	
D-0044	Glaser-Dirks DG-100 Elan	E219G185	
D-0045-BU	Rolladen-Schneider LS6-c	6278	
D-0047	Schempp-Hirth Duo Discus	468	
D-0048	SZD-51-1 Junior	B-1851	HB-3012
D-0049	Glasflügel H301B Libelle	88	
D-0050	Rolladen-Schneider LS8-a	8231	F-CGZY
D-0051	Schempp-Hirth Discus-2b	176	
D-0052	Rolladen-Schneider LS4	4605	
D-0053	Schempp-Hirth Cirrus	26	
D-0054	Scheibe SF-27B	6201	
D-0055	Schempp-Hirth Nimbus 2c	227	HB-1533
D-0057	Rolladen-Schneider LS4-a	4677	
D-0058	Schleicher Ka 6E	4180	
D-0059	Schleicher Ka 6E	4213	
D-0060	PZL PW-5 Smyk	17.06.018	
D-0061	Rolladen-Schneider LS8-18	8077	F-CGZP
D-0062	Scheibe Bergfalke III	5628	
D-0064	Akaflieg Braunschweig SB-5B Sperber	5045/A	
D-0065	Grunau Baby IIB (Permit 4.99)	94	D-7215
			PH-215
D-0066	Scheibe SF-27A	6108	
D-0067	Scheibe Spatz B	533	
D-0068	Schempp-Hirth Cirrus	31	
D-0069	Schleicher ASK 13	13088	
D-0070	Rolladen-Schneider LS1-0	4	
D-0071	Glaser-Dirks DG-300 Elan	3E326	
D-0072	Schleicher Ka 6E	4214	
D-0073	LET L-13 Blanik	173207	CS-PAW
D-0075-6B	Schleicher Ka 6E	4216	
D-0077	Schleicher K 8B	8745	
D-0079	Schleicher Ka 6E	4232	
D-0080	Schleicher ASK 13	13116	
D-0081	Schleicher ASK 13	13122	
D-0082-FAY	Glasflügel H201B Standard Libelle	14	
D-0083	Rolladen-Schneider LS3	3036	HB-1361
D-0084	Focke-Wulf Weihe 50	8	LX-CAF
D-0086	Schleicher Ka 6E	4233	
D-0087	Glaser-Dirks DG-100	14	HB-1285
D-0088	Bölkow Phoebus C	845	
D-0090-SI	Rolladen-Schneider LS8-18	8439	
D-0092	Schleicher Ka 6E	4238	
D-0093	Schleicher K 8B	8669	
D-0094	Schempp-Hirth Discus b	446	
D-0095	Schleicher ASK 13	13126	
D-0096	Schleicher ASK 13	13129	
D-0097	Schleicher ASK 13	13133	
D-0098	Schleicher Ka 6E	4253	
D-0099	Schleicher Ka 6E	4254	
D-0101	Schempp-Hirth Cirrus	30	
D-0102	Schleicher K 8B	8668	
D-0103	Schleicher K 8B	8671	
D-0104-IYA	Schempp-Hirth Discus CS	045CS	
D-0106	Schleicher K 8B	8540/A	OE-0871
D-0107	Glasflügel H304	211	
D-0108	Schempp-Hirth Discus CS	059CS	
D-0109	Schempp-Hirth Standard Cirrus	122	
D-0110	Schleicher K 8B	8327	D-KIFA
D-0111	Glasflügel H401 Kestrel	3	
D-0112-8Z	Rolladen-Schneider LS8-18	8303	
D-0113	Schleicher Ka 6E	4154	
D-0114-IEL	Glasflügel H201B Standard Libelle	211	
D-0116-SM	Rolladen-Schneider LS8-18	8304	
D-0117	Nord 1300 (Grunau Baby IIB)	117	F-CRNX
			F-CBFF
D-0118	Glaser-Dirks DG-300 Elan	3E417	
D-0119	Rolladen-Schneider LS4	4544	
D-0120	Schleicher ASK 13	13681AB	
D-0121-W	Rolladen-Schneider LS1-0	6	
D-0122	Schleicher K 8B	8788/AB	
D-0123-57	Bölkow Phoebus C	870	
D-0124	Schleicher ASW 20CL	20843	D-KAMC
			D-3365
D-0125	Schleicher Rhönbussard	125	
D-0126	Schleicher K 8B	219/61	
D-0127	Focke-Wulf Kranich III	87	
D-0128-28	Schleicher ASW 28	28052	
D-0129	Schleicher K 8B	8115/SH	
D-0130-K	Bölkow Phoebus B-1	722	OE-5210
D-0131-HEM	Glaser-Dirks DG-300 Club Elan	3E351C40	
D-0132	Akaflieg Braunschweig SB-5E Sperber	AB5004	
D-0133	Schempp-Hirth Ventus c	305	
D-0135	Bölkow Phoebus C	860	
D-0136-36	Rolladen-Schneider LS1-0 (Reservation .01)	11	
D-0137-R4	Rolladen-Schneider LS4	4607	
D-0138-IYB	Schempp-Hirth Discus CS	027CS	
D-0139-1M	Glasflügel H201B Standard Libelle	222	
D-0140	Glasflügel H201 Standard Libelle	236	
D-0141	Glasflügel H201B Standard Libelle	237	
D-0142	Rolladen-Schneider LS1-b	25	
D-0143	Schleicher Ka 6E	4256	
D-0144	Schleicher ASK 13	13096	
D-0145	Schleicher ASK 13	13134	
D-0146	Schempp-Hirth Discus CS	064CS	
D-0147	Grob G.102 Astir CS Jeans	2106	
D-0148	Schleicher ASK 13	13135	
D-0149	Schleicher ASK 13	13138	
D-0150	Vogt Lo 150 Zwergreiher	AB.1	
D-0151	Schleicher ASK 13	13141	
D-0154	Schempp-Hirth Cirrus (Reservation)	40	
D-0155	Bölkow Phoebus C	868	
D-0156	Rolladen-Schneider LS1-C	10	
D-0157	Rolladen-Schneider LS4-b	4761	
D-0158-KG	Rolladen-Schneider LS4	4378	
D-0159-IMW	Glasflügel H304	212	
D-0161	Schleicher ASW 15	15004	

D-0162	Schleicher K 8B	8786	
D-0163	Schleicher Ka 6E	4266	
D-0164	Schleicher Ka 6E	4274	
D-0165	Rolladen-Schneider LS4	4608	
D-0166	DG Flugzeugbau DG-500 Elan Orion	5E169X24	
D-0167	Schleicher Ka 6E	4269	
D-0169-FJ	Rolladen-Schneider LS8-18	8316	
D-0171	Rolladen-Schneider LS4	4609	
D-0172	Schleicher Ka 6CR Rhönsegler	6656/Si	
D-0173	Rolladen-Schneider LS4	4610	
D-0174	Glasflügel H201 Standard Libelle	185	
D-0175	Bölkow Phoebus C	878	
D-0176	Glasflügel H201 Standard Libelle	51	
D-0177	Standard Austria SH-1	74	
D-0178	LET L-23 Super Blanik	049201	
D-0179-06	Schempp-Hirth Duo Discus	28	
D-0180	Rolladen-Schneider LS1-0	19	
D-0181	Rolladen-Schneider LS1-0	18	
D-0182	Rolladen-Schneider LS1-0	9	
D-0183-3H	Rolladen-Schneider LS4	4611	
D-0184	Schempp-Hirth Cirrus	43	
D-0185	Scheibe SF-27A	6109	
D-0187	Schempp-Hirth Cirrus	56	
D-0188	Schempp-Hirth Mini-Nimbus HS-7	06	HB-1391 D-3791
D-0190	Schempp-Hirth Standard Cirrus	128	
D-0191	Rolladen-Schneider LS4	4583	
D-0192	Grob G 102 Club Astir IIIb	5568Cb	HB-1618
D-0193	Glaser-Dirks DG-300 Club Elan	3E427C72	
D-0194	Akaflieg Braunschweig SB-5B Sperber	5048/A	
D-0195	Schleicher Ka 6E	4281	
D-0196	Schleicher Ka 6E	4265	
D-0197-W	Schleicher ASW 24	24205	
D-0198	Schleicher Ka 6E	4273	
D-0199	Schleicher ASK 13	13157	
D-0200-00	Schleicher ASW 15	15179	
D-0201	Schleicher Ka 6E	4271	
D-0202	Schleicher K 8B	8779	
D-0203	Schleicher Ka 6E	4275	
D-0204	Glasflügel H401 Kestrel	52	
D-0205	Rolladen-Schneider LS6-c	6311	
D-0206	Schleicher K 7 Rhönadler	AB/7281	
D-0208	Schleicher ASK 13	13071/A	
D-0209	Schleicher K 8B	05	D-KAMB D-8877
D-0210-11	Schempp-Hirth Duo Discus	30	
D-0212	Schleicher K 8B	8740	
D-0213-LM	Glaser-Dirks DG-500 Elan Trainer	5E21T3	
D-0214	Schleicher Rhönlerche II (Reservation - cld?)	3088/Br	
D-0215	Bölkow Phoebus B-1	877	
D-0216	Bölkow Phoebus B-2	873	
D-0217	Schleicher K 8B	8288 El	
D-0218-L5	Schleicher ASW 24	24186	
D-0219-CI	Glaser-Dirks DG-300 Elan Acro	3E445A8	
D-0220	Schleicher ASK 13	13292	
D-0221	Rolladen-Schneider LS4-a	4671	
D-0222	Rolladen-Schneider LS1-0	28	
D-0223	Schleicher Ka 6E	4282	
D-0224	Schleicher ASW 15	15006	
D-0225	Schleicher ASW 15	15007	
D-0226	Glaser-Dirks DG-500/22 Elan	5E16S5	
D-0228	Schleicher ASK 13	13156	
D-0229	Schleicher Ka 6E	4288	
D-0230	Schleicher Ka 6E	4280	
D-0231	Schempp-Hirth Discus CS	056CS	
D-0232	Schleicher ASK 13	13161	
D-0233	Schleicher Ka 6E	4270	
D-0234	Schempp-Hirth Duo Discus	98	
D-0235	Schleicher ASK 13	13165	
D-0236	Schleicher K 8B	8782	
D-0237	Schleicher Ka 6E	4283	
D-0238	Schleicher ASK 13	13162	
D-0239	Schleicher ASK 13	13163	
D-0240	Schleicher ASK 13	13164	
D-0241	DG Flugzeugbau DG-800S	8-209S39	
D-0242	Schleicher ASK 13	13300/AB	
D-0243	Glasflügel H201B Standard Libelle	56	
D-0244	Schleicher ASK 21	21667	
D-0245	Glaser-Dirks DG-500 Elan Trainer	5E26T6	
D-0246	Bölkow Phoebus C	881	
D-0248	Akaflieg Braunschweig SB-5E Sperber	5033A	
D-0249	Schempp-Hirth Duo Discus	124	
D-0250	Schempp-Hirth Cirrus	63	
D-0251	Rolladen-Schneider LS1-0	8	
D-0252	Schempp-Hirth Discus CS	058CS	
D-0254-31	Rolladen-Schneider LS6-b	6164	
D-0255-IBE	Schempp-Hirth Duo Discus	31	
D-0256	SZD-32A Foka 5	W-519	DDR-2256 DM-2256
D-0257	Schleicher ASK 13	13167	
D-0258-58	Schleicher ASK 21	21403	
D-0260	Schleicher ASK 13	13168	
D-0261	Glaser-Dirks DG-500 Elan Trainer	5E57T24	
D-0266	Schleicher ASK 13	13174	
D-0267	Schleicher ASK 13	13176	
D-0268	Glaser-Dirks DG-300 Elan	3E324	OE-5472 D-8300

D-0269	Schleicher ASK 13	13179	
D-0270	Schleicher ASK 13	13180	
D-0271	Schleicher ASK 13	13181	
D-0272	Rolladen-Schneider LS4-a	4679	
D-0273	Schleicher K 8B	8798	
D-0274	Schempp-Hirth Ventus 2b	41	
D-0275	Rolladen-Schneider LS4	4101	
D-0276	Schleicher Ka 2B Rhönschwalbe	937/61	
D-0277	Glasflügel H206 Hornet	46	I-CRBV
D-0278	Glasflügel H401 Kestrel	39	
D-0281	Glasflügel H401 Kestrel	43	
D-0282-FVC	Glaser-Dirks DG-500/22 Elan	5E8S2	
D-0284	Schleicher ASK 13	13151	
D-0286	Schleicher K 8B	8771/AB	
D-0287-D9	Rolladen-Schneider LS8-a	8182	
D-0288	PIK-16C Vasama	06	OH-288 OH-VAF
D-0290	Schempp-Hirth Cirrus	66	
D-0291	VFW Fokker FK-3	0002	
D-0293	VFW Fokker FK-3	0004	
D-0294	Rolladen-Schneider LS4-b	4751	
D-0295	Akaflieg Braunschweig SB-5E Sperber	5041/A	
D-0296	Schleicher ASW 24	24130	
D-0298	Schempp-Hirth Discus CS	091CS	
D-0299	Schempp-Hirth Ventus c	590	
D-0300	Glasflügel H304	256	
D-0301	Focke-Wulf Weihe 50	SB.01	
D-0302	Glaser-Dirks DG-300 Club Elan	3E423C71	
D-0303	Schleicher K 8B	8684/A	
D-0304	Glasflügel H201B Standard Libelle	57	
D-0305	Glaser-Dirks DG-300 Elan	3E425	
D-0306	Schleicher K 8B	8668 El	
D-0307	Glaser-Dirks DG-500 Elan Trainer	5E81T35	
D-0308	Scheibe Bergfalke IV	5811	
D-0309-WS	Rolladen-Schneider LS6-b	6175	
D-0310	Schempp-Hirth Cirrus	72	
D-0311	Scheibe SF-27A	6112	
D-0312-BB	Glasflügel H401 Kestrel	47	
D-0313	Glasflügel H101 Salto	3	
D-0314	Rolladen-Schneider LS4-b	4907	
D-0315	Schempp-Hirth Standard Cirrus	108	
D-0316	Schempp-Hirth Standard Cirrus	109	
D-0317-PV	Schleicher ASK 21	21592	
D-0318	Schempp-Hirth Standard Cirrus	111	
D-0319	Schempp-Hirth Standard Cirrus	112	
D-0320	Rolladen-Schneider LS4	4160	
D-0321	Schempp-Hirth Standard Cirrus	115	
D-0322	Rolladen-Schneider LS6	6177	
D-0323	Rolladen-Schneider LS3-a	3130	OO-ZWS
D-0324	Schempp-Hirth Discus CS	029CS	
D-0325	Scheibe Bergfalke III	5635	
D-0326	Schempp-Hirth Discus CS	170CS	
D-0327-GM	Glaser-Dirks DG-500 Elan Trainer	5E119T50	
D-0328	Schempp-Hirth Standard Cirrus	135	
D-0330	Glaser-Dirks DG-300 Elan	3E345	HB-3005
D-0331	Rolladen-Schneider LS3-a	3142	PH-629
D-0332	Schleicher K 8B	8791AB	
D-0333-GT	Glasflügel H201 Standard Libelle	69	
D-0335	Schleicher ASK 13	13184	
D-0336	Schleicher Ka 6E	4309	
D-0337	Glaser-Dirks DG-300 Elan	3E277	
D-0338	Schleicher ASK 13	13185	
D-0339	Schleicher Ka 6E (Permit)	4306	
D-0340	Glasflügel H304	259	OH-638
D-0341-HR	Schempp-Hirth Duo Discus	32	
D-0342	Schleicher Ka 6E	4310	
D-0343	Schleicher ASK 13	13192	
D-0344	Glaser-Dirks DG-300 Club Elan	3E279C5	
D-0345	Schleicher ASK 13	13193	
D-0349	Schleicher Ka 6E	4313	
D-0350	Schleicher K 8B	8807	
D-0351	Schleicher Ka 6E	4318	
D-0352	Schleicher ASK 13	13204	
D-0353-G9	Rolladen-Schneider LS4-b	4947	
D-0354	Schleicher ASK 13	13206	
D-0355	Glasflügel H201B Standard Libelle	277	
D-0356	Schleicher Rhönlerche II	AB 94/59	
D-0357	Glaser-Dirks DG-300 Club Elan	3E282C7	
D-0358	Glasflügel H401 Kestrel	11	
D-0359	Glaser-Dirks DG-300 Club Elan	3E283C8	
D-0360	Scheibe L-Spatz 55	507/614	
D-0361	Glaser-Dirks DG-300 Elan	3E22	
D-0362	Schempp-Hirth Standard Cirrus	174	
D-0364-HN	Schempp-Hirth Standard Cirrus	155G	
D-0365	Grunau Baby IIB	33	OE-0368
D-0366	Schleicher ASK 21	21671	
D-0367	Schleicher ASK 13	13186	
D-0368	Glasflügel H201B Standard Libelle	77	
D-0369	Glasflügel H201 Standard Libelle	289	
D-0370	Glaser-Dirks DG-300 Elan	3E96	HB-3037
D-0371	Glasflügel H201 Standard Libelle	291	
D-0373	Vogt LO-100 Zwergreiher	01	
D-0374-UX	Schempp-Hirth Discus CS	065CS	
D-0375	Scheibe Bergfalke IV	5814	("D-KAAO")
D-0376	Scheibe Bergfalke IV	5818	("D-KAAQ")
D-0377	SZD-24-4A Foka 4	W-237	OY-XEB
D-0378	Rolladen-Schneider LS8	unkn	

D-0379	Rolladen-Schneider LS1-C	95	
D-0381	Schempp-Hirth Janus Ce	301	
D-0382	Rolladen-Schneider LS1-C	30	
D-0383	Rolladen-Schneider LS1-c	31	
D-0384	Rolladen-Schneider LS1-c	32	
D-0386	Scheibe SF-27A	6093	
D-0387	Rolladen-Schneider LS4-b	4961	
D-0388	Schempp-Hirth Standard Cirrus	3	
D-0389	Schempp-Hirth Cirrus	85	
D-0390	Rolladen-Schneider LS4	4115	
D-0391	Schleicher Ka 6CR Rhönsegler	6399	
D-0392	Glasflügel H-101 Salto	2	
D-0393	Rolladen-Schneider LS4	4379	
D-0394 -RH	Rolladen-Schneider LS4-b	4962	
D-0395	Rolladen-Schneider LS6	6183	
D-0397	Glasflügel H401 Kestrel	16	
D-0398	Glasflügel H401 Kestrel	17	
D-0399	Rolladen-Schneider LS1-e	92	
D-0400	Schempp-Hirth Duo Discus	239	
D-0401-IST	Rolladen-Schneider LS4	4388	
D-0402	Rolladen-Schneider LS1-d (Reservation 10.99)	34	
D-0403-P5	Glaser-Dirks DG-500/22 Elan	5E17S6	
D-0404	Rolladen-Schneider LS4-a	4681	
D-0405 -CF	Rolladen-Schneider LS4-b	4682	
D-0406	Rolladen-Schneider LS4-a	4683	
D-0409	Schempp-Hirth Duo Discus	127	
D-0410-KJ	Glasflügel Standard Libelle 201B	49	OO-ZGP
D-0411	Rolladen-Schneider LS4-b	4684	
D-0412	Rolladen-Schneider LS4-a	4697	
D-0413	Schleicher ASK 13	13207	
D-0414	Schleicher ASW 27	27042	
D-0415-AS	Rolladen-Schneider LS4-b	4685	
D-0416	Schleicher K 8B	8812	
D-0417-MB	Schempp-Hirth Ventus 2a	100	
D-0418	Schleicher ASW 15	15035	
D-0419	Schleicher ASK 13	13217	
D-0420	DG Flugzeugbau DG-500 Elan Orion	5E164X19	S5-7500
D-0421	Schleicher K 8B	8813	
D-0422	Schleicher ASK 13	13218	
D-0423	Rolladen-Schneider LS1-d	42	
D-0424	Glaser-Dirks DG-200/17	2-139/1736	
D-0425	Glaser-Dirks DG-200/17	2-140/1737	
D-0426-WO	Schempp-Hirth Standard Cirrus	4	
D-0427-FD	Schempp-Hirth Standard Cirrus	5	
D-0428	Schempp-Hirth Standard Cirrus	6	
D-0429	Schempp-Hirth Standard Cirrus	7	
D-0430	HpH Glasflügel 304C	63-C	
D-0431	Schleicher ASW 15	15183	
D-0432 -NM	Rolladen-Schneider LS1-d	44	
D-0433	Glasflügel H401 Kestrel	57	
D-0434	Glasflügel H401 Kestrel	59	
D-0435	Schleicher K 8B	8578/A	
D-0436-OD	SZD-48-3 Jantar Standard 3	B-1946	DDR-2436
D-0437	Rolladen-Schneider LS1-d	41	HB-1158
D-0438	Glasflügel H201 Standard Libelle	91	
D-0439	Rolladen-Schneider LS1-d	48	
D-0440	Rolladen-Schneider LS1-d	38	
D-0441-RC	Rolladen-Schneider LS4-a	4698	
D-0442	Rolladen-Schneider LS8-18	8383	
D-0445	Glasflügel H201 Standard Libelle	285	
D-0446	Schleicher Ka 6E	4326	
D-0447	Bölkow Phoebus C	920	
D-0448	Schleicher K 8B	8601/A	
D-0449	Rolladen-Schneider LS1-c	96	
D-0450	Rolladen-Schneider LS1-c	90	
D-0451	Glasflügel H401 Kestrel	51	
D-0452	Schempp-Hirth Duo Discus	141	
D-0454	SZD-9bis Bocian 1D (Reservation 10.99)	P-350	OE-0451
D-0458	Rolladen-Schneider LS1-c	109	
D-0460	Schleicher ASW 15	15036	
D-0461	Schleicher ASK 13	13219	
D-0462	DG Flugzeugbau DG-500 Elan Orion	5E204X48	
D-0463	Schleicher Ka 6E	4327	
D-0464	Rolladen-Schneider LS4	4052	
D-0465	Schleicher ASK 13	13221	
D-0466	Schleicher ASK 13	13223	
D-0468	Schleicher ASK 13	13225	
D-0469	Schleicher ASK 13	13226	
D-0470	Rolladen-Schneider LS1-c	100	
D-0472	Schleicher Ka 6E	4308	
D-0473-C6	Rolladen-Schneider LS4-a	4699	
D-0474	Glasflügel H401 Kestrel	56	
D-0475	Glasflügel H401 Kestrel	25	
D-0476	Rolladen-Schneider LS1-c	103	
D-0477	Rolladen-Schneider LS4	4248	F-CATY(2) I-GATS D-9108
D-0478	Schleicher ASK 13	13017	OO-ZXQ PL-61 (Belgian Air Cadets)
D-0479	Schempp-Hirth Cirrus	90	
D-0480	Rolladen-Schneider LS4-a	4700	
D-0481	Schempp-Hirth Cirrus	92	
D-0482	Glasflügel H201B Standard Libelle	115	
D-0483	Rolladen-Schneider LS4-a	4701	
D-0484	Schempp-Hirth Standard Cirrus	26	
D-0485	Schempp-Hirth Duo Discus	33	
D-0486	Rolladen-Schneider LS4-b	4946	
D-0487	Schempp-Hirth Standard Cirrus	29	
D-0488-BL	Schleicher ASK 13	13215	
D-0489	Rolladen-Schneider LS1-c	56	
D-0491	Schleicher ASK 13	13227	
D-0492	Schleicher ASK 13	13228	
D-0494	Rolladen-Schneider LS4-a	4702	
D-0495	Schleicher ASW 15	15045	
D-0496	Glasflügel H401 Kestrel	50	
D-0497	Rolladen-Schneider LS4-a	4703	
D-0498	Schleicher ASK 13	13230	
D-0499	Schleicher ASK 13	13231	
D-0500	Glasflügel H201B Standard Libelle	95	
D-0501	Glasflügel H201 Standard Libelle	207	
D-0503	Rolladen-Schneider LS4-a	4704	
D-0504	Schempp-Hirth Cirrus-VTC	115Y	
D-0505	Schempp-Hirth Cirrus-VTC	116Y	
D-0506	Schempp-Hirth Cirrus-VTC	117Y	
D-0508	Schleicher ASW 15	15057	
D-0509	Schleicher Ka 6E	4334	
D-0510	Glaser-Dirks DG-300 Elan	3E290	
D-0511	Glaser-Dirks DG-300 Club Elan	3E292C13	
D-0513	Schleicher ASK 13	13233	
D-0514	Schleicher ASK 13	13234	
D-0515	Schleicher ASK 13	13235	
D-0516	Schleicher ASW 15	15051	
D-0517	Glasflügel H401 Kestrel	20	
D-0518	Schleicher ASK 21	21620	
D-0519	Rolladen-Schneider LS1-c	104	
D-0520-GW	Glasflügel H304	251	
D-0521	Glasflügel H401 Kestrel	45	
D-0522	Glasflügel H201 Standard Libelle	120	
D-0523	Scheibe Bergfalke IV	5803	
D-0524	Scheibe Bergfalke IV	5804	
D-0525	Scheibe Bergfalke IV	5805	
D-0526	Rolladen-Schneider LS4-a	4705	
D-0528-2R	Glasflügel H201B Standard Libelle	260	
D-0529	Schempp-Hirth Standard Cirrus	37	
D-0530	Rolladen-Schneider LS1-f	393	F-CEKJ
D-0531	Rolladen-Schneider LS6-18W	6351	
D-0532	Scheibe L-Spatz 55	716	OE-0521
D-0533	Glasflügel H401 Kestrel	38	
D-0534	Schleicher K 8B	8819	
D-0535	Schleicher ASK 13	13236	
D-0536 -Z	Schleicher ASW 15	15052	
D-0537	Schleicher ASK 13	13237	
D-0538	Schleicher ASK 13	13240	
D-0539	Schleicher Ka 6E	4340	
D-0540	Schleicher ASW 15	15055	
D-0542-CW	Schleicher ASW 24B	24236	
D-0544	Schempp-Hirth Ventus 2b	3	
D-0545	Schleicher Ka 6E	4339	
D-0546	Vogt LO-100 Zwergreiher	204	OE-0446
D-0547-CA	Schleicher Ka 6E	4342	
D-0548	Schleicher K 8B	8828	
D-0549	Schleicher K 8B	8829	
D-0550	Schleicher ASK 13	13248	
D-0551	Schleicher ASK 13	13249	
D-0552	Schleicher ASK 13	13250	
D-0554	Glasflügel H201 Standard Libelle	171	
D-0555	Schleicher ASK 13	13072/1	
D-0556	Schempp-Hirth Cirrus	93	
D-0557-EA	Schempp-Hirth Standard Cirrus	117	
D-0558-HO	Schempp-Hirth Duo Discus	204	
D-0559	Bölkow Phoebus C	935	
D-0560	Schleicher K 8B	225/61	
D-0561	Schleicher K 8B	8687/AB	
D-0562	Schempp-Hirth Discus CS	066CS	
D-0564	Schempp-Hirth Janus Ce	294	
D-0565	Rolladen-Schneider LS1-c	99	
D-0567	Rolladen-Schneider LS4-b	4796	
D-0568	Rolladen-Schneider LS4-b	4797	
D-0570	Rolladen-Schneider LS4-b	4798	
D-0571	Bölkow Phoebus C	938	
D-0572	Siebert SIE-3 (Reservation 7.99)	3021	
D-0573	Rolladen-Schneider LS4-b	4799	
D-0574	FFA Diamant 16.5	067	
D-0576	Schleicher K 7 Rhönadler	7191/A	
D-0578	Rolladen-Schneider LS4-a	4800	
D-0579	Rolladen-Schneider LS4-b	4926	
D-0580	Glaser-Dirks DG-100G Elan	E145G113	
D-0581	Schempp-Hirth Standard Cirrus	54	
D-0582-VL	Schempp-Hirth Standard Cirrus	55	
D-0583	Siebert SIE-3	3004	
D-0584	Bölkow Phoebus C	953	
D-0585-BU	Schempp-Hirth Discus CS	030CS	
D-0586	Schempp-Hirth Cirrus	98	
D-0588	Schempp-Hirth Standard Cirrus	185	
D-0589	Schleicher ASK 13	13645AB	JA2357
D-0590-2C	Schempp-Hirth Standard Cirrus	191	
D-0591	Grob G.103C Twin III	36004	
D-0592	Bölkow Phoebus A-1	711	
D-0593	Schempp-Hirth Standard Cirrus	58	
D-0594	Schempp-Hirth Standard Cirrus	64	
D-0595	Schempp-Hirth Standard Cirrus	69	
D-0597	Schleicher Ka 6CR Rhönsegler	1114	
D-0598	Glasflügel H401 Kestrel	26	

D-0599	Glasflügel H201 Standard Libelle	154	
D-0600	Rolladen-Schneider LS1-c	102	
D-0601	Siebert SIE-3	3017	
D-0603	Glasflügel H203 Standard Libelle	1	
D-0604	Rolladen-Schneider LS4-b	41033	
D-0606	Schleicher Ka 6E	4346	
D-0608	Schleicher ASW 15	15020	
D-0609	Schempp-Hirth Ventus c	378	
D-0610	SZD-50-3 Puchacz	B-1327	DDR-3610
D-0611-FU	Glaser-Dirks DG-100G Elan	E144G112	
D-0612	Schleicher Ka 6E	4347	
D-0613	Schleicher ASK 13	13255	
D-0614	Schleicher K 8B	8833	
D-0615	Schleicher ASW 15	15066	
D-0616	Rolladen-Schneider LS6	6100	HB-1889
D-0617	Schleicher K 8B	8835	
D-0618	Schleicher ASK 13	13258	
D-0619	Schleicher ASK 13	13259	
D-0620-VIP	Schleicher ASW 15	15087	
D-0621	Schleicher ASK 13	13262	
D-0622	Schleicher K 8B	8837	
D-0623	Rolladen-Schneider LS4	4564	D-3392
D-0624	Schleicher ASK 13	13267	
D-0625	Schempp-Hirth Standard Cirrus G	56	
D-0626	Schleicher ASK 21	21559	
D-0627	Schleicher ASW 15	15078	
D-0628	Schleicher K 8B	8840	
D-0629	Schleicher K 8B	8842	
D-0630	Schleicher ASK 13	13269	
D-0631	Schleicher ASK 13	13270	
D-0632	Schleicher K 8B	8844	
D-0633	Schleicher ASW 15	15081	
D-0634	Scheibe SF-34	5102	4X-GGM D-3336
D-0635	Schleicher ASK 13	13272	
D-0636	Schleicher ASW 15	15083	
D-0637	Schleicher K 8B	8845	
D-0638	SZD-50-3 Puchacz	B-1403	DDR-3637
D-0639	Schleicher ASK 13	13276	
D-0640-TG	Glaser-Dirks DG-100G	88G9	HB-1339
D-0641	Schleicher ASK 21	21566	
D-0642-H3	Schleicher ASW 15	15088	
D-0643	Schleicher ASK 13	13277	
D-0644	Schleicher ASK 13	13278	
D-0645	Schleicher ASK 13	13288	
D-0646	Schleicher ASK 13	13282	
D-0647	Glasflügel H201B Standard Libelle	157	
D-0648	Schempp-Hirth Cirrus	100	
D-0649	Rolladen-Schneider LS6-a	6125	
D-0650	Schleicher ASK 21	21567	
D-0651	Grob G.102 Standard Astir III	5637S	N102FK
D-0652	Schempp-Hirth Standard Cirrus	76	
D-0653	Siebert SIE-3	3005	
D-0654	Schleicher ASW 15	15095	
D-0655	Schleicher Ka 6E	4357	
D-0656	Rolladen-Schneider LS1-d	112	
D-0657	Schleicher ASW 15	15101	
D-0658	Schleicher ASK 13	13289	
D-0660	Schleicher ASW 15	15100	
D-0661-KV	Rolladen-Schneider LS6-c	6257	
D-0662-6F	Rolladen-Schneider LS6	6000	
D-0663	Schleicher ASK 13	13291	
D-0664	Rolladen-Schneider LS1-d	73	
D-0665	Glaser-Dirks DG-303 Club Elan Acro	3E455C79A13	
D-0666	Glasflügel H201B Standard Libelle	167	
D-0667-T	Rolladen-Schneider LS1-c	57	
D-0668	Rolladen-Schneider LS1-d	63	
D-0669-F	Rolladen-Schneider LS1-d	62	
D-0670	Rolladen-Schneider LS1-d	64	
D-0671	Glasflügel H201 Standard Libelle	172	
D-0674	Rolladen-Schneider LS1-c	58	
D-0675	Schleicher ASK 21	21569	
D-0676-M3	Rolladen-Schneider LS1-c	76	
D-0677	Schempp-Hirth Standard Cirrus	82	
D-0678	Schempp-Hirth Standard Cirrus (Reservation)	83	
D-0679	Rolladen-Schneider LS1-c	116	
D-0680	Schleicher ASK 21	21555	
D-0681	Rolladen-Schneider LS1-c	71	
D-0682	Focke-Wulf Kranich III	55	
D-0683-R2	Rolladen-Schneider LS1-c	74	
D-0684	Rolladen-Schneider LS1-d	68	
D-0685	Rolladen-Schneider LS1-c	60	
D-0686	Rolladen-Schneider LS1-c	66	
D-0687-JZ	Schempp-Hirth Standard Cirrus	86	
D-0689	Schempp-Hirth Standard Cirrus	88	
D-0691	Schempp-Hirth Standard Cirrus	92	
D-0692	Rolladen-Schneider LS4-b	4853	
D-0693	Siebert SIE-3	3007	
D-0694	Rolladen-Schneider LS1-d	65	
D-0696	Schempp-Hirth Janus	45	SE-UMC N468F
D-0698	Schleicher ASK 21	21556	
D-0699-VS	Rolladen-Schneider LS4-b	4963	
D-0700	Focke-Wulf Weihe 50	01	HB-554
D-0701	Glasflügel H201B Standard Libelle	184	
D-0703	Schempp-Hirth Standard Cirrus	181	
D-0704	Schempp-Hirth Standard Cirrus	555	

D-0705	Schempp-Hirth Standard Cirrus	183	
D-0706	Schempp-Hirth Standard Cirrus	184	
D-0707	Schleicher ASK 13	13287	
D-0708	Schleicher ASW 15	15107	
D-0709	Schleicher Ka 6E	4363	
D-0710	Schempp-Hirth Duo Discus	18	
D-0711	Schempp-Hirth Discus CS	166CS	
D-0713	Schleicher ASW 19B	19268	BGA 2499/DZD
D-0714	Schleicher K 8B	8857	
D-0715	Schleicher ASW 15	15114	
D-0716	Schleicher ASW 15	15115	
D-0717	SZD-30 Pirat	S-07.25	DDR-1717 DM-1717
D-0718	Schleicher Ka 2 Rhönschwalbe	40	
D-0719	Schempp-Hirth Standard Cirrus	107	
D-0721	Schleicher ASK 21	21350	
D-0722	SZD-42-2 Jantar 2B	B-939	HB-1522
D-0723	Rolladen-Schneider LS4-b	4802	
D-0724	Rolladen-Schneider LS4-b	4803	
D-0725-MD	Rolladen-Schneider LS1-d (See also D-1065)	153	F-CDAZ F-CBAZ
D-0727	Rolladen-Schneider LS1-c	55	
D-0728	Rolladen-Schneider LS1-d	67	
D-0729	SZD-30 Pirat	B-319	DDR-1729 DM-1729
D-0733	SZD-30 Pirat	B-316	DDR-1733 DM-1733
D-0735	Schleicher ASK 21	21557	
D-0736	Schempp-Hirth Standard Cirrus	104	
D-0738	Schleicher ASK 21	21575	
D-0739	Schempp-Hirth Cirrus-VTC	137Y	OE-0970
D-0740	LSD Ornith (Permit 3.99)	V-1	
D-0742-42	Glasflügel H201B Standard Libelle	204	
D-0743	Glasflügel H201 Standard Libelle	205	
D-0744	Schleicher ASK 21	21570	
D-0745	Schleicher ASK 13	13302	
D-0746	Schleicher ASK 13	13303	
D-0747	Schleicher ASW 15	15120	
D-0749-49	Schleicher K 8B	8861	
D-0750	Rolladen-Schneider LS4	4546	D-0115
D-0751	SZD-30 Pirat	B-345	DDR-1751 DM-1751
D-0752	Schleicher ASK 13	13309	
D-0753	Schleicher ASW 15	15124	
D-0754	Schleicher ASK 13	13304	
D-0755	Schleicher ASK 13	13310	
D-0756	Schleicher ASW 15	15125	
D-0757	Schleicher ASK 13	13311	
D-0758	Schleicher ASW 15	15126	
D-0759-H1	Schleicher ASW 27	27044	
D-0760-M1	Schleicher Ka 6E	4374	
D-0761	Schleicher ASK 13	13318	
D-0762	Schleicher ASK 13	13321	
D-0764	Rolladen-Schneider LS1-d	85	
D-0765	Rolladen-Schneider LS1-c	78	
D-0766-66	Schleicher ASH 25	25013	
D-0767	Scheibe L-Spatz (Permit .01)	577	
D-0769	Glasflügel H201B Standard Libelle	298	
D-0770	Glasflügel H201 Standard Libelle	299	
D-0771	Glasflügel H201B Standard Libelle	300	
D-0772	Schempp-Hirth Standard Cirrus	159	
D-0774	Schleicher ASK 21	21096	
D-0775	Schleicher ASW 20L	20555	
D-0776	Schleicher ASW 20	20556	
D-0777	Glasflügel H401 Kestrel	36	
D-0778-EK	Schempp-Hirth Discus CS	077CS	
D-0779	Schempp-Hirth Standard Cirrus	164	
D-0780	Rolladen-Schneider LS1-c	107	
D-0781	Rolladen-Schneider LS1-d	98	
D-0783	Schempp-Hirth Standard Cirrus	192	
D-0787	Rolladen-Schneider LS1-d	121	
D-0788-R5	Slingsby T.59D Kestrel 19 (Permit)	1847	
D-0790	SZD-48-1 Jantar Standard 2	B-1004	SP-3176
D-0792	Schleicher ASW 15	15142	
D-0793	Schleicher ASW 15	15144	
D-0795	Glasflügel H301 Libelle	36	OE-0796
D-0796	Schleicher ASW 15	15148	
D-0797	SZD-30 Pirat	B-440	DDR-1797 DM-1797
D-0798	Schleicher K 8B	8871	
D-0799	Schleicher ASW 15	15150	
D-0800	Rolladen-Schneider LS4-b	4820	
D-0801	SZD-30 Pirat	B-444	DDR-1801 DM-1801
D-0802	Schleicher ASW 15	15154	
D-0803	Schleicher ASW 15	15155	
D-0804	DG Flugzeugbau DG-1000S	10-46S45	
D-0805	Schleicher K 8B	8874	
D-0806	Schleicher ASK 13	13346	
D-0807	SZD-51-1 Junior	B-1924	DDR-2807
D-0808	Schleicher ASW 20L	20417	
D-0809	Rolladen-Schneider LS1-c	101	
D-0811	Grunau Baby IIB	29	
D-0812	Rolladen-Schneider LS1-d	120	
D-0813	Siebert Sie 3	3016	D-0810
D-0814	Schempp-Hirth Standard Cirrus	157G	
D-0815	Glasflügel H401 Kestrel	62	

D-0816	Schleicher K 8B	923	
D-0817	Rolladen-Schneider LS1-c	118	
D-0818	Rolladen-Schneider LS8-18	8409	
D-0819	Grob G.103A Twin II Acro	3756-K-51	
D-0821	Schleicher Ka 6CR Rhönsegler	6201	RAFGGA 529
D-0822-PP	Schempp-Hirth Discus b	30	OH-730
D-0824	Schleicher ASK 13	13351	
D-0825	Bölkow Phoebus C	924	OE-0820
D-0826	Schleicher ASK 13	13352	
D-0827-WT	Schleicher ASW 27	27011	
D-0828-YH	Schleicher ASW 28-18	28728	
D-0829	Schleicher ASK 13	13345	
D-0831	SZD-30 Pirat	B-509	DDR-1831
			DM-1831
D-0833	Rolladen-Schneider LS1-c	114	
D-0834	Rolladen-Schneider LS1-d	125	
D-0835	Grunau Baby IIB	3	
D-0836	Schempp-Hirth Standard Cirrus	226	
D-0837	Rolladen-Schneider LS1-ef	106	
D-0838	Glasflügel H-101 Salto	8	
D-0840	LET L-13 Blanik	175107	
D-0841-MO	Rolladen-Schneider LS4-b	4948	
D-0844-S1	Schempp-Hirth Discus CS	169CS	
D-0845	Glasflügel H201B Standard Libelle	305	
D-0846	Schleicher K 8B (Permit 12.99)	8881/AB	
D-0847	Glasflügel H401 Kestrel	46	
D-0848	Schleicher K 8B	8878	
D-0849	Schleicher ASK 13	13358	
D-0850	Schleicher K 8B	8875	
D-0852	Schleicher ASK 13	13360	
D-0853	Schleicher ASK 13	13361	
D-0854	Schleicher ASW 15	15173	
D-0855	Schleicher ASK 13	13362	
D-0856	Schleicher ASW 15	15175	
D-0857	Akaflieg Braunschweig SB-7A (Permit)	1	
D-0858	Schleicher ASK 13	13341	
D-0859	Schleicher ASW 15	15176	
D-0860	Schleicher ASW 15	15177	
D-0861	Schleicher ASW 15	15178	
D-0862	Schempp-Hirth Discus CS	179CS	
D-0863	SZD-30 Pirat	B-585	DDR-1863
			DM-1863
D-0864	Schleicher ASW 15	15181	
D-0865	Schleicher ASK 13	13368	
D-0866	Bölkow Phoebus C-1 (Permit .01)	808	I-SEGL
D-0867	Schleicher ASK 13	13369	
D-0868	Schleicher ASW 15B	15184	
D-0869	Schleicher K 8B	8887	
D-0870	Schleicher ASW 15B	15185	
D-0871	Schleicher K 8B	8889	
D-0872	DG Flugzeugbau DG-500 Elan Orion	5E183X34	
D-0873	LET L-13 Blanik	175130	
D-0874	Rolladen-Schneider LS1-c	127	
D-0875	SZD-30 Pirat	S-01.05	DDR-1875
			DM-1875
D-0876	Schleicher ASW 15B	15192	
D-0877	Schleicher ASK 21	21561	
D-0878	Neukom Elfe S4A	62	HB-1305
D-0881	Schempp-Hirth Discus CS	178CS	
D-0882	SZD-30 Pirat	S-01.28	DDR-1882
			DM-1882
D-0883	Schleicher ASW 20	20559	
D-0884	Schleicher ASW 20	20557	
D-0885	Schleicher ASW 20	20561	
D-0886-SL	Schleicher ASW 27	27122	
D-0887	Schempp-Hirth Discus b	193	
D-0888	Glasflügel H201 Standard Libelle	278	
D-0889	Schempp-Hirth Discus b	201	
D-0890	Schempp-Hirth Standard Cirrus	210	
D-0891	Glasflügel H201B Standard Libelle	313	
D-0892	Rolladen-Schneider LS1-c	122	
D-0893-SH	Schempp-Hirth Discus b	203	
D-0894-4R	Rolladen-Schneider LS4	4387	
D-0895	Schleicher ASW 15B	15197	
D-0896	Schleicher ASW 15B	15199	
D-0897	Schleicher ASW 15B	15200	
D-0898	Rolladen-Schneider LS4-b	4794	
D-0899-LY	Rolladen-Schneider LS8-a	8284	
D-0901	Schleicher K 8B (Reservation 2.00)	8895	
D-0902	DG Flugzeugbau DG-800S	8-218S44	HB-3324
D-0904	Schleicher K 8B	8897	
D-0905	Schleicher ASK 13	13391	
D-0906	Schleicher ASW 15B	15209	
D-0908	Schleicher ASK 13	13392	
D-0909	Schempp-Hirth Discus b	188	
D-0910	Glasflügel H303 Mosquito	101	OE-5388
D-0911-HI	Glasflügel H201B Standard Libelle	306	
D-0912	Rolladen-Schneider LS1-c	129	
D-0913	Glasflügel H201B Standard Libelle	250	
D-0914 -WB	Schempp-Hirth Janus C	239	
D-0915	Glasflügel H401 Kestrel	65	
D-0916	Schleicher ASK 13	13286AB	
D-0918	Siebert SIE-3	3019	
D-0920-TK	Glasflügel H201B Standard Libelle	315	
D-0921-EP	Schempp-Hirth Discus b	215	
D-0922	Rolladen-Schneider LS1-d	119	
D-0923	Rolladen-Schneider LS1-c	132	
D-0924	Start & Flug H-101 Salto	10	
D-0925	Schempp-Hirth Standard Cirrus	212	
D-0926-2E	Schempp-Hirth Standard Cirrus	213	
D-0927	Schempp-Hirth Standard Cirrus	218	
D-0928	Schempp-Hirth Standard Cirrus	405G	F-CEFJ
D-0930	Schempp-Hirth Discus b	196	
D-0931	Schleicher Ka 6CR Rhönsegler	897	
D-0932	Schleicher ASK 13	13393	
D-0933-2H	Schempp-Hirth Discus b	209	
D-0934	Schleicher K 8B	8898	
D-0935	Rolladen-Schneider LS8-18	8271	
D-0936	DG Flugzeugbau DG-800S	8-26S3	
D-0937	Schempp-Hirth Ventus c	382	
D-0938	Darmstadt D-38	39	
D-0941-A4	Schleicher ASW 15B	15206	OE-0941
D-0942	Schleicher K 8B	8899	
D-0943	Schleicher K 8B	8901	
D-0944	Schleicher ASK 13	13395	
D-0945	Schleicher ASW 15B	15219	
D-0946	Schleicher K 8B	8902	
D-0947	Glaser-Dirks DG-300 Elan Acro	3E460A16	
D-0948	Schleicher ASK 13	13397	
D-0949	Schleicher ASW 15B	15221	
D-0950	Glasflügel H304	262	
D-0951-ES	Schleicher ASW 15B	15222	
D-0952	Glasflügel H401 Kestrel	60	
D-0953	Schempp-Hirth Standard Cirrus	224G	
D-0954-WI	Schempp-Hirth Standard Cirrus	230G	
D-0955	Avialsa-Scheibe A.60 Fauconnet	131K	F-CDLI
D-0956	Schempp-Hirth Standard Cirrus	232G	
D-0957	Glasflügel H401 Kestrel	69	OE-0950
D-0958	Start & Flug H-101 Salto	11	
D-0959	Vogt LO-100 Zwergreiher	04	
D-0960-HE	DG Flugzeugbau DG-800S	8-37S8	HB-3165
			D-8180
D-0961	Schleicher ASK 13	13246AB	
D-0963	Rolladen-Schneider LS1-c	134	
D-0965	Rolladen-Schneider LS6-18W	6340	
D-0966	Glasflügel H201B Standard Libelle	330	
D-0967	Schempp-Hirth Standard Cirrus	240G	
D-0969-AC	Schempp-Hirth Standard Cirrus	242G	
D-0971	Schempp-Hirth Discus b	224	
D-0972	Rolladen-Schneider LS6-c	6341	
D-0973	Rolladen-Schneider LS4-b	4805	
D-0974	Bölkow Phoebus C	874	OE-0974
			OE-0876
D-0975	Schempp-Hirth Standard Cirrus	227	
D-0976	Schempp-Hirth Standard Cirrus	229	
D-0977	LET L-13 Blanik (Reservation)	174921	
D-0979	Glasflügel H401 Kestrel	66	
D-0980-AC	Schempp-Hirth Discus CS	031CS	
D-0981	Schleicher K 8B	8903	
D-0982	Schleicher ASK 13	13398	
D-0983-ZE	Schempp-Hirth Ventus c	515	
D-0984	Schleicher ASW 15B	15223	
D-0985	Schleicher ASK 21	21576	
D-0986	Schleicher Ka 6E	4390	
D-0987	Schleicher ASW 15B	15227	
D-0989	Schleicher K 8B	8910	
D-0990	Schleicher ASK 21	21456	
D-0991	Rolladen-Schneider LS6-c-18	6348	
D-0992	Rolladen-Schneider LS1-c	139	
D-0993	Glaser-Dirks DG-300 Elan	3E173	HB-1869
D-0994	Schleicher K 8B	8915	
D-0995	Schleicher ASW 15B	15239	
D-0996	Schleicher K 8B	8914	
D-0997	Schleicher ASW 15B	15240	
D-0998	Schleicher ASW 17	17011	
D-0999	Glasflügel H401 Kestrel	54	
D-1001	Pilatus B4-PC11AF	171	S5-3045
			SL-3045
			YU-4222
D-1002	Scheibe SF-27A	6046	
D-1003	Rolladen-Schneider LS8-18	8306	
D-1004-MG	Schempp-Hirth Discus b	220	
D-1005	SZD-9bis Bocian 1E	P-717	DDR-3005
			DM-3005
D-1006	DG Flugzeugbau DG-1000S	10-19S19	
D-1007	Glasflügel H401 Kestrel	24	HB-1001
D-1008	Schleicher Ka 6E	4008	
D-1009	Jastreb Glasflügel 304B	323	
D-1010-CM	Jastreb Glasflügel 304B	324	
D-1011	Schleicher K 8B	8742	
D-1012	Scheibe SF-27A	6033	
D-1013	Grunau Baby III (Reservation 1.99)	76	
D-1014	Scheibe Bergfalke III	5569	
D-1015-GL	Schempp-Hirth Discus b	189	
D-1016	Schempp-Hirth Ventus b/16.6	115	HB-1742
D-1017-4T	Glaser-Dirks DG-300 Elan	3E92	OY-XLU
D-1018	Grunau Baby IIB	05	
D-1019	Scheibe L-Spatz 55	R228/H248	OE-0530
D-1020-F	Schleicher Ka 6CR Rhönsegler	6589	
D-1021	Jastreb Glasflügel 304B	326	
D-1022	Rolladen-Schneider LS1-c	133	
D-1023	Glaser-Dirks DG-300 Club Elan	3E391C59	
D-1024	Schleicher Ka 2 Rhönschwalbe	80	
D-1025-IW	Schleicher ASH 25	25001	

D-1026	Schleicher K 8B	8385/A	
D-1027	Glaser-Dirks DG-600	6-27	
D-1028-TOM	Schempp-Hirth Discus b	198	
D-1029-B7	SZD-55-1	551192047	I-NTRE
D-1030	Rolladen-Schneider LS1-c	123	
D-1031	Rolladen-Schneider LS1-d	135	
D-1032-W8	Schempp-Hirth Nimbus 3D	1/3	D-KAYY
D-1033	Glasflügel H-101 Salto	18	
D-1034	Schleicher ASW 24	24141	
D-1035	Schempp-Hirth Ventus 2c	44/130	
D-1036	Scheibe Spatz A	V-1	
D-1037	Schleicher Ka 6CR Rhönsegler	6312	
D-1038	SZD-9bis Bocian 1E	P-459	DDR-3038
			DM-3038
D-1039	Rolladen-Schneider LS6	6101	I-FAMF
			D-1094
D-1040	Schempp-Hirth Ventus c	348	
D-1041	DG Flugzeugbau DG-1000S	10-31S30	
D-1042	LET L-13 Blanik	173046	
D-1043-IYD	Schempp-Hirth Duo Discus	121	
D-1044	Schleicher ASW 19B	19004	D-3751
D-1045	Neukom Elfe S4	28	HB-1035
D-1046	Neukom Elfe S4A	75	HB-1040
D-1047	Glasflügel H401 Kestrel	84	OE-0969
D-1048	Schempp-Hirth Discus b	237	
D-1049	DG Flugzeugbau DG-1000S	10-41S40	
D-1050	Schleicher Ka 6CR Rhönsegler	948	
D-1051-P	Glasflügel H201B Standard Libelle	293	HB-1054
D-1052	Grunau Baby III	E-2	
D-1053	Glasflügel H201B Standard Libelle	288	HB-1056
D-1054-BEB	DG Flugzeugbau DG-1000S	10-33S32	
D-1055	DG Flugzeugbau DG-1000S	10-38S37	
D-1056-H4	Glaser-Dirks DG-300 Club Elan	3E404C63	
D-1057-4A	Rolladen-Schneider LS4	4584	
D-1058	Rolladen-Schneider LS4	4585	
D-1059	DG Flugzeugbau DG-1000S	10-32S31	
D-1060	Vogt LO-100 Zwergreiher	AB-34	
D-1061	Rolladen-Schneider LS4-b	4952	
D-1062	Schempp-Hirth Duo Discus	54	
D-1063	DG Flugzeugbau DG-1000S	10-49S48	
D-1064	Schleicher K 8B	8410	
D-1065	Rolladen-Schneider LS1-c	"530"	
	(C/n incorrect, believed to be 153 in which case this must be ex D-0725, F-CDAZ, F-CBAZ.; but D-0725 still current as LS1-d)		
D-1066	DG Flugzeugbau DG-1000S	10-6S6	(SE-UMY)
D-1067-9C	Rolladen-Schneider LS8-18	8312	
D-1068-M2	Schempp-Hirth Duo Discus	52	
D-1069	Schempp-Hirth Standard Cirrus	228	
D-1070	Glaser-Dirks DG-300 Elan	3E5	
D-1071	DG Flugzeugbau DG-1000S	10-35S34	
D-1073	DG Flugzeugbau DG-1000S	10-42S41	
D-1074	Schempp-Hirth Standard Cirrus	239	
D-1075-GA	Schempp-Hirth Standard Cirrus	246	
D-1076	Rolladen-Schneider LS4	4602	
D-1077	Schleicher Ka 6CR Rhönsegler	6340/SIE	
D-1078	Musger Mg.19 Steinadler	026	OE-0373
D-1079	SZD-9bis Bocian 1D	P-364	OE-0499
D-1080	Göppingen Gö IV Gövier II	1	
D-1081	Rolladen-Schneider LS8-18	8461	
D-1082	Neukom S4 Elfe	4/X	HB-1084
D-1083	Schleicher Ka 6CR Rhönsegler	6285	
D-1084	Rolladen-Schneider LS4	4603	
D-1085	Glaser-Dirks DG-200/17C	2-141CL11	
D-1086	Grob G.103 Twin Astir	3136	D-1000
D-1087-F4	Schempp-Hirth Duo Discus	58	
D-1088	Schleicher Ka 6CR Rhönsegler	6526	
D-1089	Rolladen-Schneider LS4	4604	
D-1090	Glasflügel H301 Libelle	57	
D-1091	Schempp-Hirth Discus b	227	
D-1092	Schleicher ASH 25 (Reservation 3.95)	unkn	
	(Believed to be in museum?)		
D-1093	Scheibe Bergfalke IV	5825	
D-1094-SHA	Schempp-Hirth Duo Discus	140	
D-1095	Schleicher ASK 13	13170	D-1006
D-1096	Glasflügel H201B Standard Libelle	349	
D-1097	Glasflügel H201B Standard Libelle	350	
D-1098-EM	Akaflieg Braunschweig SB-5E Sperber	5027/1	
D-1099	DG Flugzeugbau DG-1000S	10-55S54	
D-1100	DG Flugzeugbau DG-1000S	10-22S22	
D-1101	Schleicher ASW 19B	19055	
D-1102	Rolladen-Schneider LS1-c	142	
D-1104	Pilatus B4-PC11AF	005	HB-1104
D-1105	Akaflieg Braunschweig SB-5B Sperber	5005	
D-1106	Schempp-Hirth Nimbus 3/24.5	17	
D-1107	Grunau Baby III	001	
D-1108-DL	Rolladen-Schneider LS4-b	4953	
D-1109-5B	Glasflügel H201B Standard Libelle	358	
D-1110	Schleicher ASW 20L	20150	
D-1111	Schleicher K 8B	8667/AB	
D-1112	SZD-55-1	551198104	
D-1113	Akaflieg Braunschweig SB-13 (Permit 8.99)	1	
D-1114	LET L-13 Blanik	175107	
D-1115	Pilatus B4-PC11AF	043	HB-1119
D-1116	Grunau Baby III	01	
D-1118	Rolladen-Schneider LS3	3195	N9TE
D-1119-OU	Schleicher Ka 6CR Rhönsegler	6606	
	(Same marks and code worn by ASW 28 demonstrator 4.05)		

D-1120	PZL-Swidnik PW-6U	78.03.06	
D-1121	Schleicher K 8B	3	
D-1122	Rolladen-Schneider LS4	4430	
D-1123	Rolladen-Schneider LS4-b	41029	
D-1124	Schleicher ASW 24	24001	
D-1125	Schempp-Hirth Standard Cirrus	263G	
D-1126	SZD-30 Pirat	B-503	D-1626
			DDR-1826
			DM-1826
D-1127	Schleicher K 7 Rhönadler	7026	
D-1128	Akaflieg München Mü.28	V-1	
D-1129-3M	Rolladen-Schneider LS8-a	8124	OY-CIX
D-1130	Schleicher ASK 21	21606	
D-1131	Akaflieg Stuttgart FS.31 (Permit)	V-1	
D-1132	Scheibe Bergfalke II	162	
D-1133	Scheibe L-Spatz III	816	
D-1134	Schleicher ASK 21	21775	
D-1135	Glaser-Dirks DG-100G Elan	E213G179	
D-1136	Scheibe Bergfalke II	163	
D-1137-LB	Rolladen-Schneider LS4-b	4806	
D-1140	Schempp-Hirth Standard Cirrus	270	
D-1141	Grunau Baby IIB	9	D-6170
			D-6028
D-1142	Schleicher ASK 21	21274	
D-1144	Schleicher ASW 19	19144	PH-579
D-1145	Scheibe Bergfalke II	147/U	
D-1146	Dittmar Condor IV/3	28/53	OE-0869
			D-1147
D-1147-73	Schempp-Hirth Discus 2b	168	
D-1148	Scheibe Bergfalke III	5566	
D-1149	Schempp-Hirth Standard Cirrus	253G	
D-1150	Rolladen-Schneider LS4	4508	
D-1151	Scheibe Mü.13E Bergfalke	310	D-1699
D-1152	Rolladen-Schneider LS8-a	8014	
D-1153	Rolladen-Schneider LS4-b	4875	
D-1154	Schleicher ASK 21	21194	N174KS
D-1155	Schempp-Hirth Janus C	152	LN-GDF
			BGA2823/ENR
D-1156	Fauvel AV.36C	37	
D-1157	Schleicher K 8B	8577	
D-1158-L1	Rolladen-Schneider LS8-18	8467	
D-1159	Schempp-Hirth Duo Discus	168	
D-1160	Schempp-Hirth Duo Discus	166	
D-1161-3Y	Rolladen-Schneider LS8-a	8251	
D-1162	Rolladen-Schneider LS1-c	147	
D-1163-IBG	Rolladen-Schneider LS8-a	8204	
D-1164	Scheibe Bergfalke III	5545	
D-1165	Schleicher ASK 21	21510	
D-1166	Schempp-Hirth Ventus b/16.6	139	HB-1693
D-1167	Scheibe Mü.13E Bergfalke II	176	(D-0759)
			D-1167
D-1168-RB	Schempp-Hirth Ventus-2c (Permit 3.04)	87	
D-1169	Glasflügel H401 Kestrel	72	
D-1170-GE	Glasflügel H401 Kestrel	75	
D-1171	Glasflügel H205 Club Libelle	144	OE-5065
D-1172	DG Flugzeugbau DG-800S	8-70S18	
D-1173	Glaser-Dirks DG-500 Elan Trainer	5E39T13	
D-1174-Gi	Schempp-Hirth Discus CS	063CS	
D-1175	Schleicher K 8B	8930Br	
D-1176	Scheibe SF-27A	6027	
D-1177	Akaflieg Braunschweig SB.11	01	
D-1178	Glasflügel H201B Standard Libelle	133	HB-2056
	(Formerly Aeberli 201M Libelle)		HB-1007
D-1179	Rolladen-Schneider LS6-c	6213	
D-1180	LET L-13 Blanik	026835	(D-1311)
			LY-GCS
			DOSAAF
D-1181	Schempp-Hirth Duo Discus	409	
D-1182	SZD-48-3 Jantar Standard 3	B-1364	
D-1183	Scheibe Specht	01	
D-1184-G1	Glaser-Dirks DG-300 Elan	3E222	
D-1185	Glaser-Dirks DG-300 Elan	3E8	OH-789
			D-1300
D-1186	Scheibe Bergfalke II	319	
D-1187	Marganski MDM-1 Fox	219	
D-1188	Focke-Wulf Kranich III	85	
D-1189	Glaser-Dirks DG-300 Elan	3E225	
D-1190	Schempp-Hirth Standard Cirrus	255G	
D-1191	Schempp-Hirth Standard Cirrus	262G	
D-1192	Akaflieg München Mü.13E Bergfalke	1	
D-1193	Schleicher Ka 6CR Rhönsegler	6445	
D-1194	Valentin Mistral C	MC 069/86	
D-1195	Schleicher K 7 Rhönadler	7258	
D-1196	Scheibe SF-27A	6091	
D-1197	Grunau Baby IIB	3	
D-1198	Schleicher K 8B	8487	
D-1199-IFF	Glaser-Dirks DG-300 Club Elan	3E368C49	
D-1200	Scheibe SF-26A Standard	5007	
D-1201	Fauvel AV-36CR	86	
D-1202	Schempp-Hirth Nimbus 2	68	HB-1202
D-1203	SZD-30 Pirat	B-446	DDR-1803
			DM-1803
D-1204	Scheibe Spatz A	1	
D-1205	Glasflügel Hornet	54	PH-441
D-1206	Schempp-Hirth Ventus 2b	17	
D-1207	Schempp-Hirth Nimbus 2	19	
D-1208	Schempp-Hirth Duo Discus	91	

D-1209	LET L-13 Blanik	175303	
D-1210	Rolladen-Schneider LS1-e	155	
D-1211-NU	Schempp-Hirth Discus-2b	200	
D-1212	Schleicher Ka 6CR Rhönsegler	6483	
D-1213	Glasflügel H201B Standard Libelle	538	HB-1210
D-1214	Scheibe Bergfalke III	5555	
D-1215	Glaser-Dirks DG-300 Elan	3E226	
D-1216-H2	Schempp-Hirth Discus CS	295CS	
D-1217	SZD-9bis Bocian 1E	P-494	DDR-3217 DM-3217
D-1218	Neukom Elfe S-4A	81	HB-3079
D-1219	Schempp-Hirth Ventus-2c (Permit 12.03)	84	
D-1220	Schleicher K 8B	8906/AB	
D-1221	Schleicher ASW 12BV	12014	N12AJ
D-1222	Scheibe SF-27A	6004	
D-1223-FA	Glasflügel H401 Kestrel	13	N19GW CF-YAW
D-1225	Akaflieg Braunschweig SB-12	1 AB	
D-1226	SZD-32A Foka 5	W-471	DDR-2226 DM-2226
D-1227-KR	Neukom Elfe S-4A	51	HB-1228
D-1228-9T	Rolladen-Schneider LS8B	8444	
D-1229	Grob G.103A Twin II Acro	3757-K-52	
D-1230	Grob G.103A Twin II Acro	3767-K-53	
D-1231	Schleicher Ka 6CR Rhönsegler	6025	
D-1232	Rolladen-Schneider LS4-b	4967	
D-1233	Glaser-Dirks DG-500 Elan Trainer	5E76T32	
D-1234	Scheibe Bergfalke II	326	
D-1235	Rolladen-Schneider LS4	4622	
D-1236	Schleicher ASK 21	21514	
D-1237	Scheibe Bergfalke III	5562	
D-1238	Pilatus B4-PC11	074	
D-1239	Schleicher Ka 6CR Rhönsegler	6496	
D-1240	Schleicher K 8B	8611	D-KOSV D-1240
D-1241	DG Flugzeugbau DG-300 Elan Acro	3E492A31	
	(Also listed as D-1243, but Foka may still be current)		
D-1242	Schempp-Hirth Ventus c	366	
D-1243	SZD-32A Foka 5	W-472	DDR-2243 DM-2243
D-1244	Schleicher K 7 Rhönadler	7217	
D-1245-YP	Glasflügel Standard Libelle 201B	333	OE-0945
D-1247	Rolladen-Schneider LS4-a	4624	
D-1248-GO	Schleicher ASH 25	25131	
D-1249-AII	Rolladen-Schneider LS6	6128	
D-1250	Scheibe L-Spatz 55	545	
D-1251	Schempp-Hirth Standard Cirrus	383	HB-1212
D-1252-4B	Schleicher ASK 21	21469	
D-1253	Rolladen-Schneider LS4-b	4968	
D-1254	Rolladen-Schneider LS4-b	4969	
D-1256	Schleicher ASW 24	24099	
D-1257	Schleicher ASH 25	25102	
D-1258	Schleicher ASK 21	21471	
D-1259	Scheibe L-Spatz 55	548	
D-1260	Schleicher ASK 21	21472	
D-1261-GK	Grunau Baby IIB	2	
D-1262	Glaser-Dirks DG-300 Elan	3E103	
D-1263	Glaser-Dirks DG-100G Elan	E182G148	
D-1264	Schleicher ASW 24	24105	
D-1265	Schleicher ASW 24	24108	
D-1266	Schleicher K 8B	8247/A	
D-1267	Schleicher K 8B	8510/A	
D-1268	Bölkow Phoebus A-1	759	
D-1269-XK	Schleicher ASW 19B	19361	
D-1270	Schleicher ASW 20L	20562	
D-1271	Schempp-Hirth Nimbus 4	7	
D-1272	Schempp-Hirth Ventus-2c (Permit 9.03)	83	
D-1273	Rolladen-Schneider LS1-d	87	OO-ZNV D-4440
D-1274	Scheibe Bergfalke II	4	
D-1275-NV	Schleicher ASH 25	25108	
D-1277-PA	Schempp-Hirth Ventus-2bx	151	
D-1278	Schleicher ASW 24	24104	
D-1279	Grob G.103A Twin II Acro	3768-K-54	
D-1280	Grob G.103A Twin II Acro	3769-K-55	
D-1281	Rolladen-Schneider LS4-b	4909	
D-1282	Schleicher Ka 6CR Rhönsegler	6522/Si	
D-1283	Schleicher Ka 6CR Rhönsegler	6012	D-8866
D-1284	Scheibe SF-27A	6041	
D-1285	Schleicher ASW 24	24110	
D-1286	Rolladen-Schneider LS4-a	4661	
D-1287	Akaflieg Braunschweig SB-5B Sperber	5044	
D-1288	Neukom Elfe S4A	74	HB-1280
D-1289	DG Flugzeugbau DG-800S	8-252S46	
D-1290-AM	Rolladen-Schneider LS4	4590	
D-1291	Rolladen-Schneider LS4-b	4753	
D-1292	Schleicher ASK 23B	23124	
D-1293	Rolladen-Schneider LS6-b	6131	
D-1294	Scheibe L-Spatz 55	552	
D-1295-9W	Neukom Elfe S4A	64	HB-1297
D-1296	Scheibe SF-27A	6080	
D-1297	Rolladen-Schneider LS4-a	4755	
D-1298-98	Rolladen-Schneider LS4-b	4756	
D-1299	Rolladen-Schneider LS4-a	4757	
D-1300	LET L-13 Blanik	026351	HB-1303
D-1301	LET L-23 Super Blanik	917913	
D-1302-2	Bölkow Phoebus C	825	

D-1303	Glasflügel Mosquito	01	
D-1304	Scheibe Bergfalke III	5608	
D-1306	Start & Flug H101 Salto	55	
D-1307	Schleicher K 8B	8594	
D-1308	Bölkow Phoebus B-1	736	
D-1310-BE	Rolladen-Schneider LS8-18	8393	
D-1311	LET L-13 Blanik (Reservation 11.99)	026835	LY-GCS DOSAAF
D-1312	Neukom Elfe S4A	77	HB-1312
D-1313	Schleicher ASK 13	13686AB	
D-1314-AI	Neukom Elfe S4A	76	HB-1311
D-1315	Pilatus B4-PC11AF	127	BGA 4755 D-3055 D-5787 PH-578
D-1316	LET L-13 Blanik	173332	D-1313
D-1317	Scheibe Bergfalke II	E-1	
D-1318	Schleicher K 8B	8112	
D-1319	SZD-30 Pirat	B-318	DDR-1719 DM-1719
D-1320	Schleicher ASW 20L	20560	
D-1321	Rolladen-Schneider LS4-b	4954	
D-1322	Schleicher ASW 19B	19360	
D-1323-MZ	Rolladen-Schneider LS7	7026	
D-1324	Scheibe Bergfalke III	5619	
D-1325	Schleicher ASH 25	25240	
D-1327	Grob G.102 Club Astir IIIB	5596CB	
D-1328	Rolladen-Schneider LS7-WL	7024	
D-1329	Rolladen-Schneider LS7-WL	7023	
D-1330	Schleicher Ka 6CR Rhönsegler	6528	
D-1331	Scheibe Bergfalke III	5582	
D-1332	Grob G.103 Twin II	3749	
D-1334	Grob G.103 Twin II	3761	
D-1335	Schleicher ASK 13	13687AB	
D-1336	Schleicher Ka 6CR Rhönsegler	6595	
D-1337	Schleicher K 7 Rhönadler	7011	
D-1338	Schleicher ASK 21	21571	
D-1340	Rolladen-Schneider LS6-b	6135	
D-1341	Scheibe SF-27A	6063	
D-1342-9B	Rolladen-Schneider LS4-a	4662	
D-1343	Scheibe Bergfalke III	5620	
D-1344	Grunau Baby IIB	001	
D-1345	SZD-30 Pirat	B-529	DDR-1845 DM-1845
D-1346	Schleicher Ka 6CR Rhönsegler	6632	
D-1347	Schempp-Hirth Ventus c	613	
D-1348	Olympia-Meise	1	D-1347
D-1350	SZD-30 Pirat	B-569	DDR-1850 DM-1850
D-1351	Bölkow Phoebus C	817	
D-1352	Schempp-Hirth Discus CS	032CS	D-1321
D-1353	Scheibe Bergfalke III	5615	
D-1354-TL	Eiri PIK-20D	20528	HB-1350
D-1355	Schleicher ASK 13	13659AB	
D-1356	Rolladen-Schneider LS3	3001	HB-1352
D-1357	Glaser-Dirks DG-300 Elan	3E227	
D-1358-IXL	Rolladen-Schneider LS4	4642	
D-1359	SZD-9bis Bocian 1E	P-546	DDR-3359 DM-3359
D-1360	Rolladen-Schneider LS4-a	4737	
D-1361	Schleicher ASK 13	13691AB	
D-1362	Scheibe SF-27A	6077	
D-1363	Glaser-Dirks DG-300 Elan	3E18	
D-1364	Scheibe L-Spatz 55	579	
D-1365	Rolladen-Schneider LS4-a	4663	
D-1366	Schleicher ASK 13	13019	
D-1367	Rolladen-Schneider LS4	4591	
D-1368	Rolladen-Schneider LS3	3057	HB-1368
D-1369	Rolladen-Schneider LS4-a	4735	
D-1370-WJ	Rolladen-Schneider LS4-a	4734	
D-1371-IKX	Rolladen-Schneider LS4	4594	
D-1372	Glaser-Dirks DG-300 Elan	3E174	
D-1373	Glaser-Dirks DG-300 Elan	3E178	
D-1374	Rolladen-Schneider LS8-a	8046	
D-1376	SZD-30 Pirat	S-01.22	DDR-1876 DM-1876
D-1377-LD	Schempp-Hirth Duo Discus	153	
D-1378	Schleicher ASK 13	13041	
D-1379	Schleicher Ka 2B Rhönschwalbe	3	
D-1380	Schempp-Hirth Nimbus-4D	12	
D-1381	Rolladen-Schneider LS4-a	4730	
D-1382	Rolladen-Schneider LS4-a	4729	
D-1383	Schempp-Hirth Duo Discus	230	
D-1384	Akaflieg Braunschweig SB-5B	5006	
D-1385-DT	Schempp-Hirth Ventus b/16.6	255	
D-1386-UG	DG Flugzeugbau DG-800S	8-256S50	
D-1387	Rolladen-Schneider LS4-a	4647	
D-1388	Glaser-Dirks DG-100G	87G8	HB-1338
D-1390	Schleicher ASK 13	13653AB	
	(C/n same as BGA4683, ex RAFGGA509, which is current but based at RAFBruggen. Dual identity?)		
D-1391-YZ	Schleicher ASK 21	21126	
D-1392	Rolladen-Schneider LS4-b	4759	
D-1393	Schleicher ASK 13	13683AB	
D-1394	Schempp-Hirth Standard Cirrus	67	OE-0867
D-1395	Schleicher K 8B	876	
D-1396-96	Scheibe SF-27A	6059	

D-1397	Rolladen-Schneider LS3-a	3239	HB-1397
D-1398	Schleicher ASH 26 (Museum) (Reservation -cld?)	unkn	
D-1399	Schempp-Hirth Ventus 2c	27/72	
D-1400	Schleicher ASW 20	20118	HB-1450
D-1401	Grunau Baby IIB (Reservation 5.99)	001	
D-1402	Schleicher ASK 21	21162	
D-1403	Schleicher ASW 19B	19387	
D-1404	Schleicher ASW 19B	19388	
D-1405	Glasflügel H301 Libelle	79	
D-1406	SZD-30 Pirat	S-03.49	DDR-1909 DM-1909
D-1407	Schleicher K 8B	8317/A	
D-1408	Glasflügel H201 Standard Libelle	18	
D-1409	Schleicher Ka 2B Rhönschwalbe	243	
D-1410-Y7	Rolladen-Schneider LS8-18	8462	
D-1411	SZD-30 Pirat	B-474	DDR-1811 DM-1811
D-1412	Schempp-Hirth Duo Discus	233	
D-1413	Scheibe L-Spatz	002	
D-1414-AJ	Rolladen-Schneider LS1-c	105	
D-1415	Scheibe L-Spatz 55	524	
D-1416	Glaser-Dirks DG-200	2-30	HB-1415
D-1417	Schempp-Hirth Ventus b/16.6	183	
D-1418	Schempp-Hirth Discus CS	067CS	
D-1420	DFS Olympia-Meise	unkn	
D-1421	Scheibe L-Spatz 55	3	
D-1422	SZD-36A Cobra 15	W-673	HB-1223
D-1423	Scheibe Specht	848	
D-1424	Glasflügel H201B Standard Libelle	10	OE-0906
D-1425	Rolladen-Schneider LS4-a	4651	
D-1426	Scheibe SF-27A	6007	
D-1427	Scheibe Bergfalke II/55	229	
D-1428	Schleicher K 8B	8550	
D-1429-KG	Rolladen-Schneider LS8-a	8183	
D-1430	Schleicher ASW 20CL	20810	ZK-GRZ D-3430
D-1431	Schleicher ASK 21	21574	
D-1432	Schleicher ASW 20L	20240	
D-1433	Schleicher ASW 19B	19213	
D-1434	Bölkow Phoebus A-1	710	
D-1435-L4	Rolladen-Schneider LS4-b	4931	
D-1436	Grob G.103 Twin Astir	3159	HB-1436
D-1437	Rolladen-Schneider LS8-18	8205	
D-1438	Scheibe Bergfalke III	4/5609	
D-1439	Grob G.102 Astir CS 77	1748	HB-1435
D-1440	LET L-23 Super Blanik	917901	
D-1441	Scheibe Bergfalke III (Reservation -cld?)	5531	
D-1442	Rolladen-Schneider LS4-a	4666	
D-1443-SV	Schempp-Hirth Ventus 2b	19	
D-1444-A9	Glaser-Dirks DG-300 Elan	3E172	OY-XOE
D-1445-T	Rolladen-Schneider LS4-a	4667	
D-1446	Schempp-Hirth Mini-Nimbus B	43	HB-1404
D-1447	Scheibe L-Spatz 55	931	
D-1448	Schleicher ASW 27	27083	
D-1449	Scheibe L-Spatz 55	01	
D-1450	Schleicher Ka 6E	4184	
D-1451	Scheibe L-Spatz 55	618	
D-1452	Scheibe Bergfalke II	334	
D-1453-CM	Schleicher ASH 25	25015	
D-1455	Rolladen-Schneider LS8-18	8414	
D-1456	Schleicher ASK 21	21341	
D-1457	Schleicher Ka 6 Rhönsegler	306	
D-1459	Grunau Baby III (Reservation 1.00)	EB-02	
D-1460	SZD-30 Pirat	B-582	DDR-1860 DM-1860
D-1462-HL	Rolladen-Schneider LS6-18W	6279	
D-1463	Schleicher ASK 21	21342	
D-1464	Schleicher K 7 Rhönadler	366	
D-1465	Scheibe Bergfalke III	5607	
D-1466	Scheibe Zugvogel IIIA	1031	
D-1467	Rolladen-Schneider LS3-a	3228	HB-1461
D-1468	Scheibe L-Spatz 55	536	
D-1469	Glaser-Dirks DG-100G Elan	E2	HB-1465
D-1470	Schleicher K 8	351/57	
D-1471	Scheibe Bergfalke III	5614	
D-1472	Rolladen-Schneider LS4-b	4929	
D-1473-SH	Schleicher ASK 21	21165	
D-1474	Schleicher ASK 21	21166	
D-1475-UG	Schleicher ASK 21	21167	
D-1476-GO	Schempp-Hirth Discus 2B	52	
D-1477	SZD-30 Pirat	B-406	DDR-1777 DM-1777
D-1478	Schleicher Ka 6CR Rhönsegler	6586/Si	
D-1479	Rolladen-Schneider LS4-b	4930	
D-1480	SZD-51-1 Junior	B-2137	
D-1481-IT	Schleicher ASK 21	21343	
D-1482	Schleicher K 8B	8631	
D-1483-GB	Schleicher ASK 21	21127	
D-1485	Glaser-Dirks DG-200	2-16	HB-1408
D-1486-A7	Glaser-Dirks DG-500 Elan Orion	5E152X9	
D-1488-LR	Rolladen-Schneider LS4-b	4970	
D-1489	Schleicher ASK 21	21345	
D-1490	Grunau Baby IIB	002	OE-0190
D-1492	Rolladen-Schneider LS7-WL	7057	
D-1493	Schleicher ASK 23B	23097	
D-1494-G4	Rolladen-Schneider LS4-a	4808	
D-1495-CE	Rolladen-Schneider LS4-b	4809	
D-1497-MI	Rolladen-Schneider LS4-b	4971	
D-1498	SZD-30 Pirat	B-441	DDR-1798 DM-1798
D-1500	Scheibe Bergfalke II/55	255	
D-1501	Glaser-Dirks DG-100G Elan	E149G116	
D-1502	Neukom Elfe S4A	60	HB-1205
D-1503	Rolladen-Schneider LS8-18	8468	
D-1504	Schempp-Hirth Discus b	524	
D-1506	LET L-23 Super Blanik	917909	
D-1507	Rolladen-Schneider LS8-a	8008	
D-1508	Rolladen-Schneider LS8-a	8009	
D-1509-PE	Rolladen-Schneider LS4-b	4932	
D-1510-KK	Rolladen-Schneider LS8-a	8107	
D-1511	SG-38 Schulgleiter	0011	DDR-551
D-1512	Scheibe Bergfalke II	01/53	
D-1513	Schleicher ASK 21	21288	LN-GIA
D-1514	Scheibe L-Spatz 55	750	
D-1515	Bölkow Phoebus C	839	
D-1516	Schleicher ASK 21	21358	
D-1517	Scheibe L-Spatz 55	2/A	
D-1518	Rolladen-Schneider LS4-a	4668	
D-1519	Scheibe Bergfalke III	5584	
D-1520	Scheibe Spatz B (Reservation - cld?)	3	
D-1521	Schleicher ASK 21	21221	
D-1522	Olympia-Meise	E-002	
D-1523	SZD-55-1	551195065	
D-1524	Schempp-Hirth Duo Discus	10	
D-1525	Scheibe L-Spatz 55	556	
D-1526-AG	Schempp-Hirth Discus b	493	
D-1527-JO	Schempp-Hirth Discus b	278	I-NEWS
D-1528	Scheibe L-Spatz III	829	
D-1529	Schleicher ASH 25	25027	
D-1530	Grunau Baby IIb	536	
D-1531	Scheibe Zugvogel IIIA	1037	
D-1532-IGW	SZD-55-1	551195074	
D-1533	Schleicher ASK 21	21355	
D-1534-3A	Schempp-Hirth Discus 2A	25	
D-1536	Schleicher K 7 Rhönadler	537	
D-1537	Bölkow Phoebus A-1	753	
D-1540	Schleicher ASK 21	21359	
D-1541	Schleicher ASK 23B	23101	
D-1542	Schleicher K 8B	582	
D-1543	Glasflügel H201B Standard Libelle	309	HB-1548
D-1544	Schleicher ASK 21	21613	
D-1545	Schleicher ASK 21	21360	
D-1547	Glaser-Dirks DG-100G	E40G22	HB-1547
D-1548-IJT	SZD-55-1	551195075	
D-1549	Scheibe SF-27A	6085	
D-1550	Schleicher ASK 23B	23102	
D-1551	Schleicher Ka 6CR Rhönsegler	571	
D-1552-H3	Glaser-Dirks DG-100G Elan	E110G80	HB-1652
D-1553	SZD-30 Pirat	B-357	DDR-1753 DM-1753
D-1554	Grob G.103A Twin II Acro	3803-K-70	
D-1555	Grob G.103A Twin II Acro	3808-K-71	
D-1556	Grob G.102 Standard Astir III	5604S	
D-1557	Bölkow Phoebus A-1	754	
D-1558	Schempp-Hirth Ventus 2c	78/. . .	
D-1559	Schleicher ASW 27	27101	
D-1560-B9	Rolladen-Schneider LS4-a	4669	
D-1561	Scheibe Zugvogel IIIA	1045	
D-1562	Scheibe Zugvogel IIIB	1072	
D-1563	Schleicher K 7 Rhönadler	564	
D-1564	Scheibe Zugvogel IVA	1509	
D-1565-K6	Schempp-Hirth Discus CS	082CS	
D-1566	Glaser-Dirks DG-300 Elan	3E76	
D-156-S2	Schempp-Hirth Discus CS	079CS	
D-1568	Schleicher Ka 6BR Rhönsegler	482	
D-1569	Schleicher K 7 Rhönadler	479	
D-1570	Glasflügel Hornet C	99	OH-570
D-1571	Scheibe L-Spatz 55	3/809	
D-1572	Glaser-Dirks DG-300 Club Elan	3E307C20	
D-1573	Schleicher K 8B	8391/A	
D-1574	Schleicher ASW 20L	20570	
D-1575-TV	Schleicher ASW 20	20571	
D-1576-EE	Schleicher ASK 21	21107	
D-1577	Schleicher ASW 19B	19364	
D-1578	Schleicher ASW 24	24062	
D-1579	Schleicher ASK 21	21422	
D-1580	Schleicher ASW 24	24048	
D-1581	Scheibe L-Spatz 55	684	
D-1583	Schleicher ASK 21	21423	
D-1584-24	Schleicher ASW 24	24050	
D-1585	Schleicher ASK 21	21615	(JA2538)
D-1586	Schleicher ASW 24	24051	
D-1587-STI	Schempp-Hirth Discus CS	172CS	
D-1588	SZD-30 Pirat	B-431	DDR-1788 DM-1788
D-1589	Schleicher Ka 6CR Rhönsegler	622	
D-1590	Schempp-Hirth Discus CS	168CS	
D-1591	Scheibe Zugvogel IVA	1511	
D-1592-II	Rolladen-Schneider LS4-b	4773	
D-1593	Rolladen-Schneider LS4-b	4774	
D-1594-DE	Schempp-Hirth Ventus 2bXR (Permit)	142	
D-1596-LD	Schempp-Hirth Duo Discus	61	
D-1597	Rolladen-Schneider LS4-b	4940	
D-1598-LSF	Rolladen-Schneider LS4-b	4777	

D-1599-JT	Rolladen-Schneider LS4-b	4778	
D-1600	Scheibe Bergfalke III	5550	
D-1601	Scheibe Bergfalke III	5527	
D-1602	Glaser-Dirks DG-300 Club Elan	3E374C53	
D-1603	Scheibe Bergfalke III	5606	
D-1604	Rolladen-Schneider LS4	4069	HB-1603
D-1605	Scheibe L-Spatz 55	004	
D-1606-01	Schleicher ASW 24	24052	
D-1607	Schleicher ASK 21	21425	
D-1608-V1	Rolladen-Schneider LS4-b	41012	
D-1609-XF	Schleicher ASW 24	24065	
D-1610	Schleicher ASK 21	21435	
D-1611	Schleicher ASH 25	25078	
D-1612	Schleicher K 8B (Probably ex BGA3914, D-1612 originally with c/n 4)	AB 4/95	
D-1613	Schleicher Ka 6CR Rhönsegler	6635/Si	
D-1614	Schleicher K 8B	745	
D-1615	Rolladen-Schneider LS4-b	41030	
D-1616	Glasflügel H303 Mosquito B	187	OE-5243
D-1617	SZD-30 Pirat	B-397	D-1728 DDR-1768 DM-1768
D-1618-GJ	Schempp-Hirth Discus 2B	70	
D-1619-R	Schleicher ASH 26	26149	
D-1620	SZD-50-3 Puchacz	B-1337	DDR-3620
D-1621	Schleicher ASK 21	21745	
D-1622	Scheibe Bergfalke II/55	309	
D-1623	SZD-48-3 Jantar Standard 3	B-1966	
D-1624	SZD-48-3 Jantar Standard 3	B-1970	
D-1625	Scheibe Spatz B	696	
D-1626	Rolladen-Schneider LS4-b	41031	
D-1628	Schleicher K 7 Rhönadler	769	
D-1629	Scheibe L-Spatz 55	712	
D-1630	Schleicher Ka 6CR Rhönsegler	6444	
D-1631	LET L-13 Blanik	173353	
D-1632	Akaflieg Stuttgart FS.32 (Permit)	V-1	
D-1633	Glaser-Dirks DG-300 Elan (Permit)	3E61/17	
D-1634	Kurz Me 163B replica (Reservation 10.99)	1	(D-ESJK)
D-1635	Schleicher Ka 6CR Rhönsegler	6159	OE-0635
D-1637	Schleicher ASW 20	20602	
D-1638	Schleicher ASK 21	21136	
D-1640	Schleicher ASK 21	21771	
D-1641	Schleicher K 8B	8514	
D-1642	SZD-30 Pirat	B-563	DDR-1842 DM-1842
D-1643	LET L-23 Super Blanik	948120	
D-1644	Rolladen-Schneider LS4-b	4781	
D-1645-101	Schempp-Hirth Ventus 2a	20	
D-1646-W8	Rolladen-Schneider LS8B	8435	
D-1647	Schleicher ASK 21	21110	
D-1648	Schleicher ASW 20	20575	
D-1649	Schleicher ASW 20L	20577	
D-1650	Schleicher ASK 21	21112	
D-1651	Scheibe Bergfalke III	5601	
D-1652	Schleicher ASK 21	21134	
D-1653-A5	Schempp-Hirth Duo Discus	323	
D-1654	SZD-50-3 Puchacz	B-1538	DDR-3654
D-1655	Schleicher Ka 3 (Permit .02)	01	
D-1656	SZD-50-3 Puchacz	B-1541	DDR-3657
D-1657-GY	Schleicher ASW 20C	20822	
D-1658	Grunau Baby IIB	01A	
D-1659	SZD-50-3 Puchacz	B-1543	DDR-3659
D-1660	Rolladen-Schneider LS4	4122	
D-1661	Schempp-Hirth Discus b	135	
D-1662	Schleicher Ka 6CR Rhönsegler	896	
D-1663	Schleicher K 8B	816	
D-1664	SZD-30 Pirat	B-588	DDR-1864 DM-1864
D-1665	Schleicher Ka 6CR Rhönsegler	852	
D-1666	SZD-30 Pirat	W-411	D-6710 DDR-1710 DM-1710
D-1667	Glasflügel H101 Salto	67	
D-1668	Schempp-Hirth Ventus C	419	OY-XRE
D-1669	SZD-32A Foka 5	W-429	OE-0892 SP-2533
D-1671	SZD-30 Pirat	B-400	DDR-1771 DM-1771
D-1672	SZD-30 Pirat	B-401	DDR-1772 DM-1772
D-1674	Rolladen-Schneider LS7-WL	7036	
D-1675	Rolladen-Schneider LS7	7037	
D-1677-77	Rolladen-Schneider LS4	4418	
D-1678	Rolladen-Schneider LS7-WL	7038	
D-1679	Schleicher K 8B	909	
D-1681-CW	Rolladen-Schneider LS8-a	8085	
D-1684	Rolladen-Schneider LS7	7039	
D-1685	Grob G.102 Club Astir IIIB	5520CB	
D-1686	Scheibe L-Spatz 55	851 K	
D-1687	Scheibe L-Spatz 55	820 K	
D-1688-CM	Rolladen-Schneider LS8	8011	
D-1689	Rolladen-Schneider LS4-b	4928	
D-1690	SZD-30 Pirat (Rebuilt from D-2787 ex DDR/DM-1787 and adopted its c/n B-430 officially)	B-433	DDR-1790 DM-1790
D-1693	SZD-30 Pirat	B-436	DDR-1793 DM-1793
D-1694	Scheibe SF-27A	6018	
D-1695	SZD-30 Pirat	B-438	DDR-1795 DM-1795
D-1696	Schempp-Hirth Standard Cirrus	G54M	D-KING
D-1697	Schleicher ASK 21	21580	
D-1698-6W	Rolladen-Schneider LS8-a	8206	
D-1699	SZD-41A Jantar Standard	B-802	OE-5143
D-1700	Glaser-Dirks DG-100G Elan	E65G40	
D-1701	Glaser-Dirks DG-100G Elan	E67G42	
D-1702-AF	SZD-30 Pirat	W-403	DDR-1706 DM-1706
D-1703	Glaser-Dirks DG-300 Elan	3E23	
D-1705	Grob G.102 Astir CS	1238	D-7319
D-1706	Bölkow Phoebus C	823	
D-1707	Glaser-Dirks DG-300 Elan	3E325	
D-1708	Scheibe L-Spatz 55	748	(D-8397) D-1708
D-1709	SZD-30 Pirat	W-405	DDR-1708 DM-1708
D-1710	SZD-30 Pirat	W-416	DDR-1715 DM-1715
D-1711	Scheibe SF-34	5118	
D-1712	SZD-30 Pirat	W-412	DDR-1711 DM-1711
D-1713-YT	Rolladen-Schneider LS7	7051	
D-1716	Scheibe L-Spatz 55	689	
D-1717	Akaflieg München Mü.17 (Reservation)	03	
D-1718	SZD-30 Pirat	W-413	DDR-1712 DM-1712
D-1720	Schleicher Ka 6 Rhönsegler	267	
D-1722-FA	Schleicher ASW 20L	20481	HB-1728 OE-5289
D-1723-6C	SZD-30 Pirat	B-305	DDR-1722 DM-1722
D-1725-25	Schempp-Hirth Discus b	343	
D-1726	SZD-30 Pirat	B-307	DDR-1726 DM-1726
D-1727-IGA	Glasflügel H304 (Built from spares)	9265	
D-1728-E1	Schleicher ASW 28-18 (Permit 3.04)	28510	
D-1729- IYY	Schleicher ASW 20C	20713	
D-1730	Schleicher ASW 20C	20714	
D-1731	Schleicher ASW 20CL	20728	
D-1732	Schleicher K 8B	13/117	
D-1733	SZD-30 Pirat	W-414	DDR-1713 DM-1713
D-1734	SZD-30 Pirat	B-298	DDR-1724 DM-1724 SP-2531
D-1735	Scheibe Bergfalke II/55	314	
D-1736	SZD-30 Pirat	W-417	DDR-1716 DM-1716
D-1737	Scheibe Bergfalke III	5554	
D-1738	Scheibe L-Spatz 55	766	
D-1739	Glaser-Dirks DG-300 Elan	3E33	HB-1739
D-1740-AS	Akaflieg München Mü.17	02	
D-1741	Schleicher K 7 Rhönadler	1030	
D-1742	Schleicher K 7 Rhönadler	1031	
D-1743	SZD-30 Pirat	B-331	DDR-1742 DM-1742
D-1744-CJ	Schempp-Hirth Duo Discus	74	
D-1745	Schleicher K 7 Rhönadler	1032	
D-1746	Rolladen-Schneider LS4-b	41056	
D-1747	Rolladen-Schneider LS4	4445	
D-1748	Schleicher Ka 6CR Rhönsegler	1069	
D-1749	Schleicher K 8B	136	
D-1750	Schempp-Hirth Ventus c (M)	33/467	
D-1751	Schempp-Hirth Discus b	312	
D-1752-EA	Schempp-Hirth Discus b	322	
D-1753	Fauvel AV-36C1	V-1/250	
D-1754-AC2	Schempp-Hirth Janus C	263	
D-1755	Rolladen-Schneider LS8-a	8015	
D-1756	Schleicher Ka 6BR Rhönsegler	362	
D-1757	Schleicher K 8B	8034	D-KIBO D-1757
D-1758	Schleicher Ka 6CR Rhönsegler	6003	
D-1759-UK	Schempp-Hirth Discus b	330	
D-1760	Schempp-Hirth Discus b	338	
D-1762-GH	Schempp-Hirth Duo Discus	147	
D-1763	Schleicher ASH 25	25021	
D-1764	SZD-30 Pirat	B-395	DDR-1766 DM-1766
D-1765	Schleicher K 8B	8040	
D-1766	Scheibe Bergfalke II	181	
D-1767	Schempp-Hirth Standard Cirrus	474	I-ZANI
D-1768	SZD-30 Pirat	B-367	DDR-1764 DM-1764
D-1769	Schleicher Ka 6CR Rhönsegler	6035	
D-1770	Schempp-Hirth Ventus 2b	58	
D-1771	Grunau Baby III	01	D-1271 D-1078
D-1772	Schempp-Hirth Duo Discus	122	
D-1773	SZD-48-3 Jantar Standard 3	B-1447	HB-1772
D-1774	Schleicher K 8B	8038	
D-1775	Glaser-Dirks DG-500 Elan Orion	5E149X7	
D-1776	SZD-30 Pirat	B-402	DDR-1773 DM-1773
D-1777	Akaflieg Braunschweig SB-5B Sperber	5047	

D-1778	SZD-30 Pirat	B-407	DDR-1778 DM-1778
D-1779	Schleicher K 8B	8572	
D-1780	DG Flugzeugbau DG-800S	8-41S10	
D-1781	Schleicher K 7 Rhönadler	1095	
D-1783	Schleicher ASK 13	13220AB	D-0462 ?
D-1784	Scheibe L-Spatz 55	653	
D-1785	Schempp-Hirth Duo Discus	92	
D-1786	Schempp-Hirth Duo Discus	158	
D-1787-BP	Rolladen-Schneider LS8-a	8156	
D-1788	Schempp-Hirth Ventus b/16.6	196	HB-1743
D-1789	Schempp-Hirth Ventus 2b	25	
D-1790	Scheibe SF-27A	6054	
D-1791	Rolladen-Schneider LS4-a	4399	
D-1792	Rolladen-Schneider LS4	4400	
D-1793-R6	Rolladen-Schneider LS4	4401	
D-1794	Rolladen-Schneider LS1-c	146	
D-1795	Akaflieg Braunschweig SB-5B Sperber	AB5054	
D-1796	LET L-13 Blanik	175230	
D-1798	Rolladen-Schneider LS1-c	130	
D-1799	SZD-30 Pirat (Permit)	B-435	DDR-1792 DM-1792
D-1800	Schleicher ASK 13	13674AB	
D-1801	SZD-30 Pirat	S-01.27	DDR-1881 DM-1881
D-1802	Schleicher ASK 21	21130	
D-1803	Schleicher ASW 20	20605	
D-1804	Schleicher ASK 21	21145	
D-1805	Rolladen-Schneider LS1-c	145	
D-1806	Scheibe Bergfalke II/55	364	
D-1807	Schleicher K 8B	8695A	C-GVWD
D-1808	Schleicher Ka 6E	4204	OH-652
D-1809	SZD-30 Pirat	B-461	DDR-1805 DM-1805
D-1810	Bölkow Phoebus A-1	853	D-2002
D-1811	Schleicher ASH 25	25058	
D-1812	DG Flugzeugbau DG-800S	8-110S26	HB-3250
D-1813	Glaser-Dirks DG-100G Elan	E118G87	
D-1814	Schleicher K 7 Rhönadler	7207	
D-1815-SD9	SZD-55-1	551194068	
D-1816-EY	Schempp-Hirth Discus b	339	
D-1817	Schleicher ASW 19B	19417	HB-1815
D-1818	Schleicher ASK 18	18017	F-CERC
D-1819	SZD-30 Pirat	B-479	DDR-1815 DM-1815
D-1820	SZD-30 Pirat	B-471	DDR-1810 DM-1810
D-1821	SZD-30 Pirat	S-01.09	DDR-1871 DM-1871
D-1822-9F	Schleicher ASK 21	21169	
D-1823	Schleicher ASK 21	21170	
D-1824	Schleicher ASW 19B	19391	
D-1825	Schempp-Hirth Standard Cirrus	217	SE-TKU
D-1826	Schleicher K 8B	8165/03	
D-1827	SZD-30 Pirat	B-517	DDR-1837 DM-1837
D-1828	Schempp-Hirth Janus C	240	
D-1829	Schleicher Ka 6CR Rhönsegler	6228	
D-1830-9M	Grob G.103C Twin III Acro	34128	
D-1831	Schempp-Hirth Duo Discus	55	
D-1832-N	Rolladen-Schneider LS8-a	8019	
D-1833	Glaser-Dirks DG-600	6-18	PH-833
D-1834	SZD-30 Pirat	B-516	DDR-1836 DM-1836
D-1835	Schleicher Ka 6CR Rhönsegler	6242	
D-1836	Schleicher Ka 6CR Rhönsegler	6187	
D-1837	Schleicher K 8B	189/60	
D-1838	Schempp-Hirth Discus b	165	HB-1838
D-1839	Scheibe Spatz B	01/517	
D-1840	Schleicher K 8B	8334/A	
D-1841	SZD-30 Pirat	B-561	DDR-1841 DM-1841
D-1842	Rolladen-Schneider LS4-a	4744	
D-1844-9L	Rolladen-Schneider LS4-a	4743	
D-1845-ZG	Rolladen-Schneider LS4-a	4742	
D-1846	Rolladen-Schneider LS4-a	4741	
D-1847	SZD-30 Pirat	B-531	DDR-1847 DM-1847
D-1849	SZD-30 Pirat	B-530	DDR-1846 DM-1846
D-1851	Scheibe SF-27A	6001	
D-1852	Grob G.103C Twin III Acro	34111	
D-1853	Grob G.103C Twin III Acro	34124	
D-1854	Schleicher Ka 6CR Rhönsegler	6225	
D-1855	Schleicher Ka 6CR Rhönsegler	6338Si	
D-1857	Scheibe L-Spatz III	801	
D-1858	Schleicher Ka 6CR Rhönsegler	6316	
D-1859	Schleicher Ka 6CR Rhönsegler	6355	
D-1860	Scheibe SF-27A	6005	
D-1861	Glaser-Dirks DG-600-18	6-101S56	SE-UKP
D-1862	Grob G.103A Twin II Acro	3809-K-72	
D-1863-G1	Grob G.103A Twin II Acro	3810-K-73	
D-1865	Scheibe L-Spatz 55	765	
D-1866	Scheibe Bergfalke II/55	387	
D-1867	SZD-30 Pirat	B-577	DDR-1857 DM-1857
D-1868	Rolladen-Schneider LS6-18W	6366	

D-1870-MH4	Grob G.103C Twin III Acro	34112	
D-1871-MH	Rolladen-Schneider LS8-a	8184	
D-1872	Glaser-Dirks DG-300 Elan	3E24	
D-1873	SZD-30 Pirat	S-01.08	DDR-1870 DM-1870
D-1874	SZD-30 Pirat	S-01.23	DDR-1877 DM-1877
D-1875	Schempp-Hirth Ventus 2c	94	
D-1876	Schempp-Hirth Ventus 2a	82	
D-1877	Grob G.103C Twin III Acro	34126	
D-1878	Schleicher ASW 28-18	28707	
D-1879	Schempp-Hirth Discus CS	008CS	
D-1880-MB	Schempp-Hirth Janus C	262	
D-1881	Schleicher K 8B	995	
D-1882	Schleicher K 8B	8452	
D-1885	Schleicher K 8B	8456	
D-1886	Scheibe L-Spatz	201	
D-1887	Schleicher K 7 Rhönadler	7028	
D-1888	Glasflügel H-101 Salto	66	
D-1889	Rolladen-Schneider LS4	4587	HB-1882
D-1890	Schleicher K 8B	8133	
D-1891	Schleicher Ka 2B Rhönschwalbe	2007	
D-1892	SZD-30 Pirat	S-03.07	DDR-1892 DM-1892
D-1893	Scheibe SF-26A Standard	5014	
D-1894	SZD-30 Pirat	B-513	DDR-1834 DM-1834
D-1895	SZD-30 Pirat	S-03.08	DDR-1893 DM-1893
D-1896	Rolladen-Schneider LS8-a	8108	
D-1897	SZD-30 Pirat	S-03.21	DDR-1896 DM-1896
D-1898-B2	SZD-30 Pirat	S-03.22	DDR-1897 DM-1897
D-1899	SZD-30 Pirat	B-544	DDR-1849 DM-1849
D-1900	Schleicher ASK 13	13678AB	
D-1901	Habicht E	AB/KSZ1	
D-1902	Schleicher K 8B	8031	
D-1903	Scheibe Zugvogel IIIB	1078	
D-1904	SZD-30 Pirat	S-03.25	DDR-1900 DM-1900
D-1905	Schleicher K 7 Rhönadler	7131	
D-1906-3F	Schleicher K 8B	8273/A	
D-1908-K3	Schempp-Hirth Discus CS	128CS	
D-1909	SZD-30 Pirat	S-03.46	DDR-1906 DM-1906
D-1910	Rolladen-Schneider LS6	6123	HB-1911
D-1911	Schleicher ASW 27	27205	
D-1912	Schleicher ASK 13	13641AB	
D-1913	Glaser-Dirks DG-600	6-21	
D-1914	Glaser-Dirks DG-600	6-22	
D-1915	SZD-30 Pirat	S-04.21	DDR-1914 DM-1914
D-1916	SZD-30C Pirat	P-809	DDR-1916 DM-1916
D-1917	Schleicher Ka 6E	4189	
D-1918	Schleicher Ka 6BR Rhönsegler	439	ZS-GPK D-1918 HB-918
D-1919	Rolladen-Schneider LS8B	8456	
D-1920	Schleicher Ka 6CR Rhönsegler	6069	
D-1921	Schempp-Hirth Ventus 2a	99	
D-1922	Rolladen-Schneider LS8B	8455	
D-1923-SM	Rolladen-Schneider LS8-18	8157	
D-1924	Schleicher ASK 21	21325	
D-1925	Schleicher K 7 Rhönadler	296	
D-1926	SZD-30 Pirat (Permit .02)	S-04.20	DDR-1913 DM-1913
D-1927	Schleicher ASW 27	27135	
D-1929	Scheibe Bergfalke II/55	385	
D-1931-YS	Schempp-Hirth Discus CS	040CS	
D-1932-6D	Schempp-Hirth Duo Discus	162	
D-1933	Rolladen-Schneider LS6-18W	6369	
D-1934	SZD-30 Pirat	S-03.44	DDR-1904 DM-1904
D-1935	Schleicher Ka 6CR Rhönsegler	6278	
D-1936	DFS Olympia Meise	1 Burg Feuerstein	
D-1937	Schleicher Ka 6E	4193	
D-1938	Schleicher Ka 6CR Rhönsegler	6307	
D-1939	Grunau Baby IIB	0123	
D-1940	Schleicher ASK 21	21698	
D-1941	Schleicher Ka 6CR Rhönsegler	6224/A	
D-1942	Schempp-Hirth Discus b	222	HB-1968
D-1943-20	Schleicher Ka 6E	4170	
D-1944	Scheibe Specht	862	
D-1945	Rolladen-Schneider LS3-17	3348	PH-1088 OO-ZZH HB-1509
D-1946	SZD-30 Pirat	S-03.43	DDR-1903 DM-1903
D-1947	Schleicher ASK 21	21363	
D-1948	DFS Olympia Meise (Permit)	09	
D-1950-UD	Glasflügel H201B Standard Libelle	429	F-CEBO
D-1951	Akaflieg Braunschweig SB-5E Sperber	5037	
D-1952	Schleicher K 7 Rhönadler (Reservation)	7110	
D-1954	Schleicher Ka 6CR Rhönsegler	6277	

D-1955	Pilatus B4-PC11	019	
D-1956	Glaser-Dirks DG-100G Elan	E56G32	
D-1957	Vogt LO-100 Zwergreiher	1	
D-1959	Schleicher Ka 2B Rhönschwalbe	245	D-4350
D-1960	Schleicher K 10A	10004	
D-1961-VT	Rolladen-Schneider LS8-a	8185	
D-1963	Schleicher K 8B	8080/5	
D-1964	Scheibe L-Spatz 55	776	
D-1965	Schleicher K 7 Rhönadler	7051	
D-1966	Glaser-Dirks DG-300 Club Elan	3E356C43	
D-1967	Glaser-Dirks DG-300 Club Elan	3E357C44	
D-1968	Schempp-Hirth Discus CS	302CS	
D-1969-SG	Glaser-Dirks DG-300 Elan	3E359	
D-1970	Scheibe SF-27A	6064	
D-1971	Schempp-Hirth Discus CS	041CS	
D-1972	Grunau Baby III	1	OY-XBC D-3669 D-1049
D-1973-6X	Schleicher ASW 24	24134	
D-1974	Schleicher K 8B	8388/A	
D-1975	SZD-51-1 Junior	B-2133	
D-1976	SZD-51-1 Junior	unkn	
D-1977	Grunau Baby III	04	
D-1978	SZD-30 Pirat	S-01.24	DDR-1878 DM-1878
D-1979	Glaser-Dirks DG-200	2-77	
D-1980	Scheibe L-Spatz	535	
D-1981-6H	Rolladen-Schneider LS1-d	192	F-CEHA
D-1982	Grunau Baby IIB	16	
D-1983	Schempp-Hirth Standard Cirrus	419	
D-1984-SN	Schempp-Hirth Standard Cirrus	278G	
D-1985	SZD-30 Pirat	S-02.41	DDR-1885 DM-1885
D-1986	Schempp-Hirth Standard Cirrus	285G	
D-1987	Schempp-Hirth Cirrus-VTC	131Y	
D-1989	Rolladen-Schneider LS1-c	152	
D-1990	Schempp-Hirth Standard Cirrus	275G	
D-1992	Glasflügel H201B Standard Libelle	382	
D-1993-93	Rolladen-Schneider LS4-b	4852	
D-1994	Schempp-Hirth Standard Cirrus	287G	
D-1995	Marganski MDM-1 Fox	208	OE-5625
D-1996	Schempp-Hirth Standard Cirrus	307G	
D-1997	Glasflügel H201 Standard Libelle	194	HB-1006
D-1998	Glasflügel H401 Kestrel	82	
D-2000	Glaser-Dirks DG-600/18	6-37	HB-1960
D-2001	Schleicher ASK 13	13359	
D-2002	Schleicher ASK 21	21604	
D-2003	Schleicher ASK 21	21732	
D-2004	Scheibe Bergfalke III	5537	D-1001
D-2005	Vogt LO-100 Zwergreiher	AB 103	
D-2006	SZD-9bis Bocian 1E	P-718	DDR-3006 DM-3006
D-2007	Schleicher ASW 15B	15414	
D-2008	Schleicher K 8B	001AB	
D-2009	Schempp-Hirth Discus 2B	47	
D-2010	Schleicher K 8B	8490	
D-2011	Focke-Wulf Kranich III	66	
D-2012	Akaflieg Braunschweig SB-5B	5022/13A	
D-2013	Akaflieg Braunschweig SB-5E Sperber	13	
D-2014	Schleicher K 8B	03	
D-2015	Glaser-Dirks DG-100G Elan	E163G129	
D-2016-FWS	Schempp-Hirth Nimbus 2B	116	D-7258
D-2017	SZD-41A Jantar Standard	B-748	DDR-2417 DM-2417
D-2018-ZZ	Rolladen-Schneider LS8-18	8287	
D-2019	Schleicher Ka 6CR Rhönsegler	566	
D-2020	Schleicher ASW 20	20327	
D-2021	Schleicher K 8B	687	
D-2022	Scheibe L-Spatz 55	12	
D-2023-WK	Schleicher ASK 23B	23138	
D-2024	Glasflügel H303 Mosquito B	192	
D-2025-HR	Schleicher ASW 15B	15389	
D-2026	Rolladen-Schneider LS8B	8448	
D-2027	Vogt LO-100 Zwergreiher	12	
D-2028-D3	Schempp-Hirth Discus b	342	
D-2029	Rolladen-Schneider LS4-b	41052	
D-2030	Schleicher Ka 6CR Rhönsegler	1115	
D-2031	Schleicher K 7 Rhönadler	7010	
D-2032	Start & Flug H101 Salto	9	OY-MZX
D-2033	Schempp-Hirth Cirrus	71	
D-2035	Schempp-Hirth Ventus-2b	161	
D-2036	Schleicher ASW 20C	20722	
D-2037	Scheibe SF-27A	6309	D-KOBF
D-2039	Schleicher ASK 13	13319AB	
D-2040	Start & Flug H-101 Salto	V-1	
D-2041	Rolladen-Schneider LS1-c	51	
D-2042-SL	Bölkow Phoebus C (Permit 4.99)	940	
D-2043-ML	Schempp-Hirth Discus CS	242CS	
D-2044	Glasflügel H204 Standard Libelle	1	
D-2045	Rolladen-Schneider LS1-d	173	
D-2046	Rolladen-Schneider LS1-c	160	
D-2047	Schleicher K 8B	8907/AB	
D-2048	Glasflügel H401 Kestrel	37	
D-2049	SZD-30 Pirat	B-343	DDR-1749 DM-1749
D-2050	Pilatus B4-PC11	042	
D-2051	Schempp-Hirth Standard Cirrus	283G	

D-2052	Schempp-Hirth Standard Cirrus	291	
D-2054-OX	Schempp-Hirth Standard Cirrus	293	
D-2055	Schempp-Hirth Janus C	261	
D-2056	Schempp-Hirth Janus Ce	284	
D-2058	Schempp-Hirth Standard Cirrus	300	
D-2059-KP	Schempp-Hirth Standard Cirrus (Permit)	303	
D-2060	Stamer-Lippisch Zögling	AB001M	
D-2061-LB	Schempp-Hirth Discus 2A	7	
D-2062	SZD-24C Foka	W-148	DDR-2036 DM-2036
D-2063	Schempp-Hirth Standard Cirrus	311	
D-2064-CB	Schempp-Hirth Duo Discus	62	
D-2066	Schleicher ASK 13	13408	
D-2067-BT	Schleicher ASW 15B	15237	
D-2068-W2	Schempp-Hirth Duo Discus	123	
D-2069-WU	Schleicher ASW 15B	15245	
D-2070	Schleicher ASW 15B	15247	
D-2071	Schleicher ASW 15B	15248	
D-2072	Schleicher ASW 15B	15235	
D-2073	Schleicher ASW 15B	15251	
D-2074	Schleicher ASK 13	13418	
D-2075	Schleicher K 8B	8920	
D-2076	Schleicher ASW 15B	15252	
D-2077	Schleicher K 8B	8921	
D-2078	Schleicher ASK 13	13415	
D-2079	Schleicher ASW 15B	15254	
D-2080-BV	Schempp-Hirth Ventus 2c	62/181	
D-2082	Schempp-Hirth Duo Discus	209	
D-2083	Start & Flug H101 Salto	19	
D-2084	Schempp-Hirth Ventus 2b	46	
D-2085	Glasflügel 604	9	
D-2086-TX	Glasflügel H401 Kestrel	83	
D-2087	Glasflügel H401 Kestrel	85	
D-2088	Rolladen-Schneider LS6-c	6280	
D-2089	Rolladen-Schneider LS1-c	149	
D-2090	Rolladen-Schneider LS1-d	182	
D-2092	Schempp-Hirth Janus B	83	HB-1488
D-2093	LET L-13 Blanik	025412	
D-2095	SZD-24-4A Foka 4	W-306	DDR-2045 DM-2045
D-2096	Rolladen-Schneider LS1-d	169	
D-2098	Glasflügel H201B Standard Libelle	404	
D-2099	Schleicher Ka 6E	4097	
D-2100	Bölkow Phoebus B-1	929	
D-2101	Schempp-Hirth Standard Cirrus	351	
D-2102-SA	Schempp-Hirth Standard Cirrus	274	
D-2103	Schempp-Hirth Standard Cirrus	290	
D-2104	Schempp-Hirth Standard Cirrus	301	
D-2105	SZD-51-1 Junior	B-1922	DDR-2805
D-2106-63	Rolladen-Schneider LS6-c	6265	SE-URR
D-2107	Glaser-Dirks DG-300 Elan (Permit)	3E355	I-VIEL
D-2108-A2	Rolladen-Schneider LS4	4419	
D-2109	Glasflügel 604	10	I-ALTI D-2109
D-2110-IHO	Caproni Vizzola A.21S Calif	224	
D-2111-VV	Schempp-Hirth Ventus 2a	1	
D-2112-XT	Rolladen-Schneider LS8-18	8207	
D-2113	Rolladen-Schneider LS4-b	41028	
D-2114 -1H	Schempp-Hirth Duo Discus	38	
D-2115	Schleicher ASK 13	13420	
D-2116	Schleicher K 8B	8922	
D-2117	Schleicher ASW 15B	15257	
D-2118	SZD-41A Jantar Standard	B-854	DDR-2418 DM-2418
D-2119- 7	Glasflügel H201B Standard Libelle	244	OE-0919
D-2120	Schleicher ASK 13	13421	
D-2121	Schleicher ASW 15B	15261	
D-2122	Rolladen-Schneider LS1-f	405	F-CEKU
D-2123	Glasflügel H201B Standard Libelle	196	HB-1009
D-2124	Schempp-Hirth Discus 2B	65	
D-2125	SZD-24-4A Foka 4	W-337	DDR-2225 DM-2225
D-2126-K2	Schleicher ASW 15B	15263	
D-2127	Schleicher K 8B	8924	
D-2128-28	Schempp-Hirth Duo Discus	65	
D-2129	Schleicher K 8B	8925	
D-2130	Schleicher ASW 15B	15265	
D-2132	Glaser-Dirks DG-300 Elan	3E415	
D-2133-B3	SZD-48-3 Jantar Standard 3	B-1943	DDR-2433
D-2134	Rolladen-Schneider LS6-c-18	6379	
D-2135	Schleicher ASK 13	13428	
D-2136	Schleicher K 8B	8928	
D-2137-2K	Schleicher ASK 13	13429	
D-2138	Glaser-Dirks DG-100G Elan	E166G132	
D-2139	Schleicher ASK 13	13430	
D-2140-SB	Schempp-Hirth Discus 2A	9	
D-2141	Schleicher ASW 15B	15275	
D-2142	Schleicher Ka 6CR Rhönsegler	6139	OO-ZHT
D-2143	Schempp-Hirth Discus b	536	
D-2144-B5	Rolladen-Schneider LS4-b	4884	
D-2145	Scheibe Bergfalke IV	5828	
D-2146	SZD-32A Foka 5	W-485	DDR-2246 DM-2246
D-2147	Schempp-Hirth Discus 2a	209	
D-2148	Rolladen-Schneider LS4-b	4885	
D-2149-49	Schempp-Hirth Duo Discus	34	
D-2150	Schempp-Hirth Standard Cirrus	354	

D-2151	Schempp-Hirth Standard Cirrus	355	
D-2152	Schempp-Hirth Standard Cirrus	361	
D-2153	Schleicher ASK 21	21480	I-IVWG
D-2154-YX	Rolladen-Schneider LS6-c	6295	
D-2155	Schleicher ASK 21	21477	I-IVWD
D-2156	Schempp-Hirth Ventus 2b	83	
D-2157	Scheibe Bergfalke IV	5829	
D-2158	Schempp-Hirth Ventus-2c	86	
D-2159	Glasflügel H201B Standard Libelle	435	
D-2160	Glasflügel H201B Standard Libelle	436	
D-2161-NG	Rolladen-Schneider LS4-b	4887	
D-2162-TB	Schempp-Hirth Duo Discus	293	
D-2163-2J	Glasflügel H401 Kestrel	88	
D-2164	Glasflügel H401 Kestrel	89	
D-2165	Glasflügel H401 Kestrel	90	
D-2166	Glasflügel H401 Kestrel	91	
D-2167	Schleicher ASW 24	24209	
D-2168	Schempp-Hirth Duo Discus	36	
D-2169	Pilatus B4--PC11AF	121	HB-1137
D-2170	Schempp-Hirth Janus	59	I-ANUS
D-2171	Rolladen-Schneider LS4-b	41013	
D-2172	Schempp-Hirth Janus B	141	I-IVDG
D-2173	Schempp-Hirth Standard Cirrus	360G	
D-2174	Scheibe Bergfalke III	5647	
D-2175	LET L-23 Super Blanik	938102	OE-5561
D-2176	Schempp-Hirth Discus CS	047CS	
D-2177	SZD-48-3 Jantar-Standard 3	B-1953	I-KASA
D-2178	Schleicher ASK 13	13447	
D-2179	Schleicher ASW 15B	15201	D-0899
D-2180-AH	Schleicher ASW 15B	15300	
D-2181	Schleicher ASW 15B	15301	
D-2182	Schleicher ASK 13	13452	
D-2183	Schleicher ASW 15B	15302	
D-2184	Schleicher K 8B	8945	
D-2185	Schleicher ASW 15B	15303	
D-2186	Schleicher ASW 15B	15304	
D-2187	Schleicher ASK 13	13453	
D-2188	Schleicher ASK 13	13454	
D-2189	Schleicher ASK 13	13455	
D-2190	Schleicher ASK 13	13456	
D-2191	Glaser-Dirks DG-200	2-4	OE-5108
D-2192	Start & Flug H-101 Salto	28	
D-2193	Start & Flug H-101 Salto	29	
D-2195-CD	Rolladen-Schneider LS4-b	41040	
D-2196	Glasflügel H401 Kestrel	92	
D-2197-HG	Glasflügel H401 Kestrel	93	
D-2198	Rolladen-Schneider LS6-c	6293	
D-2199	Glasflügel H401 Kestrel	96	
D-2200	Glaser-Dirks DG-500/22 Elan	5E11S3	
D-2201	Schleicher ASK 21	21728	
D-2202	SZD-38A Jantar 1	B-642	DDR-2402 DM-2402
D-2204-1E	Schleicher ASW 22 (Permit 5.99)	22011	
D-2205	SZD-32A Foka 5	W-518	DDR-2255 DM-2255
D-2206	SZD-59 Acro (Permit 4.99)	B-2176	SP-3629
D-2207	SZD-32A Foka 5	W-520	DDR-2257 DM-2257
D-2208	Glasflügel H401 Kestrel	97	
D-2209	Rolladen-Schneider LS8 (Permit)	8005	
D-2211	Start & Flug H101 Salto	31	
D-2212	Pilatus B4-PC11AF	130	
D-2213	Start &Flug H101 Salto	22	(PH-1259) D-2213
D-2214	Glasflügel H201B Standard Libelle	477	
D-2215	Glasflügel H201B Standard Libelle	478	
D-2216	Glasflügel H201B Standard Libelle	479	
D-2217	Pilatus B4-PC11	89	
D-2218	Start & Flug H101 Salto	33	
D-2219	LET L-13 Blanik	025428	
D-2220	Start & Flug H101 Salto	35	
D-2221	Start & Flug H101 Salto	36	
D-2223	Rolladen-Schneider LS1-c	170	
D-2225	Rolladen-Schneider LS1-f	251	
D-2226	Glasflügel H401 Kestrel	74	OE-0953
D-2228	LET L-13 Blanik	173335	
D-2229	SZD-32A Foka 5	W-445	DDR-2206 DM-2206
D-2230	SZD-24-4A Foka 4	W-354	DDR-2230 DM-2230
D-2231	SZD-24-4A Foka 4	W-383	DDR-2232 DM-2232
D-2232	SZD-24-4A Foka 4	W-344	DDR-2233 DM-2233
D-2233	Schleicher K 8B	994	HB-689
D-2234	Rolladen-Schneider LS1-f	195	
D-2236	Schleicher Ka 6CR Rhönsegler	6502	
D-2237	Schempp-Hirth Standard Cirrus	600	
D-2238-N4	Schempp-Hirth Standard Cirrus	422G	
D-2239	Rolladen-Schneider LS8-18	8453	
D-2240	Rolladen-Schneider LS1-c	184	
D-2241	Rolladen-Schneider LS1-c	267	
D-2242	Rolladen-Schneider LS1-f	185	
D-2243	SZD-32A Foka 5	W-526	DDR-2263 DM-2263
D-2244	Rolladen-Schneider LS1-f	259	
D-2245	Rolladen-Schneider LS1-f	255	
D-2246	Rolladen-Schneider LS1-f	263	
D-2247	Schleicher ASW 28	28062	
D-2248	Rolladen-Schneider LS1-f	318	
D-2249-RR	Schempp-Hirth Duo Discus	325	
D-2250	Rolladen-Schneider LS1-f	283	
D-2251	Rolladen-Schneider LS1-f	308	
D-2252	Rolladen-Schneider LS1-f	289	
D-2253	Rolladen-Schneider LS1-f	355	
D-2254	Rolladen-Schneider LS1-f	374	
D-2256-FP	Rolladen-Schneider LS1-f	314	
D-2257	SZD-32A Foka 5	W-513	DDR-2252 DM-2252
D-2258	Rolladen-Schneider LS4	4538	
D-2259	Schleicher Ka 6E	4291	I-BZJR
D-2261	Rolladen-Schneider LS1-f	350	
D-2262	Rolladen-Schneider LS4	4540	
D-2263-DE	Glasflügel H401 Kestrel	87	D-KOWA D-2263
D-2264	Glasflügel H401 Kestrel	127	
D-2265	Glasflügel H401 Kestrel	128	
D-2266	Glasflügel H401 Kestrel	129	
D-2267	Caproni-Vizzola A-21S Calif	230	
D-2268	Scheibe Bergfalke III	5655	
D-2269	Schleicher ASK 13	13601AB	
D-2270	SZD-51-1 Junior	B-2149	
D-2271	SZD-24-4A Foka 4	W-338	DDR-2227 DM-2227
D-2272	SZD-32A Foka 5	W-525	DDR-2262 DM-2262
D-2274	Grob G.102 Speed Astir IIB	4090	
D-2275	Grob G.102 Speed Astir II	4006	BGA2484/DYK
D-2276	Grob G.103 Twin Astir	3203	
D-2277-TH	Rolladen-Schneider LS4-b	4896	
D-2278	Darmstadt D-37	38	D-KEDD
D-2279	Rolladen-Schneider LS4	4541	
D-2280	Schleicher K 8B	8715	OY-BXW
D-2282	Schempp-Hirth HS-7 Mini-Nimbus	14	OE-5122
D-2283	Schleicher ASW 22	22018	
D-2284	Schleicher ASW 22	22019	
D-2285	DG Flugzeugbau DG-300 Elan	3E476	
D-2286	Glaser-Dirks DG-100G Elan	E138G106	S5-3024 YU-4346
D-2288	Schempp-Hirth Standard Cirrus	665	
D-2289-PU	Schempp-Hirth Standard Cirrus	502	
D-2290	SZD-32A Foka 5	W-425	DDR-2200 DM-2200
D-2291-H1	Schempp-Hirth Discus CS	198CS	
D-2292	Schempp-Hirth Standard Cirrus	386G	
D-2295-F2	Bölkow Phoebus C	1001	
D-2296-OL	Rolladen-Schneider LS4-b	4889	
D-2297	SZD-32A Foka 5	W-486	DDR-2247 DM-2247
D-2298-RCA	Schempp-Hirth Ventus 2c	43/127	
D-2299	Rolladen-Schneider LS1-c	244	
D-2300	Pilatus B4-PC11AF	097	
D-2301	Pilatus B4-PC11AF	238	
D-2302	Schleicher ASK 13	13457	
D-2303	Schleicher ASW 15B	15315	
D-2304	Schleicher K 8B	8951	
D-2305-W2	Schempp-Hirth Duo Discus	144	
D-2306	SZD-36A Cobra 15	W-646	DDR-2309 DM-2309
D-2307	Schleicher ASW 15B	15319	
D-2308	Schleicher ASW 15B	15320	
D-2309	Schleicher K 8B	8954	
D-2310	Schleicher ASK 21	21778	
D-2311-J	Schleicher ASW 15B	15322	
D-2312	Schempp-Hirth Duo Discus	281	
D-2313	Schleicher ASW 15B	15324	
D-2314-14	Schleicher ASW 15B	15325	
D-2315	Rolladen-Schneider LS4-b	41020	
D-2316	Schleicher K 8B	8961	
D-2317	Schleicher ASK 13	13463	
D-2318	Schleicher ASW 15B	15328	
D-2319	Schleicher K 8B	8960	
D-2320	Schleicher K 8B	8963	
D-2321	Schleicher K 8B	8959	
D-2322-KS	Schleicher ASW 22BL	22040	
D-2323	LET L-23 Super Blanik	938101	
D-2324	Schleicher K 8B	8965	
D-2325-CK	Schempp-Hirth Discus 2b	197	
D-2326	Schleicher ASK 13	13464	
D-2327	Schleicher ASW 15B	15333	
D-2328	LET L-23 Super Blanik	928004	D-8064
D-2329	Schleicher ASW 15B	15334	
D-2331	Schleicher ASW 17	17027	
D-2332	Schleicher ASK 13	13466	
D-2333	Schleicher K 8B	8967	
D-2334	Schleicher ASW 15B	15331	
D-2335	Schleicher ASW 15B	15337	
D-2336	Schleicher ASW 15B	15338	
D-2337	Schleicher ASW 15B	15339	
D-2339	Schleicher ASW 15B	15341	
D-2340	Schleicher ASW 15B	15336	
D-2341-XY	Schleicher ASW 15B	15342	
D-2342	Schleicher ASK 13	13469	
D-2343	Rolladen-Schneider LS6-18W	6343	

D-2344	Schleicher K 8C	81001	
D-2345	LET L-23 Super Blanik	938104	
D-2346-2P	Schleicher ASW 15B	15357	
D-2347	Schleicher ASK 13	13470	
D-2348	Schempp-Hirth Discus 2B	151	
D-2349	Schleicher ASW 15B	15345	
D-2350-K8	Schleicher ASW 17	17029	
D-2351	Schleicher K 8B (Reservation 8.99)	8964	
D-2352-XC	Schempp-Hirth Duo Discus	42	
D-2353	Schleicher ASK 13	13473	
D-2354	Schleicher ASK 13	13465	
D-2355	Schleicher ASW 15B	15343	
D-2356-R	Schleicher ASW 15B	15351	
D-2357	Schleicher ASW 15B	15352	
D-2358	Rolladen-Schneider LS4-b	4890	
D-2360	Rolladen-Schneider LS4-b	41055	
D-2361	Schleicher ASW 15B	15354	
D-2362	Schleicher K 8B	8969	
D-2364	Schleicher ASK 13	13477	
D-2365-AB	Rolladen-Schneider LS8-a	8081	
D-2366-PM	Rolladen-Schneider LS8-a	8283	
D-2368-II	Schleicher ASW 15B	15360	
D-2369-YO	Rolladen-Schneider LS8-a	8158	
D-2370	Schleicher ASW 15B	15362	
D-2371-CY	Schleicher ASW 28-18 (Permit 9.03)	28504	
D-2372	Schleicher ASW 15B	15364	
D-2373	Schleicher ASK 13	13481	
D-2374	Rolladen-Schneider LS4-b	4891	
D-2375	Schleicher ASW 15B	15365	
D-2376	Schempp-Hirth Duo Discus	53	
D-2377	Schleicher ASK 13	13483	
D-2378	SZD-9bis Bocian 1E	P-568	DDR-3378 DM-3378
D-2379	Schleicher ASW 15B	15368	
D-2380	Schleicher ASW 15B	15369	
D-2381	SZD-36A Cobra 15	W-651	DDR-2312 DM-2312
D-2382	Schleicher ASW 15B	15372	
D-2383	Schleicher K 8B	8971	
D-2384-WT	Schleicher ASW 17	17034	
D-2385	Schleicher ASW 15B	15373	
D-2386	Schleicher ASW 15B	15216	
D-2387	Grob G.103 Twin Astir	3251	
D-2388	Grob G.103 Twin Astir Trainer	3252-T-29	
D-2389	Rolladen-Schneider LS6-b	6126	OO-ZRQ
D-2390	Grob G.103 Twin Astir	3257	
D-2391	Grob G.102 Astir CS Jeans	2246	
D-2392	Grob G.102 Astir CS 77	1833	
D-2393	Grob G.102 Astir CS 77	1834	
D-2394	Grob G.103 Twin Astir Trainer	3265-T-32	
D-2395	Grob G.102 Club Astir II	5001C	
D-2396	LET L-23 Super Blanik	938103	
D-2398-3RD	SZD-48-3 Jantar Standard 3	B-1664	DOSAAF
D-2400	Glasflügel H201B Standard Libelle	493	
D-2401	Glasflügel H201B Standard Libelle	494	
D-2402	Glasflügel H401 Kestrel	105	
D-2403-VY	Glasflügel H201B Standard Libelle	499	
D-2404	Glasflügel H201B Standard Libelle	500	
D-2405	Glasflügel H201B Standard Libelle	501	
D-2407	Glasflügel H201B Standard Libelle	507	
D-2408	Schleicher ASK 21	21172	
D-2409	Schleicher ASK 21	21191	
D-2410	Schempp-Hirth Duo Discus	199	
D-2411	Grunau Baby IIb	284	DDR-1084 DM-1084
D-2412	Glasflügel H201B Standard Libelle	518	
D-2413	Glasflügel H201B Standard Libelle	521	
D-2414	Slingsby T-59D Kestrel 19 (Permit .01)	1852	
D-2415	Glasflügel H401 Kestrel	106	
D-2416	Glasflügel H201B Standard Libelle	497	
D-2417	Glasflügel H401 Kestrel	107	
D-2418	Schempp-Hirth Discus CS	150CS	
D-2419	Glasflügel H201B Standard Libelle	532	
D-2420	Glasflügel H201B Standard Libelle	533	
D-2421	Glasflügel H201B Standard Libelle	534	
D-2422	Glasflügel H201B Standard Libelle	535	
D-2423	Rolladen-Schneider LS4-b	4979	
D-2424	Glasflügel H201B Standard Libelle	537	
D-2425-LY	Glasflügel H401 Kestrel	108	
D-2428	Rolladen-Schneider LS8B	8451	
D-2429	SZD-42-2 Jantar 2B	B-951	DDR-2429 DM-2429
D-2430	Rolladen-Schneider LS1-f	297	
D-2431-8V	Rolladen-Schneider LS8-18	8252	
D-2432	Rolladen-Schneider LS1-f	280	
D-2433-33	Glasflügel H201B Standard Libelle	502	PH-481
D-2434	Glasflügel H205 Club Libelle	36	
D-2435	Rolladen-Schneider LS8-18 (Permit 3.99)	8025	
D-2436	Glasflügel H205 Club Libelle	38	
D-2437	Glasflügel H205 Club Libelle	39	
D-2438	Glasflügel H205 Club Libelle	40	
D-2439	Pilatus B4-PC11AF	153	
D-2440	Glasflügel H205 Club Libelle	64	
D-2441-LI	Glasflügel H205 Club Libelle	65	
D-2442	Schleicher ASW 24	24004	
D-2443-RW	Schempp-Hirth Duo Discus	171	
D-2444	Glasflügel H205 Club Libelle	68	

D-2445	Glasflügel H205 Club Libelle	69	
D-2446	Glasflügel H205 Club Libelle	76	
D-2447	Glasflügel H205 Club Libelle	77	
D-2448	Glasflügel H205 Club Libelle	78	
D-2449	Glasflügel H205 Club Libelle	79	
D-2450	Glasflügel H205 Club Libelle	141	
D-2451	Glasflügel H205 Club Libelle	86	
D-2452	Glasflügel H205 Club Libelle	87	
D-2453-53	Glasflügel H205 Club Libelle	90	
D-2454	SZD-38A Jantar 1	B-640	DDR-2404 DM-2404
D-2455	Glasflügel H205 Club Libelle	92	
D-2456-56	Glasflügel H205 Club Libelle	93	
D-2457	Glasflügel H205 Club Libelle	94	
D-2459	Glasflügel H205 Club Libelle	96	
D-2460-TZ	Glasflügel H205 Club Libelle	124	
D-2462-T3	Glasflügel H205 Club Libelle	100	
D-2463	Glasflügel H205 Club Libelle	101	
D-2464	Glasflügel H205 Club Libelle	102	
D-2465	Rolladen-Schneider LS8-a	8026	
D-2467	Glasflügel H205 Club Libelle	113	
D-2468	Glasflügel H205 Club Libelle	114	
D-2469	Glasflügel H205 Club Libelle	115	
D-2471-3A	Glasflügel H205 Club Libelle	117	
D-2472	Glasflügel H205 Club Libelle	118	
D-2474	Glasflügel H205 Club Libelle	120	
D-2475	Glasflügel H205 Club Libelle	121	
D-2476	Rolladen-Schneider LS4-b	4893	
D-2477	Schempp-Hirth Janus	12	
D-2478	Glasflügel H205 Club Libelle	137	
D-2479	Schempp-Hirth Discus 2a	211	
D-2480	Schempp-Hirth Janus (Permit)	55	
D-2481	Rolladen-Schneider LS6-a	6061	
D-2482	Schleicher ASW 24	24066	
D-2483	Schleicher ASW 24	24067	
D-2484-GF	SZD-48-3 Jantar Standard 3	B-1944	DDR-2434
D-2485	Schleicher ASW 24	24068	
D-2486	Schleicher ASW 20L	20413	
D-2487	Schleicher ASK 21	21049	
D-2488	Schleicher ASK 21	21050	
D-2489	Schleicher ASK 21	21051	
D-2490-2W	Schleicher ASW 20L	20424	
D-2491	Schleicher ASW 20L	20425	
D-2492-Z3	Schleicher ASK 21	21055	
D-2493	Schleicher ASW 19B	19337	
D-2494-SM	Schleicher ASW 19B	19338	
D-2495-WF	Schleicher ASK 21	21057	
D-2496	Rolladen-Schneider LS8-a	8027	
D-2498	Schleicher ASW 20	20433	
D-2499	Schleicher ASW 20L	20414	
D-2500	Glasflügel H401 Kestrel	104	PH-477
D-2501	Vogt LO-100 Zwergreiher	1/2	
D-2502-RP	Schempp-Hirth Duo Discus	290	
D-2503-6R	Rolladen-Schneider LS6	6062	
D-2506	Glaser-Dirks DG-100G Elan	E82G57	
D-2507	Glaser-Dirks DG-100G Elan	E73G48	
D-2508	Glaser-Dirks DG-100G Elan	E84G58	
D-2509	Rolladen-Schneider LS4-b	41016	
D-2510	Schleicher ASW 20C	20749	
D-2511	Schleicher ASW 20C	20737	
D-2512	Scheibe Bergfalke IV	5815	
D-2513	Schleicher ASK 21	21441	
D-2514-G3	Schleicher ASW 24	24071	
D-2515	Rolladen-Schneider LS4	4252	
D-2517	Neukom Elfe S-4D	413AB	
D-2518	Schempp-Hirth Duo Discus	45	
D-2519	Schempp-Hirth Discus CS	244CS	
D-2520	Schempp-Hirth Janus C	178	
D-2521-DD	Schempp-Hirth Discus CS	086CS	
D-2522	Schempp-Hirth Duo Discus	255	
D-2523	Schempp-Hirth Ventus a/16.6	16	
D-2525	Glaser-Dirks DG-300 Elan	3E111	
D-2526	Rolladen-Schneider LS4	4348	
D-2527	Schempp-Hirth Discus CS	110CS	
D-2528	Rolladen-Schneider LS4	4373	
D-2530	Schleicher ASH 25	25003	
D-2531	Grob G.102 Astir CS Jeans	2121	
D-2532	Grob G.102 Astir CS Jeans	2122	
D-2533	Grob G.102 Astir CS Jeans	2124	
D-2534	Grob G.102 Astir CS Jeans	2125	
D-2535	Rolladen-Schneider LS4-b	4980	
D-2537	Grob G.102 Astir CS Jeans	2129	
D-2538	SG-38 Schulgleiter	44	
D-2540	Grob G.102 Astir CS Jeans	2133	
D-2541	Grob G.102 Astir CS Jeans	2134	
D-2542	Rolladen-Schneider LS6-c	6249	
D-2543	SZD-24-4A Foka 4	W-304	DDR-2043 DM-2043
D-2544	Grob G.102 Astir CS Jeans	2139	
D-2545	Grob G.102 Astir CS 77	1732	
D-2546	Grob G.102 Astir CS 77	1737	
D-2547	Grob G.102 Astir CS Jeans	2146	
D-2548	Grob G.102 Astir CS Jeans	2147	
D-2549	Grob G.102 Astir CS Jeans	2148	
D-2550	Schempp-Hirth Discus CS	108CS	
D-2551	Rolladen-Schneider LS1-d	194	OO-ZMV
D-2552	*Test Registration for Grob G.103 Twin Astir*		

D-2553	SZD-41A Jantar Standard	B-803	
D-2554	Glasflügel H303 Mosquito B	193	
D-2556	Neukom Elfe S-4D	418AB	
D-2557	Glasflügel Hornet C	94	
D-2559	Glasflügel H303 Mosquito B	190	
D-2560	Glasflügel H303 Mosquito B	147	
D-2561	LET L-13 Blanik	026017	
D-2563	Rolladen-Schneider LS3-a	3242	
D-2564	Rolladen-Schneider LS3-a	3207	
D-2565	Rolladen-Schneider LS3-a	3144	
D-2566	Rolladen-Schneider LS3-a	3127	
D-2567-DX	Rolladen-Schneider LS1-a	17	HB-946
D-2568	Rolladen-Schneider LS3-a	3134	
D-2569-VK	Rolladen-Schneider LS6	6065	
D-2570	Rolladen-Schneider LS3-a	3101	
D-2572	Schempp-Hirth Discus b	489	
D-2573	Glaser-Dirks DG-200/17	2-97/1725	
D-2574	Schempp-Hirth Discus CS	151CS	
D-2575	Schempp-Hirth Duo Discus	66	
D-2576	Glaser-Dirks DG-100	25	
D-2577	Glaser-Dirks DG-100	26	
D-2579	Rolladen-Schneider LS8-a	8132	
D-2580	Glaser-Dirks DG-100	41	
D-2581-3M	Schempp-Hirth Discus CS	107CS	
D-2582	Glaser-Dirks DG-100	54	
D-2583	Glaser-Dirks DG-100	56	
D-2584	Rolladen-Schneider LS6-c	6262	
D-2585	Glaser-Dirks DG-100	62	
D-2586-DS	Schleicher ASW 24	24076	
D-2587	Glaser-Dirks DG-100	65	
D-2588	Schempp-Hirth Duo Discus	19	
D-2589	Glaser-Dirks DG-100	67	
D-2590	Schleicher ASK 21	21448	
D-2592-H5	Glaser-Dirks DG-100G	80G4	
D-2595	Glaser-Dirks DG-100 Elan	E6	
D-2596	Glaser-Dirks DG-200/17	2-65/1704	
D-2597	Glaser-Dirks DG-200	2-66	
D-2598	SZD-55-1	551195076	BGA 4150
D-2599	Grob G.103A Twin II Acro	3656-K-25	
D-2600-MD	Schempp-Hirth Discus 2B	34	
D-2601	Grob G.102 Standard Astir III	5538S	
D-2602	Rolladen-Schneider LS3	3124	
D-2603	Grob G 103 Twin Astir	3153	F-CFBV
D-2604	Schempp-Hirth Ventus 2a	12	
D-2605	Schleicher ASW 20L	20438	
D-2607	Schleicher ASW 20	20439	
D-2608	Schleicher ASW 20L	20442	
D-2609	Rolladen-Schneider LS3-a	3067	
D-2610	Rolladen-Schneider LS3-a (Permit)	3068	
D-2611	SZD-36A Cobra 15	W-650	DDR-2311
			DM-2311
D-2612	Schleicher ASK 21	21404	
D-2613	SZD-50-3 Puchacz	B-1330	DDR-3613
D-2614	Schleicher ASW 24	24034	
D-2615-WR	Schempp-Hirth Ventus 2a	53	
D-2616	Schleicher ASK 21	21407	
D-2617	Schleicher ASK 21	21408	
D-2618	Rolladen-Schneider LS3	3074	
D-2619-MN	Rolladen-Schneider LS3-a	3158	
D-2620	Glaser-Dirks DG-100G Elan	E142G110	
D-2621	Rolladen-Schneider LS3	3093	
D-2622	Rolladen-Schneider LS3	3173	
D-2623	Schempp-Hirth Discus CS	152CS	
D-2624	Rolladen-Schneider LS3-a	3463	
D-2625	Rolladen-Schneider LS4	4003	
D-2626-MSI	Rolladen-Schneider LS3-a	3464	
D-2627	Rolladen-Schneider LS3-17	3334	
D-2628	SZD-50-3 Puchacz	B-1389	DDR-3628
D-2629	Schleicher ASK 21	21411	
D-2630-EX	Schempp-Hirth Ventus 2a (Permit .02)	48	
D-2631	Schleicher ASK 21	21412	
D-2632	Rolladen-Schneider LS3	3237	
D-2633-KM	Schleicher ASH 25	25063	
D-2634	Rolladen-Schneider LS3	3236	
D-2636	Rolladen-Schneider LS3	3317	
D-2637	Rolladen-Schneider LS3-a	3318	
D-2638-NF	Rolladen-Schneider LS8-a	8028	
D-2639	Schleicher ASW 24	24040	
D-2640	Rolladen-Schneider LS4	4429	
D-2641	Schempp-Hirth Discus CS	157CS	
D-2642	Schleicher ASW 20L	20126	
D-2643	Schleicher ASW 19B	19232	
D-2644	Schempp-Hirth Discus 2B	155	
D-2645	Schleicher ASW 19B	19238	
D-2646	Schleicher ASW 19B	19235	
D-2647	Schleicher ASK 13	13600	
D-264-NO	Schleicher ASW 19B	19236	
D-2649	Schleicher ASW 20	20119	
D-2650	Schleicher ASW 20L	20123	
D-2651	Schleicher ASW 20L	20128	
D-2652	Schleicher ASK 13	13603	
D-2653	Schleicher ASW 19B	19244	
D-2654	Schleicher ASW 20	20133	
D-2655	SZD-50-3 Puchacz	B-1539	DDR-3655
D-2656	Schleicher ASW 19B	19249	
D-2657	Schleicher ASW 20	20127	
D-2658	Schleicher ASW 20L	20137	
D-2659	Schempp-Hirth Ventus 2a	90	
D-2660-H6	Glaser-Dirks DG-600 (Permit)	6-75	
D-2661	Schleicher ASW 20	20140	
D-2662	Glasflügel H303 Mosquito	98	
D-2663	Schleicher ASK 13	13476	
D-2665	Rolladen-Schneider LS3	3120	
D-2666	Rolladen-Schneider LS6-c18	6221	F-CGUM
D-2667	Grob G.103 Twin II	3562	
D-2668	Grob G.103 Twin II	3563	
D-2669	Rolladen-Schneider LS4-b	4981	
D-2670-70	Grob G.103A Twin II Acro	3653-K-22	
D-2671	Schempp-Hirth Duo Discus	69	
D-2672-BF	Schleicher ASW 19	19206	
D-2673	Schleicher ASW 19B	19207	
D-2674	Schleicher ASW 20	20084	
D-2675	Schleicher ASW 20	20085	
D-2676	Schleicher ASW 19B	19211	
D-2677	Schleicher ASK 13	13595	
D-2678-FLO	Rolladen-Schneider LS8-a	8029	
D-2680	Schleicher ASW 19	19216	
D-2681	Schempp-Hirth Discus CS	155CS	
D-2682	Schleicher ASW 19	19217	
D-2683	Schleicher ASW 20	20096	
D-2684-GY	Schempp-Hirth Discus CS	062CS	
D-2685	Schleicher ASW 20	20097	
D-2686	Schleicher ASW 20	20098	
D-2687	Schleicher ASW 19B	19223	
D-2688	Schleicher ASW 19	19225	
D-2689	Schleicher ASW 20	20107	
D-2690-GM	Schempp-Hirth Ventus 2b	13	
D-2692-BU	Schleicher ASW 20	20393	
D-2693	Schleicher ASW 20L	20394	
D-2694	Glaser-Dirks DG-100G Elan	E135G103	HB-1694
D-2695	Schleicher ASW 20	20399	
D-2696	Schleicher ASW 20L	20498	HB-2168
			HB-1613
D-2697	Schleicher ASW 24	24157	
D-2699	Rolladen-Schneider LS4	4157	
D-2700-AG	Rolladen-Schneider LS4	4165	
D-2701	Neukom S4D Elfe	410AB	
D-2702	SZD-32A Foka 5	W-427	DDR-2202
			DM-2202
D-2703	SZD-30 Pirat	W-398	DDR-1703
			DM-1703
D-2704-KR	SZD-36A Cobra 15	W-611	DDR-2304
			DM-2304
D-2705	Schempp-Hirth Ventus-2b	147	
D-2706	Rolladen-Schneider LS4	4265	
D-2707	Rolladen-Schneider LS4	4297	
D-2708	Glaser-Dirks DG-300 Club Elan	3E336C31	
D-2709	Glaser-Dirks DG-300 Club Elan	3E342C34	
D-2710	Schleicher Ka 6CR Rhönsegler	6372/Si	D-5428
D-2711	Rolladen-Schneider LS4	4218	
D-2712	Schleicher ASK 18	18049	
D-2714	Schleicher ASW 20	20109	
D-2715-T5	Schleicher ASW 27	27160	
D-2716	Schleicher ASW 19	19219	
D-2717	Rolladen-Schneider LS1-d	16	HB-956
D-2718	Schleicher ASW 19B	19327	
D-2719	Schleicher ASK 21	21043	
D-2720	Schleicher ASW 20L	20400	
D-2721	SZD-30 Pirat	B-303	DDR-1721
			DM-1721
D-2722	Schleicher ASW 24	24140	
D-2723	Grob G.103 Twin II	3528	
D-2724	Schleicher ASK 21	21651	
D-2725-HJ	Schleicher ASW 19B	19344	
D-2726	Schleicher ASW 20	20445	
D-2728-BA	Glasflügel H303 Mosquito B	179	
D-2730	Glasflügel H303 Mosquito B	127	
D-2731	Glasflügel H303 Mosquito B	151	
D-2732	Rolladen-Schneider LS1-f	444	
D-2733-6G	Rolladen-Schneider LS1-f	445	
D-2735	Glaser-Dirks DG-300 Elan	3E77	
D-2736	Glaser-Dirks DG-300 Elan	3E78	
D-2737	Rolladen-Schneider LS1-f	316	
D-2738-9C	Rolladen-Schneider LS8-a	8083	
D-2739-EM	Rolladen-Schneider LS1-f	332	
D-2740	Glaser-Dirks DG-300 Elan	3E79	
D-2741	Rolladen-Schneider LS1-f	345	
D-2742	Rolladen-Schneider LS1-f	346	
D-2743	Glaser-Dirks DG-300 Elan	3E83	
D-2744	Schleicher ASK 21	21599	
D-2745	Rolladen-Schneider LS1-f	356	
D-2746	Glaser-Dirks DG-300 Elan	3E104	
D-2747	SZD-30 Pirat	B-341	DDR-1747
			DM-1747
D-2748	Rolladen-Schneider LS1-f	414	
D-2749	Glaser-Dirks DG-300 Elan	3E84	
D-2750-WT	Glaser-Dirks DG-300 Elan	3E86	
D-2751	Glaser-Dirks DG-300 Elan	3E87	
D-2752	SZD-30 Pirat	B-352	DDR-1752
			DM-1752
D-2753	Schleicher ASW 27	27053	
D-2754	SZD-30 Pirat	B-358	DDR-1754
			DM-1754
D-2755	Rolladen-Schneider LS4	4018	

D-2756	Rolladen-Schneider LS3-17	3449	
D-2757	Schempp-Hirth Discus b	388	
D-2758	Rolladen-Schneider LS3-17	3418	
D-2759-2M	Rolladen-Schneider LS1-f	348	
D-2760	Rolladen-Schneider LS1-f	347	
D-2761-IBD	Schempp-Hirth Discus CS	035CS	
D-2762-2J	Rolladen-Schneider LS1-f	323	
D-2763	Rolladen-Schneider LS1-f	336	
D-2764	Rolladen-Schneider LS4-b	4784	
D-2765	Rolladen-Schneider LS6-c	6323	
D-2766	Rolladen-Schneider LS1-f	339	
D-2767	Rolladen-Schneider LS1-f	340	
D-2768-KP	Rolladen-Schneider LS1-f	341	
D-2769	Rolladen-Schneider LS1-f	343	N2234W D-2769
D-2770-CG	Glaser-Dirks DG-100G Elan	E143G111	
D-2771	Rolladen-Schneider LS1-f	315	
D-2772-7A	Rolladen-Schneider LS1-f	304	
D-2773	Rolladen-Schneider LS1-f	305	
D-2774	Rolladen-Schneider LS4-a	4786	
D-2775	Rolladen-Schneider LS4-a	4787	
D-2776	Rolladen-Schneider LS1-f	301	
D-2777	Schempp-Hirth Standard Cirrus	238	CF-DMW
D-2779	Schempp-Hirth Standard Cirrus	480	
D-2780	SZD-30 Pirat	B-412	DDR-1783 DM-1783
D-2782-L2	Schempp-Hirth Duo Discus	64	
D-2783	Schempp-Hirth Nimbus 2	77	
D-2785	Schempp-Hirth Discus b	465	
D-2786-AT	Rolladen-Schneider LS8-a	8208	
D-2788	SZD-51-1 Junior	B-2190	
D-2789-GE	Schempp-Hirth Nimbus 2	118	
D-2790	Schempp-Hirth Nimbus 2	119	
D-2791-GI	Rolladen-Schneider LS8-a	8235	
D-2792-BF	Schempp-Hirth Nimbus 2B	164	
D-2793	Schempp-Hirth HS-7 Mini-Nimbus	55	
D-2794	Schempp-Hirth HS-7 Mini-Nimbus	56	
D-2795	Rolladen-Schneider LS4-b	4996	
D-2796-96	Schempp-Hirth Nimbus 2C	205	
D-2797	Rolladen-Schneider LS4-b	4983	
D-2798	Schempp-Hirth Nimbus 2C	217	
D-2799	Schempp-Hirth Nimbus 2C	218	
D-2800	Glaser-Dirks DG-600/18	6-32	
D-2801	Glaser-Dirks DG-300 Elan	3E93	
D-2802	SZD-51-1 Junior	B-1844	DDR-2801
D-2803-S8	Glaser-Dirks DG-100G Elan	E64G39	BGA4920/JZU HB-1579
D-2804	Rolladen-Schneider LS3	3038	
D-2805	Rolladen-Schneider LS3	3039	
D-2806	SZD-51-1 Junior	B-1923	DDR-2806
D-2807-I	SZD-51-1 Junior	B-1919	DDR-2802
D-2808	Rolladen-Schneider LS3	3042	
D-2809	SZD-51-1 Junior	W-961	DDR-2800
D-2810	Rolladen-Schneider LS3	3044	
D-2811	Rolladen-Schneider LS3	3045	
D-2812	SZD-30 Pirat	B-475	DDR-1812 DM-1812
D-2813	Rolladen-Schneider LS3	3047	
D-2814-PR	Schempp-Hirth Nimbus 3/24.5	42	OY-XPR N254E
D-2815	Schempp-Hirth Janus C	182	
D-2816	Schempp-Hirth Ventus b/16.6	179	
D-2817	Rolladen-Schneider LS3	3053	
D-2819	Rolladen-Schneider LS4-b	4941	
D-2820	Rolladen-Schneider LS4-b	4789	
D-2822	Rolladen-Schneider LS4-b	4790	
D-2823-MH	Rolladen-Schneider LS4-b	4791	
D-2824	Rolladen-Schneider LS3	3061	
D-2825	Rolladen-Schneider LS3	3117	
D-2826	Schleicher ASK 21	21517	
D-2827	Akaflieg München Mü.27 (Permit)	V1	
D-2828	Glaser-Dirks DG-300 Elan	3E81	HB-1791
D-2829	Schempp-Hirth Nimbus 2B	173	
D-2831	Schempp-Hirth Nimbus 2B	184	
D-2832-32	Schempp-Hirth Nimbus 2C	185	
D-2833	Rolladen-Schneider LS4	4040	
D-2834-XS	Rolladen-Schneider LS8-a	8033	
D-2836	Rolladen-Schneider LS8B	8449	
D-2837	SZD-30 Pirat	B-323	DDR-1737 DM-1737
D-2838	ICA/Brasov IS.28B2	237	
D-2839	Rolladen-Schneider LS6-c	6269	
D-2842-42	Rolladen-Schneider LS8-a	8160	
D-2844	Rolladen-Schneider LS3-a	3266	
D-2845	ICA/Brasov IS.28B2	312	
D-2846-GN	Rolladen-Schneider LS3-a	3258	
D-2847	Rolladen-Schneider LS3-a	3209	
D-2849	Rolladen-Schneider LS3-a	3171	
D-2850-TM	Rolladen-Schneider LS4-a	4792	
D-2851	Rolladen-Schneider LS4-a	4793	
D-2852	Bölkow Phoebus B-1	815	OE-0852
D-2853	Schleicher ASW 19B	19318	
D-2854	Schleicher ASK 21	21021	
D-2855	Schleicher ASK 21	21025	
D-2856	Schleicher ASW 19B	19319	
D-2857-A8	Rolladen-Schneider LS8-a	8161	
D-2858	Glaser-Dirks DG-300 Elan	3E129	
D-2859	SZD-30 Pirat	B-581	DDR-1859 DM-1859
D-286-FV	Rolladen-Schneider LS3-a	3107	
D-2861-14	Glasflügel Hornet C	96	
D-2863	Rolladen-Schneider LS3-a	3285	
D-2864	Rolladen-Schneider LS3-a	3168	
D-2865-LR	Rolladen-Schneider LS3-a	3333	
D-2866	SZD-30 Pirat	S-01.03	DDR-1866 DM-1866
D-2869	Rolladen-Schneider LS3-17	3340	
D-2870-GZ	Glaser-Dirks DG-300 Elan	3E132	
D-2871-XS	Glaser-Dirks DG-300 Elan	3E136	
D-2872	Glaser-Dirks DG-300 Elan	3E453	
D-2873	Schleicher ASW 20L	20446	
D-2874	Schleicher ASW 20	20447	
D-2875	Schleicher ASW 20	20449	
D-2876-OD	Schempp-Hirth Discus b	557	
D-2877	Glasflügel Hornet C	100	OY-XKN
D-2879	Schempp-Hirth Nimbus 2C	204	
D-2880	DG Flugzeugbau DG-800S	8-28S5	
D-2881-JA	Schempp-Hirth Mini-Nimbus C	142	
D-2882-SK	Schleicher ASW 19B	19308	
D-2883	Schleicher ASW 20	20318	
D-2884	Schleicher Ka 6E	4093	HB-885
D-2885	Schleicher ASK 21	21014	
D-2886	Schleicher ASW 20L	20320	
D-2888	Eiri PIK-20D	20570	
D-2889	Rolladen-Schneider LS3-17	3369	
D-2891	Grob G.103A Twin II Acro	3811-K-74	
D-2893	Rolladen-Schneider LS3-17	3397	
D-2894-VIN	Rolladen-Schneider LS3-a	3257	
D-2895	Rolladen-Schneider LS3-17	3409	
D-2896	Rolladen-Schneider LS4	4284	
D-2897	Rolladen-Schneider LS7	7091	
D-2898	SZD-30 Pirat	S-03.23	DDR-1898 DM-1898
D-2899	Rolladen-Schneider LS4	4300	
D-2900-T2	Glaser-Dirks DG-300 Club Elan	3E354C42	
D-2901	Grob G.102 Astir CS 77	1839	
D-2902	Grob G.102 Astir CS 77	1840	
D-2903-AF	Schempp-Hirth Duo Discus	195	
D-2904	Rolladen-Schneider LS7	7094	
D-2905	Grob G.102 Speed Astir IIB	4063	
D-2906	Schleicher ASK 21	21512	
D-2907	Grob G.102 Speed Astir IIB	4065	
D-2908-08	Schleicher ASK 21	21773	
D-2909	Grob G.102 Speed Astir IIB	4067	
D-2910	SZD-30 Pirat	S-04.11	DDR-1910 DM-1910
D-2911	Pilatus B4-PC11AF	235	
D-2912	Grob G.103 Twin II	3541	
D-2913	Grob G.103A Twin II Acro	3544-K-1	
D-2914	Grob G.103 Twin II	3545	
D-2915	Grob G.103A Twin II Acro	3546-K-3	
D-2916	Grob G.103 Twin II	3548	
D-2917	Grob G.102 Standard Astir II	5050S	
D-2918	Grob G.102 Club Astir II	5060C	
D-2919	Grob G.102 Club Astir II	5056C	
D-2920	Grob G.102 Standard Astir II	5051S	
D-2921	Schleicher ASK 21	21668	
D-2922	Rolladen-Schneider LS4-b	41051	
D-2923	Schempp-Hirth Ventus b/16.6	187	
D-2924	Schempp-Hirth Ventus b/16.6	185	
D-2925-4N	Schempp-Hirth Duo Discus	75	
D-2926	Schempp-Hirth Duo Discus	216	
D-2927	Schempp-Hirth Ventus b/16.6	200	
D-2928-SW	Rolladen-Schneider LS7-WL	7095	
D-2929	Akaflieg Stuttgart FS.29 (Permit)	V-1	
D-2930	Scheibe SF-30A Club-Spatz	6805	
D-2931	Rolladen-Schneider LS4-b	4911	
D-2932	Schempp-Hirth Standard Cirrus	384	
D-2933	LET L-13 Blanik	175121	OE-0933
D-2934	Schleicher K 8B	AB8962	
D-2935	Schempp-Hirth Duo Discus	97	
D-2936-V2	Grob G.103C Twin III	36007	
D-2937	LET L-13 Blanik	025901	
D-2939	Rolladen-Schneider LS1-f	268	
D-2942	Rolladen-Schneider LS4	4131	
D-2943-AR	Rolladen-Schneider LS8-a	8186	
D-2944-YV	Schempp-Hirth Discus b	100	
D-2948-L6	Schempp-Hirth Standard Cirrus	314	
D-2949-KK	Rolladen-Schneider LS6-18W	6354	
D-2950	Rolladen-Schneider LS6-18W	6355	
D-2951	Glasflügel H201B Standard Libelle	413	
D-2953	Rolladen-Schneider LS1-c	197	
D-2955	Schempp-Hirth Standard Cirrus	316G	
D-2956	Schempp-Hirth Standard Cirrus	317G	
D-2957	Schempp-Hirth Standard Cirrus	325G	
D-2958	Schempp-Hirth Standard Cirrus	328G	
D-2959	Schempp-Hirth Standard Cirrus	329G	
D-2960	Schleicher K 8B	8927AB	
D-2961-4H	Glaser-Dirks DG-500 Elan Trainer	5E91T39	
D-2962-BK	Glasflügel H201B Standard Libelle	410	
D-2964	Glaser-Dirks DG-100G Elan	E99G69	
D-2965-WL	Schempp-Hirth Standard Cirrus	321	
D-2966	Schempp-Hirth Duo Discus	236	
D-2968-ICE	Schempp-Hirth Duo Discus	94	

D-2970	Glaser-Dirks DG-100G Elan	E212G178	
D-2971	Rolladen-Schneider LS2 (Permit)	243	
D-2972	Glasflügel H201B Standard Libelle	415	
D-2973-FZ	Glasflügel H201B Standard Libelle	417	
D-2974	Glasflügel H201B Standard Libelle	418	
D-2975	Rolladen-Schneider LS1-d	126	
D-2977	Rolladen-Schneider LS1-c	166	
D-2978	Schleicher ASK 13	13434	
D-2979	Schleicher ASK 13	13435	
D-2980	Schleicher ASW 15B	15277	
D-2981	Schleicher ASW 15B	15278	
D-2982-CU	Schleicher ASW 15B	15279	
D-2983	Schleicher ASK 13	13432	
D-2985	Schempp-Hirth Discus b	101	
D-2986	Schleicher ASW 15B	15284	
D-2987	Schleicher ASW 15B	15285	
D-2988	Schempp-Hirth Janus C	232	HB-1897
D-2990	Schleicher ASK 13	13444	
D-2991	Schleicher ASK 21	21676	
D-2993-1D	Rolladen-Schneider LS8-a	8109	
D-2994	Glaser-Dirks DG-300 Elan Acro	3E431A2	
D-2995	Start & Flug H-101 Salto	25	
D-2996	Start & Flug H-101 Salto	26	
D-2998	Rolladen-Schneider LS1-c	165	
D-2999-PP	Schempp-Hirth Standard Cirrus	343G	
D-3000	Schempp-Hirth Standard Cirrus	235G	
D-3001	Rolladen-Schneider LS1-c	154	
D-3002-IK	Schempp-Hirth Standard Cirrus	332	
D-3003	Schempp-Hirth Standard Cirrus	334	
D-3004	Schempp-Hirth Discus 2b	1	D-6111
D-3005-LI	Schempp-Hirth Standard Cirrus	347G	
D-3006	Grob G.102 Club Astir IIIB	5620CB	D-4726
D-3007	Schempp-Hirth Standard Cirrus	350	
D-3008	SZD-9bis Bocian 1E	P-720	DDR-3008 DM-3008
D-3009	Schempp-Hirth Nimbus 2	37	
D-3010	Test Registration for Glaser-Dirks production		
D-3012	Schempp-Hirth Cirrus-VTC	140Y	
D-3013	Schempp-Hirth Discus b	104	
D-3014	Vogt LO-100 Zwergreiher	EB 01	
D-3015	Schleicher Ka 6BR-PE Rhönsegler	342	
D-3016	Siebert SIE-3	3022	
D-3017	Glasflügel H203 Standard Libelle	2	
D-3018	SZD-9bis Bocian 1E	P-727	DDR-3014 DM-3014
D-3019	Glasflügel H201B Standard Libelle	424	
D-3020	Glasflügel H201B Standard Libelle	425	
D-3021	Rolladen-Schneider LS7-WL	7072	HB-3021
D-3022	Schleicher K 8B	587	
D-3023	Rolladen-Schneider LS1-c	150	
D-3024-S1	Schempp-Hirth Discus b	105	
D-3025	Kaiser KA-1	0101	
D-3026	Schleicher K 7 Rhönadler	7005	
D-3027	Schleicher K 8B	8222	
D-3028	Schleicher K 8B	8418	
D-3029	Glasflügel H304	263	
D-3030	Schempp-Hirth Nimbus 2	60	
D-3031	Glaser-Dirks DG-100G Elan	E211G177	
D-3032	Glaser-Dirks DG-300 Club Elan Acro	3E507C87A40	
D-3033	Start & Flug H101 Salto	21	
D-3034	Schleicher K 8B	8530	
D-3035	Schleicher K 7 Rhönadler	7251	
D-3036	Schleicher K 8B	8716	
D-3037	Schleicher Ka 6CR Rhönsegler	6540	
D-3038	Grob G.102 Astir CS	1178	
D-3039	Schleicher Ka 6CR Rhönsegler	6627	
D-3040	Schleicher Ka 6CR Rhönsegler	6660AB	
D-3041	Glaser-Dirks DG-300 Elan	3E119	
D-3043	Glaser-Dirks DG-100G Elan	E209G175	
D-3044-HD	Schempp-Hirth Duo Discus	222	
D-3045	Bölkow Phoebus C	1002	
D-3046	Rolladen-Schneider LS1-f	188	
D-3047	SZD-9bis Bocian 1D	F-802	OH-292 OH-KBW
D-3048	SZD-9bis Bocian 1E	P-469	DDR-3046 DM-3046
D-3049	Schempp-Hirth Ventus b/16.6	69	
D-3050	Akaflieg Braunschweig SB-5E Sperber	AB5053	
D-3051-KD	Schempp-Hirth Nimbus 3/24.5	12	
D-3052	Glaser-Dirks DG-300 Elan	3E142	
D-3053	Grunau Baby IIB	1	
D-3054	Bölkow Phoebus B-1	949	
D-3055	Glaser-Dirks DG-300 Elan	3E358	OE-5485
D-3056-CI	Grob G.103 Twin II	3510	
D-3057	SZD-9bis Bocian 1E	P-475	DDR-3054 DM-3054
D-3058	Grob G.102 Standard Astir II	5046S	
D-3059	SZD-9bis Bocian 1E	P-444	DDR-3019 DM-3019
D-3060	HpH Glasflügel 304CZ	44-17	
D-3061	Glaser-Dirks DG-300 Elan	3E152	
D-3062	Glaser-Dirks DG-100G Elan	E208G174	
D-3063-KGN	Schleicher ASW 28-18 (Permit 10.03) (Reserved as BGA 5082)	28505	
D-3065	SZD-9bis Bocian 1E	P-479	DDR-3063 DM-3063
D-3066	Grob G.103 Twin II	3516	
D-3067	Grob G.102 Standard Astir II	5049S	
D-3068-FF	Grob G.103 Twin II	3518	
D-3069	Grob G.103 Twin II	3519	
D-3070	Rolladen-Schneider LS1-d	193	
D-3071	Schempp-Hirth Duo Discus	72	
D-3072	Rolladen-Schneider LS8B	8458	
D-3073	Grob G.103A Twin II Acro	3626-K-13	
D-3077	Rolladen-Schneider LS1-f	306	
D-3078	Grob G.103A Twin II Acro	3637-K-18	
D-3079	SZD-9bis Bocian 1E	P-756	DDR-3070 DM-3070
D-3080	Rolladen-Schneider LS8-a	8167	SE-ULX
D-3081-HH	Schleicher ASW 20C (Permit)	20838	
D-3082	Schleicher ASK 23	23045	
D-3083	Schleicher ASK 23	23046	
D-3084	SZD-55-1	551191027	HB-3084
D-3085	Schempp-Hirth Standard Cirrus B	598	OO-ZCJ (1)
D-3086-LA	Rolladen-Schneider LS8-a	8016	
D-3088	Schempp-Hirth Standard Cirrus	548	
D-3089-H0	Schempp-Hirth Nimbus 3	11	
D-3090	Schleicher Rhönlerche II (Permit .04)	557	D-3021
D-3091	Glaser-Dirks DG-100G Elan	E178G144	
D-3092	Schempp-Hirth Standard Cirrus	623	
D-3093	Schempp-Hirth Standard Cirrus	504	
D-3094-i8	Schempp-Hirth Ventus 2c	49/150	
D-3095-E8	Schempp-Hirth Standard Cirrus	557	
D-3096-ZE	Schempp-Hirth Standard Cirrus	558G	
D-3097	Glaser-Dirks DG-100G Elan	E125G93	
D-3098	Schempp-Hirth Standard Cirrus	503	
D-3099	Schempp-Hirth Standard Cirrus	407G	I-ACOB
D-3100	Vogt LO-100 Zwergreiher	AB/117	
D-3101	Schempp-Hirth Standard Cirrus	435G	
D-3102	Schempp-Hirth Nimbus 2	64	
D-3103	Neukom S-4D Elfe	419AB	
D-3104	Schempp-Hirth Standard Cirrus	427	
D-3105	Schempp-Hirth Standard Cirrus	428	
D-3106	Schempp-Hirth Standard Cirrus	441G	
D-3107	Schempp-Hirth Ventus-2b	87	N21TK
D-3108	Schempp-Hirth Ventus c	302	
D-3109	Glasflügel H201B Standard Libelle	570	
D-3110	Rolladen-Schneider LS4	4745	OE-5459 D-1841
D-3111	SZD-50-3 Puchacz	B-1085	DDR-3601
D-3112	Schempp-Hirth Janus	02	
D-3113	Schleicher ASW 27	27154	
D-3114	Rolladen-Schneider LS4-b	41023	
D-3115	Glaser-Dirks DG-100G Elan	E146G114	
D-3116	Schleicher ASW 20L	20220	D-KGPF D-3156
D-3117-SP	Sportine Aviacija 17A	130	BGA 4954/KBE
D-3118-8W	Rolladen-Schneider LS8-a	8133	
D-3119	SZD-9bis Bocian 1E	P-499	DDR-3219 DM-3219
D-3120	Schempp-Hirth Discus CS	310CS	
D-3121	Schempp-Hirth Janus B	145	
D-3123	Schempp-Hirth Duo Discus	71	
D-3124-BG	Rolladen-Schneider LS4	4422	
D-3125-Y2K	Schempp-Hirth Discus 2b	48	BGA4781/JUA
D-3126	Rolladen-Schneider LS1-f	325	
D-3128-19	Rolladen-Schneider LS1-f	423	
D-3129	Rolladen-Schneider LS1-f	424	
D-3130	Rolladen-Schneider LS1-f	425	
D-3131-DV	Rolladen-Schneider LS1-f	426	
D-3132	Rolladen-Schneider LS1-f	427	
D-3133-UX	Rolladen-Schneider LS1-f (Permit)	299	
D-3134-PS	Rolladen-Schneider LS1-f	354	
D-3135	Rolladen-Schneider LS1-f	357	
D-3136	Rolladen-Schneider LS1-f	370	
D-3137	Schempp-Hirth Duo Discus	274	
D-3138	Glaser-Dirks DG-100G Elan	E114G83	
D-3139	Glaser-Dirks DG-100G Elan	E113G82	
D-3140	Glaser-Dirks DG-100G Elan	E117G86	
D-3141	Schleicher ASK 21	21284	
D-3142	Schleicher ASK 23B	23055	
D-3143-BO	Schempp-Hirth Ventus b/16.6	147	SE-TYY
D-3144	Rolladen-Schneider LS4-b	4991	
D-3145-CW	Rolladen-Schneider LS1-f	411	
D-3146	Schleicher ASK 21	21628	
D-3147-MB	Schempp-Hirth Ventus 2ax	145	
D-3148	Schempp-Hirth Ventus b/16.6	111	
D-3149	Rolladen-Schneider LS1-f	441	
D-3150	Schleicher ASW 20CL	20839	
D-3151	Schempp-Hirth Nimbus 3/24.5	30	
D-3152	Schempp-Hirth Ventus b/16.6	117	
D-3153-OC	Rolladen-Schneider LS4-b	4992	
D-3154-AL	Schleicher ASW 20	20218	
D-3155	Schleicher ASW 20L	20219	
D-3156	DG Flugzeugbau DG-800S	8-78S21	
D-3157	Schleicher ASW 20	20226	
D-3158	Schleicher ASW 20	20227	
D-3159	Schempp-Hirth Duo Discus	164	
D-3160-E3	Rolladen-Schneider LS4-b	4993	
D-3161	Schleicher ASW 19B	19278	
D-3163-ILO	Schleicher ASW 20	20230	
D-3164	Schempp-Hirth Janus B	113	
D-3165	Schempp-Hirth Nimbus 2C	219	
D-3166	Schempp-Hirth Nimbus 2C	228	

D-3167-V3	Schempp-Hirth Nimbus 2B (Permit)	168	
D-3169	Swift S-1	122	HB-3169
D-3170	SZD-42-2 Jantar 2B	B-875	
D-3172-ZU	Schleicher ASK 21	21280	
D-3173-FC	Glaser-Dirks DG-300 Elan	3E151	
D-3174-6	Schempp-Hirth Standard Cirrus G	702	
D-3175	DG Flugzeugbau DG-300 Elan	3E470	
D-3177	Glaser-Dirks DG-300 Elan	3E149	
D-3178	Schleicher ASW 20L	20237	
D-3179-SB	Rolladen-Schneider LS4-b	4994	
D-3180-KW	PZL PW-5 Smyk	17.08.011	
D-3181	Schleicher ASW 20	20241	
D-3182	SZD-9bis Bocian 1E	P-588	DDR-3382 DM-3382
D-3183	Glaser-Dirks DG-300 Elan	3E148	
D-3184	Rolladen-Schneider LS3-a	3243	
D-3185	Schleicher ASW 24B	24235	
D-3186	Rolladen-Schneider LS3-17	3251	
D-3187	Rolladen-Schneider LS6-c	6281	
D-3188-AW	Schempp-Hirth Ventus b/16.6	127	
D-3189-B	Rolladen-Schneider LS8-a	8237	
D-3190-90	Schempp-Hirth Nimbus 3/24.5	40	
D-3191	Schempp-Hirth Ventus b	128	
D-3192-1C	Schempp-Hirth Ventus b/16.6	130	
D-3193	Schempp-Hirth Mini-Nimbus C	133	
D-3194-CC	Schempp-Hirth Mini-Nimbus C	134	
D-3195	Schempp-Hirth Mini-Nimbus C	135	
D-3196-FE	Glaser-Dirks DG-500/22 Elan	5E94S14	
D-3198-KB	Rolladen-Schneider LS4-b	4995	
D-3199-4	Neukom S-4D Elfe	407AB	
D-3200	LET L-13 Blanik	027068	DDR-3201 DM-3201
D-3201	Schleicher ASK 13	13091	
D-3203	LET L-13 Blanik	027361	DDR-3203 DM-3203
D-3204	Glaser-Dirks DG-100	27	
D-3205	Focke-Wulf Kranich III	70	
D-3206	SZD-9bis Bocian 1E	P-508	DDR-3226 DM-3226
D-3207	Scheibe Bergfalke III	5629	
D-3208	FES 530/II Lehrmeister (Reservation 9.99)	0152	DM-3152
D-3209	Schleicher ASK 13	13090	
D-3210	Schleicher Ka 6CR Rhönsegler	6005	
D-3211	Schleicher Ka 6CR Rhönsegler	6253/Si	
D-3212	Glaser-Dirks DG-300 Elan	3E147	
D-3213-SM	Glaser-Dirks DG-300 Elan	3E145	
D-3214	Scheibe Spatz A	02	
D-3215	Schleicher K 8B	992	
D-3216	Scheibe L-Spatz 55	564	
D-3217	Schleicher Ka 6CR Rhönsegler	998	
D-3218	Scheibe L-Spatz 55	736	
D-3219	Schleicher Ka 6 Rhönsegler	221	
D-3221	Scheibe Bergfalke II/55	273	
D-3222	Scheibe SF-27A	6023	
D-3223	Schempp-Hirth Duo Discus	205	
D-3224	Schleicher ASK 23	23021	
D-3225	Scheibe L-Spatz 55 (Reservation - cld?)	628	D-KAPY
D-3226	SZD-9bis Bocian 1E	P-507	DDR-3225 DM-3225
D-3227	Schleicher Ka 6BR Rhönsegler	414	
D-3228	Glaser-Dirks DG-300 Elan	3E144	
D-3230-30	Schempp-Hirth Discus 2b	171	
D-3231	SZD-9bis Bocian 1E	P-517	DDR-3235 DM-3235
D-3232	Schleicher K 8B	635	
D-3233	SZD-9bis Bocian 1E (Reservation 1.00)	P-525	DDR-3238 DM-3238
D-3234	Schleicher K 8B	736	
D-3235-JP	Schempp-Hirth Nimbus 3/24.5	24	
D-3236	Schleicher Ka 6CR Rhönsegler	10	
D-3237	Schleicher ASK 21	21091	
D-3238	Schleicher ASK 21	21072	
D-3239	SZD-24-4A Foka 4	W-352	DDR-2239 DM-2239
D-3240	Glasflügel H301 Libelle	3	
D-3242	Schleicher Ka 6CR Rhönsegler	6341/Si	
D-3243	SZD-9bis Bocian 1E	P-529	DDR-3242 DM-3242
D-3244	Rolladen-Schneider LS4-a	4733	
D-3245	Schleicher Ka 6CR-PE Rhönsegler	6293/Bi	
D-3246	Glasflügel H201B Standard Libelle	472	
D-3247-II	Schleicher ASK 21	21074	
D-3248	SZD-9bis Bocian 1E	P-533	DDR-3246 DM-3246
D-3249	Schleicher ASW 20L	20456	
D-3250	Schleicher ASK 13	13022	
D-3251	SZD-9bis Bocian 1E	P-537	DDR-3250 DM-3250
D-3252-VS	Rolladen-Schneider LS1-f	279	
D-3253-53	Rolladen-Schneider LS1-f	273	
D-3254	Schleicher ASK 21	21707	
D-3255	Rolladen-Schneider LS8-18	8440	
D-3256	Glasflügel H201B Standard Libelle	543	
D-3257	Glasflügel H201B Standard Libelle	544	
D-3259	Scheibe Bergfalke III	5657	
D-3261	Schempp-Hirth Standard Cirrus B	398	
D-3262	Schempp-Hirth Standard Cirrus	420	
D-3263	Schempp-Hirth Standard Cirrus	445	
D-3265	Schempp-Hirth Discus CS	305CS	
D-3266	SZD-9bis Bocian 1E	P-493	DDR-3216 DM-3216
D-3267	Schempp-Hirth Standard Cirrus	526	
D-3268-Ei	Schempp-Hirth Ventus 2a	54	
D-3269	Schempp-Hirth Standard Cirrus	517G	
D-3270	Schempp-Hirth Ventus 2a	30	HB-3218
D-3271	Schempp-Hirth Standard Cirrus	575	
D-3272	Schempp-Hirth Standard Cirrus	578	
D-3273	Grob G.102 Astir CS	1033	
D-3274	Grob G.102 Astir CS	1034	
D-3275	Grob G.102 Astir CS	1035	
D-3276	Grob G.102 Astir CS	1036	
D-3277-IY	Grob G.102 Astir CS	1037	
D-3278	Schleicher ASK 21	21292	
D-3279	Grob G.102 Astir CS	1039	
D-3280	Grob G.102 Astir CS	1040	
D-3281	SZD-9bis Bocian 1E	P-577	DDR-3381 DM-3381
D-3282	Grob G.102 Astir CS	1042	
D-3283	Grob G.102 Astir CS	1056	
D-3284	Grob G.102 Astir CS	1057	
D-3285	SZD-9bis Bocian 1E	P-492	DDR-3215 DM-3215
D-3286-DL	Grob G.102 Astir CS	1062	
D-3287	SZD-51-1 Junior	B-1785	HB-1931
D-3288-LC	Grob G.102 Astir CS	1064	
D-3289	Grob G.102 Astir CS	1065	
D-3290-WF	Glaser-Dirks DG-300 Elan	3E141	
D-3291	Grob G.102 Astir CS	1067	
D-3292-BU	Grob G.102 Astir CS	1068	
D-3293	Schleicher ASW 20	20404	
D-3294-GT3	Schleicher ASK 21	21044	
D-3295	Schleicher ASW 20L	20402	OY-XXF D-3295
D-3296	Schleicher ASK 21	21045	
D-3298-S9	Glasflügel H303 Mosquito B	143	
D-3299	Glasflügel H303 Mosquito B	107	
D-3300	Glaser-Dirks DG-300 Club Elan	3E269C1	
D-3301	Grob G.102 Astir CS	1069	
D-3302	Grob G.102 Astir CS	1070	
D-3303	Grob G.102 Astir CS	1071	
D-3304	SZD-55-1	551196086	
D-3305	Grob G.102 Astir CS	1073	
D-3306	Grob G.102 Astir CS	1074	
D-3307	Grob G.102 Astir CS	1075	
D-3308	SZD-9bis Bocian 1E	P-558	DDR-3368 DM-3368
D-3309-C7	Schempp-Hirth Discus b	548	
D-3310	Schleicher ASK 23B	23061	
D-3311	Schempp-Hirth Discus 2B	100	
D-3312-B1	AMS Flight/Rolladen-Schneider LS4-b	unkn	
D-3313	Glaser-Dirks DG-100G	90G10	
D-3314	Glaser-Dirks DG-100	92	
D-3315	Glaser-Dirks DG-100	94	
D-3316	Glaser-Dirks DG-100	23	
D-3317	Glaser-Dirks DG-200/17C	2-129CL06	
D-3318	Glaser-Dirks DG-200/17C	2-131CL08	
D-3319-IW	Schleicher ASW 19B	19286	
D-3320	Glaser-Dirks DG-100G Elan	E90G62	
D-3321	Glaser-Dirks DG-500 Elan Trainer	5E77T33	
D-3322	Grob G.103 Twin II	3606	
D-3323-JO	Schleicher ASW 20L	20138	
D-3324	Glaser-Dirks DG-300 Elan	3E69	
D-3326-S3	Glaser-Dirks DG-500 Elan Trainer	5E84T36	
D-3327	Schleicher ASW 19B	19254	
D-3328	SZD-9bis Bocian 1E	P-510	DDR-3228 DM-3228
D-3329-3B	Schleicher ASW 19B	19256	
D-3330	Schleicher ASW 20	20124	
D-3331	SZD-9bis Bocian 1E	P-600	DDR-3391 DM-3391
D-3333	Start & Flug H101 Salto	51	
D-3335	Pilatus B4-PC11AF	308	
D-3336	Schleicher ASW 24B	24239	
D-3339	Scheibe SF-34	5106	
D-3340	Schempp-Hirth Duo Discus	70	
D-3342	Scheibe SF-34	5108	
D-3343	SZD-9bis Bocian 1E	P-589	DDR-3383 DM-3383
D-3344	Rolladen-Schneider LS8B	8457	
D-3345	LET L-13 Blanik	025605	OY-VXH
D-3346	LET L-13 Blanik	026807	
D-3348	LET L-13 Blanik	026527	
D-3349	SZD-9bis Bocian 1E	P-596	DDR-3389 DM-3389
D-3351	Glaser-Dirks DG-300 Elan	3E73	
D-3352	Schempp-Hirth Duo Discus	253	
D-3353	LET L-13 Blanik	026858	
D-3354	Schleicher ASK 21	21285	
D-3355-H9	Rolladen-Schneider LS4	4035	
D-3356	Schleicher ASW 27B	27185	OK-7272
D-3357-4A	Rolladen-Schneider LS8-a	8187	
D-3358-1A	Rolladen-Schneider LS4	4031	
D-3359-EVA	Rolladen-Schneider LS4	4036	
D-3360	Rolladen-Schneider LS4	4046	

D-3361	Rolladen-Schneider LS8-18	8432	
D-3363	Schempp-Hirth Mini-Nimbus C	112	
D-3364	Schempp-Hirth Duo Discus	154	
D-3365	SZD-9bis Bocian 1E	P-550	DDR-3363 DM-3363
D-3366	Rolladen-Schneider LS4-b	4998	
D-3367	SZD-9bis Bocian 1E	P-547	DDR-3360 DM-3360
D-3368	Schempp-Hirth Mini-Nimbus C	115	
D-3369-H2	Schempp-Hirth Duo Discus	73	
D-3370	Schleicher ASK 21	21295	
D-3371	Schempp-Hirth Nimbus 2C	193	
D-3372	Schleicher ASK 21	21296	
D-3373-ZB	Schempp-Hirth Ventus 2c	35/91	
D-3374	Schleicher ASW 20L	20244	
D-3375	Schleicher ASW 19B	19283	
D-3376	SZD-9bis Bocian 1E	P-564	DDR-3374 DM-3374
D-3377	Schleicher ASW 19B	19274	
D-3378	Schleicher ASW 20L	20250	
D-3379	Schleicher ASW 20	20252	
D-3380	Schleicher ASW 19B	19292	
D-3381	Schleicher Ka 6E	4034	OH-338 OH-RSX
D-3382	Schempp-Hirth Duo Discus	283	
D-3383	Schleicher ASW 20	20295	
D-3384-3G	Schleicher ASW 19B	19299	
D-3385	Glaser-Dirks DG-300 Elan	3E188	
D-3386	Schleicher ASW 20	20298	
D-3387	Schleicher ASW 19B	19301	
D-3388	Glasflügel H303 Mosquito	84	
D-3389-CO	Glasflügel H303 Mosquito	85	
D-3391-91	Rolladen-Schneider LS4	4563	
D-3392-92	Rolladen-Schneider LS4-b	4895	
D-3393	SZD-9bis Bocian 1E	P-634	DDR-3397 DM-3397
D-3394	Rolladen-Schneider LS7	7065	
D-3395	Rolladen-Schneider LS7-WL	7066	
D-3396	Rolladen-Schneider LS4-b	4810	
D-3397-BE	Rolladen-Schneider LS4-a	4811	
D-3398	Glaser-Dirks DG-300 Club Elan	3E454C78	
D-3399	Schleicher ASW 19	19095	
D-3401	Schleicher Ka 6CR Rhönsegler	6208	HB-774
D-3402	Schleicher K 8B	8481SH	HB-819
D-3403	Glasflügel H304	245	F-CEBR
D-3404	Glaser-Dirks DG-600	6-34	
D-3405	Rolladen-Schneider LS6	6080	
D-3406-4M	Rolladen-Schneider LS4	4565	
D-3407	SZD-9bis Bocian 1E	P-719	DDR-3007 DM-3007
D-3408	Rolladen-Schneider LS4	4567	
D-3409	SZD-9bis Bocian 1E	P-486	DDR-3209 DM-3209
D-3410	Schleicher ASW 20CL	20768	
D-3411	Schleicher ASK 23B	23003	
D-3412	Schleicher ASW 20C	20769	
D-3413	Schleicher ASW 20C	20770	
D-3414	Schleicher ASK 21	21230	
D-3415	Schleicher ASK 21	21229	
D-3416-B1	Schleicher ASW 20CL	20773	
D-3417	Schleicher ASK 21	21233	
D-3418	Schleicher ASW 20C	20784	
D-3419-19	Schleicher ASW 20C	20777	
D-3420	Schleicher ASW 20CL	20783	
D-3421	Schleicher ASW 20CL	20788	
D-3423	Schleicher ASW 20C	20789	
D-3424	Schempp-Hirth Duo Discus	174	
D-3426	Schleicher ASW 20CL	20794	
D-3427	Schleicher ASK 23	23017	
D-3428-UF	Schleicher ASW 20C	20796	
D-3429	Schleicher ASK 21	21247	
D-3430	SZD-9bis Bocian 1E	P-512	DDR-3230 DM-3230
D-3431	Schleicher ASW 20C	20811	
D-3432	SZD-48-3 Jantar Standard 3	B-1942	DDR-2432
D-3433	Schleicher ASK 21	21257	
D-3434	Schleicher ASK 23B	23025	
D-3435	SZD-48-3 Jantar Standard 3	B-1945	DDR-2435
D-3437	Rolladen-Schneider LS4	4443	
D-3439	SZD-9bis Bocian 1E	P-526	DDR-3239 DM-3239
D-3440	Rolladen-Schneider LS4	4447	
D-3441-B4	Rolladen-Schneider LS8-a	8163	
D-3442	Rolladen-Schneider LS4	4455	
D-3443-1N	Rolladen-Schneider LS4	4454	
D-3444-S6	Rolladen-Schneider LS4	4449	
D-3445	Rolladen-Schneider LS4	4457	
D-3446	Rolladen-Schneider LS4-b	4813	
D-3447-L4	Rolladen-Schneider LS4-a	4814	
D-3449	Rolladen-Schneider LS4	4495	
D-3451	Schleicher ASK 21	21548	
D-3452	Rolladen-Schneider LS4	4464	
D-3453	Rolladen-Schneider LS4-b	4816	
D-3454	Rolladen-Schneider LS4-a	4817	
D-3455	Rolladen-Schneider LS4	4475	
D-3456-01	Glaser-Dirks DG-100G Elan	E130G98	LX-CDE(1)
D-3457	Schempp-Hirth Standard Cirrus	622	HB-1284

D-3458-WY	Schempp-Hirth Ventus 2c	58/169	
D-3459-AN	Rolladen-Schneider LS4	4480	
D-3460	Glaser-Dirks DG-500 Elan Trainer	5E130T56	
D-3461-34	Schleicher ASK 21	21386	
D-3462	Schleicher ASK 21	21387	
D-3463	Schleicher ASK 21	21550	
D-3464-64	Schleicher ASK 21	21388	
D-3466	Schleicher ASW 24	24018	
D-3467	Schleicher ASK 21	21389	
D-3468	Schleicher ASK 21	21390	
D-3469	Schleicher ASK 21	21391	
D-3471-FGT	Schempp-Hirth Discus CS	270CS	
D-3472	Schempp-Hirth Duo Discus	112	
D-3475	Schleicher ASK 21	21393	
D-3476	Schleicher ASK 21	21396	
D-3477-FR	Schleicher ASH 25	25049	
D-3478	Rolladen-Schneider LS4	4512	
D-3479	Rolladen-Schneider LS4	4513	
D-3480-MM	Schempp-Hirth Ventus c	546	
D-3481	Schleicher ASW 24	24214	
D-3482	Schleicher ASK 21	21584	
D-3483	Rolladen-Schneider LS6-c	6197	
D-3484	Rolladen-Schneider LS4	4531	
D-3485	Rolladen-Schneider LS4	4530	
D-3486-MO	Rolladen-Schneider LS8-a	8135	
D-3487	Rolladen-Schneider LS4	4528	
D-3488-FA	Schempp-Hirth Discus CS	127CS	
D-3489-E3	Rolladen-Schneider LS4	4526	
D-3490	Schleicher ASK 21	21260	
D-3491	Schleicher ASW 20BL	20677	
D-3492	Schleicher ASK 23	23027	
D-3493	Schleicher ASW 20C	20824	
D-3494	Schleicher ASW 19B	19418	
D-3495	Schleicher ASW 20CL	20820	
D-3496	Schleicher ASK 23	23033	
D-3497	Schleicher ASK 23	23040	
D-3498-YP	Schleicher ASK 23	23044	
D-3499	Schempp-Hirth Ventus 2c	34/90	
D-3500	Grob G.102 Speed Astir IIB	4082	
D-3501	Schempp-Hirth Duo Discus	407	
D-3502	Rolladen-Schneider LS4-b	4821	
D-3503	Rolladen-Schneider LS4-b	4822	
D-3505	Schleicher ASW 20CL	20736	
D-3507	Schleicher ASW 20C (Permit)	20724	
D-3508-F1	Rolladen-Schneider LS4	4213	
D-3509	Rolladen-Schneider LS4-b	4823	
D-3510-SM	Grob G.103A Twin II Acro	3657-K-26	
D-3511	Grob G.102 Club Astir IIIB	5571CB	
D-3512	Grob G.102 Club Astir IIIB	5572CB	
D-3513	SZD-9bis Bocian 1E	P-726	DDR-3013 DM-3013
D-3514	Rolladen-Schneider LS3-17	3154	
D-3515	Rolladen-Schneider LS4	4524	
D-3516	Rolladen-Schneider LS4	4521	
D-3517	Rolladen-Schneider LS3-17	3226	OO-YPR D-4573
D-3518-J2	Schempp-Hirth Discus b	448	
D-3519	Schempp-Hirth Janus C	148	OO-ZCE
D-3521-FH	Schempp-Hirth Duo Discus	78	
D-3522-HM	Schleicher ASW 22	22035	
D-3523	Rolladen-Schneider LS3-17	3330	
D-3524	Schleicher ASW 19B	19379	
D-3525	Schleicher ASW 19B	19380	
D-3526	Rolladen-Schneider LS4-b	4824	
D-3527	Rolladen-Schneider LS4-b	4912	
D-3528	Rolladen-Schneider LS4-a	4826	
D-3529-IX	Schempp-Hirth Discus b	471	
D-3530	Rolladen-Schneider LS3-17	3322	
D-3531	Schempp-Hirth Nimbus 3/24.5	41	
D-3532	SZD-9bis Bocian 1E	P-514	DDR-3232 DM-3232
D-3533	Schempp-Hirth Ventus b/16.6	145	
D-3534	SG-38 Schulgleiter	8	
D-3535	Glasflügel H201B Standard Libelle	142	
D-3538	Rolladen-Schneider LS3-a	3434	
D-3539	Rolladen-Schneider LS4-b	4841	
D-3540	SZD-9bis Bocian 1E	P-461	DDR-3040 DM-3040
D-3541-LS	Rolladen-Schneider LS4	4570	
D-3542-VV	Rolladen-Schneider LS4	4571	
D-3544	Schleicher ASK 21	21297	
D-3545-45	Rolladen-Schneider LS3-17	3282	
D-3546	Schleicher ASW 20C	20805	
D-3547	Rolladen-Schneider LS8-a	8071	
D-3548	SZD-9bis Bocian 1E	P-527	DDR-3240 DM-3240
D-3549	Schleicher Ka 6 Rhönsegler	198	
D-3550	Glasflügel H303 Mosquito B	194	
D-3551	Schempp-Hirth Ventus b/16.6	76	
D-3552	Schempp-Hirth Ventus a/16.6	1	
D-3553	Rolladen-Schneider LS4	4071	
D-3554	Vogt LO-100 Zwergreiher	101AB	
D-3555	Schleicher Ka 6CR Rhönsegler	788	
D-3556-EP	Rolladen-Schneider LS4	4360	
D-3557	Rolladen-Schneider LS4	4408	
D-3559	Rolladen-Schneider LS4	4104	
D-3560	Schleicher Ka 6BR Rhönsegler	360	

D-3561-T	Rolladen-Schneider LS4	4078	
D-3562	Schleicher ASW 20C	20750	
D-3563	Schleicher ASW 19B	19405	
D-3564	Rolladen-Schneider LS4-b	4877	
D-3565	Schleicher K 8B	480	D-KAMP
			D-3565
D-3566-X2	Grob G.103A Twin II Acro	3814-K-75	
D-3567-LT	Grob G.103A Twin II Acro	3827-K-84	
D-3568	SZD-9bis Bocian 1E	P-753	DDR-3068
			DM-3068
D-3569	Grob G.103A Twin II Acro	3826-K-83	
D-3570	Schleicher K 8	519	
D-3571-2M	Rolladen-Schneider LS8-a	8086	
D-3572	Bölkow Phoebus B-1	721	SE-TII
D-3573	Schleicher ASW 20C	20848	
D-3574-YX	Rolladen-Schneider LS4	4070	
D-3575	Rolladen-Schneider LS4-b	41050	
D-3576-YP	Rolladen-Schneider LS4	4111	
D-3577	Rolladen-Schneider LS4	4109	
D-3578	Rolladen-Schneider LS4	4110	
D-3579	Grunau Baby IIB (Reservation 4.99)	11	
D-3580	DG Flugzeugbau DG-300 Elan Acro	3E479A22	
D-3581-ii	Rolladen-Schneider LS4	4331	
D-3582	Rolladen-Schneider LS4-a	4818	
D-3583-11	Rolladen-Schneider LS4-b	4819	
D-3584	Schleicher Rhönlerche II	55	
D-3585	Glaser-Dirks DG-300 Elan	3E44	
D-3587-PE	Schleicher ASW 24	24210	
D-3588	SZD-50-3 Puchacz	B-2112	
D-3589	Schleicher ASK 21	21299	
D-3590	SZD-9bis Bocian 1E	P-599	DDR-3390
			DM-3390
D-3591	Schleicher K 7 Rhönadler	1034	
D-3592	Rolladen-Schneider LS4-b	4844	
D-3593	Schleicher K 8B	8030	
D-3594	Schleicher K 8B	8008	
D-3595	Schleicher Rhönlerche II	2	
D-3596	Rolladen-Schneider LS8-a	8048	
D-3597	Schleicher K 7 Rhönadler	7041	
D-3598	Rolladen-Schneider LS8-a	8042	
D-3599	Grob G.103C Twin III Acro	34149	D-KGSL
D-3600	Schempp-Hirth Janus C	189	
D-3601	Schleicher K 7 Rhönadler	7043	
D-3602	Schleicher K 8B	8070	
D-3603	SZD-50-3 Puchacz	B-1087	DDR-3603
D-3604	Schempp-Hirth Discus 2B	16	
D-360-70	Rolladen-Schneider LS8-a	8049	
D-3606	Schleicher ASW 28	28024	
D-3607-2V	Schempp-Hirth Duo Discus	419	
D-3608	Rolladen-Schneider LS4-b	41024	
D-3609	Rolladen-Schneider LS4-b	4828	
D-3610	DG Flugzeugbau DG-1000S	10-50S49	
D-3611	SZD-50-3 Puchacz	B-1328	DDR-3611
D-3612	Rolladen-Schneider LS4-a	4829	
D-3613	Rolladen-Schneider LS4-b	4830	
D-3614	Schleicher K 8B	8310	
D-3615	Schleicher Ka 6CR Rhönsegler	6238	
D-3616	Rolladen-Schneider LS4	4580	
D-3617	SZD-50-3 Puchacz	B-1388	DDR-3627
D-3618-PV	Schleicher ASW 28-18	28501	
D-3619	Schleicher K 10A	10002	
D-3620	SZD-50-3 Puchacz	B-1344	DDR-3625
D-3621	Schleicher Ka 3	102	D-4047
D-3622	Schleicher K 8B	8398	
D-3623	Schleicher K 8B	8408	
D-3624	Schleicher ASW 24	24035	
D-3626-GP	Rolladen-Schneider LS8-a	8087	
D-3627-5	Schleicher ASW 27	27130	
D-3628	Rolladen-Schneider LS4	4582	
D-3629	Schleicher K 10A	10012	
D-3630	SZD-50-3 Puchacz	B-1465	DDR-3639
D-3631	SZD-50-3 Puchacz	B-1400	DDR-3634
D-3632	Scheibe L-Spatz III	812	
D-3633	Schleicher K 8B	8532	
D-3634	Schleicher K 8B	8531	
D-3635	SZD-24-4A Foka 4	W-294	
D-3637	Grunau Baby IIB	04304	
D-3638	Schleicher ASK 21	21282	
D-3639	SZD-24-4A Foka 4	W-239	
D-3640-E5	Schempp-Hirth Duo Discus	242	
D-3641	Schleicher ASW 20CL	20752	
D-3642-ZI	Rolladen-Schneider LS1-f	159	OO-ZZI
			D-2427
D-3643	Schleicher K 7 Rhönadler	7274	
D-3644	SZD-50-3 Puchacz	B-1474	DDR-3644
D-3645	Schleicher K 8B	8635	
D-3646-EW	Bölkow Phoebus A-1	764	
D-3647	Schleicher K 8B	8633	
D-3648	Schleicher Ka 6CR Rhönsegler	6567	
D-3649	SZD-50-3 Puchacz	B-1480	DDR-3648
D-3650	Rolladen-Schneider LS6-a	6036	
D-3651	SZD-50-3 Puchacz	B-1535	DDR-3651
D-3652	SZD-50-3 Puchacz	B-1542	DDR-3658
D-3654	Focke-Wulf Weihe 50	3	D-5097
D-3655	SZD-50-3 Puchacz	B-1540	DDR-3656
D-3656	LET L-13A Blanik	026719	S5-7113
			YU-5369
D-3657	Schleicher Ka 6E	4084	
D-3658	Schleicher K 8B	8711	
D-3659-BY	Rolladen-Schneider LS4	4389	
D-3660	Schempp-Hirth Discus 2B	(22)/158	(D-KJSM)
D-3661	SZD-30 Pirat	W-318	
D-3662	Fauvel AV-36C	573	
D-3663-MB	Glaser-Dirks DG-100	74	HB-1327
D-3664	Schleicher Ka 6CR Rhönsegler	6621Si	
D-3665	SZD-50-3 Puchacz	B-1552	DDR-3661
D-3667	Scheibe L-Spatz III (Reservation)	241	
D-3668	Rolladen-Schneider LS4	4572	
D-3669	Rolladen-Schneider LS4	4573	
D-3670	Schleicher ASK 13	13082	
D-3671	SZD-50-3 Puchacz	B-1394	DDR-3631
D-3672	Rolladen-Schneider LS4	4574	
D-3673	Schempp-Hirth Ventus 2a	106	
D-3674	Grob G.103C Twin III Acro (Permit)	34186	
D-3676	SZD-50-3 Puchacz	B-1387	DDR-3626
D-3677	Schleicher ASW 22	22021	F-CBFF(2)
			D-2282
D-3678	Rolladen-Schneider LS4	4166	
D-3679-WH	Schleicher ASK 21	21588	
D-3680-LW	Rolladen-Schneider LS8-a	8110	
D-3681	Rolladen-Schneider LS4	4241	
D-3682-CA	Rolladen-Schneider LS6-c	6328	
D-3683	Schempp-Hirth Standard Cirrus	465G	
D-3684	SZD-50-3 Puchacz	B-1331	DDR-3614
D-3685	SZD-9bis Bocian 1E	P-522	DDR-3385
			DM-3385
D-3686	Rolladen-Schneider LS1-f	198	
D-3687	SZD-50-3 Puchacz	B-1479	DDR-3647
D-3688-8	Schempp-Hirth Standard Cirrus	447	
D-3689-GM	Schempp-Hirth Standard Cirrus	457	
D-3691-AV	Schempp-Hirth Standard Cirrus	464G	
D-3692	Schempp-Hirth Standard Cirrus	467G	
D-3693	Schleicher ASW 15B	15268	HB-1093
D-3694	Glasflügel H401 Kestrel	109	
D-3695-JG	Grob G.103C Twin III Acro	34133	
D-3696	Grob G.103C Twin III Acro	34131	
D-3697-ES	Grob G.103C Twin III Acro	34127	
D-3699	Scheibe Bergfalke IV	5841	
D-3700	Scheibe Bergfalke IV	5842	
D-3701	Scheibe Bergfalke IV	5843	
D-3702	Schempp-Hirth Discus CS	226CS	
D-3703	Glasflügel H401 Kestrel	110	
D-3704	Glasflügel H201B Standard Libelle	552	
D-3705-TP	Schempp-Hirth Standard Cirrus	471G	
D-3706	Schempp-Hirth Standard Cirrus	472G	
D-3707	Glasflügel H201B Standard Libelle	561	
D-3708-M5	Rolladen-Schneider LS4-b	4846	
D-3709	Pilatus B4-PC11A	115	
D-3710	LET L-13 Blanik	026018	
D-3712	Glasflügel H401 Kestrel	112	
D-3713	Rolladen-Schneider LS3-a	3283	
D-3715	Glasflügel H201B Standard Libelle	568	
D-3716	Glasflügel H201B Standard Libelle	565	
D-3717-8E	Rolladen-Schneider LS1-f	295	
D-3719	Rolladen-Schneider LS1-f	375	F-CEHZ
D-3720	Schleicher ASW 20	20346	
D-3721	Schleicher ASK 21	21723	
D-3722	Glaser-Dirks DG-300 Elan	3E232	
D-3723	Rolladen-Schneider LS4-b	4848	
D-3725-PW	Rolladen-Schneider LS8-a	8053	
D-3726	Rolladen-Schneider LS4-b	4849	
D-3727	Glaser-Dirks DG-100	9	
D-3728	Glaser-Dirks DG-100	10	
D-3729	Pilatus B4-PC11	137	
D-3730	Rolladen-Schneider LS4-b	4850	
D-3731	Glaser-Dirks DG-100 Elan	E162	HB-1731
D-3732-T9	Glaser-Dirks DG-100	19	
D-3733	Glaser-Dirks DG-300 Elan	3E116	
D-3734	Glaser-Dirks DG-100	21	
D-3735	Swift S-1	115	HB-3135
D-3736	Glaser-Dirks DG-100	28	
D-3737	Glaser-Dirks DG-100	29	
D-3738-YW	Schleicher ASW 20BL	20695	
D-3739	Glaser-Dirks DG-100	32	
D-3740	Glaser-Dirks DG-100	38	
D-3741	Glaser-Dirks DG-100G Elan	E39G21	
D-3742	SZD-50-3 Puchacz	B-1472	DDR-3642
D-3743	Schleicher ASK 18	18016	
D-3744	Schleicher ASK 13	13524	
D-3745	Schleicher ASK 18	18018	
D-3746	Schleicher ASK 13	13525	
D-3747	Schleicher ASK 18	18019	
D-3748-6D	Schleicher ASK 18	18020	
D-3749	Schleicher ASW 19B	19002	
D-3750	Schleicher ASW 19	19003	
D-3752	Schleicher ASW 15B	15451	
D-3753	Schleicher ASK 13	13533	
D-3754	Schleicher ASW 19	19005	
D-3755	Schleicher ASW 19	19006	
D-3756	Schleicher ASK 13	13534	
D-3757-B-10	Rolladen-Schneider LS4-b	4854	
D-3758-TF	Schleicher ASW 15B	15453	
D-3759	Rolladen-Schneider LS8-18	8313	
D-3760	Schleicher ASK 13	13535	

D-3761	Schleicher ASW 19	19008	
D-3762	Schleicher ASW 19	19009	
D-3763	Schleicher ASK 13	13536	
D-3764 -6Z	Rolladen-Schneider LS8-a	8055	
D-3765-ICH	Schleicher ASW 24	24081	
D-3766-PS	Schleicher ASK 21	21453	
D-3768	Glaser-Dirks DG-100G Elan	E32G17	
D-3769	Glaser-Dirks DG-100 Elan	E29	
D-3770	SZD-30 Pirat (Reservation 10.99)	B-398	D-5769 DDR-1769 DM-1769
D-3771	Glaser-Dirks DG-100 Elan	E25	
D-3772-DE	Schempp-Hirth Ventus 2b	84	
D-3773	Glaser-Dirks DG-100 Elan	E23	
D-3774	Glaser-Dirks DG-100G Elan	E21G11	
D-3775	Glaser-Dirks DG-100G Elan	E22G12	
D-3776	Rolladen-Schneider LS4-b	4855	
D-3777	Glasflügel H205 Club Libelle	80	
D-3778	Grob G.102 Club Astir III	5550C	
D-3779	Grob G.103 Twin II	3668	
D-3780	Grob G.103A Twin II Acro	3677-K-28	
D-3781-RO	Grob G.103 Twin II	3659	
D-3782	Schempp-Hirth Janus B	86	
D-3783	Schempp-Hirth Nimbus 2B	144	
D-3784	Schempp-Hirth Nimbus 2B	146	
D-3785	Schempp-Hirth Janus	39	
D-3786	SZD-30 Pirat	B-429	DDR-1786 DM-1786
D-3787	Schempp-Hirth Janus	35	
D-3788	Schempp-Hirth Janus	09	
D-3790	Grob G.102 Club Astir III	5577C	
D-3791	Schleicher ASK 21	21454	
D-3792	Schleicher ASW 24	24085	
D-3793-RCD	Schleicher ASK 21	21457	
D-3795-PK	Schempp-Hirth HS-7 Mini-Nimbus	23	
D-3796	Glaser-Dirks DG-200/17C	2-111CL03	
D-3797	Glaser-Dirks DG-200/17	2-110/1718	
D-3798	Glaser-Dirks DG-200/17C	2-108CL01	
D-3799-YI	Schempp-Hirth Discus 2A	33	
D-3800	Test Registration for Glaser-Dirks production		
D-3801	Glaser-Dirks DG-100	103	
D-3802-B8	Glaser-Dirks DG-100G	98G14	
D-3803	Glaser-Dirks DG-100G	97G13	
D-3804	Glaser-Dirks DG-200/17	2-124/1720	
D-3806	Glaser-Dirks DG-100G	101G15	
D-3807	SZD-50-3 Puchacz	B-1093	DDR-3607
D-3808	Glaser-Dirks DG-200/17	2-100/1712	
D-3809-LL	Glaser-Dirks DG-200/17	2-102/1713	
D-3810	Glaser-Dirks DG-200/17	2-103/1714	
D-3811	Glaser-Dirks DG-200/17	2-107/1717	
D-3812	Glaser-Dirks DG-100	63	BGA 4872 PH-543
D-3813-HM	Grob G.102 Astir CS Jeans	2190	
D-3814	Grob G.102 Astir CS Jeans	2191	
D-3815	Grob G.102 Astir CS Jeans	2192	
D-3816-H3	Rolladen-Schneider LS4-b	41018	
D-3817	Grob G.102 Astir CS Jeans	2195	
D-3818	SZD-30 Pirat	B-492	DDR-1818 DM-1818
D-3819	Grob G.102 Astir CS Jeans	2199	
D-3820-IKM	Grob G.102 Speed Astir II	4002	
D-3821-HA	Schleicher ASK 21	21646	
D-3822	Grob G.102 Astir CS Jeans	2203	
D-3826-CH	Grob G.102 Astir CS Jeans	2212	
D-3827	SZD-30 Pirat	B-506	DDR-1827 DM-1827
D-3828	Grob G.102 Astir CS Jeans	2215	
D-3829	SZD-50-3 Puchacz	B-1390	DDR-3629
D-3830	Grob G.102 Astir CS Jeans	2217	
D-3831	Grob G.102 Astir CS Jeans	2218	
D-3832-SK	Rolladen-Schneider LS8-a	8089	
D-3833	Grob G.102 Speed Astir II	4003	
D-3834-SL	Schempp-Hirth Janus Ce	279	
D-3835	Grob G.102 Speed Astir II	4007	
D-3836-AV	Schempp-Hirth Duo Discus	177	
D-3837	Rolladen-Schneider LS1-f	337	HB-1237
D-3838	Glaser-Dirks DG-300 Club Elan Acro	3E435C73A4	OE-5532
D-3839	Grob G.102 Speed Astir II	4013	
D-3840-E	Schempp-Hirth Ventus 2c	22/58	
D-3841-WD	Schleicher ASW 19B	19092	
D-3842	Schleicher ASW 19B	19093	
D-3843	Schleicher ASK 13	13565	
D-3845	Schleicher ASK 21	21447	
D-3846	Schleicher ASW 24	24087	
D-3847	Schleicher ASW 19	19098	
D-3848	Schleicher ASW 19	19099	
D-3849-II	Schleicher ASW 19	19100	
D-3850	Schleicher ASW 17	17052	
D-3851-B2	Schleicher ASK 21	21459	
D-3852	Schleicher ASW 24	24093	
D-3854	Schleicher ASK 13	13570	
D-3855-55	Schleicher ASW 19B	19103	
D-3856	Grunau Baby IIB	03	D-5739
D-3857-57	Schleicher ASK 21	21047	D-8807
D-3858	Schleicher ASK 13	13571	
D-3859-L8	Rolladen-Schneider LS8-a	8188	
D-3860-BW1	Schempp-Hirth Duo Discus	46	
D-3861	Schleicher ASW 20	20005	
D-3863	Schleicher ASW 19	19107	
D-3864	Schleicher ASK 13	13572	
D-3865-VT	Rolladen-Schneider LS4	4022	
D-3866	Schleicher ASK 21	21173	
D-3867	Schleicher ASK 21	21178	
D-3868	Schleicher ASK 21	21177	
D-3869	Rolladen-Schneider LS4	4045	
D-3870	Bölkow Phoebus C	939	
D-3871	Bölkow Phoebus C-2 (Permit)	954	
D-3872	Rolladen-Schneider LS7	7145	
D-3874	Grob G.102 Astir CS Jeans	2011	
D-3876	Grob G.102 Astir CS Jeans	2027	
D-3877	DG Flugzeugbau DG-500 Elan Orion	5E162X17	
D-3879	SZD-9bis Bocian 1E	P-575	DDR-3379 DM-3379
D-3880	Rolladen-Schneider LS4-b	4858	
D-3881	Grob G.102 Astir CS Jeans	2035	
D-3882	DG Flugzeugbau DG-300 Club Elan Acro	3E477C85A21	
D-3883-83	Schempp-Hirth Discus b	92	
D-3884	Grob G.102 Astir CS Jeans	2039	
D-3885-7G	Grob G.102 Astir CS Jeans	2041	
D-3886	Grob G.102 Astir CS Jeans	2042	
D-3888	Grob G.102 Astir CS Jeans	2049	
D-3889	Grob G.102 Astir CS Jeans	2050	
D-3890	Grob G.102 Astir CS Jeans	2052	
D-3891	Grob G.102 Astir CS Jeans	2063	
D-3892	Grob G.102 Astir CS Jeans	2054	
D-3893	Rolladen-Schneider LS3-a	3153	
D-3895	Rolladen-Schneider LS3	3104	
D-3896	Rolladen-Schneider LS3	3078	
D-3897	Rolladen-Schneider LS7	7149	
D-3898	Rolladen-Schneider LS3	3164	
D-3900	Rolladen-Schneider LS3	3106	
D-3901	SZD-9bis Bocian 1E	P-706	DDR-3001 DM-3001
D-3902	Schempp-Hirth Discus 2B	36	
D-3903	Rolladen-Schneider LS7	7150	
D-3904	Glaser-Dirks DG-500 Elan Orion	5E158X15	
D-3907	SZD-30 Pirat	S-03.47	DDR-1907 DM-1907
D-3908	Rolladen-Schneider LS4	4279	
D-3909	Rolladen-Schneider LS4	4283	
D-3910	Rolladen-Schneider LS4	4289	
D-3911	Schleicher ASW 19B	19367	OO-YNP D-8630
D-3912	Rolladen-Schneider LS3	3208	
D-3913	Schleicher ASK 21	21465	
D-3914	Schleicher ASK 21	21462	
D-3915	SZD-9bis Bocian 1E	P-728	DDR-3015 DM-3015
D-3916	Rolladen-Schneider LS3-AKE (Permit .02)	3341	
D-3917	Rolladen-Schneider LS3-AKE (Permit 2.99)	3342	
D-3918	Schempp-Hirth Discus CS	069CS	
D-3919	Rolladen-Schneider LS7	7152	
D-3920	Rolladen-Schneider LS3-a	3156	
D-3921	Rolladen-Schneider LS3-a	3296	
D-3922	Rolladen-Schneider LS3-a	3188	
D-3923	Grob G.102 Club Astir IIIB	5652CB	
D-3925	Rolladen-Schneider LS3-a	3151	
D-3926	Rolladen-Schneider LS3-a	3155	
D-3927	Rolladen-Schneider LS3-a	3161	
D-3928	Schleicher ASK 21	21397	
D-3929	Schleicher ASK 21	21398	
D-3930	Schleicher ASK 21	21399	
D-3931	Schleicher ASK 21	21401	
D-3932	Schleicher ASK 21	21402	
D-3933	Rolladen-Schneider LS3-17	3294	
D-3934-ET	Rolladen-Schneider LS8-18	8286	
D-3935	Rolladen-Schneider LS3-a	3408	
D-3936	Rolladen-Schneider LS3-a	3407	
D-3937	Rolladen-Schneider LS3-17	3268	
D-3938	Glaser-Dirks DG-200/17	2-191/1764	
D-3939	Schleicher ASW 22	22020	
D-3940	Darmstadt D-40 (Permit .02)	41	
D-3941	SZD-9bis Bocian 1E	P-464	DDR-3041 DM-3041
D-3942	Rolladen-Schneider LS3-a	3202	
D-3943	SZD-9bis Bocian 1E	P-530	DDR-3243 DM-3243
D-3945	Grob G.103 Twin Astir	3083	
D-3946	Grob G.103 Twin Astir	3085	
D-3947	Grob G.103 Twin Astir	3086	
D-3948	Schempp-Hirth Ventus 2a	38	
D-3949-CL	Schempp-Hirth Duo Discus	220	
D-3950-E2	Schempp-Hirth Duo Discus	51	
D-3951	Grob G.103 Twin Astir Trainer	3095	
D-3952-H1	Glaser-Dirks DG-300 Elan	3E468	
D-3953	Grob G.103 Twin Astir	3097	
D-3954	Grob G.103 Twin Astir	3084	
D-3956	Grob G.103 Twin Astir	3099	
D-3957	Grob G.103 Twin Astir	3100	
D-3958-LX	Schempp-Hirth Duo Discus	224	
D-3959-PC	Schleicher ASH 25	25018	
D-3960-YJ	Schempp-Hirth Discus CS	072CS	
D-3961-PR	Schempp-Hirth Discus 2b	117	
D-3962	Rolladen-Schneider LS8-a	8189	

D-3963	Rolladen-Schneider LS8-a	8090	
D-3964	Grob G.103 Twin II	3597	
D-3965	Grob G.103 Twin II	3598	
D-3966	Grob G.103 Twin II	3599	
D-3967	Schleicher ASK 13	13268AB	
D-3968-FE	Schempp-Hirth Duo Discus	298	
D-3969	Schleicher ASW 15B	15421	
D-3970-GB	Schleicher ASW 15B	15422	
D-3971	Schleicher ASK 13	13503	
D-3972	Schleicher ASW 15B	15423	
D-3973	Schleicher ASW 15B	15424	
D-3974	Schleicher ASW 15B	15425	
D-3976	Rolladen-Schneider LS8-a	8239	
D-3978	Schleicher ASK 13	13154	D-0226
D-3979	Schleicher ASW 15	15084	
D-3980	Schleicher ASW 15B	15426	
D-3981-81	Schleicher ASW 15B	15434	
D-3982	Schleicher ASK 13	13505	
D-3983	Schleicher ASW 15B	15431	
D-3984	Schleicher ASW 15B	15432	
D-3986	Schleicher ASK 13	13507	
D-3987	Schleicher ASK 13	13508	
D-3988	SZD-50-3 Puchacz	B-2110	
D-3989	Schleicher ASK 21	21508	
D-3990	Schleicher ASW 15B	15435	
D-3992-AI	Schempp-Hirth Duo Discus	176	
D-3993	Pilatus B4-PC11AF	310	
D-3994	Schleicher ASK 21	21509	
D-3995	Grob G.102 Club Astir IIIB	5546CB	
D-3996	Grob G.102 Club Astir IIIB	5549CB	
D-3998-8Y	Rolladen-Schneider LS1-f	262	
D-3999	Schleicher K 8B	8968AB	
D-4000	Scheibe SF-27A	6022	
D-4001	Glasflügel H401 Kestrel	64	PH-400 D-0972
D-4002-WO	Schempp-Hirth Ventus-2cx (Permit 6.03)	82	
D-4003	Schleicher Rhönlerche II	1119	
D-4004-FW	Schleicher ASW 19B	19112	
D-4005	Glaser-Dirks DG-300 Elan Acro	3E451A11	S5-3333
D-4006	Glasflügel H205 Club Libelle	5	
D-4007	Focke-Wulf Kranich III	56	
D-4008-BK	Schleicher Ka 6BR Rhönsegler	491	OE-5008
D-4009	Glaser-Dirks DG-300 Elan Acro	3E446A9	
D-4010-K5	Schempp-Hirth Duo Discus	100	
D-4011	Schleicher K 8B	126	
D-4012	Glasflügel H401 Kestrel	15	I-JOJO
D-4013	Schempp-Hirth Ventus b/16.6	270	
D-4014	Schempp-Hirth Discus b	57	
D-4015	Schempp-Hirth Janus B	212	
D-4016	Start & Flug H-101 Salto	49	
D-4018	Rolladen-Schneider LS4-b	4972	
D-4020-GD	Schempp-Hirth Duo Discus	183	
D-4021	Schempp-Hirth Duo Discus	202	
D-4022-29	Schleicher Ka 6CR Rhönsegler	6409	
D-4023	SZD-9bis Bocian 1E	P-448	DDR-3023 DM-3023
D-4024	Schleicher Rhönlerche II	3037	
D-4025	Schleicher ASW 15	15145	HB-1025
D-4026	Scheibe SF-27A	6030	
D-4027	SZD-9bis Bocian 1E	P-452	DDR-3027 DM-3027
D-4028-1G	Schempp-Hirth Ventus 2b	52	
D-4029	Rolladen-Schneider LS4-b	4860	
D-4030	Rolladen-Schneider LS4-b	4973	
D-4031	Schleicher K 7 Rhönadler	890	
D-4032	Schleicher ASK 21	21780	
D-4033	SZD-9bis Bocian 1E	P-457	DDR-3033 DM-3033
D-4035	Grob G.103C Twin III Acro	34148	
D-4036	Schleicher Ka 6CR Rhönsegler	1110	
D-4037	Scheibe SF-27A	6016	
D-4038	Schleicher Ka 2 Rhönschwalbe	125	
D-4039	Schleicher K 7 Rhönadler	7083	
D-4040-E5	Glaser-Dirks DG-500 Elan Trainer	5E112T46	
D-4041	Schleicher Ka 6BR Rhönsegler	358	
D-4043	Rolladen-Schneider LS4	4616	
D-4044	Rolladen-Schneider LS4	4274	
D-4045	Schleicher Rhönlerche II	132	
D-4046-K7	Rolladen-Schneider LS4	4617	
D-4047	SZD-9bis Bocian 1E	P-470	DDR-3047 DM-3047
D-4048-48	Schempp-Hirth Discus b	18	
D-4049	Schleicher Ka 6 Rhönsegler	280	
D-4050	Glasflügel Mosquito B	181	OH-569
D-4051	Schleicher ASK 21	21491	
D-4052	Schempp-Hirth Duo Discus	81	
D-4053	Scheibe SF-27A	6107	
D-4054	Schleicher Ka 6BR Rhönsegler	525	
D-4055	Rolladen-Schneider LS4	4619	
D-4056-MH	Rolladen-Schneider LS4	4620	
D-4057	Akaflieg Braunschweig SB-5E Sperber	5042	BGA4302/HYC D-2009 BGA3447/FQS RAFGGA200 D-2009
D-4058	Rolladen-Schneider LS6-c	6218	
D-4059	Glasflügel H201B Standard Libelle	286	HB-1059

D-4061	Schempp-Hirth Ventus b/16.6	35	
D-4062	Schleicher K 8B	8417	
D-4063	Rolladen-Schneider LS6-c	6237	
D-4064-8T	Rolladen-Schneider LS8-18	8240	
D-4065	Siebert SIE-3 (Permit 11.99)	3013	OY-XGZ D-0778
D-4066	DG Flugzeugbau DG-800S (Permit 7.03)	8-298S54Y1	
D-4067	Schleicher Ka 6CR Rhönsegler	6226Si	
D-4068	Schleicher K 8B	755	
D-4069	Schleicher K 7 Rhönadler	Liz.172/60	
D-4070	Scheibe L-Spatz 55	718	
D-4071-6	Schleicher ASW 28-18	28506	
D-4072-8	Schleicher K 8B	8256	
D-4073	Rolladen-Schneider LS8-a	8017	
D-4074	Grob G.103C Twin III Acro	34139	
D-4075	Schleicher Ka 6E	4140	
D-4076	Schleicher K 7 Rhönadler	833	
D-4077	Schleicher Ka 6CR Rhönsegler	1070	
D-4078	Schleicher K 8B	1146	
D-4079	Schleicher Ka 6E	4036	
D-4080	Schleicher ASK 23B	23145	
D-4082-NI	Grob G.103C Twin III Acro	34137	
D-4083	Schleicher Ka 6CR Rhönsegler	1074	
D-4084	Rolladen-Schneider LS6-c	6238	
D-4085-WS	SZD-48-1 Jantar Standard 2	B-1221	OE-5303
D-4086-25	Rolladen-Schneider LS6-c	6239	
D-4087	Schleicher ASW 20L	20359	
D-4088	Schleicher ASK 21	21029	
D-4090	Schleicher ASW 20	20360	
D-4091-91	Schempp-Hirth Discus b	562	
D-4092	Rolladen-Schneider LS6-c	6219	
D-4094-XF	Schempp-Hirth Duo Discus	107	
D-4095	Rolladen-Schneider LS6-c	6240	
D-4097	Schleicher Ka 6CR Rhönsegler	6272	
D-4098-8B	Rolladen-Schneider LS8-a	8320	
D-4099-2ND	SZD-48-3 Jantar Standard 3 (Permit 10.99)	B-1448	
D-4101	Glaser-Dirks DG-303 Elan Acro	3E444A7	LX-CRP
D-4102-LW	Glaser-Dirks DG-100G Elan	E165G131	
D-4103	Rolladen-Schneider LS4-b	4862	
D-4104	Rolladen-Schneider LS4-b	4974	
D-4105-05	Rolladen-Schneider LS4	4351	
D-4107	Rolladen-Schneider LS6-c	6241	
D-4108	Schempp-Hirth Duo Discus	143	
D-4109	Schempp-Hirth Duo Discus	194	
D-4110	Rolladen-Schneider LS4-b	4863	
D-4111-HP	Schempp-Hirth Ventus 2b (Permit .05)	128	
D-4113	PZL PW-5 Smyk	17.03.009	PH-1063
D-4114	Schleicher ASW 19B	19350	
D-4115-HR	Schempp-Hirth Ventus 2a	27	D-4111 (1)
D-4116	Schleicher Rhönlerche II (Reservation 12.02)	3072Br	BGA4116/HQH (BGA4097) HB-877
D-4117	Schleicher K 8B	8583	
D-4118	Schleicher K 8B	8606	
D-4119	Rolladen-Schneider LS8-a	8164	
D-4120	Schleicher Ka 6CR Rhönsegler	6566	
D-4121	Schleicher Ka 6CR Rhönsegler	6593	
D-4122	Schleicher Ka 6CR Rhönsegler	6582	
D-4123	Scheibe SF-34B	5122	
D-4124-4A	Rolladen-Schneider LS4-b	4942	
D-4125	Schleicher Ka 6CR Rhönsegler	6612	
D-4126	Schleicher Ka 6CR Rhönsegler	6610	
D-4127	Schleicher Ka 6E	4107	
D-4128	Schleicher Ka 6E	4100	
D-4129	Schleicher Ka 6CR Rhönsegler	6654	
D-4130	Glaser-Dirks DG-100G Elan	E189G155	
D-4131	Schempp-Hirth Standard Austria S	16	HB-676 D-8437
D-4132-GL	Schleicher Ka 6CR Rhönsegler	6509Si	
D-4133	Schleicher ASK 13	13067	
D-4134	Schleicher ASK 13	13066	
D-4135	Schleicher ASK 13	13075	
D-4136	Schleicher K 8B	8746	
D-4137	Scheibe Bergfalke III	5510	
D-4138	Scheibe Zugvogel IIIA	1056	
D-4139	Schempp-Hirth Discus CS	112CS	
D-4140	Schleicher ASK 13	13620AB	
D-4141	Schleicher ASW 19B	19085	
D-4142	Schleicher ASK 13	13621AB	
D-4143	Glaser-Dirks DG-500 Elan Trainer	5E106T42	
D-4145	Pilatus B4-PC11AF	197	
D-4146	Pilatus B4-PC11AF	202	
D-4147	Schempp-Hirth Ventus c	285	
D-4148	Rolladen-Schneider LS4-b	41025	
D-4149	Schempp-Hirth Discus CS	247CS	
D-4150-50	Schempp-Hirth Duo Discus	278	
D-4151	SZD-41A Jantar Standard	B-739	
D-4152	Schempp-Hirth Mini-Nimbus C	152	
D-4153	Schempp-Hirth Duo Discus	85	
D-4155	Grob G.103 Twin Astir	3049	OY-XIC
D-4156-3S	Rolladen-Schneider LS8-a	8209	OO-YBM
D-4157	SZD-41A Jantar Standard	B-879	
D-4158	Glaser-Dirks DG-100G Elan	E190G156	
D-4159	Glaser-Dirks DG-100G Elan	E191G157	
D-4160	Schempp-Hirth Discus b	416	
D-4161	Schleicher Ka 6CR Rhönsegler	6299	
D-4162	SZD-41A Jantar Standard	B-857	

D-4163	Grob G.102 Astir CS	1103	
D-4164	Grob G.102 Astir CS	1104	
D-4165	Grob G.102 Astir CS	1105	
D-4166-D6	Grob G.102 Astir CS	1106	
D-4168	Grob G.102 Astir CS	1108	
D-4169	Schempp-Hirth Duo Discus	179	
D-4170	Grob G.102 Astir CS	1110	
D-4171	Grob G.102 Astir CS	1111	
D-4172	Scheibe SF-34B	5137	
D-4173	Glaser-Dirks DG-100G Elan (Permit .05)	E173G139	
D-4174	Rolladen-Schneider LS4-b	4975	
D-4175	Scheibe SF-34B	5135	
D-4176	Glaser-Dirks DG-500/20 Elan	5E159W7	
D-4177	Glaser-Dirks DG-300 Club Elan Acro	3E463C83A18	
	(C/n conflicts with HB-3190, one is probably -A17)		
D-4178	Glaser-Dirks DG-100G Elan	E199G165	
D-4180	Grob G.102 Astir CS	1136	
D-4181	Grob G.102 Astir CS	1134	
D-4182	DG Flugzeugbau DG-500 Elan Orion	5E177X29	S5-7515
D-4183	Schleicher ASK 21	21531	
D-4184	Rolladen-Schneider LS4	4184	N29798
D-4185	Glasflügel H304	243	
D-4186	Glasflügel H304	244	
D-4187	Grob G.102 Astir CS 77	1754	I-IVBD
D-4188	Rolladen-Schneider LS4	4034	
D-4189	Rolladen-Schneider LS4-b	41014	
D-4190	Rolladen-Schneider LS4	4041	
D-4191	Schempp-Hirth Standard Cirrus	408G	HB-1191
D-4192-2H	Schleicher ASK 21	21532	
D-4194	Schleicher ASK 21	21533	
D-4195	Schleicher ASK 21	21534	
D-4196	Grob G.102 Astir CS	1222	
D-4197	Grob G.102 Astir CS	1223	
D-4198	Grob G.102 Astir CS	1224	
D-4199-WS	Schempp-Hirth Duo Discus	387	
D-4200	SZD-55-1	551197097	
D-4201	Scheibe SF-34B	5123	
D-4202-SIK	Scheibe SF-34B	5124	
D-4203	Scheibe SF-34B	5128	
D-4204	Grob G 102 Astir CS	1230	
D-4205	Schleicher ASK 21	21536	
D-4206	Grob G.102 Astir CS	1232	
D-4208	Schleicher ASK 21	21537	
D-4209	Grob G.102 Astir CS	1235	
D-4210	Grob G.102 Astir CS	1241	
D-4211	Grob G.102 Astir CS	1242	
D-4212	Schempp-Hirth Duo Discus	12	
D-4213	Schempp-Hirth Duo Discus	105	
D-4214	Grob G.102 Astir CS	1245	
D-4215	Grob G.102 Astir CS	1315	
D-4216	Schempp-Hirth Standard Cirrus	429	HB-1217
D-4217	Grob G.102 Astir CS	1317	
D-4218	Schempp-Hirth Duo Discus	169	
D-4219	Grob G.102 Astir CS	1319	
D-4220	Schleicher ASK 21	21525	
D-4221	Grob G.102 Astir CS	1322	
D-4222-UX	Grob G.104 Speed Astir IIC	4501	
D-4223	Schleicher ASW 20L	20302	
D-4224	Schleicher ASW 20	20297	
D-4225	Schleicher ASW 20L	20321	
D-4226	Schleicher ASW 20	20303	
D-4227	Schempp-Hirth Discus CS	279CS	
D-4228	Schleicher ASW 20L	20306	
D-4229	SZD-24-4A Foka 4	W-345	DDR-2229
			DM-2229
D-4230	Rolladen-Schneider LS4-b	4976	
D-4231	Schempp-Hirth Duo Discus	82	
D-4232	Schleicher ASK 21	21527	
D-4233	Scheibe SF-34B	5130	
D-4234	Scheibe SF-34B	5129	
D-4235	Rolladen-Schneider LS4	4019	
D-4236	Akaflieg Braunschweig SB-5B Sperber	5024A	
D-4238-RF	Rolladen-Schneider LS4	4125	
D-4241	SZD-9bis Bocian 1E	P-528	DDR-3241
			DM-3241
D-4242	Schleicher ASW 17	17042	OH-471
D-4243	Rolladen-Schneider LS4	4132	
D-4244-WS	Rolladen-Schneider LS4	4167	
D-4245-KF	Rolladen-Schneider LS4	4127	
D-4246	Rolladen-Schneider LS4	4144	
D-4247	Rolladen-Schneider LS4	4135	
D-4248	Rolladen-Schneider LS4	4130	
D-4249	Grunau Baby III	83	Belg: PL38
D-4250-II	Rolladen-Schneider LS4	4322	
D-4251	Schleicher ASK 21	21528	
D-4252	Rolladen-Schneider LS4	4179	
D-4253	Grob G.102 Astir CS	1246	
D-4254	SZD-32A Foka 5	W-515	DDR-2254
			DM-2254
D-4255	Grob G.102 Astir CS	1249	
D-4257	Schempp-Hirth Ventus 2b	81	
D-4258	Grob G.102 Astir CS	1252	
D-4259	Schleicher ASK 21	21530	
D-4260	Grob G.102 Astir CS	1254	
D-4261	SZD-32A Foka 5	W-524	DDR-2261
			DM-2261
D-4262	Grob G.102 Astir CS	1385	
D-4263-KD	Schempp-Hirth Duo Discus	389	
D-4264	Grob G.102 Astir CS	1390	
D-4265	Grob G.102 Astir CS	1391	
D-4266	Rolladen-Schneider LS4	4201	N42RL
D-4267	Grob G.102 Astir CS	1401	
D-4268	Grob G.102 Astir CS	1402	
D-4270	Grob G.102 Astir CS	1404	
D-4271	Grob G.102 Astir CS	1405	
D-4272	Schleicher ASW 22BL	22085	
D-4273	Grob G.102 Astir CS	1417	
D-4274	Grob G.102 Astir CS	1420	
D-4275-5A	Grob G.102 Astir CS	1421	
D-4276	Grob G.102 Astir CS	1422	
D-4277-EH	Grob G.102 Astir CS	1423	
D-4278	Schleicher ASK 23B	23131	
D-4279	Grob G.103C Twin III Acro	34101-K-331	
D-4280	Grob G.103A Twin II Acro	34077-K-307	
D-4281	Grob G.103A Twin II Acro	34078-K-308	
D-4282-MP	Rolladen-Schneider LS8-a	8018	
D-4283	Schleicher ASW 20L	20455	I-GHES
			D-3248
D-4284	Rolladen-Schneider LS4-b	4831	
D-4285-BS	Schleicher ASK 21	21539	
D-4286	Rolladen-Schneider LS3-a	3183	
D-4287-SI	Rolladen-Schneider LS4	4323	
D-4288	Schempp-Hirth Nimbus 2B	141	HB-1657
			D-7851
D-4289-89	Rolladen-Schneider LS4-b	4833	
D-4290	Schleicher ASK 21	21647	
D-4291	Rolladen-Schneider LS3-a	3256	
D-4292	Rolladen-Schneider LS3-17	3371	
D-4293-BJ	Rolladen-Schneider LS4	4275	
D-4294	Rolladen-Schneider LS4	4273	
D-4296	Rolladen-Schneider LS4-b	4835	
D-4297-8M	Rolladen-Schneider LS4-b	4836	
D-4298	Rolladen-Schneider LS4-b	4837	
D-4299	SZD-48-1 Jantar Standard 2	B-1222	
D-4300	DG Flugzeugbau DG-500 Elan Orion	5E199X43	S5-7518
D-4301	Schleicher Rhönlerche II	407	
D-4302-H4	Glaser-Dirks DG-300 Elan	3E97	
D-4303	Glaser-Dirks DG-300 Elan	3E395	
D-4304	Glasflügel H304	203	
D-4305-8N	Grob G.103C Twin III	36011	
D-4306	Schleicher K 8	481	
D-4307-FZ	Glaser-Dirks DG-300 Elan	3E380	
D-4308	Grunau Baby IIB	1	D-8807
D-4309	Rolladen-Schneider LS6-c-18	6367	
D-4310	Schleicher ASW 20	20610	
D-4311	DG Flugzeugbau DG-1000S	10-3S3	
D-4312	Schleicher Rhönlerche II	1021	
D-4313-3W	Glaser-Dirks DG-300 Elan	3E175	
D-4314	Schempp-Hirth Duo Discus	226	
D-4315	Schleicher K 8B	1019	
D-4316	Pilatus B4-PC11	234	HB-1316
D-4317	Schempp-Hirth Discus CS	142CS	
D-4319	Schleicher K 8	472	
D-4320	Grob G.103C Twin III Acro	34203	
D-4321-AZ	Schempp-Hirth Discus CS	149CS	
D-4322	Schleicher Rhönlerche II	3025	
D-4323	Schleicher K 7 Rhönadler	7117	
D-4324	Schleicher K 7 Rhönadler	7189	
D-4325	Schempp-Hirth Ventus 2a (Permit .02)	32	
D-4326-PY	Schleicher ASW 20	20611	
D-4327	Grunau Baby III	1	
D-4328	Scheibe L-Spatz 55	634	
D-4329	Schleicher K 8B	920	
D-4330	Schleicher ASW 24	24211	
D-4331	Rolladen-Schneider LS4-b	4839	
D-4332	Glaser-Dirks DG-500 Elan Orion	5E156X13	S5-7505
D-4333	Steinlehner/Huber SH-2H (Permit)	01	
D-4335	Schleicher K 8B	8376	
D-4336	Schleicher K 7 Rhönadler	500	
D-4337	Schleicher ASK 21	21542	
D-4338	Schleicher Ka 6CR Rhönsegler	6447	
D-4339	Schleicher ASK 21	21543	
D-4340	Glaser-Dirks DG-100G Elan	E106G75	
D-4341	Schempp-Hirth Discus 2B	122	
D-4342	Schempp-Hirth Ventus 2b	77	
D-4345	Schleicher K 8B	8444	D-KOBC
			D-4345
D-4346	Schempp-Hirth Discus CS	254CS	
D-4347	Schleicher Ka 6CR Rhönsegler	6389	
D-4348-BI	Schempp-Hirth Discus CS	111CS	
D-4349	Schleicher Ka 6 Rhönsegler	187	
D-4350	Schempp-Hirth Discus CS	116CS	
D-4351	Schleicher Ka 6 Rhönsegler	130	
D-4352	Schleicher K 8B	8670	
D-4353	Schleicher K 8B	8690	
D-4354-AF	Schempp-Hirth Discus b	141	
D-4355	Glaser-Dirks DG-100G Elan	E222G188	
	(C/n also quoted for I-LYNO)		
D-4356-F	SZD-30 Pirat	B-576	DDR-1856
			DM-1856
D-4357	Schleicher K 7 Rhönadler	7212	
D-4358	Schempp-Hirth Janus C	230	
D-4359	Schempp-Hirth Discus b	155	
D-4360	Schempp-Hirth Discus b	143	

D-4361	Schleicher K 8	P1	
D-4363	Schempp-Hirth Ventus 2c	4/7	
D-4364	Schleicher ASK 21	21727	
D-4365	Schleicher Ka 6CR Rhönsegler	618	
D-4366	Bölkow Phoebus A-1	765	
D-4367	Rolladen-Schneider LS8-a	8165	
D-4368	Schleicher Ka 6E	4114	
D-4369	Schleicher K 8B	740	
D-4370	Schleicher Ka 6CR Rhönsegler	6414Si	
D-4371	Schleicher ASW 20	20421	I-EREL
D-4372	Schleicher Ka 6E	4155	
D-4373	Schleicher K 8B	738	
D-4374	Rolladen-Schneider LS6-c	6282	
D-4375	SZD-9bis Bocian 1E	P-565	DDR-3375 DM-3375
D-4376	Rolladen-Schneider LS8-a	8241	
D-4377	SZD-9bis Bocian 1E	P-567	DDR-3377 DM-3377
D-4378	Schleicher Rhönlerche II	804	
D-4380-80	Schempp-Hirth Discus 2B	77	
D-4381	Schleicher K 8B	918	
D-4382	Schleicher K 8B	8696	
D-4384	Schleicher Ka 6CR Rhönsegler	967	
D-4385	Schleicher Rhönlerche II	940	
D-4386	Schleicher ASK 13	13016	
D-4387-ED	Rolladen-Schneider LS4-b	4878	
D-4388	Schleicher Ka 6CR Rhönsegler	1066	
D-4390-90	Schempp-Hirth Discus 2B	136	
D-4391	Schleicher K 7 Rhönadler	7001	
D-4393	Schempp-Hirth Discus b	164	
D-4394	Schleicher K 8B	8009	
D-4395-M4	Schempp-Hirth Discus b	174	
D-4396	Pilatus B4-PC11AF	241	
D-4398	Rolladen-Schneider LS4-b	4913	
D-4399	Schleicher Ka 6CR Rhönsegler	6221/B	
D-4400	Schleicher Ka 6E	4157	
D-4402-MD	Schempp-Hirth Discus b	173	
D-4403	Schleicher K 7 Rhönadler	7249	
D-4404-WB	SZD-48-3 Jantar Standard 3	B-1349	SP-3249
D-4405	Schleicher Ka 6CR Rhönsegler	6508	
D-4406	Rolladen-Schneider LS1-d	257	
D-4407	Schempp-Hirth Discus 2B	121	
D-4408	Rolladen-Schneider LS8-18	8298	
D-4409	Schleicher K 8B	114	
D-4410	Grunau Baby IIB	AB-1	
D-4411	Schleicher K 8B	8313	
D-4412	Rolladen-Schneider LS4-b	4851	
D-4413-7J	Glasflügel H206 Hornet C	97	
D-4414	LET L-23 Super Blanik	917811	
D-4415	FFA Diamant 18	057	
D-4416	SZD-41A Jantar Standard	B-747	DDR-2416 DM-2416
D-4417	Schleicher Ka 6E	4188	
D-4418-E4	Schempp-Hirth Discus CS	113CS	
D-4419	Grob G.103C Twin III	36012	D-5291
D-4420	Schleicher K 8B	8616	
D-4421	Schleicher ASK 13	13081	
D-4422	Schleicher Ka 6CR Rhönsegler	6643	
D-4423	Schleicher ASK 13	13076	
D-4424-GF	SZD-42-2 Jantar 2B	B-865	DDR-2423 DM-2423
D-4425	Schleicher ASW 15	15001	
D-4426	Schleicher K 8B	8414	
D-4427-YW	Schleicher ASW 27	27159	
D-4428-VT	Grob G.103C Twin III Acro	34158	
D-4429	Schempp-Hirth Discus CS	024CS	
D-4430-KE	Glasflügel H303 Mosquito	31	
D-4431	Glasflügel H303 Mosquito	30	
D-4432	Rolladen-Schneider LS4-b	41041	
D-4433	Vogt LO-100 Zwergreiher	AB 33	
D-4434	Glasflügel H303 Mosquito B	116	
D-4435	Glasflügel H303 Mosquito B	117	
D-4436	Schleicher ASK 21	21594	
D-4437-SH	Schempp-Hirth Discus 2b	169	
D-4438	Glasflügel H303 Mosquito B	124	
D-4439	Glasflügel H303 Mosquito B	144	
D-4440-Y4	Schempp-Hirth Discus 2A	3	
D-4441-ZB	Rolladen-Schneider LS8-18	8480	
D-4442	Rolladen-Schneider LS4	4116	
D-4443	Akaflieg Braunschweig SB-5E Sperber	AB5059	
D-4444	Rolladen-Schneider LS8-18	8396	
D-4445-LS	Rolladen-Schneider LS6E (Permit)	6364	
D-4446	Glasflügel H303 Mosquito	13	
D-4447	Glasflügel H303 Mosquito	23	
D-4448	Glasflügel H206 Hornet	88	
D-4449	Glasflügel H206 Hornet	89	
D-4450	Rolladen-Schneider LS4-b	4876	
D-4451	Rolladen-Schneider LS4-a	4676	D-0157
D-4452-DOC	Schempp-Hirth Discus 2B	141	
D-4453	Glasflügel H303 Mosquito	78	
D-4454	SG-38 Schulgleiter	1310/691	
D-4455	Glasflügel H303 Mosquito	100	
D-4456	Glaser-Dirks DG-300 Elan	3E196	
D-4457	Glaser-Dirks DG-300 Elan	3E198	
D-4458-L2	Glasflügel H206 Hornet	83	
D-4459	Glasflügel H206 Hornet	69	
D-4460	Glasflügel H303 Mosquito B	131	
D-4461	Glasflügel H206 Hornet	60	
D-4462	Glasflügel H206 Hornet	61	
D-4463	Schleicher ASK 21	21071	
D-4464	Schleicher ASK 21	21076	
D-4465	Schleicher ASK 21	21077	
D-4466	Grob G.102 Astir CS	1167	
D-4467	Schleicher ASK 13	13554	
D-4468	Schleicher ASK 13	13555	
D-4469	Schleicher ASW 19B	19063	
D-4470	Schempp-Hirth Discus b	23	
D-4471	Schleicher ASK 13	13557	
D-4472	Schleicher ASW 19	19071	
D-4473	Schleicher ASW 19B	19072	
D-4474	Schleicher ASW 19	19073	
D-4475	Schleicher ASK 13	13558	
D-4476	Schempp-Hirth Discus 2B	152	
D-4477	Rolladen-Schneider LS8-a	8282	
D-4479	Schleicher ASK 13	13560	
D-4480	Schleicher ASK 13	13564	
D-4481	Schleicher ASW 19	19077	
D-4482	Schleicher ASW 19	19078	
D-4483	Schleicher ASK 13	13561	
D-4484	Schleicher ASW 19B	19079	
D-4485	Schleicher ASW 19	19080	
D-4486	Glaser-Dirks DG-100G Elan	E217G183	I-LUKO
D-4487	Rolladen-Schneider LS4-b	4943	
D-4488	Schempp-Hirth Duo Discus	50	
D-4489	Pilatus B4-PC11	102	PH-489
D-4490	Schleicher ASK 13 (Reservation 4.99)	13563	
D-4491-FK	Schleicher ASK 21 (Permit)	21661	
D-4492-1Z	Schleicher ASK 21	21063	
D-4493	Schleicher ASW 19B	19352	
D-4494	Schleicher ASW 19	19087	
D-4495-S4	Schempp-Hirth Duo Discus	96	
D-4496	Grob G.102 Speed Astir II	4016	
D-4497-7	Grob G.102 Speed Astir II	4015	
D-4498	Schempp-Hirth manufacturer's test mark		
D-4499	Schempp-Hirth manufacturer's test mark		
D-4500	Grob G.102 Speed Astir IIB	4029	
D-4501	Grob G.102 Speed Astir II	4008	
D-4502-ZY	Schempp-Hirth Janus CT	13/272	
D-4503	Schempp-Hirth Discus CS	014CS	
D-4505	Grob G.102 Speed Astir II	4024	
D-4506	Schleicher ASW 19B	19136	
D-4507	Schempp-Hirth Duo Discus	245	
D-4508	Schempp-Hirth Discus CS	022CS	
D-4509-FI	Schempp-Hirth Discus CS	013CS	
D-4510	Glaser-Dirks DG-200	2-39	
D-4511	Glaser-Dirks DG-200	2-80	
D-4512	Schleicher ASK 21	21497	
D-4513	Schleicher ASK 21	21498	
D-4515-JT	SZD-48-1 Jantar Standard 2	B-996	
D-4516	Schempp-Hirth Duo Discus	108	
D-4517-EX	Schempp-Hirth Discus CS	025CS	
D-4519-K1	Schempp-Hirth Duo Discus	289	
D-4521	Schleicher ASK 21	21204	
D-4522	Schleicher ASW 20CL	20729	
D-4524	Schleicher ASK 13	13540	
D-4525-TD	Schleicher ASW 19B	19025	
D-4526	Schleicher ASW 19	19018	
D-4527	Schleicher K 8C	81012	
D-4528	Schleicher ASW 19	19028	
D-4529	Schempp-Hirth Discus CS	055CS	
D-4532	Schleicher ASW 19	19029	
D-4533	Schleicher ASK 18	18031	
D-4534	Schleicher ASK 13	13543	
D-4535	Schleicher ASW 24B	24234	
D-4536	Schleicher ASW 19B	19037	
D-4538	Schleicher ASK 13	13546	
D-4540	Glasflügel H303 Mosquito B	196	
D-4542-42	Schempp-Hirth Discus 2B	83	
D-4543	Rolladen-Schneider LS4	4247	
D-4544	Rolladen-Schneider LS4	4478	
D-4545-RY	Rolladen-Schneider LS4	4350	
D-4546	Grob G.103A Twin II Acro	3730-K-46	
D-4547-47	Schempp-Hirth Ventus 2a	55	
D-4548	Rolladen-Schneider LS4-b	41034	
D-4549	Grob G.102 Club Astir IIIB	5580CB	
D-4550	Grob G.102 Standard Astir II	5002S	
D-4551	Grob G.103 Twin II	3731	
D-4552	Glaser-Dirks DG-200	2-5	I-RATA D-4509
D-4553-TK	Rolladen-Schneider LS8-a	8112	
D-4554	Schempp-Hirth Discus CS	101CS	
D-4558-SG	Grob G.102 Astir CS 77	1741	
D-4560	Grob G.102 Astir CS 77	1747	
D-4561	Grob G.102 Astir CS Jeans	2165	
D-4563	Grob G.102 Astir CS 77	1756	
D-4564	Grob G.102 Astir CS Jeans	2167	
D-4565	Grob G.103 Twin Astir	3007	N59PE N70759
D-4566	Glaser-Dirks DG-500 Elan Orion	5E137X3	
D-4567	Grob G.102 Astir CS Jeans	2168	
D-4570-6B	SZD-59 Acro	X-150	SP-3570 SP-P570
D-4571-27	SZD-55-1	551196087	
D-4572-NA	Rolladen-Schneider LS8-a	8113	

D-4573	Rolladen-Schneider LS1-f	392	F-CEKI
D-4574	Schempp-Hirth Discus CS	126CS	
D-4575	Rolladen-Schneider LS3-a	3252	
D-4576	Schleicher ASK 21	21538	
D-4577	Glaser-Dirks DG-300 Club Elan	3E296C14	
D-4578-WE	Glaser-Dirks DG-300 Club Elan	3E297C15	
D-4579	Rolladen-Schneider LS3-a	3417	
D-4580	Rolladen-Schneider LS3-17	3381	
D-4581	Glaser-Dirks DG-300 Club Elan	3E298C16	
D-4582	Schleicher ASK 23B	23126	
D-4583	Rolladen-Schneider LS4	4120	HB-1583
D-4584	Schempp-Hirth Ventus 2b	118	
D-4585	Rolladen-Schneider LS3-a	3432	
D-4586	Rolladen-Schneider LS7-WL	7021	
D-4587-NC	Rolladen-Schneider LS8-18	8253	
D-4588	Rolladen-Schneider LS3-17	3331	
D-4589	Schempp-Hirth Janus B	184	
D-4590	Schempp-Hirth Janus C	191	
D-4591-KS	Schempp-Hirth Nimbus 3/24.5	61	
D-4592	Rolladen-Schneider LS3-a	3370	
D-4593	Glaser-Dirks DG-300 Elan	3E214	
D-4594-EZ	Rolladen-Schneider LS8-a	8254	
D-4595	Glaser-Dirks DG-300 Elan	3E216	
D-4596-XW	Schleicher ASK 21	21499	
D-4597	Neukom S-4D Elfe	408AB	
D-4598	Neukom S-4D Elfe	411AB	
D-4599	Schleicher ASK 21	21607	HB-3159
D-4600	Neukom S-4 Elfe	50	
D-4601	Scheibe L-Spatz 55	656/56	
D-4602	Schleicher Ka 6CR Rhönsegler	6503	
D-4603	Schleicher K 8	391	
D-4605	Schleicher K 8B	8235	
D-4606	Glaser-Dirks DG-300 Elan	3E241	
D-4607	Schleicher Ka 6CR Rhönsegler	6523Si	
D-4608	Schleicher K 8B	107	
D-4611	Schleicher ASK 21	21502	
D-4612	Schleicher K 7 Rhönadler	7177	
D-4613-8H	Rolladen-Schneider LS4-b	4944	
D-4614	Schleicher Ka 6CR Rhönsegler	6056	
D-4615	Scheibe Bergfalke II/55	386	
D-4616	Glaser-Dirks DG-300 Elan Acro	3E441A6	
D-4617-CP	Rolladen-Schneider LS8-18	8255	
D-4618	Schleicher K 8B	8722	
D-4619	Schleicher Ka 6E	4033	
D-4621	Akaflieg Braunschweig SB-5E Sperber	5011A	
D-4622	SZD-50-3 Puchacz (Reservation 2.99)	B-1341	DDR-3622
D-4623	Schleicher K 7 Rhönadler	7275	
D-4624	Schempp-Hirth Ventus-2ax	78	D-6578
D-4625	Schleicher ASK 21	21500	
D-4627	Schleicher ASW 24	24125	
D-4628	Schleicher K 8B	154/59	
D-4630	Schempp-Hirth Ventus 2c	71	
D-4631	Schleicher ASK 13	13663AB	
D-4632	Schleicher ASK 13	13664AB	
D-4633-2C	Glaser-Dirks DG-100G Elan	E215G181	
D-4635	SZD-50-3 Puchacz	B-1401	DDR-3635
D-4636	SZD-50-3 Puchacz	B-1402	DDR-3636
D-4637	Glaser-Dirks DG-300 Elan	3E239	
D-4638	Schleicher ASH 25	25115	
D-4639	Schleicher ASK 21	21493	
D-4640	Schleicher K 7 Rhönadler	981	
D-4641	Schleicher K 7 Rhönadler	7034	
D-4642	Grunau Baby III	AB 01	
D-4643	Rolladen-Schneider LS1-f	468	SE-TRL
D-4644	Rolladen-Schneider LS4	4067	SE-TXB
D-4645	Glaser-Dirks DG-100G Elan	E201G167	
D-4646	Schleicher Rhönlerche II	66/57	
D-4647-4H	Schempp-Hirth Duo Discus	287	
D-4648	Schleicher ASK 21	21495	
D-4649	Schleicher ASW 12BV (Permit .01)	12007	D-0074
D-4650	Schempp-Hirth Nimbus 2C	177	VH-GLN ZS-GKT D-6564
D-4651	Schempp-Hirth Discus CS	298CS	
D-4652-GF	Schleicher Ka 6E	4083	
D-4654	Scheibe L-Spatz 55	613	
D-4655	Schleicher K 8B	8270	
D-4658	Schleicher ASK 21	21494	
D-4659	Schleicher Ka 6E	4030	
D-4660	Schleicher K 8B	907	
D-4661	Rolladen-Schneider LS8-a	8013	
D-4662	Glaser-Dirks DG-300 Elan	3E327	
D-4663	Schempp-Hirth Discus b	131	
D-4664-YY	Schempp-Hirth Ventus c	309	
D-4665	Schleicher Ka 6E	4145	
D-4666	Grob G.103 Twin Astir	3129	HB-1426
D-4667	Glaser-Dirks DG-300 Club Elan	3E323C26	
D-4668	Schleicher ASK 13	13101	
D-4669	Scheibe L-Spatz 55	752	
D-4670	Rolladen-Schneider LS4-a	4670	D-6796
D-4672	Schleicher K 8B	8137	
D-4673	Schempp-Hirth Discus b	133	
D-4675-Y4	Rolladen-Schneider LS8-a	8256	
D-4676	Schempp-Hirth Duo Discus	212	
D-4677	Schleicher K 7 Rhönadler	7256	
D-4678	Schempp-Hirth Discus b	132	
D-4679	Schleicher ASK 18 (Museum) (Reservation - cld?)	unkn	
D-4680-B6	Schleicher ASK 21	21626	
D-4681	Schleicher ASK 13	13025	
D-4682	Schempp-Hirth Discus CS	195CS	
D-4683	Schleicher Ka 6CR Rhönsegler	6212	
D-4685	Schleicher ASK 21	21506	
D-4686	Darmstadt D-36 (Permit)	V-2	
D-4687	Schleicher ASW 20L	20579	
D-4688	Schleicher ASW 27	27133	
D-4690-MR	Schempp-Hirth Discus CS	196CS	
D-4691-JE	Schleicher ASW 20L	20581	
D-4692	Schleicher Ka 6CR Rhönsegler	6297	
D-4693-6M	Rolladen-Schneider LS8-a	8190	
D-4694-WG	Schempp-Hirth Discus 2B	78	
D-4695-JF	Schleicher ASH 25	25125	
D-4696	Akaflieg Braunschweig SB-5B Sperber	5007	
D-4697	Scheibe L-Spatz 55	4	D-KONK
D-4698	Schleicher Ka 6E	4150	
D-4699	Schleicher Ka 6E	4144	
D-4701	Glaser-Dirks DG-100G Elan	E194G160	
D-4703	Glaser-Dirks DG-300 Club Elan	3E273C4	
D-4704	Schleicher Ka 6CR Rhönsegler	6435	
D-4705-F3	Schleicher ASW 24	24203	
D-4706	Schleicher Ka 6CR Rhönsegler	6437	
D-4707	Schempp-Hirth Duo Discus	41	
D-4708	Schleicher ASK 21	21361	
D-4709	Schleicher ASK 21	21705	
D-4710	Schleicher K 8B	8614	
D-4711	Schempp-Hirth Standard Cirrus	466G	
D-4712	Schleicher K 8B	8756	
D-4713	Glaser-Dirks DG-300 Elan	3E154	
D-4714	Schleicher K 8B	8632	
D-4715	Schleicher ASK 21	21364	
D-4716	Schleicher Ka 6E	4060	
D-4717	Schleicher ASK 13	13011	
D-4718-PG	Rolladen-Schneider LS8-18	8404	
D-4719	Scheibe SF-27A	6071	
D-4720-PE	Schempp-Hirth Ventus 2a	92	
D-4721-DG	DG Flugzeugbau DG-500 Elan Orion	5E238X74	
D-4722	Schleicher Ka 6CR Rhönsegler	6604	
D-4723-TA	Schempp-Hirth Ventus 2b	101	
D-4724	Schleicher K 8B	987	
D-4725	Akaflieg Braunschweig SB-5B Sperber	5031A	
D-4727	Schempp-Hirth Duo Discus	270	
D-4728	Schleicher ASK 21	21674	
D-4729	Schleicher Ka 6CR Rhönsegler	6052Si	
D-4730	Bölkow Phoebus C	806	
D-4731	Schleicher Ka 6E	4185	
D-4733	Schempp-Hirth Discus b	469	
D-4734	Glaser-Dirks DG-100G Elan	E197G163	
D-4735	Rolladen-Schneider LS8-a	8073	
D-4736-LM	Schempp-Hirth Cirrus-VTC	150Y	
D-4737	Schempp-Hirth Cirrus-VTC	151Y	
D-4738	Schleicher ASK 21	21367	
D-4740	Schempp-Hirth Standard Cirrus	395	
D-4741	Scheibe Zugvogel IIIA	1098A	D-1896
D-4742	Schempp-Hirth Standard Cirrus	410G	
D-4743	Schempp-Hirth Standard Cirrus	400	
D-4744	Schempp-Hirth Standard Cirrus	411	
D-4745	Schleicher ASK 21	21329	
D-4746	Schempp-Hirth Standard Cirrus	433G	
D-4747	Schempp-Hirth Standard Cirrus K (Permit)	437G	
D-4748	Schempp-Hirth Standard Cirrus	397	
D-4749	Schempp-Hirth Standard Cirrus	415	
D-4750	Schleicher ASK 21	21339	
D-4751	Schempp-Hirth Cirrus-VTC	160Y	
D-4752	Schempp-Hirth Standard Cirrus	560G	
D-4753	Start & Flug H-101 Salto	72	
D-4754	Rolladen-Schneider LS4-b	41004	
D-4755	Glaser-Dirks DG-300 Elan	3E46	HB-1757
D-4756	SZD-30 Pirat	B-360	DDR-1756 DM-1756
D-4757-LP	Glaser-Dirks DG-300 Elan	3E169	
D-4758	Grob G.104 Speed Astir II	4025	OE-5408 D-4503
D-4759	Scheibe Bergfalke IV	5852	
D-4760	Scheibe Bergfalke IV	5853	
D-4761	Scheibe Bergfalke IV	5854	
D-4762	Schleicher ASK 21	21330	
D-4763	Scheibe Bergfalke III	AB5653	
D-4765	Eiri PIK-20D	20534	
D-4766	Eiri PIK-20D	20556	
D-4767-LE	Eiri PIK-20D	20555	
D-4769	Schleicher ASK 21	21371	
D-4770	Schempp-Hirth Ventus 2c	63/	
D-4771-AC	Grob G.103 Twin II	3521	
D-4772-LVB	Schempp-Hirth Duo Discus	150	
D-4773	Grob G.103 Twin II	3524	
D-4775	SZD-30 Pirat	B-404	DDR-1775 DM-1775
D-4776	Eiri PIK-20D	20623	
D-4777	Schleicher Ka 6CR Rhönsegler	6426Si	
D-4778	Schleicher ASK 21	21331	
D-4779	Eiri PIK-20D	20522	
D-4780	Schleicher ASK 21	21332	
D-4781-BS	Eiri PIK-20D	20503	(OH-509)
D-4782	Eiri PIK-20D	20535	
D-4783	Grob G.102 Astir CS	1470	

D-4784	Grob G.102 Astir CS	1477	
D-4785	Schleicher ASK 21	21372	
D-4786	Schleicher ASK 21	21286	
D-4787	Grob G.102 Astir CS	1481	
D-4788	Schempp-Hirth Discus b	21	
D-4790	Valentin Kiwi S	001	D-KELT
D-4791	Schempp-Hirth Duo Discus	79	
D-4792	Grob G.102 Astir CS	1489	
D-4793	Schleicher ASK 23	23056	
D-4794	Schempp-Hirth Discus 2B	149	
D-4795	Schleicher ASK 13	13526	JA2189
D-4796	Grob G.102 Astir CS	1495	
D-4798	Schleicher ASK 21	21287	
D-4799-RC	Schempp-Hirth Duo Discus	93	
D-4800	Grob G.102 Astir CS 77	1624	
D-4801	Grob G.102 Astir CS 77	1623	
D-4802	Grob G.102 Astir CS 77	1601	
D-4803	Grob G.102 Astir CS 77	1602	
D-4804	Grob G.102 Astir CS 77	1603	
D-4805	Grob G.102 Astir CS 77	1604	
D-4806	Grob G.102 Astir CS	1520	
D-4807	SZD-30 Pirat	B-463	DDR-1807 DM-1807
D-4808	Grob G.102 Astir CS 77	1622	
D-4809	Grob G.102 Astir CS 77	1608	
D-4810	Schempp-Hirth Duo Discus	299	
D-4811-H	Grob G.102 Astir CS 77	1610	
D-4812-GN	Schempp-Hirth Duo Discus	149	
D-4813	Grob G.102 Astir CS 77	1642	
D-4814-F	Rolladen-Schneider LS8-a	8091	
D-4815	Grob G.102 Astir CS 77	1619	
D-4816-16	Schleicher ASK 21	21333	
D-4817	Schempp-Hirth Janus	44	
D-4818	Schempp-Hirth HS-7 Mini-Nimbus	13	
D-4820	SZD-30 Pirat	B-498	DDR-1821 DM-1821
D-4821	Schleicher ASW 20CL	20857	
D-4822	Grob G.102 Astir CS 77	1644	
D-4823	SZD-30 Pirat	B-500	DDR-1823 DM-1823
D-4824	Schempp-Hirth Duo Discus	89	
D-4825	Grob G.102 Astir CS 77	1655	
D-4826	Schleicher ASK 21	21334	
D-4827	Schleicher ASW 20CL	20858	
D-4829	Grob G.102 Astir CS Jeans	2022	
D-4830	Grob G.102 Astir CS Jeans	2021	
D-4831	Glaser-Dirks DG-300 Elan	3E131	
D-4832	Grob G.102 Astir CS Jeans	2019	
D-4833	Schleicher ASK 21	21337	
D-4834	Grob G.102 Astir CS Jeans	2017	
D-4835	Grob G.102 Astir CS Jeans	2016	
D-4836	Schleicher ASK 21	21336	
D-4837	Schempp-Hirth Discus CS	222CS	
D-4838-WL	Schempp-Hirth Discus CS	224CS	
D-4839	Grob G.103 Twin Astir	3043	
D-4840	Grob G.103 Twin Astir	3045	
D-4841	Grob G.103 Twin Astir	3047	
D-4842	Grob G.103 Twin Astir	3048	
D-4843-PC	Schempp-Hirth Discus 2a	198	
D-4844	Grob G.103 Twin Astir	3053	
D-4845	Grob G.103 Twin Astir	3054	
D-4846	Schempp-Hirth Discus 2b	126	
D-4847	Schempp-Hirth Janus B	194	
D-4849	Schempp-Hirth Janus B	146	D-3090
D-4850	DG Flugzeugbau DG-500 Elan Orion	5E240X76	
D-4851	Grob G.103 Twin Astir	3065	
D-4853-B2	Rolladen-Schneider LS8-18	8412	
D-4855	Grob G 103 Twin Astir	3060	D-4850
D-4857	SZD-51-1 Junior	511199243	
D-4858-4D	Grob G.103 Twin Astir	3073	
D-4859	Schleicher ASW 20CL	20859	
D-4861-FT	Grob G.103 Twin Astir	3076	
D-4863-JD	Schleicher ASW 19B	19420	
D-4864	Schempp-Hirth Discus b	200	I-MBIG D-8111
D-4865-05	Schleicher ASK 21	21265	
D-4866	Grob G.103 Twin II	3593	
D-4867-20	Schempp-Hirth Discus CS	216CS	
D-4868	Grob G.103 Twin II	3595	
D-4869	Grob G.102 Speed Astir IIB	4102	
D-4870-DW	Schleicher ASH 25	25010	
D-4872	Rolladen-Schneider LS8-a	8115	
D-4873	Grob G.102 Speed Astir IIB	4038	
D-4874	Grob G.102 Speed Astir IIB	4046	
D-4875-L	Grob G.102 Speed Astir IIB	4071	
D-4876	Grob G.102 Speed Astir IIB	4030	
D-4877	Grob G.102 Speed Astir IIB	4039	
D-4878	Grob G.102 Speed Astir IIB	4048	
D-4879	Grob G.102 Speed Astir IIB	4047	
D-4880	Akaflieg Braunschweig SB-5E Sperber	5039A	
D-4881	Grob G.103 Twin II	3501	
D-4882	Schempp-Hirth Duo Discus	311	
D-4883	Grob G.102 Standard Astir II	5005S	
D-4884	Schempp-Hirth Ventus 2c	33/87	
D-4885	Grob G.102 Standard Astir II	5006S	
D-4886	Grob G.102 Club Astir II	5008C	
D-4887	Grob G.102 Club Astir II	5009C	

D-4888	Grob G.102 Astir CS Jeans	2068	
D-4889	Schleicher ASK 21	21338	
D-4890	Grob G.102 Astir CS Jeans	2154	
D-4891	Grob G.102 Astir CS Jeans	2152	
D-4892	Glaser-Dirks DG-300 Elan	3E113	OE-5371
D-4895	Grob G.102 Astir CS Jeans	2149	
D-4896	Grob G.102 Astir CS 77	1733	
D-4897	Grob G.102 Astir CS 77	1738	
D-4898-JY	Schleicher ASK 21	21385	
D-4899	Grob G.102 Astir CS 77	1740	
D-4901	Schempp-Hirth Duo Discus	295	
D-4903	Schempp-Hirth Mini-Nimbus C	129	
D-4904	Schleicher ASH 25	25141	
D-4905	Valentin Mistral C	MC 002/77	
D-4906	Valentin Mistral C	MC 003/77	
D-4907	Valentin Mistral C	MC 005/77	OO-ZJT D-4900
D-4909	Glaser-Dirks DG-100G Elan	E180G146	
D-4910	Valentin Mistral C	MC 010/77	
D-4911	DG Flugzeugbau DG-1000S	10-20S20	
D-4912	Glaser-Dirks DG-300 Elan	3E234	
D-4913-N1	Glaser-Dirks DG-300 Elan	3E120	
D-4914	Glaser-Dirks DG-300 Elan	3E236	
D-4916	Valentin Mistral C	MC 016/78	
D-4917-MB	Schempp-Hirth Discus 2B	125	
D-4918	Schleicher ASK 21	21376	
D-4919	Valentin Mistral C	MC 019/79	
D-4922	Valentin Mistral C	MC 023/79	
D-4923	Schleicher ASK 23B	23106	
D-4924	Schleicher ASW 24	24003	
D-4926	Valentin Mistral C	MC 026/80	
D-4928	Valentin Mistral C	MC 028/81	
D-4929	Valentin Mistral C	MC 029/81	
D-4930	Valentin Mistral C	MC 030/81	
D-4931	Valentin Mistral C	MC 031/81	
D-4932	Valentin Mistral C	MC 032/81	
D-4933	Rolladen-Schneider LS6-18W	6370	
D-4934-IL	Valentin Mistral C	MC 034/81	
D-4935	Schleicher ASK 21	21383	
D-4936	Schempp-Hirth Discus CS	219CS	
D-4937-VA	Valentin Mistral C	MC 037/81	
D-4938	Valentin Mistral C	MC 038/81	
D-4939	Valentin Mistral C	MC 039/81	
D-4940	Schleicher ASK 21	21378	
D-4942-UD	Rolladen-Schneider LS6-18W	6363	
D-4943	Valentin Mistral C	MC 043/81	
D-4944	Valentin Mistral C	MC 044/81	
D-4945-5S	Valentin Mistral C	MC 045/82	
D-4946	Valentin Mistral C	MC 046/82	
D-4947	Valentin Mistral C (Reservation)	MC 047/82	
D-4949	Valentin Mistral C	MC 049/82	
D-4950	Schempp-Hirth Duo Discus	80	
D-4951	Valentin Mistral C	MC 051/83	
D-4952	Glaser-Dirks DG-100G Elan	E177G143	
D-4953	Valentin Mistral C	MC 055/85	
D-4955-55	Schleicher ASK 21	21242	
D-4956	Valentin Mistral C	MC 056/86	
D-4957	Schempp-Hirth Discus b	394	
D-4958	Valentin Mistral C	MC 058/85	
D-4960	Valentin Mistral C	MC 060/85	
D-4961	DG Flugzeugbau DG-500 Elan Orion	5E165X20	
D-4962	Valentin Mistral C	MC 062/85	
D-4963	Valentin Mistral C	MC 063/83	
D-4964	Valentin Mistral C	MC 064/85	
D-4966-ET	Rolladen-Schneider LS4	4490	
D-4967	Rolladen-Schneider LS4	4491	
D-4968-BW	Rolladen-Schneider LS4	4492	
D-4969	Rolladen-Schneider LS4	4493	
D-4970	Rolladen-Schneider LS4	4494	
D-4971	Rolladen-Schneider LS4	4496	
D-4972	Rolladen-Schneider LS4	4497	
D-4973	*Test Registration for Rolladen-Schneider LS4-a*		
D-4974	Schleicher ASK 21	21381	
D-4975	*Test Registration for Rolladen-Schneider LS4-b*		
D-4976	Schleicher ASK 13	13699AB	
D-4978	Grunau Baby III	004A	
D-4979	Glaser-Dirks DG-100G Elan	E187G153	
D-4980	Glasflügel Mosquito	89	N302C N39JH
D-4981	Schempp-Hirth Nimbus 2B	152	
D-4982	Rolladen-Schneider LS4-a	4686	
D-4983	Schempp-Hirth HS-7 Mini-Nimbus	20	
D-4984	Schempp-Hirth HS-7 Mini-Nimbus	21	
D-4985	Grob G.103C Twin III Acro	34151	
D-4986	Schempp-Hirth HS-7 Mini-Nimbus	57	
D-4988	Schempp-Hirth HS-7 Mini-Nimbus	65	
D-4989	Rolladen-Schneider LS4-a	4687	
D-4990	Schempp-Hirth Mini-Nimbus B	75	
D-4991	Schempp-Hirth Mini-Nimbus B	76	
D-4992	Schempp-Hirth Mini-Nimbus B	77	
D-4993	Rolladen-Schneider LS4-a	4688	
D-4994	Valentin Mistral C	MC 007/77	
D-4995-AO	Schempp-Hirth Discus CS	218CS	
D-4997	Schleicher K 8B	8868AB	
D-4998	Valentin Mistral A	V-1	
D-4999	Rolladen-Schneider LS4-a	4689	
D-5000	Schmetz Condor IV/2	005	

D-5001	Rolladen-Schneider LS4-a	4690	
D-5002	Neukom S-4D Elfe	414AB	
D-5003	Glaser-Dirks DG-500 Elan Trainer	5E47T17	
D-5004-GL	Rolladen-Schneider LS4-a	4692	
D-5005-HR	Glaser-Dirks DG-500 Elan Trainer	5E48T18	
D-5006-SV	Rolladen-Schneider LS4-a	4693	
D-5007	Glaser-Dirks DG-500 Elan Trainer	5E9T1	
D-5008	Rolladen-Schneider LS4-a	4695	
D-5009	Schleicher K 7 Rhönadler	7239	
D-5010	Schleicher ASK 13	13672AB	
D-5011	LET L-13A Blanik	978503	
D-5012	Schempp-Hirth HS.7 Mini-Nimbus	12	HB-1386
D-5014	Schempp-Hirth Duo Discus	412	
D-5015	Neukom Elfe S-4A	58	HB-1097
D-5016	Schleicher Ka 6CR Rhönsegler	6067	
D-5017	SZD-9bis Bocian 1E	P-734	DDR-3017 DM-3017
D-5018	Schleicher Ka 6CR Rhönsegler	904	
D-5019	Schleicher K 8B	215/61	
D-5020	Grob G.103C Twin III	36013	
D-5021	Grob G.102 Club Astir IIIB	5542CB	OH-640
D-5022	Glaser-Dirks DG-100G Elan	E121G90	
D-5023	Schleicher K 8B	198/60	D-KIFU D-5023
D-5024	SZD-9bis Bocian 1E	P-449	DDR-3024 DM-3024
D-5025	Rolladen-Schneider LS4	4281	
D-5026	LET L-13 Blanik	026227	OH-491
D-5027	Schleicher K 8B	1145	
D-5028	Rolladen-Schneider LS6-c	6283	
D-5029	Schleicher K 7 Rhönadler	7027/A	BGA3218/FFD D-5029
D-5030	Glaser-Dirks DG-100G Elan	E161G128	
D-5031	Schleicher Ka 6CR Rhönsegler	905	
D-5032	SZD-24-4A Foka 4	W-248	
D-5034	Schempp-Hirth Discus CS	220CS	
D-5035	Glaser-Dirks DG-500 Elan Trainer	5E117T49	
D-5036-36	Schempp-Hirth Discus b	494	
D-5037	Schleicher ASK 21	21706	
D-5038	Rolladen-Schneider LS6	6194	
D-5039	Glaser-Dirks DG-300 Elan	3E295	
D-5040	Rolladen-Schneider LS7-WL	7053	
D-5041	Schleicher K 8B	8445	HB-754
D-5042	Schleicher K 8B	199/60	
D-5043	Glaser-Dirks DG-100	33	OE-5048
D-5044 -ZD	Schempp-Hirth Discus b	246	
D-5045	Schleicher K 8B	913	
D-5046	LET L-13 Blanik	173033	OE-5044
D-5047	Glaser-Dirks DG-500 Elan Orion	5E134X1	
D-5049	Schleicher ASK 21	21748	
D-5050	Schleicher ASK 23B	23150	
D-5051	Schleicher Rhönlerche II	3020	
D-5052-AA	Schempp-Hirth Nimbus 3/24.5	1	EC-EBP D-2111
D-5053	Schleicher K 7 Rhönadler	7144	
D-5054	Schleicher K 7 Rhönadler	983	
D-5055	Schempp-Hirth Ventus c	389	
D-5057-UB	Schempp-Hirth Discus b	273	
D-5058	DG Flugzeugbau DG-505 Elan Orion	5E245X77	
D-5059	Schempp-Hirth Ventus c	336	F-WGLL (?)
D-5060	Schleicher Ka 6CR Rhönsegler	966	
D-5063	Schempp-Hirth Ventus a/16.6	82	
D-5064	Schempp-Hirth Discus b	286	
D-5066	Glasflügel H401 Kestrel	2	
D-5067	Schleicher K 8B (Reservation)	8520	
D-5069-69	Glasflügel H206 Hornet	29	OE-5060
D-5070-B2	Schempp-Hirth Discus CS	071CS	OY-XXI D-3934
D-5072	Schleicher ASK 21	21248	
D-5073	Schleicher ASK 23	23018	
D-5074	Schleicher ASK 21	21249	
D-5075	Schempp-Hirth Discus b	289	
D-5076	Rolladen-Schneider LS8-a	8410	
D-5077	Glaser-Dirks DG-100	83	
D-5078	Schempp-Hirth Discus b	284	
D-5079	Schleicher Ka 2B Rhönschwalbe	2001	
D-5080	Schempp-Hirth Janus C	249	
D-5081	Schleicher K 8B	8509SH	
D-5082	Schempp-Hirth Discus b	285	
D-5083	Schleicher K 8B	193/60	
D-5084-GX	Schempp-Hirth Janus C	251	
D-5085-U2	Schempp-Hirth Discus 2B	93	
D-5086	Schleicher Ka 6CR Rhönsegler	1156	
D-5087	Dittmar Condor IV	21/53	
D-5088	Schempp-Hirth Janus C	248	
D-5089	Rolladen-Schneider LS6-c	6274	
D-5090	Schleicher K 8B	8425	
D-5091	Schempp-Hirth Ventus-2cx	89	
D-5092	Schempp-Hirth Duo Discus	249	
D-5093	Glaser-Dirks DG-300 Elan	3E139	OE-5379
D-5094	Grob G.102 Astir CS 77	1613	PH-569
D-5095	Schempp-Hirth Discus b	288	
D-5096	Schleicher K 8B	1014	
D-5097	Schempp-Hirth Discus b	260	
D-5098	Schempp-Hirth Discus b	239	
D-5099	Schleicher Ka 6CR Rhönsegler	6454	
D-5100	Schempp-Hirth Discus 2B	56	
D-5101	Schempp-Hirth Discus b	501	

D-5102-SD	Rolladen-Schneider LS4-a	4708	
D-5103	Schleicher K 7 Rhönadler	1141	
D-5104	Rolladen-Schneider LS4-b	4709	
D-5105	Schleicher K 8B	131	
D-5106	Schleicher K 8B	8591	
D-5107	Rolladen-Schneider LS4-a	4710	
D-5108	Schleicher K 8	217/61	
D-5109	Rolladen-Schneider LS4-a	4711	
D-5110	Schleicher Ka 6E	4035	
D-5111	Schleicher K 8B	8336/A	
D-5112	Glaser-Dirks DG-100G Elan	E134G102	
D-5113	SZD-51-1 Junior	B-1781	
D-5114-HI	Rolladen-Schneider LS4-a	4712	
D-5115-T1	Rolladen-Schneider LS4-a	4713	
D-5116	Schleicher K 7 Rhönadler	174/60	D-5011
D-5118	Schleicher K 7 Rhönadler	1036	
D-5119-5M	Rolladen-Schneider LS4-a	4714	
D-5121	Schleicher Ka 6CR Rhönsegler	993	
D-5122	Rolladen-Schneider LS4-a	4716	
D-5123	Schleicher ASK 21	21513	
D-5124-9G	Schleicher ASW 24	24114	
D-5125	Schleicher ASK 13 (Permit .04)	13425	JA2151
D-5126	Schleicher ASH 26	26072	
D-5128-L4	Schempp-Hirth Duo Discus	251	
D-5129	Schleicher ASK 21	21501	
D-5130	Schleicher K 7 Rhönadler	7252	
D-5131	Schleicher K 8B	1061	
D-5132	Schleicher K 7 Rhönadler	1090	
D-5133	Schleicher ASK 21	21492	
D-5134-L6	Schleicher K 8B	8946	PH-402
D-5135	Schleicher K 8B	8564	
D-5136	Eiri PIK-20D	20569	OE-5132
D-5137	Schleicher ASK 21	21490	
D-5138	Schleicher K 8B	8066	
D-5139	Schleicher ASW 24	24112	
D-5140-ZY	Grob G.103A Twin II Acro	3844-K-90	
D-5141	Grob G.103A Twin II Acro	3856-K-102	
D-5142	Schleicher Ka 6E	4116	
D-5143	Glaser-Dirks DG-300 Elan	3E199	
D-5144 -FF	Glaser-Dirks DG-300 Elan	3E200	
D-5145	Schleicher Ka 6CR Rhönsegler	6009	
D-5146	Schleicher K 8B (Reservation)	221/61	
D-5147-EF	Schleicher Ka 6CR Rhönsegler	6460	
D-5148	Glaser-Dirks DG-300 Elan	3E201	
D-5149	Grunau Baby IIB	5	
D-5150	Glaser-Dirks DG-300 Elan	3E302	
D-5152	Schleicher K 8B	8097	
D-5154	Schleicher ASK 21	21595	
D-5155	Schleicher K 8B	8107	
D-5156	Schempp-Hirth Mini-Nimbus HS-7	38	OE-5157
D-5157	Glaser-Dirks DG-100	99	OE-5128
D-5158	Bölkow Phoebus C	934	HB-1173
D-5161	Rolladen-Schneider LS7-WL	7044	
D-5163	Rolladen-Schneider LS7	7046	
D-5165	Schleicher Ka 6CR Rhönsegler	1117	
D-5166-TJ	Schempp-Hirth Janus Ce	285	
D-5167	Rolladen-Schneider LS4	4468	
D-5168	Rolladen-Schneider LS4-b	41042	
D-5169	Schleicher K 8B	8312	
D-5171	Schleicher K 7 Rhönadler	1143	
D-5172	Rolladen-Schneider LS4-a	4750	
D-5173	Rolladen-Schneider LS4-a	4749	
D-5174-WT	Rolladen-Schneider LS4-a	4748	
D-5176	SZD-24-4A Foka 4	W-249	
D-5177	Schleicher Ka 2B Rhönschwalbe	1134	
D-5178	Schempp-Hirth Discus CS	103CS	
D-5179	Schleicher Ka 6CR Rhönsegler	1127	
D-5180	Rolladen-Schneider LS4	4595	
D-5181	Schleicher Ka 6CR Rhönsegler	1129	
D-5182	Schleicher K 7 Rhönadler	7030	
D-5183	Schleicher K 8B	191/60	
D-5184	Rolladen-Schneider LS1-c	124	OO-ZZQ D-0886
D-5185	Rolladen-Schneider LS4-a	4747	
D-5186	Scheibe Zugvogel IIIA	1064	
D-5187	Rolladen-Schneider LS4-a	4746	
D-5188	Schleicher Ka 6CR Rhönsegler	6467Si	
D-5189-RW	Schempp-Hirth Discus CS	104CS	
D-5191	Schleicher K 8B	8028	D-KEBT D-5191
D-5193	Scheibe SF-27A	6048	
D-5194-8B	Glaser-Dirks DG-100G Elan	E131G99	
D-5195	Schempp-Hirth Nimbus-2B	65	V5-GOD HB-1204 D-3687
D-5197	Schleicher Ka 6CR Rhönsegler	552	
D-5198-3T	Grob G.103C Twin III Acro	34113	
D-5199	Grob G.103C Twin III Acro	34102	
D-5200-1Z	Grob G.103C Twin III Acro	34109	
D-5201	Schleicher K 7 Rhönadler	7012	
D-5202-CF	SZD-36A Cobra 15	W-563	DDR-2302 DM-2302
D-5203	Schempp-Hirth Cirrus	61	
D-5205-MV	Schleicher ASH 25	25009	F-CGKY (F-CIVH) F-CGKY F-WGKY D-5242

D-5207	Schleicher K 8B	8096/A	
D-5208	Grob G.103C Twin III	36009	
D-5210	DG Flugzeugbau DG-1000S	10-44S43	
D-5211	Schleicher K 8B	8092	
D-5212	Glaser-Dirks DG-500 Elan Trainer	5E45T15	
D-5213	Schleicher Ka 2B Rhönschwalbe	2002	
D-5215	Grob G.103C Twin III Acro	34104	
D-5216	Schleicher K 8B	8087/A	
D-5217	Schleicher ASW 17	17004	OE-0939
D-5218	Scheibe SF-27A	6076	
D-5220	Schleicher K 8B	8378	
D-5221	Grunau Baby IIB	6	
D-5222-AH	Schleicher ASW 27	27071	
D-5223	Schleicher ASK 23B	23141	
D-5224	Schleicher ASW 20L	20246	OE-5224
D-5225	Schleicher ASH 25	25011	
D-5226	Schleicher Ka 6CR Rhönsegler	6158	
D-5227	Schempp-Hirth Standard Cirrus B	682	OE-5227
			OE-5088
D-5228	Schempp-Hirth Discus b	72	
D-5229	Schleicher K 8B	8061	D-KARB
			D-5229
D-5230	Schempp-Hirth Discus b	81	
D-5231	Schempp-Hirth Ventus c	296	
D-5233-1W	Grob G.103C Twin III Acro	34116	
D-5234	Schleicher K 8B	8062	
D-5238	Schleicher K 7 Rhönadler	7260	
D-5240	Scheibe Bergfalke II/55	362	
D-5241-AX	Schleicher ASW 24	24091	
D-5244	Grob G 103 Twin Astir	3195	PH-840
			D-5955
D-5245	Schleicher Ka 6CR Rhönsegler	6090Si	
D-5246	Rolladen-Schneider LS4-a	4727	
D-5247	Rolladen-Schneider LS4-a	4726	
D-5248-P8	Rolladen-Schneider LS4-b	4783	
D-5249	Rolladen-Schneider LS4-a	4724	
D-5250	Schleicher K 7 Rhönadler	7063	
D-5251	Schleicher K 8B	8237	
D-5252	Glaser-Dirks DG-500/22 Elan	5E5S1	
D-5253	Rolladen-Schneider LS4	4589	
D-5254	Rolladen-Schneider LS4-a	4723	
D-5255	Rolladen-Schneider LS4-a	4739	
D-5256-LL	Rolladen-Schneider LS4	4596	
D-5257	Rolladen-Schneider LS4-a	4721	
D-5258	Rolladen-Schneider LS4	4597	
D-5260-FO	Schempp-Hirth Nimbus 2C	230	OE-5260
D-5262-DT	Grob G.103C Twin III Acro	34108	
D-5263	Rolladen-Schneider LS4	4598	
D-5264	Rolladen-Schneider LS4-a	4719	
D-5265	Rolladen-Schneider LS4-a	4718	
D-5266	Schleicher Rhönlerche II	3027	
D-5267-WG	Schleicher Ka 6CR Rhönsegler	6127Si	
D-5268	Grob G.103A Twin II Acro	3624-K-11	OE-5269
D-5269	Bölkow Phoebus A-1	719	
D-5270-57	DG Flugzeugbau DG-800S	8-60S17	
D-5272	Schleicher Ka 6CR Rhönsegler	6125Si	
D-5274-L3	Schempp-Hirth Duo Discus	132	
D-5275-MH	Rolladen-Schneider LS7-WL	7101	
D-5276	Schleicher K 8B	8148	
D-5277	Schempp-Hirth Ventus b/16.6	197	
D-5280-FS	Glaser-Dirks DG-300 Elan	3E249	
D-5281	Schleicher Ka 6CR Rhönsegler	6135	
D-5282	Schleicher ASK 13	13085	
D-5283	Schleicher Ka 6CR Rhönsegler	6137	
D-5284-GB	Glaser-Dirks DG-300 Club Elan	3E352C41	
D-5285	Rolladen-Schneider LS4	4414	
D-5286-AP	Rolladen-Schneider LS4	4412	
D-5287	Glaser-Dirks DG-100G Elan	E35G19	OE-5282
D-5288	Glaser-Dirks DG-300 Elan (Permit .05)	3E367	
D-5289	Schleicher Ka 6CR Rhönsegler	6375Si	
D-5291	Siebert Sie 3	3024	PH-529
D-5293	Schleicher K 8B	8192/A	
D-5294	Grob G.103C Twin III	36003	
D-5295	Schleicher ASW 27	27023	
D-5297-97	Schleicher ASK 21	21643	
D-5298	Schleicher ASW 24B	24246	
D-5299	Schempp-Hirth Duo Discus	403	
D-5300	Schleicher Ka 6CR Rhönsegler	6170	
D-5302	Glaser-Dirks DG-100G Elan	E220G186	
D-5303	Schleicher K 7 Rhönadler	7272	
D-5304-S8	HpH Glasflügel 304CZ (Permit .00)	21	
D-5305	Schleicher K 8B	8177	
D-5307	Schleicher Ka 6CR Rhönsegler	6128Si	
D-5308	Schleicher K 8B	8181	
D-5310	SZD-36A Cobra 15	W-647	DDR-2310
			DM-2310
D-5311	Schleicher ASK 13	13040	
D-5312	Schleicher K 8B	8466	
D-5313	Schleicher Ka 6E	4134	
D-5314	Schempp-Hirth Discus CS	042CS	
D-5315	Schleicher K 7 Rhönadler	7279	
D-5316	Schempp-Hirth Duo Discus	231	
D-5318	Schleicher Ka 6CR Rhönsegler	6553	
D-5319	Schleicher Ka 6CR Rhönsegler	6152Si	
D-5320-NT	Schleicher ASW 24	24005	
D-5321-SS	Schleicher ASK 21	21309	
D-5322	Bölkow Phoebus A-1	724	

D-5323	Grob G.103C Twin III Acro	34130	
D-5324	Scheibe SF-34B	5141	
D-5325	Grob G.103C Twin III Acro	34115	
D-5327	Schempp-Hirth Nimbus 3/24.5	56	
D-5328	Schempp-Hirth Ventus b/16.6	180	
D-5329	Schleicher K 8B	8211	
D-5330	Schempp-Hirth Nimbus 3	54	OE-5334
D-5331	Rolladen-Schneider LS7	7107	
D-5332	Schleicher Ka 6BR Rhönsegler	369	D-0409
			HB-614
D-5333	Schleicher Ka 6CR Rhönsegler	6376	
D-5334	Schleicher ASW 20CL	20850	
D-5335	Schempp-Hirth Ventus b/16.6	8	
D-5336-B2	Schleicher ASK 23B	23080	
D-5337	Rolladen-Schneider LS7	7109	
D-5338	Schleicher K 8B	8292	
D-5339	Schleicher K 8B	8085/2	(D-KABL)
			D-5339
D-5340-IK	Schleicher ASK 13	13055	
D-5341	Schleicher K 8B	8492	
D-5343	Schleicher K 8B	8218/EI	
D-5344	Schleicher K 7 Rhönadler	7100	
D-5345	Schleicher ASW 20CL	20851	
D-5346	Schleicher K 8B	8219	
D-5347-LL	Schleicher ASW 24	24142	
D-5348-HC	Schempp-Hirth Nimbus 3/24.5	64	OE-5348
D-5349	Schleicher ASK 21	21312	
D-5351	Glaser-Dirks DG-300 Elan	3E394	
D-5352	Glaser-Dirks DG-300 Club Elan	3E397C61	
D-5353	SZD-48-3 Jantar Standard 3	B-1354	
D-5354	SZD-48-3 Jantar Standard 3	B-1409	OE-5351
D-5355	Scheibe L-Spatz III	803	
D-5356	Schleicher K 8B	8242	
D-5357	SZD-9bis Bocian 1E	P-544	DDR-3357
			DM-3357
D-5358-E	Glaser-Dirks DG-100G Elan	E38G20	OE-5350
D-5359	Schleicher ASK 21	21208	
D-5360-NH	Schleicher ASW 20CL	20727	
D-5361	Schleicher K 7 Rhönadler	7119	
D-5363	Scheibe L-Spatz	1	
D-5364	Schleicher Ka 6CR Rhönsegler	6176	
D-5365	SZD-9bis Bocian 1E	P-521	DDR-3365
			DM-3365
D-5366	Schleicher ASK 13	13119	I-UFFA
D-5367	Schleicher ASK 21	21313	
D-5368	Schleicher Ka 6CR Rhönsegler	6191Si	
D-5369	Schleicher K 7 Rhönadler	7113	
D-5371-HL	Schleicher ASK 21	21214	
D-5372	Schleicher ASW 19B	19403	
D-5375	Schleicher K 8B	8244	D-KANT
			D-5375
D-5377	Schleicher ASK 21	21712	
D-5380	Vogt LO-100 Zwergreiher	1	
D-5383	Schleicher ASK 21	21317	
D-5384-LB	Schempp-Hirth Discus CS	051CS	
D-5385	Schleicher ASK 13	13095	
D-5386	Glaser-Dirks DG-500 Elan Trainer	5E58T25	
D-5388	Schleicher K 7 Rhönadler (Reservation 10.99)	7126	
D-5389	Schleicher K 8	8282/A	
D-5390-PL	Rolladen-Schneider LS6-c	6275	
D-5391	Doppelraab 7	2	RAFGGA589
			D-5891
D-5392	Schleicher K 8B	8460	D-5100
D-5393	SZD-9bis Bocian 1E	P-610	DDR-3393
			DM-3393
D-5394	Schleicher ASK 21	21322	
D-5398	Rolladen-Schneider LS4-b	4880	
D-5399	Glaser-Dirks DG-300 Club Elan	3E402C62	
D-5400	Schleicher ASK 23B	23074	
D-5401	Schleicher ASK 21	21335	
D-5402	Schleicher Ka 2B Rhönschwalbe	272	
D-5403	Schleicher ASW 20BL	20699	
D-5404	Schleicher K 7 Rhönadler	7124/A	
D-5405	Focke-Wulf Kranich III	82	
D-5406	Vogt LO-100 Zwergreiher	17	
D-5407	Scheibe L-Spatz 55	253	
D-5408	Schempp-Hirth Discus CS	286CS	
D-5409	Schempp-Hirth Duo Discus	1	D-8111
D-5411	DG Flugzeugbau DG-1000S	10-61S56	
	(C/n clashes with 10-58S56 current as F-CGRK)		
D-5412	Doppelraab IV	EB-1	
D-5413-2T	Glaser-Dirks DG-100G Elan	E205G171	OE 5404
D-5414	Schleicher K 7 Rhönadler	7130	
D-5416	Schleicher K 8B	8757	
D-5417	Schleicher ASK 21	21637	
D-5418	Schleicher ASK 21	21324	
D-5419	Schleicher K 8B	8285	
D-5420	Schempp-Hirth Nimbus 2B	148	OO-ZYZ
D-5421	Schleicher ASK 21	21709	
D-5422	Schleicher ASK 21	21781	
D-5423	Grunau Baby IIB	2	
D-5424	Schleicher Ka 6CR Rhönsegler	6436	
D-5427	Schleicher ASK 21	21340	
D-5428	PZL PW-5 Smyk	17.04.014	OE-5628
D-5429	Schleicher ASK 21	21328	
D-5430	Glasflügel H304	232	
D-5431	Schleicher K 8B	8470	

D-5432-E1	Schleicher ASK 23B	23092	
D-5433	Glaser-Dirks DG-300 Elan	3E228	HB-1894
D-5434	Glaser-Dirks DG-300 Club Elan	3E280C6	OE-5431
D-5435	Schleicher K 8B	8276	
D-5436	Doppelraab V	1	
D-5437	Schleicher K 8B	8302	
D-5438	SZD-24-4A Foka 4	W-305	(D-2444) DDR-2044 DM-2044
D-5439	Schleicher ASK 21	21321	
D-5441	Scheibe Bergfalke III	5539	
D-5442	Grob G.103C Twin III	36001	
D-5443-WD	Schempp-Hirth Duo Discus	260	
D-5444	Glasflügel H201B Standard Libelle	519	HB-1195
D-5445	Schempp-Hirth SHK-1	27	
D-5446	Schempp-Hirth HS-7 Mini-Nimbus	07	OE-5442 HB-1392 D-3792
D-5447	Scheibe L-Spatz III	825	
D-5448	Glaser-Dirks DG-500 Elan Trainer	5E67T28	
D-5449	Schleicher Ka 6CR Rhönsegler	6633Si	
D-5451	Rolladen-Schneider LS3	3006	PH-545
D-5453	Schleicher K 7 Rhönadler	7149	
D-5454	Schleicher Ka 6CR Rhönsegler	6261	
D-5455	Schleicher Ka 2B Rhönschwalbe	189	
D-5456	Schleicher K 8B	8448	
D-5457	Grunau Baby IIB	54	
D-5458	Grunau Baby IIB	030888	BGA1289 RAFGSA
D-5459	Scheibe SF-27A	6086	
D-5460	Glaser-Dirks DG-500 Elan Trainer	5E108T44	
D-5463	Rolladen-Schneider LS8-18	8314	
D-5464	Schleicher K 7 Rhönadler	7154	
D-5465	Schleicher K 7 Rhönadler	7257	
D-5466	Schempp-Hirth Ventus 2b	66	
D-5467	Schempp-Hirth Nimbus 2B	158	OE-5467 D-2828
D-5468	Schleicher Ka 6 Rhönsegler	176	
D-5470	Glasflügel Standard Libelle 201B	524	PH-470
D-5471-71	Schempp-Hirth Ventus 2b	51	
D-5474-D7	Schempp-Hirth Janus Ce	275	
D-5475-OS	Schempp-Hirth Discus b	390	
D-5476	Schempp-Hirth Discus b	66/392	
D-5477	Scheibe L-Spatz 55	588	
D-5480	Akaflieg Braunschweig SB-5B Sperber	5013/A	
D-5481	Schleicher Ka 2B Rhönschwalbe	213	
D-5483	Schleicher Ka 2B Rhönschwalbe	197	
D-5485	Schleicher Ka 6CR Rhönsegler	6468/Si	
D-5486	Scheibe L-Spatz 55	02	
D-5487	Schleicher K 8B	8321/A	D-KANC D-5487
D-5488	Glaser-Dirks DG-500 Elan Trainer	5E120T51	
D-5489	Schleicher Ka 6BR Rhönsegler	531	
D-5491-6K	Schleicher ASK 21	21652	
D-5493	Schempp-Hirth Discus CS	184CS	
D-5494-CA	Schempp-Hirth Discus CS	182CS	
D-5495	LET L-13 Blanik	026808	
D-5496	Schempp-Hirth Discus 2B	112	
D-5499	Rolladen-Schneider LS4-b	4934	
D-5500	Ahrens LY-542K Stösser (Permit .05)	V-1	D-7128 D-0026 D-5440
D-5501	LET L-23 Super Blanik	938110	OK-3201
D-5502	Schleicher K 7 Rhönadler	7159	
D-5503	Schleicher Ka 2B Rhönschwalbe	224	
D-5504	Schleicher K 8B	8337/A	
D-5505	Scheibe L-Spatz 55 (Permit)	4/58	OO-ZVU D-5505
D-5507	Glaser-Dirks DG-300 Club Elan	3E383C55	
D-5508-K2	Glaser-Dirks DG-300 Club Elan	3E388C57	
D-5509	Neukom S-4D Elfe	422AB	
D-5510	Rolladen-Schneider LS4-b	4881	
D-5511	Schleicher ASK 13	13028	
D-5512	Rolladen-Schneider LS6-18W	6384	
D-5513-FY	SZD-55-1	551193051	PH-993
D-5514	Schleicher ASK 13	13205	D-0353
D-5515	Grunau Baby III	1	
D-5516	SZD-48-1 Jantar Standard 2	W-897	OE-5216
D-5517	Valentin Mistral C	MC 036/81	OE-5517 D-4936
D-5518	SZD-55-1	X-144	SP-3501 SP-P501
D-5519	Schleicher Ka 6CR Rhönsegler	6419	
D-5520	Schleicher Ka 6CR Rhönsegler	6515	
D-5521	Schleicher K 7 Rhönadler	7122	
D-5522	Rolladen-Schneider LS1-d	136	OY-XCI D-2048
D-5524	Schleicher Ka 6E	4147	
D-5526	Glaser-Dirks DG-300 Elan	3E231	OE-5412
D-5527	Schleicher ASW 27B	27220	
D-5528	Grob G.103C Twin III Acro	34177	
D-5529	Rolladen-Schneider LS4	4117	
D-5530-30	Schleicher ASK 23B	23146	
D-5531-LX	SZD-41A Jantar Standard	B-933	OE-5231
D-5532	Grob G.103C Twin III Acro	34147	
D-5533	Schleicher Ka 2B Rhönschwalbe	253	
D-5534	Glaser-Dirks DG-300 Elan	3E72	OE-5513 D-3350

D-5535	Schleicher Ka 6CR Rhönsegler	6505	
D-5536	Schempp-Hirth Ventus 2b	35	
D-5537	Schleicher Ka 6CR Rhönsegler	6257Si	
D-5539-R2	Schempp-Hirth Discus 2B	110	
D-5540	Rolladen-Schneider LS4-b	41049	
D-5541	Rolladen-Schneider LS7-WL	7165	OY-XZZ
D-5543	Schempp-Hirth Standard Cirrus	46	PH-559 D-0566
D-5545	Schleicher Ka 6 Rhönsegler	292	
D-5546-E8	Schempp-Hirth Duo Discus	333	
D-5548-A2	Schempp-Hirth Duo Discus	117	
D-5550	SG-38 Schulgleiter	0010	
D-5551	Scheibe Specht (Reservation)	02/55	D-0314 OE-0319
D-5552	Schempp-Hirth Discus b	492	
D-5553-22	Rolladen-Schneider LS6-b	6138	
D-5554	Schleicher Ka 6BR Rhönsegler	355	
D-5555	Schempp-Hirth Ventus-2ax	149	
D-5556	Rolladen-Schneider LS8-18	8361	
D-5557	Schleicher Ka 6E	4130	
D-5560	Scheibe L-Spatz 55	721	
D-5561	Glasflügel H303 Mosquito B	178	HB-1517
D-5562-AB	Rolladen-Schneider LS8-18	8362	
D-5563	Schleicher K 8B	8372	
D-5564	Glaser-Dirks DG-300 Club Elan	3E316C25	
	(See also HB-1984, same c/n quoted, both current)		
D-5565	Glaser-Dirks DG-500 Elan Orion	5E140X5	
D-5566	Glaser-Dirks DG-300 Elan	3E398	
D-5569	Schleicher K 8B	8566	
D-5570	Schleicher Ka 6E	4006	
D-5571	Rolladen-Schneider LS6-b	6143	
D-5573	Glaser-Dirks DG-101G Elan	E66G41	HB-1586
D-5574	Schleicher K 8B	8569	
D-5575-4X	Schleicher Ka 6CR Rhönsegler	6588	
D-5576	Schleicher Ka 6CR Rhönsegler	6313	
D-5577	Schleicher K 7 Rhönadler	7172	
D-5578	Glasflügel H301B Libelle	42	
D-5580	Schempp-Hirth Janus CT	17/280	
D-5581	DG Flugzeugbau DG-1000S	10-17S17	
D-5582-Y	Schempp-Hirth Discus b	178	
D-5583	Schleicher K 7 Rhönadler	7176	
D-5584	Schempp-Hirth Discus b	186	
D-5585	Schempp-Hirth Standard Austria SH	48	
D-5587	Schleicher ASK 21	21158	
D-5588	Rolladen-Schneider LS4-b	4914	
D-5589-89	Schleicher ASK 21	21159	
D-5590	Schleicher Ka 6BR Rhönsegler	202	
D-5592	Scheibe SF-27A	6100	
D-5593	Schleicher K 8B	8394SH	
D-5594	Schleicher K 8B	8375	
D-5595	Marganski MDM-1 Fox	231	
D-5596	Schleicher Ka 2B Rhönschwalbe	403	
D-5599	Schleicher ASW 27	27015	
D-5600	Ahrens Delphin (Reservation - cld?)	V-1	
D-5601	Schleicher Ka 6CR Rhönsegler	6428Si	
D-5602	Scheibe SF-27A	6074	
D-5603	Glaser-Dirks DG-300 Elan	3E376	
D-5604	Glaser-Dirks DG-300 Club Elan	3E381C54	
D-5605	Schleicher ASK 21	21689	
D-5606	Schleicher K 7 Rhönadler (Reservation - cld?)	7179	
D-5608	Schempp-Hirth Duo Discus	246	
D-5609	Schleicher K 8B	8435/A	
D-5610	Scheibe SF-27A	6050	
D-5611	Bölkow Phoebus A-1	733	
D-5612	SZD-50-3 Puchacz	B-1329	DDR-3612
D-5614	Glaser-Dirks DG-200	2-164	HB-1614
D-5617	Schleicher K 8B	8416	
D-5618	Schleicher ASK 21	21717	
D-5619-JB	Glaser-Dirks DG-200/17	2-182/1760	
D-5620	Schleicher ASK 13	13680AB	
D-5621	Schleicher K 8B	8665	D-KLSV
D-5622	Schleicher ASK 13	13679AB	
D-5623	Schleicher Ka 6CR Rhönsegler	6323	
D-5624	Schleicher ASK 13	13689AB	
D-5625	Schleicher ASK 21	21081	
D-5626	Schleicher ASK 21	21082	
D-5627-HS	Schleicher ASW 19B	19354	
D-5628	Schleicher ASK 21	21083	
D-5629	Schleicher ASK 21	21084	
D-5630	Schleicher K 7 Rhönadler	413	
D-5631	Schleicher Ka 6BR Rhönsegler	416	
D-5632	SZD-50-3 Puchacz	B-1396	DDR-3632
D-5633	Schleicher ASK 21	21722	
D-5634	Schleicher ASH 26	26174	
D-5635	LET L-13 Blanik	026925	OE-5130
D-5636	Schleicher ASW 27	27045	OE-5636
D-5637	Schleicher Ka 6BR Rhönsegler	397	
D-5638	Schleicher K 8B	8472	
D-5639	Schleicher K 7 Rhönadler	7178/A	
D-5640	Schleicher Ka 6BR Rhönsegler	383	
D-5641	Schempp-Hirth Discus 2B	88	
D-5642	Glaser-Dirks DG-100G Elan	E167G133	
D-5643	Scheibe L-Spatz 55 (Reservation 1.00)	1/59	
D-5644	Schleicher Ka 6CR Rhönsegler	6347Si	
D-5645	Schleicher K 8	451	
D-5646	Schleicher Ka 6E	4039	
D-5647	DG Flugzeugbau DG-303 Elan Acro	3E475A20	OE-5641

D-5648	Rolladen-Schneider LS8-18	8351	
	Also currently quoted as Schleicher ASW-28	28016	
D-5649	Scheibe L-Spatz 55	3	
D-5650	Rolladen-Schneider LS1-f	312	
D-5651	Schleicher Ka 6CR Rhönsegler	1071	
D-5652	Schleicher Ka 6CR Rhönsegler	6360	
D-5653-AH	Rolladen-Schneider LS8-a	8403	
D-5654	Schleicher Ka 6CR Rhönsegler	6352	
D-5656	Schleicher ASK 13	13618	
D-5657-57	Schempp-Hirth Discus CS	097CS	
D-5658	Schleicher ASK 21	21593	
D-5659	Schleicher K 7 Rhönadler	502	
D-5660	SZD-50-3 Puchacz	B-1551	DDR-3660
D-5661	Glaser-Dirks DG-500 Elan Trainer	5E116T48	
D-5662	Schleicher Ka 6CR Rhönsegler	6424	
D-5663	Schleicher ASK 21	21125	HB-1663
D-5664-ZL	Rolladen-Schneider LS8-a	8358	
D-5665	Schleicher K 8B	216	
D-5666	Schempp-Hirth Discus CS	156CS	
D-5668-B1	Schempp-Hirth Ventus c	356	HB-1946
D-5670-D2	Schempp-Hirth Discus 2B	39	
D-5671	Schleicher K 8B	8436	
D-5673	Rolladen-Schneider LS6	6144	
D-5674	Schleicher K 8	508	
D-5676	Schleicher ASK 23B	23135	
D-5677	Schleicher K 8	514	
D-5680	Schleicher Ka 6CR Rhönsegler	6381	
D-5684	Schleicher Ka 6BR Rhönsegler	483	
D-5686	Schleicher K 8	512	
D-5688	Schleicher K 7 Rhönadler	548	
D-5692	Schleicher K 8B	545	
D-5694	Rolladen-Schneider LS4	4427	
D-5695	Bölkow Phoebus A-1	749	
D-5699	Schleicher K 7 Rhönadler	577	
D-5700	Schempp-Hirth Ventus c	334	OO-PPC
D-5701	Schleicher ASK 13	13001	
D-5702	Glaser-Dirks DG-600	6-30	
D-5703	Nord 1300 (Grunau Baby IIB)	120	F-CRLT
D-5704	Schleicher K 8B	134/59	
D-5705	Schempp-Hirth Duo Discus	285	
D-5706	Rolladen-Schneider LS4-b	41044	
D-5708-GG	Rolladen-Schneider LS8-18	8363	
D-5709	Schleicher K 7 Rhönadler	578	
D-5710	Glaser-Dirks DG-300 Elan	3E180	
D-5711	Schleicher ASK 21	21774	
D-5712	Schempp-Hirth Discus 2B	143	
D-5713	Schleicher ASW 19B	19395	
D-5715	Schleicher K 8B	107/58	
D-5716-IT	Glaser-Dirks DG-300 Elan	3E185	
D-5717	Schleicher K 7 Rhönadler	605	
D-5718	Schleicher ASW 28-18 (Permit 4.04)	28709	
D-5720	Glasflügel 604	6	I-ETAB
D-5721-21	Schleicher ASK 21	21714	
D-5722	Glaser-Dirks DG-100G Elan	E192G158	
D-5725	Glaser-Dirks DG-300 Elan	3E163	
D-5727-HK	Schleicher K 8B	153/59	
D-5728	Schleicher K 8B	685	
D-5729-NM	Glaser-Dirks DG-300 Elan	3E186	
D-5731	Schleicher K 8B	138/59	OE-5413 D-5731
D-5732	Schleicher K 8B	8023/SH/A	
D-5733	Glaser-Dirks DG-300 Elan	3E189	
D-5734	Schempp-Hirth Duo Discus	109	
D-5736	Schleicher K 7 Rhönadler	701	
D-5737	Schleicher Ka 6CR Rhönsegler	6562	
D-5738	Schleicher K 8B	8465	
D-5739	Glaser-Dirks DG-300 Elan	3E190	
D-5741	Rolladen-Schneider LS4	4625	
D-5742	Grob G.102 Astir CS Jeans	2172	PL-. . (Belgian Air Cadets)
D-5743	Rolladen-Schneider LS4	4626	
D-5747	Glasflügel BS.1	13	
D-5748	Schleicher K 8B (Reservation - cld?)	737	
D-5750-RR	Grob G.103C Twin III	36010	
D-5751	Rolladen-Schneider LS4	4629	
D-5752-B52	Schleicher ASK 21	21683	
D-5755	SZD-30 Pirat	B-359	DDR-1755 DM-1755
D-5757	Schleicher Ka 6CR Rhönsegler	718	
D-5758	Rolladen-Schneider LS4	4630	
D-5760	Schleicher K 8B	850	
D-5761	Akaflieg Braunschweig SB-5E Sperber	5016	
D-5762	SZD-30 Pirat	B-365	DDR-1762 DM-1762
D-5763	Schleicher ASW 28	28043	
D-5764	Schleicher K 8B	163/60	
D-5765	Schleicher K 8	110/58	
D-5766	Schleicher ASW 20	20603	OH-666
D-5767	Rolladen-Schneider LS4	4631	
D-5770	Schempp-Hirth Discus CS	043CS	
D-5772	Schleicher K 8	158/59	
D-5773	Schleicher K 7 Rhönadler	77/57	
D-5774	Rolladen-Schneider LS8-18	8285	
D-5776-RA	Schempp-Hirth Duo Discus	133	
D-5777	Schleicher K 8B	640	D-KOBU D-5747
D-5778	Schleicher K 7 Rhönadler	778	
D-5779	Schleicher K 7 Rhönadler	7218	
D-5780	Scheibe SF-27A	6087	
D-5781	Schleicher K 7 Rhönadler	832	
D-5782	Schleicher K 8 (Permit .05)	170/60	
D-5783	Rolladen-Schneider LS7	7061	
D-5784-IMM	Rolladen-Schneider LS7-WL	7062	
D-5787	Start & Flug H-101 Salto	68	
D-5790	Schempp-Hirth Ventus c	579	OY-XSS
D-5791	SZD-30 Pirat (cld 1.93 ?)	B-434	DDR-1791 DM-1791
D-5792	Rolladen-Schneider LS7	7064	
D-5793	Vogt LO-100 Zwergreiher	21	D-4093
D-5794	Schleicher Ka 6CR Rhönsegler	848	
D-5796	Schleicher K 7 Rhönadler	866	
D-5797	Rolladen-Schneider LS6-18W	6358	
D-5798	Schleicher K 8	168/60	
D-5799	Schleicher ASK 13	13032	
D-5801-Y5	Rolladen-Schneider LS8-18	8333	
D-5802	Schleicher K 8B (Reservation)	841	
D-5803	Schleicher K 8B	842	
D-5804	SZD-51-1 Junior	B-1920	DDR-2804
D-5805	Glaser-Dirks DG-300 Elan	3E106	
D-5806	Schleicher K 8B	877	
D-5807	Pilatus B4-PC11AF	111	HB-3221
D-5808-AA	Rolladen-Schneider LS8-a	8406	
D-5809	Schempp-Hirth Duo Discus	405	
D-5810	Schleicher ASK 21	21696	
D-5811	Schleicher ASW 24	24213	
D-5812	Rolladen-Schneider LS8-18	8343	
D-5813	VEB LOM 57 Libelle	015	
D-5814	Schleicher K 8B	8428/A	
D-5815	Glaser-Dirks DG-500 Elan Trainer	5E86T37	
D-5816	Schempp-Hirth Ventus 2a	112	
D-5817-6F	SZD-30 Pirat	B-485	DDR-1817 DM-1817
D-5818	Schleicher Ka 6CR Rhönsegler	6650	
D-5819	Schleicher ASW 27	27179	
D-5820	Schleicher K 7 Rhönadler	7220	
D-5821	Schleicher Ka 6CR Rhönsegler	6425	
D-5822	SZD-30 Pirat	B-499	DDR-1822 DM-1822
D-5823-C2	Schleicher K 8B	8501	
D-5824	Schleicher K 8B	AB8980	
D-5825	Schleicher Ka 6CR	6099Si	D-5812
D-5826	Rolladen-Schneider LS8-18	8407	
D-5827-LT	Schleicher ASW 27	27178	
D-5828	Rock Geier IIB	03	
D-5829	DG Flugzeugbau DG-500 Elan Orion	5E232X70	
D-5830	Rolladen-Schneider LS3-a	3454	F-CESS
D-5831	Glaser-Dirks DG-100G Elan	E93G64	
D-5832	Schleicher ASK 13	13012	
D-5833	SZD-30 Pirat	B-512	DDR-1833 DM-1833
D-5834	Schleicher ASW 24B	24227	
D-5835	Schleicher K 8B	8429SH	
D-5836	Schleicher Ka 6CR Rhönsegler	6579	
D-5837	Scheibe SF-27A	6067	
D-5838	Glaser-Dirks DG-100G Elan	E92G63	
D-5839	SZD-55-1	551196092	
D-5840	Rolladen-Schneider LS6	6108	
D-5841	Schleicher Ka 6CR Rhönsegler	6577	
D-5842	Glaser-Dirks DG-100G Elan	E89G61	
D-5843	Scheibe SF-27A	6068	
D-5844	Schleicher K 7 Rhönadler	7265	
D-5845	Scheibe SF-27A	6069	
D-5846	Glasflügel H304	224	
D-5847	Glasflügel H304	225	
D-5849	Schleicher Ka 6E	4139	
D-5850	Glasflügel BS.1	6	
D-5851	Schleicher ASK 21	21753	
D-5852	Schleicher K 8B	8737/A	
D-5854	Schleicher Ka 6CR Rhönsegler	6637	
D-5855	Scheibe Zugvogel IIIA	1055	
D-5856	Schleicher Ka 6CR Rhönsegler (Permit .02)	6290	
D-5857	Schleicher ASK 13	13068	
D-5858	Schleicher K 8B	8748	
D-5859-ISY	Neukom S-4D Elfe	415AB	
D-5860	Rolladen-Schneider LS6-b	6110	
D-5861	Glaser-Dirks DG-100G Elan	E88G60	
D-5862	Focke-Wulf Weihe 50 (Reservn - cld?) (Now in Wasserkuppe museum)	unkn	
D-5863	Schleicher Ka 6CR Rhönsegler	6378	
D-5864-64	Rolladen-Schneider LS4-b	41035	
D-5865	Glasflügel H304	258	
D-5866	Grob G.103C Twin III Acro	34195	
D-5867	Glaser-Dirks DG-100G Elan	E98G68	
D-5868-B5	Rolladen-Schneider LS8-18	8364	
D-5869	Glasflügel H301 Libelle	15	HB-794
D-5870	Grob G.102 Astir CS	1021	
D-5871	Grob G.102 Astir CS	1022	
D-5872	Glaser-Dirks DG-100G Elan	E96G66	
D-5875	Grob G.102 Astir CS (Permit)	1026	
D-5876	Grob G.102 Astir CS	1027	
D-5877-CK	Glaser-Dirks DG-202	2-169	
D-5878	Grob G.102 Astir CS	1029	
D-5879	Grob G.102 Astir CS	1030	
D-5880-NY	Grob G.102 Astir CS	1031	

D-5881	Grob G.102 Astir CS	1032	
D-5883	SZD-30 Pirat	S-01.29	DDR-1883 DM-1883
D-5884	Glaser-Dirks DG-200/17C	2-170CL16	
D-5885-8X	Schempp-Hirth Ventus 2a	56	
D-5886	Rolladen-Schneider LS1-f	256	
D-5888	SZD-30 Pirat	S-02.44	DDR-1888 DM-1888
D-5889	HBV Diamant	008	HB-889
D-5890	Rolladen-Schneider LS6-b	6111	
D-5891-EY	Glasflügel H201B Standard Libelle	503/A	
D-5895-BT	Schempp-Hirth Janus B	157	
D-5896-FJ	Schempp-Hirth Nimbus 3/24.5	25	
D-5898	Rolladen-Schneider LS3-a	3284	
D-5899	Schleicher ASK 21	21711	
D-5900	Grob G.103C Twin III Acro	34185	
D-5901-81	Rolladen-Schneider LS3-a	3160	
D-5902	Rolladen-Schneider LS4	4137	
D-5903	Rolladen-Schneider LS4	4153	
D-5904-BG	Rolladen-Schneider LS4	4118	
D-5905	Glaser-Dirks DG-300 Elan	3E233	
D-5906	Rolladen-Schneider LS6-c	6276	
D-5907	Glasflügel H303 Mosquito B	152	
D-5908-HJ	Schempp-Hirth Ventus 2b	116	
D-5909	Schleicher ASW 19B	19330	
D-5910	Grob G.103 Twin II	3640	
D-5911	Grob G.103 Twin II	3641	
D-5912	Rolladen-Schneider LS4-b	41037	
D-5913	Grob G.102 Astir CS 77	1822	
D-5914 -EP	Grob G.102 Astir CS 77	1823	
D-5915	Grob G.102 Astir CS Jeans	2232	
D-5916	Grob G.102 Astir CS Jeans	2236	
D-5917-E1	Schleicher ASW 28	28027	
D-5918	Grob G.102 Astir CS Jeans	2238	
D-5919	Grob G.102 Astir CS 77	1824	
D-5920	Grob G.102 Speed Astir IIB	4028	
D-5922	Schempp-Hirth Discus 2B	105	
D-5923	Schleicher ASK 21	21108	
D-5924	Glaser-Dirks DG-100G Elan	E122G91	
D-5925	Rolladen-Schneider LS8-18	8365	
D-5926	Glaser-Dirks DG-100G Elan	E124G92	
D-5927	Glasflügel H304	239	
D-5928	Glasflügel H304	240	
D-5929	Glasflügel H304	242	
D-5930-A4	Schempp-Hirth Ventus 2b	107	
D-5931	Glasflügel H304	236	
D-5933	Schleicher ASW 20CL	20756	
D-5934	Schleicher ASW 19B	19407	
D-5935	Schleicher ASW 20L	20759	
D-5936	Schleicher ASW 20BL	20647	
D-5940	Scheibe Bergfalke IV	5863	
D-5941-TY	Schempp-Hirth Discus 2B	153	
D-5942	Schleicher ASK 21	21587	
D-5944	Valentin Mistral C	MC 057/85	OO-ZHI D-4957
D-5945	Grob G.102 Astir CS 77	1828	
D-5947	Grob G.102 Astir CS Jeans	2242	
D-5948	Grob G.102 Astir CS Jeans	2243	
D-5950	Grob G.102 Astir CS 77	1825	
D-5952	SZD-48-3 Jantar Standard 3	B-1952	CCCP-1952
D-5954	Grob G.103 Twin Astir	3194	
D-5955	SZD-55-1	551193059	SP-3602
D-5956	Grob G.103 Twin Astir	3196	
D-5959	FFA Diamant 18	75	OO-ZDI
D-5960	Grob G.103 Twin Astir	3207	
D-5963	Grob G.103 Twin Astir Trainer	3211-T-24	
D-5967	Grob G.103 Twin Astir	3225	
D-5968	Grob G.103 Twin Astir	3227	
D-5969	Grob G.103 Twin Astir	3230	
D-5970	Rolladen-Schneider LS6-c-18	6359	
D-5971-JA	Grob G.103 Twin Astir	3246	
D-5974	Schleicher ASW 19B	19257	
D-5975	Schleicher ASW 20L	20145	
D-5976	Schleicher ASW 19B	19258	
D-5977	Schleicher ASW 19B	19260	
D-5978	Schleicher ASW 19B	19261	
D-5983	Schleicher ASW 24	24223	ZK-GRC
D-5986	Rolladen-Schneider LS4	4288	
D-5988	Rolladen-Schneider LS4	4341	
D-5990-DM	Eiri PIK-20D	20523	
D-5991-PK	Schempp-Hirth Janus C	133	
D-5994	Schleicher ASH 25	25159	
D-5995	Rolladen-Schneider LS4	4042	
D-5997	Rolladen-Schneider LS4	4030	
D-5998-VE	Rolladen-Schneider LS4	4214	
D-5999	Glaser-Dirks DG-200/17	2-168/1754	D-1532 HB-1634
D-6000	Schempp-Hirth Discus b	158	SE-UEZ
D-6001	Schempp-Hirth Mini-Nimbus B	70	
D-6002	Schleicher K 8B	8145/A	
D-6003	Schleicher Rhönlerche II	10	
D-6004	Grunau Baby III	02	
D-6005	Schleicher K 7	7071	OY-XDT D-5265
D-6006	SZD-9bis Bocian 1E	P-716	DDR-3004 DM-3004
D-6007	Glasflügel H304	249	

D-6008	Glaser-Dirks DG-300 Elan	3E26	
D-6009	Glaser-Dirks DG-300 Elan	3E29	
D-6010	Schleicher K 7 Rhönadler	7167/AB	
D-6011	Schempp-Hirth Discus b	308	
D-6012	SZD-9bis Bocian 1E	P-725	DDR-3012 DM-3012
D-6014	Eiri PIK-20D	20654	OH-600
D-6015	Akaflieg Braunschweig SB-8	V-1	
D-6016-M2	Schempp-Hirth Duo Discus	238	
D-6017	Schleicher K 8B	8287	
D-6018	Focke-Wulf Kranich III	53	
D-6019-PC	Schleicher ASW 19B	19389	
D-6020	DG Flugzeugbau DG-500/20 Elan	5E171W9	
D-6021	Schleicher K 8B	8248/2	
D-6022	Schleicher Ka 6CR Rhönsegler	6057	
D-6023	Glaser-Dirks DG-500/22 Elan	5E63S10	
D-6024	Schleicher ASW 24	24038	OE-5464
D-6025	Schleicher Ka 6CR Rhönsegler	6557Si	
D-6026	Cumulus CU-II F	01	
D-6027	Schleicher K 8B	8169	
D-6028	Schleicher K 8B	8224	
D-6029-57	Schempp-Hirth Ventus 2a	146	
D-6030	Schleicher K 8B	1	
D-6032	Glaser-Dirks DG-100	17	HB-1276
D-6033	Schleicher Rhönlerche II	84	
D-6034	Schempp-Hirth Ventus c	289	
D-6036	Schleicher K 8B	8215	
D-6037	Schleicher ASK 21	21634	
D-6038	Schleicher K 8B	8397	
D-6040	Rolladen-Schneider LS1-b	33	HB-983
D-6041	Rolladen-Schneider LS4	4627	D-5746
D-6042	Rolladen-Schneider LS7	7157	
D-6043	Dittmar Condor IV	13	LV-EHB
D-6044	Focke-Wulf Kranich III	64	
D-6046	Olympia-Meise	1/95	BGA2080 D-6220
D-6047	Rolladen-Schneider LS6	6116	
D-6048	Kranich 2B-1 (Quoted as amateur-build c/n NIE1994) (Rebuild with wings from BGA1258)	065	BGA1092 SE-SPN Fv8204
D-6049-H2	Rolladen-Schneider LS7	7160	
D-6050	Schleicher K 7 Rhönadler	7064/A	
D-6051-28E	Schleicher ASW 28-18 (Permit 5.04)	28712	
D-6052	Schleicher ASK 13	13020	
D-6053	Schleicher Ka 6CR Rhönsegler	6590	
D-6054	Grunau Baby III	AB-01-53	BGA1754 RAFGSA D-6054
D-6055	Schempp-Hirth Ventus b/16.6	250	
D-6056	Schleicher ASK 13	13027	
D-6057	Grob G.102 Club Astir IIIB	5515CB	
D-6058	Grob G.102 Club Astir III	5518C	
D-6059	Cumulus CU-III F	02	
D-6060	Schleicher ASK 13	13506AB	
D-6061	Doppelraab V	532	D-6062
D-6062	Rolladen-Schneider LS6	6118	
D-6064	Doppelraab V (Permit 8.99)	534	
D-6065	Schempp-Hirth Ventus b/16.6	249	
D-6066	Schleicher K 8B	8700	
D-6067	Schleicher K 7 Rhönadler	02/62	
D-6070	Schleicher K 7 Rhönadler	7074	
D-6071	Focke-Wulf Kranich III	68	
D-6072	Schleicher Ka 6CR Rhönsegler	6292	
D-6073	Focke-Wulf Kranich III	71	
D-6074	Schleicher ASK 21	21467	
D-6075	Schleicher ASW 24	24094	
D-6076	Schleicher ASW 24	24097	
D-6077	DG Flugzeugbau DG-1000S	10-40S39	
D-6078	Schempp-Hirth Duo Discus	436	
D-6080	Schleicher K 7 Rhönadler	7229	
D-6083	Schleicher K 8B	8720	
D-6085-14	Akaflieg Braunschweig SB-10 (Permit .02)	01	
D-6087-NW	Schleicher ASW 24	24098	
D-6088	Schleicher ASH 25	25089	
D-6089-89	Schleicher Ka 6CR Rhönsegler	6484Si	
D-6090	Glaser-Dirks DG-200/17	2-173/1756	
D-6092-N9	Schleicher ASW 24	24100	
D-6093-YK	Schleicher ASH 25	25101	
D-6094	Schempp-Hirth Nimbus 3/24.5	72	
D-6096	SZD-9bis Bocian 1E	P-484	DDR-3096 DM-3096
D-6098	SZD-9bis Bocian 1E	P-485	DDR-3098 DM-3098
D-6099-99	Schleicher K 8B	8071	
D-6100	Glaser-Dirks DG-100G	86G7	
D-6101	Start & Flug H-101 Salto	70	
D-6102	Grob G.102 Astir CS	1001	
D-6103	Schleicher ASK 21	21772	
D-6104	Schleicher Ka 6CR Rhönsegler (Reservn - cld?)	61/09/Sie	
D-6105	Grob G.102 Standard Astir III	5535S	
D-6106	Grob G.103 Twin II	3642	
D-6107	Scheibe Bergfalke III	5570	
D-6108	SG-38 Schulgleiter	14	
D-6110	Grob G.103C Twin III Acro	34179	
D-6111-D2c	Schempp-Hirth Discus-2c (Permit 9.04)	1	
D-6113	Schleicher ASK 13	13619AB	
D-6115	Schleicher Ka 6E	4166	

D-6116	Grob G 102 Club Astir IIIb	5516Cb	OE-5275
D-6118	Schleicher Ka 6CR Rhönsegler	6636	
D-6120	Schleicher ASW 20CL	20865	
D-6121	Schleicher ASK 21	21616	(JA2539)
D-6122-ACD	Schempp-Hirth Duo Discus	68	
D-6123	Schleicher Ka 6CR Rhönsegler	6162	
D-6124	Schleicher K 8B	8331SH	
D-6125	Schleicher Ka 2 Rhönschwalbe	105	
D-6126	Schleicher ASH 26	26059	
D-6127	Schempp-Hirth Cirrus	14	
D-6128	Schleicher ASK 21	21085	
D-6130	Schleicher K 8B	8183	
D-6133-JU	Schleicher K 8B	18/8132	D-3033
D-6135	Schleicher Ka 6E	4164	
D-6136	Schleicher ASK 21	21623	
D-6138	Schleicher ASW 24	24156	
D-6139	Schleicher ASW 24	24158	
D-6140	Schleicher ASW 24	24159	
D-6141	Schleicher Ka 2 Rhönschwalbe (Reservation)	79	
D-6142	Schleicher ASW 24	24161	
D-6143	Scheibe L-Spatz 55	03	
D-6144	Schleicher ASK 21	21426	
D-6146-J6	Schleicher ASK 21	21428	
D-6147	Rolladen-Schneider LS6-c	6277	
D-6148	Doppelraab 7	01	
D-6149	Schleicher ASW 24	24163	
D-6150	Doppelraab 7	0110	
D-6151	Schleicher ASW 24	24164	
D-6153-NI	Schleicher ASK 21	21461	
D-6154	Scheibe Bergfalke III	5563	
D-6155	Schleicher ASK 21	21633	
D-6156	Scheibe Zugvogel IIIB	1106	
D-6157	Schleicher ASW 24	24169	
D-6158	Grob G.102 Standard Astir III	5522S	
D-6159	Schempp-Hirth Discus b	80	I-AYEZ D-5241
D-6161	Schempp-Hirth Discus CS	263CS	OK-9307
D-6162	Grunau Baby IIB	1	
D-6163	Schleicher Ka 6CR Rhönsegler	6026	D-KODY D-6163
D-6164	Schleicher Rhönlerche II	3080Br	
D-6165	Glaser-Dirks DG-300 Elan	3E401	
D-6166	Rolladen-Schneider LS4-b	4955	
D-6167	Schempp-Hirth Janus B	68	PH-616
D-6168	Grunau Baby III (Reservation 11.99)	4	
D-6169	SZD-50-3 Puchacz	B-2053	
D-6170	Schleicher Ka 6CR Rhönsegler (Reservation)	6163	HB-756
D-6171	Schempp-Hirth Discus b	42	
D-6172	Schleicher ASW 24	24170	
D-6174	Schleicher K 10A	10001	
D-6175	Rolladen-Schneider LS6-c (W/o 10.9.02)	6235	
D-6176	Grunau Baby IIB	03	
D-6177	Schempp-Hirth Standard Cirrus B	686	I-SAIL
D-6178	Schleicher K 8B	8046	
D-6179-M6	Schleicher ASK 21	21429	
D-6180	Schleicher ASW 24	24059	
D-6181	Bölkow Phoebus A-1	788	
D-6182-FT	Schleicher ASW 24	24060	
D-6183-BK	Schleicher ASH 25	25076	
D-6184-GT	Schleicher ASK 21	21432	
D-6185	Schleicher ASK 21	21433	
D-6186	Rolladen-Schneider LS6/18W	6287	BGA4427/JDH D-9128
D-6188	Grob G.103C Twin III Acro	34143	
D-6189	Schleicher ASK 21	21701	
D-6190	Grob G.103 Twin II	3734	
D-6191	Rolladen-Schneider LS6	6119	
D-6194	Schleicher K 8B	8065	D-6121
D-6196	Focke-Wulf Kranich III	76	
D-6199-YX	Rolladen-Schneider LS4-b	4915	
D-6200	Fauvel AV-36 (Permit .00)	222	BGA2500 D-6200
D-6201	Pilatus B4-PC11AF	257	OO-ZNU LX-CVA
D-6202	SZD-48-1 Jantar Standard 2	B-1209	OE-5302
D-6203-TG	Glasflügel H304	233	
D-6205-IWS	Schempp-Hirth Janus C	208	
D-6207	SZD-9bis Bocian 1D	P-362	DDR-3207 DM-3207
D-6208	SZD-51-1 Junior	B-1930	I-KASB
D-6210	Rolladen-Schneider LS6-c	6204	
D-6211	DG Flugzeugbau DG-1000S	10-54S53	
D-6212	Vogt LO-100 Zwergreiher	14	
D-6213	Schleicher Rhönlerche II	311	
D-6214	SZD-36A Cobra 15	W-668	HB-1214
D-6215-GD	Schleicher ASW 24	24181	
D-6216	Rolladen-Schneider LS6-c	6207	
D-6217	Glaser-Dirks DG-200/17	2-91/1708	
D-6218	Glaser-Dirks DG-200	2-76	
D-6219	Schleicher K 7 Rhönadler	5	
D-6220	Glaser-Dirks DG-200/17	2-81/1702	
D-6221	Glaser-Dirks DG-200	2-78	
D-6222-AH	Schleicher Ka 6BR Rhönsegler	395	
D-6223	Glaser-Dirks DG-200	2-79	
D-6224	Grunau Baby III	1	
D-6225	Grunau Baby IIb	0001	
D-6226	Schleicher Ka 6BR Rhönsegler	418	

D-6227	Focke-Wulf Kranich III (Reservation)	88	
D-6228	Focke-Wulf Kranich III	90	
D-6229	Scheibe L-Spatz 55	01	
D-6230	Glaser-Dirks DG-300 Elan	3E53	
D-6232	Schleicher Ka 6CR Rhönsegler	6185	
D-6233-GT	Schleicher ASW 28	28049	
D-6234	Schleicher ASK 21	21437	
D-6235	Schleicher ASK 21	21449	
D-6236	Schleicher ASK 21	21450	
D-6237	Schleicher K 7 Rhönadler (Reservation - cld?)	394	
D-6238	Schleicher Ka 6CR Rhönsegler	6574	
D-6239	Schleicher ASW 24	24167	
D-6240	Schleicher K 8	510	
D-6241-MT	Schleicher ASW 24	24191	
D-6242	Schleicher K 8	04	
D-6243	Schleicher K 8B (Reservation - cld?)	515	
D-6244	Schleicher ASW 28-18 (Permit 9.04)	28715	
D-6245	Schleicher ASW 24	24198	
D-6248	Schleicher K 8B	1016	
D-6249	SZD-9bis Bocian 1E (Reservation 2.99)	P-536	DDR-3249 DM-3249
D-6250	Schleicher Ka 6CR Rhönsegler	600	
D-6253	Schleicher ASW 24	24042	
D-6255	Schleicher ASK 21	21416	
D-6256	Schleicher K 7 Rhönadler	7098	
D-6260	Glaser-Dirks DG-600	6-16	
D-6261	Schleicher K 8B	589	
D-6262	Rolladen-Schneider LS6	6043	
D-6263-AD	Rolladen-Schneider LS6-a	6044	
D-6264	Grob G.102 Standard Astir III	5528S	
D-6266	Scheibe SF-34B	5133	
D-6267	Schleicher Rhönlerche II	615	
D-6268	Schempp-Hirth Ventus 2c	13	
D-6269	Schleicher Ka 6E	4020	
D-6270	Schleicher ASW 24	24197	
D-6271	Schleicher K 8B	8415	
D-6272	SZD-55-1	551196088	
D-6273	Schleicher K 8B	734	
D-6274	Focke-Wulf Kranich III	62	
D-6276	Grob G.103C Twin III Acro	34170	
D-6277-FB	Grob G.103C Twin III Acro	34106	
D-6278	Scheibe Zugvogel IVA	1512	
D-6280	Schleicher Ka 6CR Rhönsegler	783	
D-6281	Rolladen-Schneider LS8-b	8419	PH-1281 OY-TTX D-5326
D-6282	Grob G.103C Twin III Acro	34153	
D-6283	Grob G.103C Twin III Acro	34145	
D-6284	Grob G.103C Twin III Acro	34142	
D-6285-LS	Grob G.103C Twin III Acro	34144	
D-6286	Grob G.103C Twin III Acro	34150	
D-6287	Schleicher ASK 21	21069	
D-6288	Schleicher Ka 6CR Rhönsegler	825	
D-6290	Schleicher Ka 6CR Rhönsegler	809	
D-6291	Schleicher K 7 Rhönadler	792	
D-6292	Lanaverre Standard Cirrus CS11/75L	14	F-CEVO
D-6295	Scheibe L-Spatz 55	554	
D-6296	Schleicher K 8B	1	
D-6297-WH	Schempp-Hirth Discus 2B	42	
D-6298	Schempp-Hirth Duo Discus	126	
D-6299	Akaflieg Braunschweig SB-5C (Reservation 11.99)	V-1	
D-6300	Akaflieg Braunschweig SB-5E	6	
D-6301	Neukom S-4D Elfe (Permit .00)	402AB	
D-6302	Schleicher ASW 20L	20101	
D-6304	Schleicher K 7 Rhönadler	888	
D-6305	Schleicher K 8B	5/142/59	
D-6307	SZD-36A Cobra 15	W-628	DDR-2307 DM-2307
D-6308	SZD-36A Cobra 15	W-617	DDR-2308 DM-2308
D-6309	Glaser-Dirks DG-300 Elan Acro	3E429A1	
D-6310-KB	DG Flugzeugbau DG-1000S	10-16S16	
D-6311	Schleicher Ka 6E	4191	
D-6312	Schempp-Hirth Nimbus 3D	12/61	
D-6313	Rolladen-Schneider LS4	4313	
D-6314	Rolladen-Schneider LS8-a	8141	
D-6315-WM	Rolladen-Schneider LS8-a	8142	
D-6317	Schleicher Ka 6CR Rhönsegler	1068	
D-6318-EP	Schempp-Hirth Nimbus 4	9/28	
D-6319	Schleicher Ka 6CR Rhönsegler	1044	
D-6320	Schleicher ASW 20L	20608	HB-1679
D-6321	Schleicher ASK 21	21586	
D-6322	Schleicher Rhönlerche II (Reservation - cld?)	1048	
D-6323	LET L-23 Super Blanik	948126	
D-6324	Schleicher K 8B	1103	
D-6326	Schleicher K 7 Rhönadler	1135	
D-6327	Schleicher ASW 27	27229	
D-6328	Schleicher ASW 28-18	28517	
D-6330	SZD-51-1 Junior	B-2152	
D-6331	Schleicher Rhönlerche II	3007	
D-6332	Schleicher K 7 Rhönadler	422/58	D-5633
D-6335-DS	Rolladen-Schneider LS4	4486	
D-6336-MY	Rolladen-Schneider LS6	6027	
D-6337	LET L-23 Super Blanik	907627	
D-6338	LET L-23 Super Blanik	907628	
D-6340	Grunau Baby III	75	
D-6341	Schleicher K 8B	8294	

D-6342	Schleicher Ka 6CR Rhönsegler	6487Si	
D-6345	Glasflügel H201B Standard Libelle	128	I-AVSC
D-6346	Schleicher K 8B	8359	
D-6347	Schleicher Ka 6CR Rhönsegler	6600	
D-6348	Schleicher K 8B	223/61	
D-6350	Bölkow Phoebus B-1	800	
D-6351	SZD-9bis Bocian 1E	P-538	DDR-3351 DM-3351
D-6352	Schleicher Ka 6CR Rhönsegler (Reservation 8.99)	6306	
D-6354	Scheibe L-Spatz 55 (Reservation)	E-2	D-1354
D-6355	Schleicher K 8B	8381	
D-6358	Schleicher K 7 Rhönadler	7203	
D-6359	Glaser-Dirks DG-500 Elan Orion	5E135X2	
D-6360	Schleicher K 8B	8453	
D-6361	Schleicher K 8B	8547	
D-6362	Schleicher K 8B (Reservation)	8454	
D-6363	Schleicher Ka 6CR Rhönsegler	6497	
D-6364	Schempp-Hirth Discus b	517	
D-6366-F6	Rolladen-Schneider LS6-18W	6356	HB-3177
D-6367	Grunau Baby III	2	
D-6368	Schleicher K 8B	8455	
D-6370	Rolladen-Schneider LS6	6088	
D-6371-09	Rolladen-Schneider LS6 (Permit .02)	6089	
D-6373	SZD-24-4A Foka 4	W-241	
D-6374	Schleicher K 8B	8584	
D-6376	Rolladen-Schneider LS4-b	4965	
D-6377	Schleicher Ka 6CR Rhönsegler	6533Si	
D-6378	Rolladen-Schneider LS6-a	6092	
D-6380	Schleicher Ka 6CR Rhönsegler	857	
D-6381	Schleicher Ka 6CR Rhönsegler	6547	
D-6383	Schleicher Ka 6CR Rhönsegler	6490Si	
D-6385	Scheibe SF-27A	6062	
D-6386	Schleicher K 7 Rhönadler	979	
D-6388	Schleicher ASK 21	21475	I-IVWB
D-6392	Schleicher ASK 21	21090	
D-6394-X11	Schempp-Hirth Standard Cirrus	593	
D-6395	Schempp-Hirth Standard Cirrus	596	
D-6396	Scheibe Bergfalke II/55	307	
D-6397-K7	Grob G.103A Twin II Acro	34041-K-272	
D-6398	Grob G.103A Twin II Acro	34039-K-270	
D-6399	Schleicher Ka 6CR Rhönsegler	1005	
D-6400	Bölkow Phoebus B-1	715	
D-6402	Grob G 102 Speed Astir IIB	4085	PH-1128 D-2593 N166SS D-2593
D-6403	Glaser-Dirks DG-200/17	2-188/1762	
D-6404	Schleicher Ka 6BR Rhönsegler	357	
D-6406	Rolladen-Schneider LS7	7125	
D-6407	Rolladen-Schneider LS7	7126	
D-6408	Schleicher Ka 6CR Rhönsegler	6124Si	D-4671
D-6409	Glaser-Dirks DG-100G (Permit .01)	105G16	LX-CCW D-6101
D-6410	Rolladen-Schneider LS7	7129	
D-6411	Rolladen-Schneider LS4	4173	
D-6412	Grob G.103A Twin II Acro	34059-K-289	
D-6413	Scheibe Bergfalke II/55	244	OE-0413
D-6414	Rolladen-Schneider LS7-WL	7131	
D-6415	Rolladen-Schneider LS4	4043	
D-6416-MS	Schleicher ASW 24	24180	
D-6418	Schempp-Hirth Standard Cirrus	308G	D-2062
D-6420-8M	Schempp-Hirth Janus Ce	298	
D-6421	Grob G.103A Twin II Acro	34064-K-294	
D-6423-MR	Rolladen-Schneider LS6-c	6224	
D-6424	Schleicher ASW 24B	24237	
D-6425	Rolladen-Schneider LS6-c	6226	
D-6426	Glaser-Dirks DG-300 Elan	3E377	I-PBEI
D-6427	Schempp-Hirth Standard Cirrus	19	
D-6428	Rolladen-Schneider LS4	4023	
D-6429-DC	Grob G.103A Twin II Acro	34065-K-295	
D-6430-1D	Glaser-Dirks DG-100G Elan	E141G109	
D-6432	Rolladen-Schneider LS4	4028	
D-6433	Glasflügel H205 Club Libelle	44	
D-6435	Grob G.103 Twin II	3574	
D-6437	Grob G.103 Twin II	3610	
D-6441-WM	Schempp-Hirth Nimbus 2B	171	
D-6443	Schempp-Hirth Mini-Nimbus B	68	
D-6444-H	Glasflügel H205 Club Libelle	45	HB-1244
D-6445	Grob G.103A Twin II Acro	34066-K-296	
D-6446	Grob G.103A Twin II Acro (Reservation)	34067-K-297	
D-6447	Schleicher K 8B	8290/EI	
D-6448	Schleicher ASK 21	21682	
D-6449	Schleicher ASK 21	21418	
D-6450-50	Schleicher ASW 24	24043	
D-6451-U2	Schleicher ASW 24	24046	
D-6452	Schleicher ASK 21	21421	
D-6453	Schleicher Ka 6CR Rhönsegler	6155	
D-6454	Schleicher K 8B	134/04	
D-6456	Glasflügel H401 Kestrel	122	
D-6457	Schleicher ASW 27	27052	
D-6459-5D	Schleicher ASK 21	21743	
D-6460-TX	Rolladen-Schneider LS6	6001	
D-6461	Rolladen-Schneider LS4	4436	
D-6462	Caproni Vizzola A-21S Calif	217	I-VIZP
D-6463-PS	Rolladen-Schneider LS8-18	8327	
D-6464	Grob G 103 Twin Astir	3233	PH-689 PH-659
D-6465	Schempp-Hirth Standard Austria S	15	OO-ZLI
D-6466	Scheibe LCF-2	1	
D-6467	Grob G.102 Club Astir IIIB	5503CB	
D-6468-NA	Grob G.103A Twin II Acro	3638-K-19	
D-6469-69	Grob G.103A Twin II Acro	3639-K-20	
D-6471	Schleicher Ka 6CR Rhönsegler	6317/Si	
D-6472-G2	Rolladen-Schneider LS6-c	6228	
D-6473-GT	Schempp-Hirth Duo Discus	203	
D-6474	Rolladen-Schneider LS1-f	364	
D-6475	Schempp-Hirth Ventus b/16.6	262	PH-773
D-6476-8W	Rolladen-Schneider LS1-f	288	
D-6477	Rolladen-Schneider LS1-f	368	
D-6478-BJ	Rolladen-Schneider LS1-f	287	
D-6479-1W	Rolladen-Schneider LS1-f	369	
D-6480-BX	Rolladen-Schneider LS1-f	373	
D-6481	Schleicher ASW 27	27017	
D-6482	Rolladen-Schneider LS1-f	407	
D-6485	Schleicher ASK 13	13489	
D-6486	Glaser-Dirks DG-100 Elan	E5	
D-6488	Rolladen-Schneider LS8-18	8294	
D-6489	Schleicher ASK 13	13648AB	
D-6490	Schempp-Hirth Duo Discus	101	
D-6491-WS	Schempp-Hirth Standard Cirrus	586	
D-6492	Schempp-Hirth Standard Cirrus	597	
D-6495-GW	Schempp-Hirth Nimbus 2	99	
D-6497	Rolladen-Schneider LS1-f	386	
D-6498	Glasflügel H206 Hornet	40	
D-6499	Schleicher ASW 20CL	20735	
D-6500	Schleicher K 8B	8086	D-KOCE D-4047
D-6501	Rolladen-Schneider LS6-c	6232	
D-6502-WG	Rolladen-Schneider LS6-c	6233	
D-6503	Grob G.102 Astir CS	1006	
D-6504-CW	Glasflügel H201B Standard Libelle	559	PH-504
D-6505	DG Flugzeugbau DG-500 Elan Orion	5E230X68	
D-6506-AV	Grob G.102 Astir CS	1010	
D-6507	Schleicher ASK 21	21579	
D-6508-DL	Schempp-Hirth Duo Discus	235	
D-6509	Grob G.102 Astir CS	1013	
D-6510	DG Flugzeugbau DG-1000S	10-45S44	
D-6512	Glasflügel H205 Club Libelle	107	
D-6513-BB	Schleicher ASW 19B	19414	
D-6514	Schempp-Hirth Ventus c	380	OY-XRX
D-6515	Schleicher ASK 23	23020	
D-6516	Schleicher ASK 21	21250	
D-6517	Schleicher ASK 23	23019	
D-6518	Schleicher ASW 20C	20803	
D-6519	Schleicher ASW 20CL	20804	
D-6520-HG	Schleicher ASW 20L	20552	D-KHHG OE-9394 OE-5294
D-6521-ISV	Rolladen-Schneider LS1-f	479	
D-6522-22	Schempp-Hirth Ventus 2c	24/65	
D-6523	Rolladen-Schneider LS1-f	481	
D-6524-SC	Schleicher ASW 19B	19300	
D-6525	Schleicher ASW 20	20305	
D-6527-HF	Rolladen-Schneider LS8B	8436	
D-6528	Schleicher ASW 28	28065	
D-6529	Schleicher ASW 19B	19306	
D-6530	Schleicher ASK 21	21013	
D-6531-AU	Schleicher ASW 19B	19307	
D-6533-UP	Schleicher ASW 20L	20307	
D-6534	Schleicher ASW 20	20283	
D-6535	Schleicher ASW 20L	20281	
D-6536-2	Schleicher ASK 21	21004	
D-6537	Schleicher ASK 21	21005	
D-6538	Schleicher ASW 20L	20285	
D-6541	Schleicher ASK 13	13617	
D-6542	Schleicher ASW 20L	20287	
D-6543	Schleicher ASW 20L	20290	
D-6544	SZD-9bis Bocian 1E	P-531	DDR-3244 DM-3244
D-6546	Glaser-Dirks DG-200/17	2-135/1733	
D-6547	Glaser-Dirks DG-100G Elan	E48G27	
D-6549	Schleicher ASW 19B	19298	
D-6550	Schleicher ASW 20	20231	
D-6551	Schleicher ASW 20	20291	
D-6552	Schleicher ASK 21	21011	
D-6553-53	Schleicher ASW 20CL	20808	
D-6556	Schleicher ASK 21	21122	HB-1656
D-6560	Rolladen-Schneider LS3-17	3368	
D-6561-ISE	Rolladen-Schneider LS6-18W	6360	
D-6562	Rolladen-Schneider LS3-17	3425	
D-6563	SZD-48-3 Jantar Standard 3	B-1753	DOSAAF PH-648
D-6564	Schleicher ASW 20L	20125	
D-6565	Rolladen-Schneider LS7	7134	
D-6566-6A	Rolladen-Schneider LS6-a	6140	HB-1922
D-6567	Glaser-Dirks DG-100G Elan	E52G30	
D-6568	Schempp-Hirth Ventus c	505	
D-6569	Schempp-Hirth Discus b	370	
D-6570	Schleicher K 7 Rhönadler	283	
D-6571	Schempp-Hirth Janus Ce	274	
D-6572	Rolladen-Schneider LS4	4029	
D-6573	Rolladen-Schneider LS4	4044	
D-6574	Schempp-Hirth Discus CS	019CS	
D-6575-B6	Schempp-Hirth Discus CS	020CS	
D-6576-S4	Rolladen-Schneider LS4	4032	

D-6577	Schleicher ASW 20	20276	N320CF
D-6580	DG Flugzeugbau DG-800S	8-42S11	
D-6581	Rolladen-Schneider LS4	4021	
D-6582	Scheibe L-Spatz 55	302	
D-6583	Schempp-Hirth Discus CS	129CS	
D-6585	Rolladen-Schneider LS4	4432	
D-6586	Rolladen-Schneider LS4-a	4433	
D-6587	Eiri PIK-20D	20600	
D-6588	Rolladen-Schneider LS6	6021	
D-6590	Schempp-Hirth Ventus c	491	
D-6592	Rolladen-Schneider LS4	4507	
D-6593-WX	Rolladen-Schneider LS6	6018	
D-6594	Rolladen-Schneider LS6-a	6019	
D-6595	Glaser-Dirks DG-500 Elan Orion	5E139X4	
D-6596-MT	Rolladen-Schneider LS6-a	6020	
D-6600	Caproni-Vizzola A.21S Calif	238	F-CEUD
D-6601	Schempp-Hirth Janus B	69	D-4989
D-6602-CF	Schleicher ASW 24	24220	
D-6603	Schempp-Hirth Standard Cirrus B	687	
D-6605-AM	Glaser-Dirks DG-300 Club Elan	3E414C68	
D-6606-JK	Schempp-Hirth Mini-Nimbus B	72	
D-6607	Schempp-Hirth Standard Cirrus	633	OE-5062
D-6608	SZD-50-3 Puchacz	B-1094	DDR-3608
D-6609	Glaser-Dirks DG-300 Club Elan	3E406C65	
D-6610	Schleicher Ka 6BR Rhönsegler	368	
D-6611	Schleicher Ka 6E	4183	
D-6612-PX	Schempp-Hirth Discus b	197	OO-ZPX
D-6613	Schleicher ASW 20C	20742	D-KFDW D-5358
D-6614	Caproni-Vizzola A-21S Calif	231	
D-6615-PGO	Caproni-Vizzola A-21S Calif	239	
D-6616	Caproni-Vizzola A-21S Calif	246	
D-6617	Caproni-Vizzola A-21S Calif	248	
D-6618	SZD-50-3 Puchacz	B-1335	DDR-3618
D-6619	SZD-50-3 Puchacz	B-1336	DDR-3619
D-6620	Schleicher K 7 Rhönadler	7115	
D-6621	Schleicher ASK 21	21151	BGA3712/GBW ZD651 BGA2891/ERM
D-6622	Glasflügel H303 Mosquito B	162	
D-6623-HG	DG Flugzeugbau DG-800S	8-190S36	
D-6624	Schleicher ASW 20C	20763	
D-6625	Schleicher ASW 20CL	20755	
D-6626	Schleicher ASW 20	20337	
D-6627	Grob G.102 Club Astir IIIB	5505CB	
D-6628	Grob G.102 Club Astir IIIB	5506CB	
D-6629	Grob G.102 Club Astir IIIB	5507CB	
D-6630	SZD-50-3 Puchacz	B-1392	DDR-3630
D-6633	Schempp-Hirth Mini-Nimbus C	114	D-3392
D-6634	Schleicher Ka 6CR Rhönsegler	826	
D-6636	SZD-50-3 Puchacz	B-1092	DDR-3606
D-6640	Schleicher ASW 19B	19385	HB-1692
D-6641	Schleicher ASK 21	21739	
D-6643	Grob G.103 Twin II	3614	
D-6644-44	Grob G.102 Astir CS Jeans	2143	
D-6645	Glaser-Dirks DG-200	2-40	
D-6646	Glaser-Dirks DG-200	2-44	
D-6647	Glaser-Dirks DG-200	2-45	
D-6648	Gomolzig A.21S Calif	258GO	
D-6649	Rolladen-Schneider LS4-b	4949	
D-6650-GY	Schleicher ASW 28-18	28508	
D-6651-PM	Rolladen-Schneider LS3	3096	
D-6652	Rolladen-Schneider LS3	3088	
D-6653	Rolladen-Schneider LS3	3092	
D-6655	Scheibe Bergfalke IV	5864	SE-TSD
D-6656-56	Schleicher ASK 21	21318	
D-6658	Rolladen-Schneider LS3	3056	
D-6659	Rolladen-Schneider LS3	3184	
D-6660	Marganski MDM-1 Fox	230	
D-6661-A6	Rolladen-Schneider LS6-18W	6377	
D-6662	Glaser-Dirks DG-200	2-47	
D-6663	Glaser-Dirks DG-200	2-49	
D-6664	Schleicher ASW 24	24204	
D-6665	Glaser-Dirks DG-200	2-51	
D-6666	Rolladen-Schneider LS4-b	41019	
D-6668	Neukom S-4D Elfe	403AB	
D-6669	Neukom S-4D Elfe	404AB	
D-6670	Schleicher K 8	517	
D-6671	Scheibe Zugvogel II	1022	OE-0493
D-6672	Schempp-Hirth Mini-Nimbus C	122	
D-6673-4V	Rolladen-Schneider LS4	4079	
D-6674	Rolladen-Schneider LS4	4244	
D-6675-2H	Rolladen-Schneider LS4	4272	
D-6676	Rolladen-Schneider LS4	4164	
D-6677	Grob G.102 Astir CS	1187	
D-6678-T3	Grob G.103C Twin III Acro	34197	
D-6679	Grob G.103C Twin III Acro	34202	
D-6680	Rolladen-Schneider LS4	4000	
D-6681	Gomolzig A.21S Calif	259GO	
D-6682	Gomolzig A.21S Calif	260GO	
D-6685	Rolladen-Schneider LS4	4403	
D-6686-AP	Rolladen-Schneider LS6-a (Permit)	6029	D-6556
D-6687-DH	Schempp-Hirth Duo Discus	272	
D-6688-88	Rolladen-Schneider LS8-18	8428	
D-6690	Glasflügel H303 Mosquito B	105	
D-6691-DW	Schempp-Hirth Nimbus 2C	196	
D-6692	Schempp-Hirth Janus C	87	
D-6693	Schempp-Hirth Ventus 2a	113	
D-6695	Eiri PIK-20D	20590	
D-6696	Rolladen-Schneider LS8-18	8479	
D-6697	Eiri PIK-20D	20604	
D-6698	Eiri PIK-20D	20596	
D-6699-SF	Rolladen-Schneider LS8-a	8281	
D-6700	Eiri PIK-20D	20560	
D-6704	Eiri PIK-20D	20574	
D-6705	Schleicher Ka 6CR Rhönsegler	964	
D-6707-FG	SZD-32A Foka 5	W-440	DDR-2204 DM-2204
D-6708	Eiri PIK-20D	20578	
D-6709-TM	Schleicher ASK 21	21688	
D-6710	Schempp-Hirth Duo Discus	452	
D-6711	Schleicher ASW 19	19040	
D-6712	Schleicher ASW 19	19043	
D-6713-EL	Schleicher ASW 19	19044	
D-6714-1D	Schleicher ASW 19B	19045	
D-6715	Schleicher ASW 19	19046	
D-6717-MG	Rolladen-Schneider LS8-18	8390	
D-6718-MI	Rolladen-Schneider LS8-18	8348	
D-6719	Schempp-Hirth Ventus b/16.6	71	
D-6720	Schempp-Hirth Discus-2a	183	
D-6721	Schleicher ASW 19B	19049	
D-6722	Schleicher ASW 19B	19050	
D-6723	Schleicher ASK 13	13551	
D-6725	Schleicher ASW 19B	19027	
D-6726	Schleicher ASK 18	18041	
D-6727	Schleicher ASK 13	13552	
D-6728	SZD-30 Pirat	B-309	DDR-1728 DM-1728
D-6729-W4	Schleicher ASW 19	19057	
D-6730	SZD-30 Pirat	S-03.29	
D-6731	Glasflügel H303 Mosquito	81	
D-6732	Glasflügel H303 Mosquito	86	
D-6733	Schempp-Hirth HS-7 Mini-Nimbus	51	
D-6734-MC	Schleicher ASW 28	28023	
D-6735	Schempp-Hirth Nimbus 2B	163	
D-6737	Schempp-Hirth Mini-Nimbus B	89	
D-6739	Schempp-Hirth Janus B	78	
D-6740	Schempp-Hirth Mini-Nimbus C	98	
D-6741	SZD-30 Pirat	B-330	DDR-1741 DM-1741
D-6742	Schempp-Hirth Mini-Nimbus C	100	
D-6743	Schempp-Hirth Mini-Nimbus C	101	
D-6744	Schleicher ASW 20	20407	
D-6746	Schleicher ASK 21	21048	
D-6748	Schleicher ASW 20L	20411	
D-6749	Schleicher ASW 20	20412	
D-6750	Schleicher Ka 6CR Rhönsegler	898	
D-6751	Grob G.103 Twin Astir Trainer	3248-T-28	
D-6752	Grob G.102 Astir CS 77	1816	
D-6753	Schleicher ASK 21	21600	
D-6757	Grob G.102 Astir CS Jeans	2225	
D-6758	SZD-30 Pirat	B-362	DDR-1758 DM-1758
D-6761	Rolladen-Schneider LS4	4632	
D-6762	Grob G.102 Astir CS Jeans	2228	
D-6763-DF	Schempp-Hirth Nimbus 2C	206	
D-6764	Schempp-Hirth Mini-Nimbus C	151	
D-6765	Schempp-Hirth Janus C	127	
D-6767	Schempp-Hirth Ventus b/16.6	21	ZS-GPI D-KERA D-6767
D-6768	SZD-55-1	551195077	
D-6769-69	Schempp-Hirth Duo Discus	4	
D-6770-RM	Rolladen-Schneider LS4	4634	
D-6771	Schleicher K 8	2/60	
D-6772	Rolladen-Schneider LS4	4635	
D-6773	Rolladen-Schneider LS4	4636	
D-6774	Rolladen-Schneider LS3-17	3293	
D-6776	Rolladen-Schneider LS3-a	3400	
D-6777	Schempp-Hirth Ventus 2c	50/151	HB-3303
D-6781	Glaser-Dirks DG-200	2-24	
D-6783	Glaser-Dirks DG-200	2-28	
D-6784	SZD-30 Pirat	B-413	DDR-1784 DM-1784
D-6786	Rolladen-Schneider LS4	4637	
D-6787	Glaser-Dirks DG-200	2-41	
D-6788	Glaser-Dirks DG-100 Elan	E14	
D-6789	Glaser-Dirks DG-100 Elan	E10G4	
D-6790	Schempp-Hirth Discus 2B	35	
D-6791	Glaser-Dirks DG-200	2-71	
D-6792	Glaser-Dirks DG-200	2-72	
D-6793	Glaser-Dirks DG-200	2-70	
D-6794	Glaser-Dirks DG-100G Elan	E42G23	
D-6795	Schleicher Ka 6CR Rhönsegler	6530	OE-0795
D-6799	SZD-30 Pirat	B-442	DDR-1799 DM-1799
D-6800	Glaser-Dirks DG-300 Club Elan	3E337C32	
D-6801	Pilatus B4-PC11	170	
D-6802-PI	Rolladen-Schneider LS4	4640	
D-6803	Rolladen-Schneider LS4	4641	
D-6804	Schleicher ASW 20	20206	
D-6806	SZD-30 Pirat	B-462	DDR-1806 DM-1806
D-6807-1R	Schleicher ASW 20	20209	

D-6808	Schleicher ASW 20L	20210	
D-6809	Schleicher ASW 19B	19270	
D-6810	Schempp-Hirth Duo Discus	247	
	(For conversion to Duo Discus T c/n 6/247)		
D-6811	Schempp-Hirth Discus CS	176CS	
D-6812	Schleicher ASW 19B	19273	
D-6813-OD	Schleicher ASW 20	20216	
D-6814-9	Rolladen-Schneider LS8-a	8326	
D-6815	Rolladen-Schneider LS8-a	8329	
D-6816	Schleicher K 7 Rhönadler (Permit)	7069	D-6016
D-6817-JH	Schleicher ASW 27	27080	
D-6818	Grob G.102 Speed Astir IIB	4104	OO-ZPF
	(Restored? Still listed in Belgium)		D-6818
D-6819	Schempp-Hirth Ventus 2b	143	
D-6820	Grob G.102 Speed Astir IIB	4105	
D-6822	Schleicher ASW 28-18 (Permit 11.04)	28722	
D-6823	Grob G.102 Standard Astir II	5032S	
D-6824	Schempp-Hirth Nimbus 2	113	OO-ZBT
D-6825	Schleicher Ka 6CR Rhönsegler	6116	
D-6827	Rolladen-Schneider LS3-a	3114	
D-6828	Rolladen-Schneider LS3-a	3125	
D-6829	Grob G.102 Standard Astir III	5526S	HB-1580
D-6830	Rolladen-Schneider LS3	3335	
D-6831	Rolladen-Schneider LS3-a	3116	
D-6832	Rolladen-Schneider LS3	3337	
D-6833	Rolladen-Schneider LS3 (Permit .00)	3338	
D-6834-SM	Schempp-Hirth Discus 2A	74	
D-6835	Rolladen-Schneider LS3-a	3143	
D-6836	Glasflügel H304	206	
D-6837	Glasflügel H304	207	
D-6838	Glasflügel H304	213	D-KBOO
D-6840	Schleicher ASW 27	27054	
D-6841-TSX	Schleicher ASW 27	27056	
D-6842	Schempp-Hirth Duo Discus	191	
D-6844	Schempp-Hirth Duo Discus	359	
D-6845	Glaser-Dirks DG-100 Elan	E62	
D-6847	Glaser-Dirks DG-100G Elan	E63G38	
D-6849	Schempp-Hirth Janus C	123	
D-6850-G3	Eiri PIK-20D	20598	
D-6852	SZD-30 Pirat	B-572	DDR-1852
			DM-1852
D-6853	Schleicher ASW 20	20582	
D-6854	Schleicher ASK 21	21116	
D-6855	Schleicher ASK 21	21117	
D-6856	Schleicher ASW 22	22010	
D-6857	Schleicher ASK 21	21118	
D-6858WM	Schleicher ASW 20L	20590	
D-6859	Schleicher ASW 20	20586	
D-6861	Schleicher K 8B	140	
D-6863	Glasflügel H304/17	214	
D-6864	Schleicher ASK 13	13511	
D-6865	SZD-30 Pirat	S-01.02	DDR-1865
			DM-1865
D-6866	Schleicher ASW 15B	15438	
D-6867	Schleicher ASW 15B	15439	
D-6870	Schleicher ASK 18	18008	
D-6872	SZD-30 Pirat	S-01.10	DDR-1872
			DM-1872
D-6874	Schleicher ASK 13	13514	
D-6875	Schleicher ASK 13	13515	
D-6876	Schleicher ASK 13	13516	
D-6877	Schleicher ASW 15B	15444	
D-6879	Schleicher ASK 13	13517	
D-6882	Schleicher ASK 13	13518	
D-6883	Rolladen-Schneider LS3	3014	OO-ZBO
D-6884	Schleicher K 8C	81007	
D-6885	Schleicher ASW 15B	15446	
D-6886	Schleicher ASK 13	13519	
D-6888	Schleicher ASK 18	18015	
D-6890-B1	Schempp-Hirth Janus B	92	
D-6891	Schempp-Hirth Janus B	93	
D-6892	Schleicher K 8B	8182	
D-6893	Schleicher ASK 13	13630AB	
D-6896	Rolladen-Schneider LS6	6006	OH-689
D-6897-L	Schleicher ASW 27	27036	
D-6899	Schleicher ASW 15B	15346	OE-0999
D-6900	Glasflügel H201B Standard Libelle	38	
D-6902	SZD-30 Pirat	S-03.42	DDR-1902
			DM-1902
D-6903	FFA Diamant 18	076	
D-6904	Schempp-Hirth Ventus a/16.6	3	
D-6905	Grob G.103A Twin II Acro	3857-K-103	
D-6906	Grob G.103 Twin II	3862	
D-6907-B9	Rolladen-Schneider LS8-18	8139	F-CJCD
D-6908	Grob G.103 Twin II	3864	
D-6909	Grob G.103A Twin II Acro	3859-K-105	
D-6910	DG Flugzeugbau DG-1000S	10-25S25	
D-6911	Schleicher ASW 20C	20786	
D-6912	Schleicher AS-22-2	22201	
D-6913	Schleicher ASW 20C	20780	
D-6914	Schleicher ASW 20C	20781	
D-6916	Rolladen-Schneider LS1-f	367	
D-6917	Rolladen-Schneider LS1-f	428	
D-6918	Rolladen-Schneider LS1-f	429	
D-6919	Rolladen-Schneider LS1-f	430	
D-6920	Rolladen-Schneider LS1-f	431	
D-6921-2F	Rolladen-Schneider LS1-f	432	

D-6922	Rolladen-Schneider LS3-17	3359	
	(C/n also recorded as N412H)		
D-6924	Rolladen-Schneider LS4-b	41022	
D-6926	Rolladen-Schneider LS8-18	8311	
D-6927	Rolladen-Schneider LS4	4361	
D-6928-2G	Schleicher ASW 28	28009	
D-6931	Rolladen-Schneider LS3-17	3329	
D-6933	Rolladen-Schneider LS3-17	3302	
D-6934	DFS Olympia Meise	01	
D-6936-MF	Rolladen-Schneider LS8-18	8437	
D-6937	Rolladen-Schneider LS3-a	3175	
D-6938-KN	Rolladen-Schneider LS3-a	3165	
D-6939	Grob G.103A Twin II Acro	3772-K-58	
D-6940	DG Flugzeugbau DG-1000S	10-15S15	
D-6941	Grob G.103A Twin II Acro	3775-K-61	
D-6942	Rolladen-Schneider LS3-a	3169	
D-6943	Rolladen-Schneider LS3-a	3174	
D-6944	Glasflügel H201B Standard Libelle	43	HB-944
D-6945-TT	Schempp-Hirth Discus CS	119CS	
D-6947	Schempp-Hirth Discus CS	123CS	
D-6948	Schempp-Hirth Discus CS	124CS	
D-6949	Rolladen-Schneider LS3-a	3181	
D-6950	Grob G.102 Club Astir IIIB	5597CB	
D-6952	Grob G.103 Twin II	3765	
D-6954	Schempp-Hirth Discus CS	125CS	
D-6956	Schleicher ASW 20	20280	
D-6958	Schleicher ASW 20	20289	
D-6959	Schleicher ASW 20	20282	
D-6960-DN	Schleicher ASW 20	20293	
D-6963	Schempp-Hirth Discus CS	255CS	
D-6965	Schempp-Hirth Ventus 2c	32/84	
D-6966	Schleicher Ka 6CR Rhönsegler	6544	
D-6968	Schleicher Ka 6CR Rhönsegler	6580	C-GLHB
D-6969	Schleicher ASK 21	21503	
D-6970-70	Grob G.102 Astir CS	1116	
D-6972	Grob G.102 Astir CS	1118	
D-6973	Grob G.102 Astir CS	1119	
D-6974-VA	Schempp-Hirth Duo Discus	178	
D-6975	Grob G.102 Astir CS	1121	
D-6977-2Z	Schempp-Hirth Discus a	41	HB-1823
D-6978-GA	Grob G.102 Astir CS	1124	
D-6979	Grob G.102 Astir CS	1125	
D-6980	Grob G.102 Astir CS	1127	
D-6981	Grob G.102 Astir CS	1128	
D-6983	Grob G.102 Astir CS	1102	
D-6987	Schleicher ASK 23B	23028	OH-698
D-6989	Grob G.102 Astir CS	1089	
D-6990-ZZ	Grob G.102 Astir CS	1091	
D-6991-PH	Schleicher ASK 21	21563	PH-991
D-6992	Grob G.102 Astir CS	1093	
D-6993	Grob G.102 Astir CS	1099	
D-6995	Grob G.102 Astir CS	1016	
D-6996-EZ	Schempp-Hirth Ventus 2a	57	
D-6999	Grob G.102 Astir CS	1020	
D-7000	Rolladen-Schneider LS6-c	6310	D-7900
D-7001	SZD-9bis Bocian 1E	P-713	DDR-3002
			DM-3002
D-7002	DFS Kranich III (Permit)	57	
D-7003	SZD-9bis Bocian 1E	P-714	DDR-3003
			DM-3003
D-7004	SG-38 Schulgleiter (Permit .05)	AB 002/OSC	
D-7005	Schempp-Hirth Ventus a	5	
D-7006	Schleicher ASH 25	25158	
D-7007	Schempp-Hirth Mini-Nimbus C	126	
D-7008	Schempp-Hirth Discus-2b	203	
D-7009	Schleicher K 8B	1108	
D-7010	SZD-9bis Bocian 1E	P-722	DDR-3010
			DM-3010
D-7012	Schempp-Hirth Janus C	111	
D-7013	SZD-9bis Bocian 1E	P-489	DDR-3212
			DM-3212
D-7014	Greif II	V-2	
D-7015	Schleicher K 8B	8291/EI	
D-7016	Schleicher K 8B	925	
D-7017	Glasflügel H304	254	
D-7018-R2	Schempp-Hirth Duo Discus	240	
D-7019	Schleicher ASK 21	21573	
D-7020	Schleicher K 8B	8271SH	
D-7021	Schleicher ASK 21	21562	
D-7022	Schleicher K 8	442	
D-7023	Rolladen-Schneider LS4-b	4898	
D-7024	Schleicher ASK 21	21015	
D-7025	Schleicher ASK 21	21016	
D-7026-5H	Rolladen-Schneider LS4-b	4899	
D-7027	Schleicher ASK 21	21018	
D-7028	Schleicher ASW 19B	19310	
D-7029	Rolladen-Schneider LS4-b	4900	
D-7030	SZD-9bis Bocian 1E	P-454	DDR-3030
			DM-3030
D-7031	Schempp-Hirth Ventus b	41	
D-7032	Schempp-Hirth Nimbus 3/24.5	4	
D-7033	DFS Reiher III	AB R1/OSC	
D-7034-6W	Schempp-Hirth Discus CS	050CS	
D-7035	Schempp-Hirth Nimbus 4T	4	
D-7036	Schleicher Ka 6CR Rhönsegler	806	
D-7037	Glasflügel H201B Standard Libelle	23	OE-5037
D-7038	SG-38 Schulgleiter	AB-002S	

D-7039	Schleicher Ka 2B Rhönschwalbe	229	
D-7040	Rolladen-Schneider LS4-b	4901	
D-7041-WS	Schempp-Hirth Discus CS	280CS	
D-7042	Schleicher Ka 2B Rhönschwalbe	2008/A	
D-7043	VFW Fokker FK-3 V-1	0001	
D-7044	Rolladen-Schneider LS4-b	4902	
D-7045	Schleicher Ka 6E	4201	
D-7046	Schleicher ASK 21	21215	
D-7047	Schleicher ASW 19B	19404	
D-7048	Schleicher ASK 21	21216	
D-7049	Rolladen-Schneider LS4-b	4903	
D-7050	Glasflügel H303 Mosquito	57	
D-7051	SG-38 Schulgleiter	ABX/OSC	
D-7053	Schleicher ASH 25	25133	
D-7054	Schleicher ASK 21	21518	
D-7055	SG-38 Schulgleiter	AB001/OSC	
D-7056	Schleicher K 8B	583	
D-7057	SZD-9bis Bocian 1E	P-477	DDR-3057 DM-3057
D-7058-W1	Schempp-Hirth Discus CS	044CS	
D-7059	Schleicher Rhönbussard	485	BGA395/AGX G-ALKY (RAF) BGA395
D-7060	Schleicher K 7 Rhönadler	7139	
D-7061	Göppingen Gö IV Gövier III	411	OE-0891 D-9009
D-7063	Schleicher ASH 25	25144	
D-7064	Schleicher ASH 25	25146	
D-7066	Schleicher ASK 23B	23132	
D-7067	Rolladen-Schneider LS4	4461	
D-7068	Rolladen-Schneider LS1-c	111	HB-1068
D-7069-SP	Rolladen-Schneider LS4	4485	
D-7070	Schleicher ASK 21	21654	
D-7071	SZD-9bis Bocian 1E	P-757	DDR-3071 DM-3071
D-7073	Schempp-Hirth Ventus a/16.6	23	
D-7074	SZD-9bis Bocian 1E	P-763	DDR-3074 DM-3074
D-7076	SZD-9bis Bocian 1E	P-765	DDR-3076 DM-3076
D-7077	Schleicher ASW 28	28064	
D-7078	Grunau Baby IIb	AB-04	
D-7079	Schleicher Rhönlerche II	220	D-7070
D-7080	Focke-Wulf Weihe 50	1/A	
D-7081	Schleicher ASK 21	21031	
D-7082	Schleicher ASW 20	20370	
D-7084	Schleicher ASW 20L	20371	
D-7086	Schleicher K 8	5	
D-7087	Schleicher ASK 21	21583	
D-7088	Schleicher K 8	94	
D-7089	Schleicher K 8B	563	D-5678
D-7090	Schleicher Ka 6CR Rhönsegler	6548	
D-7091	Doppelraab VI	02	
D-7092	Grob G.103C Twin III	36014	
D-7093	SZD-9bis Bocian 1E	P-483	DDR-3093 DM-3093
D-7094	Grob G.103C Twin III Acro	34193	
D-7095	Schleicher K 7 Rhönadler	604	
D-7097	Rolladen-Schneider LS4	4519	
D-7098-GB	Rolladen-Schneider LS4	4520	
D-7099	Glaser-Dirks DG-100G Elan	E104G77	
D-7100	Glaser-Dirks DG-100	1	
D-7103	Schempp-Hirth Janus B	62	
D-7104	Schleicher K 8B	8401	
D-7106	Rolladen-Schneider LS1-c	254	
D-7107	Glaser-Dirks DG-100	51	
D-7108	Schleicher K 8B	220/61	
D-7109	Schleicher ASK 21	21649	
D-7110	Cumulus Cu-II F	3/54	
D-7111	Schempp-Hirth Nimbus 2	21	(F-C . . .) D-1988
D-7112-E2	Glaser-Dirks DG-100	42	
D-7113	Glaser-Dirks DG-100	47	
D-7115	Schleicher K 7 Rhönadler	501	
D-7116-GK	SZD-50-3 Puchacz	B-1333	DDR-3616
D-7117-TJ	Schempp-Hirth Janus B	58	
D-7118	Schleicher K 7 Rhönadler	744	
D-7119	Schleicher ASK 21	21686	
D-7121	Schleicher ASK 21	21603	
D-7122	Schleicher ASW 22	22001	
D-7123	Schempp-Hirth Ventus 2b	95	
D-7124	Akaflieg Braunschweig SB-5E Sperber	5019/A	
D-7126	Schleicher K 8B	8229/A	
D-7128-AH	Schempp-Hirth Mini-Nimbus B	66	
D-7129	SZD-51-1 Junior	B-2151	
D-7130	Schleicher K 8B	8662	
D-7131-31	Schleicher ASK 23B	23147	
D-7132	Schleicher K 8B	688	
D-7133	Schempp-Hirth Ventus 2c	81	
D-7135	Schleicher ASK 21	21672	
D-7138	Scheibe L-Spatz 55 (C/n incorrect?)	549	
D-7139	Schleicher K 8B	813	
D-7140	Schleicher K 8B	8426/A	
D-7141	Schleicher Rhönlerche II	3015	
D-7142	Glasflügel H201B Standard Libelle	529	OY-VXR
D-7143	Schleicher Ka 6CR Rhönsegler	1158	
D-7144	Schleicher Rhönlerche II	3002	
D-7147	Schleicher ASK 13	13652AB	
D-7149-49	Schleicher Ka 6E	4181	
D-7150	Schleicher K 7 Rhönadler	7088	
D-7153	Schleicher Ka 6CR Rhönsegler	6500	
D-7154	Schleicher Ka 6CR Rhönsegler	6193Si	
D-7155	Schleicher Ka 6CR Rhönsegler	6126Si	
D-7156	Grunau Baby IIB	01	D-1356
D-7158	Schleicher Ka 6CR-PE Rhönsegler	717	
D-7159-TD	Schempp-Hirth Discus CS	092CS	
D-7161	Schleicher ASW 24B	24244	
D-7162	Schempp-Hirth Mini-Nimbus B	64	
D-7163	Vogt LO-100 Zwergreiher	07	
D-7164	Schempp-Hirth Discus CS	095CS	
D-7165	Schleicher Ka 6CR Rhönsegler	6478	
D-7166-E2	Schempp-Hirth Discus CS	096CS	
D-7167	Schempp-Hirth Discus CS	201CS	
D-7168-EC	Schempp-Hirth Discus CS	204CS	
D-7169-CF	Schempp-Hirth Discus CS	203CS	
D-7170	Scheibe L-Spatz 55	709	
D-7171	Schleicher Ka 6E	4225	
D-7172	Scheibe SF-27A	6088	
D-7173	SZD-51-1 Junior	B-2144	
D-7174-i7	Schempp-Hirth Ventus 2b	47	
D-7175	Schempp-Hirth Discus b	94	
D-7176-XD	Schempp-Hirth Discus b	71	
D-7177	Glasflügel H401 Kestrel	61	OO-ZPC
D-7178	Schempp-Hirth Discus b	85	
D-7179-WP	Schempp-Hirth Discus b	84	
D-7181	Schleicher Ka 6CR Rhönsegler	6117	
D-7184-B11	Schleicher Ka 6CR Rhönsegler	6361	
D-7185	Schleicher Ka 6CR Rhönsegler	6374/Si	
D-7186	Scheibe Bergfalke II	327	
D-7187	Glasflügel H401 Kestrel	99	HB-1181
D-7189	Schleicher K 7 Rhönadler	7225	
D-7190	Schleicher Ka 6CR Rhönsegler	6434	
D-7191	Rolladen-Schneider LS6-c	6344	
D-7192	Schleicher K 8B	8228/A/SH	
D-7194-MT	Glaser-Dirks DG-300 Elan	3E220	
D-7197	Schleicher Ka 6CR Rhönsegler	6466	
D-7198	Glaser-Dirks DG-300 Elan	3E221	
D-7199	Schleicher K 7 Rhönadler	690	
D-7200	Schempp-Hirth Cirrus	19	
D-7201-W1	Schempp-Hirth Discus b	459	D-0299
D-7202	Glaser-Dirks DG-200/17C	2-133CL09	
D-7206	Schempp-Hirth Duo Discus	6	
D-7207	Schempp-Hirth Duo Discus	7	
D-7208	Bölkow Phoebus A-1 (Reservation 3.99)	767	
D-7209	Scheibe L-Spatz 55	714	
D-7210	Schleicher ASK 13	13014	
D-7211	Schleicher Ka 6CR Rhönsegler	859	
D-7212	Schleicher K 8B	8717	
D-7213	SZD-9bis Bocian 1E	P-490	DDR-3213 DM-3213
D-7214	Schleicher Ka 6E	4195	
D-7215	Pilatus B4-PC11AF	101	D-3690 PH-488
D-7216	Schleicher ASK 21	21578	
D-7218	Schleicher ASW 28-18	28731	
D-7219	Glaser-Dirks DG-200	2-17	
D-7220	Schleicher Ka 6E	4119	
D-7221	Schempp-Hirth Ventus b	97	
D-7222	Schleicher Ka 6CR Rhönsegler	6617	
D-7223	Grob G.102 Astir CS	1138	
D-7224-24	Grob G.102 Astir CS	1139	
D-7225	Grob G.102 Astir CS	1140	
D-7226	Grob G.102 Astir CS	1137	
D-7227	Grob G.102 Astir CS	1143	
D-7228-SD	Grob G.102 Astir CS	1144	
D-7230	Grob G.102 Astir CS	1043	
D-7231	Grob G.102 Astir CS	1046	
D-7232	Grob G.102 Astir CS	1047	
D-7233	SZD-9bis Bocian 1E	P-515	DDR-3233 DM-3233
D-7234	Grob G.102 Astir CS	1050	
D-7235-H2	Grob G.102 Astir CS	1051	
D-7237	Grob G.102 Astir CS	1053	
D-7239	Grob G.102 Astir CS	1055	
D-7240	Schempp-Hirth Standard Cirrus	628	
D-7242	Schempp-Hirth Standard Cirrus	630	
D-7243	Schempp-Hirth Standard Cirrus B	631	
D-7244	Schempp-Hirth Standard Cirrus B	636	
D-7246	Schempp-Hirth Janus B	104	
D-7249	Schempp-Hirth Janus C	18	
D-7252	Grob G.102 Astir CS	1157	
D-7253	Grob G.102 Astir CS	1159	
D-7254-TY	Grob G.102 Astir CS	1153	
D-7256	Grob G.102 Astir CS	1158	
D-7257	Schempp-Hirth Janus	19	
D-7258-6E	SZD-32A Foka 5	W-521	DDR-2258 DM-2258
D-7259-WS	Glasflügel H206 Hornet	56	
D-7261	Glaser-Dirks DG-100	55	
D-7264	Glaser-Dirks DG-100 (Reservation 9.99)	60	
D-7265	Glaser-Dirks DG-100	61	
D-7266	Schleicher ASW 24	24144	
D-7268	Schleicher ASW 24	24151	

D-7270	Grob G.102 Astir CS	1146	
D-7271	Grob G.102 Astir CS	1147	
D-7272	Grob G.102 Astir CS	1148	
D-7273	Grob G.102 Astir CS	1149	
D-7275	Grob G.102 Astir CS	1202	
D-7276	Grob G.102 Astir CS	1203	
D-7277	Grob G.102 Astir CS	1204	
D-7278	Grob G.102 Astir CS	1205	
D-7279	Grob G.102 Astir CS	1206	
D-7280-HSN	Schleicher ASH 25	25138	
D-7282-VG	Glaser-Dirks DG-500 Elan Orion	5E154X11	
D-7283	Grob G.102 Astir CS	1210	
D-7286	Grob G.102 Astir CS	1213	
D-7287	Grob G.102 Astir CS	1214	
D-7288	Schleicher K 8C	81011	OY-XME D-3765
D-7291	Grob G.102 Astir CS	1218	
D-7295	DG Flugzeugbau DG-500/20 Elan	5E173W10	
D-7296	Grob G.102 Astir CS	1175	
D-7299	Grob G.102 Astir CS	1179	
D-7300	Grob G.102 Astir CS	1180	
D-7301	Grob G.102 Astir CS	1184	
D-7303	Grob G.102 Astir CS	1176	
D-7304	Grob G.102 Astir CS	1177	
D-7305	Grob G.102 Astir CS	1188	
D-7306	Glasflügel H206 Hornet	63	HB-1306
D-7309	Marganski MDM-1 Fox	210	OE-5624
D-7310	Grob G.102 Astir CS	1193	
D-7311-DU	Schempp-Hirth Duo Discus	184	
D-7312	Schempp-Hirth Ventus-2cx	85	
D-7313	Grob G.102 Astir CS	1196	
D-7314	Grob G.102 Astir CS	1197	
D-7315	Glasflügel H205 Club Libelle	164	
D-7321	Schleicher ASK 21	21713	
D-7322	Schleicher ASW 22	22036	
D-7326	Grob G.102 Astir CS	1304	
D-7327	Schleicher ASW 19B	19355	
D-7328	Schleicher ASW 20	20497	
D-7329	Schleicher ASW 19B	19358	
D-7330	Glasflügel H206 Hornet	66	
D-7331	Rolladen-Schneider LS1-f	482	
D-7332-BB	Rolladen-Schneider LS1-f	483	
D-7333	Rolladen-Schneider LS1-f	484	
D-7334	Rolladen-Schneider LS1-f	485	
D-7336	Schempp-Hirth Janus	23	
D-7337	Schleicher ASK 21	21786	
D-7339-GM	Rolladen-Schneider LS6-c	6254	
D-7340	Schempp-Hirth Standard Cirrus	671	
D-7341-DE	LET L-13 Blanik	026649	
D-7343	Schleicher Ka 6CR Rhönsegler	6661AB	
D-7344	Schempp-Hirth Standard Cirrus B	659	
D-7345	Schempp-Hirth Standard Cirrus B	604	
D-7346	Grunau Baby V	530	LX-CAC
D-7347	Schempp-Hirth Ventus c	308	OH-734
D-7348	Schempp-Hirth Discus-2b	193	
D-7351-LD	Rolladen-Schneider LS6-c	6256	
D-7353	Schempp-Hirth Janus B	61	
D-7354	Rolladen-Schneider LS4-b	4916	
D-7355	Grob G.102 Astir CS	1314	
D-7356	Grob G.102 Astir CS	1261	
D-7357	Grob G.102 Astir CS	1262	
D-7359	Grob G.102 Astir CS	1264	
D-7360-WS	Schempp-Hirth Ventus 2b	36	
D-7361	SZD-9bis Bocian 1E	P-548	DDR-3361 DM-3361
D-7362	SZD-9bis Bocian 1E	P-549	DDR-3362 DM-3362
D-7363	Grob G.102 Astir CS	1268	
D-7365	Grob G.102 Astir CS	1270	
D-7368	Grob G.102 Astir CS	1273	
D-7369	Grob G.102 Astir CS	1274	
D-7372-HF	Grob G.102 Astir CS	1278	
D-7373	Grob G.102 Astir CS	1280	
D-7374-HF	DG Flugzeugbau DG-800S	8-113S29	
D-7375	Grob G.102 Astir CS	1275	
D-7376	Grob G.102 Astir CS	1186	OE-5255
D-7379	Grob G.102 Astir CS	1293	
D-7381	Grob G.102 Astir CS	1335	
D-7383	LET L-13A Blanik	978504	
D-7384	Grob G.102 Astir CS	1346	
D-7385	Grob G.102 Astir CS	1347	
D-7388	Grob G.102 Astir CS	1359	
D-7389	Grob G.102 Astir CS	1360	
D-7391	Grob G.102 Astir CS	1364	
D-7393	Grob G.102 Astir CS	1366	
D-7395	SZD-9bis Bocian 1E	P-612	DDR-3395 DM-3395
D-7397	Bölkow Phoebus B3	1003	
D-7398	Schleicher ASW 15	15060	OH-398 OH-RWB
D-7399	Schempp-Hirth Janus	30	
D-7401	Pilatus B4-PC11AF	228	
D-7405-GT	Schleicher ASW 27	27047	
D-7406-EE	Grob G.102 Astir CS	1378	
D-7407	Grob G.102 Astir CS	1398	
D-7408-ACM	Schempp-Hirth Duo Discus	363	
D-7409	Grob G.102 Astir CS	1382	
D-7410	Grob G.102 Astir CS	1388	
D-7411	Grob G.102 Astir CS	1389	
D-7413-HN	Schempp-Hirth Discus CS	130CS	
D-7414	Rolladen-Schneider LS1-c	46	OE-0819
D-7415	Glasflügel H206 Hornet	81	
D-7416	Glasflügel H206 Hornet	82	
D-7417-BG	Sportine Aviacija LAK-17A	125	BGA4940/KAQ
D-7418	Glaser-Dirks DG-200	2-26	
D-7419	Glaser-Dirks DG-200	2-83	
D-7420	Glaser-Dirks DG-200/17	2-84/1703	
D-7422	Neukom S-4D Elfe	417AB	
D-7423-AV	Glasflügel H401 Kestrel	79	
D-7424	Grob G.102 Club Astir IIIB	5645CB	
D-7426	Grob G.102 Astir CS	1436	
D-7427	Grob G.102 Astir CS	1437	
D-7428	Grob G.102 Astir CS	1438	
D-7430	Grob G.102 Astir CS	1441	
D-7432-32	Schleicher ASK 23B	23161	
D-7437	Rolladen-Schneider LS8-a	8068	
D-7439	Grob G.102 Astir CS	1468	
D-7440	Grob G.102 Astir CS	1469	
D-7442	Grob G.102 Astir CS	1419	
D-7443	Grob G.102 Astir CS	1425	
D-7444	Glasflügel H303 Mosquito B	191	
D-7445	Grob G.102 Astir CS	1454	
D-7446	Grob G.102 Astir CS	1455	
D-7448	Grob G.102 Astir CS	1457	
D-7449	Grob G.102 Astir CS	1458	
D-7453	Schempp-Hirth Ventus 2c	38/112	
D-7457	Grob G.102 Astir CS	1516	
D-7458-WY	Schempp-Hirth Duo Discus	2	
D-7462	Grob G.102 Astir CS	1504	
D-7463	Grob G.102 Astir CS	1528	
D-7464	Grob G.102 Astir CS	1529	
D-7465	Grob G.102 Astir CS	1530	
D-7466	Schempp-Hirth Mini-Nimbus C	116	HB-1466
D-7470	Grob G.102 Astir CS 77	1639	
D-7471	Schleicher ASK 21	21639	
D-7473	Glasflügel H303 Mosquito	19	PH-566
D-7474-OG	Schempp-Hirth Ventus 2b	62	
D-7475	Grob G.103 Twin Astir	3002	
D-7476	DG Flugzeugbau DG-1000S	10-56S55	
D-7477-4B	Rolladen-Schneider LS4-b	4956	
D-7478	SZD-22C Mucha Standard	790	HB-747
D-7479	SZD-22C Mucha Standard	599	OE-0536
D-7480-13	Grob G.103 Twin Astir	3026	
D-7481	Schleicher ASK 21	21521	
D-7482	Schleicher ASK 21	21522	
D-7483	Schleicher ASK 21	21523	
D-7484-LL	Grob G.103 Twin Astir	3011	
D-7485	Glasflügel H303 Mosquito	102	
D-7487	Schleicher ASK 21	21731	
D-7489	Glasflügel H303 Mosquito	44	
D-7490	Glasflügel H303 Mosquito	45	
D-7493	Grob G.102 Astir CS Jeans	2003	
D-7496-DS	Grob G.102 Astir CS Jeans	2005	
D-7498-NA	Grob G.102 Astir CS 77	1661	
D-7499	Grob G.104 Speed Astir IIB	4061	HB-1499
D-7500	Pilatus B4-PC11AF	181	
D-7501	Schleicher Ka 6CR Rhönsegler	6356	
D-7502	Schleicher ASH 25	25152	
D-7503	Scheibe L-Spatz 55	670	
D-7504	Schleicher ASK 21	21677	
D-7505	Schleicher K 8B	8593	
D-7507	Schleicher ASK 13	13693AB	
D-7508	Schempp-Hirth HS-7 Mini-Nimbus	22	
D-7510	Pilatus B4-PC11	185	
D-7511	Grob G.102 Astir CS Jeans	2007	
D-7512	Grob G.102 Astir CS Jeans	2008	
D-7514-GA	Schempp-Hirth Nimbus 2C	190	F-CEDN F-WEDN
D-7516	Grob G.102 Astir CS Jeans	2012	
D-7517	Grob G.102 Astir CS Jeans	2013	
D-7518	Grob G.102 Astir CS Jeans	2010	D-7514
D-7519	Grob G.102 Astir CS Jeans	2015	
D-7520	Glasflügel H303 Mosquito B	164	
D-7521	Schleicher ASK 21	21710	
D-7522	Schleicher ASK 13	13692AB	
D-7523	Grob G.103 Twin Astir	3017	
D-7524	Schleicher ASW 24	24165	OE-5507
D-7527	Schleicher ASW 27	27021	
D-7528	Grob G.103 Twin Astir	3033	
D-7529	Grob G.102 Astir CS Jeans	2087	
D-7530	Grob G.102 Astir CS Jeans	2088	
D-7533	Grob G.102 Astir CS Jeans	2091	
D-7536-YA	Grob G.102 Astir CS Jeans	2095	
D-7537	Grob G.102 Astir CS Jeans	2096	
D-7538	Grob G.102 Astir CS Jeans	2097	
D-7540	Schleicher ASW 20L	20329	
D-7541-IWO	Schleicher ASW 20L	20330	
D-7542	Schleicher ASW 20L	20331	
D-7543	Schleicher ASW 20	20332	
D-7545-FGE	Schleicher ASW 19	19108	
D-7546	Schleicher ASW 19	19109	
D-7547	Schleicher ASW 20	20004	
D-7548	Schleicher ASW 19	19111	
D-7550	Schleicher ASW 19	19113	

D-7551	Eiri PIK-20D	20649	OH-551
D-7553	Schleicher ASK 13	13575	
D-7554	Schleicher ASK 13	13576	
D-7555-8M	Rolladen-Schneider LS8-18	8413	
D-7557-9M	Schempp-Hirth Duo Discus	291	
D-7558	Schleicher ASK 13	13578	
D-7559	Schleicher ASW 19	19127	
D-7561	Schleicher ASK 13	13580	
D-7564	Schleicher ASW 19	19132	
D-7565	Schleicher ASW 19	19133	
D-7566	Schleicher ASK 13	13581	
D-7567-L7	Schleicher ASW 19B	19134	
D-7569	Schleicher ASW 20	20021	
D-7570-HN	Schleicher ASW 19B	19114	
D-7571	Schleicher ASW 19B	19143	
D-7572	Schleicher ASW 20	20022	
D-7573-AX	Schleicher ASW 19	19145	
D-7575	Rolladen-Schneider LS7-WL	7032	
D-7576	SZD-48-3 Jantar Standard 3	B-1716	DOSAAF
D-7577	Grob G.102 Astir CS Jeans	2057	
D-7578	Grob G.102 Astir CS Jeans	2058	
D-7580	Grob G.102 Astir CS Jeans	2064	
D-7581	Grob G.102 Astir CS Jeans	2065	
D-7582	Grob G.102 Astir CS Jeans	2067	
D-7583	Grob G.102 Astir CS Jeans	2069	
D-7585	Grob G.102 Astir CS Jeans	2072	
D-7588	Grob G.102 Astir CS Jeans	2075	
D-7590	Grob G.102 Astir CS Jeans	2077	
D-7592-3H	Grob G.102 Astir CS Jeans	2082	
D-7593	Grob G.102 Astir CS Jeans	2083	
D-7594	Grob G.102 Astir CS Jeans	2085	
D-7595	Grob G.102 Astir CS Jeans	2086	
D-7597-F1	Glasflügel H206 Hornet C	93	
D-7598	Glasflügel H303 Mosquito B	161	
D-7599	Glasflügel H303 Mosquito B	163	
D-7600	Grob G.103A Twin II Acro	3867-K-108	
D-7601	Grob G.103 Twin II	3866	
D-7602	SZD-50-3 Puchacz	B-1086	DDR-3602
D-7604	Schempp-Hirth Duo Discus	248	
D-7605	Glasflügel Hornet C	98	PH-605
D-7606	Rolladen-Schneider LS4	4315	
D-7607	Rolladen-Schneider LS4	4316	
D-7608	Rolladen-Schneider LS4	4317	
D-7611	Glaser-Dirks DG-200/17	2-87/1705	
D-7612-CB	Akaflieg Berlin B-12T (Permit)	001	
D-7613-VV	Schempp-Hirth Duo Discus	148	
D-7614-MM	Rolladen-Schneider LS8-a	8203	
D-7615	Schleicher ASW 20C (Permit .05)	20778	
D-7616	Schleicher ASW 20	20334	
D-7617	Schleicher ASW 19B	19313	
D-7618	Schleicher ASW 20L	20335	
D-7619-RP	Schleicher ASW 19B	19311	
D-7621	SZD-50-3 Puchacz	B-1340	DDR-3621
D-7622-7W	Glaser-Dirks DG-600	6-76	
D-7623	SZD-50-3 Puchacz	B-1342	DDR-3623
D-7624	Schempp-Hirth Duo Discus	192	
D-7626	Grob G.102 Astir CS 77	1700	
D-7628	Grob G.102 Astir CS Jeans	2100	
D-7629	Grob G.102 Astir CS Jeans	2101	
D-7635	Grob G.102 Astir CS Jeans	2105	
D-7636-116	Schleicher ASK 21	21591	
D-7637	Grob G.102 Astir CS Jeans	2109	
D-7639	Grob G.102 Astir CS Jeans	2112	
D-7640	Grob G.102 Astir CS Jeans	2114	
D-7641	Grob G.102 Astir CS Jeans	2127	
D-7642	Grob G.102 Astir CS Jeans	2116	
D-7643	SZD-50-3 Puchacz	B-1478	DDR-3646
D-7644	SZD-55-1	551195066	
D-7646	Schleicher ASW 20L	20217	
D-7648	Schleicher ASW 20	20259	
D-7649	Schleicher ASW 20L	20260	
D-7653-53	Schleicher ASK 21	21650	
D-7655-H3	Schleicher ASW 19	19183	
D-7658	Schleicher ASW 20L	20050	
D-7659	Schleicher ASW 20	20071	
D-7660-ITT	Schleicher ASW 19	19196	
D-7662	Schleicher ASW 20	20075	
D-7663	Schleicher ASW 20	20077	
D-7664	Schleicher ASK 13	13592	
D-7667	Schleicher ASW 20	20080	
D-7668-IL	Schleicher ASW 19B	19201	
D-7669	Schleicher ASW 20	20081	
D-7670	Schleicher ASW 20	20070	
D-7671	Schleicher ASK 13	13593	
D-7672	Schleicher ASK 13	13589	
D-7673	Schleicher ASW 17	17054	
D-7674-7F	Schleicher ASW 20	20087	
D-7675	Schleicher ASW 20 (Reservation)	20069	
D-7676	Schleicher ASW 20	20074	
D-7677	Grob G.102 Astir CS 77	1844	HB-1506
D-7678	Schleicher ASW 19B	19205	
D-7679	Schleicher ASW 20	20094	
D-7680	Glasflügel H206 Hornet C	90	
D-7682	Glasflügel H303 Mosquito B	158	
D-7683	Glasflügel H206 Hornet C	92	
D-7684-61	Schleicher ASW 20	20051	
D-7685	Grob G.102 Astir CS 77	1752	
D-7686	Grob G.102 Astir CS 77	1760	
D-7690	Grob G.102 Astir CS 77	1784	
D-7691	Grob G.102 Astir CS 77	1785	
D-7692	Grob G.102 Astir CS 77	1792	
D-7693	Grob G.102 Astir CS 77	1793	
D-7694	Grob G.102 Astir CS 77	1799	
D-7697-i2	Schempp-Hirth Discus b	194	
D-7698	Schleicher ASK 21	21589	
D-7700-EKW	Schleicher ASH 25	25170	(D-KKEW)
D-7701	Neukom S-4D Elfe	406AB	
D-7702	Glaser-Dirks DG-200	2-8	
D-7703	Glaser-Dirks DG-200	2-10	
D-7704-PK	Schempp-Hirth Discus CS	269CS	
D-7705	SZD-48-3 Jantar Standard 3	B-1573	SP-3341
D-7706	Rolladen-Schneider LS3	3210	
D-7707	Schleicher ASW 20L	20584	
D-7708-MB	Schleicher ASK 21	21160	
D-7709	Schempp-Hirth Ventus 2b	134	
D-7710	Schleicher ASW 19B	19378	
D-7711	Scheibe Bergfalke IV	5816	SE-TLF
D-7712	Schleicher Ka 3	E1	D-9046
D-7713	SZD-30 Pirat	W-415	DDR-1714
			DM-1714
D-7714	Glasflügel H201B Standard Libelle	255	F-CDPY
D-7715	Schempp-Hirth Ventus b/16.6	176	
D-7716	Schempp-Hirth Ventus b/16.6	177	
D-7717	Glasflügel H304	215	D-6862
D-7718-T1	Rolladen-Schneider LS8-a	8057	
D-7719	Schleicher ASW 19B	19340	OH-626
D-7720	Schempp-Hirth Ventus b/16.6	174	
D-7721	Schleicher ASK 21	21762	
D-7722	Rolladen-Schneider LS3	3003	
D-7723	Rolladen-Schneider LS3	3004	
D-7724-IGM	Schempp-Hirth Discus CS	276CS	
D-7725	Schleicher ASH 25	25032	
D-7726	Rolladen-Schneider LS3	3007	
D-7727	Neukom Elfe S4A	87	
D-7728-D1	Schempp-Hirth Duo Discus	189	
D-7729-TE	Schleicher ASW 28	28042	
D-7730	FFA Diamant 18	077	HB-202
			HB-2020
D-7731-A3	Rolladen-Schneider LS3	3064	
D-7733	Rolladen-Schneider LS3-a	3110	
D-7734	Rolladen-Schneider LS3	3105	
D-7735	Rolladen-Schneider LS3	3108	
D-7736-B5	Schleicher ASK 21	21658	
D-7737	Rolladen-Schneider LS7-WL	7000	
D-7738	SG-38 Schulgleiter	1310/585	(DDR-)269
D-7739-TM	Rolladen-Schneider LS3	3126	
D-7740	Neukom S-4D Elfe	405AB	
D-7741	Rolladen-Schneider LS1-f	443	
D-7742	Rolladen-Schneider LS5 (Permit)	5001	
D-7743	SZD-30 Pirat	B-332	DDR-1743
			DM-1743
D-7744	Schempp-Hirth Cirrus-VTC	177	
D-7745	Rolladen-Schneider LS3-a	3404	OO-ZLS
D-7746	SZD-48-3 Jantar-Standard 3	B-1346	OO-ZPS
			(OO-ZTD)
			SP-3232
D-7747-TB	Glasflügel H201B Standard Libelle	59	I-TRIK
D-7748	Rolladen-Schneider LS6-c	6248	SE-UKK
D-7750	Rolladen-Schneider LS3-a	3075	
D-7751	Rolladen-Schneider LS4	4303	
D-7752-152	Rolladen-Schneider LS4	4183	
D-7753	Rolladen-Schneider LS4	4304	
D-7754-FR	Rolladen-Schneider LS4	4305	
D-7755	Rolladen-Schneider LS8-a	8279	
D-7756	Grob G.102 Astir CS Jeans	2176	
D-7759	Grob G.102 Astir CS Jeans	2184	
D-7760-MY	Schempp-Hirth Standard Cirrus	545	OE-5030
D-7761-77	Grob G.102 Astir CS Jeans	2186	
D-7762	Grob G.102 Astir CS Jeans	2187	
D-7763	Grob G.102 Astir CS Jeans	2188	
D-7764-U2	Schempp-Hirth Discus 2B	90	
D-7765-58	Grob G.102 Astir CS Jeans	2220	
D-7766	Grob G.102 Astir CS Jeans	2221	
D-7767	Grob G.102 Astir CS Jeans	2222	
D-7768	Scheibe SF-27A	6020	OE-0768
D-7769	Grob G.102 Astir CS Jeans	2223	
D-7770-VW	Schleicher ASW 27	27072	
D-7771	Akaflieg Braunschweig SB-5E	AB5043	
D-7772	Grob G.102 Astir CS 77	1796	
D-7773-JU	Glasfaser Albatros (Reservation 3.99)	1	
D-7774	Grob G.102 Astir CS 77	1806	
D-7775-OU	Streifeneder Falcon	1	
D-7776	Glasflügel H303 Mosquito B	140	C-GDFZ
D-7777-HL	Glasflügel H201B Standard Libelle	547	
D-7778	Grob G.103 Twin Astir Trainer	3106	
D-7779-WU	Schempp-Hirth Discus b (Permit 3.99)	574	
D-7780	Grob G.103 Twin Astir	3109	
D-7781	Grob G.103 Twin Astir Trainer	3112-T-9	
D-7782	Grob G.103 Twin Astir Trainer	3115	
D-7784	SZD-30 Pirat	B-403	DDR-1774
			DM-1774
D-7785	Grob G.102 Astir CS 77	1651	HB-1385
D-7786	Grob G.103 Twin Astir	3138	
D-7788-RE	Rolladen-Schneider LS4-b	4917	

D-7790	Schempp-Hirth Duo Discus	296	
D-7791	Grob G.103 Twin Astir	3148	
D-7792-YJ	Grob G.103 Twin Astir	3149	
D-7794	SZD-30 Pirat	B-437	DDR-1794 DM-1794
D-7795	Grob G.103 Twin Astir	3150	
D-7797-WP	Grob G.103 Twin Astir	3167	
D-7799	Pilatus B4-PC11AF	322	
D-7800-FL	Rolladen-Schneider LS6	6073	
D-7801-2X	Rolladen-Schneider LS3-a	3206	
D-7802	Rolladen-Schneider LS6	6074	
D-7803	Rolladen-Schneider LS6-a	6075	
D-7805	Rolladen-Schneider LS4-b	41038	
D-7806	Schleicher ASK 23B	23143	
D-7807	Grob G.103 Twin Astir	3170	
D-7808-IF	SZD-55-1	551196080	
D-7809	Rolladen-Schneider LS8-a	8349	
D-7810	Grob G.103 Twin Astir Trainer	3174-T-17	
D-7811-EZ	Rolladen-Schneider LS6-a	6121	
D-7812	Schleicher ASK 21	21582	
D-7813	Grob G.103 Twin Astir	3178	
D-7816	Schempp-Hirth Discus b	184	
D-7817	Glasflügel H206 Hornet	51	
D-7818	Glasflügel H206 Hornet	44	
D-7819-KX	Glasflügel H206 Hornet	43	
D-7820	Glasflügel H206 Hornet	42	
D-7821	Glasflügel H206 Hornet	45	
D-7822	Glasflügel H206 Hornet	41	
D-7823	Glasflügel H206 Hornet (Permit .00)	5	
D-7824	SZD-30 Pirat	B-501	DDR-1824 DM-1824
D-7825	Rolladen-Schneider LS4	4364	
D-7826	Rolladen-Schneider LS4	4365	
D-7828	Rolladen-Schneider LS4	4366	
D-7829	Rolladen-Schneider LS4	4367	
D-7830	SZD-30 Pirat	B-508	DDR-1830 DM-1830
D-7831-OK	Rolladen-Schneider LS8-a	8366	
D-7832	SZD-30 Pirat	B-510	DDR-1832 DM-1832
D-7833	Glasflügel H206 Hornet	26	
D-7834	Glasflügel H206 Hornet	35	
D-7835	Glasflügel H206 Hornet	36	
D-7836	Glasflügel H206 Hornet	37	
D-7837	Glasflügel H206 Hornet	34	
D-7838-B3	Schleicher ASK 21	21238	
D-7839-JV	Schleicher ASW 19B	19412	
D-7840	Schleicher ASW 20BL	20661	
D-7841	Glasflügel H206 Hornet	55	
D-7842	Schempp-Hirth Discus b	374	HB-3058
D-7844	Scheibe Bergfalke III	5654	
D-7845-ISH	Glasflügel H206 Hornet (Permit)	84	
D-7848	Schempp-Hirth Janus	36	
D-7851	SZD-30 Pirat	B-573	DDR-1853 DM-1853
D-7852	Schempp-Hirth Standard Cirrus	700	
D-7854	Schempp-Hirth Standard Cirrus B	701	
D-7855-B6	Grob G.102 Astir CS	1532	
D-7856	Glasflügel H303 Mosquito	28	
D-7857	Glasflügel H303 Mosquito	35	
D-7858	SZD-30 Pirat	B-578	DDR-1858 DM-1858
D-7859	Glasflügel H303 Mosquito B	104	
D-7861	Schleicher ASW 27	27063	
D-7865	Schempp-Hirth Mini-Nimbus C	125	
D-7866	Rolladen-Schneider LS8-a	8280	
D-7867	Glaser-Dirks DG-200	2-36	
D-7868	Glaser-Dirks DG-200	2-38	
D-7869	Glasflügel H303 Mosquito	93	
D-7870-GC	Schempp-Hirth Discus b	457	
D-7872	Rolladen-Schneider LS3-a	3109	
D-7873	Schleicher ASW 22	22039	
D-7874	SZD-30 Pirat	S-01.12	DDR-1874 DM-1874
D-7875	Rolladen-Schneider LS4-b	4882	
D-7876	Schleicher ASK 21	21198	
D-7877	Rolladen-Schneider LS3	3217	
D-7878-PP	Rolladen-Schneider LS3	3111	
D-7879	Rolladen-Schneider LS3-a	3084	
D-7880-JT	Rolladen-Schneider LS4	4549	
D-7881	Rolladen-Schneider LS3-a	3097	
D-7882	Rolladen-Schneider LS4	4550	
D-7883-1P	Schleicher ASW 27	27006	
D-7884	Rolladen-Schneider LS3-a	3112	
D-7885	Rolladen-Schneider LS3-a	3113	
D-7886	Glasflügel H303 Mosquito B	114	
D-7887	Focke-Wulf Weihe 50	02	
D-7888	Schleicher K 8B	8931	OE-0972
D-7890	Rolladen-Schneider LS3-a	3304	
D-7891	SZD-30 Pirat	S-03.06	DDR-1891 DM-1891
D-7892	Rolladen-Schneider LS3-17	3115	
D-7894	Grob G.103A Twin II Acro	3773-K-59	
D-7895	Grob G.103 Twin II	3778	
D-7896	Grob G.102 Club Astir IIIB	5603CB	
D-7898	Rolladen-Schneider LS4	4552	
D-7899	Rolladen-Schneider LS3-a	3060	

D-7901	Rolladen-Schneider LS3	3011	
D-7902	Rolladen-Schneider LS3	3012	
D-7904	Rolladen-Schneider LS4	4554	
D-7905	Rolladen-Schneider LS3	3015	
D-7906	Rolladen-Schneider LS3	3016	
D-7907	Rolladen-Schneider LS3	3017	
D-7908	Rolladen-Schneider LS3	3018	
D-7909	Rolladen-Schneider LS3	3019	
D-7910	Rolladen-Schneider LS3	3020	
D-7911-ILA	SZD-48-3 Jantar Standard 3	B-1951	CCCP-1951
D-7912	Schempp-Hirth Discus 2B	61	
D-7913-JP	Grob G.103A Twin II Acro	3786-K-64	
D-7914	Grob G.103 Twin II	3789	
D-7915	Grob G.102 Club Astir IIIB	5602CB	
D-7917	Rolladen-Schneider LS3	3027	
D-7918	Rolladen-Schneider LS4	4555	
D-7919	Rolladen-Schneider LS4	4556	
D-7920-6A	Rolladen-Schneider LS3	3030	
D-7921	Rolladen-Schneider LS3	3031	
D-7922	Schleicher ASK 23B	23136	
D-7923	Schleicher ASK 21	21635	
D-7924	Grob G.103A Twin II Acro	3801-K-68	
D-7925	Rolladen-Schneider LS8-18	8310	
D-7926	Schempp-Hirth HS-7 Mini-Nimbus	45	
D-7927	DG Flugzeugbau DG-500 Elan Orion	5E217X57	
D-7928-K7	Schleicher ASW 28	28011	
D-7930	Neukom S-4D Elfe	420AB	
D-7931	Bölkow Phoebus C	931	
D-7933	Schleicher ASW 19	19148	
D-7934	Schleicher ASW 20	20031	
D-7935	Schleicher ASW 20	20057	
D-7936	Schleicher ASW 19	19149	
D-7937-CG	Schempp-Hirth Discus 2B	154	
D-7942	LET L-23 Super Blanik	917810	
D-7945	Schleicher ASW 20	20036	
D-7946	Schleicher ASW 19	19155	
D-7949	Schleicher ASK 13	13584	
D-7950	Rolladen-Schneider LS4-b	4950	
D-7951	Schleicher ASW 20	20039	
D-7952	Schleicher ASW 20	20043	
D-7953	Schleicher ASW 19B	19165	
D-7956	Schleicher ASW 19	19167	
D-7957	Schleicher ASK 13	13585	
D-7959	Schleicher ASW 19	19170	
D-7960	Schleicher ASW 19	19169	
D-7961	Schleicher ASK 13	13587	
D-7962	Schleicher ASK 13	13588	
D-7963	Schleicher ASW 19	19181	
D-7966-B8	Schleicher ASW 19	19172	
D-7967	Schleicher ASW 19	19171	
D-7970	Schleicher ASW 19B	19175	
D-7971-IST	Schleicher ASW 19B	19176	
D-7972-GA	Schleicher ASW 19B	19195	
D-7975	Schleicher ASW 19	19177	
D-7976	Schleicher ASW 20	20066	
D-7977	Schleicher ASW 20	20055	
D-7979	Schleicher ASW 20	20023	
D-7980	Schleicher ASW 19B	19180	
D-7981-M3	Schleicher ASW 19	19182	
D-7982-HA	Glasflügel H303 Mosquito B	122	
D-7984	Schleicher ASW 19	19197	
D-7985	Grob G.103A Twin II Acro	3623-K-10	
D-7986	Grob G.102 Club Astir IIIB	5508CB	
D-7987	Schleicher ASK 23B	23057	
D-7988	Glasflügel H303 Mosquito B	132	
D-7989	Schleicher ASK 21	21289	
D-7990	Schleicher ASW 19B	19150	
D-7991	Akaflieg Braunschweig SB-5E Sperber	5050AB	
D-7992	Schempp-Hirth Mini-Nimbus C	154	
D-7993	Schempp-Hirth Nimbus 2C	213	
D-7994	Schempp-Hirth Nimbus 2C	215	
D-7995-MK	Schempp-Hirth Nimbus 2C	214	
D-7996-RH	Schempp-Hirth Mini-Nimbus C	156	
D-7998	Schleicher ASK 23B	23051	
D-8000	Vogt LO-100 Zwergreiher	AB 38	
D-8001	SZD-9bis Bocian 1E	P-705	DDR-3000 DM-3000
D-8002	DFS Habicht E replica	ABH 1/OSC	
D-8003-800	DG Flugzeugbau DG-800S	8-3S1	
D-8004	Glasflügel H304	208	
D-8005	Focke-Wulf Weihe 50	164	
D-8006-9B	Rolladen-Schneider LS3-a	3170	
D-8007	Glaser-Dirks DG-600	6-39	
D-8008	SZD-9bis Bocian 1E	P-721	DDR-3009 DM-3009
D-8009	Glasflügel H304	221	
D-8010	Glaser-Dirks DG-300 Elan	3E62	
D-8011	Glaser-Dirks DG-300 Elan	3E57	
D-8013	Schleicher K 8B	10	
D-8014	Schempp-Hirth Ventus-2a	160	
D-8015	Glaser-Dirks DG-100G Elan	E171G137	
D-8016-IXI	Rolladen-Schneider LS4-a	4652	
D-8018	SZD-9bis Bocian 1E	P-443	DDR-3018 DM-3018
D-8019	Glaser-Dirks DG-100G Elan	E170G136	
D-8021	Schleicher Ka 6CR Rhönsegler	6284	
D-8022	Scheibe Bergfalke II/55	238	

D-8026	Akaflieg Braunschweig SB-5B Sperber	5012/A	
D-8027	Schempp-Hirth Discus 2B	84	
D-8028-28	Schleicher ASW 28	28001	
D-8029-TEX	DG Flugzeugbau DG-800S	8-208S38	
D-8030	Rolladen-Schneider LS4-a	4655	
D-8031	Rolladen-Schneider LS4-a	4656	
D-8032	Schleicher Ka 6CR Rhönsegler	556	
D-8033	Schleicher Ka 6E	4152	
D-8034	Rolladen-Schneider LS4-a	4657	
D-8035	Schleicher ASK 21	21657	
D-8037-YN	Schempp-Hirth Discus 2B	108	
D-8039	SZD-9bis Bocian 1E	P-460	DDR-3039
			DM-3039
D-8040-40	Glaser-Dirks DG-500 Elan Trainer	5E111T45	
D-8041	Schleicher Ka 6CR Rhönsegler	150/59	
D-8042-CH	Rolladen-Schneider LS4-a	4658	
D-8043	Schleicher Ka 6CR Rhönsegler	6190Si	
D-8044	SZD-9bis Bocian 1E	P-467	DDR-3044
			DM-3044
D-8045	SZD-9bis Bocian 1E	P-468	DDR-3045
			DM-3045
D-8047-8S	Rolladen-Schneider LS8-a	8035	
D-8048-BC	DG Flugzeugbau DG-800S	8-27S4	
D-8049	Scheibe L-Spatz 55	624	
D-8050	Schempp-Hirth Duo Discus	5	
D-8051	Schleicher Ka 6E	4120	
D-8052-RT	Schempp-Hirth Ventus 2b	139	
D-8053	Rolladen-Schneider LS6-b	6148	
D-8054	Sportine Aviacija 19	09	
D-8055	Glaser-Dirks DG-500 Elan Trainer	5E125T54	
D-8057-34	Glaser-Dirks DG-100	43	OE-5057
D-8058	SZD-9bis Bocian 1E	P-478	DDR-3058
			DM-3058
D-8059	Allstar SZD-59 Acro	590.A.04.002	
D-8060-60	Schempp-Hirth Discus b	480	
D-8062	Grob G.103A Twin II Acro	33966-K-199	
D-8064	Göppingen Gö III Minimoa	184	N2664B
			HB-626
			D-8064
D-8065	ICA-Brasov IS.28B2	358	SE-USS
			YR-1992
D-8066-S8	Glaser-Dirks DG-300 Elan	3E182	ZK-GSS
D-8068	SZD-42-2 Jantar 2B	B-871	DOSAAF
D-8069	Grob G.103A Twin II Acro	34013-K-246	
D-8070	Vogt LO-100 Zwergreiher	AB-36	
D-8071-RA	Schempp-Hirth Discus b	565	
D-8072	Grob G.103A Twin II Acro	33967-K-200	
D-8073	SZD-9bis Bocian 1E	P-762	DDR-3073
			DM-3073
D-8077	SZD-9bis Bocian 1E	P-766	DDR-3077
			DM-3077
D-8078	Glasflügel H201B Standard Libelle	2	
D-8079	Doppelraab IV	AB-01	
D-8080	Glasflügel H201B Standard Libelle	1	
D-8081-PL	Schleicher ASW 24	24077	HB-3030
D-8082	DG Flugzeugbau DG-500 Elan Orion	5E207X50	S5-7521
D-8083	DG Flugzeugbau DG-808S (Permit 5.03)	8-299S55	
D-8084-ALB	Schempp-Hirth Discus 2A	28	
D-8085	Schleicher Ka 6CR Rhönsegler	6148	
D-8086	Schempp-Hirth Duo Discus	110	
D-8087	Grob G.103A Twin II Acro	33973-K-206	
D-8088	Schempp-Hirth Janus Ce	292	
D-8089	DG Flugzeugbau DG-808S	8-300S56X3	
D-8091	Rolladen-Schneider LS4-b	4864	
D-8092-F3	Rolladen-Schneider LS4-b	4865	
D-8093	Rolladen-Schneider LS4-b	4866	
D-8094	Rolladen-Schneider LS4-b	4867	
D-8095-M6	Rolladen-Schneider LS4-b	4868	
D-8097	Grob G.103A Twin II Acro	33974-K-207	
D-8098	Rolladen-Schneider LS4-b	4869	
D-8099	Rolladen-Schneider LS4-b	4870	
D-8100	Schleicher ASK 13	13058	
D-8101	Scheibe Bergfalke III	5509	
D-8102	Vogt LO-100 Zwergreiher	AB-37	
D-8104	Rolladen-Schneider LS4-b	4872	
D-8105	Rolladen-Schneider LS4-b	4873	
D-8106	Schempp-Hirth Nimbus 2B	138	OE-5106
D-8108-K1	Schempp-Hirth Duo Discus	8	
D-8109	Scheibe Bergfalke II	172	
D-8110	Rolladen-Schneider LS6-b	6156	
D-8111-DUO	Schempp-Hirth Duo Discus (Reservation .05)	450	
D-8112	Grob G.102 Club Astir IIIB	5634CB	
D-8113-K2	Neukom S-4D Elfe	425AB	
D-8115	Schleicher ASW 27	27051	
D-8116	Schleicher K 8B	8777	I-BAUU
D-8117	Rolladen-Schneider LS6-b	6158	
D-8118	Vogt LO-100 Zwergreiher	11	
D-8120	Scheibe L-Spatz 55	737	
D-8121	Schleicher ASK 21	21618	
D-8122	Schleicher ASH 25	25162	OH-854
			D-7021
D-8124	Schleicher ASK 21	21227	
D-8125	Schempp-Hirth Discus CS	144CS	
D-8126-AX	Schempp-Hirth Discus CS	145CS	
D-8127	Schempp-Hirth Discus CS	140CS	
D-8128	Schleicher ASW 28-18	28507	
D-8129-2M	Schempp-Hirth Duo Discus	196	

D-8133	Schleicher Ka 6E	4182	
D-8134	Schleicher Ka 2B Rhönschwalbe	199	
D-8136-2X	Schempp-Hirth Duo Discus	83	
D-8138-WA	Schempp-Hirth Duo Discus	90	
D-8140-YB	Schempp-Hirth Discus 2B	5	
D-8141	Akaflieg Stuttgart FS.25	V-1	
D-8148	Scheibe Bergfalke II	174	
D-8150	Grob G.103A Twin II Acro	33989-K-222	
D-8152	FES 530/II Lehrmeister	152	(D-3208)
			DM-3152
D-8153-53	Schleicher ASK 21	21473	
D-8159	Scheibe Bergfalke II	4	
D-8160	Scheibe L-Spatz 55	583	
D-8161	Rolladen-Schneider LS4	4395	(PH-1233)
			D-8161
			D-5499
D-8163	Standard Austria Series 1	12	OE-0663
D-8164	Schleicher Ka 6CR Rhönsegler	716	
D-8165-EM	Bölkow Phoebus C	783	
D-8166	Schempp-Hirth Ventus 2a	86	
D-8170-70	Glasflügel H301B Libelle	82	
D-8171	Pilatus B4-PC11AF	90	HB-1129
D-8173	Rolladen-Schneider LS3	3091	D-7732
D-8176-SM	Rolladen-Schneider LS7-WL	7084	
D-8177	Schleicher K 8B	8049/1	
D-8178	Rolladen-Schneider LS7	7085	
D-8179	Rolladen-Schneider LS7	7086	
D-8180	Göppingen Gö III Minimoa	324	PH-848
			N37JK
			BGA1738/CRC
D-8181	Rolladen-Schneider LS7-WL	7088	
D-8182-UG	Rolladen-Schneider LS7-WL	7089	
D-8183-TH	Schleicher ASW 24B	24242	
D-8184	Göppingen Gö IV Gövier III	409	OO-ZHW
			D-5946
			D-6041
			D8102
D-8187	Grunau Baby III (Reservation)	"XYZ"	
D-8188	Schleicher ASH 25	25248	
D-8191	Schleicher ASK 21	21627	
D-8192-LB	Rolladen-Schneider LS7	7114	
D-8193-L7	Rolladen-Schneider LS7-WL	7115	
D-8194	Schleicher ASW 27	27088	
D-8196	Glaser-Dirks DG-100G Elan	E132G100	
D-8197	Rolladen-Schneider LS7-WL	7118	
D-8198	Scheibe Bergfalke II/55	212	
D-8199	Grob G.103A Twin II Acro	34001-K-234	
D-8201	Rolladen-Schneider LS7	7087	OH-820
D-8202	Scheibe Bergfalke II	3	
D-8203-VI	Grob G.103A Twin II Acro	34008-K-241	
D-8204-GH	SZD-48-1 Jantar Standard	W-893	OE-5204
D-8206	Rolladen-Schneider LS7	7122	
D-8207	Schempp-Hirth Duo Discus	49	
D-8208-KWI	Rolladen-Schneider LS7-WL	7124	
D-8209	Scheibe L-Spatz 55	695	
D-8210	Schleicher K 8B	975	
D-8211	Scheibe L-Spatz	570	
D-8212	Rolladen-Schneider LS6-c	6286	
D-8214	Schleicher Ka 6E	4199	
D-8216	Schleicher K 8B	8567	
D-8219-YU	Schleicher ASW 19B	19218	
D-8220-HW	Schleicher ASH 25	25155	
D-8221	SZD-32A Foka 5	W-469	DDR-2221
			DM-2221
D-8222	SZD-9bis Bocian 1E	P-502	DDR-3222
			DM-3222
D-8223	Hütter H.28 II	01	
D-8225-SD	Schempp-Hirth Discus b	345	
D-8226	Schempp-Hirth Discus b	356	
D-8227	Schempp-Hirth Ventus c	482	
D-8228-5G	Schempp-Hirth Discus b	24/317	
D-8230-IMK	Schempp-Hirth Discus b	329	
D-8231	SZD-9bis Bocian 1E	P-513	DDR-3231
			DM-3231
D-8232	SZD-24-4A Foka 4	W-347	DDR-2234
			DM-2234
D-8233	Schempp-Hirth Discus CS	312CS	
D-8234	SZD-9bis Bocian 1E	P-516	DDR-3234
			DM-3234
D-8235	Schleicher ASK 21	21598	
D-8236	Akaflieg Braunschweig SB-5E Sperber	5008	
D-8237	SZD-9bis Bocian 1E	P-524	DDR-3237
			DM-3237
D-8238	Schleicher ASK 21	21602	
D-8240	Scheibe Bergfalke II/55	251	
D-8241	Schleicher Rhönlerche II	232	
D-8242	SZD-9bis Bocian 1E	P-534	DDR-3247
			DM-3247
D-8244	Grob G.102 Standard Astir III	5536S	OE-5276
D-8245	SZD-9bis Bocian 1E	P-532	DDR-3245
			DM-3245
D-8246	SZD-30 Pirat	S-01.04	(D-8861)
			DDR-1867
			DM-1867
D-8249-FX	SZD-32A Foka 5	W-499	DDR-2249
			DM-2249
D-8251	Rolladen-Schneider LS4-b	41006	

D-8252	Rolladen-Schneider LS4-b	41007	
D-8253	Schleicher ASW 20CL	20785	
D-8254 -WC	Schleicher ASW 20BL	20666	
D-8255	Schleicher ASW 27B	27210	
D-8256	Vogt LO-100 Zwergreiher	05A	
D-8258	Schempp-Hirth Discus b	552	
D-8259	Schempp-Hirth Discus b	553	
D-8260	Schempp-Hirth Discus b	554	
D-8261-3Y	Schempp-Hirth Discus-2b	207	
D-8262	Scheibe L-Spatz 55	595	
D-8263	Scheibe Spatz B	AB-01	
D-8264	SZD-32A Foka 5	W-527	DDR-2264
			DM-2264
D-8266	Scheibe Specht (Reservation 1.99)	816	
D-8268	Valentin Mistral C	MC 068/86	
D-8269	Scheibe Specht	AB-01	
D-8270-70	Schempp-Hirth Discus 2B	45	
D-8271	Scheibe L-Spatz 55	1	
D-8275	Schleicher ASW 20CL	20846	
D-8277	SZD-48-1 Jantar Standard 2	B-1166	OE-5277
D-8280	Schleicher Rhönlerche II	363	
D-8281	Schleicher Ka 6BR Rhönsegler	346	
D-8282	Schempp-Hirth Discus CS	049CS	
D-8283	Schempp-Hirth Discus CS	159CS	
D-8284-5W	Schempp-Hirth Discus CS	163CS	
D-8285	Schleicher Rhönlerche II	AB-08	
D-8286	Rolladen-Schneider LS4-b	4883	
D-8290-29	Schempp-Hirth Ventus b/16.6	33	
D-8291	Schempp-Hirth Duo Discus	136	
D-8295	Schleicher K 7 Rhönadler	434	
D-8296	DG Flugzeugbau DG-300 Elan Acro	3E469A19	
D-8297	DG Flugzeugbau DG-300 Elan	3E472	
D-8299-CO	Glaser-Dirks DG-600	6-13	HB-1957
D-8300	SZD-36A Cobra 15	W-558	DDR-2300
			DM-2300
D-8301	Schleicher Rhönlerche II	04	
D-8302	Schempp-Hirth Nimbus 4D	2/8	
D-8303	Glaser-Dirks DG-300 Club Elan	3E462C82	
D-8304-DA	HpH Glasflügel 304CZ	33	
D-8305	SZD-51-1 Junior	B-2148	
D-8306	Dittmar Condor IV/3	47	
D-8308-BP	DG Flugzeugbau DG-800S	8-100S24	
D-8310	Scheibe L-Spatz 55	545	
D-8311	Schleicher ASK 21	21155	
D-8312	Schleicher Ka 6BR Rhönsegler	496	
D-8313	SZD-36A Cobra 15	W-638	DDR-2313
			DM-2313
D-8314	Scheibe L-Spatz 55	666	
D-8316	Schleicher K 8B	516	
D-8317-5Z	Scheibe L-Spatz 55	677	
D-8318-8C	Schleicher ASW 19B	19424	
D-8319	Schleicher ASW 19B	19421	OO-ZQR
			D-8319
D-8321	Schleicher ASK 21	21135	HB-1677
D-8322	Glaser-Dirks DG-500/20 Elan	5E144W6	
D-8325	Schleicher ASK 23B	23144	
D-8326	Schleicher ASH 26	26110	
D-8327	Schleicher Ka 6CR Rhönsegler	6479	
D-8328-MO	Schleicher ASW 28	28021	
D-8330	Schleicher Rhönlerche II	469	
D-8332	Scheibe Zugvogel III	1038	
D-8333-38	Schempp-Hirth Ventus b/16.6	190	
D-8334	Schleicher K 8B	639	
D-8336	Glaser-Dirks DG-100	79	HB-1336
D-8338	Scheibe L-Spatz 55	AB 04	
D-8340	Schleicher K 7 Rhönadler	E 3	
D-8342	Schleicher Ka 6CR-PE Rhönsegler	679	
D-8344-LG	Schempp-Hirth Duo Discus	406	
D-8345	Schleicher ASW 15B	15376	I-FLIK
D-8347	Scheibe Sperber	2	
D-8348	Glasflügel H304	220	
D-8349	Schleicher ASW 15B	15358	OO-YLB
			D-2348
D-8350	SZD-55-1	551196083	
D-8351	Scheibe Zugvogel IIIA	1052	
D-8353	SZD-9bis Bocian 1E	P-540	DDR-3353
			DM-3353
D-8356	Scheibe Zugvogel IIIA	1051	
D-8357	Scheibe L-Spatz 55	717	
D-8358	Doppelraab IV (Reservation 4.99)	02	
D-8360	Schleicher ASW 27	27014	
D-8361	Schleicher K 8B	840	
D-8363	Schempp-Hirth Duo Discus	104	
D-8364	Scheibe SF-27A	6066	
D-8365	Schleicher Rhönlerche II	3060	OB-813
			OB-I-813
D-8367	Schempp-Hirth Discus CS	003CS	OK-0367
D-8368	Scheibe L-Spatz	E-1	
D-8369	Nabern FS-24 Phönix T	405	
D-8370	SZD-9bis Bocian 1E	P-560	DDR-3370
			DM-3370
D-8371	SZD-9bis Bocian 1E	P-561	DDR-3371
			DM-3371
D-8373	Schleicher ASK 23 (Museum) (Reservation - cld?)	unkn	
D-8374	Schleicher Ka 6CR Rhönsegler	965	
D-8376	SZD-9bis Bocian 1E	P-566	DDR-3376
			DM-3376

D-8377	Schempp-Hirth Discus CS	214CS	
D-8381	Schleicher Ka 6CR Rhönsegler	999	
D-8383	Scheibe SF-27A (Permit .00)	6092	
D-8384	DG Flugzeugbau DG-800S	8-109S25	
D-8386	Schleicher K 7 Rhönadler	1006	
D-8387	Schleicher Ka 6CR Rhönsegler	AB-04/201	
D-8389	Rolladen-Schneider LS8-18	8389	
D-8390	Schorndorf/Schleicher Ka 6BS	E1	
D-8391-EN	Rolladen-Schneider LS8-18	8391	
D-8392	Schleicher K 8B	1060	
D-8393-LR	Schleicher Ka 6CR Rhönsegler	1109	
D-8394	Scheibe Bergfalke II/55	344	
D-8397-FF	Rolladen-Schneider LS8-18	8397	
D-8399	Schleicher ASK 21	21301	
D-8400	Schleicher Ka 6CR Rhönsegler	1116	
D-8401	Schleicher K 8B	1101	
D-8402-GG	Rolladen-Schneider LS8-18	8402	
D-8403-84	Schleicher ASK 21	21302	
D-8404	Scheibe L-Spatz 55	751	
D-8405	Schleicher ASK 23B	23073	
D-8406	SZD-41A Jantar Standard	B-697	DDR-2406
			DM-2406
D-8407	Grob G.102 Standard Astir II	5017S	HB-1528
D-8408	Schleicher Ka 6CR Rhönsegler	6011	
D-8409	Schleicher Ka 6CR Rhönsegler	6031Si	
D-8410	Schleicher K 8B	1107	
D-8412	Schleicher K 8B	8007	
D-8414	Schleicher ASW 24B	24248	
D-8415	Hütter H-30 GFK	1	
D-8417	Schleicher K 8B	8041	
D-8418	Schleicher ASK 21	21678	
D-8419	Scheibe L-Spatz 55	585	
D-8421	Schleicher K 8B	8421	D-KOCA
D-8423	Test registration for Schempp-Hirth Duo Discus		
D-8424	Schleicher Ka 6CR Rhönsegler	6045	
D-8426-GN	SZD-48-1 Jantar Standard 2	W-847	DDR-2426
			DM-2426
			SP-3118
D-8427-ZJ	SZD-48-1 Jantar Standard 2	W-855	DDR-2427
			DM-2427
			(SP-3083)
D-8428-S5	Schleicher ASW 28-18	28702	
	(For motor conversion later)		
D-8434	Scheibe Bergfalke III	5507	
D-8435	Schempp-Hirth Duo Discus	197	
D-8437	Schleicher ASW 20C	20841	
D-8438	Schleicher K 8B	8011	
D-8439	Schleicher K 8B	281/A/3	
D-8440-GU	SZD-48-1 Jantar Standard 2	B-1052	DDR-2430
			DM-2430
D-8441	Rolladen-Schneider LS4	4536	
D-8443	Scheibe Bergfalke II/55	366	
D-8444	Schleicher Ka 6CR Rhönsegler	6063	
D-8445	Vogt LO-100 Zwergreiher (Reservation)	203	BGA3378/FMV
			OE-0445
D-8446	Schleicher K 8B	103/98	
D-8447	Vogt LO-100 Zwergreiher	205	
D-8448	Nabern FS-24 Phönix T	407	
D-8450	Schleicher K 8B	8168	
D-8451-20	Schleicher Ka 6CR Rhönsegler	6113	
D-8455	Grob G.102 Astir CS	1290	PH-551
D-8460	Schleicher ASK 21	21303	
D-8461	Schleicher K 8B	1054	
D-8462	Schleicher ASK 21	21305	
D-8463	Schleicher K 7 Rhönadler	7087	
D-8464	Schleicher ASK 21	21306	
D-8466	Schleicher ASK 23B	23076	
D-8467	Rock Geier IIB	E 1	
D-8468	Schempp-Hirth Janus C	193	
D-8469	Test Registration for Schempp-Hirth Discus a		
D-8471	Schleicher K 8B	8262	
D-8474	Schleicher K 8B	122	
D-8475	Doppelraab VI	03	
D-8477	Schleicher Ka 6CR Rhönsegler	6181	
D-8480	Scheibe SF-26A Standard	5025	
D-8481	Schleicher Ka 6CR Rhönsegler	6196	
D-8482	Scheibe Zugvogel IIIB	1086	
D-8483	Schleicher Ka 6CR Rhönsegler	6227Si	
D-8485	Schleicher Ka 6CR Rhönsegler	6234	
D-8486	Schleicher ASK 23B	23105	(LN-GCM)
			D-8486
			HB-1976
D-8488	Grob G.102 Speed Astir IIB	4043	
D-8489	Scheibe Zugvogel IIIB	1090	
D-8490	Rolladen-Schneider LS4	4534	
D-8494	Rolladen-Schneider LS4	4047	
D-8495	Scheibe Bergfalke III	5516	
D-8496	Schleicher Ka 6CR-PE Rhönsegler	6223Bi	
D-8497	Schleicher K 7 Rhönadler	7162	
D-8498	Neukom S-4D Elfe	424AB	
D-8499	Schleicher Ka 6CR Rhönsegler	6300	
D-8500	Rolladen-Schneider LS8-a	8500	
D-8502-GI	Schempp-Hirth Ventus 2b	5	
D-8503	Rolladen-Schneider LS8-18	8315	
D-8504	Kranich II	24	
D-8505	Rolladen-Schneider LS6-a	6060	
D-8506	Focke-Wulf Kranich III	74	

D-8507	Focke-Wulf Kranich III	84	F-CCBR
D-8508	Schleicher K 7 Rhönadler	7076	
D-8509	Rolladen-Schneider LS6	6059	
D-8510	Scheibe L-Spatz 55	69	
D-8512	Schleicher K 8B	997	
D-8513	Glasflügel H201B Standard Libelle	12	
D-8514	Schempp-Hirth Discus CS	205CS	
D-8516	Schempp-Hirth Discus CS	213CS	
D-8518	Schleicher ASW 27	27082	
D-8520	Rolladen-Schneider LS1-f	478	OY-XNM D-6520
D-8521	Scheibe SF-27A	6078	
D-8522	Schleicher K 8B	8019	
D-8523	Schleicher K 8B	8072	
D-8525	Schleicher K 8B	8236	
D-8528	Rolladen-Schneider LS4	4474	
D-8530	Schleicher K 8B	919	
D-8531	Schleicher Rhönlerche II (Reservation - cld?)	3	
D-8532	Glaser-Dirks DG-500 Elan Trainer	5E69T29	
D-8533	Schleicher Rhönlerche II	01	
D-8534	Schleicher K 8B	8360	
D-8535	Schleicher Ka 6BR Rhönsegler	387	
D-8537	Schempp-Hirth Nimbus 2B	117	PH-537 (PH-439)
D-8540	Schleicher Ka 6CR Rhönsegler	6638	
D-8541	Schleicher K 8B	8585	
D-8543	Focke-Wulf Kranich III	59	
D-8545	Schleicher ASW 24	24207	
D-8548-HH	Rolladen-Schneider LS4	4431	
D-8551	Grob G.102 Astir CS Jeans	2196	OO-ZJS
D-8552	Schleicher Ka 2B Rhönschwalbe	1012	
D-8554	Scheibe Bergfalke II/55	363	
D-8555	Grob G.103C Twin III Acro	34198	
D-8556	Glasflügel H304	228	
D-8557-FI	Glasflügel H304	229	
D-8558-D5	Schempp-Hirth Ventus 2b	6	
D-8560	Schempp-Hirth Discus CS	309CS	
D-8561	Schleicher Rhönlerche II	34/55	
D-8564	L-10 Libelle	1	
D-8565	Schleicher Ka 6E	4051	
D-8566	Schleicher Ka 6 Rhönsegler	278	
D-8567	Schleicher K 8B	8059	
D-8568	Schleicher Ka 6CR Rhönsegler	6291	
D-8569	Olympia-Meise	3	
D-8570-GG	Bölkow Phoebus C	802	
D-8572	Schempp-Hirth Discus a	533	
D-8575	SZD-48-3 Jantar Standard 3	B-1890	SP-3541
D-8577-HZ	Schempp-Hirth Ventus 2a	34	
D-8578	Schleicher K 8	115/58	
D-8579	Schleicher Ka 6CR Rhönsegler	002 AB	
D-8580	DG Flugzeugbau DG-800S	8-92S23	
D-8582	Schleicher ASW 20CL	20767	
D-8584	Neukom Elfe S4	15	
D-8585	Grunau Baby III	AB 1	
D-8586	SZD-51-1 Junior	B-2019	SP-3583
D-8588-ALI	Rolladen-Schneider LS8-18	8339	
D-8590	Scheibe L-Spatz (Wfu)	508B	
D-8593	Schleicher Ka 6CR Rhönsegler	6061	
D-8595	Schleicher ASK 23B	23134	
D-8598	Schleicher K 8B	01	
D-8599	Schleicher Ka 6CR-PE Rhönsegler	858	
D-8600-1E	Glaser-Dirks DG-600	6-7	
D-8602	Schleicher K 8B	8275	
D-8603	Glaser-Dirks DG-600	6-35	
D-8604	SZD-50-3 Puchacz	B-1088	DDR-3604
D-8605	Schempp-Hirth Discus 2B	150	
D-8606	Schleicher Ka 6 Rhönsegler	248	
D-8607	Schleicher Ka 6CR-PE Rhönsegler	6229Bi	
D-8608	Schleicher Ka 6CR Rhönsegler	6432Si	
D-8609-HR	Rolladen-Schneider LS8-18	8103	OE-5645
D-8610	Schleicher K 8B	8488	
D-8611	Schleicher ASK 13	13056	
D-8612	Schleicher Ka 2B Rhönschwalbe	003	
D-8614	Schleicher K 8C	81009	PH-432
D-8616	Schleicher K 8B	1055	
D-8618	Schleicher K 8B	8511	
D-8619	Schleicher Ka 6CR Rhönsegler	6470Si	
D-8620	Schleicher Ka 6CR Rhönsegler	6494	
D-8621	Schempp-Hirth SHK-1	47	HB-862
D-8622	Schleicher Ka 6BR Rhönsegler	386	
D-8624	SZD-50-3 Puchacz	B-1343	DDR-3624
D-8626	Schleicher Ka 6CR Rhönsegler	6644	
D-8627	Schleicher K 8B	8570	
D-8628-LI	Schleicher ASK 21	21120	
D-8629	Schleicher ASK 21	21121	
D-8631	Schleicher ASW 20	20585	
D-8632	Schleicher ASW 20	20591	
D-8633	Bölkow Phoebus A-1	731	
D-8637	Schleicher Ka 6CR Rhönsegler	6546	
D-8640	SZD-50-3 Puchacz	B-1470	DDR-3640
D-8642	Schleicher ASW 15B	15398	
D-8643	Schleicher ASK 13	13494	
D-8644	Schleicher ASW 15B	15409	
D-8645	Schleicher ASW 15B	15400	
D-8646	Schleicher ASW 15B	15402	
D-8647	Schleicher ASW 15B	15401	
D-8648	Schleicher ASK 13	13501	

D-8649-R9	Rolladen-Schneider LS4-b	4918	
D-8650	Schleicher ASW 15B	15403	
D-8652	Schleicher K 8C	81004	
D-8653	Schleicher ASW 15B	15410	
D-8654	Schleicher ASW 17	17040	
D-8655	Schleicher ASW 15B	15412	
D-8657	Schleicher K 8B	8973	
D-8658	Schleicher ASW 15B	15411	
D-8659	Schleicher ASK 13	13500	
D-8660	Schleicher ASW 15B	15415	
D-8665	Schleicher ASW 15B	15420	
D-866-IDA	Rolladen-Schneider LS1-f	378	
D-8667-CN	Rolladen-Schneider LS1-f	334	
D-8668-KB	Rolladen-Schneider LS1-f	330	
D-8669	Rolladen-Schneider LS1-f	327	
D-8670-EX	Schempp-Hirth Standard Cirrus	522	OE-5360 PH-509
D-8671-BV	Rolladen-Schneider LS1-f	298	
D-8672	Rolladen-Schneider LS1-f	277	
D-8676	Glaser-Dirks DG-100	13	
D-8679	Rolladen-Schneider LS1-f	381	
D-8681	Grob G.102 Astir CS	1003	
D-8682	Grob G.102 Astir CS	1004	
D-8684	Glasflügel H205 Club Libelle	72	
D-8685	Glasflügel H205 Club Libelle	73	
D-8686	Glasflügel H205 Club Libelle	74	
D-8688	Scheibe Bergfalke III	5651	
D-8690	Glasflügel H401 Kestrel	125	
D-8691	Glasflügel H401 Kestrel	126	
D-8694	Grob G.103A Twin II Acro	3689-K-40	
D-8695	Grob G.102 Club Astir IIIB	5554CB	
D-8698	Grob G.103A Twin II Acro	3690-K-41	
D-8700	Grob G.102 Speed Astir IIB	4094	VH-IUF
D-8701	Schempp-Hirth Standard Cirrus	566G	
D-8702	LET L-13 Blanik	026356	
D-8703-BY	Schempp-Hirth Duo Discus	265	
D-8704	Grob G.102 Club Astir IIIB	5566CB	
D-8709	Schleicher ASW 20CL	20719	
D-8710	DG Flugzeugbau DG-1000S	10-47S46	
D-8711	Rolladen-Schneider LS4	4014	
D-8712-1R	Rolladen-Schneider LS4	4015	
D-8713-PF	Rolladen-Schneider LS4	4557	
D-8714	Rolladen-Schneider LS1-f	453	
D-8715	Schempp-Hirth Discus 2B	71	
D-8716-AT	Grob G.102 Speed Astir IIB	4050	
D-8717	Grob G.102 Speed Astir IIB	4052	
D-8718	Grob G.102 Speed Astir IIB	4053	
D-8719	Grob G.102 Speed Astir IIB	4054	
D-8720-AW	Grob G.102 Speed Astir IIB	4055	
D-8721	Grob G.102 Speed Astir IIB	4056	
D-8722	Grob G.102 Speed Astir IIB	4072	
D-8723	Schleicher ASK 23	23152	
D-8724-55	Schleicher ASW 24	24150	I-GLID
D-8725	SZD-30 Pirat	B-306	DDR-1725 DM-1725
D-8726-AK	Akaflieg München Mü.26	V-1	D-0726
D-8727	Schleicher ASW 27	27100	OK-2727
D-8728	Schleicher ASW 28-18	28726	
D-8729	Grob G.103 Twin II	3535	
D-8732	SZD-30 Pirat	B-315	DDR-1732 DM-1732
D-8733	Schempp-Hirth Duo Discus	156	
D-8735	Schleicher Ka 6E	4156	
D-8737	Grob G.102 Speed Astir IIB	4092	
D-8739	Grob G.102 Speed Astir IIB	4095	
D-8741	Grob G.102 Standard Astir II	5003S	
D-8742	Grob G.102 Club Astir II	5012C	
D-8745	Grob G.102 Speed Astir IIB	4099	
D-8746	Schempp-Hirth Nimbus 2C	221	
D-8747	Schempp-Hirth Nimbus 2C	222	
D-8748	Grob G.103 Twin II	3549	
D-8750	Grob G.103 Twin II	3525	
D-8752	Grob G.103 Twin II	3527	
D-8754	Schleicher K 8B	8419	
D-8755	Grob G.103A Twin II Acro	3559-K-5	
D-8756	Grob G.103 Twin II	3532	
D-8757	Schleicher ASK 23B	23066	OH-757
D-8759	Grob G.102 Club Astir II	5061C	
D-8760	Schleicher Ka 2 Rhönschwalbe	72	
D-8761	Grob G.103 Twin II	3554	
D-8762-M3	Grob G.103 Twin II	3555	
D-8766	Grob G.103 Twin II	3560	
D-8767	PIK-16C Vasama	26	
D-8770	Schleicher Ka 6CR Rhönsegler	6281	
D-8773	Scheibe Zugvogel I	1002	
D-8774	Schleicher K 8B (Reservation 2.99)	02	
D-8775	Schleicher ASW 20L	20372	
D-8776	Schleicher Ka 2 Rhönschwalbe	106	
D-8777	Scheibe L-Spatz 55	553	
D-8778	Schleicher K 8B	8332SH	
D-8780	SZD-30 Pirat	B-409	DDR-1780 DM-1780
D-8781	Schleicher ASW 20L	20377	
D-8782	Schleicher K 8B	8338/A	
D-8783	Schleicher K 8B	8356	
D-8784	Schleicher ASK 21	21640	
D-8785	Scheibe L-Spatz 55	550	

D-8787	Scheibe Zugvogel IIIB	1093	
D-8788	Schleicher Rhönlerche II	115	
D-8790	Glasflügel H201B Standard Libelle	4	
D-8791	Schleicher K 8B	8389/A	
D-8792	Schleicher ASW 20L	20368	
D-8794	Grob G.103 Twin II	3529	
D-8795	Grob G.103 Twin II	3561	
D-8796	SZD-30 Pirat	B-439	DDR-1796 DM-1796
D-8797	Grob G.103 Twin II	3534	
D-8798-R1	Schleicher ASK 21	21032	
D-8800-A6	Schempp-Hirth Nimbus 2B	175	
D-8801	Schleicher ASK 21	21036	
D-8802	SZD-24-4A Foka 4	W-370	DDR-2231 DM-2231
D-8803	SZD-24-4A Foka 4	W-353	DDR-2240 DM-2240
D-8805	Schleicher K 8B	8278	
D-8806	Scheibe L-Spatz 55	1	
D-8808-B7	Schleicher Ka 6CR Rhönsegler	313	
D-8809	Schleicher ASW 19B	19324	
D-8810	Schleicher ASW 20L	20383	
D-8811	Rolladen-Schneider LS8-a	8278	
D-8812	Scheibe Bergfalke II	167	
D-8813	Scheibe Spatz A	4	
D-8815-MAC	Schempp-Hirth Ventus 2a	115	
D-8816	Scheibe Bergfalke III	5585	
D-8817	Rolladen-Schneider LS6-18W	6374	
D-8818	SZD-9bis Bocian 1E	P-563	DDR-3373 DM-3373
D-8819	Schleicher K 7 Rhönadler	7253	
D-8820	Scheibe Zugvogel IIIB	1103	
D-8821	Scheibe L-Spatz 55	640	
D-8822	Schleicher ASW 20L	20389	
D-8823	Schleicher Ka 6CR Rhönsegler	6370Si	
D-8824	Scheibe Zugvogel IIIB	1028	
D-8825	Schleicher ASK 21	21037	
D-8827	Schleicher ASW 20L	20390	
D-8828	Schleicher K 8B (Reservation 1.00)	454	
D-8829	SZD-30 Pirat	B-507	DDR-1829 DM-1829
D-8830	Grob G.103C Twin III Acro	34196	
D-8831	Schleicher ASW 19B	19347	
D-8832	Schleicher ASW 20	20391	
D-8833	Rolladen-Schneider LS4-b	4906	
D-8836	Schleicher K 7 Rhönadler	694	
D-8837-OK	SZD-48-3 Jantar Standard 3	B-1363	SP-3266
D-8838	Schleicher K 8B	8634	
D-8840	Schleicher Ka 6CR Rhönsegler	6100	D-6215
D-8841	Schleicher Ka 6CR Rhönsegler	1073	OO-ZMZ OO-ZMS D-5367
D-8842	Scheibe L-Spatz 55	700	
D-8843-YY	PZL PW-5 Smyk	17.07.016	
D-8844-ET	Glaser-Dirks DG-300 Club Elan	3E288C12	
D-8845	Grob G.102 Club Astir IIIB	5510CB	
D-8846	Grob G.102 Club Astir IIIB	5511CB	
D-8847	Grob G.102 Club Astir IIIB	5512CB	
D-8849	Vogt LO-100/150 Zwergreiher	13	
D-8850	SZD-42-2 Jantar 2B	B-1491	
D-8851	SZD-30 Pirat	B-575	DDR-1855 DM-1855
D-8852	Schleicher K 8B	03	
D-8853	Schleicher K 8B	977	
D-8854	Scheibe Bergfalke III	5617	
D-8855	Schleicher ASW 20L	20565	
D-8856	Schleicher K 8B	AB8856	
D-8858	Scheibe L-Spatz 55	741	
D-8859	Schempp-Hirth Duo Discus	371	
D-8860-CC	Schleicher Ka 6CR Rhönsegler	1075	
D-8861	Rolladen-Schneider LS4	4359	F-CFZC
D-8862	Glaser-Dirks DG-300 Elan	3E265	LN-GLU
D-8863-A5	Rolladen-Schneider LS4	4371	
D-8864	Rolladen-Schneider LS4	4372	
D-8865	Rolladen-Schneider LS4	4381	
D-8866	AB Flygindustri DFS Weihe	224	BGA1297/BWR G-ASCV SE-STN Fv8306
D-8869	Schleicher ASK 21	21641	
D-8872	Rolladen-Schneider LS4	4450	
D-8873	Rolladen-Schneider LS4	4451	
D-8874-N3	Rolladen-Schneider LS4-a	4452	
D-8875	Rolladen-Schneider LS4	4453	
D-8876	Akaflieg München Mü.13D	1	
D-8877	Schempp-Hirth Nimbus 2B	161	
D-8878	Glaser-Dirks DG-300 Elan	3E164	
D-8879	Schleicher Ka 6CR Rhönsegler	6095Si	
D-8880	Grunau Baby III	1-52	
D-8881-SZ	Schleicher ASW 19B	19056	OE-5519 D-6718
D-8882	Schleicher Ka 6CR Rhönsegler	6543	
D-8883	SZD-30 Pirat	S-01.26	DDR-1880 DM-1880
D-8884	SZD-30 Pirat	S-01.30	DDR-1884 DM-1884
D-8885	Scheibe L-Spatz 55	781	

D-8886-TL	Schleicher K 7 Rhönadler	7114	
D-8887	SZD-30 Pirat	S-02.43	DDR-1887 DM-1887
D-8888	Schleicher ASK 21	21406	
D-8889	Scheibe Bergfalke III	5543	
D-8890-i7	Schempp-Hirth Discus b	37	
D-8892	Schleicher Ka 6CR Rhönsegler	6427Si	(D-KAIA) D-8892
D-8893	Schleicher Ka 2 Rhönschwalbe (Reservation)	25	
D-8895	Schleicher Ka 6E (Permit .05)	4005	
D-8896-MH	Schleicher ASW 27	27005	
D-8897	Schleicher ASW 20L	20204	HB-1477
D-8898	Schleicher ASW 20	20589	HB-1659
D-8899	Schleicher Ka 1	33	
D-8900	Bölkow Phoebus C	854	XB-ABO N8541
D-8901	Scheibe L-Spatz 55	575	
D-8902	Schleicher Ka 6CR Rhönsegler	6482	
D-8903	Schleicher ASW 27	27033	
D-8904	Schleicher K 7 Rhönadler	7264	
D-8905-FV	Akaflieg Karlsruhe AK-5 (Permit)	501	
D-8906	Schleicher Ka 6CR Rhönsegler	6597	
D-8907	Bölkow Phoebus C (Reservation 2.99)	890	D-6964 OE-0964
D-8908	Schleicher K 8	108/58/A	
D-8909	Schleicher ASW 24B	24238	
D-8910	Schleicher Ka 2 Rhönschwalbe	02	
D-8911	SZD-30 Pirat	S-04.12	DDR-1911 DM-1911
D-8912	Schleicher Ka 6CR Rhönsegler	6410	
D-8913	Scheibe L-Spatz 55	675	
D-8914	Rolladen-Schneider LS4-b	41036	
D-8917	Schempp-Hirth Standard Cirrus	543G	
D-8918	Schempp-Hirth Standard Cirrus	549	
D-8920	Rolladen-Schneider LS1-f	281	
D-8923	Rolladen-Schneider LS1-f	300	
D-8924	LET L-13 Blanik	026360	
D-8925-3Z	Rolladen-Schneider LS4	4559	
D-8926	Glasflügel H205 Club Libelle	81	
D-8927	Glasflügel H205 Club Libelle	82	
D-8929	Glasflügel H205 Club Libelle	133	PH-534
D-8930-BT	Rolladen-Schneider LS8-18	8438	
D-8932	SZD-30 Pirat	S-04.19	DDR-1912 DM-1912
D-8933-3J	Rolladen-Schneider LS1-f	359	
D-8934	Rolladen-Schneider LS1-f	417	
D-8935	Rolladen-Schneider LS1-f	307	
D-8936	Rolladen-Schneider LS1-f	418	
D-8939-AY	Rolladen-Schneider LS1-f	421	
D-8941	Rolladen-Schneider LS1 (Permit)	454	
D-8943-CT	Glasflügel H206 Hornet	38	
D-8946	Akaflieg Braunschweig SB-5E Sperber	AB5057	
D-8947	Akaflieg Braunschweig SB-5E Sperber	AB5058	
D-8948	Glasflügel H304	222	
D-8949-SD	Glasflügel H304 (Reservation - cld?)	223	
D-8952	Schleicher K 8B	8912/AB	
D-8954	Schleicher ASW 20L	20416	
D-8955	Schleicher ASK 21	21061	
D-8956	Glaser-Dirks DG-300 Elan	3E206	
D-8958	Rolladen-Schneider LS4	4560	
D-8960-HN	Rolladen-Schneider LS4	4562	
D-8961	Rolladen-Schneider LS1-f	460	
D-8962	Rolladen-Schneider LS1-f	461	
D-8963	Schleicher ASK 13	AB13644	
D-8964	Schleicher ASK 13	AB13649	
D-8965	Glaser-Dirks DG-300 Elan	3E208	
D-8966-9R	Rolladen-Schneider LS4	4250	
D-8967	Glaser-Dirks DG-300 Elan (Reservation)	3E209	
D-8968	Glaser-Dirks DG-300 Elan	3E210	
D-8969	Glaser-Dirks DG-300 Elan	3E218	
D-8970-A7	Glaser-Dirks DG-300 Elan	3E213	
D-8971-CP	Rolladen-Schneider LS1-f	470	
D-8972-TW	Rolladen-Schneider LS1-f	471	
D-8973	Rolladen-Schneider LS4	4522	
D-8974	Grob G.103C Twin III Acro	34199	
D-8975	Grob G.103 Twin II	3647	
D-8976	Grob G.103 Twin II	3667	
D-8977	Schempp-Hirth Discus b	70	
D-8978	Schleicher ASK 23B	23116	
D-8979	Schleicher ASK 21	21451	
D-8980	Rolladen-Schneider LS1-f	487	
D-8982	Rolladen-Schneider LS1-f	489	
D-8984	Schleicher ASK 13	13399	
D-8985	SG-38 Schulgleiter	E-1	
D-8987	Glaser-Dirks DG-200/17	2-73CL24	
D-8988	Rolladen-Schneider LS8-18	8429	
D-8989	Grob G.102 Club Astir IIIB	5541CB	
D-8992	Rolladen-Schneider LS4	4294	
D-8993-IWR	Rolladen-Schneider LS6	6052	
D-8994	Rolladen-Schneider LS1-f	442	
D-8995	Schempp-Hirth Nimbus 2B	154	I-AKOB
D-8996	Glasflügel Mosquito	15	OO-ZDD
D-8997	Rolladen-Schneider LS6	6051	
D-8998	Rolladen-Schneider LS6	6050	
D-8999	Schleicher ASK 21	21777	
D-9000	Rolladen-Schneider LS4-b	4752	

D-9001	SZD-24C Foka	W-144	I-FOKA HB-715
D-9002	Glasflügel H303 Mosquito	40	OY-XHO
D-9003	Scheibe Spatz A	505	
D-9004-B3	Schleicher ASW 28-18	28502	
D-9005	Schleicher Ka 6CR Rhönsegler	6476	
D-9006-K6	Glaser-Dirks DG-300 Elan	3E257	OY-XYI
D-9007	Grob G.102 Astir CS	1443	D-9000
D-9008	Glasflügel H201B Standard Libelle	426	PH-467
D-9009	Grob G.102 Club Astir IIIB	5501CB	
D-9010	Rolladen-Schneider LS6-c	6198	
D-9011-NH	Rolladen-Schneider LS6-c	6199	
D-9012	Schleicher K 8B	8099	
D-9013	Rolladen-Schneider LS6-c	6200	
D-9014	Rolladen-Schneider LS4-b	4763	
D-9015	Rolladen-Schneider LS4-b	4772	
D-9016	Rolladen-Schneider LS4-b	4764	
D-9017-3M	Rolladen-Schneider LS4-b	4765	
D-9018-PM	Rolladen-Schneider LS4-b	4766	
D-9019	Rolladen-Schneider LS4-b	4767	
D-9020-PI	Rolladen-Schneider LS4-a	4768	
D-9021	Schleicher ASK 21	21729	
D-9022	Glaser-Dirks DG-600/18	6-61	HB-3033
D-9023-JT	Schempp-Hirth Ventus 2b	141	
D-9024	Schleicher ASW 24	24075	OY-HEX D-9022
D-9025	Schleicher Rhönsperber replica	AB-02	
D-9026	Göppingen Gö.1 Wolf replica	AB-1	
D-9028	Schleicher Ka 6E	4187	
D-9029-TS	Schempp-Hirth Duo Discus	418	
D-9030	Schleicher Ka 6CR Rhönsegler	6038	
D-9031	SZD-9bis Bocian 1E	P-455	DDR-3031 DM-3031
D-9032	SZD-9bis Bocian 1E	P-456	DDR-3032 DM-3032
D-9033-DR	Schempp-Hirth Discus b	505	
D-9034	Scheibe Bergfalke II/55	379	
D-9035	Schleicher K 8B	8491	
D-9036	Schleicher K 8B	8753	
D-9037	Schleicher Ka 6CR Rhönsegler	6450	
D-9039	Schleicher Ka 6CR Rhönsegler	6096/Si	
D-9040	Bölkow Phoebus C-1	787	OO-ZHM D-9204
D-9041-YD	Schempp-Hirth Duo Discus	135	
D-9042	SZD-24-4A Foka 4	W-299	DDR-2042 DM-2042
D-9044	Schleicher K 7 Rhönadler	7142	
D-9048	Schleicher K 8B	8104	
D-9051	Schleicher Ka 2 Rhönschwalbe	88	
D-9055	SZD-55-1XM	551198105XM	
D-9057	Schleicher Ka 6CR Rhönsegler	6093Si	
D-9060	Schleicher K 8B	116	
D-9062	SG-38 Schulgleiter	BWLV-15	
D-9064	Schleicher ASK 13	13098	
D-9065	Schleicher ASK 21	21638	
D-9067	SZD-30 Pirat	B-396	DDR-1767 DM-1767
D-9070-70	Schempp-Hirth Discus b	500	
D-9071	Schleicher K 8B	8487	D-KOPF
	(Same c/n quoted as D-1198)		D-1071
D-9074	Scheibe L-Spatz 55	567	(D-KOHN(2))
D-9075	Schleicher Ka 6 Rhönsegler	194	
D-9076	Schleicher Ka 6CR Rhönsegler	6359	
D-9077	Schempp-Hirth Ventus c	432	
D-9079	Scheibe Bergfalke II/55	224	
D-9080	Schleicher ASK 21	21590	
D-9082	Schleicher K 8B	8042	
D-9083	Doppelraab IV	E-1	
D-9084	Schleicher Ka 2B Rhönschwalbe	190	
D-9088-8T	Schempp-Hirth Duo Discus	17	
D-9090	Schleicher K 8B	8010	
D-9091	Scheibe Spatz A	001 TAB	
D-9093-AL	Schleicher ASW 27	27024	
D-9095	Schempp-Hirth Duo Discus	63	
D-9096	Schempp-Hirth Discus 2b	138	
D-9097	Schleicher K 8	3	
D-9098	Scheibe Bergfalke II/55	357	
D-9099	Rolladen-Schneider LS7	7054	
D-9100	SZD-30 Pirat	B-443	DDR-1800 DM-1800
D-9101-01	Start & Flug H-101 Salto	71	
D-9102	Rolladen-Schneider LS4	4376	
D-9103	Schempp-Hirth Ventus c	568	HB-3103
D-9104	Rolladen-Schneider LS4	4156	
D-9106	Rolladen-Schneider LS4	4195	
D-9109	Schleicher K 8	455	
D-9115	Scheibe L-Spatz 55	678	
D-9116	Schleicher Ka 6BR Rhönsegler	530	
D-9117	Schleicher Ka 6CR Rhönsegler	553	
D-9119	Schleicher ASK 21	21124	
D-9120	Bölkow Phoebus A-1	709	
D-9122	Schempp-Hirth Discus CS	135CS	
D-9123-JB	Schempp-Hirth Discus CS	136CS	(PH-1000)
D-9124-FB	Schempp-Hirth Discus CS	133CS	
D-9125	Schempp-Hirth Discus CS	137CS	
D-9127	Schempp-Hirth Discus b	12	
D-9128-BK	Schleicher ASW 28	28022	
D-9129	Rock Geier II	1	
D-9130	Glasflügel H303 Mosquito B	106	
D-9131	Schleicher Ka 6CR Rhönsegler	6564	
D-9133	Schleicher K 8B	714	
D-9134	Scheibe Bergfalke II/55	AB 350	
D-9135	Schleicher Rhönlerche II	885/1/58	
D-9140	Scheibe Spatz A	V-1	
D-9141	SZD-24-4A Foka 4	W-225	
D-9142	Schempp-Hirth Duo Discus	125	
D-9143-LR	Rolladen-Schneider LS4	4405	
D-9145-AR	Rolladen-Schneider LS4	4407	
D-9146	Schleicher K 8B	882	
D-9147	Schleicher K 8B	111	
D-9149-LT	Schempp-Hirth Duo Discus	39	
D-9152-DM	Schleicher ASW 28	28060	
D-9155	Schleicher K 8B	233/1	
D-9156	Schleicher K 7 Rhönadler	7032	
D-9157	Schleicher K 8B	AB.05	
D-9158	Schleicher Ka 6CR Rhönsegler	6184	
D-9159	Scheibe Bergfalke II/55	346	
D-9160	Scheibe Bergfalke II/55	380	
D-9161	Schleicher K 8B	3/8196	
D-9163	Schleicher Ka 2B Rhönschwalbe	E 1	
D-9165	Schleicher Ka 6CR Rhönsegler	6220	
D-9167	Schleicher Ka 6CR Rhönsegler	6318Si	
D-9173	Schleicher K 8B	8358	
D-9174	Schleicher K 8B	8374	
D-9176	Focke-Wulf Kranich III	58	
D-9177	Scheibe Bergfalke III	5524	
D-9180	Schleicher Ka 6E	4028	
D-9181	Schleicher ASK 21	21622	
D-9182	Schleicher Ka 6CR Rhönsegler	6504	
D-9184	Schleicher Ka 6CR Rhönsegler	6507	
D-9185	Scheibe SF-27A	6038	
D-9186	Schleicher Ka 6CR Rhönsegler	6489Si	
D-9188	Schleicher Ka 6CR Rhönsegler	6514	
D-9189	Scheibe Bergfalke III	5528	
D-9190	Neukom S-4A Elfe	66	HB-1229
D-9191	Schleicher Ka 6E	4040	
D-9192	Rock Geier II	V-2	
D-9193	Schleicher Ka 6CR Rhönsegler	6304	
D-9194-WF	Schempp-Hirth Duo Discus	15	
D-9195	SZD-30 Pirat	W-397	OY-DXH
D-9196	LET L-13 Blanik	173343	
D-9197	Schempp-Hirth SHK-1	30	LX-CAR OE-5090 D-9197
D-9199	Bölkow Phoebus A-1	752	
D-9201-01	Schleicher Ka 6CR Rhönsegler	6578	
D-9204-RD	Schempp-Hirth Duo Discus	172	
D-9205	Bölkow Phoebus A-1	768	
D-9206	Schleicher Ka 6CR Rhönsegler	6123Si	
D-9207	Schleicher Ka 6CR Rhönsegler (Reservation 1.00)	6599	
D-9208	LET L-13 Blanik	170718	DDR-3208 DM-3208 OK-0901
D-9211	Schleicher K 8B	8644/A	
D-9212-AK	Schempp-Hirth Discus 2A	4	
D-9213	Glasflügel H201B Standard Libelle	412	
D-9214-T	Bölkow Phoebus C	784	
D-9216	Schleicher K 8B	8732	
D-9218	Schleicher K 8B	8300/A	
D-9219	Scheibe SF-27A	6099	
D-9220	Schleicher ASK 13	13092	
D-9221	Rolladen-Schneider LS1-d	181	
D-9222-WM	Schempp-Hirth Ventus 2a (Permit .02)	2	
D-9223	SZD-41A Jantar Standard	B-815	LX-CRP
D-9224-WF	Schempp-Hirth Standard Cirrus	368	
D-9225	SZD-9bis Bocian 1E	P-506	DDR-3224 DM-3224
D-9227	Scheibe Bergfalke IV	5832	
D-9228	Schempp-Hirth Standard Cirrus	375G	
D-9229	SZD-9bis Bocian 1E	P-511	DDR-3229 DM-3229
D-9230	SZD-41A Jantar Standard	B-932	OE-5230
D-9231	Rolladen-Schneider LS1-d	246	
D-9233	Glasflügel H401 Kestrel	101	
D-9234	Glasflügel H201B Standard Libelle	491	
D-9235	Schempp-Hirth Standard Cirrus	374G	
D-9236	Glasflügel H201B Standard Libelle	484	
D-9238	Glasflügel H201B Standard Libelle	486	
D-9239	Glasflügel H401 Kestrel	70	HB-1239
D-9240	Start & Flug H101 Salto	40	
D-9241	Start & Flug H101 Salto	41	
D-9242-AH	Schleicher ASW 27	27040	HB-3242
D-9243	Start & Flug H101 Salto	38	
D-9244	Rolladen-Schneider LS1-d	260	
D-9246	Schempp-Hirth Standard Cirrus	413	
D-9247	Rolladen-Schneider LS1-d	3	OE-5247
D-9250-HI	Glasflügel H201B Standard Libelle	513	
D-9251	Glasflügel H201B Standard Libelle	515	
D-9252	Glasflügel H201B Standard Libelle	516	
D-9253	SZD-32A Foka 5	W-514	DDR-2253 DM-2253
D-9254	Schempp-Hirth Cirrus	17	HB-925
D-9255	Schleicher K 8B	8949/A	
D-9256	Schempp-Hirth Cirrus-VTC	154Y	

D-9257	Schempp-Hirth Cirrus-VTC	155Y	
D-9259-IGL	Start & Flug H101 Salto	46	
D-9261	Schleicher Ka 6CR Rhönsegler	6486Si	D-KOFA D-4637
D-9262-EF	Rolladen-Schneider LS1-f	274	
D-9264	Glasflügel H201B Standard Libelle	569	
D-9265	Schleicher ASK 13	13479	
D-9266	Schleicher ASW 15B	15374	
D-9268	Schleicher ASW 15B	15377	
D-9269	Schleicher ASW 15B	15378	
D-9270	Schleicher ASW 15B	15387	
D-9271	Schempp-Hirth Nimbus 4	6	
D-9272	Schleicher ASK 13	13480	
D-9273	Schleicher ASW 15B	15381	
D-9274	Schleicher ASW 17	17036	
D-9275	Schleicher ASK 13	13490	
D-9276	Schleicher ASW 15B	15386	
D-9277	Schleicher ASK 13	13491	
D-9278	Schleicher ASW 15B	15379	
D-9280	Schleicher ASK 18	18001	
D-9281	Schleicher ASW 15B	15390	
D-9283	Schleicher ASW 15B	15392	
D-9284-W21	Schleicher ASW 17	17035	
D-9285-FK	Schleicher ASW 15B	15395	
D-9286	Schleicher ASW 15B	15396	
D-9287	Rolladen-Schneider LS6	6049	
D-9288-4M	Schleicher ASW 15B	15393	
D-9289	Schleicher ASW 28	28047	
D-9290	Rolladen-Schneider LS1-f	321	
D-9291	Rolladen-Schneider LS1-f	326	
D-9293-CF	Rolladen-Schneider LS1-f	176	
D-9294-VS	Schempp-Hirth Ventus 2a	4	
D-9296-PM	Rolladen-Schneider LS1-f	296	
D-9297	Grunau Baby III	1	D-4684 D-5043
D-9298	Glasflügel H401 Kestrel	115	
D-9299	Glasflügel H401 Kestrel	116	
D-9300	SZD-50-3 Puchacz	B-1082	DDR-3600
D-9301	SZD-50-3 Puchacz	B-1634	SP-3402
D-9302	Schleicher Ka 6CR Rhönsegler	6398	
D-9303-MV	Glaser-Dirks DG-300 Elan Acro	3E452A12	
D-9304	Glasflügel H304	201	
D-9305	Glaser-Dirks DG-300 Club Elan	3E284C9	
D-9306	Glaser-Dirks DG-300 Club Elan	3E287C11	
D-9307	Scheibe Bergfalke III	5538	
D-9309	Akaflieg Braunschweig SB-5B Sperber	5015	
D-9311	Schleicher Ka 6CR Rhönsegler	6397	
D-9312-CZ	Schleicher K 8B	8226	
D-9313	Schleicher Ka 6CR Rhönsegler	6401	
D-9314	Schleicher K 8B	8392/SH	
D-9315	Bölkow Phoebus A-1	702	
D-9316-MO	Schleicher ASW 27	27076	
D-9317	Schleicher Rhönlerche II (Reservation)	102	
D-9320	Bölkow Phoebus B-1	707	
D-9321	Scheibe Bergfalke III	5533	
D-9322	Schleicher K 8B	8617/SH	
D-9323	Glasflügel H301 Libelle	9	
D-9325	Schleicher K 7 Rhönadler	7204	
D-9328	Schleicher K 8B	8174/A	
D-9330	Schleicher ASK 21	21551	
D-9331	Schleicher ASH 25	25057	
D-9333	Schleicher K 8C	AB81008	
D-9334	Scheibe SF-27A	6011	
D-9336	Glasflügel BS-1	14	
D-9338	Schempp-Hirth SHK-1	21	
D-9339-LD	Schempp-Hirth Duo Discus	367	
D-9340	Schleicher Ka 6CR Rhönsegler	953	
D-9343	Scheibe SF-27A (Permit .00)	6072	
D-9348	Schleicher Ka 6CR Rhönsegler	6443	
D-9349	Glasflügel H304	204	
D-9350	Rolladen-Schneider LS3-a	3233	PH-638
D-9352	Glaser-Dirks DG-300 Elan	3E134	
D-9355	Schleicher Ka 6E	4012	
D-9357	SZD-24-4A Foka 4	W-251	
D-9359	Akaflieg Braunschweig SB-5B Sperber	5014	
D-9360	Scheibe Bergfalke III	5557	
D-9361	Scheibe Bergfalke III	5556	
D-9363	Schempp-Hirth Discus b	38	
D-9365	Schleicher Ka 6E	4001	
D-9366	Schempp-Hirth SHK-1	06	
D-9367	SZD-9bis Bocian 1E	P-554	DDR-3367 DM-3367
D-9369	Schleicher Ka 6CR Rhönsegler	6488Si	
D-9370	Scheibe L-Spatz 55	511	
D-9371	Bölkow Phoebus B-1	720	
D-9372	Schleicher Ka 6CR Rhönsegler	6499	
D-9373	Glaser-Dirks DG-300 Elan	3E181	
D-9378-S7	Glasflügel H301 Libelle	20	
D-9380	SZD-9bis Bocian 1E	P-576	DDR-3380 DM-3380
D-9382	Scheibe L-Spatz III	818	
D-9383	Akaflieg Braunschweig SB-5B Sperber	5029	
D-9384	SZD-9bis Bocian 1E	P-590	DDR-3384 DM-3384
D-9385	Scheibe Bergfalke III	5575	
D-9386	Schleicher K 8B	8225/A	
D-9387	Schempp-Hirth Discus CS	227CS	

D-9388	Schempp-Hirth Discus CS	228CS	
D-9389-AF	Schempp-Hirth Discus CS	232CS	
D-9390	Schempp-Hirth Discus CS	231CS	
D-9391	Schleicher ASW 20CL	20720	
D-9392	Schleicher ASK 21	21193	
D-9393	Schleicher ASW 20CL	20721	
D-9395	Schempp-Hirth Janus Ce	303	
D-9396	Schempp-Hirth Discus CS	234CS	
D-9397	Schleicher Ka 6CR Rhönsegler	6550	
D-9398	Scheibe SF-27A	6052	
D-9399	Schleicher Ka 6CR Rhönsegler	6563	
D-9401	Schleicher Ka 6CR Rhönsegler	6561	
D-9402	Scheibe Bergfalke II/55	208	HB-569
D-9403	Schleicher ASK 13	13006	
D-9404	Schleicher K 8B	8691	
D-9405	Schleicher Ka 6CR Rhönsegler	6576	
D-9406	SZD-38A Jantar 1	B-639	DDR-2403 DM-2403
D-9407	SZD-41A Jantar Standard	B-696	DDR-2407 DM-2407
D-9408	Schleicher Ka 6CR Rhönsegler	6592	
D-9409	Schleicher K 8B	8698	
D-9410-AT	Glaser-Dirks DG-300 Elan	3E285	OY-XPI
D-9411-PV	Scheibe SF-27A	6081	
D-9412	Glasflügel H301 Libelle	45	
D-9413	Rolladen-Schneider LS1-f	311	
D-9414	Schleicher ASK 13	13039	
D-9415	Glasflügel BS.1	10	
D-9416	Glasflügel BS.1	11	
D-9417	Scheibe Bergfalke III	5611	
D-9418	Scheibe SF-27A	6104	
D-9419	Scheibe L-Spatz III	830	
D-9420	Schempp-Hirth Discus 2B (For conversion to Discus 2T c/n 3/69)	69	
D-9421	SZD-42-1 Jantar 2	B-778	DDR-2421 DM-2421
D-9422	Schempp-Hirth Cirrus	16	
D-9424	Scheibe Bergfalke III	5610	
D-9425	SZD-41A Jantar Standard	B-899	DDR-2425 DM-2425
D-9427 -Y	Glaser-Dirks DG-200/17C	2-157CL13	
D-9428-JM	Glasflügel H201B Standard Libelle	110	SE-TIT
D-9429	Glaser-Dirks DG-100G Elan	E81G56	
D-9430	Scheibe Bergfalke III	5618	
D-9431	Glasflügel H304	234	
D-9432	Glasflügel H206 Hornet	1	
D-9433	Schempp-Hirth Standard Cirrus	487G	
D-9435-FF	Rolladen-Schneider LS1-f	162	
D-9436	SZD-48-3 Jantar Standard 3	B-1969	
D-9439	Rolladen-Schneider LS1-f	319	
D-9440	Schempp-Hirth Duo Discus	160	
D-9442	Glasflügel H401 Kestrel	118	
D-9443	Schempp-Hirth Standard Cirrus	479	PH-508
D-9444	Glasflügel H205 Club Libelle	6	
D-9445	Glasflügel H205 Club Libelle	7	
D-9446	LET L-13 Blanik	026056	
D-9447-M	Glasflügel H201B Standard Libelle	592	
D-9448	Glasflügel H201B Standard Libelle	593	
D-9449	Glasflügel H201B Standard Libelle	594	
D-9450	Rolladen-Schneider LS1-f	186	
D-9451	Glasflügel H205 Club Libelle	8	
D-9452	Glasflügel H205 Club Libelle	9	
D-9453	Rolladen-Schneider LS1-f	302	
D-9454	Start & Flug H101 Salto	59	
D-9455-HI	Schempp-Hirth Duo Discus	95	
D-9456	Rolladen-Schneider LS1-f	174	
D-9457	Schempp-Hirth Standard Cirrus	519G	
D-9459	Rolladen-Schneider LS1-f	317	
D-9461-CS	Schleicher ASH 26	26092	
D-9463-i6	Glasflügel H205 Club Libelle	10	
D-9464	Glasflügel H205 Club Libelle	11	
D-9465	Glasflügel H205 Club Libelle	12	
D-9466-ZY	Glasflügel H205 Club Libelle	13	
D-9467	Glasflügel H205 Club Libelle	14	
D-9468	Rolladen-Schneider LS1-f	282	
D-9469	Glasflügel H205 Club Libelle	15	
D-9470	Glasflügel H205 Club Libelle	16	
D-9471	Glasflügel H205 Club Libelle	17	
D-9473	Glasflügel H205 Club Libelle	19	
D-9474	Glasflügel H205 Club Libelle	20	
D-9475	Glasflügel H205 Club Libelle	21	
D-9478	Glasflügel H205 Club Libelle	24	
D-9479	Rolladen-Schneider LS1-f	249	
D-9480	Schempp-Hirth Nimbus 2	90	
D-9481	Glasflügel H205 Club Libelle	25	
D-9482	Glasflügel H205 Club Libelle	26	
D-9484	Rolladen-Schneider LS1-f	360	
D-9485	Rolladen-Schneider LS1-f	361	
D-9486	Rolladen-Schneider LS1-f	362	
D-9487	Glasflügel H205 Club Libelle	27	
D-9488	Rolladen-Schneider LS1-f	372	
D-9489	Schempp-Hirth Standard Cirrus	523	
D-9490	Schleicher ASK 21	21684	
D-9491	Schleicher ASW 17	17038	
D-9492-1B	Schempp-Hirth Discus CS	002CS	D-0866 OK-0366 ?
D-9493	Glasflügel H205 Club Libelle	32	

D-9494	Glasflügel H205 Club Libelle	33	
D-9495	Glasflügel H205 Club Libelle	34	
D-9496	Schleicher ASW 20CL	20779	D-KAWH
			D-8786
D-9497	Schempp-Hirth Standard Cirrus	540G	
D-9498	Rolladen-Schneider LS1-f	328	
D-9499-Y9	Schleicher ASW 24	24074	
D-9500	Start & Flug H101 Salto	64	
D-9510	Marganski MDM-1 Fox	214	
D-9511	Schempp-Hirth Ventus-2c	90	
D-9512	Grob G.104 Speed Astir IIB	4076	HB-1512
D-9520	Grob G.104 Speed Astir IIB	4098	HB-1520
D-9521	Schleicher ASK 21	21630	
D-9522	Schleicher ASK 21	21653	
D-9528-1B	Schleicher ASW 28	28018	
D-9539	Scheibe Bergfalke IV	5866	SE-TSI
D-9555	Marganski MDM-1 Fox	209	OE-5626
D-9559	SZD-59 Acro	590.A.04.001	
D-9560	Schempp-Hirth Discus-2b	205	
D-9567	Rolladen-Schneider LS6-a	6064	OO-YLS
			D-2567
D-9571	Glasflügel H304	238	HB-1571
D-9590	Swift S1	116	HB-3138
D-9595-AD	Schempp-Hirth Ventus 2a	49	
D-9599	Schempp-Hirth Ventus 2c	68	
D-9600	Glaser-Dirks DG-600/18	6-107	HB-3092
D-9605-FT	Akaflieg Karlsruhe AK-5B (Permit)	502(formerly 1)	
D-9608-FA	Akaflieg Karlsruhe AK 8	801	(D-0820)
D-9609	SZD-48-3 Jantar Standard 3	B-1947	RA-1947
			D-5647
			DOSAAF
D-9611	Schempp-Hirth Discus a	1	HB-1783
			D-6111
D-9614	Schempp-Hirth Discus-2b	192	
D-9622	Eiri PIK-20D	20629	PH-622
D-9628-SEI	Schleicher ASW 28	28053	
D-9646	Grob G 102 Astir CS 77	1798	PH-646
D-9664	Rolladen-Schneider LS3-17 (Permit .00)	3461	F-CESV
D-9669	Rolladen-Schneider LS8-a	8074	
D-9676	LET L-13 Blanik (Permit .02)	026249	
D-9680	Schleicher ASW 27	27077	
D-9688	Grob G.103 Twin Astir	3134	F-CFBQ
D-9696-BK	Schempp-Hirth Ventus 2b	50	
D-9707-W7	Schempp-Hirth Discus 2B	146	
D-9708-Y6	Rolladen-Schneider LS8-18	8463	D-9239
D-9710	Rolladen-Schneider LS10-a (Permit 10.03)	10001	
D-9727 -K	Schleicher ASW 27	27050	
D-9728	Schleicher ASW 28	28054	
D-9733-33	Akaflieg Stuttgart FS 33 Gavilán (Permit)	33-1	
D-9760	Schempp-Hirth Discus b	9	HB-1760
D-9777	Schleicher ASW 17	17006	OO-VAT
			PL-69
			OO-ZUU
D-9801	Rolladen-Schneider LS8-a	8099	
D-9802	Schleicher ASK 21	21680	
D-9804	Rolladen-Schneider LS4	4514	HB-1804
D-9808-VH	DG Flugzeugbau DG-800S (Permit 2.03)	8-290S53X1	
D-9814-10	Akaflieg Braunschweig SB14 (Permit 1.03)	1	
D-9821	Schleicher ASK 21	21673	
D-9827	Schleicher ASW 27	27073	
D-9828-D2	Schempp-Hirth Duo Discus	362	
D-9888	Rolladen-Schneider LS8-a	8123	
D-9889	Schempp-Hirth Discus 2a	208	
D-9899	Marganski MDM-1 Fox	227	
D-9901	Rolladen-Schneider LS6-c-18	6382	
D-9902-BW1	Schempp-Hirth Duo Discus	321	
D-9903	SZD-41A Jantar Standard	B-693	D-2305
			DDR-2405
			DM-2405
D-9904	Glasflügel H201B Standard Libelle	295	D-3060
			HB-1060
D-9906	Schleicher ASK 21	21741	
D-9908-Y	Schempp-Hirth Ventus 2a	144	
D-9910-BW2	Schempp-Hirth Discus 2B	113	
D-9911-B	Schempp-Hirth Ventus 2b	119	
D-9913-5K	Grob G.102 Astir CS	1117	OY-XIY
			D-6971
D-9919	Schleicher K 8B	4	D-1919
D-9921	Schleicher ASK 21	21276	OY-XOC
D-9922	Schleicher ASH 26	26189	
D-9923-KV	Schempp-Hirth Discus-2b	202	
D-9928-LL	Schleicher ASW 28	28030	
D-9930	DG Flugzeugbau DG-1000S	10-30S29	
D-9938	VT-116 Orlik II ZK	151403	OK-5516 ?
D-9944	Rolladen-Schneider LS8B	8441	
D-9950	SZD-50-3 Puchacz	B-1534	DDR-3650
D-9959	SZD-59 Acro	B-2179	
D-9966	DG Flugzeugbau DG-800S	8-56S15	
D-9970	B-5 (Permit 6.99)	01	
D-9977-77	Schleicher ASW 27	27075	
D-9990-000	DG Flugzeugbau DG-1000S	10-1S1	
D-9994	SZD-9bis Bocian 1E	P-640	OE-0994
D-9995-i1	DG Flugzeugbau DG-1000S	10-4S4	
D-9998	Schempp-Hirth Ventus-2a	155	
D-9999-MH	Schempp-Hirth Duo Discus	129	

EC - SPAIN

The official Spanish register published is now being published and although a few unidentified sales to Spain still remain there are far fewer than in the past. A number of inactive aircraft are still officially registered and status reports on those damaged or wfu would be welcome.

Regn.	Type	C/n	Prev.Id.
EC-AAP	Piper L-14 Army Cruiser	5-3007	CU-P18
			NC41594
			(45-55531)
EC-ACA	de Havilland DH.87A Hornet Moth (Stored)	8039	EC-CAI
			EC-EBE
			EC-W51
EC-ACB	Miles M.3 Falcon (Museum)	197	EC-CAO
			EC-BDD
EC-ACJ	Auster J/1 Autocrat (Stored)	1960	EC-DAZ
			G-AHCF
EC-ACU	Miles M.38 Messenger 2A (Stored)	6360	EC-UAU
			(EC-EAL)
			G-AJEZ
EC-ADA	Piper PA-12 Super Cruiser	12-3535	
EC-ADG	Auster J/1 Autocrat (Stored)	2216	G-AJAL
EC-ADS	Piper J-3C-65 Cub Special (Damaged 22.2.97)	22467	
EC-ADU	Stinson 108-3 Voyager	4386	N6386M
EC-ADY	Stinson 108-3 Voyager	4344	N6344M
EC-AEE	Stinson 108-3 Voyager	4394	N6394M
EC-AFB	Cessna 170	19169	F-OAGF
			N11B
			N9708A
EC-AFC	Piper PA-12 Super Cruiser	12-1641	
EC-AFF	Stinson 108-3 Voyager	5183	N4183C
EC-AFG	Stinson 108-3 Voyager	4366	N6366M
EC-AGH	Piper PA-20 Pacer 125	20-648	
EC-AGJ	North American Navion 4	4-1519	F-OAIP
			N4519K
EC-AGM	Macchi MB.308	5807/34	I-MACC
EC-AGZ	Slingsby T-45 Swallow	1614	
EC-AHB	Percival P.34A Proctor 3	H.463	G-AMCO
			LZ681
EC-AHD	Piper J-3C-65 Cub Special	22468	NC3401N
EC-AHG	Piper PA-12 Super Cruiser	12-2451	OO-XAZ
			NC2290M
EC-AHL	CASA C-1.131L Jungmann (Rebuild)	unkn	EE.3-205
EC-AIA	Slingsby T-45 Swallow (Stored dismantled)	1656	
EC-AIF	Boeing Stearman E75 (Museum)	75-5513	N4657V
			42-17350
EC-AIJ	Piper PA-18A-135 Super Cub	18-2479	N10F
EC-AIQ	Piper PA-18-150 Super Cub	18-4615	F-BHAB
			N10F
EC-AIS	Auster J/1 Autocrat	2190	G-AIGH
EC-AIU	de Havilland DH.82A Tiger Moth (Rebuild)	3657	MM30-116
			F-AQJX
EC-AIY	Piper J-3C-65 Cub	12639	HB-ODO
			44-80343
EC-AJE	Piper PA-18A-135 Super Cub	18-2935	N10F
EC-AJF	Piper PA-18A-135 Super Cub	18-2883	N10F
EC-AJM	Boeing Stearman E75	75-5498	N4889V
	(Reserved as N126SE)		42-17335
EC-AJR	Auster Mk.5	1505	EC-WJR
			TJ517
EC-AJU	Grumman G.44A Widgeon	734	N41971
EC-AJY	Piper J-3C-65 Cub (Museum)	12965	HB-OCM
			44-80669
EC-AJZ	Fairchild F.24W-41A Argus II	663	HB-EAP
			FZ723
			43-14697
EC-AKD	Piper J-3C-65 Cub	11691	G-AISP
			43-30400
EC-AKE	Auster Mk.5	1526	HB-EOB
			TJ479
EC-AKK	AISA I-11B Peque	005-1-70	
EC-AKL	AISA I-11B Peque	006-1-70	
EC-AKO	de Havilland DH.89A Dragon Rapide (Dismantled)	6345	G-AERN
EC-AKQ	Piper J-3C-65 Cub	11190	HB-ONR
			43-29899
EC-AKU	Auster Mk.4	865	G-ALVV
			MT143
EC-ALD	Auster J/1 Autocrat	1967	G-AGXS
EC-ALK	Piper PA-18A-150 Super Cub (Cr 26.3.04)	18-3791	N10F
EC-ALP	CASA C-1.133C Jungmeister (Museum)	041/1023	ES1-17
EC-ALS	Aerodiffusion Jodel D.112	E.5	
EC-ALU	Aerodiffusion Jodel D.112	E.8	
EC-AMK	Piper PA-18A-150 Super Cub	18-4859	N10F
EC-ANB	Aerodiffusion Jodel D.112	E.17	
EC-AND	Aerodiffusion Jodel D.112 (Stored dismantled)	E.19	
EC-ANH	Piper PA-20 Pacer 135 (Wfu)	20-847	F-OAKO
			N10F
EC-ANI	Auster Mk.5	1262	HB-EOG
			RT635
EC-ANM	North American Navion D-16	4-753	EC-WNM
			N8753H
EC-AOM	Aerodiffusion Jodel D.112	E.32	
EC-AOR	Aerodiffusion Jodel D.112	E.37	
EC-AOU	Aerodiffusion Jodel D.112 (Stored dismantled)	E.41	
EC-AOV	Aerodiffusion Jodel D.112 (Stored dismantled)	E.42	
EC-AOY	Jodel D.1190-S	E-56	
	(Current but believed b/u Sywell 4.98)		

EC-APB	Beech 35-C33A Debonair	CE-70	D-ECMO
EC-APH	Omnipol Super Aero 45	04-005	
EC-API	Cessna 182 Skylane	33615	N5615B
EC-APJ	PZL-101-G2 Gawron	101701	SP-PBK SP-PAG
EC-APK	Aerodiffusion Jodel D.112	E.45	
EC-APO	Aerodiffusion Jodel D.112	E.54	
EC-APR	Schleicher Ka 6CR Rhönsegler (Museum)	784	
EC-APS	Schleicher Ka 6CR Rhönsegler	727	
EC-AQA	AISA I-11B Peque	54	L.8C-54
EC-AQB	Douglas C-47A-20-DK	12844	EC-WQB N54705 42-92983
EC-AQJ	PZL-101-G2 Gawron	30019	SP-CED
EC-AQS	Piper PA-25-235 Pawnee	25-430	N10F
EC-AQV	Piper PA-25-235 Pawnee	25-432	N10F
EC-ARD	Piper PA-25-150 Pawnee	25-446	N6336Z
EC-ARG	Piper PA-25-150 Pawnee (2-seater)	25-464	N6351Z
EC-ARX	Piper PA-25-150 Pawnee (Wfu ?)	25-629	N10F
EC-ARY	Piper PA-25-150 Pawnee	25-645	N10F
EC-ASA	Piper PA-25-150 Pawnee	25-491	N10F
EC-ASB	Piper PA-25-150 Pawnee	25-651	N10F
EC-ASJ	Beech C-45H (Museum)	AF-752	N9962Z 52-10822
EC-ASO	Edgar Percival EP-9 Prospector	25	G-APCT G-43-4
EC-ASU	Piper PA-18A-150 Super Cub (Badly damaged 3.7.94)	8-4607	CN-TEH F-DAEN N10F
EC-ASV	Piper PA-18A-150 Super Cub	8-5408	CN-TEC F-DAFC N10F
EC-ASY	Piper PA-18A-135 Super Cub (Crashed 7.79 but still extant)	8-2937	CN-TEB F-DABP N10F
EC-ATJ	Aerodiffusion Jodel D.112	.50	
EC-ATS	Aerodiffusion Jodel D.1190-S	.58	
EC-ATZ	Dornier Do.28A-1	3045	EC-WTZ
EC-AUD	Agusta-Bell 47G-3B (W/o 30.8.02)	1520	
EC-AUE	Agusta-Bell 47G-3B	1521	
EC-AUF	Beech H35 Bonanza	D-5105	HB-EBA D-EJIN N12B
EC-AUI	Piper PA-25-235 Pawnee	25-2179	N6617Z N10F
EC-AUK	Mooney M.20C Mark 21	2395	N6668U
EC-AUL	Aerodiffusion Jodel D.1190-S	E.59	
EC-AUO	Piper PA-25-235 Pawnee	25-2315	N10F
EC-AUQ	CEA Jodel DR.1050 Ambassadeur	421	EC-WUQ
EC-AUT	Piper PA-25-235 Pawnee	25-2327	N10F
EC-AUU	Piper PA-25-235 Pawnee	25-2330	N10F
EC-AVB	Piper PA-25-150 Pawnee	25-725	N10F
EC-AVC	Piper PA-25-150 Pawnee	25-726	N10F
EC-AVE	Aerodiffusion Jodel D.1190-S (Stored dismantled)	E.60	
EC-AVF	Cessna 182F Skylane	18254594	N3194U
EC-AVG	Aerodiffusion Jodel D.1190-S	E.62	
EC-AVH	Tipsy T.66 Nipper Mk.2	63	OO-FOL
EC-AVI	Hughes 269A (W/o 13.6.98?)	43-0201	
EC-AVJ	Cessna 170B	20573	N2421D
EC-AVK	Cessna 182F Skylane	18254426	N3526Y
EC-AVL	Cessna F172E	F172-0027/17250582	
EC-AVM	Dornier Do.27Q-5	2038	OE-DCA OE-VAK
EC-AVO	Piper PA-25-235 Pawnee	25-2428	N6829Z N10F
EC-AVQ	Aerodiffusion Jodel D.1190-S	E.68	
EC-AVR	Aerodiffusion Jodel D.1190-S	E.65	
EC-AVU	Aerodiffusion Jodel D.1190-S	E.66	
EC-AVX	Aero Commander 520	10	EC-WVX F-BBDY N4109B
EC-AXA	Zlin Z.326A Akrobat	861	EC-WXA
EC-AXD	Zlin Z.326A Akrobat	898	EC-WXD
EC-AXG	Aerodiffusion Jodel D.1190-S	E.67	
EC-AXL	Zlin Z.326A Akrobat	899	
EC-AXO	Piper PA-25-235 Pawnee	25-2582	N6886Z N10F
EC-AXQ	Piper PA-28-180 Cherokee B	28-1732	N7725W
EC-AXT	Aerodiffusion Jodel D.1190-S	E.73	
EC-AXV	Beech 95-B55 Baron (Wfu)	TC-730	
EC-AYM	Piper PA-25-235 Pawnee B	25-3068	N10F
EC-AYV	Piper PA-25-235 Pawnee B (Wfu)	25-3065	N10F
EC-AYX	Aerodiffusion Jodel D.1190-S	E.78	
EC-AZE	Piper PA-25-235 Pawnee B	25-3103	N10F
EC-AZF	Piper PA-25-235 Pawnee B	25-3114	N7203Z
EC-AZI	Agusta-Bell 47G-4	2509	MM80412
EC-AZJ	Piper PA-25-235 Pawnee B (Damaged 29.6.00)	25-3130	N10F
EC-AZL	Piper PA-25-235 Pawnee B	25-3123	N10F
EC-AZQ	Stinson 108-3 Voyager	unkn	L.2-17
EC-AZV	Piper PA-23-250 Aztec C	27-2846	N5762Y N10F
EC-AZY	Cessna F172F	F172-0161	EC-WZY
EC-BAH	Aerodiffusion Jodel D.1190-S	E.86	
EC-BAI	Aerodiffusion Jodel D.1190-S	E.87	
EC-BAK	Piper PA-22-150 Tri-Pacer	22-5427	SE-CDB N7747D

EC-BAM	Piper PA-28-180 Cherokee C	28-2206	N11C N8107W
EC-BAN	Grumman G.164 Agcat	334	N605U
EC-BAP	Gardan GY-80 Horizon 160	95	
EC-BAS	Aerodiffusion Jodel D.1190-S	E.101	(D-ELCO)
EC-BAT	Aerodiffusion Jodel D.1190-S	E.102	
EC-BBB	Cessna F172F	F172-0175	EC-WBB
EC-BBE	Piper PA-23-250 Aztec C	27-2914	N5784Y
EC-BBG	Bölkow BO.208C Junior	512	D-ENCO
EC-BBI	Piper PA-25-235 Pawnee B	25-3280	N7332Z
EC-BBJ	Cessna F172G	F172-0193	EC-WBJ
EC-BBL	MS.886 Rallye 150	440	
EC-BBM	Aerodiffusion Jodel D.1190-S	E.83	
EC-BBO	Aerodiffusion Jodel D.1190-S	E.85	
EC-BBS	Piper PA-18-150 Super Cub	18-8264	N7147Z
EC-BBU	Mooney M.20E Super 21	720	
EC-BBX	Piper PA-30 Twin Comanche	30-642	N7576Y
EC-BBZ	Piper PA-23-250 Aztec C	27-2938	N5805Y
EC-BCA	Cessna F172G	F172-0215	EC-WCA
EC-BCB	Beech D95A Travel Air	TD-635	D-GARE
EC-BCG	Piper PA-25-235 Pawnee B (Crashed 22.6.03)	25-3454	N7458Z
EC-BCL	Aerodiffusion Jodel D.1190-S	E.92	
EC-BCN	Slingsby T-45 Swallow	1488	
EC-BCO	Slingsby T-45 Swallow	1490	
EC-BCP	Piper PA-25-235 Pawnee B	25-3398	N7423Z
EC-BCR	Piper PA-25-235 Pawnee B	25-3487	N7479Z
EC-BCT	Beech A23 Musketeer	M-765	D-EMNE
EC-BCV	Agusta-Bell 47G-4	2513	
EC-BCX	Piper PA-25-235 Pawnee B	25-3493	N7483Z
EC-BDA	Piper PA-25-235 Pawnee B	25-3640	N7574Z
EC-BDB	Piper PA-25-235 Pawnee B	25-3414	N7431Z
EC-BDJ	SOCATA MS.893A Rallye Commodore 180	10571	
EC-BDN	Piper PA-28-180 Cherokee C	28-2816	N11C N8852J
EC-BDP	Aerodiffusion Jodel D.1190-S	E.90	
EC-BDQ	Aerodiffusion Jodel D.1190-S	E.93	
EC-BDR	Aerodiffusion Jodel D.1190-S	E.94	
EC-BDS	Zlin Z.526A Akrobat	1001	EC-WDS
EC-BDV	Zlin Z.526A Akrobat (Dismantled)	1004	EC-WDV
EC-BEI	Cessna 182J Skylane	18256945	N2845F
EC-BEK	Aerodiffusion Jodel D.1190-S	E.103	
EC-BEL	Aerodiffusion Jodel D.1190-S	E.109	
EC-BEM	Mooney M.20E Super 21	1081	
EC-BEP	Beech A23-19 Musketeer Sport III	MB-161	HB-ENY
EC-BEQ	Piper PA-28-180 Cherokee C	28-4008	N11C
EC-BEU	Fauvel AV-361 (Originally listed as Bergfalke c/n 5568 - see EC-BEY)	152	
EC-BEV	Scheibe Bergfalke III	5561	
EC-BEY	Scheibe Bergfalke III (Crashed 31.5.03 Quero)	5568	
EC-BEZ	Scheibe Bergfalke III	5559	
EC-BFD	Scheibe L-Spatz 55	808	
EC-BFE	Scheibe L-Spatz 55 (Preserved)	809	
EC-BFF	Scheibe L-Spatz 55 (Stored)	810	
EC-BFG	Scheibe L-Spatz 55	811	
EC-BFN	Grumman G.164 Agcat	399	N663U
EC-BFO	Piper PA-28-180 Cherokee C (Damaged 18.12.03)	28-3077	N9046J
EC-BFU	Hughes 269B	116-0275	
EC-BFX	Hughes 269B	106-0268	
EC-BFY	Hughes 269B	106-0269	
EC-BFZ	Aerodiffusion Jodel D.1190-S	E.104	
EC-BGA	Cessna F150G	F150-0104	
EC-BGC	Piper PA-28-180 Cherokee C	28-3254	N9186J
EC-BGD	Piper PA-25-235 Pawnee B (Dbr 7.5.02)	25-4009	N4498Y N10F
EC-BGG	Cessna A188 Agwagon	188-0172	N9722V
EC-BGH	Piper PA-28-140 Cherokee	28-22148	N11C
EC-BGI	Piper PA-25-235 Pawnee B	25-3761	N7791Z N10F
EC-BGJ	Piper PA-25-235 Pawnee B	25-3762	N7792Z N10F
EC-BGK	Piper PA-25-235 Pawnee B	25-3842	N4459Y N4495Y N10F
EC-BGM	Piper PA-25-235 Pawnee B	25-3926	N7747Z
EC-BGN	Piper PA-25-235 Pawnee B	25-3759	N7790Z N10F
EC-BGO	Cessna F150G	F150-0105	
EC-BGP	Piper PA-25-235 Pawnee B	25-3924	N7744Z
EC-BGQ	Piper PA-25-235 Pawnee B	25-3775	N7793Z N10F
EC-BGS	Piper PA-25-235 Pawnee B	25-3779	N7795Z N10F
EC-BGT	Piper PA-25-235 Pawnee B	25-4012	N4499Y N10F
EC-BGV	Piper PA-25-235 Pawnee B	25-4015	N4500Y N10F
EC-BGX	Piper PA-14 Family Cruiser	14-177	F-BLXZ OO-ARY
EC-BHF	Slingsby T-45 Swallow	1540	
EC-BHI	Slingsby T-45 Swallow (Stored)	1544	
EC-BHK	Slingsby T-45 Swallow	1546	
EC-BHM	Slingsby T-45 Swallow	1547	
EC-BHN	Slingsby T-45 Swallow (Stored)	1549	
EC-BHO	Slingsby T-45 Swallow (Museum)	1548	
EC-BHR	Slingsby T-45 Swallow	1552	
EC-BHU	Slingsby T-45 Swallow	1555	

EC-BHV	Slingsby T-45 Swallow (Stored)	1556	
EC-BHZ	Slingsby T-45 Swallow	1559	
EC-BJE	Beech A23-24 Musketeer Super III	MA-75	D-EKWA
EC-BJJ	Cessna F172H	F172-0338	
EC-BJL	Cessna A188 Agwagon	188-0224	N9774V
EC-BJM	Scheibe Bergfalke III	5534	
EC-BJN	Scheibe Bergfalke III	5546	
EC-BJO	Scheibe Bergfalke III (Dismantled)	5548	
EC-BJP	Beech A23-19 Musketeer Sport	MB-117	D-EJVA
EC-BJR	Piper PA-30 Twin Comanche B	30-1266	N8153Y
EC-BJS	Piper PA-25-235 Pawnee C (W/o 7.94)	25-4215	N4557Y
EC-BJU	Piper PA-23-250 Aztec C (Wfu)	27-3603	N6339Y
EC-BJX	Beech D95A Travel Air	TD-696	D-GARU
EC-BJY	SIAI-Marchetti S.205-20/R	362	EC-WJY
EC-BKB	AISA I-11B Peque	unkn	L.8C-4
EC-BKF	AISA I-11B Peque	unkn	L.8C-14
EC-BKG	Beech D95A Travel Air	TD-689	D-GARO
EC-BKH	AISA I-11B Peque (Museum)	unkn	L.8C-16
EC-BKK	AISA I-11B Peque	unkn	L.8C-21
EC-BKN	Piper PA-18-150 Super Cub	18-4061	54-2661
EC-BLX	AISA I-11B Peque (W/o 2.9.94?)	unkn	L.8C-123
EC-BLY	AISA I-11B Peque	unkn	L.8C-132
EC-BLZ	Aerodiffusion Jodel D.1190-S	E.110	
EC-BMA	Beech A23-24 Musketeer Super III	MA-218	D-EJVE
EC-BMC	Agusta-Bell 47G-4	2520	
EC-BMF	Piper PA-25-235 Pawnee C	25-4365	N4645Y
EC-BMG	SIAI-Marchetti S.205-20/R	4-107	EC-WMG
EC-BMH	SIAI-Marchetti S.205-20/R	4-115	EC-WMH
EC-BMK	Piper PA-28-180 Cherokee C	28-3973	N9774J
EC-BMN	Piper PA-25-235 Pawnee C	25-4323	N10F
EC-BMO	Piper PA-32-300 Cherokee Six	32-40132	N4136W
EC-BMP	Bölkow Phoebus A-1	708	D-1206
EC-BMR	Cessna 182K Skylane	18258034	N3034Q
EC-BNB	Piper PA-25-235 Pawnee C	25-4369	N4649Y
EC-BND	Piper PA-32-260 Cherokee Six	32-927	N5509J
EC-BNE	Cessna F172H	F172-0460	EC-WNE
			(G-AVIS)
EC-BNK	Piper PA-28R-180 Cherokee Arrow	28R-30056	N11C
EC-BNO	Beech A23-24 Musketeer Super III	MA-219	D-EJVI
EC-BNP	Piper PA-23-250 Aztec C	7-2963	YV-T-HTH
			N10F
EC-BNV	Cessna 182L Skylane	18258852	N42099
EC-BNY	Piper PA-28R-180 Cherokee Arrow	28R-30302	N11C
EC-BOF	Piper PA-28-140 Cherokee (On rebuild)	28-24125	N11C
EC-BOG	Piper PA-25-235 Pawnee C	25-4449	N4714Y
EC-BOH	Piper PA-28R-180 Cherokee Arrow (Stored)	28R-30440	N11C
EC-BOI	DHC-1 Chipmunk 22	C1/0147	D-EJAN
			G-AOJV
			WB699
EC-BOJ	Aerodiffusion Jodel D. 1190 -S	E.115	
EC-BOK	SOCATA MS.893A Rallye Commodore 180	10749	
EC-BOL	Slingsby HP-14C	1637	BGA1402
EC-BOM	SZD-24A Foka 4 (Stored)	W-366	
EC-BON	SZD-24A Foka 4 (Museum)	W-367	
EC-BOR	SIAI-Marchetti S.205-20/R	4-200	
EC-BOT	Piper PA-25-260 Pawnee C	25-4514	N4756Y
EC-BOX	Bölkow Phoebus C	841	
EC-BOY	Sportavia/ Fournier RF-4D	4067	
EC-BPD	Piper PA-28R-180 Cherokee Arrow	28R-30672	N11C
EC-BPI	Brockmeier/Schleicher Rhönlerche II	3081/Br	
EC-BPN	AISA I-11B Peque	unkn	L.8C-11
EC-BPR	AISA I-11B Peque	unkn	L.8C-87
EC-BPT	AISA I-11B Peque	unkn	L.8C-129
EC-BPV	Brockmeier/Schleicher Rhönlerche II	3082/Br	
	(Wreck noted at Cuatro Vientos 1994)		
EC-BPX	Brockmeier/Schleicher Rhönlerche II	3083/Br	
EC-BPY	AISA I-11B Peque	unkn	L.8C-134
EC-BPZ	Aerodiffusion Jodel D.1190-S	E.117	
EC-BQC	Piper PA-30 Twin Comanche B	30-1723	N8571Y
EC-BQD	Piper PA-28R-180 Cherokee Arrow	28R-30709	N4960J
EC-BQE	Piper PA-28-140 Cherokee	28-24604	N7260J
EC-BQN	SIAI-Marchetti S.205-20/R	4-162	
EC-BQO	SIAI-Marchetti S.205-20/F	4-163	
EC-BQP	SIAI-Marchetti S.205-20/R	4-160	
EC-BQR	Aerodiffusion Jodel D.1190-S	E.118	
EC-BRA	Piper PA-23-250 Aztec D	27-4127	N6849Y
			N9667N
EC-BRB	Aerodiffusion Jodel D.1190-S	E.119	
EC-BRD	Beech D55 Baron	TE-689	N7856R
EC-BRE	Piper PA-23-250 Turbo Aztec D	27-4120	N6784Y
EC-BRF	Piper PA-28-140 Cherokee B	28-25164	
EC-BRI	Hughes 269C	30-0015	
EC-BRK	Aerodiffusion Jodel D.1190-S	E.125	
EC-BRM	Beech 95-B55 Baron	TC-1290	
EC-BRT	Reims FR172F Rocket	FR17200109	
EC-BRV	Piper PA-25-260 Pawnee C	25-4969	N8549L
EC-BRZ	Aerodiffusion Jodel D.1190-S	E.120	
EC-BSG	Piper PA-30 Twin Comanche C	30-1919	N8763Y
	(Damaged 2.3.97)		
EC-BSH	SIAI-Marchetti S.205-20/F	4-273	
EC-BSI	Piper PA-28R-200 Cherokee Arrow	28R-35215	N9494N
EC-BSJ	Piper PA-25-260 Pawnee C	25-4861	N9715N
EC-BSL	Beech E33 Bonanza	CE-279	N2887A
EC-BSM	Piper PA-25-260 Pawnee C	25-4972	N8552L
EC-BSN	Piper PA-23-250 Aztec D	27-4289	N6932Y
	(Wreck noted 1.7.04)		
EC-BSO	Piper PA-30 Twin Comanche C	30-1945	N8787Y

EC-BSR	Piper PA-23-250 Aztec D (Wfu, stored)	27-4301	N6997Y
			N9698N
EC-BSS	Aerodiffusion Jodel D.1190-S	E.121	
EC-BST	Aerodiffusion Jodel D.1190-S	E.122	
EC-BSU	Aerodiffusion Jodel D.1190-S	E.123	
EC-BSV	Piper PA-28R-200 Cherokee Arrow	28R-35343	N11C
EC-BSX	Dornier Do.27Q-5 (Wfu, stored)	2094	D-EFKA
EC-BSZ	Piper PA-23-250 Aztec D	27-4364	N6993Y
EC-BTA	Cessna T.337D Turbo Skymaster	33701090	N86129
EC-BTD	Piper PA-28R-200 Cherokee Arrow	28R-35271	N2727R
EC-BTH(2)	Schleicher ASK 21	21323	
EC-BTK(2)	Stinson 108-3 Voyager (Museum)	4226	N6226M
			NC6226M
EC-BTM	AISA I-11B Peque	106	L.8C-106
EC-BTN(2)	Robin DR.400/180R Remorqueur	1759	
EC-BTQ(2)	Robin DR.400/180R Remorqueur	1760	
EC-BTX	AISA I-11B Peque	unkn	L.8C-67
EC-BTY	AISA I-11B Peque	unkn	L.8C-68
EC-BUB	AISA I-11B Peque	unkn	L.8C-77
EC-BUC(2)	Schleicher ASK 21	21352	
EC-BUD	AISA I-11B Peque	unkn	L.8C-84
EC-BUF(2)	Schleicher ASK 21	21351	
EC-BUI (2)	Schleicher ASK 21	21348	
EC-BUK(2)	Schleicher ASK 21	21353	
EC-BUO(2)	Schleicher ASK 21	21347	
EC-BUR	AISA I-11B Peque	unkn	L.8C- ?
EC-BUT	AISA I-11B Peque	unkn	L.8C-121
EC-BUV	AISA I-11B Peque	unkn	L.8C-127
EC-BUY	AISA I-11B Peque (Damaged 17.7.04)	206	L.8C-128
EC-BVE	Agusta-Bell 47G-4A	2532	
EC-BVG	Dornier Do.27Q-5	2060	D-EANL
			(D-ENAH)
EC-BVH	Cessna F172H	F172-0480	F-OCLX
EC-BVI	Piper PA-25-260 Pawnee C	25-5154	N9718N
EC-BVJ	Zlin Z.526F Trenér Master	1122	
EC-BVK	Zlin Z.526F Trenér Master (Stored)	1123	
EC-BVL	Reims/Cessna F337E Super Skymaster	F33700007	
	(Reims-assembled 337E with US c/n 33701236)		
EC-BVO	Aerodiffusion Jodel D. 1190-S	E.126	
EC-BVQ	Piper PA-28-140 Cherokee B	28-26212	N11C
EC-BVS	Piper PA-25-260 Pawnee C	25-5248	N9660N
EC-BVU	SIAI-Marchetti S.205-20/R	4-274	
EC-BVY	Piper PA-28R-200 Cherokee Arrow	28R-35711	N11C
EC-BXA	Cessna 177B Cardinal	17701478	N30813
EC-BXB	Piper PA-23-250 Aztec D (Wrecked)	27-4530	N13896
EC-BXD	Piper PA-18-150 Super Cub	18-8829	N4499Z
			N9728N
EC-BXH	Macchi AL.60B-2	30/6210	D-EIRF
			I-MACW
EC-BXM	Canadair CL.215-1A10	1010	CF-TXD
EC-BXN	Canadair CL.215-1A10	1013	CF-TXF
EC-BXO	Piper PA-22-160 Tri-Pacer	22-4987	N7127D
EC-BXS	Reims/Cessna F150K	F15000644	F-BSIH
EC-BXT	Piper PA-25-260 Pawnee C	25-5283	N8796L
EC-BXU	Sportavia/ Fournier RF-5	5081	
EC-BXX	Piper PA-25-260 Pawnee C (W/o 29.9.99?)	25-5259	N8774L
EC-BXY	Piper PA-28-180 Cherokee F	28-7105044	N11C
EC-BXZ	Piper PA-25-260 Pawnee C	25-5256	N8771L
EC-BYA	Beech C23 Sundowner	M-1291	N9237Q
EC-BYO	Cessna A188 Agwagon A	188-0443	(CN-TEM)
			N8193V
EC-BYP	Piper PA-28-180 Cherokee F	28-7105047	N11C
EC-BYQ	Cessna 207 Skywagon 207 (Wfu)	20700198	N1598U
EC-BYR	LET L-13 Blanik	174802	
EC-BYS	LET L-13 Blanik	174803	
EC-BYT	Reims/Cessna F177RG Cardinal RG	F177RG0030	
	(Reims-assembled 177RG with c/n 177RG0193)		
EC-BYU	SZD-30 Pirat	B-311	
EC-BYY	Piper PA-25-260 Pawnee C	25-5305	N9742N
EC-BYZ	Piper PA-25-260 Pawnee C	25-5333	N9651N
EC-BZA	Piper PA-25-260 Pawnee C	25-5340	N.....
			PT-DVD
			N9678N
EC-BZB	Piper PA-28-140 Cherokee E	28-7225217	N11C
EC-BZC	LET L-13 Blanik	174825	
EC-BZE	LET L-13 Blanik (W/o 26.6.99?)	174827	
EC-BZF	Bell OH-13H Sioux	1880	56-2168
EC-BZG	Bell OH-13H Sioux	1934	56-2222
EC-BZH	Bell OH-13H Sioux	1955	56-2243
EC-BZI	Bell OH-13H Sioux	2052	57-1814
EC-BZK	Piper PA-28-140 Cherokee D	28-7125534	N11C
EC-BZM	Piper PA-25-260 Pawnee C	25-5387	N8925L
EC-BZT	Brockmeier /Schleicher Rhönlerche II	3090/Br	
	(Wreck noted at Cuatro Vientos 1994)		
EC-BZX	Reims/Cessna F177RG Cardinal RG	F177RG0042	
	(Reims-assembled 177RG with US c/n 177RG0206)		
EC-CAA	Sud Avn SA.319B Alouette III	1904	
EC-CAB	Cessna A188A Agwagon	18800661	N1561M
EC-CAC	Piper PA-23-250 Aztec E	27-4770	N14212
	(Badly damaged 30.9.04)		
EC-CAF	Hughes 369HS	12-0366S	
EC-CAG	Reims/Cessna F177RG Cardinal RG	F177RG0041	
	(Reims-assembled 177RG with US c/n 177RG0205)		
EC-CAH	Reims/Cessna F150L (Wreck)	F15000774	F-WLIQ
EC-CAL	Reims/Cessna F150L (Wreck)	F15000765	F-WLIP
EC-CAN	SAAB-Scania MFI-10B Vipan	02	SE-CPH
			Fv54381

EC-CAQ	Piper PA-25-260 Pawnee C	25-5461	N9672N
EC-CAV	Piper PA-28-140 Cherokee E	28-7225329	N11C
EC-CAY	Piper PA-28R-200 Arrow	28R-7235284	N11C
EC-CAZ	Piper PA-28-140 Cherokee E	28-7225526	N11C
EC-CBR	Beech A24R Sierra	MC-126	N9786L
EC-CBS	Hirth Hi.27 Akrostar Mk.II	4008	D-EMBD
EC-CBT	Piper PA-28-235 Cherokee Charger	28-7310012	N11C
EC-CBU	Piper PA-28-180 Cherokee Challenger	28-7305015	N11C
	(Damaged 10.4.04)		
EC-CCB	LET L-13 Blanik	175225	
EC-CCD	Beech 65-80 Queen Air	LD-91	D-ILDO
	(Wfu, noted 2.01)		SE-EXU
			D-ILDO
EC-CCE	Cessna 414	414-0391	N1611T
EC-CCI	Reims/Cessna F150L	F15000987	
EC-CCJ	LET L-13 Blanik	025305	
EC-CCK	LET L-13 Blanik	025306	
EC-CCL	Enstrom F-28A	101	
EC-CCM	Piper PA-28-140 Cherokee E	28-7225568	N11C
EC-CCO	Reims/Cessna F337E Super Skymaster	F33700005	G-AXWN
	(Reims-assembled 337E with US c/n 33701218)		
EC-CCR	Beech 58 Baron	TH-280	
EC-CCT	Beech 65-80 Queen Air	LD-47	SE-EWU
			D-ILDA
			SE-EDD
			D-IGWS
EC-CCV	Piper PA-28-140 Cherokee	28-7325270	N11C
EC-CCZ	Reims FR172J Rocket (Ditched 7.12.04)	FR17200405	
EC-CDD	Cessna 421B Golden Eagle	421B0348	N7563Q
EC-CDE	Beech 95-B55 Baron (Also SpAF: E20-10)	TC-1554	
EC-CDF	Beech 95-B55 Baron (Also SpAF: E20-11)	TC-1555	
EC-CDH	Beech 95-B55 Baron (Also SpAF: E20-13)	TC-1582	
EC-CDK	Beech C90 King Air (Also SpAF: E.22-3)	LJ-608	
EC-CDL	Cessna A188B Agwagon C	18800872	N4472Q
EC-CDM	Rockwell S.2R Thrush Commander	1729R	N5529X
EC-CDP	Reims/Cessna F150L	F15000906	
EC-CDS	Piper PA-31 Turbo Navajo B	31-7300951	N7561L
EC-CDU	Scheibe L-Spatz 55	674	
EC-CDX	Bell 47G-5A	25108	
EC-CDZ	Piper PA-23-250 Aztec E	27-7305111	N40296
EC-CEB	SOCATA MS.894E Minerva 220GT	12135	F-OCTF
EC-CED	Piper PA-28-140 Cherokee	28-7325505	N11C
EC-CEE	LET L-13 Blanik	025509	
EC-CEG	Bell 47G-5A	25120	
EC-CEI	Cessna TU206D Turbo Skywagon 206	U206-1311	G-AZVU
			4X-ALK
			N72180
EC-CEJ	LET L-13 Blanik	025510	
EC-CEK	SOCATA MS.893E Rallye 180GT Gaillard	12307	F-OCUI
EC-CEL	SOCATA Rallye 100S Sport	2336	F-OCUF
EC-CEM	Piper PA-28-140 Cherokee	28-7325498	
EC-CEO	Piper PA-28-140 Cherokee	28-7325547	N9503N
EC-CEQ	Piper PA-36-285 Pawnee Brave	36-7360016	N9542N
EC-CES	Piper PA-28-180 Cherokee Challenger	28-7305498	N9510N
EC-CET	SZD-30 Pirat	B-550	
EC-CEU	SZD-30 Pirat	B-551	
EC-CEY	Piper PA-34-200 Seneca	34-7350311	N56279
EC-CFM	Dornier Do.27A-5	122	L.9-59
			55+15
			AC+916
			AS+916
			PA+114
EC-CFN	Dornier Do.27B-1 (Museum)	129	L.9-60
			55+21
			MA+391
			DE+391
			PB+108
			PB+105
EC-CFO	Dornier Do.27B-1	149	L.9-61
			55+30
			SA+114
			SA+721
			PL+112
			PC+106
EC-CFP	Dornier Do.27A-1	166	L.9-62
			55+39
			AC+920
			AS+920
EC-CFQ	Dornier Do.27B-1 (Stored)	244	L.9-63
			55+86
			GB+387
			PG+106
EC-CFS	Dornier Do.27B-1	193	L.9-65
			55+60
			MD+386
			EC+386
			QB+403
EC-CFU	Dornier Do.27A-1D (Stored)	359	L.9-67
			56+65
			ND+106
			AC+932
			AC+938
			AS+938
EC-CFV	Piper PA-28-180 Cherokee Challenger	28-7305502	N9511N
EC-CFZ	Beech 58 Baron	TH-353	N2867W
EC-CGC	LET L-13 Blanik	025521	
EC-CGD	LET L-13 Blanik	025522	
EC-CGE	Piper PA-34-200 Seneca	34-7350324	N56378
EC-CGH	Piper PA-34-200 Seneca	34-7450013	N56644
EC-CGI	Piper PA-28-180 Cherokee Challenger	28-7305599	N9556N
	(W/o 7.12.03)		
EC-CGJ	CASA/SIAT 223-A1 Flamingo	056	
EC-CGL	CASA/SIAT 223-A1 Flamingo	058	
EC-CGM	CASA/SIAT 223-A1 Flamingo	059	
EC-CGT	Piper PA-28-180 Cherokee Challenger	28-7305598	N9555N
EC-CGU	Piper PA-28-180 Cherokee Challenger	28-7305576	N9549N
EC-CGV	Piper PA-28-180 Cherokee Challenger	28-7305583	N9552N
EC-CGX	Schempp-Hirth Cirrus VTC	145	
EC-CHE	Beech A100 King Air (Also SpAF: E23-2)	B-195	
EC-CHF	Piper PA-28-140 Cherokee	28-7425011	N9583N
EC-CHG	LET L-13 Blanik	025629	
EC-CHH	SEMCO TC-4A HAFB	SEM-88	
EC-CHJ	Reims/Cessna FRA150L Aerobat	FRA1500210	F-BUUA
			F-WLIQ
EC-CHM	SOCATA Rallye 100S Sport	2418	F-OCVQ
EC-CHN	Dornier Do.27A-5	408	L.9-68
			56+94
			PB+221
EC-CHO	Dornier Do.27A-5 (Stored)	428	L.9-69
			57+02
			PK+220
EC-CHQ	Dornier Do.27A-5	445	L.9-71
			57+17
			PC+221
			PC+106
EC-CHY	Piper PA-28-235 Charger	28-7310100	N11C
EC-CIA	Glasflügel H201B Standard Libelle	488	
EC-CIB	SOCATA MS.893E Rallye 180GT Gaillard	12383	F-OCVX
EC-CIC	Piper PA-31-350 Navajo Chieftain	31-7405412	N66901
			N9774N
EC-CIF	Piper PA-18-150 Super Cub	18-7409029	
EC-CIG	Piper PA-23-250 Aztec E (Wfu, stored)	27-7405309	N40568
EC-CIK	Cessna A188B Agtruck	18801393T	N9149G
EC-CIL	Schempp-Hirth Cirrus VTC	149	
EC-CIN	SZD-30 Pirat (Dismantled)	S-01.13	
EC-CIO	SZD-30 Pirat	B-549	
EC-CIP	SZD-30 Pirat	S-01.19	
EC-CIQ	SOCATA MS.880B Rallye Club	2413	F-OCVO
EC-CIR	LET L-13 Blanik	025602	
EC-CIS	LET L-13 Blanik	025601	
EC-CIT	LET L-13 Blanik	025628	
EC-CIU	LET L-13 Blanik	025613	
EC-CIV	LET L-13 Blanik (Stored)	025612	
EC-CIX	SOCATA MS.893E Rallye 180GT Gaillard	12382	F-OCVU
EC-CIY	Piper PA-31-350 Navajo Chieftain	31-7405181	N66875
EC-CJB	SOCATA Rallye 100S Sport	2417	F-OCVP
EC-CJC	SOCATA MS.880B Rallye Club	2412	F-OCVN
EC-CJF	Reims/Cessna F337G Skymaster	F33700063	F-BSIH
	(Reims-assembled 337G with US c/n 33701513)		F-WLIQ
EC-CJJ	SOCATA Rallye 100S Sport	2420	F-OCYC
EC-CJK	SOCATA Rallye 100S Sport	2419	F-OCYB
EC-CJL	Piper PA-31-350 Navajo Chieftain	31-7405198	N66907
EC-CJM	Scheibe L-Spatz 55	671	
EC-CJO	SOCATA MS.880B Rallye Club	2459	F-OCYF
EC-CJQ	SOCATA MS.893E Rallye 180GT Gaillard	12434	F-OCYE
EC-CJR	Emmert Rehaz U.L-Spatz	6	
EC-CJS	Piper PA-28-180 Cherokee Archer	28-7405089	N9516N
EC-CJT	Piper PA-28-151 Cherokee Warrior	28-7415101	N9640N
EC-CJV	Piper PA-28-140 Cherokee	28-7425246	N9538N
EC-CKA	SZD-30 Pirat (C/n now quoted as S-01.36)	S-01.41	
EC-CKC	Piper PA-18-150 Super Cub	18-7409057	N9671N
EC-CKE	LET L-13 Blanik	026005	
EC-CKF	LET L-13 Blanik	025912	
EC-CKJ	Glasflügel H201B Standard Libelle	571	
EC-CKK	Britten-Norman BN-2A-27 Islander	714	G-BBZX
EC-CKL	Britten-Norman BN-2A-27 Islander	715	G-BBZY
EC-CKN	Piper PA-23-250 Aztec E	27-7405427	N54120
EC-CKO	Schempp-Hirth Cirrus VTC	153	
	(Reserved as BGA5123/KJG 9.04)		
EC-CKP	SAN Jodel D.140E Mousquetaire IV	194	F-BOPJ
EC-CKQ	SOCATA Rallye 100S Sport	2394	F-OCYZ
			F-BUZU
EC-CKS	SOCATA MS.894A Minerva 220	11998	F-OCZD
EC-CKT	Schleicher ASW 17	17003	D-0877
EC-CKU	Piper PA-28-180 Cherokee Archer	28-7405086	EC-YYS
			N9509N
EC-CKY	Piper PA-36-285 Pawnee Brave	36-7460025	N9532N
EC-CKZ	Cessna 182P Skylane	18262820	N52752
EC-CLA	Piper PA-28-140 Cherokee	28-7425165	N9624N
EC-CLC	Piper PA-36-285 Pawnee Brave	36-7460027	N9535N
EC-CLF	SOCATA MS.893E Rallye 180GT Gaillard	12491	F-OCSZ
EC-CLG	Beech F33A Bonanza (Also SpAF: E.24B-30)	CE-517	
EC-CLK	Beech F33A Bonanza (Also SpAF: E.24B-34)	CE-529	
EC-CLM	Beech F33A Bonanza (Also SpAF: E.24B-36)	CE-531	
EC-CLT	Piper PA-28-151 Warrior	28-7415213	N9528N
	(Wreck noted 1.7.04)		N41435
EC-CLU	Piper PA-28-140 Cherokee	28-7425418	N9543N
EC-CLX	Piper PA-28-140 Cherokee B	28-25530	N8886N
EC-CLY	SOCATA Rallye 100S Sport	2362	F-OCYU
			F-BUVY
EC-CLZ	Reims FR172J Rocket	FR17200464	F-BSGV
EC-CMA	Piper PA-28-180 Cherokee Archer	28-7405135	N9569N
EC-CMB	Aérospatiale SA.341G Gazelle	1166	F-WXFQ
EC-CMC	Reims/Cessna F150L	F15001137	F-BSGR
			(HB-CEE)
EC-CMF	Cessna A188B Agtruck	18801772T	N53335

EC-CMJ	Piper PA-28-140 Cherokee	28-7525053	N9621N
EC-CMK	SOCATA Rallye 100S Sport	2367	F-OCYY
			F-BUXD
EC-CML	SOCATA Rallye 100S.Sport	2365	F-OCYX
			F-BUXB
EC-CMM	Piper PA-28-180 Cherokee Archer	28-7405141	N9572N
EC-CMN	Rockwell S.2R Thrush Commander	2088R	N17532
	(Reserved as F-GIEN 6.04)		
EC-CMO	Piper PA-28-151 Cherokee Warrior	28-7515125	N9620N
			N32320
EC-CMP	Reims/Cessna FR. I72J Rocket	0521	F-BSGN
EC-CMR	Piper PA-28R-180 Cherokee Arrow	28R-30686	PH-ATU
			N4944J
EC-CMX	Cessna 182P Skylane	18263181	N7398N
EC-CNC	Cessna 310Q	310Q1123	N1272G
EC-CNE	Piper J-3C-65 Cub	11680	HB-OCS
			D-EBYK
			HB-OCS
			43-30389
EC-CNI	Reims/Cessna FRA150L Aerobat	FRA1500257	F-BJDD
EC-CNL	SZD-30 Pirat	S-02.39	
EC-CNM	LET L-13 Blanik (Stored)	026108	
EC-CNN	LET L-13 Blanik	026109	
EC-CNO	LET L-13 Blanik (Stored)	026119	
EC-CNP	LET L-13 Blanik	026120	
EC-CNQ	SZD-30 Pirat	S-01.18	
EC-CNR	SZD-30 Pirat	S-01.20	
EC-CNS	SZD-30 Pirat	S-01.38	
EC-CNU	SZD-30 Pirat (W/o 12.1.02)	S-02.06	
EC-CNV	SZD-30 Pirat	S-02.37	
EC-CNY	SZD-30 Pirat	S-02.46	
EC-CNZ	LET L-13 Blanik	025829	
EC-COA	Beech 95-B55 Baron (Also SpAF: E.20-12)	TC-1808	
	(Crashed 24.6.02)		
EC-COD	Beech 95-B55 Baron (Also SpAF: E.20-15)	TC-1834	
EC-COF	Beech 95-B55 Baron (Also SpAF: E.20-17)	TC-1844	
EC-COG	Beech 95-B55 Baron (Also SpAF: E.20-18)	TC-1850	
	(C/ns of -COF, -COG now revised as shown)		
EC-COH	Beech 95-B55 Baron (Also SpAF: E.20-19)	TC-1856	
EC-COQ	Beech F33A Bonanza (Also SpAF: E.24B-46)	CE-584	
EC-COR	Beech F33A Bonanza (Also SpAF: E.24B-47)	CE-585	
EC-COS	Beech F33A Bonanza (Also SpAF:E.24B-48)	CE-588	
EC-COT	Beech F33A Bonanza (Also SpAF: E.24B-49)	CE-590	
EC-COU	Beech F33A Bonanza (Also SpAF: E.24B-50)	CE-593	
EC-COV	Beech F33A Bonanza (Also SpAF: E.24B-51)	CE-586	
EC-COX	Beech F33A Bonanza (Also SpAF: E.24B-52)	CE-587	
EC-COY	Beech F33A Bonanza (Also SpAF: E.24B-53)	CE-589	
EC-CPA	LET L-13 Blanik	025911	
EC-CPB	LET L-13 Blanik	026006	
EC-CPC	LET L-13 Blanik	026019	
EC-CPD	LET L-13 Blanik	026020	
EC-CPE	LET L-13 Blanik	026034	
EC-CPG	Reims/Cessna F337G Skymaster	F33700071	F-BJDG
	(Reims-assembled 337G with US c/n 33701592)		
EC-CPJ	LET L-13 Blanik (Stored damaged)	026033	
EC-CPK	LET L-13 Blanik	026045	
EC-CPN	LET L-13 Blanik (Stored)	026059	
EC-CPO	Douglas C-47D	17094/34361	T.3-50
	(Still regd but wfu at Luis Urilla/AENA		N86442
	Museum, Malaga)		45-1091
EC-CPP	Dornier Do.28A-1	3002	D-IHIL
EC-CPQ	Reims/Cessna F150L	F15001139	F-BSGO
EC-CPR	Piper PA-36-285 Pawnee Brave	36-7560008	N9909P
EC-CPS	Reims/Cessna FRA150L Aerobat	FRA1500255	F-BJDC
EC-CPT	Reims/Cessna FRA150L Aerobat	FRA1500259	F-BJDE
			(TR-LTP)
EC-CPU	Reims/Cessna FRA150L Aerobat	FRA1500252	F-BJDA
			(I-AFAE)
EC-CPV	Reims/Cessna F150M	F15001181	F-BPPY
EC-CPX	Piper PA-36-285 Pawnee Brave	36-7560016	N53401
			N31S
			N9910P
EC-CQB	Cessna 182P Skylane	18263609	N6026J
EC-CQC	SZD-30 Pirat (Stored)	S-03.33	
EC-CQE	SZD-30 Pirat	S-03.39	
EC-CQN	LET L-13 Blanik	026131	
EC-CQU	Piper PA-36-285 Pawnee Brave	36-7560015	N9745N
	(Badly damaged 13.7.04)		
EC-CQX	Piper PA-28-180 Cherokee Archer	28-7505183	N9627N
EC-CRI	AISA I-115	54	E.9-54
EC-CRK	Cessna 207 Skywagon 207	20700230	N1630U
EC-CRL	Reims/Cessna F177RG Cardinal RG	F177RG0096	N14499
			(N14491)
EC-CRM	LET L-13 Blanik	026132	
EC-CRO	Piper PA-36-285 Pawnee Brave	36-7560026	N9736N
EC-CRP	Piper PA-28-140 Cherokee	28-7525267	N9648N
EC-CRQ	Piper PA-28-151 Cherokee Warrior	28-7515356	N9619N
EC-CRT	AISA I-115	197	E.9-197
EC-CRU	Piper PA-36-285 Pawnee Brave	36-7560038	N9654N
EC-CRY	Piper PA-23-250 Aztec E (Derelict)	27-7554041	N54249
EC-CRZ	Reims FR172J Rocket	FR17200446	CS-APE
	(Damaged 3.5.94)		F-BSGZ
EC-CSA	AISA I-115	9	E.9-9
EC-CSD	AISA I-115	132	E.9-132
EC-CSF	AISA I-115	165	E.9-165
EC-CSI	Cessna 310Q	310Q1043	CS-APP
			N69956

EC-CSM	SZD-30 Pirat (Dbr 7.8.99)	S-02.40	
EC-CSN	SZD-30 Pirat	S-04.27	
EC-CSO	SZD-30 Pirat (Dismantled)	S-04.07	
EC-CSP	SOCATA Rallye 100S Sport	2559	F-ODAR
EC-CSQ	Piper PA-28R-200 Cherokee Arrow II	28R-7535058	N32451
EC-CSR	LET L-13 Blanik	026153	
EC-CSS	LET L-13 Blanik	026152	
EC-CST	Piper PA-28R-200 Cherokee Arrow II	28R-7535319	N9580N
EC-CSU	Piper PA-28-180 Cherokee Archer	28-7505236	N9576N
EC-CSX	Piper PA-28-140 Cherokee	28-7525251	N9633N
EC-CSY	Reims/Cessna F172M	F17201111	CS-APF
	(Damaged 27.11.94)		F-BSGP
EC-CTB	Reims/Cessna FRA150L Aerobat	FRA1500212	N14492
EC-CTC	Reims FR172J Rocket	FR17200544	F-BPQQ
EC-CTF	Reims FR172J Rocket	FR17200448	EC-535
			CS-APR
			F-BSGR
EC-CTG	Piper PA-31P Pressurized Navajo	31P-7530017	N54946
EC-CTH	Reims/Cessna F150L	F15001048	CS-APH
			F-BSGN
EC-CTI	Cessna 210L Centurion	21060139	EC-532
			N59169
EC-CTK	Piper PA-34-200T Seneca II	34-7670055	N4493X
EC-CTL	Cessna TU206F Turbo Stationair	U20602629	PH-AOD
			N1596F
			N59182
EC-CTM	Reims FR172J Rocket	FR17200538	F-BJDT
EC-CTN	Piper PA-28-140 Cherokee (W/o 7.5.99?)	28-7625035	N9615N
EC-CTO	Aero Commander 680F (Damaged 6.2.03)	1195-100	OE-FAI
EC-CTP	Piper PA-28-140 Cherokee Cruiser	28-7625036	N9619N
EC-CTX	Eiri PIK-20	20089	
EC-CTY	Piper PA-28-151 Cherokee Warrior	28-7515448	N9612N
EC-CUB	Piper PA-28-151 Cherokee Warrior	28-7415218	EC-YYR
			N9530N
EC-CUC	Reims/Cessna F150M	F15001237	F-BJDK
EC-CUD	Piper PA-36-285 Pawnee Brave	36-7560127	N9707N
EC-CUE	Piper PA-28-151 Cherokee Warrior	28-7515449	N9613N
EC-CUG	Cessna 421B Golden Eagle	421B0936	EC-5310
			N5386J
EC-CUI	Schempp-Hirth Standard Cirrus B	652	
EC-CUJ	Schempp-Hirth Nimbus II	104	
EC-CUK	SOCATA MS.893E Rallye 180GT Gaillard	12640	F-ODAY
EC-CUL	Reims/Cessna FA150K Aerobat	FA1500069	D-ECHK
EC-CUN	Cessna A188B Agtruck	18802427T	N4909R
EC-CUO	SIAI-Marchetti S.205-18/F	216	F-BNLM
EC-CUP	Sportavia RF-5B Sperber	51058	D-KKOA
EC-CUR	Piper PA-28R-200 Cherokee Arrow II	28R-7535243	N9618N
			N3995X
			YV-TAST
			N9521N
EC-CUT	Cessna 340	340-0303	ECT-538
			N69449
EC-CUU	Piper PA-36-285 Pawnee Brave	36-7660007	
	(W/o 1.6.04)		
EC-CUV	Piper PA-36-285 Pawnee Brave	36-7660012	
EC-CUX	Piper PA-36-285 Pawnee Brave	36-7560065	N9954P
	(W/o 25.7.02?)		
EC-CVB	AISA I-115	124	E.9-124
EC-CVC	AISA I-115	136	E.9-136
EC-CVD	Piper PA-25-260 Pawnee D	25-7405725	N9598P
EC-CVE	Piper PA-32R-300 Cherokee Lance	32R-7680079	N8148C
EC-CVF	Cessna 210L Centurion	21060563	N94254
EC-CVG	Reims/Cessna F177RG Cardinal RG	F177RG0126	F-BJDH
			F-WLIQ
EC-CVI	Schempp-Hirth Standard Cirrus	658	
EC-CVK	Sud Avn SA.318C Alouette Astazou	2415	
EC-CVL	Piper PA-36-285 Pawnee Brave	36-7560011	N9906P
	(W/o 3.11.98?)		
EC-CVN	Reims FR172J Rocket	FR17200533	N94722
EC-CVO	Dornier Do.27B-1	151	OO-PAN
	(Derelict at Cuatro Vientos 1996)		D-EKOV
			55+31
			ND+205
			PF+107
			PD+102
EC-CVP	Reims/Cessna FRA150M Aerobat	FRA1500271	F-BJDF
EC-CVQ	Reims/Cessna FRA150M Aerobat	FRA1500277	F-BJDG
EC-CVR	Piper PA-34-200T Seneca II	34-7570312	N7623C
			N9594N
EC-CVS	SOCATA Rallye 100S Sport	2542	F-ODAV
EC-CVT	PZL-104 Wilga 35A	86282	SP-WFG
	(Remains reported at Cordoba In 1991)		
EC-CVU	PZL-104 Wilga 35A	86278	SP-WFF
	(Remains reported at Oviedo in 1983)		
EC-CVV	Cessna 414 (W/o 9.5.98?)	414-0631	ECT-555
			N69816
EC-CVX	Reims FR172G Rocket	FR17200218	CS-AKW
EC-CVY	Reims FR172J Rocket	FR17200385	CS-AJT
EC-CXA	Piper PA-28-181 Cherokee Archer II	28-7690191	N9531N
EC-CXB	Cessna 310R	310R0010	ECT-552
			ECT-5310
			N1326G
EC-CXC	Reims/Cessna F337F Super Skymaster	F33700042	CS-AHH
	(Reims-assembled 337F with US c/n 33701381)		
EC-CXD	Piper PA-18-150 Super Cub	18-7609036	N54107
EC-CXE	Piper PA-25-260 Pawnee D	25-7405621	N9535P
EC-CXG	Cessna A188B Agtruck	18802553T	N4816Q

EC-CXH	Cessna A188B Agtruck	18802510T	N4758Q
EC-CXI	Cessna A188B Agtruck	18802507T	N4749Q
EC-CXK	Piper PA-28-140 Cherokee Cruiser	28-7625157	N9537N
	(Wreck stored, Tenerife)		
EC-CXL	Piper PA-25-260 Pawnee D	25-7405614	N9528P
	(W/o 11.4.03 Cordoba)		
EC-CXM	Piper PA-28R-200 Cherokee Arrow II	28R-7335117	CS-AOL
			N11C
EC-CXN	Piper PA-28-140 Cherokee Cruiser	28-7625131	N9523N
EC-CXO	Piper PA-25-260 Pawnee D	25-7405723	N9588P
EC-CXP	Cessna F172H	F172-0367	CS-AKU
EC-CXQ	Cessna 172C (Crashed 30.3.01)	17249438	CS-AKO
			N1838Y
EC-CXR	Piper PA-28-151 Cherokee Warrior	28-7615301	N9583N
EC-CXT	LET L-13 Blanik	026305	
EC-CXU	LET L-13 Blanik	026308	
EC-CXZ	SOCATA Rallye 150T	2655	F-ODAX
EC-CYA	SOCATA Rallye 235E Gabier	12796	F-ODDY
EC-CYB	Cessna 207 Skywagon 207 (W/o 13.10.96)	20700271	N1671U
EC-CYC	Bellanca 7GCBC Citabria	832-75	OE-AOV
EC-CYD	Beech A36 Bonanza	E-788	ECT-012
			N6787S
EC-CYE	Piper PA-28-151 Cherokee Warrior	28-7615281	N9573N
			N75288
EC-CYF	Piper PA-31P Pressurized Navajo	31P-7630017	N57554
EC-CYG	Reims FR172J Rocket (W/o 27.8.98?)	FR17200537	F-BJDE
EC-CYH	Rockwell Commander 112A	296	N1296J
EC-CYL	SOCATA Rallye 100S Sport (W/o ?)	2813	F-ODDV
EC-CYO	SOCATA Rallye 235E Gabier	12801	F-ODDU
EC-CYP	LET L-13 Blanik	026245	
EC-CYR	Cessna A188B Agtruck	18802769T	N731BN
EC-CYS	Cessna A188B Agtruck (Damaged 6.7.99)	18802355T	N4836R
EC-CYT	LET L-13 Blanik	026646	
EC-CYU	SZD-30 Pirat (Displayed Barcelona Airport)	S.07.19	
EC-CYV	SZD-30 Pirat	S-07.20	
EC-CYX	SZD-30 Pirat	S-07.24	
EC-CYY	SZD-30 Pirat	S-07.21	
EC-CYZ	SZD-30 Pirat	S-07.22	
EC-CZA	SZD-30 Pirat	S-07.23	
EC-CZB	SOCATA MS.893E Rallye 180GT Gaillard	12741	F-ODEH
EC-CZC	Grumman G.164A Agcat	1294	
EC-CZD	Piper PA-25-260 Pawnee D	25-7756029	N82486
EC-CZF	Reims/Cessna F177RG Cardinal RG	F177RG0067	CS-AJH
EC-CZG	Reims FR172J Rocket	FR17200558	F-BOFC
			(D-EOGV)
EC-CZH	Piper PA-28R-200 Cherokee Arrow II	28R-7635077	N9627N
EC-CZI	Cessna 310R	310R0638	N98895
EC-CZJ	Piper PA-28R-200 Cherokee Arrow II	28R-7635318	N9592N
EC-CZL	Piper PA-18-150 Super Cub	18-7709055	N83522
EC-CZM	Piper PA-36-300 Pawnee Brave	36-7760023	N9659N
EC-CZN	Piper PA-28-140 Cherokee Cruiser	28-7625225	N9588N
EC-CZO	Piper PA-28-181 Cherokee Archer II	28-7790353	N9605N
EC-CZP	Piper PA-28-140 Cherokee Cruiser (Stored)	28-7725099	N9551N
EC-CZQ	Piper PA-34-200T Seneca II	34-7670162	N8617E
EC-CZR	Reims FR172JRocket	FR17200534	F-BJDD
EC-CZS	Cessna A188B Agtruck (W/o 25.8.03)	18802882T	N731GJ
EC-CZT	Cessna 182P	18263956	N9895E
	(Reims-assembled with "c/n" 0023)		
EC-CZU	Zlin Z.526L (Wfu)	1160	
EC-CZV	Aerotek Pitts S-2A	2135	
EC-CZX	Reims/Cessna F150M	F15001345	F-BJDH
EC-CZY	Grumman G.164A Agcat	240	N670Y
EC-CZZ	Reims FR172J Rocket	FR17200550	F-BOFB
			(D-EEVQ)
EC-DAA	Cessna 310R	310R0618	N98855
EC-DAB	Grumman AA-5A Cheetah	AA5A-0346	
EC-DAC	Grumman AA-5A Cheetah	AA5A-0347	
EC-DAD	Piper PA-28-140 Cherokee Cruiser	28-7725181	N9615N
EC-DAE	Reims FR172J Rocket	FR17200539	F-BJDJ
EC-DAF	Piper PA-28-161 Cherokee Warrior II	28-7716229	N9537N
EC-DAG	SOCATA Rallye 100ST	2944	F-ODHD
EC-DAH	CASA C-1.131E Jungmann (Stored)	2041	E.3B-273
EC-DAI	CASA C-1.131E Jungmann	1067	E.3B-421
EC-DAJ	CASA C-1.131E Jungmann	2061	E.3B-457
EC-DAK	CASA C-1.131E Jungmann (Damaged 12.94)	2022	E.3B-463
EC-DAL	CASA C-1.131E Jungmann (Damaged 22.3.03)	2065	E.3B-472
EC-DAM	CASA C-1.131E Jungmann	2160	E.3B-488
EC-DAO	CASA C-1.131E Jungmann	2107	E.3B-511
EC-DAP	CASA C-1.131E Jungmann (Cr. 23.1.97)	2147	E.3B-547
EC-DAQ	CASA C-1.131E Jungmann (Stored)	2183	E.3B-578
EC-DAR	CASA C-1.131E Jungmann	2174	E.3B-581
EC-DAS	CASA C-1.131E Jungmann (Stored)	2186	E.3B-583
EC-DAU	CASA C-1.131E Jungmann	2103	E.3B-608
	(Possibly ex E.3B-508, see EC-DAX)		
EC-DAV	CASA C-1.131E Jungmann	2217	E.3B-617
EC-DAX	CASA C-1.131E Jungmann	unkn	E.3B-567
	(Now quoted as ex E.3B-608, see EC-DAU)		
EC-DAY	Reims FR172J Rocket	FR17200545	F-BJDZ
			(D-EESK)
EC-DAZ	Piper PA-28-140 Cherokee Cruiser	28-7725276	N9544N
EC-DBA	Piper PA-28-140 Cherokee Cruiser	28-7725277	N9545N
EC-DBF	SOCATA MS.893E Rallye 180GT Gaillard	12980	F-ODHG
EC-DBG	SOCATA MS.893E Rallye 180GT Gaillard	12981	F-ODHH
EC-DBH	Piper PA-28-140 Cherokee Cruiser	28-7725281	N9547N
EC-DBI	SOCATA Rallye 235E Gabier	12802	F-ODEG
EC-DBJ	Piper PA-28-140 Cherokee Cruiser	28-7725280	N9546N

EC-DBL	Reims/Cessna F172N	F17201562	ECT-537
			F-BJDJ
EC-DBP	Piper PA-28-140 Cherokee Cruiser	28-7725100	N9552N
EC-DBQ	Piper PA-25-260 Pawnee D	25-7756026	N82479
EC-DBR	Piper PA-36-300 Pawnee Brave	36-7760139	N82667
EC-DBS	Reims/Cessna F150M	F15001369	
EC-DBT	Reims/Cessna F150M	F15001362	
EC-DBU	Piper PA-28-181 Cherokee Archer II	28-7890126	N9629N
	(Crashed 10.4.04)		
EC-DBX	SOCATA Rallye 150T	2970	F-ODHF
EC-DBZ	Reims/Cessna F337F Skymaster	F33700031	G-BDVK
	(Reims-assembled 337F with US c/n 33701353)		F-OCZZ
			F-BSIZ
EC-DCA	Piper PA-28-161 Cherokee Warrior II	28-7816149	N9635N
EC-DCF	Piper PA-36-300 Pawnee Brave	36-7860015	N9666N
EC-DCG	SOCATA Rallye 180T Galérien	3091	
EC-DCH	SOCATA Rallye 180T Galérien	3027	
EC-DCI	Cessna A188B Agtruck	18803082T	N731QX
	(Reims-assembled with "c/n" 0001)		
EC-DCJ	SOCATA Rallye 235E Gabier	12870	
EC-DCM	SOCATA Rallye 235E Gabier	12871	
EC-DCO	Reims/Cessna FR172K Hawk XP	FR17200604	F-BNGX
			(F-GAQF)
EC-DCP	Reims/Cessna FR172K Hawk XP	FR17200598	F-GAST
EC-DCR	Reims/Cessna F172N	F17201595	F-BNGY
	(W/o 14.6.90)		(F-GAQJ)
EC-DCS	SOCATA Rallye 100ST	3002	
EC-DCU	Piper PA-36-285 Pawnee Brave	36-7660062	N57753
EC-DCV	SOCATA MS.893E Rallye 180GT Gaillard	13052	
EC-DCX	Piper PA-25-260 Pawnee D	25-7856050	N4154E
EC-DCY	Thunder AX7-77A HAFB	145	
EC-DCZ	Thunder AX7-77A HAFB	149	
EC-DDA	Piper PA-25-260 Pawnee D	25-7856051	N4157E
EC-DDB	Piper PA-28-161 Cherokee Warrior II	28-7816589	N9586N
EC-DDC	SOCATA MS.883 Rallye 115	1360	F-BRMN
EC-DDD	Morane-Saulnier MS.885 Super Rallye	153	F-BMHL
			HB-EDT
EC-DDE	Piper PA-28-161 Cherokee Warrior II	28-7816588	N9585N
EC-DDF	Thunder AX7-77A HAFB	035	G-BDAZ
EC-DDG	Rockwell S.2R Thrush Commander	2456R	N8846Q
EC-DDI	SOCATA Rallye 150ST	3139	
EC-DDJ	Piper PA-28-181 Cherokee Archer II	28-7890506	N9594N
EC-DDK	Reims/Cessna F182Q Skylane II	F18200047	F-BNGT
			F-BJDK
EC-DDL	Piper PA-32R-300 Lance	32R-7780238	N2267Q
EC-DDM	SOCATA MS.893E Rallye 180GT Gaillard	13131	
EC-DDN	AISA I-115 (Museum)	196	E.9-196
EC-DDO	Grumman AA-5B Tiger	AA5B-0705	N28892
EC-DDP	Grumman AA-5A Cheetah	AA5A-0550	N26704
EC-DDT	Piper PA-28R-201T Turbo Cherokee Arrow III		
		28R-7703345	N44942
EC-DEC	Reims/Cessna F150M	F15001360	F-BNGV
EC-DED	Reims FR172J Rocket	FR17200567	F-BSGV
			F-BJDH
			F-BLIK
EC-DEE	Reims/Cessna F172N	F17201517	N96092
EC-DEF	Cessna 337D Super Skymaster	33700987	N2687S
EC-DEH	Piper PA-38-112 Tomahawk	38-78A0457	N9676N
EC-DEI	AISA I-115	53	E.9-53
EC-DEJ	AISA I-115	123	E.9-123
EC-DEK	Agusta-Bell 206B Jet Ranger	8568	
EC-DEL	Reims/Cessna F177RG Cardinal RG	F177RG0173	ECT-012
			F-BPQQ
EC-DEN	Piper PA-38-112 Tomahawk	38-78A0452	N9673N
EC-DEO	AISA I-115	194	E.9-194
EC-DEP	Piper PA-28-161 Warrior II	28-7816661	N9622N
EC-DEQ	Cessna 401B (W/o 31.10.99?)	401B0115	D-IEPC
			N7975Q
EC-DER	Grumman AA-5A Cheetah	AA5A-0629	N26756
EC-DET	Cessna Turbo 310R	310R0644	N98907
EC-DEU	Piper PA-38-112 Tomahawk (Stored)	38-78A0589	N9664N
EC-DEV	Piper PA-36-375 Brave (Crashed 1.10.99)	36-7802017	N9727N
EC-DEX	Reims/Cessna F182Q Skylane	F18200088	F-BNGR
EC-DEY	Aérospatiale SA.315B Lama	2398	F-BXAX
EC-DEZ	Thunder AX7-77A HAFB	177	
EC-DFB	Robin R.1180T Aiglon	216	F-GBMR
EC-DFD	Cessna A188B Agtruck	18803306T	N1962J
	(Reims-assembled with "c/n" 0017)		
EC-DFF	Piper PA-25-260 Pawnee D	25-7856056	(AN-BUW)
EC-DFG	Schleicher ASW 17	17055	
EC-DFH	Cameron V-77 HAFB	470	
EC-DFI	SOCATA Rallye 180T Galérien (Dam.18.12.94)	3203	
EC-DFJ	Cessna A188B Agtruck (Crashed 14.5.98)	18803305T	N1961J
	(Reims-assembled with "c/n" 0016)		
EC-DFK	Piper PA-28-161 Warrior II	28-7916041	N9506N
EC-DFM	SOCATA MS.893E Rallye 180GT Gaillard	13130	
EC-DFN	Piper PA-25-260 Pawnee D	25-7956005	N9771N
EC-DFQ	Piper PA-25-260 Pawnee D	25-7856054	(AN-BUV)
			N4169E
EC-DFT	SZD-45A Ogar	B-818	
	(Incorrectly officially recorded as c/n B-820)		
EC-DFU	Piper PA-38-112 Tomahawk	38-78A0597	N9671N
EC-DFV	Schempp-Hirth Standard Cirrus	197	BGA1679
EC-DFX	Rolladen-Schneider LS3A	3182	
EC-DFZ	Thunder AX7-77 HAFB	191	
EC-DGA	Piper PA-38-112 Tomahawk	38-78A0767	N9686N

EC-DGG	Piper PA-34-200T Seneca II	34-7670161	HB-LHU N8567E
EC-DGH	Piper PA-28RT-201T Turbo Arrow IV	28R-7931124	N9632N
EC-DGI	Piper PA-36-375 Brave	36-7902007	N9737N
EC-DGJ	Piper PA-28-181 Archer II	28-7990034	N9647N
EC-DGK	Agusta-Bell 47G-2	210	(F-BTSR) ALAT Fr.AF
EC-DGM	Robin R.2100A	168	F-BXQY
EC-DGN	Cessna T188C AgHusky	T18803334T	N2029J
EC-DGO	Piper PA-44-180 Seminole	44-7995213	N3064K
EC-DGP	Piper PA-25-235 Pawnee D	25-7856029	N9179T
EC-DGQ	Piper PA-28RT-201 Arrow IV	28R-7918056	N3050R
EC-DGR	Reims/Cessna FRA150M Aerobat	FRA1500316	F-BXXK
EC-DGS	SOCATA Rallye 180T Galérien (Crashed 7.99)	3204	
EC-DGT	Scheibe SF-25C Falke	44123	D-KACK
EC-DGX	Piper PA-28-181 Archer II	28-7990344	N9626N
EC-DGY	Thunder AX6-56 Bolt HAFB	188	
EC-DHA	Sud Avn SA.316B Alouette III	2207	HB-XKI FAP9406
EC-DHB	Grumman GA-7 Cougar	0086	N796GA
EC-DHC	Cameron V-56 HAFB	271	(EP-FHK)
EC-DHD	Piper PA-34-200T Seneca II	34-7770218	N3130Q
EC-DHF	Piper PA-31T Cheyenne II	31T-7920073	N23699
EC-DHG	Piper PA-28-161 Warrior II	28-7916450	N9539N
EC-DHH	Piper PA-38-112 Tomahawk	38-78A0593	N9666N
EC-DHJ	Lake LA-4-200 Buccaneer	948	N2964P
EC-DHK	Piper PA-38-112 Tomahawk	38-79A0237	N9709N
EC-DHL	Piper PA-32-300 Cherokee Six	32-7940214	N2838A N9592N
EC-DHN	Piper PA-28-161 Warrior II	28-7916506	N9576N
EC-DHS	Scheibe SF-28A Tandem-Falke	57106	D-KDGG
EC-DHT	Hiller UH-12E	5108	(SE-HVD) EC-DHT
EC-DHU	Aerotek Pitts S-2A (Museum)	2181	
EC-DHV	Cameron V-56 HAFB	545	
EC-DHX	Cameron V-56 HAFB	546	
EC-DIA	Boeing 747-256B	22238	
EC-DIB	Boeing 747-256B	22239	
EC-DIC	Cessna F172H	F172-0336	
EC-DID	CASA C-1.131E Jungmann	2119	E.3B-319
EC-DIE	Schempp-Hirth Nimbus IIC	223	
EC-DIF	Grob G.102 Astir CS	1086	
EC-DIG	Scheibe Bergfalke II	164	
EC-DII	SOCATA Rallye 100ST	3039	
EC-DIJ	SOCATA Rallye 150ST	3138	(D-EEUM)
EC-DIK-JJ	Schempp-Hirth Mini-Nimbus HS-7	58	PH-606
EC-DIL	Piper PA-28-181 Archer II	28-7990486	N9621N N2841V
EC-DIM	Thunder AX7-77 HAFB	204	
EC-DIN	Cessna 337G Skymaster	33701788	N53693 N2876P
EC-DIP	Thunder AX7-77 HAFB	201	
EC-DIQ	Sud Avn SA.318C Alouette Astazou	2416	
EC-DIS	Piper PA-25-235 Pawnee	25-8056002	N9769N
EC-DIT	Piper PA-25-235 Pawnee	25-8056003	N9770N
EC-DIU	Piper PA-28RT-201 Arrow IV	28R-7918266	N8111Q N9642N
EC-DIV	Piper PA-25-260 Pawnee D	25-7956035	N9772N
EC-DIZ	Thunder AX8-105 HAFB	237	
EC-DJA	Schleicher ASW 20	20294	
EC-DJB	Cameron N-77 HAFB	572	
EC-DJD	Piper PA-38-112 Tomahawk	38-79A1011	N9716N
EC-DJE	Cessna 210N Centurion	21063385	N5355A
EC-DJF	Piper PA-25-260 Pawnee D	25-7956037	N9775N
EC-DJG	Piper PA-36-375 Brave	36-7902047	N9742N
EC-DJH	Piper PA-25-260 Pawnee	25-8056010	N2407Q
EC-DJJ	Piper PA-28-161 Warrior II	28-8016183	N9536N
EC-DJK	Piper PA-28-161 Warrior II	28-8016184	N9537N
EC-DJL	CASA C-1.131E Jungmann	unkn	E.3B-534
EC-DJP	Piper PA-25-260 Pawnee	25-8056012	N9772N
EC-DJQ	Reims/Cessna FR172K Hawk XP (Wfu)	FR17200648	F-WZIA
EC-DJT	Scheibe SF-28A Tandem-Falke (Damaged 7.8.99)	57110	D-KDGV
EC-DJV	Piper PA-38-112 Tomahawk (W/o 28.6.97)	38-79A1176	N9724N
EC-DJX	Piper PA-28RT-201T Turbo Arrow IV	28R-7931194	N9523N
EC-DJY	Cessna T188C AgHusky	T18803461T	N2425J
EC-DJZ	Piper PA-28-161 Warrior II	28-8016267	N9645N
EC-DKA	Piper PA-18-150 Super Cub	18-8009013	N9174T
EC-DKB	Piper PA-28-181 Archer II	28-8090248	N9504N
EC-DKC	Piper PA-28-181 Archer II	28-8090249	N9512N
EC-DKD	Cessna 337G Skymaster	33701797	N53706
EC-DKE	Bölkow Phoebus A-1	717	
EC-DKF	Scheibe SF-27A	6058	
EC-DKG	Schleicher K 8B	8396SH	
EC-DKJ	Scheibe SF-28A Tandem-Falke	57114	D-KDGV
EC-DKK	SAN Jodel D.140E1 Mousquetaire IV	38	F-BIZR
EC-DKL	Cameron N-77 HAFB	653	
EC-DKM	ICA/Brasov IS-28M2	28	
EC-DKN	Reims/Cessna F152 (Damaged, wfu?)	F15201686	N1660C
EC-DKP	Cessna 402C	402C0275	N2757A
EC-DKX	CASA C-1.131E Jungmann	2016	E.3B-412
EC-DKZ	Cessna 210N Centurion	21063653	(N4868C)
EC-DLA	Piper PA-28RT-201T Turbo Arrow IV	28R-8031113	N82377 N9564N
EC-DLB	Piper PA-38-112 Tomahawk (Damaged 17.9.03)	38-79A1174	N24702
EC-DLK	Westland-Bell 47G3B1 (Soloy)	WA/329	G-BHBU XT170
EC-DLL	Piper PA-38-112 Tomahawk (Wreck noted 1.7.04)	38-79A1179	N9650N
EC-DLM	Piper PA-18-150	18-2546	D-EMMX ALAT 52-6228
EC-DLO	Cessna R172K Hawk XP	R1723324	N758SM
EC-DLP	Cameron N-77 HAFB	534	
EC-DLQ	Thunder-Colt 56A HAFB	065	
EC-DLR	Reims/Cessna FR172K Hawk XP	FR17200593	F-ODHP F-GAGP
EC-DLS	Reims/Cessna F337G Skymaster (Reims-assembled 337G with US c/n 33701679)	F33700078	N65327 F-BRGQ
EC-DLT	Piper PA-28-161 Warrior II	28-8016330	N9557N
EC-DLV	Zlin Z.50L	0022	
EC-DLX	Zlin Z.50L	0023	
EC-DLY	Zlin Z.50L	0024	
EC-DLZ	Cameron D-50 Hot Air Airship	752	
EC-DMB	Scheibe L-Spatz 105	1	OO-ZMG D-5166 D-3578
EC-DMC	Reims/Cessna F152	F15201783	F-WZII
EC-DMD	Scheibe SF-25E Super Falke	4319	ECT-029 OY-XGX D-KECV
EC-DME	Reims/Cessna F152	F15201784	F-WZIJ
EC-DMF	Piper PA-25-235 Pawnee	25-8056036	N9770N
EC-DMI	Scheibe L-Spatz 55	747	
EC-DMK	CASA C-1.131E Jungmann (C/n now quoted as 1049)	2049	E.3B-344
EC-DMM	Cameron D-96 Hot Air Airship	675	
EC-DMO	Piper PA-36-375 Brave	36-7802058	N3921E
EC-DMQ	Grob G.103 Twin Astir	3553	
EC-DMR	Cessna 172RG Cutlass RG	172RG0547	(N5496V)
EC-DMU	Scheibe SF-25E Super Falke	4358	D-KOOA
EC-DMY	SOCATA Rallye 235E Gabier	13149	F-ODNG N358RA
EC-DMZ	Thunder AX6-56 Bolt HAFB	294	
EC-DNA	Thunder AX7-77 HAFB	309	
EC-DND	Reims/Cessna FR182 Skylane RG	FR18200021	N9012F
EC-DNE	Schempp-Hirth Standard Cirrus	134	
EC-DNG	Cessna 172RG Cutlass RG	172RG0526	(N5417V)
EC-DNI	Schleicher ASW 20L	20408	
EC-DNJ	Piper PA-28-161 Warrior II	28-8116142	N9512N
EC-DNL	Agusta A.109A Hirundo	7182	N4210P
EC-DNM	Agusta A.109A Hirundo	7222	N4210X
EC-DNN	Cessna 152-II	15284203	N4645L
EC-DNO	SOCATA TB-10 Tobago	171	ECT-040 F-ODNM
EC-DNP	Boeing 747-256B	22764	N8296V
EC-DNS	Thunder AX6-56 HAFB	291	
EC-DNT	Cessna F172G	F172-0293	D-ENDI
EC-DNU	Aérospatiale AS.350B Ecureuil	1475	F-WZFH
EC-DNV	Cessna R172K Hawk (W/o 22.2.04)	R1723401	N758VT
EC-DNX	Reims/Cessna F172N	F17201987	N1660C (D-EOCT)
EC-DOA	Piper PA-36-300 Brave (Cr 6.2.01)	36-8060006	N9740N
EC-DOB	Fournier RF-9	6	F-BZCX F-ODNP
EC-DOD	Thunder AX7-77 HAFB	346	
EC-DOF	Thunder AX3-17/5C Sky Chariot HAFB	296	G-BILC
EC-DOG	Cessna 152-II	15284365	N6151L
EC-DOI (2)	Cessna TU206G Turbo Stationair 6-II	U20606369	D-EHTT N7566Z
EC-DOJ	Piper PA-32RT-300T Turbo Lance II	32R-7887284	N30693
EC-DOK	Piper PA-38-112 Tomahawk	38-81A0020	N25621
EC-DOL	Agusta-Bell 206B Jet Ranger III	8615	
EC-DOM	Piper PA-25-260 Pawnee	25-8156002	N90831
EC-DON	AISA I-115	138	E.9-138
EC-DOP	Piper PA-38-112 Tomahawk II	38-81A0109	N26030
EC-DOT	Piper PA-28RT-201 Arrow IV	28R-8118020	N9610N
EC-DOU	SZD-42-2 Jantar 2B	B-1074	
EC-DOV	Thunder AX8-90 HAFB	336	SE-ZYC(2)
EC-DOX	Piper PA-28-181 Archer II	28-8190194	N9525N
EC-DOY	Scheibe SF-25C Falke	4129	D-KLDF
EC-DOZ	Thunder AX6-56Z HAFB	232	G-BGYO
EC-DPA	Grob G.103A Twin II Acro	3679-K-30	
EC-DPB	Grob G.103A Twin II Acro	3680-K-31	
EC-DPC	Grob G.103A Twin II Acro	3681-K-32	
EC-DPD	Grob G.103A Twin II Acro	3682-K-33	
EC-DPE	Grob G.103A Twin II Acro	3683-K-34	
EC-DPF	Grob G.103A Twin II Acro	3684-K-35	
EC-DPG	Grob G.103A Twin II Acro	3685-K-36	
EC-DPH	Grob G.103A Twin II Acro (Dbr 21.8.02)	3686-K-37	
EC-DPI	SOCATA Rallye 180T Galérien (W/o 19.7.02)	3349	F-OGLA
EC-DPJ	SOCATA Rallye 180T Galérien	3350	F-OGLB
EC-DPK	SOCATA Rallye 180T Galérien	3351	F-OGLC
EC-DPL	SOCATA Rallye 180T Galérien	3352	F-OGLD
EC-DPM	SOCATA Rallye 235C	13353	F-OGLE
EC-DPN	SOCATA Rallye 235C	13354	F-OGLF
EC-DPO	SOCATA Rallye 235C (Fuselage replaced with c/n "13365" which may be a spare from the end of production. Stored.)	13355	F-OGLG
EC-DPP	SOCATA Rallye 235C (Wreck noted 3.05)	13356	F-OGLH
EC-DPQ	Piper PA-28-181 Archer II	28-8190059	N9605N
EC-DPR	Cameron V-56 HAFB	750	
EC-DPS	Cameron D-38/50 Hot Air Airship	751	
EC-DPT	Avialsa-Scheibe A.60	27	F-CCQE

EC-DPU	ICA/Brasov IS-29-D2	150	
EC-DPV	ICA/Brasov IS-28-B2	260	
EC-DPX	ICA/Brasov IS-28-M2	36	
EC-DPY	Piper PA-25-260 Pawnee	25-8156001	N90829
EC-DQA	Hughes 369D	61-0995D	N1108N
EC-DQB	SOCATA TB-10 Tobago	157	F-ODNX
			F-GCOP
EC-DQH	Schleicher ASW 19	19007	
EC-DQI (2)	Cessna TU206G Turbo Stationair 6-II	U20606010	N4743Z
EC-DQM	Cameron V-77 HAFB	789	
EC-DQN	Raven S-55A HAFB	835	
EC-DQS	SOCATA MS.880B Rallye Club	1954	F-BTJK
EC-DQU	Cessna L-19A Bird Dog (O-1A)	unkn	U.12-11
			51-12688
EC-DQV	Beech 95-B55 Baron	TC-2338	N3716B
EC-DQX	Cessna L-19A Bird Dog (O-1A)	unkn	U.12-5
			51-11931
EC-DQY	Cessna L-19A Bird Dog (O-1A)	unkn	U.12-6
			51-11929
EC-DQZ	Cessna L-19A Bird Dog (O-1A)	unkn	U.12-13
			51-4720
EC-DRC	SOCATA MS.893E Rallye 180GT Gaillard	13128	F-GBXB
	(W/o 5.9.04)		D-EEUD
EC-DRD	SOCATA Rallye 110ST Galopin (Wfu)	3357	F-OGLM
EC-DRE	SOCATA Rallye 110ST Galopin	3358	F-OGLO
EC-DRF	SOCATA TB-9 Tampico	262	F-OGLI
EC-DRG	Aérospatiale AS.350B Ecureuil	1597	
EC-DRJ	Robinson R-22	0259	N9076H
EC-DRK	Robinson R-22	0236	N9074F
EC-DRL	Piper PA-38-112 Tomahawk II	38-81A0021	N25622
EC-DRM	SOCATA MS.893E Rallye 180GT Gaillard	13198	F-GBKO
EC-DRN	Cessna L-19A-1 Bird Dog (O-1A)	23563	U.12-10
			51-12299
EC-DRO	CASA C.212 Aviocar	247	
EC-DRP	Grob G.109 (W/o 13.5.00)	6106	D-KHAA
EC-DRQ	SOCATA MS.880B Rallye Club	1662	F-BSKU
EC-DRT	Cameron O-77 HAFB	784	
EC-DRV	Reims/Cessna F152	F15201916	F-WZNC
EC-DRX	SOCATA TB-10 Tobago	295	F-OGLP
EC-DRZ	Cessna F172H	F172-0424	D-ELGT
EC-DSA	Aero Commander 680T	1564-20	I-ARBO
			N1199Z
EC-DSD	Piper PA-28-161 Warrior II	28-8116182	N9522N
EC-DSG	Cessna T188C AgHusky (W/o 23.8.98?)	T18803923T	N9994J
EC-DSK	SOCATA TB-10 Tobago (Wreck noted 3.05)	308	F-OGLQ
EC-DSL	Piper PA-38-112 Tomahawk II	38-82A0088	N9659N
EC-DSM	Piper PA-28-161 Warrior II	28-8116183	N9523N
EC-DSN	Thunder AX7-77A HAFB	454	
EC-DSQ	Agusta-Bell 47G-2	271	F-BIND
			F-OBND
			I-ELIT
EC-DSR	Cameron D-50 Hot Air Airship	892	
EC-DSU	MBB Bö.105S (Catalunya "02")	S-623	D-HDSS
EC-DSY	Reims/Cessna F152	F15201789	F-WZIL
EC-DSZ	Grob G.109	6122	D-KCVO
EC-DTA	Piper PA-28RT-201 Arrow IV	28R-8118038	N8315H
			N9624N
EC-DTB	SOCATA Rallye 235E Gabier	13018	F-GBXD
EC-DTD	Hughes 369D (Damaged 30.6.94)	1172D	
EC-DTE	MBB Bö.105C	S-576	D-HDPY
EC-DTF	MBB Bö.105C	S-599	D-HDQV
EC-DTG	Piper PA-23-250 Aztec C	27-3180	D-IDAX
			LN-KAG
			N10F
EC-DTH	Thunder/Colt AS-90 Hot Air Airship	451	
EC-DTJ	Piper PA-36-375 Brave	36-8102014	N6172A
	(Damaged 4.1.97)		
EC-DTK	Cameron D-50 Hot Air Airship	854	
EC-DTM	PADC/ MBB Bö.105C	S.9-402	D-HDNS(3)
			RP-C214
			(D-HDMA)
EC-DTN	SOCATA Rallye 180T Galérien	3373	F-ODQB
EC-DTQ	Piper PA-28RT-201T Turbo Arrow IV	28R-8331051	N9546N
EC-DTS	Partenavia P.68 Observer	324-17-OB	
EC-DTT	Grob G.102 Astir IIIB (Stored)	5583CB	
EC-DTV	CASA C.212-200	301	
EC-DTX	Schleicher ASW 20	20711	
EC-DTY	Piper PA-25-260 Pawnee C (W/o 16.8.02?)	25-4509	SE-FCY
EC-DTZ	Piper PA-25-260 Pawnee C	25-5301	SE-FYA
EC-DUA	Agusta-Bell 206B Jet Ranger	8665	
EC-DUC	Reims/Cessna F172N (Crashed 22.6.02)	F17201818	D-EJCA(2)
EC-DUD	Grumman G.164B Agcat	733B	
EC-DUH	Bell 47G-2	1969	F-BUYV
			74+32
			AS+387
EC-DUI	Hoffmann H-36 Dimona	3608	OE-9202
			(D-KAHG)
EC-DUJ	CASA C.101CC (Displayed at CASA factory)	98	
EC-DUN	North American T.6G Harvard	unkn	E.16-201
	(Museum, painted as E.16-201)		Fr.AF
			52-8216
EC-DUP	MBB Bö.105C	S-614	D-HDSJ
EC-DUQ	CASA C.212-200	270	
EC-DUR	Aérospatiale SA.341J Gazelle	1185	F-WTNA
EC-DUU(2)	Schleicher ASK 21	21346	
EC-DUY	MBB Bö.105C	S-628	D-HDSX
EC-DUZ	MBB Bö.105C	S-629	D-HDSY

EC-DVA	Hoffmann H-36 Dimona (Damaged)	3536	OE-9237
EC-DVF	Schleicher Ka 6CR Rhönsegler	6302	D-....
			OO-ZME
EC-DVH	CAARP CAP.10B	189	
EC-DVI	SOCATA MS.893E Rallye 180GT Gaillard	12122	F-BTVE
EC-DVJ	Hoffmann H-36 Dimona (Stored)	3671	D-KCED
EC-DVK	MBB Bö.105C	S-630	(N5489A)
			D-HDSZ
EC-DVL	MBB Bö.105C	S-631	(N5489C)
			D-HDTA
EC-DVP	Cameron 0-65 HAFB	1124	
EC-DVQ	CASA C.101CC	107	
EC-DVR	Agusta A.109A	7231	
EC-DVS	Robin DR.400/180R Remorqueur	1682	
EC-DVU	Grob G.103A Twin II Acro	33919-K-154	
EC-DVV	Grob G.103A Twin II Acro	33918-K-153	
EC-DVX	Grob G.103A Twin II Acro	33920-K-155	
EC-DXA	Rockwell Commander 690A	11328	D-IHVB
			N81449
EC-DXC	MBB Bö.105C	S-690	D-HDVD
EC-DXD	MBB Bö.105C	S-697	D-HDVK
EC-DXG	Aero Commander 680V	1711-86	N535SM
EC-DXH	MBB Bö.105C	S-698	D-HDVL
EC-DXI	MBB Bö.105C	S-699	D-HDVM
EC-DXJ	Hispano HA.220D Super Saeta	22/114	A.10C-109
			C.10C-109
EC-DXL	Wassmer WA.421-250	409	F-BPTL
EC-DXM	Aérospatiale SA.365C2 Dauphin 2	5007	PH-SSL
			G-BKXV
			PH-SSL
			F-WIPF
			N90045
EC-DXN	Aérospatiale AS.350B Ecureuil	1387	
EC-DXO	Ultramagic V-65 HAFB	65/04	
EC-DXP	Ultramagic V-65 HAFB	65/07	
EC-DXQ	Ultramagic V-77 HAFB	77/04	
EC-DXR	Hispano HA.200 Super Saeta (Museum)	20/56	A.10B-50
			C.10C-50
EC-DXU	Vickers V.806 Viscount (Wfu)	264	G-AOYO
EC-DXY	Reims/Cessna F152 (Dismantled)	F15201793	F-WZIU
EC-DXZ	Bell 206B Jet Ranger II	1051	HB-XFH
			F-BVUE
			HP-1533-71
			N58156
EC-DYD	Bell 47G-2	1620	D-HKBM
			74+29
			AS+389
			YA+028
			PA+118
			AS+383
EC-DYI	Ultramagic H-77 HAFB	77/13	
EC-DYJ	Ultramagic V-65 HAFB	65/06	
EC-DYK	Aérospatiale AS.350B Ecureuil	1863	
EC-DYL	Piper PA-28-140 Cherokee E	28-7225250	G-AZVZ
			N11C
EC-DYM	MBB Bö.105C (W/o 25.1.02?)	S-700	D-HDVN
EC-DYN	MBB Bö.105C	S-707	D-HDVU
EC-DYQ	Agusta-Bell 206B Jet Ranger III	8677	HB-XML
EC-DYR	Continental El Tomcat 6B (Bell OH-13H)	CCI-74-8	CS-HAS
			N9026T
EC-DYS	SOCATA MS.893E Rallye 180GT Gaillard	12313	F-BUNZ
EC-DYT	Cessna 340A	340A0687	G-VELT
			HB-LLZ
			N5462G
EC-DYU	Aérospatiale SA.365C-1 Dauphin 2	5053	PH-SSC
			LV-APO
			PH-SSC
			N3610B
EC-DYV	Ultramagic V-77 HAFB	77/06	
EC-DZD	Ultramagic F01 Bottle F56 SS HAFB	F01/01	
EC-DZE	Agusta-Bell 47G-4A	2535	I-CRIT
EC-DZF	Reims/Cessna F172M	F17201210	LN-NFE
			SE-GKB
EC-DZI	Agusta-Bell 47G-4A (W/o 6.3.94)	2536	I- ITOX
EC-DZJ	Bell 47G-3B (OH-13S)	3905	FAMET/
			HE.7B-29
			65-13009
EC-DZK	Agusta-Bell 47G-3B-1	1614	FAMET/
			HE.7B-32
EC-DZL	Agusta-Bell 47G-3B-1	1613	FAMET/
			HE.7B-31
EC-DZM	Agusta-Bell 47G-3B-1	1509	FAMET
			Z..7B-18
EC-DZN	Ultramagic H-65 HAFB	65/05	
EC-DZO	Ultramagic V-65 HAFB	65/11	
EC-DZP	Ultramagic V-77 HAFB	77/07	
EC-DZR	Piper PA-32-300 Cherokee Six D	32-7140028	CS-AFV
	(W/o 22.10.95)		N8635N
EC-DZS	Ultramagic V-77 HAFB	77/10	
EC-DZT	Agusta A.109A	7159	HB-XIU
EC-DZU	Valentin Taifun 17E (Stored)	1060	D-KFHA
EC-DZV	Cessna 310Q	310Q0039	D-ICAA
			PH-PLW
			(PH-ADZ)
			D-ICAA
			N7539Q
EC-DZX	Aérospatiale AS.355F1 Ecureuil 2	5243	F-WYMT
	(W/o 29.3.01, scrapped)		

EC-DZY	Aérospatiale SA.315B Lama	2381	F-BVUD
EC-DZZ	Piper PA-36-375 Brave	36-7802048	N3912E
EC-EAA	Piper PA-36-375 Brave	36-7802020	HP-1060
			YS-666A
			N9741N
EC-EAB	Cessna 402	402-0167	G-BAWZ
			N99JH
			G-BAWZ
			5Y-ANJ
			OY-AHP
			N4067Q
EC-EAE	Piper PA-38-112 Tomahawk II	38-82AO090	N9661N
EC-EAG	Aero Commander 680W	680W-1776-14	N680W
			N121AB
			N13TV
			N4988E
EC-EAI	Reims/Cessna F150K	F15000532	N8892
EC-EAJ	Ultramagic V-77 HAFB	77/09	
EC-EAL	Westland-Bell 47G-3B-1	WA/431	D-HAFH
			XT542
EC-EAR	Ultramagic V-65 HAFB	65/13	
EC-EAT	Ultramagic H-77 HAFB	77/08	
EC-EAX	Agusta-Bell 47G-3B	1510	HE.7B-19
			751-9
			Z..7B-19
EC-EAY	Agusta-Bell 47G-3B	1511	HE.7B-20
			751-10
			Z.7B-20
EC-EBB	Aérospatiale SA.365C Dauphin 2	5013	F-GBOU
EC-EBD	Grumman G.164D Turbo-Agcat	15D	G-BIVO
			N8311K
EC-EBE	Grumman G.164D Turbo-Agcat	07D	G-TCAT
			N816 IK
EC-EBF	Agusta-Bell 206B Jet Ranger II	8704	
EC-EBI	Sud Avn SA.316B Alouette III	1498	RJAF-314
EC-EBK	Colt 56A HAFB	930	
EC-EBL	Ultramagic H-77 HAFB	77/14	
EC-EBQ	Piper PA-36-375 Brave	36-7802031	N3863E
EC-EBS	Ultramagic V-65 HAFB	65/9	
EC-EBT	Ultramagic H-77 HAFB	77/11	
EC-EBU	Piper PA-36-300 Brave	36-8160012	N2346Y
EC-ECC	Ultramagic H-65 HAFB	65/17	
EC-ECE	Cessna T188C AgHusky (Dbr 13.3.01)	T18803935T	N9348K
EC-ECF	Grumman G.164A Agcat	1426	N8597H
EC-ECG	Ultramagic H-65 HAFB	65/15	
EC-ECH	MBB Bö.105CB (Ditched 29.10.02)	S-667	N.....
			(D-HDUI)
EC-ECI	MBB Bö.105CB	S-720	D-HDRH(2)
EC-ECJ	Aérospatiale AS.350B Ecureuil (W/o 13.8.94)	2031	
EC-ECK	Cessna 402	402-0284	D-IFAK
			N8436F
EC-ECL	Hoffmann H-36 Dimona	36218	
EC-ECT	Bell 206B Jet Ranger II	2237	D-HIPI (2)
			N16824
EC-ECV	Valentin Taifun 17E	1079	D-KLPA
EC-ECX	Piper PA-36-375 Brave	36-7902046	N999NA
	(Damaged 31.8.94)		N3658E
EC-ECZ	Grumman G.164B Agcat	686B	N8401K
EC-EDA	Grumman G.164B Agcat	695B	N695GA
EC-EDB	Reims/Cessna F337G Skymaster	F33700067	OO-EDU
	(Reims-assembled 337G with US c/n 33701564)		F-BVSX
	(Damaged 8.8.02)		
EC-EDC	Dassault Falcon 20	6	N750SS
			N497
			N65311
			C-GOQG
			(N21DT)
			N21JM
			N20JM
			N805F
			F-BMKH
			F-WMKH
EC-EDD	Grumman G.164B Agcat	116B	G-BEIJ
			N48685
EC-EDH	Robinson R-22	0071	N90348
EC-EDJ	Grumman G.164C Agcat	36C	N2734A
EC-EDN	Cessna 501 Citation I/SP	501-0010	VH-POZ
			(N500MD)
			N7WF
			EP-PBC
			N7WF
			N36859
EC-EDP	Grumman G.164B Agcat	318B	G-BFJO
			N6814Q
EC-EDQ	Eiri PIK-30	726	
EC-EDR	Grumman G.164B Agcat	343B	N6504K
EC-EDS	Grumman G.164B Agcat	262B	N25CD
EC-EDU	Grumman G.164C Agcat	7C	N6597K
EC-EDV	Grumman G.164 Agcat	214	N403Y
EC-EDX	Grumman G.164B Agcat	782B	N3633Z
EC-EDY	Grumman G.164B Agcat	790B	
EC-EDZ	Grumman G.164C Agcat	43C	N8085K
EC-EEA	Robin ATL	47	F-GFOX
EC-EEC	Sud Avn SA.316B Alouette III	1912	CC-CJB
			PH-SCI
			5N-AKD
			PH-SCI

EC-EED	SOCATA MS.894A Minerva 220	11718	CS-AGV
EC-EEH	MBB-Kawasaki BK.117A-3	7091	D-HBPL
EC-EEI	Bell 206L-3 Long Ranger III	51161	N3198T
EC-EEJ	Westland-Bell 47G-3B1	WA/314	D-HFFF
			XT155
EC-EEL	Ultramagic V-77 HAFB	77/12	
EC-EEN	Agusta-Bell 204B	3002	HB-XCG
			I-AGUG
EC-EEQ	Bell 212	30612	D-HOBB(2)
			EC-DYP
			D-HOBB(2)
			LN-OSM
EC-EER	Piper PA-36-375 Brave (W/o 1.7.98?)	36-8002029	N2453V
EC-EES	Bell 206L Long Ranger (Damaged 19.9.00)	45153	N16942
EC-EEV	Valentin Taifun 17E	1102	D-KFAC
EC-EEX	Piper PA-36-375 Brave (Cr 1.9.04)	36-7902028	N3983E
EC-EEZ	Bell 47G-5	7802	G-BLDF
			N8558F
EC-EFC	MBB-Kawasaki BK.117A-3	7120	D-HBCO
			(N9019V)
EC-EFF	Hoffmann H-36 Dimona II (Stored)	36230	OE-9289
EC-EFG	Hoffmann H-36 Dimona II	36223	OE-9291
EC-EFH	Rockwell Commander 690A	11130	N111VS
			N294BC
			N570H
EC-EFI (2)	Ultramagic M-160 HAFB	160/01	
EC-EFL(2)	Piper PA-34-200T Seneca II	34-7970246	N29691
EC-EFM	Piper PA-28RT-201T Turbo Arrow IV	28R-7931292	N46008
			XB-BKM
			N9627N
EC-EFN	Cessna 210M Centurion	21062158	N8866A
EC-EFO	Piper PA-34-200T Seneca II	34-7770092	N549BR
			N73GH
			N8584F
EC-EFP	Hoffmann H-36 Dimona (Stored)	36214	OE-9270
EC-EFQ	Lanaverre CS-11/75L Standard Cirrus	667	F-CEMV
EC-EFT	CASA C-1.131E Jungmann (Museum)	2226	E.3B-607
EC-EFV	Cameron N-77 HAFB	1064	
EC-EFY	SAN Jodel D.140C Mousquetaire III	162	F-BMFY
EC-EFZ	Ultramagic H-56 HAFB	56/2	
EC-EGA	Ultramagic V-65 HAFB	65/12	
EC-EGB	Ultramagic V-77 HAFB	77/15	
EC-EGC	Ultramagic H-56 HAFB	56/3	
EC-EGD	Cessna TU206G Turbo Stationair 6-II	U20606043	G-HCHU
			HB-CHU
			G-BKKJ
			N4890Z
EC-EGE	Ultramagic V-65 HAFB	65/16	
EC-EGG	Ultramagic H-56 HAFB	56/4	
EC-EGJ	Brditschka HB23/2400 (Dismantled)	23023-S-5	
EC-EGK	Brditschka HB23/2400	23021-S-4	
EC-EGP	CASA C-1.131E Jungmann	2222	E.3B-603
EC-EGS	HS.125 Series 600A	256034	EC-115
			N600SB
			N600FL
			N90BL
			N90B
			N39BH
EC-EGT	HS.125 Series 1A-522	25080	N23KL
			C-GLEO
			EI-BGW
			G-BDYE
			3D-AAB
			VQ-ZIL
EC-EGU	Cessna T188C AgHusky	T18803437T	N2200J
EC-EGV	Aérospatiale SA.365C Dauphin 2	5032	F-GBTB
EC-EGX	Piper PA-28RT-201T Turbo Arrow IV	28R-7931102	N2165U
EC-EGZ	Sud Avn SA.316B Alouette III	2319	HB-XRY
			N9005D
EC-EHB	Piper PA-36-375 Brave	36-8102001	N2364Y
EC-EHC	Dassault Falcon 20DC	46	N46VG
			(N144FE)
			N7FE
			N23555
			CF-ESO
			F-WMKG
EC-EHE	Beech A36 Bonanza	E-115	OO-KRZ
			D-EKRZ
EC-EHF	BAe.125 Series 600A	256011	N81D
			N42622
			VR-BGS
			N555GB
			N555CB
			N6001H
			N24BH
EC-EHI	Cessna T210M Turbo Centurion	21061956	N1749M
EC-EHK	Cessna TU206G Turbo Stationair 6-II	U20606260	N6386Z
EC-EHL	Cessna Turbo 310R	310R0101	N134SW
			G-BMHE
			ZS-JCF
			N69593
EC-EHN	Piper PA-36-375 Brave	36-7802022	N3830E
EC-EHP	Cessna 402B (Wfu, Valencia)	402B1232	N720J
			N4186G
EC-EHR	Centrair ASW-20F	20175	F-CEUM
EC-EHV	Bell UH-1B (204)	953	N88389
			63-8728

EC-EIB	Piper PA-36-285 Pawnee Brave	36-7360029	N56123
EC-EIF	Grumman G.164B Agcat	740B	N3629B
EC-EIH	Rockwell Commander 690A	11212	N690BT C-GIAA N9165N
EC-EIJ	Maule MX-7-180 Star Rocket	11033C	N5672A
EC-EIL	Rockwell Commander 690	11007	N171TT N711TT N9207N ZS-NHG N9207N
EC-EIN	Air Tractor AT-502 (W/o 6.8.02?)	502-0021	
EC-EIO	Air Tractor AT-502	502-0019	
EC-EIP	Piper PA-36-375 Brave	36-8002008	N2322Y ZK-EQJ
EC-EIQ	Reims/Cessna F150L (Dismantled)	F15000900	D-ECUD(2)
EC-EIT	Ultramagic M-65 HAFB	65/23	
EC-EIX	Rockwell S.2R Thrush Commander	2171R	N4963X
EC-EIY	Air Tractor AT-501	501-0016	N10018
EC-EIZ	Air Tractor AT-401	401-0679	N73173
EC-EJA	Piper PA-36-300 Brave	36-8160022	N2393Y
EC-EJB	Douglas C-47 (Derelict, .02)	4479	EC-177 (N514GL) N330 (5N-ARC) N330 F-OART N2077A HK-1201 C-1201 41-18417
EC-EJC	Ayres S.2R-T34 Turbo Thrush	6017	N4009W
EC-EJD	Cessna T188C AgHusky	T18803686T	N3898J
EC-EJF	Air Tractor AT-401	401-0685	
EC-EJG	Cessna 172N	17273863	N6324J
EC-EJH	Cessna TU206G Turbo Stationair 6-II (Ditched 23.11.04)	U20604172	N756LH
EC-EJI	Piper PA-28RT-201T Turbo Arrow IV	28R-8131192	N8425D
EC-EJJ	Ayres S.2R-T15 Turbo Thrush (W/o 10.7.94)	T15-006	N40184
EC-EJL	Glasflügel H205 Libelle	165	F-CEQP
EC-EJO	Bell 206B Jet Ranger II	2864	HB-XLD
EC-EJP	Air Tractor AT-301	301-0665	N73120
EC-EJR	Piper PA-36-375 Brave	36-8002041	N2318Y
EC-EJS	Ultramagic V-65 HAFB	65/14	
EC-EJT	Ultramagic V-65 HAFB	65/08	
EC-EJV	Piper PA-34-200T Seneca II	34-7970030	N2215D
EC-EJX	Piper PA-36-375 Brave (Dam. 27.7.02)	36-7902039	N3992E
EC-EJY	Piper PA-36-375 Brave	36-7902010	N3972E
EC-EKB	Bell UH-1B (204)	345	N4991D 61-765
EC-EKC	Bell UH-1B (204)	684	N394HP 62-12533
EC-EKD	Cessna 172N	17270671	G-BNSK N739NJ
EC-EKE	Schempp-Hirth Discus b	232	
EC-EKF	Reims/Cessna F172P (Damaged 11.5.97)	F17202189	HB-CGP
EC-EKG	Cessna 402B Utililiner II	402B1209	N321RF N321PC (N4163G)
EC-EKH	Piper PA-28RT-201T Turbo Arrow IV	28R-8131008	N8277Y
EC-EKI	Cessna 150J	15069733	N51055
EC-EKJ	Cessna 172N	17270334	N738YD
EC-EKK	Dassault Falcon 20C	106	N31V N9300M F-GBPG N987F F-WJMM
EC-EKL	Ultramagic V-77 HAFB	77/16	
EC-EKN	Cessna U206F Stationair	U20603721	N7952N
EC-EKO	Bell 206B Jet Ranger II	2406	N50006
EC-EKP	Grob G.102 Astir CS (Damaged 30.7.04)	1517	D-7453
EC-EKR	Piper PA-36-285 Pawnee Brave	36-7660049	N57728
EC-EKS	Ultramagic M-77 HAFB	77/23	
EC-EKV	Cessna T210N Turbo Centurion II	21063817	N6166C
EC-EKX	Reims/Cessna F172M	F17201180	D-EDJO
EC-EKY	Maule M-5-180C	8012C	N5642T
EC-EKZ	Maule M-5-210C Strata Rocket	6007C	N51467
EC-ELB	Bell 47G-5A	25103	CS-HAG
EC-ELH	Mooney M.20J Model 201	24-1322	N1171U
EC-ELI	Cessna 152-II	15285289	G-BNSJ N65576
EC-ELL	Piper PA-36-375 Brave	36-8202011	N2351X
EC-ELO	Aérospatiale AS.350B1 Ecureuil	2129	
EC-ELP	Cessna 172N	17268568	C-GSOG N733UW
EC-ELQ	Cessna 150M	15078731	C-GYEE (N704MY)
EC-ELR	Ultramagic H-56 HAFB	56/05	
EC-ELT	BAe.146 Series 200QT	E-2102	EC-198 G-5-102 G-BOKZ G-5-102
EC-ELU	Piper PA-36-375 Brave	36-8002017	TI-APF N9734N
EC-ELX	Piper PA-36-375 Brave (Reserved as F-OJMD 10.04)	36-8002021	C-GJEB N2410V
EC-ELZ	Piper PA-38-112 Tomahawk	38-78A0299	N9257T
EC-EMB	Piper PA-34-200T Seneca II	34-7870034	N9052K
EC-EMC	Piper PA-36-375 Brave	36-8002022	C-GJFZ N2411V
EC-EMD	McDonnell-Douglas DC-8-62F	46023	EC-217 N731PL JA8035
EC-EME	Cessna 172N	17271082	D-EGGQ N1653E
EC-EMF	Agusta-Bell 206B Jet Ranger II	8715	
EC-EMH	Cessna 402B	402B0534	N101GP
EC-EML	Piper PA-36-375 Brave (Damaged 3.10.00)	36-8202008	N2346X
EC-EMM	Cessna 172N	17268338	D-EGGO(2) N733JV
EC-EMP	Cessna 172M	17262854	D-EGGP N13569
EC-EMQ	Ultramagic M-77 HAFB	77/26	
EC-EMR	Ultramagic S-105 HAFB	105/02	
EC-EMS	Ultramagic S-90 HAFB	90/01	
EC-EMX	McDonnell-Douglas DC-8-62	45921	EC-230 N729PL N756UA SE-DBG
EC-EMZ	Pilatus PC-6/B1-H2 Turbo-Porter	672	F-GHAS C-GXIK N62149 XW-PEF HB-FEI
EC-ENA	Ayres S.2R-R1820	001DC	N40225
EC-ENB	Ayres S.2R-R1820	015DC	N3086L
EC-ENC	Cessna T188C AgHusky (Dam. 15.10.03)	T18803697T	N3933J
EC-END	Air Tractor AT-401	401-0698	N1007G
EC-ENE	Cessna 172N	17268844	N734GN
EC-ENF	Cessna T.188C AgHusky	T18803942T	N9414K
EC-ENG	Piper PA-28-161 Cadet	2841027	N9619N
EC-ENH	Cessna Turbo 310R	310R1309	N6171X
EC-ENI	Schempp-Hirth Ventus b/16.6	172	D-7717
EC-ENJ	Bell 47G-5	7938	N1477W
EC-ENK	Thunder AX7-77 HAFB	1174	
EC-ENL	Air Tractor AT-401	401-0700	N1005A
EC-ENM	Air Tractor AT-503	503-0001	N7309X
EC-ENN	Air Tractor AT-502	502-0007	N7315N
EC-ENO	Rockwell S.2R Thrush Commander	2101R	N4911X
EC-ENP	Cessna 152	15284480	N4709M
EC-ENR	Piper PA-28RT-201T Turbo Arrow IV	28R-8131137	N8385A
EC-ENV	Maule M-5-235C Lunar Rocket	7164C	N6129M
EC-ENX	Bell UH-1B (204) (Wrecked)	977	N5598G 63-12916
EC-ENY	Piper PA-36-375 Brave	36-8202009	N2349X
EC-EOA	Cessna 172P	17275892	N65794
EC-EOB	Maule M-5-180C	8005C	N5635U
EC-EOC	Ultramagic H-77 HAFB	77/27	
EC-EOD	Cessna 177RG Cardinal RG	177RG0912	N7857V
EC-EOE	Robinson R-22 Beta	0695	HB-XSF
EC-EOF	Aérospatiale SA.315B Lama	2261	F-GEJS N13583 (N515HA) N13583
EC-EOI	Bell UH-1B (204)	408	N5023U 62-1888
EC-EOP	Schleicher ASW 20 (W/o 20.4.02)	20020	D-7568
EC-EOR	Ultramagic S-105 HAFB	105/05	
EC-EOS	Piper PA-28-161 Cadet (Stored)	2841064	N9629N
EC-EOT	Cessna 172N (Dbr 6.4.00)	17273765	N5367J
EC-EOU	SOCATA TB-10 Tobago (Wreck noted 5.01)	634	F-GFFE N20FD
EC-EOV	Cessna 337G Skymaster	33701779	N53681
EC-EOX	Bell UH-1B (204)	1214	N90632 64-14090
EC-EPC	Ultramagic M-77 HAFB	77/33	
EC-EPE	Ultramagic M-77 HAFB	77/34	
EC-EPG	Robin ATL	76	F-GFSA
EC-EPH	Maule MX.7-180 Star Rocket	11039C	N6114M
EC-EPI	Ultramagic M-65 HAFB	65/29	
EC-EPJ	Cessna 152	15284583	N5408M
EC-EPK	Cessna 402B	1036	N98666
EC-EPO	Glaser-Dirks DG-400	4-223	(D-KIDG)
EC-EPP	Cessna T.337H Turbo Skymaster	01837	N1345L
EC-EPQ	Piper PA-36-375 Brave	36-8102012	C-GJFT N6167A
EC-EPR	Piper PA-34-200T Seneca II	34-7870191	N9479C
EC-EPS	Cessna 172M	17261304	N20458
EC-EPT	Cessna 172N (Wfu, stored)	17267611	N73685 N739QB
EC-EPU	Grob G.103 Astir Trainer	3237	F-CFHC
EC-EPV	Ultramagic F02 Pegaso Truck SS HAFB	F02/01	EC-197
EC-EPX	Piper PA-34-220T Seneca III	34-8233029	D-GBON N8464B
EC-EPY	Mooney M.20J Model 205	24-3112	N1010H
EC-EPZ	Piper PA-32-301T Turbo Saratoga	32-8024001	N9326C
EC-EQA	Cessna 150J	15070498	N60683
EC-EQB	Cessna 150M (Damaged 9.9.94)	15078829	N704SC
EC-EQD	Bell 47G-5A	25057	FAP-650 N2975W
EC-EQF	Bell 47G-5A (Stored)	25065	FAP-654 N2981W
EC-EQG	Reims/Cessna F172N (Damaged 8.8.03)	F17202008	G-WAGY
EC-EQJ	Cessna 411	411-0198	YV-455CP

EC-EQK	Cessna 310R	310R1610	N36873
EC-EQL	Bell 47G-3B1	6524	FAP-621 66-621
EC-EQM	Cessna 152	15281103	N49017
EC-EQN	Cessna 152	15280727	D-EMBP N152LK (N25544)
EC-EQO	Cessna 152	15282262	D-EMFO(2) N68330
EC-EQP	Dassault Falcon 20	149	EC-263 N568Q (N4359F) N1818S N4359F F-WNGO
EC-EQR	Robinson R-22M Mariner	1043M	
EC-EQS	Robin DR.400/180 Régent	1221	
EC-EQT	Cessna 172M	17261170	N20297
EC-EQV	Piper PA-34-200T Seneca II	34-7770006	N5266F
EC-EQY	MBB Bö.105CBS	S-810	D-HDZT
EC-EQZ	SOCATA TB-9 Tampico	926	
EC-ERA	Piper PA-18-150 Super Cub	18-8929	N4508Y
EC-ERB	Grumman G.164B Agcat	814B	
EC-ERC	Piper PA-28-181 Cherokee Archer II	28-7790257	N8539F
EC-ERD	Aérospatiale AS.350B Ecureuil	1530	G-JORR G-BJMY
EC-ERE	Aérospatiale AS.350B Ecureuil (Damaged 27.8.02)	1865	D-HGBA
EC-ERG	Cessna 152	15279558	N714ZH
EC-ERH	Cessna 402B	402B1086	N543GB N543GA (N1927G)
EC-ERI	Piper PA-36-285 Pawnee Brave (Damaged 5.2.97)	36-7360035	N56297
EC-ERK	Bell UH-1E (204)	6069	N151LC BuA151875
EC-ERL	Beech F33A Bonanza	CE-1245	N3084D
EC-ERM	Cessna U206F Stationair (Dam. 10.1.03)	U20602291	N987CA
EC-ERN	Piper PA-38-112 Tomahawk	38-78A0719	N2501A
EC-ERO	CASA C-1.131E Jungmann	2012	E.3B-408
EC-ERP	CASA C-1.131E Jungmann	unkn	E.3B-321
EC-ERQ	Beech 200 Super King Air (W/o 9.10.97)	BB-218	EC-351 N575HA N575HW N9209Q
EC-ERS	Cessna 340A	340A0524	N4277C
EC-ERT	Cessna 172N	17271250	N2362E
EC-ERU	Cessna 172N	17273475	N4928G
EC-ERV	Cessna 152	15281957	N67644
EC-ERY	Sikorsky S-76 Arriel 1S	760037	EC-364 F-GHUI N9007F PH-NZM N4254S
EC-ERZ	Aérospatiale AS.350B Ecureuil	2261	
EC-ESB	Hoffmann H-36 Dimona	36209	OE-9268
EC-ESD	Cessna 150M	15079292	N714MY
EC-ESH	Reims/Cessna FA150L Aerobat	FA1500099	D-ECPK
EC-ESI	Scheibe SF-25E Super Falke	4341	D-KDCR
EC-ESK	SOCATA TB-20 Trinidad	747	F-GFQN
EC-ESL	Piper PA-36-285 Pawnee Brave (W/o 7.5.98?)	36-7660087	C-GJIK N57774
EC-ESM	Cessna U206F Stationair	U20601902	D-EGJR N50045
EC-ESN	Piper PA-36-285 Pawnee Brave	36-7560066	C-GUAR N9955P
EC-ESO	Cessna 152	15281549	N65433
EC-ESP	Piper PA-38-112 Tomahawk	38-79A0460	N2463F
EC-ESU	Beech F33A Bonanza	CE-1410	N56620
EC-ESX	MBB-Kawasaki BK.117B-1	7176	D-HBHS
EC-ESY	Grob G.102 Speed Astir IIB	4106	D-6819
EC-ETC	Cessna 172N	17269216	D-EFZN(2) N734YG
EC-ETE	Piper PA-28-181 Cherokee Archer II (Accident 9/3/03 Cerdanya)	28-7790459	N3461Q
EC-ETG	Soloy-Hiller UH-12J3	5067	N4027K
EC-ETJ	Ultramagic M-160 HAFB	160/02	
EC-ETK	Ultramagic M-77 HAFB	77/39	
EC-ETN	Glaser-Dirks DG-200	2-86	F-CAYB F-WAQA
EC-ETO	Grob G.102 Astir CS	1486	D-4790
EC-ETP	Ultramagic H-65 HAFB	65/27	
EC-ETQ	Ultramagic V-77 HAFB	77/35	
EC-ETR	Ultramagic M-77 HAFB	77/37	
EC-ETS	Cessna T188C AgHusky (W/o 8.9.04)	T18803872T	N9937J
EC-ETT	CASA C-1.131E Jungmann	unkn	E.3B-397
EC-ETU	Cessna 337G Skymaster	33701573	N6AX
EC-ETV	SOCATA TB-20 Trinidad	743	F-GFQK
EC-ETX	Cessna 182P Skylane	18264317	N1404M
EC-ETY	Thunder AX7-77 HAFB	1360	
EC-EUA	Ultramagic S-105 HAFB	105/08	
EC-EUB	Lanaverre CS-11/75L Standard Cirrus	10	F-CEVK
EC-EUG	Air Tractor AT-501 (Damaged 10.9.94)	501-0083	
EC-EUH	Air Tractor AT-501	501-0082	
EC-EUI	Ultramagic H-65 HAFB	65/25	
EC-EUK	Cessna 172N (W/o 29.8.03)	17271869	N5441E
EC-EUM	Piper PA-36-285 Pawnee Brave	36-7660033	N57709
EC-EUN	Piper PA-34-200T Seneca II (W/o 29.8.03)	34-7970213	N2193Z
EC-EUO	Cessna T210M Turbo Centurion	21062810	N6660B
EC-EUP	Reims/Cessna F150M (Damaged)	F15001192	D-EIWD
EC-EUQ	Thunder AX8-105 HAFB	1644	
EC-EUR	Wassmer WA.26P	23	F-CDSB
EC-EUS	SOCATA TB-9 Tampico	1028	
EC-EUT	Bell 206L-3 Long Ranger III	51337	N8212U
EC-EUV	Cessna 172N (Damaged 21.6.97)	17272980	N1237F
EC-EUX	Cessna 172M	17264726	N61682
EC-EUY	Cessna 152	15283383	N48864
EC-EVA	Aérospatiale AS.350B Ecureuil	1345	HB-XMA D-HLTH
EC-EVF	Ultramagic M-77 HAFB (Quoted officially as 77/79, new canopy?)	77/49	
EC-EVG	PZL M-18A Dromader (W/o 15.7.97)	1Z020-21	N21MX
EC-EVH	PZL M-18A Dromader	1Z020-10	N81695
EC-EVI	PZL M-18A Dromader	1Z020-09	N8169Q
EC-EVJ	Grumman G-159 Gulfstream 1	39	EC-376 N39TG N40Y
EC-EVK	Consolidated PBY-5A Catalina (Stored, Madrid)	2008	EC-359 C-GFFH N6458C BuA46644
EC-EVL	PZL M-18A Dromader	1Z012-27	N46831
EC-EVM	Aérospatiale AS.350B Ecureuil	2312	
EC-EVN	Robinson R-22 Beta	0854	OY-HFA
EC-EVO	PZL M-18A Dromader (Damaged 23.7.94)	1Z020-16	N81702
EC-EVP	PZL M-18A Dromader (W/o 26.7.99?)	1Z020-12	N8170Q
EC-EVQ	PZL M-18A Dromader	1Z019-08	N8085K SP-DBR
EC-EVS	Bell 204 (UH-1B)	893	EC-463 N400SD N9378A 63-8668
EC-EVV	ICA-Brasov IS.28B2	339	
EC-EVX	SOCATA TB-10 Tobago	649	F-GENZ
EC-EVZ	Hughes 369HS	125-0785S	G-WHYZ 5B-CGZ N9265F
EC-EXA	Ultramagic M-77 HAFB	77/52	
EC-EXB	Grumman G-159 Gulfstream 1	153	EC-433 N153TG N80AC N733NM N733G
EC-EXE	Bell 206B Jet Ranger II	1073	HB-XXA G-BKDD C-FDVB CF-DVB N83159
EC-EXF	McDonnell-Douglas DC-9-87	49832	EC-295
EC-EXG	McDonnell-Douglas DC-9-87	49833	EC-296
EC-EXI	Ultramagic S-105 HAFB	105/09	
EC-EXJ	Mooney M.20J Model 201	24-1689	EC-447 N10882
EC-EXK	Mooney M.20J Model 201 (W/o 27.1.03 ?)	24-1690	EC-448 N10898
EC-EXL	Cessna 152	15284055	N4980H
EC-EXM	McDonnell-Douglas DC-9-87	49835	EC-298
EC-EXN	McDonnell-Douglas DC-9-87	49836	EC-299
EC-EXO	Bell 204	202	EC-436 N18SX N18SP N3145F 60-3556
EC-EXP	Cessna U206F Stationair	U20602398	N206CT
EC-EXQ	Grumman G-159 Gulfstream 1 (Wfu)	142	EC-461 N142TG N10ZA N764G
EC-EXR	McDonnell-Douglas DC-9-87	49834	EC-297
EC-EXS	Grumman G-159 Gulfstream 1 (Wfu)	64	EC-460 N64TG N49401 CF-COL N4466P N764G
EC-EXT	McDonnell-Douglas DC-9-87	49837	EC-300
EC-EXU	Cessna T210N Turbo Centurion II	21063389	N5360A
EC-EXZ	PZL M-18A Dromader	1Z021-06	EC-450 SP-DCC
EC-EYA	Cameron V-56 HAFB	2216	
EC-EYB	McDonnell-Douglas DC-9-87	49838	EC-301
EC-EYD	Fleet 2 (Museum)	324	EC-500 LV-ZCD LV-PBC R-69
EC-EYE	PZL M-18A Dromader	1Z022-02	SP-DCR
EC-EYF	PZL M-18A Dromader	1Z021-03	EC-453 SP-DBZ
EC-EYG	PZL M-18A Dromader	1Z021-04	SP-DCA
EC-EYH	PZL M-18A Dromader	1Z022-01	SP-DCP
EC-EYI	PZL M-18A Dromader	1Z021-23	SP-DCG
EC-EYJ	PZL M-18A Dromader (W/o 6.8.94)	1Z021-29	SP-DCN
EC-EYL	Cessna 150L (Damaged 2.1.94)	15075347	N11355
EC-EYN	Piper PA-38-112 Tomahawk	38-79A0184	N2435C
EC-EYO	Piper PA-36-375 Brave (Damaged 4.5.97)	36-8202006	N2337X

EC-EYQ	Piper PA-36-375 Brave	36-8102021	N99NA N6186A
EC-EYT	Cessna 210L Centurion	21060803	D-EOGY N1783X
EC-EYU	CASA C-1.131E Jungmann	unkn	E.3B-340
EC-EYV	Piper PA-34-220T Seneca III	34-8233109	OE-FYB N8161K
EC-EYX	McDonnell-Douglas DC-9-87	49839	EC-302
EC-EYY	McDonnell-Douglas DC-9-87	49840	EC-303
EC-EYZ	McDonnell-Douglas DC-9-87	49841	EC-304
EC-EZA	McDonnell-Douglas DC-9-87	49842	EC-305
EC-EZB	Avialsa-Scheibe A.60	58	F-CCVK
EC-EZC	Schempp-Hirth Discus bT	35/344	
EC-EZD	Swearingen SA.226TC Metro II	TC-314	EC-488 N232AM
EC-EZE	Swearingen SA.226TC Metro II	TC-319	EC-487 N233AM
EC-EZF	Ultramagic M-77 HAFB	77/43	
EC-EZH	Ultramagic V-65 HAFB	65/35	
EC-EZI	Ultramagic M-77 HAFB	77/42	
EC-EZL	Piper PA-32-300 Cherokee Six	32-7840113	N9709C
EC-EZM	Valentin Taifun 17E	1086	G-BMXF D-KHVA
EC-EZN	Beech 65-A80 Queen Air (W/o 9.1.99?)	LD-205	EC-EEO(1) G-ASXV OO-ATO G-ASXV
EC-EZO	Grumman G.159 Gulfstream 1 (Wfu)	41	EC-494 N41TG N9ZA N7PG
EC-EZP	Aérospatiale AS.350B Ecureuil	2413	EC-562 F-WYMC
EC-EZQ	Piper PA-38-112 Tomahawk	38-79A0754	N2539L
EC-EZS	McDonnell-Douglas DC-9-87	49843	EC-306
EC-EZV	Piper PA-38-112 Tomahawk	38-78A0310	N9273T
EC-EZX	Piper PA-28-181 Archer II	28-7990301	N2138R
EC-EZY	Piper PA-28RT-201T Turbo Arrow IV	28R-8231002	N8448B
EC-EZZ	Piper PA-28-181 Archer II	28-8190295	EC-572 N8420F
EC-FAA	SOCATA MS.893E Rallye 180GT Gaillard	12605	F-BXDY
EC-FAB	Piper PA-28R-201T Turbo Cherokee Arrow III	28R-7703139	N5650V
EC-FAG	Cessna 310R (Wreck noted 2.01)	310R1255	N6056X
EC-FAH	Douglas C-47A	9336	EC-530 F-BVJH F-OCKH F-BRGO Fr.AF F-BFGA 42-23474
EC-FAI	Robinson R-22 Alpha	0427	G-GAZE N8522K
EC-FAJ	Maule MX.7-180 Star Rocket	11074C	EC-599
EC-FAK	Piper PA-38-112 Tomahawk	38-78A0465	N2441E
EC-FAN	Cessna T210M Turbo Centurion	21062564	N761VY
EC-FAO	Bell 206L-3 Long Ranger III	51289	N206WC C-FFCE
EC-FAT	PZL M-18A Dromader	1Z022-03	EC-471 SP-DCS
EC-FAU	PZL M-18A Dromader	1Z022-04	EC-4 . . SP-DCT
EC-FAV	PZL M-18A Dromader	1Z021-27	EC-458 SP-DCL
EC-FAX	PZL M-18A Dromader	1Z021-24	EC-4 . . SP-DCH
EC-FAZ	Piper PA-36-375 Brave	36-7802007	N102RS SE-GVM
EC-FBA	Piper PA-36-375 Brave (Dam. 15.10.03)	36-7802045	N3873E
EC-FBB	Ultramagic F-04 Bird SS HAFB	F04/01	
EC-FBC	CASA/Nurtanio CN.235-100 (W/o 29.8.01)	033	
EC-FBE	Piper PA-36-375 Brave (Damaged 18.6.97)	36-8202002	N2323X
EC-FBF	PZL M-18A Dromader	1Z021-28	EC-4 . . SP-DCM
EC-FBG	PZL M-18A Dromader	1Z021-30	EC-4 . . SP-DCO
EC-FBH	PZL M-18A Dromader (Damaged 21.7.94)	1Z021-22	EC-4 . . SP-DCF
EC-FBI	PZL M-18A Dromader	1Z021-26	EC-4 . . SP-DCK
EC-FBJ	PZL M-18A Dromader (Damaged 26.8.94)	1Z021-25	EC-4 . . SP-DCI
EC-FBK	Piper PA-36-375 Brave	36-7802071	N3959E
EC-FBL	Bell 212	30558	EC-553 LN-OQZ (G-BGFE) LN-OQZ N83079
EC-FBM	Bell 212	30574	EC-552 LN-ORG (LN-OQV) N58025
EC-FBN	PZL M-18A Dromader (Damaged 2.8.03)	1Z021-20	SP-DCD
EC-FBO	PZL M-18A Dromader	1Z021-21	SP-DCE
EC-FBT	Robinson R-22 Beta	1593	
EC-FBU	Ultramagic S-105 HAFB	105/15	
EC-FBV	PZL M-18A Dromader	1Z020-27	N2178Q

EC-FBY	Mooney M.20K Model 231	25-0290	N231KU
EC-FBZ	Robinson R22 Beta	1496	EC-557
EC-FCA	Ultramagic N-77 HAFB	77/54	
EC-FCB	Airbus A320-211	158	EC-579 F-WWIC
EC-FCC	Cessna 402B	402B1013	N113JG N87184
EC-FCD	Rolladen-Schneider LS1D	205	F-CDVI
EC-FCF	SOCATA TB-20 Trinidad	957	F-GKUJ
EC-FCH	Cessna 152 (W/o 26.2.01)	15282310	N864WC N68474
EC-FCJ	Ultramagic N-77 HAFB	77/44	
EC-FCK	Ultramagic N-77 HAFB	77/62	
EC-FCM	Agusta-Bell 47G-2 (Wrecked)	267	D-HAVO 74+25 AS+067
EC-FCN	Piper PA-38-112 Tomahawk	38-78A0703	EC-FBW N2472A
EC-FCO	Bell 206L-3 Long Ranger III	51179	N52CH
EC-FCP	Agusta-Bell 206B Jet Ranger II	8006	G-BPIB D-HABI SX-HAA
EC-FCR	Cessna 150E	15060906	G-AWPX 5N-AFR N11B N6206T
EC-FCS	Colt 77A HAFB	1788	
EC-FCT	Continental El Tomcat 6C	CC7.77.7	N9098T
EC-FCV	Ultramagic N-65 HAFB	65/36	
EC-FCX	PZL M-18A Dromader	1Z020-08	N2178F
EC-FCY	Piper PA-28R-201T Turbo Arrow III	28R-7803166	N3329M
EC-FCZ	Grob G.102 Astir CS	1355	D-7394
EC-FDA	Airbus A320-211	176	EC-581 F-WWIO
EC-FDB	Airbus A320-211	173	EC-580 F-WWIL
EC-FDC	Schleicher ASW 15B	15330	D-2323
EC-FDD	Beech F33A Bonanza	CE-1571	N81728
EC-FDE	Piper PA-34-200T Seneca II	34-7970421	N2958Y
EC-FDF	Piper PA-28-181 Archer II	28-8090122	N21AG N81038
EC-FDI	Wassmer WA.26P	59	F-CDXR
EC-FDJ	Ultramagic V-65 HAFB	65/38	
EC-FDK	Piper PA-28RT-201 Arrow IV (Damaged 9.9.02)	28R-7918200	N2887W
EC-FDM	PZL M-18A Dromader	1Z022-16	SP-DBV
EC-FDN	PZL M-18A Dromader (W/o 11.9.01)	1Z022-18	SP-DCY
EC-FDO	PZL M-18A Dromader (W/o 3.2.97)	1Z022-20	SP-DCX
EC-FDP	PZL M-18A Dromader	1Z022-17	SP-DCZ
EC-FDQ	PZL M-18A Dromader	1Z022-21	SP-DCV
EC-FDR	PZL M-18A Dromader	1Z022-22	SP-DAA
EC-FDS	PZL M-18A Dromader	1Z022-23	SP-DAB
EC-FDT	PZL M-18A Dromader	1Z022-24	SP-DAC
EC-FDU	PZL M-18A Dromader	1Z022-25	SP-DAD
EC-FDV	PZL M-18A Dromader	1Z022-26	SP-DAE
EC-FDX	Thunder AX7-77 HAFB	1822	
EC-FDY	Thunder AX7-77 HAFB	1893	
EC-FEA	Piper PA-28R-200 Cherokee Arrow II	28R-7435239	N42682
EC-FEC	Cessna 150H	15068793	N23208
EC-FED	Cessna 152	15283528	N53272
EC-FEG	Cessna T210N Turbo Centurion II	21064713	N1639U N17CD N1639U
EC-FEH	Cessna 150L (Damaged 14.8.04)	15073157	N92AV N5257Q
EC-FEI	Cessna 340 (W/o 5.9.98?)	340-0113	EC-644 N888CW N4569Q
EC-FEJ	Cessna 152	15283173	N47118
EC-FEK	Cessna 172RG Cutlass RG	172RG1088	N9939B
EC-FEL	Agusta-Bell AB.412	25576	EC-607
EC-FES	Cessna 550 Citation II	550-0678	EC-777
EC-FEU	Robin ATL	109	F-GGHC
EC-FEV	Bell 206B Jet Ranger II	1162	C-GZPX N59388
EC-FEX	Robinson R-22 Beta (W/o 22.6.02?)	1293	C-GZAR
EC-FEY	McDonnell-Douglas DC-9-87	53208	EC-634
EC-FEZ	McDonnell-Douglas DC-9-87	53207	EC-633
EC-FFA	McDonnell-Douglas DC-9-87	53209	EC-635
EC-FFD	Cessna 421B Golden Eagle (On rebuild)	421B0485	N421CC (N41159)
EC-FFG	Cessna 152	15284573	N5384M
EC-FFH	McDonnell-Douglas DC-9-87	53211	EC-637
EC-FFI	McDonnell-Douglas DC-9-87	53210	EC-636
EC-FFJ	Mooney M.20J Model 205	24-3217	EC-665 N9133N
EC-FFP	Piper PA-28RT-201T Turbo Arrow IV	28R-8131043	N83093
EC-FFQ	Bell 206L-3 Long Ranger III	51463	N6635Y
EC-FFR	Ultramagic N-77 HAFB	77/66	
EC-FFS	Ultramagic V-65 HAFB	65/22	
EC-FFT	Ultramagic V-65 HAFB	65/39	
EC-FFU	Ultramagic N-77 HAFB	77/67	
EC-FFV	MBB Bö.105S	S-852	D-HFHJ
EC-FFX	Cessna 411	411-0085	N7385U
EC-FGA	Ultramagic V-65 HAFB	65/40	
EC-FGB	Ultramagic 180 HAFB	180/03	
EC-FGC	Aérospatiale AS.350B Ecureuil	2250	

EC-FGE	SOCATA TB-10 Tobago (Stored)	1239	F-GKVF
EC-FGF	Cessna 172N	17271103	N1708E
EC-FGH	Airbus A320-211	223	EC-585 F-WWIA
EC-FGI	Cessna 172N	17271255	N2374E
EC-FGJ	Cessna T210N Turbo Centurion II	21064334	N6317Y
EC-FGK	Piper PA-38-112 Tomahawk (W/o 11.4.01)	38-78A0040	N9329T
EC-FGL	Bell 206L-3 Long Ranger III	51379	N65108 C-FIPJ
EC-FGM	McDonnell Douglas DC-9-88	53193	EC-751 N19B
EC-FGO	Piper PA-28-161 Warrior II	28-8216212	N363FT N9600N
EC-FGP	Cessna 152 (Dbr 5.4.02)	15281421	N49972
EC-FGR	Airbus A320-211	224	EC-586 F-WWIM
EC-FGV	Airbus A320-211	207	EC-584 F-WWDQ
EC-FGY	Colt 180A HAFB	1701	
EC-FGZ	Aérospatiale SA.316B Alouette III	5305	EC-738 PH-SLD 5N-AKW F-WTNI
EC-FHC	Piper PA-32R-300T Turbo Lance II (W/o 24.12.98, noted derelict 12.99)	32R-7887193	N21156
EC-FHD	McDonnell-Douglas DC-9-87	53212	EC-638
EC-FHE	Reims/Cessna F177RG Cardinal RG	F177RG0163	OO-DFV PH-AXS
EC-FHF	SOCATA TB-9 Tampico	1317	F-GKVL
EC-FHG	McDonnell Douglas DC-9-88	53194	EC-752
EC-FHH	Piper PA-28R-180 Cherokee Arrow	28R-30537	N505FP N4644J
EC-FHK	McDonnell-Douglas DC-9-87	53213	EC-639
EC-FHL	SZD-50-3 Puchacz (Damaged 2.3.03)	B-2042	
EC-FHM	SZD-48-3 Jantar Standard 3	B-1960	
EC-FHO	SZD-51-1 Junior	B-1998	
EC-FHP	SZD-48-3 Jantar Standard 3	B-1962	
EC-FHQ	SZD-51-1 Junior	B-1999	
EC-FHT	Grob G.103 Twin II	3573	D-0651 D-6434
EC-FHV	Piper PA-28-161 Cherokee Warrior II	28-7816361	N3610M
EC-FHX	Bell 206B Jet Ranger II	3786	G-OCAP G-OACS G-OCAP N18096
EC-FHY	Piper PA-34-200T Seneca II	34-7870184	N9365C
EC-FHZ	Piper PA-28R-200 Cherokee Arrow B	28R-7135127	EC-757 N8591N
EC-FIB	Aérospatiale AS.350B2 Ecureuil	2558	EC-853
EC-FID	Piper PA-34-200T Seneca II	34-7970269	N2832Y
EC-FIF	Piper PA-34-220T Seneca III	34-8333072	OY-CEJ N4300D N9639N
EC-FIG	McDonnell Douglas DC-9-88	53195	EC-753
EC-FIH	McDonnell Douglas DC-9-88	53196	EC-754
EC-FII	Colt 69A HAFB	1930	
EC-FIJ	Piper PA-18A Super Cub	18-1729	EC-820 N136AA XB-PUU N1897A
EC-FIK	CASA 1-131E3	312	E.3B-312
EC-FIM	SOCATA TB-9 Tampico Club (Stored)	1338	F-GKVN
EC-FIO	Grumman G-159 Gulfstream 1	40	EC-494 N40AG N8ZA N6PG
EC-FIP	Britten-Norman BN-2A-26 Islander	623	EC-844 G-AYJE CR-CAS G-AYJE (EI-AVE) G-AYJE
EC-FIQ	Britten-Norman BN-2A-26 Islander	161	EC-843 G-BNXB V2-LAF VP-LAF G-51-161
EC-FIR	Ultramagic H-77 HAFB	77/58	
EC-FIS	Ultramagic H-77 HAFB	77/64	
EC-FIT	SZD-51-1 Junior	B-1921	
EC-FIZ	Glaser-Dirks DG-600 (W/o 2.1.04)	6-80S54	
EC-FJA	Sud Avn SA.319B Alouette III (Damaged 23.6.03)	2297	EC-746 Chile Navy N-68 N49517
EC-FJB	Beech 95-B55 Baron (Derelict)	TC-1689	EC-741 N25712
EC-FJD	Ultramagic V-77 HAFB	77/71	
EC-FJE	McDonnell Douglas DC-9-88	53197	EC-755
EC-FJF	Cessna 414	414-0523	N4212C
EC-FJG	Piper PA-36-300 Pawnee Brave (Damaged 8.8.01)	36-7660118	TG-SAN
EC-FJH	Rolladen-Schneider LS7	7159	
EC-FJJ	Sikorsky S-61N	61299	EC-862 LN-ORE
EC-FJL	PZL M-18A Dromader	1Z022-29	SP-DEC
EC-FJM	PZL M-18A Dromader	1Z022-27	SP-DEA
EC-FJN	Beech B95A Travel Air	TD-516	EC-828 N1570S
EC-FJO	PZL M-18A Dromader	1Z022-28	SP-DEB
EC-FJS	Cessna 172P	17274320	N51564
EC-FJT	Cessna 414	414-0174	N3LS N8244Q
EC-FJU	Sportavia-Pützer RF-5B Sperber	1008	EC-650 D-KILL EAF:660
EC-FJV	Aérospatiale AS.350B2 Ecureuil	2580	
EC-FJY	Schempp-Hirth Standard Cirrus	431G	
EC-FKA	Piper PA-28R-201 Arrow III	28R-7837054	N6136H
EC-FKE	Ultramagic S-105 HAFB (Reserved for OO- registry)	105/19	
EC-FKK	Cessna 401	401-0279	EC-EXH(1) HI-517 N32CM N2777 N8431F
EC-FKM	Piper PA-28RT-201T Turbo Arrow IV	28R-7931094	N2132U
EC-FKN	Piper PA-36-375 Brave	36-7802012	N3812E
EC-FKO	Piper PA-28R-180 Cherokee Arrow	28R-30658	N4936J
EC-FKP-2F	Rolladen-Schneider LS-7	7022	
EC-FKR	Piper PA-28R-200 Cherokee Arrow II	28R-7535254	N1429S
EC-FKU	Air Tractor AT-502	502-0125	N4548Y
EC-FKV	Air Tractor AT-502 (W/o 1.6.99?)	502-0162	N1529N
EC-FKX	Air Tractor AT-502	502-0168	N15337
EC-FKY	Thunder AX7-77 HAFB	1806	
EC-FKZ	Ayres S.2R-T34 Turbo Thrush	6032	N4012S C-GDHB N4012S
EC-FLA	Ayres S.2R-T34 Turbo Thrush	T34-005	N40172
EC-FLB	Robin R.3000/160	154	
EC-FLC	Wassmer WA.28 Espadon	108	F-CEOC
EC-FLH	American AG-5B Tiger (W/o 1.3.00?)	10091	EC-928 N1195F
EC-FLI	Piper PA-36-300 Pawnee Brave	36-7760080	N59670
EC-FLJ	Piper PA-36-375 Brave	36-7902014	N3979E
EC-FLK	McDonnell-Douglas DC-9-88	53304	EC-946
EC-FLL	SOCATA MS.880B Rallye Club	2556	F-BVZY
EC-FLM	Piper PA-30 Twin Comanche	30-657	LV-IMD LV-PCK
EC-FLN	McDonnell-Douglas DC-9-88	53303	EC-945
EC-FLO	Reims FR172J Rocket	FR17200402	EC-963 F-BUMN
EC-FLP	Airbus A320-211	266	EC-881 F-WWBO
EC-FLQ	Airbus A320-211	274	EC-882 F-WWBR
EC-FLR	Robinson R-22 Beta	2032	EC-951
EC-FLS	Ultramagic V-65 HAFB	65/46	
EC-FLU	Piper PA-28RT-201T Turbo Arrow IV	28R-7931159	EC-969 N2138Z
EC-FMB	Robinson R-22 Beta	2045	
EC-FMC	Consolidated PBY-5A Catalina (Coded '72',; stored, Ocana. Under restoration)	2134	EC-940 C-FIZZ CF-IZZ F-ZBAZ CF-IZZ F-ZBAZ CF-IZZ BuA64064
EC-FMD	SOCATA MS.894E Minerva 220GT	12148	F-BUVD
EC-FME	Aérospatiale AS.350B2 Ecureuil	2448	F-GKLR
EC-FMF	Grob G.102 Astir CS	1479	D-. . . . PH-571
EC-FMG	Cameron A-120 HAFB	2645	
EC-FMH	Piper PA-28RT-201T Turbo Arrow IV	28R-7931054	N3003N
EC-FMI	Centrair ASW-20F	20529	OO-ZYT BGA3313/FKC OO-ZMA
EC-FMK	Ultramagic H-77 HAFB	77/75	
EC-FMR	Robinson R-22 Beta	2047	
EC-FMT	Maule MXT-7-180 Star Rocket	14007C	EC-707
EC-FMU	PZL M-18A Dromader (W/o 16.8.02?)	1Z021-07	SP-FCM SP-DCW
EC-FMV	PZL M-18A Dromader	1Z022-30	SP-FCN
EC-FMX	Piper PA-34-200T Seneca II	34-7970396	N606RH N50MF N9605N
EC-FMZ	Sikorsky S-61N	61361	LN-ORH
EC-FNB	Aerojean/Fournier RF-5-AJI	E-003	
EC-FNC	Aerojean/Fournier RF-5-AJI	E-002	
EC-FND	McDonnell-Douglas DC-9-88	53305	EC-964
EC-FNG	Ultramagic S-130 HAFB	130/03	
EC-FNH	SOCATA MS.893A Rallye Commodore 180	11875	F-BTID
EC-FNJ	Ultramagic V-77 HAFB	77/81	
EC-FNK	Ultramagic S-160 HAFB	160/06	
EC-FNL	Ultramagic F-08 Church SS HAFB	F08/01	
EC-FNM	Boeing Stearman PT-17 (Museum)	75-8089	EC-973 (LV-HDT) LQ-HDT LV-HDT Navy 0325 / 1-E-74 BuA38468
EC-FNN	MBB Bö.105S	S-869	D-HMBL (D-HFNA)
EC-FNO	MBB Bö.105S	S-870	D-HMBM (D-HFNB)

EC-FNQ	Hughes 269C	128-0743	G-OSHE N58204
EC-FNR	Airbus A320-211	323	EC-885 F-WWBM
EC-FNT	Piper PA-28-161 Warrior II	28-7916153	N2243D
EC-FNV	Colt 77A HAFB	1738	
EC-FNY	Grob G.103 Twin Astir (Damaged 9.7.94)	3036	D-4838
EC-FNZ	Grob G.102 Speed Astir	4037	D-4872
EC-FOA	Aérospatiale AS.350B1 Ecureuil	2626	F-WYMK
EC-FOB	Ultramagic M-77 HAFB	77/78	
EC-FOD	Piper PA-36-300 Pawnee Brave	36-7760069	N59660 CF-JLO N69897
EC-FOE	Piper PA-36-375 Brave (Reserved as F-OJRD 10.04)	36-8202015	N2370X
EC-FOF	McDonnell-Douglas DC-9-88	53307	EC-966
EC-FOG	McDonnell-Douglas DC-9-88	53306	EC-965
EC-FOI	Aerojean/Fournier RF-5-AJI	E-0004	
EC-FOJ	Aerojean/Fournier RF-5-AJI	E-0005	
EC-FOK	Beech 35-33 Debonair	CD-617	N260LB N9780Y
EC-FOL	Bell 206L-3 Long Ranger III	51417	N6605R
EC-FOM	Ultramagic M-77 HAFB	77/77	
EC-FON	Mooney M.20J Model 205	24-3260	EC-980
EC-FOO	Cessna 172N	17271847	N5409E
EC-FOP	Cessna 152 (Damaged 31.1.94)	15284679	N4276R XB-CFH (N6338M)
EC-FOQ	Aérospatiale AS.350B2 Ecureuil	2639	
EC-FOR	American AG-5B Tiger	10099	N100AG
EC-FOS	Ultramagic V-65 HAFB	65/44	
EC-FOV	Cessna 177B Cardinal (W/o 13.8.98)	17702476	N13908
EC-FOX	Aérospatiale SA.365C2 Dauphin 2	5024	EC-136 CC-CGV
EC-FOZ	McDonnell-Douglas DC-9-88	53308	EC-987
EC-FPA	Cessna 421B Golden Eagle	421B0530	EC-138 N69897 CF-JLO N69897
EC-FPB	Piper PA-38-112 Tomahawk	38-78A0728	N801DV N2519A
EC-FPC	Fairchild Swearingen SA.226TC Metro IV	TC-408	EC-243 N252AM N1013F
EC-FPD	McDonnell-Douglas DC-9-88	53309	EC-988
EC-FPE	Cessna 152	15284717	N4276M XB-CFJ (N6416M)
EC-FPF	SOCATA TBM-700	12	F-OHBD
EC-FPJ	McDonnell-Douglas DC-9-88	53310	EC-989
EC-FPL	SOCATA TB-10 Tobago	1483	
EC-FPM	SOCATA TB-10 Tobago	1484	
EC-FPN	SOCATA TB-10 Tobago	1485	
EC-FPO	SOCATA TB-10 Tobago	1486	
EC-FPP	SOCATA TB-10 Tobago	1492	
EC-FPQ	Cessna 150L	15074733	N7838G
EC-FPS	Aérospatiale SA.315B Lama	2402	HB-XVN N62338
EC-FPT	Ultramagic H-42 HAFB	42/01	
EC-FPU	Scheibe Bergfalke II	245	D-1211
EC-FPX	Grob G.102 Astir CS 77	1620	D-7461
EC-FPY	Ultramagic M-77 HAFB	77/84	
EC-FQA	Cessna 337G Skymaster	33701713	N53575
EC-FQD	Cessna 172P	17275140	N55239
EC-FQE	Cessna 172N (Dismantled)	17273515	N4968G
EC-FQF	Ultramagic M-65 HAFB	65/43	
EC-FQG	Ultramagic N-180 HAFB	80/04	
EC-FQH	Aérospatiale AS.350B2 Ecureuil	2674	
EC-FQJ	Agusta A.109C	7664	N1YU
EC-FQK	Cessna 177B Cardinal	17702738	N1496C
EC-FQL	Cessna 177RG Cardinal RG	177RG0515	EC-157 N2115Q
EC-FQM	Robinson R-22 Beta	2206	EC-259
EC-FQN	American AG-5B Tiger	10132	EC-278
EC-FQR	Cessna R172K Hawk XP	R1723167	N758KX
EC-FQS	Cessna 150L	15074851	N10421 (N45RG) N10421
EC-FQT	Grob G.103 Twin Astir (Dbr 22.7.98)	3116	D-7783
EC-FQU	Bölkow Phoebus C	912	F-CDOH
EC-FQV	Hughes 269C	35-0406	N7401F
EC-FQY	Airbus A320-211	356	EC-886 F-WWIH
EC-FQZ	Ultramagic S-160 HAFB	160/10	
EC-FRA	Westland-Bell 47G3B1 (Crashed 8.7.95)	WA/396	D-HAFL XT237
EC-FRB	Aviat Pitts S-2B	5263	N473
EC-FRC	Ultramagic M-105 HAFB	105/23	
EC-FRD	Robinson R-22 Beta	0675	G-BNVF
EC-FRE	Piper PA-38-112 Tomahawk	38-79A0223	N2544C
EC-FRF	Schempp-Hirth Standard Cirrus	661	D-2286
EC-FRH	Ultramagic V-65 HAFB	65/41	
EC-FRI	Ultramagic S-160 HAFB	160/11	
EC-FRJ	Piper PA-28-140 Cherokee	28-7325592	EC-289 N56255
EC-FRL	Piper PA-28R-180 Cherokee Arrow	28R-31044	N7643J
EC-FRM	PZL M-18 Dromader	1Z013-02	EC-365 YN-BZJ
EC-FRN	PZL M-18 Dromader	1Z012-19	EC-364 YN-CAE
EC-FRO	Robinson R-22 Beta (Cr 18.3.04)	2234	N2351P
EC-FRS	Bell 206L-1 Long Ranger II	45412	HK-3166X C-GMFQ N1081Y
EC-FRT	Colt 77A HAFB	2302	
EC-FRU	Bell 206B Jet Ranger II	4268	
EC-FRV	Grumman G.1159 Gulfstream II	237	EC-363 XA-SDM XA-BAL XA-MIX N25BH N816GA
EC-FRX	Hughes 369D	116-0029D	EC-316 N4320K G-BESS
EC-FRY	Bell 206L-3 Long Ranger III	51330	N43904 JA9859
EC-FSD	Cessna TR182 Turbo Skylane RG	R18201004	N739TV
EC-FSE	Robinson R-22 Beta	0963	G-BPOF
EC-FSF	Piper PA-31P Pressurized Navajo	31P-7730012	N821BJ N277BW N82608
EC-FSG	CASA C-1.131E Jungmann	2124	E.3B-544
EC-FSH	CASA C-1.131E Jungmann	2220	E.3B-601
EC-FSI	CASA C-1.131E Jungmann (Damaged)	2164	E.3B-548
EC-FSJ	Air Création Safari GT BI Fun 18	94105	
EC-FSK	SOCATA TB-10 Tobago	1555	
EC-FSL	SOCATA TB-10 Tobago	1556	
EC-FSM	SOCATA TB-10 Tobago	1557	
EC-FSN	SOCATA TB-10 Tobago	1559	
EC-FSO	SOCATA TB-10 Tobago	1560	
EC-FSP	SOCATA TB-10 Tobago (Damaged 24.2.03)	1561	
EC-FSQ	Robinson R-22 Beta (Dbr 8.8.99)	2097	EC-986
EC-FSR	Cessna 172M (Wfu, noted 2.01)	17262684	N13341
EC-FSS	CASA C-1.131E Jungmann (Damaged 30.1.05)	2231	E.3B-319
EC-FSU	Cessna T210N Turbo Centurion II (Damaged 26.5.04, under repair)	21063741	N5404C N109TA
EC-FTA	Cessna 414 (Damaged 14.2.97)	414-0647	N414TJ N69976
EC-FTB	Sikorsky S-61N	61741	LN-OSY OY-HDS LN-OSY
EC-FTC	American AG-5B Tiger (W/o 19.12.98?)	10148	EC-311
EC-FTE	SOCATA TB-10 Tobago	1566	
EC-FTF	SOCATA TB-10 Tobago (Dam. 13.2.97)	1567	EC-395
EC-FTG	SOCATA TB-10 Tobago	1570	
EC-FTH	SOCATA TB-10 Tobago	1571	
EC-FTJ	SOCATA TB-10 Tobago	1573	
EC-FTK	SOCATA TB-10 Tobago	1574	
EC-FTM	Bell 206L-4 Long Ranger IV (W/o 30.1.04)	52024	
EC-FTO	Ultramagic F-09 Water Bottle SS HAFB	F09/01	
EC-FTQ	PZL M-18A Dromader (W/o 22.7.04)	1Z023-28	SP-DDH
EC-FTR	Boeing 757-256	26239	EC-420
EC-FTS	McDonnell-Douglas DC-9-83	49621	EC-479 EC-EJU EC-149
EC-FTX	Aérospatiale AS.355N Ecureuil 2	5550	F-WYMU
EC-FTZ	CASA C-1.131E Jungmann	2170	E.3B-556
EC-FUC	American AG-5B Tiger	10169	EC-488
EC-FUE	Ultramagic S-90 HAFB	90/07	
EC-FUF	Aérospatiale AS.350B Ecureuil	2596	EC-427 (D-HFSC)
EC-FUG	Piper PA-28-140 Cherokee (W/o 11.6.99?)	28-21412	N4657R
EC-FUH	Aérospatiale AS.355N Ecureuil 2	5554	F-WYMB
EC-FUI	Ultramagic M-77 HAFB	77/89	
EC-FUJ	Beech 65-B80 Queen Air (Wreck noted 3.05)	LD-408	EC-508 N5130Q C-FCGV CF-CGV
EC-FUK	Ultramagic S-160 HAFB	160/12	
EC-FUN	Ultramagic M-105 HAFB	105/24	
EC-FUO	Ultramagic M-65 HAFB	65/52	
EC-FUP	Ultramagic M-65 HAFB	65/47	
EC-FUQ	Ultramagic M-77 HAFB	77/92	
EC-FUR	Rockwell Commander 112TC	13085	N4593W
EC-FUS	Cameron DP-70 Hot Air Airship	1130	G-BMEZ
EC-FUU	CASA C-1.131E Jungmann	2167	E.3B-554
EC-FUY	Agusta A.109C	7670	EC-453 N1TV
EC-FUZ	Piper PA-28-140 Cherokee	28-22772	G-AVGB N11C
EC-FVD	Ultramagic S-130 HAFB	130/04	
EC-FVE	Ultramagic M-77 HAFB	77/93	
EC-FVF	Ultramagic M-77 HAFB	77/94	
EC-FVG	SOCATA MS.893A Rallye Commodore 180	11636	F-BSFI
EC-FVH	Thunder AX7-77A HAFB	2519	
EC-FVI	Rolladen-Schneider LS6C	6319	
EC-FVK	Mudry CAP.10B (To F-WQPH 7.01)	264	EC-391
EC-FVL	Ultramagic M-77 HAFB (W/o 23.4.04)	77/97	
EC-FVN	Robinson R-22 Beta (Wreck noted 1.03)	0606	EC-562 G-DLTI N2540J
EC-FVO	Sikorsky S-61N	61756	EC-575 LN-OSX
EC-FVP	Cessna 172N	17270627	N739LL

EC-FVQ	Ultramagic S-105 HAFB	105/25	
EC-FVS	Bell 206B Jet Ranger II	4012	N323BH
			C-FDBJ
EC-FVU	Hispano HA-200	20/73	E.14A- . . .
EC-FVY	BAe.146 Series 200QT	E-2117	EC-615
			G-TNTO
			F-GTNT
			G-BPBS
EC-FVZ	SZD-50-3 Puchacz	B-2087	
EC-FXA	McDonnell-Douglas DC-9-83	49938	EC-592
			SE-DPU
			VH-LNH
			XA-RTK
EC-FXC	Ultramagic S-160 HAFB	160/13	
EC-FXE	Schleicher K 7 Rhönadler	930	D-6310
EC-FXF	Ultramagic M-77 HAFB	77/57	
EC-FXH	Aérospatiale AS.350B2 Ecureuil	2638	EC-545
			(OY-HDO)
EC-FXK	Ultramagic F-10 Bird SS HAFB	F10/01	
EC-FXL	Robinson R-22 Beta	0938	EC-570
			I-INTA
EC-FXM	Ultramagic M-77 HAFB	77/86	
EC-FXP	Boeing 737-4Y0	24706	EC-644
	(Reserved as F-GRNH 10.04)		9M-MJD
EC-FXR	Cessna 152	15285137	EC-519
			N6112Q
EC-FXS	Piper PA-28-161 Warrior II	28-8316003	EC-518
			N82811
EC-FXT	Cessna 152	15279718	EC- . . .
	(Badly damaged 3.4.97)		N757GA
EC-FXY	McDonnell-Douglas DC-9-83	49627	EC-646
			EC-EOZ
			EC-215
EC-FXZ	Beech F33A Bonanza	CE-521	EC-683 ?
			E.24B-32
			EC-CLI
EC-FYD	Ultramagic S-90 HAFB	90/09	
EC-FYH	Ultramagic M-105 HAFB	105/27	
EC-FYO	Beech F33A Bonanza	CE-532	EC-688 ?
			E.24B-37
			EC-CLN
EC-FYP	Cessna 172RG Cutlass RG	172RG0770	F-GIHS
			N6547V
EC-FYQ	Ultramagic N-180 HAFB	180/07	
EC-FYR	Ultramagic S-105 HAFB	105/26	
EC-FYS	Ultramagic M-77 HAFB	77/96	
EC-FYT	Robin ATL	35	EC-568
			F-GFOK
			F-WFOK
EC-FYU	Cessna 172N	17268333	N733JQ
EC-FYV	MBB Bö.105CBS-5 (Catalunya "01")	S-896	D-HMBT(5)
EC-FYX	Thunder AX7-77A HAFB	2590	
EC-FZB	Swearingen SA.226TC Metro	TC-221	EC-666
			OO-JPI
EC-FZC	McDonnell-Douglas DC-9-83	49790	EC-742
			EC-ESJ
			EC-307
EC-FZD	Cessna 172RG Cutlass RG	172RG0187	N6498R
EC-FZE	BAe.146 Series 200QT	E-2105	EC-719
			G-TNTP
			HA-TAB,
			G-BOMI
			G-5-105
EC-FZF	PZL M-18A Dromader	1Z015-14	EC-684
	(Ditched 22.9.99, scrapped?)		D-FOHY
			DDR-TKY
EC-FZG	PZL M-18A Dromader	1Z019-26	D-FOLR
			DDR-TLR
EC-FZI	Cessna 172N	17271135	N2056E
EC-FZJ	Sikorsky S-61N	61758	EC-717
			LN-OQE(2)
EC-FZK	Aerojean/Fournier RF-5-AJI (W/o 26.3.98?)	E-007	
EC-FZL	Aerojean/Fournier RF-5-AJI (Stored)	E-008	
EC-FZM	Aerojean/Fournier RF-5-AJI (Stored)	E-009	
EC-FZN	Colt 120A HAFB	2560	
EC-FZO	Cessna 152	15282427	N69005
EC-FZP	Cessna 525 CitationJet	525-0065	EC-704
			N2649Y
EC-FZR	Ultramagic V-77 HAFB	77/80	
EC-FZS	Beech F33A Bonanza	CE-525	EC-621
			EC-CLJ
			E.24B-33
EC-FZU	Sport Aircraft Tango II	3901	
EC-FZV	Rans S-12 Airaile	S-12-119	
EC-FZY	Rolladen-Schneider LS3A	3230	D-4290
EC-GAA	Bell 205A-1	30134	EC-756
			D-HOEB
			N58087
EC-GAB	PZL M-18A Dromader	1Z024-02	SP-DDL
EC-GAC	Ultramagic M-77 HAFB	77/106	
EC-GAH	PZL M-18A Dromader (W/o 3.8.00?)	1Z020-01	D-FOLU
			DDR-TLU
EC-GAI	PZL M-18A Dromader (W/o 10.8.95?)	1Z021-16	D-FOMJ
			DDR-TMJ
EC-GAK	Cessna 172N	17269089	EC-752
			N734SZ

EC-GAL	Colt 69A HAFB	1867	
EC-GAM-730	Glasflügel H201B Standard Libelle	430	F-CEBP
EC-GAN	Swearingen SA.226TC Metro II	TC-203	EC-701
			OY-BYH
			N5303M
EC-GAO	Sud Avn SA.316B Alouette III	2324	EC-801
			F-WQDG
			Rwanda:10K04
EC-GAQ	PZL M-18A Dromader	1Z021-08	D-FOMB
			DDR-TMB
EC-GAR	PZL M-18A Dromader	1Z019-27	D-FOLS
			DDR-TLS
EC-GAS	Bell 205A-1	30081	EC-844
			F-GKCD
			VH-NGN
			C-GFHQ
			VH-NSN
			C-GFHQ
			VH-UHN
EC-GAT	McDonnell-Douglas DC-9-83	49709	EC-835
			F-GGMC
			N6203D
EC-GAU	Robinson R-22 Beta	0015	EC-824
	(Damaged 10.11.04)		N9017K
EC-GAV	Piper PA-31 Turbo Navajo	31-579	EC-411
			E.18-1
			N6641L
EC-GAX	Cessna 177RG Cardinal RG	177RG0038	EC-707
			N8038G
EC-GBA	McDonnell-Douglas DC-9-83	49626	EC-805
			EI-CGS
			EC-EMG
			EC-223
			N2606Z
EC-GBB	Beech 200 Super King Air	BB-182	EC-727
			N922JB
			N155BT
			N155PT
EC-GBC	Aerojean/Fournier RF-5-AJI (Stored)	E-010	
EC-GBD	SNCASE SE.3130 Alouette II	1916	F-GJLN
			V-64
EC-GBE	Agusta-Bell AB.412 (W/o 14.11.04)	25503	EC-757
			Fv.11339
			I-MGPE
EC-GBF	Convair CV-580	458	EC-830
			OO-DHB
			(OO-VGB)
			N537SA
			N583PL
			N5829
			N8421H
			VH-BZH
EC-GBI	Swearingen SA.226AT Merlin IV	AT-041	EC-867
			OO-JPA
			N6FJ
			SAAF-14
			N5362M
EC-GBL	Piper PA-28-161 Warrior II	2816113	N9252N
EC-GBM	Piper PA-28-161 Warrior II	2816114	N92516
EC-GBO	Piper PA-28-161 Warrior II	2816115	N9252K
EC-GBP	Canadair CL.215-1A10	1031	EC-957
			UD.13-3
EC-GBQ	Canadair CL.215-1A10 (Cancelled?)	1033	EC-958
			UD.13-5
EC-GBR	Canadair CL.215-1A10	1051	EC-983
			UD.13-11
EC-GBS	Canadair CL.215-1A10	1052	EC-984
			UD.13-12
EC-GBT	Canadair CL.215-1A10	1054	EC-985
			UD.13-14
EC-GBZ	Thunder AX7-77 HAFB	3464	
EC-GCC	Ultramagic V-77 HAFB	77/87	
EC-GCD	Ultramagic M-77 HAFB	77/110	
EC-GCE	CASA C-1.131E Jungmann	2161	E.3B-545
EC-GCF	SOCATA MS.892A Rallye Commodore 150	10591	EC-813
			(D-EAGW)
			OO-ADY
			F-BOVB
EC-GCH	FLS OA-7 Optica (Damaged 30.8.95 Valencia)	022	EC-438
			G-BOPP
EC-GCN	Bell 206B Jet Ranger II	2545	EC-938
			G-WOSP
			N18096
EC-GCP	Beech F33A Bonanza	CE-530	EC-842
			EC-CLL /
			E.24B-35
EC-GCQ	Agusta A.109C	7665	EC-895
			N1ZL
EC-GCU	Bell 206L-LT Twin Ranger	52105	EC-843
			N4261U
EC-GCV	McDonnell-Douglas DC-9-82	53165	EC-894
			N834AU
EC-GCX	Cessna 177RG Cardinal RG	177RG0567	EC-814
			N2167Q

EC-GCZ	Aérospatiale SA.365C2 Dauphin 2	5037	EC-887 PH-SSH EC-DVZ PH-SSH G-BLFN PH-SSH 5N-ALI PH-SSH (PH-BOL) F-WXFG
EC-GDB	Agusta-Bell 206B Jet Ranger II	8095	F-GJAU F-OGUL F-GAJL G-AWRV
EC-GDC	Piper PA-28-140 Cherokee Fliteliner	28-7125346	EC-718 N521FL
EC-GDF	Piper PA-28R-201T Turbo Arrow III	28R-7803097	EC-913 YV-1431P
EC-GDG	Swearingen SA.226TC Metro III (W/o 18.2.98?)	TC-220	EC-930 N220AT C-GFAP N443JA N5370M
EC-GDH	Piper PA-28-151 Cherokee Warrior	28-7415142	EC-968 N41227
EC-GDJ	Bell UH-1H (205) (W/o 19.3.98?)	5320	EC-951 N82818 66-00837
EC-GDK	Bell UH-1H (205)	5639	EC-948 N82814 66-01156
EC-GDL	Aérospatiale AS.350B2 Ecureuil	2879	
EC-GDM	Bell UH-1H (205)	5398	N205UD 66-00915
EC-GDN	Bell UH-1H (205) (Crashed 18.6.00)	5721	N6190P 66-16027
EC-GDO	Bell UH-1H (205)	8800	N205UE 66-16606
EC-GDP	Aérospatiale AS.350B2 Ecureuil	2886	
EC-GDQ	Ultramagic V-90 HAFB	90/13	
EC-GDT	Robinson R-22 Beta	2056	EC-986 G-BWMR
EC-GDU	Beech F33A Bonanza	CE-574	EC-935 EC-COM/ E.24B-42
EC-GDV	Swearingen SA.226AT Merlin IV (W/o 10.10.01)	AT-043	EC-975 F-GGAF N814MM N5371M ZS-LID SAAF-15 N5371M
EC-GDX	Eipper Quicksilver MXL-II	1691	
EC-GDY	Convair CV-580	25	EC-943 OO-DHG N73117
EC-GDZ	Cessna 337G Skymaster (W/o 6.96)	33701687	EC-852 N53532
EC-GEB	Cessna 152	15283355	EC-914 N48642
EC-GEC	Cessna 152	15280337	EC-915 N24720
EC-GEG	Piper PA-28-161 Warrior II	28-8516003	EC-936 N4377F (EC- . . .) N4377F
EC-GEI	Ultramagic V-77 HAFB	77/112	
EC-GEK	Ultramagic S-90 HAFB	90/10	
EC-GEL	Ultramagic M-77 HAFB	77/101	
EC-GEM	Cameron Beer-Mug SS Balloon	2739	
EC-GEN	Fairchild Swearingen SA.227AC Metro III	AC-688	EC-126 N727C N688NE N2701X
EC-GER	Wassmer WA.26P Squale	74	F-CDZI
EC-GES	Cessna 172RG Cutlass RG (Reims-assembled 172RG with "c/n" 0002) (Damaged 31.3.99)	172RG0008	EC-981 CS-AQZ N4650R
EC-GET	Mainair Gemini/Flash IIA	783-0290-7/ W576	EC-BT4
EC-GEV	Sport Aircraft Tango II	6871	
EC-GEX	Ultramagic N-180 HAFB	180/08	
EC-GEY	Hispano HA.200 Saeta (W/o 31.10.96)	20/79	A.10B-73
EC-GEZ	Eipper Quicksilver MX-Sprint IIR	447	
EC-GFA	Ultramagic S-130 HAFB	130/08	
EC-GFB	Ultramagic M-77 HAFB	77/115	
EC-GFC	Ultramagic M-105 HAFB	105/32	EC-025
EC-GFD	Rolladen-Schneider LS6C	6251	SE-UKM
EC-GFF	Ultramagic F-13 Pig SS HAFB	F13/01	
EC-GFG	Cessna 172K (Wfu, dismantled)	17258536	G-BVBC N84587
EC-GFH	Piper PA-28-161 Cherokee Warrior II	28-7716101	EC-998 G-MERV N2364Q
EC-GFI	Ultramagic H-77 HAFB	77/113	
EC-GFK	Swearingen SA.226AT Merlin IV	AT-062	EC-125 OY-FFD N548SM OY-FFD (OY-NPB) (OO-VGD) YU-ALF D-IFAD (F-GBBB) D-IFAD N5456M
EC-GFL	Robinson R-22 Beta	1949	OY-HFN
EC-GFN	Schleicher ASH 26E	26070	
EC-GFO	Robin HR.200/120B	296	F-WZZZ
EC-GFQ	PZL M-18A Dromader	1Z025-25	N9279F
EC-GFR	PZL M-18A Dromader	1Z025-26	N81458
EC-GFS	Cessna F172H	F172-0635	D-EFHD
EC-GFT	Piper PA-28-140 Cherokee	28-24823	EC-162 N1899J
EC-GFV	Ultramagic F-12 Soap Powder Box SS HAFB	F12/01	
EC-GFX	Air Tractor AT-802	802-0027	N6065G
EC-GFZ	Ultramagic N-180 HAFB	180/11	
EC-GGA	Eipper Quicksilver MX-Sprint II	238	
EC-GGB	Douglas DC-7CF (Stored)	45112	EC-888 N90802 G-AOIB
EC-GGC	Douglas DC-7CF (Stored)	45215	EC-889 N9734Z SE-CCF
EC-GGF	Piper PA-23-250 Aztec E	27-4810	EC-800 E.19-4 N14240
EC-GGG	Rans S-6ES Coyote II	S-6A-106	
EC-GGH	Ultramagic H-77 HAFB	77/121	
EC-GGI	Robinson R-44 Astro (Crashed 23.9.00)	0209	EC-192 G-BWIF
EC-GGJ	Colt 69A HAFB	3767	EC-191
EC-GGM	Reims/Cessna F150L	F15001107	F-BVSH
EC-GGP	Ultramagic M-77 HAFB	77/88	
EC-GGQ	Air Tractor AT-802	802-0028	N60660
EC-GGR	Ultramagic N-180 HAFB	180/09	
EC-GGS	Airbus A340-313	125	EC-154 F-WWJB
EC-GGT	Mooney M.20J Model 205	24-3076	G-BPGA
EC-GGU	Air Création Safari GT BI Mild 16S	9506084	
EC-GGV	McDonnell-Douglas DC-9-83	49791	EC-166 EC-FVX EC-546 VR-BMJ F-ODTN
EC-GHA	Piper PA-44-180T Turbo Seminole	44-8107006	N9153D EC-720 N83SM N8231L
EC-GHE	McDonnell-Douglas DC-9-83	49398	EC-245 HB-IUK SE-DPS EI-CBE EC-EXX EC-479 EI-CBE G-PATA (G-LOGI)
EC-GHG	Ultramagic M-105 HAFB	105/35	
EC-GHH	McDonnell-Douglas DC-9-83	49578	EC-291 EC-FSZ EC-390 SE-DHD
EC-GHI	Air Tractor AT-502B	502B-0360	N6095Z
EC-GHN	Convair CV-580	186	EC-255 OO-DHH N73156
EC-GHQ	Ultramagic M-77 HAFB	77/117	
EC-GHS	Partenavia P.68 Observer	329-20-OB	G-OBSV
EC-GHU	Aero Commander 680	483-153	EC-252 D-IDIH
EC-GHV	Christen Pitts S-2B	5048	EC-253 N5326C
EC-GHX	Airbus A340-313	134	EC-155 F-WWJR
EC-GHY	Aérospatiale AS.355F1 Ecureuil 2	5089	EC-293 N866MP
EC-GHZ	Beech 200 Super King Air	BB-555	EC-795 D-IFOR
EC-GIC	Bell 212	30775	LN-OQD
EC-GID	Bell 212	31150	OY-HCS
EC-GIE	Cessna 525 CitationJet	525-0133	EC-261 N52038
EC-GIG	Robinson R-22 Beta	1200	N3176S JA7785 N8054U
EC-GIH	Ultramagic S-90 HAFB	90/19	
EC-GII	Robinson R-22 Beta	2348	HA-MIP N83090
EC-GIJ	Beech 65-B90 King Air	LJ-382	EC-939 F-WQCC F-GLED EC-860 N25DC N922K

EC-GIM	Sport Aircraft Tango II-GT	8861	
EC-GIN	CASA C-1.131E Jungmann	2208	E.3B-591
EC-GIO	CASA C-1.131E Jungmann	2153	E.3B-542
EC-GIP	CASA C-1.131E Jungmann (Stored)	2171	E.3B-557 ?
EC-GIQ	CASA C-1.131E Jungmann	2192	E.3B-573
EC-GIR	CASA C-1.131E Jungmann (Stored)	2239	E.3B-620
EC-GIS	CASA C-1.131E Jungmann	2229	E.3B-610
EC-GIT	CASA C-1.131E Jungmann	2245	E.3B-626
EC-GIU	Bell UH-1H (205)	5265	EC-356 N12UH 66-00782
EC-GIV	Bell UH-1H (205)	12481	N11UH 70-15871
EC-GIX	Cameron C-80 HAFB	3573	
EC-GIY	Aérospatiale AS.350B Ecureuil	2175	EC-267 OY-HEP
EC-GIZ	Bell UH-1H (205)	5631	EC-297 N6738B 66-01148
EC-GJA	Bell UH-1H (205)	5387	EC-298 N205UD N8154L 66-904
EC-GJB	Bell UH-1H (205)	9262	EC-299 N8154S 66-17068
EC-GJC	Bell 407	53015	EC-239
EC-GJF	Cessna 501 Citation I/SP	501-0107	(N75471) 3A-MTB N54TB N501LS N107CC N1UL (N33VV) (N333BG) N3204M
EC-GJG	Robin R.1180TD Aiglon	246	EC-319 F-GCRB
EC-GJJ	Reims/Cessna F172L	F17200823	D-ECQM
EC-GJL	Agusta-Bell 205A (W/o 14.6.02?)	4010	HE.10A-5 HD.10A-5 Z.10-5 EC-SSH EC-BDF-R
EC-GJM	Fairchild SA.227BC Metro	BC-772B	EC-307 N702AM XA-RWK N2756T
EC-GJN	Sport Aircraft Tango II-GT	2883	
EC-GJO	Sport Aircraft Tango II-GT	2895	
EC-GJP	Robinson R-44 Astro (W/o 14.2.99?)	0277	
EC-GJQ	Air Création Safari GT BI XP15S	494003	
EC-GJR	Rans S-12XL Airaile	S-12-155	
EC-GJS	Beech F33A Bonanza	E-576	E24B-43 EC-CON
EC-GJT	Airbus A340-313	145	EC-156 F-WWJF
EC-GJX	Fairchild SA.227DC Metro IV	DC-855B	EC-362 N454LA N3026U
EC-GJZ	Swearingen SA.26AT Merlin IIB	T26-149	EC-202 N829HS N329HS N642PB N642RB N193G N25AC
EC-GKA	Piper PA-23-250 Aztec E	27-4807	E.18-2
EC-GKB	Schempp-Hirth Nimbus 3DM	17/40	F-CFUL D-KFUL
EC-GKC	Sport Aircraft Tango II (W/o 15.12.01)	5894	
EC-GKH	Convair CV-580	135	OO-DHD N536SA N582PL N5812 N7600 CF-ECS PH-CGK PJ-CVB
EC-GKN	Ultramagic M-77 HAFB	77/122	
EC-GKO	Ultramagic H-77 HAFB	77/124	
EC-GKP	Schleicher ASW 20C/TOP	20748	D-KCAS(3) D-8859
EC-GKQ	Ultramagic H-77 HAFB	77/61	
EC-GKR	Fairchild Swearingen SA.227AC Metro IV (W/o 12.4.02)	AC-620	N174SW
EC-GKT	Sport Aircraft Tango II-GT	T1922	
EC-GKY	Bell UH-1H (205)	13274	HE.10B-37 72-21575
EC-GKZ	Bell UH-1H (205)	13275	HE.10B-38 72-21576
EC-GLA	Piper PA-23-250 Aztec E	27-4811	EC-516 E.19-5 N14241
EC-GLB	Ultramagic M-65 HAFB	65/63	
EC-GLE	Airbus A340-313	146	EC-157 F-WWJD

EC-GLF	Cessna 172N	17270201	N738SM
EC-GLG	Cessna 150M Commuter	15078171	N9221U (F-GRSO) G-BTSO
EC-GLJ	Piper PA-23-250 Aztec E	27-4812	E.19-6 N14242
EC-GLK	Aerotek Pitts S-2A	2009	N9WK
EC-GLL	Cessna 172N	17268321	N733JB
EC-GLN	Glasflügel H201B Standard Libelle	203	OY-MGX
EC-GLO	Cessna 172N	17269275	N737AT
EC-GLP	Piper PA-28-161 Warrior II	28-8116163	G-BOPL N8342J
EC-GLR	Bell UH-1H (205)	5881	66-16187
EC-GLS	Bell 212	31155	EC-367 OY-HCU
EC-GLV	Bell 212	30587	N605LH JA9517 N58086
EC-GLX	Hispano HA-200D Saeta (W/o 13.5.00)	20/88	A.10B-82 C.10B-82
EC-GLY	Colt 90A HAFB	2295	G-BUOU
EC-GLZ	Colt 77A HAFB	3942	
EC-GMA	Hispano HA-200A Saeta (Damaged 11.99, stored)	20/65	AE.10B-59 C.10B-59 E.14B-59
EC-GMB	Glaser-Dirks DG-202-17	2-145/1743	D-1159
EC-GMC	LAK-12 Lietuva	6179	DOSAAF ?
EC-GMD	Beech A45 Mentor	X-100	E.17-20
EC-GME	Piper PA-28-140 Cherokee	28-7525228	N33696
EC-GMG	Fairchild Swearingen SA.226TC Metro III	TC-371	OY-BJT SE-IMD OY-BJT N1010B
EC-GMJ	Cessna 182J Skylane (W/o 24.6.00)	18256994	N2894F
EC-GMK	Cameron C-80 Concept HAFB	3717	
EC-GML	Robinson R-22B2 Beta (Dbr 20.8.03)	2650	
EC-GMM	Cessna 182P (Mod.)	18263823	N6754M
EC-GMN	Ultramagic M-77 HAFB	77/123	
EC-GMQ	Ultramagic N-210 HAFB	210/04	
EC-GMR	Air Création Safari GT-BI Fun 18	191004	EC-BD6
EC-GMS	Cameron A-120 HAFB	4011	
EC-GMU	Airbus A310-304	451	N571SW C-GCIV N815PA F-WWCY
EC-GMV	Cedimex Rans S-12XL-582 Airaile	S-12-160	
EC-GMX	Air Tractor AT-802A (Dbr 13.7.99)	802A-0039	N5001X
EC-GMZ	Eurocopter EC-135T1	0016	D-HECG
EC-GNA	Eurocopter EC-135T1	0017	D-HECH
EC-GND-CX	Grob G.102 Astir CS	1399	D-4272
EC-GNE	Rolladen-Schneider LS3A	3200	D-7804
EC-GNF	Ultramagic M-77 HAFB	77-127	
EC-GNG	McDonnell-Douglas DC-10-30 (Stored)	46953	YV-139C EC-CSK
EC-GNH	Cessna 177 Cardinal	17700244	N2844X
EC-GNK	Dassault Falcon 2000	37	F-WWMH
EC-GNL	Schempp-Hirth Nimbus 4 DM	23/33	
EC-GNN	Robinson R-22B2 Beta	2679	
EC-GNP	CASA C-1.131L Jungmann	2135	E.3B-509
EC-GNQ	Bell 206BJet Ranger III (W/o 27.12.04)	4230	N4382M
EC-GNR	Bell 206-LT Twin Ranger	52051	N41060
EC-GNS	Cessna 172N	17273683	N4843J
EC-GNT	Air Tractor AT-802	802-0046	N5007H
EC-GNV	Reims/Cessna F172N	F17201925	F-GCHQ
EC-GNX	Ultramagic N-210 HAFB	210/05	
EC-GNY	McDonnell-Douglas DC-9-83	49396	(SE-DHB) N396GE SX-BFO SE-DHB EC-FIX EC-389 SE-DHB
EC-GNZ	Boeing 737-4Y0	25178	D-ABAD N601TR
EC-GOD	Bell UH-1H (205)	4787	N92820 65-09743
EC-GOE	Bell UH-1H (205)	5272	N19UH 66-00789
EC-GOF	Bell UH-1H (205) (Crashed 4.8.00)	5580	N15UH 66-01097
EC-GOG	Bell UH-1H (205)	9960	N17UH 67-17762
EC-GOI	Eipper Quicksilver MX-II	5008	
EC-GOK	Mitsubishi MU-2B-35	635	OY-ARV LN-MTU OY-ARV N485AH XA-DID N485MA
EC-GOL	Cameron C-80 Concept HAFB	3563	
EC-GOM	McDonnell-Douglas DC-9-83	49579	EC-EIG EC-148
EC-GOP	Bell 412HP	36031	N4603T
EC-GOQ	Air Création Safari GT-BI Fun 18	195046	EC-CA8
EC-GOS	Air Tractor AT-802	802-0042	N5005M
EC-GOT	Airbus A310-324	455	N572SW C-GCIT N818PA F-WWCU

EC-GOU	McDonnell-Douglas DC-9-83	53198	SE-DLS
EC-GOV	Cessna 560 Citation Ultra	560-0419	N5233J
EC-GOX	Schleicher ASW 20	20134	3A-MAJ D-3325
EC-GOY	Beech C90 King Air	LJ-527	N55SG N55SQ N55SC
EC-GOZ	Reims FR172J Rocket	FR17200485	F-GLMH F-BVBS
EC-GPA	Bell 412HP	36071	N7238Y OE-XPR N194SP OE-XPP D-HHQQ N2084D
EC-GPB	Airbus A340-313	193	F-WWJR
EC-GPE	Swearingen SA.266TC Metro II	TC-273	OY-JER N5472M
EC-GPF	Reims/Cessna F337G Skymaster (Reims-assembled 337G with US c/n 33701477)	F33700059	D-IOMS (N1877M)
EC-GPG	Ultramagic S-90 HAFB	90/25	
EC-GPH	Beech E55 Baron	TE-1188	N38287
EC-GPJ	Reims/Cessna F172N	F17201561	D-EKSM
EC-GPL	PZL PW-5 Smyk	17.05.004	
EC-GPQ	Cessna 337G Skymaster	33701815	N617L N76L N1323L
EC-GPR	Cessna R172K Hawk XP	R1722544	N736HR
EC-GPS	Fairchild Swearingen SA-227AC Metro III	AC-722	N439MA
EC-GPT	Ultramagic M-65C HAFB	65/65	
EC-GPU	Ultramagic M-65C HAFB	65/66	
EC-GPV	Cameron C-80 Concept HAFB	4176	
EC-GPY	Piper PA-32R-301 Saratoga	32R-8513012	HB-PIO N81708
EC-GPZ-AJ	PZL PW-5 Smyk	17.07.023	
EC-GQA	Embraer EMB.120 Brasilia	120027	EC-GMT N14033 LN-KOD PT-SIW
EC-GQB	Cessna 205	205-0277	OO-SPI OE-DHW N8277Z
EC-GQC	Piper PA-28R-200 Cherokee Arrow B (W/o 18.8.99)	28R-7135011	C9-NPV ZS-NBG (ZS-MXS) N2106T XB-POH
EC-GQD	Cessna 150F	15061943	N8643S
EC-GQE	Piper J-3C-65 Cub	10780	G-AKAA 43-29489
EC-GQF	Aérospatiale/Alenia ATR-72-202	489	F-WWLJ
EC-GQG	McDonnell-Douglas DC-9-83	49577	EC-FSY EC-463 EC-EHT EC-147
EC-GQH	Bell 206B Jet Ranger II	578	HB-XDH EC-ENU HB-XDH OY-HSD HB-XDH (OY-HSW) HB-XDH
EC-GQJ	LET L-23 Super Blanik	917818	
EC-GQK	Airbus A340-313	197	F-WWJL
EC-GQL	DHC-4 Caribou (Wfu, stored)	258	T.9-1
EC-GQM	DHC-4 Caribou (Wfu, stored)	289	T.9-11
EC-GQN	DHC-4 Caribou (Wfu, stored)	290	T.9-12
EC-GQO	BAe.146-200QC	E-2086	D-ADEI SE-DEI G-5-086 G-BNUA G-5-086
EC-GQQ	Reims/Cessna F177RG Cardinal RG	F177RG0151	G-BFAC N177AB G-BFAC D-EDIS
EC-GQR	Ultramagic S-105 HAFB	105/44	
EC-GQY	Ultramagic M-77 HAFB	77/137	
EC-GRA	Agusta A.109C	7676	EC-GJD EC-380 N45FB N1VN
EC-GRB	CASA 1-131E	unkn	E.3B-415
EC-GRC	Piper PA-36-375 Brave	36-7802047	N3903E
EC-GRD	Ultramagic M-160 HAFB	160/09	
EC-GRE	Airbus A320-211	134	EC-FAS EC-575 F-WWIZ
EC-GRF	Airbus A320-211	136	EC-FBQ EC-576 F-WWDC
EC-GRG	Airbus A320-211	143	EC-FBS EC-577 F-WWDJ
EC-GRH	Airbus A320-211	146	EC-FBR EC-578 F-WWDM
EC-GRI	Airbus A320-211	177	EC-FEO EC-582 F-WWIP
EC-GRJ	Airbus A320-211	246	EC-FKH EC-589 F-WWII
EC-GRK	McDonnell-Douglas DC-9-87	49827	EC-EUE EC-290
EC-GRL	McDonnell-Douglas DC-9-87	49828	EC-EUD EC-291
EC-GRM	McDonnell-Douglas DC-9-87	49829	EC-EUC EC-292
EC-GRN	McDonnell-Douglas DC-9-87	49830	EC-EUL EC-293
EC-GRO	McDonnell-Douglas DC-9-87	49831	EC-EVB EC-294
EC-GRP	Aérospatiale/Alenia ATR-72-202	488	F-WWLI
EC-GRQ	Ultramagic M-105 HAFB	105/45	
EC-GRR	Cessna R172K Hawk XP	R1722270	N4077V
EC-GRS	Ultramagic F-14 Beer Bottle SS HAFB	F14/01	
EC-GRT	Reims/Cessna F172P	F17202230	HB-CID
EC-GRU	Aérospatiale/Alenia ATR-72-202	493	F-WWLN
EC-GRV	Ultramagic V-77 HAFB	77/136	
EC-GSA	Colt 77A HAFB	4214	
EC-GSB	PZL PW-5 Smyk	17.09.020	
EC-GSC	Cedimex Rans S-6ES-582 Coyote II	S-6A-118	
EC-GSJ	Convair 580	130	OO-HUB C-GGWG N5813 N8419H
EC-GSK	Bell 412	33092	SE-HVL N3205S 5N-AQS
EC-GSL	IAI-1124A Westwind	353	C-GRGE(2) N89UC N89UH N86UR N90CH N379JR 4X-CTU
EC-GSM	Cessna 172N (Officially reg with c/n 17270157)	17270175	D-EEKS(2) N738RJ
EC-GSN	Cameron C-60 Concept HAFB	3640	
EC-GSO	Bell UH-1H (205)	5466	N1217A 66-00983
EC-GSP	Bell UH-1H (205)	8853	N1206P 66-16659
EC-GSQ	Beech B300 Super King Air	FL-128	N128FL D-CDDD N3157D
EC-GSR-H	Schempp-Hirth Standard Cirrus	15	D-0454
EC-GSS	Cessna A188B	18802700T	PH-YTA N4966Q
EC-GST	Dynali Chickinox Kot-Kot	2797-E1W	
EC-GSV	Schleicher ASW 17	17013	OO-ZXF D-2112
EC-GTF	Reims/Cessna F172M	F17200908	OH-CFZ SE-FZC
EC-GTH	Grob G.109	6038	PH-789 OE-. . . PH-789 HB-2058 D-KGRO
EC-GTJ	Embraer EMB.120RT Brasilia (W/o 14.1.02)	120024	N72157 LN-KOC PT-SIT
EC-GTL	Ultramagic H-77 HAFB	77/139	
EC-GTM	Beech 1900C	UB-30	N7210R
EC-GTN	Ultramagic N-210 HAFB	210/06	
EC-GTO	McDonnell-Douglas DC-9-81 (Stored)	49570	HB-INX
EC-GTP-Q5	Schleicher ASW 19B	19331	HB-1562
EC-GTQ	Ultramagic H-65 HAFB	65/71	
EC-GTS	Cessna 500 Citation I	500-0037	N407SC N109AL SE-DPL N109AL N7CC
EC-GTT	Cedimex Rans S-12XL-503 Airaile	S-12-198	
EC-GTU	Colt 77A HAFB	4295	
EC-GTV	Reims/Cessna F152	F15201606	D-EGUN (2)
EC-GTX	SOCATA TB-10 Tobago	886	SE-KBI
EC-GTY	PZL PW-5 Smyk	17.09.010	
EC-GTZ	PZL PW-5 Smyk	17.10.005	
EC-GUA	PZL PW-5 Smyk	17.10.006	
EC-GUB	PZL PW-5 Smyk	17.10.007	
EC-GUC	Robinson R-22 Beta	2222	EC-GPO
EC-GUD	Beech 1900C-1	UC-156	N156YV
EC-GUE	MBB Bö.105C	S-188	EC-234 N3531T
EC-GUF	Air Tractor AT-802	802-0059	N51198
EC-GUH	Aérospatiale AS.355F2 Ecureuil 2	5474	N6040U
EC-GUN	Centrair 101A Pégase	101A-0314	F-CGSZ
EC-GUO	Boeing 737-4Q8	26285	N402KW
EC-GUP	Airbus A340-313X	217	F-WWJG
EC-GUQ	Airbus A340-313X	221	F-WWJA
EC-GUS	Fairchild Swearingen SA.227AC Metro III	AC-648	N2685L
EC-GUT(2)	Bell UH-1H (205)	13367	N21UH 73-21679

EC-GUU	Ultramagic H-77 HAFB	77/142	
EC-GUV	Cessna 172M	17262078	
EC-GUZ	Aérospatiale AS.355F2 Ecureuil 2	5454	N26ET
			PT-HXV
			N84CC
EC-GVA	Cameron N-77 HAFB	4343	
EC-GVC	Cessna 172M	17263446	N5232R
EC-GVD	Cessna 172P	17275947	N66010
EC-GVE	Fairchild Swearingen SA.227AC Metro III	AC-669	N2702Z
EC-GVF	Robinson R-22 Beta	1486	G-LOGS
EC-GVG	Robinson R-44 Astro	0454	
EC-GVH	Aérospatiale AS.355N Ecureuil 2	5656	
EC-GVI	McDonnell-Douglas DC-9-83	49936	EI-CPA
			TC-INB
			G-HCRP
			N3001D
EC-GVJ	Ultramagic S-105 HAFB	105/46	
EC-GVK	Ultramagic M-77 HAFB	77/146	
EC-GVL	Ultramagic M-77 HAFB	77/147	
EC-GVM	Ultramagic N-250 HAFB	250/07	
EC-GVN	Air Tractor AT-802	802-0065	N5059X
EC-GVO	McDonnell-Douglas DC-9-83	49642	N462GE
			SE-DHF
			EC-GHJ
			EC-323
			EC-GBY
			EC-807
			EI-CGR
			F-GMCD
			EC-EMT
			EC-257
			XA-TUR
			EC-EKT
			EC-190
			SE-DHF
			(EC-EFL)
EC-GVP	Bell 212	30572	LN-OQG
			SE-JCF
			LN-OQG
			N58024
EC-GVQ	SOCATA TB-200 Tobago XL	1770	F-OHTJ
EC-GVR	Robinson R-22 Beta (Damaged 16.6.04)	1489	HB-XYZ
			N40233
EC-GVS	Glaser-Dirks DG-100G Elan	E-20	HB-1518
EC-GVT	Ultramagic V-65 HAFB	65/78	
EC-GVV	Bell 212	30584	N58121
			HK-3729X
			N58121
			YS-1003P
			N58121
			C-FADC
			N58121
EC-GVX	Reims/Cessna FTB337G Super Skymaster	FTB3370004	F-GGTO
			FAP3703
			CS-AKK
EC-GVY	Cameron A-180 HAFB	4365	
EC-GXA	Bell 212	30812	LN-OQJ
EC-GXB	Schempp-Hirth Janus C	110	HB-1557
EC-GXC	Reims/Cessna FTB337G Super Skymaster	FTB3370013	CS-AUX
			FAP3712
			CS-APM
EC-GXD	Cedimex Rans S-12 Airaile	S-12-187	
EC-GXE	Fairchild Swearingen SA.227AC Metro III	AC-694B	N457AM
EC-GXF	Bell UH-1H (205)	12604	N22UH
			70-16299
EC-GXG	Bell 212	30759	N21601
			C-GJDC
			N21601
			HC-BJQ
			N49688
EC-GXH	Piper PA-36-300 Pawnee Brave	36-7860024	TG-LID
			N3658E
EC-GXI	Piper PA-36-300 Pawnee Brave	36-7760128	TG-. . .
			N82647
EC-GXJ	Fairchild Swearingen SA.226TC Metro II	TC-374	OY-AUO
			D-IAEF
			OY-AUO
			SE-IKP
			LN-SAP
			OY-AUO
			N10104
EC-GXK	Ultramagic S-90 HAFB	90/26	
EC-GXL	Ultramagic V-77 HAFB	77/149	
EC-GXM	Ultramagic V-77 HAFB	77/150	
EC-GXN	Siren PIK-30	728	F-CFPK
EC-GXO	Cedimex Rans S-6ES-503 Coyote II	S-6A-121	
EC-GXP	Fairchild 24R Argus (Dismantled)	946	E.19-4
			N14240
EC-GXQ	Beech T.34 Mentor	X-104	EC-750
			E.17-24/"79- 24"
EC-GXS	Schempp-Hirth Discus CS	249CS	
EC-GXU	McDonnell-Douglas DC-9-83	49622	EC-FTT
			EC-485
			EC-FNU
			EC-206
			EC-EJZ
			EC-382
			EC-EJZ
			EC-179

EC-GXV	Piper PA-28-140 Cherokee	28-20004	D-ELVU
			N6004W
EC-GXY	Aérospatiale AS.365N1 Dauphin 2	6242	N12AE
			N365AS
			F-WYME
EC-GYA	SOCATA Rallye 180T Galérien	2774	F-GARS
			F-ODEI
EC-GYC	SOCATA TB-200 Tobago XL	1811	F-GRBQ
EC-GYD	Piper PA-31P Pressurized Navajo	31P-7300123	N888PD
	(W/o 1.9.04)		(N831SF)
			N888PD
			N7650L
EC-GYG	Ultramagic S-160 HAFB	160/20	
EC-GYH	Ultramagic S-105 HAFB	105/48	
EC-GYI	Canadair CL.600-2B19 Regional Jet	7249	C-GDDM
			C-FMMQ
EC-GYJ	Thunder AX7-77 SI HAFB (Not confirmed)	4451	
EC-GYL	Fokker F.27 Friendship 500	10381	G-BVOM
	(Wfu, stored Madrid)		PH-FND
			PT-LZN
			F-BPNH
			PH-FND
EC-GYM	Fokker F.27 Friendship 500	10427	G-BVRN
	(Wfu)		PH-FPB
			HL5211
			(HL5207)
			PH-FPB
EC-GYN	Ultramagic M-90 HAFB	90/27	
EC-GYQ	Cessna T188C	18803490T	. . . . . .
			(N2637J)
EC-GYS	Road Air Flamingo	030	
EC-GYT	Eipper Quicksilver MX-II Sprint	209	
EC-GYU	Cessna 337E Super Skymaster	33701203	N86480
EC-GYX	Air Tractor AT-401	401-1068	
EC-GYY	Piper PA-36-300 Pawnee Brave	36-7460031	TG-LAJ
EC-GYZ	Piper PA-36-300 Pawnee Brave	36-7760119	TG-WAO
EC-GZA	Canadair CL.600-2B19 Regional Jet	7252	C-GDDO
EC-GZB-ZB	Grob G.104 Speed Astir IIB	4044	OO-ZFY
			D-3836
EC-GZC	Beech 65-B80 Queen Air	LD-228	G-WJPN
			N197MC
			N34LT
			N6876Q
			YV-TANK
			N6876Q
EC-GZD	Airbus A320-214	879	F-WWDD
EC-GZF	Reims/Cessna F150G	F150-0156	OE-AVS
EC-GZG	Beech 1900C	UC-161	N55635
EC-GZJ	Aerojean/Fournier RF-5-AJ1	E-011	
EC-GZK	Ultramagic S-130 HAFB	130/15	
EC-GZM	Ultramagic M-56 HAFB	56/14	
EC-GZN	Hispano HA.220D Super Saeta	22/103	A.10C-98
			C.10C-98
EC-GZO	Air Tractor AT-802	802-0071	N5166B
EC-GZQ	Cedimex Rans S-12XL-503 Airaile	S-12-200	
EC-GZR	Ultramagic H-77 HAFB	77/156	
EC-GZS	Ultramagic V-77 HAFB	77/154	
EC-GZT	Ultramagic M-90 HAFB	90/28	
EC-GZV	Ultramagic N-210 HAFB	210/09	
EC-GZX	Ultramagic V-77 HAFB	77/56	
EC-HAA	Boeing 757-256 (PP-VTS res .04)	26249	
EC-HAB	Airbus A320-214	994	F-WWBM
EC-HAF	Airbus A320-214	1047	F-WWIE
EC-HAG	Airbus A320-214	1059	F-WWIP
EC-HAJ	Aérospatiale AS.355N Ecureuil 2	5665	
	(W/o 21.5.01)		
EC-HAK	Embraer EMB.120ER Brasilia	120008	N212AS
			PT-SIC
EC-HAM	Comper CLA.7 Swift	S.32/5	G-ABUU
EC-HAO	Agusta A.109C	7642	D-HAAC(2)
			N1FD
EC-HAP	CASA C.212-400 Aviocar	465	EC-011
EC-HAQ	Robin DR.400/180 Régent	1301	F-GBAN
EC-HAR	Cessna 172P	17274314	N172U
			N51455
EC-HAS	Cessna 172M	17262738	N13417
EC-HAT	Cessna 172N	17269055	N81709
			C-GYWU
			(N734RM)
EC-HAY	Ultramagic N-300 HAFB	300/01	
EC-HAZ-69	Grob G.104 Speed Astir IIB	4012	OO-ZKT
			D-3837
EC-HBA	Ultramagic F-19 Bottle SS HAFB	F19/01	
EC-HBB	Ultramagic F-19 Bottle SS HAFB	F19/02	
EC-HBD	Schleicher ASW 19	19266	OY-XTP
			D-3588
			OE-5206
EC-HBE	Ultramagic H-77 HAFB	77/158	
EC-HBF	Swearingen SA.226AT Merlin IV	AT-074	EC-GDR
			EC-702
			OY-CHA
			N1006Y
			C-GDEF
			N1006Y
EC-HBI	SOCATA MS.893A Rallye Commodore 180	10795	F-BPGJ
EC-HBJ	Agusta A.109C	7646	D-HBRK
			N1YE
EC-HBK	Ultramagic V-77 HAFB	77/155	

EC-HBL	Boeing 737-85P	28381	N1787B
EC-HBM	Boeing 737-85P	28382	N1787B
EC-HBN	Boeing 737-8SP	28383	N1786B
EC-HBP	McDonnell-Douglas MD-83	49629	HB-IKP F-WQFO EC-FVC EC-525 VR-BMI EC-EOY EC-269
EC-HBQ	Agusta A.109A-II	7399	I-SOCC N1VG (D-HEEP) (D-HARK) N1VG
EC-HBS	Ultramagic H-65 HAFB	65/73	
EC-HBU	Aérospatiale/Alenia ATR-72-212A	459	N12903 F-WWLE
EC-HBY	Aérospatiale/Alenia ATR-72-212A	578	F-WWEA
EC-HCA	Piper PA-34-200 Seneca	34-7250191	9A-BPW RC-BPW YU-BPW D-GEAR N4978T
EC-HCB	Rans S-12 Airaile	S-12-138	EC-BY9
EC-HCC	Bell 206B	4505	C-GBUQ (N82404)
EC-HCD	Ultramagic F-21 Cepsa SS HAFB	F21/01	
EC-HCE	Aérospatiale AS.355N Ecureuil 2	5669	
EC-HCF	Embraer EMB.120RT Brasilia	120007	N211AS PT-SIB
EC-HCG	Aérospatiale/Alenia ATR-72-212A	580	F-WWEC
EC-HCH	Fairchild Swearingen SA.227ACMetro III	AC-658B	N2692P
EC-HCI	Grob G.102 Astir CS77	1708	D-3311
EC-HCJ	SOCATA TB-10 Tobago	245	F-GEFL 6V-AFG F-OBLK
EC-HCL	Aérospatiale AS.365N2 Dauphin 2	6416	SE-JAE F-WYMM
EC-HCM	Beech 1900C-1	UC-124	N122GP (N529LX)
EC-HCS	Reims FR172H Rocket	FR17200320	D-EEXP
EC-HCT	Bell 206L-4 Long Ranger IV	52062	G-BXMP N58968 G-OCOP N58968
EC-HCU	Fairchild Swearingen SA.226TC Metro II (Damaged)	TC-390	N19WP C-FBWY N244AM N1012B
EC-HCV	Piper PA-34-200 Seneca	34-7350268	D-GMWU N55991
EC-HDA	Cameron N-77 HAFB	4536	
EC-HDB	Cameron C-60 Concept HAFB	4550	
EC-HDC	Cameron N-77 HAFB	4560	
EC-HDD	Bell UH-1H	13551	HE.10B-51 Z.10B-51 EC-STK 73-22068
EC-HDH	BAe.146-200QT	E-2056	G-TNTA G-5-056 (G-OTNT) N146QT N146FT G-5-056
EC-HDI	Grob G.102 Astir CS	1002	D-8680
EC-HDK	Airbus A320-214	1067	F-WWBF
EC-HDM	Boeing 757-256 (PP-VTT res .04)	26250	
EC-HDN	Airbus A320-214	1087	F-WWIY
EC-HDO	Airbus A320-214	1099	F-WWDR
EC-HDP	Airbus A320-214	1101	F-WWDB
EC-HDQ	Airbus A340-313X	302	F-WWJU
EC-HDR	Boeing 757-256	26251	
EC-HDS	Boeing 757-256	26252	
EC-HDT	Airbus A320-214	1119	F-WWBO
EC-HDU	Boeing 757-256	26253	
EC-HDV	Boeing 757-256	26254	N1786B
EC-HDX	Ultramagic M-65 HAFB (Also reported current as JA-A1196)	65/88	
EC-HDZ	Schleicher ASW 15B	15215	D-0940
EC-HEA	Sud Avn SA.319B Alouette III (W/o 5.8.03)	2256	EC-FYI HD.16-7 Z.16-7 EC-STO
EC-HEB	Ultramagic H-77 HAFB	77/132	
EC-HEC	Ultramagic M-90 HAFB	90/32	
EC-HED	Ultramagic H-77 HAFB	77/165	
EC-HEE	Aérospatiale AS.355N Ecureuil 2	5645	F-OHVD
EC-HEF	Scheibe SF-28A Tandem-Falke	5768	D-KACU(2)
EC-HEI	Aérospatiale/Alenia ATR-72-212A	570	F-WWEG
EC-HEJ	Aérospatiale/Alenia ATR-72-212A	565	F-WWEE
EC-HEK	Canadair CL.600-2B19 Regional Jet	7320	C-GFCN C-FMLQ
EC-HEL	Air Tractor AT-802	802-0068	N5066S
EC-HEM	Cameron C-80 Concept HAFB	4535	
EC-HEN	Cameron C-60 Concept HAFB	4502	
EC-HEO	Ultramagic V-77 HAFB	77/144	
EC-HEP	Cameron C-80 Concept HAFB	4537	
EC-HEQ	Cessna 337 Super Skymaster (Believed w/o 14.4.04)	33700239	G-ATID N6239F
EC-HER	Grob G.102 Astir CS	1291	D-7377
EC-HET	Canadair CL.215 1A-10	1034	I-SISB UD.13-6
EC-HEU	Canadair CL.215 1A-10	1038	I-SISC UD.13-10
EC-HEV	Robinson R-44 Astro	0610	
EC-HEY	Cameron C-60 Concept HAFB (Also quoted as EC-HEY(2) with c/n 4904 - but see EC-HTN))	4355	
EC-HEZ	Aérospatiale/Alenia ATR-72-212A	582	F-WWEL
EC-HFA	Cessna 500 Citation (Damaged 10.4.03)	500-0209	N800AV (N919AT) N209MW
EC-HFC(2)	SOCATA MS.893A Rallye Commodore 180 (Damaged 11.7.03)	12634	D-EFGN
EC-HFD	Bell 412EP	36183	N52247
EC-HFF	Cessna 182M	18259371	N70805
EC-HFG	Ultramagic M-77 HAFB	77/161	
EC-HFH	Ultramagic S-130 HAFB	130/20	
EC-HFI	Ultramagic S-105 HAFB	105/54	
EC-HFJ	Air Tractor AT-402A	402A-1056	N5020A
EC-HFK	Embraer EMB.120RT Brasilia	120063	N7215U C-FZWF LN-KOE PT-SKG
EC-HFL	Scheibe Bergfalke II-55	0209	D-1907
EC-HFN	Ultramagic M-77 HAFB	77/99	
EC-HFO	Ultramagic M-77 HAFB	77/166	
EC-HFP	McDonnell-Douglas DC-9-82	53148	HL7548 HL7204
EC-HFS	McDonnell-Douglas DC-9-82	49517	EI-CTE B-540L B-2133
EC-HFT	McDonnell-Douglas DC-9-82	49521	EI-CTF B-2137
EC-HFU	Ultramagic S-130 HAFB	130/19	
EC-HFV	Bell 212	30818	N25UH XA-TJN HK-. . . N69AL XA-SQH N4426L XA-JEK N84FC C-GSHM N84FC
EC-HFX	Bell 212	30639	G-BCMC 9Y-THL HK-4103X G-BCMC (EC-GHO) EC-294 G-BCMC EC-GCS EC-932 G-BCMC 9Y-THL G-BCMC 9M-ATU VR-BFI G-BCMC N18090
EC-HFZ	Embraer EMB.120ER Brasilia	120261	LX-LGK PT-SUH
EC-HGA	McDonnell-Douglas DC-9-83 (Stored)	53052	N942AS
EC-HGF	Reims/Cessna F172M	F17201404	D-ELJB
EC-HGG	Reims/Cessna F172N	F17201560	D-EMDU(2)
EC-HGI	Cessna 550 Citation II	550-0596	D-CAWA N96TD (N13026)
EC-HGJ	McDonnell-Douglas DC-9-82	49519	EI-CTQ B-2135
EC-HGL	Sukhoi SU-31 (Damaged)	04-02	RA-0402
EC-HGM	Ultramagic M-77 HAFB	77/105	
EC-HGN	Ultramagic M-77 HAFB	77/169	
EC-HGO	Boeing 737-85P	28384	N1786B
EC-HGP	Boeing 737-85P	28385	N1786B
EC-HGQ	Boeing 737-85P	28386	N1786B
EC-HGR	Airbus A319-111	1154	D-AVYY
EC-HGS	Airbus A319-111	1180	D-AVWR
EC-HGT	Airbus A319-111	1247	D-AVYV
EC-HGU	Airbus A340-313X	318	F-WWJL
EC-HGV	Airbus A340-313X	329	F-WWJP
EC-HGX	Airbus A340-313X	332	F-WWJR
EC-HGY	Airbus A320-214	1200	F-WWII
EC-HGZ	Airbus A320-214	1208	F-WWIM
EC-HHA	Airbus A320-214	1221	F-WWBF
EC-HHD	Agusta A.109A-II	7357	VP-CCK VR-CCK N109JD N90GA
EC-HHE	Ultramagic N-180 HAFB	180/16	
EC-HHF	McDonnell-Douglas DC-9-82	49509	EI-CTP B2125
EC-HHI	Canadair CL.600-2B19 Regional Jet	7343	C-GFKQ
EC-HHJ	Reims/Cessna FR172H	FR1720316	D-EEXO

EC-HHL	Ultramagic S-90 HAFB	90/33	
EC-HHN	Embraer EMB.120RT Brasilia	120103	N127AM
			PT-SMV
EC-HHO	Beech 200 Super King Air	BB-262	N92V
			N18762
EC-HHP	McDonnell-Douglas DC-9-82	49501	EI-CTV
			B2107
EC-HHQ	Agusta A.109E Power	11058	
EC-HHR-MF	Schempp-Hirth Discus 2b	49	
EC-HHS	Dassault Falcon 50	204	EC-GPN
			VP-CGP
			VR-CGP
			F-GKAR
			F-WWHD
EC-HHT	Eurocopter EC.120BColibri	1060	
EC-HHV	Canadair CL.600-2B19 Regional Jet	7350	C-GFKR
EC-HHX	Cessna 172RG Cutlass RG	172RG0006	N4631R
	(Badly damaged 4.9.04)		
EC-HHY	Cessna 172RG Cutlass RG	172RG0393	N4827V
EC-HHZ	Aérospatiale SN.601 Corvette	15	F-GNAF
			D6-ECB
			F-GEQF
			N17AJ
			SE-DEN
			F-GDUB
			OO-MRE
			OO-MRA
			SE-DEN
			F-WIFA
EC-HIA	Aérospatiale SN.601 Corvette	19	F-GEPQ
			F-SEBH
			F-GDRC(1)
			TZ-PBF
			F-BVPL
			F-OCJL
			F-BVPL
EC-HIB	Cessna 172N	17270400	D-EFSB(2)
			N739AY
EC-HIC	Reims/Cessna F172H	F17200721	D-ECHC
EC-HID	Cessna 172N	17273303	D-EBER(3)
			N4677G
EC-HIE	Reims/Cessna F172N	F17201932	D-EHGP
EC-HIH	Ultramagic M-56C HAFB	56/15	
EC-HII	Piper PA-28-180 Cherokee D	28-5389	CS-ADX
			N7972N
EC-HIJ	Reims/Cessna F172N	F17201827	D-EIYG
EC-HIK	Cessna 172N	17268670	N104ES
			N733ZC
EC-HIL	Eurocopter EC.120B Colibri	1075	
EC-HIM	Aérospatiale AS.365N2 Dauphin 2	6478	SE-JCE
			F-WYMM
EC-HIN	Cessna 525 CitationJet	525-0197	N525KH
			N5151S
EC-HIO	Agusta A.109A-II	7319	I-CARR
EC-HIP	Boeing 757-256	29306	
EC-HIQ	Boeing 757-256	29307	
EC-HIR	Boeing 757-256	29308	N1795B
EC-HIS	Boeing 757-256	29309	
EC-HIT	Boeing 757-256	29310	
EC-HIU	Boeing 757-256	29311	
EC-HIV	Boeing 757-256	29312	
EC-HIX	Boeing 757-256	30052	
EC-HIY	Reims/Cessna F172P	F17202098	D-EIKK
			(D-ELNU)
EC-HJA	Reims/Cessna F172H	F17200690	D-EBJK(2)
			HB-CYB
EC-HJB	McDonnell- Douglas DC-9-82	49507	EI-CUF
			B-2123
EC-HJC	Swearingen SA.226TC Metro II	TC-318	OY-JEO
			N5476M
EC-HJF	Aérospatiale AS.355N Ecureuil 2	5660	
EC-HJG	Cessna 152	15284041	N4948H
EC-HJH	BAe.146 Series 200QC	E-2112	G-BOMK
			RP-C482
			F-GTNU
			G-5-112
			EC-231
			G-BOMK
EC-HJI	Aérospatiale/AleniaATR-72-512	562	F-WWLZ
EC-HJK	Road Air Flamingo	041	
EC-HJM	SOCATA TB-20 Trinidad	412	SE-IZV
			N141SW
			F-GDGK
EC-HJN	Piper PA-36-285 Pawnee Brave (Cr 8.7.03)	36-7560099	N9984P
EC-HJP	Boeing 737-85P	28535	N1800B
			N1786B
EC-HJQ	Boeing 737-85F	28387	N1786B
EC-HJR	Ultramagic M-90 HAFB	90/36	
EC-HJS	Ultramagic S-105 HAFB	105/56	
EC-HJT	Ultramagic H-77 HAFB	77/168	
EC-HJU	Convair CV-580	147	OO-DHF
			C-GQHA
			N5838
			N73158
			N2006
			N200A
			N100A
			N7600

EC-HJX	Piper PA-28-151 Cherokee Warrior	28-7515332	N33366
EC-HJY	Glasflügel H201B Standard Libelle	523	PH-469
EC-HKB	Grob G.102 Astir CS Jeans	2032	D-3878
EC-HKC	Piper PA-28 Cherokee 140	28-7225484	F-BTYE
EC-HKD	Piper PA-28 Cherokee 140	28-7325275	F-BUIH
EC-HKE	Cessna 150L (W/o 2.5.04)	15074858	N10432
EC-HKF	Ultramagic N-250 HAFB	250/10	
EC-HKG	Cameron C-80 HAFB	4739	
EC-HKH	Cessna 172N	17270379	D-EOEL(2)
			N739AA
EC-HKO	Airbus A319-111	1362	D-AVWJ
EC-HKP	McDonnell-Douglas DC-9-83	49624	EI-CGI
			EC-EKM
			EC-279
			EC-EKM
			EC-178
EC-HKQ	Boeing 737-85P	28388	
EC-HKR	Boeing 737-85P	28536	N1787B
EC-HKS	Boeing 767-3Q8ER	27686	
EC HKT	Air Tractor AT-802	802-0080	N90115
EC-HKU	Cessna 414	414-0038	N43ML
			D-IAML
			OE-FIR
			N8138Q
EC-HKV	Piper PA-36-300 Pawnee Brave	36-7360047	N6402P
	(Crashed 28.8.01)		C-GJQI
			N56702
			CF-GPK
EC-HKX	PZL M-18ADromader	1Z021-10	D-FOMD
			DDR-TMD
EC-HLA	Airbus A310-324	489	OE-LAA
			F-WWCK
EC-HLD	Convair CV-580	52	OO-DHE
			C-GDTE
			N5845
			N73125
EC-HLE	Piper PA-28R-200 Cherokee Arrow II	28R-7235051	N4439T
EC-HLF	Robin R.2160 Alpha Sport	164	SX-ACJ
			(F-GOJC)
			TS-AJC
			TU-TJC
			F-ODJC
EC-HLG	Grob G.102 Astir CS	1250	D-4256
EC-HLH	Ultramagic H-77 HAFB	77/172	
EC-HLI	Ultramagic S-105 HAFB	105/57	
EC-HLJ	Ultramagic S-105 HAFB	105/62	
EC-HLK	Piper PA-18-150 Super Cub	18-5388	D-EODA,
			ALAT
			N10F
EC-HLL	Schleicher K 7	7003	HB-716
EC-HLO	Piper PA-28-140 Cherokee	28-20032	N6032W
			(N141DC)
			(N140HY)
			N6032W
EC-HLQ	Piper PA-34-200T Seneca II	34-7670336	N4387F
EC-HLR	Robinson R-22 Beta	0555	D-HUBY
			N555GH
			(D-HEMD)
			D-HOSE(3)
EC-HLS	Ultramagic S-90 HAFB	90/39	
EC-HLT	Cessna 172N	17267862	F-GFYY
			N75630
EC-HLU	Eurocopter EC.120B Colibri	1106	F-WQDQ
EC-HLV	Piper PA-28R-200 Cherokee Arrow II	28R-7435019	N794AM
			C-GTOY
			N111RW
			N56620
EC-HLY	Glaser-Dirks DG-400	4-21	D-KOTZ
EC-HLZ	Road Air Flamingo	039	
EC-HMA	Beech C90 King Air	LJ-577	N57KA
EC-HMB	Robin DR.400/180 Régent	1094	F-BXVG
EC-HMC	Cessna 337G Skymaster	33701725	N53587
EC-HMD	Air Tractor AT-802	802-0088	N9049K
EC-HMF	Robin HR.200-120B	349	
EC-HMG	Robin R.2120	350	
EC-HMH	Piper PA-28-161 Cadet	2841345	D-EJLD
			N92155
			N623FT
			(F-GJOT)
			(F-GIEU)
EC-HML	Beech 65-88 Queen Air	LP-2	N88338
EC-HMM	Piper PA-28-181 Cherokee Archer II	28-7890428	D-EMFK
			N9566N
EC-HMN	Ultramagic M-65 HAFB	65/93	
EC-HMO	Piper PA-18-150 Super Cub	18-8547	D-EGCF
			SE-GCE
			Fv51238
EC-HMP	Cessna 172M	17265188	N64356
EC-HMQ	Reims/Cessna F172N	F17201709	F-GBFS
EC-HMS	Convair CV-580	459	OO-DHL
			C-GGWF
			N5811
			N8420H
			VH-BZ I
EC-HMY	Embraer EMB.120RT Brasilia	120009	N214AS
			PT-SID
EC-HMZ	Air Tractor AT-802	802-0095	N9087Y

EC-HNC	McDonnell-Douglas DC-9-83	49620	D-ALLV
			EI-BTV
			EC-EZU
			EC-531
			EI-BTV
EC-HNF	Piper PA-32R-300 Lance	32R-7680047	D-ELDH
			N7538C
EC-HNH	Rockwell Commander 690	11058	N690PJ
			N2069B
			CX-BOE
			N690JC
			N11VS
			N9148N
EC-HNI	Ultramagic S-90 HAFB	90/37	
EC-HNJ	Air Tractor AT-802	802-0096	N9075U
EC-HNK	Air Tractor AT-802	802-0097	N9094Z
EC-HNL	Cameron N-77 HAFB	4847	
EC-HNM	Cessna 340	340-0517	N1712G
EC-HNN	Piper PA-28R-180 Cherokee Arrow	28R-30184	D-EFMF(2)
			N3861T
EC-HNP	Reims/Cessna F177RG Cardinal RG	F177RG0131	D-EFMW
EC-HNQ	Ultramagic H-77 HAFB	77/171	
EC-HNR	Ultramagic S-90 HAFB	90/43	
EC-HNT	MBB Bö.105S	S-414	D-HDMA(2)
			(D-HDMM)
EC-HNU	Dassault Falcon 900EX	62	F-WWFM
EC-HNV	SOCATA MS.893E Rallye 180GT Gaillard	12523	D-EHLV
			F-BVNP
EC-HNX	SOCATA MS.893E Rallye 180GT Gaillard	12682	D-EBWD
			F-ODDJ
EC-HNY	Boeing 717-2CM	55059	N6203U
EC-HNZ	Boeing 717-2CM	55060	N9010L
EC-HOA	Boeing 717-2CM	55061	
EC-HOB	Dassault Falcon 900EX	43	F-WQBK
			F-GSDP
			F-WWFE
EC-HOC	Cessna F172G	F172-0296	D-ENSE
EC-HOD	Reims/Cessna F172M	F17201016	D-EJXB
EC-HOE	Piper PA-18-150 Super Cub	18-6629	D-EJEP
			N9365D
EC-HOF	Piper PA-36-300 Pawnee Brave	36-8160009	CS-AVU
	(Cr 21.7.00)		N3107H
			TG-BOM
EC-HOG	Reims/Cessna FTB337G Super Skymaster		
		FTB3370028	CS-DBV
			FAP3727
			CS-ABL
EC-HOJ	Robinson R-44 Astro	0490	G-FLYZ
EC-HOK	Piper PA-34-200 Seneca	34-7350320	F-BUTT
			F-ETAP
EC-HOL	Piper PA-34-220T Seneca	34-8233172	N1982J
			D-GIBI
			N8245J
			N9541N
			N8241T
EC-HOM	Piper PA-28-161 Cadet	2841305	D-EJTK
			N9262N
			N9206B
EC-HON	Bell 206B Jet Ranger II	2201	EC-GEH
			EC-972
			VH-HJG
			N995KP
			N2276K
			N77AH
EC-HOO	Cessna 172RG Cutlass RG	172RG0780	D-EMRK
			N6610V
EC-HOP	Cessna 172N	17272917	D-EGLY(2)
			N7370D
EC-HOQ	Lake LA-4-200 Buccaneer	650	G-OSMR
			EI-BNB
			N1057L
EC-HOR	Air Tractor AT-802	802-0098	N9107X
EC-HOS	Ultramagic M-105 HAFB	105/69	
EC-HOT	Cessna 172P	17274044	F-GGBU
			N5284K
EC-HOU	Robinson R-22 Beta	2077	F-GMPE
EC-HOV	McDonnell-Douglas DC-9-82	49416	HL7543
			HL7275
EC-HOX	Bell 212	32254	4X-BCF
			IDFAF-068
EC-HOY	Bell 212	32225	4X-BCN
			4X-BCJ
			IDFAF-069
EC-HOZ	Piper PA-34-200T Seneca II	34-7570092	N33127
EC-HPA	Robinson R-22B2 Beta	3100	
EC-HPB	MBB Bö.105S	S-672	D-HEIM(2)
			N4573T
			D-HDUN
			N4573T
			D-HDUN
EC-HPC	Piper PA-34-200T Seneca II	34-7570011	D-GBMW
			OY-PET
			N32174
EC-HPD	Sukhoi SU-26	06-02	HB-MST
			RA-0602
EC-HPE	Air Création XP-GTE-582S	00001/SF	
EC-HPF	Cameron N-77 HAFB	4888	
EC-HPG	Ultramagic N-250 HAFB	250/09	
EC-HPH	Cessna 172N (W/o 25.1.03)	17270202	N738SN
EC-HPI	Cameron N-77 HAFB	4738	
EC-HPJ	Bell 212	32217	4X-BCI
			IDFAF-051
EC-HPK	Air Tractor AT-401	401-1120	
EC-HPL	Ultramagic S-160 HAFB	160/22	
EC-HPM	Airbus A321-231	1276	F-WWID
			D-AVZO
EC-HPN	Piper PA-28-151 Cherokee Warrior	28-7415276	N41574
EC-HPO	Ultramagic N-210 HAFB	210/11	
EC-HPQ	Cessna 500 Citation	500-0157	EC-HFY
			CS-DCA
			N190AB
			PH-CTD
EC-HPR	Canadair CL.600-2B19 Regional Jet	7430	C-GHDM
			C-FMMW
EC-HPS	SOCATA MS.893A Rallye Commodore 180	11840	D-ELLR
EC-HPT	SOCATA MS.893E Rallye 180GT Gaillard	12275	F-BUNA
			(D-EKHL)
EC-HPU	Boeing 767-3Q8ER	30048	
EC-HPV	Sukhoi SU-31	04-03	RA-02217
EC-HPX	Sukhoi SU-29	80-05	RA-1278
EC-HPY	SOCATA TB-20 Trinidad	346	F-GDNH
EC-HPZ	SOCATA TB-9 Tampico	1387	F-GLFD
EC-HQA	SOCATA MS.894A Minerva 220	11829	F-BSMK
EC-HQB	SOCATA MS.893E Rallye 180GT Gaillard	12233	F-BUGM
EC-HQC	SOCATA MS.893A Rallye Commodore 180	11052	F-BRKZ
	(Originally built as MS.894A Minerva 220)		
EC-HQD	Robin R.2112 Alpha	130	
EC-HQE	Robin R.2100A	126	F-GAVS
EC-HQF	Airbus A340-313X	378	F-WWJI
EC-HQG	Airbus A320-214	1379	F-WWIO
EC-HQH	Airbus A340-313X	387	F-WWJI
EC-HQI	Airbus A320-214	1396	F-WWIX
EC-HQJ	Airbus A320-214	1430	F-WWBR
EC-HQK	Airbus A320-214	1454	F-WWBZ
EC-HQL	Airbus A320-214	1461	F-WWDD
EC-HQM	Airbus A320-214	1484	F-WWDM
EC-HQN	Airbus A340-313	414	
EC-HQO	Cessna 310Q	310Q0286	N7786Q
EC-HQP	Reims/Cessna F172M	F17200978	D-EGBF
EC-HQQ	Reims/Cessna F172N	F17201970	D-EDOV
EC-HQR	Cessna 172N	17269265	N737AH
EC-HQS	Eurocopter EC-120B Colibri	1145	
EC-HQT	Airbus A300B4-103F	124	G-TNTS
			G-CEXC
			N407U
			N220EA
			F-GBNO
EC-HQU	Cessna 172L	17260658	N19675
EC-HQY	Beech 95-B55 Baron	TC-1248	D-IHLW
			OE-FNE
EC-HQZ	Airbus A321-231	1333	D-AVZB
EC-HRA	Robinson R-22	0154	F-GJHB
			G-BJBR
			N9041N
EC-HRC	Lindstrand LBL-90A HAFB	718	
EC-HRD	Ultramagic S-160 HAFB	160/26	
EC-HRE	Reims/Cessna F172N	F17201832	D-EGGA(2)
EC-HRF	SOCATA MS.893A Rallye Commodore 180	10948	F-BREG
EC-HRG	Airbus A321-231	1366	D-AVZC
EC-HRH	Cessna 500 Citation	500-0116	D-IATC
			EC-CJH
			N116CC
EC-HRI	Grob G.103A Acro	3632-K-14	D-3074
EC-HRJ	Piper Aerostar 602P	62P-0897-8165027	D-IFFF
	(Major damage 19.10.04)		N602CP
			D-IFFF
			N6893X
EC-HRK	SOCATATB-20 Trinidad	2024	F-OILP
EC-HRL	Aérospatiale AS.365C2 Dauphin 2	5055	PH-SSY
			EC-GVU
			PH-SSY
			EC-FOY
			EC-137
			CC-CJA
EC-HRM	Ultramagic S-105 HAFB	105/68	
EC-HRN	Cessna 172RG Cutlass RG	172RG0021	D-EGIH(3)
			N4745R
EC-HRO	Cessna 550 Citation Bravo	550-0938	N5VN
			N51038
EC-HRP	Airbus A320-232	1349	F-WWBD
EC-HRQ	HS.125 Series 700B	257166	F-GRON
			F-BYFB
			G-5-18
EC-HRR	Cessna TU206G Turbo Stationair 6	U20604283	N756QY
EC-HRS	Ultramagic H-77 HAFB	77/186	
EC-HRT	Rolladen-Schneider LS-7WL	7130	BGA3738/GCZ
EC-HRU	Ultramagic S-105 HAFB	105/74	
EC-HRV	Reims/Cessna F172M	F17201375	D-EEIF
EC-HRX	Cessna F172E	F172-0053	D-EFQU
EC-HRY	Reims/Cessna FR172E	FR1720051	F-BPES
EC-HRZ	Ultramagic S-105 HAFB	105/73	
EC-HSA	Eipper Quicksilver MX-II Sprint	145	unkn
EC-HSB	Robinson R-22 Beta	1704	N4063T

EC-HSC	Cessna F172H	F172-0418	D-ECEQ(2)
EC-HSD	Aérospatiale AS.35B3 Ecureuil	3340	F-WQOS F-WQDQ
EC-HSE	Airbus A320-214	1229	EC-HHB F-WWIH
EC-HSF	Airbus A320-214	1255	EC-HHC F-WWIX
EC-HSG	Cessna 172RG Cutlass RG	172RG0249	D-EJMH(2) N5128U
EC-HSH	Canadair CL.600-2B19 Regional Jet	7466	C-GHWD C-FMKZ
EC-HSI	Cessna 402C	402C0409	D-IGEO N6785Z
EC-HSJ	SOCATATB-10 Tobago	49	F-GCEA
EC-HSK	Piper PA-28-140 Cherokee	28-23488	SE-FCB N9944W
EC-HSM	Cessna 172N	17268875	N302DP (N734HW)
EC-HSN	Robinson R-44 Raven	0856	
EC-HSO	Embraer EMB.120RT Brasilia	120214	F-GHEY PT-SSI
EC-HSP	Piper PA-28RT-201 Arrow IV	28R-7918074	D-EEJN HB-PDM N3048J
EC-HSQ	Piper PA-34-220TSeneca III	34-8133006	OY-CRB N8329B
EC-HSR	Piper PA-28-161 Warrior II	28-8016286	PH-KDM OO-HLT N81748
EC-HSS	Ultramagic H-77 HAFB	77/187	
EC-HST	Rockwell Commander 114	14299	D-EIXR N4979W
EC-HSU	Ultramagic H-77 HAFB	77/185	
EC-HSV	Boeing 767-3Q8ER	29387	
EC-HSX	Mooney M.20J Model 201	24-0947	HB-DGF SE-GXS (N3813H)
EC-HSY	Piper PA-34-200TSeneca II	34-8170043	N8297T (D-G . . .) N8297T
EC-HSZ	Piper PA-28R-200 Cherokee Arrow	28R-7235020	HB-OKH N4370T
EC-HTA	Airbus A320-214	1516	F-WWIK
EC-HTB	Airbus A320-214	1530	F-WWIO
EC-HTC	Airbus A320-214	1540	F-WWIU
EC-HTD	Airbus A320-214	1550	F-WWDC
EC-HTG	Piper PA-28-181 Archer II	28-8190109	D-EHAH(3) N8308D
EC-HTH	Glaser-Dirks DG-400	4-5	D-KEBM(2) (D-KGGJ)
EC-HTJ	Bell 212	30648	PK-HMC PK-DBZ N59580
EC-HTK	Cessna 337G Skymaster	33701622	N3371M OB-1664 YV-234P YV-TAMH (N53436)
EC-HTL	Cessna 172RG Cutlass RG	172RG0226	TC-FHT N5092U
EC-HTM	Glaser-Dirks DG-100	59	OE-5071
EC-HTN	Cameron C-60 Concept HAFB	4904	(EC-HEY(2))?
EC-HTO	Piper PA-A-36-375 Pawnee Brave	AR36-8002016	CS-AVN LV-ODG
EC-HTP	Cessna 421CGolden Eagle	421C0261	D-IAAF SE-LCP N421JK 5Y-TRI G-DEDE N6148G
EC-HTQ	Robinson R-44 Raven	0993	
EC-HTR	Beech 400A Beechjet	RK-293	N4293K
EC-HTS	Embraer EMB.120RT Brasilia	120168	N168CA PT-SQG
EC-HTT	Robinson R-44 Clipper	0435	CS-HEH G-BXUN
EC-HTU	CASA C.212-400MP Aviocar	470	
EC-HTV	Bell 212	30665	N212HS C-FJKL N70202 XC-GUS
EC-HTX	Bell 212	31151	N8169Q XC-FAW
EC-HTY	Cessna 172RG	172RG0407	
EC-HTZ	Canadair CL.600-2B19 Challenger	7493	C-GIHJ C-FMNB
EC-HUA	Reims/Cessna F172M	F17200952	D-ECWS
EC-HUC	Reims/Cessna FR172K Hawk XP	FR1720631	D-EKAA
EC-HUD	Cessna 172N	17268212	D-EKGR(2) SE-GUM N733DJ
EC-HUE	Piper PA-36-285 Pawnee Brave	36-7360055	N56542
EC-HUF	Ultramagic S-160 HAFB	160/21	
EC-HUH	Airbus A321-211	1021	EC-HAC D-AVZQ
EC-HUI	Airbus A321-211	1027	EC-HAE D-AVZL
EC-HUJ	Airbus A320-214	1292	EC-HKL F-WWBT
EC-HUK	Airbus A320-214	1318	EC-HKM F-WWDK
EC-HUL	Airbus A320-214	1347	EC-HKN F-WWDY
EC-HUM	Schempp-Hirth Ventus B	74	D-9621 HB-1621
EC-HUN	Cessna 207A Skywagon (Wfu)	20700367	CS-AUL D-EDOO N1767U
EC-HUO	Piper J-3C-90 Cub (f/n 11896) (Regd with c/n 11496 ex 43-30205 with which it exchanged identities)	12068	D-EMUX(2) OO-DAA (OO-DAB) 44-79772
EC-HUQ	Piper PA-28-161 Warrior III	2842108	N5108B N4147U (G-BZMU) N4147U
EC-HUS	Bell 212	30655	D-HAFS(2) ZK-HNK EI-BAM G-BCPY
EC-HUU	Piper PA-28R-200 Cherokee Arrow II	28R-7535317	N1540X
EC-HUV	Cessna 172N	17270374	N738ZV
EC-HUX	Robinson R-44 Astro	0376	D-HIKK
EC-HUY	Piper PA-34-200T Seneca II	34-7570013	D-GATB N32273
EC-HUZ	Boeing 717-23S	55066	
EC-HVA	Robin DR.500/200i Président	0033	
EC-HVD	Boeing 747-256B	22454	TF-ATL EC-DLC
EC-HVE	Ultramagic S-105 HAFB	105/77	
EC-HVF	Cessna T207A Turbo Stationair 8	20700727	PH-DPX D-EBMO OE-KMG(1) N9769M
EC-HVL	Cameron N-77HAFB	10096	
EC-HVM	Ultramagic M-65C HAFB	65/99	
EC-HVN	Ultramagic M-65C HAFB	65/100	
EC-HVO	Ultramagic M-65C HAFB	65/101	
EC-HVP	Cessna 172RG Cutlass	172RG0549	D-ECMV(2) (N5514V)
EC-HVQ	Cessna 525 CitationJet CJ	525-0436	N5141F
EC-HVS	SOCATA Rallye 235E-D	13154	D-EDGR
EC-HVV	Dassault Falcon 100	193	OH-AMB N3BY N259FJ F-WZGY
EC-HVZ	Airbus A300B4-203	227	N223KW N203PA F-WZMC
EC-HXA	Airbus A320-232	1497	F-WWID
EC-HXB	Cessna 172N	17267788	TC-DBP N416CA N75533
EC-HXC	Cessna 172N	17271807	TC-DBL (D-EUCB) N5270E
EC-HXD	Reims/Cessna F150M	F15001313	TC-DBG D-EIBT (D-EIFY)
EC-HXE	Reims/Cessna F172M	F17200959	D-EDAZ(3)
EC-HXF	Reims/Cessna F172N	F17202001	D-EKNF PH-AYK
EC-HXG	Air Tractor AT-802	802-0113	N91442
EC-HXH	Robinson R-44 Astro	0448	CS-HEI G-BXXM
EC-HXI	Eurocopter EC.120B Colibri	1193	
EC-HXJ	Air Tractor AT-802	802-0114	N9143Y
EC-HXL	Bell 222	47570	TC-HLS N35GH N356H JA9915 N3208N
EC-HXM	Canadair CL.600-2B19 Regional Jet	7514	C-GIQL C-FMLU
EC-HXN	Tecnam P.92S Echo	P-92-ES-005	
EC-HXP	Ultramagic N-210 HAFB	210/16	
EC-HXQ	Piper PA-28-181 Archer II	28-7990518	OY-RLN G-BTKY N2877D
EC-HXR	Agusta-Bell AB.212	5522	D-HAFG(3) RSAF1413
EC-HXS	Aérospatiale AS.350B3 Ecureuil	3439	F-WQDA F-WQDH
EC-HXV	Bell 212	30647	FAP: 74-614
EC-HXX	Bell 412SP	33062	N4014U TG-WOO H-126 TG-WOO
EC-HXY	Fairchild Swearingen SA.227AC Metro III	AC-461B	N25LD EC-FSV EC-437 N120FA F-GGLF OY-CHB N222JC NIO9TA

EC-HXZ	Bell 412	33106	PK-HMT
EC-HYA	Cessna 172N	17270143	D-EOYY N738PZ
EC-HYB	Yakovlev Yak-55	870302	LY-EGJ 15 (blue) DOSAAF
EC-HYC	Airbus A320-214	1262	EC-HKI F-WWDB
EC-HYD	Airbus A320-214	1288	EC-HKK F-WWBO
EC-HYE	Reims/Cessna FR172H Rocket	FR1720231	D-ECKZ
EC-HYF	Partenavia P.68	10	OH-PVA
EC-HYG	Canadair CL.600-2B19 Regional Jet	7529	C-GIXG C-FMLI
EC-HYH	Ultramagic N-250 HAFB	250/03	
EC-HYI	Dassault Falcon 2000	150	F-WWVH
EC-HYK	Robinson R-22 Beta	1998	CS-HDL G-BUER
EC-HYL	Glaser-Dirks DG-400	4-72	D-KLWM HB-2095
EC-HYM	Bell 412	33045	C-FTDM TG-WOJ H-124 TG-WOJ
EC-HYN	Yakovlev Yak-52	822403	LY-ZRD DOSAAF-75
EC-HYP	Piper PA-34-200T Seneca	34-7770343	N84SA D-GANY D-IANY N38821
EC-HYQ	Eurocopter EC.120B Colibri	1237	
EC-HYR	Eurocopter EC.120B Colibri	1238	
EC-HYS	Cessna 172K	17258446	D-EHTI(2) N5132G (N84372)
EC-HYT	Cessna 172RG Cutlass RG	172RG0544	D-EGQR N5480V
EC-HYU	Sukhoi SU-26M	04-02	RA-44542
EC-HYX	Yakovlev Yak-52	822105	LY-JDJ
EC-HYY	North American T-6G Texan (Rebuilt using parts from F-BMJO - flew as a Zero Replica In 1987 as F-WZBN with c/n SAM2-049. Now painted "15049/1")	182-736	F-AZAS F-WZBN F-AZAS F-BMJP Fr.AF 51-15049
EC-HYZ	Cessna 172P	17276143	G-BYEN PH-ILU N97003
EC-HZB	Beech 95-B55 Baron	TC-1287	SE-EXL
EC-HZC	Tecnam P.92 Echo	P-92-E-011	
EC-HZD	Bell 412SP	33056	N4031F N911FD N2071Y
EC-HZF	Slepcev Storch SS Mk.4	084	VH-AYQ
EC-HZG	Bell 212	32224	4X-BCO 4X-BCK IDFAF067
EC-HZH	Fairchild Swearingen SA.227AC Metro III	AC-720	N2724S XA-TGD N2724S
EC-HZI	Cessna 172RG Cutlass RG	172RG0247	D-EJGL N5120U
EC-HZJ	Beech 58 Baron	TH-461	CS-ART D-IFBF
EC-HZL	Ultramagic N-180 HAFB	180/28	
EC-HZM	Piper PA-34-200 Seneca	34-7250169	F-GFJE TU-TFU N4838T
EC-HZO	Cessna F150J	F150-0393	D-EONE
EC-HZP	Robinson R-22B2 Beta	2598	EC-GHR
EC-HZQ	Yakovlev Yak-52	822102	LY-ROS
EC-HZR	Canadair CL.600-2B19 Regional Jet	7547	C-GJFR C-FMML
EC-HZS	Boeing 737-86Q	30276	N747BX N1786B
EC-HZT	Ultramagic H-77 HAFB	77/133	
EC-HZU	Airbus A320-214	1578	F-WWBO
EC-HZV	Eurocopter EC.120B Colibri	1254	
EC-HZX	Eurocopter EC.120B Colibri	1255	
EC-HZY	Eurocopter EC.120B Colibri	1242	
EC-HZZ	Eurocopter EC.120B Colibri	1249	
EC-IAA	Canadair CL.600-2B19 Regional Jet	7563	C-GJIZ C-FMLV
EC-IAB	Cessna 525 CitationJet	525-0037	HB-VKB N1820E
EC-IAC	Cedimex Rans S-6ES-582 Coyote II	S-61-129	
EC-IAE	Reims/Cessna FR172K Hawk XP	FR17200663	D-EINT
EC-IAF	Boeing 747-256B	22455	TF-ATM EC-DLD
EC-IAH	Beech 1900C-1	UC-166	N166GL
EC-IAI	Yakovlev Yak-52	833006	LY-CRI DOSAAF-16
EC-IAJ	Yakovlev Yak-52	855705	LY-KGB DOSAAF-55
EC-IAK	Yakovlev Yak-55	880510	LY-DER DOSAAF-43
EC-IAL	Yakovlev Yak-52	833903	LY-RON DOSAAF-147
EC-IAM	Yakovlev Yak-52	844504	LY-TRO DOSAAF-79
EC-IAN	Yakovlev Yak-52	844310	LY-IBL DOSAAF-55
EC-IAO	Yakovlev Yak-52	822808	LY-NCE DOSAAF-140
EC-IAP	Yakovlev Yak-52	822109	LY-EDU DOSAAF-36
EC-IAQ	Yakovlev Yak-52	877912	LY-IZP DOSAAF-99
EC-IAR	Yakovlev Yak-52	822011	LY-CAT DOSAAF-
EC-IAS	Yakovlev Yak-52	833312	LY-CEO DOSAAF-66
EC-IAT	Cessna 182P Skylane	18262266	D-EGFY N58737
EC-IAU	Ultramagic M-65C HAFB	65/108	
EC-IAV	Bell 212	30534	N7964J P2-HCO VH-HCO N7964J
EC-IAX	Cessna 550 Citation II (Reservation: Stored as N205SC)	550-0196	N205SC N205SG (N31F) N6567C N98784
EC-IAY	Piper PA-28-180 Cherokee C	28-2765	D-EHOV N8813J
EC-IAZ	Airbus A320-232	1631	F-WWDP
EC-IBA	Cessna 500 Citation	500-0178	HB-VKK D-FBCK D-IKFJ N178CC
EC-IBB	Aérospatiale AS.350B3 Ecureuil	3488	
EC-IBC	Sud Avn SA.316B Alouette III	1324	HB-XQD A-324
EC-IBD	Bombardier BD.700-1A10 Global Express	9060	C-GGJH
EC-IBE	Road Air Flamingo	021	
EC-IBF	Grob G.102 Astir CS	1155	D-7251
EC-IBG	Piper PA-28-161 Cadet	2841025	G-BPJS N9154Z
EC-IBH	Piper PA-28-161 Cadet	2841061	G-BWOH D-ENXG N9142S
EC-IBK	Beech B300 Super King Air	FL-328	N4328W
EC-IBL	Colt 77A HAFB	10160	
EC-IBM	Canadair CL.600-2B19 Regional Jet	7591	C-GJQZ
EC-IBN	Aérospatiale AS.355N Ecureuil 2	5696	
EC-IBO	Aérospatiale AS.355N Ecureuil 2	5697	
EC-IBP	Ultramagic M-77 HAFB	77/198	
EC-IBQ	Ultramagic S-105 HAFB	105/94	
EC-IBR	Ultramagic S-105 HAFB	105/96	PH-DME C-GERC
EC-IBS	DHC-8 Series 315	560	PH-DME C-FERC
EC-IBT	DHC-8 Series 315	561	PH-DMI C-FCSG
EC-IBU	Robinson R-44 Raven	1141	
EC-IBV	Aérospatiale AS.350B3 Ecureuil	3489	F-WQPQ
EC-IBX	SNCASE SE.3130 Alouette II	1474	F-GPLU ALAT
EC-IBY	Pilatus PC-6/B2-H4	815	HB-FKF G-OAPA
EC-IBZ	Piper PA-25 Pawnee	25-66	N6059Z
EC-ICA	DHC-8 Series 315	562	PH-DML C-FDHO
EC-ICB	Piper PA-36-375 Pawnee Brave	36-7902005	TG-VEE N3963E
EC-ICC	Eurocopter EC.120B Colibri	1274	
EC-ICD	Boeing 737-81Q	30785	N308TA N1786B
EC-ICE	Reims/Cessna F172N	F17201879	N47PT F-WBQT F-GBQT
EC-ICF	Airbus A340-313X	459	F-WWJU
EC-ICG	Piper Aerostar 602P	62P-0628-7962386	N286CB VH-PHC N8226J
EC-ICH	Piper PA-34-200T Seneca	34-7970424	SE-LAV OH-PBK N2965Q
EC-ICI	SOCATA Rallye 100ST (Accident 9.3.03 nr Castejon)	2295	F-BULM
EC-ICL	Airbus A320-232	1682	F-WWBD
EC-ICM	Yakovlev Yak-52	833401	
EC-ICN	Airbus A320-214	1717	F-WWDC
EC-ICO	CASA 1-131E	2159	E.3B-. . .
EC-ICP	Schleicher ASW 20	20040	OE-5145
EC-ICQ	Airbus A320-211	199	EC-FGU EC-583 F-WWDI
EC-ICR	Airbus A320-211	240	EC-FIA EC-587 F-WWIP

EC-ICS	Airbus A320-211	241	EC-FIC EC-588 F-WWDD
EC-ICT	Airbus A320-211	264	EC-FKD EC-880 F-WWBN
EC-ICU	Airbus A320-211	303	EC-FML EC-883 F-WWDT
EC-ICV	Airbus A320-211	312	EC-FMN EC-884 F-WWIS
EC-ICX	DHC-8 Series 315	563	PH-DMM C-FDHU
EC-ICY	Cessna 172RG Cutlass	172RG1074	D-EOMZ N9905B
EC-IDA	Boeing 737-85Q	32773	N73791
EC-IDB	Airbus A330-243	461	F-WWKL
EC-IDC	Canadair CL.600-2B19 Regional Jet	7622	C-GJYV C-FMLT
EC-IDD	Ultramagic V-65 HAFB	65/109	
EC-IDE	Ultramagic M-65 HAFB	65/110	
EC-IDF	Airbus A340-313X	474	F-WWJG
EC-IDG	Aérospatiale/Alenia ATR-42-300	130	F-WQNE(2) F-WQOH(2) LZ-ATB F-WQLG D-BFFF F-WWEC
EC-IDH	Piper PA-A-36-375 Pawnee Brave	AR36-8002025	CS-AVO LV-OGC
EC-IDI	SOCATA Rallye 180TS Galérien	3025	D-EGYT
EC-IDJ	Cessna 172N	17271569	D-EADS N3492E
EC-IDK	DHC-8 Series 315	564	PH-DMP C-FDHV
EC-IDL	Piper PA-28R-200 Cherokee Arrow B	28R-7135075	D-EMDP N5071S
EC-IDM	Aérospatiale AS.355N Ecureuil 2	5698	F-WQPS
EC-IDN	Ultramagic M-77 HAFB	77/204	
EC-IDO	Ultramagic M-105 HAFB	105/98	
EC-IDP	Piper PA-28-180 Cherokee C	28-2768	SE-EPY N11C
EC-IDR	Piper PA-28-161 Warrior	2816070	D-EUUL N9144D
EC-IDS	Piper PA-34-200T Seneca II	34-7870429	G-BNEI N3058K VP-LBC N9646N
EC-IDT	Boeing 737-86Q	30281	N73793
EC-IDU	Aérospatiale AS.355F1 Ecureuil 2	5289	SE-JFE 9M-DPK 9V-BNI 9M-AYW F-ODVY F-WZFQ
EC-IDV	Piper PA-28-161 Warrior	2816023	G-BNOL
EC-IDX	Piper PA-34-220T Seneca III	3433120	G-BOCW N9612N
EC-IDY	Piper PA-34-220T Seneca III	3433122	G-BOCY N9614N
EC-IDZ	Air Création Safari GT BI F18	192021	
EC-IEA	Tecnam P.92ES Echo	P-92-ES-017	
EC-IEB	Cessna 525A CitationJet 2	525A-0064	N5135K
EC-IEC	Ultramagic M-65 HAFB	65/111	
EC-IED	Piper PA34-200 Seneca	34-7350123	G-BASX N15781
EC-IEE	Ultramagic N-250 HAFB	250/19	
EC-IEF	Airbus A320-214	1655	F-WWDY
EC-IEG	Airbus A320-214	1674	F-WWIL
EC-IEH	Cessna 172N Skyhawk II	17273212	D-ESMW(2) N6380F
EC-IEI	Airbus A320-214	1694	F-WWBT
EC-IEJ	Airbus A320-232	1749	F-WWBO
EC-IEK	Cessna 152	15284684	D-ESBC N6344M
EC-IEL	Aérospatiale SA.365C3 Dauphin 2	5017	F-GHXF LV-AID F-ODJL (F-GFIA) F-ODJL F-GBGV F-WTNW
EC-IEO	Cessna 172M	17265632	D-EEPS(3) N172WM N6893H
EC-IEQ	Airbus A320-214	1767	F-WWBV
EC-IER	Piper PA-28R-180 Cherokee Arrow	28R-30458	SE-FDG N4587J
EC-IES	Cameron N-77 HAFB	10256	
EC-IET	Cameron N-77 HAFB	10257	
EC-IEU	Bell 205A-1	30083	PT-HCR N8117J
EC-IEV	Cessna 208B Caravan I	208B0936	N40753
EC-IEY	Piper PA-28-161 Warrior	2842137	N53436
EC-IEZ	Boeing 737-33A	23628	N167AW (N3282G)
EC-IFA	Bell 212	30689	XC-GUJ
EC-IFB	Bell 222UT	47572	TC-HKL N32GH (N326H) N3209D
EC-IFD	Reims/Cessna F150K	F15000619	D-ECDA(2)
EC-IFE	Robinson R-44 Astro	0506	PH-ESP
EC-IFF	Piper PA-28-140 Cherokee Fliteliner	28-7125194	D-EHGL OE-DFB N415FL
EC-IFG	Ultramagic M-77 HAFB	77/199	
EC-IFH	Cameron N/Z-77 HAFB	10237	
EC-IFI	Cameron N-65 HAFB	10238	
EC-IFJ	Hispano HA-220	22/107	A.10C-102 C.10C-102
EC-IFK	DHC-8 Series 315	574	PH-DMX C-GFEN
EC-IFL	Vulcanair P.68C	412	
EC-IFM	Ultramagic M-77 HAFB	77/205	
EC-IFO	Ultramagic M-65 HAFB	65/116	
EC-IFP	Piper PA-28-161 Warrior II	28-8116103	D-ERAC N83079
EC-IFQ	Eurocopter EC.120B Colibri	1296	F-WQQT F-WQDK
EC-IFS	Bombardier BD.700-1A10	9089	C-GHZH
EC-IFU	Eurocopter EC.135P2	0223	
EC-IFV	Boeing 737-33A	23626	N165AW N3261W
EC-IFX	Partenavia P.68B	204	CS-AYQ G-BNXN CN-TCD HB-LLV
EC-IGA	Ultramagic M-77 HAFB	77/200	
EC-IGB	Reims/Cessna F172N	F17201717	D-EOZU
EC-IGC	Piper PA-23-250 Aztec C	27-2700	N53JM N5593Y
EC-IGD	SEEMS MS.893A Rallye Commodore 180	10478	F-BMVE
EC-IGE	DHC-8 Series 315	576	PH-DMY C-FCSG
EC-IGF	Piper PA-28R-201 Cherokee Arrow	28R-7737124	D-ENTS(2) G-BPDN N38959
EC-IGG	Robinson R-22B2 Beta	3288	N83754
EC-IGH	Robinson R-44 Raven	1189	N70704
EC-IGI	Piper PA-34-200 Seneca	34-7450016	G-SSFC G-BBXG N56647
EC-IGJ	Reims/Cessna FRA150L Aerobat (Dbr 20.10.04)	FRA1500232	PH-VBI OO-KMM (OO-HMM) (OO-WMM) N199ER PH-VBI OO-WAG (PH-VBH)
EC-IGK	Airbus A321-211	1572	EC-HTF D-AVZ I
EC-IGL	Cessna 172N Skyhawk II	17267794	G-JVMD G-BNTV N75539
EC-IGM	Aérospatiale SA.365N3 Dauphin 2	6616	
EC-IGO	Canadair CL.600-2B19 Regional Jet	7661	C-FVAZ
EC-IGP	Bell 212	30915	N5009N HK-3899X N1074C
EC-IGQ	Bell 212	30936	N5010F
EC-IGR	Bell 212	30989	N1074C HK-3900X N1074C
EC-IGS	DHC-8-315	586	C-FWBB
EC-IGT	Cessna T337G Super Skymaster	P337-0157	CC-CEA CC-PDN N60S
EC-IGU	Ultramagic N-250 HAFB	250/21	
EC-IGV	Air Tractor AT-802	802-0137	N8508Q
EC-IGX	Air Tractor AT-802	802-0115	N91465
EC-IGZ	Douglas DC-8-73CF	46133	N961R N801WA (N6165A)
EC-IHA	Piper PA-28-161 Cadet	2841293	N9202N
EC-IHC	Diamond DA 20-A1 Katana	10037	OE-ADM N10UV C-GKAI
EC-IHD	Cessna 208B Caravan I (Damaged 28.2.05)	208B0934	D-FOKM N5267D
EC-IHE	Ultramagic S-160 HAFB	160/31	
EC-IHF	Reims/Cessna F172N	F17201704	D-EHGY(2)
EC-IHG	Antonov An-2TP	1G238-20	J5- . . . SP-FBH SP-FBR
EC-IHH	Aérospatiale AS.350B2 Ecureuil	3581	
EC-IHJ	Air Tractor AT-802	802-0138	N8505Z
EC-IHK	Cessna 152	15281456	N64873
EC-IHL	Reims FR172J Rocket	FR17200460	F-BVBA
EC-IHM	Cessna F172H	F172-0634	D-EBUO
EC-IHN	Reims/Cessna F172N	F17201927	D-EKON(2)
EC-IHP	American AA-1 Yankee	AA1-0385	D-ELXC (N6185L)

EC-IHQ	Eurocopter EC.120B Colibri	1315	F-WQDX
			F-WQDE
EC-IHR	Robinson R-22 Beta	0897	CS-HBM
			G-RCGI
EC-IHS	Piper PA-34-200 Seneca	34-7250309	N1401T
EC-IHT	Piper PA-34-200 Seneca	34-7250163	N4877T
EC-IHU	Tecnam P.92JS Echo	016	
EC-IHX	Aérospatiale AS.350B3 Ecureuil	3587	F-WQRN
	(Code "6")		F-WQDM
EC-IHY	Cessna 421C Golden Eagle	421C1033	N2008K
			N929AK
			N442MM
			D-IRRR
			N6794S
EC-IHZ	Air Tractor AT-802	802-0119	N9148N
EC-IIA	DHC-8 Series 315	587	C-GDIU
EC-IIB	DHC-8 Series 315	588	C-GDIW
EC-IIC	Gates Learjet 35A	35A-346	(N34LZ)
			I-DLON
			N35AJ
			C-GMGA
			N3803G
EC-IID	Piper PA-28R-180 Cherokee Arrow	28R-30881	D-EAEN
			F-OCRF
			TR-LOA
			N7514J
EC-IIE	Robinson R-44 Raven	1240	
EC-IIF	Piper PA-28-161 Cadet	2841038	N9158J
EC-IIG	Airbus A321-211	1554	EC-HTE
			D-AVZG
EC-IIH	Airbus A340-313X	483	F-WWJI
EC-III	Boeing 737-86Q	30284	
EC-IIJ	Aérospatiale AS.350B3 Ecureuil	3585	
EC-IIK	Piper PA-28-161 Warrior II	2816028	G-BNOR
EC-IIL	Piper PA-28-161 Warrior II	2816033	G-BNOW
EC-IIM	Piper PA-34-220T Seneca III	3433115	G-BOCV
EC-IIN	Mooney M.20J Model 201	24-0494	N201XJ
			PH-SIN
			N201XJ
EC-IIO	Ultramagic M-90 HAFB	90/53	
EC-IIP	Piper PA-42-1000 Cheyenne 400	42-5527018	D-IIAQ
			N124DP
			N4112Z
EC-IIQ	Piper PA-28-181 Archer II	28-8490038	D-ELOE
			N9570N
			N4334L
EC-IIR	Embraer EMB-135BJ Legacy	145540	PT-S . .
EC-IIS	Diamond DA 20-A1 Katana	10116	N543ND
			N543SS
EC-IIT	Diamond DA 20-A1 Katana	10118	N545ND
			N545SS
EC-IIU	Cameron N-77 HAFB	10337	
EC-IIV	SOCATA TB-20 Trinidad	707	F-GFQD
EC-IIX	Robinson R-44 Raven	0952	D-HALZ
EC-IIY	Piper PA-34-200T Seneca II	34-7670337	ZS-MNU
			"ZS-MNC"
			N4458F
EC-IIZ	Airbus A320-231	1862	F-WWDZ
EC-IJB	Tecnam P.92JS Echo	020	
EC-IJC	Ultramagic H-77 HAFB	77/201	
EC-IJD	DHC-8 Series 315	589	C-GDKL
EC-IJE	Canadair CL.600-2B19 Regional Jet	7700	C-GZJZ
			C-FMMW
EC-IJF	Canadair CL.600-2B19 Regional Jet	7705	C-GZKC
			C-FMKW
EC-IJG	Vol 9/Best Off Sky Ranger	SKR 0104112	
EC-IJH	Airbus A330-322	076	D-AERG
			F-WWKY
EC-IJI	Piper PA28R-200 Arrow II	28R-7335013	D-EEPD
			N15072
EC-IJN	Airbus A321-211	1836	D-AVZN
EC-IJO	Beech 1900D	UE-300	F-GRPM
			N22120
EC-IJP	DHC-8 Series 315	582	PH-DMZ
			C-FDHV
EC-IJQ	Road Air Flamingo	043	
EC-IJR	Agusta A.109E Power	11137	
EC-IJS	Canadair CL.600-2B19 Regional Jet	7706	C-GZKD
EC-IJU	Airbus A321-231	1843	D-AVZR
EC-IJV	Piper PA-28-161 Warrior II	28-7716104	D-EGFF
			N9624N
EC-IJY	Cameron A-210 HAFB	10054	
EC-IJZ	Piper PA-34-200T Seneca II	34-8070049	ZS-LVZ
			N8131F
EC-IKA	DHC-8 Series 315	590	C-GDLD
EC-IKB	Eurocopter EC.135T2	0250	D-HTSF
			D-HECK
EC-IKC	Yakovlev Yak-52	866511	
EC-IKD	Ultramagic H-77 HAFB	77/196	
EC-IKE	Ultramagic S-105 HAFB	105/89	
EC-IKF	Piper PA-28-161 Warrior II	2816017	G-BNOI
			N9122N
EC-IKG	Piper PA-28-161 Warrior II	2816031	G-BNOU
EC-IKH	Piper PA-28-161 Warrior II	2816046	G-BOKN
			N9609N
EC-IKI	Piper PA-28-161 Warrior II	2816054	G-BOKU
EC-IKJ	Cessna 172S	172S8421	F-GPPL
			LN-PWN
			(SE-LPY)
			LN-PWD
			N7257R
EC-IKK	Aérospatiale/Alenia ATR-72-201	198	F-WQND(2)
			F-WQOG(2)
			F-WQOX
			SX-BSX
			F-WQJU
			EC-GQU
			F-WQGC
			B-22702
			F-WWEL
EC-IKL	Tecnam P.96 Golf	P-96-G-016	
EC-IKM	Cessna 208B Caravan I	208B0948	D-FMCG
EC-IKN	Agusta A.109A - II	7391	I-AGSL
EC-IKO	MBB Bö.105CBS-4	S-661	D-HGYN
			(D-HDUC)
EC-IKP	Grumman G.1159C Gulfstream IV	1109	N101GA
			V8-007
			V8-SR1
			V8-AL1
			N1761D
EC-IKQ	Aérospatiale/Alenia ATR-72-201	477	F-WQNM
			HS-PGF
			F-WWEI
EC-IKR	Eurocopter EC.135P2	0235	
EC-IKS	Aérospatiale AS.355N Ecureuil 2	5710	
EC-IKT	MBB Bö.105CBS-4	S-615	D-HEMS
			(D-HDSK)
EC-IKV	Eurocopter EC.130B4 Ecureuil	3753	
EC-IKX	Eurocopter EC.135P2	0222	G-79-07
			D-HEC .
EC-IKY	Eurocopter EC.135T2	0255	D-HECO
EC-IKZ	Canadair CL.600-2B19 Regional Jet	7732	C-GZUR
			C-FMMY
EC-ILA	Agusta A.109E Power	11028	F-GSMP
EC-ILB	Ultramagic M-65 HAFB	65/115	
EC-ILC	Mainair Blade 503	1057-1195-7-W855	EC-CH2
EC-ILD	Aérospatiale AS.350B2 Ecureuil	2598	HB-XUU
			F-WYME
EC-ILE	Beech B200 Super King Air	BB-1792	N5092K
EC-ILF	Canadair CL.600-2B19 Regional Jet	7746	C-FZQR
			C-FMNW
EC-ILG	Airbus A321-211	1233	G-VKIS
			D-AVZD
EC-ILH	Airbus A320-214	1914	F-WWDU
EC-ILI	Scheibe SF-25C Falke	44133	OE-9147
			D-KDDH
EC-ILJ	Cessna 421C Golden Eagle	421C0272	LZ-CCA
			N6390G
EC-ILK	Bombardier Learjet 45	45-064	N800UA
			N800MA
EC-ILL	Reims/Cessna F182Q	F1820072	SE-GYI
EC-ILM	Cessna 421C Golden Eagle	421C0045	N89Q
			OY-BZN
			(D-IABI)
			OY-BZN
			SE-INC
			LN-VIH
			N112GA
			D-ICST
			N9844B
EC-ILN	Aérospatiale SA.365N1 Dauphin 2	6234	LV-WLU
			F-WQDH
			F-ZVLP
EC-ILO	Airbus A321-211	1681	D-AVZW
EC-ILP	Airbus A321-211	1716	D-AVZT
EC-ILQ	Airbus A320-214	1736	F-WWDJ
EC-ILR	Airbus A320-214	1793	F-WWIM
EC-ILS	Airbus A320-214	1809	F-WWBC
EC-ILT	Reims/Cessna FT337GP Super Skymaster	FP3370021	I-BFIZ
	(Reims assembled P337G with US c/n P3370279)		G-BFIZ
EC-ILU	Cessna 172RG Cutlass RG	172RG0560	D-EDMS
			PH-AXE
			N5534V
			(N5434K)
EC-ILV	Robinson R-22B2 Beta	3411	
EC-ILX	Boeing 737-86N	28618	OK-TVQ
			N1786B
EC-ILY	Rolladen-Schneider LS3A	3205	F-CESG
EC-ILZ	Cameron A-210 HAFB	10076	
EC-IMA	Airbus A321-211	1219	G-VATH
			D-AVZB
EC-IMB	Airbus A320-214	1933	F-WWII
EC-IMC	Schleicher ASH 26E	26206	
EC-IMD	Partenavia P.68B	67	I-TIZY
EC-IME	Aérospatiale SA.315B Lama	2463	XC-BOI
			N47291
EC-IMF	Cessna 550 Citation II	550-0443	D-CGAS
			OY-CYT
			N777FB
			N777FE
			N1220S
EC-IMG	Eipper Quicksilver MXL-Sport IIR	0073	EC-CB6

EC-IMH	Aérospatiale/Alenia ATR-72-202	367	F-GJRQ
			HS-PGB
			F-WQAJ
			F-GKOK
			F-WWEX
EC-IMI	Ultramagic M-65 HAFB	65/119	
EC-IMJ	Ultramagic T-150 HAFB	150/02	
EC-IMK	Cameron A-250 HAFB	3823	SE-ZGP
EC-IML	Piper PA-28-180 Cherokee D	28-4838	SE-FDN
EC-IMM	Piper PA-28RT-201 Arrow IV	28R-7918242	F-GCTI
			N2969V
EC-IMN	Ultramagic T-150 HAFB	150/01	
EC-IMO	Ultramagic M-77 HAFB	77/215	
EC-IMP	BA Swallow 2	475	G-AEVZ
EC-IMQ	Piper PA-28-161 Warrior II	2816026	G-BNOO
EC-IMR	Piper PA-28-161 Warrior II	2816045	G-BOKM
EC-IMS	Cessna 170A	19097	N9536A
EC-IMT	Piper PA-28RT-201 Arrow IV	28-7918165	LX-FLY
			N2839K
EC-IMU	Airbus A320-214	1130	SE-RCD
			G-VKID
			F-WWIR
EC-IMV	Partenavia P.68C	290	TF-VEJ
			N714G
			N4496M
EC-IMX	Embraer EMB.120 Brasilia	120158	P4-RAL
			N312FV
			N131AM
			PT-SPW
EC-IMY	Boeing 727-225	21293	N8875Z
EC-IMZ	Bell 407	53547	C-GLZA
			(N2531Z)
EC-INA	Schleicher ASH 26E	26207	
EC-INB	Airbus A321-231	1946	D-AVXD
EC-INC	Beech 76 Duchess	ME-382	N7WZ
			G-DUCH
			N38033
EC-INE	Diamond DA 40 Star	40228	
EC-INF	Canadair CL.600-2B19 Regional Jet	7785	C-GYVM
			C-FMOI
EC-INH	Air Tractor AT-802	802-0139	N8507V
EC-INI	Ultramagic N-210 HAFB	210/21	
EC-INJ	Cessna 501 Citation I/SP	501-0086	N11SQ
			N501JP
			N501CW
			N32SX
			N583MP
			(N711AE)
			N88CF
			N8LG
			N3195M
EC-INK	de Havilland DH.60GIII Moth	5895	EC-ADE
	(Rebuilt in UK and returned to Spain 10.96,		EC-BAZ
	re-regd 7.03)		30-83
			EM-O . .
			G-ACXK
EC-INL	Aérospatiale AS.350B Ecureuil	3224	F-GMRP
EC-INM	Airbus A320-232	1979	F-WWBE
EC-INN	Bell 212	31146	SE-JLP
			HL-9213
			N5756W
EC-INO	Airbus A340-642	431	F-WWCI
EC-INP	Boeing 737-804	32903	SE-DZN
EC-INQ	Boeing 737-4Q8	25169	G-BSNW
EC-INR	Cameron N-77 HAFB	10392	
EC-INS	Gates Learjet 55B	55B-133	N810V
			N700R
			N55LF
			N155LJ
			N155PL
EC-INV	Aérospatiale/Alenia ATR-72-201	274	N274AT
			F-WWLC
EC-INX	CASA C.212-400MP	472	
EC-INY	Eurocopter EC.135T2	0275	
EC-INZ	Airbus A320-214	2011	F-WWBR
EC-IOA	Manuel Perez Rainbow	MPR 02-0001	
EC-IOB	Airbus A330-642	440	F-WWCL
EC-IOC	Robinson R-22 Mariner	1718M	G-PIKE
EC-IOD	Partenavia P.68C	229	G-BIFZ
EC-IOE	Air Tractor AT-802 (Cr 15.6.04)	802-0149	N8509Q
EC-IOF	Tecnam P.92ES Echo	P-92-ES-02	
EC-IOG	Reims/Cessna F172N	F17201523	D-EGQD
EC-IOH	Airbus A320-232	1998	F-WWIV
EC-IOI	Aérospatiale AS.350B3 Ecureuil (Code '80')	3640	
EC-IOJ	Aérospatiale AS.350B3 Ecureuil	3701	
EC-IOK	Cessna 421B	421B0398	HB-LRL
			N205PV
			N203PV
			(N41010)
EC-IOL	Air Tractor AT-301	301-0652	N600AB
			C-GTSE
EC-IOM	Agusta-Bell AB.212	5504	D-HAFV(2)
			I-AGUV
EC-ION	Eurocopter EC.135T2	0272	
EC-IOO	Boeing 747-341	24106	TF-ATH
			N830DS
			PP-VOA
			N6046P

EC-IOP	Vulcanair P.68 Observer 2	424-24/OB2	
EC-IOQ	Vulcanair P.68 Observer 2	422-22/OB2	
EC-IOR	Boeing 737-382	24449	LY-BAG
			CS-TID
EC-IOS	Piper PA-28-161 Warrior II	2816029	G-BNOS
EC-IOT	Piper PA-28-161 Warrior II	2816052	G-BOKS
EC-IOU	Boeing 737-4Y0	24689	PK-MBK
			EC-GVB
			PT-TDD
			EC-EXY
			EC-403
EC-IOV	DHC-8 Series 315	581	PH-DEJ
			C-FDHU
EC-IOX	Cessna 172P	17275025	OO-NZB
			G-BNYW
			N54655
EC-IOY	Cedimax Rans S-6ES-912	S6AV-0006	
EC-IOZ	Raytheon 390 Premier	RB-61	N61161
EC-IPA	SOCATA MS.893A Rallye Commodore 180	10647	F-BNSG
EC-IPB	Piper PA-34-200 Seneca	34-7350116	D-GBFW
			N15992
EC-IPC	Aérospatiale AS.350B3 Ecureuil	3710	
EC-IPE	Cameron Z-210 HAFB	10258	G-LGLG
EC-IPG	Vulcanair P.68 Observer 2	421-21/OB2	
EC-IPH	Tecnam P.92JS Echo	032	
EC-IPI	Airbus A320-232	2027	F-WWDP
EC-IPJ	Aérospatiale/Alenia ATR-72-202	307	F-GKOC
			F-WWEGG
EC-IPK	Diamond DA 20-A1	20129	G-BWFE
EC-IPL	Reims/Cessna FTB337G Super Skymaster		
		FTB3370020	FAP3719
EC-IPM	Bell 412	33050	C-GJKT
			TG-WOL
			H-123
			TG-WOL
EC-IPN	Boeing 747-212	21938	LV-YPC
			N924PG
			LY-YPC
			HL7453
			9V-SQM
EC-IPO	Cessna 421B Golden Eagle	421B0509	N630CP
			EC-FLT
			EC-955
			N630CP
			N69860
EC-IPP	Ultramagic H-31 HAFB	31/04	
EC-IPQ	Reims/Cessna F337G Skymaster	F33700056	G-NYTE
	(Reims-assembled 337G with US c/n 33701465)		G-BATH
			N10631
EC-IPR	Tecnam P.92 Echo Super	P-92-SP-014	
	(Wreck noted 3.05)		
EC-IPS	Boeing 737-33A	23827	CS-TMZ
			PT-TEX
			CS-TIN
			9H-ACS
			CS-TIN
			9H-ACS
			CS-TKD
			(LN-NOR)
			CS-TKD
			G-BNXW
			LN-NOR
			G-BNXW
			LN-NOR
			G-BNXW
			LN-NOR
EC-IPT	Airbus A310-325	642	N642KS
			A4O-OO
			HB-IPM
			F-WWCX
EC-IPU	Air Tractor AT-802	802-0150	N8509X
EC-IPV	Fokker F.28-0100	11451	PH-ZDJ
			PT-MRJ
			PH-EZT
EC-IPX	Tecnam P.92 Echo (Wreck noted 3.05)	unkn	
EC-IPY	Ultramagic M-77 HAFB	77/227	
EC-IPZ	Piper PA-31T2 Cheyenne IIXL	31T-8166056	D-ICGA
			N550TL
			N550T
			N9165Y
			(N715CA)
EC-IQA	Boeing 767-33AER	27310	N310AN
			VN-A768
			OO-SBY
EC-IQB	Air Création Safari GT BI Fun 18	194040	
EC-IQC	Air Tractor AT-802A (Amphibian)	802A-0155	N8512Q
EC-IQD	Diamond DA 40-180 Star	40229	
EC-IQE	Diamond DA 40-180 Star (Cr 23.3.04)	40239	
EC-IQF	Ultramagic T-180 HAFB	180/39	
EC-IQG	Cessna 152	15283177	N47131
EC-IQH	Cessna 152	15284065	N5138H
EC-IQI	Cessna 152	15281027	N48884
EC-IQJ	Ultramagic M-77 HAFB	77/229	
EC-IQK	Cedimax Rans S-12XL-582	S12AV-301	
EC-IQL	Piper PA-28-161 Warrior II	2816032	G-BNOV
EC-IQM	Piper PA-28-161 Warrior II	2816049	G-BOKO
			N9610N

EC-IQN	Piper PA-28-161 Warrior II	2816050	G-BOKP N9611N
EC-IQO	Piper PA-28-161 Warrior II	2816051	G-BOKR
EC-IQQ	Ultramagic T-180 HAFB	180/37	
EC-IQR	Airbus A340-642	460	F-WWCO
EC-IQS	SOCATA MS.893A Rallye Commodore 180	10687	F-BONG
EC-IQT	Ultramagic M-77 HAFB	77/70	
EC-IQU	Tecnam P.92 Echo S	P-92-ES-032	
EC-IQV	Piper PA-28R-180 Cherokee Arrow	28R-30548	D-ENBG N4654J
EC-IQX	Piper PA-46-350P Malibu Mirage	4622181	N9255H
EC-IQY	Cessna 182H Skylane	18256192	D-ECWI N2092X
EC-IQZ	Eurocopter EC.135P2	0293	
EC-IRA	Boeing 737-4Y0	24692	N692HE (PK-MBN) N692HE PP-VQT PT-TED EI-CBT N6069D (HR-SHM)
EC-IRB	Cessna 525 CitationJet CJ	525-0516	
EC-IRC	Kubicek BB-26 HAFB	256	OK-0256
EC-IRD	SAAB-Scania SF.340A	340A-081	OH-SAC N374DC F-GELG SE-E81
EC-IRE	Diamond DA 20-A1 Katana	10307	G-BXTR N607DA
EC-IRF	Ultramagic M-77 HAFB	77/235	
EC-IRG	SOCATA MS.894A Minerva 220	12079	F-BULA (D-ENMJ)
EC-IRH	Piper PA-28R-200 Cherokee Arrow	28R-35089	D-EBIM(2) 9XR-BM D-EBIM(2) N9380N
EC-IRI	Canadair CL.600-2B19	7851	C-GZNF C-FMMX
EC-IRJ	Piper PA-28-181 Archer II	28-8190218	D-EIGT N8379Z
EC-IRK	Reims/Cessna F150G	F150-0088	D-EKGB OE-AVK
EC-IRL	Robinson R-44 Raven II	10157	
EC-IRM	Robin DR.500/200i Président	25	F-GTZJ
EC-IRN	Ultramagic M-77 HAFB	77/239	
EC-IRO	Piper PA-28-181Cherokee Archer II	28-7690103	D-ECFC(2) N8124C
EC-IRP	Cessna 172N Skyhawk	17271494	PH-GVE N3296E
EC-IRQ	Agusta A.109E Power	11205	
EC-IRR	SAAB-Scania SF.340A	144	OH-SAF N375DC F-GHMK SE-F43
EC-IRS	Fairchild Swearingen SA-227BC Metro III	BC-786B	N61AJ XA-SCS N3200K
EC-IRT	Aérospatiale AS.350B3 Ecureuil	3717	
EC-IRV	Cessna 208B Grand Caravan	208B1038	N5174W
EC-IRX	Diamond DA 20-A1	10075	OE-VPZ N520SS
EC-IRY	Tecnam P.92 Echo S	P-92-ES-033	
EC-IRZ	Gulfstream V	582	N271JG N582GA
EC-ISA	Eurocopter EC.120B Colibri	1330	F-WQRX
EC-ISB	Aérospatiale AS.355N Ecureuil 2	5715	
EC-ISC	Piper PA-34-200T Seneca	34-7770403	ZS-MFP
EC-ISD	Cessna 337G Skymaster	33701650	YV-669P YV-TASP N53477
EC-ISE	Boeing 737-86Q	30290	N1786B
EC-ISF	Cameron Z-210 HAFB	10286	G-CBKX
EC-ISG	Ultramagic M-65C HAFB	65/127	
EC-ISH	Pilatus PC-12/45	498	HB-FPG
EC-ISI	Airbus A320-214	2123	F-WWIE
EC-ISJ	Piper PA-28-181 Cherokee Archer II (Dismantled - may be used in rebuild of EC-ETE)	28-7790478	PH-DVE N4581Q
EC-ISK	Lindstrand LBL-180A HAFB	824	G-CBNS
EC-ISM	Cessna 404 Titan	404-0614	5Y-LEA 5Y-EAG N31PG (N2684Y)
EC-ISN	Boeing 737-86Q	30291	
EC-ISO	Tecnam P.92 Echo S	P-92-ES-013	
EC-ISP	Cessna 501 Citation I/SP	501-0084	G-CITI VP-CDM VR-CDM G-CITI (N11JC) (N463CJ) N3160M
EC-ISQ	Cessna 560XL Citation Excel	560-5353	N5250E N678QS
EC-ISR	SOCATA TB-20 Trinidad	325	D-EPUK OO-RDL (D-EEKX)
EC-ISS	Cessna 525A CitationJet 2	525A-0415	N26SW N252DE
EC-IST	Schweizer S.269C	S-1850	N69A
EC-ISU	Tecnam P.96 Golf	P96-G-029	
EC-ISV	DHC-6 Twin Otter Series 200	205	OY-PAE LQ-JMM LV-JMM LV-PMP
EC-ISX	Aérospatiale/Alenia ATR 42-300	242	N242AT F-WWEW
EC-ISY	Boeing 757-256	26241	N26ND EC-FXV EC-617 EC-FUB EC-422
EC-ISZ	Aérospatiale AS.355N Ecureuil 2	5723	
EC-ITA	Ultramagic M-77 HAFB	77/210	
EC-ITB	Robin HR.200/100 Club	66	OO-VSC
EC-ITC	Robinson R-22B2 Beta	3508	N75297
EC-ITD	Robinson R-44 Raven II (W/o 20.12.04)	10201	
EC-ITE	DG Flugzeugbau DG-800B	8-258B166	D-KIAJ(3)
EC-ITF	Kubicek BB-26 HAFB	252	OK-0252
EC-ITH	Cessna 172	unkn	
EC-ITJ	Eurocopter EC.135T2	0306	
EC-ITK	Cameron DP-80 Hot Air Airship	2344	G-BTBR
EC-ITL	Ultramagic M-77 HAFB	77/230	
EC-ITM	Tecnam P.92 Echo Super	P.92-SP-017	
EC-ITN	Airbus A321-211	2115	D-AVXG
EC-ITO	SOCATA MS.892A Rallye Commodore 150	11707	F-BSKI
EC-ITP	Fairchild Swearingen SA.227BC Metro III	BC-789B	XA-SES N3003T
EC-ITQ	Diamond DA40D Star	D4.041	OE-UDV
EC-ITR	Westland-Bell 47G-3B1	WA/514	G-BGMU XT807
EC-ITS	Reims/Cessna F172M	F17200930	D-ECUT(2)
EC-ITT	Glaser-Dirks DG-200	2-56	I-ANNC
EC-ITU	Canadair CL.600-2B19 Regional Jet	7866	C-GZSQ C-FMNW
EC-ITV	Partenavia P.68C-TC	239-05/TC	SP-KWA VH-TCU
EC-ITX	Cessna 172R	17280778	N9552F
EC-ITY	Cessna 172R	17280546	N23862 N4115W
EC-ITZ	Ultramagic T-180 HAFB	180/40	
EC-IUA	Boeing 747-230B (Stored)	23509	D-ABZE N6038E
EC-IUB	Piper PA-34-220T Seneca III	3449280	N53199 N5365M
EC-IUC	Boeing 737-86N	28612	TC-SUA N1786B
EC-IUD	Cessna 172N Skyhawk	17270396	G-BOMT N739AU
EC-IUE	Kubicek BB-22 HAFB	265	OK-0265
EC-IUF	Ultramagic M-65C HAFB	65/128	
EC-IUG	Glaser-Dirks DG-400	4-90	HB-2082 (PH-742)
EC-IUJ	Air Tractor AT-802A	802A-0154	C-GYZB N51101
EC-IUK	Piper PA-28-161 Warrior II	2842178	N53665
EC-IUL	Piper PA-28-140 Cherokee D	28-7125045	D-EHFD N1730T
EC-IUM	Robinson R-22B2 Beta	2802	CS-HEF
EC-IUN	Eurocopter EC.135T2	0317	
EC-IUO	Aérospatiale AS.350B2 Ecureuil	2393	EC-HYV OE-OXT F-WYMN
EC-IUP	SAAB-Scania SF.340A	340A-083	OH-SAD N376DC F-GFBZ SE-E83
EC-IUQ	Bombardier CL.700-1A10 Global Express	9007	N907GX M28-001 C-GCRW M28-001 C-GCRW
EC-IUR	Cessna 150M	15076120	EC-HZK N66555
EC-IUS	Agusta A.109E Power	11229	
EC-IUT	Flight Design CT-2K	03-06-01-AR	
EC-IUU	Tecnam P.92JS Echo	035	
EC-IUV	Beech 200 Super King Air	BB-366	D-IBHK N1230
EC-IUX	Beech B200 Super King Air	BB-1840	N816LD
EC-IUY	Ultramagic M-77 HAFB	77/241	
EC-IUZ	Eurocopter EC.120B Colibri	1366	
EC-IVA	Cameron C-70 Concept HAFB	10520	
EC-IVB	Cameron C-70 Concept HAFB	10526	
EC-IVC	Partenavia P.68B	160	N200VE YV-1538P
EC-IVD	SAAB-Scania SF.340A	340A-117	EC-INU OH-SAE N378DC F-GHDB SE-F17
EC-IVG	Airbus A320-232	2168	F-WWDA
EC-IVH	Canadair CL.600-2B19 Regional Jet	7915	C-FADU
EC-IVI	Piper PA-28-161 Warrior II	2842172	N53532 N9512N

EC-IVJ	Cessna 525 CitationJet CJ	525-0429	N429PK
EC-IVK	Reims/Cessna F177RG Cardinal RG	F177RG0139	HZ-VIP
			N31062
EC-IVL	Air Tractor AT-802	802-0159	N85152
EC-IVM	Air Tractor AT-802A Amphibian	802A-0168	N85210
EC-IVN	Ultramagic T-180 HAFB	180/41	
EC-IVO	Fokker F.28-0100	11452	PH-RRN
			PT-WHK
			PH-RRN
			PT-MCN
			PH-EZU
EC-IVP	Aérospatiale/Alenia ATR-42-300	231	F-GKND
EC-IVQ	Grob G.104 Speed Astir IIB	4045	D-4504
			HB-1502
EC-IVR	Boeing 737-4Q8	24352	OO-RMV
			TF-FIA
EC-IVS	Reims/Cessna F150L	F15000889	OO-WIE
EC-IVT	Robinson R-44 Raven II	10307	
EC-IVU	PZL M-18A Dromader	1Z018-18	N7015H
EC-IVV	Boeing 737-883	28323	EI-CXU
			LN-RPD
			SE-DYA
			N1786B
EC-IVX	Air Tractor AT-502B	502B-0349	N60762
EC-IVY	Grob G.102 Standard Astir II	5017S	D-8407
			HB-1528
EC-IVZ	Piper PA-46-500TP Malibu Meridian	4697170	N3046P
EC-IXA	Grob G-103A Twin II Acro	3544-K-1	D-2913
EC-IXB	Kubicek BB-30 HAFB	295	OK-0295
EC-IXC	Kubicek BB-30 HAFB	296	OK-0296
EC-IXD	Airbus A321-211	2220	D-AVZR
EC-IXE	Boeing 737-883	30468	EI-CXT
			OY-KKT
			LN-RPR
			SE-DTP
			N1787B
EC-IXF	Maule MX-7-235 Star Rocket	4059C	
EC-IXG	Air Tractor 802A	802A-0169	
EC-IXH	Aérospatiale AS.355F1 Ecureuil 2	5009	D-HFAI(2)
			N5774M
			HC-BFC
			N5774M
EC-IXI	Aérospatiale AS.355N Ecureuil 2	5725	
EC-IXJ	Air Tractor AT-401	401-0795	N4549B
EC-IXK	Aérospatiale AS.350B Ecureuil	3801	F-WQDA
EC-IXL	Fairchild Swearingen SA.226AC Metro III	AC-689	D-COLC
			N706C
			N689NE
			N2705F
EC-IXM	SOCATA MS.893A Rallye Commodore 180	11821	D-EOBI
EC-IXN	Ultramagic M-90 HAFB	90/64	
EC-IXO	Boeing 737-883	30467	EI-CXP
			LN-RPO
			SE-DTN
EC-IXP	Piper PA-31 Navajo C	31-7812095	SE-IAC
EC-IXQ	Reims/Cessna FTB337G Super Skymaster	FTB3370018	CS-DPB
			FAP:3717
			CS-AAT
EC-IXR	Reims/Cessna FTB337G Super Skymaster	FTB3370019	CS-DPC
			FAP:3718
			CS-AAV
EC-IXS	Piper PA-28-161 Warrior III	2842204	N53599
EC-IXT	Piper PA-28-161 Warrior III	2842205	N30910
EC-IXU	Bell 412	33037	N177EH
			N177LG
			N177EH
			N412S
			N412SA
			XC-HAN
			N413CH
EC-IXV	Bell 412	33068	N422EH
EC-IXX	Bell 412	33043	N419EH
EC-IXY	Airbus A321-211	1006	G-OOAI
			D-AVZJ
EC-IXZ	Beech A36TC	EA-31	I-CINO
			N817BK
			N6695Z
EC-IYA	ICP Bingo	02-09-52-074	EC-014 ?
EC-IYB	Airbus A330-202	205	I-VLEC
			F-WQQM
			N205KB
			C-GGWA
			F-WWKK
EC-IYC	Aérospatiale/Alenia ATR-72-212A	709	F-WWEI
EC-IYD	Tecnam P.96-G Golf	P96-G-032	
EC-IYE	Aérospatiale/Alenia ATR-42-300	025	EC-HVR
			F-GLIB
			F-GHME
			DQ-FEK
			F-WWED
EC-IYF	Cessna 172R	17280057	N375ES
EC-IYG	Airbus A320-232	2210	F-WWBG
EC-IYH	Aérospatiale/Alenia ATR-72-202	330	F-WQUI
			SX-BAP
			F-GKOH
			F-WWLL
EC-IYI	Boeing 737-883	30194	EI-CXW
			LN-RPP
			SE-DTO
			N1787B
EC-IYJ	Reims/Cessna F172N	F17201940	D-EOVV(2)
EC-IYK	Reims/Cessna F172M	F17201101	D-EDXN
EC-IYL	Air Tractor AT-401	401-0739	N89KC
EC-IYM	Air Tractor AT-401	401-0836	N1518V
EC-IYN	Airbus A330-202	211	I-VLED
			C-GGWB
			F-WWKL
EC-IYO	Bell 212	30946	C-GZMZ
			B-7701
			B-721
EC-IYP	Bell 212	30533	C-FZPX
			PK-HCK
			G-BGMI
			EP-HCB
			VR-BEE
			N2916W
EC-IYS	Boeing 737-4Y0	24690	N254RY
			EC-HVY
			PP-NAC
			EC-GUI
			EI-CDU
			SE-DRR
			PT-TDC
			EC-GHK
			EC-308
			PT-TDA
			EC-FBP
			EC-603
			TC-AFL
EC-IYT	Aérospatiale AS.350B3 Ecureuil	3805	
EC-IYU	Piper PA-28-161 Warrior II	2816044	G-BOKL
EC-IYV	Piper PA-34-220T Seneca III	3433113	G-BOCT
EC-IYX	Piper PA-34-220T Seneca III	3433121	G-BOCX
EC-IYY	Piper PA-34-220T Seneca III	3433155	G-BSOY
			OY-CEU
EC-IYZ	Bell 407	53599	
EC-IZA	Ultramagic M-77 HAFB	77/252	
EC-IZB	Bell 407	53601	
EC-IZC	Tecnam P.92 Echo	P-92-E-014	
EC-IZD	Airbus A320-214	2207	F-WWDS
EC-IZE	Eurocopter EC.135T2	0309	
EC-IZF	Kubicek BB20GP HAFB	293	OK-0293
EC-IZG	Boeing 737-46J	27213	SX-BMB
			D-ABAG
EC-IZH	Airbus A320-214	2225	F-WWID
EC-IZI	Ultramagic N-180 HAFB	180/43	
EC-IZJ	ICP Bingo	03-04-52-104	EC-DZ3
EC-IZK	Airbus A320-232	2223	F-WWDO
EC-IZL	Boeing 747-287B	22592	LV-OOZ
EC-IZM	Boeing 737-33A	24027	F-GFUD
EC-IZN	Ultramagic M-105 HAFB	105/116	
EC-IZO	Aérospatiale/Alenia ATR-72-212A	711	F-WWEK
EC-IZP	Canadair CL.600-2B19 Regional Jet	7950	C-FBFI
			C-FMLQ
EC-IZR	Airbus A320-214	2242	F-WWDA
EC-IZS	Robinson R-22B2 Beta	2979	D-HALA(2)
			PH-HVZ
EC-IZT	Vol 9/Best Off Sky Ranger	SKR0306347	
EC-IZU	Ultramagic M-105 HAFB	105/117	
EC-IZV	Piper PA-28-180 Cherokee Challenger	28-7305490	OY-SVD
			SE-GDK
EC-IZX	Airbus A340-642	601	F-WWCS
EC-IZY	Airbus A340-642	604	F-WWCH
EC-IZZ	Ultramagic S-105 HAFB	105/108	
EC-JAA	DG Flugzeugbau DG-1000S	10-51S50	
EC-JAB	Airbus A320-214	2227	F-WWIG
EC-JAC	Air Tractor AT-802A	802A-0177	N8525Z
EC-JAD	Aérospatiale/Alenia ATR-42-300	321	F-GHPY
			F-WWES
EC-JAF	Cessna U206G Stationair 6	U206-06011	I-PAVR
			(D-EOMG)
			M4746Z
EC-JAG	Ted Smith Aerostar 601	61-0307-109	N26LL
EC-JAH	Aérospatiale/Alenia ATR-72-212A	712	F-WWEL
EC-JAI	Air Tractor AT-802	802-0176	N8524J
EC-JAJ	SOCATA TB-9 Tampico	227	G-BJOT
EC-JAK	Kamov KA.32A11BC	9624/8811/11	
EC-JAL	Kamov KA.32A11BC	9625/8812/12	
EC-JAM	Aérospatiale AS.365N1 Dauphin 2	6325	I-TTLL
			F-WTNV
EC-JAN	DG Flugzeugbau DG-500MB	5E213B12	HB-2365
EC-JAO	Ultramagic M-77 HAFB	77/245	
EC-JAP	Boeing 737-85P	33971	
EC-JAQ	Aérospatiale AS.350B Ecureuil	1352	F-GKCG
			N300HS
			XC-HEU
			N1350N
EC-JAR	Bell 407	53370	N54LM
			N60419
			C-GLZQ
EC-JAS	Cessna 177RG Cardinal RG	177RG0890	N90GS
			N7609V
EC-JAT	Air Tractor AT-802A Amphibian	802A-0179	N8516X

EC-JAU	Air Tractor AT-401	401-1149	
EC-JAV	Tecnam P.92JS Echo	038	
EC-JAX	Cessna 421C Golden Eagle	421C0337	HB-LQT F-GATY (N37396)
EC-JAY	Air Tractor AT-401	401-1150	
EC-JAZ	Airbus A319-111	2264	D-AVWQ
EC-JBA	Airbus A340-642	606	F-WWCV
EC-JBB	Dassault Falcon 900	182	N168HT F-WWFB
EC-JBC	Ultramagic T-180 HAFB	180/46	
EC-JBD	Embraer EMB-120ER Brasilia	120012	D-CAOB(2) N120AM PT-SIG
EC-JBE	Embraer EMB-120RT Brasilia	120013	D-CAOA(2) N122AM PT-SII
EC-JBF	Ultramagic M-65-C HAFB	65/138	EC-041
EC-JBG	Cessna 152	15280160	D-ENGN N24225
EC-JBH	Dassault Falcon 200	511	F-WQBK VT-TTA (F-GNMF) F-OLET F-WGTF F-OGSI F-WWGR
EC-JBI	Aérospatiale/Alenia ATR-72-212A	713	F-WWEM
EC-JBJ	Boeing 737-85P	33972	
EC-JBK	Boeing 737-85P	33973	
EC-JBL	Boeing 737-85P	33974	
EC-JBM	Air Tractor AT-502B	502B-0687	N8520K
EC-JBN	Aérospatiale/Alenia ATR-42-300	218	F-GHPK F-WWEC
EC-JBO	Tecnam P.92 Echo (Also believed to have Italian c/n 258 ex- D-MOHT)	P-92-E-006	EC-DM7
EC-JBP	Piper PA-18-150 Super Cub	18-8309001	N45540 IDFAF117
EC-JBQ	Ultramagic M-77 HAFB	77/255	
EC-JBR	Piper PA-28-161 Warrior II	2816053	G-BOKT
EC-JBS	Piper PA-34-220T Seneca III	3433089	G-BOCP
EC-JBT	Beech 1900D	UE-308	N22841
EC-JBU	Bell 407	53241	I-FREC C-GBLC (N42978)
EC-JBV	Bell 407	53613	C-FBXL (N8061T)
EC-JBX	Aérospatiale/Alenia ATR-42-300	254	N255AE N254AT F-WWEJ
EC-JBY	Reims/Cessna F172M	F17200935	D-ECUY
EC-JBZ	Reims/Cessna F172L	F17200896	D-EGSB F-BTUT
EC-JCA	Piper PA-28RT-201T Turbo Arrow IV	28R-803116	D-EJKK N8219N
EC-JCB	Robinson R-22B2 Beta	3672	
EC-JCC	Cessna 421C Golden Eagle	421C-0099	LN-BAU OE-FCA D-IACS N578AC D-IFLS OE-FLS N98800
EC-JCD	Aérospatiale/Alenia ATR-72-201	452	F-WQND HS-PGC F-WWEW
EC-JCE	Bell 412	33087	C-FBWY N9043S N301FD N3176M
EC-JCF	Aérospatiale/Alenia ATR-72-212A	595	OY-CIO F-WWEB
EC-JCG	Canadair CL.600-2B19 Regional Jet	7973	C-FCEU C-FMNB
EC-JCH	Ultramagic M-65 HAFB	65/130	
EC-JCI	Piper PA-28-161 Warrior II	28-8316044	PH-SVF N4305D N4293C
EC-JCJ	SZD-50-3 Puchacz	B-1537	SP-3691 D-4653 DDR-3653
EC-JCK	Cameron N-77 HAFB	10643	
EC-JCL	Canadair CL.600-2B19 Regional Jet	7975	C-FCID C-FMKW
EC-JCM	Canadair CL.600-2B19 Regional Jet	7981	C-FCNN C-FMLS
EC-JCN	Flight Design CT-2K	04-03-04-AR	
EC-JCO	Canadair CL.600-2B19 Regional Jet	7984	C-FCRX C-FMMT
EC-JCP	Robinson R-22 Beta	2737	
EC-JCQ	Tecnam P.2002JF Sierra	005	
EC-JCR	Aérospatiale/Alenia ATR-72-212A	468	OY-CIM F-WWLV
EC-JCS	Flight Design CT-2K	03-07-06-AR	
EC-JCT	Mooney M.20K Model 231	25-0827	N5763A
EC-JCU	Fairchild Swearingen SA.227AC Metro IV	AC-679B	N6UB VH-UUC N364AE
EC-JCV	Swearingen SA.226AT Merlin IVA	AT-038	SX-BGT EC-FUX EC-509 OO-JPN N5FJ SAAF:12 N5360M
EC-JCY	Airbus A340-642	617	F-WWCL
EC-JCZ	Airbus A340-642	619	F-WWCP
EC-JDB	Ultramagic V-77 HAFB	77/246	
EC-JDE	SOCATA TB-9 Tampico	879	D-EANL(3)
EC-JDG	Eurocopter EC.135T2	0354	
EC-JDH	Boeing 747-287B	21726	LV-MLP
EC-JDI	Robin ATL	100	F-GFST
EC-JDK	Airbus A320-214	1769	9H-ADY F-WWDK
EC-JDL	Airbus A319-111	2365	D-AVYN
EC-JDM	Airbus A321-211	2357	D-AVZV
EC-JDN	Fokker F.28-0100	11322	F-OLLD F-WLLD F-GLLP PT-MRD PH-LNE
EC-JDO	Airbus A320-214	2114	OY-VKN F-WWDZ
EC-JDQ	Aérospatiale AS.365N Dauphin 2	unkn	EC-IZQ
EC-JDR	Airbus A320-214	2347	F-WWBG
EC-JDS	Ultramagic H-65 HAFB	65/139	
EC-JDT	Robinson R-44 Raven	unkn	
EC-JDU	Boeing 737-86N	32655	
EC-JDV	Dassault Falcon 20E-5	237/476	HB-VJV VR-BKH VR-CBT N4227Y D-CITY (D-CALM) (D-CHCH) F-WPXF
EC-JDX	Aérospatiale/Alenia ATR-72-201	234	F-GHPV
EC-JDY	Beech 1900C-1	UC-91	N91YV S9-CAF N91YV
EC-JDZ	SOCATA TB-9 Tampico	286	D-EORP HB-EQO
EC-JEA	Aérospatiale AS.350B3 Ecureuil	3819	SE-JHX
EC-JEC	Piper PA-18-150 Super Cub	18-5353	F-BSEB ALAT N10F
EC-JED	Cessna 411A	411A0272	D-IHAM(2) N2620 (N3272R)
EC-JEE	Canadair CL.600-2B19 Regional Jet	7989	C-FCZD C-FMOS
EC-JEF	Canadair CL.600-2B19 Regional Jet	80089	C-FDKH C-FMMQ
EC-JEG	Bombardier BD-100-1A10 Challenger 300	20025	N125LJ C-GZEB
EC-JEH	Aérospatiale/Alenia ATR-72-212A	716	F-WWET
EC-JEI	Airbus A319-111	2311	D-AVYG
EC-JEJ	Airbus A321-211	2381	D-AVZI
EC-JEN	Canadair CL.600-2B19 Regional Jet	7958	C-FBQO C-FMNY
EC-JEO	Tecnam P.96 Golf	unkn	
EC-JEP	Tecnam P.2002JF Sierra	A006 ?	
EC-JEV	Aérospatiale/Alenia ATR-72-212	717	
EC-JEX	Boeing 737-86N	32659	
EC-JFB	Boeing 737-86N	32658	
EC-JFD	Cessna 525 CitationJet	525-0448	N448JC
EC-JFF	Airbus A320-214	2388	F-WWIH
EC-JFG	Airbus A320-214	2143	F-WWBV
EC-JFH	Airbus A320-214	2104	(EC-IQK) F-WWBE
EC-JFN	Airbus A320-214	2391	F-WWDB
EC-JFO	Pilatus PC-12/45	549	G-CCPU HB-FQE
EC-JFR	Boeing 747-228B	22272	F-GCBB N1289E (F-GCBB)
EC-JFX	Airbus A340-642	672	F-WWCB
EC-JFZ	Piper PA-28-181 Archer II	28-7990548	HB-PMZ N2910G
EC-JGA	Diamond DA 40 Star	40067	G-MOPB
EC-JGB	Beech B200 Super King Air	unkn	

UNIDENTIFIED AIRCRAFT

The following aircraft are thought to have been exported to Spain but no Spanish marks are yet known and any positive identifications would therefore be most welcome. Many overseas-registered aircraft are now operated in Spain and may not be required to take up local marks; some of these may be included below.

EC-J . .	Aérospatiale AS.350B3 Ecureuil	3785	N18HX
EC- . . .	Aérospatiale/Alenia ATR-72-201	196	PH-XLH F-WQGO B-22701 F-WWEI
EC- . . .	Agusta-Bell 206B Jet Ranger II	8620	G-BPIC D-HEAS I-CELT
EC-J . .	Airbus A320-211	234	JY-JAR CS-TNC F-WWDF N493GX F-WWDF
EC- . . .	Airbus A320-214 (Stored pending delivery)	2248	F-WWIK
EC-J . .	Airbus A321-211	2472	D-AVXA
EC- . . .	Air Command 532	PFA G/04-1147	G-BRKZ
EC-J . .	Air Tractor AT-802A	802A-0178	N85253
EC-J . .	Air Tractor AT-802A	802A-0190	N85230
EC- . . .	Antonov An-2R (Reported at Malaga still as LY-AHH)	1G212-34	LY-AHH CCCP32729
EC- . . .	Avialsa-Scheibe A.60	87K	F-CDBO
EC- . . .	Bede BD-5B	22	N522PR
EC- . . .	Beech 23 Musketeer	M-116	N2393Z
EC-J . .	Bell 412	33126	C-FAKF N412PK N412PD
EC-J . .	Bellanca 8KCAB Decathlon	508-79	N5044U
EC-J . .	Boeing 737-832	30826	N3775
EC-I . .	Boeing 747-412 (Still regd in Singapore)	24061	9V-SMA N5573B
EC-J . .	Boeing 747-287B	22593	LV-OPA
EC-I . .	Boeing Stearman A75N1	75-862	SE-BOF N56561 41-802
EC- . . .	Cameron SS Packet HAFB (Believed operated in Spain but EC- marks NTU)	560	G-BHJV
EC- . . .	Cameron V-31 HAFB (Believed "not registered" - Hoppers possibly exempt at the time)	867	
EC- . . .	Cameron R-60 HAFB	2057	
EC- . . .	Cameron C-60 HAFB	3477	
EC- . . .	Cameron C-80 Concept HAFB	4729	
EC- . . .	CASA 1-131E (painted as E.3B-179)	unkn	
EC-J . .	Centrair 101A Pégase	101A-0274	PH-804
EC-J . .	Cessna 172S	172S9678	N6135G
EC-I . .	Cessna 180	31554	N3050R 4X-CHB HB-CRB N4565B
EC- . . .	Cessna T206H Turbo Stationair	T20608429	N2163S
EC-J . .	Cessna 208B Grand Caravan	208B1024	G-WIKY N5117U
EC-J . .	Cessna T303 Crusader	T30300058	N1306C
EC- . . .	Reims/Cessna F337F Super Skymaster (Reims-assembled 337F with US c/n 33701357)	F33700033	F-BSHU
EC-J . .	Cessna 337G Skymaster	33701538	CC-PGH
EC-J . .	Cessna 421	421-0189	F-GCFV N4589L
EC-J . .	Cessna 560 Citation Ultra	560-0506	G-OGRG G-RIBV N50820
EC- . . .	Colt AS-56 Hot Air Airship	751	G-BMJP (PH-OET) G-BMJP
EC- . . .	Colt 77A HAFB	2025	
EC-I . .	Eurocopter EC.135T2	0313	
EC- . . .	Eurocopter EC.135T2	0345	
EC-J . .	Eurocopter EC.135T2	0358	
EC-J . .	Eurocopter EC.135T2	0366	
EC-J . .	Eurocopter EC.135T2	0377	
EC-I . .	Grob G.103 Twin Astir	3153	F-CFBV
EC-J . .	Grob G.109B	6242	G-BZLY D-KLMG G-BZLY OE-9230
EC-J . .	Gulfstream G200	103	N203GA
EC- . . .	Hughes 369D	108-0363D	N501RR N501RB N501RP
EC- . . .	Kamov KA.32T	unkn	
EC- . . .	LET L-23 Super Blanik	907807	
EC-J . .	Mitsubishi MU.300 Diamond 1A	A.084SA	N160H N160S N840TJ (N84DT) (N484VS) N484DM
EC-J . .	Piper PA-18A-150 Super Cub	18-5428	(LV-FPF)
EC- . . .	Piper PA-18-150 Super Cub	18-8548	D-E . . . N4296Z
EC- . . .	Piper PA-23-250 Aztec C	27-3426	EC-831 N6198Y
EC- . . .	Piper PA-23-250 Aztec C	27-4126	N6789Y EC-HEX N6789Y
EC-J . .	Piper PA-28-161 Cherokee Warrior II	28-7816652	SE-IAL
EC-J . .	Piper PA-28-161 Warrior II	2816019	G-BNOK N9122U
EC-J . .	Piper PA-28-180 Cherokee E	28-5727	D-EHGC(2) N3688R
EC-J . .	Piper PA-28-181 Cherokee Archer II	28-7690149	SE-GNE
EC-J . .	Piper PA-28-181 Archer II	28-8190164	D-ENCH(3) N8295H N9518N
EC-J . .	Piper PA-34-220T Seneca III	3433111	G-BOCR
EC-J . .	Piper PA-34-220T Seneca III	3433112	G-BOCS
EC-J . .	Piper PA-34-220T Seneca III	3433114	G-BOCU
EC- . . .	Piper PA-34-220T Seneca II	3448018	N141JL VH-YSE N92216
EC- . . .	Piper PA-36-375 Pawnee Brave	36-7802019	N2393Y 4X-AQJ N66602 YS-665A N9731N
EC- . . .	Piper PA-36-375 Brave	36-8102009	N6150A
EC- . . .	PZL-106BT-601 Turbo Kruk	10890228	SP-WAB
EC- . . .	PZL-106BT-601 Turbo Kruk	10890229	SP-WAC
EC- . . .	Quad City Challenger II	CH2-1189-0481	C-ICPZ
EC- . . .	Raven S-60A HAFB	S60A-384	N2790Y
EC-J . .	Robinson R-44 Raven	0965	N519KD
EC-J . .	Robinson R-44 Raven	1446	
EC- . . .	Rutan VariEze	1959	F-PYYZ
EC-I . .	SAAB-Scania SF.340A (Probably ntu, current as SE-KPE)	340A-055	SE-KPE LN-NVE SE-E55
EC- . . .	Scheibe SF-25D Falke	4834D	D-KHEQ
EC-J . .	Schempp-Hirth Ventus b/16.6	153	OO-ZLC D-2521
EC-I . .	Schleicher ASW 24	24075	OY-HEX D-9022
EC-J . .	Sikorsky S-76C-2	760576	N7107J
EC-J . .	Sikorsky S-76C-2	760578	N7105G
EC- . . .	SOCATA MS.880B Rallye Club	1187	F-BPHM
EC-I . .	SOCATA MS.893A Rallye Commodore 180	10793	D-EGPT F-BPGT
EC- . . .	SOCATA Rallye 100ST	2918	F-GARG
EC-J . .	SOCATA Rallye 180TS Galérien	3334	D-EFRM
EC- . . .	Stemme S-10V (Former c/n 14-007) (Cuatro Vientos Museum still as D-KGCL)	14-060M	D-KGCL(2)
EC- . . .	SNCASE SE.3130 Alouette II	1557	F-GPLO ALAT
EC- . . .	Sud Avn SA.316B Alouette III	1669	PK-TRZ PK-OAC 9M-ASX VR-HGJ
EC- . . .	Sud Avn SA.316B Alouette III	1760	PK-TPW PH-NNU
EC- . . .	Sud Avn SA.316B Alouette III	1799	PK-TRY PK-OAE PK-DAJ N9702
EC-I . .	Sukhoi SU-26	03-04	N215YA 24 Black DOSAAF
EC- . . .	Sukhoi SU-31	02-05	ZU-AVG
EC-J . .	Tecnam P.2002JF Sierra (Was noted painted as EC-JEV in error, probably EC-JEP)	A006	
EC- . . .	Ultramagic N-300 HAFB	300/ . . .	
EC- . . .	Ultramagic V-105 HAFB	105/ . . .	

HOMEBUILT AIRCRAFT AND MICROLIGHTS

EC-YAA	Monnet Sonerai II	1	
EC-YAB	AX-9-140 Tramontana HAFB	001	
EC-YAC	Hosta JG-50A	001	
EC-YAD	Vidal JG-77A	001	
EC-YAE	Mendez JG-77C	001	
EC-YAF	Monnet Moni	203	ECT-440
EC-YAG	Roger / Druine D.31 Turbulent	01	ECT-706
EC-YAH	Rotorway Executive (Stored)	3589	
EC-YAI	Rotorway Executive	31416	EC-199
EC-YAJ	Sallen 2-seat	001	
EC-YAK	Pendulaire	101	
EC-YAL	Copa	6/88	
EC-YAM	Copa	7/88	
EC-YAN	Eipper Quicksilver MXL-II	1361	
EC-YAO	Eipper Quicksilver MXL-II	1403	
EC-YAQ	Pitts S-1D Special	JFG 82/01	PP-ZZZ
EC-YAR	Eipper Quicksilver MXL-II	1521	
EC-YAS	Sallen Mach 10	16/87	
EC-YAT	Sallen Mach 15	1/89	
EC-YAU	Dynali Chickinox Kot Kot	31310417	

EC-YAV	Scheibe SF-25C Falke ? now "Singilia"	10/86	
EC-YAX	Light Aero Avid Flyer	20/88	
EC-YAY	Light Aero Avid Flyer	6/89	
EC-YAZ	Light Aero Avid Flyer	23/88	
EC-YBA	Light Aero Avid Flyer	44/89	
EC-YBB	Dynali Chickinox Kot Kot	6/90	
EC-YBC	Weedhopper	11/84	
EC-YBD	Rans S-6 Coyote II	79/90	
EC-YBE	Rans S-4 Coyote I	77/90	
EC-YBF	Brügger MB-2 Colibri	11/86	EC-386
EC-YBG	Flying Master	34/90	
EC-YBH	Comco Ikarus Fox-C22	10/90	
EC-YBI	Eipper Quicksilver MXL-II	70/90	
EC-YBJ	Cosmos Bidulum 50	28/90	
EC-YBK	Sallen Mach 15 Gyrocopter	29/90	ECT-444 ?
EC-YBL	LET L-13E Blanik M	28/89	EC-CQV
EC-YBM	Air Création GT BI Safari Quartz	8/90	
EC-YBN	Air Création Racer 12SX	43/90	
EC-YBO	Air Création GT BI Safari	25/90	
EC-YBP	Nicollier HN.700 Ménestrel II (Damaged 22.2.98)	18/90/001E	EC-605
EC-YBQ	Air Command 532 Elite	102/90	
EC-YBR	Rans S-4 Coyote I	16/91	
EC-YBS	Air Création Safari GT Quartz 16SX	38/90	EC-611
EC-YBT	Air Création Safari GT BI Fun 18	62/90	
EC-YBU	Air Création Racer Quartz 12SX	72/90	WAC-72
EC-YBV	Rans S-4 Coyote I	50/91	
EC-YBX	Eipper Quicksilver MXL-II	84/90	
EC-YBY	Light Aero Avid Flyer STOL	22/88	
EC-YBZ	VA-12C	21/89	
EC-YCA	Rotorway Executive	95/90	EC-656
EC-YCB	Cosmos Chronos 14	116/90	
EC-YCC	Light Aero Avid Flyer	17/88	
EC-YCD	Chickinox Tandem	21/91	
EC-YCE	Chickinox Tandem	20/91	
EC-YCF	Chickinox Monoplaza	53/90	
EC-YCG	Denney Kitfox	17/89	EC-661
EC-YCH	Sadler Vampire SV-2	11/91	
EC-YCI	AISA I-11B Peque (Replica)	7/89	
EC-YCJ	Rans S-7 Courier	17/91	EC-837
EC-YCK	Sirocco E	1/91	
EC-YCL	Pterodactyl Ascender	29/91	EC-724
EC-YCM	Air Command 582 Gyrocopter	114/90	
EC-YCN	Circa-Nieuport II	20/87	EC-201
EC-YCO	Eipper Quicksilver MXL-II	95/90	
EC-YCP	Light Aero Avid Flyer STOL	25/88	
EC-YCQ	Kolb Mk.II Twinstar	1/90	
EC-YCR	Air Création Safari GT BI	1	
EC-YCS	Air Création Safari Quartz 16SX	74/90	
EC-YCT	Chickinox Tandem	88/90	
EC-YCU	Air Création GT BIPlus 20	76/90	
EC-YCV	Kolb Twinstar Mk.II	55/90	EC-405
EC-YCX	Rans S-7 Courier	78/90	
EC-YCY	Rans S-10 Sakota	80/90	
EC-YCZ	Rans S-12 Airaile	38/91	
EC-YDA	TSA10 Flying Master	66/91	
EC-YDB	Rans S-4 Coyote I	139/91	
EC-YDC	Rans S-6 Coyote II	71/91	
EC-YDD	Sallen Mach 07 Gyrocopter	27/90	
EC-YDE	Rans S-6 Coyote II	80/91	
EC-YDF	Pendular Trike	13/91	
EC-YDG	Rans S-12 Airaile	83/91	
EC-YDH	Eipper Quicksilver MX-II	97/90	
EC-YDI	Volero Trike	27/91	
EC-YDJ	Air Création GT BI Quartz 16SX	63/91	
EC-YDK	Light Aero Avid Flyer	7/90	
EC-YDL	Zenair CH-701 STOL	154/91	EC-915 ?
EC-YDM	Safari GT BI Fun 18	3/91	
EC-YDN	Air Création Racer Fun 14	40/91	
EC-YDO	Eipper Quicksilver GT-500	68/91	
EC-YDP	Condor	119/90	
EC-YDQ	Rans S-6 Coyote II	58/91	
EC-YDR	Colibri JL 12SX	73/90	
EC-YDS	Dynali Chickinox Tandem	98/91	
EC-YDT	Light Aero Avid Flyer STOL	20/90	
EC-YDU	Rans S-6 Coyote II	117/91	
EC-YDV	Renegade Spirit	67/90	
EC-YDX	Aériane Sirocco	45/91	
EC-YDY	Eipper Quicksilver MX-II	22/91	
EC-YDZ	Dynali Chickinox Kot-Kot	63/90	
EC-YEA	Safari GT BI Quartz 18 BI	64/90	
EC-YEB	Safari GT BI Plus 20	88/91	
EC-YEC	Colomban MC-15 Cri-Cri	15/87	EC-598
EC-YED	Safari GT BI Plus 20	113/91	
EC-YEE	Ultravia Pelican Club	33/89	EC-723
EC-YEF	Racer Fun 14	148/91	
EC-YEG	Rans S-4 Coyote I	97/91	
EC-YEH	Quad City Challenger II	116/91	EC-921 ?
EC-YEI	Flying Master	59/90	
EC-YEJ	Aériane Sirocco	66/90	EC-645
EC-YEK	Vector 610	113/90	
EC-YEL	Light Aero Avid Flyer STOL	40/89	
EC-YEM	Light Aero Avid Flyer STOL	31/89	
EC-YEN	Quad City Challenger II	62/91	EC-871 ?
EC-YEO	Light Aero Avid Flyer STOL	14/90	
EC-YEP	Light Aero Avid Flyer STOL	106/90	
EC-YEQ	Air Création Racer 12SX	42/92	

EC-YER	Quad City Challenger II Special	118/90	
EC-YES	Safari GT BI Fun	8/91	
EC-YET	Tierra II	110/91	
EC-YEU	Safari GT BI	61/91	
EC-YEV	Dynali Chickinox Kot-Kot	163/91	
EC-YEX	Rans S-4 Coyote I	144/91	
EC-YEY	Ménestrel II	002-E/58/90	
EC-YEZ	Rans S-6 Coyote II	139/91	
EC-YFA	Rans S-6 Coyote II	84/91	
EC-YFB	Kolb Twinstar Mk.II	115/90	
EC-YFC	Renegade Spirit (W/o 7.8.96)	2/89	
EC-YFD	Mini Maxi	56/90	EC-910
EC-YFE	Bragg	101/90	EC-143
EC-YFF	Van's RV-6A	44/90	EC-118
EC-YFG	Fischer FP-404 Classic	22/90	EC-398
EC-YFH	Capella XS	87/91	EC-200
EC-YFI	Ultravia Pelican Club	108/90	EC-846
EC-YFJ	Light Aero Avid Flyer	33/91	
EC-YFK	Rans S-12 Airaile	23/92	
EC-YFL	Rans S-12 Airaile	158/91	
EC-YFM	Air Création GT BI Fun 18	43/91	
EC-YFN	Air Command 582	165/91	
EC-YFO	Rans S-12 Airaile	123/91	
EC-YFP	Light Aero Avid Flyer STOL	115/91	
EC-YFQ	Rans S-6 Coyote II	33/92	
EC-YFR	Air Création GT BI Fun 18	145/91	
EC-YFS	Rans S-12 Airaile	74/92	
EC-YFT	Air Création GT BI Quartz SX-16	8/92	
EC-YFU	Air Création Racer Quartz SX12	121/91	
EC-YFV	Air Création Safari GT BI Quartz	105/91	
EC-YFX	Air Création GT BI Fun 18	104/91	
EC-YFY	Air Création Safari GT BI Fun 18	166/91	
EC-YFZ	Colibri JL2 Quartz SX-16	133/91	
EC-YGA	Air Création Racer Fun 14	53/91	
EC-YGB	Air Création Safari GT BI Quartz	131/91	
EC-YGC	Kolb Twinstar Mk.II	4/90	
EC-YGD	Kolb Twinstar Mk.II	3/90	
EC-YGE	Sport Aircraft Tango II	24/92	
EC-YGF	Air Création GT BI Quartz SX-16	168/91	
EC-YGG	Air Création Racer Quartz SX-12	124/91	
EC-YGH	Air Création GT BI Fun 18	54/91	
EC-YGI	Rans S-12 Airaile	70/91	
EC-YGJ	Rans S-10 Sakota	49/91	
EC-YGK	Cosmos Atlas 21	136/92	
EC-YGL	Rans S-6 Coyote II	132/92	
EC-YGM	Rans S-14	110/92	
EC-YGN	Rans S-6 Coyote II	52/92	
EC-YGO	Racer SX-12	2/92	
EC-YGP	Synairgie Jaguar 16	21/92	
EC-YGQ	Light Aero Avid Flyer STOL (Damaged 7.04)	30/89	
EC-YGR	Eipper Quicksilver Sprint II	21/93	
EC-YGS	Air Création GT BI Fun 18	175/92	
EC-YGT	Air Création Safari GT BI Plus 20	2/91	
EC-YGU	Rans S-6 Coyote II	5/93	
EC-YGV	Capella XSX	11/92	
EC-YGX	Minimax Fun-18	93/90	
EC-YGY	Zenair STOL	108/91	
EC-YGZ	TEAM Hi-Max	36/90	
EC-YHA	Rans S-6 Coyote II	153/91	
EC-YHB	Rans S-12 Airaile	169/91	
EC-YHC	Cosmos Echo-12	131/92	
EC-YHD	JN-1	57/90	
EC-YHE	Rans S-12 Airaile	106/92	
EC-YHF	Doleal DJP-03	35/89	
EC-YHG	Light Aero Avid Flyer STOL	51/90	
EC-YHH	Van's RV-4	1800	EC-447
EC-YHI	Rans S-12 Airaile	167/91	
EC-YHJ	Mainair Gemini/Flash IIA (See EC-YHO)	"93088"	
EC-YHK	Dynali Chickinox Kot-Kot	82/90	
EC-YHL	Eipper Quicksilver MX-II	93062	EC-671 ?
EC-YHM	Eipper Quicksilver MX-II	125/92	EC-675 ?
EC-YHN	Denney Kitfox IV	55/92	
EC-YHO	Mainair Gemini/Flash IIA (This and EC-YHJ are probably c/ns 603-1187/W391 and 604-1187/W392, order unknown)	"50/93"	
EC-YHP	Air Création Safari GT BI Quartz	3/92	
EC-YHQ	Air Création Safari GT 1+1 Plus	56/93	
EC-YHR	Rans S-6 Coyote II	140/93	
EC-YHS	Lohele Sport Parasol	93119	
EC-YHT	TEAM Mini-Max	39/90	
EC-YHU	Light Aero Avid Flyer	40/90	
EC-YHV	Light Miniature LM-1	75/90	EC-710 ?
EC-YHX	Monnett Moni	35/88	
EC-YHY	Air Création Safari GT BI Quartz 18	22/93	
EC-YHZ	Bidulum-50 Turbo 17	60/92	
EC-YIA	Rans S-6 Coyote II	76/92	
EC-YIB	Cosmos Bidulum	123/92	
EC-YIC	Drifter ARV-582	142/92	
EC-YID	Pelican Club	23/89	
EC-YIE	Dynali Chickinox Kot-Kot	71/90	
EC-YIF	Vector 610	140/92	
EC-YIG	Rans S-12 Airaile	143/92	
EC-YIH	Sky Walker II-300	11/93	
EC-YII	Sky Walker II-300	99/91	
EC-YIJ	Capotilo	93112	
EC-YIK	Rans S-6 Coyote II	52/93	
EC-YIL	Air Création Racer Quartz SX12	94/92	

EC-YIM	Volero	93131	
EC-YIN	Drifter ARV-503	22/92	
EC-YIO	T-Bird II	101/91	
EC-YIP	TEAM Mini-Max	80/92	
EC-YIQ	Rans S-6 Coyote II	47/93	
EC-YIR	Denney Kitfox	128/91	
EC-YIS	Tierra II	119/92	
EC-YIT	Cosmos	93087	
EC-YIU	Neico Lancair 360	9/92	EC-537
EC-YIV	Sky Walker II-300	49/92	
EC-YIX	Teulai	26/90	EC-274
EC-YIY	Light Aero Avid Master	17/92	
EC-YIZ	Light Aero Avid Master	59/93	
EC-YJA	Eipper Quicksilver Sprint II-BI	93093	
EC-YJB	Rans S-6 Coyote II	115/92	
EC-YJC	Air Création Safari GT 1+1 Plus 17	137/92	
EC-YJD	Rans S-12 Airaile	44/92	
EC-YJE	Denney Kitfox	92/91	
EC-YJF	Rans S-6 Coyote II	93073	
EC-YJG	Rans S-4 Coyote I	107/91	
EC-YJH	Air Création Safari GT-BI	26/93	
EC-YJI	Fisher FP-404 Classic	37/92	
EC-YJJ	CFM Streak Shadow	K.218	
EC-YJK	Rans S-14	93081	
EC-YJL	Rans S-6 Coyote II	41/93	
EC-YJM	Cosmos Chronos	69/92	
EC-YJN	Pelican Club	22/89	
EC-YJO	Pirriqui	93085	
EC-YJP	Preceptor Ultra-Pup	95/92	EC-108 ?
EC-YJQ	Rans S-12 Airaile	93130	
EC-YJR	Dynali Chickinox Tandem	122/92	
EC-YJS	Fisher FP-202 Super Koala	12/87	
EC-YJT	Cobra	161/91	
EC-YJU	Eipper Quicksilver Sprint II-BI	93100	
EC-YJV	Mosler N-32 Pup	23/90	
EC-YJX	Air Création Safari GT-BI Fun 18	162/91	
EC-YJY	Denney Kitfox	72/92	
EC-YJZ	Challenger II	93108	
EC-YKA	Rans S-6ES Coyote II	93099	
EC-YKB	TEAM Hi-Max	93127	
EC-YKC	Air Création Racer Fun 14	93114	
EC-YKD	Dynali Chickinox Kot-Kot	40/92	
EC-YKE	Titan Tornado	144/92	
EC-YKF	Rans S-6ES Coyote II	48/93	
EC-YKG	Icaro Quartz SX16	94077	
EC-YKH	Palomo	94030	
EC-YKI	TEAM Minimax Max	37/91	
EC-YKJ	Rans S-6ES Coyote II	27/93	
EC-YKK	Pendular Trike	94050	
EC-YKL	Hazard 15M	133/92	
EC-YKM	Rans S-4 Coyote I	93086	
EC-YKN	Aero Designs Pulsar XP	7/92	
EC-YKO	Light Aero Avid Flyer	117/92	
EC-YKP	MXP-640	93140	
EC-YKQ	Pendular Biplaza Cosmos	93134	
EC-YKR	Drifter ARV-582	93095	
EC-YKS	Neico Lancair 360	19/93	EC-537 ?
EC-YKT	Volero Cosmos Chronos	94087	
EC-YKU	Mosler Ultra Pup	94061	
EC-YKV	Stolp Starduster Too (Damaged 6.6.04) (Possibly c/n ACA-38, ex N9771A)	36/92	EC-373 ?
EC-YKX	Burumballeta	9/88	EC-836
EC-YKY	Rans S-6ES Coyote II	57/93	
EC-YKZ	Tope 90	28/91	
EC-YLA	Terra-Bird 1	109/92	
EC-YLB	Rans S-6 Coyote II	93071	
EC-YLC	Rans S-4 Coyote I	122/91	
EC-YLD	Rans S-6 Coyote II	93068	
EC-YLE	Rans S-10 Sakota	94024	
EC-YLF	Phase II Chronos 16	95011-871	
EC-YLG	Eipper Quicksilver MX-II	94065	
EC-YLH	Bidulum Atlas-21	94067	
EC-YLI	TEAM Mini Max	72/91	
EC-YLJ	Rio Profil-27	44/93	
EC-YLK	Light Aero Avid Flyer	94019	
EC-YLL	Sky Walker	94096	
EC-YLM	Rans S-6 Coyote II	45/92	
EC-YLN	Villapar	60/93	
EC-YLO	Monnett Moni	93089	EC-788
EC-YLP	Anajopi GT-BI Hermes Turbo 16	35/92	
EC-YLQ	Dynali Chickinox Kot-Kot	82/92	
EC-YLR	Rans S-14	94118	EC-280 ?
EC-YLS	Flying Ghost	107/92	
EC-YLT	Pendular Fun 18	93125	
EC-YLU	Murphy Renegade Spirit	93133	
EC-YLV	Weedhopper	81/92	
EC-YLX	Polaris Cross Country Arie	94063	
EC-YLY	Rans S-12 Airaile	93082	
EC-YLZ	Gaviota	119/91	
EC-YMA	Weedhopper AX-3	94091	
EC-YMB	DTA / Hermes 17	95040-900	
EC-YMC	TEAM Z-Hi-Max	41/92	
EC-YMD	Capela XSX	53/93	
EC-YME	Rans S-12 Airaile	94010	
EC-YMF	Denney Kitfox	149/91	EC-466 ?
EC-YMG	Rans S-6 Coyote II	118/91	
EC-YMH	Solar Wings Pegasus XL	95047-907	

EC-YMI	Rans S-6 Coyote II	73/92	
EC-YMJ	Air Création Safari GT BI Fun 18	94044	
EC-YMK	Air Création Safari GT BI Fun 18	94043	
EC-YML	Cabanas Fun 18	94108	
EC-YMM	Autogyro TM-1	93067	
EC-YMN	Rans S-10 Sakota	94023	EC-901 ?
EC-YMO	Air Création Safari GT BI Fun 18	35/93	
EC-YMP	Denney Kitfox	6/93	
EC-YMQ	Maxair Drifter	95031-891	
EC-YMR	TEAM Mini-Max	94057	
EC-YMS	Eipper Quicksilver MX-II	93092	
EC-YMT	Rans S-6ES Coyote II	94102	
EC-YMU	Neico Lancair 320 Mk II	94008	
EC-YMV	Barom AGC-1 Pacific Wings	93083	
EC-YMX	Preceptor N-3 Pup	95036-896	EC-108 ?
EC-YMY	Formula Uno	94042	
EC-YMZ	Formula Uno	94117	
EC-YNA	Maxair 582 Drifter	95064-924	
EC-YNB	Rans S-12 Airaile	65/92	
EC-YNC	Pegasus Quasar	94066	
EC-YND	Rans S-4 Coyote I	94069	
EC-YNE	Neico Lancair 360	124/92	
EC-YNF	Echo-12 Trike	95037-897	
EC-YNG	Cosmos Chronos-14	95017-877	
EC-YNH	Cosmos Bidulum-50	95018-878	
EC-YNI	Cosmos Bidulum-50	95043-903	
EC-YNJ	Rans S-12 Airaile	94047	
EC-YNK	Neico Lancair 360	129/92	
EC-YNL	Volairo Cosmos	94112	
EC-YNM	Evans VP-1 Volksplane	4/81	
EC-YNN	Sky Jet II	94016	
EC-YNO	Sky Jet II	94015	
EC-YNP	Rutan Long-Ez	2/85	EC-676 ?
EC-YNQ	Eipper Quicksilver MX-II	93136	
EC-YNR	Preceptor Vagabond	96017-967	
EC-YNS	Rans S-6ES Coyote II	95068-928	
EC-YNU	AX-2 Le Guepard Autogyro	95050-910	
EC-YNV	Poisck 06A	95004-864	
EC-YNX	Commander 582 Elite gyrocopter	94026	
EC-YNY	Sport Aircraft Tango II-GT	94005-865	
EC-YNZ	Rans S-6ES Coyote II	93117	
EC-YOA	Precepter Maverick	96058-1008	
EC-YOB	TEAM Mini-Max	96021-971	EC-748 ?
EC-YOC	Air Création Safari GT BI Fun 18	94060	
EC-YOD	Vol 9/Best Off Sky Ranger 912	95046-906	
EC-YOE	TEAM Mini-Max	95002-862	
EC-YOF	Strojnic S-2A	21/88	
EC-YOG	Van's RV-6	1/92	EC-432 ?
EC-YOH	Bragg A-3	94055	
EC-YOI	Maupin Woodstock 1	159/91	
EC-YOJ	TEAM Mini-Max	92/90	
EC-YOK	Bifly Sport	18/93	
EC-YOL	Polaris Cross-Country	94072	
EC-YOM	Murphy Maverick	93137	
EC-YON	Dynali Chickinox Tandem	94110	
EC-YOO	Comco Ikarus Sherpa II	94011	
EC-YOP	T-Bird II	94051	
EC-YOQ	Fisher FP-404 Classic	94076	
EC-YOR	ESO Pendular	93094	
EC-YOS	Colometa	96003-953	
EC-YOT	Air Création Safari 1+1 Plus 20	94029	
EC-YOU	Dynali Chickinox	96005-955	
EC-YOV	Air Command 582 Elite	96081-1031	
EC-YOX	Van's RV-6	95056-916	
EC-YOY	Denney Kitfox IV	78/92	
EC-YOZ	Air Création Safari GT BI Quartz 16SX	96006-956	
EC-YPA	Rans S-6 Coyote II	96035-985	
EC-YPB	Dynali Chickinox	95042-902	
EC-YPC	Formula I	94113	
EC-YPD	Rans S-14 Airaile	96063-1013	
EC-YPE	Rans S-6 Coyote II	95057-917	
EC-YPF	Challenger II	96091-1041	
EC-YPG	Navegante Aereo Stranger 16	95026-886	
EC-YPH	Glasair II-SFT	95049-909	
EC-YPI	Rans S-6XL Coyote II	95065-925	
EC-YPJ	Polaris Skin	97017-1077	
EC-YPK	Air Création Safari GT BI Fun 18	95058-918	
EC-YPL	TEAM Mini-Max	94022	
EC-YPM	Air Création 1+1 Plus	96089-1039	
EC-YPN	Light Aero Avid Flyer	94020	
EC-YPO	Kolb Twinstar Mk II	17/93	
EC-YPP	Air Command 582 Elite	96085-1035	
EC-YPQ	Rans S-6ES Coyote II	96043-993	
EC-YPR	Rans S-9 Chaos	96083-1033	
EC-YPS	Rans S-10 Sakota	94027	
EC-YPT	Preceptor Ultra Pup	95072-932	
EC-YPU	TEAM Mini-Max	15/90	
EC-YPV	Sky Walker II-300	96106-1056	
EC-YPX	Sport Aircraft Tango I	95053-913	
EC-YPY	Sky Walker	96015-965	
EC-YPZ	Campana	96042-992	
EC-YQA	Jodel D.18	46/90	EC-929?
EC-YQB	Sport Aircraft Tango II-GT	96074-1024	
EC-YQC	Albatros Gyrocopter	97024-1084	
EC-YQD	Monnett Moni	97018-1078	
EC-YQE	Synairgie	97014-1074	
EC-YQF	Rans S-6 Coyote II	93122	

EC-YQG	Rotorway Exec 162F	96008-958	
EC-YQH	VM.002 (W/o 27.10.02)	96002-970	
EC-YQI	Interair F-2-55	95009-869	
EC-YQJ	Rans S-14 Airaile	97032-1092	
EC-YQK	Rans S-5 Coyote I	97033-1093	
EC-YQL	Challenger II	95052-912	
EC-YQM	Air Command 582 Elite	96051-1001	
EC-YQN	Genesis	95073-933	
EC-YQO	Titan Tornado	unkn	
	(Officially listed as CGS Hawk Classic c/n 96011-961 but correct type confirmed as above 8.03)		
EC-YQP	Rans S-10 Sakota	94035	
EC-YQQ	Sky Jet II	97012-1072	
EC-YQR	Sport Aircraft Tango I	94097	
EC-YQS	Albatros SX	97025-1085	
EC-YQT	Rans S-6ES Coyote II	96044-994	
EC-YQU	TEAM Mini-Max	94078	
EC-YQV	Straton D-8	96087-1037	
EC-YQX	Cedimex Rans S-12 Airaile	96067-1017	
EC-YQY	Eipper Quicksilver MXL-II Sport	96107-1057	
	(Originally listed as a Tecnam P.96 Golf)		
EC-YQZ	Rotorway Exec 152F	97019-1079	
EC-YRA	TEAM Mini-Max	111/91	
EC-YRB	Taylorcraft LM.2X 2P	100/91	
EC-YRC	Büttner Funplane	97029-1089	
	(originially listed as a DTA Trike)		
EC-YRD	Rans S-6 Coyote II	97056-1116	
EC-YRE	Terra T-Bird 2	96070-1020	
EC-YRF	Cross Country Gryps 18.5	95023-883	
EC-YRG	Sky Walker	96071-1021	
EC-YRH	Air Création GT BI Quartz 18SX	96090-1040	
EC-YRI	Murphy Renegade Spirit	94095	
EC-YRJ	Dynali Chickinox Kot-Kot	97050-1119	
EC-YRK	Eipper Quicksilver MX-II	97039-1099	
EC-YRL	LG.1 Eclipse	97052-1112	
EC-YRM	Cosmos Hermes 2-seat	94034	
EC-YRN	Air Création Safari GT BI Fun 18	94100	
EC-YRO	Vol 9/Best Off Sky Ranger	96033-983	
EC-YRP	Vol 9/Best Off Sky Ranger	94120	
EC-YRQ	CGS Hawk Classic	95071-931	
EC-YRR	AER Pendular	94006	
EC-YRS	Rans S-6ES Coyote II	97006-1066	
EC-YRT	Bidulum-50 Magnum 21	2/93	
EC-YRU	Challenger II	97063-1123	
EC-YRV	Murphy Maverick	96002-952	
EC-YRX	Aviatika MAI-89	96046-996	
EC-YRY	Raven Mk.2	152/91	
EC-YRZ	Murphy Maverick	96099-1049	
EC-YSA	Murphy Maverick	97007-1067	
EC-YSB	Neico Lancair 320	95012-872	
EC-YSC	Rans S-6ES Coyote II	96032-982	
EC-YSD	Puddle Jumper	96049-999	
EC-YSE	Solar Wings Pegasus	97021-1081	
EC-YSF	Nicollier HN-700 Menstrel II	17/90	
EC-YSG	Monnett Monerai	1	
EC-YSH	Van's RV-4	95024-884	
EC-YSI	V.M.	30/91	
EC-YSJ	Rans S-6ES Coyote II	93097	
EC-YSK	Eipper Quicksilver MX-II	126/92	
EC-YSL	Capela	29/92	
EC-YSM	Cosmos Chronos 14	96048-998	
EC-YSN	Monnett Moni	5/84	
EC-YSO	Murphy Maverick	96009-959	
EC-YSP	Brügger MB-2 Colibri	20	EC-241
	(C/n now quoted as 1/82)		
EC-YSQ	Eipper Quicksilver MX-II	95048-908	
EC-YSR	Cosmos Phase II Chronos 16	97066-1126	
EC-YSS	Vol 9/Best Off Sky Ranger 912	95088-948	
EC-YST	Cosmos Hermes 16	97053-1113	
EC-YSU	Cobra	24/93	
EC-YSV	Rans S-12 Airaile	97051-1111	
EC-YSX	Cosmos Chronos 14	97054-1114	
EC-YSY	Cosmos Chronos 16	95003-863	
EC-YSZ	ELA 04-B	98052-1213	
EC-YTA	Capela	96105-1055	
EC-YTB	Denney Kitfox IV - 1200	93105	
EC-YTC	CASA C-1.131E Jungmann	98027-1188	
	(Built from spares)		
EC-YTD	Solar Wings Pegasus XL-Q	98032-1193	
EC-YTE	Rans S-5 Coyote I	98014-1175	
EC-YTF	Colyear Martin M3-S100	98012-1173	
EC-YTG	Eipper Quicksilver MXL-IIRB Sport	98057-1218	
EC-YTH	Rans S-10 Sakota	97062-1122	
EC-YTI	Bidulum 50 Chronos 14	98018-1179	
EC-YTJ	Eipper Quicksilver GT-500	98017-1178	
EC-YTK	Pegasus Quantum	98030-1191	
	(Originally listed as Solar Wings Pegasus XL-Q)		
EC-YTL	Pelican GS	93120	
EC-YTM	Dyn'Aero MCR-01	97098-1158	
	(Dyn'Aero c/n 53)		
EC-YTN	Preceptor N-3 Pup	94101	
EC-YTO	Capella XS	97075-1135	
EC-YTP	Rans S-7 Courier	94028	
EC-YTQ	Pegasus Quantum II	98072-1233	
EC-YTR	Pegasus Quantum 15	98058-1219	
EC-YTS	Sky Walker II-300	97027-1087	
EC-YTT	Cosmos Bidulum II	98048-1209	

EC-YTU	Cosmos Bidulum	97091-1151
EC-YTV	Cosmos Chronos 14	98008-1169
EC-YTX	Eipper Quicksilver MXL-IIRB Sport	98035-1196
EC-YTY	Nieuport II	10/88
EC-YTZ	Preceptor N-3 Pup	97096-1156
EC-YUA	Challenger II	97086-1146
EC-YUB	Raj Hamsa X'Air	98067-1228
EC-YUC	Max Trainer	94070
EC-YUD	Eipper Quicksilver MXL-IIRB Sport	98005-1166
EC-YUE	Aviatika MAI-890	97070-1130
EC-YUF	Fisher FP-404 Classic II	95015-875
EC-YUG	Buse'Air 150	98074-1235
EC-YUH	Aviasud Mistral	96103-1053
EC-YUI	Pegasus Quantum Super Sport Q2	98001-1162
EC-YUJ	RAF-2000	96050-1000
EC-YUK	Taylorcraft BC-12D	98026-1187
EC-YUL	Aviatika MAI-890	96080-1030
	(Originally listed as Zenair CH-601 Zodiac)	
EC-YUM	Rotorway Exec 162F	97044-1104
EC-YUN	Rans S-7 Courier	98050-1211
EC-YUO	Bidulum 50	98079-1240
EC-YUP	Terra T-Bird 2	98013-1174
EC-YUQ	Denney Kitfox III	66/92
EC-YUR	Rans S-14 Airaile	98066-1227
EC-YUS	Rans S-6XL Coyote II	98025-1186
EC-YUT	Cosmos	98033-1194
EC-YUU	Dyn'Aero MCR-01	99003-1277
EC-YUV	Air Création Safari GT BI Quartz 16SXS	16/93
EC-YUX	Pelican Club	103/92
EC-YUY	Air Création Safari GT BI Quartz 16SXS	15/93
EC-YUZ	Air Création Safari GT BI Plus 17	53/92
EC-YVA	Rans S-6ES Coyote II	93098
EC-YVB	Colibri JL1 Quartz 12SX	64/92
EC-YVC	JF1 SX12	96034-984
EC-YVD	Colibri II XP15	97069-1129
EC-YVE	Colibri JL1	52/92
EC-YVF	Loehle Sport Parasol	98108-1269
EC-YVG	Tecnam P.92 Echo	97085-1145
EC-YVH	Air Création Safari GT BI Quartz 16SX	97002-1062
EC-YVI	TEAM Mini-Max	146/92
EC-YVJ	Rans S-6ES Coyote II	97028-1088
EC-YVK	Rans S-14 Airaile	98036-1197
EC-YVL	Zenair CH-601 Zodiac	98103-1264
EC-YVM	Zenair CH-601HDS Zodiac	96102-1052
EC-YVN	Pegasus Quasar	98084-1245
EC-YVO	Pegasus Quantum 15	98073-1234
EC-YVP	Pegasus Q2	98097-1258
EC-YVQ	Bü.133C Jungmeister	97008-1068
EC-YVR	Rans S-7 Courier	98064-1225
EC-YVS	Slepcev Storch Mk 4	97009-1069
EC-YVT	Rans S-14 Airaile	114/92
EC-YVU	Love Spirit	99012-1286
EC-YVV	Murphy Renegade Spirit	95083-943
EC-YVX	Rans S-6-116 Coyote	94063
EC-YVY	Madero Corby	96110-1060
EC-YVZ	Rans S-10 Sakota	98/92
EC-YXA	Zenair CH-601 Zodiac	98054-1215
EC-YXB	Zenair CH-601 Zodiac	98055-1216
EC-YXC	Sport Aicraft Tango GT-i	98037-1198
EC-YXD	VPM M-18 Spartan	98070-1231
EC-YXE	Oroneta Racer GT	98105-1266
EC-YXF	Rans S-14 Airaile	94013
EC-YXG	ELA 05B Gyrocopter	99016-1290
EC-YXH	Air Création Safari GT 1+1 Fun 18	98060-1221
EC-YXI	Buse'Air 150	98095-1256
EC-YXJ	Zenair CH-601 Zodiac	99023-1297
EC-YXK	D.R.P. Trike	99071-1345
EC-YXL	Buccaneer II-B2B	98068-1229
EC-YXM	Mistral	98043-1204
EC-YXN	Murphy Maverick	99060-1334
EC-YXO	Rans S-6ES Coyote II	98015-1176
EC-YXP	Pober Pixie	50/92
EC-YXQ	Rans S-14 Airaile	98101-1262
EC-YXR	Stolp SA300 Starduster Too	99050-1159
EC-YXS	Aeros	98082-1243
EC-YXT	Skystar Kitfox IV	97099-1159
EC-YXU	Lancair 320	86/91
EC-YXV	JFR Gyrocopter	99015-1289
EC-YXX	Cosmos Bidulum Chronos 14	97071-1131
EC-YXY	TEAM Mini-Max	98002-1163
EC-YXZ	Rans S-6 Coyote II	94074
EC-YYA	Biplano II	97092-1152
EC-YYB	Hispano Canelas Ranger	7/87
EC-YYC	Rans S-14 Airaile	99070-1344
EC-YYD	Dyn'Aero MCR-01	99069-1343
EC-YYE	Eipper Quicksilver MXL-IIRB Sport	99100-1374
EC-YYF	Dynali Chickinox Kot-Kot	99082-1356
EC-YYG	Xisvi	98078-1239
	(Also noted as "Cosmos")	
EC-YYH	JRB-2	9804901210
EC-YYI	Asso V	97064-1124
EC-YYJ	Rans S-6 Coyote II	96072-1022
EC-YYK	Eipper Quicksilver MXL-II Sport	98109-1270
EC-YYL	Eipper Quicksilver MXL-II Sport	98112-1273
EC-YYM	Eipper Quicksilver MXL-II Sport	99002-1276
EC-YYN	Eipper Quicksilver MXL-II Sport	98110-1271
EC-YYO	Eipper Quicksilver MXL-II Sport	99001-1275

EC-YYP	Eipper Quicksilver MXL-II Sport	98111-1272	
EC-YYQ	Murphy Maverick	99086-1360	
EC-YYR	Echo 12 Trike	99040-1314	
EC-YYS	Aero Boero	00021-1410	
EC-YYT	Robin ATL	97060-1120	
EC-YYU	CAG Toxo	95039-899	
EC-YYV	CAG Toxo	96014-964	
EC-YYX	Colibri JL2	128/92	
EC-YYY	Air Création Twin 503 Fun 18	99115-1389	
EC-YYZ	Colibri I+I XPI2	99027-1301	
EC-YZA	LM-1	99039-1313	
EC-YZB	Buse'Air 150	98098-1259	
EC-YZC	L.M.	99018-1382	
EC-YZD	Van's RV-6	97016-1076	
EC-YZE	Rans S-6ES Coyote II	99041-1315	
EC-YZF	Pulsar X-13	97055-1115	
EC-YZG	TL Ultralight TL-96 Star	00017-1406	
EC-YZH	Preceptor N-3 Pup	99091-1365	
EC-YZI	Buse'Air 150	99084-1358	
EC-YZJ	Tecnam P.92 Echo	97084-1144	
EC-YZK	Rans S-6ES Coyote II	98011-1172	
EC-YZL	Dynali Chickinox Tandem	98046-1207	
EC-YZM	SG Aviation Storm 300	99059-1333	
EC-YZN	Buse'Air 150	99077-1351	
EC-YZO	Buse'Air 150	99087-1361	
EC-YZP	Rans S-6ES Coyote II	96064-1014	
EC-YZQ	Tecnam P.92 Echo	99097-1371	
EC-YZR	Nike Vega	99068-1342	
EC-YZS	Sky Walker	00048-1437	
EC-YZT	Zenair CH-601 Zodiac	98069-1230	
EC-YZU	Tecnam P.92 Echo	99101-1375	
EC-YZV	Rans S-12S Super Airaile	009/1398	
EC-YZX	Eipper Quicksilver MXL-II	99088-1362	
EC-YZY	Viper Hazard-12 582	99078-1352	
EC-YZZ	Vol Mediterrani VM-1 Esqual (Prototype)	00058-1447	
EC-ZAA	M3 Gyrocopter	00033-1422	
EC-ZAB	Bidulum Fun 18	98062-1223	
EC-ZAC	ELA 05 BC 125	99093-1367	
EC-ZAD	Raj Hamsa X'Air 582	00062-1451	
EC-ZAE	JS Single-seat Gyrocpter	00029-1418	
EC-ZAF	Dyn'Aero MCR-01 VLA	00073-1462	
	(Dyn'Aero c/n 123)		
EC-ZAG	Ultralair Weedhopper Europa II	00025-1414	
EC-ZAH	Fantasy Air Allegro ST	00050-1439	
EC-ZAI	Rans S-6ES Coyote II	99114-1388	
EC-ZAJ	Moragon UL 2	99073-1347	
EC-ZAK	Sky Jet-II	00055-1444	
EC-ZAL	Pendular Racer	99042-1316	
EC-ZAM	Aeromaster	00003-1392	
EC-ZAN	Raj Hamsa X'Air	00015-1404	
EC-ZAO	Cosmos Bidulum 50	99029-1303	
EC-ZAP	Jodel D.1120S	00053-1442	
EC-ZAQ	Zenair CH-601 Zodiac	99111-1385	
EC-ZAR	CGS Hawk Classic single seat	00075-1464	
EC-ZAS	CGS Hawk Classic two seat	00074-1463	
EC-ZAT	Tecnam P.92S Echo	00076-1465	
EC-ZAU	Tecnam P.92S Echo	99095-1369	
EC-ZAV	Tecnam P.92S Echo (Damaged 17.12.00)	00096-1485	
EC-ZAX	Tecnam P.92S Echo	00092-1481	
EC-ZAY	Tecnam P.92S Echo	00027-1416	
EC-ZAZ	Tecnam P.92S Echo	99098-1372	
EC-ZBA	Tecnam P.92S Echo	00093-1482	
EC-ZBB	Rans S-12XL Airaile	00071-1460	
EC-ZBC	Volero Ghost 16	00047-1436	
EC-ZBD	J-300 Joker	99090-1364	
EC-ZBE	Aviaexport MAI-89	99030-1304	
EC-ZBF	Zenair CH-601 Zodiac	98104-1265	
EC-ZBG	Buse'Air 150	99013-1287	
EC-ZBH	Air Command 912 two-seater	00078-1467	
EC-ZBI	TL Ultralight TL-96 Star	00081-1479	
EC-ZBJ	Air Création Racer XP11	00031-1420	
EC-ZBK	Aero Designs Pulsar	93103	
EC-ZBL	Fly Unlimited	99036-1310	
EC-ZBM	TL Ultralight TL-96 Star	00049-1438	
EC-ZBN	Sky Walker	99083-1357	
EC-ZBO	Cosmos Chronos 16	00085-1474	
EC-ZBP	Lockwood Drifter 912	96097-1047	
EC-ZBQ	Dyn'Aero MCR-01	00057-1446	
EC-ZBR	Comco Ikarus Fox-C22	00012-1401	
EC-ZBS	Cosmos Chronos 16	00035-1424	
EC-ZBT	Sky Walker II	00019-1408	
EC-ZBU	Raj Hamsa X'Air	00065-1454	
EC-ZBV	YC-100 Hirondelle	99113-1387	
EC-ZBX	Dyn'Aero MCR-01	00069-1458	
EC-ZBY	Eipper Quicksilver MXL-II	96096-1046	
EC-ZBZ	Sport Aircraft Tango I	00010-1399	
EC-ZCA	Colibri 2000	00046-1435	
EC-ZCB	Air Création Safari GT BI Plus 20	00082-1471	
EC-ZCC	Poisk-06 Fun 18	00094-1483	
EC-ZCD	Tecnam P.96 Golf	00123-1512	
EC-ZCE	Synairgie Volero	97050-1110	
EC-ZCF	Air Création Buggy XP12	00115-1504	
EC-ZCG	Light Aero Avid Flyer STOL	00114-1503	
EC-ZCH	Air Création Safari GT BI SX16	00083-1472	
EC-ZCI	Murphy Renegade Spirit	99028-1302	
EC-ZCJ	Air Création Buggy XP12	00110-1499	
EC-ZCK	Rutan Cozy Classic	95035-895	

EC-ZCL	Tecnam P.92S Echo	99096-1370	
EC-ZCM	Rans S-7 Courier	00098-1487	
EC-ZCN	CASA C-1.131E Jungmann	00040-1429	
EC-ZCO	Air Création Buggy XP12	00109-1498	
EC-ZCP	Murphy Renegade Spirit	97082-1142	
EC-ZCQ	Vol Mediterrani VM-1 Esqual	00079-1468	
EC-ZCR	CP.301C Emeraude (W/o 15.6.02)	41/90	
EC-ZCS	Capella XSX TD	98088-1249	
EC-ZCT	Eipper Quicksilver MXL-II	98099-1260	
EC-ZCU	Rans S-6-116 Coyote II	94062	
EC-ZCV	Bicicleta Aerea	99020-1294	
EC-ZCX	Raj Hamsa X'Air	00038-1427	
EC-ZCY	Light Aero Avid Flyer	01003-1540	
EC-ZCZ	Jodel D.92 Bébé	96001-951	
	(Originally listed with c/n 778)		
EC-ZDA	Vol 9/Best Off Sky Ranger	01021-1558	
EC-ZDB	Rans S-4 Coyote	00119-1508	
EC-ZDC	TL Ultralight TL-96 Star	00145-1534	
EC-ZDD	Terra Bird II	98046-1207B	
EC-ZDE	Dyn'Aero MCR-01	00051-1440	
EC-ZDF	TL Ultralight TL-96 Star	00077-1466	
EC-ZDG	Tecnam P.92 2000RG	01057-1570	
EC-ZDH	Europa Avn Europa	95025-88	
	(True c/n is 187, builder E. Sanchez)		
EC-ZDI	Moragon UL 2	01013-1550	
EC-ZDJ	Rans S-6 Coyote II	94092	
EC-ZDK	Sky Walker 300-II	00005-1394	
EC-ZDL	TL Ultralight TL-96 Star	01005-1542	
EC-ZDM	Eipper Quicksilver MXL FJC	01064-1577	
EC-ZDN	Eipper Quicksilver Sport	01008-1545	
EC-ZDO	MAI MD-20	01007-1544	
EC-ZDP	MAI MD-20	01006-1543	
EC-ZDQ	Monnet Sonerai II	98093-1254	
EC-ZDR	Vol Mediterrani VM-1 Esqual	00101-1490	
EC-ZDS	Falcon XP	97045-1105	
EC-ZDT	Light Aero Avid Flyer STOL	67/92	
EC-ZDU	Zenair CH-601 Zodiac	00099-1488	
EC-ZDV	TL Ultralight TL-96 Star	01045-1598	
EC-ZDX	Air Création Racer Quartz 12SX	00136-1525	
EC-ZDY	Tecnam P.96 Golf	01012-1549	
EC-ZDZ	Vol 9/Best Off Sky Ranger	00013-1402	
EC-ZEA	Rans S-12 Airaile	01023-1560	
EC-ZEB	J-6 Karatoo	93078	
EC-ZEC	Light Aero Avid Flyer STOL	42/90	
EC-ZED	Compac 110	97041-1101	
EC-ZEE	Light Aero Avid Flyer STOL	00102-1491	
EC-ZEF	Rans S-12XL Airaile	01019-1556	
EC-ZEG	Campana 912	96045-995	
EC-ZEH	Tecnam P.96 Golf	01028-1581	
EC-ZEI	Sky Walker II-300	01051-1564	
EC-ZEJ	Challenger II Special	00103-1492	
EC-ZEK	Tecnam P.96 Golf	01016-1553	
EC-ZEL	Tecnam P.92 Ilusion	01052-1565	
EC-ZEM	Magni M-14 Scout	01032-1585	
EC-ZEN	Antares Pendular-Stream 16	00121-1510	
EC-ZEO	Max Air Drifter	98006-1167	
EC-ZEP	Moragon UL 2	99075-1349	
EC-ZEQ	Pottier P.180S	112/91	
EC-ZER	Tecnam P.96 Golf 100	01070-1607	
EC-ZES	Sport Aircraft Tango II-GT	01050-1563	
EC-ZET	Moragon UL 2	01076-1613	EC-001
	(Originally listed as a Moragon M1)		
EC-ZEU	Magni M-16 Tandem	01046-1599	
EC-ZEV	Zenair CH-601HD Zodiac	00146-1535	
EC-ZEX	Lucentum	01078-1615	
EC-ZEY	Moragon UL 2	01061-1574	
EC-ZEZ	Tecnam P.92 Echo	00095-1484	
EC-ZFA	Gemini Ultra	01026-1579	
EC-ZFB	CAG Toxo II	00127-1516	
EC-ZFC	Comco Ikarus C-42 Cyclone	01033-1586	
EC-ZFD	Comco Ikarus C-42 Cyclone	01034-1587	
EC-ZFE	Mignet HM-1000 Balérit	01042-1595	
EC-ZFF	Vol Mediterrani VM-1 Esqual	00100-1489	
EC-ZFG	Jodel D.18	99038-1312	
EC-ZFH	Hawk Plus single-seater	01074-1611	
EC-ZFI	Comco Ikarus C-42 Cyclone	01096-1633	
EC-ZFJ	Moragon UL 2	01073-1610	
EC-ZFK	Aeriane Swift	01069-1606	
EC-ZFL	Leza-Lockwood Drifter 912	00087-1476	
EC-ZFM	Moragon UL 2	01038-1591	
EC-ZFN	Eipper Quicksilver MXL-II Sport	00122-1511	
EC-ZFO	Comco Ikarus C-32 Fox Tristar	00139-1628	
EC-ZFP	Moragon UL 2	01092-1629	
EC-ZFQ	Fantasy Air Allegro 2000	01035-1588	
EC-ZFR	Air Création Racer Fun 14	99110-1384	
EC-ZFS	Platzer Kiebitz P-25	12/89	
EC-ZFT	Vol Mediterrani VM-1 Esqual	01030-1583	
EC-ZFU	Mignet HM-1000 Balerit	01093-1630	
EC-ZFV	Raj Hamsa X'Air	98076-1237	
EC-ZFX	Vol Mediterrani VM-1 Esqual (RG)	01120-1657	
EC-ZFY	Eipper Quicksilver GT-500	00113-1502	
EC-ZFZ	Cosmos BI TOP 14.9	98085-1246	
EC-ZGA	Zenair CH-601 Zodiac	00014-1403	
EC-ZGB	Tecnam P.92 Super	02022-1686	
EC-ZGC	Murphy Rebel Elite	00036-1425	
EC-ZGD	Rans S-6 Coyote II	98075-1236	
EC-ZGE	Brügger MB-2 Colibri	1/81	

EC-ZGF	Volero Pendular	01106-1643	
EC-ZGG	Neico Lancair 360	97037-1097	
EC-ZGH	Air Création Mild Twin 503	00104-1493	
EC-ZGI	Air Création Racer SX12	00112-1501	
EC-ZGJ	Magni M-16 Tandem Trainer	01039-1592	
EC-ZGK	Tecnam P.96 Golf 100	02014-1678	
EC-ZGL	Zenair CH-701 STOL	01067-1604	
EC-ZGM	Tecnam P.92 2000RG	01048-1601	
EC-ZGN	Zenair CH-601UL Zodiac	01113-1650	
EC-ZGO	ELA 07	02016-1680	
EC-ZGP	ELA 07	02021-1685	
EC-ZGQ	Vol Mediterrani VM-1 Esqual	01031-1584	
EC-ZGR	Capella XL	95019-879	
EC-ZGS	Light Aero Avid Flyer Magnum	02041-1705	
EC-ZGT	Cosmos Pendular	01058-1571	
EC-ZGU	Moragon UL 2	02024-1688	
EC-ZGV	Magni M-16 Tandem Trainer	02030-1694	
EC-ZGX	Rans S-12 Airaile	02015-1679	
EC-ZGY	Vol Mediterrani VM-1 Esqual	02036-1700	
EC-ZGZ	Tecnam P.96 Golf 100	01124-1661	
EC-ZHA	TEAM Mini Max V Max	00089-1478	
EC-ZHB	Alpe 101	95080-940	
EC-ZHC	Tecnam P.96 Golf 100	01124-1662	
EC-ZHD	Pendular Trike	02005-1669	
EC-ZHE	Hummel Bird	97095-1155	
EC-ZHF	Zenair CH-601 Zodiac	00072-1461	
EC-ZHG	TL Ultralight TL-96 Star	01085-1622	
EC-ZHH	Aviasud Mistral Standard	02045-1709	
EC-ZHI	Sport Aircraft Tango I	01090-1627	
EC-ZHJ	Adventure Air Adventurer	96012-962	
EC-ZHK	Zenair CH-601 Zodiac	01100-1637	
EC-ZHL	Moragon M 1	02054-1718	
EC-ZHM	Moragon M 1	02060-1724	
EC-ZHN	Nicollier HN-700 Menestral	00067-1456	
EC-ZHO	Raj Hamsa X'Air	01121-1658	
EC-ZHP	Moragon M 1	02055-1719	
EC-ZHQ	Neico Lancair 320	61/93	
EC-ZHR	Raj Hamsa X'Air	02034-1698	
EC-ZHS	Eipper Quicksilver MX-II Sprint	00108-1497	
EC-ZHT	Viper 2200/Cosmos 13	02008-1672	
EC-ZHU	Vol Mediterrani VM-1 Esqual	02023-1687	
EC-ZHV	Air Command Tomatito	00141-1530	
EC-ZHX	Rans S-4 Coyote I	02009-1673	
EC-ZHY	Tecnam P.92 Echo Super	02068-1728	
EC-ZHZ	Rans S-12 Airaile	02071-1731	
EC-ZIA	Robin ATL L (C/n also quoted as 02013-1677)	121	F-GGHQ
EC-ZIB	Robin ATL L (C/n also quoted as 02056-1720)	130	F-GIKT
EC-ZIC	QuikKit Glass Goose (W/o 16.6.04)	99024-1298	
EC-ZID	Eipper Quicksilver MX-II	97090-1150	
EC-ZIE	Vol Mediterrani VM-1 Esqual	02091-1755	
EC-ZIF	Challenger II	102/92	
EC-ZIG	Jabiru UL	99103-11377	
EC-ZIH	Kiebitz B/450	01072-1609	
EC-ZII	Light Aero Avid Flyer STOL	97088-1148	
EC-ZIJ	Dragon Light 200	01010-1547	
EC-ZIK	CAG Toxo	02067-1736	
EC-ZIL	Zenair CH-601 Zodiac	01114-1651	
EC-ZIM	Monnett Moni	17/84	
EC-ZIN	Vol Mediterrani VM-1 Esqual	02093-1757	
EC-ZIO	CAG Toxo	02051-1715	
EC-ZIP	Bragg	02072-1732	
EC-ZIQ	Vol Mediterrani VM-1 Esqual	01123-1660	
EC-ZIR	Aviatika MAI-890	02105-1769	
EC-ZIS	Min-Dango Volero-Cosmos P-19	01110-1647	
EC-ZIT	ATEC Zephyr 2000	02106-1770	
EC-ZIU	Zenair CH-801	02050-1714	
EC-ZIV	TL Ultralight TL-96 Star	02006-1670	
EC-ZIX	ATEC Zephyr 2000	02107-1771	
EC-ZIY	ATEC Zephyr 2000 (Crashed 6.3.04)	02122-1786	
EC-ZIZ	CASA C-1.131E Jungmann	02074-1738	
EC-ZJA	TEAM Mini-Max 1600R	02109-1773	
EC-ZJB	TL Ultralight TL-2000 Sting	03015-1804	
EC-ZJC	Kiebitz P-5	00148-1537	
EC-ZJD	Dynali Chickinox	94105	
EC-ZJE	Evektor EV-97 Eurostar 2000R	03023-1812	
EC-ZJF	ELA 07-912	02123-1787	
EC-ZJG	ICP MXP.740 Savannah	02086-1750	
EC-ZJH	Viper Hazard-12	03003-1792	
EC-ZJI	Viper Hazard-12	03001-1790	
	(W/o 4.8.03 - type quoted as Colyaer Mascato S100)		
EC-ZJJ	Viper Hazard-15	03002-1791	
EC-ZJK	Magni M-16 Tandem Trainer	03014-1803	
EC-ZJL	Flamingo	02094-1758	
EC-ZJM	Rans S-16 Shekari	01065-1578	
EC-ZJN	Dallach D-7 Fascination	03013-1802	
EC-ZJO	Gemini Thruster	02049-1713	
EC-ZJP	Raptor Gyrocopter	02100-1764	
EC-ZJQ	ELA 07-912	03004-1793	
EC-ZJR	ATEC Zephyr 2000	03026-1782	
EC-ZJS	Sky Walker II-300	114/91	
EC-ZJT	Leza-Lockwood Drifter ARV-582	00007-1396	
EC-ZJU	Martin III Seaplane	03028-1783	
EC-ZJV	Moragon UL 2	01002-1539	
EC-ZJX	ELA 07-R100	03024-1813	
EC-ZJY	Sport Aircraft Tango II two-seat	01089-1626	
EC-ZJZ	Eipper Quicksilver MXL-II	02110-1774	
EC-ZKA	Raj Hamsa X'Air	03032-1815	
EC-ZKB	J1B	48/91	
EC-ZKC	Raj Hamsa X'Air	01004-1541	
EC-ZKD	TEAM Mini-Max	98106-1267	
EC-ZKE	ATEC Zephyr 2000	03011-1800	
EC-ZKF	Slepcev Storch SS4UL	03031-1814	
EC-ZKG	ELA 07-912S	02087-1751	
EC-ZKH	ELA 07-912S	02082-1746	
EC-ZKI	ELA 07-914	03007-1796	
EC-ZKJ	Jet Fox 97	03012-1801	
EC-ZKK	Colibri JL I+I XP12	02113-1777	
EC-ZKL	Moragon M-3	02084-1748	
EC-ZKM	Tecnam P.96 Golf 100	03037-1820	
EC-ZKN	Vol Mediterrani VM-1 Esqual	02037-1701	
EC-ZKO	ATEC Zephyr 2000	03036-1819	
EC-ZKP	Cedimax Rans S-6ES Coyote II	02125-1789	
EC-ZKQ	Texan Top Class	03067-1850	
EC-ZKR	Evektor EV-97 Eurostar	03022-1811	
EC-ZKS	Piper J-3C Cub	98096-1247	
EC-ZKT	Zenair CH-601 Zodiac	02052-1716	
EC-ZKU	Tecnam P-2002 Sierra	03058-1841	
EC-ZKV	ATEC Zephyr 2000	03030-1788	
EC-ZKX	TL Ultralight TL-2000 Sting	03070-1853	
EC-ZKY	TL Ultralight TL-2000 Sting	03064-1847	
EC-ZKZ	Tecnam P-2002 Sierra	03062-1845	
EC-ZLA	ATEC Zephyr 2000	03042-1825	
EC-ZLB	Magni M-16 Tandem Trainer	03063-1846	
EC-ZLC	Air Création Mild Twin 503	03054-1837	
EC-ZLD	Aerotec Vampir	02053-1717	
EC-ZLE	Fantasy Air Allegro 2000	01109-1646	
EC-ZLF	Moravan Zlin Savage	03010-1799	
EC-ZLG	Aeromoragón Moragón M-1	03043-1826	
EC-ZLH	Avid Flyer	99056-1330	
EC-ZLI	FC-15 Alondra	99062-1336	
EC-ZLJ	Direct Fly Asso V	02112-1776	
EC-ZLK	TL Ultralight TL-2000 Sting	03075-1858	
EC-ZLL	Mustang II	00106-1495	
EC-ZLM	Titan Tornado	02042-1706	
EC-ZLN	Rutan VariEze	03045-1828	
EC-ZLO	Sonex	01111-1648	
EC-ZLP	Fisher Super Koala	13/87	
EC-ZLQ	ATEC Zephyr 2000	03044-1827	
EC-ZLR	Breezer	02035-1699	
EC-ZLS	Zenair CH-701 STOL	03049-1832	
EC-ZLT	ATEC Zephyr 2000	03076-1859	
EC-ZLU	Bicicleta Aerea	99010-1284	
EC-ZLV	Pottier P-130 UL	03018-1807	
EC-ZLX	Quicksilver MXL-II	03081-1864	
EC-ZLY	ICP MXP-740 Savannah	03091-1874	
EC-ZLZ	Alpi Avn Pioneer 200	02080-1744	
EC-ZMA	Moravan Zlin Savage	02075-1739	
EC-ZMB	Air Création GT BI SX-16	01017-1554	
EC-ZMC	Magni M-16 Tandem Trainer	03019-1808	
EC-ZMD	Quicksilver MXL-II Sport	03052-1835	
EC-ZME	ELA 07-115	04020-1904	
EC-ZMF	TL Ultralight TL-232 Condor	02032-1696	
EC-ZMG	Sport Aircraft Tango I	03048-1831	
EC-ZMH	Zenair CH-601 XL Zodiac	03093-1876	
EC-ZMI	Raj Hamsa X'Air	00124-1513	
EC-ZMJ	Zenair CH-601 XL Zodiac	03071-1854	
EC-ZMK	ELA 07-115	04032-1916	
EC-ZML	Vol Mediterrani VM-1 Esqual	04021-1905	
EC-ZMM	Vol Mediterrani VM-1 Esqual	04029-1913	
EC-ZMN	Tecnam P-2002 Sierra	04015-1899	
EC-ZMO	Tecnam P-2002 Sierra	04025-1909	
EC-ZMP	Tecnam P-2002 Sierra	04030-1914	
EC-ZMQ	Bello I	04007-1891	
EC-ZMR	RLR	03053-1836	
EC-ZMS	Air Création Buggy Kiss 450	03057-1840	
EC-ZMT	Zenair CH-601 Zodiac	03050-1833	
EC-ZMU	ELA 07-R115	04058-1942	
EC-ZMV	Rans S-12 Airaile	57/92	
EC-ZMX	Tecnam P-2002 Sierra	04053-1937	
EC-ZMY	F.C.B.	01014-1551	
EC-ZMZ	Tecnam P-2002 Sierra	04031-1915	
EC-ZNA	Tecnam P-2002 Sierra	04022-1906	
EC-ZNB	Tecnam P-2002 Sierra	04014-1898	
EC-ZNC	Tecnam P-2002 Sierra	04024-1908	
EC-ZND	Zenair CH-601 Zodiac	02104-1768	
EC-ZNE	Zenair CH-701 STOL	04027-1911	
EC-ZNF	Avid Flyer STOL	03060-1843	
EC-ZNG	Autogiro B II C	04041-1925	
EC-ZNH	Neico Lancair 360	01097-1634	
EC-ZNI	Tecnam P.96 Golf 100	04052-1936	
EC-ZNJ	Zenair CH-601 XL Zodiac	04005-1889	
EC-ZNK	Raj Hamsa X'Air	03073-1856	
EC-ZNL	Capella XSX TR	02073-1737	
EC-ZNM	Rans S-12XL Airaile	02018-1682	
EC-ZNN	HFL Stratos	04018-1902	
EC-ZNO	Technoflug Piccolo B	04042-1926	
EC-ZNP	ATEC Zephyr 2000	03074-1857	
EC-ZNQ	ELA 07-R115	04070-1954	
EC-ZNR	Comco Ikarus C-42 Cyclone	02028-1692	
EC-ZNS	Tecnam P-2002 Sierra	04051-1935	
EC-ZNT	Van's RV-4	01068-1605	
EC-ZNU	Vol Mediterrani VM-1 Esqual	02003-1667	
EC-ZNV	King Cobra Biplaza	96040-990	
EC-ZNX	ATEC Zephyr	04047-1931	

EC-ZNY	Air Création Racer 503 SL XP11	04012-1896
EC-ZNZ	Autogiro MT-2	04039-1923
EC-ZOA	Denney Kitfox III	03033-1816
EC-ZOB	ATEC Zephyr 2000	04079-1963
EC-ZOC	Loehle Mustang 5151	97097-1157
EC-ZOD	Girabet	04050-1934
EC-ZOE	Raj Hamsa X'Air	03072-1855
EC-ZOF	Tecnam P-2002 Sierra	04040-1924
EC-ZOG	Air Création Safari GT BI XP15	02111-1775
EC-ZOH	CASA C 1.131 Jungmann	02081-1745
EC-ZOI	Ragwing Special	03101-1884
EC-ZOJ	Raj Hamsa X'Air	04034-1918
EC-ZOK	ELA 07-115	04095-1979
EC-ZOL	Evektor EV-97 Eurostar 2000R	04054-1938
EC-ZOM	Alto Jabiru 3300	04028-1912
EC-ZON	Kappa KP-2 UR Sova	04065-1949
EC-ZOO	Dynali Chickinox Kot-Kot	03082-1865
EC-ZOP	Moravan Zlin Savage	04001--1878
EC-ZOQ	Quicksilver MXL-II Sport	02098-1762
EC-ZOR	Ekolot JK-05 Junior	04059-1943
EC-ZOS	JLA Savannah	04072-1956
EC-ZOT	Tecnam P-2002 Sierra	04101-1985
EC-ZOU	Zenair CH-601 XL Zodiac	04090-1974
EC-ZOV	Quicksilver MXL-II Sport	04063-1947
EC-ZOX	Test Alpin 2	04062-1946
EC-ZOY	ZH-XL	04064-1948

The following temporary registrations are also known - many have probably been re-regd in the above sequence but others are recent sightings:-

EC-002	Vol Mediterrani VM-1 Esqual (Noted 8.03)		
EC-004	Sinus 912 (Type unconfirmed, noted 9.7.04)		
EC-043	Rans S-12XL Airaile		
EC-044	Rans S-6 Coyote IIXL		
EC-047	ICP Bingo		
EC-108	N-3 Pup (See EC-YMX)		
EC-152	Brügger MB-2 Colibri		
EC-160	Pterodactyl Ascender		
EC-161	Pterodactyl Ascender (Type unconfirmed, noted 22.8.04)		
EC-164	Juvenavia Vulcano (Stored incomplete)		
EC-173	Rand-Robinson KR-2		
EC-175	Neico Lancair 360		
EC-249	TEAM Mini-Max		
EC-250	Air Command Gyrocopter (to EC-ZHV?)		
EC-300	Rans S-6 Coyote II		
EC-303	Pober Pixie		
EC-365	Light Aero Avid Flyer)		
EC-369	Light Aero Avid Flyer) (Probably re-registered in EC-YE. range)		
EC-370	Light Aero Avid Flyer)		
EC-414	Christen Eagle (Type unconfirmed)		
EC-432	Van's RV-6 (See EC-YOG)		
EC-444	Aviatika 890U Mai		
EC-459	Type unknown		
EC-466	Denney Kitfox III (See EC-YMF)		
EC-506	Rans S-6 Coyote II (W/o 19.6.94)		
EC-565	Light Aero Avid Flyer		
EC-573	Type unknown		
EC-579	Rotorway Executive 90 (Damaged 6.10.94)		
EC-581	Saltapraos		
EC-601	Light Aero Avid Flyer		
EC-659	Sky Walker		
EC-676	Rutan Long-Ez (See EC-YNP)		
EC-693	Consolidated PBY-5A Catalina (Cuatro Vientos Museum)	1960	EC-314 C-FFFW N45998 CF-FFW N6070C BuA46596
EC-703	Rand-Robinson KR-2		
EC-711	Denney Kitfox		
EC-718	Eipper Quicksilver MXL-II Sport	029	
EC-741	Aero Designs Pulsar (See EC-CE8)		
EC-748	TEAM Mini-Max (See EC-YOB)		
EC-826	Rans S-6 Coyote II TD/912		
EC-847	Air Création		
EC-901	Rans S-10 Sakota (See EC-YMN)		
EC-914	Rans S-12 Airaile		
EC-926	Eipper Quicksilver MX		
EC-927	Rans S-12 Airaile		
EC-929	Jodel D.18		
EC-937	Cameron RX-100 HAFB (Cuatro Vientos Museum)	2666	G-BTXP
EC-1592	Magni M-16TTGyro		

MICROLIGHTS

EC-AA1	Ultralight Soaring Wizard J3	
EC-AA2	Pterodactyl Ascender 1	
EC-AA3	Pterodactyl Ascender 1	
EC-AA4	Ultralight Soaring Wizard	
EC-AA5	King Cobra	
EC-AA7	Cobra	
EC-AA8	Condor III-2	
EC-AA9	Weedhopper JC-24C	
EC-AB1	Ultralight Soaring Wizard T-38B	66023
EC-AB2	Ultralight Soaring Wizard T-38B	66024
EC-AB3	King Cobra	
EC-AB4	Eipper Quicksilver MX-II	1222
EC-AB5	Condor III 40	
EC-AB7	King Cobra	
EC-AB8	Mistral 2-seater	
EC-AB9	Dragon Light 150	016
EC-AC1	Dragon 150	
EC-AC2	Southdown Puma Sprint	
EC-AC3	Condor III 440	
EC-AC4	Eipper Quicksilver MX-IIAA	1909
EC-AC5	Wizard T-38	
EC-AC6	Eipper Quicksilver MX-II	1910
EC-AC7	Eipper Quicksilver MX-II	1940
EC-AC8	Aquillon Etoile	B-19
EC-AC9	Eipper Quicksilver MX-II	1943
EC-AD1	Terratorn Tierra II	
EC-AD2	Wizard T-38	66018
EC-AD3	Rotec Rally III	
EC-AD4	Lazair II	B0-37
EC-AD5	Jordan Aviation Duet	5
EC-AD6	Wizard T-38	66069
EC-AD7	Eipper Quicksilver MX-II	2000
EC-AD8	Wizard J-3	
EC-AD9	Pterodactyl Ascender 2+2	83042092
EC-AE1	Eipper Quicksilver MX	4261
EC-AE2	Eipper Quicksilver MX	3839
EC-AE3	Eipper Quicksilver MX-I	3829
EC-AE4	PumAll	109
EC-AE5	Eipper Quicksilver MX-II	2082
EC-AE6	Eipper Quicksilver MX	3693
EC-AE7	Eipper Quicksilver MX-L	1386
EC-AE8	Eipper Quicksilver MX	1809
EC-AE9	Wizard T-38	44013
EC-AF1	Wizard T-38B	
EC-AF2	Sport Aircraft Tango II-GT	108502
EC-AF4	Pterodactyl Ascender II	
EC-AF5	Eipper Quicksilver MX-II	1955
EC-AF6	Tango B-84	12841
EC-AF7	Pterodactyl Ascender 2+2	1376
EC-AF8	Pterodactyl Ascender 2+2	1407
EC-AF9	Eipper Quicksilver MX-II	1781
EC-AG1	Pterodactyl Ascender II	
EC-AG2	Aériane Sirocco	
EC-AG3	Eipper Quicksilver MX-II	1447
EC-AG4	Sorrell SNA-8 Hiperlight	125
EC-AG5	Sorrell SNA-8 Hiperlight	134
EC-AG6	Challenger II	
EC-AG7	Challenger II	
EC-AG8	Interair F2	15/85
EC-AG9	Wizard T-38	66036
EC-AH1	Spilfire F2/55	85/16
EC-AH2	Cosmos Hermes	
EC-AH3	Sport Aircraft Tango II	10842
EC-AH4	Sky Jet IV	OLB/00501
EC-AH5	Luroplane 3-por-2	
EC-AH6	Humbert La Moto del Cielo	8806
EC-AH7	Interair F-2/55	SF-007
EC-AH8	Interair F-2/55	SF-001
EC-AH9	Interair F-2/55	SF-006
EC-AI1	Interair F-2/55	85/00
EC-AI2	Interair F-2/55	SF-003
EC-AI3	Challenger	100B118103
EC-AI4	Sky Jet II	MLB/0512A
EC-AI5	Cosmos Bidulum 53	
EC-AI6	Sport Aircraft Tango II	5861
EC-AI7	Sky Jet II A3	0101/85
EC-AI9	Sport Aircraft Tango II-GT	10863
EC-AJ1	Interair F-2/55	87/1
EC-AJ2	Cosmos Bidulum 46	3585302
EC-AJ3	Sport Aircraft Tango II	12855
EC-AJ4	Sky Jet	00505A
EC-AJ5	Hummer B	
EC-AJ8	Eipper Quicksilver MX-II	28AD
EC-AJ9	Sport Aircraft Tango II-GT	2871
EC-AK1	Sport Aircraft Tango II-GT	4871
EC-AK3	Zodiac Twinstar	116
EC-AK4	Aviasud Mistral	06.87/042
EC-AK5	Aviasud Mistral	017
EC-AK6	Eipper Quicksilver MX-II	2240
EC-AK7	Cosmos Pendular	3585110
EC-AK8	Sport Aircraft Tango II	2872
EC-AK9	Sport Aircraft Tango II	9874
EC-AL1	Sport Aircraft Tango II-GT	6875
EC-AL2	Sport Aircraft Tango II	1882
EC-AL3	Eipper Quicksilver MX-II	2216
EC-AL4	Aviasud Mistral	034
EC-AL5	Comco Ikarus Fox-C22	8803-3120
EC-AL6	Comco Ikarus Fox-C22	8803-3121
EC-AL7	Air Création Safari GT BI Plus 20	042
EC-AL8	Humbert La Moto del Cielo	8823
EC-AL9	Sport Aircraft Tango II	5856
EC-AM1	Sport Aircraft Tango II	4873
EC-AM2	Sport Aircraft Tango II	6876

EC-AM3	Rotec Panther 2	25733	
EC-AM4	Sport Aircraft Tango II-GT	3887	
EC-AM5	Eipper Quicksilver MX-II	1225	
EC-AM6	Sport Aircraft Tango II-GT	4882	
EC-AM7	Sallen Mach-15 Gyrocopter	129	
EC-AM8	Sallen Mach-15 Gyrocopter	119	
EC-AM9	Eipper Quicksilver MX-II	1994	
EC-AN1	Eipper Quicksilver MXL-II	3721	
EC-AN3	Sallen Mach-15 Gyrocopter	123	
EC-AN4	Sallen Mach-15 Gyrocopter	134	
EC-AN5	Sallen Mach-15 Gyrocopter	121	
EC-AN6	Hispano Lights Colometa 52A	1511-8852002	
EC-AN7	Sport Aircraft Tango II-GT	9872	
EC-AN8	Sallen Mach 15 Gyrocopter	132	
EC-AN9	Eipper Quicksilver MX-II	2217	
EC-A01	Sallen Mach-10 Gyrocopter	110	
EC-A02	Dynali Chickinox Tandem	2944381	
EC-A03	Sport Aircraft Tango II-GT	7871	
EC-A04	Sallen Mach-15 Gyrocopter	120	
EC-A05	Sallen Mach-15 Gyrocopter	114	
EC-A06	Sallen Mach-15 Gyrocopter	130	
EC-A07	Sallen Mach-15 Gyrocopter	133	
EC-A08	Sallen Mach-15 Gyrocopter	136	
EC-AO9	Sallen Mach-15 Gyrocopter	137	
EC-AP1	Sport Aircraft Tango II-GT	6891	
EC-AP2	Sport Aircraft Tango II-GT	2885	
EC-AP4	Sport Aircraft Tango II-GT	3884	
EC-AP5	Sport Aircraft Tango II-GT	3881	
EC-AP6	Sport Aircraft Tango II-GT	3871	
EC-AP7	Hispano Lights Colometa 52A	04049052003	
EC-AP8	Hispano Lights Colometa 52A	04049052004	
EC-AP9	Sport Aircraft Tango II	3895	
EC-AQ1	Sport Aircraft Tango II	3894	
EC-AQ2	Sport Aircraft Tango II	1895	
EC-AQ3	Sport Aircraft Tango II	4893	
EC-AQ4	Sport Aircraft Tango II	6892	
EC-AQ5	Sport Aircraft Tango II	5856	
EC-AQ6	Sallen Mach-15 Gyrocopter	127	
EC-AQ7	Sport Aircraft Tango II-GT	1903	
EC-AQ8	Sport Aircraft Tango II	9877	
EC-AQ9	Sport Aircraft Tango II	1902	
EC-AR1	Sport Aircraft Tango II	4891	
EC-AR2	Sport Aircraft Tango II-GT	5891	
EC-AR3	Sport Aircraft Tango II	6893	
EC-AR4	Sport Aircraft Tango II	2901	
EC-AR5	Sport Aircraft Tango II-GT	12854	
EC-AR6	Sport Aircraft Tango II	3905	
EC-AR8	Hispano Lights Colometa 52V	09049052005	
EC-AR9	Sport Aircraft Tango II-GT	5892	
EC-AS1	Sport Aircraft Tango II	1905	
EC-AS2	Eipper Quicksilver MX-II	2327	
EC-AS3	Sport Aircraft Tango II-GT	5895	
EC-AS4	Sport Aircraft Tango II	3902	
EC-AS5	Sallen Mach 15 Gyrocopter	131	
EC-AS7	Sport Aircraft Tango II	1901	
EC-AS8	Sport Aircraft Tango II	2902	
EC-AS9	Sport Aircraft Tango II	2905	
EC-AT2	Sport Aircraft Tango II	5903	
EC-AT3	Sport Aircraft Tango II	1893	
EC-AT4	Sport Aircraft Tango II	3904	
EC-AT5	Hispano Lights Colometa 52A	05119052006	
EC-AT6	Sport Aircraft Tango II	12852	
EC-AT7	Aerial Arts Chaser S	CH-779	EC-280
EC-AT8	Dynali Chickinox Kot-Kot	31191855	
EC-AU1	Dynali Chickinox Tandem II	292796	
EC-AU2	Sport Aircraft Tango II	4903	
EC-AU3	Sport Aircraft Tango II	9842	
EC-AU4	Dynali Chickinox Kot-Kot	31139741	
EC-AU5	Sport Aircraft Tango II	1913	
EC-AU6	Sport Aircraft Tango II	6904	
EC-AU7	Sallen Mach-15 Gyrocopter	138	
EC-AU8	Sallen Mach-15 Gyrocopter	118	
EC-AU9	Sallen Mach-10 Gyrocopter	115	
EC-AV1	Sport Aircraft Tango II	2882	
EC-AV2	Sport Aircraft Tango II	4905	
EC-AV3	Sport Aircraft Tango II	2904	
EC-AV4	Sport Aircraft Tango II	1912	
EC-AV5	Sport Aircraft Tango II	3876	
EC-AV6	Dynali Chickinox Kot-Kot	31256693	EC-606 ?
EC-AV7	Sallen Mach 15 Gyrocopter	15-142	
EC-AV8	Sport Aircraft Tango II	4904	
EC-AV9	Sport Aircraft Tango II	9876	
EC-AX1	Sport Aircraft Tango II	6902	
EC-AX2	Sport Aircraft Tango II-GT	5901	
EC-AX3	Dynali Chickinox Tandem	219154	
EC-AX4	Sport Aircraft Tango II-GT	2913	
EC-AX5	Sport Aircraft Tango II-GT	2911	
EC-AX6	Sport Aircraft Tango II-GT	2912	
EC-AX7	Sport Aircraft Tango II	4902	
EC-AX8	Sport Aircraft Tango II-GT	5904	
EC-AX9	Eipper Quicksilver MX-II	3876	
EC-AY1	Dynali Chickinox Kot-Kot	329846	
EC-AY2	Dynali Chickinox Tandem	2106128	
EC-AY3	Sport Aircraft Tango II	5851	
EC-AY4	Sallen Mach-15 Gyrocopter	15-143	
EC-AY6	Sport Aircraft Tango II-GT	3912	
EC-AY7	Sallen Mach 10 Gyrocopter	10-111	
EC-AY8	Sport Aircraft Tango II-GT	2915	
EC-AY9	Sport Aircraft Tango II-GT	1914	
EC-AZ1	Sallen Mach 15 Gyrocopter	128	
EC-AZ2	Sport Aircraft Tango II-GT	3911	
EC-AZ3	Sport Aircraft Tango II-GT	4911	
EC-AZ4	Sport Aircraft Tango II-GT	1885	
EC-AZ5	Sport Aircraft Tango II	3853	
EC-AZ6	Eipper Quicksilver MXL -II	140	
EC-AZ7	Dynali Chickinox Kot-Kot	31086928	
EC-AZ8	Dynali Chickinox Monoplaza	11087812	
EC-BA1	Air Création Safari GT-BI Fun 18	191003	
EC-BA2	Air Création Safari GT-BI Fun 18	191007	
EC-BA3	Sport Aircraft Tango II	6903	
EC-BA4	Sport Aircraft Tango II	5893	
EC-BA5	Eipper Quicksilver MXL	3722	
EC-BA6	Eipper Quicksilver MX-Sprint II	212	
EC-BA7	Eipper Quicksilver MX-Sprint II	292	
EC-BA8	Sport Aircraft Tango II	4901	
EC-BA9	Air Création Safari GT-BI Fun 18	191006	
EC-BB1	Sport Aircraft Tango II	4894	
EC-BB2	Air Création Safari GT-BI Fun 18	192013	
EC-BB3	Eipper Quicksilver MXL-Sport II	78	
EC-BB4	Sallen Mach-15 Gyrocopter	15-144	
EC-BB5	Eipper Quicksilver MX-Sprint II	137	
EC-BB6	Dynali Chickinox	31220684	
EC-BB7	Eipper Quicksilver MXL-II	1353	
EC-BB8	Air Création Safari GT-BI Fun 18	192014	
EC-BB9	Sallen Mach-15 Gyrocopter	112	
EC-BC1	Eipper Quicksilver MXL-II	1212	
EC-BC2	Sallen Mach-10	140	
EC-BC3	Sallen Mach-15 Gyrocopter	15-145	
EC-BC4	Eipper Quicksilver MXL	1689	
EC-BC5	Sport Aircraft Tango II	4884	
EC-BC6	Sport Aircraft Tango II	6851	
EC-BC7	Eipper Quicksilver MX-II	237	
EC-BC8	Sport Aircraft Tango II	5912	
EC-BC9	Sport Aircraft Tango II-GT	5913	
EC-BD1	Eipper Quicksilver MX-II	210	
EC-BD2	Sallen Mach-15 Gyrocopter	15-146	
EC-BD3	Sport Aircraft Tango II-GT	2914	
EC-BD4	Sport Aircraft Tango II-GT	4912	
EC-BD5	Sport Aircraft Tango II-GT	3913	
EC-BD7	Dynali Chickinox Kot-Kot	354134	
EC-BD8	Eipper Quicksilver MXL	222	
EC-BD9	Eipper Quicksilver MX-II	1315	
EC-BE1	Air Création Safari GT-BI Fun 18	192017	
EC-BE2	Eipper Quicksilver MXL	1685	
EC-BE3	Sport Aircraft Tango II-GT	5914	
EC-BE4	Eipper Quicksilver MXL-II	143	
EC-BE5	Sallen Mach-15 Gyrocopter	15-147	
EC-BE6	Air Création Safari GT-BI Fun 18	191010	
EC-BE8	Air Création Safari GT-BI Fun 18	191002	
EC-BE9	Air Création Safari GT-BI Fun 18	192015	
EC-BF1	Air Création Safari GT-BI Quartz 16 SXE	292008	
EC-BF2	Eipper Quicksilver MX Sprint II	144	
EC-BF3	Eipper Quicksilver MXL	3260	
EC-BF4	Dynali Chickinox Tandem	258186	
EC-BF5	Air Création Safari GT-BI Quartz 16 SXE	292007	
EC-BF6	Sallen Mach-15 Gyrocopter	15-126	
EC-BF7	Sallen Mach-15 Gyrocopter	15-149	
EC-BF8	Eipper Quicksilver MX	142	
EC-BF9	Sport Aircraft Tango II-GT	1891	
EC-BG1	Sport Aircraft Tango II-GT	1926	
EC-BG2	Air Création GT BI Fun 18	19001	
EC-BG3	Air Création GT BI Quartz 16SXE	291002	
EC-BG4	Sport Aircraft Tango II-GT	4914	
EC-BG5	Ultraligeros Espana Volero Jaguar-16	V-1921	
EC-BG6	Dynali Chickinox Kot-Kot	31060000	
EC-BG7	Sport Aircraft Tango II-GT	T2922	
EC-BG8	Sport Aircraft Tango II-GT	1921	
EC-BG9	Sport Aircraft Tango II-GT	1911	
EC-BH1	Dynali Chickinox Kot-Kot	2592E106	
EC-BH2	Dynali Chickinox Kot-Kot	32144536	
EC-BH3	Ultraligeros Espana Volero Jaguar-16	V-3922	
EC-BH4	Ultraligeros Espana Volero Jaguar-16	V-3921	
EC-BH5	Ultraligeros Espana Volero Jaguar-16	V-3924	
EC-BH6	Ultraligeros Espana Volero Jaguar-16	V-3923	
EC-BH7	Fly-Master TSA-10	003	
EC-BH8	Eipper Quicksilver MX-II	3269	
EC-BH9	Sallen Mach 15 Gyrocopter	15-148	
EC-BI1	Sport Aircraft Tango GT-II	T2921	
EC-BI2	Air Création Safari GT BI Fun 18	192025	
EC-BI3	Ultraligeros Espana Volero Jaguar-16	V-1923	
EC-BI4	Ultraligeros Espana Volero Jaguar-16	V-4921	
EC-BI5	Ultraligeros Espana Volero Jaguar-16	V-3925	
EC-BI6	Sport Aircraft Tango II-GT	T2923	
EC-BI7	Air Création Safari GT-BI Quartz 16 SXE	291005	
EC-BI8	Eipper Quicksilver MX-Sprint IIR	0138	
EC-BJ1	Air Création Safari GT-BI Fun 18	192029	
EC-BJ2	Air Création Safari GT-BI Fun 18	192024	
EC-BJ4	Air Création Safari GT-BI Fun 18	191012	
EC-BJ5	Sport Aircraft Tango II-GT	T1925	
EC-BJ7	Air Création Safari GT-BI Fun 18	192031	
EC-BJ8	Eipper Quicksilver MX-II	5007	
EC-BK1	Eipper Quicksilver MX-II	5009	
EC-BK2	Sallen Mach-15 Gyrocopter	15-150	
EC-BK3	Dynali Chickinox Kot-Kot	31216262	

EC-BK4	Dynali Chickinox Kot-Kot	31126409
EC-BK5	Air Création Safari GT-BI Fun 18	192032
EC-BK6	Ultraligeros Espana Volero Jaguar-16	V-1915
EC-BK7	Air Création Safari GT-BI Fun 18	192018
EC-BK8	Cedimex Rans S-12 Airaile	S-12-100
EC-BK9	Air Création Safari GT-BI Fun 18	192020
EC-BL1	Ultraligeros Espana Volero Jaguar-16	V-1914
EC-BL2	Ultraligeros Espana Volero Jaguar-16	V-1924
EC-BL3	Air Création Safari GT-BI Fun 18	192022
EC-BL4	Air Création Safari GT-BI Fun 18	193033
EC-BL5	Carlos Perez Fly-Master TSA-10	000
EC-BL6	Eipper Quicksilver MX-Sprint IIR	0349
EC-BL7	Eipper Quicksilver MX-Sprint II	0289
EC-BL8	Carlos Perez Fly-Master TSA-10	016
EC-BL9	Carlos Perez Fly-Master TSA-10	012
EC-BM1	Carlos Perez Fly-Master TSA-10	015
EC-BM2	Air Création Safari GT-BI Fun 18	192028
EC-BM3	Sport Aircraft Tango II-GT	T-2925
EC-BM4	Sport Aircraft Tango II-GT	T-2924
EC-BM5	Eipper Quicksilver MX	0082
EC-BM6	Carlos Perez Fly-Master TSA-10	009
EC-BM7	Eipper Quicksilver MX-Sprint II	0364
EC-BM8	Carlos Perez Fly-Master TSA-10	007
EC-BM9	Ultraligeros Espana Volero Jaguar-16	V-4923
EC-BN1	Sallen Mach-15 Gyrocopter	15-151
EC-BN2	Eipper Quicksilver MX-Sprint IIR	390
EC-BN3	Ultraligeros Espana Volero Jaguar-16	V-1925
EC-BN4	Eipper Quicksilver GT-500	0068
EC-BN5	Eipper Quicksilver GT-500	0088
EC-BN6	Ultraligeros Espana Volero Jaguar-16	V-1922
EC-BN7	Ultraligeros Espana Volero Jaguar-16	V-2922
EC-BN8	Ultraligeros Espana Volero Jaguar-16	V-2924
EC-BN9	Dynali Chickinox Kot-Kot	1393-E-11
EC-BO1	Air Création Safari GT-BI Fun 18	193034
EC-BO2	Eipper Quicksilver GT-500	0089
EC-BO3	Cedimex Rans S-12 Airaile	S-12-115
EC-BO4	Cedimex Rans S-12 Airaile	S-12-108
EC-BO5	Cedimex Rans S-12 Airaile	S-12-103
EC-BO6	Eipper Quicksilver MXL-Sport IIR	0328
EC-BO7	Air Création Safari GT BI Quartz 16 SXE	292003
EC-BO8	Cedimex Rans S-12 Airaile	S-12-117
EC-BO9	Eipper Quicksilver MX-Sprint IIR	0312
EC-BP1	Eipper Quicksilver MX-Sprint II	0365
EC-BP2	Eipper Quicksilver MX-Sprint IIR	0309
EC-BP3	Ultraligeros Espana Volero Jaguar-16	V-1916
EC-BP4	Cedimex Rans S-12 Airaile	S-12-114
EC-BP5	Eipper Quicksilver MXL-Sport IIR	0353
EC-BP6	Air Création Safari GT-BI Quartz	293010
EC-BP7	Ultraligeros Espana Volero Jaguar-16	V-4925
EC-BP8	Cedimex Rans S-12 Airaile	S-12-112
EC-BP9	Air Création Safari GT-BI XP15	193036
EC-BQ1	Air Création Safari GT-BI Quartz 16 SXE	91004
EC-BQ2	Eipper Quicksilver MX-Sprint IIR	350
EC-BQ3	Eipper Quicksilver GT-500	0074
EC-BQ4	Eipper Quicksilver MX-Sprint IIR	0388
EC-BQ5	Cedimex Rans S-12 Airaile	S-12-118
EC-BQ6	Carlos Perez Fly-Master TSA-10	014
EC-BQ7	Eipper Quicksilver MX-Sprint IIR	0363
EC-BQ9	Mainair Gemini/Flash IIA	934-01937-W732
EC-BR1	Mainair Gemini/Flash IIA	914-07927-W713
EC-BR2	Mainair Gemini/Flash IIA	871-12917-W666
EC-BR3	Mainair Gemini/Flash IIA	847-07917-W641
EC-BR4	Aviasud Mistral 582	157
EC-BR5	Eipper Quicksilver MX-Sprint II	0392
EC-BR6	Air Création Safari GT-BI Fun 18S	191011
EC-BR7	Air Création Safari GT-BI SX16	291006
EC-BR8	Eipper Quicksilver MX-Sprint II	0391
EC-BR9	Cedimex Rans S-12 Airaile	S-12-102
EC-BS1	Sallen Mach-15 Gyrocopter	15-154
EC-BS2	Air Création Safari GT-BI Quartz 16 SXS	293012
EC-BS3	Sport Aircraft Tango II-GT	3915
EC-BS4	Eipper Quicksilver MXL-II	1693
EC-BS5	Dynali Chickinox Kot-Kot	3119196
EC-BS6	Air Création Safari GT-BI Fun 18	193038
EC-BS7	Eipper Quicksilver MX-Sprint IIR	0362
EC-BS8	Cedimex Rans S-12 Airaile	S-12-113
EC-BS9	Air Création Safari GT-BI Fun 18	193037
EC-BT1	Air Création Safari GT-BI Quartz 16 SXS	294015
EC-BT2	Air Création Safari GT-BI Quartz 16 SXS	293013
EC-BT3	Mainair Gemini/Flash IIA	952-06937-W747
EC-BT5	Mainair Gemini/Flash IIA	782-02907-W575
EC-BT6	Air Création Safari GT-BI Fun 18	194040
EC-BT7	Eipper Quicksilver MXL-Sport IIR	0409
EC-BT8	Cedimex Rans S-12 Airaile	S-12-111
EC-BT9	Dynali Chickinox Kot-Kot	31149060
EC-BU1	Sport Aircraft Tango II	3862
EC-BU2	Eipper Quicksilver MXL-Sport IIR	0354
EC-BU3	Cedimex Rans S-12 Airaile	S-12-131
EC-BU4	Mainair Gemini/Flash IIA	987-04947-W783
EC-BU5	Cedimex Rans S-12 Airaile	S-12-132
EC-BU6	Mainair 582 Blade	1005-0894/-W801
EC-BU7	Air Création Safari GT-BI Fun 18	194041
EC-BU8	Ultraligeros Espana Volero Jaguar-16	V-2923
EC-BU9	Ultraligeros Espana Volero Jaguar-16	V-1931
EC-BV1	Eipper Quicksilver MX-Sprint IIR	446
EC-BV2	Eipper Quicksilver MXL-Sport II	0142
EC-BV3	Aviasud Mistral Twin	146

EC-BV4	Weedhopper AX-2	B-3043109	
EC-BV5	Cedimex Rans S-12 Airaile	S-12-133	
EC-BV6	Cedimex Rans S-12 Airaile	S-12-105	
EC-BV7	Cedimex Rans S-12 Airaile	S-12-129	
EC-BV8	Sport Aircraft Tango II-GT	4915	
EC-BV9	Dynali Chickinox Kot-Kot	5192-E-108	
EC-BX1	Air Création Safari GT-BI Fun 18	194044	
EC-BX2	Air Création Safari GT-BI SX16	293011	
EC-BX3	Cedimex Rans S-12 Airaile	S-12-121	
EC-BX4	Eipper Quicksilver MXL-Sport IIR	0393	
EC-BX5	Cedimex Rans S-12 Airaile	S-12-104	
EC-BX6	Eipper Quicksilver MX-Sprint IIR	211	
EC-BX7	Cedimex Rans S-6 Coyote II	S-6A-100	
EC-BX8	Cedimex Rans S-12 Airaile	S-12-130	
EC-BX9	Eipper Quicksilver GT-500	0082	
EC-BY1	Cedimex Rans S-12 Airaile	S-12-136	
EC-BY2	Cedimex Rans S-12 Airaile	S-12-135	
EC-BY4	Carlos Perez Fly-Master TSA-10	011	
EC-BY5	Cedimex Rans S-12 Airaile	S-12-106	
EC-BY6	Cedimex Rans S-6 Coyote II	S-6A-101	
EC-BY7	Cedimex Rans S-6 Coyote II	S-6A-102	
EC-BY8	Cedimex Rans S-12 Airaile	S-12-124	
EC-BZ2	Eipper Quicksilver MXL-II	1214	
EC-BZ3	Eipper Quicksilver MX-II	3763640	
EC-BZ4	Cedimex Rans S-6 Coyote II	S-6A-104	
EC-BZ5	Eipper Quicksilver MXL-Sport IIR	0350	
EC-BZ6	Cedimex Rans S-12 Airaile	S-12-122	
EC-BZ7	Cedimex Rans S-12 Airaile	S-12-127	
EC-BZ8	Cedimex Rans S-6 Coyote II	S-6A-103	
EC-BZ9	Dynali Chickinox Kot-Kot	1392-E-103	
EC-CA1	Cedimex Rans S-12 Airaile	S-12-141	
EC-CA2	Eipper Quicksilver GT-500	0079	
EC-CA3	Eipper Quicksilver MXL-II	1603	
EC-CA4	Air Création Safari GT-BI Fun 18	194045	
EC-CA5	UltraLigeros Espana Volero	V-1932	
EC-CA6	Cedimex Rans S-6 Coyote II	S-6A-105	
EC-CA7	Cedimex Rans S-12 Airaile	S-12-140	
EC-CA9	Sallen Mach-10	10-155	
EC-CB1	Sallen Mach-15 Gyrocopter	15-152	
EC-CB2	Aviasud Mistral	139	
EC-CB3	Eipper Quicksilver MXL-Sport IIR	0541	
EC-CB4	Sport Aircraft Tango II-GT	6894	
EC-CB5	Cedimex Rans S-6ES Coyote II	S-6A-108	
EC-CB7	Weedhopper AX-3	C-3123195	
EC-CB8	Eipper Quicksilver MXL Sport IIR	0583	
EC-CB9	Eipper Quicksilver MX Sprint IIR	315	
EC-CC1	Air Création Safari GT-BI Fun 18	192019	
EC-CC2	Air Création Safari GT-BI Fun 18	194043	
EC-CC3	Air Création Safari GT-BI Fun 18	191008	
EC-CC4	Sport Aircraft Tango II-GT	T-1951	
EC-CC5	Air Création Safari GT-BI XP15S	494004	
EC-CC6	Carlod Perez Fly Master TSA-10	010	
EC-CC7	Carlos Perez Fly Master TSA-10	002	
EC-CC8	Cedimex Rans S-12 Airaile	S-12-142	
EC-CC9	Cedimex Rans S-12 Airaile	S-12-146	
EC-CD1	Cedimex Rans S-6ES Coyote II	S-6A-111	
EC-CD2	Eipper Quicksilver MXL Sport II	0072	
EC-CD3	Eipper Quicksilver MXL-II	1357	
EC-CD4	Rans S-12 Airaile	S-12-116	
EC-CD5	Air Création Safari GT-BI M16	394001	
EC-CD6	Cedimex Rans S-12 Airaile	S-12-144	
EC-CD7	Cedimex Rans S-6ES Coyote II	S-6A-110	
EC-CD8	Hispano Aeronautica Canelas Ranger	S-93-02	
EC-CD9	Cedimex Rans S-12 Airaile	S-12-134	
EC-CE1	Cedimex Rans S-12 Airaile	S-12-137	
EC-CE2	Cedimex Rans S-6 Coyote II	S-6A-109	
EC-CE3	Cedimex Rans S-6ES Coyote II	S-6A-107	
EC-CE4	Eipper Quicksilver MXL Sport II	141	
EC-CE5	Air Création Safari GT-BI Fun 18	194042	
EC-CE7	Eipper Quicksilver MX Sprint IIR	0463	
EC-CE8	Aero Designs Pulsar II	0130	
EC-CE9	Mainair Blade 582	994-0694-7-W791	G-MYSH
EC-CF1	UltraLigeros Espana Volero	V-1934	
EC-CF2	Dynali Chickinox Kot-Kot	5192-E-109	
EC-CF3	Cedimex Rans S-12 Airaile	S-12-147	
EC-CF4	Mainair Blade 503	1073-0296-7-W875	
EC-CF5	UltraLigeros Espana Volero	V-2921	
EC-CF6	Eipper Quicksilver MXL Sport IIR	0327	
EC-CF7	Eipper Quicksilver MXL Sport IIR	0326	
EC-CF8	Eipper Quicksilver MXL-II	1690	
EC-CF9	Eipper Quicksilver GT-500	0043	
EC-CG1	Eipper Quicksilver GT-500	0070	
EC-CG2	Eipper Quicksilver MXL Sport IIR	0259	
EC-CG3	Eipper Quicksilver MXL Sport IIR	0593	
EC-CG4	Eipper Quicksilver MXL Sport IIR	0325	
EC-CG5	Eipper Quicksilver MXL Sport IIR	0410	
EC-CG6	Eipper Quicksilver MXL Sport IIR	0352	
EC-CG7	Dynali Chickinox Kot-Kot	2395-E-2	
EC-CG8	Dynali Chickinox Tandem	1195-E-1	
EC-CG9	Cedimex Rans S-12 XL Airaile	S-12-150	
EC-CH1	Cedimex Rans S-12 Airaile	S-12-145	
EC-CH3	Cedimex Rans S-12XL Airaile	S-12-153	
EC-CH4	Cedimex Rans S-12XL Airaile	S-12-166	
EC-CH5	Cedimex Rans S-12XL Airaile	S-12-165	
EC-CH6	Cedimex Rans S-12XL Airaile	S-12-157	
EC-CH7	Cedimex Rans S-12XL Airaile	S-12-162	
EC-CH8	Cedimex Rans S-6ES Coyote II	S-6A-117	

EC-CH9	Cedimex Rans S-12XL Airaile	S-12-172
EC-CI1	Eipper Quicksilver Sprint II	0045
EC-CI2	Sallen Mach-10	10-116
EC-CI3	Cedimex Rans S-12XL Airaile	S-12-154
EC-CI4	Cedimex Rans S-6ES Coyote II	S-6A-116
EC-CI5	Cedimex Rans S-6ES Coyote II	S-6A-112
EC-CI6	Eipper Quicksilver MX Sprint IIR	0492
EC-CI7	Cedimex Rans S-12XL Airaile	S-12-159
EC-CI8	Sport Aircraft Tango II-GT	6872
EC-CI9	Cedimex Rans S-12XL Airaile	S-12-151
EC-CJ1	Cedimex Rans S-12XL Airaile	S-12-173
EC-CJ2	Cedimex Rans S-6ES Coyote II	S-6A-120
EC-CJ3	Road Air Flamingo	004
EC-CJ4	Road Air Flamingo	003
EC-CJ5	Road Air Flamingo	005
EC-CJ6	Sport Aircraft Tango II-GT	2892
EC-CJ7	Eipper Quicksilver GT-500	0305
EC-CJ8	Cedimex Rans S-12XL Airaile	S-12-156
EC-CJ9	Dynali Chickinox Kot-Kot	31980
EC-CK1	Cedimex Rans S-6ES Coyote II	S-6A-115
EC-CK2	Cedimex Rans S-12XL Airaile	S-12-170
EC-CK3	Sport Aircraft Tango II-GT	1881
EC-CK4	Sport Aircraft Tango II-GT	9875
EC-CK5	Sport Aircraft Tango II-GT	6873
EC-CK6	Cedimex Rans S-12XL-582	S-12-171
EC-CK7	Dynali Chickinox Kot-Kot	1392-E-104
EC-CK8	Ultralair Weedhopper AX3	B-4033202
EC-CK9	Cedimex Rans S-6ES-503 Coyote II	S-6A-125
EC-CL3	Cedimex Rans S-6ES-582 Coyote II	S-6A-114
EC-CL4	Cedimex Rans S-12XL-582	S-12-168
EC-CL5	Cedimex Rans S-12 Airaile	S-12-174
EC-CL6	Cedimex Rans S-6ES-582 Coyote II	S-6A-113
EC-CL7	Eipper Quicksilver MXL-IIR Sport	673
EC-CL8	Cedimex Rans S-12XL Airaile	S-12-176
EC-CL9	Road Air Flamingo	009
EC-CM1	Road Air Flamingo	010
EC-CM2	Road Air Flamingo	002
EC-CM3	Road Air Flamingo	007
EC-CM4	Road Air Flamingo	006
EC-CM5	Cedimex Rans S-6ES-582 Coyote II	S-6A-124
EC-CM6	Sport Aircraft Tango II-GT	3896
EC-CM7	Eipper Quicksilver MXL-II Sport	081
EC-CM8	Road Air Flamingo	012
EC-CM9	Road Air Flamingo	011
EC-CN1	Cedimex Rans S-6ES-503 Coyote II	S-6A-123
EC-CN2	Air Création Safari GT BI Fun 18	196047
EC-CN3	Road Air Flamingo	008
EC-CN4	Eipper Quicksilver MXL-II Sport	123
EC-CN5	Eipper Quicksilver MXL-II Sport	0075
EC-CN6	Eipper Quicksilver MXL-IIR Sport	587
EC-CN7	Road Air Flamingo	016
EC-CN8	Cedimex Rans S-12 Airaile	S-12-126
EC-CN9	Cedimex Rans S-6ES-503 Coyote II	S-6A-122
EC-CO1	Micro Aviation Pulsar II	0133
EC-CO2	Micro Aviation Pulsar II	0129
EC-CO3	Cedimex Rans S-6ES-582	S-6A-135
EC-CO4	Cedimex Rans S-6ES-503 Coyote II	S-6A-137
EC-CO5	Cedimex Rans S-6ES-503 Coyote II	S-6A-138
EC-CO6	Mainair Blade	1058-1195-7-W856
	(Type confirmed but regd as Gemini/Flash IIA)	
EC-CO7	Mainair Blade	1102-1296-7-W905
	(Type confirmed but regd as Gemini/Flash IIA)	
EC-CO8	Eipper Quicksilver MXL-II	1694
EC-CO9	Eipper Quicksilver MXL-II	1692
EC-CP1	Eipper Quicksilver MXL-II	1688
EC-CP2	Eipper Quicksilver MXL-II Sport	224
EC-CP3	Eipper Quicksilver MXL-IIR Sport	355
EC-CP4	Eipper Quicksilver MXL-IIR Sprint	493
EC-CP5	Cedimex Rans S-12XL-503	S-12-169
EC-CP6	Cedimex Rans S-6ES-503 Coyote II	S-6A-136
EC-CP7	Eipper Quicksilver MXL-II Sport	0223
EC-CP8	Eipper Quicksilver GT-500	0304
EC-CP9	Eipper Quicksilver MXL-IIR Sport	0584
EC-CQ1	Road Air Flamingo	015
EC-CQ2	Cedimex Rans S-12 Airaile	S-12-180
EC-CQ3	Cedimex Rans S-12 Airaile	S-12-158
EC-CQ4	UltraLigeros Espana Volero	V1918
EC-CQ5	Cedimex Rans S-6ES-582 Coyote II	S-6A-139
EC-CQ7	Cedimex Rans S-12XL-582 Airaile	S-12-186
EC-CQ8	Cedimex Rans S-12XL-503 Airaile	S-12-184
EC-CQ9	Cedimex Rans S-12XL-582 Airaile	S-12-177
EC-CR1	Cedimex Rans S-6ES-582 Coyote II	S-6A-127
EC-CR2	Sport Aircraft Tango II-GT	5911
EC-CR3	Vol 9/Best Off Sky Ranger	SK-1210695
EC-CR4	Cedimex Rans S-12XL-503 Airaile	S-12-181
EC-CR6	Cedimex Rans S-12XL-503 Airaile	S-12-189
EC-CR7	Eipper Quicksilver MXL-II Sport	408
EC-CR8	Cedimex Rans S-6A-503 Coyote II	S-6A-133
EC-CR9	Vol 9/Best Off Sky Ranger	SK-1210795
EC-CS1	Cedimex Rans S-12XL-582 Airaile	S-12-192
EC-CS2	Cedimex Rans S-12 Airaile	S-12-178
EC-CS3	Cedimex Rans S-12XL-582 Airaile	S-12-179
EC-CS4	Eipper Quicksilver MX-II	1882
EC-CS5	Road Air Flamingo	014
EC-CS6	Air Création Safari GT BI Fun 18	193035
EC-CS7	Pampa's Bull Flightstar	PB-FSB046
EC-CS8	Cedimex Rans S-6ES-582 Coyote II	S-6A-145
EC-CS9	Cedimex Rans S-6ES-503 Coyote II	S-6A-146
EC-CT1	Cedimex Rans S-12XL-582 Airaile	S-12-188
EC-CT2	Dynali Chickinox Kot-Kot	4595
EC-CT3	Eipper Quicksilver MXL-IIR Sport	672
EC-CT4	Eipper Quicksilver GT-500	0039
EC-CT5	Cedimex Rans S-12XL-582 Airaile	S-12-190
EC-CT6	Sport Aircraft Tango II-GT	2903
EC-CT7	Mainair Blade	1085-0596-7-W88
	(Type confirmed but regd as Gemini/Flash IIA)	
EC-CT8	Cedimex Rans S-6ES-582 Coyote II	unkn
EC-CT9	Sport Aircraft Tango II-GT	2903
EC-CU1	Eipper Quicksilver MX-II Sprint	208
EC-CU2	Cedimex Rans S-12XL-503 Airaile	S-12-183
EC-CU3	Cedimex Rans S-12XL-503 Airaile	S-12-182
EC-CU4	Eipper Quicksilver MXL-II Sport	0585
EC-CU5	Cedimex Rans S-6ES-503 Coyote II	S-6A-141
EC-CU6	Cedimex Rans S-6ES-503 Coyote II	S-6A-148
EC-CU7	Road Air Flamingo	018
EC-CU8	Sport Aircraft Tango II-GT	4872
EC-CU9	Sport Aircraft Tango I	5864
EC-CV1	Cedimex Rans S-12XL-503 Airaile	S-12-194
EC-CV2	Micro Aviation Pulsar II	0136
EC-CV3	Cedimex Rans S-6ES-503 Coyote II	S-6A-143
EC-CV4	Cedimex Rans S-6ES-582 Coyote II	S-6A-144
EC-CV5	Air Création Clipper XP 582S	97110
EC-CV6	Cedimex Rans S-12XL-503 Airaile	S-12-193
EC-CV7	Dynali Chickinox Kot-Kot	31061814
EC-CV8	Eipper Quicksilver GT-500	319
EC-CV9	Cedimex Rans S-12XL-582 Airaile	S-12-191
EC-CX1	Cedimex Rans S-12XL-582 Airaile	S-12-196
EC-CX2	Road Air Flamingo	023
EC-CX3	Eipper Quicksilver MXL-II Sport	324
EC-CX5	Cedimex Rans S-6ES-503 Coyote II	S-6A-132
EC-CX6	Cedimex Rans S-6ES-582 Coyote II	S-6A-149
EC-CX7	Cedimex Rans S-12XL-582 Airaile	S-12-185
EC-CX8	Eipper Quicksilver MXL-IIR Sport	0411
EC-CX9	Road Air Flamingo	001
EC-CY1	Cedimex Rans S-6ES-503 Coyote II	S-6A-134
EC-CY2	Cedimex Rans S-12XL-503 Airaile	S-12-195
EC-CY3	Cedimex Rans S-6ES-503 Coyote II	S-6A-140
EC-CY4	Cedimex Rans S-12XL-582 Airaile	S-12-202
EC-CY5	Air Création Safari GT BI Quartz 16 SXS	292009
EC-CY6	Eipper Quicksilver MX-II Sprint	141
EC-CY7	Cedimex Rans S-6ES-582 Coyote II	S-6A-151
EC-CY8	Road Air Flamingo	017
EC-CY9	Eipper Quicksilver MX-IIR Sprint	464
EC-CZ1	Cedimex Rans S-6ES-582 Coyote II	S-6A-150
EC-CZ2	Eipper Quicksilver MX-II	2214
EC-CZ3	Cedimex Rans S-12XL-582 Airaile	S-12-206
EC-CZ4	Eipper Quicksilver MXL-II Sport	125
EC-CZ5	Eipper Quicksilver MXL-IIR Sport	674
EC-CZ6	Eipper Quicksilver MXL-II Sport	225
EC-CZ7	Cedimex Rans S-12XL-503 Airaile	S-12-201
EC-CZ8	Cedimex Rans S-12XL-582 Airaile	S-12-203
EC-CZ9	Cedimex Rans S-6ES-503 Coyote II	S-6A-154
EC-DA1	Cedimex Rans S-12XL-582 Airaile	S-12-207
EC-DA2	Eipper Quicksilver MX-II Sprint	0534
EC-DA3	Cedimax Rans S-12 Airaile	S-12-109
EC-DA4	Eipper Quicksilver MXL-IIRB Sport	1687
EC-DA5	Cedimex Rans S-12XL-503 Airaile	S-12-199
EC-DA6	Cedimex Rans S-12XL-582 Airaile	S-12-208
EC-DA7	Dynali Chickinox Kot-Kot	2797 E2W
EC-DA8	Eipper Quicksilver MXL-II Sport	221
EC-DA9	Eipper Quicksilver MX-II Sprint	0533
EC-DB1	Road Air Flamingo	019
EC-DB2	Cedimex Rans S-6ES-582 Coyote II	S-6A-153
EC-DB4	Cedimex Rans S-12 Airaile	S-12-139
EC-DB5	Cedimex Rans S-12XL-503 Airaile	S-12-210
EC-DB6	Eipper Quicksilver GT-500	0086
EC-DB7	Air Création XP GTE 503S	98002 SF
EC-DB8	Air Création Mild GTE 503S	98004 SF
EC-DB9	Air Création XP GTE 503S	98001 SF
EC-DC1	Cedimex Rans S-6ES-582 Coyote II	S-6A-142
EC-DC2	Cedimex Rans S-6ES-582 Coyote II	S-6A-119
EC-DC3	Cedimex Rans S-12XL-582 Airaile	S-12-211
EC-DC4	Road Air Flamingo	033
EC-DC5	Cedimex Rans S-12XL-582 Airaile	S-12-164
EC-DC6	Road Air Flamingo	034
EC-DC7	Cedimex Rans S-12XL-582 Airaile	S-12-205
EC-DC8	Cedimex Rans S-6ES-582 Coyote II	S-6A-128
EC-DC9	Cedimex Rans S-6ES-503 Coyote II	S-6A-157
EC-DD1	Cedimex Rans S-12 Airaile	S-12-213
EC-DD2	Eipper Quicksilver MXL-II Sport	5996
EC-DD3	Cedimex Rans S-12XL-503 Airaile	S-12-214
EC-DD4	Air Création Safari Quartz GT BI SXS	99003 SF
EC-DD5	Cedimex Rans S-6ES-582 Coyote II	S-6A-156
EC-DD6	Vol 9/Best Off Sky Ranger	SK-0516697
EC-DD7	Road Air Flamingo	038
EC-DD8	Air Création Mild GTE 503SL	99001 SF
EC-DD9	Cedimex Rans S-12XL-582 Airaile	S-12-215
EC-DE1	Cedimex Rans S-6ES-503 Coyote II	S-6A-131
EC-DE2	Cedimex Rans S-12XL-503 Airaile	S-12-212
EC-DE3	Cedimex Rans S-12XL-582 Airaile	S-12-209
EC-DE4	Cedimex Rans S-12XL-582 Airaile	S-12-204
EC-DE5	Cedimex Rans S-12XL-503 Airaile	S-12-218
EC-DE6	Cedimex Rans S-6ES-582 Coyote II	S-6A-159
EC-DE7	Sport Aircraft Tango II	5905

EC-DE8	Eipper Quicksilver MXL-II Sport	782
EC-DE9	Sallen Mach-15	15-157
EC-DF1	Cedimex Rans S-12XL-582 Airaile	S-12-216
EC-DF2	Eipper Quicksilver MXL-II Sport	784
EC-DF3	Eipper Quicksilver MXL-II Sport	783
EC-DF4	Road Air Flamingo	040
EC-DF5	Cedimex Rans S-12XL-582 Airaile	S-12-217
EC-DF6	Eipper Quicksilver MX-II Sprint	139
EC-DF7	Eipper Quicksilver GT-500	318
EC-DF8	Eipper Quicksilver GT-400	1421
EC-DF9	Sport Aircraft Tango II-GT	T1924
EC-DG1	Air Création Mild GTE 503SL	99004 SF
EC-DG2	Cedimex Rans S-6ES-582 Coyote II	S-6-AV-0001
EC-DG3	Air Création Safari GT BI Fun 18	192023
EC-DG4	Tecnam P.92 Echo S	P-92-ES-011
EC-DG5	Tecnam P.92 Echo S	P-92-ES-012
EC-DG6	Tecnam P.92 Echo S	P-92-ES-009
EC-DG7	Road Air Flamingo	037
EC-DG8	Road Air Flamingo	045
EC-DG9	Tecnam P.92 Echo S	P-92-ES-013
EC-DH1	Cedimex Rans S-6ES-582 Coyote II	S-6-AV-0002
EC-DH2	Tecnam P.92 Echo S	P-92-ES-008
EC-DH3	Road Air Flamingo	013
EC-DH4	Road Air Flamingo	029
EC-DH5	Vol 9/Best Off Sky Ranger 912	SKR 0005057
EC-DH6	Vol 9/Best Off Sky Ranger 912	SKR 0102091
EC-DH7	Vol 9/Best Off Sky Ranger 912	SKR 0010069
EC-DH8	Vol 9/Best Off Sky Ranger 912	SKR 1215696
EC-DH9	Vol 9/Best Off Sky Ranger 912	SKR 9905019
EC-DI1	Vol 9/Best Off Sky Ranger 912	SKR 0005047
EC-DI2	Sport Aircraft Tango I	1876
EC-DI3	Air Création Safari GT BI Fun 18	192027
EC-DI4	Eipper Quicksilver GT-500	040
EC-DI5	Eipper Quicksilver MXL-II Sport	785
EC-DI6	Eipper Quicksilver MX-II Sprint	549
EC-DI7	Micro Aviation Pulsar II	138
EC-DI8	Micro Aviation Pulsar II	137
EC-DI9	Vol 9/Best Off Sky Ranger 582	SKR 0002043
EC-DJ1	Road Air Flamingo	044
EC-DJ2	Micro Aviation Pulsar II	140
EC-DJ3	Micro Aviation Pulsar II	131
EC-DJ4	Tecnam P.92 Echo S	P-92-ES-001
EC-DJ5	Tecnam P.92 Echo S	P-92-ES-016
EC-DJ6	Tecnam P.92 Echo S	P-92-ES-006
EC-DJ7	Tecnam P.92 Echo S	P-92-ES-007
EC-DJ8	Cedimex Rans S-6ES-HKS-700E Coyote II	S-6A-160
EC-DJ9	Micro Aviation Pulsar II	139
EC-DK1	Tecnam P.92 Echo S	P-92-ES-014
EC-DK2	Tecnam P.92 Echo	P-92-E-010
EC-DK3	Road Air Flamingo	032
EC-DK4	Tecnam P.92 Echo	P-92-E-009
EC-DK5	Tecnam P.92 Echo S	P-92-ES-015
EC-DK6	Eipper Quicksilver GT-500	0085
EC-DK7	TL Ultralight TL-96 Star	TL-96-01-010
EC-DK8	TL Ultralight TL-96 Star	TL-96-01-006
EC-DK9	TL Ultralight TL-96 Star	TL-96-01-012
EC-DL1	TL Ultralight TL-96 Star	TL-96-01-004
EC-DL2	Vol 9/Best Off Sky Ranger 582	SKR 0107119
EC-DL3	Road Air Flamingo	046
EC-DL4	TL Ultralight TL-96 Star	TL-96-01-007
EC-DL5	Tecnam P.92 Echo S (Crashed 12.12.04)	P-92-ES-010
EC-DL6	Tecnam P.92 Echo S	P-92-ES-018
EC-DL7	Tecnam P.92 Echo	P-92-E-007
EC-DL8	Tecnam P.92 Echo S	P-92-ES-020
EC-DL9	TL Ultralight TL-96 Star	TL-96-01-009
EC-DM1	TL Ultralight TL-96 Star	TL-96-02-014
EC-DM2	TL Ultralight TL-96 Star	TL-96-01-008
EC-DM3	Tecnam P.92 Echo S	P-92-ES-019
EC-DM4	Tecnam P.96 Golf	P-96-6-010
EC-DM5	Tecnam P.96 Golf (Dismantled)	P-96-G-012
EC-DM6	Tecnam P.92 Echo S	P-92-ES-021
EC-DM8	Tecnam P.96 Golf	P-96-G-013
EC-DM9	Tecnam P.92 Echo S	P-92-ES-022
EC-DN1	Vol 9/Best Off Sky Ranger 912	SKR 0112147
EC-DN2	TL Ultralight TL-96 Star	TL-96-01-013
EC-DN3	TL Ultralight TL-96 Star	TL-96-02-011
EC-DN5	Tecnam P.96 Golf	P-96-G-014
EC-DN6	Mainair Blade 912	1200-0699-7-W1003
EC-DN7	Tecnam P.92 Echo	P-92-E-008
EC-DN8	Albin Feito Moragon M-1	M-1-02-001
EC-DN9	Albin Feito Moragon M-1	M-1-02-002
EC-DO1	Albin Feito Moragon M-1	M-1-02-003
EC-DO2	Tecnam P.96 Golf	P-96-G-011
EC-DO3	TL Ultralight TL-96 Star	TL-96-02-017
EC-DO4	Tecnam P.96 Golf	P-96-G-015
EC-DO5	TL Ultralight TL-96 Star	TL-96-02-015
EC-DO6	Eipper Quicksilver MX-II Sprint	213
EC-DO7	TL Ultralight TL-96 Star	TL-96-02-016
EC-DO8	TL Ultralight TL-96 Star	TL-96-02-018
EC-DO9	TL Ultralight TL-96 Star	TL-96-01-002
EC-DP1	Micro Aviation Pulsar II	135
EC-DP2	Albin Feito Moragon M-1	M-1-02-004
EC-DP3	Albin Feito Moragon M-1	M-1-02-005
EC-DP4	Tecnam P.96 Golf	P-96-G-017
EC-DP5	Tecnam P.92 Echo S	P-92-ES-024
EC-DP6	Manuel Perez Rainbow	MPR 02-0002
EC-DP7	Road Air Flamingo	042

EC-DP8	Tecnam P.92 Echo S	P-92-ES-023
EC-DP9	Cedimex Rans S-12XL-582 Airaile	S-12-AV002
EC-DQ1	TL Ultralight TL-96 Star	TL-96-01-003
EC-DQ2	TL Ultralight TL-96 Star	TL-96-02-021
EC-DQ3	Tecnam P.92 Echo S	P-92-ES-025
EC-DQ4	Albin Feito Moragon M-1	M-1-02-006
EC-DQ5	Tecnam P.96 Golf	P-96-G-018
EC-DQ6	Cedimex Rans S-12 Airaile	S-12-300
EC-DQ7	Air Création Clipper XP 582S	00001 JL
EC-DQ8	Air Création Clipper XP 582S	02005 JL
EC-DQ9	Air Création Clipper XP 582S	99001 JL
EC-DR1	Cedimex Rans S-12XL-582 Airaile	S-12-AV001
EC-DR2	Air Création Clipper XP 582S	01001 JL
EC-DR3	Air Création Clipper XP 582S	02006 JL
EC-DR4	Mainair Blade	1341-0902-7-W . . . .
EC-DR5	Cedimex Rans S-6ES-582 Coyote II	S-6-AV-0005
EC-DR6	Albin Feito Moragon M-1	M-1-03-008
EC-DR7	Albin Feito Moragon M-1	M-1-03-007
EC-DR8	Tecnam P.92 Echo S	P-92-ES-026
EC-DR9	Tecnam P.96 Golf	P-96-G-019
EC-DS1	Manuel Perez Rainbow	MPR 02-0004
EC-DS2	Tecnam P.92 Echo S	P-92-ES-027
EC-DS3	Tecnam P.92 Echo	190
EC-DS4	Air Création Clipper XP 582S	00004 JL
EC-DS5	TL Ultralight TL-96 Star	TL-96-03-024
EC-DS6	TL Ultralight TL-96 Star	TL-96-02-019
EC-DS7	Tecnam P.96 Golf	P-96-G-021
EC-DS8	Tecnam P.92 Echo Super	P-92-SP-011
EC-DS9	Road Air Flamingo	031
EC-DT1	Air Création Clipper XP 582S	00002 JL
EC-DT2	TL Ultralight TL-96 Star	TL-96-02-020
EC-DT3	TL Ultralight TL-96 Star	TL-96-02-024
EC-DT4	Tecnam P.96 Golf	P-96-G020
EC-DT5	TL Ultralight TL-96 Star	TL-96-02-023
EC-DT6	Tecnam P.92 Echo S	P-92-ES-029
EC-DT7	Tecnam P.92 Echo Super	P-92-SP-012
EC-DT8	Tecnam P.96 Golf	P-96-G-023
EC-DT9	Tecnam P.92 Echo Super	P-96-SP-014
EC-DU1	Tecnam P.92 Echo Super	P-96-SP-010
EC-DU2	Tecnam P.96 Golf	P-96-G-024
EC-DU3	Road Air Flamingo	022
EC-DU4	Tecnam P.92 Echo Super	P-92-SP-015
EC-DU5	Tecnam P.92 Echo S	P-92-ES-030
EC-DU6	Tecnam P.92 Echo S	P-92-ES-031
EC-DU7	Vol 9/Best Off Sky Ranger	SKR 0209241
EC-DU9	Tecnam P.96 Golf	P-96-G-026
EC-DV1	Air Création Fun 18 Twin 503SL	01002SF
EC-DV2	Air Création Fun 18 Twin 503SL	02007JL
EC-DV3	Aeromoragón Moragón M-1	M-1-03-011
EC-DV4	TL Ultralight TL-96 Star	TL-96-01-005
EC-DV5	Vol 9/Best Off Sky Ranger	SKR 0303343
EC-DV6	Aeromoragón Moragón M-1	M-1-03-012
EC-DV7	Aeromoragón Moragón M-1	M-1-03-013
EC-DV8	Tecnam P.96 Golf	P-96-G-027
	(Reported 9.04 as P.2002JF Sierra)	
EC-DV9	Tecnam P.92 Echo S	P-92-ES-035
EC-DX1	Tecnam P.92 Echo S	P-92-ES-034
EC-DX2	Tecnam P.96 Golf	P-96-G-025
EC-DX3	Flight Design CT-2K	02-01-01-AR
EC-DX4	Tecnam P.92 Echo Super	P-92-SP-016
EC-DX5	Tecnam P.96 Golf	P-96-G-022
EC-DX6	Flight Design CT-2K	01-06-03-AR
EC-DX7	Flight Design CT-2K	02-06-05-AR
EC-DX8	Flight Design CT-2K	00-10-04-AR
EC-DX9	Tecnam P.96 Golf	P-96-G-028
EC-DY1	Tecnam P.92 Echo S	P-92-ES-037
EC-DY2	Tecnam P.92 Echo S	P-92-ES-036
EC-DY3	Manuel Perez Rainbow MPR	03-0005
EC-DY4	Manuel Perez Rainbow MPR	03-0010
EC-DY5	Manuel Perez Rainbow MPR	02-0007
EC-DY6	Manuel Perez Rainbow MPR	03-0011
EC-DY7	Manuel Perez Rainbow MPR	03-0009
EC-DY8	Aeromoragón Moragón M-1	M-1-03-014
EC-DY9	TL Ultralight TL-96 Star	TL-96-03-025
EC-DZ1	ICP Bingo	03-03-52-096
EC-DZ2	ICP Super Bingo	03-03-52-099
EC-DZ4	ICP Bingo	03-04-52-101
EC-DZ5	ICP Bingo	03-04-52-102
EC-DZ6	ICP Bingo	02-12-52-083
EC-DZ7	ICP Bingo	02-06-52-060
EC-DZ8	ICP Bingo	03-07-52-120
EC-DZ9	Road Air Flamingo	047
EC-EA1	Flight Design CT-2K	02-06-04-AR
EC-EA2	ICP Bingo	03-03-52-098
EC-EA3	Aeromoragón Moragón M-1	M-1-03-016
EC-EA4	Aeromoragón Moragón M-1	M-1-03-015
EC-EA5	ICP Bingo	03-03-52-095
EC-EA6	ICP Bingo	02-07-52-061
EC-EA7	ICP Bingo	01-12-52-039
EC-EA8	ICP Bingo	03-02-52-092
EC-EA9	ICP Bingo	03-01-52-090
EC-EB1	ICP Bingo	02-09-52-073
EC-EB2	ICP Bingo	02-02-52-054
EC-EB3	ICP Bingo	01-05-52-016
EC-EB4	Flight Design CT-2K	03-05-06-AR
EC-EB5	ICP Bingo	02-12-52-086
EC-EB6	Tecnam P.96 Golf	P-96-G-030

EC-EB7	ICP Bingo	03-01-52-087	
EC-EB8	ICP Bingo	03-04-52-103	
EC-EB9	Tecnam P.92 Echo	P-92-E-013	
EC-EC1	Tecnam P.92 Echo Super	P-92-SP-018	
EC-EC2	ICP Bingo	03-05-52-109	
EC-EC3	Tecnam P.96 Golf	P-96-G-031	
EC-EC4	Mainair 503 Blade	1143-0198-7-W946	
	(Registered as Mainair Gemini/Flash II but exported from UK as above in 1998)		
EC-EC5	ICP Bingo	02-11-52-081	
EC-EC6	Quicksilver MX-Sprint-IIR	552	
EC-EC7	Quicksilver MX-Sprint-IIR	550	
EC-EC8	Air Création Clipper XP 582S	99002 SF	
EC-EC9	Air Création GTE Kiss 450	00003 SF	
EC-ED1	Air Création GTE Kiss 450	03001 SF	
EC-ED2	Air Création Twin 503SL Fun 18	03004 SF	
EC-ED3	Vol 9/Best Off Sky Ranger	SKR 0309374	
EC-ED4	Tecnam P.96 Golf	P-96-G-033	
EC-ED5	ICP Bingo	01-12-52-042	
EC-ED6	Tecnam P.92 Echo Super	P-92-SP-019	
EC-ED7	Aeromoragón Moragón M-1	M1-04-018	
EC-ED8	Air Création Twin 503SL Fun 18	03005 JL	
EC-ED9	Quicksilver MXL-Sport-IIR	682	
EC-EE1	Air Création Clipper XP 582S	03002SF	
EC-EE2	Manuel Perez Rainbow	MPR-0013	
EC-EE3	Manuel Perez Rainbow	MPR-0015	
EC-EE4	Tecnam P.92 Echo Super	P-92-SP-020	
EC-EE5	ICP Bingo	02-02-52-048	
EC-EE6	Tecnam P.92 Echo Super	P-92-SP-022	
EC-EE7	Tecnam P.92 Echo Super	P-92-SP-021	
EC-EE8	Flight Design CT-2K	03-07-07-AR	
EC-EE9	Manuel Perez Rainbow	MPR 0016	
EC-EF1	Air Création GTE Clipper/ Kiss 450	03003 SF	
EC-EF2	Vol 9/Best Off Sky Ranger	SKR 0403465	
EC-EF3	Tecnam P.96 Golf	P-96-G-034	
EC-EF4	Aeromoragón Moragón M-1	M1-04-019	
EC-EF5	Tecnam P.92 Echo Super	P-92-SP-023	
EC-EF6	Tecnam P.92 Echo	P-92-E-015	
EC-EF7	Tecnam P.92 Echo	P-92-E-016	
EC-EF8	Vol 9/Best Off Sky Ranger	SKR 0102090	
EC-EF9	Tecnam P.92 Echo	P-92-E-017	
EC-EG1	Manuel Perez Rainbow	MPR 02-0003	
EC-EG2	ICP Bingo	04-01-52-140	
EC-EG3	ICP Bingo	04-01-52-142	
EC-EG4	ICP Bingo	04-01-52-160	
EC-EG5	Quicksilver MXL-Sport-II	0124	
EC-EG6	Tecnam P.92 Echo S	P-92-ES-039	
EC-EG7	ICP Bingo	04-05-52-152	
EC-EG8	Tecnam P.96 Golf	P-96-G-035	
EC-EG9	ICP Bingo	04-10-52-161	
EC-EH1	Tecnam P.92 Echo S	P-92-ES-038	
EC-EH2	Tecnam P.92 Echo S	P-92-ES-040	
EC-EH4	Aeromoragón Moragón M-1	unkn	
EC- . . .	Powerchute Kestrel	00366	G-MWGS
EC- . . .	Mainair Gemini/Flash IIA	291-285-3-W27	G-MMUY
EC- . . .	Solar Wings Pegasus XL-R	SW-WA-1379	G-MVGP
EC- . . .	Solar Wings Pegasus Quasar IITC	6564	G-MYJV
EC- . . .	Solar Wings Pegasus Quatum 15	6651	G-MYLM
EC- . . .	Tecnam P.96 Golf	unkn	
	(Built using parts from EC-DM5)		
EC- . . .	Velocity XL RG	SLL 1	N67AG

EK - ARMENIA

Regn.	Type	C/n	Prev.Id.
EK-10151	McDonnell-Douglas DC-10-15	42858	N301FV
			SX-CVH
			N48258
			PP-OOO
			V2-LEX
			N1003L
			(PP-AJN)
			N1003L
			N19B
			(XA-MEX)
EK-11001	Antonov An-12TB	5343408	UN-11001
	(Identity unconfirmed, also quoted as c/n 8346106 ex CCCP11204)		EX-11001
EK-11010	Antonov An-12TB	3341110	CCCP11010
EK-11028	Antonov An-12BK	7345310	CCCP11028
EK-11029	Antonov An-12B	7344908	RA-11029
			CCCP11029
EK-11304	Antonov An-12BP	0901304	4L-11304
EK-11351	Antonov An-12BP	4341910	UR-11351
EK-11660	Antonov An-12BP	5343209	CCCP11660
EK-11997	Antonov An-12BP (Damaged 3.11.03)	6344407	CCCP11997
EK-12148	Antonov An-12BP	unkn	
EK-12222	Antonov An-12	unkn	
	(Possibly c/n 00347606,ex CCCP-11341(2), and to ST-SAF)		
EK-12333	Antonov An-12BP	8346006	LZ-BRA
			LZ-ITB
			RA-11368
			SovAF 75 red
			CCCP11521
EK-12555	Antonov An-12BP	8345607	RA-11367
	(Also carries regn RDPL-34142)		
EK-12777	Antonov An-12 (To EX-029 ?)	unkn	
EK-13399	Antonov An-26	47302606	RA-13399
			CCCP13399
EK-32001	Airbus A320-211	0397	(F-OIBB)
			N320AW
			C-GVXA
			N541LF
			(C-FNVT)
			F-WWBM
EK-32007	Airbus A320-211	0726	P4-VNF
			N726NS
			VH-HYN
			F-WWBP
EK-32008	Airbus A320-211	0229	N229AN
			VH-HYL
			F-WWIN
EK-32009(2)	Airbus A320-211	0547	F-WQSB
			VH-HYO
			F-WWIU
EK-32010	Airbus A320-211	0632	VH-HYS
			F-WWBI
EK-320 . .	Airbus A320-211	0142	D-AKFX
			VH-HYJ
			F-WWDI
EK-46369	Antonov An-24B	07305910	RA-46369
			CCCP46369
EK-46419	Antonov An-24B	87303704	RA-46419
			CCCP46281
EK-46513	Antonov An-24RV	37308409	UR-46513
			RA-46513
			CCCP46513
EK-46581	Antonov An-24B	97304910	RA-46581
			CCCP46581
EK-46630	Antonov An-24RV	37308809	UR-46630
			CCCP46630
EK-46656	Antonov An-24RV	47309302	RA-46656
			CCCP46656
EK-46711	Antonov An-24B	99902109	RA-46711
EK-46741	Antonov An-12	8345408	RA-46741
	(C/n also reported as 8345406)		
EK-46839	Antonov An-24T	7910201	RA-46839
			Sov AF?
EK-47812	Antonov An-24RV	17307004	RA-47812
			CCCP47812
EK-47835	Antonov An-24B	17307307	RA-47835
			CCCP47835
EK-48026	Antonov An-32B	32-09	ArmeniaAF
EK-48138	Antonov An-32B (Identity unconfirmed)	32-01	RA-48138
EK-49273	Antonov An-24T	7910405	RA-49273
EK-49275	Antonov An-24T	9911102	RA-49275
EK-65044	Tupolev Tu-134A-3	49450	65044
			CCCP65044
EK-65072	Tupolev Tu-134A-3	49972	CCCP65072
EK-65575	Tupolev Tu-134A	62350	RA-65575
			ES-AAL
			CCCP65768
EK-65650	Tupolev Tu-134A-3 (Stored)	0351006	CCCP65650
EK-65822	Tupolev Tu-134A-3 (Stored)	09071	CCCP65822
EK-65831	Tupolev Tu-134A-3 (Stored)	17102	CCCP65831
EK-65848	Tupolev Tu-134A-3 (Wfu)	23136	CCCP65848

EK-74701	Boeing 747-238B	21352	YA-EAG N161UA VH-EBM N8295V
EK-76445	Ilyushin Il-76TD	1023410330	4L-76445 RA-76445
EK-76446	Ilyushin Il-76TD	1023412418	RA-76446
EK-85166	Tupolev Tu-154B1 (Stored)	76A-166	CCCP85166
EK-85200	Tupolev Tu-154B	77A-200	CCCP85200
EK-85279	Tupolev Tu-154B1 (Stored)	78A-279	CCCP85279
EK-85403	Tupolev Tu-154B2	80A-403	CCCP85403
EK-85442	Tupolev Tu-154B2	80A-442	CCCP85442
EK-85536	Tupolev Tu-154B2	82A-536	CCCP85536
EK-85566	Tupolev Tu-154B2	82A-566	CCCP85566
EK-86117	Ilyushin Il-86	51483209085	CCCP86117
EK-86118	Ilyushin Il-86	51483209086	CCCP86118
EK-86724	Ilyushin Il-76M	073410284	EP-TPZ EK-86724 CCCP86724
EK-86817	Ilyushin Il-76M	063407191	EP-TPO EK-86817 CCCP86817
EK-87316	Yakovlev Yak-40 (Stored)	9331529	RA-87316 CCCP87316
EK-87359	Yakovlev Yak-40	9340831	EP-TQA ER-87359 RA-87359 UN-87359 CCCP87359
EK-87536	Yakovlev Yak-40	9520142	EP-TQS EP-DMS ? EK-87536 CCCP87536
EK-87662	Yakovlev Yak-40	9240625	RA-87662 UN-87662 CCCP87662
EK-88157	Yakovlev Yak-40 (Stored)	9611146	CCCP88157
EK-88167	Yakovlev Yak-40 (Stored)	9610147	CCCP88167
EK-88199	Yakovlev Yak-40	9630149	EP-TQU EK-88199 88199 CCCP88199
EK-88250	Yakovlev Yak-40 (Stored)	9640452	RA-88250
EK-88262	Yakovlev Yak-40K	9711752	88262
EK-98116	Antonov An-24T (Identity unconfirmed)	7910403	CCCP98116 Sov.AF?
EK-	McDonnel-Douglas DC-8-62	45953	N66656 PP-DGP PP-DGX N66656 OB-1323 OB-R-1323 N807AX JA8031

ER - MOLDOVA

Regn.	Type	C/n	Prev.Id.
ER-ACI	Antonov An-12BP	6343707	UR-PWH
ER-ADD	Antonov An-12BP	2340403	UR-11961 CCCP11961
ER-ADE	Antonov An-12BP	2340503	D2-FCU
ER-ADK	Antonov An-12BP	5342802	UN-11005 CCCP11905
ER-ADN	Antonov An-12BP	3341606	RA-11328 CCCP11328 Sov.AF 23 red
ER-AEJ	Antonov An-72	36572094889	ER-ACA(1) ER-72977 HK-3808X CCCP72977
ER-AEN	Antonov An-74	36547095898	ER-ACN RA-74009 MOLD-74009 CCCP74009
ER-AEW	Antonov An-32 (Reserved as ZS-PHR 5.04)	26-01	RA-48090 CCCP48090
ER-AEZ	Antonov An-24 RV (Reserved as ZS-... 5.04)	47309705	D2-FVL ER-AEH YR-AMK
ER-AFB	Antonov An-24RV	87310810b	4L-48116 UK-08823 CCCP08823
ER-AFD(2)	Antonov An-26B	173109-10	UN-26054 CCCP26054
ER-AFE	Antonov An-26B	173109-05	RA-26050 CCCP26050
ER-AFI	Antonov An-32	32-05	ER-ADI UR-48140 RA-48140
ER-AFL	Antonov An-26B	117-05	RA-26082 CCCP26082
ER-AFM	Antonov An-32B	33-05	ER-ACM HK-4021X RA-48002
ER-AFN	Antonov An-26B	273126-02	TL-ACZ RA-26093 CCCP26093
ER-AFQ	Antonov An-26B	273125-03	RA-26124 UR-26124 CCCP26124
ER-AFU	Antonov An-26B	126-03	RA-26125 CCCP26125 OB-1348 CCCP26125
ER-AFV	Antonov An-26B	138-07	?
ER-AFY	Antonov An-24RV	47309809	YR-AMY J5-GBE(2) YR-AMY
ER-AFZ	Antonov An-72	36572070698	ER-72933 CCCP72933
ER-AIA	Antonov An-2R	1G193-50	CCCP68080
ER-AIC	Antonov An-2T	1G73-20	Soviet AF
ER-AIP	Antonov An-28	1AJ004-06	SP-GCA
ER-AJA	Antonov An-28 (Stored)	1AJO03-07	RA-27843 CCCP27843
ER-AJC	Antonov An-28	1AJO03-12	RA-28748 CCCP28748
ER-AJE	Antonov An-28 (Stored)	1AJO06-12	RA-28701 CCCP28701
ER-AJH	Antonov An-28	1AJO04-07	RA-28758 CCCP28758
ER-AJI	Antonov An-28	1AJO04-01	RA-28752 CCCP28752
ER-AJL	Antonov An-28	1AJO05-14	UR-28781 CCCP28781
ER-AJR	PZL-104 Wilga 35A	18840788	
ER-AJS	PZL-104 Wilga 35A	85258	
ER-AJU	PZL-104 Wilga 35A	85257	
ER-ARA	AUS-N-7 AX-7 HAFB	1030895	
ER-ATA	Stranger	96.008	
ER-ATB	Stranger	96.009	
ER-AWC	Antonov An-24RV	27307504	RA-46846 CCCP46846
ER-AWD	Antonov An-24RV	1117306907	RA-47805 CCCP47805
ER-AWF	Antonov An-72	36572070696	ER-72932 CCCP72932
ER-AWK	Antonov An-32B	3202	N6505 ER-AWK OB-1610 UR-48130 CCCP48130
ER-AWL	Antonov An-32B	31-10	S9-GRJ ER-AEX(1) RA-48076 48076 CCCP48076
ER-AWR	Antonov An-24RV	37308605	LZ-MNE UR-46608 CCCP46608
ER-AWV	Antonov An-26	4104	D2-FDA RA-26574 CCCP26574
ER-AWW	Antonov An-26	8004	RA-26246 CCCP26165(1)
ER-AWY	Antonov An-32	21-03	RA-48972 CCCP48972
ER-AXA	Antonov An-12V	01347907	LZ-BRW RA-11112(2) CCCP11112(2)
ER-AXE	Antonov An-12BK	7345201	
ER-AXG yellow	Antonov An-12BK	00347407	SovAF 12
ER-AXH black	Antonov An-12BP	5343208	SovAF 661 CCCP11661
ER-AXM	Antonov An-12BP	2340806	LZ-SFN LZ-FEA LZ-PHA RA-11307 SovAF
ER-AXQ	Antonov An-12BK	8345805	CCCP12153
ER-AXV	Airbus A320-211	0622	F-WQSG VH-HYR F-WWBU
ER-AXW	Airbus A320-211	0662	F-WQSE VH-HYT F-WWDM
ER-AXY	Antonov An-12	9346904	LZ-SFT RA-13341 CCCP13341
ER-AXZ	Antonov An-12BK	8346106	UkrAF 03 blue

ER-AZA	Antonov An-26 (Stored)	77305509	RA-26227 CCCP26227 CCCP59502 PeruAF:376
ER-AZB	Antonov An-24RV	27307506	RA-46848 CCCP46848
ER-AZC	Antonov An-26	5602	RA-26228 CCCP27216 PeruAF:378
ER-AZD	Antonov An-24TV	1021911	RomAF:1911 YR-AMS Rom AF:1911
ER-AZE	Antonov An-26	2206	RomAF:206 UR-26229 26229 CCCP26229 RomAF:206
ER-AZF	Antonov An-26	07309510	UR-KRB
ER-AZG	Antonov An-24RV	57310105	YR-ARA YR-BMA
ER-AZH	Antonov An-24RV	57310405	YR-ARB YR-RRB YR-BMG
ER-AZI	Antonov An-32B	28-05	UR-48055 CCCP48055
ER-AZK	Antonov An-26B	14310	RA-26594 CCCP26594
ER-AZL	Antonov An-24RV	47309406	RA-46668 CCCP46668
ER-AZM	Antonov An-24RV	27308007	RA-46479 CCCP46479
ER-AZN	Antonov An-24RV	37308801	RA-46624 CCCP-46624
ER-AZO	Antonov An-26B	10606	EX-26036 CCCP26036
ER-AZP	Antonov An-24RV	17307002	RA-47810 CCCP47810
ER-AZR	Antonov An-26B	8205	UR-BWY UR-26670 CCCP26670
ER-AZT	Antonov An-26B	9005	UR-26689 CCCP26689
ER-AZV	Antonov An-24RV	27307506	RA-46848 CCCP46848
ER-EMA	Embraer EMB-120RT Brasilia	120223	N246CA PT-SSS
ER-IBD	Ilyushin Il-76T	073411338	RA-76507 CCCP76507
ER-IBE	Ilyushin Il-76MD	0043454615	CU-T1419 CU-C1258 CU-T1258
ER-IBF	Ilyushin Il-76T	073410300	HA-TCI RA-76430 CCCP86729
ER-IBG	Ilyushin Il-76T	unkn	
ER-IBL	Ilyushin Il-76TD	0053463908	RA-76659 CCCP76659
ER-IBN	Ilyushin Il-76TD	0033448390	RA-76848 Ukr.AF 76567 CCCP76567
ER-IBO	Ilyushin Il-76TD	0043452546	RA-76591 CCCP76591
ER-IBP	Ilyushin Il-76T	093418556	RA-76516 CCCP76516
ER-IBT	Ilyushin Il-76TD	0033447364	RA-76368 UR-76561 CCCP7656
ER-IBV	Ilyushin Il-76T	0003423699	RA-76521 CCCP76521
ER-IBW	Ilyushin Il-76T	093418543	RA-76759 CCCP-76759 YI-AKS Iraqi AF:2068
ER-IBY	Ilyushin Il-76TD	0053460832	RA-76482 CCCP76482
ER-ICB	Ilyushin Il-18D	187010603	RA-74296 CCCP74296 CCCP75473
ER-ICG	Ilyushin Il-18V	184007301	YR-IMG
ER-ICJ	Ilyushin Il-18D (W/o 27.1.04)	186009102	YR-IMJ
ER-JGD	Yakovlev Yak-40	9421334	RA-88307 VN-A441
ER-JON	Yakovlev Yak-52	9010711	DOSAAF 68? yellow
ER-LGA	Learjet 35A	35A-406	I-KELM N35Q N764G
ER-MGE	Mil Mi-8T	10720	RomAF:720
ER-MGF	Mil Mi-8PS	10728	RomAF:728 RomAF:01 RomAF:728
ER-MGP	MiL Mi-14PS	75097	
ER-MHA	Mil Mi-8 MTV-1	95626	RA-25481
ER-MHD	Mil Mi-8 MTV-1	95864	Mold.AF: 02black LZ-... CCCP27030
ER-MHE	Mil Mi-8 MTV-1	95865	CCCP27031
ER-MHF	Mil Mi-8 MTV-1	95862	CCCP27028
ER-MHG	Mil Mi-8 MTV-1	95861	CCCP27027
ER-MHH	Mil Mi-8 MTV-1	96121	RA-25746(2)
ER-MHL	Mil Mi-8 MTV-1	95721	RA-25105
ER-MHM	Mil Mi-8 MTV-1	95881	RA-27047
ER-MHZ	Mil Mi-8 MTV-1	96078	RA-22503
ER-MUC	Aviatika MAI-890	101	ZU-BLW
ER-MUS	Aviatika MAI-890	163	
ER-SBA	SAAB 2000	038	HB-IZV SE-038
ER-SFA	SAAB 2000	056	HB-IYA SE-056
ER-SFB	SAAB 2000	022	HB-IZL SE-022
ER-SGB	SAAB-Scania SF.340B	182	HB-AKF SE-F82
ER-SGC	SAAB-Scania SF.340B	160	HB-AKA SE-F60
ER-TAI	Tupolev Tu-154B2	82A-546	UR-85546 ER-TAI UR-85546 YL-LAE CCCP85546
ER-TCF	Tupolev Tu-134A-3	62390	ER-AAZ ER-65686 CCCP65686
ER-WOA	PZL-104 Wilga 35A	128456	
ER-XVC	X-32 Bekas	324	
ER-XVL	X-32 Bekas	336	
ER-YCA	Yakovlev Yak-42D	4520424306017	RA-42435
ER-YCD	Yakovlev Yak-42	11140105	RA-42549 CCCP42549
ER-YGD	Yakovlev Yak-40	9831458	RA-87970 CCCP87970
ER-YGR	Yakovlev Yak-40	9521640	HA-LJG ER-JGA RA-87514 CCCP87514
ER-01762	Antonov An-2P	1G107-09	CCCP01762
ER-07206	Antonov An-2TP	1G146-35	CCCP07206
ER-07863	Antonov An-2	1G170-22	CCCP07863
ER-15796	Mil Mi-2	522850033	CCCP15796
ER-19282	Kamov Ka-26	7001606	CCCP19282 YR-19282 CCCP19282
ER-19292	Kamov Ka-26	7101805	CCCP19292
ER-19296	Kamov Ka-26	7101809	19296 CCCP19296
ER-19298	Kamov Ka-26	7101903	CCCP19298 YR-19298. CCCP19298
ER-19316	Kamov Ka-26	7203105	YR-CYV ER-19316 YR-CZM YR-19316 CCCP19316
ER-19328	Kamov Ka-26	7303310	YR-CZE CCCP19328 YR-19328 CCCP19328
ER-19329	Kamov Ka-26	7303401	YR-CYI ER-19329 YR-CXI ER-19329 CCCP19329
ER-19343	Kamov Ka-26	7303509	YR-CTA ER-19343 YR-CYL ER-19343 YR-CZH 19343 CCCP19343
ER-19345	Kamov Ka-26	7303601	YR-CYC ER-19345 YR-CZI YR-19345 ER-19345 CCCP19345
ER-19347	Kamov Ka-26	7303603	YR-19347 CCCP19347
ER-19360	Kamov Ka-26	7202401	CCCP19360
ER-19370	Kamov Ka-26	7202509	CCCP19370
ER-19381	Kamov Ka-26	7202705	YR-CZK YR-19381 CCCP19381
ER-19385	Kamov Ka-26	7202709	CCCP19385
ER-19387	Kamov Ka-26	7202801	YR-CXF ER-19387 YR-19387 CCCP19387
ER-19416	Kamov Ka-26	7404410	YR-CZA YR-19416 ER-19416 CCCP19416
ER-19475	Kamov Ka-26	7303904	CCCP19475
ER-19476	Kamov Ka-26	7303905	CCCP19476

ER-19486	Kamov Ka-26	7404101	YR-19486
			CCCP19486
ER-19500	Kamov Ka-26	7404206	CCCP19500
ER-19502	Kamov Ka-26	7404208	CCCP19502
ER-19503	Kamov Ka-26	7404301	CCCP19503
ER-19505	Kamov Ka-26	7404315	YR-CXJ
			YR-19505
			CCCP19505
ER-19506	Kamov Ka-26	7404316	YR-CYF
			ER-19506
			YR-CZU
			YR-19506
			CCCP19506
ER-19507	Kamov Ka-26	7404317	YR-CZF
			ER-19507
			YR-CZF
			YR-19507
			ER-19507
			CCCP19507
ER-19521	Kamov Ka-26	7404513	CCCP19521
ER-19534	Kamov Ka-26	7404607	CCCP19534
			YR-19534
			CCCP19534
ER-19611	Kamov Ka-26	7405014	CCCP19611
ER-19622	Kamov Ka-26	7405110	CCCP19622
ER-20121	Mil Mi-2	543022063	CCCP20121
ER-20164	Mil Mi-2	523430034	CCCP20164
ER-20170	Mil Mi-2	523427034	CCCP20170
ER-20223	Mil Mi-2	527012011	CCCP20223
ER-20257	Mil Mi-2	547215071	CCCP20257
ER-20289	Mil Mi-2	527408111	CCCP20289
ER-20293	Mil Mi-2	527428111	CCCP20293
ER-20680	Mil Mi-2	526645050	CCCP20680
ER-20726	Mil Mi-2	527543032	CCCP20726
ER-20727	Mil Mi-2	527544032	CCCP20727
ER-20728	Mil Mi-2	527545032	CCCP20728
ER-20739	Mil Mi-2	547636052	EW-20739
			ER-20739
			CCCP20739
ER-20740	Mil Mi-2	527637052	CCCP20740
ER-20819	Mil Mi-2	528023013	CCCP20819
ER-20820	Mil Mi-2	528024013	CCCP20820
ER-20821	Mil Mi-2	528025013	CCCP20821
ER-20830	Mil Mi-2	548103033	CCCP20830
ER-23211	Mil Mi-2	5210132037	CCCP23211
ER-23237	Mil Mi-2	5210238057	CCCP23237
ER-23238	Mil Mi-2	5210239057	CCCP23238
ER-23264	Mil Mi-2	5210338087	CCCP23264
ER-23265	Mil Mi-2	5210339087	CCCP23265
ER-23313	Mil Mi-2	529144045	CCCP23313
ER-23334	Mil Mi-2	529223055	CCCP23334
ER-23429	Mil Mi-2	529344085	CCCP23429
ER-23469	Mil Mi-2	526208069	CCCP23469
ER-23470	Mil Mi-2	526209069	CCCP23470
ER-23471	Mil Mi-2	526210069	23471
			CCCP23471
ER-24073	Kamov Ka-26	6900602	CCCP24073
ER-26046	Antonov An-26B	108-07	CCCP26046
ER-26059	Antonov An-26B	111-04	UR-26059
			ER-26059
			CCCP26059
ER-26068	Antonov An-26B	113-08	CCCP26068
ER-26204	Antonov An-26B	141-03	UR-26204
			ER-26204
			CCCP26204
ER-32274	Antonov An-2TP	1G96-36	CCCP32274
ER-32424	Antonov An-2	1G101-05	CCCP32424
ER-33645	Antonov An-2R	1G233-35	YR-33645
			ER-33645
			CCCP33645
ER-33646	Antonov An-2R	1G233-36	YR-SRE
			ER-33646
			YR-33646
			ER-33646
			CCCP33646
ER-33648	Antonov An-2R	1G233-38	CCCP33648
ER-35531	Antonov An-2P	1GI14-43	CCCP35531
ER-35538	Antonov An-2P	1GI14-50	CCCP35538
ER-46417	Antonov An-24B (Wfu ?)	87304102	UR-46417
			ER-46417
			CCCP46417
ER-46508	Antonov An-24RV	37308404	CCCP46508
ER-46599	Antonov An-24B (Wfu ?)	97305109	CCCP46500
ER-46685	Antonov An-24RV	47309710	CCCP46685
ER-47698	Antonov An-24RV (Stored)	27307605	CCCP47698
ER-65036	Tupolev Tu-134A (Stored)	48700	CCCP65036
ER-65050	Tupolev Tu-134A (Stored)	49756	CCCP65050
ER-65051	Tupolev Tu-134A-3 (Stored)	49758	CCCP65051
ER-65071	Tupolev Tu-134A-3 (Stored)	49915	CCCP65071
ER-65094	Tupolev Tu-134A-3 (Wfu ?)	8360255	CCCP65094
ER-65140	Tupolev Tu-134A-3 (Wfu ?)	60932	CCCP65140
ER-65707	Tupolev Tu-134A-3 (Stored)	63435	CCCP-65707
ER-65791	Tupolev Tu-134A-3 (Wfu ?)	63110	CCCP65791
ER-75929	Ilyushin Il-18D	187010505	CCCP75929
			CCCP74251

ES - ESTONIA

Regn.	Type	C/n	Prev.Id.
ES-ABC	Boeing 737-5Q8	26324	
ES-ABD	Boeing 737-5Q8	26323	
ES-ABG	Boeing 737-505	25790	LN-BRU
			(LN-KKM)
			N651LF
			LN-BRU
			(SE-RAN)
			LN-BRU
ES-ABH	Boeing 737-53S	29074	F-GJNT
			N1786B
ES-ABI	Boeing 737-5L9	29234	OY-APP
			N1786B
ES-ACA	Aero Commander 500	803-80	OH-ACA
			N8464C
ES-AKE	Douglas C-47B	16697/33445	9Q-CUK
			N99665
			CAF:12906
			KP227
			44-77113
ES-ANS	Cessna 172R	17280581	N7274K
ES-BAB	Antonov An-2T	1G160-38	DOSAAF-O9
ES-BAH	Antonov An-2R	1G172-34	RA-40726
			CCCP40762
ES-CAB	Antonov An-2R	1G219-07	CCCP32608
ES-CAC	Antonov An-2R	1G206-45	CCCP17940
ES-CAD	Antonov An-2R	1G194-36	CCCP68096
ES-CAJ	Antonov An-2TP	1G137-49	CCCP70175
ES-CAK	Antonov An-2TP	1G137-35	CCCP70161
ES-DAA	Antonov An-28	1AJ007-16	RA-28731
			CCCP28731
ES-DAB	Antonov An-28	1AJ005-13	RA-28780
			CCCP28780
ES-ECA	Cessna 310K	310K0161	SE-GTY
			LN-TSA
			N7061L
ES-ECB	Cessna F150J	F150-0452	OH-CBO
ES-ECD	Cessna F172G	F172-0254	OH-CEM
ES-ECE	Reims/Cessna F172P	F17202196	OH-BFO
			SE-IPN
			G-BKWH
ES-ECG	Reims/Cessna F172L	F17200873	OH-CFP
ES-ECM	Cessna 150J	15069492	N50699
ES-ECN	Reims/Cessna F150L	F15000891	OH-CFT
ES-ECP	Cessna 150M	15076454	ES-FCB
			OH-CMZ
			N8AZ
			(N3302V)
ES-EPA	Piper PA-31 Navajo C	31-7612088	SE-KZA
			PH-TUR
			D-IBRU
			N62859
ES-FCC	Cessna 172M	17262412	OH-CVX
			C-FIGO
			N12967
ES-FPC	Piper PA-28-140 Cherokee B	28-26267	OH-PCC
			N5544U
ES-FPM	Piper PA-34-200T Seneca II	34-8070191	D-GLHW
			N14EG
			N8191J
ES-FPW	Piper PA-28R-200 Cherokee Arrow	28R-35289	OH-PJW
ES-HPK	Robinson R-22 Beta	0639	G-LAND
ES-HPL	Robinson R-22 Beta	1007	G-PPLH
ES-JPL	CEA Jodel DR.1050 Ambassadeur (Modified)	204	OH-JOB
ES-JRS	SAN Jodel D.117 Grand Tourisme	B729	F-BIDV
ES-LLB	LET L-410UVP-E20C	912608	OK-WDG
			CCCP67678
ES-LLC	LET L-410UVP-E20C	912609	OK-WDH
			CCCP67679
ES-LTA	Tupolev Tu-134A	8360195	RA-65091
			LY-ABG
			CCCP65091
ES-NAA	Antonov An-2	1G224-21	FLARF02809
			RA-40444
			CCCP40444
ES-NOB	Antonov An-72	36572070695	CCCP72931
ES-NOD	Antonov An-28	1AJ002-06	UR-28808
			CCCP28808
ES-NOG	Antonov An-72	36572080786	RA-72942
			CCCP72942
ES-NOH	Antonov An-72	36572095909	EL-ALX
ES-NOI	Antonov An-72	36572096914	RA-72982
			Russian AF
ES-NOK	Antonov An-72	36572080780	RA-72939
	(Operating as United Nations UN-090)		CCCP72939
ES-NOP	Antonov An-72	36572010905	"01-01"
ES-NOW	Antonov An-28	1AJ002-07	FLARF02726
			(RA-28809)
			CCCP28809
ES-NYA	Yakovlev Yak-18T	22203044761	DOSAAF
ES-NYC	Yakovlev Yak-18T	22202044533	UR-BEM
ES-NYY	Yakovlev Yak-52	845005	DOSAAF
ES-PAE	Yakovlev Yak-52	9111412	CCCP05050
	(Reserved as SE-LVH 7.04)		

ES-PAH	Piper PA-31-350 Navajo Chieftain	31-7405156	SE-GDI
ES-PCO	Cessna 172R	17281181	N21283
ES-PJG	BAe. Jetstream Series 3103	701	ES-LJD OY-SVR D-CONA(3) (PH-KJH) G-31-701
ES-PLB	LET L-410UVP	851413	LY-AVY CCCP67509
ES-PLI	LET L-410UVP	851438	LY-AIL RA-67531 CCCP67531
ES-PLW	LET L-410UVP (T)	810726	ES-EPA 53+01 LSK 313
ES-PLY	LET L-410UVP	810727	ES-EPI 53+02 LSK-316
ES-PMC	Mil Mi-8TB	10579	93+71 LSK-755
ES-PMD	Mil Mi-8T	10595	D-HOXE DDR-SPE DM-SPE
ES-PM .	Mil Mi-8T	10596	D-HOXF DDR-SPF DM-SPF
ES-PSF	Schweizer 269C	S-1774	SE-JCZ N69A
ES-PVS	Bombardier Learjet 60	60-190	EI-IAU N190LJ N5012K
ES-RAB	PZL- 04 Wilga 35A	107370	DOSAAF
ES-RAC	PZL-104 Wilga 35A	128435	DOSAAF
ES-RAF	PZL-104 Wilga 35A	17820668	DOSAAF
ES-RID	SOCATA MS.894A Minerva 220	11939	D-EDCJ
ES-RWA	PZL-104 Wilga 35A	96284	ES-RAE DOSAAF
ES-RWE	PZL-104 Wilga 35A	17820681	DOSAAF
ES-SAE	PZL-104 Wilga 35A	140523	DOSAAF
ES-TAB	PZL-104 Wilga 35A	15800578	DOSAAF
ES-TAD	PZL-104 Wilga 35A	128433	DOSAAF-15
ES-TAE	PZL-104 Wilga 35A (Wfu?)	18840779	DOSAAF
ES-TLC	Aero L-39 Albatros	533223	?
ES-TWG	PZL-104 Wilga 35A	18840781	DOSAAF
ES-UBA	Evektor EV-97R Eurostar	2003-1609	
ES-UBC	Evektor EV-97R Eurostar (on floats)	2002-1506	
ES-UCA	Comco Ikarus C-42 Cyclone	0107-6367	
ES-UCB	Comco Ikarus C-42 Cyclone	0208-6469	
ES-UFM	Urban Air UFM-13 Lambada	39/13	
ES-UHA	X-32 Bekas	346	
ES-UJF	Advanced Light Aircraft JF-91	unkn	I-2763
ES-UNA	Murphy Renegade II	223	OH-U161
ES-UNU	Murphy Renegade Spirit	108	
ES-VCW	Cessna 172M	17260805	OH-CTZ C-GEXJ N19852
ES-XAB	Mil Mi-2	54 7845 102	Est AF:12 yellow ES-XAB Est AF:12 yellow
ES-XYK	Yakovlev Yak-18T	5201207	CCCP . . . . .
ES-XYL	Yakovlev Yak-52 (Reserved as SE-LXB 7.04)	833205	DOSAAF
ES-XYP	Yakovlev Yak-52 (Reserved as SE-LUV 7.04)	844707	DOSAAF
ES-YLF	Aero L-39C Albatros	433141	
ES-YLI	Aero L-39C Albatros	433142	
ES-YLN	Aero L-39C Albatros (Coded '08')	533637	
ES-YLP	Aero L-39C Albatros	533620	
ES-YLR	Aero L-39C Albatros	533628	
ES-YLS	Aero L-39C Albatros	533638	
ES-YLT	Aero L-29 Delfin	094112	Estonia AF Soviet AF
ES-YLU	Aero L-29 Delfin	194445	Estonia AF Soviet AF
ES-YLX	Aero L-39C Albatros	432905	Khyrg.AF 105
ES-YLZ	Aero L-39C Albatros	432939	
ES-YYC	Yakovlev Yak-52	9010912	
ES-YYU	Yakovlev Yak-52	unkn	
ES- . . .	Antonov An-2T	1G160-28	DOSAAF
ES-U . .	Beaver RX-650	0003	OH-U211
ES-U . .	Beaver RX-650	0009	OH-U268
ES- . . .	Beech 35 Bonanza	D-302	N2895V NC2895V
ES- . . .	Berkut 540	19	N223ES
ES- . . .	Cessna 172R	17280581	N7274K
ES- . . .	Comco Ikarus Fox C-22	8903-3194	OH-U132
ES-H . .	Eurocopter EC.130B4 Ecureuil	3694	F-GIYK
ES- . . .	PZL-104 Wilga 35	96286	DOSAAF
ES- . . .	PZL-104 Wilga 35	139464	DOSAAF
ES- . . .	Rotorway Scorpion 133	1342	N613EL
ES- . . .	SOCATA MS.893A Rallye Commodore 180	11030	D-E . . . F-BRDZ
ES- . . .	SOCATA MS.893A Rallye Commodore 180	11891	OY-ANS SE-FSH
ES- . . .	Super Aero 45	03-007	OH-EFC OY-EFC (G-BFAZ) D-GGAM D-EGAM

BALLOONS

ES-HAA	Interavia TA-80 Balloon	0270292	
ES-HAH	Interavia TA-80 Balloon	0260292	
ES-HAR	Interavia TA-80 Balloon	0221191	
ES-HAS	Interavia TA-80 Balloon	0270999	

MICROLIGHTS

ES-KAK	Bogdola Janos Powered Hang Glider	BB	
ES-KAN	Ferrari Tirelli II	unkn	
ES-KAS	Poisk-06 Hang Glider	R-1205	
ES-KAT	Powered Hang Glider	unkn	
ES-KEV	Powered Hang Glider MD-20	3139	
ES-KHK	Poisk-06 Powered Hang Glider	R-0210	
ES-KLM	Powered Hang Glider	unkn	
ES-KLY	Powered Hang Glider MD-20	3033	
ES-KRG	Poisk-06 Hang Glider	R-2518	
ES- . . .	Southdown Puma Sprint	T45	OH-U151

GLIDERS

ES-1000	LAK-12 Lietuva	653	
ES-1001	LAK-12 Lietuva	6165	
ES-1002	LAK-12 Lietuva	6156	
ES-1004	SZD-48-3 Jantar Standard 3	B-1454	DOSAAF
ES-1005-EV	SZD-48-1 Jantar Standard 2	B-1225	DOSAAF
ES-1006	SZD-48-1 Jantar Standard 2	B-1164	DOSAAF
ES-1007	SZD-41A Jantar Standard	B-912	DOSAAF
ES-1009	SZD-48-3 Jantar Standard 3	B-1702	DOSAAF
ES-1010	Schleicher ASW 15	15092	
ES-1019	LET L-13 Blanik	172307	
ES-1021	LET L-13 Blanik	173614	
ES-1024	LET L-13 Blanik	026214	
ES-1025	LET L-13 Blanik	026439	
ES-1501	SZD-36A Cobra 15	W-602	DOSAAF
ES-1602	SZD-30 Pirat	S-05.22	DOSAAF
ES-2001	LET L-13 Blanik	026437	
ES-2003	LET L-13 Blanik	026706	
ES-2004	LET L-13 Blanik	026707	
ES-2006	LET L-13 Blanik	174518	
ES-2010	LET L-13 Blanik	026951	
ES-2021	SZD-48-3 Jantar Standard 3	B-1651	DOSAAF
ES-2023-KJ	SZD-48-3 Jantar Standard 3	B-1703	DOSAAF
ES-2024	SZD-48-3 Jantar Standard 3	B-1884	DOSAAF
ES-20 . .	SZD-48-1 Jantar Standard 2	B-1229	DOSAAF
ES-3117	LET L-13 Blanik	027317	
ES-3119	LET L-13 Blanik	027319	
ES-3120	LET L-13 Blanik	027320	
ES-3276	SZD-48-3 Jantar Standard 3	B-1576	ES-2022 DOSAAF
ES-4112	LET L-13 Blanik	026919	ES-2012
ES-5304	Amateur Powered Seaplane	20122.01H (4276)	

EW - BELARUS

Regn.	Type	C/n	Prev.Id.
EW-001PA	Boeing 737-8EV	33079	N375BC
EW-215KB	LET L-410UVP	820904	UR-67344
			CCCP67344
EW-250PA	Boeing 737-524	26319	N427LF
			XU-756
			N19634
EW-251PA	Boeing 737-5Q8	27634	PT-SSC
EW-01406	Antonov An-2TP	1G230-46	CCCP01406
EW-06076	Mil Mi-26 T	34001212466	
EW-06077	Mil Mi-26 T	34001212467	
EW-07428	Antonov An-2P	1G151-03	CCCP07428
EW-07772	Antonov An-2TP	1G161-47	CCCP07772
EW-07778	Antonov An-2TP	1G161-53	CCCP07778
EW-07793	Antonov An-2P	1G162-43	CCCP07793 ?
EW-07815	Antonov An-2R (Wfu ?)	1G169-30	CCCP07815 ?
EW-07887	Antonov An-2	1G170-49	CCCP07887
EW-11365(2)	Antonov An-12BP	5343109	Sov.AF 09 yel.
EW-11371(2)	Antonov An-12BP	4342108	Sov.AF 08 yel.
EW-14126	Mil Mi-2	5210838029	CCCP14126
EW-14158	Mil Mi-2	5210443117	CCCP14126
EW-14159	Mil Mi-2	5210444117	CCCP14158
EW-14199	Mil Mi-2	5410940069	CCCP14199
EW-14200	Mil Mi-2	5410941069	CCCP14200
EW-14213	Mil Mi-2	5211048119	CCCP14213
EW-14214	Mil Mi-2	5211049119	CCCP14214
EW-14216	Mil Mi-2	5211101119	CCCP14216
EW-14251	Mil Mi-2	5211138050	CCCP14251
EW-14255	Mil Mi-2	5211142060	CCCP14255
EW-14256	Mil Mi-2	5211143060	CCCP14256
EW-15624	Mil Mi-2	5210039126	CCCP15624
EW-16051	Antonov An-2R	1G164-04	CCCP16051 ?
EW-17844	Antonov An-2R	1G204-45	CCCP17844
EW-17869	Antonov An-2R	1G205-10	CCCP17869
EW-17870	Antonov An-2R	1G205-11	CCCP17870
EW-17892	Antonov An-2R	1G205-33	CCCP17892
EW-17893	Antonov An-2R	1G205-34	CCCP17893
EW-17979	Antonov An-2R	1G210-03	CCCP17979
EW-17981	Antonov An-2R	1G210-05	CCCP17981
EW-17983	Antonov An-2R	1G210-07	CCCP17983
EW-19280	Kamov Ka-26	7001210	CCCP19280
EW-19613	Kamov Ka-26	7505112	CCCP19613
EW-20371	Mil Mi-2	529818066	CCCP20371
EW-20737	Mil Mi-2	527634052	CCCP20737
EW-20913	Mil Mi-2	528545024	CCCP20913
EW-20961	Mil Mi-2	549517115	CCCP20961
EW-23232	Mil Mi-2	5210233057	CCCP23232
EW-23291	Mil Mi-2	529112025	CCCP23291
EW-24061	Kamov Ka-26	00304	CCCP24061
EW-24082	Kamov Ka-26	6900901	CCCP24082
EW-24086	Kamov Ka-26	7000905	CCCP24086
EW-24325	Kamov Ka-26	7706117	CCCP24325
EW-26079	Antonov An-26B (Cancelled?)	116-08	CCCP26079 ?
EW-26112	Antonov An-26B	121-09	CCCP26112
EW-26127	Antonov An-26B	127-01	CCCP26127
EW-32634	Antonov An-2R	1G219-33	CCCP32634
EW-32673	Antonov An-2R	1G211-32	CCCP32673 ?
EW-32674	Antonov An-2R (Stored)	1G211-33	CCCP32674
EW-32685	Antonov An-2R	1G211-44	CCCP32685
EW-32686	Antonov An-2R	1G211-45	CCCP32686
EW-32744	Antonov An-2R	1G212-49	CCCP32744
EW-33303	Antonov An-2R	1G225-20	CCCP33303 ?
EW-33533	Antonov An-2R	1G229-25	CCCP33533
EW-33582	Antonov An-2R	1G230-19	CCCP33582
EW-33583	Antonov An-2R	1G230-20	CCCP33583
EW-40495	Antonov An-2R	1G225-12	CCCP40495
EW-40499	Antonov An-2R	1G225-16	CCCP40499 ?
EW-40541	Antonov An-2TP	1G83-44	CCCP40541
EW-40606	Antonov An-2R	1G213-01	CCCP40606
EW-40622	Antonov An-2R	1G213-29	CCCP40622
EW-40658	Antonov An-2R	1G214-16	CCCP40658
EW-40678	Antonov An-2R	1G214-36	CCCP40678
EW-40739	Antonov An-2R	1G172-11	CCCP40739
EW-40809	Antonov An-2R (Stored)	1G173-36	CCCP40809
EW-40840	Antonov An-2R	1G174-18	CCCP40840
EW-40929	Antonov An-2R (Stored)	1G216-09	CCCP40929
EW-40931	Antonov An-2R	1G216-11	CCCP40931
EW-40986	Antonov An-2R	1G217-26	CCCP40986
EW-43951	Antonov An-2R	1G210-28	CCCP43951
EW-46250	Antonov An-24B (Cancelled?)	77303208	?
EW-46304	Antonov An-24B	97305204	CCCP46304
EW-46359	Antonov An-24B	07305809	UR-46359
			EW-46359
			RA-46359
			CCCP46359
EW-46375	Antonov An-24B	07306008	CCCP46375
EW-46404	Antonov An-24B (Cancelled?)	77303909	46404
			CCCP46404
EW-46483	Antonov An-24RV	27308101	CCCP46483
EW-46498	Antonov An-24RV	27308301	CCCP46498
EW-46607	Antonov An-24RV (Wfu ?)	37308604	CCCP46607
EW-46615	Antonov An-24RV	37308702	CCCP46615
EW-46631	Antonov An-24RV	37308810	CCCP46631
EW-46829	Antonov An-24RV	17306706	CCCP46829
EW-46835	Antonov An-24RV	17306802	CCCP46835
EW-47291	Antonov An-24B	07306601	CCCP47291
EW-47697	Antonov An-24RV	27307604	CCCP47697
EW-47808	Antonov An-24RV	17306910	CCCP47808
EW-47825	Antonov An-24B	17307206	TC-ANK
			EW-47825
			CCCP47825
EW-54612	Antonov An-2R	1G180-56	CCCP54612 ?
EW-54876	Antonov An-2R	1G185-36	CCCP54876
EW-54894	Antonov An-2R	1G186-42	CCCP54894
EW-54901	Antonov An-2R	1G186-49	CCCP54901
EW-54905	Antonov An-2R	1G186-53	CCCP54905
EW-54906	Antonov An-2R	1G186-54	CCCP54906
EW-54912	Antonov An-2R	1G186-60	CCCP54912
EW-54924	Antonov An-2R	1G187-17	CCCP54924
EW-56371	Antonov An-2R	1G180-50	CCCP56371
EW-62521	Antonov An-2R	1G175-44	CCCP62521
EW-62618	Antonov An-2R	1G178-03	CCCP62618 ?
EW-62621	Antonov An-2R	1G178-13	HA-MKH
			EW-62621
			CCCP62621
EW-62660	Antonov An-2R	1G178-52	CCCP62660
EW-62696	Antonov An-2R	1G179-26	CCCP62696
EW-63955	Tupolev Tu-134A (Wfu ?)	63955	CCCP63955
			Sov.AF
EW-65049	Tupolev Tu-134A (Wfu ?)	49755	CCCP65049
EW-65082	Tupolev Tu-134A-3	60081	CCCP65082
EW-65085	Tupolev Tu-134A	60123	CCCP65085
EW-65106	Tupolev Tu-134A	60315	CCCP65106
EW-65108	Tupolev Tu-134A (Wfu ?)	60332	CCCP65108
EW-65133	Tupolev Tu-134A-3	60645	CCCP65133
EW-65145	Tupolev Tu-134A	60985	65145
			CCCP65145
EW-65149	Tupolev Tu-134A-3 (Wfu ?)	61033	CCCP65149
EW-65663	Tupolev Tu-134A (Wfu ?)	51109	CCCP65663
EW-65676	Tupolev Tu-134A (Wfu ?)	1351502	CCCP65676
EW-65754	Tupolev Tu-134A	62154	CCCP65754
EW-65764	Tupolev Tu-134A-3 (Wfu ?)	62305	UR-65764
			CCCP65764
EW-65772	Tupolev Tu-134A	62472	CCCP65772
EW-65821	Tupolev Tu-134A (Wfu ?)	08060	CCCP65821
EW-65892	Tupolev Tu-134A (Wfu ?)	38050	CCCP65892
			HA-LBL
			CCCP65892
EW-65957	Tupolev Tu-134A (Wfu ?)	2351802	CCCP65957
EW-65974	Tupolev Tu-134A (Wfu)	3352004	CCCP65974
EW-68086	Antonov An-2R (Stored)	1G193-56	CCCP68086
EW-70316	Antonov An-2P	1G140-20	CCCP70316
EW-70383	Antonov An-2P	1G141-37	CCCP70383
EW-71168	Antonov An-2R	1G200-11	CCCP71168
EW-71170	Antonov An-2R	1G200-13	CCCP71170
EW-76709	Ilyushin Il-76MD	0063473173	CCCP76709
EW-76710	Ilyushin Il-76TD	0063473182	CCCP76710
EW-76711	Ilyushin Il-76MD	0063473187	CCCP76711
EW-76712	Ilyushin Il-76MD	0063473190	RA-76712
			CCCP76712
EW-76734	Ilyushin Il-76MD	0073476312	CCCP76734
EW-76735	Ilyushin Il-76TD	0073476314	RA-76735
			CCCP76735
EW-76737	Ilyushin Il-76TD	0073477323	RA-76737
			CCCP76737
EW-78765	Ilyushin Il-76MD	0083486590	CCCP78765
EW-78769	Ilyushin Il-76MD	0083487607	CCCP78769
EW-78779	Ilyushin Il-76TD	0083489662	CCCP78779
EW-78787	Ilyushin Il-76MD	0083490698	CCCP78787
EW-78792	Ilyushin Il-76TD	0093490718	RA-78792
			CCCP78792
EW-78799	Ilyushin Il-76TD	0093491754	CCCP78799
EW-78801	Ilyushin Il-76TD	0093492763	CCCP78801
EW-78808	Ilyushin Il-76MD	0093493794	CCCP78808
EW-78819	Ilyushin Il-76MD	0093495883	CCCP78819
EW-78826	Ilyushin Il-76MD	1003499991	CCCP78826
EW-78827	Ilyushin Il-76TD	1003499997	CCCP78827
EW-78828	Ilyushin Il-76MD	1003401004	CCCP78828
EW-78836	Ilyushin Il-76MD	0093499986	CCCP78836
EW-78839	Ilyushin Il-76MD	1003402047	CCCP78839
EW-78843	Ilyushin Il-76MD	1003403082	CCCP78843
EW-78848	Ilyushin Il-76MD	1003405159	CCCP78848
EW-78849	Ilyushin Il-76TD	1013405192	CCCP78849
EW-81531	Antonov An-2R	1G208-35	CCCP81531 ?
EW-81539	Antonov An-2R	1G208-43	CCCP81539
EW-82853	Antonov An-2R	1G168-23	CCCP82853
EW-82854	Antonov An-2R (Stored)	1G163-24	CCCP82854
EW-84682	Antonov An-2R (Stored)	1G191-60	CCCP84682
EW-84725	Antonov An-2R	1G201-43	CCCP84725
EW-84730	Antonov An-2R	1G201-48	CCCP84730
EW-85122	Tupolev Tu-154B (Wfu ?)	75A-122	CCCP85122
EW-85411	Tupolev Tu-154B2 (Wfu)	80A-411	CCCP85411
EW-85419	Tupolev Tu-154B2 (Wfu)	80A-419	CCCP85419
EW-85465	Tupolev Tu-154B2 (Wfu)	80A-465	CCCP85465
EW-85486	Tupolev Tu-154B2 (Wfu ?)	81A-486	CCCP85486
EW-85509	Tupolev Tu-154B2	81A-509	UN-85509
			CCCP85509
EW-85538	Tupolev Tu-154B2	82A-538	4K-85538
			EW-85538
			CCCP85538
EW-85545	Tupolev Tu-154B2	82A-545	CCCP85545

EW-85580	Tupolev Tu-154B2 (Wfu)	83A-580	CCCP85580
EW-85581	Tupolev Tu-154B2	83A-581	CCCP85581
EW-85582	Tupolev Tu-154B2 (Wfu)	83A-582	CCCP85582
EW-85591	Tupolev Tu-154B2	83A-591	CCCP85591
EW-85593	Tupolev Tu-154B2 (Wfu)	83A-593	CCCP85593
EW-85703	Tupolev Tu-154M	91A-878	CCCP85703
EW-85706	Tupolev Tu-154M	91A-881	CCCP85706
EW-85741	Tupolev Tu-154M	91A-896	ES-LTR CCCP85741
EW-85748	Tupolev Tu-154M	92A-924	CCCP85748
EW-85815	Tupolev Tu-154M	95A-1010	
EW-87320	Yakovlev Yak-40 (Wfu ?)	9331929	CCCP87320
EW-87330	Yakovlev Yak-40	9510139	CCCP87330
EW-87419	Yakovlev Yak-40 (Wfu ?)	9421134	CCCP87419
EW-87577	Yakovlev Yak-40	9220922	RA-87577 EW-87577 CCCP87577
EW-87657	Yakovlev Yak-40 (Wfu ?)	9020409	I-JAKA CCCP87657
EW-87658	Yakovlev Yak-40	9240225	HA-LJD CCCP87658
EW-88161	Yakovlev Yak-40	9611546	CCCP88161
EW-88187	Yakovlev Yak-40 (Wfu ?)	9620748	88187 CCCP88187
EW-88202	Yakovlev Yak-40	9630449	CCCP88202
EW-96225	Antonov An-2TP	1G72-09	CCCP96225
EW-.	PZL-104 Wilga 35A	21930950	
EW-.	PZL-104 Wilga 35A	21930949	

BALLOONS

EW-0165L	Hot Air Balloon
EW-0355L	Hot Air Balloon

F - FRANCE

CNRAC REGISTER (HISTORIC AND VINTAGE AIRCRAFT)

Regn.	Type	C/n	Prev.Id.
F-AZAA	Morane-Saulnier MS.130 Et-2 (Painted as French Navy "F28" - currently stored)	02	F-APEK
F-AZAB	Salmson/CFAD 7 Cri-Cri Major (Reservation)	9	F-BFNG
F-AZAC(2)	SNCASO SO.1221 Djinn	010/FC-18	F-BNDL F-BHHK F-WHHK
F-AZAD(2)	Procaer F-400 Cobra (Reservation)	02	(I-COBR)
F-AZAE	Morane-Saulnier MS.733 Alcyon (Reservation)	165	Fr.Navy
F-AZAF	Morane-Saulnier MS.733 Alcyon (Reservation)	190	Fr.Navy
F-AZAH	Morane-Saulnier MS.315	254	F-BBZO
F-AZAJ	Morane-Saulnier MS.138 Ep-2	3220/138	F-AQDN
F-AZAK	Morane-Saulnier MS.230	403	F-BEJO
F-AZAN	Morane A-1 Replica	01	
F-AZAO	Morane A-1 Replica	3	
F-AZAP	Morane A-1 Replica	02	
F-AZAT	North American Harvard IV	CCF4-550	F-BRGB (N73687) D-FABA AA+635 53-4631
F-AZAU	North American AT-6G Texan	182-800	F-BNAU Fr.AF 51-15113
F-AZAV	Albatros C-1 Replica (Constructed from de Havilland DH.82A Tiger Moth components)	005	F-WZBH
F-AZAZ	Morane-Saulnier MS.185	3672/01	F-AJRQ
F-AZBA	Bleriot XI Replica (Ditched 26.7.98, for rebuild)	1	F-PERV F-WERV
F-AZBD	Latécoère Laée 17P Replica (Formerly Norseman c/n 778 ex.F-BSTC/F-OBTC/RNoAF/44-70513. W/o in 1987 - wreck at La Ferté-Alais)	01	
F-AZBE	North American AT-6C Harvard IIA (Painted to represent NA-64 Yale)	88-12127	F-WJBI F-BJBI BAF:H-29 EX633 41-33606
F-AZBF	SE-5A Replica	MF-01	
F-AZBG	SFCA/Peyrot Taupin G	10	F-PMEM F-APGB
F-AZBI	Spalinger S.18-III Glider	201	OO-ZPG HB-416
F-AZBJ	SG-38 Primary Glider (DFS 108-14)	19	F-WRRK
F-AZBK	North American AT-6G Texan (Flew as a Zero Replica as F-WZBK in 1987 with c/n SAM2-367)	182-54	F-WZBK F-AZBK F-BVQD (PH-. . .) F-BVQD Fr.AF 51-14367
F-AZBL	North American SNJ-5 Texan (Flew as a Zero Replica as F-WZBM in 1987 with c/n SAM2-669)	88-17667	F-WZBM F-AZBL N9801C BuA90669 42-85886
F-AZBM	Piper J-2 Cub (Formerly Piper L-4H Cub c/n 12332 ex.F-BDTH/44-80036)	unkn	F-WZBM
F-AZBN	Noorduyn UC-64A Norseman (Stored outside at La Ferté-Alais)	774	CN-TEE EC-ANO I-AIAK YE-AAD I-AIAK 44-70509
F-AZBO	Caudron C.635 Simoun (Reservation)	342	F-DADY
F-AZBP	Breguet XIVP Replica	02	
F-AZBQ	North American T-6G Texan	182-535	F-BOEO Fr.AF 51-14848
F-AZBS	Bücker Bü .133C Jungmeister	16	F-BOHK HB-MIQ U-69
F-AZBU	Bücker Bü .131 Jungmann	83	F-BOHF HB-UTS A-70
F-AZBV	Nord 1002 Pingouin	125	F-BDXV Fr.Mil
F-AZBX	Nord 1002 Pingouin (Reservation)	282	F-BDJU Fr.Mil
F-AZBZ	CASA I-131E Jungmann	2150?	E3B-549
F-AZCA	de Havilland DH.89A Dragon Rapide	6541	F-BGON G-ALZF X7381
F-AZCB	Dassault MD-311 Flamant	291	Fr.AF
F-AZCC	Pilatus P2-05	37	U-117
F-AZCE	Pilatus P2-06 (Painted in Japanese marks)	72	U-152
F-AZCF	Fairchild F.24W-41A Argus II (Identity as quoted is suspect - another possibility is that "314" as quoted is part of a serial number 314499)	314	VH-AVN G-AKJM EV806 42-13578
F-AZCG	Pilatus P2-05	26	U-106

F-AZCH	DHC-1 Chipmunk 22	C1/0702	OY-ALW
	(Painted as "WB557")		P-132
F-AZCI	Fairchild F.24R-46A Argus III (Painted as "AZ-CI")	998	F-BEXC
	(c/n quoted as "33038AC1679" - while the		KK380
	above is thought correct another possible		44-83037
	identity is c/n 999 ex.F-BFPD)		
F-AZCK	Boeing Stearman A75-N1	75-1653	N64926
			41-8094
F-AZCM	North American/CCF Harvard 4	CCF4- . .?	G-BJMS
	(Painted as Swiss AF "U-301")		MM53802
F-AZCN	SE-5 Replica (Stampe conversion)	2	F-WZCN
F-AZCP	Morane-Saulnier MS.502 Criquet	320	F-BBUS
F-AZCQ	North American T-6G Texan	168-140	E.16-191
			49-3037
F-AZCR	Holste MH-52 (Reservation)	4	F-BEAC
			F-WEAC
F-AZCS	de Havilland DH.82A Tiger Moth (Reservation)	unkn	
F-AZCT	Caudron C-275 Luciole	7474	F-BBCF
			F-APLM
F-AZCV	North American T-6G Texan	182-142	E.16-193
			51-14456
F-AZCX	Morane-Saulnier MS.341/3 (Reservation)	4234	F-ANVS
F-AZCY	SE-5 Replica (Stampe conversion)	3	
F-WZCZ	Nord N.1101 Noralpha	77	CEV
F-AZDA	Morane-Saulnier MS.500 Criquet	226	F-BBUG
	(Painted as "2E+RA")		
F-AZDB	Polikarpov Po-2W	0045	YU-CNS
F-AZDD	Dassault MD.312 Flamant	216	Fr.AF
	(Painted as "312-DK")		
F-AZDE	Dassault MD.312 Flamant (Wfu)	251	Fr.AF
F-AZDF	Dassault MD.454A Mystere IVA	315	Fr.AF
	(Painted as "1-DF")		
F-AZDG	Erco 415C Ercoupe	3782	F-WZDG
			F-BDPQ
			NC3157H
F-AZDH(2)	de Havilland DH.82A Tiger Moth (Reservation)	unkn	
F-AZDI	Boeing Stearman E75/N2S-5	75-5238	N5817N
			BuA61116
			42-17075
F-AZDO	Auster J/1 Autocrat (Painted "V-J1")	2202	F-BFXO
			G-AIPU
F-AZDP	Douglas AD-4 Skyraider	7449	F-WZDP
	(Painted as "124143/205-RM")		TR-KFP
			(N91909)
			Fr.AF'14'
			BuA124143
F-AZDQ	Douglas AD-4 Skyraider	unkn	F-WZDQ
	(Painted as "126956"/"VMC-1"/"RM")		TR-K . .
			Fr.AF '45'
			BuA126956
F-AZDR	Dassault MD.312 Flamant (Coded "V" Fr.AF)	160	Fr.AF
F-AZDT	Bücker Bü.133E Jungmeister replica	3F	
F-AZDU	North American AT-6D Harvard III	88-14948	F-WZDU
			G-AZJD
			F-BJBF
			H-9
			SAAF7509
			EX959
			41-33932
F-AZDV	Morane-Saulnier MS.500 Criquet (Reservation)	591	(F-BMHX)
	(Painted as "AZ+DV")		F-BDHX
F-AZDX	Boeing B-17G-VE	8246	F-BGSP
	(Painted as 48846 "Pink Lady")		ZS-DXM
			F-BGSP
			44-8846A
F-AZDY	Dassault MD.312 Flamant (Reservation)	156	CEV
F-AZDZ	Auster J/2 Arrow	2354	F-BFVJ
			OO-ABP
F-AZEA	Stampe SV.4B	unkn	
F-AZEB	Utva Aero 3F	unkn	YU-DAJ
			YU-CWA
			JRV40156
F-AZEC	Utva Aero 3F	65	YU-CYF
			JRV40165
F-AZEE	Boeing Stearman A75N1 (PT-17)	75-3286	F-WZEE
	(Painted as RAF "FK107")		C-GBLQ
			N65335
			BuA28011
			41-25848
F-AZEF	North American T-6G Texan	182-74	Fr.AF
			51-14387
F-AZEG	Chance Vought F4U-5NL Corsair	unkn	FAH-605
	(Painted as "P"/"22")		NX4901E
			BuA124724
F-AZEH	Dassault MD.311 Flamant (Reservation, wfu)	274	Fr.AF
F-AZEI	de Havilland DH.82A Tiger Moth	84882	G-APIG
			T6553
F-AZEJ	Beech E-18S	BA-359	F-BTCS
			N23J
F-AZEK	SIPA S.903	99	F-BEJZ
			F-BGHY
F-AZEL	Dassault MD.312 Flamant	177	F-WZEL
			Fr.AF
F-AZEM	Bücker Bü .131D Jungmann	5	
F-AZEN	Dassault MD.312 Flamant	250	Fr.AF
	(Cld 26.1.95. Currently stored in Cyprus)		
F-AZEO	Dassault MD.312 Flamant	210	Fr.AF
F-AZER	Dassault MD.311 Flamant	276	(N276DF)
			Fr.AF
F-AZES	Dassault MD.312 Flamant (Code: "319-CG")	226	Fr.AF
F-AZEU(2)	DHC-1 Chipmunk T.20	C1/0299	FAP1307
F-AZEX	Stampe & Renard/ Stampe SV.4B	"1194"	
F-AZEY	Nord 3202	20	F-WZBY
			ALAT
F-AZEZ	North American T-6G Texan	182-361	Fr.AF
			51-14674
F-AZFA	Auster J/2 Arrow	2377	OO-ABV
F-AZFB	Yakovlev Yak-11 (Reservation)	25III/06	EAF- ?
F-AZFE	Dassault MD.312 Flamant	237	Fr.AF
F-AZFF	LET L-13 Blanik	026750	OO-ZHG
			LX-CAH
F-AZFG	Yakovlev Yak-18A	1609	EAF-640
F-AZFH	Brooks Pitts S-1S Special	K.027	F-WZAF
			N835
F-AZFJ	Yakovlev Yak-11	25III/02	EAF- ?
F-AZFL	Nord 3202	92	ALAT
F-AZFM	Nord 3400	122	ALAT
F-AZFN	Douglas AD-4 Skyraider	7609	ChadAF
	(Painted as 125716 "22-DG")		Fr.AF
			BuA125716
F-AZFO(2)	Nord 1201 Norécrin (Reservation)	6	F-BDSA
F-AZFP(2)	SPAD S-XIIIC1	4371	
F-AZFR	Soko J20 Kraguj	37	(F-AZGR)
			JRV30153
F-AZFS	Dassault MD-312 Flamant	217	Fr.AF
F-AZFT	Nord 3202	34	F-WYAY
			ALAT
F-AZFU	Nord 3202	37	F-WYAZ
			ALAT
F-AZFX	Dassault MD-311 Flamant	282	Fr.AF
F-AZFY	Moynet 360-6 Jupiter (Reservation)	03	F-BLKY
	(c/n quoted officially as "360.6")		F-WLKY
F-AZFZ	Payen PA-349 (Reservation)	01	
F-AZGB	North American T-6D Harvard IV	CCF4-175	N175JR
			CF-UNL
			RCAF20384
F-AZGC	EKW C-3605 (Wfu ?)	273	F-WZII
			C-493
F-AZGD	EKW C-3605 (Wfu ?)	330	F-WZIG
			C-550
F-AZGE	Dassault MD-312 Flamant	158	Fr.AF
F-AZGF	Nord 3202	80	G-BEFH
			N2255N
			ALAT
F-AZGG	CASA I-131E Jungmann	unkn	E3B-540
F-AZGI	CASA I-131E Jungmann	unkn	E3B-532
	(Painted in Sp.AF c/s as 781/13")		
F-AZGJ	Boeing Stearman E75	"75-SA28"	
F-AZGK(2)	Stinson V-77 Reliant	77-177	N77DB
			NC77DB
F-AZGL	CASA I-131E Jungmann (Reservation)	"1022"	
F-AZGM	Boeing Stearman A75-N1	75-589	G-BPEX
			N65D
			N61304
			40-2032
F-AZGO	DHC-1 Chipmunk T.20	C1/0346	F-WZGO
			FAP1308
F-AZGP	OGMA/DHC-1 Chipmunk T.20	OGMA-23	FAP1333
F-AZGQ	OGMA/DHC-1 Chipmunk T.20	OGMA-15	FAP1325
F-AZGR(2)	Boeing Stearman B75N1	75-2650	N62418
			BuA04320
F-AZGS	North American T-6G Texan	168-556	Fr.AF
	(Painted as 49-3432)		49-3432
F-AZGT	Nord 3202	94	F-WZBB
	(w/o 14.7.91)		ALAT
F-AZGU(3)	de Havilland DH.115 Vampire T.55	989	U-1229
	(Painted as "U-1229")		
F-AZGV	Payen PA-49 (Reservation)	B-02	
F-AZGX	Dassault MD.311 Flamant (Reservation)	290	Fr.AF
F-AZGY	Starck AS-70	unkn	
F-AZGZ	Pitts S-1S Special	288H	
F-AZHA	Nord NC.856A-1 Norvigie	25	F-BYCM
			F-BJLH
			ALAT
F-AZHB	Antonov An-2	17309	LSK-452
F-AZHC	Bücker Bü.133E Jungmeister	F5-2009	
F-AZHD	North American NA-68 (Replica)	SA-30	
	(Painted as Fr.Navy "11F2"/"79413")		
F-AZHE	North American NA-68 (Replica)	SA-31	
	(Painted as Fr.Navy "14.F.7")		
F-AZHG	Pilatus P3-03 (Painted as "A-805")	322-4	A-805
F-AZHH	de Havilland DH.100 Vampire FB.6	708	J-1199
F-AZHI	de Havilland DH.100 Vampire FB.6 (Reservation)	652	J-1143
F-AZHJ	de Havilland DH.100 Vampire FB.6	668	J-1159
F-AZHK	Douglas AD-4N Skyraider	61/7802	N91989
			Fr.AF
			BuA127002
F-AZHL	Morane-Saulnier MS.315	350	F-BCNT
F-AZHM	Antonov An-2 (Wrecked)	17311	D-FONH
			DDR-SKH(2)
			LSK453
F-AZHN	North American T-28C	226-124	N2800Q
	(Painted as "140547"/"ER")		BuA140547

F-AZHO	Nord 3202	95	F-WZBC F-AZAC ALAT (F-BNRN) ALAT
F-AZHP	S.0.4050 Vautour IIN	348	CEV-"DP" Fr.AF
F-AZHR	North American T-28	135/174-602	Fr.AF 51-7749
F-AZHT	Pilatus P.3-03	324-6	(F-AZGU) A-807
F-AZHU	de Havilland DH.115 Vampire T.55	870	U-1210
F-AZHV	de Havilland DH.115 Vampire T.55 (Reservation)	983	U-1223
F-AZHX	de Havilland DH.100 Vampire FB.6 (Painted as VZ192-"4-LH")	624	J-1115
F-AZHY	de Havilland DH.100 Vampire FB.6 (Coded DY-6)	610	J-1101
F-AZIA	Boisavia B.605 Mercurey (Reservation)	5	F-BHGA
F-AZIB	North American T-6G Texan	182-585	F-BMJQ Fr.AF 51-14898
F-AZIC	Boeing Stearman PT-13D	75-5540	G-BTZM N4738V 42-17377
F-AZIG	CCF Harvard Mk.4	CCF4-128	CF-UVQ RCAF20337
F-AZIH	Standard Austria (Reservation)	8	HB-680
F-AZII	Piper J-2 Cub (Identity uncertain)	5418	
F-AZIJ	Nord 3202	85	G-BRVA G-BIZL N2255Y ALAT
F-AZIK	de Havilland DH.100 Vampire FB.6	700	J-1191
F-AZIL	Nord 3202	18	ALAT
F-AZIM	Yakovlev Yak-3 (Same c/n quoted as F-AZIS)	9/04623	RomaniaAF
F-AZIN	Blériot XI	225	G-AVXV
F-AZIO	Yakovlev Yak-11	Y-5434	
F-AZIP	Boeing Stearman PT-17	75-341	N58712 AN-BLL N58712 40-1784
F-AZIQ	CASA I-131E Jungmann (Reservation .02)	unkn	E3B-625
F-AZIR	Yakovlev Yak-11	25-III-21	
F-AZIS	Yakovlev Yak-3 (Same c/n quoted as F-AZIM)	9/04623	RomaniaAF
F-AZIT	Nord 3202 (Painted as "AIT")	74	ALAT
F-AZIU	North American T-6G Texan	182-38	Fr.AF 51-14351
F-AZIV	Nord 3400	123	ALAT
F-AZIX	SNCASO SO.1221S Djinn (Reservation .00)	FR-3	ALAT '3'/ CELAG
F-AZIY	Nord 3202	15	F-WZBA ALAT
F-AZIZ	Luscombe 8A Silvaire	3071	G-OWIZ N71644 NC71644
F-AZJA	Grumman TBM-3E Avenger	85869	N9927Z BuA85869
F-AZJB	Yakovlev Yak-11	25III/03	EAF-533 ?
F-AZJC	WACO UPF-7	5495	N29998 NC29998
F-AZJD	Dewoitine D.27-SA	SA-290/322	F-AZBF (F-AZBC) HB-RAC U-290
F-AZJE	Aero 3	unkn	YU-CXO JRV40174
F-AZJF	Hirth Hi.27 Akrostar II	4003	F-WZJF HB-MSA D-EBAZ
F-AZJH	Morane-Saulnier MS.181 (Reservation)	unkn	
F-AZJI	North American T-6G Texan	182-407	Fr.AF 51-14720
F-AZJJ	North American P-51D-NA Mustang	122-41046	N335J N6317T CF-MWM RCAF9231 44-74506
F-AZJK	Nord 3202	64	ALAT
F-AZJL	DHC-1 Chipmunk 22 (Painted as WP900-"V-15")	C1/0771	G-BWRX WP900
F-AZJN	Auster J/IN Alpha	unkn	
F-AZJO	Nord 3202	101	F-WZBE F-AZAI F-BNRP ALAT
F-AZJP	Beech D-17S	6738	(F-AZGU) N1126V N4926V XB-LEQ NC67718 BuA23721 44-76056 (BuA23721)
F-AZJQ	DHC-1 Chipmunk 22	C1/0829	WP967
F-AZJR	Boeing Stearman E75 (Painted as USN "4273"/"741")	75-5656	(F-AZJS) N5358N 42-17493
F-AZJS	North American T-6 Harvard (Reservation)	unkn	

F-AZJT	Nord 3202BIB	71	F-WZBD F-AZAD ALAT
F-AZJU	CASA C.352L (Now regd as Junkers Ju 52/3m) (Painted as Luftwaffe "N9+AA")	24	G-BECL T2B-212
F-AZJV	DHC-1 Chipmunk	OGMA-65	CS-AZP FAP1375
F-AZJX	Aero 45	4904	F-GFYA I-CRES
F-AZJY	Caudron-Renault JN760-C1	01	(F-PNJY) F-WNJY
F-AZJZ(2)	Hiller UH-12A (Reservation .01)	158	ALAT F-BEEF
F-AZKA	SZD-24C Foka	W-177	OO-ZJ L SP-2093
F-AZKB	SAAB S.91BSafir	91295	F-BHAG SE-XAE
F-AZKC	SNCAN/Stampe SV.4A (Reservation .01)	65	F-BABI Fr.mil
F-AZKD	Piaggio FWP.149D (Painted as "141"/"Z-KD")	141	D-EEWR (G-BLOW) D-EEWR 91+20 YA+457 YA+010 KB+118
F-AZKE	Aeronca C-3 (Reservation .01)	A-517	N14631 NC14631
F-AZKF	de Havilland DH.115 Vampire T.55	DH-37	HB-RVK U-1233
F-AZKG	North American T-28 Trojan	174-111	N14119 Fr.AF 51-3573
F-AZKH	Fouga CM.170 Magister	219	F-GJIR Fr.AF
F-AZKI	Scottish Aviation Bulldog T.Mk1	BH120-273	XX615
F-AZKJ	Scottish Aviation Bulldog T.Mk1	BH120-248	XX555
F-AZKL	Yakovlev Yak-50 (Reservn 7.04)	842703	DOSAAF
F-AZKM	North American OV-10B Bronco (Painted as "99+24" "Ville de Ravensburg")	338-9	99+24 D-9553 BuA 158300
F-AZKN	Morane-Saulnier MS.733 Alcyon	165	Fr.Navy
F-AZKP	AIAA/Stampe SV.4A	1143	F-BANX Fr.mil
F-AZKQ	North American T-6 Harvard IV (Also reserved as F-AZQK)	"53796"	
F-AZKR	Fouga CM.170 Magister (Reservation .02)	565	F-WIMK Fr.AF
F-AZKS	Morane-Saulnier MS.733 Alcyon	83	F-BLXN Fr.Mil
F-AZKT	Dassault MD.312 Flamant	260	Fr.AF
F-AZKV	Nord 1200 (Reservation)	unkn	
F-AZKY(2)	Douglas AD-4N Skyraider (Reservation) (Painted as "126937")	7798	Fr.AF BuA126998
F-AZKZ	Morane-Saulnier MS.317	6549/295	F-AZKS F-BGUU Fr.Mil
F-AZLA	Beech D-17S	4829	N1255N NC221 BuA33030
F-AZLC	WACO UPF-7	5711	(F-AZJC) N32079 NC32079
F-AZLD	Stampe SV.4B	01-97	
F-AZLE	SNCAN/Stampe SV.4C	551	F-BDCV
F-AZLF	CASA I-131E Jungmann	2036	E3B-. . .
F-AZLG	Nord 3400 (Reservation)	89	ALAT
F-AZLH	Alpavia/ Fournier RF-3	10	F-BLER
F-AZLI	DHC-1 Chipmunk T.10	C1/0915	WZ877
F-AZLJ	North American NA-154Navion 4 (Registered as a model L-17A)	NAV-4-277	F-BIPP OO-DEN OO-TWX NC91470
F-AZLK	Scottish Aviation Bulldog T.Mk1	BH120-321	XX663
F-AZLL	Lockheed 12A	1287	F-BJJY G-AGTL N33615 BuA0294
F-AZLO	DHC-1 Chipmunk 22 (Stored)	C1/0529	WG479
F-AZLP	Beech-SFERMA PD-146 Marquis 60A	10	F-BLLP
F-AZLT	Morane-Saulnier MS.760AParis	32	Fr.Navy
F-AZLY	Yakovlev Yak-3UA (Permit 1.02) (Conversion from Yak-11 with original c/n)	172890	
F-AZLZ	Scottish Aviation Bulldog T.Mk1	BH120-217	XX531
F-AZMA	Nord 3202	65	G-BMBF N2254X EPNER ALAT
F-AZMB	Caudron G-III	SA-33	
F-AZMC	OGMA/DHC-1 Chipmunk T.20	OGMA-11	FAP1321
F-AZMD	Morane-Saulnier MS.504 Criquet	600/01	F-BCME
F-AZME	Messerschmitt Me 108 (Reservation .00)	unkn	
F-AZMF	Pilatus P3-05	466-15	A-828
F-AZMG	Soko 522 Ikarus	068	JRV60168
F-AZMH	Mooney M.20B Mark 21	1778	HB-DUM
F-AZMI	Hunting Jet Provost T.3A	PAC/W/9269	G-BVBE XM461

F-AZMJ(2)	Focke-Wulf FW.44JStieglitz	2782	OH-SZF SZ-15
F-AZMK	Hiller UH-12B (Reservation 1.01)	667	(F-BNGL) ALAT
F-AZML	North American AT-6D Harvard III (Stored)	88-15564	F-BJBD BAF: H-6 SAAF:7555 EZ174 41-34047
F-AZMM	Nord 3400	29	ALAT
F-AZMO	Fouga CM.175 Zephyr	14	F-WQCG Fr.Navy
F-AZMP	North American T-6G-NF Texan	168-160	F-WZMP (F-AZMP) SpAF AE.6-188 49-3056
F-AZMQ	SNCASO SO.1221SDjinn (Reservation .01)	95/FR-145	ALAT: 95/F-MCDL
F-AZMR	Nord 1002	216	F-BFKR Fr.Mil
F-AZMS	Morane-Saulnier H	Sams 22.01	
F-AZMT	de Havilland DH.82A Tiger Moth (Identity unconfirmed)	85983	F-BGEK EM752
F-AZMV	Pitts BS-1SSpecial	001	F-BVKB F-WVKB
F-AZMX	Cessna 305C/L-19E Bird Dog	24557	F-GFCX F-GECD ALAT
F-AZMZ	Boeing Stearman E75 (Salis rebuild, modified) (May have used parts of F-AZJR?)	75-SA98	unkn
F-AZNA	Nord 2504 Noratlas (Reservation)	001	(F-GFTS) Fr.Navy F- WIFU
F-AZNB	CASA 1-1131E Jungmann	2149	E3B- . . .
F-AZNE	DHC-1 Chipmunk T.20	C1/0255	FAP1302
F-AZNH	Hurel-Dubois HD-34	01	F-BHOO F-WHOO
F-AZNJ	Albert A-110 (Reservn 7.04)	17	F-A . . .
F-AZNN	Yakovlev Yak-11 (Painted as "14")	25III/05	EAF- ?
F-AZNP	Blériot XI-2 Replica	01.98	
F-AZNR	Nord 1110	150	F-WJDQ Fr.Mil
F-AZNV	Breguet 905SA	24	F-CCIV
F-AZNX	Beech C-45B	5990	Fr.AF: 140 RCAF: HB140 43-35553
F-AZOA	Scottish Aviation Bulldog T.Mk1	BH120-334	XX688
F-AZOB	Scottish Aviation Bulldog T.Mk1	BH120-218	XX532
F-AZOD	Scottish Aviation Bulldog T.Mk1	BH120-255	XX559
F-AZOE	Mudry CAP.20E (Reservn 12.04)	02	F-TFVV F-BTAI F-ZWRP F-BOPV
F-AZOG	Scottish Aviation Bulldog T.Mk1	BH120-254	XX558
F-AZOH	Morane-Saulnier MS.733 Alcyon	63	F-BKOH Fr.AF
F-AZOK	Yakovlev Yak-11 (Painted as "37")	25III/19	EAF- ?
F-AZOL	Aichi Type 99 Val Replica (Converted from Vultee BT-13)	308	N63163 40-917
F-AZOM	AIAA/Stampe SV.4C	1146	F-BAOM Fr.Mil
F-AZOO	de Havilland DH.100 Vampire FB.6 (Painted "DU-J")	636	J-1127
F-AZOP	de Havilland DH.100 Vampire FB.6 (Painted "DU-M")	701	J-1192
F-AZOT	SNCAN/Stampe SV.4C	334	F-BCOT
F-AZOU	North American T-6 Harvard (Quoted c/n is conversion contract number but correct c/n believed to be182-072. Given as ex 51-14317 but this was sold to Japan and above believed correct. Painted as "51149") (Reservn 12.03)	"AF33-038-21174"	Tunis.AF:Y-61.. Fr.AF 51-14385 51-14385
F-AZOY	Mudry CAP.20 (Reservn 12.04)		F-TFVW F-BTAE
F-AZOZ	Scottish Aviation Bulldog T.Mk1	BH120-221	XX535
F-AZPB	CASA I-131E Jungmann	1036	F-WZPB E3B- . . .
F-AZPD	DHC-1 Chipmunk T.10	C1/0027	WB575
F-AZPE	Yakovlev Yak-18	EM-019	SP-APR(2)
F-AZPF	Fouga CM.175 Zephyr	28	Fr.Navy
F-AZPG	Blériot XII-2	SA-29	
F-AZPH	SNCAN/Stampe SV.4C	309	F-BCLI
F-AZPI	Fouga CM.175 Zephyr	5	Fr.Navy
F-AZPK	Pilatus P.2-05	31	OO-PTO U-111 A-111
F-AZPL	Nord NC.854	10	F-BDZT F-BZBL F-BDZT
F-AZPN	CSS-13 (Polikarpov Po.2)	8-0518	SP-APB(3) SP-AEP(2)
F-AZPO	CSS.13 (Polikarpov Po.2)	49-026	"PLW-5" SP-ANB(1)
F-AZPP	de Havilland DH.82A Tiger Moth (As "T8857")	PH-001	
F-AZPS	Bellanca 7KCAB Citabria	202	C-FDSF CF-DSF
F-AZPT	Boeing Stearman A75N1 (Reservation)	unkn	
F-AZPU	Pilatus P.3-05	465-14	HB-RCC A-827

F-AZPV	SNCASO SO.1221S Djinn (Reservation .04)	1102/FR-12	F-BHZK ALAT 'BSB'
F-AZPX	SNCASO SO.1221S Djinn (Reservation .04)	FR-127-77	ALAT
F-AZPY	Yakovlev Yak-18A	710	HB-RBD EAF-710
F-AZPZ	Fouga CM.170 Magister	413	F-GNBG Fr.AF
F-AZQK	North American T-6 Harvard IV (Also reserved as F-AZKQ)	"53796"	
F-AZQL	Morane-Saulnier MS.131	4	
F-AZQQ	Pilatus P.3-05	502-51	HB-RCI A-864
F-AZQZ	DHC-1 Chipmunk 22	C1/0916	WZ878
F-AZRA	Fieseler Fi.156C3 Storch (Built as MS.505 Criquet. Painted as 2E+RA)	2039/14	F-BBAT Fr.mil
F-AZRB	North American AT-6D Harvard (Painted as "90747/3")	88-17955	N3651F BuA90747 42-86174
F-AZRC	Nord N.3400	78	ALAT
F-AZRD	North American AT-6D Harvard (Painted as '14906/RD')	88-14510	F-BJBM 42-44467
F-AZRF	Pilatus P.3-05	507-56	A-869
F-AZRH	Nord 260	3	F-BKRH
F-AZRJ	Grumman F8F-2 Bearcat (Reservation) (Painted as Fr.Navy "9384"/"P")	D.1122	N200N N618F N1029B BuA121748
F-AZRM	Scottish Aviation Bulldog T.Mk1	BH120-274	XX616
F-AZRO	Fieseler Fi.156C3 Storch (Reservation .00) (This is quoted with same details as F-AZRA above, one may be c/n 4362 ex NX436FS)	2039	
F-AZRP	Morane-Saulnier MS.733 Alcyon (Reservation .02)	147	F-BNEH Fr.Mil
F-AZRS	Cessna 195B	7980	N3095B
F-AZSA	Morane-Saulnier MS.733 Alcyon	149	F-GIQK F-BMQK Fr.AF
F-AZSB	North American P-51 Mustang (Painted as "411622""NookyBooky IV")	unkn	N2251D 44-74427
F-AZSC	North American AT-6D-NTTexan	88-15943	C.6-154 41-34671
F-AZSI	SIPA S.903 (Reservation)	unkn	
F-AZSM	DHC-1 Chipmunk 22	C1/0789	WP914
F-WZSN	North American T-6 Harvard	unkn	F-AZSN
F-AZSP	Morane-Saulnier MS.733 Alcyon	123	F-BLYI Fr.Mil
F-AZSR	North American T-6G Texan (Painted as Navy "05-SF")	197-75	Fr.AF 53-4579
F-AZST	Boeing Stearman PT-18	75-2184	N61860 41-8625
F-AZSV	AIAA/Stampe SV.4C1 (Reservn 12.03)	1018	F-PRSV ? CN-TUI F-BDKQ
F-AZTB	MS.505 CriquetV (C/n officially quoted as 23/20)	602/23	F-BEJN F-ZJPJ F-BEJN Fr.mil
F-AZTC	Taylorcraft BC-12D1	10176	G-BTJZ N44376 NC44376
F-AZTD	Mudry CAP.20	07	OO-TDO F-BTDO
F-AZTE	Douglas C-47A	9172	F-WZTE F-GDPP (F-ODQE) TL-AAX TL-JBB F-BRGN Fr.AF G-AGZF WZ984 G-AGZF 42-23310
F-AZTF	Scottish Aviation Bulldog T.Mk1	BH120-309	XX639
F-AZTG	North American T-6 Harvard (Reservation)	unkn	
F-AZTJ	Beagle A.61 Terrier 2	B.604	G-ASAK WE591
F-AZTM	de Havilland DH.82A Tiger Moth	85946	F-BGCS Fr.AF DF210
F-AZTT	CASA I-131E Jungmann	2241	E3B- . . .
F-AZUJ	Potez 60 Sauterelle (Reservation .04)	3862	F-PNUJ F-ANUJ
F-AZUL	CASA I-131EJungmann	2114	E3B- . . .
F-AZUR	DHC-1 Chipmunk 22	C1/0580	WK562
F-AZUT	SNCAN/Stampe SV.4B (Reservn 7.04)	444	F-BCXJ
F-AZUV	CASA I-131E Jungmann	2190	OE-AUV D-EHFT(2) E3B-580
F-AZVA	DHC-1 Chipmunk 22	C1/0188	WB739
F-AZVG	Dassault MD.312 Flamant	189	Fr.AF
F-AZVM	Nord 2501 Noratlas	105	Fr.AF'63-VM'
F-AZVN	North American T-6G-NT Texan (Painted as RCAF 983)	168-87	TunisianAF: Y-61501 MoroccanAF: 49-2983 49-2983

F-AZVO	Caudron 270 Luciole	6607/32	G-BDFM F-BBPT Fr.AF F-ALVO
F-AZVS	CASA I-131E Jungmann	1035	E3B- . . .
F-AZVV	Nord 1101 Noralpha (Reservation .00)	15	F-BYAX CEV F-BBAJ
F-AZVZ	Mudry CAP.20 (Reservation .02)	6	F-GIPA F-TFVZ F-BTAH F-TFVZ
F-AZXI	Piper PA-22-150 Tripacer (Reservation .04)	22-4476	F-GHXI PH-RCH D-EANA N5801D
F-AZXM	DHC-1 Chipmunk 22	C1/0863	WZ845
F-AZXU	Morane-Saulnier MS.733 Alcyon	141	F-BLXU Fr.Mil
F-AZYA	Yakovlev Yak-11	172624	OO-YAK EgyptAF:079
F-AZYD	Yakovlev Yak-50 (Reservation 6.04)	3208	DOSAAF
F-AZYJ	Yakovlev Yak-9U-M	0470403	N9250
F-AZYK	Yakovlev Yak-18A (Reservn, but see LY-XPA)	2624	
F-AZYO	Yakovlev Yak-50	3201	
F-AZYS	Chance Vought F4U-7 Corsair (Painted as FR.Navy "133704"/ "14.F.6")	124541	Fr.Navy?
F-AZYT	North American T-6G Texan	unkn	41-32360
F-AZYU	Utva-66F1	0807	YU-DLI JRV51104
F-AZYV	Nord 1101 Noralpha	13	F-BYAV CEV
F-AZZE	Fouga CM.170 Magister	435	F-GKYH F-WKYH Fr.AF
F-AZZG	SG-38 Schulgleiter	20.24	
F-AZZO	Morane-Saulnier MS.733 Alcyon	108	F-BMMU Fr.Mil
F-AZZZ	Morane-Saulnier MS.733 Alcyon	139	F-BKOK Fr.AF
F-AZ . .	Grumman TBM-3E Avenger	3920	F-WQON C-GFPR N3357G BuA53858
F-AZ . .	North American T-28DFennec	174-111	N14119 Fr.AF 51-3573

METROPOLITAN FRANCE

F-AJAC	Albert 110 (Under restoration .99)	16	
F-AJFZ	Albert A.61 (Under restoration .99)	1	
F-AMJP	Potez 43.1 (Under restoration .99)	3322	
F-BAGK	AIAA/Stampe SV.4C	1110	Fr.Mil
F-BAHF	AIAA/Stampe SV.4C	1121	Fr.Mil
F-BAHG	AIAA/Stampe SV.4C	1122	Fr.Mil
F-BAHL	AIAA/Stampe SV.4C	1124	Fr.Mil
F-BAHV	AIAA/Stampe SV.4C	1130	Fr.Mil
F-BANI	AIAA/Stampe SV.4C	1140	Fr.Mil
F-BAOL(3)	SNCAN/Stampe SV.4C	207	F-BHEY ALAT F-BBLB
F-BAQC	Poullin PJ.5B (Cub Conversion)	6	F-PAQC
F-BARP	Morane-Saulnier MS.505 Criquet	496/10	
F-BASF	Beech P35 Bonanza	D-7077	F-OBSF N9548Y
F-BASJ(3)	Morane-Saulnier MS.733 Alcyon	13	(F-BDZC(2)) F-BDZY
F-BAUA	Beech D50 Twin Bonanza	DH-39	F-OAUA
F-BAVB	Morane-Saulnier MS.505 Criquet	633	Fr.Mil
F-BAVN	Agusta-Bell 47G-2	066	F-OAVF
F-BAVZ	Ryan Navion F	911	N8911H
F-BAYP	PA-18A-150 Super Cub (Damaged 24.6.00)	18-5486	N6192D
F-BBBL	SNCAN/Stampe SV.4A	156	CEV F-BFCE CEV
F-BBEG	Nord N.1203 Norécrin VI	295	
F-BBER	Nord N.1203 Norécrin VI	332	
F-BBEZ	Nord N.1203 Norécrin VI	344	
F-BBIK	Piper J-3C-65 Cub	11173	Fr.Mil 43-29882
F-BBJZ	Nord NC.858S Norvigie	140	
F-BBOL	Cessna 182D	18253391	F-OBTL N8991X
F-BBON	SNCAN/Stampe SV.4C	322	
F-BBPY	Bell 47G	490	F-OAPY OO-SHZ OO-UBC
F-BBQP	SNCAN/Stampe SV.4C	191	
F-BBQZ	Piper J-3C-65 Cub	12625	44-80329
F-BBTD	Piper J-3C-65 Cub	13148	HB-OVU 45-4408

F-BBUJ	Morane-Saulnier MS.505 Criquet	263/23	
F-BBUU	SNCAN/Stampe SV.4A	85	Fr.Mil
F-BBVI	SNCAN/Stampe SV.4A	16	Fr.Mil
F-BBVM	SNCAN/Stampe SV.4A	199	
F-BBXU(3)	Morane-Saulnier MS.317	6522/268	F-BBZU
F-BBZR	Morane-Saulnier MS.317	6512/258	
F-BCBC	Morane-Saulnier MS.317	323	
F-BCBN	Piper PA-25-235 Pawnee B	25-3744	F-OCHN N7624Z
F-BCCB	Beech S35 Bonanza	D-7345	F-OCCB
F-BCDC	Piper PA-30 Twin Comanche (Wrecked)	30-389	F-OCDC N7380Y N10F
F-BCDX	Piper J-3C-65 Cub (Officially quoted with f/n 10353)	10528	43-29237
F-BCGS	SNCAN/Stampe SV.4C	281	
F-BCJJ	Piper PA-32-260 Cherokee Six	32-226	F-OCJJ N3800W (ZK-CNS)
F-BCLH	SNCAN/Stampe SV.4C	308	
F-BCNL	Morane-Saulnier MS.317	6527/273	
F-BCOP	SNCAN/Stampe SV.4C	328	
F-BCPF	Piper J-3C-65 Cub	13251	45-4511
F-BCPK	Piper J-3C-65 Cub	13147	45-4407
F-BCPN	Piper J-3C-65 Cub	11801	OO-REA 43-30510
F-BCPY	Piper J-3C-65 Cub	11531	43-30240
F-BCPZ	Piper PA-12 Super Cruiser seaplane	12-3485	NC4057H
F-BCQB	SNCAN/Stampe SV.4A	364	
F-BCQM	SNCAN/Stampe SV.4C	398	
F-BCQT	SNCAN/Stampe SV.4C	411	
F-BCUV	SNCAN/Stampe SV.4A	419	F-BCTC
F-BCXD	SNCAN/Stampe SV.4A	438	
F-BCZE	SNCAN/Stampe SV.4C	262	F-BCKH
F-BCZQ	Gardan GY-80 Horizon 160	7	F-OCBQ
F-BCZR	Piper PA-24-260 Comanche	24-4196	F-OCER N8751P N10F
F-BDCM	SNCAN/Stampe SV.4C	542	
F-BDGL	SNCAN/Stampe SV.4C	493	
F-BDHC(4)	AIAA/Stampe SV.4A	1125	F-BAHN Fr.Mil
F-BDII	SNCAN/Stampe SV.4C	487	
F-BDJJ	SNCAN/Stampe SV.4A	516	F-BDGV
F-BDJP	Stampe SV.4C	591	F-GLHI (2) N591SV F-BGIX ALAT F-BDEL
F-BDME	SNCAN/Stampe SV.4A	635	
F-BDMI	SNCAN/Stampe SV.4A	639	
F-BDNF	SNCAN/Stampe SV.4A	661	
F-BDNM	SNCAN/Stampe SV.4A1	668	
F-BDNN	SNCAN/Stampe SV.4C	669	
F-BDNU	SNCAN/Stampe SV.4C	676	
F-BDOE	SNCAN/Stampe SV.4C	685	
F-BDOX	SNCAN/Stampe SV.4C	370	
F-BDOY	Zodiac-Vernanchet HG 380 Free Balloon	205/8888	
F-BDTA	Piper J-3C-65 Cub	10174	43-1313
F-BDTI	Piper J-3C-65 Cub	13181	45-4441
F-BDTS	Piper J-3C-65 Cub	12526	44-80230
F-BDTT	Piper J-3C-65 Cub	12488	44-80192
F-BDTX	Piper J-3C-65 Cub	12804	44-80508
F-BDUV	Piper J-3C-65 Cub	11653	OO-AVL 43-30362
F-BDXM	Morane-Saulnier MS.506L Criquet (Lycoming conversion)	635	F-WDXM F-BDHM
F-BDZP	Nord NC.854	6	
F-BEAU	Piper PA-20-135 Pacer	20-1057	N10F
F-BEGD	Piper J-3C-65 Cub	9676	43-815
F-BEGG	Piper J-3C-65 Cub	12886	44-80590
F-BEGU	Piper J-3C-65 Cub	10384	F-OTAN-2 F-BEGU 43-29093
F-BEHG	Morane-Saulnier MS.733 Alcyon	6	Fr.AF
F-BEHM	Macchi MB.308	53/5826	F-OAHM I-LAGI
F-BEJF	Morane-Saulnier MS.505 Criquet	654/4	
F-BEJZ(3)	Piper J-3C-65 Cub	11457	F-BFCX 43-30166
F-BEKZ	Piper J-3C-65 Cub	11889	Fr.AF 44-79593
F-BEOF	Nord N.1203 Norécrin VI	108	
F-BEOM	Nord N.1203 Norécrin VI	127	
F-BEPO	GY-30 Supercab (Stored)	01	F-WEPO
F-BEPY	AIAA/Stampe SV.4A	1056	Fr.Navy
F-BERB	SAN Jodel D.140 Mousquetaire	33	F-OBRB
F-BERY	Nord N.1203 Norécrin III	353	
F-BETD	Piper PA-12 Super Cruiser	12-3557	
F-BETK	Piper J-3C-65 Cub	13241	NC74120 45-4501
F-BETR	Piper J-3C-65 Cub	12164	44-79868
F-BETY	Piper J-3C-65 Cub	13177	45-4437
F-BEUS	Nord N.1203 Norécrin VI	180	
F-BEYR	SIPA S.903	15	
F-BEZG	Nord NC.858S	100	
F-BEZX	Nord NC.858S	116	

F-BFAM	Piper PA-24-250 Comanche	24-2802	F-OCCC
			N4636S
			LV-PQE
			N7591P
F-BFAR	Wassmer WA.41 Baladou	105	
F-BFBO	Piper J-3C-65 Cub	13153	NC74119
			45-4413
F-BFBP	Piper J-3C-65 Cub	13195	NC74118
			45-4455
F-BFBQ	Piper J-3C-90 Cub	12443	44-80147
	(Officially quoted as c/n 12959 which is HB-OGL)		
F-BFDS	Jodel D.112 Club	485	
F-BFES	Piper PA-18A-150 Super Cub	18-3293	F-DAES
			N3295B
F-BFFJ	Piper J-3C-65 Cub	12679	44-80383
F-BFFN	Piper J-3C-65 Cub	13348	NC74115
			45-4608
F-BFFP	Piper PA-11 Cub Special (Damaged 23.6.99)	11-867	
F-BFFU	Piper PA-11 Cub Special	11-939	
F-BFFV	Piper PA-11 Cub Special	11-940	
F-BFHH	Piper PA-18 Super Cub 95	18-1537	ALAT
			51-15537
F-BFKL(3)	Holste MH.1521M Broussard	38	ALAT
F-BFLC	C.A.B .GY-20 Minicab	3	
F-BFMA	Piper PA-11 Cub Special	11-946	
F-BFMG	Piper PA-11 Cub Special	11-945	
F-BFML	Piper J-3C-65 Cub	12229	44-79933
F-BFMQ	Piper J-3C-65 Cub	12527	44-80231
F-BFOL	Beech D35 Bonanza	D-3606	F-OBOL
			OO-YAC
			(OO-SCF)
F-BFON	Boisavia B.601 Mercurey	01	F-WFON
F-BFOP	SNCAN/Stampe SV.4C	494	CEV
F-BFOZ	Piper J-3C-65 Cub	12696	N74123
			44-80400
F-BFPM	Stinson 108-3 Voyager	108-5080	N4080C
F-BFPX	Aeronca 7AC Champion	2192	OO-TWG
F-BFQD	Piper J-3C-65 Cub (Coded "YC")	13028	OO-SUD
			44-80732
F-BFQG	Piper J-3C-65 Cub	13289	45-4549
F-BFQL	Piper J-3C-65 Cub	12788	NC74124
			44-80492
F-BFQN	Piper J-3C-65 Cub	11725	N79815
			43-30434
F-BFQO	Piper PA-12 Super Cruiser	12-3492	N79814
	(Badly damaged 29.5.03)		NC79814
			NC4059H
F-BFUB	AIAA/Stampe SV.4C	1087	Fr.Mil
F-BFYD	Piper J-3C-65 Cub	"8979"	Fr.Mil
	(Quoted c/n is believed in error)		42-38410
F-BFYI	Piper J-3C-65 Cub	13054	OO-AVJ
			44-80758
F-BFYM	Piper J-3C-65 Cub (W/o 16.11.01)	12166	OO-PCR
			44-79870
F-BFZA	Piper PA-18 Super Cub 95	18-1338	ALAT
			51-15338
F-BFZK	Morane-Saulnier MS.317	6525/271	Fr.Mil
F-BFZN	SNCAN/Stampe SV.4C	71	Fr.Mil
F-BGGE	SNCAN/Stampe SV.4C	531	Fr.Mil
F-BGGP	SNCAN/Stampe SV.4C	41	Fr.Mil
F-BGGQ	SNCAN/Stampe SV.4C	54	Fr.Mil
F-BGJR	Nord N.1203 Norécrin VI	375	
F-BGKL	Jodel D.112 Club	618	
F-BGKX	Morane-Saulnier MS.317	6518/264	Fr.Mil
F-BGOF	Bell 47G-2	1319	
F-BGOZ	Cessna 170A	19959	
F-BGPA	Piper J-3C-65 Cub	8531	OO-AVC
			42-36407
F-BGPO	Beech A35 Bonanza	D-1503	HB-ECB
F-BGPP	Beech 35 Bonanza	D-677	HB-ECS
			NC90572
F-BGPT	Piper PA-18 Super Cub 125	18-1137	N1327A
F-BGQC	Piper J-3C-65 Cub	9001	Fr.Mil
			42-38432
F-BGQM	Piper J-3C-65 Cub	9920	43-1059
F-BGQY	Piper PA-12 Super Cruiser	12-1118	G-AJGY
F-BGSD	Aero Commander 560A	366	
F-BGTB	Cessna 310	35474	CN-TTB
			N5274A
F-BGTP	Piper J-3C-65 Cub	11967	F-BDRT
			OO-GAG
			44-79671
F-BGUV	Morane-Saulnier MS.317	6551/297	Fr.Mil
F-BGUZ	Morane-Saulnier MS.317	6560/306	Fr.Mil
F-BGXC	Piper J-3C-65 Cub	11446	43-30155
F-BGXS	Piper J-3C-65 Cub	10535	43-29244
F-BGZM(2)	Boisavia B.606 Mercurey	3	F-BHCH
F-BHCK	Jodel D.112 Club	483	
F-BHCR	Jodel D.112 Club	206	
F-BHDB	Bell 47G	19	OO-CSC
			N165B
F-BHDG	Wassmer Jodel D.112 Club	265	
F-BHDM(2)	Boisavia B.601L Mercurey	110	F-BIRF(2)
F-BHFK(2)	Nord 1203 Norécrin	230	F-BEUU
F-BHGN	Jodel D.112 Club	379	
F-BHGX	Leopoldoff L.55 Colibri	5	
F-BHHD(3)	AIAA/Stampe SV.4C	119	F-BAHC
F-BHHF(2)	Morane-Saulnier MS.317	312	F-BCBR
F-BHHO	Piper PA-18-150 Super Cub	18-5319	N10F
F-BHHP(2)	Piper PA-22-135 Tri-Pacer	22-2013	(F-BMXY)
			F-DAFE
			OO-HAA
			N3771A
F-BHHQ(2)	Piper J-3C-65 Cub	10272	(F-GJMQ)
			C-GVGM
			N46784
			NC46784
			43-1411
			(42-60221)
F-BHHV(2)	SNCAN/Stampe SV.4C	361	F-BGRN
			F-BCOJ
F-BHHX	Beech C35 Bonanza	D-2691	HB-EBC
F-BHKF	Wassmer Jodel D.112 Club	333	
F-BHKR	Wassmer Jodel D.112 Club	347	
F-BHLP	Nord N.1203 Norécrin VI	141	F-OBLP
			CN-TYN
			F-BEQI
F-BHLT	SAN Jodel D.140A Mousquetaire	25	F-OBLT
F-BHMM	Beech C-45G	AF-465	F-WHMM
	(Under restoration 10.02)		(OO-GET) ?
			51-11908
F-BHOR	Rockwell Commander 112	0284	N1284J
F-BHOT	SNCASO SO.1221-S Djinn	1006/FR-25	F-WHOT
F-BHOY	Rousseau Piel CP.301B Emeraude	107	
F-BHPY	Jodel D.112 Club	550	
F-BHQO	Bell 47G-2	684	F-OAQO
F-BHQP	CEA Jodel DR.1051 Sicile	538	
F-BHTF	Nord N.1203 Norécrin III (Wfu)	358	
F-BHTO	Wassmer Jodel D.112 Club	518	
F-BHTP	Wassmer Jodel D.112 Club	519	
F-BHXK	SAN Jodel D.112 Club (ex D.117)	512	
F-BHXL	SAN Jodel D.117 Grand Tourisme	588	
F-BHXM	SAN Jodel D.117 Grand Tourisme	591	
F-BHYX	Jodel D.112 Club	555	
F-BHYZ	Wassmer Jodel D.120 Paris-Nice	69	
F-BIAL	Beech D50 Twin Bonanza (USArmy c/s)	DH-104	
F-BIAV	Passot Jodel D.112 Club	708	
F-BIBC	Jodel D.117 (Being rebuilt)	606	
F-BIBH	Jodel D.119D	626	
F-BIBI	SAN Jodel D.117 Grand Tourisme	612	
F-BICB	Agusta-Bell 47G-2	062	F-BHEO
F-BICE	Cessna 170B	26436	N2893C
F-BIDB	SAN Jodel D.117A Grand Tourisme	691	
F-BIDQ	SAN Jodel D.117 Grand Tourisme	721	
F-BIEI	Bell 47G-2 (W/o 5.7.01)	1275	F-ZBA .
			F-BGSS
F-BIEJ	Bell 47G	1285	Fr.Mil
F-BIEQ	Bell 47G-2	1465	F-ZBAI
			F-BHKZ
F-BIEV	SNCASO SO.1221-S Djinn	1019/FR-58	PB+158
			PB+120
F-BIEX	Jodel D.112 Club	568	F-BIKX
F-BIFB	Cessna 305C Bird Dog (L-19)	24582	ALAT
F-BIFH	Hiller UH-12B	273	Fr.AF
			51-16119
F-BIFN	Agusta-Bell 47G-2	209	Fr.Mil
F-BIFS	Hiller UH-12B	249	Fr.AF
			51-16095
F-BIFT	Aérospatiale SA.315B Lama	05	
F-BIGF	Jodel D.112D Club	850	
F-BIGH	Jodel D.119 (ex D.112 Club)	857	
F-BIHC	Dornier Do.28A-1 (Restoration?)	3024	F-OBHC
			D-IDTF
F-BIHJ	Piper PA-24-260 Comanche B	24-4455	N8994P
F-BIHT	CEA DR.250/160 Capitaine	71	F-OCHT
F-BIKS	Wassmer Jodel D.112 Club	571	
F-BIMQ	Piel CP.301A Emeraude	244	
F-BINC	SAN Jodel D.140C Mousquetaire III	104	(D-EFVK)
			F-BINC
F-BINY	CEA DR.253 Régent	101	F-WINY
F-BIOE	SAN Jodel D.117 Grand Tourisme	755	
F-WIPA	Bell 47GRP	"01"	
F-BIPJ(3)	Morane-Saulnier MS.505 Criquet	149	F-BAOU
F-BIPS	Morane-Saulnier MS.733 Alcyon (Wfu)	5	Fr.Mil
F-BIPU	Jodel D.112 Club	5	F-BIRU
F-BIPY	SNCASO SO.1221-S Djinn	1033/FR-83	
F-BIQA	Wassmer Jodel D.112 Club	572	
F-BIQL	Wassmer Jodel D.112 Club	581	
F-BIRL	Jodel D.112 Club	654	
F-BIRV	SNCAN/Stampe SV.4C	697	CEV
F-BISI	Piel CP.301A Emeraude	268	(D-EHBI)
F-BISN	Piel CP.301A Emeraude	284	
F-BITA	SAN Jodel DR.1050 Ambassadeur	52	
F-BITS	SAN Jodel DR.100A Ambassadeur	56	
F-BIUI	Jodel D.119	955	
F-BIUR	Rousseau Piel CP.301B Emeraude	116	
F-BIVI	SAN Jodel DR.100A Ambassadeur	65	
F-BIXA	Wassmer Jodel D.120 Paris-Nice	116	
F-BIXM	Wassmer Jodel D.112 Club	892	
F-BIXN	Wassmer Jodel D.112 Club	1001	
F-BIZE	SAN Jodel D.140C Mousquetaire III	01	
F-BIZF	SAN Jodel D.140 Mousquetaire	20	
F-BIZH	SAN Jodel D.140A Mousquetaire	43	
F-BIZP	SAN Jodel D.140C Mousquetaire III	29	

F-BJAC	Piper PA-22-150 Tri-Pacer	22-5147	ALAT/F-MKAD
			N10F
F-BJAG	Piper PA-24-250 Comanche	24-359	N10F
F-BJAX	Scintex Piel CP.301C-1 Emeraude	567	
F-BJCL	Jodel DR100A Ambassadeur	8	
	(Damaged 22.4.03, probable write-off)		
F-BJDC	Agusta-Bell 47G	052	ALAT
F-BJDE	Agusta-Bell 47G	067	ALAT
			F-BHPC
F-BJDR	SAN Jodel D.140C Mousquetaire III	26	
F-BJDU	Gardan GY-80 Horizon 150	01	F-WJDU
F-BJEC	Cessna 182B Skylane	52214	N7214E
F-BJEE	Cessna 182B Skylane	52201	(N7201E)
F-BJFR	Scintex Piel CP.301C-1 Emeraude	547	
F-BJFU	Scintex Piel CP.301C-1 Emeraude (Wfu)	554	
F-BJGM	Wassmer WA.41 Baladou	168	
F-BJGS	Piper PA-23-235 Apache	27-516	N4924P
F-BJIC	Wassmer Jodel D.112A Club	1005	
F-BJIK	Wassmer Jodel D.112A Club	1010	
F-BJIY	Wassmer Jodel D.112A Club	1014	
F-BJJA	SAN Jodel DR.1050 Ambassadeur	92	
F-BJJG	SAN Jodel DR.1050 Ambassadeur	115	
F-BJJK	SAN Jodel DR.1050 Ambassadeur	194	
F-BJJR	SAN Jodel DR.1050 Ambassadeur	107	
F-BJJV	Cessna 172B (Dismantled)	17248393	N7893X
F-BJJX	Jodel D.127	1048	
F-BJLK	Cessna 172B	17248217	N7717X
F-BJLL	CEA Jodel DR.1050 Ambassadeur	13	
F-BJLP	CEA Jodel DR.1051-M1 Sicile Record	25	
F-BJMD	Scintex ML.250 Rubis	03	
F-BJMG	Scintex ML.250 Rubis	103	
F-BJMQ	Scintex CP.1310-C3 Super Emeraude	911	
F-BJMR	Scintex CP.1310-C3 Super Emeraude	921	
F-BJMT	Scintex CP.1315-C3 Super Emeraude	922	
F-BJOA	Jodel D.128	974	
F-BJOO	Procaer F-15A Picchio	12	
F-BJOQ	Piel CP.301A Emeraude	349	
F-BJOV	CEA Jodel DR.1050 Ambassadeur	24	
F-BJOZ	CEA Jodel DR.1050 Ambassadeur	30	
F-BJPE	Wassmer Jodel D.112 Club	1018	
F-BJPI	Wassmer Jodel D.112 Club	1020	
F-BJPV	Wassmer Jodel D.112 Club	1065	
F-BJPY	Wassmer Jodel D.112A Club	1066	
F-BJPZ	Wassmer WA.40 Super IV	6	
F-BJQK	SNCASE SE.313B Alouette II	1979	Cambodian AF
F-BJQT	SAN Jodel D.140B Mousquetaire II	64	
F-BJQZ	SAN Jodel D.140B Mousquetaire II	70	
F-BJRG	Cessna 172B	17248424	N7924X
F-BJRI	Cessna 182D Skylane	18253401	(N9001X)
F-BJRN	Cessna 210A	21057828	N9528X
F-BJRQ	Cessna 170B	26377	F-OAQV
			N2834C
F-BJRV	Cessna 172B	17248592	N8092X
F-BJUB	CEA Jodel DR.1050 Ambassadeur	43	
F-BJUK	Piper PA-18-150 Super Cub	18-7549	N3812Z
F-BJUM	Procaer F.15A Picchio	11	
F-BJUN	Nord NC.858 (Reservation)	27	F-BFIV
F-BJUR	Cessna 172B	17248725	N8225X
F-BJVD	Scintex Piel CP.301-C2 Emeraude	576	
F-BJVE	Scintex Piel CP.301-C2 Emeraude	577	
F-BJVJ	Scintex CP.1310-C3 Super Emeraude	900	
F-BJVM	Scintex Piel CP.301-C3 Emeraude	591	
F-BJVX	Scintex CP.1315-C3 Super Emeraude	912	
F-BJVY	Scintex CP.1315-C3 Super Emeraude	913	
F-BJVZ	Scintex CP.1315-C3 Super Emeraude	914	
F-BJYP	SAN Jodel DR.1050 Ambassadeur	254	
F-BJYV	SAN Jodel DR.1050 Ambassadeur	258	
F-BJZF	CEA Jodel DR.1050 Ambassadeur	213	
F-BJZG	CEA Jodel DR.1050 Ambassadeur	214	
F-BKAF	Wassmer WA.40 Super IV	18	
F-BKAI	Wassmer Jodel D.112 Club	1069	
F-BKAU	Wassmer Jodel D.112 Club (Stored dismantled)	1076	
F-BKBA	Cessna 172C	17248784	N8284X
F-BKBB	Cessna 182D Skylane	18253628	N9228X
F-BKBE	Piper PA-18-150 Super Cub	18-7658	N10F
	(Damaged 14.12.99)		
F-BKBZ	SAN Jodel DR.1050 Ambassadeur	268	
F-BKCF	Wassmer Jodel D.112 Club	1080	
F-BKCQ	Wassmer Jodel D.119		
F-BKCT	Wassmer WA.40 Super IV	34	
F-BKDA	Morane-Saulnier MS.881 Rallye	1	
F-BKDD	Morane-Saulnier MS.880B Rallye Club	15	
F-BKDF	Morane-Saulnier MS.880B Rallye Club	17	
F-BKDV	Morane-Saulnier MS.880B Rallye Club	69	
F-BKEH	Morane-Saulnier MS.885 Super Rallye	54	
F-BKEO	Morane-Saulnier MS.885 Super Rallye	55	
F-BKEQ	Morane-Saulnier MS.885 Super Rallye	58	
F-BKFA	Beech S35 Bonanza	D-7432	HB-EFA
F-BKFC	Piper PA-23-250 Aztec C (Wfu, stored)	27-3922	N6616Y
F-BKGL	CEA Jodel DR.1050-M1 Sicile Record	233	
F-BKGU	Cessna 172C (Dismantled)	17249387	N1687Y
F-BKHC	SANJodel DR.1051 Sicile	385	
F-BKHD	SAN Jodel DR.1050 Ambassadeur	366	
F-BKHF	SAN Jodel DR.1050 Ambassadeur	370	
F-BKHP	SAN Jodel DR.1050 Ambassadeur	368	
F-BKIJ	CEA Jodel DR.1050 Ambassadeur	305	
F-BKIT	CEA Jodel DR.1051-M1 Sicile Record	329	

F-BKIU	CEA Jodel DR.1050 Ambassadeur	313	
F-BKJE	Wassmer WA.40 Super IV	38	
F-BKJZ	Wassmer Jodel D.112 Club	1128	
F-BKKP	Morane-Saulnier MS.880B Rallye Club	172	
F-BKKU	Morane-Saulnier MS.886 Super Rallye	319	
F-BKLA	Morane-Saulnier MS.885 Super Rallye	95	
F-BKLG	Morane-Saulnier MS.885 Super Rallye	121	
F-BKLK	Morane-Saulnier MS.885 Super Rallye	131	
F-BKLN	Morane-Saulnier MS.885 Super Rallye	138	
F-BKLS	Morane-Saulnier MS.885 Super Rallye	167	
F-BKLT	Morane-Saulnier MS.885 Super Rallye	156	
F-BKLV	Morane-Saulnier MS.885 Super Rallye	162	
F-BKLZ	Morane-Saulnier MS.885 Super Rallye	157	
F-BKMR	Agusta-Bell 206B Jet Ranger	8313	
F-BKND	Wassmer WA.40A Super IV	50	
F-BKNO	Piper J-3C-65 Cub	12784	F-BBOO
			OO-AVT
			44-80488
F-BKNT	Wassmer Jodel D.112 Club	1169	
F-BKOD	Morane-Saulnier MS.733 Alcyon	46	Fr.AF
F-BKOG	Morane-Saulnier MS.733 Alcyon (Reservation)	61	Fr.Mil
F-BKOI	Morane-Saulnier MS.733 Alcyon	74	Fr.AF
F-BKOJ	Morane-Saulnier MS.733 Alcyon	138	Fr.AF
F-BKOZ	Morane-Saulnier MS.733 Alcyon	45	Fr.AF
			F-BHCV
			Fr.AF
F-BKPK	CEA Jodel DR.1050 Ambassadeur (Stored)	332	
F-BKPN	CEA Jodel DR.1050-MI Sicile Record	336	
F-BKPS	CEA Jodel DR.1051 Sicile	324	
F-BKQN	Cessna 182F Skylane	18254493	N3593Y
F-BKQQ	Cessna 182E Skylane	18253793	N9393X
F-BKQU	Pilatus PC-6A/H2 Porter	534	
F-BKRA	Cessna 182E Skylane	18254163	N3163Y
F-BKRF	Cessna 172C	17249241	N1541Y
F-BKRG	Cessna 182E Skylane	18253914	N2914Y
F-BKRL	Piper PA-23-250 Aztec B	27-2082	N5068Y
F-BKRM	Cessna 310F	310-0074	HB-LBK
			N6774X
F-BKRU	Piper PA-18 Super Cub 95	18-1456	ALAT
			51-15456
F-BKRZ	Cessna 182A Skylane	51468	F-DAFU
			N2168G
F-BKSB	SAN Jodel D.140B Mousquetaire II	85	
F-BKSD	SAN Jodel D.140C Mousquetaire III	91	
F-BKSH	SAN Jodel D.140B Mousquetaire II	94	
F-BKSJ	SAN Jodel D.140C Mousquetaire III	97	
F-BKSK	SANJodel D.140BMousquetaire II	99	
F-BKSR	SAN Jodel D.140C Mousquetaire III (W/o 25.1.02)	106	
F-BKSS	SAN Jodel D.140C Mousquetaire III	107	
F-BKTD	SEEMS MS.880B Rallye Club	328	
F-BKTK	Morane-Saulnier MS.880B Rallye Club	215	
F-BKTX	Morane-Saulnier MS.880B Rallye Club	288	
F-BKTZ	SEEMS MS.880B Rallye Club	315	
F-BKUC	Morane-Saulnier MS.885 Super Rallye	234	(D-ELVO)
F-BKUU	Morane-Saulnier MS.885 Super Rallye	268	
F-BKVN	Beech P35 Bonanza	D-7114	
F-BKVY	SAN DR.1050-M Excellence	394	(G- . . . .)
			F-BKHX
F-BKXK	Morane-Saulnier MS.885 Super Rallye	232	F-OBXK
F-BKYB	SEEMS MS.880B Rallye Club	308	
F-BKZB	SEEMS MS.880B Rallye Club	337	
F-BKZG	SEEMS MS.880B Rallye Club	341	
F-BLAO	CEA Jodel DR.1051 Sicile	416	
F-BLAS	CEA Jodel DR.1051 Sicile	420	
F-BLAT	CEA Jodel DR.1051 Sicile	425	
F-BLAY	CEA Jodel DR.1051 Sicile	427	
F-BLBN	SEEMS MS.885 Super Rallye	5352	
F-BLBU	SEEMS MS.885 Super Rallye	384	
F-BLBV	SEEMS MS.885 Super Rallye	383	
F-BLCM	Piper PA-18-150 Super Cub	18-5347	ALAT
			N10F
F-BLDC	SAN Jodel D.150A Mascaret	05	
F-BLDN	SAN Jodel D.150A Mascaret	21	
F-BLDS	SAN Jodel D.150A Mascaret	23	
F-BLEB	Piper PA-23-250 Aztec B	27-2434	N5394Y
			N10F
F-BLEC	Cessna 182F Skylane	18254872	N3472U
F-BLEP	Alpavia/ Fournier RF-3	8	
F-BLEV	Morane-Saulnier MS.733 Alcyon	68	Fr.AF
F-BLEY	Piper PA-18-150 Super Cub (Damaged 6.4.02)	18-5344	ALAT
F-BLFK	Wassmer Jodel D.112 Club	1177	
F-BLFP	Wassmer WA.40A Super IV	59	
F-BLFT	Wassmer WA.40A Super IV	55	
F-BLFX	Wassmer Jodel D.112 Club	1179	
F-BLGA	SOCATA Rallye 180T Galerien	3303	
F-BLGB	SOCATA Rallye 180T Galerien	3304	
F-BLGC	SOCATA Rallye 180T Galerien	3305	
F-BLGD	Beech 35-C33 Debonair	CD-867	
F-BLGN	Agusta-Bell 47G-2	283	
F-BLGO	Procaer F.15A Picchio	10	D-EBBE
F-BLGV	Cessna 182F Skylane	18254703	N3303U
F-BLHA	Mooney M.20C Mark 21	2485	
F-BLHD	Cessna 172D	17250009	N2409U
F-BLHJ	Piper PA-24-250 Comanche	24-3507	N8253P
F-BLHP	Piper PA-18-150 Super Cub	18-5355	ALAT
			N10F
F-BLIK	SOCATA Rallye 180T Galerien	3306	

F-BLIL	SOCATA Rallye 180T Galerien	3307	
F-BLIM	SOCATA Rallye 180T Galerien	3308	
F-BLIN	SOCATA Rallye 180T Galerien	3309	
F-BLIO	SOCATA Rallye 180T Galerien	3310	
F-BLIP	SOCATA Rallye 180T Galerien	3311	
F-BLIQ	SOCATA Rallye 180T Galerien	3312	
F-BLIS	SOCATA Rallye 180T Galerien	3314	
F-BLIT	SOCATA Rallye 180T Galerien	3315	
F-BLIV	SOCATA Rallye 180T Galerien	3316	
F-BLJL	SANJodel DR.1050 Ambassadeur	469	
F-BLJM	SANJodel DR.1050 Ambassadeur	470	
F-BLJN	SANJodel DR.1050M Excellence	474	
F-BLJO	SANJodel DR.1050M Excellence	475	
F-BLJT	SAN Jodel DR.1050M Excellence	484	
F-BLJV	SAN Jodel DR.105-M Excellence	482	
F-BLKD	Cessna FP172D Skyhawk Powermatic	FP172-0003/P17257179	F-WLKD
F-BLKK	SAN Jodel D.140R Abeille	501	F-WLKK
F-BLKL	Morane-Saulnier MS.760C Paris III	01	F-WLKL
F-BLKM(2)	Bücker Bü 133E Jungmeister	39	F-BLGM HB-MIB U-92
F-BLKU	Gardan GY-80 Horizon 180	07	
F-BLLJ	Piper PA-23-250 Aztec C	27-3756	N6462Y
F-BLMF	CEA Jodel DR.1050 Ambassadeur	434	
F-BLMI	CEA Jodel DR.1051 Sicile	438	
F-BLMK	CEA Jodel DR.1051 Sicile	440	
F-BLMO	CEA Jodel DR.1051 Sicile	445	
F-BLMR	CEA Jodel DR.1051 Sicile	441	
F-BLMS	CEA Jodel DR.1051 Sicile	448	
F-BLNA	Wassmer Jodel D.112 Club	1204	
F-BLNH	Wassmer WA.40A Super IV	63	
F-BLNM	Wassmer Jodel D.112 Club	1207	
F-BLNS	Wassmer Jodel D.112 Club	1210	
F-BLNY	Wassmer WA.40A Super IV	72	
F-BLOB	Mooney M.20C Mark 21 (Wrecked)	2613	
F-BLOD	Piper PA-22-150 Caribbean (Converted to PA-20 taildragger standard)	22-7482	G-ARFA N3566Z
F-BLOK	Mooney M.20E Super 21	229	
F-BLON	Cessna 206 Super Skywagon	206-0081	N5081U
F-BLOQ	Piper PA-25-235 Pawnee	25-2400	N6824Z
F-BLOR	Piper PA-28-160 Cherokee	28-302	N10108 LV-PRZ
F-BLOU	Gardan GY-80 Horizon 160	5	
F-BLPE	Gardan GY-80 Horizon 150	20	
F-BLPJ	Gardan GY-80 Horizon 160	44	
F-BLPK	Gardan GY-80 Horizon 160 (Dismantled)	41	
F-BLPM	Gardan GY-80 Horizon 160	06	
F-BLPQ	Gardan GY-80 Horizon 160	48	
F-BLPV	Gardan GY-80 Horizon 160	59	
F-BLPY	Gardan GY-80 Horizon 160	63	
F-BLQU	Nord 1101 Noralpha	136	N6171X F-BLQU Fr.Mil
F-BLRB	CEA Jodel DR.1051 Sicile	507	
F-BLRK	CEA Jodel DR.1051 Sicile	518	
F-BLRL	CEA Jodel DR.1050 Ambassadeur	516	
F-BLRN	CEA Jodel DR.1051 Sicile	514	
F-BLRQ	CEA Jodel DR.1051-M1 Sicile Record	524	
F-BLRR	CEA Jodel DR.1050 Ambassadeur	522	
F-BLRU	CEA Jodel DR.1050 Ambassadeur	525	
F-BLRY	CEA Jodel DR.1051 Sicile	523	
F-BLSB	SEEMS MS.885 Super Rallye	388	
F-BLSI	SEEMS MS.892A Rallye Commodore 150	10453	
F-BLSK	SEEMS MS.892A Rallye Commodore 150	10450	
F-BLSO	SEEMS MS.892A Rallye Commodore 150	10485	
F-BLTS(2)	Aérospatiale AS.350B Ecureuil	1175	
F-BLVC	Gardan GY-80 Horizon 160	32	
F-BLVG	Gardan GY-80 Horizon 160	72	
F-BLVI	Gardan GY-80 Horizon 160	31	
F-BLVQ	Gardan GY-80 Horizon 160	81	
F-BLVR	Gardan GY-80 Horizon 160	82	
F-BLVU	Gardan GY-80 Horizon 160	85	
F-BLVV	Gardan GY-80 Horizon 160	76	
F-BLXB	Alpavia/ Fournier RF-3	19	
F-BLXC	Alpavia/ Fournier RF-3	14	
F-BLXE	Alpavia/ Fournier RF-3	13	
F-BLXF	Alpavia/ Fournier RF-3	20	
F-BLXG	Alpavia/ Fournier RF-3	15	
F-BLXH	Alpavia/ Fournier RF-3	16	
F-BLXP	Morane-Saulnier MS.733 Alcyon	95	Fr.Mil
F-BLYE	Morane-Saulnier MS.733 Alcyon (Dism, stored)	107	Fr.Mil
F-BLYR	Cessna 182G Skylane	18255263	N2063R
F-BLYU	Nord 1101 Noralpha	18	Fr.Mil
F-BLZC	CEA Jodel DR.1051 Sicile	531	
F-BLZS	CEA Jodel DR.1050 Ambassadeur	550	
F-BMAB	Wassmer Jodel D.112 Club	1214	
F-BMAC	Wassmer Jodel D.112 Club	1215	
F-BMAN	Wassmer Jodel D.112 Club	1221	
F-BMBM	SAN Jodel D.140C Mousquetaire III	129	
F-BMBS	SAN Jodel D.140C Mousquetaire III	126	
F-BMBV	SAN Jodel D.140C Mousquetaire III	134	
F-BMBX	SAN Jodel D.140C Mousquetaire III	142	
F-BMBY	SAN Jodel D.140C Mousquetaire III	137	
F-BMBZ	SAN Jodel D.140C Mousquetaire III	115	
F-BMCA	Piper PA-24-250 Comanche	24-3288	N8099P N10F (N8043P)

F-BMCB	Cessna 182F Skylane	18254698	N3298U
F-BMCP	Cessna F172E	F172-0061	
F-BMCQ	Cessna 206 Super Skywagon	206-0003	N5003U
F-BMCR	Cessna F172E	F172-0062	
F-BMCT	Beech 95-B55 Baron	TC-524	HB-GBO
F-BMCU	Piper PA-18 Super Cub 95	18-1429	OO-MJD (OO-HNB) ALAT 51-15429
F-BMDL	Alpavia/ Fournier RF-3	33	
F-BMDM	Alpavia/ Fournier RF-3	34	
F-BMDY	Alpavia/ Fournier RF-3	49	
F-BMEE	SOCATA MS.893E Rallye 180GT Gaillard	12435	
F-BMFF	SAN Jodel D.140C Mousquetaire III	140	
F-BMFK	SAN Jodel D.140C Mousquetaire III	147	
F-BMFS	SAN Jodel D.140C Mousquetaire III	157	
F-BMFT	SAN Jodel D.140C Mousquetaire III	158	
F-BMFV	SAN Jodel D.140C Mousquetaire III	159	
F-BMFX	SAN Jodel D.140C Mousquetaire III	161	
F-BMGB	CEA Jodel DR.1051-M1 Sicile Record	570	
F-BMGE	CEA Jodel DR.1051 Sicile	562	
F-BMGG	CEA Jodel DR.1051 Sicile	574	
F-BMGH	CEA Jodel DR.1051 Sicile	567	
F-BMGK	CEA Jodel DR.1050 Ambassadeur	572	
F-BMGL	CEA Jodel DR.1050-M1 Sicile Record	576	
F-BMGQ	CEA Jodel DR.1051-M1 Sicile Record	583	
F-BMHM	Piper J-3C-65 Cub (Quoted officially with c/n 11157 - f/n 11735 confirms the true c/n as 11907)	11907	Fr.Mil 44-79611
F-BMII	Wassmer WA.40A Super IV	80	
F-BMIL	Wassmer Jodel D.112 Club	1261	
F-BMIN	Wassmer WA.40A Super IV	81	
F-BMJB	Scintex CP.1310-C3 Super Emeraude	926	
F-BMJC	Scintex CP.1315-C3 Super Emeraude	930	
F-BMJD	Scintex CP.1310-C3 Super Emeraude	932	
F-BMJF	CAARP CP.1315-C3 Super Emeraude	933	
F-BMJM	CAARP CP.1330 Super Emeraude	942	
F-BMJN	Piper PA-18 Super Cub 95	18-1419	ALAT 51-15419
F-BMJR	Piper PA-28-140 Cherokee	28-20191	5T-TJI HB-OLF N6174W
F-BMJU	Morane-Saulnier MS.733 Alcyon	189	Fr.Navy
F-BMJV	Piper PA-18 Super Cub 95 (Damaged 19.6.99)	18-1356	ALAT 51-15356
F-BMKD	Sportavia/ Fournier RF-4D	4007	
F-BMKL	AIAA/Stampe SV.4C	1078	F-BCDN Fr.Mil
F-BMKP	Piper PA-28R-180 Cherokee Arrow	28R-30086	(F-GBOP) F-OCKP N3774T
F-BMLA	Cessna F172E	F172-0066	
F-BMLC	Cessna 336 Skymaster	336-0193	N3893U
F-BMLJ	Mooney M.20E Super 21	425	
F-BMLS	Cessna F172E	F172-0073	
F-BMLT	Piper PA-24-250 Comanche	24-3573	N8322P
F-BMMA	SNCAN/Stampe SV.4A	630	Fr.Mil F-BDGA
F-BMMG	SNCAN/Stampe SV.4A	153	Fr.Mil F-BBAK
F-BMMH	SNCAN/Stampe SV.4A	247	Fr.Mil F-BCKE
F-BMMR	Morane-Saulnier MS.733 Alcyon (Dismantled)	100	Fr.Mil
F-BMMY	Morane-Saulnier MS.733 Alcyon	128	Fr.Mil
F-BMMZ	Morane-Saulnier MS.733 Alcyon (Reservation)	130	Fr.Mil
F-BMNC	SEEMS MS.881 Rallye 105	408	
F-BMNE	GEMS MS.881 Rallye 105	410	
F-BMNL	SEEMS MS.893A Rallye Commodore 180	10489	
F-BMNO	SEEMS MS.892A Rallye Commodore 150	10492	
F-BMNQ	SEEMS MS.892A Rallye Commodore 150	10494	
F-BMNR	SEEMS MS.892A Rallye Commodore 150	10495	
F-BMNS	SEEMS MS.893A Rallye Commodore 180	10496	
F-BMNT	SEEMS MS.893A Rallye Commodore 180	10497	
F-BMNU	SEEMS MS.892A Rallye Commodore 150	10498	
F-BMOE	Wassmer Jodel D.120A Paris-Nice	268	
F-BMOU	Wassmer Jodel D.112 Club	1300	
F-BMOY	Wassmer Jodel D.112 Club	1301	
F-BMPK	CEA Jodel DR.1050-M1 Sicile Record	602	
F-BMPM	CEA Jodel DR.1051-M1 Sicile Record	606	
F-BMPR	CEA Jodel DR.1051-M1 Sicile Record	613	
F-BMQC	Morane-Saulnier MS.733 Alcyon	200	Fr.Mil
F-BMQQ	Zlin Z.326 Trenér Master	890	
F-BMQS	Zlin Z.326 Trenér Master	894	
F-BMQU	Zlin Z.326 Trenér Master	900	
F-BMQV	Zlin Z.326 Trenér Master	901	
F-BMRC	Piper PA-28-235 Cherokee	28-10272	N8800W
F-BMRH	Cessna 210E Centurion	21058625	N4925U
F-BMRI	Cessna 310 I	310I0198	N8198M
F-BMRL	Cessna F172F	F172-0108	
F-BMRP	Cessna 182H Skylane	18255947	N1847X
F-BMRT	SNCAN/Stampe SV.4A	686	Fr.Mil
F-BMRV	Mooney M.20E Super 21	512	
F-BMSK	Dornier Do.28A-1	3055	D-IBOR
F-BMSN	Cessna 182G Skylane	18255120	N3720U
F-BMSO	Cessna 182H Skylane	18256106	N2006X
F-BMSS	Dassault Falcon 20F	2/402	F-WMSS
F-BMSY	Piper PA-24-260 Comanche	24-4050	N8633P N10F

F-BMSZ	Piper PA-18-150 Super Cub	18-8156	N5409Y
F-BMTD	Alpavia/ Fournier RF-3	55	
F-BMTE	Alpavia/ Fournier RF-3	60	
F-BMTK	Alpavia/ Fournier RF-3	70	
F-BMTU	Alpavia/ Fournier RF-3	87	
F-BMUB	Gardan GY-80 Horizon 160	86	
F-BMUC	Gardan GY-80 Horizon 160	87	
F-BMUE	Gardan GY-80 Horizon 160	89	
F-BMUF	Gardan GY-80 Horizon 160 (Stored)	90	
F-BMUI	Gardan GY-80 Horizon 160	103	
F-BMUT	Gardan GY-80 Horizon 180	140	
F-BMUX	Gardan GY-80 Horizon 160D	154	
F-BMUZ	Gardan GY-80 Horizon 180	146	
F-BMVC	SEEMS MS.892A Rallye Commodore 150	10461	
F-BMVK	SEEMS MS.892A Rallye Commodore 150	10509	
F-BMVS	SEEMS MS.892A Rallye Commodore 150	10511	
F-BMVV	GEMS MS.892A Rallye Commodore 150	10538	
F-BMYJ	Wassmer WA.40A Super IV	90	
F-BMYM	Wassmer WA.41 Baladou	94	
F-BMZD	CEA Jodel DR.1050-M1 Sicile Record	629	
F-BMZE	CEA DR.250 Capitaine	19	
F-BMZF	CEA DR.250 Capitaine	5	
F-BMZH	CEA DR.250/160 Capitaine	7	
F-BMZK	CEA DR.250/160 Capitaine	14	
F-BMZN	CEA DR.250/160 Capitaine	21	
F-BMZO	CEA DR.250/160 Capitaine	2	
F-BMZP	CEA DR.250/160 Capitaine	4	
F-BMZS	CEA DR.250 Capitaine	23	
F-BMZT	CEA DR.250A/160 Capitaine	3	
F-BMZU	CEA DR.250/160 Capitaine	34	
F-BMZX	CEA DR.250/160 Capitaine	26	
F-BMZY	CEA DR.250/160 Capitaine	24	
F-BMZZ	CEA DR.250 Capitaine	1	
F-BNAA	Cessna 210E Centurion	21058697	N4997U
F-BNAB	Piper PA-24-260 Comanche	24-4156	N8709P
F-BNAE	Cessna U206 Super Skywagon	U206-0403	N8003Z
F-BNAF	Piper PA-30 Twin Comanche	30-17	N7016Y
F-BNAJ	Zlin Z.326 Trenér Master	906	
F-BNAQ	Cessna 210E Centurion	21058678	N4978U
F-BNBA	SEEMS MS.892A Rallye Commodore 150	10514	
F-BNBJ	GEMS MS.892A Rallye Commodore 150	10542	
F-BNBN	GEMS MS.892A Rallye Commodore 150	10549	
F-BNBT	GEMS MS.892A Rallye Commodore 150	10557	
F-BNCJ	Wassmer Jodel D.112 Club	1311	
F-BNCM	Wassmer Jodel D.112 Club	1313	
F-BNCO	Wassmer Jodel D.112 Club	1315	
F-BNCQ	Wassmer WA.40A Super IV (Dismantled)	101	
F-BNCU	SNCAN/Stampe SV.4C	447	(F-GDXM)
			F-BCXM
F-BNDD(4)	Holste MH.1521M Broussard	240	Fr.AF
F-BNDT	Cessna F172G	F172-0198	
F-BNDU	Cessna F172G	F172-0202	
F-BNEA	Morane-Saulnier MS.733 Alcyon (Dism, stored)	53	Fr.Mil
F-BNEC	Morane-Saulnier MS.733 Alcyon	129	Fr.Mil
F-BNEL	Morane-Saulnier MS.733 Alcyon	159	Fr.Mil
F-BNEX	Holste MH.1521C Broussard	108	Fr.AF
F-BNFC	Cessna 175A Skylark	56689	HB-CRI
			N7989T
F-BNFF	Cessna F150F	F150-0001/15062312	F-WLIK
			(N3512L)
F-BNFJ	Cessna 182J Skylane	18256710	N2610F
F-BNFN	Cessna F172G	F172-0256	
F-BNFQ	Piper PA-28-140 Cherokee	28-20635	N6550W
			N11C
F-BNFS	Piper PA-32-260 Cherokee Six	32-191	N3376W
F-BNFX	Piper PA-28-180 Cherokee C	28-2489	N8316W
F-BNGL	Hiller UH-12B	667	ALAT
F-BNGM	Hiller UH-12B	699	ALAT
F-BNGP	CEA DR.220 2+2	01	F-WNGP
F-BNHE	Wassmer WA.41 Baladou	109	
F-BNHO	Wassmer Jodel D.112 Club	1345	
F-BNHS	Wassmer WA.41 Baladou	113	
F-BNIA	Mooney M.20E Super 21	624	
F-BNIF	SAN Jodel D.140C Mousquetaire III	168	
F-BNII	SAN Jodel D.140C Mousquetaire III	171	
F-BNIL	SAN Jodel D.140E Mousquetaire IV	174	
F-BNIR	SAN Jodel D.140E Mousquetaire IV	177	
F-BNIV	SAN Jodel D.140E Mousquetaire IV	182	
F-BNIZ	SAN Jodel D.140E Mousquetaire IV	184	
F-BNJE	CEA DR.250/160 Capitaine	38	
F-BNJF	CEA DR.250/160 Capitaine	39	
F-BNJI	CEA DR.250/160 Capitaine	44	
F-BNJK	CEA DR.250/160 Capitaine	45	
F-BNJO	CEA DR.250/160 Capitaine	56	
F-BNJQ	CEA DR.250/160 Capitaine	55	
F-BNJX	CEA DR.250/160 Capitaine	63	
F-BNKM	Cessna F172G	F172-0205	
F-BNKO	Piper PA-24-260 Comanche B	24-4334	N8887P
			N10F
F-BNKS	Piper PA-28-140 Cherokee	28-21180	N11C
F-BNLC	Cessna 185B Skywagon	185-0533	TR-LLR
			F-OBZU
			N2533Z
F-BNLH	Cessna T210F Turbo-System Centurion	T210-0074	N6174R
F-BNLR	Piper PA-18 Super Cub 95	18-2076	(F-BNOH)
			R-65
			52-2476
F-BNMG	Cessna 172C	17249164	HB-CRU
			N1464Y
F-BNMJ	Beech A23-19 Musketeer Sport III	MB-116	
F-BNMP	Piper PA-18-150 Super Cub	18-1022	ALAT
			51-15325
F-BNMR	Piper PA-18 Super Cub 95	18-1388	ALAT
			51-15388
F-BNMT	Beech D95A Travel Air	TD-577	HB-GBU
F-BNMY	Zlin Z.526A Akrobat	1005	
F-BNNK	SOCATA MS.892A Rallye Commodore 150	10590	
F-BNNU	SOCATA MS.893A Rallye Commodore 180	10577	
F-BNNX	SOCATA MS.893A Rallye Commodore 180	10578	
F-BNOA	Mooney M.20E Super 21	919	
F-BNOB	Mooney M.20E Super 21	960	
F-BNOF	Jodel D.112D Club	1380	
F-BNOI	Beech 35-C33A Debonair	CE-39	
F-BNOK	Beech 95-C55 Baron	TE-54	
F-BNOL	Beech S35 Bonanza	D-7498	(F-ODOL)
			HB-EFC
F-BNOM	Beech 35-C33 Debonair	CD-1029	
F-BNOR	Beech 35-C33 Debonair	CD-942	HB-ENI
F-BNOS	Beech S35 Bonanza	D-7944	HB-EFG
F-BNOZ	CEA DR.250/160 Capitaine	28	
F-BNPB	Piper PA-30 Twin Comanche	30-701	TJ-ADC
			N7665Y
F-BNPI	Piper PA-18-150 Super Cub	18-5396	ALAT
			N10F
F-BNPM	CEA DR.220 2+2	2	F-WNPM
F-BNPQ	Bell 47J	1425	F-OBPQ
			I-AGUS
F-BNPR	Piper PA-23-250 Aztec C	27-3297	N6091Y
F-BNPS	Agusta-Bell 206A Jet Ranger	8021	(G-AVSV)
F-BNQA	Gardan GY-80 Horizon 180	150	
F-BNQB	Gardan GY-80 Horizon 180	169	
F-BNQC	Gardan GY-80 Horizon 180	133	
F-BNQI	Gardan GY-80 Horizon 180	158	
F-BNQJ	Gardan GY-80 Horizon 180	170	
F-BNQL	Gardan GY-80 Horizon 180	155	
F-BNQO	Gardan GY-80 Horizon 150D	168	
F-BNQQ	Piper PA-18 Super Cub 95	18-1601	ALAT
			51-15601
F-BNQT	Gardan GY-80 Horizon 180	174	
F-BNQV	Gardan GY-80 Horizon 180	177	
F-BNQX	Gardan GY-80 Horizon 180	178	
F-BNQY	Gardan GY-80 Horizon 180	164	
F-BNQZ	Gardan GY-80 Horizon 180	161	
F-BNRI	Beech A23-24 Musketeer Super III	MA-105	
F-BNRK	Beech V35 Bonanza	D-8238	
F-BNRM	Cessna 210E Centurion	21058693	F-OCGG
			N4993U
F-WNRQ(2)	Cessna 305C Bird Dog (L-19) (Coded AJO)	24519	ALAT
F-BNRR	Zlin Z.326 Trenér Master	913	F-WNRR
			F-BNRR
F-BNRX	Fournier RF-6B-100 (Reservation)	14	HB-EZP
			F-GANP
			D-EGRF
			(F-GADM)
F-BNRY	Nord NC.856A Norvigie	85	ALAT
F-BNRZ(2)	SNCAN/Stampe SV.4C	357	F-BCOF
F-BNSC	SOCATA MS.893A Rallye Commodore 180	10641	
F-BNSD	SOCATA MS.893A Rallye Commodore 180	10644	
F-BNSI	SOCATA MS.893A Rallye Commodore 180	10642	
F-BNSN	SOCATA MS.893A Rallye Commodore 180	10600	
F-BNSQ	SOCATA MS.893A Rallye Commodore 180	10580	
F-BNST	SOCATA MS.893A Rallye Commodore 180	10583	
F-BNSV	SOCATA MS.893A Rallye Commodore 180	10596	
F-BNSX	SOCATA MS.893A Rallye Commodore 180	10597	
F-BNSZ	SOCATA MS.893A Rallye Commodore 180	10599	
F-BNTC	Piper PA-32-260 Cherokee Six	32-607	N3695W
F-BNTG	Beech A23-24 Musketeer Super III	MA-33	
F-BNTL	Beech 35-C33 Debonair	CD-1049	
F-BNTM	Piper PA-32-300 Cherokee Six	32-40086	N4046W
F-BNTO	Agusta-Bell 47G-2	061	F-OATO
F-BNTP	Cessna F172G	F172-0239	
F-BNVA	CEA DR.250/160 Capitaine	64	
F-BNVB	CEA DR.220 2+2	3	
F-BNVC	CEA DR.250/160 Capitaine	67	
F-BNVE	CEA DR.250/160 Capitaine	61	
F-BNVL	CEA DR.250/160 Capitaine	72	
F-BNVO	CEA DR.220 2+2	8	
F-BNVS	CEA DR.250/160 Capitaine	78	
F-BNVT	CEA DR.220 2+2	9	
F-BNVU	CEA DR.250/160 Capitaine	80	
F-BNVY	CEA DR.220 2+2	11	
F-BNXB	SOCATA MS.893A Rallye Commodore 180	10652	
F-BNXD	AIAA/Stampe SV.4C	1090	Fr.Navy
F-BNXL	SOCATA MS.893A Rallye Commodore 180	10608	
F-BNXM	SOCATA MS.892A Rallye Commodore 150	10633	
F-BNXP	SOCATA MS.880B Rallye Club	839	
F-BNXY	SOCATA MS.880B Rallye Club	832	
F-BNYB	Gardan GY-80 Horizon 180	162	
F-BNYC	Gardan GY-80 Horizon 160D	152	
F-BNYE	Gardan GY-80 Horizon 180	185	
F-BNYI	Gardan GY-80 Horizon 180	189	
F-BNYJ	Gardan GY-80 Horizon 180	201	
F-BNYN	Gardan GY-80 Horizon 180	202	
F-BNYO	Gardan GY-80 Horizon 160D	219	

F-BNYQ	Gardan GY-80 Horizon 180	191	
F-BNYR	Gardan GY-80 Horizon 180	193	
F-BNYU	Gardan GY-80 Horizon 180	165	
F-BNZB	Wassmer Jodel D.112 Club	1348	
F-BNZH	Wassmer WA.41 Baladou	120	
F-BNZU	Wassmer Jodel D.120A Paris-Nice	323	
F-BNZV	Wassmer WA.41 Baladou	125	
F-BOAF	Piper PA-28-180 Cherokee B	28-1130	F-OCAF N7183W
F-BOBE	Wassmer WA.41 Baladou	131	
F-BOBF	Wassmer WA.40A Super IV	132	
F-BOBK	Wassmer WA.41 Baladou	135	
F-BOBN	Wassmer WA.41 Baladou	137	
F-BOBP	Wassmer WA.41 Baladou	129	
F-BOBQ	Wassmer WA.41 Baladou	140	
F-BOBV	Wassmer WA.41 Baladou	145	
F-BOBX	Wassmer Jodel D.120 Paris-Nice	334	
F-BOCA	CEA DR.250B/160 Capitaine	82	
F-BOCF	CEA DR.220 2+2	14	
F-BOCG	CEA DR.250/160 Capitaine	85	
F-BOCJ	CEA DR.220 2+2	16	
F-BOCL	CEA DR.220 2+2	18	
F-BOCM	CEA DR.250/160 Capitaine	88	
F-BOCR	CEA DR.220 2+2	24	
F-BOCT	CEA DR.220 2+2	26	
F-BODD	SOCATA MS.893A Rallye Commodore 180	10661	
F-BODE	SOCATA MS.892A Rallye Commodore 150	10658	
F-BOEI	Piper PA-32-260 Cherokee Six	32-690	N3769W
F-BOER	Piper PA-18 Super Cub 95	18-1442	ALAT 51-15442
F-BOFA	SOCATA MS.893A Rallye Commodore 180	10825	F-OCMA
F-BOFD	Wassmer WA.54 Atlantic	133	F-ODBD
F-BOFE	Cerva CE.43 Guepard	465	F-ODAI
F-BOFF	CEA DR.221 Dauphin	49	F-WOFF
F-BOFG	CEA DR.253 Régent	01	F-WOFG
F-BOFS	CEA DR.360 Chevalier	01	F-WOFS
F-BOFV	Agusta-Bell 47G-2	169	ALAT
F-BOFY	Piper PA-18 Super Cub 95	18-1378	F-BOMY ALAT 51-15378
F-BOGA	Cessna F150G	F150-0092	
F-BOGE	Cessna F150G	F150-0094	
F-BOGF	Cessna F172G	F172-0314	
F-BOGH	Cessna F150G	F150-0103	
F-BOGO	Cessna F172H	F172-0362	
F-BOGP	Cessna F172H	F172-0371	
F-BOGT	Cessna F172H	F172-0340	
F-BOGV	Cessna F150G	F150-0178	
F-BOGX	Cessna F150G	F150-0179	
F-BOGZ	Cessna F172H	F172-0333	
F-BOHH	Nord 262-A35	49	F-WOFX
F-BOHJ	Piper PA-18-150 Super Cub	18-5324	ALAT N10F
F-BOHK(2)	Wassmer WA.40A Super IV	127	F-BOBA
F-BOHP	Holste MH.1521C.1 Broussard	10	Fr.AF
F-BOHT	Mooney M.20F Executive	670170	N9593M
F-BOHV	Piper PA-23-250 Aztec C	27-3442	N6215Y
F-BOHX	Cessna T210G Turbo-System Centurion	T210-0241	N6841R
F-BOID	Beech M35 Bonanza	D-6434	HB-EID
F-BOIS	Cessna F172E	F172-0082	F-OCIS
F-BOJK	SIAI-Marchetti S.205-18/F	240	(OO-HAP)
F-BOJN	Mooney M.20F Executive	670026	
F-BOJP	Mooney M.20F Executive	670216	N9639M
F-BOJQ	Piper PA-18-180M Super Cub	18-5325	F-WOJQ F-BOJQ ALAT N10F
F-BOJU	Cessna 182K Skylane	18257740	N2540Q
F-BOJX	Piper PA-30 Twin Comanche B	30-1318	N8199Y
F-BOJZ	Cessna 401	401-0072	N3272Q
F-BOKA	CEA DR.250/160 Capitaine	89	
F-BOKF	CEA DR.220 2+2	35	
F-BOKG	CEA DR.220 2+2	36	
F-BOKH	CEA DR.220 2+2	37	
F-BOKJ	CEA DR.220 2+2	39	
F-BOKK	CEA DR.220 2+2	40	
F-BOKN	CEA DR.220 2+2	43	
F-BOKO	CEA DR.220A 2+2	52	
F-BOKS	CEA DR.220 2+2	48	
F-BOKX	CEA DR.220A 2+2	54	
F-BOKY	CEA DR.220A 2+2	55	
F-BOKZ	CEA DR.221 Dauphin	56	
F-BOLC	Piper PA-23-250 Aztec C	27-3382	N6172Y N10F
F-BOLE	Piper PA-28-140 Cherokee	28-22847	N4442J
F-BOLN	SIAI-Marchetti S.205-20/R	363	
F-BOLO	Mooney M.20E Super 21	1177	OO-WIA
F-BOLP	Beech 35-C33A Debonair	CE-147	
F-BOLR	Cessna 310L	310L0104	N3254X
F-BOLS	Aero Commander 200D (W/o 24.9.00)	351	N2978T
F-BOLU	Piper PA-30 Twin Comanche B	30-1438	N8370Y N10F
F-BOLV	Mooney M.20F Executive	670296	
F-BOLZ	Piper PA-30 Twin Comanche B	30-1233	N8135Y (CF-U . C)
F-BOMB	Piper PA-18 Super Cub 95	18-1640	ALAT 51-15640

F-BOMC	Piper PA-18 Super Cub 95	18-1636	ALAT 51-15636
F-BOMF	Piper PA-18 Super Cub 95	18-1435	ALAT 51-15435
F-BOMH	Piper PA-18 Super Cub 95 (On rebuild)	18-2097	ALAT 52-2497
F-BOMI	Piper PA-18 Super Cub 95	18-1359	ALAT 51-15359
F-BOMK	Piper PA-18 Super Cub 95	18-1455	ALAT 51-15455
F-BOML	Piper PA-18 Super Cub 95	18-1367	ALAT 51-15367
F-BOMM	Piper P-A-18-95 Super Cub	18-1397	ALAT 51-15397
F-BOMP	Piper PA-18 Super Cub 95	18-1409	ALAT 51-15409
F-BOMT	Piper PA-18 Super Cub 95	18-1506	ALAT 51-15506
F-BOMV	Piper PA-18 Super Cub 95	18-1465	ALAT 51-15465
F-BOMX	Piper PA-18 Super Cub 95	18-1368	ALAT 51-15368
F-BONA	SOCATA MS.892A Rallye Commodore 150	10706	
F-BONE	SOCATA MS.893A Rallye Commodore 180	10686	
F-BONH	SOCATA MS.893A Rallye Commodore 180	10688	
F-BONI	SOCATA MS.893A Rallye Commodore 180 (Dismantled, stored)	10691	
F-BOOF	Beech V35A Bonanza	D-8635	
F-BOOQ	Piper PA-18 Super Cub 95	18-1648	ALAT 51-15648
F-BOOR	Piper PA-18 Super Cub 95	18-2108	ALAT 52-2508
F-BOOV	Piper PA-18 Super Cub 95	18-1594	ALAT 51-15594
F-BOOX	Piper PA-18 Super Cub 95	18-1616	ALAT 51-15616
F-BOOZ	Beech 95-C55 Baron	TE-286	
F-BOPA	SAN Jodel D.140R Abeille	522	
F-BOPF	SAN Jodel D.150 Mascaret	61	
F-BOPG	SAN Jodel D.140E Mousquetaire IV	188	
F-BOPH	SAN Jodel D.140E Mousquetaire IV	191	
F-BOPK	SAN Jodel D.140R Abeille	523	
F-BOPO	SAN Jodel D.140R Abeille	526	
F-BOPS	SAN Jodel D.140E Mousquetaire IV	190	
F-BOPT	SAN Jodel D.140R Abeille	528	
F-BOPY	Beech V35 Bonanza	D-8383	
F-BOPZ	SAN Jodel D.140E Mousquetaire IV	189	F-WOPZ
F-BOQA	Cessna F172H	F172-0383	
F-BOQB	Cessna F150G	F150-0117	
F-BOQD	Cessna F172H	F172-0369	
F-BOQF	Cessna F150G	F150-0208	
F-BOQH	Cessna F150G	F150-0210	
F-BOQJ	Cessna F150G	F150-0212	
F-BOQK	Cessna F150G	F150-0213	
F-BOQN	Cessna R172E (Converted to Reims FR172 Rocket prototype FR1720001)	R172-0256	
F-BOQO	Cessna F150G	F150-0133	
F-BOQP	Cessna F172H	F172-0402	
F-BOQS	Cessna F150H (Damaged 14.12.99)	F150-0227	
F-BOQV	Cessna F172H	F172-0452	
F-BOQY	Cessna F172H	F172-0483	
F-BORA	Sportavia/ Fournier RF-4D	4012	
F-BORB	Sportavia/ Fournier RF-4D	4014	
F-BORC	Sportavia/ Fournier RF-4D	4015	
F-BORI	Sportavia/ Fournier RF-4D	4017	
F-BOSJ	Mooney M.20F Executive	670260	G-AVHD
F-BOSK	Club Aerostatique de France Free Balloon HG 600m3	8810	
F-BOSO	Piper PA-28-180 Cherokee C	28-3931	(G-AVBR) N9679J
F-BOSX	SIAI-Marchetti S.205-20/R	376	
F-BOSY	Beech 65-A90 King Air	LJ-128	D-IMTW
F-BOTB	SOCATA MS.893A Rallye Commodore 180	10671	
F-BOTC	SOCATA MS.893A Rallye Commodore 180	10672	
F-BOTD	SOCATA MS.893A Rallye Commodore 180	10673	
F-BOTF	SOCATA MS.893A Rallye Commodore 180	10675	
F-BOTG	SOCATA MS.893A Rallye Commodore 180 (Dism)	10676	
F-BOTH	SOCATA MS.893A Rallye Commodore 180	10677	
F-BOTI	SOCATA MS.893A Rallye Commodore 180	10678	
F-BOTJ	SOCATA MS.893A Rallye Commodore 180	10679	
F-BOTK	SOCATA MS.893A Rallye Commodore 180	10680	
F-BOTL	SOCATA MS.893A Rallye Commodore 180	10681	
F-BOTM	SOCATA MS.893A Rallye Commodore 180	10682	
F-BOTN	SOCATA MS.893A Rallye Commodore 180	10683	
F-BOTP	SOCATA MS.893A Rallye Commodore 180	10669	
F-BOTQ	SOCATA MS.892A Rallye Commodore 150	10712	
F-BOTU	SOCATA MS.893A Rallye Commodore 180	10696	
F-BOTX	SOCATA MS.880B Rallye Club	881	
F-BOUA	Piper PA-18 Super Cub 95	18-1417	ALAT 51-15417
F-BOUB	Piper PA-18 Super Cub 95	18-1422	ALAT 51-15422
F-BOUE	Piper PA-18 Super Cub 95	18-1470	ALAT 5I-15470
F-BOUH	Piper PA-18 Super Cub 95	18-1519	ALAT 51-15519

F-BOUK	Piper PA-18 Super Cub 95	18-1605	ALAT 51-15605
F-BOUY	Piper PA-18 Super Cub 95	18-1611	ALAT 51-15611
F-BOUZ	Piper PA-18 Super Cub 95	18-1634	ALAT 51-15634
F-BOVA	SOCATA MS.892A Rallye Commodore 150	10711	
F-BOVH	SOCATA MS.893A Rallye Commodore 180	10718	
F-BOVI	SOCATA MS.880B Rallye Club	1142	
F-BOVJ	SOCATA MS.880B Rallye Club	892	
F-BOVM	SOCATA MS.880B Rallye Club	1114	
F-BOVP	SOCATA MS.880B Rallye Club	1107	
F-BOVY	SOCATA MS.880B Rallye Club	895	
F-BOXB	Sportavia/ Fournier RF-4D	4042	
F-BOXD	Sportavia/ Fournier RF-4D	4044	
F-BOXI	Sportavia/ Fournier RF-4D	4061	
F-BOXJ	Sportavia/ Fournier RF-4D	4062	
F-BOXR	Cessna T210G Turbo-System Centurion	T210-0248	N6848R
F-BOXT	Piper PA-28-140 Cherokee	28-23133	N9669W
F-BOXU	Piper PA-28R-180 Cherokee Arrow	28R-30290	N3947T
F-BOYC	Wassmer WA.40A Super IV	147	
F-BOYG	Wassmer WA.41 Baladou	149	
F-BOYJ	Wassmer WA.41 Baladou	151	
F-BOYK	Wassmer WA.41 Baladou	152	
F-BOYR	Wassmer WA.41 Baladou	156	
F-BOYY	Wassmer WA.421-250	407	
F-BOZB	CEA DR.221 Dauphin	59	
F-BOZF	CEA DR.253 Régent	102	
F-BOZG	CEA DR.220A 2+2	63	
F-BOZH	CEA DR.221 Dauphin	64	
F-BOZJ	CEA DR.250/160 Capitaine	95	
F-BOZK	CEA DR.221 Dauphin	66	
F-BOZM	CEA DR.253 Régent	105	
F-BOZN	CEA DR.250/160 Capitaine	96	
F-BOZO	CEA DR.221 Dauphin	69	
F-BOZP	CEA DR.221 Dauphin	71	
F-BOZQ	CEA DR.221 Dauphin	72	
F-BOZS	CEA DR.221 Dauphin	74	
F-BOZT	CEA DR.220A 2+2	75	
F-BOZV	CEA DR.221 Dauphin	77	
F-BOZX	CEA DR.221 Dauphin	78	
F-BPAB	Gardan GY-80 Horizon 180	218	
F-BPAD	Gardan GY-80 Horizon 160D	137	
F-BPAI	SOCATA MS.880B Rallye Club	1253	
F-BPAJ	Gardan GY-80 Horizon 180	243	
F-BPAM	SOCATA MS.880B Rallye Club	1260	
F-BPAN	SOCATA MS.880B Rallye Club	1257	
F-BPAR	SOCATA MS.893A Rallye Commodore 180	10916	
F-BPAS	SOCATA MS.893A Rallye Commodore 180	11021	
F-BPAU	SOCATA MS.893A Rallye Commodore 180	11025	
F-BPAY	SOCATA MS.893A Rallye Commodore 180	10940	
F-BPBA	SOCATA MS.893A Rallye Commodore 180	10716	
F-BPBG	SOCATA MS.880B Rallye Club	1120	
F-BPBO	SOCATA MS.892A Rallye Commodore 150	10783	
F-BPBQ	SOCATA MS.893A Rallye Commodore 180	10733	
F-BPBT	SOCATA MS.893A Rallye Commodore 180	10730	
F-BPBX	SOCATA MS.893A Rallye Commodore 180	10738	
F-BPCA	CEA DR.253 Régent	108	
F-BPCC	CEA DR.253 Régent	109	
F-BPCE	CEA DR.253 Régent	110	
F-BPCG	CEA DR.221 Dauphin	84	
F-BPCH	CEA DR.220A 2+2	91	
F-BPCJ	CEA DR.221 Dauphin	86	
F-BPCK	CEA DR.221 Dauphin	87	
F-BPCN	CEA DR.221 Dauphin	117	
F-BPCO	CEA DR.221 Dauphin	92	
F-BPCT	CEA DR.221 Dauphin	97	
F-BPCY	CEA DR.221 Dauphin	101	
F-BPDA	SOCATA MS.893A Rallye Commodore 180	10734	
F-BPDK	SOCATA MS.893A Rallye Commodore 180	10773	
F-BPDP	SOCATA MS.893A Rallye Commodore 180	10790	
F-BPDR	SOCATA MS.880B Rallye Club	1140	
F-BPDT	SOCATA MS.880B Rallye Club	1146	
F-BPEF	Cessna F172H	F172-0467	
F-BPEI	Cessna F172H	F172-0501	
F-BPEJ	Cessna F150H	F150-0282	
F-BPEK	Cessna F150H	F150-0287	
F-BPEO	Cessna F172H	F172-0496	
F-BPEP	Cessna F172H	F172-0493	
F-BPEQ	Cessna F150H	F150-0305	
F-BPEU	Cessna F150H	F150-0311	
F-BPEV	Cessna F150H	F150-0385	
F-BPEX	Cessna F150H	F150-0388	
F-BPFH	Piper PA-23-250 Aztec C	27-3834	N6541Y
F-BPFJ	SIAI-Marchetti S.205-18/R	4-119	
F-BPFO	Beech 95-C55 Baron	TE-167	HB-GCO
F-BPFP	Sud Avn SA.318C Alouette Astazou	2006/15	
F-BPFR	Beech 35-C33A Debonair	CE-85	HB-EKZ
F-BPFS	Cessna 337C Super Skymaster	33700839	N2539S
F-BPFX	Piper PA-28R-180 Cherokee Arrow	28R-30434	N4571J
F-BPGA	SOCATA MS.880B Rallye Club	1147	
F-BPGC	SOCATA MS.893A Rallye Commodore 180	10799	
F-BPGP	SOCATA MS.880B Rallye Club	1173	
F-BPGU	SOCATA MS.880B Rallye Club	1176	
F-BPGV	SOCATA MS.893A Rallye Commodore 180	10796	
F-BPHF	SOCATA MS.892A Rallye Commodore 150	10777	
F-BPHG	SOCATA MS.880B Rallye Club	1169	
F-BPHK	SOCATA MS.880B Rallye Club	1186	
F-BPHL	SOCATA MS.892A Rallye Commodore 150	10784	
F-BPHN	SOCATA MS.880B Rallye Club	1134	F-BPBN
F-BPHU	SOCATA MS.880B Rallye Club	1221	
F-BPHY	SOCATA MS.893A Rallye Commodore 180	10816	
F-BPIC	Piper PA-30 Twin Comanche B	30-1251	F-OCIP N8140Y
F-BPIF	Piper PA-18 Super Cub 95 (Quoted officially as c/n 18-1384,but the f/n is 18-1359)	18-1462	ALAT 51-15462
F-BPIK	Piper PA-30 Twin Comanche B	30-1582	N8548Y N10F
F-BPIR	Piper PA-30 Twin Comanche B	30-1412	N8549Y N10F
F-BPIS	Beech 95-C55 Baron	TE-301	HB-GCX
F-BPIT	Beech 35-C33 Debonair	CD-852	HB-EKP
F-BPIU	Cessna 182L Skylane	18258690	N3390R
F-BPIX	Cessna 310N	310N0140	N5040Q
F-BPJC	SIAI-Marchetti S.205-20/R	4-209	
F-BPJE	Piper PA-32-300 Cherokee Six	32-40388	N4148R
F-BPJF	Beech 95-B55 Baron	TC-1143	
F-BPKB	CEA DR.221 Dauphin	104	
F-BPKC	CEA DR.221 Dauphin	105	
F-BPKD	CEA DR.253 Régent	114	
F-BPKE	CEA DR.221 Dauphin	106	
F-BPKF	CEA DR.221 Dauphin	107	
F-BPKG	CEA DR.221 Dauphin	90	
F-BPKH	CEA DR.221 Dauphin	108	
F-BPKI	CEA DR.221 Dauphin	109	
F-BPKP	CEA DR.221 Dauphin	115	
F-BPKQ	CEA DR.253 Régent	119	
F-BPKS	CEA DR.221 Dauphin	116	
F-BPKU	CEA DR.221 Dauphin	119	
F-BPKX	CEA DR.221 Dauphin	120	
F-BPKY	CEA DR.315 Petit Prince	302	
F-BPKZ	CEA DR.253 Régent	122	
F-BPLG	Sportavia/ Fournier RF-4D	4123	
F-BPLJ	Sportavia/ Fournier RF-4D	4125	
F-BPLO	Sportavia/ Fournier RF-4D	4134	
F-BPLR	Sportavia/ Fournier RF-5	5067	
F-BPLZ	Sportavia/ Fournier RF-5	5079	
F-BPMB	SOCATA MS.893A Rallye Commodore 180	10755	
F-BPME	SOCATA MS.893A Rallye Commodore 180	10760	
F-BPMG	SOCATA MS.893A Rallye Commodore 180	10762	
F-BPMH	SOCATA MS.893A Rallye Commodore 180	10763	
F-BPMI	SOCATA MS.893A Rallye Commodore 180	10764	
F-BPMJ	SOCATA MS.893A Rallye Commodore 180	10765	
F-BPMK	SOCATA MS.893A Rallye Commodore 180	10766	
F-BPML	SOCATA MS.893A Rallye Commodore 180	10767	
F-BPMM	SOCATA MS.893A Rallye Commodore 180	10770	
F-BPMN	SOCATA MS.893A Rallye Commodore 180	10771	
F-BPMV	SOCATA MS.892A Rallye Commodore 150	10778	
F-BPMZ	SOCATA MS.892A Rallye Commodore 150	10807	
F-BPNM	Zlin Z.326 Trenér Master	928	
F-BPNR	Zlin Z.326 Trenér Master	933	
F-BPOA	CEA DR.220A 2+2	121	
F-BPOB	CEA DR.315 Petit Prince	303	
F-BPOE	CEA DR.315 Petit Prince	305	
F-BPOH	CEA DR.315 Petit Prince	306	
F-BPOJ	CEA DR.253 Régent	127	
F-BPOL	CEA DR.253 Régent	128	
F-BPON	CEA DR.221 Dauphin	124	
F-BPOO	CEA DR.340 Major	301	
F-BPOQ	CEA DR.360 Chevalier	310	
F-BPOR	CEA DR.315 Petit Prince	309	
F-BPOZ	CEA DR.253 Régent	116	
F-BPPH	Sud Avn SA.316B Alouette III	2245	
F-BPPO	Piper PA-24-250 Comanche	24-1988	F-OBPO N10F
F-BPQE	SOCATA MS.892A Rallye Commodore 150	10781	
F-BPQF	SOCATA MS.892A Rallye Commodore 150	10782	
F-BPRC	CEA DR.315 Petit Prince	316	
F-BPRF	CEA DR.315 Petit Prince	319	
F-BPRG	CEA DR.253 Régent	134	
F-BPRI	CEA DR.315 Petit Prince	321	
F-BPRJ	CEA DR.315 Petit Prince	318	
F-BPRK	CEA DR.360 Chevalier	323	
F-BPRM	CEA DR.315 Petit Prince	325	
F-BPRO	CEA DR.315 Petit Prince	326	
F-BPRP	CEA DR.315 Petit Prince	327	
F-BPRR	CEA DR.221 Dauphin	127	
F-BPRT	CEA DR.221 Dauphin	128	
F-BPRU	CEA DR.315 Petit Prince	330	
F-BPSC	SOCATA MS.893A Rallye Commodore 180	10824	
F-BPSE	SOCATA MS.892A Rallye Commodore 150	10810	
F-BPSL	SOCATA MS.894A Minerva 220	11010	
F-BPST	SOCATA MS.880B Rallye Club	1236	
F-BPTA	Wassmer WA.41 Baladou	160	
F-BPTC	Wassmer WA.421-250	411	
F-BPTF	Wassmer WA.41 Baladou	162	
F-BPTG	Wassmer WA.421-250	417	
F-BPTK	Wassmer WA.41 Baladou	165	
F-BPTN	Wassmer WA.421-250	424	
F-BPTO	Wassmer WA.421-250	425	
F-BPTX	Wassmer WA.51 Pacific	04	
F-BPTY	Wassmer WA.51 Pacific	10	
F-BPUG	Fokker F.27 Friendship 500	10379	PH-FNB

F-BPUH	Fokker F.27 Friendship 500 (Stored)	10382	PH-FNE
F-BPUJ	Fokker F.27 Friendship 500 (Stored)	10390	PH-FNN
F-BPVI	Wassmer WA.421-250	415	F-OCOK
F-BPVJ	Boeing 747-128B (Preserved, Le Bourget)	20541	N28903
			(F-BPVI)
F-BPVZ	Boeing 747-228F	21787	
F-BPXN	SOCATA ST-60 Rallye 7-300	01	
F-BPXT	SOCATA MS.894A Minerva 220	11036	F-WPXT
F-BPXU	CAARP CAP.20	01	F-WPXU
F-BPXV	Fournier RF-6B-100 (Stored dismantled)	01	F-WPXV
F-BPXZ	Robin HR.100/200B Royale	01	F-WPXZ
F-BPYH	SOCATA MS.893A Rallye Commodore 180	10917	
F-BPYJ	SOCATA MS.880B Rallye Club	1247	
F-BPYM	SOCATA MS.880B Rallye Club	1245	
F-BPYN	SOCATA MS.880B Rallye Club	1250	
F-BPYO	SOCATA MS.880B Rallye Club	1249	
F-BPYQ	SOCATA MS.894A Minerva 220	11016	
F-BPYS	SOCATA MS.880B Rallye Club	1251	
F-BPYT	SOCATA MS.880B Rallye Club	1255	
F-BPYU	SOCATA MS.893A Rallye Commodore 180	10932	
F-BPYX	SOCATA MS.893A Rallye Commodore 180	10923	
F-BPZP	Wassmer WA.421-250	430	
F-BRAE	Piper PA-28R-180 Cherokee Arrow	28R-30703	N4956J
F-BRAG	Bölkow BO.208C Junior (Stored)	680	D-EGZN
F-BRAH	Cessna 182M Skylane	18259320	N70598
F-BRAI	Cessna P206C Super Skylane	P206-0516	N8716Z
F-BRAJ	Agusta-Bell 206A Jet Ranger	8110	
F-BRAK	Beech 95-B55 Baron	TC-1170	
F-BRAU	Beech V35 Bonanza	D-8381	HB-EFL
			N4809J
F-BRAY	Piper PA-32-260 Cherokee Six	32-265	6V-AAY
			F-OCHD
			N3404W
F-BRAZ	Beech 36 Bonanza	E-110	
F-BRBB	Cessna F172H	F172-0567	
F-BRBD	Cessna F172H	F172-0542	
F-BRBE	Cessna F172H	F172-0612	
F-BRBI	Reims FR172F Rocket	FR17200099	
F-BRBN	Cessna F150J	F150-0520	
F-BRBV	Reims/Cessna F172H	F17200682	
F-BRBZ	Reims/Cessna F172H (Derelict)	F17200673	
F-BRCD	CEA DR.315 Petit Prince	336	
F-BRCE	CEA DR.340 Major	337	
F-BRCF	CEA DR.340 Major	340	
F-BRCI	CEA DR.315 Petit Prince	341	
F-BRCL	CEA DR.315 Petit Prince	344	
F-BRCN	CEA DR.315 Petit Prince	346	
F-BRCO	CEA DR.340 Major	348	
F-BRCP	CEA DR.380 Prince	356	
F-BRCQ	CEA DR.340 Major	347	
F-BRCR	CEA DR.315 Petit Prince	349	
F-BRCY	CEA DR.340 Major	353	
F-BRCZ	CEA DR.340 Major	354	
F-BRDB	SOCATA MS.892A Rallye Commodore 150	10910	
F-BRDG	SOCATA MS.893A Rallye Commodore 180	10975	
F-BRDI	Gardan GY-80 Horizon 180	250	
F-BRDJ	SOCATA MS.880B Rallye Club	1295	
F-BRDL	SOCATA MS.893A Rallye Commodore 180	10754	
F-BRDM	SOCATA MS.893A Rallye Commodore 180	10759	
F-BRDQ	SOCATA MS.880B Rallye Club	1285	
F-WRDT	SOCATA MS.892A Rallye Commodore	10951	F-BRDT
	(SACMA engine)		
F-BREB	SOCATA MS.893A Rallye Commodore 180	10964	
F-BREE	SOCATA MS.880B Rallye Club	1291	
F-WREI	Gardan GY-80 Horizon 180	242	F-BREI
F-BREL	SOCATA MS.893A Rallye Commodore 180	10956	
F-BREN	SOCATA MS.893A Rallye Commodore 180	10651	F-OCHZ
F-BRER	SOCATA MS.893A Rallye Commodore 180	10946	
F-BRET	SOCATA MS.893A Rallye Commodore 180	10967	
F-BRFA	CEA DR.340 Major	355	
F-BRFF	CEA DR.315 Petit Prince	359	
F-BRFH	CEA DR.315 Petit Prince	361	
F-BRFL	CEA DR.315 Petit Prince	366	
F-BRFO	CEA DR.315 Petit Prince	369	
F-BRFP	CEA DR.315 Petit Prince	370	
F-BRFS	CEA DR.253B Régent	145	
F-BRFT	CEA DR.340 Major	373	
F-BRFU	CEA DR.315 Petit Prince	374	
F-BRFX	CEA DR.315 Petit Prince	375	
F-BRFY	CEA DR.253B Régent	140	
F-BRGB	SOCATA MS.880B Rallye Club	1296	F-BREJ
F-BRGD	Aero Resources Super J-2	043	F-WRGD
			N4333G
F-BRGN(4)	Gardan GY-100/135 Baghera	1	F-WRGA
			F-BRGA
F-BRGQ	SIAI-Marchetti S.208	2-48	OO-BMW
F-BRGS	SOCATA MS.893A Rallye Commodore 180	11064	D-EBVQ
F-BRGT	Piper PA-28R-200 Cherokee Arrow	28R-35820	TJ-AEC
			N11C
			N5042S
F-BRGV	SAN Jodel D.140C Mousquetaire III	96	5T-TJP
			F-OCAN
F-BRHA	Mooney M.20E Super 21	810	F-OCHA
			N5891Q
F-BRHM	Bölkow BO.208C Junior	687	D-EEAJ
F-BRHT	Piper PA-28R-180 Cherokee Arrow (Wfu?)	28R-30693	N4946J
F-BRIA	SOCATA Rallye 150SV Garnement	3366	F-OGLX

F-BRIB	Piper PA-28-235 Cherokee	28-10583	N9002W
F-BRIC	SEEMS MS.885 Super Rallye	5277	PH-MSC
F-BRIE	Aermacchi AL.60B-2	88/6268	
F-BRII	Cessna U206D Skywagon 206	U206-1318	N72204
F-BRIL	Mooney M.20F Executive	690050	
F-BRIO	Beech 95-B55 Baron	TC-1201	N164V
F-BRIR	Piper PA-32-300 Cherokee Six B	32-40635	N4261R
F-BRIZ	Beech E33A Bonanza	CE-271	(ZS-FLZ)
F-BRJL	SOCATA MS.892A Rallye Commodore 150	10972	
F-BRJO	Gardan GY-80 Horizon 180	240	
F-BRJP	Gardan GY-80 Horizon 180	255	
F-BRJX	SOCATA MS.892A Rallye Commodore 150	10970	
F-BRKA	SOCATA MS.893A Rallye Commodore 180	10937	
F-BRKB	SOCATA MS.893A Rallye Commodore 180	10949	
F-BRKC	SOCATA MS.893A Rallye Commodore 180	10957	
F-BRKD	SOCATA MS.893A Rallye Commodore 180	10958	
F-BRKE	SOCATA MS.893A Rallye Commodore 180	10959	
F-BRKF	SOCATA MS.893A Rallye Commodore 180	10960	
F-BRKG	SOCATA MS.893A Rallye Commodore 180	10961	
F-BRKH	SOCATA MS.893A Rallye Commodore 180	10965	
F-BRKI	SOCATA MS.893A Rallye Commodore 180	10998	
F-BRKK	SOCATA MS.893A Rallye Commodore 180	10977	
F-BRKL	SOCATA MS.893A Rallye Commodore 180	10978	
F-BRKP	SOCATA MS.893A Rallye Commodore 180	10985	
F-BRKR	SOCATA MS.893A Rallye Commodore 180	10987	
F-BRKS	SOCATA MS.893A Rallye Commodore 180	10995	
F-BRKT	SOCATA MS.893A Rallye Commodore 180	10996	
F-BRKU	SOCATA MS.893A Rallye Commodore 180	10997	
F-BRKV	SOCATA MS.893A Rallye Commodore 180	11046	
F-BRLB	SOCATA MS.893A Rallye Commodore 180	11054	
F-BRLF	SOCATA MS.880B Rallye Club	1319	
F-BRLI	Gardan GY-80 Horizon 180	259	
F-BRLM	SOCATA MS.880B Rallye Club	1336	
F-BRLO	SOCATA MS.892A Rallye Commodore 150	10993	
F-BRLQ	SOCATA MS.893A Rallye Commodore 180	11415	
F-BRLV	SOCATA MS.893A Rallye Commodore 180	11058	
F-BRLZ	SOCATA MS.880B Rallye Club (W/o)	1347	
F-BRMG	SOCATA MS.893A Rallye Commodore 180	11413	
F-BRMJ	SOCATA MS.894A Minerva 220	11077	
F-BRMK	SOCATA MS.892A Rallye Commodore 150	11406	
F-BRMO	SOCATA MS.883 Rallye 115	1362	
F-BRMU	SOCATA MS.883 Rallye 115	1380	
F-BRNA	Zlin Z.526 Trenér Master	1063	
F-BRND	Zlin Z.526 Trenér Master	1080	
F-BRNO	Beech 65-B90 King Air	LJ-482	HB-GEE
F-BRNQ	Piper PA-28R-200 Cherokee Arrow	28R-35714	N4988S
F-BRNU	Piper PA-23-250 Aztec C	27-3284	6V-ABJ
			7T-VBG
			N6082Y
F-BROA	CEA DR.360 Chevalier	376	
F-BROC	CEA DR.360 Chevalier	379	
F-BROE	CEA DR.315 Petit Prince	381	
F-BROF	CEA DR.315 Petit Prince	394	
F-BROJ	CEA DR.315 Petit Prince	388	
F-BROK	CEA DR.340 Major	389	
F-BROR	CEA DR.340 Major	392	
F-BROS	CEA DR.340 Major	393	
F-BROT	CEA DR.380 Prince	395	
F-BROV	CEA DR.380 Prince	399	
F-BROX	CEA DR.360 Chevalier	400	
F-BROY	CEA DR.315 Petit Prince	365	F-OCMY
F-BRPD	Piper PA-28-140 Cherokee B	28-25740	N8877N
F-BRPQ	Cessna T337D Turbo Super Skymaster	33700995	N2695S
F-BRPS	Reims FR172F Rocket	FR17200083	
F-BRPX	Piper PA-23-250 Aztec D	27-4285	N6928Y
F-BRQD	SAN Jodel D.140C Mousquetaire III	131	F-OCOD
			TT-AAB
			F-OCAX
F-BRQI	Sud Avn SA.316B Alouette III	1915	FAP9399
F-BRQM	Piper PA-18-150 Super Cub	18-5322	(F-BRQH)
			ALAT
F-BRQN	Piper PA-18-150 Super Cub	18-5328	(F-BRQG)
			ALAT
			N10F
F-BRRK	SOCATA MS.893A Rallye Commodore 180	11439	
F-BRRL	SOCATA MS.892A Rallye Commodore 150 (Wfu)	11428	
F-BRRM	SOCATA MS.880B Rallye Club	1395	
F-BRRP	SOCATA MS.893A Rallye Commodore 180	11418	
F-BRRR	SOCATA MS.880B Rallye Club (Wfu 7.00)	1403	(D-ECCG)
F-BRRY	SOCATA MS.880B Rallye Club	1558	
F-BRRZ	SOCATA MS.893A Rallye Commodore 180	11436	
F-BRSC	Beech 60 Duke	P-66	
F-BRSG	Cessna 182N Skylane	18260154	N92328
F-BRSH	Cessna 414	414-0064	N8164Q
F-BRSV	Bellanca 17-30 Viking 300	30051	N6684V
F-BRTB	CEA DR.315 Petit Prince	401	
F-BRTD	CEA DR.380 Prince	403	
F-BRTE	CEA DR.340 Major	402	
F-BRTF	CEA DR.340 Major	382	
F-BRTG	CEA DR.315 Petit Prince	404	
F-BRTJ	CEA DR.220A-B 2+2	133	
F-BRTK	CEA DR.315 Petit Prince	408	
F-BRTL	CEA DR.340 Major	413	
F-BRTM	CEA DR.253B Régent	152	
F-BRTN	CEA DR.380 Prince	410	
F-BRTO	CEA DR.315 Petit Prince	411	
F-BRTP	CEA DR.315 Petit Prince	412	

F-BRTR	CEA DR.315 Petit Prince	415	
F-BRTV	CEA DR.380 Prince	398	
F-BRTZ	CEA DR.253B Régent	150	
F-BRUA	Beech P35 Bonanza	D-7241	HB-EKI
F-BRUB	Piper PA-28R-200 Cherokee Arrow	28R-35239	N2645R
F-BRUC	Beech 95-B55 Baron	TC-1298	
F-BRUE	Piper PA-28R-200 Cherokee Arrow	28R-35364	N2949R
F-BRUH	Beech E33 Bonanza	CD-1230	N7770R
F-BRUM	Cessna T210J Turbo-System Centurion	T210-0395	N2245R
F-BRUS	Piper PA-30 Twin Comanche C	30-1816	HB-LFG
			N8673Y
F-BRUU	Wassmer WA.421-250	418	
F-BRUV	Bellanca 17-30A Viking 300	30269	
F-BRVB	CEA DR.315 Petit Prince	438	
F-BRVD	CEA DR.380 Prince	418	
F-BRVH	CEA DR.220A-B 2+2	134	
F-BRVI	CEA DR.360 Chevalier	427	
F-BRVJ	CEA DR.340 Major	430	
F-BRVK	CEA DR.315 Petit Prince	431	
F-BRVL	CEA DR.340 Major	432	
F-BRVP	CEA DR.340 Major	435	
F-BRVT	Robin DR.300/108 2+2 Tricycle	493	
F-BRVV	Robin DR.300/108 2+2 Tricycle	489	
F-BRXC	Reims FR172G Rocket	FR17200197	
F-BRXF	Reims/Cessna F172H	F17200705	
F-BRXG	Reims FR172G Rocket	FR17200204	
F-BRXK	Reims/Cessna F150K	F15000615	
F-BRXN	Cessna U206E Stationair	U20601674	N9474G
F-BRXO	Reims/Cessna F150K	F15000624	
F-BRXU	Reims/Cessna F150K	F15000630	
F-BRXX	Reims/Cessna F150K	F15000632	
F-BRYA	SOCATA MS.893A Rallye Commodore 180	11468	
F-BRYL	SOCATA MS.880B Rallye Club	1523	
F-BRYU	SOCATA MS.880B Rallye Club	1515	(G-AXHH)
F-BRZA	CEA DR.315 Petit Prince	445	
F-BRZB	CEA DR.315 Petit Prince	441	
F-BRZE	CEA DR.315 Petit Prince	450	
F-BRZK	CEA DR.360 Chevalier	456	
F-BRZM	CEA DR.360 Chevalier	458	
F-BRZN	CEA DR.340 Major	459	
F-BRZO	CEA DR.315 Petit Prince	461	
F-BRZQ	CEA DR.315 Petit Prince	463	
F-BRZT	CEA DR.253B Régent	165	
F-BRZY	CEA DR.220A-B 2+2	139	
F-BSAE	SOCATA MS.880B Rallye Club (Wrecked)	1537	
F-BSAF	SOCATA MS.880B Rallye Club	1539	
F-BSAG	SOCATA MS.880B Rallye Club	1543	
F-BSAN	SOCATA MS.893A Rallye Commodore 180	11487	
F-BSAO	SOCATA MS.883 Rallye 115	1551	(D-EDDH)
F-BSAV	SOCATA MS.893A Rallye Commodore 180	11457	
F-BSAX	SOCATA MS.880B Rallye Club	1576	
F-BSAY	SOCATA MS.880B Rallye Club	1556	(G-AXHI)
F-BSBA	CEA DR.220A-B 2+2	141	
F-BSBG	CEA DR.315 Petit Prince	472	
F-BSBI	CEA DR.340 Major	473	
F-BSBM	CEA DR.253B Régent	170	
F-BSBN	CEA DR.315 Petit Prince	480	
F-BSBR	CEA DR.315 Petit Prince	488	
F-BSBS	CEA DR.315 Petit Prince	491	
F-BSBT	Robin DR.300/108 2+2 Tricycle	492	
F-BSBV	Robin DR.300/108 2+2 Tricycle	494	
F-BSBX	Robin DR.300/108 2+2 Tricycle	499	
F-BSBY	CEA DR.315 Petit Prince	495	
F-BSBZ	CEA DR.360 (convtd from DR.340 Major .95)	482	
F-BSCD	SOCATA MS.893A Rallye Commodore 180	11486	
F-BSCK	SOCATA MS.893A Rallye Commodore 180	11073	
F-BSCM	SOCATA MS.880B Rallye Club	1598	
F-BSDA	SOCATA MS.893A Rallye Commodore 180	11465	
F-BSDB	SOCATA MS.893A Rallye Commodore 180	11467	
F-BSDC	SOCATA MS.893A Rallye Commodore 180	11475	
F-BSDD	SOCATA MS.893A Rallye Commodore 180	11476	
F-BSDE	SOCATA MS.893A Rallye Commodore 180	11477	
F-BSDF	SOCATA MS.893A Rallye Commodore 180	11478	
F-BSDG	SOCATA MS.893A Rallye Commodore 180	11479	
F-BSDH	SOCATA MS.893A Rallye Commodore 180	11480	
F-BSDI	SOCATA MS.893A Rallye Commodore 180	11481	
F-BSDK	SOCATA MS.893A Rallye Commodore 180	11483	
F-BSDL	SOCATA MS.893A Rallye Commodore 180	11484	
F-BSDM	SOCATA MS.893A Rallye Commodore 180	11499	
F-BSDN	SOCATA MS.893A Rallye Commodore 180	11500	
F-BSDR	SOCATA MS.880B Rallye Club	1604	
F-BSEA	Beech E33A Bonanza	CE-249	HB-EHI
F-BSEC	Piper PA-18-150 Super Cub	18-5371	ALAT
			N10F
F-BSEH	Piper PA-28R-200 Cherokee Arrow	28R-35233	HB-OZS
			N2628R
F-BSEN	Beech 95-B55 Baron	TC-1328	HB-GEL
F-BSEO	Piper PA-23-250 Aztec D	27-4428	N13778
F-BSEP	Cessna 150F	15062954	G-ATLS
			(N8854G)
F-BSES	SNCASO SO.1221-S Djinn	1001/FR7	G-AXFO
			F-BHOI
			F-WHOI
F-BSFE	SOCATA MS.880B Rallye Club	1613	
F-BSFF	SOCATA MS.880B Rallye Club	1614	
F-BSFQ	SOCATA MS.880B Rallye Club	1688	
F-BSFX	SOCATA ST-10 Diplomate	114	

F-BSFY	SOCATA ST-10 Diplomate	115	
F-BSGB	Agusta-Bell 206B Jet Ranger	8325	
F-BSGC	CAARP CAP.10B	04	
F-BSGK	Dornier Do.27A-4	451	57+23
			PB+223
F-BSGM	Dornier Do.27A-4	524	57+63
			GB+375
F-BSGN	Deveque Free Balloon HG RD 700	8	
F-BSGS	Wassmer WA.421-250	428	
F-BSHB	Reims/Cessna F177RG Cardinal RG	F177RG0001/ 177RG0004	F-WLIR
			N8004G
F-BSHD	Reims FR172H Rocket	FR17200255	
F-BSHM	Reims/Cessna FA150K Aerobat	FA1500077	
F-BSHQ	Reims/Cessna F177RG Cardinal RG	F177RG0016/ 177RG0133	
F-BSHV	Reims/Cessna F177RG Cardinal RG (Dismantled)	F177RG0032/ 177RG0195	
F-BSIA	Bell 47G-2	1629	ALAT
			Fr.AF
			N2848B
F-BSIB	Reims/Cessna F150K	F15000637	
F-BSIG	Reims/Cessna F150K	F15000643	
F-BSIH	CEA Jodel DR.1050-M1 Sicile Record	634	HB-EEU
F-BSIN	Reims/Cessna F150K	F15000649	
F-BSIO	Reims/Cessna F150K	F15000650	
F-BSIR	Reims/Cessna F150K	F15000653	
F-BSIS	Reims FR172H Rocket	FR17200242	
F-BSIT	Reims/Cessna F150K	F15000654	
F-BSIU	Reims/Cessna F150K	F15000655	
F-BSIX	Reims/Cessna F150K (Fuselage stored at Cosne-s-Loire 15.10.03)	F15000657	
F-BSIY	Reims/Cessna F150K	F15000658	
F-BSJA	CEA DR.380 Prince	486	
F-BSJB	Robin DR.300/108 2+2 Tricycle	500	
F-BSJF	Robin DR.300/108 2+2 Tricycle	503	
F-BSJG	Robin DR.300/108 2+2 Tricycle	504	
F-BSJH	Robin DR.300/108 2+2 Tricycle	505	
F-BSJJ	Robin DR.300/108 2+2 Tricycle	506	
F-BSJN	Robin DR.300/108 2+2 Tricycle	512	
F-BSJQ	Robin DR.300/108 2+2 Tricycle	509	
F-BSJR	Robin DR.300/108 2+2 Tricycle	514	
F-BSJT	CEA DR.360 Chevalier	532	
F-BSJU	Robin DR.300/108 2+2 Tricycle	518	
F-BSJV	CEA DR.360 Chevalier	533	
F-BSJZ	CEA DR.315 Petit Prince	522	
F-BSKC	SOCATA MS.893A Rallye Commodore 180	11642	
F-BSKF	SOCATA MS.892A Rallye Commodore 150	11704	
F-BSKH	SOCATA MS.892A Rallye Commodore 150	11706	
F-BSKK	SOCATA MS.880B Rallye Club (Wrecked)	1701	
F-BSKM	SOCATA MS.880B Rallye Club	1694	
F-BSKN	SOCATA MS.892A Rallye Commodore 150	11764	
F-BSKP	SOCATA MS.894A Minerva 220	11627	
F-BSKV	SOCATA MS.880B Rallye Club	1692	
F-BSKY	SOCATA MS.880B Rallye Club	1696	
F-BSLC	Robin DR.300/108 2+2 Tricycle	527	
F-BSLF	Robin DR.300/108 2+2 Tricycle	537	
F-BSLJ	Robin DR.300/108 2+2 Tricycle	540	
F-BSLQ	Robin DR.300/108 2+2 Tricycle	552	
F-BSLR	Robin DR.300/108 2+2 Tricycle	551	
F-BSLT	CEA DR.253B Régent	184	
F-BSLU	Robin DR.300/108 2+2 Tricycle	557	
F-BSLX	Robin DR.300/108 2+2 Tricycle (Wfu)	559	
F-BSLY	Robin DR.300/140 Major	560	
F-BSLZ	Robin DR.300/108 2+2 Tricycle	561	
F-BSMA	SOCATA MS.893A Rallye Commodore 180	11768	
F-BSMB	SOCATA MS.893A Rallye Commodore 180	11769	
F-BSMC	SOCATA MS.893A Rallye Commodore 180	11770	
F-BSME	SOCATA MS.892A Rallye Commodore 150	11716	
F-BSMG	SOCATA MS.880B Rallye Club	1805	
F-BSMH	SOCATA MS.880B Rallye Club	1806	
F-BSMO	SOCATA ST-10 Diplomate	131	
F-BSMZ	SOCATA MS.892A Rallye Commodore 150	11817	
F-BSNA	Wassmer WA.51A Pacific	13	
F-BSND	Wassmer WA.421-250	427	
F-BSNE	Wassmer WA.51A Pacific	16	
F-BSNJ	Enstrom F-28A	264	F-GATB
			3A-MJC
			(OO-BAO)
F-BSNL	Wassmer WA.52 Europa	24	
F-BSNM	Wassmer WA.51A Pacific	25	
F-BSNO	Wassmer WA.421-250	422	
F-BSNR	Wassmer WA.52 Europa	29	
F-BSNT	Wassmer WA.52 Europa	31	
F-BSOA	Robin DR.300/108 2+2 Tricycle	562	
F-BSOC	Robin DR.300/108 2+2 Tricycle	564	
F-BSOD	Robin DR.300/108 2+2 Tricycle	565	
F-BSOE	Robin DR.300/108 2+2 Tricycle	566	
F-BSOF	Robin DR.300/108 2+2 Tricycle	567	
F-BSOI	Robin HR.100/200B Royal	04	
F-BSOK	Robin DR.300/120 Petit Prince	574	
F-BSON	CEA DR.315 Petit Prince	579	
F-BSOP	Robin DR.300/120 Petit Prince	580	
F-BSOR	Robin DR.300/108 2+2 Tricycle	582	
F-BSOT	Robin DR.300/120 Petit Prince	585	
F-BSOU	CEA DR.315 Petit Prince	587	
F-BSOY	Robin HR.100/200B Royal	07	

F-BSPJ	Robin DR.300/108 2+2 Tricycle	612	
F-BSPK	Robin DR.300/140 Major	614	
F-BSPL	Robin DR.300/180R Remorqueur	591	
F-BSPM	Robin DR.300/120 Petit Prince	617	
F-BSPN	Robin DR.300/120 Petit Prince	618	
F-BSPO	Robin DR.300/120 Petit Prince	620	
F-BSPQ	Robin DR.300/120 Petit Prince	621	
F-BSPS	Robin DR.300/108 2+2 Tricycle	622	
F-BSPT	Robin DR.300/108 2+2 Tricycle	627	
F-BSPU	Robin HR.100/200B Royal	111	(D-EBAX)
F-BSPY	Robin DR.300/125 Petit Prince	30	
F-BSQJ	Cerva CE-43 Guepard	03/433	F-WSQF
F-BSQR	Robin HR.200/100 Club	01	F-WSQR
F-BSRE	Cessna 414	414-0156	N8226Q
F-BSRN	Agusta-Bell 206A Jet Ranger II	8278	
F-BSRQ	Cessna 185 Skywagon	185-0106	TR-LLQ
			F-OBVN
			N9906X
F-BSRS	Piper PA-18-150 Super Cub	18-4894	TR-LNS
			F-OAYV
F-BSST	Cessna 210L Centurion (Wrecked)	21061044	D-EARK
			N2077S
F-BSTD	Cessna 421B Golden Eagle	421B0106	N8076Q
F-BSTL(2)	SNCAN/Stampe SV.4C	458	F-BCVZ
F-BSUS	SIAI-Marchetti S.208	2-20	OO-HIJ
F-BSVI	SOCATA MS.880B Rallye Club	1735	
F-BSVO	Beech A23-19 Musketeer Sport III	MB-34	HB-ENR
F-BSVP	SOCATA MS.894A Minerva 220	11677	
F-BSVR	SOCATA MS.893A Rallye Commodore 180	11666	
F-BSVS	SOCATA MS.893A Rallye Commodore 180	11715	
F-BSVU	SOCATA MS.893A Rallye Commodore 180	11744	
F-BSVV	SOCATA MS.893A Rallye Commodore 180	11745	
F-BSVX	SOCATA MS.893A Rallye Commodore 180	11746	
F-BSVY	SOCATA MS.893A Rallye Commodore 180	11747	
F-BSVZ	SOCATA MS.893A Rallye Commodore 180	11749	
F-BSXD	SOCATA MS.880B Rallye Club	1762	
F-BSXE	SOCATA MS.894A Minerva 220	11872	
F-BSXK	SOCATA ST-10 Diplomate	133	
F-BSXL	SOCATA MS.880B Rallye Club	1799	
F-BSXP	SOCATA MS.892A Rallye Commodore 150 (Wfu)	11818	
F-BSXT	SOCATA MS.880B Rallye Club	1803	
F-BSXU	SOCATA MS.880B Rallye Club	1804	
F-BSXV	SOCATA MS.880B Rallye Club	1802	
F-BSYO	SOCATA MS.880B Rallye Club (Derelict)	1791	F-BSKO
F-BSYU	Gardan GY-80 Horizon 180	229	OO-UIL
F-BSZA	SOCATA MS.880B Rallye Club	1813	
F-BSZG	SOCATA MS.880B Rallye Club	1858	
F-BSZM	SOCATA ST-10 Diplomate	134	
F-BTAJ	Beech 58 Baron	TH-199	
F-BTAN	SIAI-Marchetti S.205-18/R	4-169	OO-HED
F-BTAU	DHC-6 Twin Otter 200	153	N246GW
			(N33TW)
			N246GW
F-BTBB	Robin DR.300/120 Petit Prince	636	
F-BTBC	Robin DR.300/120 Petit Prince	637	
F-BTBD	Robin DR.300/108 2+2 Tricycle	638	
F-BTBE	Robin DR.300/120 Petit Prince	640	
F-BTBJ	Robin DR.300/120 Petit Prince	654	
F-BTBK	Robin DR.300/120 Petit Prince	655	
F-BTBO	Robin DR.300/180R Remorqueur	660	
F-BTBS	Robin DR.300/120 Petit Prince	664	
F-BTBV	CEA DR.360 Chevalier	666	
F-BTBZ	Robin DR.300/180R Remorqueur	671	
F-BTCG	Pilatus PC-6/A-H2 Porter	551	I-SORE
F-BTCN	Piper PA-28R-200 Cherokee Arrow B	28R-7135182	N2289T
F-BTCQ	Piper PA-34-200 Seneca	34-7250019	N2396T
F-BTCR	Beech 95-B55 Baron	TC-1351	HB-GES
F-BTCZ	Cessna 182P Skylane	18260951	N7311Q
F-BTDD	McDonnell-Douglas DC-10-30	46963	
F-BTDE	McDonnell-Douglas DC-10-30	46853	N54639
			(F-BTDE)
F-BTDG	Boeing 747-3B3	22514	
F-BTDH	Boeing 747-3B3	22515	
F-BTDM	Mudry CAP.10B	29	
F-BTDN	Mudry CAP.10B	30	
F-BTDY	Cessna 421B Golden Eagle	421B0233	G-AZPT
			N5990M
F-BTEM	Reims/Cessna FT337GP Super Skymaster	FP33700012	D-IAPV
	(Reims-assembled P337G Pressurized Skymaster US c/n P3370159)		
F-BTEN	Agusta-Bell 47G-2	251	74+11
			AS+373
			LA+102
			AS+052
F-BTEX	SOCATA MS.893E Rallye 180GT Gaillard	12438	D-EGHH
			F-BVHX
F-BTEY	Piper PA-23 Apache	23-52	F-OCST
			OO-EHG
			HB-LBT
			OO-CHF
			N1075P
F-BTFA	Reims/Cessna FA150L Aerobat	FA1500121	F-WLIO
			(G-AZBJ)
			F-BSHP
F-BTFH	Reims/Cessna F150L	F15000789	
F-BTFI	Reims/Cessna F150L	F15000802	
F-BTFJ	Reims/Cessna F150L	F15000781	
F-BTFL	Reims/Cessna F172L	F17200864	
F-BTFM	Reims FR172H Rocket	FR17200317	
F-BTFN	Reims/Cessna F150L	F15000782	
F-BTFV	Reims/Cessna F172L	F17200886	
F-BTFY	Reims/Cessna F150L	F15000834	
F-BTGR	Agusta-Bell 47G-2	198	F-MJAF
F-BTGT	Piper PA-23-250 Aztec C	27-3270	5R-MCE
			N6072Y
F-BTGU	Piper PA-28-140 Cherokee E	28-7225124	N11C
F-BTHC	SOCATA MS.880B Rallye Club	1902	
F-BTHG	SOCATA MS.883 Rallye 115	1392	
F-BTHM	SOCATA MS.883 Rallye 115	1644	
F-BTHO	SOCATA MS.883 Rallye 115	1646	
F-BTHV	SOCATA ST-10 Diplomate	142	
F-BTIA	SOCATA ST-10 Diplomate	143	
F-BTIC	SOCATA MS.880B Rallye Club	1905	
F-BTIE	SOCATA MS.880B Rallye Club	1903	
F-BTIG	SOCATA MS.893A Rallye Commodore 180	11892	
F-BTIK	SOCATA MS.880B Rallye Club (Wfu)	1922	
F-BTIV	SOCATA MS.880B Rallye Club (Dam 10.6.03)	1958	
F-BTJP	SOCATA MS.880B Rallye Club	1967	
F-BTJV	SOCATA MS.893A Rallye Commodore 180	11979	
F-BTJZ	SOCATA MS.880B Rallye Club	2046	
F-BTKA	Robin DR.300/125 Petit Prince	670	
F-BTKC	Robin DR.400/120 Petit Prince	696	
F-BTKE	Robin DR.300/120 Petit Prince	695	
F-BTKF	CEA DR.360 Chevalier	698	
F-BTKG	Robin DR.300/120 Petit Prince	700	
F-BTKH	Robin DR.400/120 Petit Prince	701	
F-BTKK	Robin DR.300/108 2+2 Tricycle	711	
F-BTKN	Robin DR.400/160 Chevalier	715	
F-BTKP	Robin HR.100/210 Safari	143	
F-BTKQ	Robin DR.300/108 2+2 Tricycle	717	
F-BTKR	Robin DR.400/180 Régent	699	(D-ENTJ)
F-BTKT	Robin DR.400/120 Petit Prince	723	
F-BTKU	Robin DR.400/120 Petit Prince	719	
F-BTKX	Robin DR.400/120 Petit Prince	732	
F-BTLD	Wassmer WA.54 Atlantic	52	
F-BTLE	Wassmer WA.52 Europa	55	
F-BTLI	Wassmer WA.52 Europa	58	
F-BTLJ	Wassmer WA.52 Europa (Wrecked)	77	
F-BTLK	Wassmer WA.52 Europa	60	
F-BTLR	Wassmer WA.52 Europa	75	
F-BTLU	Cerva CE.43 Guepard	436	
F-BTLV	Wassmer WA.52 Europa	84	
F-BTLY	Cerva CE.43 Guepard	437	
F-BTME	Beech 99	U-79	N551GP
			N100GP
F-BTMH	Piper PA-34-200 Seneca	34-7250135	F-BTDY
			N4566T
F-BTMN	Beech 36 Bonanza	E-43	HB-EHG
F-BTMS	Piper PA-23-250 Aztec E	27-7305053	N9738N
F-BTPA	SOCATA MS.893A Rallye Commodore 180	11981	
F-BTPB	SOCATA MS.893A Rallye Commodore 180	11982	
F-BTPC	SOCATA MS.893A Rallye Commodore 180	11983	
F-BTPD	SOCATA MS.893A Rallye Commodore 180	11984	
F-BTPE	SOCATA MS.893A Rallye Commodore 180	11985	
F-BTPH	SOCATA MS.893A Rallye Commodore 180	11988	
F-BTPI	SOCATA MS.893A Rallye Commodore 180	11989	
F-BTPJ	SOCATA MS.893A Rallye Commodore 180	11990	
F-BTPM	SOCATA MS.880B Rallye Club	2047	
F-BTPS	SOCATA MS.893A Rallye Commodore 180	11993	
F-BTPY	SOCATA MS.880B Rallye Club	2111	
F-BTQF	Piper PA-28R-200 Cherokee Arrow II	28R-7235162	F-BTMU
F-BTQH	Piper PA-28R-200 Cherokee Arrow II	28R-7235174	N11C
F-BTQJ	Piper PA-28R-200 Cherokee Arrow II	28R-7235169	N11C
F-BTQM	Beech C23 Sundowner	M-1388	
F-BTQP	Beech 65-90 King Air	LJ-40	I-GNIS
			HB-GCH
F-BTQY	Cessna 182P Skylane	18261517	N21249
F-BTRB	SOCATA MS.887 Rallye 125	2040	
F-BTRN	SOCATA ST-10 Diplomate	151	
F-BTRO	SOCATA MS.880B Rallye Club	2085	(D-EMJD)
F-BTRZ	SOCATA ST-10 Diplomate	155	
F-BTSF	Agusta-Bell 47G-2	080	ALAT
F-BTSH	Bell 47G	709	ALAT
			Fr.AF
			Fr.Navy
F-BTSI	Bell 47G-2	1632	ALAT
			N2851B
F-BTSJ	Agusta-Bell 47G-2	131	ALAT
F-BTSM	Agusta-Bell 47G-2	117	ALAT
F-BTSN	Agusta-Bell 47G-2	126	ALAT
F-BTSQ	Agusta-Bell 47G-2	168	ALAT
F-BTSV	Agusta-Bell 47G-2	199	ALAT
F-BTSX	Agusta-Bell 47G-2	147	ALAT
F-BTUB	Reims/Cessna F150L	F15000858	
F-BTUF	Reims FR172H Rocket	FR17200335	
F-BTUH	Reims/Cessna F172L	F17200885	
F-BTUK	Reims/Cessna F172L	F17200888	
F-BTUL	Reims/Cessna F172L	F17200889	
F-BTUM	Reims/Cessna F172L	F17200890	
F-BTUN	Reims/Cessna F172L	F17200891	
F-BTUP	Reims/Cessna F172L	F17200894	
F-BTUQ	Reims/Cessna F150L	F15000837	
F-BTUY	Reims/Cessna F172L	F17200901	
F-BTUZ	Reims/Cessna F172L	F17200903	
F-BTVC	SOCATA MS.880B Rallye Club	2107	

F-BTVG	SOCATA MS.893E Rallye 180GT Gaillard	12124	
F-BTVI	SOCATA MS.893E Rallye 180GT Gaillard	12126	
F-BTVJ	SOCATA MS.893E Rallye 180GT Gaillard	12127	
F-BTVN	SOCATA MS.880B Rallye Club	2120	
F-BTXD	SNCAN/Stampe SV.4A	595	CN-TTG
			F-BDEP
F-BTXS	Robin DR.300/120 Petit Prince	720	F-BTKS
F-BTYI	Piper PA-34-200 Seneca	34-7350077	F-BTMY
			F-BTMX
F-BTYK	Piper PA-34-200 Seneca	34-7250091	N4416T
F-BTYL	Beech V35B Bonanza	D-9468	
F-BTYQ	Piper PA-23-250 Aztec E	27-7304972	F-BTMV
			N9728N
F-BTYS	Beech F33A Bonanza	CE-433	(D-EHWB)
F-BTZF	Robin DR.400/160 Chevalier	754	
F-BTZI	Robin DR.400/120 Petit Prince	756	
F-BTZM	Robin DR.400/180 Régent	768	
F-BTZN	Robin DR.400/120 Petit Prince	769	
F-BTZO	Robin DR.400/140 Major	770	
F-BTZP	Robin DR.400/2+2 Tricycle	773	
F-BTZT	Robin HR.100/210 Safari	152	
F-BTZY	Robin DR.400/140 Major	799	
F-BTZZ	Robin DR.400/160 Chevalier	802	
F-BUAV	Sud Avn SA.316B Alouette III	1683	HC-BMP
	(Awaiting rebuild with parts of c/n 1281, 9.02)		F-BUAV
			FAP9345
F-BUAZ	SNCAN/Stampe SV.4A	19	F-BBAB
F-BUBC	Reims FR172J Rocket	FR17200363	
F-BUBF	Reims/Cessna F150L (W/o 5.5.02)	F15000841	
F-BUBI	Reims/Cessna F172L	F17200892	
F-BUBK	Reims/Cessna F150L	F15000846	
F-BUBM	Reims/Cessna F150L	F15000849	
F-BUBN	Reims/Cessna F150L	F15000854	
F-BUBQ	Reims/Cessna F172L	F17200898	
F-BUBS	Reims/Cessna F150L	F15000855	
F-BUBT	Reims/Cessna FRA150L Aerobat	FRA1500199	
F-BUBX	Reims/Cessna F150L	F15000860	
F-BUCE	SOCATA MS.880B Rallye Club (To TU- ?)	2116	
F-BUCG	SOCATA MS.880B Rallye Club	2222	
F-BUCI	SOCATA MS.880B Rallye Club	2227	
F-BUCL	SOCATA MS.880B Rallye Club	2221	
F-BUCQ	SOCATA MS.880B Rallye Club	2242	
F-BUCT	SOCATA MS.893E Rallye 180GT Gaillard	12179	
F-BUCY	SOCATA MS.880B Rallye Club	2223	
F-BUDJ	Mudry CAP.10B	41	
F-BUDL	Mudry CAP.10B	44	
F-BUDM	Mudry CAP.10B	45	
F-BUDQ	Mudry CAP.10B	49	
F-BUDU(2)	Wassmer WA.40 Super IV	36	F-BIUB
			F-OBUB
F-BUDZ(2)	Christen Pitts S-2B	5131	F-WVDZ
F-BUED	Reims FR172J Rocket	FR17200371	
F-BUEG	Reims/Cessna F177RG Cardinal RG	F177RG0085	
F-BUEJ	Reims/Cessna F150L	F15000995	
F-BUEL	Reims/Cessna F150L	F15000997	
F-BUEM	Reims/Cessna F150L	F15000998	
F-BUEO	Reims/Cessna F172M	F17201136	
F-BUEQ	Reims/Cessna F172M	F17201025	
F-BUER	Reims/Cessna F172M	F17201026	
F-BUES	Reims/Cessna F172M	F17201027	
F-BUET	Reims/Cessna F172M	F17201028	
F-BUEY	Reims/Cessna F172M	F17201032	
F-BUGI	SOCATA MS.893E Rallye 180GT Gaillard	12229	
F-BUGK	SOCATA MS.893E Rallye 180GT Gaillard	12231	
F-BUGL	SOCATA MS.893E Rallye 180GT Gaillard	12232	
F-BUGO	SOCATA MS.893E Rallye 180GT Gaillard	12265	
F-BUGP	SOCATA MS.893E Rallye 180GT Gaillard	12266	
F-BUGU	SOCATA MS.880B Rallye Club	2258	
F-BUHA	Robin DR.400/120 Petit Prince	782	
F-BUHB	Robin DR.400/140 Major	783	
F-BUHC	Robin DR.400/180 Régent	785	
F-BUHD	Robin DR.400/2+2 Tricycle	787	
F-BUHE	Robin DR.400/140B Major	788	
F-BUHI	Robin DR.400/120 Petit Prince	792	
F-BUHJ	Robin DR.400/140 Major	793	
F-BUHL	Robin DR.400/160 Chevalier	795	
F-BUHN	Robin DR.400/2+2 Tricycle	801	
F-BUHO	Robin HR.100/210 Safari	158	
F-BUHP	Robin DR.400/140 Major	804	
F-BUHQ	Robin DR.400/120 Petit Prince	805	
F-BUHR	Robin DR.400/125 Petit Prince	806	
F-BUHT	Robin DR.400/140 Major	808	
F-BUHU	Robin DR.400/180 Régent	809	
F-BUHX	Robin DR.400/120 Petit Prince	810	
F-BUIJ	Piper PA-34-200 Seneca	34-7350204	F-ETAA
F-BUIQ	Piper PA-39 Twin Comanche C/R	39-80	N14473
			G-AYKO
			N8921Y
F-BUIR	Beech 60 Duke	P-87	TU-TEV
			(HB-GDX)
			N2850B
F-BUJC	SOCATA MS.880B Rallye 100ST	2289	
F-BUJF	SOCATA MS.893E Rallye 180GT Gaillard (Wfu)	12268	
F-BUJH	SOCATA MS.880B Rallye Club	2259	
F-BUJR	SOCATA MS.880B Rallye Club	2284	
F-BUKF	Wassmer WA.52 Europa	95	
F-BUKI	Wassmer WA.54 Atlantic	92	

F-BUKJ	Wassmer WA.52 Europa	98	
F-BUKK	Wassmer WA.54 Atlantic	99	
F-BUKL	Wassmer WA.52 Europa	101	
F-BUKS	Wassmer WA.52 Europa	108	
F-BUKT	Wassmer WA.54 Atlantic	94	
F-BUKV	Wassmer WA.52 Europa	118	
F-BULD	SOCATA MS.893E Rallye 180GT Gaillard	12305	
F-BULK	SOCATA Rallye 100S Sport	2293	
F-BULL	SOCATA Rallye 100S Sport	2294	
F-BULO	SOCATA Rallye 100S Sport	2297	
F-BULT	Procaer F.15A Picchio	15	I-LINV
F-BULU	SOCATA MS.880B Rallye Club	2303	
F-BULX	SOCATA MS.893E Rallye 180GT Gaillard	12274	
F-BUMA	Reims/Cessna F150L	F15001090	
	(Replacement fuselage fitted)		
F-BUMB	Reims FR172J Rocket	FR17200423	
F-BUMC	Reims/Cessna F150L	F15000863	
F-BUMD	Reims/Cessna F172L	F17200904	
F-BUME	Reims/Cessna F150L	F15000999	
F-BUMF	Reims FR172J Rocket	FR17200403	
F-BUMJ	Reims/Cessna F177RG Cardinal RG	F177RG0091	
F-BUMK	Reims/Cessna F177RG Cardinal RG	F177RG0071	(G-BAIV)
F-BUML	Reims/Cessna FRA150L Aerobat	FRA1500198	
F-BUMS	Reims/Cessna F150L	F15001007	
F-BUMT	Reims/Cessna F172M	F17201002	
F-BUMU	Reims/Cessna F172M	F17201004	
F-BUMV	Reims/Cessna F172M	F17201005	
F-BUMX	Piper PA-25-235 Pawnee C	25-5412	N8947L
F-BUMY	Reims/Cessna F172M (Dismantled)	F17201014	
F-BUNB	SOCATA MS.893E Rallye 180GT Gaillard	12276	(D-EKHM)
F-BUND	SOCATA MS.893E Rallye 180GT Gaillard	12278	
F-BUNG	SOCATA MS.893E Rallye 180GT Gaillard	12306	
F-BUNH	SOCATA MS.880B Rallye Club	2347	
F-BUNL	SOCATA Rallye 100S Sport	2340	
F-BUNM	SOCATA MS.880B Rallye Club	2352	
F-BUNP	SOCATA Rallye 100S Sport	2337	
F-BUNQ	SOCATA Rallye 100ST	2338	
F-BUNS	SOCATA Rallye 100S Sport	2342	
F-BUOF	Piper PA-25-235 Pawnee C	25-4382	4X-APR
			N4660Y
F-BUOG	Piper PA-18-150 Super Cub	18-8057	F-OCSG
			TT-BAA
			F-OCCE
			N4062Z
F-BUOJ	Piper PA-28-180 Cherokee Challenger	28-7305463	F-ETAE
F-BUOL	Piper PA-28-140 Cherokee E	28-7225130	HB-OML
			N15778
F-BUON	Beech C23 Sundowner	M-1448	
F-BUOS	Beech 58 Baron	TH-401	(D-IDUA)
F-BUOT	Piper PA-28-180 Cherokee Challenger	28-7305508	F-ETAK
F-BUOV	Grumman AA-5 Traveler	AA5-0410	N7110L
F-BUPA	Robin DR.400/120 Petit Prince	817	
F-BUPC	Robin DR.400/120 Petit Prince	821	
F-BUPE	Robin DR.400/140 Major	823	
F-BUPK	Robin DR.400/180 Régent	831	
F-BUPL	Robin DR.400/120 Petit Prince	832	
F-BUPO	Robin DR.400/120 Petit Prince	838	
F-BUPQ	Robin DR.400/120 Petit Prince	842	
F-BUPS	Robin DR.400/140 Major	852	
F-BUPT	Robin DR.400/140 Major	854	
F-BUPU	Robin DR.300/120 Petit Prince	635	PH-SRE
F-BUQB	Robin HR.200/120B	03	F-WUQB
F-BUQE	Piper PA-25-235 Pawnee C	25-4445	4X-APS
F-BUQF	Robin HR.200/120B Club	04	(D-ENQF)
			F-BUQF
			F-WUQF
F-BUQG	Robin HR.200/120	05	F-WUQG
F-BUQH	Robin HR.200/100 Club	06	F-WUQH
F-BUQL	Robin HR.200/100 Club	08	
F-BUQP	Aérospatiale SN.601 Corvette	4	F-WUQP
F-BUQY	Montgolfière Moderne MM18 O-56 HAFB	01	F-WUQY
F-BURE	Reims/Cessna F337G Skymaster	F33700062	
	(Reims-assembled 337G with US c/n 33701512)		
F-BURL	Reims/Cessna F150L	F15001019	
F-BURM	Reims/Cessna F177RG Cardinal RG	F177RG0084	
F-BURN	Reims/Cessna F150L	F15001028	
F-BURO	Reims/Cessna F172M	F17201048	
F-BURP	Reims FR172J Rocket	FR17200443	
F-BURQ	Reims FR172J Rocket	FR17200451	
F-BURU	Reims/Cessna F177RG Cardinal RG	F177RG0087	
F-BURV	Reims/Cessna F172M	F17201068	
F-BUSB	Robin DR.400/180 Remorqueur	862	
F-BUSC	Robin HR.100/210 Safari	170	
F-BUSE	Robin DR.400/160 Chevalier	865	
F-BUSF	Robin DR.400/2+2 Tricycle	869	
F-BUSG	Robin DR.400/160 Chevalier	871	
F-BUSH	Robin DR.400/140 Major	872	
F-BUSI	Robin HR.200/100 Club	10	
F-BUSM	Robin DR.400/180 Régent	878	
F-BUSN	Robin DR.400/140 Major	894	
F-BUSP	Robin HR.100/210 Safari	179	
F-BUSU	Robin DR.400/180 Régent	881	
F-BUSY	Robin DR.400/2+2 Tricycle	877	
F-BUTG	Cessna U206F Stationair (Dam. 8.10.00)	U20602123	N71140
F-BUTJ	Piper PA-28R-200 Cherokee Arrow II	28R-7335406	F-ETAI
F-BUTL	Piper PA-28R-200 Cherokee Arrow II	28R-7335010	N15063
F-BUTZ	Beech 95-C55 Baron (W/o 17.1.01)	TE-105	D-ILVA

F-BUUC	Piper PA-28-140 Cherokee F	28-7325567	N9506N
F-BUUD	Piper PA-28-140 Cherokee F	28-7325569	N9507N
F-BUUE	Piper PA-34-200 Seneca	34-7350336	F-ETAR
F-BUUH	Piper PA-28-180 Cherokee Archer	28-7405006	F-ETAT
F-BUUI	Piper PA-28R-200 Cherokee Arrow II	28R-7435012	F-ETAU
F-BUUK	Cessna 310Q	310Q0275	5H-MOW
			5Y-AOF
			N7775Q
F-BUUN	Piper PA-28-180 Cherokee Challenger	28-7305597	N56467
F-BUUO	Rockwell S.2R-600 Thrush Commander	1902R	
F-BUVK	SOCATA MS.894A Minerva 220	12090	
F-BUVL	SOCATA MS.893E Rallye 180GT Gaillard	12327	
F-BUVR	SOCATA MS.880B Rallye Club	2334	
F-BUVT	SOCATA MS.880B Rallye Club	2331	
F-BUVU	SOCATA MS.880B Rallye Club	2357	
F-BUVV	SOCATA MS.880B Rallye Club	2358	
F-BUVZ	Piper PA-30 Twin Comanche B	30-1379	TR-LKK
			N8253Y
F-BUXA	SOCATA Rallye 100S Sport	2364	
F-BUXB	Bell 47G-2	2445	G-BBKW
			N6770D
			ZK-HAQ
			N6770D
F-BUXC	SOCATA Rallye 100S Sport	2366	
F-BUXG	SOCATA MS.880B Rallye Club	2373	
F-BUXI	SOCATA MS.880B Rallye Club (Written off)	2389	
F-BUXK	SOCATA MS.893E Rallye 180GT Gaillard	12208	
F-BUXM	SOCATA MS.893E Rallye 180GT Gaillard	12210	
F-BUXP	SOCATA MS.893E Rallye 180GT Gaillard	12329	
F-BUXV	SOCATA MS.880B Rallye Club	2397	
F-BUXZ	SOCATA MS.880B Rallye Club	2404	
F-BUYJ	Cessna 182P Skylane	18262479	N52244
F-BUYK	Piper PA-23-250 Aztec E	27-7405263	F-ETAW
			N40528
F-BUYX	Bell 47G-2	2007	74+38,
			AS+399
			YA+033 ?
F-BUYY	Beech 95-B55 Baron	TC-1700	
F-BUZA	SOCATA MS.893E Rallye 180GT Gaillard	12213	
F-BUZB	SOCATA MS.893E Rallye 180GT Gaillard	12314	
F-BUZE	Piper PA-28R-200 Cherokee Arrow	28R-35188	OO-LGH
			N9472N
F-BUZF	Bellanca 17-31ATC Turbo Viking	75-31119	N9744E
F-BUZG	SOCATA MS.880B Rallye Club	2401	
F-BUZH	SOCATA MS.880B Rallye Club	2402	
F-BUZK	SOCATA MS.880B Rallye Club	2405	
F-BUZL	SOCATA MS.893E Rallye 180GT Gaillard	12212	
F-BUZN	SOCATA MS.893E Rallye 180GT Gaillard	12320	
F-BUZQ	SOCATA MS.893E Rallye 180GT Gaillard	12380	
F-BUZR	SOCATA MS.892E Rallye 150GT	12237	
F-BUZS	SOCATA MS.880B Rallye Club	2453	
F-BUZY	SOCATA MS.880B Rallye Club	2407	
F-BVAB	SOCATA MS.880B Rallye Club	2411	
F-BVAD	SOCATA MS.893E Rallye 180GT Gaillard	12381	
F-BVAI	SOCATA MS.880B Rallye Club	2416	
F-BVAK	SOCATA MS.880B Rallye Club	2430	
F-BVAR	SOCATA MS.880B Rallye Club	2461	
F-BVAS	SOCATA MS.880B Rallye Club	2455	
F-BVAU	SOCATA MS.880B Rallye Club	2431	F-BVAL
F-BVAV	SOCATA MS.893E Rallye 180GT Gaillard	12375	
F-BVAX	SOCATA MS.893E Rallye 180GT Gaillard	12385	
F-BVBI	Reims/Cessna F172M	F17201109	
F-BVBK	Reims/Cessna F150L	F15001065	
F-BVBL	Reims/Cessna F150L	F15001077	
F-BVBM	Reims FR172J Rocket	FR17200469	
F-BVBN	Reims FR172J Rocket	FR17200480	
F-BVBP	Reims/Cessna F172M	F17201057	
F-BVBQ	Reims FR172J Rocket	FR17200488	
F-BVBR	Reims FR172J Rocket	FR17200476	
F-BVBT	Reims FR172J Rocket	FR17200458	
F-BVBU	Reims/Cessna F150L	F15001082	
F-BVBV	Reims/Cessna F150L	F15001104	
F-BVBX	Reims/Cessna F150L	F15001114	
F-BVCA	Robin DR.400/2+2 Tricycle	897	
F-BVCB	Robin DR.400/2+2 Tricycle	907	
F-BVCE	Robin DR.400/140 Major	899	
F-BVCF	Robin DR.400/180 Régent	903	
F-BVCJ	Robin DR.400/180 Régent	898	
F-BVCK	Robin DR.400/180 Régent	912	
F-BVCL	Robin DR.400/140 Major	909	
F-BVCN	Robin HR.200/100 Club	22	
F-BVCR	Robin DR.400/2+2 Tricycle	915	
F-BVCV	Robin DR.400/140 Major	919	
F-BVCY	Robin DR.400/125 Petit Prince	923	
F-BVDA	Robin DR.400/180 Régent	922	
F-BVDC	Robin DR.400/140 Major	927	
F-BVDD	Robin DR.400/2+2 Tricycle	930	
F-BVDI	Robin DR.400/140 Major	911	
F-BVDJ	Robin DR.400/180 Régent	910	
F-BVDL	Robin DR.400/2+2 Tricycle	934	
F-BVDP	Robin DR.400/180 Régent	941	
F-BVDR	Robin DR.400/140 Major	939	
F-BVEA	Beech B24R Sierra 200	MC-235	
F-BVED	Beech 58 Baron	TH-443	
F-BVEE	Piper PA-34-200 Seneca (Dam. 1.10.00)	34-7450060	F-ETAY
F-BVEJ	Aerotek Pitts S-2A	2067	F-WVEJ
			G-BCGF
			N80038
F-BVEK	Cessna F172G (Wrecked)	F172-0217	CN-TZG
F-BVEL	Agusta-Bell 206B Jet Ranger	8402	
F-BVER	Mooney M.20C Aerostar 200	700045	F-OCRO
			N9432V
F-BVEY	Beech F33A Bonanza	CE-489	
F-BVFF	Aérospatiale/BAC Concorde 101	15	F-WJAN
F-BVFO	Agusta-Bell 47G	096	ALAT
			Fr.AF
F-BVFR	Agusta-Bell 47G-2	143	F-BTSR
			(F-BTSL)
			ALAT
F-BVFU	Bell 47G	1313	ALAT
F-BVFY	Agusta-Bell 47G-2	211	G-AWSK
			AAF: 3B-XB
F-BVFZ	Mooney M.20E Super 21	341	N6981U
F-BVGB	Airbus A300B2-1C (Stored, Hurn)	06	F-WVGB
F-BVGC	Airbus A300B2-1C (Stored, Hurn)	07	F-WVGC
F-BVHB	SOCATA MS.887 Rallye 125	2173	
F-BVHD	SOCATA MS.880B Rallye 100T	2503	
F-BVHG	SOCATA MS.893E Rallye 180GT	12439	
F-BVHH	SOCATA MS.893E Rallye 180GT	12440	
F-BVHI	SOCATA MS.893E Rallye 180GT	12441	
F-BVHK	SOCATA MS.893E Rallye 180GT	12443	
F-BVHM	SOCATA MS.893E Rallye 180GT	12317	F-BUZE
F-BVHR	SOCATA MS.893E Rallye 180GT	12446	
F-BVHS	SOCATA MS.893E Rallye 180GT	12447	
F-BVHT	SOCATA MS.893E Rallye 180GT	12448	
F-BVHV	SOCATA MS.880B Rallye 100T	2514	
F-BVHZ	SOCATA MS.880B Rallye 100S	2422	
F-BVIA	Reims/Cessna F172M	F17201128	
F-BVIB	Reims/Cessna FRA150L Aerobat	FRA1500235	
F-BVID	Reims/Cessna F172M	F17201168	
F-BVIE	Reims/Cessna F172M	F17201185	
F-BVIF	Reims/Cessna F172M	F17201200	
F-BVIH	Reims/Cessna F150L	F15001087	
F-BVII	Reims/Cessna F172M	F17201134	
F-BVIJ	Reims/Cessna F177RG Cardinal RG	F177RG0081	(G-BAOR)
F-BVIK	Reims/Cessna F177RG Cardinal RG	F177RG0103	
	(Fuselage stored)		
F-BVIM	Reims/Cessna F177RG Cardinal RG	F177RG0111	
F-BVIP	Reims/Cessna F177RG Cardinal RG	F177RG0104	
F-BVIR	Reims/Cessna F177RG Cardinal RG	F177RG0089	(D-EJXO)
F-BVIS	Reims FR172J Rocket	FR17200491	
F-BVIT	Reims/Cessna F337G Skymaster	F33700066	
	(Reims-assembled 337G with US c/n 33701560)		
F-BVIX	Reims/Cessna F172M	F17201239	
F-BVIY	Reims/Cessna F177RG Cardinal RG	F177RG0107	
F-BVIZ	Reims/Cessna F177RG Cardinal RG	F177RG0110	
F-BVJA	Piper PA-28-140 Cherokee Cruiser	28-7425145	N9615N
F-BVJG	Cessna 337D Super Skymaster	33701048	OO-DMN
F-BVJJ	Piper PA-34-200 Seneca	34-7450090	F-ETAZ
F-BVJN	Grumman AA-1B Trainer	AA1B-0369	N8869L
F-BVJS	Grumman AA-5 Traveler	AA5-0551	
F-BVJU	Cessna 185A Skywagon	185-0500	TR-LKR
			F-OBYQ
			N2500Z
F-BVJY	Cessna A188B Agtruck	18801389T	N9133G
F-WVKE	Aérospatiale SA.365 Dauphin	004	
F-WVKI	Aérospatiale AS.350 Ecureuil	002	
F-BVKQ	Bell 47G	722	Fr.Mil
F-BVLA	SOCATA MS.880B Rallye Club	2515	
F-BVLD	SOCATA MS.880B Rallye Club	2476	
F-BVLE	SOCATA MS.880B Rallye Club	2502	
F-BVLF	SOCATA MS.894E Minerva 220GT	12199	
F-BVLH	SOCATA MS.893E Rallye 180GT Gaillard	12450	
F-BVLI	SOCATA MS.887 Rallye 125	2168	
F-BVLN	CEA DR.253B Régent	189	OO-RJB
F-BVLZ	SOCATA MS.894A Minerva 220	12081	
F-BVMB	Robin DR.400/2+2 Tricycle	949	
F-BVMC	Robin DR.400/180 Régent	955	
F-BVMD	Robin DR.400/140 Major	957	
F-BVMF	Robin DR.400/120 Petit Prince	945	
F-BVMG	Robin DR.400/140 Major	887	(G-BBOG)
F-BVMH	Robin DR.400/160 Chevalier	958	
F-BVMK	Robin DR.400/120 Petit Prince	961	
F-BVML	Robin DR.400/2+2 Tricycle	972	
F-BVMP	Robin DR.400/180 Régent	908	
F-BVMQ	Robin DR.400/140 Major	967	
F-BVMR	Robin DR.400/140 Major	882	(G-BBOF)
			(D-EFDC)
F-BVNE	MS.880B Rallye Club	2520	
F-BVNG	MS.880B Rallye Club	2537	
F-BVNJ	MS.880B Rallye Club	2540	
F-BVNK	MS.893E Rallye 180GT Gaillard	12495	
F-BVNX	MS.893E Rallye 180GT Gaillard	12528	
F-BVNZ	MS.880B Rallye Club	2543	
F-BVOB	Piper PA-28-180 Cherokee Archer	28-7405113	F-ETBJ
F-BVOE	SNCAN/Stampe SV.4C	605	F-BDFA
F-BVOF	Piper PA-28-140 Cherokee	28-22046	6V-ACN
			5T-TAJ
			F-OCJC
			N7492R
F-BVOI	Piper PA-28-180 Cherokee Archer	28-7405131	F-ETBV
			N9565N
F-BVOJ	Piper PA-28-180 Cherokee Archer	28-7405133	F-ETBW
F-BVOL	Piper PA-28-180 Cherokee Archer	28-7405149	F-ETBZ
F-BVON	Piper PA-34-200 Seneca	34-7450159	F-ETBT

F-BVOP	Piper PA-28-180 Cherokee Archer	28-7405117	F-ETBL
F-BVOR	SOCATA ST-10 Diplomate	109	TU-TFR
			F-OCPF
F-BVOS	Beech V35B Bonanza	D-9286	TN-AEP
			F-BVOS
			TR-LSC
			F-OCRY
F-BVOZ	Piper PA-18 Super Cub 95	18-3162	OO-FBA
			OL-L84
			L-84
			53-4762
F-BVPG	Aérospatiale SN.601 Corvette	25	F-WNGU
F-BVPK	Aérospatiale SN.601 Corvette	7	N611AC
			F-OBZR
F-BVPN	Dassault Falcon 20E	311/515	F-WRQS
F-BVPR	Dassault Falcon 10	5	F-WVPR
			F-BVPR
			(F-V10F)
			F-WLCT
F-BVRC	Piper PA-28R-200 Cherokee Arrow II	28R-7435174	F-ETBI
F-BVRF	Enstrom F-28A	213	
F-BVRN	Grumman AA-1B Trainer	AA1B-0399	N8899L
F-BVRT	Beech 58 Baron	TH-488	
F-BVRX	Cessna 182P Skylane	18263110	N7326N
F-BVSA	Reims FR172J Rocket	FR17200502	
F-BVSC	Reims FR172J Rocket	FR17200506	
F-BVSD	Reims/Cessna F150L	F15001110	F-WLIT
F-BVSE	Reims/Cessna FTB.337G Super Skymaster	0001	F-WLIP
F-BVSG	Reims FR172J Rocket	FR17200508	
F-BVSJ	Reims/Cessna F172M	F17201187	
F-BVSK	Reims FR172J Rocket	FR17200511	
F-BVSL	Reims/Cessna F177RG Cardinal RG	F177RG0112	
F-BVSM	Reims/Cessna F177RG Cardinal RG	F177RG0113	
F-BVSN	Reims/Cessna F177RG Cardinal RG	F177RG0102	(G-BBNW)
F-BVSO	Reims/Cessna F172M	F17201190	
F-BVSP	Reims/Cessna FRA150L Aerobat	FRA1500248	
F-BVSR	Reims/Cessna F172M	F17201195	
F-BVST	Reims FR172J Rocket	FR17200513	
F-BVSU	Holste MH.1521 Broussard	022	ALAT
F-BVSV	Reims/Cessna F150L	F15001117	
F-BVTB	Beech C90 King Air	LJ-579	D-INAF
F-BVTF	Piper PA-28-180 Cherokee Archer	28-7405142	F-ETBP
F-BVTH	Piper PA-28-151 Cherokee Warrior	28-7415145	N9508N
F-BVTK	Piper PA-28-140 Cherokee Cruiser	28-7425255	N9549N
F-BVTL	Piper PA-28-180 Cherokee Archer	28-7405125	F-ETBM
F-BVTM	Piper PA-28-180 Cherokee Archer	28-7405147	F-ETBX
F-BVTN	Piper PA-28R-200 Cherokee Arrow II	28R-7435225	F-ETBY
F-BVTP	Piper PA-23-250 Aztec C	27-3901	N6598Y
F-BVTQ	Piper PA-28-180 Cherokee Archer	28-7405153	F-ETBU
F-BVTT	Piper PA-28R-200 Cherokee Arrow II	28R-7435202	F-ETBO
F-BVTX	Piper PA-23-250 Aztec D	27-4560	N94476
			HP-575
			(PT-DPD)
			N13927
F-BVUC	Piper PA-23-250 Aztec E	27-7305225	G-BCDX
			N40495
			N40504
F-BVUH	Beech C23 Sundowner	M-1408	F-BUIZ
			N58156
F-BVUJ	Piper PA-28-180 Cherokee Archer	28-7405144	F-ETBQ
F-BVUK	Piper PA-28-140 Cherokee Cruiser	28-7425262	N9532N
F-BVUM	Mooney M.20E Chaparral	700032	F-OCRM
F-BVUN	Bell 206A Jet Ranger	247	D-HAMO
F-BVUP	Piper PA-34-200 Seneca	34-7450199	F-VAAC
F-BVUS	Piper PA-28-151 Cherokee Warrior	28-7415462	N9620N
F-BVUV	Cessna 310Q	310Q1095	N1244G
F-BVVA	Piper PA-28-180 Cherokee Archer	28-7505061	N9631N
F-BVVB	Piper PA-28-151 Cherokee Warrior	28-7515165	N9636N
F-BVVC	Cessna 210L Centurion	21061114	N2153S
F-BVVI	Grumman AA-5 Traveler	AA5-0686	
F-BVVJ	Grumman AA-5B Tiger	AA5B-0008	N1508R
F-BVVT	Bellanca 7GCBC Citabria	845-75	OE-VPY
F-BVVX	Piper PA-28-235 Cherokee E	28-7110019	6V-ACO
			N11C
F-BVVY	Piper PA-28-180 Cherokee D	28-5336	6V-ADS
			TU-TEW
			N7925N
F-BVXB	Reims/Cessna F172M	F17201204	
F-BVXC	Reims/Cessna F150L	F15001123	
F-BVXD	Bell 47G	1458	F-SE . . /CNET
F-BVXE	Robin HR.100/250TR	502	D-EFIT
			F-BVDS
F-BVXF	Reims/Cessna F150L	F15001129	
F-BVXG	Reims/Cessna F150L	F15001131	
F-BVXN	Reims/Cessna F172M	F17201277	
F-BVXO	Reims FR172J Rocket	FR17200509	(D-EIQT)
F-BVXQ	Reims FR172J Rocket	FR17200528	(F-BSGY)
F-BVXR	Reims/Cessna F172M	F17201347	D-EBJA
F-BVXT	Reims/Cessna F150M	F15001187	
F-BVXX	Reims FR172J Rocket	FR17200523	
F-BVYC	Robin HR.200/100 Club	51	
F-BVYD	Robin DR.400/2+2 Tricycle	987	
F-BVYF	Robin DR.400/160 Chevalier	980	
F-BVYI	Robin HR.100/250TR	504	
F-BVYK	Robin DR.400/140 Major	995	
F-BVYR	Robin DR.400/120 Petit Prince	984	
F-BVYS	Robin HR.200/100 Club	60	

F-BVYT	Robin DR.400/180 Régent	993	
F-BVYU	Robin HR.200/100 Club	57	
F-BVYV	Robin HR.200/100 Club	58	
F-BVYZ	Robin DR.400/140 Major	1003	
F-BVZC	SOCATA MS.893E Rallye 180GT Gaillard	12490	
F-BVZI	SOCATA MS.893E Rallye 180GT Gaillard	12488	
F-BVZU	SOCATA MS.893E Rallye 180GT Gaillard	12562	
F-BXAM	Cessna U206F Stationair	U20602751	N35844
F-BXAP	Beech C90 King Air	LJ-522	D-IHVB
F-BXAT	Cessna 172K (Damaged 12.2.00)	17258289	N79964
F-BXAU	Cessna 182P Skylane	18263417	N9651G
F-BXBC	Montgolfière-Moderne MM20 O-65 HAFB	9	
F-BXBF	Montgolfière-Moderne MM18 O-65 HAFB	14	
F-BXBS	Montgolfière-Moderne MM20 O-70 HAFB	25	
	(Also has Cameron c/n 222)		
F-BXCE	Cerva CE-43 Guepard (CE-44 prototype)	459	F-WXCE
	(Derelict Pontoise)		
F-BXCF	Wassmer WA.54 Atlantic	132	
F-BXCH	Wassmer WA.54 Atlantic	146	
F-BXCI	Cerva CE-43 Guepard	460	
F-BXCL	Wassmer WA.54 Atlantic	139	
F-BXCM	Wassmer WA.54 Atlantic	140	
F-BXCO	Cerva CE-43 Guepard	461	
F-BXCP	Holste MH.1521M Broussard	149	ALAT
F-BXCV	Cerva CE-43 Guepard	474	
F-BXDJ	SOCATA Rallye 100ST	2617	
F-BXDM	SOCATA MS.893E Rallye 180GT Gaillard	12636	
F-BXDN	SOCATA MS.893E Rallye 180GT Gaillard	12578	
F-BXDO	SOCATA MS.893E Rallye 180GT Gaillard	12579	
F-BXDP	SOCATA MS.893E Rallye 180GT Gaillard	12580	
F-BXDQ	SOCATA MS.893E Rallye 180GT Gaillard	12581	
F-BXDR	SOCATA MS.893E Rallye 180GT Gaillard	12602	
F-BXDS	SOCATA MS.893E Rallye 180GT Gaillard	12603	
F-BXEC	Robin DR.400/140 Major	954	
F-BXED	Robin DR.400/2+2 Tricycle	983	
F-BXEE	Robin DR.400/140 Major (Dismantled)	999	
F-BXEK	Robin DR.400/120 Petit Prince	1011	
F-BXEN	Robin HR.200/120B	62	
F-BXEO	Robin DR.400/2+2 Tricycle	1017	
F-BXEQ	Robin DR.400/140 Major	1019	
F-BXET	Robin DR.400/2+2 Tricycle	1024	
F-BXEU	Robin DR.400/140 Major	1023	
F-BXEV	Robin HR.200/120B	65	
F-BXEX	Robin HR.200/120	52	(G-BCMX)
F-BXEZ	Robin DR.400/2+2 Tricycle	1026	
F-WXFK	Aérospatiale AS.332C Super Puma	2006	
F-BXGG	Robin HR.100/250TR Président	516	
F-BXGJ	Robin HR.100/250TR Président	518	
F-BXGN	Robin HR.100/250TR Président	522	
F-BXGQ	Robin HR.100/250TR Président	542	
F-BXGS	Robin HR.100/250TR Président	544	
F-BXGT	Robin HR.100/250TR Président	545	
F-BXGU	Robin HR.100/250TR Président	546	
F-BXGX	Robin HR.100/250TR Président	548	
F-BXGY	Robin HR.100/250TR Président	549	
F-BXHD	Mudry CAP.10B	60	
F-BXHE	Mudry CAP.10B	61	
F-BXHF	Mudry CAP.10B	63	
F-BXHG	Mudry CAP.10B	64	
F-BXHL	Mudry CAP.10B	69	
F-BXHN	Mudry CAP.10B	71	
F-BXHO	Mudry CAP.10B	75	
F-BXHR	Mudry CAP.10B	79	
F-BXHS	Mudry CAP.10B	81	
F-BXHT	Mudry CAP.10B	82	
F-BXHU	Mudry CAP.10B	83	
F-BXHV	Mudry CAP.10B	85	
F-BXHX	Mudry CAP.10B	90	
F-BXIB	Reims/Cessna F172M	F17201307	
F-BXID	Reims/Cessna F177RG Cardinal RG	F177RG0128	
F-BXIE	Reims/Cessna F177RG Cardinal RG	F177RG0130	
F-BXIF	Reims/Cessna F150M	F15001179	
F-BXIG	Reims/Cessna F150M (W/o 1.8.03)	F15001162	
F-BXII	Reims/Cessna F150M	F15001202	(OE-ATZ)
F-BXIL	Reims/Cessna FTB.337G Super Skymaster	0034	
F-BXIN	Reims/Cessna F172M	F17201331	
F-BXIP	Reims FR172J Rocket	FR17200553	(F-BPQQ)
F-BXIT	Reims/Cessna F172M	F17201345	
F-BXIU	Reims/Cessna F172M	F17201351	
F-BXIV	Reims/Cessna F172M	F17201349	
F-BXIX	Reims/Cessna F172M	F17201357	
F-BXIY	Reims/Cessna F172M	F17201359	
F-BXJB	Robin DR.400/180 Régent	1032	
F-BXJF	Robin DR.400/2+2 Tricycle	1035	
F-BXJI	Robin DR.400/180 Régent	1040	
F-BXJK	Robin HR.200/120B	69	
F-BXJN	Robin DR.400/140 Major	1048	
F-BXJO	Robin DR.400/2+2 Tricycle	1046	
F-BXJP	Robin DR.400/180 Régent	1045	
F-BXJQ	Robin HR.200/100 Club	71	
F-BXJS	Robin HR.200/IOOS Club	73	
F-BXJU	Robin DR.400/120 Petit Prince	1054	
F-BXJV	Robin DR.400/180 Régent	1056	
F-BXJX	Robin DR.400/140 Major	1058	
F-BXJZ	Robin DR.400/2+2 Tricycle	1059	
F-BXLF	Beech 58 Baron	TH-647	
F-BXLM	Mooney M.20E Chaparral	21-1177	

F-BXLQ	Reims/Cessna FT337GP Super Skymaster (Reims-assembled P337G Pressurized Skymaster c/n P3370150)	FP33700009	N14491
F-BXLV	Agusta-Bell 206B Jet Ranger	8508	
F-BXLZ	Piper PA-34-200 Seneca	34-7450216	F-VAAF
F-BXMA	SOCATA MS.893E Rallye 180GT Gaillard	12607	
F-BXMB	SOCATA MS.892E Rallye 150GT	2628	
F-BXML	Cessna F172G	F172-0225	OO-WIG PH-AFF
F-BXMP	SOCATA MS.880B Rallye Club	2560	
F-BXMS	SOCATA Rallye 235E Gabier	12691	
F-BXMT	SOCATA Rallye 235E Gabier	12692	
F-BXMU	SOCATA MS.880B Rallye Club	2589	
F-BXMV	SOCATA MS.892E Rallye 150GT	12500	
F-BXNB	Reims/Cessna F177RG Cardinal RG	F177RG0134	
F-BXNC	Reims/Cessna F337G Skymaster (Reims-assembled 337G with US c/n 33701614)	F33700074	F-WLIN
F-BXNE	Reims/Cessna F177RG Cardinal RG	F177RG0132	
F-BXNG	Reims/Cessna F150M	F15001248	
F-BXNH	Reims/Cessna F150M	F15001244	
F-BXNM	Reims FR172J Rocket (Wrecked)	FR17200531	
F-BXNN	Reims/Cessna F150M	F15001207	(G-BDEO)
F-BXNO	Reims/Cessna F150M	F15001232	
F-BXNQ	Reims/Cessna F150M	F15001211	
F-BXNR	Reims/Cessna F150M	F15001282	
F-BXNS	Reims/Cessna F150M	F15001150	(D-EDNW)
F-BXNT	Reims/Cessna F150M	F15001167	
F-BXNU	Reims/Cessna F150M	F15001246	
F-BXNX	Reims/Cessna F150M	F15001218	(I-BONJ)
F-BXNZ	Reims/Cessna F150M	F15001239	
F-BXOB	Piper PA-28R-200 Cherokee Arrow II	28R-7435198	OO-FEY N41551
F-BXON	Beech E90 King Air	LW-161	
F-BXOR	Beech 58 Baron	TH-679	
F-BXPF	Bell 206A Jet Ranger	306	G-AWRI
F-BXPM	Piper PA-28R-200 Cherokee Arrow II	28R-7335127	LX-SIM N16323
F-BXPO	Cessna 340A	340A0053	N98599
F-BXPP	Piper PA-23-250 Aztec E	27-7654053	F-VAAI N9663N
F-BXPQ	Piper PA-28-151 Cherokee Warrior	28-7615122	N9521N
F-BXPR	Rockwell Commander 114	14054	F-WXPR N4724W
F-BXPS	Rockwell Commander 112TC	13026	F-WXPS
F-BXPX	Piper PA-39 Twin Comanche C/R	39-51	TR-LPH (F-OCOO) N8894Y
F-BXPY	Beech C90 King Air	LJ-684	
F-BXQC	Zlin Z.526 Trenér Master	1289	D-EKOM
F-BXQD	Reims/Cessna F172M	F17201412	
F-BXQG	Reims/Cessna F177RG Cardinal RG	F177RG0141	F-WLIO
F-BXQH	Reims/Cessna F150M	F15001253	
F-BXQI	Reims/Cessna F172M	F17201386	
F-BXQK	Reims/Cessna F172M	F17201388	
F-BXQM	Reims/Cessna F150M	F15001296	(F-BXZD)
F-BXQN	Reims/Cessna F150M	F15001300	
F-BXQO	Reims/Cessna F150M	F15001297	
F-BXQP	Reims/Cessna F150M	F15001284	
F-BXQQ	Reims/Cessna F172M	F17201434	
F-BXQT	Reims/Cessna F150M	F15001307	
F-BXQV	Reims/Cessna F172M	F17201464	
F-BXQX	Reims/Cessna F177RG Cardinal RG	F177RG0145	
F-BXQZ	Reims/Cessna F150M	F15001291	
F-BXRA	Robin DR.400/160 Chevalier	1062	
F-BXRB	Robin DR.400/140 Major	1063	
F-BXRD	Robin DR.400/140B Major	1064	
F-BXRG	Robin DR.400/160 Chevalier	1066	
F-BXRJ	Robin HR.200/100 Club	74	
F-BXRL	Robin HR.100/210 Safari	206	
F-BXRM	Robin DR.400/140 Major	1071	
F-BXRN	Robin DR.400/120 Petit Prince	1073	
F-BXRO	Robin DR.400/2+2 Tricycle	1074	
F-BXRP	Robin DR.400/160 Chevalier	1076	
F-BXRR	Robin DR.400/140B Major	1081	
F-BXRS	Robin DR.400/160 Chevalier	1082	
F-BXRU	Robin DR.400/2+2 Tricycle	1084	
F-BXRV	Robin DR.400/160 Chevalier	1086	
F-BXRX	Robin DR.400/2+2 Tricycle	1085	
F-BXRY	Robin DR.400/2+2 Tricycle	1089	
F-BXRZ	Robin DR.400/140B Major	1087	
F-BXSC	Piper PA-28-181 Archer II	28-7690068	
F-BXSD	Piper PA-28R-200 Cherokee Arrow II	28R-7635100	(F-OCHB) F-BXSD
F-BXSE	Piper PA-32R-300 Cherokee Lance	32R-7680073	
F-BXSG	Cessna A185F Skywagon (Reims-assembled with "c/n" 0002)	18502844	N1466F
F-BXSK	Piper PA-31T Cheyenne	31T-7620020	
F-BXSL	Beech C90 King Air	LJ-648	
F-BXSM	Piper PA-32R-300 Cherokee Lance	32R-7680156	
F-BXSO	Beech A36 Bonanza	E-806	
F-BXSP	Beech V35B Bonanza	D-9615	N4372W
F-BXSQ	Piper PA-34-200T Seneca II (Stored unmarked since 6.99, but reserved as F-OHCR)	34-7670160	
F-BXSS	Robin DR.400/2+2 Tricycle	1109	
F-BXTD	SOCATA Rallye 100ST	2621	
F-BXTE	SOCATA Rallye 150ST	2662	
F-BXTL	SOCATA MS.880B Rallye Club	2622	
F-BXTM	SOCATA MS.880B Rallye Club	2623	

F-BXTP	SOCATA Rallye 150ST	2668	
F-BXTS	SOCATA Rallye 150ST	2667	
F-BXTT	SOCATA MS.880B Rallye Club	2627	
F-BXTU	SOCATA MS.880B Rallye Club	2717	
F-BXTV	SOCATA MS.880B Rallye Club	2670	
F-BXTZ	SOCATA MS.893E Rallye 180GT Gaillard	12676	
F-BXUD	Cameron V-56 HAFB	229	
F-BXUS	Chaize CS.2000F12 HAFB	006	
F-BXUX	Cameron O-77 HAFB	354	
F-BXUZ	Thunder AX7/65 HAFB	128	
F-BXVF	Robin DR.400/140B Major	1097	
F-BXVJ	Robin HR.100/285 Tiara	536	
F-BXVK	Robin HR.200/100 Club	80	
F-BXVM	Robin DR.400/2+2 Tricycle	1101	
F-BXVO	Robin HR.200/lOOS Club	79	
F-BXVP	Robin DR.400/120 Petit Prince	1104	
F-BXVQ	Robin HR.200/100 Club	85	
F-BXVT	Robin DR.400/120 Petit Prince	1105	
F-BXVY	Robin DR.400/180 Régent	1111	
F-BXXG	Bell 47G-2	1638	ALAT N2857B
F-BXXH	Agusta-Bell 47G-2	055	ALAT
F-BXXJ	Agusta-Bell 47G-2	106	ALAT
F-BXXK	Agusta-Bell 47G	069	ALAT F-BHPG
F-BXXL	Agusta-Bell 47G-2	114	ALAT
F-BXXO	Agusta-Bell 47G-2	189	ALAT
F-BXXP	Bell 47G-2	1627	ALAT Fr.AF N2846B
F-BXXQ	Bell 47G-2	1639	ALAT Fr.AF N2858B
F-BXXR	Mudry CAP.10B	32	D-EGTR F-BUDB
F-BXXS	Agusta-Bell 47G	078	ALAT
F-BXXU	Agusta-Bell 47G-2	154	ALAT
F-BXXX	Agusta-Bell 47G-2	186	ALAT
F-BXXY	Agusta-Bell 47G-2	203	F-MJAO ALAT
F-BXXZ	Bell 47G-2 (Badly damaged near Fabregues, Spain 27.10.01)	1636	D-HAFU F-BILG Fr.Mil N2855B
F-BXYD	SOCATA Rallye 150ST	2693	
F-BXYE	SOCATA Rallye 235E Gabier	12699	
F-BXYH	SOCATA MS.880B Rallye Club	2720	
F-BXYI	SOCATA MS.880B Rallye Club	2721	
F-BXYJ	SOCATA MS.893E Rallye 180GT Gaillard	12570	Fr.AF
F-BXYS	SOCATA Rallye 235E Gabier	12709	
F-BXYU	SOCATA Rallye 235E Gabier (Dam 11.3.04)	12711	
F-BXYV	SOCATA Rallye 235E Gabier	12712	
F-BXYY	SOCATA Rallye 235E Gabier	12769	
F-BXZD	Reims/Cessna F150M	F15001245	
F-BXZF	Reims/Cessna F172M	F17201268	
F-BXZG	Reims/Cessna F150M	F15001278	
F-BXZH	Beech N35 Bonanza	D-6636	I-SCAI HB-EIH
F-BXZI	Cessna 182P Skylane (Reims-assembled with "c/n" 0046)	18264310	N1393M
F-BXZJ	Reims/Cessna F172M	F17201403	
F-BXZL	Reims/Cessna F172M	F17201245	
F-BXZM	Reims/Cessna F172M	F17201247	
F-BXZO	Reims/Cessna F172M	F17201274	
F-BXZP	Reims/Cessna F172M	F17201283	
F-BXZQ	Reims/Cessna F172M	F17201285	
F-BXZR	Reims/Cessna F172M	F17201292	
F-BXZS	Reims/Cessna F172M	F17201301	
F-BXZT	Reims/Cessna F172M	F17201330	(G-BDEP) (OY-BIB)
F-BXZU	Bell 47G-2	1623	ALAT Fr.AF N2842B
F-BXZX	Reims/Cessna F172M	F17201367	
F-BXZZ	Reims/Cessna F172M	F17201383	
F-BYAJ	Aerotek Pitts S-2A	2195	G-BGSD N31458
F-BYAO	Fokker F.27 Friendship 100	10127	F-WYAO F-BYAO VH-EWA VH-TFH PH-FAX
F-BYAS	Mooney M.20J Model 201	24-0380	
F-BYAX	Nord N.1101 Noralpha	15	CEV F-BBJJ
F-BYCK	Wassmer WA.54 Atlantic	124	HB-DCN F-BUKY
F-BYCZ	Aérospatiale SA.315B Lama	2395	OE-EXW
F-WZAV	Bede BD-5J	50005	N150BD
F-WZAZ	Stampe SV.4L (Lycoming conversion)	01	
F-WZCG	Mudry CAP.X	02	
F-WZCH	Mudry CAP.232	001	F-WWZH F-WZCH
F-WZCI	Mudry CAP.231EX	01	
F-WZCJ	Sukhoi SU.26MX	unkn	
F-WZCY	Sud Avn SA.330 Puma	02	F-ZWWO
F-WZJF	Microjet 200	01	

F-WZJI	Aérospatiale AS.355 Ecureuil 2	002	
F-WZJY	Robin R.3000/140PRV	001	
F-WZLK	Aérospatiale AS.332L2 Super Puma	2298	
F-WZLQ(2)	Fouga CM-170 Magister	126	Fr.AF
F-BZZZ	Bellanca 8KCAB Decathlon	173-75	F-BZAA
			F-WZAA
F-GAAB	Reims/Cessna FRA150M Aerobat	FRA1500290	
F-GAAC	Reims/Cessna F177RG Cardinal RG	F177RG0142	
F-GAAE	Reims/Cessna F177RG Cardinal RG	F177RG0147	
F-GAAF	Reims/Cessna F177RG Cardinal RG	F177RG0148	
F-GAAH	Reims/Cessna F177RG Cardinal RG	F177RG0153	
F-GAAJ	Reims/Cessna F172M	F17201462	
F-GAAK	Reims/Cessna F172M	F17201465	
F-GAAN	Reims/Cessna FT337GP Super Skymaster	FP33700016	
	(Reims-assembled P337G Pressurized Skymaster US c/n P3370229)		
F-GAAO	Reims/Cessna F177RG Cardinal RG	F177RG0150	
F-GAAV	Reims/Cessna F150M	F15001324	
F-GAAY	Reims/Cessna F150M	F15001327	
F-GABB	Robin DR.400/2+2 Tricycle	1114	
F-GABD	Robin DR.400/2+2 Tricycle	1118	
F-GABE	Robin DR.400/180 Régent	1119	
F-GABG	Robin DR.400/2+2 Tricycle	1121	
F-GABH	Robin DR.400/120 Petit Prince	1122	
F-GABJ	Robin DR.400/2+2 Tricycle	1125	
F-GABK	Robin DR.400/2+2 Tricycle	1126	
F-GABM	Robin HR.200/100S Club	94	
F-GABN	Robin DR.400/140B Major 80	1132	
F-GABQ	Robin DR.400/180 Régent	1135	
F-GABT	Robin DR.400/180 Régent	1138	
F-GABZ	Robin DR.400/160 Chevalier	1142	
F-GACF	SOCATA MS.880B Rallye Club	2780	
F-GACJ	SOCATA Rallye 100ST	2761	
F-GACK	SOCATA Rallye 100ST	2762	
F-GACL	SOCATA MS.880B Rallye Club	2781	
F-GACM	SOCATA MS.880B Rallye Club	2782	
F-GACO	SOCATA MS.880B Rallye Club	2778	
F-GACP	SOCATA Rallye 235E Gabier	12763	
F-GACR	SOCATA Rallye 235E Gabier	12764	
F-GACS	SOCATA MS.893E Rallye 180GT Gaillard	12724	
F-GADC	Fournier RF-6B-100	15	
F-GADE	Fournier RF-6B-100	6	
F-GADH	Fournier RF-6B-100	10	
F-GADI	Fournier RF-6B-100	9	
F-GADJ	Fournier RF-6B-100	11	
F-GADK	Fournier RF-6B-100	12	
F-GADL	Fournier RF-6B-100	13	
F-GADM	Fournier RF-6B-100	29	
F-GADN	Fournier RF-6B-100	16	
F-GADQ	Fournier RF-6B-100	19	
F-GADS	Fournier RF-6B-100	20	
F-GADT	Fournier RF-6B-100	21	
F-GADV	Fournier RF-6B-100	23	
F-GADY	Fournier RF-6B-100	25	
F-GAED	Robin DR.400/140B Major 80	1146	
F-GAEE	Robin DR.400/160 Chevalier	1147	
F-GAEF	Robin DR.400/160 Chevalier	1148	
F-GAEG	Robin DR.400/120 Petit Prince	1149	
F-GAEJ	Robin DR.400/180 Régent	1156	
F-GAEK	Robin DR.400/120 Petit Prince	1151	
F-GAEP	Robin DR.400/140B Major 80	1159	
F-GAEQ	Robin HR.200/100S Club	99	
F-GAET	Robin DR.400/140B Major 80	1164	
F-GAEX	Robin DR.400/140B Major 80	1168	
F-GAEZ	Robin DR.400/2+2 Tricycle	1170	
F-GAFG	SOCATA MS.880B Rallye Club	2815	
F-GAFN	SOCATA MS.893E Rallye 180GT Gaillard	12738	
F-GAFP	SOCATA MS.880B Rallye Club	2852	
F-GAFQ	SOCATA MS.892E Rallye 150GT	12823	
F-GAFU	SOCATA MS.880B Rallye Club	2850	
F-GAFV	SOCATA MS.880B Rallye Club	2851	
F-GAGA	Reims/Cessna F177RG Cardinal RG	F177RG0154	
F-GAGD	Reims/Cessna F177RG Cardinal RG	F177RG0157	
F-GAGE	Reims/Cessna F177RG Cardinal RG	F177RG0158	
F-GAGG	Reims/Cessna F177RG Cardinal RG	F177RG0160	
F-GAGI	Reims/Cessna F150M	F15001276	(G-BDPE)
F-GAGL	Reims/Cessna F150M	F15001337	
F-GAGN	Reims/Cessna F172M	F17201387	
F-GAGO	Reims/Cessna F150M	F15001317	
F-GAGR	Reims FR172J Rocket	FR17200583	
F-GAGS	Reims FR172J Rocket	FR17200563	
F-GAGT	Reims/Cessna F172M	F17201494	
F-GAGV	Reims/Cessna F172N	F17201583	
F-GAGX	Reims/Cessna F172M	F17201498	
F-GAGY	Reims/Cessna FR172K Hawk XP	FR17200601	
F-GAHA	Robin DR.400/140B Major 80	1169	
F-GAHB	Robin DR.400/140B Major 80	1171	
F-GAHC	Robin DR.400/2+2 Tricycle	1172	
F-GAHE	Robin DR.400/2+2 Tricycle (Damaged 28.3.99)	1174	
F-GAHG	Robin DR.400/140B Major 80	1176	
F-GAHH	Robin DR.400/2+2 Tricycle	1177	
F-GAHK	Robin DR.400/140B Major 80	1180	
F-GAHM	Robin DR.400/120 (Originally DR.400/140B)	1183	
F-GAHN	Robin DR.400/140B Major 80	1184	
F-GAHP	Robin DR.400/2+2 Tricycle	1186	
F-GAHQ	Robin DR.400/2+2 Tricycle	1187	
F-GAHR	Robin DR.400/180 Régent	1188	
F-GAHS	Robin DR.400/2+2 Tricycle	1189	
F-GAHV	Robin DP.400/2+2 Tricycle	1191	
F-GAHX	Robin DR.400/2+2 Tricycle	1192	
F-GAHY	Robin DR.400/160 Chevalier	1193	
F-GAHZ	Robin HR.200/100 Club	103	
F-GAIB	Wassmer WA.54 Atlantic	149	
F-GAIC	Wassmer WA.81 Piranha	803	F-WAIC
F-GAIE	Wassmer WA.54 Atlantic	150	
F-GAIF	Wassmer WA.81 Piranha	804	
F-GAIG	Wassmer WA.80 Piranha	806	
F-GAIK	Wassmer WA.81 Piranha	808	
F-GAIQ	Wassmer WA.81 Piranha	815	
F-GAIT	Wassmer WA.81 Piranha	820	
F-GAIU	Wassmer WA.81 Piranha	822	
F-GAJB	Piper PA-28-151 Cherokee Warrior	28-7615188	F-GALE
			N9550N
F-GAJF	Piper PA-28R-200 Cherokee Arrow II	28R-7635357	
F-GAJM	Hughes 269C	114-0373	
F-GAJQ	Grumman G.164A Agcat	1277	N8903H
F-GAJU	Grumman AA-1B Trainer	AA1B-0664	
F-GAKB	SOCATA MS.880B Rallye Club	2887	
F-GAKD	SOCATA Rallye 235E Gabier	12830	
F-GAKG	SOCATA MS.893E Rallye 180GT Gaillard	12790	
F-GAKK	SOCATA MS.880B Rallye Club	2946	
F-GAKO	SOCATA MS.880B Rallye Club	2894	
F-GAKV	SOCATA MS.893E Rallye 180GT Gaillard	12792	
F-GAKX	SOCATA MS.880B Rallye Club	2912	
F-GALA	Piper PA-28-181 Cherokee Archer II	28-7690210	N9541N
F-GALC	Piper PA-28-181 Cherokee Archer II	28-7690147	N9517N
F-GALD	Piper PA-31T Cheyenne	31T-7620032	
F-GALH	Piper PA-28R-200 Cherokee Arrow II	28R-7635283	N75194
F-GALN	Beech 200T Super King Air	BB-186/BT-1	
F-GALP	Beech 200T Super King Air	BB-203/BT-2	
F-GALQ	Agusta-Bell 47G-2	108	I-MICO
			ALAT
F-GALY	Piper PA-23-250 Aztec E	27-7654101	F-VAAL
			N62633
F-GAMC	IRMA/Sud Avn SA.316B Alouette III	5310	HC-BNU
			F-GAMC
F-GAMD	Bell 47G-2	2005	G-BAZO
			9J-RAD
			VP-RAD
			ZS-HBE
			N5187B
F-GAME	Piper PA-38-112 Tomahawk	38-78A0655	PH-SRT
			N9704N
F-GAMG	Hughes 369D	106-0009D	
F-GAMJ	Cessna U206G Stationair II	U20603638	F-WAMJ
			F-GAMJ
			N7369N
F-GAMO	Beech 58 Baron	TH-818	
F-GAMT	Enstrom F.280C Shark	1062	
F-GAMX	Cessna 182J Skylane	18256812	CS-AGM
			F-OCKG
			5N-AFU
			N2712F
F-GANB	Fournier RF-6B-100	30	
F-GANC	Fournier RF-6B-100	31	
F-GAND	Fournier RF-6B-100	32	
F-GANE	Fournier RF-6B-100	33	
F-GANF	Fournier RF-6B-120	44	F-WANF
F-GANG	Fournier RF-6B-100	35	
F-GANH	Fournier RF-6B-100	36	
F-GANK	Fournier RF-6B-100	41	
F-GANL	Fournier RF-6B-100 (Dismantled)	40	
F-GANQ	Chaize CS.2200F12 HAFB	061	
F-GANU	Bell 47G-2	1633	G-BEUG
			EP-HAV
			N6764
			Fr.AF
			N2852B
F-GANX	Bell 47G-2	2434	G-BBUK
			N6751D
F-GANY	Bell 47G-2	1635	G-BEUH
			EP-HAW
			N6765
			Fr.AF
			N2854B
F-GANZ	Cessna 172RG Cutlass RG	172RG0638	N6348V
F-GAOB	Robin DR.400/180 Régent	1195	
F-GAOD	Robin DR.400/2+2 Tricycle	1201	
F-GAOE	Robin HR.200/100S Club	104	
F-GAOG	Robin DR.400/120A Petit Prince	1213	
F-GAOH	Robin DR.400/2+2 Tricycle	1217	
F-GAOJ	Robin HR.200/100 Club	105	
F-GAOK	Robin DR.400/2+2 Tricycle	1218	
F-GAOM	Robin DR.400/2+2 Tricycle	1220	
F-GAON	Robin DR.400/140B Major 80	1238	
F-GAOP	Robin DR.400/120 Petit Prince	1540	
F-GAOQ	Robin DR.400/2+2 Tricycle	1239	
F-GAOU	Robin DR.400/160 Chevalier	1226	
F-GAOV	Robin DR.400/140B Major 80	1232	
F-GAOX	Robin DR.400/2+2 Tricycle	1240	
F-GAOY	Robin DR.400/2+2 Tricycle	1253	
F-GAPF	Piper PA-28R-201 Cherokee Arrow III	28R-7737064	N9504N
F-GAPI	Aerotek Pitts S-2A	2089	N28MC
F-GAPL	Piper PA-25-235 Pawnee C	25-4714	N4907Y

F-GAPM	Cessna A188B AgTruck	18802851T	N731EY
F-GAPZ	Beech A36 Bonanza	E-1086	
F-GAQB	Reims/Cessna F150M	F15001414	
F-GAQC	Reims/Cessna F150M	F15001420	
F-GAQG	Reims/Cessna FR172K Hawk XP	FR17200605	
F-GAQL	Reims/Cessna F182Q Skylane	F18200036	
F-GAQO	Reims/Cessna F172M	F17201501	
F-GAQP	Reims/Cessna F172M	F17201391	
F-GAQQ	Reims FR172J Rocket	FR17200580	
F-GAQR	Reims/Cessna F182Q Skylane	F18200053	
F-GAQT	Reims FR172J Rocket	FR17200566	
F-GAQV	Reims/Cessna F150M	F15001311	
F-GAQY	Reims/Cessna F177RG Cardinal RG	F177RG0144	
F-GAQZ	Reims/Cessna F172M	F17201496	
F-GARD	SOCATA MS.893E Rallye 180GT Gaillard	12960	
F-GARH	SOCATA MS.880B Rallye Club	2919	
F-GARI	SOCATA MS.880B Rallye Club	2920	
F-GARO	SOCATA MS.880B Rallye Club	2939	
F-GARP	SOCATA MS.880B Rallye Club	2940	
F-GARQ	SOCATA MS.880B Rallye Club	2941	
F-GASB	Reims/Cessna F172M	F17201508	
F-GASE	Reims/Cessna F172M	F17201390	
F-GASF	Reims/Cessna F172M	F17201507	
F-GASH	Reims/Cessna F172M	F17201511	
F-GASK	Reims/Cessna F150M	F15001323	
F-GASM	Reims/Cessna F150M	F15001401	
F-GASO	Reims/Cessna F172N	F17201522	
F-GASS	Reims/Cessna F150M	F15001378	
F-GASV	Reims/Cessna F152	F15201435	(F-GAQH)
F-GASX	Reims/Cessna F172N	F17201574	
F-GASY	Reims/Cessna F150M	F15001386	F-WZDR
F-GASZ	Reims/Cessna F152	F15201429	F-WZDA
			(N70791)
F-GATD	Piper PA-28-181 Cherokee Archer II	28-7890138	N9631N
F-GATE	Piper PA-28R-201T Turbo Arrow III	28R-7803039	N9636N
F-GATJ	Cessna 210K Centurion	21059380	OO-HGO
			OO-PAG
			N9480M
F-GATT	Grumman AA-5B Tiger	AA5B-0651	
F-GATU	Grumman AA-5A Cheetah	AA5A-0532	
F-GAUA	Mudry CAP.20LS-200	02	
F-GAUH	Mudry CAP.10B	106	
F-GAUL	Mudry CAP.20LS-200	6	
F-GAUM	Mudry CAP.21	2	
F-GAUN	Mudry CAP.20LS-200	9	
F-GAUO	Mudry CAP.10B	140	(PT-LCJ)
F-GAUP	Mudry CAP.21 (Assembled from kit)	1	
F-GAUR	Mudry CAP.10B	105	
F-GAUT	Mudry CAP.10B	174	
F-GAUY	Mudry CAP.10B	177	
F-GAVA	Robin DR.400/2+2 Tricycle	1254	
F-GAVC	Robin DR.400/180 Régent	1223	(F-BNPC)
F-GAVH	Robin DR.400/160 Chevalier	1262	
F-GAVI	Robin DR.400/2+2 Tricycle	1263	
F-GAVJ	Robin DR.400/160 Chevalier	1265	F-WAVJ
			F-GAVJ
F-GAVK	Robin DR.400/2+2 Tricycle	1270	
F-GAVL	Robin DR.400/2+2 Tricycle	1271	
F-GAVM	Robin DR.400/180 Régent	1272	
F-GAVN	Robin DR.400/2+2 Tricycle	1273	
F-GAVO	Robin R.2100	125	
F-GAVP	Robin DR.400/2+2 Tricycle	1275	
F-GAVQ	Robin DR.400/2+2 Tricycle	1278	
F-GAVU	Robin DR.400/160 Chevalier	1229	
F-GAVV	Robin DR.400/120 Petit Prince	1280	
F-GAVX	Robin DR.400/2+2 Tricycle	1281	
F-GAXA	Robin R.2160 Alpha Sport	112	
F-GAXB	Robin R.2160 Alpha Sport	113	
F-GAXC	Robin R.2160 Alpha Sport	144	
F-GAXD	Robin R.2160 Alpha Sport	142	
F-GAXE	Robin R.2160 Alpha Sport	143	
F-GAXF	Robin R.2160 Alpha Sport	141	
F-GAXG	Robin R.2160 Alpha Sport	145	
F-GAXH	Robin R.2160 Alpha Sport	146	
F-GAXI	Robin R.2160 Alpha Sport	147	
F-GAXJ	Robin R.2160 Alpha Sport	148	
F-GAXM	Robin R.2160 Alpha Sport	151	
F-GAXN	Robin R.2160 Alpha Sport	152	
F-GAXO	Robin R.2160 Alpha Sport	153	
F-GAXP	Robin R.2160 Alpha Sport	154	
F-GAXQ	Robin R.2160 Alpha Sport	155	
F-GAYH	SOCATA MS.880B Rallye Club	2955	
F-GAYJ	SOCATA Rallye 235E Gabier	12877	
F-GAYN	SOCATA Rallye 100ST	2967	
F-GAYO	SOCATA Rallye 100ST	2998	
F-GAYY	SOCATA MS.880B Rallye Club (Wfu)	3004	
F-GAYZ	SOCATA MS.880B Rallye Club	3005	
F-GAZN	Chaize CS.2000F12 HAFB	012	
F-GAZP	Cameron O-77 HAFB	462	
F-GAZV	Cameron V-65 HAFB	488	
F-GAZX	Cameron V-77 HAFB	489	
F-GAZY	Cameron O-77 HAFB	416	
F-GBAB	Robin DR.400/2+2 Tricycle	1284	
F-GBAI	Robin DR.400/2+2 Tricycle	1289	
F-GBAJ	Robin R.2100A	132	
F-GBAK	Robin DR.400/2+2 Tricycle	1292	
F-GBAM	Robin R.1180T Aiglon	215	F-WZAO

F-GBAP	Robin DR.400/2+2 Tricycle	1302	
F-GBAQ	Robin DR.400/2+2 Tricycle	1305	
F-GBAR	Robin DR.400/2+2 Tricycle	1307	
F-GBAX	Robin DR.400/180R Remorqueur	1312	
F-GBAY	Robin DR.400/2+2 Tricycle	1316	
F-GBBY	Cessna U206G Stationair 6	U20604375	(N756UV)
	(Reims-assembled with "c/n" 0007)		
F-GBCB	SOCATA Rallye 100ST	3029	
F-GBCH	SOCATA Rallye 180T Galérien	3134	
F-GBCI	SOCATA Rallye 100ST	3032	
F-GBCJ	SOCATA MS.880B Rallye Club	3033	
F-GBCP	SOCATA MS.893E Rallye 180GT Gaillard	13109	
F-GBCQ	SOCATA Rallye 100ST	3036	
F-GBCR	SOCATA MS.880B Rallye Club	3037	
F-GBCT	SOCATA Rallye 180T Galérien	3047	
F-GBCU	SOCATA Rallye 180T Galérien	3168	
F-GBCV	SOCATA Rallye 180T Galérien	3169	
F-GBCX	SOCATA Rallye 180T Galérien	3170	
F-GBCY	SOCATA Rallye 180T Galérien	3171	
F-GBCZ	SOCATA Rallye 180T Galérien	3172	
F-GBDQ	Piper PA-25-235 Pawnee B	25-3984	N7782Z
F-GBDR	Beech F33A Bonanza	CE-740	N98170
F-GBDX	Grumman AA-5B Tiger	AA5B-0936	
F-GBED	Ayres S.2R Thrush Commander	1819R	G-BCKB
			N5619X
F-GBEG	Bell 47G-2	2588	G-LIFT
			N6783D
			CF-UAI
			N6783D
F-GBEH	Grumman AA-5B Tiger	AA5B-1092	OO-RTA
			OO-HRT
F-GBEM	Reims/Cessna FR172K Hawk XP	FR17200626	LX-JED
F-GBEN	Holste MH.1521M Broussard	224	Fr.AF
	(Plate on aircraft quotes c/n 253)		
F-GBEQ	Piper PA-28-161 Warrior II	28-8416103	
F-GBEU	Bell 47G-2	1995	N5159B
F-GBEV	Cameron N-65 HAFB	1351	
F-GBEY(2)	Cameron V-77 HAFB	630	
F-GBEZ	SOCATA MS.880B Rallye-Club	1205	F-BPQZ
F-GBFA	Reims/Cessna F152	F15201478	
F-GBFB	Reims/Cessna F152	F15201491	
F-GBFD	Reims/Cessna F150M	F15001356	
F-GBFG	Reims/Cessna F172N	F17201688	
F-GBFL	Reims/Cessna F152	F15201482	
F-GBFN	Reims/Cessna F172N	F17201694	
F-GBFP	Reims/Cessna F172N	F17201720	
F-GBFQ	Reims/Cessna F152	F15201488	
F-GBFT	Reims/Cessna F172N	F17201659	
F-GBFV	Reims/Cessna F172N	F17201727	
F-GBFX	Reims/Cessna F152	F15201486	
F-GBGE	SOCATA Rallye 235E Gabier	12729	F-WBGE
			F-GBGE
			F-OAGE
			ZS-JSP
			F-ODCM
F-GBGF	Cessna 210L Centurion	21059607	D-ECTP
			(N5107Q)
F-GBGM	Cessna A185F Skywagon (Stored)	18503636	N8236Q
F-GBGQ	Grumman AA-5 Traveler	AA5-0202	N9991Q
			CS-AHM
F-GBGZ	Cessna T210L Turbo Centurion	21060901	PH-ATO
			N5300V
F-GBHA	SOCATA TB-10 Tobago	5	
F-GBHB	SOCATA TB-10 Tobago	6	F-WBHB
F-GBHE	SOCATA TB-9 Tampico	9	
F-GBHG	SOCATA TB-10 Tobago	13	
F-GBHK	SOCATA TB-10 Tobago	21	
F-GBHL	SOCATA TB-10 Tobago	22	
F-GBHM	SOCATA TB-10 Tobago	28	
F-GBHO	SOCATA TB-10 Tobago	31	
F-GBHS	SOCATA TB-10 Tobago	33	
F-GBHU	SOCATA TB-10 Tobago	36	
F-GBHZ	SOCATA TB-10 Tobago	77	
F-GBIA	Robin DR.400/140B Major 80	1321	
F-GBIC	Robin DR.400/2+2 Tricycle	1309	
F-GBIE	Robin DR.400/2+2 Tricycle	1313	
F-GBIF	Robin R.2100A	158	
F-GBIH	Robin DR.400/160 Major	1327	
F-GBIK	Robin R.2100A	156	
F-GBIM	Robin DR.400/180 Régent	1337	
F-GBIO	Robin DR.400/2+2 Tricycle	1333	
F-GBIP	Robin R.1180T Aiglon	221	
F-GBIQ	Robin R.2160 Alpha Sport	162	
F-GBIR	Robin DR.400/180 Régent	1330	
F-GBIT	Robin DR.400/180 Régent	1335	
F-GBIU	Robin DR.400/140B Major 80	1338	
F-GBIV	Robin DR.400/120A Petit Prince	1339	
F-GBIX	Robin DR.400/180 Régent (marked 'Major')	1340	
F-GBIY	Robin DR.400/180 Régent	1344	
F-GBJA	Reims/Cessna F152	F15201492	
F-GBJF	Reims/Cessna F152	F15201485	
F-GBJG	Reims/Cessna F150M	F15001377	
F-GBJH	Reims/Cessna F182Q Skylane	F18200093	
	(W/o 10.2.05)		
F-GBJJ	Reims/Cessna F152	F15201544	
F-GBJK	Reims/Cessna F152	F15201548	
F-GBJM	Reims/Cessna F152	F15201552	

F-GBJQ	Reims/Cessna F172N	F17201771	
F-GBJR	Reims/Cessna F152	F15201538	
F-GBJS	Reims/Cessna F152	F15201610	
F-GBJV	Reims/Cessna F152	F15201581	
F-GBJX	Reims/Cessna F152	F15201568	
F-GBJY	Reims/Cessna F172N	F17201778	
F-GBJZ	Reims/Cessna F172N	F17201779	
F-GBKB	SOCATA Rallye 100ST	3059	
F-GBKC	SOCATA Rallye 100ST	3062	
F-GBKE	SOCATA Rallye 100ST	3063	
F-GBKF	SOCATA Rallye 100ST (Dismantled)	3064	
F-GBKG	SOCATA Rallye 100T	3065	
F-GBKL	SOCATA Rallye 235E Gabier	13020	
F-GBKS	SOCATA Rallye 150ST	3142	
F-GBKT	SOCATA Rallye 110ST Galopin	3214	
F-GBLF	Beech A36 Bonanza	E-1443	
F-GBLH(2)	Robin DR.400/180 Régent	790	D-EDGP
F-GBLJ	Piper PA-28-161 Warrior II	28-7916190	
F-GBLL(4)	Piper PA-28RT-201T Turbo Arrow IV	28R-7931269	N2944N
F-GBLT	Hughes 269C	19-0757	N58205
F-GBLU	Beech C90 King Air	LJ-822	(F-GNCY)
			F-GBLU
F-GBLZ	Cessna TU206G Turbo Stationair 6	U20605151	(N4894U)
F-GBML	Mooney M.20J Model 201	24-0530	
F-GBMM	Piper PA-38-112 Tomahawk	38-79A0531	N2456G
F-GBMO	Piper PA-28-181 Archer II	28-7990361	N9638N
F-GBMP	CEA DR.250/160 Capitaine	37	F-OCMP
			SE-CIP
			F-BNJP
F-GBMQ	Aérospatiale AS.350B Ecureuil	1042	F-WZFV
F-GBMT	Piper PA-30 Twin Comanche B	30-1488	N8342Y
F-GBMZ	Cessna 310R-II	310R1592	
F-GBOE	SNCASE SE.3130 Alouette II	1844	D-HOFE
F-GBOH	Bell 47G-2	2195	HB-XFB
			OE-AXL
			HB-XFB
			N90799
			HB-XAX
F-GBOJ	Bell 47G-2	1621	D-HAIN
			74+30
			AS+384
F-GBOM	Reims/Cessna F172M (Damaged 4.9.99)	F17201401	OO-WAW
F-GBOO	Bell 47G-2	2435	D-HEBA
F-GBOQ	Grumman AA-5B Tiger	AA5B-1083	
F-GBOR	Cameron O-65 HAFB	426	
F-GBOV	Piper PA-38-112 Tomahawk	38-78A0801	N9718N
F-GBOY	Piper PA-28-161 Warrior II	28-7916494	
F-GBPA	Piper PA-28R-201T Turbo Cherokee Arrow III		
		28R-7703190	OO-AWD
			OO-HCI
			N38230
F-GBPB	Beech 65-90 King Air	LJ-98	OY-ANP
			N158G
			N158GD
F-GBPF	Cessna 310R-II	310R1665	(N2638U)
F-GBPI	Piper PA-28RT-201T Turbo Arrow IV	28R-7931145	N29214
			N9640N
F-GBPK	Piper PA-44-180 Seminole	44-7995308	
F-GBPL	Mooney M.20K Model 231	25-0339	N231PJ
F-GBPN	Cessna A185F Skywagon	18503819	N4623E
F-GBPO	Bell 47G-2	2424	N6761D
F-GBPR	Bell 47G-2	2179	N5188B
F-GBPU	Piper PA-38-112 Tomahawk	38-79A1105	
F-GBPX	Piper PA-38-112 Tomahawk	38-79A1037	
F-GBPY	Piper PA-34-200T Seneca II	34-7970284	N9562N
F-GBPZ	Beech C90 King Air	LJ-860	
F-GBQA	Reims/Cessna F182Q Skylane	F18200103	
F-GBQB	Reims/Cessna F182Q Skylane	F18200104	
F-GBQD	Reims/Cessna F152	F15201587	
F-GBQE	Reims/Cessna F152	F15201593	
F-GBQF	Reims/Cessna F152	F15201599	
F-GBQG	Reims/Cessna F152	F15201620	
F-GBQH	Reims/Cessna F172N	F17201807	
F-GBQI	Reims/Cessna F172N	F17201822	
F-GBQJ	Reims/Cessna FR182 Skylane RG	FR18200027	(PH-AYA)
F-GBQL	Reims/Cessna F150M	F15001344	
F-GBQO	Reims/Cessna F152	F15201665	
F-GBQQ	Reims/Cessna F172N	F17201848	
F-GBQR	Reims/Cessna F182Q Skylane	F18200121	
F-GBQS	Reims/Cessna F172N	F17201878	
F-GBQU	Reims/Cessna F172N	F17201905	
F-GBQX	Reims/Cessna F172N	F17201899	
F-GBQY	Reims/Cessna F152	F15201641	
F-GBQZ	Reims/Cessna F172N	F17201902	
F-GBRF	Dassault Falcon 10	38	N20EE
			N20ET
			N2OES
			N127FJ
			F-WJMM
F-GBRK	Piper PA-28-161 Warrior II	28-7916448	
F-GBRL	Beech F33A Bonanza	CE-867	
F-GBRN	Robin HR.200/100 Club	46	D-EEWJ
F-GBRO	Bell 47G-2	2559	N8421E
F-GBRU	Fairchild F.27J	43	N2771R
			EL-AHI
			N2771R
F-GBSB	SOCATA MS.892E Rallye 150GT	13228	

F-GBSC	SOCATA MS.893E Rallye 180GT Gaillard	13229	
F-GBSF	SOCATA Rallye 110ST Galopin	3234	
F-GBSG	SOCATA Rallye 110ST Galopin	3235	
F-GBSL	SOCATA Rallye 110ST Galopin	3254	
F-GBSN	SOCATA Rallye 110ST Galopin	3256	
F-GBSO	SOCATA Rallye 110ST Galopin	3257	
F-GBSP	SOCATA Rallye 110ST Galopin	3264	
F-GBSQ	SOCATA Rallye 110ST Galopin	3265	
F-GBSS	SOCATA Rallye 110ST Galopin	3267	
F-GBST	SOCATA Rallye 110ST Galopin	3268	
F-GBSU	SOCATA Rallye 110ST Galopin	3269	
F-GBSV	SOCATA Rallye 110ST Galopin	3270	
F-GBSX	SOCATA Rallye 110ST Galopin	3271	
F-GBSZ	SOCATA Rallye 110ST Galopin	3273	
F-GBTD	Cessna T210N Turbo Centurion II	21063179	N6970N
F-GBTJ	Piper PA-28RT-201T Turbo Arrow IV	28R-7931282	N9608N
F-GBTK	Piper PA-28-161 Warrior II	28-8016333	
F-GBTM	Dassault Falcon 20GF	397	F-WBTM
			F-GBTM
			F-WRQP
F-GBTN	Reims/Cessna F172N	F17201834	LX- III
F-GBTP	Piper PA-34-200 Seneca	34-7250286	TR-LRA
			N1299T
F-GBTS	Reims/Cessna F182P Skylane	F18200004	OO-WAS
			F-GAAA
F-GBTU	Piper PA-28-161 Warrior II	28-7916581	N8073S
			N9603N
F-GBTX	Reims/Cessna F172M	F17201492	F-ODEK
F-GBTZ	Robin DR.400/2+2 Tricycle	1347	
F-GBUF	Robin DR.400/120A Petit Prince	1355	
F-GBUH	Robin DR.400/2+2 Tricycle	1359	
F-GBUJ	Robin DR.400/120 Petit Prince	1361	
F-GBUL	Robin DR.400/2+2 Tricycle (Dismantled)	1356	
F-GBUO	Robin DR.400/180 Régent	1370	
F-GBUP	Rohin DR.400/140B Major 80	1364	
F-GBUQ	Robin DR.400/120A Petit Prince	1371	
F-GBUR	Robin DR.400/120 Petit Prince	1374	
F-GBUT	Robin DR.400/180 Régent	1377	
F-GBUU	Robin DR.400/140B Major 80	1379	
F-GBUV	Robin DR.400/2+2 Tricycle	1376	
F-GBUY	Robin DR.400/2+2 Tricycle	1382	
F-GBVB	Robin R.1180T Aiglon II	226	
F-GBVF	Robin DR.400/2+2 Tricycle	1390	
F-GBVG	Robin R.1180T Aiglon II	230	
F-GBVH	Robin DR.400/120A Petit Prince	1394	
F-GBVJ	Robin DR.400/2+2 Tricycle	1399	
F-GBVK	Robin DR.400/2+2 Tricycle	1393	
F-GBVL	Robin DR.400/120A Petit Prince	1406	
F-GBVM	Robin R.1180T Aiglon II	229	
F-GBVN	Robin DR.400/180 Régent	1408	
F-GBVP	Robin DR.400/120A Petit Prince	1407	
F-GBVR	Robin DR.400/120 Petit Prince	1415	
F-GBVS	Piper PA-30 Twin Comanche B	30-1293	I- KLKL
			N8178Y
F-GBVT	Robin DR.400/140B Major 80	1416	
F-GBVV	Robin DR.400/180R Remorqueur	1412	
F-GBVX	Robin DR.400/120A Petit Prince	1419	
F-GBXF	SOCATA Rallye 235CA Gaucho	13078	
F-GBXN	SOCATA Rallye 110ST Galopin	3291	
F-GBXO	SOCATA Rallye 110ST Galopin	3292	
F-GBXQ	SOCATA Rallye 110ST Galopin	3294	
F-GBXR	SOCATA Rallye 110ST Galopin	3295	
F-GBXS	SOCATA Rallye 110ST Galopin	3296	
F-GBXV	SOCATA Rallye 235E Gabier	13338	
F-GBZH	Cameron V-77 HAFB	524	
F-GBZI	Cameron N-31 HAFB	525	
F-GBZN	Thunder AX7/65 Bolt HAFB	209	
F-GBZS	Cameron V-65 HAFB	555	
F-GBZY	Cameron V-77 HAFB	566	
F-GCAA	Robin DR.400/160 Chevalier	1410	
F-GCAB	Robin R.1180T Aiglon II	233	
F-GCAG	Robin R.1180T Aiglon II	235	
F-GCAH	Robin DR.400/160 Chevalier	1423	
F-GCAL	Robin DR.400/120 Petit Prince	1424	
F-GCAM	Robin DR.400/160 Chevalier	1422	
F-GCAO	Robin DR.400/2+2 Tricycle	1428	
F-GCAQ	Robin DR.400/120 Petit Prince	1433	
F-GCAR	Robin R.1180T Aiglon II	240	
F-GCAT	Robin DR.400/120 Petit Prince	1436	
F-GCAU	Robin R.1180T Aiglon II	241	
F-GCAV	Robin DR.400/120 Petit Prince	1432	
F-GCBD	Boeing 747-228B Combi	22428	N1305E
F-GCBF	Boeing 747-228F	22794	N4506H
			(F-GCBF)
F-GCBG	Boeing 747-228F	22939	N4544F
F-GCBH	Boeing 747-228B	23611	N6046P
F-GCBI	Boeing 747-228B Combi	23676	N6009F
F-GCBJ	Boeing 747-228B	24067	N6018N
F-GCBK	Boeing 747-228F	24158	N6055X
F-GCBL	Boeing 747-228F	24735	
F-GCBM	Boeing 747-228F	24879	
F-GCCD	Partenavia P.6BB	75	PH-RVR
F-GCCE	Cessna U206G Stationair 6	U20604818	N734BD
	(Reims-assembled with "c/n" 0015)		
F-GCCF	Piper PA-38-112 Tomahawk	38-79A0738	N9674N
F-GCCJ	Bell 47G	723	ALAT
F-GCCK	Bell 47G	1316	ALAT

F-GCCL	Agusta-Bell 47G	047	ALAT
F-GCCM	Agusta-Bell 47G	085	ALAT
F-GCCN	Agusta-Bell 47G	087	ALAT
F-GCCT	Cessna 210N Centurion II	21062969	N6198N
F-GCCU	Piper PA-25-235 Pawnee D	25-7405726	N9591P
F-GCCV	Piper PA-28-181 Archer II	28-8090005	N8073Z
			N9612N
F-GCEB	SOCATA TB-10 Tobago	50	
F-GCEE	SOCATA TB-10 Tobago	75	
F-GCEI	SOCATA TB-10 Tobago	96	
F-GCEJ	SOCATA TB-10 Tobago	91	
F-GCEL	SOCATA TB-10 Tobago (Wrecked)	97	
F-GCEM	SOCATA TB-10 Tobago	112	
F-GCEO	SOCATA TB-9 Tampico	120	
F-GCER	SOCATA TB-10 Tobago	70	
F-GCEU	SOCATA TB-10 Tobago	93	
F-GCEX	SOCATA TB-10 Tobago (W/o 28.1.02)	98	
F-GCEZ	SOCATA TB-9 Tampico	123	
F-GCFA	Beech A36 Bonanza	E-1602	
F-GCFJ	Piper PA-38-112 Tomahawk	38-79A1021	N9712N
F-GCFL	Piper PA-38-112 Tomahawk	38-79A1147	N9680N
F-GCFN	Piper PA-38-112 Tomahawk	38-79A1148	N9681N
F-GCFP	Piper PA-38-112 Tomahawk	38-79A1157	N9699N
F-GCFQ	Aérospatiale AS.350B Ecureuil	1200	
F-GCFU	Piper PA-28-161 Warrior II	28-8016089	OO-HLD
			N8097D
F-GCFX	Piper PA-28-181 Archer II	28-8090266	N8177S
F-GCFZ	Agusta-Bell 206B Jet Ranger III	8578	
F-GCGA	Beech C90 King Air	LJ-894	
F-GCGD	Piper PA-38-112 Tomahawk	38-80A0074	
F-GCGJ	Cessna 210N Centurion (W/o 17.5.03)	21063941	(N7350C)
F-GCGL	SNCASE SE.313B Alouette II	1157	TR-LVA
			AAF: 3D-XW
F-GCGM	SNCASE SE.313B Alouette II	1906	TR-LVB
			AAF: 3D-XJ
F-GCGQ	Boeing 727-227	20609	N411BN
F-GCGZ	Aérospatiale AS.350B Ecureuil	1068	TJ-AFU
			F-WZFR
F-GCHA	Reims/Cessna F152	F15201648	
F-GCHB	Reims/Cessna F152	F15201649	
F-GCHC	Reims/Cessna F152	F15201650	
F-GCHD	Reims/Cessna F152	F15201651	
F-GCHE	Reims/Cessna F172N	F17201888	
F-GCHF	Reims/Cessna FR182 Skylane RG	FR18200044	
F-GCHH	Reims/Cessna F152	F15201693	
F-GCHJ	Reims/Cessna F152	F15201702	
F-GCHL	Reims/Cessna F152 (Dbr 16.9.00, stored)	F15201708	
F-GCHM	Reims/Cessna F172N	F17201913	
F-GCHO	Reims/Cessna F172N	F17201917	
F-GCHP	Reims/Cessna F152	F15201748	
F-GCHR	Reims/Cessna F172N	F17202009	
F-GCHS	Reims/Cessna F152	F15201717	
F-GCHT	Reims/Cessna F152	F15201722	
F-GCHU	Reims/Cessna F152	F15201703	
F-GCHZ	Reims/Cessna F152	F15201730	
F-GCIA	Robin DR.400/120 Petit Prince	1444	
F-GCIG	Robin DR.400/160 Chevalier	1453	
F-GCIH	Robin DR.400/120 Petit Prince	1454	
F-GCII	Robin DR.400/120 Petit Prince	1455	
F-GCIJ	Robin DR.400/120 Petit Prince	1456	
F-GCIK	Robin DR.400/120 Petit Prince	1459	
F-GCIL	Robin DR.400/160 Chevalier	1457	
F-GCIM	Robin DR.400/120 Petit Prince	1469	
F-GCIN	Robin DR.400/160 Chevalier	1467	
F-GCIP	Robin DR.400/120 Petit Prince	1458	
F-GCIQ	Robin DR.400/120 Petit Prince	1475	
F-GCIR	Robin DR.400/160 Chevalier	1473	
F-GCIS	Robin DR.400/120 Petit Prince	1468	
F-GCIT	Robin DR.400/120 Petit Prince	1474	
F-GCIU	Robin DR.400/120 Petit Prince	1479	
F-GCIX	Robin DR.400/120 Petit Prince	1480	
F-GCIY	Robin DR.400/120 Petit Prince	1488	
F-GCJB	Mooney M.20K Model 231	25-0248	N231GU
F-GCJC	Aérospatiale AS.350B Ecureuil	1257	
F-GCJD	Piper PA-28-161 Warrior II	28-8016251	N8148U
F-GCJE	Piper PA-44-180 Seminole	44-8095025	
F-GCJG	Piper PA-28-181 Archer II	28-8090219	N8146N
F-GCJK	Piper PA-28-181 Archer II	28-8090103	OO-HLF
			N8093Z
F-GCJL	Boeing 737-222	19067	N9029U
F-GCJM	Piper PA-28RT-201T Turbo Arrow IV	28R-7931245	OO-HCZ
			N2948B
			N9581N
F-GCJO	Fairchild-Hiller FH.227B	530	N703U
F-GCJP	Partenavia P.68B	190	
F-GCJU	Wassmer WA.54 Atlantic	144	G-MPWA
			F-GBIS
			F-OBUS
F-GCKB	Cameron V-65 HAFB	594	
F-GCKE	Thunder AX7/65Z HAFB	249	
F-GCKI	Thunder AX3/21C Sky Chariot HAFB	276	
F-GCKQ	Cameron V-56 HAFB	650	
F-GCKU	Cameron V-77 HAFB	665	
F-GCKV	Cameron N-77 HAFB	666	
F-GCKZ	Balloon Works Firefly 7 HAFB	"10177"	
F-GCLD	Beech C90 King Air	LJ-637	N95DD
			N95BD
			N7311R

F-GCLH	Piper PA-31T Cheyenne II	31T-8020044	N2330V
F-GCLI	Piper PA-28-161 Warrior II	28-8016236	OO-HLO
			N8141Y
F-GCLJ	Beech 76 Duchess	ME-347	
F-GCLR	Piper PA-28-161 Warrior II	28-8016228	OO-HLL
			N3578X
F-GCLT	Reims/Cessna F172N	F17201894	XT-ABM
			F-ODKN
F-GCLU	Piper PA-28-181 Archer II	28-8090213	OO-HLP
			N81419
F-GCLV	Piper PA-28-181 Archer II	28-8090312	N8216V
F-GCLX	Cessna 172RG Cutlass RG	172RG0553	(N5526V)
F-GCLZ	Piper PA-38-112 Tomahawk	38-80A0069	
F-GCMB	Piper PA-28R-201T Turbo Cherokee Arrow III		
		28R-7703087	N3055Q
F-GCMC	Piper PA-28-181 Archer II	28-8090218	OO-HLS
			N8146B
F-GCMI	Piper PA-28-161 Warrior II	28-8016287	OO-HLU
			N81762
F-GCMP	Agusta-Bell 206B Jet Ranger III	8592	(G-LOCK)
F-GCMT(2)	Beech B24R Sierra	MC-158	G-BAXM
F-GCNB	Reims/Cessna F172N	F17201995	
F-GCNC	Reims/Cessna F152	F15201729	D-EEFY
F-GCND	Reims/Cessna F152	F15201779	
F-GCNG	Reims/Cessna F152	F15201781	
F-GCNJ	Reims/Cessna F152	F15201751	
F-GCNK	Reims/Cessna F172N	F17202019	
F-GCNN	Reims/Cessna FR182 Skylane RG	FR18200050	
F-GCNO	Reims/Cessna F152	F15201764	
F-GCNP	Reims/Cessna F152 (Dismantled)	F15201765	
F-GCNQ	Reims/Cessna F172N	F17202017	PH-AYF
F-GCNS	Reims/Cessna F152	F15201800	
F-GCNT	Reims/Cessna F172N	F17202039	
F-GCNU	Reims/Cessna F172N	F17202037	(OY-BNS)
F-GCNV	Reims/Cessna F172P	F17202076	
F-GCNZ	Reims/Cessna F182Q Skylane	F18200150	
F-GCOA	SOCATA TB-10 Tobago	124	
F-GCOJ	SOCATA TB-9 Tampico	155	
F-GCOM	SOCATA TB-10 Tobago	161	
F-GCOQ	SOCATA TB-10 Tobago	172	
F-GCOS	SOCATA TB-10 Tobago (Derelict)	174	
F-GCOU	SOCATA TB-9 Tampico	202	
F-GCOX	SOCATA TB-9 Tampico	224	
F-GCOY	SOCATA TB-9 Tampico	233	
F-GCPB	Piper PA-28RT-201T Turbo Arrow IV	28R-8031124	N82318
F-GCPF	Piper PA-28-161 Warrior II	28-7916587	OO-HCG
			N8073T
			N9604N
F-GCPJ	Piper PA-32R-301 Saratoga SP	32R-8013120	N8252G
			N9578N
F-GCPO	Piper PA-34-200T Seneca II	34-8070358	N8266V
F-GCQA	Cessna 172RG Cutlass	172RG0007	N4648R
F-GCQB	SOCATA MS.880B Rallye Club	853	F-BODP
F-GCQE	Piper PA-28-181 Archer II	28-8090370	N9582N
			N82525
F-GCQF	Reims/Cessna F172M	F17200947	LX-AIJ
F-GCQH	Cessna 335	335-0059	F-WCQH
			F-GCQH
			N6801C
F-GCQI	Agusta-Bell 47G-2	027	(F-GDQI)
			I- COLO
			IDFAF
			Fr.AF
F-GCQJ	Piper PA-28RT-201 Arrow IV	28R-8118023	N82910
F-GCQM	Agusta-Bell 47G-2	148	F-BXXE
			ALAT
F-GCQO	Reims FR172J Rocket	FR17200376	TU-TGC
F-GCQR	Aérospatiale SA.365C2 Dauphin 2	5054	
F-GCQZ	Aérospatiale AS.350B Ecureuil	1562	
F-GCRA	Robin R.1180TD Aiglon	245	
F-GCRD	Robin R.1180TD Aiglon	248	
F-GCRE	Robin R.1180TD Aiglon	249	
F-GCRF	Robin R.1180TD Aiglon	250	
F-GCRG	Robin R.1180TD Aiglon	251	
F-GCRH	Robin R.1180TD Aiglon	252	
F-GCRJ	Robin R.1180TD Aiglon	254	
F-GCRL	Robin R.1180TD Aiglon	256	
F-GCRM	Robin R.1180TD Aiglon	257	
F-GCRN	Robin R.1180TD Aiglon	258	
F-GCRP	Robin R.1180TD Aiglon	260	
F-GCRQ	Robin R.1180TD Aiglon	261	
F-GCRR	Robin R.1180TD Aiglon	263	
F-GCRS	Robin DR.400/120 Petit Prince	1485	
F-GCRU	Robin DR.400/120 Petit Prince	1481	
F-GCRV	Robin DR.400/120 Petit Prince	1487	
F-GCRX	Robin DR.400/120 Petit Prince	1491	
F-GCRY	Robin DR.400/120 Petit Prince	1492	
F-GCRZ	Robin DR.400/120 Petit Prince	1496	
F-GCSD	Cessna 172RG Cutlass RG	172RG0248	N5125U
	(Reims-assembled with "c/n" 0008)		
F-GCSE	Cessna TU206G Turbo Stationair 6	U20605777	(N5463X)
F-GCSF	Cessna 207A Stationair 8	20700585	N73397
F-GCSG	Cessna T210N Turbo Centurion II	21063870	N6338C
F-GCSH	Cessna TR182 Turbo Skylane RG (Wrecked)	R18201051	N756EL
F-GCSI	Piper PA-38-112 Tomahawk	38-80A0073	N9652N
F-GCSL	Boeing 737-222	19066	N9028U
F-GCSM	Cessna 172RG Cutlass RG	172RG0548	(N5511V)

F-GCSO	Beech 95-B55 Baron	TC-2311	
F-GCSP	Cessna 172RG Cutlass RG	172RG0563	N5539V
F-GCSV	Cessna P210N Pressurized Centurion II	P21000528	N731QL
F-GCTD	Piper PA-28-161 Warrior II	28-7916212	OO-WPC
			OO-HCT
			N9554N
F-GCTF	Piper PA-39 Twin Comanche C/R	39-54	G-AZMW
			(D-GMWB)
			N8897Y
F-GCTK	Cessna 172RG Cutlass RG	172RG0566	N5543V
F-GCTO	Aérospatiale AS.350B Ecureuil	1361	
F-GCTQ	Piper PA-28-181 Archer II	28-8090297	OO-HLZ
			(OO-HCZ)
			N82002
F-GCTR	Beech E90 King Air	LA-115	
F-GCTU	Piper PA-38-112 Tomahawk	38-80A0085	N9694N
F-GCTV	Piper PA-38-112 Tomahawk	38-80A0087	N9695N
F-GCTX	Piper PA-38-112 Tomahawk	38-80A0088	N9696N
F-GCUA	Robin DR.400/120 Petit Prince	1498	
F-GCUB	Robin DR.400/180 Régent	1500	
F-GCUE	Robin DR.400/160 Chevalier	1503	
F-GCUF	Robin DR.400/160 Chevalier	1504	
F-GCUG	Robin DR.400/120 Petit Prince	1511	
F-GCUI	Robin DR.400/160 Chevalier	1518	
F-GCUK	Robin DR.400/120 Petit Prince	1515	
F-GCUM	Robin DR.400/180 Régent	1521	
F-GCUS	Robin DR.400/120 Petit Prince	1509	
F-GCUT	Robin DR.400/120 Petit Prince	1507	
F-GCUU	Robin DR.400/120 Petit Prince	1533	
F-GCVA	Mooney M.20K Model 231	25-0508	
F-GCVC	Cessna A185F Skywagon	18504045	N6463E
F-GCVF	Agusta-Bell 206B Jet Ranger III	8607	
F-GCVS	Cessna A185F Skywagon	18504190	N61440
F-GCVV(2)	SNCASE SE.3130 Alouette II	1010/10	Fr.AF
F-GCVX(2)	Cessna A185F Skywagon	18503383	N7379H
F-GCVY	Agusta-Bell 206B Jet Ranger III	8623	
F-GCXA	Thunder AX7/65Z HAFB	293	
F-GCXC	Thunder AX7/65Z HAFB	305	
F-GCXF	Chaize CS.2200F12 HAFB	027	
F-GCXH	Thunder AX7/77 Bolt HAFB	326	
F-GCXM	Cameron O-77 HAFB	721	
F-GCXP	Thunder AX7/65 HAFB	335	
F-GCXU	Deveque HG RD 700 Free Balloon	11	
F-GCXX	Chaize CS.2200F12 HAFB	037	
F-GCYD	Reims/Cessna F152	F15201836	
F-GCYL	Reims/Cessna F172P	F17202086	
F-GCYQ	Reims/Cessna FR182 Skylane RG	FR18200064	
F-GCYR	Reims/Cessna F172P	F17202104	
F-GCYT	Reims/Cessna F152	F15201851	
F-GCYY	Reims/Cessna F172P	F17202066	
F-GCZA	Thunder AX7/77 HAFB	371	
F-GCZB	Thunder AX6/56 HAFB	370	
F-GCZG	Thunder AX7/77 S1 HAFB	415	
F-GCZR	Cameron O-56 HAFB	840	
F-GCZS	Cameron D-50 Hot Air Airship	818	G-BJXY
F-GCZX	Leys HG VL-248 Free Balloon	01	F-WCZX
F-GCZZ	Cameron V-56 HAFB	704	
F-GDAA	Cessna U206G Stationair 6	U20606082	N5228Z
F-GDAB	Cessna 172RG Cutlass RG	172RG0808	N9381B
F-GDAF	Enstrom F.280C Shark	1206	N5697T
F-GDAI	Piper PA-28-161 Warrior II	28-8116185	N8360V
F-GDAJ	Piper PA-28-181 Archer II	28-8090315	OO-HKC
			N8218A
F-GDAK	Beech F90 King Air	LA-141	
F-GDAP	Cessna U206G Stationair 6	U20605967	N6605X
F-GDAT	Piper PA-28-161 Warrior II	28-8116106	N8311V
F-GDBA	SOCATA TB-21 Trinidad TC	01	F-WDBA
F-GDBG	SOCATA TB-10 Tobago	279	
F-GDBK	SOCATA TB-10 Tobago	274	
F-GDBP	SOCATA TB-9 Tampico	347	
F-GDBS	SOCATA TB-9 Tampico	365	
F-GDBU	SOCATA TB-9 Tampico	361	F-WGPL
F-GDBZ	SOCATA TB-9 Tampico	373	
F-GDCE	Piper PA-28-181 Cherokee Archer II	28-7890538	OO-MLT
			N39524
F-GDCH	Piper PA-28-161 Warrior II	28-7916418	D-EIRI
			N29077
F-GDCI	Embraer EMB.110P2 Bandeirante	110333	PT-SDJ
F-GDCJ	Aérospatiale SA.330J Puma	1665	F-GDFO
F-GDCM	Sud Avn SA.318C Alouette Astazou	1950	D-HI FO
F-GDCV	SOCATA TB-10 Tobago	204	F-ODOD
			F-GDBD
F-GDDB	Reims/Cessna F152	F15201859	
F-GDDD	Reims/Cessna F152	F15201849	
F-GDDH	Reims/Cessna F172P	F17202130	
F-GDDJ	Reims/Cessna F152	F15201864	
F-GDDL	Reims/Cessna FR182 Skylane RG	FR18200062	
F-GDDM	Reims/Cessna F152	F15201834	
F-GDDN	Reims/Cessna F172P	F17202106	(G-BIYL)
			D-EEBT
F-GDDO	Reims/Cessna F152	F15201891	
F-GDDP	Reims/Cessna F152	F15201887	
F-GDDQ	Reims/Cessna F152	F15201888	
F-GDDR	Reims/Cessna F172P	F17202134	
F-GDDS	Reims/Cessna F152	F15201862	(D-EANL)
F-GDDT	Reims/Cessna F172P	F17202123	(D-EEJR)
F-GDDV	Reims/Cessna F152	F15201871	D-EAND

F-GDDX	Reims/Cessna F152	F15201905	
F-GDDY	Reims/Cessna F152	F15201917	
F-GDDZ	Reims/Cessna F172P	F17202132	
F-GDEA	Robin DR.400/120 Petit Prince	1531	
F-GDEB	Robin DR.400/180 Régent	1532	
F-GDEC	Robin DR.400/120 Petit Prince	1534	
F-GDED	Robin DR.400/180 Régent	1536	
F-GDEE	Robin DR.400/120 Petit Prince	1538	
F-GDEH	Robin DR.400/120 Petit Prince	1556	
F-GDEJ	Robin DR.400/160 Chevalier	1561	
F-GDEM	Robin DR.400/120 Petit Prince	1563	
F-GDEN	Robin DR.400/120 Petit Prince	1573	
F-GDEO	Robin DR.400/120 Petit Prince	1580	
F-GDEP	Robin DR.400/180 Régent	1577	
F-GDEQ	Robin DR.400/120 Petit Prince	1566	D-EGDV
F-GDES	Robin DR.400/120 Petit Prince	1581	
F-GDET	Robin DR.400/120 Petit Prince	1539	
F-GDEU	Robin DR.400/120 Petit Prince	1567	
F-GDEV	Robin R.1180TD Aiglon	278	
F-GDEY	Robin DR.400/120 Petit Prince	1592	
F-GDEZ	Robin DR.400/120 Petit Prince	1579	
F-WDFJ	Dassault Falcon 20G	362	F-GDFJ
			F-WDFJ
			F-WATF(1)
			F-WZAS
F-GDFM	Aérospatiale AS.350B Ecureuil	1007	G-BGHG
			F-GBBK
F-GDFN	Piper PA-34-200T Seneca II	34-7970169	N159CB
			N3066V
F-GDFP	Cessna T303 Crusader	T30300127	(N4933C)
F-GDFQ	Piper PA-38-112 Tomahawk II	38-81A0028	N25634
F-GDFU	Cessna 210N Centurion II	21064215	(N5467Y)
F-GDFX	Aérospatiale SA.315B Lama	2629	
F-GDGC	SOCATA Rallye 110ST Galopin	3347	
F-GDGF	SOCATA Rallye 110ST Galopin	3364	
F-GDGG	SOCATA TB-20 Trinidad	422	
F-GDGI	SOCATA Rallye 110ST Galopin	3377	
F-GDGJ	SOCATA Rallye 110ST Galopin	3378	
F-GDGL	SOCATA TB-9 Tampico	359	
F-GDGM	SOCATA TB-20 Trinidad	383	
F-GDGP	SOCATA TB-10 Tobago	392	
F-GDGQ	SOCATA TB-20 Trinidad	449	
F-GDGU	SOCATA TB-20 Trinidad	406	
F-GDGZ	SOCATA TB-20 Trinidad	419	
F-GDHD	Britten-Norman BN-2A-9 Islander	591	F-WDHD
			9Q-CMJ
			G-BENU
F-GDHI	Cessna 172RG Cutlass RG	172RG0819	(D-EANK)
			N9421B
F-GDHL	SNCASE SE.3130 Alouette II	1325	D-HHAA
			75+33
			PK+201
			PL+131
			PH+135
F-GDHM	SNCASE SE.3130 Alouette II	1545	D-HHAB
			76+00
			PZ+201
			PN+131
F-GDHO	SNCASE SE.3130 Alouette II	1891	D-HOBY
F-GDHT	SNCASE SE.313B Alouette II	1854	D-HHAH
			76+05
			PY+212
			PO+140
F-GDHX	Aérospatiale AS.350B Ecureuil	1662	
F-GDHY	Piper PA-28R-201T Turbo Arrow III	28R-7803333	HB-PCD
			N36688
F-GDIA	Reims/Cessna F152	F15201895	
F-GDIB	Reims/Cessna F172P	F17202141	
F-GDID	Reims/Cessna F152	F15201911	
F-GDIE	Reims/Cessna F152	F15201898	
F-GDIH	Reims/Cessna F172P	F17202138	
F-GDII	Reims/Cessna F172P	F17202155	
F-GDIJ	Reims/Cessna F152	F15201902	
F-GDIK	Reims/Cessna F152	F15201817	
F-GDIL	Reims/Cessna F152	F15201828	F-WZIX
F-GDIO	Reims/Cessna F152	F15201892	
F-GDIP	Reims/Cessna F152	F15201927	
F-GDIQ	Reims/Cessna F152	F15201903	
F-GDIT	Reims/Cessna F172P	F17202180	
F-GDIV	Reims/Cessna F172P	F17202177	
F-GDIX	Reims/Cessna F172P	F17202162	
F-GDIY	Reims/Cessna F172P	F17202191	
F-GDIZ	Reims/Cessna F152	F15201923	F-WZND
F-GDJB	SOCATA Rallye 150SV Garnement	3330	F-ODNH
F-GDJD	SOCATA Rallye 235E Gabier	13346	TU-VBK
			F-ODNZ
F-GDJE	Robin DR.400/120 Petit Prince	1527	D-EGWU
F-GDJF	Piper PA-28-161 Warrior II	28-8316042	N9631N
F-GDJN	Agusta-Bell 47G-2	269	I-ESTA
F-GDJO	Agusta-Bell 47G-2	121	I-CIDI
			IDFAF
			Fr.AF
F-GDJR	Bell 47G	1974	I-ONGO
			SE-HBH
			N2869B
F-GDJS	Beech B200 Super King Air	BB-1116	(D-ILOC)
F-GDJT	Cessna 172RG Cutlass RG	172RG1022	N9768B

F-GDJV	SNCASE SE.313B Alouette II	1680	D-HICU
F-GDJZ	Piper PA-28-161 Cherokee Warrior II	28-7816484	OO-AFL OO-HCM N9499C
F-GDKA	Robin DR.400/120 Petit Prince	1587	
F-GDKD	Robin DR.400/120 Petit Prince	1608	
F-GDKE	Robin DR.400/120 Petit Prince	1598	
F-GDKF	Robin DR.400/120 Petit Prince	1602	
F-GDKG	Robin DR.400/120 Petit Prince	1609	
F-GDKH	Robin DR.400/120 Petit Prince	1610	
F-GDKI	Robin DR.400/120 Petit Prince	1611	
F-GDKJ	Robin DR.400/120 Petit Prince	1612	
F-GDKL	Robin DR.400/160 Chevalier	1613	
F-GDKM	Robin DR.400/120 Petit Prince	1615	
F-GDKN	Robin DR.400/160 Chevalier	1616	
F-GDKP	Robin DR.400/120 Petit Prince	1620	
F-GDKQ	Robin DR.400/120 Petit Prince	1621	
F-GDKR	Robin DR.400/120 Petit Prince	1623	
F-GDKS	Robin DR.400/120 Petit Prince	1627	
F-GDKT	Robin DR.400/180 Régent	1624	
F-GDKX	Robin DR.400/120 Petit Prince	1636	
F-GDKY	Robin DR.400/180 Régent	1626	
F-GDKZ	Robin DR.400/160 Chevalier	1637	
F-GDLC	SOCATA TB-10 Tobago	199	F-BNGQ PH-AFM F-BNGZ
F-GDLE	Beech 200 Super King Air	BB-230	G-BEHR
F-GDLG	Piper PA-28R-200 Cherokee Arrow II	28R-7235308	OO-LDH PH-LDH N1508T
F-GDLH	Cessna 421B Golden Eagle	421B0320	3A-MDB F-BTQR N5950M
F-GDLI	CEA DR.220	29	(G- . . . .) F-BOCV
F-GDLJ	Piper PA-38-112 Tomahawk	38-80A0078	OO-TIC PH-TMP OO-HKF N9660N
F-GDLK	Piper PA-44-180 Seminole	44-7995209	OO-ALK OO-HCR N2210K
F-GDLM	Cessna TR182 Turbo Skylane RG	R18201115	G-OAST (N756MM)
F-GDLN	Piper PA-28RT-201 Arrow IV	28R-7918186	OO-PAR N2871N
F-GDLR	Dassault Falcon 10	121	HB-VFT (HB-VFS) F-WPUU
F-GDLS	Piper PA-38-112 Tomahawk	38-80A0093	OO-HKI N9685N
F-GDLV	Aérospatiale AS.355F Ecureuil 2	5265	F-WZKM
F-GDLX	Piper PA-44-180T Turbo Seminole	44-8107035	OO-GMH OO-HKR N8322X
F-GDLY	SOCATA Rallye 150SV Garnement	3345	TU-VBI F-ODNY
F-GDLZ	Piper PA-28RT-201 Arrow IV	28R-8218003	G-BJXE N8460L
F-GDMG	Bell 47G-2	1626	D-HABA F-BBOK F-OBOK Fr.Mil N2845B
F-GDMH	Agusta-Bell 47G-2	122	D-HAMG D-HNFC OE-AXT (OE-AXI) G-AYOF F-OCGB Fr.AF
F-GDMJ	Agusta-Bell 47G-2	242	D-HANY AAF: 3B-XI
F-GDMN	Piper PA-28-140 Cherokee Cruiser	28-7725108	G-BEMV N9561N
F-GDMP	Sportavia/ Fournier RF-5	5002	D-KIGA
F-GDMQ	SOCATA TB-20 Trinidad	282	F-OGLN
F-GDMS	Aérospatiale AS.355F Ecureuil 2	5063	
F-WDMT(2)	Microjet MJ.200B	3	
F-WDMU	Nord 1101 Noralpha	132	CAN: CAN-9
F-WDMX	Microjet MJ-200B	2	
F-GDNA	SOCATA TB-20 Trinidad	320	
F-GDNC	SOCATA TB-20 Trinidad	327	
F-GDNE	SOCATA TB-20 Trinidad	332	
F-GDNF	SOCATA TB-20 Trinidad	344	
F-GDNG	SOCATA TB-20 Trinidad	345	
F-GDNJ	SOCATA TB-20 Trinidad	402	
F-GDNK	SOCATA TB-20 Trinidad	403	
F-GDNL	SOCATA TB-20 Trinidad	434	
F-GDNM	SOCATA TB-20 Trinidad	435	
F-GDNN	SOCATA TB-20 Trinidad	436	
F-GDNO	SOCATA TB-20 Trinidad	437	
F-GDNP	SOCATA TB-20 Trinidad	438	
F-GDNQ	SOCATA TB-20 Trinidad	439	
F-GDNR	SOCATA TB-20 Trinidad	440	
F-GDNT	SOCATA TB-20 Trinidad	471	
F-GDNU	SOCATA TB-20 Trinidad	472	

F-GDNV	SOCATA TB-20 Trinidad	548	(F-OINV) F-GDNV
F-GDNX	SOCATA TB-20 Trinidad	549	(F-OINX) F-GDNX
F-GDNZ	SOCATA TB-20 Trinidad	551	
F-GDOA	Reims/Cessna F152	F15201924	
F-GDOC	Reims/Cessna F152	F15201926	
F-GDOE	Reims/Cessna F152	F15201931	
F-GDOF	Reims/Cessna F152	F15201913	
F-GDOG	Reims/Cessna F152	F15201897	
F-GDOH	Reims/Cessna F172P	F17202207	
F-GDOK	Reims/Cessna F152	F15201938	
F-GDOL	Reims/Cessna F172P	F17202210	
F-GDOM	Reims/Cessna F172P	F17202216	
F-GDON	Reims/Cessna F172P	F17202203	
F-GDOR	Reims/Cessna F152	F15201948	
F-GDOX	Reims/Cessna F152	F15201946	
F-GDOY	Reims/Cessna F172P	F17202218	(F-WDOY)
F-GDPB	Piper PA-25-235 Pawnee B (Two-seat)	25-3109	F-WDPB N7202Z
F-GDPC	Cessna 305C/L-19E Bird Dog	24728	F-WDPC ALAT
F-GDPF	Cessna 305C/L-19E Bird Dog	24705	ALAT
F-GDPN	Piper PA-25-235 Pawnee B (Officially quoted as 25-3262)	25-3292	(F-BJQH) F-OGIG F-BOAT F-OCGT N7342Z
F-GDPO	Agusta-Bell 47G-2	265	HB-XHX D-HEKG 74+23 AS+065
F-GDPU	Piper PA-31 Turbo Navajo	31-367	HP- . . . ? I- CGAI N9244Y
F-GDPX	Holste MH.1521M Broussard (Plate on aircraft quotes c/n 108)	170	F-WDPX F-GDPX Fr.AF
F-GDQB	Agusta-Bell 47G-2	158	HB-XOP OE-AXY (F-BXZU) Fr.AF ALAT
F-GDQC	Bell 47G-4	3329	N1152W HC-AXA N1152W
F-GDQF	Piper PA-34-200T Seneca II (Damaged, .04)	34-7770337	HB-LIY N38751
F-GDQL(2)	SNCASE SE.313B Alouette II	1250	Gendarmerie/ F-MJBI Fr.AF
F-GDQN	Sud Avn SA.318C Alouette Astazou	2059	C-FZHM CF-ZHM F-BRPG
F-GDQR	Sud Avn SA.318C Alouette Astazou	2262	C-FMQP CF-MQP
F-GDQX	Agusta-Bell 206B Jet Ranger II	8517	3A-MFC F-BXSV
F-GDRA	Reims/Cessna F152	F15201880	N9073F
F-GDRE	Hughes 269C	43-0201	N8964F
F-GDRF	Agusta-Bell 47G-2	039	ALAT
F-GDRG	Piper PA-23-250 Aztec E	27-7305213	(D-IHBR) LX-HBR D-IHBR N40489
F-GDRH	Piper PA-28-161 Warrior II	28-7916003	PH-SBV N39735
F-GDRI	Morane-Saulnier MS.733 Alcyon	71	F-BLYA Fr.AF
F-GDRO	Morane-Saulnier MS.733 Alcyon	97	F-BLXQ Fr.Mil
F-GDRQ	Aérospatiale AS.350B Ecureuil	1832	
F-GDRR	SNCASE SE.3130 Alouette II	1671	Gendarmerie/ F-MJAV F-MJBB
F-GDRS	Reims/Cessna F152	F15201460	D-EAAQ
F-GDRU	Robin DR.400/2+2	1000	F-BXEA
F-GDRV	Bell 47G-2	1968	D-HORN 74+31 AS+386
F-GDRX	Reims/Cessna F172M	F17200969	D-ECZL
F-GDSE	Piper PA-28-181 Cherokee Archer II	28-7790451	N3336Q
F-GDSF	CEA DR.250/160 Capitaine	97	OY-DNW
F-GDSI	Cameron O-77 HAFB	1157	
F-GDSJ	Cameron O-84 HAFB	607	N389CB
F-GDSN	Holste MH.1521M Broussard	247	Fr.AF
F-GDSP	Cameron O-77 HAFB	1255	
F-GDSR	Piper PA-28RT-201T Turbo Arrow IV	28R-7931155	D-EELW N2124Z
F-GDST	Cessna 172RG Cutlass RG	172RG0831	N9469B
F-GDSV	Beech 58 Baron	TH-667	TJ-AFD F-ODAZ
F-GDTA	Mudry CAP.10B	179	
F-GDTB	Mudry CAP.10B	180	
F-GDTF	Mudry CAP.10B	181	
F-GDTG	Mudry CAP.10B	191	
F-GDTJ	Mudry CAP.10B	204	

F-GDTM	Mudry CAP.21	14	
F-GDTN	Mudry CAP.10B	73	OO-LAT
F-GDTO	Mudry CAP.10B	218	
F-GDTQ	Mudry CAP.10B	227	
F-GDTR	Mudry CAP.21 (W/o 1.5.01)	16	
F-GDTT	Mudry CAP.230	05	
F-GDTV	Mudry CAP.10B	231	
F-GDTX	Mudry CAP.10B	225	
F-GDTY	Mudry CAP.10B	226	
F-GDTZ	Mudry CAP.10B	230	
F-GDUE(2)	SNCASE SE.313B Alouette II	1457/243	Fr.AF
F-GDUF(2)	SNCASE SE.313B Alouette II (W/o 12.6.97 ?)	1727/336	Fr.AF
F-GDUP	Aermacchi AL.60C5	68/6248	TL-KAO I- MANH CF-XKU
F-GDUQ	Aermacchi AL.60C5	95/6275	TL-KAM I- MANJ
F-GDUR	Chaize CS.2200F12 HAFB	062	
F-GDUS	Fokker F.28 Fellowship 2000	11053	5N-ANB PH-ZAX PH-EXF
F-GDUT	Fokker F.28 Fellowship 2000	11091	5N-ANH PH-EXT
F-GDVY	Robin DR.400/140B Major 80	714	F-BTKM
F-GDXA	Aérospatiale AS.350B Ecureuil	1610	
F-GDXD	Cameron N-105 HAFB	1122	
F-GDXE	Cameron N-105 HAFB	1125	
F-WDXH	Fouga CM-170 Magister	2	Fr.AF
F-GDXJ	Bell 47G-2	1317	HB-XIE (F-BVFX) Fr.Mil
F-GDXK	Thunder AX7-77Z HAFB	830	
F-GDXN	Chaize CS.3000F16 HAFB	063	
F-GDXO	Chaize CS.2200F12 HAFB	064	
F-GDXQ	Thunder AX7-77 HAFB	805	
F-GDXR	Aérospatiale AS.350B Ecureuil	1912	F-OGNB
F-GDYA	Robin DR.400/180 Régent	1639	
F-GDYC	Robin DR.400/120 Petit Prince	1641	
F-GDYD	Robin DR.400/180 Régent	1642	
F-GDYE	Robin DR.400/120 Petit Prince	1643	
F-GDYF	Robin R.3000/140	002	F-WZJZ
F-GDYG	Robin DR.400/120 Petit Prince	1648	
F-GDYH	Robin DR.400/120 Petit Prince	1649	
F-GDYK	Robin DR.400/120 Petit Prince	1661	
F-GDYN	Robin DR.400/120 Petit Prince	1663	
F-GDYP	Robin DR.400/120 Petit Prince	1667	
F-GDYQ	Robin R.3000/120	105	F-WDYQ F-WEIA(1)
F-GDYR	Robin DR.400/120 Petit Prince	1669	
F-GDYT	Robin DR.400/180 Régent	1675	
F-GDYU	Robin DR.400/120 Petit Prince	1654	
F-GDYX	Robin DR.400/120 Petit Prince	1673	
F-GDYY	Robin DR.400/160 Chevalier	1674	
F-GDZB	Chaize CS.2200F12 HAFB	040	
F-GDZG	Thunder AX7-77SI HAFB	471	
F-WDZI	Chaize CS.2300F24 HAFB	039	
F-GDZM	Cameron V-56 HAFB	930	
F-GDZO	Cameron V-65 HAFB	946	
F-GDZR	Cameron V-77 HAFB	890	(F-GEAB)
F-GDZS	Thunder AX7-65Z HAFB	518	
F-GDZU	Cameron V-65 HAFB	950	
F-GDZX	Chaize CS.2200F12 HAFB	046	
F-GDZY	Aerostat Solaire Malleray	01	F-WDZY
F-GEAC	Ballonfabrik Augsburg HG K.630N Free Balloon	13336	
F-GEAE	Charles et Robert AX-3 HAFB	01	F-WEAE
F-GEAG	Cameron V-77 HAFB	349	
F-GEAL(2)	Christen Pitts S-2B	5197	
F-GEAO	Balloon Works Firefly 8-24 HAFB	F8-023	N37228
F-GEAP	Chaize CS.2200F32 HAFB	047	
F-GEAR	Chaize CS.2200F32 HAFB	048	
F-GEAS	Chaize CS.2200F12 CMM HAFB	049	
F-GEAT	Chaize CS.3000F16 HAFB	050	
F-GEAV	Bell 206B Jet Ranger II	1207	G-BBOS VR-BID G-BBOS
F-GEAZ	Chaize CS.3000F16 HAFB	057	
F-GEBA	Piper PA-28-181 Cherokee Archer II	28-7890196	PH-LIA OO-HCK N9889K
F-GEBD	Beech A36 Bonanza	E-1592	D-EKBH
F-GEBE	Cessna 310Q	310Q0731	N4568L
F-GEBI	Thunder AX7-65 HAFB	630	
F-GEBL	Thunder AX10-160 HAFB	643	
F-GEBM	Piper PA-18-150 Super Cub	18-1294	CS-ALJ FAP3205
F-GEBO	Reims/Cessna F172M	F17201364	D-EEGN
F-GEBQ	Piper PA-38-112 Tomahawk	38-78A0293	D-EGXB N9678N
F-GEBS	Pilatus PC-6/B1-H2 Turbo-Porter	702	HB-FFK
F-GEBT	Cessna 172RG Cutlass RG (Dam. 25.5.02)	172RG0648	N6385Y
F-GEBV	SAN Jodel D.140C Mousquetaire III	128	CN-TZH
F-GEBX	Thunder AX8-105 HAFB	640	
F-GEBY	Thunder AX10-160A HAFB	677	
F-GECF	Marks reserved for Ecole de Conduite France		
F-GECG	Thunder AX7-77 HAFB	675	
F-GECH	Thunder AX7-65Z HAFB	674	
F-GECJ	Thunder AX7-77 HAFB	688	

F-GECL	Mooney M.20J Model 201	24-1531	N57942
F-GECM	Aérospatiale AS.350B Ecureuil	1792	
F-GECO	Chaize CS.3000F16 HAFB	059	
F-GECT	Aérospatiale SA.315B Lama (W/o 18.10.00)	2666	
F-GECX	Thunder AX7-77 HAFB	741	
F-GECY	Robin DR.400/160 Chevalier	888	F-BUSQ
F-GECZ	Thunder AX7-77 HAFB	723	
F-GEDF	Aérospatiale AS.350B Ecureuil	1820	
F-GEDG	Piper PA-18A-150 Super Cub	18-2849	CN-TDE F-DADF
F-GEDH	Piper PA-18A-150 Super Cub (Officially quoted with f/n 18-490 - marks originally allotted to c/n 18-4606)	18-558	PH-AAT R-207 51-15672 N7187K
F-GEDJ	Piper PA-18A-150 Super Cub	18-6373	CN-TDB F-DAFQ N10F
F-GEDL	Mooney M.20E Chaparral	21-0059	HB-DFG C-GNFJ N7179V
F-GEDN	SNCASE SE.3130 Alouette II	1262/156	Fr.AF
F-GEDO	Piper PA-28-161 Warrior II	28-7916004	PH-SBW N39736
F-GEDT	Deveque HG RD 700 Free Balloon	12	
F-GEDU	Piper PA-32-300 Cherokee Six	32-7440007	TZ-ACK 5U-AAQ 6V-ADM N56601
F-GEDX	Cessna 210R Centurion II	21064970	(N7596U)
F-GEEB	Thunder AX7-65 HAFB	543	
F-GEEC	Cameron O-65 HAFB	967	
F-GEEI	Thunder AX7-65 HAFB	573	
F-GEEK(2)	Piper PA-28-161 Warrior II	28-8516012	N4380F
F-GEEM	Cameron O-105 HAFB	1145	
F-GEEO	Pilatus PC-6/B1-H2 Turbo-Porter	676	HB-FEO
F-GEEP	Cameron O-77 HAFB	1147	
F-GEEQ	Chaize CS.2200F12 HAFB	058	
F-GEER	Chaize CS.2000F12 HAFB	065	
F-GEES	Durondeau L-180 HAFB	15	
F-GEEU	Chaize CS.3000F16 HAFB	067	
F-GEEV	Chaize CS.2200F12 HAFB	068	
F-GEEX	Chaize CS.2200F32 HAFB	069	
F-GEEY	Chaize CS.3000F16 HAFB	071	
F-GEFA	Piper PA-28RT-201T Turbo Arrow IV	28R- 8231036	N8176V N9643N
F-GEFC	Sportavia/ Fournier RF-5	5087	F-OCPQ
F-GEFD	Morane-Saulnier MS.880B Rallye Club	77	HB-EDF
F-GEFH	Reims/Cessna F172M	F17201258	D-EESB
F-GEFI	Aérospatiale AS.350B Ecureuil	1787	D-HHCC
F-GEFT	Piper PA-31 Turbo Navajo	31-678	N4683Y D-IBRO F-BRQJ N6799L N9714N
F-GEFU(2)	Cessna 172N	17272605	N6112D
F-GEFZ	Cessna 425 Corsair	425-0059	LN-AFB SE-IFM (N6777L)
F-WEGB	Aérospatiale/Alenia ATR-42-200 (Stored)	002	
F-GEGG	Thunder AX8-105 HAFB	1052	
F-GEGI	Cameron A-105 HAFB	1339	
F-GEGJ	Thunder AX7-77Z HAFB	941	
F-GEGM	Thunder AX10-160A HAFB	943	
F-GEGN	Thunder AX7-77 HAFB	985	
F-GEGO	Piper PA-28-181 Cherokee Archer II	28-7790320	TU-TMH F-ODFO N1639H
F-GEGP	Thunder AX8-9OA HAFB	995	
F-GEGV	Thunder AX7-77Z HAFB	1047	
F-GEGX	Thunder AX7-65Z HAFB	1046	
F-GEGZ	Thunder AX7-77Z HAFB	1041	
F-GEHB	Aérospatiale SA.341G Gazelle	1099	N266E
F-GEHC	Aérospatiale SA.341G Gazelle	1417	N341AT N49536
F-GEHF	Aérospatiale SA.341G Gazelle	1320	N905XX N905X N49508
F-GEHM	Aérospatiale AS.350B Ecureuil	1722	
F-GEHN	Aérospatiale AS.350B Ecureuil	1027	F-ODIO
F-GEHO	SNCASE SE.313B Alouette II	1628	Gendarmerie/ F-MJAO ALAT
F-GEHV	Aérospatiale AS.350B Ecureuil	1454	N5786B
F-GEHX	Cessna 177B Cardinal	17702665	F-OGHX N20379
F-GEHZ	Aérospatiale AS.350B Ecureuil	1291	N803DB N3611T
F-WEIA	Robin R.3000Z	001	
F-GEIB	Robin DR.400/180 Régent	1676	
F-GEIC	Robin DR.400/120 Petit Prince	1678	
F-GEID	Robin DR.400/120 Petit Prince	1677	
F-GEIF	Robin DR.400/180 Régent	1690	
F-GEIH	Robin DR.400/180 Régent	1689	
F-GEIJ	Robin DR.400/180R Remorqueur	1709	F-WEIJ F-BEIJ
F-WEIK	Robin R.3000/180R	107	
F-GEIL	Robin DR.400/180R Remorqueur	1693	

F-GEIM	Robin DR.400/180R Remorqueur	1694	
F-GEIO	Robin DR.400/120 Petit Prince	1699	
F-GEIR	Robin DR.400/120 Petit Prince	1704	
F-GEIS	Robin DR.400/120 Petit Prince	1705	
F-GEIT	Robin DR.400/180R Remorqueur	1710	
F-GEIU	Robin DR.400/120 Petit Prince	1712	
F-GEIV	Robin R.3000/120	111	
F-GEIY	Robin R.3000/120	113	
F-GEIZ	Robin R.3000/140	114	
F-GEJC	SNCASE SE.313B Alouette II	04	
	(Restored .01, c/n previously quoted as 1004 ex FrAF)		
F-GEJD	Cessna 172RG Cutlass RG	172RG1158	D-EBDO N9428D
F-GEJJ	Beech A36TC Bonanza	EA-9	N6652Z
F-GEJK	Cessna 305C/L-19E Bird Dog (Stored)	24588	ALAT
F-GEJO	Piper PA-28-181 Archer II	28-8690018	(F-GFEG) N9097C
F-GEJQ	Piper PA-28-181 Archer II	2890030	N9123P
F-GEJV	Beech A100 King Air	B-129	N235B
F-GEJZ	Reims/Cessna F172M	F17201099	TU-TGT F-OCVT
F-GEKA	Robin R.3000/120	115	
F-GEKC	Robin DR.400/120 Petit Prince	1722	
F-GEKD	Robin DR.400/120 Petit Prince	1728	
F-GEKE	Robin DR.400/160 Chevalier	1729	
F-GEKG	Robin DR.400/180 Régent	1732	
F-GEKH	Robin DR.400/120 Petit Prince	1733	
F-GEKI	Robin DR.400/120D	1734	
F-GEKJ	Robin R.3000/120	119	
F-GEKL	Robin DR.400/120 Petit Prince	1736	
F-GEKN	Robin DR.400/120 Petit Prince	1739	
F-GEKO	Robin DR.400/120 Petit Prince	1740	
F-GEKP	Robin DR.400/160 Chevalier	1741	
F-GEKT	Robin DR.400/120 Petit Prince	1745	
F-GEKV	Robin DR.400/120 Petit Prince	1746	
F-GEKY	Robin DR.400/180R Remorqueur	1748	
F-GELB	Agusta-Bell 47G-2	103	D-HFLA ALAT
F-GELC	Agusta-Bell 47G	019	ALAT
F-GELF	Robinson R-22A Alpha	0444	N8555A
F-GELH	Fouga CM.170 Magister (Stored)	102	Fr.AF
F-GELJ	SNCASE SE.313B Alouette II	85/1100	Fr.AF
F-GELK	Reims/Cessna F172N	F17201811	D-EGLC
F-GELL	Beech E90 King Air	LW-88	9Q-CTQ N1TQ N1LQ N1LC N9OCJ
F-GELM	Piper PA-34-200T Seneca II	34-7870040	N9833K
F-GELN	Bell 47G-4A	7668	N1438W
F-GELT	Dassault Falcon 100	211	F-WZGT
F-GELU	Piper PA-34-200 Seneca	34-7350147	N16463
F-GELX(2)	Piper PA-32R-301T Turbo Saratoga SP	32R-8529005	N4385D
F-GELY	Beech A-36 Bonanza	E-458	TN-ACZ CR-LMX N2893W
F-GEMO	Airbus A310-304	504	F-WWCF
F-GENA	SOCATA TB-20 Trinidad	450	
F-GENB	SOCATA TB-20 Trinidad	460	
F-GENC	SOCATA Rallye 110ST Galopin	3384	
F-GENH	SOCATA TB-20 Trinidad	498	
F-GENJ	SOCATA TB-20 Trinidad	499	
F-GENK	SOCATA TB-10 Tobago	506	
F-GENR	SOCATA TB-20 Trinidad	513	F-OGMS
F-GENS	SOCATA TB-20 Trinidad	588	
F-GENT	SOCATA TB-9 Tampico	587	
F-GENY	SOCATA TB-10 Tobago	640	
F-GEOE	Aérospatiale AS.350B1 Ecureuil	2024	
F-GEOF	Hughes 269C	S-1183	D-HIVE
F-GEON	Piper PA-28R-201T Turbo Cherokee Arrow III	28R-7703293	G-OTUX SE-GPZ
F-GEOO	Piper PA-34-200T Seneca II	34-7870299	G-BMHP 4X-CAW N36160
F-GEOP	Thunder AX7-65Z HAFB	1088	
F-GEOQ	Piper PA-28R-201 Arrow III	28R-7837214	G-HIFI G-BFTB N9652C
F-GEOR	Mudry CAP.10B	77	G-WIXY F-BXHQ
F-GEOS	Cameron O-65 HAFB	1517	
F-GEOT	Reims/Cessna FR172K Hawk XP	FR17200649	OO-VNX OO-HNX
F-GEOU	Beech C90 King Air	LJ-941	N3804C
F-GEOV(2)	Piper PA-28R-201 Arrow III	28R-7837062	N4YN N6207H
F-GEOY(2)	Sud Avn SA.316B Alouette III	5397	F-ODRU D2-ESI F-WTNF
F-GEPA	Chaize CS.3000F16 HAFB	074	
F-GEPB	Aérospatiale AS.350B Ecureuil	1893	
F-GEPK	Piper PA-28RT-201T Turbo Arrow IV	28R-8031155	N8249Q
F-GEPN	Aérospatiale SA.365C2 Dauphin 2	5073	EC-DUT D-HELY
F-GEPO	Beech 58 Baron	TH-112	G-AYGZ
F-GEPR	Wassmer WA.40A Super IV	82	OO-ROY
F-GEPT	SOCATA TB-10 Tobago	342	F-OGKD
F-GEPZ	SOCATA MS.892A Rallye Commodore 150	11948	TU-TKY F-BTJU
F-GEQH(2)	Bell 47G-2	2420	N1044L CF-DTR
F-GEQI (2)	Aérospatiale SA.330J Puma	1590	F-ODJE
F-GEQJ	Aérospatiale/Alenia ATR-42-300	008	PH-ATR F-WWED
F-GEQL(3)	Cessna TR182 Turbo Skylane RG	R18201327	N9193Y
F-GEQN(2)	Bell 47	26	N106L N106B NC106B
F-GEQO(2)	SOCATA TB-9 Tampico	294	6V-AFE
F-GEQS(2)	SNCASE SE.3130 Alouette II	1142	ALAT Fr.AF
F-GEQT	Cessna 172RG Cutlass RG	172RG0419	N4933V
F-GEQV	Cessna 172N	17271921	N5691E
F-GEQX	Piper PA-28-161 Cherokee Warrior II	28-7716080	N1038Q
F-GEQZ	SOCATA MS.880B Rallye-Club	1273	F-BRDN
F-GERB	Cessna U206D Skywagon 206	U206-1385	LN-LJQ N72376
F-GERE	Cessna 305C/L-19E Bird Dog	24514	ALAT
F-GERF	Sportavia/ Fournier RF-5	5021	D-KAHF
F-GERJ	Aérospatiale SA.365N Dauphin 2	6066	F-ODRA F-WXFH
F-GERM	Piper PA-28RT-201T Turbo Arrow IV	28R-8131122	N8382V
F-GERR	Thunder AX7-77 HAFB	977	
F-GERS	Beech 200 Super King Air	BB-753	N3705B
F-GERX	Thunder AX7-77 HAFB	1107	
F-GERZ	Thunder AX7-77Z HAFB	1102	
F-GESF	Cameron A-105 HAFB	1549	
F-GESJ	Beech E90 King Air	LW-97	F-WZIG(2) D-IDTB F-ODID TR-LRX
F-GESK	Thunder AX7-77 HAFB	775	
F-GESN	Piper PA-28R-200 Cherokee Arrow II	28R-7535364	N3948X
F-GESR	SNCASE SE.3130 Alouette II	1551	LQ-HIS
F-GEST	Aérospatiale SA.341G Gazelle	1113	EC-CUA F-BVRU
F-GESX	Piper PA-28RT-201T Turbo Arrow IV	28R-8431006	N4330Y
F-GETA	Boeing 747-3B3	23413	N6009F (F-GDUE)
F-GETB	Boeing 747-3B3	23480	(F-GDUF) N6018N
F-GETC	Reims/Cessna F177RG Cardinal RG	F177RG0050	F-GETZ LX-RST G-AZKU
F-GETF	Piper PA-23-250 Aztec F	27-7854011	G-BFKN N63890
F-GETG	Piper PA-28RT-201 Arrow IV	28R-8218009	N8040A
F-GETH	Piper PA-28RT-201T Turbo Arrow IV	28R-8031064	N8156Y
F-GETI	Beech F90 King Air	LA-19	N90NS N90MT N6686A
F-GETK	Piper PA-28-181 Archer II	28-8490059	N4350J
F-GETL	Reims/Cessna F177RG Cardinal RG	F177RG0065	F-OCTL
F-GETQ	Piper PA-34-200T Seneca II	34-7870437	N30JA
F-GETR	Aérospatiale AS.355F Ecureuil 2	5060	F-OBUU
F-GETT	Piper PA-18 Super Cub 95	18-3230	OO-ACC OL-L56 L-156 53-4830
F-GETV	Thunder AX6-56 HAFB	845	
F-GETY	Thunder AX7-77 HAFB	799	
F-GETZ	Piper PA-28-181 Cherokee Archer II	28-7890085	N47511
F-GEUA	Reims/Cessna F172P	F17202225	
F-GEUB	Reims/Cessna F172P	F17202228	
F-GEUC	Reims/Cessna F172P	F17202231	
F-GEVA	SOCATA TB-20 Trinidad	552	
F-GEVB	SOCATA TB-10 Tobago	561	
F-GEVC	SOCATA TB-10 Tobago	562	
F-GEVE	SOCATA TB-10 Tobago	564	
F-GEVF	SOCATA TB-10 Tobago	565	
F-GEVG	SOCATA TB-10 Tobago	566	
F-GEVH	SOCATA TB-10 Tobago	567	
F-GEVI	SOCATA TB-10 Tobago	568	
F-GEVJ	SOCATA TB-20 Trinidad	691	
F-GEVK	SOCATA TB-20 Trinidad	734	
F-GEVL	SOCATA TB-20 Trinidad	735	
F-GEVM	SOCATA TB-20 Trinidad	736	
F-GEVO	SOCATA TB-20 Trinidad	752	
F-GEVP	SOCATA TB-20 Trinidad	753	
F-GEVQ	SOCATA TB-20 Trinidad	796	
F-GEVR	SOCATA TB-20 Trinidad	797	
F-GEVS	SOCATA TB-20 Trinidad	798	
F-GEVT	SOCATA TB-20 Trinidad	799	
F-GEVU	SOCATA TB-20 Trinidad	800	
F-GEVV	SOCATA TB-20 Trinidad	801	
F-GEVX	SOCATA TB-20 Trinidad	802	
F-GEVY	SOCATA TB-20 Trinidad	803	
F-GEVZ	SOCATA TB-20 Trinidad	804	
F-GEXA	Boeing 747-4B3	24154	
F-GEXB	Boeing 747-4B3M	24155	
F-GEXC	Hughes 269C	94-0352	N9584F
F-GEXL	Beech 200 Super King Air	BB-202	N2425X D-IBVW

F-GEXM	Piper PA-28RT-201T Turbo Arrow IV	28R-7931107	N3033U
F-GEXN	Hughes 269C	27-0578	D-HDAN(2) D-HMAP
F-GEXO	Thunder AX7-77 HAFB	963	
F-GEXQ	Agusta-Bell 47G-2	241	D-HIFA LN-ORT I- LOBY
F-GEXV	Beech A100 King Air	B-199	N110TD N600AC G-BBVL N85TC G-BBVL
F-GEYB	Raven Europe S-55A HAFB	E-4	
F-GEYD	Raven Europe FS-57A HAFB	E-6	
F-GEYE	Raven Europe S-55A HAFB	E-7	
F-GEYG	Raven Europe S-55A HAFB	E-9	
F-GEYH	Raven Europe S-55A HAFB	E-010	
F-GEYI	Raven Europe RX-65 HAFB	E-012	F-WEYI F-GEYI F-WEYI
F-GEYJ	Raven Europe S-55A HAFB	E-013	
F-GEYK	Raven Europe S-55A HAFB	E-015	
F-GEYN	Raven Europe S-55A HAFB	E-019	
F-GEYR	Raven Europe S-55A HAFB	E-1	
F-GEYT	Raven Europe S-55A HAFB	E-021	
F-GEYU	Raven Europe S-60A HAFB	E-023	
F-GEYV	Raven Europe S-60A HAFB	E-027	
F-GEYX	Raven Europe FS-57A HAFB	E-028	
F-GEYY	Raven Europe S-55A HAFB	E-029	
F-GEZA(1)	Raven Europe S-55A HAFB (Ntu ?)	E-026	
F-GEZA(2)	Kubicek BB-20 HAFB (Now current?)	179	F-GIBT(3) OK-0179
F-GEZB	Raven Europe S-55A HAFB	E-036	
F-GEZG	Raven Europe S-60A HAFB	E-055	
F-GEZI	Raven Europe S-55A HAFB	E-060	
F-GEZJ	Raven Europe S-55A HAFB	E-061	
F-GEZK	Raven Europe S-60A HAFB	E-068	
F-GEZM	Raven Europe RX-7 HAFB	E-064	
F-GEZN	Raven Europe RX-7 HAFB	E-097	
F-GEZO	Raven Europe FS-57A HAFB	E-103	
F-GEZP	Raven Europe RX-7 HAFB	E-079	
F-GEZQ	Raven Europe S-55A HAFB	E-104	
F-GEZR	Raven Europe FS-57A HAFB	E-098	
F-GEZS	Thunder AX7-77Z HAFB	678	
F-GEZT	Raven Europe S-66A HAFB	E-091	
F-GEZU	Raven Europe RX-7 HAFB	E-075	
F-GEZX	Raven Europe FS-57A HAFB	E-101	
F-GEZY	Raven Europe S-52A HAFB	E-102	
F-GEZZ	Raven Europe RX-7 HAFB	E-108	
F-GFAB	Aérospatiale AS.355F Ecureuil 2	5165	F-ODOM
F-WFAD	Ballon Commemoratif Dollfuss	unkn	
F-GFAQ	Aérospatiale AS.350B1 Ecureuil	2048	
F-GFAU	Beech 58 Baron	TH-1281	N1829D
F-GFAV	Robinson R-22 Beta	0560	
F-GFAX	Piper PA-28-161 Warrior II	28-8016090	OO-FLF OO-HLE, N8097E
F-GFBB	Aérospatiale AS.350B Ecureuil	1831	
F-GFBE	Sportavia/ Fournier RF-5	5044	TR-LAO F-OCOM
F-GFBH(3)	Thunder AX7-77 HAFB	1874	
F-GFBI (2)	Piper PA-44-180 Seminole	4495010	D-GFPA N92076
F-GFBJ	Grumman G.164A Agcat	1124	N5168
F-GFBM	Aérospatiale SA.365C2 Dauphin 2	5070	F-OAYC
F-GFBR	Cessna 172RG Cutlass RG	172RG0668	N6406V
F-GFBT	Beech V35B Bonanza	D-9727	N4079S
F-GFBU	Cessna 177RG Cardinal RG	177RG0671	N2724V
F-GFBV	Hughes 269C	15-0383	D-HMAU
F-GFCC	Pilatus PC-6/B1-H2 Turbo-Porter	572	C-GWZO N2852T
F-GFCF	Hughes 269C	119-0853	N58390
F-GFCG	Cessna 210N Centurion	21064148	OO-BIA N5275Y
F-GFCH	Aérospatiale SA.365C2 Dauphin 2	5072	F-OCCD F-WTNY
F-GFCI	Aérospatiale SA.341G Gazelle	1206	N3WU N3WL N55931
F-GFCJ	Cessna 310R	310R1519	D-ILCF N5229C
F-GFCK	Hughes 269C	104-0366	N9289F
F-GFCM	Aérospatiale SA.315B Lama	2226	G-BLLX ZK-HDX
F-GFCQ	Grumman G-159 Gulfstream 1	140	N92SA N92K N300A N760G
F-GFCS	Aérospatiale AS.350B1 Ecureuil	1970	
F-GFCT	Cessna 172N	17267974	N75817
F-GFCU	Cessna 172N	17269612	N737RH
F-GFCZ	Cessna 172M	17267413	N73380
F-GFDC	Pilatus PC-6/B1-H2 Turbo-Porter	656	ZK-PTP F-OCQV VH-SMA HB-FDC
F-GFDE	Cessna T207A Turbo Stationair 8	20700654	N75921

F-GFDH	Aérospatiale SN.601 Corvette	13	N601AN F-BVPD
F-GFDI	Thunder AX7-77 HAFB	1187	
F-GFDJ	Beech E90 King Air	LW-86	N410PB (N505N) N410PB (N429K) N410PD N410FD N3126W
F-GFDL	Aérospatiale AS.350B Ecureuil	1824	D-HHKK
F-GFDO	Agusta-Bell 206B Jet Ranger II	8531	G-BEKH
F-GFDP	Bell 47G	D-6	G-ARIA N4929V YI-ABY NC152B
F-GFDQ	CEA DR.360 Chevalier	524	OO-MAS
F-GFDS	Robin DR.400/120 Petit Prince	1528	EC-EAU F-OCJD
F-GFDT	Cameron O-77 HAFB	1651	
F-GFDY	Bell 206B Jet Ranger II	3600	G-OUPP N206SH N2261L
F-GFEA	Piper PA-31T Cheyenne	31T-7620011	N76PT N54990
F-GFEC	Aérospatiale SA.365C2 Dauphin 2	5071	F-ODBV F-GDCT
F-GFEE	Piper PA-28R-180 Cherokee Arrow	28R-30350	5R-MEE N3995T
F-GFEF	Grumman G-159 Gulfstream 1	122	N707MP N152SR N153SR N738G
F-GFEH	Robinson R-22 Beta	0769	
F-GFEO	Embraer EMB.120 Brasilia	120062	PT-SKF
F-GFET	SOCATA TB-10 Tobago	659	N20HY
F-GFEX	Aérospatiale AS.355F Ecureuil 2	5217	ZS-HKZ
F-GFEY	Aérospatiale AS.355F Ecureuil 2	5046	N57826
F-GFFA	Robinson R-22B Beta	0665	
F-GFFC	Grumman AA-5A Cheetah	AA5A-0573	TU-TMW F-OCBJ F-GBDJ
F-GFFD	Pilatus PC-6/B2-H2 Turbo-Porter	708	HB-FFD
F-GFFH	Robinson R-22 Beta (Noted 6.03)	unkn	
F-GFFI	Cameron A-140 HAFB	1561	
F-GFFJ	Ultramagic V-77 HAFB	77/18	
F-GFFM	Cameron N-160 HAFB	1622	G-BOGH
F-GFFO	Cessna 150M	15078660	N704JZ
F-GFFQ	SOCATA TB-20 Trinidad	647	N20GM
F-GFFT	SOCATA TB-20 Trinidad	672	N20LK
F-GFFU	Aérospatiale AS.350B Ecureuil	2083	
F-GFFV	Bell 47G-2	1987	N2874B
F-GFFX	Thunder AX8-9OA SIII HAFB	1890	
F-GFFY	Chaize CS.2200F12 HAFB	080	
F-GFFZ	Cessna 172RG Cutlass RG	172RG0375	N4754V
F-GFGA	Cessna P210N Pressurized Centurion II	P21000279	N210WC N4748K
F-GFGC	Robinson R-22B Beta	0687	
F-GFGH	SOCATA Rallye 235E Gabier	13337	F-ODNQ
F-GFGI (2)	Hughes 269C	117-0646	F-GDCF OE-CXN
F-GFGJ	Cessna U206G Stationair 6	U20604302	N756RT
F-GFGL	Beech 58 Baron (Reservation only - status uncertain)	TH-360	TR-LSG F-OCTZ
F-GFGN	Piper PA-28-181 Archer II	2890056	
F-GFGO	Piper PA-28-181 Archer II	2890060	
F-GFGQ(2)	Cessna 172N	17271595	N3576E
F-GFGS	Cessna 182N Skylane	18260799	D-EFWG N9255G
F-GFGX	Piper PA-28-181 Cherokee Archer II	28-7690275	N9697K
F-GFHA	Robinson R-22 Beta	0591	N24702
F-GFHC	Beech C90 King Air	LJ-717	N200BX
F-GFHI	Cessna 172RG Cutlass RG	172RG0332	N4595V
F-GFHL	Bell 47G-2	2433	N5828K C-FLMZ CF-LMZ
F-GFHM(2)	Aérospatiale AS.350B Ecureuil	1560	F-WYMB MAAW H-05 D-HEZE
F-GFHN(2)	Bell 47G-2	1489	N2805B
F-GFHQ	Beech 65-B90 King Air	LJ-347	N777SB N1TV N3290A N38RH N76AS N76RJ N333JJ D-IEVV
F-GFHS	Sud Avn SA.318C Alouette Astazou	2233	N4683
F-GFHT	Cessna 172N	17271679	N4938E
F-GFHU	Thunder AX7-77 HAFB	1253	
F-GFHX	Piper PA-12 Super Cruiser	12-3534	CN-TBS F-BFBK NC4102H
F-GFIC	Grumman G-159 Gulfstream 1	49	N456 N749G
F-GFIE	Piper PA-28-181 Archer II	2890071	

F-GFIF	Cessna 310R-II	310R0586	G-BEMA
			N87476
F-GFII	Hughes 369D	129-0628D	N58357
F-GFIO	SNCAN Stampe SV.4C	695	F-BDOO
F-GFIP	Thunder AX8-105 HAFB	1262	
F-GFIR	Beech C90 King Air	LJ-434	C-GRCN
			N14GA
			OE-FDU
			HB-GDU
F-GFIT	Piper PA-28RT-201 Arrow IV	28R-8018023	N35747
F-GFIU	Piper PA-32R-301 Saratoga SP	32R-8113044	N8340D
F-GFIX	Thunder AX8-9OA HAFB	1239	
F-GFIY	Chaize CS.3000F16 HAFB	084	
F-GFIZ	Piper PA-28RT-201T Turbo Arrow IV	28R-7931213	N2825N
F-GFJA	Piper PA-32R-300 Cherokee Lance	32R-7680224	OO-BEL
			OY-BLR
F-GFJG	Cessna TR182 Turbo Skylane RG	R18201854	N5306T
F-GFJH	Aérospatiale/Alenia ATR-42-300	049	
F-GFJI	Reims/Cessna FRA150L Aerobat	FRA1500139	TU-TFT
			F-OCPM
F-GFJJ(2)	Piper PA-28-181 Archer II	28-7990157	N321DG
F-GFJO	Bell 47G-2	2251	C-FKMX
			CF-KMX
F-GFJR	Cessna 425 Corsair	425-0032	N6773B
F-GFJY(2)	Piper PA-28-181 Archer II	28-8490111	N132AV
			N9637N
F-GFJZ	Thunder AX8-105 HAFB	1240	
F-GFKA	Airbus A320-111	005	F-WWDI
F-GFKB	Airbus A320-111	007	F-WWDJ
F-GFKD	Airbus A320-111	014	F-WWDO
F-GFKE	Airbus A320-111	019	
F-GFKF	Airbus A320-111	020	
F-GFKG	Airbus A320-111	021	
F-GFKH	Airbus A320-211	061	
F-GFKI	Airbus A320-211	062	
F-GFKJ	Airbus A320-211	063	
F-GFKK	Airbus A320-211	100	
F-GFKL	Airbus A320-211	101	
F-GFKM	Airbus A320-211	102	
F-GFKN	Airbus A320-211	128	
F-GFKO	Airbus A320-211	129	
F-GFKP	Airbus A320-211	133	
F-GFKQ	Airbus A320-111	002	F-WWDA
F-GFKR	Airbus A320-211	186	
F-GFKS	Airbus A320-211	187	
F-GFKT	Airbus A320-211	188	
F-GFKU	Airbus A320-211	226	
F-GFKV	Airbus A320-211	227	
F-GFKX	Airbus A320-211	228	
F-GFKY	Airbus A320-211	285	
F-GFKZ	Airbus A320-211	286	
F-GFLA	SOCATA TB-10 Tobago	85	F-ZVLA
F-GFLC	Piper PA-28-181 Archer II	28-8490047	TJ-AHB
			N4338E
F-GFLJ(2)	Nord 1101 Noralpha	141	N72SL
			F-BLTS
			Fr.Mil
F-GFLM	Bell 47G-2	1631	F-GBLM
			G-BEUE
			EP-HAU
			N6763
			Fr.AF
			N2850B
F-GFLU	CEA DR.253 Régent	113	G-AWCD
F-GFLZ(2)	Piper PA-28-181 Archer II	28-8690049	N9082Z
F-GFMB	Beech C23 Sundowner 180	M-1501	TU-TGL
F-GFMC	Chaize CS.3000F16 HAFB	076	
F-GFMD	Dassault Falcon 10	136	F-WZGS
			I- MUDE
			F-WZGH
F-GFMF	Chaize CS.2200F12 HAFB	082	
F-GFMG	Robin DR.300/120 Petit Prince	615	F-ZVMG
F-GFMK	Bell 206B Jet Ranger II	2386	N777TE
F-GFML	SOCATA MS.893E Rallye 180GT Gaillard	12386	F-ZVML
F-GFMM	Robin DR.400/2+2 (Damaged 11.8.00)	1451	F-ZVMM
			F-GCIE
F-GFMO	Piper PA-28-181 Archer II	28-8390011	N8300Z
F-GFMQ	SOCATA ST-10 Diplomate	147	F-BTJM
F-GFMT	Cessna 172N	17268481	N733RC
F-GFMU	Cessna F172H	F172-0404	LX-AVB
			D-EMFC
F-GFMV	Beech 58 Baron	TH-745	OO-DUK
			F-ODCZ
F-GFMX	Agusta-Bell 206B Jet Ranger II	8305	OE-BXP
F-GFNC	Robin ATL	03	F-WFNC
F-GFNE	Robin ATL	05	F-WFNE
F-GFNF	Robin ATL	06	F-WFNF
F-GFNG	Robin ATL	07	F-WFNG
F-GFNH	Robin ATL	08	F-WFNH
F-GFNL	Robin ATL	12	F-WFNL
F-GFNM	Robin ATL	13	F-WFNM
F-GFNP	Robin ATL	20	F-WFNP
F-GFNQ	Robin ATL	17	F-WFNQ
F-GFNS	Robin ATL	18	F-WFNS
F-GFNT	Robin ATL	19	F-WFNT
F-GFNX	Robin ATL	24	F-WFNX
F-GFNY	Robin ATL	21	F-WFNY

F-GFNZ	Robin ATL	25	F-WFNZ
F-GFOC	Robin ATL	27	F-WFOC
F-GFOD	Robin ATL	28	F-WFOD
F-GFOE	Robin ATL	29	F-WFOE
F-GFOF	Robin ATL	30	F-WFOF
F-GFOG	Robin ATL	31	F-WFOG
F-GFOJ	Robin ATL	34	F-WFOJ
F-GFOL	Robin ATL	36	F-WFOL
F-GFOM	Robin ATL	37	
F-GFOO	Robin ATL	39	
F-GFOQ	Robin ATL	41	
F-GFOR	Robin ATL	42	
F-GFOS	Robin ATL	43	
F-GFOT	Robin ATL	44	
F-GFOU	Robin ATL	45	
F-GFOV	Robin ATL	46	
F-GFPA	Aérospatiale SA.365C2 Dauphin 2	5063	F-ODNK
			F-GCTL
F-GFPC	Chaize CS.2200F12 HAFB	085	
F-GFPD(2)	Piper PA-25-235 Pawnee	25-2685	N6940Z
F-GFPF	Dassault Falcon 10	68	N80MP
			N91DH
			N11DH
			(N7NL)
			N7NP
			N152FJ
			F-WLCV
F-GFPH	Piper PA-23-235 Apache	27-602	F-OBYY
			F-BMLL
			N4319Y
F-GFPJ	Piper PA-18-135 Super Cub	18-3188	OO-WIK
	(Quoted officially with f/n 18-3191)		OO-HBB
			OL-L01
			L-114
			53-4788
F-GFPM	Aérospatiale AS.350B Ecureuil	1833	
F-GFPN	Robinson R-22 Beta	0848	
F-GFPP	Beech A36 Bonanza	E-1454	N6027M
F-GFPQ	Sud Avn SA.318C Alouette Astazou	2247	C-FQMQ
			CF-QMQ
F-GFPS	Beech 76 Duchess	ME-209	N6626W
F-GFPX	Thunder AX10-160 HAFB	1295	
F-GFPY	CEA DR.315 Petit Prince	332	F-BPRY
F-GFPZ	Mudry CAP.20	5	Fr.AF: F-TFVY
			F-BTAG
			F-TFVY
F-GFQA	SOCATA TB-20 Trinidad	571	F-OGMT
F-GFQC	SOCATA TB-9 Tampico	699	
F-GFQE	SOCATA Rallye 180T Galérien	3386	
F-GFQF	SOCATA TB-20 Trinidad	709	
F-GFQH	SOCATA TB-10 Tobago	733	
F-GFQJ	SOCATA TB-20 Trinidad	741	
F-GFQO	SOCATA TB-10 Tobago	657	(N20HQ)
F-GFQU	SOCATA TB-10 Tobago	769	
F-GFQV	SOCATA TB-10 Tobago	661	(N20JQ)
F-GFQX	SOCATA TB-10 Tobago	663	(N20JY)
F-GFQY	SOCATA TB-20 Trinidad	779	
F-GFRA	Robin ATL	50	
F-GFRF	Robin ATL	55	
F-GFRH	Robin ATL	57	
F-GFRJ	Robin ATL	59	
F-GFRK	Robin ATL	60	
F-GFRM	Robin ATL	62	
F-GFRN	Robin ATL	63	
F-GFRO	Robin ATL	64	
F-GFRP	Robin ATL	65	
F-GFRR	Robin ATL	67	
F-GFRS	Robin ATL	69	
F-GFRT	Robin ATL	70	
F-GFRU	Robin ATL	71	
F-GFRY	Robin ATL	75	
F-GFRZ	Robin ATL	82	
F-GFSC	Robin ATL	79	
F-GFSD	Robin ATL	84	
F-GFSE	Robin ATL	85	
F-GFSF	Robin ATL	86	
F-GFSJ	Robin ATL	90	
F-GFSK	Robin ATL	91	
F-GFSL	Robin ATL	92	
F-GFSN	Robin ATL	94	
F-GFSR	Robin ATL	98	
F-GFSS	Robin ATL	99	
F-GFSU	Robin ATL	101	
F-GFSX	Robin ATL	104	
F-GFSY	Robin ATL	105	
F-GFSZ	Robin ATL	111	F-WFSZ
F-GFTE	Cessna 177B Cardinal	17702568	N19393
F-GFTF	Piper PA-34-200 Seneca	34-7350303	LX- IER
			OO- ITF
			N56197
F-GFTK	Ayres S.2R Thrush Commander	2518R	N4008D
F-GFTN	Piper PA-28R-201T Turbo Arrow IV	28R-7931103	N3024U
F-GFTR	Robin DR.400/180 Régent	1858	
F-GFTU	Agusta-Bell 47G-2	250	EC-DXB
			D-HIRT
			74+10
			AS+051

F-GFTV	Beech A36 Bonanza	E-1640	N6730L
F-WFTX	Fouga CM.170 Magister	522	Fr.AF
F-GFTY	Piper PA-25-235 Pawnee	25-2741	N6991Z (N585Z) N6991Z
F-GFTZ	Piper PA-28-161 Warrior II	28-8216093	N8053R
F-GFUE	Boeing 737-33A	24387	
F-GFUF	Boeing 737-33A	24388	
F-GFUG	Boeing 737-4B3	24750	
F-GFUH	Boeing 737-4B3	24751	
F-GFUM	Pilatus PC-6/B2-H2 Turbo Porter	740	HA-YDB
F-GFUO	Piper PA-25-235 Pawnee	25-2141	N6585Z
F-GFUP	Piper PA-25-235 Pawnee	25-2841	N7061Z
F-WFUQ	Fouga CM-170 Magister	523	Fr.AF
F-GFUR	Robin ATL	80	
F-GFUS	Cameron N-90 HAFB	2376	
F-GFUV	Piper PA-31T Cheyenne	31T-7720063	N3948A YV-279CP N82185
F-GFUX	Ultramagic Label Rouge HAFB	6/01	
F-GFUY	Beech A36 Bonanza	E-2640	
F-GFVA	Cessna 305C/L-19E Bird Dog	24522	ALAT
F-GFVB	Cessna 305C/L-19E Bird Dog	24534	ALAT
F-GFVD	Cessna 305C/L-19E Bird Dog	24539	ALAT
F-GFVF	Cessna 305C/L-19E Bird Dog	24545	ALAT
F-GFVL	Thunder AX7-77Z HAFB	1242	
F-GFVN	Beech F90 King Air	LA-166	HB-GHM N6133H
F-GFVP	Wassmer Jodel D.120A Paris-Nice	217	OO-PCJ LX-OUF(1) F-BKNF
F-GFVV	Holste MH.1521M Broussard	298	Fr.AF
F-GFVZ	Robin DR.400/180 Régent	1113	F-BXVZ
F-GFXA	Robin DR.400/120 Petit Prince	1749	
F-GFXB	Robin DR.400/160 Chevalier	1750	
F-GFXC	Robin DR.400/120 Petit Prince	1752	
F-GFXD	Robin DR.400/120 Petit Prince	1751	
F-GFXE	Robin DR.400/180 Régent	1755	
F-GFXF	Robin DR.400/120 Petit Prince	1753	
F-GFXG	Robin DR.400/180 Régent	1756	
F-GFXH	Robin DR.400/120 Petit Prince	1757	
F-GFXJ	Robin DR.400/120 Petit Prince	1772	
F-GFXK	Robin DR.400/180 Régent	1763	
F-GFXL	Robin DR.400/160 Major	1761	
F-GFXN	Robin DR.400/120 Petit Prince	1768	
F-GFXO	Robin DR.400/120 Petit Prince	1770	
F-GFXP	Robin DR.400/120 Petit Prince	1771	
F-GFXQ	Robin R.3000/120	127	
F-GFXS	Robin DR.400/180 Régent	1774	
F-GFXT	Robin DR.400/100 Cadet	1775	F-WFXT
F-GFXV	Robin DR.400/180 Régent	1777	
F-GFXX	Robin DR.400/160 Chevalier	1779	
F-GFXY	Robin DR.400/180 Régent	1780	
F-GFXZ	Robin DR.400/120 Petit Prince	1782	
F-GFYD	Zlin Z.526F Trenér Master	1176	F-BTGD F-WTGD
F-GFYJ(2)	Cessna T210N Turbo Centurion II	21063648	N4860C
F-GFYK	Piper PA-28-180 Cherokee C	28-3282	F-OCJV N9219J
F-GFYQ	Thunder AX7-77 HAFB	1366	
F-GFYR	Hughes 369D	39-0483D	N58262
F-GFYT	Piper PA-28-161 Cadet	2841060	
F-GFYV	Piper PA-28-161 Cadet	2841059	
F-GFZA	Piper PA-28-181 Archer II	28-8390074	TJ-AGW N82608 N9516N
F-GFZC	Aérospatiale AS.350B Ecureuil	2163	
F-GFZD	Aérospatiale AS.350B Ecureuil	2195	
F-GFZF	Sud Avn SA.318C Alouette Astazou	2352	D-HHFS SX-HAN
F-GFZG	Piper PA-28-140 Cherokee E	28-7225350	PH-LAM N11C
F-GFZH	Reims/Cessna FTB.337 Super Skymaster (W/o 15.4.04)	0035	F-BXNL
F-GFZI	Zodiac MGZ 2-2-S Free Balloon	002	
F-GFZJ	SOCATA TB-20 Trinidad	626	(F-GFPO) N800X
F-GFZK	Piper PA-28-180 Cherokee Archer	28-7505247	6V-AFS OO-KIS OO-HAP N3919X
F-GFZL	Cessna 172F	17253259	TN-AAS (F-GELD) TN-AAS F-OCGC (N5637R)
F-GFZN	Robinson R-22 Beta	1004	
F-GFZO	Morane-Saulnier MS.733 Alcyon	140	F-BNEE Fr.Mil
F-GFZP	Balloon Works Firefly 7 HAFB	F7-479	
F-GFZQ	SNCASE SE.313B Alouette II	1813	F-MJBO
F-WFZR(2)	Chaize CS-500F12 HAFB	EX-001	
F-GFZS	Thunder AX7-77 HAFB	718	
F-GFZV	Piper PA-28-181 Archer II	2890117	
F-GFZX	Piper PA-28R-201T Turbo Cherokee Arrow III	28R-7703319	N43938 (N748SB) N43938

F-GGAA	Schweizer 269C	S-1308	
F-GGAC	Piper PA-28-181 Archer II	2890067	
F-GGAD	Zlin Z.526F Trenér Master	1177	(F-GGAA) F-BTGE F-WTGE
F-GGAE	Piper PA-28-161 Cadet	2841062	
F-GGAG	Bell 47G-2	665-10	CF-HFX
F-GGAJ	Cessna T210N Turbo Centurion II	21063891	N6445C
F-GGAL	Cessna 650 Citation III	650-0117	N1321N
F-GGAM	Beech 65-90 King Air	LJ-32	F-BTOK PH-FSS HB-GCF
F-GGAO	Aérospatiale AS.350B Ecureuil	2208	
F-GGAP	Chaize 3000 Ovmi Gas Balloon	001	F-WGAP
F-GGAR(2)	Aérospatiale AS.350B Ecureuil	1841	F-WYMC HB-XPG
F-GGAU	Reims/Cessna F172N	F17201867	D-EKAU
F-GGAX	Agusta-Bell 206B Jet Ranger II	8020	D-HOOL SE-HPD
F-GGAY	Piper PA-28-181 Cherokee Archer II	28-7790461	N3493Q
F-GGBA	Piper PA-28RT-201T Turbo Arrow IV	28R-8431002	N4324P N9547N
F-GGBD	Piper PA-32R-301T Turbo Saratoga SP	32R-8129110	N8442U
F-GGBI	Thunder AX7-77 HAFB	1481	
F-GGBK	Rockwell S.2R Thrush Commander	1426R	
F-GGBM	Cameron N-77 HAFB	2067	
F-GGBN	Hughes 269C	20-0894	D-HKAG
F-GGBO	Holste MH.1521C-1 Broussard	262	F-WGBO Fr.AF
F-GGBQ	Piper PA-28-140 Cherokee Cruiser	28-7625059	N921C N4580X
F-GGBR	SOCATA Rallye 150SV Garnement	3365	F-OGLV
F-GGBX	SNCASE SE.3130 Alouette II	1373	ALAT
F-GGBY	SNCASE SE.313B Alouette II	1332	ALAT
F-GGBZ(2)	Cessna 172N	17268486	N733RH
F-GGCD	Chaize CS-2200F12 HAFB	81	
F-GGCE	Piper PA-28RT-201T Turbo Arrow IV	28R-8031111	N45KC N9566N
F-GGCF	Piper PA-28RT-201T Turbo Arrow IV	28R-7931310	N8094Q
F-GGCG	SNCASE SE.313B Alouette II	1172	ALAT
F-GGCH	Piper PA-31T Cheyenne II	31T-8120056	N51TW N2572Y
F-GGCI	SNCASE SE.313B Alouette II	1050	ALAT
F-GGCN	Holste MH.1521C1 Broussard	6	Fr.Mil
F-GGCQ	SNCASE SE.313B Alouette II	1348	ALAT
F-GGCR	Raven Europe FS-57A HAFB	E-092	
F-GGCS	Cessna 152	15283555	N4622B
F-GGCT	Cessna 152	15280130	N757ZH
F-GGCV	Cessna 172RG Cutlass RG	172RG1111	N9997B
F-GGCX	Cessna 172RG Cutlass RG	172RG1134	N9360D
F-GGCZ	Cessna 172RG Cutlass RG	172RG0708	N6447V
F-GGDB	Piper PA-28RT-201 Arrow IV	28R-7918160	N2824R
F-GGDC	Piper PA-28-161 Cadet	2841063	
F-GGDE	Cessna A185F Skywagon	18504075	N60925
F-GGDF	Thunder AX7-65 HAFB	818	
F-GGDG	SNCASE SE.313B Alouette II	1104	ALAT Fr.AF
F-GGDH	SNCASE SE.313B Alouette II	1103	ALAT
F-GGDI	Hughes 369D	67-0149D	N444HM ZK-HJQ
F-GGDK	Thunder AX7-77 HAFB	1342	
F-GGDL	Piper PA-28-181 Archer II	28-8190242	N83912
F-GGDN	Thunder AX7-77 HAFB	1504	
F-GGDO	Thunder AX7-77Z HAFB	1515	
F-GGDQ	Robinson R-22 Beta	1042	
F-GGDS	Chaize CS2000F12 HAFB	095	
F-GGDT	Hughes 369D	67-0154D	N81418 TG-REY YS-1014P
F-GGDU	Bell 47G-2	1540	N5185B
F-GGDX	Cessna A185F Skywagon (Reserved as F-OMMP 8.04)	18503538	N767RC N2901Q
F-GGDY	Hughes 269C	41-1043	D-HMIG
F-GGEA	Airbus A320-111	010	F-WWDL
F-GGEB	Airbus A320-111	012	F-WWDM
F-GGEC	Airbus A320-111	013	F-WWDN
F-GGEE	Airbus A320-111	016	F-WWDQ
F-GGEF(2)	Airbus A320-111	004	F-WWDC
F-GGEG(2)	Airbus A320-111	003	F-WWDB
F-GGFC	Robinson R-22 Beta (Damaged 23.11.99)	0822	
F-GGFF	SNCAN Stampe SV.4C	610	F-BDFF
F-GGFG	Robinson R-22 Beta	1055	N8045U
F-GGFK(2)	Colt Montgolfier SS HAFB	1281	G-BPHV
F-GGFL	Robinson R-22 Beta	1045	
F-GGFN	Bell 47G	1708	OO-MMT PH-AAH D-HABO
F-GGFR	Cessna 310R	310R2103	(F-GFGD) N6830Q
F-GGFT	Piper PA-28-161 Cadet	2841075	
F-GGFV	Piper PA-28-161 Cadet	2841077	
F-GGFX	Piper PA-28-161 Cadet	2841078	
F-GGFY	Piper PA-28-161 Cadet	2841079	
F-GGFZ	Robinson R-22 Beta	0838	3A-MTU
F-GGGA	Cessna F.550 Citation	F550-0586	N1301N
F-WGGC	Fouga CM-170 Magister	459	Fr.AF
F-WGGD	Holste MH.1521M Broussard	290	Fr.AF

F-WGGE	Mudry CAP.20	4	Fr.AF: F-TFVX F-BTAF
F-GGGJ	Colt 90A HAFB	1553	
F-WGGK	Holste MH.1521M Broussard	127	ALAT
F-GGGL	Mooney M.20J Model 205	24-3027	
F-GGGN	Cessna T210N Turbo Centurion II	21064426	N6537Y
F-GGGO	Colt 90A HAFB	1565	
F-GGGP	Beech A36 Bonanza	E-2200	N216JP N7212L
F-WGGQ	Holste MH.1521M Broussard (Stored)	143	ALAT
F-GGGR	Boeing 727-2H3	20822	PH-AHD N191CB TS-JHP
F-GGGS	Robin HR.100/250TR	553	(F-ODSX) 6V-AEK F-ODFX
F-GGGT	Cessna F550 Citation II	0611	
F-GGGZ	Piper PA-38-112 Tomahawk	38-81A0022	HB-PFT
F-GGHA	Robin ATL	106	
F-GGHD	Robin ATL	110	
F-GGHE	Robin ATL	81	F-WZZX (PH-ATL)
F-GGHG	Robin ATL	117	
F-GGHH	Robin ATL	118	
F-GGHI	Robin DR.400/180R Remorqueur	1833	
F-GGHJ	Robin DR.400/140B Major 80	1832	
F-GGHK	Robin DR.400/140B Major 80	1834	
F-GGHL	Robin DR.400/180 Régent	1835	
F-GGHM	Robin ATL	119	
F-GGHO	Robin R.3000/140	133	
F-GGHP	Robin ATL	120	
F-GGHR	Robin DR.400/180 Régent	1844	
F-GGHT	Robin DR.400/180 Régent	1846	
F-GGHU	Robin DR.400/180 Régent	1848	
F-GGHV	Robin DR.400/120 Dauphin 2+2	1849	
F-GGHX	Robin DR.400/120 Dauphin 2+2	1850	
F-GGHY	Robin DR.400/160 Major	1853	
F-GGIB	SOCATA TB-20 Trinidad	777	
F-GGIC	SOCATA TB-20 Trinidad	778	
F-GGID	SOCATA TB-20 Trinidad	790	
F-GGIE	SOCATA TB-20 Trinidad	854	
F-GGIF	SOCATA TB-20 Trinidad	855	
F-GGIG	SOCATA TB-20 Trinidad	859	
F-GGIH	SOCATA TB-20 Trinidad	990	
F-GGII	SOCATA TB-20 Trinidad	991	
F-GGIJ	SOCATA TB-20 Trinidad	996	
F-GGIK	SOCATA TB-10 Tobago	785	
F-GGIO	SOCATA TB-20 Trinidad	791	
F-GGIP	SOCATA TB-20 Trinidad	794	
F-GGIR	SOCATA TB-9 Tampico	809	
F-GGIU	SOCATA TB-9 Tampico	885	
F-GGIV	SOCATA TB-9 Tampico	890	
F-GGIX	SOCATA TB-20 Trinidad	898	
F-GGIY	SOCATA TB-10 Tobago	906	
F-GGJB	Robin DR.400/120 Petit Prince	1788	
F-GGJC	Robin DR.400/120 Petit Prince	1791	
F-GGJD	Robin DR.400/180 Régent	1789	
F-GGJF	Robin DR.400/180 Régent (W/o 18.8.02)	1796	
F-GGJG	Robin DR.400/120 Petit Prince	1799	
F-GGJH	Robin DR.400/160 Chevalier	1795	
F-GGJI	Robin DR.400/120 Dauphin 2+2	1801	
F-GGJJ	Robin DR.400/180 Régent	1804	
F-GGJL	Robin DR.400/180 Régent	1807	
F-GGJM	Robin R.3000/140	131	
F-GGJO	Robin DR.400/120 Dauphin 2+2	1814	
F-GGJP	Robin DR.400/180 Régent	1811	
F-GGJQ	Robin DR.400/120 Dauphin 2+2	1813	
F-GGJR	Robin DR.400/120 Dauphin 2+2	1815	
F-GGJS	Robin DR.400/120 Dauphin 2+2	1816	
F-GGJT	Robin DR.400/180 Régent	1820	
F-GGJU	Robin DR.400/120 Dauphin 2+2	1822	
F-GGJV	Robin DR.400/180 Régent	1840	
F-GGJX	Robin DR.400/120 Dauphin 2+2	1823	
F-GGJY	Robin DR.400/160 Major	1824	
F-GGKB	Piper J-3C-65 Cub	14986	N42690 NC42690
F-GGKC(2)	Piper J-3C-65 Cub	5037	N30655 NC30655
F-GGKH	Holste MH.1521C Broussard (Plates on aircraft quote c/ns 35 and 232)	32	F-WGKH Fr.AF
F-GGKK	Holste MH.1521C-1 Broussard	211M	F-WGKK Fr.AF
F-GGKL	Holste MH.1521C-1 Broussard	255	F-WGKL Fr.AF
F-WGKN	Holste MH.1521M Broussard	261	Fr.AF
F-GGKR	Holste MH.1521M Broussard	316	F-WGKR Fr.AF
F-GGKU	Aérospatiale SA.342 Gazelle	1186	TT-OAG F-WTNC
F-GGKV	Aérospatiale SA.342 Gazelle	1378	TT-OAF
F-GGKX	Aérospatiale SA.330B Puma	1021	TT- . . . ALAT
F-GGKY	Aérospatiale SA.330 Puma	1200	TT- . . . ALAT
F-GGKZ	Robinson R-22 Beta	1146	

F-GGLA	Beech 200 Super King Air	BB-744	F-GGPJ (N713JS) (N700CR) N152WC N3702M
F-GGLB	Bell 47G-2 (Dbr 15.9.03)	1056	N10194
F-GGLH	Robinson R-22 Beta	1065	N8046U
F-GGLI	Cessna 152	15281685	N66950
F-GGLL	Piper PA-28-161 Warrior II	28-8116012	N8255A
F-GGLM	Thunder AX7-77Z HAFB	1450	
F-GGLN	Beech 200 Super King Air	BB-439	N500JA C-FMCF N110MJ N110JJ
F-GGLO	Piper PA-18-150 Super Cub	18-5329	TR-LBY F-BLOV ALAT N10F
F-GGLP	Beech A36 Bonanza	E-1595	N19WH N66775
F-GGLS	Morane-Saulnier MS.885 Super Rallye	125	D-EMTE
F-GGLU	Morane-Saulnier MS.880B Rallye Club	68	D-EDRC F-BKDU
F-GGLV	Beech A100 King Air	B-150	N51BL N54MG N54KA
F-GGLY	Cameron N-90 HAFB	2124	
F-GGLZ(2)	Holste MH.1521M Broussard	102	ALAT
F-WGMG	RJ-03A Roitelet Helicopter	unkn	
F-GGMH	Piper PA-28-181 Archer II	2890166	
F-GGMJ	Mooney M.20J Model 205	24-3045	N205DD
F-GGMK	Piper PA-18-150 Cub	1809051	N9522N
F-WGMO(2)	AS.300	008	
F-WGMQ	Aérospatiale AS.350Z Ecureuil	1013	F-WYMZ N134BH N90001
F-GGMT	Aerotek Pitts S.2A	2272	
F-GGMU	Piper PA-28RT-201T Turbo Arrow IV	28R-8031014	N8114P
F-GGMV	Beech 200 Super King Air	BB-616	SE-IUN N123AF N6693F
F-GGMY	Piper PA-28-181 Archer II	28-7990375	6V-AEP N2235X
F-GGNA	SOCATA TB-20 Trinidad	807	
F-GGNB	SOCATA TB-20 Trinidad	808	
F-GGNC	SOCATA TB-20 Trinidad	816	
F-GGND	SOCATA TB-20 Trinidad	817	
F-GGNE	SOCATA TB-20 Trinidad	818	
F-GGNF	SOCATA TB-20 Trinidad	819	
F-GGNG	SOCATA TB-10 Tobago	945	
F-GGNH	SOCATA TB-10 Tobago	946	
F-GGNJ	SOCATA TB-10 Tobago	1172	
F-GGNK	SOCATA TB-10 Tobago	1173	
F-GGNM	SOCATA TB-10 Tobago	1175	
F-GGNO	SOCATA TB-20 Trinidad	1213	
F-GGNP	SOCATA TB-20 Trinidad	1264	
F-GGNQ	SOCATA TB-20 Trinidad	1265	
F-GGNR	SOCATA TB-20 Trinidad	1266	
F-GGNS	SOCATA TB-20 Trinidad	1267	
F-GGNT	SOCATA TB-20 Trinidad	1284	
F-GGNU	SOCATA TB-20 Trinidad	1285	
F-GGNV	SOCATA TB-20 Trinidad	1286	
F-GGNX	SOCATA TB-20 Trinidad	1287	
F-GGNY	SOCATA TB-20 Trinidad	1301	
F-GGNZ	SOCATA TB-20 Trinidad	1302	
F-GGOB	Grob G.115A	8027	F-WGOB D-EGVV
F-GGOD	Grob G.115A	8036	F-WGOD D-EGVV
F-GGOH	Grob G.115A	8076	D-EGVV
F-GGOJ	Grob G.115A	8064	D-EIAW
F-GGOK	Grob G.115A	8096	
F-GGOL	Grob G.115A	8103	
F-GGOP	Grob G.115A	8106	
F-GGOQ	Grob G.115A	8107	
F-GGPI	Agusta-Bell 206B Jet Ranger II	8169	G-BPHF SE-HGS D-HARU
F-GGPL(2)	Mooney M.20J Model 201	24-1632	
F-GGPO	Piper PA-28-161 Cadet	2841103	
F-GGPQ	SOCATA TB-20 Trinidad	972	
F-GGPR	Beech 200 Super King Air	BB-681	LN-AXA (LN-AAX) N200NF D-ILBO N6751T
F-GGPS	Aerotek Pitts S-2B	5015	N66LF N53206
F-WGPU(2)	Fouga CM.170R Magister	014	Fr.AF
F-GGPX	Cameron 105SS Paint-Tin HAFB	2239	
F-GGPY	Aérospatiale AS.350B Ecureuil	2361	
F-GGQA	Robin DR.400/120 Dauphin 2+2	1851	
F-GGQB	Robin DR.400/140B Major 80	1852	
F-GGQD	Robin DR.400/120 Dauphin 2+2	1878	
F-GGQE	Robin DR.400/120 Dauphin 2+2	1877	
F-GGQF	Robin DR.400/160 Major	1856	
F-GGQG	Robin ATL	124	

F-GGQH	Robin R.3000/140	134	
F-GGQI	Robin ATL	125	
F-GGQJ	Robin ATL	126	
F-GGQK	Robin DR.400/180 Régent	1860	
F-GGQL	Robin DR.400/120 Dauphin 2+2	1859	
F-GGQM	Robin DR.400/120 Dauphin 2+2	1863	
F-GGQN	Robin DR.400/180 Régent	1867	
F-GGQO	Robin DR.400/100 Cadet	1864	
F-GGQP	Robin DR.400/100	1865	
F-GGQQ	Robin DR.400/180R Remorqueur	1868	
	(Wreck noted at St Girons 9.03)		
F-GGQR	Robin DR.400/120 Dauphin 2+2	1866	
F-GGQS	Robin ATL	127	
F-GGQU	Robin DR.400/100 Cadet	1871	
F-GGQX	Robin DR.400/120 Dauphin 2+2	1879	
F-GGQY	Robin DR.400/180 Régent	1873	
F-GGQZ	Robin DR.400/140B Major 80	1880	
F-GGRC	Chaize CS.2200F12 HAFB	092	
F-GGRF	Cameron A-120 HAFB	2242	
F-GGRK	Cessna 310R	310R0141	(F-GGRF)
			F-ODRK
			F-BXAK
			N5021J
F-GGRL	Mooney M.20J Model 201	24-1622	
F-GGRN	Piper PA-28R-201 Arrow III	28R-7837283	N36544
F-GGRQ	Ultramagic H-77 HAFB	77/47	
F-GGRT	Chaize CS.3000F16 HAFB	086	
F-GGRU	Cameron N-65 HAFB	2287	
F-GGRV	Piper PA-31T Cheyenne	31T-7720036	N41RC
			N1RA
			YV-123CP
F-GGRX	Piper PA-28R-201 Arrow	2837035	N9187Z
F-GGRY	Piper PA-28-161 Cadet	2841104	
F-GGSD	Cameron O-77 HAFB	1410	
F-GGSG	Cameron O-77 HAFB	1429	
F-GGSH	Schweizer 269C	S-1271	D-HDAM
F-GGSI	Piper PA-28-161 Warrior II	28-8116172	N8346F
F-GGSJ	Chaize CS.3000F16 HAFB	077	
F-GGSK	Piper PA-23-250 Aztec F	27-7854125	TJ-AFR
			N63996
F-GGSL	Robin DR.400/140B Major 80	1861	
F-GGSM	Aerotek Pitts S-2A	2151	N31502
F-GGSN	Robin DR.400/100 Cadet (marked '2+2')	1862	
F-GGSO	Cameron A-140 HAFB	2270	
F-GGSP	SOCATA TB-10 Tobago	271	D-EEVU
F-GGSR(2)	Hughes 269C	28-0667	D-HMAR
			D-HOYH
F-GGSY	Cessna 150M	15078308	N9359U
F-GGTB	Aerotek Pitts S-2A	2160	N31429
F-WGTF/G/H	*Re-useable test registrations for Falcon 20/TPE 731*		
	modifications by Europe Falcon Service		
F-GGTJ	Aérospatiale SA.342J Gazelle	1473	C-GVWC
	(Formerly SA.341G, converted 3.92)		F-WXFX
F-GGTK	Piper PA-28R-201 Cherokee Arrow III	28R-7737162	N47453
F-GGTL	Piper PA-46-310P Malibu	46-8508077	N6915C
F-WGTM(2)	Aérospatiale AS.355F Ecureuil 2	5264	G-BOSK
			D-HERP
F-GGTN	Reims/Cessna FTB.337G Super Skymaster	0003	FAP3702
			CS-AAW
F-GGTO	Reims/Cessna FTB.337G Super Skymaster	0004	FAP3703
			CS-AKK
F-GGTQ(2)	Aérospatiale AS.350D Ecureuil	1147	N35978
F-GGTR	Aerotek Pitts S-2A	2171	N31439
F-GGTS	Cameron O-77 HAFB	1460	
F-WGTX	Heli Atlas	01	
F-WGTY	Heli Atlas	02	
F-WGTZ	Heli Atlas	unkn	
F-GGUY	Cameron Concept 80 HAFB	3424	
F-GGVA	Cameron O-77 HAFB	1659	
F-GGVB	Dassault Falcon 50	11	N5739
			N203BT
			N501NC
			N50FH
			F-WZHE
F-GGVC	Cessna U206F Stationair	U20602674	N33214
F-GGVD	Colt 21A HAFB	1609	
F-GGVG	Swearingen SA.226TB Merlin IIIB	T-293	D-IBBB(2)
			N5469M
F-GGVI	SNCAN/Stampe SV.4C	429	F-BCVI
F-GGVK	Schweizer 269C	S-1449	D-HITA
F-GGVL	Piper PA-28-161 Cadet	2841105	
F-GGVQ	Boeing 737-2K2C	20944	VT-EKD
			PH-TVE
F-GGVS	Cameron N-90 HAFB	2312	
F-GGVT	Cameron N-105 HAFB	2303	
F-GGVU	Cameron N-90 HAFB	2318	
F-GGVZ	Piper PA-28-181 Archer II	28-8190289	N9195Y
			HR-AIR
			N8421H
F-GGXA	Robin DR.400/120 Dauphin 2+2	1897	
F-GGXB	Robin ATL	128	
F-GGXC	Robin DR.400/120 Dauphin 2+2	1888	
F-GGXD	Robin DR.400/120 Dauphin 2+2	1882	
F-GGXE	Robin DR.400/180R Remorqueur	1883	
F-GGXF	Robin ATL	129	
F-GGXG	Robin DR.400/180 Régent	1891	
F-GGXI	Robin DR.400/120 Dauphin 2+2	1895	

F-GGXJ	Robin DR.400/140B Major 80	1896	
F-GGXK	Robin DR.400/120 Dauphin 2+2	1881	
F-GGXO	Robin DR.400/120 Dauphin 2+2	1905	
F-GGXP	Robin DR.400/180 Régent	1907	
F-GGXQ	Robin DR.400/140B Major 80	1928	
F-GGXS	Robin DR.400/140B Major 80	1913	
F-GGXU	Robin DR.400/100 Cadet	1909	
F-GGXX	Robin ATL L	131	
F-GGXY	Robin DR.400/140B Major 80	1923	
F-GGXZ	Robin DR.400/180 Régent	1924	
F-GGYA	Mudry CAP.10B	232	
F-GGYB	Mudry CAP.10B	233	
F-GGYC	Mudry CAP.10B	235	
F-GGYD	Mudry CAP.10B	234	
F-GGYE	Mudry CAP.10B	237	
F-GGYF	Mudry CAP.10B	238	
F-GGYG	Mudry CAP.10B	239	
F-GGYI	Mudry CAP.10B	240	
F-GGYJ	Mudry CAP.10B	243	
F-GGYK	Mudry CAP.10B	247	
F-GGYL	Mudry CAP.10B	245	
F-GGYQ	Mudry CAP.231	14	F-WGZD
F-GGYT	Mudry CAP.10B	252	
F-GGYU	Mudry CAP.10B	253	
F-GGYV	Mudry CAP.10B	254	
F-GGYZ	Mudry CAP.231	20	
F-GGZB	Piper PA-28-181 Cherokee Archer II	28-7890105	N47624
F-GGZI	Gardan GY-80-160 Horizon	47	OO-GOD
			F-OCCV
F-GGZJ	Cessna 172N	17269362	N737EN
F-GGZL	Thunder AX7-77 HAFB	1829	
F-GGZN	Piper PA-32R-301 Saratoga SP	32R-8313030	TR-LBD
			N8246A
F-GGZO	Reims/Cessna F172N	F17201997	D-EIZO
F-GGZQ	Piper PA-38-112 Tomahawk	38-79A0485	N2571F
F-GGZS	Thunder AX8-105 HAFB	1505	
F-GGZU	Ultramagic S-105 HAFB	105/14	
F-GGZX	Christen A-1 Husky	1159	
F-GGZY	Schweizer 269C	S-1487	
F-GGZZ	Piper PA-32-300 Cherokee Six	32-7440110	N42160
F-GHAC	Mooney M.20J Model 201	24-1637	
F-GHAF(2)	Hughes 269C	61-1060	D-HIRN
			N5016R
F-WHAG	Raven Europe Aeroglobe Balloon	001	
F-GHAI	Bell 47G-2	1502	N2828B
F-GHAK	Aérospatiale AS.350B Ecureuil	1631	LN-OPQ
			SE-HSK
			LN-OPQ
			(D-HKXP)
			OE-KXP
			D-HLTJ
F-GHAM	Robin ATL	103	
F-GHAN	Sud Avn SA.318C Alouette Astazou	2185	LV-ARI
			ZS-HKX
			CF-CWN
			N8659
F-GHAV	Reims FR172J Rocket	FR17200489	N26674
			F-BVBH
F-GHAX	Chaize CS.2200F12 HAFB	089	
F-GHAY	Chaize CS.2200F12 HAFB	087	
F-GHBA	Piper PA-28-161 Cadet	2841162	
F-GHBB	Beech C90 King Air	LJ-510	D-ILHB
F-GHBC	Chaize CS.3000F16 HAFB	073	F-WHBC
F-GHBD	Beech C90 King Air	LJ-545	D-ILHD
F-GHBF	Robinson R-22M Mariner	1034M	
F-GHBJ	Mooney M.20K Model 252 TSE	25-1127	
F-GHBN	Cessna 172N	17271123	N2026E
F-GHBO	Cameron N-77 HAFB	1643	
F-GHBP	Cameron D-96 Hot Air Airship	536	SE-ZAD
			G-BHBJ
F-GHBQ	Piper PA-28-181 Archer II	28-8290018	N8406B
F-GHBR	Aérospatiale AS.350B Ecureuil	1600	(F-GHC0)
			F-GGBR
			N58030
F-GHBS	Mooney M.20F Executive	670142	D-EBBM(2)
			N9565M
F-GHBV	Aérospatiale AS.350B Ecureuil	1544	N323LB
F-GHBX	Thunder AX7-77 HAFB	1808	
F-GHBY	Piper J-3C-65 Cub	unkn	F-BFBY
			"43-17737"
F-GHCC	Aérospatiale SA.315B Lama	2474	N49504
F-GHCE	Bell 206B Jet Ranger II	2092	N16701
F-GHCG	Mooney M.20J Model 205	24-3075	N205RS
F-GHCI	Aérospatiale SA.315B Lama	1819/11	(F-ODSK)
			TR-LXB
			F-GAMF
			F-ZBAM
F-GHCM	Cessna T303 Crusader	T30300003	N9335T
F-GHCV	Beech 200 Super King Air (Reservation)	unkn	
F-GHCX	Wassmer Jodel D.120 Paris-Nice	305	F-BNCX
F-GHCY	SNCASE SE.313B Alouette II (Reservation)	unkn	
F-GHDD	Piper PA-28-161 Cadet	2841262	
F-GHDE	Ultramagic V-77 HAFB	77/24	
F-GHDH	Cessna 172P	17276254	N93ER
			(N98073)
F-GHDI	Ultramagic M77 Air Balloon	77/38	
F-GHDJ	Ultramagic HAFB (Reservation)	unkn	

F-GHDL	Robinson R-22 Beta	1171	
F-GHDM	Piper PA-28-161 Cadet	2841263	
F-GHDN(2)	Cameron A-180 HAFB	2455	G-BTAO
F-GHDO	Beech 65-B90 King Air	LJ-206	3X- . . . F-BTAK HB-GDG
F-GHDU	Piper PA-28R-201 Cherokee Arrow III	28R-7703233	N38520
F-GHDV	Cameron N-77 HAFB	1773	
F-GHDX	Dassault Falcon 10	140	N88WL N70WC N205FJ F-WZGL
F-GHDY	Balloon Works Firefly F7-15 HAFB	F7-725	
F-GHED	McDonnell-Douglas DC-9-83 (MD-83)	49576	EI-BWE EC-EFK
F-GHEL	Mooney M.20J Model 205	24-3028	N205MJ
F-GHEM	Beech C90 King Air	LJ-760	N700JP N707CB (N9OAJ) N707CB N319D
F-GHEN	Cessna U206G Stationair	U20603587	G-BOSC 5N-ASU N7256N
F-GHEO	Cessna R182 Skylane RG	R18200453	N9833C
F-GHEV	Cessna 172N	17269730	N737WK
F-GHFC	Cessna 172P	17274447	N52229
F-GHFE	Beech C90 King Air	LJ-544	(F-GHFC) D-ILHC
F-GHFG	Holste MH.1521M Broussard	104	Fr.AF
F-GHFI (2)	Aérospatiale SA.315B Lama	2476	D-HLEO F-GHCN G-BLXJ N403AH N47309
F-GHFJ	Aérospatiale AS.350B Ecureuil	2127	LN-OTP
F-GHFR	Aérospatiale AS.350B Ecureuil	1374	N5779W
F-GHGB	Holste MH.1521C1 Broussard	256	Fr.AF
F-GHGM(2)	Rockwell S.2R-600 Thrush Commander	1821R	CS-APO N5621X
F-GHGZ	Cessna 208 Caravan I	20800188	
F-GHHA	Colt 240A HAFB	1924	
F-GHHB	Robinson R-22B Beta	0783	
F-GHHF	Aérospatiale AS.350B Ecureuil	2145	N373RE N6024V
F-GHHJ	Cameron N-90 HAFB	2511	
F-GHHQ	Bell 205A-1	30092	C-GVHX N8189J
F-GHHR	Bell 205A-1	30223	C-GFHN LN-OQP C-GIGC
F-GHHT	Robinson R-22 Beta	1815	
F-GHHU	Zlin Z.526 Trenér Master	1081	F-BRNE
F-GHHV	Beech A100 King Air	B-91	N9050V
F-GHHX	Thunder AX7-77A HAFB	1954	
F-GHHZ	Thunder AX7-77Z HAFB	1935	
F-GHIA	Embraer EMB.120RT Brasilia	120154	PT-SPT
F-GHIB	Embraer EMB.120RT Brasilia	120162	PT-SQA
F-GHIE	Robinson R-22 Mariner (W/o 4.6.02?)	1307M	
F-GHIG	SNCASO SO.1221 Djinn	97/FR147	ALAT
F-GHIH	Piper J-3C-65 Cub Special	20546	N7242H NC7242H
F-GHIK	Robinson R-22 Beta	1750	
F-GHIO	Bell 206B Jet Ranger II	2895	YU-HDG N1067F
F-GHIP	Piper L-4B Cub	9357	N1138V 43-496 (42-59306)
F-WHIQ	Holste MH.1521M Broussard	291	Fr.AF
F-GHIS	Hughes 269C	74-0325	N58161
F-GHIU	Beech 58 Baron	TH-986	N2046E N46E N2046E
F-GHIV	Beech F90 King Air	LA-22	N4269Y N444EM N4269Y D-ICET
F-GHIX	Piper PA-28-181 Archer II	28-8390042	N42940
F-GHIY	Piper PA-28-181 Archer II	28-8490067	N131AV N9592N N43570
F-GHJB	Agusta-Bell 47G-2	210	EC-DGK F-BTSR ALAT Fr.AF
F-GHJC	Chaize CS.2200F12 HAFB	78	
F-GHJG	Piper PA-28-181 Archer II	28-7990073	N22244
F-GHJI	Piper PA-28-181 Archer II	28-7990023	N39958
F-GHJJ	Chaize CS.2200F12 HAFB	091	
F-GHJK	Reims/Cessna F150L	F15000819	HB-CWH
F-GHJL	Dassault Falcon 10	58	N500FF N458A N58AS N76FJ N143FJ F-WJMM
F-GHJM	Cessna 207A Stationair 8 (Wrecked)	20700635	F-OGJM (N75576)
F-GHJO	Cessna 152	15284330	C-GGEB (N5517L)
F-GHJT	Piper PA-28-181 Archer II	28-8090087	N8086L
F-GHJU	Cessna 402C	402C0274	N6652C YV-472C YV-278CP N2741A
F-GHJV	Piper PA-31T Cheyenne	31T-7720067	N900SF N999WS N82186
F-GHKB	Piper PA-28-161 Cadet	2841253	
F-GHKD	Cessna 152	15280899	N25989
F-GHKE	Cessna 152	15280176	N24254
F-GHKG	Beech V35B Bonanza	D-9488	D-EAPM CS-AOK N2881W
F-GHKH	Chaize CS.2200F12 HAFB	107	
F-GHKI	Piper PA-28-161 Warrior II	28-8516009	N4379S
F-GHKJ	Piper PA-28-161 Warrior II	28-8216061	N8461Z
F-GHKO	Cameron N-105 HAFB	3103	OO-BBQ G-BUYZ
F-GHKR	Cameron Hex Glass 84 SS HAFB	3272	OO-BHG
F-WHKS	Bell 222A	47040	F-WQAA F-WKHS F-WYMA SE-HSF N1085G
F-GHKU	Mudry CAP.10B	211	F-ZVMU
F-GHKV	Beech 58 Baron	TH-1537	N31425
F-GHKY	Cessna R182 Skylane RG	R18200728	N736GF
F-GHKZ	Robin DR.400/140B Major 80	924	F-BVCZ
F-GHLB	Beech 200 Super King Air (Reserved as N349JW, 4.99)	BB-349	D-IEXD N80GA G-BFEA G-BRON G-BFEA
F-GHLD	Beech 200 Super King Air (Cr. 17.12.98)	BB-233	(N823AL) (N37KG) N50JD
F-GHLE	Piper PA-28RT-201T Turbo Arrow IV	28R-8431012	N4334K N9561N
F-GHLF	Hughes 369E	0361E	
F-GHLJ	Chaize CS 2200F12 HAFB	099	
F-GHLK	Piper PA-28-181 Archer II	28-7990391	N3065Y
F-GHLL	Balloon Works Firefly 7 HAFB	F7-603	N9041B
F-GHLO	Rockwell S.2R Thrush Commander	1920R	EC-CKM N17535
F-GHLQ	Piper J-3C-65 Cub	15243	N42908 NC42908
F-GHLR	Bell 206B Jet Ranger II	2718	N2761B
F-GHLS	Aérospatiale AS.355N Ecureuil 2	5579	B-HJK VR-HJK F-OHNB
F-GHLU	Cessna 152	15280860	N25923
F-GHLX(2)	Bell 47G-2	1388	C-FVTS CF-VTS RCAF1388 RCN . . . .
F-GHLY	Piper PA-28-161 Warrior II	2816055	
F-GHLZ	Piper PA-38-112 Tomahawk	38-78A0642	N2327A
F-GHMA	Cessna 210L Centurion	21060907	N5319V
F-GHMB	Mooney M.20K Model 231	25-0740	N5634Q
F-GHMC	Aérospatiale AS.355F Ecureuil 2	5108	(F-GHCH) N57902
F-GHMH	Robinson R-22 Beta	1144	
F-GHMM(2)	Ultramagic M-105 HAFB	105/112	
F-GHMQ	Aérospatiale AS.350B2 Ecureuil	2525	
F-GHMR	Thunder AX8-9OA3 HAFB	1428	
F-GHMS	Cessna T210L Turbo Centurion	21060012	N210ES N59003
F-GHMV	Cameron O-65 HAFB	2112	
F-GHMX(3)	Cameron A-230 HAFB (Reservation)	unkn	
F-GHNA	Piper PA-30 Twin Comanche C	30-1873	N8720Y
F-GHNB	Cameron V-90 HAFB	2502	
F-GHNF	Colt 240A HAFB	1229	G-BOOS
F-GHNG	Thunder AX10-180 HAFB	626	G-BLUG
F-GHNH	Thunder AX10-180 HAFB	625	G-BLUF
F-GHNI	Thunder AX10-180 HAFB	627	G-BLUH
F-GHNK	Thunder AX10-180 HAFB	939	G-BNHW
F-GHNN	Thunder AX10-160 HAFB	565	G-BLKH
F-GHNO	Thunder AX10-160 HAFB	563	G-BLKF
F-GHNP(2)	Grumman G.164B Agcat	768B	EC-EIE N3632D
F-GHNQ	Thunder AX10-160 HAFB	554	G-BLHA
F-GHNR(2)	Piper PA-38-112 Tomahawk	38-78A0563	D-EAJZ N9654N
F-GHNS	Cameron O-84 HAFB	404	G-BNUK F-GCKY N149CB
F-GHNX	Chaize CS.2200F12 HAFB	109	
F-GHNY	Cessna 152	15284287	N5292L
F-GHNZ	Cessna 152	15279559	N714ZJ
F-GHOC	Beech 200 Super King Air	BB-406	G-OEMS N222PA
F-GHOD	Robinson R-22 Beta	1157	
F-GHOE	Aérospatiale AS.350B Ecureuil	1019	CS-HBJ D-HMFG G-BNAS C-GMLT

F-GHOF	Raven Europe FS-57A HAFB	E-131	
F-GHOG	Cessna 172N	17270189	N738RY
F-GHOH	Schweizer 269C	S-1272	D-HDAS
F-GHOI	McDonnell-Douglas DC-10-30	46870	OY-KDA
F-GHOK	Robinson R-22 Beta	1591	
F-GHOM	SNCASE SE.3130 Alouette II	1510	ALAT
F-GHON	AIAA/ Stampe SV.4C	1147	F-BAON
F-GHOO	Schweizer 269C	S-1302	
F-GHOP	Cessna 172RG Cutlass RG	172RG0338	3A-MOP F-GCGO N4606V
F-GHOR	Cameron O-65 HAFB	1732	
F-GHOV	SNCAN Stampe SV.4C	341	F-BCOV
F-GHOY(2)	Aérospatiale AS.332L1 Super Puma	9005	
F-GHOZ	Cameron O-160 HAFB	1308	G-BMOZ
F-GHPB	Dassault Falcon 10	215	
F-GHPD	SNCASE SE.3130 Alouette II	1319	ALAT
F-GHPE	Cessna 150L	15072136	N6636G
F-GHPH	Aérospatiale AS.350B2 Ecureuil	2365	
F-GHPI	Aérospatiale/Alenia ATR-42-300	214	F-WWEB
F-GHPJ	Robin DR.400/120 Dauphin 2+2	1874	
F-GHPM	Mooney M.20J Model 201	24-1640	
F-GHPN	Piper PA-28-161 Cadet	2841252	
F-GHPP	Piper PA-32R-301 Saratoga SP	3213022	
F-GHPQ	Piper PA-28-161 Warrior II	28-7916492	N2867M
F-GHPS	Aeritalia/SNIAS ATR-42-300	006	B-2206 F-GGFA OH-LTA F-WWEB
F-GHPT	Piper PA-28-181 Archer II (W/o 18.5.02)	2890081	
F-GHQA	Airbus A320-211	033	F-GGEF(1)
F-GHQB	Airbus A320-211	036	F-GGEG(1)
F-GHQC	Airbus A320-211	044	F-GGEH(1)
F-GHQD	Airbus A320-211	108	
F-GHQE	Airbus A320-211	115	
F-GHQF	Airbus A320-211	130	
F-GHQG	Airbus A320-211	155	
F-GHQH	Airbus A320-211	156	
F-GHQI	Airbus A320-211	184	
F-GHQJ	Airbus A320-211	214	
F-GHQK	Airbus A320-211	236	
F-GHQL	Airbus A320-211	239	
F-GHQM	Airbus A320-211	237	
F-GHQO	Airbus A320-211	278	
F-GHQP	Airbus A320-211	337	
F-GHQQ	Airbus A320-211	352	
F-GHQR	Airbus A320-211	377	
F-GHRG	Piper PA-46-310P Malibu	46-8608067	N9099N
F-GHRH	Aérospatiale AS.350B Ecureuil	2504	F-WZKI
F-GHRI	Thunder AS-261 Hot Air Airship	1380	F-WGGM G-BPLD
F-GHRJ	Piper PA-28-181 Cherokee Archer II	28-7790360	N1950H
F-GHRK	DHC-6 Twin Otter 200	144	N202E (N871SA) N202E
F-GHRL	Piper PA-32R-301T Turbo Saratoga SP	32R-8429011	HB-PIA N43537
F-GHRM	Chaize CS.2200F12 HAFB	103	
F-GHRN	Chaize CS.2200F12 HAFB	102	
F-GHRP	SAN Jodel D.140E Mousquetaire IV	155	OO-JOS
F-GHRQ	Cameron O-105 HAFB	2459	
F-GHRR	Piper PA-46-310P Malibu	46-8608058	F-ODRR N9535N
F-GHRT	Cessna 310Q	310Q0936	F-ODRT TT-BAE F-BUYQ N69714
F-GHRY	Aérospatiale AS.365N2 Dauphin 2	6412	LX-HUF F-GHRY
F-GHSH	Piper PA-25-260 Pawnee D	25-7656044	N54895
F-GHSJ	Cessna P210N Pressurized Centurion II	P21000493	(F-GFMJ) CN-TCZ F-GCSY N731MH
F-GHSL	Robinson R-22M Mariner	0955M	
F-GHSM	SOCATA MS.880B Rallye Club	1559	F-GBSM F-BRYV
F-GHSP	Cessna 172N	17272830	N6486D
F-GHSQ	Piper PA-25-235 Pawnee	25-2754	C-FRHP CF-RHP N7002Z
F-GHSR	Robinson R-22 Beta	1347	
F-GHSS	Schweizer 269C	S-1301	
F-GHST	Bell 206B Jet Ranger II	1104	D-HOCH SE-HLL LN-OSV G-BBES N18092
F-GHSV	Beech 200 Super King Air	BB-622	N212BF N7009J N7009
F-GHSX	Piper PA-25-235 Pawnee	25-2387	N6765Z
F-GHSZ	Piper PA-28-151 Cherokee Warrior	28-7415698	N44663
F-GHTA	Piper PA-31T Cheyenne II	31T-7820015	N107BK N82217
F-GHTB	Robin HR.200/120B Club	23	HB-EXD
F-GHTC	Piper PA-28-161 Cadet	2841011	

F-GHTE	Diamond DA20-A1-100 Katana	10257	G-BXPB
F-GHTF	Aérospatiale AS.350B Ecureuil (Reservation)	unkn	
F-GHTH	Hughes 269C	47-0586	N7484F
F-GHTI	Cessna 421A (Wfu, stored)	421A0158	(F-GGFI) N777GP N3358Q
F-GHTJ(2)	CEA DR.250/160 Capitaine	41	F-OCIA
F-GHTL	Beech A36 Bonanza	E-799	N2545B
F-GHTM	Cessna TR182 Turbo Skylane RG	R18201528	N5263S
F-GHTN	SNCASE SE.3130 Alouette II	1401	ALAT
F-GHTO	SNCASE SE.3130 Alouette II	1021	ALAT
F-GHTQ(2)	Piper PA-25-235 Pawnee C	25-5074	N8637L
F-GHTR	Beech F33A Bonanza	CE-1054	N72167
F-GHTS	Cameron O-105 HAFB	1932	
F-GHTU	SNCASE SE.3160 Alouette III	1429	ALAT
F-GHTY	Piper PA-28RT-201 Arrow IV	28R-8118013	N8282Z
F-GHTZ	Mooney M.20K Model 231	25-0322	N231NG
F-GHUE	Robinson R-22 Beta	1831	
F-GHUH	Holste MH.1521C Broussard	275	ALAT
F-GHUJ	Holste MH.1521M Broussard	295	ALAT
F-GHUM	Aérospatiale AS.350B Ecureuil	1448	F-ODQT F-WIPB F-WZLF
F-GHUN	Aérospatiale SA.315B Lama	2359	N7CH N18857
F-GHUT	Aérospatiale AS.350B2 Ecureuil	2545	
F-GHUV	Beech E90 King Air	LW-278	YV-195CP N4757C N700MA
F-GHUY	Cessna 421B Golden Eagle (W/o 18.2.02)	421B0417	I- MAME N41049
F-GHUZ	Piper PA-28R-201 Arrow III	28R-7837020	N47972
F-GHVB	Cameron O-84 HAFB	1979	
F-GHVF	Fairchild Swearingen SA.227AT Merlin IVC	AT-423	N10NB N807M
F-GHVH	Fairchild PC-6/B2-H2 Turbo-Porter	2072	N530RQ FAB-. . . N5306F
F-GHVI	Piper PA-28-161 Cadet	2841165	
F-GHVJ	Mooney M.20J Model 201 (Wfu?)	24-1560	N5812Z
F-GHVL	Boeing 737-53A (Reservation)	unkn	
F-GHVP	Chaize CS2200F12 HAFB	104	HB-BSJ
F-GHVQ	SNCASE SE.313B Alouette II	1398	(F-GHSY) ALAT
F-GHVV	Beech 200 Super King Air	BB-676	N970AA N676DP G-ONCA N1362B 9Y-TGR
F-GHVX	Cessna 152	15285449	N93255
F-GHVY	Cessna 152	15284585	N5426M
F-GHVZ	Cessna 152	15285056	N4735Q
F-GHXC	Aérospatiale AS.350B Ecureuil	1093	N3594N
F-GHXD	Rockwell Commander 114	14134	N5463X (N58230) N5463X YS-217P
F-GHXE	Christen A-1 Husky	1161	
F-GHXJ	Thunder AX8-90 HAFB	2126	
F-GHXK	Boeing 737-2A1C	21599	N171AW YS-08C N1247E
F-GHXL	Boeing 737-2S3	21775	G-BMOR EI-BPR (EI-BRR) G-BMOR
F-GHXM	Boeing 737-53A	24788	
F-GHXQ(2)	Piper PA-28-181 Archer II	28-8090007	N2966W
F-GHXR	Aérospatiale SA.360C Dauphin	1010	(F-GHXQ) G-BRMP N49513
F-GHXT	Cameron A-105 HAFB	1755	
F-GHYC	Schweizer 269C	S-1532	N86G
F-GHYF	Piper PA-28-161 Warrior II	28-8516052	N69086
F-GHYG	Aérospatiale SA.315B Lama	2383	N85356 F-BV VQ
F-WHYH	Zeppy II Airship	01	
F-GHYJ	Cameron O-77 HAFB	2632	
F-GHYL	Aérospatiale AS.350BA Ecureuil	2632	
F-GHYN(2)	Douglas DC-8-55F (Reservation 1.04)	45819	(F-GIYJ) Fr.AF:F-RAFC F-BNLD TU-TXK Fr.AF:F-RAFC F-BNLD TU-TXG F-BNLD
F-GHYP	Hughes 269C	120-1012	N6593G YV-206CP YV-2092P N1094T
F-GHYQ(2)	Robin DR.400/120 Dauphin 2+2	2203	F-GMKK
F-GHYS	Agusta-Bell 47G-2	261	D-HCXB OE-CXB D-HCXB OE-CXB, D-HAKM, 74+19, AS+376, LA+105, AS+061

F-GHYT	Robinson R-22 Beta	1752	
F-GHYX	Piper PA-28-181 Archer II	28-8190101	N8302S
F-GHYZ	Piper PA-28-181 Archer II	28-7990370	N2229X
F-GHZA	SOCATA TB-20 Trinidad	917	
F-GHZC	SOCATA TB-20 Trinidad	953	
F-GHZG	SOCATA TB-9 Tampico	931	
F-GHZH	SOCATA TB-20 Trinidad	966	
F-GHZI	SOCATA TB-9 Tampico	940	
F-GHZK	SOCATA TB-9 Tampico	944	
F-GHZM	SOCATA TB-9 Tampico	993	
F-GHZO	SOCATA TB-20 Trinidad	1017	
F-GHZS	SOCATA TB-9 Tampico	1015	
F-GHZU	SOCATA TB-20 Trinidad	1023	
F-GHZX	SOCATA TB-9 Tampico	1050	
F-GIAB	Piper PA-28-161 Cadet	2841066	
F-GIAD	Aérospatiale AS.350B Ecureuil	2112	
F-GIAF(2)	SOCATA MS.893E Rallye 180GT	12725	(F-GTCO)
	(Reservation 1.04)		F-ZBDR
			F-GAFJ
F-GIAM	Cessna 340A	340A0746	N2671X
F-GIAO(2)	Hughes 269C	16-0465	D-HABS
			SE-HHB
			G-BDOX
F-GIAQ(2)	Cessna 152	15279649	N757DD
F-GIAS	Cessna 421C Golden Eagle	421C0300	N421YA
			N8179G
F-GIAV	Cameron O-77 HAFB	1922	
F-GIAY	Piper PA-32R-301 Saratoga SP	32R-8313024	N4313T
			N9518N
F-GIBA	Cessna 172N	17273006	N1470F
F-GIBD	Robin HR.100/210 Safari	154	5T-TJB
			F-BUHG
F-GIBE	Piper PA-28-161 Cadet	2841132	
F-GIBF(2)	Ultramagic S-130 HAFB	130/24	
F-GIBI	Aérospatiale AS.355F Ecureuil 2	5027	D-HAST(2)
			F-ODNS
F-GIBJ	Robin DR.400/120 Petit Prince	830	6V-AFP
			F-BUPJ
F-GIBK	Aérospatiale SA.315B Lama	2287/41	F-GEHY
			N65181
F-GIBM	Aérospatiale AS.350B Ecureuil	1424	N5784Y
F-GIBN	Holste MH.1521CBroussard	261	Fr.AF
F-GIBO	Cameron N-90 HAFB	2560	
F-GIBP	Zlin Z.526F Trenér Master	1082	F-BRNF
F-GIBQ	Piper PA-28-161 Cadet	2841324	N92156
F-GIBT(3)	Kubicek BB-20 HAFB (Res .02; now F-GEZA ?)	179	OK-0179
F-GIBU	Aérospatiale SA.342J Gazelle	1470	HB-XMU
			N9000A
F-GIBV	Pilatus PC-6/B1-H2 Turbo-Porter	651	D-FLEV(2)
			OH-POB
			HB-FCZ
			ST-ADH
			HB-FCZ
F-GIBX	Piper PA-28-161 Cadet	2841323	N92155
F-GIBZ	Cameron N-65 HAFB	1439	OO-BON
F-GICA	Beech B300 Super King Air	FA-146	
F-GICJ	Cessna P210N Pressurized Centurion II	P21000678	(F-GFTY)
			N5358W
F-GICK	American AG-5B Tiger	10111	
F-GICP	Piper PA-28RT-201T Turbo Arrow IV	28R-8431004	N4327B
F-GICQ	Beech A36 Bonanza	E-2569	N8043E
F-GICR	Beech A36 Bonanza	E-2354	N3094T
F-GICU	Robin DR.400/180R Remorqueur	1483	EC-DKY
			D-EGPE
F-GICX	Hughes 269C	95-0432	F-BXOU
F-GICY	PZL-104 Wilga 80	CF14800562	SP-TWS
F-GICZ	Maule MX-7-180 Star Rocket	11069C	G-MORL
F-GIDA	Robin DR.400/180 Régent	1838	
F-GIDD	Piper PA-28R-201 Arrow	2837060	(N181ND)
F-GIDF	Piper PA-44-180 Seminole	44-8195005	N89PG
			(N256EP)
			N256ER
			N252ER
			N9628N
F-GIDG	Cessna 182P Skylane	18261311	TJ-AET
			TL-AAL
			N20942
F-GIDI	Piper PA-28-181 Archer II	28-8290099	HB-PIE
			D-EIIT
			N9638N
F-GIDK	Douglas C-47B	16604/33352	F-GIAZ
			C-GSCC
			C-GGJH
			CAF12965
			RCAF1000
			KN655
			44-77020
F-GIDR	Aérospatiale AS.350B Ecureuil	1993	N350TC
			N6008J
F-GIDS	Pilatus PC-6/B1-H2 Turbo-Porter	584	HB-FBZ
			P2-SEA
			P2-PNO
			P2-PNG(1)
			VH-PNG
			HB-FBZ
F-GIEA	Piper PA-28-161 Cadet	2841106	
F-GIEB	Piper PA-28-161 Cadet	2841107	

F-GIEC	Piper PA-28-181 Archer II	2890105	N91634
F-GIED	Piper PA-28-161 Cadet	2841108	
F-GIEE	Piper PA-28-161 Cadet	2841109	
F-GIEF	Piper PA-28-161 Cadet	2841147	
F-GIEG	Piper PA-28-161 Cadet	2841149	(F-GIEH)
F-GIEH	Piper PA-28-161 Cadet	2841161	
F-GIEI	Piper PA-28-161 Cadet	2841164	
F-GIEJ	Piper PA-28-161 Cadet	2841169	
F-GIEK	Piper PA-28-161 Cadet	2841170	
F-GIEM	Piper PA-28-161 Cadet	2841267	
F-GIEN(2)	Rockwell S.2R Thrush Commander	2088R	EC-CMN
			N17532
F-GIEO	Piper PA-28-161 Cadet	2841269	
F-GIEP	Piper PA-28-161 Cadet	2841270	
F-GIEQ	Piper PA-28-161 Cadet	2841271	
F-GIEV	Partenavia P.68C	253	PH-EMC
			G-OLES
			G-JAJV
			OO-TJG
			(OO-XJG)
F-GIFA	Beech A36 Bonanza	E-1485	N6038M
F-GIFC	Beech 65-B90 King Air	LJ-456	D-ILTY
F-GIFE	Piper PA-28R-201 Arrow III	28R-7837128	N3623M
F-GIFG	Beech A36 Bonanza	E-1814	N3825Z
F-GIFI	Cessna 172R	17280433	
F-GIFK	Beech F90 King Air	LA-62	(F-HAAG(1))
			F-GIFK
			D-ICBD
			N714D
F-GIFM	Beech F33A Bonanza	CE-1612	
F-GIFN	Piper PA-28-161 Cadet	2841133	
F-GIFS	Cameron N-105 HAFB	2903	
F-WIFS	Aérospatiale AS.332L2 Super Puma	2167	
F-GIFZ	Holste MH.1521M Broussard	315	Fr.AF
F-GIGC	Cessna 310R	310R1824	N2640X
F-GIGD	Cessna 310R	310R1825	N2737T
F-GIGE	Cessna 172N	17271560	N3473E
F-GIGF	Cessna 150L	15074507	N19585
F-GIGH	Piper PA-18-150 Super Cub	1809027	
F-GIGJ	Fouga CM.170 Magister	561	F-WIGJ(2)
			Fr.AF
F-GIGK	Cessna P210N Pressurized Centurion II	P21000198	N521BB
			N6685P
F-GIGL	Robinson R-22 Beta	0873	
F-GIGQ	Colt 105A HAFB	2280	
F-GIGR	Ultramagic S90 HAFB	90/05	
F-GIGS	Thunder AX7-77 HAFB	1944	
F-GIGT	Aérospatiale AS.355F1 Ecureuil 2	5023	N355F
F-GIGX	Piper PA-25-260 Pawnee C	25-4477	N4730Y
F-WIGY	Fouga CM.170 Magister (Reserved as F-GLHO)	331	Fr.AF
F-GIHC	Hughes 369E	0376E	
	(Crashed into sea near Grand Turk, Turks & Caicos Islands 4.2.00)		
F-GIHD	Aérospatiale AS.350B Ecureuil	1100	N3598X
F-GIHE	Robinson R-22 Beta	0905	
F-GIHG	Robinson R-22 Beta	0904	
F-GIHH	Robinson R.22 Beta	0814	N26417
F-GIHJ	Aérospatiale AS.350B Ecureuil	1531	XA-MVA
F-GIHM	Pilatus PC-6/B1-H2 Turbo-Porter	581	HS-TFD
			HS-SKE
			HS-CHE
			XW-PFB
			N13200
F-GIHN	Hughes 269C	65-0417	F-BXOS
F-GIHO	Morane-Saulnier MS.733 Alcyon	155	F-BMQB
			Fr.AF
F-GIHP	Schweizer 269C	S-1429	N429MS
F-GIHQ	Robin ATL	68	HB-SCA
F-GIHT(2)	Mudry CAP.10B	25	Fr.AF
F-GIHU(2)	Aérospatiale AS.355F2 Ecureuil 2	5313	XC-EDM
			F-WYMA
F-GIIC(2)	Thunder AX8-90SII HAFB	2343	
F-GIID	Cameron N-90 HAFB	2953	
F-GIIE	Sud Avn SA.316B Alouette III	1885	(F-GIDD)
			Zimbabwe/
			RhAF
			N4965
F-GIIF	Robinson R-22 Beta	2245	
F-GIIG	Morane-Saulnier MS.885 Super Rallye	42	HB-EDP
F-GIII	Piper PA-31T Cheyenne II	31T-8020037	N805SW
F-GIIK	Hughes 269C	16-0460	F-BXPJ
F-GIIL	Cessna 172N	17272705	N6300D
F-GIIM	Colt 90A HAFB	2370	
F-GIIN	Cameron N-105 HAFB	3021	
F-GIIO	Piper PA-28-181 Archer II	2890190	
F-GIIQ	Cessna 172M	17266422	N80177
F-WIIR	Ballon Assimilable 1840m BCB	001	
F-GIIS	Reims/Cessna F172P	F17202115	TU-TMG
			F-OCGJ(2)
F-GIIT	Cameron Concept 80 HAFB	3088	
F-GIIU	Chaize JZ25F16 HAFB	120	
F-GIIV	Cameron V-77 HAFB	1514	OO-BOR
F-GIIZ	Aerotek Pitts S-2A	2112	G-ODAH
			G-BDKS
F-GIJA	SNCASE SE.313B Alouette II	1570	ALAT
F-GIJB	Beech 200 Super King Air	BB-13	N83MA
			N595A
			N200PB

F-GIJC	Mooney M.20K Model 231 (Wfu?)	25-0555	N1022G
F-GIJH	Robin DR.300/125	651	F-ODJH
			F-BTBH
F-GIJI	Mooney M.20J Model 205	24-3092	
F-GIJJ(2)	SNCASE SE.313 Alouette II	1019	ALAT
F-GIJK(2)	SNCASE SE.313B Alouette II	1087	F-MJAH
			F-MJSA
F-GIJM	Agusta-Bell 206B Jet Ranger III	8612	F-GCTJ
F-GIJO	Piper PA-28-180 Cherokee E	28-5776	TR-LWU
			HB-OZY
			N3673R
F-GIJP	Aérospatiale AS.350B Ecureuil	1672	HK-3152X
			F-WZKH
F-GIJQ	Aérospatiale AS.350B Ecureuil	1647	EI-BYT
			(F-GIIC)
			EI-BYT
			G-JRBI
			EI-BNO
			G-BKJY
F-GIJZ	Maquette Frederic St.Denis	unkn	
	(Apparently a model or mock-up: does anyone know more?)		
F-GIKA	Robin DR.400/140B Major 80	1911	
F-GIKB	Robin DR.400/140B Major 80	1912	
F-GIKC	Robin DR.400/120 Dauphin 2+2	1919	
F-GIKD	Robin DR.400/180 Régent	1914	
F-GIKE	Robin DR.400/120 Dauphin 2+2	1929	
F-GIKG	Robin DR.400/140B Major 80	1930	
F-GIKI	Robin DR.400/120 Dauphin 2+2	1931	F-WIKI
			F-GIKI
F-GIKJ	Robin DR.400/160 Major	1941	
F-GIKK	Robin DR.400/120 Dauphin 2+2	1942	
F-GIKL	Robin ATL L	132	
F-GIKM	Robin DR.400/120 Dauphin 2+2	1945	
F-GIKN	Robin DR.400/140B Major 80	1946	
F-GIKO	Robin DR.400/120 Dauphin 2+2	1947	
F-GIKP	Robin DR.400/120 Dauphin 2+2	1948	
F-GIKQ	Robin DR.400/120 Dauphin 2+2	1965	
F-GIKR	Robin ATL L	134	
F-GIKS	Robin DR.400/180 Régent	1950	
F-GIKV	Robin DR.400/180 Régent	1951	
F-GIKX	Robin DR.400/180 Régent	1952	
F-GIKY	Robin DR.400/120 Dauphin 2+2	1954	
F-GIKZ	Robin DR.400/120 Dauphin 2+2	1961	
F-GILM	Aérospatiale SN.601A Corvette	32	EC-DUF
			OY-ARA
			SE-DED
			OY-ARA
			F-BTTQ
			F-WNGR
F-GILQ	Schweizer 269C-1	0036	
F-GILR	Robin R.2160D Acrobin	C209	HB-KBN
			N216MH
F-GILS	Robinson R-22 Beta	0601	G-BNBT
			N2530W
F-GILT	Piper PA-28-161 Cadet	2841067	
F-GIMA	Cessna 414A Chancellor II	414A0446	N2732F
F-GIMB	Cameron V-65 HAFB	2055	
F-GIML	Beech E90 King Air	LW-180	N2180L
F-GIMM	Piper PA-28RT-201T Turbo Arrow IV	28R-8231067	N8261X
			N9583N
F-WIMN	Fouga CM-170 Magister	440	Fr.AF
F-WIMQ	Fouga CM.170 Magister	438	Fr.AF
F-GIMT	Thunder AX8-90S1 HAFB	2418	
F-GIMZ	Aérospatiale SA.315B Lama	2642	YV-350CP
			YV-428A
F-GINH	SOCATA MS.893A Rallye Commodore 180	10605	HB-EDZ
F-GINJ	Beech 58 Baron	TH-539	F-OANJ(2)
			5T-CJS
			F-BVUZ
F-GINM	Robin DR.400/180 Régent	861	D-EDHN
F-GINP	Thunder AX7-65SI HAFB	446	G-LING
F-GINQ	Aérospatiale SA.330JPuma	1583	LX-HUL
			PT-HAA
			LX-HUL
			F-GHRY
			I-EHPJ
			PH-SSB
			PK-TRF
			PH-SSB
			F-WXFM
F-GINR	Bell 47G	32	N112B
			NC112B
F-GINS	Schroeder Fire Balloons G30/24 HAFB	193	
F-GINT	Chaize JZ.25F16 HAFB	131	
F-GINU	Piper PA-32R-301 Saratoga SP	3213035	
F-GINX	Chaize JZ.25F16 HAFB	132	
F-GIOG	Fokker F.28-0100	11364	(F-GIOH)
			PH-EZA
F-GIOI	Fokker F.28-0100	11433	PH-MXA
			PH-NXA
F-GIOT	Thunder AX7-77 HAFB	1474	
F-GIPA	Mudry CAP.20	6	F-TFVZ
			F-BTAH
			F-TFVZ
F-GIPB(2)	Aérospatiale SA.315B Lama	2379	CP-2401
			F-BVEU
F-GIPC	Piper PA-32R-301 Saratoga SP	32R-8313005	N82778

F-GIPE	Mooney M.20J Model 205	24-3066	
F-GIPF	Cameron O-65 HAFB	1925	
F-GIPG	Beech 65-90 King Air	LJ-83	N827T
			(YV-980P)
			N827F
F-GIPH	Dassault Falcon 10	194	N61FC
			N100FJ
			N260FJ
			F-WZGZ
F-GIPI	Aérospatiale SA.365C3 Dauphin 2	5020	(F-GIIP)
			G-BGKM
			F-WMHI
F-GIPJ	Aérospatiale SA.365N Dauphin 2 (Reservation)	unkn	
F-GIPM	Beech A36 Bonanza	E-2405	N3108F
F-GIPR	Piper PA-28-181 Archer II	28-8190312	N8433F
F-GIPS	Thunder AX7-77 HAFB	1807	
F-GIPT	Mooney M.20K Model 231	25-0172	N231RK
F-GIPU	Mudry CAP.10B	16	Fr.AF
F-GIPX	Thunder AX10-180SIII HAFB	3449	
F-GIPY	Aérospatiale AS.350B1 Ecureuil	2033	F-GHFY
			LN-OCA
F-GIPZ	SNCASE SE.313B Alouette II	"076"	Fr.AF
F-GIQA	Cessna 172N	17273536	N5087G
F-GIQI	Cameron Z-105 HAFB	10157	LX-BIQ
F-GIQM	Cessna 152	15280306	N24518
F-GIQN	Cessna 152	15282366	N68766
F-GIQO	Cessna 172N	17268742	I-NCCD
			N734CD
F-GIQQ	CASA C.212 (Permit 6.00)	387	Fr.AF/F-ZVMR
F-GIQR	Piper PA-28R-180 Cherokee Arrow	28R-30757	HB-OZL
			N7415J
F-GIQS	Ultramagic V-77 HAFB (Reservation)	77/112	
F-GIQT	HOAC DV-20 Katana	20078	D-EHLK
F-GIQU	Aérospatiale SA.315B Lama (Reservation .99)	2449	I-CTEC
F-GIRD	Beech 76 Duchess	ME-387	N3809N
F-GIRE	Wörner K-1000/3-Stu Gas Balloon	0323	
F-GIRF	Aérospatiale AS.350B2 Ecureuil	2411	
F-GIRG	Thunder AX8-105S2 HAFB	2402	
F-GIRH	Aérospatiale SN.601 Corvette	14	SP-FOA
	(Reservation, stored as SP-FOA)		F-BVPS
F-GIRI	Mooney M.20E Super 21	1978	HB-DUV
F-GIRJ	Piper PA-18 Super Cub	18-1010	SX-ADP
	(Quoted with f/n 18-1079)		RHAF115313
			51-15313
F-GIRP	Piper PA-28-161 Cherokee Warrior II	28-7816124	N2291F
			C-GIYC
			N9627N
F-GIRQ	Cessna 172R	17280293	N9520P
F-GIRR	Cameron V-65 HAFB	1723	
F-GIRT	Bell 206B Jet Ranger II	1924	F-OGNI
			N49716
F-GIRV	Piper PA-28-181 Archer II	28-8590018	G-BPRW
			N43823
F-GISA	Boeing 747-428	25238	
F-GISB	Boeing 747-428	25302	
F-GISC	Boeing 747-428	25599	
F-GISD	Boeing 747-428	25628	
F-GISE	Boeing 747-428	25630	
F-GISF to GISZ	Boeing 747-428 reservations for Air France (Combi)		
F-GITA	Boeing 747-428	24969	
F-GITB	Boeing 747-428	24990	N6009F
F-GITC	Boeing 747-428	25344	
F-GITD	Boeing 747-428	25600	
F-GITE	Boeing 747-428	25601	
F-GITF	Boeing 747-428	25602	
F-GITH	Boeing 747-428ER	32868	
F-GITI	Boeing 747-428ER	32869	
F-GITJ	Boeing 747-428	32871	
F-GITK to GITZ	Boeing 747-428 reservations for Air France (Passenger)		
F-GIUA(2)	Boeing 747-428ERF	32866	N5017Q
F-GIUB	Boeing 747-428ERF	33096	
F-GIUC	Boeing 747-428ERF	32867	
F-GIUD	Boeing 747-428ERF	32870	
F-GIUE	Boeing 747-428ERF (Reservation 6.04)	33097	
F-GIUF to GIUZ	Boeing 747-428ERF reservations for Air France (Cargo)		
F-GIVA	Piper PA-28-181 Archer II	2890108	
F-GIVB	Maule MX.7-235 Star Rocket	10083C	N9208V
F-GIVD(2)	Dassault Falcon 50EX (Reservation)	251	N870
			VP-CLN
			VR-CLN
			(F-GOND)
			F-WOND
F-GIVH	Bell 206B Jet Ranger II	4176	
F-GIVK	Embraer EMB.120RT Brasilia	120112	C-FKOE
			LN-KOB
			PT-SNE
F-GIVL	Aérospatiale AS.355N Ecureuil 2	5603	
F-GIVN	Bell 47G-2 (Wrecked)	2323	N7084M
F-GIVO	Ultramagic V-56 HAFB	56/13	
F-GIVS	Cessna U206G Stationair 6	U20604881	HB-CKO
	(Soloy Turbine Pac conversion)		N56HT
			(N734VR)
F-GIVU	SNCASE SE.3130 Alouette II	1473	Fr.AF
F-GIVV	Cessna 340A	340A1520	N34DA
			(N6871L)

F-GIVY	Robinson R-44 Astro	0035	
F-GIVZ	Robinson R-22B2 Beta	2689	
F-GIXA	Boeing 737-2K2C	20836	PH-TVC F-GGZA PH-TVC LV-MDB PH-TVC
F-GIXB	Boeing 737-33A	24789	F-OGSD F-GFUI
F-GIXC	Boeing 737-38B	25124	F-OGSS N4320B N1792B
F-GIXD	Boeing 737-33A	25744	N3213T
F-GIXE	Boeing 737-3B3	26850	N854WT F-GIXE
F-GIXF	Boeing 737-3B3	26851	N4361V
F-GIXG	Boeing 737-382	24364	F-OGSX CS-TIA
F-GIXH	Boeing 737-3S3	23788	5W-FAX N851LF G-NAFH G-BOYN EC-ECQ EC-277 G-BOYN EC-ECQ N271LF
F-GIXI	Boeing 737-348	23809	F-OGSY EC-FQP EC-279 EI- BUD N1786B
F-GIXJ	Boeing 737-3Y0	23685	G-MONH
F-GIXL	Boeing 737-348	23810	F-OHCS EC-FSC EC-375 EI- BUE N1787B
F-GIXM	Boeing 737-36E	25159	F-WIXM (F-GLXO) N315FL EC-FFN EC-703
F-GIXO	Boeing 737-3Q8	24132	N241LF EC-FET EC-593 EC-EIR EC-160
F-GIXR	Boeing 737-3H6QC	27125	9M-MZA (9M-MFZ)
F-GIXS	Boeing 737-3H6QC	27347	9M-MZB
F-GIXQ, GIXT	Reserved for S.E.A./Europe Airpost		
F-GIXU	Fairchild F.24R-46A Argus III	1063	F-BEXU F-OAAS F-BEXU KK445 44-83102
F-GIXX	Pilatus PC-6/B2-H2 Turbo-Porter	564	N17XX N777XX N187H
F-GIXY	Mudry CAP.232	19	
F-GIXZ	Robin DR.315 Petit Prince	364	OO-NEW F-BRFK
F-GIYA	Reims/Cessna F152	F15201854	HB-CKD F-GCYO
F-GIYB	Aérospatiale AS.355F1 Ecureuil 2	5142	N5793Z
F-GIYC(2)	Cameron N-120 HAFB	10252	
F-GIYD	Cessna 152	15282164	C-GYRP N68175
F-GIYE	Sud Avn SA.316B Alouette III	1452	A-452
F-GIYF	Aérospatiale SA.365C3 Dauphin 2	5068	VH-HCF 9M-WYN
F-GIYG	Aérospatiale AS.350B Ecureuil	1410	HB-XLZ
F-GIYL	Piper PA-28-180 Cherokee D	28-4540	HB-OZM N5245L
F-GIYN	Robinson R-22B2 Beta	2925	
F-GIYO	Cessna 172RG Cutlass RG	172RG0558	D-EDYO N5532V
F-GIYP	Robinson R-22 Beta	1399	
F-GIYX	Reims/Cessna F177RG (Reservation)	F177RG0114	F-BVIN
F-GIYY	Bell 47G-3B (Reservation 5.99) (Possibly Bell TH-13T Soloy N873M c/n 3476 ex 65-8043)	"68043"	
F-GIYZ	Cameron A-105 HAFB	2931	
F-GIZA	Bell 47G-2 (Shelby Aero Rebuild)	SA-53	N1775
F-GIZB	Beech C90 King Air	LJ-955	N768SB N678SB
F-GIZD	Reims/Cessna F172M	F17201355	I- CCAV
F-GIZE	CAARP CAP.10B	5	Fr.AF
F-GIZG	Aérospatiale AS.350B3 Ecureuil	3084	
F-GIZH	Cessna 172R	17280427	N9509Q
F-GIZI	Cessna 172R	17280435	N9328F
F-GIZJ	Cameron-Thunder AX9-140A SII HAFB	4566	G-BYLU
F-GIZK	Cessna 182S	18280909	N72761
F-GIZL	Mudry CAP.10B	18	Fr.AF
F-GIZN(2)	Hughes 269C	100-0058	D-HART
F-GIZO	Robinson R-22 Beta	1814	F-ODZO
F-GIZR	Enstrom F.28A	223	OO-NMT G-RONT

F-GIZS(2)	Hughes 269C	72-0148	OH-HIY G-BAFC
F-GIZT	Ultramagic M-90 HAFB	90/35	
F-GIZV	Bell 47G-2	2219	(F-GMPZ) G-ASYW VR-BBA CP-704 VP-TCF CP-671 VR-BBA
F-GIZX	Ultramagic H-77 HAFB	77/176	
F-GIZY	Ultramagic H-77 HAFB	77/162	
F-GJAB	Aérospatiale AS.350B Ecureuil	1174	N3599U
F-GJAC	Holste MH.1521C Broussard	180	Fr.AF
F-GJAD	Beech E90 King Air	LW-3	N888BH N9493Q
F-GJAH	Cessna 172N	17272635	N6208D
F-GJAK	Embraer EMB.120RT Brasilia	120215	PT-SSJ
F-GJAM	Aérospatiale AS.350B1 Ecureuil	1866	D-HILF
F-GJAN	SOCATA TB-20 Trinidad	965	
F-GJAP	Aérospatiale SN.601 Corvette	31	EC-DYE F-WZSB N602AN F-BTTK F-WNGZ
F-GJAR	Cessna 172N	17269835	N738AX
F-GJAS	Aérospatiale SN.601 Corvette	8	6V-AEA F-WPTT
F-GJAT	Piper PA-34-200T Seneca II	34-7670342	D-GIRK D-IFFP PH-WON N4564F
F-GJAV	Cameron A-160 HAFB	1931	G-BPYF
F-GJAX	Aérospatiale AS.355N Ecureuil 2	5543	I- IIII F-WYMH
F-GJAZ	Leys HG VL-248 Free Balloon	2	
F-GJBA	Mooney M.20J Model 205	24-3132	N10675
F-GJBB	Colt 77A HAFB	1757	
F-GJBC	Pilatus PC-6/B2-H2 Turbo-Porter	868	
F-GJBD	Robinson R-22 Beta	1400	
F-GJBE	Robinson R-22 Beta	1348	
F-GJBF	Holste MH.1521C-1 Broussard (Could possibly be c/n 013 ex. F-ZWTL)	13	Fr.AF
F-GJBH	Sud Avn SA.319B Alouette III	2102	(F-GGPU) Fr.AF
F-GJBI	Robinson R-22 Beta	1782	N40790
F-GJBK	Bell 47G-2	2428	N2883B
F-GJBM	SOCATA TB-10 Tobago	304	F-OIBM F-GDBM
F-GJBN	SNCASE SE.313B Alouette II	1619	ALAT
F-GJBP	Pilatus PC-6/B2-H4 Turbo-Porter	716	HB-FFL 9N-AAW HB-FFL
F-GJBQ	Nord 1101 Noralpha	177	F-ZJBQ
F-GJBS	Beech B200 Super King Air	BB-1181	N6725Y
F-GJBZ	Dassault Falcon 50EX	269	(F-GPBG) F-WWHT
F-GJCB	Piper PA-28R-201 Arrow III	28R-7837053	HB-PBR N6135H
F-GJCG	Cessna R182 Skylane RG	R18200340	N4234C
F-GJCI	Cessna 152	15280674	N25467
F-GJCJ	Robinson R-22 Beta (Noted 6.03)	unkn	
F-GJCL	Piper PA-28RT-201T Turbo Arrow IV	28R-8131004	N8275A
F-GJCM	Aérospatiale AS.350B1 Ecureuil	1988	LN-OMQ
F-GJCN	Cessna 152	15283979	N4806H
F-GJCO	Cessna 152	15281503	N64969
F-GJCP	Aérospatiale AS.350B1 Ecureuil	2172	JA9788
F-GJCQ	Aérospatiale SA.315B Lama	2526	
F-GJCR	Beech E90 King Air	LW-251	N7ZU N483 TG-BET
F-GJCS	Piper PA-28R-201 Cherokee Arrow III	28R-7737016	N1915H
F-GJCT	Cessna 172N	17268897	N734JU
F-GJCU	Cameron N-105 HAFB	3964	
F-GJCV	SNCASE SE.3130 Alouette II	1344	ALAT
F-GJCX(2)	Chaize JZ.25F12 HAFB	139	
F-GJCZ	Robinson R-44 Astro	0496	
F-GJDA	Pilatus PC-6A/B2-H2 Turbo Porter	721	HA-YDA
F-GJDB	Dassault Falcon 20	76	(F-GGFO) N776DS N937GC N970F F-WMKF
F-GJDC	Piper PA-28-161 Warrior II	2816100	N9222F
F-GJDD	Mooney M.20K Model 231	25-0776	(F-GJLU) LX-MLL N5696U
F-GJDF	Aérospatiale AS.350B2 Ecureuil	2642	F-WYMO
F-GJDG	Cessna F500 Citation	0312	N82AT N33MQ (N233ME) N33ME N5312J
F-GJDH	Piper PA-28-151 Cherokee Warrior	28-7415335	N41854
F-GJDJ	Cameron A-105 HAFB	2450	
F-GJDK(3)	Cessna 421A	421A0080	CN-TBH CN-MBD N2980Q

F-GJDN	Robin DR.400/120	1018	F-BXER
F-GJDP	Cessna T303 Crusader	T30300032	N19HK
			N45526
			C-GNTK
			(N9636T)
F-GJDT	Hughes 269C	99-0822	PH-HFH
F-GJDU	Cameron N-90 HAFB	3326	
F-GJDV	Aérospatiale SA.365N Dauphin 2	6065	I- SINV
F-GJDX	Robin DR.400/140B Major 80	781	F-BTZU
F-GJDZ	Cameron O-77 HAFB	2590	
F-GJEF	Piper PA-28-181 Archer II	2890189	N9232N
F-GJEG	SNCASE SE.3130 Alouette II	1229	V-45
			HB-XBK
			V-45
F-GJEH	Aviat Pitts S.2B	5255	N98AV
F-GJEI	Bell 47G-2	2426	N2889B
F-GJEJ	Beech K35 Bonanza	D-5912	HB-EGW
	(c/n correct but quoted as "D-59A2")		D-EGWA
			HB-EGW
F-WJEL	SOCATA TB-200 (Prototype)	1214	F-GKEC
F-GJEM	Piper J-3C-65 Cub	12963	HB-ONK
			44-80667
F-GJEN	Piper PA-28-181 Archer II	28-7990201	N3024H
F-GJEP	Christen Pitts S-2B	5156	
F-GJER	Maule MX-7-235 Star Rocket	10071C	N6127Q
F-GJET	Cessna 182Q	18266805	D-EWED
			N96676
F-GJFA	Beech B200 Super King Air	BB-1270	N30391
F-GJFC	Beech B200 Super King Air	BB-1347	
F-GJFE	Beech B200 Super King Air	BB-1399	
F-GJFF to H	Reserved for DGAC/SFACT		
F-GJFI	Cessna 208B Grand Caravan	208B0230	N208GC
			(N4909B)
F-GJFN	Beech F33A Bonanza	CE-896	HB-EWA
F-GJFO	Thunder AX7-65Z HAFB	1743	
F-GJFP	Cessna T210R Turbo Centurion II	21064913	N6148U
F-GJFR	Cessna 172P	17274712	N53258
F-GJFS	Chaize CS.4000F16 HAFB	101	
F-GJFT	Mooney M.20J Model 201	24-1134	N1085D
F-GJFU	Aérospatiale AS.355F1 Ecureuil 2	5079	G-BUZI
			N57894
F-GJFV	Bell 206B Jet Ranger II	2567	N501WN
			N5010N
F-GJGG	Balloon Works Firefly F7B-15 HAFB	F7B-346	
F-GJGH	Piper PA-28R-201T Turbo Cherokee Arrow III	28R-7703396	N47548
F-GJGI	Chaize CS.2200F12 HAFB	112	
F-GJGK	Mooney M.20J Model 205	24-3178	N9119N
F-GJGM	Mudry CAP.232	07	
F-GJGN	Mooney M.20J Model 205	24-3200	
F-GJGQ	Schweizer S.269C	S.1545	PH-KBS
			N41S
F-GJGR	Beech A36 Bonanza	E-2221	N7223R
F-GJGT	Aérospatiale SA.342J Gazelle	1094	C-GSDZ
			N14416
F-GJGU	Aérospatiale AS.355F1 Ecureuil 2	5095	N7090T
			C-FMHP
			C-FVHQ
			N321HC
F-GJGV	Bell 206B Jet Ranger II	913	G-BALC
F-GJGX	Chaize JZX.22F12 HAFB	152	
F-GJGY	Ultramagic M-145 HAFB	145/10	
F-GJGZ	Cameron N-77 HAFB	2705	
F-GJHA	Cessna F150G	F150-0089	OO-SIQ
F-GJHD	Piper PA-28R-201T Turbo Cherokee Arrow III	28R-7703135	G-RYAN
			G-BFMN
			OO-DGP
			N5622V
F-GJHF	Piper PA-38-112 Tomahawk	38-78A0357	TJ-AHE
			F-OBNV
			N9667N
F-GJHP	Schweizer 269C	S-1402	N424MS
F-GJHR	Piper PA-28-181 Archer II	28-8090071	N876HR
			N8077T
F-GJHT	Piper PA-38-112 Tomahawk	38-79A0278	N2340D
F-GJHU	SAN Jodel D.140C Mousquetaire III	153	D-EIFI
F-GJHY	Agusta-Bell 206B Jet Ranger II	8426	EC-CPF
			F-BXAJ
F-GJHZ	Piper PA-46-310P Malibu	46-8508090	I-LRNZ
			I-DANB
			N2484X
F-GJIB	SNCASE SE.313B Alouette II	1627	FAP9209
			76+30
F-GJID	Aerostar S-57A HAFB	3187	
F-GJIF	Ultramagic H-77 HAFB	77/126	
F-GJIH	Piper PA-28-236 Dakota	28-8111060	D-ENIH
			N8365D
F-GJII	Cameron V-77 HAFB	1915	OO-BRP
			(OO-BRR)
F-GJIJ	Fouga CM.170 Magister	482	Fr.AF
F-GJIM	Aérospatiale AS.350B Ecureuil	1489	N5434T
			XA-. . .
F-GJIN	Ultramagic M-77 HAFB	77/104	
F-GJIO	Ultramagic N-180 HAFB	180/19	

F-GJIP	Aérospatiale AS.350B3 Ecureuil	3820	
F-GJIQ	SNCASE SE.3160 Alouette III (Reservn 8.00)	1184	F-WQLS
			ALAT
F-GJIR(2)	Eurocopter EC.120BColibri	1327	
F-GJIT	Piper PA-23-250 Aztec F	27-7954087	F-OGIT
			N6771A
F-GJIU	Ultramagic H-77 HAFB	77/178	
F-GJIV	Ultramagic H-77 HAFB	77/170	
F-GJIX	Chaize JZ.25F16 HAFB	149	
F-GJIY	Aérospatiale AS.350B Ecureuil	1731	G-PLMC
			G-BKUM
F-GJIZ	Chaize JZ.22F24 HAFB	151	
F-GJJA	Cameron N-77 HAFB	2473	
F-GJJB	Thunder AX7-65 HAFB	1473	
F-GJJC	Piper PA-28RT-201T Turbo Arrow IV	28R-8531004	N4391D
			N9528N
F-GJJD	Cameron A-105 HAFB	2537	
F-GJJE	Chaize JZ.22F12 HAFB	141	
F-GJJH	Aérospatiale AS.350B2 Ecureuil	2584	
F-GJJI	Fouga CM.170 Magister	500	Fr.AF
F-GJJM	Holste MH.1521M Broussard	292	Fr.AF
F-GJJN	Reims/Cessna F406 Caravan II	F406-0088	
F-GJJQ	Lindstrand LBL-180 HAFB	051	
F-GJJR	Piper PA-28RT-201T Turbo Arrow IV	28R-8431016	N4340K
F-GJJT	Chaize CS.2200F12 HAFB	106	
F-GJJU	Aérospatiale AS.365N	6157	JA9637
F-GJJX	Cessna 150M (Reservation .99)	15078807	ZS-JWW
	(Now reserved as F-OHLM?)		(N704RE)
F-GJJY	Cessna U206F Stationair	U20602855	TR-LDV
			TN-AET
			N1170Q
F-GJJZ	Aérospatiale AS.355N Ecureuil 2	5694	
F-GJKA	Cameron N-77 HAFB	527	LX-PIN
F-GJKB	Chaize JZ.30F16 HAFB	136	
F-GJKD	Robinson R-44 Astro	0114	D-HKAZ
			(ES- . . .)
			D-HKAZ
F-GJKE	Cameron N-65 HAFB	1861	LX-OKE
F-GJKF	Aérospatiale AS.350B3 Ecureuil	3309	
F-GJKG	SOCATA TB-20 Trinidad	1181	PH-JED
			F-GKUP
F-GJKJ	Aérospatiale AS.355N Ecureuil 2	5607	N336FP
			N614LH
			JA6785
F-GJKL	Sud Avn SA.316B Allouette III	5277	F-ODLH
			N1037S
			TG-TEK
F-GJKO	Aérospatiale AS.350B3 Ecureuil	3350	
F-GJKQ	Airbus A310-304 (Reservation)	571	TU-TAC
			F-WWYM
			F-GHYM
F-GJKR	Airbus A310-304 (Reservation)	651	TU-TAD
			F-WWCC
F-GJKS	Airbus A310-304 (Reservation)	652	TU-TAE
			F-WWCH
F-GJKT(2)	Airbus A310-304 (Reservation)	671	TU-TAF
			F-WWCM
F-GJKU	Cessna 172R	17280869	N2432F
F-GJKX	Ultramagic H-65 HAFB	65/84	(F-GIZM)
F-GJKY	Aérospatiale AS.350B3 Ecureuil	3441	
F-GJKZ	Bell 214B-1	28066	C-GTWG
			N4410N
			JA9304
			N2179R
F-GJLC(2)	Cessna F172H	F172-0441	CN-TTU(2)
F-GJLE	Colt 105A HAFB	1596	
F-GJLF	Mooney M.20M Model 257 TLS	27-0066	
F-GJLG	Cessna 172P	17275063	N54836
F-GJLK	SNCASE SE.3130 Alouette II (W/o 23.7.98)	1914	V-62
F-GJLM	Robin DR.400/180 Régent	1286	F-GBAG
F-GJLO	SOCATA MS.893A Rallye Commodore 180	11411	D-EAGQ
F-GJLP	Holste MH.1521C1 Broussard	279	Fr.AF
F-GJLR	Piper PA-28-161 Warrior II	28-7916231	N2236K
F-GJLS	Cessna 172R	17280173	N9893F
F-GJLT	Holste MH.1521C Broussard (Stored)	44C	F-BJLT
	(Plate on aircraft quotes c/n 85)		
F-GJLV	Ultramagic M-130 HAFB	130/29	
F-GJLX	Hughes 369D	91-1058D	(F-GHLX)
			N16DK
			N5107J
F-GJLY	Ultramagic M-105 HAFB	105/70	
F-GJLZ	Cessna P210N Pressurized Centurion II	P21000423	N7757K
F-GJMA	Dassault Falcon 10	116	N525RC
	(Dbr 27.9.96? CofA expired 10.97)		N925DS
			(N927DS)
			N4DS
			N189FJ
			F-WNGL
F-GJMB	SOCATA TB-20 Trinidad	909	
F-GJMC	SOCATA TB-20 Trinidad	910	
F-GJMD	SOCATA TB-20 Trinidad	911	
F-GJME	SOCATA TB-20 Trinidad	unkn	
F-GJMF	SOCATA TB-20 Trinidad	unkn	
F-GJMG	Mooney M.20M Model 257 TLS	27-0032	
F-GJMJ	Beech B200 Super King Air	BB-1032	I- CUVI
			N6494S
F-GJML	Chaize CS.2200F12 HAFB	108	

F-GJMN	Fouga CM.170 Magister	424	F-WQCE
			Fr.AF
F-GJMO	Robinson R-22M Mariner	1296M	
F-GJMP	Bell 47G-2	7525	CF-CIU
F-GJMQ(2)	Reims/Cessna F172L (Reservation 10.00)	F17200893	F-BTUO
F-GJMS	Piper PA-28-181 Archer II	28-8490103	N133AV
F-GJMT(2)	Diamond DA42 Twin Star	42.009	
F-GJMU	Rockwell S.2R Thrush Commander	1689R	EC-CMS
			N5589X
F-GJMX(2)	Piper PA-11 Cub Special	11-1060	F-BFMX
F-GJMY	Cameron A-105 HAFB	2277	
F-GJMZ	Mooney M.20M Model 257 TLS	27-0152	N9162D
F-GJNA	Boeing 737-528	25206	
F-GJNB	Boeing 737-528	25227	
F-GJNC	Boeing 737-528	25228	
F-GJND	Boeing 737-528	25229	
F-GJNE	Boeing 737-528	25230	
F-GJNF	Boeing 737-528	25231	
F-GJNG	Boeing 737-528	25232	
F-GJNH	Boeing 737-528	25233	
F-GJNK	Boeing 737-528	25236	
F-GJNL	Boeing 737-5H6 (Reserved as LV-BAR 3.05)	26448	9M-MFC
F-GJNM	Boeing 737-528	25237	(F-GJNL)
F-GJNN	Boeing 737-528	27304	
F-GJNO	Boeing 737-528	27305	
F-GJNX	Boeing 737-5H6	26454	9M-MFE
F-GJNZ	Boeing 737-5H6	26450	9M-MFD
F-GJOL	Wassmer WA.41 Baladou	163	TU-TLY
			F-OCOL
F-GJOM	Piper PA-28-181 Archer II	2890143	
F-GJOZ	SOCATA TB-10 Tobago	319	HB-EQU
F-GJPG	SNCASE SE.3130 Alouette II	1716	F-MJAN
F-GJPH(2)	Aérospatiale AS.350B3 Ecureuil	3824	
F-GJPI (2)	Aérospatiale AS.350B3 Ecureuil	3484	
F-GJPJ	Piper PA-28-161 Warrior II	28-8516001	N4376U
F-GJPN	Fairchild Swearingen SA.227AC Metro III	AC-757B	N57NE
F-GJPO	Piper PA-28RT-201T Turbo Arrow IV	28R-7931039	N2227L
F-GJPP	Cameron N-90 HAFB	1952	
F-GJPT	Cessna 310R	310R1817	N310LC
F-GJPV	Robinson R-22 Beta	1836	(F-GIVM)
			N23104
F-GJPX	SNCASE SE.3130 Alouette II (Permit .02)	1489	Fr.AF
F-GJPZ	Aérospatiale SA.365N Dauphin 2	6115	LN-OLN
			G-BLUO
F-GJQA	Robin DR.400/140B Major 80	1955	
F-GJQB	Robin DR.400/140B Major 80	1956	
F-GJQC	Robin DR.400/140B Major 80	1970	
F-GJQE	Robin DR.400/120 Dauphin 2+2	1966	
F-GJQF	Robin R.3000/140	143	
F-GJQG	Robin DR.400/180R Remorqueur	1963	
F-GJQH	Robin DR.400/180R Remorqueur	1964	
F-GJQI	Robin ATL L	133	
F-GJQJ	Robin DR.400/180 Régent	1967	
F-GJQK	Robin DR.400/120 Dauphin 2+2	1962	
F-GJQL	Robin DR.400/120 Dauphin 2+2	1968	
F-GJQN	Robin DR.400/180 Régent	1976	
F-GJQO	Robin DR.400/140B Major 80	1978	
F-GJQP	Robin DR.400/140B Major 80	1979	
F-GJQQ	Robin DR.400/140B Dauphin 4	1986	
F-GJQR	Robin DR.400/140B Major 80	1971	
F-GJQS	Robin DR.400/140B Major 80	1977	
F-GJQT	Robin DR.400/120 Dauphin 2+2	1987	
F-GJQU	Robin DR.400/120 Dauphin 2+2	1983	
F-GJQV	Robin DR.400/120 Dauphin 2+2	1975	
F-GJQX	Robin DR.400/120 Dauphin 2+2	1993	
F-GJQY	Robin DR.400/160 Major	1988	
F-GJQZ	Robin DR.400/120 Dauphin 2+2	1989	
F-GJRA	Holste MH.1521C Broussard	282	Fr.AF
F-GJRB	SOCATA TB-10 Tobago	228	SE-GFV
			F-ODOE
F-GJRC	Piper J-3C-90 Cub	12028	(F-GJPR)
			HB-OIR
			44-79732
F-GJRE	Piper PA-28RT-201 Arrow IV	28R-8118059	N8354D
F-GJRF	CASA C.212-200CB	150	TR-LZJ
			F-WIPE
F-GJRG	Thunder AX7-77SI HAFB	1627	OO-BTA
F-GJRJ	Piper PA-28-181 Archer II	2890144	
F-GJRK	Beech C90 King Air	LJ-710	3A-MON(3)
			D-IAFH
F-GJRL	Thunder AX7-65 HAFB	1695	
F-GJRM	Piper 28-236 Dakota	28-8211033	N8200K
F-GJRP	Aérospatiale AS.350B Ecureuil	1926	D-HOST
F-GJRR	Piper PA-28RT-201T Turbo Arrow IV	28R-7931294	N8072D
F-GJRS	Piper PA-34-200T Seneca II	34-7670322	N3892F
F-GJRY	Cameron N-105 HAFB	10304	
F-GJRZ	Cessna 152	15279724	D-EFRZ
			N757GG
F-GJSE	Aérospatiale AS.355NEcureuil 2	5225	(F-GTRE)
			N908BA
			N5802X
F-GJSG	Piper PA-18 Super Cub 95	18-5648	HB-OPW
			N10F
F-GJSI	Schweizer 269C	S-1390	
F-GJSJ	Cameron Z-105 HAFB	10429	
F-GJSL	Aérospatiale SA.342J Gazelle	1052	C-GPGO
			N8350

F-GJSN	Aérospatiale AS.355N Ecureuil 2	5701	
F-GJSO	Cameron Z-105 HAFB	10376	
F-GJSQ	Cessna 172N	17272306	N1837C
F-GJSS	Schweizer 269C	S-1578	N110LU
F-GJSU	Piper PA-23-250 Aztec E	27-4776	F-ODSU
			TU-TJY
			TU-TIC
			N14219
F-GJSY	Nord 262-A20 (Reservation 11.02)	38	F-BPNU
			F-WOFA
F-GJSZ	Aérospatiale AS.350B2	9058	
F-GJTC	Christen Pitts S-2B	5162	
F-GJTD	Cessna 150M	15075860	TR-LTD
			N66132
F-GJTR	Eurocopter EC.120B	1360	
F-GJTU	Aérospatiale AS.350B3	3449	EP-...
			F-GNMI
F-GJTV	Dassault Falcon 50 (Reservation)	unkn	
F-WJTX/Y	Reserved for Transair France		
F-GJTZ	Cessna 172L	17260417	N7117Q
F-GJUA	Boeing 737-548	25165	LN-TUX
			SE-DUT
			EI-CDT
			PT-MNC
			EI-CDT
F-GJUB to K	Reserved for Boeing 737-500s for Air France		
F-GJUM	Ultramagic S-105 HAFB	105/01	EC-EGR
F-GJUP	Cameron N-133 HAFB	2563	
F-GJUS	Cameron O-84 HAFB	175	N83CB
F-GJUV	Piper PA-28-181 Archer II	28-8490060	N4350K
F-GJUX	Thunder AX7-77 HAFB	1745	
F-GJVA	Airbus A320-211	144	F-WWDK
F-GJVB	Airbus A320-211	145	F-WWDL
F-GJVE	Airbus A320-211	215	
F-GJVF	Airbus A320-211	244	
F-GJVG	Airbus A320-211	270	
F-GJVU	Airbus A320-212	436	G-BXAT
			F-GJVY
			(PH-GCL)
			F-WWDE
F-GJVW	Airbus A320-211	491	N131LF
			F-WWBS
F-GJVX	Airbus A320-211	420	PH-GCX
			N486GX
			F-WWIE
F-GJXA	SOCATA TB-20 Trinidad	1303	
F-GJXB	SOCATA TB-20 Trinidad	1304	
F-GJXC	SOCATA TB-10 Tobago	1496	
F-GJXD	SOCATA TB-10 Tobago	1497	
F-GJXE	SOCATA TB-10 Tobago	1498	
F-GJXF	SOCATA TB-10 Tobago	1500	
F-GJXG	SOCATA TB-10 Tobago	1504	
F-GJXH	SOCATA TB-10 Tobago	1505	
F-GJXI	SOCATA TB-10 Tobago	1591	
F-GJXJ	SOCATA TB-10 Tobago	1592	
F-GJXK	SOCATA TB-10 Tobago	1593	
F-GJXM	SOCATA TB-10 Tobago	1426	
F-GJXN	SOCATA TB-10 Tobago	1427	
F-GJXO	SOCATA TB-10 Tobago	1428	
F-GJXP	SOCATA TB-10 Tobago	1429	
F-GJXQ	SOCATA TB-10 Tobago	1430	
F-GJXR	SOCATA TB-10 Tobago	1431	
F-GJXS	SOCATA TB-10 Tobago	1432	
F-GJXT	SOCATA TB-10 Tobago	1433	
F-GJXU	SOCATA TB-10 Tobago	1491	
F-GJXV	SOCATA TB-10 Tobago	1493	
F-GJXX	Cessna 560 Citation V	560-0070	(N2725A)
F-GJXY	SOCATA TB-10 Tobago	1494	
F-GJXZ	SOCATA TB-10 Tobago	1495	
F-GJYA	Aérospatiale AS.355N Ecureuil 2	5535	N66ED
			N113LP
F-GJYC(2)	Robinson R-44 Raven	1260	
F-GJYD	Cessna 550 Citation II	550-0415	N1949M
			N1949B
			OH-CUT
			D-CNCI
			N12165
F-GJYF	Cameron O-90 HAFB	4001	
F-GJYL	Aerotek Pitts S-2A	2092	HB-MSD
			N8ED
F-GJYN	Robinson R-44 Astro	0418	
F-GJYP	SOCATA TB-20 Trinidad	2145	
F-GJYY	Reims/Cessna F152	F15201660	(F-GJMX)
			HB-CCM
F-GJYZ	Hughes 269C	65-0419	F-BXOT
F-GJZB	Robin DR.400/180 Régent	1982	
F-GJZD	Robin DR.400/140 Major	1994	
F-GJZE	Robin DR.400/120 Dauphin 2+2	2005	
F-GJZF	Robin DR.400/140B Major 80	1999	
F-GJZG	Robin DR.400/120 Dauphin 2+2	2003	
F-GJZH	Robin DR.400/120 Dauphin 2+2	2002	
F-GJZI	Robin DR.400/140B Dauphin 4	2016	
F-GJZJ	Robin DR.400/120 Dauphin 2+2	2018	
F-GJZK	Robin DR.400/180 Régent	2000	
F-GJZL	Robin DR.400/120 Dauphin 2+2	2009	
F-GJZM	Robin DR.400/120 Dauphin 2+2	2010	

F-GJZO	Robin DR.400/120 Dauphin 2+2	2023	
F-GJZP	Robin DR.400/120 Dauphin 2+2	2028	
F-GJZQ	Robin DR.400/160 Major	2030	
F-GJZR	Robin DR.400/120 Dauphin 2+2	2034	
F-GJZS	Robin DR.400/120 Dauphin 2+2	2033	
F-GJZT	Robin DR.400/140B Dauphin 4	2025	
F-GJZU	Robin DR.400/120 Dauphin 2+2	2031	
F-GJZV	Robin DR.400/160 Major	2032	
F-GJZX	Robin DR.400/140B Dauphin 4	2041	
F-GJZY	Robin R.3000/160 (Damaged, .03)	149	
F-GKAC	Cameron N-77 HAFB	1958	
F-GKAD	SOCATA TB-20 Trinidad	954	
F-GKAF(2)	Balloon Works Firefly F8B-15 HAFB	410	OO-BWK
			N2523K
F-GKAH	Cessna 172N	17273807	N5477J
F-GKAJ	Mudry CAP.10B	27	Fr.AF
F-GKAM	Mudry CAP.10B	114	HB-SAM
F-GKAO	Piper PA-28-181 Cherokee Archer II	28-7690349	HB-PBE
			N6134J
F-GKAP	Piper PA-28-161 Warrior II	28-8216072	N847AH
			N84727
F-GKAV	Colt 21A HAFB	1742	
F-GKAX	Cessna 152	15285711	F-OGUT
			N566V
			(N94541)
F-GKBB	Cessna 172RG Cutlass RG	172RG0222	N5085U
F-GKBE	Aérospatiale AS.350B Ecureuil	2503	
F-GKBF	Aérospatiale AS.350B3 Ecureuil	3305	
F-GKBG	Rockwell 112 Commander	198	N1198J
F-GKBI	Cameron O-65 HAFB	2729	
F-GKBJ	Piper PA-12 Super Cruiser	12-3521	F-BFBJ
			NC4084H
F-GKBL	Cessna 172RG Cutlass RG	172RG0609	N6289V
F-GKBN	Cameron A-105 HAFB	3289	
F-GKBO	Robin DR.400/140B Dauphin 4	2156	HB-KDG
F-GKBS	SNCASE SE.313B Alouette II	1442	ALAT
F-GKBU	SNCASE SE.3130 Alouette II	1743	Fr.AF
F-GKBV	Partenavia P.68B	13	F-OHCT
			F-WQHL
			G-MOET
			G-HPVC
			OH-PVB
F-GKCA	Piper PA-18-150 Super Cub	18-8604	F-OCFI
F-GKCB	Piper PA-28RT-201T Turbo Arrow IV	28R-8131136	N83843
F-GKCF	Aérospatiale AS.350D Ecureuil	1452	N5797D
F-GKCH	Cameron O-84 HAFB	2552	
F-WKCI	Airbus A320-212 (Temp regd 10.02)	132	F-GKCI
			C-GVXH
			F-GLGN
			N482GX
			F-WWIY
F-GKCK	SNCASE SE.316V Alouette III	1256	ALAT
F-GKCM	Cameron Bouchon 116 HAFB	2021	
F-GKCN	Aérospatiale AS.350D Ecureuil	1098	N3596D
F-GKCO	Cessna 172R	17280055	F-WKCO
			N374ES
F-GKCQ	Thunder AX10-180A HAFB	1791	
F-GKCR	Piper PA-28RT-201T Turbo Arrow IV	28R-8131078	N8339H
F-GKCU	Aérospatiale SA.365N Dauphin 2	6011	PH-SEC
			F-GJEO
			F-ZWVT
			F-WZLG
			N6003L
			F-WZLG
F-GKCV	Beech 200 Super King Air	BB-251	I- BMPE
			HB-GGO
			N256TW
			N18251
F-GKDA	Piper PA-24-260 Comanche C	24-4847	5U-BAX
			5N-AHS
			N9348P
F-GKDB	Dassault Falcon 20E	271/493	(F-GHPO)
			7T-VRP
			F-WNGN
F-GKDE	Reims/Cessna F152	F15201653	HB-CCK
F-GKDF	Mooney M.20M Model 257 TLS	27-0109	
F-GKDG	Cameron O-65 HAFB	4908	
F-GKDK	Bell 206BJet Ranger II (Reservation .00)	unkn	
F-WKDL	SOCATA TBM-700 (also carries "221" on tail)	03	
F-GKDM	Pilatus PC-6/B1-H2 Turbo-Porter	670	S2-ACD
			AP-AVU
			HB-FES
F-GKDP	Helibras HB.350B Esquilo (Possible w/o 29.7.98)	1522	YV-569CP
			PT-HLX
F-GKDT	Aérospatiale SA.315B Lama	2562	HB-XUC
			XC-CAM
F-GKDU	Cessna R182 Skylane RG	R18200316	N182KP
			(N3701C)
F-GKEA	Beech F33A Bonanza	CE-1628	
F-GKEB	SNCAN Stampe SV.4C	618	F-BDFN
F-GKEC(2)	Piper PA-28-181 Cherokee Archer II	28-7890218	N6221H
F-GKEF	Piper PA-28-181 Archer II	28-8290031	N8445U
F-GKEI	Fouga CM.170 Magister	479	Fr.AF
	(Previously reserved as F-GLEZ and F-GLSA, ntu)		
F-GKEJ	Piper PA-38-112 Tomahawk II	38-82A0077	G-BPOW
			N2592V

F-GKEL	Beech A100 King Air	B-228	N23868
			ZS-XGB
			N23868
F-GKEM	Fokker F.27 Friendship 500	10596	TR-LCQ
			PH-FTX
			CN-CDC(2)
			PH-FTX
			N272SA
			N334MV
			PH-FTX
			PH-EXM
F-GKEN	Piper PA-23-250 Aztec E	27-4784	F-ODLN
			F-BTMQ
			F-BTDZ
			N14226
F-GKEP	Eurocopter EC.130B (Reservation 1.01)	3257	F-WQES
F-GKER	Cameron A-140 HAFB	2181	
F-GKET	Robin DR.300/108	599	F-BMRQ
			OO-JMM
F-GKEV	Cameron N-90 HAFB	2342	
F-GKEX	Dassault Falcon 2000EX (Reservation .01)	001	F-WMEX
F-GKFA	Raven Europe RX-7 HAFB	E-164	
F-GKFB	Raven Europe FS57A HAFB	E-172	
F-GKFD	Raven Europe S-60A HAFB	E-185	
F-GKFE	Raven Europe S-60A HAFB	E-177	
F-GKFF	Raven Europe FS-57A HAFB	E-195	
F-GKFH	Raven Europe FS-57A HAFB	E-203	
F-GKFI	Raven Europe RX-7 HAFB	E-215	
F-GKFJ	Raven Europe RX-8 HAFB	E-223	
F-GKFK	Raven Europe FS-57A HAFB	E-210	
F-GKFL	Raven Europe S-49A HAFB	E-216	
F-GKFM	Raven Europe S-66A HAFB	E-225	
F-GKFO	Raven Europe FS-57A HAFB	E-228	
F-GKFP	Raven Europe FS-57A HAFB	E-229	
F-GKFQ	Raven Europe FS-57A HAFB	E-230	
F-GKFR	Raven Europe S-66A HAFB	E-231	
F-GKFS	Raven Europe S-60A HAFB	E-232	
F-GKFT	Raven Europe FS-57A HAFB	E-237	
F-GKFU	Raven Europe S-52A HAFB	E-204	
F-GKFX	Raven Europe S-49A HAFB	E-239	
F-GKFY	Raven Europe RX-8 HAFB	E-241	
F-GKFZ	Raven Europe W-49A HAFB	E-242	
F-GKGA	Aérospatiale SN.601 Corvette	11	F-WFPD
			EI-BNY
			F-BTTV
			F-ODKS
			TR-LWY
			F-BTTS
			N613AC
			(F-WIFU)
F-GKGE	SNCASE SE.3130 Alouette II	1541	ALAT
F-GKGF	Colt 90A HAFB	3888	
F-GKGG	Cessna A185F Skywagon	18503341	C-GYVZ
F-GKGJ	SNCAN Stampe SV.4C1	517	F-BDIA
F-GKGN	Grumman-American AA-5B Tiger	AA5B-0089	G-BDGN
			N6147A
F-GKGQ	SNCAN/Stampe SV.4C	54	F-BGGQ
			Fr.Mil
F-GKGR	Agusta-Bell 206B Jet Ranger II	8294	YU-HAP
F-GKGU	Cessna 172R	17280338	
F-GKGX	Cessna 172R	17280343	N9512W
F-GKGZ	Aerotek Pitts S-2A	2149	TU-TNY
			N31501
F-GKHA	Aérospatiale AS.350B2 Ecureuil	2359	
F-GKHB	Schweizer 269C	S-1438	(N431MS)
F-GKHD	Fokker F.28-0100	11381	HB-IVI
			PH-JXY
F-GKHE	Fokker F.28-0100	11386	HB-IVK
			PH-JXK
F-GKHF	SNCAN/Stampe SV.4C (Reservation .99)	300	F-BBAM
F-GKHG	Enstrom 280C Shark	1034	G-KLAY
			G-BGZD
F-GKHH	Eurocopter EC.120B Colibri	1122	
F-GKHI	Cessna 172N	17272688	N6281D
F-GKHJ	Dassault Falcon 900	11	N251SJ
			F-GLGY
			UN-09002
			F-WEFX
			LX-AER
			F-WWFK
F-GKHM	SNCASE SE.3160 Alouette III	1088	ALAT
F-GKHR	SIAI S.205-20/R	4-211	OO-DLX
F-GKHT	Robin DR.400/120D	1726	HB-KBB
F-GKHU	Robin DR.400/120D	1723	HB-KBA
F-GKHV	Cameron Camembert SS HAFB	2516	
F-GKIA	Pilatus PC-6/ B2-H2 Turbo Porter	689	VH-MKT
			A14-689
			HB-FEB
F-GKIC	Piper PA-46-350P Malibu Mirage	4622051	N927DC
			N91631
F-GKID	Cessna 500 Citation I	500-0319	N94MA
			D-ICUW
			N22LH
			N5319J
			HZ-NC1
			N5319J
F-GKII	Beech 200 Super King Air	BB-515	N200HC

F-GKIJ	Piper PA-44-180 Seminole	44-7995193	N3010H
F-GKIM	Robin DR.400/160 Major	2039	F-GJKM
F-GKIR	Cessna 500 Citation I	500-0361	N90EB N5361J C-GOIL N5361J D-IKPW N5361J
F-GKIT	Cameron V-77 HAFB	2230	
F-GKIV	Zlin Z.526F Trenér Master	1079	F-BRNC
F-GKIZ	Beech 350 Super King Air	FL-23	N1543Q
F-GKJB	Aérospatiale SN.601 Corvette	20	TR-LZT F-BTTN N616AC F-WNGS
F-GKJE	Aérospatiale AS.350B Ecureuil	1144	N350AJ N350S N3604D
F-GKJF	Cameron A-105 HAFB	2678	
F-GKJI (2)	Mudry CAP.10B	20	Fr.AF
F-GKJJ	Cameron A-180 HAFB	2564	(F-GHMX)
F-GKJN	Chaize CS.3000F16 HAFB	098	
F-GKJT	Holste MH.1521M Broussard	106	Fr.AF
F-GKJZ	Chaize JZ40F16 HAFB	111	
F-GKKA	Mudry CAP.10B	257	
F-GKKC	Mudry CAP.10B	59	D-EDKG F-BXHC
F-GKKI	Mudry CAP.231EX	02	G-BVXL F-GKKF F-WGZC
F-GKKM	Mudry CAP.10B	270	
F-GKKZ	Mudry CAP.10B	113	HB-SAL
F-GKLK	Schweizer 269C (Reservation?)	unkn	
F-GKLL	Aérospatiale AS.350B Ecureuil	1202	SE-HKH
F-GKLM	Beech F33A Bonanza	CE-1687	
F-GKLS(2)	Agusta-Bell 206B Jet Ranger II	8441	G-JERY G-BDBR
F-GKLT	Piper PA-28-181 Archer II	2890124	F-ODLT
F-GKMA	Aérospatiale AS.350B Ecureuil	2285	
F-GKMB	Aérospatiale AS.350B Ecureuil	2304	F-WYMD
F-GKMF	Balloon Works Firefly F8 HAFB	F8-362	
F-GKMO	Ultramagic M-77C HAFB	77/250	
F-GKMP(2)	Aérospatiale AS.350B3 Ecureuil	3828	F-WQDD F-WQDQ
F-GKMJ	Cameron N-77 HAFB	2530	
F-GKMM	Ultramagic M-65 HAFB	65/76	
F-GKMS(2)	Christen A-1 Husky	1168	N9601C
F-GKMT	Chaize JZ25F16 HAFB	119	F-WKMT
F-GKMU	Westland SA.341G Gazelle 1 (Also quoted as c/n 1181 ex C-FEDG) (No longer current?)	WA/1141	Q P-1 G-BBSJ G-17-11
F-GKMV	Mooney M.20J Model 205	24-3210	
F-GKMX	Piper PA-28-161 Warrior II	28-8616048	N9084Z N9509N
F-GKMY	McDonnell-Douglas DC-10-30	47815	SE-DFF N5464M G-BGXI
F-GKMZ	Mudry CAP.232	09	
F-GKNB	Aérospatiale/Alenia ATR-42-300	226	
F-GKNC	Aérospatiale/Alenia ATR-42-300	230	
F-GKOR	Cameron O-105 HAFB	2171	
F-GKOT	SNCASE SE.3130 Alouette II	1243	ALAT Fr.AF
F-GKOX	Cameron A-210 HAFB	10612	
F-GKOY	Piper PA-28-161 Cadet	2841334	(N9217N)
F-GKPA	Mooney M.20J Model 205	24-3166	N1079Y
F-GKPC	Aérospatiale/Alenia ATR-72-201	171	F-WWEA
F-GKPD	Aérospatiale/Alenia ATR-72-201	177	F-WWEH
F-GKPE	Aérospatiale/Alenia ATR-72-201	192	F-WWEE
F-GKPF	Aérospatiale/Alenia ATR-72-201	222	
F-WKPG	SOCATA TBM-700 (also carries "212" on tail)	002	
F-GKPH	Aérospatiale/Alenia ATR-72-201	352	F-WWEJ
F-GKPP	Morane-Saulnier MS.760B Paris 2 (W/o 10.91, used as spares but still regd.)	098	3A-MPP HB-VEP F-BOHN D-INGA
F-GKPR	Christen Pitts S-2B	5120	N6033Z
F-GKPS	Piper PA-28RT-201 Arrow IV	28R-7918128	N28456
F-WKPX	Fokker F.27 Friendship 100	10121	OO-SVM F-GAOT N1036U VH-TFF PH-FAR
F-GKPY	Fokker F.27 Friendship 100	10224	LX-LGA PH-FEO
F-GKQA	Robin DR.400/120 Dauphin 2+2	2040	
F-GKQB	Robin DR.400/140B Dauphin 4	2042	
F-GKQC	Robin DR.400/120 Dauphin 2+2	2043	
F-GKQE	Robin DR.400/100 Cadet	2049	
F-GKQG	Robin DR.400/160 Major	2064	
F-GKQH	Robin DR.400/120 Dauphin 2+2	2053	
F-GKQI	Robin DR.400/180 Régent	2048	
F-GKQJ	Robin DR.400/180 Régent	2046	
F-GKQK	Robin DR.400/140B Dauphin 4	2056	
F-GKQM	Robin DR.400/120 Dauphin 2+2	2057	
F-GKQN	Robin DR.400/160 Major	2058	
F-GKQO	Robin DR.400/180 Régent	2087	
F-GKQP	Robin DR.400/120 Dauphin 2+2	2060	
F-GKQQ	Robin DR.400/140B Dauphin 4	2077	
F-GKQR	Robin DR.400/120 Dauphin 2+2	2062	
F-GKQS	Robin DR.400/120 Dauphin 2+2	2068	
F-GKQU	Robin DR.400/180 Régent	2065	
F-GKQV	Robin DR.400/120 Dauphin 2+2	2037	
F-WKQX	Robin X-4	001	
F-GKQY	Robin DR.400/120 Dauphin 2+2	2069	
F-GKQZ	Robin DR.400/120 Dauphin 2+2	2070	
F-GKRB	Robin R.3000/160	141	
F-GKRD	Robin DR.400/120 Dauphin 2+2	1992	
F-GKRL	Aérospatiale AS.350B3 Ecureuil	3473	
F-GKRM	Balloon Works Firefly F7B HAFB	F7B-316	
F-GKRN	SOCATA TB-21 Trinidad TC	520	I- SERN F-ODQO
F-GKRO	Holste MH.1521C1 Broussard	154	Fr.AF
F-GKRP	Mooney M.20J Model 205	24-3211	
F-GKRQ	Reserved for Kit Aircraft		
F-GKRR	Piper PA-31T Cheyenne II	31T-8120015	N107TT HK-2617P N2411X
F-GKRY	Cameron N-105 HAFB	10577	
F-GKSB	Raven-Europe RX-8 HAFB (Envelope destroyed 3.9.03)	E-220	
F-GKSC	Thunder AX8-105Z HAFB	1763	
F-GKSF	Aérospatiale SA.315B Lama	2471	N471E TG-WAV
F-GKSJ	Balloon Works Firefly F7B-15 HAFB	F7B-326	
F-GKSM	Cessna 182P Skylane	18264935	N1373S
F-GKSP	Beech C90B King Air	LJ-1409	(F-GKDG)
F-GKSS	Beech 58 Baron	TH-154	3A-MON F-BSRF
F-GKTA	Boeing 737-3M8	24413	OO-LTH
F-GKTB	Boeing 737-3M8	24414	OO-LTI
F-GKTC	Robinson R-22 Beta	1369	
F-GKTM	Cameron A-210 HAFB	4660	
F-GKTN	Cameron A-120 HAFB	4659	
F-GKTO	DHC-6 Twin Otter 300	523	TR-LAL F-GAMR
F-GKTP	Cameron A-105 HAFB	4351	
F-GKTR	Bell 47G-2	2457	C-FCAD CF-CAD
F-GKTS	Aérospatiale AS.355F1 Ecureuil 2	5081	HB-XPF F-GDFH
F-GKUB	SOCATA TB-20 Trinidad	1124	
F-GKUD	SOCATA TB-9 Tampico Club	1128	
F-GKUE	SOCATA TB-9 Tampico Club	1129	
F-GKUF	SOCATA TB-9 Tampico Club	1147	
F-GKUG	SOCATA TB-9 Tampico Club	1148	
F-GKUH	SOCATA TB-9 Tampico Club	1149	
F-GKUI	SOCATA TB-10 Tobago	1150	
F-GKUM	SOCATA TB-20 Trinidad	1177	
F-GKUN	SOCATA TB-9 Tampico Club	1168	
F-GKUO	SOCATA TB-9 Tampico Club	1171	
F-GKUQ	SOCATA TB-9 Tampico	1180	
F-GKUR	SOCATA TB-20 Trinidad	1195	
F-GKUS	SOCATA TB-10 Tobago	1208	
F-GKUT	SOCATA TB-10 Tobago	1169	
F-GKUU	SOCATA TB-9 Tampico	1182	
F-GKUV	SOCATA TB-9 Tampico	1194	
F-GKUY	SOCATA TB-9 Tampico	1179	
F-GKVE	SOCATA TB-20 Trinidad	1245	
F-GKVH	SOCATA TB-9 Tampico Club	1270	
F-GKVI	SOCATA TB-9 Tampico Club	1311	
F-GKVK	SOCATA TB-9 Tampico Club	1290	
F-GKVO	SOCATA TB-20 Trinidad	1330	
F-GKVS	SOCATA TB-9 Tampico Club	1310	
F-GKVT	SOCATA TB-9 Tampico Club	1312	
F-GKVU	SOCATA TB-9 Tampico Club	1313	
F-GKVV	SOCATA TB-9 Tampico Club	1314	
F-GKVY	SOCATA TB-9 Tampico Club	1347	
F-GKVZ	SOCATA TB-20 Trinidad	1329	N5559U
F-GKXA	Airbus A320-211	287	
F-GKXB	Airbus A320-212	235	F-OHFX CS-TND N494GX F-WWDM
F-GKXC	Airbus A320-214	1502	F-WWIG
F-GKXD	Airbus A320-214	1873	F-WWDV
F-GKXE	Airbus A320-214	1879	F-WWDX
F-GKXF	Airbus A320-214	1885	"F-WWGKXF"
F-GKXG	Airbus A320-214	1894	F-WWDV
F-GKXH	Airbus A320-214	1924	F-WW..
F-GKXI	Airbus A320-214	1949	F-WW..
F-GKXJ	Airbus A320-214	1900	F-WW..
F-GKXK	Airbus A320-214 (Reservation)	2140	F-WWBR
F-GKXL to GKXZ Reserved for A.320s for Air France			
F-GKYC	Aérospatiale SA.341G Gazelle	1414	EC-EET F-GDFR I- ETBA F-WIPJ
F-GKYF	Fouga CM.170 Magister	315	F-WKYF Fr.AF
F-GKYG	Aérospatiale AS.350B Ecureuil	1536	JA9315
F-GKYL	Piper PA-28RT-201T Turbo Arrow IV	28R-7931288	N4511U

F-GKYN	Aérospatiale/Alenia ATR-42-300	095	(OY-FKA)
			F-GKYN
			F-ODUL
F-GKYY	Beech 300 Super King Air	FL-357	N61907
F-GKZA	Beech 58 Baron	TH-1401	(F-GHHA)
			N104MK
			N6753K
F-GKZB	Beech 58 Baron	TH-1608	(F-GHYB)
F-GKZE	Beech 58 Baron	TH-1494	5V-MCB
F-GKZF	Beech 58 Baron	TH-1486	5V-MCA
F-GKZT	Beech 58 Baron	TH-1557	G-BSDY
			N1557M
F-GKZU	Beech 58 Baron	TH-1459	F-GMRD
			3A-MON
			N851BE
F-GLAB	SOCATA TB-9 Tampico Club	1074	
F-GLAE	SOCATA TB-9 Tampico Club	1051	
F-GLAF	SOCATA TB-9 Tampico Club	1093	
F-GLAG	SOCATA TB-9 Tampico Club	1094	
F-GLAH	SOCATA TB-20 Trinidad	1076	
F-GLAI	SOCATA TB-9 Tampico Club	1087	
F-GLAK	SOCATA TB-9 Tampico Club	1108	
F-GLAL	SOCATA TB-9 Tampico Club	1091	
F-GLAO	SOCATA TB-9 Tampico Club	1106	
F-GLAP	SOCATA TB-9 Tampico Club	1034	
F-GLAQ	SOCATA TB-9 Tampico Club	1035	
F-GLAR	SOCATA TB-9 Tampico Club	1165	
F-GLAS	SOCATA TB-10 Tobago	1166	
F-GLBM	SOCATA TBM-700	22	F-OHBF
F-GLBZ	SOCATA TBM-700	32	N356M
F-GLCA	Raven Europe FS-57A HAFB	E-244	
F-GLCB	Raven Europe S-49A HAFB	E-252	
F-GLCD	Raven Europe FS-57A HAFB	E-256	
F-GLCF	Raven S-57S Fraise HAFB	3001	
F-GLCG	Raven Europe S-60A HAFB	E-262	
F-GLCH	Raven Europe FS-57A HAFB	E-264	
F-GLCI	Raven Europe S-60A HAFB	E-266	
F-GLCJ	Raven Europe S-66A HAFB	E-269	
F-GLCK	Raven Europe FS-57A HAFB	E-276	
F-GLCL	Raven Europe RX-7 HAFB	E-261	
F-GLCM	Raven Europe FS-57A HAFB	E-273	
F-GLCN	Raven Europe S-52A HAFB	E-259	
F-GLCO	Raven Europe S-55A HAFB	E-277	
F-GLCP	Raven Europe S-52A HAFB	E-278	
F-GLCQ	Raven Europe S-55A HAFB	E-285	
F-GLCR	Raven Europe FS-57A HAFB	E-286	
F-GLCT	Raven Europe S-60A HAFB	E-295	
F-GLCU	Raven Europe S-55A HAFB	E-299	
F-GLCV	Raven Europe S-60A HAFB	E-300	
F-GLCY	Raven Europe S-55A HAFB	E-298	
F-GLCZ	Raven Europe S-71A HAFB	E-290	
F-GLDA	Robin DR.400/160 Major	2074	
F-GLDB	Robin DR.400/120 Dauphin 2+2	2072	
F-GLDC	Robin DR.400/120 Dauphin 2+2	2082	
F-GLDD	Robin DR.400/120 Dauphin 2+2	2083	
F-GLDE	Robin DR.400/140B Dauphin 4	2075	
F-GLDF	Robin DR.400/140B Dauphin 4	2091	
F-GLDG	Robin DR.400/140B Dauphin 4	2092	
F-GLDI	Robin DR.400/140B Dauphin 4	2086	
F-GLDJ	Robin DR.400/120 Dauphin 2+2	2094	
F-GLDK	Robin DR.400/120 Dauphin 2+2	2090	
F-GLDL	Robin R.3000/160	155	
F-GLDM	Robin DR.400/180 Régent	2093	
F-GLDN	Robin DR.400/140B Dauphin 4	2096	
F-GLDO	Robin DR.400/120 Dauphin 2+2	2099	
F-GLDP	Robin DR.400/120 Dauphin 2+2	2097	
F-GLDS	Robin DR.400/100 Cadet	2101	
F-GLDT	Robin DR.400/120 Dauphin 2+2	2102	
F-GLDU	Robin DR.400/120 Dauphin 2+2	2103	
F-GLDV	Robin DR.400/180 Régent	2120	
F-GLDX	Robin DR.400/120 Dauphin 2+2	2110	
F-GLDY	Robin DR.400/160 Major	2117	
F-GLDZ	Robin DR.400/180 Régent	2105	
F-GLEA	Cessna 172N	17272260	N9425E
F-GLEB	American AG-5B Tiger	10100	N100AG
F-GLEC	Aérospatiale SN.601 Corvette	30	(F-GKGB)
			EC-DUE
			OO-MRC
			TR-LAH
			OO-MRC,
			F-BTTP
			F-WNGQ
F-GLED(2)	SNCASE SE.3130 Alouette II	1425	ALAT
F-GLEE(2)	Agusta A.109E Power	11603	
F-GLEF(3)	Agusta A.109E Power	11027	
F-GLEG	Agusta A.109E Power	11030	
F-GLEH	Agusta A.109E Power	11037	
F-GLEJ	Mooney M.20K Model 252 TSE	25-1100	N252GD
			N252ZD
F-GLEK	Ultramagic N-180 HAFB	180/20	
F-GLEL	Cameron V-77 HAFB	2467	
F-GLEM	Piper PA-28-181 Archer	28-7990494	N2852K
F-GLEO	Reims/ Cessna F172M	F17201196	OO-WAJ
F-GLEP	Cameron A-180 HAFB	4510	
F-GLEQ	Agusta A.109E Power (Reservn 11.03)	unkn	
F-GLER	Cameron A-180 HAFB	4511	(F-GLEF)
F-GLET	Robinson R-22 Beta	1957	
F-GLEU	Pilatus PC-6/B1-H2 Turbo-Porter	627	I- SAEZ
			D-FLEV
			N4229S
			9M-APQ
			5Y-AHY
			HB-FDE,
			ST-ADJ(1)
			HB-FDE
F-GLEX	Chaize JZ.40F16 HAFB	160	
F-GLEY	Agusta-Bell 206B Jet Ranger III	8558	3A-MRG
			(F-GBLB)
F-GLFA	SOCATA TB-9 Tampico Club	1363	
F-GLFC	SOCATA TB-200 Tobago XL	1376	
F-GLFI	SOCATA TB-9 Tampico Club	1436	
F-GLFM	Aérospatiale AS.350BA Ecureuil	1395	F-WZJD(2)
			SE-HRR
			G-PDCC
			G-PORR
			F-WZFF
F-GLFS	SOCATA TB-20 Trinidad	1364	
F-GLFV	SOCATA TB-9 Tampico Club	1471	
F-GLFX	SOCATA TB-9 Tampico Club	1575	
F-GLFY	SOCATA TB-9 Tampico Club	1582	
F-GLFZ	SOCATA Rallye 235C	13075	
F-GLGC	Piper PA-31-350 Chieftain	31-8052149	N3279H
			V2-LCC
			VP-LCC
F-GLGF	Robin DR.315 Petit Prince	484	OO-BIB
F-GLGG	Airbus A320-211	203	ZS-NZP
			F-WWDN
F-GLGH	Airbus A320-211	220	ZS-NZR
			F-WWIJ
F-GLGK	SOCATA MS.880B Rallye-Club	1584	LX-FBA
			F-BSCL
F-GLGL	Piper PA-28RT-201 Arrow IV	28R-7918250	N108CC
			N9624N
F-GLGM	Airbus A320-212	131	N481GX
			F-WWIX
F-GLGN	Airbus A320-212	132	N482GX
			F-WWIY
F-GLGR	Reims/Cessna FA152 Aerobat	FA1520384	(F-GLYB)
			3A-MPC
			F-GDOP
F-GLGT	Piper PA-32R-301 Saratoga II HP	3213081	N9249G
F-GLGV	SIGA MA-26 Pilatre de Rozier HAFB	128	
F-GLHA	Robin DR.400/120 Petit Prince	794	F-BUHK
F-GLHD	Aérospatiale SA.315B Lama	2647	VT-VKT
			F-GDJH
F-GLHF	Fouga CM.170 Magister	406	F-WLHF
			Fr.AF
F-GLHG	Piper PA-28R-200 Cherokee Arrow II	28R-7635051	N4461X
F-GLHJ	Dassault Falcon 2000	12	I-SNAW
			F-WWMM
F-GLHK	Mooney M.20M Model 257 TLS	27-0176	
F-GLHL	Agusta-Bell 47J	1135	
F-GLHO	Fouga CM.170 Magister (Reservation .99)	331	F-WIGY
			Fr.AF
F-GLHP	Aérospatiale AS.350B2 Ecureuil	2609	
F-GLHT	Bell 407	53294	N4442F
F-GLHY	Agusta-Bell 47G-4A	2544	D-HOOD
F-GLHZ	Rockwell Commander 112	173	N1184J
F-GLIC	Cameron A-180 HAFB	3344	G-BWBR
F-GLID	Bell 47G-2	2416	C-FLMD
			CF-LMD
F-GLIE	SOCATA TB-20 Trinidad	994	G-PLYD
F-GLIF	Beech 200 Super King Air	BB-192	F-OGPQ
			OY-CBV
			LN-KCI
			OY-CBV
			(EI-BGR)
			SE-GRP
F-GLIG	Robin DR.400/180 Régent (Reservation 3.00)	741	TT-DEA
			TL-AAO
F-GLIJ	Canadair CL.600-2B19 Regional Jet	7081	C-F . . .
F-GLIK	Canadair CL.600-2B19 Regional Jet	7084	C-FMMT
F-GLIL	SIGA MA-35 Pilatre de Rozier HAFB	150	
F-GLIN	Lindstrand LBL-105AHAFB	680	
F-GLIO	Cessna R182 Skylane RG	R18201815	N510DC
			N5101T
F-GLIQ	Cameron C-80 HAFB	3584	
F-GLIR	Fokker F.28-0100	11509	PH-EZF
F-GLIS	Fokker F.28-0070	11540	PH-RRS
			(F-GLIS)
			PH-EZS
F-GLIT	Fokker F.28-0070	11541	PH-RRT
			(F-GLIT)
			PH-EZN
F-GLIU	Fokker F.28-0070	11543	PH-RRU
			(F-GLIU)
			PH-EZM
F-GLIV	Fokker F.28-0070	11556	PH-RRV
			(F-GLIV)
			PH-RRV
F-GLIX	Fokker F.28-0070	11558	PH-RRW
			(F-GLIX)
			PH-RRW
F-GLIY	Canadair CL.600-2B19	7053	C-FMMQ

F-GLIZ	Canadair CL.600-2B19	7057	C-FMMY
F-GLJB	SNCASE SE.3130 Alouette II	1073	ALAT
F-GLJC	Piper PA-22-150 Caribbean	22-6854	N2857Z
F-GLJF	Schweizer 269C	S-1550	N41S
F-GLJH	Cameron N-120 HAFB	3416	G-BWJL
F-GLJJ	Cameron N-120 HAFB	3713	
F-GLJL	Beech 95-B55 Baron	TC-1718	HB-GDX
F-GLJM	Cameron N-77 HAFB	2659	
F-GLJN	SOCATA MS.880B Rallye Club	2427	EC-CJN F-OCVV
F-GLJP	Agusta-Bell 206B Jet Ranger II	8315	(F-GGPD) YU-HAV
F-GLJR	Cameron A-105 HAFB	3367	
F-GLJT	Cameron N-105 HAFB	10043	
F-GLKA	Robin DR.400/180R Remo 180	2108	
F-GLKB	Robin DR.400/180R Remo 180	2109	
F-GLKD	Robin DR.400/140B Dauphin 4	2121	
F-GLKE	Robin DR.400/180 Régent	2119	
F-GLKF	Robin DR.400/120 Dauphin 2+2	2122	
F-GLKG	Robin DR.400/180 Régent	2116	
F-GLKH	Robin R.3000/160	158	
F-GLKI	Robin DR.400/140B Dauphin 4	2111	
F-GLKK	Robin DR.400/180 Régent	2130	
F-GLKL	Robin DR.400/160 Major	2129	
F-GLKO	Robin DR.400/120D Petit Prince	1604	HB-EQY
F-GLKP	Robin DR.400/180R Remo 180	2131	
F-GLKQ	Robin DR.400/120D Petit Prince	1605	HB-EQZ
F-GLKR	Robin DR.400/120 Dauphin 2+2	2134	
F-GLKS	Robin DR.400/120 Dauphin 2+2	2126	
F-GLKT	Robin DR.400/180 Régent	2136	
F-GLKU	Robin DR.400/120 Dauphin 2+2	2140	
F-GLKV	Robin DR.400/120 Dauphin 2+2	2139	
F-GLKX	Robin DR.400/120 Dauphin 2+2	2141	
F-GLKZ	Robin DR.400/120 Dauphin 2+2	2128	
F-GLLA	Beech C90A King Air	LJ-1093	HB-GHN N70PJ HB-GHN D-IDSR N720DK N7204V
F-GLLB	Piper PA-28-161 Warrior III	2842005	
F-GLLF	Cessna 172S	172S8092	N681SP
F-GLLH	Beech B200 Super King Air	BB-1109	N900ED N900FD N6580B (YV-554CP)
F-GLLR	Piper PA-32-300 Cherokee Six	32-7640093	N75183
F-GLLY	Ultramagic S-130 HAFB (Reservation .99)	130/. .	
F-GLMA	CEA DR.250/160 Capitaine	99	OO-LIP D-EDLC
F-GLMC	Wassmer Jodel D.120 Paris-Nice	82	F-BIKL
F-GLME	Thunder AX7-65 HAFB	2064	
F-GLMF	Holste MH.1521M Broussard	289	ALAT
F-GLMI	Bell 407 (Reservation)	53117	N14054
F-GLMK	Thunder AX10-180A S3 HAFB	2183	
F-GLMR	Balloon Works Firefly 7B-15 HAFB	F7B-336	
F-GLMS	Piper J-3C-65 Cub (L-4H)	12192	OO-GMS (OO-LSD) PH-CMS D-EGUL G-ANXP N79819 NC78919 44-79896
F-GLMX	McDonnell-Douglas DC-10-30	47814	LN-RKC N5463Y G-BGXH
F-GLND	Beech 1900D	UE-196	N3234G
F-GLNE	Beech 1900D	UE-197	N3234U
F-GLNF	Beech 1900D	UE-69	YR-RLA YR-AAK N82896
F-GLNG	Aérospatiale AS.350B Ecureuil	1415	F-OGNY N114CT N5784R
F-GLNH	Beech 1900D	UE-73	YR-RLB YR-AAL N82923
F-GLNI	BAe.146 Series 200QC	E-2188	G-BTDO G-6-188
F-GLNK	Beech 1900D	UE-269	N11017
F-GLNM	Cessna 340A	340A0351	G-BPNM N989HC N999HC (N37331)
F-GLNU	Aérospatiale AS.365N3 Dauphin 2	6327	ZS-HVI
F-GLNY	Agusta-Bell 47G-2	260	9H-AAF 74+18 AS+060
F-GLNZ	SOCATA TB-10 Tobago	179	I- ODNZ F-GAKU OO-DAL
F-GLOA	Cessna 172RG Cutlass RG	172RG0168	N6336R
F-GLOB	Cameron O-65 HAFB	2798	
F-GLOF	Schweizer 269C	S-1588	N69A
F-GLOH	Wassmer WA.54 Europa	93	F-BXOH(3) F-BUKX F-OCUY
F-GLOK	Cessna 172P	17275517	N64080
F-GLOL	Ultramagic M-130 HAFB	130/37	
F-GLOM	Cameron A-105 HAFB	2956	
F-GLOO	Reims/Cessna F172N	F17201690	OO-VTG
F-GLOP(2)	Aérospatiale AS.350BA Ecureuil	1897	D-HFSH D-HBEN
F-GLOR(2)	Eurocopter EC.135T1	0041	
F-GLOT	Mudry CAP.21	6	F-ODOT
F-GLOU	Robinson R-44 Astro	0032	I- OOOI
F-GLOV	Boeing 767-304ER	28039	G-OBYA D-AGYA
F-GLPA	Robinson R-22 Beta	0670	G-BNRZ
F-GLPD(2)	Robinson R-22 Beta	2235	OK-XIE N2347V
F-GLPF	Cameron O-105 HAFB	2856	
F-GLPH	Aérospatiale AS.365N2 Dauphin 2	6439	F-WTNC
F-GLPJ	Beech 1900C	UC-40	OY-BVG OH-BPA OY-BVG N31101
F-GLPK	Beech 1900C	UC-74	N15528
F-GLPL	Beech 1900C	UC-92	
F-GLPM	Cessna 340A	340A0451	N6263X
F-GLPN	Cessna 207A Stationair 8 (Soloy Pac convn)	20700595	N73469
F-GLPO	Cessna 152	15280278	N24481
F-GLPR	Cessna 172N	17267672	N73778
F-GLPT	Swearingen SA.226T(B) Merlin IIIB	T-298	VH-AWU N5495M
F-GLPV	SNCASE SE.3130 Alouette II	1443	F-MJAZ
F-GLQJ	Piper PA-28R-201T Turbo Arrow III	28R-7803366	F-OGQJ N22081
F-GLQQ	Piper J-3C-65 Cub	7396	C-GUQQ N126RB N40637 NC40637
F-GLRC	SNCASE SE.313BAlouette II (Crashed 23.9.02)	1117	F-MJAW
F-GLRD	Chaize CS.2200F12 HAFB	113	
F-GLRE	Fouga CM.170 Magister	217	Fr.AF
F-GLRF	SIGA MA-26 Pilatre de Rozier HAFB	114	
F-GLRG	Embraer EMB.120ER Brasilia	120149	PH-MGX OO-DTK PT-SPO
F-GLRJ	Chaize CS.2200F12 HAFB	114	
F-GLRK	Ultramagic N-180 HAFB	180/26	
F-GLRM	Cameron O-65 HAFB	2689	
F-GLRN	Diamond DA 20-100 Katana	10111	N537SS
F-GLRO	Robin DR.400/120D Dauphin 2+2	1688	HB-KAR
F-GLRP	Piper PA-31T Cheyenne II	31T-8120064	F-ZBFZ F-WFLQ HK-2906P HK-2906X N9141Y
F-GLRS	SNCASE SE.313B Alouette II	1346	ALAT
F-GLRV	Piper J-3C-65 Cub	9440	N48526 NC48526 43-579 (42-59389)
F-GLRZ	Beech C90A King Air	LJ-1296	(F-GJDK) F-OGRZ
F-GLSB	Cameron V-77 HAFB	3257	
F-GLSD	Airship Industries Skyship SKS 600BL (Reservation .02)	1215-06	N606SA JA1004 VH-HAN (G-SKSK)
F-GLSF	Robinson R-22 Beta	1813	(F-GHJY)
F-GLSM	Mooney M.20C Ranger	20-0024	N7790M
F-GLSO	Ultramagic M-130 HAFB	130/31	
F-GLSP	Ultramagic H-77 HAFB	77/193	
F-GLSR	Beech A36 Bonanza	E-2120	OO-PBC F-GIBC N67578
F-GLSS	Cameron N-77 HAFB	1887	OO-BJR
F-GLST	Piper PA-28-161 Warrior II	28-7916306	N3036T
F-GLSV	Galaxy 7 HAFB	GLX-1737	
F-GLTC	Cessna T210F Turbo-System Centurion	T210-0188	CN-TZS N6788R
F-GLTD	Ultramagic S-90 HAFB	90/47	
F-GLTH	Aérospatiale AS.350B Ecureuil	2701	
F-GLTI	Ultramagic H-77 HAFB	77/ 232	
F-GLTK	Cessna 550 Citation II	550-0609	N344A D-CHOP N609TC (N1242A)
F-GLTO	Fouga CM.170 Magister	471	F-WFPK Fr.AF
F-GLTR	Cessna 172R	17280833	
F-GLTZ	Piper PA-18A-150 Super Cub	18-5136	N7062B
F-GLUB	Piper J-3C-65 Cub	16395	N92002 NC92002
F-GLUC	Raven-Europe S-55A HAFB	E-400	
F-GLUD	Robin DR.400/120 Dauphin 2+2	2165	
F-GLUF	Jum J'Aie	001	
F-GLUI (2)	Sky 105-24 HAFB (Originally c/n 085, ntu)	143	
F-GLVA	Robin DR.400/180 Régent	2146	
F-GLVB	Robin DR.400/120 Dauphin 2+2	2148	
F-GLVD	Robin DR.400/120 Dauphin 2+2	2147	
F-GLVE	Robin DR.400/120 Dauphin 2+2	2151	

F-GLVF	Robin DR.400/120 Dauphin 2+2	2150	
F-GLVG	Robin DR.400/120 Dauphin 2+2	2153	
F-GLVI	Robin DR.400/120 Dauphin 2+2	2138	
F-GLVJ	Robin DR.400/120 Dauphin 2+2	2142	
F-GLVK	Robin DR.400/140B Dauphin 4	2158	
F-GLVL	Robin DR.400/140B Dauphin 4	2154	
F-GLVN	Robin DR.400/140B Dauphin 4	2163	
F-GLVO	Robin DR.400/180 Régent	2155	
F-GLVP	Robin DR.400/140B Dauphin 4	2164	
F-GLVQ	Robin DR.400/120 Dauphin 2+2	2166	
F-GLVR	Robin DR.400/120 Dauphin 2+2	2168	
F-GLVS	Robin DR.400/120 Dauphin 2+2	2169	
F-GLVT	Robin DR.400/140B Dauphin 4	2170	
F-GLVU	Robin DR.400/140B Dauphin 4	2171	
F-GLVV	Robin DR.400/160 Major	2172	
F-GLVX	Robin DR.400/140B Dauphin 4	2175	
F-GLVY	Robin DR.400/120 Dauphin 2+2	2173	
F-GLVZ	Robin DR.400/160 Major	2174	
F-GLXD	Aérospatiale SA.315BLama	2610	
F-GLXF	Boeing 737-219	22657	G-BJXJ
	(Stored)		N851L
			N6066Z
			(ZK-NAT)
F-GLXI	Boeing 737-4Y0	26066	TC-JDZ
F-GLXJ(2)	Boeing 737-4Y0	25177	G-OBMM
F-GLXL	SNCASE SE.3130 Alouette II	1612	76+25
			QW+218
			QW+743
F-GLXQ	Boeing 737-4Y0	24688	OO-VEO
			SX0BLN
			EI-TVC
			EC-GYK
			G-OABF
			EC-FZT
			EC-739
			9M-MJI
			(G-OAAB)
F-GLXZ	SOCATA TB-200 Tobago XL	1448	F-ODXZ
F-GLYC	Cessna 560 Citation V	560-0205	
F-GLYG	Robinson R-22 Beta	0947	G-BPUK
F-GLYN	Robin DR.400/180R Remorqueur	1306	HB-EYN
F-GLYS	McDonnell-Douglas DC-10-30	46872	F-ODLX
			(F-GKMR)
			SE-DFE
			(SE-DEB)
F-GLZA	Airbus A340-311	005	F-WWCA
F-GLZB	Airbus A340-311	007	
F-GLZC	Airbus A340-311	029	
F-GLZG	Airbus A340-311	049	
F-GLZH	Airbus A340-311	078	
F-GLZI	Airbus A340-311	084	
F-GLZJ	Airbus A340-313X	186	(F-GLZN)
F-GLZK	Airbus A340-313X	207	
F-GLZL	Airbus A340-313X	210	
F-GLZM	Airbus A340-313X	237	
F-GLZN	Airbus A340-313X	245	
F-GLZO	Airbus A340-313X	246	
F-GLZP	Airbus A340-313X	260	
F-GLZQ	Airbus A340-313X	289	
F-GLZR	Airbus A340-313X	307	
F-GLZS	Airbus A340-313X	310	
F-GLZT	Airbus A340-313X	319	
F-GLZU	Airbus A340-313X	377	
F-GLZV, X, Y, Z	Reserved for A.340s for Air France		
F-GMAB	Piper PA-28-140 Cherokee Cruiser	28-7625052	C-GGVB
F-GMAC	Cameron Concept 60 HAFB	3058	
F-GMAF	Robin DR.400/140B Dauphin 4	2104	
F-GMAH	Balloon Works Firefly F7B HAFB	F7B-345	
F-GMAK	Cameron N-105 HAFB	3920	
F-GMAN	Cameron A-105 HAFB	4361	
F-GMAP	Cameron C-80 Concept HAFB	3380	
F-GMAS	Commander Aircraft 114B	14552	N60096
F-GMAT	Aérospatiale AS.350B3 Ecureuil	3202	
F-GMAX	Ultramagic V-105 HAFB (Reservation .99)	105/12	
F-GMAY	Aérospatiale SA.365N Dauphin 2	6137	
F-GMBA	Aérospatiale AS.355N Ecureuil 2	5320	N35EC
			YV-O-KWH-5
			F-WZKO
F-GMBB	Cessna P210NPressurized Centurion	P21000380	D-EAOH
			N4953K
F-GMBC	Piper PA-46-310P Malibu	46-8408039	G-BORP
			N4346M
F-GMBD	Piper PA-28-181 Archer II	2890062	HB-PLK
F-GMBE	Reims/Cessna FTB.337G Super Skymaster	0017	(F-GGTP)
			FAP3716
			CS-AAO
F-GMBF	Robinson R-22M Mariner	2193M	F-OGUV
			(F-GMAL)
F-GMBH	Aérospatiale AS.350B3 Ecureuil	3125	
F-GMBI	SIGA MA-30 Pilatre de Rozier HAFB	107	
F-GMBJ	Chaize CS.2200F12 HAFB	143	
F-GMBL	Aérospatiale AS.355N Ecureuil 2	5358	(N75EC)
			YV-O-KWH-6
F-GMBM	Robin DR.400/140B Dauphin 4	2219	
F-GMBO	Aérospatiale AS.350B2 Ecureuil	2253	SE-HUS
F-GMBP(2)	Ultramagic S-130 HAFB	130/18	
F-GMBS	Chaize CS.3000F16 HAFB	115	
F-GMBV	Aérospatiale AS.350BA Ecureuil	1709	3A-MMC
			F-WZFU
F-GMBX	Lindstrand LBL-77A HAFB	515	
F-GMBY	Cessna 182P	18264498	I-BLAC
			N1948M
F-GMCA	Cameron N-77 HAFB	2714	
F-GMCE	Robinson R-22 Beta	2071	N23263
F-GMCF	Piper PA-28-181 Archer II	28-8290155	N8244D
F-GMCG	Christen Pitts S-2B	5243	
F-GMCH	Type unknown	1370	
F-GMCI	Cessna 550 Citation II	550-0050	F-ODUT
			N250CF
			(N259CF)
			D-CJJJ
			N362DJ
			N102FC
			(N3298M)
F-GMCJ	Eurocopter EC.135T1	0020	
F-GMCM	Piper PA-28RT-201T Turbo Arrow IV	28R-8531010	N6914K
F-GMCN	Piper PA-32R-301 Saratoga II HP	3213049	N9221G
F-GMCO	Thunder AX6-56A HAFB	163	G-BRNY
F-GMCY	Nord 1101 Noralpha	67	CEV
F-GMEF	Piper PA-38-112 Tomahawk II	38-81A0057	N25701
F-GMEG	Piper PA-38-112 Tomahawk	38-80A0168	N25417
F-GMEL	Pilatus PC-6/B2-H2 Turbo-Porter	536	N4915
F-GMEM	Durondeau E220 HAFB	008	OO-BPN
			(F-GMEM)
			OO-BPN
F-GMEN	Aérospatiale AS.350B3 Ecureuil	3115	
F-GMEP	Colt 69A HAFB	1960	
F-GMER	Cameron C-80 Concept HAFB	4655	
F-GMES	Robin ATL (Reservation)	73	F-GFRV
F-GMEU	SIGA MA-26 Pilatre de Rozier HAFB	102	F-WMEU
F-GMEV	SIGA MA-30 Pilatre de Rozier HAFB	132	
F-GMEY	Beech F33A Bonanza	CE-1434	PH-MEY
			N5534Y
F-GMEZ	Cameron N-105 HAFB	4607	
	(Later reserved with c/n 4693 - as replacement?)		
F-GMFA	Raven Europe S-60A HAFB	E-110	
F-GMFB	Raven Europe RX-7 HAFB	E-111	
F-GMFD	Raven Europe FS-57A HAFB	E-122	
F-GMFF	Raven Europe FS-57A HAFB	E-129	
F-GMFG	Raven Europe RX-7 HAFB	E-156	
F-GMFH	Raven Europe RX-7 HAFB	E-162	
F-GMFJ	Raven Europe FS-55A HAFB	E-135	
F-GMFL	Raven Europe RX-7 HAFB	E-138	
F-GMFN	Raven Europe S-60A HAFB	E-139	
F-GMFO	Raven Europe FS-57A HAFB	E-144	
F-GMFP	Raven Europe RX-7 HAFB	E-133	
F-GMFS	Raven Europe S-60A HAFB	E-163	
F-GMFT	Raven-Europe S-55A HAFB	E-157	
F-GMFU	Raven Europe FS-57A HAFB	E-158	
F-GMFX	Raven Europe S-52A HAFB	E-200	
F-GMFY	Raven Europe S-55A HAFB	E-161	
F-GMFZ	Raven Europe FS-57A HAFB	E-150	
F-GMGB	Beech B200 Super King Air	BB-1390	(F-GLOP)
			F-ODZK
			N8043B
F-GMGD	Dragonfly 333	3330093003	
F-GMGE	Dragonfly 333	3330093004	
F-GMGF	Cessna P210N Pressurized Centurion II	P21000253	I- NCVH
			N4665K
F-GMGG	Christen A-1 Husky	1091	HB-KCR
F-GMGK	Aérospatiale/Alenia ATR-72-202	365	F-WQIX
			F-OHAT
			F-WWEM
F-GMGM	SOCATA Rallye 100ST	2582	Fr.Navy-82
F-GMGN	SOCATA Rallye 100ST	2585	Fr.Navy-85
F-GMGO	Aerostar RX-8 HAFB	3296	
F-GMGP	Robin DR.400/140B Dauphin 4	2231	
F-GMGS	Aerostar RX-8 HAFB	3258	
F-GMGT	Aerostar S-60A HAFB	3221	
F-GMGU	Raven S-57A HAFB	3195	
F-GMGY	SIGA Pilatre de Rozier MA-26 HAFB	151	
F-GMGZ	SIGA Pilatre de Rozier MA-26 HAFB	152	
F-GMHA	Robinson R-22 Beta (Accident 16.8.99)	2059	
F-GMHB	SIAI-Marchetti SF.260	358	Phil.AF
F-GMHC	Eurocopter EC.135T1	0036	
F-GMHE	Eurocopter EC.135T1	0048	
F-GMHF	Eurocopter EC.135T1	0056	
F-GMHG	Eurocopter EC.135T1	0066	
F-GMHH	Robin HR.100/210 Safari	155	3A-MUZ
	(Wfu 1.00, to UK .04)		F-BUHH
F-GMHI	Aérospatiale SA.365N1 Dauphin 2	6037	PH-SED
			F-GNXB
			5N- . . .
			F-GDXB
			(F-ODSA)
			F-WTNV
F-GMHJ	Eurocopter EC.135T1	0032	
F-GMHK	Eurocopter EC.135T1	0081	D-HBYH
F-GMHM	SIGA MA-26 Pilatre de Rozier HAFB	101	
F-GMHR	Aérospatiale AS.350B Ecureuil	1921	OY-HEJ
F-GMHS	Ultramagic N-180 HAFB	180/10	
F-GMHT	Robinson R-22	unkn	
	(HS.748 Series 2A reservation .02)		
F-GMHU to F-GMHX	Reserved for West Air France		

F-GMHY	Bell 47G	673	F-GGSU
			F-BMHY
			Fr.Mil
F-GMHZ	Eurocopter EC.120BColibri	1178	
F-GMIA	Mooney M.20J Model 205	24-3358	
F-GMIB	Robin DR.500/200i Président	0002	
F-GMID	Hughes 369D	106-0007D	D-HDEK(3)
			(OK- . . .)
			D-HDEK(3)
			CS-HDE
			D-HDEK(3)
			OE-DXN
F-GMIF	Cessna 207A Stationair 7 (Soloy Pac convn)	20700416	HB-CJF
			N7138J
			N21190
			C-GBUZ
			N7352U
F-GMIL	Robinson R-44 Astro	0283	
F-GMIM	Schweizer 269C	S-1239	D-HJON
F-GMIN	Cameron A-210 HAFB	4258	
F-GMIS	Cessna U206F Stationair	U20602194	F-MJAD
			F-MJAJ
			F-BRGM
			N7411Q
F-GMIX	SOCATA TB-20 Trinidad	693	I- SDMB
			F-ODRQ
F-GMIZ	Aérospatiale SA.365C1 Dauphin 2	5018	
F-GMJA	Cessna 177B Cardinal	17702254	N35188
F-GMJB	Thunder AX7-77 HAFB	2281	
F-GMJC	Eurocopter EC.135T1	0026	
F-GMJE	Robin DR.360 Chevalier	702	OO-FFI
			OO-BOB
			D-ENTG
F-GMJF	Rockwell Commander 112	289	N1289J
F-GMJG	Pilatus PC-6/B2-H2 Turbo Porter	659	HB-FEF
			F-GIMU
			HB-FEF
			EC-EHK
			HB-FEF
F-GMJH	Cameron Z-210 HAFB	10273	
F-GMJI	Robinson R-44 Raven	0850	D-HALV
F-GMJL	Aérospatiale SA.341G Gazelle	1245	G-BKLT
	(W/o 18.6.98)		(F-GMJL)
			(F-GGGB)
			G-BKLT
			N15WC
			N47261
F-GMJR	Rockwell Commander 112TC	13072	N24WE
F-GMKA	Robin HR.200/120B	263	
F-GMKB	Robin HR.200/120B	253	
F-GMKC	Robin HR.200/120B	252	
F-GMKD	Robin HR.200/120B	256	
F-GMKE	Robin HR.200/120B	257	
F-GMKF	Robin HR.200/120B	258	
F-GMKG	Robin HR.200/120B	259	
F-GMKH	Robin HR.200/120B	261	
F-GMKI	Robin DR.400/120 Dauphin 2+2	2206	
F-GMKJ	Robin DR.400/180 Régent	2204	
F-GMKL	Robin R.2160 Alpha Sport	265	
F-GMKM	Robin DR.400/140B Dauphin 4	2202	
F-GMKN	Robin DR.400/120 Dauphin 2+2	2199	
F-GMKO	Robin DR.400/140B Dauphin 4	2179	
F-GMKP	Robin DR.400/120 Dauphin 2+2	2182	
F-GMKR	Robin DR.400/180 Régent	2186	
F-GMKS	Robin DR.400/120 Dauphin 2+2	2177	
F-GMKT	Robin DR.400/180 Régent	2183	
F-GMKV	Robin DR.400/160 Major	2195	
F-GMKX	Robin DR.400/140B Dauphin 4	2194	
F-GMKY	Robin DR.400/180 Régent	2210	
F-GMKZ	Robin DR.400/180R Remo 180	2189	
F-GMLA	Cessna 172S	172S8715	N789SP
F-GMLC(2)	Robinson R-22 Beta	unkn	
F-GMLG	Ultramagic S-105 HAFB	105/63	
F-GMLI	McDonnell-Douglas DC-9-83	53014	SE-RDL
			TF-MDC
			D-ALLQ
F-GMLJ	Cessna 414	414-0635	I-CCEE
			N69826
F-GMLK	McDonnell-Douglas MD-83	49672	F-WMLK
			EI-CNO
			EC-FTU
			EC-487
			EC-EJQ
			EC-150
F-GMLL	Ultramagic H-77 HAFB	77/177	
F-GMLM	Cessna 182F Skylane	18254683	F-BKQM
			N3283U
F-GMLN	Cameron N-90 HAFB	4146	
F-GMLO	Robin DR.400/180 Régent	2063	G-FILO
F-GMLQ	Cameron N-77 HAFB	3859	
F-GMLT	Beech 200T Super King Air	BT-34	N56361
	(Converted from B200 c/n BB-1426 on production line)		
F-GMLV	SOCATATBM-700	219	
F-GMLZ	Robinson R-22 Beta	0565	G-IEPF
			N2419X
F-GMMA	Pilatus PC-6/B1-H2 Turbo-Porter	714	HA-YDC
	(Damaged by fire Granville 13.11.03)		
F-GMMB	Hughes 269C	129-0874	D-HHUT
			SE-HKN
F-GMMD	Cameron O-105 HAFB	3852	
F-GMMF	Chaize JZ.35F16 HAFB	133	
F-GMMG	Cameron N-105 HAFB	4318	
F-GMMJ	Chaize JZ.25F16 HAFB	121	
F-GMMK	Aérospatiale SA.365C2 Dauphin 2	5010	PH-SSK
			5N-BAO
			PH-SSK
			EC-800
			PH-SSK
			RP-C1248
			PH-SSK
			F-GFAP
			PH-SSK
			5N-ALZ
			PH-SSK
			N9006N
			F-WZAY
F-GMMN	Robin DR.400/180 Régent	2426	
F-GMMO	Lindstrand LBL-69A HAFB	313	
F-GMMR	CEA Jodel DR.1051 Sicile	308	OO-GUY
			F-BKIN
F-GMMS	Mooney M.20R Ovation	29-0144	
F-GMMT	Ultramagic M-90 HAFB	90/15	
F-GMNA	Raven Europe FS-57A HAFB	E-307	
F-GMNB	Raven Europe S-71A HAFB	E-310	
F-GMND	Raven Europe S-52A HAFB	E-316	
F-GMNE	Raven Europe S-60A HAFB	E-334	
F-GMNF	Raven Europe FS-57A HAFB	E-317	
F-GMNG	Raven Europe RX-8 HAFB	E-328	
F-GMNH	Raven Europe S-49A HAFB	E-335	
F-GMNI	Raven Europe S-55A HAFB	E-326	
F-GMNJ	Raven Europe S-60A HAFB	E-336	
F-GMNK	Raven Europe S-60A HAFB	E-324	
F-GMNM	Raven Europe FS-57A HAFB	E-340	
F-GMNN	Raven Europe FS-57A HAFB	E-346	
F-GMNP	Raven Europe S-55A HAFB	E-348	
F-GMNQ	Raven Europe FS-57A HAFB	E-308	
F-GMNR	Raven Europe FS-57A HAFB	E-354	
F-GMNS	Raven Europe S-52A HAFB	E-301	
F-GMNT	Raven Europe FS-57A HAFB	E-329	
F-GMNU	Raven Europe S-60A HAFB	E-355	
F-GMNV	Raven Europe FS-57A HAFB	E-352	
F-GMNX	Raven Europe S-52A HAFB	E-359	
F-GMNY	Raven Europe RX-7 HAFB	E-366	
F-GMOA	Robin DR.400/120 Petit Prince	978	LX-RCA
			F-BVMT
F-GMOE	Dassault Falcon 2000	001	(F-GMIR)
			F-WNAV
			F-WNEW
F-GMOF	Aérospatiale SN.601 Corvette	12	TJ-AHR
			TR-LYM
			F-BVPC
F-GMOI	Cameron A-210 HAFB	4257	
F-GMOM	Eurocopter EC.135T1	0023	
F-GMON	Eurocopter EC.135T1	0024	
F-GMOP	Piper PA-23 Apache (Reservation)	unkn	
F-GMOR	Cameron C-60 Concept HAFB	2976	
F-GMOT	Dassault Falcon 50	111	N50AH
			VR-CDF
			F-GKTV
			N297W
			F-WZHZ
F-GMOU	Reims/Cessna F152	F15201925	HB-CKR
			F-GDOB
F-GMPB	Cessna 182S	18280217	N2627A
F-GMPD	SIGA MA-26 Pilatre de Rozier HAFB (Res .99)	unkn	
F-GMPF	Maule MX-7-235 Star Rocket	10060C	D-ENLR
			N61113
F-GMPG	Fokker F.28-0100	11362	F-GIOF
			PH-EZT
F-GMPH	Piper PA-28-181 Archer II	2843085	
F-GMPJ	American AG-5B Tiger	10170	
F-GMPL	Bell 206B Jet Ranger II	4393	
F-GMPM	Beech C90B King Air	LJ-1303	(F-GIAO)
			N80513
F-GMPN	SOCATA MS.893E Rallye 180GT Gaillard	12264	3A-MPO
			F-BUGN
F-GMPP	Beech M35 Bonanza	D-6451	(F-GNTP)
			I- TINE
			HB-EBH
			D-EBBA
F-GMPV	Mudry CAP.10B	260	
F-GMPY	Piper PA-28-151 Cherokee Warrior	28-7615037	HB-PAK
			N9637N
F-GMQA	SOCATA TB-10 Tobago	1594	
F-GMQB	SOCATA TB-10 Tobago	1595	
F-GMQC	SOCATA TB-20 Trinidad	1620	
F-GMQD	SOCATA TB-20 Trinidad	1621	
F-GMQE	SOCATA TB-20 Tri nidad	1622	
F-GMQF	SOCATA TB-20 Trinidad	1623	
F-GMQG	SOCATA TB-20 Trinidad	1624	
F-GMQH	SOCATA TB-10 Tobago	1734	
F-GMQI	SOCATA TB-10 Tobago	1735	
F-GMQJ	SOCATA TB-10 Tobago	1736	
F-GMQK	SOCATA TB-20 Trinidad	1737	

F-GMQL	SOCATA TB-20 Trinidad	1738	
F-GMQM	SOCATA TB-20 Trinidad	1739	
F-GMQN	SOCATA TB-20 Trinidad	1740	
F-GMQO	SOCATA TB-20 Trinidad	1741	
F-GMRA	Robin DR.400/140B Dauphin 4	2253	
F-GMRB	Maule MX-7-235 Star Rocket	10119C	
F-GMRC	Robinson R-22 Beta	2072	N23269
F-GMRE	Reims/Cessna FR182 Skylane RG	FR18200016	HB-CCG
			D-EGTN
F-GMRF	SIAI-Marchetti SF.260	unkn	
F-GMRG	Mudry CAP.232	12	
F-GMRJ	Cameron A-120 HAFB	4477	
F-GMRM	Piaggio P.180 Avanti	1027	
F-GMRN	Beech E90 King Air	LW-304	G-SANB
			G-BGNU
F-GMRR	Robin DR.400/140B Dauphin 4	2430	
F-GMRS	McDonnell-Douglas DC-10-30 (Reservation)	unkn	
F-GMRT	SIGA MA-26 Pilatre de Rozier HAFB	115	
F-GMRV	Robin DR.400/160 Major	1933	6V-AGB
F-GMSB	Mooney M.20MTLS	27-0126	OO-LSD
F-GMSC	Aérospatiale AS.355N Ecureuil 2	5582	
F-GMSD	SIGA MA-30 Pilatre de Rozier HAFB	143	
F-GMSE	Piper PA-28RT-201T Turbo Arrow IV	28R-8131042	OO-GCI
			N83090
F-GMSG	Bell 407	53261	N407FG
			C-GDUS
F-GMSH	Hughes 269C	71-1071	D-HDEL
			N5045J
F-GMSI	Schweizer 269C-1	0050	
F-GMSJ(2)	Piper PA-22-160 Tri-Pacer	22-6232	CN-TTF
F-GMSL	Robinson R-22 Beta	2216	(F-GMBL)
F-GMSO	Ultramagic M-130 HAFB (Reservation .01)	130/. .	
F-GMSP	Ultramagic M-90 HAFB	90/48	
F-GMSR	Cessna 180E	18051093	F-BFVX
			F-OBVX
			N8693X
F-GMSV	Sky 105-24 HAFB	081	
F-GMTA	SNCASE SE.3160 Alouette III	1535	F-WQFJ
			A-535
F-GMTB	Ultramagic M-105 HAFB	105/85	
F-GMTF	Eurocopter EC-135T1	0012	
F-GMTH	Aérospatiale AS.350B Ecureuil	2700	
F-GMTL	Ultramagic H-77 HAFB	77/128	
F-GMTO	Swearingen SA.226AT Merlin IVA	AT-031	N22KW
			N95KY
			N5FW
			N44AG
			N5346M
F-GMTP	SIGA Pilatre de Rozier MA-26 HAFB	154	
F-GMTT	Schröder Fire Balloons G HAFB	364	
F-GMUG	Ultramagic M-145 HAFB	145/16	
F-GMUL	CEA Jodel DR.1050 Ambassadeur	15	HB-EUF
			F-BJHI
F-GMUP	Cessna F150J	F150-0431	HB-CJE
			LX-AVA
			D-EBML
F-GMUT	Cameron A-120 HAFB	10156	
F-GMUZ	Piper PA-28RT-201T Turbo Arrow IV	28R-8131143	N8396H
F-GMVB(2)	SAAB 2000	019	SE-019
F-GMVC(2)	SAAB 2000	021	SE-021
F-GMVD(2)	SAAB 2000	034	SE-034
F-GMVE	SAAB 2000	040	SE-040
F-GMVG	SAAB 2000	049	SE-049
F-GMVS	Pilatus PC-6/B1-H2 Turbo Porter	518	N6251U
			PH-OTB
F-GMVT	Robinson R-44 Astro	0453	
F-GMVU	SAAB 2000	045	LX-RAC
			F-GMVF
			SE-045
F-GMXA	Robin DR.400/140B Dauphin 4	2211	
F-GMXB	Robin DR.400/120 Dauphin 2+2	2212	
F-GMXD	Robin DR.400/140B Dauphin 4	2214	
F-GMXE	Robin DR.400/180 Régent	2208	
F-GMXF	Robin DR.400/180 Régent	2218	
F-GMXG	Robin DR.400/120 Dauphin 2+2	2223	
F-GMXH	Robin DR.400/120 Dauphin 2+2	2132	F-WLKJ
F-GMXI	Robin DR.400/160 Major	2220	
F-GMXJ	Robin DR.400/120 Dauphin 2+2	2221	
F-GMXK	Robin HR.200/120B	266	
F-GMXL	Robin HR.200/120B	267	
F-GMXM	Robin DR.400/120 Dauphin 2+2	2226	
F-GMXN	Robin DR.400/180 Régent	2222	
F-GMXO	Robin DR.400/180 Régent	2224	
F-GMXP	Robin DR.400/120 Dauphin 2+2	2227	
F-GMXQ	Robin HR.200/120B	272	
F-GMXR	Robin DR.400/120 Dauphin 2+2	2230	
F-GMXS	Robin DR.400/140B Dauphin 4	2233	
F-GMXU	Robin HR.200/120B	277	
F-GMXV	Robin DR.400/180 Régent	2237	
F-GMXX	Robin DR.400/180 Régent	2238	
F-GMXY	Robin DR.400/140B Dauphin 4	2239	
F-GMYA to Z	Reserved for Airbus A321-100s for Air France but not used?		
F-GMZA	Airbus A321-111	498	D-AVZK
F-GMZB	Airbus A321-111	509	D-AVZN
F-GMZC	Airbus A321-111	521	D-AVZW
F-GMZD	Airbus A321-111	529	D-AVZA
F-GMZE	Airbus A321-111	544	D-AVZF

F-GMZF	Airbus A321-111 (Reservation)	unkn	
F-GNAG	Beech A36 Bonanza	E-1653	CP-1566
F-GNAI	Aérospatiale SA.365C3 Dauphin 2	5026	G-BJKB
			N3601T
F-GNAL	Piper PA-32R-300 Cherokee Lance	32R-7680422	N414AL
			N9626N
F-GNAM	Piper PA-28-181 Archer II	2890014	N9108Z
F-GNAP	Reims/Cessna F150L	F15000843	F-BUBG
F-GNAR	Beech F33A Bonanza	CE-1735	
F-GNAS	CEA DR.253B Régent	157	CN-TAS
			F-BIFA
			D-EFCW
F-GNAT	Bell 47J	1134	MM80219
F-WNAV	Dassault Falcon 2000	1	(F-WNEW)
F-GNBC	Mooney M.20R Ovation	29-0034	
F-GNBD	Piper PA-28-181 Archer II	28-8090311	HB-PFD
			N8216T
F-GNBE	Piper PA-32RT-300 Lance II	32R-7885042	N9299C
F-GNBF	Sud Avn SA.316B Alouette III	1383	A-383
F-GNBH	Eurocopter EC-120BColibri	1307	
F-GNBI	Grob G.115B (Reservation)	8010	D-ENZM
F-GNBK	Mooney M.20J Model 201	24-0417	F-GKDC
			N201AN
F-GNBM	Robinson R-22 Mariner	unkn	
F-GNBP	Aérospatiale AS.350BA Ecureuil	1357	(F-GTBP)
			(F-GMLD)
			3A-MLD
			F-GCQD
F-GNBR	Beech 1900D	UE-327	N23154
F-GNBT	Aérospatiale AS.350B3 Ecureuil	3095	
F-GNBV	Cameron Z-105 HAFB	10554	
F-GNCA	Cameron N-77 HAFB	3035	
F-GNCB	Thunder AX7-77A HAFB	2202	
F-GNCC	Cessna U206F Stationair	U20602126	F-MJAA
			F-BRGI
			N71171
F-GNCD	Schweizer 269C	S-1362	G-FPEL
F-GNCE	Chaize JZX.18F12 HAFB	118	F-WNCE
F-GNCG	Ultramagic M77 HAFB	77/107	
F-GNCH	Piper PA-28-181 Archer III	2843074	
F-GNCI	SIGA MA-30 Pilatre de Rozier HAFB	139	
F-GNCK	Wassmer WA.51A Pacific	72	HB-DCK
F-GNCL	SOCATA TB-20 Trinidad	960	G-BRIN
F-GNCM	Piper PA-28-161 Cadet	2841292	N9202H
F-GNCN	Ultramagic S-90 HAFB	90-12	
F-GNCO	Dassault Falcon 900EX (Reservation 6.01) (Also reserved as F-GOEA)	97	F-WNCO
F-GNCP	Cessna F550T Citation II	0004	N312GA
			C-GPAW
			N98786
F-GNCR	SNCASE SE.313B Alouette II (Reservation 4.00)	1539	F-WQLV
			ALAT
F-GNCS	Thunder AX8-9OSI HAFB	2503	G-DAFL
F-GNCT	Sud Avn SA.318C Alouette Astazou	2265	TJ-AHP
			F-GBGX
			VR-HGX
F-GNCV	Mudry CAP.10B	303	
F-GNDD	Ultramagic M-77 HAFB	77/189	
F-GNDE	Robinson R.22 Beta	2443	N999MK
			N8311E
F-WNDF	Fournier RF-47	01	
F-GNDH	Piper PA-34-200T Seneca II	34-8070359	D-GMFG
			N8248V
F-GNDI	Reserved for Dassault Aviation		
F-GNDJ	Piper PA-25-235 Pawnee C	25-5323	N8819L
F-GNDL	Mudry CAP.10B	269	
F-GNDM	Firefly 9B-15 HAFB	F9B-2005	
F-GNDP	Robin DR.400/120 Petit Prince	2073	
F-GNDR	Ultramagic S-90 HAFB	90/06	
F-GNDT	Cessna 340A	340A1008	TR-LCL
			G-SILV
			D-IHOS
			(N4272C)
F-GNDV	Sud Avn SA.318C Alouette Astazou	1988	F-GBDV
			F-ZBDB
F-GNDX	Cameron C-80 HAFB	4124	
F-GNDZ	Dassault Falcon 10	17	EC-949
			F-GHDZ
			N33HL
			N27DA
			N29966
			VH-FFB
			OH-FFB
			F-WLCS
F-GNEB	Cessna U206F Stationair II	U20603364	OO-SPA
			(N8507Q)
F-GNEC	Cameron V-90 HAFB	3022	
F-GNEE	Beech C90B King Air	LJ-1328	N90HB
			N8250K
F-GNEG	Beech B200 Super King Air	BB-1377	HB-GIR
			N56881
			(N65N)
F-GNEM	McDonnell-Douglas DC-10-30	46892	TU-TAM
			HS-TGB
			TU-TAM
			(TU-TBD)

F-GNEN	Piper PA-28-161 Warrior II	28-8016245	F-ZBEN D-EINK N9614N
F-GNET	Balloon Works Firefly 7 HAFB (Reservation .99)	unkn	
F-GNEV	Mudry CAP.10B	115	Fr.AF
F-GNEX	Lindstrand LBL-77AHAFB	706	
F-GNFA	Cameron O-77 HAFB	4449	
F-GNFB	Piper PA-14 Family Cruiser	14-133	F-BFFB
F-GNFE	Mudry CAP.10B	22	Fr.AF
F-GNFG	Chaize JZ.25F12 HAFB	134	
F-GNFJ	SNCASE SE.3130 Alouette II	1908	V-59
F-GNFL	Piper PA-31 Turbo Navajo B	31-7400986	I- ELET N7598L
F-GNFP	Bell 206B Jet Ranger II	1148	(F-GKLS) G-HUMT ZS-HDY
F-GNFR	Piper L-4H Cub (Identity highly suspect)	11114	EC-AKP HB-OUC EC-AKP HB-OFC 43-29823
F-GNGC	Schweizer 269C	S-1632	
F-GNGE	Ultramagic M-77C HAFB	77/216	
F-GNGF	Cameron O-105 HAFB	3023	F-BUWW
F-GNGG	Mooney M.20J Model 205	24-3216	F-GMOC N8VH F-GKBT
F-GNGI	Chaize JZ.30F16 HAFB	185	
F-GNGS	Schweizer 269C	S-1389	G-BRFP N41S
F-GNGU	Grumman G.159 Gulfstream 1	101	4X-ARV F-GFGU N300SB N222H N716G
F-GNHB	SOCATA Rallye 235F	3388	
F-GNHD	SOCATA TB-200 Tobago XL	1459	
F-GNHE	SOCATA Rallye 235F	3389	
F-GNHF	SOCATA TB-10 Tobago	1315	(SX- . . .) F-GNHF F-OGSE
F-WNHG	SOCATA TB-200 Tobago XL	1633	F-GNHG
F-GNHI	Partenavia P.68B	169	G-WICK G-BGFZ
F-GNHL	SOCATA Rallye 235F	3392	
F-GNHM	SOCATA Rallye 235F	3393	
F-GNHN	SOCATA Rallye 235F	3391	
F-GNHP	SOCATA TBM-700	102	
F-GNHQ	SOCATA TB-9 Tampico	1450	SE-KNT
F-GNHS	SOCATA TB-200 Tobago XL	1761	
F-GNHZ	SOCATA TB-9 Tampico	1185	F-WWRH F-WNGQ (D-ENVY(2)) F-WNGQ (D-ENVY(2))
F-GNIF	Airbus A340-313X	168	(F-GLZL)
F-GNIG	Airbus A340-313X	174	
F-GNIH	Airbus A340-313X	373	
F-GNII	Airbus A340-313X	399	
F-GNJA	HOAC DV-20 Katana	20011	
F-GNJB	HOAC DV-20 Katana	20076	OE-ADV
F-GNJC	HOAC DV-20 Katana	20031	OE-ASC N25DV
F-GNJD	HOACDV-20 Katana	0153	D-ENON
F-GNJE	Diamond DA 20-A1 Katana	10135	N202EC
F-GNJF	Diamond DA 20-A1 Katana	10119	N546SS
F-GNJG	Diamond DA 20-A1 Katana	10225	OE-AID N225DA
F-GNJH	Diamond DA 20-A1-100 Katana	10090	OE-AAO N527SS
F-GNJI	Diamond DA20-A1-100 Katana	10125	OE-AIH N553SS
F-GNJJ	Diamond DA20-A1-100 Katana	10027	N607F
F-GNJK	Diamond DA20-A1-100 Katana	10072	N127MF N177AA
F-GNJL	Diamond DA 40 Star	40006	OE-KPB OE-VPB
F-GNJM	Diamond DA 40 Star	40013	OE-DAF OE-VPN
F-GNJO	Diamond DA 40 Star	40031	
F-GNJP	Diamond DA 40 Star	40038	
F-GNJQ	Diamond DA 40 Star	40040	
F-GNJR	Diamond DA 40 Star	40064	
F-GNJS	Diamond DA 40 Star	40075	
F-GNJT	Diamond DA 40 Star	40076	
F-GNJU	Diamond DA 40D Star (Reservation .05)	D4.122	OE-VPW
F-GNJV(2)	Diamond DA 40D Star	D4.009	
F-GNJX	Diamond DA 40 Star	40026	OE-DLF
F-GNJY	Diamond DA 40 Star	40008	OE-KPN OE-VPN
F-GNJZ	Diamond DA 40D Star (Permit 11.02)	D4.002	
F-GNLA	Aérospatiale SA.315B Lama	2165/32	F-GJRT Fr.AF ALAT
F-GNLB	Sud Avn SA.318C Alouette Astazou	2163	EC-FZH F-GDQP C-FBMU CF-BMU

F-GNLG	Fokker F.28-0100	11363	D-ADFE F-GIOF PH-EZV
F-GNLH	Fokker F.28-0100	11311	D-ADFB F-GIOC PH-EZE
F-GNLI	Fokker F.28-0100	11315	D-ADFC F-GIOD PH-EZF
F-GNLJ	Fokker F.28-0100	11344	D-ADFD F-GIOE PH-EZD
F-GNLK	Fokker F.28-0100	11307	D-ADFA F-GIOB PH-EZX
F-GNLL	Aérospatiale AS.350B3 Ecureuil	3294	F-WQDC
F-GNLO	Eurocopter EC.135T1	0005	SE-JUP D-HQQQ
F-GNLP	Aérospatiale AS.350B Ecureuil	1848	HB-XRO D-HONY
F-GNLT	Aérospatiale SA.365N Dauphin 2	6069	JA9585
F-GNLV	SIGA MA-26 Pilatre de Rozier HAFB	103	(F-GNBR)
F-GNLZ	Sky 77-24 HAFB	183	
F-GNMA	Beech C90A King Air	LJ-1299	N8253D
F-GNMD	Piper PA-18-150 Super Cub	18-8209009	TR-LAX N91243
F-GNMF	Dassault Falcon 900	47	(F-GOFC) F-WQBJ A6-ZKM F-WWFA
F-GNMH	Nord 260 (Reservation)	8	CEV: 'MC' F-BLHO LN-LME F-BLHO
F-GNMJ	Beech B36TC Bonanza	EA-517	D-ENMS (D-EOPL) D-ENMS N8217W
F-GNMN	Canadair CL.600-2B19 Regional Jet	7003	(N915CA) (D-ACLD) C-GVRJ "D-ARJA" (D-ARJD) C-GVRJ
F-GNMO	Robinson R.22 Beta	1437	OO-VCF N40244
F-GNMP	Beech C90 King Air	LJ-828	(F-GPJC) I-BOMY F-GFME N6037C
F-GNNA	Robin DR.400/120 Petit Prince	2236	
F-GNNB	Robin HR.200/120B	278	
F-GNNC	Robin HR.200/120B	279	
F-GNND	Robin DR.400/160 Major	2241	
F-GNNE	Robin DR.400/140B Dauphin 4	2247	
F-GNNF	Robin HR.200/120B	280	
F-GNNH	Robin HR.200/120B	281	
F-GNNI	Robin DR.400/120 Dauphin 2+2	2252	
F-GNNJ	Robin DR.400/180R Remo 180	2254	
F-GNNK	Robin DR.400/125	2258	F-WNNK
F-GNNL	Robin DR.400/140B Dauphin 4	2256	
F-GNNM	Robin DR.400/160 Major	2259	
F-GNNN	Robin DR.400/180 Régent	2264	
F-GNNO	Robin HR.200/120B	283	
F-GNNP	Robin DR.400/140B Dauphin 4	2257	
F-GNNQ	Robin HR.200/120B	284	
F-GNNS	Robin DR.400/120 Dauphin 2+2	2262	
F-GNNT	Robin HR.200/120B	285	
F-GNNU	Robin DR.400/120 Dauphin 2+2	2263	
F-GNNX	Robin DR.400/120 Dauphin 2+2	2265	
F-GNNY	Robin DR.400/120 Dauphin 2+2	2267	
F-GNNZ	Robin DR.400/120 Dauphin 2+2	2270	
F-GNOA	Beech 1900D (Reservation .99)	UE-51	N51YV
F-GNOE	Beech B300 Super King Air	FL-183	HB-GJL
F-GNOL	Agusta-Bell 47G-2	205	EC-DUK D-HIPO IDFAF Fr.AF
F-GNOM	Cameron O-84 HAFB	4624	
F-GNOO	Cameron Concept C-60 HAFB	3176	
F-GNOR	Cameron O-105 HAFB	3984	
F-GNOT	SIGA MA-26 Pilatre de Rozier HAFB	157	
F-GNOU	SIGA MA-26 Pilatre de Rozier HAFB	113	
F-GNOV	Aerotek Pitts S-2A	2202	OO-NOV N31469
F-GNPC	Ultramagic N-160 HAFB	160/15	
F-GNPD	Beech 200 Super King Air	BB-199	LN-PAD OY-AUK N83DS N33DS N32KA N525BC
F-GNPF	SNCASE SE.313B Alouette II	1507	ALAT
F-GNPJ	Robin DR.400/140B Dauphin 4	2261	
F-GNPP	Chaize JZ.30F16 HAFB	129	
F-GNPS	Robinson R-22 Beta	2582	

F-GNPU(2)	Piper PA-23-250Aztec D	27-4209	F-GFPU N250GM D-IFMS N6864Y
F-GNPV	Piper PA-32R-301T Turbo Saratoga SP	32R-8329012	N4291Z
F-GNPY	SNCASE SE.313B Alouette II	1343	ALAT
F-GNPZ	SNCASE SE.3130 Alouette II (Reservation)	1382	ALAT
F-GNQA	Diamond DA20-A1-80 Katana	10038	N401PF C-FWKI
F-GNQB	Diamond DA20-A1-80 Katana	10226	N226DA
F-GNQC	Diamond DA20-A1-80 Katana	10094	N199D
F-GNRA	Raven Europe RX-7 HAFB	E-368	
F-GNRB	Raven Europe RX-8 HAFB	E-369	
F-GNRD	Raven Europe RX-7 HAFB	E-349	
F-GNRE	Raven Europe RX-8 HAFB	E-376	
F-GNRF	Raven Europe RX-8 HAFB	E-378	
F-GNRG	Raven Europe RXS-8 HAFB	E-382	
F-GNRH	Raven Europe S-66A HAFB	E-381	
F-GNRI	Raven Europe FS-57A HAFB	E-394	
F-GNRJ	Raven Europe S-55A HAFB	E-391	
F-GNRK	Raven Europe FS-57A HAFB	E-404	
F-GNRL	Raven Europe FS-57A HAFB	E-398	
F-GNRM	Raven Europe RXS-8 HAFB	E-392	
F-GNRO	Raven Europe S-52A HAFB	E-407	
F-GNRQ	Raven Europe S-55A HAFB	E-402	
F-GNRS	Raven Europe S-55A HAFB	E-353	
F-GNRV	Raven Europe S-55A HAFB	E-380	
F-GNRY	Raven Europe FS-57A HAFB	E-396	
F-GNRZ	Raven Europe S-60A HAFB	E-397	
F-GNSA	Beech 58 Baron	TH-1701	
F-GNSB	Beech 58 Baron	TH-1702	
F-GNSC	Beech 58 Baron	TH-1703	
F-GNSD	Beech 58 Baron	TH-1704	
F-GNSE	Beech 58 Baron	TH-1705	
F-GNSF	Beech 58 Baron	TH-1706	
F-GNSG	Beech 58 Baron	TH-1734	
F-GNSH	Beech 58 Baron	TH-1736	
F-GNSI	Beech 58 Baron	TH-1510	N3178P
F-GNSJ	Beech 58 Baron	TH-1515	N3076B
F-GNSK	Beech 58 Baron	TH-2004	N4104H
F-GNSL	Beech 58 Baron	TH-2006	N3216S
F-GNSM	Beech 58 Baron	TH-2033	N51030
F-GNSN	Beech 58 Baron	TH-2062	N61732
F-GNSO	Beech 58 Baron	TH-2080	N62030
F-GNTV	Cameron N-77 HAFB	3900	
F-GNUA	Robinson R-22M Mariner	2025M	F-OGUA
F-GNUJ	Robin ATL L	22	EC-FKB F-GFNU F-WFNU
F-GNUT	Chaize CS.2200F12 HAFB	168	
F-GNVM	Eurocopter EC.130B4 Ecureuil	3648	F-WQDD
F-GNVN	Mudry CAP.10B	278	Fr.AF
F-GNVS	Aérospatiale SA.365N Dauphin 2	6138	JA9610
F-GNVV	Chaize JZ.25F16 HAFB	126	
F-GNXX	Ultramagic M-105 HAFB	105/37	
F-GNYD	Fouga CM.170 Magister (Reservation)	232	Fr.AF
F-GNYG	Raven-Europe FS-57A HAFB	E-408	
F-GNYK	Robinson R-44 Clipper	0319	N7132M
F-GNYN	Fouga CM.170 Magister	532	Fr.AF
F-GNYQ	Robinson R-44 Astro	0388	
F-GNYR	Cessna 208B Grand Caravan	208B1039	D-FOXI
F-GNZA	Morane-Saulnier MS.885 Super Rallye	274	F-BHZA F-OBZA
F-GNZC	Cessna R182 Skylane RG	R18201199	TR-LZC (N756ZA)
F-GNZK	Cessna 414	414-0277	G-AZZK N1562T
F-GNZS	SIGA MA-30 Pilatre de Rozier HAFB	153	
F-GOAD	Piper J-3C-65 Cub (Reservation)	10293	HB-OCW HB-OUF 43-1432
F-GOAF	Boeing 737-242C	19847	N847TA F-GGPA (F-GFVK) C-FNAB CF-NAB N6241
F-GOAG	Pilatus PC-6/B1-H2 Turbo Porter	658	D-FDHP HB-FDH
F-GOAL	Dassault Falcon 50	131	F-WGTF (F-GPLH) I- ADAG HZ-BB2 F-WPXD
F-GOAM	Beech A36 Bonanza	E-2427	3A-MAR N3084W
F-GOAP	Cessna 172R	17280423	N9540Q
F-GOAS	Mudry CAP.10B	133	F-WQHT Fr.AF
F-GOAT	Cessna 402C Utiliner	402C0015	TT-DAQ TT-BAC(3) G-OFAR (N4656A)
F-GOAV	Reims/Cessna F152	F15201757	HB-CNT
F-GOAZ	SIGA MA-22 Pilatre de Rozier HAFB	105	
F-GOBA	Robinson R-44 Raven	1308	
F-GOBC	Cameron A-120 HAFB	4148	OO-BUA LX-PFX

F-GOBI	Ultramagic S-130 HAFB	130/25	
F-GOBJ	Mooney M.20M Model 257 TLS	27-0199	LX-PAL
F-GOBL	Robin ATL L	96	F-GFSP
F-GOBM	Cessna F150G	F150-0215	F-BOQM
F-GOBO	SIGA MA-26 Pilatre de Rozier HAFB	125	
F-GOBP	CASA C.212-CB	10	TC-AOS EC-CRX EC-102
F-GOBQ	Morane-Saulnier MS.317 (Reservation .00)	6565/311	F-BCBQ
F-GOBR(3)	Pilatus PC-6/B2-H4 Turbo Porter	944	
F-GOBS	Chaize JZ.30F16 HAFB	146	
F-GOBU	Lindstrand LBL-90A HAFB	582	D-OCLO G-CLAG
F-GOBV	Wörner FKP-380/STU Gas Balloon (Res .01)	6202	
F-GOBX	Wörner FKP-380/STU Gas Balloon	6205	
F-GOBY	Cameron O-90 HAFB	2813	G-OREY
F-GOCB	Mudry CAP.10	28	Fr.AF
F-GOCC	Pilatus PC-6/B1-H2 Turbo Porter	667	SE-IRR C-GXIJ N62156 XW-PFQ HB-FDR
F-GOCD	Chaize JZ25F16 HAFB	127	
F-GOCE	Cameron N-77 HAFB	3630	
F-GOCF	Beech 200 Super King Air	BB-397	LX-GDB D-IAMW F-GFIV PH-SLG (N . . . .) PH-SLG 5N-ALF PH-SLG
F-WOCM(2)	Chaize JZ.15S16 HAFB	161	
F-GOCO	Cameron A-90 HAFB (Reservn 10.04)	unkn	
F-GOCP	Cameron V-90 HAFB	3415	
F-GOCS	SOCATA MS.880B Rallye Club	1579	OO-CCS F-BSCB
F-GOCV	Aérospatiale SA.341G Gazelle	1010	F-GFFN D-HMTB F-GBOP D-HMTB
F-GODA(2)	Piper PA-18-150 Super Cub	18-4892	TR-LDA TR-LME F-OAXG
F-GODC	Cameron V-90 HAFB	3325	
F-GODM	Grob G.115	8067	LX-AVF (D-EGVV)
F-GODR	Mudry CAP.232 (Dbf 15.12.95)	03	
F-GODV(2)	Mudry CAP.232	32	
F-GODZ	Pilatus PC-6/340 Porter	340	(N340N) ST-AFR HB-FAR
F-GOEA	Dassault 900EX (Res .01, also as F-GNCO)	97	F-WNCO
F-GOEM	Aérospatiale SA.315B Lama (Reservation 3.01)	2498	I-MROS G-BMUC N49529
F-GOES	Reims/Cessna FRA150L Aerobat (Reservn)	FRA1500179	TT-CAJ F-OCTP
F-GOFA	Scintex Piel CP.301C Emeraude	511	F-BJFA
F-GOFC(2)	Piper PA-38-112 Tomahawk	38-79A0003 N9690N	OO-BFC
F-GOFD	Chaize JZ.25F16 HAFB	135	
F-GOFE	Robinson R-22 Beta	2357	OO-CMQ
F-GOFF	SOCATA TB-20 Trinidad	306	HB-EQS
F-GOFJ	Cameron N-77 (Reservation 7.01)	2507	LX-BTL LX-BIL(2)
F-GOFL	Cameron A-160 HAFB	4159	
F-GOFP	Reims/Cessna F152	F15201752	6V-AGK F-GCNL
F-GOFR	Ultramagic M-105 HAFB	105/104	
F-GOFY	Cameron N-77 HAFB	3052	
F-GOGC	Cameron O-84 HAFB	4379	
F-GOGG	Balloon Works Firefly 7-15 HAFB	F7-1037	
F-GOGI	Cameron SS HAFB	"447"	
F-GOGM	Robinson R-44 Raven II	10304	N7531S
F-GOGN	CASA C.212-200CB	92	(F-GOBP) TC-AOC
F-GOGO	Cameron A-105 HAFB	3207	
F-GOGT	Fouga CM.170 Magister	545	Fr.AF
F-GOHA	Embraer EMB.135ER	145189	
F-GOHB	Embraer EMB.135ER	145198	
F-GOHC	Embraer EMB.135ER	145243	
F-GOHD	Embraer EMB.135ER	145252	PT-SJJ
F-GOHE	Embraer EMB.135ER	145335	PT-SNB
F-GOHF	Embraer EMB.135ER	145347	PT-SNN
F-GOIG	SOCATA TB-20 Trinidad	2183	
F-GOIK	SOCATA TB-10 Tobago	2203	
F-GOIL to F-GOIZ Reserved for SOCATA , 4.02			
F-GOJB	Mudry CAP.231EX	04	OO-CAP F-GNCF F-WZCF
F-GOJE	Cameron N-56 HAFB	645	OO-CLA
F-GOJF	Robinson R-44 Raven	1215	
F-GOJH	Cameron A-210 HAFB	2451	G-BTCK
F-GOJL	Schweizer 269C	S-1525	D-HHAK
F-GOJM	Cameron O-90 HAFB	3336	
F-GOJO	SIGA MA-35 Pilatre de Rozier HAFB	146	

F-GOJP	Chaize JZ.22F12 HAFB	157	
F-GOJR	Chaize CS.2200F12 HAFB	123	
F-GOJS(2)	Tecnam P.92JS Echo	39	
F-GOKQ	Robin DR.400/120 Dauphin 2+2	2185	3A-MKQ
			F-GMKQ
F-GOLA	Thunder AX7-77A HAFB	4230	
F-GOLB	Colt Bibendum 110 SS HAFB	4221	G-BXNR
F-GOLC	Thunder AX10-160 HAFB	4260	
F-GOLF	Cessna 310R	310R1638	N179MP
			N2634N
F-GOLH	Eurocopter EC.130B4 Ecureuil	3882	(F-GSNB)
			F-WWXA
F-GOLJ	Cessna 421C Golden Eagle	421C1252	D-INOS
			N6787L
F-GOLL	Zlin Z.726K Universal	1069	OK-DXA
			OK-YRB
			OK-95
F-GOLP	Aérospatiale AS.355N Ecureuil 2	5588	
F-GOLR	Cameron N-90 HAFB	10154	
F-GOLT	Robinson R-44 Raven II	10187	
F-GOLY	Cameron N-77 HAFB	4075	LX-BIL(3)
F-GOMA	BAe.146 Series 200QC	E-2211	G-BVCD
			G-6-211
F-GOMB	Pilatus PC-6/B2-H4 Turbo Porter	819	HB-FMG
			FAC-111
			HB-FHR
F-GOMC	Zlin Z.526F Trenér Master	1078	F-BRNB
F-GOME	Pilatus PC-6/B2-H2 Turbo Porter	543	N4911
F-GOMF	Cessna 210 (Reservation)	"0012"	
F-GOMH	Holste MH.1521M Broussard	64	Fr.AF
F-GOMJ	Christen Pitts S-2B	5176	EC-EXV
			N6081F
F-GOML	Aviat Pitts S-2B	5213	G-GOMD
			F-GOMD
			N319JM
F-GOMM	Cessna 414	414-0831	I- CCMM
			N98745
F-GOMP	PIper PA-28R-201 Arrow	2844001	
F-GOMS	Robin DR.400/120 Dauphin 2+2	2316	
F-GONA	Cameron N-105 HAFB (Reservation .99)	1446	PH-ISO
F-GONB	Aérospatiale SA.330JPuma	1571	F-WQPM
			LX-HUC
			PT-HAO
			LX-HUC
F-GONC	Cessna T210N Turbo Centurion II	21064544	F-GHNC
			N9543Y
F-GONG	SAN Jodel D.140R Abeille	506	OO-VVN
F-GONI	SNCASE SE.313BAlouette II	1520	Fr.AF
F-GONS	Thunder AX7-77 SI HAFB	4204	F-GHHY
F-GONZ	Robinson R-22B2 Beta	2693	
F-GOOB	Beech 1900C	UC-153	N153YV
			F-GNPM
			N153YV
F-GOOD	SOCATA TB-20 Trinidad	2142	
F-GOOF	Robin DR.400/140B Dauphin 4	2561	
F-GOOG	Cameron A-105 HAFB	4645	
F-GOOI	Cameron C-60 Concept HAFB	3160	LX-OOI
F-GOOM	Piper PA-28-151 Cherokee Warrior	28-7515020	F-OGOM
			N44739
F-GOOO	Beech 300 Super King Air	FA-175	N175NJ
			JA8868
			N1558Y
F-GOPA	Chaize JZ.30F16 HAFB	128	
F-GOPB(2)	Cameron A-210 HAFB	3672	
F-GOPC	Robinson R-22 Mariner	1648M	3A-MBC
F-GOPE	Beech 1900D	UE-103	N82930
			(F-GMSA)
F-GOPF	Chaize JZ.30F16 HAFB	163	
F-GOPG	Eurocopter EC.135T1	0062	D-HECP
			D-HECK
F-GOPH	Schweizer 269C	S-1416	D-HEHE
			N919FH
			N7508D
F-GOPI	SIGA MA-26 Pilatre de Rozier HAFB	108	
F-GOPJ	Aérospatiale AS.365N3 Dauphin 2 (Res 10.04)	6705	
F-GOPL	SIGA MA- Pilatre de Rozier HAFB (Res. .00)	unkn	
F-GOPM	Dassault Falcon 20E	302/510	F-WQBM
			N84V
			OE-GDP(1)
			D-COMM
			F-WRQP
F-GOPP	Chaize JZ.30F16 HAFB	150	
F-GOPR	Piper PA-23-250 Aztec E	27-4727	G-AZWW
			N14161
F-GOPS	Cameron A-210 HAFB	10529	
F-GOPX	CAARP CAP.10	01	F-ZAGO
			F-BOPX
F-GOPY	Bell 206B Jet Ranger II	2584	G-RSMA
			G-SHZZ
			G-BNUW
			N5018B
F-GORA	Robin DR.400/160 Chevalier	2271	
F-GORB	Robin DR.400/140B Dauphin 4	2272	
F-GORC	Robin DR.400/120 Dauphin 2+2	2276	
F-GORD	Robin DR.400/180 Régent	2277	
F-GORG	Robin DR.400/140B Dauphin 4	1034	F-BXJE
F-GORH	Robin DR.400/160 Chevalier	2279	
F-GORI	Robin DR.400/120 Dauphin 2+2	2283	
F-GORJ	Robin DR.400 NGL Régent 3	2278	
	(Appears to be development aircraft for DR.500 Président)		
F-GORK	Robin DR.400/140B Dauphin 4	2286	
F-GORL	Robin DR.400/140B Dauphin 4	2288	
F-GORM	Robin DR.400/120 Dauphin 2+2	2289	
F-GORN	Robin DR.400/120 Dauphin 2+2	2300	
F-GORO	Robin DR.400/180 Régent	2292	
F-GORP	Robin DR.400/120 Dauphin 2+2	2295	
F-GORQ	Robin DR.400/120 Dauphin 2+2	2297	
F-GORR	Robin DR.400/140B Dauphin 4	2298	
	(Badly damaged on landing at Grenoble-St Geoirs 28.10.02)		
F-GORS	Robin HR.200/120B	292	
F-GORT	Robin DR.400/180 Régent	2299	
F-GORU	Robin HR.200/120B	294	
F-GORY	Robin DR.400/180 Régent	2301	
F-GORZ	Robin DR.400/120 Dauphin 2+2	2284	
F-GOSA(2)	General Avia F.22 Pinguino (Reservation .99)	016	
F-GOSB	Beech B300 Super KIng Air	FL-301	N4211V
F-GOSC	Ultramagic M-210 HAFB	210/13	
F-GOSD	Piper PA-46-310P Malibu	46-8508099	N88PL
			N9605N
F-GOSE	Piper PA-46-310P Malibu	4608010	N770MR
			N146DS
			G-DODS
			N9100N
F-GOSF	Beech A36 Bonanza	E-3259	N41020
F-GOSH	Cameron V-90 HAFB	10223	
F-GOSM	Aérospatiale AS.350B3 Ecureuil	3524	
F-GOSN	Cessna 152	15285410	C-GOSM
	(Reservation 10.04)		N93126
F-GOSP	Pilatus PC-6/B2-H4 Turbo Porter	699	HB-FEZ
F-GOST	Cessna A152 Aerobat	A1520774	N7587B
F-GOTA(2)	Aérospatiale SA.365N Dauphin 2	6147	TN-AES
F-GOTC	Mudry CAP.232	15	
F-GOTE	Cameron A-180 HAFB	3144	G-TATE
F-GOTG	Cessna U206FStationair	U20603430	I-AMCK
			N8574Q
F-GOTL	Robin ATL (Reservation 8.01)	83	HB-SCC
			F-WZZZ
			HB-SCC
F-GOTO	Reims FR172J Rocket	FR17200532	TR-LTO
F-GOTT	Cessna T207 Turbo Skywagon	20700323	
	(Soloy Pac conversion)		
F-GOTU	Hughes 369E	0248E	C-FXQH
			N132KC
			N16028
F-GOUD	Cameron Nivea SS HAFB	4576	
F-GOUE	SIGA MA-26 Pilatre de Rozier HAFB	112	
F-GOUH	Piper PA-34-220TSeneca III	34-8133161	D-GEUH
			N8413K
			ZP-TVM
			N8413K
F-GOUM	Mudry CAP.10B	122	Fr.AF
F-GOUN	Mudry CAP.10B (Reservation .99)	129	Fr.AF
F-GOUP	Mudry CAP.10B	138	Fr.AF
F-GOVA	Robin DR.400/120 Dauphin 2+2	2303	
F-GOVB	Robin DR.400/120 Dauphin 2+2	2304	
F-GOVC	Robin HR.200/120B	297	
F-GOVD	Robin DR.400/180 Régent	2106	G-MRSL
			G-BUAP
F-GOVE	Robin DR.400/120 Dauphin 2+2	2307	
F-GOVF	Robin DR.400/120 Dauphin 2+2	2315	
F-GOVG	Robin DR.400/140B Dauphin 4	2314	
F-GOVJ	Robin HR.200/120B	301	
F-GOVK	Robin HR.200/120B	303	
F-GOVL	Robin DR.400/120 Dauphin 2+2	2312	
F-GOVM	Robin DR.400/160 Chevalier	2317	
F-GOVO	Robin DR.400/120 Dauphin 2+2	2322	
F-GOVP	Robin DR.400/180 Régent	2328	
F-GOVQ	Robin DR.400/160 Chevalier	2321	
F-GOVR	Robin DR.400/140B Major 80	1345	I- GUCC
			F-GBUC
F-GOVS	Robin DR.400/180 Régent	2323	
F-GOVT	Robin DR.400/140B Dauphin 4	2325	
F-GOVU	Robin DR.400/120 Dauphin 2+2	2326	
F-GOVV	Robin DR.400/180 Remo 180	2331	
F-GOVX	Robin DR.400/120 Dauphin 2+2	2330	
F-GOXD	Robin DR.400/180RP Remorqueur 212	1817	OO-CXD
			HB-KBU
			D-EAJD
F-GOYA	Dassault Falcon 900EX	11	F-WWFI
F-GOYC	Robinson R-44 Astro	0511	
F-GOYD	Fouga CM.170 Magister (Reservation)	203	Fr.AF
F-GOYE	Pilatus PC-6/B2-H2 Turbo Porter	517	N617SA
			XW-PDG
			HB-FCI
			D-ENLJ
F-GOZI	SAAB 2000	012	HB-IZI
			SE-012
F-GOZJ	SAAB 2000 (Reservation 3.04)	015	HB-IZJ
			SE-015
F-GOZO	Mudry CAP.231	8	F-WQOM
			CN-ABK
F-GOZY	Aérospatiale AS.350B3 Ecureuil	3535	
F-GOZZ	Robin DR.400/160 Chevalier	2306	

F-GPAA	Dassault Falcon 20/ CC117 ECM	103/423	G-FRAV CAF117505 CAF20505 F-WMKH
F-GPAB	Dassault Falcon 20F	254	G-FRAC (N910FR) C-FYPB CF-YPB N4423F F-WNGO
F-GPAC	Beech B200 Super King Air	BB-920	SE-LMM (N83TJ) PK-YPS N83TJ C-GSCM
F-GPAD	Dassault Falcon 20E	280/503	(F-GPAE(2)) G-FRAE N910FR I-EDIS F-WPXK
F-GPAF	Piper PA-34-200T Seneca II	34-7670005	N3953X
F-GPAI	Ultramagic S-90 HAFB	90/17	
F-GPAJ	Christen Pitts S-2B	5286	(N98AV)
F-GPAL	SOCATA Rallye 100ST	2583	F-WQFQ Fr.Navy 83
F-GPAR	Robinson R-22 Beta	2439	(F-GLHI)
F-GPAS	Beech 200 Super King Air	BB-209	D-IACS ZP-TTC ZP-PTC EB-001 N5450M N545GM
F-GPAU	Mudry CAP.231	22	CN-ABM
F-GPBA	Cessna 172N	17272517	C-FEIQ N5322D
F-GPBB	Piper PA-28-181 Archer III	2843196	N41332 N9503N
F-GPBC	SNCASE SE.313B Alouette II	1635	ALAT
F-GPBF	Piper PA-31T Cheyenne II	31T-7920094	OH-PYE SE-ICS
F-GPBH	Agusta A.109E Power	11606	
F-GPBI	Piper PA-32R-301T Saratoga II TC	3257098	OK-LAB OY-JAG N9515N
F-GPBJ	Lindstrand LBL-77A HAFB	272	
F-GPBO	Aérospatiale SA.316B Lama (Reservation .99)	1414	A-414
F-GPBZ	Piper PA-24-260 Comanche B	24-4766	HB-PBZ 5U-AAG F-OCLU N9298P N10F
F-GPCA	Cameron N-105 HAFB	3421	
F-GPCB	Beech 58 Baron	TH-1467	HB-GHX N72281
F-GPCC	Mooney M.20K Model 231	25-0359	N231QJ
F-GPCD	Aérospatiale AS.350BA Ecureuil	2658	F-ODYY
F-GPCE	Cameron N-105 HAFB	3720	
F-GPCH	Beech 58 Baron (Reservation)	TH-404	F-BUYT
F-GPCJ	Fouga CM.170 Magister	369	Fr.AF
F-GPCL	Robinson R-22 Beta	1379	G-BSIN N4015H
F-GPCP	SNCASE SE.313B Alouette II	1046	ALAT
F-GPCS	Lindstrand LBL-105A HAFB	327	
F-GPCT	Cameron A-120 HAFB	4151	
F-GPCV	SNCASE SE.3130 Alouette II	1384	ALAT
F-GPDA	Durondeau L-300 HAFB	22	
F-GPDB	Cameron A-120 HAFB	4473	
F-GPDC	HS.748 Series 2A	1612	G-AZSU A2-ABB G-AZSU VP-BCM
F-GPDD	Chaize JZX.25F16 HAFB	167	
F-GPDF	Aérospatiale AS.350B3 Ecureuil	3290	
F-GPDH	Eurocopter EC.120B Colibri	1334	
F-GPDI	Cameron A-180 HAFB (Reservation .02)	unkn	
F-GPDL	Reims/Cessna F150M	F15001229	TN-ADL F-BXNK
F-GPDM	Ultramagic S-90 HAFB	90/16	
F-GPDO	Cessna 152 (Reservn .04)	unkn	
F-GPDR	SIGA MA-26 Pilatre de Rozier HAFB	100	
F-GPDT	Robin DR.500/200i Président	0014	
F-GPDU	SIGA MA-35 Pilatre de Rozier HAFB	129	
F-GPDV	Kubicek BB-37 HAFB	276	OK-0276
F-GPEE	Cameron N-90 HAFB	4573	
F-GPEG	SIGA MA.26 Pilatre de Rozier HAFB	158	
F-GPEH	SIGA MA-26 Pilatre de Rozier HAFB	140	
F-GPEL	Piper PA-28-161 Warrior II	28-8216114	HB-PIM D-EFFJ N9629N
F-GPEP	SNCASE SE.313BAlouette II	1322	ALAT
F-GPEQ	Cessna 210L Centurion	21060712	F-ZBEQ OO-DIL N1677X
F-GPER	SIGA MA-26 Pilatre de Rozier HAFB	148	
F-GPFA	Cessna 172S	172S8159	N7280N
F-GPFC	Cessna 525 CitationJet	525-0101	
F-GPFD	Dassault Falcon 100	221	OE-GHA F-WZGH
F-GPFJ	Ultramagic S-90 HAFB	90/54	
F-GPFL	Eurocopter EC.135T1	0227	
F-GPFN	Schweizer 269C	S-1627	
F-GPGC	Bell 206LT Twin Ranger	52069	N41061
F-GPGF	Cameron C-80 Concept HAFB	10416	
F-GPGG	Cameron O-90 HAFB	10074	
F-GPGH	Beech B300 Super King Air	FL-120	D-CBBB(2) N1512H
F-GPGM	SNCASE SE.3160 Alouette III (Damaged)	1536	A-536
F-GPGO	Cameron 105 Ronald SS HAFB	4047	
F-GPGP	SNCASE SE.3130 Alouette II	1475	ALAT
F-GPGT	Eurocopter EC.120BColibri (Reservation .02)	unkn	
F-GPHB	Balloon Works Firefly 7-15 HAFB	F7-911	
F-GPHC(2)	Cessna T206H Stationair TC	T20608078	N4206V
F-GPHD	Fouga CM.170 Magister (Reservation)	445	Fr.AF
F-GPHE	Aérospatiale AS.350B3 Ecureuil	3313	
F-GPHF(2)	Mooney M.20J Model 205	24-3290	D-ENHF(2)
F-GPHG	SIGA MA-18 Pilatre de Rozier HAFB	104	
F-GPHH	Aérospatiale SA.341JGazelle (Reservation .02)	"57"	
F-GPHI	Aérophile 5500 Tethered Gas Balloon	1	
F-GPHK	BAe. 146-300 (Reservation .02)	E-3202	G-BTUY G-NJIC B17811 B-1781 G-BTUY G-6-202
F-GPHL	Robin DR.400/120 Dauphin 2+2	2428	
F-GPHP	Piper PA-38-112 Tomahawk	38-80A0102	D-EKEF(2) N9691N
F-GPHR	Piper PA-28 (Reservation .02)	unkn	
F-GPHS	Robinson R-44 Astro	0124	
F-GPHU	Fouga CM.170 Magister (Permit 5.00)	374	F-WIGZ Fr.AF
F-GPHV	Cameron N-77 HAFB	3821	
F-GPIA	Aérospatiale/Alenia ATR-42-300	018	TR-LEW F-GIIA F-ODGM F-WDGM
F-GPIC	SIGA MA-26 Pilatre de Roxier HAFB	119	
F-GPIF	Robinson R-44 Raven II	10272	
F-GPIK	Partenavia P.68B (Reservation .02)	152	G-KWIK
F-GPIP	Cameron Z-77 HAFB (Reservation 3.04)	4947	
F-GPJA	Beech 58 Baron	TH-1532	G-BPJA N3102A
F-GPJB	Robin DR.400/120 Dauphin 2+2	2235	
F-GPJC(2)	Chaize JZX.20F12 HAFB	155	
F-GPJD	Beech E90 King Air	LW-328	N551M N797PA N1AM
F-GPJE	Aérospatiale SA.365N Dauphin 2	6151	HB-XDJ F-OHCF F-WYMB JA9625
F-GPJF	Sud Avn SA.316B Alouette III	1353	CN-HTA F-GOLE ALAT
F-GPJG	Robinson R-44 Astro	0567	
F-GPJH	Colt 77AHAFB (Reservation .02)	unkn	
F-GPJL	Robin DR.400/180 Régent	2349	
F-GPJN	Colt 105A HAFB	4783	
F-GPJO	SIGA MA-30 Pilatre de Rozier HAFB	130	
F-GPJR	Robinson R-44 Astro	0036	HB-XZX
F-GPJS	Stinson SR-10C Reliant	3-5846	F-BBCS
F-GPJT	Cessna 172N (Reservation .01, ntu) (Also reserved as F-GVJP)	17273282	OO-CIR N172N C-GBJJ (N4656G)
F-GPJY	Robinson R-44 Astro	0439	G-WYMR
F-GPKB	Aérophile 5500 Tethered Gas Balloon	3	
F-GPKC	Sud Avn SA.318CAlouette Astazou	2112	ALAT
F-GPKD	SAAB-Scania 340B	173	HB-AKD SE-F73 (F-GVAB)
F-GPKF	Robin DR.400/140B Dauphin 4	2385	
F-GPKL	Piper PA-46-350P Malibu Mirage	4622194	
F-GPKU	Cessna 152	15282981	F-OGKU N46006
F-GPLA	Aérospatiale SN.601 Corvette	28	F-BTTL (OO-TTL) F-BTTL F-WNGX
F-GPLB	SIGA MA-26 Pilatre de Rozier HAFB	122	
F-GPLC	Piper PA-28-235 Cherokee Pathfinder	28-7710021	5Y-GWB N2929Q
F-GPLD	Durondeau L220 HAFB	018	OO-BRS
F-GPLE	Aérospatiale AS.350B2 Ecureuil	3881	F-WQDH
F-GPLF	Cessna 525 CitationJet	525-0291	N51744
F-GPLI	SNCASE SE.313B Alouette II	1458	ALAT
F-GPLK	Beech C90A King Air	LJ-1391	3A-MRL HB-GJE
F-GPLL	SIGA MA-30 Pilatre de Rozier HAFB	155	
F-GPLM	Durondeau L-220 HAFB (Permit 7.00)	13	
F-GPLS	Cameron V-90 HAFB	4439	
F-GPLX	SIGA MA-35 Pilatre de Rozier HAFB	134	
F-GPMA	Airbus A319-113	598	D-AVYD
F-GPMB	Airbus A319-113	600	D-AVYC
F-GPMC	Airbus A319-113	608	D-AVYE
F-GPMD	Airbus A319-113	618	D-AVYJ

F-GPME	Airbus A319-113	625	D-AVYQ
F-GPMF	Airbus A319-113	637	D-AVYT
F-GPMG	Airbus A319-113	644	D-AVYA
F-GPMH	Airbus A319-113	647	D-AVYD
F-GPMI	Airbus A319-113	660	D-AVYC
F-GPNA	Aérospatiale AS.355F1 Ecureuil 2	5207	N5802B
F-GPNJ	Dassault Falcon 900EX	50	F-WWFS
F-GPNK	Fokker F.28-0100	11324	SE-DUC PH-CFB (PH-LNR) PH-EZG (G-FIOU) PH-EZG
F-GPNL	Fokker F.28-0100	11325	SE-DUD PH-CFC (PH-LNT) PH-EZI (G-FIOV) PH-EZI

F-GPNM to GPNZ Reserved for Air France Regional Airlines 9.02

F-GPOA	Aérospatiale/Alenia ATR-72-202	204	F-ORAC (XU-RAC) F-GKJK F-WQAG ZS-NDI F-WWER (N7270) F-WWER
F-GPOB	Aérospatiale/Alenia ATR-72-202	207	F-ORAN (XU-RAN) F-WQAH ZS-NDJ F-WWEF (N7271) F-WWEF
F-GPOC	Aérospatiale/Alenia ATR-72-202	311	B-22707 F-WWED
F-GPOD	Aérospatiale/AleniaATR-72-202	361	B-22711 F-WWEX

F-GPOE to GPOH Reserved for ATR-72s for Europe Airpost

F-GPOL	Kubicek BB-30Z HAFB	275	OK-0275
F-GPOM	Robin DR.400/120 Dauphin 2+2	2481	
F-GPOP	Mudry CAP.10B	10	Fr.AF
F-GPOR	Thunder AX8-84 HAFB	853	
F-GPOS	Cameron V-65 HAFB	4271	LX-BOS
F-GPOX	Ultramagic S-130 HAFB	130/42	
F-GPPA(2)	Holste MH.1521M Broussard (Reservation .99)	38	F-BFKL ALAT
F-GPPB	Ultramagic S-90 HAFB	90/44	
F-GPPC	Chaize CS.2200F12 HAFB	184	
F-GPPE	Agusta A.109A	7173	F-WQBP (F-GRMA) F-WQBP(2) F-GRMK G-HWBK
F-GPPF	Dassault Falcon 50	65	N1EV N50LV D-BFFB N65HS N90FJ N50FJ F-WZHT
F-GPPH	Bell 206B Jet Ranger II	3661	(F-GNPH) 3A-MLS C-GWPI ZK-HSP
F-GPPM	CAARP CAP.10	1	Fr.AF
F-GPPS	Mudry CAP.231	6	F-WQOK CN-ABI
F-GPPZ	Schröder Fire Balloons G HAFB	560	
F-GPRC	Mudry CAP.232 (W/o 24.10.95)	02	
F-GPRD	Chaize JZ.22F12 HAFB	140	
F-GPRE	Eurocopter EC.120B Colibri	1123	
F-GPRF	Cessna 152	15284714	N6410M
F-GPRH	Beech 300LW Super King Air	FA-226	F-OHRT N80907
F-GPRI	Aérophile 5500 Tethered Gas Balloon	014	
F-GPRJ	Raven Europe S-40A HAFB	E-312	
F-GPRM	Cessna U206F Stationair (Wreck noted 9.5.03)	U20602125	CN-TFL F-GPCM F-MJAF F-BRGH N71163
F-GPRO	Pilatus PC-6/B1-H2 Turbo Porter	524	HB-FHL OO-POF F-BKRR
F-GPRR	Aérospatiale AS.350B3 Ecureuil	3776	
F-GPRT	Cessna 152	15279995	OO-GPJ N757TQ
F-GPSA	Dassault Falcon 50	123	N211EF VH-SFJ (F-GDSC) F-WZHH
F-GPSB	Chaize JZ.22F12 HAFB	162	
F-GPSI	Robinson R-44 Astro	0882	
F-GPSK	Cameron N-90 HAFB	4242	
F-GPSL	Cameron V-77 HAFB	4243	
F-GPSN	Fairchild Swearingen SA.227AC Metro III	AC-758B	N58NE
F-GPSO	SOCATA Rallye 100ST	2584	Fr.Navy 84
F-GPSP	Cessna TR182 Turbo Skylane RG	R18200860	LX-GHL N737NK
F-GPST	Cameron C-80 Concept HAFB	10004	
F-GPTB	Canadair CL.600-2B19 Regional Jet	7177	
F-GPTC	Canadair CL.600-2B19 Regional Jet	7182	
F-GPTD	Canadair CL.600-2B19 Regional Jet	7184	
F-GPTE	Canadair CL.600-2B19 Regional Jet	7183	
F-GPTF	Canadair CL.600-2B19 Regional Jet	7197	C-FMLB
F-GPTG	Canadair CL.600-2B19 Regional Jet	7223	
F-GPTJ	Canadair CL.600-2B19 Regional Jet	7323	C-FMLV
F-GPTK	Canadair CL.600-2B19 Regional Jet	7332	C-FMND
F-GPTL	Beech A100 King Air (Reservation)	B-109	N78MK N78CA N51VK N51V N1GX N1GT
F-GPTM	Canadair CL.600-2B19 Regional Jet	7020	EC-GTG F-GNME C-FMMB
F-GTPT	Boeing 747-400 (Reservation 10.04 for Corsair)	unkn	
F-GPUB	Beech B36TCBonanza	EA-317	D-EFMT
F-GPUC	Cessna 152	15285282	N64903
F-GPUH	SNCASE SE.3130 Alouette II	1523	ALAT
F-GPUJ	Cessna 525A Citation	0169	N5262W
F-GPUM	Aérospatiale SA.330J Puma	1652	HB-XUV I- EHPD
F-GPUY	Cameron N-105 HAFB	4693	
F-GPVF	McDonnell-Douglas DC-10-30 (Reservation)	unkn	
F-GPVH	Agusta A.109E Power	11607	
F-GPVM	Robinson R-44 Astro	0056	
F-GPXA	Fokker F.28-0100	11487	PH-EZW
F-GPXB	Fokker F.28-0100	11492	PH-EZK
F-GPXC	Fokker F.28-0100	11493	PH-EZY
F-GPXD	Fokker F.28-0100	11494	PH-EZO
F-GPXE	Fokker F.28-0100	11495	PH-EZP
F-GPXF	Fokker F.28-0100	11330	F-WQJX N133ML SE-DUG PH-CFH (PH-LNY) (G-FIOA) PH-EZB
F-GPXG	Fokker F.28-0100	11387	SX-BGL (F-GNAN) F-WQJJ HL7207 PH-KXB
F-GPXH	Fokker F.28-0100	11476	SX-BGM (F-GNAO) F-WQJK HL7212 PH-EZY
F-GPYA	Aérospatiale/Alenia ATR-42-512	457	(G-ZAPJ) F-WWET
F-GPYB	Aérospatiale/Alenia ATR-42-512	480	F-WWLZ
F-GPYC	Aérospatiale/Alenia ATR-42-512	484	F-WWEB
F-GPYD	Aérospatiale/Alenia ATR-42-512	490	F-WWLJ
F-GPYF	Aérospatiale/Alenia ATR-42-512	495	F-WWLM
F-GPYK	Aérospatiale/Alenia ATR-42-512	537	F-WWLC
F-GPYL	Aérospatiale/Alenia ATR-42-512	542	F-WWLH
F-GPYM	Aérospatiale/Alenia ATR-42-512	520	F-WWLR
F-GPYN	Aérospatiale/Alenia ATR-42-512	539	F-WWLO
F-GPYO	Aérospatiale/Alenia ATR-42-512	544	F-WWLH
F-GPYP	Canadair CL.600-2B19 Regional Jet	7126	C-FMML
F-GPYY	Beech 1900C-1	UC-115	N115YV

F-GPZG to GPZZ Reserved for Air Liberté, now not to be used?

TEMPORARY REGISTRATIONS:

The F-WQ . . series is used mainly for delivery or ferry flights. Some marks are often re-used. At the time of going to press the following are thought to be currently in use:

F-WQB . mainly used by Dassault
F-WQD . , F-WQE . mainly used by Eurocopter
F-WQF . , H ., I ., J ., L ., M ., N ., Q ., S ., U . mainly used by Airbus and SNIAS/EADS
F-WQO . , F-WQP . being used by CAP Aviation

We have listed here a number of ATR-42s, which tend to retain their marks for longer, together with other aircraft for which no subsequent identity is yet known.

F-WQIN	Fokker F.27 Friendship 600 (Stored)	10401	9Q-CBP PH-FNZ PT-LDT N379BS C9-AMD CR-AMD PH-FNZ
F-WQJN	Aérospatiale/Alenia ATR-42-300 (Stored, storm damaged 12.99)	083	YR-ATY F-WQBV N4207G F-WWEI
F-WQNC	Aérospatiale/Alenia ATR-72-202 (Permit 11.04)	296	VP-BNH VR-BNH OY-CIJ F-WWLV

F-WQNJ	Aérospatiale/Alenia ATR-42-500 (Permit 10.04)	510	VP-BVE
			N16450
			F-WWLB
F-WQNM	Aérospatiale/Alenia ATR-42-300 (Permit 10.04)	178	EK-42023
			F-OHRP
			F-WQNJ
			C-GICX
			N2411G
			F-WWEK
F-WQNQ	Aérospatiale/Alenia ATR-72-212 (Permit 10.04)	422	OY-CIW
			F-WQNR
			HS-PGJ
			F-OHLB
			F-WWLZ
F-WQPF	Antonov An-2 (Permit 3.01)	1G240-33	SP-FAF
			(F-GROM)
			SP-FAF
F-WQRQ	SOCATA TB-20 Trinidad (SMA diesel engine) (Permit 8.02)	1809	G-OSMA
			F-WWRS
F-WQRS	Airbus A321-211 (Stored 1.03)	1012	G-CBOI
			OO-SUC
			D-AVZH
F-WQSB	Airbus A320-211 (Stored 5.03)	547	VH-HYO
			F-WWIU
F-WQSC	Sikorsky S-76C (Permit 12.02)	760269	F-WJDI
			N3123U
F-WQSR(3)	Aérospatiale AS.365N2 Dauphin 2 (Permit 11.040)	6418	D2-EVE
			F-GHRZ
			LX-HUI
			F-GHRZ
F-WQSX(2)	Airbus A320-214	937	SU-LBC
			F-WWIS
F-WQTB	Airbus A310-322	404	F-WIHT
			HB-IPG
			F-WWCD
F-WQUD	Reims/Cessna F406 Caravan II	F406-0043	D-INUS
F-WQVF	Conair/Fokker F.27-600 Firefighter (Permit 12.04, stored Bergamo)	10432/003	F-ZBFF
			C-FGDS
			OY-CCM
			CN-CDA
			PH-FPG
F-WQVG	Conair/Fokker F.27-600 Firefighter (Permit 12.04, stored Bergamo)	10440/002	F-ZBFG
			C-FBDY
			VH-TQR
			PH-EXB
F-GRAA	Cessna 172M (Reservation .00)	unkn	
F-GRAC	Aérospatiale AS.350BA Ecureuil	1652	(F-GPUM)
			SX-HBP
F-GRAD	Piper PA-28-180 Cherokee Challenger	28-7305060	F-OGFW
F-GRAE(2)	Eurocopter EC.120B Colibri	1049	
F-GRAF	Cessna 172R	17280232	(N415ES)
F-GRAG(2)	Piper PA-18-135 Super Cub	18-2539	OO-VVP
			OO-HMB
			ALAT
			52-6221
F-GRAH	Durondeau L-300 HAFB	023	
F-GRAI	Reims F406 Caravan II	F406-0061	N406CT
			F-GURA
			F-OGVS
			N3121X
F-GRAJ	Pilatus PC-12/45	406	
F-GRAK	Bell 412EP	36191	N70722
F-GRAL	Cameron O-105 HAFB	3908	
F-GRAM	Chaize CS.2200F12 HAFB	144	
F-GRAP	Lindstrand LBL-105A HAFB	208	
F-GRAS	Cameron V-77 HAFB	3930	
F-GRAT	Cameron V-90 HAFB	4771	
F-GRAU	Aérospatiale SA.365C3 Dauphin 2	5023	G-BGNM
			EC-DOQ
			G-BGNM
			EC-DOQ
			G-BGNM
			EC-DOQ
			G-BGNM
			EC-DOQ
			G-BGNM
			(G-BGPU)
F-WRAV	Raven Europe EU-250 Balloon	E-309	
F-GRAX	Dassault Falcon 900	120	VP-BNJ
			VR-BNJ
			F-WWFN
F-GRAZ	Scintex ML.250 Rubis (Reservation .99)	101	F-BJME
F-GRBD	SOCATA TB-9 Tampico	1092	EC-EYM
			F-GKUK
F-GRBG	SOCATA TB-9 Tampico	1348	EC-FLE
			F-GKVX
F-GRBH	SOCATA TB-10 Tobago	1807	
F-GRBJ	SOCATA TB-20 Trinidad	1822	
F-GRBK	SOCATA TB-20 Trinidad	1825	F-WWRB
F-GRBL	SOCATA TB-20 Trinidad	1827	
F-GRBO	SOCATA TB-200 Tobago XL	1812	
F-GRBT	SOCATA TB-20 Trinidad	1109	I- FMLV
			F-ODTY
F-GRBW	SOCATA TB-20 Trinidad	1874	
F-GRBZ	SOCATA TB-20 Trinidad	2105	
F-GRCC	SIGA MA-26 Pilatre de Rozier HAFB	123	(F-GNUI)
F-GRCE	Bell 206B Jet Ranger II	1679	F-BXLG
			N90070
F-GRCG	Cameron A-210 HAFB	4728	
F-GRCH	Cessna 500 Citation	500-0201	N690EA
			(F-. . . .)
			N690EA
			(F-GIHU)
			N690EA
			XC-GUO
F-GRCJ	Antonov An-2 (See F-OHRJ)	unkn	
F-GRCL	Moniot APM-20 Lionceau	12	
F-GRCM	Schweizer 269C (Reservation)	unkn	
F-GRCP	Pilatus PC-6/B2-H2 Turbo Porter	2071	N392AC
			N392CA
			OB-. . . .
			N5305F
F-GRCS	Balloon Works Firefly F9B-15 HAFB (Permit)	F9B-027	(F-GRCZ)
F-GRCT	Thunder Ax10-180A HAFB	1723	G-PICT
F-GRDC	Chaize JZ.25F16 HAFB	147	
F-GRDD	Chaize CS.2200F12 HAFB	165	
F-GRDF	Chaize CS.2200F12 HAFB	158	
F-GRDJ	Piper PA-36-285 Pawnee Brave	36-7660123	N57803
F-GRDM	Aérospatiale AS.355N Ecureuil 2	5690	
F-GRDN	Bell 206B Jet Ranger II	1172	G-SHCC
			N280C
F-GRDO	Cameron Z-105 HAFB	10599	
F-GRDR	Cessna 150L	15074024	G-BSBY
			N18662
F-GRDX	Aérophile 5500 Tethered Gas Balloon	4	(F-GSMA)
F-GREB	Mooney M.20M Model 257 TLS	27-0025	OO-GJS
			(OO-MEY)
			(OO-GJS)
			F-GJSM
			N10901
F-GREC	Hughes 269C	S-1711	N41S
F-GREF	Cameron N-65 HAFB	3024	
F-GREL	Mooney M.20J Model 205	24-3403	N2138W
F-GREM	Chaize JF.30F16 HAFB	175	
F-GREN	Schröder Fire Balloons 50/24HAFB	886	
F-GREP	Robin DR.400/160 Major	2439	
F-GRES	Holste MH.1521M Broussard	124	Fr.AF
F-GREV	Cameron N-77 HAFB	1704	LX-REV
F-GREY	Robinson R-44 Astro	0090	
F-GRGA	Embraer EMB.145	145008	PT-SYE
F-GRGB	Embraer EMB.145	145010	PT-SYG
F-GRGC	Embraer EMB.145	145012	PT-SYI
F-GRGD	Embraer EMB.145	145043	PT-SZI
F-GRGE	Embraer EMB.145EU	145047	PT-SZM
F-GRGF	Embraer EMB.145EU	145050	PT-SZP
F-GRGG	Embraer EMB.145EU	145118	PT-SCU
F-GRGH	Embraer EMB.145EU	145120	PT-SCW
F-GRGI	Embraer EMB.145EU	145152	PT-SED
F-GRGJ	Embraer EMB.145EU	145297	PT-SKO
F-GRGK	Embraer EMB.145EU	145324	PT-SMQ
F-GRGL	Embraer EMB.145EU	145375	PT-SOZ
F-GRGM	Embraer EMB.145MP	145418	PT-STP
F-GRGP	Embraer EMB.135ER	145188	
F-GRGQ	Embraer EMB.135ER	145233	PT-SHX
F-GRGR	Embraer EMB.135ER	145236	PT-SIB
F-GRHA	Airbus A319-111	0938	D-AVYS
F-GRHB	Airbus A319-111	0985	D-AVYO
F-GRHC	Airbus A319-111	0998	D-AVYW
F-GRHD	Airbus A319-111	1000	D-AVYP
F-GRHE	Airbus A319-111	1020	D-AVYX
F-GRHF	Airbus A319-111	1025	D-AVYE
F-GRHG	Airbus A319-111	1036	D-AVYS
F-GRHH	Airbus A319-111	1151	D-AVWK
F-GRHI	Airbus A319-111	1169	D-AVYX
F-GRHJ	Airbus A319-111	1176	D-AVWN
F-GRHK	Airbus A319-111	1190	D-AVYQ
F-GRHL	Airbus A319-111	1201	D-AVWT
F-GRHM	Airbus A319-111	1216	D-AVYF
F-GRHN	Airbus A319-111	1267	D-AVWB
F-GRHO	Airbus A319-111	1271	D-AVWC
F-GRHP	Airbus A319-111	1344	D-AVYQ
F-GRHQ	Airbus A319-111	1404	D-AVYB
F-GRHR	Airbus A319-111	1415	D-AVYF
F-GRHS	Airbus A319-111	1444	D-AVWA
F-GRHT	Airbus A319-111	1449	D-AVWD
F-GRHU	Airbus A319-111	1471	D-AVYR
F-GRHV	Airbus A319-111	1505	D-AVYF
F-GRHX	Airbus A319-111	1524	D-AVWC
F-GRHY	Airbus A319-111	1616	D-AVWG
F-GRHZ	Airbus A319-111	1622	D-AVYO
F-GRIB	Robinson R-22M2 Mariner	3080M	
F-GRIC	Cameron N-90 HAFB	4143	CS-BAR
F-GRIF	Robinson R-22 Beta	0526	(F-GPPP)
			HB-XZZ
			N999PS
			TG-. . .
			N23667
F-GRIM	Chaize JZ.30F16 HAFB	159	
F-GRIP	Robin DR.400/180 Régent	2527	
F-GRIS	Cameron N-90 HAFB	3811	
F-GRIV	Piper PA-28RT-201T Turbo Arrow IV	28R-8031091	D-EIIV(2)
			LX-FRL
			N8190B

F-GRIX	SIGA MA-26 Pilatre de Rozier HAFB	118	
F-GRIZ	Piper PA-28-160 Cherokee	28-8	F-BLIX
	(Reservation .00)		F-OCIX
			N5007W
F-GRJA	Canadair CL.600-2B19 Regional Jet	7070	C-FMKW(3)
F-GRJB	Canadair CL.600-2B19 Regional Jet	7076	C-FMLS(3)
F-GRJC	Canadair CL.600-2B19 Regional Jet	7085	C-F . . .
F-GRJD	Canadair CL.600-2B19 Regional Jet	7088	C-FMLU(4)
F-GRJE	Canadair CL.600-2B19 Regional Jet	7106	C-FMNQ(4)
F-GRJF	Canadair CL.600-2B19 Regional Jet	7108	C-FMLU(5)
F-GRJG	Canadair CL.600-2B19 Regional Jet	7143	C-FMMQ
F-GRJH	Canadair CL.600-2B19 Regional Jet	7162	C-F . . .
F-GRJI	Canadair CL.600-2B19 Regional Jet	7147	C-FZAL
			C-FMMY(4)
F-GRJJ	Canadair CL.600-2B19 Regional Jet	7190	C-GBFF
F-GRJK	Canadair CL.600-2B19 Regional Jet	7219	C-FMMQ
F-GRJL	Canadair CL.600-2B19 Regional Jet	7221	
F-GRJM	Canadair CL.600-2B19 Regional Jet	7222	
F-GRJN	Canadair CL.600-2B19 Regional Jet	7262	C-FMLT
F-GRJO	Canadair CL.600-2B19 Regional Jet	7296	
F-GRJP	Canadair CL.600-2B19 Regional Jet	7301	
F-GRJQ	Canadair CL.600-2B19 Regional Jet	7321	C-FMLS
F-GRJR	Canadair CL.600-2B19 Regional Jet	7375	C-FMKW
F-GRJT	Canadair CL.600-2B19 Regional Jet	7389	C-FMOS
F-GRLB	Eurocopter EC.130B4 Ecureuil	3515	
F-GRLC	Piper PA-28RT-201T Turbo Arrow IV	28R-7931100	I-ARLC
			N2158U
F-GRLO	SIGA MA-30 Pilatre de Rozier HAFB	111	
F-GRLT	Mooney M.20K Model 231	25-0141	N40WE
			N4758Y
			YV-1805P
F-GRMB	Beech A36 Bonanza	E-2292	F-GRST
			F-ODST
			D-EBVS(2)
F-GRMF	Schweizer 269C	S-1395	D-HEYN
			HB-XUP
F-GRMM to GRMO Reserved for AOM (formerly Minerve)			
F-GRMP	Cessna 310R	310R1250	(F-GFZR)
			TJ-AHA
			PH-VWM
			N98997
F-GRMR	Robin DR.400/160 Major	2429	
F-GRMS	SNCASE SE.313B Alouette II	1568	Fr.AF
F-GRMT	Robinson R-22B2 Beta	3629	
F-GRNB	Boeing 737-85F	28824	N500GX
			N1782B
			N1787B
F-GRND	Boeing 737-85F	28827	
F-GRNE	Boeing 737-85F	30568	
F-GRNF	Boeing 737-329	23774	N774CT
			D-ADIE
			OO-SDY
F-GRNG	Boeing 767-38E	24798	N798AW
	(Reservation 10.04)		HL7264
F-GRNH	Boeing 737-4Q8	24706	EC-FXP
			EC-644
			9M-MJD
F-GRNO	Embraer EMB.120RT Brasilia	120144	PT-OZM
	(Reservation .99)		F-GGTE
			PT-SPK
F-GRNT	Swearingen SA.226T(B) Merlin IIIB	T-312	N84GA
			N90NB
			(N52SJ)
			N90NB
F-GRNV	Boeing 737-329	24356	CN-RDA
			OO-SYB
F-GRNX	Boeing 737-46B (Reservation 9.01)	25262	PH-AAU
			D-ABCC
			OO-ILJ
F-GRNY	Aérophile 5500 Tethered Gas Balloon	2	
F-GROA	Robin DR.400/180 Régent	2423	
F-GROK	Cameron N-65 HAFB	4654	
F-GROL	Kubicek BB-60 HAFB	280	OK-0280
F-GROM	Cameron N-77 HAFB	4838	
F-GROP	Schröder Fire Balloons 40/24 HAFB	446	D-OGVE
F-GROS	Cameron N-77 HAFB	4677	
F-GROT	Mudry CAP.10B	11	Fr.AF
F-GROU	Mudry CAP.10B	24	F-WQCM
			Fr.AF
F-GROV	Piper PA-28RT-201T Turbo Arrow IV	28R-8131009	N8277H
F-GROY	Ultramagic S-90 HAFB	90/41	
F-GROZ	Cameron A-340HL HAFB	10544	
F-GRPA	Mudry CAP.232	06	
F-GRPB	Cameron N-105 HAFB	4861	
F-GRPC	Nord 1101 Noralpha (Reservation .99)	113	F-BFNJ
			F-ZJPS
F-GRPG	Ultramagic S-90 HAFB	90/ 60	
F-GRPL	Ultramagic M90 HAFB	90/46	
F-GRPS	Piper PA-31T Cheyenne II	31T-7820010	LX-GPP
			3A-MSB
			F-GGAT
			D-IFPD
			N333PD
			N82211
F-GRPV	Diamond DA20-A1 Katana	10036	(F-GYBQ(1))
	(Reservation .05)		N236BR
			C-GKAN

F-GRRA	Mudry CAP.10B	119	Fr.AF
F-GRRB	Aérospatiale SA.315B Lama	2475	CNET/F-SEBO
F-GRRE	Moniot APM-20 Lionceau	5	
F-GRRF	Moniot APM-20 Lionceau	6	
F-GRRG(2)	Moniot APM-20 Lionceau	7	
F-GRRH	Moniot APM-20 Lionceau	8	
F-GRRI	Moniot APM-20 Lionceau	9	
F-GRRK	Moniot APM-20 Lionceau	10	
F-GRRL	Moniot APM-20 Lionceau	11	
F-GRRN	Moniot APM-20 Lionceau	15	
F-GRRO	Moniot APM-20 Lionceau	14	
F-GRRR	Robinson R-22M2 Mariner	3073M	
F-GRRT	Mudry CAP.10B	116	(F-GIPQ)
			Fr.AF
F-GRRU	Sikorsky S-76A	760186	LX-HUE
			ZS-RKH
			LX-HUE
			F-GDHU
			F-WZSB
			F-GDHU
F-GRRX	Moniot APM-20 Lionceau	4	
	(C/n as given, but earlier quoted as c/n 13, rebuild of c/n 1)		
F-GRSD	Airbus A320-214	653	F-WWIF
			F-GJDY
			F-WWIF
F-GRSE	Airbus A320-214	657	F-WWIR
F-GRSF	SIGA MA-22 Pilatre de Rozier HAFB	106	
F-GRSI	Airbus A320-214	973	F-WWBR
F-GRSJ(2)	Cameron A-120 HAFB	10103	
F-GRSK	Grumman G.164 AgCat (Reservation .99)	unkn	
F-GRSL	Mudry CAP.231	17	HB-MSR
			F-GGYX
F-GRSN	Airbus A320-214	1692	F-WWIN
F-GRSO(2)	Beech 200CSuper King Air	BL-11	(F-GYMD)
			(5B-CJM)
			PH-SKP
			F-GIMD
			N41JK
			(5H-. . .)
			I-MADY
			D-INEF
F-GRSP	CEA DR.250/160 Capitaine	13	OO-BOY
F-GRSQ	Airbus A330-243	501	F-WWKG
F-GRTA	Euravial RF-47	3	F-WWNG
F-GRTC	Aquila AT-01	AT01-111	
F-GRTE(2)	Aérospatiale AS.350B3 Ecureuil (Res 12.04)	unkn	
F-GRUB	Pilatus PC-6/ B2-H4 Turbo Porter	940	HB-FMJ
F-GRUI	Lindstrand LBL-69A	761	
F-GRUN	Boeing 747-400 (Reservn 10.04 for Corsair)	unkn	
F-GRVA	Ultramagic V-105 HAFB	105/36	
F-GRVB	Robinson R-44 Astro	0042	D-HTUT
F-GRVC	Aérospatiale SA.341G Gazelle	1164	JRV126 . .
			JRV12013
F-GRVD	Ultramagic M-105 HAFB	105/86	
F-GRVK	Sud Avn SA.316B Alouette III	1184	ALAT
F-GRVN	Piper J-3C-65 Cub	11343	F-BHEB
			F-OAEB
			43-30052
F-GRVZ	Pilatus PC-6/B2-H4 Turbo-Porter	901	
F-GRXA	Airbus A319-111	1640	D-AVYJ
F-GRXB	Airbus A319-111	1645	D-AVYC
F-GRXC	Airbus A319-111	1677	D-AVWF
F-GRXD	Airbus A319-111	1699	D-AVYG
F-GRXE	Airbus A319-111	1733	D-AVWT
F-GRXF	Airbus A319-111	1938	D-AVWG
F-GRXG	Airbus A319-115LR	2213	D-AVYM
F-GRXH	Airbus A319-115LR	2228	D-AVWC
F-GRXI	Airbus A319-115LR	2279	D-AVYF
F-GRXJ	Airbus A319-115LR	2456	D-AVYX
F-GRXK to GRXZ Reserved for Airbus A319s for Air France			
F-GRYD	Fouga CM.170 Magister (Reservation)	393	Fr.AF
F-GRYL	Beech 1900D	UE-301	N22161
F-GRYR	Raven Europe S-55A HAFB	E-357	
F-GRZA	Canadair CL.600-2C10 Regional Jet 700	10006	C-GHCE
F-GRZB	Canadair CL.600-2C10 Regional Jet 700	10007	C-GHCF
F-GRZC	Canadair CL.600-2C10 Regional Jet 700	10008	C-GHCO
F-GRZD	Canadair CL.600-2C10 Regional Jet 700	10016	C-GJEZ
F-GRZE	Canadair CL.600-2C10 Regional Jet 700	10032	C-G . . .
F-GRZF	Canadair CL.600-2C10 Regional Jet 700	10036	C-G . . .
F-GRZG	Canadair CL.600-2C10 Regional Jet 700	10037	C-GIBT
F-GRZH	Canadair CL.600-2C10 Regional Jet 700	10089	C-G . . .
F-GRZI	Canadair CL 600-2C10 Regional Jet 700	10093	C-GI
F-GRZJ	Canadair CL 600-2C10 Regional Jet 700	10096	C-GI
F-GRZK	Canadair CL 600-2C10 Regional Jet 700	10098	C-GI
F-GRZL to GRZZ Reserved for Brit'air			
F-GSAC	Pilatus PC-6/B2-H4 Turbo-Porter	902	HB-FIJ
F-GSAG	Nord 1203 Norécrin (Ntu, dismantled)	104	F-BEOQ
F-GSAK	SAAB S.91B Safir	91229	F-BHAK
F-GSAM	Lindstrand LBL-120A	448	
F-GSAO	SOCATA TB-20 Trinidad	1801	
F-GSAS	Aérospatiale AS.355F1 Ecureuil 2	5159	N5796B
F-GSAT	Pilatus PC-6/B2-H4 Turbo Porter	904	HB-FLC
F-GSAU	Aérospatiale AS.355N Ecureuil 2	5570	D-HSMM
			CS-HDP
			N888B
			N6097C

F-GSAV	SIGA MA.18 Pilatre de Rozier HAFB (Res .04)	161	
F-GSBA	Robin DR.400/140B Dauphin 4	2342	
F-GSBB	Robin DR.400/120 Dauphin 2+2	2334	
F-GSBC	Robin DR.400/180 Régent	2340	
F-GSBD	Robin DR.400/180 Régent	2329	
F-GSBE	Robin DR.400/120 Dauphin 2+2	2337	
F-GSBF	Robin DR.400/120 Dauphin 2+2	2335	
F-GSBG	Robin DR.400/180 Régent	2336	
F-GSBH	Robin DR.400/180 Régent	2341	
F-GSBI	Robin DR.400/120 Dauphin 2+2	2352	
F-GSBJ	Robin DR.400/140B Dauphin 4	2350	
F-GSBK	Robin DR.400/120 Dauphin 2+2	2351	
F-GSBL	Robin HR.200/120B	314	
F-GSBM	Robin DR.400/180 Régent	2353	
F-GSBN	Robin DR.400/120 Dauphin 2+2	2355	
F-GSBO	Robin DR.400/180 Régent	2358	
F-GSBP	Robin DR.400/120 Dauphin 2+2	2356	
F-GSBQ	Robin DR.400/120 Dauphin 2+2	2374	
F-GSBR	Robin DR.400/140B Major	2344	
F-GSBS	Robin DR.400/140B Major	2357	
F-GSBT	Robin DR.400/120 Dauphin 2+2	2359	
F-GSBU	Robin DR.400/140B Dauphin 4	2369	
F-GSBV	Robin DR.400/180 Régent	2364	
F-GSBX	Robin DR.400/180 Régent	2366	
F-GSBY	Robin HR.200/120B	319	
F-GSBZ	Robin DR.400/180 Régent	2362	
F-GSCB	Piper PA-18-135 Super Cub (Officially quoted with f/n 18-4577 as c/n)	18-4006	TC-CUB Turkish AF 54-2606
F-GSCC	Mudry CAP.10B	127	F-WQCN Fr.AF
F-GSCD	SAN Jodel D.140E Mousquetaire IV	180	D-EDHL
F-GSCE	Aérospatiale AS.350BA Ecureuil	9009	
F-GSCH	Schröder Fire Balloons G HAFB	480	
F-GSCI	SIGA MA-30 Pilatre de Rozier HAFB	121	
F-GSCP	Cessna 172R	17280170	N9890F
F-GSDB	Piper PA-28R-200 Cherokee Arrow	28R-35039	TU-TMT F-BVFT TU-TFA N9339N
F-GSDF	Eurocopter EC.130B4 Ecureuil	3539	F-WQDB
F-GSDL	Mooney M.20R Ovation (W/o 13.2.01)	29-0027	
F-GSDR	Ultramagic M-77 HAFB	77/130	
F-GSDV	Commander Aircraft 114B	14601	N6018F
F-GSEB	Beech B200 Super King Air	BB-1110	TR-LDU N110GA CN-TNB F-GGAR N7045C HZ-MW2 N200MW
F-GSED	Robinson R-44 Raven II	10205	
F-GSEE	Robin DR.400/140B Dauphin 4	2360	
F-GSEH	Aérospatiale AS.350B3 Ecureuil	3827	
F-GSEM	Schröder Fire Balloons G30/24 HAFB	1070	
F-GSER	Dassault Falcon 50	2	F-BINR F-RAFJ F-BINR F-WINR
F-GSEU	Airbus A330-243	635	F-WWYO
F-GSEV	Piper PA-28-181 Archer II	2890091	OO-MTW N9151Z
F-GSEX	Boeing 747-312	23028	F-WSEX N117KC VH-INK N117KC (9V-SKC) (9V-SQV)
F-GSFF	Cameron C-80 Concept HAFB	4608	
F-GSFG	Cameron N-105 HAFB	4828	
F-GSFM	Cameron N-90 HAFB	4923	
F-GSFO	Reims/Cessna F152	F15201774	D-EGNW
F-GSFP	CEAJodel DR.1051-M1 Sicile Record (Reservation 2.02)	626	F-BMEM F-OCEM
F-GSFR	Cameron N-77 HAFB	3783	
F-GSFT	SIGA MA-26 Pilatre de Rozier HAFB	120	
F-GSFV	Chaize CS.3000F16	116	
F-GSGD	Robin DR.400/160 Major	2504	
F-GSGE	Cameron Z-120 HAFB	10628	
F-GSGF	Kubicek BB-45 HAFB	52	OO-BBT OK-6052
F-GSGG	Aérospatiale SA.332C Super Puma	2033	HB-XVY N5795P N300US N5795P
F-GSGP	Cameron N-90 HAFB	10254	
F-GSGS	Piper PA-46-350P Malibu Mirage	4622154	D-EBPA N92421
F-GSGT	Cessna U206 Super Skywagon	U206-0364	6V-AHC 6V-ABV F-OCEJ N2164F
F-GSGZ	Mudry CAP.232	08	
F-GSHA	Schweizer 269C	S-1401	D-HOBO HB-XVK N86G
F-GSHB	Robinson R-22M Mariner	2101M	3A-MJM

F-GSHC	Piper PA-34-220TSeneca III	3433156	N300AN N9174N
F-GSHD	Fouga CM.170 Magister (Reservation)	529	Fr.AF
F-GSHG	Fouga CM.170 Magister (Permit 5.00)	045	G-FUGA G-BSCT Fr.AF
F-GSHJ	Robinson R-44 Raven	1279	
F-GSHK	Airbus A320-231	326	SU-RAB F-WWDK
F-GSHL	Piper PA-34-220T Seneca V	3449044	D-IOSH
F-GSHM	Piper PA-34-220T Seneca V	3449045	D-IOSI (2)
F-GSIB	Cameron N-77 HAFB	2065	G-BRIB
F-GSIC	Hughes 369D	50-0717D	D-HLIA N1099Z
F-GSID	Cameron O-120 HAFB	3420	HB-QAI
F-GSIM	Diamond DA42 Twin Star (Res 2.05)	42.010	OE-VPY
F-GSIN	Beech 200 Super King Air	BB-239	N517JM G-WWHL G-BLAE I- ELCO N517JM N17649
F-GSIR	Thunder AX8-105SII HAFB	3591	
F-GSIS	SIGA MA-35 Pilatre de Rozier HAFB	133	
F-GSIT	SIGA MA-30 Pilatre de Rozier HAFB	124	
F-GSIU	Robin R.2000/120	312	
F-GSIX	Piper PA-32-260 Cherokee Six	32-59	HB-OLZ N3313W
F-GSJB	Ultramagic S-105 HAFB	105/59	
F-GSJC	Piper PA-34-220TSeneca III	3433159	D-GIPA
F-GSJD	Beech 58P Baron	TJ-74	G-PAPU G-NIPU N1PU N313A N1PU N1PT N1899L
F-GSJF	Sky 77/24 HAFB	128	
F-GSJL	Beech B90 King Air (Reservation)	LJ-393	N221NC N800CT N300CT N757K
F-GSJO	Cameron Z-120 HAFB	10359	
F-GSJR	Piper PA-46-350P Malibu Mirage	4636112	
F-GSJS	Bell 206L-4 Long Ranger IV	52059	N96V N90C N62LH
F-GSJT	Aérospatiale AS.350BA Ecureuil	1192	F-ODLL (N215EH) N3602V
F-GSKA to GSKF	Reserved for DC-10-30s for Sky Jet		
F-GSKY	Boeing 747-312	23244	TF-ATG N680SW 9V-SKK ZS-OKK 9V-SKK N124KK (9V-SKK)
F-GSLA(2)	SOCATA TB-20 Trinidad	2205	
F-GSLB	Cameron C-80 Concept HAFB	4910	
F-GSLC	Thunder AX8-90 SI HAFB	1624	G-SLCI
F-GSLP	SNCASE SE.313BAlouette II	1554	ALAT
F-GSLT	Robinson R-44 Astro	0470	
F-GSLZ	Dassault Falcon 100	208	F-WQBJ N71M I-OANN F-GELS F-WZGO
F-GSMA	Aérophile 5500 Tethered Gas Balloon (Originally allocated to c/n 4 which is F-GRDX)	5	
F-GSMB	Eurocopter EC.135T1	0031	(F-GTIL) VP-CEO
F-GSMC	Cessna F500 Citation	0308	F-GMLH (F-GIRS) N6525J N70TG N38CJ N308CC (N5308J)
F-GSMD	Piper PA-28-181 Archer III	2843066	N9282N
F-GSME	SIGA MA-26 Pilatre de Rozier HAFB	138	
F-GSMJ	Cameron N-90 HAFB	2979	HB-BXU
F-GSMK	Reims/Cessna F150K	F15000534	HB-CUR
F-GSMM	Cameron C-70 Concept HAFB	10112	
F-GSMN	CEAJodel DR.1050 Sicile (Reservation .01)	437	D-ELMN F-BLMN
F-GSMR	Piper PA-34-200T Seneca II	34-8070208	D-GORS N8195L
F-GSMU	Eurocopter EC.135T1	0043	
F-GSMV	Robin DR.400/180 Régent	2361	
F-GSNA	Dassault Falcon 900EX	145	
F-GSNG	Cameron C-80 Concept HAFB	4911	
F-GSOE	Aérospatiale AS.350B3 Ecureuil	9100	
F-GSOL	Cameron N-90 HAFB	3769	
F-GSON	Cameron N-90 HAFB	4373	
F-GSPA	Boeing 777-228	29002	
F-GSPB	Boeing 777-228	29003	

F-GSPC	Boeing 777-228	29004	
F-GSPD	Boeing 777-228ER	29005	
F-GSPE	Boeing 777-228ER	29006	
F-GSPF	Boeing 777-228ER	29007	
F-GSPG	Boeing 777-228ER	27609	
F-GSPH	Boeing 777-228ER	28675	
F-GSPI	Boeing 777-228ER	29008	
F-GSPJ	Boeing 777-228ER	29009	
F-GSPK	Boeing 777-228ER	29010	
F-GSPL	Boeing 777-228ER	30457	N50281
F-GSPM	Boeing 777-228ER	30456	
F-GSPN	Boeing 777-228ER	29011	
F-GSPO	Boeing 777-228ER	30614	
F-GSPP	Boeing 777-228ER	30615	
F-GSPQ	Boeing 777-228ER	28682	
F-GSPR	Boeing 777-228ER	28683	
F-GSPS	Boeing 777-228ER	32306	
F-GSPT	Boeing 777-228ER	32308	
F-GSPU	Boeing 777-228ER	32309	
F-GSPV	Boeing 777-228ER	28684	
F-GSPX	Boeing 777-228ER	32698	
F-GSPY	Boeing 777-228ER	32305	
F-GSPZ	Boeing 777-228ER	32310	
F-GSQA	Boeing 777-228ER	32723	N5017Q
F-GSQB	Boeing 777-228ER	32724	N5018Q
F-GSQC	Boeing 777-228ER	32727	
F-GSQD	Boeing 777-228ER	32726	
F-GSQE	Boeing 777-228ER	32851	
F-GSQF	Boeing 777-228ER	32849	N50217
F-GSQG	Boeing 777-228ER	32850	N5028Y
F-GSQH	Boeing 777-228ER	32711	
F-GSQI	Boeing 777-228ER	32725	N60697
F-GSQJ	Boeing 777-228ER (Reservn 3.05)	32852	
F-GSQK to GSQZ Reserved for Boeing 777-328s for Air France			
F-GSRA	Robin DR.400/140B Dauphin 4	2372	
F-GSRB	Robin R.2160 Alpha Sport	320	
F-GSRC	Robin DR.400/120 Dauphin 2+2	2370	
F-GSRE	Robin DR.400/160 Chevalier	2386	
F-GSRF	Robin DR.400/120 Dauphin 2+2	2390	
F-GSRG	Robin DR.400/120 Dauphin 2+2	2373	
F-GSRH	Robin R.2160 Alpha Sport	325	
F-GSRI	Robin DR.400/160 Chevalier	2394	
F-GSRJ	Robin DR.400/120 Dauphin 2+2	2380	
F-GSRK	Robin DR.400/120 Dauphin 2+2	2395	
F-GSRL	Robin DR.400/180 Régent	2368	
F-GSRM	Robin DR.400/200R Remo 200	2287	F-WGXT
	(Formerly DR.400/185V6 test aircraft)		
F-GSRN	Robin DR.400/120 Dauphin 2+2	2396	
F-GSRO	Robin DR.400/120 Dauphin 2+2	2377	
F-GSRP	Robin DR.400/120 Dauphin 2+2	2397	
F-GSRQ	Robin DR.400/120 Dauphin 2+2	2400	
F-GSRR	Robin DR.400/140B Dauphin 4	2393	
F-GSRS	Robin DR.400/120 Dauphin 2+2	2378	
F-GSRT	Robin DR.400/180 Régent	2399	
F-GSRU	Robin DR.400/120 Dauphin 2+2	2404	
F-GSRV	Robin DR.500/200i Président	0009	
F-GSRX	Robin HR.200/120B	330	
F-GSRY	Robin HR.200/120B	327	
F-GSRZ	Robin HR.200/120B	328	
F-GSSA(2)	Lindstrand LBL-77AHAFB	748	
F-GSSB	Thunder AX7-77A HAFB	4065	
F-GSSC	Robin DR.400/120 Dauphin 2+2	2338	
F-GSSF	Chaize JZ.40F16 HAFB	154	(F-GPSF)
F-GSTA	Airbus A300-608ST Beluga "1"	001/655	F-WAST
F-GSTB	Airbus A300-608ST Beluga "2"	002/751	F-WSTB
F-GSTC	Airbus A300-608ST Beluga "3"	003/765	F-WSTC
F-GSTD	Airbus A300-608ST Beluga "4"	004/776	F-WSTD
F-GSTE	Schröder Fire Balloons G HAFB	679	
F-GSTF	Airbus A300-600ST Beluga "5"	005/796	F-WSTF
F-GSTH	Aérospatiale AS.355N Ecureuil 2	5649	
F-GSTJ	Fournier/Euravial RF.47	02	F-WWTJ
F-GSTM	Mudry CAP.10B	128	Fr.AF
F-GSTT	Robin DR.400/120 Dauphin 2+2	1906	G-BPTT
F-GSTY	Robin DR.400/120 Dauphin 2+2	1876	D-EDTY
F-GSTZ	Mauls MX-7-180 Star Rocket	11045C	OO-LVL
F-GSUK	Sukhoi SU-31 (Reservation 12.04)	unkn	
F-GSUN	Boeing 747-312	23030	N119KE
			(9V-SKE)
			(9V-SQX)
F-GSUP	Mudry CAP.10B	7	Fr.AF
F-GSUR	Robin DR.400/120 Dauphin 2+2	2524	
F-GSVA	Piper PA-28-181 Archer II	28-8190111	HB-PFX
			N8309K
F-GSVC	Beech 1900D (Reservation)	UE-340	N23317
F-GSVI	SIGA MA-26 Pilatre de Rozier HAFB	110	
F-GSVM	Balloon reservation		
F-GSVU	Airbus A319-133CJ	1256	(F-GVBG)
			D-AVYZ
			(VP-BCS)
			D-AVYZ
			F-WWIF
			D-AVYZ
F-GSYA	Aerospatiale AS.365N2 Dauphin 2	6220	JA9913
F-GSYD	Fouga CM.170 Magister	455	F-WSYD
			Fr.AF
F-GSYL	Cameron N-105 HAFB	4509	
F-GSYR	Cameron Z-120 HAFB	10609	

F-GSYS	Piper PA-34-220TSeneca V	3449091	G-CBOB
			N9ZB
			(G-CBOB)
			N61HB
			N9500N
F-GSZA	SOCATA TB-200 Tobago XL	1597	F-OHDL
F-GSZB	SOCATA TB-20 Trinidad	1886	
F-GSZC	SOCATA TB-10 Tobago	1823	
F-GSZD	SOCATA TB-20 Trinidad	1904	
F-GSZF	SOCATA TB-20 Trinidad	1910	
F-GSZG	SOCATA TB-20 Trinidad	1437	CS-DAM
			F-GLFJ
F-GSZH	SOCATATB-10 Tobago	1928	
F-GSZI	SOCATA TB-20 Trinidad	1916	(N678TB)
F-GSZJ	SOCATA TB-20 Trinidad (formerly T-tail version)	1227	F-WHGQ
F-GSZM	SOCATATB-9 Tampico GT	2011	
F-GSZN	SOCATA TB-20 Trinidad	2037	
F-GSZP	SOCATA TB-20 Trinidad	2059	
F-GSZS	SOCATATB-20 Trinidad	2138	
F-GSZU	SOCATATB-9 Tampico	2146	
F-GSZV	SOCATATB-9 Tampico	2143	
F-GSZX	SOCATATB-9 Tampico	1833	5N-. . .
			F-OIDF
F-GSZY	SOCATATB-10 Tobago	1892	
F-GTAD	Airbus A321-111	777	D-AVZI
F-GTAE	Airbus A321-211	796	D-AVZN
F-GTAH	Airbus A321-211	1133	D-AVZD
F-GTAI	Airbus A321-211	1299	D-AVZP
F-GTAJ	Airbus A321-211	1476	D-AVZP
F-GTAK	Airbus A321-211	1658	D-AVZP
F-GTAL	Airbus A321-211	1691	D-AVZY
F-GTAM	Airbus A321-211	1859	D-AVZY
F-GTAN to GTAZ Reserved for A.321s for Air France			
F-GTBA	Aérospatiale AS.350B2 Ecureuil	2577	F-OGRY
F-GTBB	Aerostar S-49A HAFB	S49A-3031	D-OAUR
			D-Aurora
F-GTBE(2)	Aérospatiale AS.350B2 Ecureuil	3215	
F-GTBF	Hughes 269C	77-0616	G-BXHI
			G-GBHH
			TF-HRH
			TF-HHO
			N45CD
			N9250F
			(N51CC)
F-WTBM	SOCATA TBM-700	01	
	(Listed erroneously as F-WTBN in DGAC records and marks therefore re-allocated as in next entry)		
F-GTBM(2)	Cameron C-70 Concept HAFB	10250	
F-GTBR	Robin DR.500/200i Président	0008	
F-GTBS	Thunder AX7-77A HAFB	4292	
F-GTBY	Partenavia P.68B	43	F-BXLI
F-GTCB	Boeing 727-200 (Reservation)		
F-GTCC	Airbus A300B4-203 (Reservation .99)	219	N474AS
			RP-C3005
			F-WZMV
F-GTCF	Piper PA-34-220TSeneca V	3449145	N9521N
			N41638
F-GTCG	Chaize JZ22F12 HAFB	145	
F-GTCH	Aérospatiale AS.365N3 Dauphin 2 (Res 11.04)	6710	
F-GTCM	Schweizer 300CB	0072	N69A
F-GTCN	SOCATA MS.893E Rallye 180GT	12532	F-ZBBX
	(Reservation .02)		F-BVZL
F-GTCP	Cameron N-90 HAFB	10271	
F-GTCR	Beech C90A King Air	LJ-1660	N4470M
F-GTCS	Piper PA-32R-301T Saratoga II TC	3257038	N9503N
	(Written-off 25.3.04)		
F-GTCT	Hughes 369E	0033E	D-HMEB
			OE-XFB
			D-HGTJ
			G-TMJH
F-GTDB	Wassmer WA.52 Europa	78	D-EINA
F-GTDC	Airbus A300B4-203 (Reservation .99)	unkn	
F-GTDD	Robin DR.400/180 Régent	2398	
F-GTDM	Cessna U206F Stationair	Us0602340	OO-HPD
			(F-GNMS)
			OO-HPD
			(PH-TXM)
			OO-HPD
			N88JP
			(N2095U)
F-GTDN	SIGA MA-40 Pilatre de Rozier HAFB	109	D-OTAB(2)
F-GTDR	Robinson R-22M2 Mariner	2604M	(F-GRLB)
F-GTDS(2)	Cessna T303 Crusader	T30300025	F-GJMK
			N9550T
F-GTDV	Aérophile 5500 Tethered Gas Balloon	015	
F-GTEA	Wassmer WA.51 Pacific (Reservn .04)	06	F-BTEA
F-GTEB	Robinson R-22B2 Beta	3517	
F-GTEF	Beech 200 Super King Air	BB-560	LN-MAA
			N200NA
			N72GA
			C-FDLO
			N38DD
F-GTEM	Beech 300 Super King Air	FL-80	PH-BRN
			N8275D
F-GTET	Cameron Z-150 HAFB	10246	
F-GTEZ	Piper PA-28-181 Archer II	2890165	D-ETAP
			N9195B

F-GTFA	Robin DR.400/160 Chevalier	2376	
F-GTFM	Piper PA-46-310P Malibu (Reservn .04)	46-8408041	D-EKVH
			HB-PKB
			(D-EIDN)
			HB-PKB
			D-ERAS
			HB-PKB
			(D-ERAS)
			HB-PKB
			D-ELBU
			N43467
F-GTFP	Sud Aviation SA.318CAlouette Astazou	2157	ALAT
F-GTGA	Aérospatiale AS.350B3 Ecureuil	3466	
F-GTGB	Eurocopter EC.120BColibri	1186	
F-GTGE	Cameron N-105 HAFB	4749	
F-GTGR	Robinson R-44 Raven II	10499	
F-GTGT	Robinson R-22 Beta	2296	N679BH
			LQ-BJY
F-GTGV	Raven RXS-8 HAFB	RXS8-3102	
F-GTGX	Diamond DA42 Twin Star (Reservn 12.04)	unkn	
F-GTHA	Pilatus PC-6/B2-H4 Turbo Porter	939	HB-FMF
			N939WA
			HB-FMF
F-GTHB	Robin DR.300/108 2+2	510	OO-FWB
			F-BSLB
F-GTHC	Diamond DA 20-A1 Katana	10309	N309DA
F-GTHD	Fouga CM.170 Magister (Res 1.99, stored)	530	Fr.AF
F-GTHH	Cessna 172S (Reservation .00)	unkn	
F-GTHL	SNCASE SE.313B Alouette II (Reservation 8.02)	1359	F-ODZR
			ALAT
F-GTHR	Aérospatiale AS.350B2 Ecureuil	2629	HB-XQU
			OE-XHK
F-GTIE	Aérospatiale AS.350B3 Ecureuil	3410	
F-GTIM	Lindstrand LBL-69A HAFB	491	
F-GTIS	Wörner FKP-380/STU Gas Balloon	6206	
F-GTIV	Cameron N-77 HAFB	4606	
F-GTJA	Ultramagic M-105 HAFB	105/107	
F-GTJB	Cameron A-250 HAFB	3928	
F-GTJC	Cessna 172S	172S8277	N7273H
F-GTJF	Dassault Falcon 50	246	TC-YSR
			N246FJ
			F-WWHF
F-GTJH	Cameron Z-120 HAFB	10587	
F-GTJM	SOCATA TBM-700	145	
F-GTJP	Robinson R-44 Astro	0590	
F-GTJR	Robin DR.400/120 Dauphin 2+2	2459	
F-GTKJ	Beech 1900D	UE-348	N23406
F-GTLC	Ultramagic N-210 HAFB	210/08	
F-GTLF	Hughes 369E	0344E	LN-OMZ(2)
			SE-JAR
			OH-HET
F-GTLG	Reims/Cessna FR182 Skylane RG	FR1820056	N111ES
			F-GCYB
F-GTLL	SNCASE SE.313B Alouette II	1181	ALAT
F-GTLP	Agusta A.109C (W/o 1.11.02)	7612	D-HLAT
			3A-MIS
F-GTLR	Robinson R-44 Astro	0433	G-XPTS
F-GTLY	McDonnell-Douglas DC-10-30	46954	F-ODLY
			F-GKMS
			SE-DFH
			ZK-NZS
			CC-CJS
			ZK-NZS
			(N85NA)
			ZK-NZS
F-GTLZ	McDonnell-Douglas DC-10-30	46869	F-ODLZ
	(Reservation .99)		SE-DFD
			(SE-DEA)
F-GTMA	Chaize JZ.25F12 HAFB	148	
F-GTMC	SNCASE SE.3130 Alouette II	1668	ALAT
F-GTMD	Cessna 525 CitationJet	525-0312	
F-GTME	CEA DR.253B Régent	179	F-OCQE
F-GTMF	Ultramagic M-130 HAFB	130/40	
F-GTML	Piper PA-32R-301T Turbo Saratoga SP	32R-8029109	CN-TKA
			F-GDQA
			OO-JSM
			N82542
F-GTMP	Robin DR.400/120 Dauphin 2+2	2444	
F-GTMR	Robin DR.500/200i Président	20	
F-GTNI	Schröder Fire Balloons G 30/24 HAFB	906	D-OTNI
F-GTNY	Schröder Fire Balloons Gas Bottle SS HAFB	680	
F-GTOD	Dassault Falcon 10	155	N725PA
			(N110TP)
			D-CIEL
			(N220FJ)
			F-WZGC
F-GTOJ	Mudry CAP.232	38	F-WQOM
F-GTOL	Ultramagic M-145 HAFB	145/35	
F-GTOM	Boeing 747SP-44	21253	LX-ACO
	(Reserved as ZS-OTW 8.01)		CN-RMS
			ZS-SPD
F-GTOU	Cameron C-80 HAFB	4177	
F-GTOY	Aérospatiale AS.350B Ecureuil	1030	C-FBKW
			N7091U
			C-FBKW
			N90033
F-GTPA	Robin DR.400/180 Régent	2405	

F-GTPB	Robin DR.400/180 Régent	2406	
F-GTPC	Robin DR.400/120 Dauphin 2+2	2402	
F-GTPD	Robin DR.400/120 Dauphin 2+2	2417	
F-GTPE	Robin DR.400/160 Major	2413	
F-GTPF	Robin DR.400/120 Dauphin 2+2	2416	
F-GTPG	Robin DR.400/160 Major	2409	
F-GTPH	Robin DR.400/180 Régent	2410	
F-GTPI	Robin DR.400/140B Dauphin 4	2422	
F-GTPJ	Robin DR.400/140B Dauphin 4	2432	
F-GTPK	Robin DR.400/140B Dauphin 4	2421	
F-GTPL	Robin DR.400/160 Major	2408	
F-GTPM	Robin DR.400/120 Dauphin 2+2	2425	
F-GTPN	Robin DR.400/180 Régent	2435	
F-GTPO	Robin HR.200/120B	340	
F-GTPP	Robin DR.400/160 Major	2411	
F-GTPR	Robin HR.200/120B	333	
F-GTPS	Robin DR.400/120 Dauphin 2+2	2427	
F-GTPT	Robin DR.400/180 Régent	2440	
F-GTPU	Robin DR.400/160 Major	2424	
F-GTPV	Robin DR.400/180 Régent	2438	
F-GTPX	Robin DR.400/180 Régent	2436	
F-GTPY	Robin DR.400/120 Dauphin 2+2	2437	
F-GTPZ	Robin DR.400/160 Major	2403	
F-GTQB	SOCATA TB-20 Trinidad	2095	N221H
F-GTQC	SOCATA TB-20 Trinidad	2130	F-OIUH
F-GTQD	SOCATA TB-20 Trinidad	2132	F-OIUJ
F-GTQF	SOCATA TB-10 Tobago	2094	
F-GTQG to F-GTQZ Reserved for SOCATA 11.02			
F-GTRA	Ultramagic S-105 HAFB (Envelope destr. 3.02)	105/51	
F-GTRB	Fairchild Swearingen SA-227AC Metro III	AC-519	EC-GJV
			F-GHVE
			HB-LNE
			N31083
F-GTRC	Kubicek BB-22 HAFB	278	OK-0278
F-GTRD	Aérospatiale AS.350B2 Ecureuil	9063	
F-GTRE(2)	Aérospatiale AS.355N Ecureuil 2	9610	
F-GTRG	Robinson R-44 Raven II	10154	N75284
F-GTRI	Ultramagic M-105 HAFB	105/115	
F-GTRJ	Agusta A.109C	7623	I-CRBM
			I-CRBN
F-GTRK	Aérospatiale AS.350B3 Ecureuil	9048	
F-GTRO	Cameron A-250 HAFB	10317	
F-GTRQ	SIGA MA-26 Pilatre de Rozier HAFB	135	
F-GTRS	Aérospatiale AS.355N Ecureuil 2	5686	
F-GTRY	Cessna 525 CitationJet	525-0359	
F-GTSG	Embraer EMB.120ER Brasilia	120087	PH-BRS
			OO-DTG
			PT-SME
F-GTSH	Embraer EMB.120RT Brasilia	120104	OO-DTH
			PT-SMW
F-GTSI	Embraer EMB.120RT Brasilia	120123	OO-DTJ
			PT-SNP
F-GTSJ	Embraer EMB.120RT Brasilia	120176	OO-DTL
			PT-SQO
F-GTSK	Embraer EMB.120RT Brasilia	120213	OO-MTD
			(OO-DTM)
			PT-SSH
F-GTSN	Embraer EMB.120ER Brasilia	120099	LX-RGI
			F-GFER
			PT-SMR
F-GTSO	Embraer EMB.120ER Brasilia	120097	(F-GVMA)
			LX-NVL
			F-GFEQ
			PT-SMP
F-GTTB	Aerospatiale AS.350B Ecureuil	9078	
F-WTTH	Aérospatiale SA.365N4/Eurocopter EC.155B Dauphin 2 (Reservation .01)	6530	F-WQEZ
F-GTTZ	Aérospatiale AS.365N3 Dauphin 2	9001	F-WQEG
F-GTUI	Boeing 747-422	26875	N186UA
F-GTVC	Beech 1900D	UE-349	N23430
F-GTVE	Aerosopatiale AS.355F2 Ecureuil 2	5378	DQ-FGH
			F-WYMT
F-GTVM	Beech 58 Baron	TH-1944	N3234X
F-GTVY	Robin DR.400/140B Dauphin 4	2019	F-GJZN
F-GTXU	Robin DR.400/120 Dauphin 2+2	2419	
F-GTXV	Robin DR.400/120 Dauphin 2+2	2420	
F-GTYA	SOCATA TB-20 Trinidad	2150	(F-GMQP)
F-GTYB	SOCATA TB-20 Trinidad	2153	
F-GTYC	SOCATA TB-20 Trinidad	2154	
F-GTYD	SOCATA TB-20 Trinidad	2157	
F-GTYE	SOCATA TB-20 Trinidad	2159	
F-GTYF	SOCATA TB-20 Trinidad	2162	
F-GTYG	SOCATA TB-20 Trinidad	2163	
F-GTYH	SOCATA TB-20 Trinidad	2170	
F-GTYI	SOCATA TB-20 Trinidad	2185	
F-GTYJ	SOCATA TB-20 Trinidad	2186	
F-GTYK to F-GTYS Reserved for S.E.F.A.			
F-GTYT	Cameron N-90 HAFB	4461	
F-GTYU to F-GTYZ Reserved for S.E.F.A.			
F-GTZC	Robin DR.500/200i Président	22	
F-GTZD	Robin DR.400/160 Major	2442	
F-GTZE	Robin HR.200/120B	342	
F-GTZH	Robin DR.400/120 Dauphin 2+2	2455	
F-GTZI	Robin DR.400/120 Dauphin 2+2	2443	
F-GTZK	Robin DR.400/120 Dauphin 2+2	2451	
F-GTZL	Robin DR.400/160 Major	2460	
F-GTZN	Robin HR.200/120B	351	

F-GTZO	Robin DR.400/120 Dauphin 2+2	2458	
F-GTZP	Robin DR.400/140B Dauphin 4	2461	
F-GTZQ	Robin DR.400/180 Régent	2446	
F-GTZR	Robin DR.400/140B Dauphin 4	2463	
F-GTZS	Robin DR.400/120 Dauphin 2+2	2464	
F-GTZT	Robin DR.400/180 Régent	2452	
F-GTZU	Robin DR.400/120 Dauphin 2+2 (Dismantled .03)	2486	
F-GTZX	Robin DR.400/180 Régent	2469	
F-GTZY	Robin DR.400/160 Major	2445	
F-GTZZ	Robin DR.400/180 Régent	2462	
F-GUAA	Airbus A321-211	808	G-JSJX D-AVZP
F-GUAB	SOCATA TB-10 Tobago	1721	
F-GUAC	SOCATA TB-10 Tobago	1720	
F-GUAF	SOCATA TB-20 Trinidad	2181	
F-GUAH	Robinson R-44 Raven II	10110	
F-GUAJ	Dassault Falcon 50	169	I-SNAB F-WPXD
F-GUAL	Robin HR.100-210	169	F-OCQU
F-GUAM	Embraer EMB.145MP	145266	PT-SIY
F-GUAN	Cessna FA150K Aerobat	FA1500019	OH-CBV
F-GUAR	Piper PA-28-161 Cherokee Warrior II (Reservation 8.04)	28-7816576	PH-ANI N31685
F-GUAS	Pilatus PC-6/B2-H2 Turbo Porter	557	N184L ST-AGR N184L
F-GUAT	Mudry CAP.10B	8	Fr.AF
F-GUAY	Cameron N-105 HAFB	4694	
F-GUBA	Embraer EMB.145MP	145398	PT-SQV
F-GUBB	Embraer EMB.145MP	145419	PT-STQ
F-GUBC	Embraer EMB.145MP	145556	PT-SZP
F-GUBD	Embraer EMB.145MP	145333	PT-SMZ
F-GUBE	Embraer EMB.145MP	145668	PT-S . .
F-GUBF	Embraer EMB.145MP	145669	PT-S . .
F-GUBG	Embraer EMB.145MP	145890	PT-SYD

F-GUBH to F-GUBZ Reserved for Regional Airlines

F-GUCA	Aérospatiale AS.350B3 Ecureuil	3558	F-WQDC
F-GUCC	Cameron C-60 Concept HAFB	3880	LX-OIO
F-GUCE	Robinson R-44 Astro	0551	
F-GUCF	Mudry CAP.231 (Reservation 12.04)	09	CN-ABL
F-GUCG	SNCASE SE.313B Alouette II	1506	ALAT
F-GUCP	Robinson R-22B2 Beta	3374	EI-CZI N71849
F-GUCT	Cessna F172H (Reservation .04)	F172-0489	D-ENFA(3)
F-GUDC	Dassault Falcon 2000EX	49	F-WWGN
F-GUDJ	Piper PA-36-285/400 Pawnee Brave	36-7560109	N9993P
F-GUDM	Lindstrand LBL-120AHAFB	760	
F-GUEA	Embraer EMB.145MP	145342	PT-SNI
F-GUFD	Embraer EMB.145MP	145197	
F-GUFP	Beech B200 Super King Air	BB-1698	N32287
F-GUFR	SIGA MA-30 Pilatre de Rozier HAFB	116	
F-GUGA	Airbus A318-111	2035	D-AUAD
F-GUGB	Airbus A318-111	2059	D-AUAF
F-GUGC	Airbus A318-111	2071	D-AUAG
F-GUGD	Airbus A318-111	2081	D-AUAH
F-GUGE	Airbus A318-111	2100	D-AUAI
F-GUGF	Airbus A318-111	2109	D-AUAJ
F-GUGG	Airbus A318-111	2317	D-AUAA
F-GUGH	Airbus A318-111	2344	D-AUAF
F-GUGI	Airbus A318-111	2350	D-AUAG

F-GUGJ to F-GUGZ Reserved for Airbus A318s for Air France

F-GUHD	Fouga CM.170 Magister (Reservation)	533	Fr.AF
F-GUIG	Lindstrand LBL-180A HAFB	932	
F-GUIL	Mooney M.20J Model 205	24-3131	F-GJIL
F-GUIX	Cessna 172R	17280207	N9402F
F-GUJA	Embraer EMB.145MP	145407	
F-GUJB	Robinson R-44 Raven	0826	D-HALR
F-GUJF	Sud Avn SA.318C Alouette Astazou	2096	ALAT
F-GUJL	SIGA MA-22 Pilatre de Rozier HAFB	126	
F-GUKQ	Robin DR.400/120 Dauphin 2+2	2453	
F-GULC	Robin HR.100-210	unkn	
F-GULF	Eurocopter EC.120B Colibri	1082	
F-GULL	Robin DR.400/180 Régent	2475	
F-GULM	Beech C90AKing Air	LJ-1226	N369B XA-RQM N2854B
F-GULP	Aérospatiale AS.350BA Ecureuil	1737	D-HFSC(2) SE-HNF
F-GUMA	Embraer EMB.145 (Reservation 2.00)	145405	
F-GUMC	Ultramagic N-300 HAFB	300/12	
F-GUMD	Piper PA-28-181 Archer III	2843243	N9524N
F-GUMR	Piper PA-32-301 Saratoga	32-8106040	(I- . . . .) F-GIMR TJ-AHF F-OBNX N8334B

F-GUNA to F-GUNZ Reserved for Airbus A318s for Air France

F-GUPB	Sud Avn SA.316B Alouette III	1779	EC-HXK F-BSUQ HC-BOX F-BSUQ
F-GUPC	Robinson R-22B2 Beta	3461	
F-GUPE	Beech 1900D	UE-248	N10882
F-GUPF	Aérospatiale AS.350B1 Ecureuil	1191	F-GIPN N3599X
F-GUPI	Robin DR.400/140B Dauphin 4	2519	
F-GUPM	Beech C90A King Air (Reservation .01)	LJ-1209	N53TJ N3030C N1571T
F-GUPP	Piper PA-28-161 Warrior III	2842155	N5349V
F-GUPS	Cameron A-120 HAFB	10248	
F-GUPT	Embraer EMB.145MP	145294	PT-SKL
F-GUPV	Robin DR.400/180 Régent	2478	(F-GNVP)
F-GURB	Robinson R-44 Raven II	10393	
F-GURJ	SNCASE SE.313B Alouette II	1741	ALAT
F-GURM	Robinson R-22 Beta	2507	G-BWAK N83311
F-GURS	Cessna 337G Skymaster	33701612	N53419
F-GURU	Sky 105-24 HAFB	152	
F-GUSB	Ultramagic M-77C HAFB	77/237	
F-GUSE	Aérospatiale AS.350B3 Ecureuil	9046	
F-GUSF	SIAI-Marchetti SF.260WL	440	BF8451 LARAF-440 I-RAIG
F-WUSH	Ballon Helium Globe Trott'Air 2	001	
F-GUSL	Aérospatiale AS.350B2 Ecureuil	9040	
F-GUST	Cessna 421B Golden Eagle	421B0968	OE-FMZ D-IGPZ G-BLAZ ZS-JOL N87534
F-GUTB	Cessna 182S	18280745	N2459F
F-GUTO	Piper PA-28-151 Cherokee Warrior	28-7615020	N4495X
F-GUTR	DHC-6 Twin Otter 300 (Reservation .01)	380	C-GHBP 6V-ADD
F-GUVA	Diamond DA40D Star	D4.012	
F-GUVB	Diamond DA40D Star	D4.014	
F-GUVC	Diamond DA40D Star (Permit)	D4.015	
F-GUVD	Diamond DA40D Star	D4.016	
F-GUVE	Diamond DA40D Star	D4.045	
F-GUVF	Diamond DA40D Star	D4.019	
F-GUVH	Diamond DA40D Star	D4.063	
F-GUVI	Diamond DA40D Star	D4.117	OE-VPW
F-GUVJ	Diamond DA40D Star	D4.119	OE-VPY
F-GUVK	Diamond DA40D Star	D4.121	
F-GUVL	Diamond DA40D Star	D4.110	
F-GUVM	Diamond DA40D Star	D4.139	
F-GUVN	Diamond DA40D Star	D4.140	
F-GUVO	Diamond DA40D Star	D4.141	
F-GUVQ	Diamond DA40D Star	D4.131	

F-GUVP to F-GUVZ Reserved for SCAPAerosport for Diamond DA 40TDIs

F-GUXA	Robin DR.400/120 Dauphin 2+2	2467	
F-GUXB	Robin DR.400/160 Major	2468	
F-GUXC	Robin DR.400/120 Dauphin 2+2	2465	
F-GUXD	Robin DR.400/140B Dauphin 4	2484	
F-GUXE	Robin DR.400/160 Major (Damaged 8.12.03)	2480	
F-GUXF	Robin DR.400/120 Dauphin 2+2	2473	
F-GUXG	Robin DR.500/200i Président	30	
F-GUXH	Robin DR.400/160 Major	2483	
F-GUXI	Robin DR.400/120 Dauphin 2+2	2476	
F-GUXJ	Robin DR.400/140B Dauphin 4	2489	
F-GUXK	Robin DR.400/180 Régent	2488	
F-GUXL	Robin DR.400/120 Dauphin 2+2	2491	
F-GUXN	Robin DR.400/140B Dauphin 4	2493	
F-GUXO	Robin DR.400/180 Régent	2496	
F-GUXP	Robin DR.400/180 Régent	2487	
F-GUXQ	Robin DR.400/120 Dauphin 2+2	2497	
F-GUXR	Robin DR.400/180 Régent	2498	
F-GUXS	Robin HR.200/120B	354	
F-GUXU	Robin R.2120U	368	
F-GUXV	Robin DR.400/120 Dauphin 2+2	2507	
F-GUXX	Robin R.2120U	347	F-WZZX
F-GUXZ	Robin DR.500/200i Président	34	
F-GUYA	Robin DR.400/160 Major	2492	
F-GUYC	Schröder Fire Balloons G 30/24	964	
F-GUYD	Fouga CM.170 Magister (Reservation)	465	Fr.AF
F-GUYH	Boeing 737-329	23771	F-WQUE CN-RDB OO-SDV
F-GUYS	Cameron C-90 Concept HAFB	10528	
F-GUYY	Cessna 172RG Cutlass RG	172RG0828	(F-OIII) 5V-TPI F-GDAC (N94618)
F-GUZE	Aérospatiale AS.355N Ecureuil 2	5548	N548JR XA-BBE F-WYML
F-GUZZ	Beech D-17S	4823	G-BUXU N9113H BuA.33024
F-GVAD	Robin DR.400/140B Major	1717	HB-KAZ
F-GVAF	Robinson R-44 Raven II	10234	G-SBRB
F-GVAG	Cameron Z-160 HAFB	10567	
F-GVAK	Robin DR.400/180 Régent	2456	
F-GVAL	Ultramagic S-90 HAFB	90/29	
F-GVAM	Lindstrand LBL-69A HAFB	752	
F-GVAQ	Aquila AT-01 (A-210)	AT01-104	F-WQQS D-EZUM(1)
F-GVAR	Aérospatiale SA.365N1 Dauphin 2	6256	JA6694 N29TH N6024P

F-GVAS	SNCASE SE.313B Alouette II	1060	ALAT
F-GVAT	Ultramagic N-180 HAFB	210/12	(F-GVAA)
F-GVAV	Robin DR.400/180R Remo 180	2466	
F-GVBA	SIGA MA-35 Pilatre de Rozier HAFB	145	
F-GVBB	SIGA MA-26 Pilatre de Rozier HAFB	142	
F-GVBC	Robinson R-22B2 Beta	3139	(F-GUDB)
F-GVBG	Airbus A319-133CJ (Reservation .00)	unkn	
F-GVBH	Robinson R-22B2 Beta	3425	N71938
F-GVBP	Ultramagic T-180 HAFB	180/30	
F-GVBR	Embraer EMB.120RTBrasilia	120014	LX-PTU
			(F-HAOC)
			LX-PTU
			OY-JRT
			F-WQGG
			F-GFIN
			PT-SIJ
F-GVCA	Lindstrand LBL-69A HAFB	790	
F-GVCB	SNCASE SE.313B Alouette II	1539	CN-HTL
			ALAT
F-GVCE	Aérospatiale AS.350B3 Ecureuil	3227	
	(Also reserved as F-GKCE)		
F-GVCH	Lindstrand LBL-90A HAFB	697	
F-GVCM	Ultramagic H-77 HAFB	77/174	(F-GUCM)
F-GVCP	Reims/Cessna F152	F15201615	D-EGUX
F-GVCT	Piper PA-38-112 Tomahawk II	38-82A0105	HB-PGV
F-GVDA	Dassault Falcon 2000	121	VP-BNT
	(Reservation .04)		F-ORAX
			F-WQBN
			HZ-KSDA
			F-WWVQ
F-GVDB	Cameron Z-90 HAFB	4945	
F-GVDC	Cameron Z-77 HAFB (Reservation 11.04)	10673	
F-GVDH	Robinson R-44 Raven II	10143	N75240
F-GVDL	SIGA MA-30 Pilatre de Rozier HAFB	127	
F-GVDM	Cameron N-90 HAFB	10149	
F-GVDT	SIGA MA-26 Pilatre de Rozier HAFB	149	
F-GVDV	Jodel D.140E Mousquetaire IV	193	D-EKGG
F-GVEP	Beech C90 KIng Air	LJ-683	N269SC
			PT-MPC
			N1583L
			(N711BE)
			N1583L
F-GVFA	Cessna 172R	17280868	N2448L
F-GVFE	Aérospatiale AS.365N Dauphin 2	6219	N29EH
			HL9234
F-GVFF	Mudry CAP.231	23	CN-ABN
F-GVFP	Aquila AT-01	AT01-119	
F-GVGH	Cessna T182T	T18208131	N51338
F-GVGS	Embraer EMB.145MP	145385	PT-SQJ
F-GVHD	Embraer EMB.145MP	145178	
F-GVHF	Aérospatiale AS.355N Ecureuil 2	5571	G-BZPO
			HS-YHF
			F-OHEZ
			F-WYMC
F-GVHS	Diamond DA20-A1 Katana	10287	N287DA
F-GVIB	Chaize JZ.25F24 HAFB	169	
F-GVIE	Lindstrand LBL-77A HAFB	712	
F-GVIF	Aérospatiale AS.365N Dauphin 2	6063	CamAF:XU-009
			N21277
			JA6665
			N7138H
			VR-BLI
			XT-BBG
			XT-MAO
			F-WKQI
F-GVIG	Bell 47G-2	2018	D-HFWP
			ST-AIU
			D-HOCA
F-GVIN	Cameron N-90 HAFB	4731	G-VINS
F-GVIP	Aérospatiale SA.365C1 Dauphin 2	5045	RP-C365
F-GVIT	SIGA MA-30 Pilatre de Rozier HAFB	117	
F-GVJA	Aérospatiale AS.365N Dauphin 2	5689	
F-GVJB	Pilatus PC-12/45	359	HB-FSN(3)
F-GVJC	Robinson R-44 (Reservation 11.04)	unkn	
F-GVJL	SNCASE SE.3130 Alouette II (Reservation .00)	1620	ALAT
F-GVJM	Piper PA-28-181 Archer III	2843101	OY-JAE
F-GVJP	Cessna 172N (Reservation .01, ntu)	17273282	OO-CIR
	(Also reserved as F-GPJT)		N172N
			C-GBJJ
			(N4656G)
F-GVKM	Diamond DA42 Twin Star (Reservn 3.05)	42.012	
F-GVLA	Hughes 269C	120-1003	C-GLTM
F-GVLD	SOCATATB-20 Trinidad	1088	N21FR
			SE-KBG
F-GVLH	Robinson R-44 (Reservation 12.04)	unkn	
F-GVLL	Sud Avn SA.316B Alouette III	1081	F-GSOS
			ALAT
F-GVMC	Cameron A-140 HAFB	1550	LX-BUS(2)
F-GVMD	Robinson R-44 Astro	0699	
F-GVMH	Robinson R-22 Beta (Reservation 9.04)	"0826"	
F-GVML	Bombardier BD.700-1A10 Global Express	9081	C-GXTX
			G-CBNR
			G-52-25
			C-GHGC
			(F-GVML)
			C-GHGC
F-GVMT	SIGA MA-22 Pilatre de Rozier HAFB	147	

F-GVNH	Robinson R-22B2 Beta (Reservation .04)	3655	
F-GVNT	Lindstrand LBL-180A HAFB	071	G-EVNT
F-GVOB	Bell 206B Jet Ranger II	2624	N921RB
			N5016G
F-GVOL	Ultramagic M-130 HAFB	130/17	
F-GVOS	SIGA MA-30 Pilatre de Rozier HAFB	136	
F-GVOZ	Piper PA-28-181 Archer II	2890061	HB-PLJ
			N9136B
F-GVPP	Robinson R-44 Raven II	10104	G-ILTY
F-GVPR	Aérospatiale AS.355N Ecureuil 2	5726	
F-GVPT	Cessna 172S	172S9322	N5338D
F-GVRF	CEA Jodel DR.1051 Sicile	511	OO-LRF
			F-BLRF
F-GVRG	Cessna F150H (Reservation .04)	F150-0232	D-EGDU
F-GVRH	Robinson R-22B2 Beta	3655	G-CCYW
F-GVRJ	Diamond DA 40D Star	D4.103	
F-GVRM	Beech 65-A90 King Air	LJ-121	N948RM
	(W/o 24.12.04)		N666FG
			(D-I . . .)
			N666FG
			F-GERH
			HB-GCU
			D-ILNA
F-GVSB	Robinson R-44 Raven	1258	
F-GVTA	Eurocopter EC.120B Colibri	1258	
F-GVTF	Pilatus PC-6/B2-H4 Turbo Porter	915	HB-FMI
			F-OGXM
F-GVTH	McDonnell-Douglas DC-9-21	47308	"F-WTVH"
			F-WQPC
			OY-KGF
F-GVTO	Lindstrand LBL-69A HAFB	757	
F-GVUE	Robinson R-44 Astro	0621	
F-GVUN	American AG-5B Tiger	10078	D-EPOS(1)
			N1194G
F-GVUS	Chaize JZ.25F12 HAFB	177	
F-GVVV	Airbus A300B4-103	069	5V-TTT
	(Stored St Nazaire in derelict state 9.03)		(PH-FNQ)
			N471AS
			G-BYYS
			RP-C3002
			F-WZEB
F-GVYH	Robinson R-22B2 Beta	3768	
F-GVZA	Aérospatiale/Alenia ATR-42-512	503	F-WQLJ
			N14445
			F-WWEN
F-GVZF	Aérospatiale/Alenia ATR-72-212	461	F-OGXF
			F-WWLP
F-GVZX	Aérospatiale/Alenia ATR-42-300	011	F-WVZX
			SP-EEA
			F-WQGF
			D-BAAA
			F-ODSA
			F-WWEQ
F-GVZY	Aérospatiale/Alenia ATR-42-300	080	F-WVZY
			SP-EEC
			F-WQID
			D-BCCC
			F-WWEF
F-GVZZ	Aérospatiale/Alenia ATR-42-300	055	SP-EEB
			F-WQGI
			D-BBBB
			F-ODSB
			F-WWEJ

F-WW . .)
F-WZ . .) These series are used as temporary registrations for test flights and deliveries. As the majority of applications are likely to be short-lived we are not attempting to provide a 'current' list but would welcome reports of confirmed usage.

F-GXAA	Chaize CS.3000F16 HAFB	198	
F-GXAC(2)	Pilatus PC-6/B2-H4 Turbo Porter	710	OO-NAC
	(Reservation 2.04)		HB-FFP
			OO-FWJ
			HB-FFP
F-GXAL	Cameron V-90 HAFB	4818	
F-GXBA	Chaize JZ.22F12 HAFB	125	F-WMTZ
F-GXBB	Robin DR.400/180 Régent	2499	
F-GXBC	Chaize JZ.22F24 HAFB (Reservation 11.04)	200	
F-GXBJ	Reims/Cessna F150M	F15001203	F-BXIJ
F-GXBM	Cameron Z-105 HAFB	10542	
F-GXBR	Robin DR.400/120 Dauphin 2+2	2485	
F-GXCB	Aérospatiale AS.350B3 Ecureuil	3544	
F-GXCF	Aquila AT-01 (Reservation .04)	AT01-127	
F-GXCG	Chaize JZ.22F12 HAFB	173	
F-GXCP	Mudry CAP.232	40	
F-GXCT	Lindstrand LBL-120A HAFB	994	
F-GXDB	Mudry CAP.232	33	
F-GXDI	Sky 105-24 HAFB	059	G-BXDW
F-GXDM	Cameron N-77 HAFB	10107	
F-GXEB	Chaize CS.3000F16 HAFB	110	OO-BBE
F-GXEK	Robin DR.400/120 Dauphin 2+2	2523	
F-GXES	Piper PA-42 Cheyenne III	42-8001043	D-IYES
			OY-YES
			N809AA
			HB-LRI
			N48WA
			N4089T
F-GXFL	Chaize JZ.30F16 HAFB	182	

F-GXFM	Cameron A-340 HAFB (Reservation 12.04)	10650	
F-GXFP	Sud Avn SA.318C Alouette Astazou (Reservation .04)	1952	ALAT
F-GXGA	Robin DR.400/180 Régent	2509	
F-GXGB	Robin DR.400/120 Dauphin 2+2	2512	
F-GXGC	Robin DR.500/200i Président	35	
F-GXGE	Robin DR.400/120 Dauphin 2+2	2514	
F-GXGH	Robin DR.400/120 Dauphin 2+2	2518	
F-GXGI	Robin DR.400/180 Régent	2520	
F-GXGL	Robin DR.400/140B Dauphin 4	2521	
F-GXGM	Robin DR.400/160 Major	2522	
F-GXGX	Cameron N-90 HAFB	4917	
F-GXHV	Chaize JZ.30F16 HAFB (Reservation 6.04)	193	
F-GXIL	Cameron N-90 HAFB (Reservation 7.04)	3080	G-RIZI
F-GXJA	Robin DR.400/160 Major	2474	
F-GXJL	Ultramagic N-180 HAFB	180/23	
F-GXJM	Chaize JZ.30F16 HAFB	164	
F-GXJP	Aérospatiale AS.350B3 Ecureuil	9055	
F-GXJR	Robin DR.400/120 Dauphin 2+2	2525	
F-GXLB	Chaize JZ.22F12 HAFB	181	
F-GXLL	Cameron N-65 HAFB	3037	LX-BCC
F-GXLS	Aérophile 5500 Tethered Gas Balloon	010	
F-GXMA	Piper PA-23 Apache (Reservation 11.01)	23-618	I-GEMA N6467C YV-P-EPY YV-T-ATP N10F
F-GXMC	Dassault Falcon 50	190	CS-TMJ I-CAFÉ F-WWHG
F-GXMD	Lindstrand LBL-105AHAFB	968	
F-GXMG	Chaize CS.3000F16 HAFB	190	
F-GXML	Chaize JZ.40F16 HAFB (Reservation 5.04)	192	
F-GXMQ	Hughes 269C	71-1086	OO-VMR D-HESY
F-GXMV	Aquila AT-01	AT01-126	
F-GXNA	SIGA MA-22 Pilatre de Rozier HAFB	144	
F-GXNN	Cameron Z-90 HAFB (Reservation 12.04)	10649	
F-GXOB	Aérospatiale AS.350B3 Ecureuil	3259	F-GUZZ (F-GNMB)
F-GXOL	Robin DR.400/120 Dauphin 2+2	2539	
F-GXPE	Aérospatiale AS.350B2 Ecureuil	9031	
F-GXPF	Chaize JZ.18F24 HAFB	170	
F-GXPP	Robin DR.400/140B Dauphin 4	2500	
F-GXRA	Chaize CS.3000F16 HAFB	183	
F-GXRC	Robinson R-22B Beta	3419	
F-GXRD	Robinson R-22B Beta	3420	
F-GXRE	Robinson R-44 Raven	1301	N71957
F-GXRF	Robinson R-44 Raven	1302	
F-GXRJ	Piper PA-34-220T Seneca III	3433130	HB-LQR
F-GXRR	Eurocopter EC.135T2 (Reservation 11.04)	0411	
F-GXRS	Chaize JZ.30F16 HAFB	156	
F-GXTB	Embraer EMB.135LR (Reservation .01)	unkn	
F-GXTJ	Chaize JZ.25F24 HAFB	172	
F-GXXL	SNCASE SE.313B Alouette II (Reservation .00)	1190	(F-GUSS) (F-GLRU) ALAT
F-GXYZ	Robin DR.400/120 Dauphin 2+2	2545	
F-GXZC	Chaize JZ.22F12 HAFB	179	
F-GYAA	Reims/Cessna F150M	F15001172	OO-SEW (YU-CCW) F-BVXJ
F-GYAC	Robin DR.400/160 Major	2533	
F-GYAF	Pilatus PC-6/B2-H4 Turbo Porter (Res 4.04)	810	HB-FGI
F-GYAI	Airbus A320-211	293	(F-GYAG) 9H-ABQ F-WWDZ
F-GYAK	Robin R.2120U	377	
F-GYAN	Airbus A321-111	535	HB-IOE D-AVZC
F-GYAO	Airbus A321-111	642	F-WQQV HB-IOG D-AVZH
F-GYAP	Airbus A321-111	517	HB-IOA D-AVZS
F-GYAQ	Airbus A321-111	827	HB-IOI D-AVZY
F-GYAR	Airbus A321-111	891	HB-IOJ D-AVZJ
F-GYAS	Airbus A319-115CJ	1999	D-AVYQ
F-GYAT	Cessna 404 Titan	404-0640	F-ZBDW F-BIPJ N5293J
F-GYAV	Robin DR.400/120 Dauphin 2+2	2566	
F-GYBA	Agusta A.109E Power (Permit 9.00)	11086	F-WYBA
F-GYBB	Robin DR.400/120 Dauphin 2+2	2548	
F-GYBQ(2)	Diamond DA20-A1 Katana (Reservn .054)	10261	OE-VPZ C-FXVI N264DA
F-GYCA	Dassault Falcon 20E-5	240/478	HB-VMN N240AT I-SNAG F-WLCX
F-GYCB	Schweizer 269C	S-1740	D-HCWK N41S
F-GYCC	Hughes 369E	0325E	D-HASP I-BNAR
F-GYCE	Beech B90 King Air (Reservation .04)	LJ-363	F-GICE N303WJ N43TC N81648 N95GR N959B
F-GYCG	Robin DR.400/180 Regent	2568	
F-GYCT	Lindstrand LBL-180A HAFB	1009	
F-GYDB	SIGA MA-26 Pilatre de Rozier HAFB	137	
F-GYDC	Mudry CAP.10C	308	
F-GYDD	Robin DR.400/140B Dauphin 4	2571	
F-GYDG	Aérospatiale AS.350BA Ecureuil	1300	F-OGXC F-GJHI
F-GYDH	Robinson R-44 Astro	1082	
F-GYDJ	Aérospatiale AS.350B3 Ecureuil	3719	F-GURR
F-GYDM	Lindstrand LBL-120A HAFB (Reservation 2.04)	263	(F-GUMP) G-BWDM
F-GYDX	Cameron V-77 HAFB (Reservation 2.04)	660	G-BIDU
F-GYES	Aérospatiale AS.355F1 Ecureuil 2	5042	G-KGMT G-PASE N57818
F-GYFA	Cessna 182S (Reservation .00)	unkn	
F-GYFK	Airbus A320-214	533	F-WQSY B-652L B-2224 HB-IJA F-WWIF
F-GYFL	Airbus A320-214	548	F-WQSZ B-653L B-2214 HB-IJC F-WWIJ
F-GYFM	Airbus A319-112	1068	F-WQRR G-CBOH OO-SSB D-AVWD
F-GYFN	Airbus A319-112 (Reservation 10.03)	1086	F-OHJX F-WIHF OO-SSC D-AVWL
F-GYGA	Robin DR.400/140B Dauphin 4	2567	
F-GYGD	SIGA MA.40 Pilatre de Rozier HAFB	156	
F-GYHB	Robinson R-22B2 Beta	3248	
F-GYIT	Mudry CAP.10C	312	
F-GYJL	Sud Avn SA.316B Alouette III	1527	ALAT
F-GYJM	Airbus A319-112	1145	F-WQRT G-CBOJ OO-SSF D-AVWH
F-GYJR	Robin DR.400/180 Régent	2526	
F-GYKA	Mudry CAP.10C	300	
F-GYKB	Robin DR.400/120 Dauphin 2+2	2540	
F-GYKC	Robin DR.400/140B Dauphin 4	2550	
F-GYKF	Robin DR.400/160 Major	2517	
F-GYKG	Robin DR.400/120 Dauphin 2+2	2547	
F-GYKH	Robin DR.400/160 Major	2541	
F-GYKI	Robin DR.400/140B Dauphin 4	2552	
F-GYKJ	Robin DR.400/180 Régent	2528	
F-GYKL	Robin DR.400/160 Major	2530	
F-GYKM	Robin DR.400/180 Régent	2536	
F-GYKN	Robin DR.400/120 Dauphin 2+2	2557	
F-GYKQ	Robin DR.400/120 Dauphin 2+2	2565	
F-GYKR	Mudry CAP.10C	314	
F-GYKS	Mudry CAP.10C	313	
F-GYKX	Robin DR.400/120 Dauphin 2+2	2558	
F-GYKY	Robin DR.400/140B Dauphin 4	2542	
F-GYKZ	Robin DR.400/140B Dauphin 4	2546	
F-GYLB	Eurocopter EC.120B Colibri	1340	
F-GYLC	Robin DR.400/140B Dauphin 4	2551	
F-GYLE	Eurocopter EC.120B Colibri	1182	
F-GYLR	Mudry CAP.10B	309	
F-GYMA	Cameron N-90 HAFB	3994	G-BWYC
F-GYMH	Cameron N-90 HAFB (Reservation 12.04)	3072	LX-GSM
F-GYMM	Robin DR.400/140B Major	2161	HB-KDH
F-GYMY	Eurocopter EC.120B Colibri	1311	
F-GYNN	Piper PA-28-181 Archer III	2843172	OO-KJA N4118T C-GDGG
F-GYOL	Dassault Falcon 50	88	LZ-010 F-GYOL F-WQBK N588FJ VP-CRT VR-CRT F-WQCP N188FJ XA-OVR N92FJ F-WZHU
F-GYOT	Robinson R-44 Astro	1068	
F-GYPB	Dassault Falcon 20E5	307	F-GKIS OE-GLL I-GCAL, HB-VDV F-WRQT
F-GYPE	Embraer EMB.135LR	145492	PT-SXL
F-GYPG	Robin DR.400/160 Major	2490	

F-GYPH	Aérospatiale AS.365N3 Dauphin 2	6694	F-WWOG
F-GYPM	Beech A36 Bonanza 36	E-3522	N936B
F-GYPP	Chaize JZ.40F16 HAFB	194	
F-GYPQ	Piper PA-46-350P Malibu Mirage	4622013	I-OBER
			N9154N
F-GYPR	Robin DR.400/160 Major	2532	
F-GYRA	Schweizer 269C	S-1604	N86G
F-GYRE	Aérospatiale AS.350B3 Ecureuil	3818	
F-GYRL	Robin DR.400/ 140B Major	2554	
F-GYRO	Mudry CAP.232	25	
F-GYRR	Aérospatiale AS.350B3 Ecureuil	3861	
F-GYSL	Dassault Falcon 20F	341	F-OHCJ
			VR-CDT
			N31IJS
			N78BC
			N51IWR
			N511WP
			N66GA
			N20FJ
			N4462F
			F-WMKF
F-GYSO	Robinson R-44 Raven II	10204	
F-GYTE	Piper PA-22-150 Tri-Pacer (Reservation .02)	22-3215	F-BATE(2)
			F-OATF
F-GYVC	Robin DR.400/120 Dauphin 2+2	2563	
F-GYVE	Eurocopter EC.120B Colibri	1226	
F-GYVM	SNCASE SE.313B Alouette II	1411	ALAT
F-GYXU	Robin DR.400/120 Dauphin 2+2	2494	
F-GYXV	Robin DR.400/120 Dauphin 2+2	2495	
F-GYYY(3)	Airbus A310-204	486	5B-DAX
			F-WWBN
F-GYZA	Mudry CAP.10C	305	
F-GYZB	Mudry CAP.10B	306	
F-GYZC	Mudry CAP.10C	310	
F-GYZD to F-GYZZ Reserved for DGAC / S.E.F.A.			
F-GZAA	Schröder Fire Balloons G26/24 HAFB	1123	
F-GZAB	Ultramagic M-130 HAFB	130/28	
F-GZAC	Aérospatiale AS.350B3 Ecureuil	9047	
F-GZAF	Lindstrand LBL-77A HAFB	1010	
F-GZAG	Diamond DA 20-A1-80 Katana	10175	C-FCAD
F-GZAL	Robin DR.400/120 Dauphin 2+2	2502	
F-GZAM	Cameron Z-90 HAFB	10589	
F-GZAS	Eurocopter EC.120BColibri	1375	
F-GZAT	Beech 200 Super King Air (Reservation .01)	BB-561	F-GULJ
			G-VICW
			G-ECAV
			N36GA
			N963JC
F-GZBA	Wassmer Jodel D.120A Paris-Nice	273	OO-MOI
			F-BMOI
F-GZBB	Robin DR.400/160 Major	2537	
F-GZBC	Piper PA-46-350P Malibu Mirage	4636132	N9898M
F-GZPM	Cameron Z-105 HAFB	10555	
F-GZBR	Sud Avn SA.316B Alouette III	1096	ALAT
F-GZCA	Airbus A330-203	422	
F-GZCB	Airbus A330-203	443	
F-GZCC	Airbus A330-203	448	
F-GZCD	Airbus A330-203	458	F-WWJH
F-GZCE	Airbus A330-203	465	F-WWKM
F-GZCF	Airbus A330-203	481	
F-GZCG	Airbus A330-203 (Stored pending delivery)	498	F-WWKI
F-GZCH	Airbus A330-203	500	
F-GZCI	Airbus A330-203	502	F-WWKJ
F-GZCJ	Airbus A330-203	503	
F-GZCK	Airbus A330-203	516	
F-GZCL	Airbus A330-203	519	
F-GZCM	Airbus A330-203	567	F-WWYT
F-GZCN	Airbus A330-203	584	
F-GZCO	Airbus A330-203	657	
F-GZCP	Airbus A330-203	660	
F-GZCQ to GZCZ Reserved for Airbus A330s for Air France			
F-GZDF	Cameron Z-250 HAFB (Reservation 11.04)	10663	
F-GZDJ	Grumman G.164B Agcat	622B	N8227K
F-GZDL	Aquila AT-01	AT01-120	
F-GZDO	Pilatus PC-6/B1-H2 Turbo Porter	705	N705SA
			HS-CHV
			N62162
			XW-PGN
			HB-FFG
F-GZED	Aerotek Pitts S-2A	2063	N33RS
F-GZEN	Cessna 177 (Reservation .01)	17700111?	N8211G?
	(May be Reims/Cessna F177RG c/n F177RG0111, F-BVIM)		
F-GZEP	Cameron Colt 77A HAFB	10305	
F-GZFA	Chaize JZ.22F24 HAFB	176	
F-GZFS	SNCASE SE.313B Alouette II	1386	ALAT
F-GZGM	Hughes 369E	0309E	HA-MSH
F-GZGP	Piper PA-28-181 Archer II	28-8290065	D-EDTX
			N8467E
F-GZHH	Cameron Z-150 HAFB	10347	
F-GZIF	Robin R.1180T Aiglon	244	F-GCIF
F-GZIG	SAN Jodel D.140A Mousquetaire	46	OO-LCA
			F-BIZK
F-GZIN	SIGA MA-26 Pilatre de Rozier HAFB	159	
F-GZIT	Cameron V-90 HAFB	4878	
F-GZJF	SNCASE SE.313B Alouette II (Reservn .04)	1163	Fr.Navy
F-GZJH	Cameron Z-250 HAFB	10412	

F-GZJM	Swearingen SA226-T Merlin III	T-264	N422AG
			LX-LAP
			BelgAF:CF-04
			N5378M
			(N100JB)
			N5378M
F-GZJP	Aérospatiale AS.350B3 Ecureuil	3332	HB-ZCI
			F-WQDD
F-GZJX	Diamond DA42 Twin Star (Reservn 12.04)	unkn	
F-GZJY	Lindstrand LBL-69A HAFB (Reservn 7.04)	715	G-BZJY
F-GZLC	Cessna 550 Citation II	550-0190	F-BTEL
			N98715
F-GZLG	SIGA MA.30 Pilatre de Rozier HAFB (Res 1.04)	160	
F-GZMB	SIGA MA-40 Pilatre de Rozier HAFB	131	
F-GZMD	Lindstrand LBL-77A HAFB	666	
F-GZNM	SIGA MA-26 Pilatre de Rozier HAFB	141	
F-GZOB	Colt 69A HAFB	2601	
F-GZOO	Aérospatiale AS.350B2 Ecureuil	9012	
F-GZPB	Aérospatiale AS.355N Ecureuil 2	5738	F-WQDI
			F-WQDJ
F-GZPC	Cameron Z-105 HAFB	10678	
F-GZPE(2)	Piaggio P.180 Avanti	1064	
F-GZPP	Cameron N-133 HAFB	10387	
F-GZRB	SOCATA TBM-700	166	F-OHBZ
			OH-TJJ
			F-OHBZ
F-GZSB	Cameron O-90 HAFB	10594	
F-GZTL	Mooney M.20M TLS Model 257	27-0240	N424AT
F-GZUJ	Cessna 525A CitationJet CJ2	525A-200	N5203S
F-GZUT	Cameron C-80 HAFB	10397	
F-GZVE	Diamond DA 40D Star	D4.114	
F-GZYA	Robin DR.400/140B Dauphin 4	2124	HB-KDA
F-GZZB	Beech E90 King Air	LW-296	F-GETJ
	(Reservation .01)		N207CP
			N4424V
			YV-207CP
F-GZZZ(3)	Airbus A320-211	030	VH-HYH
			F-WWDI
F-HAAA	Beech E90 King Air	LW-175	F-BXSN
F-HAAC	Robin DR.400/120 Dauphin 2+2	2576	
F-HAAD	Robin DR.400/120 Dauphin 2+2	2577	
F-HAAE	Robin DR.400/120 Dauphin 2+2	2578	
F-HAAG(2)	Beech 200 Super King Air	BB-722	3A-MBD
			9Q-CFE
			OO-CFE
F-HAAM	Cessna 172S	172S8743	N35234
F-HABI	Diamond DA40DStar	D4.066	
F-HABJ	Diamond DA40DStar	D4.067	
F-HABK	Diamond DA40D Star	D4.071	
F-HABL	Diamond DA40D Star	D4.076	
F-HABM	Diamond DA40D Star	D4.077	OE-VPW
F-HABN	Diamond DA40D Star	D4.083	OE-VPW
F-HABO	Diamond DA40DStar	D4.132	
F-HABP	Diamond DA40D Star	D4.133	
F-HABQ	Diamond DA40D Star	D4.134	
F-HABR	Diamond DA40D Star	D4.136	OE-VPW
F-HACA	Cessna 550 Citation II	550-0182	N107CF
			(F- . . . .)
			N165MC
			N30XX
			F-GEFB
			N78TF
			F-GCSZ
			(F-BKFB)
			N88830
F-HACC	Cessna 172S	172S9753	N65766
F-HACF	Aquila AT-01	AT01-125	
F-HACL	Diamond DA20-A1 Katana	10041	OE-VPZ
			C-GRAY
			N843DF
			C-FWKM
F-HACV	Robin DR.400/120 Dauphin 2+2	2572	
F-HADP	Robin DR.400/180 Régent	2564	
F-HADR	Beech C90A King Air	LJ-1583	N902PL
F-HAEA	Aérospatiale AS.350B3 Ecureuil	3428	F-WWOP
F-HAEG	Aquila AT-01	AT01-123	D-EAQA
			(D-EFTT)
F-HAFG	Robin DR.400/140B Dauphin 4	2580	
F-HAFH	Eurocopter EC.120B Colibri	1395	F-WQDG
F-HAFL	Cessna 172S	172S8457	F-OJHG
			F-GTHG
			N2466G
F-HAFP	Cessna 172S	172S9384	N5358S
F-HAFR	Robin R.2120U	367	
F-HAIR	Dassault Falcon 50	37	F-GMCU
			I-SAME
			(I-CAIK)
			F-WZHM
F-HAJA	Cessna 172R	172R81161	N53413
F-HAJD	Cessna 525 Citation	525-0523	N51246
F-HALB	Eurocopter EC.120B Colibri	1394	F-WQDL
F-HALE	Piaggio P.180 Avanti	1060	I-FXRF
F-HALL	Aérospatiale AS.350B2 Ecureuil	2105	HB-ZCE
			D-HUBW
			G-PLME
			G-BONN

F-HALM	Dassault Falcon 50	134	F-GOCT N134FJ
F-HALS	Beech 1900D	UE-379	N31525
F-HAMV	Robin R.2120U	373	F-WQOZ
F-HAND	Aerospatiale AS.355N Ecureuil 2	5621	D-HLSM HS-YHG F-OHKG
F-HAOA	Cessna 525 CitationJet	525-0024	N525DJ F-GNCJ N13291
F-HAPB	Cessna T182T Turbo Skylane	182T08024	N3530T
F-HAPE	Beech 1900D	UE-367	N30515
F-HAPF	Robin R.2120U	366	
F-HAPP	Cessna 525A CirationJet CJ2	525A-0009	N525LC N5235G
F-HAPY	Cessna 182S	18280334	D-EEKB N9510P
F-HARA	Robin DR.400/140B Dauphin 4	2559	
F-HARJ	Cessna 172R	17280087	OY-PBS N5260M
F-HASC	Cessna 525 CitationJet	525-0177	G-OWRC G-OCSB N1280A (RP-C717) N1280A N5163C
F-HAXA	Dassault Falcon 900EX	12	F-WQBL N912EX (N900SB) N900EX N913FJ F-WWFJ
F-HAXY	Boeing 757-2K2	26635	F-WAXY N512TZ PH-TKC
F-HBAB	Airbus A321-211	823	F-WBAB G-VOLH D-AVZX
F-HBAC	Airbus A320-214	888	EC-GZE F-WWDG
F-HBAR	Robin DR.400/180 Régent	2549	
F-HBBB	Embraer EMB-120ER Brasilia	120209	EC-HUP F-GHEX PT-SSD
F-HBBM	Dassault Falcon 50	16	F-WQBL (F-GYBM) D-BFAR D-BIRD (N50M) F-WZHH
F-HBCA	Beech 1900D	UE-188	SE-KXV N1564J
F-HBCI	Robin DR.500/200i Président	41	
F-HBED	Eurocopter EC.120BColibri	1362	
F-HBFP	Hawker 800XP	258689	N36689
F-HBIL	Airbus A330-243	320	
F-HBOL	Dassault Falcon 900EX	107	F-WWFE
F-HCAT	Airbus A330-243	285	F-WWKB
F-HCDP	Robinson R-44 Raven (Reservation 3.05)	1152	HB-ZDZ
F-HCFX	Cessna 172S	172S9747	N65744
F-HCIR	Cirrus SR20	1464	N618CD
F-HEAD	Eurocopter EC.135T2	0285	
F-HEOL	Cessna 525A CitationJet CJ2	525A-0219	N5247U
F-HERO	Eurocopter EC.135T2	0274	
F-HHAM	Beech C90A King Air	LJ-1361	N5521T
F-HJAC	Boeing 747-312	23243	(F-OJAC) 9V-SKJ N123KJ (9V-SKJ)
F-HJCM	Beech C90A King Air	LJ-1098	N294TT F-GFCO N7218V
F-HJPC	Aérospatiale AS.350B Ecureuil	1153	F-GINV
F-HLCA	Eurocopter EC.135T2	0244	F-WLCA D-HKBS
F-HLCB	Eurocopter EC.135T2	0268	
F-HLCC	Eurocopter EC.135T2	0291	
F-HLIM	Cessna 560 Citation V (Reservn 2.05)	560-0683	N51042
F-HSEA	Boeing 747-422 (Reservn 2.05)	26877	F-WSEA N188UA
F-HSEX	Boeing 747-422 (Reservn 2.05)	26878	N189UA
F-HSUN	Boeing 747-422 (Reservn 12.04)	26880	N191UA
F-HUTC	Schweizer 269C-1	0167	

FRANCE d'OUTREMER

F-OAIZ	Raven-Europe S.60A HAFB	E-040	
F-OBJR	SOCATA MS.893E Rallye 180GT Gaillard	12647	F-BXMR
F-OBYN	Piper PA-31-350 Chieftain	31-8152005	N4046M
F-OCEY	Piper PA-38-112 Tomahawk	38-78A0692	N2442A
F-OCFA	Piper PA-23-250 Aztec C	27-2788	N10F (N5674Y)
F-OCFE	Cessna 150E	15061471	N4071U
F-OCFK	Cessna 310P	310P0053	N5753M
F-OCFL	Piper PA-23-250 Aztec C *(Accident 16.12.03)*	27-3856	VH-SVZ N6560Y
F-OCFN	Piper PA-28-140 Cherokee	28-24166	N11C
F-OCFP	Piper PA-31 Turbo Navajo	31-370	VH-SVY N9279Y
F-OCGU	Cessna U206A Super Skywagon	U206-0492	N8092Z
F-OCLJ	Piper PA-32-260 Cherokee Six	32-1015	
F-OCMJ	Cessna 182J	18257111	N3011F
F-OCNX	Cessna 172K	17258463	N84411
F-OCOY	Britten-Norman BN-2AIslander	131	G-51-53
F-OCPR	Piper PA-28-140 Cherokee C	28-26922	N11C
F-OCPT	SOCATA MS.893A Rallye Commodore 180	11665	
F-OCQG	Sud Avn SA.318C Alouette Astazou	2219	
F-OCQO	Reims/Cessna F337F Super Skymaster (Reims-assembled 337F with US c/n 33701385)	F33700045	
F-OCQQ	Robin DR.400/180 Régent	740	
F-OCQX	Robin DR.400/180 Régent	916	
F-OCQZ	DHC-6 Twin Otter 300	412	
F-OCSO	Piper PA-23-160 Apache G	23-1988	CF-NMP N4463P
F-OCSP	SOCATA MS.894A Minerva 220	11997	(D-EMJJ)
F-OCUX	Reims/Cessna F172M	F17201009	
F-OCXA	Cessna 177B Cardinal	17702092	ZK-DSF
F-OCXB	Cessna 310Q	310Q1075	ZK-DRK N1222G
F-OCXP	Britten-Norman BN-2A-21 Islander	483	G-BDLF
F-OCXQ	Aérospatiale SA.342J Gazelle	1602	
F-OCXS	Hughes 369HS	106-0865S	
F-OCXU	Piper PA-28-161 Cherokee Warrior II	28-7816534	N9572N
F-ODBN	DHC-6 Twin Otter 300	470	
F-ODDZ	Cessna U206E Stationair	U20601633	5R-MEV (N9433G)
F-ODFC	Reims/Cessna F150M	F15001338	
F-ODGD	Cessna 152	15283539	ZK-EOZ (N53379)
F-ODGF	Cessna 152	15283590	ZK-ETB (N4710B)
F-ODGH	Cessna 207A Stationair 8	20700650	ZK-EOE N85020 (N75894)
F-ODGJ	Hughes 269C	70-0937	ZK-HPM
F-ODGK	Hughes 369HS	85-0763S	ZK-HPE (N222PF) N900Q
F-ODGQ	Aérospatiale AS.350B Ecureuil	2263	
F-ODGS	Piper PA-31T Cheyenne	31T-7720041	TS-LAZ LN-PAE (N82144)
F-ODGT	Piper PA-28-161 Warrior II	28-8616050	N9294A N9511N
F-ODGV	Robin ATL L	97	F-GFSQ
F-ODHL	Robin R.2112 Alpha	123	
F-ODHS	Cessna U206G Stationair II	U20603900	N7362C
F-ODIN	Cessna TU206G Turbo Stationair 6	U20604722	(N732TZ)
F-ODIV	Piper PA-38-112 Tomahawk	38-80A0058	N9656N
F-ODIX	Beech 58 Baron	TH-1016	
F-ODJD	SOCATA MS.893E Rallye 180GT Gaillard (Floats)	13202	
F-ODJJ	Cessna 172G	17254376	5R-MDR N11B (N4307L)
F-ODKR	Cessna TU206G Turbo Stationair 6	U20604562	N9757M
F-ODLB	Cessna 150K	15071137	ZS-FXM N5637G
F-ODLC	Aérospatiale SA.315B Lama	2635	
F-ODLF	Beech 58 Baron	TH-310	ZS-PTE N1041W
F-ODLI	Aérospatiale AS.350B1 Ecureuil	2063	F-WYMC
F-ODLJ	Aérospatiale SA.365C3 Dauphin 2	5079	D-HMKB
F-ODLP	Piper PA-31 Turbo Navajo B	31-756	F-BTCX N7234L
F-ODLR	Piper PA-28-161 Cadet	2841153	(F-GHBI)
F-ODLS	Piper PA-28-181 Archer II	2890084	F-GFYB
F-ODLU	Aérospatiale AS.350B1 Ecureuil	2242	
F-ODMM	Piper PA-31T Cheyenne II	31T-8020084	N2592V
F-ODMN	Aérospatiale SA.365C1 Dauphin 2	5047	F-GCJR
F-ODNL	Mudry CAP.10B	70	HB-SAI
F-ODNR	Mudry CAP.10B	139	
F-ODPA	Centrair ASW-20F	20151	
F-ODQI	Piper PA-31-350 Navajo Chieftain	31-7305065	F-BUOI F-ETAH
F-ODSE	Chaize CS.3000F16 HAFB	079	
F-ODSM	Piper PA-28R-201 Cherokee Arrow III	28R-7737084	N38223
F-ODSR	Aérospatiale SN.601 Corvette	35	YV-01CP YV-589CP F-GDAZ PH-JSC
F-ODSZ	SOCATA TB-10 Tobago	660	SE-IMZ N20HZ
F-ODTD	Raven-Europe S.60A HAFB	E-049	
F-ODTI	SNCASE SE.3130 Alouette II	1852	F-GBOC D-HOFO
F-ODTU	Raven Europe FS-83A HAFB	E-076	
F-ODTV	Raven Europe S-60A HAFB	E-077	
F-ODUN	Dornier 228-212 *(Stored)*	8197	D-CATS(1) D-CBDH(3)
F-ODUO	Piper PA-28-181 Archer II	28-8490065	N4355B
F-ODUS	Aérospatiale AS.350B Ecureuil	2098	

F-ODUY	Piper PA-28-181 Archer II	2890092	N9152X
F-ODVF	Airbus A310-304	445	
F-ODVG	Airbus A310-304	490	
F-ODYB	Dornier 228-212	8191	D-CORK
			D-CBDA(4)
F-ODYD	Aérospatiale/Alenia ATR-42-300	221	
F-ODYE	Aérospatiale/Alenia ATR-42-300	335	F-WWLW
F-ODYF	Britten-Norman BN-2A-26 Islander	309	G-BADK
			G-51-309
F-ODYG	Cessna 402B	402B0931	ZK-KAN
			N87138
F-ODYH	Cessna 402B	402B0585	ZK-DSB
			N1457G
F-ODYJ	SOCATA TB-10 Tobago	1193	
F-ODYL	SOCATA TB-10 Tobago	1192	
F-ODYM	Robinson R-22 Mariner	1908M	
F-ODYN	Cessna 152	15282982	C-GRXZ
			N46008
F-ODYO	Piper PA-28-151 Cherokee Warrior	28-7515153	ZK-DUV
			N9628N
F-ODYQ	SOCATA TB-20 Trinidad	1118	VH-LQJ
F-ODYU	Aérospatiale AS.350BA Ecureuil	1998	ZK-HZH
F-ODZH	Dornier 228-202K *(wfu?)*	8077	N2255Y
			VH-NSZ
			G-BMND
			D-CESI
			D-IESI
F-ODZJ	Boeing 737-53A	24877	F-GHXN
F-ODZP	SNCASE SE.3130 Alouette II	1573	ALAT
F-ODZQ	Robinson R-22 Beta	2094	N23340
F-ODZR	SNCASE SE.3130 Alouette II	1359	ALAT
F-ODZT	Schweizer 269C	S-1650	N86G
F-ODZV	Aérospatiale AS.355F2 Ecureuil 2	5310	JA9611
F-ODZX	Aerotek Pitts S-2A	2122	N5SV
F-ODZY	Boeing 737-33A	27452	
F-ODZZ	Boeing 737-39M	28898	N35153
			N1786B
F-OFDF	Airbus A330-223	253	HB-IQD
			F-WWKM
F-OGBL	Piper PA-23-160 Apache G	23-2006	N4484P
F-OGDS	Cessna 150H	15067214	N6414S
F-OGES	DHC-6 Twin Otter 300 *(W/o 24.3.01)*	254	N302MA
F-OGEV	Cessna 150K	15071815	N6315G
F-OGFC	Cessna P206E Super Skylane	P20600627	N5727J
F-OGFF	Piper PA-28-180 Cherokee F	28-7105138	
F-OGFR	Piper PA-28-140 Cherokee E	28-7225294	
F-OGGT	Beech 58 Baron	TH-514	
F-OGGX	Beech C23 Sundowner	M-1649	
F-OGHN	Piper PA-28R-200 Cherokee Arrow II	28R-7635342	
F-OGHQ	Cessna 177B Cardinal	17702522	N17238
F-OGHT	Hughes 269C	117-0643	F-GATL
F-OGHZ	Piper PA-28-181 Cherokee Archer II *(Cr.)*	28-7690351	N6142J
F-OGIC	Cessna A185F Skywagon	18503348	N6990H
F-OGIO	Piper PA-32-301 Saratoga	32-8006078	N82425
F-OGIU	Cessna A188B Agtruk *(W/o 17.1.03)*	18802399T	N4880R
F-OGJF	Piper PA-28-181 Archer II	28-8090333	
F-OGJG	Piper PA-28-236 Dakota	28-8011119	
F-OGJJ	Robin R.2160 Alpha Sport	184	
F-OGJT	Piper PA-23-250 Aztec E	27-7305050	N40245
F-OGJU	Piper PA-32-301 Saratoga	32-8106006	N8290U
F-OGKO	Piper PA-28-151 Cherokee Warrior	28-7715109	N5358F
F-OGKQ	Cessna 172P	17276311	N98571
F-OGNG	Cessna 152	15283030	N46319
F-OGNJ	Piper PA-28-161 Cherokee Warrior II	28-7816079	N47475
F-OGNK	Piper PA-23-250 Aztec F	27-7854054	N63917
F-OGNP	Cessna T188C AgHusky	T18803636T	N3372J
F-OGOB	Cessna 152	15281780	N67363
F-OGOC	Cessna 172M	17263038	N13913
F-OGOG	Reims/Cessna F406 Caravan II	F406-0026	
F-OGOL	Dornier 228-202K	8139	D-CACC
			(D-CBDS)
F-OGON	Grumman G.164B Agcat	54B	- ? -
			N48503
F-OGOQ	Dornier 228-201	8056	7P-LAL
			D-CAMI
F-OGOU	Aérospatiale AS.355F2 Ecureuil 2	5051	N281DB
			C-GLCA
			N281DB
			N5778C
F-OGOZ	Dornier 228-202K	8161	D-CBDR(2)
F-OGPB	Hughes 269C	76-0521	N42JW
F-OGPJ	Piper PA-28-161 Warrior II	28-7916379	V2-LCA
			VP-LCA
			N9507N
F-OGPM	Beech 58 Baron	TH-345	N1896W
F-OGPP	Piper PA-23-250 Aztec F	27-7654152	C-GPXX
			N9701N
F-OGPS	Aérospatiale AS.350B2 Ecureuil	2412	
F-OGPV	Piper PA-28-181 Archer II	28-8190091	N82978
F-OGQQ	Airbus A310-304	592	F-WWCN
F-OGQR	Airbus A310-304	593	F-WWCP
F-OGQT	Airbus A310-304	622	F-WWCD
F-OGRA	Piper PA-28-181 Archer II	28-8090354	N8233S
F-OGRB	Piper PA-23-250 Aztec F	27-7754102	N6570X
			- ? -
			N63771
F-OGRH	Piper PA-28-161 Cherokee Warrior II	28-7716282	N38864
F-OGRI	Aérospatiale AS.350B Ecureuil	1282	F-GHHK
			N3610U
F-OGRN	Ayres S.2R-T34 Turbo Thrush	T34-163	N3096S
F-OGRP	Aérospatiale AS.355F1 Ecureuil 2	5085	N900HH
			N57876
F-OGRT	Boeing 737-341	26854	(PP-VPC)
F-OGRV	Cessna 150L	15075755	N65980
F-OGRX	SOCATA TB-9 Tampico Club	1349	
F-OGSB	Raven Europe S-60A HAFB	E-191	
F-OGSK	Raven Europe S-66A HAFB	E-246	
F-OGSL	Raven Europe S-60A HAFB	E-235	
F-OGSU	Raven Europe S-60A HAFB	E-263	
F-OGUK	Piper PA-28-180 Cherokee G	28-7305323	CF-CCP
F-OGUR	Piper PA-28R-201 Arrow III	28R-7837041	C-FGWJ
			N9852K
F-OGUS	Aérospatiale AS.350B Ecureuil	1379	F-GIHA
			N5449C
F-OGUZ	Aérospatiale AS.350B2 Ecureuil	2684	(D-HWPA)
F-OGVA(2)	Dornier 228-212	8236	D-CBDB(7)
F-OGVB	GAF N-24A Nomad	0076FA	N4816C
	(Dismantled)		VH- IIK
F-OGVE(2)	Dornier 228-212	8237	D-CBDD(7)
F-OGVF	Cessna 150M	15078963	N704XU
F-OGVI (2)	Cessna U206G Stationair 6	U20604849	N734LN
F-OGVK	Cessna 150M	15078184	N9234U
F-OGVM	Cessna A188B Agtruck	18802804T	N731DA
F-OGVN	Partenavia P.68B *(Wrecked)*	155	F-GBLY
F-OGVO	Hughes 269C	86-0539	N911PD
			TF-ELI
			N911PD
F-OGVQ	Cessna TU206G Turbo Stationair 6	U20604854	N734NZ
			XB-ANA
			N734NZ
F-OGVT	Cessna 172N	17268788	N143ER
			N734EB
F-OGVX	Partenavia P.68B	39	G-BFVO
			SE-FUK
F-OGXA	Britten-Norman BN-2A-26 Islander	788	D-IHUG
			PH-PFS
			G-BDRV
F-OGXB	Britten-Norman BN-2A-2 Islander	303	D-IHVH
			G-AZUS
			G-51-303
			(N58JA)
F-OGXD	Cessna U206G Stationair 6	U20605007	N4622U
F-OGXE	Robin R.2160 Alpha Sport	290	F-GORE
F-OGXH	Reims FR172J Rocket	FR17200408	F-BUMI
F-OGXL	Cessna U206G Stationair 6	U20604129	F-GOSA
			OO-MTC
			N756JN
F-OGXN	CAARP CAP.10B	4	Fr.AF
F-OGXT	Piper PA-28-236 Dakota	28-7911116	N3009T
F-OGXU	Hughes 269C	118-0734	N58281
F-OGXX	Cessna 208B Grand Caravan	208B0557	(F-OHXI)
			N1268N
F-OGYC	Airbus A320-212	569	(JY-CAS)
			F-WWDG
F-OGYO	Airbus A310-324	568	F-WGYO
			OE-LAC
			F-WWCE
F-OGYP(2)	Airbus A310-324	442	N812PA
			F-WWCZ
F-OGYQ	Airbus A310-324	453	N817PA
			F-WWCK
F-OHAA	Dornier 228-212	8198	D-CDWK
			D-CBDK(4)
F-OHAF	Dornier 228-212	8199	D-CLOG
			D-CBDZ(2)
F-OHAJ	Piper PA-28R-201 Arrow III	28R-7837014	N47911
F-OHAK	Cessna 152	15285907	N95499
F-OHAL	Robin DR.400/160 Chevalier	812	F-BUHY
F-OHAM	Aérospatiale AS.350BA Ecureuil	2633	F-WYMP
F-OHAO	Aérospatiale AS.355F2 Ecureuil 2 *(Resvn)*	unkn	
F-OHAP	Piper PA-28-161 Warrior II	28-8516022	N43820
F-OHAV	Cessna 404 Titan	404-0216	HB-LOY
			OY-GAZ
			LN-MAI
			(SE-GYF)
			N88676
F-OHAY	Cessna U206G Stationair 6	U20604683	N732JK
F-OHAZ	Cessna 172N	17271145	N2077E
F-OHCB	Piper PA-28R-200 Cherokee Arrow II	28R-7635100	F-BXSD
			N9642N
F-OHCE(2)	Raven-Europe S-60A HAFB	E-288	
F-OHCH	Raven Europe S-60A HAFB	E-320	
F-OHCI	Raven-Europe S-60A HAFB	E-314	
F-OHCP	Beech 200 Super King Air	BB-831	F-ODUA
			N43WB
			N78011
			N7801L
F-OHCR	Piper PA-34-200T Seneca II	34-7670160	F-BXSQ
	(Reservation, not yet taken up)		
F-OHCU	Aérospatiale AS.350B3 Ecureuil	3288	F-GLJE
F-OHED	Aérospatiale AS.350B2 Ecureuil	2597	
F-OHEN	Aérospatiale AS.355F2 Ecureuil 2	5515	
F-OHEO	Aérospatiale AS.350B2 Ecureuil	2679	
F-OHFK	Sud Avn SA.316B Alouette III	1510	JRV23157

F-OHFO	Dassault Falcon 50EX	267	(D-BETI)
			F-WWHR
F-OHFR(2)	Airbus A320-212	189	G-UKLL
			C-GRYY
			G-BWCP
			N483GX
			F-WWDC
F-OHFU	Airbus A320-212	190	PH-DVR
			(SE-DVH)
			G-UKLJ
			G-BWKN
			N484GX
			F-WWDD
F-OHFV	Aérospatiale/Alenia ATR-42-300	012	F-WQJB
	(W/o in Kosovo 13.11.99)		N12MQ
			N420MQ
			F-WWED
F-OHFZ	Aérospatiale/Alenia ATR-72-212	469	HS-PGH
			F-OHLC
			F-WWLW
F-OHGB	Airbus A320-211	289	A40-MC
			TC-ONC
			9H-ABX
			F-WWBX
F-OHGC	Airbus A320-211	407	CS-TNF
			F-WWDH
F-OHGH	Robinson R-44 Clipper	0446	
F-OHGL	Aérospatiale/Alenia ATR-42-320	323	F-WWET
F-OHGT	Aérospatiale/Alenia ATR-72-212A *(Stored)*	698	F-WWEU
F-OHJD	Aérospatiale/Alenia ATR-42-500	556	F-WW . .
F-OHJF	DHC-6 Twin Otter 300	500	N929MA
F-OHJG	DHC-6 Twin Otter 300	603	Fr.AF
			C-GRQZ
F-OHJJ	Aérospatiale/Alenia ATR-42-512	614	F-WWLU
F-OHJK	Beech B200 Super King Air	BB-1544	N1094S
F-OHJM	Dornier 328-300	3129	D-BDXL(1)
F-OHJN	Aérospatiale/Alenia ATR-72-210	535	F-WWEC
F-OHJO	Aérospatiale/Alenia ATR-72-212A	553	F-WWLC
F-OHJP	Cessna R182 Skylane RG	R18200128	N7363Y
F-OHJR	Piper PA-23-250 Aztec E	27-7554087	VH-WJJ
			N54785
F-OHJS	Aérospatiale/AleniaATR-72-212A	696	F-WWES
F-OHJT	Aérospatiale/AleniaATR-72-212A	590	
F-OHJU	Aérospatiale/Alenia ATR-72-212A	563	F-WWEA
F-OHJX	Airbus A319-112	1086	F-WIHF
			OO-SSC
			D-AVWL
F-OHJY	Airbus A319-112	1124	F-WIHG
			OO-SSE
			D-AVYV
F-OHKG to OHKZ	*Reservations for Eurocopter*		
F-OHLJ	Airbus A300B4-203 *(Reservation .00)*	125	N472AS
			(F-GTDC)
			N472AS
			RP-C3003
			F-WZEO
F-OHLL	Airbus A300B4-203 *(Reservation .00)*	219	N474AS
			(F-GTCC)
			N474AS
			RP-C3005
			F-WZMV
F-OHLM	Cessna 150M	15078807	(F-GJJX)
	(Identity not confirmed; reservation .00)		ZS-JWW
			(N704RE)
F-OHLP	Airbus A340-211	014	F-WQRG
			OO-SCW
			F-GNIB
			F-WWJF
F-OHLQ	Airbus A340-212	022	F-WQRF
			OO-SCX
			F-GNIC
			(OO-SLH)
			F-WWJM
F-OHMB	Airbus A320-231	376	F-WWIK
F-OHMC	Airbus A320-231	386	F-WWBI
F-OHMD	Airbus A320-231	433	F-WWDC
F-OHME	Airbus A320-231	252	XA-RZU
			F-WWBD
F-OHMF	Airbus A320-231	259	XA-RYQ
			F-WWBK
F-OHMG	Airbus A320-231	260	XA-RYS
			F-WWBL
F-OHMH	Airbus A320-231	261	XA-RYT
			F-WWBM
F-OHMI	Airbus A320-231	275	XA-RJW
			F-WWIG
F-OHMJ	Airbus A320-231	276	XA-RJX
			F-WWIM
F-OHMK	Airbus A320-231	296	XA-RJY
			F-WWIH
F-OHML	Airbus A320-231	320	XA-RJZ
			F-WWBI
F-OHMM	Airbus A320-231	321	XA-RKA
			F-WWBK
F-OHMN	Airbus A320-231	353	XA-RKB
			F-WWDV
F-OHNE	Aérospatiale AS.355N Ecureuil 2	5584	
F-OHNR	Aérospatiale AS.350BA Ecureuil	2922	
F-OHNS	Aérospatiale AS.350BA Ecureuil	2925	
F-OHNV(2)	Aérospatiale AS.350BA Ecureuil	2981	
F-OHNX	Aérospatiale AS.350B Ecureuil	1612	
F-OHOD	Aérospatiale AS.365N3 Dauphin 2 *(Res .04)*	9000	D2-E . .
F-OHOR	Aérospatiale AS.350B3 Ecureuil	3307	
F-OHOV	Aérospatiale SA.365N4/Eurocopter EC.155B	6583	
	Dauphin *(Reservation .00)*		
F-OHPD	Airbus A300B4-203	305	N209PA
	(Wfu and stored)		F-WZMV
F-OHPJ(2)	Airbus A340-313X	173	F-WWJG
F-OHPK	Airbus A340-212	176	F-WWJE
F-OHPL	Airbus A340-313X	187	F-WWJO
F-OHPM	Airbus A340-313X	196	F-WWJI
F-OHPR	Airbus A310-325	702	F-WWCG
F-OHPS	Airbus A310-325	704	F-WWCL
F-OHPT	Airbus A310-304	526	F-WHPT
			D-AIDK
			F-WWCC
F-OHQB	Ayres S.2R-T34	226	N2264K
F-OHQC	Ayres S.2R-T34	227	N2269V
F-OHQD	Ayres S.2R-T34	243DC	N2045D
F-OHQE	Cessna A188B AgTruck	18802623T	N4887Q
F-OHQI	Cessna 172R	17280214	N9403F
F-OHQK	Dornier 228-212	8238	D-CBDU(7)
F-OHQL(2)	Aérospatiale/Alenia ATR-42-512	524	F-WWEF
F-OHQM(2)	Cessna 208B Grand Caravan	208B0726	
F-OHQN(2)	Cessna 208B Grand Caravan	208B0715	N1258H
			N52627
F-OHQO	Pilatus PC-6/B2-H4 Turbo Porter	924	
F-OHQQ	Cessna A188B AgTruck	18803900T	N9971J
F-OHQS	Cessna 182S *(Res. as N9525P 1.04)*	18280177	N9525P
F-OHQT	Hughes 269C *(Reservation)*	34-0288	YV-245E
			N9574F
F-OHQU	Cessna 208B Grand Caravan	208B0725	N12326
F-OHQV	Aérospatiale/Alenia ATR-42-512	571	F-WWEM
F-OHQX	Pilatus Britten-Norman BN-2A-26 Islander	3009	"F-OHQW"
			D-IORC
			OY-CEG
			G-BLNR
			RP-C184
F-OHQY	Pilatus Britten-Norman BN-2B-20 Islander	2251	V2-LFE
			9M-TAC
			G-BTLW
F-OHRA	Piper PA-32-300 Cherokee Six B	32-40635	F-BRIR
			N4261R
F-OHRB	Nord 262C Frégate	74	F-BSUF
F-OHRE	Piper PA-28-181 Archer II	28-8590087	N2537Y
F-OHRJ	Antonov An-2 *(See F-GRCJ)*	unkn	
F-OHRN	Aérospatiale/Alenia ATR-42-320	268	F-WQNF
			G-BUEA
			F-WWEW
F-OHRR	Grumman G.164 AgCat	216	N406Y
F-OHRS	Grumman G.164 AgCat	671	YU-BGX
F-OHRX	Beech 1900D	UE-282	N11296
F-OHRY	Grumman G.164B AgCat	132B	N6605Q
F-OHRZ	Grumman G.164A AgCat	1383	N8506H
F-OHSA	Piper PA-23-250 Aztec C	27-3862	5R-MCP
			N6565Y
F-OHSB	Aérospatiale SA.365C3 Dauphin 2	5014	G-BFVW
			F-WXFO
F-OHSD	Airbus A330-202	507	F-WWYS
F-OHSE	Aérospatiale AS.350B2 Ecureuil	2291	VH-EEA
			ZK-IWI
F-OHSF	Aérospatiale/Alenia ATR-72-212A	650	F-WWEC
F-OHSM	Aérospatiale AS.355F2 Ecureuil 2	5510	OE-BXV(3)
			F-WYMA
F-OHSN	Aérospatiale AS.355N Ecureuil 2	9606	
F-OHSP	Aérospatiale AS.355N Ecureuil 2	9607	
F-OHVY	Eurocopter EC.120B Colibri *(Reservation .02)*	unkn	
F-OHXY	Cessna 172S	172S9310	N53212
F-OHYA	Cessna U206F Stationair	U20603130	N52EC
			(N8269Q)
F-OHZM	Airbus A330-301	183	F-WWKP
F-OHZN	Airbus A330-301	184	F-WWKG
F-OHZO	Airbus A330-301	188	F-WWKQ
F-OHZP	Airbus A330-301	191	F-WWKR
F-OHZQ	Airbus A330-301	189	F-WWKS
F-OHZR	Airbus A330-301	198	F-WWKT
F-OHZS	Airbus A330-301	200	F-WWKH
F-OHZT	Airbus A330-301	203	F-WWKI
F-OIAB	Cessna 172N	17268209	VH-KJJ
			N1748C
			(N733DF)
F-OIAC	Piper PA-34-200 Seneca	34-7350277	VH-RRS
			OY-DZP
			HB-LEK
			N56054
F-OIAF	Eurocopter EC.120B Colibri	1094	
F-OIAG	Aérospatiale AS.350B2 Ecureuil	2170	
F-OIAH	Aérospatiale AS.350B2 Ecureuil	9004	
F-OIAI	Robinson R-44 Astro *(Damaged 30.12.03)*	0800	
F-OIAJ	Aérospatiale AS.350BA Ecureuil	1296	- ? -
			F-OIAE
			ZK-HLX
			F-ODGE
F-OIAK	Aérospatiale AS.350B3 Ecureuil	3653	

F-OIAM	Aérospatiale/Alenia ATR-42-320	403	F-WWLD
F-OIAP	Cessna 182P Skylane	18262717	VH-IRN N52619
F-OIAS	Robinson R-44 Raven II	10326	
F-OIAT	Mooney M.20J Model 205	24-3370	
F-OIAU	Aérospatiale AS.350B2 Ecureuil	2978	
F-OIAV(2)	DHC-6 Twin Otter Srs 300 *(Reservation 8.00)* *(Originally reserved for c/n 559)*	703	YJ-RV8 F-ODGL G-MAIL (G-BHTO)
F-OIAX	Cessna 172S	172S9213	ZK-JOL N5281R
F-OIAY(2)	DHC-6 Twin Otter Srs.300	507	P2-KSR N720CA C-GPJB
F-OIBD	Robinson R-22B2 Beta	2921	
F-OIBH	Piper PA-28-140 Cherokee Cruiser *(Res.04)*	28-7425434	N44628
F-OICF	Beech 58 Baron *(Reservation .00)*	unkn	
F-OICG	Aérospatiale/Alenia ATR-42-300	003	F-GEGE F-WEGE PH-HWJ F-GEGC F-WEGC
F-OICL	Aérospatiale AS.350B2 Ecureuil	9025	
F-OICP	Robinson R-22B2 Beta	3467	N75125
F-OICR	Aérospatiale SA.330J Puma	1301	(F-GJOD) (F-OPLH) F-GPLH(2) PT-HUC F-GBET HC-BNQ F-GBET PT-HSE F-GBET PT-HPW C-GSLA N55929 C-GUMP N330RM
F-OIEL	Aérospatiale AS.350B Ecureuil	9052	
F-OIFB	Cessna 182Q Skylane	18267570	TU-TLZ TU-TXZ (F-OBYY) N5204N
F-OIFR(2)	Cessna A188B Agtruck	18802379T	N4860R
F-OIGC to OIGZ *Reservations for SOCATA*			
F-OIJA	Cessna 172SP	172S08154	N954SP
F-OIJB	Aérospatiale/Alenia ATR-42-500	579	F-WWLF F-WWEZ
F-OIJC	Cessna 172SP	172S08303	N2461N
F-OIJD	Piper PA-28-181 Archer III	2843371	N9522N N41848
F-OIJE	Embraer EMB.145MP	145360	PT-SNZ
F-OIJF	Embraer EMB.145MP	145362	PT-SON
F-OIJG	Aérospatiale/Alenia ATR-72-212A	654	F-WWEI
F-OIJH	Aérospatiale/Alenia ATR-72-212A	682	F-WWEE
F-OIJI	DHC-6 Twin Otter Srs.310	277	HB-LSU VH-TGG N8861
F-OIJL	DHC-6 Twin Otter Srs.310	281	HB-LSV N616BA VH-TGH N8336
F-OIJO	Cessna 208B Grand Caravan	208B0961	N4109K N5262W
F-OIJR	Piper PA-34-220T Seneca V	3449216	F-WIJR N9525N
F-OIJS	Britten-Norman BN-2B-20 Islander	2294	VH-CSS G-BWJO
F-OIJT	Piper PA-23-250 Aztec F	27-7854129	N6513A
F-OIJX	Cessna A188B Agwagon	18803839	N9693J
F-OIJY	DHC-6 Twin Otter Srs.300	797	D-IFLY(6) 9Q-CJD C-GDIU
F-OIKA to OILZ *Reserved / used by SOCATA for overseas deliveries*			
F-OIMB to OIMZ *Reserved / used by SOCATA for overseas deliveries*			
F-OIMA	Short SD.3-60 *(Reservation .00)*	SH.3751	N948RR G-BVMX G-BPFS G-REGN G-OCIA G-BPFS
F-OINC	Beech B200 Super King Air	BB-1244	F-GSFA G-RIOO N251DL N72357
F-OIOL	Bell 412	33160	N4380K F-GKAK N3207D
F-OIOM	Aérospatiale SA.315B Lama	2423	EC-DNZ N47065
F-OIPA	Robin DR.400/200R Remo 200	2375	
F-OIPB	Pilatus PC-6/B1-H2 Turbo Porter	661	HB-FKQ A14-661 HB-FDM
F-OIPM	Robinson R-44 Raven	0765	C-GMDV

F-OIQA	Piper PA-31-350 Navajo Chieftain	31-7952191	N9020S N3534L
F-OIQB	Aérospatiale/Alenia ATR-42-512	621	F-WWEE
F-OIQC	Aérospatiale/Alenia ATR-42-512	627	F-WWCH
F-OIQD	Aérospatiale/Alenia ATR-42-512	631	F-WWLL
F-OIQF	DHC-6 Twin Otter Srs 300	815	N45KH ET-AIM C-GDCZ
F-OIQK	Beech 200C Super King Air *(Reservn 12.04)*	BL-149	N36949
F-OIQL	Beech 200C Super King Air *(Reservn 12.04)*	BL-148	N36948
F-OIQN	Aérospatiale/Alenia ATR-72-212A *(Res 4.05)*	719	F-WWET
F-OIRA(2)	Aérospatiale/Alenia ATR-72-212A	697	F-WWET
F-OIRB	Aérospatiale/Alenia ATR-72-212A	573	F-WWEK
F-OISB	Eurocopter EC.120B	1379	F-WWPC
F-OISC	Aérospatiale AS.350B2 Ecureuil	3925	
F-OISD	Aérospatiale AS.350B2 Ecureuil	3933	
F-OISE	Eurocopter EC.155B1 Dauphin	6697	
F-OITA	Partenavia P.68C *(Reservation 5.01, ntu)*	365	V2-LDC
F-OITB	Partenavia P.68C *(Reservation 5.01, ntu)*	302	V2-LEG N5390X
F-OITC	Partenavia P.68C *(Reservation 5.01 but wfu)*	280	V2-LCM
F-OITM	Cessna 172 *(Reservation 11.04)*	unkn	
F-OITQ	Aérospatiale/Alenia ATR-42-512	622	
F-OIUA to OIUZ *Reserved / used by SOCATA for overseas deliveries*			
F-OIVJ	SOCATA TB-20 Trinidad *(Reservation 1.01)*	691	F-GEVJ
F-OIVR	Cessna A188B Agtruck	18803491T	LX-AHN CN-THN LX-AHN N2640J
F-OIVU	Airbus A321-211	1017	G-OOAJ D-AVZM
F-OIYA	Aérospatiale/Alenia ATR-72-212	479	F-WWEL
F-OIYB	Aérospatiale/Alenia ATR-72-212	481	F-WWEQ
F-OIYL	Aérospatiale AS.350B2 Ecureuil	9008	
F-OIZO	Robinson R-22M2 Mariner	3296M	
F-OJBA to OJBZ *Reserved / used by SOCATA for overseas deliveries*			
F-OJCL	Robinson R-44 Astro	0943	
F-OJGF	Airbus A340-313X	385	(OO-SQA) F-WWJC
F-OJHH	Airbus A310-304	586	EP-MHH TC-JDD F-WWCK
F-OJHI	Airbus A310-304	537	EP-MHI TC-JDC F-WWCO
F-OJIJ	Piper PA-32-300 Cherokee Six	32-40451	F-BPIJ N4134R
F-OJJG	Cessna 182P	18262700	F-BVEG N52601
F-OJLC	Pilatus PC-6/B2-H4 Turbo Porter *(Reservn .02)*	unkn	
F-OJLE	Cessna 210 *(Reservation .00)*	unkn	
F-OJMD	Piper PA-36-375 Brave *(Reservation 10.04)*	36-8002021	EC-ELX C-GJEB N2401V
F-OJRD	Piper PA-36-375 Brave *(Reservation 10.04)*	36-8002015	EC-FOE N2370X
F-OJSB	Airbus A320-214	2152	
F-OJSE	Airbus A330-202	510	F-WWYT
F-OJSN	Piper PA-32-301 Saratoga	32-8006042	F-GCSN (OO-HKB) N8199H
F-OJTN	Airbus A340-313X	395	C-GZIA F-WWJF
F-WKAF	Reims/Cessna F182Q Skylane (Diesel engined) *(Permit 10.02)*	F18200167	F-OKAF F-GCYP
F-OKAY	Aérospatiale SA.365N Dauphin 2	6113	N28EH HL9229 F-WYMW
F-OKJP	Cessna 182J Skylane	18257250	F-BUTC N3150F
F-OKLG	Aérospatiale AS.350B3 Ecureuil	3616	
F-OKLN	Reims/Cessna F172N	F17201998	D-EKLN
F-OKRM	Airbus A320-211	615	F-WQSD VH-HYQ F-WWBR
F-OKTB	SOCATA TB-20 Trinidad	2210	VH-ITB F-OIMP
F-OKVL	Aérospatiale/Alenia ATR-72-201	215	(F-OHCE) F-WWEK
F-OLAG	Reims/Cessna F150L	F15001120	F-BVBY
F-OLIE	Robinson R-22B2 Beta	3193	
F-OLLL	Fokker F.28-0100 *(Reservation .04)*	11264	PT-MQU PH-THY PK-JGA PH-EZL
F-OLLM	Fokker F.28-0100 *(Reservation .04)*	11301	PT-MQM PH-LMV PK-JGE PH-LMV
F-OLLN	Fokker F.28-0100 *(Reservation .04)*	11341	PT-MRX PH-LNH XA-RKM PH-LNH
F-OLLO	Fokker F.28-0100 *(Reservation .04)*	11462	PT-MRS PH-EZX
F-OLLP	Fokker F.28-0100 *(Reservation .04)*	11470	PT-MRO PH-EZR

F-OLLQ	Fokker F.28-0100 *(Reservation .04)*	11472	PT-MRP PH-EZU
F-OLLR	Fokker F.28-0100 *(Reservation .04)*	11473	PT-MRQ PH-EZV
F-OLOV	Airbus A340-313E *(Reservation 12.04)*	668	(F-OJET) (F-ONUI) F-WWJD
F-OLVR	Aérospatiale AS.355N Ecureuil 2	9609	
F-OMAY	Boeing 777-2Q8ER *(Reservation .05)*	29402	
F-OMEA	Airbus A330-243	527	F-WWKZ
F-OMEB	Airbus A330-243	529	F-WWYB
F-OMEC	Airbus A330-243	532	F-WWYC
F-OMGL	Robinson R-44 Raven II	10567	(F-OKTA)
F-OMMP	Cessna A185F Skywagon *(Reservation 8.04)*	18503538	F-GGDX N767RC N2901Q
F-OMPC	Cessna 172 *(Reservation .04)*	unkn	
F-OMSA	Airbus A330-301	54	F-WMSA N54AN EI-SHN F-WWKJ
F-OMTA	Boeing 737-300 *(Reservation .01 for MTA)*	unkn	
F-OMTB	Boeing 737-300 *(Reservation .01 for MTA)*	unkn	
F-ONAT	Schröder Fire Balloons GHAFB	743	
F-ONLY	Cessna 404 Titan	404-0692	F-ZBDX F-GCQM N6764C
F-OOUA	Airbus A319-112	588	N588MX HB-IPW D-AVYB
F-OPAR	Boeing 777-2Q8ER	29908	EI-CRS
F-OPTP	Airbus A330-223	240	HB-IQB F-WWKZ
F-ORAV	Dassault Falcon 2000	171	(HZ-KSDD) F-WWVK
F-ORGC	Robin R.2160 Alpha Sport	149	5R-MLU F-GAXK
F-ORME	Airbus A321-231	1878	D-AVZA
F-ORMF	Airbus A321-231	1953	D-AVXF
F-ORMG	Airbus A321-231	1956	D-AVZE
F-ORMH	Airbus A321-231	1967	D-AVZI
F-ORMI	Airbus A321-231	1977	D-AVZU
F-ORMJ	Airbus A321-231	2055	D-AVZE
F-ORUN	Boeing 777-2Q8ER	28676	EI-CRT (HL . . . .)
F-OSAM	Aérospatiale SA.365N Dauphin 2 *(Permit for ferry 4.01)*	6102	N798LF N798LL N365ME N365DU 9V-BNN F-WXFC
F-OSEA	Airbus A340-313X	438	(F-GTUC) F-WWJV
F-OSPJ	Reims/Cessna F406 Caravan II	F406-0091	
F-OSUN	Airbus A340-313X	446	(F-GTUD) F-WWJA
F-OTDH	Cessna U206F Stationair	U20602794	N35912
F-OTZA	Robin R.2160 Alpha Sport	341	F-GTZA
F-OVFB	Aérospatiale AS.355N Ecureuil 2	5720	
F-OVLU	Robin R.2160 Alpha Sport	115	OO-VLU
F-OXDB	Robinson R-44 Raven II	10117	N75150

CNRA REGISTER (Homebuilt Aircraft)

F-PAAC(2)	Stern ST-87 Europlane	27	
F-PAAF(2)	Cassutt III	284	
F-WAAH	FM.100 Banbi *(Noted 6.01)*	unkn	
F-PAAS	Piel CP.320 Super Emeraude *(Reservation)*	426	
F-PABD	Péna Bilouis	03	
F-PABF	Pottier P.230S Panda	443	
F-PABJ	Pottier P.220S Koala	245	
F-PABK	Jodel D.18	457	
F-PABL	Nicollier HN-434 Super Ménestrel	17	
F-PABN	Jodel D.113	1744	
F-PABR	Morin M-85 *(Reservation .04)*	14	
F-PABY	RSA/Pottier P.130L Bleu Citron	1030	
F-PACA	Jodel D.18	206	
F-PACB	Pottier P.230S Panda	1	
F-PACD	Pottier P.230S Panda	468	
F-PACE	Jodel D.18	147	
F-PACF	Aeronca !!AC Chief	1602	OO-TWT
F-PACG	SNCAN/Stampe SV-4	220	CN-MAR Fr.AF
F-PACI	Guy Paci GP.01 Caracara	01	
F-PACK	Jodel D.113V	1802	
F-PACL	Dyn'Aéro MCR-4S 2002	23	
F-PACM	Jodel D.18	169	
F-PACO	Druine D.5 Turbi	67	
F-PACS	Pottier P.230S Panda *(Reservation)*	unkn	
F-PACT	Pietenpol Aircamper *(Reservation .03)*	3095	
F-PACV	Vandamme TPL-1	01	
F-PADB	Nicollier HN.700 Ménestrel II	79	
F-PADD	Dyn'Aéro MCR-01 Sportster	261	
F-PADE	Jodel D.18	327	
F-PADF	Dyn'Aéro MCR-4S 2002 *(Reservation .04)*	44	
F-PADJ	Pottier P.80S	56	
F-PADS	Dyn'Aéro MCR-4S 2002	08	
F-PADV	Pottier P.130L Coccinelle *(Reservation)*	1104	
F-PADY	Jodel D.112 Club	1626	
F-PAEA(2)	Sequoia F.8L Falco *(Reservation 11.04)*	1380	
F-PAED	Rutan Cozy *(Reservation)*	CC-1037	
F-PAEL	Dyn'Aéro MCR-4S 2002	6	F-WAEL
F-WAEO	Revolution Mini-500	0230	
F-PAFE	Rutan Long-Ez *(Reservation)*	1673	
F-PAFK	Kessler FK-001	01	
F-PAGA	Pottier P.180S	167	
F-PAGB	Jurca MJ.77 Gnatsum	15	
F-PAGD	Auster J/1 Autocrat	2218	G-AJID
F-PAGE	Nicollier HN-434 Super Ménestrel	61	F-WAGE
F-PAGG	Gouvin GG-01 Scorpion *(Reservation)*	01	
F-PAGI	Piel CP.320-100 Super Emeraude	446	
F-PAGM	Jodel D.19	120T	
F-PAHM	Acrolaram *(Reservation)*	01	
F-PAHS	Dyn'Aéro MCR-01 Sportster	180	
F-PAIA	Nicollier HN-700 Ménestrel II	124	
F-PAII	WagAero Aero Trainer *(Reservation)*	3724	
F-PAIR	Del-Vion DVD-01 (Mod. Jodel D.20) *(Reservation .03)*	04	
F-PAJB	Dyn'Aéro MCR-01	77	
F-PAJC	Pottier P.250S	405	
F-PAJD	Didier AH-01 *(Also reported as Wag Aero Wag-a-Bond)*	02	
F-PAJN	Ollivier CO-04 Collivier	01	
F-PAJO	Europa Aviation Europa XS	413	
F-PAJP	Cariou CL-3	19	
F-PAKT	Kieger AK-01T	03	
F-PAKV	Europa Aviation Europa XS *(Reservation .04)*	564	
F-PALB	Jodel DR.1054M Ambassadeur	848	
F-PALC	Heintz Tri-Z	3-1356	
F-PALE	Jodel D.18 *(Reservation .01)*	335	
F-PALF	Dyn'Aéro MCR-4S 2002	21	
F-PALG	Microcopter MC-1 *(Reservation .04)*	01	
F-PALI	Europa Aviation Europa	332	
F-PALM	Dyn'Aéro MCR-01	152	
F-PALP	Jodel D.140E Mousquetaire IV *(Reservation .02)*	407	
F-PALS	Jeannet JH-01 Le Courlis	01	F-WALS ?
F-PALU	Colomban MC-100 Banbi	04	
F-PAMA	Rotorway Exec 162 HDF	6682	
F-PAMB	G.802B Gerfaut *(Reservation)*	02	
F-PAMC	Nicollier HN-700 Ménestrel II	103	
F-PAMD	Brügger MB-2 Colibri	261	
F-PAMI (2)	Piel CP.320 Super Emeraude *(Reservation .04)*	470	
F-PAML	Pottier P.180S	202	
F-PAMT	Rand-Robinson KR-1	5469	
F-PAMV	Dyn'Aéro MCR-4S 2002	38	
F-PAND	Nicollier HN-700 Ménestrel II *(Reservation .01)*	68	
F-PANG	Jurca MJ.77 Gnatsum	04	
F-PANZ	Jodel D.113	1794	
F-PAOI	Mauboussin M.202S	001	F-WAOI F-BAOI
F-PAOL	Dyn'Aéro MCR-01 ULC	253	
F-PAOM	Clave Goéland *(Reservation)*	06	
F-PAPA	Colomban MC-15 Cri-Cri	224	
F-PAPC	Zenair CH-601HD Zodiac	6-1604	F-WAPC
F-PAPE	Blavier 8C2	01	F-WAPE
F-PAPF	Faure JPF-4 *(F-WAPF noted as Marquion Gyro 7.01)*	01	
F-PAPI	Caudron C.272/5 Luciole	6799	F-PMMI F-AMMI
F-PAPY	Pottier P.80SM	59	
F-PARA	Ameur Balbuzard *(Replaced by 2nd prototype which was then w/o ?)*	01	F-WARA
F-PARB	Jodel DR.1054M	862	
F-PARD	Pottier P.180S *(Reservation)*	21	
F-PARI	Richet Cobra 200DR	01	
F-PARJ	Kieger AK-2R	01	
F-PARK	Pottier P.180S	112	F-PYZQ
F-PARL	Nicollier HN.453RL Super Ménestrel	01	
F-PARM	Nicollier HN.700 Ménestrel	27	
F-PARS	Pottier P.230S Panda	421	
F-PARV	Colomban MC-100 Banbi *(Reservation .03)*	93	
F-PASB	Steen Aero Skybolt	341	
F-PASD	WagAero Sport Trainer	3122	
F-PASE	Saint-Ex AT-02	01	
F-PASM	Rutan VariEze	1794	F-WASM
F-PASO	Jodel D.150/120	142	
F-PASP	Dyn'Aéro CR.100T	35	
F-PASR	Rolland RS-3000	01	
F-PASS	Colomban MC-15 Cri-Cri	308	
F-PAST	Croses EC-6 Criquet	06	
F-PATH	WagAero Observer *(Reservation .01)*	2442	
F-PATM	Autogyre Libellule	01	
F-PATO	Pottier P.230S Panda	*03*	
F-PATR	Feugray TR-200	04	F-WATR
F-PAUR	Van's RV-4	309	
F-PAVC	Notteghem Occitan Club	04	
F-WAVL	Murphy Rebel *(Reservation 7.04)*	525R	
F-PAVM	Jodel D.19	22T	
F-PAVO	Colomban MC-100 Banbi	40	
F-PAVU	Jodel D.112 Club *(Reservation)*	1709	
F-PAVX	Nicollier HN.700 Ménestrel II	15	
F-PAXF	Aero Designs Pulsar	101F	F-WRXF

F-PAXV	Jodel D.150C/120 Mascaret (Lycoming O-320)	149	G-BZXH
			F-PBUS
F-PAYC	Pottier P.80S	68	
F-PAYE	Jodel D.113	1780	
F-PAYM	Piel CP.1320 Super Emeraude *(Reservation .99)*	36	
F-PAYS	Pottier P.60A Minacro	14	
F-PBAA	Dyn'Aéro MCR-4S 2002	18	
F-PBAB	Colomban MC-15 Cri-Cri *(Reservation .02)*	126	
F-PBAG	Pottier P.60 Minacro	15	
F-PBAL	Ameur MP.100 Balbuzard *(Project abandoned)*	MP100/01	
F-PBAM	Nicollier HN.700 Ménestrel II	02	
F-PBAR(2)	Jodel D.19	09-T	
F-PBAT	Stampe LBP	01	
F-PBAY	Farman 404 *(Under rebuild .99)*	7358.1	F-AMGY
F-PBBF	Jodel D.112 Club	01	F-BBBF
			F-WBBF
F-PBBG	Europa Aviation Europa	36	F-WBBG
F-PBBK	Aero 101C	01	F-BBBK
F-PBBM	Rutan Cozy	436	
F-PBBR	Piel CP.320 Super Emeraude	443	
F-WBBY	Tesson La Persévérance *(Reservation)*	01	
F-PBCA	Rutan Cozy *(Reservation)*	CC-1021	
F-PBCB	Nicollier HN.700 Ménestrel II	116	
F-PBCH	Piel CP.320 Super Emeraude	452	
F-PBCI	Nicollier HN-700 Ménestrel II *(Reservation)*	120	
F-PBCJ	Pottier P.130L	1000	
F-PBCL	Nicollier HN.700 Ménestrel II	97	
F-PBCM	Fairchild 24 Argus (UC-61)	01-1996	
	(Possibly a rebuild of 43-14531 c/n 495)		
F-PBCO	Ollivier DR.100 Collivier	01	
F-PBCQ	Coq *(Reservation)*	unkn	
F-PBCT	Piel CP.751B Beryl II	37	
F-PBDB	Bauer-Declerck DB-8/1650P (HAFB?)	01	
F-WBDO	Bulle d'Orage Montgolfiere	01	
F-PBDR	Jodel D.18	98	
F-PBDS	Aeronca 7AC Champion	2501	F-WBDS
			F-BLLI
			N83821
			NC83821
F-PBEC	F-8L-BX Falco	233-1	F-BNAS
	(Rebuild of Aeromere Falco F-8L c/n 233)		LX-AIY
			I- LEPG
			(D-EBQE)
F-PBEJ	Jacquot Véloce *(Reservation .01)*	01	
F-PBEK	Jodel DR.1053M *(Reservation .02)*	882	
F-PBER	WAR FW-190A Replica	339	
F-PBFJ	Péna Bilouis	1	
F-PBFT	Nord NC.856N Norvigie *(Reservation)*	2	F-BBBY
F-PBGD	Starck AS.70 Jac	07	
F-PBGS	Starck AS.70L Jac	12	
F-PBGT(2)	Air Camper J-3 Torpedo *(Reservation)*	2533	
F-WBGX(2)	Stolp SA.300Starduster Too	36	G-BPCE
	(Reservation, from storage at Barcelona)		N8HM
F-PBHC	Mauboussin 125 Corsaire	208	F-BBHC
F-PBIP	Thomson Cassutt *(Reservation .04)*	402	
F-PBIS	Junqua RJ-03 Ibis	02	
F-PBIX	Druine Fradon D.60 Condor	01	F-BBIX
F-PBJC	Fournier RF-5	A-03	
F-PBJL	Rutan VariEze	1449	
F-PBJP	Jodel D.112 Club	1630	
F-PBJR	Pottier P.180S	132	
F-PBKL	Van's RV-7 *(Reservation .02)*	70925	
F-PBKR	Dyn'Aéro MCR-4S 2002	45	
F-PBLA	Quercy CQR-01	18	
F-PBLB	Geronimo LB-1	01	
F-PBMC	WAR F-4U Corsair	559/512	
F-PBMD	Nicollier HN.700 Ménestrel II	29	
F-PBME	Pottier P.230S Panda *(Reservation .99)*	473	
F-PBMG	Mugnier L'Embellie Balloon	01	
F-PBMJ	Rutan Long-Ez	184	
F-PBML	Van's RV-4 *(Reservation 5.04)*	4220	
F-PBMS	Heintz Zenith CH250-160	2-1605	
F-PBNF	Colomban MC-15 Cri-Cri	578	
F-PBNO	Jodel DR.1053M	832	
F-PBNP	Jodel DR.1050M	701	
F-PBNS	Piel CP.80 *(Reservation .99)*	64	
F-PBNV	Max Plan MP-207 Busard *(Reservation .02)*	44	
F-PBOB(2)	Pottier P.80S	66	
F-PBOI	Jodel D.92 Bébé	40	
F-PBOS	Jodel D.92 Bébé	23	
F-PBOV	Jodel D.112 Club	27	
F-PBOX	Jodel D.92 Bébé	115	
F-PBOZ	Jodel D.92 Bébé	97	
F-PBPC	Dyn'Aéro MCR-01	46	F-WBPC
F-PBPF	Jodel D.150 Mascaret *(Reservation)*	147	
F-PBPY	Jodel D.92 Bébé	38	
F-PBRD	Club des Ballons Libre du Nord XW-340	01	
F-PBRG	Apodo *(Reservation)*	01	
F-PBRI	Bücker Bü.133C Jungmeister	2008	F-AZLB
			F-AZEU
F-PBRL	Pottier P.230S Panda	426	
F-PBRU	Brügger MB.8 *(Reservation .99)*	01	
F-PBRV	Jodel DR.1051 *(Reservation .02)*	913	
F-PBSC	Amphibie Esperanza 4	05	
F-PBSE	Bücker 131SA Jungmann	2224	N52DM
	(Presumably CASA I-131E from c/n)		E3B-624
F-PBSG	Viking Dragonfly Mk.2	824	

F-PBSH	Nicollier HN.700 Ménestrel II	113	
F-PBSM	Junqua RJ-03 Ibis	21	F-WBSM
F-PBSQ	Druine D.3 Turbulent *(Reservation)*	127	
F-PBSS	Colomban MC-15 Cri-Cri	579	
F-PBSY	Adam RA.14 Loisirs *(Dismantled)*	121	F-WBSY
F-PBTO	Jodel D.18	192	
F-PBUG	Jodel DH.251	1	
F-PBUL	Balatchev Centaure *(Reservation .99)*	01	
F-PBXM	Jodel D.921 Bébé *(Transferred to 91-UT but current)*	198	
F-PBXS	Druine D.31 Turbulent	03	
F-PBXU	Jodel D.92 Bébé	126	
F-PBYM	Starck AS.80 Holiday	NJ-1	
F-PBZE	Piel CP.320 Super Emeraude	429	
F-PBZH	Brändli BX-2 Cherry *(Reservation)*	94	
F-PBZT	Jodel D.112 Club	unkn	
F-PCAA	Pottier P.180S	169	
F-PCAB	WAR P-47D Thunderbolt	60	F-WCAB
F-PCAC	Nicollier HN.434 Super Ménestrel	14	F-WCAC
F-PCAD	Jodel D.18	89	
F-PCAK	Dyn'Aéro MCR-01 Sportster	84	
F-PCAL	Jodel D.18	122	F-WCAL
F-PCAN	Midgy LD.261	2	F-BCAN
F-PCAO	Jodel D.18	79	
F-PCAP	Mudry CAP.10	A5	
F-PCAR	Carriou CL-8 RSA Club	01	F-PSAG ?
F-PCAT	Pottier P.180S	90	F-WCAT
F-PCBA	ACBA-10 *(Reservation 11.04)*	01	
F-PCBC	Colomban MC-15 Cri-Cri	360	
F-PCBD	Jodel D.18 *(Reservation)*	367	
F-PCBJ	Bachoffer BA-01 *(Reservation)*	01	
F-PCBL	CBLN XW 500 HAFB	01	
F-PCBM	Autoplan CBM-01	01	
F-PCBN	Jodel D.119D (formerly D.113, D.112)	4	F-WCBN
F-PCBY	Rutan Long-Ez	1803	
F-PCBZ	Jodel D.19	145T	
F-PCCA	Jodel DR.100T	803	
F-PCCL	Nicollier HN-700 Ménestrel II	33	
F-PCCM	Croibier-Muscat CCM 01	01	
F-PCCU	Jodel D.112 Club	40	
F-PCDB	Speedy RG *(Destroyed 9.9.95)*	01	
F-PCDO	Jodel D.140R Abeille	454	
F-PCDQ	Chapeau JC.1 Levrier	01	F-WCDQ
F-PCDY	Jodel D.128	973	
F-PCEA	Jodel D.18	177	
F-PCEK	Mauboussin 123C Corsaire	179	F-BCEK
F-PCES	Mauboussin 125 Corsaire	177	F-BCES
F-PCET	Vintras ET-01	01	
F-PCFD	Viking Dragonfly Mk.2	572	F-WCFD
F-PCFH	Colomban MC-15 Cri-Cri *(Reservation)*	470	
F-PCFK	Paumier MP.02 Baladin	09	
F-PCFM	Jodel D.19	146T	
F-PCGB	Viking Dragonfly Mk.2	802	
F-PCGG	Rutan Long-Ez	1655	
F-PCGJ	Jodel D.19	123T	
F-PCGK	Jodel D.112 Club	1679	
F-PCGL	Lepeintre KAP-10 *(Reservation 11.04)*	01	
F-PCGO	Jodel DH.251	07	
F-PCGS	Pottier P.180S	89	
F-PCGT	Zenair CH-601 Zodiac	6-2060	
F-PCGV	Dyn'Aéro MCR-01 Club	166	
F-PCHA	Jodel D.140R Abeille	429	
F-PCHB	Brändli BX-2 Cherry	141	
F-PCHJ	Jodel D.18	368	
F-PCHM	Jodel D.119T	1831	
F-PCHN	Pechon JP-01 *(Reservation)*	01	
F-PCHP	Rutan Cozy *(Reservation .02)*	182	
F-PCHR	SIPA S.903 *(Reservation)*	01	
F-PCHV	Borel Erbé *(Reservation .02)*	01	
F-PCIM	Starck AS.57	11	F-BCIM
F-PCIO	Mauboussin 127 Corsaire	181	F-BCIO
F-PCIP	Mauboussin 123C Corsaire	183	F-BCIP
F-PCIR	Jodel D.92 Bébé	826	
F-PCJA	Péna Bilouis *(Reservation .03)*	33	
F-PCJB	Gardan GY-21 Minicab	27	
F-PCJC	Viking Dragonfly Mk.1	1115	
F-PCJG	Grinvalds G-801 Orion	54	
F-PCJH	Brügger MB-2 Colibri	269	
F-PCJL	Jodel D.19	156T	
F-PCJM	Nicollier HN.700 Ménestrel II	147	
F-PCJP	Pocino PJ-1A Toucan	01	
F-PCJS	Stern ST-87 Europlane *(Reservation .03)*	53	
F-PCLB	Dyn'Aéro MCR-01	60	
F-PCLC	Colomban MC-15 Cri-Cri *(Reservation .03)*	241	
F-PCLD	Quaissard Monogast	5	
F-PCLF	Colomban MC-15 Cri-Cri	533	
F-PCLG	Jodel D.113 *(Reservation .99)*	1673	
F-PCLM	Jodel D.19T	260-T	
F-PCLR	Croses LC-6 Criquet *(Reservation)*	60	
F-PCLS	Nicollier HN.700 Ménestrel II	119	
F-PCMB	Jodel D.19	170-T	
F-PCMC	Péna Le Dahu	05	
F-PCME	Notteghem Occitan 01 Club	05	
F-PCMG	Ollivier CO-02 Collivier	01	
F-PCMH	Jodel D.18	105	
F-PCMJ	Jodel D.18	16	
F-PCML	Canu 3J	01	
F-PCMM	Piper J-3C-65 Cub *(Rebuilt)*	S.1	

F-PCMN	Jodel D.113	1629	
F-WCMO	Jodel D.20	12	
F-PCMS	Jodel DR.1050M	791	
F-PCMT	Jodel D.19	95	
F-PCMV	Cassutt IIIM	646	
F-PCNC	Chambon PC-80	01	
F-PCOL	Fournier RF-5	2A	
F-PCOM	Viking Dragonfly Mk.2F	825	
F-PCOO	Grandjean DG.01 Alcyon	21	F-WCOO
F-PCOS	Jodel D.92 Bébé	141	
F-PCOU	Pecou SP-230	001	
F-PCOZ	Rutan Cozy	CC-1042	
F-PCPA	Jodel D.18	143	
F-PCPC	Jodel D.18	240	
F-PCPD	Jodel D.18	49	
F-PCPJ	Jodel D.113	1639	
F-PCPL	Pottier P.60A Minacro	17	F-WCPL
F-PCPR	Jurca MJ.5 Sirocco	25	
F-PCPS	Pottier P.70S	29	(F-PROO)
F-PCQR(2)	Val Lot JG-01	01	
F-PCRA	Van's RV-4	714	
F-PCRH	Henetier Gold HCR-2900 (HAFB?)	01	
F-PCRI	Colomban MC-15 Cri-Cri	405	
F-PCRM	Roussoulieres CR-02 Charly *(Reservation)*	01	
F-PCRP	Colomban MC-15Z Cri-Cri *(Reservation .03)*	289	
F-PCRQ	Quercy CQR.01 Cadi	01	
F-PCRT	Jodel DR.1053MV	772	
F-PCRY	Brändli BX-2 Cherry	113	
F-PCSA	Marie JPM-01 Médoc	22	
F-PCSB	Deramecourt 1900 HAFB	01	
F-PCSC	Pecou SP-250	001	
F-PCSE	Nicollier HN-700 Ménestrel II *(Reservation .04)*	216	
F-PCSJ	Jodel D.19 *(Transferred to 37-QU but current)*	261-T	F-WCSJ
F-PCSM	Stern ST-87C Europlane	18	
F-PCST	Rotorway Exec 162HDF	6035	
F-PCSY	Bücker Bü.131D Jungmann	01	F-BCSY
F-PCTF	Van's RV-4	3903	
F-PCTL	Colomban MC-100 Banbi	10	
F-PCTR	Colomban MC-15 Cri-Cri *(Reservation .03)*	494	
F-PCTS	Jodel D.113T *(Reservation .03)*	35	
F-PCTY	Nicollier HN-433 Ménestrel	67	
F-PCUB	Wag-A-Bond *(Reservation)*	412	
F-PCUO	Jodel DR.1053M	906	
F-WCUV	Mignet HM.290 *(Reservation)*	419	
F-PCUX	Jodel D.112 Club	181	
F-PCYG	Monnett Sonerai II LS *(Reservation)*	836	
F-PCYM	Jodel D.18	133	F-WCYM
F-WCZD	CJ-200	01	
F-PCZF	Brochet MB-72 *(Reservation)*	01	F-BCZF F-WCZF
F-PCZO(2)	Jodel D.113T *(Reservation 10.03)*	31T	
F-PDAB	Rutan Cozy	E-717	
F-PDAC	Arlais-Chasle AC-210	001	
F-PDAF	Jodel D.18 *(Reservation)*	unkn	
F-PDAI	Dyn'Aéro MCR-01 ULC	224	
F-PDAM	Duruble RD-03 Edelweiss *(Reservation)*	47	
F-PDAN	Jodel DH.251 *(Reservation)*	05	
F-PDAT	Humbert Tetras	07	
F-PDAX	Jodel D.113	1588	
F-PDBB	WagAero Sportsman 2+2	568	
F-PDBG	Deborde-Rolland Cobra 201AC	01	F-WDBG F-PDBG
F-PDBP	SNCAN/Stampe SV.4C *(Reservation .01)*	479	F-BDBP
F-PDCB	Jodel DR.1051M	770	
F-PDCC	Dyn'Aéro MCR-01 Club	171	
F-PDCM	Jodel D.113	1687	
F-PDDA	Jodel D.140E Mousquetaire	472	
F-PDDL	Jodel DR.100 Ambassadeur	894	
F-PDDR	Didier AH-01	01	
F-PDEL	Jodel D.18	05	
F-PDEM	Viking Dragonfly *(Reservation)*	1009	
F-PDES	Pottier P.180S	130	F-WDES
F-PDFL	Dyn'Aéro MCR-01 ULC	168	
F-PDGL	Canadian Home Rotors Baby Belle *(Type now renamed CHR Safari)*	0361N	
F-PDGM	Jodel D.140C Mousquetaire III	445	
F-PDHE(2)	SIPA 200 Minijet	7	F-BDHE
F-PDHF	Jodel D.92 Bébé	W6	
F-PDHI	Jodel D.92 Bébé	603	
F-PDHK	Jodel D.92 Bébé	M.11	F-WDHK
F-PDHT	Dyn'Aero MCR--01 Sportster	197	
F-PDHV	Verhees Delta	01	F-WDHV
F-PDID	Aeronca 0-58B-L3 Grasshopper *(Res., c/n quoted as '30123')*	8092	F-BELT 42-36123
F-PDJC	Jodel DR.1051T *(Reservation)*	875	
F-PDJV	Delvion DV-01 Zephyr	01	
F-PDKG	Aurensan KG-1 *(Reservation .99)*	01	
F-PDKL	Aurensan KG-1 *(Reservation .99)*	01	
F-PDKY	Jodel D.112 Club	42	
F-PDLC	Jodel D.18	14	
F-PDLF	Junqua RJ-03 Ibis *(Reservation .99)*	31	
F-PDLQ	Marie JPM-01 Médoc	38	
F-PDMA	Jodel DR.1051	858	
F-PDMC	Nicollier HN.700 Ménestrel II	67	
F-PDMI	Stampe DL *(Reservation 9.04)* (Believed to be rebuild of SV.4A F-BDLI c/n 639)	01	
F-PDMM	Europa Aviation Europa	257	

F-PDNE	Le Goeland *(Also currently marked 57-PH)*	02	F-WDNE
F-PDOE	Dyn'Aéro MCR-4S 2002	09	F-WDOE
F-PDOF	Leopoldoff L-3 Colibri *(Reservation)*	127	F-BGFS
F-PDOG	Dyn'Aéro MCR-01	18	F-WQUF
F-PDOL	CAP Dole	01	
F-PDOM	Jodel D.140E Mousquetaire IV *(Reservation .03)*	488	
F-PDOZ	Dyn'Aéro MCR-4S 2002	07	
F-PDPY	Junqua RJ-03 Ibis *(Reservation .03)*	41	
F-PDPZ	Holleville RH.1 Bambi	01	F-WDPZ
F-PDRA	Jodel-Miettaux DM02 Bébé Special	01	
F-PDRJ	Andrieux JA-3 SP	01	
F-PDRV	Van's RV-4	3809	
F-PDSD	Jodel D.18	116	
F-PDSL	Van's RV-8 *(Reservation 9.04)*	81963	
F-PDTC	Jodel DR.1050M Sicile Record	781	
F-PDTL	Brügger MB-2 Colibri	249	
F-PDUD	Zenair CH-701 STOL	7-1543	
F-PDVD	Poullin PJ.5A (Cub conversion) *(F/n 11614 - thus formerly L-4H c/n 11788 ex.43-30497)*	1	F-WDVD
F-PDVL(2)	Delvion DVD-01 *(Reservation .04)*	05	
F-PDVN	Marie JPM-01 Médoc	44	
F-PDVO	Poulin PJ.5A	03	
F-PDVP	Poulin PJ.5A	4	
F-PDVR	Lucas L-9	01	
F-PDVV	Jodel D.112 Club	A.103	
F-PDYT	Turquetil TYT-01 *(Reservation 12.04)*	01	
F-PDZN	Junqua RJ-03 Ibis Canard	23	
F-PEAC	Jodel D.153D1 Mascaret *(Reservation 7.03)*	133	
F-PEAH	Colomban MC-15 Cri-Cri	69	
F-PEAK	BRT Eider	02	
F-PEAL	Dyn'Aéro MCR-01	57	
F-PEAM	Jodel D.18	252	
F-PEAZ(2)	Duruble RD-03 *(Reservation 6.04)*	13	
F-PEBP	Jodel D.113	1707	
F-PEBZ	Brochet MB-50 Pipistrelle	52	F-PHBZ
F-PECA	Péna Le Joker	02	
F-PECB	Sable-Bouchon SB-2	01	
F-PECH	Colomban MC-100 Banbi	01	F-WECH
F-PECM	Colomban MC-100 Banbi *(Reservation .02)*	87	
F-PECQ	Nicollier HN-434 Super Ménestrel	02	
F-PECS	Jodel D.18	18	
F-PEDF	Nicollier HN-700 Ménestrel II	54	
F-PEDP	Murphy Rebel	416	
F-PEDR	Jodel D.129F *(Reservation .01)*	1735	
F-PEEP	DH-251 *(Reservation .04)*	17	
F-PEER	Rotorway Exec 162HDF	6704	
F-PEGA	Pégase 01 *(Reservation .02)*	01	
F-PEGH	Jodel D.113	1650	
F-PEGL	Jodel D.140C Mousquetaire III *(Reservation)*	453	
F-PEGR	Jodel D.18	428	
F-PEGY	Jodel D.19	101	
F-PEHO	Jodel D.92 Bébé *(Reservation as OH-XJA .05)*	43	
F-PEHV	Gardan GY-201 Minicab	A-216	
F-PEJC	Rutan Cozy Mk.4	83	F-WEJC
F-PEJH	Dyn'Aéro CR.100C	28	
F-PEJM	Enfissi EJM-002	01	
F-PEJR	Rand-Robinson KR-2	7854	
F-PELB	Dyn'Aéro MCR-01 VLA	94	F-WELB
F-PELD	Jurca MJ.2H Tempête	48	
F-PELR	Jodel D.19	364-T	
F-PEMA	Stolp SA.750 Acroduster Too *(Reservation 6.03)*	634	
F-PEMJ	Jurca MJ.5L2 Sirocco	45	
F-PEMY	Jodel D.18	162	
F-PENA	Péna Bilouis	01	
F-PENO	Jodel D.19	13T	F-WENO
F-PEOO	SFAN-4 *(Reservation .99)*	01	F-PFOO F-WFOO
F-PEPE	Jodel D.116T *(Formerly reserved as Anquetil JA-1 Kiout)*	01	F-WEPE
F-PEPM(2)	Nicollier HN.700 Ménestrel II	26	
F-PEPS	Pottier P-220D Koala *(Reservation)*	415	
F-PERB	Rhone et Sud-Est J-3 Cub	01	
F-PERD	Jodel D.119T Club (conv from D.112)	202	
F-PERG	C.A.B. GY-20 Minicab	A-162	
F-PERK	Jodel D.113V (ex D.112, D.127, D.119V)	196	
F-PERL	Jodel D.92 Bébé	213	
F-PERT	Jodel D.116 Club (ex D.112)	54	
F-PERU	Jodel D.112 Club	47	F-WERU
F-PERZ	Jodel D.112 Club	231	
F-PESG	Jodel D.20	19	
F-PESK	Pottier P.180SP	33	
F-PESL	Nicollier HN-434 Super Ménestrel	21	
F-PESM	Jodel D.121 (ex D.11, D.115)	64	
F-PESR	Rolland RS-1600 (HAFB?)	01	
F-PESV	Van's RV-4 *(Reservation .99)*	3594	
F-PESY	Jodel D.92 Bébé	175	F-WESY
F-WETE	Dyn'Aéro MCR-01 *(Reservation .01)*	28	
F-PETI	Colomban MC-100 Banbi	03	
F-PEUP	SAN B-1(Formerly SAN B-101, modified Cub) *(Reservation .02)*	101	F-PFUP F-WFUP
F-PEVF	Jodel D.112 Club	275	
F-PEVH	Jodel D.92 Bébé	332	
F-PEVL	Jodel D.112 Club	221	
F-PEVN	Jodel D.126 (ex D.112)	12	
F-PEVT	Jodel D.92 Bébé	A.8	
F-PEVX	Jodel D.112 Club	A.193	
F-PEVY(2)	Boudeau MB.16 Mickevy	01	

F-PEYA	Jodel DR.1053M	849	
F-PEYO	Jodel D.140E Mousquetaire IV *(Reservation .03)*	471	
F-PEZE	Rutan VariEze	2194	
F-PEZI	Lacroix LNB-12 Autoplan	01	
F-PFAB	Jodel D.19	390T	F-WFAB
F-PFAD	Nicollier HN-700 Ménestrel II	96	
F-PFAG	Notteghem Occitan Club	12	
F-PFAI	Dyn'Aéro MCR-01UL	23	F-WFAI
	(Also recorded as Colomban MC-100 and as MCR-01 c/n 01, regd. 3.6.97)		
F-PFAK(2)	Péna Capena C	16	
F-PFAM	Pottier P.130L *(Reservation .99)*	1047	
F-PFAR	Bagimer II Alouette	01	F-WFAR
F-PFAX	Rand-Robinson KR-2 *(Reservation)*	01	
F-PFBA	Sequoia F.8L Falco	1266	F-WFBA
F-PFBB	Adam RA.14 Loisirs	01	F-WFBB
F-PFBE	Jodel D.112 Club	1719	
F-PFBM	Rutan Cozy	E-736	
F-PFBR	Grinvalds G-801 Orion *(Wfu)*	38	
F-PFCA	Jodel D.112 Club	1648	
F-PFCL	CQR-01 Quercy *(Reservation .04)*	05	
F-PFCR	Jodel D.119T	09A	
F-PFCZ	Jodel D.112 Club	32	
F-PFDA	Gatard Statoplan AG 01 Alouette	01	F-WFDA
F-PFEN	Jodel D.112 Club	111	
F-PFET	Jodel D.112 Club	112	
F-PFEX	SFAN-2 *(Reservation .01)*	102	F-PEEX
F-WFFF	Dyn'Aéro MCR-01 *(Reservation)*	121	
F-PFFG	Elisport CH-7 Kompress *(Reservation 12.04)*	108	
F-PFGJ	Coupe JC-3	04	
F-PFGR	Dyn'Aero MCR-4S 2002 *(Reservation .04)*	33	
F-PFGT	Europa Aviation Europa	145	F-WFGT
F-PFHC	Dyn'Aéro CR.100C	27	
F-PFHM	Nicollier HN-700 Ménestrel II	32	
F-PFHN	Nicollier HN-500 Bengali	01	
F-PFHV	Colomban MC-15 Cri-Cri	304	
F-PFIF	Rutan Cozy *(Reservation)*	597	
F-PFIL	CQR-01 Quercy *(Reservation 11.04)*	16	
F-PFIN	Jodel D.112 Club	1770	
F-PFIZ	Jodel DR.1055M Enigma (Nosewheel mod.)	889	
F-PFJB	Freslon Omega	01	
F-PFJC	Quercy CQR-01	02	
F-PFJD	Darcissac-Grinvalds DG-87 Goeland	01	F-WFJD
F-PFJG	Grinvalds G-801 Orion *(Reservation .01)*	04	
F-PFJJ	Rutan Long-Ez	1358	
F-PFJL	Colomban MC-15 Cri-Cri	175	
F-PFJP	Stolp SA.300 Starduster Too	265	
F-PFJR	Dyn'Aéro MCR-4S 2002	22	
F-WFKA	Allard D-40 Puck	unkn	
F-PFKC	Mignet HM.360	1	F-WFKC
F-PFKL	Dyn'Aéro MCR-01	138	
F-PFKR(2)	Replica FKD-8 *(Reservation .01)*	01	
F-PFKU	WAR F-4UCorsair *(Reservation .99)*	242	
F-PFLB	Caudron C.601 Aiglon	7102/18	F-BFLB
			F-ANXX
F-PFLC	Jodel D.113	1789	
F-PFLL	Croses LC-6 *(Reservation) (Damaged 27.1.01)*	87	
F-PFLM	Rutan VariEze	1928	
F-PFLO	Jodel D.18 *(Reservation .99)*	04	
F-PFLX	Trotobas Le Felix TF-01 *(Reservation)*	01	
F-PFLY	Jodel D.112 Club	1785	
F-PFMJ	Lucas L-7	01	
F-PFML	Jodel D.113 *(Reservation .02)*	1822	
F-PFMP	Rutan Cozy	20	
F-PFMR	Pietenpol Aircamper	0041	
F-PFMT	Croses LC-6M Criquet	28	
F-PFMX	Jurca MJ.5F1 Sirocco *(Reservation .99)*	14	
F-PFNE	Colomban MC-15 Cri-Cri *(Reservation)*	553	
F-PFOI	Heintz Zenith 130 FLR	33	
F-PFOX(2)	Rand-Robinson KR-2	01	
F-PFPB	Flamant-Peignant-Pijean (autogiro?) *(Res.)*	01	
F-PFPS	Viking Dragonfly Mk.3	101	
F-PFPV	Jodel D.18	237	
F-PFPZ	Stern ST-87 Europlane	06	
F-PFQA	Piper J-3C-65 Cub	9929	(F-BFQA)
	(Quoted officially with f/n 9761)		43-1068
F-PFRA	SAN.01 Piper Cub	01	F-BFRA
F-PFRC	Nicollier HN.434 Super Ménestrel	82	
F-PFRE	Stark AS.80 Holiday *(ex c/n 01)*	5201	F-WFRE
F-PFRG	Dyn'Aero MCR-4S 2002	34	
F-PFRI (2)	Canadian Home Rotors FR-001 Safari*(Res .02)*	S-2105	
F-PFSB	Dyn'Aéro MCR-01	41	F-WSLL
F-PFSU	EAA Acrosport II	1654	
F-PFSV	Jodel D.140E Mousquetaire IV	415	
F-PFTN	Dyn'Aero MCR-01 Sportster	250	
F-PFTY	Jurca MJ-12 *(Reservation .99)*	03	
F-PFVA	Potez 36/13	3203	F-PEVA
			F-AMEI
F-PFVG	Brditschka HB-207 Alpha	207-030	
F-PFVS	Soccol VS.01 Gascon	01	
F-PFVV	Adam RA-14 Loisirs *(Reservation .99)*	35bis	F-PEVV
F-PFXG	Pottier P.220S Koala	409	
F-PFYC	Chasle YC-15 Tourbillon II	01	
F-PFYU	WagAero Sport Trainer *(Reservation 6.03)*	4320	
F-PFYY	Piel CP.30 Emeraude	01	F-PFVY
F-PGAC	Dyn'Aéro MCR-01	03	
F-PGAD	SIPA S.903	40	F-PGAO
			F-BGAO

F-PGAF	Jodel D.113 *(Reserved originally as D.119A)*	1733	
F-PGAG	Colomban MC-15 Cri-Cri	571	
F-PGAH	SIPA S.903	33	F-BGAH
F-PGAJ	Stoddard-Hamilton Glastar GS-1	5047	F-WGAJ
F-PGAK	Van's RV-6 *(Reservation .03)*	24408	
F-PGAM	Brochet MB.80	3	F-WGAM
			F-BGLC
F-PGAP	Safari FR-001	2108	
F-PGAR	Jodel DR.1051	910	
F-PGAS	Pottier P.180S	115	
F-PGAT	Jodel D.19 *(Reservation)*	267-T	
F-PGAY	Jurca MJ.77 Gnatsum	10	
F-PGBC	Stoddard-Hamilton Glastar GS-1	5074	F-WSLC
F-PGBJ	Jodel D.112 Club	1610	
F-PGBL	Dyn'Aéro MCR-01	136	
F-PGBS	Pottier P.60A Minacro	09	
F-WGBT	Jurca MJ.54 Silas *(Reservation)*	01	
F-PGCC	Brändli BX-2 Cherry	22	
F-PGCD	Nord NC.856A	33	ALAT
F-PGCF	Gyrostar	01	
F-PGCG	Jodel D.112 Club *(Reservation .03)*	1801	
F-PGCI	Guilie CAP TR	01	
F-PGCR	Stolp SA.300 Starduster Too	254	
F-PGCT	Adam RA-14 Loisirs	111	
F-PGDB	Dyn'Aéro MCR-01	148	F-WGDB
F-PGDF	Pottier P.230S Panda	423	
F-PGDG	Nicollier HN-700 Ménestrel II	25	
F-PGDL	DG-01 Leader	01	
F-PGDU	Dyn'Aéro MCR-4S 2002	05	
F-PGEL	Colomban MC-15 Cri-Cri	201	
F-PGEV	Rutan Long-Ez	2106L	
F-PGFO	Jodel D.92 Bébé	121	
F-PGFY	Fournet F-50 *(Reservation .04)*	01	
F-PGGG	Grinvalds G-801 Orion *(Res., or F-PGGR?)*	13	
F-PGGO	Coupe JC.200	4	
F-PGGP	Jodel D.18	413	
F-PGGT	Jodel DR.1053M	742	
F-PGGZ	Jodel D.92 Bébé	34	
F-PGHG	Pottier P.230S Panda	455	
F-PGHS	Mignet HM.293A *(Reservation)*	01	
F-PGIC	Aero 101	3	F-BGIC
F-PGIE	Jodel D.18	08	F-WGIE
F-PGIL	Jurca MJ.2D Tempête	82	
F-PGIR(2)	Giron PG-01 *(Reservation 12.04)*	01	
F-PGJB	Rand-Robinson KR-2	8006	
F-PGJJ	Dyn'Aéro MCR-01 Sportster	202	
F-PGJL	Rutan Cozy Mk.4	162	F-PCOQ
F-PGJV	Zenair CH-701 STOL *(Reservation .03)*	7-5186	
F-PGJY	Rutan Cozy	337	
F-PGKH	Piper J-3 Marabout *(CofA exp 7.00, stored)*	EN2	F-BGKH
	(f/n 8456 - L-4A c/n 8321 ex.42-15202)		ALAT
F-PGKL	Europa Aviation Europa XS	395	F-WGKL
F-PGLA	Brochet MB.83 *(Reservation .04)*	01	F-BGLA
F-PGLF	Brochet MB.83D	6	F-BGLF
F-PGLH	Brochet MB-83D	8	F-BGLH
F-PGLM	Jodel D.18	310	
F-PGLP	Junqua RJ-03 Ibis *(Reservation .02)*	39	
F-PGLX	Jodel D.113	55	
F-PGMB	Marie JPM.01 Médoc	06	
F-PGMF	Jodel D.18	163	
F-PGMH	Jodel D.18	75	
F-PGMI	Jurca MJ.77 Gnatsum *(Reservation)*	21	
F-WGML	Jurca MJ.100D Spitfire	2	
F-PGMN	C.A.B. GY-201 Minicab *(ex c/n 16)*	A.124	F-BGMN
F-PGMS	Rutan Long-Ez	358	
F-PGNA	Jodel D.11 T28	07A	
F-PGOA	Pottier P.180S	76	
F-PGOM	Pottier P.180S *(Reservation .99)*	200	
F-PGPB	Jodel D.19 *(Reservation .04)*	331T	
F-PGRA	Velocity Standard RG	179	F-WGRA
F-PGRB	Nicollier HN.434 Super Ménestrel	22	
F-PGRD	Fournier RF-47 *(Reservation .04)*	06	
F-PGRE	Jodel D.112 Club	115	
F-PGRF	Fournier RF-47 *(Reservation)*	04	
F-PGRG	Dyn'Aéro CR.100	05	
F-PGRK	Starck AS-80 Holiday	56	
F-PGRP	Jodel DB-1101	001	
F-PGRS	Stern ST-87 *(Reservation)*	43	
F-PGSG	Pottier P.230S Panda	444	
F-PGSH	Pereira Osprey GP-4 *(Reservation)*	71	
F-PGSI	Fournier RF-47 *(Reservation .01)*	05	
F-PGSJ	Fisher Horizon 2	AH-0082	
F-PGSP	Marie JPM-01 Médoc *(Reservation .01)*	53	
F-PGSY	Dyn'Aéro MCR-01	97	
F-PGTC	Piel CP.1320 Super Emeraude	05	
F-PGTE	Jodel D.112 Club	137	
F-PGTL	Guilliot DG-1	01	
F-PGTM	Junqua RJ-03 Ibis	01	
F-PGTU	Ambrosini F.4 Rondone 1	019	F-BGTU
F-PGTY	Jurca MJ.2 Tempête	54	
F-PGUE	Jodel DR.1054F Ambassadeur	878	
F-PGUI	Evans VP-1 Volksplane	V-1382-GD	
F-PGUY	Nicollier HN.434 Super Ménestrel	03	
F-PGVR	Piel CP.30A Emeraude	2	F-WGVR
F-PGYA	Mignet HM.293	JH-3/37	F-WGYA
F-PGYB	Jodel D.112 Club	122	
F-PGYN	Jodel D.92 Bébé	124	

F-PGYR	Druine D.5 Turbi	02	F-WGYR
F-PHAI	Dyn'Aéro MCR-01 ULC	311	
F-PHAM	Stolp SA.300 Starduster Too	785	N6099
F-PHAT	Van's RV-6	25304	
F-PHBL	Innovator Mosquito *(Reservation .04)*	1005	
F-PHBT	Feugray TR-200	06	
F-PHCB	Jodel D.19	268	
F-PHCC	Hennetier Gold 2190	01	
F-PHCD	Deschamps / Charles Dolfus HG-760 Balloon	01	
F-PHCH	Nicollier HN-700 Ménestrel II	61	
F-PHDF	Rotorway Exec 162HDF	6281	F-WHDF
F-PHDH	Hammentien DH-500	01	
F-PHDJ	Pottier P.220S Koala	410	
F-PHDP	Jurca MJ.77 Gnatsum	11	
F-PHDS	Quercy CQR-01	17	
F-PHEL	Zenair CH-601HDS Zodiac	"601"	
F-PHEM	Colomban MC-15Z Cri-Cri	205	
F-PHEU	Rolland RS-3000 HAFB	03	
F-PHFB	Jodel D.112 Club	268	
F-PHFG	Couyaud GC-01	01	
F-PHFK	Caudron C.232 *(Reservn., probably ntu)*	6486/1	F-AJSS
F-PHFL	Jodel D.112 Club	184	
F-PHGF	Rotorway Exec 162HDF *(Reservation 6.04)*	6121	
F-PHGP	Rotorway Exec 162HDF	3034	
F-PHGT	Leopoldoff L.55 Colibri	2	F-BHGT
F-PHHH	Dyn'Aéro MCR-4S 2002	19	
F-PHIF	Dyn'Aéro MCR-01 *(Reservation 6.03)*	20	
F-PHII	Dynali H-2	01	
F-PHIL	Piel CP.615A Super Diamant	55	
F-PHIM	Stoddard-Hamilton Glastar *GS-1*	5525	
F-PHJB	Jodel D.112 Club	374	
F-PHJJ	Jodel D.113 Club (ex D.112)	A.204	
F-PHJK	Jodel D.112 Club	212	
F-PHJL	Jodel D.112 Club	159	
F-PHJN	Jodel D.112 Club (ex D.118, D.121)	104	
F-PHJO	Jodel D.112 Club	281	
F-PHJP	Jodel D.112 Club	211	
F-PHJS	Jodel D.92 Bébé	349	
F-PHJX	Jodel D.112 Club	A.386	
F-PHJY	Jodel D.112 Club	328	
F-PHKV	Windex 1200C	007	F-WHKV
F-PHLA	Jodel D.112 Club	304	
F-PHLB	Jodel D.112 Club	A.14	F-WHLB
F-PHLC	Jodel D.119C (ex D.112, D.113C)	329	
F-PHLF	Jodel D.112 Club	284	
F-PHLJ	Jodel D.92 Bébé	350	
	(Transferred to W62-AAB but regn still current)		
F-PHLL	Druine Martin (D.61 Condor variant)	02	F-WBIY
F-PHLM	Piel CP.30 Emeraude	4	
F-PHLN	Piel CP.301 Emeraude	5	
F-PHLO	Piel CP.30 Emeraude	10	
F-PHLP	Jodel D.112 Club	383	
F-PHLQ	Jodel D.112 Club	282	
F-PHLR	Jodel D.112 Club	290	F-WHLR
			F-PHLR
F-PHLS	Jodel D.112 Club	136	F-WHLS
F-PHMC	Croses LC-6W Criquet	122	
F-PHME	Nicollier HN.700 Ménestrel II	181	
F-PHMH	Rutan Cozy	E-706	
F-PHMN	Colomban MC-15 Cri-Cri	120	
F-PHMP	Pottier P.270S	432	
F-PHMR	Dyn'Aéro MCR-01 Sportster	228	
F-PHOK	Jodel D.113	1751	
F-PHOQ	Rippert A.1-65 Cub	1	F-BEKV
	(Converted fromPiper L-4 c/n 12154)		44-79858
F-PHOT(2)	Dyn'Aéro MCR-01 Club 912F	103	F-WHOT
	(Originally allocated to MCR-01 c/n 172)		F-WWUQ
F-PHPC	Piel CP.615 Super Diamant	50	
F-PHPG	Helicoptère Autour 01	01	
F-PHQA	Jodel D.92 Bébé	263	
F-PHQC	Jodel D.112 Club	317	
F-PHQE	Jodel D.119 (ex D.121)	44	
F-PHQG	Leopoldoff L.4 Colibri (ex L.3 rebuilt)	24	F-APZN
F-PHQH	Larrieu JL.2	01	F-WHQH
	(converted from D.112 c/n 77)		F-BGMA
F-PHQI	Piel CP.301 Emeraude	38	
F-PHQK	Jodel D.119A	472	(F-BHAE)
F-PHQN	Delassalle-Planchais LD45-4	04	
F-PHQO	Chatelain AC.5 Bijou	01	
F-PHQP	Jodel D.92 Bébé	390	
F-PHQS	Jodel D.112 Club	468	
F-PHQZ	Druine D.5 Turbi	48	
F-PHRC	Europa Aviation Europa	108	F-PSLO
			F-WSLO
F-PHRP	Rigault RPH-01 *(Reservation 10.03)*	01	
F-PHRS	Piel CP.320 Super Emeraude	420	
F-PHSJ	OGMA/Auster D.5/160 *(Reservation .02)*	136	CR-GAX
F-PHUD	Jodel D.112 Club	398	
F-PHUF	Camandre 1 (Cub conversion)	01	
F-PHUL	Jodel D.112 Club	360	
F-PHUM	Jodel D.112 Club	404	
F-PHUP	Jodel D.112 Club	375	
F-PHUQ	Jodel D.119 (ex D.112)	291	
F-PHUS	Jodel D.112 Club	220	
F-PHUV	Jodel D.119	A.392	
F-PHVI	Boisavia B.601 Mercurey *(Reservation .02)*	23	F-BHVI
F-PHYN	Brügger MB-2 Colibri	21	

F-PHZC	Adam RA.15/1 Major	1	
	(Possibly rebuild of F-PEPD, F-WEPD ?)		
F-PHZD	Piel CP.30 Emeraude	75	
F-PHZG	Jodel D.112 Club	213	
F-PHZM	Jodel D.113 (ex D.119)	318	
F-PHZN	Potez 36/14	3207	F-AMEM
F-PHZO	Piel CP.301 Emeraude	11	
F-PHZX	Jodel D.113 (ex D.119)	A.97	
F-PHZY	Marabout M (Cub conversion)	01	
F-PIAB	Rutan Cozy	45	
F-PIAC	Sequoia F.81L Falco *(Reservation .02)*	1394	
F-PIAF	Viking Dragonfly Mk.2	1024	
F-PIAN	Boisavia B.601L Mercurey	25	(F-GLNA)
			F-BIAN
F-PICG	Rand-Robinson KR-2	7499	
F-PICK	Dyn'Aéro MCR-01	147	F-WICK
F-PICL	Canadian Home Rotors Baby Belle	0366N	
	(Type now known as CHR Safari)		
F-PICM	ICAM 77 HAFB	1	
F-PICO	Jodel D.18	60	
F-PICR	Aero Designs Pulsar XP *(Reservation .04)*	unkn	
F-PIDZ	Jodel D.119V	1772	
F-PIED	Pottier P.180S	111	
F-PIEL	Piel CP.320 Super Emeraude *(Reservation)*	416	
F-WIFE	Pottier P.180S	27	
F-WIGE	Stoddart-Hamilton GlaStar GS-1 *(Reservation 6.04)*	5336	
F-PIFS	Soubrane Acro 200	01	
F-PIGT	Taillefer DT-01 (Modified Jodel DR.250, 180hp)	01	
F-PIHH	Jodel D.112 Club (ex D.123)	279	
F-PIHI	Piel CP.301 Emeraude	34	
F-PIHL	Croses EC-1	02	F-WIHL
F-PIHV	Jodel D.112 Club (ex D.119)	619	
F-PIHX	Jodel D.113 (ex D.119)	621	
F-PIHY	Jodel D.119	653	
F-PIID	Jodel D.112 Club	660	
F-PIIE	Jodel D.92 Bébé	292	
F-PIIM	Jodel D.112 Club	749	
F-PIIO	Jodel D.112 Club (ex D.119)	319	
F-PIIS	Druine D.5 Turbi	26	
F-PIIT	Gardan GY-201 Minicab	217	
F-PIIX	Piel CP.30 Emeraude	19	
F-PIJH	Jurca MJ.5G2 Sirocco	60	
F-PILA	Guimbal G2 Cabri	01	
F-PILD	Neico Lancair 320	640	F-WILD
F-PILO	Jodel D.112 Club	1769	F-WILO
F-PILP	Jodel D.119	1746	
F-PIMA	Jodel D.113	1760	
F-PIML	Rutan Cozy *(Reservation)*	1-737	
F-PINB	Jodel D.112 Club	769	
F-PIND	Jodel D.92 Bébé	371	
F-PINE	Jodel D.112 Club (ex D.124)	782	
F-PINI	Jodel D.119 (ex D.112)	57	
F-PINJ	Piel CP.310 Emeraude (ex CP.301)	49	
F-PINK	Piel CP.301 Emeraude	08	
F-PINM	Gardan GY-201-90 Minicab	A144	
F-PINP	Jodel D.119 (ex D.112) *(W/o 10.2.01)*	387	
F-PINR	Piel CP.310 Emeraude (ex CP.308)	27	
F-PINV	Jodel D.92 Bébé	391	
F-PINY	Jodel D.119 (ex D.112)	449	
F-WIOI	Wadsworth PW-01 *(Reservation)*	01	
F-PIOL	Jurca MJ.2P Tempête	47	
F-PION	Colomban MC-15 Cri-Cri *(Reservation .01)*	362	
F-PIOU	Rolland RS-3000 HAFB	04	
F-PIPA	Jodel D.112 Club	1814	
F-PIPE	Jodel D.113	1725	
F-PIPO	Jodel D.19	359T	
F-PIPR	Altair 2PL *(Reservation)*	01	
F-PIRA	Pereira Osprey 2	752	F-WIRA
F-PIRE	Dyn'Aéro MCR-01 Sportster	238	
F-PIRI	Jodel D.150/120	146	
F-PITR	Techaero Feugray TR-200 *(Reservation)*	09	
F-PITS	Cousin DFC-01 Optima *(Reservation)*	01	
F-PITY	Brditschka HB-207 Alpha *(Reservation 9.04)*	57	
F-PITZ	Pottier P.130L Coccinelle *(Reservation 10.04)*	1063	
F-PIUS	Dyn'Aéro CR.100	22	F-WWUV
			Fr.AF:FTGCJ
F-PIUT	Dyn'Aéro MCR-01 Club	158	
F-PIVA	Colomban MC-15 Cri-Cri	428	
F-PIVS	Van's RV-4 *(Reservation .04)*	4429	
F-PIVX	Nicollier HN-700 Ménestrel II	unkn	
F-PIXL	Dyn'Aéro MCR-4S 2002	15	F-WIXL
F-PIXX	Jodel D.140C Mousquetaire III	433	
F-PIYA	Druine D.5 Turbi	46	
F-PIYB	C.A.B. GY-201 Minicab	A.159	
F-PIYC	Jodel D.113 (ex D.112)	713	
F-PIYF	Jodel D.92 Bébé	151	
F-PIYJ	Jodel D.119	864	
F-PIYM	Jodel D.112 Club	748	
F-PIYN	Piel CP.301 Emeraude	178	
F-PIYO	Jodel D.119	739	
F-PIYP	Jodel D.92 Bébé	398	
F-PIYR	Jodel D.119G (ex D.112)	676	
F-PIYS	Jodel D.112 Club *(Accident 14.3.03)*		513
F-PIYT	Jodel D.119	102	
F-PIYV	Brochet MB.76	23	
F-PIYY	Piel CP.315 Emeraude	16	
F-PIYZ	Jodel D.113 (ex D.119)	620	

F-PJAB	Jabiru J400	102	
F-PJAC	Jodel D.92 Bébé	657	
F-PJAG	Jodel DR.1050MT	792	
F-PJAI	Jabiru J400 *(Reservation 11.04)*	172	
F-PJAK	Rutan Cozy *(Crashed 17.5.00, restored)*	190	F-WJAK
F-PJAM	Nicollier HN.700 Ménestrel II	65	
F-PJAR	Du Dognon 01	01	
F-PJAS	Dyn'Aéro MCR-01 Sportster	24	
F-WJAV	Murphy Rebel *(Reservation .04)*	532	
F-PJAY	Jodel D.113.3L *(Reservation .03)*	1753	
F-PJBC	Jodel DR.1051 Ambassadeur	788	
F-PJBD	Morin M-82	02	
F-PJBG	Jurca MJ.5 Sirocco	19	
F-PJBL	Jodel D.18 *(Reservation)*	11	
F-PJBM	Dyn'Aéro MCR-01 Club	167	
F-PJBR	Jodel DR.1051M	827	
F-PJBS	WagAero Sport Trainer	3303	
F-PJBV	Jodel D.18	349	
F-PJBY	Blenet RB-1 Joze	01	F-WJBY
F-PJCA	Jodel D.112 Club	943	
F-PJCB	Piel CP.750A Beryl II *(Reservation)*	06	
F-PJCD	Jurca MJ.2 Tempête	66	
F-PJCH	Steen Skybolt *(Reservation .04)*	320	
F-PJCK	Aero Club Lons/Leglise L-400	01	
F-PJCL	Dyn'Aéro MCR-01	65	
F-PJCM	Piel CP.215 Pinocchio (built as CP.211, CP.212)	01	
F-PJCN	Adam RA.14 Loisirs	110	
F-PJCX	Jodel D.119 (ex D.112)	671	
F-PJDH	Mauboussin 123C Corsaire	159	F-ARDR
F-PJDL	Grinvalds G-801 Orion	16	F-WJDL
F-PJDP	Jodel D.113	1803	
F-PJDR	Dyn'Aéro MCR-01	07	F-WJDR
F-PJDV	Van's RV-4 *(Reservation)*	44062	
F-PJDY(2)	Mignet HM.390 Auto-Ciel *(Reservation)*	1 bis	
F-PJDZ	Nord NC.858	64	F-BFSK
F-PJEA	Dyn'Aéro MCR-01	80	
F-PJEB	Rutan VariEze	1962	
F-PJET	Rutan Cozy *(Reservation 5.03)*	452	
F-PJFB	Jodel DR.1051 *(Reservation .04)*	892	
F-PJFK	Notteghem Occitan	02	
F-PJFM	Dyn'Aero MCR-01 M *(Reservation .04)*	254	
F-PJFT	Van's RV-6	22419	
F-PJGC	Jodel D.119	529	F-WJGC
F-PJGE	Piel CP.301A Emeraude	3	
F-PJGI	Adam RA.14 Loisirs	45	
F-PJGJ	Jodel D.119 (ex D.112)	952	
F-PJGM	Jodel D.112 Club *(Stored)*	682	
F-PJGO	Jodel D.119	975	
F-PJGP	Gatard Statoplan AG 02 Poussin	02	
F-PJGQ	Damoure-Fabre-Lacroix DFL-6 Saphir	01	F-WJGQ
F-PJGR	Jodel D.112 Club	147	
F-PJGS	Jodel D.119	994	
F-PJGZ	Jodel D.112 Club	403	
F-PJHB	Caudron C.431 Rafale replica *(Reservation)*	01	
F-PJHG	Pottier P.80S	69	
F-PJHJ	Pottier P.80S	156	
F-PJHM	Jodel D.18	469	
F-PJIC	Jodel DR.1056M Ambassadeur	886	
F-PJIM	Stolp SA.300 Starduster Too	2105	
F-PJJB	Robin CR.100	06	
F-PJJC	Rutan Cozy *(Reservation)*	CC-1056	
F-PJJG	Jurca MJ.5H1 Sirocco	52	
F-PJJP	Rutan Cozy	819	
F-PJJR	Jurca MJ.55	01	
F-PJKB	Jodel D.119 (ex D.111)	790	
F-PJKD	Druine D.31 Turbulent	93	
F-PJKG	CEA Jodel DR.101 Ambassadeur	31	
F-PJKL	Piel CP.301 Emeraude	192	
F-PJKM	Jodel D.119L (ex D.112)	617	
F-PJKN	Jodel D.112 Club	963	
F-PJKP	Jodel D.121 (ex D.112)	191	
F-PJKR	Piel CP.315 Emeraude (ex CP.301, CP.305)	343	
F-PJKV	Paumier MP-21 Baladin	01	
F-PJKY	Jodel D.112 Club *(Cancelled?)*	1037	
F-PJLB	Rutan Long-Ez	1344	
F-PJLC	JLC-01 Abeille *(Reservation)*	01	
F-PJLG	Nicollier HN-700 Ménestrel II	76	
F-PJLH	Taylor Coot Amphibian *(Reservation .99)*	106	
F-WJLM	Piel CP.1320 Saphir	1	
F-PJLO	Nicollier HN.434 Super Ménestrel	53	
F-PJLS	Jodel D.19	399T	
F-PJLT	Pottier P.270S *(Reservation .99)*	436	
F-PJLV	Pottier P.270S	441	
F-PJMA	Dyn'Aéro MCR-01 VLA	54	F-WSLK
F-PJMC	Jodel D.119	390	F-PIHO
F-PJMD	Jodel DR.1053M	726	
F-PJMF	Van's RV-8 *(Reservation .02)*	81724	
F-PJMK	Van's RV-8 *(Reservation .04)*	unkn	
F-PJML	Colomban MC-15 Cri-Cri *(Reservation)*	unkn	
F-PJMP	Nicollier HN-434 Super Ménestrel	48	
F-PJMR	EAA Acrosport II	1079	
F-PJMS	Sauval SE-5A *(Reservation .99)*	01	
F-PJMT	Jodel D.18	45	F-WJMT
F-PJNL	DS-150 *(Reservation)*	unkn	
F-PJOB	Lucas L.5-200	2	F-WJOB
F-PJOC	Gravereau Box'Air Racer	01	F-WJOC ?
F-PJOD	Jodel DR.1054 Ambassadeur	857	

F-PJOE	Jurca MJ.2E Tempête	96	
F-PJOH	Rutan Cozy *(Reservation .99)*	CC-1021	
F-PJOJ	C.A.B. GY-201 Minicab *(ex c/n 722)*	A.204	
F-PJOK	Péna Le Joker	01	F-WJOK
F-PJOO	Joordens M-5JJ *(Reservation .02)*	01	
F-PJOR	Nicollier HN-434 Super Ménestrel	74	
F-PJOS	Piel CP.301A Emeraude	445	
F-PJPB	Nicollier HN-434 Super Ménestrel	73	
F-PJPC	CAPENA	05	
F-PJPD	Marie JPM-01 Médoc	21	F-WJPD
F-PJPF	WAR FW-190 Replica	184	
F-PJPG	Croses EC-6 Criquet	47	
F-PJPL	Pottier P.70S	30	
F-PJPS	EAA Acrosport II	602	
F-WJPY	Dyn'Aéro MCR-01 *(Noted 7.01)*	unkn	
F-PJQA	Junqua RJ.02 Volucelle	01	F-WJQA
F-PJRA	Jodel DR.1050M	760	
F-PJRC	Chalard JRC-01	01	
F-PJRD	Jodel D-20	04	
F-PJRH	Marcel 01	01	
F-PJRM	Colomban MC-15 Cri-Cri	294	
F-PJRP	Croses LC-6 Criquet	100	
F-PJSA	Legrand-Simon LS.60	01	F-BJSA F-WJSA
F-PJSB	Schepers Job/ Magni M-16 Trainer gyrocopter	01	
F-PJSE	Juste JSE-18 *(Reservation .02)*	01	
F-PJSF	Jodel D.18	371	
F-PJSM	Godbille GJJ	01	F-WJSM
F-PJST	Rand-Robinson KR-2S *(Reservation .99)*	447	
F-PJSX	Jurca MJ.5K2 Sirocco	01	F-WJSX
F-PJTA	Jodel D.18	189	
F-PJUL	Jodel D.18	418	
F-PJUP	Schwind Autogyre JS-01 *(Reservation)*	01	
F-PJVD	Van's RV-7A *(Reservation .03)*	70290	
F-PJVJ	Jodel D.11 D1	1585	
F-PJVM	Nicollier HN-700 Ménestrel II	85	
F-PJXA	Jodel D.112 Club	941	
F-PJXB	Jodel D.92 Bébé	422	
F-PJXC	Jodel D.112 Club	971	
F-PJXD	Jodel D.112 Club	1054	
F-PJXE	Jodel D.112 Club	1041	
F-PJXF	Jodel D.119	1032	
F-PJXG	Jodel D.119	984	
F-PJXH	Jodel DR100A Ambassadeur	202	
F-PJXJ	Jodel D.112 Club	1034	
F-PJXN	Jodel D.112 Club	1101	
F-PJXO	Jodel D.119	1087	
F-PJXP	Piel CP.60 Diamant	01	F-WJXP
F-PJXR	Jodel D.112 Club	1107	
F-PJXS	Jodel D.112 Club	214	
F-PJXV	Jodel D.112 Club	1104	
F-PJXX	Jodel D.119	451	
F-PJXZ	Piel CP.301 Emeraude	200	
F-PJYA	Natin JNB-01	01	
F-PJYB	Colomban MC-15 Cri-Cri	57	
F-PKAD	Rutan Long-Ez	1059	
F-PKAM	Fournier RF-47 *(Reservation .04)*	07	
F-PKAS	Deramecourt D20/3000P HAFB	01	
F-PKBM	Flamme PF-01	01	
F-PKCF	Piel CP.1320 Saphir	57	
F-PKEN	Jodel D.119	1551	
F-PKER	Gasnier "De Kerdonis" GG-01	01	
F-PKFC	Jodel D.112 Club	972	
F-PKFG	Jodel D.112 Club	950	
F-PKFI	Druine D.31 Turbulent	115	
F-PKFJ	Piel CP.301 Emeraude	32	
F-PKFL	Jodel D.112 Club	391	
F-PKFN	Mignet HM.380B	12	F-WKFN
F-PKFO	Jodel D.92 Bébé	446	
F-PKFT	Jodel D.112 Club	985	
F-PKFU	Lucas L.4 Baby	01	F-WKFU
F-PKFY	Jodel D.112 Club	1050	
F-PKFZ	C.A.B. GY-201-90 Minicab	A.233	
F-PKGQ	Jodel DRM (converted DR.1050/239)	01	F-BKGQ
F-PKIT	Dyn'Aéro MCR-01	01	
F-WKJR	Wheeler Express *(Reservation .03)*	70	
F-PKLE	Pottier P.220S Koala *(Reservation .99)*	461	
F-PKMB	Jodel D.112 Club	1085	
F-PKMC	Jodel D.112 Club	271	
F-PKMD	Jodel D.119	1044	
F-PKMF	Jodel D.112 Club	986	
F-PKMG	Piel CP.301A Emeraude	353	
F-PKMH	Jodel D.119 (ex D.112)	777	
F-PKMJ	Jodel D.119 (ex D.112)	1135	
F-PKMK	Jodel D.119	1154	
F-PKMN	Jodel D.119	678	
F-PKMP	Jodel D.113 (ex D.112)	793	
F-PKMR	Jodel D.119	741	
F-PKMT	Druine D.31 Turbulent	248	
F-PKMV	Damoure-Fabre DF-5C	01	
F-PKMX	Piel CP.316 Emeraude	352	F-WKMX
F-PKOR	Fournier RF-47 *(Reservation .04)*	08	
F-PKPL	Jodel DR.1050 Ambassadeur	778	
F-PKRJ	Light Aero Avid Flyer	798	F-PRKJ F-WRKJ
F-PKRL	Europa Aviation Europa XS *(Reservation .04)*	447	
F-PKSE	Jodel D.112 Club	1765	

F-PKUE	Dyn'Aéro MCR-01	72	F-WQUR
F-PKUJ	Europa Aviation Europa	297	F-WQUJ
F-PKVB	Piel CP.301 Emeraude	93	
F-PKVC	Tipsy T.66 Nipper III	7	OO-NIG
F-PKVD	Jodel D.112 Club	1182	
F-PKVI	Jodel D.92 Bébé	460	
F-PKVH	Junca-Steiner JS *(Reservation)*	01	
F-PKVU	Druine D.31 Turbulent	96	
F-PKVX	Jodel D.112 Club	1195	
F-PKVZ	Piel CP.325 Super Emeraude	359	F-WKVZ
F-PKXA	Piel CP.301A Emeraude	322	
F-PKXC	Jodel D.119	1139	
F-PKXL	Jodel D.112 Club	1224	
F-PKXR	Jodel D.113	1142	
F-PKXV	Jodel D.112 Club	1201	
F-PKXX	Piel CP.601 Diamant	5	
F-PKXY	Aero 20	1	F-WKXY
F-PLAB	Jodel D.19	253-T	
F-WLAC	Europa Aviation Europa Classic *(Reservation .03)*	320	
F-PJAF	Colomban MC-15 Cri-Cri *(Reservation 7.04)*	108	TR-LAF
F-PLAH	OGMA/Auster D.5/160 *(Reservation .03)*	140	CR-GBI CR-CAQ
F-PLAJ	Jaillet AJ-160	01	
F-PLAL	Leblanc L-06 *(Dismantled, noted 10.03)*	01	
F-PLAM	Lamaziere AL-01 *(Reservation .99)*	01	
F-PLAN	Dyn'Aéro MCR-4S 2002	32	
F-PLAR	Tipsy T.66 Nipper Mk.III *(Reservation .02)*	61	F-OBYV
F-PLAT	Berger BG-180 *(Reservation .03)*	01	
F-PLAU	Péna Bilouis	27	
F-PLAY	Piel CP.320 Super Emeraude	439	
F-PLBC	Pottier P.220S Koala	469	
F-PLBM	Jodel D.119	1763	(F-PBPM)
F-PLBT	Wittman W8 Tailwind	522	
F-PLCA	Druine-Lucas D.31 LP1 Turbulent	01	F-WLCA
	(Originally regd as Druine-Colombier D.31 Turbulent c/n 392)		
F-PLCB	Jodel D.18	444	
F-PLCD	Ollivier C0-03 Collivier	01	
F-PLCL	Piel CP.90 Pinocchio II	7	
F-PLCR	EAA Acro Sport II *(Reservation .04)*	1913	
F-PLDA	CAP X-2 *(Reservation 3.04)*	01	
F-PLDH	Dyn'Aéro MCR-01 Sportster	71	
F-PLDJ	Dyn'Aéro MCR-4S 2002	27	
F-PLDS	Rutan Cozy *(Reservation)*	CC-1038	
F-PLDV	Pottier P.240S	01	
F-PLEA	Dyn'Aéro CR.100	26	
F-PLEF	Brügger MB-2 Colibri	242	
F-PLEJ	Godbille JG.IB	01	
F-PLEM	Dyn'Aéro MCR-01 Sportster	216	
F-WLEO	Viking Dragonfly Mk.I	1116	
F-PLEZ	Rutan Long-Ez	1580	
F-PLFC	Lucas L-5 *(Reservation, actually wears F-WLMC)*	61	
F-PLFD	Denney Kitfox III	1095	
F-PLFG	CQR-01 Quercy *(Reservation 10.04)*	15	(F-PQFG)
F-PLGC	Tormancy LR-01	01	
F-PLGJ	Steen Skybolt	173	
F-PLGL	Jurca MJ.2 Tempête	44	F-WLGL
F-PLGO	Nicollier HN.700 Ménestrel II	128	
F-PLGR	ARSA Club LGR-61	01	
F-PLGZ	Jodel D.18	402	
F-PLHB	Alpha HB-207 *(Reservation)*	207-019	
F-PLHF	Pottier P.220S Koala	413	
F-PLHM	Viking Dragonfly I *(Reservation .00)*	372	F-WLHM
F-PLHR	Jodel D.112	1779	
F-PLIC	Rolland RS-3000 HAFB?	02	
F-PLII	Bonsergent Bons-77 HAFB?	01	
F-PLIL	Lilles JCL-01 Laser 2000	01	
F-PLIZ	Dyn'Aéro MCR-4S 2002	29	
F-PLJB	Nicollier HN.434 Super Ménestrel	31	
F-PLJC	Jodel D.113	1635	
F-PLJM	Jodel D.19	424-T	
F-PLJP	Jodel D.140E Mousquetaire IV	452	
F-PLJR	Stern ST-87 Europlane	34	
F-PLKE	Europa Aviation Europa XS	389	F-WLKE
F-PLKP	Jodel DR.200P	01	F-BLKP F-WLKP
F-PLKQ	CPG 150 *(Reservation .99)*	01	
F-PLLB	Jodel D.18 *(Reservation 4.04)*	211	
F-PLMB	Leopoldoff LMB	04.98	
F-PLMC	Lucas L-5	61	F-WLMC (F-PLFC)
F-PLMJ	Pottier P.270S	438	
F-PLMK	Laigniel-Mathely-Klinka LMK-1 Oryx	01	F-WLMK
F-PLMP	Heinz Zenith 100	2-128	
F-PLMS	Lucas L-5	46	
F-PLNA	Monobi MC-210 *(Reservation .99)*	01	
F-PLOC	Canadian Home Rotors Safari FR-001	2109	
F-PLOI	Bauer-Declerck DB-8/1650 (HAFB?)	2	
F-PLPG	Denize RD-20 Raid-Driver	27	F-WLPG
F-PLPH	EAA Acrosport 2	1222	
F-PLPL	Lusley PL16/2000	01	
F-PLPP	Jodel D.18	106	
F-PLPR	Pottier P.180S	135	
F-PLRJ	Gombert Péna "Le Dahu"	01	
F-PLRL	Sangler LRL-01 *(Reservation 11.04)*	01	
F-WLRY	Jodel D.20 Jubilé *(Reservation 5.04)*	007	
F-PLSA	Nicollier HN-700 Ménestrel II	142	
F-PLSD	Nicollier HN-700 Ménestrel II	104	

F-PLSG	Nicolas NG-01	01	
F-PLUA	Druine D.31B Turbulent	249	
F-PLUB	Jurca MJ.2D Tempête	3	
F-PLUC	Dyn'Aéro MCR-4S 2002	26	
F-PLUF	Jodel D.119	1132	
F-PLUG(2)	Akrotech Giles G-202	029	F-WLUG
F-PLUI	Jodel D.119	1226	
F-PLUK	Jodel D.113 (ex D.112)	1186	
F-PLUL	Jodel D.113 (ex D.119)	1027	
F-PLUM	Jodel D.119 (ex D.112)	187	
F-PLUN	Piel CP.301D Emeraude	361	
F-PLUP	Jodel D.112 Club	1193	
F-PLUQ	Jodel D.119	995	
F-PLUR	Jodel D.113E (ex D.119A)	1230	
F-PLUS	Jodel D.119	530	
F-PLUU	Jodel D.112 Club	1244	
F-WLUV	Bensen B.8ML Gyrocopter (ex B.7M)	01	
F-PLVR	Dyn'Aéro MCR-01	08	
F-PLYM	Duruble RD-03 Edelweiss	23	
	(Previously listed as Duruble RD-02 Edelweiss c/n 02)		
F-PLYT	Heintz Zenith	122	
F-PMAA	Piel CP.323 Super Emeraude	428	
F-PMAB	Jodel D.112	163	HB-SUF
F-PMAC	Jodel D.114 3L	1670	
F-PMAG	Colomban MC-15 Cri-Cri	356	
F-PMAH	Dyn'Aéro MCR-01 *(Reservation .02)*	144	
F-PMAK	Jodel DR.1050M1 Sicile Record *(Reservation .99)*	887	
F-PMAR	Nicollier HN-700 Ménestrel II	14	
F-PMAT	Rutan Cozy	E-707	
F-PMAX	Stolp SA.750 Acroduster Two	529	
F-PMAY	Colomban MC-15 Cri-Cri	499	
F-PMAZ	Jodel D.18	53	
F-PMBC	Nord NC.856G Norvigie *(Reservation .00)*	02	
	(Rebuilt by GPPA, Angers from c/n 38 F-MMCB)		
F-PMBE	Jodel D.140C Mousquetaire III *(Reservation .01)*	462	
F-PMBG	Jodel D.18 *(Reservation 3.04)*	151	
F-PMBL	Marie JPM-01 Médoc *(Reservation .99)*	51	
F-PMBS	WagAero Sport Trainer	2196	
F-PMCA	Pitts S-1DSpecial	7-0342	
F-PMCB	Nord NC.854CM	01	
F-PMCC	Piel CP.320 Super Emeraude	431	
F-PMCD	Luscombe 8A Silvaire	895	C-FRNJ CF-RNJ NC22069
F-PMCE	Jodel D.18	352	
F-PMCF	Laigniel-Mathely-Klinka LMK-1	01-LPCA	
F-PMCG	WagAero Wagabond *(Reservation .99)*	1007	
F-PMCH	Nicollier HN-700 Ménestrel II *(Reservation .01)*	180	
F-PMCL	Nicollier HN-700 Ménestrel II	133	
F-PMCM	Jodel D.140E Mousquetaire IV	460	
F-PMCR	Pottier P.180S	176	(F-PEUG)
F-PMCS	Jurca MJ.5 Sirocco	127	
F-PMDA	Jodel DA-01 *(Reservation)*	01	
F-PMDC	Dyn'Aéro MCR-01 Sportster	133	
F-PMDJ	Aurore Mini Bulle MB-2 *(Reservation .02)*	192	
F-WMDK	WAR F-4U Corsair *(Reservation)*	477	
F-PMDL	Jodel DR.1053 Ambassadeur	852	F-WMDL
F-PMDS	deHavilland DH.82A Tiger Moth *(Reservation .99; officially registered* *with c/n "7400")*	83741	F-WMDS F-BGZY (G-ATWI) F-BGZY (F-OAPT) T7400
F-PMEB	Jodel D.112 Club	1245	
F-PMED	Jodel D.119	1092	
F-PMEE	Jodel D.113	1235	
F-PMEH	Croses EC-6 Criquet	37	
F-PMEN	Jodel D.119	219	
F-PMEO	Jodel D.119C *(W/o 10.2.01)*	1249	
F-PMER	Jodel D.112 Club	1136	
F-PMES	Leger RL-3	01	
F-PMET	Lederlin 380L	01	
F-PMEU	Jodel D.112 Club	1328	
F-PMEZ	Jodel D.119	718	
F-PMFH	Viking Dragonfly Mk 2	MH-5015-V	
F-PMGA	Nicollier HN-700 Ménestrel II	71	
F-PMGE	Mayence MP-01	01	
F-PMGG	Nicollier HN-700 Ménestrel II *(Reservation .02)*	125	
F-PMGT	Rutan Cozy	627	
F-PMGV	Jodel D.140E Mousquetaire IV	463	
F-PMIC	BRT Eider	01	
	(Previously reserved as Murphy Rebel)		
F-PMIE	Péna Bilouis *(Reservation .99)*	30	
F-PMIK	Péna Bilouis *(Reservation .03)*	31	
F-PMIL	Junqua RJ-03	25	
F-PMIP	Evans VP-1 *(Reservation .02)*	2315	
F-PMJC	Jodel D.140R Abeille	416	
F-PMJD	Europa Aviation Europa XS *(Reservation 6.03)*	571	
F-PMJF	Jurca MJ.5 Sirocco *(Reservation, abandoned)*	94	
F-PMJG	Kelly Hatz CB-1 *(Reservation .99)*	326	
F-PMJL	Brügger MB.2 Colibri *(Reservation 3.04)*	22	
F-PMJP	Rutan Cozy Mk IV	32	
F-PMJR	Jodel D.19	279-T	
F-PMJS	Sequoia F.8L Falco	965	
F-PMKI	E Racer Mk.1	ER-263	
F-PMLC	Pottier P.230S Panda *(Reservation)*	448	
F-PMLD	Jodel DH.251 *(Reservation)*	06	

F-PMLG	Fournier RF-5	A-04	F-WMLG
	(Originally c/n 5084)		F-BSGA
F-PMLH	Europa Aviation Europa XS	560	F-WMLH
F-PMLO	Colomban MC-15 Cri-Cri	482	
F-PMLR	Van's RV-8	80592	
F-PMLS	Melos DFB-1A	01	
F-PMLT	Nicollier HN.701TM Ménestrel II	166-01	
F-PMMB	Stern ST-87 Europlane *(Reservation .99)*	35	
F-PMMC	Jodel D.112 Club	1784	
F-PMMM	Jurca MJ-2 Tempête *(Reservation .03)*	22	
F-PMMR	Jodel DR.1050 Ambassadeur	861	
F-PMNA	Hubert GH-2600	01	
F-PMOA	Jodel D.18 *(Reservation)*	450	
F-PMOF	Junqua RJ-03 Ibis *(Reservation .02)*	34	
F-PMOH	Jodel D.112 Club *(Reservation)*	1327	
F-PMON	Jodel D.1103T *(Reservation .01)*	01	
F-PMOS	Nicollier HN.700 Ménestrel II *(Reservation .99)*	43	
F-PMPF	Dyn'Aéro MCR-01 M	222	
F-PMPG	Pottier P.180S	133	
F-PMPJ	Jodel D.113-3L *(Accident 27.2.00)*	1723	
F-PMPL	Jodel D.92 Bébé	509	
F-PMPM	Marie JPM-01 Médoc *(Reservation 12.03)*	52	
F-PMPY	Jodel DR.1051M *(Reservation 4.03)*	895	
F-PMPZ	Rutan VariEze *(Reservation)*	1736	
F-PMQJ	Jodel D.128 *(Reservation .99)*	1764	
F-PMQT	Duruble RD-03 Edelweiss *(Reservation .00)*	49	
F-PMRA	Rotorway Exec 162HDF	6631	
F-PMRD	Duruble RD-03 Edelweiss *(Reservation)*	26	
F-PMRG	DG-250 *(Reservation .03)*	01	
F-PMRJ	Jodel D.140E Mousquetaire IV	430	
F-PMRN	Nicollier HN.700 Ménestrel II	182	
F-PMRR	Rutan Cozy	CC-1051	
F-PMRV	Van's RV-4	3466	
F-PMRY	Nicollier HN.700 Ménestrel II	63	
F-PMSA	MSA 1800/20 (HAFB?)	01	
F-PMSC	Omega CS-900 *(Reservation)*	01	
F-PMSD	Jodel DR.1054M *(Reservation .02)*	850	
F-PMSE	Jodel D.112 Club	1700	
F-PMSJ	Molière MLR 102Blue Djinn	01	
F-PMSZ	Nicollier HN.700 Ménestrel II	163	
F-PMTB	Marie JPM-01 Médoc	34	
F-PMTR	Dyn'Aéro MCR-01 Sportster	256	
F-PMTS	Stern ST-87 Europlane	30	
F-PMTY	EAA Acrosport II	2063	
F-PMVA	Maurel MG-1008 *(Reservation .01)*	01	
F-PMVM	Jodel D.18	439	
F-PMVT	Maunoury DM-01 *(Reservation .99)*	01	
F-PMXA	Jodel D.112 Club	1291	
F-PMXB	Jodel D.119D	1337	
F-PMXF	Jodel D.119	1335	
F-PMXH	Jodel D.112 Club	1191	
F-PMXK	Chatelain AC.9	01	
F-PMXL	Vintras-Bouiller VB.20 Isard	01	F-WMXL
F-PMXO	Jurca MJ.2D Tempête	20	
F-PMXQ	Chasle YC-12 Tourbillon	01	F-WMXQ
F-PMXT	Piel CP.301 Emeraude	366	
F-PMXU	Jodel D.92 Bébé	494	
F-WMXZ	Fourneron CF-2 Gyrocopter	02	
F-PMYB	Dyn'Aéro MCR-01	68	F-WMYB
F-PMYD	Rutan Long-Ez	1797L	F-WMYD
F-PMYG	Notteghem Occitan Club *(Reservation)*	03	
F-PMYV	Piel CP.605 Diamant *(Reservation)*	34	
F-PMZO	Jurca MJ-2 Tempête *(Reservation .01)*	88	
F-PNAC	Jodel D.113 *(Reservation)*	1619	
F-PNBC	Nicollier HN-700 Ménestrel II	70	
F-PNBG	Piel CP.1321B Super Emeraude	40	
F-PNCE	Dyn'Aéro MCR-01 Club	142	
F-PNCF	Nord NC.856A Norvigie	13	F-WNCF
			F-BMSD
F-PNCH	Charmont M500NC	01	
F-PNDF	Fournier RF-47	01	F-WNDF
F-PNDL	Colomban MC-100 Banbi	06	
F-PNEP	Nicollier HN-434 Super Ménestrel *(Reservation .01)*	70	
F-PNEU	Jodel D.113 *(W/o .02?)*	1773	
F-PNEV	Dyn'Aéro MCR-4S	01	
F-WNGE	Neico Lancair 235 *(Reservation .03)*	167	
F-PNGT	Leduc RL-19 *(Reservation .99)*	1	F-PAGT
F-PNHJ	Nicollier HN.700 Ménestrel II	137	
F-PNIC	Nicollier HN-434 Super Ménestrel	50	F-WNIC
F-PNJD	Lucas L-5	19	
F-PNJL	Neico Lancair LC.30 *(Reservation)*	225	F-WNJL
F-PNJP	Kurun JPR-01	01	
F-PNKU	Fouga CM-8R Sylphe IIIB	1	F-CRRE
F-PNLG	Jodel D.92	41	
F-PNLY	Coupe C-423G	02	F-WNLY
F-PNMI	Jodel D.112 Club	522	F-BHVE
F-PNOA	Murphy Rebel *(Reservation .03)*	524	
F-PNOC	Dyn'Aéro MCR-01 Sportster *(Reservation .03)*	195	
F-PNOG	ACBA-8 Midour 2 (ACBA-7 modified)	01	F-PRNG
F-PNOI	Dyn'Aéro MCR-01	111	F-WNOI
F-WNOK	Dyn'Aéro MCR-01	162	
F-PNRJ	Jodel D.19	110T	
F-PNSF	Jodel D.140E Mousquetaire IV *(Reservation 11.04)*	927	
F-PNUB	Jodel D.119	1289	
F-PNUF	Jodel D.119A	983	
F-PNUG	Jodel D.112 Club	1155	
F-PNUH	Jodel D.113 (ex D.119)	1325	
F-PNUI	Jodel D.112 Club	1194	
F-PNUL	Jodel D.119D	1383	
F-PNUN	Piel CP.605B Diamant (ex CP.603)	10	F-WNUN
F-PNUT	Piel CP.319 Emeraude	367	
F-PNVL	Dyn'Aéro MCR-01 Sportster *(Reservation .03)*	45	
F-PNVO	Nevereau/Stampe SV.4C	01	F-WNVO
	(Originally SNCAN-built SV.4C c/n 590 F-BDEK)		
F-POAD	Babin BJ-3	01	
F-POAI	Jodel D.18	87	F-WOAI
F-POAM(2)	Grinvalds G-802B Orion *(Reservation .04)*	06	
F-POBG	Jodel D.18	166	F-WOBG
F-POBJ	Jodel D.18	461	
F-POBY	Jurca MJ.5 Sirocco	50	
F-POCC	Notteghem Occitan Club	01	
F-POCF	Rutan VariEze	2109	
F-POCH	Colomban MC-200 Banbi *(Reservation .03)*	86	
F-POCM	Jodel D.119T	1819	F-WOCM
F-POCT	CQR Occitan Club *(Reservation .01)*	09	
F-POCU	SNCAN/Stampe SV.4C	229	F-BOCU
F-PODB	Cabrix *(Reservation .00)*	01	
F-POEL	Pottier P.230S Panda *(Reservation)*	456	
F-POEM	Jodel D.113 3L *(W/o 25.5.02)*	1609	
F-POET	Heintz CH-180 Zenith *(Reservation)*	18-841	
F-POFC	ACBM-01 *(Reservation .03)*	01	
F-POFG	Farigoux FG-01 Origan	01	
F-POIA	Jodel D.92 Bébé	466	
F-POIB	Jodel D.112 Club	1377	
F-POIC	Jodel D.119 (ex D.112)	1275	
F-POID	Jodel D.119	1133	
F-POIF	Jodel D.112 Club	965	
F-POIH	Jodel D.119	714	
F-POII	Jodel D.119DA	1287	
F-POIL	Jurca MJ.5G2 Sirocco	17	F-WOIL
F-POIP	Jurca MJ.5 Sirocco	11	
F-POIS	Dyn'Aéro MCR-01 Club	217	
F-POIX	Piel CP.301A Emeraude	356	
F-POIZ	Piel CP.301A Emeraude	196	
F-POJP	Pottier P.230S Panda	430	
F-POLC	Van's RV-8 *(Reservation .03)*	81939	
F-POLE	Bushby Midget Mustang II	1708	
F-POLI	Van's RV-6	24044	
F-POLO (2)	Jodel DR.1053	865	
	(Previously reserved for Brügger MB-2 Colibri c/n 196)		
F-POLU	Deramecourt D16/1600 HAFB	01	
F-POLV	Pottier P.230S Panda *(Reservation)*	431	
F-POMD	Jurca MJ.5 Sirocco *(Reservation .04)*	189	
F-POMF	Jodel D.18	125	F-WOMF
F-PONG	Nicollier HN-700 Ménestrel II *(Reservation .01)*	189	
F-PONT	Pontier DePonAl D-520 *(Reservation .00)*	01	
F-PONY	Stolp SA.750 Starduster Too	585	F-WONY
F-POOF	Barry MB-02 Souricette *(Reservation .02)*	54	
F-POOL	Dyn'Aéro MCR-4S 2002	36	F-WWUU
F-POOO	Nord NC.854S	78	F-BFSZ
F-POOS	Van's RV-4 *(Reservation .00)*	4369	
F-POPB	Jodel D.140E Mousquetaire IV *(Damaged 21.6.03)*	461	
F-POPF	LMK-1 Oryx *(Reservation .04, see F-PSJM)*	03	
F-POPG	LMK-1 Oryx	02-LPCA	
F-POPI	Colomban MC-15 Cri-Cri *(Reservation)*	286	
F-POPN	Jodel D.140E Mousquetaire IV	486	
F-POQR	Jodel D.113T *(Reservation .01)*	1817	
F-PORM	Lucas L-5	03	
F-POSE	Potez 60 Sauterelle	4184	F-WOSE
			F-AOSE
F-POSO	Rutan Cozy Mk.4	443	
F-POST	Breguet 14P *(Reservation .99)*	150-AB	
F-POTE	Pottier P.180S	180	F-WOTE
F-POTT	Bourgue PB-04 *(Reservation 3.04)*	01	
F-POUA	Barry Souricette *(Reservation)*	168	
F-POUF	Jodel DH.251PR	03	
F-POUN	Pottier P.220S Koala *(Reservation)*	414	
F-POUS	Gatard AG-02 Poussin *(Reservation .99)*	53	
F-PPAC	Pottier P.130L Coccinelle *(Reservation .03)*	1051	
F-PPAF	Colomban MC-15 Cri-Cri *(Reservation .00)*	580	
F-PPAH	Pottier P.60A Minacro *(Reservation .03)*	06	
F-PPAN	Nord NC.858S *(Reservation .02)*	74	F-BFSU
F-PPAP	Fisher Celebrity *(Dismantled)*	56	F-WPAP
F-PPAT	Jabiru SK-80 *(Reservation .99)*	101	F-WPAT
F-PPBH	Pottier P.230S Panda	449	
F-PPCC	Piel CP.301 Emeraude	338	
F-PPCM	Zenair CH-300 Tri-Z	3.97	
F-PPCO	Rotorway Exec 162 HDF	6509	
F-PPCY	Boland 48.12 Hot Air Bag Balloon	01	
F-PPDI	Nicollier HN-700 Ménestrel II	123	
F-PPDM	Brändli BX-2 Cherry *(Reservation .02)*	147	
F-PPDY	Dyn'Aéro MCR-01	101	F-WPDY
F-PPEJ	Jodel D.113VTC	27-A	
F-PPER	Seguineau CL-2200/12 (HAFB ?) *(Reservation 11.04)*	01	
F-PPHC	Nicollier HN-700 Ménestrel II	115	
F-PPHJ	Jodel D.113A	1790	
F-PPHM	Piper J-3C-65 Cub	12961	F-BCPX
			44-80665
F-PPIA	Chasle LMC-1	04	
F-PPJB	Jodel D.18	235	
F-PPJG	Lucas L-7 *(Reservation 3.04)*	20	
F-PPJJ	Jodel D.18 *(Same c/n quoted as SE-XMF)*	274	
F-PPJM	Jodel D.119 *(Reservation)*	1599	
F-PPJR	Renaud 01	01	

F-PPLS	Colomban MC-15 Cri-Cri *(Reservation .00)*	322	
F-PPMD	Piel CP.1321 Super Emeraude	70	
F-PPMF	Stern ST-87 Europlane	36	
F-PPMU	Pottier P.180S	110	
F-PPOT	Rutan Long-Ez	1950-L	
F-PPOU	Mignet HM.383 *(Reservation 5.03)*	112	
F-PPPD	Jodel D.119 (ex D.121)	1405	
F-PPPK	Druine D.31 Turbulent	207	
F-PPPL	Leglaive Miniplane *(Wfu)*	1	
F-PPPO	Druine D.31 Turbulent	316	
F-PPPP	Jurca MJ.2E Tempête	26	
F-PPPS	Jodel D.113 (ex D.119)	1427	
F-PPPV	Jodel D.92 Bébé (ex D.95)	532	
F-PPPX	Jodel D.119	1039	
F-PPRB	Jodel D.112 Club	1767	
F-PPRC	Péna Bilouis	26	
F-PPRJ	Pottier P.230S Panda *(Reservation .03)*	496	
F-PPRP	Piel CP.320 Super Emeraude	434	
F-PPRQ	Jodel D.120	257	F-BMOX
	(Previously rebuilt with c/n 283)		F-BMAX
F-PPSA	Sens AS-05	01	
F-PPSE	Leys VL1050 Le Petit Prince Balloon	01	
F-PPTL	Dyn'Aéro CR.100C *(Reservation .99)*	30	
F-PPVD	Dufour Bil'Aero OD-01	1	
F-PPVJ	Pottier P.60A Minacro *(Reservation .01)*	02	
F-PPYL	Luciani PL-160	01	
F-PPYS	Jodel D.112 Club	1778	
F-WPZA	Rebas-Courcel Gyrocopter *(Reservation)*	01	
F-PPZB	Jurca MJ.2D Tempête	13	F-WPZB
F-PPZD	Jurca MJ.5F1 Sirocco	26	
F-PPZF	Jodel D.119 (ex D.112)	1426	
F-PPZG	Barbaro RB-60	01	
	(Rebuilt 1976-86 with fuselage of Auster J/5 F-BEAV c/n 2028)		
F-PPZI	Gazuit-Valladeau GV-1031	01	F-WPZI
F-PPZK	Jodel D.112 Club	1414	
F-PPZL	Jodel D.119	1290	
F-PPZM	Croses EAC-3 *(Reservation)*	5	
F-PPZP	Jodel D.113 (ex D.119)	1419	
F-PPZX	Druine D.31B2 Turbulent	60	
F-PQCD	CQR-01 Quercy *(Reservation .04)*	19	
F-PQNO	Dyn'Aéro MCR-01	14	F-WSLI
F-PQUA	Dyn'Aéro MCR-01	21	F-WQUA
F-PQUA(2)	Aurore Souricette	168	F-WQUA
F-PQUB	KIS TR-1	034	F-WQUB
F-PQUC	Dyn'Aéro MCR-01	26	F-WQUC
F-WQUD	Dyn'Aéro MCR-01 *(Reservation)*	10	
F-PQUE	Dyn'Aéro MCR-01	25	F-WQUE
F-WQUF	Dyn'Aéro MCR-01 *(Reserved as F-PDOG)*	18	
F-PQUG	Dyn'Aéro MCR-01	16	F-WQUG
F-PQUK	Murphy Rebel	490	F-WQUK
F-PQUL	Europa Aviation Europa	184	F-WQUL
F-PQUM	Dyn'Aéro MCR-01	70	F-WQUM
F-PQUN	Dyn'Aéro MCR-01	04	F-WQUN
F-PQUO	Light Aero Avid Flyer IV	1507	F-WQUO
F-PQUP	Dyn'Aéro MCR-01	09	F-WQUP
F-PQUS	Jodel D.20 *(To 55-JT but still regd)*	11	F-WQUS
F-PQUT	Jodel D.20	09	F-WQUT
F-PQUU	Neico Lancair 320	691	F-WQUU
F-PQUV	Dyn'Aéro MCR-01	42	F-WQUV
F-PRAA	Jodel D.19	288	
F-PRAB	Jodel D.18	90	
F-PRAC	Pottier P.180S	206	
F-PRAD	Colomban MC-15 Cri-Cri	389	
F-PRAE	Jodel D.19T	220-T	
F-PRAF	Jodel D.18	47	
F-PRAG	Rutan Cozy	279	
F-PRAH	Jurca MJ.53 Autan	1	
F-PRAI	Jodel D.18V	227	
F-PRAJ	Jodel D.18	131	
F-PRAK	Piel CP.402 Donald	9	
F-PRAL	Pottier P.180S	195	F-WRAL
F-PRAM	Jodel D.19	196-T	
F-PRAO	Jodel D.18	315	
F-PRAP	GR.90 Condor *(Reservation)*	01	
F-PRAQ	Jodel D.19T	24	
F-PRAR	Rutan Long-Ez	2039L	F-WRAR
F-PRAS	Viking Dragonfly Mk.3	966	
F-PRAT	Jodel D.113	1671	
F-PRAU	Jodel D.113	1550	
F-PRAV	Jodel DR.1053M	795	
F-PRAX	Jodel D.19	271	
F-PRAZ	Gardan GY-201 Minicab	A-243	
F-PRBA	Druine D.31 Turbulent	414	F-WRBA
F-PRBB	Bücker Bü .131 Jungmann	R-1	F-WRBB
	(Believed to be a rebuild of CASA I-131E Jungmann ex E3B-459, G-BECY)		
F-PRBC	Jodel D.119	1675	
F-WRBD	Quickie Quickie Q-1	31154-84	
F-PRBE	Stolp SA.750 Acroduster Too	224	
F-PRBF	Jodel D.18	311	
F-PRBI	Olagnier Pélican	01	
F-PRBJ	Avaram	01	
F-PRBK	Evans VP-1 Volksplane	2344	
F-PRBL	Deborde-Rolland Cobra 200A	01	
F-PRBM	Piel CP-750A Beryl	14	
F-PRBN	Croses EC-3 Pouplume	58	
F-PRBO	Jodel D.19	309	
F-PRBP	Rutan Long-Ez	2080L	

F-PRBQ	Cassutt IIIM	169	
F-PRBR	Jodel D.18	176	
F-PRBS	Sens 01 *(formerly LC-3 Sagittaire c/n 23)*	01	
F-PRBT	Colomban MC-15 Cri-Cri	301	D-GLMH
			F-PZIX
F-PRBU	Zenair CH-600 Zodiac	6-1	
F-PRBV	Gatard AG.02 Poussin	33	
F-PRBX	Jodel D.113	1654	
F-PRBZ	Colomban MC-15 Cri-Cri	471	
F-PRCA	Jodel D.92 Bébé	692	
F-PRCB	K&S Jungster 1J1	8001-RL	
F-PRCC	Viking Dragonfly Mk.3	0538	
F-PRCD	Jurca MJ.53 Autan	02	
F-WRCE	Pottier P.180S	007	
F-PRCG	Pottier P.180S	92	
F-PRCH	Piel CP.1320 Saphir	34	
F-PRCJ	Jodel D.18	96	
F-PRCK	Lucas L-5-03	47	F-WRCK
F-PRCL	Brügger MB.2 Colibri	71	
F-PRCM	Piel CP.80	73	
F-PRCN	Jodel D.119D	1642	
F-PRCO	Jodel D.18	56	
F-PRCP	Stern ST-87 Europlane	01	
F-PRCR	Jodel D.19	297	
F-PRCS	Taylor JT.2 Titch	F4	
F-PRCT	CAP-XB	01	F-WRCT
F-PRCU	Jeoffroy JJ-01	01	F-WRCU
	(Modified Jodel DR.1052 c/n 773)		
F-PRCV	Nicollier HN-700 Ménestrel II	17	
F-PRCY	Lucas L-5	44	
F-PRDA	Jodel D.19T	318-T	
F-PRDB	Brügger MB.2 Colibri	171	F-WRDB
F-PRDC	Jodel D.18	126	
F-PRDD	Ferrière LF-04	01	
F-PRDE	Jodel D.18	134	
F-PRDF	Jodel D.18	281	
F-PRDG	Colomban MC-15 Cri-Cri	314	
F-PRDH	Jodel D.150/120	129	
F-PRDI	Stern ST-85 Evasion	01	F-WRDI
F-PRDJ	WagAero Sport Trainer	842	F-WRDJ
F-PRDK	Rutan Long-Ez	1197	
F-PRDL	Rutan Cozy	E-731	F-WRDL
F-WRDM	Deborde-Rolland Cobra 260	01	
F-PRDN	Daurelle AD-02	01	
F-PRDP	Nicollier HN-700 Ménestrel II	6	
F-PRDR	Pottier P.180S	185	
F-PRDS	Rutan Long-Ez	1859L	F-WRDS
F-WRDT	Jurca MJ.10 Spitfire	1	
F-PRDU	Denize RD-105 Raid Driver	24	
F-PRDV	Croses EC-6 Criquet	84	
F-PRDX	Nicollier HN-434 Super Ménestrel	29	
F-PRDY	Nicollier HN-700 Ménestrel II	38	
F-PRDZ	Jodel D.18	269	
F-WREA	DGH-02 Gyrocopter	2	
F-WREB	Tadrent TA-01 Gyrocopter	01	
F-WREC	Quetzal Gyrocopter	01	
F-WRED	Averso AX-02 Gyrocopter	22	
F-WREE	CFB-01 Gyrocopter	01	
F-PREF	Nicollier HN.434 Super Ménestrel	75	
F-WREF	Bensen-B-8 Gyrocopter	8-104-100	
	(Same c/n as quoted for F-WYUV)		
F-WREG	La Colombe Gyrocopter *(former c/n 01)*	02	
F-PREH	Druine D.5 Turbi	25	
F-WREI	Rouet JR Guêpe Gyrocopter	01	
F-WREJ	Averso AX-02 Gyrocopter	20	
F-PREK	Humbert Moto du Ciel DA	8807	
F-WREL	Fauvette Gyrocopter	01	
F-WREM	Averso AX-02 Gyrocopter	23	
F-WREN	Averso AX-02 Gyrocopter	24	
F-WREO	Averso AX-02 Gyrocopter	21	
F-WREP	Bensen B-8 Gyrocopter	104-OF	
F-WREQ	Averso AX-02 Gyrocopter	26	
F-WRER	Averso AX-02 Gyrocopter	25	
F-PRES	Jodel D.19	I99-T	
F-WRET	Auque AM-01 Gyrocopter	01	
F-PRET(2)	Murphy Rebel	526R	
F-WREU	Elixir Gyrocopter	1	
F-PREU(2)	Pottier P.220S Koala	463	
F-WREV	Vigneron POMV Gyrocopter	01	
F-PREV(2)	Rutan VariEze	1961	
F-WREX	Averso AX-02 Gyrocopter	28	
F-WREY	TUR-1 Gyrocopter	001	
F-WREZ	Averso AX-02 Gyrocopter	29	
F-WRFA	Light Aero Avid Flyer	539	
F-WRFB	Light Aero Avid Amphibian	78-A	
F-PRFC	Light Aero Avid Flyer	695	F-WRFC
F-WRFD	Light Aero Avid Flyer	646	
F-WRFF	Light Aero Avid Flyer	543	
F-WRFG	Light Aero Avid Flyer	479	
F-WRFH	Aviasud Mistral Mk.10	130	
F-WRFI	Light Aero Avid Amphibian	63	
F-PRFK	Neico Lancair 235	197	F-WRFK
F-PRFL	Christen Eagle 2	TA-3	F-WRFL
F-PRFM	Light Aero Avid Flyer Mk.IV	729	F-WRFM
F-WRFN	Light Aero Avid Flyer	797	
F-WRFO	Light Aero Avid Flyer	537	
F-PRFP	Light Aero Avid Flyer Mk.IV	727	F-WRFP

F-WRFQ	Light Aero Avid Flyer	728	
F-PRFR	Neico Lancair 235	195	F-WRFR
F-WRFS	Rans S-10 Sakota	05-911-33	
F-WRFT	Rans S-10 Sakota	04-911-29	
F-WRFU	Light Aero Avid Flyer	645	
F-PRFV	Light Aero Avid Flyer	723	F-WRFV
F-PRFX	Light Aero Avid Flyer	536	F-WRFX
F-PRFY	Light Aero Avid Flyer	690	F-WRFY
F-WRFZ	Christen Eagle 2	MG-2	
F-WRGA	Franck Gyrocopter	002	
F-WRGB	Doucet DP-1 Gyrocopter	01	
F-WRGC	Averso AX-02 Gyrocopter	27	
F-WRGD	Herzig HF-1 Gyrocopter	01	
F-WRGE	Averso AX-02 Gyrocopter	31	
F-WRGF	Averso AX-02 Gyrocopter	30	
F-WRGG	GA-LAPA-1 Gyrocopter	01	
F-WRGH	Radas RR-2 Gyrocopter	01	
F-WRGI	Rabillard CR-02 Gyrocopter	01	
F-WRGJ	Sagittaire Gyrocopter	02	
F-WRGK	Cartier-Traverse CT1 Gyrocopter	01	
F-WRGL	Chauvin & Changeur CHA-2 Gyrocopter	01	
F-WRGM	Playe PL-B-1 Gyrocopter	01	
F-WRGN	Flying Dream Gyrocopter	01	
F-WRGO	Averso AX-06 Guepard Gyrocopter	01	
F-WRGP	Weinbrenner J.W.Gyrocopter	004	
F-WRGQ	Nieddu NA-01 Gyrocopter	01	
F-WRGR	Averso AX-02 Gyrocopter / Snoopy	1	
F-WRGS	Ceyrat JC Gyrocopter	01	
F-WRGT	Colibri Gyrocopter	02	
F-WRGU	Averso AX-02 Gyrocopter	32	
F-WRGV	Maisonhaute MB-1 Gyrocopter	01	
F-WRGX	Max-1 Gyrocopter	1	
F-WRGY	Averso AX-06 Guepard Gyrocopter	2	
F-WRGZ	DGH-02 Gyrocopter	1	
F-WRHA	Gisquet JG-1 Gyrocopter	01	
F-WRHB	Roum TOW Gyrocopter	01	
F-WRHC	Ledent LL-1 Gyrocopter	01	
F-WRHD	Eclair Gyrocopter	01	
F-WRHE	Soubsol S-1S Gyrocopter	01	
F-PRHF	Gyrocopter Mk.1	01	F-WRHF
F-WRHG	B.TPR Gyrocopter	01	
F-WRHH	Doleac DJP-03 Gyrocopter	02	
F-WRHI	Mehault MN-1 Gyrocopter	01	
F-WRHJ	GRB Gyrocopter	01	
F-WRHK	Averso AX-02 Gyrocopter	33	
F-WRHL	Jeanneau JC-0001 Gyrocopter	01	
F-WRHM	JG-01 Gyrocopter	01	
F-WRHN	Mammouth Gyrocopter	01	
F-WRHO	Tadrent AT-1 Gyrocopter	01	
F-WRHP	Pellefigue PJF Gyrocopter	01	
F-WRHQ	DGH-03 Gyrocopter	01	
F-WRHR	Duflos DR-01 Gyrocopter	01	
F-WRHS	Averso AX-02 Gyrocopter	34	
F-WRHT	La Gazelle 01 Gyrocopter	01	
F-WRHU	Boillon RB-03 Gyrocopter	1	
F-WRHV	Lacoste HL-01 Gyrocopter	1	
F-WRHX	DGH-03 Gyrocopter	03	
F-WRHY	RM-02 Gyrocopter	1	
F-WRHZ	Averso AX-02 Gyrocopter	01	
F-PRIA	Pitts S-1D Special	7-0503	
F-PRIB	Brügger MB-2 Colibri	240	F-WRIB
F-PRIC	Pottier P.80S	024	
F-PRID	Heintz Zenith	2-124	
F-PRIE	Jodel D.19	1681	
F-PRIF	Jodel DR.1050	739	
F-PRIG	Nicollier HN-700 Ménestrel II	81	
F-PRIH	Rutan Long-Ez	2203	
F-PRII	Péna Capena	9	
F-PRIJ	Pottier P.60 Minacro	03	
F-PRIK	Colomban MC-15 Cri-Cri	67	F-WRIK
F-PRIL	Colomban MC-15 Cri-Cri	492	
F-PRIM	Zenair CH-600 Zodiac	6-1003	
F-PRIN	Piel CP.90 Pinocchio II	10	F-WRIN
F-PRIO	Jodel D.18	342	
F-PRIP	Darcissac-Grinvalds DG-87 Goëland	02	
F-PRIR	Vare JCV-24 Tangara	01	F-WRIR
F-PRIS	Rutan Long-Ez	1272	
F-PRIU	Nicollier HN-700 Ménestrel II	05	
F-PRIV	Damoure-Fabre-Lacroix DFL-6 Saphir	3	
F-PRIX	Pottier P.180S	20	F-WRIX
F-PRIZ	Jodel D.92 Bébé	811	
F-PRJA	Jodel D.18	46	
F-PRJD	Alexandre Dewoitine D-501	01	F-WRJD
	(Constructed from Mauboussin-Beaujard 130 F-PCIZ c/n 01, formerly Mauboussin 129/48 F-BCIZ c/n 226)		
F-PRJE	Jurca MJ.5H1 Sirocco	21F	
F-PRJF	Colomban MC-12 Cri-Cri	21	
F-PRJG	Piel CP-320 Super Emeraude	437	
F-PRJI	Jodel D.18	48	
F-PRJJ	Leopoldoff L-55 Colibri	LF-01-93	F-WVZR
	(Rebuild of Leopoldoff L-56 F-BHGU c/n 03)		
F-PRJL	Deborde-Rolande Cobra L-160 *(Reservn)*	01	
F-PRJM	Jess Canard *(Reservation)*	1	
F-PRJN	Jodel DR100MJJ	01	
F-PRJO	Jodel D.150 Mascaret	119	
F-PRJP	Jodel D.18 *(To 89-KG but still regd)*		214
F-PRJQ	Colomban MC-15 Cri-Cri	56	

F-PRJR	Max Plan MP.205 Busard	25	F-WRJR
F-PRJS	Rutan Long-Ez	2073-L	
F-PRJT	Jodel D.18	301	
F-PRJU	Viking Dragonfly Mk.3	1133	
F-PRJV	Jodel D.9 Bébé	83	
F-PRJX	Pottier P.230S Panda	409	
F-PRJY	Zenair CH-701 STOL *(Reservation)*	1302	
F-PRJZ	Marie JPM-01 Médoc	36	
F-WRKA	Light Aero Avid Flyer	696	
F-WRKB	Light Aero Avid Flyer	687	
F-WRKC	Denney Kitfox	410	
F-WRKD	Light Aero Avid Flyer	725	
F-WRKG	Neico Lancair 320	547	
F-PRKI	Neico Lancair 320	552	F-WRKI
F-PRKJ	Light Aero Avid Flyer *(Reserved as F-PKRJ)*	798	F-WRKJ
F-PRKK	Light Aero Avid Flyer IV	1097	F-WRKK
F-WRKL	Light Aero Avid Flyer	981	
F-WRKM	Light Aero Avid Flyer	472	
F-WRKN	Light Aero Avid Flyer	726	
F-WRKO	Light Aero Avid Flyer	799	
F-WRKP	Light Aero Avid Flyer	692	
F-PRKQ	Light Aero Avid Flyer IV	1099	F-WRKQ
F-PRKR	Light Aero Avid Flyer	696	F-WRKR
F-WRKS	Murphy Rebel	136	
	(Appears to have become F-WSDO, then C-FJCS)		
F-WRKT	Light Aero Avid Flyer	1095	
F-WRKU	Murphy Rebel	141	
F-WRKV	Light Aero Avid Flyer	1212	
F-WRKX	Light Aero Avid Flyer	724	
F-PRKY	Ultravia Pelican Club PL	438	F-WRKY
F-PRKZ	Neico Lancair 360 *(Same c/n quoted for PH-HAN)*	248	F-WRKZ
F-PRLA	Laplace RL-221	01	
F-PRLB	Jodel D.113	1702	
F-PRLC	Brändli BX-2 Cherry	110	
F-PRLD	Peters PGK-1 Hirondelle	183	F-WRLD
F-PRLE	Nicollier HN.434 Super Ménestrel	27	F-WRLE
F-PRLF	Nicollier HN.700 Ménestrel II	50	
F-PRLG	Colomban MC-15 Cri-Cri	23	F-WRLG
F-PRLH	Deborde-Rolland Cobra 202 *(Reservation)*	01	
F-WRLI	Steen Skybolt CJ-250	325	
F-PRLJ	CJL-100	01	
F-PRLK	Brändli BX-2 Cherry	145	
F-PRLL	Jodel D.113	1666	
F-PRLM	Pottier P.70S	38	
F-PRLN	Stolp SA-750 Acroduster Too	528	
F-PRLO	Stolp Starduster Too ? *(Reservation)*	unkn	
F-PRLP	Marie JPM-01 Médoc	26	
F-PRLR	Brändli BX-2 Cherry	111	
F-PRLS	Zenair CH-701 STOL	7-1349	
F-PRLT	Darcissac-Grinvalds DG-87 Goeland	03	
F-PRLU	Jodel D.113	1637	
F-PRLV	Couderc Vagabond *(Reservation)*	001	
F-PRLX	Jodel D.18	386	
F-PRLY	Decolro DRC-01	01	
F-PRLZ	Kieger AK-01	2	
F-PRMA	Nicollier HN.434 Super Ménestrel	23	
F-PRMB	Jodel D.150	123	
F-PRMC	Microgy MK-20	01	
F-PRMD	Pottier P.230S Panda	442	
F-PRME	Rutan Cozy	455	
F-PRMG	Stern ST-87C Europlane	11	
F-PRMH	Pottier P.220S Koala	446	
F-PRMI	Helicoptere Cicare CH-7 Angel *(Reservation)*	unkn	
F-PRMJ	Jodel D.18	320	
F-PRMK	Nicollier HN.700 Ménestrel II	53	
F-PRML	Viking Dragonfly Mk.2	950	
F-PRMM	Colomban MC-15 Cri-Cri	200	
F-PRMN	Brügger MB.2 Colibri	123	
F-PRMO	Lucas L-6B	01	
F-PRMR	Stern-Mallick SM Vega	01	
F-PRMS	Grinvalds G-801 Orion	21	F-WRMS
F-PRMT	Filcoa J-6 Karatoo	2907885	
F-PRMU	Piel CP.1320 Saphir	32	F-WRMU
F-PRMV	Piel CP.320 Super Emeraude	409	
F-PRMX	Rutan Long-Ez	2179	
F-PRMY	Piel CP.1321 Saphir	37	
F-PRMZ	WagAero Sportsman 2+2	885	
F-PRNA	Jodel D.140E Mousquetaire IV	431	
F-PRNB	Nicollier HN-434 Super Ménestrel	45	
F-PRNC	Zenair CH-600 Zodiac	6-3	
F-PRND	Protech PT-2	1070	
F-PRNE	Jodel DR.1053P	735	F-WRNE
F-PROB	Rutan VariEze	1432	OO-101 (OO-76)
F-PROC	Pottier P.80S	65	
F-PROD	Jodel D.113	1721	
F-PROF	Salvato SVO-01	01	
F-PROI	Heintz Zenith 100	2.127	
F-PROM	Tissot-Charbonnier TC-180 Océanair *(Reservation .03)*	02	
F-PROO(2)	Brügger MB-2 Colibri *(Reservation)*	275	
F-PROP	Dyn'Aéro MCR-01 Sportster *(Reservation .04)*	265	
F-PROQ	Pottier P.180S	171	
F-PROS	Lucas L.5	033	
F-PROU	Piel CP.322-120 Super Emeraude	424	
F-PROV	Colomban MC-15 Cri-Cri	311	
F-PROY	Jodel D.113 (regd as D.119)	1605	
F-WRPA	Berset BR-01 Gyrocopter	01	

F-PRPB	Jodel D.18	343	
F-PRPC	Pottier P.70S	15	
F-WRPH	Lucas LP-01 Gyrocopter	01	
F-PRPJ	Colomban MC-12 Cri-Cri	151	
F-PRPL	Jodel DR.1055M	811	
F-PRPM	Jodel D.140R Abeille *(Damaged 22.9.02)*	400	
F-PRPT	Nicollier HN-700 Ménestrel II	16	
F-PRPY	Colomban MC-12 Cri-Cri	24	
F-WRQA	Duquenne DM-01 Gyrocopter	1	
F-WRQB	Carbonnel CR-01 Gyrocopter	1	
F-WRQC	Averso AX-02 Gyrocopter	02	
F-WRQD	Averso AX-02G Gyrocopter	03	
F-WRQE	Vassot PV-01 Gyrocopter	001	
F-WRQF	Gyrolet 1 Gyrocopter	01	
F-WRQG	Labussiere LC-01 Gyrocopter	01	
F-WRQH	Doleac DJP-03C Gyrocopter	01	
F-WRQI	Bonnot BP-01 Gyrocopter	01	
F-WRQJ	Libellule Gyrocopter	1	
F-WRQK	Raspberry Gyrocopter	1	
F-WRQL	Doleac DJP-Max Gyrocopter	1	
F-WRQM	Hanneton Gyrocopter	1	
F-WRQN	Dupin Bizuth Gyrocopter	DD-01	
F-WRQO	Guepard Gyrocopter	01	
F-WRQP	Caylus Gyrocopter	2	
F-WRQQ	Aquila Gyrocopter	1	
F-WRQR	Pennec-Peden PP-01 Gyrcopter	01	
F-WRQS	Icarus Gyrocopter	01	
F-WRQT	Boinon GB Gyrocopter	01	
F-WRQU	Bonnafous BC Gyrocopter	02	
F-WRQV	Cherokee Gyrocopter	FK-500	
F-WRQX	Averso AX-02G Gyrocopter	GM-01	
F-WRQY	Averso AX-02 Gyrocopter	MM-01	
F-WRQZ	Bonnafous BC-2 Gyrocopter	02	
F-PRRD	Rutan Cozy	E-751	
F-PRRG	Jodel D.18	180	
F-PRRK	Rand-Robinson KR-1 *(Reservation)*	4928	
F-PRRM	Gravereau GD-2001 Milan Royale	01	
F-PRRV	Gerfan RV02	01	F-WRRV
F-PRSA	Jodel D.18	23	
F-PRSC	Rutan Cozy	593	
F-PRSG	Jodel D.119	1385	
F-PRSH	Jodel D.18	277	
F-PRSJ	Rolland RC-65	01	
F-PRSK	Van's RV-6 *(Reservation)*	23914	
F-PRSM	Dyn'Aéro MCR-4S 2002	28	
F-PRSV	Dumortier/Stampe SV.4YD *(Reservation 4.04)* (Also reserved as F-AZSV ?)	01	
F-PRSZ	Piel CP.320 Super Emeraude	427	
F-PRTD	Coupe JC-380D	8	F-WRTD
F-PRTE	Dyn'Aéro MCR-4S 2002 *(Reservation 7.04)*	31	
F-PRTJ	Godbille JG-03	01	
F-PRTR	Dyn'Aéro MCR-4S 2002	02	
F-PRUD	Nickel-Foucard NF-02 Asterix	01	
F-PRUQ	Aeromarine Skyote	63	
F-PRVI	Pottier P.180S	94	
F-PRVJ	Rutan Cozy	384	
F-PRVL	Van Lith IX bis	01	F-PYSZ F-WYSZ
F-PRVS	Van's RV-6	22239	
F-WRXA	Rans S-6ES SQFT Coyote II	0192262	
F-PRXB	Aero Designs Pulsar	07-F	F-WRXB
F-PRXC	Light Aero Avid Flyer	1219	F-WRXC
F-PRXD	Stoddard Hamilton Glasair II-RG	1060	F-WRXD
F-WRXE	Light Aero Avid Flyer	1214	
F-WRXF	Aero Designs Pulsar *(Reserved as F-PAXF)*	101	
F-WRXG	Murphy Rebel	14 . ?	
F-WRXH	Light Aero Avid Flyer	977	
F-PRXI	Light Aero Avid Flyer	795	F-WRXI
F-PRXJ	Aero Designs Pulsar 582	255-2F	F-WRXJ
F-WRXK	Light Aero Avid Flyer	1096	
F-PRXL	Light Aero Avid Flyer	976	F-WRXL
F-WRXM	Light Aero Avid Flyer Mk.IV	1094	
F-PRXN	Light Aero Avid Flyer Mk.IV *(Wrecked)*	1098	F-WRXN
F-WRXO	Rans S-9 Chaos	0790092	
F-WRXQ	Light Aero Avid Flyer	1220-D	
F-WRXR	Denney Kitfox	785	
F-WRXS	Light Aero Avid Flyer	1372	
F-PRXT	CFM Streak Shadow SA	K192-SA	F-WRXT
F-WRXU	Light Aero Avid Flyer	800	
F-WRXV	Light Aero Avid Flyer	1370	
F-PRXX	Aero Designs Pulsar	12-F	
F-PRXY	Murphy Rebel	263	F-WRXY
F-WRXZ	Dyn'Aéro CR.100C	05	
F-WRYA	Roitelet Gyrocopter	CA-01	
F-WRYB	Averso AX-02 Gyrocopter	GC-01	
F-WRYC	Rodriguez RH Gyrocopter	01	
F-WRYD	Ricard Jokari Gyrocopter	1	
F-WRYE	Averso AX-02 Gyrocopter	JB	
F-WRYF	Kimpe KM Gyrocopter	1	
F-PRYG	Jodel DR.1050	814	
F-WRYH	Portespane Gyrocopter	03	
F-WRYI	Delsol MD Gyrocopter	2703	
F-WRYJ	Pasquier PJ Gyrocopter	01	
F-WRYK	Vimon-Hoffmann VHB-1 Gyrocopter	01	
F-WRYL	AB-01 Gyrocopter	01	
F-WRYM	REL Gyrocopter	01	
F-WRYN	Dieudonne RD Gyrocopter	01	
F-WRYO	Bimbo Gyrocopter	01	
F-PRYP	Potez 60 Sauterelle	P-1991-1	
F-WRYQ	Elite 80 Gyrocopter	01	
F-WRYR	Gyrolet 3 Gyrocopter	01	
F-WRYS	Mistral 01 Gyrocopter	01	
F-WRYT	AST-1 Gyrocopter	01	
F-WRYU	Esposito GSE-01 Gyrocopter	01	
F-WRYV	Callauzene JC Gyrocopter	01	
F-WRYX	Le Gaulois 01 Gyrocopter	01	
F-WRYY	Dal-Bor 01 Gyrocopter	01	
F-WRYZ	MS-01 Abeille Gyrocopter	01	
F-PRZB	Brochet MB-50 Pipistrelle	8	F-PHZB
F-PRZZ	Rutan Cozy	414	
F-PSAB	Jodel D.20 Jubilé	01	F-WSAB
F-PSAC	Jodel D.18 *(Reservation)*	257	
F-PSAD	Delustre DD-100 *(Reservation)*	001	
F-PSAF	Mignet HM.360	166	
F-PSAG	RSA Carriou CL-3 *(Reservn, to F-PCAR?)*	01	
F-PSAM	Piel CP.322 Super Emeraude *(Reservation)*	451	
F-PSAR	Jodel D.119	1756	
F-PSAT	Murphy Rebel	523	
F-PSBC	Pottier P.230S Panda	422	
F-PSBI	Soyer-Barritault SB-1/160	01	F-WSBI
F-PSBR	Marie JPM 01 Tanagra	19	
F-PSCA	Thebault M500 CR	01	
F-PSCC	Cassutt 3M	582	
F-PSCF	Rutan Cozy	128	
F-PSCH	Pottier P.190S	01	
F-PSCJ	Pottier P.180S	52	
F-PSCK	Chudzik CC-02 *(Reservation .00)*	01	
F-PSCM	Nicollier HN-434 Super Ménestrel *(Reservation .02)*	30	
F-PSCZ	Europa Aviation Europa	192	F-WSCZ
F-PSDA	Light Aero Avid Amphibian	75	F-WSDA
F-WSDB	Light Aero Avid Flyer	1371	
F-WSDC	Light Aero Avid Flyer *(Also marked 25-MN)*	423	
F-WSDD	Light Aero Avid Flyer	1369	
F-WSDE	Rans S-6ES Coyote II	0193428	
F-WSDF	Light Aero Avid Flyer	980	
F-PSDG	Light Aero Avid Flyer IV	1210	F-WSDG
F-PSDH	Light Aero Avid Flyer	1315	F-WSDH
F-WSDI	Light Aero Avid Flyer	481	
F-WSDJ	Light Aero Avid Flyer	540	
F-WSDK	Light Aero Avid Flyer	1405	
F-WSDL	Light Aero Avid Flyer	1406	
F-PSDM	Fisher Celebrity	054	F-WSDM
F-PSDN	Light Aero Avid Magnum	26	F-WSDN
F-PSDO	Murphy Rebel	0136-R	F-WSDO
F-PSDP	Light Aero Avid Magnum	07	F-WSDP
F-PSDQ	Aero Designs Pulsar	111-F	F-WSDQ
F-PSDR	Aero Designs Pulsar 582	106-F	F-WSDR
F-WSDS	Light Aero Avid Flyer Bandit	1403	
F-PSDT	Jodel D.20 (Tricycle u/c)	14	F-WSDT(2)
F-PSDU	Murphy Rebel	269	F-WSDU
F-PSDV	Neico Lancair 320	651	F-WSDV
F-PSDX	Denney Kitfox IV Speedster	ACS-093/4152518	F-WSDX
F-PSDY	Murphy Rebel	352	F-WSDY
F-PSDZ	Aero Designs Pulsar	114-F	F-WSDZ
F-PSEA	Tissot-Charbonnier TC-160 Océanair	01	
F-PSEC	Jodel-Huguene y DH-251 *(Reservation .03)*	11	
F-PSFE	Jodel D.112 Club	1729	
F-PSFG	Tech'Aero Feugray TR-200	05	
F-PSFS	Bonnet BLJ-01	01	
F-PSGG	Grinvalds G-801 Orion	48	
F-PSHB	Jurca MJ-51 Sperocco *(Reservation .03)*	01	
F-WSHK	Monnet Sonerai 2S *(Reservation .02)*	3169023	
F-PSHR	Dyn'Aéro MCR-01	119	
F-PSIC	Jodel DR.1050M	821	
F-PSIR	Fournier RF-7	03	
F-WSIT	Europa Aviation Europa Classic *(Reservation .04)*	289	
F-PSJB	Croses LC-6 Criquet	63	
F-PSJC	Sens JCS-01 *(Reservation 10.03)*	001	
F-PSJH	JR-01 Mancha	01	
F-PSJM	LMK-1 Oryx *(Reservation, cancelled)* (Project possibly restored as F-POPF .04)	LPCA-03	
F-PSJP	DRLS 250 *(Reservation .99)*	01	
F-WSKA	Light Aero Avid Flyer	1404	
F-PSKC	Murphy Rebel	415	F-WSKC
F-WSKD	Wheeler Express	1133	
F-WSKE	Denney Kitfox	4156	
F-PSKF	Light Aero Avid Flyer IV	1218	F-WSKF
F-PSKG	Dyn'Aéro CR.100	24	F-WSKG
F-WSKH	Light Aero Avid Flyer	1502	
F-PSKI	Murphy Rebel	434	F-WSKI
F-PSKJ	Denney Kitfox Vixen 912	KCV-024	F-WSKJ
F-WSKK	Stoddard-Hamilton Glasair IIFT	2249-FT	
F-PSKL	Stoddard-Hamilton Glasair IIS-RG	2250-RG	F-WSKL
F-WSKM	Stoddard-Hamilton Glasair IIRG	unkn-RG	
F-PSKN	Stoddard-Hamilton Glasair IIS-FT	2305-FT	F-WSKN
F-WSKO	Stoddard-Hamilton Glasair IITD*(Res as F-PSUZ)*	1109-TD	
F-WSKP	Rans S-10 Sakota	988030	
F-PSKQ	Murphy Rebel	262	F-WSKQ
F-WSKR	Aero Designs Pulsar	320-2J	
F-WSKS	Light Aero Avid Flyer Speedwing	1415	
F-PSKT	Ultravia Pélican PL-914	624	F-WSKT
F-WSKU	Light Aero Avid Flyer	978	
F-PSKV	Dyn'Aéro CR.100C	25	F-WSKV

F-PSKX	Murphy Rebel *(Rebuild of c/n 256)*	538	F-WSKX
	(W/o 20.8.03)		C-FPNT
F-WSKY	Akrotech G-202 *(Reservation)*	030	
F-PSKZ	Light Aero Avid Flyer IV	1501	F-WSKZ
F-PSLA	Dyn'Aéro MCR-01 VLA	52	F-WSLA
F-WSLB	Akrotech G-202 *(W/o 3.5.98)*	27	
F-WSLD	Dyn'Aéro MCR-01 *(Reservation)*	8	
F-PSLF	Dyn'Aéro MCR-01	17	F-WSLF
F-PSLG	Dyn'Aéro MCR-01	05	F-WSLG
F-PSLH	Europa Aviation Europa	273	F-WSLH
F-WSLI	Dyn'Aéro MCR-01 *(Reserved as F-PQNO)*	14	
F-PSLJ	Stoddart-Hamilton Glastar GS-1	5079	F-WSLJ
F-PSLM	Rand-Robinson KR-2	66	
F-PSLN	Europa Aviation Europa	98	F-WSLN
F-PSLP	Pottier P.230S Panda	427	
F-PSLQ	Dyn'Aéro MCR-01	30	F-WSLQ
F-PSLR	Dyn'Aéro MCR-01	33	F-WSLR
F-PSLS	Dyn'Aéro MCR-01	44	F-WSLS
F-WSLT	Rans S-7 Courier *(Reservation)*	1295167	
F-PSLU	Light Aero Avid Magnum	97	F-WSLU
F-WSLV	Akrotech G-202 *(Reservation)*	K-04	
F-PSLX	Dyn'Aéro MCR-01	37	F-WSLX
F-PSLY	Europa Aviation Europa	275	F-WSLY
F-PSLZ	Dyn'Aéro MCR-01	39	F-WSLZ
F-PSMA	Aero Designs Pulsar	352	
F-PSMB	Nicollier HN-700 Ménestrel II	88	
F-PSMJ	Piel CP.1320 Saphir *(Reservation)*	25	
F-PSML	Jodel DR.1050-M1 *(Reservation .00)*	893	
F-PSMR	Jodel D.20	06	F-WSMR
F-PSMU	Europa Aviation Europa XS	439	
F-PSOK	Mraz M.1D Sokol *(Reservation .01)*	298	HB-TAY
F-PSPA	Alexandre SPAD VII *(Reservation 7.04)*	01	
F-PSPF	Rouet MR-01	01	
F-PSPL	Druine D.5 Turbi	77	
F-PSRD	Nicollier HN-700 Ménestrel II	127	
F-PSRG	EAA Acrosport II	964	
F-PSSA	Jodel D.119	1278-1	
F-WSSB	Bensen B-8MV Gyrocopter	unkn	
F-WSSC	Bensen B-8 Gyrocopter	unkn	
F-WSSE	Laboye-Bensen Gyrocopter	1	
F-PSSF	Druine D.31 Turbulent	182	
F-WSSG	Bensen-Testa 70 Gyrocopter	001	
F-PSSH	Jodel D.119V	1428	
F-WSSL	Raybout D-2 Autogyre	01	
F-PSSN	Jodel D.119	1399	
F-PSSO	Leblanc L.52	1	
F-WSSP	Bensen/Nuville JN-2 Gyrocopter	01	
F-PSSQ	Duranton DE Junior	01	
F-PSSR	Druine D.5 Turbi	50	F-WSSR
			F-PSSR
F-PSSS	Seckler SS-02 *(Reservation)*	01	
F-WSSS	Bensen B-8M Gyrocopter *(Cld?)*	3213	
F-WSSU	Bensen B.8MC Gyrocopter	01	
F-PSSV	Jodel D.119	1413	
F-PSSX	Gazuit-Valladeau GV-1031	02	F-BSSX
			F-WSSX
F-WSTA	Ameur Aviation Altania *(Reservation .99)*	001	
F-PSTC	Ultimate 20.300T *(Reservation)*	130 393 004	
F-PSTE	Dyn'Aéro MCR-01 Club	128	F-WWUV
F-PSTF	Dyn'Aéro MCR-4S 2002	39	F-WWUU
F-PSTO	Jodel D.113T	01	
F-PSUA	Europa Aviation Europa	310	
F-WSUD	Dyn'Aéro MCR-01 *(Reservation .00)*	unkn	
F-PSUN	Jurca MJ.77 Gnatsum	09	
F-PSUR	Brugger MB.2 Colibri	177	
F-PSUZ	Stoddard-Hamilton Glasair II-TD	1109TD	F-WSKO
F-PSVR	Jodel DR.100	843	
F-WSYB	Gyrol L-2 Autogyre	002	
F-PSYC	Jodel D.119	1432	
F-PSYD	Jodel D.112 Club *(Stored)*	1472	
F-PSYE	Starck AS.80 Holiday	58	
F-PSYH	Druine D.5 Turbi	27	
F-WSYJ	Bensen B.8M Gyrocopter	01	
F-PSYN	Mignet HM.360	128	F-WSYN
F-PSYP	Jodel D.112 Club	1447	
F-WSYR	Campbell Cricket Gyrocopter	CA/342	G-AYHJ
F-WSYS	Bensen B-8M Gyrocopter	01	
F-PSYT	Roy Mignet GR	01	F-WSYT
F-WSYZ	Bensen B-8M	01	
F-WSZA	Bouget-Capdeville BC-1 Gyrocopter	01	
F-WSZB	Scheila Gyrocopter	001	
F-WSZC	Fardeau Gyrocopter	001	
F-WSZD	Colin CX Gyrocopter	01	
F-WSZE	Gamin H-16 Gyrocopter	01	
F-WSZF	Lion Gyrocopter	001	
F-WSZG	Cobra Gyrocopter	01	
F-WSZH	Marquion-Dreyer MD-05B Gyrocopter	001	
F-WSZI	BouilinBJM-III Gyrocopter	001	
F-WSZJ	Averso AX-02 Gyrocopter	LJS-01	
F-WSZK	Averso AX-02 Gyrocopter	unkn	
F-WSZL	Rapetout Gyrocopter	01	
F-WSZM	Albatros Gyrocopter	02	
F-WSZN	Arc en Ciel Gyrocopter	01	
F-WSZO	Dieudonne RD-02 Gyrocopter	01	
F-WSZP	GS-01 Gyrocopter	01	
F-WSZQ	Maury M-1 Gyrocopter	001	
F-WSZR	Martins OM Gyrocopter	01	
F-WSZS	Rivollier-Bernardi RB Gyrocopter	01	
F-WSZU	Averso AX-02 Gyrocopter	001	
F-WSZV	Faure JPF-002 Gyrocopter	002	
F-WSZX	Libellule Gyrocopter	01	
F-WSZY	Colibri Gyrocopter	01	
F-WSZZ	Palombe Gyrocopter	01	
F-PTAH	Startrap FG-01 *(Dismantled)*	01	
F-PTAJ	Piel CP.615 Super Diamant	57	
F-PTAM	Rutan Long-Ez *(Reservation)*	1515	
F-PTAT	W.A.R. FW.190A Replica	117	F-WTAT
F-PTAV	Pottier P.230S Panda	452	
F-PTBG	Van's RV-4	2841	
F-WTBS	Steen Skybolt	478	
F-PTCA	Stern ST-87 Europlane *(Reservation .99)*	47	
F-PTCC	Stern ST-87 Europlane	32	
F-PTCD	Ameur Avn Baljims 1A	01	
F-PTCM	Jurca MJ.77 Gnatsum *(Reservation)*	02	
F-PTCR	Dyn'Aéro CR.120 *(Reservation)*	02	
F-PTDD	G-802 Gerfaut *(Reservation .99)*	04	F-WTDD
F-PTDM	Jurca MJ.2H Tempête	10	
F-WTEA	Queniet QG-01 Gyrocopter	04	
F-WTEB	Descatha DB Gyroglider	01	
F-WTEC	Bensen B-8M Gyrocopter	01	
F-WTED	Danis DB Giroplaneur	01	
F-WTEE	Danis DB Giroplaneur Nautic	03	
F-WTEF	Danis DB Giroplaneur Nautic	02	
F-WTEG	Danis DB Autogire	01	
F-PTEJ	Jurca MJ.5-K2 Sirocco	16	
F-PTEK	Jodel D.112 Club	1459	
F-WTEM	Bensen B.8MG Gyrocopter	1	
F-PTER	Jurca MJ.2D Tempête	34	
F-WTEY	Bensen B.8MB Gyrocopter	01	
F-WTEZ	Bensen B.8MT Gyrocopter	01	
F-PTEZ(2)	Potez 60-EF	01	
F-PTGI	Dyn'Aéro MCR-01	115	
F-PTIC	Secat S-5 *(Reservation .03)*	01	F-PIIC
			F-WCDS
F-PTIM	Bartoli BR-01	01	
F-PTIO	Dyn'Aéro MCR-01 Sportster	186	
F-PTIS	Tissot-Charbonnier TC-120 Oceanair	1	
F-PTIT	Dyn'Aéro MCR-01 Club GD	02	
F-PTJB	G-802B Gerfaut *(Reservation .99)*	03	
F-PTJC	Rutan Cozy *(Reservation)*	E-716	
F-PTJD	Pottier P.70S *(Reservation .01)*	42	
F-PTJM	Rutan VariEze	1756	
F-PTLC	WagAero Sport Trainer	1240	
F-PTLF	G-802L Gypaete *(Reservation .99)*	01	
F-PTMV	Rutan Cozy	CC-1058	
F-PTNF	Tipsy Nipper Marquis *(Damaged 13.7.03)*	01	
F-PTOP	Jodel DR.1050M *(Reservation)*	783	
F-PTOY	Clenet DC-01 Baboo *(Reservation)*	01	
F-PTRA	Jodel DH.251	08	
F-PTRB	Bodenan CRD-01 *(Reservation)*	01	
F-PTRC	Parker Teenie Two	15-1838	
F-PTRD	Rotorway Exec 162HDF *(Reservation 6.04)*	6792	
F-PTSH	Jodel D.140R Abeille	434	
F-PTSL	Sequoia F.8L Falco *(Reservation .04)*	1350	(F-PFSL)
F-PTSM	Pennec & Lucas PL-5 Dieselis *(Reservation .04)*	14	
F-PTVC	Tissot & Charbonnier TC-160 Océanair *(Reservn 12.04)*	04	
F-PTVH	Dyn'Aéro CR.100C	29	
F-PTXA	Jodel D.119	1276	
F-PTXC	Croses EC.8 Tourisme	18	F-WTXC
F-PTXE	Vintras JPV.30 Joker	01	F-WTXE
F-PTXG	Heintz Zenith	16	
F-WTXI	Bensen B.8M Gyroplaneur	01	
F-PTXM	Jurca MJ.2D Tempête	21	
F-WTXN	Bensen-Sica SP-01 Gyrocopter	01	
F-PTXO	Druine D.31 Turbulent	359	
F-PTXP	Jodel D.119A	1341	
F-WTXQ	Bensen B.8MB Gyrocopter	01	
F-PTXR	Jodel D.119	1502	
F-PTXU	Piel CP.320A Super Emeraude	83	F-WTXU
F-WTXV	Bensen JC-01 Gyrocopter	01	
F-WTXZ	Rouaux RB-01 Gyrocopter	01	
F-WTYB	Bonnafous B-5 Gyrocopter	01	
F-WTYC	Le Roitelet Gyrocopter	01	
F-WTYE	FGA Gyrocopter	01	
F-WTYF	Flying Dream Gyrocopter	02	
F-WTYG	Vignan JPV Corfou Gyrocopter	01	
F-WTYH	Despaux DR Gyrocopter	01	
F-WTYI	BMW Gyrocopter	01	
F-WTYJ	Lacombe Gyrocopter	01	
F-WTYK	Colibri Gyrocopter	01	
F-WTYL	Mondary JM Gyrocopter	01	
F-WTYM	Zéphir Gyrocopter	01	
F-WTYN	Tête Brûlée Gyrocopter	01	
F-WTYO	Averso AX-02 Gyrocopter	01	
F-WTYP	Tigre Opter Gyrocopter	07	
F-WTYQ	Phénix Gyrocopter	01	
F-WTYR	OK Gyrocopter	01	
F-WTYS	AG-15 Gyrocopter	15	
F-WTYT	Puente PR Gyrocopter	01	
F-WTYU	Aubin DA Gyrocopter	01	
F-WTYV	Ousset OA Gyrocopter	01	
F-WTYX	Galaxy Gyrocopter	01	
F-WTYY	Averso AX-02 Gyrocopter	01	
F-WTYZ	Weinbrenner Gyrocopter	05	

F-WTZA	Mila 01 Gyrocopter	01	
F-WTZB	Beltrando BD-01 Gyrocopter	01	
F-WTZC	Python Gyrocopter	01	
F-WTZD	Dilal Gyrocopter	01	
F-WTZE	Picsou Gyrocopter	01	
F-WTZF	GJ Gyrocopter	02	
F-WTZG	Glemet GJL Gyrocopter	01	
F-WTZH	Dessart-Larioze DL Gyrocopter	01	
F-WTZI	Enfossi EJM Gyrocopter	01	
F-WTZJ	VHM Gyrocopter	01	
F-WTZK	Averso AX-02 Gyrocopter	01	
F-WTZL	Evenot EL-02 Gyrocopter	01	
F-WTZM	Derlan Gyrocopter	01	
F-WTZN	Michelot DM Gyrocopter	01	
F-WTZO	Kloeti RK Gyrocopter	01	
F-PTZP	Magni M-18 Gyrocopter	01	F-WTZP
F-WTZQ	Colombie OC Gyrocopter	01	
F-WTZR	Raoul Gyrocopter	01	
F-WTZS	Berger BX Guepard Gyrocopter	01	
F-WTZT	Romagnoli RJ Gyrocopter	01	
F-WTZU	Le Loup Gyrocopter	01	
F-WTZV	Maffre Gyrocopter	01	
F-WTZX	Tiercelin GT Gyrocopter	01	
	(Noted marked as Averso AX07, 8.99)		
F-WTZY	Navarro Gyrocopter *(Reservation)*	01	
F-WTZZ	Ducos G-3 Gyrocopter *(Reservation)*	01	
F-PUAV	Dyn'Aéro MCR-4S 2002	46	F-WWUY
F-PUCE	Dyn'Aéro MCR-01	36	F-WUCE
F-PUCH	Brändli BX-2 Cherry *(Reservation)*	151	
F-PUCK	Motopompe *(Reservation)*	01	
F-PUCY	Bonnavaud LB-01	01	
F-PUFB	Nicollier HN.343 Ménestrel *(Noted 7.01)*	unkn	
F-PUIG	Brügger MB-2 Colibri	102	
F-PUJG	Colomban MC-15 Cri-Cri (Res)	110	
F-PULC	Nicollier HN.700 Ménestrel II	37	
F-PULL	Piel CP.320 Super Emeraude *(Reservation .01)*	460	
F-PULP	Ferrier AAL-01	01	
F-PULS	Aero Designs Pulsar	109-F	F-WSKB
F-PULY	CAR-01 *(Reservation .04)*	22	
F-PUMA	Piel CP.320 Super Emeraude	440	
F-PUNK	Jurca MJ.52 Zephyr *(Reservation .99)*	01	
F-PUPY	Preceptor Ultra Pup *(Reservn., or F-PUPI ?)*	129	
F-WUQQ	Scorpion Gyrocopter	01	
F-PURG	Jodel D.119A *(Reservation)*	1699	F-PHUG
F-PURL	Rutan Long-Ez *(Reservation .04)*	127	
F-WURR	Murphy Rebel *(Reservation .99)*	268R	
F-PURU	Dyn'Aéro MCR-01 Sportster	218	
F-WUSA	Bervat Gyrocopter *(Reservation)*	01	
F-WUSB	Ferrie FB Gyrocopter *(Reservation)*	01	
F-WUSC	Durand DC Gyrocopter *(Reservation)*	01	
F-WUSD	Gurau GG Gyrocopter *(Reservation)*	01	
F-WUSE	Gayaud GR Gyrocopter *(Reservation)*	01	
F-WUSF	Kerchaun KD Gyrocopter *(Reservation)*	01	
F-WUSG	Palavadeau Bensen 002 Gyrocopter *(Res.)*	02	
F-WUSH	Delfour DC Gyrocopter *(Reservation)*	01	
F-WUSI	Averso AX Gyrocopter *(Reservation)*	06	
F-WUSJ	Max Gyrocopter *(Reservation)*	001	
F-WUSK	Averso Guepard Gyrocopter *(Reservation)*	01	
F-WUSL	Fior Gyrocopter *(Reservation)*	01	
F-WUSM	Averso AX-02 Gyrocopter *(Reservation)*	01	
F-WUSN	Averso AX-02 Gyrocopter *(Reservation)*	01	
F-WUSO	VHB-1 Supercopter *(Reservation)*	01	
F-WUSP	Bonnafous BC03 Gyrocopter *(Reservation)*	01	
F-WUSQ	Daubert DF Gyrocopter *(Reservation)*	01	
F-WUSR	Magni Gyrocopter *(Reservation)*	01	
F-WUSS	Aerogi Gyrocopter *(Reservation)*	01	
F-WUST	Snoopy Gyrocopter *(Reservation)*	01	
F-WUSU	Equilibre 2 Gyrocopter *(Reservation)*	01	
F-WUSV	Odorico R-003 Gyrocopter *(Reservation)*	03	
F-WUSX	Delawind Gyrocopter *(Reservation)*	01	
F-WUSY	Rangers Gyrocopter *(Reservation)*	001	
F-WUSZ	Pisoni P-01 Gyrocopter *(Reservation)*	01	
F-WUTA	Sorrano GSXR Gyrocopter *(Reservation)*	01	
F-WUTB	Moustique Gyrocopter *(Reservation)*	001	
F-WUTC	Averso Guepard Gyrocopter *(Reservation)*	01	
F-WUTD	Lopez Gyrocopter *(Reservation)*	001	
F-WUTE	Faulcon Gyrocopter *(Reservation)*	01	
F-WUTF	Averso AX-2 Guepard Gyrocopter *(Res.)*	01	
F-WUTG	Averso AX-2 Guepard Gyrocopter *(Res.)*	01	
F-WUTH	Progressor Pou Gyrocopter *(Reservation)*	01	
F-WUTI	Maya Gyrocopter *(Reservation)*	001	
F-WUTJ	Jacquelin JMJ Gyrocopter *(Reservation)*	001	
F-WUTK	Lignac J'Ais'Quim'Faut Gyrocopter *(Res.)*	001	
F-WUTL	Betaille BG Gyrocopter *(Reservation)*	01	
F-WUTM	Creusot HC Gyrocopter *(Reservation)*	01	
F-WUTN	Martins OM-02 Gyrocopter *(Reservation)*	unkn	
F-WUTO	Benus Gyrocopter *(Reservation)*	002	
F-WUTP	Techer JYT Gyrocopter *(Reservation)*	01	
F-WUTQ	Petitgirard VP-01 Gyrocopter *(Reservation)*	01	
F-WUTR	Kloeti RK-02 Gyrocopter *(Reservation)*	02	
F-WUTS	Averso AX-02 Guepard Gyrocopter *(Res.)*	01	
F-WUTT	Schaeffer MS-01 Gyrocopter *(Reservation)*	01	
F-WUTU	Magni M-16 Trainer Gyrocopter *(Reservn)*	01	
F-WUTV	Averso AX-02 Guepard Gyrocopter *(Res.)*	01	
F-WUTX	Air Command 582 Gyrocopter *(Reservn)*	KC-164	
F-WUTY	Cena CP-003 Gyrocopter *(Reservation)*	03	
F-WUTZ	Averso AX-02 Guepard Gyrocopter *(Res.)*	01	

F-WUUA	Bensen B-8 Gyrocopter *(Reservation)*	01	
F-WUUB	Berva Gyrocopter *(Reservation)*	03	
F-WUUC	Colibri 2 Gyrocopter *(Reservation)*	01	
F-WUUD	Sundarp MS-1 Gyrocopter *(Reservation)*	01	
F-WUUE	(Agnelet) Autogyre *(Reservation)*	01	
F-WUUF	Mosquito Killer Gyrocopter *(Reservation)*	001	
F-WUUG	Fourlade JF Dominator Gyrocopter *(Res.)*	01	
F-WUUH	Gabi Gyrocopter *(Reservation)*	02	
F-WUUI	X2 Gyrocopter *(Reservation)*	001	
F-WUUJ	Vil Coyote Gyrocopter *(Reservation)*	unkn	
F-WUUK	Magni M-14 Gyrocopter *(Reservation)*	01	
F-WUUL	Magni M-18 Gyrocopter *(Reservation)*	01	
F-WUUM	Magni M-16 Gyrocopter *(Reservation)*	01	
F-WUUN	Monoplace CBGyrocopter *(Reservation .99)*	01	
F-WUUO	Gisquet JG Gyrocopter *(Reservation .99)*	01	
F-WUUP	Magni M-16 Gyrocopter *(Reservation .99)*	01	
F-WUUQ	Mourier Gyrocopter *(Reservation .99)*	01	
F-WUUR	Polge Gyrocopter *(Reservation .99)*	01	
F-PUYJ	Dyn'Aéro MCR-4S 2002	40	
F-PUZL	Light Aero Avid Amphibian	61	F-WRFE
F-PVAC	Van's RV-6A	25387	
F-PVAJ	Jodel D.113	1669	
F-PVAL	Disdier JD-01 *(Reservation)*	01	
F-PVAP	Jodel DR.1052M Ambassadeur *(Reservation .99)*	851	
F-PVAR	Van's RV-6A *(Reservation 5.04)*	60542	
F-PVBC	Druine D.5 Turbi	97	
F-PVBG	Van's RV-6 *(Reservation 7.04)*	22593	
F-PVBN	Pamany PL-4A *(Reservation)*	420	
F-PVBR	Weinbrenner HJW-01 *(Reservation .02)*	001	
F-PVDB	Vandenbrock VDB-01 Gyrocopter	01	
F-PVDD	Stern ST-87 Europlane *(Reservation .02)*	12	
F-PVDG	Piel CP.320 Super Emeraude	442	
F-PVDM	Piel CP.618A Super Diamant	59	
F-PVDN	Dyn'Aéro CR.100	14	
F-PVDV	Delvion DVDiesel	01	
F-PVGB	Autogyre PVGB-01	01	
F-PVGR	WAR FW.190A Replica *(Reservation .02)*	368	
F-PVGS	Changeur-Gianinetti Cg-01	01	
F-PVIB	Jodel D.140 Mousquetaire *(Reservation .01)*	457	
F-PVIC	Dyn'Aéro MCR-4S 2002	30	
F-PVIL	Velocity Standard RG	046	
F-PVIN	Stolp SA.750 Acroduster Too	150	
F-PVIP	Van's RV-4	730	
F-PVIR	Quercy AR	07	
F-PVIT	Beck BK Sut Evolution *(Reservation .02)*	03	
F-PVIV	Albouy M5PA	01	
F-PVJB	Wittmann W-10 Tailwind *(Reservation 11.04)*	1212	
F-PVJC	Van's RV-6	24287	
F-PVJF	Viking Dragonfly Mk 1 *(Reservation)*	1017	
F-PVJM	Piel CP.615C Super Diamant *(Reservation .04)*	75	
F-PVLS	Piel CP.320 Super Emeraude	435	
F-PVLT	Notteghem Occitan Club	06	F-WVLT
F-PVMA	Jurca MJ.5L2 Sirocco *(Reservation)*	113	
F-PVMC	Rutan Cozy	E-747	
F-PVMM	Lucas L-8	01	
F-PVMR	Dyn'Aéro MCR-01	139	
F-PVMT	Marie JPM-01 Médoc *(Reservation .00)*	50	
F-PVNK	Dyn'Aéro MCR-01 Sportster *(Reservation 9.04)*	201	
F-PVQB	Delattre/Potez 60 Sauterelle	1	
F-PVQE	Piel CP.310 Emeraude	364	
F-PVQG	Pottier P.70	01	
F-WVQH	Laboye HL-01 Gyrocopter	01, or 2 ?	
F-PVQN	Druine D.5 Turbi	9	
F-PVQP	Jurca MJ.2D Tempête	17	
F-PVQQ	Chatelain AC.11	01	
F-PVQR	Roloff RLU-1 Breezy	FE1/01	
F-PVQS	Heintz Zenith 100LR	03	F-WVQS
F-PVQT	Heintz Zenith	7	
F-PVQU	Heintz Zenith 130	22MF	
F-PVQV	Heintz Zenith 125 FLR	04	
F-PVQX	Leger JCL 01 *(To 37- . .)*	1	F-WVQX
F-WVQZ	Geiser G-10 Motodelta	01	
F-PVRD	Druine D.31 Turbulent	395	F-WVRD F-PZRD
F-PVRO	Colomban MC-15 Cri-Cri	379	
F-PVSG	Dyn'Aéro MCR-4S 2002 *(Reservation .04)*	25	
F-PVSM	Dyn'Aéro MCR-01	89	
F-PVVA	ACBA-7 Midour	03	
F-PVVP	ACBA-7 Midour	02	
F-PVYN	Jodel D.18T	483	
F-WWMU	Ameur Altania	unkn	
F-WWNA	Murphy Rebel 912	485	
F-WWNB	Murphy Rebel 912	486	
F-WWNO	Sauper ADV.01 Papango	01	
F-WWUU	Dyn'Aéro MCR-01	69 (and others)	
F-PXAD	ACALLA-Jodel D.140E Mousquetaire	428	
F-PXAK	Jodel D.112 Club	1660	
F-PXAV	BK Sud Eleisson	01	
F-PXDV	Landray GL.1	01	F-WXDV
F-PXEC	Rotorway Exec 162HDF	6651	
F-PXGX	Guillaumaud GX-01 *(Reservation)*	01	F-WXGX
	(Probably Guillaumaud Glasair II N111XG c/n 3071)		
F-PXJB	Rutan VariEze	1763	
F-PXJJ	Nicollier HN-700 Ménestrel II *(Reservation .02)*	172	
F-PXKA	Jurca MJ.2D Tempête	8	

F-PXKB	Gatard Statoplan AG-02 Poussin	19	F-WXKB
F-PXKC(2)	Jurca MJ.2A Tempête	42	F-WXKC
			(F-PYBR(1))
F-PXKE	Mudry CAP.10B	A-1	
F-PXKI	Jurca MJ.5 Sirocco	27	
F-PXKJ	Jodel D.112 Club	1488	
F-PXKK	Croses LC.10 Criquet	01	F-WXKK
F-WXKM	Eysseric F Gyrocopter	01	
F-WXKN	Bos AB-01 Gyrocopter	01	
F-PXKO	Brügger MB-2 Colibri	46	
F-WXKP	Rigaud RD Gyrocopter	06	
F-PXKQ	Heintz Zenith 90LR	20	F-WXKQ
F-PXKS	Jodel D.92 Bébé	486	
F-WXKT	Averso Epervier XA Gyrocopter	01	
F-PXKU	Jurca MJ.2 Tempête	4	F-WXKU
F-PXKV	Coupe JC-01	001	
F-PXKY	Jodel D.92 Bébé	648	(F-PXKC)
F-PXMC	Dyn'Aéro MCR-01	40	
F-PXTA	Stoddard-Hamilton Grastar GS-1	5719	F-WASK
F-PXXL	Gatard AG-02 Poussin *(Reservation)*	35	
F-PXYZ	Jurca MJ.2 Tempête	101	
F-PYAE	Jodel D.113 (ex D.119)	1026	F-POAE
F-PYAF	Jodel D.18 *(Reservation)*	248	
F-PYAM	Colomban MC-15 Cri-Cri	513	
F-PYAN	Jodel D.18 *(Reservation)*	329	
F-PYAS	Max Plan MP-207 Busard	19	
F-PYAT	Dyn'Aéro MCR-01	92	
F-PYAV	Quercy CQR-01	06	
F-PYBA	Jodel D.92 Bébé	658	
F-PYBB	Gatard AG 04 Pigeon	1	F-WYBB
F-PYBC	Heintz Zenith 100	28	
F-PYBD	Heintz Zenith 100BF	47	
F-PYBE	Lucas L-5	02	F-WYBE
F-PYBG	Croses-Bujon BEC-9 Paras-Cargo *(on rebuild)*	01	
F-PYBH	Piel CP.80 *(Dismantled)*	08	
F-PYBJ	Jodel D.119	1517	
F-PYBK	Piel CP.80	12	
F-PYBL	Jodel D.92 Bébé	638	
F-PYBN	Heintz Zenith 105	21	
F-PYBP	Piel CP.80	06	F-WYBP
F-PYBQ	Starck Nickel SN.01	1	F-WYBQ
	(Conversion of Starck AS.37 c/n 14)		
F-PYBR(2)	Heintz Zenith 100MF	5	
F-PYBV	Terrade AT Diamant	01	
	(Jodel derivative built from D.120s F-BHYD and F-BNHK)		
F-PYBX	Jurca MJ.5G1 Sirocco	15	
F-PYBZ	Dyke JD-2 Manta	1239	F-WYBZ
F-PYCC	Quercy CQR-01	08	
F-PYCG	Pottier P.180S	209	F-WYCG
F-PYCR	Dyn'Aéro MCR-01 Sportster	49	
F-WYDA	Megret-Amy ML-02 Gyrocopter	02	
F-WYDB	Ferrer La Darnaga Gyrocopter	01	
F-WYDC	Faure Bensen B.8 JPF Gyrocopter	01	
F-WYDE	Py MP-01 Alouette Gyrocopter	01	
F-WYDF	Chamanier AC-01 Gyrocopter	01	
F-WYDG	Sudres GS PPMB Gyrocopter	01	
F-WYDH	Faure AF-01 Gyrocopter	01	
F-WYDJ	Massemin JM-01 Gyrocopter	01	
F-WYDK	Debout AD-01 Gyrocopter	01	
F-WYDL	Callaugene JC-01 Gyrocopter	01	
F-WYDM	Lapierre Bensen RL-01 Gyroglider	01	
F-WYDN	Clerc JMC-01 Gyrocopter	01	
F-WYDO	Audrouhin AAG Gyrocopter	01, later 3	
F-WYDP	Bastet RB-01 Gyrocopter	01	
F-WYDQ	Bensen B.8MS Gyrocopter	01	
F-WYDR	Lix-01 Gyrocopter	01	
F-WYDS	Bensen B.8MH Gyrocopter	01	
F-WYDT	Henric CH-01 Gyrocopter	01	
F-WYDU	Bensen AR-01 Gyrocopter	01	
F-WYDV	Schleiss PS-01 Gyrocopter	01	
F-WYDX	Dabian GD-01 Gyrocopter	01	
F-WYDZ	Canville JMC-01 Gyrocopter	01	
F-PYEA	Colomban MC-15 Cri-Cri	4	F-WYEA
	(Formerly MC-11, MC-12B)		
F-PYEB	Pottier P.80S	01	
F-PYEC	Rand-Robinson KR-2	4391	F-WYEC
F-PYEE	Jurca MJ.5H2 Sirocco	35	
F-PYEF	Pottier P.70S	25	F-WYEF
F-PYEG	Heintz Zenith 125	31	
F-PYEI	Evans VP-1 Volksplane	2069	
F-PYEJ	Jurca MJ.5K1 Sirocco	41	
F-WYEN	Mignet HM.293	31	
F-PYEP	Jodel D.112 Club	1401	
F-PYEQ	Evans VP-1 Volksplane	V-2251	
F-PYER	Jodel D.112 Club	1434	
F-PYET	Jodel DR.1051M1 Sicile	700	
F-PYEU	Druine D.31 Turbulent	379	
F-WYEY(2)	Dyn'Aéro MCR-01 *(Reservation .99)*	92	
F-PYEZ	Brügger MB-2 Colibri *(accident 30.8.87)*	100	
F-PYFA	Jurca MJ.2 Tempête	29	
F-PYFB	Piel CP.70 Béryl	03	
F-PYFD	Jurca MJ.2D Tempête	52	
F-PYFE	Brügger MB-2 Colibri	88	F-WYFE
F-PYFH	Delaunay JDA-01	01	
F-PYFO	Milon PMB-78 Faucon	01	
F-PYFP	Rutan Vari-Viggen SP	072	F-WYFP
F-PYFQ	Max Plan MP.205 Busard	17	

F-PYFR	Jodel D.119	1514	
F-PYFS	Jodel D.92 Bébé	686	
F-PYFT	Croses LC-6 Criquet	72	
F-PYFU	Delemontez-Cauchy DC-01	01	
F-PYFV	Croses LC-6 Criquet	22	
F-PYFX	Jurca MJ.2 Tempête	59	
F-PYFZ	Croses LC-6 Criquet	42	
F-WYGA	Carayon LC-01 Gyrocopter	01	
F-WYGB	Dedieu DF-01 Gyrocopter	01	
F-WYGD	St.Lary ISL-01 Gyrocopter	01	
F-WYGF	Laugier AL-01 Gyroglider	01	
F-WYGH	Audrouhin AAG-01 Gyrocopter	01	
F-WYGI	Daubian GD-02 Roitelet Gyrocopter	01	
F-WYGJ	Bordes RB-01 Gyrocopter	01	
F-WYGK	Odorico RO-01 Eole Gyrocopter	01	
F-WYGL	Bex DB-01 Gyrocopter	01	
F-WYGM	Rodriguez JCR-01 Gyrocopter	01	
F-WYGO	Durieux MD-01 Gyrocopter	01	
F-WYGP	Bensen B.8MP Gyrocopter	577	
F-WYGQ	Bor BJ-01 Gyrocopter	01	
F-WYGR	Bournery DB-47 Gyrocopter	01	
F-WYGS	Pequignot MP-01 Gyrocopter	01	
F-WYGT	Forich JCF-01 Gyrocopter	01	
F-WYGU	Bensen B.8MP Gyrocopter	01	
F-WYGV	Averso-Loupiac AL-01 Gyrocopter	01	
F-WYGX(2)	Montbazon BLVM-01 Gyrocopter	01	
F-WYGY	Bouchiba JB-01 Gyrocopter	01	
F-WYGZ	Meyrou JBM-01 Gyrocopter	01	(F-WYGX)
F-PYHB	Jurca MJ.5K1 Sirocco	7	
F-PYHC	Mignet HM.360 *(Transferred to 28-OO but still regd)*	97	
F-PYHD	Mignet HM.293W *(Transferred to 76-KY but still regd)*	01	F-WYHD
F-PYHG	Nickel *(Transferred to ULM register 10.04)*	1	
F-PYHI	Croses LC-6 Criquet	23	
F-PYHK	Jurca MJ.2D Tempête	49	
F-PYHM	Piel CP.751 Béryl	4	F-WYHM
F-PYHO	Jodel DR.1051-M1 Sicile Record	713	
F-PYHQ	Croses-Noel CN-1	01	
F-PYHR	Rutan VariEze *(C/n also quoted for HB-YDE)*	1991	
F-PYHS	Rutan VariEze	1697	F-WYHS
F-PYHT	Rutan VariEze	1384	
F-PYHV	Jodel D.119	1573	
F-PYHX	St Germain Raz-Mut	55	
F-PYHY	Jodel D.119-3L	1504	F-WYHY
F-PYHZ	Rutan VariEze	1694	(F-PYHG(1))
F-PYIB	Rutan VariEze	1609	F-WYIB
F-PYIC	Heintz-Zenith 100LR	84	
F-PYIE	Piel CP.1320 Saphir	3	F-WYIE
F-PYIF	Mudry CAP.10A	A.2	
F-PYIG	Pottier P.80S	8	
F-PYIH	Heintz Zenith 125	15	
F-PYII	Pottier P.70S	02	F-WYII
F-PYIJ	Colomban MC-15 Cri-Cri (ex MC-12)	14	F-WYIJ
F-PYIK	Pottier P.170S *(Wfu)*	004	
F-PYIM	Lucas LL-5	1	F-WYIM
			F-PYIM
			F-WYIM
F-PYIN	Tsilefski TG-01 Malech	01	
F-PYIP	Rutan VariEze	1457	
F-PYIS	Pottier P.70S	32	
F-PYIT	Duruble RD-03 Edelweiss 150	1	F-WYIT
F-PYIV	Brügger MB-2 Colibri	107	
F-PYIX	Piel CP.607 Diamant	11	
F-PYIY	Cassutt IIIM	548	
F-PYIZ	Cassutt IIIM	585	
F-PYJA	Croses LC-6 Criquet	75	
F-PYJC	Pottier P.100TS	01	F-WYJC
F-PYJF	Fere F.3	1	
F-PYJG	Jurca MJ.2 Tempête	7W6	
F-PYJI	Dessevres-Coupe JCD	1	F-WYJI
F-PYJJ	Brügger MB-2 Colibri	149	
F-PYJK	Heintz Zenith 120	77	
F-PYJM	Minina MG.2	1	
F-PYJN	Jodel D.119	1555	
F-PYJO	Rutan VariEze	1775	
F-PYJP	Piel CP.80	51	
F-PYJR	Pottier P.80S	23	
F-PYJS	Piel CP.1320 Saphir	14	
F-PYJU	Pottier P.80S	19	
F-PYJV	Brügger MB-2 Colibri *(Accident 10.8.03)*	114	
F-PYJX	Boyer BF	02	F-WYJX
F-PYJY	Gardan-Laverlochere GL.10	01	
F-PYJZ	Nicollier HN433 Ménestrel	37	F-WYJZ
F-PYKA	Nicollier HN433 Ménestrel	43	F-WYKA
F-PYKB	Brügger MB-2 Colibri	145	
F-PYKC	Jodel D.112 Club	1570	
F-PYKD	Croses LC.6 Criquet	83	
F-PYKE	Chasle YC.10 Migrateur	01	F-WYKE
F-PYKK	Piel CP.801 Racer	17	
F-PYKO	Colomban MC-15 Cri-Cri	08	
F-PYKP	Pottier P.70S	011	
F-PYKQ	Rutan VariEze	1989	
F-PYKR	Piel CP.80	15	
F-PYKS	Brügger MB-2 Colibri	66	
F-PYKT	Pottier P.180S	012	F-WYKT
F-PYKU	Jodel DR.1052	704	
F-PYKX	Jodel D.92 Bébé	615	
F-PYLD	Jodel D.113	1574	

F-PYLF	Croses LC.6 Criquet	79	
F-PYLG	Pottier P.170B (ex P.170S)	012	
F-PYLH	Colomban MC-15 Cri-Cri (ex MC-12)	6	
F-PYLJ	Piel CP.80	66	
F-PYLK	Piel CP.70 Beryl	06	F-WYLK
F-PYLL	Jodel D.92 Bébé	713	
F-PYLM	Stark AS-37B *(Originally c/n '77')*	36	
F-PYLP	Jodel DR.1050M Excellence	718	
F-PYLQ	Jurca MJ5-G2 Sirocco	47	F-WYLQ
F-PYLX	Pottier P.180S	06	
F-PYLY	Rutan VariEze	2043	
F-PYLZ	Pottier P.80S	44	F-WYLZ
F-PYMD	Dyn'Aéro MCR-01C	102	F-WWUU
F-PYMV	Stern ST-87 Europlane *(Damaged .03)*	33	
F-PYNA	Grinvalds G-801ST Orion	28	F-WYNA
F-PYNC	Jodel D.92 Bébé	729	
F-PYND	Cavarroc RC-01	01	
F-PYNE	Jodel D.92 Bébé	766	
F-PYNG	Jodel D.18 *(To ULM register)*	91	
F-PYNH	Brügger MB-2 Colibri	116	
F-PYNJ	Jodel D.18	20	
F-PYNK	Colomban MC-15 Cri-Cri	135	
F-PYNL	Jodel D.112 Club	1645	
F-PYNM	Cassutt IIIM	282	
F-PYNN	Colomban MC-15 Cri-Cri	269	
F-PYNO	Rutan Long-Ez	1595	
F-PYNP	Jodel D.18	137	
F-PYNQ	Jodel DR.1050M	753	
F-PYNR	Colomban MC-15 Cri-Cri	262	
F-PYNS	Feugray TR-200 *(Accident 5.6.93)*	1	
F-PYNT	Colomban MC-15 Cri-Cri	47	
F-PYNU	Jodel D.112 Club	1616	
F-PYNX	Jodel D.18	119	
F-PYNY	Piel CP.320A Super Emeraude	412	
F-PYNZ	Pottier P.180S	139	F-WYNZ
F-PYOB	Pottier P.80S	38	
F-PYOC	Collard CSR-1 Tsétsé	01	F-WYOC
F-PYOD	Rutan VariEze	1385	
F-PYOF	Rutan Long-Ez	1047	
F-PYOG	Evans VP-1 Volksplane	V-2589	
F-PYOL	Gros-Bredelet GB-01	01	
F-PYOM	Pottier P.70S	40	
F-PYON	Jodel DR.1050 Ambassadeur	723	
F-PYOO	Rutan VariEze	2164	
F-PYOP	Rutan VariEze	2042	
F-PYOQ	Rutan Long-Ez	355	F-WYOQ
F-PYOT	Piel CP.320 Super Emeraude	386	
F-PYOU	Jodel D.112 Club	1386	
F-PYOX	Jodel D.113	1444	
F-PYOY	Heintz Zenith 100	52	
F-PYPB	Pottier P.80S	40	
F-PYPC	Pottier P.180S	36	F-WYPC
F-PYPD	Marquion RM-01 Helicopter	01	
F-PYPE	Courtes JCC-01	1	
F-PYPF	Stolp SA-750 Acroduster Too	359	
F-PYPH	Jurca MJ.5G Sirocco *(accident 8.6.89)*	30	F-WYPH
F-PYPI	Pottier P.180S	41	
F-PYPJ	Pottier P.180S	51	
F-PYPK	Mudry-Canu CAP.10B	A-4	F-WYPK
	(Built using parts of CAP.10B F-BUDN c/n 46, 1983)		
F-PYPL	Fournier RF-7	02	
F-PYPM	Colomban MC-15 Cri-Cri	20	
F-PYPN	Colomban MC-15 Cri-Cri	74	
F-PYPO	Brügger MB-2 Colibri *(Stored)*	87	
F-PYPP	Evans VP-1 Volksplane	2258	F-WYPP
F-PYPQ	Piel CP.80SC *(accident 24.5.93)*	02	
F-PYPR	Jurca MJ.5L2 Sirocco	37	
F-PYPT	Jodel D.119	1563	
F-PYPY	Rutan Long-Ez	1163	F-WYPY
F-PYPZ	Piel CP.605C Diamant	45	
F-PYQA	Stern/Staudt ST-80 Balade	01	
F-PYQC	Proust Lespace Helicopter	001	F-WYQC
F-PYQD	Colomban MC-15 Cri-Cri	177	
F-PYQE	Rutan Long-Ez	809	
F-PYQF	Jodel D.92 Bébé	725	
F-PYQG	Croses LC-6 Criquet	69	
F-PYQI	Pottier P.180S *(accident 30.4.90)*	34	
F-PYQJ	Jodel D.112 Club	1521	
F-PYQK	Colomban MC-12 Cri-Cri	46	
F-PYQM	Jodel D.18	01	(F-WZDH)
F-PYQN(2)	Rutan VariEze	2134	
F-PYQO	Piel CP.605B Super Diamant	21	
F-PYQP	Colomban MC-15 Cri-Cri	10	
F-PYQQ	WAR P-47 Thunderbolt	71	
F-PYQS	Lendepergt LP-01 Sibylle	01	
F-PYQT	Quaissard GQ Monogast	01	F-WYQT
F-WYQU	Quickie Q2 *(Reservation)*	01	
F-PYQV	Brochet MB-72	9	F-BGTG
F-PYQX	Mignet HM-384	1235	
F-PYQY	Jodel D.119TK	04	

The following registration batches, suffixed (2), were originally used by ULMs but were re-allocated as shown from 1985 onwards:

F-WYRA(2)	Bensen-Francois B-PF Gyrocopter	1	
F-WYRB(2)	Averso AAD La Guepe Gyrocopter	01	
F-WYRC(2)	Gros GG-01 Gyrocopter	01	
F-WYRD(2)	Phoenix Gyrocopter	01	
F-WYRE(2)	Lejeune RL Gyrocopter	02	
F-WYRF(2)	Raymond RR-01 Gyrocopter	01	
F-WYRG(2)	Varga VJM-01 Gyrocopter	01	
F-WYRH(2)	Bensen-Germain BG Gyrocopter	1	
F-WYRI (2)	Rameil RF-01 Gyrocopter	01	
F-WYRJ(2)	Rodrigue-Souza SDDS Gyrocopter	001	
F-WYRK(2)	Bensen-SENA CP Gyrocopter	01	
F-WYRL(2)	Roy RJ-01 Gyrocopter	01	
F-WYRM(2)	Santos Marques SM Gyrocopter	1	
F-WYRN(2)	Castagnet SLC-11 Gyrocopter	1	
F-WYRO(2)	Beillard Avril Gyrocopter	001	
F-WYRP(2)	Bouchiba JB Gyrocopter	03	
F-WYRQ(2)	Bensen-Ruchonnet B.8M-BR Gyrocopter	1	
F-WYRR(2)	Doleac DJP-01 Space Gyrocopter	01	
F-WYRS(2)	Averso AX Le Guepard Gyrcopter	02	
F-WYRT(2)	Bot BF-2 Gyrocopter	1	
F-WYRU(2)	Fournier FAA Gyrocopter	01	
F-WYRV(2)	Cros CM-01 Gyrocopter	01	
F-WYRX(2)	Dougnac CD-01 Libellule Gyrocopter	01	
F-WYRY(2)	Labit LR Gyrocopter	2	
F-WYRZ(2)	Baudry-Bourgon-Bouchet-Lachaise BBBL	1	
F-PYSA(2)	Piel CP.80	59	
F-PYSB(2)	Parker Teenie Two	5-1203	
F-PYSC(2)	Jodel D.119 (ex D.112)	1579	
F-PYSE(2)	Pottier P.180S	48	
F-PYSF(2)	Rutan Long-Ez	1433	
F-PYSG(2)	Brügger MB-2 Colibri	175	
F-PYSH(2)	Colomban MC-15 Cri-Cri	127	
F-PYSJ(2)	Pottier P.80S	50	
F-PYSK(2)	Colomban MC-15 Cri-Cri	336	
F-PYSL(2)	Jurca MJ.5K1 Sirocco	57	
F-PYSM(2)	Rutan VariEze	2048	
F-PYSN(2)	Colomban MC-15 Cri-Cri	65	
F-PYSO(2)	Piel CP.1320D Saphir	18	
F-PYSS(2)	Piel CP.70 Béryl	7	
F-PYST(2)	Pottier P.70S	47	
F-PYSU(2)	Jodel D.92 Bébé	746	
F-PYSV(2)	Stolp SA.300 Starduster Too	1677	
F-PYSY(2)	Rutan Long-Ez	1094	
F-PYTA(2)	Mignet HM.8	L-1	
F-PYTB(2)	Sauzeau Eres-II Coquin	01	F-WYTB
F-PYTC(2)	Colomban MC-15 Cri-Cri	104	
F-PYTD(2)	Lucas L-5	4	
F-PYTG(2)	Leglaive-Gautier LG-150	01	F-WYTG
F-PYTH(2)	Colomban MC-15 Cri-Cri	156	
F-PYTI (2)	Jodel DR.1051M	762	
F-PYTJ (2)	Descatoire CD-01 Astuss	01	
F-PYTL(2)	Pottier P.80S	48	
F-PYTM(2)	Jodel D.18 *(accident 18.3.90)*	9	
F-PYTN(2)	Jurca MJ.5K1 Sirocco	92	
F-PYTO(2)	Jodel DR.1050M	745	
F-PYTP (2)	Piel CP.751B Béryl	02	
F-PYTQ (2)	Péna Capena	02	
F-PYTR (2)	Brügger MB-2 Colibri	115	
F-PYTU (2)	Mudry CAP.10B	A-3	
F-PYTV (2)	Rutan VariEze	2008	F-WYTV
F-PYTX (2)	Colomban MC-15 Cri-Cri	248	
F-PYTY (2)	Colomban MC-15 Cri-Cri	278	
F-PYTZ (2)	Rutan Long-Ez	2117	
F-WYUA	Bensen B.8MJ Gyrocopter	01	
F-WYUB	Franclet PF-01 Gyrocopter	01	
F-WYUC	Soulignac BS-01 Gyrocopter	01	
F-WYUD	Loupiac AL Gyrocopter	02	
F-WYUE	Sers AS-01 Gyrocopter	01	
F-WYUF	Antome Gyrocopter	01	
F-WYUG	Durand Gyrocopter	01	
F-WYUH	Baldy LB-01 Gyrocopter	01	
F-WYUI	Ocon AO-01 Gyrocopter	01	
F-WYUJ	Idrac A-1 Gyrocopter	02	
F-WYUK	Galea BG-01 Gyrocopter	01	
F-WYUL	Jurquet JJ-01 Gyrocopter	01	
F-WYUM	Puente Gyrocopter	01	
F-WYUN	Chrysalide Gyrocopter	01	
F-WYUO	Bonnafous-Chapuis BC-1 Gyrocopter	1	
F-WYUP	Paques PB-8 Gyrocopter	1	
F-WYUQ	Doucet DR-01 Gyrocopter	01	
F-WYUR	Bensen DB Gyrocopter	001	
F-WYUS	Bensen-Clisson BC-1 Gyrocopter	01	
F-WYUT	Bensen LG Gyrocopter	1	
F-WYUU	Bensen-Miquel B-CM Gyrocopter	1	
F-WYUV	Bensen B-8 Gyrocopter *(same c/n as F-WREF)*	8-104100	
F-WYUX	Zago AZ-01 Gyrocopter	01	
F-WYUY	Rives RR-01 Gyrocopter	01	
F-WYUZ	Andre JPA-01 Gyrocopter	001	
F-PYVB (2)	Jodel DR.1050M	765	
F-PYVC (2)	Piel CP.321 Super Emeraude	400	
F-PYVD (2)	Colomban MC-15 Cri-Cri	16	
F-PYVE (2)	WAR P-47D Thunderbolt	95	F-WYVE
F-PYVG (2)	Jodel D.113 (ex D.112)	1231	
F-PYVH (2)	Rutan Long-Ez	1218	
F-PYVI (2)	K & S Jungster 1	J1-76003R	F-WYVI
F-PYVJ (2)	Verges VJ-01 Gringo	01	
F-PYVK (2)	Colomban MC-15 Cri-Cri	160	
F-PYVL (2)	Pottier P.180S	97	
F-PYVM (2)	Jodel D.19	01	
F-PYVN (2)	Colomban MC-15 Cri-Cri	194	F-WYVN
F-PYVO (2)	Pottier P.180S	46	F-WYVO
F-PYVP (2)	Viking Dragonfly Mk.2	511	

F-PYVQ (2)	Colomban MC-15 Cri-Cri	77	
F-PYVS (2)	Adam RA.14 Loisirs	17	F-PGKC
F-PYVT (2)	Jurca MJ.2E Tempête	18	LX-PUT F-PNUD
F-PYVV (2)	Brügger MB-2 Colibri	104	
F-PYVY (2)	Jodel D.18	06	
F-PYVZ (2)	Colomban MC-15 Cri-Cri	400	
F-PYXA (2)	Pitts S-1D Special	7-0492	F-WYXA
F-PYXB (2)	Starck AS.71	32R	F-WYXB
F-PYXC (2)	Kreimendahl Shoestring	054	F-WYXC "F-WXYC"
F-PYXD (2)	Pottier P.180S	119	
F-PYXE (2)	Nicollier HN434 Super Ménestrel	1	
F-PYXF (2)	Pottier P.180S	24	
F-PYXG (2)	Colomban MC-15 Cri-Cri	180	
F-PYXH (2)	Jodel DR.1050M	733	
F-PYXJ (2)	Rutan VariEze	2092	
F-PYXK (2)	Jodel D.150-B3 Mascaret	106	
F-PYXM (2)	Rutan Long-Ez	1688	
F-PYXN (2)	Piel CP.320 Super Emeraude	415	
F-PYXO (2)	Piel CP.80	20	
F-PYXP (2)	Jodel D.18	80	
F-PYXS (2)	Heintz Zenith 150 Tri-Z	3-111	F-WYXS
F-PYXT (2)	Viking Dragonfly Mk-3TH	551	
F-PYXU (2)	Jodel DR.1050M	769	
F-PYXX (2)	Jodel D.19	2	
F-PYXY (2)	Colomban MC-15 Cri-Cri	264	F-WYXY
F-PYXZ (2)	Jodel D.92 Bébé	17	
F-PYYA (2)	Coupe-Brault JCFB 01	1	
F-PYYB (2)	Piel CP.80	62	
F-PYYC (2)	Pottier P.180S *(Wreck noted 9.03)*	91	F-WYYC
F-PYYF (2)	Piel CP.320 Super Emeraude	383	
F-PYYG (2)	Van's RV-4	474	F-WYYG
F-PYYI (2)	Rutan Long-Ez	1575	
F-PYYJ (2)	Colomban MC-15 Cri-Cri	344	
F-PYYK (2)	Colomban MC-15 Cri-Cri	86	
F-PYYL (2)	Jodel D.92 Bébé *(accident 14.1.90)*	645	
F-PYYM (2)	Piel CP.801	72	
F-PYYN (2)	Brügger MB-2 Colibri	228	
F-WYYO (2)	Feugray TR260 Faucon	001-J	
F-WYYP (2)	Jodel D.18 *(Dismantled)*	82	
F-PYYR (2)	Croses LC-6 Criquet	62	
F-WYYS (2)	HLM-01 Helicopter	01 or 02 ?	
F-PYYT (2)	Viking Dragonfly Mk2	103	F-WYYT
F-PYYX (2)	Pottier P.180S	98	
F-PYYY (2)	Druine D.31 Turbulent	356	
F-PYZB (2)	Rutan VariEze	2013	
F-PYZC (2)	Legallois RL	1	
F-PYZD (2)	Rutan Long-Ez	624	F-WYZD
F-PYZE (2)	Pottier P.180S *(W/o 21.10.00)*	80	
F-PYZF (2)	Rutan Long-Ez	734	
F-PYZG (2)	Rutan Long-Ez *(accident 16.6.90)*	1703	
F-PYZH (2)	Jodel DR.1050M	766	F-WYZH
F-PYZI (2)	Stolp SA.300 Starduster Too	1690	
F-PYZJ (2)	Jodel DR.1050M	764	
F-PYZK (2)	Minina MG.3 Harmattan	001	
F-PYZL (2)	Pottier P.180S	66	F-WYZL
F-PYZO (2)	Viking Dragonfly Mk.2	1007	
F-PYZP (2)	Jodel D.119V	1569	
F-PYZR (2)	Brugger MB.2 Colibri	168	
F-PYZS (2)	Piel CP.80	18	
F-PYZT (2)	Chaboud CJC-01	01	
F-PYZU (2)	Rutan VariEze	1850	
F-PYZV (2)	Monnet Moni	327	F-WYZV
F-PYZX (2)	Pottier P.80S	57	
F-PYZY (2)	Pottier P.180S	67	
F-PZAG	Jurca MJ.2H Tempête	30	
F-PZAM	Dyn'Aéro MCR-01 Sportster	193	
F-PZAR	Darcissac-Grinvalds DG-87 Goëland *(Wfu)*	04	
F-PZAV	Van's RV-4	4238	
F-PZAZ	Piel CP.320 Super Emeraude	454	
F-PZBA	Jodel D.18	247	
F-PZBB	Jodel D.19	108T	
F-WZBC (3)	SOFCA Paramoteur Agrion	0001	
F-WZBD (3)	SOFCA Paramoteur Agrion	1	
F-WZBG (2)	SOFCA Paramoteur Agrion	002	
F-WZBH (2)	SOGCA Paramoteur Agrion	003	
F-PZBM	Colomban MC-15 Cri-Cri	429	F-WZBM
F-PZBO	Piel CP.1321 Saphir	24	
F-PZBP	Jodel D.113	1161	
F-PZBQ	Jodel D.119T	05-A	F-WZBQ (F-PART)
F-PZBR	De La Calle CRT-01 Amphibian	01	F-WZBR
F-PZBS	Colomban MC-15 Cri-Cri	417	
F-PZBT	Pottier P.180S	44	
F-WZBU	Feugray (Tech'Aero) TR.300 *(Reservation)*	3	
F-PZBV	Rutan VariEze	1939	F-WZBV
F-PZBX	Rutan Long-Ez	1565	F-WZBX
F-PZBY	Jodel DR.1053M	746	
F-PZBZ	Jodel D.18 *(W/o 21.6.03, wreck noted 9.03)*	183	
F-WZEA	Borel JPB-30 Gyrocopter	01	
F-WZEB	Mompo AM-01 Gyrocopter	01	
F-WZEC	Le Bauzec Moustique Gyrocopter	01	
F-WZED	Combon-Bonnafous BCGyrocopter	02	
F-WZEE	Averso Train'Air XA-03 Gyrocopter	03	
F-WZEF	Doleac DJP-2 Gyrocopter	01	
F-WZEG	Revol RG Gyrocopter	01	
F-WZEH	Savez SGB Gyrocopter	01	
F-WZEI	Cobra Gyrocopter	01	
F-WZEJ	Verdan VG-1 Gyrocopter	01	
F-WZEK	Domme JD Gyrocopter	01	
F-WZEL	Naja Gyrocopter	01	
F-WZEM	Poma Gyrocopter	001	
F-WZEN	Moustic Gyrocopter	01	
F-WZEO	Strupp Gyrocopter	01	
F-WZEP	Lix Condor Gyrocopter	002	
F-WZEQ	Durant DJL Gyrocopter	03	
F-WZER	Chanet JCC.2000 Gyrocopter	1	
F-WZES	Gregnanin GE Gyrocopter	01	
F-WZET	Franck Gyrocopter	001	
F-WZEU	Mono 87 Gyrocopter	001	
F-WZEV	HRP Gyrocopter	01	
F-WZEX	Stuani SR-1 Gyrocopter	01	
F-WZEY	Weinbrenner JW Gyrocopter	03	
F-WZEZ	Bouche BB Gyrocopter	01	
F-PZGL	Valladeau RV-12 (Polikarpov 1-15 replica)	01	
F-WZGM	Carro Quickie 1 *(Reservation)*	C-1	
F-PZGN	Wittmann W.8 Tailwind	622	
F-PZGO	Colomban MC-15 Cri-Cri	207	
F-PZGP	Pottier P.180S	159	
F-PZGQ	Adam RA-14 Loisirs	132	F-PAHD
F-PZGR	Jodel D.112 Club	1678	
F-PZGS	Pottier P.180S	161	F-WZGS
F-PZGT	Loriot DG-01	01	
F-PZGU	Brändli BX-2 Cherry *(Reservation)*	58	
F-PZGV	Chasle YC-320 *(Reservation)*	001	
F-PZGX	Rand-Robinson KR-2	7975	
F-PZGZ	Denize RD.205 Raid Driver	2	
F-WZHA	AB-53 Gyrocopter	0	
F-WZHB	Averso AX-02 Gyrocopter	17	
F-WZHC	Averso AX-02 Gyrocopter	19	
F-WZHD	Pouilles GP Gyrocopter	01	
F-WZHE	Hoffmann VHB-1 Gyrocopter	01	
F-WZHF	Huvier HR-1 Gyrocopter	02-M	
F-WZHG	AU SR Gyrocopter	01	
F-WZHH	Vandenbulke VG-1 Gyrocopter	01	
F-WZHI	Faucher PF-1 Gyrocopter	001	
F-WZHJ	Darrozes MD Gyrocopter	01	
F-WZHK	Le Bigourdin Gyrocopter	1	
F-WZHL	Colibri Gyrocopter	01	
F-WZHM	Bensen-Vandamme B-VG Gyrocopter	01	
F-WZHN	Tessier YT-1 Gyrocopter	2	
F-WZHO	Revol GR Gyrocopter	02	
F-WZHP	AX-1 Gyrocopter	01	
F-WZHQ	Bonnafous BC-2 Gyrocopter	02	
F-WZHR	Krauss BK-1 Gyrocopter	1	
F-WZHS	Krauss GK-1	1	
F-WZHT	Averso AX-02 Gyrocopter	18	
F-WZHU	JF-1 Gyrocopter	01	
F-WZHV	Aubert AJL-2 Gyrocopter	001	
F-WZHX	Courgey HC-1 Gyrocopter	001	
F-WZHY	Ingrassia IS-1 Gyrocopter	1	
F-PZHZ	Mercier IX Gyrocopter	01	F-WZHZ
F-WZID	2CV'Eau Volante	unkn	
F-PZIG	Jurca MJ.2P Tempête *(Reservation)*	28	
F-PZIK	Desjardins D-01 Ibis	01	F-WZIK
F-PZIL	Piel CP.605B Super Diamant	48	
F-PZIM	Croses LC-6 Criquet	97	
F-PZIO	Croses LC-10 Criquet	32	
F-PZIP	Piel CP.803	70	
F-PZIQ	Colomban MC-15 Cri-Cri	282	F-WZIQ
F-PZIT	Evans VP-1 Volksplane *(Stored)*	V-1583	
F-PZIU	Pottier PRM.180	045	
F-PZIV	Colomban MC-15 Cri-Cri	41	F-WZIV
F-WZJF	Marmande Aero Microjet 200	01	
F-WZJG	Auricoste AA-01 Gyrocopter	unkn	
F-PZLD	Salis AJBS 10 (Modified CAP 10)	01	F-WZLD
F-WZLH(3)	Rotorway Executive	938	
F-WZLI (3)	Geiser Zeppy Airship	01	
F-PZLJ	Jodel D.112 Club	125	F-PKMM
F-PZLL	Constantini STC-1 Magic	1	
F-PZLM	Serleg 225EX Amphibian	001	F-WZLM
F-WZLN(2)	Lanot Aquitain	003	
F-WZLP(2)	Lanot Aquitain	002	
F-WZLS(4)	Grillon 120	01	(F-GESP)
F-WZLU	Gardan GY-120 Microlight	001	
F-WZLY	Hornet S-10	unkn	
F-WZLZ	Loravia ULI-2	01	
F-PZMA	Heintz Zenith 100CP	2123	
F-PZMB	Jodel D.92 Bébé	730	
F-PZMC	Gatard AG-02 Poussin	34	
F-PZMD	Pottier P.180S	47	
F-PZMF	Colomban MC-15 Cri-Cri	51	
F-WZMG	Rutan Defiant	119	
F-PZMH	Pottier P.180S *(Wfu)*	144	F-WZMH
F-PZMJ	Dupau MD-12 Papillon	01	
F-PZMK	Dedon Quickie 2	02-F	
F-PZML	Colomban MC-15 Cri-Cri	440	
F-PZMM	Rutan VariEze *(Reservation, ex OO-104?)*	1847	
F-PZMN	Colomban MC-15 Cri-Cri	68	
F-PZMO	Kieger AK-01	01	
F-PZMP	Grinvalds G-801 Orion *(accident)*	9	
F-PZMQ	Taylor JT.2 Titch	108	
F-PZMR	Colomban MC-100 Banbi	83	F-GUMR

F-PZMU	Jodel D.18	34	
F-PZMV	Nicollier HN-700 Ménestrel II	001	
F-WZNL	Capdevielle CPCL Gyrocopter	1	
F-WZNM	Sudre SRE Gyrocopter	01	
F-WZNN	Guillaume DG Gyrocopter	01	
F-WZNO	Darmanne Gyrocopter	01	
F-WZNP	Fournier FAA Gyrocopter	02	
F-WZNQ	GG-200 Gyrocopter	01	
F-WZNR	Averso AX-02 Gyrocopter	8	
F-WZNS	Lambour-Deudon LLD Gyrocopter	1	
F-WZNT	Duhamel-Greaux-Huber DGH-01 Gyrocopter	01	
F-WZNU	Duhamel-Greaux-Huber DGH-02 Gyrocopter	01	
F-PZNV	Nicollier HN. *(Noted 7.01)*	unkn	
F-WZNX	Coqu Bensen B-8 Gyrocopter	C-1	
F-WZNY	Averso AX-02 Gyrocopter	10	
F-WZNZ	Averso AX-02 Gyrocopter	11	
F-WZOA(2)	Hard HP Gyrocopter	01	
F-PZOB(1)	Le Ventilateur ULM	01	
F-PZOB(2)	Van's RV-4 *(Reservation)*	3091	
F-WZOC(2)	Mono LG Gyrocopter	01	
F-WZOD(2)	Blandy AB-1 Gyrocopter	01	
F-WZOE(2)	Lejeune RL-2 Gyrocopter	03	
F-WZOF(2)	HIR-1 Gyrocopter	01	
F-WZOG(2)	Bluebird Gyrocopter	01	
F-WZOH(2)	Redbird Gyrocopter	01	
F-WZOI (2)	Averso AX-02 Gyrocopter	1	
F-WZOJ(2)	Bensen B-8JLG Gyrocopter *(w/o 27.1.91?)*	1	
F-WZOK(2)	HTV Gyrocopter	2	
F-WZOL(2)	Liberty Gyrocopter	01	
F-WZOM(2)	Cena CP-02 Gyrocopter	1	
F-WZON(2)	Averso AX-02 Gyrocopter	2	
F-WZOO(2)	Beart JMB-1 Gyrocopter	01	
F-WZOP(2)	Averso AX-02 Gyrocopter	4	
F-WZOQ(2)	Gil Gyrocopter	01	
F-WZOT(2)	Cros CM-2 Gyrocopter	02	
F-WZOU(2)	Chevallot Bensen B-8	CD-01	
F-WZOV(2)	Bourgue BP-01 Gyrocopter	01	
F-WZOY(2)	Barbier CB Gyrocopter	01	
F-WZOZ(2)	Averso AX-02 Gyrocopter	5	
F-PZPA (2)	Chambon-Koenig CK-01 Profil	001	F-WZPA
F-PZPD (2)	Gatard AG-02CR Poussin	40	
F-WZPE	Kreimendahl K-10 Shoestring *(Stored dismantled)*	48	
F-PZPF (2)	Colomban MC-15 Cri-Cri	84	
F-PZPG(2)	Jodel D.112 Club	767	F-PCDV
F-PZPH (2)	Pottier P.180S *(accident 31.12.89)*	99	
F-PZPI (2)	Pottier P.180S	25	
F-PZPJ (2)	Brügger MB-2 Colibri	172	
F-PZPK (2)	Colomban MC-15 Cri-Cri	81	
F-PZPM (2)	Dopouridis DV.219 (Jodel variant)	01	F-WZPM
F-PZPN (2)	Rutan Long-Ez	2115	
F-PZPO (2)	Jurca MJ.7 Gnatsum	2	F-WZPO
F-PZPP (2)	Jodel D.19	15T	F-WZPP
F-PZPQ (2)	Daurelle AD-01	01	
F-PZPR (2)	Colomban MC-15 Cri-Cri	306	
F-PZPS (2)	Jodel D.18	124	
F-PZPT (2)	Jodel DR.100 Ambassadeur	763	
F-PZPV (2)	Pottier P.180S	32	F-WZPV
F-PZPY (2)	Croses LC-6 Criquet	59	
F-PZPZ (2)	Landray GL-07	01	
F-WZQA(2)	Bernardeau Bensen B-8B Gyrocopter	B-1	
F-WZQB(2)	Portal-Revertegat HRP Gyrocopter	02	
F-WZQC(2)	Averso AX-02 Gyrocopter	6	
F-WZQD(2)	Bourdon B-2 Gyrocopter	01	
F-WZQE(2)	Sanchez SB-01 Gyrocopter	1	
F-WZQF(2)	Baldy LB-02 Gyrocopter	1	
F-WZQG(2)	Bastien BH-2 Gyrocopter	01	
F-WZQH(2)	Doleac Aircopter DJP Max	03	
F-WZQI (2)	Tenneguin TT-01 Gyrocopter	01	
F-WZQK(2)	Lettinger LC Gyrocopter	01	
F-WZQL(2)	Passot MP-02 Morgon Gyrocopter	2	
F-WZQM(2)	Averso AX-04 Le Guépard Gyrocopter	01	
F-WZQN(2)	Averso AX-05 Léopard Gyrocopter	01	
F-WZQO(2)	Phénix Gyrocopter	SC-01	
F-WZQP(2)	Romero JR-1 Gyrocopter	001	
F-WZQQ(2)	Kraetter AK Gyrocopter	1	
F-WZQR(2)	Tenneguin TT-02 Gyrocopter	01	
F-WZQS(2)	Bourgues BP-02 Gyrocopter	1	
F-WZQT(2)	Fortunato ERF Gyrocopter	01	
F-WZQU(2)	Averso AX-02 Gyrocopter	7	
F-WZQV(2)	Pate NP-001 Gyrocopter	001	
F-WZQX(2)	Bond Gyrocopter	007	
F-WZQY(2)	Mousticq Gyrocopter	01	
F-WZQZ(2)	Bensen B-8 Gyrocopter	104-V1	
F-PZRC	Brügger MB-2 Colibri	51	
F-PZRF	Jodel D.112 Club	1602	
F-PZRH	Croise AC-1 (1/2 scale Spitfire)	01	
F-PZRI	Evans VP-2B Volksplane	2130	
F-PZRJ	Christen Eagle II	01	
F-PZRM	Brügger MB-2 Colibri	108	
F-PZRN	Pottier P.80S	015	
F-PZRO	Pottier P.180S	77	
F-PZRP	Rutan Long-Ez	621	
F-PZRQ	Lucas L-5	24	F-WZRQ
F-PZRR	Croses LC-6 Criquet	104	
F-PZRT	Jodel DR.1050M *(Reservation)*	721	
F-PZRU	Rutan VariEze *(Reservation)*	1843	
F-PZRX	Rutan Long-Ez	2114	
F-PZRY	Albarde Ruty	01	F-WZRY
F-PZRZ	Evans VP-2 Volksplane	2201	
F-PZSF (2)	Pottier P.80S	28	
F-PZSH (2)	Jodel D.112 Club	453	
F-PZSI (2)	Max Plan MP-207 Busard	20	F-WZSI
F-WZSK(2)	Quenaud 50	01	
F-PZSL (2)	Colomban MC-15 Cri-Cri	270	
F-PZSM (2)	Jodel DR.1053M Sicile Record	737	
F-PZSN (2)	Colomban MC-15 Cri-Cri	25	
F-PZSP (2)	Colomban MC-15 Cri-Cri	39	
F-PZSS (2)	Brügger MB-2 Colibri	85	
F-PZST (2)	Colomban MC-15 Cri-Cri	147	
F-PZSU (2)	Druine D.31B2 Turbulent	409	
F-PZSV (2)	Jodel DR.100A	754	
F-PZSZ (2)	Pottier P.80S	58	
F-PZTA (2)	Fournier RF-5	01	F-WZTA
F-PZTB (2)	Jodel DR.1050M1 Sicile Record	744	
F-PZTC (2)	Péna Capena (Modified CAP-20)	01	F-WZTC
F-PZTD (2)	Colomban MC-15 Cri-Cri	64	F-WZTD
F-PZTE (2)	Jurca MJ.2E Tempête	43	
F-PZTF (2)	Pottier P.70S	49	
F-PZTG (2)	Colomban MC-15 Cri-Cri	113	
F-PZTI (2)	Colomban MC-15 Cri-Cri	63	
F-PZTL (2)	Piel CP.320A Super Emeraude	382	
F-PZTM (2)	Rutan VariEze	277	
F-PZTN (2)	Pottier P.80SR	14	F-WZTN
F-PZTO (2)	Colomban MC-15 Cri-Cri	85	
F-PZTP (2)	Colomban MC-15 Cri-Cri	66	
F-PZTQ (2)	Taylor JT-2 Titch Mk.3	CB-5	
F-PZTR (2)	Colomban MC-15 Cri-Cri	121	
F-PZTS (2)	Evans VP-2 Volksplane	V2-1521	F-WZTS
F-WZTT (2)	Watson Windwagon	JW-573	F-PZTT
F-PZTU (2)	Colomban MC-15 Cri-Cri	27	F-WZTU F-PZTU
F-PZTV (2)	Pottier P.180S	42	
F-PZTY (2)	Pottier P.70S	28	
F-PZTZ (2)	Druine D.31 Turbulent	358	
F-WZUA(2)	Light Aero Avid Flyer	CP84-1	
F-WZUB(2)	Light Aero Avid Flyer	263	
F-WZUD(2)	Light Aero Avid Flyer	264	
F-WZUE(2)	Janowski J-5 Marco	F-2	
F-WZUF(2)	Light Aero Avid Amphibian *(now 37-QV?)*	24	
F-WZUG(2)	Light Aero Avid Flyer	327	
F-WZUH(2)	Light Aero Avid Flyer	422	
F-WZUI (2)	Light Aero Avid Amphibian	25	
F-WZUJ(2)	Janowski J-5 Marco	6	
F-WZUK(2)	Light Aero Avid Flyer	323	
F-WZUL(2)	Janowski J-5 Marco	8	
F-WZUM(2)	Light Aero Avid Flyer	476	
F-WZUN(2)	Light Aero Avid Flyer	541	
F-WZUO(2)	Light Aero Avid Flyer	538	
F-WZUP(2)	Light Aero Avid Flyer	421	
F-WZUQ(2)	Light Aero Avid Flyer	473	
F-WZUR(2)	Light Aero Avid Flyer	471	
F-WZUS(2)	Light Aero Avid Flyer	542	
F-WZUT(2)	Light Aero Avid Flyer	424	
F-WZUU(2)	Light Aero Avid Flyer	319	
F-PZUV	Light Aero Avid Flyer	475	F-WZUV(2)
F-WZUX(2)	Light Aero Avid Amphibian	41	
F-PZUY	Light Aero Avid Flyer	647	F-WZUY(2)
F-WZUZ(2)	Light Aero Avid Flyer	694	
F-WZVA(2)	Bensen GGMS Gyrocopter	01	
F-WZVB(2)	Sicard JMS-01 Gyrocopter	01	
F-WZVC(2)	Onyx Gyrocopter	01	
F-WZVD(2)	Hernando FH-1 Gyrocopter	1	
F-WZVE(2)	Condomine YC-2 Gyrocopter	1	
F-WZVF(2)	Mouchel BM-01 Gyrocopter	01	
F-WZVG(2)	Cauchy CM-01 Gyrocopter	01	
F-WZVH(2)	Flip Gyrocopter	1	
F-WZVI (2)	Hostein AH-01 Gyrocopter	01	
F-WZVJ(2)	Laboye-Meygret LMN-1 Gyrocopter	01	
F-WZVK(2)	Viala HTV Gyrocopter	1	
F-WZVL(2)	Bouchiba JB Gyrocopter	2	
F-WZVM(2)	Mace MA-01 Gyrocopter	01	
F-WZVN(2)	Proust DP-3 Gyrocopter	1	
F-WZVO(2)	Odorico OR-02 Gyrocopter	02	
F-WZVP(2)	Beaudoin GB-01 Beaugiro	01	
F-WZVQ(2)	Zamponi CZ-01 Gyrocopter *(Wrecked)*	01	
F-WZVR(2)	Pascal JP-01 Gyrocopter	01	
F-WZVS(2)	Seidner AS-100 Gyrocopter	01	
F-WZVT(2)	Passot MP-01 Gyrocopter	1	
F-WZVU(2)	Lejeune RL-01 Gyrocopter	01	
F-WZVV(2)	Lambelin Bensen BML Gyrocopter	001	
F-WZVX(2)	Desauge Bensen JD Gyrocopter	01	
F-WZVY(2)	Oudoul GO Gyrocopter	1	
F-WZVZ(2)	Dumon B-RD Gyrocopter	1	
F-PZXD (2)	ACBA-4 Pipit Véloce	01	
F-PZXE (2)	Croses EC-7 Tous Terrains	01	F-PPPM ?
F-PZXF (2)	Jodel D.119T	1562	
F-PZXH (2)	Nicollier HN-434 Super Ménestrel	36	
F-PZXI (2)	Lucas L-5	28	F-WZXI
F-PZXJ (2)	Colomban MC-15 Cri-Cri	268	F-WZXJ
F-PZXK (2)	Rutan Cozy	310	
F-PZXM (2)	Colomban MC-15 Cri-Cri	443	
F-PZXN (2)	Pottier P.180S	88	F-WZXN
F-PZXO (2)	Jodel D.18	07	
F-PZXQ (2)	Rutan VariEze	2200	

F-PZXR (2)	Jodel D.18	92	
F-PZXT (2)	Descubes III	01	
F-PZXU (2)	Colomban MC-15 Cri-Cri	352	
F-PZXV (2)	Colomban MC-15 Cri-Cri *(Reservation)*	247	
F-WZXX (2)	Dirigeable DIPA Aeromodelisme Balloon	unkn	
F-WZXY (2)	Dirigeable DIPA Aeromodelisme Balloon	unkn	
F-PZXZ (2)	Viking Dragonfly Mk.2 (SB-2)	771	
F-WZYA	Portespane DP Requin Blanc Gyrocopter	01	
F-PZYB	Averso AX-02 Guepard Gyrocopter	09	F-WZYB
F-WZYC	Deluc MD-2 Black Panther Gyrocopter	01	
F-WZYE	Carletti Bensen B-8AC Gyrocopter	01	
F-WZYF	Casset RC-01 Gyrocopter	01	
F-WZYG	Lagarde AL-01 Gyrocopter	01	
F-WZYH	Laboye Bensen B-8LH Gyrocopter	006	
F-WZYI	CD Gyrocopter	01	
F-WZYJ	Averso AX-02 Gyrocopter	12	
F-PZYK	Jodel DR.1054M (ex DR.1051)	757-13A	
F-WZYL	Telegoni ATM-01 Gyrocopter	1	
F-WZYM	Meygret CHM-2 Gyrocopter	01	
F-WZYN	Fuertes JF-1 Gyrocopter	1	
F-WZYO	Gerard Bensen G-800MV Gyrocopter	GR-01	
F-WZYP	Averso AX-02 Gyrocopter	13	
F-WZYQ	Averso AX-02 Gyrocopter	14	
F-WZYR	Averso AX-02 Gyrocopter	15	
F-WZYS	Benoit L-1 Gyrocopter	1	
F-WZYT	Arnould JPA-001 Gyrocopter	001	
F-WZYU	Averso AX-02 Gyrocopter	16	
F-WZYV	Rabillard CR-1 Gyrocopter	01	
F-WZYX	Duhamel-Greaux-Hubert DGH-03 Gyrocopter	01	
F-WZYY	Paraire PG Gyrocopter	01	
F-WZYZ	Arnaud AR-1 Gyrocopter	01	
F-PZZL	Piel CP.615 Diamant	46	
F-PZZM	Jodel D.18	216	
F-PZZO	Brändli BX-2 Cherry	28	F-WZZO
F-PZZP	Jodel D.18	141	
F-PZZQ	Jurca MJ.5 Sirocco	46	
F-PZZR	Lannier LA Bengali	01	
F-PZZS	Colomban MC-15 Cri-Cri	94	F-WZZS
F-PZZZ	Neico Lancair 320	400	

GLIDERS AND MOTOR GLIDERS

The most recently reported tail codes are shown next to the registration where space permits.

F-CAAB	Scheibe SF-28A Tandem-Falke	5772	PH-635 PH-TER D-KCLB
F-CAAZ	Eiri PIK-20E	20274	
F-CABI	Glaser Dirks DG-200	2-117	
F-CABK-FS	Schleicher ASW 19B	19309	
F-CABY	Breguet 900	1	
F-CACC-T73	Grob G.103 Twin Astir II	3515	OH-644 D-3063
F-CACI- K06	Glaser Dirks DG-200/17	2-121/1724	
F-CACL	Wassmer WA.22A Super Javelot	115	Fr.AF
F-CACM	Wassmer WA.22A Super Javelot (Wfu)	124	Fr.AF
F-CACN	ICA/Brasov IS.28B2	224	
F-CADC	Air 100	12	
F-CADN	Grob G.102/77J Astir Jeans	2099	
F-CADO	Grob G.102/77J Astir Jeans	2103	
F-CADQ(2)	Grob G.102/77J Astir Jeans	2248	D-2396
F-CADS(2)	Grob G.102/77J Astir Jeans	unkn	
F-CADT(2)	Rolladen-Schneider LS4	4212	BGA2933/ETF N3UK
F-CAEA	Wassmer WA.22 Super Javelot	126	Fr.AF
F-CAEC	Grob G.102/77J Astir CS Jeans	2135	
F-CAEM	Grob G.102/77J Astir CS Jeans	2061	D-7579
F-CAEN	Rolladen-Schneider LS6	6067	F-WAEN(2) D-1504
F-CAEO	Rolladen-Schneider LS1C	113	D-1044
F-CAEQ-37	Rolladen-Schneider LS4	4264	D-5530
F-CAES	Wassmer WA.30 Bijave	162	Fr.AF
F-CAFA	Scheibe SF-28A Tandem-Falke	5747	HB-2029 D-KOEY
F-CAFI	Carmam M.100S Mésange	57	OO-ZFE F-CDDN
F-CAFJ-L11	Rolladen-Schneider LS1D	137	OO-ZMH
F-CAFK	SZD-50-3 Puchacz	B-2060	
F-CAFL	Scheibe SF-28A Tandem-Falke	5712	OE-9069 D-KDAL(1)
F-CAFO(2)	Caudron C.800	10312/352	F-CADI
F-CAFZ	Wassmer WA.22A	151	Fr.AF
F-CAGI	Wassmer WA.22A	153	Fr.AF
F-CAGJ	Schleicher K 8B	972	D-4383
F-CAGK	Wassmer WA.30 Bijave	231	Fr.AF
F-CAGL	Fauvel AV.22S	2	F-CCGL
F-CAGU	Breguet 904S Nymphale	11	F-CCFU
F-CAHJ	Fournier RF-9	1	
F-CAHL(2)	Fournier RF-9	9	
F-CAHM(2)	Fournier RF-9	3	
F-CAHP(2)	Fournier RF-9	5	
F-CAHY	Fournier RF-9	2	
F-CAIA	Issoire D.77 Iris	01	F-WAQA
F-CAIC-IC	Schempp-Hirth Ventus a	298	F-WAIC N125SG
F-CAID	Scheibe SF-28A Tandem-Falke	5761	HB-2007 (D-KACN)
F-CAJB-T74	Grob G.103 Twin Astir II	3206	OO-ZMA
F-CAJC(2)	SZD-51-1 Junior	B-2020	
F-CAJE	Nord 2000	35	F-CAJD
F-CAJJ	Caudron C.800	9780/120	
F-CAKO-8X	Rolladen-Schneider LS4A	4674	D-0124
F-CALA	Schleicher ASK 14	14032	D-KOHC
F-CALB	Scheibe SF-25B Falke	46128	D-KADD
F-CALG	Schleicher ASK 14	14050	G-AYRN (D-KISA(2))
F-CAMF	Avialsa-Scheibe A.60	4	
F-CAOB(2)	Schempp-Hirth Janus CM	37/290	D-KAOK(2)
F-CAOT	Stemme S-10	10-53	D-KGCI (3)
F-CAPF	Caudron C.800 (Being restored)	181/9841	
F-CAPX	Wassmer WA.21 Javelot II	51	Fr.AF
F-CAQA(4)	Scheibe SF-25C Falke 2000	44324	F-WAQA(4) D-KOOQ
F-CAQB-2A	SZD-42-1 Jantar 2A	B-784	F-WAQB LX-CMD F-WAQB
F-CAQC	Schleicher ASW 17	17051	F-WAQC
F-CAQE	ICA/Brasov IS.28B2	118	F-WAQE
F-WAQG	Carmam C-38	25	
F-WAQH(5)	A.S.D.Glider	1	
F-WAQI	KV-3A	01	
F-CAQJ	Carmam C-38	03	F-WAQJ
F-CAQN(2)	Grob G.109B	6239	F-WAQN
F-CAQO	Grob G.109B	6333	F-WAQO
F-CAQP	Grob G.109B	6374	F-WAQP
F-CAQQ	Scheibe SF-25C Falke	4483	F-WAQQ OY-VXV (D-KEIC(1))
F-CAQS(2)	Scheibe SF-28A Tandem-Falke	5799	OY-XJB (D-KDCZ)
F-CAQT	Scheibe SF-28A Tandem-Falke	5741	HB-2023 (D-KOEB(2))
F-CAQU	Loravia SFL-25R Remorqueur (Converted SF-25C Falke for glider towing)	4813	F-WAQU(2) D-KBAV
F-CAQV(2)	Scheibe SF-25A Falke	4545	F-WAQV(2) D-KANY
F-CAQX	Scheibe SF-25C Falke	4404	F-WAQX(2) D-KAAM
F-WAQY(2)	Centrair 201C Marianne	201C-095	
F-CAQZ	Scheibe SF-25E Super Falke	4364	D-KNIY(2)
F-CARA -MV	Schempp-Hirth Nimbus IIB	162	PH-599
F-CARB	Schempp-Hirth Nimbus 3	21	Fr.AF
F-CARD	Sportavia/ Scheibe SF-25B Falke	4863	F-WARD D-KAEB
F-CARH	Fournier RF-10	02	F-WARH
F-WARI	Fournier RF-10	03	
F-CARJ	Fournier RF-10	4	F-WARJ
F-CARK	Schleicher ASW 22A	22022	D-9394
F-CARL(2)	Scheibe SF-28A Tandem-Falke	5717	D-KOAI
F-CARM	Schempp-Hirth Janus C	91	D-3198
F-CARN	Grob G.102 Astir CS	1494	HB-1375
F-CARP	Scheibe SF-25B Falke	46205	D-KASW (D-KAST)
F-CARS	Scheibe SF-25E Super Falke	4348	D-KDGA
F-CASB	Air 102	36	
F-CASD	Schleicher ASK 14	14026	D-KOIA
F-WASE	KV-5	001	
F-CASF	Grob G.103 Twin II	3674	D-8697
F-CASH-3W	Schleicher ASH 25	25127	
F-CATA	Grob G.103 Twin Astir	3168	D-7805
F-CATC	Rolladen-Schneider LS4	4051	D-4189
F-CATD(2)	Schleicher ASH 25E	25030	D-4705
F-CATE(2)	Valentin Taifun 17E	1041	HB-2099 D-KDSF
F-CATI-4W	Rolladen-Schneider LS4	4558	D-8922
F-CATT-2	Rolladen-Schneider LS6C	6227	D-6426
F-CATU-T72	Grob G.103 Twin Astir II	3236	
F-CAUB(2)	Caudron C.800	310/9970	F-CAUA
F-CAVY	Schleicher K 8B (Dismantled)	8170	
F-CAXA	Schempp-Hirth Janus CE	183	OO-ZXA
F-CAYD-JB	Glaser Dirks DG-200/17	2-112/1719	
F-CAYU	Air 102 (Dismantled)	39	
F-CBAN	Caudron C.800	9985/325	F-CBXA
F-CBBA	IAR-Brasov IS.28M2	53	
F-CBBC	IAR-Brasov IS.28M2	61	
F-CBBD	IAR-Brasov IS.28B2	345	
F-CBBF	IAR-Brasov IS.28M2	51	
F-CBBG	IAR-Brasov IS.28M2	55	
F-CBBN(2)	Schleicher K 8B	8755	D-1039
F-CBCA	Glaser Dirks DG-200/17	2-127/1729	
F-WBCB	Stralpes ST-II Minimus	01	
F-CBCC(2)	Glaser Dirks DG-200/17	2-172/1755	
F-CBCD	Stralpes ST-15 Crystal	01	F-WBCD
F-CBCE	Stralpes ST-15 Crystal	1	F-WBCE
F-CBCF	Stralpes ST-15 Crystal	2	F-WBCF
F-WBCG	Stralpes ST-15 Crystal	3	
F-CBCI	Stralpes ST-15 Crystal	8	
F-CBCJ-CJ	Stralpes ST-15 Crystal	9	
F-CBCK	Stralpes ST-15 Crystal	10	
F-CBCN	Stralpes ST-15 Crystal	6	
F-CBCO(2)	Stralpes ST-15 Crystal	7	
F-CBDA-YV	Schleicher ASW 20L	20460	

F-CBDB	Schleicher ASW 22	22024	F-WBDB
F-CBDC(2)	Schleicher ASW 20L (Code 'DC')	20319	
F-CBDD-A2	Schleicher ASW 20BL	20648	F-WBDD
F-CBDE-1Z	Schleicher ASW 22	22016	F-WBDE
F-CBDF	Schleicher ASW 20	20576	
F-CBDH	Schleicher ASW 20CL	20710	F-WBDH
F-CBDI -GP	Schleicher ASW 20CL	20744	F-WBDI
F-CBDM	Schleicher ASW 20CL	20743	F-WBDM
F-CBDN	Schleicher ASW 20C	20761	F-WBDN
F-CBDP	Schleicher ASK 21	21105	F-WBDP
F-CBDQ	Schleicher ASK 21	21209	
F-CBDR	Schleicher ASK 21	21146	F-WBDR
F-CBDS	Schleicher ASK 21	21183	
F-CBDT	Schleicher ASK 21	21184	
F-CBDU	Schleicher ASK 21	21186	
F-CBDV	Schleicher ASK 21	21187	
F-CBDX	Schleicher ASK 21	21188	
F-CBDY	Schleicher ASK 21	21202	
F-CBDZ	Schleicher ASK 21	21203	
F-CBET(2)	Rolladen-Schneider LS6B	6202	
F-CBFR	Nord 2000 (Being restored)	13/10343	
F-CBGE	Nord 2000	48/10378	
F-CBGV	Wassmer WA.20 Javelot 1	3	
F-CBGZ -7	Wassmer WA.20 Javelot 1	7	
F-CBHD	Air 100	13	
F-CBHF	Air 100	7	
F-CBHN	Stralpes ST-15 Crystal	5	
F-CBJR(2)	Scheibe SF-25B Falke	46161	LX-CAB
			D-KOXY
			(D-KBIF)
F-CBLA	Centrair C-201A Marianne	201A-027	
F-CBLB(2)	Centrair C-201A Marianne	201A-028	
F-CBLC	Centrair C-201A Marianne	201A-029	
F-CBLD(2)	Centrair C-201A Marianne	201A-032	
F-CBLF	Centrair C-201A Marianne	201A-031	
F-CBLG	Centrair C-201A Marianne	201A-033	
F-CBLH	Centrair C-201A Marianne	201A-034	
F-CBLJ	Centrair C-201A Marianne	201A-036	
F-CBLK(2)-U2	Centrair C-201A Marianne	201A-038	
F-CBLL(2)	Centrair C-201A Marianne	201A-039	
F-CBLM(2)	Centrair C-201A Marianne	201A-040	
F-CBLN(2)	Centrair C-201A Marianne	201A-041	
F-CBLO	Centrair C-201A Marianne	201A-042	
F-CBLP	Centrair C-201B Marianne	201B-043	
F-CBLR(2)	Centrair C-201A Marianne (W/o 26.7.02)	201A-045	
F-CBLS(2)	Centrair C-201B Marianne	201B-046	
F-CBLT(2)	Centrair C-201B Marianne	201B-047	
F-CBLU(2)	Centrair C-201B Marianne	201B-048	F-WBLU
F-CBLV(2)	Centrair C-201B Marianne	201B-051	
F-CBLY(2)	Centrair C-201B Marianne	201B-050	
F-CBLZ	Centrair C-201B Marianne	201B-059	
F-CBMA	Castel C.310P	117	
F-CBNV(2)	Schempp-Hirth Nimbus 2	52	F-CEDB
F-CBOT	Sportavia-Pützer RF-5B Sperber	51055	D-KENT
F-CBPE	Schempp-Hirth Ventus-2c	5/8	OE-5597
F-CBPF(2)	Fournier RF-9	4	EC-DML
			F-ODPB
			F-WDPB
F-CBPJ-PJ	Glaser Dirks DG-200	2-52	
F-CBPM	Schleicher ASH 25	25038	F-WBPM
			D-4756
F-CBPR	Wassmer WA.28E	117	D-4231
F-CBQO	Wassmer WA.20 Javelot 1	1	
F-CBRS	Fauvel AV.36	119	
F-CBRX	Fauvel AV.36 (Being restored)	123	
F-CBSM	Fauvel AV.36	138	
F-CBUU	Wassmer WA.22A	152	Fr.AF
F-CBVV	Wassmer WA.30	175	Fr.AF
F-CBYV	Caudron C.800	9891/231	
F-CBZU	Schleicher Ka 6E	4211	
F-CBZX	Schleicher Ka 6CR Rhönsegler	6609	
F-CCAA(2)	Schempp-Hirth Janus B	08	HB-1325
			D-3115
F-CCAB	Rolladen Schneider LS-1D	26	
F-WCAF	Carmam JP.15/34	01	
F-WCAR	Carmam JP.15/36 Aiglon	02	
F-CCAV	Schleicher Ka 6CR Rhönsegler	6545	
F-CCBC	Wassmer WA.28 Espadon	01	F-WCBC
F-CCBD	Eiri PIK-20E-II	20294	F-WCBD
			OH-577
F-CCBT-N56	Schempp-Hirth Nimbus IIC	56	OO-HZG
F-CCCB	Wassmer WA.22 Super Javelot	01	F-WCCB
F-CCCL	Breguet 901S Mouette	9	
F-CCCM	Breguet 901S Mouette	10	
F-CCCP	Breguet 901S Mouette	13	
F-CCCQ	Breguet 901S Mouette	14	
F-CCCU	Breguet 901S Mouette	18	
F-CCCX	Breguet 901S Mouette	20	
F-CCDK	Scheibe Bergfalke II/55	207	
F-CCEA	Wassmer WA.20 Javelot	01	F-WCEA
F-CCEE	Wassmer WA.21 Javelot II	2	
F-CCEO	Wassmer WA.21 Javelot II	18	
F-CCER	Wassmer WA.21 Javelot II	24	
F-CCEU	Wassmer WA.21 Javelot II	30	
F-CCEX	Wassmer WA.21 Javelot II	32	
F-CCFA	FFA Diamant 18	70	
F-WCFC	Carmam JP.15/36 Aiglon	04	

F-CCFE	Wassmer WA.21 Javelot II	45	TU-TPB
			F-CCKJ
F-CCFF	Issoire E.78 Silène	01	
F-CCFK	Breguet 904S Nymphale (Dismantled)	1	
F-CCFN	Breguet 904S Nymphale	4	
F-CCFP	Breguet 904S Nymphale (Dismantled)	6	
F-CCFQ	Breguet 904S Nymphale	7	
F-CCFR	Breguet 904S Nymphale	8	
F-CCFY	Breguet 904S Nymphale	14	
F-CCFZ	Breguet 904S Nymphale	15	
F-CCGE	Breguet 901S1	34	
F-CCGK	Fauvel AV.22S	1	
F-CCHD	Wassmer WA.21 Javelot II	8	
F-CCHG	Wassmer WA.21 Javelot II	19	
F-CCHK	Wassmer WA.21 Javelot II	28	
F-CCHR-WH	Schempp-Hirth Janus B	03	D-3110
F-CCJX	Schleicher ASK 21	21040	(F-CBDQ)
			F-WCJX
F-CCJY	Scheibe SF-28A Tandem-Falke	5763	D-KACP
F-CCKE	Wassmer WA.21 Javelot II	39	
F-CCKI	Wassmer WA.21 Javelot II	43	
F-CCKL	Wassmer WA.21 Javelot II (Dismantled)	47	
F-CCKQ	Wassmer WA.21A Javelot II	53	
F-CCLI	Avialsa-Scheibe A.60 Fauconnet (Under restoration)	13	
F-CCLL	Avialsa-Scheibe A.60 Fauconnet	16	
F-CCLM	Wassmer WA.22 Super Javelot	63	
F-CCLN	Wassmer WA.22 Super Javelot	61	
F-CCLO	Wassmer WA.22 Super Javelot	02	
F-CCLS	Wassmer WA.22 Super Javelot	66	
F-CCLZ	Wassmer WA.22 Super Javelot	70	
F-CCME	Wassmer WA.30 Bijave	8	
F-CCMH	Wassmer WA.30 Bijave	11	
F-CCMI	Wassmer WA.30 Bijave	13	
F-CCMY	Wassmer WA.30 Bijave	31	
F-CCNB	Wassmer WA.30 Bijave (Dismantled)	52	
F-CCNC	Wassmer WA.30 Bijave	53	
F-CCNH	Wassmer WA.30 Bijave	58	
F-CCNI	Wassmer WA.30 Bijave	59	
F-CCNJ	Wassmer WA.30 Bijave	60	
F-CCNL	Wassmer WA.30 Bijave (Dismantled)	62	
F-CCNM	Wassmer WA.30 Bijave	63	
F-CCNN	Wassmer WA.30 Bijave	64	
F-CCNP	Wassmer WA.30 Bijave	66	
F-CCNQ	Wassmer WA.30 Bijave	67	
F-CCNR	Wassmer WA.30 Bijave	68	
F-CCNU	Wassmer WA.30 Bijave	71	
F-CCNZ	Wassmer WA.30 Bijave	75	
F-CCOC	Wassmer WA.22 Super Javelot	75	
F-CCOD	Wassmer WA.22 Super Javelot (Dismantled)	76	
F-CCOH	Wassmer WA.22 Super Javelot	80	
F-CCOI	Wassmer WA.22 Super Javelot	81	
F-CCOL	Wassmer WA.22 Super Javelot	84	
F-CCOQ	Wassmer WA.30 Bijave	30	
F-CCOR	Wassmer WA.22 Super Javelot	86	
F-CCOS	Wassmer WA.22 Super Javelot	87	
F-CCOT	Wassmer WA.22 Super Javelot	88	
F-CCOU	Wassmer WA.22 Super Javelot	89	
F-CCPI	Carmam M.100S Mésange	10	
F-CCPT	Scheibe Zugvogel IIIB	1084	
F-CCPV	Standard Austria S	42	
F-CCQC	Avialsa-Scheibe A.60 Fauconnet	25	
F-CCQD	Avialsa-Scheibe A.60 Fauconnet	26	
F-CCQF	Avialsa-Scheibe A.60 Fauconnet	28K	
F-CCQK	Avialsa-Scheibe A.60 Fauconnet	33K	
F-CCRB	Wassmer WA.22A Super Javelot	94	
F-CCRC	Wassmer WA.30 Bijave	34	
F-CCRD	Wassmer WA.30 Bijave	35	
F-CCRI	Wassmer WA.30 Bijave	38	
F-CCRJ	Wassmer WA.30 Bijave	33	
F-CCRL	Wassmer WA.30 Bijave	40	
F-CCRM	Wassmer WA.30 Bijave	41	
F-CCRN	Wassmer WA.30 Bijave	42	
F-CCRO(2)	Mouisset AP	01	
F-CCRS	Wassmer WA.30 Bijave	46	
F-CCRU	Wassmer WA.30 Bijave	47	
F-CCRZ	Wassmer WA.22A Super Javelot	97	
F-CCSY	Carmam M.100S Mésange	35	
F-CCTA	Wassmer WA.30 Bijave	77	
F-CCTE	Wassmer WA.30 Bijave	80	
F-CCTH	Wassmer WA.30 Bijave	83	
F-CCTK	Wassmer WA.30 Bijave	85	
F-CCTP	Wassmer WA.30 Bijave	89	
F-CCTR	Wassmer WA.30 Bijave	91	
F-CCTZ	Wassmer WA.30 Bijave	98	
F-CCUC	Siren C.30S Edelweiss	3	
F-CCUM	Siren C.30S Edelweiss	15	
F-CCUV	Siren C.30S Edelweiss	24	
F-CCVF	Avialsa-Scheibe A.60 Fauconnet	53K	
F-CCVO	Avialsa-Scheibe A.60 Fauconnet	62	
F-CCVQ	Avialsa-Scheibe A.60 Fauconnet	64	
F-CCVX	Avialsa-Scheibe A.60 Fauconnet	70	
F-CCXJ	Carmam M.100S Mésange	45	
F-CCXX	Carmam M.200 Foehn	7	
F-CCXY	Carmam M.200 Foehn (Dismantled)	9	
F-CCXZ	Carmam M.200 Foehn	10	
F-CCYA	Wassmer WA.30 Bijave	97	
F-CCYB	Wassmer WA.30 Bijave	99	

F-CCYD	Wassmer WA.30 Bijave	101	
F-CCYF	Wassmer WA.30 Bijave	103	
F-CCYM	Wassmer WA.30 Bijave	110	
F-CCYO	Wassmer WA.30 Bijave	112	
F-CCYP	Wassmer WA.30 Bijave	115	
F-CCYQ	Wassmer WA.30 Bijave	114	
F-CCYS	Wassmer WA.30 Bijave	116	
F-CCYT	Wassmer WA.30 Bijave	117	
F-CCYU	Wassmer WA.30 Bijave	118	
F-CCYV	Wassmer WA.30 Bijave	119	
F-CCYX	Wassmer WA.30 Bijave	120	
F-CCYZ	Wassmer WA.30 Bijave	122	
F-CCZC	Wassmer WA.30 Bijave (Dismantled)	125	
F-CCZE	Wassmer WA.30 Bijave (Dismantled)	127	
F-CCZI	Wassmer WA.30 Bijave	130	
F-CCZJ	Wassmer WA.30 Bijave	131	
F-CCZK	Wassmer WA.30 Bijave	132	
F-CCZM	Wassmer WA.30 Bijave	133	
F-CCZO	Wassmer WA.30 Bijave	135	
F-CCZU	Wassmer WA.30 Bijave	138	
F-CCZX	Wassmer WA.22A Super Javelot	108	
F-CCZZ	Wassmer WA.22A Super Javelot	105	
F-CDAF	Glasflügel H201B Standard Libelle	557	
F-CDAH	Schempp-Hirth SHK-1	15	
F-CDAI	Siren C.30S Edelweiss	28	
F-CDAK	Siren C.30S Edelweiss	30	
F-CDAL	Siren C.30S Edelweiss	31	
F-CDAM	Siren C.30S Edelweiss	32	
F-CDAU	Siren C.30S Edelweiss (Dismantled)	40	
F-CDAV	Siren C.30S Edelweiss	41	
F-CDAY	LCA-Scheibe 10 Topaze	001	F-WDAY
F-CDBG	Avialsa-Scheibe A.60 Fauconnet	79K	
F-CDCB	Wassmer WA.30 Bijave	143	
F-CDCC	Wassmer WA.30 Bijave	144	
F-CDCE	Wassmer WA.30 Bijave	146	
F-CDCF	Wassmer WA.22A Super Javelot	109	
F-CDCI	Wassmer WA.22A Super Javelot	111	
F-CDCL	Wassmer WA.30 Bijave	150	
F-CDCP	Wassmer WA.30 Bijave	156	
F-CDCQ	Wassmer WA.30 Bijave	157	
F-CDCV	Wassmer WA.30 Bijave	161	
F-CDCZ	Wassmer WA.30 Bijave	166	
F-CDDC	Carmam M.200 Foehn	12	
F-CDDD	Carmam M.200 Foehn	13	
F-CDDU	Carmam M.200 Foehn	26	
F-CDED	Wassmer WA.22A Super Javelot	122	
F-CDEE	Wassmer WA.22A Super Javelot	123	
F-CDEF	Wassmer WA.30 Bijave	169	
F-CDEG	Wassmer WA.30 Bijave	170	
F-CDEH	Wassmer WA.30 Bijave	172	
F-CDEK	Wassmer WA.22A Super Javelot	127	
F-CDEQ	Wassmer WA.30 Bijave	177	
F-CDES	Wassmer WA.22A Super Javelot	130	
F-CDET	Wassmer WA.30 Bijave	180	
F-CDFK	Avialsa-Scheibe A.60 Fauconnet	108K	
F-CDFM	Avialsa-Scheibe A.60 Fauconnet	110K	
F-CDFQ	Avialsa-Scheibe A.60 Fauconnet	114	
F-CDFR	Avialsa-Scheibe A.60 Fauconnet	115K	
F-CDFT-M7	Avialsa-Scheibe A.60 Fauconnet	117	
F-CDFZ	Avialsa-Scheibe A.60 Fauconnet	122	
F-CDGA	Siren C.30S Edelweiss	42	
F-CDGC	Siren C.30S Edelweiss	44	
F-CDGN	Rocheteau-Scheibe CRA.60	12K	
F-CDHC	Carmam M.200 Foehn	30	
F-CDHE	Carmam M.200 Foehn	31	
F-CDHO	Carmam M.200 Foehn	40	
F-CDHQ	Carmam M.100S Mésange	67	
F-CDHS	Carmam M.200 Foehn	43	
F-CDHT	Carmam M.100S Mésange	69	
F-CDID	Wassmer WA.22A Super Javelot	136	
F-CDIE	Wassmer WA.30 Bijave	191	
F-CDIH	Wassmer WA.30 Bijave	194	
F-CDIJ	Wassmer WA.30 Bijave (Dismantled)	195	
F-CDIL	Wassmer WA.30 Bijave	197	
F-CDIN	Wassmer WA.22A Super Javelot	141	
F-CDIP	Wassmer WA.30 Bijave	200	
F-CDIQ	Wassmer WA.30 Bijave	201	
F-CDIS	Wassmer WA.30 Bijave	203	
F-CDIT	Wassmer WA.22A Super Javelot	142	
F-CDIZ	Wassmer WA.22A Super Javelot	146	
F-CDJA	Wassmer WA.30 Bijave	208	
F-CDJB	Wassmer WA.22A Super Javelot	147	
F-CDJC	Wassmer WA.30 Bijave	209	
F-CDJE	Wassmer WA.30 Bijave	211	
F-CDJF	Wassmer WA.30 Bijave	212	
F-CDJG	Wassmer WA.30 Bijave	213	
F-CDJM	Wassmer WA.30 Bijave	217	
F-CDJN	Wassmer WA.22A Super Javelot	150	
F-CDJO	Wassmer WA.30 Bijave	218	
F-CDJQ	Wassmer WA.30 Bijave	220	
F-CDJR	Wassmer WA.30 Bijave	221	
F-CDJX	Wassmer WA.30 Bijave (Dismantled)	225	
F-CDKF	Carmam M.100S Mésange	74	
F-CDKI	Carmam M.200 Foehn (Dismantled)	51	
F-CDKK	Carmam M.100S Mésange	77	
F-CDKN	Carmam M.200 Foehn	53	
F-CDKV	Carmam M.200 Foehn	56	
F-CDLC	Avialsa-Scheibe A.60 Fauconnet (Being restored)	125K	
F-CDLG	Avialsa-Scheibe A.60 Fauconnet	129K	
F-CDLR	Avialsa-Scheibe A.60 Fauconnet	140	
F-CDMB	Wassmer WA.30 Bijave	234	
F-CDMC	Wassmer WA.30 Bijave	235	
F-CDMJ	Wassmer WA.30 Bijave	240	
F-CDMN	Wassmer WA.30 Bijave	242	
F-CDMP	Wassmer WA.30 Bijave	244	
F-CDMT	Wassmer WA.30 Bijave	247	
F-CDMU	Wassmer WA.26P Squale	07	
F-CDMV	Wassmer WA.30 Bijave	248	
F-CDMY	Wassmer WA.26P Squale	08	
F-CDNH	Avialsa-Scheibe A.60 Fauconnet	155K	
F-CDNX	Rocheteau-Scheibe CRA.60	08	
F-CDNY	Rocheteau-Scheibe CRA.60	09	
F-CDOC	Bölkow Phoebus C	889	
F-CDOF	Bölkow Phoebus C	902	
F-CDOG	Bölkow Phoebus C	906	
F-CDOJ	Bölkow Phoebus C	915	
F-CDOL	Bölkow Phoebus CWB	925	
F-CDOO	Bölkow Phoebus C	932	
F-CDOP	Bölkow Phoebus C	926	
F-CDOQ	Bölkow Phoebus CWB	937	
F-CDOR	Bölkow Phoebus CWB	941	
F-CDOS	Bölkow Phoebus B1	943	
F-CDOU-C80	Jastreb Standard Cirrus G/81	227	
F-CDOV	Jastreb Standard Cirrus G/81	229	
F-CDOX-C82	Jastreb Standard Cirrus G/81	239	
F-CDOY	Jastreb Standard Cirrus G/81	240	
F-CDPC	Glasflügel H201 Standard Libelle	70	
F-CDPD	Schempp-Hirth L265 Cirrus	29	
F-CDPF-701	Glasflügel H201 Standard Libelle	150	
F-CDPG-702	Glasflügel H201B Standard Libelle	151	
F-CDPH-703	Glasflügel H201B Standard Libelle	152	
F-CDPR	Glasflügel H201B Standard Libelle	226	
F-CDPS-707	Glasflügel H201 Standard Libelle	227	
F-CDPT-7230	Glasflügel H201B Standard Libelle	230	
F-CDPU	Glasflügel H201 Standard Libelle	231	
F-CDPX	Glasflügel H201 Standard Libelle	247	
F-CDQA	Wassmer WA.30 Bijave	251	
F-CDQG	Wassmer WA.26P Squale	11	
F-CDQO	Wassmer WA.26P Squale	17	
F-CDQU	Wassmer WA.30 Bijave	257	
F-CDQX	Wassmer WA.30 Bijave	259	
F-CDQZ	Wassmer WA.30 Bijave	261	
F-CDRA	Schleicher Ka 6E	4278	
F-CDRD	Schleicher Ka 6E	4293	
F-CDRH	Schleicher Ka 6E	4298	
F-CDRI	Schleicher Ka 6E	4299	
F-CDRK	Schleicher Ka 6E	4302	
F-CDRL	Schleicher Ka 6E	4289	
F-CDRM	Schleicher Ka 6E	4290	
F-CDRN	Schleicher Ka 6E	4303	
F-CDRT	Schleicher Ka 6E	4319	
F-CDRU	Schleicher Ka 6E	4320	
F-CDRX	Schleicher Ka 6E	4323	
F-CDRZ	Schleicher ASK 14	14035	D-KECH
F-CDSA	Wassmer WA.30 Bijave	262	
F-CDSD	Wassmer WA.26P Squale	25	
F-CDSJ	Wassmer WA.26P Squale	30	
F-CDSK	Wassmer WA.30 Bijave	264	
F-CDSN	Wassmer WA.26P Squale	32	
F-CDSP	Wassmer WA.26P Squale	34	
F-CDSQ	Wassmer WA.30 Bijave	266	
F-CDSU	Wassmer WA.30 Bijave	270	
F-CDTA	Schleicher Ka 6E	4322	
F-CDTC	Schleicher Ka 6E	4328	
F-CDTG	Schleicher Ka 6E	4332	
F-CDTM	Schleicher Ka 6E	4350	
F-CDTN	Schleicher Ka 6E	4351	
F-CDTP	Schleicher Ka 6E	4354	
F-CDTQ	Schleicher ASK 13	13275	
F-CDTR	Schleicher Ka 6E	4355	
F-CDTS	Schleicher Ka 6E	4356	
F-CDTT	Schleicher Ka 6E	4358	
F-CDTU	Schleicher Ka 6E	4359	
F-CDTV	Schleicher ASW 15	15117	
F-CDTY	Schleicher Ka 6E	4361	
F-CDUA	Wassmer WA.30 Bijave	271	
F-CDUB	Wassmer WA.30 Bijave	272	
F-CDUC	Wassmer WA.30 Bijave	273	
F-CDUD	Wassmer WA.26P Squale	39	
F-CDUE	Wassmer WA.26P Squale	40	
F-CDUJ	Wassmer WA.26P Squale	44	
F-CDUN	Wassmer WA.26P Squale	47	
F-CDUO	Wassmer WA.30 Bijave	274	
F-CDUP	Wassmer WA.30 Bijave	275	
F-CDUR	Wassmer WA.26P Squale	48	
F-CDUS	Wassmer WA.26P Squale	49	
F-CDUU	Wassmer WA.26CM	03	
F-CDUX	Wassmer WA.30 Bijave	278	
F-CDVC	Rolladen-Schneider LS1C	47	
F-CDVE-L04	Rolladen-Schneider LS1C	201	
F-CDVJ-L7	Rolladen-Schneider LS1C	206	
F-CDVN	Rolladen-Schneider LS1D	210	
F-CDVQ-L16	Rolladen-Schneider LS1C	213	

F-CDVT	Rolladen-Schneider LS1D	141	
F-CDVV	Rolladen-Schneider LS1D	156	
F-CDVW-L22	Rolladen-Schneider LS1C	157	
F-CDVY-L34	Rolladen-Schneider LS1D	190	
F-CDVZ-L25	Rolladen-Schneider LS1D	191	
F-CDXC	Wassmer WA.26P Squale (Dismantled)	54	
F-CDXD	Wassmer WA.26CM	05	
F-CDXH	Wassmer WA.26CM	09	
F-CDXL	Wassmer WA.26P Squale	56	
F-CDXN	Wassmer WA.30 Bijave	280	
F-CDXO	Wassmer WA.26P Squale	57	
F-CDXS	Wassmer WA.26P Squale	60	
F-CDXV	Wassmer WA.26P Squale	62	
F-CDYA	Schleicher ASK 13	13296	
F-CDYB	Schleicher ASK 13	13297	
F-CDYC	Schleicher ASK 13	13298	
F-CDYD	Schleicher ASK 13	13299	
F-CDYG	Schleicher Ka 6E	4367	
F-CDYI	Schleicher Ka 6E	4369	
F-CDYL	Schleicher Ka 6E	4372	
F-CDYM	Schleicher ASK 13	13316	
F-CDYO	Schleicher ASK 13	13322	
F-CDYP	Schleicher ASK 13	13323	
F-CDYS	Schleicher ASK 13	13326	
F-CDYU	Schleicher ASW 15	15123	
F-CDYX	Schleicher ASK 13	13332	
F-CDYY	Schleicher ASK 13	13336	
F-CDYZ	Schleicher ASK 13	13334	
F-CDZD	Wassmer WA.26P Squale	69	
F-CDZJ	Wassmer WA.26P Squale	75	
F-CDZK	Wassmer WA.28 Espadon	93	
F-CDZM	Wassmer WA.28 Espadon	91	
F-CDZO	Wassmer WA.28 Espadon	95	
F-CDZR	Wassmer WA.28F	98	
F-CDZT	Wassmer WA.28 Espadon	100	
F-CDZZ-W15	Wassmer WA.28 Espadon	105	
F-CEAA	Schleicher ASK 13	13337	
F-CEAB	Schleicher ASK 13	13338	
F-CEAC	Schleicher ASK 13	13339	
F-CEAD	Schleicher ASK 13	13340	
F-CEAE	Schleicher ASK 13	13343	
F-CEAF	Schleicher ASK 13	13344	
F-CEAG	Schleicher ASK 13	13347	
F-CEAI	Schleicher ASK 13	13349	
F-CEAJ	Schleicher ASK 13	13350	
F-CEAK	Schleicher ASK 13	13353	
F-CEAL	Schleicher ASK 13	13355	
F-CEAM	Schleicher ASK 13	13356	
F-CEAO	Schleicher Ka 6E	4379	
F-CEAP	Schleicher ASK 13	13365	
F-CEAT	Schleicher ASK 13	13371	
F-CEAU	Schleicher Ka 6E	4380	
F-CEAV	Schleicher ASK 13	13372	
F-CEAX	Schleicher ASK 13	13373	
F-CEAY	Schleicher ASK 14	14062	D-KICI
F-CEAZ	Schleicher ASW 15	15171	
F-CEBB-715	Glasflügel H201 Standard Libelle	302	
F-CEBC-716	Glasflügel H201 Standard Libelle	303	
F-CEBE-718	Glasflügel H201B Standard Libelle	318	
F-CEBG-720	Glasflügel H201B Standard Libelle	320	
F-CEBH	Glasflügel H201 Standard Libelle	321	
F-CEBJ-723	Glasflügel H201B Standard Libelle	360	
F-CEBK	Glasflügel H201B Standard Libelle	361	
F-CEBN	Glasflügel H201B Standard Libelle	427	
F-CEBQ	Glasflügel H201 Standard Libelle	431	
F-CEBS-M21	Glasflügel H304	246	
F-CEBU	Glasflügel H304	252	
F-CEBV	Jastreb Standard Cirrus G/81	242	
F-CEBX	Jastreb Standard Cirrus G/81 (Dismantled)	243	
F-CECC	Schleicher ASK 13	13381	
F-CECD	Schleicher ASK 13	13382	
F-CECE	Schleicher Ka 6E	4381	
F-CECF	Schleicher Ka 6E	4382	
F-CECG	Schleicher ASW 17	17005	
F-CECH	Schleicher Ka 6E	4383	
F-CECI-R25	Schleicher ASK 13	13383	
F-CECJ	Schleicher ASK 13	13384	
F-CECK	Schleicher ASK 13	13385	
F-CECL	Schleicher ASK 13	13387	
F-CECN	Schleicher Ka 6E	4386	
F-CECO	Schleicher ASK 13	13389	
F-CECQ	Schleicher ASK 13	13390	
F-CECS-K89	Schleicher Ka 6E	4389	
F-CECT	Schleicher ASK 13	13402	
F-CECU	Schleicher ASK 13	13405	
F-CECY	Schleicher ASK 13	13407	
F-CEDA-N1	Schempp-Hirth Nimbus II	8	
F-CEDC	Schempp-Hirth Nimbus II	53	
F-CEDD-N6	Schempp-Hirth Nimbus II	54	
F-CEDF-N8	Schempp-Hirth Nimbus IIC	71	
F-CEDG-N9	Schempp-Hirth Nimbus IIC	73	
F-CEDH-N10	Schempp-Hirth Nimbus IIC	74	
F-CEDJ-N12	Schempp-Hirth Nimbus IIC	92	
F-CEDK-N14	Schempp-Hirth Nimbus IID	112	
F-CEDL-N15	Schempp-Hirth Nimbus IID	120	
F-CEDM-N17	Schempp-Hirth Nimbus IIB	137	F-WEDM
F-CEDO-W	Schempp-Hirth Ventus a	25	F-WEDO

F-CEDQ-14	Schempp-Hirth Ventus b	52	F-WEDQ
F-CEDS-28	Schempp-Hirth Ventus b	44	F-WEDS
F-CEDT	Schempp-Hirth Ventus bT	31/202	F-WEDT
F-CEDU	Schempp-Hirth Ventus b	95	F-WEDU
			D-4305
F-CEDV	Schempp-Hirth Ventus b	235	F-WEDV
F-CEDX	Glasflügel H303B Mosquito	128	
F-CEDZ-M05	Glasflügel H303B Mosquito	154	
F-CEEA	LCA-Scheibe 10 Topaze	1	
F-CEEC	LCA-Scheibe 10 Topaze	3	
F-CEED	LCA-Scheibe 10 Topaze	4	
F-CEEE	LCA-Scheibe 11 Topaze	5	
F-CEEG	LCA-Scheibe 10 Topaze	7	
F-CEEL	LCA-Scheibe 11 Topaze	12	
F-CEEM	LCA-Scheibe 11 Topaze	13	
F-CEEN	LCA-Scheibe 11 Topaze	14	
F-CEEO	LCA-Scheibe 11 Topaze	15	
F-CEEQ	LCA-Scheibe 11 Topaze	17	
F-CEET	LCA-Scheibe 11 Topaze	20	
F-CEEY	LCA-Scheibe 11 Topaze	24	
F-CEFB-EA	Schempp-Hirth CS-11 St.Cirrus	326G	
F-CEFD-C05	Schempp-Hirth CS-11 St.Cirrus	342G	
F-CEFE	Schempp-Hirth CS-11 St.Cirrus	344G	
F-CEFF-CI	Schempp-Hirth CS-11 St.Cirrus	371G	
F-CEFG-C10	Schempp-Hirth CS-11 St.Cirrus	387G	
F-CEFH	Schempp-Hirth CS-11 St.Cirrus	401G	
F-CEFK	Schempp-Hirth CS-11 St.Cirrus	406G	
F-CEFQ-C13	Schempp-Hirth CS-11 St.Cirrus	453G	
F-CEFS-C22	Schempp-Hirth CS-11 St.Cirrus	462G	
F-CEFU	Schempp-Hirth CS-11 St.Cirrus	468G	
F-CEFV	Schempp-Hirth CS-11 St.Cirrus	469G	
F-CEFZ	Schempp-Hirth CS-11 St.Cirrus	512G	
F-CEGA	Schleicher ASK 13	13404	
F-CEGC	Schleicher ASK 13	13410	
F-CEGD	Schleicher ASK 13	13412	
F-CEGE	Schleicher ASW 15B	15269	
F-CEGG	Schleicher ASW 15B	15271	
F-CEGH	Schleicher ASW 15B	15272	
F-CEGI	Schleicher ASW 15B	15273	
F-CEGK	Schleicher ASK 13	13411	
F-CEGM-A13	Schleicher ASW 15B	15281	
F-CEGN	Schleicher ASW 15B	15297	
F-CEGO	Schleicher ASW 15B	15291	
F-CEGP	Schleicher ASW 15B	15292	
F-CEGQ	Schleicher ASW 15B	15293	
F-CEGS	Schleicher ASW 15B	15295	
F-CEGT-A13	Schleicher ASW 15B	15296	
F-CEGU	Schleicher K 8B	8933	
F-CEGV	Schleicher K 8B	8934	
F-CEGX	Schleicher K 8B	8935	
F-CEGZ	Schleicher Ka 6E	4186	
F-CEHC	Rolladen-Schneider LS1D	216	
F-CEHD	Rolladen-Schneider LS1D	217	
F-CEHF	Rolladen-Schneider LS1D	219	
F-CEHG	Rolladen-Schneider LS1D	220	
F-CEHI-L32	Rolladen-Schneider LS1D	222	
F-CEHJ	Rolladen-Schneider LS1D	223	
F-CEHK	Rolladen-Schneider LS1D	224	
F-CEHL	Rolladen-Schneider LS1D	225	
F-CEHM-L35	Rolladen-Schneider LS1D (Dismantled)	226	
F-CEHO-L39	Rolladen-Schneider LS1D	228	
F-CEHR-L48	Rolladen-Schneider LS1D	231	
F-CEHS-L43	Rolladen-Schneider LS1D	232	
F-CEHT	Rolladen-Schneider LS1D	233	
F-CEHU	Rolladen-Schneider LS1D	234	
F-CEHV	Rolladen-Schneider LS1D	235	
F-CEHY	Rolladen-Schneider LS1D	237	
F-CEIB-SG	Rolladen-Schneider LS4	4012	
F-CEIC	Rolladen-Schneider LS4	4013	
F-CEID-FL	Rolladen-Schneider LS4	4020	
F-CEIE	Rolladen-Schneider LS4	4053	
F-CEIF-SC	Rolladen-Schneider LS4	4056	
F-CEIG-V08	Rolladen-Schneider LS4	4057	
F-CEII-V10	Rolladen-Schneider LS4	4059	
F-CEIJ-V11	Rolladen-Schneider LS4	4138	
F-CEIK-V12	Rolladen-Schneider LS4	4139	
F-CEIL	Rolladen-Schneider LS4	4245	
F-CEIM-RF	Rolladen-Schneider LS4	4140	
F-CEIN-FF	Rolladen-Schneider LS4	4141	
F-CEIP-V20	Rolladen-Schneider LS4	4231	
F-CEIQ-RM	Rolladen-Schneider LS4	4292	
F-CEIR-TC	Rolladen-Schneider LS4	4232	
F-CEIS-V22	Rolladen-Schneider LS4	4233	
F-CEIT-V23	Rolladen-Schneider LS4	4234	
F-CEIV-V25	Rolladen-Schneider LS4	4236	
F-CEIX	Rolladen-Schneider LS4	4237	
F-CEIY-V27	Rolladen-Schneider LS4	4238	
F-CEIZ-V49	Rolladen-Schneider LS4	4239	
F-CEJA	Schleicher K 8B	8936	
F-CEJB	Schleicher K 8B	8937	
F-CEJC	Schleicher K 8B	8939	
F-CEJD	Schleicher K 8B	8940	
F-CEJE	Schleicher K 8B	8938	
F-CEJG-SG	Schleicher ASW 17	17022	
F-CEJH	Schleicher K 8B	8956	
F-CEJI	Schleicher K 8B	8957	
F-CEJJ	Schleicher ASK 13	13461	

F-CEJK	Schleicher ASK 13	13462	
F-CEJM	Schleicher ASW 15B	15349	
F-CEJN-A24	Schleicher ASW 15B	15350	
F-CEJP	Schleicher K 8B	8976	
F-CEJQ	Schleicher K 8B	8977	
F-CEJR	Schleicher ASK 13	13497	
F-CEJS	Schleicher K 8B	8979	
F-CEJT	Schleicher ASK 13	13509	
F-CEJU	Schleicher ASK 13	13520	
F-CEJV	Schleicher K 8B	8982	
F-CEJW	Schleicher ASK 13	13521	
F-CEJX	Schleicher ASK 13	13522	
F-CEJY	Schleicher K 8B	8984	
F-CEJZ	Schleicher K 8B	8983	
F-CEKA	Rolladen-Schneider LS1F	376	
F-CEKC	Rolladen-Schneider LS1F	380	
F-CEKD	Rolladen-Schneider LS1F	387	
F-CEKE-L54	Rolladen-Schneider LS1F	388	
F-CEKF-L55	Rolladen-Schneider LS1F	389	
F-CEKL-L61	Rolladen-Schneider LS1F	396	
F-CEKM-L62	Rolladen-Schneider LS1F	397	
F-CEKO	Rolladen-Schneider LS1F	399	
F-CEKP	Rolladen-Schneider LS1F	400	
F-CEKR	Rolladen-Schneider LS1F	402	
F-CEKS-F1	Rolladen-Schneider LS1F	403	
F-CEKT-LT	Rolladen-Schneider LS1F	404	
F-CEKV-L72	Rolladen-Schneider LS1F	439	
F-CEKY	Rolladen-Schneider LS1F	451	
F-CELB	Glasflügel H201B Standard Libelle	531	
F-CELC-758	Glasflügel H201B Standard Libelle	558	
F-CELD	Wassmer WA.26P Squale	64	F-CDXY
F-CELE	Glasflügel H201B Standard Libelle	590	
F-CELF	Glasflügel H201 Standard Libelle	428	
F-CELG	Glasflügel H201B Standard Libelle	600	
F-CELH-709	Glasflügel H201B Standard Libelle	599	
F-CELJ-740	Glasflügel H201B Standard Libelle	589	
F-CELK-MF	Glasflügel H303B Mosquito	156	
F-CELL-M07	Glasflügel H303B Mosquito	168	
F-CELM-M08	Glasflügel H303B Mosquito	169	
F-CELN	Glasflügel H303B Mosquito	175	
F-CELO	Glasflügel H303B Mosquito	176	
F-CELP	Glasflügel H303B Mosquito	182	
F-CELR-738	Glasflügel H201B Standard Libelle	598	
F-CELS-M²	Glasflügel H303B Mosquito	188	
F-CELT-M14	Glasflügel H303B Mosquito	189	
F-CELU	Glasflügel H303B Mosquito	197	
F-CELV	Glasflügel H303B Mosquito	198	
F-CELY	Glasflügel H303B Mosquito	202	
F-CEMC	Grob/Schempp-Hirth CS-11 St.Cirrus	552G	
F-CEMD-C32	Grob/Schempp-Hirth CS-11 St.Cirrus	562G	
F-CEMJ-C38	Grob/Schempp-Hirth CS-11 St.Cirrus	584G	
F-CEMM-C41	Schempp-Hirth CS-11/75 St.Cirrus	589	
F-CEMO	Schempp-Hirth CS-11/75 St.Cirrus	617	
F-CEMS	Schempp-Hirth CS-11/75 St.Cirrus	649	
F-CEMU	Schempp-Hirth CS-11/75 St.Cirrus	657	
F-CENA	LCA-Scheibe 12	26	
F-CENB	LCA-Scheibe 12	27	
F-CENF	LCA-Scheibe 12	31	
F-CEOE	Wassmer WA.28F	110	
F-CEOF	Wassmer WA.28 Espadon	111	
F-CEOG	Wassmer WA.28 Espadon	112	
F-CEOH	Wassmer WA.28 Espadon	113	
F-CEPA	Schempp-Hirth Janus A	05	F-WEPA
F-CEPB	Schempp-Hirth Janus	14	
F-CEPC-3C	Schempp-Hirth Janus A	17	
F-CEPD	Schempp-Hirth Janus A	21	
F-CEPE	Schempp-Hirth Janus A	22	
F-CEPF-33	Schempp-Hirth Janus A	33	
F-CEPG	Schempp-Hirth Janus A	32	
F-CEPH	Schempp-Hirth Janus A	38	
F-CEPI-J46	Schempp-Hirth Janus B	46	
F-CEPJ	Schempp-Hirth Janus B	67	
F-CEPL	Schempp-Hirth Janus B	82	
F-CEPM-J20	Schempp-Hirth Janus B	84	
F-CEPN	Schempp-Hirth Janus B	85	
F-CEPO	Schempp-Hirth Janus B	94	
F-CEPP	Schempp-Hirth Janus B	95	
F-CEPQ	Schempp-Hirth Janus B	100	
F-CEPR-PR	Schempp-Hirth Janus B	102	
F-CEPS-J22	Schempp-Hirth Janus B	101	
F-CEPT	Schempp-Hirth Janus B	105	
F-CEPU-J107	Schempp-Hirth Janus B	107	
F-CEPV	Schempp-Hirth Janus B	108	
F-CEPX	Schempp-Hirth Janus B	109	
F-CEPY	Schempp-Hirth Janus B	114	
F-CEPZ	Schempp-Hirth Janus B	115	
F-CEQC	Glasflügel H205 Libelle	146	
F-CEQD	Glasflügel H205 Libelle	147	
F-CEQE-H05	Glasflügel H205 Libelle	148	
F-CEQG	Glasflügel H205 Libelle	150	
F-CEQH	Glasflügel H205 Libelle	151	
F-CEQI	Glasflügel H205 Libelle	152	
F-CEQJ	Glasflügel H205 Libelle	156	
F-CEQK	Glasflügel H205 Libelle	157	
F-CEQN	Glasflügel H205 Libelle	161	
F-CEQO	Glasflügel H205 Libelle	162	
F-CEQQ	Glasflügel H205 Libelle	166	

F-CEQR	Glasflügel H205 Libelle	167	
F-CEQT	Glasflügel H205 Libelle	169	
F-CEQU	Glasflügel H205 Libelle	170	
F-CEQV	Glasflügel H303 Mosquito	16	
F-CEQX-M2	Glasflügel H303 Mosquito	41	F-WEQX
F-CEQY	Lanaverre CS-11/75L Standard Cirrus	37	
F-CEQZ	Lanaverre CS-11/75L Standard Cirrus	38	
F-CERA	Schleicher ASK 13	13523	
F-CERB	Schleicher ASK 13	13531	
F-CERD	Schleicher ASK 13	13532	
F-CERE	Schleicher ASK 13	13541	
F-CERG	Schleicher K 8B	8985	
F-CERI	Schleicher ASK 18	18032	
F-CERJ	Schleicher ASK 18	18033	
F-CERL	Schleicher ASK 18	18035	
F-CERM	Schleicher ASW 19	19041	
F-CERN	Schleicher ASK 13	13544	
F-CERO	Schleicher ASK 13	13573	
F-CERP-X01	Schleicher ASW 20	20024	
F-CERS-F04	Schleicher ASW 19	19241	
F-CERU	Schleicher ASW 19B	19326	
F-CERV-X99	Centrair ASW-20F	20500	
F-CERX-X1	Centrair ASW-20F	20513	
F-CERY-X117	Centrair ASW-20F	20517	
F-CESA	Rolladen-Schneider LS1F	469	
F-CESB	Rolladen-Schneider LS1F	455	
F-CESD	Rolladen-Schneider LS3	3203	
F-CESE-S02	Rolladen-Schneider LS3A	3303	
F-CESF-S03	Rolladen-Schneider LS3A	3204	
F-CESH	Rolladen-Schneider LS3A	3157	
F-CESI-S06	Rolladen-Schneider LS3A	3187	
F-CESJ-S07	Rolladen-Schneider LS3A	3383	
F-CESL-S09	Rolladen-Schneider LS3A	3385	
F-CESM-S10	Rolladen-Schneider LS3A	3419	
F-CESO-S14	Rolladen-Schneider LS3A	3438	
F-CESQ	Rolladen-Schneider LS3A	3452	
F-CESR	Rolladen-Schneider LS3A-17	3453	
F-CEST-S17	Rolladen-Schneider LS3A	3455	
F-CESU-S19	Rolladen-Schneider LS3A	3460	
F-CESX-V60	Rolladen-Schneider LS4B	41053	
F-CETG	Carmam JP.15/36A Aiglon	9	
F-CETI	Carmam JP.15/36A Aiglon	11	
F-CETL	Carmam JP.15/36A Aiglon	14	
F-CETY	Carmam JP.15/36AR Aiglon	29	
F-CEUC	Caproni A.21S Calif	237	
F-CEUE	Caproni A.21S Calif	240	
F-CEUF	Caproni A.21S Calif	241	
F-CEUJ	Centrair ASW-20FL	20174	
F-CEUK	Centrair ASW-20F	20168	
F-CEVA	Schempp-Hirth CS-11/75 Standard Cirrus	698	
F-CEVF	Lanaverre CS-11/75L Standard Cirrus	5	
F-CEVI	Lanaverre CS-11/75L Standard Cirrus	8	
F-CEVL-C11	Lanaverre CS-11/75L Standard Cirrus	11	
F-CEVM	Lanaverre CS-11/75L Standard Cirrus	12	
F-CEVN-C68	Lanaverre CS-11/75L Standard Cirrus	13	
F-CEVP-C70	Lanaverre CS-11/75L Standard Cirrus	23	
F-CEVQ-C71	Lanaverre CS-11/75L Standard Cirrus	24	
F-CEVU	Lanaverre CS-11/75L Standard Cirrus	29	
F-CEVV-C76	Lanaverre CS-11/75L Standard Cirrus	30	
F-CEVY-RR	Lanaverre CS-11/78L Standard Cirrus	32	F-WEVY
F-CEVZ-C7	Lanaverre CS-11/75L Standard Cirrus	34	
F-CEXA-R01	Grob G.102 Astir CS	1459	
F-CEXB	Grob G.102 Astir CS	1522	
F-CEXC	Grob G.102 Astir CS	1523	
F-CEXD-R04	Grob G.102 Astir CS	1524	
F-CEXE	Grob G.102 Astir CS	1525	
F-CEXF	Grob G.102 Astir CS	1526	
F-CEXG-R08	Grob G.102 Astir CS	1527	
F-CEXK	Grob G.102 Astir CS	1535	
F-CEXL	Grob G.102 Astir CS	1536	
F-CEXM-R14	Grob G.102/77 Astir CS	1688	
F-CEXN	Grob G.102/77 Astir CS	1697	
F-CEXO-R20	Grob G.102/77 Astir CS	1706	
F-CEXP	Grob G.102/77 Astir CS	1699	
F-CEXQ-R26	Grob G.102/77 Astir CS	1730	
F-CEXR-R29	Grob G.102/77 Astir CS	1743	
F-CEXS-R30	Grob G.102/77 Astir CS	1759	
F-CEXT-R38	Grob G.102/77 Astir CS	1775	
F-CEXU-R31	Grob G.102/77 Astir CS	1773	
F-CEXV-R32	Grob G.102/77 Astir CS	1779	
F-CEXX	Grob G.102/77 Astir CS	1774	
F-CEXY	Grob G.102/77 Astir CS	1794	
F-CEXZ-R35	Grob G.102/77 Astir CS	1795	
F-CEYA	Scheibe SF-28A Tandem-Falke	5756	D-KMOS (D-KMGF)
F-CEYB	Scheibe SF-28A Tandem-Falke	5781	D-KCIR(2)
F-CEYC	Scheibe SF-28A Tandem-Falke	5783	(D-KDFM(1))
F-CEYE	Scheibe SF-28A Tandem-Falke	5785	(D-KDFQ(1))
F-CEYF-L72	Scheibe SF-28A Tandem-Falke	5786	(D-KDFW(1))
F-CEYG	Scheibe SF-28A Tandem-Falke	5787	(D-KDFY(1))
F-CEYH	Scheibe SF-28A Tandem-Falke	5788	(D-KDFZ(1))
F-CEYI	Scheibe SF-28A Tandem-Falke	5789	(D-KDFX(3))
F-CEYJ	Scheibe SF-28A Tandem-Falke	5790	(D-KDFY(3))
F-CEYK	Scheibe SF-28A Tandem-Falke	5792	(D-KDCJ(1))
F-CEYL	Scheibe SF-28A Tandem-Falke	5793	(D-KDCK(1))
F-CEYM	Scheibe SF-28A Tandem-Falke	5794	(D-KDCQ(1))
F-CEYN	Scheibe SF-28A Tandem-Falke	5795	(D-KDCU(2))

F-CEYO	Scheibe SF-28A Tandem-Falke	5796	(D-KDCW)
F-CEYP	Scheibe SF-28A Tandem-Falke	5797	(D-KDCX)
F-CEYQ	Scheibe SF-28A Tandem-Falke	5798	(D-KDCY)
F-CEYS	Scheibe SF-28A Tandem-Falke	57101	(D-KDBR(1))
F-CEYT	Scheibe SF-28A Tandem-Falke	57104	(D-KDBY(1))
F-CEYU	Scheibe SF-28A Tandem-Falke	57105	(D-KDBU(2))
F-CEYV	Scheibe SF-28A Tandem-Falke	5734	HB-2022
			(D-KOED(1))
F-CEYY	Scheibe SF-28A Tandem-Falke	57109	(D-KDGS(1))
F-CEZA	Scheibe Bergfalke IV	5861	
F-CEZB	Scheibe Bergfalke IV	5865	
F-CFAA-JD	Schempp-Hirth HS-7 Mini-Nimbus	17	F-WFAA
F-CFAB-101	Schempp-Hirth HS-7 Mini-Nimbus	130	
F-CFAC-L'OR	Schempp-Hirth Janus B	121	
F-CFAD	Schempp-Hirth Janus B	124	
F-CFAE-E	Schempp-Hirth Janus B	128	
F-CFAF-AF	Schempp-Hirth Janus B	131	
F-CFAG	Schempp-Hirth Janus B	135	
F-CFAH	Schempp-Hirth Janus B	137	
F-CFAI	Schempp-Hirth Janus B	139	
F-CFAJ-J39	Schempp-Hirth Janus B (Damaged 13.3.03)	153	
F-CFAL	Schempp-Hirth Janus C	154	
F-CFAM-M	Schempp-Hirth Janus C	155	
F-CFAN-J43	Schempp-Hirth Janus C	159	
F-CFAO-PT	Schempp-Hirth Janus C	160	
F-CFAP	Schempp-Hirth Janus C	164	
F-CFAQ	Schempp-Hirth Janus C	173	
F-CFAR-IN	Schempp-Hirth Janus C	166	
F-CFAS	Schempp-Hirth Janus B	175	
F-CFAT	Schempp-Hirth Janus B	180	
F-CFAU-J50	Schempp-Hirth Janus B	192	
F-CFAV-T	Schempp-Hirth Janus CT	3/195	F-WFAV
			D-KFAV
			F-WFAV
F-CFAX-73	Schempp-Hirth Janus B	204	
F-CFAY -J53	Schempp-Hirth Janus B	207	
F-CFAZ-AZ	Schempp-Hirth Janus B	221	
F-CFBA-T01	Grob G.103 Twin Astir	3055	
F-CFBB-T02	Grob G.103 Twin Astir	3082	
F-CFBC-T03	Grob G.103T Twin Astir Trainer	3124	
F-CFBD	Grob G.103 Twin Astir	3119	
F-CFBE-T05	Grob G.103 Twin Astir	3120	
F-CFBH-T08	Grob G.103 Twin Astir	3123	
F-CFBI	Grob G.103 Twin Astir	3131	
F-CFBJ-T10	Grob G.103 Twin Astir	3132	
F-CFBK-T11	Grob G.103 Twin Astir	3133	
F-CFBL	Grob G.103 Twin Astir	3114	
F-CFBM-T13	Grob G.103 Twin Astir	3135	
F-CFBN-T14	Grob G.103 Twin Astir	3158	
F-CFBO-T15	Grob G.103 Twin Astir	3128	
F-CFBR-T18	Grob G.103 Twin Astir	3161	
F-CFBS-T19	Grob G.103 Twin Astir	3162	
F-CFBT-T20	Grob G.103 Twin Astir	3125	
F-CFBU-T21	Grob G.103 Twin Astir	3183	
F-CFBX-T23	Grob G.103 Twin Astir	3281	
F-CFBZ-T25	Grob G.103T Twin Astir Trainer	3201	
F-CFCB-R15	Grob G.102/77J Astir Jeans	2079	
F-CFCC-R16	Grob G.102/77J Astir Jeans	2084	
F-CFCD-R21	Grob G.102/77J Astir Jeans	2111	
F-CFCE-R17	Grob G.102/77J Astir Jeans	2094	
F-CFCF	Grob G.102/77J Astir Jeans	2098	
F-CFCH-R24	Grob G.102/77J Astir Jeans	2115	
F-CFCI-R25	Grob G.102/77J Astir Jeans	2123	
F-CFCJ	Grob G.102/77J Astir Jeans	2144	
F-CFCK-R28	Grob G.102/77J Astir Jeans	2145	
F-CFCL-R36	Grob G.102/77J Astir Jeans	2163	
F-CFCM-R37	Grob G.102/77J Astir Jeans	2177	
F-CFCO-R40	Grob G.102/77J Astir Jeans	2179	
F-CFCQ	Grob G.102/77J Astir Jeans	2200	
F-CFCR-R43	Grob G.102/77J Astir Jeans	2201	
F-CFCS-R44	Grob G.102/77J Astir Jeans	2204	
F-CFCU-R46	Grob G.102/77J Astir Jeans	2231	
F-CFCX	Grob G.102C Club Astir II	5021C	
F-CFCY-R49	Grob G.102C Club Astir II	5022C	
F-CFCZ-R60	Grob G.102C Club Astir II	5023C	
F-CFDA	Jastreb Standard Cirrus G/81	256	F-WFDA
F-CFDB-C89	Jastreb Standard Cirrus G/81	257	F-WFDB
F-CFDC	Jastreb Standard Cirrus G/81	260	F-WFDC
F-CFDE	Scheibe SF-34B	5140	
F-CFDF	Schempp-Hirth Discus CS	017CS	
F-CFDG-Z19	Rolladen-Schneider LS6C	6301	
F-CFDH	Schempp-Hirth Discus b	509	
F-CFDI-D28	Schempp-Hirth Discus b	513	
F-CFDJ-D29	Schempp-Hirth Discus CS	175CS	
F-CFDK-D30	Schempp-Hirth Discus CS	180CS	
F-CFDL-D31	Schempp-Hirth Discus CS	221CS	
F-CFDM	Schempp-Hirth Discus b	139	D-4693
F-CFDN-D33	Schempp-Hirth Discus CS	235CS	
F-CFDO-DE	Schempp-Hirth Discus 2a	20	D-2778
F-CFDP	Schempp-Hirth Discus 2b	31	
F-CFDQ-DA	Schempp-Hirth Discus 2a	27	D-4096
F-CFDR	Schempp-Hirth Discus 2T	32/181	
F-CFDS-ET	Schempp-Hirth Discus 2a	173	
F-CFEB	Issoire E-78B Silène	5	
F-CFER	Issoire E-78B Silène	10	
F-CFFA-X02	Centrair ASW-20FL	20101	
F-CFFD-X04	Centrair ASW-20F	20104	
F-CFFF	Centrair ASW-20F	20106	
F-CFFH	Centrair ASW-20F	20111	
F-CFFI-JM	Centrair ASW-20F	20112	
F-CFFN-X18	Centrair ASW-20FL	20117	
F-CFFP	Centrair ASW-20F	20120	
F-CFFS-X24	Centrair ASW-20FL	20124	
F-CFFT	Centrair ASW-20FL	20125	
F-CFFU-X26	Centrair ASW-20F	20126	
F-CFFV-X29	Centrair ASW-20F	20129	
F-CFFY-X34	Centrair ASW-20F	20134	
F-CFFZ	Centrair ASW-20F	20135	
F-CFGE	Pottier 15/34 Kit Club	50-38	
F-CFGI	Pottier 15/34 Kit Club	50-44	
F-CFGK	Pottier 15/34 Kit Club	50-48	
F-CFHB	Grob G.103 Twin Astir	3229	
F-CFHD	Grob G.103 Twin Astir	3234	
F-CFHE-T30	Grob G.103 Twin Astir	3241	
F-CFHF-T31	Grob G.103 Twin Astir	3244	
F-CFHG-T32	Grob G.103T Twin Astir Trainer	3243	
F-CFHH-T33	Grob G.103 Twin Astir	3250	
F-CFHI -T34	Grob G.103 Twin Astir	3255	
F-CFHJ-T35	Grob G.103T Twin Astir Trainer	3283	
F-CFHK	Grob G.103T Twin Astir Trainer	3282	
F-CFHM	Grob G.103 Twin Astir II	3530	
F-CFHO-T40	Grob G.103 Twin Astir II	3566	
F-CFHQ-T42	Grob G.103 Twin Astir II	3568	
F-CFHR	Grob G.103 Twin Astir II	3569	
F-CFHS	Grob G.103 Twin Astir II	3578	
F-CFHT	Grob G.103 Twin Astir II	3579	
F-CFHU	Grob G.103 Twin Astir II	3580	
F-CFHV	Grob G.103 Twin Astir II	3581	
F-CFHX-T48	Grob G.103 Twin Astir II	3582	
F-CFHY-T49	Grob G.103 Twin Astir II	3583	
F-CFHZ	Grob G.103 Twin Astir II	3584	
F-CFIA	Grob G.102/77 Astir CS	1801	
F-CFIB-R51	Grob G.102/77 Astir CS	1802	
F-CFID	Grob G.102/77 Astir CS	1810	
F-CFIE-R54	Grob G.102/77 Astir CS	1811	
F-CFIF-R55	Grob G.102/77 Astir CS	1815	
F-CFIG-R56	Grob G.102/77 Astir CS	1821	
F-CFII -R58	Grob G.102S Speed Astir	5034S	
F-CFIJ	Grob G.102S Speed Astir	5035S	
F-CFIK	Grob G.102S Speed Astir	5036S	
F-CFIL	Grob G.102S Speed Astir	5037S	
F-CFIM	Grob G.102S Speed Astir	5038S	
F-CFIN-R73	Grob G.102S Speed Astir	5039S	
F-CFIO	Grob G.102S Speed Astir	5042S	
F-CFIP-R75	Grob G.102S Speed Astir II	5043S	
F-CFIQ-R76	Grob G.102 Astir CS 77	1817	
F-CFIR-W	Grob G.102 Astir CS 77	1637	PH-572
F-CFJA	Scheibe SF-28A Tandem-Falke	57115	(D-KDGX(2))
F-CFJB	Scheibe SF-28A Tandem-Falke	57117	(D-KOOH(1))
F-CFJC-RF	Scheibe SF-28A Tandem-Falke	57119	(D-KNAU(1))
F-CFJD	Scheibe SF-28A Tandem-Falke	57121	D-KNIH
F-CFJE	Scheibe SF-28A Tandem-Falke	5769	D-KACV
F-CFJF	Scheibe SF-28A Tandem-Falke (W/o 6.2.00)	5726	D-KOAO
F-CFJG	Scheibe SF-28A Tandem-Falke	5725	D-KOAM
F-CFJH	Scheibe SF-28A Tandem-Falke	5709	D-KHOS
F-CFJJ	Scheibe SF-28A Tandem-Falke	5720	D-KOAL
F-CFJK	Scheibe SF-28A Tandem-Falke	5705	F-WFJK
			D-KHOO
F-CFJL	Scheibe SF-28A Tandem-Falke	5737	D-KOEG
F-CFKA-T51	Grob G.103 Twin Astir II	3585	
F-CFKB-T52	Grob G.103 Twin Astir II	3586	
F-CFKC-T53	Grob G.103 Twin Astir II	3587	
F-CFKD	Grob G.103 Twin Astir II	3588	
F-CFKE-T55	Grob G.103 Twin Astir II	3589	
F-CFKF-T56	Grob G.103 Twin Astir II	3590	
F-CFKG	Grob G.103 Twin Astir II	3591	
F-CFKH	Grob G.103 Twin Astir II	3592	
F-CFKI	Grob G.103 Twin Astir II	3627	
F-CFKJ-T60	Grob G.103 Twin Astir II	3628	
F-CFKK-T61	Grob G.103 Twin Astir II	3629	
F-CFKL-T62	Grob G.103 Twin Astir II	3630	
F-CFKM	Grob G.103 Twin Astir II	3631	
F-CFKN	Grob G.103 Twin Astir II	3693	
F-CFKO-T65	Grob G.103 Twin Astir II	3694	
F-CFKP-T66	Grob G.103 Twin Astir II	3695	
F-CFKQ-T67	Grob G.103 Twin Astir II	3704	
F-CFKR-T68	Grob G.103 Twin Astir II	3705	
F-CFKS	Grob G.103 Twin Astir II	3706	
F-CFKT	Grob G.103 Twin Astir II	3707	
F-CFKU-T71	Grob G.103 Twin Astir II	3715	
F-CFKV-T75	Grob G.103 Twin Astir II	3759	
F-CFKY-T77	Grob G.103 Twin Astir II	3834	
F-CFKZ-T78	Grob G.103 Twin Astir II	3835	
F-CFLC	Centrair ASW-20FL	20138	
F-CFLE	Centrair ASW-20F	20142	
F-CFLF-X43	Centrair ASW-20F	20143	
F-CFLG	Centrair ASW-20F	20144	
F-CFLH	Centrair ASW-20FL	20146	
F-CFLI- LI	Centrair ASW-20FL	20148	
F-CFLJ	Centrair ASW-20F	20147	
F-CFLK-X49	Centrair ASW-20F	20149	
F-CFLM	Centrair ASW-20F	20152	
F-CFLN-X53	Centrair ASW-20FL	20153	
F-CFLP-AV	Centrair ASW-20F	20157	

F-CFLQ	Centrair ASW-20FL	20158	
F-CFLT-X61	Centrair ASW-20FL	20161	
F-CFLX-X86	Centrair ASW-20FL	20186	
F-CFMA	Grob G.102C Club Astir II	5024C	
F-CFMC-R63	Grob G.102C Club Astir II	5053C	
F-CFMD	Grob G.102C Club Astir II	5054C	
F-CFMF-R66	Grob G.102C Club Astir IIIB	5509CB	
F-CFMG-R67	Grob G.102C Club Astir IIIB	5544CB	
F-CFMI-R69	Grob G.102C Club Astir IIIB	5565CB	
F-CFMJ	Grob G.102C Club Astir IIIB	5582CB	
F-CFMK-FY	Grob G.102/77J Astir Jeans	2240	D-5946
F-CFML-R86	Grob G.102/77J Astir Jeans	2245	
F-CFMM-R47	Grob G.102/77J Astir Jeans	2093	D-7535
F-CFMN	Grob G.102/77J Astir Jeans	2055	D-7576
F-CFMO	Grob G.102/77J Astir Jeans	2023	D-4828
F-CFMQ	Grob G.102/77J Astir Jeans	2092	D-7534
F-CFMR	Grob G.102/77J Astir Jeans	2159	D-4555
F-CFMT	Grob G.102/77J Astir Jeans	2071	HB-1399
F-CFMU	Grob G.102/77J Astir Jeans	2102	D-7630
F-CFNB	Pottier 15/34 Kit Club	50-59	
F-CFPD	Siren PIK-20E2-F	710	
F-CFPE	Siren PIK-30	713	
F-CFPG	Siren PIK-30	723	
F-CFPH	Siren PIK-30	724	
F-CFPJ	Siren PIK-30	727	
F-CFPO	Siren PIK-30	712	F-WFPO
F-CFQG-B43	Centrair 101A Pégase	101A-043	
F-CFQH	Centrair 101A Pégase	101A-037	
F-CFQK-B47	Centrair 101A Pégase	101A-047	
F-CFQL	Centrair 101A Pégase	101A-049	
F-CFQN-B51	Centrair 101A Pégase	101A-051	
F-CFQO-B52	Centrair 101A Pégase	101A-052	
F-CFQP	Centrair 101A Pégase	101A-053	
F-CFQS	Centrair 101A Pégase	101A-059	
F-CFQT	Centrair 101A Pégase	101A-044	
F-CFQZ	Centrair 101A Pégase	101A-067	
F-CFRA	Centrair 101A Pégase	101A-001	F-WFRA
F-CFRB	Centrair 101A Pégase	101A-005	
F-CFRC-B06	Centrair 101A Pégase	101A-006	
F-CFRD	Centrair 101A Pégase	101A-007	
F-CFRE-RE	Centrair 101A Pégase	101A-008	
F-CFRF	Centrair 101A Pégase	101A-009	
F-CFRG	Centrair 101A Pégase	101A-010	
F-CFRH-B14	Centrair 101A Pégase	101A-014	
F-CFRI	Centrair 101A Pégase	101A-011	
F-CFRJ	Centrair 101A Pégase	101A-013	
F-CFRK	Centrair 101A Pégase	101A-015	
F-CFRL	Centrair 101A Pégase	101A-018	
F-CFRM	Centrair 101A Pégase	101A-019	
F-CFRO	Centrair 101A Pégase	101A-017	
F-CFRQ	Centrair 101A Pégase	101A-021	
F-CFRT-B22	Centrair 101A Pégase	101A-022	
F-CFRU-B25	Centrair 101A Pégase	101A-025	
F-CFRV-B30	Centrair 101A Pégase	101A-030	
F-CFSC	Centrair ASW-20F	20521	
F-CFSG	Centrair ASW-20F	20525	
F-CFTA	Centrair ASW-20FL	20107	EI-126 F-CFFG
F-CFTB	Grob G.103 Twin Astir II	3212	
F-CFTC	Schleicher K 8B	8422	
F-CFTD	Scheibe SF-28A Tandem-Falke	5719	D-KOAK
F-CFTE	Scheibe Bergfalke IV	5844	
F-CFTH	Schleicher K 8B	8450SH	HB-823
F-CFTJ	Scheibe SF-28A Tandem-Falke (Damaged 3.9.03)	5738	D-KOEH
F-CFTK	Scheibe SF-28A Tandem-Falke	5758	HB-2032 D-KMGH
F-CFTL-R23	Grob G.102/77J Astir Jeans	2113	3A-MCG F-CFCG
F-CFTM	Scheibe SF-28A Tandem-Falke	5702/V-2	D-KAOQ
F-CFTN	Scheibe SF-28A Tandem-Falke	5762	OY-XHG D-KAWU (D-KACO(2))
F-CFTO	Schempp-Hirth Nimbus 3/24.5	33	BGA3102/FAH N17UF
F-CFTU	Scheibe SF-28A Tandem-Falke	5722	D-KAUM
F-CFUA	Schempp-Hirth Nimbus 3	35	
F-CFUB-17	Schempp-Hirth Nimbus 3/24.5	38	F-WFUB
F-CFUC	Schempp-Hirth Nimbus 2	176	D-6851
F-CFUF	Schempp-Hirth Nimbus 3DM	10/28	D-KCUF
F-CFUG-CLM	Schempp-Hirth Nimbus 3D	6/33	D-1753
F-CFUH	Schempp-Hirth Nimbus 3DM	8/24	D-KFUH
F-CFUI-EN	Schempp-Hirth Nimbus 3D	8/41	D-4518
F-CFUJ-SFA	Schempp-Hirth Nimbus 3D	7/35	
F-CFUN	Schempp-Hirth Nimbus 3/24.5	50	F-WFUN
F-CFUO-N41	Schempp-Hirth Nimbus 3DT	55	
F-CFUP-UP	Schempp-Hirth Nimbus 3DT	60	
F-CFUR	Schempp-Hirth Nimbus 3/24.5	34	D-1151 N88SA
F-CFUS-US	Schempp-Hirth Nimbus 4DT	1/1	D-KFUS D-2111
F-CFUT-EK	Schempp-Hirth Nimbus 3D	10/50	D-2872
F-CFUV-MX	Schempp-Hirth Nimbus 4D	3/11	D-8563
F-CFUX	Schempp-Hirth Nimbus 4DM	6/14	D-KLUX
F-CFUZ-EN	Schempp-Hirth Nimbus 4D	6/36	
F-CFVA-PP	Glaser-Dirks DG-400	4-52	F-WFVA
F-CFVC	Glaser-Dirks DG-400	4-109	F-WFVC

F-CFVD	Glaser-Dirks DG-400	4-110	F-WFVD
F-CFVF	Glaser-Dirks DG-400	4-122	F-WFVF
F-CFVG	Glaser-Dirks DG-400	4-140	F-WFVG
F-CFVI	Glaser-Dirks DG-400	4-172	
F-CFVJ	Glaser-Dirks DG-400	4-173	
F-CFVL-K31	Glaser-Dirks DG-300 Elan	3E88	F-WFVL
F-CFVM	Glaser-Dirks DG-300 Elan	3E137	F-WFVM
F-CFVN	Glaser-Dirks DG-300 Elan	3E153	F-WFVN
F-WFVO	Glaser-Dirks DG-300 Elan	3E171	
F-CFVP	Glaser-Dirks DG-300 Elan	3E170	F-WFVP
F-CFVR	Glaser-Dirks DG-300 Elan	3E212	F-WFVR
F-CFVS-K38	Glaser-Dirks DG-300 Elan	3E229	F-WFVS
F-CFVT	Glaser-Dirks DG-300 Elan	3E245	F-WFVT
F-CFVU	Glaser-Dirks DG-300 Elan	3E276	F-WFVU
F-WFXA	Centrair 101C Pégase	101C-901	
F-CFXC-B72	Centrair 101A Pégase	101A-072	
F-CFXF	Centrair 101A Pégase	101A-075	
F-CFXG-B76	Centrair 101A Pégase	101A-076	
F-CFXJ-B93	Centrair 101A Pégase	101A-093	
F-CFXK	Centrair 101A Pégase	101A-085	
F-CFXM	Centrair 101A Pégase	101A-0106	
F-CFXN	Centrair 101A Pégase	101A-0104	
F-CFXO-RD	Centrair 101A Pégase	101A-0103	
F-CFXP	Centrair 101A Pégase	101A-0101	
F-CFXQ	Centrair 101A Pégase	101A-0113	
F-CFXR-B114	Centrair 101A Pégase	101A-0114	
F-CFXS	Centrair 101A Pégase	101A-0115	
F-CFXT	Centrair 101A Pégase	101A-0116	
F-CFXV-XV	Centrair 101A Pégase	101A-0134	
F-CFXX	Centrair 101A Pégase	101A-0133	
F-CFXY	Centrair ASW-20F	20531	
F-CFXZ-B135	Centrair 101A Pégase	101A-0135	
F-CFYA-T79	Grob G.103 Twin Astir II	3838	
F-CFYB-T80	Grob G.103 Twin Astir II	3766	
F-CFYC-T82	Grob G.103A Twin II Acro	33951-K-184	
F-CFYD-T83	Grob G.103A Twin II Acro	33952-K-185	
F-CFYE	Grob G.103A Twin II Acro	33963-K-196	
F-CFYF-T85	Grob G.103A Twin II Acro	33968-K-201	
F-CFYG	Grob G.103A Twin II Acro	34052-K-282	
F-CFYH-SH	Grob G.103A Twin II Acro	34058-K-288	
F-CFYI	Grob G.103 Twin Astir II	3570	D-6640
F-CFYJ	Grob G.103 Twin Astir II	3596	D-3963
F-CFYK-T91	Grob G.103 Twin Astir II	3556	D-8764
F-CFYL-R3	Grob G.103A Twin II Acro	3845-K-91	PH-744
F-CFYM	Grob G.103A Twin II Acro	33965-K-198	D-8067
F-CFYN	Grob G.103 Twin Astir II	3594	D-4867
F-CFYP	Grob G.103 Twin Astir II	3675	D-8703
F-CFYQ	Grob G.103 Twin Astir II	3188	HB-1442
F-CFYR	Grob G.103 Twin Astir II	3663	D-2600
F-CFYS-T99	Grob G.103 Twin Astir	3078	D-3949
F-CFYT	Grob G.103A Twin II Acro	3732-K-47	D-1604 PL-90 D-6189
F-CFYU	Grob G.103 Twin Astir	3071	D-4856
F-CFZA-J	Rolladen-Schneider LS4	4336	
F-CFZB-V31	Rolladen-Schneider LS4	4358	
F-CFZD-V32	Rolladen-Schneider LS4	4397	
F-CFZE-V33	Rolladen-Schneider LS4	4409	
F-CFZF	Rolladen-Schneider LS4	4425	
F-CFZH-V36	Rolladen-Schneider LS4	4476	
F-CFZI	Rolladen-Schneider LS4	4487	
F-CFZJ-V38	Rolladen-Schneider LS4	4488	
F-CFZK-V40	Rolladen-Schneider LS4	4499	
F-CFZL	Rolladen-Schneider LS4	4500	
F-CFZM-C43	Rolladen-Schneider LS4	4509	
F-CFZN-V43	Rolladen-Schneider LS4	4517	
F-CFZO-VM	Rolladen-Schneider LS4	4535	
F-CFZP-L1	Rolladen-Schneider LS4	4645	
F-CFZQ	Rolladen-Schneider LS4	4644	
F-CFZR-V43	Rolladen-Schneider LS4	4643	
F-CFZS-KE	Rolladen-Schneider LS4	4680	
F-CFZT	Rolladen-Schneider LS4	4639	
F-CFZU-V78	Rolladen-Schneider LS4	4678	
F-CFZV	Rolladen-Schneider LS4	4707	
F-CFZX	Rolladen-Schneider LS4	4779	
F-CFZY-V16	Rolladen-Schneider LS4	4142	3A-MCD
F-CFZZ-V55	Rolladen-Schneider LS4B	4938	BGA4018/HLA
F-CGAB	Valentin Taifun 17E	1027	F-WGAB D-KCCF
F-CGAC	Valentin Taifun 17E	1037	F-WGAC D-KDSE
F-CGAD	Valentin Taifun 17E	1049	F-WGAD D-KDSO
F-CGAF	Valentin Taifun 17E	1073	F-WGAF D-KHVA
F-CGAG	Valentin Taifun 17E	1100	F-WGAG D-KHVA
F-CGAK	Hoffmann H-36 Dimona	3524	F-WGAK
F-CGAM	Hoffmann H-36 Dimona	36206	F-WGAM
F-CGAN	Hoffmann H-36 Dimona	36237	F-WGAN
F-CGAP	Hoffmann H-36 Dimona	36225	F-WGAP
F-CGAQ	Hoffmann H-36 Dimona	36226	F-WGAQ
F-CGAT	Hoffmann H-36 Dimona	36258	F-WGAT
F-CGAU	Hoffmann H-36 Dimona	36260	F-WGAU
F-CGAV	Hoffmann H-36 Dimona	36265	F-WGAV
F-CGBA-B136	Centrair 101A Pégase	101A-0136	
F-CGBB-TB	Centrair 101A Pégase	101A-0137	

F-CGBC-TC	Centrair 101A Pégase	101A-0138	
F-CGBD-TD	Centrair 101A Pégase	101A-0139	
F-CGBE	Centrair 101A Pégase	101A-0140	
F-CGBF	Centrair 101B Pégase	101B-0143	F-WGBF
F-CGBG	Centrair 101BC Pégase	101B-0148	F-WGBG
F-CGBH-B144	Centrair 101A Pégase	101A-0144	
F-CGBI	Centrair 101A Pégase	101A-0145	
F-CGBJ-B146	Centrair 101A Pégase	101A-0146	
F-CGBK-AD	Centrair 101A Pégase	101A-0147	
F-CGBO	Centrair 101A Pégase	101A-0153	
F-CGBP-BP	Centrair 101A Pégase	101A-0171	
F-CGBQ	Centrair 101A Pégase	101A-0158	
F-CGBR	Centrair 101A Pégase	101A-0159	
F-CGBS	Centrair 101A Pégase	101A-0160	
F-CGBT	Centrair 101A Pégase	101A-0162	
F-CGBV	Centrair 101A Pégase	101A-0164	
F-CGBX	Centrair 101A Pégase	101A-0165	
F-CGBZ-B169	Centrair 101A Pégase	101A-0169	
F-CGCA-BYO	Schleicher ASW 20C	20762	F-WGCA
F-CGCB	Schleicher ASW 20L	20381	
F-CGCC	Schleicher ASK 21	21244	
F-CGCD	Schleicher ASW 22	22046	F-WGCD
F-CGCE	Schleicher ASH 25	25006	F-WGCE
F-CGCG	Schleicher ASK 21	21245	
F-CGCH	Schleicher ASK 21	21269	
F-CGCI	Schleicher ASK 21	21264	
F-CGCJ-CJ	Schleicher ASK 21	21270	
F-CGCK	Schleicher ASK 21	21277	
F-CGCL	Schleicher ASK 21	21298	
F-CGCM	Schleicher ASK 21	21344	
F-CGCN	Schleicher ASW 20C	20817	
F-CGCO	Schleicher ASW 20C	20818	
F-CGCQ-G1	Schleicher ASW 20CL	20860	
F-CGCR-S1	Schleicher ASW 20CL	20829	F-WGCR
F-CGCT	Schleicher ASK 23	23034	F-WGCT
F-CGCU	Schleicher ASK 23	23053	F-WGCU
F-CGCV	Schleicher ASK 23B	23063	F-WGCV
F-CGCX	Schleicher ASK 23B	23064	F-WGCX
F-CGCY-A18	Schleicher ASW 15	15170	Fr.AF
F-CGCZ	Schleicher ASK 23B	23072	F-WGCZ
F-CGDB	Aerostructure-Fournier RF-10	8	F-WGDB
F-CGDC	Aerostructure-Fournier RF-10	9	F-WGDC
F-CGDD	Aerostructure-Fournier RF-10	10	F-WGDD
F-CGDE	Aerostructure-Fournier RF-10	14	
F-CGEB-B170	Centrair 101A Pégase	101A-0170	
F-CGEC	Centrair 101A Pégase	101A-0172	
F-CGED-E	Centrair 101A Pégase	101A-0173	
F-CGEF-B174	Centrair 101A Pégase	101A-0174	
F-CGEG-B180	Centrair 101A Pégase	101A-0180	
F-CGEH-EZ	Centrair 101A Pégase	101A-0167	
F-CGEI	Centrair 101A Pégase	101A-0181	
F-CGEJ	Centrair 101A Pégase	101A-0183	
F-CGEL-B192	Centrair 101A Pégase	101A-0192	
F-CGEM-EM	Centrair 101A Pégase	101A-0191	
F-CGEN-B196	Centrair 101A Pégase	101A-0196	
F-CGEO	Centrair 101A Pégase	101A-0194	
F-CGEP	Centrair 101A Pégase	101A-0193	
F-CGEQ	Centrair 101A Pégase	101A-0197	
F-CGER	Centrair 101A Pégase	101A-0195	
F-CGET-B206	Centrair 101A Pégase	101A-0206	
F-CGEU	Centrair 101A Pégase	101A-0210	
F-CGEV-B212	Centrair 101A Pégase	101A-0212	
F-CGEX-ii	Centrair 101A Pégase	101A-0215	
F-CGEY	Centrair 101A Pégase	101A-0216	
F-CGFB-B213	Centrair 101B Pégase	101B-0213	F-WGFB
F-CGFC-B217	Centrair 101A Pégase	101A-0217	
F-CGFD	Centrair 101A Pégase	101A-0211	
F-CGFE-E	Centrair 101A Pégase	101A-0219	
F-CGFF-Z	Centrair 101A Pégase	101A-0220	
F-CGFG-B222	Centrair 101A Pégase	101A-0221	
F-CGFH	Centrair 101A Pégase	101A-0222	
F-CGFI	Centrair 101A Pégase	101A-0223	
F-CGFJ	Centrair 101A Pégase	101A-0226	
F-CGFK	Centrair 101A Pégase	101A-0232	
F-CGFL	Centrair 101A Pégase	101A-0227	
F-CGFM-JC	Centrair 101A Pégase	101A-0228	
F-CGFN-B231	Centrair 101A Pégase	101A-0231	
F-CGFO	Centrair 101A Pégase	101A-0229	
F-CGFP-B230	Centrair 101A Pégase	101A-0230	
F-CGFQ	Centrair 101A Pégase	101A-0233	
F-CGFR	Centrair 101A Pégase	101A-0234	
F-CGFS-AA	Centrair 101A Pégase	101A-0235	
F-CGFT	Centrair 101A Pégase	101A-0236	
F-CGFU	Centrair 101A Pégase	101A-0237	
F-CGFV	Centrair 101A Pégase	101A-0238	
F-CGFX	Centrair 101A Pégase	101A-0239	
F-CGFY-B241	Centrair 101A Pégase	101A-0241	
F-CGFZ-T	Centrair 101A Pégase	101A-0242	
F-CGGA-EH	Schempp-Hirth Discus b	35	F-WGGA
F-CGGB-IL	Schempp-Hirth Discus b	36	F-WGGB
F-CGGC	Schempp-Hirth Discus b	89	F-WGGC
F-CGGE	Schempp-Hirth Discus b	102	F-WGGE
F-CGGF-SJ	Schempp-Hirth Discus b	117	F-WGGF
F-CGGG-3G	Schempp-Hirth Discus b	129	F-WGGG
F-CGGH	Schempp-Hirth Discus b	163	F-WGGH
F-CGGI	Schempp-Hirth Discus b	177	F-WGGI
F-CGGK	Schempp-Hirth Discus b	191	F-WGGK
F-CGGL-D13	Schempp-Hirth Discus b	192	F-WGGL
F-CGGM-D14	Schempp-Hirth Discus b	213	F-WGGM
F-CGGO	Schempp-Hirth Discus b	148	F-WGGO
F-CGGP	Schempp-Hirth Discus bT	33/335	
F-CGGQ-D16	Schempp-Hirth Discus b	340	
F-CGGR	Schempp-Hirth Discus b	91	D-5239
F-CGGS	Schempp-Hirth Discus CS	037CS	
F-CGGU	Schempp-Hirth Discus CS	105CS	
F-CGGV	Schempp-Hirth Discus CS	106CS	
F-CGGY-D24	Schempp-Hirth Discus CS	117CS	
F-CGGZ	Schempp-Hirth Discus CS	118CS	
F-CGHB-E5	Centrair 101BC Pégase	101BC-0504	F-WGHB
F-CGHC	Centrair 101BC Pégase	101BC-0507	
F-CGHD	Centrair 101BC Pégase	101BC-0509	
F-CGHF	Centrair 101BC Pégase	101BC-0508	
F-CGHG-E12	Centrair 101D Pégase	101D-0512	
F-CGHJ-E14	Centrair 101D Pégase	101D-0514	
F-CGHK	Centrair 101D Pégase	101D-0517	
F-CGHL	Centrair 101D Pégase	101D-0515	
F-CGHM	Centrair 101D Pégase	101D-0516	
F-CGHO	Centrair 101D Pégase	101D-0521	
F-CGHQ	Centrair 101D Pégase	101D-0522	
F-CGHR-F	Centrair 101D Pégase (W/o 24.7.02)	101D-0520	
F-CGHS	Centrair 101D Pégase	101D-0524	
F-CGIA	Schempp-Hirth Janus A	41	D-3786
F-CGIB	Wassmer WA.30 Bijave	222	F-CDJS
F-CGIC	Wassmer WA.22A	119	Fr.AF
F-CGKA	Schleicher ASW 20CL	20856	
F-CGKB	Schleicher ASW 20CL	20847	
F-CGKC	Schleicher ASK 21	21414	
F-CGKD	Schleicher ASK 21	21427	
F-CGKF	Schleicher ASK 21	21445	
F-CGKG	Schleicher ASW 24	24007	F-WGKG
F-CGKH	Schleicher ASW 24	24008	F-WGKH
F-CGKI-GN	Schleicher ASW 24	24053	F-WGKI
F-CGKK	Schleicher ASW 24	24056	F-WGKK
F-CGKL-EV	Schleicher ASW 24E	24814	D-KAXG
F-CGKM -GAI	Schleicher ASW 24	24102	
F-CGKN	Schleicher ASW 24	24084	F-WGKN
F-CGKO-88	Schleicher ASW 24	24088	
F-CGKP-ES	Schleicher ASW 24	24095	
F-CGKQ	Schleicher ASW 24 (Damaged 10.5.03)	24103	
F-CGKS	Schleicher ASW 20	20583	D-4690
F-CGKT	Schleicher ASH 25	25022	F-WGKT
F-CGKU	Schleicher ASH 25	25028	F-WGKU
F-CGKV-IA	Schleicher ASH 25E	25046	F-WGKV
			D-KFAX(2)
F-CGKZ-3Z	Schleicher ASH 25	25094	
F-CGLA	Schempp-Hirth Ventus b	236	F-WGLA
F-CGLB	Schempp-Hirth Ventus b	238	F-WGLB
F-CGLC	Schempp-Hirth Ventus b	245	F-WGLC
F-CGLD-Y12	Schempp-Hirth Ventus b	260	F-WGLD
F-CGLF	Schempp-Hirth Ventus b	269	F-WGLF
F-CGLH-IW	Schempp-Hirth Ventus b	291	F-WGLH
F-CGLI	Schempp-Hirth Ventus b/16.6	313	F-WGLI
F-CGLJ-EQ	Schempp-Hirth Ventus 2a	72	
	(F-WGLJ, Schempp-Hirth Ventus b/16.6 c/n 315 also believed current)		
F-CGLK-DER	Schempp-Hirth Ventus b/16.6	316	F-WGLK
F-CGLM	Schempp-Hirth Ventus b/16.6	339	F-WGLM
F-CGLN	Schempp-Hirth Ventus b/16.6	361	F-WGLN
F-CGLO	Schempp-Hirth Ventus c	433	F-WGLO
F-WGLQ	Schempp-Hirth Ventus cM	6/417	D-KGLQ
F-CGLS-EN	Schempp-Hirth Ventus 2a	07	D-8559
F-CGLT	Schempp-Hirth Ventus 2a	08	D-8560
F-CGLV	Schempp-Hirth Ventus 2b (W/o 4.6.98)	29	
F-CGLX	Schempp-Hirth Ventus 2b	69	
F-CGLY	Schempp-Hirth Ventus c	425	F-WGLY
F-WGMA	Centrair 201 Marianne	201-001	
F-CGMB	Centrair 201 Marianne	201-002	F-WGMB
F-CGMC	Centrair 201B1 Marianne	201-003	F-WGMC
F-CGMD-Z04	Centrair 201B1 Marianne	201-004	
F-CGME	Centrair 201B1 Marianne	201-005	
F-CGMF	Centrair 201B1 Marianne	201-006	
F-CGMH-E8	Centrair 201B1 Marianne	201-008	
F-CGMI	Centrair 201B1 Marianne	201-009	
F-CGMJ	Centrair 201B1 Marianne	201-010	
F-CGMK	Centrair 201B1 Marianne	201-011	F-WGMK
F-CGMO	Centrair 201B1 Marianne	201-016	
F-CGMP	Centrair 201B1 Marianne	201-017	F-WGMP
F-CGMQ	Centrair 201B1 Marianne	201-018	F-WGMQ
F-CGMR	Centrair 201B1 Marianne	201-019	F-WGMR
F-CGMS	Centrair 201B1 Marianne	201-020	F-WGMS
F-CGMT	Centrair 201B1 Marianne	201-021	F-WGMT
F-CGMU	Centrair 201B1 Marianne	201-022	F-WGMU
F-CGMX-X	Centrair 201B1 Marianne	201-024	
F-CGMY	Centrair 201B1 Marianne	201-025	
F-CGMZ	Centrair 201B Marianne	201-026	F-WGMZ
F-CGNA	Centrair 101A Pégase	101A-0248	
F-CGNB-B240	Centrair 101A Pégase	101A-0240	
F-CGNC	Centrair 101A Pégase	101A-0256	
F-CGND	Centrair 101A Pégase	101A-0246	
F-CGNE	Centrair 101A Pégase	101A-0249	
F-CGNF	Centrair 101A Pégase	101A-0247	
F-CGNH	Centrair 101A Pégase	101A-0257	
F-CGNI	Centrair 101A Pégase	101A-0258	
F-CGNJ-B259	Centrair 101A Pégase	101A-0259	
F-CGNK-LV	Centrair 101A Pégase	101A-0270	

F-CGNL-NL	Centrair 101A Pégase	101A-0271	
F-CGNN	Centrair 101A Pégase	101A-0263	
F-CGNO	Centrair 101A Pégase	101A-0272	
F-CGNP-Y31	Centrair 101A Pégase	101A-0266	
F-CGNR	Centrair 101C Pégase	101C-0903	
F-CGNS	Centrair 101C Pégase	101C-0904	
F-CGNV	Centrair 101A Pégase	101A-0277	
F-CGNX-AY	Centrair 101B Pégase	101B-0279	
F-CGNZ-SJ	Centrair 101A Pégase	101A-0281	
F-CGOB	Centrair 101A Pégase	101A-0316	
F-CGOC-U2	Centrair 101A Pégase	101A-0317	
F-CGOD-OD	Centrair 101A Pégase	101A-0318	
F-CGOE-F	Centrair 101A Pégase	101A-0320	
F-CGOF	Centrair 101A Pégase	101A-0326	
F-CGOG-B327	Centrair 101A Pégase	101A-0327	
F-CGOH	Centrair 101A Pégase	101A-0328	
F-CGOJ	Centrair 101A Pégase	101A-0330	
F-CGOK-SN	Centrair 101A Pégase	101A-0324	
F-CGOL	Centrair 101A Pégase	101A-0331	
F-CGOM-3M	Centrair 101A Pégase	101A-0332	
F-CGON-AF	Centrair 101A Pégase	101A-0333	
F-CGOP	Centrair 101A Pégase	101A-0335	
F-CGOQ-B336	Centrair 101A Pégase	101A-0336	
F-CGOR-BOF	Centrair 101A Pégase	101A-0337	
F-CGOS-OM	Centrair 101A Pégase	101A-0338	
F-CGOT	Centrair 101A Pégase	101A-0339	
F-CGOU-721	Centrair 101A Pégase	101A-0340	
F-CGOV-ED	Centrair 101A Pégase	101A-0341	
F-CGOX-33	Centrair 101A Pégase	101A-0342	
F-CGOZ	Centrair 101A Pégase	101A-0354	
F-CGPA-5N	Rolladen-Schneider LS3A	3162	
F-CGPN	Wassmer WA.22A	155	Fr.AF
F-CGQA-J57	Schempp-Hirth Janus C	224	
F-CGQC	Schempp-Hirth Janus CM	229/28	
F-CGQD	Schempp-Hirth Janus B	231	
F-CGQE-AJ	Schempp-Hirth Janus CM	234/29	F-WGQE D-KHIA(5)
F-CGQF	Schempp-Hirth Janus CM	246/31	F-WGQF
F-CGQG	Schempp-Hirth Janus CM	33/250	F-WGQG D-KGQG
F-CGQH	Schempp-Hirth Janus C	258	
F-CGQI	Schempp-Hirth Janus CM	34/259	F-WGQI D-KGQI
F-CGQJ-VA	Schempp-Hirth Janus C	267	
F-CGQK	Schempp-Hirth Janus CT	12/271	F-WGQK D-KGQK
F-CGQL	Schempp-Hirth Janus CE	287	
F-CGQM	Schempp-Hirth Janus CE	295	
F-CGQO	Schempp-Hirth Janus CE	293	D-7460
F-CGQP	Schempp-Hirth Janus C	219	D-4148
F-CGQQ-Q2	Schempp-Hirth Janus CE	306	
F-CGQR	Schempp-Hirth Janus CE	307	
F-CGQS-D34	Schempp-Hirth Discus CS	262CS	
F-CGRD	Glaser-Dirks DG-400	4-203	
F-CGRE	Glaser-Dirks DG-400	4-215	
F-CGRG	Glaser-Dirks DG-400	4-243	
F-CGRH	Glaser-Dirks DG-400	4-257	
F-CGRI	Glaser-Dirks DG-400	4-283	D-KSPL
F-CGRJ	Glaser-Dirks DG-400	4-262	
F-CGRK	DG Flugzeugbau DG-1000S	10-58S56	
F-CGRL	PZL-Swidnik PW-5 Smyk	17.13.001	
F-CGRP	Glaser-Dirks DG-600	6-59	
F-CGRR	Glaser-Dirks DG-600	6-60	
F-CGRT	Glaser-Dirks DG-600M	6-83M29	
F-CGRV	Glaser-Dirks DG-400	4-112	N62JW
F-CGRX	Glaser-Dirks DG-800	8-23A20	D-KAPS
F-CGRY	Glaser-Dirks DG-800S	8-73S19	D-8081
F-CGRZ	HOAC HK-36TTC Super Dimona	36524	
F-CGSA	Centrair 101A Pégase	101A-0282	
F-CGSB	Centrair 101A Pégase	101A-0288	
F-CGSC	Centrair 101A Pégase	101A-0287	
F-CGSD	Centrair 101A Pégase	101A-0292	
F-CGSF	Centrair 101A Pégase	101A-0291	
F-CGSG-B294	Centrair 101A Pégase	101A-0294	
F-CGSH-B295	Centrair 101A Pégase	101A-0295	
F-CGSJ	Centrair 101A Pégase	101A-0297	
F-CGSK-B298	Centrair 101A Pégase	101A-0298	
F-CGSL	Centrair 101A Pégase	101A-0300	
F-CGSM(2)	Centrair 101A Pégase	101A-0301	
F-CGSN	Centrair 101A Pégase	101A-0302	
F-CGSO-B30	Centrair 101A Pégase (W/o 12.6.02)	101A-0303	
F-CGSP-B304	Centrair 101A Pégase	101A-0304	
F-CGSQ	Centrair 101A Pégase	101A-0305	
F-CGSR-FS	Centrair 101A Pégase	101A-0306	
F-CGSS	Centrair 101A Pégase	101A-0308	
F-CGST	Centrair 101A Pégase	101A-0309	
F-CGSU-PstV	Centrair 101A Pégase	101A-0310	
F-CGSV	Centrair 101A Pégase	101A-0269	
F-CGSX-AC	Centrair 101A Pégase	101A-0312	
F-CGSY	Centrair 101A Pégase	101A-0313	
F-CGTB	Centrair 201B Marianne	201B-062	
F-CGTC	Centrair 201B Marianne	201B-063	
F-CGTD	Centrair 201B Marianne	201B-065	
F-CGTE	Centrair 201B Marianne	201B-067	
F-CGTF	Centrair 201B Marianne	201B-071	
F-CGTG-CA	Centrair 201B Marianne	201B-073	
F-CGTH	Centrair 201B Marianne	201B-075	

F-CGTI	Centrair 201B Marianne	201B-076	
F-CGTK	Centrair 201B Marianne	201B-079	
F-CGTL	Centrair 201B Marianne	201B-080	
F-CGTM-P22	Centrair 201B Marianne	201B-030	
F-CGTN	Centrair 201B Marianne	201B-083	
F-CGTO	Centrair 201B Marianne	201B-084	
F-CGTP	Centrair 201B Marianne	201B-087	
F-CGTQ	Centrair 201B Marianne	201B-089	
F-CGTR	Centrair 201B Marianne	201B-091	
F-CGTS	Centrair 201B Marianne	201B-092	
F-CGUA-Z06	Rolladen-Schneider LS6A	6093	F-WGUA
F-CGUB	Rolladen-Schneider LS6	6097	F-WGUB
F-CGUD	Rolladen-Schneider LS6	6130	F-WGUD
F-CGUE-CA	Rolladen-Schneider LS6B	6137	F-WGUE
F-CGUG-D	Rolladen-Schneider LS6B	6142	F-WGUG
F-CGUH-72	Rolladen-Schneider LS6B	6179	F-WGUH
F-CGUJ	Rolladen-Schneider LS6C	6206	
F-CGUK	Rolladen-Schneider LS6C	6208	
F-CGUL	Rolladen-Schneider LS6C	6222	
F-CGUN-Z01	Rolladen-Schneider LS6B	6087	F-WGUN
F-CGUO-Z15	Rolladen-Schneider LS6C	6243	
F-CGUP	Rolladen-Schneider LS6C	6244	
F-CGUQ	Rolladen-Schneider LS6C	6255	
F-CGUR-3A	Rolladen-Schneider LS6C	6268	
F-CGUS	Rolladen-Schneider LS6C	6312	
F-CGUT-RC	Rolladen-Schneider LS6C	6300	
F-CGUU-Z21	Rolladen-Schneider LS6C	6304	
F-CGUV-Z22	Rolladen-Schneider LS6C	6305	
F-CGUX	Rolladen-Schneider LS6C	6320	
F-CGUY-Z27	Rolladen-Schneider LS6C	6321	
F-CGUZ-Z28	Rolladen-Schneider LS6C (Wreck noted 10.00)	6322	
F-CGVA	Grob G.102 Astir CS	1063	D-3287
F-CGVL	Schempp-Hirth Ventus 2b	45	
F-CGVN	Wassmer WA.30 Bijave	206	Fr.AF
F-CGVO	Centrair C-201B Marianne	201B-064	
F-CGVV-2V	Rolladen-Schneider LS7	7106	D-9777 D-5330
F-CGXA	Grob G.103C Twin III	36002	
F-CGXC	Grob G.103C Twin III Acro	34122	D-3698
F-CGXD-TD	Grob G.103C Twin III Acro	34136	D-4034
F-CGXE	Grob G.103C Twin III Acro	34138	D-4343
F-CGXF-106	Grob G.103C Twin III Acro (W/o 1.4.02)	34140	D-4344
F-CGXG	Grob G.103C Twin III	36008	D-8940
F-CGXH	Grob G.103C Twin III Acro	34178	
F-CGXI-T109	Grob G.103C Twin III Acro	34184	
F-CGXJ-SJ	Grob G.103C Twin III Acro	34114	D-1833
F-CGYB	Rolladen-Schneider LS7	7014	F-WGYB D-4644
F-CGYC	Rolladen-Schneider LS7	7015	F-WGYC D-4643
F-CGYD	Rolladen-Schneider LS7	7103	
F-CGYE-007	Rolladen-Schneider LS7	7120	
F-CGYF-EB	Rolladen-Schneider LS7	7155	
F-CGYG-Y55	Rolladen-Schneider LS4B	4988	
F-CGYH-V56	Rolladen-Schneider LS4B	4989	
F-CGYI-V57	Rolladen-Schneider LS4B	4999	
F-CGYJ	Rolladen-Schneider LS4B	41003	
F-CGYL	Stemme S-10	10-33	D-KGCI (2)
F-CGYM	Stemme S-10V (Originally built as S-10 c/n 10-55)	14-055M	D-KGCU(2)
F-CGYP	Stemme S-10VT (Permit 3.00)	11-025	
F-CGZA-Z29	Rolladen-Schneider LS6C-18	6327	
F-CGZB	Rolladen-Schneider LS6C-18	6325	
F-CGZC	Rolladen-Schneider LS6C-18	6326	D-7141
F-CGZD	Rolladen-Schneider LS6C-18	6335	D-1681
F-CGZE	Rolladen-Schneider LS6-18W	6368	
F-CGZF-Z34	Rolladen-Schneider LS6C-18	6376	
F-CGZK-2M	Rolladen-Schneider LS8A	8041	D-3571
F-CGZL-ER	Rolladen-Schneider LS8A	8043	D-3626
F-CGZM-EU	Rolladen-Schneider LS8A (W/o 12.3.02)	8045	
F-CGZO	Rolladen-Schneider LS8A	8063	
F-CGZQ	Rolladen-Schneider LS8A	8082	
F-CGZR	Rolladen-Schneider LS8A	8137	
F-CGZT-T	Rolladen-Schneider LS8A	8143	
F-CGZU	Rolladen-Schneider LS8A	8170	
F-CGZV-GA5	Rolladen-Schneider LS8A	8191	
F-CGZX-V92	Rolladen-Schneider LS8A	8192	
F-CGZZ	Rolladen-Schneider LS8-18	8257	D-6597
F-CHAA-GA2	Schleicher ASW 24	24106	
F-CHAB	Schleicher ASW 24	24107	
F-CHAC-SM	Schleicher ASW 24	24117	
F-CHAD	Schleicher ASW 24	24126	
F-CHAE-CG	Schleicher ASW-24	24127	
F-CHAF	Schleicher ASW 24	24145	
F-CHAG	Schleicher ASW 24E	24843	
F-CHAH	Schleicher ASW 24E	24852	
F-CHAI	Schleicher ASW 24	24147	
F-CHAJ-GA3	Schleicher ASW 24	24148	
F-CHAL	Schleicher ASH 25	25121	
F-CHAM	Schleicher ASK 21	21504	
F-CHAN	Schleicher ASK 21	21505	
F-CHAO	Schleicher ASH 25	25092	
F-CHAP-AP	Schleicher ASH 25	25099	
F-CHAQ	Schleicher ASH 25	25123	
F-CHAR	Schleicher ASH 25	25137	
F-CHAS	Schleicher ASK 23B	23009	BGA2999/EVZ
F-CHAT	Schleicher ASH 25	25080	F-WHAT

F-CHAV-8	Schleicher ASH 25	25136	
F-CHAX -AX	Schleicher ASH 25	25065	D-5282 (D-KFAX(1))
F-CHAZ	Schleicher ASH 25	25156	
F-CHBA	Swift S-1A	0108	
F-CHBC	Schleicher ASH 25E	25055	F-WHBC D-KBBC
F-CHBJ	Glaser-Dirks DG-200/17	2-122/1726	3A-MBJ
F-CHBL	Rolladen-Schneider LS4	4435	D-3441
F-CHBY	Schleicher ASK 21	21619	
F-CHCA	Sportavia/ Scheibe SF-25B Falke	4827	D-KHEG
F-CHCB	Scheibe SF-25E Super Falke	4351	D-KDGK
F-CHCC	Scheibe SF-25E Super Falke	4365	D-KIOK(2)
F-CHCD	Scheibe SF-25D Falke	4825D	D-KHEE
F-CHCE	Scheibe SF-25B Falke	4630	D-KOKE (D-KIMJ)
F-CHCF	Sportavia/ Scheibe SF-25C Falke	4242	D-KAJD
F-CHCH	Scheibe SF-25B Falke	AB46302	D-KAFI (2)
F-CHCI	Scheibe SF-25E Super Falke	4329	D-KDFO
F-CHCJ	Scheibe SF-25E Super Falke	4361	D-KLUE
F-CHCK	Scheibe SF-25B Falke	46177	D-KAGK
F-CHCL	Scheibe SF-25D Falke	AB46305	D-KOAN
F-CHCM	Scheibe SF-25B Falke	46173	D-KURT OE-9038 D-KIBS
F-CHCN	Scheibe SF-25C Falke 1700	44107	D-KMJG
F-CHCO	Scheibe SF-25E Super Falke	4321	G-BDZS (D-KECX)
F-CHCP	Scheibe SF-25E Super Falke	4356	D-KOOZ(2)
F-CHCR	Scheibe SFL-25R Falke	4619	D-KEGA
F-CHCS	Scheibe SF-25E Super Falke	4317	D-KLUH
F-CHCT	Scheibe SF-25B Falke	46146	D-KCAM
F-CHCU	Scheibe SFL-25R Falke	4694	D-KOSH
F-CHCV	Scheibe SFL-25R Falke	46187	D-KASB
F-CHDA	Centrair 101A Pégase	101A-0355	
F-CHDB	Centrair 101A Pégase	101A-0356	
F-CHDC-C	Centrair 101A Pégase	101A-0357	
F-CHDD	Centrair 101A Pégase	101A-0358	
F-CHDF	Centrair 101A Pégase	101A-0360	
F-CHDG	Centrair 101A Pégase	101A-0361	
F-CHDH	Centrair 101A Pégase	101A-0362	
F-CHDI -Si	Centrair 101A Pégase	101A-0363	
F-CHDJ	Centrair 101A Pégase	101A-0366	
F-CHDK	Centrair 101A Pégase	101A-0367	
F-CHDL-L	Centrair 101A Pégase	101A-0369	
F-CHDM	Centrair 101A Pégase	101A-0370	
F-CHDN-SN	Centrair 101A Pégase	101A-0372	
F-CHDO-B01	Centrair 101A Pégase	101A-0373	
F-CHDP	Centrair 101A Pégase	101A-0374	
F-CHDQ	Centrair 101A Pégase	101A-0375	
F-CHDR	Centrair 101A Pégase	101A-0376	
F-CHDS	Centrair 101A Pégase	101A-0349	
F-CHDT	Centrair 101A Pégase	101A-0377	
F-CHDU-B01	Centrair 101A Pégase	101A-0364	
F-CHDX	Centrair 101A Pégase	101A-0368	
F-CHDY-SY	Centrair 101A Pégase	101A-0371	
F-CHDZ	Centrair 101A Pégase	101A-0379	
F-CHEA	Centrair 101A Pégase	101A-0380	
F-CHEB	Centrair 101A Pégase	101A-0378	
F-CHEC	Centrair 101A Pégase	101A-0381	
F-CHED	Centrair 101A Pégase	101A-0382	
F-CHEE	Centrair 101A Pégase	101A-0383	
F-CHEF-AB	Centrair 101A Pégase	101A-0384	
F-CHEG	Centrair 101A Pégase	101A-0385	
F-CHEH	Centrair 101A Pégase	101A-0386	
F-CHEI-EI	Centrair 101A Pégase	101A-0387	
F-CHEJ-C	Centrair 101A Pégase	101A-0388	
F-CHEK	Centrair 101A Pégase	101A-0389	
F-CHEL-L	Centrair 101A Pégase	101A-0390	
F-CHEM-EG	Centrair 101A Pégase	101A-0391	
F-CHEN	Centrair 101A Pégase	101A-0393	
F-CHEO-77	Centrair 101A Pégase	101A-0395	
F-CHEP-B396	Centrair 101A Pégase	101A-0396	
F-CHEQ	Centrair 101A Pégase	101A-0397	
F-CHER-VO	Centrair 101A Pégase	101A-0398	
F-CHES	Centrair 101A Pégase	101A-0399	
F-CHEU-401	Centrair 101A Pégase	101A-0401	
F-CHEV	Centrair 101A Pégase	101A-0402	
F-CHEX	Centrair 101A Pégase	101A-0405	
F-CHEY	Centrair 101A Pégase	101A-0406	
F-CHEZ -5	Centrair 101A Pégase	101A-0407	
F-CHFA-SD	Centrair 101A Pégase	101A-0466	
F-CHFD	Centrair 101A Pégase	101A-0469	
F-CHFE-FE	Centrair 101A Pégase	101A-0470	
F-CHFF	Centrair 101A Pégase	101A-0471	
F-CHFG	Centrair 101A Pégase	101A-0472	
F-CHFH	Centrair 101A Pégase	101A-0474	
F-CHFI	Centrair 101A Pégase	101A-0473	
F-CHFK-B480	Centrair 101A Pégase	101A-0480	
F-CHFL	Centrair 101A Pégase	101A-0481	
F-CHFM	Centrair 101A Pégase	101A-0482	
F-CHFN-N	Centrair 101A Pégase	101A-0483	
F-CHFP	Centrair 101A Pégase	101A-0486	
F-CHFQ	Centrair 101A Pégase	101A-0487	
F-CHFR-CL	Centrair 101A Pégase	101A-0488	
F-CHFS-I	Centrair 101A Pégase	101A-0489	
F-CHFT	Centrair 101A Pégase	101A-0494	

F-CHFU	Centrair 101A Pégase	101A-0496	
F-CHFV	Centrair 101A Pégase	101A-0497	
F-CHFX	Centrair 101A Pégase	101A-0498	
F-CHFY-FY	Centrair 101A Pégase	101A-0499	
F-CHFZ-BBX	Centrair 101A Pégase	101A-0600	
F-CHGA	Centrair 101A Pégase	101A-0601	
F-CHGB	Centrair 101A Pégase	101A-0602	
F-CHGC	Centrair 101A Pégase	101A-0603	
F-CHGD-D	Centrair 101A Pégase	101A-0604	
F-CHGE-GE	Centrair 101A Pégase	101A-0605	
F-CHGF	Centrair 101A Pégase	101A-0606	
F-CHGG	Centrair 101A Pégase	101A-0490	
F-CHGH	Centrair 101A Pégase	101A-0607	
F-CHGI	Centrair 101A Pégase	101A-0612	
F-CHGJ-V	Centrair 101A Pégase	101A-0614	
F-CHGK	Centrair 101A Pégase	101A-0615	
F-CHGL-AA	Centrair 101A Pégase	101A-0616	
F-CHGM-BAF	Centrair 101A Pégase	101A-0617	
F-CHGN	Centrair 101A Pégase	101A-0618	
F-CHGO	Centrair 101A Pégase	101A-0622	
F-CHGP	Centrair 101A Pégase	101A-0621	
F-CHGQ-IS	Centrair 101A Pégase	101A-0623	
F-CHGR	Centrair 101A Pégase	101A-0624	
F-CHGS-GS	Centrair 101A Pégase	101A-0625	
F-CHGT-B626	Centrair 101A Pégase (W/o 25.4.02)	101A-0626	
F-CHGU	Centrair 101A Pégase	101A-0627	
F-CHGV	Centrair 101A Pégase	101A-0630	
F-CHGX-S8	Centrair 101A Pégase	101A-0629	
F-CHGY	Centrair 101A Pégase	101A-0631	
F-CHGZ	Centrair 101A Pégase	101A-0632	
F-CHHA	Scheibe SF-25B Falke	46144	D-KJHM OE-9138 D-KCAK
F-CHHB-Y2	Schempp-Hirth Janus C	187	D-7718
F-CHHC	Glaser-Dirks DG-800	8-31A23	
F-CHHD	SZD-51-1 Junior	B-2138	
F-CHHE	Schleicher Ka 6E	4240	HB-961
F-CHHF	Caproni A-21S Calif	218	HB-1180
F-CHHG	Schleicher K 8B	883	HB-682
F-CHHH	Grob G.102/77 Astir CS	1808	HB-1470
F-CHHI	Schleicher ASK 13	13232	D-0512
F-CHHJ	Grob G.102/77J Astir CS Jeans	2239	D-5943
F-CHHK	Scheibe SF-28A Tandem-Falke	5749	D-KOFF
F-CHHM	Marganski MDM-1 Fox	221	
F-CHHN	Schleicher Ka 6E	4041	D-1932
F-CHHO	Schleicher ASH 25	25002	D-2522
F-CHHP	Grob G.102 Astir Jeans 77J	2234	D-5949
F-CHHR	Grob G.102 Astir Jeans 77J	2237	D-5917
F-CHHS	Schempp-Hirth Discus CS	210CS	OY-XUV
F-CHHU	Schleicher K 8B (Reservation 3.01)	8522	D-7193
F-CHHY	Glaser-Dirks DG-400	4-6	D-KINS
F-CHIA	Schleicher ASK 21	21526	
F-CHIB	Schleicher ASK 21	21540	
F-CHIC	Schleicher ASK 21	21549	
F-CHID	Schleicher ASK 21	21547	
F-CHIE	Schleicher ASK 21	21080	PH-711
F-CHIF-SA	Schleicher ASW 24	24176	
F-CHIG	Schleicher ASW 24	24178	
F-CHII	Schleicher ASH 25	25107	D-1272
F-CHIL	Schleicher ASK 21	21553	
F-CHIM	Schleicher ASK 21	21614	
F-CHIN	Schleicher ASK 21	21625	
F-CHIS-JC	Schleicher ASW 19B	19128	D-7560
F-CHIT	Schleicher ASH 25	25100	
F-CHIU	Schleicher ASH 25	25157	
F-CHJB	Glaser-Dirks DG-500T Elan Trainer	5E22T4	
F-CHJC	Glaser-Dirks DG-500T Elan Trainer	5E27T7	
F-CHJD-DG1	Glaser-Dirks DG-500T Elan Trainer	5E49T19	
F-CHJE-DG2	Glaser-Dirks DG-500T Elan Trainer	5E73T30	
F-CHJF	Glaser-Dirks DG-500M Elan	5E83M35	
F-CHJG-DD	Glaser-Dirks DG-500T Elan Trainer	5E88T38	
F-CHJH	Glaser-Dirks DG-500/22 Elan	5E102S15	
F-CHJI	Glaser-Dirks DG-500 Elan Trainer	5E129T55	
F-CHJJ	DG Flugzeugbau DG-500 Elan Orion	5E168X23	(D-0168)
F-CHJK	DG Flugzeugbau DG-500 Elan Orion	5E172X25	
F-CHJM	Schempp-Hirth Nimbus 3DM	6/20	D-KAJM
F-CHJN-NJ	Glaser-Dirks DG-500M Elan	5E96M42	OH-857
F-CHJO-DG3	DG Flugzeugbau DG-500 Elan Orion	5E218X58	
F-CHJP	DG Flugzeugbau DG-500MB	5E242MB19	
F-CHKA	Centrair 101A Pégase	101A-0408	
F-CHKB-KB	Centrair 101A Pégase	101A-0410	
F-CHKC	Centrair 101A Pégase	101A-0412	
F-CHKD	Centrair 101A Pégase	101A-0411	
F-CHKE	Centrair 101A Pégase	101A-0413	
F-CHKF	Centrair 101A Pégase	101A-0414	
F-CHKG-B415	Centrair 101A Pégase	101A-0415	
F-CHKH	Centrair 101A Pégase	101A-0416	
F-CHKI	Centrair 101A Pégase	101A-0417	
F-CHKJ-AM	Centrair 101A Pégase	101A-0418	
F-CHKK-K	Centrair 101A Pégase	101A-0419	
F-CHKL	Centrair 101A Pégase	101A-0409	
F-CHKM	Centrair 101A Pégase	101A-0420	
F-CHKN	Centrair 101A Pégase	101A-0421	
F-CHKO-B422	Centrair 101A Pégase	101A-0422	
F-CHKP-B423	Centrair 101A Pégase	101A-0423	
F-CHKQ	Centrair 101A Pégase	101A-0424	
F-CHKR	Centrair 101A Pégase	101A-0428	

F-CHKS-KS	Centrair 101A Pégase	101A-0429	
F-CHKT-KT	Centrair 101A Pégase	101A-0430	
F-CHKU	Centrair 101A Pégase	101A-0431	
F-CHKV	Centrair 101A Pégase	101A-0432	
F-CHKX-X	Centrair 101A Pégase	101A-0433	
F-CHKY	Centrair 101A Pégase	101A-0434	
F-CHLA-3A	Centrair 101A Pégase	101A-0436	
F-CHLB-B43	Centrair 101A Pégase	101A-0438	
F-CHLC	Centrair 101A Pégase	101A-0439	
F-CHLD	Centrair 101A Pégase	101A-0440	
F-CHLE-B02	Centrair 101A Pégase	101A-0441	
F-CHLF-Y	Centrair 101A Pégase	101A-0443	
F-CHLG	Centrair 101A Pégase	101A-0442	
F-CHLH	Centrair 101A Pégase	101A-0444	
F-CHLI	Centrair 101A Pégase	101A-0446	
F-CHLJ	Centrair 101A Pégase	101A-0445	
F-CHLK	Centrair 101A Pégase	101A-0447	
F-CHLL	Centrair 101A Pégase	101A-0452	
F-CHLM-EO	Centrair 101A Pégase	101A-0453	
F-CHLN	Centrair 101A Pégase	101A-0454	
F-CHLO	Centrair 101A Pégase	101A-0455	
F-CHLP	Centrair 101A Pégase	101A-0456	
F-CHLQ	Centrair 101A Pégase	101A-0457	
F-CHLR-BNO	Centrair 101A Pégase	101A-0458	
F-CHLS	Centrair 101A Pégase	101A-0459	
F-CHLT	Centrair 101A Pégase	101A-0460	
F-CHLU-S1	Centrair 101A Pégase	101A-0461	
F-CHLV	Centrair 101A Pégase	101A-0462	
F-CHLX	Centrair 101A Pégase	101A-0463	
F-CHLY	Centrair 101A Pégase	101A-0464	
F-CHLZ	Centrair 101A Pégase	101A-0465	
F-CHMB-7A	Schleicher ASW 24	24175	
F-CHMD-MD	Schleicher ASH 25	25193	
F-CHMP	Schleicher ASH 25	25181	
F-CHNA	Grob G.102 Astir CS	1456	D-7447
F-CHNB	Scheibe SF-25B Falke	46116	D-KABN
F-CHNC	Rolladen-Schneider LS4	4510	3A-MSS
F-CHND	Schempp-Hirth Janus C	165	HB-1672
F-CHNE-87	Bölkow Phoebus C	910	
F-CHNF	Sportine Aviacija LAK-17A	148	
F-CHNG	Sportine Aviacija LAK-19	012	
F-CHNN	Wassmer WA.30 Bijave	168	Fr.AF
F-CHNO	Sportine Aviacija LAK-19	014	
F-CHNP	Sportine Aviacija LAK-19	015	
F-CHNX-17	LAK-17 Nida	126	
F-CHOA	Grob G.103C Twin IIISL	35051	D-KPIC
F-CHPA	Grob G.102 Astir CS	1017	D-6996
F-CHPB	Rolladen-Schneider LS4B	41010	BGA4281
F-CHPC	Bréguet 904S Nymphale (Reservation .99)	9	F-CCFS
F-CHPG	Schempp-Hirth Duo Discus (W/o 11.7.00)	198	
F-CHPH	Wassmer WA.22A Super Javelot	137	Fr.AF
F-CHPV	Caproni-Vizzola A-21S Calif	46	
F-CHQB	HOAC HK-36TTC Super Dimona	36558	
F-CHQC	HOAC HK-36TTC Super Dimona	36607	
F-CHQD	HOAC HK-36TTC Super Dimona	36610	
F-CHQE	HOAC HK-36TTC Super Dimona	36612	OE-9409
F-CHQF	HOAC HK-36TTC Super Dimona	36611	
F-CHQG	HOAC HK-36TTC Super Dimona	36687	
F-CHQH to F-CHQZ Reserved for HK-36 Super Dimonas			
F-CHRA	Schleicher ASK 14	14023	D-KEBB
F-CHRC	Schempp-Hirth Ventus c	376	F-WHRC
F-CHRD	Glaser-Dirks DG-505MB	5E150MB1	D-KTDG
F-CHRE	Wassmer WA.22A Super Javelot	134	FrAF
F-CHRF	Bréguet 901S Mouette	2	F-ZABX
F-CHRG	Rolladen-Schneider LS8A	8149	
F-CHRI	Schleicher ASK 13	13446	D-2992
F-CHRK	Schleicher ASK 13	13545	F-CERK
F-CHRS	Wassmer WA.30 (Dismantled)	165	Fr.AF
F-CHRT	Rolladen-Schneider LS6C	6273	PH-972
F-CHRZ	PZL PW-6U (Permit 11.02)	78.03.03	
F-CHSA	Grob G.102 Astir CS	1256	D-7350
F-CHSB	Schleicher ASK 13	13670AB	D-5800
F-CHSC	Scheibe SF-25E Super Falke	4323	G-WOLD G-BOVM N250BA (D-KECZ)
F-CHSE-GA	Schleicher ASK 13	13175	D-0265
F-CHSF	Schleicher K 8B	8206	D-8465
F-CHSG	Stralpes ST-15 Crystal	4	
F-CHSM	Rolladen-Schneider LS6-18W	6380	
F-CHSN	SZD-55-1	551191031	F-WHSN
F-CHSO-5.5	SZD-55-1	551192042	F-WHSO
F-CHSP	SZD-55-1	551193056	F-WHSP
F-CHTA-CHN	Schempp-Hirth Duo Discus	09	
F-CHTB	Schempp-Hirth Duo Discus	40	
F-CHTC	Schempp-Hirth Duo Discus	67	
F-CHTD	Schempp-Hirth Duo Discus	88	
F-CHTE	Schempp-Hirth Duo Discus	106	
F-CHTF	Schempp-Hirth Duo Discus	120	
F-CHTG	Schempp-Hirth Duo Discus	134	
F-CHTH	Schempp-Hirth Duo Discus	221	
F-CHTI	Schempp-Hirth Duo Discus	145	
F-CHTJ	Schempp-Hirth Duo Discus	151	
F-CHTK-K	Schempp-Hirth Duo Discus	155	
F-CHTL	Schempp-Hirth Duo Discus	167	
F-CHTM	Schempp-Hirth Duo Discus	190	
F-CHTN	Schempp-Hirth Duo Discus	237	

F-CHTO	Schempp-Hirth Duo Discus	252	
F-CHTP-BL	Schempp-Hirth Duo Discus	342	
F-CHTQ	Schempp-Hirth Duo Discus	264	
F-CHTR	Schempp-Hirth Duo Discus	268	
F-CHTS	Schempp-Hirth Duo Discus	276	
F-CHTT	Schempp-Hirth Duo Discus	279	
F-CHTU-TU	Schempp-Hirth Duo Discus T	34/308	
F-CHTV-CW	Schempp-Hirth Duo Discus	304	
F-CHTX	Schempp-Hirth Duo Discus	303	
F-CHTY	Schempp-Hirth Duo Discus	331	
F-CHTZ	DG Flugzeugbau DG-800B (Permit 7.00)	8-201B123	
F-CHUA	Centrair 101A Pégase	101A-0633	
F-CHUB-B628	Centrair 101A Pégase	101A-0628	
F-CHUC	Centrair 101A Pégase	101A-0634	
F-CHUD-DD	Centrair 101A Pégase	101A-0635	
F-CHUE	Centrair 101A Pégase	101A-0636	
F-CHUF-B22	Centrair 101A Pégase	101A-0637	
F-CHUG to CHUZ Reserved for Centrair 101A Pégase production			
F-CHVE-4W	Schempp-Hirth Janus C	144	BGA3857/HDG D-3666
F-CHVZ	Rolladen-Schneider LS4	4489	Fr.mil
F-CHXA	Aeromot AMT.100 Ximango (W/o 17.8.02)	100023	PT-PMV
F-CHXB	Aeromot AMT.100 Ximango	100022	PT-PMU
F-CHXC	Aeromot AMT.100 Ximango	100025	PT-PMX
F-CHXD	Aeromot AMT.100 Ximango	100027	PT-PMZ
F-CHXE	Aeromot AMT.100 Ximango	100031	PT-POO
F-CHXF	Aeromot AMT.100 Ximango	100032	PT-POP
F-CHXG	Aeromot AMT.200 Super Ximango	200040	
F-CHYA	DG Flugzeugbau DG-800B	8-131B60	
F-CHYB	DG Flugzeugbau DG-800B	8-269B177	
F-CHYC-YB	DG Flugzeugbau DG-800S	8-255S49	
F-CHYB to CHYZ Reserved for Aerosport			
F-CHZA to CHZZ Reserved for Centrair SNC-34C Alliance production			
F-CIAC	Schempp-Hirth Ventus 2c	75	
F-CIAF	Bölkow Phoebus C	898	HB-960
F-CIAI	Grob G.102 Astir CS 77	1750	D-4565
F-CIAJ	Schleicher ASK 14	14051	D-KISE
F-CIAO	Rolladen-Schneider LS6-18W	6365	D-1049
F-CIBA-V60	Rolladen-Schneider LS8A	8250	
F-CIBB-GA6	Rolladen-Schneider LS8A	8262	
F-CIBC-GA7	Rolladen-Schneider LS8-18	8321	
F-CIBD	Rolladen-Schneider LS8-18	8356	
F-CIBN	Scheibe SF-25E Falke	4803	D-KBAQ
F-CIBO	Grob G.102/77J Astir Jeans	2128	D-2536
F-CIBZ	Grob G.102 Astir CS	1381	D-7408
F-CICA	PZL PW-5 Smyk	17.02.004	
F-CICB-EZ	PZL PW-5 Smyk	17.07.012	
F-CICC-EY	PZL PW-5 Smyk	17.07.013	
F-CICD-FH	PZL PW-5 Smyk	17.09.011	
F-CICE	PZL PW-5 Smyk	17.10.022	
F-CIDA to CIDZ Reservations for Schempp-Hirth Duo Discus, .01			
F-CIDB-DB	Schempp-Hirth Duo Discus	337	
F-CIDC	Schempp-Hirth Duo Discus	353	
F-CIDD	Schempp-Hirth Duo Discus	341	
F-CIDE	Schempp-Hirth Duo Discus	372	
F-CIDF	Schempp-Hirth Duo Discus	382	
F-CIDG	Schempp-Hirth Duo Discus	394	
F-CIDH	Schempp-Hirth Duo Discus	417	
F-CIDI	Schempp-Hirth Duo Discus	416	
F-CIDJ	Schempp-Hirth Duo Discus	446	
F-CIDN	Schempp-Hirth Janus C	151	(F-CJDN) D-5719 PH-719
F-CIED	Glaser-Dirks DG-500 Elan Trainer	5E20T2	D-0262
F-CIEE	Grob G.102 Astir CS Jeans	2162	D-4557
F-CIEL	Swift S-1A	106	SP-3574
F-CIGA	Glaser-Dirks DG-300 Elan	3E70	D-3325
F-CIGC	Schleicher K 8B	506	HB-620
F-CIGV	Schleicher ASK 13	13422	D-2122
F-CIHB	Centrair SNC-34C Alliance	34003	
F-CIHC	Centrair SNC-34C Alliance	34001	
F-CIHD	Centrair SNC-34C Alliance	34004	
F-CIHE	Centrair SNC-34C Alliance	34005	
F-CIHF	Centrair SNC-34C Alliance	34006	
F-CIHG	Centrair SNC-34C Alliance	34007	
F-CIHH	Centrair SNC-34C Alliance	34008	
F-CIHI	Centrair SNC-34C Alliance	34009	
F-CIHJ	Centrair SNC-34C Alliance	34010	
F-CIHK	Centrair SNC-34C Alliance	34011	
F-CIHL	Centrair SNC-34C Alliance	34012	
F-CIHM	Centrair SNC-34C Alliance	34014	
F-CIHN-A15	Centrair SNC-34C Alliance	34015	
F-CIHO	Centrair SNC-34C Alliance	34016	
F-CIHP	Centrair SNC-34C Alliance	34017	
F-CIHQ	Centrair SNC-34C Alliance	34018	
F-CIHS	Centrair SNC-34C Alliance	34020	
F-CIHU	Centrair SNC-34C Alliance	34022	
F-CIHV	Centrair SNC-34C Alliance	34023	
F-CIHX	Centrair SNC-34C Alliance	34024	
F-CIHY-RB	Centrair SNC-34C Alliance	34025	
F-CIHZ	Centrair SNC-34C Alliance	34027	
F-CIIT	Schempp-Hirth Nimbus 4D	4/20	
F-CIJA	Schempp-Hirth Ventus 2c	23/59	
F-CIJB	Schempp-Hirth Ventus 2c	26/71	
F-CIJC	Schempp-Hirth Ventus 2cM (Converted from former Ventus 2c c/n 39/113)	57113	
F-CIJD-74	Schempp-Hirth Ventus 2cT	27/96	

F-CIJE-HB	Schempp-Hirth Ventus 2c M	35/119	
	(Converted from former Ventus 2c c/n 40/119)		
F-CIJF	Schempp-Hirth Ventus 2cT	42/137	
F-CIJG	Schempp-Hirth Ventus 2c	55/164	
F-CIJH	Schempp-Hirth Ventus 2cT	46/145	
	(Converted from former Ventus 2c c/n 47/145)		
F-CIJI-GA8	Schempp-Hirth Ventus 2b	122	
F-CIJJ	Schempp-Hirth Ventus 2cT	67/206	
F-CIJK	Schempp-Hirth Ventus 2cT	75/...	
F-CIJL	Schempp-Hirth Ventus 2cT	103/...	
F-CIJN-EP	Schempp-Hirth Ventus 2cT	77/...	
F-CILA	Schempp-Hirth Duo Discus	214	
F-CILC	Schleicher ASH 25	25130	BGA3800/HAZ
			G-BTYJ
F-CILH	Schempp-Hirth Janus CM	36/269	G-LOAF
			OH-830
F-CIMC	Schleicher ASK 21	21700	
F-CIME	Schempp-Hirth Duo Discus	218	
F-CIMJ	Schempp-Hirth Duo Discus	3	D-7459
F-CIML	Schempp-Hirth Janus C	217	D-7180
F-CIMM	Rolladen-Schneider LS8-18	8270	D-0285
F-CIPH	Schleicher ASK 14	14015	D-KILY
F-CIPV	Schleicher ASK 21	21104	HB-1640
F-CIRC	Schleicher K 8B	8384SH	(F-CLLA)
			HB-806
F-CIRH	Stemme S-10V	14-028M	OY-JAX
	(Converted from S-10 c/n 10-28)		(G-CHLT)
			D-KGCL(1)
F-CIRS	Schempp-Hirth Duo Discus	130	
F-CIRV	Schleicher ASK 21.	21308	I-SIRV
F-CITS	Schleicher ASK 21	21744	
F-CITT	Schleicher ASK 21	21779	
F-CITU	Schleicher ASK 21	21763	
F-CITV	Schleicher ASK 21	21764	
F-CITX	Schleicher ASK 21	21750	
F-CITY	Schleicher ASK 21	21756	
F-CITZ	Schleicher ASK 21	21761	
F-CIVH-VH	Schleicher ASH 25	25005	OO-ZUZ
F-CIVY	Schleicher ASK 21	21156	D-4721
F-CIZY	Scheibe SF-25C Falke 1700	4453	D-KOZY
F-CJAA-EC	Schempp-Hirth Nimbus 4T (Permit 3.00)	32	
F-CJAB	Schempp-Hirth Nimbus 4D	10/53	
F-CJAC to F-CJAY	Reserved for Schempp-Hirth Nimbus production		
F-CJAN	Schempp-Hirth Janus C	257	OY-XRR
F-CJAZ	Schempp-Hirth Nimbus 4D	8/39	D-8157
F-CJBA	Centrair SNC-34C Alliance	34028	
F-CJBB	Centrair SNC-34C Alliance	34029	
F-CJBC	Centrair SNC-34C Alliance	34030	
F-CJBD	Centrair SNC-34C Alliance	34031	
F-CJBE	Centrair SNC-34C Alliance	34032	
F-CJBF	Centrair SNC-34C Alliance	34033	
F-CJBG	Centrair SNC-34C Alliance	34034	
F-CJBH	Centrair SNC-34C Alliance	34035	
F-CJBI	Centrair SNC-34C Alliance	34036	
F-CJBJ-S11	Centrair SNC-34C Alliance	34038	
F-CJBK	Centrair SNC-34C Alliance	34037	
F-CJBL	Centrair SNC-34C Alliance	34039	
F-CJBM	Centrair SNC-34C Alliance	34040	
F-CJBN	Centrair SNC-34C Alliance	34042	
F-CJBO-S12	Centrair SNC-34C Alliance	34043	
F-CJCN	Schleicher ASK 21	21621	HB-3178
F-CJCM	Castel C.25S	60	F-CRNK
	(Also reserved as F-CRMC(2))		
F-CJCR-L38	Rolladen-Schneider LS1D	227	D-7111
			F-CEHN
F-CJCT	Breguet 901S Mouette	17	F-CCCT
F-CJCV	Schleicher ASW 20BL	20667	D-6988
			OE-5363
F-CJDB	Grob G.102 Standard Astir II	5045S	HB-1530
F-CJDI	Schempp-Hirth Nimbus-2C	81	F-CEDI
F-CJEF-S6	SZD-51-1 Junior	W-950	HB-1895
F-CJEM	Schleicher ASK 21	21439	HB-3023
F-CJFB	Avialsa-Scheibe A.60 Fauconnet	59K	OO-ZCX
			F-CCVL
F-CJGC	Schempp-Hirth Duo Discus	225	
F-CJHA	Grob G.102 Astir CS	1100	D-6994
F-CJHD	Castel C.311P	16	(F-CARC)
			F-CALS
F-CJIM-S7	SZD-51-1 Junior	B-1500	HB-1797
F-CJJC	Schleicher ASW 27	27139	
F-CJJH	Sportine Aviacija LAK-17a	159	
F-CJLD-FD	Schleicher ASW 28 (Permit 5.02)	28026	
F-CJLS	Grob G.109B	6394	HB-2111
F-CJMC-EF	Schempp-Hirth Discus 2A	24	
F-CJOE	Scheibe SF-25B Falke	4668	D-KAPD
F-CJPB	Rolladen-Schneider LS-3-17	3450	D-6929
F-CJPC	Schleicher ASW 27	27162	
F-CJPG	Schleicher ASH 25E	25119	F-CHHL
			HB-2197
F-CJPH-TZ	Sportine Aviacija LAK-19	005	
F-CJRG	Schleicher ASK 21	21734	
F-CJSD	Schempp-Hirth Ventus 2cT	89/...	
F-CJUB	Schempp-Hirth Duo Discus	432	
F-CJVO-95	Schleicher ASW 28	28025	
F-CJZA	Start + Flug H 101 Salto	27	BGA 4902
			D-2997
F-CJZV	Schleicher ASW 27	27131	

F-CLCC	Schleicher ASW 27	27190	
F-CLCD	Schleicher ASW 28	28017	D-5938
F-CLCV	Schleicher ASW 24	24064	D-6186
F-CLFM-27	Schleicher ASW 27	27105	D-7627
F-CLIT	Götz/Schleicher K 8B	8528Gö	HB-829
F-CLMP	Schleicher ASK 21	21137	D-4311
F-CLRC	Schleicher ASH 25	25233	
F-CNPU	CARMAM JP.15/36AR	054	(F-GNPU)
			Fr.AF
F-CNPX	Grob G.103 Twin Astir (Reservation 1.01)	unkn	
F-CNVV	Schleicher ASW 28 (Permit 2.02)	28019	D-5972
F-COQX	Avialsa-Scheibe A.60 Fauconnet	45	D-....
			F-CCQX
F-CPPM	Scheibe SF 28A Tandem-Falke	5718	D-KEPM
			HB-2034
			D-KAZE(1)
			(D-KOAJ)
F-CPZT-AZ	Schempp-Hirth Ventus c	347	(F-CRZT)
			D-9438
			D-KBHK(1)
			D-5470
			PH-943
			D-5470
F-CXXL	Schempp-Hirth Janus C	255	D-5068

GLIDERS/MOTOR-GLIDERS WITH RESTRICTED CofA

F-CRAG(2)	Pottier JP15/34R Kit Club	60-43	
F-CRAH(2)	Boulay Condor	01	
F-CRBA(2)	Rutan 77-6	F1	
F-CRBG(2)	Fournier RF-9	13	
F-CRBJ	Castel C.301S	1127	F-CAKD
F-CRBL	Fauvel AV.36 (Modified)	131	F-CBSF
F-CRBM(2)	Sirius C (Homebuilt)	19	
F-CRDQ	Castel 25S	139	F-CAMX
F-CRDU(2)	ACBA 3A	01	
F-CREB	Peyronnenc PP.1	01	F-WREB
F-CREV(2)	Nord 1300	228	F-CREU
			F-CBXE
F-CREZ(2)	Rolladen/Mudry LS1-SP-1	01	F-CREK(2)
			F-WRKE
F-CRFK	Emouchet SA.104	282	F-CCFC
F-CRFU	Nord 1300	197	
F-CRGC	Fauvel AV-222 Buse	07	F-WRGC
F-CRGF	Fournier RF-9	12	
F-CRGL	Nord 1300	94	F-CBXR
F-CRHL	Nord 1300	60	F-CBXV
F-CRHT	Castel C.301S	1133	F-CBXO
F-CRHX	Castel 25S	150	
F-CRJM(2)	Castel C.301S (Being restored)	1050	F-CRHQ
			F-CBLA
F-CRLA(2)	Avia 152A (Reservation .02)	301	(F-AZVI)
F-CRLO	Nord 1300	123	F-CAGX
F-CRMB	Sablier 18 (Reservation .99)	01	
F-CRML	Castel 25S	115	F-CBOU
F-CRMU(2)	Castel 25S	172	F-CRMA
			F-CBAP
F-CRND(2)	Pottier 15/34R	60-60	
F-CRNR	Nord 1300	65	F-CAAN
F-CROF	Emouchet SA.103	94	F-CBJB
F-CROI (2)	Fouga CM.8W	01	
F-CROL(2)	Neukom AN-20B (Stored)	7	
F-CRPY	Fouga Sylphe IIIB	01	
F-CRQX	Fauvel AV.361	323	
F-CRRA	Scheibe Mü.13D	03	
F-CRRI	Bouley Menin BM 1	01	F-WRRI
F-CRRJ	Vaysse TCV 03	PS-1	
F-CRRL	Compact	1	
F-CRRM	Fauvel AV.451	13	F-WRRM
F-CRRN	Emouchet SA.104	233	F-CRNJ
			F-CBJH
F-CRRO	Mouisset	01	
F-CRRP	Rambaud Fournier RF-9	03-A	F-CAHK
F-CRRY	Fauvel AV.45	01	(F-PYEY)
			F-WCAG
			F-CCAG

GOVERNMENT-OPERATED AIRCRAFT: SECURITÉ CIVILE, FIRE SERVICE AND CUSTOMS

F-ZBAA(4)	Conair Turbo-Firecat *(Code "T.22")*	456/027	F-WEOL
	(Grumman US-2B Tracker conversion)		C-FQCW
			F-WEOL
			F-ZBAA(4)/T.14
			F-WEOL
			C-GYQN
			BuA136547
F-ZBAB(3)	Reims/Cessna F406 Vigilant	F406-0025	F-GEUL
			F-WZDV
F-ZBAC(3)	Aérospatiale AS.355F2 Ecureuil 2	5026	C-GFSI
F-ZBAD(3)	Aérospatiale AS.355F2 Ecureuil 2	5156	N5796A

F-ZBAN(2)	SNCASE SE.316B Alouette III	1115	F-RAFQ
F-ZBAP(3)	Conair Turbo Firecat *(Code "T- 12")*	567/026	F-ZBDA
	(Grumman US-2BTracker conversion)		F-WEOK
			C-FOKN
			F-WEOK
			F-ZBDA/T.12
			F-WEOK
			C-GYQS
			BuA136658
F-ZBAR(3)	Canadair CL.215 1A-10 *(Code "P.21") (Museum)*	1021	
F-ZBAU(2)	Conair Firecat *(Code "T.2")*	DH-32/009	F-WZLQ
	(Grumman CS-2F1 Tracker conversion)		C-FOPW
			CF-OPW
			RCN1533
F-ZBAW	Sud Avn SA.316B Alouette III	2306	
F-ZBAZ(2)	Conair Turbo Firecat *(Code "T.01")*	DH-57/008	F-WEOL
	(Grumman CS-2F1 Tracker conversion)		C-FVPK
	(Damaged 19.9.98, repair under consideration)		F-WEOL
			F-ZBAZ/T.01
			F-WZLS
			(F-WZLR)
			C-FOPZ
			CF-OPZ
			RCN1558
F-ZBBB(2)	Reims/Cessna F406 Vigilant	F406-0039	F-WZDS
F-ZBBL(2)	Conair Turbo Firecat *(Code "T-19")*	626/024	F-WEOK
	(Grumman US-2A Tracker conversion)		C-FTFC
			F-WEOJ
			F-ZBBL/T.10
			F-WDQD
			C-GHPV
			BuA136717
F-ZBBN(2)	Aérospatiale AS.350B1 Ecureuil	1951	F-ZKBT
			D-HHZZ(2)
F-ZBBV	Canadair CL.215 1A-10 *(Code "P.46")*	1046	C-GAOS
	(Static display)		
F-ZBCE	Reims/Cessna F406 Vigilant	F406-0042	F-GKRA
			F-WKRA
			F-GKRA
F-ZBCF	Reims/Cessna F406 SurMar	F406-0077	F-WZDZ
F-ZBCG	Reims/Cessna F406 PolMar II	F406-0066	F-WZDT
F-ZBCH	Reims/Cessna F406 SurMar	F406-0075	
F-ZBCI	Reims/Cessna F406 Vigilant	F406-0070	
F-ZBCJ	Reims/Cessna F406 Vigilant	F406-0074	F-WZDJ
F-ZBCZ	Conair Turbo Firecat *(Code "T-23")*	DH-94/036	F-ZBCA
	(Grumman CS2F-3 Tracker conversion)		(F-ZBBF)
			C-FKUF
			CAF12195
			RCN1595
F-ZBDE	SNCASE SE.3160 Alouette III	1630	FAP9331
F-ZBDI	Sud Avn SA.316B Alouette III	1878	FAP9388
F-ZBDJ	Sud Avn SA.316B Alouette III	1879	FAP9389
F-ZBDL	SNCASE SE.3160 Alouette III	1611	XC-FAR
F-ZBDV	Aérospatiale AS.350BA Ecureuil	1157	F-GCFR
F-ZBEA	Aérospatiale AS.350B Ecureuil	1003	F-GBBQ
			F-WZAL
F-ZBEF	Aérospatiale AS.355F2 Ecureuil 2	5236	
F-ZBEG(2)	Canadair CL.415 6B-11 *(Code "P.39")*	2015	C-FXBH
F-ZBEH(2)	Conair Turbo Firecat *(Code "T-20")*	410/035	F-WEOJ
	(Grumman US-2A Tracker conversion)		C-FCAD
			N435DF
			BuA136501
F-ZBEJ	Aérospatiale AS.355F1 Ecureuil 2	5003	F-WZKI
F-ZBEK	Aérospatiale AS.355F2 Ecureuil 2	5298	
F-ZBEL	Aérospatiale AS.355F2 Ecureuil 2	5299	
F-ZBEO	Canadair CL..415 6B-11 *(Code "P.36")*	2011	C-FWPD
F-ZBEP	Reims/Cessna F406 Vigilant	F406-0006	
F-ZBER	Cessna 404 Titan	404-0608	F-GAMZ
			LN-KAG
			SE-IBL
			(N2683Y)
F-ZBES	Reims/Cessna F406 Vigilant	F406-0017	
F-ZBET	Conair Turbo Firecat *(Code " T-15")*	703/028	F-WEOJ(3)
	(Grumman US-2A Tracker conversion)		C-GHYH
			F-ZBET/T.15
			F-WEOJ
			C-GHYH
			BuA147559
F-ZBEU(2)	Canadair CL..4156B-11 *(Code "P.42")*	2024	C-FZDE
F-ZBEW	Conair Turbo Firecat *(Code "T-11")*	621/025	F-WEOL
	(Grumman US-2B Tracker conversion)		C-FSPK
			F-WEOL
			F-ZBEW/T.11
			F-WEOJ
			C-GYQY
			BuA136712
F-ZBEY	Conair Turbo Firecat *(Code "T-07")*	400/017	C-FYHB
	(Grumman US-2A Tracker conversion)		F-WEOK
			F-ZBEY/T.7
			F-WDQD
			C-GRXU
			BuA136491
F-ZBFA	Reims/Cessna F406 PolMar I	F406-001	F-GGRA(2)
			F-GGAN
			F-GFLT
			F-WZLT
F-ZBFC	Aérospatiale AS.350B1 Ecureuil	2109	

F-ZBFD	Aérospatiale AS.350B1 Ecureuil	2114	F-GIRO
F-ZBFE	Conair Turbo Firecat *(Code "T-17")*	656/032	F-WEOK(3)
	(Grumman US-2A Tracker conversion)		C-FFQM
			N437DF
			BuA136747
F-ZBFH	Aérospatiale AS.350BA Ecureuil	2110	JA9771
F-ZBFJ	Beech B200 Super King Air *(Code "B.98")*	BB-1102	(F-GKDO)
			D-IWAN
			HB-GHI
			N147D
F-ZBFK	Beech B200 Super King Air *(Code "B.96")*	BB-876	F-GHSC
			N52BC
F-ZBFM	SNCASE SE.3160 Alouette III	1280	ALAT
F-ZBFN	Canadair CL.415 6B-11 *(Code "P.33")*	2006	C-FVUK
F-ZBFP	Canadair CL.415 6B-11 *(Code "P.31")*	2002	C-FBET
F-ZBFS	Canadair CL.415 6B-11 *(Code "P.32")*	2001	C-GSCT
F-ZBFV	Canadair CL.415 6B-11 *(Code "P.37")*	2013	C-FWPE
F-ZBFW	Canadair CL.415 6B-11 *(Code "P.38")*	2014	C-FWZH
F-ZBFX	Canadair CL.415 6B-11 *(Code "P.34")*	2007	C-FVUJ
F-ZBFY	Canadair CL.415 6B-11 *(Code "P.35")*	2010	C-FVDY
F-ZBGA	Reims/Cessna F406 SurMar	F406-0086	F-WWSR
F-ZBGB	Cessna T206H Turbo Stationair	T20608446	F-GXRH
			N2107Q
F-ZBGC	Cessna T206H Turbo Stationair	T20608445	F-GXRG
			N2106R
F-ZBGD	Reims/Cessna F406 PolMar III	F406-0090	F-WWNP
			(F-ZBGB)
F-ZBMA	Conair Turbo Firecat *(Code "T-24")*	461/021	C-GFZG
	(Grumman US-2B Tracker conversion)		F-ZBEX
			F-WEOL
			F-ZBEX/T.9
			F-WDSX(2)
			C-GQCW
			N4477Z
			BuA136552
F-ZBMB	Beech B200 Super King Air *(Code "B.97")*	BB-1379	F-GJFD
F-ZBM .	DHC-8 Dash Eight Srs 402 *(Reservation .05)*	4040	C-FBAM
			N532DS
			LN-RDW
			N384BC
			C-FDHZ
F-ZBM .	DHC-8 Dash Eight Srs 402 *(Reservation .05)*	4043	C-FBSG
			N535DS
			LN-RDN
			C-FWBB
F-ZBPA	MBB-Kawasaki BK.117C-2/Eurocopter EC.145	9006	D-HJFA
F-ZBPB	MBB-Kawasaki BK.117C-2/Eurocopter EC.145	9007	D-HJFB
F-ZBPC	MBB-Kawasaki BK.117C-2/Eurocopter EC.145	9009	D-HJFD
F-ZBPD	MBB-Kawasaki BK.117C-2/Eurocopter EC.145	9010	D-HJFE
F-ZBPE	MBB-Kawasaki BK.117C-2/Eurocopter EC.145	9011	D-HJFF(3)
F-ZBPF	MBB-Kawasaki BK.117C-2/Eurocopter EC.145	9012	D-HJFG
F-ZBPG	MBB-Kawasaki BK.117C-2/Eurocopter EC.145	9013	D-HJFH
F-ZBPH	MBB-Kawasaki BK.117C-2/Eurocopter EC.145	9015	D-HJFJ
F-ZBPI	MBB-Kawasaki BK.117C-2/Eurocopter EC.145	9016	D-HJFK
F-ZBPJ	MBB-Kawasaki BK.117C-2/Eurocopter EC.145	9017	D-HJFL
F-ZBPK	MBB-Kawasaki BK.117C-2/Eurocopter EC.145	9020	D-HJFO
F-ZBPL	MBB-Kawasaki BK.117C-2/Eurocopter EC.145	9021	D-HJFP
F-ZBPM	MBB-Kawasaki BK.117C-2/Eurocopter EC.145	9022	D-HJFQ
F-ZBPN	MBB-Kawasaki BK.117C-2/Eurocopter EC.145	9023	D-HJFR
F-ZBPO	MBB-Kawasaki BK.117C-2/Eurocopter EC.145	9025	D-HJFT
F-ZBPP	MBB-Kawasaki BK.117C-2/Eurocopter EC.145	9030	D-HJFU
F-ZBPQ	MBB-Kawasaki BK.117C-2/Eurocopter EC.145	9031	D-HJFV
F-ZBPR	MBB-Kawasaki BK.117C-2/Eurocopter EC.145	9034	D-HJFW
F-ZBPS	MBB-Kawasaki BK.117C-2/Eurocopter EC.145	9042	D-HRWA
F-ZBPT	MBB-Kawasaki BK.117C-2/Eurocopter EC.145	9043	D-HRWB
F-ZBPU	MBB-Kawasaki BK.117C-2/Eurocopter EC.145	9045	D-HRWD
F-ZBPV	MBB-Kawasaki BK.117C-2/Eurocopter EC.145	9046	D-HRWE
F-ZBPW	MBB-Kawasaki BK.117C-2/Eurocopter EC.145	9048	D-HRWF
F-ZBPX	MBB-Kawasaki BK.117C-2/Eurocopter EC.145	9049	D-HRWG
F-ZBPY	MBB-Kawasaki BK.117C-2/Eurocopter EC.145	9050	D-HRWH
F-ZBPZ	MBB-Kawasaki BK.117C-2/Eurocopter EC.145	9056	D-HRWI
F-ZBQA	MBB-Kawasaki BK.117C-2/Eurocopter EC.145	9057	D-HRWJ
F-ZBQB	MBB-Kawasaki BK.117C-2/Eurocopter EC.145	9058	D-HRWO
F-ZBQC	MBB-Kawasaki BK.117C-2/Eurocopter EC.145	9059	D-HRWP
F-ZBQD	MBB-Kawasaki BK.117C-2/Eurocopter EC.145	9060	D-HRWR
F-ZBQE	MBB-Kawasaki BK.117C-2/Eurocopter EC.145	9062	D-HRWS
F-ZBQF	MBB-Kawasaki BK.117C-2/Eurocopter EC.145	9064	D-HRWT

A total of 32 Eurocopter EC.145s are on order for the Securité Civile

F-ZB . . .	Aérospatiale SA.365N Dauphin 2	6091	F-GFBX
			OY-HMZ
			F-GEDQ
			F-WYME
			TF-SIF
			F-WXFJ

GENDARMERIE AIRCRAFT

In most cases only the last 3 letters of the " Registration" are actually carried on the aircraft.

F-MCSC(2)	Aérospatiale AS.350B Ecureuil	1691	F-MJCE(1)
F-MCSF	Aérospatiale AS.350B1 Ecureuil	2225	F-MJBZ(1)
F-MCSG	SNCASE SE.3160 Alouette III	1160	F-MJBU(1)
			F-MCSK
			F-MCSH(1)
			F-MJBE(2)

F-MCSL	Aérospatiale AS.350B1 Ecureuil	2096	F-MJCS(1)
			F-ZKCP
F-MCSM	Aérospatiale AS.350B1 Ecureuil	2222	F-MJCZ(1)
F-MCSN	Aérospatiale AS.350B1 Ecureuil	2423	F-MJCZ(2)
F-MCZA	Aérospatiale AS.350B Ecureuil	1692	F-MJCF(1)
F-MJAA(2)	Aérospatiale AS.550U2 Fennec	2815	CEV
F-MJBA(2)	MBB-Kawasaki BK.117C-2/Eurocopter EC.145	9008	D-HMBG
			F-MJBA(2)
			D-HJFC
F-MJBB(3)	MBB-Kawasaki BK.117C-2/Eurocopter EC.145	9014	D-HJFI
F-MJBC(2)	MBB-Kawasaki BK.117C-2/Eurocopter EC.145	9018	D-HJFM
F-MJBD(2)	MBB-Kawasaki BK.117C-2/Eurocopter EC.145	9019	D-HJFN
F-MJBE(2)	MBB-Kawasaki BK.117C-2/Eurocopter EC.145	9024	D-HJFS
F-MJBF	MBB-Kawasaki BK.117C-2/Eurocopter EC.145	9035	D-HJFX
F-MJBG	MBB-Kawasaki BK.117C-2/Eurocopter EC.145	9036	D-HJFY
F-MJBH	MBB-Kawasaki BK.117C-2/Eurocopter EC.145	9037	D-HJFZ
F-MJBP	Sud Avn SA.319B Alouette III	2057	
F-MJBQ	Sud Avn SA.319B Alouette III	1956	ZaireAF:9T-HT6
F-MJBS	Sud Avn SA.319B Alouette III	2202	F-BVVH
F-MJBU(2)	Sud Avn SA.316B Alouette III	2330	F-MCSG
			F-BYAQ
F-MJBW	SNCASE SE.3160 Alouette III	1120	ALAT
F-MJBX	Sud Avn SA.316B Alouette III	1693	ALAT
F-MJBZ(2)	Sud Avn SA.319B Alouette III	2338	Fr.AF
F-MJCA	Aérospatiale AS.350BA Ecureuil	1028	F-GBLQ
F-MJCB	Aérospatiale AS.350B Ecureuil	1574	
F-MJCC(2)	Aérospatiale AS.350B Ecureuil	1916	
F-MJCD	Aérospatiale AS.350B Ecureuil	1576	
F-MJCE(2)	Aérospatiale AS.350B Ecureuil	1812	F-MCSC(2)
			F-MJCM(1)
F-MJCF(2)	Aérospatiale AS.350B Ecureuil	1810	F-MCSA(2)
			F-MJCK(1)
F-MJCG	Aérospatiale AS.350B Ecureuil	1753	
F-MJCH	Aérospatiale AS.350B Ecureuil	1756	
F-MJCJ	Aérospatiale AS.350B Ecureuil	1809	
F-MJCK(2)	Aérospatiale AS.350B Ecureuil	1953	
F-MJCL	Aérospatiale AS.350B Ecureuil	1811	
F-MJCM(2)	Aérospatiale AS.350B Ecureuil	1952	
F-MJCN	Aérospatiale AS.350B Ecureuil	2044	
F-MJCO	Aérospatiale AS.350B Ecureuil	1917	
F-MJCP	Aérospatiale AS.350B Ecureuil	2045	
F-MJCQ	Aérospatiale AS.350B Ecureuil	2057	
F-MJCR	Aérospatiale AS.350B Ecureuil	2088	
F-MJCS(2)	Aérospatiale AS.350B Ecureuil	1575	F-MCSE(3)
			F-MJCC(1)
F-MJCT	Aérospatiale AS.350B Ecureuil	2104	
F-MJCU	Aérospatiale AS.350B Ecureuil	2117	
F-MJCV	Aérospatiale AS.350B Ecureuil	2118	
F-MJCW	Aérospatiale AS.350B Ecureuil	2218	
F-MJCX	Aérospatiale AS.350B Ecureuil	2219	
F-MJCY	Aérospatiale AS.350B Ecureuil	2221	
F-MJCZ(3)	Aérospatiale AS.350BA Ecureuil	1467	F-GHCO
			(F-GHBR)
			LN-OTC

MICROLIGHTS / ULMs

Registration is by the prefix number of the Département in which the owner lives, administered on a regional basis. Département names are now given below as a reference aid. The F-J... marks are portable radio call-signs rather than aircraft registrations, they may therefore remain with an owner and be transferred to other aircraft. We have moved these into the second column for ease of reference, with an alphabetical index at the end.
No complete ULM listing is as yet available and what follows is made up largely of reported sightings. As in the main register the letter W is used for test flying, although it may be applied before, after, or in the middle of the registration! A number of companies now have re-usable test marks of various types as indicated within the list. Only confirmed types are now included and the editor would welcome any additional reports and sightings. We are still recording ULMs that have been withdrawn from use or have had accidents, simply because otherwise there is no other source which gives all this information in one place.
Where c/ns are quoted for weight-shift machines these usually apply to the trike unit, however registrations are usually carried on the wings which in some cases may frequently be exchanged between trikes and checks should be carried out wherever possible.

01 : Ain

01-R		Rans S-6 Coyote		
01-T		Zenith Baroudeur		
01-AD		Perouges X-15		
WAV-01		Murphy Rebel		
W01-BM		Fox Tristar		
01-BP		Air Création GT BI Quartz		
01-CG		Airplumb		
01-CQ		Weedhopper		
01-CR		Weedhopper		
01-DA	F-JAFY	Dynali Chickinox		
01-DE		Aviasud Mistral		
01-DJ		Air Création		
01-DT		Aviasud Mistral		
01-DZ		Aviasud Mistral		
01-EB		Dynali Chickinox		
01-EJ		Eipper Quicksilver GT		
01-FA	F-JAGS	C A Minifox		
01-FY		Weedhopper AX-3		
01-GB		Denney Kitfox		
01-W-GE		Tecnam P.96 Golf		
01-GI		Dynali Chickinox		
01-GX		Air Création		
01-HC		Aviasud Mistral		
01-HF		Micro Aviation Pulsar 2		
		(WHF-01 noted as Avid Champion, .00)		
01-HT		Weedhopper AX-3	C3113174	
01-HU		Air Création GTE Clipper		
01-HV		Dynali Chickinox		
01-II		Best Off Sky Ranger		
01-IJ		Arrow Caprice 21		
01-IO		Microleve floatplane		
01-IR	F-JCOS	Rans S-6ES Coyote II		
01-JM		Cosmos		
01-JS		Soubeyrat Albatros paramotor		
01-KF	F-JCKL	Rans S-6ESD Coyote II		
01-KG	F-JCKM	Rans S-7 Courier		
01-KH	F-JCKO	Rans S-6ESD Coyote IIXL		
01-KI		Rans S-6 Coyote II		
01-KM	F-JCBH	Rans S-6ES Coyote II		
01-KP		Pegasus Quantum Super Sport	7279	
01-LB	F-JCUM	Tecnam P.92 Echo		
01-LG		Air Création		
01-LJ		Rans S-6 Coyote II		
01-MB		Tecnam P.92S Echo		
01-MC	F-JEIU	Rans S-7 Courier		
01-MN	F-JEJI	Rans S-9 Chaos		
01-MO	F-JEMR	Rans S-6 Coyote tailwheel		
01-MQ		Flight Design CT		
01-MR	F-JEIK	Tecnam P.92 Echo		
01-NH		Flight Design CT		
01-NI		Flight Design CT		
01-NL		unidentified paramotor		
01-NM		Rans S-9 Chaos		
01-NN		Flight Design CT-2K		
01-NP	F-JEKH	Tecnam P.96 Golf		
01-NS	F-JBUW	Pegasus XL		
01-OD		Pipistrel/Zen ULM Sinus		
W01-OF	F-JELH	ATEC Zephyr	01	
01-OI		Rans S-6 Coyote II		
01-OJ		Flight Design CT		
01-OL	F-JEKV	Tecnam P.92-S Echo		
01-OQ	F-JELJ	Tecnam P.92 Echo		
01-OR	F-JELS	Tecnam P.96 Golf	18?	
W01-OS		ATEC Zephyr		
01-OT	F-JELC	Flight Design CT		
W-PA-01		Icarus Jet Fox 97		
01-PB		Jodel D.18V	84	F-PYYQ
01-PM		Zenair CH-601 Zodiac		
01-PQ		Air Création		
01-PR	F-JENY	Tecnam P.96 Golf 100		
01-PS		Tecnam P.96 Golf *(Damaged)*		
01-QB	F-JEOD	Tecnam P.96 Golf 100		
01-QC	F-JFFQ	Tecnam P92S Echo		
		(Also carried marks 77-AHP internally 8.03)		
01-QI		DTA Dynamic (also reported as Rans S-6ES Coyote)		
01-QM	F-JBJI	Tecnam P.92 Echo		
01-QQ	F-JEPH	Tecnam P.92S Echo		
01-RL		Flight Design CT-2K		
01-RP		Tecnam P.92S Echo		
01-RT	F-JERU	Tecnam P.92 Echo Super		
01-SH	F-JETJ	Tecnam P.92S Echo Jabiru		
01-TE	F-JEVV	Tecnam P.2002 Sierra		
01-WUL		Twin Weedhopper		

02 : Aisne

02-J		Cosmos		
02-BO		Humbert Moto du Ciel		
02-BX		Mignet HM.1000 Balèrit		
02-CA		Ghost 12		
02-CN		Cosmos		
02-CO	F-JAOP	JCC Aviation J-300 Joker Kit		
02-DA		Cosmos SM		
02-DG		Lascaud Bifly		
02-DL		Air Création Quarrtz		80-BZ
02-DM		Sunny		
02-EF		Barry Souris Bulle		
02-GH		Light Aero Avid Flyer		
02-GS		Mignet HM.1000 Balèrit	35	
02-GV		Piel Onyx		
02-GY		Zenair CH-701 STOL		
02-HB		III Sky Arrow 500TF		
02-HI		Light Aero Avid Flyer		
02-HQ		Rans S-12 Airaile		
02-IZ		TEAM Mini-MAX		
02-JH		Buse'Air 150		
02-JD		Buse'Air 150GT		
02-JM	F-JFZK	Rans S-6 Coyote II		
02-JO	F-JFHD	Zenair CH-701 STOL		
02-KF		Cosmos / Chronos		
02-KJ		Air Création Fun		
02-KV		Air Création Racer		
02-KY		Rans S-6 Coyote II		
02-LE		Fantasy Air Allegro		
02-LU		DTA Dynamic 450		
02-LW		Ranger 582/ Top 12.9		
02-LZ		Air Création		
WUL-02		Ultravia Pelican *(Special marks? Used .92)*		

03 : Allier

3-B		Eipper Quicksilver MX	
03-AD		Zenith Baroudeur	
03-AF		Zenith Baroudeur	
03-AJ		Air Création GT BI Quartz	
03-AQ	F-JABA	Aermas 386	
03-AZ		Pegasus	
03-BC		Air Création	
03-BG		Air Création SX	
03-BS	F-JECR	Jodel D.19UL	
03-CG		Dynali Chickinox	
03-CO		Air Création	
03-DD		Synairgie	
03-DE		Synairgie, also reported as Quicksilver	
03-DG		Dynali Chickinox	
03-DL		Tandem Air Sunny	
03-ET		Tandem Air Sunny	
03-FV		Sunny (side-by-side seating)	
03-FX		Synairgie	
03-IH		Aviasud AE-209 Albatross	10
03-II		Airwave Rave Jet Pocket paraglider	
03-IT		Air Création	
03-JE		Air Création GTL 503SL	
03-RA		Rans S-5 Coyote	

04 : Alpes-de-Haute-Provence

04-AQ		Weedhopper Europa	
04-AS		Air Création	
04-AZ		Micro Avn Pulsar	
04-BA		Cosmos Bidulm	
04-BF		Mignet HM.1000 Balèrit	70
04-BP	F-JCTJ	Mignet HM.1100 Cordouan	
04-BQ		Cosmos	
04-CH		Urban Air Lambada	
W04-DT		Dynamic 912	
04-FU		Aviasud Mistral	
04-HM		Mignet HM.14 Pou-du-Ciel	
04-NH		Air Création	
04-SH		Quicksilver	
04-UL		Twin Weedhopper	

05 : Hautes-Alpes

05-I		Noin CLN-1 Sirius	01
05-AB		Noin CLN-1 Sirius	02
05-BD		Noin CLN-1 Sirius	
05-BP		Cosmus Bidulm	
05-BQ		Cosmos	
05-CG		Aquilair Swing	
05-CO		Claude Noin Choucas	01
05-DE		Air Création Clipper	
05-DI		Best Off Sky Ranger	
05-DP		Raj Hamsa X'Air	
05-DX		Filcoa JB Kitten	
05-EH		Best Off Sky Ranger	
05-EL		B&F Funk FK-9	
05-EN		Cosmos	
05-FF		Aquilair Swing	
05-FU		Zenair CH-701 STOL	
05-GU		B&F Funk FK-9 Mk.III	
W05-HA		Aerojames Isatis 01	
05-HB		Aquilair Swing 14.9	
5-KZ		Skyranger	
05-PR		Weedhopper	
05-PV		Rans S-6 Coyote II	
05-UG		Best Off Sky Ranger	

06 : Alpes-Maritimes

06-C		ULAC X-99 (2-seater)	163
06-M		Eipper Quicksilver MX	
06-N		Ultrasport Eagle XL (also reported as Pioneer Flightstar)	
06-AE		Arrow F2 Foxcat (2-seater)	
06-AF		Skycraft AJS.2000	
06-AG		Mustang	
06-AR		Weedhopper	
06-BA		Synairgie Skyranger (floats)	
06-BG		Dynamic 503	
06-CA		PGO Cobra	
06-CD		Murphy Renegade Floatplane	
06-CR		European Aerolights Maestro II	
06-CZ		Air's Maestro	
06-DA		Rans S-6 Coyote II	
06-DD		Air's Maestro (floats)	
06-DG		Aviasud Albatross	
06-DJ		Hydroplum (?)	
W06-DR		Buse'Air 150	
06-DY		Best Off Sky Ranger	
06-EC	F-JJDZ	Denney Kitfox	518
WEL-06		Espace Liberté Country	
06-FM		Pendulaire	
06-GS		Evektor EV-97 Eurostar	2002-08-03
06-MA		Light Aero Avid Flyer ?	
06-SW		Zenith *(W/o 29.7.01)*	

07 : Ardèche

07-B		Butterfly	
07-F		Air Création Quartz	
07-M		Titan Tornado	
07-AA		Air Création	
07-AQ		Quartz SX	
07-AX		Air Création	
07-BB		Air Création SX	
07-BC		Air Création Racer SX 12	
07-BL		Air Création Quartz	
07-BM		Aviasud Mistral	50
07-BO		Air Création	
07-CS		Air Création SX-12	
07-CY		Air Création	
07-DG		Butterfly	
07-DH		Air Création Fun	
07-DT		Air Création Fun 447 Racer	
07-DU		ICP Super Bingo	02 05 52 055
07-EC		Weedhopper Europa	
07-EI		Air Création Fun	
07-EQ		Air Création Safari	
07-ES		Weedhopper	
07-FQ		Rans S-6 Coyote II	
07-FU		Air Création Quartz	
07-GA		Air Création Clipper XP	
07-GH		Air Création XS	
07-GL		Air Création Racer 503	
07-GQ		Air Création	
07-GT		Air Création Fun GTE *(To OO-D09)*	139
07-HC		Air Création XP12 Buggy	
07-HD		Air Création Buggy Fun	
07-HJ		Air Création XP15	
07-HM	F-JCUE	Fly Synthesis Storch	
07-IH		Air Création Kiss	
07-IM		Air Création GTE / XP15 *(W/o 6.8.03)*	
07-JC		Air Création GTE Kiss	
07-JE		Air Création Clipper 912 / iXess 15 GTE	A03028-1075
07-JF		Air Création Clipper 912 / iXess	
07-JS		Air Création Clipper iXess	
07-KI		Air Création Tanarg iXess	A5054-5057(wing)

08 : Ardennes

8-D		Air Création Quartz		
08-BH		Anax Imperator		
08-BI		Cosmos Chronos		
		(Seen .03 but also reported as a Best Off Sky Ranger)		
08-BO		Air Création GT BI / XP		
08-BQ		Weedhopper AX-3	B112968	
08-BU		Rabs S-12 Airaile		
08-CD		Didier Pti'Tavion		
08-CM		Air Création Clipper / XP		
08-CR	F-JBOM	Weedhopper AX-3 Sport		
08-CT		Unidentified (Souricette?)		
08-CV		Air Création XP GT BI		
08-DR		European Airwings Springbok 2000		
08-DT		Air Création GT BI / Fun		
08-DU	F-JGGI	Aerotrophy Trophy 2000TT		
08-DW	F-JGGV	Ekolot JK.03 Beetle/ Aerotrophy 4000		
08-EB		ATEC Zephyr		
08-EE	F-JGGU	TL Ultralight TL-2000 Sting		
08-EG	F-JGHH	Unknown, Kitfox type *(Dismantled)*		
08-EH		Air Création GTE Clipper Mild		
08-EK	F-JGHA	WDFL Fascination		
08-EL		Air Création GTE XP		
08-EM		Sauper J.300 Joker		
08-EN		Rans S-10 Sakota	0494.172	W08-EN OO-135
08-ER		Didier Titan		
08-ET		Pipistrel/Zen ULM Sinus		
08-EU		Unidentified flexwing		
08-EX		Weedhopper	9102555	
08-FB		Ekolot JK05 Junior	05 02 06	
08-FO	F-JGIE	Ekolot JK05 Junior	05 03 07	
08-FP		Ekolot JK05 Junior	05 03 06	
8-TA		Rans S.6 Coyote		

09 : Ariège

09-AB	F-JIBB	Humbert Tetras	
09-AC		Tempest (Modified)	
09-AN		Urban Air Lambada	
09-AQ		Air Création GT BI	
09-AZ		Dynali Chickinox	
09-FC		Denney Kitfox	

10 : Aube

10-C		Huntair Pathfinder	
10-E		Huntair Pathfinder	
10-G		Vector 600	
10-R		Eipper Quicksilver MX	
10-T		Zenith	021
10-Z		Dynali Chickinox	
10-AC		RP.82 Oméga	
10-AL		Aviasud Mistral	
10-AV		Eipper Quicksilver II	
10-BB		Humbert	
10-BG		Previot Helios IV	
10-DH		Safari	
10-DP		Eipper Quicksilver GT500S	
10-DS		Prevot Helios 5TR	
10-EE		Eipper Quicksilver GT500S	

10-EK		Prevot Helios 5TR		
10-ER		Quicksilver GT500		
10-FJ		Aviakit Hermés		
10-FN		Quicksilver GT500		
10-FY	F-JBYR	Aviakit Hermés		
10-GA		Quicksilver MXL-3		
10-GH	F-JGGA	Quicksilver GT500		
10-GI		Quicksilver GT500		
10-GJ		Light Aero Avid Flyer		
10-GL		Light Aero Avid Lite		
10-GM		Humbert Moto-du-Ciel		
10-GS-W		SG Aviation Storm 300		
10-HB		Air Création		
10-HC		Aviakit Vega 2000		
10-HF		Eurofly Sky Raider *(actually marked W-HF-01 !)*		
10-HN	F-JEJC	Fantasy Air Cora CT		
10-HQ		Aviakit Vega 2000		
10-HT		Aviakit Vega 2000		
10-IB	F-JGGN	Zenair CH-701 STOL		
10-IS		Ecofly Norman Mini Explorer		
10-IY		Light Aero Avid Flyer		
10-LA		Zenair MXD 740		
10-SR		Eipper Quicksilver GT500		

11 : Aude

11-AJ		Weedhopper		
11-BY		Ikarus C-22 Extreme		
11-CH		Buse'Air 150		
11-DB		Sunwheel		
11-DM		Aviasud Sirocco		
11-DO	F-JCVU	DTA Dynamic		
11-DP	F-JCXQ	Eipper Quicksilver GT500		
11-DQ		Air Création GTE		
11-ES		Zenair CH-701 STOL		44-RI
11-FA	F-JJIC	B&F Funk FK-9 Mk.III	09-172	
11-FR	F-JCXS	Zenair CH-601HD Zodiac		23-MX
11-UG		DT Dynamic 450		

12 : Aveyron

12-AB		Aero Services Guepard 912S		
12-AE		Aero Services Guepy 582		
12-AF		Weedhopper		
12-AJ		Air Création Kiss Buggy Twin		
12-AU		Weedhopper		
12-BB		Ultralair Weedhopper		
12-BD	F-JLDD	Aero Services Guepard 912S		
12-BE		Aviasud Mistral		
12-BU		Cosmos		
12-BV		Cosmos Echo 12		
12-CF		Weedhopper		
12-CI		Aviasud Albatros AE.209		
12-CT		Aero Services Guepard		
12-CZ		Croses Air Plume		26-CL
12-DR		Fly Synthesis Storch		
12-PL		Aero Services Guepy Club 582T		
12-RJ		Aero Services Guepard 912S		

13 : Bouches-du-Rhône

13-AX		Zenith Barodeur		
13-CH		Croses Airplume	15	
13-CZ		Filcon J-6 Karatoo		
13-DD		J-3 Kitten		
13-DN		Air's Maestro		
13-DQ		Air Création SX II		
13-DT		Aviasud Mistral		
13-DX		Air Création		
13-DZ		Cosmos Chronos		
13-EC		Zenith Baroudeur		
13-EO		Air Création		
13-GD		Oméga paraglider		
13-HW		PGO Cobra		64-JL
13-IO		Zenith Baroudeur		
13-JF		Air Création Clipper GTE		
13-JM		Best Off Sky Ranger		
13-LD		Air Création		
13-LZ	F-JJCW	Best Off Sky Ranger		
13-MB		Zenair CH.601 Zodiac UL Exclusive		
13-MH	F-JCCK	Fantasy Air Allegro SW		
13-MO	F-JJCH	Fantasy Air Allegro		
13-MW		Aviasud Albatros		
13-OP		Jodel D.18	329	F-PAON

14 : Calvados

14-F		Condor		
14-I		Air Création		
14-K		Lega Avia		
14-AB		Air Création Quartz		
14-AG		Super O		
14-BC		Air Création Trike		
14-BE		Air Création XS		
14-BS		Air Création Trike		33-AP
14-BV		Air Création GT BI Fun		
14-CA		Cosmos		
14-CB		Mignet HM.1000 Balèrit	51	
14-CD		Cosmos		
14-CF		JCC Aviation J.300 Joker		
14-DF		Air Création GT BI		
14-DH		ACGE		
14-DI		Weedhopper AX-3		
14-DM		Weedhopper		
14-FI		Weedhopper AX-3		
W14-FP		Mignet HM.293M Pou du Ciel	600	F-PVQM F-WVQM
14-FR		ATEC Zephyr 2000		
14-GD		Rans S-6S Coyote		
14-GI	F-JHIK	Aeropro Eurofox		
14-GM		Air Création Fun		

15 : Cantal

15-BM	F-JDEP	Air Création Buggy		
15-BX		Air Création		
15-FP		Air Création Twin GTE XP15		
15-KM		Corsair JPX Souricette		

16 : Charente

16-AC		Ultrastar		
16-AK		Ultrastar		
16-AT		Dragon		
16-BF		Weedhopper AX-3		
16-BL	F-JKRH	Tecnam P.92 Echo		
16-BN		Mignet HM.360	158	F-PYKI
16-CP	F-JKSB	Microaviation Rotavia Storch		
16-DA		Squale		
16-DB		Magni M-14 Scout 2000 Gyro		
16-DH		Micro Aviation Pulsar		
16-DX		Piel CP.150 Onyx		
16-ED		Cobra		
16-EM	F-JKFE	Type unknown		
16-GD	F-JBOV	Tecnam P.92 Echo *(also marked 55-IE)*		
W16-JE		Magni M-20 Talon	409	
16-LD	F-JKQJ	Dyn'Aéro MCR-01C	145	

17 : Charente-Maritime

17-G		Mignet HM.1000 Balèrit 3X		
17-L		Huntair Pathfinder		
17-S		Trike 44PM	8300351	
17-X		Eipper Quicksilver MX-II		
17-AA		Léger Frères		
17-AS		Mignet HM.1000 Balèrit 3X		
17-AU		Zenith Baroudeur LS-120		
(2)		Jodel D.18	193	F-PSCG
17-BB		Quartz		
17-BD		Air Création		
17-BJ		Cosmos Chronos 16		
17-CB		Zenith Baroudeur		
17-CC		Weedhopper AX-3		
W17-CP		unidentified gyrocopter		
17-CV		Mignet HM.1000 Balèrit 3X *(sold as 95-GU?)*	24	
17-CY		Weedhopper AX-3		
17-DA		Mustang	044	
17-DB		Denney Kitfox		
17-DC		Top Concept Hurricane *(Replaced? Noted 2002 as Bu.133 replica)*		
17-DG		Mignet HM.1000 Balèrit 3X *(sold as 52-BF ?)*	28	
17-DJ		Weedhopper Europa 1		
17-DM		Weedhopper Europa 2		
17-DY		Air Création Quartz		
17-EA		Weedhopper AX-3		
17-EE		Weedhopper AX-3		
17-EF		Weedhopper Europa 2		
17-EJ		Micro Aviation Pulsar III		
17-FN		Mignet HM.1000 Balèrit 3X	64	
17-FR		Weedhopper AX-3		
17-FU		Weedhopper AX-3		
17-GD		Le Petaplume		
17-GE		Buccaneer II Floatplane		
17-GF	F-JAMJ	Mignet HM.1000 Balèrit	80	
17-HS		Mignet HM.1000 Balèrit		
17-HU		Zenair ZH.701		
17-HZ		Europa		
17-JJ		Skyranger		
17-JL		Mignet HM.1000 Balèrit		
17-JY		Mignet HM.1000 Balèrit	122	
17-KB		Air Création GTE Mild		
17-KD		Weedhopper		
17-LG	F-JCIZ	Mignet HM.1100 Cordouan		
17-LL		Mignet HM.1100 Cordouan		
17-LN		Mignet HM.1100 Cordouan	04	
17-LY		WDFL D4 Fascination		
17-MC		Chereau J-300 Joker		
17-ME	F-JCZS	Mignet HM.1100 Cordouan	8	
17-MJ		Weedhopper AX-3		
17-PJ		Jodel D.92 Bébé	88	F-PJKS

18 : Cher

18-AM		Club ASL18		
18-AS		Aériane Sirocco		
18-BB		Dynali Chickinox		
18-CB		Cosmos La Mouette		
18-CF		Cosmos		
18-CO		Air Création		
18-CU		Air Création		
18-DC		Cosmos		
18-DF		Air Création Quartz		

18-DO		Cosmos		
18-DP		Dynali Chickinox		
18-EO	F-JART	JCC Aviation J-300 Joker		
18-ER		Quicksilver GT500		
18-EX		Rans S-6 Coyote II		
18-FA		Air Création Fun		
18-FX		Aquilair		
18-GH		Cosmos / Top 14.9		
18-GS		Cosmos		
18-HA	F-JFRN	JCC Aviation J-300 Joker		18-BJ
18-HE	F-JFRR	B&F Funk FK-9 Mk III		
18-HF	F-JFQV	Flight Design CT 180	00-05-02-96	
18-HM		Dyn'Aéro MCR-01		
18-JM	F-JPAS	Aviasud Mistral		

19 : Corrèze

19-W		Trike		
19-DE		Quartz Trike		
19-EB		MD.03 (Biplane Amphibian)	01	

20 : Corse (2A : Basse-Corse, 2B : Haute-Corse)

20-H		Aériane Sirocco		
20-GS	F-JBXV	SG Aviation Storm 300 Special		
2A-G		Cosmos		
2A-AU		Synairgie 2-seater		
2B-H		Tisserand Hydroplum (prototype)		
2B-AA		Hydroplum Amphibian		

21 : Côte d'Or

21-AH		Cosmos Profile		
21-AJ		Mono Dragster		
21-AK		Aériane Sirocco		
21-AN		Chapelet		
21-AP		JC.24 Weedhopper		
21-AR		Pendulaire		
21-BC		La Mouette Cosmos		
21-BN		Croses Air Plume		
21-CB		Cosmos		
21-DR		Rans S-6ESDCoyote II		
21-EQ		Cosmos		
21-FH		Cosmos		
21-GB		Trike		
21-GG		Cosmos		
21-HC		Chariot		
21-HE		Dynali Chickinox		
21-HS		Air Création		
21-HT		Air Création		
21-HV		Cosmos		
21-IM		Cosmos		
21-IU		Rans S-6 Coyote II		
21-JR		Cosmos Bi Place/Chronos 16	21100	
21-JS		Cosmos Phase 2		
21-KJ		Air Création Ibis Quartz		
21-KL		Cosmos		
21-KM		Cosmos / La Mouette		
21-LC		Cosmos		
21-LD		Cosmos / Chronos 16		
21-LH		Cosmos		
21-LI		Rans S-14 Airaile		
21-LU		Cosmos		
21-MG		Cosmos		
21-MV		Pegasus Quasar		
21-NB		Cosmos		
21-NJ		III Sky Arrow 500TF	017	
21-NM		Cosmos Phase 2		
21-NN		Cosmos Phase 2 *(W/o 17.8.02)*		
21-NO	F-JCLP	Rans S-7 Courier		
21-NP		Zenair CH.601 Zodiac		
21-NQ		Cosmos	21230	
21-NY		Air Création XP GT BI		
21-OH		Cosmos Phase 2 Top 12.9		
21-OJ		Cosmos		
21-OR		Rans S-6ESDCoyote II		
21-OT		Ecolight X'Air		
21-PG		Rans S-6 Coyote II		
21-PO		Cosmos		
21-PU		ICP MXP-740 Savannah	06-98-50-089	
21-QD		Cosmos Bi Place/Chronos 16	B21262	
21-QF		Cosmos / Top 12.9	B21448	
21-QG		Tecnam P.92 Echo		
21-QK		Dyn'Aéro MCR-01	74	
21-QM		Cosmos / Chronos		
21-QP	F-JGTP	Dyn'Aéro MCR-01 *(to OO-D34)*	112	
21-QS		Dyn'Aéro MCR-01 ULC	169	
21-RA		Cosmos Mono / Topless	M0037	
21-RK		Dyn'Aéro MCR-01		
21-RM		Cosmos Bi Place/Chronos 16	21399	
21-RX		Dyn'Aéro MCR-01	170	
21-RY	F-JGNS	Fantasy Air Allegro SW	00-114	
21-SB		Rans S-7 Courier		
21-SC		Air Création XP		
21-SD		Humbert Tetras		
21-SG	F-JGOA	Dyn'Aéro MCR-01		
21-SI		Air Création GTi Clipper XP		
21-SJ		Cosmos Phase 2	21337	
21-SM		Cosmos / Top 14.9	B21467	
21-SP		Dyn'Aéro MCR-01E	01	
21-ST		Fly Synthesis Storch		
21-TL	F-JGQU	Dyn'Aéro MCR-01 ULC		
21-TM		Cosmos / Top 12.9		
21-TN		Cosmos / Top 14.9		
21-TV		Aquilair Swing L951 582 *(W/o 19.10.03)*		
21-UA	F-JGRL	Fantasy Air Allegro SW		
21-UB		Cosmos		
21-UO		Dyn'Aéro MCR-01	249	
21-VE		Dyn'Aero MCR-01		
21-VF	F-JGYN	Dyn'Aero MCR-01 Diesel (Siemens VDO)		
21-YC		Dyn'Aéro MCR-01 UL	305	

22 : Côtes-d'Armor

W22-C		SCA Lone Ranger		
22-M		Veliplane		
22-AP		Weedhopper		
22-AR		Air Création		
22-CK		Air Création Racer		
22-DE		Humbert Moto-du-Ciel		
22-DN		Rans S-6 Coyote II		
22-EA	F-JCDE	Rans S-6ESD Coyote II		
22-EL		Rans S-6 Coyote II		
22-FJ		Mignet HM.1100 Cordouan	21	
22-FO		Air Création Kiss		
22-FT		Quicksilver GT.500		
22-FX		Zenith ?		
22-GL		ICP Bingo 4S	03 08 52 159	
22-GV		Rans S-12 Airaile		

23 : Creuse

23-AF		Kolb Twinstar (?)		
23-AW		Weedhopper		
23-BH		AX-3		
23-BL		Joellev (Joker?)		
23-CA		(trike?)/ Air Création Quartz		
23-CD	F-JIFL	Sauper J300 Joker		

24 : Dordogne

24		Aériane Sirocco 377		
24-R		Zenith Baroudeur		
24-AB		Eipper Quicksilver MX-II		
24-AP		Air's Maestro		
24-AS		Eipper Quicksilver MX-II		
24-AX		Eipper Quicksilver MX-II		
24-BD		Soprano		
24-BE		J-3 Kitten		
24-BH		de Havilland DH.82A Tiger Moth (Scale Replica)		
24-BT		Top Concept Hurricane		
24-CG		Toper Tielman ?		
24-CO		Delpech MD.04 Airland		
24-CT	F-JASX	TEAM Mini-MAX		
24-DF		Top Concept Hurricane		
24-DQ		Quicksilver *(wing ex 24-BD)*		
24-EE		Top Concept Hurricane		
24-EF		Air Création GTE XP		
24-FL		Hurricane		
24-GH		Weedhopper		
24-GY	F-JKAH	ICP MXP-740 Savannah	12-97-50-072	27-LE
24-HB		Mignet HM.1100 Corduan	17	17-NF
24-HE		Air Création XS		
24-HF		Weedhopper		
24-HG		Weedhopper		
24-HH		Eipper Quicksilver MXL III Sport		
24-HI		Raj Hamsa X'Air		
24-HL		Air Création GT BI		
24-HV		Weedhopper		
24-IL		Top Concept Hurricane		
24-IN		Raj Hamsa X'Air		
24-JH		Air Création XP		
24-JM	F-JHYF	Xxtrim		
24-KI		Aeropro Eurofox		

25 : Doubs

25-J		ASW Microstar		
25-R		Kalbermatten Mini Spitfire		
25-AN		Ikarus Comco Fox-C22		
25-BD		SEP		
25-BM		Air Composite		
25-BX		Cosmos		
25-CD		Zenith Baroudeur		
25-CE		Air Création GTBI XP		
25-CI		Cosmos Chronos	B025	
25-CQ		Cosmos		
25-CR		Cosmos Chronos		
25-DF		Cosmos Chronos		
25-DG		Air Création		
25-DJ		Cosmos		
25-DQ		Air Création XP / Select		
25-DR		Rans S-6 Coyote II		
25-DV		Moto du Ciel		
25-ED		Air Création		
25-EG		Airborne Australia Cosmos Chronos		
25-EQ		Rans S-6 Coyote II		
25-FP		Air Création SX-II		
25-GE		Cosmos Chronos		
25-GV		Comco Ikarus Fox-C22		
25-HL		Air Création GTE Clipper XP		

25-HN		Air Création SX II		
25-HO		Comco Ikarus Fox-C22		
25-HV		Cosmos Merlin		D-MMWW ?
		(Now reported as Sun & Moon Titan or as a Magic!)		
25-IC		Rans S-6ESD Coyote II		
25-IE		Rans S-6ESD Coyote II		
25-IJ		Zenair CH-701 STOL		
25-IT	F-JCLN	Air Création Clipper		
25-IV		B&F Funk FK-9	81	
25-JE		Air Création Clipper		
25-JI	F-JGNC	Comco Ikarus Fox-C22		
25-JM		Cosmos		
25-JQ		Comco Ikarus Fox-C22		
25-JS		Aviakit Hermes Adventure		
25-KB	F-JDFK	Humbert Tetras		
25-KC		Skyfly S-34 Skystar	017	
25-KE		Ecolight AFM		
25-LB		Air Création GT 582		
25-MF		Air Création		
25-MN		Light Aero Avid Flyer *(Also marked F-WSDC)*	423	
25-MX		Noin Exel		
25-NB	F-JBRU	Rans S-6 Coyote II		
25-NG		SG Avn Storm 300S		
25-NH		Buse'Air		
25-NQ	F-JGPH	Best Off Sky Ranger		
25-NX		Air Création Racer SX II		
25-NY	F-JGPX	Zenair CH-701 / Dedalius Pegastol wing		
25-OD		Jodel D.18	33	F-PYXL
25-OG	F-JGPJ	ATEC Zephyr		
25-PA		B&F Funk FK-9 TG		
25-PH		Jodel D.18	370	F-PRSB
25-PU		Jodel D.92 Bébé	775	
25-QF		Apollo Fox		
25-QG		Jabiru (tailwheel)		

26 : Drôme

26-G		Air Création		
26-AJ		Quartz 18		
26-AP		Air Création Alpair Chariot		
26-AS		Air Création		
26-BL		Air Création		
26-BO		Air Création XP		
26-BP		Air Création		
26-BU		Air Création SX		
26-CR		Air Création Alpair Chariot		
26-DD		Air Création Fun		
26-DE		Air Création XS		
26-EC		Air Création		
26-EE		Cosmos		
26-EJ		Air Création Fun		
26-ER		Air Création		
26-ES		Weedhopper	B1062930	
		(Also carries c/n B3043088)		
26-EV		Quicksilver GT-500		
26-FF		Air Création S		
26-FG		Air Création SX		
26-FK		Weedhopper		
26-FR		Air Création Fun		
26-FS		Air Création Fun		
26-FY		Weedhopper		
26-GB		Bifly	1	
26-GD		Air Création XP		
26-GE		Weedhopper		
26-GQ		Air Création Safari		
26-GS		Air Création Quartz		
26-GT		Aviasud		
26-GU		Air Création GT BI SX		
26-GV		Air Création		
26-GX		Mignet HM.1000 Balèrit		
26-HG		Air Création		
26-HL		Aviasud Xpair 65 *(W/o 27.4.03)*		
26-HP		Air Création XP		
26-IB		Airwave		
26-IL	F-JCTY	Zenair CH-701 STOL		
26-IR		Weedhopper	B1061140	
26-IV		Flexwing		13-CR
26-JE		Air Création		
26-JH		Air Création Mild		
26-JO		Sirius		
26-JS		Air Création / Pegasus		07-T
26-JV		Air Création Racer XP		
26-JX		Air Création		
26-KB		DTA Dynamic 15		
26-KN		ULM Evasion		
26-KR		III Sky Arrow		
26-KZ		Aviasud Albatros		
26-LA		Denney Kitfox III		
26-LB		Air Création		
26-LF		Air Création		
26-LK		Air Création XP		
W26-LL		Air Création		
26-LO		Aero Services Guepard		
26-LS		"Sunny"		
26-MD		Light Aero Avid Flyer		
26-ME	F-JAWB	Air Création GT BI SX		
26-MO		Best Off Sky Ranger		
26-MP		Dynamic 15		
W26-MQ		Jodel D.9 (?)		
26-MR		Air Création Kiss 450B	A01058-1051	
26-MS		Air Création		
26-MT		Air Création GT BI		
26-NB		Cosmos Bi Place	21460	
26-RC		Asso Aeri Asso V Champion V		

27 : Eure

27-H		Synairgie Puma BI		
27-AC		Aerospecial Airpuce		
27-BG		Eipper Quicksilver MXL-II		
27-CG		JPK		
27-DG		Cosmos		
27-DH		Synairgie		
27-DV		Air Création		
27-DY		Synairgie		
27-EM		Puma		
27-EV		Dynali Chickinox Kot-Kot III		
27-EX		Cosmos/La Mouette		
27-FB		Synairgie		
27-FI		Puma		
27-FK		Mignet HM.360	01	F-WNUQ
27-FO		Synairgie Puma		
27-FS		Air's Maestro 2		
27-FT		Synairgie Puma		
27-FZ		Cosmos		
27-GA		Weedhopper		
27-GO		Air Création Safari		
27-GP		Allegro 1		
27-GQ		Air Création		
27-GT		Air's		
27-GU		Air Création XS		
27-GW		Puma		
27-GZ		Aviasud Mistral		
27-HD		Cosmos		
27-HM		Weedhopper		
27-HN		Air Création		
27-HS		Europa		
27-HU		Best Off Sky Ranger		
27-HZ		ICP MXP-740 Savannah	A6 07-93-50-008	
27-IC		Mignet HM.1000 Balèrit		
27-IH		Aviasud Albatross		
27-IK		Evasion		
27-IN		Cosmos		
27-JF		Best Off Sky Ranger		
27-JG		RC.01 Courtonne		
27-JN		Zeff		
27-KS	F-JCLG	Zenair CH.701 STOL	A6-04-91-1060	
27-LB		Best Off Sky Ranger		
27-LH		Aviasud Albatros 582		
27-LM		Dynamic 15/582	20/2000	
27-LQ	F-JFVP	Comco Ukarus Fox C-22		
27-MA		ICP MXP.740 Savannah	12-96-50-049	
27-MB		Brügger MB.2 Colibri	180	F-PYOI
27-MC		ICP MXP.740 Savannah	01-98-50-077	*(see 27-MO)*
27-ML		Rans S.6 Coyote II		
27-MO	F-JFVD	ICP MXP.740 Savannah	08-99-50-126	
27-MQ		Synairgie		
27-NC		Synairgie		
27-NI	F-JFVJ	ICP MXP.740 Savannah	08-99-50-125	
27-NQ		Air Création XS		
27-NR		Air Création XS Twin / Kiss		
27-NT		ICP MXP.740 Savannah	02-00-51-002 K4	
27-NW		Cosmos		
27-NY		Rans S-6 Coyote II		
27-OB	F-JCLG	ICP MXP.740 Savannah	05-00-51-012 K4	
27-OG		Micro Aviation Pulsar III		
27-OH	F-JFVN	ICP MXP.740 Savannah	10-00-51-026	
27-OM		Aviakit Vega		
27-PE		ICP MXP.740 Savannah		
27-PL		ICP MXP.740 Savannah	01-10-51-100	
27-PQ		Fly Synthesis Storch		
27-PX		ICP Super Bingo 582	01 12 52 040	
27-QE		ICP Super Bingo	01 12 52 046	
27-QF		ICP Super Bingo 582	01 12 52 045	
27-QN		(trike) / Chronos		
27-QY		ICP MXP.740 Savannah	01 12 51 127	
27-RA		ICP Super Bingo	02 11 52 080	
27-RM	F-JFVW	ICP Bingo 4S/ HKS700E	03 06 52 116	

28 : Eure-et-Loir

28-C		Langlois Eldor		
28-D		Pendulaire Azur (Also reported as Mustang)		
28-R		Air Création		
28-U		Skycraft AJS.2000		
28-V		Eipper Quicksilver MX		
28-AC		Aiglon 01		
28-AO		Charcoal Raven X	HN003	
28-BG		Allegro		
28-BJ		Air's Maestro 2		
28-BL		Air's Maestro		
28-DE		Weedhopper JC-24	9072521	
28-DQ		Weedhopper JC-24		
28-EP		Renegade 503		
28-EV		Air Création		
28-EY		Pegasus		
28-FC		Comco Ikarus Fox-C22		

28-FJ		Allegro II		
28-FM		Springbok		91-IF
28-FN		Top Commander Tempest		
28-FP		Air Création		
28-FQ		Air Création /Cosmos		
28-FT		Comco Ikarus Fox-C22		
28-GJ	F-JALL	JCC Aviation J-300 Joker		
28-GN		Weedhopper		
28-GS		Renegade 503		
28-GT		Air Création GT Fun		
28-HO		Air's Maestro 2		
28-HP		Aviasud Mistral		
28-HS		Epervier		
28-HY		Aviasud Albatros		
28-IM		Weedhopper		
28-IP		Air Création		
28-JF		Air Création		
28-JL		Renegade 503		
28-JS		Aviasud Mistral		
28-KA		Weedhopper AX-3		
28-KD		Rans S-6 Coyote II		
28-KN		Falcon Daxiwing		
28-KW		Murphy Renegade Spirit		
28-KZ		European Airwings Sprinbok 3000		
28-LB		Comco Ikarus Fox-C22		
28-LH		Rans S-6 Coyote II		
28-LI		Comco Ikarus Fox-C22	9411-3637	
28-LJ		Weedhopper AX-3		71-CO
28-LV		Synairgie		
28-LW	F-JBJE	Humbert Tetras		
28-ME		Rans S-6 Coyote II		
28-MO		Comco Ikarus Fox-C22		
28-MS		Aquilair Swing		
28-MZ	F-JFOK	Rans S-6 Coyote II		
28-NA		Aviasud Mistral		
28-ND		European Airwings Maestro II		
28-NE		Air Création		
28-NM		Comco Ikarus C-42 Cyclone		
28-NN		Air Création Clipper GTE XP		
28-NQ		Air Création Clipper GTE XP		
28-NR		Rans S-6 Coyote II		
28-NV		Air Création GT		
28-NX		B&F Funk FK-9	76	
28-NZ		B&F Funk FK-9TG	67	
28-OO		Mignet HM.360	97	F-PYHC
28-PE		B&F Funk FK-9TG	74	
28-PG		Rans S-6 Coyote II		
28-PL	F-JFQS	Rans S-7 Courier		
28-PM		Comco Ikarus Fox C-22	9511-3696	
28-PO		Air Création Clipper GTE		
28-PP		III Sky Arrow 500TF	040	
28-PT		Air Création Quartz		
28-QC		Air Création Clipper GTE		
28-QD		Air Création Clipper GTE		
28-QE		Air Création GT BI / XP		
28-QP		Rans S-6ESD Coyote IIXL		
28-QQ	F-JCQT	B&F Funk FK-9TG Mk.II	093-TG912	
28-RC	F-JDAS	Rans S-7 Courier		
28-RJ		B&F Funk FK-9 Mk.II		
28-RL	F-JFGF	Weedhopper		
28-RR		Comco Ikarus C-42 Cyclone		
28-RV		Zenair CH.701 STOL		
28-RX		Air Création		
28-SA		Comco Ikarus Fox C-22	9501-3638	
28-SK	F-JBGS	Comco Ikarus C-42 Cyclone		
28-SL	F-JFOR	Rans S-6 Coyote II		
28-SM		Air Création GTE		
28-SN		Air Création XP		
28-SO		Air Création		
		Also reported as Rans S-6 Coyote, .04		
28-ST		Comco Ikarus Fox C-22		
28-SX		Air Création		
28-SY		Humbert Tetras		
28-TA		Rans S-6 Coyote II		72-CL
28-TC	F-JDCX	Rans S-6 Coyote II		
28-TD		Denney Kitfox	785	
28-TK		Air's Maestro 2		
28-TQ		Rans S.6 Coyote II		
28-TU		Air Création Buggy		
28-UC		Aviasud Mistral		
28-UK		Eipper Quicksilver MX		
28-UO		Fly Synthesis Storch		
28-UT		Air Création Buggy		
W28-UV	F-JFUM	Fantasy Air Allegro		
28-UW		Air Création GT BI		
28-UY		Comco Ikarus C-42 Cyclone		
28-VI		Pulsar 582		
28-VN		Cosmos		
28-VP	F-JFOU	Humbert Tetras		
28-VS	F-JFSV	Tecnam P.92S Echo		
28-VV	F-JFSW	Evektor EV.97 Eurostar	2001-10-14	
28-WF		Comco Ikarus Fox C-22		
28-WH		Air Création Clipper / Kiss		
28-WN		Air Création XP		
28-WS		Aero Services Guepy Jabiru 80		
28-WT		Pipistrel/Zen ULM Sinus		
28-XH		Cosmos XP		
28-XL		Comco Ikarus C-42 Cyclone		
28-XN	F-JFNQ	Pipistrel/Zen ULM Sinus		
28-XP		Fly Synthesis Storch XS		
28-XV		Fly Synthesis Storch *(W/o 9.6.02)*		
28-XY		Fly Synthesis Storch		I-5330
28-YA		Remos G3 Mirage		
28-YE		Fly Synthesis Storch XS		
28-YM		Light Aero Avid Flyer		
28-YO		Zenair CH-601 Zodiac	6-9110	
28-YT		Air Création Twin / iXess		
28-YV		Magni M-16 Gyro		
28-YW		Air Création SX		
28-ZA		Fly Synthesis Wallaby		
28-ZD	F-JFAK	Aviakit Vega		
28-ZE	F-JPAF	ICP Super Bingo	03 01 52 089	
28-ZF		Weedhopper		
28-ZN		Aero Services Guepy Club 582T		
28-AAD	F-JFQT	Aero Services Guepard		
28-AAM		Impulse 100		

29 : Finistère

29-H		Eipper Quicksilver MX		
29-AA		Bidulum		
29-AF		Air Création		
29-AX		Air Création		
29-AZ		Flipper		
29-BI		Air Création		
29-BK		Air Création		
29-CD		Cosmos Echo 12		
29-CF		Rans S-6E Coyote II		
29-CG		Rans S-6 Coyote II		
29-CH		Rans S-12 Airaile		
29-CR		Air Création		
29-CS		Mignet HM.14 Pou-du-Ciel		
29-CZ		Weedhopper AX-3		
29-DJ		Rans S-6 Coyote II		
29-DL		Air Action Quicky		
29-EM		TEAM Mini-MAX		
29-EX	F-JHMS	Rans S-6 Coyote II		
29-FJ		Air Création *(Damaged 30.6.01)*		
29-FM		Chereau J-300 Joker		
29-FO		Rans S-6 Coyote II		
29-FY		Rans S-6 Coyote II		
29-GH		Cosmos Phase 2	916	
29-GI		Aero Services Guepy		
29-GX		Chapelet Lazer		
29-GY		Air Création Buggy		
29-HC		Rans S-6 Coyote II (Diesel)		
29-HD		Aviasud Mistral		
29-HS		Rans S-6 Coyote II		
29-IA	F-JHOO	Brugger Colibri ULM		
29-IC		Zenair CH-601UL Zodiac 'Quick'		
29-PO		Cosmos		
29-PQ		Air Création Kiss		

30 : Gard

30-U		Funfly		
30-AD		Eipper Quicksilver MX-II		
30-AO		Sirocco		
30-BM		JC-24 Weedhopper Europa II		
30-BN		Air Création XS		
30-BX		Dynali Chickinox		
W30-CE	F-JAAS	AX-3 Weedhopper Ultracam		
30-CH		Pegasus		
30-CN		Dynali Chickinox		
30-CP		Tefou Trike		17-AR
30-CT		Air Création Quartz SX		
30-CX		Air Création		
30-DC		Dynali Chickinox		
30-DD		Quicksilver MX		
30-DE		Air Création		
30-DF		Mignet HM.1000 Balèrit	55	
30-DH		JC-24 Weedhopper Europa II		
30-DK		Air Création		
30-DN		Weedhopper	B1072931	
30-DP		Rans (exact type unknown)		
30-DQ		Beaufils SE-5A Replica	A4850	
30-DS		Air Création		
30-EB		Dynali Chickinox		
30-ED		Air Création		
30-EF		Air Création Plus		
30-EG		Air Création Quartz		
30-EP		Aviasud Albatros		
30-EY		(Cessna 150 Replica)		
30-FD		Rossi 503S Pegasus		
30-FJ		Criquet		
30-FN		Air Création GTI		
30-FT		Air Création		
30-FU		Quicksilver GT		
30-FV		Aquilair		
30-FY		La Mouette		
30-GB		Air Création SX		
W30-GE		Solar Wings Pegasus Quasar IITC	6662	G-MYOD
30-GX		Fly Synthesis Storch		
30-HN	F-JCUO	Zenair CH.701 STOL		
30-IF		Air Création		

30-JA		Jabiru UL30-KA	
30-JJ	F-JJEY	Slepcev (type) Storch	
30-JL		Air Création	
30-JO		Fly Synthesis Storch	
30-JP		X'Air	
30-JY	F-JJEW	Jabiru UL	
30-JZ		Jabiru	

31 : Haute-Garonne

31-T		Eipper Quicksilver MX	
31-AA		Pegasus Quantum	
31-AH		Humbert Tetras 912B	
31-AI	F-JIAI	B&F Funk FK-9	09-116
31-AM		Humbert Tetras 912B	
31-AO	F-JIAO	B&F Funk FK-14 Polaris	
31-BH		Urban Air UFM-13 Lambada	
31-BI	F-JIBI	B&F Funk FK-9 Mk.III	09-03-153
31-BM		Pipistrel/Zen ULM Sinus	
31-BP	F-JIBP	B&F Funk FK-9 Mk.III	
31-BQ	F-JIBQ	B&F Funk FK-9 Club Mk.IV	
31-BR		Aeroservices Guepard 912	
31-BS		B&F Funk FK-9 Mk.III *(Damaged 30.5.01)*	
31-BU	F-JIBU	B&F Funk FK-12 Comet	012-058
31-BV	F-JIBV	B&F Funk FK-14 Polaris	014-010
31-CD		Weedhopper	
31-DE	F-JIDE	B&F Funk FK-12 Comet	012-012
31-DL		Eipper Quicksilver MX	
31-DR		Unidentified amphibian	
31-DT		Le Raitelet	CQR/1
31-DV		Eipper Quicksilver MX-II	1053
31-EJ		Eipper Quicksilver	
31-EN		JC-31D Weedhopper	
31-ET		Dallach Voltige	
31-EW		Humbert Tetras	
W31-FE		Le Gallen LLG.24	01
31-GS		Kitfox Koala	
31-GX		Denney Kitfox	
31-HA		Denney Kitfox	
31-HC		Dragon Light *(Dismantled .03)*	007
31-HI		Denney Minifox	
31-IJ		ULM Services Frelon	
31-IQ		Micro Avn Pulsar III	
31-JE		Aviasud Mistral *(Damaged 11.6.01)*	
31-JT		Delpech MD.04 Airland *(W/o 23.5.03)*	
31-JV		Air Création XPII	
31-JZ		Tecnam P.92 Echo	
31-KP		Best Off Sky Ranger 503	
31-KR		Zenair CH-701 STOL (tailwheel)	
31-KT		Humbert Tetras	
31-LR		MXP-740 Savannah	
31-OO		Zenith Baroudeur Aeronautique 2000	
31-RP		Humbert Tetras 912BS	
31-PQ		Humbert Tetras	
W31-SP		Unidentified gyrocopter *(W/o 18.10.03)*	
31-TA		ICP MXP-740 Savannah	
31-TH		Aviasud AE.209 Albatros	
31-TK		Rans S-6 Coyote II	
31-TU		Air Création Clipper GTE	
31-UM		Weedhopper AX-3	
31-UZ		B&F Funk FK-9 MkIII	
31-VD		Guepard AX-02	
31-VE	F-JIVE	B&F Funk FK-9TG Mk.III	09-03-112
31-VK		Air Copter DJP3	
31-VP	F-JIVP	B&F Funk FK-9 Mk.III	09-03-128

32 : Gers

32-AH		Cosmos	
32-AP		Deluc Gyrocopter	
32-AR		Best Off Sky Ranger	
32-BT		Moto du Ciel	
32-CV	F-JBCC	Ultralair JC.24 Weedhopper Sport	9122574
32-DA		Weedhopper JC-31	
32-HL		Henri Lascombes autogyro	
32-MD		Deluc Gyrocopter (2-seat)	
32-RE		Deluc Gyrocopter	

33 : Gironde

33-BL		Bombardier		
33-CO		Mustang		
33-CQ		Eipper Quicksilver MX		
33-CS		Eipper Quicksilver MX		
33-CU		Mustang		
33-CY		Mustang		
33-DD		Eipper Quicksilver MX-II		
33-DU		Aériane Sirocco	54	
33-DX		Top Concept Hurricane		
33-EB		Air's Allegro/La Mouette Hermes 16		
33-EG		Bidulum 43		
33-ES		JC.31 Weedhopper		
33-FC		Cobra		
33-FL		PGO Cobra		
33-FR		Eipper Quicksilver MX-II	1848	
33-FT		Pou du Ciel MF-02		
33-FZ		Mignet HM.14		
33-GJ		Aviasud Mistral		
33-GK		PGO Cobra		
33-GM		Mignet HM.1000 Balèrit	14	
33-GX		Mignet HM.1000 Balèrit	23	
33-HQ		Top Concept Hurricane		
33-IM		Landray GL-3	01	F-PYIL
33-IN		Gipsy *(W/o 30.10.98)*		
33-KF		Hurricane		
33-LL		Dynamic 503		
33-MQ		Air Création GT BI		
33-MT	F-JKAG	Mignet HM.1100 Cordouan	15	
33-PC	F-JKBM	Barry Souris Bulle		
33-PM		LUAL L11	01	
33-PW	F-JKCI	B&F Funk FK.14 Polaris		
33-QM		Humbert Tetras	"9417"?	
33-RB		Aero Services Guepard 912S		
33-RJ		Fly Synthesis Storch HS		
33-RK		Rans S-12 Airaile *(Damaged 12.6.03)*		
33-RR		Kappa KP2U Sova		
33-RS		Aeroprakt A22 Vision		
33-RV		Ozone paramotor		
33-SW		Aerotrophy Eurofox		
33-TG		Ozone paramotor		
33-TO		Aeroprakt A22 Vision		
33-TP		TL Ultralight TL-2000 Sting carbon		
33-UX		ELA-7C gyrocopter		

34 : Hérault

34-E		J-3		
34-F		Humbert Moto du Ciel		
34-V		Eipper Quicksilver		
34-AC		Aériane Sirocco		
34-AL		Aeropiel CP.150G Onyx		
34-AM		Mignet HM.14		
34-BB		Aériane Sirocco		
34-BC		Distri Snap Epsilon		
34-BD		Mignet HM.1000 Balèrit 3X		
34-BO		Weedhopper		
34-BR		Air's Maestro		
34-CC		Eipper Quicksilver MX		
34-CD		Quicksilver		
34-CE		Eipper Quicksilver MX-II		
34-DJ		Renegade		
34-DU		Air's Allegro		
34-DV		Air's Allegro		
34-DX		Air's Maestro		
34-DY		Air's Allegro		
34-EA		Air's Maestro		
34-EB		Air's Allegro		
34-EF		Eipper Quicksilver MX		
34-EG		J-3 Kitten		
34-EH		Eipper Quicksilver MX		
34-EL		JC-31 Weedhopper		
34-EP		Dynali Chickinox		
34-EQ		Dynali Chickinox		
34-ER		Eipper Quicksilver MX-II		
34-EY		Weedhopper JC-24 Sport		
34-FB		Top Concept Hurricane		
34-FI		Eipper Quicksilver MX-II		
34-FJ		Thruster TST		
34-FL		Eipper Quicksilver GT-400		
34-WFM		Air Création GT BI Quartz		
34-FP		Air Création		
34-FQ		Eipper Quicksilver MX		
34-GC		La Mouette Cosmos		
34-GD		Cobra		W34-GD
34-GG		Weedhopper		
34-GJ		Weedhopper 1		
34-GQ		AX-3 Weedhopper Twin		
34-GU		AX-3 Weedhopper		
34-GV		Eipper Quicksilver MX-II		
34-G .		Air Création GT-BI X5		
34-HB		Aeriane Sirocco		
34-HC		AX-3 Weedhopper Amphibian		
34-HF		Weedhopper		
34-HL		Eipper Quicksilver MX-II	1262	
34-HU		Tempête		
34-HX		AX-3 Weedhopper		
34-IC		AX-3 Weedhopper		
34-ID		Weedhopper		
34-IE		Weedhopper		
34-IH		AX-3 Weedhopper		
34-II		AX-3 Weedhopper		
34-IK		Weedhopper		
34-IM		AX-3 Weedhopper		
34-IT		AX-3 Weedhopper		
W34-JP		Campana		
34-KD	F-JJKN	Top Fun		
34-KN		Air Création		
34-MB		TEAM Mini-MAX		
34-MJ		Rans S-6 Coyote II		
34-MN		Mignet HM.1000 Balèrit		
34-MP		Air Création GTE		
34-NB		Rans S-6 Coyote II		
34-NI		Weedhopper *(W/o 6.8.01)*		
34-NP		Weedhopper		
34-OO		Air Création XPClipper		
34-PH		Humbert Tetras		
34-PN		Aviasud Albatros		

34-PY		Humbert Tetras		
34-QO		Aviasud Albatros		
34-RB		Aviasud Albatros		
34-RU		Denis Chevillet Micro B		
34-SA		Flight Design CT		
34-SB	F-JBGD	Best Off Sky Ranger		
W34-SX		Trim		
34-VC		TL Ultralight TL-2000 Sting carbon		
34-VN		Advance Sigma paramotor		

35 : Ille-et-Vilaine

35-E		ULM 35/Djinn 300		
35-AK		Mignet HM.14		
35-AY		Air Création		
35-AZ		Air Création GT BI		
35-BC		Air Création GT BI		
35-BD		Mignet HM.1000 Balèrit 3X	60	
35-BF		Weedhopper AX-3		
35-BH		Air Création GT BI		
35-BM		Weedhopper		
35-BO		Croses Criquet	60	
35-BV		Air Création GT BI Quartz		
35-BY		TL Ultralight TL-32 Typhoon Sprint		
35-CI	F-JBGG	JCC Aviation J-300 Joker		
35-CK		Air Création		
35-CP		Rans S-12 Airaile		
35-DA		Air Création		
35-DB		Cobra		
35-DC		Air Création		
35-DD		Cosmos		
35-DP		Light Aero Avid Flyer	980	
35-DR		Air Création SX		
35-DW		Air Création SX		
35-EA		Rans S-6 Coyote II		
35-EE		Air Création Racer		
35-EF		Rand-Kar X'Air		
35-EO		Air Création Fun		
35-EP		Synairgie		
35-EV		Rans S-6 Coyote II		
35-EZ		TL Ultralight TL-2000 Sting carbon		
35-FL		Rans S-6 Coyote II		

36 : Indre

36-AA		Trike		
36-AD		Trike		
36-AG		Air Création GT BI Quartz		
36-AI		Humbert Moto du Ciel		
36-AJ		Trike		
36-AL		Air Création GT BI Quartz		
36-BA		Air Création GT BI Quartz		
36-BF		Air Création GT BI Quartz		
36-BO		Air Création GT BI Quartz		
36-BX		Breezy RLU.1		
36-CC		Trike		
36-CE		Hovey Delta Hawk II (2-str)		
36-CI		Puma		
36-DS		Air Création Quartz		
36-DT		Air Création Fun / GT Mild		
36-EJ		Air Création		
36-EK		Ikel		
36-ER		Pegasus Quantum		
36-ES		Humbert Moto du Ciel		
36-EY		Cosmos Trike		
36-FF		Synairgie Puma *(Also reported as Colibri Air)*		
36-FH		Synairgie		
36-FJ		Air Création Fun		
36-FM		Syna Aero Euro		
36-FN		Puma		
36-FO		Air Création		
36-FP		Synairgie		
36-FQ		Air Création		
36-FT		Puma		
36-GN		Puma B1 *(now Air Création XP ?)*		
36-HM		Synairgie		
36-HH		Croses Pou-type		
36-HR		Air Création XS		
36-HX		Synairgie		
36-HZ		Air Création Mild		
36-JW		Cosmos		
36-KC		Air Création		
36-KE	F-JFTU	Humbert Tetras		
36-KI		Aviakit Hermes 2		
36-KL		Air Création XP		
36-KT	F-JFOW	Humbert Tetras		
36-KV		CRI 01 gyrocopter		F-WZKV
36-LB		Corrado		
36-LH		Tecnam P.92 Echo Super		
36-LK		TEAM Mini-MAX		
36-LM		unidentified gyrocopter *(W/o 17.11.02)*		
36-LN	F-JFQZ	Aviakit Vega		
36-LQ		Air Création		
36-LS	F-JFSL	European Airwings Maestro II		
36-LT		Raj Hamsa X'Air (Reported as Air Création XP 5.03)		
36-LV	F-JFSM	B&F Funk FK-9 Mk.III	09-147	
36-LW		Zephr		
36-LY		III Sky Arrow 500TF		
36-MA		Raj Hamsa X'Air		
36-MC	F-JFUP	Dyn'Aéro MCR-01	14	
36-ME		Humbert Tetras		
36-MH		Air Création		
36-MK		Best Off Sky Ranger		

37 : Indre-et-Loire

37-B		Trike		
37-H		Veliplane		
37-N		Trike		
37-X		Aeropiel CP.150 Onyx	48	
37-AA		RH.02		93-AD
37-AD		Azur		
37-AK		Synairgie		
37-AX		Synairgie		
37-BI		Weedhopper	8032376	
37-BP		Plus		
37-BR		Air Création Quartz		
37-BS		Air Création		
37-BT		Air Création		
37-BU		Air Création		
37-CA		Air Création		
37-CB		Air Création GT BI		
37-CC		JCC Aviation J-300 Joker		
37-CD		Air Création Quartz X5		
37-CE		Air Création		
37-CH		France Air Ceyx 2200/18 *(Damaged 17.4.03)*		
37-CL		Air Création GT BI		
37-CO		PGO Cobra		
37-CP		Mudry Baroudeur	319	
37-CS		Air Création		
37-CU		Patrifor		
37-DI		Safari		
37-DJ		Air Création Quartz		
37-DK		JCC Aviation J-300 Joker		
37-DP		Air Création Quartz		16-DP
37-DS		Aquilair / Cosmos Chronos		
37-DT		Air Création Quartz		
37-DU		Air's Maestro 2		
37-DX	F-JBRN	JCC Aviation J-300 Joker		
37-EA		Kolb Twinstar		
37-EB		Safari		
37-EC		Pagojet		
37-EP		Air Création GT BI Quartz SX		
37-ES		JCC Aviation J-300 Joker		
37-EU		Safari		
37-FA		Weedhopper AX-3		
37-FB		L.X.P.		
37-FK		Air Création Quartz X5		
37-GB		Cosmos Trike		
37-GP		Pagojet		
37-GR	F-JAOU	JCC Aviation J-300 Joker		
37-GS		Air's Maestro 2		61-CA
37-HC		Air's Maestro 2		
37-HD		Air Création Quartz		
37-HI		B&F Funk FK-9 Mk.III		
37-HL	F-JATT	JCC Aviation J-300 Joker		
37-HU		Ultrastar		
37-HZ		Onyx Biplane		
37-IQ		Air Création GTE XP		
37-JD		Aviasud Albatros AE-209	57	
37-JE		Cosmos		
37-JF		Weedhopper		
37-JU		Air Création GT-BI		
37-JW		Colibri		
37-KA		JCC Aviation J-300 Joker		
37-KD		Weedhopper		
37-KN	F-JFOT	Air Création GTE Clipper XP		
37-KP		Best Off Sky Ranger		
37-KS		Caprice 21		
37-KU	F-JFSC	Aviasud Mistral		
37-KY	F-JFSU	Air Création GTE Clipper XP		
37-LA		Best Off Sky Ranger		
37-LB		Fly Synthesis Storch		
37-LE		Cosmos		
37-LR		Synairgie		
37-LS		Fly Synthesis Storch		
37-LH		Pelican		
37-LK		Air Création GT-BI		
37-LN		Weedhopper		
37-LS		Fly Synthesis Storch *(W/o 17.11.02)*		
37-MH		SMAN Pétrel		
37-MK		"AN VIA IT"		
37-ML		European Airwings Springbok 2000		
37-MN		Air Création Racer XP II		
37-MR		Air Création Clipper		
37-MX	F-JCUF	JCC Aviation J-300 Joker		
37-MY		TL Ultralight TL.232 Condor		
37-NE		European Airwings Springbok 2000		
37-NH		Aviasud Mistral *(Damaged 5.8.01)*		
37-NJ		Dynamic IS 503		
37-NO		Air Création XP		
37-NU		Fly Synthesis Storch		
37-PH		Humbert Tetras		
37-PI		unidentified gyrocopter		
37-PN	F-JFSA	Raj Hamsa X'Air 602T		
37-PQ		Synairgie (Cosmos wing)		

37-PT		X'Air 602		
37-PX		DT Dynamic 582		
37-QA		Pegasus		
37-QB		Sauper J-300 Joker		
37-QE		Cosmos		
37-QI		Piel CP.462		
37-QL		Raj Hamsa X'Air		
37-QN		Synairgie		
37-QR		Comco Ikarus Fox C-22		
37-QU		Jodel D.19	261T	F-PCSJ
				F-WCSJ
37-QV		Light Aero Avid Amphibian	24	F-WZUF(2)
37-QZ		Air Création GTE Clipper	A99B8-9135	
37-RC		Best Off Sky Ranger		
37-RI		Air Création Clipper / XP *(for sale)*		
37-RO		Best Off Sky Ranger		
37-RR		Air Service Guepy Jabiru 80		
37-RS		Sauper J-300 Joker		
37-RU		Best Off Sky Ranger		
37-RV		Flight Design CT-2K		
37-RX		Air Création Clipper		
37-RZ		Ekolot JK05 Junior		
37-SK		DTA Dynamic 503		91- . .
37-SQ		B&F Funk FK-9		
37-SS		Aero Services Guepy Jabiru 2/2		
37-SV		Sauper J-300 Joker 3		
37-TB		Sauper J-300 Joker		
W37-TF		Alpi Aviation Pioneer 300		
37-TG	F-JGXG	Sauper J300 Joker (72-GL internally)		
37-TS		Air Création Clipper/ Kiss		
37-TX		Air Création Clipper / iXess		
37-UA		Weedhopper		
37-UQ		Air Création Clipper / iXess		

38 : Isère

38-V		JC-31 Weedhopper		
38-AQ		Aerosport Puma	S.195/365	G-MBBU
38-AV		Croses Air Plume	18	
38-BG		Solar Wings Puma		55-Y
38-BH		Cosmos Elf		
38-BT		CFM Shadow		
38-CE		Cosmos Chronos		
38-CM	F-JAVL	SMAN Pétrel, *noted 4.00*	045 ?	54-PL
				56-CM
38-CQ		Air Création Racer A6		
38-CR		Cosmos		
38-DQ		Weedhopper		
38-ER		Pegasus Quantum		
38-ET		Rans S-6 Coyote II		
38-EU		Rans S-6 Coyote II		
38-FC		Weedhopper	B1101148	72-ED
38-FR		Rans S-6ES Coyote II *(W/o 4.1.03)*		
38-FT		Pendulaire		
38-FU		Pendulaire		
38-GY		CP.152B Onyx	140	
38-HV		Rans S-6 Coyote II		
38-IA		Air's Maestro 2		
38-ID		Quicksilver MXE Sport		
38-IO		Air Création		
38-IZ		unidentified paramotor		
38-JA		TEAM Mini-MAX 1500R		
38-JG		Best Off Sky Ranger		
38-JH		Rans S-6 Coyote II		
38-KA	F-JEJM	Aviakit Hermés (Code "FB")	FR977R5	
38-KC		Humbert Tetras		
38-KK		Air Création		
38-KQ		TEAM Mini-MAX		
38-LC		Rans S-6ESDCoyote II		
38-LM		Light Aero Avid Flyer	692	
38-NL	F-JEPL	Best Off Sky Ranger (skis)		36-KM

39 : Jura

39-J		Safari		
39-AF		Eipper Quicksilver MX-II	1776	
39-BL		JC.31 Weedhopper		
39-BP		Cosmos/Atlas		
39-BV		Renegade 503		
39-BY		Renegade 503		
39-CC		Renegade 503	328	
39-ED		Koenig AK 09 Faucon		
39-ER		ICP MXP.740 Savannah		
39-FC	F-JCZX	Light Aero Avid Flyer		
39-FO	F-JCYT	Humbert Tetras		
39-FR	F-JGOJ	ICP MXP.740 Savannah	06 96 50 036	
		(Reported 8.01 as 39-RF)		
39-GS		Zenair CH-601UL Zodiac		
39-IT		Dynali Chickinox		

40 : Landes

40-D		Aerodyne Vector		
40-J		Aériane Sirocco		
40-L		JC.24 Weedhopper		
40-M		Eipper Quicksilver MX		
40-S		Dynali Chickinox		
40-AP		Trike		
40-AX		Trike		
40-EJ	F-JKCH	Best Off Sky Ranger		
40-ET		DTA Dynamic 15		
40-EU		Air Création		
40-EW		Tucan Fly		
40-EX		Jodel D.195		
40-EZ		Weedhopper (2-str)		
40-FI		B&F Funk FK-9 Mk.III	09-129	
40-UL		Twin Weedhopper		

41 : Loir-et-Cher

41-G		Pelican		
41-K		Antar		
41-AH		Labasse Griffon 41		
41-BI		Air Création Quartz		
41-BY		AX-3		
41-CD		Air Création GT BI Quartz		
41-CK		(trike)/ Air Création Kiss		
41-CO		AX-3		
41-DB		Air Création GT BI Quartz		
41-DJ		Synairgie		
41-ED		Air Création Quartz		
41-EX		AX-3		
41-GD		Air Création Clipper GTE / XP		
41-GE		Pendulaire XP		
41-GR		J-300 Joker		
41-GX		Rans S-7 Courier		
41-HA		Maestro		
41-HG		Fly Synthesis Storch HS		
41-HN		Best Off Sky Ranger		
41-HS		Tecnam P.92S Echo		
41-HT	F-JFPD	Flight Design CT	99 05 02 53	
		(Also reported as AX-3 .03)		
41-HX	F-JFPF	Arno J-300 Joker		
41-JA	F-JFPN	B&F Funk FK-9 Mk.III		
41-JK		unidentified gyrocopter		
W41-JL		Boutin Air Copter		
41-JP		European Airwings Springbok		39-GA
41-JX		J-300 Joker		
41-JY	F-JFNO	Raj Hamsa X'Air-F		
41-KD		AX-3		
41-KP		B&F Funk FK-9 Mk.III	111	
41-KS		"Aiglons"		
41-KU		Comco Ikarus C-42 Cyclone		
41-LI		TL Ultralight TL-2000 Sting carbon		
41-LL		Air Création GT BI Fun		
41-ME		Sauper ADV-01 Papango		

42 : Loire

42-M		Zenith Baroudeur		
42-N		JC.31C Weedhopper		
42-0		Zenith Baroudeur		
42-AJ		Zenith Baroudeur		
42-BA		HFL Stratos 300		
42-BY		Weedhopper		
42-CA		Cosmos Pegasus Q		
42-CK		Weedhopper		
42-CN		Humbert		
42-CY		Air Création Quartz		
42-DM		Aviasud Mistral		
42-DX		Best Off Sky Ranger		
42-ET		DTA Dynamic 503		
42-EU		Solar Wings Pegasus		
42-FU		TL Ultralight TL-232 Condor		
42-HC		ICP MXP.740 Savannah	01 05 51 079	
42-JC		Aquilair Chronos 16		

43 : Haute-Loire

43-J		J-3 Kitten		
43-N		Aquila S-440		
43-BMW		Air Création GT BI Quartz		
43-BS		Denney Kitfox		
43-BT		Helios		
43-CF		Cosmos		
43-DA		Aquilair Swing (also rep. as Cosmos wing)		
43-DD	F-JEAC	Rans S-6 Coyote II		
43-DK		Aquilair Swing		
43-GT		Aquilair Swing /Cosmos Ghost 16 wing		55-GI (wing)
43-IJ		Aquilair Swing 14		
43-JI		Aquilair Swing/ Ghost 16		

44 : Loire-Atlantique

44-L		Cosmos Chronos		
44-0		Concept		
44-S		Vector		
44-AF		Weedhopper		
44-AM		Dragon 150		
44-CD		Polaris		
44-DB		Cyclone Ax-3		
44-DL		Sirocco		
44-DU		Huiles Loto		
44-EB		*wreck noted, 1.02*		
44-FT		Cosmos Chronos		
44-FV		La Mouette Cosmos		
44-GB		AX-3		
44-GO		Cosmos		
44-HF		Cosmos Chronos		
44-HJ		Cosmos		
44-HK		Cosmos		

44-HR		"La Poste"		
44-HS		Cosmos		
44-HY		AX-3		
44-IC		Cosmos		
44-IL		Cosmos		
44-IU		Cosmos		
44-JM		Weedhopper AX-3		
44-KB		Rand-Kar X-Air		
44-KC		AX-3		
44-KU		Weedhopper		
44-LA		AX-3		
44-LF		Chronos		
44-LK		Cosmos		
44-LO		Rans S-6 Coyote II		
44-LS		Chronos		
44-LO		Rans S-6 Coyote II		
44-MB		Rans S-6 Coyote II		
44-MK		Cosmos		
44-MS		Aviasud Albatros		
44-MT		Air Création Mild		
44-ND		Rand-Kar X-Air		
44-NP		Barry Souricette		
44-OB		Cosmos		
44-OE	F-JHTP	Zenair CH-701 STOL		F-JBWZ
44-OK		Quicksilver GT500		
44-OL		Rand-Kar X-Air		
44-OO		AX-3		
44-OU		Rand-Kar X-Air		
44-OV		Rand-Kar X-Air		
44-PH		Rand-Kar X-Air		
44-PN		Rans S-6 Coyote II		
44-PO		Buse'Air 150		
44-PR		AX-3		
44-PX		HMD.380		
44-PY		Aviasud Albatros		
44-QE		ICP MXP.740 Savannah		
44-RH		Solar Wings Pegasus Quantum 15	6952	G-MYVF
44-RM		Cosmos		
44-RN		Aviasud Albatros		
44-RV		Rand-Kar X-Air		
44-SF		Rand-Kar X-Air		
44-SY		Chapelet Lazar		
44-TF		Rand-Kar X-Air F		
44-UH	F-JHTC	Cosmos Phase 2		
44-UJ		Raj Hamsa X'Air		
44-UQ		Trophy TT2000		
44-XD	F-JHWF	Rans S-12 Airaile *(New c/s F-JPAI ?)*		
44-XH		Brügger MB.2 Colibri		
44-XO	F-JHVR	X'Air 804T		
44-YH		Humbert Tetras		
44-ZG		Gyrocopter		
44-ZH		Magni M-16 gyro		
44-ZJ		Aerotrophy TL Sting		
44-ZP		Chapelet		
44-ZR		Magni M-18 gyro		
44-AAI		Eurowing Goldwing		
44-AAL		Fly Synthesis Storch CL *(W/o 17.11.02)*		
44-ABB		Aero 4000		
44-ABS		Chapelet Lazer/ Avant		
44-ABV	F-JHYL	TL Ultralight TL-2000 Sting		
44-ABY	F-JGAZ	Light Aero Avid Flyer IV		55-QH
44-ACB		Raj Hamsa X'Air Hanuman		
44-ACC		Zenair CH-601 Zodiac		
44-ACO		Raj Hamsa X'Air-F		
44-ACQ		unidentified gyrocopter		
44-ADF		Raj Hamsa X'Air-F		
44-ADS		Raj Hamsa X'Air Hanuman		

45 : Loiret

45-AG		Synairgie		
45-AP		Mustang		
45-BP		Air Création Racer SX 12		
45-BV		Synairgie		
45-CU		Piel CP.15 B	50	
45-DB		AX-3		
45-ED		Air Création		
45-EH		Cosmos		
45-EP		JCC Aviation J-300 Joker		
45-EX		SCEP Mustang		
45-FM		Air Création Quartz		
45-FO		Air Création		
45-GC		Mustang		
45-GG		AX-3		
45-GH		C A Bidulm		
45-GR		Air Création GT BI Quartz		
W-45-HY		Air Création XP		
45-JA		Air Création		
45-JI		Air Création Clipper		
45-KB		Synairgie		
45-KC		Air Création GT BI 16 SX		
45-KG		Mignet HM.293 Pou du Ciel		
45-KL		III Sky Arrow 501TF		
45-LF		Air Création (wing?)		
45-LG		Zenair CH-701 STOL		
45-LN		Cosmos		
45-LP		Aeros Stranger		77-VE
45-MA		SE.5 replica		
45-MB		"Wild Bird"		
45-MJ		Air Création Clipper		
45-NA		Zenair CH-701 STOL		
45-ND		III Sky Arrow 500TF		
45-NN		Zodiac Ultrastar	104	
45-NP	F-JFPQ	Dyn'Aero MCR-01	121	
45-NQ		Air Création Buggy Twin / Kiss		
45-PT		Cosmos Phase 2	21455	
45-QH		Cosmos		
45-QI		Air Création Buggy XP		
45-QJ	F-JFGH	B&F Funk FK-9 Mk.III (taildragger)		
W45-QK		Barry Souricette		
45-QN		TL Ultralight TL-2000 Sting carbon		
45-QW		ICP Super Bingo	02 09 52 070	
45-RF		Pipistrel/Zen ULM Sinus		
45-RG		Air Création / iXess		
45-RL		Action paramotor		
45-RQ		ATEC Zephyr 2000C		
45-SA		Urban Air Lambada		
45-YF		Air Création		

46 : Lot

46-AR		PGO Avn AJS 2000 Cobra		
46-BO		Aerolas Airland *(W/o 1.8.99)*		
46-CI		Rand-Kar X'Air 602T *(W/o 9.6.03)*		
46-FC		Synairgie		
46-IE		Synairgie		
46-PN		Humbert Tetras		

47 : Lot-et-Garonne

47-P		La Mouette Cosmos		57-AK
47-BJ		Atlas Wing		
47-BL		Air Création		
47-BY		ADR-20		
47-CK		Air Création Kiss		
47-CR		Cosmos		
47-DG		Mignet HM.14		
47-EB		Air Création GT BI Quartz		
47-EC		Air Création GT BI Quartz		
47-EI		Air Création Racer		
47-EO		Top Concept Hurricane *(W/o 9.7.01)*		
47-FK		La Moto du Ciel		
47-FN	F-JBBZ	Rans S-6 Coyote II		
47-FW		Air Création GT BI Quartz		
47-FY		Cosmos Chronos 16		
47-GE		Dauphin/Synairgie		
47-GG		Buccaneer II Amphibian		
47-GH		Air Création Racer		
47-GM		Aero Designs Pulsar		
47-GN		Air Création Racer		
47-GU		Weedhopper	B1081143	
47-GW		Air Création GT		
47-GY		Air Création GT		
47-HB		Weedhopper	0011129	
47-HD		Air Création GT BI X5		
47-HF		Air Création		
47-HQ		Rans S-6 Coyote II		
47-HY		Rans S-6 Coyote II *(To OO-C71)*	0295752ES	
47-IN		Buccaneer S2B		
47-JA		Rans S-6 Coyote II		
47-JC		Rans S-6 Coyote II		
47-JI		Synairgie		
47-JM		Air Création		
47-JP		Air Création		
47-KO		Mignet HM.1000 Balerit		
47-LW		Air Création GTE		
47-MA		Best Off Sky Ranger		
47-MB		Kappa KP2U Sova		
47-MC		Mignet HM.1100 Cordouan	11	
47-MJ		Best Off Sky Ranger		
47-ML		Air Création Racer	447	
47-MM		Top Concept Hurricane		wing of 16-CM
47-MQ	F-JKCR	Kappa KP2U Sova		
47-MV		Air Création		
47-MW	F-JKDA	Vol Mediterrani VM-1 Esqual		
47-MY		Rans S-7		
47-NA		Best Off Sky Ranger		
47-NB	F-JKDB	Kappa KP2U Sova		
47-NG		Kappa KP2U Sova		
47-NH		Kappa KP2U Sova		
47-NI		Buccaneer S2B		
47-NJ		Best Off Sky Ranger		
47-NZ		Air Création		
47-OE	F-JKEH	Kappa KP2U Sova		
47-OG		Comco Ikarus C-42 Cyclone (or 47-QG ?)		
47-OR		Air Création		
47-OY		Aeropro Eurofox		
47-PG		Best Off Sky Ranger		

48 : Lozère

48		Dragon 150		

49 : Maine-et-Loire

49-A		Air Création GT BI Quartz		
49-AL		Air Création GT BI Quartz		
49-BF		Ropulcia Colt		
49-BG		Microbel Must		

49-BP		Microbel Must		
49-BV		Synairgie		
49-CK		Unidentified flexwing		
49-DA		Chaser Microbel		
49-EU		Aerial Arts Chaser 377		
49-FO		CP.152B Onyx	50	
49-GB		Fulmar (?) Pendulaire *(W/o 15.4.01)*		
49-GE		Air Création Quartz		
49-HE	F-JHWX	Humbert Tetras		
49-HF		Air Création		
49-HO		Synairgie		
49-IB		Best Off Sky Ranger		
49-KL		Air Création		
49-KU	F-JHWS	Pipistrel Sinus		
49-LO	F-JHZC	TL Ultralight TL-2000 Sting carbon		
49-LP		Best Off Sky Ranger		
49-VU		Air Création GT BI Quartz		
49-RJ		Lemonnier Springbok 2000		

50 : Manche

50-U		Aerodyne Vector 627SR		
50-AF		Aerodyne 627SR Vector TM		40-D
50-AG		Air Création Quartz 180SX		
50-AI		Aerodyne Vector 627SR		
50-AJ		Air Création		
50-AN		Quartz X5		
50-AO		Air Création		
50-AQ		Quartz X5		
50-AV		Lemmonier Maestro		
50-BH		Fischer FP-202 Super Koala		
50-BI		Air Création		
50-BL		Air Création		
50-CG		Aviasud Mistral		
50-CJ		SE-5A Replica		
50-CN		Air Création GT BI SX		
50-CR		Air Création		
50-CU		Air Création		
50-CX		Air Création SX		
50-CY		Dynali Chickinox		
50-DF		Air Création		
50-DI		Air Création SX		
50-DP		Air Création GT BI		
50-DY		Air Création		
50-DZ		Air Création		
50-ED		Parapente		
50-EI		Air Création		
50-EN		Humbert Tetras		
50-EQ		Moto du Ciel		
50-EX		Air Création SXI		
50-FA		Air Création		
50-FB		Air Création		
50-FD		Croses Criquet ULM	114	
50-FH		Mustang		
50-FI		Pegasus		
50-FM		Air Création GT BI		
50-FN		Air Création Mild		
50-FO		Avions Guepard 912		
50-FR		Air Création Quartz		
50-FU		Air Création (Also reported as Mustang 3.04)		
50-FX		Chapelet BB		
50-FZ		Air Création		76-FE
50-GA		Synairgie trike		
50-GB		Air Création		
50-GC		Air Création GT BI		
50-GE		Aquilair (or Air Création ?)		
50-GJ		Weedhopper AX-3		
50-GK		Air Création SX		
50-GL		Air Création SX		
50-GO		Rans S-6 Coyote II		
50-GQ		Humbert Tetras (Also reported as Gyrocopter)		
50-GS		Air Création		
50-GT		Air Création		
50-GU		Air Création GT BI		50-DS
50-HB		Air Création		
50-HC		Air Création Quartz		
50-HJ		Air Création		
50-HL	F-JHGQ	Mustang	c/n 86 063	
50-HN		Air Création Quartz		
50-HP		Air Création		
50-HQ		Magni Gyro		
50-HS		Air Création GT BI		
50-HU		Dynali Chickinox		
50-HV		Air Création		
50-HX	F-JHGO	Zenair CH-601UL Zodiac		78-MT
50-HY		Air Création Fun		
50-IA		Best Off Sky Ranger		
50-IB		Air Création Twin		
50-ID		Air Création		
50-IE		Dynamic 582 / 16		
50-II		Air Création		
50-IK		Aviasud Mistral		
50-IL		Air Création XS		
50-IT		B&F Funk FK-9TG		
50-IV		Air Création SX		
50-IX		Air Création		
50-IY		Humbert Tetras		
50-JB	F-JHHI	Xxtrim		
50-JC		Air Création SX		
50-JE	F-JHGU	Best Off Sky Ranger		
50-JF		Excel		
50-JH		Air Création Quartz		
50-JL		Air Création XP		
50-JQ		Air Création XP		
50-JR		Aquilair		
50-JS	F-JHHT	Humbert Tetras		
50-JU		Profe Tukan		
50-KA		Croses ULM Pou du Ciel		
50-KC		Delta DTA trike } *both recorded 28.3.04 in*		
50-KC		Air Création SX } *different locations!*		
50-KH		Humbert Tetras 912CS		
50-KK		Best Off Sky Ranger		
50-KL		Air Création XP		
50-KN		Delta DTA (Now reported as Air Création trike)		
50-KP		Avant		
50-KU		Air Création XP		
50-LE	F-JHIW	ATEC Zephyr 2000		OK-DUA-04
50-LJ	F-JKDF	DTA Dynamic 15		
50-UC		Zenair CH-701 STOL		

51 : Marne

51-AA		Egrett Sophie		
51-AU		Jean Francois Mustang	86-055	
51-AV		Mustang		
51-BD		Cosmos Profil		
51-BF		Air Création		
51-BU		Mustang		
51-CL		Air Création SX		
51-DC		Humbert Moto-du-Ciel		
51-DJ		Breezy RLU.1 ("Pegase" ?)		
51-DN		Air Création Fun GT		
51-DS		Air Création		
51-EQ		Mignet HM.1000 Balèrit	41	
51-ES		Weedhopper		
51-ET		Rans S-12 Airaile		
51-EW		Air Création XP GT BI		
51-EX		Air Création Racer		
51-EY		Air Création		
51-FA		Aviasud Albatros	166	
51-FR		Cosmos		
51-FY	F-JBGL	Humbert Tetras		
51-GF		Aviasud Albatros		
51-GH		Gyrocopter		
51-GI		Air Création Safari		
51-GK		Dédé		02-AB
51-GL		TEAM Mini-MAX		
51-GP		Mignet HM.293 Pou du Ciel		
51-GQ		Air Création GTE SX		
51-GT		Interplane Skyboy		
51-HA		X'Air		
51-HE		X'Air		
51-HM		Jupiter		
51-HN		Helios		
51-HR		Cosmos		
51-HV		X'Air		
51-HW		Aeriane P-Swift		
51-IA		Air Création XP		
51-IB		Zenair CH-601 Zodiac		
51-IL		Ultralair JC-24 Weedhopper Sport		
51-IS		Zenair CH-701 STOL		
51-IT		Mustang		
W51-IX		Magni Gyrocopter		
51-JA		Cosmos		
51-JH		Air Création GT BI Buggy / XP		
51-JK		Ecolight X'Air		
51-JO	F-JGGQ	Micro Aviation Pulsar III - 912		
51-KM		Cosmos		
51-KQ		Evektor EV-97 Eurostar		
51-PX		Autogyro, type unknown		
51-SD		Air Création		
51-SR		Cosmos		

52 : Haute-Marne

52-AD		Cosmos		
52-AH		Cosmos		
52-AL		Cosmos		
52-AP		Cosmos		
52-AT		Cosmos		
52-AW		Cosmos		
52-AX		Cosmos		
52-BC		Cosmos		
52-BE		Air Création GT BI SX		
52-BF		Mignet HM.1000 Balèrit	28	17-DG
52-BG		Air Création GT BI SX		
52-BH		Weedhopper		
52-BL		Weedhopper		
52-BQ		Synairgie		
52-BR		Cosmos		
52-CA		Air Création		54-FV
52-CE		Air Création		
52-CI		Air Création		
52-CK		Air Création Fun		
52-CL		Cosmos		
52-CO		Air Création		

52-CQ		Air Création SX		
52-EC		Cosmos		
52-GG		Cosmos		
WHM-52		Mignet HM.1100 Cordouan		

53 : Mayenne

53-AJ		Mignet HM.1000 Balèrit		
53-DD		Tertraedre		
53-EB		Cosmos Chronos		
53-EH		Pegasus		
53-FG		ICP MXP-740 Savannah		77-YC
53-UV		Rans S-6 Coyote II		

54 : Meurthe-et-Moselle

54-V		Cosmos 250/Azure		
54-AC		Eipper Quicksilver MX		
54-AK		AEIM Epsilon		
54-AP		Kolb Ultrastar		
54-RR	F-JGBM	Mustang	920601	
54-AT		"Fujicolor"		
54-BH		Air Création XP GT BI		
54-BX		Huntair Pathfinder		
54-CC		Rans S-6 Coyote II		
54-CK		Guerpont Biplum		
54-DT	F-JAYT	Humbert Moto-du-Ciel		
54-EP		Eipper Quicksilver		
54-EX		Cosmos		
54-FF	F-JGBT	Weedhopper		
54-FX		Pegasus / Air Création		
54-GI	F-JAGP	Humbert Moto-du-Ciel		
54-GR		Murphy Renegade Spirit		
54-GS		Huntair Pathfinder *(Wrecked)*		
54-HD		Air Création XS		
54-HF		Nostalgair N3 Pup (Also reported as J-3 Kitten)		
54-HG		Cosmos Echo 12		
54-HJ		SMAN Petrel		
54-HL		Weedhopper JC.31		
54-HN		Humbert Moto-du-Ciel		
54-IA		Humbert Moto-du-Ciel		
54-IB		Cosmos		
54-IR		La Mouette		
54-JE	F-JAPR	Aviasud Albatros AE.209		
54-JL		Murphy Renegade Spirit	241	
54-JM		Air Création Mild GT		
54-JN		Piel CP.150 Onyx		
54-JS		AX-3		
54-KA		Ultralair AX-3 Weedhopper	0062663	LX-XGK
54-KG		Air's Maestro		
54-KK		Denney Kitfox		
54-KN	F-JBWK	ASL.18		
54-KP		Guerpond Autoplum 4-01	01	
54-KS		Murphy Renegade Spirit		
54-KU		Air Création Clipper		
54-KV		Air Création		
54-KX	F-JBMJ	Rans S-6XL Coyote II		
54-LA		Air Création Clipper XP GTE		
54-LB		Air Création Clipper GTE XP		
54-LD		Air Création GT		
54-LI		Air Création Clipper GTE		
54-LR		Air Création XP GTE		
54-LT	F-JBRX	Denney Kitfox		
54-LX		Air Création XP		
54-ME		Air Création XP Clipper GTE		
54-MH		Air Création Quartz		
54-MI		X'Air		
54-MP		Air Création XP Racer		
54-MS		Aviasud Albatros		
54-ND		Ecolight X'Air		
54-NN		Cosmos		
54-NO		Raj Hamsa X'Air		
54-NT		Air Création La Mouette/Ghost 14		
54-NV		Cosmos		
54-NX		Air Création XP Clipper		
54-NY		Trophy TT2000 STOL	9709007	
54-OA	F-JCPV	Micro Aviation Pulsar 2		
54-OD	F-JCSK	Humbert Tetras		
W54-OE		WagAero CUBy II		
54-OO		Air Création XB Vue 582 Max		
54-OP		Air Création GT		
54-OR		Air Création		
54-OY		Dynali Chickinox		
54-PA		Air Création XP		
54-PK		Cosmos		
54-PL	F-JAVL	SMAN Pétrel	045	38-CM/56-CM
54-PY		Humbert Tetras 912BS		
54-QA		Air Création XP Clipper		
54-QB		Air Création XP GTE Mild		
54-QD		Air Création XP GT BI		
54-QH		Light Aero Avid Flyer		
54-QL		Cosmos		
54-QM	F-JGPW	Fly Synthesis Storch		
54-QP		Humbert Tetras		
54-QT	F-JGAY	III Sky Arrow 500TF	040	
54-QV		Aviakit Vega 2000		
54-QX		Humbert Moto-du-Ciel (Also reported as Patrouiller)		
54-RJ		Dynali Chickinox		
54-RO		DTA Dynamic 582	00032	
W54-RQ		Scheibe SF-24 Motorspatz?		
54-RV		SE.5A Replica		
54-RY	F-JCBU	Pipistrel Sinus		
54-SA		Mignet HM.1000 Balèrit	078	ALAT/F-MUCB
54-SE		Humbert Tetras		
54-SF		Croses LC-6 Criquet	38	
54-SH		Cosmos Top 12.9		
54-SK		Weedhopper 2-str		
54-SL		Pottier P.130UL Bleu Citron	1022	
54-SP		Huntair Pathfinder		57-FC
54-SR		Jetfox		
54-SS		Flight Design CT-2K		
54-TA		Humbert Tetras		
54-TL		Aerotrophy Trophy 2000		
54-TN		Air Création Mild		
54-TO		Best Off Sky Ranger		05-CF
54-TP		Rans S-6 Coyote II		
54-TY	F-JGDI	Pipistrel/Zen ULM Sinus		
54-UC	F-JGDE	Light Aero Avid Flyer	AF692	
54-US		B&F Funk FK-12 Comet	051	D-M . . .
54-UU	F-JGDP	Humbert Tetras		
54-VO		Rans S-6 Coyote II		
54-VP	F-JGEO	Merlin		
54-XH	F-JGEM	Evektor EV-97 Eurostar	2002-15-21	
54-YH		Humbert Moto-du-Ciel		
54-YM		TEAM Mini-MAX		28-EM (?)
54-YY	F-JGFI	B&F Funk FK-9 Club		
W54-ZC		Comco Ikarus Fox-C22		
54-ZD	F-JGFK	Best Off Sky Ranger		
54- . .		Interplane Skyboy		

55 : Meuse

55-N		Aviasud Sirocco		
55-AB		Weedhopper		
55-AD		Ultralair JC.31C Weedhopper		
55-AU		Huntair Pathfinder		
55-CE		Mignet HM.1000 Balèrit	18	
55-CL		Aviasud Mistral		
55-CT		Ultralair JC.24 Weedhopper Sport		
55-CU		Dynali Chickinox		
55-CX		Denney Kitfox		
55-DB		Sky System		
55-DN		Air Création		
55-DP		Weedhopper	9042500	
55-DU		Cosmos Chronos		
55-EB		Huntair Pathfinder		
55-EG		Dynali Chickinox		
55-EI		Ultralair JC24 Weedhopper Sport *"La Poste" titles*	B2032997	
55-EV		Mignet HM.293A Pou-du-Ciel		
55-FA		Rans S-6ESD Coyote II		
55-FC	F-JBZI	Mignet HM.293 Pou-de-Ciel		
55-FE		Eipper Quicksilver GT-500-R582 *(Built by ULM Air Champagne)*	0060	
55-FG		Synergie		
55-FH		Air Création GT BI Fun / Quartz		
55-FM		Air Création		
55-FO	F-JAPB	Humbert Tetras		
55-FR	F-JBME	Ultravia PL-914 Pelican Super Sport		
55-FS		Moto-du-Ciel		
55-FT		Cosmos Chronos 12		
55-FX		Eipper Quicksilver GT-500		
55-GC		Dynali Chickinox		
55-GF	F-JGEW	Rans S-6ESD Coyote II		(ex F-JAMV)
55-GM		Micro Aviation Pulsar II		
55-GO		Cosmos		55-EH
55-GR		Cosmos		
55-GS	F-JCKR	Rans S-7 Courier		
55-GT		HM.293A Pou-du-Ciel		55-FC
55-HA		Light Aero Avid Flyer		
55-HE		Cosmos		
55-HG		Ecolight X'Air		
55-HH		Light Aero Avid Flyer	801	F-WRKH
55-HN	F-JBAL	Humbert Moto-du-Ciel		
55-HQ		Aquilair Swing 14		
55-HV		Jodel D.9 Bébé		
55-HW		Humbert Moto-du-Ciel		
55-HY		Mignet HM.1100 Cordouan	11	
55-IE	F-JBOV	Tecnam P.92 Echo *(also marked 16-GD)*		
55-IG		Dyn'Aéro MCR-01 ULC		
55-II		Dynali Chickinox		
55-IO		Fly Synthesis Storch		
55-IU		Air Création Clipper GTE XP		
55-IX	F-JGBR	Flight Design CT-180	99-04-03-52	
55-IY		Ecolight X'Air		
55-JC		Best Off Sky Ranger		
55-JO		Zenair CH.701 STOL II		
55-JP		Cosmos / La Mouette		
55-JT		Jodel D.20	11	F-PQUS
55-KH		Dynali Chickinox		
55-KJ		Aquilair Swing 14R		
55-KL		Air Création iXess		
55-MG		Micro Aviation Pulsar II		

56 : Morbihan

56		Zenith Baroudeur		
56-G		Zenith Baroudeur		

56-J		Veliplane		
56-K		Zenith Baroudeur		
56-L		Zenith Baroudeur		
56-N		SMAN	01	
56-U		Wida		
56-X		Danis Jumbo		
56-AJ		Weedhopper		
56-AR		SMAN Pétrel	01	
56-AV		SMAN Pétrel	001	
56-BA		SMAN Pétrel		
56-BK		Air Création Biplace		
56-BS		Denney Kitfox		
56-CH		SMAN Pétrel	044	
56-CQ	F-JBWG	Sauper J-300 Joker		
56-CR		Air Création		
56-DR	F-JBSW	SMAN Pétrel	061	
56-DV		Air Création XS		
56-EZ		Air Création		
56-GD		Magni M-14 Scout 2000 Gyro		
56-GI		Fly Synthesis Storch		
56-GK	F-JOAH	Tecnam P.92 Echo Super		
56-GL	F-JHQI	Raj Hamsa X'Air		
56-HG		Ekolot JK05 Junior	05.02.11	
56-HM		Air Création SX III		

57 : Moselle

57-F		Aériane Sirocco 377		
57-N		Lang JL-1		
57-P		Huntair Pathfinder		
57-AM		Dynali Chickinox		
57-BC	F-JBJQ	Moto-du-Ciel		
57-BD		Huntair Pathfinder		
57-BK		Aviasud Mistral		
57-BM		Air Création Quartz		
57-BO	F-JGEN	"Profil"		
57-BP		Huntair Pathfinder		
57-DN		Sunny		
57-ER		Humbert Moto-du-Ciel		
57-FL		Cosmos Chronos		
57-FS		Weedhopper	B1091145	
57-GG		Synairgie		
57-GP		Air Création		
57-GQ	F-JAVT	Aviasud Mistral		
57-GV		Tandem Air Sunny Sport RV		
57-HE		Synairgie		
57-HT		Rans S-14		
57-HX	F-JAZB	Ultralair JC.24 Weedhopper Sport	C2043015	
57-IT		Humbert Moto-du-Ciel		
57-IX		Huntair Pathfinder		57-D
57-JB		Weedhopper AX-3		
57-JC		Weedhopper AX-3		
57-JD		Cosmos Chronos 16		
57-JF		AX-3 Weedhopper		
57-JJ		Weedhopper	B3013088	
57-JK		Dynali Chickinox		
57-KA		Kolb Ultrastar		
57-KC		Dynali Chickinox		
57-KF		Rans S-6 Coyote II		
57-KL		Weedhopper AX-3		
57-LA		Ultralair JC.24 Weedhopper Sport		
57-LI		Solar WingsPegasus Quasar		
57-LK		Cosmos		
57-LL		Air Création		
57-LP		Cosmos		
57-LQ		Rans S-6 Coyote II		
57-LR	F-JBLU	Air Création GTE Clipper XP		
57-LT		Euronef ATTL-1		
57-LX		Technoflug Piccolo	103	D-MTOH
57-LY		Air's Maestro		
57-MD		Comco Ikarus Fox-C22		
57-MJ		Rans S-6 Coyote II		
57-MK		Solar Wings Pegasus XL-Quantum 15 (Also reported as Quasar, .01)		
57-ML		Aviakit Hermes		
57-MN		Murphy Renegade Spirit		
57-MS	F-JGDT	Rans S-6 Coyote II		
57-MV		TEAM Mini-MAX 1600R SpeedMax		
57-MY		Platzer Kiebitz		
57-NL		Rans S-6 Coyote II		
57-NM		Air Création GTE Clipper (Also reported as Murphy Renegade Spirit, .01)		
57-NS		Air Création XP		
57-NX		Let-Mont Tulak		
57-OG		Mignet HM.293 Pou du Ciel		
57-OH		Rans S-6 Coyote II		
57-OK		Comco Ikarus Fox-D	8510-FD34	LX-XOE D-MBOE
57-OL		Fantasy Air Allegro SW		
57-ON		Air Création Racer		
57-OO		Ultralair JC.24 Weedhopper Sport	1012867	55-DM
57-OP		P90 Cobra		
57-OY		Euroala Jet Fox 91		
57-PD		Mignet HM.1000 Balèrit	13	
57-PE		Light Aero Avid Flyer		
57-PH		Le Goeland	02	F-PDNE F-WDNE
57-PI		Dynali Chickinox		
57-PJ		"E.C.L." Pou-type	116	
57-PK		Albatross		
57-PM	F-JBZG	Aerotech Storch		
57-PN		Cosmos Phase 2	21086	
57-PO		Ecolight X'Air		
57-PP		Cosmos		
57-PQ		Air Création XP		
57-PR		Cosmos		
57-PU		Humbert Tetras		
57-PX	F-JGAF	Denney Kitfox		
57-PY		Dynali Chickinox Kot-Kot		
57-QA		Jet Fox		
57-QC	F-JGAV	Humbert Tetras		
57-QD		Aviakit Hermés		
57-QF		Aerostar Air Light Wild Thing WT-01	98 08 057	
57-QI		Humbert Tetras		
57-QL	F-JGAL	Best Off Sky Ranger		
57-QM	F-JGAH	TL Ultralight TL-232 Condor		
57-QP		Humbert Tetras		
57-QR		Zenair CH.701 STOL		
57-QU		DTA Dynamic 15		
57-QX		Rans S-6 Coyote II		
57-RF		Rans S-6 Coyote II		
57-RL		Humbert Tetras		
57-RN		Weedhopper	7032296	
57-RO		Rand-Kar X'Air 502T *(W/o 6.7.03)*		
57-RV	F-JGEQ	Aero Services Guepy		
57-SB		Fly Synthesis Storch		
57-SH		Rans S-12 Airaile		
57-SL		Air Création Racer		
57-SQ	F-JGCO	Humbert Tetras	791	
57-SR		Autoplum		W57-SR
57-SS	F-JGER	Stern Schmetterling 2000		W57-SS
57-TK		Platzer Kiebitz B9		
57-TT		Raj Hamsa X'Air		
57-UB		Best Off Sky Ranger		
57-UC	F-JGEP	Zenair CH-701 STOL		
W57-YR		Wezel / AlbastarApis 2	W002	

58 : Nièvre

58-AA		Aeromas 386		
58-AG		Eipper Quicksilver MX	5805	
58-AH		Eipper Quicksilver MX-II	1178	
58-AI		Eipper Quicksilver MX		
58-AS		Eipper Quicksilver MX		
58-AV		Zenith Baroudeur		
58-BB		Weedhopper		
58-BY		Galaxy		
58-CJ		Air Création Quartz		
58-CN		Air Création		
58-EE		Dynamic 582 DT/15		
58-EI		Air Création GT BI / XP		
58-EK		Dynamic 582 DT/15		
58-ER		Humbert Tetras		
58-FF		Buse'Air 150		
58-FM		Quicksilver		
58-FQ		Fly Synthesis Storch "Plasir III"		
58-FS		Rans S-6 Coyote II		
58-ID		Air Création		
58-JE		Raj Hamsa X'Air Hanuman		
58-QY		Mignet HM. Pou du Ciel		
58-WF		Zenair CH-601 Zodiac		

59 : Nord

59-B		Quicksilver MX		
59-C		Air Création		
59-H		Dynali Chickinox Kot-Kot *(not airworthy)*		
W59-AA		Rans S.6 Coyote II		
59-AM		JC-24 Weedhopper		
59-AN		JC-31C Weedhopper Europa II		
59-AR		JC-24 Weedhopper		
59-AS		JC-24 Weedhopper		
59-AW		Zenair CH-601 Zodiac		
59-BA		Zodiac Ultrastar	127	
59-BF		AX-3 Cyclone (The Squadron SE.5A Replica "59BF" noted in the UK in 1985 and painted as "F760", is believed to have been a US-registered ultralight)		
59-BQ		Weedhopper		
59-BU		Weedhopper		
59-BZ		Lemonnier Maestro	86.102	
59-CA		Dynali Chickinox		
59-CK		Weedhopper		
59-DD		Kolb Twinstar		
59-DJ		Weedhopper	9041112	55-DY?
59-DP		Quicksilver GT-500		
59-DT		Cosmos		
59-DV		Rans S-12 Airaile		
59-DY		AX-3 Weedhopper		
59-EA		Weedhopper 1		
59-EB		Weedhopper		
59-EE		Premier Cyclone AX-3 / 503		
59-EF		Air Création		
59-EP		Aerolac MD04 Airland		
59-ES		Dynali Chickinox		
59-ET		Dynali Chickinox		
59-EX		Dynali Chickinox		
59-EZ		Marquart Charger *(Weedhopper 8.02?)*		

59-FD		Air Création Quartz		
59-FJ		Dynali Chickinox Kot-Kot		
59-FQ		Cosmos/Top 14.9		
59-FU		Weedhopper		
59-FZ		Dynali Chickinox Kot-Kot		
59-GB		Dynali Chickinox		
59-GC		Weedhopper		
59-GD		Cyclone Ax-359-GP Quartz		
59-GQ		Weedhopper		
59-GT		Mignet HM.293A Pou du Ciel		55-FC
59-HB		Macair 1142 Merlin		
59-HC		Aviasud Mistral		
59-HG		Dynali Chickinox		OO-. . .
59-HI		Dynali Chickinox Kot-Kot		
59-HP		Dynali Chickinox		
59-HV		Air Création		
59-HX		Weedhopper JC-24D Sport *(Stored)*	B1071142	
59-IE		Humbert Moto du Ciel		
59-IG		Dynali Chickinox Kot-Kot		
59-IL		Eipper Quicksilver GT500		
59-IN		Eipper Quicksilver Mk.IIHP		
59-IO		Eipper Quicksilver MX		
59-IP		Mignet HM.293 Pou-du-Ciel		
59-IT		Dynali Chickinox		
59-IW	F-JAMH	SMAN Pétrel		
59-IY		Air Création GT BI SX		
59-JE		Dynali Chickinox Kot-Kot		
59-JG		Weedhopper		
59-JH		Weedhopper AX-3		
59-JO		Citizen Flyer Twin JL9		
59-KC		Cosmos GT		
59-KG		Weedhopper		
59-KK		Epervier		
59-KN		Mignet HM.1000 Balèrit	46	
59-KP		Eipper Quicksilver GT500		
59-KU		Aviasud AE209 Albatros	46	PH-2M5
59-LJ		TEAM Mini-MAX		
59-LV		Cosmos		
59-LY		Rans S-12 Airaile		
59-LZ		Aviasud AE209 Albatros *(To OO-D37)*	50	
59-MB		Aviasud AE209 Albatros	51	
59-MH		Zenair CH.701		
59-MI		Zenair CH.701 STOL		
59-MJ		Zenair CH.701 STOL	003	(OO-B67)
59-MN		F.2 Foxcat *(Damaged, stored)*		
59-MO		Rans S-6 Coyote II	0192261	OO-A52
59-MP		Rans S-6 Coyote II		
59-MQ		Cyclone AX-3 / 503		
59-MT		Zenair CH.701 STOL *(To OO-E23)*		
59-MU		Zenair CH.701 STOL*(painted 59/72014)*	7-2014?	
59-MW		Zenair CH.701 STOL		
59-MX		Fly Synthesis/Rodaro Storch	22?	
59-MZ		Rans S-6 Coyote II		
59-NA		Dynali Chickinox Kot Kot		
59-NE		DTA Dynamic Guepy		
59-NG		Dynali Chickinox Tandem		
59-NI		Zenair CH-701 STOL		
59-NJ		Rans S-6 Coyote II *(To OO-E14)*	0593502	
59-NK		Rans S-6ESD Coyote II	0891214	OO-A60
59-NL		AMF Chevvron 2-32	031	OO-A29
59-NM		Cosmos Chronos 16		
59-NP		Cosmos		
59-NQ		Aviatika Locafly		
59-NS		Synairgie		
59-NU		Mignet HM.1000 Balèrit	92	
59-NV		Rans S-6 Coyote II *(To OO-D28)*	0894667	
59-OJ		Zenair CH.601 Zodiac		
59-OK		Zenair CH.601 Zodiac		
59-OL		Rans S-6 Coyote II		
59-OO		Air Création		
59-OP		Rans S-6 Coyote II		
59-OR		Fly Synthesis Storch		
59-OS		Zenair CH-601 Zodiac		
59-OV		Rans S-12 Airaile	0792245	OO-B08
59-PB		Dynali Chickinox		
59-PD		Mignet HM.1000 Balèrit	111	
59-PG		Rans S-6 Coyote II		
59-PK		Zenair CH.701 STOL		
59-PM		Aviasud Mistral		
59-PN		Aviasud Mistral	195	D-MNAT
		(Also wears regn OO-C22)		
59-PP		Macair 1142 Merlin		
59-PQ		Dynali Chickinox Kot-Kot		
59-PS		Eipper Quicksilver GT-500	202	OO-B01
59-PV	OQ-AYW	Rans S-6 Coyote II (tailwheel)		
59-QC		Zenair CH-601 Zodiac UL		
59-QD		Rans S-6 Coyote II		
59-QE	F-JFIR	Rans S-6 Coyote II		
59-QF		Zenair CH-701 STOL		
59-QI		Solar Wings Pegasus Chaser		
59-QJ		Zenair CH-701 STOL		
59-QM		Rans S-6 Coyote II	1091222	OO-A53
59-QP		Zenair CH-601 Zodiac		
59-QQ		Ultravia Pelican		
59-QR		AES Sky Ranger		
59-QS		Rans S-6ES Coyote II *(To OO-C06)*	295732ES	OO-C06
59-QT		Zenair CH-701 STOL		

59-QX		Dynali Chickinox		
59-QY		Mignet HM.293 Pou du Ciel		
59-RA		Rans S-6 Coyote II		
59-RC		Aviasud AE.209 Albatros		
59-RE		Rans S-6 Coyote II		
59-RJ		Air Création GTE Clipper *(To OO-D96)*		
59-RL		Weedhopper AX-3		59-RH?
59-RN		Evans VP-2 Volksplane		
59-RR		Rans S-6 Coyote II		
59-RT		Zenair CH-701 STOL		
59-RU		Zenair CH-701 STOL		
59-RY		Mignet HM.1000 Balèrit	115	
59-RZ		Croses Airplume	23	OO-833
59-SA		Rans S-6 Coyote II		
59-SE		Dynali Chickinox Kot-Kot		
59-SF		Mignet HM.1000 Balèrit	119	
59-SH	F-JCPP	Zenair CH-601HD Zodiac	6-1780	59-OJ C-FMXN
59-SJ		Rans S-6 Coyote II		
59-SN		Zenair CH-701 STOL *(To OO-C72)*	7-2886	
59-SR		Zenair CH-601 Zodiac		
59-SW		Zenair CH-701 STOL		
59-TD		Fly Synthesis Storch *(To OO-D59)*	155	
59-TF		Murphy Renegade Spirit	PFA/188-11562	G-MWHK
59-TH	F-JCBU	Rans S-7 Courier		
59-TL		Zenair CH.601 Zodiac UL *(Damaged 2.7.01)*		
59-TM	F-JDEI	Zenair CH.601 Zodiac UL		
59-TN	OQ-AXH	Rans S-6 Coyote II		
59-TT		Rans S-6ES Coyote II	Co.930201	
		(Also registered OO-A98 and based in Belgium)		
59-TZ	F-JCCR	Air Création Fun GT BI		
59-UA		Mignet Proto		
59-UB	F-JFKJ	Zenair CH-601 Zodiac		
59-UC	F-JCLU	Zenair CH-701 STOL		
59-UD		Aérianne Swift	45	
59-UE		Air Création XP		
59-UG		Mignet HM.1000 Balèrit	127	
59-UI		Air Création Racer XS		
59-UJ		Rans S-6 Coyote II		
59-UK		Rans S-6 Coyote II	11961068	OO-D52
		(Restored ?)		59-UK
59-UO		Air Création Fun GT		
59-US		Air Création Fun GT		
59-UU		Air Création GTE		
59-UX		Air Création Fun		59-GR
59-VB		DPM Cosmos	21225	
59-VC		TEAM Mini-MAX		
59-VF		Solar Wings Pegasus Quantum		
59-VH		Solar Wings Pegasus Quantum		
59-VJ		Air Création GTE Clipper		
59-VM		Rans S-12 Airaile		
59-VN		Zenair CH-601 Zodiac		
59-VO		Fly Synthesis Storch		W59-VO
59-VQ		TL Ultralight TL-132 Condor	94016	
59-VT		Zenair CH-601UL Zodiac		
59-VV		Zenair CH-601 Zodiac		
59-VX		Zenair CH-601TD Zodiac *(To OO-D60)*	6-9130	
59-VZ		Dynali Chickinox		74-AQ
59-WA		Rans S-6 Coyote II *(To OO-D06)*	*07971139*	
59-WC		Aviasud AE.209 Albatros	28	
59-WD		Air Création XS GT BI		
59-WE		Rans S.6 Coyote II *(To OO-D50)*	06971124	
59-WF	F-JDCH	Zenair CH.601HD Zodiac	6-3592	
59-WI	F-JDBB	Mignet HM.1100 Cordouan	05	
59-WK	F-JFKS	Rans S-7 Courier		
59-WM		Aquilair Swing 14		
59-WO		Fisher FP.404		
59-WP		Dynali Chickinox Tandem		
59-WW		Zenair CH.601 Zodiac		
59-XA		ICP Torino MXP-740 Savannah	09-97-50-060	
59-XD		Fly Synnthesis Storch		
59-XH		Aquilair Swing 14		
59-XI		Air Création Clipper GTE		
59-XJ		JC.31 Weedhopper *(To OO-D02)*	3788844	
59-XS		Zodiac CH.701 STOL *(To OO-D22)*	7-9000	
59-XT		Rans S-12 Airaile		
59-XU		Zenair CH-601 Zodiac		
59-XX		Best Off Sky Ranger		
59-XZ	F-JFJE	Zenair CH-601 Zodiac		
59-YA		Fly Synthesis Storch		
59-YD		Zenair CH-601TDO Zodiac	6-9009	
59-YF		Air Création	A98-101	
59-YI		Zodiac CH.701 STOL		
59-YJ		Mignet HM.1100 Cordouan	9	
59-YK		Fly Synthesis Storch *(To OO-D74)*	232	
59-YM		Solar Wings Pegasus		
59-YN		Rans S-6ES Coyote II *(To OO-D05)*	06981238	
59-YP		Rans S-6 Coyote II		
59-YS		Rans S-12 Airaile		
59-ZB		SE.5A replica		
59-ZF		Zenair CH-601 Zodiac		
59-ZI		Aviasud AE.208 Albatros *(To OO-D24)*	129	
59-ZK		Air Création XP		
59-ZN		Quicksilver GT500		
59-ZR		Mignet HM.293 Pou du Ciel		
59-ZS		SE.5A replica		
59-ZV		Fly Synthesis Storch *(To OO-D31)*	243	

59-ZW		Fly Synthesis Storch *(To OO-D30)*	245	
59-ZY		Fly Synthesis Storch		
W59-AAB		Sauper J-300 Joker		
59-AAC		Air Création Quartz		
59-AAG	F-JFHX	Rans S-6 Coyote II		
59-AAH	F-JFHD	Zenair CH.701 STOL		
59-AAI		Rans S-6 Coyote II		
59-AAJ		Fly Synthesis Storch *(To OO-D66)*	250	
59-AAM		Fly Synthesis Storch		
59-AAN		Pegasus Quantum Super Sport		
59-AAQ		Rans S-6 Coyote II		
59-AAU		Quad City Challenger		
59-AAV		Zenair CH-601 Zodiac		
59-AAW		Zenair CH-601 Zodiac		
59-AAX		Fly Synthesis Storch		
59-AAY		Air Création Fun		35-CC
59-ABA		Fly Synthesis Storch HS		
59-ABE		Rans S-12 Airaile		
59-ABL		Rans S-6 Coyote II		
59-ABM	F-JFHU	Souricette		
59-ABO		Zenair CH-601 Zodiac *(W/o 17.8.03)*		
59-ABU	F-JAPY	Zenair CH-601 Zodiac		
59-ABW	F-JCTP	Aviasud AE-209 Albatros	105	D-MAMT 83-GO
59-ACA	F-JABY	Zenair CH-601 Zodiac		
59-ACB		Rans S-6 Coyote II		
59-ACE		Fly Synthesis Storch		
59-ACG	F-JFIZ	Zenair CH-601 Zodiac		
59-ACI		Zenair CH-601XL Zodiac		
59-ACL		Zenair CH-601 Zodiac		
59-ACU		X'Air		
59-ACV		Zenair CH-701 STOL		
59-CAB		B&F Funk FK-9 Mk.III		
59-CAC		B&F Funk FK-9 Mk.III		
59-CAD		Rans S-10 Sakota		
59-CAF	F-JFHT	B&F Funk FK-9 Mk.III	09-03-130	
59-CAI		Jodel D.9 Bébé		
59-CAL		Gyrocopter, type unknown		
59-CAM		Eurofox		W59-CAM
59-CAN		Jodel D.18		
59-CAP		B&F Funk FK-9 Mk.III		
59-CAQ		Croses LC-6 (Pou du Ciel)		
59-CAR		Dyn'Aéro MCR-01	125	
59-CAT		Rans S-7 Courier		59-WCAT
59-CAU		RSA / Pottier P.130UL Bleu Citron		
59-CAV		European Airwings Springbok 2000		
59-CAW		Ultravia Pelican Sport		
59-CBD		Aviakit Vega JC		
59-CBF		B&F Funk FK-9 Mk.III		
59-CBG		Best Off Sky Ranger		
W59-CBJ		Biplane pusher, type unknown		
59-CBO		Zenair CH-601 Zodiac		
59-CBP		Pipistrel/Zen ULM Sinus		
59-CBQ		Aeropro Eurofox *(Damaged)*		
59-CBS		Mignet HM.1100 Balerit	83	ALAT: FMUCD
59-CBZ		B&F Funk FK-9 Mk.III		
59-CCA		Air Création		
59-CCB		Raj Hamsa X'Air		
59-CCC	F-JFKV	Fly Synthesis Storch		
59-CCG		Zenair CH-601 Zodiac		
59-CCI		Air Création XP		
59-CCM		Zenair CH-601XL Zodiac		
59-CCR	F-JDET	DTA Dynamic Guepy 582		63-M ?
59-CCU		Weedhopper		
59-CDL		Leopoldoff L-3 Colibri *(Wreck noted 7.04)*	127	(F-PDOF) F-BGFS
59-CDN		Zenair CH-601 Zodiac		
59-CDP		Aviasud Albatros		
59-CDX		Air Création Kiss (To OO-D97)	AO1195-1208	
59-CEC		Rans S-6 Coyote II		
59-CEH		Air Création Clipper GTE		
59-CEI		Dynali Chickinox *(Wears both marks)*	5092B109	OO-A91
59-CEJ		B&F Funk FK-12 Comet	12-034	
59-CEN		Best Off Sky Ranger		
59-CEQ	F-JFKZ	Evektor EV.97 Eurostar	2001.10.14	
59-CER		European Airwings Springbok *(Dam. 30.6.02)*		
W59-CEU		Alpi Aviation Pioneer 200		
59-CEV		Zenair CH-601 Zodiac		
59-CEZ		Evektor EV.97 Eurostar	2002.14.18	OK-DUU 33
59-CFA		Pottier P.130 Bleu Citron		
59-CFD		TL Ultralight TL-2000 Sting carbon		
59-CFF		Zenair CH-601XL Zodiac		
59-CFT		DTA Dynamic 15		
59-CFZ		Zenair CH-601XL Zodiac	6-9315	
59-CGA		Zenair CH-601XL Zodiac		
59-CGC		Rans S-6 Coyote II		
59-CGD		unidentified flexwing		59-AJ
59-CGG		Zenair CH-601 Zodiac		
59-CGJ	F-JFLM	Kappa KP2 UR Sova		
59-CGP		Zenair CH-701 STOL		
59-CHI		Zenair CH-601 Zodiac		
59-CHN		Magni M-16 Tandem Trainer gyro		
59-CHP		B&F Funk FK-12 Comet	12-059	
59-CIN		Zenair CH-701 STOL		
59-CIO		Zenair CH-601XL Zodiac		
59-CIV		Air Création iXess		
59-CKA		Evektor EV-97 Eurostar		
59-CKH		Rans S-6 Coyote (tailwheel)		
59-CLP		TL Ultralight TL-2000 Sting		

60 : Oise

60-AQ		Quartz Air Création SX		
60-AU		Veliplane		
60-BC		Air Création Fun		
60-BH		Air Création		
60-BJ		Synairgie		
60-BL		Mainair Gemini		
60-CI		Air Création Quartz		
60-DK		Air Création Fun GT BI		
60-FQ		Cosmos		
60-GV		Aviasud AE.209 Albatros		
60-HX		Humbert Tetras		
60-JB		Dyn'Aéro MCR-01		
60-KB	F-JFZI	Jodel D.18	191	54-VF W54-VF

61 : Orne

61-L		Zodiac Ultrastar 500	145	
61-AE		Air Création		
61-AH		Air Création		
61-AN		Dynali Chickinox		
61-AP		Aviasud Mistral		
61-AS		Eipper Quicksilver MX-II		
61-AX		Quartz		
61-BG		X5 Racer		
61-BK		JCC Aviation J-300 Joker		
61-BN		Dynali Chickinox (previously reported as Thruster)		
61-BT		Air Création GT BI		
61-CB		Dynali Chickinox		
61-CF		Aviasud Mistral		
61-CH		Air Création		
61-DB		Dynali Chickinox		
61-DD		Air Création Mild		
61-DH		Air Création GT		
61-DS		Air Création GT BI Quartz		
61-EC		Biplume		
61-EF	F-JBSA	Buse'Air 150		
61-EH		Buse'Air 150		
61-EL		Dynali Chickinox		
61-EP		Air's Allegro 2		
61-ER		Dynali Chickinox		
61-ET		Air Création GT Mild		
61-EV		Air Création SX		
61-FG	F-JHGX	Humbert Tetras *(ex F-JCAJ)*		
61-FM		Air Création GT BI		
61-FO		Air Création GT XS		
61-FR		J-6 Karatoo		
61-FU		Raj Hamsa X'Air		
61-GJ		ICP MXP-740 Savannah		
61-GK		Air Création / Fun		
61-HB		ATEC Zephyr		
61-HO		Windlass Trike		
61-HS		Ray Hamsa X'Air		
61-IA	F-JHHY	Pipistrel/Zen ULM Sinus		
61-II		Aero Services Guepy 582		
61-IK		Comco Ikarus C-42 Cyclone		
61-MH		Synairgie Puma Bi		

62 : Pas-de-Calais

62-P		UTA Djins 300		
62-BN		Eipper Quicksilver		
62-CD		JC-24 Weedhopper AX-3		
62-CE		Cosmos		
62-CU		Cosmos Chronos		
62-DC		Air Création Fun		
62-DG		Weedhopper		
62-DW		Air Création Fun		
62-ED		Rans S-6 Coyote II		
62-EE		Rans S-6 Coyote II		
62-EG		J-3 Kitten		
62-EJ		Cosmos Later reported on AX-3 Cyclone		
62-EK	F-JFJT	Synairgie		
62-FH		Synairgie		
62-FJ		Eipper Quicksilver		
62-FQ		Dynali Chickinox		
62-FS		Weedhopper		
62-FT		AES Sky Ranger		
62-FX	F-JBUL	Zenair CH-701 STOL		
62-GF		Synairgie Dauphin		
62-GI		Best Off Sky Ranger		
62-GJ		Best Off Sky Ranger	SR05-17057	
62-GK		Zenair CH.601 Zodiac		
62-GM		Light Aero Avid Flyer		
62-GN		Rans S-6 Coyote II		
62-GP		Synairgie		
62-GS		Rans S-6 Coyote II		
62-GW		Air Création		
62-GY		Synairgie		
62-HA		Light Aero Avid Light		
62-HB		Micro Aviation Pulsar III		
62-HC		Best Off Sky Ranger		
62-HH	F-JFHL	Zenair CH.601 Zodiac		

62-AAA		B&F Funk FK-9 Mk.III		
W62-AAB		Jodel D.92 Bébé	350	F-PHLJ
62-AAC		Jodel D.9 Bébé		F-P
62-AAD		Jodel D.92 Bébé	751	RF-PFGP
W62-AAH		Mignet HM.293 *(W/o 8.7.03)*		
62-AAL		Air Création Twin SL		
62-AAT		Magni M-16 Gyro		
62-AAV		Air Création Kiss 450B	A01026-1015	
62-AAW	F-JFJO	Zenair CH.601 Zodiac		
62-ABB	F-JFKG	Buse'Air 150GT		
62-ABF		Air Création Quartz		
62-ABK		Air Création Kiss		
62-ABL		Air Création GTE Kiss		
62-ABN	F-JFKE	Zenair CH.601 Zodiac	6-9237	
62-ABP		Synairgie Puma		
62-ABS		Air Création XP		
62-ABT		Humbert Tetras BS *(W/o 22.6.03)*		
62-ABV		Best Off Sky Ranger		
62-ACE	F-JFLJ?	Aero Services Guepard 912S		
62-ACG		Air Création XP		
62-ACH		Jodel D.92 Bébé		
62-ACI		Flight Design CT-2K		W62-ACI
62-ACJ		Zenair CH-601 Zodiac	6-9226	
62-ADB		Zenair CH-601 Zodiac		
62-ADD		Air Création		
62-ADE		Unidentified gyrocopter		
62-ADF		Unidentified gyrocopter		
62-ADG		Aero Services Guepy 582		
62-ADS		Zenair CH-601 Zodiac (USN c/s)		
62-ADT		Humbert Tetras		
62-ADZ		DTA Dynamic 15		
62-AEA		Zenair CH-601 Zodiac		
62-AEF	F-JFKE	Zenair CH-601 Zodiac		
62-AEG		Zenair CH-601 Zodiac		
62-AEK		Air Création GT BI XP		
62-AEN		Air Création Kiss		
62-AFJ		ICP MXP-740 Savannah		

63 : Puy-de-Dôme

63-AH		Pendulaire		
63-AK		Pendulaire		
63-AQ		Pendulaire		
63-CB		Air Création Cosmos		
63-CC		JCC Aviation J-300 Joker		
63-CS		Air Création Quartz		
63-EA		Air Création SX		
63-EG		Air Création		
63-EN		Titan Tornado		
63-FJ	F-JAZN	Denney Kitfox		
63-GE		Denney Kitfox		
63-GG		Rans S-6 Coyote II		
63-JC		Air Création Safari GT BI 503		
63-KD		Light Aero Avid Flyer *(Damaged 24.8.01)*		
63-LI		Air Création Twin GTE		
63-MI		Air Création Twin		
		(Also reported as Humbert Tetras w/o 26.4.02)		

64 : Pyrénées-Atlantiques

64-AX		Pendulaire		
64-DR		Air's Maestro 2		
64-FM		Air Création GTB		
64-GJ		Cosmos *(W/o 5.8.01)*		
64-GN		Aeriane		
64-HD		Aurore Souris Bulle		
64-IA		SE5A replica		
64-JO	F-JKCW	B&F Funk Fk.9 Mk.III	180	
64-JP	F-JKDI	Best Off Sky Ranger		
64-JW		Air Création SX		
64-KA		Tecnam P.92S Echo	675	
64-KH	F-JKFV	J-3		
64-K I		Aurore Mini-Bulle *(Dbr 28.5.03)*		
64-KX	F-JKGM	B&F Funk FK-9		
64-AUI		Aurore Mini-Bulle		
64-WAU		Aurore Mini-Bulle *(same aircraft as above?)*		

65 : Hautes-Pyrénées

65-N		Eipper Quicksilver MX		
65-AG		Chasle YC.100 Hirondelle		
65-CO		Air Création XS		
65-CV		Aviasud Albatros AE-209 *(error for 66-CV?)*	107	
W65-DY		Morin M.80 (builder Dufau)		
65-ED	F-JBCP	Campana Observer		
65-EM		Titan Tornado 912		
65-GZ		Quicksilver MXII Sprint		
65-HF		Raj Hamsa X'Air		
65-HG		Rans Coyote I		
65-HH		Air Création Grif Spyder SP		
65-HL		Air Création Fun		
65-HU	F-JIHU	B&F Funk FK-9 Mk.III		
65-IA		Henri Lascombes autogyro		
65-IV		Air Création Grif Spyder		
65-JD		Aviasud Sirocco		

66 : Pyrénées-Orientales

66-AD		Zenith Baroudeur		
66-AJ		Weedhopper		
66-BN		Eipper Quicksilver GT		
66-BX		Weedhopper		
66-CH		Weedhopper		
66-CQ		Weedhopper		
66-CR		Air Création Quartz		
66-CT		Weedhopper		
66-CU		Weedhopper		
66-DB	F-JAOB	Weedhopper		
66-DD		Air Création GT18 Quartz		
66-DK	F-JBDW	Pelican		
66-DO		Ultralair Weedhopper JC.31 Premier AX-3 *(W/o 7.8.02)*		
W66-DT		Hélios		
66-EX		Weedhopper		
66-FK		Air Création Clipper Quartz		
66-FU	F-JCXR	Type unknown		
66-GB		Zenair CH- ?		
66-GD		Best Off Sky Ranger		
66-GG		Storch		
66-GH		Denney Kitfox	693	
66-GI		Weedhopper		
66-GM		Air Création Quartz		
66-HJ		Air's Maestro 2		
66-JA		DTA Dynamic 582 *(W/o 12.7.03)*		
66-QC		Weedhopper		

67 : Bas-Rhin

67-V		Pioneer Flightstar		
67-AG		Falcon		
67-AK		Zenith Baroudeur		
67-AQ		Mustang		
67-AV		Mustang		
67-BJ		La Mouette		
67-BK		Pioneer Flightstar		
67-CL		Pioneer Flightstar		
67-DS	F-JCOO	Rans S-6 Coyote II		
67-EF		Sky Pup		
67-EI		Denney Kitfox		
67-EK		Weedhopper AX-2		
67-EL		Koenig AK.09 Faucon		
67-EM	F-JAKQ	Rans S-6 Coyote II		
67-ES		Weedhopper		
67-FG		Epervier		
67-FK		Croses Criquet Léger	86	
67-FM		Rans S-12 Airaile		
67-GO		Airwave/CEM Rave paraglider		
67-GU		JCC Aviation J-300 Joker ?		
67-GZ	F-JBTG	Rans S-6 Coyote II		
67-HB		Rans S-12 Airaile		
67-HG		Mignet HM.1000 Balèrit	114	
		(Same c/n quoted for 68-HC. Order unknown)		
67-HM		Cosmos Chronos		
67-HP		Rans S-6 Coyote II		
67-HT		Mignet HM.293 Pou-du-Ciel		
67-IA		Tipsy T.66 Nipper 2	59	D-ECPU(1) LX-AIG
67-IB		Mignet HM.293 Pou-du-Ciel		
67-IH		Interplane Skyboy		
67-IR		Interplane Skyboy		
67-IS		Rans S-6 Coyote II		
67-JC		Voilerie du Vent Phebus		
67-JD		Rans S-6ESD Coyote II		
67-JE		Sky Ranger		
67-JL		Mignet HM.1000 Balèrit		
67-JM		Avion JC Nacelle		
67-KU		Fantasy Air Allegro ST	98-101	
67-KW		Voilerie du Vent Phebus		
67-KZ	F-JBLQ	Rans S-6 Coyote II		
67-LE		Weedhopper		
67-LG	F-JCFN	Murphy Maverick 503		
67-LQ		Pioneer Flightstar		
67-MN	F-JGTU	Fantasy Air Allegro SW	99-107	
67-MP		Euro III		
67-MT	F-JGSI	Fantasy Air Allegro SW		
67-MV		TEAM Speed-Max		W-67-MV
67-MY		Platzer Kiebitz		
67-NN		Voilerie du Vent Phebus		
67-NT		Zenair CH-701 STOL		
67-NU		Rans S-6 Coyote II		
67-OL		Fantasy Air Allegro SW	01-118	
67-OS		single-seat biplane		
67-PE	F-JGTO	Fantasy Air Allegro SW	01-120	
67-PF	F-JGTN	Mignet HM.1100 Cordouan	08	
67-PK		(trike?)/ Zenith wing		
67-PL	F-JGTQ	Aviakit Vega		
67-QE		Fantasy Air Allegro SW	02-124	
67-QI		Fantasy Air Allegro		
67-QS	F-JGUC	Impulse Finesse Max		
67-QY	F-JGUF	WDFL Fascination		
67-RO		Pioneer Flightstar		
W67-UQ		B-87 Experimental		
67-VB		Fantasy Air Allegro	04-133	

68 : Haut-Rhin

68-AO		Skycraft AJS2000 *(Also reported as Rans S-6)*		
68-BO		Comco Ikarus Fox II	8604-3015	D-MJGH
68-BY		Aerotec VM18		
68-CE		Best Off Sky Ranger		
68-CN		Weedhopper		

68-CQ		Weedhopper		
68-DJ		Ultralair JC.24 Weedhopper Sport		
68-DQ		Ultralair JC.24 Weedhopper Sport		
68-EJ		Cosmos Trike		
68-EL		Weedhopper		
68-FE		Weedhopper AX.3		
68-FF		Cosmos Trike		
68-FH		Rans S-6 Coyote II		
68-FI		Aviasud AE.209 Albatros		
68-FS		Croses Criquet UL		
68-GB		Aviasud Albatros		
68-GH		Rans S-12 Airaile *(Also regd D-MNBI)*	1292-356	
68-GK		Best Off Sky Ranger		
68-GM		Best Off Sky Ranger		
68-GP		DTA Feeling		
68-HC		Mignet HM.1000 Balèrit *(Same c/n quoted for 67-HG. Order unknown)*	114	
68-HK		Comco Ikarus Fox-C22		
68-HV		Weedhopper AX-3		
68-HY		Cosmos		
68-IL		Air Création		
68-IN		Light Aero Avid Lite		
68-IO		Skyboy		
68-IP		Air Création XP		
68-IQ		Best Off Sky Ranger		
68-JA		Mignet HM.293 Pou-du-Ciel		
68-JM		Best Off Sky Ranger		
68-KH		Cosmos Phase 2	21005	
68-KK		Best Off Sky Hanger		
68-KR	F-JDAB	Humbert Tetras		
68-KS		Quicksilver ?		
68-KV		Phantom 1		
68-LC		Best Off Sky Ranger		
68-LD		Aquilair XP		
68-LF		Weedhopper AX-3		
68-LM		Humbert Moto-du-Ciel *(W/o 2.5.02)*		
68-MS		"Petit Chef" (based on Sunwheel?)		
68-MU	F-JGBZ	Aviasud Sirocco		
68-MZ		Aero Services Guepy 582		
68-NW		Aviasud AE-209 Albatros		
68-OH		DEA Yuma		
68-OK		DEA Yuma		
68-OP	F-JGTW	Aviakit Vega UL		
W68-QA		Barry Souricette		
68-TN		Light Aero Avid Flyer		

69 : Rhône

69-M		Southdown Puma		
69-AE		Weedhopper JC-31		
69-AK		J-3 Kitten		
69-AR		Cosmos		
69-AU		Croses Air Plume	19	
69-BI		Aerial Arts Chaser		
69-BO		Croses Air Plume		
69-BX		Microbel Must		
69-CA		Pendulaire		
69-CX		Solar Wings Pegasus XL-Q		
69-EG		Synairgie Trike		
69-EI		Weedhopper		
69-EJ		Cosmos		
69-EQ		Biplum		
69-ER		Tandem Air Sunny		
69-ET		Weedhopper		
69-EX		Weedhopper		
69-GB		Aviasud AE.209 Albatros		
69-GD		Weedhopper AX-3		62-DG
69-GI		TEAM Mini-MAX		
69-GV		Aviasud AE.209 Albatros		
69-HV		Air Création		
69-IJ		Air Création		
69-JB		Cosmos		
69-ME		Flight Design CT		
69-MJ		DTA Dynamic		
69-NI		Dynamic 15		
69-NM		Humbert Tetras 912BS		
69-NQ		Cosmos		
69-OD		DTA Dynamic 450		
69-OF		DTA Dynamic 15/430		
69-OH		Exalt Air		
69-OK		DTA Dynamic 450		
69-OU		ICP Super Bingo		
69-PK	F-JETO	B&F Funk FK-9 Club Mk.IV		

70 : Haute-Saône

70-AB		Eipper Quicksilver MX		
70-AX		Raven		
70-BO		Cosmos		
70-BS		Cosmos Chronos		
70-CN		Air Composite		
70-DK		Humbert Moto-du-Ciel		
70-DR		Dynamic 15		
70-DS		Humbert Moto-du-Ciel		
70-EH		Zenair CH.601 Zodiac		
70-EI		Air Création DT Mild		
70-EP		Humbert Tetras		
70-EY		Air Création		
70-FG	F-JHMZ	Best Off Sky Ranger		
70-FH	F-JGQD	Jodel D.18		
70-FJ		Jodel D.20	20	
70-HH		Light Aero Avid Flyer		

71 : Saône-et-Loire

71-F		Southdown Puma		
71-N		Croses Airplume (Mavic ?)		
71-AE		Mustang		
71-AF		Air's Maestro		
71-AH		Mustang		
71-BA		Europa Malik		
71-BB		Cosmos		
71-BJ		Cosmos		
71-BK		Aviasud Mistral		
71-BL		Aviasud Mistral		
71-CJ		Aviasud Mistral	100	
71-CP		Aviasud Mistral	110	
71-CT		Croses LC-6		
71-CV		Mignet HM.1000 Balèrit 3X		
71-DE		Synairgie		
71-DL		Air Création		
71-EA		Croses (Pou du Ciel)		
71-EG		Air Création GT		
71-EH		Weedhopper		
71-ES		Air Création GT BI		
71-ET		Air Création XP		
71-FC	F-JBWE	Tecnam P.92 Echo	100	
71-FG		Air Création Clipper GTE		
71-FH		Rans S-6 Coyote II		
71-FO		Cosmos		
71-FR		Mustang		
71-GH		Weedhopper	6081068	
71-GL	F-JGXE	SG Aviation Storm 300		
71-GP	F-JGMO	Azurlog Caprice 21		
71-HA	F-JGOY	SG Aviation Storm 300 Special		
71-KD		Voyageur 172		

72 : Sarthe

72-K		Aerokart		
72-L		JC-24 Weedhopper		
72-AA		JC-24 Weedhopper		
72-AM		Air Création Safari		
72-BC		Mignet HM.1000 Balèrit 3X	20	
72-BJ		JC-24 Weedhopper Europa 2		
72-BK		JC-24 Weedhopper Europa 1		
72-BN		Skywalker		
72-CA		Solar Wings Pegasus XL-R	SW-WA-1253 / SW-TB-1248	
72-DJ		Air Création Quartz		
72-EB		Air Création GT BI 16 SX		
72-EG		Air Création XS		
72-FS	F-JBHV	Aviasud Albatros		
72-FV	F-JBIS	Humbert Tetras		
72-GA		Air Création SX		
72-GB		Maxair Drifter XP503		
72-GL	F-JGXG	Sauper J-300 Joker *(internal marking, ex or to?)*		37-TG
72-GV		JCC Aviation J-300 Joker		
72-HB		Air Création GT BI		
72-HU	F-JHUA	Raj Hamsa X'Air		
72-IB	F-JHVF	Raj Hamsa X'Air		
72-I I		Aero Services Guepy		
72-IT	F-JHWJ	Jodel D.18	17	F-PRJK
72-IU		(trike) / Air Création XP		
72-JB	F-JHXP	European Airwings Springbok 2000		
72-JD		Raj Hamsa X'Air		
72-JF		Air Création		
72-JL	F-JHYV	B&F Funk FK-9 Mk.III	09-111	
72-JT		Fly Synthesis Texan Top Class		

73 : Savoie

73-AB		Air's Maestro (Single-seat)		
73-AN		Air's Allegro		
73-BU		Renegade 503		
73-CI		Weedhopper		
73-DG		Rans S-6 Coyote II	0293-44 .	
73-EF	F-JBEC	Rans S-6 Coyote II		
73-EK		Air Création		
73-EN		Zenair CH-701		
73-ER	F-JBOK	Rans S-6ESD Coyote II		
73-FU	F-JCQU	Rans S-6ES Coyote II		
73-HL		Rans S-7 Courier		
73-HR		Aviasud AE.532 Mistral		
73-HS	F-JEKE	Ikarusflug Eurofox	Farman No.15	
73-HX		Noin Sirius		
73-IB	F-JELU	Pipistrel/Zen ULM Sinus		
73-IK		Pipistrel/Zen ULM Sinus		
73-JE		Pipistrel/Zen ULM Sinus		
73-JH		Pipistrel/Zen ULM Virus		
73-JL		Air Création Fun		
73-JR		Aviasud AE.532 Mistral		
W73-KC		Mignet HM.293 *(W/o 10.12.03)*		
73-KO		Alpi Aviation Pioneer 200		
73-MN		Air Création		
73-NT		Alpi Aviation Pioneer 300S		

74 : Haute-Savoie

74-Y		Aériane Sirocco		
74-AM		Zodiac Ultrastar	122	

74-CK		Weedhopper	8032378	
74-CQ		Paraplane		
W74-DG		Paraplane		
74-CH		Weedhopper		
74-DO		Sirius		
74-DP		Croses Airplume	21	
74-DX		Denney Minifox	519	
74-EG		Denney Minifox		
74-EO		Rans S-6 Coyote II		
74-EV		Mignet HM.14		
74-FH		Albatros		
74-GB		Cosmos Profil/La Mouette		
74-GJ		Micro Aviation Pulsar III		
74-GQ		Ultralair Weedhopper JC-31		
74-GU		Top Concept Hurricane		
74-HG		Synairgie		
74-HK		Technic'air F40GT parachute		
74-IC		Ushuaia floatplane		
74-KF	F-JCWA	Rans S-6ESD Coyote II		
74-LP		Aurore Souricette		
74-ME		Humbert Tetras		
74-NF		Mignet HM.100 Balèrit	102	
74-OX		Air Création Clipper		
74-PF		Rans S-6ESD Coyote II		
74-PG		Urban Air UFM-10 Samba *(W/o 11.6.02?)*		

75 : Paris

75-H		Eipper Quicksilver MX		
75-Y		Aériane Sirocco		
75-AJ		Guerpont Biplum		
75-DN		Doutart Le Chevron Volant		
75-EI		Zenith Baroudeur	016	
75-FL		Mignet HM.100 Balèrit		
75-GF		Air Création		
75-GG		Air Création Racer SX 12		
75-GIW		Inovatic		
75-GJ		Zenith Baroudeur		
75-GV		J.2		
75-HP		Pegasus Le Volant (Previously reported as Air Création Le Volant and Synairgie Puma B1, presumably representing trike changes)		
75-HV		Synairgie		
75- I I		Air's Maestro		
75-KC		Cosmos		
75-KG		JCC Aviation J.300 Joker		
75-KM		Johnathan Souricette		
75-KN		JCC Aviation J.300 Joker		
75-KT		SIT Systems Alto Paramotor		
75-KU		Adventure paraglider		
75-LG		Barodeur		
75-LQ		Best Off Sky Ranger		
75-LP		Souris Bulé		
75-MH		Aero Kuhlmann SCUB	2	
75-MI	F-JBVS	Scub MTR-75		
75-MT		Rans S-6 Coyote II		
75-NK		Weedhopper		
75-NM		III Sky Arrow 450		
75-OF		unidentified gyrocopter		
75-OH		Humbert Moto du Ciel		
75-OJ	F-JBSN	Pulsar III 95	135	
75-PB		Light Aero Avid Flyer		
75-PV		Rans S-6 Coyote II		
75-PW		Fantasy Air Allegro		
75-PY		Aquilair		
75-PZ	F-JFDV	Rans S-6 Coyote II		
75-QG		Cosmos		
75-QL		Raj Hamsa X'Air		
75-RG		Air Création Fun		

76 : Seine-Maritime

76-AX		Vector		
76-CG	F-JAEN	Weedhopper		
76-DG		Air Création SX		
76-DL		Synairgie		
76-EG		Foxi Puma 14		
76-EN		Sybairgie Puma Bi		
76-FA		Synairgie		
76-FK		AX.3		
76-FU		AX.3		
76-GD		Synairgie		
76-GK		Air Création Mild		
76-HR		Air Création XP		
76-HS		Weedhopper		
76-IH		Zenair CH-701 STOL		
76-IL	F-JFWP	Croses LC-6 UL		
76-IM		Aviasud Mistral		
76-IS		Air Création		
76-IX		X'Air 602T		
76-JB		Air Création Kiss		
76-JG		ICP MXP.740 Savannah	11 00 51 031	
76-JM		III Sky Arrow 500TF		
76-JV	F-JHTY	Rans S-6 Coyote II	0492293	
76-KB		Raj Hamsa X'Air		
76-KJ		Air Création Clipper / iXess		
76-KN		Air Création iXess		
76-KT		Michelet autogyro		
76-KV		Zenair CH-601XL Zodiac		
76-KY		Mignet HM.293W	01	F-PYHD
76-LJ		Raj Hamsa X'Air		
76-OG		Air Création		

77 : Seine-et-Marne

77-N		Veliplane		
77-BA		Veliplane		
77-BH		Comco Ikarus Fox-C22		
77-BJ		Falcon		
77-BN		Veliplane		
77-BS		Croses Airplume	10	
77-BT		Profile Trike		
77-CH		Zenith Baroudeur		
77-CK		Veliplane		
77-CL		Veliplane		
77-CU		Zenith Baroudeur Aeronautique 2000		
77-DC		Veliplane		
77-DG		Air Création		
77-DH		Dynamic		
77-DI		Veliplane		
77-DK		Rans S-7 Courier		
77-DN		Mignet HM.1000 Balèrit	02	
77-DQ		Aviasud Mistral		
77-DU		Zenith Baroudeur		
77-DY		Zenith Baroudeur		
77-EA		Zenith Baroudeur		
77-EE		Zenith Baroudeur		
77-EG		Air Création		
77-ES		Etendard 493 (also reported as Air Création)		
77-FD		Trike		
77-FH		Saphir		
77-FZ		Air Création SXN		
77-GD		Mainair Gemini/Flash IIA		
77-GN		Propulsar		
77-GP		Paraman Powerchute (Now reported as Aquilair IP)		
77-GS		Mainair Gemini/Flash IIA		
77-HH		Mainair Gemini/Flash IIA		
77-ID		Air Création		
77-IK		Air's Maestro		
77-IM		Cosmos (Mainair wing?)		
77-IS		Powerchute		
77-JA		Zenith Baroudeur		
77-JF		Air Création GT BI Quartz		
77-JH		La Mouette Cosmos		
77-JV		Zenith Baroudeur		
77-KA		Air's Maestro		
77-KC		Challenger		
77-KD		Eipper Quicksilver GT-500		
77-LB		Air Création Cosmos		
77-LC		Zenith Baroudeur		
W77-LD		Zenith Baroudeur		
77-LF		C.Jupitor		
77-LL		Rans S-6 Coyote II		
77-LQ		Air Création/ Cosmos Chronos		
77-LY		Air Création Safari GT BI		
77-MD		TEAM Mini-MAX		
77-MH		Air Création Cosmos Chronos 16		
77-MK	F-JFBY	B R Ghost 18		
77-MJ		Weedhopper		
77-MQ		(powered parachute)		
77-MS		Air Création Fun GT		
77-MU		Air Création Fun GT BI		
77-MX		Air Création Cosmos		
77-NB		Chronos		
77-NS		Cosmos Chronos 16		
77-NX		Adventure 210 paraglider		
77-OH		Zenith		
77-PJ		Dynali Chickinox		
77-PK		Dynali Chickinox		
77-PV		Jonathan Souricette		
77-QY		Mustang		
77-RK		Aviatika MAI-980		
77-RS		Rans S-6 Coyote II		
77-RT		Rans S-6 Coyote II		
77-SK		Rans S-6 Coyote II		
77-SL		Rans S-6ESD Coyote II		
77-ST		Aviasud AE209 Albatros	107	
77-SV		Weedhopper AX-3		
77-TK		Rans S-7 Courier		
77-TX		Rans S-6ESD Coyote II		
77-TY		Rans S-6ESD Coyote II		
77-UD		Rans S-12 Airaile		
77-UE		Air Création Fun GT BI/ Cosmos Chronos 16		
77-US		Cosmos Aeros		
77-UY		Alexandre		
77-XK		Micro Avn Pulsar		
77-XP		Cosmos		
77-XQ		C Roger		
77-XY		Air Création / Cosmos		
77-VC		Raj Hamsa X'Air		
77-VD		Humbert Tetras		
77-VF		Cosmos		
77-VH		Saphir		
77-VL	F-JCUQ	Air Création Clipper		
77-VQ		Raj Hamsa X'Air		
77-YA		Zenith Baroudeur		

77-YF		Cosmos		
77-YI		Pegasus		
77-YN		Comco Ikarus C-42 Cyclone		
77-YP		Cosmos		
77-YZ		Air Création XP		
77-ZD	F-JFAE	Tecnam P.92 Echo		
77-ZV	F-JFAI	Tecnam P.92S Echo		
77-ZW		Rans S-6 Coyote II		81-BE ?
77-ZY		Pocino SE.5A replica *(Painted "D3540")*	21	
77-AAE		Barry MB-01 Souricette		
77-AAI		Gyrocopter "Andre Terrasson"		
77-AAY		Souricette		
77-ABF	F-JFAY	Quicksilver GT500		
77-ABG		Cosmos		
77-ABH		Cosmos		
77-ABK		Air Création		
77-ABP		Rans S-6 Coyote II		
77-ACB		Fantasy Air Allegro		
77-ACF		J3 Chicken		
77-ACG		European Airwings Maestro II		
77-ACX		Cosmos Phase 2		
77-ADF		DT Dynamic 450		
77-ADH		DT Dynamic		
77-ADO		Air Création Veliplane GTE XP		
77-ADQ		DT Dynamic 450		
77-ADU		DT Dynamic 450		
77-ADW	F-JFBQ	Flight Design CT-2K		
77-AEB		DT Dynamic 450		
77-AEC		Zenair CH-601 Zenith		
77-AEL	F-JFBO	Flight Design CT-2K/912S		
77-AEP		Dynali Chickinox		
77-AES		Jabiru		
77-AEW		Magni M-16 Gyro		
77-AFI		Challenger		02-CV
77-AFK		Pegasus Quantum Super Sport		
77-AFL	F-JFBQ	Flight Design CT-2K		
77-AFM		Cosmos Chronos		
77-AFN		Zenair CH-601 Zenith		
77-AFP		Cosmos		
77-AFT		Tecnam P.96 Golf		
77-AFW		Air Création / Chronos II		
77-AFX		Best Off Sky Ranger		
77-AGA		Light Aero Avid Flyer		
77-AGD		Quicksilver GT500		
77-AGF		Pegasus		
77-AGH		Rans S-6 Coyote II		
77-AGJ		Comco Ikarus C-42		
77-AGR		Synairgie		
77-AGS		Air Création "ITIN"		
W77-AHH		Air Création GTE Kiss 13 *(W/o 1.6.03)*		
77-AHK		Best Off Sky Ranger		
77-AHO		Air Création GT		
77-AHP		Tecnam P.92S Echo (Carried marks internally, 01-QC externally)		01-QC
77-AHR		Cosmos		
77-AJA		Air Création Clipper/ XP		
77-AJC	F-JDEK	Best Off Sky Ranger		

78 : Yvelines

78-Q		Weedhopper		
78-AI		Veliplane		
78-AS		AILE Patrilor 3		
78-BK		Jokair Maestro		
78-CM		Mignet Touraco		
78-DM		Zenith Baroudeur		
78-DN		Veliplane Mustang		
78-DS		Air's Maestro		
78-FG		Safari		
78-FY		Eipper Quicksilver MXL-II		
78-GK		Aviasud Mistral		
F-78HV		Murphy Renegade Spirit		
78-JE		Icarus Comco Fox-C22		
78-JK		Cosmos		
78-JR		Powerchute		
78-KJ		Weedhopper		
78-KR		Zodiac Ultra Star		
78-KV		Weedhopper AX-3 (or Baroudeur?)		70-CF
78-KY		Maestro		
78-MI		Rans S-6 Coyote II		
78-NK		GB 14 Bis		
78-PJ		Cosmos		
78-QF		Best Off Sky Ranger		
78-QV		Serval		
78-QY		Zenair CH-601 Zodiac	6-9017	
78-RE	F-JFCE	Espace Liberté Yuma	FELS 03 06 00	
78-RU		Asso Aeri Champion V		
78-SM		Xxtrim		

79 : Deux-Sèvres

79-R		Mustang		
79-S		Quartz		
79-X		Trike		
79-AB		Aviasud Mistral		
79-BC		Pottier P.320 UL	1	
79-BE		Air Création XS		
79-BF		Air Création XS		
79-BG		Air Création XS		
79-BJ		Air Création Quartz		
79-BM		Air Création Quartz		
79-BN		JC-24 Weedhopper		
79-BP	F-JKRX	Ikarusflug Dynamic WT9		
79-BU		Air Création		
79-BS		Air Création XS		
79-BY		Air Création		
79-CK		Air Création		
79-CB		Air Création XS		
79-DH		Pottier P.320 UL		
79-DK		Air Création		
79-EF		Air Création		
79-EG	F-JKTA	Pottier P.320 UL	2	
79-EQ	F-JBUE	Rans S-6 Coyote II		
79-EY		Weedhopper		
79-FA		TL Ultralight TL-232 Condor		
79-FC		Light Aero Avid Flyer		
79-FE		Air Création Quartz		
79-FJ		Air Création		
79-FM		Weedhopper AX-3		
79-FR		Air Création		

80 : Somme

80-C		Weedhopper		
80-D		Air Création		
80-AB		Aviasud Mistral		
80-BI		Synairgie		
80-BO		Synairgie		
80-BU		Synairgie Puma Bi		
80-CB		Weedhopper AX-3		
80-CC		Best Off Sky Ranger		
80-CE		Synairgie Dauphin		
80-CG		Synairgie/Air Action		
80-CH		Synairgie/Air Action		
80-CK		Synairgie Dauphin		
80-CL		Cyclone AX-3		
80-CP		Synairgie Dauphin		
80-CR		Quartz ZSX		
80-CS		Best Off Sky Ranger		
80-DF		Cyclone AX-3	C3073132	
80-DK		Lorafly		
80-DL		Best Off Sky Ranger		
80-DM		Air Création SX		
80-DW		Air Création Fun GTE		
80-DX		Best Off Sky Ranger		
80-EB		Air Création Fun GTE Mild		
80-EH		"Little Mouse" (Homebuilt - Souricette?)		
80-EM		Mignet HM.293 Pou du Ciel		
80-EO		Cyclone AX-3	C3083143	
80-EP		Air Création XP		
80-EQ		Air Création Fun		
80-ER		Air Création GTE		
80-ES		Air Création Fun GTE Mild		
80-ET		Air Création Fun GTE Mild		
80-EU		Air Création		
80-EV	F-JBAS	Rans S-6 Coyote		
80-FE		Cosmos Top 12.9/Ranger 582		
80-FO		Air Création		
80-FQ		Air Création Quartz		
80-FS		Sky Ranger		
80-FT		Air Création Clipper GTE		
80-GA		Best Off Sky Ranger		
80-GB		Cyclone AX-3	C3123184	
80-GE		Best Off Sky Ranger		
80-GF		Air Création Quartz		
80-GI		Air Création		
80-GJ		Air Création GTE		
80-GN		Air Création Buggy		
80-GO		Guepy 582		
80-GP		Air Création		
80-GY	F-JCMV	Cosmos	21320	
80-GZ		Air Création		
80-HD		Air Création XP12	A98/009	
80-HF		Mignet HM.293A Pou du Ciel		
80-HG		Mignet HM.293A Pou du Ciel		
80-HI		Rans S-12 Airaile		
80-HJ		Cosmos		
80-HL		Air Création GTE		
80-HM		Synairgie Puma		
80-HQ		Cosmos		
80-IC		Air Création Kiss		
80-ID		Air Domi Trophy TT2000		
80-IF		Air Création Fun 18QC	A99072-9077	
W80-IK		Gyrocopter		
80-IL		Jodel D.92 Bébé	354	F-PFRB
80-IM		Quicksilver GT-500		
80-IO		Cualt 200		
80-IV	F-JFXQ	Air Création GTE XP15	A99137-9140	
80-IX		Air Création Kiss 450B	A00185-181	
80-JF		Air Création		
80-JG		Air Création XP		
80-JN		Air Création Clipper		
80-JU		Best Off Sky Ranger		
80-KM		Air Création Mild		
80-KY		Air Création GTE		
80-LT		Air Création XP		
80-LV		Air Création iXess		

80-LX		Air Création Mild		
80-MB		Best Off Sky Ranger		
80-ME		Air Création iXess		
80-MI		Air Création XP		
80-MJ		Air Création iXess		
80-MS		Pegasus XL		
80-VA		Synairgie		

81 : Tarn

81-S		Air Création		
81-U		Air Création		
81-V		Zenith Baroudeur		
81-AC		Aviasud AE.532 Mistral		
81-AL		Aviasud AE.209 Albatros		
81-CT	F-JAUK	Chereau J-300 Joker		
81-DE		Airplume	32	
81-FC	F-JBHY	Chereau J-300 Joker		
81-HC		Aviasud AE.532 Mistral		
81-HP		Mignet HM.1000 Balèrit		
81-LG		Aquilair		
81-MS		Mignet HM.293		
81-PW		Pegasus		
81-QE	F-JIQE	Dynamic		
81-QF		Rajhamsa X'Air		
81-UC		Air Création		

82 : Tarn-et-Garonne

W82-AE		Aviasud AE.532 Mistral		
82-AF		Dynali Chickinox		
82-AG		Weedhopper JC-31D		
82-AH		Best Off Sky Ranger		
82-AJ		Buse'Air		
82-AP		Zenair CH-601 Zodiac		
82-AU		Best Off Sky Ranger		
82-AW		Zenair CH-601 Zodiac		
82-BC		Synairgie/Best Off Sky Ranger		
W82-BQ		Croses Criquet L		
82-CE		Best Off Sky Ranger		
82-CG		Pipistrel/Zen ULM Sinus		
82-DM		Top Concept Hurricane		
82-EE		Best Off Sky Ranger		
82-FO		Best Off Sky Ranger		
82-JB		Tecnam P.92 Echo		
82-PC		Trike / Atlas wing		
82-WA		Zenair CH-601 Zodiac		

83 : Var

83-D		Best Off Sky Ranger		
83-H		Aériane Sirocco		
83-T		Eipper Quicksilver MX		
83-AE		Aériane Sirocco (also reported as Gyrocopter 7.01)		
83-AG		CFM Shadow (also reported as Storch IIS)		
83-AH		Dyn'Aéro MCR-01		
83-AK		Aviasud Mistral (also reported as Best Off Sky Ranger and as Zenair CH-701)		
83-AP		Air's Maestro (Two-seat)		
83-AU	F-JJKJ	Ultravia Pelican Sport		
83-AW		Flight Design CT-180UL		
83-AX		Best Off Sky Ranger (floatplane)		
83-BB		Aviasud Mistral		
83-BC		KFM		
83-BE		Nike Aeronautica		
83-BG		Aériane Sirocco		
83-BJ		Sky Ranger *(wreck noted 4.02)*		
83-BN		*Rans S-6 Coyote II*		
83-BP		Aviasud Mistral		
83-BQ		Aviasud Mistral		
83-BV		Patrilor		
83-CB		Aviasud Mistral		
83-CC		Air's Maestro		
83-CF		Avcan		
83-CI		Aviasud AE.209 Albatros		
83-CJ		Aviasud Mistral		
83-CK		Air Création		
83-CL	F-JCQO	Aviasud AE.209 Albatros 912		
83-CP		Aviasud Mistral		
83-CR		Best Off Sky Ranger *(W/o 19.7.03)*		
83-CT		Air's Maestro (Seaplane)		
83-DA		Aviasud Mistral		
83-DB		ULM Rapid		
83-DG		Weedhopper		
83-DN		Aviasud Mistral		
83-DO		Aviasud Mistral		
83-DV		PGO Cobra		
83-DY		Aviasud Mistral		
83-EB		Murphy Renegade Spirit UK *(Wears both UK and French marks)*	PFA188-12791	G-BWPE
83-EG		Denney Kitfox III	993	
83-EP		Mignet HM.1000 Balèrit	45	
83-EU		Aviasud Albatross	95	
83-EV		Aviasud Albatross 62-CV	32	
W83-FI		Croses Airplume		
W83-FJ		Fly Synthesis Storch		
83-FS		Air Création Clipper / XP		
83-FY		Air Création Kiss		
83-FZ		Magni gyrocopter		
83-GD		Rans S-6 Coyote II		
83-GF		Best Off Sky Ranger		
83-GJ		Zenair CH-601 Zodiac		
83-GP		Best Off Sky Ranger		
83-GR	F-JCGI	Best Off Sky Ranger		
83-HF		Air Création		
83-HR	F-JDBG	Mignet HM.1100 Balerit	07	
83-IA		Air Création 503SL		
83-IC		Pipistrel/Zen ULM Sinus		
W83-IG		Gatard Statoplan AG.02 Poussin	01	F-PHUO
83-JB		Tecnam P.92 Echo		
83-JD		Air Création XP		
83-JF	F-JJJB	Pipistrel/Zen ULM Sinus		
83-JG		Aviasud Albatros 582	CAP-28	
83-JP	F-JJAI	Aero Service Guepard 912		
83-LW		Ekolot JK05 Junior		
83-MB		Best Off Sky Ranger		
83-MD		Humbert Tetras		
83-MM		Cosmos		
83-MU		unidentified gyrocopter		
83-MZ		Dyn'Aéro MCR-01		
83-NG		ICP MXP.740 Savannah	01-10-51-099	
83-NV		Flight Design CT-180		
83-PA		EVP-1		
83-PF		Eipper Quicksilver		
83-PM		Asso Aeri V Champion V		
83-PU	F-JCMB	Kolb Firestar		
83-RM		Best Off Sky Ranger		
83-SA		III Sky Arrow 500TF		
83-SD		III Sky Arrow 500TF		
83-SE		III Sky Arrow 500TF	070/98.017	
83-SG		Gyrocopter		
83-SJ	F-JBQT	Best Off Sky Ranger		
83-SL		Humbert Tetras *(W/o 6.7.03)*		
83-SU		Fly Synthesis Storch		
83-TM	F-JJHI	Light Aero Avid Flyer IV "Tundra"		
83-UA		Slepcev Storch		
83-VD		Rans S-6 Coyote II		
83-VG	F-JJDT	Aero Service Guepard 912		

84 : Vaucluse

84-J		Huntair		
84-0		Airplast Prima		
84-Y		Albatross Delta Pilot		
84-AE		Pipistrelle		
84-AJ		Croses Airplume		
84-AL		Aviasud Mistral		
84-AP		Weedhopper Europa II		
84-AS		Eipper Quicksilver MX		
84-AT		Weedhopper JC.31		
84-BA		Moto du Ciel		
84-BB		Croses Airplume		
84-BY		AMF Chevvron Amphibian		
84-CB		Weedhopper AX-3		
84-CC		Weedhopper JC.31		
84-CW		Air Micro		
84-DF		Albatros		
84-DG		Air Création		
84-DI		Rans S-6 Coyote II		
84-DO		Air Création GT BI		
84-EA		Dynali Chickinox		
84-EL		Marquion Gyrocopter		
84-EM		Gyrocopter AX-06?		
84-EN		Gyrocopter AX-06?		
84-EW		Aquilair Swing		
84-EY		Cierva C.30 autogyro replica		
84-FH		Zenair CH-601 Zodiac		
84-GY		Mignet HM.14		

85 : Vendée

85-A		Allegro		
85-AA		Quartz		
85-AD		Agriplane Condor		
85-AE		Weedhopper		
85-AL		Quartz		
85-AT		Weedhopper Europa II		
85-AV		Weedhopper		
85-AX		Allegro		
85-BF	F-JATC	SMAN Pétrel Amphibian	026	
85-BH		Synairgie Puma		
85-BJ		Synairgie Puma		
85-BK		Weedhopper		
85-BL		Weedhopper		
85-BT		Weedhopper		
85-BX		Weedhopper		
85-BY		Weedhopper		
85-CD		Trike		
85-CL		Air Création		
85-CV		Air Création		
85-CX		Air Création		
85-DC		Air Création Quartz		
85-DD		Weedhopper		
85-DG		Weedhopper		
85-DJ		Moto du Ciel		
85-DS		Hermes		
85-EL		Quicksilver GT-500		
85-EN		Quicksilver MXL-III Sport		
85-EP		Air Création Quartz		

85-ES		Synairgie Puma		
85-EU		AX-3		
85-EX		Best Off Sky Ranger		
85-FB		Synairgie Trike		
85-FJ		Best Off Sky Ranger		
85-FN		Kitfox		
85-FR		SMAN Pétrel		
85-FT		Technic' ULM (Maestro Quatro?)		
85-GA	F-JCJS	Humbert Tetras		
85-GU		Humbert Tetras ?		
85-HP		(Trike?)/ Air Création Mild		
85-HQ	F-JHVJ	Aero Services Guepy 582		
W85-IM		Evektor EV.97 Eurostar	2001-14-10 *(or 10-14?)*	
85-IQ		3XTrim		
85-JB		Air Création Kiss		
85-JM		3XTrim		
85-JT		"TL-S"		
85-JX		Aerotrophy Trophy 2000		
85-KC		Humbert Tetras		
85-KE		Buse'Air 150		
85-KG		Light Aero Avid Flyer IV		
85-KH		Best Off Sky Ranger		
85-KQ		Aerotrophy A22 Vision		
85-KT		TL Ultralight TL-2000 Sting carbon		
85-LN	F-JHYC	Evektor EV-97 Eurostar	2001-13-08	85-11
85-LN		Evektor EV-97 Eurostar	2003-16-21	
85-LS	F-JHAA	3XTrim		
85-LW		Aeropro Eurofox		

86 : Vienne

86-AA		Aile Stryker 19	
86-AO		Air Création	
86-BA		Air Création Buggy / iXess	
86-BJ		Zenith Barodeur	
86-BS		Magni M-16 Gyro	
86-BX		Quasar	
86-CN		Air Création Quartz	
86-CT		Zodiac Ultrastar	
86-DU		Zodiac Twinstar	
86-EC		Dynali Chickinox	
86-EN		X5	
86-GK		Weedhopper	
86-GR		Air Création SX	
86-JJ		Synairgie	
86- . .		Aviasud Albatros AE-209	24

87 : Haute-Vienne

87-M		Eipper Quicksilver	
87-AY		Aviasud Albatros	
87-BY		Dyn'Aéro MCR-01	90
87-JM		B&F Funk FK-9	

88 : Vosges

88-I		Humbert 02 Moto du Ciel	
88-AJ		Humbert Moto du Ciel	WHB-1
88-AK		Humbert Moto du Ciel	
88-AN		Humbert Moto du Ciel	POP-01
88-CE		Cosmos	
88-CI		Air Création Fun	
88-CL		Weedhopper	
88-DD		Weedhopper	
88-DE		Denney Kitfox	
88-DF		Moto du Ciel	
88-DM	F-JBPJ	Humbert Tetras	
88-DN		Humbert Tetras	
88-DT		Humbert Tetras	
88-EC		Humbert Moto du Ciel	
88-ED		Humbert Moto du Ciel	
88-EE		Humbert Tetras	
88-EG		ACV Guepy	
88-EQ		Humbert Tetras	
88-ES		Gemini	
88-ET	F-JASO	Humbert Tetras	
88-EX		Weedhopper	
88-FB		Humbert Tetras	
88-FE	F-JBZE	Humbert Moto du Ciel	
88-FF		Air Création	
88-FY	F-JGCD	ACV Guepy 582	
88-GA	F-JCXX	Humbert Tetras	
88-GB	F-JBDP	Humbert Moto du Ciel	
88-GD		Humbert Tetras	
88-GI		Mignet HM.1000 Balèrit	114
88-GJ		Cosmos	
88-GP		Humbert Moto du Ciel	
88-GS		Best Off Sky Ranger	
88-GT		Humbert Tetras	
88-HE		Raj Hamsa X'Air	
88-HF		Humbert Tetras	
88-HI		Humbert Tetras *(W/o 12.5.03)* (Earlier reported as Moto du Ciel)	
88-HL	F-JGCM	Espace Liberté Yuma	FELS 05 06 2001
88-HM	F-JGDS	Jodel D.20 Legende	17
88-HP		Air Création GT BI	
88-HQ		Humbert Moto du Ciel	
88-IB	F-JGEI	Humbert Tetras 912CSL	
88-KJ		Best Off Sky Ranger	

89 : Yonne

89-AA		Etendard		
89-BC		Air Création Quartz		
89-BH		Air Création Quartz		
89-BI		Air Création		
89-BM		Air Création		
89-BS		Air Création Quartz		
89-CF		Air Création		
89-CM		Air Création		
89-DD		Air Création		
89-DY		Air Création		
89-EB		Air Création		
89-EC		Air Création		
89-EH		Air Création		
89-EK		Air Création		
89-FH		Air Création Clipper		
89-FJ		Weedhopper		
89-FY		Rans S-6 Coyote II		
89-GK		Buse'Air 150		
89-GO		Cosmos		
89-HM		Zenair CH-601 Zodiac		
89-HN		Zenair CH-601 Zodiac		
89-HO		Zenith Barodeur		
89-HR		Buse'Air 150		
89-HV		Tecnam P.92 Echo	341-10	
89-IK		Mignet HM.293 Pou du Ciel		
89-IV		Buse'Air 150		
89-JA		Best Off Sky Ranger		
89-JB		Air Création / Cosmos		
89-JG		Aviakit Vega		
89-JI		Chapelet Lazer		
89-JK		European Airwings Springbok 2000		
89-JT		Air Création Clipper/ Kiss		
89-JU		Aviakit Vega *(Damaged 24.6.01)*		
89-KB		Air Création GT		
89-KC		Quicksilver MX-L		
89-KG	F-JGPZ	Jodel D.18	214	F-PRJP
89-KM		Cosmos		
89-LC		Light Aero Avid Flyer		
89-LG		Aviasud AE.209Albatros		
W89-LU		Denney Kitfox	CFX 01	

90 : Territoire-de-Belfort

90-AS		Cosmos
90-BG		Cosmos
90-BK		Weedhopper Europa II
90-CC	F-JGCV	Humbert Tetras
90-CG		Humbert Tetras
90-CI		Ikarusflug Eurofox Savane
90-CK		Macair Merlin
90-CL		Aviasud Albatros
90-CR		Rans S-6-116 Super Coyote II
90-DG		Rans S-6 Coyote II
90-DH		J-6 Karatoo (also reported as Let-Mont Tulak)
90-DK		Cosmos
90-DM	F-JGNX	Pipistrel/Zen ULM Sinus
90-DN		Cosmos
W90-DQ		Gyrocopter *(W/o 12.5.03)*

91 : Essonne

91-M		Ulac Aviation X99	169
91-N		Landray GL.4 Visa	
91-O		Eipper Quicksilver	
91-S		Aviasud Sirocco "Antar"	
91-V		Aviasud Sirocco "Antar"	
91-X		Aviasud Sirocco "Antar"	
91-Y		Aviasud Sirocco "Antar"	
91-AK		Trike	
91-BL		Veliplane	
91-BN		FT-91 Renegade	
91-CB		FT-91 Renegade	
91-CF		Eipper Quicksilver	
91-CV		Mervay	
91-DU		FT-91 Renegade	
91-ED		Quartz 2 XS	
91-FN		Eipper Quicksilver MX	
91-FT		Renegade Spirit 503	
91-GF		Eipper Quicksilver MX	
91-GH		La Mouette	
91-GK		Air Création	
91-GQ		Maestro	
91-HA		Chariot	
91-HC		Aviasud AE.532 Mistral	
91-HF		Papillon II	
91-HY		Allegro 2-seater	
91-IJ		Air Création SX	
91-IO		Cyclone AX-3	
91-JE		Barry Souricette	
91-JM		Sky Ranger	
91-JN		Barry Souricette	
91-KC		Ultralair AX3-14	
91-KH		Dynamic 503	
91-KI		Aviakit Vega 2000C	
91-KJ		Aero Kuhlmann SCUB / AK	
91-KP		Sky Ranger	
91-KV		Cosmos	
91-KX		Cosmos	

91-LA		Pulsar / La Mouette		
91-LE		Sky Ranger		
91-LL		Aquilair Swing 14		
91-LN		Swift motorglider		
91-LO		Cosmos		
91-LP		Comco Ikarus Fox C-22		
91-LU		Air Création GTE Mild		
91-MO		Zenith Barodeur		
91-MP		Best Off Sky Ranger		
91-MU		unidentified paramotor		
91-NC		AX-3		
91-NG		Air Domi Trophy TT2000		
91-NM	F-JFAH	Avid Amphibian		
91-OA		Air Création Mild		
91-OY		Cosmos		
91-PT		Barry Souris Bulle		
91-QE		Air Création GT BI		
91-QI		DTA Dynamic		
91-QO		Air Création Quartz		
91-QR		Zenair CH-701 STOL		
91-QT		Zenair CH-701 STOL		
91-RK	F-JFBZ	Pipistrel/Zen ULM Sinus		
91-RY	F-JFBW	Fly Synthesis Storch		
91-SJ		Air Création		
91-TB		Landray GL-06 Papillon		
91-TQ		ICP Super Bingo	02 06 52 059	
91-UM		Cosmos		
91-UT		Jodel D.921	198	F-PBXM
91-VG		Zlin Savage		
91-VN		Air Création GTE		
91-WC		Barry Souricette		

92 : Hauts-de-Seine

92-K		Pulsar III		
92-AD		Veliplane Trike		
92-AE		Veliplane		
92-AK		Veliplane		
92-AN		Eipper Quicksilver MX		
92-AR		Kolb Ultrastar		
92-AU		Eipper Quicksilver MX II		
92-BK		Zenith Baroudeur		
92-BM		Zenith Baroudeur		
92-BS		Zenith Baroudeur		
92-BU		Zenith Baroudeur		
92-CH		Kolb Ultrastar		
92-CT		Aviasud Mistral		
92-CU		CFM Shadow Series B	010	G-MNES
92-CX		Air's Maestro		
92-DF		Zenith Baroudeur	123	
92-DN		Zenith Baroudeur		56-G
92-EB		Air Création		
92-EP		Air Création		
92-EQ		Zenith Baroudeur		
92-EV		Veliplane		
92-FF		JC.31 Weedhopper		
92-FG		GT-BI Quartz		
92-FN		Zenith Baroudeur		
92-FP		Zenith Baroudeur		
92-GA		Cosmos		
92-GD		Air's Maestro		
92-GM		Quartz		
92-GN		Air's Maestro II		
92-GP		Cosmos		
92-GS		Air Création/ Cosmos 14		
92-GU		Aviasud Mistral		83-DA
92-HD		Weedhopper		
92-HE		Air Création Cosmos		
92-HJ		Solar Wings Pegasus Quantum		
92-HO		Jonathan		
92-HQ		Weedhopper		
92-HU		Air Création Fun GT		
92-HV		Aviasud Albatros	383	
92- I I		Air Création Ghost 12		
92-IO		Weedhopper AX-3		
92-IR		Rans S 6ESD Coyote II		
92-IY		TEAM Mini-MAX		
92-JA		Air Création Cosmos Chronos		
92-JC		DTA Dynamic		
92-JP		Cosmos Chronos		
92-KM		Comco Ikarus C-42		
92-KU		Cosmos Chronos (also reported as Weedhopper)		
92-LK		Magni gyrocopter		

93 : Seine-Saint-Denis

93-AJ		Mignet HM.293		
93-AK		ULAC X99		
93-BB		Zenith Baroudeur ('Thompson' ?)		
93-BG		Aériane Sirocco		
93-BY		Air Création		
93-CU		Cosmos Trike		
93-EO		Best Off Sky Ranger		
93-ET		Rans S-6ESD Coyote II		
93-FG		Cosmos		
93-FH		Cosmos Chronos		
93-FJ		Aviasud Albatros AE-209	28	65-CV
93-FK		Rans S-6 Coyote II		
93-FM		Curtiss Jenny replica		
93-FR		ICP MXP-740 Savannah	06-96-50-036	
93-FV		Best Off Sky Ranger		
93-GI		Cosmos		
93-GN		Air Création Clipper GTE		
93-HG		Cosmos/ Top 12.9		
93-JP		Air Création Cosmos		
93-LO		Air Création Quartz		

94 : Val-de-Marne

94-AQ		Air Création		
94-AX		Aviasud Sirocco		
94-BD		Aviasud Sirocco		
94-BE		Coutrot Pou du Ciel		
94-CH		Pacific		
94-DT		JCC Aviation J-300 Joker		
94-EC		Quartz X5		
94-EF		Mainair Gemini/Flash IIA		
94-EH		Veliplane		
94-EV		Air Création Cosmos		
94-EX		Weedhopper AX-3		
94-FA		Zenith Baroudeur		
94-FB		Air Création Cosmos Chronos/Fun GT BI		
94-FG		Mignet HM.1000 Balèrit	71	
94-FU		Aviasud AE.209 Albatros		
94-GK		Air Création Fun GTE (Also reporteed as Cosmos Chronos 16, w/o 14.9.02)		
94-HD		Cosmos		
94-HF		unidentified gyrocopter		
94-HP		Weedhopper		
94-HR		Echo 12		
94-HS		Fly Synthesis Storch		
94-IJ		Tecnam P.92 Echo		
94-JH		Air Création XP		

95 : Val d'Oise

95-M		Veliplane		
95-O		Bee		
95-AM		Air Création		
95-AN		Air Création		
95-BP		Zenith Baroudeur		
95-CH		ASEA 3-axis		
95-CY		Aviasud Mistral		
95-DD		Quartz SX		
95-DN		Doutart Chevron Volant		
95-EA		Quartz		
95-EH		Quartz X5		
95-EV		Zenith Baroudeur		
95-FM		Aviasud Mistral	121	
95-GJ		Air Création		
95-GS		Cyclone AX-3 / 503		
95-GU		Mignet HM.1000 Balèrit	24	17-CV
95-HA		Air Création Cosmos		
95-HI		Weedhopper Europa II		
95-HN		Air Création Fun GT BI		
95-HP		Air Création Cosmos		
95-HX		Air Création Cosmos		
95-IA		Air Création Clipper		
95-IH		Croses ULM Criquet		
95-II	F-JBSN	Micro Aviation Pulsar 2		
95-IK		Aquilair Swing 14		
95-IN		Air Création Fun GT		
95-IX		Sirius		
95-JF		Rans S-6ESD Coyote II		
95-KD	F-JBZU	III Sky Arrow 500TF	033	
95-KV	F-JFAJ	Buse Air 150GT	41	
95-LB		Gyrocopter		
95-LC		Air Command Gyrocopter		
95-ME		Gyrocopter		
95-MG		Humbert Moto du Ciel		
95-MU		Best Off Sky Ranger (also reported as Aquilair)		
95-NA		Gyrocopter		
95-NI		III Sky Arrow 500TF		
95-NN		Zenair CH-601 Zodiac *(W/o 18.10.02)*		
95-NP		Jabiru		
95-NQ		Air Création		
95-NX		Spratt 103		
95-OB		Storch IIS		
95-OD		Rans S-6 Coyote II		
95-OG	F-JFTX	Evektor EV-97 Eurostar		
95-ON		Dyn'Aéro MCR-01	208	
95-OT		B&F Funk FK-14 Polaris		
95-OV		Humbert Tetras		
95-QE		Espace Liberté Yuma		

97 : Overseas Départements (Part of the EU - of those listed below, 971 is Guadeloupe, 974 is La Réunion and 975 is St Pierre et Miquelon)

AD-97-1		Weedhopper Amphibian		
97-BA		Air's Maestro		
971-AL		Buccaneer		
974-D		Mustang		
974-J		Quartz 18		
974-AA		Quartz		
974-DH		Zenair CH-701 STOL		
974-DQ		Murphy Renegade Spirit		
974-FQ		B&F Funk FK-12 Comet		
975-ZZ		Rans S-6 Coyote II		

Test Registrations

WAA-01		Jodel D.20 ULM	8
WAU		Barry MB-02 Mini-Bulle	2
WAAB	F-JFQJ	Sauper Aviation J-300 Joker	
WAAC		Jabiru UL/ Jabiru engines/ CAG Toxo	
WC-S9		Cosmos Helios S9	
WDT 211		DTA Dynamic 15	
WEHA1		Humbert Tetras 912CS	
WEHA2		Humbert Tetras 912CSL	
WEL01		Espace Liberté Yuma	

Aircraft transferred from the CNRA register, new ULM registrations not yet known:

17- ?	Jodel D.20	02	F-PMJA
21- ?	Jodel D.19	416T	
25- ?	Jodel D.18	43	F-PZPB(2) F-WZPB
27- ?	Liberty APL-01	01	
31- ?	Druine D.31 Turbulent	49	F-PVQC
33- ?	Jodel D.18	333	F-PCPG
43- ?	Zenair CH-600 Zodiac	6-1001	F-PZXL(2) F-WZXL
47- ?	Jodel D.18	112	F-PZPX(2)
55- ?	Jodel D.18	412	F-PLCT
56- ?	Jodel D.92 Bébé	719	F-PZRA
59- ?	Jodel D.18	91	F-PYNG
62- ?	Brügger MB-2 Colibri	55	F-PYEH
70- ?	Jodel D.18	388	F-PMAS
79- ?	Rans S-6 Coyote II S-116	07961016	F-PSLE F-WSLE
80- ?	Jodel D.92 Bébé	801	F-PJPR
84- ?	Dyn'Aéro MCR-01	88	F-PIAM
91- ?	Light Aero Avid Flyer	979	F-PRKF F-WRKF
?	Jodel D.92 Bébé	UAC.33	F-PBOL

Cross-reference for observed F-J . . . tie-ups (see note at start of this section):

F-JAAS	30-CE	F-JABA	03-AQ
F-JABY	59-ACA	F-JAEN	76-CG
F-JAFY	01-DA	F-JAGP	54-GI
F-JAGS	01-FA	F-JAKQ	67-EM
F-JALL	28-GJ	F-JAMH	59-IW
F-JAMJ	17-GF	F-JAOB	66-DB
F-JAOP	02-CO	F-JAPB	55-FO
F-JAPR	54-JE	F-JAPY	59-ABU
F-JART	18-EO	F-JASO	88-ET
F-JASX	24-CT	F-JATC	85-BF
F-JATT	37-HL	F-JAUK	81-CT
F-JAVL	38-CM/54-PL	F-JAVT	57-GO
F-JAYT	54-DT	F-JAZB	57-HX
F-JAZN	63-FJ	F-JBAL	55-HN
F-JBAS	80-EV	F-JBBZ	47-FN
F-JBCC	32-CV	F-JBCP	65-ED
F-JBDP	88-GB	F-JBDW	66-DK
F-JBEC	73-EF	F-JBER	54-KK
F-JBGD	34-SB	F-JBGG	35-CI
F-JBGL	51-FY	F-JBGS	28-SK
F-JBGT	67-GZ	F-JBHV	72-FS
F-JBHY	81-FC	F-JBIS	72-FV
F-JBJE	28-LW	F-JBJI	01-QM
F-JBJQ	57-BC	F-JBLQ	67-JZ
F-JBLU	57-LR	F-JBME	55-FR
F-JBMJ	54-KX	F-JBOK	73-ER
F-JBOM	08-CR	F-JBOV	16-GD/55-IE
F-JBPJ	88-DM	F-JBQT	83-SJ
F-JBRN	37-DX	F-JBRU	25-NB
F-JBRX	54-LT	F-JBSA	61-EF
F-JBSN	75-OJ/95-II	F-JBSW	56-DR
F-JBTG	67-GZ	F-JBUE	79-EQ
F-JBUL	62-FX	F-JBUW	01-NS
F-JBVS	75-MI	F-JBWE	71-FC
F-JBWG	56-CQ	F-JBWZ	44-OE
F-JBXV	20-GS	F-JBYR	10-FY
F-JBZE	88-FE	F-JBZG	57-PM
F-JBZI	55-FC	F-JBZU	95-KD
F-JCBH	01-KM	F-JCBU	59-TH/54-RY
F-JCCR	59-TZ	F-JCDE	22-EA
F-JCFN	67-LG	F-JCGI	83-GR
F-JCJS	85-GA	F-JCKL	01-KF
F-JCKM	01-KG	F-JCKO	01-KH
F-JCKR	55-GS	F-JCLG	27-KS/27-OB
F-JCLN	25-IT	F-JCLP	21-NO
F-JCLU	59-UC	F-JCMB	83-OU
F-JCMV	80-GY	F-JCOO	67-DS
F-JCOS	01-IR	F-JCPP	59-SH
F-JCPV	54-OA	F-JCQO	83-CL
F-JCQS	28-PL	F-JCQT	28-QQ
F-JCQU	73-FU	F-JCSK	54-OD
F-JCTJ	04-BP	F-JCTY	26-IL
F-JCUE	07-HM	F-JCUF	37-MX
F-JCUM	01-LB	F-JCUO	30-HN
F-JCUQ	77-VL	F-JCVU	11-DO
F-JCWA	74-KF	F-JCWG	06-BZ
F-JCXQ	11-DP	F-JCXR	66-FU
F-JCXS	11-FR	F-JCXX	88-GA
F-JCYT	39-FO	F-JCZX	39-FC
F-JDAB	68-KR	F-JDAS	28-RC
F-JDBB	59-WI	F-JDBG	83-HR
F-JDCH	59-WF	F-JDCX	28-TC
F-JDEI	59-TM	F-JDEK	77-AJC
F-JDEP	15-BM	F-JDET	59-CCR
F-JDFK	25-KB	F-JEAC	43-DD
F-JECR	03-BS	F-JEIK	01-MR
F-JEIU	01-MC	F-JEJC	10-HN
F-JEJI	01-MN	F-JEJM	38-KA
F-JEKE	73-HS	F-JEKH	01-NP
F-JEKV	01-OL	F-JELC	01-OT
F-JELH	01-OF	F-JELJ	01-OQ
F-JELS	01-OR	F-JELU	73-IB
F-JEMR	01-MO	F-JENY	01-PR
F-JEOD	01-QB	F-JEPH	01-QQ
F-JEPL	38-NL	F-JERU	01-RT
F-JETJ	01-SH	F-JEVV	01-TE
F-JFAE	77-ZD	F-JFAH	91-NM
F-JFAI	77-ZV	F-JFAJ	95-KV
F-JFAK	28-ZD	F-JFAY	77-ABF
F-JFBO	77-AEL	F-JFBQ	77-ADW/AFL
F-JFBW	91-RY	F-JFBY	77-MK
F-JFBZ	91-RK	F-JFCE	78-RE
F-JFCO	62-AAW	F-JFDV	75-PZ
F-JFFQ	01-QC/77-AHP	F-JFGF	28-RL
F-JFGH	45-QJ	F-JFHD	59-AAH/02-JO
F-JFHL	62-HH	F-JFHT	59-CAF
F-JFHU	59-ABM	F-JFHX	59-AAG
F-JFIR	59-QE	F-JFIZ	59-ACG
F-JFJE	59-XZ	F-JFJO	62-AAW
F-JFJT	62-EK	F-JFKE	62-ABN/AEF
F-JFKG	62-ABB	F-JFKJ	59-UB
F-JFKS	59-WK	F-JFKV	59-CCC
F-JFKZ	59-CEQ	F-JFLJ ?	62-ACE
F-JFLM	59-CJG	F-JFNO	41-JY
F-JFNQ	28-XN	F-JFOK	28-MZ
F-JFOR	28-SL	F-JFOT	37-KN
F-JFOU	28-VP	F-JFOW	36-KT
F-JFPD	41-HT	F-JFPF	41-HX
F-JFPN	41-JA	F-JFPQ	45-NP
F-JFQS	28-PL	F-JFQT	28-AAD
F-JFQV	18-HF	F-JFQZ	36-LN
F-JFRN	18-HA	F-JFRR	18-HE
F-JFSA	37-PN	F-JFSC	37-KU
F-JFSL	36-LS	F-JFSM	36-LV
F-JFSU	37-KY	F-JFSV	28-VS
F-JFSW	28-VV	F-JFTU	36-KE
F-JFTX	95-OG	F-JFUM	28-UV
F-JFVD	27-MO	F-JFVJ	27-NI
F-JFVN	27-OH	F-JFVP	27-LQ
F-JFVW	27-RM	F-JFWP	76-IL
F-JFXQ	80-IV	F-JFZI	60-KB
F-JFZK	02-JM	F-JGAF	57-PX
F-JGAH	57-QM	F-JGAL	57-QL
F-JGAV	57-QC	F-JGAZ	44-ABY
F-JGBM	54-AR	F-JGBR	55-IX
F-JGBT	54-FF	F-JGBZ	68-MU
F-JGCD	88-FY	F-JGCM	88-HL
F-JGCO	57-SQ	F-JGCV	90-CC
F-JGDE	54-UC	F-JGDI	54-TY
F-JGDP	54-UU	F-JGDS	88-HM
F-JGDT	57-MS	F-JGEM	54-XH
F-JGEN	57-BO	F-JGEO	54-VP
F-JGEP	57-UC	F-JGEQ	57-RV
F-JGER	57-SS	F-JGEW	55-GF
F-JGFI	54-YY	F-JGFK	54-ZD
F-JGGA	10-GH	F-JGGI	08-DU
F-JGGN	10-IB	F-JGGQ	51-JO
F-JGGU	08-EE	F-JGGV	08-DW
F-JGHA	08-EK	F-JGHH	08-EG
F-JGIE	08-FO	F-JGMO	71-GP
F-JGNC	25-JI	F-JGNS	21-RY
F-JGNX	90-DM	F-JGOA	21-SG
F-JGOJ	39-RF	F-JGOY	71-HA
F-JGPH	25-NQ	F-JGPJ	25-OG
F-JGPW	54-QM	F-JGPX	25-NY
F-JGPZ	89-KG	F-JGQD	70-FH
F-JGQU	21-TL	F-JGRL	21-UA
F-JGSI	67-MT	F-JGTN	67-PF
F-JGTO	67-PE	F-JGTP	21-QP
F-JGTQ	67-PL	F-JGTU	67-MN
F-JGTW	68-OP	F-JGUC	67-QS
F-JGUF	67-QY	F-JGXE	71-GL
F-JGYN	21-VF	F-JHAA	85-LS
F-JHGQ	50-HL	F-JHGU	50-JE
F-JHGX	61-FG	F-JHHI	50-JB
F-JHHQ	14-FR	F-JHHT	50-JS
F-JHHY	61-IA	F-JHIK	14-GI
F-JHIW	50-LE	F-JHMS	29-EX
F-JHMZ	70-FG	F-JHOO	29-IA
F-JHQI	56-GL	F-JHTC	44-UH
F-JHTP	44-OE	F-JHTY	76-JV
F-JHUA	72-HU	F-JHVF	72-IB
F-JHVJ	85-HQ	F-JHVR	44-XO
F-JHWF	44-XD	F-JHWJ	72-IT
F-JHWS	49-KU	F-JHWX	49-HE
F-JHXP	72-JB	F-JHYC	85-LN
F-JHYF	24-JM	F-JHYL	44-ABV
F-JHYV	72-JL	F-JHZC	49-LO

F-JIAI	31-AI	F-JIAO	31-AO
F-JIBB	09-AB	F-JIBI	31-BI
F-JIBP	31-BP	F-JIBQ	31-BQ
F-JIBU	31-BU	F-JIBV	31-BV
F-JIDE	31-DE	F-JIFL	23-CD
F-JIHU	65-HU	F-JIQE	81-QE
F-JIVE	31-VE	F-JIVP	31-VP
F-JJAI	83-GP	F-JJCH	13-MO
F-JJCK	13-MH	F-JJCW	13-LZ
F-JJDZ	06-EC	F-JJEW	30-JY
F-JJEY	30-JJ	F-JJHI	83-TM
F-JJIC	11-FA	F-JJJB	83-JF
F-JJKJ	83-AU	F-JJKN	34-KD
F-JKBM	33-PC	F-JKCH	40-EJ
F-JKCI	33-PW	F-JKCR	47-MQ
F-JKCW	64-JO	F-JKDA	47-MW
F-JKDB	47-NB	F-JKDF	50-LJ
F-JKDI	64JP	F-JKEH	47-OE
F-JKFE	16-EM	F-JKFV	64-KH
F-JKGM	64-KX	F-JKQJ	16-LD
F-JKRH	16-BL	F-JKRX	79-BP
F-JKSB	16-CP	F-JKTA	79-EG
F-JLDD	12-BD	F-JOAH	56-GK
F-JPAF	28-ZE	F-JPAI	44-XD
F-JPAS	18-JM		

Registration/call-sign tie-ups unknown:

F-JBBO	Humbert Moto du Ciel		
F-JBCM	Rans S-6 Coyote II		
F-JBGG	Sauper Avn J.300 Joker	(37- ?)	
F-JBQI	HM.1000 Balerit		117
F-JCQJ	Rans S-6 Coyote II		
F-JETP	B&F Funk FK-9 Mk.IV		
F-JFVR	AMF Chevvron 2-32C		
F-JHPQ	Buse'Air 180		
F-JHXD	Jabiru		
F-JIBI	*Used by B&F (Funk) on FK-9 and FK-14 demonstrators*		
F-JIBY	Dyn'Aéro MCR-01		
F-JIMW	Mitchell Wing or similar		
F-JIPF	B&F Funk FK-9		
F-JITM	B&F Funk FK-14 Polaris		
'QO'	Jodel D.18		

Type unidentified:

F-JCWG 06-BZ — F-JGHH 08-EG

See also end of Belgian ULM section for OQ- call signs used by French aircraft.

Finally, a series of "registrations" is now known for radio contolled model hot air balloons. The following have been noted so far:

F-LBC6

F-LBC9 — F-LBC10

HA - HUNGARY

Regn.	Type	C/n	Prev.Id.
HA-AAI	Gerle II	F-04	
HA-ABA	Antonov An-2P	1G234-23	
HA-ABC	Antonov An-2P	1G235-20	
HA-ABD	Antonov An-2P	1G235-21	
HA-ABG	Antonov An-2R	1G151-13	CCCP07438
HA-ABJ	Antonov An-2	1G201-40	RA-84722 CCCP84722
HA-ABK	Antonov An-2	1G235-37	DOSAAF'12'
HA-ABN	Antonov An-2	1G152-47	RA-07519 CCCP07519
HA-ABP	Antonov An-2R	1G185-52	RA-54885 CCCP54885
HA-ABR	Antonov An-2	1G174-08	RA-40830 CCCP40830
HA-ABS	Antonov An-2T	1G76-15	RA-09681 CCCP09681
HA-ACD	Partenavia P.68C	278	N17VK PH-GRO G-BMLR OY-BYS D-GOBY
HA-ACF	Cessna 421	421-0048	N4048L N209PP N4048L
HA-ACG	Cessna 402B	402B1222	N4421Z C-GYJQ (N4176G)
HA-ACL	Dornier Do.28D-2 Skyservant (Walter M601 turbo conversion)	4125	D-IDRC 58+50
HA-ACM	Dornier Do.28D-2 Skyservant (Walter M601 turbo conversion)	4134	D-IDRD 58+59
HA-ACN	Cessna 402B	402B1037	OO-SVD (OO-SVO) G-BENE N98668
HA-ACO	Dornier Do.28D-2 Skyservant (Walter M601 turbo conversion)	4335	G-BWCN 5N-AYE D-ILID 9V-BKL D-ILID
HA-ACQ	Partenavia P.68C	367	D-GERI
HA-ACU	Dornier Do.28D-2/TP Skyservant (Walter M601 turbo conversion)	4121	D-IDRS 58+46
HA-ACX	Beech B24R Sierra	MC-237	HB-EWM
HA-ACY	Dornier Do.28G92 Skyservant (Walter M601 turbo conversion)	4320	KAF-113
HA-ACZ	Dornier Do.28D-2/TP Skyservant (Walter M601 turbo conversion)	4199	F-GHYI 59+24
HA-ANC	Antonov An-2T	1G27-21	
HA-ANG	Antonov An-2P	1G132-53	
HA-ANI	Antonov An-2P	1G132-55	
HA-ANK	Antonov An-2P	1G174-42	
HA-ANM	Antonov An-2P	1G187-35	
HA-ANO	Antonov An-2P (Accident 10.99)	1G188-33	
HA-ANP	Antonov An-2P	1G224-09	
HA-ANR	Antonov An-2TD	1G224-10	
HA-ANS	Antonov An-2P	1G230-21	
HA-ANT	Antonov An-2P	1G230-22	
HA-ANV	Antonov An-2P	1G231-48	
HA-ANX	Antonov An-2P	1G232-57	
HA-ANZ	Antonov An-2P	1G232-56	
HA-APA	Piper PA-28R-200 Cherokee Arrow II	28R-7535328	OY-BLM (SE-GLK)
HA-APC	Piper PA-28R-200 Cherokee Arrow B	28R-7135009	SE-FPN
HA-APF	Piper PA-28-140 Cherokee	28-23765	SE-FAE
HA-APG	Piper PA-32-300 Cherokee Six	32-40333	C-FYDY
HA-APH	Piper PA-28-180 Cherokee C	28-2381	N5863W
HA-API	Piper PA-32-300 Cherokee Six	32-40220	N4149W
HA-APJ	Piper PA-28-140 Cherokee F	28-7325128	SE-GAS
HA-APK	Piper PA-28-140 Cherokee C	28-26700	D-EEFI N5868U
HA-APL	Piper PA-28-140 Cherokee B	28-25362	D-EBTB N8166N
HA-APN	Piper PA-28-181 Archer II	28-8090277	D-EAHP(2) N8179X
HA-APO	Piper PA-28R-200 Cherokee Arrow II	28R-7335188	D-EDMH N55158
HA-APR	Piper PA-46-310PMalibu	46-8408030	OY-JEK N4337G
HA-ARA	Aero Commander 500A	1113-55	SE-GUR N1527T G-ASIO N4441 N6236X
HA-BCA	Mil Mi-2 (Preserved)	516301099	
HA-BCB	Mil Mi-2 (Wrecked)	516302099	
HA-BCD	Mil Mi-2 (Wfu)	517537032	
HA-BCE	Mil Mi-2	5111201011	
HA-BCF	Mil Mi-2	5111202011	
HA-BCG	Mil Mi-2	511543080	DOSAAF-42
HA-BCH	Mil Mi-2	543723084	DOSAAF-41
HA-BCI	Mil Mi-2 (Wfu 10.97)	562247032	D-HVAD 94+81 LSK-377

HA-BCJ	Mil Mi-2	562818043	D-HVAA 94+64 NVA-423
HA-BCK	Mil Mi-2 (W/o 28.12.99)	562946063	D-HVAB 94+65 LSK-503
HA-BCL	Mil Mi-2	563820114	D-HVAC 94+53 LSK-306
HA-BCM	Mil Mi-2 (Reservation)	unkn	
HA-BCR	Mil Mi-2	546743080	DOSAAF-O9
HA-BCT	Mil Mi-2	547716062	RA-20761 CCCP20761
HA-BDA	Aérospatiale AS.350B2 Ecureuil	2472	F-WYME
HA-BDB	Aérospatiale AS.350B2 Ecureuil	2607	
HA-BDC	Aérospatiale AS.350B Ecureuil	1715	OO-VCZ D-HLOS
HA-BFA	Mil Mi-2	545049017	UR-14351 CCCP14351
HA-BFC	Mil Mi-2	549245065	UR-23337 CCCP23337
HA-BFG	Mil Mi-2 (W/o 18.5.96 ?)	5210003106	UR-15618 CCCP15618
HA-BFK	Mil Mi-2	525916128	UR-23513 CCCP23513
HA-BFM	Mil Mi-2 (Reservation)	unkn	
HA-BFN	Mil Mi-2 (Reservation)	unkn	
HA-BFO	Mil Mi-2 (Reservation)	unkn	
HA-BFP	Mil Mi-2 (Reservation)	unkn	
HA-BFR	Mil Mi-2	528021013	UR-20817 EW-20817 CCCP20817
HA-BFS	Mil Mi-2 (Reservation)	unkn	
HA-BFT	Mil Mi-2	526534020	UR-20657 CCCP20657
HA-BFU	Mil Mi-2	525108017	UR-14360 CCCP14360
HA-BFV	Mil Mi-2 (Wfu, CoA exoired 2.97)	529812056	UR-20365 CCCP20365
HA-BFY	Mil Mi-2	5411038109	DOSAAF
HA-BFZ	Mil Mi-2	526442010	CCCP20653
HA-BGC	Mil Mi-2	543722084	Sov.mil:31 red
HA-BGE	Mil Mi-2	568942124	Slovak:8942 Czech:8942
HA-BGF	Mil Mi-2	518215053	Slovak:8215 Czech:8215
HA-BGH(2)	Mil Mi-2 (Stored)	518918104	HAF: 8918
HA-BGI	Mil Mi-2	547744082	UkraineAF SovietAF
HA-BGJ	Mil Mi-2	5110717098	Czech:0717
HA-BGK	Mil Mi-2	518915104	HAF: 8915
HA-BGL	Mil Mi-2 (W/o 31.3.05)	519415095	HAF: 9415
HA-BGM	Mil Mi-2 (Stored)	519414095	HAF: 9414
HA-BGN	Mil Mi-2	518345093	HAF: 8345
HA-BGO	Mil Mi-2 (Crashed 19.8.02)	548633044	(HA-BGH) (HA-BGD) RA-01149 Sov.mil
HA-BNA	Britten-Norman BN-2A-27 Islander	816	YR-BNT Rom.AF:816 YR-BNT G-BEGP
HA-DAD	Antonov An-2R	1G122-14	RA-02603 CCCP02603
HA-DAE	Antonov An-2R	1G164-06	RA-16053 CCCP16053
HA-DAF	Antonov An-2R	1G169-26	RA-07811 CCCP07811
HA-ELA	WagAero CUBy II	AAH-O10	
HA-FAA	Reims/Cessna FA.337G Super Skymaster (Reims-assembled 337G with US c/n 33701609)	F33700073	OE-FAH (F-BJDI)
HA-FAB	Fokker F.27 Friendship 500	10370	HB-ISY F-BPUB PH-FMS
HA-FAC	Fokker F.27 Friendship 500	10341	PH-FLM PT-LAL N272FA PH-EXM VH-EWO OY-STO PH-FLM
HA-FAD(2)	Fokker F.27 Friendship 500	10449	PH-JLN D-AAAF PH-JLN F-BSUN PH-FPZ
HA-FAE	Fokker F.27 Friendship 500F	10425	HB-IVQ PH-FOZ G-BVZW 9Q-CBU PH-FOZ VH-EWS F-BYAF OY-APA (OY-DKR) PH-FOZ

HA-FAF	Fokker F.27 Friendship 500F	10632	PH-FYC F-WQKM PH-FYC PT-LAJ PH-FSJ PH-EXB
HA-FAG	Cessna 421C Golden Eagle	421C0008	N156RH F-GKRH D-IBUS N87542
HA-FAH	Fokker F.27 Friendship 500F	10634	PH-FHL PT-LAK PH-FSL (N426SA) PH-EXJ
HA-FBA	Zlin Z.43	0060	
HA-FBI	Zlin Z.43	0075	
HA-HSA	Mil Mi-8T	7970	UR-22623 CCCP22623
HA-HSB	Kamov Ka.32T	2991101	UR-CBK
HA-HSC	Kamov Ka.32T	2788617	
HA-HSD	Kamov Ka.32T	1788613	
HA-HUY	Yakovlev Yak-52	899912	LY-AFR DOSAAF-99
HA-HUZ	Yakovlev Yak-52	9011001	LY-AMC DOSAAF-106
HA-JAA	Yakovlev Yak-52	899802	DOSAAF-74
HA-JAB	Yakovlev Yak-18T	22202023842	FLA-02160 CCCP44420
HA-JAC	Yakovlev Yak-18T	22202034139	RA-44506 HA-JAC FLA-02159
HA-JAD	Yakovlev Yak-18T	5200509	FLA-02161
HA-JAE	Yakovlev Yak-52	9011011	DOSAAF-113
HA-JAJ	Yakovlev Yak-18T	22202040216	DOSAAF
HA-JAL	Yakovlev Yak-18T	22202047216	DOSAAF
HA-JAO	Yakovlev Yak-52	unkn	
HA-JAS	Cessna 177RG Cardinal RG	177RG1193	C-GLMD N52394
HA-JAT	Yakovlev Yak-52	unkn	
HA-JAV	Yakovlev Yak-52	856008	DOSAAF
HA-JAX	Yakovlev Yak-52	unkn	
HA-JAY	Yakovlev Yak-52	877412	LY-JAN Ukr.AF 24red DOSAAF-24yel
HA-JDA	Cessna 172M	17264977	C-GKHH N64032
HA-JDC	Reims/Cessna F150L	F15000728	OE-CVW HB-CVW
HA-JDE	SOCATAMS.893A Rallye Commodore 180	10800	D-ELSJ
HA-JDG	Cessna F150H	F150-0313	D-EDDH
HA-JDH	Reims/Cessna F150M	F15000734	D-ECLQ
HA-JDI	SOCATA MS.894A Minerva 220	11076	D-EKMI F-BRMI
HA-JDJ	Cessna 182E	18254279	OE-DDC N3279Y
HA-JDL	IAR-823	41	Rom.AF
HA-JDM(2)	IAR-823	42	Rom.AF
HA-JDN	IAR-823	44	Rom.AF
HA-JDO	Cessna F.172D	17250001/F172-0003	OE-DCW F-WLIS (N2401U)
HA-JDP	SOCATAMS.894A Minerva 220	11625	D-EFAA F-BSFA
HA-JDQ	Cessna 150C	15059991	OE-AYI N7891Z
HA-JDR	Cessna 182S	18280385	D-EMGL
HA-JDT	Cessna 150 (Reservation)	17802	OE-AFD N6402T
HA-JDU	Reims/Cessna F177RG Cardinal RG	F177RG0063	N43AG D-EANY N10632
HA-JDV	Reims/Cessna F150K	F15000547	D-ECCD
HA-JDW	Mooney M.20J Model 201	24-1005	D-ELIW(3) (N3996H)
HA-JDX	Piper PA-38-112 Tomahawk	38-80A0067	HB-PHE D-ECIZ N9721N
HA-JDY	SOCATAMS.893A Rallye Commodore 180	11779	D-EGOH F-BSZC
HA-JDZ	Cessna F172G (Reservation)	F172-0300	D-EGAC
HA-JUA	Reims/Cessna F177RG Cardinal RG	F177RG0140	F-BOEL F-ODEA F-BXQL
HA-JUV	Cessna 177 Cardinal	17700885	D-EDVY N29435
HA-LAC(2)	LET L-410UVP-E3	871828	Rus.AF: 21 red
HA-LAD	LET L-410UVP-E8A	902516	
HA-LAE	LET L-410UVP-E8A	902517	
HA-LAF	LET L-410UVP-E8A	902518	
HA-LAG(2)	LET L-410UVP	800425	CCCP67159
HA-LAK(2)	LET L-410UVP-E	861606	UN-67566 RA-67566 CCCP67566
HA-LAO	LET L-410UVP-E	902501	RA-67648 CCCP67648

HA-LAQ	LET L-410UVP-E4	841332	HAF-332
			HA-YFB
HA-LAR	LET L-410UVP-E4 (W/o 27.1.05)	871923	HAF-923
HA-LAV	LET L-410UVP	892215	SP-KTA
			HA-LAV
			RA-67604
			CCCP67604
HA-LAY	LET L-410UVP	841326	LZ-MNG
			UR-67100
			CCCP67100
HA-LAZ	LET L-410UVP-E	902504	SP-KTB
			HA-LAZ
			RA-67651
			CCCP67651
HA-LCN	Tupolev TU-154B-2	78A-326	
HA-LCR	Tupolev TU-154B-2 (Badly damaged 5.7.00)	82A-543	
HA-LCU	Tupolev TU-154B-2	82A-531	CCCP85531
HA-LCV	Tupolev TU-154B-2	82A-544	CCCP85544
HA-LCX	Tupolev TU-154M	88A-788	RA-85650
			CCCP85650
HA-LCY	Tupolev TU-154M	unkn	
HA-LDB	LET L.200D Morava	171127	
HA-LDC	LET L.200D Morava	171130	
HA-LDF	LET L.200D Morava	171408	
HA-LDG	LET L.200D Morava	171411	S5-CAH
			SL-CAH
			YU-BBF
HA-LEB	Boeing 737-2M8	22090	OO-TEO
			TC-AJK
			OO-TE0
			4X-ABM
			OO-TE0
HA-LEJ	Boeing 737-3Q8	26303	
HA-LEV	Boeing 737-4YO	24904	TC-JDE
HA-LFM	Aérospatiale SA.341G Gazelle	1301	G-OCMJ
			G-HTPS
			G-BRNI
			YU-HBI
HA-LFN	Soko/Aérospatiale SA.341G Gazelle	045	JRV . . . .
HA-LFO	Soko/Aérospatiale SA.341G Gazelle	022	JRV . . . .
HA-LFP	Soko/Aérospatiale SA.341G Gazelle	008	JRV12616
HA-LFR	Soko/Aérospatiale SA.341G Gazelle	021	HA-VLA
			YU-HDN
			JRV . . . .
HA-LFS	Agusta-Bell 206A Jet Ranger II	8108	PH-HHG
			OH-HRJ
			HB-1
HA-LFU	Bell 206BJet Ranger II	2512	HA-LFT
			N4353F
			HA-LFE
			G-BNXF
			N206E
			N12TE
HA-LFV	Soko/Aérospatiale SA.341G Gazelle	084	JRV12705
HA-LFX	Soko/Aérospatiale SA.341G Gazelle	090	
HA-LFY	Soko/Aérospatiale SA.341G Gazelle	095	
HA-LFZ	Sud Avn SA.318C Alouette Astazou	2043	ALAT
HA-LGA	Tupolev TU-154M	78A-283	RA-85283
			CCCP85283
HA-LGB	Tupolev TU-154M	92A-905	RA-85723
			CCCP85723
HA-LGC	Tupolev TU-154M	92A-913	RA-85731
			EP-LAX
			RA85731
			CCCP85731
HA-LGD	Tupolev TU-154M	92A-976	RA-85792
			EP-LAZ
			RA-85792
		85792	
HA-LHA	Boeing 767-27GER	27048	
HA-LHB	Boeing 767-27GER	27049	
HA-LIX	Lisunov Li-2	18433209	
HA-LJB	Yakovlev Yak-40	9640851	CCCP87214
HA-LJC	Yakovlev Yak-40	9440937	4K-87218
			HA-LJC
			CCCP87218
			OK-EEF
HA-LJG	Yakovlev Yak-40	9521640	ER-JGA
			RA-87514
			CCCP87514
HA-LKB	Boeing 737-86Q	30294	OK-TVC
HA-LKO	Boeing 737-5Y0	25185	N185FR
			PT-SSL
			G-OBMR
			XA-RJS
HA-LKP	Boeing 737-5Y0	25289	TC-JDV
			(EI-CFU)
HA-LMA	Fokker F.28-0070	11564	PH-EZR
HA-LMB	Fokker F.28-0070	11565	PH-EZX
HA-LMC	Fokker F.28-0070	11569	PH-EZA
HA-LME	Fokker F.28-0070	11575	PH-WXB
			I-REJU
			PH-EZB
HA-LMF	Fokker F.28-0070	11571	PH-RVE
			(I-REJB)
			PH-EZE
HA-LNA	Canadair CL.600-2B19 Regional Jet	7676	C-FMKZ
HA-LNB	Canadair CL.600-2B19 Regional Jet	7686	C-FMNW

HA-LNC	Canadair CL.600-2B19 Regional Jet	7784	
HA-LND	Canadair CL.600-2B19 Regional Jet	7807	
HA-LOA	Boeing 737-7Q8	28254	
HA-LOB	Boeing 737-7Q8	29346	
HA-LOC	Boeing 737-8Q8	32797	
HA-LOD	Boeing 737-6Q8	28259	
HA-LOE	Boeing 737-6Q8	28260	
HA-LOF	Boeing 737-6Q8	29348	N1786B
HA-LOG	Boeing 737-6Q8	28261	
HA-LOH	Boeing 737-6Q8	30667	
HA-LOI	Boeing 737-8Q8	29350	
HA-LOJ	Boeing 737-7Q8	29349	
HA-LOK	Boeing 737-8Q8	30669	
HA-LOL	Boeing 737-7Q8	29352	
HA-LOM	Boeing 737-8Q8	30672	
HA-LON	Boeing 737-7Q8	29353	
HA-LOP	Boeing 737-7Q8	29354	
HA-LOR	Boeing 737-7Q8	29355	
HA-LOS	Boeing 737-7Q8	29359	
HA-LOT	Boeing 737-8Q8 (Reservation 4 .05)	30684	
HA-LPA	Airbus A320-233	839	EI-DFV
			VP-BVC
			F-WWBE
HA-LPB	Airbus A320-232	1635	EI-DFT
			N635VX
			F-WWDT
HA-LPC	Airbus A320-233	892	EI-DGF
			VP-BVD
			F-WWDF
HA-LPD	Airbus A320-233	1902	EI-DGB
			F-WQTK
			N902VX
			F-WWDG
HA-LPE	Airbus A320-233	1892	EI-DFU
			F-WQTJ
			N892VX
			F-WWBU
HA-LPF	Airbus A320-233	1834	EI-DGC
			F-WQTI
			N834VX
			F-WWBF
HA-LRA	Yakovlev Yak-40	9440837	OK-EED
HA-MAB	Antonov An-2 (Reservation)	unkn	
HA-MAC	Antonov An-2 (Reservation)	unkn	
HA-MAD	Antonov An-2 (Reservation)	unkn	
HA-MAE	Antonov An-2 (Reservation)	unkn	
HA-MAF	Antonov An-2R	1G190-45	LY-ACN
			CCCP84613
HA-MAG	Antonov An-2P	1G114-36	RA-35524
			CCCP35524
HA-MAH	Antonov An-2R	1G178-39	RA-62647
			CCCP62647
HA-MAL	Antonov An-2R	1G225-15	RA-40498
			CCCP40498
HA-MAM	Antonov An-2R	1G208-44	CCCP81540
HA-MAR	Antonov An-2R	1G205-39	RA-17898
			CCCP17898
HA-MAS	Antonov An-2 (Reservation)	unkn	
HA-MAT	Antonov An-2 (Reservation)	unkn	
HA-MAV	Antonov An-2R	1G211-15	RA-43996
			CCCP43996
HA-MAW	Antonov An-2R	1G166-57	RA- . . . . .
			CCCP . . . . .
HA-MAX	Antonov An-2R	1G167-59	RA-82845
			CCCP82845
HA-MAY	Antonov An-2R	1G185-40	CCCP54880
HA-MBA	Antonov An-2R	1G161-06	
HA-MBB	Antonov An-2R	1G161-07	
HA-MBC	Antonov An-2R	1G161-08	
HA-MBD	Antonov An-2R	1G161-09	
HA-MBE	Antonov An-2R	1G161-10	
HA-MBF	Antonov An-2R	1G161-11	
HA-MBG	Antonov An-2R	1G163-29	
HA-MBJ	Antonov An-2R	1G166-28	
HA-MBK	Antonov An-2R	1G166-29	
HA-MBL	Antonov An-2R	1G166-30	
HA-MBN	Antonov An-2R (Wfu)	1G166-32	
HA-MBO	Antonov An-2R	1G166-33	
HA-MBP	Antonov An-2R	1G167-46	
HA-MBR	Antonov An-2R (Wfu)	1G168-14	
HA-MBT	Antonov An-2R	1G172-53	
HA-MBV	Antonov An-2R	1G172-54	
HA-MBZ	Antonov An-2R	1G191-14	RA-84636
			CCCP84636
HA-MCB(2)	Kamov Ka.26	7303410	RA- . . . . .
HA-MCD(2)	Kamov Ka.26	7404717	RA-19558
			CCCP19558
HA-MCE(2)	Kamov Ka.26	7605519	RA- . . . . .
HA-MCF(2)	Kamov Ka.26	7505306	RA- . . . . .
HA-MCH	Kamov Ka.26	7404620	CCCP19 . . .
HA-MCI	Kamov Ka.26	7303406	D-HOAV
			DDR-SPV
			DM-SPV
HA-MCJ	Kamov Ka.26	7303502	CCCP19 . . .
HA-MCK	Kamov Ka.26	7404408	CCCP19414
HA-MCL	Kamov Ka.26	7404420	CCCP19 . . .
HA-MCM	Kamov Ka.26 (Cr 31.7.04)	7202904	CCCP19 . . .
HA-MCN	Kamov Ka.26	7102104	CCCP19 . . .

HA-MCO	Kamov Ka.26 (Stored)	7101804	CCCP-19291
HA-MCP	Kamov Ka.26	7404619	D-HOAR DDR-SPR DM-SPR
HA-MDA	Antonov An-2R	1G176-23	
HA-MDB	Antonov An-2R	1G176-24	
HA-MDE	Antonov An-2R	1G177-20	
HA-MDF	Antonov An-2R	1G181-37	
HA-MDG	Antonov An-2R	1G181-38	
HA-MDH	Antonov An-2R	1G181-39	
HA-MDI	Antonov An-2R	1G181-40	
HA-MDK	Antonov An-2R	1G181-42	
HA-MDM	Antonov An-2R	1G183-20	
HA-MDN	Antonov An-2R (Wfu)	1G183-21	
HA-MDO	Antonov An-2R	1G185-43	
HA-MDP	Antonov An-2R (Wfu)	1G185-44	
HA-MDQ	Antonov An-2R (Wfu)	1G185-45	
HA-MDR	Antonov An-2R	1G185-46	
HA-MDS	Antonov An-2R	1G185-47	
HA-MDT	Antonov An-2R	1G185-53	
HA-MDU	Antonov An-2R	1G186-02	
HA-MDV	Antonov An-2R	1G186-03	OK-MDV HA-MDV
HA-MDX	Antonov An-2R	1G186-05	
HA-MDY	Antonov An-2R	1G186-06	
HA-MDZ	Antonov An-2R	1G186-04	
HA-MEA	Antonov An-2R	1G186-07	
HA-MEB	Antonov An-2R	1G186-08	
HA-MEC	Antonov An-2R	1G187-28	
HA-MED	Antonov An-2R	1G187-29	
HA-MEF	Antonov An-2R	1G187-30	
HA-MEG	Antonov An-2R	1G187-31	
HA-MEI	Antonov An-2R	1G190-18	
HA-MEJ	Antonov An-2R	1Gl90-19	
HA-MEK	Antonov An-2R	1G190-20	
HA-MEL	Antonov An-2R	1G190-21	
HA-MEM	Antonov An-2R	1G190-22	
HA-MEN	Antonov An-2R	1G190-23	
HA-MEO	Antonov An-2R	1G190-24	
HA-MES	Antonov An-2R	1G194-28	
HA-MEX	Antonov An-2R	1G217-53	
HA-MEY	Antonov An-2R	1G217-54	
HA-MEZ	Antonov An-2R	1G127-27	RA- . . . . . CCCP . . . . .
HA-MFA	Z-137T Agro Turbo	026	OM-UJJ OK-UJJ
HA-MFC	Z-137T Agro Turbo	030	OM-UJN OK-UJN
HA-MFD	Z-137T Agro Turbo	034	OM-VIK OK-VIC
HA-MFG	Z-37T Agro Turbo	036	OK-WIC
HA-MFH	LET Z-37P Cmelák	17-07	OK-CKV
HA-MFI	LET Z-37P Cmelák	17-13	OK-CIO
HA-MFJ(2)	LET Z-37P Cmelák	13-10	OM-AIR OK-AIR
HA-MFK	LET Z-37 Cmelák	unkn	
HA-MFL	LET Z-37P Cmelák	11-21	OM-AJA OK-AJA HA-MGX
HA-MFO	LET Z-37P Cmelák	16-22	OK-CJF
HA-MFR	Z-137T Agro Turbo	053	
HA-MFX	LET Z-37 Cmelák	08-24	OM-YJP OK-YJP
HA-MGA	LET Z-37A Cmelák	10-03	OK-ZJS
HA-MGD(2)	LET Z-37A Cmelák	17-19	OK-DJR
HA-MGE(2)	Z-137T Agro Turbo	045	OK-XJB
HA-MGF	LET Z-37T Agro Turbo	023	OM-SJB OK-SJB
HA-MGH(2)	LET Z-37T Agro Turbo	021	OK-SJN
HA-MGJ(2)	Z-137T Agro Turbo	025	OK-UJI
HA-MGN(2)	Z-137T Agro Turbo	035	OK-VID
HA-MGO	LET Z-37AC-2 Cmelák	10-12	OK-ZXW OK-ZJW
HA-MGP(2)	LET Z-37 Cmelák	09-13	OK-ZJR
HA-MGR	LET Z-37AC-2 Cmelák	16-28	OK-CJJ
HA-MGS(2)	LET Z-37T Agro Turbo	005	OK-PJC
HA-MGV(2)	LET Z-37T Agro Turbo	009	OK-RJC
HA-MGY	LET Z-37T Agro Turbo (Sold to OK, not yet regd)	008	OK-RJB
HA-MGZ	LET Z-37T Agro Turbo (Sold to OK, not yet regd)	015	OK-RJI
HA-MHN	Antonov An-2R (Wfu)	1G126-02	
HA-MHQ	Antonov An-2R	1G145-42	
HA-MHS	Antonov An-2R	1G145-44	
HA-MHT	Antonov An-2R	1G155-11	
HA-MHU	Antonov An-2R (Stored)	1G155-12	
HA-MHV	Antonov An-2R	1G154-05	
HA-MHW	Antonov An-2R	1G158-60	
HA-MIA	Hiller UH-12E	1329	N14CU N13CU 61-3143
HA-MIB(2)	Rogerson-Hiller UH-12E (W/o 15.5.93)	5224	
HA-MIC	Rogerson Hiller UH-12E (W/o 5.5.00)	5225	
HA-MID	Hiller UH-12E (Wreck)	HA3018	G-BLDM N118HA G-BCXK N118HA
HA-MIF	Robinson R-22 Beta	1872	N700VG N23159
HA-MIG	Hiller UH-12D	1145	N16MQ

HA-MIH	Rogerson-Hiller UH-12E	5226	
HA-MIJ	Hiller UH-12E	2262	G-BDOI XS166
HA-MIK	Enstrom F-28A	124	G-BASB
HA-MIL	Enstrom 280 Shark	1021	G-BTLF N43RG
HA-MIM	Hiller UH-12E4 (Crashed 27.7.00)	2315	OH-HKT G-BPKP S3-BAS S2-ABE AP-ATV
HA-MIO	Robinson R-22 Beta	2256	N2354F
HA-MIR	Enstrom F-28C	138	G-OSWA G-BZZZ G-BBBZ
HA-MIT	Enstrom 280C Turbo Shark	1138	N51732
HA-MIV	Robinson R-44 Astro (W/o 23.2.01)	0666	D-HKAA(2)
HA-MIW	Robinson R-44 Astro	0543	D-HALF
HA-MIX	Robinson R-44 Astro	0650	D-HKUL
HA-MIZ	Robinson R-22B2 Beta	unkn	
HA-MJA	Piper PA-25-235 Pawnee	25-2908	YU-BOK N7110Z
HA-MJB	Piper PA-25-235 Pawnee	25-2403	YU-BKH YU-BBA N6828Z
HA-MJC	Piper PA-25-235 Pawnee C	25-3178	YU-BDB N7272Z
HA-MJE	Cessna A188B Agtruck	18802833T	YU-B . . N73IEF
HA-MJG	Piper PA-36-300 Brave	36-7860088	9A-BLT RC-BLT YU-BLT N9686N
HA-MJH	Piper PA-36-300 Brave	36-7860075	9A-BLP RC-BLP YU-BLP N9702N
HA-MJI	Piper PA-25-235 Pawnee	25-8056006	9A-BMN RC-BMN YU-BMN N9777N
HA-MKA	Antonov An-2R	1G186-29	OM-JIR OK-JIR
HA-MKB	Antonov An-2R	1G190-15	OM-KIU OK-KIU
HA-MKC	Antonov An-2R	1G186-30	OM-JIS OK-JIS
HA-MKE	Antonov An-2R	1G158-34	UR-07714 CCCP07714
HA-MKF	Antonov An-2	1G233-43	OM-248 OM-UIN OK-UIN
HA-MKG	Antonov An-2	1G158-16	(HA-DAG) ? CCCP07696
HA-MKI	Antonov An-2R	1G153-36	LY-ANV CCCP05723
HA-MMC	Kamov Ka.26 (Wfu)	7001002	
HA-MMD	Kamov Ka.26 (Wfu)	7001003	
HA-MME	Kamov Ka.26	7001102	
HA-MMF	Kamov Ka.26	7001103	
HA-MMG	Kamov Ka.26	7001105	
HA-MMK	Kamov Ka.26	7303301	
HA-MMO	Kamov Ka.26	7303304	
HA-MMQ	Kamov Ka.26	7404305	
HA-MMS	Kamov Ka.26	7303307	
HA-MMT	Kamov Ka.26 (Wfu, stored)	7303906	
HA-MMW	Kamov Ka.26 (Wfu)	7303909	
HA-MMX	Kamov Ka.26	7404302	
HA-MMY	Kamov Ka.26	7404303	
HA-MMZ	Kamov Ka.26 (Wfu, stored)	7404304	
HA-MNA	Kamov Ka.26 (Wfu)	7404306	
HA-MNB	Kamov Ka.26	7404307	
HA-MNE	Kamov Ka.26 (Wfu, stored)	7404418	
HA-MNF	Kamov Ka.26 (Wfu, stored)	7505001	
HA-MNH	Kamov Ka.26 (Wfu)	7505010	
HA-MNI	Kamov Ka.26 (Wfu)	7505011	
HA-MNL	Kamov Ka.26	7505203	
HA-MNM	Kamov Ka.26	7505204	
HA-MNO	Kamov Ka.26	7505205	
HA-MNQ	Kamov Ka.26 (Wfu)	7605402	
HA-MNT	Kamov Ka.26	7605603	
HA-MNU	Kamov Ka.26	7605607	
HA-MNV	Kamov Ka.26	7605608	
HA-MNW	Kamov Ka.26	7605609	
HA-MNX	Kamov Ka.26 (Wfu)	7605610	
HA-MNY	Kamov Ka.26	7605611	
HA-MPA	Kamov Ka.26 (Wfu)	7706108	
HA-MPB	Kamov Ka.26	7706109	
HA-MPC	Kamov Ka.26 (Wfu)	7706110	
HA-MPD	Kamov Ka.26	7706111	
HA-MPE	Kamov Ka.26 (Wfu)	7706112	
HA-MPG	Kamov Ka.26	7706306	
HA-MPI	Kamov Ka.26 (Wfu)	7706307	
HA-MPJ	Kamov Ka.26 (Wfu)	7806308	
HA-MPL	Kamov Ka.26	7806310	
HA-MPM	Kamov Ka.26 (Wfu)	7806311	
HA-MPN	Kamov Ka.26	7806312	
HA-MPO	Kamov Ka.26 (Wfu)	7806314	

HA-MPR	Kamov Ka.26	7806315	
HA-MPS	Kamov Ka.26	7806316	
HA-MPT	Kamov Ka.26	7806317	
HA-MPV	Kamov Ka.26	7806319	
HA-MPY	Kamov Ka.26 (Wfu)	7806402	
HA-MPZ	Kamov Ka.26	7806403	
HA-MRA	Kamov Ka.26	7806404	
HA-MRB	Kamov Ka.26	7806408	
HA-MRC	Kamov Ka.26	7806409	
HA-MRD	Kamov Ka.26 (Wfu)	7806410	
HA-MRE	Kamov Ka.26	7806502	
HA-MRF	Kamov Ka.26	7806503	
HA-MRG	Kamov Ka.26 (Wfu)	7806506	
HA-MRH	Kamov Ka.26	7806507	
HA-MRI	Kamov Ka.26	7806508	
HA-MRJ	Kamov Ka.26 (Cr 10.9.04)	7001401	HAF-401
HA-MRK	Kamov Ka.26	7001402	HAF-402
HA-MRL	Kamov Ka.26 (Wfu)	7001405	HAF-405
HA-MRM	Kamov Ka.26 (Wfu)	7001406	HAF-406
HA-MRN	Kamov Ka.26	7001506	HAF-506
HA-MRO	Kamov Ka.26 (Wfu, stored)	7001604	HAF-604
HA-MRP	Kamov Ka.26	7101701	HAF-701
HA-MRQ	Kamov Ka.26	7001510	HAF-510
HA-MRS	Kamov Ka.26	7001501	HAF-501
HA-MRV	Kamov Ka.26	7001601	HAF-601
HA-MRW	Kamov Ka.26	7001509	HAF-509
HA-MRX	Kamov Ka.26 (Wfu)	7001602	HAF-602
HA-MRY	Kamov Ka.26	7001403	HAF-403
HA-MRZ	Kamov Ka.26	7001508	HAF-508
HA-MSI	Hughes 369E	0310E	
HA-MSL	Hughes 269C (W/o 8.1.05)	30-0890	D-HRIO
			D-HMAX
			PH-HCH
			TF-ATH
HA-MSR	Hughes 269C	117-0650	SE-HNH
			OY-HSG
			SE-HNH
			OY-HCG
			HB-XHF
HA-MST	Hughes 269C	110-0067	PH-HIH
			(PH-HHH)
			N9640F
			C-. . . .
			N9640F
HA-MSU	Hughes 269B	116-0277	SE-HCU
HA-MSX	Schweizer 269C	S-1293	SE-HSU
			LN-OTM
			SE-HSU
			N69A
HA-MSZ	Hughes 269C	11-0084	SE-HDL
HA-MTG	PZL M-18 Dromader	1Z006-01	
HA-MTP	PZL M-18 Dromader	1Z007-20	
HA-MTY(2)	PZL M-18A Dromader	1Z017-21	OM-SGC
			OK-SGC
HA-MUI	PZL M-18 Dromader	1Z009-10	
HA-MUR	PZL M-18 Dromader	1Z011-10	
HA-MVA	PZL M-18 Dromader	1Z007-06	SP-FCE
			SP-DBY
			SP-PBC
			OK-LZP
HA-MVB	PZL M-18A Dromader	1Z017-15	OM-SGN
			OK-SGN
HA-MVE	PZL M-18A Dromader	1Z017-20	OM-SGB
			OK-SGB
HA-MZB	Kamov Ka.26	7404710	LY-HAC
			CCCP19551
HA-MZC	Kamov Ka.26	7605514	LY-HAF
			CCCP24336
HA-MZD	Kamov Ka.26	7303501	LY-HAA
			CCCP19335
HA-MZE	Kamov Ka.26	7304004	LY-HAB
			CCCP19481
HA-MZF	Kamov Ka.26	7504904	LY-HAE
			CCCP19577
HA-MZG	Kamov Ka.26	7101705	HAF-705
HA-MZH	Kamov Ka.26	7202510	LY-HAL
			CCCP19371
HA-MZI	Kamov Ka.26	7303408	
HA-MZJ	Kamov Ka.26	7404716	RA-19557
			CCCP19557
HA-MZK	Kamov Ka.26	7404010	
HA-MZL	Kamov Ka.26	7202805	
HA-MZM	Kamov Ka.26	7404416	
HA-MZN	Kamov Ka.26	7404712	LY-HAD
			CCCP19553
HA-MZO	Kamov Ka.26	7505111	
HA-MZP	Kamov Ka.26	7605416	
HA-MZR	Kamov Ka.26	7505114	
HA-MZS	Kamov Ka.26	7505105	
HA-MZT	Kamov Ka.26	7605420	
HA-MZU	Kamov Ka.26	7705911	
HA-MZV	Kamov Ka.26	7404516	
HA-MZW	Kamov Ka.26	7304006	
HA-MZX	Kamov Ka.26	7102003	UR-19261
HA-OME	Super Aero 045	unkn	
HA-PAO	CSS-13 (Polikarpov Po-2)	0448	HAF-'48'
HA-PET	Extra EA.330/L	002	D-EPET(2)

HA-PPY	Soko 341GGazelle	021	HA-LFR
	(Also has Aérospatiale c/n 1118)		HA-VLA
			YU-HDN
			JRV
HA-PYC	PZL-101 Gawron	119292	
HA-PZK	PZL-101 Gawron (Derelict 6.97)	21012	
HA-RBT	Robinson R-44 Raven II	10484	D-HXZY
HA-RTL	Hughes 369D	69-0532D	N54WK
			N58346
HA-SABA	Neico Lancair IV	HSH-LIV-0001	
HA-SABC	Van's RV-4	779	N13HW
HA-SAC	Zlin Z.526A Akrobat	1019	
HA-SAM	Zlin Z.526F Trenér Master	1099	
HA-SAU	Zlin Z.526F Trenér Master (Crashed 3.02)	1292	
HA-SAV	Zlin Z.526F Trenér Master	1293	
HA-SBA	PZL-101A Gawron	107199	
HA-SBB	PZL-101A Gawron	107200	
HA-SBC	PZL-101A Gawron	107201	
HA-SBD	PZL-101A Gawron	107230	
HA-SBE	PZL-101A Gawron	107231	
HA-SBF	PZL-101A Gawron	107232	
HA-SBG	PZL-101A Gawron	107233	
HA-SBH	PZL-101A Gawron	107234	
HA-SBI	PZL-101A Gawron	107235	
HA-SBK	PZL-101A Gawron	107237	
HA-SBL	PZL-101A Gawron	119294	
HA-SBM	PZL-101A Gawron	119295	
HA-SBN	PZL-101A Gawron	119296	
HA-SBP	PZL-101A Gawron	107236	HA-YGA
HA-SDA	Zlin Z.726 Universal	1333	
HA-SDE	Zlin Z.726 Universal	1357	
HA-SDF	Zlin Z.726 Universal	1358	
HA-SDG	Zlin Z.726 Universal	1359	
HA-SEA	PZL-104 Wilga 35A	96315	
HA-SEB	PZL-104 Wilga 35A	118374	
HA-SEC	PZL-104 Wilga 35A (Crashed 14.7.02)	129451	
HA-SED	PZL-104 Wilga 35A	149544	
HA-SEF	PZL-104 Wilga 35 (Dismantled)	59064	Police R-07
HA-SEH	PZL-104 Wilga 35A	17820684	
HA-SEJ	PZL-104 Wilga 35A	18840772	
HA-SEK	PZL-104 Wilga 35A (Accident 7.99)	19870852	
HA-SEL	PZL-104 Wilga 35A	19880864	
HA-SEM	PZL-104 Wilga 35A	19880865	
HA-SEN	PZL-104 Wilga 35A	19880866	
HA-SEO	PZL-104 Wilga 35A (W/o 15.7.96)	19880867	
HA-SEP	PZL-104 Wilga 35A	19880868	
HA-SER	PZL-104 Wilga 35A	20890876	
HA-SES	PZL-104 Wilga 35A	20890875	
HA-SET	PZL-104 Wilga 35A	20900899	
HA-SEU	PZL-104 Wilga 35A	CF15810606	YU-DHU
HA-SEV	PZL-104 Wilga 80	CF15810611	YU-DHX
HA-SEW	PZL-104 Wilga 35A	15800576	DOSAAF'45'
HA-SEZ	PZL-104 Wilga 80	CF21940948	SP-WDS
			EC-GCO
			EC-803
HA-SFA	Zlin Z.42M	0175	
HA-SFE	Zlin Z.42M	0179	
HA-SFG	Zlin Z.42M	0180	
HA-SFJ	Zlin Z.142	0219	
HA-SFK	Zlin Z.142	0220	
HA-SFL	Zlin Z.142	0223	
HA-SFM	Zlin Z.142	0224	
HA-SFN	Zlin Z.142	0225	
HA-SFO	Zlin Z.142	0226	
HA-SFR	Zlin Z.142	0236	
HA-SFS	Zlin Z.142	0237	
HA-SFU	Zlin Z.142	0239	
HA-SFV	Zlin Z.142	0240	
HA-SFX	Zlin Z.142	0243	
HA-SFY	Zlin Z.142	0255	
HA-SFZ	Zlin Z.142	0241	
HA-SGA	Zlin Z.142	0256	
HA-SGC	Zlin Z.142	0273	
HA-SGD	Zlin Z.142	0274	
HA-SGE	Zlin Z.142	0275	
HA-SGF	Zlin Z.142	0282	
HA-SGH	Zlin Z.142	0313	
HA-SGI	Zlin Z.142	0314	
HA-SGJ	Zlin Z.142	0315	
HA-SGK	Zlin Z.142	0346	
HA-SGL	Zlin Z.142	0374	
HA-SGM	Zlin Z.142	0419	
HA-SGN	Zlin Z.142	0420	
HA-SGR	Zlin Z.142	0459	
HA-SGU	Zlin Z.142	0483	
HA-SGV	Zlin Z.142	0484	
HA-SGX	Zlin Z.142	0486	
HA-SGY	Zlin Z.142	0487	
HA-SGZ	Zlin Z.142	0516	
HA-SIF	Zlin Z.50LS	0033	
HA-SIH	Zlin Z.50LS	0050	
HA-SIJ	Zlin Z.50LS	0056	
HA-SJA	Reims FR172J Rocket	FR17200412	D-ECXQ
HA-SJB	Cessna 150D	15060596	OE-AYN
			N4596U
HA-SJC	Cessna 172N	17269115	N734UB
HA-SJD	Cessna 172N	17269825	N738AM
HA-SJE	Cessna 172N	17268295	N733GY

HA-SJF	Cessna 172N	17273311	N4685G
HA-SJG	Cessna 152	15284015	N4909H
HA-SJH	Cessna 152	15285024	N6477P
HA-SJI	Cessna 152	15284544	N5338M
HA-SJK	Cessna 152	15284860	N4960P
HA-SJL	Cessna 172M	17265068	N64179
HA-SJM	Cessna 172M	17261908	N12251
HA-SJN	Cessna R172K Hawk XP	R1722349	N9729V
HA-SJO	Cessna 172N	17271843	N5398E (N944SA) N5398E
HA-SJP	Cessna 177RG Cardinal RG	177RG1226	N52644
HA-SJQ	SOCATA MS.883 Rallye 115	1531	SE-KNN OY-DJO
HA-SJR	SOCATA MS.893E Rallye 180GT Gaillard	12531	F-BVZK
HA-SJS	Cessna 150	17389	N5889E
HA-SJT	Cessna 150G	15066914	N3014S
HA-SJU	Cessna 150M	15076687	N4056V
HA-SJV	Cessna 150M	15076400	N3142V
HA-SJW	Cessna 150H	15068122	N22184
HA-SJX	Cessna 172N	17270653	N31EF N739MQ
HA-SJY	Cessna 172N	17268609	N733WP
HA-SJZ	Reims/Cessna F150K	F15000486	F-BRBJ
HA-SKA	Cessna 210H Centurion	21059024	C-GKPG N6124F
HA-SKC	Cessna P206E Super Skylane (Damaged)	P20600618	N5718J
HA-SKD(2)	Cessna 172N	17270586	N739JT
HA-SKE	Cessna 150G	15066532	N8632J
HA-SKF	Cessna 150M	15077223	N63275
HA-SKG	Cessna 182A Skylane	34371	N72DC N9971B
HA-SKI	Cessna 150G	15065401	N2201J
HA-SKJ	Cessna 185C Skywagon	185-0712	F-BMCV N5812T
HA-SKL	Cessna 172M	17264904	N61944
HA-SKM	Cessna 172K	17258947	N800TS (N7247G)
HA-SKN	Cessna R172K Hawk XP	R1722402	SE-IYV N736BS
HA-SKO	Cessna 172N	17269692	SE-KLM N737UU
HA-SKP	Reims/Cessna F172H	F17200739	OO-NZV
HA-SKQ	Reims FR172G Rocket	FR17200192	D-EUPC OE-DUC HB-CUC
HA-SKR	Cessna 175C Skylark	17557110	N8510X
HA-SKS	Cessna 152	15285904	N95491
HA-SKT	Cessna 182Q Skylane	18266280	N759UX
HA-SKU	Piper PA-28-140 Cherokee E	28-7225304	C-FTVX CF-TVX
HA-SKV	Cessna 152	15285545	C-FAFS N93742
HA-SKW	Cessna 210	57526	F-BFRQ(2) F-OBRQ N6526X
HA-SKX	Cessna U206 Super Skywagon	U206-0433	OO-SPR LN-HHL N8033Z
HA-SKY	Cessna T210K Turbo Centurion (W/o 14.6.01)	21059306	LN-RTG SE-FTC G-AYCL (N9406M)
HA-SKZ	Cessna 210MCenturion	21062785	N6554B
HA-SLA	Reims/Cessna F150L (Crashed 6.4.97)	F15000788	OO-CLO F-BTFF
HA-SLB	Cessna 172N	17272218	OO-GAL N9306E
HA-SLC	Morane-Saulnier MS.885 Super Rallye	142	D-EJPW HB-EDM
HA-SLD	Cessna 150M	15077875	N7986U
HA-SLE	Cessna 172L	17259309	N1201H CF-AZC (N7609G)
HA-SLF	Cessna F172F	F172-0140	OO-CMT (HB-CMT)
HA-SLG	Cessna 172C	17248772	N8272X
HA-SLH	Cessna 182P Skylane	18263126	SE-GGE (N7342N)
HA-SLJ	Cessna 150F	15062039	OO-SPC PH-ICA N8739S
HA-SLK	Reims/Cessna FR172K Hawk XP	FR17200643	D-EIYP
HA-SLM	Cessna 182P	18262838	D-ELOM(3) N52778
HA-SLN	Reims/Cessna F150L	F15000661	D-ECGB
HA-SLO	Cessna 152	15280886	9A-DBB N25968
HA-SLP	Reims/Cessna F150L	F15000722	OE-ALS
HA-SLR	Cessna 172N	17269338	OY-JRA N737DM
HA-SLS	UTVA-66	0872	JRV 51247
HA-SLT	Reims/Cessna F150L	F15000922	OO-KAI PH-KAG OO-WIJ
HA-SLU	Reims/Cessna F152 (Wrecked)	F15201780	OE-CFL
HA-SLV	Holste MH.1521M Broussard	303	F-GGKP Fr.AF
HA-SLY	Reims/Cessna F172K	F17200800	D-ECHN
HA-SLZ	Cessna F172G	F172-0262	N600MK OO-VEV F-BNLB
HA-SUA	Reims/Cessna F150L	F15000955	OE-ATG
HA-SUB	Cessna 152	15282919	VH-MXV (N89929)
HA-SUD	Cessna 182C	52912	VH-TMC N11B N9012T
HA-SUE	Diamond DA20-A1 Katana	10021	OK-KAT N322FT
HA-SUF	Diamond DA 40D Star	D4.011	
HA-SUG	Diamond DA 40D Star	D4.049	
HA-SUH	Reims FR172H Rocket	FR17200323	D-EEXQ
HA- SUI	Diamond DA20-A1	10047	N232JA N103KS C-GKAX
HA-SUK	Reims/Cessna F152	F15201772	D-EIBS
HA-SUM	Cessna 172S	172S9470	N261SP
HA-SUN	Cessna 172	28311	N5711A
HA-SUP	Robin (Dbf 23.8.04)	1552 ?	
HA-SUZ	Cessna 182P (Reims-assembled with "c/n" 0007)	18263835	OE-DGR N6786M
HA-SVA	Cessna TU206E Turbo Stationair	U20601615	4X-CAZ G-OFEK (4X- . . .) G-OFEK N9415G
HA-SVB	Reims/Cessna F150J	unkn	
HA-SVF	Reims/Cessna F150J	F1500525	SE-FKF
HA-SVL	Cessna 150M	15077990	?
HA-TCB	Ilyushin IL-76TD	1013408257	UR-78736 CCCP78736(2)
HA-TCG	Ilyushin IL-76TD	23436048	RA-76382 UR-76382 CCCP76382
HA-TCH	Ilyushin IL-76T	0083483513	UR-76434 76434 CCCP78751
HA-TCJ	Ilyushin IL-76T	0083484527	UR-76437 CCCP76437 CCCP78754
HA-TCK	Ilyushin IL-76T	1023409280	4K-AZ11 RA-76354
HA-TCL	Antonov An-32 (Officially quoted as ex ER-APA)	3009	ER-ADB UR-48073 48073 CCCP48073
HA-TCN	Antonov An-26	97307705	UR-26244 UkrAF: 20 blue
HA-TCP	Antonov An-26	12703	UR-26129 CCCP26129
HA-TRA	Zlin Z.226MS Trenér	322	
HA-TRD	Zlin Z 226T Trenér 6	350	
HA-TRE(2)	Zlin Z 326 Trenér Master	918	F-BSTA TR-LMX
HA-TRM	Zlin Z.226MS Trenér	369	
HA-TRT	Zlin Z.326 Trenér Master	833	
HA-TUA	Reims FR172HRocket	FR17200294	D-ECQZ
HA-TUB	Cessna 182D (Crashed 31.1.02)	18253201	D-ESWW OE-DDA N8801X
HA-TUC	Reims FR172H Rocket	FR17200309	F-BTFD
HA-TUD	Grob G.115	8065	D-ELWZ
HA-TUE	SOCATAMS.880B Rallye-Club	1268	HB-EEQ
HA-TUG	Scottish Avn Bulldog 101	BH100/181	Fv.61063 G-AZWJ
HA-TUH	Scottish Avn Bulldog 120/121	BH100/189	Fv.61071 G-BACR
HA-TUI	Scottish Avn Bulldog 120/121	BH120/219	XX533
HA-TUJ	Scottish Avn Bulldog 101	BH100/104	Fv.61004 G-AYZL
HA-TUN	Cessna 150M	15078359	OO-HVC N9411U
HA-TUP	Cessna 182P Skylane (Reims-assembled with 'c/n' 0006)	18263805	F-BXAL N6702M
HA-TUR	Piper PA-28-161 Cherokee Warrior II	28-7816189	D-ERSA N9736K
HA-TUS	Cessna 175	55612	OE-DKG N7312M
HA-TUT	Cessna 172P	17274510	D-EFZQ N52414
HA-TUW	SOCATA TB-9 Tampico Club	1274	D-ETGM I-IAEX
HA-TUY	SOCATARallye-180T-D Galérien	2976	D-ECYR(3)
HA-VEA	SOCATAMS.894A Minerva 220	11045	HB-ERR F-BRJJ
HA-VEB	Cessna 182G	18255832	F-BMEA F-OCEA N11B N3432S
HA-VEC	Reims FR172J Rocket	FR17200481	D-EIQW
HA-VED	SOCATA MS.893A Rallye Commodore 180	10650	OO-RED
HA-VEF	SOCATA MS.893E Rallye 180GT Gaillard	12865	OO-LVG F-GAKJ
HA-VEG	SOCATAMS.893A Rallye Commodore 180	11463	D-ECCR

HA-VEH	SOCATA MS.880BRallye Club	2350	OE-DDH
			D-EAKZ
			F-BUNJ
HA-VEI	Fuji FA.200-160 Aero Subaru	150	OO-YAP
			N19AP
			OO-YAP
HA-VEJ	Reims/Cessna FRA150L Aerobat	FRA1500186	SE-FZF
HA-VEK	Morane-Saulnier MS.885 Super Rallye	48	D-EEKM
			HB-EDQ
			OO-TEL
			F-BKEU
HA-VEL	Cessna F172H	F172-0534	D-EJBT
			D-ELNM
HA-VEM	Cessna F172F	F172-0173	D-EHNY
HA-VEN	Cessna 150F	15064094	OO-VLA
			N7994F
HA-VEO	Morane-Saulnier MS.885 Super Rallye	12	D-EOEB
			F-BKEB
HA-VEP	SOCATAMS.880BRallye Club	1259	OE-CMV
			F-BPAL
HA-VER	Reims FR172G Rocket	FR17200203	OE-DLV
HA-VEQ	Reims FR172F Rocket	FR17200145	F-BRBO
HA-VES	SOCATA TB-9 Tampico	127	(SE-. . .)
			LN-KLE
			F-GCOE
HA-VET	Luscombe 8E Silvaire	2891	N71464
			NC71464
HA-VEU	Cessna 150H	15068194	N22288
HA-VEW	Cessna 150F	15064526	D-ELLY
			(D-ECJH)
			C-FUTL
			CF-UTL
			N3126X
HA-VEX	Cessna 172N	17273261	OO-LXV
			N7575F
HA-VEY	SOCATATB-9 Tampico	244	D-EFAV(2)
HA-VEZ	IAR-823	43	RomAF
HA-VOC	Dornier Do 28D-2	4331	TC-FBC
			D-IDWM
			CN-. . .
			TC-IDWM
HA-XAD	A-01 Famadár	01/1986	
HA-XAE	Vector 610	1394	
HA-XAJ	Rubik R-32	01	
HA-XAK	Light Aero Avid Flyer STOL	823	
HA-XAU	Rotorway Executive 90	5085	
HA-XAW	Taylorcraft LM-2X-2P	AR 92/1	
HA-XAX	Rotorway Executive 90	6100	
HA-XBF	RAF-2000GTX	H2-92-3-57	
HA-XBG	Rotorway Executive 90	5130	
HA-XBM	V-001 Vereb	001	
HA-XBO	S-52 Hummingbird helicopter (Cld, for sale)	09	
HA-XBW	WW001 Shark	unkn	
HA-YAB	Yakovlev Yak-18T	12-35	RA-44777
HA-YAC	Yakovlev Yak-18T	14-35	RA-44532
HA-YAD	Yakovlev Yak-18T	22202054812	RA-81584
HA-YAE	Yakovlev Yak-18T	11-35	RA-44000
HA-YAF	Yakovlev Yak-18T	08-34	RA-44480
HA-YAG	Yakovlev Yak-18T	05-36	RA-01555
HA-YAH	Yakovlev Yak-18T	unkn	
HA-YAI	Yokovlev Yak-18T	22202052122	RA-44538
HA-YAJ	Yakovlev Yak-18T	01-33	LY-APP
			LY-AOG
HA-YAK	Yakovlev Yak-18T	22202044785	LY-AFS
			DOSAAF
HA-YAL	Yakovlev Yak-18T	7201513	
HA-YAM	Yakovlev Yak-18T	22202047812	RA-44504
			LY-AMJ
			DOSAAF
HA-YAN	Yakovlev Yak-18T	10-34	
HA-YAO	Sukhoi SU-29	001-01	RA-44479
HA-YAP	Yakovlev Yak-18T	22202034023	RA-44545
HA-YAR	Sukhoi SU-29	75-03	RA-01609
HA-YAS	Sukhoi SU-29	77-05	
HA-YAT	Sukhoi SU-29	78-02	RA-01610
			RA-7802
HA-YAU	Yakovlev Yak-18T	15-35	RA-44527
HA-YAV	Yokovlev Yak-18T	22202047817	RA-01153
HA-YBA	Piper Aerostar 601P	61P-0780-8063393	N3831Y
			D-IFWF
			N3636D
HA-YCD	Piper PA-23-250 Aztec E	27-4700	OH-PKS
			SE-FYI
HA-YCE	Piper PA-23-250 Aztec E	27-7405341	N5132G
			C-GRFF
			N40594
HA-YCF	Piper PA-23-250 Aztec E	27-4684	D-IDMV
			N14081
HA-YCG	Piper PA-23-250 Aztec	27-334	9A-BAG
			RC-BAG
			YU-BBC
			N6830Z
HA-YCH	Piper PA-34-200 Seneca	34-7350290	D-GIFT
			N56156
HA-YCI	Piper PA-34-200 Seneca	34-7350259	D-GBFM
			N55602
HA-YCK	Piper PA-34-220T Seneca V	3449070	D-GIMR
			N41278
HA-YDE	Pilatus PC-6/B2-H2 Turbo-Porter	814	
HA-YDF	Technoavia SMG-92 Finist	01-005	
HA-YDG	Technoavia SMG-92 Finist (W/o 3.2.02)	00-004	RA-44485
HA-YDH	Technoavia SMG-92 Finist	01-007	
HA-YDI	Technoavia SMG-92 Finist	01-009	
HA-YDN	Technoavia SMG-92 Finist	unkn	
HA-YFC	LET L-410-FG	851528	
HA-YFD	LET L-410UVP-E17	892324	
HA-YHA	Antonov An-2R	1G151-53	
HA-YHB	Antonov An-2PF	1G181-44	
HA-YHC	Antonov An-2PF	1G181-45	
HA-YHD	Antonov An-2PF	1G187-36	
HA-YHE	Antonov An-2PF	1G187-37	
HA-YHF	Antonov An-2PF	1G224-13	
HA-YHG	Antonov An-2PF	1G234-08	
HA-YLR	Yakovlev Yak-40 (To museum)	9541044	
HA-YMA	Maule M-7-235C Super Rocket	4079C	
HA-YMB	Maule M-7-235C Super Rocket	4081C	
HA-YMC	Maule M-5-235C Lunar Rocket	7336C	SE-IGD
HA-YTV	Kamov Ka.26	7001504	HAF-504
HA-. . .	Beech 200 Super King Air	BB-306	N500HY
			N274K
HA-. . .	Bell 206L-3 Long Ranger III	51040	D-HAPY(2)
HA-. . .	Cessna F150J (Possibly to HA-SVB)	F150-0444	D-EABO
HA-. . .	Cessna 152 (For spares use?)	15281190	OO-KPM
			N49201
HA-. . .	Cessna F172H	F172-0353	OO-LKC
			F-BOQE
HA-. . .	Cessna 172P	17275867	N65763
HA-. . .	Enstrom F-28A	251	G-BPPL
HA-. . .	Extra EA.300/S	1032	
HA-. . .	Mitsubishi MU-2B-20	191	SE-GHG
			N99EE
			N112MA
HA-. . .	Piper PA-18-150 Super Cub	18-8062	D-EFBU
			N4068Z
HA-. . .	Piper PA-38-112 Tomahawk	38-79A0994	N9972G
			4R-ATB
			G-BJVR
			N9655N
HA-. . .	Piper PA-31 Turbo Navajo	31-442	N14111
			N3181D
			G-IGON
			D-IGON
			(D-IHFP)
			N6479L
HA-. . .	Piper PA-31T Cheyenne II	31T-7820011	N250CT
			N884CA
			(N8RS)
			N88NW
			N777TH
			N378HC
			N82212
HA-. . .	Robin DR.400/180R Remorqueur (See HA-SUP)	1552	D-EVCH
			"D-EVHB"
			PH-VHB
			D-ECDC(2)
HA-. . .	Rotorway Exec 162F	6525	N162TM
HA-. . .	Sukhoi SU-29	74-05	N229JD

BALLOONS ANDAIRSHIPS

HA-X01	SCB AX-6 Bottle SS Balloon	SCBO90/1991	
HA-X02	Kubicek BBJäger SSHAFB	138	
HA-X03	Tomi C-45 HAFB	054/2002	
HA-X04	Tomi M-50 Mobile Phone SSHAFB	055/2002	
HA-002	Tomi AX-10 HAFB	BAV064/1989	
HA-003	Sup-Air E-AX-10 HAFB	1994/SA2	
HA-005	Lindstrand LBL-203P Tethered Gas Balloon	101	
HA-301	SCB AX-3 Sky Walker Balloon	SCB096/1991	
HA-401	SCB SX-4 Sky Rider Balloon	SCBO91/1991	
HA-502	Supa Air D (AX-5) Balloon	005/1991	
HA-603	SCB AX-6 HAFB	SCB093/1991	
HA-604	SCB AX-6 HAFB	SCB106/1993	
HA-605	Tomi AX-6 HAFB	28/1996	
HA-606	Ultramagic M-65C HAFB	65/105	
HA-703	MHSZ AX-7 HAFB	10/1982	
HA-704	Colt 77A HAFB	759	
HA-705	RSZ-05 HAFB	BAV021/1986	
HA-707	Tomi AX-7 HAFB	BAV023/1986	
HA-708	Tomi AX-7 HAFB	BAV024/1986	
HA-710	Tomi AX-7 HAFB	BAV031/1987	
HA-711	Tomi AX-7 HAFB	BAV032/1987	
HA-712	Tomi AX-7 HAFB	BAV052/1988	
HA-713	Mecsek AX-7 HAFB	BAV056/1988	
HA-714	Tomi AX-7 HAFB	BAV057/1988	
HA-715	Tomi AX-7 HAFB	BAV062/1989	
HA-716	RSZ-05/1 HAFB	1989/001	(G-BRSZ)
			HA-716
HA-717	Tomi AX-7 HAFB	BAV073/1989	
HA-718	Tomi AX-7 HAFB	BAV077/1989	
HA-719	Tomi AX-7 HAFB	SCB086/1990	
HA-720	Tomi AX-7 HAFB	SCB087/1990	
HA-721	SCB AX-7 HAFB	SCB094/1991	

HA-722	SCB AX-7 HAFB	SCB092/1991	
HA-723	Tomi AX-7 HAFB	36/1997	
HA-724	SCB AX-7 HAFB	SCB098/1991	
HA-725	Tomi AX-7 HAFB	004/92	
HA-726	Tomi AX-7 HAFB	005/92	
HA-727	Tomi AX-7 HAFB	006/92	
HA-728	SCB AX-7 HAFB	SCB100/1992	
HA-729	SCB AX-7 HAFB	SCB104/1993	
HA-731	Tomi AX-7 HAFB	8/1993	
HA-732	Tomi AX-7 HAFB	9/1993	
HA-733	Tomi AX-7 HAFB	11/1993	
HA-735	SCB AX-7 HAFB	SCB107/1994	
HA-736	Tomi AX-7 HAFB	17/1994	
HA-737	Tomi AX-7 HAFB	15/1994	
HA-738	Tomi AX-7 HAFB	16/1994	
HA-739	Cameron C-60 HAFB	3342	
HA-740	Tomi AX-7 HAFB	20/1995	
HA-741	Kubicek BB-22 HAFB	40	
HA-742	Tomi AX-7 HAFB	002/95	
HA-743	Tomi AX-7 HAFB	22/1995	
HA-744	Ultramagic H-77 HAFB	77/114	
HA-745	Tomi AX-7 HAFB	23/1995	
HA-746	SCB AX-7 HAFB	SCB111/1995	
HA-747	Tomi AX-7 HAFB	39/1997	
HA-749	Ultramagic H-77 HAFB	77/152	
HA-750	Tomi AX-7 HAFB	42/1998	
HA-751	Tomi AX-7 HAFB	45/1999	
HA-752	Cameron N-77 HAFB	961	D-OBIS (1)
			D-Kurbis(2)
HA-752	Tomi AX-7 HAFB	52/2001	
HA-752	Tomi AX-7 HAFB	. . /2001	
HA-754	Colt 77AHAFB	1190	
HA-755	Tomi AX-8 HAFB	57/2003	
HA-756	Kubicek BB- HAFB	292	OK-0292
HA-807	Tomi AX-8 HAFB	3/1981	
HA-808	Tomi AX-8 HAFB	4/1980	
HA-813	Tomi AX-8 HAFB	3/1982	
HA-815	Tomi AX-8 HAFB	5/1982	
HA-819	Tomi AX-8 HAFB	1/1983	
HA-820	Tomi AX-8 HAFB	1/1984	
HA-821	RSZ-03/1 HAFB	KÖ ÉV 1/1986	
HA-822	Tomi AX-8 HAFB	BAV004/1983	
HA-823	Tomi AX-8 HAFB	BAV008/1984	
HA-824	Tomi AX-8 HAFB	BAV010/1985	
HA-825	RSZ-03/1 HAFB	1985/MMRK/01	
HA-826	Tomi AX-8 HAFB	BAV012/1985	
HA-827	Tomi AX-8 HAFB	BAV019/1986	
HA-828	Tomi AX-8 HAFB	BAV020/1986	
HA-829	RSZ-03/1 HAFB	1986/001	
HA-830	RSZ-03/1 HAFB	1988/001	
HA-831	RSZ-03/1 HAFB	1990/001	
HA-832	Tomi AX-8 HAFB	BAV030/1986	
HA-833	Tomi AX-8 HAFB	BAV022/1986	
HA-834	Tomi AX-8 HAFB	BAV039/1987	
HA-835	Tomi AX-8 HAFB	BAV049/1988	
HA-836	Tomi AX-8 HAFB	BAV050/1988	
HA-837	Tomi AX-8 HAFB	BAV051/1988	
HA-838	Tomi AX-8 HAFB	BAV058/1988	
HA-839	Tomi AX-8 HAFB	BAV083/1990	
HA-840	Tomi AX-8 HAFB	BAV071/1989	
HA-841	Tomi AX-8 HAFB	BAV072/1989	
HA-842	RSZ-03/1 HAFB	1990/003	
HA-843	RSZ-03/1 HAFB	1990/002	
HA-844	Tomi AX-8 HAFB	BAV085/1990	
HA-845	RSZ-03/1 HAFB	1991/001	
HA-846	RSZ-03/1 HAFB	1990/004	
HA-847	RSZ-03/1 HAFB	1991/002	
HA-848	RSZ-03/1 HAFB	1991/004	
HA-849	SCB AX-8 HAFB	SCB095/1991	
HA-850	SCB AX-8 HAFB	SCB097/1991	
HA-851	Tomi AX-8 HAFB	003/1991	
HA-852	SCB AX-8 HAFB	SCBO99/1992	
HA-853	SCB AX-8 HAFB	SCB101/1992	
HA-854	SCB AX-8 HAFB	SCB102/1993	
HA-855	Tomi AX-8 HAFB	007/1993	
HA-856	SCB AX-8 HAFB	SCB103/1993	
HA-857	Tomi AX-8 HAFB	10/1993	
HA-858	Tomi AX-8 HAFB	13/1994	
HA-859	Tomi AX-8 HAFB	18/1994	
HA-860	SCB AX-8 HAFB	SCB109/1995	
HA-861	SCB AX-8 HAFB	SCB110/1995	
HA-862	Tomi AX-8 HAFB	25/1995	
HA-863	Tomi AX-8 HAFB	26/1995	
HA-864	Tomi AX-8 HAFB	27/1996	
HA-865	Tomi AX-8 HAFB	32/1996	
HA-866	Tomi AX-8 HAFB	31/1996	
HA-867	Tomi AX-8 HAFB	33/1996	
HA-868	Tomi AX-8 HAFB	29/1996	
HA-869	Tomi AX-8 HAFB	37/1997	
HA-870	SCB AX-8 HAFB	SCB112/1997	
HA-871	Supair/B HAFB	1999/SA-1	
HA-872	Cameron N-105 HAFB	1893	D-Seidenschnitt
HA-873	Schröder Fire Balloons G HAFB	551	D-OWEW
HA-874	Supair/B HAFB	2000/SA-1	
HA-875	Thunder AX8-105 SII HAFB	2586	D-OLVE
HA-876	Tomi AX-8 HAFB	48/2000	
HA-877	Ultramagic S-90 HAFB	90/51	
HA-878	Schröder Fire Balloons G3000/24 HAFB	133	
HA-879	Cameron Z-90 HAFB	10046	LX-BLB
HA-902	Pecs AX-9 HAFB	1/1982	
HA-903	RSZ-04/1 HAFB	BAV011/1985	
HA-904	Tomi AX-9 HAFB	BAV063/1989	
HA-905	Tomi AX-9 HAFB	BAV070/1989	
HA-906	Tomi AX-9 HAFB	SCB089/1990	
HA-907	SCB AX-9 HAFB	SCB088/1991	
HA-908	SCB AX-9 HAFB	SCB089/1991	
HA-909	RSZ 04/1 HAFB	1991/01	
HA-910	Sup-Air C HAFB	1994/SA1	
HA-911	Kubicek BB-37 HAFB	41	
HA-912	Tomi AX-9 HAFB	30/1996	
HA-913	Tomi AX-9 HAFB	40/1997	
HA-914	Cameron A-180 HAFB	3425	D-OMNI
HA-915	Supair/C HAFB	2000/SA-2	
HA-916	Schröder Fire Balloons G HAFB	442	D-ORSY
HA-917	Tomi AX-9 HAFB	49/2000	
HA-918	Tomi AX-8 HAFB	50/2000-01	
HA-920	Tomi AX-9 HAFB	053/2002	
HA-921	Colt 120A HAFB	1733	D-Brandenburg
		G-BSJF	
HA-922	SUP-Air/C Balloon	unkn	
HA-B-401	Cameron DP-90 Hot Air Airship	3233	
HA-B-601	Jakab Airship	L.I./1996	

GLIDERS AND MOTORGLIDERS

HA-X001	KM400	unkn	
HA-1001	Brditschka HB-21/2400	21029	OE-9226
HA-1002	Brditschka HB-21/2400	21018	OE-9306
			PH-677
HA-1003	Doppelraab/Hankur 1	1051/02	D-KKKK
			D-6210
			(D-KBOP)
			D-6210
HA-1004	Brditschka HB-21/1600	21008	OE-9131
HA-1039	R-16 Lepke	E-1000	
HA-1200	Scheibe SF-25C Falke	44119	OE-9128
			D-KNOB
HA-1201	Sportavia/ Scheibe SF-25C Falke 1700	4205	D-KAOJ
HA-1202	Scheibe SF-25C Falke 1700	4434	D-KMSW
HA-1205	Scheibe SF-25C Falke 1700	44158	D-KEFH
HA-1206	Scheibe SF-25BFalke	4669	D-KAPF
HA-1207	Brditschka HB-3B	057	OE-9053
HA-1208	Scheibe SF-25C Falke 1700	44156	D-KEFF
HA-1209	Jastreb-VTC Sole-77	192	YU-6011
			YU-XAA
HA-1210	Grob G.109	6041	D-KEAN(3)
HA-1211	Scheibe SF-25BFalke	4686	D-KBAH(2)
			(D-KBIT)
HA-1212	Sportavia/ Scheibe SF-25B/DFalke	4843	D-KHFA
HA-1213	Scheibe SF-25BFalke	44369	D-KNAV
HA-1214	Valentin Taifun 17E	1050	I-KLIX
			D-KLIX
HA-1215	Grob G.109	6078	D-KCBF
			OE-9274
			D-KCBF
HA-1216	Hoffman H-36 Dimona	3666	D-KDTZ
HA-1217	Scheibe SF-25BFalke	4656	D-KABC
HA-1218	Hoffman H-36 Dimona	36253	D-KFRK
HA-1219	Scheibe SF-25C Falke 1700	44151	G-BXXC
			D-KEFA(2)
HA-1220	Scheibe SF-25B Falke	46153	OE-9037
			(D-KCAS)
HA-1221	Sportavia/ Scheibe SF-25C Falke 1700	4235	D-KAOV
HA-1222	Hoffman H-36 Dimona	36234	D-KLDS
HA-1223	Scheibe SF-25C Falke	4445	OE-9058
			(D-KDAE)
HA-1225	Sportavia/ Scheibe SF-25B Falke	4824	D-KHED
HA-1227	Scheibe SF-25E Falke	4312	D-KDDB(2)
HA-1228	Scheibe SF-25C Falke 1700	44234	D-KDCI
HA-1229	Scheibe SF-25C Falke 1700	44186	D-KDEP
HA-1231	Scheibe SF-25C Falke	unkn	
HA-1232	Scheibe SF-25D Falke	4639D	D-KHOF
HA-1233	Sportavia/Scheibe SF-25C Falke	4226	D-KEAG
HA-1234	Scheibe SF-25C Falke 1700	44220	D-KDFQ
HA-1235	Scheibe SF-25D Falke 1700	46212D	D-KAAP
HA-12 . .	Scheibe SF-25C Falke	46217C	SE-UBS
			LN-GMJ
			D-KAAS
HA-1929	Zögling RRG-1	BR-01	
HA-2336	R-07 Vocsok 81	F-01	
HA-3175	Schempp-Hirth Nimbus 3/24.5	36	D-3175
HA-3176	Schempp-Hirth Nimbus 4T	1/1	D-KBXX
HA-3409	E-31 Esztergom	E-1289	
HA-3426	E-31 Esztergom	E-1306	
HA-3429	E-31 Esztergom	E-1309	
HA-3430	E-31 Esztergom	E-1310	
HA-3445	Grob G.102 Astir CS77	1783	HB-1445
HA-3456	Grob G.102 Astir CS77	1782	HB-1456
HA-3457	Grob G.102 Astir CS77	1380	HB-1333
HA-3458	Schleicher ASW 15B	15417	D-8662
HA-3459	Schleicher ASW 15B	15241	D-2065
HA-3471	Grob G.102 Astir CS77	1809	HB-1471
HA-3472	Grob G.102 Astir CS77	1751	PH-639

HA-3474	Schleicher ASW 15B	15375	D-9267
HA-3500	LET L-33 Solo	960404	
HA-3600	PZL PW-5 Smyk	17.08.018	
HA-4000	Scheibe L-Spatz 55	572	
HA-4001	Glaser-Dirks DG-400	4-77	D-KHMZ
HA-4002	Schleicher K 8B	8561/A	D-2359
			D-KOBE
			D-5359
HA-4003	Schleicher K 8B	120/58	D-8574
HA-4004	SZD-36A Cobra 15	W-569	PH-836
			D-0929
HA-4005	SZD-36A Cobra	W-759	SP-3585
			SP-2926
HA-4006	SZD-36A Cobra	W-621	D-1158
			HB-1153
HA-4008	Schleicher K 8B	8582	D-4008
HA-4011	Scheibe L-Spatz 55	569	
HA-4012	Schleicher K 8B	113	D-9063
HA-4013	Schleicher K 7 Rhönadler	304	D-6206
HA-4014	Schleicher K 8B	518	OE-5421
HA-4015	Schleicher K 8B	8896	D-0903
HA-4059	R-22 Futár	E-741	
HA-4133	R-22g Junius 18	E-1026	
HA-4155	Cinke (Wfu)	E-1088	
HA-4210	Scheibe L-Spatz 55	04	OE-0403
HA-4211	R-22SV Super Futár	E-1152	HB-670
			OE-0404
HA-4215	R-22SV Super Futár	E-1157	
HA-4225	SZD-22C Mucha Standard	748	
HA-4234	SZD-22C Mucha Standard	779	
HA-4235	SZD-22C Mucha Standard	787	
HA-4239-yp	SZD-24-4C Foka	W-201	
HA-4240	SZD-24 Foka 4A	W-207	
HA-4244	SZD-24-4A Foka 4	W-231	
HA-4247	SZD-24-4A Foka 4	W-330	
HA-4248	SZD-24-4A Foka 4	W-371	
HA-4249	SZD-24-4A Foka 4	W-372	
HA-4250	SZD-32A Foka 5	W-419	
HA-4251	SZD-32A Foka 5	W-473	
HA-4252	SZD-32A Foka 5	W-516	
HA-4253	SZD-32A Foka 5	W-512	
HA-4254	SZD-32A Foka 5	W-517	
HA-4255-ab	SZD-32A Foka 5 (Wfu)	W-528	
HA-4256	SZD-36A Foka 5	W-548	
HA-4257	SZD-36A Foka 5 (Cr 6.4.01)	W-549	
HA-4258	SZD-32A Foka 5	W-550	
HA-4260	SZD-32A Foka 5	W-552	
HA-4261	SZD-32A Foka 5	W-553	
HA-4262	SZD-32A Foka 5	W-465	YR-183
HA-4263	SZD-32A Foka 5	W-464	YR-182
HA-4264	Schleicher K 8B	814	HB-673
HA-4265	Schleicher K 8B	8787	D-0264
HA-4266	Scheibe L-Spatz 55	659	OE-5011
HA-4267	Scheibe L-Spatz 55	R250/H264	OE-0831
HA-4268	Schleicher K 8B	8027	D-4002
HA-4269	Scheibe Zugvogel IIIA	1062	OE-0591
HA-4270	Avialsa-Scheibe A.60 Fauconnet	32	F-CCQJ
HA-4271	Scheibe L-Spatz 55	R844/H193	OE-0500
HA-4272	Schleicher K 8B	8493	HB-822
HA-4273	Schleicher K 8B	741	D-4371
HA-4274	Schleicher K 8B	1192	HB-720
HA-4276	VTC-75 Standard Cirrus	246	
HA-4277	VTC-75 Standard Cirrus	247	
HA-4279	VTC-75 Standard Cirrus	249	
HA-4280	VTC-75 Standard Cirrus	250	
HA-4281	VTC-75 Standard Cirrus	282	
HA-4282	VTC-75 Standard Cirrus	283	
HA-4283	VTC-75 Standard Cirrus	294	
HA-4284-50	VTC-75 Standard Cirrus	295	
HA-4285	VTC-75 Standard Cirrus	362	
HA-4287	VTC-75 Standard Cirrus	364	
HA-4288	VTC-75 Standard Cirrus	365	
HA-4289	VTC-75 Standard Cirrus	366	
HA-4290	VTC-75 Standard Cirrus	367	
HA-4291	VTC-75 Standard Cirrus	368	
HA-4292	VTC-75 Standard Cirrus	369	
HA-4293	VTC-75 Standard Cirrus	370	
HA-4295	VTC-75 Standard Cirrus	248	HA-4278
HA-4296	Schleicher K 8B	8411	HB-792
HA-4298	SZD-36A Cobra	W-582	D-5410
			OH-419
HA-4299	Schleicher ASW 15	15040	D-0467
HA-4306	SZD-30 Pirat	B-328	OE-0713
HA-4307	SZD-36 Cobra 15	W-771	
HA-4308	SZD-36 Cobra 15	W-768	
HA-4311-57	SZD-36 Cobra 15	W-566	
HA-4312-66	SZD-36 Cobra 15	W-661	
HA-4313	SZD-36 Cobra 15	W-726	
HA-4314	SZD-36 Cobra 15	W-688	
HA-4315	SZD-36 Cobra 15 (Wfu)	W-773	
HA-4316	SZD-36 Cobra 15	W-774	
HA-4317	SZD-36 Cobra 15	W-784	
HA-4318	SZD-36 Cobra 15	W-785	
HA-4319-49	SZD-36 Cobra 15	W-799	
HA-4321	VTC-75 Cirrus 17	142	
HA-4322	VTC-75 Cirrus 17	143	
HA-4323	VTC-75 Cirrus 17	144	
HA-4324	VTC-75 Cirrus 17	146	

HA-4325	VTC-75 Cirrus 17	147	
HA-4326-VZ	VTC-75 Cirrus 17	161	
HA-4328	Schempp-Hirth Standard Cirrus	615	
HA-4329	SZD-30 Pirat	S-07.04	
HA-4330	SZD-30 Pirat	S-03.27	
HA-4331	SZD-30 Pirat	S-04.03	
HA-4333	SZD-30 Pirat	S-04.24	
HA-4334	SZD-30 Pirat	S-04.50	
HA-4335	SZD-30 Pirat	S-04.49	
HA-4336	SZD-30 Pirat	S-05.19	
HA-4337	SZD-30 Pirat	S-05.37	
HA-4338	SZD-30 Pirat	S-05.38	
HA-4339	SZD-30 Pirat	S-05.39	
HA-4340	SZD-30 Pirat	S-05.40	
HA-4341	SZD-30 Pirat	S-05.41	
HA-4342	SZD-30 Pirat	S-05.42	
HA-4343	SZD-30 Pirat	S-05.43	
HA-4344	SZD-30 Pirat	S-05.44	
HA-4345	SZD-30 Pirat	S-07.05	
HA-4347-V	SZD-30 Pirat	S-07.07	
HA-4348	SZD-30 Pirat	S-07.08	
HA-4353-TZ	SZD-38A Jantar 1	B-673	
HA-4354-VL	SZD-38A Jantar 1	B-674	
HA-4356	SZD-38A Jantar 1	B-687	
HA-4357	SZD-38A Jantar 1	B-688	
HA-4358	SZD-30 Pirat	S-07.01	
HA-4359	SZD-30 Pirat	S-07.02	
HA-4360	SZD-41A Jantar Standard	B-690	
HA-4361	SZD-41A Jantar Standard	B-692	
HA-4362	SZD-30 Pirat	S-07.26	
HA-4363	SZD-36A Cobra 15	W-800	
HA-4364	SZD-30 Pirat	S-08.17	
HA-4365	SZD-30 Pirat	S-08.18	
HA-4366	SZD-30 Pirat (Cr 6.4.01)	S-08.19	
HA-4368	SZD-30 Pirat	S-08.21	
HA-4369-9L	SZD-30 Pirat	S-08.22	
HA-4370-1S	SZD-30 Pirat	S-08.23	
HA-4371	SZD-30 Pirat	S-08.24	
HA-4372	SZD-30 Pirat	S-08.25	
HA-4373	SZD-30 Pirat	S-08.26	
HA-4374	SZD-30 Pirat	S-08.27	
HA-4375	SZD-30 Pirat	S-08.28	
HA-4376	SZD-30 Pirat (Wfu)	S-08.16	
HA-4377	SZD-30 Pirat	S-08.29	
HA-4378	SZD-30 Pirat	S-08.30	
HA-4379	SZD-30 Pirat	S-08.31	
HA-4380	SZD-30 Pirat	S-08.32	
HA-4381-MZ	SZD-30 Pirat	S-08.33	
HA-4382-4T	SZD-30 Pirat	S-08.34	
HA-4383	SZD-30 Pirat	S-08.35	
HA-4384	SZD-30 Pirat	S-08.36	
HA-4385	SZD-30 Pirat	S-08.37	
HA-4386	SZD-30 Pirat	S-08.38	
HA-4388	SZD-30 Pirat (Dismantled)	S-08.40	
HA-4389	SZD-30 Pirat	S-08.41	
HA-4390	SZD-30 Pirat	S-08.42	
HA-4391	SZD-30 Pirat	S-08.43	
HA-4392	SZD-30 Pirat	S-08.44	
HA-4393	SZD-30 Pirat	S-08.45	
HA-4394	SZD-30 Pirat C	P-801	
HA-4395	SZD-30 Pirat C	P-832	
HA-4396-8Z	SZD-30 Pirat C	P-835	
HA-4397	VTC-75 Cirrus 17	178	YU-4302
HA-4398	SZD-36A Cobra 15	W-573	OE-0938
HA-4399	SZD-30 Pirat	B-568	OE-0973
HA-4400-TE	SZD-48-1 Jantar Standard 2	B-1184	
HA-4401-TF	SZD-48-1 Jantar Standard 2	B-1224	
HA-4402	SZD-48-1 Jantar Standard 2	B-1223	
HA-4403	SZD-41A Jantar Standard	B-737	
HA-4404-TI	SZD-41A Jantar Standard	B-740	
HA-4406	Eiravion PIK-20D	20614	
HA-4407	Eiravion PIK-20D	20610	
HA-4408	Eiravion PIK-20D	20612	
HA-4409	Eiravion PIK-20D	20611	
HA-4410	Eiravion PIK-20D	20627	
HA-4411	Eiravion PIK-20D	20633	
HA-4412	Eiravion PIK-20D	20634	
HA-4413	Eiravion PIK-20D	20647	
HA-4414	Eiravion PIK-20D	20551	BGA2272
HA-4415	Eiravion PIK-20D	20667	
HA-4416	SZD-48-1 Jantar Standard	B-1096	
HA-4417	SZD-48-1 Jantar Standard	B-1051	
HA-4418-HE	SZD-42-2 Jantar 2B	B-943	
HA-4419-HH	SZD-42-2 Jantar 2B	B-945	
HA-4420	SZD-42-2 Jantar 2B	B-950	
HA-4421	SZD-42-2 Jantar 2B	B-1127	
HA-4422-IV	SZD-42-2 Jantar 2B	B-1129	
HA-4423-AA	SZD-42-2 Jantar 2B (Destroyed 8.99?)	B-1307	
HA-4424-EI	SZD-42-2 Jantar 2B	B-1130	
HA-4425	SZD-48-1 Jantar Standard 2	B-1136	
HA-4426-AR	SZD-48-1 Jantar Standard 2	B-1185	
HA-4427	SZD-48-1 Jantar Standard 2	B-1188	
HA-4428-HK	SZD-42-2 Jantar 2B	B-1309	
HA-4429	SZD-48-1 Jantar Standard	B-1189	
HA-4432	IAR-Brasov IS.29D2	133	
HA-4433	IAR-Brasov IS.29D2	161	
HA-4435	IAR-Brasov IS.29D2 (Wrecked)	164	
HA-4436	IAR-Brasov IS.29D2	165	

HA-4437	IAR-Brasov IS.29D2	166	
HA-4438	IAR-Brasov IS.29D2	167	
HA-4439	IAR-Brasov IS.29D2	168	
HA-4440	IAR-Brasov IS.29D2	169	
HA-4441	IAR-Brasov IS.29D	170	
HA-4442	IAR-Brasov IS.29D2	171	
HA-4443	IAR-Brasov IS.29D2	172	
HA-4444	IAR-Brasov IS.29D2	173	
HA-4445	IAR-Brasov IS.29D2	174	
HA-4446	IAR-Brasov IS.29D2	175	
HA-4447	IAR-Brasov IS.29D2	176	
HA-4449	IAR-Brasov IS.29D2	178	
HA-4450-NV	SZD-42-2 Jantar 2B	B-1308	
HA-4451	SZD-42-2 Jantar 2B	B-1132	
HA-4452	SZD-42-2 Jantar 2B	B-1133	
HA-4453	SZD-42-2 Jantar 2B	B-1310	
HA-4454	SZD-42-2 Jantar 2B	B-1322	
HA-4455-XK	SZD-42-2 Jantar 2B	B-1324	
HA-4456-YL	SZD-42-2 Jantar 2B	B-1487	
HA-4457-AZ	SZD-42-2 Jantar 2B	B-1488	
HA-4459	SZD-48-3 Jantar Standard 3	B-1453	
HA-4460	SZD-48-3 Jantar Standard 3	B-1571	
HA-4461-TH	SZD-48-3 Jantar Standard 3	B-1652	
HA-4462-II	SZD-42-2 Jantar 2B	B-1674	
HA-4463	SZD-48-3 Jantar Standard 3	unkn	
HA-4464	LAK-12 Lietuva	6122	
HA-4465-KT	LAK-12 Lietuva	6132	
HA-4466	LAK-12 Lietuva	6134	
HA-4467-GTi	SZD-48-3 Jantar Standard 3	B-1906	
HA-4468	SZD-48-3 Jantar Standard 3	B-1907	
HA-4469-VV	SZD-42-2 Jantar 2B	B-1680	
HA-4470	SZD-48-3 Jantar Standard 3	B-1452	HA-4458
HA-4471-BM	Schempp-Hirth Discus CS	093CS	
HA-4472-KB	Schempp-Hirth Discus CS	094CS	
HA-4473	Schempp-Hirth Discus CS	098CS	
HA-4474-RD	SZD-48-1 Jantar Standard 2	B-1234	DOSAAF
HA-4478	IAR-Brasov IS.29D2	182	
HA-4479	IAR-Brasov IS.29D2	183	
HA-4481	IAR-Brasov IS.29D2	199A	
HA-4482-MP	Schempp-Hirth Discus CS	215CS	
HA-4483	Schempp-Hirth Ventus 2b	40	
HA-4484	SZD-48-1 Jantar Standard 2	B-985	
HA-4485	Schempp-Hirth Nimbus 2	20	D-2091
HA-4488	SZD-48-1 Jantar Standard 2	B-1026	OE-5296
			OE-5155
HA-4489-PJ	SZD-48-3 Jantar Standard 3	B-1959	PH-917
HA-4490	Schempp-Hirth Ventus b/16.6	28	PH-704
HA-4491	Eiri PIK-20B	20025	OY-XHH
			OH-453
HA-4492	Grob G.102 Astir CS	1216	D-7289
HA-4494	SZD-48 Jantar Standard 2	W-879	OE-5187
HA-4495	Schempp-Hirth Ventus 2a	110	
HA-4496	Grob G.102 Astir CS	1497	D-4797
HA-4498	Schleicher K 8B	8171	D-5296
HA-4499	Rolladen-Schneider LS8-18	8379	
HA-4500	H205 Glasflugel Libelle	111	BGA2188/DKZ
			RAFGSA774
HA-4502	Grob G.102 Astir CS 77	1800	PH-657
HA-4503	Schempp-Hirth Discus 2b	98	D-7072
HA-4504	Schempp-Hirth Ventus cM	70/534	D-KEDV
HA-4505	Rolladen-Schneider LS8-18	8420	
HA-4506	SZD-48 Jantar Standard 2	W-890	OE-5198
HA-4507	Eiri PIK-20E	20231	OO-ELG
			D-KLMO
HA-4509	LAK-17A	135	
HA-4510-BB	Glasflügel H304C	56-C	
HA-4511	LAK-17A	136	
HA-4513	Schempp-Hirth Discus 2b	unkn	
HA-4515	SZD-48-1 Jantar Standard 2	B-1101	OO-YEA
			LX-EBO
			HB-1555
HA-4518	Grob G.102 Astir CS	1269	D-7364
HA-4521	Schempp-Hirth Ventus bT	81	N201GF
HA-4525	Schempp-Hirth Discus 2a	199	
HA-5000	IAR-Brasov IS.28B2	240	
HA-5001	IAR-Brasov IS.28B2	243	
HA-5002	IAR-Brasov IS.28B2 (Dismantled)	244	
HA-5003	IAR-Brasov IS.28B2	252	
HA-5004	IAR-Brasov IS.28B2	272	
HA-5005	IAR-Brasov IS.28B2	273	
HA-5006	IAR-Brasov IS.28B2	274	
HA-5007	IAR-Brasov IS.28B2	275	
HA-5008	IAR-Brasov IS.28B2	278	
HA-5009	IAR-Brasov IS.28B2	279	
HA-5010	IAR-Brasov IS.28B2	280	
HA-5011	IAR-Brasov IS.28B2	289	
HA-5012	IAR-Brasov IS.28B2	229	
HA-5013	IAR-Brasov IS.28B2	241	
HA-5015	IAR-Brasov IS.28B2	303	
HA-5016	IAR-Brasov IS.28B2	304	
HA-5017	IAR-Brasov IS.28B2	323	
HA-5018	IAR-Brasov IS.28B2	331	
HA-5019	IAR-Brasov IS.28B2	333	
HA-5020	IAR-Brasov IS.28B2	334	
HA-5021	IAR-Brasov IS.28B2	335	
HA-5022	IAR-Brasov IS.28B2	328	
HA-5023	IAR-Brasov IS.28B2	329	
HA-5024	IAR-Brasov IS.28B2	330	

HA-5026	IAR-Brasov IS.28B2	337	
HA-5027	IAR-Brasov IS.28B2	338	
HA-5028	IAR-Brasov IS.28B2	340	
HA-5030	IAR-Brasov IS.28B2	332	
HA-5031	IAR-Brasov IS.28B2	343	
HA-5032	IAR-Brasov IS.28B2	344	
HA-5033	IAR-Brasov IS.28B2	346	
HA-5034	IAR-Brasov IS.28B2	347	
HA-5035	R-IIb Cimbora 84	F-03	
HA-5036	IAR-Brasov IS.28B2	348	
HA-5037	IAR-Brasov IS.28B2	349	
HA-5038	IAR-Brasov IS.28B2	352	
HA-5040	IAR-Brasov IS.28B2	350	
HA-5050	Schleicher K 7 Rhönadler	693	HB-660
HA-5051	Schleicher K 7 Rhönadler	1084	HB-694
HA-5052	Schleicher K 7 Rhönadler	464	D-9110
HA-5053	Schleicher K 7 Rhönadler	7059/A	OY-XTD
			D-5472
HA-5054	Schleicher K 7 Rhönadler	7016	D-7146
HA-5055	Schleicher K 7 Rhönadler	7086	D-8880
HA-5060	Schleicher Ka 6CR Rhönsegler	6384	OY-XLE
			D-0071
			OO-ZAA
HA-5087	Schleicher K 7 Rhönadler	211	D-5037
HA-5090	Schleicher K 7 Rhönadler	7090	D-2000
HA-5100	Grob G.103 Twin Astir	3186	HB-1448
HA-5175	LET L-13 Blanik	027359	
HA-5176	LET L-13 Blanik	027360	
HA-5177	LET L-13 Blanik	170511	DOSAAF
HA-5190	LET L-13 Blanik	170210	OK-9834
HA-5192	LET L-13 Blanik	026244	
HA-5193	LET L-13 Blanik	026804	
HA-5195	SZD-9bis Bocian 1E	P-442	
HA-5196	SZD-9bis Bocian 1E	P-687	
HA-5198	LET L-13J Blanik	173405	OK-6911
HA-5200	LET L-23 Super Blanik	897517	
HA-5201	LET L-23 Super Blanik	897519	
HA-5202	LET L-23 Super Blanik	897520	
HA-5304	R-26S Góbé	E-1172	
HA-5311	R-26S Góbé	E-1179	
HA-5313	R-26S Góbé	E-1182	
HA-5314	R-26S Góbé	E-1183	
HA-5315	R-26S Góbé	E-1184	
HA-5316	R-26S Góbé	E-1185	
HA-5317	R-26S Góbé	E-1186	
HA-5319	R-26S Góbé	E-1188	
HA-5321	R-26S Góbé	E-1190	
HA-5322	R-26S Góbé	E-1191	
HA-5323	R-26S Góbé	E-1192	
HA-5326	R-26S Góbé	E-1195	
HA-5328	R-26S Góbé	E-1197	
HA-5329	R-26S Góbé	E-1198	
HA-5330	R-26S Góbé	E-1199	
HA-5331	R-26S Góbé	E-1200	
HA-5334	R-26S Góbé	E-1203	
HA-5335	R-26S Góbé	E-1204	
HA-5336	R-26S Góbé	E-1205	
HA-5337	R-26S Góbé	E-1206	
HA-5339	R-26S Góbé	E-1208	
HA-5340	R-26S Góbé	E-1209	
HA-5341	R-26S Góbé	E-1210	
HA-5343	R-26S Góbé	E-1212	
HA-5344	R-26S Góbé	E-1213	
HA-5346	R-26S Góbé	E-1215	
HA-5347	R-26S Góbé	E-1216	
HA-5349	R-26S Góbé	E-1218	
HA-5350	R-26S Góbé	E-1219	
HA-5353	R-26S Góbé	E-1222	
HA-5355	R-26S Góbé	E-1224	
HA-5357	R-26S Góbé	E-1226	
HA-5358	R-26S Góbé	E-1227	
HA-5360	R-26S Góbé	E-1229	
HA-5362	R-26S Góbé	E-1231	
HA-5363	R-26S Góbé	E-1232	
HA-5365	R-26S Góbé	E-1234	
HA-5366	R-26S Góbé	E-1235	
HA-5367	R-26S Góbé	E-1236	
HA-5370	R-26S Góbé	E-1239	
HA-5372	R-26S Góbé	E-1241	
HA-5374	R-26S Góbé	E-1243	
HA-5376	R-26S Góbé	E-1245	
HA-5377	R-26S Góbé	E-1246	
HA-5378	R-26S Góbé	E-1247	
HA-5379	R-26S Góbé	E-1248	
HA-5380	R-26S Góbé	E-1249	
HA-5382	R-26S Góbé	E-1251	
HA-5384	R-26S Góbé	E-1253	
HA-5385	R-26S Góbé	E-1254	
HA-5386	R-26S Góbé	E-1255	
HA-5387	R-26S Góbé	E-1256	
HA-5388	R-26S Góbé	E-1257	
HA-5390	R-26S Góbé	E-1259	
HA-5391	R-26S Góbé	E-1260	
HA-5392	R-26S Góbé	E-1261	
HA-5393	R-26S Góbé	E-1262	
HA-5395	R-26S Góbé	E-1264	
HA-5396	R-26S Góbé	E-1265	
HA-5397	R-26S Góbé	E-1266	

HA-5398	R-26S Góbé	E-1267	
HA-5399	R-26S Góbé	E-1268	
HA-5400	R-26S Góbé	E-1269	
HA-5401	R-26S Góbé	E-1270	
HA-5402	R-26S Góbé	E-1271	
HA-5403	R-26S Góbé	E-1272	
HA-5404	R-26S Góbé	E-1273	
HA-5405	R-26S Góbé	E-1274	
HA-5407	R-26S Góbé	E-1276	
HA-5408	R-26S Góbé	E-1277	
HA-5500	R-26SU Góbé	A800001	
HA-5501	R-26SU Góbé	A800002	
HA-5502	R-26SU Góbé	A800003	
HA-5503	R-26SU Góbé	A800004	
HA-5504	R-26SU Góbé	A800005	
HA-5505	R-26SU Góbé	A800006	
HA-5506	R-26SU Góbé	A800007	
HA-5507	R-26SU Góbé	A800023	
HA-5508	R-26SU Góbé	A800024	
HA-5509	R-26SU Góbé	A800025	
HA-5510	R-26SU Góbé	A800026	
HA-5511	R-26SU Góbé	A800027	
HA-5512	R-26SU Góbé	A800028	
HA-5513	R-26SU Góbé	A800029	
HA-5514	R-26SU Góbé	A800030	
HA-5515	R-26SU Góbé	A800031	
HA-5516	R-26SU Góbé	A800032	
HA-5517	R-26SU Góbé 82	A800033	
HA-5518	R-26SU Góbé 82	A800034	
HA-5519	R-26SU Góbé 82	A800035	
HA-5520	R-26SU Góbé 82	A800036	
HA-5521	R-26SU Góbé 82	A800037	
HA-5522	R-26SU Góbé 82	A800038	
HA-5523	R-26SU Góbé 82	A800039	
HA-5524	R-26SU Góbé 82	A800040	
HA-5525	R-26SU Góbé 82	A800041	
HA-5526	R-26SU Góbé 82	A800042	
HA-5527	R-26SU Góbé 82	A800043	
HA-5528	R-26SU Góbé 82	A800044	
HA-5529	R-26SU Góbé 82	A800045	
HA-5531	R-26SU Góbé 82	A800047	
HA-5532	R-26SU Góbé 82	A800048	
HA-5533	R-26SU Góbé	A800049	
HA-5534	R-26SU Góbé	A800050	
HA-5535	R-26SU Góbé	A800051	
HA-5536	R-26SU Góbé	A800052	
HA-5537	R-26SU Góbé	A800053	
HA-5538	R-26SU Góbé	A800054	
HA-5539	R-26SU Góbé	A800055	
HA-5540	R-26SU Góbé	A800056	
HA-5541	R-26SU Góbé	A800057	
HA-5542	R-26SU Góbé	A800058	
HA-5543	R-26SU Góbé	A800059	
HA-5544	R-26SU Góbé	A800060	
HA-5545	R-26SU Góbé (Wfu)	A800061	
HA-5546	R-26SU Góbé	A800062	
HA-5547	R-26SU Góbé	A800064	
HA-5548	R-26SU Góbé	A800066	
HA-5549	R-26SU Góbé	A800067	
HA-5550	R-26SU Góbé	A800068	
HA-5551	R-26SU Góbé	A800069	
HA-5558	R-26SU Góbé	A800070	
HA-5559	R-26SU Góbé	A800073	
HA-5560	R-26SU Góbé	A800063	BGA3473/FRU
HA-5561	R-26SU Góbé	A800071	
HA-5562	R-26SU Góbé	A800072	
HA-5563	R-26SU Góbé	AA800065	OE-5451
HA-7007	Grob G.103 Twin III Acro	34000-K-233	D-8155
HA-7019	A-15	0305	
HA-7020	A-15	0306	
HA-7022	Swift S-1A	113	
HA-7023	Marganski MDM-1 Fox	235	
HA-5060	Schleicher Ka 6CR Rhönsegler	6384	OY-XLE
			D-0071
			OO-ZAA
HA-	Schempp-Hirth Ventus bT	81	N201GF
HA-	Schempp-Hirth Ventus b/16.6	268	F-CGLE
HA-	Schleicher ASW 15B	19296	OO-ZCY
			D-7940
HA-	Schleicher K 7 Rhönadler	7059/A	OY-XTD
			D-5472

MICROLIGHTS (Alphabetical series)

HA-YABC	KSML-IM Nyirseg -2	001/P	
HA-YABD	CFM Shadow Series BD	093	G-MVLN
HA-YABH	Apollo CX/R Okoplan	MZ16/90	
HA-YABJ	Denney Kitfox III	972	
HA-YABK	Denney Kitfox III	973	
HA-YABL	Apollo CX Racer GT/R	MZ48/91	
HA-YABM	Apollo CX Racer GT/R	MZ49/91	
HA-YABP	Apollo CX Racer GT/R	MZ42/91	
HA-YABR	Apollo CX Racer GT/R	MZ58/90	
HA-YABV	Aviatek MAI-890 Junior	07	
HA-YABY	Light Aero Avid Flyer	824	
HA-YACA	Light Aero Avid Flyer Mk.IV	1166	
HA-YACB	Light Aero Avid Flyer D	1167	
HA-YACF	Apollo CX Tandem/R	MZ89040	
HA-YACG	Apollo CX Racer GT/R	MZ118/91	
HA-YACH	Apollo CX Racer GT/R	MZ107/91	
HA-YACI	Apollo CXM Racer GT	180495	
HA-YACJ /57-05	Apollo CX Racer GT/R	MZ47/92	
HA-YACK	Apollo CX Racer GT/R	MZ92/91	
HA-YACL	Apollo CX Racer GT	MZ16/92	
HA-YACN	Denney Kitfox IV	1780	
HA-YACO	Apollo CX Racer GT/R	MZ111/91	
HA-YACP	Apollo CXM Racer GT/R	MZ51/91	
HA-YACR	Apollo CXM Racer GT/R	100693	
HA-YACT	GAK-22 Dino	001-93	HA-XBP
HA-YACZ	Aerostar WT-01 Wild Thing	001	YR-6107
HA-YAME	Fly Synthesis Storch	238/A29G	
HA-YCAB	BB-01 Bence	BB 01-09	
HA-YCAD	Apollo C17 Jet Star/R	090699	
HA-YCTS	Flight Design CTSW	04.06.05	
HA-YEAF	Apollo Star-Bi ke/R	SB 002/92	
HA-YEAO	BB-01 Bence	BB 01-08	
HA-YEAR	Apollo CXM Tandem/R	MZ74/92	
HA-YEAS	Kolibri AK-3	06	
HA-YEAV	TLUltralight TL-32 Typhoon	93A038	
HA-YFKC	B&F Funk FK-12 Comet	012-053	
HA-YFKM	B&F Funk FK-9 Mk.III	09-03b-171	
HA-YFKP	B&F Funk FK-14 Polaris	014-042	
HA-YGAB	Apollo CX Racer GT/R	MZ45/91	
HA-YGAC	Apollo CX Racer GT/R	MZ119/91	
HA-YHAB	Apollo CXM Racer GT/R	MZ73/92	
HA-YHAD	Apollo CXM Racer GT/R	010793	
HA-YHAE	Apollo CXM Racer GT/R	050293	
HA-YHAG	Apollo C15 Racer GT/R	200694	
HA-YHAI	Apollo CXMD GTA	140898	
HA-YHST	TLUltralight TL-96 Star (Cr 6.9.04)	01S/01	
HA-YIMI	Apollo Fox UL	240300	
HA-YJAB	Kolibri AK-3	002	
HA-YNAH	Apollo CX Racer GT/R	MZ33/89	
HA-YNAK	Apollo CX Aircross/R	AT 001005/87	
HA-YNAL	Apollo CX Racer GT/R	MZ112/91	
HA-YNAM	Apollo CX Racer GT/R	MZ116/91	
HA-YNAN	Apollo CX Racer GT/R	MZ27/91	
HA-YNAO	Apollo CXM Racer GT/A	MZ49/91	
HA-YNAQ	RAF-2000GTX	H2-92-3-56	
HA-YNAT	Apollo Fox	01	
HA-YNAU	Apollo Fox	040700	
HA-YNAV	Apollo Fox	210600	
HA-YNAZ	Apollo Fox	100700	
HA-YNBA	Apollo Classic	1009/00	
HA-YNBC	Apollo Fox	150201	
HA-YNBD	Apollo Fox	130301	
HA-YNBE	Apollo Fox	120501	
HA-YNBG	Apollo Fox	270801	
HA-YNBH	Apollo Fox	040302	
HA-YNBI	Apollo Fox	unkn	
HA-YNBK	Apollo Fox	unkn	
HA-YNBM	Apollo Fox	unkn	
HA-YNBN	Apollo Fox	unkn	
HA-YOAB	Apollo CX Racer GT/R	MZ06/90	
HA-YOAD	Apollo CXM Aircross	MZ28/92	
HA-YOAE	Fantasy Air Cora Legato	C-010796	
HA-YRAA	Apollo CX Aircross	AT 01016	
HA-YRAB	Apollo CXM Racer GT/R	100194	
HA-YRAC	Apollo CXM Racer GT/R	110194	
HA-YRAF	Apollo CX Racer GT/R	MZ87/91	
HA-YRAG	Apollo CX Tandem/R	MZ89/0710	
HA-YRAH	Apollo CXM Racer GT	MZ68/1992	
HA-YRAI	Kolibri AK-4	008	
HA-YRAJ	Diamond DA 20 Katana	10185	N185DA
	(Midwest Hawk AE110 Wankel engine test-bed)		
HA-YRAK	Apollo CXM GT/R	090594	
HA-YRAM	JORA	003/94	
HA-YROP	Denney Kitfox	003/1994	
HA-YSAA	Apollo CX Racer GT/R	MZ46/89	
HA-YSAC	Apollo CX Racer GT/R	MZ28/91	
HA-YSAE	Apollo CX Racer GT/R	MZ30/91	
HA-YSAF	Apollo CX Racer GT/R	MZ23/90	
HA-YSAH	Apollo CX Racer GT/R	MZ51/90	
HA-YSAL	Apollo CX Racer GT/R	MZ88/91	
HA-YSAP	Apollo CX Racer GT/R	MZ115/91	
HA-YSAQ	Apollo CX Racer GT/R	MZ39/92	
HA-YSAT	Apollo CX Racer GT/R	MZ89/91	
HA-YSAU	Apollo CX Racer GT/R	MZ104/91	
HA-YSAV	Apollo CX Racer GT/R	MZ05/91	
HA-YSAX	Apollo CX Tandem/R	MZ45/90	
HA-YSAZ	Tandem Air Sunny Sport 582UL	43/93	
HA-YSBD	Apollo CXM Racer GT/R	MZ69/92	
HA-YSBE	Apollo CXM GT/A	171195	
HA-YSKA	Hirth Göbler F30EP	H001	
HA-YTAA	KSML-IM Nyirség-2	001	
HA-YTAB	KSML-IM Nyirség-2	002	
HA-YTAC	KSML-IM Nyirség-2	003	
HA-YTAD	KSML-IM Nyirség-2	004	
HA-YTAE	KSML-IM Nyirség-2	005	
HA-YUAB	Apollo CX Aircross 1400	3 68 2823	
HA-YUAC	Apollo CXM Racer GT/R	150693	
HA-YUAD	Apollo CX Racer GT/R	MZ37/91	
HA-YVAB	OCSI SZ-01	AA-90-01M	

HA-YVAE	Apollo CX Racer GT/R	MZ33/90
HA-YVAF	Fantasy Air Cora Legato	unkn
HA-YWAB	Apollo CX Racer GT/R	MZ108/91
HA-YWAC	Apollo CXM Racer GT/R	030193
HA-YWAD	Apollo CXM Racer/T	170194
HA-YWAE	Apollo CXM Racer	MZ70/92
HA-YWAF	Apollo CX Racer GT/R	MZ33/92
HA-YWAI	Apollo CXM Racer GT/R	190994
HA-YWOL	Zenair CH-601VZodiac	M-002
HA-YXAD	Apollo CX Racer GT/R	MZ105/91
HA-YXAE	Apollo CX Racer GT/R	MZ123/91
HA-YXAF	Apollo CXM Racer GT/R	MZ54/92
HA-YXAH	Apollo CXM Racer GT/R	1305/93
HA-YZAA	Apollo CX Tandem/R	MZ26/89
HA-YZAB	Apollo CX Racer GT/R	MZ129/90
HA-YZAC	Apollo CX Racer GT/R	MZ14/87
HA-YZAF	Apollo CX Racer GT/R	MZ55/91
HA-YZAG	Apollo CX Racer GT/R	MZ60/91
HA-YZAH	Apollo CX Racer GT/R	MZ900130
HA-YZAI	Apollo CX Racer GT/R	MZ44/91
HA-YZAJ	Apollo CX Racer GT/R	MZ61/91
HA-YZAK	Apollo CX Racer GT/R	MZ33/91
HA-YZAL	Apollo CX Racer GT/R	MZ109/91
HA-YZAM	Pipistrel-15	TRMM 0900580392
HA-YZAN	Apollo CX Racer GT/R	MZ121/91
HA-YZAO	Apollo CX Racer GT/R	MZ25/92
HA-YZAP	Apollo CX Racer GT/R	MZ125/91
HA-YZAQ	Apollo CX Aircross/R	AV 01025
HA-YZAR	Apollo C4M Racer GT/R	MZ31/92
HA-YZAS	Apollo C4M Racer GT/R	MZ41/92
HA-YZAV	Apollo C4M Racer GT/R	MZ44/92
HA-YZBA	Apollo CXM Racer GT/R	0201/93
HA-YZBD	Pipistrel-15	0870961291
HA-YZBG	Apollo CXM Racer GT/R	120495
HA-YZBH	Kolibri AK-4	010

MICROLIGHTS (Numerical series)

00-11	Air Création	25-16
00-13	Apollo CX	
03-49	Apollo CX	
03-75	Apollo	
03-76	Bence	
03-99	Moyes Litespeed	
07-115	Apollo Jet Star CX-MD	
12-1	MZ Produkt ZX	
15-10	Apollo CX	
15-12	Apollo CX	
15-18	Apollo CX	
18-001	Apollo CX	
22-45	Apollo CX Racer GT/R	MZ117/91
22-56	Apollo Racer GT	
22-57	Apollo CX-M	
25-1	Apollo CX	25-001
25-2	Apollo CX	
25-3	Apollo CX	
25-6	Apollo CX	
25-08	Apollo CX	
25-11	Apollo	
25-12	Apollo/Air Creation XP 15	
25-13	Air Création Quartz SX-II	
25-14	Apollo	
25-15	TL-22 Duo	95C04
25-16	Apollo trike	
25-25	Apollo CX	
25-30	Apollo CX	
25-56	Apollo Racer GT	
25-113	Apollo/Air Creation SX II	
29-02	Apollo CX-MD	
31-14	Apollo CX-MD	
31-15	Type unknown	
33-89	Apollo C-15	
36-24	Type unknown	
36-86	Serpa Tandem 1100	
36-92	Bence-O2/Stratus 2 SP	
40- 17	Homebuilt CX	
44-001	Apollo CX	
44-003	Apollo CX	
44-004	Apollo CX	44-004
44-005	Apollo CX	
44-006	Apollo CX	
44-007	Apollo CX	
44-008	Apollo CX	
44-009	Apollo CX	
44-011	Apollo CX	
44-012	Apollo CX	
44-22	Apollo CX	MZ 890821
44-023	Apollo CX	
45-101	Apollo CX	
45-102	Apollo CX	
45-108	Apollo CX	
45-111	Apollo CX	
45-112	Apollo CX	
57-03	Apollo CX-MD	
57-05	see HA-YACJ	
57-29	Type unknown	
57-35	Type unknown	
57-36	Type unknown	
57-62	Apollo C-15D	
59-69	Type unknown	
61-10	Apollo C15	
67-09	Apollo CX	
69-69	Type unknown	
75-07	Apollo CX	
75-10	Apollo CX	
99-02	Buckeye Dream Machine (Paraplane)	4765
99-04	Sun Flightcraft Explorer	02011016
139-12	Apollo Tandem C4	

HB - SWITZERLAND

(*) Aircraft Registered in Liechtenstein

Regn.	Type	C/n	Prev.Id.
HB-AEE	Dornier 328-100	3005	D-CITA(2)
HB-AES	Dornier 328-100	3021	D-CHIC
			D-CDXQ
			D-CAOS
			D-CDXN
			VT-VIF
			D-CDZG
			D-CDHF
HB-AFC	Aérospatiale/Alenia ATR-42-320	087	F-WQLF
			TR-LEZ
			F-WQLF
			F-OICA
			(F-OIET)
			F-WQCS
			OK-TFF
			F-WQAF
			TC-AGC
			F-WIYB
			B-2202
			F-WWEM
HB-AFD	Aérospatiale/Alenia ATR-42-320	121	(LZ-ATA)
			F-WQNA
			D-BEEE
			F-WWER
HB-AFE	Bücker Bü.131 Jungmann	36	G-ATJX
			D-EDMI
			HB-AFE
			A-88
			HB-AFE
HB-AFF	Aérospatiale/Alenia ATR-42-320	264	F-GOBK
			F-SEBK
			F-WQCH
			N99839
			F-WWLG
HB-AFG	Aérospatiale/Alenia ATR-72-201	108	F-OMAR
			F-GIGO
			F-WWEZ
HB-AFH	Aérospatiale/Alenia ATR-72-202	313	
HB-AFK	Aérospatiale/Alenia ATR-72-202	232	F-GKOB
HB-AFO	de Havilland DH.60GMoth	1878	CH-325
HB-AHF	SAAB-Scania SF.340A	026	D-CDIE
			HB-AHF
HB-ALP	Piper J-3C-100 Cub	12026	44-79730
HB-CAB	Cessna 140	10119	
HB-CAD	Cessna 140	13033	
HB-CAF	Cessna 140	12839	
HB-CAG	Cessna 140	14236	
HB-CAO	Cessna 170	18720	
HB-CAX	Cessna 170A	19644	
HB-CBA	Cessna 150D	15060123	OE-AYR
			N4123U
HB-CBF	Cessna F150F	F150-0005/15062382	
HB-CBG	Cessna 182J Skylane	18256707	N2607F
HB-CBK	Cessna F150F	F150-0026/15062986	
HB-CBS	Cessna 172	46428	N6328E
HB-CBX	Cessna F150G	F150-0069	
HB-CBZ	Cessna 182J Skylane	18257233	N3133F
HB-CCA	Reims/Cessna FR172K Hawk XP	FR17200621	(D-EIIH)
HB-CCD	Reims/Cessna F152	F15201565	
HB-CCF	Reims/Cessna F152	F15201629	
HB-CCN	Reims/Cessna F152	F15201621	
HB-CCO	Reims/Cessna F172N	F17201763	
HB-CCR	Cessna T210N Turbo Centurion II	21063489	(N5545A)
HB-CCT	Reims/Cessna F172N	F17201885	
HB-CCV(*)	Reims/Cessna F172M	F17201476	D-EKOC(2)
HB-CCZ	Reims/Cessna F152	F15201609	
HB-CDA	Reims/Cessna F150L	F15000775	
HB-CDB	Reims/Cessna F150L	F15000870	
HB-CDC	Reims/Cessna F172M	F17200945	

HB-CDE	Reims/Cessna F177RG Cardinal RG	F177RG0077	
HB-CDF	Reims/Cessna F172M	F17200926	
HB-CDH	Reims/Cessna F150L	F15000924	
HB-CDL	Reims/Cessna F172M	F17200955	
HB-CDN	Cessna F172H	F172-0570	G-AXSO
HB-CDP	Reims/Cessna F150L	F15000923	
HB-CDR	Reims/Cessna F150L	F15001105	
HB-CDS	Reims/Cessna F172M	F17201153	
HB-CDU	Cessna 182P Skylane	18262790	
HB-CEC	Cessna 182P Skylane	18262474	N52235
HB-CED	Reims/Cessna F177RG Cardinal RG	F177RG0075	(D-ECYM)
HB-CEE	Reims/Cessna F150L	F15001115	
HB-CEO	Cessna 172M	17265929	N9079H
HB-CEU	Reims/Cessna F172L	F17200879	D-EEZI
HB-CFA	Reims/Cessna F152	F15201801	D-ECEO
HB-CFB	Cessna 172RG Cutlass RG	172RG0520	N5402V
HB-CFF	Reims/Cessna F152	F15201869	
HB-CFG	Reims/Cessna F152	F15201970	
HB-CFH	Reims/Cessna F152	F15201809	D-EBHJ
			N8495L
HB-CFN	Reims/Cessna F172P	F17202113	
HB-CFO	Cessna 172RG Cutlass RG	172RG0804	N9358B
HB-CFR	Reims/Cessna F172P	F17202053	
HB-CFS	Cessna 182R Skylane	18267859	N5075H
HB-CFT	Reims/Cessna F172P	F17202133	
HB-CFW	Reims/Cessna F152	F15201907	
HB-CFY	Reims/Cessna F172M	F17201123	D-EENO
HB-CFZ	Cessna TR182 Turbo Skylane RG	R18201660	N6317S
HB-CGB	Reims/Cessna F172P	F17202137	(D-EIKH)
HB-CGD	Reims/Cessna FR182 Skylane RG	FR18200067	F-GCYM
HB-CGF	Reims/Cessna F172P	F17202040	N37797
			PH-AYN
HB-CGH	Reims/Cessna F152	F15201860	
HB-CGI	Reims/Cessna F172P	F17202129	D-EGOY
HB-CGK	Cessna 152	15284522	N5305M
HB-CGM	Reims/Cessna F177RG Cardinal RG	F177RG0136	D-EHRB
HB-CGN	Reims/Cessna F172P	F17202139	
HB-CGR	Cessna 172RG Cutlass RG	172RG0688	N6427V
HB-CGS	Cessna 172RG Cutlass RG	172RG1076	N9908B
HB-CGU	Reims/Cessna F172P	F17202194	LX- III
HB-CGW	Cessna U206G Stationair 6	U20604822	D-ELML
	(Reims-assembled with "c/n" 0016)		N1659C
			(OY-BNK)
			N734CN
HB-CGX	Cessna TR182 Turbo Skylane RG	R18201949	(N6257T)
HB-CHA	Reims/Cessna F152	F15201901	
HB-CHB	Reims/Cessna FR182 Skylane RG	FR18200043	G-ILLI
			(HB-CCU)
			N1660C
HB-CHJ	Cessna P210N Pressurized Centurion II	P21000522	D-EATD
			(F-GCQG)
			N731PG
HB-CHM	Reims/Cessna FR182 Skylane RG	FR18200035	D-EIEG
HB-CHV	Reims/Cessna F152	F15201553	F-GBJN
HB-CHW	Reims/Cessna F172P	F17202208	
HB-CHY	Reims/Cessna F172M	F17201063	D-EENZ
HB-CHZ	Cessna 210L Centurion	21061320	D-EARB
			N2534S
HB-CIA	Reims/Cessna F172P	F17202219	
HB-CIC	Cessna TR182 Turbo Skylane RG	R18201847	(D-EITW)
			N5275T
			(D-EITW)
HB-CIE	Reims/Cessna F172P	F17202221	
HB-CIF	Reims/Cessna F177RG Cardinal RG	F177RG0123	D-EFMV
			F-WLIQ
HB-CIG	Cessna P210N Pressurized Centurion	P21000069	D-EKOP
			N3890P
HB-CIH	Reims/Cessna F172P	F17202178	OE-KAB
HB-CIN	Cessna TR182 Turbo Skylane RG	R18201402	D-EGPY
			N4722S
HB-CIO	Reims/Cessna F172P	F17202235	
HB-CIP	Reims/Cessna F172P	F17202153	OO-TRG
			OO-XRG
HB-CIR	Cessna 182Q Skylane	18266647	N95832
HB-CIS	Cessna 172N	17273679	N4800J
HB-CIT	Reims/Cessna F172P	F17202248	
HB-CIU	Reims FR172J Rocket	FR17200437	D-EJXX
HB-CIV	Cessna 182R Skylane	18268557	D-EDEC(3)
			N9564X
HB-CIW	Reims/Cessna F152	F15201980	
HB-CIX	Reims/Cessna F152	F15201966	
HB-CIY	Reims/Cessna F152	F15201955	D-EFIT
HB-CJC	Cessna TR182 Turbo Skylane RG	R18201992	N6352T
HB-CJI	Cessna U206G Stationair 6	U20605938	N6527X
	(Allison turboprop conversion)		
HB-CJQ	Cessna 172N	17271531	D-EAOT
			N3397E
HB-CJR	Cessna 172P	17274303	N51370
HB-CJU	Cessna R182 Skylane RG	R18201685	N6488S
HB-CJV	Reims/Cessna F152	F15201564	D-EFGR
HB-CJW	Cessna 152	15283388	N48904
HB-CKA	Cessna 170A	19135	OO-GAY
			N11B
			N9574A

HB-CKB	Cessna 182P	18263933	D-EIGS
	(Reims-assembled with "c/n" 0021)		(D-EEOB)
			N9872E
HB-CKG	Reims/Cessna F172P	F17202251	G-BMPB
HB-CKH	Cessna P210N Pressurized Centurion II	P21000613	N734VR
HB-CKL	Reims/Cessna F182Q Skylane	F18200109	D-EIYK
HB-CKP	Reims/Cessna F152 (Taildragger conv.)	F15201944	F-GEUE
HB-CKT	Cessna 172RG Cutlass RG	172RG1163	F-GEBP
			N9441D
HB-CKU	Reims/Cessna F172P	F17202195	F-GDOQ
			F-WZDR
HB-CKV	Cessna TR182 Turbo Skylane RG	R18200898	
			N757ZH
HB-CKY	Reims/Cessna F172P	F17202211	D-EAEL(2)
HB-CLA	Cessna R182 Skylane RG	R18201701	N7181S
HB-CLB	Cessna 182Q Skylane	18267423	N4857N
HB-CLE	Reims/Cessna F182Q Skylane	F18200166	D-EOOK
			N182PL
			D-EOOK
HB-CLF	Reims/Cessna F172P	F17202169	G-BKHZ
HB-CLL	Cessna 172P	17276572	N9538L
HB-CLN	Cessna 172RG Cutlass RG	172RG0970	N9690B
HB-CLO	Cessna 172P	17276627	N9830L
HB-CLP	Cessna 172P	17276461	N99528
HB-CLS	Cessna 172P	17276640	N9855L
HB-CLT	Cessna TR182 Turbo Skylane RG	R18201656	D-EOQC(4)
			N737GQ
			C-GIQN
			(N6275S)
HB-CLU	Cessna R182 Skylane RG	R18201776	N4848T
HB-CLY	Reims/Cessna F172M	F17200976	D-ECXL
HB-CMC	Cessna 175 Skylark	56111	OY-AED
			N6611E
HB-CMK	Cessna 175B Skylark	17556791	N8091T
HB-CML	Cessna 182F Skylane	18254812	N3412U
HB-CMO	Cessna F172E	F172-0041	
HB-CMS	Cessna 150D	15060517	OE-AYT
			N4517U
HB-CMZ	Cessna 182H Skylane	18256287	N2387X
HB-CNC	Cessna 150J	15070521	N60715
HB-CNE	Reims/Cessna F150M	F15001309	
HB-CNF	Cessna F172H	F172-0653	D-EABZ
HB-CNG	Cessna 210L Centurion	21060208	OE-DFE
			(N59309)
HB-CNI	Reims/Cessna F152	F15201494	(D-EAAX)
HB-CNK	Reims/Cessna F152	F15201445	
HB-CNM	Cessna 177RG Cardinal RG	177RG1335	N53062
HB-CNN	Cessna TR182 Turbo Skylane RG	R1821045	(N756DC)
HB-CNO	Cessna 182P Skylane	18264838	N1270S
HB-CNS	Reims/Cessna F152	F15201741	
HB-CNY	Reims/Cessna F172N	F17201681	D-EIIF
HB-COE	Cessna 180	30465	N1765C
HB-COK	Cessna 170B	26445	N3402C
HB-COR	Cessna 140A	15351	N9630A
HB-CPJ	Cessna TR182 Turbo Skylane RG	R18201654	N6252S
HB-CPL	Cessna 172	29046	N6946A
HB-CPP	Cessna 172	29928	N8128B
HB-CPU	Cessna 150	17036	N5536E
HB-CPX	Cessna 182B Skylane	51964	N2664G
HB-CQA	Cessna 172N	17270725	N739QR
HB-CQB	Cessna A185F Skywagon	18504093	N60998
HB-CQC	Cessna R182 Skylane RG	R18202034	N6474T
HB-CQF	Cessna 172M	17261782	N5375Q
HB-CQI	Cessna 152	15280211	N24314
HB-CQL	Cessna 172P	17274190	N6393K
HB-CQM	Cessna 172N	17273010	N1916F
HB-CQN	Cessna 150L	15074264	N19239
HB-CQO	Cessna 150L	15074592	N21988
HB-CQP	Cessna 182S	18280200	N164GT
			N9460Z
HB-CQQ	Cessna 172R	17280102	
HB-CQR	Cessna 172R	17280506	
HB-CQS	Cessna P210N Pressurized Centurion II	P21000167	N6307P
HB-CQU	Cessna 182Q Skylane	18266611	D-EFST(3)
			N95727
HB-CQW	Cessna 172S	172S8288	
HB-CQZ	Cessna 182S	18280571	D-EMWJ
			N7276Y
HB-CRD	Cessna 172	36339	N8639B
HB-CRG	Cessna 182A Skylane	51429	N2129G
HB-CRL	Cessna 175A Skylark	56752	N8052T
HB-CRM	Cessna 175B Skylark	17556959	N8259T
HB-CRR	Cessna 150B	15059485	N7385X
HB-CRS	Cessna 172C	17249162	N1462Y
HB-CRZ	Cessna 182E Skylane	18254203	N3203Y
HB-CSD	Cessna F150G	F150-0101	
HB-CSE	Cessna F172H	F172-0329	
HB-CSF	Cessna F150G	F150-0123	
HB-CSM	Cessna F150G	F150-0189	
HB-CSR	Cessna 182H Skylane	18255849	D-EFHY
			N3449S
HB-CSS	Cessna 210F Centurion	21058757	N1857F
HB-CST	Cessna 182G Skylane	18255388	OE-DDM
			N2188R
HB-CSZ	Cessna F150H	F150-0265	
HB-CTD	Cessna F150H	F150-0296	
HB-CTF	Cessna F150H	F150-0336	

HB-CTL	Cessna 182L Skylane	18258953	(D-EFMJ)
			(D-EDCD)
			N42301
HB-CTR	Cessna F172H	F172-0582	
HB-CTS	Cessna 150F	15062938	D-ECYQ
			N8838G
HB-CTU	Cessna F150J	F150-0476	
HB-CTW	Cessna F150J	F150-0491	
HB-CUA	Reims/Cessna F150K	F15000590	
HB-CUD	Cessna F172H	F172-0560	
HB-CUE	Cessna 182M Skylane	18259376	N70814
HB-CUI	Reims/Cessna F150K	F15000618	
HB-CUQ	Reims/Cessna FA150K Aerobat	FA1500009	
HB-CVD	Reims/Cessna F150L	F15000684	
HB-CVI	Reims/Cessna F177RG Cardinal RG	F177RG0011/177RG0120	
HB-CVK	Cessna 182N Skylane	18260526	N8986G
HB-CVL	Reims/Cessna FA150K Aerobat	FA1500054	D-ECAD
HB-CVM	Reims/Cessna F172K	F17200796	
HB-CVT	Reims/Cessna F150L	F15000721	
HB-CVU	Reims/Cessna F172K	F17200783	
HB-CVV	Cessna 182L Skylane	18258763	D-EDHY
			N3463R
HB-CVZ	Cessna F150J	F150-0497	F-WLIT
			G-AXUG
			F-BRBF
HB-CWA	Reims/Cessna FRA150L Aerobat	FRA1500134	
HB-CWC	Cessna 177B Cardinal	17701690	
HB-CWD	Reims/Cessna F177RG Cardinal RG	F177RG0047	
HB-CWE	Reims/Cessna F172L	F17200829	
HB-CWI	Reims/Cessna FRA150L Aerobat	FRA1500147	
HB-CWN	Cessna 182P Skylane	18261794	
HB-CWR	Reims/Cessna F150L	F15000669	I-NOLE
HB-CWT	Reims/Cessna F150M (W/o 8.8.03)	F15001208	
HB-CWX	Cessna 182P Skylane	18263399	N9511G
HB-CWY	Cessna 182P	18263877	N6882M
	(Reims-assembled with "c/n" 0010)		
HB-CWZ	Cessna A185F	18502641	N4879C
HB-CXA	Cessna 177B Cardinal	17702234	N35150
HB-CXE	Cessna 182P	18264380	N1590M
	(Reims-assembled with "c/n" 0051)		
HB-CXF	Cessna T210L Turbo Centurion	21061259	N2378S
HB-CXK	Cessna T210L Turbo Centurion	21059922	N41CF
			N30428
HB-CXN	Reims/Cessna F150M	F15001343	
HB-CXV	Reims/Cessna F152	F15201504	
HB-CXW	Reims/Cessna F152	F15201499	
HB-CXZ	Reims/Cessna F172N	F17201630	
HB-CYC	Cessna 172RG Cutlass RG	172RG0556	N5529V
HB-CYE	Cessna 152	15284056	N4981H
HB-CYF	Reims/Cessna F152	F15201792	
HB-CYH	Cessna 172P	17274157	N5492K
HB-CYJ	Cessna P210R	P21000836	
HB-CYK	Cessna TU206G Turbo Stationair 6	U20606155	SE-III
			N6134Z
HB-CYL	Reims/Cessna FR182 Skylane RG	FR18200060	D-EGPX
HB-CYM	Cessna 182S	18280312	D-EASG
			N2002X
HB-CYN	Cessna TP206C Turbo Super Skylane	P206-0451	D-EAWB
			N8651Z
HB-CYO	Cessna 182S	18280778	N72616
HB-CYP	Reims/Cessna F152	F15201578	D-EGUE
HB-CYS	Cessna T206H Turbo Stationair	T20608324	N3552S
HB-CYT	Reims/Cessna F172M	F17201192	D-EOQH
HB-CYU	Cessna 172S	172S9323	N5328X
HB-CYV	Cessna 170B	20615	N2463D
			N550PN
			N2463D
HB-CYX	Cessna 152	15283756	D-EAAS(3)
			N51168
HB-CYY	Cessna P210N Pressurized Centurion	P21000656	N915BT
			N5219W
HB-C . .	Cessna C-37 Airmaster	368	N18049
			NC18049
HB-DAI	Nord 1203 Norécrin II	307	
HB-DBC	Ruschmeyer R.90-230RG	012	D-EEBX
HB-DBF	Ruschmeyer R.90-230RG	006	D-EEHY
HB-DBL	Saab S.91D Safir	91439	
HB-DCA	Wassmer WA.40 Super IV	45	
HB-DCB	Wassmer WA.40A Super IV	68	
HB-DCE	Wassmer WA.421/250	420	
HB-DCF	Gardan GY-80 Horizon 160	24	F-BLPG
HB-DCI	Gardan GY-80 Horizon 160	62	F-BLVM
HB-DCQ	Gardan GY-80 Horizon 150	112	F-BMUN
HB-DCR	Varga 2150A Kachina	154-80	OO-HTB
			N80716
HB-DCU	Varga 2180 Kachina	180-82	
HB-DED	Mooney M.20E Super 21	213	
HB-DEG	Mooney M.20E Super 21	345	
HB-DEK	Mooney M.20C Mark 21	2594	N6890U
HB-DEN	Mooney M.20E Super 21	714	
HB-DET	Mooney M.20E Super 21	947	
HB-DEU	Mooney M.20E Super 21	1053	
HB-DEV	Mooney M.20F Executive	670058	N3520X
HB-DEW	Mooney M.22	670002	N7706M
HB-DEZ	Mooney M.20F Executive	670187	N9610M
HB-DFA	Mooney M.20J Model 201	24-0262	

HB-DFF	Mooney M.20J Model 201	24-0545	
HB-DFI	Mooney M.20K Model 231	25-0104	
HB-DFK	Mooney M.20J Model 201	24-0796	
HB-DFL	Mooney M.20J Model 201	24-0764	N4548H
HB-DFM	Mooney M.20J Model 201	24-0775	
HB-DFN	Mooney M.20J Model 201	24-0801	
HB-DFO	Mooney M.20K Model 231	25-0129	
HB-DFP	Mooney M.20J Model 201	24-0817	
HB-DFR	Mooney M.20K Model 231	25-0027	N4564H
HB-DFS	Mooney M.20J Model 201	24-0824	
HB-DFT	Mooney M.20J Model 201	24-0837	
HB-DFU	Mooney M.20J Model 201	24-0859	
HB-DFW	Mooney M.20C Ranger	690088	N9305V
HB-DFX	Mooney M.20J Model 201	24-0967	(N3866H)
HB-DFY	Mooney M.20K Model 231	25-0366	N231QS
HB-DFZ	Mooney M.20K Model 231	25-0368	N231QU
HB-DGC	Mooney M.20K Model 231	25-0539	
HB-DGD	Mooney M.20K Model 231	25-0816	
HB-DGE	Mooney M.20K Model 231	25-0389	EI-BJD
			C-GMWH
			(N4024H)
HB-DGG	Mooney M.20J Model 201	24-0804	SE-GXF
HB-DGI	Mooney M.20K Model 231	25-0693	G-BKMC
			N1167W
HB-DGL	Mooney M.20K Model 231	25-0887	
HB-DGM	Mooney M.20K Model 252 TSE	25-1036	
HB-DGN	Mooney M.20K Model 252 TSE	25-1037	
HB-DGP	Varga 2150A Kachina	158-80	G-BLHT
			OO-RTW
HB-DGR	Mooney M.20K Model 231	25-0709	N9042G
			YV-2310P
HB-DGS	Mooney M.20J Model 201	24-1615	
HB-DGV	Mooney M.20J Model 201	24-1624	
HB-DGW	Mooney M.20J Model 201	24-1621	
HB-DGZ	Mooney M.20J Model 205	24-3035	
HB-DHA	Mooney M.20K Model 252 TSE	25-1155	
HB-DHF	Mooney M.20L PFM	26-0022	
HB-DHG	Mooney M.20K Model 252 TSE	25-1170	
HB-DHH	Mooney M.20K Model 231	25-0554	N2XK
HB-DHI	Mooney M.20J Model 201	24-1039	D-EESU
			N3683H
HB-DHK	Mooney M.20K Model 252 TSE	25-1185	
HB-DHL	Mooney M.20J Model 201	24-1685	
HB-DHO	Mooney M.20L PFM	26-0036	N155MP
HB-DHP	Mooney M.20M Model 257 TLS	27-0015	
HB-DHV	Mooney M.20M Model 257 TLS	27-0056	
HB-DHW	Mooney M.20J Model 201	24-1579	N58152
HB-DHY	Mooney M.20S	30-0015	
HB-DHZ	Mooney M.20M Model 257 TLS	27-0046	
HB-DIA	Mooney M.20J Model 205	24-3288	
HB-DIB	Mooney M.20M Model 257 TLS	27-0078	I-SEVE
			N9124N
HB-DIC	Mooney M.20J Model 205	24-3240	D-ECZL
			N9139V
HB-DIE	Mooney M.20R Ovation	29-0015	
HB-DIF	Mooney M.20M Model 257 TLS	27-0206	
HB-DIG	Mooney M.20J Model 205	24-3379	
HB-DIH	Mooney M.20J Model 205	24-3385	
HB-DIK	Mooney M.20J Model 205	24-3392	
HB-DIL	Mooney M.20R Ovation	29-0102	
HB-DUK	Mooney M.20A	1531	(N8353E)
HB-DUN	Bellanca 14-13-3 Cruisair Senior	1637	N6516N
HB-DUP	Mooney M.20A	1658	
HB-DUX	Luscombe 8A Silvaire	2835	NC71408
HB-DUZ	Gardan GY-80 Horizon 160	02	
HB-DVD	Gardan GY-80 Horizon 180	192	
HB-DVE	Gardan GY-80 Horizon 180	148	
HB-DVF	Mooney M.20F Executive	670298	N2904L
HB-DVG	Mooney M.20F Executive	670313	N2919L
HB-DVK	Mooney M.20F Executive	670348	N2989L
HB-DVM	Mooney M.20E Super 21	670003	
HB-DVN	Mooney M.20E Super 21	807	N5885Q
HB-DVV	Mooney M.20B Mark 21	1831	D-ECTO
HB-DVY	Mooney M.22	690004	N7729M
HB-DVZ	Mooney M.22	700001	N7734M
HB-DWC	Mooney M.20C Mark 21	3269	
HB-DWD	Mooney M.20E Super 21	1003	N2684W
HB-DWF	Luscombe 8A Silvaire	1230	N25354
			NC25354
HB-DWI	Mooney M.20F Executive	22-1411	
HB-EAC	Meteor FL.55B	1119	I-FELH
HB-EAI	CEA Jodel DR.1050 Ambassadeur	16	
HB-EBG	Beech G35 Bonanza	D-4523	
HB-EBK	CEA Jodel DR.1050 Ambassadeur	533	F-BLZE
HB-EBM	CEA Jodel DR.1051 Sicile	446	
HB-EBS	CEA Jodel DR.1050 Ambassadeur	231	
HB-EBZ	CEA Jodel DR.1051 Sicile	426	
HB-ECD	Beech B35 Bonanza	D-2271	
HB-ECF	Beech A35 Bonanza	D-1827	
HB-ECG	Beech A35 Bonanza	D-1828	
HB-ECX	Beech B35 Bonanza	D-2656	
HB-EDB	Robin DR.300/180R Remorqueur	613	(D-EHDV)
			F-BSPP
HB-EDD	Morane-Saulnier MS.885 Super Rallye	56	
HB-EDE	Morane-Saulnier MS.880B Rallye Club	76	
HB-EDH	Morane-Saulnier MS.885 Super Rallye	43	
HB-EDY	Morane-Saulnier MS.880B Rallye Club	207	

HB-EEI	CEA Jodel DR.1050 Ambassadeur	549	
HB-EEM	CEA Jodel DR.1050M Sicile	575	
HB-EEN	CEA Jodel DR.1050M1 Sicile Record	610	
HB-EEV	CEA DR.250/160 Capitaine	27	
HB-EEW	CEA Jodel DR.1050 Ambassadeur	568	F-OCCZ
HB-EEX	CEA DR.250/160 Capitaine	31	
HB-EEZ	CEA DR.250/160 Capitaine	48	
HB-EFB	Beech F35 Bonanza	D-4132	
HB-EFH	Beech V35 Bonanza	D-8072	
HB-EFM	Beech V35 Bonanza	D-8414	
HB-EFP	CEA Jodel DR.1050 Ambassadeur	338	
HB-EFR	CEA Jodel DR.1051 Sicile	318	F-BKPA
HB-EFS	CEA DR.220 2+2	17	F-BOCK
HB-EFT	CEA Jodel DR.1050M1 Sicile Record	619	F-BMPX
HB-EGB	Beech C35 Bonanza	D-2761	
HB-EGC	Beech C35 Bonanza	D-2766	
HB-EGE	Beech A35 Bonanza	D-2045	
HB-EGF	Beech D35 Bonanza	D-3540	
HB-EGP	Beech H35 Bonanza	D-4930	
HB-EGS	Beech D35 Bonanza	D-3637	PH-NFF
HB-EHB	Beech 35-C33 Debonair	CD-1085	
HB-EHF	Beech 35-C33A Debonair	CE-103	
HB-EHK	Beech V35B Bonanza	D-9330	D-EHKK
HB-EHN(*)	Beech V35B Bonanza	D-9180	
HB-EHO	Beech 35-33 Debonair	CD-132	OE-DNE
HB-EHP	Beech 35-A33 Debonair	CD-344	I-ZEZE HB-EIO
HB-EHR	Beech V35B Bonanza	D-9439	
HB-EHS	Beech C23 Sundowner	M-1451	
HB-EHW	Beech C23 Sundowner	M-1571	
HB-EIT	Beech 35-A33 Debonair	CD-377	
HB-EIU	Beech 35-B33 Debonair	CD-438	
HB-EIX	Beech E35 Bonanza	D-3788	N7325B
HB-EIZ	Beech P35 Bonanza	D-7105	D-EEIZ HB-EIZ
HB-EJA(*)	Beech A36 Bonanza	E-1669	
HB-EJD	Beech 77 Skipper	WA-136	
HB-EJE	Beech A36TC Bonanza	EA-118	
HB-EJJ	Morane-Saulnier MS.505 Criquet	590	F-BCMQ
HB-EJM	Beech F33A Bonanza	CE-962	
HB-EJN	Beech V35B Bonanza	D-9907	D-EOLM
HB-EJQ	Beech A36 Bonanza	E-2130	N6747J
HB-EJR	SOCATA TB-10 Tobago	370	
HB-EJV	Beech 35-C33A Debonair	CD-1028	OE-DYT D-EKVO
HB-EJW	Beech B36TC Bonanza	EA-292	N150CB N6398U YV-2305P
HB-EKC	Aero 45S	51195	
HB-EKJ	SIAI-Marchetti SF.260D	735/41-005	I-LELG
HB-EKX(*)	Beech 35-C33A Debonair	CE-78	
HB-ELD	Oberlerchner JOB 15-180/2	069	OE-DOA
HB-ELI	Piper J-3C-90 Cub	13129	44-80833
HB-ELJ	Beech 35-C33 Debonair	CD-1010	D-ECLB
HB-ELK	SIAI-Marchetti S.205-18/R	104	
HB-ELO	Piper J-3C-65 Cub	13237	45-4497
HB-ELP	SIAI-Marchetti S.205-20/R	231	
HB-ELT	SIAI-Marchetti S.205-20/R	237	
HB-ELX	SIAI-Marchetti S.205-22/R	383	
HB-EMI	Fairchild F.24W-41A Argus II	767	FZ827 43-14803
HB-EMM	Partenavia P.66B Oscar 150	18	I-BIRT
HB-EMN	Robin DR.300/235 Remorqueur (Built as /180R)	544	
HB-EMP	Robin DR.300/180R Remorqueur	550	
HB-EMQ	Robin DR.300/180R Remorqueur	571	
HB-EMR	CEA DR.250/160 Capitaine	57	F-BNJS
HB-EMW	Robin HR.100/200B Royale	114	
HB-EMX	CEA DR.250/160 Capitaine	25	F-BMZV
HB-EMZ	CEA DR.221 Dauphin	79	F-BPCB
HB-ENP	Beech A23-19 Musketeer Sport III	MB-33	
HB-ENS	Beech A23-19 Musketeer Sport III	MB-35	
HB-ENV	Beech A23-24 Musketeer Super III	MA-108	
HB-ENW	Beech A23-24 Musketeer Super III	MA-107	
HB-ENX	Beech A23-19 Musketeer Sport III	MB-141	
HB-EOF	Auster J/1 Autocrat (Dismantled)	1981	
HB-EOP	Auster J/1 Autocrat (Lycoming)	1974	
HB-EOW	Auster Mk.5	1004	NJ611
HB-EPG	Robin DR.300/180R Remorqueur	649	
HB-EPK	Partenavia P.64B Oscar 200	62	
HB-EPL	Partenavia P.66B Oscar 150	39	
HB-EPN	Ryan Navion A	881	F-BESJ N8881H
HB-EPS	S.A.I. KZ-VII Laerke	188	
HB-EQA	SOCATA MS.880B Rallye Club	1179	F-BPGZ
HB-EQB	Robin DR.400/180 Régent	1389	D-EJRZ
HB-EQC	Robin DR.400/180R Remorqueur	1028	D-EGPR
HB-EQD	Robin DR.400/180R Remorqueur	1564	
HB-EQE	Robin DR.400/180R Remorqueur	1464	
HB-EQG	Robin DR.400/180R Remorqueur	1476	
HB-EQK	Robin HR.100/250TR	537	G-BFPG ZS-JSU F-ODCS
HB-EQM	Robin DR.300/180R Remorqueur	710	D-ELAR
HB-EQN	Robin DR.400/180R Remorqueur	1569	
HB-EQR	SOCATA TB-20 Trinidad	293	F-BNGQ
HB-EQV	Robin HR.100/250TR	550	OY-POD
HB-ERB	Erco 415C Ercoupe	4367	OO-EXA
HB-ERH	Erco 415C Ercoupe	1751	D-ELEN N99128
HB-ERJ	SIAI-Marchetti SF.260C (Built as SF.260WL)	'254'	F-GMSF BFAF: 8424? LibyanARAF502
HB-ERM	SOCATA MS.893A Rallye Commodore 180	10939	
HB-ERO	Fairchild F.24R-46A Argus III	891	HB653 43-14927
HB-ERP	SOCATA MS.883 Rallye 115	1364	
HB-ERQ	Robin DR.380 Prince	546	F-BSLM
HB-ERT	SOCATA MS.894A Minerva 220	11075	
HB-ERV	SOCATA MS.893A Rallye Commodore 180	10616	F-BNNO
HB-ESB	North American Navion 4	4-331	LR-AAU
HB-ESO	North American Navion 4	4-1361	OE-DYD HB-ESO N4361K
HB-ESU	Fuji FA-200-180 Aero Subaru	192	
HB-ETD	Aeronca 7BCM Champion (C/n plate shows model 7AC)	3490	N84777 NC84777
HB-ETF	Aeronca 7AC Champion	1792	OO-TWB
HB-ETI	Comte AC-4 (Painted in original registration as CH-180)	15	CH-180
HB-ETM	SOCATA MS.894A Minerva 220	12096	
HB-ETN	Maule M-4-210 Rocket	1035	
HB-ETR	Maule M-4-210C Rocket	1033C	
HB-ETS	Maule M-4-220C Strata Rocket	2020C	
HB-ETX	Fuji FA-200-180AO Aero Subaru	246	
HB-ETY	SOCATA MS.894A Minerva 220	12089	F-BUNV
HB-EUD	Beagle A.61 Terrier 2	B.616	G-ASCE WE571
HB-EUG	CEA DR.221 Dauphin	99	F-BPCV
HB-EUI	Robin HR.100-200B Royal	129	D-EEDD
HB-EUK	CEA Jodel DR.1051M1 Sicile Record	609	F-BMPO
HB-EUL	Taylorcraft Plus D	176	LB317
HB-EUM	Robin HR.100-200D Royal	174	
HB-EUN	Robin DR.300/108 2+2	523	F-BSJM
HB-EUO	CEA Jodel DR.1050M1 Sicile Record	625	5A-CAA G-ATBR
HB-EUP	Robin DR.400/180R Remorqueur	780	
HB-EUQ	Robin DR.400/180R Remorqueur	786	
HB-EUV	Robin DR.400/180R Remorqueur	820	
HB-EUX	CEA DR.340 Major	462	D-EERT
HB-EUZ	CEA DR.250/160 Capitaine	70	F-BNVI
HB-EVP	SIAI-Marchetti S.208	1-04	
HB-EVQ	Maule M-5-235C Lunar Rocket	7282C	
HB-EVT	SIAI-Marchetti SF.260	2-57	I-RAIB
HB-EVW	Procaer F.15 Picchio	05	I-LONI
HB-EVY	Maule M-5-235C Lunar Rocket	7302C	N56364
HB-EWE	Beech 23 Musketeer	M-504	OE-DMK D-ENXU
HB-EWG	Beech F33A Bonanza	CE-513	OE-DMN D-EBNP
HB-EWH	Beech F33A Bonanza	CE-844	
HB-EWP	SIAI-Marchetti SF.260	2-29	D-EBAA
HB-EWQ	SIAI-Marchetti SF.260C	636/46-002	I-APAB
HB-EWR	Beech F33A Bonanza	CE-609	
HB-EWU	Beech A36 Bonanza	E-854	
HB-EWY	Sportavia-Pützer RS.180 Sportsman	6017	D-EFBJ
HB-EXC	Fuji FA-200-180 Aero Subaru	98	D-EMYV
HB-EXF	Robin HR.200/120 Acrobin	25	
HB-EXG	Robin DR.400/180 Régent	943	
HB-EXH	Robin HR.200/120 Acrobin	28	
HB-EXL	Robin DR.400/180R Remorqueur	959	
HB-EXQ	Robin DR.400/180R Remorqueur	1037	
HB-EXT	Robin DR.400/180R Remorqueur	1027	D-EGPQ
HB-EXU	Robin DR.400/180R Remorqueur	1199	
HB-EXV	CEA DR.250/160 Capitaine	68	F-BNJV
HB-EXW	Robin DR.400/180R Remorqueur (Damaged 8.7.04)	1257	
HB-EXX	Robin R.2160 Alpha Sport	124	
HB-EXY	Robin DR.400/180R Remorqueur	1227	
HB-EYD	SOCATA MS.893E Rallye 180GT Gaillard	12680	F-BXYZ
HB-EYK	SOCATA Rallye 235E Gabier	13114	
HB-EYN	Robin DR.400/180R Remorqueur	1306	
HB-EYO	Robin DR.400/180R Remorqueur	1372	
HB-EYP	Robin R.1180T	222	
HB-EYS	Robin DR.400/180R Remorqueur	1297	
HB-EYV	Maule M-5-235C Lunar Rocket	7300C	N56362
HB-EYX	SOCATA TB-10 Tobago	110	
HB-EYY	SOCATA TB-10 Tobago	111	
HB-EZG	PZL-104 Wilga 35A	86275	SP-WRF
HB-EZJ	Auster Mk.5 (On rebuild)	1753	G-ANHZ TW384
HB-EZN	SOCATA Rallye 180TS Galérien	3320	
HB-EZS	Maule M-5-235C Lunar Rocket	7355C	
HB-EZW	SOCATA TB-10 Tobago	351	
HB-EZX	Robin DR.400/180R Remorqueur	1349	D-EEGE
HB-EZZ	SIAI-Marchetti SF.260C	570/42-006	I-SMAB
HB-FCF	Pilatus PC-6/B1-H2 Turbo Porter	614	
HB-FCT	Pilatus PC-6/B2-H2 Turbo Porter	637	
HB-FDU	Pilatus PC-6/B1-H2 Turbo Porter	663	
HB-FFV	Pilatus PC-6/B2-H2 Turbo Porter	817	9Q-CTH(2) HB-FFV
HB-FFW	Pilatus PC-6/B2-H2 Turbo Porter	735	
HB-FGI	Pilatus PC-6/B2-H2 Turbo Porter	810	

HB-FHZ	Pilatus PC-6/B2-H2 Turbo Porter	840	ZS-MTP HB-FHZ
HB-FKC	Pilatus PC-6/B2-H4 Turbo Porter	844	
HB-FKH	Pilatus PC-6/B2-H4 Turbo Porter	865	
HB-FKL	Pilatus PC-6/B2-H4 Turbo Porter	867	
HB-FKM	Pilatus PC-6/B2-H4 Turbo Porter	873	
HB-FKP	Pilatus PC-6/B2-H4 Turbo Porter	877	
HB-FKR	Pilatus PC-6/B2-H4 Turbo Porter	872	
HB-FKT(*)	Pilatus PC-6/B2-H4 Turbo Porter	876	
HB-FLA	Pilatus PC-6/B2-H4 Turbo Porter	905	
HB-FLB	Pilatus PC-6/B2-H4 Turbo Porter	906	
HB-FLE	Pilatus PC-6/B2-H4 Turbo Porter	912	
HB-FLG	Pilatus PC-6/B2-H4 Turbo Porter	910	
HB-FLH	Pilatus PC-6/B2-H4 Turbo Porter	918	
HB-FLI	Pilatus PC-6/B2-H4 Turbo Porter	893	F-GONE
HB-FLK	Pilatus PC-6/B2-H4 Turbo Porter	779	D-FACT N119SA LV-MAF
HB-FMB	Pilatus PC-6/B2-H4 Turbo Porter	932	
HB-FMC	Pilatus PC-6/B2-H4 Turbo Porter (Crash 8.4.00)	938	
HB-FMF	Pilatus PC-6/B2-H4 Turbo Porter	939	N939WA HB-FMF
HB-FMH	Pilatus PC-6/B2-H4 Turbo Porter	894	D-FUNY
HB-FMP	Pilatus PC-6/B2-H4 Turbo Porter	935	D-FREI
HB-FOB	Pilatus PC-XII Eagle	P-02	
HB-FOD	Pilatus PC-12/45	103	HB-FOD N361DB HB-FOD ZS-NWZ
HB-FOG	Pilatus PC-12 Eagle	134	
HB-FOI	Pilatus PC-12/45	157	
HB-FOP	Pilatus PC-12/45	291	
HB-FOQ	Pilatus PC-12/45	349	
HB-FOR	Pilatus PC-12/45	257	N653CA HB-FQO
HB-FOS	Pilatus PC-12/45	366	
HB-FOT	Pilatus PC-12/45	121	ZS-PVT HB-FSB
HB-FOU	Pilatus PC-12/45	368	
HB-FOV	Pilatus PC-12/45	190	ZS-OFN HB-FSY
HB-FOW	Pilatus PC-12/45	411	
HB-FOX	Pilatus PC-12/45	334	
HB-FOY	Pilatus PC-12/45	386	
HB-FOZ	Pilatus PC-12/45	352	
HB-FPB	Pilatus PC-12/45	381	HB-FSO(4)
HB-FPC	Pilatus PC-12/45	422	VP-BBB HB-FRK
HB-FPE	Pilatus PC-12/45	479	
HB-FPJ	Pilatus PC-12/45	490	
HB-FPK	Pilatus PC-12/45	513	
HB-FPL	Pilatus PC-12/45	247	F-GTTT HB-FRR(2)
HB-FPR	Pilatus PC-12/45	544	
HB-FPS	Pilatus PC-12/45	608	
HB-FPU	Pilatus PC-12/45	625	
HB-FPX	Pilatus PC-12/45	566	

HB-FQ . , HB-FR . , HB-FS . used as delivery marks for Pilatus PC-12

HB-GBL	Beech 95 Travel Air	TD-222	N2043C
HB-GCE	Beech 95 Travel Air	TD-216	N657Q
HB-GCG	Beech 95-55 Baron	TC-76	D-ICAX I-VICO HB-GOI
HB-GDS	Beech 95-B55 Baron	TC-850	5Y-AGT VQ-ZEG ZS-DVO
HB-GEA	Beech 95-55 Baron	TC-64	N1221Z
HB-GEC	Beech 95-B55 Baron	TC-1272	
HB-GFA	Beech A60 Duke	P-172	
HB-GFF	Beech D95A Travel Air	TD-584	SE-EWT OH-BTA
HB-GGM	Beech 58P Baron	TJ-103	
HB-GGP	Beech 58P Baron	TJ-157	
HB-GGU	Beech E90 King Air	LW-315	
HB-GHD	Beech F90 King Air	LA-50	F-GCLS
HB-GHG	Beech 95-B55 Baron	TC-1616	G-BBEM
HB-GHK	Rockwell Commander 695	96023	ZS-KZV (N9943S)
HB-GHV	Beech 300 Super King Air	FA-170	
HB-GIA	Beech 95-B55 Baron	TC-1825	N7220R
HB-GIL	Beech 200 Super King Air	BB-194	N502EB N300PH N200PH
HB-GIT	Beech 300 Super King Air	FA-142	N987BT N3081Z
HB-GIX	Beech E95 Travel Air	TD-717	G-AWCW
HB-GJD	Beech 200C Super King Air	BL-7	F-GJBJ N6690E
HB-GJF(*)	Beech C90B King Air	LJ-1407	
HB-GJH	Beech C90 King Air	LJ-972	N18080
HB-GJI	Beech 200 Super King Air	BB-451	D-IBOW(3)
HB-GJJ	Beech B60 Duke	P-272	D-INMC N30MC N4470W
HB-GJK	Beech B60 Duke	P-274	D-INAR(2)
HB-GJM	Beech 200 Super King Air	BB-255	N32KD N32KC N820DY N920DY
HB-GJO	Beech 58 Baron	TH-2001	N3231F
HB-GJR	Beech B300 Super King Air	FL-340	N5070M
HB-GJS	Beech B300 Super King Air	FL-404	N6204G
HB-GOD	Beech 95 Travel Air	TD-247	
HB-GPC	Beech 58P Baron	TJ-463	
HB-GPD	Beech 58P Baron	TJ-281	N369RS N4097M ZS-MMM N123CR
HB-GPG	Beech 200 Super King Air	BB-307	N703HT N921S N23687
HB-GPH	Beech B200 Super King Air	BB-1569	EI-WHE VP-CHE N20505
HB-GPI	Beech 300LW Super King Air	FA-220	N41GA (N300LW) N41GA D-IOWB D-IOEB(2)
HB-G . .	Beech B200 Super King Air	BB-531	SE-LDM VH-XFB N2657 C-GBWO N2657
HB-HAB	Dornier Do.27H-2	2012	V-605 HB-HAB V-605
HB-HAO	Pilatus PC-7 Turbo Trainer	101	

HB-HC . , HB-HD . , Used as delivery marks for Pilatus PC-7, PC-9

HB-HEC	FFA AS.202/15 Bravo	V-3	
HB-HEF	FFA AS.202/15 Bravo	002	
HB-HEG	FFA AS.202/15 Bravo	003	
HB-HEH	FFA AS.202/15 Bravo	004	
HB-HEI	FFA AS.202/15 Bravo	006	
HB-HEM	FFA AS.202/15 Bravo	007	
HB-HEO	FFA AS.202/15 Bravo	009	
HB-HEP	FFA AS.202/15 Bravo	010	
HB-HER	FFA AS.202/15 Bravo	011	
HB-HES	FFA AS.202/15 Bravo	012	
HB-HET	FFA AS.202/15 Bravo	014	
HB-HEW	FFA AS.202/15 Bravo	018	
HB-HEY	FFA AS.202/18 Bravo	015	
HB-HEZ	FFA AS.202/15 Bravo	019	
HB-HFD	FFA AS.202/18A Bravo	023	
HB-HFF	FFA AS.202/15-1 Bravo	107	
HB-HFH	FFA AS.202/15-1 Bravo	108	
HB-HFI	FFA AS.202/15-1 Bravo	109	
HB-HFJ	FFA AS.202/18A4 Bravo	243	
HB-HFK	FFA AS.202/15-1 Bravo	112	
HB-HFV	FFA AS.202/15-1 Bravo	127	
HB-HFW	FFA AS.202/15-1 Bravo	129	
HB-HFX	FFA AS.202/15-1 Bravo	124	
HB-HFZ	FFA AS.202/18A-2 Bravo	237	
HB-HGB	FFA AS.202/15-1 Bravo	130	
HB-HKA	Dornier Do.27Q-5	2062	D-ENYQ F-OBVT F-BKVT F-GFVT OO-OJB

HB-HL . Used as delivery marks for Pilatus PC-7

HB-HMR	Pilatus PC-7 Mk II	010	
HB-HOH	Dätwyler MD-3-160	001	
HB-HOJ	Dätwyler MD-3-160	002	
HB-HOO	Pilatus PC-7 Turbo Trainer (Crash 14.1.00)	394	
HB-HOP	Junkers Ju 52/3mg4e (c/n officially quoted as 3385, which was probably a Luftwaffe aircraft)	6610	A-703 HB-HOP
HB-HOS	Junkers Ju 52/3mg4e	6580	A-701 HB-HOS A-701
HB-HOT	Junkers Ju 52/3mg4e	6595	A-702 HB-HOT A-702
HB-HOY	CASA 352A-3 (Junkers Ju 52/3m)	96	D-CIAK T.2B-165
HB-HPA	Pilatus PC-9 Turbo Trainer	001	

HB-HQ ., HB-HR ., Used as delivery marks for Pilatus PC-9 Turbo Trainer

HB-HZA	Pilatus PC-21	P01	
HB-HZB	Pilatus PC-21 (W/o 13.1.05)	P02	
HB-IAH	Dassault Falcon 900EX	28	F-WWFZ
HB-IAJ	Dassault Falcon PC-12/45	498	F-WWGC
HB-IAQ	Dassault Falcon 900EX	35	N2BD F-WWFJ
HB-IAU	Dassault Falcon 2000EX	014	F-WWGM

HB-IAW	Dassault Falcon 2000	16	F-WWMB
HB-IAX	Dassault Falcon 2000	33	F-WWME
HB-IAZ	Dassault Falcon 2000	30	F-WWMB
HB-IBH	Dassault Falcon 2000	42	F-WWMG
HB-IBX	Gulfstream IVSP	1183	VR-BDC N476GA
HB-IDJ	Canadair CL.600-2B19 Regional Jet	7136	VP-CRJ VR-CRJ N136SE C-FMNQ
HB-IEE	Boeing 757-23A	24527	HB-IHU
HB-IEJ	Gulfstream IV	1148	N427GA JA8380 N427GA
HB-IES(*)	Dassault Falcon 50	61	F-WZHI
HB-IFJ	Dassault Falcon 900EX	092	F-WWFK
HB-IFQ	Dassault Falcon 900	121	9M-BAB N478FJ F-WWFE
HB-IGH	McDonnell-Douglas DC-8-72	46067	VP-BJR VR-BJR N8966U
HB-IGI	Dassault Falcon 900EX	83	F-WWFY
HB-IGL	Dassault Falcon 900	58	OE-ILS F-WWFE
HB-IGM	Gulfstream V	5004	
HB-IGP	IAI-1126 Galaxy	013	N160HA XA-MAK N200GA N13GX 4X-CVG
HB-IGQ	Dassault Falcon 2000EX	9	(N209EX) F-WWGH
HB-IGR	Dassault Falcon 50	104	F-WZHR N105FJ N90AE F-GFGQ F-WWHK N50VG SE-DVG N351JS LX-UAE F-GUAE
HB-IGX	Dassault Falcon 900EX	86	N986EX
HB-IGY	Dassault Falcon 900EX	95	F-WWFO
HB-IHQ	Bombardier BD.700-1A10 Global Express	9011	VP-BJJ N700KJ C-GDGW
HB-IHR	Boeing 757-2G5	29379	
HB-IHS	Boeing 757-2G5	30394	
HB-IHX	Airbus A320-214	942	F-WWIU
HB-IHY	Airbus A320-214	947	F-WWIY
HB-IHZ	Airbus A320-214	1026	F-WWDD
HB-IIB	Boeing 737-3M8	24024	(OO-LTE)
HB-IIO	Boeing 737-7AK (BBJ)	29865	N1786B
HB-IIP	Boeing 737-7AK (BBJ)	29866	N1779B
HB-IIQ	Boeing 737-7CN (BBJ) (Res as D-ABPA)	30752	N1026G
HB-IIR	Boeing 737-86Q	30295	
HB-IIS	Gulfstream V	572	P4-FAZ N472GA (N223SS) N472GA
HB-IIT	Boeing 737-33V	29339	G-EZYO
HB-IIV	Canadair CL.600-2B16 Challenger	5397	VP-BCB N605PA C-GLXY
HB-IIY	Gulfstream V	638	N638GA
HB-IJI	Airbus A320-214	577	F-WWDT
HB-IJJ	Airbus A320-214	585	F-WWIV
HB-IJK	Airbus A320-214	596	F-WWBH
HB-IJL	Airbus A320-214	603	F-WWBK
HB-IJM	Airbus A320-214	635	F-WWDD
HB-IJN	Airbus A320-214	643	F-WWDI
HB-IJO	Airbus A320-214	673	F-WWBF
HB-IJP	Airbus A320-214	681	F-WWBH
HB-IJQ	Airbus A320-214	701	F-WWDL
HB-IJR	Airbus A320-214	703	F-WWDS
HB-IJS	Airbus A320-214	782	F-WWDS
HB-IJU	Airbus A320-214	1951	F-WWIJ
HB-IJV	Airbus A320-214	2024	F-WWDK
HB-IJW	Airbus A320-214	2134	F-WWBO
HB-IJX	Airbus A320-214 (Reservation .04)		
HB-IJY	Airbus A320-214 (Reservation .04)		
HB-IJZ	Airbus A320-211	211	F-GJVD
HB-IKN	McDonnell-Douglas DC-9-83	49951	G-GMJM N13627
HB-IKO	Comte AC-4	034	D-ELIS HB-IKO CH-262
HB-IKR	Gulfstream IV	1159	N458FA 9K-AJB N17583
HB-IKS	Canadair CL.600-2B16 Challenger	5042	N28UA HB-IKS C-FEUV C-GLYA
HB-IKZ	Bombardier BD.700-1A10 Global Express	9054	N700LA C-GFWY
HB-ILJ	Fokker F.27 Friendship 500	10596	F-SEBJ CN-CDC PH-FTX N334MV PH-FTX PH-EXM
HB-IMJ	Gulfstream V	517	N517GA
HB-IMY	Gulfstream IV	1084	N448GA
HB-INJ	Bombardier BD.700-1A10 Global Express	9086	C-GHZC
HB-INQ	Gulfstream V	568	N568JC N845HS N461GA
HB-INV	McDonnell-Douglas DC-9-81	49359	
HB-INW	McDonnell-Douglas DC-9-83 (Stored)	49569	(RA-. . . .) EC-HVC HB-INW
HB-INZ	McDonnell-Douglas DC-9-83 (Stored)	49572	(RA-. . . .) EC-HVX HB-INZ
HB-IOC	Airbus A321-111	520	D-AVZV
HB-IOH	Airbus A321-111	664	D-AVZL
HB-IOK	Airbus A321-111	987	D-AVZC
HB-IOL	Airbus A321-111	1144	D-AVZE
HB-IPR	Airbus A319-112	1018	D-AVYQ
HB-IPS	Airbus A319-112	734	D-AVYZ
HB-IPT	Airbus A319-112	727	D-AVYC
HB-IPU	Airbus A319-112	713	D-AVYB
HB-IPV	Airbus A319-112	578	F-WWTA D-AVYA
HB-IPX	Airbus A319-112	612	D-AVYH
HB-IPY	Airbus A319-112	621	D-AVYK
HB-IPZ	Airbus A319-113	629	D-AVYR
HB-IQA	Airbus A330-223	229	F-WWKS
HB-IQC	Airbus A330-223	249	F-WWKI
HB-IQG	Airbus A330-223	275	F-WWKF
HB-IQH	Airbus A330-223	288	F-WWKK
HB-IQI	Airbus A330-223	291	F-WWKS
HB-IQJ	Airbus A330-223	294	F-WWYJ
HB-IQK	Airbus A330-223	299	F-WWYD
HB-IQO	Airbus A330-223	343	F-WWYA
HB-IQP	Airbus A330-223	366	F-WWYZ
HB-IQZ	Airbus A330-243	369	F-WWKG
HB-ISB	Douglas DC-3C	4666	C-FTAS CF-TAS CF-CPW 41 -18541
HB-ISC	Douglas DC-3C	9995	G-BMCR N88YA N88Y NC6K NC65266 42-24133
HB-ISD	Dassault Falcon 50	159	VP-CWI VR-CWI I-LXAG LX-NUR F-WZHC
HB-ISE	Boeing 767-3Q8	27600	EI-CNS (I-VLEB) EI-CNS N6005C
HB-ISF	Dassault Falcon 2000	26	N112CD TC-CIN VP-BHC TC-CIN F-WQFL N2000A N2046 F-WWMN
HB-ITF	Gulfstream IV	1202	N369XL JY-RAY V8-009 V8-MSB N432GA
HB-ITG	Bombardier BD.700-1A10 Global Express	9036	N777GX C-GFAT
HB-ITK	Canadair CL.600-2B16 Challenger	5090	VP-CAM N400KC N818TH N818LS N404CB N601CB C-GLXF
HB-IUH	McDonnell-Douglas DC-9-81 (Stored)	53150	
HB-IUJ	Bombardier BD.700-1A10 Global Express	9095	C-GIPA
HB-IUM	McDonnell-Douglas DC-9-83	49847	D-AGWC N62020
HB-IUN	McDonnell-Douglas DC-9-83	49769	D-ALLK
HB-IUO	McDonnell-Douglas DC-9-83	49857	D-ALLN
HB-IUT	IAI-1126 Galaxy	007	N847GA (C-GRJZ) N847GA
HB-IUU	IAI-1126 Galaxy	011	"HB-IGA" N634GA HB-IUU N634GA

HB-IUW	Dassault Falcon 900	150	N335MC N150FJ F-WWFC
HB-IUX	Dassault Falcon 900EX	54	F-WWFY
HB-IVL	Gulfstream V	513	N513GA
HB-IVM	Dassault Falcon 2000	55	F-WWMM
HB-IVN	Dassault Falcon 2000	61	F-WWME
HB-IVO	Dassault Falcon 2000	62	F-WWMF
HB-IVR	Canadair CL.600-2B16 Challenger	5318	HB-IKQ C-FYYH C-GLXO
HB-IVS	Canadair CL.600-2B16 Challenger	5166	N601A 9M-NSK, N618CC C-GLWT
HB-IVX	DHC-7-102	91	VP-CDZ SU-MAC LN-WFG C-GFUM
HB-IVZ	Gulfstream V	577	N577GA
HB-IWZ	Gulfstream IV	1061	N429AL N161AK F-GPAK N457GA N17582
HB-IXF	BAe.146 Series RJ85	E-2226	G-CROS
HB-IXG	BAe.146 Series RJ85	E-2231	G-6-231
HB-IXH	BAe.146 Series RJ85	E-2233	G-6-233 G-XARJ G-6-233
HB-IXK	BAe.146 Series RJ85	E-2235	G-XAIR G-6-235
HB-IXN	Avro 146-RJ100	E-3286	G-6-286
HB-IXO	Avro 146-RJ100	E-3284	G-6-284
HB-IXP	Avro 146-RJ100	E-3283	G-6-283
HB-IXQ	Avro 146-RJ100	E-3282	G-6-282
HB-IXR	Avro 146-RJ100	E-3281	G-6-281
HB-IXS	Avro 146-RJ100	E-3280	G-6-280
HB-IXT	Avro 146-RJ100	E-3259	G-BVYS
HB-IXU	Avro 146-RJ100	E-3276	G-6-276
HB-IXV	Avro 146-RJ100	E-3274	G-6-274
HB-IXW	Avro 146-RJ100	E-3272	G-6-272
HB-IXX	Avro 146-RJ100	E-3262	G-6-262
HB-IYB	SAAB 2000	057	SE-057
HB-IYC	SAAB 2000	058	SE-058
HB-IYD	SAAB 2000	059	SE-059
HB-IYE	SAAB 2000	060	SE-060
HB-IYF	SAAB 2000	061	SE-061
HB-IYG	SAAB 2000	062	SE-062
HB-IYH	SAAB 2000	063	SE-063
HB-IYW	Avro 146-RJ100	E-3359	G-6-359
HB-IYX	Avro 146-RJ100	E-3357	G-6-357
HB-IYY	Avro 146-RJ100	E-3339	G-6-339
HB-IYZ	Avro 146-RJ100	E-3338	G-6-338
HB-IZH	SAAB 2000	011	SE-011
HB-IZJ	SAAB 2000	015	SE-015
HB-IZO	SAAB 2000	029	SE-029
HB-IZR	SAAB 2000	033	SE-033
HB-IZZ	SAAB 2000	048	SE-048
HB-JAI	Embraer EMB.145LU	145351	PT-SNQ
HB-JAL	Embraer EMB.145LU	145400	PT-SQX
HB-JAM	Embraer EMB.145LU	145420	PT-STR
HB-JAN	Embraer EMB.145LU	145434	PT-SUF
HB-JAO	Embraer EMB.145LU	145456	PT-SVB
HB-JAS	Embraer EMB.145LU	145559	PT-SZU
HB-JAT	Embraer EMB.145LU	145564	PT-SZZ
HB-JAU	Embraer EMB.145LU	145570	PT-SBC
HB-JAV	Embraer EMB.145LU	145574	PT-SBK
HB-JAW	Embraer EMB.145LU	145580	PT-SBR
HB-JAX	Embraer EMB.145LU	145588	EI-GXA HB-JAX PT-SBY
HB-JAY	Embraer EMB.145LU	145601	EI-GXB HB-JAY PT-SCK
HB-JEA	Embraer EMB.135BJ Legacy	145555	PT-SCK
HB-JEB	Gulfstream 200 (IAI 1126 Galaxy)	032	N406LM N66GX 4X-CVE
HB-JEC	Bombardier BD-100-1A10 Challenger 300	20029	N129LJ C-GZEJ
HB-JED	Embraer EMB.135BJ Legacy	145644	PT-S . .
HB-JEE	Gulfstream 550	5025	N925GA
HB-JEG	Dassault Falcon 2000EX/EASy	34	F-WWGM
HB-JEI	Dassault Falcon 900	86	F-GVAE A6-UAE F-WWFE
HB-JEJ	DHC-8 Dash Eight 315	546	SU-YAM C-FDHD
HB-JEK	DHC-8 Dash Eight 315	549	SU-YAN PK-TVM SU-YAN CGDKL
HB-JEN	Bombardier BD-700-1A10 Global Express	9015	N708KS N700KS C-GDXX

HB-JER	Bombardier BD-700-1A10 Global Express	9017	VP-BDD C-GEIR
HB-JES	Gulfstream V	556	N556AR N656GA
HB-JEZ	Cessna 750 Citation X	750-0179	N5147B OE-HFE
HB-JIA	McDonnell-Douglas MD-90-30	53552	N743BC SU-BMR N934MD TC-JHA N534MD TC-KTA N6202S
HB-JIB	McDonnell-Douglas MD-90-30	53553	N744BC SU-BMS N935MD TC-JHB N535MD TC-KTB N6203U
HB-JIC	McDonnell-Douglas MD-90-30	53576	N765BC SU-BMQ
HB-JMA	Airbus A320-313X	538	F-WWJJ
HB-JMB	Airbus A340-313X	545	F-WWJL
HB-JMC	Airbus A340-313X	546	F-WWJM
HB-JMD	Airbus A340-313X	556	F-WWJN
HB-JME	Airbus A340-313X	559	F-WWJP
HB-JMF	Airbus A340-313X	561	F-WWJQ
HB-JMG	Airbus A340-313X	562	F-WWJR
HB-JMH	Airbus A340-313X	585	F-WWJV
HB-JMI	Airbus A340-313X	598	F-WWJX
HB-JMJ	Airbus A340-313X (Reservation)		
HB-JMK	Airbus A340-313X (Reservation)		
HB-JML	Airbus A340-313X (Reservation)		
HB-JRA	Canadair CL.600-2B16 Challenger	5529	C-GJZB
HB-JRB	Canadair CL.600-2B16 Challenger	5530	C-GJZD
HB-JRC	Canadair CL.600-2B16 Challenger	5540	C-GKMU C-GLXM
HB-JRZ	Canadair CL.600-2B16 Challenger	5553	C-GLWT C-GZTU
HB-JSY	Dassault Falcon 900EX	96	N900ZA N93ZR F-WWFP
HB-JVA	Fokker F.28-0100	11460	PH-EZE N1451N
HB-JVC	Fokker F.28-0100	11501	N1468A PH-EZM
HB-JVD	Fokker F.28-0100	11498	N1466A PH-EZK
HB-JVE	Fokker F.28-0100	11459	N1450A PH-EZD
HB-JVF	Fokker F.28-0100	11466	N1454D PH-EXK
HB-JVG	Fokker F.28-0100	11478	N1458H PH-EZA
HB-JZF	Airbus A319-111	2184	G-EZEH D-AVWO
HB-JZG	Airbus A319-111	2196	G-EZEI D-AVYC
HB-JZH	Airbus A319-111	2230	G-EZEM D-AVWI
HB-JZI	Airbus A319-111	2245	G-EZEN D-AVYH
HB-JZJ	Airbus A319-111	2265	G-EZES D-AVWR
HB-J . .	Canadair CL.600-2B16 Challenger	5599	C-GLWX
HB-KAB	SOCATA TB-20 Trinidad	377	
HB-KAC	Robin R.2160D Alpha Sport	134	F-GBAU
HB-KAD	Robin DR.400/120D Petit Prince	1632	
HB-KAF	Robin R.1180TD Aiglon	283	
HB-KAH	SOCATA TB-20 Trinidad	425	
HB-KAJ	SOCATA TB-10 Tobago	431	
HB-KAL	CEA DR.250/160 Capitaine	47	F-BNJM
HB-KAM(2)	Beech F33A Bonanza	CE-1292	OY-BVO
HB-KAU	SOCATA TB-10 Tobago	515	
HB-KAW	Robin DR.400/180R Remorqueur	1707	
HB-KAY	SOCATA TB-20 Trinidad	578	
HB-KBH	SOCATA TB-20 Trinidad	700	
HB-KBJ	CEA DR.250/160 Capitaine	42	F-BNJJ
HB-KBK	Robin DR.400/180R Remorqueur	779	F-BTZQ
HB-KBM	Robin DR.400/RP Remorqueur (Porsche engine)	1785	D-EAJB(2)
HB-KBP	Robin DR.400/180R Remorqueur	1769	
HB-KBS	SOCATA TB-20 Trinidad	774	
HB-KBV	Robin DR.400/120D Dauphin 2+2	1819	
HB-KBX	Robin DR.400/120D Petit Prince	1843	
HB-KCB	Maule MX-7-235 Star Rocket	10069C	N6124C
HB-KCC	CEA Jodel DR.1050 Ambassadeur	535	D-EBEI F-BLZF
HB-KCE	Maule MX-.7-235 Star Rocket	10072C	N6117T
HB-KCF	Robin DR.400/160D Chevalier	1890	
HB-KCG	Robin DR.400/140B Major	1885	
HB-KCH	Robin DR.400/180S	1900	
HB-KCI	Christen A-1 Husky	1079	
HB-KCJ	Robin DR.400/140B Major	1916	
HB-KCK	Beech C33A Debonair (Ditched 1.4.04)	CE-67	D-ECMI
HB-KCL	Maule M-7-235 Super Rocket	4054C	N6108X
HB-KCO	Robin R.3000/160S	135	F-GGXN

HB-KCQ	Maule M-7-235 Super Rocket	4066C	N6130Q
HB-KCS	Robin DR.400/180R Remo180	1934	
HB-KCV	SOCATA TB-20 Trinidad	997	(D-EAOQ)
HB-KDB	Robin DR.400/140B Major	2125	
HB-KDC	SOCATA TB-200	1444	
HB-KDD	Robin DR.400/140B Major	2152	
HB-KDF	Maule MX-7-235 Star Rocket	10117C	
HB-KDK	Beech F33A Bonanza	CE-815	N2036M
HB-KDL	Maule MXT-7-180 Star Rocket	14054C	
HB-KDM	Maule M-7-235 Super Rocket	4110C	
HB-KDN	SOCATA TB-200 Tobago XL	1558	
HB-KDO	Robin DR.400/200R Remo 200	2133	F-WZZX F-GLKN
HB-KDP	Robin DR.400/200R Remo 200	2190	
HB-KDT	PZL-104 Wilga 80	CF14800563	I-MATE SP-TWT
HB-KDV	Robin DR.400/140B Dauphin 4	2240	
HB-KDY	Robin DR.400/200R Remo 200	2242	
HB-KEA	Robin DR.400/140B Major	2274	
HB-KEB	Robin DR.400/140B Major	2275	
HB-KEC	Robin R.3000/160	160	F-GLVM
HB-KED	Robin DR.400/180 Régent	2294	
HB-KEE(*)	Robin DR.400/180 Régent	2290	
HB-KEF	Aviat A-1 Husky	1292	
HB-KEG	Aviat A-1 Husky	1293X	
HB-KEH	Robin R.3000/160	169	
HB-KEI	SOCATA TBM-700	3	F-GJTS
HB-KEK	Aviat A-1 Husky	1278	D-EIHU
HB-KEL	Robin R.3000/160	123	
HB-KEN	Maule M-7-235C Super Rocket	25003C	N1025C
HB-KEO	Aviat A-1 Husky	1324	D-EPCD
HB-KEP	Robin R.2160 Alpha Sport	318	
HB-KEQ	Robin R.3000/160	146	F-GJZC
HB-KER	Maule MX-7-235 Star Rocket	10066C	HB-KDS (D-EVAM) N6112Y
HB-KES	Robin DR.400/180RRemorqueur (Originally built as DR.400/120, converted 1997-2001)	845	F-BUPR
HB-KET	CEA Jodel DR.250/160 Capitaine	76	D-ENVQ F-BNVQ
HB-KEV	Oberlerchner JOB 15-180/2	064	D-EKWK D-EHGE OE-CAW
HB-KEW	American 8KCAB Decathlon	763-96	N69BP
HB-KEX	Robin DR.400/140B Dauphin 4	2407	
HB-KEY	Robin DR.500/200i Président	0011	
HB-KEZ	Robin DR.500/200i Président	0012	
HB-KFA	Robin HR.200/160	331	
HB-KFB	Robin HR.200/160	332	
HB-KFC	Maule MX-7-235 Star Rocket	10053C	N5668Y
HB-KFD	Robin DR.400/140B Dauphin 4	2431	
HB-KFE	Robin DR.500/200i Président	15	
HB-KFF	Maule M-7-235CSuper Rocket	4048C	D-EHVW N6109V
HB-KFG	Beech A36TC Bonanza	EA-249	D-EAZA
HB-KFH	Robin DR.400/200RRemo 200	2450	
HB-KFI	Robin DR.400/140B Dauphin 4	2470	
HB-KFJ	Robin DR.500/200i Président	0026	
HB-KFK	Robin DR.400/180R Remorqueur	1939	D-EJFH
HB-KFL	Robin DR.400/180RRemorqueur	1908	D-EIHV
HB-KFM	SOCATA TB-20 Trinidad	1921	
HB-KFN	Robin DR.400/180 Régent	2503	
HB-KFO	Robin DR.400/140B Dauphin 4	2501	
HB-KFP	Robin DR.400/140B Dauphin 4	2506	
HB-KFQ	Robin DR.400/140B Dauphin 4	2508	
HB-KFR	SOCATA TBM-700	195	
HB-KFS	CEA DR.250/160 Capitaine	66	F-BNVD
HB-KFT	Robin DR.500/200i Président	0032	F-GUXM
HB-KFU	Robin DR.400/140B Dauphin 4	2516	
HB-KFV	Robin DR.400/140B Dauphin 4	2529	
HB-KFW	Robin DR.400/140B Dauphin 4	2535	
HB-KFX	Robin DR.400/180 Régent	2556	
HB-KFY	Robin DR.400/180 Régent	2560	
HB-KFZ	Tecnam P.92JS Echo	22	
HB-KIA	Beech A36 Bonanza	E-2522	N5664F
HB-KIE	Robin R.3000/160	144	
HB-KIF(*)	Maule MX-7-420 Starcraft	13002C	N9204Y
HB-KIJ	Robin R.3000/160	150	
HB-KIO	Maule MX-7-235 Star Rocket	10094C	
HB-KIP	Christen A-1 Husky	1153	
HB-KIQ	Maule MX-7-235 Star Rocket	10095C	
HB-KIU	Piaggio FWP.149D	175	D-EFCT 91+53 DF+394 AS+0 . . KB+141
HB-KIW	Beech F33A Bonanza	CE-1286	N1527P
HB-KIY	Robin DR.400/140B Major	2135	
HB-KOB	Beech C33A Debonair	CD-860	D-EKVE
HB-KOC	Robin DR.400/180R Remo 180	2562	
HB-KOD	SOCATA TB-10 Tobago	269	D-EESP
HB-KOE	Robin DR.400\180 Régent	2569	
HB-KOI	American Champion 7GCAA Citabria Adventure	477-2003	G-IGLS
HB-KOK	Tecnam P2002-JF Sierra	004	
HB-KOL	SOCATA TBM-700	218	N700NE F-HOPE F-GLBV
HB-K . .	SOCATA TB-9 Tampico	283	LN-KLL OY-CDA TF-BRO
HB-LAD	Piper PA-30 Twin Comanche	30-434	N7423Y N10F
HB-LBH	Piper PA-23-160 Apache	23-1625	N4144P
HB-LBI	LET L-200A Morava	170702	
HB-LBM	Cessna 310F	310-0147	N6847X
HB-LCY	Cessna 320C Skyknight	320C0054	N3054T
HB-LDH	Piper PA-23-250 Aztec C	27-3305	N6098Y
HB-LEH	Cessna 340	340-0075	D-ILEH HB-LEH N5940M
HB-LEL	Piper PA-34-200 Seneca	34-7350313	N56296
HB-LEM	Piper PA-34-200 Seneca	34-7350327	(4X-CAK) HB-LEM N56394
HB-LER	Piper PA-34-200 Seneca	34-7450014	N56645
HB-LEU	Piper PA-34-200 Seneca	34-7450076	N40751
HB-LFP	Cessna Turbo 310P	310P0207	N5907M
HB-LGH	Cessna 310Q	310Q0051	OY-AKD
HB-LHA	Cessna 335	335-0030	N2708D
HB-LHW	Cessna 402B	402B0926	N87130
HB-LIG	Piper PA-34-200T Seneca II	34-7670262	N6146J
HB-LIN	Piper Aerostar 601P	61P-571-7963248	D-IEWF N8085J
HB-LIP	Piper PA-34-200T Seneca II	34-7770198	N2798Q
HB-LKA	Piper PA-34-200T Seneca II	34-7770049	N6945F
HB-LKB	Piper PA-34-200T Seneca II	34-7870183	N9364C
HB-LKF	Cessna 340A	340A0096	OE-FBS(1) N1529G
HB-LKG	Gulfstream GA-7 Cougar	0089	N798GA
HB-LKM	Piper PA-34-200T Seneca II	34-7970106	N3056K
HB-LKU	Cessna 340A	340A0493	N6322X
HB-LLK	Piper PA-31T1 Cheyenne I	31T-7904014	N401PT
HB-LLM	Piper PA-34-200T Seneca II	34-7970108	N2077N
HB-LLX(*)	Piper PA-34-200T Seneca II	34-8070232	
HB-LMC	Piper PA-34-200 Seneca	34-7450008	OO-GPA N56622
HB-LML	Piper PA-34-200 Seneca	34-7250341	N3094T
HB-LMM	Piper PA-34-200T Seneca II	34-8170029	N8292T
HB-LMN	Cessna 340A	340A0945	N2745D
HB-LMR	Cessna 421C Golden Eagle	421C0111	N421PB
HB-LMS	Piper PA-34-220T Seneca III	34-8133105	
HB-LNN	Cessna T303 Crusader	T30300089	D-IJAA N2289C
HB-LNX	Piper PA-31T2 Cheyenne IIXL	31T-8166050	N700XL
HB-LOA	Partenavia P.68B	35	D-GITE
HB-LOE	Cessna 425 Corsair	425-0016	ZS-KST N6771L
HB-LOG	Piper PA-34-200T Seneca II	34-7870415	OE-FSS N39677
HB-LOK	DHC-6 Twin Otter 300	658	D-IASL
HB-LOO	Piper PA-23-250 Aztec B	27-2250	F-GDAG F-BMSF F-OBZY N5221Y
HB-LOR	Piper PA-23-250 Aztec E	27-7305192	D-IFGE N40474
HB-LOT	Piper PA-31 Turbo Navajo B	31-7400981	D-IDRA N7589L
HB-LPD	Cessna 421C Golden Eagle	421C0206	D-IOSR N98486
HB-LPE	Piper PA-34-200 Seneca	34-7250293	D-GOBI N1344T
HB-LPI	Cessna 340	340-0070	D-ICEF (N5929M)
HB-LPT	Cessna 414A Chancellor	414A0054	N62PC N6673C
HB-LPZ	Partenavia P.68B	44	OY-CEP OH-PVC
HB-LQJ	Piper PA-34-200 Seneca	34-7350164	D-GNUT EI-AWT N55034
HB-LQK	Piper PA-44-180T Turbo Seminole	44-8207010	N81610
HB-LQM	Piper PA-34-220T Seneca III	3433129	
HB-LQP	Piper PA-31T1 Cheyenne 1	31T-8004044	OO-JMR N180SW
HB-LQQ	Piper PA-34-200T Seneca II	34-7570281	N1544X
HB-LQV	DHC-6 Twin Otter Series 300	643	5Y-LQV HB-LQV F-GFAJ TT-EAI Chad Army 5A-DCY
HB-LQY	Piper PA-34-220T Seneca III	3448006	
HB-LQZ	Cessna 421C Golden Eagle	421C1237	N811SW G-BNEW (N2724L)
HB-LRC	Piper PA-34-220T Seneca III	3448026	N93KH
HB-LRD	Piper PA-34-220T Seneca III	3448015	N9208X
HB-LRL	Cessna 421B Golden Eagle	421B0398	N205PV N203PV (N41010)
HB-LRO	DHC-6 Twin Otter Series 300	523	F-GKTO TR-LAL F-GAMR

HB-LRR	DHC-6 Twin Otter Series 300	505	5Y-KZT
			N888WJ
			F-ODGP
			N505GH
			J6-SLH
			C-GPJA
HB-LRU	Piper PA-34-220T Seneca III	3433171	I-CGAQ
			N91970
HB-LRV	Piper PA-31T Cheyenne II	31T-7820017	N82222
HB-LRY	Piper PA-34-220T Seneca III	3433132	N9191P
HB-LSC	Piper PA-34-220T Seneca III	34-8333004	N8240G
HB-LSD	Piper PA-34-200T Seneca II	34-7970098	D-ICTM
			N2192K
HB-LSE	Cessna Turbo 310R	310R0276	D-ICYF
			(N5478J)
HB-LSG	Piper PA-60-602P Aerostar	60-8265033	D-IGGG
			N6901Z
HB-LSH	Cessna 340A	340A0477	F-GESV
			D-IAWL
			N6306X
HB-LSI	Cessna 421C Golden Eagle II	421C0140	N3913C
HB-LSK	STOL UC-1 Twin Bee	018	N9512U
HB-LSM	Cessna 340A	340A0701	N8515G
HB-LSQ	Cessna 340A	340A0661	N1891E
			D-ICMF
			N1661C
			N1891E
HB-LSR	Cessna 340	340-0180	D-IGOL(2)
			D-ICOP
			N7641Q
HB-LSS	Piper PA-34-220T Seneca III	3447015	N947G
HB-LSV	DHC-6 Twin Otter Series 300	281	N616BA
			VH-TGH
			N8336
HB-LTA	Piper PA-34-200T Seneca II	34-8070122	D-GASC
			N8156C
HB-LTD	DHC-6 Twin Otter Series 300	717	C-GIED
			HK-2547
			HK-2547X
HB-LTE	Piaggio P.180 Avanti	1042	
HB-LTG	DHC-6 Twin Otter Series 300	628	D-IFLY
			LN-BNT
HB-LTH	Piper PA-34-220T Seneca V	3449040	SP-FTS
			N321TS
HB-LTI	Piper PA-31T Cheyenne II	31T-8020091	F-GIPL
			N76SC
			N20AM
			N40TW
			N2331X
HB-LTJ	Piper PA-34-220T Seneca V	3449226	
HB-LTL	Piper PA-34-220T Seneca V	3449157	D-GPAS
			N41736
HB-LTM	Piper PA-42-1000 Cheyenne 400LS	42-5527028	N4119X
HB-LTP	Piper PA-44-180T Turbo Seminole	44-8207008	F-GJJP
			N81487
HB-LTS	Partenavia P.68B Observer	69	D-GIRO
HB-LYN	Piaggio P.180 Avanti	1066	
HB-L . .	Piper PA-31 Turbo Navajo	31-544	(N5359S)
			(SE- . . .)
			N5359S
			SE-FHS
HB-MIP	Bücker Bü.133 Jungmeister	11	D-EGDS
			G-AXIH
			HB-MIP
			U-64
"HB-MIU"(2)	Bücker Bü.133 Jungmeister	49	HB-MIL
	(Stored Basle)		U-50
HB-MIZ	Bücker Bü.133 Jungmeister	1003	U-53
HB-MKH	Bücker Bü.133 Jungmeister	40	U-93
HB-MKN	Bücker Bü.133 Jungmeister	23	U-76
HB-MKO	Bücker Bü.133C Jungmeister		
HB-MKP	Bücker Bü.133 Jungmeister	28	U-81
HB-MKR	Bücker Bü.133 Jungmeister (Dätwyler rebuild)	WD29A	HB-MIU
	(Rebuild of c/n 29 using Spanish wings)		U-82
HB-MKZ	Bücker Bü.133 Jungmeister	09	U-62
HB-MSE	Aerotek Pitts S-2S	3001	
HB-MSF	Mudry CAP.20LS-200	8	OO-BNG
HB-MSK	Hirth Hi.27 Akrostar Mk.II	4009	D-EOIG
HB-MSL	Extra EA.300	05	D-ELET(2)
HB-MSO	Sukhoi SU-26M	0604	RA-0604
HB-MSS	Sukhoi SU-26M	0704	RA-0704
HB-MSV	Mudry CAP.231	11	G-PELG
			G-OPPS
			F-GGYN
			F-WZCI
			G-OPPS
HB-MSW	Extra EA.300/200	014	G-IISI
			(HB-M . .)
			G-IISI
			D-EXWE
HB-MSX	Extra EA.300/L	026	
HB-MSY	Extra EA.300/200	028	
HB-M . .	Christen Eagle	L0026	N246RL
HB-NAB	Beagle B.121 Pup 150	043	G-35-043
HB-NBB	Slingsby T.67M Firefly	2003	G-SFTW
HB-NCB	Rockwell Commander 112	165	(N1165J)
HB-NCE	Rockwell Commander 112TC	13018	

HB-NCF	Rockwell Commander 114	14034	
HB-NCG	Rockwell Commander 112TC	13074	
HB-NCH	Rockwell Commander 114	14050	
HB-NCI	Rockwell Commander 114	14208	N4878W
HB-NCK	Rockwell Commander 112	384	N1384J
HB-NCO	Rockwell Commander 114	14183	D-EIXD
			HB-NCO
HB-NCP	Rockwell Commander 114	14374	N5806N
HB-NCR	Rockwell Commander 112TCA	13251	N4675W
HB-NCS	Rockwell Commander 114	14356	N114TC
			N5772N
HB-NCT	Rockwell Commander 112	442	N1442J
HB-NCU	Rockwell Commander 114A	14532	
HB-NCV	Rockwell Commander 114	14407	D-EJAB
HB-NCY(*)	Rockwell Commander 112A	188	OE-DYB
HB-NCZ	Rockwell Commander 114	14527	G-BGTE
			N5910N
HB-NDA	Rockwell Commander 112TC	13070	D-EIXM
			N4580W
HB-NDC	Commander Aircraft 114B	14550	N184A
HB-NDE	Rockwell Commander 114	14150	OO-EJL
			N4820W
			VH-MCN
			N4820W
HB-OAG	Piper J-3C-100 Cub	12897	44-80601
HB-OAP	Piper PA-12 Super Cruiser	12-2245	OO-XAZ
			NC2239M
HB-OBB	Piper J-3C-65 Cub (F/n 9777 quoted as c/n)	9945	43-1084
HB-OBF	Piper J-3C-85 Cub	13257	45-4517
HB-OBG	Piper J-3C-85 Cub	13231	45-4491
HB-OBL	Piper J-3C-65 Cub	12575	44-80279
HB-OBP	Piper J-3C-90 Cub	11709	43-30418
HB-OCI	Piper J-3C-65 Cub	12704	44-80408
	(Rebuild using parts and c/n of HB-OCK which was then rebuilt using parts and c/n 13249 of HB-OFG)		
HB-OCP	Piper J-3C-90 Cub	10937	43-29646
HB-OCR	Piper J-3C-90 Cub	11059	43-29768
HB-OCU	Piper J-3C-100 Cub	12842	44-80546
HB-ODC	Piper J-3C-90 Cub	12892	44-80596
HB-ODE	Piper J-3C-85 Cub	12866	44-80570
HB-ODH	Piper J-3C-90 Cub	13342	45-4602
HB-ODL	Piper PA-22-108 Colt	22-9336	D-EHRO
HB-ODN	Piper J-3C-65 Cub	10457	43-29166
HB-ODW	Piper J-3C-90 Cub	12542	HB-OEL
			44-80246
HB-ODX	Piper J-3C-65 Cub	13130	44-80834
HB-ODZ	Piper J-3C-90 Cub	MDC-1049	43-30360
	(Dätwyler rebuild, original c/n 11651)		
HB-OEI	Piper J-3C-90 Cub	11382	43-30091
HB-OEN	Piper J-3C-65 Cub	11842	44-79546
HB-OER	Piper J-3C-90 Cub	12595	44-80299
HB-OEY	Piper J-3C-90 Cub	12440	44-80144
HB-OFK	Piper J-3C-65 Cub	13131	44-80835
HB-OFP	Piper J-3C-90 Cub	12092	44-79796
HB-OFR	Piper J-3C-65 Cub	13285	45-4545
HB-OFV	Piper J-3C-65 Cub	13188	45-4448
HB-OFW	Piper J-3C-90 Cub	12273	44-79977
HB-OGA	Piper J-3C-90 Cub	13123	44-80827
HB-OGC	Piper J-3C-65 Cub	11486	43-30195
HB-OGG	Piper J-3C-65 Cub	10993	D-EHAL
			G-AIYX
			43-29702
HB-OGX	Piper PA-18 Super Cub 95	f/n 18-1622	F-BRUL
	(True c/n either 18-1623 or 18-1625)		ALAT
HB-OGZ	Piper J-3C-90 Cub	12648	44-80352
HB-OHC	Piper PA-28-180 Cherokee C	28-3623	F-OAYB
			TJ-ADI
			N9503J
HB-OHN	Piper PA-28-140 Cherokee C	28-26401	N5615U
HB-OHT	Piper PA-28-140 Cherokee C	28-26484	N5687U
HB-OHW	Piper PA-28R-200 Cherokee Arrow	28R-35609	N4968S
HB-OHX	Piper PA-28-180 Cherokee F	28-7105220	N11C
HB-OIA	Piper J-3C-90 Cub	12619	44-80323
HB-OIC	Piper J-3C-90 Cub	12372	SE-ATX
			44-80076
HB-OID	Piper PA-28R-200 Cherokee Arrow B	28R-7135226	N2389T
HB-OIN	Piper J-3C-65 Cub	12119	44-79823
HB-OIO	Piper J-3C-90 Cub	11231	43-29940
HB-OIX	Rösgen EPR.301	1	
HB-OKB	Piper PA-18-150 Super Cub	18-8884	N8573Y
HB-OKD	Piper PA-28-180 Cherokee G	28-7205182	N11C
HB-OKG	Piper PA-28-180 Cherokee G	28-7205176	N4848T
HB-OKK	Piper PA-28R-200 Cherokee Arrow II	28R-7335009	N11C
HB-OKL	Piper PA-28R-200 Cherokee Arrow II	28R-7335008	N11C
HB-OKN	Piper J-3C-90 Cub	12333	OO-SAM
			OO-AVO
			44-80037
HB-OKP	Piper J-3C-65 Cub	12810	F-BFQH
			44-80514
HB-OKT	Piper PA-28R-200 Cherokee Arrow II	28R-7435181	N9526N
HB-OKX	Piper PA-28-180 Cherokee Challenger	28-7305007	N11C
HB-OLH	Piper PA-28R-200 Cherokee Arrow II	28R-7535156	N33492
HB-OLP	Piper PA-28-140 Cherokee	28-20495	N6425W
HB-OLW	Piper PA-18-180 Super Cub	18-8337	N4171Z
HB-OLX	Piper PA-18-180 Super Cub	18-8446	N4222Z
HB-OMF	Piper PA-32-300 Cherokee Six	32-40148	N4097W
HB-OMN	Piper PA-28-140 Cherokee E	28-7225118	N15777

HB-OMP	Piper PA-28-140 Cherokee E	28-7225232	N15458 (XB-ZIP)
HB-OMS	Piper PA-28-180 Cherokee Challenger	28-7305437	N11C
HB-OMV	Piper PA-18 Super Cub 95	18-6327	D-EDOK N10F
HB-OMW	Piper PA-28-180 Cherokee Challenger	28-7305572	N9551N
HB-OMX	Piper PA-28-180 Cherokee Challenger	28-7305575	N9548N
HB-ONA	Piper J-3C-100 Cub	12867	44-80571
HB-ONB	Piper J-3C-90 Cub	12063	44-79767
HB-ONE	Piper J-3C-90 Cub	12661	44-80365
HB-ONG	Piper J-3C-90 Cub	13032	44-80736
HB-ONH	Piper J-3C-100 Cub (Damaged 18.8.04)	12519	44-80223
HB-ONW	Piper J-3C-65 Cub	12144	D-ELRO F-BFNM F-OBAX Fr.AF 44-79848
HB-ONY	Piper J-3C-100 Cub	18601	N98414 NC98414
HB-OOC	Piper PA-12 Super Cruiser (Dismantled)	12-2306	NC2653M
HB-OOF	Piper PA-16 Clipper	16-502	
HB-OPH	Piper PA-18-150 Super Cub	18-5517	N6982D
HB-OPL	Piper PA-22-150 Tri-Pacer	22-2865	N2504P
HB-OPP	Piper PA-18-150 Super Cub	18-5784	N10F
HB-OPU	Piper PA-18-150 Super Cub	18-5938	
HB-OQA	Piper PA-18-150 Super Cub	18-5375	D-ECBX ALAT N10F
HB-OQB	Piper PA-18-150 Super Cub	18-8991	(PT-IGG) N9728N
HB-OQG	Piper PA-28-151 Cherokee Warrior	28-7415089	N9629N
HB-OQK	Piper PA-28-151 Cherokee Warrior	28-7415439	N9612N
HB-OQL	Piper PA-18 Super Cub 95	18-1613	(D-EOCG) ALAT 51-15613
HB-OQN	Piper PA-28R-200 Cherokee Arrow II	28R-7435093	N54381
HB-OQO	Piper PA-28-235 Cherokee Pathfinder	28-7410096	N44559
HB-OQR	Piper PA-28R-200 Cherokee Arrow II	28R-7535011	N9591N
HB-OQS	Piper PA-28-151 Cherokee Warrior	28-7515009	N9572N
HB-OQT	Piper PA-28-180 Cherokee Archer	28-7505016	N9593N
HB-OQU(*)	Piper PA-28-140 Cherokee Cruiser	28-7525061	N9625N
HB-OQV	Piper PA-28-151 Cherokee Warrior	28-7515204	N9507N
HB-OQW	Piper PA-28-181 Cherokee Archer II	28-7690049	N9640N
HB-OQY	Piper PA-28-140 Cherokee Cruiser	28-7525190	N9605N
HB-ORA	Piper PA-18-150 Super Cub	18-7049	N10F
HB-ORH	Piper PA-18-150 Super Cub	18-7408	N10F
HB-ORK	Piper PA-18-150 Super Cub	18-7035	D-ENAG
HB-ORL	Piper PA-18-150 Super Cub	18-5301	F-BBOM F-OBDM
HB-ORM	Piper PA-18-150 Super Cub	18-7478	
HB-ORN	Piper PA-18-150 Super Cub	18-7514	N10F
HB-ORT	Piper PA-18-150 Super Cub	18-6433	D-ENAT N9068D
HB-ORV	Dätwyler/PA-18-150 Super Cub	MDC-1040	
HB-ORW	Dätwyler/PA-18-150 Super Cub	MDC-1041	
HB-ORY	Piper PA-18-180M Super Cub	18-4639	D-ENOL N10F
HB-ORZ	Piper PA-18-180M Super Cub	18-7938	N4013Z
HB-OSK	Piper J-3C-90 Cub	13139	44-80843
HB-OSM	Piper J-3C-90 Cub	12252	44-79956
HB-OSW	Piper J-3C-65 Cub	13262	45-4522
HB-OSY	Piper J-3C-90 Cub	11805	D-ECYF (SL-ABD) HB-OUG 43-30514
HB-OTB	Piper PA-24-180 Comanche	24-189	
HB-OTF	Piper PA-24-260 Comanche C	24-4915	D-EHGM N9410P
HB-OTG	Piper J-3C-100 Cub	11626	OO-FAB F-BDRQ F-OADH 43-30335
HB-OTN	Piper PA-22-108 Colt	22-8221	N10F
HB-OTR	Piper PA-22-150 Caribbean	22-7525	LN-BWE N10F
HB-OTS	Piper PA-24-250 Comanche	24-2320	N7155P
HB-OTW	Piper PA-24-250 Comanche	24-2643	N10F
HB-OUA	Piper J-3C-100 Cub (Rebuilt after accident 12.6.49 with unidentified fuselage but the original, f/n 12639, was later rebuilt as HB-ODO/EC-AIY/G-BSYO)	"12809"	44-80513
HB-OUD	Piper J-3C-90 Cub	11854	44-79558
HB-OUE	Piper J-3C-100 Cub	12315	44-80019
HB-OUN	Piper J-3C-100 Cub	12316	44-80020
HB-OUP	Piper J-3C-65 Cub	12530	44-80234
HB-OUR	Piper J-3C-100 Cub	10853	44-29562
HB-OUS	Piper J-3C-100 Cub	11502	43-30211
HB-OUV	Piper J-3C-90 Cub	11756	F-BFMP 43-30465
HB-OVC	Piper PA-12 Super Cruiser	12-540	F-BFQZ OO-PDO OO-PDC
HB-OVE	Piper J-3C-90 Cub	12264	44-79968
HB-OVF	Piper J-3C-90 Cub (Painted as "480176")	12492	F-BEGR NC74116 44-80196
HB-OVH	Piper PA-28-160 Cherokee	28-554	N5472W
HB-OVR	Piper PA-24-250 Comanche (Damaged 29.5.04)	24-1595	N6478P
HB-OVS	Piper PA-24-250 Comanche	24-3251	N8039P (ZS-CWH)
HB-OVT	Piper PA-28-180 Cherokee B	28-1174	N7312W
HB-OVW	Piper PA-24-250 Comanche	24-3498	N8296P
HB-OVX	Piper PA-28-180 Cherokee B	28-1258	N7419W
HB-OWB	Piper PA-22-108 Colt	2-9565	N5726Z
HB-OWI	Piper PA-28-180 Cherokee B	28-795	N7042W
HB-OWL	Piper PA-28-180 Cherokee B	28-1514	N7571W
HB-OWM	Piper PA-28-180 Cherokee B	28-1689	N7750W
HB-OWO	Piper J-3C-90 Cub	12132	44-79836
HB-OWS	Piper J-3C-90 Cub	11379	D-ENIX PH-NAB 43-30088
HB-OXD	Piper J-3C-90 Cub (Rebuilt Piper TG-8)	G-215	N49625 NC49625 43-3223
HB-OXI	Piper J-3C-100 Cub	12896	F-BFQM HB-OGE 44-80600
HB-OXL	Dätwyler/Piper J-3C-90 Cub	MDC-1039	
HB-OXR	Piper J-3C-100 Cub	12611	D-EMYT LX-ACL OO-VIR 44-80315
HB-OXX	Piper PA-18-150 Super Cub	18-6300	D-EDYK N10F
HB-OXY	Piper J-3C-100 Cub (c/n not confirmed - officially 12223)	13223	F-BDTO 45-4483
HB-OXZ	Piper J-3C-90 Cub	12986	F-BFMM HB-OGY 44-80690
HB-OYB	Piper PA-18-150 Super Cub	18-1192	V-652 KAB-102 HB-OOM
HB-OYH	Piper PA-28-140 Cherokee	28-20959	N6821W
HB-OYI	Piper PA-28-140 Cherokee	28-21466	N11C
HB-OYM	Piper PA-18-150 Super Cub	18-8324	N5750Y
HB-OYN	Piper PA-28-180 Cherokee C	28-3100	N9065J
HB-OYT	Piper PA-28-140 Cherokee	28-22577	N4228J
HB-OYW	Piper PA-28R-180 Cherokee Arrow	28R-30100	N3787T
HB-OYX	Piper PA-28R-180 Cherokee Arrow	28R-30065	N3756T
HB-OYZ	Piper PA-28R-180 Cherokee Arrow	28R-30014	N3710T
HB-OZB	Piper PA-28-140 Cherokee	28-24135	N1723J
HB-OZC	Piper PA-18 Super Cub 95 (Dismantled)	18-5598	D-EKAG OE-AEM 2A-AR N10F
HB-OZD	Piper PA-28-180 Cherokee D	28-4564	N5266L
HB-OZF	Piper PA-28-140 Cherokee	28-23088	N9631W
HB-OZG	Piper PA-28-140 Cherokee	28-21528	OO-DPD G-AVDD OE-DPD (OE-APD) N11C
HB-OZI	Piper PA-28R-180 Cherokee Arrow	28R-30769	N7425J
HB-OZK	Piper PA-28-180 Cherokee D	28-4702	N5393L
HB-OZT	Piper PA-28-140 Cherokee B	28-26092	N98188
HB-OZU	Piper PA-28R-200 Cherokee Arrow	28R-35221	N9454N
HB-OZV	Piper PA-28-180 Cherokee D	28-4613	N5310L
HB-OZX	Piper PA-28R-200 Cherokee Arrow	28R-35319	N2982R
HB-PAB	Piper PA-28-161 Cherokee Warrior II	28-7816495	D-ELET N9564N
HB-PAD	Piper PA-28R-200 Cherokee Arrow II	28R-7435157	N41219
HB-PAE	Piper PA-28-180 Cherokee Archer	28-7505098	N9527N
HB-PAF	Piper PA-28-180 Cherokee Archer	28-7505200	N1047X
HB-PAI	Piper PA-18-150 Super Cub	18-7509081	N66804
HB-PAL	Piper PA-28R-200 Cherokee Arrow II	28R-7635125	N7975C
HB-PAP	Piper PA-28-140 Cherokee Cruiser	28-7625115	N9514N
HB-PAR	Piper PA-18-180M Super Cub	18-7609050	N83278
HB-PAT	Piper PA-28-181 Cherokee Archer II	28-7690245	N9343K
HB-PAV	Piper PA-18-150 Super Cub	18-8055	V-654 N10F
HB-PAW	Piper PA-18-150 Super Cub	18-8192	V-655 N10F
HB-PAX	Piper PA-18-150 Super Cub	18-8193	V-656 N10F
HB-PAY	Piper PA-18-135 Super Cub	18-2548	D-ELNL ALAT 52-6230
HB-PAZ	Piper PA-32-301T Turbo Saratoga	32-8024019	G-BSMC N8190Y
HB-PBA	Piper PA-18-150 Super Cub (Quoted c/n is a spare fuselage number)	18-4922	D-ENDE (D-EIOT) RBAF
HB-PBB	Piper PA-28-151 Cherokee Warrior	28-7415062	N54437
HB-PBF	Piper PA-28R-201 Cherokee Arrow III	28R-7737012	N1764H
HB-PBH	Piper PA-28-181 Cherokee Archer II	28-7790151	N5995F
HB-PBK	Piper PA-32R-300 Lance	32R-7780141	N1174H
HB-PBO	Piper PA-28-235 Cherokee Pathfinder	28-7710022	N3063Q
HB-PBP	Piper PA-28R-201T Turbo Cherokee Arrow III	28R-7703205	N38350
HB-PBS	Piper PA-28R-201T Turbo Cherokee Arrow III	28R-7703294	N40027
HB-PBV	Piper PA-28-181 Cherokee Archer II	28-7790562	N38552
HB-PBW	Piper PA-28-181 Cherokee Archer II	28-7790603	N38899

HB-PBX	Piper PA-28R-200 Cherokee Arrow B	28R-7135207	D-ENOL N2266T
HB-PBZ	Piper PA-24-260 Comanche B	24-4766	5U-AAG F-OCLU N9298P
HB-PCA	Piper PA-28-181 Cherokee Archer II	28-7890230	N2138M
HB-PCB	Piper PA-28-181 Cherokee Archer II	28-7890389	N6989C
HB-PCC	Piper PA-28R-201T Turbo Arrow III	28R-7803321	N36329
HB-PCE	Piper PA-32-300 Cherokee Six	32-40332	F-BIEP F-OCLG N4035R
HB-PCH	Piper PA-28-161 Cherokee Warrior II	28-7816611	N36093
HB-PCI	Piper PA-28-180 Cherokee E	28-5745	D-EEFU N3648R
HB-PCM	Piper PA-18-150 Super Cub	18-7809037	N82964
HB-PCN	Piper PA-18-150 Super Cub	18-7809038	N82968
HB-PCV	Piper PA-28-140 Cherokee Cruiser	28-7725096	N9544N
HB-PCZ	Piper PA-28-181 Cherokee Archer II	28-7890529	N36763
HB-PDC	Piper PA-28R-201 Arrow III	28R-7837269	N36212
HB-PDD	Piper PA-28-181 Cherokee Archer II	28-7890528	N36744
HB-PDH	Piper PA-28-181 Archer II	28-7990159	N2141D
HB-PDI	Piper PA-28-181 Archer II	28-7990338	N2088V
HB-PDJ	Piper PA-18-150 Super Cub	1809056	F-GJOV
HB-PDL	Piper PA-18-150 Super Cub	18-7909016	N9750N
HB-PDS	Piper PA-28-236 Dakota	28-7911217	N2871Z
HB-PDU	Piper PA-28RT-201 Arrow IV	28R-7918201	N2887Y
HB-PDV	Piper PA-28-236 Dakota	28-7911246	N2920G
HB-PDW	Piper PA-28RT-201T Turbo Arrow IV	28R-7931169	N2221Z
HB-PDX	Piper PA-28RT-201T Turbo Arrow IV	28R-7931183	N28511
HB-PEA	Piper PA-28-181 Archer II	28-7990350	N2210W
HB-PEC	Piper PA-28-236 Dakota	28-7911188	N29680
HB-PEH	Piper PA-28-181 Archer II	28-7990531	N2886Z
HB-PEJ	Piper PA-32R-301 Saratoga SP	3213007	G-YUCS G-BSOL N9130Z N9590N
HB-PEL	Piper PA-28RT-201 Arrow IV	28R-7918262	N8079B
HB-PEN	Piper PA-28-236 Dakota	28-8011011	N9501N
HB-PEO	Piper PA-28RT-201 Arrow IV	28R-8018039	N8153H
HB-PER	Piper PA-28-181 Archer II	28-8090221	N8146R
HB-PES	Piper PA-32R-301 Saratoga SP	32R-8013042	N81437
HB-PEU	Piper PA-28RT-201T Turbo Arrow IV	28R-8131019	N8287X
HB-PEW	Piper PA-28-181 Archer II	28-8190005	
HB-PEX	Piper PA-28-161 Warrior II	28-8016295	N8181W
HB-PEY	Piper PA-28-161 Warrior II	28-8016323	N82112
HB-PEZ	Piper PA-28-236 Dakota	28-8011091	N81682
HB-PFA	Piper PA-28-181 Archer II	28-8090159	N8129M
HB-PFE	Piper PA-28-181 Archer II	28-8090314	N82173
HB-PFK	Piper PA-18-150 Super Cub	18-8009059	N9767N
HB-PFP	Piper PA-32RT-300 Lance II	32R-7885243	N78LD N39750
HB-PFS	Piper PA-28-181 Archer II	28-8190083	N82895
HB-PFW	Piper PA-25-260 Pawnee	25-8056047	N90819 N9770N
HB-PFY	Piper PA-32-301T Turbo Saratoga	32-8124004	N83166
HB-PFZ	Piper PA-28-236 Dakota	28-8111033	N8308L
HB-PGA	Piper PA-32R-301 Saratoga SP (W/o 13.10.01)	32R-8113045	
HB-PGB	Piper PA-28-181 Archer II	28-8190142	
HB-PGC	Piper PA-28-181 Archer II	28-8190172	
HB-PGE	Piper PA-28-181 Archer II	28-8190204	
HB-PGF	Piper PA-28RT-201T Turbo Arrow IV	28R-8131121	
HB-PGG	Piper PA-28-161 Warrior II	28-8116236	
HB-PGL	Piper PA-38-112 Tomahawk II	38-82A0011	
HB-PGM	Piper PA-28-181 Archer II	28-8190245	N8392A
HB-PGN	Piper PA-28-161 Warrior II	28-8216134	
HB-PGP	Piper PA-28-236 Dakota	28-8211030	
HB-PGR	Piper PA-28RT-201T Turbo Arrow IV	28R-8231045	
HB-PGU	Piper PA-38-112 Tomahawk II	38-82A0104	
HB-PGX	Piper PA-28-181 Archer II	28-8290121	
HB-PGY	Piper PA-28-236 Dakota	28-8311009	
HB-PGZ	Piper PA-28-236 Dakota	28-8211036	
HB-PHB	Piper PA-28-181 Archer II	28-8190208	D-EEJT N83666
HB-PHC	Piper PA-28-181 Archer II	28-8290168	
HB-PHD	Piper PA-28-161 Warrior II	28-8016246	D-EGWL N9615N
HB-PHG	Piper PA-28-181 Archer II	28-8190221	D-EFXP N8380H
HB-PHH	Piper PA-28-161 Warrior II	28-8316034	
HB-PHM	Piper PA-28-181 Archer II	28-8390038	
HB-PHO	Piper PA-28-181 Archer II	28-8390030	
HB-PHP	Piper PA-18-125 Super Cub	18-7901	(D-ELIY) EL-AEB N10F
HB-PHR	Piper PA-28-181 Archer II	28-8190141	D-EIFP N83235
HB-PHT	Piper PA-28-181 Archer II	28-7990564	OY-BRZ
HB-PHU	Piper PA-28-181 Archer II	28-8490070	N4359N
HB-PHV	Piper PA-28-161 Warrior II	28-8416082	N4329J
HB-PHW	Piper PA-28-236 Dakota	28-7911212	OY-BRW
HB-PHX	Piper PA-18-180M Super Cub	18-8431	(F-GBEE) 5R-MEC N4212Z
HB-PHZ	Piper PA-18-150 Super Cub	18-8009039	D-EMII N2320P
HB-PIC	Piper PA-18-150 Super Cub (Wrecked)	18-8309025	N91293
HB-PID	Piper PA-28-181 Archer II	28-8490084	N4365U
HB-PIG	Piper PA-28R-201 Arrow III	28R-7837261	OE-DUG N31991
HB-PIJ	Piper PA-18-135 Super Cub	18-4036	G-BLFB (G-AOSG) OO-ALH (OO-LVV) EI-291 I-EIVT MM542636 54-2636
HB-PIK	Piper PA-28R-201T Turbo Arrow III	28R-7803343	D-EKTP N36803
HB-PIL	Piper PA-28-181 Cherokee Archer II	28-7790190	9V-BHJ N9538N
HB-PIN	Piper PA-28RT-201 Arrow IV	28R-8018057	D-EIHU
HB-PIR	Piper PA-28-181 Archer II	28-8690048	N9086Z N9514N
HB-PIT	Piper PA-28RT-201T Turbo Arrow IV	28R-8031047	OY-GKF
HB-PIU	Piper PA-46-310P Malibu	46-8608047	
HB-PIV	Piper PA-28-181 Archer II	28-8190002	D-EFSP N8247C
HB-PIX	Piper PA-28RT-201 Arrow IV	28R-7918100	D-EFKI N2187Y
HB-PIZ	Piper PA-32R-301 Saratoga SP	32R-8513007	N9539N
HB-PKC	Piper PA-46-310P Malibu	46-8608033	N9296M
HB-PKD	Piper PA-46-310P Malibu	46-8608028	N9282Y
HB-PKE	Piper PA-28-181 Archer II	2890087	D-ELLT N9149Z
HB-PKF	Piper PA-28-236 Dakota	2811004	N9110R
HB-PKG	Piper PA-28-181 Archer II	2890008	N9106Z
HB-PKH	Piper PA-28RT-201T Turbo Arrow IV	28R-8231048	N8205H
HB-PKI	Piper PA-18-150 Super Cub	18-7692	D-EDFE
HB-PKK	Piper PA-28-181 Archer II	28-8690012	N90831
HB-PKM	Piper PA-28-181 Archer II	2890026	N9217T
HB-PKP	Piper PA-46-310P Malibu (Damaged 19.10.01)	46-8408022	G-SOFY N910LE N4336P
HB-PKR	Piper PA-28-181 Cherokee Archer II	28-7890544	D-EDES(3) N39624
HB-PKS	Piper PA-46-350P Malibu Mirage	4636180	
HB-PKT	Piper PA-28RT-201T Turbo Arrow IV	28R-8031129	N8235W
HB-PKU	Piper PA-32RT-300T Turbo Lance II	32R-7887046	G-WROY G-WRAY OY-BRD "OY-BRO"
HB-PKV	Piper PA-28R-201T Turbo Arrow IV	28R-8331039	G-BSRS ZS-LGJ N4307U
HB-PKX	Piper PA-28RT-201T Turbo Arrow IV	28R-8331032	G-BNIG N4299S
HB-PLC	Piper PA-28RT-201T Turbo Arrow IV	28R-8231056	N8216Q
HB-PLD	Piper PA-46-310P Malibu	4608123	
HB-PLE	Piper PA-46-310P Malibu	4608121	
HB-PLG	Piper PA-18-150 Super Cub	18-7949	I-MAMJ
HB-PLL	Piper PA-28-161 Warrior II	2816057	
HB-PLO	Piper PA-24-250 Comanche	24-269	F-BBFV F-DAFV N10F
HB-PLP	Piper PA-28-181 Archer II	2890074	
HB-PLQ	Piper PA-18-150 Super Cub	1809112	N4159Z
HB-PLR	Piper PA-28-181 Archer II	2890094	
HB-PLW	Piper PA-28-181 Archer II	2890085	
HB-PLY	Piper PA-28-181 Archer II	2890095	
HB-PLZ	Piper PA-28-181 Archer II	2890099	
HB-PMB	Piper PA-28R-201T Cherokee Arrow III	28R-7703114	N3565Q
HB-PMC	Piper PA-28-161 Warrior II	2816077	
HB-PME	Piper PA-28-161 Cadet	2841110	
HB-PMF	Piper PA-28-161 Warrior II	2816078	
HB-PMG	Piper PA-28-181 Archer II	2890109	
HB-PMH	Piper PA-28-181 Archer II	2890112	
HB-PMI	Piper PA-28-161 Cadet	2841111	
HB-PMJ	Piper PA-28-236 Dakota	2811027	
HB-PMK	Piper PA-28-181 Archer II	2890130	
HB-PMM	Piper PA-18-150 Super Cub	1809052	
HB-PMN	Piper PA-18-150 Super Cub	1809053	
HB-PMP	Piper PA-28-236 Dakota	2811030	
HB-PMR	Piper PA-28-181 Archer II	2890131	
HB-PMS	Piper PA-28R-201T Turbo Arrow III	28R-7803212	N6238C
HB-PMT	Piper PA-28-181 Archer II	2890151	
HB-PMU	Piper PA-32RT-300T Turbo Lance	32R-7887073	N36735
HB-PMV	Piper PA-28R-201T Turbo Cherokee Arrow III	28R-7703231	D-EKJW N38503
HB-PMY	Piper PA-28-181 Archer II	2890191	
HB-PNB	Piper PA-28-181 Archer III	2890218	
HB-PND	Piper PA-28-181 Archer III	2843006	
HB-PNG	Piper PA-28-161 Warrior II	2816109	
HB-PNH	Piper PA-46-350P Malibu Mirage	4636003	
HB-PNI	Piper PA-28RT-201T Turbo Arrow IV	28R-8431018	N4349D N9574N
HB-PNJ	Piper PA-28-181 Archer III	2843025	
HB-PNL	Piper PA-28-161 Warrior II	2816108	
HB-PNM	Piper PA-28-161 Warrior II	28-8616046	N7TY C-FUNY N9507N
HB-PNN	Piper PA-28-161 Warrior II	2816103	(HB-PNG)

HB-PNP	Piper PA-28RT-201T Turbo Arrow IV	28R-8131037	D-EANB N8304T
HB-PNR	Piper PA-28-161 Cadet	2841080	D-EFCF N9166Z
HB-PNT	Piper PA-28RT-201T Turbo Arrow IV	28R-8431031	G-BOGJ N4376E
HB-PNU	Piper PA-18-150 Super Cub	18-7883	D-ENSU N8019P
HB-PNV	Piper PA-25-235 Pawnee	25-8056042	I-SLAM N9770N
HB-PNX	Piper PA-32R-301T Turbo Saratoga SP	32R-8029040	N3579S SE-KKL N3579S
HB-PNZ	Piper PA-24-260 Comanche C	24-4934	F-BRUO N9426P
HB-POB	Piper PA-28R-201T Turbo Cherokee Arrow III	28R-7703245	N38571
HB-POC	Piper PA-28-161 Cadet	2841291	N9200J
HB-POD	Piper PA-18-180M Super Cub (Damaged 29.7.04)	18-7409045	I-FOSS N9746N
HB-POE	Piper PA-28-161 Cadet	2841296	N9207Z
HB-POF	Piper PA-28-161 Cadet	2841294	N9204N
HB-POG	Piper PA-18-150 Super Cub	18-2538	D-ELNK ALAT 52-6220
HB-POJ	Piper PA-28-236 Dakota	28-8411030	N4370G
HB-POK	Piper PA-28R-201T Arrow	2803005	F-GIGM N9178N
HB-POL	Piper PA-28-181 Archer II	28-8490016	N4326M
HB-PON	Piper PA-24-260 Comanche C	24-4868	N9368P
HB-POP	Piper PA-46-350P Malibu Mirage	4622077	N9185B
HB-POQ	Piper J-3C-65 Cub	17650	OE-AAS(1) N70638 NC70638
HB-POR	Piper PA-28-236 Dakota	28-8011056	N8089Y
HB-POU	Piper PA-18-180 Super Cub	18-5655	D-EIRG (SE-. . .) PH-LUB N7189D
HB-POW	Piper PA-28-181 Archer II	2890158	N91892 (OH-PBM) (SE-KMI)
HB-POX	Piper PA-28-181 Archer II	2890159	SE-KMK
HB-POY	Piper PA-46-350P Malibu Mirage	4622090	N836AJ
HB-POZ	Piper PA-18-150 Super Cub	18-8877	F-BTCO N8480Y
HB-PPB	Piper PA-28RT-201T Turbo Arrow IV	28R-7931278	N700CT N2963Q
HB-PPC	Piper PA-46-350P Malibu Mirage	4636298	N41864
HB-PPD	Piper PA-24-260 Comanche C	24-5016	D-EDAS N9498P
HB-PPF	Piper PA-28-161 Warrior III	2842011	
HB-PPG	Piper PA-28-161 Warrior III	2842012	
HB-PPH	Piper PA-46-350P Malibu Mirage	4636045	
HB-PPI	Piper PA-28-181 Archer III	2843045	
HB-PPJ	Piper PA-18-150 Super Cub	18-5342	I-EAEW D-EAEW ALAT N10F
HB-PPK	Piper PA-28-181 Archer III	2843084	
HB-PPL	Piper PA-18-150 Super Cub	18-7299	F-GERI F-OBOJ N10F
HB-PPM	Piper PA-28-181 Archer III	2843095	
HB-PPN	Piper PA-28-181 Archer III	2843140	N9509N
HB-PPQ	Piper PA-28-181 Cherokee Archer II	28-7690190	D-EFFR N8885E N9530N
HB-PPR	Piper PA-28R-201 Arrow	2844018	N9518N
HB-PPS	Piper PA-28-181 Archer III	2843259	N9519N
HB-PPT	Piper PA-28-181 Archer II	2890163	D-ETAM N9224D (SE-KMF)
HB-PPU	Piper PA-46-350P Malibu Mirage	4636227	N4140S N9508N
HB-PPV	Piper PA-28-181 Archer II	2890123	D-ELLV N9144Z
HB-PPW	Piper PA-28-181 Archer II	2890156	D-ETAF N92115
HB-PPX	Piper PA-28-181 Archer II	2890176	D-ETCE N9149G (F-GJOE)
HB-PPY	Piper PA-28-181 Archer II	2890194	D-ETCV N9227K
HB-PPZ	Piper PA-28-181 Archer II	2890146	D-EICM N9203P
HB-PQA	Piper PA-28-181 Archer III	2843398	N4176W
HB-PQB	Piper PA-28-181 Archer II	2890073	D-EIWL N9140Z
HB-PQC	Piper PA-28-161 Cadet	2841102	PH-TED C-FDYA
HB-PQD	Piper PA-28-181 Archer II	2890149	D-ELLM(2) N91739
HB-PQE	Piper PA-28R-201T Turbo Arrow III	28R-7803013	D-ENNS(2) N47762
HB-PQF	Piper PA-28-181 Archer III	2843067	D-EKIK N9279N
HB-PQG	Piper PA-28R-201T Turbo Arrow III	28R-7803047	
HB-PQI	Piper PA-28-161 Cadet	2841124	D-EFXK N9510N N9180X
HB-PQJ	Piper PA-18A-150 Super Cub	18-5877	N10F F-OBDB F-BJDB
HB-PQK	Piper PA-18-150 Super Cub	18-7323	N3487Z D-ENRY
HB-PQL	Piper PA-28-181 Archer II	2890121	D-ECWO N9183Z
HB-PQM	Piper PA-18 Super Cub 95	18-3200	D-ELSG (D-EETT) OL-L26 L-126 53-4800
HB-PQN	Piper PA-32R-300 Cherokee Lance	3246119	N4129T
HB-PQO	Piper PA-28R-201 Arrow III	28R-7837173	N6555C ZS-KYV D-EMTX
HB-PQR	Piper PA-28-181 Archer III	2843363	N4146L
HB-PQS	Piper PA-28-181 Archer III	2843069	I-PAEA N92834
HB-P . .	Piper PA-18-150 Super Cub	1809056	F-GJOV
HB-RAG	Dewoitine D.26	278	U-286
HB-RAI	Dewoitine D.26	276	U-284
HB-RAJ	CCF-4/North American Harvard IV	CCF4-384	I-RYGA 51-17202
HB-RAL	MDC-Trailer (Built from PA-18 parts by Dätwyler)	MDC-1038	
HB-RAM	Pilatus P.2-06	64	U-144
HB-RAN	Morane-Saulnier MS.733 Alcyon	134	F-BNED Fr.Mil
HB-RAO	Morane-Saulnier MS.317	329	F-BCBI
HB-RAR	Pilatus P.2-06	56	U-136
HB-RAV	Pilatus P.2-06	48	U-128
HB-RAW	Pilatus P.2-06	49	U-132
HB-RAX	Pilatus P.2-05	23	U-103
HB-RAY	Pilatus P.2-05 (For restoration)	35	U-115
HB-RAZ	Pilatus P.2-05	46	U-126
HB-RBC	Pilatus P.2-05	42	U-122
HB-RBG	Boeing Stearman E75	75-5345	N68489 42-17182
HB-RBI	EKW C-3603	327	C-547
HB-RBK	Pilatus P.3-03	327-9	A-810
HB-RBN	Pilatus P.3-03	330-12	A-813
HB-RBR	Pilatus P.3-05	508-57	A-870
HB-RBU	Pilatus P.3-05	484-33	A-846
HB-RBX	Pilatus P.3-05	493-42	A-855
HB-RBY	Pilatus P.3-05	510-59	A-872
HB-RCB	Pilatus P.3-05	497-46	LX-PAD HB-RCB A-859
HB-RCD	Pilatus P.3-05	505-54	G-BUKM A-867
HB-RCE	Pilatus P.3-05	457-6	A-819
HB-RCF	FFA D-3801 (Morane-Saulnier MS.406C) (Composite rebuild also using parts from J-276)	194	J-143
HB-RCG	Pilatus P.3-05	483-32	A-845
HB-RCH	Pilatus P.3-05	456-5	A-818
HB-RCJ	Pilatus P.3-05	467-16	A-829
HB-RCL	Pilatus P.3-05	511-60	A-873
HB-RCN	North American T-6GTexan	197-035	Fr.AF 52-8231
HB-RCQ	Pilatus P.3-05	453-2	A-815
HB-RCS	Pilatus P.3-05	490-39	A-852
HB-RCT	North American T-28B Trojan	200-337	N391W BuA138266
HB-RCV	Bleriot XI Replica	1	
HB-RCX	Yakovlev Yak-18A	607	F-AZFK EAF: . . .
HB-RCY	Pilatus P.3-05	460-9	A-822
HB-RCZ	Yakovlev Yak-18A	1410	
HB-RDE	North American B-25J Mitchell (Reservation 1.05; c/n quoted as '108-47562')	108-47662	F-AZID N9621C 45-8811
HB-RDD	Ryan ST-3KR (PT-22A)	1799	N1799 N2625R N46382 42-57503
HB-RVA	de Havilland DH.112 Venom FB.50	840	J-1630
HB-RVC	de Havilland DH.112 Venom FB.50	841	J-1631
HB-RVE	de Havilland DH.100 Vampire FB.6	993	J-1082
HB-RVF	de Havilland DH.115 Vampire T.55	868	U-1208
HB-RVH	de Havilland DH.100 Vampire FB.6	612	J-1103
HB-RVI	de Havilland DH.115 Vampire T.55	DHP.44352	U-1235
HB-RVJ	de Havilland DH.115 Vampire T.55	988	U-1228
HB-RVN	de Havilland DH.100 Vampire FB.6	706	J-1197
HB-RVP	Hawker Hunter T.Mk.68 (Identity unconfirmed - c/n quoted officially as " 41HR/003206")	HABL-003221	J-4205 G-6-412 Fv.34086 G-9-62
HB-RVQ	Hawker Hunter F.Mk.58	41H-697451	J-4084
HB-RVR	Hawker Hunter T.Mk.68	41HR/670803X	J-4201
HB-RVS	Hawker Hunter F.Mk.58 (Centre section should be 41H-697407)	XE-28/697405	"J-4015" J-4040

HB-RVT	Hawker Hunter F.Mk.58	41H-697447	J-4080
HB-RVU	Hawker Hunter F.Mk.58	41H-697453	J-4086
HB-RVV	Hawker Hunter T.Mk.68	HABL003207	J-4206
	(Officially quoted as 41HR/670841, thought		G-9-413
	to be ex J-4203, G-9-411, 7767M, WV398)		Fv.34072
			G-9-48
HB-RWW	Hawker Hunter T.Mk.68	41HR738150	J-42
HB-RXA	Bristol 171B Sycamore Mk.52	13483	D-HELM
			78+25
			GD+102
			LB+102
			CD+090
			BD+178
			G-18-156
HB-RXB	Bristol 171B Sycamore Mk.52	13475	D-HALD
	(Painted as "XG544")		78+17
			GD+112
			WE+545
			SC+206
			AS+
			CA+328
			G-18-148
HB-SAC	Gardan GY-20/1 Minicab	RHR-1	
HB-SAE	Jodel D.9 Bébé	AB-11	D-EHAX
HB-SAG	Gardan GY-20 Minicab	V-11	F-BEYG
HB-SAN	Mudry CAP.10B	147	
HB-SAP	Mudry CAP.10B	186	F-WZCG
HB-SAS	Mudry CAP.10B	182	
HB-SAV	Mudry CAP.10B	185	F-GDTE
HB-SAW	Mudry CAP.10B	209	
HB-SAX	Mudry CAP.10B	246	
HB-SBD	Mudry CAP.10B	268	
HB-SCB	Robin ATL	74	
HB-SCD	Robin ATL	107	
HB-SCF	Calair CA-25 Skyfox	CA25007	
HB-SCG	Skyfox CA25N Gazelle	CA25N027	
HB-SCL	HOAC DV-20 Katana	20046	
HB-SCM	HOAC DV-20 Katana	20074	
HB-SCN	HOAC DV-20 Katana	20124	
HB-SCO	HOAC DV-20 Katana	20115	
HB-SCP	HOAC DV-20 Katana	20077	
HB-SCS	HOAC DV-20 Katana	20131	
HB-SCT	HOAC DV-20 Katana	20112	
HB-SCU	HOAC DV-20 Katana	20143	
HB-SCV	Diamond DA 20-A1 Katana	10101	
HB-SCW	Diamond DA 20-A1 Katana	10138	
HB-SCX	Diamond DA 20-A1 Katana	10142	
HB-SCY	Diamond DA 20-A1 Katana	10264	
HB-SCZ	Diamond DA 20-A1 Katana	10298	N298DA
HB-SDA	Diamond DA 40 Star	40053	
HB-SDB	Diamond DA 40 Star	40022	
HB-SDC	Diamond DA 40 Star	40047	
HB-SDD	Diamond DA 40D Star	D4.017	
HB-SDE	Diamond DA 40D Star	D4.112	
HB-SDF	Diamond DA 40 Star	40371	
HB-SDG	Diamond DA 20-A1 Katana	10073	N518SS
HB-SDI	HOAC DV-20 Katana	20035	SE-LOL
			OE-CES
			C-FSBS
HB-SDJ	Diamond DA 40 Star	40393	
HB-SDP	Diamond DA 40D Star	D4.147	
HB-SEE	Binder CP.301S Smaragd	115	
HB-SEF	Binder CP.301S Smaragd	116	D-EDRI
HB-SEH	SAN Jodel D.140C Mousquetaire III	50	F-BHQV
			F-OBQV
HB-SEL	Binder CP.301S Smaragd	004	
HB-SEW	CEA Jodel DR.1050 Ambassadeur	223	F-BKGE
HB-SEX	Erla 5A	14	D-ENAL
			D-YBIT
HB-SEY	Wassmer Jodel D.120 Paris-Nice	154	D-EJIZ
HB-SEZ	SAN Jodel D.117 Grand Tourisme	801	F-BIOM
HB-SFA	SAN Jodel D.140E Mousquetaire IV	187	F-BOPD
HB-SFB	SAN Jodel D.140E Mousquetaire IV	176	F-BNIQ
HB-SFC	SAN Jodel D.140C Mousquetaire III	127	F-BMBL
HB-SFD	SAN Jodel D.140C Mousquetaire III	167	F-BNIE
HB-SFE	SAN Jodel D.140C Mousquetaire III	160	F-BMFU
HB-SFF	SAN Jodel D.140C Mousquetaire III	19	D-EIZD
			F-BIZD
HB-SFH	SAN Jodel D.140C Mousquetaire III	130	D-EHBG
			F-BMBN
HB-SFI	SAN Jodel D.140R Abeille	525	F-BOPM
HB-SFR	SAN Jodel D.140R Abeille	521	F-BNIY
HB-SFS	Aquila AT01	AT01-109	
HB-SOA	Gardan GY-201 Minicab (Wfu?)	A-213	
HB-SOG	Jodel D.112 Club	490	
HB-SOH	Jodel D.11	489	
HB-SOI	Druine D.31 Turbulent	00	
HB-SOK	Piel CP.301A Emeraude	74	
HB-SOU	Jodel D.112 Club	unkn	
HB-SPH	Gardan GY-201 Minicab	05	F-BFLK
HB-SPI	Brügger Kolibri MB-2	2	
HB-SPK	Diamond DA 40 Star	40046	
HB-SPM	Potez 600 Sauterelle	3998	F-PIIN
			F-AOET
HB-SPN	Slingsby T.66 Nipper Mk.III	S.132/1708	G-AXLJ
HB-SPO	SAN Jodel D.117 Grand Tourisme	605	F-BIBB
HB-SPP	SIPA S.903	48	F-BGAX

HB-SPQ	Slingsby T.66 Nipper Mk.III	S.118/1625	G-AWDB
HB-SPS	Jodel D.112 Club	350	F-BHKT
HB-SPT	SIPA S.903	88	F-BGHM
HB-SPU	SIPA S.903	76	F-BGHA
HB-SPX	Wassmer Jodel D.120 Paris-Nice	211	F-BKJM
HB-SUD	Jodel D.11	399	
HB-SUG	Gardan GY-201 Minicab	unkn	
HB-SUH	Jodel D.11	286	
HB-SUI	Gardan GY-20 Minicab	A126	
HB-SUK	Gardan GY-201 Minicab	210	
HB-SUM	Gardan GY-201 Minicab	A211	
HB-SUN	Jodel D.9 Bébé	73	
HB-SUT	Gardan GY-201 Minicab	212/1	
HB-SUU	Jodel D.112 Club	316	
HB-SUV	Jodel D.11	487-5	
HB-SUX	Gardan GY-201 Minicab	1	
HB-SUY	Jodel D.11	315-24	
HB-SVB	Druine D.31 Turbulent	287	
HB-SVC	Uetx Jodel D.11	982	
HB-SVL	Jodel D.112 Club	459	TS-ABC
			F-PHFF
HB-SVM	Uetz Jodel U.2V	22	
HB-SVT	Uetz Jodel U.2V	23	
HB-SVV	Wassmer Jodel D.112 Club	1121	F-BKJO
HB-SVX	SAN Jodel D.117A Grand Tourisme	889	F-BIXK
HB-TBD	Uetz Marabu	01	
HB-TBU	Uetz U4M Pelikan	7303	
HB-TBV	Uetz U3M Pelikan	25	
HB-TBX	Uetz U4M Pelikan	05	
HB-TBY	Uetz U4M Pelikan	27	
HB-TBZ	Uetz U4M Pelikan	29	
HB-TCB	Zlin Z.326 Trenér Master	902	F-BMQX
HB-TCC	Zlin Z.326 Trenér Master	925	F-BORV
HB-TCD	Zlin Z.143L	0022	
HB-TCE	Zlin Z.143L	0006	
HB-TCG	Zlin Z.526F Trenér Master	1238/26	I-GIRE
HB-TCH	Zlin Z.143L	0029	
HB-TRG	Zlin Z.526F Trenér Master	1232	YR-ZLR
HB-TRJ	Zlin Z.526F Trenér Master	1287	YR-ZLW
HB-TRQ	Zlin Z.526ASM Akrobat Special	1027	OK-WXB
HB-TRS	Stinson 108-3 Voyager	108-4419	F-BBSV
			HB-TRH
			N6419M
HB-TUG	DHC-1 Chipmunk 22	C1/0731	WP847
HB-TUM	OGMA/DHC-1 Chipmunk 20	OGMA-62	OO-NPO
			FAP1372
HB-UAF	Praga E-114M Air Baby	119	F-BCSN
HB-UAL	Champion 7GCB Challenger	40	
HB-UAO	Champion 7FC Tri-Traveller	446	
HB-UAW	Champion 7ECA Citabria	238	
HB-UBC	de Havilland DH.82A Tiger Moth	3956	G-AOUX
			N6652
HB-UBI	American AA-1A Trainer	AA1A-0087	N9387L
HB-UBK	Klemm Kl.35D	1918	D-EJUL
			SE-BGB
			Fv5029
HB-UBN	American AA-1A Trainer	AA1A-0166	N9266L
HB-UBP	American AA-1A Trainer	AA1A-0167	N9267L
HB-UBS	American AA-1A Trainer	AA1A-0353	
HB-UBT	American AA-1A Trainer	AA1A-0354	
HB-UBV	Grumman-American AA-5 Traveler	AA5-0036	N5836L
HB-UBW	Grumman-American AA-5 Traveler	AA5-0035	N5835L
HB-UCA	Grumman-American AA-5 Traveler	AA5-0581	N9581L
HB-UCD	Grumman-American AA-5 Traveler	AA5-0541	(N9541L)
HB-UCE	Grumman-American AA-5A Cheetah	AA5A-0054	
HB-UCF(*)	Grumman-American AA-5B Tiger	AA5B-0170	
HB-UCH	Grumman-American AA-5B Tiger	AA5B-0465	
HB-UCL	Grumman-American AA-5B Tiger	AA5B-0904	
HB-UCM	Grumman-American AA-5B Tiger	AA5B-0924	
HB-UCO	Grumman-American AA-5B Tiger	AA5B-1078	
HB-UCT	Gyroflug SC-01 Speed Canard	S-16	
HB-UCV	Gyroflug SC-01B Speed Canard	S-33	(D-EAMR)
HB-UCW	Grumman-American AA-5B Tiger	AA5B-1027	D-EEJW
			(D-EAZG)
			N4517E
HB-UCY	Gyroflug SC-01B-160 Speed Canard	S-34	
HB-UCZ	Gyroflug SC-01B-160 Speed Canard	S-35	
HB-UDA	American AG-5B Tiger	AA5B-10135	SP-FYC
HB-UDB	CASA I-131E Jungmann	2147	EC-DAP
	(Identity suspect, EC-DAP crashed		E.3B-547
	after HB-UDB registered; parts used?)		
HB-UEB	Bölkow BO.209 Monsun	124	(D-EFJB)
HB-UEC	Bölkow BO.209 Monsun	151	(D-EBJK)
HB-UEG	Bölkow BO.209 Monsun	195	(D-EAIK)
HB-UGA	Grob G.115	8011	(D-EGVV)
HB-UGB	Grob G.115	8020	(D-EGVV)
HB-UGD	Grob G.115	8023	(D-EGVV)
HB-UGE	Grob G.115A	8026	(D-EGVV)
HB-UOD	Laverda F.8L Falco IV	402	D-ELXE
HB-UOG	Aeromere F.8L Falco	230	G-AZAY
			D-EFAK
HB-UOH	Aviamilano F.8L Falco I	105	G-KYNG
			I-KYNG
			HB-UOH
			I-STRI
HB-UOK	Aviamilano F.8L Falco I	115	I-DARE
HB-UPC	Bölkow BO.208C Junior	610	(D-EJUT)

HB-UPD	Bölkow BO.208C Junior	584	D-EJMO
HB-UPE	de Havilland DH.60G-III Moth Major	5078	CH-348
HB-UPF	Bölkow BO.208C Junior	637	(D-EGFE)
HB-UPH	Bölkow BO.208C Junior	676	(D-EGZJ)
HB-UPM	de Havilland DH.82A Tiger Moth	DHNZ-135R	G-BJLI
			ZK-ATM
			NZ1455
HB-UPP	de Havilland DH.82A Tiger Moth	1000	G-BCRD
	(Dismantled, for rebuild)		N17565
			VH-FBR
			A17-565
HB-UPR	SNCAN/ Stampe SV.4A	662	F-BDNG
HB-UPS	SNCAN/ Stampe SV.4A	243	OO-EFD
			F-BCKC
HB-UPT	AIAA/ Stampe SV.4C	1113	F-BAGN
HB-UPY	de Havilland DH.82A Tiger Moth	85635	G-ANOR
			DE694
HB-UPZ	Waco YMF (F5C)	F5C-055	
HB-URD	Bücker Bü.131 Jungmann	33	A-24
HB-URF	Bücker Bü.131 Jungmann	47	A-36
HB-URH	Bücker Bü.131 Jungmann	61	A-49
HB-URM	Bücker Bü.131 Jungmann	60	A 48
HB-USD	Bücker Bü. APM 131-150 Jungmann	65	A-52
HB-UTH	Bücker Bü. APM 131-150 Jungmann	51	OE-AKH
			HB-UTH
			A-40
HB-UTN	Bücker Bü.131 Jungmann	87	A-74
HB-UUA	Bücker Bü. APM 131-150 Jungmann	8	A-1
			HB-UTE
			A-1
HB-UUC	Bücker Bü.131 Jungmann	13	A-6
HB-UUD	Bücker Bü. APM 131-150 Jungmann	16	A-9
HB-UUE	Bücker Bü.131 Jungmann	24	A-15
HB-UUF	Bücker Bü. APM 131-150 Jungmann	71	A-58
HB-UUH	Bücker Bü. APM 131-150 Jungmann	76	A-63
HB-UUI	Bücker Bü. APM 131-150 Jungmann	95	A-82
	(c/n offcially quoted as 94)		HB-USM
			A-82
HB-UUL	Bücker Bü. APM 131-150 Jungmann	29	A-20
HB-UUM	Bücker Bü. APM 131-150 Jungmann	31	A-22
			HB-UFI
			A-22
HB-UUN	Bücker Bü. APM 131-150 Jungmann	41	A-30
HB-UUO	Bücker Bü. APM 131-150 Jungmann	42	A-31
HB-UUP	Bücker Bü. APM 131-150 Jungmann	50	G-BHGZ
	(c/n officially quoted as 59)		HB-UUP
			A-39
			HB-UTF
			A-39
HB-UUR	Bücker Bü.131 Jungmann	73	A-60
HB-UUS	Bücker Bü. APM 131-150 Jungmann	79	A-66
HB-UUT	Bücker Bü.131 Jungmann	81	A-68
HB-UUU	Bücker Bü. APM 131-150 Jungmann	84	A-71
HB-UUV	Bücker Bü. APM 131-150 Jungmann	18	A-11
HB-UUW	Bücker Bü. APM 131-150 Jungmann	11	A-4
HB-UUY	Bücker Bü. APM 131-150 Jungmann	10	A-3
HB-UVB	Bücker Bü. APM 131-150 Jungmann	39	A-28
HB-UVC	Bücker Bü.131 Jungmann	66	A-53
	(c/n officially quoted as 53)		HB-HEL
HB-UVE	Bücker Bü. APM 131-150 Jungmann	69	A-56
HB-UVF	Bücker Bü. APM 131-150 Jungmann	93	A-80
HB-UVG	Bücker Bü.131 Jungmann	30	A-21
HB-UVH	CASA I-131E Jungmann	2152	E.3B-. . .
HB-UVK	CASA I-131E Jungmann	2115	I-FERT
			E.3B-519
HB-UVM	CASA I-131E Jungmann	2088	E.3B-484
HB-UVN	CASA I-131E Jungmann	2142	E.3B-522
HB-UVP	CASA I-131E Jungmann (C/n "466" quoted)	2064	E.3B-466
HB-UVR	CASA I-131E Jungmann	2240	D-EOGG
			E.3B-576
HB-UVU	CASA I-131E Jungmann	2062	D-EINA(3)
			(F-GTDB)
			EC-DMJ
			E.3B-464
HB-UVZ	Bücker Bü.131 Jungmann	43	A-32
HB-UXL	Bölkow BO.207	208	(D-EHUM)
HB-UXN	Bölkow BO.208C Junior	513	D-ENCU
HB-UXW	Bölkow BO.208C Junior	594	(D-EKDO)
HB-U . .	de Havilland DH.85 Leopard Moth	PPS.85/1/DH.7131	G-APKH
	(Reported may become HB-ODD)		
HB-VCN(2)	North American NA265-65 Sabreliner 65	465-32	N303A
			N97RE
HB-VDO	Cessna 551 Citation II/SP	551-0133	I-JESA
	(Converted from c/n 550-0088)		N222TG
	(Accident 20.1.03)		G-JRCT
			N2663N
HB-VHV	BAe.125 Series 800B	258153	G-5-627
HB-VIF	Gates Learjet 36A	36A-057	
HB-VIS	Cessna 550 Citation II	550-0447	(N447CJ)
			N12482
HB-VJB	Cessna 501 Citation I/SP	501-0067	VR-BLW
			HB-VJB
			D-IGMB
			SE-DEO
			N2959A
HB-VJI	Gates Learjet 31	31-011	N3803G
HB-VJK	Gates Learjet 35A	35A-651	
HB-VJL	Gates Learjet 35A	35A-653	
HB-VKW	BAe.125 Series 800B	258246	N387H
			G-5-782
HB-VLA	HS.125 Series 700B	257031	N89TJ
			G-5-701
			G-BFSP
			D-CBAE
			G-5-701
			G-BFSP
			G-PRMC
			G-BFSP
HB-VLE	Cessna 500 Citation I	500-0313	N313BA
			XA-SDS
			XB-DYF
			XA-KUJ
			N76GT
			(N5313J)
HB-VLF	BAe.125 Series 800	258264	N805H
			G-5-806
HB-VLG	BAe.125 Series 800	258265	N806H
			G-5-809
HB-VLQ	Cessna 550 Citation II	550-0324	N23W
			I-JESJ
			N171LE
			N5873C
HB-VLR	Gates Learjet 31A	31A-127	N80727
HB-VLZ	Cessna 560 Citation Ultra	560-0446	
HB-VMB	Bombardier Learjet 45	45-021	N5009T
HB-VMH	Cessna 550 Citation II	550-0649	N44LQ
HB-VMJ	Cessna S550 Citation SII	S550-0029	N608LB
			N185SF
			(N1260N)
HB-VML	Bombardier Learjet 45	45-084	N5009V
HB-VMO	Cessna 560XL Citation Excel	560-5061	N5200R
HB-VMR	IAI-1125A Astra SPX	115	N526GA
HB-VMT	Cessna 525 CitationJet	525-0250	N250CJ
HB-VMU	Cessna 560XL Citation Excel	560-5066	N134SW
HB-VMV	Cessna 560 Citation V	560-0166	N166JV
			ZS-NDW
			N68872
HB-VMW	Cessna 550 Citation Bravo	550-0955	N50715
HB-VMX	Cessna 550 Citation Bravo	550-0946	N52229
HB-VMY	Cessna 550 Citation Bravo	550-0964	N52234
HB-VMZ	Cessna 560XL Citation Excel	560-5067	N42PA
HB-VNA	Cessna 560 Citation Ultra	560-0280	PH-MDC
			(N51042)
			N1298G
HB-VNB	Cessna 560 Citation Ultra	560-0271	N49TT
			PH-VLG
			N1296N
HB-VNC	Cessna 560XL Citation Excel	560-5058	N555WE
			N555WF
			N5235G
HB-VND	Cessna 560XL Citation Excel	560-5106	N506AM
			N5221Y
HB-VNE	Beech 400A Beechjet	RK-318	N3185K
HB-VNG	Dassault Falcon 200	502	N64YR
			N64YP
			N232F
			N573E
			N5732
			N216FJ
			F-WPUU
HB-VNH	Cessna 560XL Citation Excel	560-5172	N5086W
HB-VNI	Cessna 560XL Citation Excel	560-5154	N154XL
HB-VNJ	Hawker 800XP	258521	N50521
HB-VNK	Cessna 525 CitationJet	525-0271	N860DB
			N860DD
HB-VNL	Cessna 525 CitationJet	525-0375	N375KH
			N5225K
HB-VNM	Dassault Falcon 20F5	426	I-BAEL
			N416RM
			N555PT
			N123WH
			N427F
			F-WJMK
HB-VNO	Cessna 525A CitationJet 2	525A-0033	N163PB
HB-VNP	Cessna 525 CitationJet	525-0499	N5200Z
HB-VNS	Cessna 560XL Citation Excel	560-5209	N501XL
HB-VNU	Cessna 500 Citation	500-0282	N510RC
			N501CW
			N501SS
			N520RB
			N26WD
			N282CC
			(N5282J)
HB-VNW	Cessna 560 Citation Ultra	560-0457	G-GRGS
			VP-CMS
			N59HA
			N51564
HB-VNZ	Cessna 550 Citation Bravo	550-0906	D-CSSS
			N850GM
			C-GLCE
			N5166T
HB-VOA	IAI-1125 Astra SPX	111	N848GA
			N297GA
			OE-GAM

HB-V . .	Cessna 525 CitationJet (Reservation)	525-0354	N821P (D-IMPP) N821P N5225K
HB-XAQ	SNCASE SE.3130 Alouette II (Not c/n 1932 as previously recorded)	1931	V-53
HB-XBA	Agusta-Bell 206B Jet Ranger III	8593	G-HYDE
HB-XBF	SNCASE SE.3130 Alouette II	1236	N92785 HB-XBF V-48
HB-XBQ	Schweizer/Hughes 269D	0024	N69A
HB-XBZ	Agusta-Bell 47G-3B1	1594	(D-HZKA) HB-XBZ
HB-XCB	Sud Avn SA.316B Alouette III (Stored, 9.99)	1259	
HB-XCJ	Aérospatiale AS.350B2 Ecureuil	2557	F-GJOK
HB-XCM	SNCASE SE.3160 Alouette III (Wreck noted 9.99)	1443	
HB-XDA	SNCASE SE.3160 Alouette III	1609	
HB-XDG	Aérospatiale SA.315B Lama	2221	F-WIEL
HB-XDI	Aérospatiale SA.315B Lama	2207	
HB-XDN	Aérospatiale SA.315B Lama	2232	
HB-XDQ	Schweizer 269C	S-1732	
HB-XEJ	Schweizer 269C	S-1733	N41S
HB-XEO	Aérospatiale SA.315B Lama (Stored, 9.99)	2321	F-BUYA
HB-XES	Enstrom F-28C	353	
HB-XFE	Aérospatiale SA.315B Lama	2436	OE-EXB HB-XFE
HB-XFQ	Schweizer 269C	S-1687	N69A
HB-XFX	Aérospatiale SA.315B Lama (W/o 10.7.04)	2445	
HB-XGJ	Schweizer 269C	S-1688	N41S
HB-XGP	Aérospatiale SA.315B Lama	2349	F-BVUG HB-XDZ
HB-XHB	Westland-Bell 47G-3B1	WA/424	G-BEPA XT512
HB-XHD	Aérospatiale SA.315B Lama	2460	OE-EXL
HB-XHN	Aérospatiale SA.315B Lama	1083/04	F-BIEC
HB-XHO	Agusta-Bell 206A Jet Ranger II	8155	OE-DXS D-HBBZ
HB-XIA	Aérospatiale SA.315B Lama	2552	
HB-XIB	Aérospatiale SA.315B Lama (W/o 28.2.99)	2531	
HB-XII	Aérospatiale SA.315B Lama	2551	
HB-XJA	Agusta A.109A-II	7317	N295CA JA9695 N1CL N109GG
HB-XJE	Westland-Bell 47G-3B1 Soloy	WA/352	D-HAHE(2) (D-HAFM) XT193
HB-XJF	McDonnell-Douglas MD-900 Explorer	00017	N9213Z
HB-XJH	Robinson R-22 Beta	2551	
HB-XJJ	SNCASE SE.313B Alouette II	1903	V-57
HB-XJK	Sud Avn SA.319B Alouette III (W/o 17.2.99)	2273	I-OYEN N1044N ZK-HNY
HB-XJN	Aérospatiale SA.315B Lama	2609	I-BREY
HB-XJP	Schweizer 269C	S-1731	
HB-XJQ	Enstrom 480	5018	
HB-XJR	Sud Avn SA.316B Alouette III (W/o 27.9.00)	1781	I-LESY HB-XOT D-HADX F-GBGJ XC-FEZ
HB-XJS	Robinson R-44 Astro	0083	D-HRHP
HB-XJW	Aérospatiale AS.350B Ecureuil (Reserved as N775MA 8.04)	1802	OE-KXB D-HHFF
HB-XJZ	Robinson R-22 Beta	2674	
HB-XKE	Kamov Ka.32A12	8709/02	
HB-XKN	Bell 206B Jet Ranger II	1205	G-BBTV N18092
HB-XLA	Agusta-Bell 206B Jet Ranger III	8616	
HB-XLL	Agusta-Bell 206B Jet Ranger III	8609	P2-XLL HB-XLL
HB-XLM	Robinson R-22	0072	
HB-XLN	Robinson R-22	0073	
HB-XLS	Enstrom 280C Shark	1211	N5695K
HB-XMC	Aérospatiale SA.315B Lama	2527	ZK-HNW
HB-XMG	Westland-Bell 47G-3B1	WA/579	XT824
HB-XMJ	Bell 206B Jet Ranger II	4302	N112AJ
HB-XMO	Enstrom 280C Shark (W/o 23.5.97)	1213	N5697N
HB-XND	Aérospatiale SA.315B Lama	2624	
HB-XNR	Enstrom 280F (Crash 26.8.99)	1512	
HB-XNS	Sud Avn SA.319B Alouette III	2389	
HB-XNU	Agusta-Bell 206B Jet Ranger II (Dbr 27.9.00)	8289	D-HASA LN-OSI D-HAWA
HB-XNW	Sud Avn SA.316B Alouette III (W/o 20.6.96)	2265	N49543
HB-XNZ	SNCASE SE.3160 Alouette III	1071	LX-EEE RDAF:M-071
HB-XOE	SNCASE SE.3160 Alouette III	1019	LX-AAA RDAF:M-019
HB-XOF	SNCASE SE.3160 Alouette III	1439	LX-OOO RDAF:M-439
HB-XOO	Sud Avn SA.319B Alouette III	1959	D-HAAK
HB-XOV	Bell 214ST	28129	N13158
HB-XOY	Aérospatiale SA.315B Lama	2508	ZK-HNV
HB-XPJ	Aérospatiale SA.315B Lama	2368	(N315TM) 9M-SAB F-GAML LN-OSO
HB-XPL	Aérospatiale SA.315B Lama	2560	OE-EXD HB-XPL I-STEC
HB-XPQ	Agusta-Bell 206B Jet Ranger III	8606	EC-EAN HB-XPQ OE-DXV
HB-XPS	Hughes 269C	S-1228	
HB-XPT	Hughes 269C	S-1229	
HB-XPU	Schweizer 269C	S-1233	
HB-XPY	Aérospatiale SA.315B Lama	2542	N9007N
HB-XQB	McDonnell-Douglas MD.600N	RN-007	N92007
HB-XQC	Bell 407	53132	
HB-XQE	Agusta A.109E Power	11016	
HB-XQJ	Aérospatiale AS.350B3 Ecureuil	3093	
HB-XQK	Robinson R-22B2 Beta	2757	
HB-XQL	Robinson R-44 Astro	0408	
HB-XQN	SNCASE SE.3160 Alouette III	1217	A-217
HB-XQO	Bell 206B Jet Ranger II (W/o 26.3.05)	3934	OE-XRH N42TM D-HMTM
HB-XQP	Bell 206L-4 Long Ranger IV	52016	D-HOBC(2)
HB-XQT	SNCASE SE.313B Alouette II	1650	F-GNPX ALAT
HB-XQV	Bell 407	53259	
HB-XQW	Aérospatiale AS.365N1 Dauphin 2	6350	N610LH JA6609
HB-XRA	Aérospatiale SA.315B Lama	1542/17	F-GHCG F-ODSJ (F-GHCG) TR-LZR TR-LUY 3D-XZ
HB-XRD	Aérospatiale SA.315B Lama	2400	OE-EXV
HB-XRE	Aérospatiale SA.315B Lama	2462	G-BMSN N47319
HB-XRF	Aérospatiale SA.315B Lama	2490	OE-KXD HB-XRF G-BMUA N49524
HB-XRL	Aérospatiale SA.315B Lama	2291	C-GDWD HB-XFO OE-EXA F-BSEJ
HB-XRN	Aérospatiale SA.315B Lama	2309	N6390
HB-XRW	Hughes 369E	0231E	
HB-XSE	Aérospatiale AS.350B1 Ecureuil	2133	
HB-XSI	Bell 206B Jet Ranger II	3091	
HB-XSK	Schweizer 269C	S-1329	
HB-XSL	Bell 206B Jet Ranger II	1516	D-HCBB N111RL N111WH
HB-XSM	Agusta-Bell 206B Jet Ranger II	8550	OE-BXW(1)
HB-XSO	Aérospatiale AS.350B1 Ecureuil	1950	D-HACC D-HAHI (2) F-WZKX
HB-XSP	Bell 206L-3 Long Ranger III	51158	N3199J
HB-XSR	Robinson R-22 Beta	0774	
HB-XSU	Aérospatiale AS.350B1 Ecureuil	2115	
HB-XSV	Aérospatiale SA.315B Lama	2421	LN-ORU N67103
HB-XSW	Aérospatiale SA.315B Lama	2563	
HB-XTA	Bell 412	33168	EI-BVL N3207Q
HB-XTB	Bell 412	33177	
HB-XTC	Aérospatiale SA.315B Lama	2521	N90016
HB-XTD	Aérospatiale SA.315B Lama	2596	N70283 XC- . . .
HB-XTM	Aérospatiale SA.315B Lama (Crash 4.3.97)	2654	LN-OMW
HB-XTN	Aérospatiale SA.315B Lama	2407	N62345
HB-XTO	Aérospatiale SA.315B Lama	2633	LN-OTE
HB-XTQ	Robinson R-22 Beta	1014	N8040A
HB-XTW	Aérospatiale SA.315B Lama (W/o 5.9.00)	2537	F-GCLB G-DASL
HB-XTY	Aérospatiale SA.315B Lama	2645	LN-OMO (LN-OLM) F-WXFG
HB-XUA	Aérospatiale SA.315B Lama	2595	F-GHCP ZK-HBR(2) XC-DOS
HB-XUE	Bell 206B Jet Ranger	3080	OE-KXR N5744M
HB-XUN	Hughes 369E	0358E	VR-BLS HB-XUN (D-HILV)
HB-XUW	Agusta-Bell 206B Jet Ranger III	8722	
HB-XUZ	Aérospatiale AS.350B2 Ecureuil	2381	
HB-XVA	Aérospatiale AS.350B2 Ecureuil	2387	F-WYME
HB-XVB	Aérospatiale AS.350B2 Ecureuil	2340	
HB-XVL	Aérospatiale SA.315B Lama	2334	F-GEOI N62250 (N502HA) N62250
HB-XVM	Aérospatiale AS.350B2 Ecureuil	2399	F-WYMO
HB-XVV	Aérospatiale SA.315B Lama	2382	OE-OXB HB-XVV JA9134 N382HS

HB-XWA	Agusta A.109K2	10001	I-RAIE
HB-XWB	Agusta A.109K2	10002	
HB-XWC	Agusta A.109K2	10003	
HB-XWD	Agusta A.109K2	10004	
HB-XWG	Agusta A.109K2	10007	
HB-XWH	Agusta A.109K2	10008	
HB-XWJ	Agusta A.109K2	10010	
HB-XWM	Agusta A.109K2	10013	
HB-XWN	Agusta A.109K2	10014	
HB-XWO	Agusta A.109K2	10015	
HB-XWP	Agusta A.109K2	10027	
HB-XXC	Sud Avn SA.316B Alouette III (Crashed 30.12.99)	1592	OE-EXT G-BMMS N4261E C-GXGW N65376 9M-ASI FM1097
HB-XXJ	Aérospatiale SA.315B Lama	1155/16	F-GFFG TR-LZQ TR-LUZ AAF:3D-XU F-WIES
HB-XXN	Bell 206B Jet Ranger II	4123	
HB-XXO	Bell 206B Jet Ranger II	3595	N22988 (N101DG) N22988
HB-XXQ	Robinson R-22 Beta	1538	
HB-XXY	Bell 206B Jet Ranger II	4131	D-HHBI
HB-XYA	Bell 206B Jet Ranger II	3067	SE-HUH G-BPZH ZK-HWL
HB-XYB	SNCASE SE.3130 Alouette II	1915	V-63
HB-XYG	Bell 214B-1	28044	LN-OPR C-GLCA N214PH N5015G
HB-XYI	Schweizer 269C	S-1538	N41S
HB-XYL	Schweizer 269C	S-1648	
HB-XYM	Hughes H.369E	0461E	
HB-XYP	McDonnell-Douglas MD.520N	LN-052	N5204P
HB-XYT	Aérospatiale SA.315B Lama	2439	D-HBRA G-BMUB N47276
HB-XYW	Bell 206B Jet Ranger II	4180	
HB-XZE	Robinson R-22HP	0316	N8415L N8327B
HB-XZF	Hughes 269C	39-0772	OY-HCW
HB-XZH	Robinson R-22 Beta	2195	N23412
HB-XZK	Robinson R-22 Beta	2213	N23488
HB-XZN	Robinson R-22 Beta	2332	N81907
HB-XZS	Robinson R-22 Beta	2368	
HB-XZU	Aérospatiale SA.315B Lama	2522	JA9190
HB-XZV	Robinson R-22 Beta	2380	N83094
HB-ZBB	Eurocopter EC.120B Colibri	1067	
HB-ZBC	Agusta A.109E Power	11032	
HB-ZBD	Eurocopter EC.120B Colibri	1009	D-HACO(2)
HB-ZBF	Westland-Bell 47G-3B1	WA/403	D-HISE OE-AXZ D-HLBS OE-AXZ HB-XIF D-HATW XT244
HB-ZBG	Aérospatiale SA.365N1 Dauphin 2	6251	N600GN
HB-ZBJ	Aérospatiale AS.350B3 Ecureuil	3204	
HB-ZBL	Sud Avn SA.316B Alouette III	1101	F-ZLAR
HB-ZBM	McDonnell-Douglas MD.520N	LN-088	N3224X
HB-ZBN	Aérospatiale AS.350B3 Ecureuil	3209	
HB-ZBO	Schweizer 269C	S-1782	N69A
HB-ZBP	Hughes 269C	23-0184	G-BAUK
HB-ZBQ	Hughes 369D	70-0748D	OE-KXW G-BNMY N1091A
HB-ZBS	McDonnell-Douglas MD.520N	LN-089	
HB-ZBU	Agusta-Bell 206B Jet Ranger 3	8649	I-SIMB I-MIST
HB-ZBY	Aérospatiale SA.365N1 Dauphin 2	6307	LX-HGR JA9902
HB-ZBZ	Bell 430	49057	N6389Z C-FOEP
HB-ZCA	Eurocopter EC.120BColibri	1092	F-WQDC
HB-ZCC	Aérospatiale AS.350B2 Ecureuil	2107	I-RECL OE-OXC
HB-ZCB	Aérospatiale AS.350B3 Ecureuil (W/o 7.9.04)	3417	G-CBBJ
HB-ZCG	Eurocopter EC.120B Colibri	1095	F-WQDH
HB-ZCH	Bell 430	49060	N2344T C-GLZS
HB-ZCL	Aérospatiale AS.350B3 Ecureuil	3303	F-WQDD
HB-ZCM	Aérospatiale AS.350B3 Ecureuil	3306	F-WQDF
HB-ZCN	Schweizer 269D	0033A	N86G
HB-ZCO	Schweizer 269C	S-1866	
HB-ZCP	Agusta A.109E Power	11075	
HB-ZCQ	Agusta A.109E Power	11093	
HB-ZCS	Aérospatiale AS.350B3 Ecureuil (W/o 22.12.03)	3265	F-WQDH
HB-ZCU	Robinson R-44 Astro	0986	

HB-ZCW	McDonnell-Douglas MD-900 Explorer	900-00019	N1884B N9021H
HB-ZCX	Aérospatiale AS.350B3 Ecureuil	3105	I-AOLA
HB-ZCY	Aérospatiale AS.350B3 Ecureuil	3399	
HB-ZCZ	Aérospatiale AS.350B3 Ecureuil	3434	
HB-ZDA	Aérospatiale AS.350B3 Ecureuil	3421	
HB-ZDB	Robinson R-22B2 Beta	3068	
HB-ZDC	Agusta A.109C	7635	OO-VXB HB-XXB
HB-ZDD	Aérospatiale AS.350B3 Ecureuil	3414	
HB-ZDE	Aérospatiale AS.350B3 Ecureuil (Damaged 18.1.04)	3442	
HB-ZDF	McDonnell-Douglas MD-900 Explorer	900-00114	N904AA N7014U
HB-ZDG	Aérospatiale SA.315B Lama (Damaged 10.7.03)	2505	(F-GTBE) D-HFWZ (D-HAWZ) (F-GHCF)
HB-ZDH	Robinson R-44 Raven	0989	N7197B
HB-ZDI	Robinson R-22B2 Beta	2337	D-HOLM
HB-ZDK	Robinson R-44 Raven	1106	
HB-ZDM	Agusta A.109E Power	11132	
HB-ZDN	Aérospatiale AS.350B1 Ecureuil	1707	D-HEND F-OJJJ F-WQDO F-GIZC F-WYMZ CS-HBP JA9355
HB-ZDO	McDonnell-Douglas MD-900 Explorer	900-00077	N70547
HB-ZDR	Aérospatiale SA.365N3 Dauphin 2	6584	F-WQDM
HB-ZDS	Eurocopter EC.120B Colibri	1248	
HB-ZDT	Agusta A.109E Power	11129	
HB-ZDV	Aérospatiale AS.350B3 Ecureuil	3531	
HB-ZDW	Robinson R-44 Raven	1147	
HB-ZDX	Aérospatiale AS.350B3 Ecureuil	3553	
HB-ZDY	Aérospatiale AS.350B3 Ecureuil	3570	
HB-ZEA	Aérospatiale AS.350B3 Ecureuil	3475	
HB-ZEB	Bell 206B Jet Ranger II	2959	I-FLOP I-MIBI (F-GOOD) I-MIBI N333WM N5763P
HB-ZEC	Aérospatiale AS.350B3 Ecureuil	3537	F-WQDL
HB-ZED	Aérospatiale AS.350B3 Ecureuil	3548	
HB-ZEF	Eurocopter EC.135T2	0259	D-HECA
HB-ZEG	Robinson R-22B2 Beta	3325	N70734
HB-ZEH	Kaman K-1200 K-Max	A94-0014	N164KA
HB-ZEI	Aérospatiale AS.350B3 Ecureuil	3610	
HB-ZEJ	Aérospatiale AS.350B3 Ecureuil	3543	F-WQDP F-GNLD F-WQDH
HB-ZEK	Aérospatiale AS.350B3 Ecureuil	3674	
HB-ZEL	Aérospatiale AS.350B3 Ecureuil	3673	
HB-ZEM	Robinson R-22B2 Beta	3389	
HB-ZEN	Eurocopter EC.135T2	0257	D-HECH
HB-ZEO	Agusta A.109E Power	11164	
HB-ZEP	Eurocopter EC.120B Colibri	1336	F-WWPO F-WQDE
HB-ZEQ	Sud Avn SA.316B Alouette III	1152	F-GOZR ALAT
HB-ZER	Eurocopter EC.120B Colibri (Damaged 13.8.03)	1346	F-WQDV
HB-ZES	Aérospatiale AS.350B3 Ecureuil	3657	F-WQDA
HB-ZET	Aérospatiale AS.350B3 Ecureuil	3715	
HB-ZEU	Aérospatiale SA.341G Gazelle	1111	D-HAAF
HB-ZEV	Robinson R-22B2 Beta	3405	
HB-ZEW	Eurocopter EC.130B4 Ecureuil	3659	F-WQDL
HB-ZEY	Eurocopter EC.130B4 Ecureuil	3541	F-GOGS F-WQDQ
HB-ZEZ	Eurocopter EC.120B Colibri	1338	
HB-ZFA	Aérospatiale AS.350B Ecureuil	1594	G-BYYH SE-JDU LN-OTO
HB-ZFB	Eurocopter EC.130B4 Ecureuil	3536	F-GNLD
HB-ZFC	Agusta A.109E Power	11165	
HB-ZFD	Aérospatiale SA.342J Gazelle	1058	F-GKRF C-FEMF
HB-ZFE	Aérospatiale AS.350B3 Ecureuil	3671	
HB-ZFF	Aérospatiale AS.350B3 Ecureuil	3600	SE-JHC
HB-ZFH	Enstrom 280C Shark	1145	N51741 C-FCJU N4426W N613LG C-GCNR
HB-ZFI	Aérospatiale AS.350B3 Ecureuil	3698	F-GSDC
HB-ZFJ	Sud Avn SA.316B Alouette III	1408	V-221
HB-ZFK	Agusta A.109C	7639	N1EQ N5QS OE-XRC
HB-ZFL	Enstrom 280FX Shark	2075	D-HFBR
HB-ZFM	Eurocopter EC.120B Colibri	1363	
HB-ZFN	Robinson R-44 Raven II	10178	
HB-ZFO	Robinson R-44 Raven II	10216	

HB-ZFP	Bell 430	49063	N430D N802DM
HB-ZFQ	Robinson R-44 Raven II	10241	
HB-ZFR	Eurocopter EC.120B Colibri	1378	
HB-ZFS	Enstrom 280FX Shark	2059	G-MEYO SX-HCN
HB-ZFT	Robinson R-22B2 Beta	3597	
HB-ZFU	Aérospatiale SA.315B Lama	2237	I-GELP TG-H-FEM-CP (TG-H-JOO-CP
HB-ZFV	Aérospatiale AS.350B3 Ecureuil	3850	SE-JLO
HB-ZFW	Robinson R-44 Raven II	10396	N73858
HB-ZFX	Kamov Ka-32A-12	8809/09	RA-31599
HB-ZFY	Eurocopter EC.120B Colibri	1396	F-WQDK
HB-ZFZ	Aérospatiale AS.350B2 Ecureuil	2158	OE-OXA F-WIPI OE-OXA F-WYMD
HB-ZGB	Bell 206L-3 Long Ranger III	51260	D-HEPY (2) C-FDFM
HB-ZGC	Agusta A.139	31010	
HB-ZGD	Agusta A.139	31014	
HB-ZGE	Agusta A.139	31015	
HB-ZGG	Robinson R-44 Raven II	10587	
HB-ZGH	Robinson R-22B2 Beta	3722	
HB-ZGI	Aérospatiale AS.350B3 Ecureuil	3832	
HB-ZGK	Kaman K-1200 K-Max	A94-0026	D-HFZA(2) N3289T
HB-ZGL	Robinson R-44 Raven II	10641	
HB-ZGN	Eurocopter EC.120B Colibri	1206	VP-BGL F-WQDN
HB-ZGZ	Robinson R-44 Raven (Reservation .05)	unkn	
HB-ZRA	MBB-Kawasaki BK.117C-2	9026	
HB-ZRB	MBB-Kawasaki BK.117C-2	9028	
HB-ZRC	MBB-Kawasaki BK.117C-2	9032	
HB-ZRD	MBB-Kawasaki BK.117C-2	9033	
HB-ZRE	MBB-Kawasaki BK.117C-2	9041	
HB-Z . .	Aérospatiale AS.350B1 Ecureuil	2174	G-MSDJ G-BPOH
HB-Z . .	Schweizer 269C	S-1873	N106JT

EXPERIMENTAL AND HOMEBUILT AIRCRAFT

HB-XVC	Brügger MB.1 Kolibri	1	
HB-YAH	Luton LA.5 Major	1	
HB-YAL	Brügger MB.2 Kolibri	43	
HB-YAN	Aero 101 (Rebuilt)	011	F-PGYO
HB-YAS	Jodel D.9 Bébé	570	
HB-YAU	Bede BD-5B	281	
HB-YAV	Brügger MB.2 Kolibri	41	
HB-YAW	Tipsy T.66 Nipper Mk.2	69	OO-WOT PH-MEV
HB-YBA	Evans VP-1 Volksplane	V-1622	
HB-YBC	Brügger MB.2 Kolibri	27	
HB-YBD	Monnet Sonerai 1	290	
HB-YBG	Rutan VariEze	1236	
HB-YBI	Prometheus PV	001	
HB-YBK	Mignet HM.380	31	
HB-YBL	Rutan VariEze	511	
HB-YBO	Rutan VariEze	1513	
HB-YBP	Rotorway Exec 90	5222	
HB-YBS	Rutan VariEze	1924	
HB-YBV	Rutan VariEze	2145	
HB-YBW	Rutan Long-Ez	353	
HB-YBX	Brändli BX-2 Cherry	001	
HB-YBY	Rutan Long-Ez	1137	
HB-YCA	Neukom AN-20B	03	
HB-YCC	Quickie Quickie	475	
HB-YCE	Rutan VariEze	2174	
HB-YCF	Rutan VariEze	2178	
HB-YCG	Rutan Long-Ez	1293	
HB-YCH	Neukom AN-20B	20-09	
HB-YCI	Rutan Long-Ez	1701	
HB-YCK	Vetro GB-3 Twin Baby	01	
HB-YCM	Rutan VariEze	2202V	
HB-YCO	Vetro	03	
HB-YCP	Neukom AN-22	001	
HB-YCU	Zenair Tri-Z	3-440	
HB-YCW	Colomban MC-15 Cri-Cri	12-0016	
HB-YCY	Brändli BX-2 Cherry	01-A	
HB-YDB	Rutan Long-Ez	1665	
HB-YDD	Rutan VariEze	2210-V	
HB-YDE	Rutan VariEze (C/n also quoted for F-PYHR)	1991	
HB-YDF	Rutan VariEze	2187	
HB-YDH	Brändli BX-2 Cherry	142	
HB-YDL	Rutan VariEze	2115	
HB-YDN	Brügger MB-2 Colibri D	225-001	
HB-YDR	AFM	01	
HB-YDS	Brändli BX-2 Cherry	3	
HB-YDT	Marco J-5	03	
HB-YDU	Brändli BX-2 Cherry	031	
HB-YDW	Brändli BX-2 Cherry	038	
HB-YDX	Brändli BX-2 Cherry	057	
HB-YDY	Brändli BX-2 Cherry	049	
HB-YEA	Stoddard-Hamilton Glasair RG	750	
HB-YEB	Neico Lancair 235	150	
HB-YEC	Colomban MC-15 Cri-Cri	134	
HB-YEE	Light Aero Avid Flyer	269	
HB-YEF	Rutan VariEze	6801D	
HB-YEG	Viking Dragonfly II	748	
HB-YEI	Mignet HM-8 Avionette	FS-01	
HB-YEK	Pottier P.180	73	
HB-YEL	WAR FW-190	289	
HB-YEM	Light Aero Avid Hauler	482	
HB-YEN	Rotorway Executive	2951	
HB-YEQ	Light Aero Avid Hauler	483	
HB-YER	Denney Kitfox II	408	
HB-YEV	Brügger MB-2 Kolibri	160	
HB-YEW	Mad Whisky	SR01	
HB-YEY	Brändli BX-2 Cherry	27	
HB-YEZ	Light Aero Avid Hauler	962	
HB-YFB	Denney Kitfox III	890	
HB-YFC	Light Aero Avid Hauler	833	
HB-YFD	TEAM Mini-MAX	352	
HB-YFE	Denney Kitfox III	971	
HB-YFF	Evans VP-1 Volksplane	V-2304	
HB-YFG	Rotorway Executive 90	5134	
HB-YFH	Denney Kitfox III	1194	
HB-YFI	Denney Kitfox IV	1193	
HB-YFK	Stoddard-Hamilton Glasair IIRG	1116	
HB-YFL	Rotorway Executive 90	28609	
HB-YFM	Air Command 532 Elite	001	
HB-YFN	Denney Kitfox III	1078	
HB-YFO	Light Aero Avid Hauler	963	
HB-YFP	Light Aero Avid Hauler	1104	
HB-YFQ	Light Aero Avid Hauler	566	
HB-YFR	Neico Lancair 320	503	
HB-YFS	Denney Kitfox IV	1856	
HB-YFT	Light Aero Avid Flyer Mk.IV	925	
HB-YFU	Denney Kitfox III	1167	
HB-YFV	Neico Lancair 320	366	
HB-YFW	Rotorway Executive 90	5156	
HB-YFX	Denney Kitfox IV	1881	
HB-YFY	Rutan Long-Ez	1279	
HB-YFZ	Denney Kitfox IV-1200	1903	
HB-YGA	Denney Kitfox IV	1581	
HB-YGC	Ultravia Pelican GS	377	
HB-YGE	Kitfox IV	ICU-97	
HB-YGF	Light Aero Avid Flyer Mk IV	778	
HB-YGG	Brändli BX-2 Cherry	112	
HB-YGH	Rotorway Executive 90	8-01	
HB-YGJ	Neico Lancair 235	227	
HB-YGK	Rotorway Executive 90	5121	
HB-YGL	Stoddard-Hamilton Glasair II-FT	1096	
HB-YGM	Denney Kitfox IV-1200 Speedster	C950 40107	
HB-YGQ	Dallach Sunrise II	00	
HB-YGR	Rotorway Executive 90	5240	
HB-YGS	Brändli BX-3	001	
HB-YGT	Denney Kitfox IV-1200	1893	
HB-YGU	Rotorway Executive 90	5201	
HB-YGV	Light Aero Avid Flyer Mk.IV	1319D	
HB-YGW	Denney Kitfox IV	S9411-0061	
HB-YGX	Denney Kitfox IV-1200 Speedster	KCS140	
HB-YHA	Mühlemann M-1	1	
HB-YHB	Velocity 173RG Elite	DMO 078	
HB-YHD	Light Aero Avid Flyer Mk IV	1240	
HB-YHH	WAR Focke Wulf FW-190	288	
HB-YHK	Light Aero Avid Hauler	534	
HB-YHL	Aero Designs Pulsar XP	363	
HB-YHM	Aero Designs Pulsar XP	346	
HB-YHP	Elisport CH-7 Angel	82	
HB-YHQ	Neico Lancair 320	870-320-691	
HB-YHR	Brändli BX-2 Cherry	150	
HB-YHS	Rotorway Executive 90	5237	
HB-YHT	Brändli BX-2 Cherry	84	
HB-YHU	Skystar Aero Designs Pulsar XP	331	
HB-YHV	Velocity 173FG	92	
HB-YHW	Aero Designs Pulsar XP	287	
HB-YHX	Stoddard-Hamilton Glasair IIRG	1100	
HB-YHZ	Light Aero Avid Flyer	1499D	
HB-YIA	Europa Aviation Europa (Reservation)	024	
HB-YIB	Europa Aviation Europa	268	
HB-YIE	Europa Aviation Europa	169	
HB-YIG	Dyn'Aero MCR-01	127	
HB-YIH	Light Aero Avid Magnum	M008	
HB-YIJ	Rotorway Exec 162F	6068	
HB-YIK	Light Aero Avid Hauler NG	964	
HB-YIL	Esprit VF-II	001	
HB-YIN	Aero Designs Pulsar XP	369	
HB-YIQ	Brditschka HB-207 Alfa	207009	
HB-YIR	Denney Kitfox Vixen	V94090017	
HB-YIS	Neico Lancair 360 Mk.II	873-320-670	
HB-YIT	Denney Kitfox V	S95010094	
HB-YIZ	Jurca MJ-10 Spitfire	MJ10-HAUG	
HB-YJA	Stoddard-Hamilton Glasair IIRG	3282	
HB-YJD	Denney Kitfox IV-1200	C94090060	
HB-YJE	Brditschka HB-207 Alfa	207016	
HB-YJF	Europa Aviation Europa (Reservation)	294	
HB-YJG	Dyn'Aero MCR-01	67	
HB-YJJ	Zenair CH-601 Zodiac	6-2216	
HB-YJK	Brinkert Mini-500 (W/o 3.11.01)	480	

HB-YJM	One Design MSW	95-0278	
HB-YJO	Stoddard-Hamilton Glastar GS-1	5561	
HB-YJP	Denney Kitfox IV-1200 Speedster	JCS136	
HB-YJQ	Dyn'Aero MCR-01	118	
HB-YJS	Brinkert Mini-500	260	
HB-YJT	Kitfox IV-1200 Speedster	GSC121	
HB-YJU	Aero Designs Pulsar XP	362	
HB-YJV	Denney Kitfox IV-1200	C96050163	
HB-YJW	Aero Designs Pulsar XP	395	
HB-YJY	Votex 322	001	
HB-YJZ	Elisport CH-7 Angel	CH70000K-41	
HB-YKA	Van's RV-4	2626	
HB-YKC	Zenair CH-701 STOL	7-3661	
HB-YKD	Van's RV-6	23949	
HB-YKE	Pottier P.180S	173	
HB-YKH	Dyn'Aero MCR-01	075	
HB-YKI	Europa Aviation Europa (Reservation)	097	
HB-YKK	Van's RV-4	2/13 EXP	
HB-YKL	Dyn'Aero MCR-01	185	
HB-YKM	Zenair CH-601HDS Zodiac	6-2235	
HB-YKN	Stoddard-Hamilton Glasair Super IISRG	2377	
HB-YKP	Glastar GS-1	5794	
HB-YKQ	Slepcev Storch	74	
HB-YKR	Elisport CH-7 Angel	68	
HB-YKS	Aceair A-200 Aeriks	001	
HB-YKV	Zenair Zodiac 601HDS	6-2209	
HB-YKW	Elisport CH-7 Kompress	080	
HB-YKY	Dyn'Aero MCR-01	50	
HB-YLA	Votec 322	02-003	
HB-YLB	Votec 322	02-004	
HB-YLC	Votec 322	02-005	
HB-YLE	Dyn'Aero MCR-01	209	
HB-YLF	Elisport CH-7	70	
HB-YLG	Potier P.180S	120	
HB-YLI	Stoddard-Hamilton Glasair III	3281	
HB-YLL	Van's RV-6	25685	
HB-YLP	Aerostyle Breezer	003	
HB-YLQ	TEAM Mini-MAX R1500	1010	
HB-Y . .	Europa Aviation Europa	PFA/247-13502	G-BYPK

BALLOONS AND AIRSHIPS

HB-BAJ	Cameron N-90 HAFB	3348	
HB-BAQ	Cameron N-133 HAFB	3359	
HB-BAS	Raven S-55A HAFB	626	
HB-BAX	Colt 77A HAFB	045	
HB-BBA	Stuttgart K-945/2-STU Gas Balloon	0283	
HB-BBE(4)	Colt 105A HAFB	1193	
	(Formerly c/ns 054,322,and 714)		
HB-BBF	Stuttgart K-1000/3-STU Gas Balloon	0284	
HB-BBG	Augsburg K-1260/3-RI Gas Balloon	10512	
HB-BBQ	Ultramagic M-130 HAFB	130/05	
HB-BBV	Cameron V-77 HAFB	649	
HB-BBW	Raven RX-7 HAFB	238	
HB-BCG	Raven S-55A HAFB	732	
HB-BCJ	Cameron N-160 HAFB	3341	
HB-BCV(2)	Thunder AX7-77Z HAFB	1301	
	(Formerly c/n 409)		
HB-BCY	Cameron O-84 HAFB	838	
HB-BDA	Cameron O-84 HAFB	883	
HB-BDD	Cameron O-84 HAFB	1068	
HB-BDJ	Cameron A-140 HAFB	3329	
HB-BDK	Colt 21A HAFB	1031	
HB-BDV	Thunder Colt AX8-105Z HAFB	425	
HB-BEA	Stuttgart K-780/2-STU Gas Balloon	0235	
HB-BEJ	Cameron N-133 HAFB	3338	
HB-BEQ(3)	Colt 210A HAFB (Reservation .01)	10061	
	(Formerly used envelopes c/ns 2635 and 4208)		
HB-BFA	Cameron N-90 HAFB	1019	
HB-BFB(3)	Cameron N-90 HAFB	3407	
	(Formerly c/ns 1016 and 2170)		
HB-BFE	Cameron N-105 HAFB	902	
HB-BFJ	Cameron O-120 HAFB	3364	
HB-BFQ	Raven-Europe S-66A HAFB	E-383	
HB-BFR	Cameron O-84 HAFB	1087	
HB-BFU(2)	Cameron N-90 HAFB	3060	
	(Formerly c/n 1083)		
HB-BFX	Colt 90A HAFB	622	
HB-BFY	Cameron N-90 HAFB	1102	
HB-BGH	Balloon Works Firefly F7B HAFB	F7B-052	G-BKOO N3609T
HB-BGN	Augsburg K-1050/3-RI Gas Balloon	43041	
HB-BGQ	Raven Europe RX-9 HAFB	E-371	
HB-BGU	Bronschhofen 1050 Gas Balloon	8403	
HB-BGV	Augsburg K-1680/4-RI Gas Balloon	10415	
HB-BGY	Aerostar S-55A HAFB	3001	
HB-BHL	Colt 90A HAFB	848	
HB-BHO	Cameron N-105 HAFB	1292	
HB-BHQ	Raven-Europe S-66A HAFB	E-395	
HB-BHR	Cameron O-84 HAFB	1989	
HB-BHS	Raven-Europe MFM FRX-65 HAFB	E-034	
HB-BJB	Bronschhofen 1050 Gas Balloon	8404	
HB-BJE	Cameron N-105 HAFB	1391	
HB-BJI	Cameron O-84 HAFB	1417	
HB-BJO	Bronschhofen 1050 Gas Balloon	8406	
HB-BJQ	Colt 21A HAFB	1030	
HB-BJS	Bronschhofen 1050 Gas Balloon	8405	
HB-BJX	Raven-Europe MFM FS-57A HAFB	E-107	
HB-BJZ(2)	Raven-Europe S-66A HAFB	E-294	
	(Formerly c/n E-069)		
HB-BKD	Cameron N-105 HAFB	1521	
HB-BKH	Cameron N-105 HAFB	1532	
HB-BKJ	Schröder Fire Balloons 26/24 HAFB	282	
HB-BKK	Cameron N-105 HAFB	1587	
HB-BKL	Cameron O-105 HAFB	1581	
HB-BKS	Bronschhofen 1350 Gas Balloon	88-401	
HB-BKV	Cameron A-105 HAFB	1637	
HB-BKW	Schröder Fire Balloons G HAFB	372	D-OGUY
HB-BLB	Bronschhofen 1050 Gas Balloon	8408	
HB-BLE	Colt 21A Cloudhopper HAFB	1110	
HB-BLF	Cameron N-145 HAFB	1684	
HB-BLJ	Cameron N-145 HAFB	1695	
HB-BLM	Raven-Europe S-60A HAFB	E-095	
HB-BLP	Cameron A-105 HAFB	1696	
HB-BLT(2)	Raven-Europe S-66A HAFB	E-265	
HB-BLU	Cameron N-105 HAFB	1743	
HB-BLY	Colt 120A HAFB	1276	
HB-BMA	Cameron V-42 HAFB	1788	
HB-BMB	Aerostar S-66A HAFB	3028	
HB-BMC	Chaize CS.3000F16 HAFB	90	
HB-BMD	Schröder Fire Balloons 26/24 HAFB	38	
HB-BME	Cameron A-250 HAFB	1697	
HB-BMG	Lindstrand LBL-240A HAFB	192	
HB-BML	Cameron N-105 HAFB	1850	
HB-BMN	Cameron SS HAFB	1797	
HB-BMR	Raven-Europe S-60A HAFB	E-116	
HB-BNB	Schröder Fire Balloons 45/24 HAFB	76	
HB-BNE	Schröder Fire Balloons 30/24 HAFB	81	
HB-BNK	Cameron N-105 HAFB	2053	
HB-BNL(2)	Cameron A-375 HAFB	4620	
	(New envelope replacing c/n 2132)		
HB-BNO	Cameron N-105 HAFB	2143	
HB-BNQ	Cameron A-300 HAFB	2156	
HB-BNR	Colt 105A HAFB	1613	
HB-BNU	Thunder AX8-105 HAFB	1640	
HB-BNY	Raven-Europe S-60A HAFB	E-155	
HB-BOD	Stuttgart K-630/1-STU Gas Balloon	0129	
HB-BOF	Stuttgart K-945/2-STU Gas Balloon	0201	
HB-BOJ	Thunder AX8-90 SI HAFB	2678/3512	
HB-BOS	Stuttgart K-945/2-STU Gas Balloon	0220	
HB-BPA	Colt 90A HAFB	1442	
HB-BPD	Cameron V-77 HAFB	1926	
HB-BPG	Thunder AX8-105 HAFB	1432	
HB-BPH	Cameron N-105 HAFB	1923	
HB-BPK	Colt 120A HAFB	3446	
HB-BPO	Cameron N-105 HAFB	2244	
HB-BPS(2)	Raven-Europe S-66A HAFB	E-171	
	(Formerly c/n E-134)		
HB-BPT	Schröder Fire Balloons 40/24 HAFB	461	
HB-BPU	Ultramagic S-130 HAFB	130/01	
HB-BPW	Cameron O-90 HAFB	1997	
HB-BPY	Raven-Europe FS-57A HAFB	E-154	
HB-BQA	Cameron A-105 HAFB	2306	
HB-BQC	Cameron N-56 HAFB	2205	
HB-BQF	Thunder AX8-105 HAFB	1653	
HB-BQH	Colt 105A HAFB	1661	
HB-BQK	Colt 120A HAFB	1681	
HB-BQM	Thunder AX10-180 HAFB	1660	
HB-BQO	Balloon Works Firefly 8 HAFB	F8-360	
HB-BQP	Schröder Fire Balloons 36/24 HAFB	123	
HB-BQW	Colt 105A HAFB	1756	
HB-BQX	Cameron N-105 HAFB	2305	
HB-BQY	Stuttgart K-1000/3-STU Gas Balloon	0327	
HB-BRC	Cameron N-120 HAFB	2272	
HB-BRE	Aerostar S-66A HAFB	3057	
HB-BRF	Stuttgart K-1260/3-STU Gas Balloon	1025	
HB-BRI	Raven-Europe S-60A HAFB	E-205	
HB-BRJ	Thunder AX9-140 SII HAFB	3616	
HB-BRK	Raven-Europe RX-8 HAFB	E-190	
HB-BRN	Cameron V-77 HAFB	5222	N29919
HB-BRO	Aerostar S-77A HAFB	3014	
HB-BRU	Cameron A-105 HAFB	2329	
HB-BRV	Schröder Fire Balloons 36/24 HAFB	136	
HB-BRZ	Cameron N-120 HAFB	2385	
HB-BSF	Cameron V-56 HAFB	2396	
HB-BSH	Thunder AX8-90 HAFB	1988	
HB-BSI	Colt 105A HAFB	10282	
	(New envelope replacing c/n 1852)		
HB-BSL	Stuttgart K-1000/3-STU Gas Balloon	1026	
HB-BSM	Colt 105A HAFB	1844	
HB-BST	Cameron O-90 HAFB	3069	
HB-BSU	Thunder AX8-105 HAFB	1842	
HB-BSY	Raven-Europe FS-57A HAFB	E-221	
HB-BSZ	Aerostar S-49A HAFB	3035	
HB-BTD	Cameron A-140 HAFB	2485	
HB-BTE	Stuttgart K-1000/3-STU Gas Balloon	1027	
HB-BTF	Cameron N-90 HAFB	2517	
HB-BTH	Balloon Works Firefly F7-15 HAFB	F7-736	
HB-BTL(2)	Thunder AX8-90 SI HAFB	4663	
	(New envelope replacing c/n 1926)		
HB-BTM	Cameron N-77 HAFB	2523	

HB-BTN(2)	Colt 120A HAFB (Replaces envelope c/n 1918)	4497	
HB-BTO(2)	Ultramagic M-105 HAFB (Formerly c/n 105/11)	105/22	
HB-BTP	Raven-Europe S-60A HAFB	E-234	
HB-BTS	Schröder Fire Balloons 36/24 HAFB	182	
HB-BTX	Ultramagic V-105 HAFB	105/16	
HB-BTZ	Aerostar S-49A HAFB	3065	
HB-BUA	Aerostar S-49A HAFB	3066	
HB-BUB	Schröder Fire Balloons 30/24 HAFB	199	
HB-BUC	Aerostar S-49A HAFB	3080	
HB-BUD	Colt 160A HAFB	1973	
HB-BUF	Colt 120A HAFB	2013	
HB-BUG	Colt 31A HAFB	2020	
HB-BUH	Cameron O-90 HAFB	2604	
HB-BUI	Cameron N-105 HAFB	2605	
HB-BUK	Raven-Europe S-49A HAFB	E-251	
HB-BUL	Raven-Europe S-60A HAFB	E-250	
HB-BUN	Thunder AX7-65 HAFB	2035	
HB-BUO	Colt 105A HAFB	2061	
HB-BUP	Cameron N-145 HAFB	2684	
HB-BUQ	Cameron N-145 HAFB	2706	
HB-BUW	Ultramagic N-180 HAFB	180/13	
HB-BUX(3)	Cameron A-180 HAFB (New envelope replacing c/ns 2682and 3694)	10165	
HB-BUZ	Raven-Europe FS-57A HAFB	E-255	
HB-BVA	Raven-Europe S-60A HAFB	E-254	
HB-BVB	Aerostar S-49A HAFB	3142	
HB-BVC	Balloon Works Firefly 8 HAFB	F8-380	
HB-BVE	Cameron O-120 HAFB	2732	
HB-BVI	Colt AS.105 Mk II Hot Air Airship	2069	G-BUAD
HB-BVK	Cameron A-105 HAFB	2740	
HB-BVL	Balloon Works Firefly 8 HAFB	F8-384	
HB-BVM	Bronschhofen 780 Gas Balloon	88-202	
HB-BVO	Schröder Fire Balloons 24/24 HAFB	254	
HB-BVP	Cameron N-105 HAFB	2752	
HB-BVS	Aerostar S-71A HAFB	3009	
HB-BVT	Raven-Europe RX-8 HAFB	E-267	
HB-BVU	Raven-Europe S-66A HAFB	E-271	
HB-BVV	Thunder AX9-140 SII HAFB	2124	
HB-BVW	Raven-Europe RX-8 HAFB	E-291	
HB-BVY	Cameron Battery SS HAFB	2762	
HB-BWA	Cameron DP-90 Hot Air Airship	2771	
HB-BWC	Cameron O-105 HAFB	2788	
HB-BWD	Ultramagic S-130 HAFB	130/06	
HB-BWF	Schröder Fire Balloons 36/24 HAFB	245	
HB-BWG	Schröder Fire Balloons 22/24 HAFB	276	
HB-BWH	Cameron V-90 HAFB	2811	
HB-BWK	Cameron N-105 HAFB	2792	
HB-BWP	Schröder Fire Balloons "Kater" SS HAFB	311	
HB-BWT	Colt 90A HAFB	2217	
HB-BWU	Balloon Works Firefly 8 HAFB	F8-390	
HB-BXA	Raven-Europe S-60A HAFB	E-303	
HB-BXC	Raven-Europe FS-57A HAFB	E-257	F-GLCE
HB-BXK	Cameron N-120 HAFB	2941	
HB-BXL	Cameron SS HAFB	2947	
HB-BXN	Cameron O-77 HAFB	2950	
HB-BXO	Chaize JZ30 F16 HAFB	117	
HB-BXP	Thunder AX9-140 SII HAFB	2304	
HB-BXR	Colt 77A HAFB	2040	
HB-BXV	Colt 120A HAFB	2303	
HB-BXX	Schröder Fire Balloons "Vase" SS HAFB	462	D-OBXX
HB-BYB	Cameron N-160 HAFB	2990	
HB-BYE	Cameron N-105 HAFB	3011	
HB-BYF	Schröder Fire Balloons G HAFB	428	
HB-BYH	Cameron N-77 HAFB	3007	
HB-BYI	Cameron A-160 HAFB	3041	
HB-BYJ	Cameron N-90 HAFB	3042	
HB-BYK	Thunder AX8-105 SII HAFB	2373	
HB-BYL	Raven Europe RXS-8 HAFB	E-333	F-WKJI
HB-BYM	Raven Europe RXS-8 HAFB	E-331	
HB-BYN	Raven Europe S-66A HAFB	E-332	
HB-BYO	Colt 77A HAFB	1912	
HB-BYQ	Cameron O-120 HAFB	3074	
HB-BYR	Thunder AX8-105 HAFB	2435	
HB-BYS	Schröder Fire Balloons 36/24 HAFB	343	
HB-BYT	Cameron N-160 HAFB	3101	
HB-BYU	Thunder AX8-9O SII HAFB	2438	
HB-BYW(2)	Cameron N-120 HAFB (New envelope replacing c/n 3119)	4678	
HB-BYX	Balloon Works Firefly F-11 HAFB	F11-001	N2594U
HB-BYY	Raven Europe S-66A HAFB	E-330	
HB-BYZ	Cameron N-120 HAFB	3165	
HB-BZE	Cameron N-105 HAFB	3183	
HB-BZG(2)	Cameron A-300 HAFB (New envelope replacing c/n 3259)	4669	
HB-BZH	Bronschhofen 1050 Gas Balloon	8411	
HB-BZI	Bronschhofen 780 Gas Balloon	88-203	
HB-BZJ	Schröder Fire Balloons G HAFB	423	
HB-BZK	Cameron N-120 HAFB	3327	
HB-BZL	Thunder AX9-120SII HAFB	2593	
HB-BZM	Colt 105A HAFB	2602	
HB-BZO	Schröder Fire Balloons G HAFB	431	
HB-BZP	Cameron O-120 HAFB	3309	
HB-BZQ	Raven Europe RX-8 HAFB	E-364	
HB-BZR	Raven Europe S-49A HAFB	E-365	
HB-BZU	Raven Europe RX-9 HAFB	E-373	

HB-BZW	Thunder AX8-105 SI HAFB	2410	D-OMAA
HB-BZX	Cameron N-145 HAFB	3310	
HB-BZY	Balloon Works Firefly 11 HAFB	F11-003	
HB-BZZ	Raven Europe S-60A HAFB	E-356	
HB-QAA	Lindstrand LBL-105A HAFB	163	
HB-QAB	Lindstrand LBL-105A HAFB	159	
HB-QAC	Lindstrand LBL-105A HAFB	160	
HB-QAD	Lindstrand LBL-105A HAFB	161	
HB-QAE	Lindstrand LBL-105A HAFB	162	
HB-QAF	Lindstrand LBL-105A HAFB	139	
HB-QAG	Lindstrand LBL-310A HAFB	355	
HB-QAH	Lindstrand LBL-120A HAFB	373	
HB-QAL	Cameron A-375 HAFB	3440	
HB-QAM(2)	Cameron A-250 HAFB (New envelope replacing c/n 3476)	4690	
HB-QAN	Cameron N-120 HAFB	3474	
HB-QAO	Cameron SS HAFB	3642	
HB-QAQ	Cameron N-120 HAFB	3562	
HB-QAS	Thunder AX9-120 SII HAFB	3597	
HB-QAT	Wörner NL-640/STU Gas Balloon	1047	
HB-QAU	Ultramagic M-130 HAFB	130/10	
HB-QAV	Ultramagic M-130 HAFB	130/07	
HB-QAW	Ultramagic M-145 HAFB	145/03	
HB-QAX	Thunder AX8-105 SI HAFB	3578	
HB-QAY	Cameron N-120 HAFB	3593	
HB-QAZ	Schröder Fire Balloons 40/24 HAFB	481	
HB-QBA	Raven-Europe S-66A HAFB	E-315	
HB-QBB	Balloon Works Firefly 10 HAFB	F10-017	
HB-QBD	Colt 160A HAFB	3577	
HB-QBF	Colt AS-105 Mk.2 Hot Air Airship	3570	
HB-QBG	Schröder Fire Balloons G HAFB	504	
HB-QBH	Lindstrand LBL-150A HAFB	348	
HB-QBI	Lindstrand LBL-120A HAFB	303	
HB-QBJ	Aerostar S-60A HAFB	3209	
HB-QBL	Lindstrand LBL-310A HAFB	330	
HB-QBN	Cameron 105SS HAFB	3680	G-LOKO
HB-QBO	Colt 120A HAFB	3670	
HB-QBP	Cameron A-160 HAFB	3675	
HB-QBQ	Cameron N-56 HAFB	3674	
HB-QBR	Chaize JZ.30F16 HAFB	137	
HB-QBS	Thunder AX9-120 SII HAFB	3718	
HB-QBT	Colt 42A HAFB	3719	
HB-QBU	Colt 31A HAFB	3681	
HB-QBW(2)	Colt AS105 Mk 2 Hot Air Airship (Rebuild of c/n 3665 with new c/n)	10259	
HB-QBY	Cameron N-145 HAFB	3340	
HB-QCA	Cameron A-180SV HAFB	3865	
HB-QCB	Cameron N-120 HAFB	3764	
HB-QCC	Cameron N-120 HAFB	3831	
HB-QCD	Thunder AX8-90 SII HAFB	3752	
HB-QCE	Cameron A-160SV HAFB	3872	
HB-QCF	Cameron N-120 HAFB	3959	
HB-QCH	Cameron N-120 HAFB	3937	
HB-QCI	Colt 120A HAFB	3840	
HB-QCJ	Thunder AX9-120 SIITV HAFB	3845	
HB-QCK	Colt 69A HAFB	2581	G-BVKY
HB-QCN	Colt 105A HAFB	3851	
HB-QCO	Thunder AX8-105A HAFB	1407	OO-BVP
HB-QCP	Cameron O-105 HAFB	3145	F-GOOR
HB-QCQ	Lindstrand LBL-120A HAFB	485	
HB-QCR	Lindstrand LBL-120A HAFB	481	
HB-QCS	Augsburg K-945/2-RI Gas Balloon	8908	
HB-QCV	Colt 180A HAFB	3949	
HB-QCX	Balloon Works Firefly 9B-15 HAFB	F9B-015	
HB-QCZ	Cameron A-160 HAFB	3998	
HB-QDA	Schröder Fire Balloons G 36/24 HAFB	1076	
HB-QDB	Sky 65-24 HAFB	058	
HB-QDD	Ultramagic V-90 HAFB	90/22	
HB-QDE	Balloon Works Firefly 9B-15 HAFB	F9B-018	
HB-QDF	Cameron N-105 HAFB	4074	
HB-QDG	Schröder Fire Balloons G HAFB	584	
HB-QDH	Cameron A-160 HAFB	4091	
HB-QDI	Aerostar S-66A HAFB	3061	
HB-QDJ	Cameron A-120 HAFB	4110	
HB-QDK	Cameron A-300 HAFB	4009	
HB-QDM	Schröder Fire Balloons G HAFB	586	
HB-QDN(2)	Cameron N-90 HAFB (Replacing envelope c/n 4097)	4428	
HB-QDO(2)	Cameron N-160 HAFB (Replacing envelope c/n 4098)	4430	
HB-QDP	Cameron A-120 HAFB	4114	
HB-QDQ	Ultramagic S-130 HAFB	130/12	
HB-QDR	Ultramagic M-90 HAFB	90/23	
HB-QDS	Aerostar RX-9 HAFB	3009	
HB-QDT	Lindstrand LNBL-105A HAFB	147	G-BVTU
HB-QDV	Cameron N-120 HAFB	4209	
HB-QDX	Cameron N-120 HAFB	4219	
HB-QDY	Ultramagic M-65C HAFB (Res. as D-OOHP 2.98)	65/70	
HB-QDZ	Sky 105-24 HAFB	091	
HB-QEA	Lindstrand LBL-150A HAFB	777	
HB-QEB	Colt 120A HAFB	4152	
HB-QEC	Lindstrand LBL-150A HAFB	502	
HB-QED	Lindstrand LBL-120A HAFB	650	
HB-QEE	Lindstrand LBL-180A HAFB	517	
HB-QEF	Lindstrand LBL-120A HAFB	753	
HB-QEG	Lindstrand LBL-150A HAFB	678	
HB-QEH	Schröder Fire Balloons G HAFB	643	

HB-QEI	Cameron O-160 HAFB	4925	
HB-QEJ	Sky 105-24 HAFB	097	
HB-QEL	Sky 105-24 HAFB	093	
HB-QEM	Sky 105-24 HAFB	094	
HB-QEN	Balloon Works Firefly 8 HAFB	F8-425	
HB-QEO	Colt 105A HAFB	4306	
HB-QEP	Cameron N-133 HAFB	4281	
HB-QEQ	Colt 120A HAFB	4283	
HB-QES	Schröder Fire Balloons G HAFB	669	
HB-QET	Cameron Concept C-60 HAFB	3453	G-BWAM
HB-QEU	Cameron O-105 HAFB	4381	
HB-QEV	Schröder Fire Balloons G HAFB	700	
HB-QEW	Cameron A-120 HAFB	4413	
HB-QEX	Schröder Fire Balloons G HAFB	702	
HB-QEY	Colt 120A HAFB	4429	
HB-QEZ	Aerostar RX-9 HAFB	3008	
HB-QFB	Sky 105-24 HAFB	127	
HB-QFC	Aerostar S-66A HAFB	3063	
HB-QFD	Aerostar RX-9 HAFB	3014	
HB-QFE	Schröder Fire Balloons G HAFB	717	
HB-QFF	Cameron A-120 HAFB	4481	
HB-QFG	Thunder AX7-77Z HAFB	795	F-GFAM
HB-QFH	Sky 105-24 HAFB	141	
HB-QFI	Colt 120A HAFB	4515	
HB-QFJ	Cameron V-65 HAFB	4542	
HB-QFK	Cameron N-120 HAFB	4527	
HB-QFL	Cameron Cows' Heads SS HAFB	4517	
HB-QFM	Aerostar RX-9 HAFB	3016	
HB-QFN	Schröder Fire Balloons G HAFB	749	
HB-QFO	Aerostar RX-9 HAFB	3017	
HB-QFP	Thunder AX9-120 SII HAFB	4617	
HB-QFQ	Cameron A-400 HAFB	4621	
HB-QFR	Schröder Fire Balloons G HAFB	778	
HB-QFS	Schröder Fire Balloons G HAFB	785	
HB-QFT	Cameron O-160 HAFB	4685	
HB-QFU	Lindstrand LBL-105A HAFB	556	
HB-QFV	Sky 90-24 HAFB	169	
HB-QFW	Colt 120A HAFB	4827	
HB-QFX	Cameron N-120 HAFB	4697	
HB-QFY	Cameron A-300 HAFB	4446	
HB-QFZ	Cameron A-160 HAFB	4727	
HB-QGA	Schröder Fire Balloons G HAFB	802	
HB-QGB	Cameron A-250 HAFB	4797	
HB-QGC	Sky 105-24 HAFB	180	
HB-QGD	Cameron A-210 HAFB	10089	
HB-QGE	Schröder Fire Balloons G HAFB	820	
HB-QGF	Cameron RX-120 Roziere Replica HAFB	4748	
HB-QGG	Cameron A-160 HAFB	4781	
HB-QGH	Cameron N-120 HAFB	4764	
HB-QGI	Schröder Fire Balloons SFErdbeere HAFB	234	D-OMEN D-OELE(2)
HB-QGJ	Schröder Fire Balloons G HAFB	845	
HB-QGK	Schröder Fire Balloons G 26/24 HAFB	846	
HB-QGL	Cameron Flying Cow SS HAFB	4799	
HB-QGM	Cameron O-84 HAFB	4845	
HB-QGN	Aerostar S-77A HAFB	S77A-3034	
HB-QGO	Schröder Fire Balloons G 34/24 HAFB	127	HB-BQV
HB-QGP	Schröder Fire Balloons G 26/24 HAFB	854	
HB-QGQ	Cameron Orange Cube SS HAFB	4859	
HB-QGR	Cameron Z-160 HAFB	4884	
HB-QGS	Schröder Fire Balloons G 34/24 HAFB	857	
HB-QGT	Colt 120A HAFB	4901	"HB-QSU"
HB-QGV	Cameron A-160 SS HAFB	4903	
HB-QGW	Colt 31A Cloudhopper HAFB	4868	
HB-QGX	Kubicek BB-37 HAFB	141	
HB-QGY	Cameron C-60 Concept HAFB	4907	
HB-QGZ	Aerostar Cell Phone SS HAFB	Cell-3001	
HB-QHA	Kubicek BB-37 HAFB	165	OK-0165
HB-QHB	Ultramagic S-105 HAFB	105/91	
HB-QHC	Colt 105A HAFB	10113	
HB-QHD	Colt 260A HAFB	10120	
HB-QHE	Kubicek BB-37 HAFB	169	OK-0169
HB-QHF	Ultramagic M-145 HAFB	145/31	
HB-QHG	Kubicek BB-45 HAFB	174	OK-0174
HB-QHH	Kubicek BB-45 HAFB	175	OK-0175
HB-QHI	Schröder Fire Balloons G 34/24 HAFB	966	
HB-QHJ	Wörner NL-1000/STU Gas Balloon (W/o 8.8.02)	1075	
HB-QHK	Schröder Fire Balloons G 30/24 HAFB	989	
HB-QHL	Schröder Fire Balloons G 40/24 HAFB	985	
HB-QHM	Ultramagic M-130 HAFB	130/35	
HB-QHN	Schröder Fire Balloons G 36/24 HAFB	977	
HB-QHO	Lindstrand LBL-90B HAFB	836	
HB-QHP	Wörner NL-1000/STU Gas Balloon	1076	
HB-QHQ	Lindstrand LBL-90B HAFB	830	
HB-QHR	Kubicek BB-45 HAFB	181	OK-0181
HB-QHS	Aerostar S-60A HAFB	S60A-3278	
HB-QHT	Colt 150A HAFB	10270	
HB-QHU	Kubicek BB-37 HAFB	186	OK-0186
HB-QHV	Cameron N-120 HAFB	10228	
HB-QHW	Schröder Fire Balloons G 36/24 HAFB	992	
HB-QHX	Kubicek BB-37 HAFB	196	OK-0196
HB-QHY	Kubicek BB-22 HAFB	194	OK-0194
HB-QHZ	Kubicek BB-45 HAFB	197	OK-0197
HB-QIA	Kubicek BB-45 HAFB	201	OK-0201
HB-QIB	Ultramagic M-145 HAFB	145/36	
HB-QIC	Kubicek BB-37 HAFB	210	OK-0210
HB-QID	Colt 105A HAFB	10319	

HB-QIE	Aerostar S-64A HAFB	S64A-3001	
HB-QIG	Kubicek BB-30Z HAFB	215	OK-0215
HB-QIH	Kubicek BB-30Z HAFB	217	OK-0217
HB-QII	Ultramagic N-180 HAFB	180/33	
HB-QIJ	Kubicek BB-26 HAFB	218	OK-0218
HB-QIK	Schröder Fire Balloons G 34/24 HAFB	1026	
HB-QIL	Schröder Fire Balloons G 30/24 HAFB	1019	
HB-QIM	Schröder Fire Balloons G 34/24 HAFB	1031	
HB-QIN	Kubicek BB-45 HAFB	222	OK-0222
HB-QIO	Ultramagic F-24 Flying Man SS	F24/01	
HB-QIP	Gefa-Flug AS.105GD Hot Air Airship	0026	
HB-QIQ	Gefa-Flug AS.105GD Hot Air Airship	0014	D-OGAC
HB-QIR	Kubicek BB-60 HAFB	231	OK-0231
HB-QIS	Cameron Z-160 HAFB	10368	
HB-QIT	Lindstrand LBL-35A HAFB	891	
HB-QIU	Kubicek BB-37 HAFB	239	OK-0239
HB-QIV	Lindstrand LBL-35A HAFB	899	
HB-QIW	UltraMagic N-250 HAFB	250/28	
HB-QIX	Kubicek BB-60 HAFB	327	OK-0327
HB-QIY	Kubicek BB- HAFB	328	OK-0328
HB-QJA	Schröder Fire Balloons G 34/24 HAFB	874	
HB-QJB	Cameron N-133 HAFB	4932	
HB-QJC	Ultramagic M-130 HAFB	130/26	
HB-QJE	Ultramagic S-90 HAFB	90/45	
HB-QJF	Schröder Fire Balloons G 45/24 HAFB	885	
HB-QJG	Cameron N-133 HAFB	4961	
HB-QJH	Colt 240A HAFB	4954	
HB-QJI	Cameron N-160 HAFB	10024	
HB-QJK	Schröder Fire Balloons G 36/24 HAFB	916	
HB-QJL	Schröder Fire Balloons G 40/24 HAFB	936	
HB-QJM	Schröder Fire Balloons G 34/24 HAFB	891	
HB-QJO	Ultramagic M-130 HAFB	130/27	
HB-QJP	Schröder Fire Balloons G 34/24 HAFB	915	
HB-QJQ	Kubicek BB-37 HAFB	159	OK-0159
HB-QJR	Schröder Fire Balloons G 36/24 HAFB	937	
HB-QJS	Kubicek BB-22 HAFB	162	OK-0162
HB-QJT	Kubicek BB-22 HAFB	156	OK-0156
HB-QJU	Colt 120A HAFB	4895	
HB-QJV	Kubicek BB-30 HAFB	149	OK-0149
HB-QJW	Kubicek BB-16 HAFB	157	OK-0157
HB-QJX	Ultramagic N-180 HAFB	180/27	
HB-QJZ	Ultramagic M-77C HAFB	77/195	
HB-QKA	UltraMagic M-90 HAFB	90/59	
HB-QKB	Cameron C-70 Concept HAFB	10400	
HB-QKD	Kubicek BB-37 HAFB	313	OK-0313
HB-QKG	Kubicek BB-20 HAFB	242	OK-0242
HB-QKH	Kubicek BB45 HAFB	243	OK-0243
HB-QKI	Kubicek BB-60 HAFB	245	OK-0245
HB-QKJ	Kubicek BB-22 HAFB	246	OK-0246
HB-QKK	Kubicek BB-60 HAFB	247	OK-0247
HB-QKL	Kunicek BB-45 HAFB	290	OK-0290
HB-QKM	Kubicek BB-37 HAFB	283	OK-0283
HB-QKN	Kubicek BB-37 HAFB	302	OK-0302
HB-QKO	Kubicek BB-60 HAFB	286	OK-0286
HB-QKP	Kubicek BB-45 HAFB	301	OK-0301
HB-QKQ	Cameron Z-275 HAFB	10571	
HB-QKR	Cameron Z-120 HAFB	10573	
HB-QKS	Cameron Z-90 HAFB	10409	
HB-QKT	Colt 120A HAFB	4709	[HB-QFW]
HB-QKU	Schröder Fire Balloons G 40/24 HAFB	1091	
HB-QKV	Ultramagic M-65C HAFB	65/140	
HB-QKX	Ultramagic M-120 HAFB	120/11	
HB-QKY	Schröder Fire Balloons G 42/24 HAFB	1124	
HB-QSA	Kubicek BB-26 HAFB	310	OK-0310
HB-QSC	Kubicek BB-60 HAFB	311	OK-0311
HB-QSG	Kubicek Church SS HAFB	200	OK-0200
HB- . . .	Thunder AX8-90 SI HAFB	10025	
HB-Q . .	Aerostar S-60A HAFB	S60A-3069	
HB-Q . .	Schröder Fire Balloons G HAFB	1117	

MOTOR-GLIDERS

HB-2001	Schleicher ASK 14	14054	(D-KISU)
HB-2004	Sportavia/ Fournier RF-4D	4097	
HB-2005	Alpavia/ Fournier RF-3	28	F-BMDI
HB-2010	Scheibe SF-25B Falke	4692	(D-KOSF)
HB-2013	Alpavia/ Fournier RF-3	29	F-BMDG
HB-2014	Schleicher ASK 14	14056	(D-KISY)
HB-2018	Sportavia-Pützer RF-5B Sperber	51010	
HB-2025	Glaser-Dirks DG-800A	8-64A38	D-KIIS
HB-2030	Schleicher ASK 16	16016	(D-KIVU)
HB-2031	Schleicher ASK 16	16017	(D-KAAQ)
HB-2033	Schleicher ASK 16	16026	(D-KITU)
HB-2036	Farner Colibri SL-1	001	
HB-2040	SZD-45A Ogar	B-660	
HB-2042	Scheibe SF-28A Tandem-Falke	5782	(D-KDFD)
HB-2045	Scheibe SF-25E Super Falke	4340	D-KIOJ HB-2045 (D-KDCN)
HB-2048	Scheibe SF-28A Tandem-Falke	5704	D-KAVM
HB-2053	Eiri PIK-20E	20260	
HB-2055	Eiri PIK-20E	20283	
HB-2061	Siren/Eiri PIK-20E-IIF	701	F-WANC

HB-2063	Grob G.109	6115	
HB-2068	Glaser-Dirks DG-400	4-8	
HB-2069	Glaser-Dirks DG-400	4-43	
HB-2070	Glaser-Dirks DG-400	4-40	
HB-2073	Glaser-Dirks DG-400	4-57	
HB-2074	Glaser-Dirks DG-400	4-49	
HB-2077-CA	Glaser-Dirks DG-400	4-61	
HB-2083	Grob G.109B	6231	
HB-2084	Grob G.109B	6220	
HB-2087	Grob G.109B	6258	
HB-2088	Grob G.109B	6270	
HB-2089	Glaser-Dirks DG-400	4-115	
HB-2092	Glaser-Dirks DG-400	4-89	
HB-2094	Valentin Taifun 17E	1029	D-KDSA
HB-2096	Hoffmann H-36 Dimona	36101	
HB-2097	Grob G.109B	6280	
HB-2098	Schempp-Hirth Ventus bT	9/136	HB-1658
HB-2100	Schempp-Hirth Ventus bT	47/242	
HB-2101	Glaser-Dirks DG-400	4-118	
HB-2103	Grob G.109B	6355	
HB-2107	Scheibe SF-25C Falke	44376	(D-KNBB)
HB-2109	Glaser-Dirks DG-400	4-135	
HB-2114	Schempp-Hirth Ventus bT	282/67	
HB-2116	Schempp-Hirth Ventus bT	303/73	D-KBHC
			D-KASE(3)
HB-2117	Valentin Taifun 17E	1080	D-KHVA(16)
HB-2119	Hoffmann H-36 Dimona	36215	
HB-2120	Schempp-Hirth Ventus bT	311/75	
HB-2121	Raab Krähe IV	Liz.015	D-KADY(2)
HB-2122	Schempp-Hirth Ventus bT	338/91	
HB-2123	Glaser-Dirks DG-400	4-31	D-KIDG(2)
HB-2126	Scheibe SF-25C Falke 2000	44436	(D-KIAC)
HB-2127	Glaser-Dirks DG-400	4-210	
HB-2128	Schempp-Hirth Ventus cT	125/399	
HB-2130	Technoflug Piccolo	010	D-KACL
HB-2131	Technoflug Piccolo	005	D-KAFT
HB-2132	Schleicher ASH 25E	25039	D-KBEB
HB-2134	Glaser-Dirks DG-400	4-227	(D-KIDG)
HB-2135	Schempp-Hirth Ventus cM	15/442	D-KCPB
HB-2136	Schleicher ASW 20L TOP	20403	HB-1569
HB-2138	Schleicher ASW 20 TOP	20053	HB-1417
HB-2139	Glaser-Dirks DG-400	4-47	ZS-VKN
			D-KBOL
HB-2140	Schleicher ASW 20BL TOP	20955	
HB-2142	Technoflug Piccolo	021	D-KCTB
HB-2145	Schempp-Hirth Ventus cT	124/398	
HB-2146	Neukom Elfe S4A/TOP	63	HB-1236
HB-2149	Technoflug Piccolo	024	D-KCFA
HB-2150	Technoflug Piccolo	037	D-KOIB (2)
HB-2151	Technoflug Piccolo	030	D-KCFG
HB-2152	Canard SC	V-01	
HB-2153	Glaser-Dirks DG-400	4-244	
HB-2154	Glaser-Dirks DG-400	4-246	
HB-2155	Hoffmann H-36 Dimona	36277	
HB-2156	Technoflug Piccolo	031	D-KCFH
HB-2157	Schempp-Hirth Discus bT	11/282	D-KCCE(2)
HB-2159	Schempp-Hirth Discus bT	12/287	D-KIDE(2)
HB-2160	Schempp-Hirth Nimbus 3DT	30	
HB-2161	Glaser-Dirks DG-400	4-253	
HB-2163	Valentin Kiwi	K3013	D-KEGX(1)
HB-2164	Schempp-Hirth Ventus cM	18/447	(D-KCPF)
HB-2167	Glaser-Dirks DG-400	4-274	
HB-2169	Schempp-Hirth Ventus bT	41/231	HB-1788
HB-2170	Schempp-Hirth Ventus cT	149/475	
HB-2172	Schleicher ASH 25E	25071	D-KBFA
HB-2173	Schempp-Hirth Ventus cT	150/476	
HB-2174	Schempp-Hirth Ventus cM	32/465	
HB-2175	Schempp-Hirth Ventus cM	16/443	D-KCPE
HB-2176	Glaser-Dirks DG-400	4-271	
HB-2177	Stemme S-10 (Crashed 17.6.96)	10-20	D-KGCI
HB-2180	Glaser-Dirks DG-500M	5E-25M13	
HB-2181	Schleicher ASW 24E	24830	
HB-2182	Schleicher ASW 24E	24831	
HB-2187	Stemme S-10	10-08	D-KKBH
HB-2188	Schempp-Hirth Discus bT	40/352	
HB-2191	Hoffmann HK-36R Super Dimona	36316	
HB-2192	Schleicher ASW 24E	24820	D-KAXH
HB-2193	Schempp-Hirth Discus bT	97/436	
HB-2194	Schempp-Hirth Discus bT	70/397	
HB-2198	Schempp-Hirth Discus bT	54/372	
HB-2199	Stemme S-10	10-21	D-KGCH
HB-2201	Glaser-Dirks DG-500M	5E-43M21	
HB-2202	Glaser-Dirks DG-400	4-282	(D-KIDG)
HB-2203	Glaser-Dirks DG-600M	6-63M14	
HB-2204	Glaser-Dirks DG-600M	6-82M28	
HB-2205	Hoffmann HK-36R Super Dimona	36338	
HB-2206	Schempp-Hirth Ventus cT	163/530	
HB-2207	Schempp-Hirth Discus bT	78/409	
HB-2208	Hoffmann HK-36R Super Dimona	36349	
HB-2211	Glaser-Dirks DG-400	4-289	
HB-2213	Valentin Kiwi	K3015	D-KEGX(3)
HB-2214	Technoflug Piccolo B	061	D-KIMW(2)
HB-2219	Grob G.103C Twin IIISL	35013	
HB-2222	Glaser-Dirks DG-600M	6-64M15	
HB-2223-AC	Schempp-Hirth Ventus cM	86/567	
HB-2224	Grob G.103C Twin IIISL	35032	
HB-2225	Technoflug Piccolo B	064	
HB-2226	Schempp-Hirth Discus bT	85/420	
HB-2229	Schempp-Hirth Ventus cT	173/564	
HB-2230	Stemme S-10	10-44	D-KGCD(4)
HB-2231	Technoflug Piccolo B	067	D-KAAL(3)
HB-2232	Schempp-Hirth Nimbus 3DT	58	
HB-2233	Schempp-Hirth Ventus cT	175/572	
HB-2235	Stemme S-10	10-48	
HB-2236	Glaser-Dirks DG-500M	5E-79M32	
HB-2237	Schempp-Hirth Ventus cT	179/594	
HB-2240	Schleicher ASW 22BE	22067	
HB-2241	Stemme S-10	10-7	D-KARD
HB-2243	Schempp-Hirth Discus bT	115/468	
HB-2245	Schempp-Hirth Ventus cM	101/593	
HB-2249	Glaser-Dirks DG-500M	5E-93M40	
HB-2251	Schempp-Hirth Ventus cT	183/601	
HB-2254	Schempp-Hirth Nimbus 4M	27/10	
HB-2255	Technoflug Piccolo B	100	D-KENZ
HB-2256	Glaser-Dirks DG-500M	5E-122M52	
HB-2258	Schempp-Hirth Ventus cM	63/524	D-KALE(2)
HB-2260	Technoflug Piccolo B	093	D-KIIB
HB-2261	Scheibe SF-25C Falke	44570	D-KTIH
HB-2262	Schleicher ASH 26E	26037	D-KHHE
HB-2263	Schempp-Hirth Ventus 2cT	9/33	D-KCUP
HB-2264	Glaser-Dirks DG-500M	5E-113M50	(D-KNDG)
HB-2266	Schleicher ASH 26E	26057	D-KLEH(1)
HB-2268	Technoflug Piccolo B	101	D-KIKC
HB-2269	Schleicher ASH 26E	26055	D-KKTG
HB-2270	Schleicher ASH 26E	26053	D-KMML(1)
			D-2270
HB-2271-38	Glaser-Dirks DG-500M	5E-148M60	
HB-2272	Technoflug Piccolo B	102	D-KAIW
HB-2273	Valentin Kiwi	3008	D-KBEI
HB-2275	Glaser-Dirks DG-800A	8-61A36	
HB-2276	Schleicher ASH 26E	26074	
HB-2279	Scheibe SF-25C Falke	44351	D-KNAI
HB-2280	Scheibe SF-25C Rotax-Falke	44595	D-KTIT(1)
HB-2281-HB	Schleicher ASH 25E	25052	D-KKHB
HB-2282	Technoflug Piccolo B	108	D-KIHI (2)
HB-2283	Schleicher ASH 26E	26088	(D-5222)
HB-2284	Schempp-Hirth Nimbus 4 DM	10/18	D-KCUC
HB-2285-N7	Glaser-Dirks DG-500M	5E-2M01	JRV . . . .
			D-5007
HB-2286	Schempp-Hirth Ventus 2cT	14/54	
HB-2288-VZ	Schleicher ASH 26E	26122	
HB-2289	Schempp-Hirth Ventus 2cT	11/42	D-KAFT(2)
HB-2290	Schempp-Hirth Ventus 2cM	32/56	D-KSEE
HB-2291	Glaser-Dirks DG-800B	8-83B20	D-KDFF(3)
HB-2292	DG Flugzeugbau DG-800B	8-93B28	D-KMEG
HB-2293	Schempp-Hirth Ventus 2cM	24/46	D-KFFH
HB-2294	Schempp-Hirth Ventus 2cM	26/48	D-KPUE
HB-2295	Technoflug Piccolo B	113	D-KKAL
HB-2297	HOAC HK-36TTC Super Dimona	36535	
HB-2298	Schempp-Hirth Ventus 2cM	40/70	
HB-2299	Technoflug Piccolo B	114	D-KKAM
HB-2300	Glaser-Dirks DG-800B	8-76B17	D-KTHG
HB-2301	Technoflug Piccolo B	112	D-KKAK
HB-2302	Technoflug Piccolo B	057	D-KIMF(2)
HB-2303	Glaser-Dirks DG-400	4-214	D-KEDI (2)
HB-2305	Stemme S-10VT	11-003	
HB-2307	Glaser-Dirks DG-800B	8-82B19	D-KIBK
HB-2308	DG Flugzeugbau DG-800B	8-122B51	
HB-2310	HOAC HK-36TTC Super Dimona	36570	
HB-2311-CD	DG Flugzeugbau DG-800B	8-118B47	D-KGJW
HB-2312	DG Flugzeugbau DG-800B	8-116B45	D-KRDS
HB-2313	DG Flugzeugbau DG-800B	8-98B33	D-KTAR
HB-2314	HOAC HK-36TTC Super Dimona	36580	
HB-2315	Schleicher ASW 24/TOP	24811	D-KKDK
HB-2316	Schleicher ASH 26E	26142	
HB-2317	Schempp-Hirth Ventus 2cM	51/105	D-7317
	(Formerly Ventus 2c c/n 37/105)		
HB-2318	Schleicher ASH 25E	25019	D-KEMU
HB-2319	DG Flugzeugbau DG-800B	8-101B35	D-KNTT
HB-2320	Glaser-Dirks DG-800B	8-50B4	D-KBDW
HB-2321	IAR IS.28M2/GR	76	YR-2512
HB-2322	DG Flugzeugbau DG-800B	8-135B64	
HB-2323	DG Flugzeugbau DG-800B	8-123B52	
HB-2324	HOAC HK-36TTC Super Dimona	36594	
HB-2325	Schempp-Hirth Ventus 2cT	32/111	
HB-2327	DG Flugzeugbau DG-800B	8-153B77	
HB-2328	HOAC HK-36TTC Super Dimona	36619	
HB-2329	Schleicher ASH 26E	26096	HB-3203
HB-2330	Schleicher ASH 26E	26033	D-KJAS
HB-2331	DG Flugzeugbau DG-800B	8-173B97	
HB-2332	DG Flugzeugbau DG-800B	8-129B58	
HB-2334	DG Flugzeugbau DG-500MB	5E-185MB2	D-KSGF
HB-2335	HOAC HK-36TC-Eco Super Dimona	36581	OE-9481
HB-2336	DG Flugzeugbau DG-800B	8-87B23	D-KFMA
HB-2237	Schempp-Hirth Ventus 2cT	45/144	
HB-2338	HOAC HK-36TTC Super Dimona	36652	
HB-2339	Schempp-Hirth Nimbus 4 DM	38/54	
HB-2340	DG Flugzeugbau DG-800B	8-117B46	D-KBPM
HB-2341	DG Flugzeugbau DG-800B	8-183B107	
HB-2342	DG Flugzeugbau DG-800B	8-188B112	
HB-2344	DG Flugzeugbau DG-800B	8-170B94	
HB-2345	Sportavia/ Fournier RF-5B	51076	D-KLEO
HB-2346	DG Flugzeugbau DG-800B	8-177B101	
HB-2347	DG Flugzeugbau DG-800B	8-182B106	

HB-2348	DG Flugzeugbau DG-800B	8-184B108	
HB-2350	Schempp-Hirth Ventus 2cM	87/. .	
HB-2351	Schleicher ASH 25M	25122	D-KASS(2)
HB-2352	DG Flugzeugbau DG-800B	8-195B117	
HB-2353	Schempp-Hirth Ventus 2cT	54/1 . .	
HB-2355	HOAC HK-36TTC Super Dimona	36674	
HB-2356	Schempp-Hirth Duo Discus T	20/275	HB-3356
HB-2357	Schempp-Hirth Nimbus 4T	8	D-KHIO
HB-2358	DG Flugzeugbau DG-500MB	5E-192MB7	
HB-2359	Schleicher ASH 25E	25061	D-KOGH
HB-2360	HOAC HK-36TTC Super Dimona	36673	
HB-2361	IAR IS.28M2/GR	75	D-KWDO
			YR-1997
HB-2362	Scheibe SF-25C Falke	44333	D-KDOW(2)
HB-2363	HOAC HK-36TTS Super Dimona	36393	OE-9493
HB-2364	Sportavia/ Scheibe SF-25B Falke	4808	D-KEBU(2)
			D-KETT(1)
			(D-KAHP)
HB-2366	DGFlugzeugbau DG-800B	8-222B136	
HB-2367	Schempp-Hirth Ventus 2cM	110/. .	
HB-2368	DGFlugzeugbau DG-800B	8-234B148	
HB-2369	DGFlugzeugbau DG-800B	8-220B134	
HB-2370	DGFlugzeugbau DG-800B (c/n unconfirmed)	8-229B143	
HB-2371	Schempp-Hirth Nimbus 4 DM	12/21	D-KMLT
HB-2372	Schempp-Hirth Nimbus 4 DM	45/. .	
HB-2373	HOAC HK-36TC Super Dimona	36633	N633TT
HB-2374	HOAC HK-36TC Super Dimona	36709	
HB-2376	HOAC HK-36TTC Super Dimona	36708	
HB-2377	HOAC HK-36TTC Super Dimona	36726	
HB-2378	Stemme S-10VT	11-037	D-KSVT
HB-2379	Schleicher ASH 25M	25226	D-KKTL
HB-2380	Technoflug Piccolo B	122	D-KJTF
HB-2381	DGFlugzeugbau DG-800B	8-243B157	
HB-2382	Schleicher ASH 25M	25228	
HB-2383	Schempp-Hirth Ventus 2cM	119/. .	
HB-2384	Schempp-Hirth Nimbus 4 DM	46/63	
HB-2385	DGFlugzeugbau DG-800B	8-274B182	
HB-2386	Schempp-Hirth Duo Discus T	56/. .	
HB-2387	Schleicher ASW 24/TOP	24853	D-KAXS(2)
HB-2388	Technoflug Piccolo B	125	
HB-2390	DGFlugzeugbau DG-800B	8-268B176	
HB-2392	Schempp-Hirth Ventus 2cM	131/. .	
HB-2393	Schleicher ASH 25M	25134	HB-3093
HB-2394	DGFlugzeugbau DG-800B	8-284B192	
HB-2396	DGFlugzeugbau DG-800B	8-2898195	
HB-2397	Schleicher ASH-26E	26204	
HB-2399-A2	Schempp-Hirth Ventus 2cxM	143/. .	D-KADP
HB-2400	DGFlugzeugbau DG-800B	8-287B193	
HB-2401	Schleicher ASH 25M	25244	
HB-2402	Stemme S-10VT	11-062	D-KLAO
HB-2403	Stemme S-10VT	11-059	D-KGAG(2)
HB-2404	Schleicher ASH-26E	26222	
HB-2408	Schempp-Hirth Ventus 2cxM	151/. .	
HB-2410	Technoflug Carat A	CA21	
HB-2415	Scheibe SF-25C Falke 1700	4443	D-KOOR
			OE-9198
			OE-9060
			(D-KDAC(1))

GLIDERS

HB-87	Grünau Baby II	90	
HB-120	Grünau Baby II	281	
HB-138	SG-38 Schulgleiter	8	D-3534 ?
HB-183	Grünau Baby II	unkn	
HB-190	RRG Zögling	HS1	
HB-223	Hütter H.28	unkn	
HB-225	Spalinger S-19	unkn	
HB-234	Grünau Baby II	unkn	
HB-255	Scheibe L-Spatz 55	512	
HB-257	Moswey IIa	unkn	
HB-280	Spalinger S-21H	280	
HB-289	Grünau Baby IIb	AB201	
HB-309	Moswey IIa	unkn	
HB-336	Spyr IV	unkn	
HB-348	Nord 1300	210	F-CRJP
			F-CAQV
HB-366	Spalinger S-22 II	unkn	
HB-369	Spyr V Replica	unkn	
HB-373	Moswey III	44	
HB-374	Moswey III	unkn	
HB-376	Moswey III	unkn	
HB-380	Moswey III	unkn	
HB-381	DFS-Meise	unkn	
HB-384	DFS-Meise	unkn	
HB-403	Grunau Baby IIb (C/n is DFS type no.)	"108-49"	
HB-411	Spalinger S-18 IIB	unkn	
HB-418	Spalinger S-16 II	unkn	
HB-437	Spalinger S-25M	unkn	
HB-442	Karpf Baby	unkn	
HB-444	Karpf Baby	unkn	
HB-458	Spalinger S-18 III	unkn	
HB-461	Karpf Zögling	unkn	
HB-465	Schleicher Ka 2 Rhönschwalbe	122	
HB-475	Kranich III	1167	LX+WJ
HB-485	Moswey III	unkn	
HB-486	Spalinger S-18 III	unkn	
HB-491	Olympia-DFS Meise	unkn	
HB-494	Karpf Baby	1	
HB-505	Karpf Baby	unkn	
HB-509	Spyr 5A	unkn	
HB-510	Spalinger S-18 III	unkn	
HB-520	Müller Moswey IVA	1	ZS-GBX
			HB-520
HB-522	Müller Moswey IVA	4/2	BGA2277/DPS
			HB-522
HB-531	Grünau Baby II	1/53	D-6344
HB-532	Fauvel AV-36	unkn	
HB-533	VT-116 Orlik II	151928	OK-8428
HB-534	Neukom Elfe M	unkn	
HB-535	Schleicher Ka 2B	unkn	
HB-538	Kranich III	78	
HB-545	Moswey III	unkn	
HB-552	Weber-Landolf-Münch WLM-1	03	
HB-556	Weihe 50	unkn	
HB-557	Slingsby T-31BCadet TX.3	704	D-1081
			PH-797
			WT909
HB-560	Fauvel AV.36 Monobloc	31	
HB-562	WLM-2	01	
HB-568	Fauvel AV.36 Monobloc	101	F-CBRA
HB-574	Schleicher Ka 6 Rhönsegler	175	
HB-575	Scheibe L-Spatz 55	573	
HB-580	Grünau Baby IIB	unkn	
HB-587	Schleicher Ka 2B Rhönschwalbe	254	
HB-588	Schleicher Ka 6 Rhönsegler	249	
HB-592	Schleicher Rhönlerche II	230	
HB-593	Scheibe L-Spatz 55	unkn	
HB-595	Schleicher Rhönlerche II	261	
HB-597	Schleicher Rhönlerche II	266	
HB-602	Schleicher Ka 6BR Rhönsegler	335	
HB-608	Schleicher Rhönlerche II	379	
HB-609	Schleicher Ka 6BR Rhönsegler	356	
HB-610	Schleicher Rhönlerche II	401	
HB-612	Scheibe L-Spatz 55	646	
HB-617	Schleicher Ka 6BR Rhönsegler	457	
HB-625	Schleicher Ka 6B Rhönsegler	495	
HB-637	Schleicher K 8B	636	
HB-643	Schleicher Ka 6CR Rhönsegler	620	
HB-645	Schleicher Ka 2B Rhönschwalbe	633	
HB-649	Schleicher Rhönlerche II	797	
HB-651	Schleicher Ka 6CR Rhönsegler	722	
HB-652	Schleicher K 7 Rhönadler	765	
HB-653	Schleicher K 7 Rhönadler	777	
HB-654	Schleicher Ka 6CR Rhönsegler	675	
HB-655	Schleicher Rhönlerche II	710	
HB-663	Schleicher K 8B	669	
HB-664	Schleicher Rhönlerche II	672	
HB-671	Schleicher K 8B	838	
HB-687	Schleicher K 7 Rhönadler	933	
HB-690	Scheibe Bergfalke II/55	340	
HB-692	Schleicher Rhönlerche II	956	
HB-693	SZD-22C Mucha Standard	F-676	
HB-695	Schleicher K 8B	1053	
HB-697	Schleicher Rhönlerche II	1120	
HB-701	Schleicher K 8B	1059	
HB-703	Schleicher Ka 6CR Rhönsegler	6006	
HB-704	Schleicher K 8B	1123	
HB-706	SZD-22C Mucha Standard	F-675	
HB-708	Schleicher Rhönlerche II	3003	
HB-710	Schleicher K 8B	8004	
HB-711	Schleicher Ka 6CR Rhönsegler	6065	
HB-712	Schleicher K 8B	8351	
HB-713	Schleicher K 8B	1106	
HB-714	SZD-24C Foka	W-142	
HB-724	Schleicher Ka 2B Rhönschwalbe	1064	
HB-730	Schleicher Ka 6CR Rhönsegler	6049	
HB-732	Scheibe L-Spatz 55	543	
HB-733	Schleicher Ka 2B Rhönschwalbe	2005	
HB-734	Götz/Schleicher K 8B	04	
HB-736	Neukom Elfe MN	unkn	
HB-737	Scheibe L-Spatz 55	551	D-1770
			D-4682
			D-4036
HB-742	Glasflügel H.301 Libelle	01	
HB-744	Slingsby T-31B Cadet TX.3	908	BGA3251/FGN
			XE795
HB-745	Scheibe SF-26A Standard	5033	
HB-748	Slingsby T.50 Skylark 4	1371	
HB-750	SZD-25A Lis	727	SP-2343
HB-752	Schleicher K 8B	8184	
HB-753	Schleicher K 8B	8263	
HB-757	Schleicher Rhönlerche II	3033	
HB-759	SZD-22C Mucha Standard	778	
HB-762	HBV Diamant	V-3	
HB-764	Schleicher K 8B	8281	
HB-765	Schleicher K 8B	8254	
HB-767	Slingsby T.50 Skylark 4	1401	
HB-768	Schleicher K 7 Rhönadler	7112	
HB-771	Schleicher Ka 6CR Rhönsegler	6236	
HB-778	Schleicher K 8B	8328	
HB-786	Schleicher Rhönlerche II	3054	
HB-787	Schleicher K 8B	8420	

HB-789	Schleicher Ka 6CR-PE Rhönsegler	6143	
HB-790	Schleicher K 8B	8409	
HB-793	Schleicher Ka 6CR Rhönsegler	6369/Si	D-4100
HB-795	Scheibe SF-26A	5051	D-1801
HB-796	Schleicher Ka 6CR Rhönsegler	6008	
HB-798	Glasflügel H.301 Libelle	47	
HB-803	Neukom Elfe Standard S2/3P	7	
HB-804	Neukom Elfe Standard S2/3V	8	
HB-807	Schleicher Rhönlerche II	3064Br	
HB-811	Götz/Schleicher K 8B	8363Go	
HB-816	Schleicher Ka 6CR Rhönsegler	682	
HB-827	Schleicher Rhönlerche II	3073Br	
HB-828	Götz/Schleicher K 8B	8504Go	
HB-830	Schleicher K 8B	8518	
HB-833	Musger Mg 23SL Arrow	25	
HB-834	Schleicher K 8B	8548	
HB-839	Schleicher Ka 6E	4025	
HB-840	Schleicher K 8B	8555	
HB-841	Neukom Elfe S3P	9	
HB-842	Neukom Elfe S2/3P	11	
HB-845	Neukom Elfe S3P	13	
HB-846	Götz/Schleicher K 8B	8527Go	
HB-847	Götz/Schleicher K 8B	8526Go	
HB-848	Schleicher Rhönlerche II	3057Br	
HB-850	Schleicher Ka 6E	4018	
HB-851	Schleicher Ka 6CR Rhönsegler	824	
HB-859	Neukom Elfe S2/3	unkn	
HB-860	Schleicher Rhönlerche II	955	
HB-871	Schleicher Ka 6CR Rhönsegler	6620	
HB-872	Neukom AN-66	14	
HB-878	Schleicher Ka 6CR Rhönsegler	6584	
HB-880	Götz/Schleicher K 8B	8640Go	
HB-884	Schleicher K 8B	8694	
HB-888	Schleicher K 8B	8692	
HB-893	HBV Diamant 16.5	017	
HB-896	Schleicher Ka 6E	4105	
HB-899	Schleicher K 8B	8728	
HB-901-NN	Neukom AN-66	20	
HB-902	Neukom Elfe S3P	18	
HB-903	Neukom Elfe S3P	17	
HB-904	Neukom AN-66B	22	
HB-909	Glasflügel H.301 Libelle	58	
HB-916	HBV Diamant 18	030	
HB-917	HBV Diamant 18	036	
HB-919	Bölkow Phoebus A-1	793	
HB-933	Bölkow Phoebus B-1	794	
HB-940	HBV Diamant 16-5	060	
HB-943	Schleicher K 8B	8601/A	
HB-945	Slingsby T-53B	1702	
HB-949	Glasflügel H201B Standard Libelle	48	
HB-953	Schleicher ASW 12	12010	
HB-957	Schiller FS-1	1	
HB-969	Schleicher Rhönlerche II	3031	
HB-970	Schleicher ASW 15	15012	
HB-972	Glasflügel H201B Standard Libelle	67	
HB-976	Glasflügel H201B Standard Libelle	164	
HB-977	Neukom Elfe S4	23	
HB-978	Schleicher Ka 6E	4312	
HB-979	Schleicher Ka 6E	4048	
HB-982	Neukom Elfe 17	46	
HB-996	Schleicher Ka 6CR Rhönsegler	6534	
HB-1004	Rolladen-Schneider LS1C	37	
HB-1008	Schleicher ASW 15	15105	
HB-1010	Glasflügel H201B Standard Libelle	202	
HB-1011	Schleicher ASW 15	15121	
HB-1014	SZD-12 Mucha 100	87	F-CCDU SP-1461
HB-1015	Schempp-Hirth Standard Cirrus	113	
HB-1016	Glasflügel H201B Standard Libelle	195	
HB-1018	Schleicher ASW 15	15111	
HB-1019	Schleicher ASW 15	15104	
HB-1029	Schleicher ASW 15	15143	
HB-1030	Schleicher ASW 15	15094	
HB-1033	Schempp-Hirth Standard Cirrus	170	
HB-1036	Glasflügel H201B Standard Libelle	201	
HB-1042	Rolladen-Schneider LS1C	84	
HB-1043	Neukom AN-17	27	
HB-1044	Neukom AN-66C	26	
HB-1052	Schleicher Ka 6CR Rhönsegler	6014	
HB-1055	Glasflügel H201B Standard Libelle	287	
HB-1058	Glasflügel H201B Standard Libelle	312	
HB-1061	Rolladen-Schneider LS1D	89	
HB-1062	Glasflügel H202 Standard Libelle	169	D-0649
HB-1064	Schleicher Ka 6E	4384	
HB-1066	Glasflügel H201B Standard Libelle	296	
HB-1070	Glasflügel H201B Standard Libelle	311	
HB-1072	LET L-13 Blanik	175106	
HB-1074	Neukom Elfe 17	8/36	
HB-1075	LET L-13 Blanik	175113	
HB-1078	Schleicher ASK 13	13675AB	
HB-1079	Neukom Elfe 17	31	
HB-1080	Neukom Elfe MK	1	
HB-1081	Neukom Elfe 17	6/39	
HB-1082	Glasflügel H201B Standard Libelle	332	
HB-1085	Glasflügel H201B Standard Libelle	407	
HB-1087	Neukom Elfe 17	11	
HB-1089	Glasflügel H201B Standard Libelle	357	
HB-1091	Glasflügel H201B Standard Libelle	397	
HB-1100	Pilatus B4-PC11AF	001	
HB-1101	Pilatus B4-PC11	002	
HB-1103	Pilatus B4-PC11	004	
HB-1105	Pilatus B4-PC11	006	
HB-1106	Pilatus B4-PC11	007	
HB-1108	Pilatus B4-PC11	009	
HB-1116	Pilatus B4-PC11	024	
HB-1122	Pilatus B4-PC11	056	
HB-1123	Pilatus B4-PC11	057	
HB-1125	Pilatus B4-PC11	064	
HB-1128	Pilatus B4-PC11	079	
HB-1130	Pilatus B4-PC11	118	
HB-1131	Pilatus B4-PC11AF	119	
HB-1132	Pilatus B4-PC11	120	
HB-1133	Pilatus B4-PC11	014	
HB-1139	Pilatus B4-PC11AF	095	
HB-1143	Pilatus B4-PC11	117	
HB-1148	Pilatus B4-PC11	143	
HB-1156	Glasflügel H201B Standard Libelle	403	
HB-1163	Neukom Elfe S4	55	
HB-1165	Neukom Elfe 17	34	
HB-1166	Neukom Elfe 17	32	
HB-1167	Neukom Elfe 17	15/35	
HB-1168	Glasflügel H201B Standard Libelle	443	
HB-1169	Neukom Elfe S4	unkn	
HB-1171	G.Steiner SB-7	701	
HB-1174	Glasflügel H401 Kestrel	95	
HB-1177	Glasflügel H201B Standard Libelle	505	
HB-1178	Neukom Elfe 17	40	
HB-1179	Schleicher ASW 15B	15306	
HB-1182	Neukom Elfe 17A	42	
HB-1185	SZD-30 Pirat	S.01-33	
HB-1186	Schempp-Hirth Nimbus 2	67	
HB-1189	Glasflügel H201B Standard Libelle	506	
HB-1190	Neukom Elfe S4	82	
HB-1192	Glasflügel H201B Standard Libelle	520	
HB-1199	Neukom Elfe S4A	47	
HB-1213	SZD-36 Cobra 15	W-667	
HB-1218	Neukom Elfe 17A	61	
HB-1219	Neukom Elfe S4A	53	
HB-1220	Neukom Elfe S4A	48	
HB-1225	Glasflügel H401 Kestrel	124	
HB-1227	Sperber	1	
HB-1230	SZD-38A Jantar 1	B-615	
HB-1231	Glasflügel H401 Kestrel	119	
HB-1232	Glasflügel H101 Salto	43	
HB-1233	Schempp-Hirth Standard Cirrus	530	
HB-1238	Rolladen-Schneider LS1F	258	
HB-1242	Schempp-Hirth Standard Cirrus	564G	
HB-1245	Schleicher Rhönlerche II	116	
HB-1247	Neukom Elfe S4A	72	
HB-1248	Schempp-Hirth Standard Cirrus	87	D-0688
HB-1249	Glasflügel H205 Club Libelle	85	
HB-1252	Pilatus B4-PC11	172	
HB-1253-333	Pilatus B4-PC11AF	175	
HB-1255	Pilatus B4-PC11A	196	
HB-1257	Pilatus B4-PC11AF	188	
HB-1260	Glasflügel H205 Club Libelle (Mod) (Cr. 12.8.97)	46	
HB-1266	Glasflügel H205 Club Libelle	59	
HB-1268	Glasflügel H205 Club Libelle	60	
HB-1273	Neukom Elfe 17A	49	
HB-1275	Neukom Elfe 17A	75	
HB-1279	Neukom Elfe S4A	70	
HB-1283	Neukom Elfe S4A	80	
HB-1292	HBV Diamant 16.5	68	
HB-1293	Schempp-Hirth Standard Cirrus	625	
HB-1294	Glasflügel H206 Hornet	30	
HB-1295	Glasflügel H206 Hornet	6	
HB-1296	Glasflügel H206 Hornet	2	
HB-1299	Standard Austria S	44	F-CCPU
HB-1301	Grob G.102 Astir CS	1126	
HB-1302	Neukom Elfe 17A	85	
HB-1305	Neukom Elfe S4A	62	
HB-1314	Pilatus B4-PC11AF	129	
HB-1317	Pilatus B4-PC11AF	242	
HB-1318	Pilatus B4-PC11	244	
HB-1319	Pilatus B4-PC11AF (Crashed 27.6.97)	247	
HB-1320	Pilatus B4-PC11AF	258	
HB-1321	Pilatus B4-PC11AF	276	
HB-1329	Glaser-Dirks DG-100	69	
HB-1334	Glaser-Dirks DG-200	2-2	
HB-1337	Grob G.102 Astir CS	1334	
HB-1340	Delphin	001	
HB-1341	Grob G.102 Astir CS	1432	
HB-1346	Glaser-Dirks DG-100	93	
HB-1347	Glaser-Dirks DG-100	96	
HB-1351	Grob G.102 Astir CS	1473	
HB-1353	Rolladen-Schneider LS3	3005	
HB-1357	Rolladen-Schneider LS3	3025	
HB-1358	Rolladen-Schneider LS3	3026	
HB-1364	Rolladen-Schneider LS3	3046	
HB-1366	Rolladen-Schneider LS3	3066	
HB-1367	Slingsby T-21BSedbergh	589	BGA3520/FTT WB926
HB-1371	Rolladen-Schneider LS3A	3201	
HB-1372	Rolladen-Schneider LS3A	3095	

HB-1373	Glasflügel H201B Standard Libelle	414	
HB-1374	Glasflügel H303 Mosquito	14	
HB-1376	Grob G.102 Astir CS	1490	
HB-1379	Schleicher ASW 19B	19110	
HB-1381	Grob G.102 Astir CS	1629	
HB-1388	SZD-41A Jantar Standard	B-796	
HB-1394	Grob G.102 Astir CS 77	1687	
HB-1395	Schempp-Hirth Mini-Nimbus HS-7	35	
HB-1398	Grob G.103 Twin Astir II	3044	
HB-1405	Schempp-Hirth Mini-Nimbus HS-7	44	
HB-1406	Grob G.103 Twin Astir II	3088	
HB-1407	Glaser-Dirks DG-200	2-14	
HB-1409	Glaser-Dirks DG-200	2-18	
HB-1410	Glaser-Dirks DG-200	2-20	
HB-1413	Schempp-Hirth Mini-Nimbus HS-7	52	BGA3489/FSL HB-1413
HB-1414	Schempp-Hirth Mini-Nimbus HS-7	46	
HB-1418	Rolladen-Schneider LS3	3312	
HB-1419	Glasflügel H303 Mosquito	91	
HB-1421-BW	Grob G.103 Twin Astir II	3090	
HB-1422	Schleicher ASW 19	19179	
HB-1423	Glasflügel H303B Mosquito	115	
HB-1425	Schempp-Hirth Mini-Nimbus C	107	
HB-1428	Glaser-Dirks DG-200	2-37	
HB-1429	Valentin Mistral C	MC 012/78	
HB-1430	Grob G.102 Astir CS 77	1726	
HB-1432	Glasflügel H303B Mosquito	118	
HB-1433	Rolladen-Schneider LS3A	3137	
HB-1434	Grob G.102 Astir CS 77	1731	
HB-1438	Grob G.102 Astir CS 77	1771	
HB-1439	Glaser-Dirks DG-100	104	
HB-1444	Glaser-Dirks DG-200	2-55	
HB-1446	Grob G.102 Astir CS 77	1772	
HB-1449	Schleicher ASW 20	20129	
HB-1452	Schempp-Hirth Mini-Nimbus C	111	
HB-1458	Grob G.102 Astir CS 77	1812	
HB-1459	Grob G.102 Astir CS 77	1804	
HB-1460	Molino PIK-20D	20646	
HB-1463	Rolladen-Schneider LS3A	3148	
HB-1464	Glaser-Dirks DG-100G	E11G5	
HB-1468	Glaser-Dirks DG-100 Elan	E13	
HB-1469	Rolladen-Schneider LS3-17	3270	
HB-1473	Grob G.103 Twin Astir II	3226	
HB-1475	Rolladen-Schneider LS3A	3240	
HB-1478	Schleicher ASW 19B	19259	
HB-1479	Schleicher ASK 18B	18039	
HB-1480	Schempp-Hirth Nimbus 2C	189	
HB-1486	Club Libelle 205	28	I-CLUC
HB-1490	Schempp-Hirth Mini-Nimbus C	131	
HB-1491	Grob G.102 Astir CS 77	1605	
HB-1496	Schempp-Hirth Nimbus 2	44	D-1229
HB-1498	Grob G.102 Speed Astir IIB	4066	
HB-1501	Rolladen-Schneider LS3-17	3238	
HB-1503	Schempp-Hirth Mini-Nimbus C	137	
HB-1504	Grob G.102 Astir CS 77	1836	
HB-1505	Pilatus B4-PC11AF	309	D-1161 HB-1505
HB-1507-T4	SZD-48-1 Jantar Standard 2	W-918	
HB-1513	Schempp-Hirth Mini-Nimbus C	146	
HB-1515	Glaser-Dirks DG-100 Elan	E-28	
HB-1519	Schleicher ASW 20	20292	
HB-1537	Schleicher ASW 19B	19320	
HB-1538	Glaser-Dirks DG-100G Elan	E31G16	
HB-1540-CT	Grob G.103 Twin Astir II	3537	
HB-1544	Glaser-Dirks DG-200/17	2-120/1725	
HB-1545	Schleicher ASK 21	21027	
HB-1546	Schempp-Hirth Nimbus 2C	231	
HB-1550	Valentin Mistral C	MC 033/81	
HB-1551	Rolladen-Schneider LS4	4010	
HB-1552	Delphin	02	
HB-1554	Schleicher ASK 21	21053	
HB-1556	Glasflügel H201B Standard Libelle	582	
HB-1560	SZD-48-1 Jantar Standard 2	B-1162	
HB-1561	Rolladen-Schneider LS4	4050	
HB-1563	Grob G.103 Twin Astir II	3600	
HB-1564	Rolladen-Schneider LS4	4025	
HB-1567-MX	Rolladen-Schneider LS4	4060	
HB-1568-SB	Schempp-Hirth Janus C	149	
HB-1570	Schempp-Hirth Ventus A	18	
HB-1574	Rolladen-Schneider LS4	4107	
HB-1575	Glaser-Dirks DG-100G Elan	E69G44	
HB-1576	Glaser-Dirks DG-100G Elan	E58G34	
HB-1577	Glasflügel H304	241	
HB-1581	Grob G.103 Twin II Acro	3654-K-23	
HB-1582	Valentin Mistral C	MC 040/81	
HB-1585	SZD-48-1 Jantar Standard 2	B-1170	
HB-1589	Schleicher ASK 21	21078	
HB-1590	Schleicher ASK 21	21101	
HB-1591	Schleicher ASK 21	21102	
HB-1592	Glaser-Dirks DG-100G Elan	E78G53	
HB-1593	Glaser-Dirks DG-200/17	2-160/1751	
HB-1594	Rolladen-Schneider LS4	4158	
HB-1595	Rolladen-Schneider LS4	4112	
HB-1598	Schempp-Hirth Mini-Nimbus C	159	
HB-1599	Schempp-Hirth Ventus b	75	
HB-1601	Schleicher ASW 20	20428	
HB-1602	Rolladen-Schneider LS4	4174	
HB-1605	Grob G.103A Twin II Acro (Cr. 10.4.99)	3678-K-29	
HB-1606	Glasflügel H304B	349	D-9375
HB-1607	Glasflügel H304	250	
HB-1609	Glaser-Dirks DG-100 Elan	E87	
HB-1610	Glasflügel H304	253	
HB-1612	Glaser-Dirks DG-100 Elan	E94	
HB-1615	Rolladen-Schneider LS1F	371	
HB-1618	Grob G.102 Club Astir IIIB	5568CB	
HB-1619	Rolladen-Schneider LS4	4080	
HB-1620	Schleicher ASK 21	21111	
HB-1622	Schleicher ASK 21	21088	
HB-1623	Schleicher ASW 20L	20578	
HB-1624	Schleicher ASK 21	21103	
HB-1629	Schleicher ASK 21	21097	
HB-1630	Schleicher ASK 21	21095	
HB-1632	Schleicher ASK 21	21092	
HB-1633	Rolladen-Schneider LS4	4133	
HB-1635	Schleicher ASK 21	21100	
HB-1636-PE	Glaser-Dirks DG-200	2-167	
HB-1638	Schempp-Hirth Nimbus 3	15	
HB-1639	Glaser-Dirks DG-200/17	2-174/1757	
HB-1641	Rolladen-Schneider LS4	4152	
HB-1642	Glaser-Dirks DG-100G Elan	E95G65	
HB-1643	Rolladen-Schneider LS4	4168	
HB-1647	Rolladen-Schneider LS4	4128	
HB-1649-AJ	Schleicher ASK 21	21114	
HB-1651-M9	Grob G.103 Twin Astir II	3703	
HB-1653	Schleicher K 8B	8012SH/A	
HB-1654	Schleicher ASK 21	21138	
HB-1655	Rolladen-Schneider LS4	4169	
HB-1660	Schleicher ASW 20L	20595	
HB-1661	Schempp-Hirth Nimbus 3/24.5	29	
HB-1662	Rolladen-Schneider LS4	4155	
HB-1664	Centrair 101AP Pégase	101A-029	
HB-1665	Centrair 101AP Pégase	101A-026	
HB-1666-1K	Centrair 101A Pégase	101A-027	
HB-1667	Centrair 101A Pégase	101A-028	
HB-1668	Rolladen-Schneider LS4	4324	
HB-1669	Schleicher ASK 21	21139	
HB-1670	Schempp-Hirth Ventus b/16.6	123	
HB-1671	Rolladen-Schneider LS4	4154	
HB-1673	Rolladen-Schneider LS4	4176	
HB-1676	Schempp-Hirth Nimbus 3/24.5	14	
HB-1678	Rolladen-Schneider LS4	4193	
HB-1680	Rolladen-Schneider LS4	4270	
HB-1681	Schempp-Hirth Nimbus 2C	200	D-3196
HB-1682	Schleicher ASK 21	21140	
HB-1683	Rolladen-Schneider LS4	4210	
HB-1684	Schempp-Hirth Ventus b	138	
HB-1685-N6	Schleicher ASK 21	21161	
HB-1686	Rolladen-Schneider LS4	4170	
HB-1687	Rolladen-Schneider LS4	4320	
HB-1688	Centrair 101A Pégase	101A-042	
HB-1689	Centrair 101A Pégase	101A-063	
HB-1690	Schleicher ASK 21	21163	
HB-1695	Rolladen-Schneider LS4	4333	
HB-1697	Grob G.103A Twin II Acro	3785-K-63	
HB-1698	Centrair 101AP Pégase	101A-060	
HB-1699	Schleicher ASK 21	21171	
HB-1700	Schleicher ASK 21	21164	
HB-1701	Schleicher ASW 22	22031	
HB-1703	Glaser-Dirks DG-100G Elan	E136G104	
HB-1704	Schempp-Hirth Janus B	174	
HB-1705	Rolladen-Schneider LS4	4332	
HB-1708	Schleicher ASK 21	21175	
HB-1710	Centrair 101A Pégase	101A-077	
HB-1714	Schleicher ASW 19B	19396	
HB-1715	Rolladen-Schneider LS4	4357	
HB-1716	Schempp-Hirth Nimbus 3/24.5	63	
HB-1720	Centrair 101A Pégase	101A-107	
HB-1722	Schleicher ASK 21	21192	
HB-1723	Rolladen-Schneider LS4	4374	
HB-1725	Centrair 101A Pégase	101A-105	
HB-1726	Grob G.103A Twin II Acro	3818-K-79	
HB-1727	Schleicher ASW 20C	20718	
HB-1729	Glaser-Dirks DG-300 Elan	3E21	
HB-1730	Schleicher ASW 19B	19399	
HB-1732	Glaser-Dirks DG-300 Elan	3E98	
HB-1733	Glaser-Dirks DG-100G Elan	E159G126	
HB-1735	Schleicher ASW 20C	20731	
HB-1736	Glaser-Dirks DG-300	3E37	
HB-1738	Schempp-Hirth Discus b	22	
HB-1741	Schempp-Hirth Ventus b/16.6	193	
HB-1745	Glaser-Dirks DG-300 Elan	3E42	
HB-1746	Grob G.103 Standard Astir	5044S	
HB-1747	Rolladen-Schneider LS4	4471	
HB-1748	Valentin Mistral C	MC052/84	
HB-1749	Rolladen-Schneider LS4	4417	
HB-1750	Schempp-Hirth Nimbus 2B	150	D-7507
HB-1751	Glaser-Dirks DG-300 Elan	3E48	
HB-1752-IB	Glaser-Dirks DG-300 Elan	3E43	
HB-1753-JP	Rolladen-Schneider LS4	4423	
HB-1754-G5	Glaser-Dirks DG-300 Elan	3E49	
HB-1755	Glaser-Dirks DG-300 Elan	3E51	
HB-1756	Glaser-Dirks DG-300 Elan	3E52	
HB-1758	Schleicher ASW 20CL	20708	D-KAAL D-7474

HB-1759	Rolladen-Schneider LS4	4458	
HB-1762	Schempp-Hirth Janus C	203	
HB-1763	Rolladen-Schneider LS4	4459	
HB-1764	Rolladen-Schneider LS4	4446	
HB-1765	Glaser-Dirks DG-300 Elan	3E58	
HB-1766	Schleicher ASK 21	21232	
HB-1767	Rolladen-Schneider LS4	4484	
HB-1768	Neukom Elfe S4A	90	
HB-1769	Schempp-Hirth Nimbus 2C	236	D-1809
HB-1773	Schleicher ASW 19B	19413	
HB-1774	Schempp-Hirth Nimbus 3/24.5	78	
HB-1775	Schleicher ASW 19B	19409	
HB-1776-BE	Glaser-Dirks DG-300 Elan	3E74	
HB-1777	Centrair 101A Pégase	101-0166	
HB-1778	Grob G.103 Twin II Acro	33950-K-183	
HB-1779	Schleicher ASK 23	23014	
HB-1782	Schempp-Hirth Mini-Nimbus C	99	D-6741
HB-1784	Schleicher ASW 20CL	20795	
HB-1786	Schleicher ASK 23	23012	
HB-1787	Schempp-Hirth Discus b	14	BGA3253/FGQ
			HB-1787
HB-1789	Glaser-Dirks DG-300 Elan	3E9O	
HB-1790	Schleicher ASK 23	23015	
HB-1792-BY	Rolladen-Schneider LS6	6026	
HB-1793	Schleicher ASK 21	21246	
HB-1794	Glaser-Dirks DG-300 Elan	3E121	
HB-1796	Schleicher ASK 23	23016	
HB-1798	Schleicher ASW 20B	20672	
HB-1799	Rolladen-Schneider LS4	4504	
HB-1800	Glaser-Dirks DG-300 Elan	3E100	
HB-1801	Schempp-Hirth Discus b	39	
HB-1802	Schempp-Hirth Discus b	25	
HB-1805	Schempp-Hirth Discus b	43	
HB-1806	Schempp-Hirth Discus b	19	
HB-1807	SZD-48-3 Jantar Standard 3	B-1463	
HB-1808	Schleicher ASW 20CL	20816	
HB-1809	SZD-51-1 Junior	B-1503	
HB-1810	Schempp-Hirth Ventus b/16.6	287	
HB-1811	Schleicher ASK 21	21258	
HB-1812	Schempp-Hirth Discus b	46	
HB-1813	Rolladen-Schneider LS6	6083	
HB-1818	Rolladen-Schneider LS4	4523	
HB-1819	Glaser-Dirks DG-300 Elan	3E135	
HB-1820-3E	Schempp-Hirth Discus b	60	
HB-1822	Schempp-Hirth Discus b	56	
HB-1824	Rolladen-Schneider LS4	4515	
HB-1825	Schleicher ASW 20CL	20821	
HB-1826	Schempp-Hirth Discus b	59	
HB-1827	Schempp-Hirth Discus b	61	
HB-1828-N1	Rolladen-Schneider LS4	4527	
HB-1830	Schempp-Hirth Discus b	73	
HB-1832	Rolladen-Schneider LS4	4551	
HB-1834	Schleicher ASK 21	21300	
HB-1835	Rolladen-Schneider LS4	4525	
HB-1836	SZD-48-3 Jantar Standard 3	B-1566	
HB-1837	Schempp-Hirth Ventus b/16.6	294	D-3086
HB-1839	Schleicher ASK 21	21283	
HB-1840	Rolladen-Schneider LS4	4537	
HB-1841	Glaser-Dirks DG-300 Elan	3E159	
HB-1842	Glaser-Dirks DG-300 Elan	3E168	
HB-1843	Glaser-Dirks DG-300 Elan	3E146	
HB-1845	Glaser-Dirks DG-300 Elan	3E150	
HB-1846	Glasflügel H-101 Salto	24	OE-5369
			D-2994
HB-1847-1F	SZD-51-1 Junior	W-940	
HB-1848	SZD-51-1 Junior	W-939	
HB-1849	Glasglügel H401 Kestrel	41	D-0277
HB-1850	Schempp-Hirth Ventus b/16.6	272	
HB-1851	SZD-48-3 Jantar Standard 3	B-1572	
HB-1852	ICA-Brasov IS.28B2	320	D-2843
HB-1854	Schleicher ASK 21	21290	
HB-1856	Schleicher ASW 19B	19423	
HB-1857	Rolladen-Schneider LS4	4577	
HB-1859	Rolladen-Schneider LS6	6079	
HB-1860	Schempp-Hirth Discus b	106	
HB-1861	Glaser-Dirks DG-300 Elan	3E166	
HB-1862	Schleicher ASK 23	23060	
HB-1865	Rolladen-Schneider LS4	4588	
HB-1866	Rolladen-Schneider LS3A	3192	
HB-1867	Schleicher ASK 23B	23071	
HB-1868	Schempp-Hirth Janus C	226	
HB-1870	Rolladen-Schneider LS4	4586	
HB-1871	Schleicher ASW 20CL	20842	
HB-1872	Glaser-Dirks DG-300 Elan	3E205	
HB-1873	Glaser-Dirks DG-300 Elan	3E191	
HB-1875	Rolladen-Schneider LS4	4592	
HB-1876	Rolladen-Schneider LS6A	6124	
HB-1877	Schempp-Hirth Discus b	116	
HB-1878	Glaser-Dirks DG-300 Elan	3E193	
HB-1879	Schleicher ASK 23B	23078	
HB-1881	Glaser-Dirks DG-300 Elan	3E197	
HB-1883	Schleicher ASK 23B	23079	
HB-1884	Schleicher ASK 21	21311	
HB-1885	Schempp-Hirth Discus b	127	
HB-1886	Rolladen-Schneider LS6	6096	
HB-1890	Schleicher ASK 23B	23081	
HB-1892	Rolladen-Schneider LS4	4621	
HB-1893	Rolladen-Schneider LS4	4618	
HB-1896	Schempp-Hirth Discus b	137	
HB-1898	Glaser-Dirks DG-300 Elan	3E211	
HB-1899	Schempp-Hirth Janus C	243	
HB-1900	Rolladen-Schneider LS6	6094	
HB-1901	Schleicher ASK 23B	23090	
HB-1902	Glaser-Dirks DG-300 Elan	3E223	
HB-1904	Schempp-Hirth Discus b	218	
HB-1905	Schempp-Hirth Janus C	228	
HB-1906	SZD-51-1 Junior	W-957	
HB-1907	Schempp-Hirth Discus b	150	
HB-1908	Schempp-Hirth Discus b	154	
HB-1909	Rolladen-Schneider LS4	4648	
HB-1910	Rolladen-Schneider LS4	4650	
HB-1912	Schempp-Hirth Discus b	159	
HB-1913	Centrair 101D Pégase	101D-0527	
HB-1915	Schempp-Hirth Discus b	183	
HB-1916	Rolladen-Schneider LS1F	331	D-2738
HB-1917	Glaser-Dirks DG-300 Elan	3E252	
HB-1918	SZD-51-1 Junior	B-1770	
HB-1919	Glaser-Dirks DG-300 Elan	3E238	
HB-1923	Glaser-Dirks DG-300 Elan	3E254	
HB-1924	Rolladen-Schneider LS6 (Cr 15.4.04)	6009	D-6590
HB-1925	Schempp-Hirth Ventus b	184	D-7721
HB-1926	Glaser-Dirks DG-300 Elan	3E253	
HB-1929	Schleicher ASH 25	25026	
HB-1933	Glaser-Dirks DG-300 Elan	3E256	
HB-1934	Glaser-Dirks DG-300 Elan	3E262	
HB-1936	Schempp-Hirth Ventus c	358	
HB-1937	Rolladen-Schneider LS4	4664	
HB-1940	Schleicher ASH 25E	25024	
HB-1941	Glaser-Dirks DG-300 Elan	3E264	
HB-1942	Rolladen-Schneider LS6B	6155	
HB-1943	Glaser-Dirks DG-300 Elan	3E318	
HB-1944	Glaser-Dirks DG-600	6-2	D-0626
HB-1945	Schempp-Hirth Ventus c	363	
HB-1948	Schempp-Hirth Discus b	208	
HB-1950	Glaser-Dirks DG-300 Elan	3E272	
HB-1951	Schempp-Hirth Discus b	281	
HB-1952	Schempp-Hirth Discus b	199	
HB-1953-RK	Schempp-Hirth Nimbus S-3D	2/8	D-1973
HB-1956	Centrair 101B Pégase	101B-0283	
HB-1958	Schempp-Hirth Discus b	228	
HB-1959	Schleicher ASK 21	21368	
HB-1961	Schempp-Hirth Discus b	24	D-4124
HB-1962	Schleicher ASK 21	21366	
HB-1963	Schempp-Hirth Ventus c	368	
HB-1965	Schempp-Hirth Discus b	229	
HB-1966	Schempp-Hirth Discus b	231	
HB-1967	Schleicher ASK 23B	23104	
HB-1969	Glaser-Dirks DG-300 Club Elan	3E299/C17	
HB-1970	Schleicher ASK 21	21384	
HB-1972	Glaser-Dirks DG-300 Elan	3E289	
HB-1973	Schempp-Hirth Discus b	236	
HB-1977	Rolladen-Schneider LS7	7020	D-4587
HB-1979	Rolladen-Schneider LS7	7012	
HB-1980	Glaser-Dirks DG-300 Elan	3E321	
HB-1981	Rolladen-Schneider LS7	7002	D-1253
HB-1982	Schleicher ASK 21	21377	
HB-1983	Glaser-Dirks DG-300 Elan	3E308	
HB-1984	Glaser-Dirks DG-300 Elan	3E316	
	(C/n 3E-316/C25 is also quoted for D-5564, both are current)		
HB-1987	SZD-51-1 Junior	B-1827	
HB-1988	Rolladen-Schneider LS7	7010	D-1275
HB-1989	Schempp-Hirth Ventus c	405	
HB-1990	Schempp-Hirth Discus b	267	
HB-1991	Glaser-Dirks DG-300 Elan	3E322	
HB-1992	Schempp-Hirth Ventus c	416	
HB-1993	Rolladen-Schneider LS7	7034	D-1671
HB-1994	Glaser-Dirks DG-500/22	5E13S4	
HB-1995	Rolladen-Schneider LS6A	6189	D-5020
HB-1996	Rolladen-Schneider LS7	7042	D-5156
HB-1998	Rolladen-Schneider LS7	7047	
HB-1999	Schempp-Hirth Janus C	253	
HB-3004	Avafiber Canard SC (Solar powered)	01	
HB-3005	Glaser-Dirks DG-300 Elan	3E345	
HB-3006	Rolladen-Schneider LS7	7063	
HB-3007	Glaser-Dirks DG-300 Elan	3E244	HB-007 ?
HB-3008	Schleicher ASW 24	24047	
HB-3009	Schleicher ASW 24	24045	
HB-3011	Rolladen-Schneider LS4	4760	
HB-3013	SZD-51-1 Junior	B-1846	
HB-3015	Schleicher ASK 23B	23047	N923KS
HB-3016	Grob G.103 Twin III Acro	34129	
HB-3017	SZD-51-1 Junior	B-1859	
HB-3018	Grob G.103 Twin III Acro	34132	
HB-3019	Rolladen-Schneider LS6B	6191	D-5026
HB-3022	Schempp-Hirth Discus b	325	
HB-3024	Schleicher ASW 24	24016	D-3463
HB-3025	Rolladen-Schneider LS4A	4770	
HB-3026	Schleicher ASK 21	21438	
HB-3027	Schempp-Hirth Discus b	309	
HB-3028	Celstar GA-1	S001	ZS-GTC
HB-3029	Schleicher ASK 21	21466	
HB-3031	Rolladen-Schneider LS6A	6010	HB-1795
HB-3032	Rolladen-Schneider LS7	7096	

HB-3034	Rolladen-Schneider LS4A	4782	
HB-3036	SZD-51-1 Junior	B-1927	
HB-3038	Schleicher ASK 21	21452	
HB-3039	Glaser-Dirks DG-600	6-49	
HB-3040-TG	SZD-55-1	551190003	
HB-3041	Schempp-Hirth Discus b	341	
HB-3043	Schempp-Hirth Discus b	385	
HB-3044	Schempp-Hirth Discus b	410	
HB-3045	SZD-55-1	551190006	
HB-3047	Schleicher ASH 25	25051	D-3460
HB-3048-NY	Rolladen-Schneider LS7	7141	
HB-3049	Schleicher ASH 25	25103	
HB-3050	Glaser-Dirks DG-500/22	5E-44T14	
HB-3051	Pilatus B4-PC11AF	282	D-2230
HB-3052	Schempp-Hirth Ventus c	499	
HB-3053	Grob G.103A Twin II Acro	3622-K-9	D-3071
HB-3054	Schleicher ASK 23B	23122	
HB-3055	Schleicher ASK 23B	23130	
HB-3056	SZD-55-1	551191012	
HB-3059	Glaser-Dirks DG-600	6-65	
HB-3062	Schempp-Hirth Discus b	354	
HB-3064	Schleicher ASH 25	25128	
HB-3068	Rolladen-Schneider LS7	7151	
HB-3070	Schleicher ASK 23B	23128	
HB-3071	Schempp-Hirth Ventus c	518	
HB-3072	Glaser-Dirks DG-300 Elan	3E419	
HB-3073	SZD-55-1	551192034	
HB-3074	Rolladen-Schneider LS4B	4842	
HB-3075	Schleicher ASK 21	21507	
HB-3076	Rolladen-Schneider LS4B	4834	
HB-3077	Schleicher ASW 24	24139	
HB-3080	SZD-55-1	551191021	
HB-3081	Schempp-Hirth Janus CE	278	
HB-3082	Rolladen-Schneider LS4B	4847	
HB-3083	Glaser-Dirks DG-500/22	5E-52S9	
HB-3085	Rolladen-Schneider LS6C	6272	
HB-3086	Schempp-Hirth Ventus c	549	
HB-3087	Schempp-Hirth Janus CE	288	
HB-3088	Schempp-Hirth Duo Discus	56	
HB-3089	Centrair 101A Pégase	101A-0426	
HB-3090	Centrair 101A Pégase	101A-0427	
HB-3091	Schleicher ASK 23B	23133	
HB-3094	Schempp-Hirth Discus CS	076CS	
HB-3095	Scheibe SF-34	5139	
HB-3097-GW	Glaser-Dirks DG-500/22 Elan	5E89S13	
HB-3098	Schempp-Hirth Discus CS	080CS	
HB-3099	Schleicher ASK 21	21546	
HB-3100	Schempp-Hirth Janus CE	289	
HB-3101	Schempp-Hirth Discus CS	083CS	
HB-3102	Grob G.103C Twin III	34171	
HB-3104	Schleicher ASW 24	24182	
HB-3105	Schempp-Hirth Discus CS	085CS	
HB-3106	SZD-55-1	551192043	
HB-3107	SZD-55-1	551192045	
HB-3108	Schempp-Hirth Discus b	450	
HB-3109	Schempp-Hirth Discus b	238	D-1029
HB-3110	Glaser-Dirks DG-600/18	6-113	
HB-3111	Glaser-Dirks DG-300 Elan Acro	3E437A5	
HB-3112	SZD-51-1 Junior	B-2016	
HB-3114	Swift S-1	109	
HB-3115	Rolladen-Schneider LS6C	6298	
HB-3117	Rolladen-Schneider LS4B	4966	
HB-3118	SZD-55-1	551192048	
HB-3120	Rolladen-Schneider LS4B	4908	
HB-3121	Schempp-Hirth Discus CS	164CS	
HB-3122	Glaser-Dirks DG-300 Elan	3E439	
HB-3123	Swift S-1	107	(D-9107)
HB-3126	Swift S-1	101	SP-3536
HB-3127	Rolladen-Schneider LS6C	6309	
HB-3128	Schleicher ASW 20FL	20116	F-CFFM
HB-3129	Glaser-Dirks DG-200/17C	2-130/CL-07	D-0695 PH-695
HB-3130	Schleicher ASW 22	22006	D-2270
HB-3131	Schempp-Hirth Duo Discus	24	
HB-3132	Schempp-Hirth Janus CE	296	
HB-3133	Rolladen-Schneider LS4B	4951	
HB-3134	Glaser-Dirks DG-500 Elan Trainer	5E104T41	
HB-3136	SZD-51-1 Junior	B-2130	
HB-3137-SR	Glaser-Dirks DG-500 Elan	5E109S16	
HB-3139	Swift S-1	105	SP-3573
HB-3141	Rolladen-Schneider LS6C	6330	
HB-3142	Schempp-Hirth Discus CS	153CS	
HB-3143	Schleicher ASK 21	21601	
HB-3144	Rolladen-Schneider LS4B	4936	
HB-3145	Rolladen-Schneider LS4B	4924	
HB-3146	Rolladen-Schneider LS6C-18	6334	D-1832
HB-3147	Centrair 101B Pégase	101B-0484	
HB-3150	Glaser-Dirks DG-500 Elan Trainer	5E123T53	
HB-3151	Glaser-Dirks DG-800S	8-29S6	D-5093
HB-3152	Glaser-Dirks DG-800S	8-30S7	D-5559
HB-3153	Schempp-Hirth Duo Discus	14	
HB-3154	Schempp-Hirth Discus b	519	
HB-3155	Glaser-Dirks DG-300 Elan	3E450	S5-3155
HB-3156	Schleicher ASW 24B	24228	D-3156
HB-3157	Scheibe SF-27A	6037	D-1205
HB-3158	Rolladen-Schneider LS6-18W	6317	D-1789
HB-3160	Schempp-Hirth Duo Discus	20	
HB-3161	Rolladen-Schneider LS6-18W	6336	D-8035
HB-3162	Schempp-Hirth Discus CS	185CS	
HB-3163	Swift S-1	120	
HB-3166	Schempp-Hirth Duo-Discus	27	
HB-3167-YL	Rolladen-Schneider LS6C-18	6347	D-1772
HB-3168	Glaser-Dirks DG-800S	8-43S12	D-5647
HB-3170	Rolladen-Schneider LS8A	8020	D-2035
HB-3171	Rolladen-Schenider LS-4B	4977	
HB-3173	Glaser-Dirks DG-800S	8-55S14	
HB-3174	Rolladen-Schneider LS4B	4986	
HB-3175	Rolladen-Schneider LS6C-18	6357	
HB-3176	Rolladen-Schneider LS4B	4985	
HB-3179	Glasflügel H304	257	D-5827
HB-3180	Glaser-Dirks DG-800S	8-57S16	
HB-3181	Schempp-Hirth Discus CS	197CS	
HB-3182	Rolladen-Schneider LS8A	8021	D-2171
HB-3183	SZD-51-1 Junior	B-2140	
HB-3185	Glaser-Dirks DG-505 Elan Orion	5E151X8	
HB-3186	Rolladen-Schneider LS8A	8078	
HB-3187	Rolladen-Schneider LS4B	4990	
HB-3188	Schleicher ASH 25	25185	
HB-3189	Schleicher ASH 26	26073	D-5775
HB-3190	Glaser-Dirks DG-303 Elan	3E464A18	
HB-3191 -IQ	Schleicher ASH 25	25020	D-2519
HB-3192	Schempp-Hirth Ventus 2c	6/9	D-2389
HB-3193	Schempp-Hirth Duo Discus	152	
HB-3194	Schempp-Hirth Ventus 2a	26	
HB-3197	Glaser-Dirks DG-505 Elan Orion	5E157X14	
HB-3198	Rolladen-Schneider LS7WL	7059	D-5775
HB-3199	Schleicher ASW 27	27027	D-7453
HB-3200	Glaser-Dirks DG-303 Elan	3E465	
HB-3201	Glaser-Dirks DG-500/20	5E124W1	D-7320 (D-0219)
HB-3202	Glaser-Dirks DG-303 Elan	3E466	
HB-3204	Glaser-Dirks DG-505 Elan Orion	5E163X18	
HB-3205	Glaser-Dirks DG-505 Elan Orion	5E146X6	D-2988
HB-3206	Rolladen-Schneider LS8A	8052	D-3719
HB-3207	Schempp-Hirth Ventus 2c	10/22	D-5206
HB-3208	Schleicher ASW 24B	24243	
HB-3209	Schleicher ASW 27	27028	D-7456
HB-3210	Rolladen-Schneider LS6C-18	6373	
HB-3211	Rolladen-Schneider LS8A	8067	
HB-3212	Centrair 101A Pégase	101A-0613	
HB-3213	Rolladen-Schneider LS8-18	8300	
HB-3214	Schmepp-Hirth Duo Discus	87	
HB-3215	Schleicher ASH 26	26094	
HB-3216	Rolladen-Schneider LS8A	8070	
HB-3217	Schempp-Hirth Ventus 2a	39	
HB-3219	Rolladen-Schneider LS6C	6375	
HB-3220	Rolladen-Schneider LS4B	41008	
HB-3222	Schempp-Hirth Nimbus 3D	9/44	D-4346
HB-3223	Schempp-Hirth Duo Discus	102	
HB-3224	Schempp-Hirth Duo Discus	99	
HB-3225	Schleicher ASK 21	21642	
HB-3226-C6	Rolladen-Schneider LS8A	8121	
HB-3227	DG-Flugzeugbau DG-505 Elan Orion	5E166X21	
HB-3228	DG-Flugzeugbau DG-505 Elan Orion	5E216X56	
HB-3229	Glaser-Dirks DG-505 Elan Orion	5E155X12	D-3680
HB-3230	Rolladen-Schneider LS8A	8098	
HB-3232	Schempp-Hirth Duo Discus	113	
HB-3233	Schempp-Hirth Duo Discus	115	
HB-3234	Schempp-Hirth Ventus 2c	20/51	
HB-3235	Schempp-Hirth Ventus 2c	19/49	
HB-3236-ZP	Schleicher ASW 27	27048	
HB-3237	Rolladen-Schneider LS8A	8127	
HB-3238	Rolladen-Schneider LS8A	8126	
HB-3239-ML	Schleicher ASW 27	27049	
HB-3240	Schleicher ASW 27	27038	
HB-3241	Marganski MDM-1 Fox	216	
HB-3243	Caproni A.21S Calif	211	D-6613 I-VIZR
HB-3244	Centrair 101A Pégase	101A-0334	F-CGOO
HB-3245	Centrair 101A Pégase	101A-0467	F-CHFB
HB-3246	Schempp-Hirth Ventus 2c	25	
HB-3248	Swift S-1	123	
HB-3249	Rolladen-Schneider LS8A	8140	
HB-3251	PZL PW-5 Smyk	17.08.019	
HB-3252	DG-Flugzeugbau DG-800S	8-111S27	
HB-3253	DG-Flugzeugbau DG-800S	8-112S28	
HB-3254	Rolladen-Schneider LS8A	8194	
HB-3255	Rolladen-Schneider LS8A	8168	
HB-3256	DG-Flugzeugbau DG-505 Elan	5E-179X30	
HB-3257	Schempp-Hirth Ventus 2b	67	
HB-3258	Schleicher ASW 27	27090	
HB-3259	Schleicher ASW 24B	24249	
HB-3260	Schempp-Hirth Duo Discus	114	D-3887
HB-3261	Schleicher ASW 27	27087	
HB-3263	Schempp-Hirth Duo Discus	182	
HB-3264	Schleicher ASW 27	27095	
HB-3265	Schleicher ASW 27	27079	
HB-3266	DG-Flugzeugbau DG-505 Elan Orion	5E-184X35	
HB-3267	Rolladen-Schneider LS8-18	8228	D-7298
HB-3269	Schleicher ASW 27	27107	
HB-3270	Schleicher ASH 25	25048	D-4959
HB-3271	Rolladen-Schneider LS4B	41027	
HB-3272-MH	Schempp-Hirth Duo Discus	207	
HB-3274-UB	Schempp-Hirth Discus 2b	19	D-7195

HB-3275	Rolladen-Schneider LS8-18	8258	D-6598
HB-3276	DG-Flugzeugbau DG-505 Elan Orion	5E176X28	D-4629
HB-3277-IY	Schempp-Hirth Duo Discus	206	
HB-3278-EQ	Schleicher ASH 25	25210	
HB-3279	Schempp-Hirth Duo Discus	213	
HB-3280	DG-Flugzeugbau DG-800S	8-138S31	
HB-3281	Schempp-Hirth Discus 2b	26	D-6683
HB-3282	DG-Flugzeugbau DG-800S	8-139S32	
HB-3283	Schempp-Hirth Discus 2b	37	
HB-3284	Rolladen-Schneider LS8-18	8265	D-4671
HB-3285-MD	DG-Flugzeugbau DG-800S	8-140S33	(D-9800)
HB-3286	DG-Flugzeugbau DG-800S	8-141S34	
HB-3287	Rolladen-Schneider LS8-18	8289	D-0089
HB-3288	Rolladen-Schneider LS8-18	8247	D-4344
HB-3289	Schleicher ASW 27	27001	D-5527
HB-3290	Schempp-Hirth Discus 2b	43	
HB-3291	Schempp-Hirth Discus 2b	44	
HB-3292	DG-Flugzeugbau DG-505 Elan Orion	5E-197X41	
HB-3293	Rolladen-Schneider LS8-18	8290	D-5808
HB-3294	Rolladen-Schneider LS8-18	8332	
HB-3295-SD	DG-Flugzeugbau DG-505 Elan Orion	5E-203X47	
HB-3296	Schempp-Hirth Duo Discus	244	
HB-3297	Rolladen-Schneider LS8-18	8328	
HB-3298	Marganski MDM-1 Fox	223	D-4034
HB-3299	Glaser-Dirks DG-800S	8-9S2	D-8027
HB-3300-GU	Schempp-Hirth Discus 2b	29	D-4093
HB-3301	Schempp-Hirth Discus 2b	58	
HB-3302	Mahrer Delphin III	03	
HB-3304	Grob G.102 Astir CS Jeans	2132	D-2539
HB-3305	Schempp-Hirth Discus 2b	79	
HB-3306	Rolladen-Schneider LS7WL	7146	D-3873
HB-3307	Pilatus B4-PC11AF	231	D-4144
HB-3308	DG-Flugzeugbau DG-800S	8-211S41	
HB-3309	DG-Flugzeugbau DG-800S	8-210S40	
HB-3310	Schempp-Hirth Nimbus 3/24.5	95	OE-5409
HB-3311	Schempp-Hirth Ventus 2c	57/168	
HB-3312	Rolladen-Schneider LS8-18	8330	
HB-3313	Rolladen-Schneider LS8-18	8331	
HB-3314	Rolladen-Schneider LS8-18	8340	
HB-3315	Rolladen-Schneider LS8-18	8274	D-2109
HB-3316	Schempp-Hirth Discus 2b	99	
HB-3317	Rolladen-Schneider LS8-18	8338	
HB-3318	Rolladen-Schneider LS8-18	8346	
HB-3319	Schempp-Hirth Ventus 2c	65	
HB-3320-	Rolladen-Schneider LS8-18	8368	
HB-3321	Schempp-Hirth Ventus 2c	66	
HB-3322	Schempp-Hirth Discus 2b	114	
HB-3323	Glasflügel H304	235	F-CELZ
HB-3324	DG-Flugzeugbau DG-800S	8-218S44	
HB-3325	Schempp-Hirth Ventus 2a	21	PH-1077
HB-3326	Schleicher ASH 25	25207	
HB-3327	Schempp-Hirth Discus 2b	104	
HB-3328	Glaser-Dirks DG-300 Elan	3E115	D-1812
			HB-1817
HB-3329	Schleicher ASW 27	27158	
HB-3330	SZD-55-1	551195079	D-4855
HB-3331	Rolladen-Schneider LS4B	41045	
HB-3332	Schempp-Hirth Ventus 2c	69	
HB-3333-AB	Rolladen-Schneider LS8-18	8369	
HB-3334	Rolladen-Schneider LS8-18	8352	
HB-3335	Schleicher ASH 25	25017	D-3125
			HB-1920
			D-3125
HB-3336	Rolladen-Schneider LS-3-17	3390	PH-679
			D-6941
HB-3337	Rolladen-Schneider LS8-18	8350	
HB-3338	Schempp-Hirth Discus b	162	D-0789
HB-3339	Schleicher ASW 28	28044	
HB-3341	Schleicher ASW 28	28039	
HB-3342	Schempp-Hirth Discus 2b	130	
HB-3343	Rolladen-Schneider LS8-18	8399	
HB-3344	Schleicher ASW 28	28035	
HB-3345	DG-Flugzeugbau DG-800S	8-254S48	
HB-3346	Rolladen-Schneider LS8-18	8398	
HB-3347	Schempp-Hirth Duo Discus	327	
HB-3348	Schleicher ASW 27	27180	
HB-3349	Schempp-Hirth Discus 2b	132	
HB-3350	Schempp-Hirth Duo Discus	334	
HB-3351	Rolladen-Schneider LS8-18	8442	
HB-3353	Schleicher ASW 22	22025	BGA3184/FDT
			D-7709
HB-3354	Glaser-Dirks DG-500 Elan Trainer	5E115T47	D-0074
HB-3355	Schempp-Hirth Discus 2b	162	
HB-3357	Rolladen-Schneider LS8-18	8447	
HB-3358	DG-Flugzeugbau DG-800S	8-285S51	
HB-3359	Rolladen-Schneider LS8-18	8445	
HB-3360	Rolladen-Schneider LS8-18	8446	
HB-3361	DG-Flugzeugbau DG-1000S	10-13S13	
HB-3362	Schempp-Hirth Duo Discus	365	(D-4263)
HB-3363	Schleicher ASW 28	28063	
HB-3364	Rolladen-Schneider LS8-18	8465	
HB-3365	Rolladen-Schneider LS7WL	7143	D-6193
HB-3367	DG-Flugzeugbau DG-1000S	10-26S26	
HB-3368	Rolladen-Schneider LS8-b	8474X	
HB-3369	Schempp-Hirth Duo Discus	366	
HB-3370	Schleicher ASW 28-18	28503	D-5370
HB-3372	SZD-51-1 Junior	511.A.03.001	
HB-3373	Schempp-Hirth Ventus 2b	11	
HB-3374	DG-Flugzeugbau DG-808S	8-290S53X1	D-9808
HB-3375-B8	Glasflügel H304C Wasp	65C	
HB-3376	Schleicher ASW 28-18	28513	
HB-3377-N8	Rolladen-Schneider LS8-18	8497	
HB-3380	Schempp-Hirth Ventus bT	190	
HB-3381	Schleicher ASW 28-18	28515	
HB-3382	Schleicher ASW 28-18	28718	D-7382
HB-3383	DG-Flugzeugbau DG-300CL Elan Acro	3E-504C86A38	
HB-3384	Schempp-Hirth Duo Discus	159	D-9209
HB-3397	Schempp-Hirth Ventus 2c	67	OO-YEU

MICROLIGHTS

Microlights may not be registered in Switzerland as a result of a national referendum. The reported allocation of U-1081 is thought to represent an example on trials with the Swiss Air Force, A number of three-axis machines classified as ULMs in other countries nevertheless appear in the Swiss homebuilt category.

I - ITALY

Regn.	Type	C/n	Prev.Id.
I-AASV	S.A.I. F.7 Rondone I	9	
I-ABCA	Beech E33A Bonanza	CE-235	HB-EHH
I-ABMT	Caproni Ca.100 Caproncine	unkn	MM55914
I-ABOU	Caproni Ca.100 Caproncine floatplane	3992	MM65156
I-ACCU	Cessna 150M	15077136	N63298
I-ACIR	Piper PA-28-140 Cherokee C	28-26747	N5953U
I-ACLG	Dornier 328-300	3133	D-BGAG
			D-BDXO
I-ACLU	Piper PA-28RT-201 Arrow IV	28R-8018021	N35720
I-ACMH	Piper PA-28-161 Warrior II	28-8216024	G-BMNM
			N8447N
I-ACMI	Partenavia P.64 Oscar	06	
I-ACMM	Piper PA-28-180 Cherokee F	28-7105230	N11C
I-ACMN	Piper PA-28-180 Cherokee G	28-7205106	N11C
I-ACMP	Piper PA-28-140 Cherokee C	28-26724	N5913U
I-ACMQ	Reims/Cessna F172L	F17200868	(I-CCAD)
I-ACMR	Cessna 172M	17263056	N4302R
I-ACMS	Piper PA-28-161 Warrior II (Wrecked)	28-8416060	N4345D
I-ACMT	SIAI-Marchetti S.205-20/R	4-113	
I-ACMV	SIAI-Marchetti S.205-20/R	4-108	
I-ACMX	Cessna 172M	17267500	N73485
I-ACNU	Partenavia P.64B Oscar B-1155	68	
I-ACOI	Bell 412	31001	
I-ACPD	Piper PA-28R-200 Cherokee Arrow II	28R-7535080	N32705
I-ACRS	Reims/Cessna F172P	F17202067	
I-ACRV	Partenavia P.66B Oscar 150	16	
I-ACSI	Macchi MB.308	101/5874	MM53055
I-ACST	Maule MXT-7-180 Star Rocket	14002C	N9213A
I-ACTD	Piper PA-34-220T Seneca III	34-8233174	N8242A
I-ACTV	Partenavia P.66B Oscar 150	01	
I-ACUD	SOCATA MS.893A Rallye Commodore 180	10692	
I-ACVB	Partenavia P.66B Oscar 100	77	
I-ACVZ	Cessna 172P	17274861	N54054
I-ADAA	Reims/Cessna F152-II	F15201914	
I-ADAC	Cessna 182R Skylane	18267826	N6327N
I-ADAP	Robinson R-22B2 Beta	2986	
I-ADDV	Aérospatiale AS.365N3 Dauphin 2	6649	
I-ADJA	Canadair CL.600-2B19 Regional Jet	7478	C-GIDJ
			C-FMNY
I-ADJB	Canadair CL.600-2B19 Regional Jet	7486	C-GIGH
			C-FMMB
I-ADJC	Canadair CL.600-2B19 Regional Jet	7494	C-GIHG
			C-FMKV
I-ADJD	Canadair CL.600-2B19 Regional Jet	7625	C-GJYW
I-ADJE	Canadair CL.600-2B19 Regional Jet	7629	C-GJYX
I-ADJF	BAe. 146-300	E-3193	G-BUHC
			EI-CTO
			G-BUHC
			G-BTMI
			(N883DV)
			G-6-193
I-ADJH	BAe. 146-300	E-3129	G-BTXN
			EI-CTM
			G-JEAL
			G-BTXN
			HS-TBM
			G-5-129
I-ADLH	Aérospatiale/Alenia ATR-42-512	445	F-OHFM
			F-WWLZ
			F-GJMV
			F-WWER

I-ADLI	Aérospatiale/Alenia ATR-42-512	515	F-OHFN
			F-WWLP
I-ADLJ	Aérospatiale/Alenia ATR-72-212A	686	F-WQMO
			F-WWEI
I-ADLK	Aérospatiale/Alenia ATR-72-212A	706	F-WWEF
I-ADLL	Aérospatiale/Alenia ATR-42-512	518	F-OHFP
			(I-ADLL)
			F-WWLX
I-ADLM	Aérospatiale/Alenia ATR-72-212	543	F-WWLB
I-ADLN	Aérospatiale/Alenia ATR-72-212	557	F-WWLV
I-ADLO	Aérospatiale/Alenia ATR-72-212A	585	F-WWEQ
I-ADLP	Aérospatiale/Alenia ATR-42-512	604	F-WQKY
			F-WWLH
I-ADLQ	Aérospatiale/Alenia ATR-42-512	606	F-WQMA
			F-WWLK
I-ADLS	Aérospatiale/Alenia ATR-72-212A	634	F-WQMB
			F-WWLL
I-ADLT	Aérospatiale/Alenia ATR-72-212A	638	F-WQME
			F-WWLN
I-ADLU	Aérospatiale/Alenia ATR-42-512	609	F-WQMH
			F-WWLP
I-ADLV	Aérospatiale/Alenia ATR-42-512	610	F-OHJI
			F-WQMI
			F-WWLQ
I-ADLW	Aérospatiale/Alenia ATR-72-212A	707	F-WWEG
I-ADLZ	Aérospatiale/Alenia ATR-42-512	611	F-WWLR
I-ADRE	S.A.I. F.7 Rondone II	020	
I-ADRY	Partenavia P.64B Oscar 200	09	
I-AEAL	Cessna 500 Citation I	500-0053	HB-VGO
			I-KUNA
			N9OWJ
			I-CITY
			N553CC
I-AEEA	Stinson L-5 Sentinel	unkn	MM52963
I-AEEE	Stinson L-5 Sentinel	unkn	MM52956
I-AEEG	Stinson L-5 Sentinel	unkn	MM56686
I-AEEI	Stinson L-5 Sentinel	unkn	MM52958
I-AEEP	Stinson L-5 Sentinel (Stored)	unkn	MM52839
I-AEEX	Stinson L-5 Sentinel (W/o 1.8.01)	unkn	MM52884
I-AEFE	Stinson L-5 Sentinel (SSVV conversion)	unkn	MM53454
I-AEFF	Stinson L-5 Sentinel	unkn	MM52967
I-AEFH	Stinson L-5B Sentinel	unkn	MM52892
I-AEFJ	Stinson L-5 Sentinel	unkn	MM52877
I-AEFO	Stinson L-5 Sentinel	unkn	MM56694
I-AEFU	Stinson L-5 Sentinel	unkn	MM52873
	(Flies marked as 298592-"5M")		42-98596
I-AEFZ	Stinson L-5 Sentinel	unkn	MM52970
I-AEGB	Stinson L-5 Sentinel	unkn	MM52863
			44-1672 .
I-AEGC	Stinson L-5 Sentinel (Wrecked)	unkn	MM52891
I-AEGD	Stinson L-5 Sentinel (SSVV conversion)	unkn	MM52847
I-AEGI	Stinson L-5 Sentinel (SSVV conversion)	unkn	MM52876
I-AEGN	Stinson L-5 Sentinel (SSVV conversion)	unkn	MM52846
	(W/o 1.8.01)		
I-AEGR	Stinson L-5 Sentinel	unkn	MM52854
I-AEGS	Stinson L-5 Sentinel	unkn	MM52979
I-AEGZ	Stinson L-5 Sentinel (SSVV conversion)	unkn	MM52952
I-AEKA	Fiat G.46-4B-V	180	I-LSBA
			I-AEKA
			MM53304
I-AEKT	Fiat G.46-4A Series 6	216	MM53491
I-AERG	SOCATA MS.892A Rallye Commodore 150	11638	
I-AERQ	SOCATA MS.892A Rallye Commodore 150	11641	
I-AESC	Piper PA-28RT-201T Turbo Arrow IV	28R-7931095	N500DS
			N500DU
			N2137U
I-AESW	SOCATA TBM-700	225	F-OIKG
I-AETB	Piper PA-18-150 Super Cub	18-7909080	N9753N
I-AFAB	Reims FR172H Rocket	FR17200281	N5448
I-AFAF	Reims/Cessna F172M	F17201281	D-EECR
I-AFCN	Aérospatiale AS.350B2 Ecureuil	1997	JA9461
I-AFET	Aérospatiale SA.315B Lama	2663	
I-AGAA	Piper J-3C-65 Cub	12079	44-79783
I-AGAE	Partenavia P.68B	183	I-GYAN
I-AGFA	Aérospatiale SA.365N1 Dauphin 2	6229	
I-AGKK	Agusta A.109K2	10021	
I-AGKL	Agusta A.109K2	10020	
I-AGMP	Agusta-MD.500N	301	
I-AGSD	Partenavia P.68TC	248-10-TC	(EC-DOI)
I-AGSE	Agusta A.109A-II	7354	
I-AGSF	Agusta-Bell AB.412	25542	
I-AGSH	Agusta A.109A-II	7384	
I-AGSN	Agusta A.109A-II	7396	
I-AGSO	Agusta-Bell AB.412	25560	
I-AGUI	Agusta-Bell AB.412	25507	Fv11337
			I-DACB
I-AGUN	Agusta-Bell 206B-1 Jet Ranger	9010	
I-AGUO	Bell 206B Jet Ranger II	1102	G-BBET
			N18091
I-AGWH	Agusta EH.101/510	510-001	
I-AIAA	Avia LM.5	5	
I-AIIA	Lake LA-4-200 Buccaneer (Sank, Lake Como 9.99)	1010	N80029
I-AICO	MBB-Kawasaki BK.117C-1	7542	D-HZBV
I-AIKE	Mudry CAP.10B	222	
I-AIMA	Maule MX-7-180 Star Rocket	11068C	N9206R
I-AINA	Cessna 172N	17269301	N737BX
I-AINB	Cessna 172RG Cutlass RG	172RG0131	N6269R

I-AINC	Cessna 172M	17264625	N61540
I-AIND	Cessna 172M	17261243	N20383
I-AINE	Aérospatiale AS.350B Ecureuil	3705	
I-AIOI	Aérospatiale AS.350B2 Ecureuil	2535	
I-AIRC	Piper PA-24-250 Comanche (Damaged)	24-1605	N6894P
			G-APZI
			EI-ALI
I-AIRG	Robinson R-22 Beta	1277	I-MIAC
			N8066V
I-AIRI	Piper PA-23-250 Aztec B	27-2010	N5098Y
			LV-PST
I-AIRJ	Dornier 328-300	3186	
I-AIRK	Aérospatiale AS.350B Ecureuil	3276	
I-AIRP	Piper PA-22-108 Colt	22-9595	N5753Z
I-AIRQ	Eurocopter EC.135P1	0101	
I-AIRR	Agusta-Bell 412	25577	HB-XVU
I-AIRT	Robinson R-22B2 Beta	3026	
I-AIRU	Sud Avn SA.316B Alouette III	1390	F-GPAH
			A-390
I-AIRW	Gates Learjet 31	31-025	N39399
I-AIRX	Dornier 328-300	3142	D-BDXS
I-AIRY	Aérospatiale AS.350B2 Ecureuil	2193	HB-XTF
			F-WZTB
I-AITE	Aeritalia-Partenavia AP.68TP-600 Viator	9006	
I-AIVO	Bell 412	33014	HB-XRP
			N2070E
			(ZK-HNF)
			N2070E
			ZS-HKG
			A2-HKG
			ZS-HKG
			N2070E
I-AKAI	Piper PA-34-200 Seneca	34-7350045	N15269
I-AKIS	Stork	001	I-5816
I-AKRM	T-30 Katana	003	
I-AKRO	Mudry CAP.10B	42	F-BUDK(1)
I-ALAA	Cessna F172H	F172-0566	
I-ALAB	Cessna F150J	F150-0442	
I-ALAD	Cessna F150J	F150-0400	
I-ALAG	Cessna F150H	F150-0382	(I-FAUL)
I-ALAJ	Reims/Cessna F150L	F15000667	
I-ALAK	Beech 95-B55 Baron	TC-1218	HB-GDR
I-ALAO	Reims FR172H Rocket	FR17200235	
I-ALAV	Reims/Cessna F150K	F15000544	
I-ALBA	Beech 35-C33 Debonair	CD-876	HB-EKO
I-ALBJ	S.A.I. F.4 Rondone 1	013	
I-ALBN	Reims/Cessna F172M	F17200954	(I-FFST)
I-ALCA	Cessna 182P Skylane	18260947	N7307Q
I-ALCH	SOCATA Rallye 235E Gabier	12907	F-GBXC
I-ALCI	Robinson R-44 Astro	0163	
I-ALCO	Aviamilano F.8L Falco	120	
I-ALDO	Piper J-3C-65 Cub	13071	HB-OES
			44-80775
I-ALEU	Cessna 172RG Cutlass RG	172RG0757	N6532V
I-ALEW	Reims/Cessna F172M	F17201309	D-EESF
I-ALFE	Aérospatiale AS.350B Ecureuil	3665	
I-ALHO	Hawker 800XP	258561	N16300
			N1630
I-ALIF	Partenavia P.57 Fachiro IIf	26	
I-ALJC	Cessna 182E Skylane	18253969	N2969Y
I-ALJG	Cessna 172D	17249643	N2143Y
I-ALJK	Cessna 337A Super Skymaster	33700471	N5371S
I-ALJM	Cessna F172G	F172-0249	
I-ALJO	Cessna F172F	F172-0131	
I-ALJP	Cessna F172G	F172-0192	
I-ALJS	Cessna 210F Centurion	21058748	N1848F
I-ALJT	Cessna F150F	F150-0030/15063079	
I-ALJZ	Cessna F172H	F172-0361	(I-AIJZ)
I-ALKA	Cessna 550 Citation II	550-0351	(N167WE)
			I-ALKA
			N99KW
I-ALKI	Cessna 210H Centurion	21058985	N5985F
I-ALLU	Tecnam P.92J Echo	027	
I-ALOO	Piper PA-28-180 Cherokee Archer	28-7505064	N32491
I-ALPC	SIAI-Marchetti SF.260C	713/47-002	
I-ALPD	SIAI-Marchetti SF.260C	714/47-003	
I-ALPG	Cessna 551 Citation II /SP	551-0355	N551AS
			N5451G
I-ALPK	Fokker F.28-0100	11244	F-WQHE
			HB-IVA
			PH-EZB
I-ALPL	Fokker F.28-0100	11250	F-WQHG
			HB-IVB
			PH-EZC
I-ALPP	Cessna F150J	F150-0434	
I-ALPQ	Fokker F.28-0100	11256	F-WQFP
			HB-IVH
			PH-EZI
I-ALPS	Fokker F.28-0100	11254	F-WQHK
			HB-IVF
			PH-EZG
I-ALPW	Fokker F.28-0100	11255	PH-FYB
			V8-RB4
			HB-IVG
			PH-EZH
I-ALPX	Fokker F.28-0100	11251	F-WQFL
			HB-IVC
			PH-EZD

I-ALPY	Piper PA-28-180 Cherokee E	28-5843	G-AYIE
			N11C
I-ALPZ	Fokker F.28-0100	11252	F-WQBP
			HB-IVD
			PH-EZE
I-ALRE	HOAC DV-20 Katana	20062	D-EDSX
I-ALRO	Beech F33A Bonanza	CE-1444	N5644J
I-ALWA	Cessna F172D	F172-0017/17250285	
I-ALWE	Aérospatiale AS.350B2 Ecureuil	2468	F-WQ . .
			C-FJXY
I-ALWI	Mudry CAP.10B	228	
I-AMAA	Reims/Cessna F172M	F17201275	D-EEVK
I-AMAB	Reims/Cessna F150M	F15001175	D-EEVF
I-AMAD	Cessna 182P	18264100	D-EGWZ
	(Reims-assembled with "c/n" 0036)		PH-MYL
			D-EJPD
			N6085F
I-AMAG	Beech F33A Bonanza	CE-650	D-ELKA
I-AMAI	Reims FR172H Rocket	FR17200298	D-ECRP
I-AMAP	Reims/Cessna F150L	F15000895	D-ECTW
I-AMAQ	Cessna 182K Skylane	18257798	D-EHSV
			N2598Q
I-AMAS	Reims FR172H Rocket	FR17200326	D-EEYL
I-AMAT	Cessna 152	15280995	D-EOHN
			N48839
I-AMAU	Piper PA-28R-200 Cherokee Arrow II	28R-7635234	N234SW
			N9377K
			G-BMJF
			ZS-JUF
			N9377K
I-AMAV	Reims/Cessna F152	F15201973	
I-AMAX	Cessna 182P Skylane	18264283	N71671
I-AMAY	Aérospatiale SA.315B Lama	2607	
I-AMAZ	Maule MXT-7-180 Star Rocket	11046C	N6116U
I-AMCB	Cessna R172K Hawk XP (Dam. 26.4.03)	R1722399	N736BP
I-AMCC	Cessna 172N	17269368	N737EU
I-AMCG	Cessna R172K Hawk XP	R1723321	N758SJ
I-AMCH	Cessna 152	15285885	N95400
I-AMCO	Cessna 172N	17269064	N734RW
I-AMCP	Cessna 152	15280197	N24289
I-AMCQ	Cessna 152	15280639	N25411
I-AMCR	Cessna 152	15285267	N6528Q
I-AMCX	Piper PA-34-220T Seneca III	34-8133004	N83262
I-AMCY	Cessna 500 Citation	500-0192	(N70WA)
			I-ACMY
			N100JJ
			N220S
			N508S
			N4TK
I-AMCZ	Cessna 152	15281481	N64931
I-AMDB	Cessna 152	15281044	N48911
I-AMDC	Cessna A152 Aerobat	A1520865	N4683A
I-AMDE	Cessna 152	15284137	N6157H
I-AMDF	Cessna 152	15280055	N757WE
I-AMDG	Cessna 150M	15076585	N3675V
I-AMDH	Cessna 172RG Cutlass RG	172RG0512	N5350V
I-AMDI	Cessna 172RG Cutlass RG	172RG0887	N9568B
I-AMDJ	Cessna 152	15281764	N67336
I-AMDK	Cessna 152	15285603	N94128
I-AMDM	Mooney M.20K Model 231	25-0424	N3570H
I-AMDY	Cessna 172RG Cutlass RG	172RG0502	N5299V
I-AMFE	Reims/Cessna F172L	F17200902	F-BUEB
I-AMGG	Agusta-Bell 47J-3	2114	3A-MGG
			Caribin. CC-. .
			MM80496
I-AMLT	Aérospatiale AS.355F1 Ecureuil 2	5014	F-GKLP
			F-OGPY
			F-GJST
			N181DB
I-AMMO	III Sky Arrow 650 TCNS	CNS027	
I-AMNB	Aérospatiale AS.350B Ecureuil	1043	3A-MNB
			I-ARIT
I-AMOK	Eurocopter EC.120B Colibri	1031	
I-AMOM	Piper PA-28RT-201T Turbo Arrow IV	28R-7931227	N2858A
I-AMON	Piper PA-28RT-201T Turbo Arrow IV	28R-8231032	N81293
I-AMRS	Neico Lancair 320	1313	
I-AMSH	Aérospatiale AS.350B2 Ecureuil	9039	F-GVBS
I-AMVD	Schweizer 269C	S-1540	HB-XYJ
			N69A
I-AMVE	Aérospatiale AS.350B2 Ecureuil	2640	F-WYMQ
I-AMVG	Aérospatiale AS.350B3 Ecureuil (W/o 9.2.01?)	3071	
I-AMVI	Schweizer 269C	S-1649	HB-XFJ
I-AMVL	Schweizer 269C	S-1566	N601LU
			(JA . . . .)
			N601LU
I-AMVM	Aérospatiale AS.350B3 Ecureuil	3409	
I-AMVO	Aérospatiale AS.350B3 Ecureuil	3571	LN-ODL
			F-WQDE
I-AMVP	Aérospatiale AS.350B Ecureuil	3821	
I-ANBE	Hughes 369D	1127D	N5183Y
I-ANCP	Partenavia P.68B	17	
I-ANDY	Piper PA-28-181 Archer II	28-8590066	N6920S
I-ANER	Laverda F.8LFalco IV	410	HB-UOE
			OY-DKH
I-ANEW	Agusta AB.139	31004	
I-ANGI	Piper PA-23-235 Apache	27-564	N4963P
I-ANIA	Agusta A.109A-II	7286	

I-ANLA	Piper PA-28RT-201T Turbo Arrow IV	28R-8331049	N43155
I-ANNE	Cessna 182M Skylane	18259398	N70864
I-ANNJ	Beech 35-33 Debonair	CD-62	
I-ANNY	Gardan GY-80 Horizon 160	23	
I-AOPA	Robin ATL L	66	F-GFRQ
I-APCE	Piper PA-28-161 Cadet	2841045	N9161Z
I-APEX	Aérospatiale SA.315B Lama	2491	F-GFCA
			N40IAH
			N218RM
			N47314
I-APGN	Raz-Mut	unkn	
I-APLI	de Havilland DH.82A Tiger Moth	86562	I-RIBU
			G-APLV
			PG653
I-APUS	Aérospatiale SA.315B Lama	2539	N9005Q
			VR-HIL
			N9005Q
I-AQLE	Partenavia P.66B Oscar 150	49	
I-AQUA	Lake LA-4-250 Renegade	10	N47LA
			I-AQVA
			N1401G
I-AQUI	Cessna 172N	17271207	N2254E
I-ARAA	Piper PA-18-150 Super Cub	18-3931	PH-LWD
			OO-LWD
			EI-234
			I-EIQF
			MM54-2531
			54-2531
I-ARAM	Bölkow BO.207	243	D-EJBO
I-ARAS	Cessna 172C	17249312	N1612Y
I-ARDA	Piper PA-24-250 Comanche	24-1305	N6324P
I-ARDO	Cessna U206F Stationair	U20602809	N35934
I-ARIF	Dassault Falcon 2000	203	F-WWVQ
I-ARME	Piper PA-22-160 Tri-Pacer	22-7357	N10F
I-ARMY	Piper PA-18-135 Super Cub	18-2002	EI-75
			I-EIDI
			MM52-2402
			52-2402
I-AROM	Cessna 501 Citation I/SP	501-0042	N420AM
			(N120DP)
			I-TOSC,
			N773FR
			N87185
I-AROO	Cessna 550 Citation II	550-0081	N254AM
			I-FBCT
			N26626
I-AROS	Piper PA-18-150 Super Cub	18-4912	N4729
			N4599A
I-ARPI	Piper PA-28RT-201T Turbo Arrow IV	28R-7931273	N2955A
I-ARRO	III Sky Arrow 650T	001	
I-ARWI	Procaer F.15A Picchio	07	
I-ASEL	Agusta-Bell 206B Jet Ranger II	8326	HB-XQI
			I-MIPE
			D-HMOS
I-ASER	Beech 400A Beechjet	RK-204	N2357K
I-ASFC	Robinson R-44 Raven II	10039	
I-ASIO	Aérospatiale SA.315B Lama	1923/21	D-HODU
I-ASKI	Piper PA-34-200 Seneca	34-7250115	N4572T
I-ASKY	Christen A-1 Husky	1155	
I-ASMI	Beech B200 Super King Air	BB-1124	LX-DUC
			D-IVHN
			N678EB
			ZS-MMO
			N200JW
			N800RD
			N30SL
			N301D
I-ASSW	Asso V Whisky	unkn	
I-ATAL	Stinson L-5 Sentinel (Euravia covn)	001	
I-ATAQ	Reims/Cessna F177RG Cardinal RG		
		F177RG0034/ 177RG0197	
I-ATAT	Partenavia P.68TC	254-14-TC	
I-ATEA	Agusta-Bell 206BJet Ranger III	8735	HB-XZB
I-ATEC	Aérospatiale AS.350BA Ecureuil	3053	S5-HCZ
			RA-04101
			F-WQDR
I-ATLR	Aérospatiale/Alenia ATR-72-212A	701	F-WWEA
I-ATMC	Aérospatiale/Alenia ATR-72-212A	588	F-WWED
I-ATPA	Aérospatiale/Alenia ATR-72-212A	626	F-WQKZ
			F-WWLC
I-ATPI	Beech F33A Bonanza	CE-464	HB-EHT
I-ATPM	Aérospatiale/Alenia ATR-72-212A	705	F-WWED
I-ATRF	Aérospatiale/Alenia ATR-42-300	034	F-WWEP
I-ATRG	Aérospatiale/Alenia ATR-42-300	042	F-WWEW
I-ATRJ	Aérospatiale/Alenia ATR-42-300	057	F-WWEL
I-ATRL	Aérospatiale/Alenia ATR-42-300	068	F-WWES
I-ATRM	Aérospatiale/Alenia ATR-42-300	114	F-WWEK
I-ATSL	Aérospatiale/Alenia ATR-72-212A	592	F-WWEM
I-ATSM	Aérospatiale/Alenia ATR-72-212A	702	F-WWEX
I-ATWO	Agusta AB.139	31002	
I-AUNI	Robinson R-22 Beta	1769	
I-AUNY	Cessna 501 Citation I/SP	501-0213	N6785D
I-AVAA	Mudry CAP.10B	38	F-BUDH
I-AVAB	Piper PA-18-150 Super Cub	18-7909097	N9750N
I-AVAM	Piper PA-18 Super Cub 95	18-7363	

I-AVEB	Mitsubishi MU.300 Diamond 1A	A.087SA	N870AM
			(PH-JSL)
			HB-VIA
			N487DM
I-AVGM	Cessna 550 Citation II	550-0492	
I-AVIF	Aérospatiale SA.315B Lama	2566	
I-AVIU	Cessna TR182 Turbo Skylane RG	R18201372	N4665S
I-AVIV	Reims/Cessna F152	F15201831	
I-AVJC	Bell 206B Jet Ranger II	1491	N100FW
			N777FW
			N777FL
I-AVJF	MBB-Kawasaki BK.117C-1	7525	D-HBKX(2)
I-AVJG	Gates Learjet 35A	35A-189	N727JP
	(W/o, Geneva 24.10.99)		N18NM
			N35KC
			N32FN
			N32TC
			(N189TC)
			N39292
			VH-AJV
			N381IG
I-AVON	Partenavia P.64B Oscar B	52	
I-AVRM	Cessna 550 Citation II	550-0491	
I-AVSS	Beech 400A Beechjet	RK-66	N6048F
			HB-VLM
			N400Y
			N400A
			(N400DT)
			N400A
I-AVVM	Cessna S550 Citation SII	S550-0062	N12715
I-AXOO	Agusta A.109C	7648	OO-AAY
			D-HMET
I-AZRO	Piper PA-28RT-201T Turbo Arrow IV	28R-8031025	N2852S
I-AZUL	SOCATA Rallye 180T Galérien	3090	F-GAYS
I-BADB	Piper PA-18-150 Super Cub	18-8764	N4426Z
I-BADC	Piper PA-18-150 Super Cub	18-8770	N4437Z
			N9723N
I-BAEB	Piper PA-18-150 Super Cub	18-7609021	N9773P
I-BAKE	Aero Designs Pulsar	01	
I-BALF	Piper PA-18-150 Super Cub	18-7609149	N9691P
I-BALG	Piper PA-18-150 Super Cub	18-7609129	I-ALGD
			N83443
I-BALK	Piper PA-18-150 Super Cub	18-7709032	N66842
I-BALM	Piper PA-18-150 Super Cub	18-7809035	N82961
I-BALN	Piper PA-18-150 Super Cub	18-7809033	N82951
I-BALP	Piper PA-18-150 Super Cub	18-8009044	N9757N
I-BALS	Piper PA-18-150 Super Cub	18-8109080	N91192
I-BALT	Piper PA-18-150 Super Cub	18-8109082	N91201
I-BALW	Christen A-1 Husky	1133	
I-BALX	Sud Avn SA.318CAlouette Astazou	2170	EC- . . .
			F-GNCU
			TJ-AHW
			TR-LPE
I-BALZ	Christen A-1 Husky	1157	
I-BAND	Cessna R172K Hawk XP	R1723081	N758GH
I-BANG	de Havilland DH.82A Tiger Moth	85482	G-APRY
			DE486
I-BARO	Sequoia F.8LFalco	503	
I-BATR	Piper PA-18-150 Super Cub	18-8699	N4377Z
I-BAZZ	S.A.I. F.4 Rondone I	021	
I-BBAK	Cessna 182R Skylane	18268475	N9936E
I-BBMM	Christen Pitts S-2B	5196	N317JK
I-BBTT	Cessna T210N Turbo Centurion	21063796	OO-TVH
			N6083C
I-BCOM	Piaggio P.180 Avanti	1040	
I-BDIJ	SNCAN/Stampe SV.4C	511	F-BDIJ
I-BEAR	Piper PA-28RT-201 Arrow IV	28R-7918129	N28471
	(Damaged 18.2.01)		
I-BEAS	Piper PA-34-220T Seneca III	34-8133248	N711KB
			(D-GKBL)
			N711KB
			N9589N
I-BEAU	Dassault Falcon 900	23	F-WWFK
I-BEBO	Piper PA-24-260 Comanche B	24-4759	N9260P
I-BECS	Schweizer 269C	S-1261	N75045
I-BEGA	Rand-Robinson KS-2S	8824-372	
I-BEKT	Beech 76 Duchess	ME-85	HB-GGR
			F-GBRO
I-BEMA	Agusta-Bell 47J-3	2070	MM80359
			Carabin. CC-5
			MM80359
			Navy 2-06
I-BEMF	Cessna 182Q Skylane	18265216	N7567S
I-BENN	Cessna 550 Citation Bravo	550-0859	(N550KH)
			N551KH
I-BENT	Cessna 560XL Citation Excel	560-5053	N5231S
I-BERL	SOCATA Rallye 100S Sport	2359	HB-ERL
			I-RALR
I-BEST	Cessna 320B Skyknight	320B0006	N9806L
I-BETO	Robinson R-22 Beta	2370	N8015S
I-BETT	Piper PA-28RT-201T Turbo Arrow IV	28R-8331023	N4293K
I-BGBG	Cessna 152	15283080	N46605
I-BGFE	Piper PA-31-350 Navajo Chieftain	31-7652043	N59772
I-BGMT	Piper PA-18-150 Super Cub	18-7545	N10F
I-BGTT	SNCASE SE.313B Alouette II	1115	F-GMJT
			(F-GMLC)
			CNET/F-SEBN
I-BIAP	Piper PA-28-140 Cherokee	28-24326	N1882J
I-BIAR	Piper PA-28-140 Cherokee	28-24336	N1891J
I-BIAT	Piper PA-28-140 Cherokee	28-24572	N7235J
I-BIFA	Enstrom 280FX Shark	2065	(JA7857)
I-BIKA	Airbus A320-214	951	F-WWBT
I-BIKB	Airbus A320-214	1226	F-WWIG
I-BIKC	Airbus A320-214	1448	F-WWBV
I-BIKD	Airbus A320-214	1457	F-WWDE
I-BIKE	Airbus A320-214	999	F-WWBZ
I-BIKF	Airbus A320-214	1473	F-WWDP
I-BIKG	Airbus A320-214	1480	F-WWDT
I-BIKI	Airbus A320-214	1138	F-WWDJ
I-BIKL	Airbus A320-214	1489	F-WWDN
I-BIKO	Airbus A320-214	1168	F-WWDL
I-BIKU	Airbus A320-214	1217	F-WWBD
I-BIMA	Airbus A319-112	1722	D-AVWP
I-BIMB	Airbus A319-112	2033	D-AVYP
I-BIMC	Airbus A319-112	2057	D-AVYC
I-BIMD	Airbus A319-112	2074	D-AVYM
I-BIME	Airbus A319-112	1740	D-AVWW
I-BIMF	Airbus A319-112	2083	D-AVYZ
I-BIMG	Airbus A319-112	2086	D-AVWD
I-BIMH	Airbus A319-112	2101	D-AVYY
I-BIMI	Airbus A319-112	1745	D-AVWZ
I-BIMJ	Airbus A319-112	1779	D-AVYG
I-BIML	Airbus A319-112 (Reservation .04)	2127	D-AVWN
I-BIMO	Airbus A319-112	1770	D-AVWC
I-BIOI	Macchi MB.308	122/5895	MM53075
I-BIRS	Partenavia P.64B Oscar B-1155	56	
I-BISB	Cessna 172P floatplane	17275014	N54630
I-BISI	Piper J-3C-65 Cub	13121	F-BCPG
			44-80825
I-BITT	Partenavia P.64B Oscar 200	01	
I-BIXA	Airbus A321-112	477	D-AVZE
I-BIXB	Airbus A321-112	524	D-AVZY
I-BIXC	Airbus A321-112	526	D-AVZZ
I-BIXD	Airbus A321-112	532	D-AVZB
I-BIXE	Airbus A321-112	488	D-AVZG
I-BIXF	Airbus A321-112	515	D-AVZQ
I-BIXG	Airbus A321-112	516	D-AVZR
I-BIXH	Airbus A321-112	940	D-AVZS
I-BIXI	Airbus A321-112	494	D-AVZI
I-BIXJ	Airbus A321-112	959	D-AVZP
I-BIXK	Airbus A321-112	1220	D-AVZC
I-BIXL	Airbus A321-112	513	D-AVZO
I-BIXM	Airbus A321-112	514	D-AVZP
I-BIXN	Airbus A321-112	576	D-AVZR
I-BIXO	Airbus A321-112	495	D-AVZJ
I-BIXP	Airbus A321-112	583	D-AVZT
I-BIXQ	Airbus A321-112	586	D-AVZU
I-BIXR	Airbus A321-112	593	D-AVZW
I-BIXS	Airbus A321-112	599	D-AVZZ
I-BIXT	Airbus A321-112	765	D-AVZW
I-BIXU	Airbus A321-111	434	D-AVZB
			F-WWID
I-BIXV	Airbus A321-112	819	D-AVZU
I-BIXZ	Airbus A321-112	848	D-AVZC
I-BJBB	Cessna 152	15284252	G-BJBB
			N5086L
I-BKAK	Rutan Long-Ez	001	
I-BKBS	MBB-Kawasaki BK.117C-1	7504	D-HOTZ
			XA- . . .
			D-HOTZ
			D-HECA(3)
			D-HMBF
I-BLAE	Piper PA-28-161 Cadet	2841054	N9163V
I-BLAS	Mudry CAP.10B	151	N151AS
			F-WZCG
I-BLBU	Aérospatiale AS.350B2 Ecureuil	3816	
I-BLDS	SG Aviation Storm 400 T1 Century	193	
I-BLEU	Agusta A.109EPower	11151	
I-BLIM	SNCASE SE.313B Alouette II	1242	F-GHUQ
			ALAT
I-BLIP	Aérospatiale SA.315B Lama	2495	
I-BLIV	Piper PA-31P Pressurized Navajo	31P-7300122	HB-LIV
			N7350L
I-BLQA	Robinson R-44 Raven	1360	
I-BLUB	Cessna 650 Citation VI	650-0216	N68269
I-BLUX	Aérospatiale AS.350B2 Ecureuil	2506	SE-JAF
			F-WYMN
I-BMBN	Beech V35 Bonanza	D-8133	N9046S
I-BMFE	Gates Learjet 25C	25C-146	N6KJ
			N9HN
			C-GRQX
			N9HN
			N9HM
			N146LJ
I-BMGF	Pilatus PC-6/B2-H4 Turbo Porter	913	HB-FLD
I-BNAP	Bredanardi NH-500D	BH-12	
I-BNBH	Hughes 269C	24-0274	
I-BNCC	Bredanardi NH-300C	003	
I-BNCD	Bredanardi NH-300C	004	
I-BNCS	Bredanardi NH-300C	019	
I-BNDB	Schweizer 269C	S-1560	N104LU
I-BNDD	Schweizer 269C	S-1599	N69A
I-BOAT	Cessna 525 CitationJet	525-0450	N5156D

I-BOBO	Piper J-3C-65 Cub	12128	I-PIST 44-79832
I-BOCA	Piper J-3C-65 Cub	20141	N6910H NC6910H
I-BODE	Stolp SA.75- Starduster	400	
I-BOGO	Reims FR172J Rocket	FR17200568	(I-AIIA) (I-CCAJ) (D-EALR) (I-CCAJ) (D-EOGV)
I-BOLK	Robin DR.400/180R Remorqueur (CofA exp. 1.6.02. Stored Rieti 7.04)	1706	
I-BONG	Reims/Cessna F150K Floatplane	F15000621	(I-ALAT)
I-BONU	Piper PA-28-161 Cadet	2841274	N91966
I-BOYA	Cessna A152 Aerobat	A1520966	G-BOYA N761ML
I-BPAA	Bredanardi NH-300C	023	I-BNCT
I-BPAC	Boeing 737-4Z9	25147	OE-LNH
I-BPAE	Piaggio P.180 Avanti	1081	
I-BPAF	Piaggio P.180 Avanti	1086	
I-BPBP	Robinson R-22 Beta	1276	I-MIBP N8076R
I-BRAL	Aérospatiale AS.350BA Ecureuil	1904	
I-BRBR	Beech 35-C33A Debonair	CE-35	HB-EKV
I-BRIG	Partenavia P.64B Oscar 200	03	
I-BRIP	Partenavia P.66B Oscar 150	43	
I-BRIS	Partenavia P.66B Oscar 100	39	
I-BRJN	Reims/Cessna F150L	F15001025	
I-BRMA	Agusta-Bell AB.412	25626	
I-BRMS	Stoddard-Hamilton Glastar GS-1	5228	
I-BRUZ	SE.5A Replica	unkn	
I-BSAB	Piper PA-46-350P Malibu Mirage	4622049	G-BSAB N9161N
I-BSAM	Robinson R-22B Beta	1076	N8048U
I-BSHV	Bell 206B Jet Ranger II (W/o 20.10.04)	909	HB-XHV D-HORY
I-BSTI	Fairchild Swearingen SA.227AC Merlin III	AC-470	(D-CBST) C-FAFM C-FJLX N470A (N470CA) N470A HB-LNB N30486
I-BSTS	Fairchild Swearingen SA.227AC Metro III	AC-603	N3117S
I-BTEC	Robinson R-22 Beta	0569	G-GSFC N2425J
I-BTRE	Piper PA-18-135 Super Cub	18-3339	EI-120 I-EIKR MM53-7739 53-7739
I-BUCK	Bücker Bü.131 Jungmann	46	HB-UTM A-35
I-BUFF	Piper PA-18S-150 Super Cub Floatplane	1809008	N9616N
I-BUNN	Reims FR172H Rocket	FR17200289	D-ECQN
I-BURI	Avia FL.54 Meteor	1126	OE-ABR I-FELO
I-BURL	Stinson L-5 Sentinel	unkn	MM52883
I-BURY	Piper PA-23-250 Turbo Aztec D	27-4400	N6628Y
I-BUSP	Airbus A300B4-203 (Stored)	067	N207EA F-GBNC F-WZEP
I-BUTT	Robinson R-22B2 Beta	3229	
I-BUZZ	Rand-Robinson KR-2	8311	
I-BVUL	Piper PA-34-200T Seneca II	34-7570128	G-BVUL OY-PEA N33531
I-BXPD	Beech P35 Bonanza	D-7025	CN-TYI
I-BXWA	Sud Avn SA.316B Alouette III (Damaged 28.2.03)	1307	F-GIBY A-307
I-BXWB	Aérospatiale SA.315BLama	2453	(OY-HVD) HB-XGG
I-BXWD	Aérospatiale SA.315BLama	2617	F-GJGF F-GHIJ N5785V
I-BXWE	Aérospatiale SA.315BLama	2470	HB-XXS OE-OXI HB-XXS YV-318A F-WTND
I-BYRA	Evans VP-1 Volksplane	unkn	
I-BZEB	Reims FR172J Rocket	FR17200490	D-EDCC(3) D-EECC(1)
I-BZEC	Reims FR172J Rocket	FR17200379	D-ECVG
I-CAAL	Robin DR.400/140 Major	863	
I-CACO	Aérospatiale SA.315BLama	2457	F-GAMB
I-CACR	Maule MX-7-180 Star Rocket	11060C	N9204U
I-CADF	Dragon Fly 333AC	EB063	
I-CAEX	Dassault Falcon 900EX	91	(F-OINA) F-WQBJ N989EX F-WWFJ
I-CAFD	Dassault Falcon 50	183	F-WWHC
I-CAKE	Pilatus PC-6/B2-H4 Turbo Porter	942	HB-FMM
I-CAMI	Aviamilano F.14 Nibbio	207	
I-CAMT	Partenavia P.66B Oscar 100	57	
I-CAMY	Mooney M.20J Model 205	24-3205	N9132N

I-CANO	Cessna U206G Stationair 6	U20606003	N4692Z
I-CAPA	Evans VP-1 Volksplane	unkn	
I-CAPC	CAP.1	unkn	
I-CAPF	Evans VP-1 Volksplane	V-2358	
I-CAPH	Evans VP-1 Volksplane	V-8-78-AC	
I-CAPJ	Ianotta I-66 San Francesco	001	
I-CAPK	Sparviero	unkn	
I-CAPM	Jodel D.92 Bébé	unkn	
I-CAPS	Brügger MB-2 Colibri	002	
I-CAPU	Evans VP-2 Volksplane	V-2294	
I-CARQ	General Avia F.22B Pinguino	010	
I-CASP	Piper PA-28R-200 Cherokee Arrow II	28R-7335155	N333RG
I-CAST	Dragon Fly 333	051	
I-CATF	Evans VP-1 Volksplane	unkn	
I-CATS	Robinson R-44 Astro	0546	
I-CATW	Reims/Cessna F150M	F15001188	
I-CAVE	Partenavia P.64B Oscar B-1155	69	
I-CAVI	Piper PA-28-180 Cherokee Archer	28-7505171	N4436X N9622N
I-CAVL	Aviamilano P.19 Scricciolo	341	
I-CAVM	Piper PA-28-161 Cadet	2841090	N9170N
I-CBJR	Cessna T210L Turbo Centurion	T21060102	OE-DGP N59118
I-CBSQ	Mooney M.20R Ovation	29-0116	N323SQ N716MA
I-CCAA	Mooney M.20E Chaparral	700028	N943IV
I-CCAB	Reims FR172H Rocket	FR17200312	
I-CCAD	Reims FR172J Rocket	FR17200357	
I-CCAE	Reims FR172J Rocket	FR17200413	
I-CCAF	Reims FR172J Rocket	FR17200404	
I-CCAH	Reims/Cessna F172M	F17201056	
I-CCAL	Reims FR172J Rocket	FR17200483	
I-CCAN	Reims FR172J Rocket	FR17200556	
I-CCAP	Reims FR172J Rocket	FR17200438	(D-EJXY)
I-CCAQ	Reims/Cessna F172M (Damaged 1.4.01)	F17201336	
I-CCAR	Reims/Cessna F172M	F17201135	(F-BSGU)
I-CCAS	Reims FR172J Rocket	FR17200527	
I-CCAT	Reims/Cessna F172M	F17201358	
I-CCAW	Reims/Cessna F172M	F17201427	
I-CCBA	Reims FR172J Rocket	FR17200541	
I-CCBC	Cessna U206F Stationair	U20603232	N8371Q
I-CCBF	Reims/Cessna F172N	F17201550	
I-CCBG	Reims/Cessna FR172K Hawk XP	FR17200599	
I-CCBI	Maule MX.7-235 Star Rocket	10075C	N92047
I-CCDC	Reims FR172J Rocket	FR17200571	
I-CCFF	Cessna 340A	340A0223	N3888G
I-CCIM	Piper PA-28-161 Cadet	2841091	N9170R
I-CCSV	Piper PA-28-161 Cadet	2841096	N9173R
I-CCWW	Piper PA-24-260 Comanche	24-4048	N8589P HB-OYA N8589P
I-CDAL	Piper PA-28R-201 Arrow	2844032	N4172U
I-CECC	SOCATA MS.883 Rallye 115	1510	F-BRYK
I-CECI	Aeromere F.8L Falco	202	
I-CEDA	SOCATA TB-10 Tobago	759	
I-CEDI	de Havilland DH.82A Tiger Moth	85374	G-AOUI DE352
I-CELF	Bell 206B Jet Ranger II	1605	N77884 N333PA N90108
I-CELJ	Piper PA-28-180 Cherokee Archer	28-7405263	N44594
I-CELU	Cessna 172RG Cutlass RG	172RG0326	N5293U
I-CELY	Piper PA-34-200T Seneca II	34-8070255	N8230V
I-CENB	Reims/Cessna F150L	F15000943	
I-CEND	Reims FR172J Rocket	FR17200401	
I-CENE	Reims/Cessna F150L	F15000986	
I-CEPI	Robin DR.380 Prince	609	
I-CERL	Piper J-3C-65 Cub	17372	HB-OWY N70386 NC70386
I-CERR	Piper PA-20 Pacer 125	20-796	HB-OON
I-CERX	Aeritalia-Fiat G.222	4043	
I-CESY	Piper PA-28-161 Cadet	2841097	N9173X
I-CFAA	Agusta-Bell AB.412	25610	
I-CFAB	Agusta-Bell AB.412	25614	
I-CFAC	Agusta-Bell AB.412	25615	
I-CFAD	Agusta-Bell AB.412	25618	
I-CFAE	Agusta-Bell AB.412EP	25918	
I-CFAF	Agusta-Bell AB.412EP	25919	
I-CFPA	Piaggio P.180 Avanti	1094	
I-CFSB	Hughes 369HS	84-0634S	I-BNAD
I-CFSC	Hughes 369HS	94-0648S	
I-CFSD	Bredanardi NH-500D	BH-01	
I-CFSE	Bredanardi NH-500D	BH-02	
I-CFSF	Bredanardi NH-500D	BH-03	
I-CFSG	Bredanardi NH-500D	BH-04	
I-CFSH	Bredanardi NH-500D	BH-05	
I-CFSI	Bredanardi NH-500D	BH-06	
I-CFSJ	Agusta-Bell 412	25561	
I-CFSK	Bredanardi NH-500D	BH-07	
I-CFSL	Bredanardi NH-500D	BH-15	
I-CFSM	Bredanardi NH-500D	BH-16	
I-CFSN	Bredanardi NH-500D	BH-17	
I-CFSO	Agusta-Bell 412	25562	
I-CFSP	Agusta-Bell 412	25563	
I-CFSW	Agusta-Bell 412	25564	
I-CFSX	Agusta-Bell 412	25572	

I-CFSZ	Canadair CL-215-1A10	1108	C-FFYO
			C-FBNJ
			C-GKEE
I-CFVA	Aérospatiale AS.350B Ecureuil	3243	
I-CGAB	Piper PA-28-140 Cherokee E	28-7225166	N11C
I-CGAD	Piper PA-28-140 Cherokee F	28-7325020	N11C
I-CGAM	Piper PA-28-151 Cherokee Warrior	28-7715151	N9523N
I-CGAO	Piper PA-18-150 Super Cub	18-8109085	(LN-FAL)
			N91205
I-CGAR	Piper PA-34-220T Seneca III	34-8233081	N8096B
I-CGAS	Piper PA-28-181 Archer II	28-8690020	N9102T
I-CGAT	Piper PA-31T Cheyenne	31T-7520033	N54964
I-CGAV	Piper PA-34-220T Seneca III	34-8433021	N4312E
I-CGAZ	Piper PA-28RT-201 Arrow IV	28R-7918247	N4507U
I-CGBB	Mooney M.20J Model 205	24-3129	N1067S
I-CGCC	Christen A-1 Husky	1158	
I-CGCL	Agusta-Bell 412	25600	
I-CGDD	Christen A-1 Husky	1181	
I-CGFE	Aérospatiale AS.365N2 Dauphin 2	6494	F-WQDI
I-CGTT	Piper PA-31T Cheyenne II	31T-7820045	N82288
I-CHEK	Piper PA-28R-201 Arrow	2844017	N4136W
I-CHIM	Aviamilano F.8L Falco	112	
I-CHNR	Beech 95 Travel Air	TD-299	N9623R
I-CHOP	Bell 206B Jet Ranger II	2523	G-BSUG
			N888GC
			N222PF
			N315GC
I-CHTH	Grumman AA-5A Cheetah	AA5A-0659	
I-CICC	Partenavia P.66B Oscar 100	13	
I-CICO	Procaer F.15B Picchio	20	
I-CIGB	Cessna 501 Citation I/SP	501-0163	(I-AGIK)
			N1354G
I-CILL	Mudry CAP.21	8	F-GDTC
I-CIOH	Aérospatiale SA.365N Dauphin 2	6004	F-WYMI
			F-WZJS
I-CIRE	Aviamilano F.8L Falco	111	
I-CITS	Robinson R-22 Beta	1374	
I-CITU	Aerotek Pitts S-2A	2199	G-BGSF
I-CJAO	Cessna U206B Super Skywagon	U206-0782	N3482L
I-CLAD	Cessna 500 Citation I	500-0223	N223P
			OH-COC
			N400SA
			N444KV
			N444LP
			N223CC
I-CLAM	Robinson R-22 Mariner	2490M	N83206
I-CLEO	Schweizer 269C	S-1490	N86G
I-CLIC	Robinson R-22B2 Beta	3093	
I-CLLO	Cessna 172M	17266468	N80240
I-CLMF	Agusta A.119 Koala	14031	N17YC
I-CLON	American AA-5B Tiger	AA5B-0432	N81110
I-CLRM	Agusta A.109E Power (Damaged 6.3.01)	11042	
I-CMAL	Cessna 560XL Citation Excel	560-5344	N51055
I-CMAO	Reims/Cessna F150L	F15000748	D-ECQB
I-CMDA	Cessna 172A	46883	HB-CMD
			OE-DGW
			N7283T
I-CMDV	Agusta A.109A	7128	
I-CMLC	Bell 206B Jet Ranger II	3394	G-BWVE
			G-BOSX
			N20681
I-CMMA	Piper PA-46-350P Malibu Mirage	4622062	N9178D
I-CMMB	Piper PA-28RT-201T Turbo Arrow IV	28R-8231029	N8101C
I-CMUT	Dassault Falcon 20F	389	F-WRQV
I-CNPG	Piper PA-28-161 Warrior II	28-7916394	N424RP
			N16PA
			N9514N
I-COAE	Agusta A.109A	7180	LX-HRG
			3A-MGI
			I-GAME
			N284CN
			D-HACP
			HB-XKZ
I-COBY	Piper PA-34-200T Seneca II	34-7670026	N9244K
			N9611N
I-COCE	Aérospatiale SA.365N Dauphin 2	6099	F-WYMD
			G-BLWC
I-COKK	Beech F33A Bonanza	CE-1307	N524PD
I-COLL	Piper PA-28-181 Archer II	28-8190074	N82854
I-COMB	Piper PA-18 Super Cub 95	18-3656	F-DADQ
I-COND	Hughes 269C	117-0644	
I-COOP	Aérospatiale SA.315B Lama	2668	
I-COPT	Eurocopter EC.120BColibri	1268	
I-CORB	Piper PA-28R-200 Cherokee Arrow II	28R-7635072	N4535X
I-CORD	Ariel 92-S	589	
I-CORR	Partenavia P.57 Fachiro IIf	33	
I-COSS	Sud Avn SA.318C Alouette Astazou	2151	F-GMLE
			F-GMLF
			9V- . . .
			F-GDQO
			C-FBMG
			CF-BMG
			F-WIEN
I-COTT	Beech 77 Skipper	WA-292	HB-EJK
I-CRAB	Reims/Cessna F150L	F15001032	
I-CRAC	Reims/Cessna F150L	F15001098	
I-CRBO	Partenavia P.66C Charlie	104	

I-CRCA	Piper PA-28-181 Archer II	2890153	N9211G
I-CRE I	Piper PA-32R-301 Saratoga II HP	3246223	N3101Q
I-CREM	Dassault Falcon 10	161	F-WWZK
			I-CREM
			N50SL
			N30CN
			N230FJ
			F-WZGM
I-CRIC	Mudry CAP.231EX	001	F-GRLR
			F-WZCI
I-CRMC	Aérospatiale AS.350B Ecureuil	1272	F-GCJZ
I-CRMD	Agusta A.109A-II	7301	
I-CRPI	Piper PA-28-180 Cherokee Archer	28-7505254	N3992X
I-CRSE	Piper PA-28RT-201T Turbo Arrow IV	28R-7931225	N2853W
I-CRSR	Sud Avn SA.316B Alouette III (Dam. 11.1.01)	1949	F-OCUR
I-CSAM	Aérospatiale AS.350B1 Ecureuil	2233	
I-CSCM	Robinson R-22B2 Beta	3365	N7507P
I-CSDI	Robinson R-44 Raven II	10469	
I-CUCC	Cessna 172M	17262671	N13326
I-CUDP	SNCASE SE.313 Alouette II	1165	F-ZBAA
			F-BIFM
			F-WIFM
I-CVDA	Piper PA-28-140 Cherokee	28-20920	HB-PEM
			D-EMHA
			N6790W
I-CVMD	Agusta A.109A	7107	N109JD
			(N1091F)
			N109JD
			I-DCMV
I-CWSA	Piper PA-18-150 Super Cub	18-8109002	N24291
I-CYRN	Partenavia P.64B Oscar B	37	
I-CZAJ	Monnet Sonerai IILS	51LS	
I-DAAD	Piper PA-28RT-201T Turbo Arrow IV	28R-7931077	N3013R
I-DACD	Agusta A.109A-II	7258	(N9047U)
I-DACE	Agusta A.109A-II (A.109K)	7340	
I-DACG	Agusta-Bell 206B Jet Ranger III	8652	
I-DACM	McDonnell-Douglas DC-9-82	49971	
I-DACN	McDonnell-Douglas DC-9-82	49972	
I-DACP	McDonnell-Douglas DC-9-82	49973	
I-DACQ	McDonnell-Douglas DC-9-82	49974	
I-DACR	McDonnell-Douglas DC-9-82	49975	
I-DACS	McDonnell-Douglas DC-9-82	53053	
I-DACT	McDonnell-Douglas DC-9-82	53054	
I-DACU	McDonnell-Douglas DC-9-82	53055	
I-DACV	McDonnell-Douglas DC-9-82	53056	
I-DACW	McDonnell-Douglas DC-9-82	53057	
I-DACX	McDonnell-Douglas DC-9-82	53060	
I-DACY	McDonnell-Douglas DC-9-82	53059	
I-DACZ	McDonnell-Douglas DC-9-82	53058	
I-DADS	SOCATATB-20 Trinidad	712	HB-KCN
			G-BNAZ
I-DAFE	Cessna 172N	17272647	N6229D
I-DAGF	Cessna 525 CitationJet	525-0347	N1133G
I-DAGI	Neico Lancair 235	1	
I-DAGS	Canadair CL.600-2B16 Challenger	5085	D-ACTE
			D-ACTU(1)
			N618CC
			C-FJPI
			C-GLXD
I-DALS	Piper PA-28-161 Warrior II	28-8016171	D-EWII,
			N8144Z
			N9525N
I-DAMS	Aérospatiale AS.365N3 Dauphin 2	6700	F-WWOX
I-DAND	McDonnell-Douglas DC-9-82	53061	
I-DANF	McDonnell-Douglas DC-9-82	53062	
I-DANG	McDonnell-Douglas DC-9-82	53176	
I-DANH	McDonnell-Douglas DC-9-82	53177	
I-DANL	McDonnell-Douglas DC-9-82	53178	
I-DANM	McDonnell-Douglas DC-9-82	53179	
I-DANP	McDonnell-Douglas DC-9-82	53180	
I-DANQ	McDonnell-Douglas DC-9-82	53181	
I-DANR	McDonnell-Douglas DC-9-82	53203	
I-DANS	Piper PA-28-161 Warrior II	28-8316054	N42952
I-DANU	McDonnell-Douglas DC-9-82	53204	
I-DANV	McDonnell-Douglas DC-9-82	53205	
I-DANW	McDonnell-Douglas DC-9-82	53206	
I-DARD	Piper PA-28-161 Warrior II	28-8216172	N8224V
I-DARJ	Aérospatiale AS.350B Ecureuil	3680	
I-DASO	Sud Avn SA.316B Alouette III	1318	F-GJCY
			ALAT
I-DAST	Aérospatiale AS.350B3 Ecureuil	3436	
I-DATA	McDonnell-Douglas DC-9-82	53216	
I-DATB	McDonnell-Douglas DC-9-82	53221	
I-DATC	McDonnell-Douglas DC-9-82	53222	
I-DATD	McDonnell-Douglas DC-9-82	53223	
I-DATE	McDonnell-Douglas DC-9-82	53217	
I-DATF	McDonnell-Douglas DC-9-82	53224	
I-DATG	McDonnell-Douglas DC-9-82	53225	
I-DATH	McDonnell-Douglas DC-9-82	53226	
I-DATI	McDonnell-Douglas DC-9-82	53218	
I-DATJ	McDonnell-Douglas DC-9-82	53227	
I-DATK	McDonnell-Douglas DC-9-82	53228	
I-DATL	McDonnell-Douglas DC-9-82	53229	
I-DATM	McDonnell-Douglas DC-9-82	53230	
I-DATN	McDonnell-Douglas DC-9-82	53231	
I-DATO	McDonnell-Douglas DC-9-82	53219	
I-DATP	McDonnell-Douglas DC-9-82	53232	

I-DATQ	McDonnell-Douglas DC-9-82	53233	
I-DATR	McDonnell-Douglas DC-9-82	53234	
I-DATS	McDonnell-Douglas DC-9-82	53235	
I-DATU	McDonnell-Douglas DC-9-82	53220	
I-DAVA	McDonnell-Douglas DC-9-82	49215	
I-DAVB	McDonnell-Douglas DC-9-82	49216	
I-DAVD	McDonnell-Douglas DC-9-82	49218	N6203D
I-DAVG	McDonnell-Douglas DC-9-82	49220	
I-DAVJ	McDonnell-Douglas DC-9-82	49431	
I-DAVL	McDonnell-Douglas DC-9-82	49433	
I-DAVM	McDonnell-Douglas DC-9-82	49434	
I-DAVN	McDonnell-Douglas DC-9-82	49435	
I-DAVP	McDonnell-Douglas DC-9-82	49549	
I-DAVR	McDonnell-Douglas DC-9-82	49550	
I-DAVS	McDonnell-Douglas DC-9-82	49551	
I-DAVT	McDonnell-Douglas DC-9-82	49552	
I-DAVU	McDonnell-Douglas DC-9-82	49794	
I-DAVV	McDonnell-Douglas DC-9-82	49795	
I-DAVW	McDonnell-Douglas DC-9-82	49796	
I-DAVX	McDonnell-Douglas DC-9-82	49969	
I-DAVZ	McDonnell-Douglas DC-9-82	49970	
I-DAWA	McDonnell-Douglas DC-9-82	49192	N19B
I-DAWB	McDonnell-Douglas DC-9-82	49197	
I-DAWC	McDonnell-Douglas DC-9-82	49198	
I-DAWD	McDonnell-Douglas DC-9-82	49199	
I-DAWE	McDonnell-Douglas DC-9-82	49193	
I-DAWF	McDonnell-Douglas DC-9-82	49200	
I-DAWG	McDonnell-Douglas DC-9-82	49201	
I-DAWH	McDonnell-Douglas DC-9-82	49202	
I-DAWI	McDonnell-Douglas DC-9-82	49194	
I-DAWJ	McDonnell-Douglas DC-9-82	49203	
I-DAWL	McDonnell-Douglas DC-9-82	49204	
I-DAWM	McDonnell-Douglas DC-9-82	49205	
I-DAWO	McDonnell-Douglas DC-9-82	49195	
I-DAWP	McDonnell-Douglas DC-9-82	49206	
I-DAWQ	McDonnell-Douglas DC-9-82	49207	
I-DAWR	McDonnell-Douglas DC-9-82	49208	
I-DAWS	McDonnell-Douglas DC-9-82	49209	
I-DAWT	McDonnell-Douglas DC-9-82	49210	
I-DAWU	McDonnell-Douglas DC-9-82	49196	
I-DAWV	McDonnell-Douglas DC-9-82	49211	
I-DAWW	McDonnell-Douglas DC-9-82	49212	
I-DAWZ	McDonnell-Douglas DC-9-82	49214	
I-DBCH	Zenair CH-701 STOL	7-1332	
I-DDAC	Tecnam P.92-2000RG VEL	003	
I-DDVE	Aérospatiale AS.365N2 Dauphin 2	6414	G-CBRA I-GRDN F-WYMJ
I-DDVF	Dassault Falcon 2000	161	F-WWVA
I-DEAS	Gulfstream V	593	(I-MPUT) N593GA
I-DEBO	Hughes 369D	39-0480D	HB-XIR
I-DEBS	SP 318 (This is a modified SA.318C Alouette Astazou helicopter)	001	
I-DECA	Piper PA-28R-200 Cherokee Arrow II	28R-7635300	N6125J
I-DECR	Piper PA-28-181 Cherokee Archer II	28-7690448	N6981J
I-DEEN	Cessna TR182 Turbo Skylane RG	R18200665	N9150R
I-DEIB	Boeing 767-33AER	27376	G-OITA VH-ITA N276AW N1794B
I-DEIC	Boeing 767-33AER	27377	G-OITB VH-ITB N361AW N6009F
I-DEID	Boeing 767-33A	27468	G-OITC (VH-ITH)
I-DEIF	Boeing 767-33A	27908	G-OITF N6055X
I-DEIG	Boeing 767-33AER	27918	G-OITG
I-DEIL	Boeing 767-33AER	28147	G-OITL
I-DELA	Mooney M.20J Model 205	24-3349	N612SB
I-DELB	Cessna 172S	172S9534	N2157D
I-DELF	Robinson R-22 Beta	1091	
I-DEMP	Boeing 747-243B (Stored)	22513	
I-DENI	MBB-Kawasaki BK.117C-1	7539	D-HMB .
I-DENY	Aérospatiale SA.315B Lama	2525	G-BMKT N9002K
I-DEPE	Pilatus Britten-Norman BN-2B-26 Islander	2253	G-BTLY
I-DEPL	Polliwagen	unkn	
I-DERI	Reims/Cessna F150L	F1500740	OE-CVY
I-DERT	SIAI-Marchetti S.205-18/R	357	
I-DEST	Piper PA-28-140 Cherokee Cruiser	28-7525085	N9503N
I-DETO	Robinson R-22B2 Beta	3598	N75341
I-DEUM	Cessna 525A CitationJet 2	525A-0095	N5221Y
I-DEVE	Dragon Fly DF333AC	EB054	
I-DIAV	Partenavia P.57 Fachiro IIf	18	
I-DIDE	Piper PA-24-250 Comanche	24-158	I-DIDJ HB-OTC N5199P
I-DIDU	Brugger MB-2 Colibri	40	
I-DIEL	Robinson R-22	0104	HB-XMK N9041Q
I-DIES	Dassault Falcon 900	30	F-WGTH HB-IAF F-WWFL
I-DIGI	Partenavia P.57 Fachiro IIf	12	

I-DINU	Robin DR.400/160 Chevalier	1711	
I-DIPA	SEEMS MS.885 Super Rallye	353	
I-DISA	Boeing 777-243ER	32855	
I-DISB	Boeing 777-243ER	32859	N5016R
I-DISD	Boeing 777-243ER	32860	
I-DISE	Boeing 777-243ER	32856	
I-DISI	Reims/Cessna F150L	F15001027	
I-DISO	Boeing 777-243ER	32857	N5014K
I-DISU	Boeing 777-243ER	32858	
I-DIZE	McDonnell-Douglas DC-9-32	47502	
I-DJET	Vulcanair P.68C	426	
I-DLAB	Piper J-3C-65 Cub (Crashed 12.9.04)	9495	43-634 (42-59444)
I-DLER	Aérospatiale AS.350B2 Ecureuil	3299	
I-DLOH	Hawker 800XP	258450	D-CTAN N41441
I-DMPL	Partenavia P.68C	350	
I-DODE	Piper J-3C-65 Cub	9664	43-803 (42-59613)
I-DOIT	Zorzoli PRG-1	02	
I-DONY	Cessna 207 Skywagon 207	20700261	F-BXAI N1661U
I-DOOD	Rotorway Exec	6276	
I-DPCA	Agusta A.109A-II	7322	MM81223
I-DPCB	Agusta A.109A-II	7323	MM81224
I-DPCC	Agusta A.109A	7226	MM80752 I-DACK N9046Z
I-DPCD	Canadair CL.215-6B11 (Code '7')	2003	C-FTUA
I-DPCE	Canadair CL.215-6B11 (Code '8')	2004	C-FTUS
I-DPCF	Canadair CL.215-6B11 (Code '23')	2059	C-GIWU
I-DPCG	Canadair CL.215-6B11 (Code '24')	2060	C-GJHU
I-DPCH	Canadair CL.215-6B11 (Code '25')	2062	C-GJLB
I-DPCJ	Agusta A.109K	10034	
I-DPCK	Canadair CL.215-6B11 (Code '22') (W/o 18.3.05)	2051	C-GHGV
I-DPCN	Canadair CL.215-6B11 (Code '9') (W/o 8.03)	2008	C-FUAK
I-DPCO	Canadair CL.215-6B11 (Code '10')	2009	C-FVRA
I-DPCP	Canadair CL.215-6B11 (Code '11')	2020	C-FYCY
I-DPCQ	Canadair CL.215-6B11 (Code '12')	2021	C-FYDA
I-DPCR(2)	Piaggio P.180 Avanti	1032	(D-IMLP)
I-DPCS(2)	Piaggio P.180 Avanti	1033	
I-DPCT	Canadair CL.215-6B11 (Code '18')	2029	C-FZYS
I-DPCU	Canadair CL.215-6B11 (Code '14')	2030	C-GALV
I-DPCV	Canadair CL.215-6B11 (Code '15')	2035	C-GCXG
I-DPCW	Canadair CL.215-6B11 (Code '16')	2036	C-GDHW
I-DPCY	Canadair CL.215-6B11 (Code '20')	2047	C-GFUS
I-DPCZ	Canadair CL.215-6B11 (Code '21')	2048	C-GGCW
I-DRAC	Cessna T310Q	310Q0078	(N7578Q)
I-DRAW	Zlin Z.50L	0011	OK-HZD
I-DREI	Aérospatiale AS.350B3 Ecureuil	3359	F-WQDR
I-DRIS	Partenavia P.66B Oscar 100	51	
I-DROB	Tecnam P.92S Echo	N.C.001	
I-DROP	Piper PA-28-140 Cherokee D	28-7125238	N5076S
I-DSAM	Aérospatiale AS.350B Ecureuil	2296	F-WYMA
I-DSPV	Neico Lancair 320	670/A	
I-DUCL	Rand-Robinson KR-2	6657/001	
I-DUEK	Aérospatiale AS.350B Ecureuil	3300	F-WQDC
I-DUPA	McDonnell-Douglas MD-11F	48426	
I-DUPE	McDonnell-Douglas MD-11F	48427	
I-DUPI	McDonnell-Douglas MD-11F	48428	
I-DUPO	McDonnell-Douglas MD-11F	48429	
I-DUPU	McDonnell-Douglas MD-11F	48430	
I-DUST	Stolp SA-700 Acroduster One	020	
I-DZPO	CASA C.212DD Aviocar	387	Fr.AF/F-ZVMR
I-EAAA	Piper PA-28RT-201T Turbo Arrow IV	28R-8331026	F-GFIM N923CC N9641N N4295T
I-EACB	Schweizer 269C-1	0059	HB-XJV
I-EADU	Robin DR.400/180R Remorqueur	800	D-EADU
I-EADV	Cessna 152	15279853	D-EADV N757MR
I-EAGR	Enstrom 280FX Shark	2027	N8624T
I-EAGS	Agusta A.109A-II	7426	N1YU
I-EAHC	Schweizer 269C	S-1821	
I-EAHS	Schweizer 269C-1	0058	
I-EANI	Piper PA-28-161 Warrior II	28-8016369	D-EANI (2) N82401
I-EASY	Rutan Long-Ez	unkn	
I-EBSS	Piper PA-28RT-201T Turbo Arrow IV	28R-8031013	D-EBSS N8106J
I-EBXK	Reims/Cessna F150M	F15001373	D-EBXK
I-ECID	Piper PA-18-150 Super Cub	18-4549	D-ECID(2) OE-CID OE-BID N10F
I-ECOA	PZL M-18B Dromader	1Z024-28	SP-DED(2)
I-ECOC	PZL M-18B Dromader	1Z024-30	SP-DEF(2)
I-ECOH	PZL M-18B Dromader	1Z024-29	SP-DEE(2)
I-ECOL	Agusta A.109C	7608	
I-ECOS	Robinson R-22 Beta	1006	N8039M
I-ECOW	PZL-104 Wilga 80	CF21990939	SP-WDG
I-ECSA	Grob G.115A	8094	
I-ECSE	Grob G.115A	8095	
I-ECSI	Reims/Cessna F152	F15201937	G-BKTT

I-ECSO	Cessna 152	15283856	G-BOTC N5385B
I-ECUR	Aérospatiale AS.355F Ecureuil 2	5285	I-BSBS F-WZKK
I-EDAI	de Havilland DH.82A Tiger Moth (Accident 6.7.96)	86560	G-AYUX F-BDOQ Fr.AF PG651
I-EDEM	Cessna 525 CitationJet	525-0155	N155CJ
I-EEGR	Piper PA-28RT-201T Turbo Arrow IV	2831037	D-EEGR N4363P
I-EEJA	Airbus A319-115LR	244	D-AVWZ
I-EEQQ	CASA I-131E Jungmann	2178	D-EEQQ HB-UVI D-EEQQ E3B-562
I-EEYA	Cessna 182P Skylane	18260833	D-EEYA N9293G
I-EEZA	Airbus A330-223	358	EI-CXF N583LF TU-TAX F-WWYO
I-EEZB	Airbus A330-223	364	EI-CXG N364LF TU-TAY F-WWKE
I-EEZC	Airbus A320-214	1852	F-WWIT
I-EEZD	Airbus A320-214	1920	F-WWDJ
I-EEZE	Airbus A320-214	1937	F-WWIO
I-EEZF	Airbus A320-214	1983	F-WWDM
I-EEZG	Airbus A320-214	2001	F-WWBB
I-EEZH	Airbus A320-214	737	F-GRSG F-WWBS
I-EEZI	Airbus A320-214	749	F-GRSH F-WWIK
I-EEZK	Airbus A320-214	1125	I-VLEA HB-IGZ F-WWIH
I-EFCN	Aérospatiale AS.350B Ecureuil	1445	
I-EFCT	Piper PA-28-180 Cherokee F	28-7105122	N5097S
I-EFLY	Aérospatiale SA.315B Lama	2497	F-GFCV N49531
I-EGDO	SOCATA Rallye 235E Gabier	12905	F-GBKZ
I-EGEB	Beech 95-B55 Baron	TC-1261	HB-GEB
I-EHAB	Agusta-Bell 412	25505	
I-EHAC	Agusta-Bell 412	25504	(G-BKNS)
I-EHRB	Cessna 182P Skylane	18264372	D-EHRB(2) D-EDRB(2) I-EKRB D-EKRB(1) N1565M
I-EIAD	Cessna 305C (L-19E) Bird Dog (Regal Air conversion) (Damaged 18.3.05)	0030	EI-5 MM61-2984 61-2984
I-EIAF	Cessna 305C (L-19E) Bird Dog (Regal Air conversion)	0011	EI-13 MM61-2965 61-2965
I-EIAG	Cessna 305C (L-19E) Bird Dog (Regal Air conversion)	0012	EI-15 MM61-2966 61-2966
I-EIAH	Cessna 305C (L-19E) Bird Dog (Regal Air conversion)	0008	EI-18 MM61-2962 61-2962
I-EIAI	Cessna 305C (L-19E) Bird Dog (Regal Air conversion)	0033	EI-20 MM61-2987 61-2987
I-EIAJ	Cessna 305C (L-19E) Bird Dog (Regal Air conversion)	0005	EI-24 MM61-2959 61-2959
I-EIAN	Cessna 305C (L-19E) Bird Dog (Regal Air conversion)	0006	EI-30 MM61-2960 61-2960
I-EIAP	Cessna 305C (L-19E) Bird Dog (Damaged) (Regal Air conversion)	0027	EI-32 MM61-2981 61-2981
I-EIAS	Cessna 305C (L-19E) Bird Dog (Regal Air conversion)	0028	EI-37 MM61-2982 61-2982
I-EIAU	Cessna 305C (L-19E) Bird Dog (Regal Air conversion)	0001	EI-39 MM61-2955 61-2955
I-EIAV	Cessna 305C (L-19E) Bird Dog (Regal Air conversion)	0004	EI-19 MM61-2958 61-2958
I-EIAW	Cessna 305C (L-19E) Bird Dog (Regal Air conversion)	0009	EI-36 MM61-2963 61-2963
I-EIAX	Cessna 305C (L-19E) Bird Dog (Regal Air conversion)	0019	EI-35 MM61-2973 61-2973
I-EIAY	Cessna 305C (L-19E) Bird Dog (Regal Air conversion)	0020	EI-41 MM61-2974 61-2974
I-EIAZ	Cessna 305C (L-19E) Bird Dog (Regal Air conversion)	0022	EI-17 MM61-2976 61-2976
I-EIBG	Cessna 305C (L-19E) Bird Dog (Regal Air conversion)	0024	EI-42 MM61-2978 61-2978
I-EIBK	Cessna 305C (L-19E) Bird Dog (Regal Air conversion)	0043	EI-44 MM61-2995 61-2995
I-EIPP	Eipper Quicksilver MX-II	001	
I-EISS	Piper L-21A Super Cub 125 (Officially regd as a PL-21A, painted as "115800". It is thought more likely to be f/n 18-965, ie c/n 18-861 ex N10544, 51-15696)	001/18-965	51-15800
I-EJRA	Cessna 402B	402B0918	N82931
I-EJVA	Piper PA-28RT-201T Turbo Arrow IV (Damaged 20.7.04)	28R-8031002	D-EJVA(2) N81042
I-EKIA	Piper PA-28R-201T Turbo Arrow III	2803002	SE-KIA
I-EKOR	Partenavia P.64B Oscar B	45	
I-ELBA	Beech 95-B55 Baron	TC-1291	HB-GEF
I-ELBR	Aérospatiale AS.350B2 Ecureuil	2502	
I-ELBY	Robinson R-22B2 Beta	2876	
I-ELDE	Westland-Bell 47G-3B1	WA/519	(D-HOAA) XT812
I-ELGF	Fokker F.28-0100	11253	PH-FYA V8-RB3 HB-IVE PH-EZF
I-ELIM	Partenavia P.68C	293	N39278
I-ELIW	Aérospatiale AS.350B3 Ecureuil	3301	F-GNPE
I-ELLY	Cessna 182Q Skylane	18265876	N759CA
I-ELOP	Agusta A.119 Koala	14044	
I-ELPA	Aérospatiale SA.315B Lama	2568	F-GCFO
I-ELPO	SIAI-Marchetti S.205-18/F	229	
I-ELSE	Piper PA-28-180 Cherokee Archer	28-7405008	N9563N
I-ELTE	Aérospatiale AS.350B Ecureuil	1477	HB-XMI
I-ELTW	Bredanardi NH.300C	022	I-BNCP
I-ELYP	Aérospatiale AS.365N3 Dauphin 2	6625	F-WQDO
I-ELYS	Bombardier Learjet 40	45-2016	N40078
I-ELZA	Laverda F.8L Falco	407	
I-EMAH	Cessna U206F Stationair	U20602309	N1958U
I-EMAS	Bell 206B Jet Ranger II	286	N4761R
I-EMCX	Embraer EMB-170ST (Reservation .03)	17000008	PT-SKA
I-EMHW	Piper PA-28R-201 Cherokee Arrow III	28R-7737125	D-EMHW N38975
I-EMIC	Piper PA-34-220T Seneca V	3449306	N3091Y
I-EMME	Aeromere F.8L Falco	225	
I-ENAL	Tecnam P.92J Echo	007	
I-ENBI	Piper PA-18-150 Super Cub	18-7868	D-ENBI
I-ENDE	Piper PA-28-140 Cherokee B	28-25320	N8070N
I-ENDO	Agusta-Bell 47J3B1	2063	OE-DXD OE-BXF(1)
I-ENRJ	Cessna 172N	17270663	N739NA
I-ENSI	Tecnam P.92 Echo 2000RG VEL	02	
I-EOLN	Reims/Cessna F182Q Skylane	F18200158	D-EOLN
I-EORG	Tecnam P.92JS Echo	-19	
I-EPEP	Aérospatiale SA.315B Lama	2661	
I-EPIA	Agusta-Bell 206B Jet Ranger III	8701	F-GEJM
I-EPIB	Bell 407	53260	C-GDSZ
I-EPIC	Agusta AB.139	31003	
I-EPTL	Piper PA-28RT-201T Turbo Arrow IV	28R-7931116	N2215V
I-EPUS	Bredanardi NH-300C	020	
I-EPWR	Agusta A.109E Power	11005	
I-EQUR	Aérospatiale AS.350B2 Ecureuil	2579	
I-ERID	Partenavia P.64B Oscar B-1155	60	
I-ERJA	Cessna 501 Citation I/SP	501-0006	N93TJ N5016P (N1236P) N121UW N121JW N358CC (N5358J)
I-ERJD	Bombardier Learjet 45	45-068	
I-ERJE	Bombardier Learjet 45	45-226	N40085
I-ERJG	Bombardier Learjet 40	45-2015	N40077
I-ERMS	Aérospatiale AS.350B3 Ecureuil	3214	
I-ERNE	Piper PA-28-161 Cadet	2841272	N91955
I-ESAU	Piper PA-30 Twin Comanche	30-203	N7221Y
I-ESER	Piper PA-28-181 Archer III	2843446	N53403 N9513N
I-ESEV	Robinson R-22B2 Beta	2669	
I-ESSE	Piper PA-32R-301T Saratoga II TC	3257285	N5347N
I-ESSO	Cessna 182L Skylane	18258957	N42309
I-ESUE	Agusta A.109E Power	11124	
I-ETAL	Reims/Cessna F150L	F15001099	HB-CEA
I-ETAR	Cessna 172M	17266658	N80580
I-ETBR	Bell 206B Jet Ranger II	484	HB-XXH C-GFAJ N112FL
I-ETEL	Aérospatiale AS.350B2 Ecureuil	9050	F-GTEC
I-ETIA	Aérospatiale SA.315B Lama	2548	
I-ETIB	Aérospatiale SA.315B Lama	2090/14	IDFAF
I-ETID	Aérospatiale SA.315B Lama	2615	F-GDFB
I-ETIK	SOCATA Rallye 235E Gabier	12831	F-GAKS
I-ETOB	Robinson R-22B2 Beta	2938	
I-ETOS	Partenavia P.68	11	
I-ETTO	Rutan VariEze	02	
I-EURY	SG Aviation Storm 400 (Also reported as Evektor EV-97 Eurostar)	226	
I-EVER	Robinson R-44 Raven	0932	
I-EVIT	Hughes 369D	39-0478D	HB-XIO

I-EWAA	Cessna 182Q Skylane	18265935	N182FM
			(N759EM)
I-EWAB	Cessna 172N	17273714	N5147J
I-EWAD	Cessna 152	15283059	N46482
I-EWAE	Cessna 172N	17272711	N6310D
I-EWAN	Piper PA-18-150 Super Cub	18-2063	PH-WAN
	(Officially quoted as 18-2076 which is the f/n)		(PH-VBF)
			(OO-WAN)
			PH-WAN
			R-77
			54-2463
I-EXMA	Embraer EMB.145LR	145250	PT-SIM
I-EXMB	Embraer EMB.145LR	145330	PT-SMW
I-EXMC	Embraer EMB.145LR	145436	PT-SUH
I-EXMD	Embraer EMB.145LR	145445	PT-SUQ
I-EXME	Embraer EMB.145LR	145282	PT-SJY
I-EXMF	Embraer EMB.145LR	145641	PT-SED
I-EXMG	Embraer EMB.145LR	145652	PT-SEM
I-EXMH	Embraer EMB.145LR	145665	PT-SEZ
I-EXMI	Embraer EMB.145LR	145286	PT-SKD
I-EXML	Embraer EMB.145LR	145709	
I-EXMM	Embraer EMB.145LR	145738	PT-SHS
I-EXMN	Embraer EMB.145LR	145750	PT-SJJ
I-EXMO	Embraer EMB.145LR	145299	PT-SKQ
I-EXMU	Embraer EMB.145LR	145316	PT-SMH
I-EZIO	Agusta-Bell 47J-3	2116	MM80488
			Caribin. CC-27
			MM80488
I-FABJ	Tecnam P.92-JS Echo (Wreck noted 7.04)	015	
I-FABR	Macchi MB.308	001	
I-FACN	Cessna 172R	17280147	
I-FADI	Piper PA-18-135 Super Cub	18-4017	OO-LWA
	(f/n 18-5261 quoted officially as c/n)		EI-274
			I-EIVA
			MM54-2617
			54-2617
I-FADL	SIAI-Marchetti S.205-20/R	4-248	
I-FAGE	Piper PA-28R-200 Cherokee Arrow II	28R-7435149	N40994
I-FAIV	Agusta-Bell 204B	3048	OE-EXO
			HB-XBO
I-FARA	Piper PA-28-140 Cherokee	28-24296	N1858J
I-FARN	Cessna 500 Citation I	500-0401	N2651
			N2617K
I-FASH	Agusta A.109E Power Elite	11153	
I-FBAX	Alenia G.222 / C-27J Spartan	4115	
I-FDAG	Robinson R-44 Raven	0951	
I-FEEV	Cessna 650 Citation III	650-0105	N67BG
			N48TT
			N15TT
			N655CC
			(N1320B)
I-FEFE	Van's RV-9	"9384"	
I-FELN	Meteor FL.54	1125	
I-FEST	Piper PA-31P Pressurized Navajo	31P-19	N12434
			CF-AYA
			N9732N
I-FEVM	Partenavia P.66B Oscar 150	19	
I-FFAE	Reims/Cessna F172M	F17201087	
I-FFAF	Reims/Cessna F150L	F15001033	
I-FFAG	Reims/Cessna F150L	F15001052	
I-FFAZ	Cessna 310Q	310Q0749	N7500Q
I-FFLJ	Cessna 120	14318	C-FFLJ
			CF-FLJ
I-FFSC	Reims FR172F Rocket (W/o 11.7.04)	FR17200135	
I-FFSD	Cessna F172H	F172-0621	
I-FFSG	Reims/Cessna FA150K Aerobat	FA1500016	
I-FFSJ	Reims/Cessna FA150K Aerobat	FA1500005	
I-FFSM	Reims FR172G Rocket	FR17200181	
I-FFSO	Reims/Cessna F150L	F15000832	F-WLIO
I-FFSP	Reims FR172H Rocket	FR17200304	
I-FFSQ	Reims/Cessna FA150L Aerobat	FA1500082	
I-FFSR	Reims/Cessna F150L	F15000696	
I-FFSV	Reims/Cessna F172L	F17200865	
I-FFSW	Reims FR172H Rocket	FR17200257	D-ECGF
I-FGEX	Van's RV-4	01	
I-FGPB	General Avia F.22C Pinguino	024	
I-FIAM	Piper PA-30 Twin Comanche B	30-1718	N8570Y
I-FICV	Dassault Falcon 900	54	F-WWFC
I-FINA	Vulcanair P.68 Observer 2	420-20/OB2	
I-FJDC	Dassault Falcon 100	203	F-WQBM
			N54FH
			N45JB
			XA-TBL
			N100CT
			VR-CLA
			N267FJ
			F-WZGJ
I-FJDN	Dassault Falcon 50EX	295	F-WWHW
I-FJJS	Cessna 172N floatplane	17268905	C-FJJS
			N702DK
			(N734KC)
I-FJTB	Cessna 550 Citation Bravo	550-0922	N51896
I-FJTC	Cessna 550 Citation Bravo	550-0988	N32FJ
			N5174W
I-FLAG	Aérospatiale AS.350B2 Ecureuil	2621	F-GPFE
			G-BWAZ
			OO-AKK
			OO-XKK
			F-WYML
I-FLAK	Agusta A.109E Power	11076	
I-FLAN	Agusta A.109E Power (W/o 9.10.01)	11038	
I-FLAO	Aérospatiale AS.350B1 Ecureuil	2097	
I-FLAP	Aérospatiale AS.350B2 Ecureuil	2487	G-BTLS
I-FLAR	Aérospatiale SA.315B Lama	2662	
I-FLAX	Aérospatiale SA.315B Lama	2029/A	F-GIXV
			F-OGVY
			3A-MLB
			VH-PDU
			P2-PDU
			VH-PDU
			VH-FJS
			F-WKQF
I-FLDA	Dragon Fly DF333AC	EB056	
I-FLIP	Robinson R-22 Beta	0812	
I-FLRI	BAe.146 Series 200	E-2220	G-BVMT
			G-6-220
I-FLUS	Aérospatiale AS.350B3 Ecureuil	3416	
I-FLYA	Cessna 501 Citation I/SP	501-0099	N3170A
I-FLYM	Mooney M.20M Model 257 TLS	27-0128	N9155G
I-FLYP	Dassault Falcon 2000	103	F-WWVX
I-FLYR	Robinson R-22B2 Beta	2734	
I-FLYV	Dassault Falcon 2000	108	F-WWVC
I-FLYW	Dassault Falcon 900EX	27	N626CC
			N900EX
			N927EX
			F-WWFY
I-FOGS	Piper PA-28-140 Cherokee D	28-7125079	N1761T
I-FORA	Rand-Robinson KR-2S	9122-646	
I-FORD	Piper PA-28-140 Cherokee C	28-26407	N5917U
I-FOSG	Turnercraft D7	unkn	
I-FREA	Bell 206B Jet Ranger II	463	N2671Q
			(N999SD)
			N267IQ
			C-FTPP
			CF-TPP
			N2264W
I-FREB	Bell 206B Jet Ranger II	3105	I-MIAB
			N5760U
I-FREH	Agusta A.109E Power	11602	
I-FREI	Agusta A.109E Power	11103	
I-FREJ	Agusta A.109E Power	11114	
I-FREK	Agusta A.109K2	10037	
I-FREL	Bell 412	33047	N2152V
I-FRES	Robinson R-22B2 Beta	3117	
I-FRRE	Christen A-1 Husky	1132	
I-FSTK	Fokker F.27 Friendship 600	10409	OY-FCM
			F-SEBG
			PH-EXX
			TY-BBI
			TY-ATM
			TY-AAG
			PH-FOH
			PK-GFE
			PH-FOH
I-FURB	Cessna 152	15280885	OY-JRC
			N25967
I-FVBD	Aérospatiale SA.315B Lama	2620	
I-FVDB	Aérospatiale SA.315B Lama	2636	
I-FVPD	Hughes 269C	120-1011	N1107U
I-FXRB	Piaggio P.180 Avanti (Damaged 31.12.02)	1035	
I-FXRC	Piaggio P.180 Avanti	1045	
I-FXRD	Piaggio P.180 Avanti	1067	
I-FXRE	Piaggio P.180E Avanti	1049	
I-FZIT	Agusta A.109E Power	11062	
I-GAGI	Aviamilano P.19 Scricciolo	320	
I-GAIB	Evans VP-1 Volksplane	unkn	
I-GALB	Bellanca 7ECA Citabria	1182-77	
I-GALD	SIAI-Marchetti S.208	4-227	OE-DLU(1)
	(Converted from S.205-22/R ET-ACT)		ET-ACT
I-GAMP	Piper PA-28-180 Cherokee Archer	28-7505231	N1465X
I-GANI	Schweizer 269C	S-1781	HB-XJY
			N69A
I-GANP	Hughes 269C	59-0785	D-HERW
I-GARC	Cessna 152	15285775	D-EZBG
			N94736
I-GASD	Cessna 650 Citation III	650-0037	N37VP
			VH-OZI
			N37CD
			N411BB
I-GASF	Schweizer 269C	S-1263	SE-HSC
			LN-OTW
			SE-HSC
			N41S
I-GATE	Agusta A.109A-II	7285	N3235A
I-GATI	Agusta-Bell 47J-3	2124	MM . . . . .
I-GATO	de Havilland DH.82A Tiger Moth	85250	DE193
I-GAUS	Partenavia P.68	02	
I-GAYD	MS.893E Rallye 180GT Gaillard	12987	F-GAYD
I-GBCG	Agusta-Bell 47G-3B1	1530	EI-39 /
			MM80343
I-GBGI	Cessna 152	15280822	N25857
I-GBSD	SOCATA MS.893E Rallye 180GT Gaillard	13230	F-GBSD
I-GBVD	Aérospatiale AS.350B Ecureuil	3689	
I-GBXK	SOCATA MS.892E Rallye 150GT Gaillard	13288	F-GBXK
I-GEAA	General Avia F.20 Pegaso	003	
I-GEAD	General Avia F.22 Pinguino	001	

I-GEAE	General Avia F.22R Pinguino Sprint	002	
I-GEAG	General Avia F.22B Pinguino	004	
I-GEAH	General Avia F.22C Pinguino	005	
I-GEAM	Piper PA-28R-200 Cherokee Arrow II	28R-7435006	N9569N
I-GEAN	General Avia F.22A Pinguino	011	
I-GEAZ	General Avia F.22C Pinguino	007	
	(Damaged 1.2.04)		
I-GEMA	Piper PA-23-150 Apache	23-618	N6467C
			YV-P-EPY
			YV-T-ATP
			N10F
I-GEMI	Agusta A.109EPower	11085	
I-GEMK	Partenavia P.68C-TC	258-16-TC	D-GEMK
I-GEOK	Tecnam P.92J Echo	010	
I-GEOR	Aeromere F.8L Falco	215	
I-GGAA	Piper PA-28-151 Cherokee Warrior	28-7415341	N41868
I-GGAB	Skystar Kitfox IV	1	
I-GGGG	Christen A-1 Husky	1052	
I-GGMS	Piper PA-34-220T Seneca V	3449016	N9284N
I-GHEP	Piper PA-31P Pressurized Navajo	31P-7630016	N540L
			N57552
I-GHIA	Piper PA-32R-300T Turbo Lance II	32R-7887154	HB-PCW
			N39710
I-GHIB	Cessna T210M Turbo Centurion	21061971	I-GHII
			N815HG
			N1997M
I-GIBR	Cessna T182T Turbo Skylane	T18208231	N2101Z
I-GICA	Robinson R-22 Mariner	2260M	
I-GICO	Aérospatiale AS.350B Ecureuil	2229	
I-GIFE	Partenavia P.68C	335	
I-GIGJ	SOCATA MS.894A Minerva 220	12196	
I-GIPA	Beech 58P Baron	TJ-148	N48TX
			N10021
I-GIPS	CASA I-131E Jungmann (Wrecked)	2116	E3B- . . .
I-GISY	Tri-R TR-4 KISCruiser	01	
I-GITA	Piper PA-28R-201 Arrow	2844011	N9280N
I-GIUN	Maule MX-7-235 Star Rocket	10080C	N6133H
			(D-EVEP)
			N6133H
I-GIWW	Cessna 550 Citation Bravo	550-0871	N871CB
I-GJUL	Partenavia P.68B	206	
I-GKBM	SR318 NC001 (SA.318C Alouette rebuild)	001/1786	F-GKBM
			F-MJAT
			F-MCSI
			F-MJAX
I-GLAK	Stoddard-Hamilton GlaStar GS-1	5086	
I-GLAM	Robinson R-22B2 Beta	2716	
I-GLAS	Piper PA-18-150 Super Cub	18-7809117	N82058
I-GLGM	Aérospatiale AS.350B2 Ecureuil	2332	F-WYMK
I-GLTS	Aérospatiale AS.350B2 Ecureuil	2627	
I-GLUE	Jodel D.18B	381	
I-GMBT	Piper PA-18-150 Super Cub	18-7421	N10F
I-GNAP	Hughes 269C	S-1312	
I-GOBJ	Dassault Falcon 20C-5	460/180	OY-BDS
			F-WMKF
I-GODF	Piper PA-32-300 Cherokee Six	32-7540169	N1524X
I-GOES	Piper PA-32-260 Cherokee Six	32-223	G-AVTK
	(Rebuilt using spare fuselage 32-856S)		I- . . . .,
			G-AVTK
			N3266W
I-GOLF	Piper PA-18-150 Super Cub	18-8871	N8465Y
I-GOLP	Mooney M.20M Model 257 TLS	27-0113	N9149Z
I-GONG	Robinson R-22 Mariner	2649M	
I-GONI	Agusta-Bell AB.412	25506	(G-BKNU)
I-GORB	Sukhoi SU-29	76-04	RA7604
I-GOSF	Cessna 525A CitationJet 2	525A-0199	N5152X
I-GPAP	Robinson R-22 Mariner	1410M	I-MIAD
			N4009A
I-GPAR	Agusta-Bell 206B Jet Ranger III	8714	
I-GPBP	Aérospatiale AS.350B2 Ecureuil	2345	I-BPGP
I-GRAB	Hughes 269C	48-0683	N58172
I-GRAD	Partenavia P.68TC	222	
I-GRAE	Aérospatiale SA.315B Lama	1807/37	HB-XYQ
			(SE-HUN)
			F-MJAX
I-GRAL	Hughes 269C	S-1299	N7506H
I-GREG	Partenavia P.66B Oscar 150	23	
I-GREN	Aérospatiale SA.315B Lama	2482	F-GELX
			N223RM
I-GRIG	Robinson R-22 Beta	1869	N23105
I-GRIM	Maule MXT-7-180 Star Rocket	14006C	
	(Damaged 18.7.04)		
I-GRIS	Reims/Cessna F172P	F17202233	PH-AVD
			PH-AXT(4)
I-GROB	Grob G.115A	8019	
I-GROC	Grob G.115A	8035	(D-EGVV)
I-GSGS	Piper PA-32R-301 Saratoga IITC	3257052	N41276
I-GUAN	Schweizer 269C	S-1825	
I-GUGU	Cessna 172M	17265576	N6770H
I-GUMA	SIAI-Marchetti S.205-20/R	4-112	
I-GUSA	Aérospatiale AS.350B Ecureuil	3672	
I-GUYD	Piper PA-28R-201 Arrow	2844009	N9278Q
I-GVWD	Robinson R-44 Raven II	10594	
I-HANS	Zlin Z.50LA	0002	D-EFHJ
			OK-IRK
			OK-FSA
			OK-072

I-HAVE	Aérospatiale AS.350B3 Ecureuil	3205	
I-HBEP	Aérospatiale AS.350B Ecureuil	3302	
I-HBFI	Agusta A.109E Power	11048	
I-HBHA	Agusta A.109K2	10023	I-ECAM
I-HBHB	Agusta A.109K2	10025	
I-HBHC	MBB-Kawasaki BK.117B-2	7251	D-HITZ
I-HBHG	MBB-Kawasaki BK.117B-2	7164	D-HBHG
			Abu Dhabi
			Police: S-716
			D-HBHG
I-HBMC	MBB-Kawasaki BK.117C-1	7528	D-HBMC
I-HBMS	MBB-Kawasaki BK.117C-1	7531	D-HMBB
I-HBZC	Agusta A.109E Power	11094	HB-ZCT
I-HDBX	MBB-Kawasaki BK.117C-1	7546	D-HDBX
I-HDBZ	MBB-Kawasaki BK.117C-1	7547	D-HDBZ(2)
I-HDPR	Agusta A.109E Power	11625	
I-HDOC	Robinson R-22B2 Beta	3493	
I-HECD	MBB-Kawasaki BK.117C-1	7500	D-HECD
I-HECE	MBB-Kawasaki BK.117B-2	7244	D-HECE(2)
			D-HDDD(3)
			D-HECE(2)
			(D-HFII)
I-HEDB	Robinson R-22 Beta	1302	N8069U
I-HEDC	Robinson R-22 Beta	1352	N8080N
I-HEDD	Aérospatiale AS.350B2 Ecureuil	2479	F-WYMU
I-HEDO	Robinson R-22 Beta	0764	
I-HEDY	Cessna 172RG Cutlass RG	172RG1045	N9799B
I-HEFA	Robinson R-22B2 Beta	3615	
I-HEFB	Robinson R-22B2 Beta	3668	
I-HEFC	Robinson R-22B Beta	3704	
I-HELD	Robinson R-22B2 Beta	3377	
I-HELI	Robinson R-22 Beta	2519	
I-HELO	Agusta A.109E Power	11605	
I-HELY	Robinson R-22 Beta	2501	
I-HENO	Hughes 369E	0281E	
I-HESP	Robinson R.22B Beta	0572	N2440Q
I-HHHH	Christen A-1 Husky	1051	N11N
I-HIFI	Eurocopter EC.135T1	0085	
I-HIGH	Reims/Cessna FT337GP Super Skymaster	FP33700007	G-HIGH
	(Reims-assembled P337GPressurized Skymaster		OO-KAL
	US c/n P3370060)		
I-HISY	Robinson R-22B2 Beta	3314	
I-HKAV	MBB-Kawasaki BK.117C-1	7540	D-HKAV
I-HMED	Eurocopter EC.135T1	0082	
I-HOLD	Aérospatiale AS.350B Ecureuil	3566	
I-HOOK	Aérospatiale AS.350B3 Ecureuil	3090	
I-HORT	Aérospatiale AS.350B Ecureuil	3699	
I-HPGF	Robinson R-44 Raven II	10488	
I-HPLC	Aérospatiale AS.350B Ecureuil	3702	
I-HPWG	Bell 206B Jet Ranger II	3297	I-MIGE
			D-HHCW
			N39105
I-HSAR	Agusta A.109E Power	11125	
I-HUFF	Robinson R-22B2 Beta	2942	
I-HUPF	Mooney M.20	1169	D-ECYR
			N6502B
I-HVEN	MBB-Kawasaki BK.117C-1	7526	D-HVEN
	(Damaged 11.6.04)		(D-HBKY)
I-HYDR	Piper PA-31T Cheyenne	31T-7520034	N54966
I-IAAA	Partenavia P.66C Charlie	01	
I-IAAF	Partenavia P.66C Charlie	06	
I-IAAG	Partenavia P.66C Charlie	07	
I-IAAH	Partenavia P.66C Charlie	08	
I-IAAK	Partenavia P.66C Charlie	11	
I-IAAL	Partenavia P.66C Charlie	12	
I-IAAM	Partenavia P.66C Charlie	13	
I-IAAN	Partenavia P.66C Charlie	14	
I-IAAO	Partenavia P.66C Charlie	15	
I-IAAR	Partenavia P.66C Charlie	18	
I-IAAS	Partenavia P.66C Charlie	19	
I-IAAT	Partenavia P.66C Charlie	20	
I-IAAU	Partenavia P.66C Charlie	21	
I-IAAX	Partenavia P.66C Charlie	24	
I-IAAZ	Partenavia P.66C Charlie (W/o 30.9.04)	26	
I-IABA	Partenavia P.66C Charlie	27	
I-IABB	Partenavia P.66C Charlie	28	
I-IABF	Partenavia P.66C Charlie	32	
I-IABG	Partenavia P.66C Charlie	33	
I-IABI	Partenavia P.66C Charlie	35	
I-IABK	Partenavia P.66C Charlie	37	
I-IABL	Partenavia P.66C Charlie	38	
I-IABN	Partenavia P.66C Charlie	40	
I-IABO	Partenavia P.66C Charlie	41	
I-IABP	Partenavia P.66C Charlie	42	
I-IABS	Partenavia P.66C Charlie	45	
I-IABT	Partenavia P.66C Charlie (W/o 20.4.04)	46	
I-IABW	Partenavia P.66C Charlie	49	
I-IABX	Partenavia P.66C Charlie	50	
I-IACB	Partenavia P.66C Charlie	55	
I-IACE	Partenavia P.66C Charlie	58	
I-IACF	Partenavia P.66C Charlie	59	
I-IACG	Partenavia P.66C Charlie	60	
I-IACJ	Partenavia P.66C Charlie	63	
I-IACK	Partenavia P.66C Charlie	64	
I-IACL	Partenavia P.66C Charlie	65	
I-IACN	Partenavia P.66C Charlie	67	
I-IACO	Partenavia P.66C Charlie	68	

I-IACQ	Partenavia P.66C Charlie	70	
I-IACT	Partenavia P.66C Charlie	73	
I-IACU	Partenavia P.66C Charlie	74	
I-IACV	Partenavia P.66C Charlie	75	
I-IACW	Partenavia P.66C Charlie	76	
I-IACZ	Partenavia P.66C Charlie	79	
I-IADA	Partenavia P.66C Charlie	80	
I-IADE	Partenavia P.66C Charlie	84	
I-IADF	Partenavia P.66C Charlie	85	
I-IADH	Partenavia P.66C Charlie	87	
I-IADI	Partenavia P.66C Charlie	88	
I-IADL	Partenavia P.66C Charlie	89	
I-IADM	Partenavia P.66C Charlie	90	
I-IADN	Partenavia P.66C Charlie	91	
I-IADO	Partenavia P.66C Charlie	92	
I-IADR	Partenavia P.66C Charlie	95	I-RAIP
I-IADS	Partenavia P.66C Charlie	97	
I-IADT	Partenavia P.66C Charlie	98	
I-IADU	Partenavia P.66C Charlie	99	
I-IADW	Partenavia P.66C Charlie	101	
I-IADX	Partenavia P.66C Charlie	102	
I-IAEA	SOCATA TB-9 Tampico Club	1143	
I-IAEC	SOCATA TB-9 Tampico Club	1202	
I-IAED	SOCATA TB-9 Tampico Club	1203	
I-IAEF	SOCATA TB-9 Tampico Club	1207	
I-IAEG	SOCATA TB-9 Tampico Club	1215	
	(Damaged 1.6.04)		
I-IAEH	SOCATA TB-9 Tampico Club	1216	
I-IAEI	SOCATA TB-9 Tampico Club	1217	
I-IAEK	SOCATA TB-9 Tampico Club	1219	
I-IAEL	SOCATA TB-9 Tampico Club	1220	
I-IAEM	SOCATA TB-9 Tampico Club	1221	
I-IAEO	SOCATA TB-9 Tampico Club (Damaged 9.2.02)	1238	
I-IAEP	SOCATA TB-9 Tampico Club	1254	
I-IAEQ	SOCATA TB-9 Tampico Club	1255	
I-IAER	SOCATA TB-9 Tampico Club	1256	
I-IAES	SOCATA TB-9 Tampico Club	1257	
I-IAET	SOCATA TB-9 Tampico Club	1260	
I-IAEU	SOCATA TB-9 Tampico Club (Damaged 23.7.01)	1261	
I-IAEW	SOCATA TB-9 Tampico Club	1263	
I-IAEY	SOCATA TB-9 Tampico Club	1281	
I-IAEZ	SOCATA TB-9 Tampico Club	1282	
I-IAFA	SOCATA TB-9 Tampico Club	1283	
I-IAFB	SOCATA TB-9 Tampico Club	1291	
I-IAFD	SOCATA TB-9 Tampico Club	1293	
I-IAFE	SOCATA TB-9 Tampico Club	1294	
I-IAFG	SOCATA TB-9 Tampico Club	1322	
I-IAFI	SOCATA TB-9 Tampico Club	1324	
I-IAFJ	SOCATA TB-9 Tampico Club	1343	
I-IAFL	SOCATA TB-9 Tampico Club	1345	
I-IAFM	SOCATA TB-9 Tampico Club	1346	
I-IAFN	SOCATA TB-9 Tampico Club	1365	
I-IAFO	SOCATA TB-9 Tampico Club	1366	
I-IAFP	SOCATA TB-9 Tampico Club	1367	
I-IAFQ	SOCATA TB-9 Tampico Club	1368	
I-IAFT	SOCATA TB-9 Tampico Club	1385	
I-IAFU	SOCATA TB-9 Tampico Club	1386	
I-IAFV	SOCATA TB-9 Tampico Club	1370	
I-IAFW	SOCATA TB-9 Tampico Club	1371	
I-IAFX	SOCATA TB-9 Tampico Club	1372	
I-IAFY	SOCATA TB-9 Tampico Club	1373	
I-IAGA	SOCATA TB-9 Tampico Club	1388	
I-IAGB	SOCATA TB-9 Tampico Club	1389	
I-IAGC	SOCATA TB-9 Tampico Club	1390	
I-IAGD	SOCATA TB-9 Tampico Club	1391	
I-IAGE	SOCATA TB-9 Tampico Club	1392	
I-IAGF	SOCATA TB-9 Tampico Club	1393	
I-IAGG	SOCATA TB-9 Tampico Club	1394	
I-IAGH	SOCATA TB-9 Tampico Club	1395	
I-IAGI	SOCATA TB-9 Tampico Club	1396	
I-IAGJ	SOCATA TB-9 Tampico Club	1397	
I-IAGK	SOCATA TB-9 Tampico Club	1410	
I-IAGL	SOCATA TB-9 Tampico Club	1411	
I-IAGM	SOCATA TB-9 Tampico Club	1412	
I-IAGN	SOCATA TB-9 Tampico Club	1413	
I-IAGO	SOCATA TB-9 Tampico Club	1414	
I-IAGP	SOCATA TB-9 Tampico Club	1415	
I-IAGQ	SOCATA TB-9 Tampico Club	1416	
I-IAGR	SOCATA TB-9 Tampico Club	1417	
I-IAGS	SOCATA TB-9 Tampico Club	1418	
I-IAGV	SOCATA TB-9 Tampico Club	1535	
I-IAGW	SOCATA TB-9 Tampico Club	1536	
I-IAGX	SOCATA TB-9 Tampico Club	1537	
I-IAGY	SOCATA TB-9 Tampico Club	1538	
I-IAGZ	SOCATA TB-9 Tampico Club	1548	
I-IAHA	SOCATA TB-9 Tampico Club	1549	
I-IAHB	SOCATA TB-9 Tampico Club	1550	
I-IAIB	General Avia F.22C Pinguino	026	
I-IAID	General Avia F.22C Pinguino	025	
I-IBAB	SIAI-Marchetti S.205-20/R	002/06-002	
I-IBAD	SIAI-Marchetti S.205-20/R	004/06-004	
I-IBAF	SIAI-Marchetti S.205-20/R	007/06-007	
I-IBAG	SIAI-Marchetti S.205-20/R	008/06-008	
I-IBAI	SIAI-Marchetti S.205-20/R	015/06-015	
I-IBAJ	SIAI-Marchetti S.205-20/R	016/06-016	
I-IBAK	SIAI-Marchetti S.205-20/R	017/06-017	
I-IBAN	SIAI-Marchetti S.205-20/R	025/06-025	

I-IBLE	Aérospatiale SA.315B Lama	2483	
I-IBLI	Robinson R-22B Beta	3667	
I-ICAB	SIAI-Marchetti S.205-20/R	011/06-011	
I-ICAF	SIAI-Marchetti S.205-20/R	014/06-014	
I-ICAK	SIAI-Marchetti S.205-20/R	021/06-021	
I-ICAL	SIAI-Marchetti S.205-20/R	022/06-022	
I-ICAO	SIAI-Marchetti S.205-20/R	029/06-029	
I-ICAQ	SIAI-Marchetti S.205-20/R	031/06-031	
I-ICAS	SIAI-Marchetti S.205-20/R	033/06-033	
I-ICBA	SIAI-Marchetti S.205-20/R	040/06-040	
I-ICES	Piper PA-28-140 Cherokee D (Dam.17.4.02)	28-7125233	N5073S
I-ICGR	Aérospatiale SA.315B Lama	2671	
I-IEAA	Partenavia P.68B	87	
I-IEAD	Partenavia P.68B	150	
I-IEAG	Partenavia P.68B	234	
I-IEAH	Partenavia P.68C	387	
I-IELE	Robinson R-44 Raven	1061	
I-IFRE	Robinson R-22 Beta	2437	
I-IFRR	Robinson R-22B2 Beta (Damaged 2.7.04)	3279	
I-IHAA	Bredanardi NH-300C	010	
I-IHAB	Bredanardi NH-300C	011	
I-IHAC	Schweizer 269C	S-1491	N41S
I-IHAD	Schweizer 269C	S-1498	N69A
I-IHAE	Schweizer 269C	S-1602	N86G
I-IJMW	Mooney M.29J Model 201	24-1633	OO-JMW
I-IKIM	Piper PA-28-181 Archer II	28-7990524	N2877W
I-ILAB	Piper PA-34-220TSeneca V	3449168	OY-LAB
			N9515N
I-ILLL	Hughes 269C	110-0985	N7011X
			YV-594CP
			YV-175E
			YV-2091P
			N1094N
I-IMEC	Reims FR172H Rocket	FR17200311	
I-IMMG	Cessna 525A CitationJet 2	525A-0038	N5235G
I-IMMI	Cessna 525 CitationJet CJ	525-0379	N5188A
I-IMPE	Piper PA-38-112 Tomahawk II	38-82A0055	N2395V
I-INAA	Piper PA-18-150 Super Cub	18-7809148	N63922
I-INAB	Piper PA-18-150 Super Cub	18-7809175	N82213
I-INAC	Piper PA-18-150 Super Cub	18-7809176	N82301
I-INAD	Piper PA-18-150 Super Cub	18-8009043	N82696
	(Bare frame noted 7.04)		
I-INGA	Piper PA-32R-301T Saratoga II TC	3257239	N5337E
I-INKA	Piper PA-28-180 Cherokee Challenger	28-7305011	N15098
I-INOT	Pilatus PC-6/B2-H4 Turbo Porter	892	HB-FKZ
I-INTR	Agusta A.129DE	29800	
I-IOIO	Zlin Z.526AFS Akrobat	1330	
I-IOLE	Cessna 172RG Cutlass RG	172RG0166	N6333R
I-IPAD	Cessna TU206G Turbo Stationair	03881	(N7341C)
I-IPAJ	Cessna TU206G Turbo Stationair 6	04152	N756KM
I-IPAK	Cessna TU206G Turbo Stationair 6	05613	N5294X
I-IPAQ	Cessna TU206G Turbo Stationair 6	04390	N756VL
I-IPAR	Cessna TU206G Turbo Stationair 6	U20604291	N756RG
I-IPIZ	Beech 400A Beechjet	RK-29	N15693
			I-IPIZ
I-IRCA	Cessna 182J Skylane	18257172	N3072F
I-IRNO	Partenavia P.66B Oscar 150	41	
I-IRPI	Aérospatiale SA.315B Lama	2672	
I-IRTO	Beech 58P Baron	TJ-252	D-IRTO
			N167TA
			N6694X
I-ISAA	SIAI-Marchetti SF.260D (Damaged 29.7.04)	830	
I-ISAB	SIAI-Marchetti SF.260D	831	
I-ISAC	SIAI-Marchetti SF.260D	832	
I-ISAD	SIAI-Marchetti SF.260D	833	
I-ISAE	SIAI-Marchetti SF.260D	834	
I-ISAF	Aérospatiale SA.315B Lama	2148	IDFAF
I-ISAG	SIAI-Marchetti SF.260D	835	
I-ISAH	SIAI-Marchetti SF.260D	836	
I-ISAI	SIAI-Marchetti SF.260D	837	
I-ISAJ	SIAI-Marchetti SF.260D	838	
I-ISAL	SIAI-Marchetti SF.260D	849	
I-ISAM	SIAI-Marchetti SF.260D	850	
I-ISAR	Aérospatiale AS.350B2 Ecureuil	2576	OE-XHG
			F-WZKH
I-ISAS	Aérospatiale AS.350B3 Ecureuil	3503	F-WQDM
I-ISBE	Agusta A.109E Power	11222	
I-ISEB	Reims/Cessna F172M	F17201133	OY-ESB
			SE-FZT
I-ISEO	Cessna F150J	F150-0471	
I-ISKY	Monnet Sonerai IIL	unkn	
I-ISOR	Cessna 402B	402B0438	
I-ITAA	Robin DR.400/180R Remorqueur	1241	
	(Damaged 20.10.04)		
I-ITAB	Robin DR.400/180R Remorqueur	1242	
I-ITAD	Robin DR.400/180R Remorqueur	1244	
I-ITAE	Robin DR.400/180R Remorqueur	1245	
I-ITAF	Robin DR.400/180R Remorqueur	1246	
I-ITAG	Robin DR.400/180R Remorqueur	1247	
I-ITAJ	Robin DR.400/180R Remorqueur (Wfu)	1249	
I-ITAK	Robin DR.400/180R Remorqueur	1250	
I-ITAO	Robin DR.400/180R Remorqueur	1350	
I-ITAP	Robin DR.400/180R Remorqueur	1351	
I-ITAQ	Robin DR.400/180R Remorqueur	1352	
I-ITAR	Robin DR.400/180R Remorqueur	1353	
I-ITAS	Robin DR.400/180R Remorqueur	1489	
I-ITAU	Robin DR.400/180R Remorqueur	1505	

I-ITAV	Robin DR.400/180R Remorqueur	1506	
I-ITAW	Robin DR.400/180R Remorqueur	1548	
I-ITAX	Robin DR.400/180R Remorqueur	1568	
I-ITAY	Robin DR.400/180R Remorqueur	1519	
I-ITAZ	Robin DR.400/180R Remorqueur	1601	
I-ITBB	Robin DR.400/180R Remo 180	2001	
I-ITBC	Robin DR.400/180R Remo 180 (Damaged 8.6.01)	2007	
I-ITBD	Robin DR.400/180R Remo 180	2008	
I-ITBE	Robin DR.400/180R Remo 180	2013	
I-ITBF	Robin DR.400/180R Remo 180	2014	
I-ITBG	Robin DR.400/180R Remo 180	2020	
I-ITSA	Piper PA-30 Twin Comanche B	30-1282	N8169Y
I-IVIV	Robinson R-44 Astro	0216	
I-IZAA	Mudry CAP.20LS-200	11	
I-IZAB	Mudry CAP.20LS-200	12	
I-IZAF	Mudry CAP.10B	95	F-WZCH
I-IZAG	Mudry CAP.10B	145	F-WZCG
I-IZAI	Mudry CAP.10B	242	
I-IZAJ	Mudry CAP.10B	251	
I-IZAK	Mudry CAP.21	4	F-GAUQ
I-IZAL	Mudry CAP.10B	255	
I-IZAM	Mudry CAP.10B	258	
I-IZAN	Mudry CAP.10B	271	
I-JADE	Robinson R-22B2 Beta	3428	
I-JALU	Piper PA-28RT-201T Turbo Arrow IV	28R-8531003	N4385N
I-JAMY	Dassault Falcon 2000	54	D-BIRD F-WWML
I-JANN	Iannotta I.66 San Francesco	unkn	
I-JANS	Sud Avn SA.316BAlouette III	1226	F-WQKO A-226
I-JANV	Iannotta I.66L San Francesco	01	
I-JARR	Sivel SD.27	001	
I-JCRT	Robinson R-22 Mariner	3004M	
I-JECT	Sukhoi SU-31M	05	RA-01088
I-JEMP	Rand-Robinson KR-2	8123	
I-JENY	Fokker DR.1 Triplane Replica	1	
I-JESB	Piper PA-18-150 Super Cub	1809009	N9617N
I-JESC	Piper PA-28R-201 Arrow	2837020	N9178R
I-JESD	Piper PA-28-181 Archer II	2890154	N9211D
I-JESO	Cessna 550 Citation II	550-0255	N28GA I-DEAF N6861L
I-JESS	Robinson R-22B Beta	3671	
I-JETA	Boeing 737-229	21839	OO-SBS LX-OOO OO-SBS LX-OOO OO-SBS
I-JETC	Boeing 737-230	23153	D-ABMA
I-JETD	Boeing 737-230	23158	D-ABMF
I-JETX	Cessna 750 Citation X	750-0184	N51896
I-JJOB	Aérospatiale SA.315B Lama	2641	F-GEPU G-BNHZ
I-JJOY	de Havilland DH.82A Tiger Moth	86550	G-APGM EI-AHM EI-AHH PG641
I-JOBE	Mooney M.20R Ovation	29-0085	N9147F
I-JOGG	Reims/Cessna F152	F15201688	N8064X
I-JOHN	Pasotti F.7 Rondone (Stored 7.04) (C/n originally quoted as 08 which was duplicated)	N8	
I-JOKE	Zlin Z.526F Trenér Master	1298	
I-JOLE	Macchi MB.308	unkn	
I-JUKY	SAN Jodel DR.1050 Ambassadeur	293	
I-JULI	Beech 95-B55 Baron(W/o 26.5.02)	TC-629	HB-GBH
I-JULY	Piper PA-32R-300 Cherokee Lance (Dism.)	32R-7680045	N7298C
I-JUNI	Schweizer 269C	S-1824	
I-JURA	Rand-Robinson KR-2	unkn	
I-KALA	Agusta A.119 Koala	14007	VH-CHI VH-FOX
I-KALU	Rutan VariEze	001	
I-KARL	Rutan Long-Ez	001	
I-KAVA	Piper PA-28-161 Cadet	2841275	N91968
I-KAWA	Schleicher 269C	S-1829	
I-KDHF	SG Aviation Storm 400 Century	185	
I-KEIT	Piper PA-23-250 Aztec E	27-7305040	N40237
I-KELE	Agusta A.109A-II	7315	
I-KEOM	Eurocopter EC.130B4 Ecureuil	3706	
I-KETO	Cessna 750 Citation X	750-0161	N5245L
I-KGKM	Aérospatiale SA.315B Lama	1241/48	Fr.AF
I-KIDA	Piper PA-28-161 Warrior II	28-7916264	N2220N
I-KIIS	Cessna T210N Turbo Centurion II	21063986	LX-III (2) TR-LBN F-GCSC (N4683Y)
I-KILE	Piper PA-28R-201 Arrow	2837050	N92067
I-KIMM	Piper PA-23-250 Aztec E	27-7405434	N54127
I-KIRO	Robinson R-22B2 Beta	3208	
I-KISE	Piper PA-34-220T Seneca IV	3448065	N9251V (N295PS) N9251R
I-KITF	Denney Kitfox (Also marked I-3667)	unkn	
I-KITO	Piper PA-24-260 Comanche B	24-4386	I-GIOV N8930P
I-KITS	SG Aviation Storm 400 T1 Century	108	
I-KJNG	Boeing Stearman E-75	005	

I-KKGR	Dyn'Aero MCR-01 (Not yet cld but same c/n is now on I-LOSG)	106	
I-KKLT	Aviat Pitts S-2B	5248	
I-KKVB	Piper PA-34-220T Seneca IV	3447012	N9262B
I-KNOT	Agusta A.119 Koala	14004	
I-KNOW	Agusta A.119 Koala (W/o 26.2.01)	14005	
I-KOAL	Agusta A.119 Koala	14003	
I-KOLA	Agusta A.119 Koala	14024	
I-KOME	Piper PA-24-250 Comanche	24-837	N6099P
I-KORR	Piper PA-32RT-300T Turbo Lance II	32R-7987102	D-EIRR N2209P
I-KQUO	Cessna 152	15282875	N89806
I-KRAM	Tecnam P.92JSEcho	030	
I-KRAY	Rand-Robinson KR-2	5412	
I-KRFN	Rand-Robinson KR-2	9478	
I-KRLI	Rand-Robinson KR-2	8191	
I-KRLS	Piper PA-28-161 Cadet	2841033	N9157J
I-KRNL	Piper PA-34-200T Seneca II	34-7870449	N21703
I-KRSC	Rand-Robinson KR-2	unkn	
I-KYKO	Christen Pitts S-2B	5167	
I-LAAC	Piper PA-28RT-201T Turbo Arrow IV	28R-8031126	N8233X
I-LAAS	Robinson R-44 Astro	0191	
I-LABO	Piper PA-18 Super Cub 95	18-2018	I-EIRI MM52-2418 52-2418
I-LACA	Piper PA-34-220T Seneca III	34-8133011	N83311
I-LACI	Piper PA-38-112 Tomahawk	38-78A0027	N9317T
I-LACO	Britten-Norman BN-2A-6 Islander	17	G-AWBY
I-LAKI	Rutan Long-Ez	83001	
I-LALE	Cessna 172K	17258379	N84208
I-LALL	Cessna 525A CitationJet 2	525A-0005	OY-LLA N372CT N552CJ N5235G
I-LALM	Robinson R-22B2 Beta	2987	
I-LAMC	Robinson R-44 Astro	0274	
I-LAMO	Aérospatiale AS.350B Ecureuil	2171	
I-LANC	Piper PA-32RT-300 Lance II	32R-7985100	N2078X
I-LAON	Agusta A.109E Power	11505	
I-LARJ	SIAI-Marchetti S.205-18/R	4-204	
I-LASA	Robinson R-22B2 Beta	2922	
I-LASC	Piper PA-28-236 Dakota	28-7911209	N2854G
I-LASD	Aérospatiale AS.350B2 Ecureuil	2410	F-GHHL
I-LASM	Aérospatiale AS.350B Ecureuil	3573	
I-LASJ	Schweizer 269C	S-1459	D-HPAP HB-XNQ D-HHOR N99DM
I-LASL	Aérospatiale AS.350B Ecureuil	3293	
I-LASP	Aérospatiale AS.350B1 Ecureuil	1822	JA9779 N6004C F-WJUL F-GJUL F-WJUL F-WYMK
I-LASS	Aérospatiale AS.350B2 Ecureuil	3513	
I-LAZZ	Aérospatiale SA.315B Lama	2653	
I-LBLZ	Piper PA-34-220TSeneca V	3449175	N4175Z
I-LDAP	Piper PA-28-181 Archer II	28-8390072	N4309N
I-LDAV	Aérospatiale SA.341G Gazelle	1034	F-BUFB F-WMHC
I-LEAN	Schweizer 269C	S-1472	
I-LEAS	Cessna 182K Skylane	18258416	N2816R
I-LECI	Piper PA-28RT-201T Turbo Arrow IV	28R-8031138	N82396
I-LECN	Piper PA-28RT-201T Turbo Arrow IV	28R-7931192	N29040
I-LEDI	Xausa X-001	unkn	
I-LELB	SIAI-Marchetti SF.260C	563/41-001	
I-LELC	SIAI-Marchetti SF.260C	566/41-002	
I-LELD	SIAI-Marchetti SF.260C	567/41-003	
I-LELF	SIAI-Marchetti SF.260C	568/41-004	
I-LELH	SIAI-Marchetti SF.260D	764	
I-LELM	SIAI-Marchetti SF.260D	765	
I-LELO	Piper PA-18-150 Super Cub	18-7809034	N82956
I-LEMO	Piper PA-24-250 Comanche	24-1278	N6298P
I-LEOG	Agusta A.109C	7602	
I-LEOZ	Partenavia P.66B Oscar 100	58	
I-LETI	Schweizer 269C	S-1276	HB-XRT N7504Z
I-LETY	Piper PA-18-150 Super Cub	18-7909095	N82384
I-LFSA	Cessna 177B Cardinal	17702080	N34906
I-LGAW	Christen Eagle	unkn	
I-LGET	Robin DR.400/180 Régent (Damaged 14.1.01)	1525	
I-LGUE	Piper PA-18-150 Super Cub	18-5263	N5761D
I-LIAB	Dassault Falcon 20	172/456	F-BRHB F-WNGM
I-LIAC	Dassault Falcon 20D	234/475	D-COLL (D-CIBM) F-WLCU
I-LIAD	Gates Learjet 35A	35A-111	OE-GMA (I-SIDU) (HB-VFE) N3815G
I-LIAO	Schweizer 269C	S-1445	
I-LIAT	Piper PA-31T1 Cheyenne I	31T-8004052	N2316X
I-LIDC	MBB-Kawasaki BK.117C-1	7529	D-HMB .
I-LIDD	Agusta A.109EPower	11107	
I-LIDY	Quickie Quickie Q.2	unkn	

I-LIGU	Aérospatiale AS.350B3 Ecureuil	3354	
I-LIMB	Piper PA-28-236 Dakota	2811035	F-GJPQ (HB-PNF)
I-LIMG	Piper PA-32RT-300T Turbo Lance II	32R-7887288	N3001A
I-LINO	Evans VP-1 Volksplane	unkn	
I-LINB	Airbus A320-231	363	G-SUEE N363RY G-IEAG F-WWBX
I-LINF	Airbus A320-231	393	G-CVYD B-HYO VR-HYO F-WWIR
I-LING	Airbus A320-231	414	5B-DBJ EI-TLR B-HYR VR-HYR F-WWIU
I-LINH	Airbus A320-231	163	G-RDVE OY-CND F-WWDU
I-LIOI	Agusta E-101	50009	
I-LIPO	Beech C90 King Air	LJ-616	SE-GXD N1MX N1MB N1970T
I-LIPS	Piper PA-22-150 Tri-Pacer	22-5488	HB-OPS
I-LITT	Robinson R-22 Beta	2345	N83081
I-LIVA	Airbus A321-231	1950	D-AVXE
I-LIVB	Airbus A321-231	1970	D-AVZK
I-LIVD	Airbus A321-231	792	D-ALAH D-AVZM
I-LIVL	Airbus A330-243	627	F-WWYE
I-LIVM	Airbus A330-243	551	F-WWKE
I-LIVN	Airbus A330-243	597	F-WWKQ
I-LIVO	Piper PA-28-181 Archer III	2843052	N92768
I-LIZZ	Piper PA-34-220T Seneca III	34-8133156	N8410D
I-LJFE	Macchi AL.60B-2	89/6269	
I-LLAG	Boeing 767-330ER	25137	N691LF D-ABUX
I-LLBB	Agusta A.109C	7625	
I-LLEA	Schweizer 269C	S-1743	
I-LLEO	Bell 206B Jet Ranger	4077	N63AJ N21463 C-FHBC
I-LLES	Hiller UH-12E	5141	I-LION
I-LMAX	Steen Skybolt	unkn	
I-LOBE	Aérospatiale AS.365N3 Dauphin 2	6699	
I-LOGI	Aérospatiale SA.315B Lama	2489	(F-GEEK) N49521
I-LONE	Jodel D.18	01	
I-LORI	Piper PA-28-151 Cherokee Warrior	28-7415666	N9555N
I-LORY	Monnett Sonerai II	1008	
I-LOSG	Dyn'Aero MCR-01	106	I-KKGR
I-LRMS	Piper PA-28-181 Cherokee Archer II	28-7890152	N47921
I-LSBB	Cessna 208BGrand Caravan	208B0712	N1268C N5246U
I-LSBC	Piper PA-18-150 Super Cub	18-8109006	HB-PFV SX-AJS HB-PFV
I-LSBD	Christen A-1 Husky	1024	N2910F
I-LSBV	Beech A36TC Bonanza	EA-144	HB-EJF
I-LSEE	Cessna 172N floatplane	17273797	N5442J
	(Damaged 4.10.04, dismantled)		
I-LSMA	Mooney M.20K Model 231	25-0862	N888DK
I-LTOP	Aérospatiale AS.355F1 Ecureuil	5106	N5792X
I-LTRY	Piper PA-28-181 Archer II	28-8590013	N4381M
I-LTTH	Agusta A.109	13753	
I-LUAN	Piper PA-31-325 Navajo C/R	31-7512027	N59950
I-LUBA	Reims/Cessna F150L	F15001103	
I-LUBB	Cessna 172P	17274485	N52294
I-LUDA	General Avia F.22B Pinguino	012	
I-LUEL	Piper PA-30 Turbo Twin Comanche C	30-1760	N8649Y N9726N
I-LUGA	Agusta-Bell 47G-2	165	MM80093
I-LUHH	Schweizer 269C	S-1645	N6145H
I-LUJJ	Schweizer 269C	S-1482	N227TA N127CP
I-LUKI	Piper PA-28RT-201 Arrow III	28R-8118067	F-GHJZ N8380Y
I-LUMM	Cessna 172P	17274307	N51388
I-LUNE	Cessna F150J	F150-0477	
I-LUPP	Cessna 182Q Skylane	18267596	N5247N
I-LUPU	Aérospatiale AS.350B Ecureuil	3803	
I-LURR	Cessna 172P	17274450	N52235
I-LURY	Sud Avn SA.316B Alouette III	1365	HB-XPB D-HFRD ZAF: 9T-HT4
I-LUXA	Aérospatiale AS.365N3 Dauphin 2	6624	F-WQDL
I-LVIA	Rotorway Exec 90	001	
I-LVNA	Aérospatiale AS.350B2 Ecureuil	3321	F-WQDD
I-LVNB	Cessna 525A CitationJet 2	525A-0073	N5165T
I-LXGR	Grumman G.1159C Gulfstream IV	1234	N924ML N475GA
I-LYDU	Piper PA-28RT-201 Arrow IV	28R-8118047	N83198
I-LYFE	Partenavia P.68	12	
I-LYNC	Fokker DR.I M Replica	01/84M	

I-MABO	Aérospatiale AS.350B3 Ecureuil	3392	
I-MADS	Piper PA-28R-201T Turbo Cherokee Arrow III	28R-7703166	N5919V
I-MAED	Cessna 172RG Cutlass RG	172RG1157	N9426D
I-MAEL	Aérospatiale SA.315B Lama	2510	F-GEEZ N49564
I-MAFE	CASA C.212-CC	273	EC-DVD (N431CA)
I-MAFI	Robinson R-22 Beta	2428	N83106
I-MAFP	Agusta A.109EPower	11121	
I-MAFR	Bredanardi NH-500D	BH-13	
I-MAGB	Schweizer 269C	S-1603	N41S
I-MAGH	Piper PA-28-181 Archer II	28-7990213	N2129J
I-MAGJ	Rockwell Commander 690A	11265	N81540 TC-RZL TurkPol:J-11265 UN-77 N81540 (LV-PUP)
I-MAGM	Agusta-Bell AB.412	25602	Fv11338 I-LEMA
I-MAGN	Magni MT-5 Autogyro (Rebuild of Termavaki JT-5)	01	OH-XYS
I-MAIK	Schweizer 269C	S-1868	N86G
I-MAIL	Robinson R-22B2 Beta	3186	
I-MAIP	Partenavia P.66B Oscar 150	10	
I-MAKO	Aérospatiale AS.350B2 Ecureuil	3693	
I-MAKT	Partenavia P.68C	209	
I-MALG	Robinson R-44 Astro	0628	
	(Also quoted as c/n 0624)		
I-MALO	Piper J-3C-65 Cub (Rebuilt)	001M	
I-MALU	Piper J-3C-65 Cub	11950	44-79654
I-MAMI	Cessna 210C	21058134	N3634Y
I-MAMM	Partenavia P.64 Oscar	07	
I-MAMO	Brügger MB-2 Colibri	231	
I-MAMY	Laverda F.8L Falco	419	
I-MAPE	Piper PA-28R-201 Arrow	2844007	N9275P
	(Registration being worn simultaneously by two aircraft of the same type, Rome-Urbe, 9.99)		
I-MAPY	Neico Lancair 320	1	
I-MARA	Macchi MB.308 (Rebuilt)	01	
I-MARJ	CEA DR.340 Major	320	F-OCMG
I-MARK	SIAI-Marchetti SF.260	2-35	
I-MARL	SIAI-Marchetti S.205-18/F	343	
I-MASE	Piper PA-23-160 Apache	23-1720	N4224P
I-MASF	SOCATA MS.880B Rallye Club	1222	
I-MASK	SOCATA MS.880B Rallye Club	1294	
I-MASQ	SOCATA MS.880B Rallye Club	1324	
I-MASV	SOCATA MS.892A Rallye Commodore 150	10992	
I-MASY	SOCATA MS.880B Rallye Club	1519	
I-MATJ	Aérospatiale AS.350B3 Ecureuil	3189	
I-MATU	Reims/Cessna FRA150L Aerobat	FRA1500204	
I-MAUL	Maule MX-7-180 Star Rocket	11036C	N61086
I-MAVV	Piper PA-28RT-201T Turbo Arrow IV	28R-8131076	D-ENET N8333A
I-MAWW	Beech 58P Baron	TJ-55	
I-MAXX	Piper PA-28RT-201T Turbo Arrow IV	28R-8031145	LY-AOH N82392
I-MCDT	Aérospatiale AS.350B2 Ecureuil	9057	F-GRME
I-MDNA	Piper PA-38-112 Tomahawk II	38-82A0048	N2326V
I-MDVC	Agusta A.109A	7225	N9046Y
I-MDVI	Partenavia P.66B Oscar 150	50	
I-MEAS	Cessna 421B Golden Eagle	421B0251	(N3367Q)
I-MEDT	Aérospatiale AS.350B2 Ecureuil	2766	F-WYMI
I-MEFA	Pilatus PC-6/B2-H4 Turbo Porter	671	HB-FFI
I-MEMA	Stinson L-5 Sentinel (Euravia)	003	
I-MENC	Cessna 172R	17280148	
I-MEPI	Piper PA-34-200T Seneca II	34-7970355	N2184K
	(Reserved as D-GHBW, .04)		
I-MERG	Partenavia P.66B Oscar 150	48	
I-MERL	Piper PA-32-300 Cherokee Six	32-7940258	N81188
I-MESO	MBB-Kawasaki BK.117C-1	7532	(ZS-. . .)
I-MEZE(2)	Rutan StagEze	001	
I-MFMM	Agusta A.109C	7605	EC-ETF 3A-MOR
I-MGAG	Aérospatiale AS.350B3 Ecureuil	3499	
I-MGIA	Robinson R-44 Clipper	0906	N7190F
I-MIAE	Aérospatiale AS.350B Ecureuil	1774	N8837K N516FB RP-C668
I-MIAS	Robinson R-22 Beta	1134	N8044X
I-MIAZ	Aérospatiale AS.350B3 Ecureuil	3469	
I-MICI	Piper J-3C-65 Cub	10900	43-29609
I-MICU	Aérospatiale SA.315B Lama	2295	F-GEJU N62886
I-MIFA	Beech 23 Musketeer	M-337	N2373J
I-MIGL	CEA DR.300/125 Petit Prince	658	
I-MIIS	Hughes 369E	0110E	N5223X
I-MILB	Reims/Cessna F172M	F17201112	D-EDXQ
I-MILI	Aeromere F.8L Falco	219	
I-MIMU	Piper PA-34-200 Seneca	34-7350330	N56424
I-MIPS	Monnet Sonerai IILS	001	
	(Believed to be N17DB, c/n 1545L exported to Italy)		
I-MIRK	Piper PA-34-200T Seneca II	34-8170053	N8306P
I-MISA	Cessna 172C	17249520	N2020Y
I-MISE	Partenavia P.66B Oscar 150	47	
I-MISS	Reims FR172J Rocket	FR17200415	
I-MITI	Piper PA-23-250 Turbo Aztec E	27-7304943	N14358

I-MLQT	Fokker F.27 Friendship 400	10295	HB-ITQ
			HA-ACK
			HB-ITQ
			PH-SFB
			N714A
			PH-FIO
I-MLRT	Fokker F.27 Friendship 500	10377	F-BPUE
			PH-FMZ
I-MLTT	Fokker F.27 Friendship 500	10378	F-BPUF
			PH-FNA
I-MLUT	Fokker F.27 Friendship 500	10369	F-BPUA
			PH-FMR
I-MLVS	Piper PA-34-220T Seneca V	3449124	N41406
I-MLVT	Fokker F.27 Friendship 500	10373	F-BPUC
			PH-FMV
I-MLXT	Fokker F.27 Friendship 500	10374	F-BPUD
			PH-FMW
I-MMAA	Robinson R-22 Beta	1164	N8062L
I-MMAC	Robinson R-22 Beta	2127	
I-MMAF	Robinson R-22 Beta	2514	
I-MMAG	Robinson R-22 Beta	2502	N83240
I-MMAH	Robinson R-22B2 Beta	2658	
I-MMAK	Robinson R-22B2 Beta	3183	
I-MMAL	Robinson R-22B2 Beta	3762	
I-MMAS	Robinson R-44 Raven II	10489	
I-MMBA	Robinson R-44 Astro	0112	
I-MMBB	Robinson R-44 Raven II	10321	N7533Z
I-MMCA	Cessna 172N	17271153	D-EOEV
			N2091E
I-MMEM	SIAI-Marchetti SF.260	2-43	
I-MMES	Robinson R.22B Beta	0551	
I-MMIK	Eurocopter EC.120B Colibri (Believed w/o)	1335	
I-MMNF	Rotorway Exec 162F	6275/02	
I-MMRR	Piper PA-28RT-201 Arrow IV	28R-8218023	N539FT
			N9519N
I-MODC	Piper PA-32-301 Saratoga	32-8506017	N2541Y
			N9597N
I-MODD	Sud Avn SA.318C Alouette Astazou	2186	F-GDQS
			C-GNQX
			N8262
I-MODJ	Bücker Bü.131 Jungmann	001	
	(Rebuild, ex I-BRIK, wfu 3.79 identity unknown ?)		
I-MODN	Piper PA-38-112 Tomahawk II	38-82A0042	N91514
I-MODU	Piper PA-28-181 Archer II	28-8190188	N83527
I-MOEN	Beech 77 Skipper	WA-135	HB-EJC
I-MOKA	SIAI-Marchetti S.205-20/R	4-159	
I-MOKE	Agusta A.109C	7660	
I-MOLG	Procaer F.15B Picchio	21	
I-MONY	Mooney M.20K Model 252 TSE	25-1217	
I-MOSS	AIAA Stampe SV.4C	1049	F-BBGQ
I-MROS	Aérospatiale SA.315B Lama	2498	G-BMUC
	(Reserved as F-GOEM 3.01)		N49529
I-MRSV	Fiat G.59B	181	MM53774
I-MSAA	BAe.146-200QT	E-2109	I-TPGS
			G-TNTD
			RP-C481
			G-TNTD
			SE-DHM
			G-BOMJ
			G-5-109
I-MSPG	Cessna F150G	F150-0119	
I-MSTR	Agusta A.109A	7227	N4256P
			I-KTRE
I-MTOP	Beech B200 Super King Air	BB-1825	N4485Z
I-MTVB	Cessna 550 Citation Bravo	550-0932	G-MIRO
			(I-MTVB)
			N5103J
I-MUNA	Agusta A.109EPower	11052	G-TVAA
I-MUNI	Mooney M.20K Model 231	25-0597	N1147P
I-MUNY	Mooney M.20K Model 231	25-0483	N94471
I-MURE	Aérospatiale SA.315B Lama	2509	N72590
I-MUSE	Partenavia P.64 Oscar	10	
I-MYCL	Mooney M.20M Model 257 TLS	27-0134	N9159Q
I-MYRO	Robinson R-22 Beta	1723	N4075S
I-NACA	Piper PA-18 Super Cub 95	18-2023	EI-92
			I-EITA
			MM52-2423
			52-2423
I-NADI	Pereira GP-2 Osprey	unkn	
I-NAIG	Robinson R-22 Beta	2440	
I-NAIS	Piper PA-24-260 Comanche B	24-4777	N9299P
			N9701N
I-NARE	Aérospatiale AS.350B Ecureuil	1266	
I-NASA	Piper PA-30 Turbo Twin Comanche C	30-1864	N8715Y
I-NATS	Dassault Falcon 2000EX	011	F-WWGJ
I-NCAA	Cessna A150M Aerobat	A1500633	N9824J
I-NCCA	Cessna 414A Chancellor	414A0282	N2618C
I-NCCD	Cessna 172N	17268742	N734CD
	(Sold? Same c/n now shown as F-GIQO)		
I-NCOP	III Sky Arrow 650 TCNS	CNS028	
I-NDIO	Aérospatiale AS.350B1 Ecureuil	2308	
I-NEGL	Cessna 421A	421A0138	OO-EDB
			OO-LFC
			HB-LFL
			(N4048L)
I-NEKI	Piper PA-32-301 Saratoga	32-8106009	N8294B
I-NENA	Piper PA-18-150 Super Cub	18-7709074	N83550

I-NEOS	Boeing 737-86N	32733	N1786B
I-NEOT	Boeing 737-86N	33004	
I-NEOU	Boeing 737-86N	29887	
I-NEOX	Boeing 737-86N	33677	
I-NERO	Reims/Cessna F150L	F15000950	
I-NERY	Aérospatiale SA.315B Lama	2437	
I-NEVY	Robinson R-44 Raven II	10468	
I-NEWA	Piper PA-28R-201T Turbo Arrow	2803004	N9176Q
I-NGPR	Piper PA-28-181 Archer II	28-8090368	N8241A
	(Damaged 31.10.04)		
I-NIGI	Agusta A.109E Power	11619	
I-NIKC	Robinson R-44 Astro	0698	
I-NIKI	Piper PA-18-150 Super Cub	18-7509064	N7480L
I-NITA	Piper J-3C-65 Cub	10905	43-29614
	(Identity quoted officially as 44-79610 = c/n 11906)		
I-NITL	Tecnam P.92JS Echo	013	
I-NJNO	Sud Avn SA.318C Alouette Astazou	1804	F-BMRG
			Cambodia AF
I-NOLB	Reims/Cessna F150K	F15000640	
I-NOLD	Reims/Cessna F150L	F15000668	
I-NOLJ	Reims/Cessna F150L	F15000948	
I-NOLL	Reims/Cessna F150L	F15000989	
I-NOLP	Reims/Cessna F150L	F15000755	
I-NOLQ	Reims/Cessna F150M	F15001217	
I-NOLS	Reims/Cessna F150L	F15001070	
I-NOLT	Reims/Cessna F150L	F15001084	
I-NOLV	Reims/Cessna F150L	F15001116	(OE-ATO)
I-NOPA	Piper PA-34-200T Seneca II	34-8170048	N8303U
I-NOWA	Aérospatiale/Alenia ATR-42-300	051	F-WWEF
I-NOWT	Aérospatiale/Alenia ATR-42-300	054	F-WWEI
I-NRDS	Agusta A.109E Power	11175	
I-NSEM	Robinson R-22 Beta	2517	N83298
I-NUBJ	Agusta-Bell 412EP	25913	
I-NUDO	Partenavia P.64B Oscar B	30	
I-NUMI	Dassault Falcon 900	89	F-WWFB
I-NUVE	Partenavia P.66B Oscar 150	05	
I-OAZA	Robinson R-44 Raven II	10348	
I-OBBY	Piper PA-32-300 Cherokee Six E	32-7340119	N55463
I-OBPC	Partenavia P.68 Observer	261-08-OB	
I-OBSR	Partenavia P.68 Observer	236-01-OB	
I-OBSW	Partenavia P.68 Observer	331-21-OB	
I-OCEA	Boeing 747-230F	21592	D-ABYO
I-OCEU	Boeing 747-230F (Reservation .04)	22668	D-ABYU
			N1785B
I-ODHK	SOCATA Rallye 235E Gabier	12881	F-ODHK
I-ODKF	SOCATA TB-10 Tobago	17	F-ODKF
I-ODLV	Robinson R-22 Beta	1035	F-ODLV
			N8043E
I-ODNV	SOCATA TB-9 Tampico	216	F-ODNV
I-ODQD	SOCATA TB-20 Trinidad	385	F-ODQD
I-ODSO	SOCATA TB-20 Trinidad	761	F-ODSO
I-OETE	Aérospatiale AS.350B Ecureuil	1103	F-WZFH
I-OGQH	SOCATA TB-10 Tobago	1007	F-OGQH
I-OHDB	SOCATA TB-20 Trinidad	1469	F-OHDB
I-OLEY	Aérospatiale SA.315B Lama	2369	
I-OMAT	Piper PA-18 Super Cub 95	18-3356	EI-134
	(Officially quoted with f/n 18-3299 as c/n)		I-EIHI
			MM53-7756
			53-7756
I-OMET	Aérospatiale AS.350B Ecureuil	2490	F-WYMQ
I-OMGA	Piper PA-32-301 Saratoga	32-8306032	N8156U
			N9512N
I-ONIL	Piper PA-28-180 Cherokee C	28-3121	HB-OYO
			N9084J
I-ONVI	Aérospatiale AS.350B3 Ecureuil	3437	
I-ONYX	Hughes 369E	0483E	OY-HEM
I-OPBS	Dyn'Aero MCR-01	43	
I-OPCV	Cessna 182N Skylane	18260467	N8927G
I-OPEF	CASA I-131EJungmann	2194	HB-UDE
			E3B- . . .
I-OPES	Avia FL.3	A.7	
I-OPIS	SAI G-97 Spotter V	1?	
I-ORAO	Aérospatiale AS.355N Ecureuil 2	5583	
I-ORAS	Agusta A.109A	7183	
I-ORBE	Piper PA-28-161 Warrior II	28-8016368	N8240X
			(N8240V)
I-ORLY	Aérospatiale SA.315B Lama	2627	
I-ORSE	Piper PA-31 Turbo Navajo	31-523	N6595L
I-OSPA	Aérospatiale AS.355N Ecureuil 2	5502	G-NMHS
			G-DPPS
			F-WYMM
I-OTEL	Cessna 501 Citation I/SP	501-0048	(I-DAEP)
			N414CC
			N87510
I-OTIS	SIAI-Marchetti S.208	4-52	MM61939
I-OXAL	SOCATA MS.893A Rallye Commodore 180	10945	
I-PABL	Cessna 550 Citation Bravo	550-1083	N5201M
I-PACC	Partenavia P.57 Fachiro IIf	28	
I-PADI	Rockwell 114 Commander	14388	G-PADY
			(G-BFXT)
			N5840N
I-PAEA	Piper PA-28-181 Archer III	2843069	N92834
I-PAFA	Parodi FA.313	001	
	(Homebuilt based on SE.3130 Alouette II)		
I-PAFI	Piper PA-28RT-201T Turbo Arrow IV	28R-8231059	N8238X
I-PAGG	Partenavia P.57 Fachiro IIf	32	
I-PAHH	Partenavia P.64 Oscar	12	

I-PAIA	SIAI-Marchetti S.205-18/R (Damaged 17.10.02)	4-292	
I-PALS	Piper PA-31T Cheyenne	31T-7620005	N54979
I-PAMR	Aérospatiale AS.350B2 Ecureuil	3547	
I-PAMY	Piper PA-28-180 Cherokee F	28-7105039	N5185S
I-PAOZ	Partenavia P.64B Oscar B	67	
I-PAPA	Macchi AL.60B-2	17/6162	
I-PARJ	Partenavia P.68	06	
I-PASC	Piper PA-28-181 Archer III	2843162	N41226
I-PATE	Aérospatiale SA.365N2 Dauphin 2	6356	
I-PATI	Aérospatiale SA.315B Lama	2651	
I-PATS	Agusta S.211A	201	
I-PAVV	Piper PA-18-150 Super Cub	18-8006	HB-OWK N6785Z
I-PAWR	Agusta A.109EPower	11510	
I-PAXE	Agusta A.109EPower	11127	
I-PAZZ	Schweizer 269C	S-1626	F-OHAR N41S
I-PCFA	Agusta A.109EPower	11055	
I-PCLE	Agusta A.109A	7164	
I-PDAC	Piper PA-34-200 Seneca	34-7450145	I-SIMO N41653
I-PDRG	SOCATA TB-21 Trinidad TC	1040	
I-PECS	Robinson R.22M2 Mariner	2710M	SX-HMR
I-PEGA	Cessna 500 Citation I	500-0081	HB-VDA N5B N581CC
I-PEKF	Airbus A320-214	1322	F-WWDS
I-PEKG	Airbus A320-214	1132	I-PEKA (HB-IJU) F-WWIS
I-PEKH	Airbus A320-214	1162	I-PEKZ I-PEKB F-WWBZ
I-PEKI	Airbus A320-214	1179	I-PEKC F-WWDQ
I-PEKL	Airbus A320-214	1244	I-PEKD F-WWIQ
I-PELE	Piper PA-28R-200 Cherokee Arrow II	28R-7635360	N6915J
I-PELL	Aérospatiale SA.315B Lama	2621	
I-PELO	SNCAN/ Stampe SV.4C	375	F-BBFI Fr.Mil
I-PENN	Partenavia P.57 Fachiro IIf	36	
I-PEPE	Piper PA-22-108 Colt	22-8242	
I-PEPI	SOCATA MS.880B Rallye Club	885	
I-PFDC	Aérospatiale AS.355N Ecureuil 2	5514	F-WYMF F-WYMB F-WYMC
I-PGAB	Cessna 172R	17280421	N26624 N41227
I-PGAC	Piper PA-34-200 Seneca	34-7350098	OE-FHZ D-GHSI N15829
I-PGAR	Piper PA-28RT-201T Turbo Arrow IV	28R-8231063	G-BNBX N8257H
I-PGCC	Pitts S-1S Special	101	
I-PIAH	Beech 200 Super King Air	BB-777	
I-PIAT	Piper PA-18-150 Super Cub	18-7509138	N9714P
I-PICC	Procaer F.15 Picchio	02	
I-PIDR	Piper PA-28-181 Archer II	28-8490083	N4365K
I-PIER	Avia LM.5	3	
I-PIKY	Piper PA-28RT-201 Arrow IV	28R-7918106	N2102Z
I-PILA	Piper PA-18-150 Super Cub	18-6696	N9453D
I-PILL	Robinson R-22 Beta	1167	N8055J
I-PINA	Rutan VariEze	1318	
I-PIOT	Piper PA-28-161 Warrior II	28-7916388	HB-PDP N2210Z
I-PITO	Aérospatiale SA.315BLama	2461	F-GIIB CS-HBR F-GKSA TG-WAT
I-PITS	Christen Pitts S-2B	5140	
I-PITT	Pitts S-1T Special	001	
I-PITU	Piper PA-28RT-201 Arrow IV	28R-7918241	D-EITU N2967A
I-PITZ	Pitts S-1C Special	007	
I-PJAR	Piaggio P.180 Avanti	1002	
I-PJAV	Piaggio P.180 Avanti	1001	
I-PJNO	Piper PA-28-181 Archer II	28-8190157	N8331A
I-PLAM	Reims/Cessna FR182 Skylane RG	FR18200037	F-BVOE (PH-AYA)
I-PLAS	Reims/Cessna FT337GP Super Skymaster (Reims-assembled P337G Pressurized Skymaster US c/n P3370051)	FP33700004	(G-BAVV)
I-PLLY	318GC (Rebuilt SA.318C Alouette Astazou)	001	
I-PLUH	Agusta A.109LUH (Allocated SAAF4114 for testing)	13651	
I-PNCA	Cessna 550 Citation II	550-0235	N67SG (N6803T)
I-PNIN	Piper PA-34-200T Seneca II	34-7570160	N33785
I-PNTG	SOCATA TB-10 Tobago	805	
I-POBA	CEA DR.1051 Sicile	543	
I-POGI	Partenavia P.66C Charlie	94	
I-POHE	Piper PA-18-150 Super Cub	18-8458	HB-POH D-EBYK(2) N4232Z
I-POMI	Cessna 320D Executive Skyknight	320D0002	N4102T
I-POMO	Piper PA-31T1 Cheyenne I	31T-7904030	N601PT
I-PONC	Reims/Cessna F172H	F17200668	
I-PONJ	Champion 7ECA Citabria	119	
I-POPA	Bell 412SP	33199	N14UV
I-POPY	Cessna T210N Turbo Centurion II	21063966	N4638Y
I-PORL	Piper PA-28-161 Cadet	2841289	N9199X
I-PORR	Cessna 152	15281301	N49482
I-POSI	Partenavia P.66B Oscar 150	22	
I-POTA	Robinson R-44 Raven	1271	N7508P
I-POWR	Agusta A.109EPower	11501	
I-POXY	Rutan Long-Ez	001	
I-PRAL	SIAI-Marchetti S.208	369	
I-PRBE	Bredanardi NH-300C	016	I-BNCO
I-PRCO	Hughes 269C	14-0268	I-BNBE
I-PREM	Piper PA-34-200TSeneca II	34-7870221	D-GFIT N215RW N9775C
I-PRIM	Partenavia P.66B Oscar 100	43	
I-PRMA	SG Aviation Storm 280S1	62	
I-PROD	General Avia F.15E Picchio	38-GA	
I-PRSC	Piper PA-34-200 Seneca	34-7450154	N41853
I-PRVV	Aérospatiale SA.315B Lama	2418	
I-PSCM	Cessna P210R Pressurized Centurion II	P21000862	D-EDDS(3) N5530A
I-PSFH	Pilatus PC-6/B2-H4 Turbo Porter	778	OY-SFH N117SA (D-FHPK) LV-MAE
I-PSMR	SOCATA MS.880B Rallye Club (CofA exp.6.5.02. Wreck at Rieti 7.04)	1133	OY-DFG
I-PTEC	Ultravia Pelican	unkn	
I-PUBB	Champion 7GCAA Citabria	125	
I-PULI	Cessna 340A	340A0019	HB-LMW D-IMJP (N98528)
I-PULL	Akrotech G-200	28	
I-PVAE	Piper PA-34-220TSeneca V	3449041	N92865
I-PVLA	Cessna 172N	17272322	HB-CLZ N4639D
I-PVLB	Cessna 172RGCutlass II RG	172RG0002	F-GGCY N4597R
I-PVLC	Cessna 172N floatplane	17272343	D-EWGN SE-INU N4732D
I-PVLD	Beech 76 Duchess	ME-170	D-GEXA N6021L
I-PVLE	Cessna 172N	17270935	HB-CJA N739ZK
I-PWER	Agusta A.109E Power	11001	
I-PYCG	47TT (1999 rebuild of Agusta-Bell 47G-3B1 MM80490)	001	
I-PYRO	SNCASE SE.3130 Alouette II	1558	F-GLNO XR376 (XJ376)
I-RAGC	Piper PA-31-350 Navajo Chieftain	31-7552024	9Q-CSI N61520
I-RAGW	Cessna 500 Citation	500-0311	LN-AAF (OY-VIP) SE-DRT N39RE N501RL OH-COL N818CD N5311J

I-RAIA to RAIZ *Test Registrations used for type certification by R.A.I.*

I-RALC	SOCATA MS.894E Minerva 220GT	12137	
I-RALE	SOCATA MS.880B Rallye Club	2052	(D-EMJB)
I-RALF	SOCATA MS.880B Rallye Club	2087	
I-RALJ	SOCATA MS.880B Rallye Club	2391	F-BUXU
I-RALK	SOCATA MS.880B Rallye Club	2410	
I-RALL	Morane-Saulnier MS.885 Super Rallye	45	(D-EMPA)
I-RALQ	SOCATA Rallye 100S Sport	2345	
I-RALS	SOCATA Rallye 100S Sport	2360	
I-RAMT	Piper PA-32RT-300T Turbo Lance II	32R-7887054	N36576
I-RAPS	Agusta A.109EPower	11160	
I-RATI	Cessna P210N Pressurized Centurion	P21000646	N210NM D-ENGL N5160W
I-RAUL	Beech F33C Bonanza	CJ-27	HB-EKH
I-RAVU	Cessna F150J	F150-0443	(G-AXBR)
I-RAWA	III Sky Arrow 650 TCNS	CNS009	
I-RAWB	III Sky Arrow 650 TCNS	CNS013	
I-RAWC	III Sky Arrow 650 TCNS	CNS014	
I-RAWD	III Sky Arrow 650 TCNS	CNS015	
I-RAWE	III Sky Arrow 650 TCNS	CNS017	
I-RAWF	III Sky Arrow 650 TCNS	CNS018	
I-RAWG	III Sky Arrow 650 TCNS	CNS019	
I-RAWH	III Sky Arrow 650 TCNS	CNS020	
I-RAWI	III Sky Arrow 650 TCNS	CNS023	
I-RAWJ	III Sky Arrow 650 TCNS	CNS024	
I-RBII	Robinson R-22B2 Beta	2733	
I-RCNF	Aero Designs Pulsar 912	01	
I-RCPM	Agusta A.109E Power	11172	
I-RDGO	Valmet L-90TP Redigo	S016	OH-VTS
I-REBY	Mudry CAP.232	30	F-GRED
I-RECE	Agusta-Bell AB.412	25571	

I-REDO	Piper J-3C-65 Cub (True c/n unknown)	"11438"	
I-REDV	Agusta A.109A Hirundo	7223	N9547S
I-REGO	Aviamilano P.19 Scricciolo	215/339	
I-REIL	Aérospatiale AS.350B2 Ecureuil	2379	
I-RELT	North American NA.265-40 Sabreliner	282-133	N41NR N65740
I-REMR	Agusta A.109EPower	11133	
I-REMU	Robin DR.400/120 Petit Prince	1910	F-GGXV
I-REMV	Agusta A.109EPower	11119	
I-RESG	Colomban MC-15 Cri-Cri	unkn	
I-RFSZ	Piper PA-28-181 Cherokee Archer II	28-7690069	N7593C
I-RGDT	Piel CP.80	80	
I-RGGG	Cessna P337G Pressurized Skymaster	P3370285	N46JA N2QN
I-RGRB	Rockwell Commander 114	14188	N4858W
I-RGSA	III Sky Arrow 650 TCNS	RG001	
I-RHOO	Agusta A.109E Power (Damaged 23.10.04)	11167	
I-RIBO	Cessna 170B	25557	HB-COD (N4613C)
I-RICI	Cessna 182R Skylane	18268105	N9909H
I-RICK	Rand-Robinson KR-2S	9270-768	
I-RIFA	Aviamilano P.19 Scricciolo	351	
I-RIFI	Reims/Cessna F150L	F15000962	
I-RIKJ	Piper PA-28-181 Archer II	28-8490068	N4359K
I-RIKK	Robinson R-22 Beta	1446	
I-RIML	Aérospatiale/Alenia ATR-42-300	206	G-BYHB HS-TRL F-WWEU
I-RIMS	Aérospatiale/Alenia ATR-42-300	190	G-BYHA HS-TRK F-WWEF
I-RJGA	Pitts S-1E Special	78001	
I-RJLJ	Mooney M.20J Model 205	24-3419	N433FM
I-RMDV	Sikorsky S-76A	760235	N760P
I-RMPW	Agusta A.109EPower	11067	
I-RMTI	Agusta-Bell 412EP	25923	
I-RNBR	Agusta-Bell 412EP	25921	
I-ROBH	Robinson R-22 Beta	1870	N23143
I-ROBJ	Piper PA-18-150 Super Cub	18-7893	N3977Z
I-ROBO	Robin R.2160D Alpha Sport	186	D-EFQM
I-ROCH	Cessna 172RG Cutlass RG	172RG0984	N9713B
I-ROCK	Parker Teenie Two	unkn	
I-ROCS	Agusta AB.139	31005	
I-RODY	Robinson R-22 Beta	1054	
I-ROLI	Piper PA-30 Twin Comanche	30-639	N7613Y
I-ROLL	SIAI-Marchetti SF.260	112	HB-EV V OO-HAZ I-SJAD
I-ROME	Van's RV-6N	3975	
I-RONY	Hawker 800XP	258506	N50166
I-ROSA	Piper PA-22-150 Tri-Pacer	22-2804	N2433P
I-ROTA	Vag-A-Bond	unkn	
I-ROYA	Mudry CAP.10B	53	F-BUDS
I-ROYJ	Piper PA-18-150 Super Cub	18-7709066	N83549
I-ROYS	Piper PA-18-150 Super Cub	18-7509124	N40575
I-ROYY	Piper PA-18-150 Super Cub	18-7509122	N40573
I-ROZO	SOCATA TB-20 Trinidad	1258	G-POZO I-POZO
I-RPLL	Cessna R172K Hawk XP	R1723290	N758RB
I-RRAA	Cessna 172N	17272073	N6839E
I-RRPG	Partenavia P.68B	193	
I-RRRR	Robinson R-22M Mariner	1305M	
I-RTAA	Partenavia P.68B	181	
I-RUFA	Aérospatiale AS.350B3 Ecureuil	3483	
I-RUIS	Robinson R-22B2 Beta	3363	N7509U
I-RVRP	Cessna 525 CitationJet CJ	525-0397	N5163C
I-RWLT	Piper PA-28-161 Archer II	28-8390085	N4313Z
I-SAAB	Cessna 172N floatplane	17269026	N734QG
I-SAAV	SIAI-Marchetti SF.260B	2-58	
I-SABR	Piper PA-28RT-201T Turbo Arrow IV	28R-8031076	N81774
I-SABY	Piper PA-28-180 Cherokee E	28-5852	N3892R
I-SADG	Aérospatiale AS.350B3 Ecureuil	3120	
I-SADP	Bredanardi NH-300C	014	
I-SALE	Laverda F.8L Falco	408	
I-SANA	Partenavia P.57 Fachiro II (CofA exp.5.2.01. Stored Rieti 7.04)	10	
I-SANW	Cessna 152	15285766	PH-ANW N94689
I-SARB	Bell 412	33078	
I-SARI	Piper J-3C-65 Cub	12612	D-ELIC SE-BFE 44-80316
I-SARY	SNCAN/ Stampe SV.4C	379	I-SARC F-BDIS
I-SASA	Piper PA-31T1 Cheyenne I	31T-8004024	
I-SATL	Partenavia P.66C Charlie	103	
I-SAXS	Piper PA-34-220T Seneca III	34-8233175	D-GENT N8249Y
I-SBIR	Cessna 152	15282029	OY-JRB N67804
I-SCAN	Heintz Zenith CH-200	unkn	
I-SCAP	Cessna 182P Skylane	18261064	N7424Q
I-SCDT	Piper PA-18-150 Super Cub	18-7909174	N9754N
I-SCDX	Reims/Cessna F152	F15201455	
I-SCTA	Agusta A.109EPower	11201	
I-SCUD	Piper PA-28-140 Cherokee D	28-7125245	N5079S
I-SDCR	Piper PA-34-200T Seneca II	34-8070254	N8230S
I-SDFC	Bombardier BD.100-1A10 Challenger 300	20013	N315LJ C-GZEI
I-SDSH	Schweizer 269C	S-1238	N207RJ F-GJBO N7508A
I-SEAE	Dassault Falcon 2000	200	F-WWVN
I-SEAL	Reims FR172H Rocket	FR17200314	D-EARY
I-SEEL	Robinson R-22 Beta	2390	N2364D
I-SEIA	Agusta A.109A-II	7388	
I-SEMA	Robinson R-22B2 Beta	3116	
I-SEMD	Robinson R-22B2 Beta	3105	
I-SEMG	Robinson R-22B2 Beta	3137	
I-SEMV	Robinson R-22B2 Beta	3213	
I-SEPA	Partenavia P.68	08	
I-SERY	Aérospatiale SA.315B Lama	2603	F-GDCY
I-SESE	Mooney M.20K Model 252 TSE	25-1219	N1068G
I-SESI	Aérospatiale SA.315B Lama	2053/20	N29907 D-HASO
I-SEXI	Aero L-29 Delfin	591235	-?-
I-SFAC	Agusta A.109E Power	11152	
I-SFTP	SIAI-Marchetti SF.260TP	661/60-004	
I-SHOW	Zlin Z.50LS	0054	
I-SIAF	SIAI-Marchetti S.205-22/R	378	
I-SIAR	SIAI-Marchetti S.205-20/R	003	
I-SIAW	SIAI-Marchetti SF.260	102	
I-SIBD	American AG-5B Tiger	10089	N11947
I-SIBM	Mudry CAP.10B	146	
I-SIBY	Robinson R-22M2 Mariner	2830M	
I-SICJ	Tecnam P.92-JS Echo	034	
I-SICY	Tecnam P.92J Echo	033	
I-SIEL	Robinson R-22B2 Beta	2719	
I-SIEM	Piper PA-28-180 Cherokee Challenger	28-7305541	N56151
I-SILK	Partenavia P.57 Fachiro IIf	23	
I-SILL	Aérospatiale AS.350B2 Ecureuil	2456	F-WYMT
I-SIMI	Piper PA-28R-180 Cherokee Arrow	28R-30600	N4697J
I-SIMJ	Cessna U206G Stationair floatplane	U20603657	LN-ALC N7426N
I-SINE	SNCASE SE.3160 Alouette III	1203	
I-SINK	SIAI-Marchetti SF.260B	3-84	
I-SINS	Aérospatiale SA.365N1 Dauphin 2	6306	
I-SINT	Aérospatiale SA.360C Dauphin	5030	
I-SISI	Piper J-3C-65 Cub	12474	44-80178
I-SISO	SOCATA MS.880B Rallye Club	894	
I-SIST	Beech 35-C33 Debonair	CD-914	HB-EJU D-EMYI
I-SIVI	Piper PA-28-161 Cadet	2841026	N9155G
I-SIVM	Mudry CAP.21DS	OK3	
I-SIXA	Fokker F.27 Friendship 500	10637	G-JEAF OY-SRD G-JEAF VH-EWW PH-EXE
I-SJAB	SIAI-Marchetti S.205-20/R	4-199	
I-SJAE	SIAI-Marchetti S.208	1-10	
I-SJAG	SIAI-Marchetti S.205-18/R	4-105	
I-SJAU	SIAI-Marchetti S.208A	1-13	
I-SJAY	SIAI-Marchetti SF.260B	3-78	
I-SJAZ	SIAI-Marchetti S.208	2-22	
I-SKIM	Cessna 182H Skylane	18256597	N8497S
I-SKIP	Sukhoi SU-26MZ	unkn	RA-44528
I-SKIT	Neico Lancair Super ES	001	
I-SKYD	Cessna 207 Skywagon	20700337	N1737U
I-SKYW	Bell 206BJet Ranger II	3968	OE-XRA N206RP C-FTOU N67CT N67AJ N3DU C-GAJR
I-SLIM	Piper PA-22-108 Colt	22-9496	N5690Z
I-SLOT	SOCATA MS.893A Rallye Commodore 180	11003	OO-DAX F-BRLU
I-SLVN	940A-Zefiro	unkn	
I-SMAA	SIAI-Marchetti SF.260C	369/42-001	
I-SMAU	Reims/Cessna F172P	F17202077	
I-SMBR	Piper PA-28-161 Warrior II	28-8016103	N8102Q
I-SMCE	SIAI-Marchetti SF.260E	784	I-RAIE I-RAIC
I-SMEB	McDonnell-Douglas DC-9-82	53064	B-28001 N6203D (N812ML)
I-SMEC	McDonnell-Douglas DC-9-83	49808	N183NA N3010G
I-SMED	McDonnell-Douglas DC-9-83	53182	N875RA N456AW
I-SMEL	McDonnell-Douglas DC-9-82	49247	HB-IKK
I-SMEM	McDonnell-Douglas DC-9-82	49248	HB-IKL
I-SMEP	McDonnell-Douglas DC-9-82	49740	
I-SMER	McDonnell-Douglas DC-9-82	49901	N6202S
I-SMES	McDonnell-Douglas DC-9-82	49902	
I-SMET	McDonnell-Douglas DC-9-82	49531	
I-SMEV	McDonnell-Douglas DC-9-82	49669	
I-SMEZ	McDonnell-Douglas DC-9-82	49903	PH-SEZ I-SMEZ N3010C (I-SMEZ)
I-SNAW	Dassault Falcn 2000	12	F-WWMM

I-SNAX	Dassault Falcon 900	69	F-WWFD
I-SNEK	Robinson R-44 Raven	1168	G-CBKH
I-SOCO	Aérospatiale SA.315B Lama	2183/39	F-GMET
			F-OCFX
I-SOFI	Aérospatiale SA.315BLama	2604	LN-OTB
			SE-HSP
			LN-OTB
I-SOFY	Robinson R-44 Raven II	10206	
I-SOGA	Piper PA-30 Twin Comanche	30-377	HB-LCP
			N7360Y
			N10F
I-SOLG	Piper PA-28-181 Archer II	28-8190086	N8293L
I-SOND	Aérospatiale SA.315B Lama	2481	N221RM
I-SORA	Piper PA-23-250 Aztec C	27-3595	N6396Y
I-SORV	Vulcanair P.68 Observer 2	423-23/OB2	
I-SOUL	Bell 206B Jet Ranger II	1599	I-MIBE
			N90104
I-SPAA	Cessna 172P	17274919	N54211
I-SPAB	Cessna 172P	17275083	N54942
I-SPAH	Cessna 150L	15074326	N19309
I-SPAI	Reims/Cessna F150L	F15000694	OE-ALR
I-SPAO	Cessna 172RG Cutlass RG	172RG0962	OO-STS
			N9677B
I-SPAP	Reims/Cessna F172N	F17201774	D-EFGT
I-SPAQ	Reims/Cessna F172N	F17201647	D-EFEH(2)
I-SPAR	Pagani Condor 150	001	
I-SPAT	Cessna 172S	172S8742	N3525L
I-SPAX	Piper PA-28RT-201T Turbo Arrow IV	28R-7931017	N2101G
I-SPBI	Robinson R-22 Beta	0746	
I-SPFO	SOCATA Rallye 235E Gabier	12872	
I-SPID	Procaer F.15B Picchio	17	
I-SPIN	Piper PA-28-161 Warrior II	28-7916498	N2875A
I-SPOT	Agusta-Bell 412	25601	
I-SPYD	Tecnam P.92J Echo	002	
	(This c/n current as I-TECK. I-SPYD is thought to be a Tecnam P.2002JF Sierra)		
I-SRAF	BAe.125-1000	259012	N512LR
			N512QS
			(N512HR)
			N512QS
			HZ-SJP2
			G-5-726
I-SRHA	Robinson R-22 Beta	1403	N40225
			(N4021A)
I-SRMA	Canadair CL-215-1A10	1004	I-SMRA
			C-FYWQ
			9A-CAB
			C-FYWQ
			CF-YWQ
			CF-PQH
I-SRMB	Canadair CL-215-1A10	1012	C-FTXE
			9A-CAC
			C-FTXE
			CF-TXE
			CF-PQQ
I-SRMC	Canadair CL-215-1A10	1076	C-GBXQ
	(Current status unknown)		C-GKEA
I-SRMD	Canadair CL-215-1A10	1097	C-GOFN
I-SSEP	North American T-6G-1-NH Texan	182-149	MM54101
	(Regd as "VR T6 SP") (Painted as "114462")		51-14462
I-SSKK	Piper PA-28RT-201T Turbo Arrow IV	28R-7931304	N8090Q
I-STAD	Vulcanair P.68 Observer 2	407-13/OB2	
I-STAF	Cessna 182N Skylane	18260209	N92453
I-STAS	Beech S35 Bonanza	D-7617	
I-STEN	Piper PA-28RT-201T Turbo Arrow IV	28R-8131120	N8380Z
I-STET	Piper PA-28R-200 Cherokee Arrow II	28R-7335016	N15099
I-STIL	T.9 Stiletto	01	
I-STRF	Asso Aeri Asso IV Whisky	39	
I-SUCK	Bell 47G-2	2149	MM80809
			57-6220
I-SUDE	SOCATA MS.880B Rallye Club	1855	
I-SUDH	SOCATA MS.892A Rallye Commodore 180	11868	
I-SUDM	SOCATA MS.893A Rallye Commodore 180	11973	
I-SUDN	SOCATA MS.892A Rallye Commodore 150	12038	
I-SUDP	SOCATA MS.894A Minerva 220	12001	
I-SUDQ	SOCATA MS.880B Rallye Club	2084	(D-EMJC)
I-SUDU	SOCATA MS.887 Rallye 125	2159	F-OCTH
I-SUDV	SOCATA MS.880B Rallye Club	2152	
I-SUDX	SOCATA MS.880B Rallye Club	2153	
I-SUDY	SOCATA MS.880B Rallye Club	2156	
I-SUED	Cessna 340A	340A1247	OE-FPN
			N444WF
			(N87453)
I-SUGA	Robinson R-22B2 Beta	3506	N75256
I-SUSY	S.A.I. F.7 Rondone II	02	
I-SVFA	Cessna 172RG Cutlass RG	172RG1062	N9867B
I-SVFB	Cessna 172RG Cutlass RG	172RG0968	N9687B
I-SVFC	Cessna 172M	17265378	N5220H
I-SVFD	Cessna 172L	17259615	N7915G
I-SVFE	Cessna 172RG Cutlass RG	172RG0903	N9590B
I-SVFF	Cessna 172M	17266963	N1268U
I-SVFG	Cessna 152	15283749	N5108B
I-SVFH	Cessna 152	15283939	N6484B
I-SVFI	Cessna 152	15282437	N69018
I-SVFL	Cessna 152	15282636	N89112
I-SWSA	Sud Avn SA.318C Alouette Astazou	2143	F-GEFF
			N6184
I-SYAW	SIAI-Marchetti S.205-20/R	4-253	
I-SYNT	Piper PA-34-200T Seneca II	34-7970258	N29472
I-SYST	Bredanardi NH-300C	021	
I-TAKA	Cessna 560XLS Citation XLS	560-5537	N5152X
I-TALE	Sud Avn SA.318C Alouette Astazou	2025	
I-TALL	Beech 58P Baron	TJ-93	HB-GGK
			I-TINT
			HB-GGK
I-TATU	Piper PA-22-108 Colt	22-9295	N5567Z
I-TEAK	Cessna 182R Skylane	18268246	N4585E
I-TEBO	Piper PA-22-150 Caribbean	22-7336	N10F
			N3423Z
I-TECC	Tecnam P.92JS Echo	unkn	
I-TECE	Tecnam P.92J Echo	unkn	
I-TECH	Eurocopter EC.120BColibri	1235	
I-TECK	Tecnam P.92J Echo	002	
I-TECM	Piper PA-34-220T Seneca III	34-8133189	N8424K
I-TECN	Tecnam P.92J Echo	001	
I-TECO	Piper PA-32R-301 Saratoga SP	32R-8113038	N31HB
			N8331R
I-TECS	Tecnam P.92 Echo 2000RG	001	
I-TEFA	Aérospatiale AS.350B Ecureuil	3697	
I-TEJF	Tecnam P.2002-JF	001	
I-TEJG	Tecnam P.92JS Echo	026	
I-TEJR	Tecnam P.2002JR Sierra	unkn	
I-TEJS	Tecnam P.92JS Echo (Damaged 2.10.04)	014	
I-TERB	BAe.146-200	E-2012	EI-DBY
			G-DEFK
			G-DEBK
			C-FHAV
			N601AW
I-TERK	BAe.146-200	E-2066	G-CCJP
			D-ALOA
			N536BA
			C-FHNX
			N356BA
			XA-RTI
			N405XV
			C-FHNX
			N405XV
			G-5-066
			N405XV
I-TERV	BAe.146-200	E-2014	EI-DBZ
			G-DEFL
			G-DEBL
			C-FHAX
			N602AW
I-TEST	Aérospatiale AS.355F1 Ecureuil 2	5119	N5791Z
I-TFSA	Piper PA-28RT-201 Arrow IV	28R-7918114	D-EMPW
			N2164Z
I-TGZA	AS-10 Microlight	C006	
I-THRS	Piper PA-28-180 Cherokee D	28-5399	N2374R
I-TIBI	Cessna T210N Turbo Centurion II	21063432	D-EIME(2)
			N5429A
I-TILE	Piper PA-28R-200 Cherokee Arrow	28R-7635395	N4067F
I-TILI	Strojnik/Pitts S-2A Special	012B	I-RATO
	(originally c/n 012, rebuilt after accident)		
I-TINI	Aviamilano F.8L Falco	118	
I-TINX	Agusta-Bell 206B Jet Ranger II	8520	HB-XFS
I-TITT	Piper PA-34-200 Seneca	34-7250351	N15048
I-TITY	Robinson R-22B2 Beta	2857	
I-TLBC	Agusta A.109A-II	7261	
I-TLCM	Dassault Falcon 900	81	N81GN
			7T-WPA
			F-WWFL
I-TLRN	Partenavia AP.68TP-600 Viator	9005	I-RAIL
I-TNAA	Aérospatiale AS.350B Ecureuil	3752	
I-TNBB	Aérospatiale AS.365N3 Dauphin 2	6609	
I-TNLD	Aérospatiale AS.350B3 Ecureuil	3383	
I-TOAD	Cessna T207A Turbo Stationair 8	20700642	G-NJAP
			(N75768)
I-TOBI	Jodel D.18B	347	
I-TOBY	Tecnam P.2002-JF	unkn	
I-TOGI	Schweizer 269C	S-1552	N69A
I-TOIO	Cessna 501 Citation I/SP	501-0252	N825HL
			N2628Z
I-TOLI	Schweizer 269C	S-1391	
I-TOLL	Mooney M.20J Model 201	24-1518	N5784R
I-TOLO	Aérospatiale AS.350B3 Ecureuil	3398	
I-TOLU	Agusta A.109A-II	7424	
I-TOMJ	Piper PA-38-112 Tomahawk	38-78A0677	N9712N
I-TOMK	Schweizer 269C	S-1562	N69A
I-TOND	Piper PA-28-161 Cadet	2841273	N91956
I-TONT	Mudry CAP.10B	190	
I-TOOT	Murphy Rebel	001	
I-TOPA	Piper PA-28-181 Archer II	28-8390027	N8328H
I-TOPB	Beech 400 Beechjet	RK-133	N133BP
			VP-BMR
			N1133T
I-TOPD	Beech 400A Beechjet	RK-163	N163BJ
			XA-JET
			N2363A
I-TOPI	Partenavia P.66B Oscar 100	38	
I-TOPZ	Vulcanair P.68C	429	
I-TORD	Cessna 152	15279668	N757DY
I-TORK	Schweizer 269C	S-1823	

I-TOSY	Cessna 172M	17262349	PH-JJG N12894
I-TOTA	CEA Jodel DR.1050 Ambassadeur	322	
I-TOTE	Piper PA-24-250 Comanche	24-1853	HB-OTE N6726P
I-TREE	Cessna 172N	17272944	N1069F
I-TREG	SOCATA MS.894A Minerva 220	12092	
I-TREH	SOCATA MS.894A Minerva 220	12093	
I-TREI	III Sky Arrow 650TC	C001	
I-TREM	III Sky Arrow 650TC	C002	
I-TREO	III Sky Arrow 650TC	C009	
I-TREP	Piper PA-42-720 Cheyenne IIIA	42-5501045	
I-TREQ	Piper PA-42-720 Cheyenne IIIA	42-5501046	
I-TRER	Piper PA-42-720 Cheyenne IIIA	42-5501047	
I-TRET	III Sky Arrow 650TC	C010	
I-TREU	III Sky Arrow 650TC	C013	
I-TREX	III Sky Arrow 650TC	C005	
I-TREY	III Sky Arrow 650TC	C012	
I-TREZ	III Sky Arrow 650TCN	CN007	
I-TRIB	Bell 47G3B1	2926	N1130W
I-TRIP	Aviamilano F.8L Falco	102	
I-TRUE	Partenavia P.64B Oscar 200	04	
I-TSNP	Robinson R-22 Beta	1411	N4009F
I-TTAM	Robinson R-44 Astro	0547	
I-TTCC	Robinson R-22 Mariner	0803M	
I-TTEB	Piper PA-28R-201T Turbo Arrow III	28R-7803071	N9854K
I-TVNW	Robinson R-44 Raven II	10016	
I-TWIN	Partenavia P.68	01	
I-UBFC	Agusta A.109E Power	11031	
I-UDDY	Reims/Cessna F172M	F17201514	F-GAQN
I-UDLB	SOCATA Rallye 110ST Galopin	3318	
I-UGON	Van's RV-6	60258	
I-ULJA	Dassault Falcon 20F	380	N3848U N289MM (N288MM) N922ML N9654N N1BX N8BX N136F F-WMKI
I-UMPL	SOCATA Rallye 110ST Galopin	3272	
I-UNIC	Cessna T206H Turbo Stationair	T20608279	N3523Z
I-UUNY	Cessna 500 Citation I	500-0358	SE-DEP N82MJ N36870 EP-PAQ N36870
I-VAAS	Piper PA-28-181 Archer II	2890187	D-ETCK N9179P
I-VAGO	Pereira Osprey Amphibian	unkn	
I-VALO	Piper PA-18A-150 Super Cub	18-4263	N2487P
I-VALP	Piper PA-18A-150 Super Cub	18-4264	N2488P
I-VALY	Reims/Cessna F172N	F17201769	D-EICL PH-AXR
I-VAMA	SOCATA Rallye 150ST	3102	
I-VANO	Mitchell-Wing B-10	unkn	
I-VANS	Van's RV-6	60217	
I-VANZ	Cessna 182P Skylane	18264562	OY-PEC N8204M
I-VAVF	Vulcanair VF.600W Mission	01	
I-VBIG	Van's RV-4	1985	
I-VBIT	Aérospatiale AS.350B Ecureuil	1553	
I-VBMR	Stewart S-51 Mustang replica	unkn	
I-VDAC	Piper PA-28RT-201 Arrow IV	28R-7918059	D-EBLH(3) N818PD N9610N
I-VEAR	Beech A36 Bonanza	E-3505	N566CB N566C
I-VEBA	Piper PA-30 Twin Comanche	30-773	N7797Y
I-VEIC	Piper PA-34-200T Seneca II	34-7770011	N5364F
I-VENT	Piper PA-28-140 Cherokee	28-24576	N7239J
I-VEPP	Reims/Cessna F172H (W/o 30.3.03)	F17200696	
I-VFOU	Agusta-Bell 412EP	25917	
I-VFOV	Agusta-Bell 412EP	25920	
I-VFOW	Agusta-Bell 412EP	25922	
I-VFOZ	Agusta-Bell 412EP	25927	
I-VGON	Van's RV-6	unkn	
I-VIBA	Piper PA-22-160 Tri-Pacer	22-6544	N9632D
I-VICC	Partenavia P.68B	16	
I-VICK	Cessna 172M	17264307	N8951V
I-VICP	Piper PA-34-200 Seneca	34-7450015	N56646
I-VICR	Partenavia P.68R	40	
I-VICT	Partenavia P.68	03	
I-VICY	Fairchild SA.227DC Metro 23	DC-849B	N451LA N3024V
I-VIER	Aérospatiale AS.350B Ecureuil	3546	F-WQDT
I-VIGI	Mitsubishi MU.300 Diamond	A.013SA	N81HH
I-VIGN	Piper PA-28RT-201 Arrow IV	28R-7918107	OY-CEI TF-TMG N2114Z
I-VIMQ	Boeing 767-3Q8ER	27993	I-PIMQ I-AIMQ EI-CMQ
I-VIMU	Aérospatiale AS.355F2 Ecureuil 2	5443	
I-VINC	Aviamilano F.8L Falco	106	
I-VINI	SOCATA MS.892A Rallye Commodore 150	11876	
I-VIOL	Aérospatiale SA.315B Lama	2501	
I-VIOU	Sud Avn SA.316B Alouette III	2179	
I-VIPK	Pajno V1	V-1	
I-VISI	Beech 35-B33 Debonair	CD-552	HB-EIW
I-VITB	Piper PA-18 Super Cub 95	18-2011	I-EIPI MM52-2411 52-2411
I-VITH	Beech 400A Beechjet	RK-309	N3239A
I-VIZZ	Zlin Z.526F Trenér Master	1162	
I-VLEF	Airbus A330-202	339	F-WQQO N339LF C-GGWD F-WWYZ
I-VLLE	Sud Avn SA.319B Alouette III	1999	HB-XUM FAP-636
I-VMAB	Rutan VariEze	unkn	
I-VOGH	Cessna 182R Skylane	18267749	N5480N
I-VOLG	Piper PA-32R-300 Cherokee Lance	32R-7680295	N75347
I-VORA	Piper PA-18-150 Super Cub	18-7909137	N9753N
I-VRCW	Cessna P210N Pressurized Centurion II	P21000790	N6504W
I-VREM	Aérospatiale AS.355F Ecureuil 2	5297	F-GEHL
I-VRGT	Agusta A.109EPower	11003	N1NQ
I-VRST	SIAI-Marchetti S.205-20/R	4-138	
I-VRVR	Aérospatiale AS.355F Ecureuil 2	5180	
I-VSEM	Robinson R-22 Beta	2563	
I-VULE	Vulcanair AP.68TP-300 Spartacus	020	
I-VULG	Vulcanair SF.600A Canguro	010	I-VULA
I-VVEE	Beech 58P Baron	TJ-320	N3707N
I-ZACM	Piper PA-28RT-201T Turbo Arrow IV	28R-8631005	N9085Z
I-ZANC	Robinson R-22 Beta	2561	
I-ZARO	Christen A-1 Husky	1042	
I-ZARY	Maule MXT-7-180 Star Rocket	14011C	N9225S
I-ZEND	Zlin Z.526F Trenér Master	1311	
I-ZEUS	Partenavia P.66B Oscar 100	44	
I-ZIAC	Eurocopter EC.120B Colibri	1380	F-WQUJ F-WQDH
I-ZKRC	Agusta-Bell 206B Jet Ranger III	8731	
I-ZOLI	Rutan Long-Ez	unkn	
I-ZUBO	Partenavia P.64B Oscar B-1155	03	
I-ZUMA	Piper PA-18 Super Cub 95	18-1993	I-EILU MM52-2393 52-2393
I-ZVPC	Zambelli PZ.150 (Modified PA-18 ?)	001	
I-ZYTT	Piper PA-34-220T Seneca V	3449300	N3010F
I-ZZIO	Robin DR.400/180R Remorqueur	990	OE-DUO D-EOKB

GLIDERS AND MOTOR-GLIDERS

I-ACOS	Bölkow Phoebus B-1	769	
I-ACRN	Scheibe Bergfalke IV	5835	
I-ACRO	Schleicher ASK 13	13195	
I-ACRQ	LET L-13 Blanik	175116	
I-ADRT	Schempp-Hirth Nimbus 2B	153	
I-AECX	Velino (Homebuilt)	101	
I-AESV	AS 10 Microlight motorglider	001	
I-AFFE	Grob G.102 Astir Club IIIB	5553CB	
I-AIRZ	Bölkow Phoebus A-1	755	D-1349
I-AJTB	Grob G.109B	6384	(F-CAQQ)
I-ALIA	Schleicher ASW 19B	19014	
I-ALOE	Glasflügel H205 Club Libelle	29	
I-ALOR	Grob G.103 Twin Astir II	3533	
I-ALZA	Schleicher ASK 21	21715	
I-ANEA	Glaser-Dirks DG-300 Elan	3E-372	
I-ANKA	Schempp-Hirth Nimbus 2	9	D-0884
I-ANTO	Schempp-Hirth Standard Cirrus (W/o 6.1.01)	510	
I-APBK	Scheibe SF-25C Falke 2000	44435	(D-KIAB(1))
I-ASAV	Glaser-Dirks DG-400	4-235	(D-KSAV) I-ASAV (D-KIDG)
I-ASEN	Glasflügel H.301 Libelle	87	
I-ASET	Schempp-Hirth Cirrus	7	
I-ASPE	Hoffmann H-36 Dimona	36241	
I-ASVV	Scheibe Zugvogel IIIA	1035	OE-0416
I-AUAA	Aeronautica Umbra AU-SF-25B Falke	001	
I-AUAD	Aeronautica Umbra AU-SF-25B Falke	006	
I-AVAD	Grob G.109B	6331	
I-AVAG	Scheibe Bergfalke III	5598	D-1289
I-AVAH	Glaser-Dirks DG-300 Elan (W/o 22.4.02)	3E-365	
I-AVAK	Glaser-Dirks DG-300 Elan	3E-306	
I-AVAR	Glaser-Dirks DG-300 Elan	3E-251	
I-AVAS	Glaser-Dirks DG-300 Elan	3E-408	
I-AVAT	Glaser-Dirks DG-300 Elan	3E-366	
I-AVCZ	Glasflügel H201B Standard Libelle	141	
I-AVVA	Hoffmann H-36 Dimona	36268	
I-AVVB	Grob G.103 Twin Astir	3166	D-7796
I-AYAX	Glaser-Dirks DG-100G Elan	E61-G37	
I-BAUU	Schleicher K 8B	8777	
I-BEPO	Schempp-Hirth Standard Cirrus	529	
I-BITO	Glasflügel H401 Kestrel	8	
I-BLEK	Alpavia/ Fournier RF-3	02	F-BLEK
I-BLOB	Glaser-Dirks DG-300 Elan	3E-430	
I-BOOK	Glaser-Dirks DG-300 Elan	3E-411	
I-BOOM	Glaser-Dirks DG-300 Elan	3E-432	

I-BOYS	Schempp-Hirth Standard Cirrus	585	
I-BOZZ	Schempp-Hirth Discus b	216	
I-BPLQ	Sportavia/ Fournier RF-4D	4136	F-BPLQ
I-BRAE	Schempp-Hirth Janus B	147	
I-BRAN	Schleicher Ka 6E	4378	
I-BREM	Grob G.109B	6442	
I-BROC	Glasflügel H.301B Libelle	96	
I-BRRR	AS 10 Microlight motorglider	0009	
I-BRUT	Glaser-Dirks DG-300 Elan	3E-409	
I-BSTR	Grob G.102 Astir III	5599S	
I-BZAF	Scheibe SF-25C Falke	4470	D-KOBL
I-BZAR	Glaser-Dirks DG-300 Elan	3E-422	
I-BZUM	Grob G.102 Astir CS 77	1714	
I-CAIO	Schleicher ASK 14	14006	D-KOIB
I-CALM	Glasflügel H206 Hornet	31	
I-CAOS	Glasflügel H401 Kestrel	40	
I-CCCP	Caproni Vizzola A.21S Calif	229	
I-CCLO	Sportavia/ Scheibe SF-25C Falke	4212	D-KAWA
I-CECJ	Glaser-Dirks DG-300 Elan	3E-384	
I-CEMM	Glaser-Dirks DG-200	2-61	D-7776
I-CENN	Schleicher ASK 13 (Stored 7.04)	13117	
I-CENO	Schleicher Ka 6E	4260	
I-CEUO	Centrair ASW-20F	20179	F-CEUO
I-CIAU	Schempp-Hirth SHK-1	18	
I-CILY	Schleicher ASW 15B	15218	
I-CINK	Glaser-Dirks DG-300 Elan	3E-235	
I-CIOK	Schleicher ASW 20	20092	
I-CIOT	Schleicher Ka 6E	4267	
I-CIUK	SZD-30 Pirat (Damaged 9.7.04)	B-566	
I-CJSA	LET L-13 Blanik	026110	
I-CLAB	Glasflügel H205 Club Libelle	41	
I-CLUB	Scheibe SF-27A	6053	
I-CNVV	Aeromere M-100S	000	
I-CRBB	Glasflügel H201B Standard Libelle	475	
I-CROZ	Scheibe Mü.13E Bergfalke	01	
I-CRVV	LET L-13 Blanik	025420	
I-CSWP	Glasflügel H401 Kestrel	1	
I-CYAO	Schempp-Hirth Cirrus	V-2	D-8437 D-9406
I-DAMJ	Schleicher ASW 15B	15430	
I-DAVY	Grob G.109B	6417	
I-DEKA	Grob G.109	6127	D-KCOT (I- . . . .)
I-DENT	Glasflügel H401 Kestrel	22	
I-DEUX	Glasflügel H206 Hornet	57	D-7260
I-DGAM	Glaser-Dirks DG-200	2-85	
I-DHEM	AS 10 Microlight motorglider	C011	
I-DIAW	Rolladen-Schneider LS3A	3410	D-4297
I-DIGY	Glaser-Dirks DG-300 Elan	3E-39	
I-DISK-LB	Schempp-Hirth Discus A	03	D-6095
I-DOSE	LET L-13 Blanik	175102	
I-DUEP	Glaser-Dirks DG-300 Elan	3E-410	
I-DUKI	Schleicher ASK 13	13148	
I-DUNO	Rolladen-Schneider LS3-17	3457	D-6684
I-DURI	Avionautica Rio CVV.8	012	
I-DURT	Schleicher ASW 24E	24848	(D-KAXS)
I-EDEC	Schleicher Ka 6CR Rhönsegler	568	
I-EDEL	Schleicher K-7	405	
I-ELAN	Glaser-Dirks DG-300 Elan	3E-75	
I-ELJO	Schleicher ASW 24	24149	
I-ENCA	Schleicher ASK 13	13280	
I-ERSI	Schempp-Hirth Standard Cirrus B	595	
I-ERST	SZD-30 Pirat	B-424	
I-EUGI	Schempp-Hirth Ventus cT	110/377	
I-EVAM	Scheibe Bergfalke IIt55 (Stored 7.04)	391	
I-FACG	Rolladen-Schneider LS4	4363	
I-FALL	Glaser-Dirks DG-300 Elan	3E-274	
I-FEVV	Schleicher ASK 13	13158	
I-FEWW	Sportavia/ Fournier RF-4D	4019	F-BORF
I-FGTM	Rolladen-Schneider LS4	4362	
I-FIUR	Glasflügel H201B Standard Libelle	72	
I-FLAV	Glasflügel H206 Hornet	4	
I-FLUG	Schleicher ASW 19B	19052	
I-FOFI-64	Schempp-Hirth Standard Cirrus	417	
I-FOLE	Meteor MS.30L Passero	50.005	
I-FOLL	Meteor MS.30L Passero	50.009	
I-FOXY	Glaser-Dirks DG-300 Elan	3E-382	
I-FRYY	Rolladen-Schneider LS4	4306	HB-1712
I-GEDE	Sportavia-Pü tzer RF-5B Sperber	51035	(D-KEAQ)
I-GELO	Grob G.109B	6273	
I-GGBP	Glaser-Dirks DG-300 Elan	3E-379	
I-GIDI	LET L-13 Blanik	171612	D-9811 OK-1811
I-GIRI	Schleicher ASK 13	13394	
I-GITO	Schleicher ASK 21	21486	
I-GLAD	Schleicher ASW 20C	20716	D-7875
I-GLOO	Schleicher ASW 15B	15242	
I-GNEO	Schempp-Hirth Standard Cirrus	473	
I-GOAL	Schleicher Ka 6E	4376	
I-GOST	Schleicher ASW 24	24146	
I-GOUP	Glasflügel H201B Standard Libelle	365	
I-GROG	Schempp-Hirth Discus A	111	
I-GRRR	Glaser-Dirks DG-300 Elan	3E-428	
I-GULP	LET L-13 Blanik	175007	
I-HEXE	Bölkow Phoebus C	942	
I-HOBO	Glaser-Dirks DG-200	2-54	
I-HOWA	Grob G.102 Astir CS	1098	

I-HVAR	EC.39D Uribel D	030	
I-IBTS	Glaser-Dirks DG-200	2-53	
I-IDEA	Schempp-Hirth Standard Cirrus	91	
I-IDOT	Schleicher Ka 6E	4353	
I-IILY	Schempp-Hirth Ventus b/16.6	122	D-3153
I-ILMA	Hoffmann H-36 Dimona	36274	
I-ILPO	Schleicher ASK 21	21239	
I-IMAA	Scheibe SF-25C Falke	44253	D-KDBI
I-IMAB	Scheibe SF-25C Falke (W/o 17.10.04)	44254	D-KDBL
I-IMAC	Scheibe SF-25C Falke	44256	D-KDBM
I-IMAF	Scheibe SF-25C Falke	44260	D-KDBP
I-IMAH	Scheibe SF-25C Falke	44306	(D-KOOE)
I-IMRH	Rolladen-Schneider LS6A	6106	
I-INES	Glasflügel H205 Club Libelle	4	
I-IOOO-VS	Rolladen-Schneider LS6A	6023	D-6334
I-IPER	Glaser-Dirks DG-300 Elan	3E-305	
I-IVAA	Schleicher ASK 13	13562	
I-IVAB	Grob G.103 Twin Astir	3145	
I-IVAC	Grob G.103 Twin Astir	3146	
I-IVAD	Grob G.103 Twin Astir	3164	
I-IVAE	Grob G.103 Twin Astir	3165	
I-IVAF	Grob G.103 Twin Astir	3180	
I-IVAG	Grob G.103 Twin Astir	3175	
I-IVAH	Grob G.103 Twin Astir	3184	
I-IVAI	Grob G.103 Twin Astir	3185	
I-IVAJ	Grob G.103 Twin Astir	3259	
I-IVAK	Grob G.103 Twin Astir	3258	
I-IVAM	Glasflügel H201 Standard Libelle	19	
I-IVAR	Grob G.103 Twin Astir	3215	
I-IVAT	Grob G.103 Twin Astir (Damaged 25.6.04)	3204	
I-IVAU	Grob G.103 Twin Astir	3276	
I-IVAV	Grob G.103 Twin Astir	3277	
I-IVAW	Grob G.103 Twin Astir	3278	
I-IVBA	Grob G.102 Astir CS 77	1734	
I-IVBC	Grob G.102 Astir CS 77	1755	
I-IVBE	Grob G.102 Astir CS 77	1765	
I-IVBF	Grob G.102 Astir CS 77	1766	
I-IVBI	Grob G.102 Standard Astir II	5026S	
I-IVBJ	Grob G.102 Standard Astir II	5027S	
I-IVBK	Grob G.102 Standard Astir II	5028S	
I-IVBL	Grob G.102 Standard Astir II	5029S	
I-IVBN	Grob G.102 Standard Astir II	5048S	
I-IVBP	Grob G.102 Standard Astir II	5524S	
I-IVBQ	Grob G.102 Standard Astir II	5525S	
I-IVCB	Caproni Vizzola A.21S Calif	251	
I-IVDB	Schempp-Hirth Janus	77	
I-IVDC	Schempp-Hirth Janus B	130	
I-IVDE	Schempp-Hirth Janus B	134	
I-IVDF	Schempp-Hirth Janus B	140	
I-IVEA	Centrair ASW-20F	20193	F-CEUV
I-IVEC-S2	Centrair ASW-20F	20195	F-CEUY
I-IVED	Centrair ASW-20F	20196	F-CEUZ
I-IVFA-C5	Rolladen-Schneider LS4	4276	
I-IVFB-C6	Rolladen-Schneider LS4	4277	
I-IVFC	Rolladen-Schneider LS4	4278	
I-IVPA-P1	Glaser-Dirks DG-300 Club Elan	3E-346/C35	
I-IVPB-P2	Glaser-Dirks DG-300 Club Elan	3E-347/C36	
I-IVPC	Glaser-Dirks DG-300 Club Elan	3E-348/C37	
I-IVPE-P5	Glaser-Dirks DG-300 Club Elan	3E-363/C48	
I-IVPF-PI	Glaser-Dirks DG-300 Club Elan	3E-375/C51	
I-IVPG-P7	Glaser-Dirks DG-300 Elan	3E-386	
I-IVPH-Z	Glaser-Dirks DG-300 Elan	3E-387	
I-IVPI	Glaser-Dirks DG-300 Elan	3E-390	
I-IVPK	Glaser-Dirks DG-300 Club Elan	3E-440/C75	
I-IVPL	Glaser-Dirks DG-300 Elan	3E-488	
I-IVSA	DG Flugzeugbau DG-500 Elan Orion	5E-210X52	
I-IVSB	DG Flugzeugbau DG-500 Elan Orion	5E-212X54	
I-IVVA	Grob G.103 Twin Astir II	3698	
I-IVVB	Grob G.103 Twin Astir II	3699	
I-IVVC	Grob G.103 Twin Astir II	3700	
I-IVVE	Grob G.103 Twin Astir II	3758	
I-IVVF	Grob G.103 Twin Astir II	3836	
I-IVVI	Grob G.103 Twin III Acro	34160	
I-IVVJ	Grob G.103 Twin III Acro	34161	
I-IVVK	Grob G.103 Twin III Acro	34162	
I-IVVL	Grob G.103 Twin III Acro	34163	
I-IVVM	Grob G.103 Twin III Acro	34164	
I-IVVN	Grob G.103 Twin III Acro	34165	
I-IVVO	Grob G.103 Twin III Acro (W/o 3.5.92)	34166	
I-IVVP	Grob G.103 Twin III Acro	34167	
I-IVVQ	Grob G.103 Twin III Acro	34168	
I-IVVR	Grob G.103 Twin III Acro	34169	
I-IVVS	Grob G.103 Twin III Acro	34181	
I-IVVT	Grob G.103 Twin III Acro (Damaged 5.9.04)	34182	
I-IVVV	Grob G.103 Twin III Acro	34188	
I-IVVW	Grob G.103 Twin III Acro (Damaged 26.10.02)	34189	
I-IVVY	Grob G.103 Twin III Acro	34191	
I-IVVZ	Grob G.103 Twin III Acro (W/o 25.11.01)	34192	
I-IVWA	Schleicher ASK 21	21474	
I-IVWC	Schleicher ASK 21	21476	
I-IVWE	Schleicher ASK 21	21478	
I-IVWF	Schleicher ASK 21	21479	
I-IVWH	Schleicher ASK 21	21481	
I-IVWI	Schleicher ASK 21	21482	
I-IVWJ	Schleicher ASK 21	21483	
I-IVWK	Schleicher ASK 21	21484	
I-IVWL	Schleicher ASK 21	21685	

I-IVWM	Schleicher ASK 21	21687	
I-IVWN	Schleicher ASK 21	21690	
I-IVWO	Schleicher ASK 21	21691	
I-IVWP	Schleicher ASK 21	21692	
I-IVWQ	Schleicher ASK 21	21693	
I-IVWR	Schleicher ASK 21	21695	
I-IVWS	Schleicher ASK 21	21697	
I-JANO	Schempp-Hirth Janus	11	D-2476
I-JOLI	Schleicher ASW 15B	15316	
I-JOSE	Schleicher ASW 20	20448	
I-JOUX	Glasflügel H201B Standard Libelle	476	
I-JUCK	Glaser-Dirks DG-300 Elan	3E-162	
I-JULO	AM-11 Motorglider	unkn	
I-JURI	Glasflügel H201 Standard Libelle	73	
I-KAIB	Scheibe SF-25B Falke	46234	D-KAIB
I-KAND	Scheibe SF-25C Falke	44425	
I-KAOS	Rolladen Schneider LS1-F	322	
I-KARO	Glasflügel H201B Standard Libelle	473	
I-KAZZ	Rolladen-Schneider LS3A	3437	D-3540
I-KBDG	Glaser-Dirks DG-400	4-165	D-KBDG
I-KCEO	Glaser-Dirks DG-400	4-193	D-KCEO
I-KCIP	Grob G.109	6016	D-KCIP(2)
I-KDFD	Scheibe SF-25C Falke 1700 (Damaged 5.9.04)	44209	D-KDFD(2)
I-KDHA	Valentin Taifun 17E	1059	D-KDHA
I-KEEN-52	Glaser-Dirks DG-300 Elan	3E-340	
I-KEOG	Grob G.109B	6307	D-KEOG
I-KFAP	Glaser-Dirks DG-400 (Reserved as D-KUKI 11.99)	4-156	D-KFAP
I-KHHB	Valentin Taifun 17E	1067	D-KHHB
I-KICO	Glasflügel H401 Kestrel	12	
I-KIKA	Glasflügel H201B Standard Libelle	35	
I-KILC	Grob G.109	6108	D-KILC
I-KIPR	Valentin Taifun 17E	1083	D-KIPR
I-KIRA	Glasflügel H201B Standard Libelle	280	
I-KLEO	Hoffmann HK-36R Super Dimona	36352	
I-KMAP	Schempp-Hirth Ventus cM	38/474	D-KMAP
I-KOKI	Glasflügel H401 Kestrel	9	
I-KOLL	Schleicher ASW 20L	20551	
I-KRYS	Glaser-Dirks DG-300 Elan	3E-255	
I-LADJ	Aeronautica Umbria AU-SF-25B Falke (Amateur-built version, not related to I-AUAA c/n 001)	001	
I-LAMP	Schleicher ASW 20	20249	
I-LARY	Schempp-Hirth SHK-1	59	
I-LAVU	Schleicher ASW 15	15056	D-0542
I-LBIS	Scheibe Bergfalke IV	5826	
I-LBOB	Schleicher ASW 20	20375	
I-LBOS	Bölkow Phoebus B-1	805	D-1458
I-LEFA	EC.39C Uribel C	024	
I-LERE	Schleicher ASW 15B	15267	
I-LFOX	Glaser-Dirks DG-200	2-60	
I-LGEP	Schempp-Hirth Discus b	408	
I-LGIO-Y	Rolladen-Schneider LS6A	6127	D-0665
I-LGVA	Glasflügel H205 Club Libelle	70	
I-LIPA	Schempp-Hirth Nimbus 2B	169	D-2206
I-LIVE	Schleicher ASW 19B	19026	
I-LJET	Schempp-Hirth SHK-1	56	
I-LMAT	Glasflügel H206 Hornet	48	
I-LMIG	Schempp-Hirth Discus b	249	
I-LOIS	Schempp-Hirth Ventus A	73	D-0150
I-LOOP	Schempp-Hirth Standard Cirrus	478	
I-LORA	Glaser-Dirks DG-200	2-25	D-6782
I-LORJ	Rolladen-Schneider LS3A	3443	D-6923
I-LRIP	Schempp-Hirth Discus b	323	
I-LUCB	Sportavia-Fournier RF-4D	4092	D-KALD
I-LUKA	Glaser-Dirks DG-200	2-92	
I-LULU	Glasflügel H201B Standard Libelle	554	
I-LUSO	Bölkow Phoebus C	928	
I-LVBG	Grob G.102 Astir CS 77	1777	I-IVBG
I-LVIG	Schleicher ASK 21 (Damaged 12.6.04)	21430	
I-LVIP	Glaser-Dirks DG-300 Elan	3E-230	
I-LVIT	Rolladen-Schneider LS6A	6076	D-3398
I-LYNO	Glaser-Dirks DG-100G Elan	E222-G188	
I-MACH	Schempp-Hirth Standard Cirrus	331	D-3024
I-MAEN	LET L-13 Blanik	173455	
I-MAGO	Bölkow Phoebus A-1	758	
I-MAIA	Rolladen-Schneider LS6A	6181	
I-MEIO	LET L-13 Blanik	026250	
I-MERY	Glaser-Dirks DG-300 Elan	3E-420	
I-MEZZ	Scheibe Bergfalke IV	5836	
I-MIGG	Glaser-Dirks DG-300 Elan	3E-412	
I-MIMO	Rolladen-Schneider LS3A	3435	D-2866
I-MISU	Aviamilano A-2	601	
I-MONJ	AS 10 Microlight motorglider	unkn	
I-MOSK	Schleicher ASW 20	20422	
I-MUGE	Grob G.103 Twin Astir	3187	D-5953
I-MVAM	Scheibe SF-25A Motorfalke	4524	D-KAJY
I-NERI	AS 10 Microlight motorglider	unkn	
I-NEVI-47	Schempp-Hirth Nimbus 2	109	D-7246
I-NEWD	Glasflügel H205 Club Libelle	56	
I-NIBO	Schleicher ASK 21	21327	
I-NIMB	Rolladen-Schneider LS3A	3431	D-4584
I-NMCV	Schempp-Hirth Standard Cirrus	461G	
I-NOIR	Schleicher ASW 15	15106	
I-NONI	Schempp-Hirth Janus C	106	D-4519
I-NOVL	LET L-13 Blanik	025421	
I-NYKE	Glaser-Dirks DG-300 Elan	3E-424	
I-NYKK	Schleicher Ka 6E	4338	D-0544

I-NYNO	Glaser-Dirks DG-100G Elan	E218-G184	
I-OASI	Glasflügel H401 Kestrel	10	
I-OCIO	Glasflügel H205 Club Libelle	55	
I-OGHY	Schempp-Hirth Standard Cirrus	553G	
I-OKAY	Schleicher ASW 20	20373	
I-OKEY	Schempp-Hirth Standard Cirrus	509	
I-OKYO	Schleicher ASW 15B	15198	
I-OOSO	Schleicher ASW 24	24136	
I-OPEL	Bölkow Phoebus C	818	
I-ORNI	Rolladen-Schneider LS3A	3459	D-3393
I-ORPO	Scheibe SF-25B Falke	4612	D-KODB
I-OSSO	Schleicher ASW 15B	15266	
I-PAIS	Schleicher ASK 21	21349	
I-PAIU	Scheibe SF-25B Falke	4682	D-KBAH
I-PAMI	Schempp-Hirth Ventus b	49	D-2925
I-PATR	Grob G.103 Twin Astir	3242	
I-PEAW	Glasflügel H201B Standard Libelle	553	
I-PECK	Schempp-Hirth Ventus c	538	
I-PHIL	Schempp-Hirth Standard Cirrus	541G	
I-PICK	Schleicher ASK 21	21405	
I-PICW	Eiri PIK-20E	20256	OH-563
I-PIKA	Hoffmann HK-36R Super Dimona	36320	
I-PIKE	Eiri PIK-20E-II	20295	OH-615
I-PINE	Glaser-Dirks DG-200	2-46	D-6661
I-PING	Scheibe Bergfalke IV	5837	
I-PINK	Schleicher ASW 19B	19178	
I-PLAN	Grob G.109	6156	D-KCEC
I-PLOC	Schleicher ASK 13	13120	
I-PLOK	Schleicher ASK 13	13213	
I-PLOQ	Schleicher ASK 13 (Dismantled)	13271	
I-PORK	Hoffman H-36 Dimona	3519	OE-9219 (D-KBIW)
I-PUCI	Glasflügel H201B Standard Libelle	316	
I-PUSC	Glasflügel H206 Hornet	32	
I-PZLO	SZD-50-3 Puchacz	B-2046	D-1107
I-RANI	EC.39C Uribel C	028	
I-RDPR	AS 10 Microlight motorglider	unkn	
I-RECM	Schleicher ASW 24	24137	
I-RFOS	Sportavia/ Fournier RF-5	5027	OH-385 OH-FKB
I-RGOT	Rolladen-Schneider LS4	4136	D-0531
I-RHEM	Aeromere M-100S	030	
I-RHEN	Schempp-Hirth Discus b	223	
I-RIZO	Eiri PIK-20D	20653	
I-ROAR	LET L-13 Blanik	175030	
I-ROKI	Glasflügel H206 Hornet	47	
I-ROPA	Schempp-Hirth Janus	13	
I-RORI	EC-39C Uribel C	021	
I-ROSL	Schleicher ASW 15B	15370	
I-RUMA	Schleicher ASW 20	20574	
I-RYZZ	Glaser-Dirks DG-300 Elan	3E-426	
I-SANO	Schleicher ASK 13	13118	
I-SCFL	Schleicher ASW 20	20316	
I-SCPV	Caproni Vizzola A-2	610	
I-SEGI	Hoffmann HK-36R Super Dimona	36301	OE-9350
I-SELL	Schleicher ASK 13	13264	
I-SELZ	Schleicher ASW 20L	20423	D-2604
I-SETA	Avionautica Rio M-IOOS	072	
I-SEXY	HBV Diamant	006	
I-SKYY	Schleicher ASW 24	24129	
I-SNOB	Schempp-Hirth Nimbus 2B	155	
I-SOLO	Glasflügel H201B Standard Libelle (W/o 7.8.76)	396	
I-SONG	Schleicher ASW 19B	19369	
I-SOUF	Schleicher ASW 24	24138	
I-STMA	Hoffmann H-36 Dimona	36117	HB-2072
I-SURC	LET L-13 Blanik	175003	
I-SYBI	Glaser-Dirks DG-300 Elan	3E-369	
I-TAFA	Grob G.103 Twin Astir	3023	
I-TASS	Rolladen-Schneider LS6	6038	D-3652
I-TEAM	Glaser-Dirks DG-200	2-33	D-7417
I-TILI	Strojnik S-2A	012B	
I-TILU	Sportavia-Pützer RF-5B Sperber	51047	D-KITZ
I-TORR	Sportavia-Fournier RF-5	5026	
I-TOTI	Slingsby T.51 Dart 17R	1511	
I-TREK	Schleicher ASW 24	24153	
I-TWJN	Grob G.103 Twin Astir II	3572	
I-TWYN	Grob G.103 Twin Astir	3058	D-4848
I-UKSI	Rolladen-Schneider LS4	4706	D-0527
I-URKA	Glasflügel H201B Standard Libelle	363	
I-USAF	Glaser-Dirks DG-300 Elan	3E-243	
I-VDAA	Schleicher ASK 21	21787	
I-VELU	Aeromere M-100S	015	
I-VIPK	Pajno V-1	V1	
I-VITA	Schempp-Hirth Cirrus	9	
I-VIUS	Glasflügel H303 Mosquito	83	
I-VIZQ	Caproni Vizzola A-21S Calif	219	
I-VLEN	Rolladen Schneider LS-1F	313	
I-VOLK	Sportavia-Fournier RF-4D	4045	
I-VOOL	LETL-13 Blanik	026841	D-3362
I-VORY	Glasflügel H201B Standard Libelle	588	
I-VVSS-55	Schleicher ASW 20L	20558	D-0882
I-ZAGO	Costr.Taliedo CAT 20	01DC	
I-ZAKK	AS 10 Microlight motorglider	C021	
I-ZAKO	Schleicher ASK 16	16018	D-KAAR
I-ZAVA	Glasflügel H205 Club Libelle	53	
I-ZBOW	Schleicher ASW 24	24128	D-6132

I-ZEDA	Schleicher ASK 21	21304	
I-ZITA	Glasflügel H206 Hornet	33	
I-ZUCK	Hoffman H-36 Dimona	36205	D-KFGT
I-ZWEI	Schempp-Hirth Janus	43	D-4816
I-ZWYK	Schempp-Hirth Discus b	332	
I-ZZIP	Eiri PIK-20D-78Ex	20586	(OH-594)

BALLOONS AND AIRSHIPS

I-AIMO(4)	Cameron O-77 HAFB (Formerly c/ns 912, 1472 and 2083)	4206	
I-AJMO	Cameron N-105 HAFB	1868	
I-ALBB	Thunder AX7-77 SI HAFB	1289	
I-APAI	Cameron V-77 HAFB	2423	
I-APIS	Cameron O-84 HAFB	2677	
I-AZIT	Cameron N-105 HAFB	4326	
I-BGAS	Ultramagic M-105 HAFB	105/101	
I-BGEJ	Cameron N-105 HAFB	2002	
I-BINN	Colt 105A HAFB (Replaces c/n 1739)	4689	
I-BOPA	Bonanno X-7 Homebuilt HAFB	009	
I-BZLA	Thunder AX7-77 HAFB	1634	
I-CCNE	Ultramagic M-130	130/16	
I-CHAR	Thunder AX7-77 HAFB	1343	
I-CHBC	Cameron O-120 HAFB	2340	
I-CING(2)	Cameron N-90 HAFB (Formerly c/n 1129)	1675	
I-DLOG	Cameron N-105 HAFB	2284	
I-DUCK(2)	Cameron O-77 HAFB	905	
I-FEED(2)	Cameron O-77 HAFB (Formerly c/n 1117)	3156	
I-FLEG	Cameron N-90 HAFB	2778	
I-FRIK(2)	Cameron O-84 HAFB (Formerly c/n 1509)	2935	
I-FRIM	Cameron O-105 HAFB	1266	
I-FROG(3)	Cameron V-77 HAFB (Formerly V-77 c/ns 848 and 1455)	2926	
I-FROK(2)	Cameron O-84 HAFB (Formerly c/n 2425)	4440	
I-FRQM	Cameron O-84 HAFB	1546	
I-GASI	Thunder AX7-77 HAFB	2116	
I-GIVJ	Cameron N-105 HAFB	3171	
I-GOOD	Aerophile 5500 Tethered Balloon	7	
I-GUFY	Cameron V-77 HAFB	2514	
I-HUSQ	Ultramagic S-90 HAFB	90/69	
I-IFIM	Cameron O-84 HAFB	2044	
I-KAMI (2)	Cameron O-84 HAFB (Formerly c/n 1507)	4205	
I-KBPC	Cameron V-77 HAFB	3312	
I-KIKE(2)	Cameron N-105 HAFB (Formerly c/n 1167)	2363	
I-KONG	Cameron O-105 HAFB	2578	
I-LAMB	Cameron O-105 HAFB	2685	
I-LBAA	Cameron O-105 HAFB	2080	
I-LBIG	Cameron N-90 HAFB	2443	
I-LBLU	Cameron O-105 HAFB	4529	
I-LBUS	Cameron A-210 HAFB	1789	
I-LDOC	Cameron O-120 HAFB	3586	
I-LEGS	Ultramagic S-90 HAFB	90/68	
I-LMAL	Cameron V-77 HAFB	2491	
I-LOSI	Cameron N-105 HAFB	2657	
I-MELS	Ultramagic M-105 HAFB	105/67	
I-MMAT	Chaize BY.14F16 HAFB	180	
I-MOVI	Cameron O-77 HAFB	2039	
I-NELL(2)	Cameron O-77 HAFB (Formerly c/n 906)	1287	
I-NIER	Colt 105A HAFB	1675	
I-NISE	Cameron N-105 HAFB	3594	
I-NORG	Gefa-Flug AS.105GD HA Airship	0021	G-BZUR D-OATY
I-NPUT	Cameron V-77 HAFB	2424	
I-OECM	Wörner NL-840/STU Gas Balloon	1068	D-OECM
I-OMFS(3)	Cameron V-77 HAFB (Formerly c/ns 1177 and 1906)	4207	
I-ORBI	Ultramagic M-130 HAFB	130/38	
I-PAAM	Bonnano X-8 Homebuilt HAFB	007	
I-PACA	Ultramagic M-105 HAFB	105/41	
I-PARK	Augsburg K-1260/3-RI Gas Balloon	10007	D-OUTE D-Auguste X
I-PERC	Ultramagic V-105 HAFB	105/33	
I-RIKY	Thunder AX7-77 HAFB	895	G-BNDU
I-ROLO	Ultramagic M-105 HAFB	105/55	
I-RORY	Cameron O-84 HAFB	1847	
I-SGMA	Cameron O-84 HAFB (Formerly c/n 2753)	4027	
I-SIFO	Ultramagic S-90 HAFB	90/30	
I-SOLL(3)	Colt 77A HAFB (Formerly c/ns 265 and 499)	810	
I-TETO	Cameron V-77 HAFB	4195	
I-VANI	Cameron N-105 HAFB	3460	
I-VESP(2)	Cameron V-31 HAFB (Formerly c/n 831)	3081	
I-VSGE	Cameron O-105 HAFB	2382	G-BSSD

The following balloons have been supplied to Italy but no marks are known:

I-	Cameron N-105 HAFB	3736	
I-	Colt Apple SS HAFB	756	G-BMKU
I-	Colt 56A HAFB	2198	
I-	Thunder AX7-77 SI HAFB	1222	
I-	Thunder AX7-77 SI HAFB	1341	
I-	Thunder AX7-77 SI HAFB	1533	

MICROLIGHTS

Most Ultralights and Microlights are now registered in a numerical series, if indeed they carry any registrations at all. The following are known so far and details of other sightings would be welcome. Clearly not all available registrations have been used or noted, therefore we list known regns of unidentified types in the hope that these may be identified in the future. Some corrections have been made to the earlier lists.

I-0001	Quicksilver MX-II Sprint	
I-0002	Polaris	
I-0003	Flexwing, type unknown	
I-0006	Polaris	
I-0012	Leonardino	
I-0020	Quicksilver GT-500	
I-0026	Golf 19	
I-0029	NIKE (Trike)	
I-0063	Quicksilver MX-II	1877
I-0082	Fisher FP-404 Classic	008
I-0083	Fisher FP-404 Classic	
I-0094	TEAM Mini-MAX Sport	
I-0097	Fokker D.VII replica	
I-0202	Blue Sky Dream (prototype glider)	
I-0214	Murphy Maverick (Wreck noted 9.99)	
I-0248	Tirelli 503 flexwing	
I-0276	Voyager	
I-0306	Type unknown	
I-0391	Pipistrone 6	
I-0514	Raj Hamsa X'Air	
I-0568	TEAM Mini-MAX floatplane	
I-0654	Sirio flexwing	
I-0717	Quicksilver GT-400	
I-0738	Flexwing, type unknown	
I-0766	Crevon motor glider (Chevvron ?)	
I-0827	Sivel T-7 Leone	
I-0847	Fly Synthesis Wallaby	
I-1197	NIKE (Trike)	
I-1203	Type unknown	
I-1209	Weedhopper	
I-1220	Type unknown	
I-1224	"Poppy"	
I-1239	Light Aero Avid Flyer	
I-1242	Sky Walker II	
I-1250	Eurofly Firefox	
I-1277	Eurofly Firefox 2000	
I-1319	Nike Aeronautica Wega	
I-1327	Aliferrari Red Devil	
I-1344	Bagaliante	
I-1364	Zenith Baroudeur	
I-1368	ICP MXP-740 Savannah	
I-1377	High wing, type unknown	
I-1385	Hovey (model?)	
I-1418	Flexwing, type unknown	
I-1446	Tirelli Top Class	
I-1447	Murphy Renegade Spirit	
I-1465	Ferrari Tucano	
I-1493	Air Command Commander Sport gyro	
I-1521	Sky Sports Europe Buccaneer II	
I-1524	Bagalini Colombo	
I-1547	Flexwing, type unknown	
I-1550	Spectrum Beaver	
I-1589	Sky Devil	
I-1608	Stern flexwing	
I-1630	Ferrari Olimpios	
I-1637	Ferrari Tucano	
I-1657	Ferrari Tucano	
I-1660	Fly Synthesis Wallaby	
I-1707	Sky Devil	
I-1710	Buccaneer II Hydro	
I-1727	Preceptor Pup N3-2	
I-1735	Quicksilver MXL-II Sport	
I-1739	Type unkn (high-wing 1-seater)	
I-1743	SE.5A replica	
I-1772	La Mouette Trike	
I-1801	Type unknown	
I-1859	Sky Devil	
I-1861	Zenair CH-701 STOL	
I-1865	Tirelli Polaris Gryps	
I-1876	TEAM Mini-MAX Sport	
I-1877	Light Aero Avid Flyer	
I-1903	Zanardo Wright Flyer 1903 RM	
I-1913	Weedhopper	
I-1921	Tirelli Motodelta	
I-1924	Ferrari Tucano	
I-1942	Fisher Classic	
I-1947	Top Concept Hurricane	
I-1948	Denney Kitfox	

I-1962	Air Light Avid Flyer		
I-1975	Piuma Originale	1	
I-1994	Denney Kitfox		
I-2010	Murphy Renegade Spirit		
I-2024	Quicksilver MX-II Sprint		
I-2025	Euroala Jetfox 97		
I-2080	Quicksilver MXL-II Sport		
I-2097	Aviatika MAI-89		
I-2099	Aviatika MAI-89		
I-2110	Fly Synthesis Storch		
I-2125	Aviasud Sirocco		
I-2128	Weedhopper Sport		
I-2136	Type unknown		
I-2142	Denney Kitfox IV		
I-2153	Type unknown (Pusher microlight)		
I-2159	Denney Kitfox		
I-2178	Elisport CH-7 Angel		
I-2179	Sky Devil		
I-2192	Bipadus		
I-2238	Light Aero Avid Flyer		
I-2249	Ferrari Tucano		
I-2285	Dragon Fly 333		
I-2301	Pottier P.(?)		
I-2332	Murphy Renegade Spirit		
I-2338	Rodaro Storch		
I-2340	Type unknown, flexwing		
I-2348	Quicksilver GT-500		
I-2258	Type unknown		
I-2290	Type unknown, flexwing		
I-2327	Ray Hamsa X'Air		
I-2350	Type unknown, flexwing		
I-2371	Denney Kitfox		
I-2381	Light Aero Avid Flyer		
I-2413	Light Aero Avid Flyer (tricycle u/c)		
I-2422	TEAM Mini-MAX		
I-2426	Skykraft		
I-2433	Tipsy T.66 Nipper	40	I-FAIB OO-ITB OY-AEV
I-2458	Type unknown		
I-2469	Rodaro Kangaroo 447		
I-2476	Scheibe Spatz (KFM motor)		
I-2479	Type unknown, flexwing		
I-2525	Piper J-3C-65 Cub	18633	I-CERE N98442
I-2537	Ferrari Tucano X-2		
I-2545	Maefin Top Fun		
I-2554	Denney Kitfox III		
I-2575	Smith Miniplane		
I-2578	Denney Kitfox		
I-2579	Euroala Jetfox JF.91S		
I-2580	Denney Kitfox		
I-2587	Martinet		
I-2590	Fly Synthesis Storch		
I-2591	Fly Synthesis Storch (This regn also given for Avid Flyer now SE-VAZ)		
I-2596	Maefin Top Fun		
I-2600	III Sky Arrow 450T		
I-2608	Cormorano		
I-2609	Light Aero Avid Flyer		
I-2614	Dynali Chickinox		
I-2621	Weedhopper Sport		
I-2630	Weedhopper		
I-2632	Eurofly Firefox 2000		
I-2636	Buccaneer II hydro		
I-2638	Macchi MB.308 (rebuild)	5819/46	I-PINI
I-2639	Rans S-9 Chaos		
I-2645	Flylab Tucano		
I-2651	Flylab Tucano		
I-2660	Maefin Top Fun		
I-2671	Rans S-6 Coyote II		
I-2692	Dragon Fly 333		
I-2699	Flylab Tucano		
I-2713	Preceptor Pup N3-2		
I-2720	Flexwing. type unknown		
I-2730	Zenair CH-701 STOL		
I-2739	Buccaneer II		
I-2744	Quicksilver GT-500		
I-2746	Polaris FIB (sold as C-IGFI, 1.00)	4158695	
I-2753	Zenair CH-701 STOL amphibian		
I-2762	HFL Stratos 300	unkn	D-MBJL
I-2808	Cormorano		
I-2811	Rans S-4 Coyote I		
I-2819	Type unknown		
I-2828	Fly Synthesis Storch 582		
I-2837	Quicksilver GT-500		
I-2858	Elisport CH-7 Angel	A031	
I-2872	Agrocopteros MXP-100		
I-2874	Light Aero Avid Flyer		
I-2884	La Mouette flexwing: 'Aviazione Sportiva' magazine titles		
I-2908	Sky Walker II		
I-2921	Light Aero Avid Flyer		
I-2927	Tango		
I-2928	Skystar Kitfox		
I-2947	Zenair CH-701 STOL (ICP-built?)		
I-2959	Fly Synthesis Wallaby		
I-2969	Pelican		

I-2977	Euroala Jetfox JF.91		
I-2986	Fly Synthesis Storch		
I-2992	Ferrari Tucano		
I-2993	Ferrari Tucano		
I-3000	III Sky Arrow 450T	48	
I-3001	Liguria Motori Curtiss Jenny (scale replica)		
I-3002	Zenair CH-701 STOL (ICP-built?)	AG-11-92-10-002	
I-3008	Quicksilver MXL II Sport		
I-3014	Kolb Twinstar II		
I-3017	Type unknown, flexwing		
I-3024	TEAM Mini-MAX Sport		
I-3032	Type unknown		
I-3037	Magni M-16 Tandem Trainer gyrocopter		
I-3050	Alpair Excelsior 90		
I-3059	Euroala Jetfox JF.91		
I-3060	Flylab Tucano (To 9H-UME)	0122	
I-3073	Maefin Top Fun		
I-3091	Flexwing, type unknown		
I-3096	Ferrari (Tucano?)		
I-3114	Fly Synthesis Storch		
I-3121	Maefin Top Fun		
I-3127	ICP MX-740 Savannah (amphibious floats)		
I-3130	Denney Kitfox		
I-3135	Magni M-16 Tandem Trainer gyrocopter		
I-3136	Cormorano		
I-3145	Zenair CH-701 STOL		
I-3146	Flylab Tucano X-2		
I-3149	La Mouette flexwing		
I-3156	Pegasus		
I-3157	Aviasud Mistral		
I-3163	Magni M-16 Tandem Trainer gyrocopter		
I-3169	Quicksilver MX-III (To SE-VGG, 4.04)	398	
I-3170	Flylab Tucano		
I-3172	Fischer FP.404 Classic		
I-3176	Elisport CH-7 Angel		
I-3182	TEAM Mini-Max		
I-3183	Ultravia Pélican 912		
I-3189	Rodaro Storch		
I-3219	Catto Goldwing		
I-3222	Tirelli Class-Atlas 21		
I-3226	Denney Kitfox IV		
I-3231	Elisport CH-7 Angel		
I-3232	Buccaneer II hydro		
I-3234	Rans S-9 Chaos		
I-3235	Fly Synthesis Storch 582		
I-3263	Denney Kitfox IV		
I-3266	Rossi Soavi		
I-3276	Euroala Jetfox JF.91		
I-3284	Fly Synthesis Storch		
I-3290	III Sky Arrow 650TC	12	
I-3292	Avia FL-3 (Said to be rebuild combining c/n A.52 I-SICI and c/n 178 I-OZZO)		
I-3293	Type unknown, flexwing		
I-3294	Elisport CH-7 Angel		
I-3296	III Sky Arrow 450T		
I-3306	Eurofly Firefox		
I-3313	Microleve MkII Corsario hydro		
I-3334	Euroala Jetfox JF.91		
I-3342	Elisport CH-7 Angel		
I-3344	M-100		
I-3348	Flylab Tucano		
I-3351	Fly Synthesis Storch HS		
I-3355	Euroala Jetfox JF.91		
I-3376	Buccaneer II hydro		
I-3378	Pipistrel/Chronos 16		
I-3381	Aer Mantova Jaguar		
I-3387	Pipistrel trike		
I-3388	Maefin Top Fun		
I-3390	Vector		
I-3391	Previsani Ali Pelo		
I-3393	Flexwing, type unknown		
I-3402	Fly Synthesis Storch		
I-3403	Fly Synthesis Storch		
I-3405	ICP MXP-740 Savannah	02-94-50-019	
I-3409	Light Aero Avid Flyer		
I-3415	ICP MXP-740 Savannah	07-93-50-008	
I-3416	Rans S-7 Courier		
I-3428	Flylab Tucano		
I-3435	WAG-Aero CUBy II		
I-3436	Fox Basic		
I-3440	Type unknown, flexwing		
I-3443	Vidor Guiseppe Asso IV Wisky		
I-3447	Tecnam P.92 Echo		
I-3449	Euroala Jetfox JF.91		
I-3452	TEAM MIni-Max Sport		
I-3453	CG-10 Ultralight		
I-3456	Flylab Tucano		
I-3465	Euroala Jetfox JF.91		
I-3466	Raj Hamsa X'Air		
I-3467	Rans S-9 Chaos		
I-3468	Jodel D.18		F- ?
I-3474	Borowsky Piccolo		
I-3481	Fly Products Swirl gyrocopter		
I-3490	Pottier P.180		
I-3496	Fly Synthesis Storch		
I-3500	Maefin Top Fun		
I-3501	Flylab Tucano		

I-3503	Magni M-16 Tandem Trainer gyrocopter		
I-3509	Tecnam P.92 Echo	15	
I-3510	Fly Synthesis Storch AS		
I-3512	Rans S-6 Coyote II		
I-3521	Zenith Baroudeur		
I-3524	Buccaneer II hydro		
I-3525	Pegasus		
I-3528	Tecnam P.92 Echo		
I-3529	Fly Synthesis Storch		
I-3541	Tecnam P.92 Echo		
I-3542	III Sky Arrow 450T		
I-3544	FGX Ultralight		
I-3551	Skystar Vixen		
I-3552	Tecnam P.92 Echo		
I-3556	'Dedalus Poppy' ?		
I-3559	Magni M-14 Scout gyrocopter		
I-3560	Flylab Tucano		
I-3563	Zenair CH-701 STOL		
I-3566	Rans S-6 Coyote II		
I-3576	Flylab Tucano		
I-3582	Tecnam P.92 Echo		
I-3584	Nando Groppo Groppino		
I-3585	Tecnam P.92 Echo		
I-3603	WAG-Aero CUBy II		
I-3615	Type unknown		
I-3617	Rodaro Kangaroo 447		
I-3619	Rans S-9 Chaos		
I-3622	Flylab Tucano		
I-3629	Tecnam P.92 Echo		
I-3634	Flylab Tucano		
I-3646	Eurofly Firefox		
I-3655	Dragon Fly 333		
I-3662	Tirelli Class-Atlas 21		
I-3665	Dragon Fly		
I-3667	Denney Kitfox (Wears both marks)		I-KITF
I-3670	Sonaca Falcon		
I-3673	Tecnam P.92 Echo		
I-3675	Aviatika MAI-890	010A	
I-3681	Zenair CH-701 STOL		
I-3686	Tecnam P.92 Echo		
I-3691	Maifin TopFun		
I-3701	TEAM Hi-MAX		
I-3709	Murphy Rebel		
I-3714	Zenair CH-701 STOL		
I-3715	Eurofly Firefox 2000		
I-3737	Jodel D.9 Bébé		
I-3739	Tirelli Class 462		
I-3740	Scheibe SF-27A (Nose-mounted König SD570 engine)	6029	D-4342
I-3745	Tecnam P.92 Echo		
I-3746	Dragon Fly 333		
I-3752	Buccaneer II hydro		
I-3753	Microleve Corsario V		
I-3754	SG Aviation Storm 280P		
I-3764	SG Aviation Storm 280Si		
I-3765	Tecnam P.92 Echo		
I-3767	Capella XL		
I-3771	ICP MXP-640T Amigo !		
I-3775	Aviatika MAI-890		
I-3782	Denney Kitfox		
I-3788	ICP MXP-741 Savannah		
I-3795	Tecnam P.92 Echo		
I-3803	Fly Synthesis Storch		
I-3807	Murphy Rebel		
I-3810	Agrocopteros MXP-100 hydro		
I-3811	Type unknown		
I-3816	Skystar Kitfox III		
I-3820	Pipistrel flexwing		
I-3822	Fly Synthesis Storch		
I-3836	TEAM Mini-MAX Sport		
I-3838	Iannotta I-66 San Francesco		
I-3842	Tecnam P.92 Echo		
I-3850	Flylab Tucano		
I-3851	Tecnam P.92 Echo		
I-3854	Blue Sky Dream glider		
I-3855	III Sky Arrow 450T		
I-3858	Dragon Fly 333		
I-3859	Type unknown, pusher		
I-3861	Type unknown, weightshift (Pegasus?)		
I-3864	Light Aero Avid Flyer		
I-3866	III Sky Arrow 450T	0015	
I-3873	Tecnam P.92 Echo		
I-3874	Druine D.31B2 Turbulent	166	F-PJGT
I-3875	Type unknown, flexwing		
I-3876	Flylab Tucano X-2	0263	
I-3882	TEAM Mini-MAX		
I-3887	Zenair CH-701 STOL		
I-3888	Denney Kitfox		
I-3890	Rans S-7 Courier		
I-3891	Sport Flight Sky Pup		
I-3896	Elisport CH-7 Kompress		
I-3898	Tecnam P.92 Echo	041	
I-3901	Sparrow Effe		
I-3903	Pipistrel/Zen Virus		
I-3905	Quicksilver GT-400		
I-3910	Volmer VJ-22 Sportsman		
I-3911	Fly Synthesis Storch		
I-3915	Dragon Fly 333		
I-3916	Tecnam P.92 Echo		
I-3925	Bipadus		
I-3926	Aero Design Pulsar XP		
I-3928	Rotorway Exec		
I-3933	Europa Aviation Top Fun S5		
I-3934	Air-Light Wild Thing		
I-3940	Aviasud Albatros		
I-3941	Cram		
I-3952	Type unknown (Grif?)		
I-3957	Jodel D.19T	172	
I-3959	Tecnam P.92 Echo		
I-3962	Murphy Renegade Spirit		
I-3964	Type unknown, pusher		
I-3965	Murphy Rebel		
I-3968	Murphy Rebel		
I-3975	Aviatika MAI-890		
I-3980	Top Fun		
I-3981	Tecnam P.92J Echo		
I-3982	Denney Kitfox III (To 9H-UMH 12.03)		
I-3985	Dragon Light		
I-3987	Zenair CH-701 STOL		
I-3992	Avia FL-3	87	I-ADOA
I-3994	GT Air		
I-3995	Euroala Jetfox JF.91		
I-3998	Dynali Chickinox		
I-3999	Tecnam P.92 Echo		
I-4000	Air Command Gyrocopter		
I-4004	Moravan Zlin Savage 912S (coded "R-G")		
I-4006	Type unknown, flexwing		
I-4014	Tecnam P.92 Echo		
I-4018	Murphy Rebel		
I-4026	Fly Synthesis Storch		
I-4037	Zenair CH-701 STOL		
I-4049	Type unknown, flexwing		
I-4050	La Mouette		
I-4053	Aviatika MAI-890U		
I-4056	Tecnam P.92 Echo		
I-4071	Air-Light Wild Thing		
I-4080	Type unknown		
I-4096	Best Off Sky Ranger		
I-4100	Buccaneer II hydro		
I-4107	Advanced Avn Cobra		
I-4109	Silver		
I-4132	Rodaro Storch		
I-4136	Sonaca Falcon		
I-4146	Tecnam P.92 Echo		
I-4155	Type unknown, flexwing		
I-4169	Type unknown, flexwing		
I-4171	Asso Aeri Asso III		
I-4182	ICP MXP-740 Savannah		
I-4186	Flylab Tucano	5	
I-4196	Type unknown		
I-4198	Murphy Renegade Spirit		
I-4215	JEOF Candiana GV 1		
I-4241	Air Création		
I-4244	Fly Synthesis Storch		
I-4256	Air Création		
I-4265	Fly Synthesis Storch		
I-4269	Fly Synthesis Storch		
I-4270	Dragon Fly 333	018-94	
I-4272	Flylab Tucano		
I-4274	Fly Synthesis Storch		
I-4275	Flylab Tucano		
I-4276	Dragon Fly 333		
I-4280	Tecnam P.92 Echo		
I-4281	Type unknown, flexwing		
I-4285	ICP MXP-640 Amigo !	07-94-45-006	
I-4293	Tecnam P.92 Echo		
I-4298	TEAM Mini-MAX Sport		
I-4306	Type unknown		
I-4309	Rans S-9 Chaos		
I-4312	Denney Kitfox		
I-4316	III Sky Arrow 450T		
I-4317	Aviatika MAI-890U		
I-4318	Aviatika MAI-890U		
I-4319	Flylab Tucano		
I-4320	Tecnam P.92J Echo	086	
I-4322	SG Aviation Storm 280SI		
I-4323	Fly Synthesis Storch		
I-4324	Fly Synthesis Storch		
I-4326	Fly Synthesis Storch		
I-4344	Tecnam P.92 Echo		
I-4340	Tecnam P.92 Echo		
I-4345	Tecnam P.92 Echo		
I-4346	Tecnam P.92 Echo		
I-4348	Tecnam P.92 Echo		
I-4350	Flylab Tucano		
I-4351	Tecnam P.92 Echo		
I-4352	Tecnam P.92 Echo		
I-4353	Tecnam P.92S Echo		
I-4355	Eurofly Firefox		
I-4358	Fly Synthesis Storch		
I-4359	Tecnam P.92 Echo		
I-4365	ICP MXP-741 Savannah	02-94-50-018	
I-4372	Fly Synthesis Storch		
I-4374	Air Command Gyrocopter	0332	

I-4385	Tecnam P.92 Echo		
I-4387	Fly Synthesis Storch 582		
I-4393	Elisport CH-7 Angel		
I-4394	SG Aviation Storm 280SI		
I-4401	Dragon Fly 333		
I-4403	Dragon Fly 333		
I-4410	Magni MT-5 gyroplane		
I-4413	Denney Kitfox		
I-4414	Aces High Cubby II		
I-4423	Flylab Tucano		
I-4426	TEAM Mini-MAX 1500R		
I-4430	Vidor Guiseppe Asso III	35	
I-4431	Skystar Vixen		
I-4432	Dragon Fly 333		
I-4434	SG Aviation Storm 300 Special		
I-4438	Tecnam P.92 Echo		
I-4443	ICP MXP-740 Savannah	AG-11-92-50-004	
I-4447	Tecnam P.92 Echo		
I-4449	Denney Kitfox III		
I-4451	Aerdelta Nike powered hang-glider		
I-4456	Zenair CH-701 STOL		
I-4457	Piper PA-17 Vagabond		
I-4460	Type unknown		
I-4462	Tecnam P.92 Echo		
I-4463	Murphy Rebel (Wreck noted 9.99)		
I-4465	Dragon Fly 333		
I-4471	Fly Synthesis Storch CL		
I-4478	Piper J-3C-65 Cub		
	(This may also be a Moravan Zlin Savage, Cub look-alike)		
I-4485	Moravan Zlin Savage 912S		
I-4486	III Sky Arrow 450T		
I-4489	Fly Synthesis Storch		
I-4490	Piper PA-17 Vagabond	17- ?	N ?
I-4492	Tecnam P.92 Echo		
I-4493	Zenair CH-601UL Zodiac		
I-4494	Tecnam P.92 Echo		
I-4496	Nando Groppo Groppino		
I-4499	Skystar Kitfox III		
I-4501	Unidentified high wing 3-axis type		
I-4503	Kronos 16		
I-4505	Meteor FL-54		
	(This was also reported as a Lombardi FL-5)		
I-4519	Dragon Fly 333		
I-4520	Dragon Fly 333		
I-4521	Flylab Tucano		
I-4522	Trike, fitted with Mainair Flash 2A wing c/n W702		
I-4523	Type unknown		
I-4531	Tecnam P.92 Echo		
I-4532	Zenair CH-701 STOL		
I-4533	Euroala Jetfox JF.91S		
I-4536	Rans S-7 Courier		
I-4537	Filippin Fire Fox		
I-4539	Dragon Fly 333	032-96	
I-4541	Tecnam P.92 Echo		
I-4542	Tecnam P.92 Echo		
I-4543	Jodel D.18		
I-4548	Fly Synthesis Storch AS		
I-4549	Smith Miniplane (USN c/s "6-B-1")		
I-4553	Quicksilver/Kong		
I-4554	Vidor Guiseppe Asso III	37	
I-4555	Salsedo Elpo 6		
I-4560	Raj Hamsa X'Air		
I-4568	Fly Synthesis Storch		
I-4575	Asso Aeri Asso V Champion		
I-4576	SG Aviation Storm 400 Special	179	
I-4579	Aliferrari Red Devil		
I-4580	Microleve Mk.II Corsario hydro		
I-4583	SG Aviation Storm 280 Si		
I-4589	Flash		
I-4590	Mainair 912 Blade	1041-0695/W839	
I-4583	SG Aviation Storm 280SI		
I-4596	Slepcev Storch		
I-4598	Type unknown		
I-4601	Quicksilver MXL-II Sport		
I-4606	Embree Monnett Sonerai IIL	114389	N348KE
I-4618	Flash		
I-4619	Biplane, type unknown		
I-4628	Tecnam P.92 Echo		
I-4632	Type unknown, flexwing		
I-4633	Magni gyrocopter		
I-4634	Tecnam P.92 Echo		
I-4640	Rans S-9 Chaos		
I-4643	Fly Synthesis Storch HS		
I-4644	Tecnam P.92 Echo		
I-4646	ICP MXP-740 Savannah		
I-4649	Zenair CH-701 STOL		
I-4651	Mainair 912 Blade	1066-0196/W868	
I-4654	Fly Synthesis Storch AS		
I-4655	Tecnam P.92 Echo		
I-4658	Fly Synthesis Storch		
I-4660	Dragon Fly 333		
I-4661	Tecnam P.92 Echo		
I-4665	Dragon Fly 333		
I-4666	Raj Hamsa X'Air		
I-4681	Tecnam P.92 Echo		
I-4682	SG Aviation Storm 280SI		
I-4683	Magni M-16 Tandem Trainer gyrocopter		
I-4684	Magni M-18 Spartan gyrocopter		
I-4685	Brugger MB-2 Colibri		
I-4686	Rans S-7 Courier		
I-4688	Tecnam P.92 Echo		
I-4689	Tecnam P.92 Echo		
I-4691	Rans S-10 Sakota		
I-4702	Dragon Fly 333		
I-4704	Tecnam P.92 Echo	0169	
I-4709	Rans S-5 Coyote I		
I-4715	TEAM Mini-MAX 1500R		
I-4717	Nando Groppo Groppino		
I-4720	Microleve II Corsario hydro		
I-4724	Fly Synthesis Storch		
I-4729	Fly Synthesis Storch		
I-4738	J-3 Kitten		
I-4739	ICP MXP-740 Savannah	02-96-50-030	
I-4743	Tecnam P.92 Echo		
I-4745	Tecnam P.92 Echo		
I-4747	Tecnam P.92 Echo		
I-4750	Tecnam P.92 Echo		
I-4752	Tecnam P.92 Echo		
I-4755	Alisport Silent		
I-4761	Vidor Guiseppe Asso III		
I-4762	Alpi Avn Pioneer 200		
I-4766	Light Aero Avid Flyer		
I-4769	Type unknown, flexwing		
I-4776	Ferrari Tucano		
I-4781	Tecnam P.92 Echo		
I-4786	SG Aviation Storm 280SL		
I-4792	Flylab Tucano		
I-4793	Fly Synthesis Storch CL		
I-4795	Type unknown, flexwing		
I-4798	Type unknown		
I-4801	Kolb Twinstar		
I-4809	Eurofly Firefox 2000		
I-4814	III Sky Arrow 450T	31	
I-4815	Asso Aeri Asso III		
I-4817	Aliferrari Red Devil		
I-4819	Tecnam P.92 Echo		
I-4827	Asso Aeri Asso III		
I-4832	GTR Special		
I-4834	Infa Air GTR-400 JPX		
I-4837	Denney Kitfox		
I-4840	Rotorway Exec 162F		
I-4842	Dragon Fly 333		
I-4847	Fly Synthesis Storch CL		
I-4856	SG Aviation Storm 280 Si		
I-4858	Slepcev Storch Mk4		
I-4859	Quicksilver GT-500		
I-4867	Slepcev Storch Mk4		
I-4868	Tecnam P.92 Echo		
I-4870	Fly Synthesis Storch		
I-4872	Iannotta I-96 San Francesco III		
I-4874	III Sky Arrow 450T		
I-4875	Eurofly Flash 912		
I-4881	Zenair CH-601 UL Zodiac		
I-4884	ICP MXP-740 Savannah		
I-4885	Tecnam P.92 Echo		
I-4886	ICP MXP-640 Amigo !	03-95-4-008	
I-4887	Fly Synthesis Storch		
I-4888	Light Aero Avid Flyer IV		
I-4892	Zenair CH-601 Zodiac		
I-4894	SG Aviation Storm 280 Si		
I-4906	Dell'Oro Gespa HM.293 Pou du Ciel		
I-4912	Type unknown, flexwing		
I-4916	Tecnam P.92 Echo		
I-4932	Vidor Guiseppe Asso III		
I-4934	Dragon Fly 333		
I-4935	Unidentified hydroplane		
I-4940	Raj Hamsa X'Air		
I-4949	Elisport CH-7 Angel		
I-4951	Fly Synthesis Storch		
I-4955	Tecnam P.96 Golf (Prototype)		
I-4962	Nando Groppo Groppino		
I-4970	SG Aviation Storm 280 Si		
I-4974	SG Aviation Storm 280 Si		
I-4975	JEOF Candiana GV 1		
I-4983	Quicksilver GT-500		
I-4984	Filippin Fire Fox		
I-4997	Eurofly Firefox		
I-4999	Eurofly Firefox		
I-5000	Revolution Mini 500		
I-5003	Monnett Sonerai II		
I-5004	SG Aviation Storm 280 si		
I-5005	Tecnam P.92 Echo		
I-5009	Monnett Sonerai S2		
I-5013	Fly Synthesis Storch		
I-5019	Dragon Fly Turbo		
I-5022	SG Aviation Storm 280 si		
I-5023	Denney Kitfox		
I-5024	III Sky Arrow 650T	106	
I-5025	Denney Kitfox		
I-5028	SG Aviation Storm 280 si		
I-5030	Flash		
I-5031	III Sky Arrow 450T	0037	
I-5033	Aero Sviluppi AS-10		
I-5034	Unidentified low wing monoplane		

I-5045	Flexwing, type unknown	
I-5055	Iannotta I-96 San Francesco III	
I-5056	Fly Synthesis Storch SS	
I-5061	Pottier P.180	
I-5063	ICP MXP-740 Savannah	12-96-50-050
I-5065	Flexwing, type unknown	
I-5067	SG Aviation Storm 280	
I-5069	Denney Kitfox IV	
I-5070	Quicksilver Mk.II	
I-5074	Denney Kitfox IV	
I-5075	Eurofly Firefox	
I-5080	Jodel D.18	
I-5082	Revolution Mini 500	
I-5091	Mainair 912 Blade	1120-0497/W923
I-5097	Raj Hamsa X'Air	
I-5101	Fly Synthesis Storch	
I-5104	Denney Kitfox	
I-5105	JEOF Candiana GV 1	
I-5106	Raj Hamsa X'Air	
I-5108	"Autocostruito"	
I-5123	Fly Synthesis Storch	
I-5124	Fly Synthesis Storch HS	
I-5128	Tecnam P.92 Echo	
I-5132	Dragon Fly 333 Turbo	
I-5133	Slepcev Storch Mk4	014
I-5138	Tecnam P.92 Echo	
I-5142	Fly Synthesis Storch	
I-5148	Raj Hamsa X'Air	
I-5150	Bagaliante	
I-5151	Loehle P-51 Mustang	
I-5155	Quicksilver MXL-II Sport	
I-5158	Dragon Fly 333	
I-5167	ICP MXP-640 Amigo ! (or ICP Zenair CH-601?)	
I-5169	Type unknown	
I-5170	Ultravia Pelican	
I-5175	Tecnam P.92 Echo	
I-5176	Tecnam P.92 Echo	
I-5181	Tecnam P.92 Echo	
I-5184	Fly Synthesis Storch	
I-5185	Tecnam P.92 Echo	
I-5204	Air Création Racer SX-II	
I-5205	SG Aviation Storm 280 si	
I-5207	Eurotecnik Eurofox	
I-5210	Type unknown	
I-5213	Fly Synthesis Storch HS	
I-5214	Tecnam P.92 Echo	
I-5225	Fly Synthesis Storch	
I-5226	SG Aviation Storm 280 Si	
I-5227	Revolution Mini 500	
I-5228	SG Aviation Storm 280TF-1	
I-5231	ICP MXP-740 Savannah	
I-5234	Slepcev Storch Mk4	
I-5235	Elisport CH-7 Angel	
I-5236	Elisport CH-7 Kompress	
I-5241	Skystar Vixen	N93VX
I-5244	Tecnam P.92 Echo	
I-5246	Flylab Tucano	
I-5249	SG Aviation Storm 280SI	
I-5250	Tecnam P.96 Golf	
I-5251	Evektor Eurostar/ Pottier P.220S Koala	
I-5254	Denney Kitfox IV	
I-5255	Dragon Fly 333	EB052
I-5257	Tecnam P.92 Echo	
I-5259	Eurofly Flash 912	
I-5263	Filippin Fire Fox	
I-5264	Eurofly Firefox	
I-5265	III Sky Arrow 450T	
I-5267	Tecnam P.96 Golf	
I-5268	Maefin Top Fun	
I-5272	Tecnam P.92J Echo	
I-5273	Flexwing, type unknown	
I-5274	Tecnam P.96 Golf	
I-5279	Eurotecnik Eurofox	
I-5282	Magni M-14 Scout gyrocopter	
I-5284	Tecnam P.92 Echo	
I-5286	Tecnam P.96 Golf 100	
I-5289	Flexwing, type unknown	
I-5290	Magni M-14 Scout gyrocopter	
I-5291	Asso Aeri Asso V Champion V	
I-5292	Asso Aeri Asso V Champion V	
I-5293	Protec Prostar PT-2	
I-5294	Raj Hamsa X'Air	
I-5295	SG Aviation Storm 280	
I-5307	Flylab Tucano	
I-5310	Type unknown	
I-5313	Tecnam P.92 Echo	
I-5317	Tecnam P.92 Echo	
I-5318	SG Aviation Storm 400 Special	
I-5321	ICP MXP-740 Savannah	
I-5323	Maefin Top Fun	
I-5324	Tecnam P.92 Echo	
I-5325	MIG 27	
I-5332	Tecnam P.92 Echo	
I-5334	SG Aviation Storm 300S	
I-5335	JEOF Candiana GV 1	
I-5339	Tecnam P.92 Echo	
I-5342	Tecnam P.92 Echo	

I-5345	J-3 Kitten	
I-5348	Tecnam P.92 Echo	
I-5352	Sivel T-7 Leone	6
I-5354	WDFL D4 BK Fascination	
I-5355	Kolb Twinstar III	
I-5356	Jodel D.18	
I-5357	ICP MXP-640 Amigo !	
I-5358	Tecnam P.96 Golf	
I-5359	WAG-Aero CUBy II (believed crashed)	
I-5363	ICP MXP-740 Savannah	
I-5365	SG Aviation Storm 280SI	
I-5371	Raj Hamsa X'Air	
I-5373	Fly Synthesis Storch	
I-5374	SG Aviation Storm 280SI	
I-5376	Flexwing, type unknown	
I-5382	Flylab Tucano	
I-5389	Zenair CH-601UL Zodiac	
I-5392	Tecnam P.92 Echo	
I-5400	Type unknown, flexwing	
I-5402	Denney Kitfox IV	
I-5403	WDFL D4 Fascination (also noted as FK-14 Polaris)	
I-5409	Unidentified high-wing monoplane	
I-5410	Iannotta I-96 San Francesco III	
I-5413	Fly Synthesis Storch AS	
I-5414	Tirelli Class / Chronos 12	
I-5419	Fly Products Swirl gyrocopter	
I-5422	Tecnam P.92 Echo	
I-5429	Raj Hamsa X'Air	
I-5430	WDFL D4 Fascination	
I-5431	SG Aviation Storm 300 (also noted as Fly Synthesis Storch)	
I-5433	Tecnam P.92S Echo 100	
I-5436	Aerotechnik EV-97 Eurostar	
I-5437	TEAM Mini-MAX Extra	
I-5442	Tecnam P.92 Echo	
I-5447	Fly Synthesis Storch	
I-5449	III Sky Arrow 450T	
I-5454	Hydravion, flexwing type unknown	
I-5458	Tecnam P.92 Echo	
I-5460	SG Aviation Storm 280	
I-5466	Eurofly Firefox	
I-5467	DEA Yuma	
I-5468	JEOF Candiana GV 1	
I-5470	Quicksilver MXL-II Sport	
I-5475	ICP MXP-640 Amigo !	12-97-45-016
I-5476	III Sky Arrow 450T	
I-5481	Tecnam P.96 Golf	
I-5483	Tecnam P.92 Echo	
I-5484	Magni M-16 Tandem Trainer gyrocopter	
I-5486	Dragon Fly 333	
I-5487	Tecnam P.92 Echo	311
I-5488	Nando Groppo Groppino	
I-5489	ICP MXP-640 Amigo !	
I-5497	Alpi Avn Pioneer 200	
I-5506	Tecnam P.92 Echo	
I-5510	Magni M-14 Scout gyrocopter (Code "48")(W/o 7.6.03)	
I-5512	Eurofly Flash	
I-5514	Unidentified low wing monoplane	
I-5517	Fly Synthesis Storch	
I-5518	Nando Groppo Groppino	
I-5521	Fly Synthesis Storch	
I-5527	WDFL D4 Fascination	
I-5532	SG Aviation Storm 300 Special	
I-5536	DEA Yuma	
I-5539	Eurofly Flash Light 582	
I-5541	Tecnam P.96 Golf	33
I-5542	III Sky Arrow 450T	
I-5544	Asso Aeri Asso VI Junior	1
I-5545	Tecnam P.92J Echo	
I-5546	Fly Synthesis Storch 582	
I-5550	Jodel D.18	
I-5555	Aerosport R-4S Hirundo	01
I-5559	ICP MXP-740 Savannah	
I-5561	Fly Synthesis Storch 582	
I-5562	Flylab Tucano	
I-5563	Tecnam P.96 Golf	
I-5567	ICP MXP-640 Amigo !	
I-5569	Asso Aeri Asso V Champion V	
I-5572	Tecnam P.92 Echo	
I-5574	Flight Design CT-2K	
I-5576	Polaris	
I-5580	Piuma Evoluzione motorglider	
I-5590	Tecnam P.96 Golf 100	
I-5592	ICP MXP-740 Savannah	03-98-50-079
I-5602	ICP MXP-640 Amigo !	05-98-45-019
I-5607	DEA Yuma	
I-5608	Fly Synthesis Storch	
I-5615	Euroala Jet Fox 97	
I-5616	Asso Aeri Asso V Champion V	
I-5619	Tecnam P.92 Echo	
I-5625	Revolution Mini 500	
I-5626	Tecnam P.96S Golf	
I-5635	Asso Aeri Asso IV Whisky	
I-5637	Toresi D-10 Tukan	
I-5639	Slepcev Storch Mk4	
I-5641	Quicksilver GT-500	
I-5642	ICP MXP-740 Savannah	
I-5643	Type unknown ("Magic Acro") low wing	

I-5644	Type unknown, flexwing		
I-5645	Unidentified biplane		
I-5646	Aerotecknik / Pottier P.220UL Eurostar		
I-5648	Skystar ?		
I-5651	ICP MXP-640 Amigo !	07-98-45-021	
I-5653	SG Aviation Storm 400 Century	04	
I-5659	Eurofly Flash 912		
I-5660	ICP MXP-740 Savannah		
I-5662	Rans S-7 Courier		
I-5663	Slepcev Storch		
I-5667	Tecnam P.92 Echo		
I-5668	Flight Design CT		
I-5671	Tecnam P.92S Echo		
I-5677	Air Création GT BI		
I-5680	Tecnam P.92 Echo		
I-5681	Elisport CH-7 Kompress		
I-5683	Monnett Sonerai II		
I-5686	Rans S-7 Courier		
I-5688	Tecnam P.92S Echo 100		
I-5689	Tecnam P.92 Echo		
I-5690	Fly Synthesis Wallaby		
I-5693	Alisport Silent (Cancelled)		
I-5700	Tecnam P.96 Golf		
I-5701	Pipistrel/Zen Sinus		
I-5702	ICP MXP-740 Savannah		
I-5710	Evektor EV-97 Eurostar	99-0404	
I-5713	Tecnam P.92 Echo		
I-5716	Rans S-7 Courier		
I-5717	Fly Synthesis Storch SS		
I-5719	ICP MXP-640 Amigo !	07-98-45-022	
I-5720	Tecnam P.92 Echo		
I-5721	Alpi Avn Pioneer 300 S		
I-5722	Farina Fox helicopter		
I-5730	SG Aviation Storm 280		
I-5731	Aerotecknik / Pottier P.220UL Eurostar		
I-5737	ICP MXP-640 Amigo ! S	10-98-55-002	
I-5739	Fly Synthesis Storch HS		
I-5740	Morava Zlin Savage 912S	004	
I-5744	Tecnam P.92 Echo		
I-5745	Magni M-20 Talon gyrocopter		
I-5746	Tecnam P.96 Golf		
I-5747	Type unknown		
I-5749	ICP MXP-740 Savannah	09-98-50-095	
I-5750	Magni gyrocopter		
I-5752	Polaris MO		
I-5757	Tecnam P.96 Golf		
I-5758	Magni M-14 Scout gyrocopter		
I-5760	ICP MXP-740 Savannah	10-98-50-097	
I-5761	Raj Hamsa X'Air		
I-5762	Tecnam P.92S Echo 100		
I-5765	Brügger MB.2 Colibri		
	(Regn also reported as Smith Miniplane)		
I-5767	Alpi Avn Pioneer 300 S	10	
I-5769	Rans S-7 Courier		
I-5770	Asso Aeri Asso V Champion V		
I-5771	Tecnam P.96 Golf 100		
I-5772	Tecnam P.92 S Echo 100		
I-5777	Eurofly Flash		
I-5780	Eurofly Firefox 2000		
I-5788	GIADA Fly Biposto (Trike)		
I-5793	Tecnam P. 96 Golf 100		
I-5800	Fly Synthesis Storch		
I-5803	Type unknown, flexwing		
I-5811	Alisport Silent In		
I-5812	Aries AP-1		
I-5815	Flight Design CT-2K		
I-5817	Avid Catalina		
I-5818	III Sky Arrow 450T	063	
I-5820	Elisport CH-7 Kompress		
I-5821	III Sky Arrow 450T		
I-5825	Tecnam P.96 Golf		
I-5826	DEA Yuma		
I-5827	ICP MXP-740 Savannah	11-98-50-102	
I-5829	Type unknown		
I-5830	Flylab Tucano		
I-5831	Motorglider, type unknown		
I-5833	Velocity S5		
I-5837	Sonex Ltd Sonex		
I-5846	Tecnam P.92S Echo		
I-5850	ICP MXP-640 Amigo !		
I-5867	SG Aviation Storm 300S		
I-5871	Aerotechnik Eurostar		
I-5873	Magni M-18 Spartan gyrocopter		
I-5876	Evektor EV-97 Eurostar		
I-5880	Tecnam P.92S Echo		
I-5882	Tecnam P.92 Echo		
I-5884	Tecnam P.92S Echo		
I-5888	Tecnam P.96 Golf 100		
I-5892	Denney Kitfox II		
I-5893	Eurofly Firefox 2000		
I-5894	Tecnam P.96 Golf 100		
I-5895	Quicksilver GT-500		
I-5901	Eurofly Flash 912		
I-5907	Tecnam P.92S Echo		
I-5908	Elisport CH-7 Angel		
I-5918	Elisport CH-7 Angel		
I-5921	Tecnam P.92 Echo		
I-5924	Elisport CH-7 Angel		
I-5930	Fly Synthesis Storch		
I-5932	Fly Synthesis Storch		
I-5935	MG 27		
I-5936	Brügger MB-2 Colibri		
I-5938	Unidentified low-wing monoplane		
I-5947	Fly Synthesis Storch		
I-5955	Pipistrel Sinus		
I-5956	Fly Synthesis Storch		
I-5960	ICP MXP-640 Amigo !		
I-5961	Fly Synthesis Storch		
I-5962	Tecnam P.92S Echo		
I-5963	ICP MXP-640 Amigo !	11-98-45-028	
I-5966	Maefin Top Fun		
I-5967	Pipistrelle trike/ Air Création wing		
I-5969	Slepcev Storch Mk4		
I-5971	Tecnam P.96 Golf 100		
I-5973	Pipistrel Spider / Top 14		
I-5975	Tecnam P.96 Golf 100		
I-5979	ICP MXP-640 Amigo !		
I-5980	Stork		
I-5981	Aerotechnik Eurostar		
I-5983	Tecnam P.92 Echo		
I-5984	Tecnam P.96SGolf	96	
I-5985	Eurofly Flash 912		
I-5986	ICP MXP-740 Savannah		
I-5987	Euroala Jetfox JF.97		
I-5989	Kappa KP 2U Sova		
I-5991	Jodel D.19		
I-6002	Tecnam P.96 Golf 100		
I-6006	Kappa KP 2U Sova		
I-6007	Pipistrel Sinus		
I-6009	Alisport Silent		
I-6012	Fisher Horizon		
I-6013	Alpi Avn Pioneer 300		
I-6014	Kappa KP 2U Sova		
I-6015	III Sky Arrow 450TS		
I-6016	IIISky Arrow 450TS		
I-6017	III Sky Arrow 450TS	067P	
I-6020	Zenair CH-701 STOL		
I-6022	Tecnam P.96 Golf 100		
I-6025	Quicksilver MXL-II Sport		
I-6027	Elisport CH-7 Angel		
I-6035	Alisport Silent		
I-6039	Tecnam P.92S Echo		
I-6043	Tecnam P.92S Echo		
I-6048	Tecnam P.92 Echo 2000RG (prototype)		
I-6051	Murphy Renegade Spirit		
I-6052	Aviotech Jabiru SK		
I-6053	Asso Aeri Asso V Champion V		
I-6056	Alpi Avn Pioneer 300S	15	
I-6060	Tecnam P.92S Echo		
I-6062	Tecnam P.96S Golf		
I-6066	Asso Aeri Asso III		
I-6069	Alisport Silent Club		
I-6075	Eurofly Firefox		
I-6076	Kappa-2U Sova		
I-6077	Kappa-2U Sova		
I-6078	Flexwing, type unknown		
I-6081	Raj Hamsa X'Air Sport		
I-6083	Fly Synthesis Storch SS		
I-6088	Eurofly Firefox 2000		
I-6089	Tecnam P.92S Echo		
I-6091	Eurofly Flash 912		
I-6092	Tecnam P.92S Echo		T7-037
I-6096	Aviotech Jabiru SK		
I-6098	SG Aviation Storm 280 Si		
I-6102	Tirelli Motodelta		
I-6104	Tecnam P.96 Golf 100		
I-6105	Tecnam P.92 Echo		
I-6107	Air Création Buggy		
I-6114	Eurofly Flash Light		
I-6117	ICP MXP-640 Amigo !	01-99-45-030	
I-6119	Eurofly Flash 912		
I-6126	Pipistrel Sinus 912		
I-6128	SG Aviation Storm 300 S		
I-6131	ICP MXP-740 Savannah	06-99-50-119	
I-6133	ICP MXP-640 Amigo !	01-99-45-029	
I-6135	Asso Aeri Asso VI Junior		
I-6136	Tecnam P.96 Golf		
I-6144	Eurofly Flash Light 582		
I-6145	Tecnam P.96 Golf 100		
I-6149	Alpi Avn Pioneer 300	19	
I-6151	Tecnam P.92S Echo		
I-6153	Flight Design CT		
I-6158	Tecnam P.92S Echo		
I-6163	Evektor EV-97 Eurostar		
I-6164	Alpi Avn Pioneer 300S (Cancelled)	16	
I-6165	Tecnam P.92S Echo		
I-6167	Euroala Jetfox 97		
I-6170	Alpi Avn Pioneer 300 Elegance	18	
I-6171	Eurofly Firefox		
I-6172	SG Aviation Storm 300 S		
I-6173	Alpi Avn Pioneer 300 Elegance	20	D-MIPO I-6173
I-6174	Asso Aeri Asso V Champion V	22	
I-6175	Fly Synthesis Storch		

I-6177	Asso Aeri Asso V Champion V		
I-6178	Asso Aeri Asso V Champion V		
I-6179	Zenair CH-701 STOL	7-9120	
I-6181	Flylab Tucano Delta 3		
I-6183	Tecnam P.96 Golf 100		
I-6184	Tecnam P.96 Golf		
I-6185	Fly Synthesis Storch		
I-6186	Fly Synthesis Storch		
I-6189	Brügger MB-2 Colibri		
I-6191	Flexwing, type unknown		
I-6194	Tecnam P.96 Golf		
I-6195	Tecnam P.96 Golf		
I-6196	SG Aviation Storm 300 Special Turbo		
I-6203	Kappa 77 KP-2U Sova		
I-6205	ICP MXP-740 Savannah	07-93-50-007	
I-6209	Eurofly Flash Light 582		
I-6210	Fly Synthesis Texan		
I-6215	Fly Synthesis Storch		
I-6218	Tecnam P.92S Echo		
I-6221	Tecnam P.96 Golf 100		
I-6222	Fly Synthesis Storch		
I-6224	Evektor EV-97 Eurostar	2000	OK-FUR 20 ?
I-6228	Flylab Tucano		
I-6231	Type unknown, flexwing		
I-6232	Type unknown (similar to J-3 Cub)		
I-6235	Fly Synthesis Texan		
I-6236	Magni M-16 Tandem Trainer gyrocopter		
I-6237	Magni M-14 Scout gyrocopter		
I-6238	Magni M-16 Tandem Trainer gyrocopter		
I-6239	SG Aviation Storm 300 Focus		
I-6243	Tecnam P.96 Golf 100		
I-6245	Alpi Avn Pioneer 300S	22	
I-6246	Eurofly Flash 912		
I-6247	Kappa 77 KP-2U Sova		
I-6248	Pipistrel Sinus		
I-6250	Fly Synthesis Texan		
I-6251	Tecnam P.92S Echo		
I-6255	Tecnam P.92S Echo		
I-6256	Asso Aeri Asso V Champion V		
I-6258	Eurofly Flash 912		
I-6261	Magni M-14 Scout gyrocopter		
I-6263	Tecnam P.96 Golf 100		
I-6267	SG Aviation Storm 280		
I-6269	Eurofly Firefox		
I-6270	SG Aviation Storm 300 Focus		
I-6272	Tecnam P.96 Golf 100		
I-6274	DEA Yuma		
I-6279	Elisport CH-7 Angel		
I-6280	Tecnam P.96 Golf 100		
I-6281	Tecnam P.96 Golf 100		
I-6283	Denney Kitfox IV		
I-6284	Tecnam P.96 Golf		
I-6285	Fly Synthesis Texan		
I-6286	SG Aviation Storm 400 Special		
I-6288	Tecnam P.92 Echo	539	
I-6290	Fly Synthesis Storch		
I-6294	Tecnam P.92 Echo		
I-6295	Tecnam P.92 Echo 2000RG		
I-6301	ICP MXP-640 Amigo ! S	03-00-55-009	
	(Now reported as Asso Aeri Asso VI Junior)		
I-6303	Alisport Professor		
I-6305	Alpi Avn Pioneer 300	2	
I-6306	Tecnam P.96 Golf 100	149	
I-6309	DEA Yuma		
I-6312	Alpi Avn Pioneer 300S (or Storm 300S ?)	23	
I-6317	Tecnam P.96 Golf		
I-6321	Evektor EV-97 Eurostar		
I-6324	Flylab Tucano		
I-6326	Evektor EV-97 Eurostar	2001-0911	
I-6328	ICP MXP-640 Amigo ! S	07-99-55-004	
I-6335	Tecnam P.92 Echo		
I-6336	Evektor EV.97 Eurostar	2001-1006	
I-6337	ICP MXP-640 Amigo !		
I-6338	Tecnam P.96 Golf 100		
I-6340	Asso Aeri Asso V Champion		
I-6343	Tecnam P.92 Echo 2000RG		
I-6345	Air Création XP		
I-6348	ICP Super Bingo		
I-6350	Magni M-16 Tandem Trainer gyrocopter		
I-6351	Tecnam P.92 Echo		
I-6355	Tecnam P.92S Echo		
I-6357	Alpi Avn Pioneer 300 Elegance	24	
I-6359	Tecnam P.92 Echo		
I-6360	Tecnam P.96 Golf 100		
I-6361	Tecnam P.96 Golf 100		
I-6363	DEA Yuma		
I-6364	SG Aviation Storm 300 S		
I-6365	Fantasy Air Allegro 2000	01-801	
I-6366	Fantasy Air Allegro 2000	02-803	
I-6368	Alpi Avn Pioneer 200	1	
I-6369	SG Aviation Storm 300 S		
I-6370	Ferrari Tucano		
I-6373	Rotorway Exec 162F		
I-6376	Evektor EV-97 Eurostar		
I-6377	Air Création Clipper		
I-6378	Avis/Aeropro Nitra		
I-6379	DEA Yuma		

I-6380	Denney Kitfox	
I-6381	Tecnam P.96 Golf 100	
I-6382	Aeropro Eurofox	
I-6387	Air Création Racer 503	
I-6390	ICP MXP-740Savannah	
I-6391	Asso Aeri Asso V Champion V	
I-6392	Robinson R-22 Beta	
I-6393	Tecnam P.96 Golf 100	
I-6394	SG Aviation 105S Rally	
I-6395	Alpi Avn Pioneer 300L	
I-6396	Tecnam P.96 Golf	
I-6402	SG Aviation Storm 300 S	
I-6403	Pipistrel Sinus	
I-6405	Fisher FP-404	
I-6406	DEA Yuma	
I-6410	Elisport CH-7 Angel	
I-6412	Tecnam P.92S Echo 100	
I-6414	Ferrari ULM Tucano	
I-6416	Magni gyrocopter	
I-6428	Euro-Fly Flash	
I-6429	Euroala Jetfox JF.91	
I-6430	Tecnam P.92S Echo 100	
I-6435	Alpi Avn Pioneer 300L	
I-6437	Alpi Avn Pioneer 300S	50
I-6438	Tecnam P.96 Golf 100	
I-6441	ICP MXP-740 Savannah	01-00-50-141
I-6442	Tecnam P.92S Echo	
I-6445	Alpi Avn Pioneer 300L	38
I-6448	Magni M-14 Scout gyrocopter	
I-6449	Magni M-16 Tandem Trainer gyrocopter	
I-6452	Pipistre/Zen Sinus	
I-6453	ICP MXP-740 Savannah amphibian	
I-6454	Tecnam P.92J Echo	
I-6455	Tecnam P.92 Echo	
I-6457	ATEC Zephyr 2000-C100	
I-6458	Tecnam P.92 Echo 2000RG	
I-6459	Flight Design CT	01-04-05-15
I-6461	Asso Aeri Asso V Champion V	
I-6463	ICP MXP-740 Savannah amphibian	
I-6467	Fly Synthesis Storch SS	
I-6469	Alpi Avn Pioneer 300L	
I-6473	Asso Aeri Asso V Champion V	
I-6475	Flylab Tucano Delta 3	350F
I-6476	Fly Synthesis Texan	
I-6477	Tecnam P.92S Echo	
I-6488	Aerotechnik EV-97 Eurostar	
I-6491	Aerotechnik EV-97 Eurostar	
I-6493	Gyrocopter	
I-6494	Flight Design CT	
I-6495	Alpi Avn Pioneer 300	29
I-6497	Alpi Avn Pioneer 200	5
I-6498	Alpi Avn Pioneer 200	6
I-6502	ICP MXP-740 Savannah	
I-6503	Tecnam P.92 Echo 2000RG	
I-6506	ATEC Zephyr 2000	
I-6513	TEAM Mini-MAX	
I-6518	Fly Synthesis Texan Top Class	
I-6520	Moravan Zlin Savage 912S	
I-6522	Alpi Avn Pioneer 200	
I-6525	Elisport CH-7 Angel	
I-6526	SG Aviation Storm 300S	
I-6528	Tecnam P.92 Echo 2000RG	
I-6529	Fly Synthesis Texan Top Class	
I-6531	Evektor EV-97 Eurostar	
I-6535	Eurofly Firefox	
I-6537	Evektor EV-97 Eurostar	
I-6540	Evektor EV-97 Eurostar	
I-6544	ICP MXP-740 Savannah 912	
I-6545	Raj Hamsa X'Air Sport	
I-6548	ICP MXP-740 Savannah	01-00-50-139
I-6549	Alpi Avn Pioneer 300S	41
I-6551	Tecnam P.92S Echo	407
I-6552	Magni gyrocopter	
I-6559	Jet Fox JF.97	
I-6560	Polaris Skin	
I-6566	Asso Aeri Asso V Champion	
I-6570	Aeropro Eurofox	
I-6572	Elisport CH-7 Kompress	
I-6574	Evektor EV-97 Eurostar	
I-6575	Asso Aeri Asso VI Junior	
I-6577	Aeropro Eurofox "Guardian Angel"	
I-6579	Alpi Avn Pioneer 300	51
I-6582	Alpi Avn Pioneer 300S	52
I-6583	ICP Bingo 503	
I-6584	Alpi Avn Pioneer 200	2
I-6588	III Sky Arrow 450TS	079S
I-6589	Tecnam P.92 Echo 2000RG	08
I-6591	III Sky Arrow 450TS	
I-6592	Eurofly Firefox	
I-6593	Magni M-16 Tandem Trainer	
I-6594	Alpi Avn Pioneer 200	12
I-6595	Eurofly Flash 912	
I-6597	Unidentified high-wing monoplane	
I-6602	Flexwing, type unknown	
I-6612	Tecnam P.96 Golf 100	
I-6613	Alpi Avn Pioneer 300	
I-6614	Rossi Soavi 1+1 Frecce Tricolori (flexwing)	

I-6615	Evektor EV.97 Eurostar	
I-6616	Elisport CH-7 Kompress	
I-6618	TL Ultralight TL-2000 Sting Carbon	
I-6622	Asso Aeri Asso VI Junior	
I-6625	Alpi Avn Pioneer 300S	53
I-6626	Alpi Avn Pioneer 300	
I-6627	Fly Synthesis Texan Top Class	
I-6628	Evektor EV-97 Eurostar	2000-0711
I-6630	Alisport Silent	
I-6632	Alpi Avn Pioneer 300	42
I-6633	Flight Design CT-2K	
I-6635	Brugger MB-2 Colibri	
I-6638	Best Off Sky Ranger	
I-6641	Air Creation / iXess	A03154-3144
I-6642	SG Aviation Storm 300S	
I-6643	Microleve Corsario Mk.II	
I-6644	Brugger MB.2 Colibri	
I-6653	Tecnam P.92J Echo Super	
I-6655	Alisport Silent In	
I-6656	Dyn'Aero MCR-01	
I-6657	Tecnam P.96 Golf	
I-6659	SG Aviation Storm 400RG Cyclone	
I-6660	ICP Bingo 503	01-05-52-023
I-6662	Alpi Avn Pioneer 300	
I-6663	Magni M-16 Tandem Trainer gyrocopter	
I-6664	TEAM Mini-MAX K-Max	
I-6665	Tecnam P.92 Echo 2000RG	
I-6666	Alpi Avn Pioneer 300	
I-6667	SG Aviation Storm 280 Si	
I-6668	Microleve Mk V	
I-6670	Alpi Avn Pioneer 200	
I-6676	Euro-Fly Flash	
I-6678	ICP Bingo 503	
I-6683	Moravan Zlin Savage	
I-6684	ICP Super Bingo	01-12-52-044
I-6688	Alpi Avn Pioneer 300	
I-6689	Evektor EV-97 Eurostar	
I-6693	Pipistrel/Zen Sinus 912	
I-6696	Piuma Veloce	
I-6697	Fly Synthesis Wallaby	
I-6699	Emmebiavio C-26	001
I-6700	Nando Groppo Dui	
I-6701	Nando Groppo Dui	
I-6706	Tecnam P.92JEcho Super	
I-6707	DEA Yuma	
I-6709	Tecnam P.92J Echo Super	
I-6711	Alpi Avn Pioneer 200	23
I-6714	Giada Fly	
I-6716	Tecnam P.92 Echo	
I-6718	Evektor EV.97 Eurostar	
I-6721	Fly Synthesis Storch	
I-6722	Weightshift, type unknown	
I-6724	ICP Bingo 503	
I-6725	SG Aviation Storm 300 Focus	
I-6728	Tecnam P.96 Golf 100	
I-6730	Alpi Avn Pioneer 300	
I-6739	Tecnam P.92J Echo Super	
I-6745	ICP MXP-740 Savannah	01-11-51-109
I-6747	Tecnam P.92 Echo	
I-6748	Flight Design CT-2SW	
I-6749	ICP MXP-640 Amigo !	03-99-45-036
I-6751	Alpi Avn Pioneer 300	
I-6753	Kappa 77 KP-2U Sova	
I-6754	Tecnam P.92S Echo	
I-6757	Alpi Avn Pioneer 200 Student	
I-6758	Tecnam P.96 Golf 100	
I-6764	Alpi Avn Pioneer 200	
I-6767	Asso Aeri Asso V Champion V	
I-6769	Tecnam P.92 Echo 2000RG	
I-6783	Tecnam P.92 Echo Super	
I-6784	ICP Bingo 503	
I-6787	Tecnam P.92 Echo	
I-6789	Microleve Corsario	
I-6790	Alpi Avn Pioneer 200	
I-6791	Moravan Zlin Savage 912S	
I-6797	Pipistrel/Zen Virus 912	
I-6799	Tecnam P.92S Echo 100	
I-6805	Alpi Avn Pioneer 300JS	
I-6806	Tecnam P.92 Echo Super	
I-6807	SG Aviation Storm RG	
I-6813	ICP Bingo 503	
I-6824	Tecnam P.92 Echo Super	
I-6825	ICP MXP-740 Savannah	
I-6826	TEAM Mini-MAX	
I-6831	Flight Design CT-2K	
I-6832	Fly Synthesis Storch CL	
I-6833	Flight Design CT-2K	
I-6836	MBAvio C.26	
I-6841	Magni M-16 Tandem Trainer gyrocopter	
I-6851	FB.5 Starlight	
I-6857	ICP Super Bingo	
I-6858	Moravan Zlin Savage 912S	
I-6861	Tecnam P.96 Golf 100	
I-6862	Microleve Corsario Mk.5	
I-6868	Magni M-18 Spartan gyrocopter	
I-6872	Kappa 77 KP2U Sova	
I-6873	Evektor EV-97 Eurostar	2002-1417

I-6874	Tecnam P.92 Echo Super		
I-6875	ICP Bingo 503	02-07-52-064	
I-6877	AeroPro Eurofox		
I-6884	Tecnam P.92S Echo 100		
I-6886	Fly Synthesis Texan		
I-6890	Evektor EV-97 Eurostar		
I-6892	Moravan Zlin Savage		
I-6895	Tecnam P.92 Echo Super		
I-6897	Alpi Avn Pioneer 300		
I-6898	Flylab Tucano		
I-6901	SG Aviation Storm 280RG		
I-6905	Nike Aeronautica Orion		
I-6906	ICP MXP-740 Savannah	02-03-51-141	
I-6910	Zenair CH-701 STOL		
I-6911	Evektor EV.97 Eurostar		
I-6914	Asso Aeri Asso V Champion V		
I-6915	Magni M-16 Tandem Trainer gyrocopter		
I-6918	BE.DI.MA. Flight Eagles UB3		
I-6919	Asso Aeri Asso VIIIB Centauro		
I-6920	Magni M-16 Tandem Trainer gyrocopter		
I-6922	ICP MXP-740 Savannah	12-00-51-039	
I-6923	Pipistrel/Zen Sinus		
I-6924	Fly Line Revenge M10		
I-6925	Magni M-16 Tandem Trainer gyrocopter		
I-6927	Tecnam P.92S Echo 100		
I-6929	AeroPro Eurofox		
I-6931	SG Aviation Rally 105		
I-6934	SG Aviation Rally 105		
	(Also reported as Fly Line Revenge M10)		
I-6936	Alpi Avn Pioneer 300S		
I-6937	Tecnam P.96 Golf 100		
I-6942	Rand-Robinson KR.2S		
I-6943	Pegasus Quantum 914		G-59-7
I-6946	Fly Synthesis Storch CL Deluxe		
I-6953	Tecnam P.92S Echo 100		
I-6954	Tecnam P.92 Echo 2000RG		
I-6956	Fly Synthesis Storch Classic		
I-6960	Tecnam P.92S Echo 100		
I-6961	Fly Synthesis Texan Top Class		
I-6965	Alpi Avn Pioneer 300		
I-6966	Alpi Avn Pioneer 300 S		
I-6970	Tecnam P.92 Echo		
I-6972	Eurofly Flash Light 582		
I-6973	Fly Synthesis Storch HS		
I-6978	Eurofly Flash		
I-6980	ICP Super Bingo		
I-6993	Eurofly Flash 618		
I-6996	Tecnam P.92 Echo		
I-6999	Tecnam P.92 Echo Super		
I-7000	Piper PA-17 Vagabond		
I-7006	Tecnam P.92 Echo		
I-7013	DEA Yuma		
I-7020	Tecnam P.92 Echo Super		
I-7024	Eurofly FB-5 Star Light		
I-7027	Aerospool WT-9 Dynamic		
I-7030	III Sky Arrow 450TS		
I-7032	Flight Design CT-2K		
I-7035	Alpi Avn Pioneer 300		
I-7038	Best Off Sky Ranger		
I-7051	Tecnam P.92 Echo Super		
I-7052	Eurofly VP trike/ Hazard		
I-7060	SG Aviation Storm 280RG		
I-7065	Tecnam P.92 Echo Super		
I-7067	Alpi Avn Pioneer 300		
I-7070	Tecnam P.92S Echo 100		
I-7074	J-3 Kitten		
I-7075	Best Off Sky Ranger		
I-7076	Flight Design CT-2K	02-06-06-26	
I-7085	ICP MXP-740 Savannah BW		
I-7090	Alpi Avn Pioneer 300		
I-7094	Pipistrel/Zen Virus		
I-7100	Asso Aeri Asso V Champion V		
I-7108	Kappa 77 KP-2U Sova		
I-7110	Skystar Pulsar XP TD		
I-7112	Aerotechnik EV-97 Eurostar		
I-7129	Aeroprakt A22 Vision		
I-7130	ICP MXP-740 Savannah		
I-7132	Alpi Avn Pioneer 200		
I-7133	Alpi Avn Pioneer 300		
I-7136	Euroala Jetfox JF.97		
I-7138	Tecnam P.92 Echo		
I-7139	Tecnam P.92 Echo		
I-7143	Flylab Tucano		
I-7146	RoDa FIB (Polaris FIB variant?)		
I-7147	Kappa 77 KP-2U Sova		
I-7150	Brügger MB-2 Colibri		
I-7155	Brügger MB-2 Colibri		
I-7171	Evektor EV-97 Eurostar	2000-0708	
I-7173	Pratico		
I-7176	ICP MXP-740 Savannah		
I-7179	SG Aviation Rally 105		
I-7187	Alpi Avn Pioneer 200		
I-7190	MBAvio C.26		
I-7201	Aeropro Eurofox		
I-7209	SG Aviation Storm 300		
I-7214	Polaris AM-FIB		
I-7220	Tecnam P.2002 Sierra		

I-7227	Aerotechnik EV-97 Eurostar	
I-7231	Fly Synthesis Texan	
I-7240	Zlin Savage	
I-7244	Alpi Avn Pioneer 200	
I-7248	Brügger MB-2 Colibri	
I-7249	Zlin Savage	
i-7251	WDFL D4 Fascination	
I-7252	ICP Bingo	
I-7257	ATEC Faeta	
I-7264	Alpi Avn Pioneer 330	
I-7280	Tecnam P.2002 Sierra	
I-7287	Alpi Avn Pioneer 200	
I-7301	Yo Yo (Type? A Robinson R-22 was similarly marked)	
I-7302	Cobra	
I-7307	Aeropro CZ Eurofox	
I-7315	Piper PA-17 Vagabond	
I-7318	Tecnam P.92 Echo	
I-7319	Eurofly Comfort Flash	
I-7320	Tecnam P.92 Echo 100	
I-7322	ICP MXP-740 Savannah	
I-7333	ICP MXP-740 Savannah	
I-7337	Fantasy	
I-7357	Replica Plans Curtiss Jenny Replica	
I-7370	BRM Land Africa	
I-7372	ICP MXP-740 Savannah	
I-7377	III Sky Arrow 450TS	
I-7393	Coavia DF-2000	
I-7394	Coavia DF-2000	
I-7413	Fly Synthesis Storch HS	
I-7429	Aerospool WT 9 Dynamic	
I-7432	Type unknown (Paraglider)	
I-7435	Fly Synthesis Texan Top Class	37
I-7454	Tecnam P.2002 Sierra	050
I-7457	In.Fa.Ir.GTR 400	
I-7491	Baglini Colombo	
I-7501	Comco Ikarus C42	
I-7533	Rans S-6 Coyote Super	
I-7548	Fantasy Air Allegro 2000	
I-7551	ELA-07 Autogyro	
I-7575	Tecnam P.2004 Bravo	
I-7625	Skystar Kitfox IV	

LN - NORWAY

Many aircraft remain currently registered with long-expired CoAs or following accidents. Details of these are now given in the register which follows.

Regn.	Type	C/n	Prev.Id.
LN-AAB(3)	SAAB S.91B Safir	91262	SE-IGL 13-73 5-53 / Fv50053
LN-AAC(4)	Piper PA-28-180 Cherokee Challenger	28-7305486	SE-GBB OY-BGH
LN-AAD(3)	Lake LA-4-200 Buccaneer	837	SE-GRL N6184V
LN-AAE(2)	Cessna 175C Skylark	17557093	SE-FTG LN-HHA (SE-FTG) D-EHVO N8393T
LN-AAG(2)	Piper PA-34-220T Seneca IV	3448070	D-GCWB N9251H
LN-AAI (2)	Cessna TU206G Turbo Stationair 6	U20606863	N200RG N9434R
LN-AAJ	Lake LA-4-200 Buccaneer (Damaged 9.8.03)	976	OY-JRH N3085P
LN-AAK	Aviat A-1AHusky	1458	N58AW
LN-AAL	Van's RV-6	21149	
LN-AAM	Piper PA-28R-200 Cherokee Arrow II	28R-7435257	D-EGMU(2) N43248
LN-AAN(2)	Stoddart-Hamilton SH-1 GlaStar	5384	(LN-GCD) (LN-AAN)
LN-AAO(2)	Dornier 228-201	8108	SE-LHD LN-AAO SE-LHD G-CAYN D-IABE D-CBDO G-MNLR D-IOHI D-COHI
LN-AAP	Beech 35-B33 Debonair	CD-745	OY-DMK SE-EKD
LN-AAQ(2)	SOCATA TB-10 Tobago	79	SE-GFO
LN-AAR(2)	Van's RV-4 (Reservation 8.02)	1486	(LN-HUS)
LN-AAS(2)	SAAB S-91ASafir	91128	SE-BNL SE-BNZ SE-BNL SE-BNZ SE-BNL
LN-AAT(2)	SAABMFI-9B Trainer	058	(LN-MFI) SE-EUD
LN-AAV	Piper J-3C-65 Cub (Reservation 4.01)	11615	SE-AUT 43-30324
LN-AAW	SOCATA TB-10 Tobago	636	SE-LAE OH-TBE F-GFQT N20FF
LN-AAX(2)	Van's RV-4 (Reservation 8.01)	unkn	
LN-AAY	Piper PA-18 Super Cub 95 (Reservation 8.01)	18-1472	D-ENLJ ALAT 51-15472
LN-AAZ	Piper PA-18A-150 Super Cub (Res. 3.03)	18-7338	SE-KBO LN-BEB SE-EIK OY-ASS N10F
LN-ABA(2)	Van's RV-6 (Temp regd 5.10.04)	24921	
LN-ABB(2)	Zenair CH-600 Zenith (Reservation 4.02)	6-1190	
LN-ABC	Van's RV-4 (Temp regd 12.2.02)	81104	
LN-ABD(3)	Piel CP.328 Super Emeraude (Temp reg 4.05)	unkn	
LN-ABE(3)	Cessna U206G Stationair 6 II	U20604218	SE-GYR N756NF
LN-ABF(2)	Van's RV-4 (Temp regd 19.8.02)	1485	
LN-ABG(2)	Jabiru 200C	0030	
LN-ABH(3)	SOCATA MS.893E Rallye 180GTGaillard	12273	OO-JMA F-BUJX
LN-ABI (2)	Piper PA-28-140 Cherokee (W/o 21.4.05)	28-24416	SE-FDB
LN-ABJ	Piper PA-34-220T Seneca III	3433090	OY-JBI D-GCPA N9135B
LN-ABK(2)	Daytona Cub	43	
LN-ABL(3)	Van's RV-6A (Reservation 9.03)	80238	
LN-ABM(3)	Europa Aviation Europa XS (Reservation .05)	unkn	
LN-ABN(3)	Reims FR172J Rocket (Res. 3.03, but cr as OO-PIO 1.7.03)	FR17200440	OO-PIO F-BURI
LN-ABO(3)	Cessna 185A Skywagon	185-0439	SE-EEM N1639Z
LN-ABP(3)	Mooney M.20J Model 201	24-0939	PH-RAN D-EAAB(2) N3788H
LN-ABQ	Reims FR172F Rocket	FR17200086	SE-FEZ
LN-ABR(2)	SOCATA MS.894AMinerva 220	11977	D-EJAA F-BTJH
LN-ABS(2)	Van's RV-4	1416	
LN-ABT(2)	Diamond DA 20-A1 Katana	10311	C-FPMF N311DA

LN-ABU(4)	Cessna 441 Conquest	441-0162	N800AB N477SJ N66CP N441CF (N2721F)
LN-ABV	Europa Aviation Europa XS (Reservation .05)	unkn	
LN-ABW(2)	SOCATARallye 110ST Galopin	3225	SE-BIW LN-BIW(5) F-GBKX
LN-ABX	Piper PA-28-140 Cherokee (Res 2.04)	28-20972	OY-BBD (SE-EOF)
LN-ABY	Pereira GP4 (Reservation 2.04)	unkn	
LN-ABZ	Piper PA-31-350 Navajo Chieftain (Panther II conversion)	31-7852132	OY-FTN 4X-CCX N7HF N27735
LN-ACA	Reims/Cessna FR172K Hawk XP	FR17200614	D-EGTF
LN-ACB	Aero Composites/Grefstad Sea Hawker	210	
LN-ACC	Piper PA-31-350 Navajo Chieftain	31-7952088	SX-BNV N112GD C-FYZF N35161
LN-ACD	Piper PA-28-140 Cherokee B (Res .05)	28-25668	SE-LBN LN-BNZ
LN-ACE(2)	Rockwell Commander 690A	11121	S5-CAI D-IGAF (N57121)
LN-ACF	Piper PA-18 Super Cub 95 (Rebuilding)	18-3232	RNoAF34832/ 'FA-F' 53-4832
LN-ACG	Piper PA-18 Super Cub 95	18-3237	RNoAF34837/ 'FA-O' 53-4837
LN-ACH	Piper PA-18 Super Cub 95	18-3238	RNoAF34838/ 'FA-P' 53-4838
LN-ACI	Piper PA-18 Super Cub 95	18-3239	RNoAF34839/ 'FA-H' 53-4839
LN-ACJ	Piper PA-18 Super Cub 95	18-3241	RNoAF34841/ 'FA-C' 53-4841
LN-ACK	Piper PA-18 Super Cub 95	18-3244	RNoAF34844/ 'FA-S' 53-4844
LN-ACL	Piper PA-18 Super Cub 95	18-3248	RNoAF34848/ 'FA-N' 53-4848
LN-ACM	Reims/Cessna F182Q Skylane (Reservation 4.04)	F18200141	SE-LDN D-EFNQ
LN-ACN(2)	Extra EA.230 Ultimate	004	OO-PAB D-ELBS
LN-ACO	Piper PA-32R-301T Saratoga II TC	3257036	D-EPGH N41277
LN-ACP	Cessna P210N Pressurized Centurion	P21000207	D-ESCR N4517K
LN-ACQ	SAAB MFI-9B Trainer	055	SE-ENH
LN-ACR	Mooney M.20K Model 231 (Reservation 7.04)	25-0875	OY-SUA SE-KZU OY-SUA N5809Y
LN-ACS	Piper PA-28-140 Cherokee B	28-26160	SE-FHC N98305
LN-ACT	Yakovlev YAK-52	867014	LY-ANS DOSAAF
LN-ACU	Cessna 172R	17280668	(LN-KFK) N460ER
LN-ACV	Piper PA-42-1000 Cheyenne 400LS	42-5527023	N722ER C-GMFI N429BX
LN-ACW	Piper PA-42-1000 Cheyenne 400LS (Reservation .05)	42-5527019	N1515H
LN-ACX	Cessna 551 Citation II /SP	551-0496	LX-PRS N999GH N8008F N232CC (N12543)
LN-ACZ	Cessna U206G Stationair 6 (Soloy) (Reservation 3.05)	U20603724	D-EATU OY-CKC N7993N
LN-ADA	Aero L-29 Delfin (Reservation 3.05)	294879	ES-YLA EstAF A-121 Sov AF
LN-ADB	Cessna 172F Skyhawk (Reservation 4.05)	17252008	SE-EAL N8108U
LN-AEA(3)	SOCATA MS.892E Rallye 150T (Crashed 6.6.02, stored)	2803	SE-GTF
LN-AEC(2)	Piper PA-28-180 Cherokee G	28-7205275	
LN-AED(9)	Cessna 172N	17268157	N733BA
LN-AEF(7)	Denney Kitfox II	462	
LN-AEG(3)	Cessna 172E	17250985	(N3785S)
LN-AEH(2)	Piper PA-18-150 Super Cub (Crashed 16.5.04, to spares)	18-8472	N4244Z
LN-AEJ	Cessna F172E (Dbr 24.1.87, stored)	F172-0036/17250691	OY-DCD
LN-AEK(3)	Piper PA-18-150 Super Cub (Now fitted with 160 hp engine)	18-8531	

LN-AEP	Cessna 170B (CoA exp 31.5.87, stored)	26196	N2552C
LN-AER(2)	Piper PA-18-150 Super Cub	18-8150	N10F
LN-AEV(4)	Grumman GA-7 Cougar	0041	N417GA C-GVOZ N751GA
LN-AEW(3)	Maule MX.7-180 Star Rocket	11025C	N5668N
LN-AEX	Piper PA-23-250 Aztec C (CoA exp 30.9.89, to Norwegian Avn Museum)	27-2538	SE-EMG
LN-AEY	Piper PA-31 Turbo Navajo	31-457	
LN-AEZ(2)	Cessna U206G Stationair 6	U20606796	N9986Z
LN-AGM	Cessna 172S Skyhawk SP	172S9674	N6106G
LN-AKE(2)	Beech 58 Baron	TH-967	OY-ARZ
LN-AKH	Van's RV-4	2751	
LN-AKT	Rutan Long-Ez	1043	
LN-AKU	Morane-Saulnier MS.885 Super Rallye (CoA exp 30.6.98, stored)	266	D-EKUE F-BKUP (D-EMVE)
LN-ALA	Cessna A185F Skywagon Floatplane	18503201	N93249
LN-ALB	Reims/Cessna F172N	F17201566	
LN-ALD	Cessna U206G Stationair Floatplane	U20603628	N7355N
LN-ALE	Reims/Cessna F172M	F17201385	N31058
LN-ALF	Relms/Cessna FA.152 Aerobat	0341	
LN-ALG	Reims/Cessna F172N	F17201668	
LN-ALH(2)	Cessna 172N	17270475	N739EB
LN-ALI (3)	Piper PA-34-200T Seneca II	34-7970259	N2822A
LN-ALK	Reims/Cessna F177RG Cardinal RG	F177RG0149	(F-BJDJ) N91049
LN-ALL	Cessna 210M Centurion (Cr 27.3.90, b/u)	21061645	N732NP
LN-ALM(3)	Bellanca 8KCAB Decathlon	553-79	SE-GXR
LN-ALO(2)	Cessna 140	9032	OY-AVO D-EKUH N89980
LN-ALP(2)	Cessna U206G Stationair 6 Floatplane (Dbr 7.8.84)	U20605175	N4951U
LN-ALR	Reims/Cessna F177RG Cardinal RG	F177RG0170	(G-. . . .)
LN-ALS	Cessna U206G Stationair 6 (Cr 21.5.86, stored for spares)	U20605230	N5349U
LN-ALT(2)	Piper PA-28-181 Archer II	28-7990435	N28924
LN-ALU(2)	Reims/Cessna F172P	F17202103	
LN-ALV(2)	Reims/Cessna F172P	F17202118	
LN-ALX(2)	Cessna U206G Stationair 6 Floatplane	U20605407	N6300U
LN-ALZ(2)	Reims/Cessna F172P	F17202125	
LN-AMY	North American AT-6D Texan	88-16849	(LN-LCS) (LN-LCN) N10595 42-85068
LN-ASA	Reims/Cessna F172M	F17201107	
LN-ASB	Reims/Cessna F172M	F17201151	
LN-ASD	Cessna 182P Skylane	18263104	(N7320N)
LN-ASF	Reims/Cessna F172M	F17201083	
LN-ASH	Reims/Cessna F172M	F17201240	
LN-ASJ	Reims/Cessna F172M Floatplane	F17201303	
LN-ASM	Cessna 182P Skylane (Reims-assembled with "c/n" 0012)	18263880	(N6887M)
LN-ASN	Reims/Cessna F172M	F17201414	
LN-ASO	Cessna 180B	50534	LN-HHO SE-CTR N5234E
LN-ASP	Reims/Cessna F172M	F17201466	
LN-ASQ	Reims/Cessna F172M (Destroyed 29.12.02)	F17201448	
LN-ASR	Cessna U206F Stationair Floatplane	U20603141	N8280Q
LN-ASS	Cessna 182P (Reims-assembled with "c/n" 0056)	18264412	SE-LOV LN-ASS N1677M
LN-AST	Reims/Cessna F172N	F17201524	
LN-ASW	Cessna A185F	18503906	I-AGEL N4918E
LN-ASY	Reims/Cessna F172N	F17201591	
LN-ATF	Rutan Long-Ez	1567	
LN-ATR	Piper PA-28-181 Archer II (W/o 15.6.93)	28-7990093	N30466
LN-AUD	Neico Lancair 320 (CoA exp 30.11.03, to be restored)	485-320-227	
LN-AWA	Beech A100 King Air (Reservation 7.04, still flying as SE-LDL)	B-213	SE-LDL F-GFEV N660CB N7243R
LN-BAK(3)	SOCATA TB-10 Tobago	619	OY-GCL D-EOQC(3) SE-IMU
LN-BAT(2)	Cessna 421B Golden Eagle	421B0915	N421L OO-DFE D-IMMI N5457J
LN-BBU	Piper PA-28-140 Cherokee	28-21094	OY-BBU N11C
LN-BDA(5)	Piper PA-28-161 Cherokee Warrior II	28-7816512	N9664C
LN-BDB(7)	Piper PA-28-140 Cherokee E	28-7225392	
LN-BDC	Cessna F172H(Cr 8.11.76,scrapped .90	F172-0588	
LN-BDD(5)	Dornier Do.27Q-5 (Cr 10.6.85, stored)	2042	(TF-FHK) LN-BDD(3) OY-AFZ D-EKOC
LN-BDF(3)	Cessna A185E Skywagon Floatplane	185-1047	N11B (N4450F)
LN-BDG	Cessna 180	32150	N3352D
LN-BDH(3)	Piper PA-28-140 Cherokee	28-23019	N9577W

LN-BDI (3)	SAAB S.91B-2 Safir (CoA exp 31.3.02, under restoration)	91328	RNoAF57328 328/'UA-I'
LN-BDJ (2)	SOCATA MS.880B Rallye-Club	1909	SE-FSL
LN-BDL (3)	Cessna 172P Skyhawk II	17274491	N52302
LN-BDM(2)	de Havilland DH.82A Tiger Moth	85294	G-ANSC DE248
LN-BDO(3)	Cessna 170B	27048	N3505D
LN-BDV(3)	Piper PA-28-180 Cherokee D (CoA exp 31.3.96, stored)	28-5394	
LN-BDX(2)	Reims/Cessna F172M (Destroyed 29.12.02)	F17200916	
LN-BDY	Piper PA-28-140 Cherokee B (CoA exp 28.2.93, under restoration)	28-25602	
LN-BDZ	Piper PA-28-140 Cherokee B	28-25644	
LN-BEA(2)	Piper J-3C-90 Cub	16353	SE-BCT
LN-BEC(4)	Cessna 172B (Reservation 4.05)	17248398	(LN-BEQ) OY-DPW SE-CYW N7898X
LN-BED(2)	Maule M-5-180C (Rebuilt with parts from LN-AEU c/n 8021C)	8061C	OY-CPM N749RC
LN-BEE(5)	SOCATA MS.893A Rallye Commodore 180 (CoA exp 31.8.96, to spares)	10929	SE-CIW
LN-BEF	Lake LA-4 Buccaneer (W/o 12.6.88, stored)	411	N7638L
LN-BEG(2)	SIAI FN-333 Riviera (CoA exp 30.6.89, restored and for sale)	009	SE-CWN I-SIAU
LN-BEH	Reims/Cessna F150L	F15000707	
LN-BEL	Cessna I50F (CoA exp 30.4.00, stored)	61903	SE-ESN N8603S
LN-BEM	Cessna U206E Skywagon 206 (Crashed 8.5.99, stored)	U20601530	N9130M
LN-BEN(2)	Cessna T210M Turbo Centurion	21061584	OH-CHP N732KY
LN-BEO(2)	Ted Smith Aerostar 601P	61P-0275-60	(LN-AAS) G-PAMS G-GAIR N90488
LN-BER(2)	Dornier DO 228-212 (Stored .01)	8192	F-ODYC D-CJKM D-CBDB(4)
LN-BET	Piper PA-32-260 Cherokee Six D	32-7100016	
LN-BEV(2)	Cessna 180H (CoA exp 28.2.94, stored)	18051550	N2750X
LN-BEW(2)	Cessna U206G Stationair 6 (W/o 13.8.86)	U20604664	N732EG
LN-BEX(2)	Cessna 177A Cardinal (Cr 6.7.84)	17701264	SE-FEF N30453
LN-BFC	Aero Commander 100 Darter (Cr 11.11.85)	254	
LN-BFD(4)	Piper PA-18-I50 Super Cub	18-7663	SE-CRY OH-CPM
LN-BFG (4)	Piper PA-38-112 Tomahawk (W/o 29.9.90)	38-79A0881	SE-ICH
LN-BFK(3)	Piper PA-28-140 Cherokee F	28-7325139	N15689
LN-BFL(5)	Piper PA-38-112 Tomahawk	38-79A1025	
LN-BFN(3)	Piper PA-28-140 Cherokee F	28-7325140	N15690
LN-BFO(3)	Piper PA-38-112 Tomahawk (Cr 17.6.99)	38-79A1026	
LN-BFQ	Cessna U206D Skywagon 206 Floatplane	U206-1352	(N72286)
LN-BFS(5)	Auster 5 (Under restoration)	1788	SE-BZL TW440
LN-BFT (3)	Piper J-3C-65 Cub (f/n 12641 officially quoted as c/n)	12811	LN-OAE 44-80515
LN-BFU(3)	Cessna U206G Stationair 6 (CoA exp 30.6.96, under restoration)	U20604763	N733EX
LN-BFV(2)	Auster J/1 Autocrat	2005	(LN-BFT) G-AGYN
LN-BFY	de Havilland DH.114 Heron 1B (Now in Sola Museum)	14015	"LN-PSG" G-AOXL (LN-BFY) G-AOXL PK-GHB
LN-BGA(2)	Piper PA-23-180 Cherokee Challenger	28-7305525	SE-GDL
LN-BGB	Cessna U206F Stationair	U20601757	
LN-BGE	Cessna 172L	17259927	N3827Q
LN-BGG	Cessna 172K	17258781	N7081G
LN-BGH	Cessna 172K	17257409	N46648
LN-BGI	Piper PA-28-151 Cherokee Warrior (CoA exp 31.8.85, stored)	28-7415068	
LN-BGK (3)	EAA Acro Sport (No CoA issued, for sale)	01	
LN-BGM	Reims/Cessna F172M	F17201070	
LN-BGO	Cessna A185F Skywagon	18502437	(N1716R)
LN-BGP	Cessna U206F Stationair (W/o 13.4.95)	U20602254	(N1548U)
LN-BGQ(2)	Piper PA-28-161 Warrior II	28-8116219	SE-IKA
LN-BGR	Cessna 150D (CoA exp 30.9.97, stored)	15060457	SE-EHL OY-TRI N4557U
LN-BGT	Piper PA-28-151 Cherokee Warrior	28-7515208	
LN-BGZ(3)	Piper PA-28RT-201 Arrow IV	28R-7918251	SE-ICR
LN-BIA(2)	Piper PA-39 Twin Comanche C/R (W/o 7.6.90)	39-129	G-AZIA N8966Y
LN-BIB(2)	SOCATA MS.893A Rallye Commodore 180 (W/o 5.12.90, broken up)	12063	
LN-BIC	Reims/Cessna F172L (Cr 2.3.89, stored)	F17200812	(D-ECHL)
LN-BID(3)	SOCATA Rallye 100ST (CoA exp 30.4.89, stored)	3045	
LN-BIE(6)	DHC-2 Beaver (Float or wheel u/c)	1056	SE-BIO C-FMAV CF-MAV
LN-BIF(3)	Fairchild PT-19A-FACornell	T43-7228	N51324 43-83641
LN-BIG(6)	Aerotek Pitts S-2A (CoA exp 30.11.82, stored)	2042	N42PS

LN-BIH(2)	Cessna 172B	17248149	SE-CXH N7649X
LN-BII (4)	SAAB S.91B Safir	91284	RNoAF0074 Fv50074
LN-BIK(2)	Cessna 180H Skywagon Floatplane	18052105	(LN-UXZ) N9005M
LN-BIL(3)	SOCATA MS.880B Rallye Club	2963	
LN-BIQ(2)	SOCATA Rallye 235E Gabier	13326	
LN-BIS(4)	SOCATA MS.880B Rallye Club	2950	
LN-BIT(2)	Piper PA-28-140 Cherokee	28-23520	N11C N9973W
LN-BIV(5)	SAAB MFI-15-200A (CoA exp 30.6.89, stored)	15801	SE-S31
LN-BIX(2)	Cessna 172N (CoA exp 31.7.97, stored)	17268317	TF-BHX N733HX
LN-BIZ	SOCATA Rallye 150T	2656	
LN-BNB(4)	Auster 5 (Reservation 3.00)	1425	(LN-HAY) (LN-NFE) LN-BNB (LN-BAK) G-ANIO TJ422
LN-BND	Piper PA-22-108 Colt (W/o 10.12.92)	22-8947	N10F
LN-BNL	Piper PA-22-108 Colt (CoA exp 31.8.92, stored)	22-9170	
LN-BNR(4)	Cessna 177RG Cardinal RG	177RG0809	TF-IOO(3) TF-SPE N7511V
LN-BNS(3)	Orlican L-40 Meta-Sokol (Damaged 29.12.02, stored)	150713	LN-BNS(1) OK-NMR
LN-BOX	Neico Lancair 320	930-320-770	
LN-BRD	Boeing 737-505	24651	(G-GFFF) LN-BRD
LN-BRE	Boeing 737-405	24643	
LN-BRH	Boeing 737-505	24828	D-ACBB LN-BRH
LN-BRI	Boeing 737-405	24644	9M-MLL LN-BRI
LN-BRK	Boeing 737-505	24274	
LN-BRM	Boeing 737-505	24645	(SE-RAF) LN-BRM
LN-BRO	Boeing 737-505	24647	(SE-RAH) LN-BRO
LN-BRQ	Boeing 737-505	25348	(SE-RAC) LN-BRQ (9M-MLL) LN-BRQ
LN-BRR	Boeing 737-505	24648	(SE-RAI) LN-BRR
LN-BRS	Boeing 737-505	24649	(SE-RAK) LN-BRS
LN-BRV	Boeing 737-505	25791	
LN-BRX	Boeing 737-505	25797	
LN-BSB	Quickie Q-1 (Temp regd 27.9.88, stored)	262	
LN-BSN	Svein Nordahl Quickie Q-1 (CoA exp 31.5.94, stored)	261	
LN-BUC	Boeing 737-505	26304	
LN-BUD	Boeing 737-505	25794	(SE-RAO) LN-BUD (LN-BUA)
LN-BUE	Boeing 737-505	27627	
LN-BUF	Boeing 737-405	25795	
LN-BUG	Boeing 737-505	27631	
LN-BWE(3)	Piper PA-23-160 Apache (Cr 12.8.00)	23-1509	N4033P
LN-BWF(3)	Cessna 180C Floatplane	50813	SE-CTY N9313T
LN-BWH(2)	Cessna 180H Skywagon Floatplane	18051995	N3495Y N29205
LN-BWL	Luscombe 8F Silvaire Floatplane	S-76	N3544G
LN-BWM(2)	Cessna 180D (CoA exp 31.8.01, under restoration)	18050986	N6486X
LN-BWO(4)	Reims/Cessna FRA150L Aerobat	FRA1500154	
LN-BWT	Aero C-104 Jungmann (Wfu)	189	OK-BFJ CzAF
LN-BWU(2)	Piper J-3C-65 Cub (CoA exp 31.12.99, under restoration)	13202	SE-CGU LN-RAI 45-4462
LN-BWV(2)	Cessna U206F Stationair (CoA exp 31.5.04, stored)	U20601994	(N51300)
LN-BWY	Reims/Cessna FRA150L Aerobat (CoA exp 31.3.80, stored)	FRA1500172	
LN-BWZ	Reims FR172J Rocket	FR17200374	
LN-DAA(2)	Cessna 172N (Rebuilt with new fuselage 1978-9)	17269065	SE-GOX N734RX
LN-DAC(3)	Cessna 182M Skylane	18259391	SE-FEO N70847
LN-DAE(2)	Reims/Cessna F172M	F17201201	(LN-BGS) D-EOQN
LN-DAG(2)	Reims/Cessna F172M	F17201219	(OY-BIN)
LN-DAH(3)	Reims/Cessna F172M	F17201471	SE-GMB
LN-DAL (3)	Reims/Cessna F172H (CoA exp 30.4.03, stored)	F17200681	SE-FMS
LN-DAO(2)	Reims/Cessna F172M (W/o 31.7.88)	F17201431	
LN-DAP(3)	MFI-9B Trainer (CoA exp 31.8.99, stored)	036	(LN-BFL) SE-ENA
LN-DAV(2)	Reims/Cessna F172M	F17201479	
LN-DAW(2)	Reims/Cessna F172N	F17201573	
LN-DAX	Piper PA-28-151 Cherokee Warrior	28-7515176	N32529

LN-DAY	Reims/Cessna F172N	F17201608	
LN-DAZ	Reims/Cessna F172N (CoA exp 29.2.00, under restoration)	F17201620	
LN-DBA(3)	Cessna 180C Floatplane (CoA exp 30.11.99, stored)	50810	SE-CXA N9310T
LN-DBC(2)	Cessna 172P	17275187	OY-CJC N55471
LN-DBG	Cessna 185 Skywagon Floatplane	185-0136	N9936X
LN-DBI (2)	Piper PA-28-140 Cherokee F (Dbr 10.85, to instructional airframe)	28-7325219	
LN-DBJ(2)	Cessna A185F Skywagon Floatplane	18503369	(N7347H)
LN-DBK(2)	Beech A23-24 Musketeer Super III (Cr 7.8.99, wreck stored)	MA-228	
LN-DBM(2)	Cessna 206 Super Skywagon	206-0117	N5117U
LN-DBQ(2)	Cessna U206G Stationair (W/o 30.9.87)	U20603563	N7206N
LN-DBR(3)	Cessna 172D	17250165	(N2565U)
LN-DBU	Cessna 172C (CoA exp 31.5.95, restn)	17249398	N1698Y
LN-DBY	Cessna 182N Skylane	18260103	N92231
LN-DDD	Rutan Defiant	0024B	
LN-DFK	Robin DR.400/180RD Remo180	2553	
LN-DFL	Diamond DA 20-A1 Katana	10289	OE-VPZ C-GSMF N289DF
LN-DHC	DHC-1 Chipmunk 22	C1/0038	WB586
LN-DRF	Viking Dragonfly Mk.2 (Temp 3.7.91, cr. 1.6.97)	594	
LN-EAA	EAA Acro Sport II (Temp reg 19.12.03)	119	
LN-EHB	Van's RV-4	2760	
LN-EIC	Piper PA-25-235 Pawnee	25-2591	SE-EIC D-EEIO SE-EIC
LN-ERA	Shirl Dickey ERacer Mk.II (Temp reg 2.7.03)	330	
LN-ESS	CASA I-131EJungmann (Painted as Sp.AF '781-25') (Reservation 12.00, but still flyingin Norway as G-BRSH)	2156	G-BRSH E3B-540
LN-FAA(2)	Piper PA-22-108 Colt (CoA exp 31.5.01, stored)	22-9353	
LN-FAB	Taylor J-2 Cub	980	
LN-FAC	BAe. Jetstream Series 3201	856	N856TE N422AM G-31-856
LN-FAD(3)	Piel CP.301C Emeraude (To Sola museum)	L-355/67	
LN-FAE(3)	Piper PA-28-151 Cherokee Warrior (W/o 5.8.86)	28-7615379	N5905F N9608N
LN-FAF	Cessna 150 (Dbr 7.85, to Nor Avn Museum)	17257	SE-CNN OY-AEF N5757E
LN-FAG(3)	Reims/Cessna F172M	F17201485	
LN-FAH(4)	Rockwell Commander 690B	11367	OY-BEJ N888TB D-IAWW N81547
LN-FAJ(2)	BAe. Jetstream Series 3102	621	G-BTXL (D-C . . .) G-BTXL G-BLDO (G-BLCY) G-31-621
LN-FAK(3)	SOCATA MS.893E Rallye 180GT Gaillard	13008	
LN-FAM(4)	BAe. Jetstream Series 3112	740	C-GJPO (N2247R) C-GJPO (N331QC) G-31-740
LN-FAO(5)	Aérospatiale/Alenia ATR-42-320	148	F-WQKX D-BGGG F-WWEU
LN-FAP(5)	Aérospatiale/Alenia ATR-42-320	110	F-WQKQ D-BDDD F-WWEG
LN-FAT(3)	SOCATA Rallye 180T Galérien	2972	
LN-FAU(3)	Reims/Cessna F172N (W/o 24.8.85)	F17201644	
LN-FAV(6)	BAe. Jetstream Series 3102	606	OY-CLB SE-KHA G-BKKY (SE-IZA) G-BKKY G-31-46
LN-FAW(3)	Reims/Cessna F172N	F17201703	
LN-FAX	Cessna U206G Stationair 6 (W/o 21.3.82, wreck stored)	U20604100	(N756HH)
LN-FAZ(2)	BAe. Jetstream Series 3112	749	C-GJPU (N839JS) G-31-749
LN-FKE(2)	Piper PA-31 Turbo Navajo	31-293	SE-FFE (SE-INR) LN-NPL SE-FFE
LN-FKL	SOCATA MS.893A Rallye Commodore 180	11471	SE-FNL OY-DJT
LN-FLY	Denney Kitfox III (Temp 21.8.92, cr 20.5.93)	1066	
LN-FMU	SAAB S.91B Safir (Painted as RNoAF "FM-U")	91267	RNoAF058 Fv.50058
LN-FOB	Piper PA-28-151 Cherokee Warrior	28-7415344	SE-GBN
LN-FOC	Cessna 210H Centurion	21059007	SE-FBY N6107F
LN-FOF(3)	Piper PA-28-180 Cherokee Challenger	28-7305404	SE-GDY
LN-FOK(3)	Piper PA-28-180 Cherokee B	28-1061	
LN-FOP(2)	Piper PA-28-140 Cherokee	28-22922	SE-EYP
LN-FSA	Piper PA 28-181 Cherokee Archer II	28-7890549	OY-BRH
LN-FSB	Piper PA-28-140 Cherokee	28-23870	OY-DNM (LN-VYR)
LN-FWA	Gulfstream Commander 690C	11681	(LN-FAN) SE-IUV N110WE ZS-KZO N5933K
LN-FWB	Gulfstream Commander 690C	11613	SE-GSS D-IBOB (N5865K)
LN-HAB(3)	Cessna 150F	15063502	N11B N6902F
LN-HAD	Piper J-4A-65 Cub Coupé (Wfu)	4-568	
LN-HAE(5)	Cessna 310R	310R0525	TF-EUT TF-ELT OY-BJN N87353
LN-HAG(6)	Pottier P.180S	148	
LN-HAH(3)	Cessna 210L Centurion	21060751	
LN-HAI (5)	Cessna U206F Stationair (Cr 21.7.04, stored)	U20603058	N4696Q
LN HAJ(2)	Light Aero Avid Magnum	43	
LN-HAK(3)	Piper PA-28-140 Cherokee (CoA exp 31.5.91, to Museum, Bodo)	28-20733	SE-EOF
LN-HAM(4)	Cessna U206F Stationair	U20602689	N33244
LN-HAN(3)	Piper PA-28-140 Cherokee	28-20353	SE-EML
LN-HAR(6)	Piper PA-18-150 Super Cub	18-1566	(LN-HHN) D-ELTB ALAT 51-15566
LN-HAS(3)	Cessna 150D (Cr 2.11.03)	15060568	LN-BIE N4568U
LN-HAU(3)	Piper PA-18A-150 Super Cub (No CoA issued, stored)	18-6642	SE-CLE N10F
LN-HAW(3)	Cessna 150F	15062678	N11B N8578G
LN-HAX	Piper J-3C-65 Cub (CoA exp 30.6.93, stored) (Officially quoted as Dätwyler c/n 12500)	12874	D-EBIW HB-ONO 44-80578
LN-HFK	SOCATA TB-10 Tobago (Cr 4.9.91, to spares)	78	SE-GFK
LN-HHA(4)	Piper PA-18-150 Super Cub (No CoA issued, stored)	18-1570	(LN-HHA(2)) D-EMTJ ALAT 51-15570
LN-HHH	Piper PA-28-140 Cherokee	28-20950	N11C
LN-HHI (3)	Piper PA-18S-135 Super Cub Floatplane	18-2094	(LN-HHE) D-ELTG ALAT 52-2494
LN-HHK(2)	Piper PA-28-180 Cherokee C (Cr 25.8.91)	28-3170	SE-EYK
LN-HHO(2)	Piper PA-18-150 Super Cub (CoA exp 30.6.81, being restored)	18-1450	D-ELTN ALAT 51-15450
LN-HHR	Piper PA-28-140 Cherokee	28-21085	N11C
LN-HHS(2)	SAAB S.91B-2 Safir (Cr 2.5.99, rebuilding)	91210	Fv50010
LN-HIH	Cessna 182M Skylane	18259653	SE-LDF (SE-LEM) OY-AGR N71528
LN-HOA(2)	Reims/Cessna F182Q Skylane (Diesel)	F18200154	
LN-HOE	Cessna U206G Stationair 6 Floatplane (CoA exp 31.5.03, stored)	U20605143	(N4885U)
LN-HOF	Reims/Cessna F172N	F17201896	
LN-HOG(2)	Cessna 172N	17272740	N6354D
LN-HOK	Rockwell Commander 114	14111	N4781W
LN-HON	Cessna U206G Stationair 6 Floatplane	U20605475	(N6397U)
LN-HOO	Cessna TU206G Turbo Stationair 6 Floatplane	U20605490	(N6493U)
LN-HOQ	Reims/Cessna F172P (Cr 13.2.88)	F17202035	
LN-HOR(2)	Piper PA-28-140 Cherokee E	28-7225264	SE-FYX
LN-HOV(2)	Rand-Robinson KR-2	10057	
LN-HOX	Reims/Cessna F172P	F17202029	
LN-HOY	Reims/Cessna F172N	F17201928	
LN-HOZ	Cessna U206G Stationair 6 Floatplane (Dbr 5.10.03, wreck stored)	U20604279	SE-GYK N756QU
LN-HPB	Rutan Long-Ez (Damaged 19.7.04)	190	
LN-HPC	Grumman-American AA-5A Cheetah	AA5A-0841	G-BGCN
LN-HPJ(2)	Cessna TP206C Turbo-System Super Skylane (CoA exp 28.2.90, stored)	P206-0502	SE-FED N8702Z
LN-HPT	Cessna 310R	310R0083	OY-BIW (SE-GKA)
LN- IGA	K & S Jungster 1 (CoA exp 31.5.98, stored)	J1-73012R	(LN-HOT(2))
LN- IGB	Condor Yak-52	888814	UR-BEO UR-BTN DOSAAF-86
LN- IKA(2)	Cessna TU206G Turbo Stationair 6	U20606251	(N6356Z)
LN- IKD(2)	Cessna 150F	15062147	(SE-ESP) N8847S
LN- IKG(2)	Cessna 172C	49042	OY-AFI N1342Y
LN- IKJ(3)	Piper J-3C-65 Cub (L-4J) (CoA not issued, under restoration)	12081	(SE-ASO) LN-IKJ(1) SE-ASO 44-79785

LN- IKO	Cessna 180B	50435	SE-CLS N5135E
LN- IKP	Piper PA-22-108 Colt (CoA expired 30.9.83, stored)	22-9128	(LN-IKI) LN-IKP SE-CZH
LN- IKQ	Reims FR172F Rocket	FR17200101	(G-AWYC)
LN- IKS	Cessna 172C (W/o 22.1.94)	17249255	N1555Y
LN- IKX	Cessna F150J	F150-0420	
LN- IKY	Cessna 172P	17274139	N5473K
LN- ILS	DHC-8 Series 103 (CoA exp 31.8.03, stored)	396	(LN-WIL)
LN-JAN	Sequoia F.8L Falco (W/o 9.5.02)	626	
LN-JBL	Cessna 172G	17254437	N4362L
LN-JET	de Havilland DH.100 Vampire Mk.6 (Painted as RNoAF "ZK-P")(CoA exp31.5.04)	655	LN-17 (LN-JET) J-1146
LN-JYS	Van's RV-4	1445	
LN-KAC	Piper PA-22-150 Tri-Pacer (Converted to PA-20 Pacer 1.97)	22-5368	SE-CDC N7658D
LN-KAD(4)	Piper PA-18-150 Super Cub	18-7809141	(OY-CGS(3)) SE-IAO
LN-KAE(3)	SOCATA TB-10 Tobago	27	F-ODKL
LN-KAF(4)	Piper PA-28-181 Cherokee Archer II	28-7690341	(LN-AED) OY-CTW N6101J
LN-KAH(3)	Auster J/1 Autocrat (CoA exp 30.9.02, stored)	2044	SE-ARM
LN-KAI (3)	Piper PA-23-250 Aztec E (CoA exp 30.4.03, stored)	27-7304954	SE-KHV OY-RPW G-BARU N14367
LN-KAJ(2)	Grumman-American AA-5 Traveler (Cr 29.9.03)	AA5-0372	(OY-GAA) (N5472L)
LN-KAK(2)	Piper J-3C-65 Cub (Float or wheel u/c)	LFS-1/56	SE-CBR
LN-KAL(3)	Aero Designs Pulsar	179	
LN-KAM(2)	Cessna F150G	F150-0111	
LN-KAN(2)	Cessna P206A Super Skylane (W/o 4.7.94)	P206-0270	N4670F
LN-KAO(2)	Cessna A185E Skywagon	185-1187	N4733Q
LN-KAP(5)	Mudry CAP.10B	130	F-GGBB Fr.AF
LN-KAQ	Champion 7ECA Citabria	540	N5107T
LN-KAT(4)	Cessna 208B Grand Caravan	208B0970	N12295 N5268E
LN-KCA	Cessna A185F Skywagon Floatplane	185-1302	N335OL
LN-KCC	Cessna 177 Cardinal (Cr 5.11.80)	17700995	N29618
LN-KCD	Cessna F150H	F150-0312	
LN-KCE	Cessna F150H	F150-0333	
LN-KCF	Cessna 180H (Cr 4.5.03)	18051952	N3452Y
LN-KCH	Piper PA-18-150 Super Cub	18-8579	(SE- . . .) N4995P
LN-KCJ	Cessna 140 (Quoted officially as c/n 11721)	8529	LN-TSV SE-AZZ LN-NAK
LN-KCL	Piper PA-28-140 Cherokee	28-23576	N11C N3527K
LN-KCM(2)	Piper PA-18A-150 Super Cub	18-5878	D-EGCI N7582D
LN-KCN	Auster 6A Tugmaster (CoA exp 31.5.04)	3743	SE-ELM VF514
LN-KCO	Piper PA-18 Super Cub 95	18-2051	(LN-BFR) R-42 52-2451
LN-KCU	Piper PA-18 Super Cub 95	18-2053	R-68 52-2453
LN-KCX	Piper PA-18 Super Cub 95	18-2062	R-76 52-2462
LN-KCY(3)	Maule M-7-235 Super Rocket	4014C	OY-CRZ HR-AKY N5657H

LN-KFA to -KFE Reserved for replicas and rebuilds

LN-KIS	Tri-R KIS TR-1	32	
LN-KJK	Cessna 208B Grand Caravan	208B0554	N1267A
LN-KKB(2)	Boeing 737 (Reservation 6.04)	unkn	
LN-KKC(2)	Boeing 737 (Reservation 6.04)	unkn	
LN-KKF	Boeing 737-3K2	24326	N730BC PH-HVM
LN-KKG	Boeing 737-3K2	24327	PH-HVN
LN-KKH	Boeing 737-3K2	24328	PH-HVT
LN-KKI	Boeing 737-3K2	24329	PH-HVV
LN-KKJ(2)	Boeing 737-36N	28564	N564SR PP-VQP PT-TEP N1786B
LN-KKK	Piper PA-34-220T Seneca V	3449010	SE-KEP N92865
LN-KKL	Boeing 737-36N	28671	N671SR PP-VPS
LN-KKM(2)	Boeing 737-3Y0	24676	HA-LES TC-SUN (PT-TEO)
LN-KKN	Boeing 737-3Y0	24910	HA-LET TC-SUR
LN-KKO	Boeing 737-3Y0	24909	HA-LED
LN-KKP	Boeing 737-3M8	25040	OO-SBX TC-BIR VR-CRC PH-YAA OO-LTK
LN-KKQ	Boeing 737-36Q	28658	EC-GMY
LN-KKR	Boeing 737-3YO	24256	OM-AAA F-GNFU EC-GFU EC-204 EC-FVJ EC-542 G-MONM
LN-KKS	Boeing 737-33A	24094	ZK-PLU F-OFGX
LN-KKT	Boeing 737 (Reservation 6.04)	unkn	
LN-KKU	Boeing 737 (Reservation 6.04)	unkn	
LN-KKV	Boeing 737 (Reservation 6.04)	unkn	
LN-KLA(3)	Piper J-3C-65 Cub (L-4J) (Cr 14.8.01, under repair)	13163	LN-MAU(1) 45-4423
LN-KLB(2)	Grumman-American AA-5B Tiger	AA5B-0729	
LN-KLC	Grumman-American AA-5A Cheetah	AA5A-0549	F-GBDK
LN-KLD(2)	SOCATA TB-9 Tampico (Converted to TB-10 Tobago, 4.93)	225	
LN-KLF(2)	Grumman-American AA-5A Cheetah	AA5A-0610	
LN-KLG(2)	Grumman-American AA-5A Cheetah	AA5A-0014	SE-GRF OY-GAH
LN-KLH(2)	Grumman-American AA-5A Cheetah	AA5A-0844	
LN-KLI (2)	Grumman-American AA-5B Tiger	AA5B-1131	
LNOKLK(3)	Piper PA-34-200T Seneca II (Reservation 3.05)	34-7570028	SE-GIC LN-KLK (LN-KLS) SE-GIC
LN-KLM	SOCATA TB-9 Tampico	303	
LN-KLP(3)	SOCATA TB-10 Tobago	390	
LN-KLQ(2)	Mooney M.20J Model 201	24-1597	OY-CGK
LN-KLW	Piel CP.301 Emeraude	1-79A	
LN-LAB(2)	Van's RV-6	22930	
LN-LAG(2)	Neico Lancair 320	1	
LN-LFB	Mooney M.20C Ranger (CoA exp 28.2.02, stored)	690028	N9157V
LN-LFG	SOCATA MS.893E Rallye 180GT Gaillard	3242	SE-GFD
LN-LFI	Piper PA-24-250 Comanche (W/o 18.10.92)	24-2898	SE-EPA N7688P
LN-LFJ	Pottier P.180S	162	
LN-LFK	SAAB S.91B-2 Safir	91341	RNoAF:57341 341/'UA-V'
LN-LFM	SOCATA MS.880B Rallye-Club	1522	OY-DJM
LN-LGB	Cessna 150G	15066260	N8360J
LN-LGC	Cessna 172B	17247960	SE-CXU N7460X
LN-LGF	Reims/Cessna F172P (W/o 29.6.88)	F17202050	(EI-BIN) (EI-BIC)
LN-LGG(2)	Reims/Cessna F172N	F17201929	SE-IFG
LN-LJB	Cessna 210G Centurion	21058936	SE-FBC N5936F
LN-LJD	Piper PA-18-150 Super Cub	18-8541	SE-GCA Fv51234 N10F
LN-LJF	Cessna F172H	F172-0572	(G-AXBI)
LN-LJJ	Piper PA-18 Super Cub 95	18-3088	OL-L14 L-14 53-4688
LN-LJK	Piper PA-18 Super Cub 95 (CoA exp 31.7.88, stored)	18-3103	OL-L29 L-29 53-4703
LN-LJM	Piper PA-18 Super Cub 95	18-3122	OL-L48 L-48 53-4722
LN-LJT	Cessna 180H Skywagon (W/o 8.9.86)	18052088	N91450
LN-LMB(2)	Piper PA-28-140 Cherokee	28-24421	
LN-LME(2)	Piper PA-28-140 Cherokee	28-24441	
LN-LMG(3)	Cessna A185F Skywagon	18503278	SE-GZN
LN-LMI (3)	C.L.Larsen Special II (Cr. 6.8.82, wfu)	02	LN-11
LN-LMJ	Cessna U206C Super Skywagon Floatplane	U206-1163	N29205
LN-LMK(5)	Piper PA-34-200T Seneca II (Cr 22.9.98, stored)	34-7870278	OY-AUC 5Y-BCW N31940
LN-LMO(4)	Grumman-American AA-5 Traveler	AA5-0262	OY-AYU
LN-LMP(4)	Reims/Cessna FRA150L Aerobat (Cr 9.9.03)	FRA1500131	SE-GFY LN-BWJ
LN-LMQ(4)	Cessna U206E Stationair	U20601608	SE-KLK LN-LMQ(2) N9408G
LN-LMR(3)	Piper PA-28R-180 Cherokee Arrow	28R-30976	
LN-LMX(2)	Aeritalia/Partenavia AP.68TP Spartacus	8006	I-RA1Z
LN-LMY(2)	SAAB S.91B-2 Safir (CoA exp 30.9.84)	91281	RNoAF:071 Fv50071
LN-LMZ(2)	Dornier Do.28A-1 (Stored, Sola Museum)	3003	D-IHOL
LN-LTH	Cessna 182E	18254027	(OY-EHL) (LN-EHL) N3027Y
LN-LTP	Van's RV-4	1403	
LN-LYR	Dornier 228-202K	8166	D-CTCA D-CBDU TC-FBP D-CBCE D-CBDW
LN-MAB(4)	Rutan Long-Ez	2072	
LN-MAE(4)	Beagle A.61 Terrier (CoA exp 31.1.89, stored)	3740	(LN-MAU) (LN-BNH) SE-ELL VF543

LN-MAJ	Cessna 310R	310R0627	(N98871)
LN-MAQ	Cessna U206G Stationair II (Floatplane) (CoA exp 31.5.04, stored)	U20603733	SE-GZY (N9933N)
LN-MAR(3)	SkyStar Denney Kitfox IV	1636	
LN-MAT(3)	Piper PA-34-200T Seneca II	34-7670341	OY-BLW
LN-MAV	Piper J-3C-65 Cub (L-4J) (CoA exp 31.12.02, on rebuild)	13157	45-4417
LN-MAX(2)	de Havilland DH.82A Tiger Moth (Constructed from the original frame of c/n 84167 but uses paperwork of c/n 85738 LN-BDO, G-ANSE, DE840)	84167	(G-ASPV) T7794
LN-MAZ	SAAB S.91D Safir	91433	G-BCFS PH-RLV
LN-MOB(5)	Beech 200 Super King Air	BB-584	(N490WP) N400WP N6679H
LN-MOC(3)	Beech B200 Super King Air	BB-1449	N200KA
LN-MOD(6)	Beech B200 Super King Air	BB-1459	N8163R
LN-MOE(3)	Beech B200 Super King Air	BB-1460	N8164G
LN-MOF(4)	Beech B200 Super King Air	BB-1461	N8261E
LN-MOG(3)	Beech B200 Super King Air	BB-1465	N8214T
LN-MOH(2)	Beech B200 Super King Air	BB-1466	N8216Z
LN-MOI (2)	Beech B200 Super King Air	BB-1470	N8225Z
LN-MOJ(4)	Beech B200 Super King Air	BB-1334	TC-SKO N5545B
LN-MOK	Cessna 182	33768	(LN-ATS) (LN-IKJ) OY-BZG D-EBRX OE-DKS(1) N5768B
LN-MOL(2)	Dornier 228-202K	8156	TF-ELA TC-FBN D-CORN(2)
LN-MOM	Piper PA-28-180 Cherokee C	28-3981	SE-EZR
LN-MON(2)	Beech B200 Super King Air	BB-1537	ZS-ARL N3237M
LN-MOO(2)	Beech B200 Super King Air	BB-1692	N29AH N772TP
LN-MOT(3)	Beech B200 Super King Air	BB-1590	D-IHUT
LN-MTC(2)	Reims/Cessna F172M	F17201261	
LN-MTD(4)	Cessna 177RG Cardinal RG (Rebuilt using front section of c/n 177RG0846 ex N7549V)	177RG0895	N7627V
LN-MTE(2)	Cessna 182N Skylane	18260245	SE-FXU OH-CDR N92525
LN-MTF(2)	Cessna R182 Skylane RG	R18200551	N1763R
LN-MTG(2)	Cessna 172P (W/o 27.8.93)	17274775	N53533
LN-MTH(2)	Cessna 172N	17272201	N8443E (OY-CYK) N8443E
LN-MTJ	Piper PA-28-161 Warrior II	28-8216021	N8330G
LN-MTM(2)	Cessna 172P	17274333	N51639
LN-MTN	Piper PA-28-140 Cherokee D	28-7125348	
LN-MTO	Cessna 140 (CoA exp 31.3.78, under restoration)	8864	LN-BNT N89815
LN-MTP(2)	Cessna 172P	17275197	N55522
LN-MTQ	Cessna A185E Skywagon (Cr 26.6.84)	18501839	N1625M
LN-MTS(3)	Cessna 182Q Skylane	18265900	N759DA
LN-MTT(2)	Cessna 172M	17263835	N20781
LN-MTU(4)	Cessna 172P	17275510	N64050
LN-MTW	Cessna 182N Skylane	18260459	N8919G
LN-MTX	Cessna 172P	17274671	N53043
LN-NAB(4)	Piper PA-31 Navajo C	31-8012029	OY-BYJ PH-URI N1002W PH-URI N3552V
LN-NAE(2)	Cessna 177RG Cardinal RG	177RG1009	N34611
LN-NAG(2)	Piper PA-28-161 Cherokee Warrior II	28-7816376	
LN-NAH(2)	Piper PA-28-181 Cherokee Archer II	28-7690194	
LN-NAK(3)	Cessna F172H (Damaged 29.10.85, stored)	F172-0604	(LN-RTJ)
LN-NAL(2)	Piper PA-28-151 Cherokee Warrior	28-7615377	
LN-NAM(2)	Piper PA-28-181 Cherokee Archer II (W/o 27.8.02)	28-7690386	
LN-NAO(3)	Piper PA-28-161 Cherokee Warrior II (Destroyed 29.12.02, to spares for -NPR, -PAL)	28-7716166	
LN-NAQ	Piper PA-28-181 Cherokee Archer II	28-7790302	
LN-NAR(2)	Piper PA-28-161 Cherokee Warrior II	28-7716054	
LN-NAS(2)	Piper PA-28-161 Cherokee Warrior II	28-7716055	
LN-NAU	Piper J-3C-65 Cub (L-4H) (CoA exp 31.7.88. Exhibited in Sola Museum)	11673	43-30482
LN-NAV(2)	Piper PA-18-90 Super Cub	18-1342	D-EAEQ ALAT 51-15342
LN-NAY	Piper PA-28-181 Cherokee Archer II	28-7790488	
LN-NAZ	Piper PA-28-161 Cherokee Warrior II	28-7816220	
LN-NEW	Piper PA-28-181 Archer III	2843454	SE-ILU N5332G N9518N
LN-NEX	Diamond DA 40D Star	D4.028	
LN-NEZ	Diamond DA 40D Star	D4.065	OE-VPW
LN-NFA(2)	Cessna 182Q Skylane (Rebuilt 1992 using fuselage from Cessna 182P D-EDVF c/n 18264428)	18266169	D-EAGW N759QF
LN-NFB(2)	Reims/Cessna F172P	F17202111	D-EGWJ

LN-NFC(2)	Cessna U206G Stationair 6 (Regd 11.96 but CoA never issued)	U20606489	D-EGOP(3) N27173 (N9437Z)
LN-NFD	Cessna A185F Skywagon Floatplane	18504152	N61342
LN-NFF	Cessna 177RG Cardinal RG	177RG1309	N8707Z
LN-NFG	Cessna 172P	17274277	N51194
LN-NFH	Piper PA-28-140 Cherokee E (CoA exp 30.6.95, stored)	28-7225299	SE-GAG
LN-NFI	Reims/Cessna F152	F15201766	D-EITF
LN-NFJ (2)	Reims/Cessna F172M	F17201483	D-EOXY (G-BDZE)
LN-NFK(3)	SOCATA MS.Rallye 235E	12798	SE-GTC
LN-NFL	Reims/Cessna F172L (Cr 29.9.98, stored)	F17200807	D-EHMS PH-JBA
LN-NFN(3)	Piper PA-23-235 Apache (CoA never issued, stored)	27-533	TF-ELL N4948P
LN-NFP(2)	Cessna 177RG Cardinal RG	177RG1336	N53070
LN-NFS	Grumman-American AA-5B Tiger	AA5B-1208	(N5481V) D-EGFC
LN-NFU	Piper PA-38-112 Tomahawk	38-79A0938	D-ELMC N9681N
LN-NFW	Reims/Cessna F172N Skyhawk II	F17201683	SE-FOT LN-FAV
LN-NFX	Cessna 172P	17274239	N50950
LN-NFY(2)	Piper PA-38-112 Tomahawk	38-79A0775	N2598L
LN-NOA(2)	Beech 200 Super King Air	BB-829	N829AJ SE-KVL C9-SWE N225JL N225HP
LN-NOK	Piper PA-18-150 Super Cub	1809054	
LN-NPJ	Auster Mk.5 (CoA exp 31.5.87, stored)	1410	SE-CDL TJ340
LN-NPK	Cessna 172B	17248518	SE-CTK N8018X
LN-NPN(2)	Piper PA-28-180 Cherokee C (W/o 13.11.78)	28-3247	SE-EYT
LN-NPO(2)	Piper PA-28-181 Archer II	28-8090012	SE-ICX
LN-NPQ(2)	Piper PA-28-181 Cherokee Archer II	28-7890340	
LN-NPR(3)	Piper PA-28R-201 Arrow III (Destroyed 29.12.02, now rebuilt)	28R-7837247	
LN-NPS(2)	Piper PA-28-161 Cherokee Warrior II	28-7816449	
LN-NPT	Piper PA-28-140 Cherokee	28-22832	
LN-NPV	Piper PA-28-140 Cherokee	28-22902	
LN-NPW	Piper PA-28-140 Cherokee	28-22917	
LN-NPX(3)	Cessna 310P	310P0229	(OY-AKB) (LN-TUV) N5729M
LN-NPZ	Piper PA-31 Navajo C	31-7512047	SE-GIY
LN-NTH	Piper PA-25-235 Pawnee C	25-4505	SE-FCX OH-PIS SE-FCX
LN-NVK	Cessna 152	15281089	OY-CTY (N48988)
LN-OAA(2)	SNCASE SE.3130 Alouette II (Res. 6.02) (Rebuild from Swedish Navy spares by KJJohansen, main frame used previously on SE-HRA, ex SE-HDD)	KJJ.001	
LN-OAB(3)	Robinson R-44 Astro	0273	OH-HES LN-OAB(2) (SE-JDH)
LN-OAC	Aérospatiale AS.350B2 Ecureuil	2511	N350R D-HMIR N6042S
LN-OAD(2)	Robinson R-22B2 Beta	2755	
LN-OAE(2)	Robinson R-44 Astro	0397	
LN-OAF(3)	Rotorway Exec 162F (Cr 1.9.03, rebuilding?)	6208	
LN-OAG(3)	Robinson R-22 Beta	2912	
LN-OAI (2)	Robinson R-44 Clipper	0608	
LN-OAJ	Robinson R-22 Beta	2051	N62900
LN-OAK(3)	Aérospatiale AS.350B3 Ecureuil	3212	
LN-OAM(2)	Robinson R-44 Astro	0452	
LN-OAN(2)	Aérospatiale AS.350B3 Ecureuil	3199	
LN-OAP(2)	Schweizer 269D	0057	N297TH
LN-OAR(2)	Bell 206BJet Ranger III (Temp wfu 29.5.04, stored)	3616	RP-C1156 N2271Z
LN-OAS(2)	Bell 206BJet Ranger III	2369	JA9200 C-GERX
LN-OAU(3)	Aérospatiale AS.350BA Ecureuil	1533	SE-HRO D-HHSB
LN-OAW(2)	Aérospatiale AS.332L Super Puma	2053	VH-LHD LN-OAW(2) OY-HMH LN-OME(1)
LN-OAX	Aérospatiale AS.355F1 Ecureuil 2	5096	SE-JDK (LN-OAU) N8794Y PT-HTW N813DB N578ST
LN-OAY	Robinson R-22B2 Beta	3025	
LN-OAZ	Robinson R-44 Clipper	0700	
LN-OBA(2)	Aérospatiale AS.332L1 Super Puma	2384	
LN-OBB(2)	Aérospatiale AS.350B3 Ecureuil	3493	SE-JLC F-WWXT
LN-OBC	Robinson R-22 Beta	1340	
LN-OBE(2)	Robinson R-44 Astro (Damaged 13.6.04)	0078	
LN-OBG(2)	Aérospatiale AS.355P1 Ecureuil 2 (CoA exp 30.6.04)	5681	F-WQDF

LN-OBI (2)	Robinson R-22B2 Beta	3311	
LN-OBL	Hughes 269C (Cr 13.7.90, stored Sweden)	70-0024	(SE-HTY) N9615F
LN-OBM	Robinson R-44 Astro	0197	
LN-OBO(3)	Robinson R-44 Raven II	10063	
LN-OBP(2)	Aérospatiale AS.350B3 Ecureuil	3575	F-WQDS
LN-OBR(2)	Eurocopter EC.120BColibri	1064	
LN-OBS	Bell 206L-3 Long Ranger III	51235	(LN-OPP) C-FBBW
LN-OBT(2)	Aérospatiale AS.350B Ecureuil	1363	F-GCQQ
LN-OBU(2)	Hughes 369E (W/o 14.12.00)	0458E	SE-JAD
LN-OBV(2)	MBB Bö.105C	S-680	D-HMUC (D-HDUV)
LN-OBW(2)	Aérospatiale AS.355N Ecureuil 2	5540	SE-JMA N355EL JA6712
LN-OBX(2)	Aérospatiale AS.332CSuper Puma	2001	I-EMEB F-WQDA C-GOOH F-WZJK
LN-OBY(2)	Bell 47G-4A (Reservation 4.03)	7746	D-HITT N7914J
LN-OBZ(2)	Robinson R-44 Raven II	10150	
LN-OCA(2)	Robinson R-44 Raven	1309	
LN-OCB	Aérospatiale AS.350B Ecureuil (W/o 28.7.88)	1786	D-HAFP
LN-OCE	Aérospatiale SA.315B Lama	2179	5V-MAF F-WKQI
LN-OCG(2)	Aérospatiale AS.350B3 Ecureuil	3455	SE-JFI
LN-OCH(2)	Rotorway Exec 162F (Cr 18.2.04, stored)	6328	N162TT
LN-OCJ(2)	Robinson R-44 Astro	0103	D-HULM(2)
LN-OCK(2)	SNCASE SE.3130 Alouette II (HKP-2)	1268	SE-HRA SwNavy 02038 SwNavy 02108
LN-OCL(2)	Aérospatiale AS.332L Super Puma	2077	G-PUMD F-WXFD
LN-OCM(2)	Aérospatiale AS.332L Super Puma	2091	G-PUME
LN-OCN(2)	Hughes 369E	0181E	SE-HSN OY-HEW
LN-OCO(2)	Aérospatiale AS.365N2 Dauphin 2	6420	OY-HLL JA6677 (OY-HLL) (SE-JGU) F-WYMR
LN-OCP(2)	Eurocopter EC.135P1	0279	G-CCLK
LN-OCQ(3)	Schweizer 269C	S-1773	G-CBYA OY-HSM N69A
LN-OCS	Emstrom 280C Shark (Reservation 4.04 but wfu)	1017	G-ECHO G-LONS G-BDIB
LN-OCT(2)	Robinson R-44 Raven II	10409	
LN-OCU(2)	Robinson R-22B2 Beta	3701	
LN-OCV(2)	Robinson R4-44	0024	G-SMJH G-NTEE
LN-OCW	Aérospatiale AS.350B-3 Ecureuil (Res 2.05)	3042	
LN-OCX(2)	Robinson R-44 Raven II	10719	
LN-OCY(2)	Robinson R-44 Raven II	10728	
LN-ODB	Aérospatiale AS.365N2 Dauphin 2	6358	G-NTWO
LN-ODC	Schweizer 269C-1	0071	N27HT (HL . . . .) N69A
LN-ODD(2)	Aérospatiale SA.315B Lama	2578	SE-HRX (LN-O . .) SE-HRX F-GEHI LN-OSQ
LN-ODE	Robinson R-22M Mariner	2198M	SE-JGN N2337X
LN-ODF	Eurocopter EC.120BColibri	1119	F-WQDP
LN-ODG	Schweizer 269C	S-1316	OH-HCF SE-HTA N41S
LN-ODH(2)	Aérospatiale AS.350B2 Ecureuil	2462	F-GRUE F-GHUP
LN-ODI	Hughes 269C	127-0654	SE-HHX
LN-ODK	Aérospatiale AS.350B3 Ecureuil	3569	F-WQDA
LN-ODN	Eurocopter EC.120B Colibri	1299	D-HAEC(2)
LN-ODQ	Aérospatiale AS.350B Ecureuil (Reservn .05)	unkn	
LN-ODR	Aérospatiale AS.350B2 Ecureuil	2364	SE-JFL JA9891
LN-ODS	Aérospatiale AS.350B3 Ecureuil	3601	F-WQDR
LN-ODT	Bell 206B-3 Jet Ranger III (Re 4.05)	unkn	
LN-OEF	Robinson R-44 Astro (CoA exp 31.8.04)	0239	
LN-OEN	Eurocopter EC.120BColibri	1146	(LN-ONE)
LN-OEO	Aérospatiale AS.365 Dauphin (Reservn .05)	unkn	
LN-OEP	Aérospatiale AS.365 Dauphin (Reservn .05)	unkn	
LN-OEQ	Aérospatiale AS.350B3 Ecureuil (Reservn .05)	unkn	
LN-OER	Aérospatiale AS.350B3 Ecureuil (Reservn .05)	unkn	
LN-OGA	Robinson R-44 Astro (Cr 30.8.03)	0057	TC-HIT G-INNS
LN-OGB	Robinson R-44 Astro	0574	SE-JDV
LN-OGC	Robinson R-44 Clipper	0819	G-TURV
LN-OGD	Robinson R-44 Raven	0725	OH-HTH FLARF 02748 N71877
LN-OGE	Hughes 369D	1200892D	N2LY (D-H . . .) SE-JCH LN-OQV N48AW
LN-OGG	Aérospatiale AS.350B1 Ecureuil	2021	SE-JLL OE-XRS F-GEOD
LN-OGH	Robinson R-44 Clipper	1135	G-KAZZ
LN-OGI	Robinson R-44 Astro	0457	G-LNTI G-TPTS
LN-OGJ	Robinson R-44 Raven II	10657	
LN-OGL	Aérospatiale AS.350B3 Ecureuil	3792	
LN-OGR	Robinson R-44 Clipper	0616	OY-HSV
LN-OHA	Aérospatiale AS.332L2 Super Puma	2396	F-WYMS
LN-OHC	Aérospatiale AS.332L2 Super Puma	2393	F-W . . .
LN-OHD	Aérospatiale AS.332L2 Super Puma	2395	F-WQDN
LN-OHE	Aérospatiale AS.332L2 Super Puma	2474	
LN-OHG	Aérospatiale AS.332L2 Super Puma	2493	
LN-OHH	Aérospatiale AS.332L2 Super Puma	2366	VN-8609
LN-OHI	Aérospatiale AS.332L2 Super Puma	2582	F-WW . .
LN-OHJ	Aérospatiale AS.332L2 Super Puma	2594	
LN-OHK	Aérospatiale AS.332L2 Super Puma	2613	
LN-OHL	Aérospatiale AS.332L2 Super Puma	2617	
LN-OKV	SNCASE SE.3130 Alouette II (HKP-2) (Reservation 3.05. Rebuild with c/n 01)	1128	(LN-OCR) SE-HRC SwNavy 02039 SwNavy 02109 N7808B YV-E-FPJ F-WIEK
LN-OLA(2)	Agusta A.109E Power	11117	
LN-OLB(2)	Aérospatiale AS.332L Super Puma	2082	OY-HMJ LN-OLB F-WKQA
LN-OLC(2)	Aérospatiale AS.332L Super Puma	2083	(LN-ONE) JA6782 LN-OLC F-WKQB
LN-OLD(2)	Aérospatiale AS.332L Super Puma	2103	OY-HMI LN-OLD
LN-OLE(2)	Aérospatiale AS.365N2 Dauphin 2	6405	VT-CKR F-WQDZ F-WQDK F-WQDG JA6671
LN-OLG(2)	Aérospatiale AS.350B2 Ecureuil	2198	
LN-OLH	Agusta A.109E Power	11135	
LN-OLI	Agusta A.109E Power	11204	
LN-OLJ	Aérospatiale AS.365N2 Dauphin 2	6404	D-HNIK N942H N653CN N365JD
LN-OLK	Bell 212 (Crashed 18.12.03)	30722	C-GOKT YV-324C C-GOKT
LN-OLL(4)	Aérospatiale AS.365N2 Dauphin 2	6424	G-BTUX
LN-OLT (2)	Aérospatiale SA.365N Dauphin 2	6140	G-BLUP
LN-OMA(2)	Aérospatiale AS.350B3 Ecureuil (Reserved as OY-HGM .04)	3677	
LN-OMB(2)	Aérospatiale AS.350B2 Ecureuil	2514	F-WYMO
LN-OMF(5)	Aerospatiale AS.332L Super Puma	2067	G-PUMK LN-OMF G-PUMK LN-OMF F-WXFP
LN-OMH(2)	Aérospatiale AS.332L Super Puma	2113	HZ-RH4 LN-OMH
LN-OMI (5)	Aérospatiale AS.332L Super Puma	2123	G-BLZJ LN-OMI G-PUMJ LN-OMI G-BLZJ LN-OMI G-BLZJ LN-OMI F-W . . .
LN-OMJ	Aérospatiale AS.365N2 Dauphin 2	6301	F-WQEZ F-WIPI G-BVME F-WKAY F-WYML
LN-OMM	Bell 214ST	28199	N3216U
LN-OMN(2)	Aérospatiale AS.365N2 Dauphin 2	6423	F-GHXG (LN-OMN) F-GHXG F-WYMS
LN-OMP(2)	Hughes 369E (W/o 21.6.01)	0177E	SE-HRB
LN-OMX(2)	Aérospatiale AS.332L-1 Super Puma	2351	G-BTNZ F-WYMA G-BTNZ
LN-OND	Aérospatiale AS.332L Super Puma	2157	G-BLXS
LN-ONE(3)	Aérospatiale AS.332L1 Super Puma	9002	F-WQEF F-WQDD
LN-ONH	Aérospatiale AS.332L2 Super Puma	2488	
LN-ONI	Aérospatiale AS.332L2 Super Puma	2500	
LN-ONN(2)	Sikorsky S-92A	920011	N7107S

LN-ONO(2)	Sikorsky S-92A	920012	(LN-ONN) N7108Z
LN-ONZ	Sikorsky S-76C+	760456	
LN-OOA	Eurocopter EC.135P1	0125	D-HECF
LN-OOB	Eurocopter EC.135P2	0165	D-H . . .
LN-OOC	Eurocopter EC.135P2	0350	
LN-OOD	Eurocopter EC.135P2	0356	
LN-OOE	Eurocopter EC.135P2	0357	
LN-OOF	Eurocopter EC.135P2	0390	
LN-OPA(2)	Aérospatiale AS.350B3 Ecureuil	3589	
LN-OPB	Aérospatiale AS.350B1 Ecureuil	1940	
LN-OPD	Aérospatiale SA.365N Dauphin 2	6067	Fr.Navy D-HJMJ F-GDPE
LN-OPE	Aérospatiale AS.350B1 Ecureuil	2183	
LN-OPF(2)	Aérospatiale AS.350B3 Ecureuil	3679	
LN-OPG(2)	Aérospatiale AS.350B3 Ecureuil	3712	
LN-OPH	Aérospatiale AS.332L1 Super Puma	2347	
LN-OPJ(2)	Aérospatiale SA.365N1 Dauphin 2	6228	9M-TAF
LN-OPK	Aérospatiale AS.350B3 Ecureuil	3091	
LN-OPL(2)	Aérospatiale SA.365N1 Dauphin 2	6346	F-WQDP F-OGSV(2) LX-HUP F-OGSV(2) JA9970
LN-OPM(2)	Aérospatiale SA.365N1 Dauphin 2	6264	CS-HCG F-WYMI F-ODUZ
LN-OPO(2)	Bell 214B	28053	N214KR JA9268 N18091
LN-OPP(3)	Aérospatiale AS.350B2 Ecureuil	2020	SE-HRT
LN-OPS(2)	Aérospatiale AS.350B Ecureuil	1849	SE-HTS D-HHTT
LN-OPT	Aérospatiale AS.350B1 Ecureuil	1881	D-HHPS
LN-OPV(2)	Aérospatiale AS.350B2 Ecureuil	2378	HB-XUS
LN-OPY(2)	Aérospatiale AS.350B3 Ecureuil	3446	
LN-OPZ(2)	Aérospatiale AS.350B3 Ecureuil	3064	SE-JCV F-WQDY
LN-OQA	Sikorsky S-92A	920013	(LN-ONO) N7116J
LN-OQB	Sikorsky S-92A (Reservation 4.04)	920018	
LN-OQC	Sikorsky S-92A (Reservation 4.04)	920020	
LN-OQM(2)	Sikorsky S-61N	61764	(D-HOSA)
LN-OQQ(3)	Sikorsky S-61N	61814	
LN-ORC(4)	Sikorsky S-61N	61817	(LN-OQU)
LN-ORF(2)	Bell 47G-4 (Reservation 9.04)	3149	N3066G
LN-ORH(4)	Aérospatiale AS.350B2 Ecureuil (W/o 10.6.02)	2843	OY-HJC
LN-ORJ(4)	Aérospatiale AS.350B1 Ecureuil	2212	N501RP C-GFIN
LN-ORK(5)	Aérospatiale AS.350BA Ecureuil	1056	SE-JDE LN-ORK F-WZFT
LN-ORM(5)	Bell 214B-1	28054	SE-HLE LN-ORM SE-HLE
LN-ORS(2)	Agusta-Bell 206A Jet Ranger (W/o 13.12.86)	8212	D-HEZF (D-HAVA)
LN-ORW(3)	Bell 204 /UH-1B (Under rebuild using parts of c/n 297, RNoAF699/SI-L, 61-0699)	1087	(LN-10) (LN-ORN) RNoAF963/JT-F 64-13963
LN-OSA(3)	Hughes 269C	40-0918	PH-HJH C-GBSA N10970
LN-OSB(3)	MBB Bö.105S	S-606	N2913Z N132EH D-HDSB
LN-OSD(2)	MBB Bö.105S (W/o 4.1.91)	S-607	N2914W D-HDSC
LN-OSE(3)	MBB Bö.105S	S-634	N2784V D-HDTD
LN-OSI (2)	MBB Bö.105CBS	S-609	N29144 D-HDSE
LN-OSJ	Sikorsky S-61N	61715	N53094
LN-OSK(2)	Hughes 369E	0261E	SE-HSR LN-OBA SE-HSR
LN-OSR(4)	Rotorway Exec 162F	6095	
LN-OSZ(2)	MBB Bö.105S	S-666	N4573A HK-3225 N4573A D-HDUH
LN-OTC(2)	Hughes 369HS	89-0112S	N2171Z VH-PMY G-AXPL
LN-OTL(4)	Bell 206B Jet Ranger II (CoA exp 23.10.01, to USA)	234	OH-HHW PH-HNH N4071G
LN-OTQ	MBB Bö.105CBS (W/o 12.4.89)	S-582	D-HDQE
LN-PAL (2)	Piper PA-28-161 Cherokee Warrior II (Damaged 29.12.02, being rebuilt)	28-7816500	
LN-PAM(2)	Piper J-3C-65 Cub (CoA exp 30.4.84, stored)	12807	SE-CGY LN-RTM 44-80511
LN-PBE	Cessna 208B Grand Caravan	208B0587	(OY-PBE) N9782X N7229Z

LN-PBF(2)	Cessna 208B Grand Caravan	208B0584	OY-PBF G-MART N1126L N52642
LN-PBJ(2)	Cessna 208B Grand Caravan	208B0859	N5188W
LN-PBK	Cessna 208B Grand Caravan	208B0914	N5196U
LN-PBN	Cessna 208B Grand Caravan	208B1089	N5060K
LN-PLH	Cessna 182S	18280524	N2346W
LN-PWA	Cessna 172R	17280168	
LN-PZL	PZL-104 Wilga 80	CF20890880	G-BXMU EC-GMH ZK-PZP SP-FWP
LN-PZM	PZL-104 Wilga 35 (Reservation 5.04)	118403	OY-CFA HB-EZI
LN-PZN	PZL-104 Wilga 35A (Reservation 5.04)	19840811	OY-CFH SP-ZOD
LN-RAA(2)	Cessna 182P Skylane (CoA exp 31.5.04)	18262731	SE-GGC N52365
LN-RAB(2)	Cessna 172P	17274101	N5412K
LN-RAF(4)	Van's RV-4	1553	
LN-RAI (2)	Cessna 172N	17272812	N6461D
LN-RAK(2)	Piper J-3C-65 Cub (L-4J) (CoA exp 31.3.77, under restoration)	12889	44-80593
LN-RAL(5)	Reims/Cessna F172H	F17200676	SE-FUI D-EBLQ
LN-RAM(3)	Reims/Cessna F172M	F17201454	SE-GMY
LN-RAN(3)	Piper PA-28-161 Cherokee Warrior II	28-7816501	LN-PAN(2)
LN-RAP(2)	Piper J-3C-65 Cub (L-4J) (Flies as "43-E")	12583	SE-CDH LN-RAP 44-80287
LN-RAR(2)	Bellanca 7GCBC Citabria	1209-80	
LN-RBI	Piper J-3C-65 Cub	12640	(SE-IML) OY-ALN D-EDUH SL-ABC SL-AAC F-BDTL 44-80344
LN-RCN	Boeing 737-883	28318	(OY-KLB) LN-RCN SE-DTK N1786B
LN-RCT	Boeing 737-683	30189	OY-KKF N1786B
LN-RCU	Boeing 737-683	30190	SE-DNZ N1786B
LN-RCW	Boeing 737-683	28308	SE-DNY N1787B
LN-RCX	Boeing 737-883	30196	SE-DYH N1787B (LN-RPO) (SE-DTS) (LN-RPO)
LN-RCY	Boeing 737-883	28324	SE-DTT N1786B
LN-RCZ	Boeing 737-883	30197	SE-DTS
LN-RDA(2)	Bombardier DHC-8Q Series 402	4013	(SE-LRA) (OY-KCB) C-GDFT
LN-RDB(2)	Bombardier DHC-8Q Series 402	4018	(OY-KCC) C-FDHU
LN-RDC(3)	Bombardier DHC-8Q Series 402	4019	(SE-LRD) (OY-KCD) C-FDHW
LN-RDD(3)	Bombardier DHC-8Q Series 402	4009	(OY-KCA) LN-RDD (SE-LRC) (OY-KCA) C-GFQL
LN-RDE(2)	Bombardier DHC-8Q Series 402	4020	(SE-LRE) (LN-RDC) C-FDHX
LN-RDF(2)	Bombardier DHC-8Q Series 402	4021	(OY-KCB) LN-RDF (SE-LRF) (LN-RDD) C-FDHZ
LN-RDG	Bombardier DHC-8Q Series 402	4022	(OY-KCC) LN-RDG (OY-KCC) (SE-LRG) (SE-LOG) C-FGNP
LN-RDH	Bombardier DHC-8Q Series 402	4023	(OY-KCD) (SE-LRH) C-FNGB
LN-RDI	Bombardier DHC-8Q Series 402	4024	(LN-RDC) (OY-KCE) C-GERL
LN-RDJ(2)	Bombardier DHC-8Q Series 402	4010	N480DC (LN-RDJ) (LN-RDA) C-GFUM
LN-RDK	Bombardier DHC-8Q Series 402	4025	(LN-RDD) C-GETI

LN-RDL	Bombardier DHC-8Q Series 402	4011	(SE-LRB) (SE-LOB) C-FDHY
LN-RDM(3)	Bombardier DHC-8Q Series 402	4033	N481DC (LN-RDM) C-GFRP
LN-RDO(2)	Bombardier DHC-8Q Series 402	4036	C-FDHD
LN-RDP	Bombardier DHC-8Q Series 402	4012	OY-KCA (SE-LRC) (SE-LOC) C-FWBB
LN-RDQ	Bombardier DHC-8Q Series 402	4008	OY-KCB (SE-LRA) (SE-LOA) C-GFOD (B-17401) C-GFEN
LN-RDR(2)	Bombardier DHC-8Q Series 402	4034	N482DC (LN-RDR) (SE-LRG) C-GFYI
LN-RDS	Bombardier DHC-8Q Series 402	4035	(SE-LRH) C-GHRI
LN-RDT(2)	Bombardier DHC-8Q Series 402	4038	N382BC (LN-RDT) (OY-KCE) C-FDHW
LN-REB	Pazmany PL-4A (Temp reg 14.10.92, no CoA issued)	682	
LN-RET	Cessna 140	8784	LN-TSI N89735
LN-RIC	Grefstad Sea Hawker (W/o 18.6.97)	91	
LN-RKF(2)	Airbus A340-313X	413	SE-REA F-WWJM
LN-RKG(2)	Airbus A340-313X	424	SE-REB F-WWJP
LN-RKH(2)	Airbus A330-343	497	(SE-REG) F-WWYP
LN-RKI	Airbus A321-232	1817	(LN-RKG) D-AVZK
LN-RKK	Airbus A321-232 (Reservation for SAS)	unkn	
LN-RKL	Airbus A321-232 (Reservation for SAS)	unkn	
LN-RLE	McDonnell-Douglas DC-9-82	49382	
LN-RLF(2)	McDonnell-Douglas DC-9-82	49383	VH-LNJ LN-RLF
LN-RLR(3)	McDonnell-Douglas DC-9-82	49437	VH-LNL LN-RLR(2)
LN-RME	Evans Volksplane VP-II (Reservn .05)	1147	
LN-RMG	McDonnell-Douglas DC-9-87	49611	
LN-RMH	McDonnell-Douglas DC-9-87	49612	N6203U
LN-RMK	McDonnell-Douglas DC-9-87	49610	
LN-RML	McDonnell-Douglas DC-9-81	53002	
LN-RMM	McDonnell-Douglas DC-9-82	53005	
LN-RMN	McDonnell-Douglas DC-9-82	53295	
LN-RMO	McDonnell-Douglas DC-9-81	53315	
LN-RMP	McDonnell-Douglas DC-9-87	53337	
LN-RMR	McDonnell-Douglas DC-9-81	53365	
LN-RMS	McDonnell-Douglas DC-9-81	53368	
LN-RMT(2)	McDonnell-Douglas DC-9-81	53001	OY-KHS (SE-DIP)
LN-RMU	McDonnell-Douglas DC-9-87	53340	SE-DMC
LN-RNC(2)	Fokker F.27-050	20176	PH-EXY
LN-RND(2)	Fokker F.27-050	20178	PH-EXZ
LN-RNE(2)	Fokker F.27-050	20179	PH-EXE
LN-RNF	Fokker F.27-050	20183	PH-EXI
LN-RNG	Fokker F.27-050	20184	PH-EXJ
LN-RNM	Fokker F.27-050	20199	(SX-BTK) PH-ZDI SE-LFP PH-EXH
LN-ROA	McDonnell-Douglas MD-90-30	53459	
LN-ROB	McDonnell-Douglas MD-90-30	53462	
LN-ROM	McDonnell-Douglas DC-9-81	53008	(LN-RLB) SE-DIY
LN-RON	McDonnell-Douglas DC-9-81	53347	(LN-RLC) SE-DMD N90125
LN-ROO	McDonnell-Douglas DC-9-81	53366	(LN-RLD) SE-DME
LN-ROP	McDonnell-Douglas DC-9-82	49384	(LN-RLI) SE-DFS
LN-ROR	McDonnell-Douglas DC-9-81	49385	(LN-RLJ) SE-DFT
LN-ROS	McDonnell-Douglas DC-9-81	49421	(LN-RLK) SE-DFU N841RA SE-DFU
LN-ROT	McDonnell-Douglas DC-9-81	49422	(LN-RLL) SE-DFR SE-DFV (SE-DFW)
LN-ROU	McDonnell-Douglas DC-9-81	49424	(LN-RLO) SE-DFX N840RA SE-DFX
LN-ROW	McDonnell-Douglas DC-9-81	49438	(LN-RLQ) SE-DFY
LN-ROX	McDonnell-Douglas DC-9-81	49603	(LN-RLU) SE-DIA N19B
LN-ROY	McDonnell-Douglas DC-9-81	49615	(LN-RLV) SE-DID N843RA SE-DID
LN-ROZ	McDonnell-Douglas DC-9-81	49608	(LN-RLW) SE-DIH
LN-RPA	Boeing 737-683	28290	
LN-RPB	Boeing 737-683	28294	N1787B
LN-RPF	Boeing 737-683	28307	N1784B N1786B
LN-RPG	Boeing 737-683	28310	
LN-RPH	Boeing 737-683	28605	N1786B
LN-RPJ	Boeing 737-783	30192	(OY-KKI) N1786B
LN-RPK(3)	Boeing 737-783	28317	N1786B
LN-RPL(3)	Boeing 737-883	30469	(OY-KKN) LN-RPL (SE-DYC) (OY-KKN) N1786B
LN-RPM(3)	Boeing 737-883	30195	(SE-DYD)
LN-RPN(2)	Boeing 737-883	30470	(SE-DYG) (LN-RPN) N1786B
LN-RPS	Boeing 737-683	28298	OY-KKC N1786B
LN-RPT	Boeing 737-683	28299	OY-KKD N1787B
LN-RPU	Boeing 737-683	28312	OY-KKP (SE-DTH) (OY-KKH) N1786B
LN-RPW	Boeing 737-683	28289	OY-KKA N5002K
LN-RPX	Boeing 737-683	28291	SE-DNN N1787B
LN-RPY	Boeing 737-683	28292	SE-DNO N1780B N1786B
LN-RPZ	Boeing 737-683	28293	OY-KKB N1787B
LN-RRK	Boeing 737-883	32278	SE-DYG
LN-RRL	Boeing 737-883	28328	(LN-RNP) SE-DYT (SE-DYD)
LN-RRM	Boeing 737-783	28314	SE-DTI N1786B
LN-RRN	Boeing 737-783	30191	SE-DTG N1786B
LN-RRO	Boeing 737-683	28288	SE-DNM N1003M
LN-RRP	Boeing 737-683	28311	SE-DTU N1786B (SE-DTG) (LN-RPC) (OY-KKG)
LN-RRR	Boeing 737-683	28309	SE-DTF N1787B
LN-RRS	Boeing 737-883	28325	(SE-DYM)
LN-RRT	Boeing 737-883	28326	(SE-DYN) (SE-DTT)
LN-RRU	Boeing 737-883	28327	(SE-DYP)
LN-RRW	Boeing 737-883	32277	SE-DTR N1787B (SE-DYR)
LN-RRX	Boeing 737-683	28296	SE-DNR N7376
LN-RRY	Boeing 737-683	28297	SE-DNS N35135 N1786B
LN-RRZ	Boeing 737-683	28295	SE-DNP N1786B
LN-RTB(2)	Piper PA-18 Super Cub 95	18-1593	ALAT 51-15593
LN-RTH(2)	Piper PA-18 Super Cub 95	18-1408	D-ENLI ALAT 51-15408
LN-RTI (2)	Rutan Defiant	0023B	
LN-RTJ (4)	Denney Kitfox II (Cr 25.9.94, stored)	463	
LN-RTQ	Cessna U206E Skywagon 206 Floatplane (W/o 2.10.89, stored)	U20601449	
LN-RTV(3)	Rockwell Lark Commander 100-180	5162	
LN-SAC	Cessna TP337G Super Skymaster (Stored)	0169	N68S
LN-SAD(3)	SAAB-MFI-15-200A Safari	15814	SE-FIR
LN-SAG(3)	Cessna 172M (W/o 1.10.83)	17263760	N1815V
LN-SAI (2)	Piper J-3C-65 Cub (L-4J)	12579	44-80283
LN-SAK(3)	SAAB S.91B-2 Safir (W/o 12.11.83)	91340	RNoAF:57340 340/'UA-U'
LN-SAL(3)	SAAB S.91B Safir (Stored)	91286	Fv50076
LN-SAM(3)	SAAB S.91B-2 Safir (Under restoration)	91342	RNoAF:57342 342/'UA-W'
LN-SAO(3)	SAAB S.91B-2 Safir	91344	RNoAF:57344 344/'UA-Y'

LN-SAP(3)	SAAB S.91B-2 Safir	91333	RNoAF:57333 333/'UA-N'
LN-SAQ	SAAB S.91B-2 Safir (W/o 15.8.87, stored Sweden)	91322	RNoAF:57322 322/'UA-C'
LN-SAS(3)	PZL-150 Koliber	19005	SE-KHG SP-PHA SP-ZKC
LN-SAU(2)	Schweizer TSC-1A1 Teal	23	G-BAVK N41S N2023T
LN-SFK	Cessna 182M Skylane	18259952	N91918
LN-SFT	Fairchild Swearingen SA.226T Merlin IIIB	T-342	N342NX 9Q-CQP G- IIIA N1008S
LN-SHA	Neico Lancair 320	582-320-329FB	
LN-SKY	Steen Skybolt (Reservn .05)	unkn	
LN-SNI	Rans S-9 Chaos	1098112	
LN-SPO	Cessna 421C Golden Eagle	421C-0804	D-IZZY N26563
LN-SUN(4)	Canadair CL.600-2B16 Challenger	5517	N517RH C-GJSO C-GLXK
LN-SUS(2)	IAI 1126 Galaxy	051	OY-RAK N293GA 4X-CVF
LN-SUV(5)	Cessna 550 Citation Bravo	550-0951	N51KR TC-TPE N5076J
LN-SUX(2)	Cessna 560XL Citation Excel	560-5271	LN-SUR
LN-SUZ(3)	Beech B200 Super King Air	BB-1547	N780CA N180CA N1117N
LN-SVO	Piper PA-28-181 Cherokee Archer II	28-7790101	OY-CTG C-GUST N5368F
LN-SXY	Neico Lancair 360	630	
LN-TAU(2)	Piper PA-25-235 Pawnee D	25-7756038	G-BFBX N82504
LN-TEK	Cessna U206F Stationair Floatplane	U20602858	C-GTHK N1179Q
LN-TEP	Cessna U206G Stationair 6 Floatplane	U20605186	N5305U
LN-TET	Piper J-3C-65 Cub	18020	LN-BWU N71006 NC71006
LN-TEX	Noorduyn AT-16-ND Harvard IIB	14A-2268	FAP1794 D-FIBU OO-AAR H-58 KF568
LN-TEZ	Fuji FA-200-160 Aero Subaru	295	G-BMLN (G-BIMR)
LN-TFC(2)	Piper PA-34-220T Seneca V	3449094	
LN-TFD(2)	Piper PA-34-220T Seneca V	3449121	N9512N
LN-TFF(2)	Slingsby T-67M/200 Firefly	2051	SE-LBF LN-TFF G-7-126
LN-TFJ	Cessna T210N Turbo Centurion II	21063655	N4879C
LN-TFM	Cessna P210N Pressurized Centurion II	P21000268	N4737K
LN-TFQ	Piper PA-28-181 Archer III	2843265	N9524N
LN-TFS	Piper PA-28-181 Archer III	2843273	
LN-TFU	Piper PA-28-181 Archer III	2843285	
LN-TFV	Piper PA-28-181 Archer III	2843293	N9522N
LN-TFW	Grob G.115D	82078	D-EZAN
LN-TFX	Grob G.115D	82067	N115MH D-EGVV
LN-TFY	Grob G.115D	82052	N115AD D-EGVV
LN-TFZ	Grob G.115D	82014	D-EXEC
LN-TOR	ProTech PT-2 Prostar (Temp reg 6.1.03)	1164	
LN-TSB	Cessna 182A	33977	N5977B
LN-TSE(3)	Cessna 150F	15062137	(SE-ESS) N8837S
LN-TSF	Cessna 180 (Crashed 12.5.96)	32473	N6576A
LN-TSG	Cessna U206 Super Skywagon	206-0388	(SE- . . .) LN-TSG N11B (N2188F)
LN-TSK(4)	SOCATA Rallye 180T Galérien	2973	SE-GTH
LN-TSL	Cessna 172 (CoA exp 31.8.04)	36540	N8840B
LN-TSP	Cessna 180A (CoA exp 31.5.00, under restoration)	50262	N5364D
LN-TST(4)	Cessna 177A Cardinal	17701343	SE-ELX N30583
LN-TSV(3)	Piper PA-28-140 Cherokee (CoA exp 30.6.99, under restoration)	28-22312	(LN-HHV)
LN-TSW	Cessna 150E	15061451	N11B (N4051U)
LN-TSX	Piper PA-18 Super Cub 95 (CoA never issued, stored)	18-1545	OO-HMV ALAT 51-15545
LN-TSZ	Piper PA-18 Super Cub 95	18-1579	OO-HMN ALAT 51-15579
LN-TUA	Boeing 737-705	28211	(LN-SUA)
LN-TUD	Boeing 737-705	28217	N1786B
LN-TUF	Boeing 737-705	28222	N1786B

LN-TUH	Boeing 737-705	29093	N1786B
LN-TUI	Boeing 737-705	29094	N1787B
LN-TUJ	Boeing 737-705	29095	
LN-TUK	Boeing 737-705	29096	
LN-TUL	Boeing 737-705	29097	
LN-TUM	Boeing 737-705	29098	
LN-TVB(3)	Beech A23 Musketeer II (Cr 3.5.81, stored)	M-788	OH-BMC N1447L
LN-TVD	Cessna 172D (CoA exp 31.8.04)	17250004	(OY-TRE) N2404U
LN-TVE(3)	Beagle A.61 Terrier 2	B.626	SE-ELR (SE-ELJ) G-ASIE G-35-11 VX924
LN-TVI (2)	Malmö MFI-9 Junior	013	(SE-EBZ)
LN-TVK	Piper PA-22-160 Tri-Pacer (Cr 16.8.88, wreck stored)	22-5680	N8425D
LN-TVO(2)	Cessna 150D (W/o 14.7.94, parts used to rebuild LN-BEH)	15060532	N4532U
LN-TVR(5)	Orlican L-40 Meta-Sokol (Destroyed 29.12.02, wreck stored)	150615	OY-ADC LN-TVR(2) OY-ADC
LN-TVS	Cessna 180 (Dbf 6.9.92)	30454	N1754C
LN-TVZ	Cessna F150J (Cr 27.9.92, displayed unmarked in shopping mall, Kjeller)	F150-0487	
LN-TWA	Piper PA-28RT-201T Turbo Arrow IV	28R-8231012	N4327X LN-TWA N8467J
LN-TWB	Piper PA-31-325 Navajo C/R	31-8212025	N4083T
LN-TWK	Reims/Cessna F406 Caravan II (Reservation, not yet taken up)	0032	PH-CLE LN-TWH PH-CLE AP-BFA N422AB G-BPSW F-WZDU
LN-TWL(2)	Beech B200 Super King Air	BB-1144	N120AJ ZS-NWT D-IBHF N62BE N221P
LN-UFO	Piper PA-28-151 Cherokee Warrior (On rebuild, reserved 2.03 but used for spares)	28-7715241	SE-GPC
LN-ULF	Cessna 182P	18264448	OY-CKL OH-CVF N1795M
LN-USA	Rutan Cozy	112	(LN-FOZ)
LN-UXA(2)	Piper PA-28-140 Cherokee	28-23020	
LN-UXB(2)	Piper PA-28-140 Cherokee (W/o 24.7.96)	28-23108	
LN-UXC(3)	Piper PA-18-150 Super Cub	18-3213	OL-L10 L-139 53-4813
LN-UXE(2)	Piper PA-28-140 Cherokee	28-23118	
LN-UXF(2)	Piper PA-28-140 Cherokee (Crashed 27.2.99, stored)	28-23168	
LN-UXK	Piper PA-28-140 Cherokee	28-23263	
LN-UXQ(2)	Grumman-American AA-5 Traveler	AA5-0198	(OY-AYS)
LN-UXR	Piper PA-28-180 Cherokee C	28-4292	
LN-UXZ(2)	Cessna U206G Stationair 6 (W/o 2.9.82)	U20605694	SE-IFI (N5378X)
LN-VIF	Cessna 180H Skywagon Floatplane	18052004	(N91217)
LN-VIG	Rutan VariEze	1879	
LN-VIK	Quickie 2	058	
LN-VIZ(2)	Beech B200 Super King Air	BB-1136	D-IDOK N62KL N62KM N83KA
LN-VYC(2)	Piper PA-38-112 Tomahawk (CoA exp 30.4.04, for spares)	38-79A0880	SE-ICO
LN-VYE	Cessna 150F (W/o 22.5.81)	15062643	N8543G
LN-VYG(2)	de Havilland DH.82A Tiger Moth (CoA exp 31.7.85, stored)	85328	LN-BDN G-ANSB DE282
LN-VYI	Piper PA-23-250 Aztec C	27-3873	
LN-VYJ	Cessna 180 (Floats or wheels u/c)	32096	OY-DGF OE-DBE HB-CPB N3298D
LN-VYN(5)	Cessna U206E Skywagon 206	U20601490	N1490M
LN-VYP	Piper PA-18-150 Super Cub (CoA exp 14.5.04, stored)	18-8328	SE-EPP
LN-VYU	Piper PA-28-140 Cherokee (W/o 13.12.82, stored)	28-23845	
LN-VYZ	Cessna F172H Floatplane	F172-0414	OY-EGT
LN-WDA	Bombardier DHC-8Q Series 402	4069	C-GERL
LN-WDB	Bombardier DHC-8Q Series 402	4070	C-GETI
LN-WDC	Bombardier DHC-8Q Series 402	4071	C-GEVP
LN-WFA	DHC-8 Series 311	342	C-FTUY EI-CIS D-BOBS C-GFHZ
LN-WFB	DHC-8 Series 311	293	PH-SDS EI-CIU PT-OKD C-GDIU

LN-WFC(3)	DHC-8 Series 311	236	D-BEYT
			C-GFCF
LN-WFE(2)	DHC-8 Series 311	491	C-GFCA
LN-WFH	DHC-8 Series 311	238	C-FZOH
			PH-SDJ
			C-GFYI
LN-WFO(2)	DHC-8 Series 311	493	C-GERC
LN-WFP(2)	DHC-8 Series 311	495	C-GFUM
LN-WFR	DHC-8 Series 311	385	N383DC
			ZS-NME
			C-GFUM
LN-WFS	DHC-8 Series 311	535	C-GEWI
LN-WFT	DHC-8 Series 315	532	C-FATN
			G-JEDC
			C-GEOA
LN-WIA	DHC-8 Series 103	359	C-GHRI
LN-WIB	DHC-8 Series 103	360	C-GFBW
LN-WIC	DHC-8 Series 103	367	C-GDNG
LN-WID	DHC-8 Series 103	369	C-FDHD
LN-WIE	DHC-8 Series 103	371	C-GFYI
LN-WIF	DHC-8 Series 103	372	C-GFOD
LN-WIG	DHC-8 Series 103	382	C-GLOT
LN-WIH	DHC-8 Series 103	383	C-GFYI
LN-WII	DHC-8 Series 103	384	C-GFOD
LN-WIJ	DHC-8 Series 103	386	C-GFQL
LN-WIK	DHC-8 Series 103	394	C-GDNG
LN-WIL(2)	DHC-8 Series 103	398	C-GFCF
LN-WIM	DHC-8 Series 103	403	C-GDIU
LN-WIN	DHC-8 Series 103	409	C-GDNG
LN-WIO	DHC-8 Series 103	417	C-GFQL
LN-WIP	DHC-8 Series 106	239	C-FXNE
			OE-LLK
			C-GETI
LN-WIR	DHC-8 Series 103	273	C-FZNU
			OE-LRT
			OE-HRT
			C-GFYI
LN-WIS	DHC-8 Series 103	247	N813AW
	(Cr 14.6.01, to spares)		C-GFRP
			N813AW
			C-GFRP
LN-WNB	Holste MH.1521M Broussard	16M	F-GHJH
			ALAT:312 BC-GI
LN-WND	Douglas C-53D	11750	N59NA
			G-BLYA
			FinAF:DO-9
			OH-LCG
			42-68823
LN-WNH	North American AT-6D Harvard	88-14552	(LN-LFW)
	(Flown as FS907/AJ)		G-SUES
			FAP1506
			74+24
			EX881
			41-33854
LN-WNO	Cessna 305C/L-19EBird Dog	24568	(LN-AAN)
	(Damaged 29.12.02, rebuilding)		F-GECB
			ALAT:F-MAMN

GLIDERS AND MOTOR-GLIDERS

LN-GAA(2)	Eiri PIK-3B	1	
LN-GAB(4)	Grob G.103 Twin II Acro	34063-K-293	
LN-GAC	Scheibe Zugvogel IIIB	1074	D-8460
	(CoA exp 31.5.96, stored)		
LN-GAD(5)	Scheibe Specht	410/1957	
LN-GAF(5)	Eiri PIK-20B	20047	SE-TVD
			OH-459
LN-GAG(2)	Schleicher K 7 Rhönadler	7266	
	(CoA exp 31.5.89, stored)		
LN-GAH(4)	Grob G.102 Astir CS	1162	D-4183
LN-GAI (2)	Scheibe Bergfalke IIa	343	
	(CoA exp 30.6.83, stored)		
LN-GAJ(3)	Rolladen-Schneider LS8A	8010	SE-UTP
			D-1646
LN-GAK(5)	Schempp-Hirth Ventus 2cM	89/. . .	D-KTAK
LN-GAL(4)	Schempp-Hirth Ventus B/16.6	47	D-6402
LN-GAM(4)	Schleicher ASK 21	21132	
LN-GAN(5)	Grob G.103C Twin III SL	35049	
LN-GAO(5)	Schempp-Hirth Duo Discus T	113	
LN-GAP(2)	Schleicher K 7 Rhönadler	7246	
LN-GAQ(2)	Schleicher K 8B (CoA exp 31.10.03)	8217	D-1900
LN-GAS(2)	LET L-13 Blanik (Cr 3.4.85)	026127	
LN-GAT(3)	Scheibe SF-28A Tandem-Falke	5765	OY-XMV
			D-KACR
LN-GAV(3)	LET L-13 Blanik	025810	
LN-GAW(4)	Aerotechnik L-13SL Vivat	930508	D-KACH(3)
LN-GAY(4)	Glasflügel H201B Standard Libelle	480	OH-429
LN-GAZ(2)	SZD-55-1	551190009	HB-3046
LN-GBA(4)	Grob G.102 Astir CS77	1625	D-4799
LN-GBB(3)	Rolladen-Schneider LS6 "BB"	6014	D-4975
LN-GBC(2)	Schleicher Rhönlerche II	3010	D-3595
	(CoA exp 31.3.88, stored)		
LN-GBD(3)	Scheibe SF-25C Falke	4499	SE-TLV
			D-KEIQ
LN-GBE(3)	Brditschka HB-21/2400	21027	SE-TUM
LN-GBF(2)	Pilatus B4-PC11	107	
LN-GBG(3)	Schleicher ASK 13	13103	
LN-GBH(5)	Rolladen-Schneider LS6 "BH"	6022	
	(CoA exp 30.9.03)		
LN-GBI(3)	Grob G.109	6036	SE-UCV
			(SE-UMI)
			D-KDMF
LN-GBK(4)	Schleicher K 8B	1	D-6077
LN-GBM(6)	LET L-13 Blanik	026124	OY-XRK
			HB-1243
LN-GBN(2)	Schleicher K 7 Rhönadler	7236	
	(CoA exp 30.4.94, stored		
LN-GBO(2)	Eiri PIK-20D (Reservn 5.02 for rebuild)	20548	
LN-GBP(4)	Scheibe SF-25CFalke 1700	44100	D-KEIR
LN-GBQ	Schleicher ASK 13	13190	
LN-GBR(3)	Schleicher K 8B	8754	
LN-GBS(2)	SZD-30 Pirat (W/o 21.9.97)	S-02.20	
LN-GBT(2)	Schleicher K 7 Rhönadler	7237	
LN-GBV(3)	Schleicher K 8B	1088	D-1731
LN-GBW(4)	Scheibe Bergfalke III	5578	SE-TEM
	(CoA exp 31.7.99, stored)		
LN-GBX	Grob G.102 Astir CS	1519	
LN-GBY	Rolladen-Schneider LS3	3065	
LN-GCA	Schleicher ASW 15	15017	OY-VJX
			D-0344
LN-GCB	Glaser-Dirks DG-500 Elan Trainer	5E-23T5	SE-UIG
LN-GCC	Schleicher ASW 19B	19370	D-7245
			D-1390
LN-GCD(2)	Schleicher ASW 27	27221	
LN-GCE	Scheibe SF-34	5107	D3341
LN-GCF	SZD-48-3 Jantar Standard 3	B-1372	HB-1737
LN-GCG	Rolladen-Schneider LS8-18	8430	
LN-GCI	Rolladen-Schneider LS8B	8415	
LN-GCJ	Schleicher ASK 21	21742	
LN-GCK	Schleicher ASW-19B	19083	SE-TTT
LN-GCM(2)	Rolladen-Schneider LS4B	41054	
LN-GCN	Glaser-Dirks DG-1000S	10-24S24	
LN-GCO	Centrair SNC-34C Alliance	34021	F-CIHT
LN-GCP	Schempp-Hirth Duo Discus T	79	
LN-GCQ	Schempp-Hirth Standard Cirrus	559G	SE-TOG
LN-GCR	Schleicher ASH-26E	26052	D-KBFL
LN-GCS	Schleicher ASK 21	21520	SE-ULE
LN-GCT	LAK-19T	004	
LN-GCU	Grob G.103C Twin IIISL	35007	D-KAME
LN-GCV	PZL PW-6U	78.03.09	
LN-GCX(2)	Rolladen-Schneider LS3	3008	HA-4512
			HB-1354
LN-GCY	Schempp-Hirth Ventus 2cxT	126	D-KGBR
LN-GCZ	Schleicher K 8B	8129/A	OY-HAX
			D-1939
LN-GDA	Brditschka HB-21	21013	PH-947
	(Reservation, stored Hamar as PH-947)		D-KIDU
			HB-2046
LN-GDB	Schleicher ASW 15B	15382	OY-XNJ
			D-9271
LN-GDD	Schempp-Hirth Duo Discus	211	
LN-GDE	Schempp-Hirth Discus 2b	170	
LN-GDM	Schempp-Hirth Nimbus 4 DM	36/51	
LN-GDW	Schempp-Hirth Discus b	163/571	
LN-GEE	SZD-45A Ogar	X-133	SP-0027
LN-GEL	LET L-23 Super Blanik	978308	
LN-GEM	Schleicher K 8B (Under restoration)	151	OY-XEM
			D-5198
LN-GER	Rolladen-Schneider LS8A	8129	
LN-GET	SZD-48-1 Jantar Standard	B-1034	SE-UMR
			OH-585
LN-GFE	Schempp-Hirth Discus b	166	SE-UFE
LN-GFI	LET L-13 Blanik	171520	LY-10013
			DOSAAF
LN-GFJ	LET L-13 Blanik	027260	LY-GAC
			DOSAAF
LN-GFK	LET L-13 Blanik	026243	OY-XGB
LN-GFN	Monnett Moni	369	
	(Temp reg 15.1.92, no CoA yet issued)		
LN-GFT	LET L-13 Blanik	026415	LY-GLC
			DOSAAF
LN-GGA(3)	Pilatus B-4/PC-11	209	
LN-GGC(2)	Bölkow Phoebus C	888	OH-379
			OH-PHC
LN-GGD(2)	Schleicher K 8B	8610	
LN-GGF(2)	Bölkow Phoebus B-1	738	HB-855
LN-GGG(4)	Schleicher K 8B (CoA exp 31.3.99, stored)	8682/A	D-5834
LN-GGH(3)	Scheibe SF-34	5109	D-1114
LN-GGI (4)	Schleicher K 8B (CoA exp 31.5.01, stored)	8412	
	(Originally quoted as c/n 12 ex OY-BXG)		
LN-GGJ	Bölkow Phoebus A-1	809	D-5488
	(CoA exp 30.11.99, stored)		
LN-GGK(2)	SZD-30 Pirat	S-07.03	
	(CoA exp 31.5.88, stored)		
LN-GGM(3)	Schempp-Hirth Nimbus II	121	OY-XGR
LN-GGN(2)	Pilatus B-4/PC-11AF	256	
LN-GGO(3)	Grob G.102 Astir CS	1198	OY-XOP
	(CoA exp 31.8.02, stored)		LN-GGO(2)
LN-GGP(2)	PIK-16C Vasama (CoA exp 31.7.99, stored)	19	OY-BXB
LN-GGR(2)	Rolladen-Schneider LS3	3052	

LN-GGS(2)	Schleicher K 8B	04	OH-319
			OH-RTN
LN-GGT	Schleicher K 8 (CoA exp 31.7.85)	521/59	
LN-GGU(2)	Grob G.102 Astir CS 77	1711	
LN-GGV(2)	Grob G.102 Astir CS 77	1640	D-7471
	(CoA exp 31.5.94, stored)		
LN-GGW(2)	Grob G.102 Astir CS	1488	
LN-GGX(2)	Grob G.102 Astir CS Jeans	2185	(OY-XMZ)
			D-7760
LN-GGY	Rolladen-Schneider LS3	3058	HB-1365
LN-GGZ	Schleicher K 8B (CoA exp 31.3.03, stored)	8913	D-0991
LN-GHA	Rolladen-Schneider LS1F	329	(LN-GHO)
			SE-TON
LN-GHB	Scheibe Bergfalke III	5583	D-5771
	(CoA exp 30.6.01, stored)		
LN-GHC	Rolladen-Schneider LS3A	3339	(D-3183)
LN-GHD	Rolladen-Schneider LS3A	3363	
LN-GHE	Schleicher K 8B (CoA exp 31.10.03, stored)	8380	D-6345
LN-GHF	Glasflügel H303 Mosquito B	180	
LN-GHG	Grob G.102 Astir CS	1182	OY-XJM
	(CoA exp 30.6.04, stored)		D-4192
LN-GHH	Schleicher Rhönlerche II (Cr 7.9.94)	104/61	D-6253
LN-GHI	Scheibe Bergfalke II/55 (CoA exp 30.6.96)	84	D-1492
LN-GHK	Rolladen-Schneider LS6	6034	
LN-GHL	Schleicher ASW 19B	19402	
LN-GHO(2)	Grob G.103 Club Astir II	5055C	D-3060
LN-GHR(2)	Slingsby T.21B Sedbergh	"FF1161"	BGA3338/FLD
	(CoA not issued)		WB987
LN-GHS(2)	Rolladen-Schneider LS6	6095	
LN-GHV	Sportavia/ Scheibe SF-25C Falke	4208	OY-XHM
			D-KAIJ
LN-GHX	Grob G.102 Astir CS (Dbr 31.5.92)	1115	OY-XKJ
			D-4175
LN-GHY	Rolladen-Schneider LS6	6107	
LN-GIA(2)	LET L-23 Super Blanik	988409	
LN-GIB	Schleicher ASK 21	21293	
LN-GIC	Schempp-Hirth Discus b (Cr 7.8.98)	153	
LN-GID	Valentin Mistral C	MC050/82	D-4950
LN-GIE(2)	Scheibe Bergfalke III	5520	SE-TBY
LN-GIF	Schleicher ASK 21	21554	
LN-GII	Schleicher ASW 19B	19272	OY-XJS
LN-GIK	Rolladen-Schneider LS4A	4720	
LN-GIL	Scheibe Bergfalke II/55 (CoA exp 30.4.99)	3	D-1683
LN-GIM	Rolladen-Schneider LS7	7028	D-1317
LN-GIN	Rolladen-Schneider LS7	7127	
LN-GIO	Lunds Tekniske Kern-Silhouette SA-60	LTSA-1	
	(CoA exp 30.4.99, stored)		
LN-GIR	Rolladen-Schneider LS7	7049	D-5175
LN-GIW	Schempp-Hirth Discus b	290	
LN-GLA	Scheibe Bergfalke IV (W/o 21.7.94)	5840	D-3698
LN-GLB	Scheibe L-Spatz	01	SE-TIP
LN-GLD	LET L-13 Blanik	026007	D-3708
	(CoA exp 31.3.87. Stored, Denmark)		
LN-GLE	Rolladen-Schneider LS4	4062	(D-5989)
LN-GLF	Rolladen-Schneider LS4	4061	(D-5988)
LN-GLG	Rolladen-Schneider LS4	4064	
LN-GLH	Rolladen-Schneider LS3A	3365	
LN-GLI	Schleicher K 7 Rhönadler (CoA exp 30.4.96)	771	D-5763
LN-GLJ	SZD-41A Jantar Standard	B-813	OY-XII
LN-GLK(2)	Scheibe SF-25B Falke (Cr 5.8.00)	4641	SE-UAM
			D-KEDF
LN-GLL	Schleicher K 7 Rhönadler	7186	D-3031
LN-GLM	Glasflügel H303 Mosquito	24	SE-TTG
LN-GLN	Scheibe Bergfalke IV	5812	D-0309
	(CoA exp 31.10.03, stored)		
LN-GLO	Jastreb Standard Cirrus G/81	278	
LN-GLS	Scheibe Bergfalke III	5542	D-6370
	(CoA exp 30.4.03, stored)		
LN-GLU(2)	LET L-23 Super Blanik	978309	
LN-GLV	Slingsby T.30B Prefect Mk.2	1132	BGA853
	(CoA exp 31.8.96, stored)		
LN-GLW	Eiri PIK-20B	20129C	OY-XIH
			OH-488
LN-GLX	Grob G.103A Twin II Acro	3878-K-116	
LN-GLZ	Grob G.103 Twin Astir	3539	OY-XOU
			D-8732
LN-GMB	Eiri PIK-20E	20289	
LN-GMC(4)	Scheibe SF-25B Falke	46202	(LN-GDX)
	(CoA exp 30.9.03)		SE-UBM
			D-KASQ
LN-GMD	Grob G.109	6001	D-KECG(2)
			D-KBGF
LN-GMF	Scheibe SF-25B Falke	46125	D-KABZ
	(CoA exp 28.2.01, stored)		
LN-GMK	Monnett Moni (CoA exp 31.8.01, stored)	00328	
LN-GMR	Valentin Taifun 17E	1053	D-KDST
LN-GMT	IAR IS.28M2	043	
LN-GMV	Eiri PIK-20E	20286	D-KARM
LN-GMY	Hoffmann H-36 Dimona	3653	SE-TUS
LN-GOD	LET L-13 Blanik (CoA exp 31.5.04)	026246	HB-1287
LN-GOL	Schleicher ASW 20	20322	SE-UGH
			OH-580
LN-GOR	LET L-13 Blanik	026610	LY-GJQ
			DOSAAF
LN-GOS	Schleicher K 7 Rhönadler	162/59	BGA2665/EGB
			D-5743
LN-GOY	Scheibe SF-36A	4104	(OY-XMI)
			D-KOOY
			(LN-GOY)
			D-KOOY
			(LN-GKN)
LN-GPA	Glaser-Dirks DG-300 Elan	3E-303	
LN-GPO	Schempp-Hirth Discus b	334	SE-UIK
LN-GPP	Grob G.103C Twin III Acro	34105	
LN-GPR	LET L-23 Super Blanik	978310	
LN-GPS	Schempp-Hirth Discus bT	155/555	
	(Possibly conversion of Discus B c/n 555 D-8261?)		
LN-GRR	Schempp-Hirth Ventus 2cT	43/139	
LN-GRY	Sportavia/ Fournier RF-5	5113	G-AZZW
LN-GSS	Schempp-Hirth Ventus 2cT	34/118	
LN-GSW	Schleicher ASW 15B	15244	OY-XBN
LN-GTE	Schleicher ASW 20	20325	OH-526
LN-GTI	Grünau Baby II b	504	(LN-GBA)
	(CoA exp 30.9.99, stored)		BGA.1560
			RAFGGA.505
LN-GTT	Rolladen-Schneider LS8A	8177	
LN-GWA(2)	PZL PW-5 Smyk	17.08.001	
LN-GWC	PZL PW-5 Smyk	17.03.018	
LN-GWS	PZL PW-5 Smyk	17.05.011	
LN-GWW	PZL PW-5 Smyk	17.05.008	
LN-HAA	SZD-22C Mucha Standard (CoA exp 31.10.93)	F-616	

BALLOONS

LN-ASU	Cameron D-77 HAFB	212	
	(CoA exp 30.6.90, stored)		
LN-ASX	Cameron O-56 HAFB (Wfu)	98	SE-ZZE
	(CoA exp 30.6.87, stored)		
LN-CAB	Aerostar Aurora 69 S53A HAFB	S53A-3080	
LN-CAC	Cameron N-90 HAFB	3438	SE-ZGI
LN-CAD	Cameron C-80 Concept HAFB	10309	
LN-CAE	Cameron C-120 Concept HAFB (Res 4.03)	unkn	
LN-CAF	Ultramagic H77 HAFB	77/256	
LN-CBA	Cameron V-77 HAFB	614	
	(CoA exp 31.8.99, stored)		
LN-CBD	Cameron O-42 HAFB	183	SE-ZZK
LN-CBE	Cameron V-77 HAFB	1101	
LN-CBF	Cameron N-105 HAFB	943	
LN-CBG	Cameron V-77 HAFB	1694	
LN-CBH	Cameron A-120 HAFB	2830	
LN-CBI	Cameron V-77 HAFB	3635	
LN-CBJ	Colt 77A HAFB (CoA exp 31.5.99, stored)	4073	
LN-CBK	Aerostar RX-7 HAFB (Dbf .89)	3086	
LN-CBM	Cameron V-77 HAFB	3715	
LN-CBS	Colt 77A HAFB	1904	
LN-CBX	Cameron O-77 HAFB	1277	SE-ZBX

MICROLIGHTS

An asterisk * after the registration indicates a Permit expired before 1.1.05

LN-YAA *	La Mouette Cosmos	N1-86	
LN-YAB(2)	Mainair Gemini/Flash II	KR-425-386-4/W-183-386-2	
LN-YAC *	Aerodyne Vector 610 (To Sola museum)	1389	
LN-YAD	Teratorn Tierra 2	844020	
LN-YAE(2)	Bautek Pico (Reservation 8.02)	unkn	
LN-YAF(2)	Denney Kitfox II	367	
LN-YAH(2)	Jabiru UL-450	528	
LN-YAI (2) *	Solar Wings Pegasus XL-R	SW-TB-1065/SW-WA-1072	
LN-YAJ *	Solar Wings Typhoon XL	N-2-85/SW-WA-1023	
	(Wing has same c/n as LN-YCB, mated with local trike)		
LN-YAK *	CFM Shadow	003/2	
LN-YAL *	Solar Wings Pegasus XL-R	SW-TB-1089/SW-WA-1137	
LN-YAM(2) *	Zodiac Ultrastar	151	
LN-YAN *	Mainair Triflyer 330/Flash IIA	355-785-1/W-28-285-1	
	(Registered as Mainair Gemini trike unit,		
	trike c/n same as LN-YBN)		
LN-YAO	Solar Wings Pegasus XL-R	SW-TB-1067/SW-WA-1316	
	(Used parts and trike c/n SW-TB-1067 from LN-YBC)		
LN-YAP *	Solar Wings Pegasus XL-R/Se	SW-TB-1156/SW-WA-1154	
	(Trike previously on LN-YCA)		
LN-YAQ *	Pioneer Flightstar	673	D-M . . .
LN-YAR(3)	Solar Wings Pegasus Flash	W-138-12-85	
LN-YAS(2) *	Solar Wings Pegasus Flash 1 (Mainair wing c/n W87)	SW-TB-1017/SW-WF-0002	
LN-YAT(2)	Solar Wings Pegasus XL (Reservation)	unkn	
LN-YAU *	Birdman Chinook WT-II	03507	
LN-YAV	Birdman Chinook WT-2S (Dbr 16.6.90)	00952	
LN-YAX *	Steinbach Firebird/Austro Sierra 170	2204	
LN-YAY(2)	ICP MXP-740 Savannah	03-12-51-262	
LN-YAZ(2)	ATEC Zephyr 2000	Z1050704A	
LN-YBA	TLUltralight TL-132 Condor	99C05	SE-YUB
LN-YBB	Solar Wings Pegasus XL-R	SW-TB-1019/SW-WA-1037	
	(Cr 24.9.01)		
LN-YBC(2)	ATEC Zephyr (Reservation .03)	unkn	
LN-YBD *	Solar Wings Pegasus Photon	SW-TP-0017/SW-WP-0017	
LN-YBE(2)	Jabiru UL430	181	

LN-YBF *	Solar Wings Pegasus XL-R	SW-TB-1051/SW-WA-1068	
LN-YBG	Solar Wings Pegasus XL-R		
	(Cr 1.7.93)	SW-TB-1052/SW-WA-1069	
	(Wing c/n also quoted for LN-YCR)		
LN-YBH(2)	ICP MXP-740 Savannah	02-07-51-154	
LN-YBI *	Solar Wings Pegasus XL-R	SW-TB-1064/SW-WA-1071	
LN-YBJ *	Rotec Panther 2 Plus	69055	
LN-YBK *	Pioneer Flightstar	669	
LN-YBL *	Thruster Gemini	086-119	
LN-YBM *	Mainair Gemini/Flash II	433-586-4/W191	
LN-YBN	Mainair Triflyer 330	KR-355-785-3/W-190-586-1	
	(Registered as Merlin Scorcher) (Cr 10.7.03)		
LN-YBO *	Mainair Merlin Solo / Flash	KR 354-785-1/W-215-686-1	
LN-YBQ	Mainair Gemini Flash II	530-387-5/W232	
LN-YBR(2)	Rans S-6S Super Six	0596991	
LN-YBS *	Ultrasport Tripacer Manta Fledge III	BF02/BF27	
LN-YBT(2)	Kompol Stratus P-2 Trike	N-001	PL-GDL
LN-YBU *	La Mouette Profil 17	V001 P003	
LN-YBV *	Pioneer Flightstar	674	
LN-YBW(2) *	Pioneer Flightstar	unkn	
LN-YBX	Mainair Gemini/Flash II	438-686-4/W-157-386-2	
LN-YBY(2) *	Rotec Rally Sport	25501	
LN-YBZ *	La Mouette Protax Maxi Hermes	15MGA-1551-H15-85141	
LN-YCA(2) *	Ultrasports Tripacer/ Hermes 15M Demon	TA12/1	
	(Trike used on LN-YAP)		
LN-YCB	Solar Wings Pegasus XL-R	SW-TB-1001/SW-WA-1023	
	(Wing c/n same as that given for LN-YAJ)		
LN-YCC *	Solar Wings Pegasus Panther /Ultrasports trike	TA 12-4/1084-1227	
LN-YCD *	Solar Wings Panther Wizard /Ultrasports trike	TA 12-5/82-00601	
LN-YCE *	Solar Wings Pegasus XL-R /Ultrasports trike	TA12-2 /84-1228XL	
LN-YCF(2)	Solar Wing /Ultrasports trike /Demon wing?	TA 12-3	LN-YCA(1)
LN-YCG *	Solar Wings Panther/Southdown Puma Sprint		
	(C/n quoted is Fuji-Robin engine serial)	- /83-00293	
LN-YCH *	Solar Wings Typhoon S4+	T7851455/82-00084	
	(C/n quoted is Fuji-Robin engine serial)		
LN-YCI *	Skyhook Pixie	T7851445/1785	
LN-YCJ *	Solar Wings Hiway Skytrike Photon	TA12-9/SW-WP-0016	
	(Appears to have been mated with Ultrasports trike after sale)		
LN-YCK *	Aerodyne Vector 610 (Displayed in mall, Sandnes)	1203-270	
LN-YCL	Zenair CH-701 STOL	7-1260	
LN-YCM	Mainair Gemini/Flash II	KR439-786-3/W-223-3609612	
LN-YCN *	Rotec Panther 2 Plus	19863	
LN-YCO *	Solar Wings Pegasus Flash 2	SW-TB-1018/SW-WF-0115	
LN-YCP *	Solar Wings Pegasus XL-R	SW-TB-1088/SW-WA-1084	
LN-YCQ *	Ultrasports Tripacer /La Mouette Profil 17	T EVE 1/W EVE 1	
LN-YCR *	Solar Wings Eagle 3XL	OL-8548948/SW-WA-1069	
	(Wing c/n also quoted for LN-YBG)		
LN-YCS *	La Mouette Protax Mini /Profil 17	BR 001/BR 1306	
LN-YCT	Mainair Gemini/Flash II W	T448-786-4/W-222-786-2	
	(Trike c/n same as LN-YCX. Crashed 10.7.04)		
LN-YCU *	Solar Wings Pegasus XL-R	SW-TB-1086/SW-WA-1082	
LN-YCV	Quad City Ultralight Challenger 1	0987-0-0230	
LN-YCX	Mainair Gemini/Flash II	448-786-4/W-300-1186-2	
	(Trike c/n same as LN-YCT)		
LN-YCY *	Mainair Merlin Scorcher	505-1286-1/W308-1286-1	
LN-YCZ	Mainair Merlin/La Mouette Cronos	352-785-2/116	
LN-YDA *	Solar Wings Pegasus XL/ Special	T-170285/WT7841143TSR	
LN-YDB *	Solar Wings Pegasus XL-R	SW-TB-1087/SW-WA-1083	
LN-YDC	Birdman Chinook WT11-1S (Reservation)	unkn	
LN-YDD *	Rotec Panther 2 Plus	69066	
LN-YDE *	Manta Fledge III /Cosmos Dragster	FC 10/125	
LN-YDF(2)	Halley Apollo Jetstar	S-04/2002	
LN-YDG *	La Mouette Minimum /Profil 15	N 201/87	
LN-YDH *	La Mouette Cosmos Azur 17	N 387 TN184 W	
LN-YDI	Mainair Merlin/Flash II	KR-353-785-1 /W211-686-1	
	(Registered as Mainair Merlin Scorcher)		
	(Wing formerly SW-WF-0123 / G-MNYY rebuilt and re-sold)		
LN-YDJ *	Mikrofly Stratus 1	GF 01/87	
LN-YDK *	Zodiac Ultrastar	127	
LN-YDL	Eipper Quicksilver MXL-II	1196	
LN-YDM *	Aerial Arts Chaser S	TR 678/ W-678-388	
	(Not a Chaser c/n, possibly local trike and Aerial Arts 130SX wing)		
LN-YDN	Pioneer Dualstar	DS 104/DS1000-DS103	
LN-YDO(2) *	Zodiac Twinstar	06	
LN-YDP *	Birdman Chinook WT-IS	03757	
LN-YDQ *	Birdman Chinook WT-IIS	03747	
LN-YDR *	Solar Wings Pegasus XL-SE	TSRSW-TB-1155/SW-WA-1153	
LN-YDS *	Mainair Merlin Scorcher	KR-356-7853/W-205-686-1	
LN-YDT *	Quad City Ultralight Challenger 2	0587 R0 257	
LN-YDU *	Hiway Skytrike 160 Mk.2/Excalibur	unkn	
LN-YDV *	Birdman Chinook WT-II	03687	
LN-YDW	Thruster Gemini TST Mk.1	867-TST-023	G-MTKC
	(Crashed 19.7.95)		
LN-YDX	Air Création Buggy 582SL/iXess	A04009-4009/T01076	
LN-YDY *	Solar Wings Pegasus TSR	T285 1328 TSR	
LN-YDZ	ATEC Zephyr 2000 (Reservn 3.05)	unkn	
LN-YEA *	La Mouette Compact/Schwartze Minimum	01-88	
LN-YEB(2)	Denney Kitfox III	899	(LN-YVW)
LN-YEC(2)	ICP MXP-740 Savannah	02-03-51-141	
LN-YED *	La Mouette Cosmos Hermes 15 Dragster	N 188 T/N 188W	
LN-YEE *	Solar Wings Pegasus XL-SE	SW-TB-1154 /SW-WA 1152	
LN-YEF(2)	ATEC Zephyr 2000C	Z1170205A	
LN-YEG *	La Mouette Cosmos Dragster Turbo 16	N-228	
LN-YEH *	Teratorn Tierra II	880313 07	
LN-YEI *	La Mouette Minimum Hermes 15	2-88	
LN-YEK *	La Mouette Cosmos Magnum 21	308/001-89	
LN-YEL	Flight Design CT 2K	03.03.04.11	

LN-YEM *	La Mouette Cosmos Turbo 15 Dragster	110	
LN-YEN(2)	Denney Kitfox IV Classic	C97010184	
LN-YEO	La Mouette Cosmos Turbo 15 Dragster	N113-88	
	(Crashed 19.3.01)		
LN-YEP *	La Mouette Cosmos Turbo 15 Dragster	N112-88	
LN-YEQ *	La Mouette Cosmos Bidulm Turbo 15	N3-88	
LN-YER *	La Mouette Cosmos Dragster Hermes 15	110-88	
LN-YES *	Mainair Gemini/Flash II	KR-441-780-4/W-222-786-2	
	(Wing has same c/n as LN-YCT)		
LN-YET *	Teratorn Tierra I	860805009	
LN-YEU *	La Mouette Minimum Profil 17	5-88	
LN-YEV *	La Mouette Minimum Hermes 16	6-88	
LN-YEW *	La Mouette Minimum Hermes 16	6-89	
LN-YEX	Mikrofly Stratus 2	MFP 02 88	
LN-YEY *	La Mouette Minimum Hermes 15	3-87	
LN-YEZ *	Teratorn Tierra II	880712021	
LN-YFA *	La Mouette Minimum Profil 17	3-87/8-88	
LN-YFB *	La Mouette Minimum Hermes 16	9-88	
LN-YFC *	La Mouette Minimum Hermes 15	10-88	
LN-YFD *	Aerial Arts Chaser 110 SX	TR 674/ W 674	
	(Not a Chaser c/n, possibly local trike and Aerial Arts 130SX wing)		
LN-YFE *	La Mouette Minimum Turbo 15	029	
LN-YFF	Fisher Super Koala (Crashed 23.8.01)	1	
LN-YFG	Aviasud Mistral (Cr 9.7.95)	12-88-71	
LN-YFH *	Air Création Safari GT-BI/Quartz 16SX	501	
LN-YFI *	La Mouette Minimum Bidulm Turbo 16	0052	
LN-YFJ *	Aerial Arts Chaser 377	CH 795	
LN-YFK *	Aerial Arts Chaser 377	CH 793	
LN-YFL	Aerial Arts Chaser 377	CH 794	
LN-YFM *	Zodiac Ultrastar	148	
LN-YFN	La Mouette Cosmos Bidulm Chronos	208	
LN-YFO *	Teratorn Tierra IA	890319039	
LN-YFP	La Mouette Cosmos Bidulm Chronos	198	
LN-YFQ	Solar Wings Pegasus XL-Q	SW-TE-0218/SW-WQ-0233	
	(Still regd but flying as LN-YOJ)		
LN-YFR *	Quad City Ultralight Challenger II	CH2-0289-CW-0398	
LN-YFS	Fisher Super Koala (Reservation)	unkn	
LN-YFT	Air Création SX GT 503/Kiss 13	104/A-00015-0019	
LN-YFU	Air Création SX GT 462	102	
LN-YFV	Air Création GT BI /Quartz SX 16	103	
LN-YFX *	Hovey Delta Bird	unkn	
LN-YFY	TEAM Mini-MAX 1100R (Cr 21.6.98)	223-4-90	
LN-YFZ *	Mikrofly Stratus 1	MFP 04 89	
LN-YGA *	Mosler N-3-2 Pup	0021 LAS-2	
LN-YGB *	S.M.A.N. Pétrel	52083	
LN-YGE	Mainair Gemini/Flash IIA	KR-297-0385-3/W31-385-1	
	(Trike c/n 297 was Mainair 440 Triflyer sold with Flash 1 wing c/n W33; while this wing was originally on LN-YTG)		
LN-YGF *	Mikrofly Stratus 1	MFP 03 89	
LN-YGG *	Kolb Twinstar Mk.2	M2-154	
LN-YGH	Furuheim Mikromoth 1-503	BF 00390	
LN-YGI	Rans S-6ES Coyote II (Cr 29.5.02)	1089.089	
LN-YGJ	Pioneer Flightstar	675	
LN-YGK	Quad City Ultralight Challenger II	H2-0388-CW-. . . .	
	(Dbr 15.11.01)		
LN-YGL	Quad City Ultralight Challenger II Special	H2-1289 CW-0493	
LN-YGM	Air Création Racer SX 12	106/90	
LN-YGN	Quad City Ultralight Challenger II Special	CH2-1289 CW-0494	
	(Cr 23.5.04)		
LN-YGO *	Zodiac Twin Star	011	
LN-YGP *	Mikrofly Stratus 1	MFP 05 90	
LN-YGQ *	Quad City Ultralight Challenger II Special	CH2-1289 CW-0492	
LN-YGR *	Rans S-5 Coyote I	90.124	
LN-YGS *	Aerial Arts Chaser S	TR 459/W 459	
	(Not a Chaser c/n. Local trike with Aerial Arts 130SX wing?)		
LN-YGT(2) *	Eipper Quicksilver GT-400S	GT2801174	
LN-YGU	Quad City Ultralight Challenger II Special	CH2-1189 CW-0478	
	(Possibly sold as N101SV?)		
LN-YGV	Mikrofly Stratus 2B	MFP 06 91	
LN-YGW *	Quad City Ultralight Challenger II Special	CH2-0890 CW-0533	
LN-YGX *	Aerial Arts Chaser S	"CH592"	
	(Possibly Chaser c/n CH792, or a local trike and Aerial Arts 130SX wing)		
LN-YGY	Rans S-6 Coyote II	0989.079	
LN-YGZ	Rans S-6ES Coyote II	0191.155	
LN-YHA	Rans S-5 Coyote I (Cr 4.8.04)	1090.148	
LN-YHB	Rans S-6 Coyote II	0191.158	
LN-YHC *	Eipper Quicksilver GT-500	0065	
LN-YHD *	Kolb Firestar	3607811 or HJD-3 ?	
LN-YHE	Rans S-12 Airaile	0491073	
LN-YHF	Quad City Ultralight Challenger II Special	CH2-0890 CW-0552	
LN-YHG *	Mikrofly Stratus 2B	MFP 07 91	
LN-YHH	Rans S-5 Coyote I	90137	
	(Wfu 5.6.04, under restoration)		
LN-YHI	Rans S-6 Coyote II (Cr 2.8.95)	0591.190	
LN-YHJ *	Rans S-12 Airaile	0591.074	
LN-YHK *	Solar Wings Pegasus Quasar	SW-TQC-0071/SW-WQQ-0465	
LN-YHL *	Eipper Quicksilver MX II	3016	SE-YAE
LN-YHM *	Teratorn Tierra I	88030718	
LN-YHN *	Mikrofly Stratus 1	MFP 08 91	
LN-YHO *	European CUBy 2	AAH0 06	
LN-YHP	Preceptor N3-2 Pup (Reservation .05)	unkn	
LN-YHQ	Light Aero Avid High Gross STOL	1471 HGS	
LN-YHR	Rans S-12 Airaile	0491.070	
LN-YHS	Fisher Classic	C-053	
LN-YHT	Quad City Ultralight Challenger II Special	CH-20688 CW-0330	
LN-YHU	Rans S-7 Courier (Cr 25.5.03)	0991.087	
LN-YHV(2)	Best Off Sky Ranger (C/n may be engine type)	912	

LN-YHW(2)	Rans S-6S Super Six	0495.795	
LN-YHX	Rans S-6 Coyote II	1091.232	
LN-YHY	Murphy Renegade II	386	
LN-YHZ *	Rans S-12 Airaile	0891.120	
LN-YIA	Rans S-7 Courier	1291.090	
LN-YIB	Mikrofly Stratus 2B	MFP 09 92	
LN-YIC	Mikrofly Stratus 2B (Cr 29.5.04)	MFP 10 92	
LN-YID *	TEAM Mini-MAX	701	
LN-YIE	Rans S-6 Coyote II (Reservation)	unkn	
LN-YIF	Trike?Turbo 15 (Reservation)	unkn	
LN-YIG	Rans S-12 Airaile	1292.352	
LN-YIH *	Rans S-6ES Coyote II	0990.140	
	(Same c/n quoted for LN-YMH)		
LN-YII *	Quad City Ultralight Challenger II Special	CH-20589 CW-0421	
LN-YIJ *	Fisher FP101 Koala	N-3	
LN-YIK	Fisher Super Koala	N-2	
LN-YIL	Edra Sao Paulo Seabird	049	
LN-YIM	Mikrofly Stratus 2B	MFP 11 92	
LN-YIN	Atlas (Reservation)	unkn	
LN-YIO	Kolb Firestar	193	
LN-YIP *	Mikrofly Stratus 1B	MFP 12 93	
LN-YIQ	Noim Sirius C	C15	(F) 05-BH
LN-YIR *	TEAM Hi-MAX	811P	
LN-YIS	TEAM Hi-MAX (Reservation)	unkn	
LN-YIT *	Teratorn Tierra 2	920627157	
LN-YIU *	Rans S-12 Airaile	0293.378	
LN-YIV	Rans S-12 Airaile	unkn	
LN-YIX	Mikrofly Twin Stratus	MFP 13 93	
LN-YIY *	TEAM Hi-MAX	232	
LN-YIZ	Rans S-12 Airaile (Cr 31.5.97)	1192.329	
LN-YJA	Mainair Sports Scorcher	639-588-6/W428-588-4	
LN-YJB(2)	Murphy Renegade Spirit (Cr 16.5.97)	336	
LN-YJC *	Rans S-12 Airaile	0493.409	
LN-YJD *	TEAM Z-Max	764P	
LN-YJE	TEAM Z-Max	763P	
LN-YJF	Rans S-6 Coyote II	0392281	
LN-YJG	TEAM Hi-MAX (Reservation .05)	unkn	
LN-YJH(2)	Rans S-6ES Coyote II	0195721ES	
LN-YJI	Skystar Denney Kitfox III	902	
LN-YJJ	Halley Apollo Fox	S-04/04	
LN-YJK *	La Mouette Cosmos Dragster Turbo 15	N115	
LN-YJL	TEAM Z-Max	525P	
LN-YJN	TEAM Z-Max (Reservation)	unkn	
LN-YJO	Teratorn Tierra II	880317106	
LN-YJP	Kolb Ultrastar (Cr 13.9.94)	150	
LN-YJS	Fisher FP404	N4-404	
LN-YKA	Type unknown (Reservation)	unkn	
LN-YKB *	Preceptor N3-2 Pup	0122	
LN-YKC	Preceptor N3-2 Pup (Reservation)	unkn	
LN-YKD	Mikrofly Twin Stratus (Cr 3.4.99)	MFP 14 96	
LN-YKE(2)	Sonex (Reservation 8.02)	unkn	
LN-YKF *	Denney Kitfox III	1065	LN-TSH
	(Permit exp 18.6.02, dismantled, stored)		
LN-YKG	Falken (Reservation)	1	
LN-YKH	Rans S-6ES Coyote II	0795.857	
LN-YKI	Edra Sao Paulo Seabird (Reservation)	unkn	
LN-YKJ	Rans S-6ES Coyote II	1295.907.ES	
LN-YKK	Spectrum Beaver RX650 (Cr 14.3.94)	027	
LN-YKL(2) *	Preceptor N3-2 Ultra Pup	LA-066-KP	(LN-YHW(1))
LN-YKM	Rans S-6 Coyote II	1095.887	
LN-YKN	Denney Kitfox IV	401-1517	(LN-AEO)
LN-YKO *	Zodiac Ultrastar	146	
LN-YKP	Rans S-6ES Coyote II	0395.775	
LN-YKQ	Rans S-6ES Coyote II	1294.710	
LN-YKR(2) *	Light Aero Avid Flyer Bandit	1417E	
LN-YKS *	Denney Kitfox III	994	
LN-YKT *	Edra Sao Paulo Seabird	077	
LN-YKU	Rans S-6ES Coyote II	0996.1036.ES	
LN-YKV	Jora (Reservation)	11/96	(OY) 9- . . .
LN-YKW	Murphy Maverick	060M	
LN-YKX	Light Aero Avid Flyer	394	LN-PET
LN-YKY	Rans S-12 Airaile (Reservation)	unkn	
LN-YKZ	Rans S-6 Super Six (Cr 9.4.00)	1292.404	
LN-YLA	TEAM Hi-MAX (Cr 16.7.99)	TA2	
LN-YLB	Rans S-6S Super Six	1295909S	
LN-YLC	Rans S-6ES Coyote II	0592301	
LN-YLD	TEAM Hi-MAX (Reservation)	unkn	
LN-YLE	La Mouette Cosmos Bidulm Chronos	0228/960 425 8	
LN-YLF	Rans S-6ES Coyote II	0495.799ES	
LN-YLG	Bailey-Moyes Dragonfly	26	
LN-YLH	Rans S-6ES Coyote II	0195720ES	
LN-YLI	Fisher FP-303 (Reservation)	unkn	
LN-YLJ	Edra Sao Paulo Seabird (Cr 7.7.04)	76	
LN-YLK	SGAvn Storm 280G	44	
LN-YLL *	Quad City Ultralight Challenger I Special	CHCW 0488-105	
	(C/n as quoted. Possibly CH2-0484-0105, ex N105PL, or possibly could be CH2-0488-CW-0305))		
LN-YLM	Rans S-6 Coyote II	1292.402	
LN-YLN	Merlin	M1138	
LN-YLO *	Merlin GT	96063	
LN-YLP	Mikrofly Twin Stratus	MFP 16/2000	
LN-YLQ	Jora UL (Cr 12.10.00)	C-106	
LN-YLR	Rans S-6ES Coyote II	912961072ES	
LN-YLS	Teratorn Tierra 1A	900121060	
LN-YLT(2)	Denney Kitfox III	995	LN-ULV
LN-YLU	Jabiru UL 450	444	
LN-YLV	Rans S-6S Super Six	11971183S	
LN-YLW(2) *	Rans S-7E Courier	0189037-515	SE-YKR
LN-YLX	Jora UL	C-108	
LN-YLY	Comco Ikarus C42B	0204-6441	
LN-YLZ	Jabiru UL 450	436	
LN-YMA *	Teratorn Tierra 1	870806017	
LN-YMB *	Teratorn Tierra 1	860404005	
LN-YM *	Teratorn Tierra 1	860302004	
LN-YMD	Jabiru UL450/2200	370	
LN-YME *	Teratorn Tierra 1A	900222065	
LN-YMF	Teratorn Tierra 2	901026091	
LN-YMG *	Teratorn Tierra 1A	880715019	
LN-YMH *	Rans S-6 Coyote II	0990.140	
	(Same c/n quoted for LN-YIH)		
LN-YMI *	Behlen Trike	19/830008	
LN-YMJ	Jabiru UL450	441	
LN-YMK	Jabiru UL 450	369	
LN-YML *	Teratorn Tierra 1	860301002	
LN-YMM	Jora UL	1797	
LN-YMN	Denney Kitfox III	1031	LN-AKF
LN-YMO	Preceptor N3-2 Ultra Pup (Cr 12.4.04)	LA065UP	
LN-YMQ	Jabiru UL450	389	
LN-YMR *	Denney Kitfox III	C97010188	
LN-YMS	Jabiru UL450	325	
LN-YMT	Murphy Rebel	297R	
LN-YMU	Murphy Maverick	002M-UL	C-FPSJ
LN-YMV	Murphy Maverick	062M	
LN-YMX *	Eipper Quicksilver MXL-2 Sport	365	
LN-YMY	Jabiru UL450	593	
LN-YMZ	Mikrofly Twin Stratus	MFP 17/2002	
LN-YNA	Mikrofly Twin Star (Reservation 7.04)	MFP 1805	
LN-YNB	Kolb Twinstar III	M3-032	N4263A
LN-YNH	Light Aero Avid Flyer (Reservation)	unkn	
LN-YNI	Take Off Merlin 1100/XP15	39900/A00117/0117	SE-VCU
	(Crashed 20.8.03)		
LN-YNK	Skystar Denney Kitfox IV	DCU-016	
LN-YNP(2)	Jabiru UL (Reservation .00)	unkn	
LN-YNT	Light Aero Avid Flyer IV	1035-859	SE-XMX
LN-YNV	Light Aero Avid Flyer IV (Reservn 3.05)	unkn	
LN-YNW	Jodel (model?) (Reservation 11.99)	unkn	
LN-YOA	Quad City Ultralight Challenger II Special	CH2-1188- CW 0371	
	(Correct c/n may be CH2-0888-0371)		
LN-YOB	Quad City Ultralight Challenger II Special	CH2-0190-CW0508	
LN-YOC	Rans S-12 Airaile	0492.210	
LN-YOD	ICP Bingo 4S	03-08-52-128	
LN-YOH	Urban Air Samba XXL	SA XL 12	
LN-YOJ *	Solar Wings Pegasus XL-Q	SW-TE-218/SW-Q-0024	
	(Trike SW-TE-218 is ex LN-YFQ which had wing SW-Q-0233)		
	(Wing SW-Q-0024 originally sold with trike SW-TE-0029 as LN-YKR(1), later sold as SE-YRC)		
LN-YOL	Rans S-12 Airaile	0493.396	
LN-YOM	Quad City Ultralight Challenger II	01871 R 0231	
	(C/n 0231 also quoted for LN-YOR and for N231SP)		
LN-YOO	Light Aero Avid Flyer IV (Cr 3.9.97)	1491 HGS	
LN-YOR	Quad City Ultralight Challenger I	0987 R 0231	
	(C/n 0231 also quoted for LN-YOM and for N231SP)		
LN-YOS *	First Strike Supercat	474	
LN-YOU *	Mainair 440 Gemini /Puma Sprint	241-384	
LN-YOY	Jora UL	008-1995	(OY) 9-187
LN-YPA	Denney Kitfox IV (Reservation .05)	1635	LN-LMA
LN-YPC	Lamco Euro Cub Mk.1	CAH-011	
LN-YPD	Polaris FIB 582	0331087	
	(C/n now shown as 0331987/03B4678)		
LN-YPE	Air Création Clipper 912/iXess	T04014	
LN-YPG *	Teratorn Tierra 1A	880714017	
LN-YPH	Rans S-6 Coyote II	1093.549	
LN-YPK	Eipper Quicksilver GT-400	GT 2801206/3590197	
LN-YPL	Comco Ikarus C42B	0205-6461	
LN-YPM	Zenair CH-701 STOL UL	7-8033	
LN-YPO	Mikrofly Twin Stratus	MFP 15 97	
LN-YPP	Teratorn Tierra 1A	880316106	
LN-YPR	Zenair CH-601 UL Zodiac	6-9402	
LN-YPS(2) *	Mainair Gemini/Flash 1	KR-294-0385-W29	
LN-YPU	Pegasus Quik 912S EXE	8110	
LN-YPW	La Mouette Cosmos Bidulm Chronos	532	(F) 05-BT
LN-YPX	Solar Wings Pegasus XL-Q	SW-WQ-0024	
	(Crashed 11.5.02)		
LN-YPZ	Rans S-6S Super Six	1294.715S	
LN-YQS *	Eipper Quicksilver MX-II	3981	
LN-YQT *	Rans S-12 Airaile	0292.189	
LN-YQW(2)	La Mouette Cosmos Chronos 14	N187T	
LN-YRB(2)	Rans S-6S Super Six (Reservation 7.99)	unkn	
LN-YRE *	Teratorn Tierra 1A	900723078	
LN-YRH *	Teratorn Tierra 1 (to museum, Sola)	860303003	
LN-YRJ	Skystar Denney Kitfox IV	DCV 018	
LN-YRO	Air Solar Wings Pegasus XL-SE/Kiss 450		
	(Crashed 21.4.04)	T01076/A02164-2145	
LN-YRR	Lamco Eurocub Mk.1	CAH 008	
	(Now recorded as c/n CAH-001)		
LN-YRS	Murphy Renegade Spirit (Cr 8.4.04)	AC-385	
LN-YRT(2)	Titan Tornado (Reservation .05)	unkn	
LN-YRV *	TEAM Z-Max	P712	(OY) 9-162
LN-YRW	Ragwing Special (Reservation)	unkn	
LN-YRY	Rans S-6S Super Six	1294.711S	
LN-YSA	III Sky Arrow 450T	030	
LN-YSB(2) *	III Sky Arrow 450T	044	
LN-YSC	III Sky Arrow 450T	036	

LN-YSD	Fisher FP-404 Classic (Reservation)	unkn	
LN-YSE	Zenair CH-701 STOL	7-1263	LN-PSB
LN-YSF	La Mouette Cosmos Dragster Hermes 16	N2 87	
LN-YSH	III Sky Arrow 450TS	069S	
LN-YSI	Light Aero Avid Flyer (Cr 4.6.98)	354	LN-HAL
LN-YSJ *	Murphy Renegade Spirit 2	379	
LN-YSK *	La Mouette Cosmos Dragster Turbo 16	189	
LN-YSL	Denney Kitfox IV	C01970185	
LN-YSN	Fisher FP-202 Super Koala	SK 082	
LN-YSP(2)	Comco Ikarus C42 Cyclone	9803-6082	
LN-YSR *	La Mouette Cosmos Dragster Turbo 16	83-2	
LN-YSS	Zenair CH-601 UL Zodiac (Reservn 3.05)	unkn	
LN-YST	Fisher Super Koala	SK 090	
LN-YSV	Asso Aeri Asso V Champion V	32	
LN-YSW *	Aériane Sirocco	11/84	
LN-YSX	Sonex	210	
LN-YTA *	Birdman Chinook WT-IIS	01212	
LN-YTB *	Birdman Chinook WT-II	03667	
LN-YTC *	Birdman Chinook WT-II	03657	
LN-YTD *	Denney Kitfox IV-1200	1725	SE-YTB
LN-YTE	Rans S-6 ES Coyote II	0191.156	
LN-YTF *	Birdman Chinook WT-IIS	00512	
LN-YTG	Mainair Gemini/Flash 2 (Original wing W-33 went to LN-YGE)	293-0385-3/W-31-385-1	
LN-YTH *	Fisher FP-202 Super Koala	2-90	
LN-YTI	Light Aero Avid Flyer	863	(LN-TTI)
LN-YTJ *	Fisher FP-202 UL Koala	2196	
LN-YTK	Halley Apollo Jet Star (Reservation .05)	unkn	
LN-YTL	Teratorn Tierra 1A Special	901025090	
LN-YTM	Rans S-6ES Coyote II	0596.992ES	
LN-YTN	Quad City Challenger 2 (Cr 1.9.90)	CH20289/CW0389	
LN-YTO	Rans S-7 Courier	0989.057	LN-ATC
LN-YTP *	Light Aero Avid Flyer Mk.4 STOL	1201	
LN-YTR	Denney Kitfox IV (Reservation)	1832	
LN-YTS(2)	Rans S-14 Airaile	0895.088	
LN-YTT *	Teratorn Tierra 1	920209017	
LN-YTU	Pegasus Quantum 912EXE	7876	
LN-YTV *	Hodge Apollo CX	AS/02/007/87	
LN-YTW *	Rans S-6 ES Coyote II (Same c/n as N42739, possibly ex and returned to?)	0191.159	
LN-YTX	TL Ultralight TL-132 Condor	95C11	SE-YTX
LN-YTY	Titan Tornado 912 (Reservation)	unkn	
LN-YTZ	ATEC Zephyr 2000 (Reservation .05)	unkn	
LN-YUA	Tornado 2 gyrocopter	'1'	(OY) 10-14
LN-YUG	Rans S-12XL Airaile	04970794	SE-YUG
LN-YUH	Halley Apollo Jet Star	01/04	
LN-YVA	Asso Aeri (Reservation .05)	unkn	
LN-YVE	Eipper Quicksilver MXL Sport	162	
LN-YVF *	Denney Kitfox III	970	(LN-SVF)
LN-YVI	Rans S-12 Airaile	0892.254	
LN-YVL	Rans S-6ES Coyote II (Cr 6.6.95)	0195.718ES	
LN-YVM	Rans S-6 Coyote II (Reservation .05)	0789.043	SE-YKS
LN-YVN	Fly Synthesis Storch CL (Reservn 3.05)	10	
LN-YVT	Light Aero Avid Flyer	158	
LN-YVV	Skystar Kitfox II	306	LN-REV
LN-YWA	Rans S-6 Coyote II (Cr 21.8.01)	0192.266	
LN-YWB	Best Off Sky Ranger	SKR.0306.348	
LN-YWH	ICP MXP-740 Savannah	11-98-50-1 04	
LN-YWM	Best Off Sky Ranger	SKR0106228	
LN-YWN	Sonex (Reservation .05)	unkn	
LN-YWW *	Lamco Eurocub Mk.1	CAH-004	
LN-YWY	Murphy Renegade Spirit	382	
LN-YXA	Halley Apollo C-15TN Jet-Star	S-01/2000	SE-VCP
LN-YXL	Denney Kitfox IV	1633	LN-BEI (2)
LN-YXR	Raj Hamsa X'Air	869	
LN-YXX *	Teratorn Tierra 1A	890820058	
LN-YYC	Polaris FIB	04B4734/0431133	
LN-YYG	Halley Apollo Fox	170701	SE-YYG
			HA-YNBF
LN-YYP	Halley Apollo Fox (Reservn 8.04)	S-06/2002	SE-YYP
LN-YYW	Rans S-12 Airaile	1294.542	
LN-YYY(2) *	Denney Kitfox III	858	LX-FOX
LN-YZC	Zenair CH-601 UL Zodiac	6-9490	(OY) 9-268
LN-YZL *	Eipper Quicksilver MX2	QS.83.3264.1	
LN-YZP	Rans S-6S Super Six	0195.716S	
LN-YZX	Omsider Mk.0	001	
LN-YZZ	Air Création Clipper XP 582SL (C/n quoted in Germany as 7954557567)	134/95	D-MMYZ

LX - LUXEMBOURG

Regn.	Type	C/n	Prev.Id.
LX-ACD(2)	Cerva CE-43 Guepard	466	F-BXCD
LX-ACE	Rutan Cozy Classic	CC.1002	N52CZ
LX-ACP	Cessna P210N Pressurized Centurion	P21000131	N33CP
			C-GRAT
			N4901P
LX-ACR	Piper PA-31T1 Cheyenne I	31T-8104067	D-IACR
			N52TW
			N2608Y
LX-AGM	Mooney M.20K Model 231	25-0636	N1154P
LX-AHZ	Cessna T210N Turbo Centurion II	21063672	I-KKIS
			N4918C
LX-AIA	Piper PA-18 Super Cub 95	18-1011	ALAT
			51-15314
LX-AIB(3)	Piper PA-28-161 Cadet	2841086	N91692
LX-AIC(2)	Reims/Cessna F172L	F17200852	
LX-AID(2)	Reims/Cessna F172N	F17201972	D-EOOT
LX-AIE(3)	Piper PA-28-161 Cadet (Damaged 20.6.01)	2841346	D-ESTG
			N92294
			N151ND
			N92294
LX-AIF(2)	Piper PA-28-161 Cadet	2841173	N9185V
LX-AIG(3)	Piper PA-28-161 Cadet	2841315	N9211Q
LX-AIL(2)	Bellanca 7ECA Scout	1055-74	N88301
LX-AIM(2)	Reims/Cessna FRA150L Aerobat	FRA1500123	OO-WIV
			D-ECGJ
LX-AIP	Reims/Cessna F152 (W/o 18.5.02)	F15201432	
LX-AIQ	Reims/Cessna F152	F15201868	
LX-AIR(2)	Piper PA-28-235 Cherokee	28-10586	N9005W
LX-AIS(2)	Reims/Cessna F152	F15201617	
LX-AIT(3)	Cessna TR182 Turbo Skylane RG	R18201415	F-GCVZ
			N4753S
LX-AIX	Reims/Cessna F182Q Skylane	F18200102	
LX-AIY	Cirrus SR20	1359	N8150C
LX-AIZ	Reims/Cessna F172N	F17201968	D-EAKU
LX-AKI	Dassault Falcon 50EX	306	
LX-ALF	Grob G.115A	8030	(OO-PHD)
			(D-EGVV)
LX-ALX	Beech B200 Super King Air	BB-951	N37HR
			RP-C969
			VH-AGB
			RP-C969
LX-APB	Beech C90A King Air	LJ-867	D-IEKG
			HB-GIH
			D-IIIS
			(D-IFQM)
LX-ARA	Beech F33A Bonanza (Damaged)	CE-861	N222FT
			N31228
			D-EHVE
LX-ARC	Hawker 800XP	258444	EC-HJL
			N40489
LX-ARS	Grumman-American AA-1B Trainer	AA1B-0556	D-EHLD
			(N1456R)
LX-ATT	Piper PA-28-181 Archer II	28-8090096	OO-PAQ
			OO-HLC
			N80922
LX-AVA(2)	Piper PA-28-181 Archer II	2890157	D-ETAH
			N9214X
LX-AVB	Piper PA-28-161 Cadet	2841261	D-ENXN
			N9194N
LX-AVC(2)	Piper PA-28-161 Warrior II	28-8016061	D-EMTJ(2)
			N4TX
			N8082Y
LX-AVG	Piper PA-28-236 Dakota	28-8611006	OY-CEC
LX-AVS	PA-32R-301T Turbo Saratoga SP	32R-8129087	F-GMCL
			N8410B
LX-AWY	Grumman AA-5 Traveler	AA5-0723	
LX-BOY	Robin HR.100/200B Royale	119	D-EOCY
LX-BSM(2)	Colomban MC-15 Cri-Cri	421	
LX-CDH	Murphy Rebel (Reservation)	unkn	
LX-COS	Dassault Falcon 900	159	LX-NAN
			F-WQPL
			LX-NAN
			N263PW
			P4-NAN
			F-WWFD
LX-DAD	Cessna T303 Crusader	T30300281	OO-DAD
			N4837V
LX-DAR	Cirrus SR22	0220	N855CD
LX-DEA	CASA C.212 (Reservation .03)	unkn	
LX-DIN	Lancair Legacy 2000	137	
LX-DIS	Cessna 140	12409	C-FELQ
			CF-ELQ
LX-DPA	Dassault Falcon 10	113	F-GFHH(2)
			(F-GFHG)
			HB-VIW
			I-CHOC
			(I-SHOP)
			F-WPXE
LX-DSL	Bombardier Learjet 45	45-158	N3019T
LX-DWT	Europa Aviation Europa XS-MG (Reservn .04)	434	
LX-EAR	Gates Learjet 31A	31A-160	VP-BMX
			N31LR
LX-EBV	Stoddard-Hamilton Glastar (Res .04)	5628	(N130EB)
LX-FAC	Piper PA-18 Super Cub 95	18-2132	52-2532

LX-FAZ	Canadair CL.600-2B16 Challenger	5307	C-GIDG (N604BA) VP-BHA VR-BHA C-FXUQ C-GLXH
LX-FBY	Canadair CL.600-2B16 Challenger	5485	N485CL C-GLXB
LX-FCA	Piper PA-32R-301T Turbo Saratoga SP	32R-8129099	N8430H
LX-FCV(6)	Boeing 747-4R7F	25866	N17856
LX-FLO	Piper PA-28-181 Archer II	28-8190084	OO-ESC OO-HKO N8291Y
LX-FMR	Dassault Falcon 50	165	HZ-SM3 F-WZHF
LX-FOX	Cessna 525 CitationJet	525-0229	LX-TRA D-IHOL(2) N5218R
LX-FTA	Dassault Falcon 900	201	N210FJ F-WWFA
LX-FUN	Piper PA-46-500TP Malibu Meridian	4697050	N123SX G-BTZP N53308 N9531N N5020Y
LX-GBY	Hawker 800XP	258392	N23569
LX-GCA	Cessna 525 CitationJet	525-0235	I-ESAI VP-BZZ N5246Z
LX-GCV(4)	Boeing 747-4R7F	25867	
LX-GDC	Canadair CL.600-2A12 Challenger	3065	N601JP (N45PA) N601JP N500PE N1623 N602CC C-GLYA
LX-GDE	Embraer EMB.120RT Brasilia	120184	LX-EAC N288UE PT-SQW
LX-GDL	Cessna 550 Citation II	550-0033	LX-JET LX-GDL (N526CA) F-WPLT F-GPLT N46DA N755CM N59MJ TR-LYE (N3252M)
LX-GDM	Dassault Falcon 50 (Reservation)	unkn	
LX-GER	Aero Designs Pulsar	379	
LX-GES	Dassault Falcon 900	78	N522KM C-GSSS N332MC N456FJ F-WWFH
LX-GEX	Bombardier BD.700-1A10 Global Express	9013	C-GZSM HB-IUR C-GDXU
LX-GHI	Short SC.7 Skyvan 3M	SH.1890	Arg.CG:PA-53 G-14-62
LX-GHL	Cessna TR182 Turbo Skylane RG (Reims-assembled with "c/n" 0002) (F-GPSP res 11.02)	R18200860	N737NK
LX-GJL	Dassault Falcon 900	197	(LX-MAM) N197FJ F-WWFQ
LX-GNG	Beech C90A King Air	LJ-1321	F-GYGL D-IOMG N8232L
LX-GOL	IAI-1125 Astra SP	059	HB-VNF D-CCAT N4341S
LX-GTX	Express Aircraft Express (Reservation .01)	unkn	
LX-HBP	Aérospatiale AS.355N Ecureuil 2	5699	
LX-HCP	Robinson R44 Clipper II	10403	N104PG
LX-HDS	Aérospatiale AS.350B3 Ecureuil	3223	ZS-RLE
LX-HEC	Aérospatiale SA.365N4 / Eurocopter EC.155B Dauphin	6600	F-WQPX
LX-HEP(2)	Bell 212	30972	N606LH JA9545 N1071G
LX-HEX	Revolution Mini-500	349	
LX-HLC	Robinson R-22 Beta	2344	D-HIPA
LX-HMD	McDonnell-Douglas MD.900	00033	D-HRTA
LX-HMS	McDonnell-Douglas MD.900	00037	HB-XQZ N9199X
LX-HPG	McDonnell-Douglas MD.900	00013	SX-HJP N9213P
LX-HRU	Aérospatiale AS.365N3 Dauphin 2	6648	
LX-HUF	Aérospatiale AS.365N2 Dauphin 2	6412	F-GHRY
LX-ICV	Boeing 747-428F	25632	(F-GIUA) N6005C
LX-IIH	Cessna 525 CitationJet CJ	525-0391	N5130J
LX-IMS	Bombardier Learjet 45	45-070	N50163
LX-INT	Rutan Cozy 111 Canard	E-711	
LX-IOI	Neico Lancair IV-P	LIV-347-FB-P	N10VJ
LX-IRE	Dassault Falcon 50EX	324	N324EX F-WWHD
LX-JCD	Cessna 560XL Citation Excel (Reserved as F-GXXX)	560-5104	(F-HACD) N5223D
LX-JCO	Mooney M.20R Ovation	29-0071	D-EICO(3)
LX-JDP	Beech 200 Super King Air	BB-303	F-GHCS(2) N18345
LX-JFA(2)	SOCATA TBM-700	63	F-GLJS
LX-JFB	SOCATA TBM-700 (Reservation)	13	F-GJPY (F-GKDJ)
LX-JFD	SOCATA TBM-700	199	F-OIKC
LX-JFE	SOCATA TBM-700	208	F-OIKE
LX-JFF	SOCATA TBM-700	212	F-OIKF
LX-JFH	Pilatus PC-12/45	522	
LX-JFI	Pilatus PC-12/45	574	
LX-JJH	Dyn'Aero MCR-01	215	
LX-JOE	Brändli BX-2 Cherry	13	F-PRLQ F-WRLQ
LX-JTB	Commander 114B	14577	D-EJTB(3)
LX-KCV(2)	Boeing 747-4R7F	25868	
LX-KEN	Cessna F172E	F172-0055	D-EMAX
LX-KEV	Pilatus Britten-Norman BN-2T Islander	2102	LX-III V2-LDF (OB-T-1282) V2-LDF VP-LMF N660J G-BIIO
LX-KIN	SOCATA TB-20 Trinidad	331	F-GDND
LX-KTY	Beech B90 King Air	LJ-339	F-WKTY (F-GKTY) N143KB N120LG N211SC N766K
LX-KVF	SOCATA TB-21 Trinidad TC	721	D-EFMV
LX-LAB	Pilatus PC-12/45	531	(LX-DOG)
LX-LAR	Gates Learjet 35A	35A-653	HB-VJL
LX-LCG	Raytheon 390 Premier	RB-51	N4251D
LX-LCL	Piper PA-28R-201T Turbo Arrow III	28R-7803083	N6050H
LX-LCO	Cessna P210N Pressurized Centurion II	P21000104	N4781P C-GVVY N478IP
LX-LCT	Mooney M.20K Model 231	25-0811	N5741A D-EMEM N574IA
LX-LCV(2)	Boeing 747-4R7F	29053	
LX-LFA	Dassault Falcon 900B	154	F-GVBF F-WQBK VP-BGF F-WQBJ VP-BJA VR-BJA F-WWFL
LX-LFB	Dassault Falcon 900	62	F-GSCN F-WQBL N62FJ F-GIVR F-WWFJ
LX-LGC(2)	Fokker F.27-050 (Res. as SE-LJG 2.05)	20168	PH-EXH
LX-LGD(3)	Fokker F.27-050 (Res. as SE-LJH 2.05)	20171	PH-EXJ
LX-LGE(3)	Fokker F.27-050 (Res. as SE-LJI 2.05)	20180	PH-EXF
LX-LGI (2)	Embraer EMB.145LU	145369	PT-SOU
LX-LGJ(2)	Embraer EMB.145LU	145395	
LX-LGK(3)	Embraer EMB.135LR	14500886	PT-SXY
LX-LGL(2)	Embraer EMB.135LR	14500893	PT-SYF
LX-LGN(2)	Boeing 737-59D (Stored, reserved as OK-WGD for 4.05)	25065	G-OBMX SE-DNE (SE-DND)
LX-LGO	Boeing 737-5C9	26438	
LX-LGP(2)	Boeing 737-5C9	26439	
LX-LGQ	Boeing 737-5C9	33802	
LX-LGR	Boeing 737-7C9	33803	
LX-LGS	Boeing 737-5C9	33956	
LX-LGU(2)	Embraer EMB.145EU	145084	PT-S . .
LX-LGV(2)	Embraer EMB.145ER	145129	PT-SDG
LX-LGW(2)	Embraer EMB.145ER	145135	PT-SDM
LX-LGX(3)	Embraer EMB.145ER	145147	PT-SDX
LX-LGY(4)	Embraer EMB.145ER	145242	PT-SIH
LX-LGZ(2)	Embraer EMB.145LR	145258	PT-SIR
LX-LLM	Beech 65-C90A King Air	LJ-1261	F-GJSD N56787
LX-LMB	Beech F33A Bonanza	CE-1578	OO-PMK F-GJGA N81701
LX-LOU	Bombardier Learjet 60	60-277	N40079
LX-LOV	Cessna 525 Citation Jet	525-0102	TC-CRO N202CJ N52038
LX-LTX	Beech E90 King Air	LW-297	SE-IKD OY-AZG
LX-LWK	Boeing Stearman A75N1	75-323	N8162G 40-1766
LX-MAC	Piper PA-18-150 Super Cub	18-5392	OO-ACN D-EIWW ALAT N10F
LX-MCV(3)	Boeing 747-4R7F	29729	
LX-MEG	SOCATA TB-10 Tobago (Reservation .04)	530	G-BMEG
LX-MEL	Dassault Falcon 900B	115	HB-IBG LX-TAG EC-FPI EC-235 F-WWFL
LX-MEN	Reims/Cessna F177RG Cardinal RG	F177RG0051	

LX-MRC	Cessna 525 CitationJet	525-0473	N5201M
LX-NCV(3)	Boeing 747-4R7F	29730	
LX-NIT	Dyn' Aero MCR-4S	37	
LX-NOP	Swearingen SA.226T Merlin 111A	T-259	RBAF CF-01 N5374M
LX-NRJ	Swearingen SA.226T Merlin 111A	T-265	RBAF CF-05 N5381M
LX-OBI	Cirrus SR22	0390	N905CD
LX-OCV(2)	Boeing 747-4R7F	29731	
LX-OKC	Piper PA-28-160 Cherokee	28-7225328	HB-OKC N11C
LX-OMC	Gates Learjet 31A	31A-167	D-CGOM N613SA I-ERJB N167LJ
LX-ONE	Gates Learjet 35A	35A-417	N281CD (N37HR) HC-BTN N90RK N97D D-CONO (N117RJ) N117FJ N934GL
LX-OUF(3)	Grumman AA-5B Tiger	AA5B-0275	G-BDYB
LX-PAA	Piper PA-18-135 Super Cub	18-3815	(PH-KNC) R-125 54-2415
LX-PAB	Cessna 305C (L-19E) Bird Dog	23312	ALAT 51-12855
LX-PAC	Cessna 305C (L-19E) Bird Dog	24566	F-GHDK ALAT
LX-PAE	North American T-6G Texan	168-587	E16-106 49-3453
LX-PAK	Bombardier BD.700-1A10 Global Express	9115	(F-GOAK) C-GKCN
LX-PAV	Piper PA-32R-301T Saratoga IITC	3257097	N9513N
LX-PBL	Beech C90A King Air	LJ-1539	D-IGAH(2) (D-IUWM) N2217Q
LX-PCT	Gates Learjet 31A	31A-112	N5082S
LX-PCV	Boeing 747-4R7F	29732	
LX-PCW	Cessna 182Q Skylane	18266467	N94630
LX-PEA	Cirrus SR20	1410	N5293W
LX-PEZ	III Sky Arrow 450T	K-118	
LX-PHM	Cirrus SR20	1347	N8124E
LX-PIX	Swearingen SA.226T Merlin IIIA	T-267	RBAF CF-06 N5382M
LX-PMD	Cirrus SR20	1331	N1133C
LX-PMR	Raytheon Premier 390	RB-64	N6164U
LX-PNC	Cirrus SR20	1408	N5347Y
LX-PRA	Bombardier Learjet 60	60-145	N145LJ
LX-PRE	Raytheon 390	RB-60	N6160D
LX-PTC	Piper PA-28RT-201T Turbo Arrow IV	28R-7931157	N100US N9645N
LX-RAD	Beech 65-A90-1 King Air (U-212G)	LM-126	N7271A 70-15892
LX-RCC	Robin DR.400/120 Dauphin 2+2	2319	
LX-RCD	Robin DR.400/180 Régent	2320	
LX-RCE	Robin DR.400/180 Régent	2313	D-ECJH
LX-RCV	Boeing 747-4R7F	30400	
LX-RED	Piper PA-60-602PAerostar	62P-0872-8165010	D-IAHT(2) N60HT D-IAPB N6890X
LX-REM	Britten-Norman BN-2T Turbine Islander	2146	G-05/OT-GLA G-DEMO G-BKEA
LX-RJE	Cirrus SR20	1354	N422M
LX-ROB	Aero L-39ZO Albatros	232302	ES-TLA
LX-ROH	Robin R.3000/160	153	(D-EKKS(2))
LX-RPL	Bombardier Learjet 60	60-212	N5012H
LX-RSO	Swearingen SA.226T Merlin 111A	T-260	RBAF CF-02 N5373M
LX-RST(3)	Piper PA-31T Cheyenne II	31T-7820027	F-GGPJ N61RA N22CA N82231
LX-SAR	SOCATA TB-20 Trinidad	2049	
LX-SCV	Boeing 747-4R7F	29733	
LX-SEA	Beech 300LW Super King Air	FA-94	F-GVPE I-AZME N25219
LX-SUD	Piper PA-22-135 Tri-Pacer (Built as PA-22 Tri-Pacer 125)	22-295	D-EFUV N983A
LX-SUP	Cessna 525 CitationJet	525-0351	VP-BRJ N5246Z
LX-SVW	Dassault Falcon 2000	133	F-WQBK HZ-KSDB F-WWVI
LX-TCV	Boeing 747-4R7F	30401	N6046P
LX-TDC	Cessna 404 Titan	404-0815	(F-GSCR) F-ZBDY F-GCVR N67664
LX-THS	Dassault Falcon 50	185	F-GKBZ N238Y N23SY C-GDCO N184FJ F-WWHE

LX-TLA	McDonnell-Douglas DC-8-62FC	45960	F-GDJM I-DIWC
LX-TLB	McDonnell-Douglas DC-8-62 (Stored)	45925	N922BV CX-BQN CX-BQN-F C-GMXR N922CL HB-IDG
LX-TOY	Pitts S-1S Special	789H	LX-POL
LX-TPL	SOCATA MS.880B Rallye-Club	2041	F-BTPL
LX-TRE	Tecnam P2002-JF Sierra	003	
LX-UCV	Boeing B747-4R7F	33827	
LX-UGO	Short SC.7 Skyvan Series 3-100 (Cr 2.12.93)	SH.1945	5T-MAN G-14-113
LX-ULI	Piper PA-28RT-201T Turbo Arrow IV	28R-8031112	N8223V
LX-UXM	Bölkow BO.207	290	HB-UXM (D-ENWO)
LX-VAN	Reims FR172H Rocket	FR17200300	LX-PCL D-ECRR
LX-VAZ	Cessna 550 Citation II	550-0622	HB-VKP N826EW N326EW (N1255J)
LX-VIP	Bombardier BD.700-1A10 Global Express	9076	N700XT C-GHER
LX-WAL	BAe. ATP	2059	SE-LHZ G-OBWN G-11-059 G-BVEO G-11-059
LX-WAM	BAe. ATP	2060	SE-LPU (SE-LNZ) G-OBWO (EI-COS) G-11-060
LX-WAN	BAe. ATP	2020	SE-LHX N851AW G-WISS N851AW G-11-20 G-WISS G-11-20 G-WISS
LX-WAO	BAe. ATP	2043	SE-LPS G-BTPM EC-GSH EC-GNI G-BTPM
LX-WGM	Murphy Renegade Spirit (Reservation)	unkn	
LX-WOW	Beech C24R Sierra	MC-754	N3846Q
LX-YSL	Cessna 525 CitationJet	525-0322	N52LT
LX-ZAZ	CASA C-1.131E Jungmann	2032	D-EKPH G-BECX E3B-430
LX- . . .	Aérospatiale AS.350B Ecureuil	1804	F-GIGA D-HOUA
LX- . . .	Beech C90A King Air	LJ-1526	N998P
LX- . . .	McDonnell-Douglas MD-900 Explorer	00071	D-HIFA(5) D-HUAX N7047K

BALLOONS AND AIRSHIPS

LX-ASS	Raven S-49AHAFB	3042	
LX-AXA	Cameron A-120 HAFB	3944	
LX-BAB	Schröder Fire Balloons G 50/24 HAFB	878	
LX-BCE	Cameron N-77 HAFB	4501	
LX-BCO	Schröder Fire Balloons G34/24 HAFB	1054	
LX-BCP(2)	Cameron V-77 HAFB	3124	
LX-BEG	Cameron N-90 HAFB	4432	
LX-BEO	Schröder Fire Balloons G22/24 HAFB	928	
LX-BES	Cameron N-90 HAFB	3618	LX-SES
LX-BIG(2)	Schröder Fire Balloons G HAFB	704	
LX-BIL(4)	Cameron N-90 HAFB	4843	
LX-BIS	Cameron N-90 HAFB	4367	
LX-BKW	Schröder Fire Balloons G26/24 HAFB	927	
LX-BLK	Cameron Z-90 HAFB	4792	
LX-BLS	Cameron Z-90 HAFB (Reservation .02)	10224	
LX-BLX	Cameron GP-65 HAFB	10114	
LX-BMG	Cameron N-77 HAFB	3059	
LX-BMK	Cameron A-105 HAFB	4935	
LX-BML	Cameron N-77 HAFB	4551	
LX-BMM	Cameron Z-77 HAFB	4719	
LX-BMN	UltraMagic M-65C HAFB	65/120	
LX-BOP	Schröder Fire Balloons G20/16 HAFB	1102	
LX-BOT	Cameron O-105 HAFB	10428	
LX-BPO	Schröder Fire Balloons G 30/24 HAFB	1045	
LX-BPT	Schröder Fire Balloons G 26/24 HAFB	850	
LX-BST	Schröder Fire Balloons G 45/24 HAFB	767	
LX-BTL	Cameron N-77 HAFB (Reserved as F-GOFJ .02, not yet taken up)	2507	LX-BIL(2)
LX-BVE	Cameron Z-90 HAFB	10420	
LX-BVI	Ultramagic M-105 HAFB	105/106	
LX-BVO	Ultramagic S-105 HAFB	105/90	
LX-BVU	UltraMagic T-150 HAFB	150/03	
LX-BWS	Cameron A-120 HAFB	4905	

LX-DBI	Cameron A-140 HAFB	2660	
LX-EUR(2)	Cameron N-77 HAFB	3320	
LX-EXP	Cameron A-105 HAFB	2728	
LX-FES	Cameron V-65 HAFB	3051	
LX-GSM	Cameron N-90 HAFB (Reserved as F-GYMH 12.04)	3072	
LX-HAI	Cameron N-90 HAFB	1869	
LX-HIT(2)	Cameron V-65 HAFB	4720	
LX-HOT(2)	Cameron O-77 HAFB	925	
LX-LUX(2)	Cameron O-105 HAFB	2500	
LX-MOB	Schröder Fire Balloons G HAFB	498	
LX-OKE(2)	Cameron N-77 HAFB	2676	
LX-OLE	Cameron N-65 HAFB	2066	
LX-RTL	Cameron N-90 HAFB	3253	
LX-TNT	Cameron N-90 HAFB	3969	
LX-TOP	Cameron A-180 HAFB	2234	
LX-ZEP	Cameron N-90 HAFB	1870	

GLIDERS AND MOTOR-GLIDERS

LX-CAC(2)	Valentin Mistral C	MC 053/84	D-0210
LX-CAM	Grob G.109B	6266	
LX-CAT(2)	Scheibe SF-25B Falke	46175	D-KAGJ
LX-CAX	Glasflügel H303 Mosquito	165	D-7521
LX-CCF	Glaser-Dirks DG-505MB	5E-219B14	
LX-CLS	Rolladen-Schneider LS4B	4879	D-5117
LX-CLV	Schleicher ASK 21	21379	
LX-CMB	Schempp-Hirth Nimbus 2B	165	D-2791
LX-CMN-MN	Rolladen-Schneider LS4	4330	D-0400
LX-CMW	Rolladen-Schneider LS4	4319	PH-732 D-2512
LX-COY-U2	Glaser-Dirks DG-400	4-162	OY-XOY
LX-CPB	Schleicher ASW 20	20257	D-7645
LX-CPG	Scheibe Bergfalke III	AB-5649	
LX-CRJ	Grob G.109B	6297	D-KEOE
LX-CVN	Hoffman H-36 Dimona	36244	D-KLSW
LX-UCL(2)	Grob G.103C Twin IIISL	35048	

MICROLIGHTS

LX-XAA	Cosmos BI 17	21300	
LX-XAE	Comco Ikarus Fox C-22	9703-3722	D-MXAE
LX-XAJ	Alpi Aviation Pioneer 300S	37	
LX-XAM	Fly Synthesis Storch 503	113/60	59-PI
LX-XAP	Sky Walker 1+1	26104	
LX-XBB	Light Aero Avid Mk.IV STOL	1583D	
LX-XCB	Zenair CH-701 STOL	7-3183	59-NI
LX-XCD	Kolb Firestar	KXP-254	
LX-XCH	Cosmos Phase II 582	21520	
LX-XDH	Type unknown		
LX-XEP	Funk FK-9 Mk3	09-03-206	
LX-XER	Continental Aerolights Eagle XL	85071015	PH-1R2
LX-XHC	Funk FK-9 Mk3	09-03-205	
LX-XHG	Jabiru 450 UL	426	
LX-XHO	Cosmos DPM	B0174	
LX-XHT	3xtrim	E33-2002	
LX-XIE	Aeroprakt A-20	033	
LX-XJG	Fantasy Air Allegro 2000	01-412	
LX-XOG	Aeroprakt A-22 Vision	02-012	D-MRSL
LX-XOK	Letov ST-4 Aztek	809609-X04	OK-CUU-20
LX-XPE	Funk FK-9 Mk3	163	
LX-XPP	Weedhopper AX-3	92810	57-EL
LX-XRE	Rans S-6 Coyote II	0494611	D-MRES
LX-XRG	Aeroprakt A-22 Vision	80	
LX-XTT	Air's Maestro	128-87	
LX-X . .	Air Création Racer /Fun 14	105	OO-C16
LX-X . .	Pegasus Quantum 15	7288	G-MZET

LY - LITHUANIA

Regn.	Type	C/n	Prev.Id.
LY-ABK(2)	Antonov An-2	1G238-11	(SE-LCG) SP-FBG
LY-ABP	Yakovlev Yak-52 (W/o 2.8.03)	800810	DOSAAF
LY-ABS	Antonov An-2	1G234-01	(SE-KZY) SP-FAN
LY-ABT	Antonov An-2	1G233-20	(SE-KZV) SP-FAG
LY-ABY	Antonov An-2TP	1G238-13	SE-LCI SP-FBI
LY-ACV	Antonov An-2	1G185-24	CCCP54864
LY-ACW	Antonov-AN-2	1G185-26	CCCP54866
LY-ADG	Antonov An-2	1G201-02	CCCP71219
LY-ADI	Antonov An-2 (Stored)	1G206-46	CCCP17941
LY-ADJ	Antonov An-2	1G206-47	CCCP17942
LY-ADM	Antonov An-2	1G211-08	CCCP43989
LY-ADR	Antonov An-2	1G220-39	CCCP40249
LY-ADW	Cessna 150M	unkn	
LY-AEI	Antonov An-2	1G168-39	CCCP82863
LY-AEJ	Antonov An-2	1G168-44	CCCP82868
LY-AEK	Antonov An-2	1G168-45	CCCP82869
LY-AEL	Antonov An-2	1G171-35	CCCP92978
LY-AEM	Antonov An-2R (Unconfirmed, SP-FLX still current)	1G178-27	SP-FLX LY-AEM CCCP62635
LY-AEN	Antonov An-2	1G182-31	HA-ABI LY-AEN CCCP56474
LY-AEO	Antonov An-2	1G185-14	CCCP54854
LY-AER	Antonov An-2	1G191-15	CCCP84637
LY-AES	Antonov An-2	1G191-16	CCCP84638
LY-AET	Antonov An-2	1G192-07	CCCP84689
LY-AEX	Antonov An-2	1G227-03	CCCP33404
LY-AFB	Yakovlev Yak-52	822610	DOSAAF-112
LY-AFD	Antonov An-2R	1G201-10	LY-APD Lith: 08 blue LY-ADW CCCP71227
LY-AFF	Yakovlev Yak-12M	512764	DOSAAF
LY-AFJ	Yakovlev Yak-52	9712003	
LY-AFO	Antonov An-2	1G211-42	LY-ADL CCCP32683
LY-AFQ	Yakovlev Yak-52	8910206	DOSAAF-138
LY-AFU	Antonov An-2R	1G178-15	LY-ACU CCCP62623
LY-AFW	Yakovlev Yak-18T	721515	
LY-AGA	PZL-104 Wilga 35A (Derelict)	unkn	
LY-AGB	PZL-104 Wilga 35A	15810581	DOSAAF
LY-AGC	PZL-104 Wilga 35A	15810596	DOSAAF
LY-AGD	PZL-104 Wilga 35A	18830743	DOSAAF
LY-AGE	PZL-104 Wilga 35A	18840793	DOSAAF
LY-AGF	Antonov An-2 (Derelict)	1G138-42	CCCP70224
LY-AGH	Antonov An-2R	1G206-51	Lith.:06blue LY-AEB CCCP17946
LY-AGI	Yakovlev Yak-52	845202	
LY-AGJ	Cessna 172L (or 150M ?)	unkn	
LY-AGL	Yakovlev Yak-55	870406	DOSAAF
LY-AGM	Cessna F172D	F172-0002/17249996	D-EDSO F-WLIP (N2396U)
LY-AGP	Boeing 737-375	23808	N808WC EC-GEU EC-136 PT-TEE (C- . . . .)
LY-AGQ	Boeing 737-524	26339	N33635
LY-AGS	SOCATA MS.893A Rallye Commodore 180	10666	D-EJCE
LY-AGT	Tupolev Tu-204C	1450741364024	RA-64024
LY-AGV	Cessna 150M	unkn	
LY-AGW	Cessna 150L	unkn	
LY-AGZ	Boeing 737-524	26340	N19636
LY-AHA	Antonov An-2R	1G206-52	LithAF 09blue LY-AEA CCCP17947
LY-AHC	Yakovlev Yak-50	853007	G-BVVO LY-AMO DOSAAF
LY-AHD	Yakovlev Yak-12A	30119	SP-CXW PLW- . . .
LY-AHG	Piper PA-28RT-201T Turbo Arrow IV	unkn	
LY-AHH	Antonov An-2R	1G212-34	CCCP32729
LY-AHJ	PZL-104 Wilga 35A (C/n previously reported as 107373)	18830737	DOSAAF
LY-AHK	PZL-104 Wilga 35A	96305	DOSAAF
LY-AHL	PZL-104 Wilga 35A	128461	DOSAAF
LY-AHM	PZL-104 Wilga 35A	128462	DOSAAF
LY-AHN	PZL-104 Wilga 35A	18840789	DOSAAF
LY-AHO	Antonov An-2	1G160-39	DOSAAF
LY-AHQ	Antonov An-2	1G194-46	DOSAAF
LY-AHR	Yakovlev Yak-50	801809	DOSAAF
LY-AHS	Yakovlev Yak-52	888815	DOSAAF
LY-AHW	Yakovlev Yak-52	844405	DOSAAF
LY-AHY	Yakovlev Yak-52	877406	DOSAAF

LY-AHZ	Yakovlev Yak-52	877608	DOSAAF
LY-AIA	Yakovlev Yak-52	899606	DOSAAF
LY-AIC	Yakovlev Yak-18T	5201508	DOSAAF
LY-AII	Yakovlev Yak-50	842608	DOSAAF-16
LY-AIJ	Yakovlev Yak-52	833707	DOSAAF
LY-AIN	Antonov An-2DT	1G174-29	DOSAAF
LY-AIO	Antonov An-2DT	1G160-43	DOSAAF
LY-AIP	Yakovlev Yak-18T	5200709	DOSAAF
LY-AIQ	Yakovlev Yak-52	833610	DOSAAF
LY-AIR	Yakovlev Yak-52	844012	DOSAAF
LY-AIW	Yakovlev Yak-52	877704	DOSAAF
LY-AIX	Yakovlev Yak-52	866802	DOSAAF
LY-AJC	PZL-104 Wilga 35A	85240	DOSAAF
LY-AJD	PZL-104 Wilga 35A	128439	DOSAAF
LY-AJE	PZL-104 Wilga 35A	139481	DOSAAF
LY-AJF	PZL-104 Wilga 35A	16810616	DOSAAF
LY-AJG	Antonov An-2	1G178-48	CCCP62656
LY-AJH	PZL-104 Wilga 35A	128434	DOSAAF
LY-AJI	Antonov An-2	1G194-44	DOSAAF-42
LY-AJJ	Antonov An-2	1G28-06	DOSAAF-08
LY-AJK	PZL-104 Wilga 35A	15810584	DOSAAF
LY-AJL	PZL-104 Wilga 35A	96290	DOSAAF
LY-AJM	PZL-104 Wilga 35A	85249	DOSAAF
LY-AJN	PZL-104 Wilga 35A	128458	DOSAAF
LY-AJO	PZL-104 Wilga 35A	16810622	DOSAAF
LY-AJP	PZL-104 Wilga 35A	139492	DOSAAF
LY-AJT	PZL-104 Wilga 35A	139494	DOSAAF
LY-AJU	PZL-104 Wilga 35A	18840784	DOSAAF
LY-AJV	PZL-104 Wilga 35A	107365	DOSAAF
LY-AJW	PZL-104 Wilga 35A	96298	DOSAAF
LY-AJX	PZL-104 Wilga 35A	96309	DOSAAF
LY-AJZ	PZL-104 Wilga 35A	17820669	DOSAAF
LY-AKB	Antonov An-2	1G230-28	RA-33586 CCCP33586
LY-AKG	Sukhoi Su-26 (C/n previously reported as 35130)	06-03	RA-0603
LY-AKJ	PZL-104 Wilga 35A	128417	DOSAAF
LY-AKK	Yakovlev Yak-52	889203	Ukr.AF 86yellow DOSAAF-135
LY-AKM	Antonov An-2	1G85-44	DOSAAF-08
LY-AKN	Yakovlev Yak-52	9011003	DOSAAF-105
LY-AKO	Piper PA-28-140 Cherokee B	28-26752	N5360S
LY-AKS	PZL-104 Wilga 35A	16820650	DOSAAF
LY-AKU	Yakovlev Yak-50	842810	DOSAAF
LY-ALB	Yakovlev Yak-18T	7201814	DOSAAF
LY-ALI	Erco Ercoupe 415C	2516	N99893 NC99893
LY-ALP	Yakovlev Yak-52	844414	DOSAAF
LY-ALQ	Yakovlev Yak-52	844010	DOSAAF
LY-ALR	Yakovlev Yak-52	833609	DOSAAF
LY-ALT	Yakovlev Yak-52	822704	DOSAAF-121
LY-ALW	Yakovlev Yak-18T	22202044595	LY-XLW LY-30
LY-ALX	Piper PA-28-140 Cherokee	28-23313	SE-FAP
LY-AMA	Yakovlev Yak-52	877111	DOSAAF-137
LY-AME	Yakovlev Yak-50	812008	DOSAAF
LY-AMG	Yakovlev Yak-18T	22202034016	DOSAAF
LY-AMK	Cessna 150L	15072219	N6719G
LY-AML	Cessna 150L	15073341	N5441Q
LY-AMM	Cessna 172I	17256618	N8418L
LY-AMT	Yakovlev Yak-55	920410	DOSAAF-35
LY-AMW	Antonov An-2	1G186-40	CCCP54892
LY-AMX	Yakovlev Yak-52	878014	DOSAAF-116
LY-AMY	Antonov An-2T	1G43-30	DOSAAF
LY-ANB	PZL-104 Wilga 35A	96292	DOSAAF
LY-ANC	PZL-104 Wilga 35A	85250	DOSAAF
LY-AND	PZL-104 Wilga 35A	85252	DOSAAF
LY-ANK	Antonov An-2	1G170-31	CCCP07872
LY-ANP	Yakovlev Yak-52	811907	DOSAAF
LY-ANS	Yakovlev Yak-52 (Damaged in Norway 07.07.01, LN-ACT res 9.04)	867014	DOSAAF
LY-ANW	Yakovlev Yak-52	9111510	YL-CAD DOSAAF-60
LY-ANY	Yakovlev Yak-52	811704	DOSAAF
LY-AOA	Cessna 150G	15064647	N3247X
LY-AON	Yakovlev Yak-52	822812	DOSAAF-143
LY-AOO	Yakovlev Yak-18T	22202040425	LY-AOG
LY-AOP	Antonov An-2 (Reserved as PR-AAG)	1G141-49	RA-70395 CCCP70395
LY-AOQ	Antonov An-2	1G170-33	CCCP07874
LY-AOS	Antonov An-2	1G187-56	CCCP54947
LY-AOY	Yakovlev Yak-52	unkn	
LY-APA	SOCATA MS.880B Rallye Club	1725	I-AERP
LY-APG	Antonov An-2	1G172-37	LithAF:20yellow LY-ACO CCCP40765
LY-APH	Antonov An-2	1G177-56	LithAF:17yellow LithAF:17blue LY-AEE CCCP-62671
LY-API	Piper PA-28-140 Cherokee E	28-7225081	C-GPZM N2663C
LY-APK	Antonov An-26B	12201	RA-26114 CCCP26114
LY-APL	Cessna 150M	15078047	N8997U
LY-APN	Antonov An-26B	12010	UR-BXF YL-LDC CCCP26109
LY-APS	Yakovlev Yak-18T	4200703	
LY-APT	Yakovlev Yak-50	791506	DOSAAF
LY-APV	Antonov An-2R	1G233-23	LY-ABJ (SE-KYZ) SP-FAI
LY-APW	Yakovlev Yak-52	9111303	DOSAAF-23
LY-AQA	Antonov An-2	1G201-09	LithAF: 03 (LY-ADX) CCCP71226
LY-AQD	Yakovlev Yak-52	844412	DOSAAF
LY-AQE	Yakovlev Yak-52	unkn	
LY-AQS	Antonov An-2 (Destined for Brazil)	1G187-56	LY-AOS CCCP-54947
LY-ARA	Beech 95-B55A Baron	TC-1389	G-AYPD
LY-ARB	Yakovlev Yak-52	unkn	
LY-ARD	SOCATA ST-10 Diplomate	unkn	
LY-ARE	Antonov An-2R	1G220-25	CCCP40235
LY-ARH	Yakovlev Yak-18T	22202040114	
LY-ARI	Aérospatiale/Alenia ATR-42-300	012A	F-WQBT OY-CIF YU-ALK VH-AQC F-WWEI
LY-ARJ	Aérospatiale/Alenia ATR-42-300	059	F-OIJJ TF-ELK F-OGNS
LY-ARK	SOCATA MS.893A Rallye Commodore 180 (This c/n still believed current as F-BRLO)	10993	
LY-ARL	Reims/Cessna F150K	F15000584	D-ECEU
LY-ARS	Piper PA-30 Twin Comanche C	30-1824	ZS-FVP V5-FVP ZS-FVP N8680Y
LY-ARU	SOCATA Rallye 235E Gabier	12836	OH-SEV OY-CAU F-GARU
LY-ARY	Aérospatiale/Alenia ATR-42 420	118	TF-ELJ C-FIQN F-WWEO
LY-ARZ	Yakovlev Yak-40	9641851	SP-FYT LY-AAZ CCCP88245
LY-ASI	Sukhoi SU-29	90-07	
LY-ASO	Mooney M.20E Super 21	519	LY-BRT N4995V (PH-BWA) D-ENNO (N79855)
LY-ATB	Cessna 172M	17264783	D-EAMU(2) N61762
LY-ATD	Partenavia P.68B	121	F-GATX G-BFET
LY-ATL	Yakovlev Yak-18T	05-40	
LY-ATM	Piper PA-38-112 Tomahawk	unkn	
LY-ATN	Yakovlev Yak-52	unkn	
LY-ATV	Cessna 421B Golden Eagle	421B0248	LY-AYT (N2137E) OY-RYT N1560T
LY-AUA	Antonov An-2	1G170-07	LY-ALA CCCP07848
LY-AUH	Antonov An-2R	1G195-33	LY-APE LithAF:10blue LY-ADU CCCP68128
LY-AUP	Antonov An-2R	1G206-49	LY-APJ LithAF:02blue LY-AED CCCP17944
LY-AVA	LET L-410UVP-E	882036	RusAF 2036
LY-AVE	Antonov An-2R	1G208-22	CCCP81522
LY-AVF	Antonov An-2R	1G161-57	CCCP07782
LY-AVI	Antonov An-2R	1G220-14	CCCP40224
LY-AVP	LET L-410UVP	851514	RA67547 CCCP67547
LY-AVR	Cessna 172RG Cutlass RG	172RG0130	D-ELCO(3) N6268R
LY-AVS	Yakovlev Yak-52	9111509	DOSAAF-59
LY-AVT	LET L-410UVP-E	882033	RusAF 2033
LY-AVV	LET L-410UVP-E	892335	RA67609 CCCP67609
LY-AVX	LET L-410UVP-E	872015	RusAF 2015
LY-AVZ	LET L-410UVP-E	892336	RA67610 CCCP67610
LY-AYY	Beech B23 Musketeer Custom	M-1266	N7652R
LY-AZK	LET L-410UVP-E	861723 ?	RA-. . . . .
LY-AZM	LET L-410UVP-E	861724 ?	RA-. . . . .
LY-AZW	Boeing 737-5Q8	27629	PT-SSB
LY-AZX	Boeing 737 5Q8	28052	PT-SSE
LY-AZY	Boeing 737-548	26287	F-GJNV EI-CDS
LY-AZZ	Yakovlev Yak-55	880509	DOSAAF
LY-BAL	Yakovlev Yak-52	878207	UkrAF: 139yellow DOSAAF-139
LY-BBB	Tecnam P.92 Echo 200RG	unkn	
LY-BIG	Antonov An-2T	1G235-23	Ukr AF:48red

LY-BJK	Yakovlev Yak-52	867002	LY-ALK DOSAAF-113
LY-BRZ	Yakovlev Yak-52	unkn	
LY-BSD	Boeing 737-2T4	22701	N4569N (N85AF)
LY-BSG	Boeing 737-2T2	22793	N457IM (C-GDPG) N1779B (C-GDPG)
LY-BSK	HS.125-700B	257212	LY-ASL OH-BAP G-5-659 OH-BAP G-5-659 G-IJET N81CN N81CH G-RACL G-5-12
LY-CPT	Yakovlev Yak-50	812107	DOSAAF
LY-DIA	Yakovlev Yak-52	844913	DOSAAF 148?
LY-DOT	Aérospatiale/Alenia ATR-42-300	176	OY-MUK EI-CBF (N426TE) F-WWEG
LY-EBE	Yakovlev Yak-50	unkn	
LY-EDO	Yakovlev Yak-52	833301	DOSAAF 55?
LY-EGO	PZL-101A Gawron	85162	SP-FGB SP-KXI (2)
LY-EKD	TL Ultralight TL-2000 Sting	unkn	
LY-EMI	Yakovlev Yak-18T	22202044623	
LY-ESK	SAAB-Scania 340B	359	N359SB SE-C59
LY-FLY	Yakovlev Yak-52	9111503	YL-CAA DOSAAF-53
LY-FUN	Yakovlev Yak-52	867211	DOSAAF
LY-GFC	Yakovlev Yak-52	9010401	DOSAAF
LY-GPI	Yakovlev Yak-50	852910	DOSAAF
LY-HAI	Kamov Ka.26	7706010	CCCP24308
LY-HAO	Mil Mi-8T	3029	
LY-HAP	Mil Mi-8T	22613	
LY-HAV	Robinson R-44 Raven II	unkn	
LY-HAW	Mil Mi-2 (possibly LY-HBW re-regd)	unkn	
LY-HBI	Mil Mi-2	525803088	YL-LHT YL-LHB CCCP15201
LY-HBN	Robinson R-44	unkn	
LY-HBQ	Kamov Ka.26	7202603	LY-HAG CCCP19403
LY-HBT	Mil Mi-17-IV	440M02	
LY-HBX	Mil Mi-2	542910043	Sov AF
LY-HBZ	Mil Mi-8T	99254392	OK-XYD RA-27015 CCCP27015
LY-HCB	Eurocopter EC.120B Colibri	unkn	
LY-HCC	Eurocopter EC.120B Colibri	unkn	
LY-HCH	Mil Mi-8T	unkn	
LY-HCR	Robinson R-44 Raven II	unkn	
LY-HCS	Mil Mi-2	518914104	HA-BGP HAF-8914
LY-HCT	Mil Mi-2	543630064	LY-HBY RA-23616 Sov AFl
LY-HDW	Schweizer 269C	S-1642	N430CK
LY-HID	Robinson R-44 Astro	0483	
LY-HMA	Mil Mi-2	548944114	YL-LHM Sov Mil
LY-HMC	Hiller UH-12B	735	SE-HMS N8506 O-7 54-2941
LY-HUB	Yakovlev Yak-52	899713	UkrAF:78yellow DOSAAF 78
LY-IAH	Piper PA-38-112 Tomahawk	38-78A0694	SE-IAH
LY-ICG	Piper PA-38-112 Tomahawk	38-79A0746	SE-ICG
LY-IOO	Yakovlev Yak-50	unkn	
LY-JJK	Yakovlev Yak-50	842801	DOSAAF-29
LY-JKA	Juka Experimental	01	
LY-JKL	Yakovlev Yak-50	unkn	
LY-KAE	Antonov An-2R (overturned in Sweden 8.03)	1G196-54	LY-KAF Lith AF: 18yellow LY-ADF CCCP-68159
LY-KAG	Antonov An-2R	1G195-22	LithAF:04blue LY-ADV CCCP68117
LY-LAK	PZL-101A Gawron	unkn	
LY-LHS	Seawind 3000 (being built in Yemen)		
LY-LJK	Sukhoi SU-31 (C/n 35125 previously reported)	01-03	
LY-LLA	Cessna 172M	17261669	D-EBKN N3549Q
LY-LLB	Reims/Cessna F152	F15201595	D-EGOR(2)
LY-LMA	Cessna A150L Aerobat	A1500433	N6156F
LY-LMB	Cessna 152	15279681	N757EM
LY-LMC	Cessna 152	15279498	N714WV
LY-LMD	Cessna 152	15280525	N25065
LY-LME	Cessna 152	15279626	N757CE
LY-LMF	Cessna 152	15279554	N714ZD
LY-LMG	Cessna 172M	17261239	C-FCZS
LY-LMH	Cessna 172M	17265307	C-GIWP
LY-LMI	Cessna 310Q	310Q0951	N1974B (N69734)
LY-LMJ	Cessna 310Q	310Q0996	N310JE N888L N888PD N69815
LY-LRJ	Gates Learjet 55	55-011	ES-PVV N200BA D-CREW N574W N411GL (N57TA) N37951
LY-MAJ	Yakovlev Yak-52	unkn	
LY-MAX	Yakovlev Yak-52	822501	DOSAAF 88?
LY-MHC	Antonov An-2R	1G215-33	LY-AVK CCCP40896
LY-NXC	Yakovlev Yak-52	9010306	UR-BBU UkrAF:03 DOSAAF 03
LY-OHO	Piper PA-22-150 Tri-Pacer	unkn	
LY-ONE	Yakovlev Yak-52	822605	DOSAAF 107?
LY-OSO	Yakovlev Yak-52	833401	DOSAAF
LY-PEP	Yakovlev Yak-18T	06-33	DOSAAF
LY-PTE	Yakovlev Yak-52	833703	DOSAAF 117?
LY-RED	Yakovlev Yak-52	unkn	
LY-RUN	SAAB-Scania 340A	086	G-RUNG F-GGBV SE-E86
LY-SBA	SAAB-Scania 340B	248	SE-G48 EC-349 N248PX EI-CFA SE-G48
LY-SBC	SAAB 2000	025	F-GTSE D-ADSE SE-025
LY-SBD	SAAB 2000	023	F-GTSD D-ADSD SE-023
LY-SBG	SAAB 2000	032	HB-IZQ SE-032
LY-SIX	Yakovlev Yak-52	899309	Ukr.AF: 109yellow DOSAAF-06
LY-SKB	Yakovlev Yak-42D	4520424811431	LY-AAX CCCP42362
LY-SKC	Yakovlev Yak-42D	4520423016269	CU-T1278
LY-SKD	Yakovlev Yak-42D	4520423914323	UN-42373 RA-42373 CCCP42373
LY-SKW	Boeing 737-382	25162	N161LF F-GNFH OY-SEF CS-TIL
LY-SKY(2)	Yakovlev Yak-52	9011108	
LY-SNW	Piper PA-28-140 Cherokee	28-20691	N6600W
LY-STB	Piper PA-46-310P Malibu	46-8408027	N43367
LY-SUN	Yakovlev Yak-52	9010408	Ukr.AF 20yellow DOSAAF-20
LY-TBW	Cessna U206G Stationair 6	U20604326	LN-FAY (N756ST)
LY-TED	Antonov An-2	1G235-51	Sov.AF-17
LY-TOP	Yakovlev Yak-52 (Identity unconfirmed)	822514	RA-44520
LY-TOY	Yakovlev Yak-55	901105	DOSAAF
LY-TRY	Yakovlev Yak-55	900908	DOSAAF
LY-TTD	Yakovlev Yak-52TW	888713	UR-BGG UkrAF 70yellow DOSAAF
LY-VSM	ATEC Zephyr 2000	unkn	
LY-VIP	Cessna 172	unkn	
LY-VTP	SG Aviation Storm 280G	unkn	
LY-YAK	Yakovlev Yak-18T	22202034006	
LY-YES	Yakovlev Yak-52	unkn	
LY-ZDV	Mitsubishi MU-2B-60 Marquise	1515SA	OH-STA (F-HASI) LX-TWO N802SM N910DA N426MA
LY-. . .	Beech 65-90 King Air	LJ-107	N78Q N7BF N157CA N1183S N1153S
LY-. . .	Cessna 150J	15069492	N50699
LY-. . .	Cessna 150M	15077397	N63563
LY-. . .	Cessna A150L Aerobat	A1500286	N5986J
LY-. . .	Decourt DMS.884-1 (Modified MS.883 c/n 1337)	1	F-BRMA
LY-. . .	Maule MXT-7-180	14067C	N317AJ

LY-...	Piper PA-22-150 Tri-Pacer (Probably LY-OHO above)	22-3901	SE-CHD OY-DUW LN-BDU
LY-H..	Mil Mi-8T	99254381	OK-XYB RA-27014 CCCP27014
LY-...	Morane-Saulnier MS.885 Super Rallye	252	SP-FRV D-EIAD F-BKUF
LY-...	Robin HR.200/100 Club	78	F-BXVI
LY-...	Yakovlev Yak-12M (Possibly LY-XKI below)	210999	G-PFKD LY-FKD SP-FKD SP-AAD PLW
LY-...	Yakovlev Yak-52	878509	

EXPERIMENTAL SERIES

LY-XAA	Lituanica		
LY-XAB	LAK-XA	004	
LY-XAC	LAK-16M	207	
LY-XAD	LAK-16M	208	
LY-XAE	BRO-11M	90010	LY-GFE
LY-XAF	LET L-13 Blanik (Experimental)	unkn	
LY-XAG	Experimental Type unknown		
LY-XAH	Experimental Type unknown		
LY-XAI	Experimental Type unknown		
LY-XAJ	Experimental Type unknown		
LY-XAL	Aventura II	unkn	
LY-XAM	Yakovlev Yak-12	212615	
LY-XAO	Brditschka HB-207 Alfa	unkn	
LY-XAP	Brditschka HB-207 Alfa	unkn	
LY-XAR	Eksperimenitis	unkn	
LY-XAT	TL Ultralight TL-132/232 Condor	95C17	SP-FPB
LY-XAU	Vladas Kensgaila Lituanica	unkn	
LY-XAV	Eksperimentinis Sraigtasparnis	VR-555	
LY-XAW	SP-2 Eksperimentinis	unkn	
LY-XAX	SZD-32 Foka 5	unkn	
LY-XAY	LET L-13 Blanik	unkn	
LY-XAZ	LET L-13 Blanik (Experimental)	unkn	
LY-XBK	Experimental Type unknown		
LY-XBR	Experimental Type unknown		
LY-XCA	Mil Mi-2U	549133035	EstAF 61yellow ES-XAD SovAF 40yellow
LY-XCB	Mil Mi-2U	549035015	ES-XAC DOSAAF 20yel
LY-XCC	Yakovlev Yak-52	unkn	
LY-XCG	Rotary Air Force RAF-2000	unkn	
LY-XCH	LET L-13 Blanik	unkn	
LY-XCR	NV-2 Nimfa	unkn	
LY-XDZ	Experimental Type unknown		
LY-XFP	LET L-13 Blanik	170406	LY-GFP DOSAAF
LY-XJB	Yakovlev Yak-12M	212615	SovAF
LY-XJK	MAI-90 Juka	01	
LY-XKD	Experimental Type unknown		
LY-XKE	LAK-16	011	LY-GKE
LY-XKI	Yakovlev Yak-12M	unkn	
LY-XKK	Moravan Zlin Z.42M	0135	SP-ALA OK-HSJ
LY-XKL	LET L-13 Blanik	026711	LY-GKL DOSAAF
LY-XKU	LET L-13 Blanik	174203	LY-GKU DOSAAF
LY-XLA	LAK-16	297	LY-GLN
LY-XLB	LAK-16A	105	LY-GLB
LY-XLC	BRO-11M	90004	LY-GMA
LY-XLD	BRO-11M	90015	LY-GMC
LY-XLE	BRO-11M	90006	LY-GLE
LY-XLF	LAK-16A	101/A	LY-GLW
LY-XLG	BRO-11M	900009	LY-GLM
LY-XLH	LAK-16	220	LY-GDM
LY-XLI	LAK-16	310	LY-GLH
LY-XLL	BRO-11M	900011	LY-GLL
LY-XLM	Zuvedra		
LY-XLR	LET L-13 Blanik	173001	YL-DBG DOSAAF
LY-XLS	BRO-11M	910087	LY-GLS
LY-XLT	LAK-16	90374	LY-GLT
LY-XLV	LAK-16A	104	LY-GLV
LY-XLX	LAK-16A	102	LY-GLX
LY-XLY	LAK-16A	103/A	LY-GLY
LY-XMA	LET L-13 Blanik	814021	
LY-XMB	BRO-11M	90025	LY-GMB
LY-XMC	Zilvinas		
LY-XMD	Gandras		
LY-XME	SAS / LET L-13 Blanik	027118	DOSAAF
LY-XMF	Kregzdute		
LY-XMG	Skraidykle		
LY-XMH	Aeroplastika LAK-X	001	
LY-XMI	SML		
LY-XMU	Aero L-29 Delfin	194434	SovAF
LY-XMV	Zlin Z.326T Trenér	823-14	DOSAAF
LY-XNB	LET L-13 Blanik	172619	DOSAAF
LY-XNN	Kompol S.C. Skraidykle		
LY-XNR	Experimental Type		
LY-XNY	Auster J/2 Arrow	2355	OY-ABY D-EGIL OY-ABY
LY-XPA	Yakovlev Yak-18A (See also F-AZYK)	2624	
LY-XRK	Yakovlev Yak-55	901110	DOSAAF 118?
LY-XRR	Aero L-29 Delfin	094003	UR-BCF
LY-XVD	Moravan Z.326A Akrobat	585-05	DOSAAF
LY-XVV	Yakovlev Yak-12M	unkn	
LY-XXL	Aerocomp Comp Air7 Turbine	17256	

GLIDERS

LY-GAC(2)	LET L-13 Blanik	174230	DOSAAF
LY-GAD	LET L-13 Blanik	174304	DOSAAF
LY-GAE	LET L-13 Blanik	027148	DOSAAF
LY-GAF	LET L-13 Blanik	027311	DOSAAF
LY-GAG	LET L-13 Blanik	174508	DOSAAF
LY-GAH	LET L-13 Blanik	174511	DOSAAF
LY-GAI	LET L-13 Blanik	174510	DOSAAF
LY-GAJ	LET L-13 Blanik	174514	DOSAAF
LY-GAK	LET L-13 Blanik	174513	DOSAAF
LY-GAL	LET L-13 Blanik	026444	DOSAAF
LY-GAM	LET L-13 Blanik	026445	DOSAAF
LY-GAN	LET L-13 Blanik	026446	DOSAAF
LY-GAO	LET L-13 Blanik	173708	DOSAAF
LY-GAP	LET L-13 Blanik	026948	DOSAAF
LY-GAQ	LET L-13 Blanik	173525	DOSAAF
LY-GAR	LET L-13 Blanik	026949	DOSAAF
LY-GAS	LET L-13 Blanik	027149	DOSAAF
LY-GAT	LET L-13 Blanik	027150	DOSAAF
LY-GAU	LET L-13 Blanik	027151	DOSAAF
LY-GAV	LET L-13 Blanik	027313	DOSAAF
LY-GAW	LAK-12 Lietuva	669	DOSAAF
LY-GAY	LAK-12 Lietuva	6102	DOSAAF
LY-GAZ	LAK-12 Lietuva	6118	DOSAAF
LY-GBA	LAK-12 Lietuva	6140	DOSAAF
LY-GBB	LAK-12 Lietuva	6147	DOSAAF
LY-GBC	LAK-12 Lietuva	6151	DOSAAF
LY-GBF	SZD-48-1 Jantar Standard 2	B-1235	DOSAAF
LY-GBG	SZD-48-3 Jantar Standard 3	B-1283	DOSAAF
LY-GBH	SZD-48-3 Jantar Standard 3	B-1422	DOSAAF
LY-GBI	SZD-48-3 Jantar Standard 3	B-1423	DOSAAF
LY-GBK	SZD-48-3 Jantar Standard 3	B-1763	DOSAAF
LY-GBL	SZD-42-2 Jantar 2B	B-868	DOSAAF
LY-GBM	SZD-50-3 Puchacz	B-1078	DOSAAF
LY-GBP	LET L-13 Blanik	174523	DOSAAF
LY-GBQ	LET L-13 Blanik	026213	DOSAAF
LY-GBR	LET L-13 Blanik	026625	DOSAAF
LY-GBV	LET L-13 Blanik	174634	DOSAAF
LY-GBW	LET L-13 Blanik	026212	DOSAAF
LY-GBX	LET L-13 Blanik	027309	DOSAAF
LY-GBY	LET L-13 Blanik	027310	DOSAAF
LY-GBZ	LET L-13 Blanik	027307	DOSAAF
LY-GCB	LET L-13 Blanik	027308	DOSAAF
LY-GCC	LET L-13 Blanik	027147	DOSAAF
LY-GCD	LET L-13 Blanik	027306	DOSAAF
LY-GCE / 2-07	LET L-13 Blanik	027305	DOSAAF
LY-GCF	LET L-13 Blanik	173806	DOSAAF
LY-GCG	SZD-48-1 Jantar Standard 2	B-1212	DOSAAF
LY-GCH	SZD-48-1 Jantar Standard 2	B-1196	DOSAAF
LY-GCI	SZD-48-3 Jantar Standard 3	B-1405	DOSAAF
LY-GCJ-W	SZD-48-3 Jantar Standard 3	B-1506	DOSAAF
LY-GCK-J	SZD-48-3 Jantar Standard 3	B-1460	DOSAAF
LY-GCL-DR	SZD-48-3 Jantar Standard 3	B-1407	DOSAAF
LY-GCM	SZD-48-3 Jantar Standard 3	B-1643	DOSAAF
LY-GCN-CN	SZD-48-3 Jantar Standard 3	B-1284	DOSAAF
LY-GCO	SZD-48-3 Jantar Standard 3	B-1765	DOSAAF
LY-GCP	SZD-48-3 Jantar Standard 3	B-1697	DOSAAF
LY-GCQ	SZD-42-2 Jantar 2B	B-946	DOSAAF
LY-GCT	Hoffman H-36 Dimona	3692	OE-9232
LY-GCV	LAK-12 Lietuva	663	DOSAAF
LY-GCW	LAK-12 Lietuva	664	DOSAAF
LY-GCY-S	LAK-12 Lietuva	6100	DOSAAF CCCP6100
LY-GCZ-O	LAK-12 Lietuva	6116	DOSAAF
LY-GDA-DA	LAK-12 Lietuva	6137	DOSAAF CCCP6137
LY-GDB-P	LAK-12 Lietuva	6131	DOSAAF CCCP6131
LY-GDC-SV	LAK-12 Lietuva	6142	DOSAAF
LY-GDD-KR	LAK-12 Lietuva	6125	DOSAAF
LY-GDE	LAK-12 Lietuva	6148	DOSAAF
LY-GDF-DF	LAK-12 Lietuva	6153	DOSAAF
LY-GDG	LAK-12 Lietuva	6154	DOSAAF
LY-GDH-DH	LAK-12 Lietuva	6155	DOSAAF
LY-GDI-DI	LAK-12 Lietuva	6163	DOSAAF
LY-GDJ-MZ	LAK-12 Lietuva	679	DOSAAF CCCP679
LY-GDK	SZD-50-3 Puchacz	B-1077	DOSAAF

LY-GDL	SZD-30 Pirat	S.06-30	DOSAAF
LY-GDQ	LAK-16	003	DOSAAF
LY-GDS	LAK-16	010	DOSAAF
LY-GDV	LAK-12 Lietuva	6227	DOSAAF
LY-GDW	Hoffman H-36 Dimona	36270	F-CGAX
LY-GDY	LAK-19	001	LY-XCE
LY-GEA-P7	LAK-17A	134	
LY-GEB	LAK-17A	unkn	
LY-GEC	LAK-17A	unkn	
LY-GED	LAK-19	unkn	
LY-GEE	LAK-19	unkn	
LY-GEN	LAK Genesis 2	01	
LY-GEP-BB	LAK-17A	131	
LY-GEQ	LAK-17A	133	
LY-GEX	LAK-17A	unkn	
LY-GFA-SV	LAK-17A	101PV	
LY-GFF	PZL PW-5 Smyk	17.08.020	
LY-GFG	LET L-13 Blanik	174638	DOSAAF
LY-GFI	LET L-13 Blanik	173462	DOSAAF
LY-GFJ	LET L-13 Blanik	173711	DOSAAF
LY-GFK	LET L-13 Blanik	173210	DOSAAF
LY-GFL	SZD-48-1 Jantar Standard 2	B-1030	DOSAAF
LY-GFM-DG	SZD-48-1 Jantar Standard 2	B-1054	DOSAAF
LY-GFN	LAK-12 Lietuva	632	DOSAAF
LY-GFQ	LET L-13 Blanik	172230	DOSAAF
LY-GFS	LET L-13 Blanik	173610	DOSAAF
LY-GFU	LET L-13 Blanik	174206	DOSAAF
LY-GFV	LET L-13 Blanik	174321	DOSAAF
LY-GFX	LET L-13 Blanik	026915	DOSAAF
LY-GFY	LET L-13 Blanik	026916	DOSAAF
LY-GFZ	LET L-13 Blanik	174128	DOSAAF
LY-GGB	LET L-13 Blanik	171011	DOSAAF
LY-GGE	LET L-13 Blanik	172949	DOSAAF
LY-GGK	LET L-13 Blanik	026449	DOSAAF
LY-GGN	LET L-13 Blanik	unkn	
LY-GGP	LET L-13 Blanik	174229	DOSAAF
LY-GGR	LET L-13 Blanik	172915	DOSAAF
LY-GGS	LET L-13 Blanik	027135	DOSAAF
LY-GGT	SZD-48-1 Jantar Standard 2	W-920	DOSAAF
LY-GGU	LET L-13 Blanik	026947	DOSAAF
LY-GGX	LET L-13 Blanik	027316	DOSAAF
LY-GGZ	LET L-13 Blanik	171116	DOSAAF
LY-GHA	LET L-13 Blanik	026946	DOSAAF
LY-GHE	SZD-48-1 Jantar Standard 2	B-1182	DOSAAF
LY-GHF	SZD-48-1 Jantar Standard 2	B-1020	DOSAAF
LY-GHG	SZD-48-1 Jantar Standard 2	B-1186	DOSAAF
LY-GHH	SZD-48-3 Jantar Standard 3	B-1696	DOSAAF
LY-GHI	LAK-12 Lietuva	6110	DOSAAF
LY-GHN	LET L-13 Blanik	172311	DOSAAF
LY-GHP	LET L-13 Blanik	027145	DOSAAF
LY-GHQ	LET L-13 Blanik	027144	DOSAAF
LY-GHR	LET L-13 Blanik	027314	DOSAAF
LY-GHS	LET L-13 Blanik	026713	DOSAAF
LY-GHT	LET L-13 Blanik	027312	DOSAAF
LY-GHW	LAK-12 Lietuva	691	DOSAAF
LY-GHX	SZD-41A Jantar Standard	B-919	DOSAAF
LY-GHY	SZD-48-3 Jantar Standard 3	B-1518	DOSAAF
LY-GHZ	LET L-13 Blanik	171003	DOSAAF
LY-GIA	LET L-13 Blanik	172209	DOSAAF
LY-GIB	LET L-13 Blanik	172306	DOSAAF
LY-GIC	LET L-13 Blanik	172519	DOSAAF
LY-GID	LET L-13 Blanik	172617	DOSAAF
LY-GIF	LET L-13 Blanik	172923	DOSAAF
LY-GIG	LET L-13 Blanik	173468	DOSAAF
LY-GIH	LET L-13 Blanik	026709	DOSAAF
LY-GII	LET L-13 Blanik	026911	DOSAAF
LY-GIJ	LET L-13 Blanik	026913	DOSAAF
LY-GIK	LET L-13 Blanik	026914	DOSAAF
LY-GIL	LET L-13 Blanik	171816	DOSAAF
LY-GIN	SZD-41A Jantar Standard	B-845	DOSAAF
LY-GIO	SZD-41A Jantar Standard	B-893	DOSAAF
LY-GIP	SZD-48-1 Jantar Standard 2	B-1022	DOSAAF
LY-GIR	LAK-12 Lietuva	642	DOSAAF
LY-GIS-BG	LAK-17A	unkn	
LY-GJB-LAK	LAK-17A	unkn	
LY-GJI	SZD-48-3 Jantar Standard 3	B-1406	DOSAAF
LY-GJJ	LET L-13 Blanik	172716	DOSAAF
LY-GJK	LET L-13 Blanik	173712	DOSAAF
LY-GJM	LET L-13 Blanik	171620	DOSAAF
LY-GJN	LET L-13 Blanik	027303	DOSAAF
LY-GJR	SZD-36A Cobra 15	W-633	DOSAAF
LY-GJU	SZD-41A Jantar Standard	B-745	DOSAAF
	(c/n unconfirmed - B-748 quoted officially, B-745 is YL-DAE)		
LY-GJY	SZD-36A Cobra 15	W-640	DOSAAF
LY-GJZ	SZD-41A Jantar Standard	B-924	LY-GJL DOSAAF
LY-GKB	LAK-12 Lietuva	6215	
LY-GKD	SZD-30 Pirat	S-06.35	DOSAAF 8-18
LY-GKF	LAK-12 Lietuva	6214	LY-GKA
LY-GKH	LET L-13 Blanik	172424	DOSAAF
LY-GKI	LET L-13 Blanik	026448	DOSAAF
LY-GKJ	LET L-13 Blanik	174317	DOSAAF
LY-GKK	LET L-13 Blanik	174318	DOSAAF
LY-GKM	LET L-13 Blanik	026714	DOSAAF
LY-GKO	LET L-13 Blanik	027156	DOSAAF
LY-GKP	LET L-13 Blanik	027157	DOSAAF
LY-GKQ	LET L-13 Blanik	172511	DOSAAF

LY-GKR	LET L-13 Blanik	173501	DOSAAF
LY-GKT	SZD-48-3 Jantar Standard 3	B-1644	DOSAAF
LY-GKV	LET L-13 Blanik	173705	DOSAAF
LY-GKW	LET L-13 Blanik	027136	DOSAAF
LY-GKX	SZD-48-1 Jantar Standard 2	B-1227	DOSAAF
LY-GKY	LAK-12 Lietuva	681	DOSAAF
LY-GKZ	LAK-12 Lietuva	8105	DOSAAF
LY-GLI	LAK-16	217	
LY-GLK	LAK-16	238	
LY-GLQ	LAK-12 Lietuva	6225	
LY-GLU	LAK-16A	001	
LY-GMF	LAK-12	unkn	
LY-GMG	SZD-48-3 Jantar Standard 3	B-1530	DOSAAF
LY-GMH	LET L-13 Blanik	unkn	
LY-GMI	LET L-13 Blanik	unkn	
LY-GMJ	LET L-13 Blanik	unkn	
LY-GMK	LET L-13 Blanik	unkn	
LY-GMM	LAK-19	unkn	
LY-GMN	LAK-17A	unkn	
LY-GMO	LAK-17A	unkn	
LY-GNK-S20	LET L-13 Blanik	unkn	
LY-GNV	LET L-13 Blanik	unkn	
LY-GPB	Bölkow Phoebus B3	unkn	
LY-GPD	SZD-41A Jantar Standard	B-923	LY-GBD DOSAAF
LY-GPS	LET L-13 Blanik	170811	DOSAAF
LY-GPV	LET L-13 Blanik (Experimental)	172811	
LY-GPW	LET L-13 Blanik	172205	DOSAAF
LY-GUA	PZL PW-5 Smyk	17.08.021	
LY-GUB	SZD-36A Cobra 15	W-728	DOSAAF
LY-GYY	LAK-19	unkn	
LY-G . .	LET L-13 Blanik	172517	
LY-G . . -S10	LET L-13 Blanik	unkn	
LY-G . .	SZD-36A Cobra 15	W-778	DOSAAF
LY-G . .	SZD-36A Cobra 15	W-780	DOSAAF
LY-G . .	SZD-36A Cobra 15	W-781	DOSAAF
LY-G . .	SZD-30 Pirat	B-547	DOSAAF
LY-G . .	SZD-30 Pirat	S-03.11	DOSAAF

BALLOONS

LY-LNL	Kubicek BB-20GP HAFB	255	OK-0255
LY-LUK	Kubicek BB-30Z HAFB	254	OK-0254
LY-OAD	Cameron A-105 HAFB	1740	D-Rhenag
LY-OAE	Cameron N-105 HAFB	2317	D-OKKK D-Schafer(2)
LY-OAF	Schröder Fire Balloons G HAFB	180	D-OALL D-Allkauf
LY-OAK	Thunder AX8-105 SII HAFB	1903	D-OKIH D-Wetterau
LY-OAL	Colt 90A HAFB	2329	D-OKIB
LY-OAM	Cameron N-90 HAFB	1534	D-OAMA D-Lottogluck
LY-OAN	Raven S-49A HAFB	3122	N9006W
LY-OAP	Cameron N-105 HAFB	1814	D-Europal(2)
LY-OAT	Cameron N-90 HAFB	1100	D-Rheingas II D-Bruhl
LY-OBA	AX-7 "Moletai" HAFB	004	
LY-OBB	Aerotechnik AB-2a HAFB	880312	
LY-OBD	Aerotechnik AB-8 HAFB	890419	
LY-OBE	Tomi AX-7 HAFB	BAV048/1988	LOD-0002
LY-OBF	Cameron O-84 HAFB	2031	LOD-0009
LY-OBG	Colt 105A HAFB	unkn	
LY-OBH	Free Balloon TA-61	0470992	
LY-OBI	Free Balloon TA-80	0410692	
LY-OBK	Cameron O-120 HAFB	3489	
LY-OBL	Free Balloon TA-61	0471032	
LY-OBM	LS-7 HAFB	LS-002	
LY-OBP	Expermental B HAFB	unkn	
LY-OBQ	Interavia 80TA Free Balloon	310492	
LY-OBT	Cameron N-70 HAFB	3244	
LY-OBU	Cameron N-77 HAFB	3258	
LY-OBV	Cameron C-80 Concept HAFB	3433	
LY-OBW	Raven RX-7 HAFB	377	
LY-OBZ	Tomi AX-7 HAFB	BAV060/1988	
LY-OCA	Cameron C-80 Concept HAFB	3605	
LY-OCB	Cameron C-80 Concept HAFB	3960	
LY-OCC	Cameron C-80 Concept HAFB	4008	
LY-OCE	Cameron C-80 Concept HAFB	4346	
LY-OCF	Kubicek BB-26 HAFB	209	OK-0209
LY-OCH	Ultramagic M-65 HAFB	65/85	
LY-OCI	Cameron A-140 HAFB	3122	D-OHSV
LY-OCJ	Thunder AX8-105 SII HAFB	2514	D-OGIM
LY-OCK	Ultramagic M-65C HAFB	unkn	
LY-OCL	Cameron A-120 HAFB	unkn	
LY-OCN	Kubicek BB-26 HAFB	unkn	
LY-OCP	Cameron C-80 Concept HAFB	10169	
LY-OCQ	Ultramagic M- HAFB	unkn	
LY-OCR	Cameron C-80 Concept HAFB (Stored, UK)	4594	
LY-OCW	Kubicek BB-26 HAFB	262	OK-0262
LY-ODA	Cameron O-105 HAFB	1459	D-Rheingas (3)
LY-ODD	Schröder Fire Balloons G HAFB	020	D-Dortmund
LY-ODE	Cameron N-105 HAFB	2886	PH-FWW

LY-ODG	Colt 90A HAFB	1137	D-OHYP PH-APL
LY-ODO	Cameron N-90 HAFB	4490	
LY-ODY	Cameron C-80 Concept HAFB	10328	
LY-OGD	Thunder AX8-90 SII HAFB	1575	D-OFCD D-Sonnenklar
LY-OKI	Colt 90A HAFB	unkn	
LY-OOD	Cameron C-80 Concept HAFB	10325	
LY-OSB	Thunder AX9-120 SII HAFB	unkn	
LY-OSC	Schröder Fire Balloons G HAFB	491	D-OSCM
LY-OYY	RSZ-05 HAFB	unkn	
LY-O . .	Cameron A-120 HAFB (Possibly now LY-OCL above)	3592	D-OJCB(2)
LY-O . .	Colt 105A HAFB (Possibly now LY-OBG above)	3940	D-OEBM(2)
LY-O . .	Thunder AX9-120 SII HAFB (Possibly now LY-OSB above)	2337	D-OSBD
LY-O . .	Thunder & Colt 105A HAFB	1799USA	N137TC
LY-O . .	Thunder AX8-105SII HAFB	4240	D-OBLC (2)

MICROLIGHTS

LY-SAC	Skraidykle	XA3-29	
LY-SAJ	Skraidykle		
LY-SAL	Skraidykle		
LY-SAM	Skraidykle		
LY-SAN	Skraidykle		
LY-SAO	Skraidykle		
LY-SAP	Skraidykle		
LY-SAQ	Skraidykle		
LY-SAR	Skraidykle		
LY-SAS	Skraidykle		
LY-SAT	Skraidykle		
LY-SAU	Skraidykle		
LY-SAV	Skraidykle		
LY-SAW	Skraidykle		
LY-SAY	Motoskraidykle		
LY-SAZ	Skraidykle		
LY-SBE	Skraidykle		
LY-SBF	Skraidykle		
LY-SBH	Skraidykle		
LY-SBI	Skraidykle		
LY-SBJ	ULSA Klubas Sakalas Motoskraidykle		
LY-SBL	ULSA Klubas Sakalas Motoskraidykle		
LY-SBM	ULSA Klubas Sakalas Motoskraidykle		
LY-SBN	ULSA Klubas Sakalas Motoskraidykle		
LY-SBO	ULSA Klubas Sakalas Motoskraidykle		
LY-SBP	ULSA Klubas Sakalas Motoskraidykle		
LY-SBR	Valdas Stanius Motoskraidykle		
LY-SBS	Skraidykle		
LY-SBT	Motoskraidykle		
LY-SBU	Skraidykle		
LY-SBV	Skraidykle		
LY-SBX	Skraidykle		
LY-SKV	Motoskraidykle		
LY-SLK	Motoskraidykle		
LY-SWE	Seawind 3000	058	
LY-UAA	Rand Kar X'Air F602T Grand Raid	648	
LY-UAB	X-32 Bekas	0373	
LY-UAC	X-32 Bekas	0379	
LY-UAD	EOL-Special UL-02	E32-2002	
LY-UDL	Dalius Liekis RK-6 Magija	unkn	
LY- . . .	AK-3 Kolibri	3	PH-2U6

LZ - BULGARIA

Regn.	Type	C/n	Prev.Id.
LZ-ACR	SOCATA TB-10 Tobago (Identity unconfirmed)	681	D-EACR(2)
LZ-ACS	Tupolev TU-134A	1351303	LZ-TUP LZ D050 LZ-TUP BAF: 050 LZ-TUP
LZ-ALA	Cirrus SR22	0488	N1355C
LZ-ANC	Antonov An-24V	67302808	
LZ-AND	Antonov An-24V	77303301	
LZ-ASA	Zlin Z.143L	0002	LZ-ITL SE-KXM OK-ZOB
LZ-ASB	Zlin Z.143L	0005	OK-OAA OK-ZOF
LZ-ASC	Zlin Z.143L	0001	OK-YOA OK-080
LZ-ASE	Cessna 414 (Accident 25.1.02)	414-0072	D-IHST HB-LGN N8172Q
LZ-ASM	Mil Mi-8	unkn	
LZ-ASN	Mil Mi-8	unkn	
LZ-ASZ	Antonov An-24B	27307903	RA-49290 LZ-ANT SP-LTS
LZ-ATR	Aérospatiale/Aeritalia ATR-42-300	151	F-WQNC(3) CU-T1453 F-WQII N433MQ (N148DD) F-WWEW
LZ-ATS	Aérospatiale/Aeritalia ATR-42-300	130	F-WQNO(2) CU-T1451 F-WQIQ N19AE N141DD F-WWEA
LZ-ASZ	Antonov An-24RV	27307903	RA-49290 LZ-ANT SP-LTS
LZ-AZC	Ilyushin IL-18D	184006903	CCCP75530
LZ-AZO	Ilyushin IL-18D	184007405	RA-75553 D-AOAO DM-STF CCCP75553
LZ-BAN	MBB Bö.105	unkn	
LZ-BAP	MBB Bö.105	unkn	
LZ-BCA	LET Z-37 Cmelák	unkn	
LZ-BCB	LET Z-37 Cmelák	unkn	
LZ-BFD	Antonov An-12	5343005	RA-98102 CCCP98102 SovietAF-17
LZ-BFG	Antonov An-12BT	6344305	LZ-BAG RA-11650 CCCP11650 YI-AES IAF-685
LZ-BFU	Ilyushin IL-18V	183005905	LZ-BEU 4W-ABO YE-AYE CCCP75870
LZ-BHA	Airbus A320-211	029	N290SE VH-HYG F-WWDF
LZ-BHB	Airbus A320-212	294	OY-CNP G-HBAP G-HAGT F-WWID
LZ-BHC	Airbus A320-212	349	OY-CNR OO-AEZ OY-CNR G-DACR G-OEXC F-WWBU
LZ-BHD	Airbus A320-212	221	CS-TQE OY-CNB G-DRVE F-GLGI ZS-NZS F-WWIK
LZ-BOD	Boeing 737-3Y0	23749	EC-FKJ EC-781 EC-ECR
LZ-BOE	Boeing 737-3Y0	23923	EC-FJZ EC-898 EI-CEE G-TEAB EI-BZP (N117AW) EI-BZP (LN-AEQ) EC-EIA EC-152

LZ-BOI	Boeing 737-530	25311	D-ABJF
LZ-BOJ	Boeing 737-3L9	23718	N377PA
			N718CT
			OO-CTX
			N2371
			PH-OZA
			G-BOZA
			OY-MMN
LZ-BOK	Boeing 737-3M8	24023	F-GFUI
			PH-TSR
			HB-IIA
			(OO-LTD)
			(OO-BTD)
LZ-BOL	Boeing 737-3M8	24024	G-OGVAI
			HB-IIB
LZ-BOM	Boeing 737-31S	29059	D-ADBO
LZ-BON	Boeing 737-31S	29060	D-ADBP
LZ-BOS	Flight Design CT-2K	unkn	
LZ-BRA	Antonov An-12BP	8345006	LZ-ITB
			RA-11368
			SovAF:75 red
			CCCP11521
LZ-BRC	Antonov An-12BP	8345510	ER-ACW
			D2-FBY
			ER-ALE
			RA-12959
			CCCP12959
LZ-BRP	Antonov An-12 BP	402408	LZ-BAF
			CCCP ?
LZ-BRV	Antonov An-12 BP	unkn	
LZ-BSK	Kamov Ka.26	unkn	
LZ-BTG	Tupolev TU-154A	75A-095	
LZ-BTJ	Tupolev TU-154B-1	78A-270	
LZ-BTK	Tupolev TU-154B	76A-144	
LZ-BTL(2)	Tupolev TU-154B	77A-208	
LZ-BTO	Tupolev TU-154B-1	78A-258	
LZ-BTP	Tupolev TU-154B-1	78A-278	
LZ-BTS	Tupolev TU-154B-2	80A-422	
LZ-BTT	Tupolev TU-154B-2	81A-483	
LZ-BTU	Tupolev TU-154B-2 (Burgas Museum)	81A-484	
LZ-BTV	Tupolev TU-154B-2	82A-569	CCCP85569
LZ-BTY	Tupolev TU-154M	89A-800	
LZ-BTZ	Tupolev TU-154M	88A-781	
LZ-BZB	Antonov An-2	unkn	
LZ-CAE	Mil Mi-8	10312	
LZ-CAF	Mil Mi-8T	10314	
LZ-CAL	Mil Mi-8	10317	
LZ-CAM	Mil Mi-8	10318	
LZ-CAR	Mil Mi-8T	8606	RA-24639
			CCCP24639
LZ-CAT	Mil Mi-8S	10319	
LZ-CAV	Mil Mi-8P	unkn	
LZ-CAX	Mil Mi-8T	7666	CCCP22847
LZ-CBA	Antonov An-26	8007	UR-26659
			CCCP26659
LZ-CBB	Antonov An-24RV	37309008	BulgAF 030
LZ-CBC	Antonov An-24B	07305810	BulgAF 040
			LZ-MNI
			BulgAF 040
LZ-CBE	Antonov An-12B	5343708	LZ-BAC
			CCCP1100 .
LZ-CBG	Antonov An-12	2340804	
LZ-CBH	Antonov An-12BP	9346807	LZ-BAH
			RA-11317
			CCCP11317
LZ-CBM	Antonov An-12BP	2340505	UR-CCP
LZ-CCE	LET L-410UVP-E3	871816	SovietAF
LZ-CCF	LET L-410UVP-E	861722	SovietAF:1722
LZ-CCK	LET L-410UVP-E	902514	LZ-KLC
			CCCP67660
LZ-CDA	Mil Mi-8MTV-1	95887	RA-27053
			CCCP27053
LZ-CDV	Mil Mi-8	unkn	
LZ-DAF	DAR-23 Accent	X002	
LZ-DAH	DAR-25 Impulse	unkn	
LZ-DAR	DAR-21 Vektor	unkn	
LZ-DAS	DAR-23 Accent	X001?	
LZ-DBB	Tecnam P.92 Echo	unkn	
LZ-DOB	Yakovl ev Yak-40	9340432	
LZ-DOC	Yakovl ev Yak-40	9340532	
LZ-DOE	Yakovl ev Yak-40	9521441	
LZ-DOF	Yakovl ev Yak-40	9521541	
LZ-DOM	Yakovl ev Yak-40	9620447	
LZ-DOR	Yakovlev Yak-40	9231623	
LZ-DOS	Yakovlev Yak-40	9231423	
LZ-EMA	Kamov Ka.26	unkn	
LZ-FAA	Mil Mi-8MT (Identity unconfirmed)	103M10	BAF:410
LZ-GPG	LET Z-37 Cmelák	14-26	
LZ-GVD	Antonov An-2	unkn	
LZ-HAF	Kamov Ka.26	unkn	
LZ-HAG	Kamov Ka.26	unkn	
LZ-HAJ	Kamov Ka.26	unkn	
LZ-HAK	Kamov Ka.26	unkn	
LZ-HAL	Kamov Ka.26	unkn	
LZ-HAM	Kamov Ka.26	unkn	
LZ-HAN	Kamov Ka.26	unkn	

LZ-HBA	BAe.146 Series 200	E-2072	VH-NJQ
			G-BNJI
			EI-CTY
			G-BNJI
			HB-IXC
			N190US
			N366PS
			G-BNJI
			G-5-072
LZ-HBB	BAe.146 Series 200	E-2073	VH-NJU
			G-VFV
			EI-JET
			G-BVFV
			HB-IXD
			N191US
			N367PS
			G-5-073
LZ-HBC	BAe.146 Series 200	E-2093	VH-JJS
			G-5-093
LZ-HMF	Tupolev TU-154M	88A-777	CU-T1275
LZ-HMH	Tupolev TU-154M	87A-754	LZ-BTH
LZ-HMI	Tupolev TU-154M	85A-706	LZ-BTI
			EP-LBG
			LZ-BTI
			EP-LBE
			LZ-BTI
LZ-HMN	Tupolev TU-154M	90A-832	LZ-BTN(2)
LZ-HMQ	Tupolev TU-154M	87A-743	LZ-BTQ
			EP-LBD
			LZ-BTQ
LZ-HMS	Tupolev TU-154M	87A-751	CU-T1265
LZ-HMY	Tupolev TU-154M	91A-875	UR-85700
			85700
			CCCP85700
LZ-HMW	Tupolev TU-154M	85A-707	LZ-BTW
			EP-LBI
			LZ-BTW
			EP-LBI
			LZ-BTW
LZ-ITA	Antonov An-12BP	3341004	
LZ-ITS	Antonov An-12BP	3341505	4R-SKL
			RA-12174
			CCCP12174
LZ-KLV	Zenair CH-701 STOL	unkn	
LZ-LCA	Tupolev TU-154M	89A-829	RA-85671
			CCCP85671
LZ-LCQ	Tupolev TU-154M	89A-802	EP-MBK
			LZ-LTD
			RA-85657
			CCCP85657
LZ-LCS	Tupolev TU-154M	86A-727	4K-727
			SP-LCA
LZ-LCT	Tupolev TU-154M	85A-717	EP-LBN
			UN-85836
			B-2602
LZ-LCV	Tupolev TU-154M	86A-733	LZ-HMP
			4K-733
			SP-LCB
LZ-LCX	Tupolev TU-154M	86A-744	LZ-LTX
			EP-LBN
			LZ-BTX
			EP-LBC
			LZ-BTX
LZ-LDK	McDonnell-Douglas DC-9-82	49432	I-DAVK
LZ-LDX	McDonnell-Douglas DC-9-81	49844	HB-ISX
LZ-LDZ	McDonnell-Douglas DC-9-81	49930	HB-ISZ
LZ-LKG	Tecnam P.92 Echo	unkn	
LZ-LSB	LET L-410UVP-E1	861802	
LZ-LTD	Tupolev TU-154M	89A-802	RA-85657
			CCCP85657
LZ-LTF	Tupolev TU-154M	88A-794	RA-85652
			CCCP85652
LZ-LTG	Tupolev TU-154M	92A-927	LZ-LTA
			RA-85744
			UN-85744
			CCCP85744
LZ-MAN	LET L-410UVP	unkn	
LZ-MBA	Bell 407	53499	N2040D
			C-GBUB
LZ-MIA	Mil Mi-2	543541054	
LZ-MIB	Mil Mi-2	544516115	
LZ-MIC	Mil Mi-2	526015029	LZ-5029
LZ-MID	Mil Mi-2	526020029	LZ-5034
LZ-MIG	Tupolev TU-154M	90A-840	
LZ-MIK	Tupolev TU-154M	90A-844	
LZ-MIL	Tupolev TU-154M	90A-845	
LZ-MIR	Tupolev TU-154M	90A-852	
LZ-MIS	Tupolev TU-154M	90A-863	
LZ-MNK	Antonov An-12BK	8345802	Ukr AF 53 red
LZ-MNL	Antonov An-26	1309	PWL-1309
LZ-MNM(2)	Antonov An-12	unkn	
LZ-MNN	Antonov An-12P	0901409	UR-11322
			EW-11322
			CCCP11322
			CCCP12777
LZ-MNO	LET L-410UVP	800507	CCCP67036
LZ-MNP	LET L-410UVP	790216	CCCP67180

LZ-MNQ	Antonov An-12BP	3341402	SovAF:70black
LZ-MNR	Antonov An-26	7504	LZ-NHC RA-26177 CCCP-26177
LZ-MNS	Antonov An-26	unkn	
LZ-MNT	Antonov An-26	unkn	
LZ-MOB	Mil Mi-26	226207	
LZ-MOC	Kamov Ka.32T	unkn	
LZ-MOM	Mil Mi-8MTV-1	unkn	
LZ-MOQ	Mil Mi-8MTV-1	unkn	
LZ-MOR	Mil Mi-8MTV-1	unkn	
LZ-MOT	Kamov Ka.32	unkn	
LZ-MOW	Mil Mi-8MTV-1	unkn	
LZ-MOX	Mil Mi-8MTV-1	unkn	
LZ-MOZ	Kamov Ka.32T	unkn	
LZ-MRC	Kamov Ka.32T	5504	RA-31003 CCCP31003
LZ-MRK	Mil Mi-8MTV-1	unkn	
LZ-MRO	Mil Mi-8MTV-1	94887	
LZ-MRT	Mil Mi-8MTV-1	94888	
LZ-MRU	Mil Mi-8MTV-1	94836	
LZ-MRW	Kamov Ka.32T	unkn	
LZ-MSF(2)	Mil Mi-8T	99150938	LZ-CAZ LZ-MSG(1) CCCP24023
LZ-MSG(2)	Mil Mi-8T	99150935	LZ-CAH LZ-MSF(1) CCCP24024
LZ-MSH	Mil Mi-2	5411114010	LZ-RMB CCCP14227
LZ-MSL	Kamov Ka.32T	22905 ?	
LZ-MSN	Mil Mi-8MTV-1	95919	UR-27083 CCCP27083
LZ-MST	Kamov Ka.32T	unkn	
LZ-NHA	Antonov An-26	4702	UR-26605 CCCP26605
LZ-NKL	Flight Design CT-2K	unkn	
LZ-OKC	Kamov Ka.26	7303501	HA-MZD LY-HAA CCCP19335
LZ-OOI	Dassault Falcon 2000	123	
LZ-RMA	LET L-410UVP-E3	902523	BAF: 069
LZ-RMC	LET L-410UVP-E12	882207	LZ-LSC
LZ-RME	LET L-410UVP-E3	902524	BAF: 064
LZ-RMF	LET L-410UVP	831104	UR-67416 CCCP67416
LZ-RMI	LET L-410UVP	831113	UR-67422 CCCP67422
LZ-RMK	LET L-410UVP	851406	UR-67502 CCCP67502
LZ-SAA	Antonov An-12	unkn	
LZ-SFA	Antonov An-12	02348007	LZ-SGA YU-AIC (JRV73311)
LZ-SFF	Antonov An-12	unkn	
LZ-SFH	Antonov An-26	3904	RA-26570
LZ-SFI	Antonov An-12	unkn	
LZ-SFK	Antonov An-12	2341901	CCCP11511
LZ-SFL	Antonov An-12	4342101	
LZ-SFR	Antonov An-12BP	401801	RA-11345 CCCP11345
LZ-SFS	Antonov An-12	6344308	SP-LZB PLW-51 SP-LZB PLW-51 SP-LZB PLW-51
LZ-SFW	Antonov An-12	unkn	
LZ-SNA	Antonov An-2	1G149-01	
LZ-SNB	Antonov An-2	1G149-02	
LZ-SNC	Antonov An-2	1G56-48	LZ-1074
LZ-SND	Antonov An-2	1G55-20	LZ-1039 LZ-916
LZ-SNG	Antonov An-2	1G82-47	
LZ-TCA	Yakovlev Yak-18T	22202050376	
LZ-TCB	Yakovlev Yak-18T	22202034068	
LZ-TCC	Yakovlev Yak-18T	13-35	
LZ-TEA	Antonov An-14	601613	LZ-7001
LZ-TEB	Antonov An-14	601610	LZ-7002
LZ-TEC	Antonov An-14	601606	LZ-7003
LZ-TED	Antonov An-14	601607	LZ-7004
LZ-TEE	Antonov An-14	601609	LZ-7005
LZ-TEF	Antonov An-14	603101	LZ-7006
LZ-TEG	Antonov An-14	003309	LZ-7007
LZ-TEK	Antonov An-14	unkn	
LZ-TUG	Tupolev TU-134A-3	49858	OK-BYT
LZ-TUH	Tupolev TU-134A	7360142	OK-HFM
LZ-TUJ	Tupolev TU-134A	7349913	OK-HFL
LZ-TUL	Tupolev TU-134A-3	4352303	
LZ-TUN	Tupolev TU-134A-3	4352307	
LZ-TUT	Tupolev TU-134B-3	63987	
LZ-TVA	Cessna 150	unkn	
LZ-UBC	TL Ultralight TL-96 Star	unkn	
LZ-UKB	Light Aero Avid Flyer (W/o 18.10.02?)	unkn	
LZ-VAA	Kamov Ka.26	unkn	
LZ-VAB	Kamov Ka.26	unkn	
LZ-VAC	Kamov Ka.26	unkn	
LZ-VAD	Kamov Ka.26	unkn	
LZ-VBA	Antonov An-2	unkn	
LZ-VDG	Rans S-12 Airaille (Type also quoted as RS-12)	unkn	
LZ-VEA	Antonov An-12BP	1340106	RA-11976 CCCP11976
LZ-VEB	Antonov An-12TB	01347701	RA-12999 CCCP12999
LZ-VEC	Antonov An-12BP (Possible w/o in accident 9.3.05)	6344610	UK-93920 CCCP93920
LZ-VED	Antonov An-12BP	02348207	3C-QQY D2-FDB RA-11526 CCCP11526
LZ-VEE	Antonov An-12BP	402410	LZ-RAA RA-11959 CCCP11959
LZ-VEF	Antonov An-12	402001	LZ-BAE CCCP11976
LZ-VLA	Antonov An-2	unkn	
LZ-VLB	Antonov An-2	unkn	
LZ-VLC	Antonov An-2	unkn	
LZ-VLD	Antonov An-2	unkn	
LZ-VPD	Antonov An-24RV	47309703	RA-46681 CCCP46681
LZ-VVI	Antonov An-24B	07306503	RA-47283 CCCP47283
LZ-YUK	Beech 200 Super King Air	BB-82	LZ-FEO LZ-RGP N788AA 8R-GFB
LZ-ZAH	Ilyushin IL-18D (Identity unconfirmed)	185008905	LZ-BEH SP-LSI PLW-102
LZ-103	PZL-101 Gawron	74123	LZ-GA. . .
LZ-104	PZL-101 Gawron	74124	LZ-GA. . .
LZ-105	PZL-101 Gawron	74125	LZ-GA. . .
LZ-106	PZL-101 Gawron	74126	LZ-GA. . .
LZ-107	PZL-101 Gawron	63108	LZ-GA. . .
LZ-108	PZL-101 Gawron	85139	LZ-GA. . .
LZ-109	PZL-101 Gawron	85140	LZ-GA. . .
LZ-110	PZL-101 Gawron	52075	LZ-GA. . . SP-CFK
LZ-111	PZL-101 Gawron	107228	LZ-GA. . .
LZ-114	PZL-101 Gawron	107226	LZ-GA. . .
LZ-115	PZL-101 Gawron	119269	LZ-GA. . .
LZ-116	PZL-101 Gawron	119270	LZ-GA. . .
LZ-117	PZL-101 Gawron	119275	LZ-GA. . .
LZ-118	PZL-101 Gawron	119257	LZ-GA. . .
LZ-121	PZL-101 Gawron	119261	LZ-GA. . .
LZ-124	PZL-101 Gawron	119266	LZ-GA. . .
LZ-125	PZL-101 Gawron	119272	LZ-GA. . .
LZ-126	PZL-101 Gawron	119256	LZ-GA. . .
LZ-127	PZL-101 Gawron	119260	LZ-GA. . .
LZ-129	PZL-101 Gawron	119263	LZ-GA. . .
LZ-130	PZL-101 Gawron	119271	LZ-GA. . .
LZ-131	PZL-101 Gawron	119267	LZ-GA. . .
LZ-132	PZL-101 Gawron	107227	LZ-112 LZ-GA. . .
LZ-133	PZL-101 Gawron	119298	LZ-GA. . .
LZ-134	PZL-101 Gawron	119273	LZ-GA. . .
LZ-138	PZL-101 Gawron	118243	LZ-GA. . .
LZ-400	PZL-104 Wilga 35	48041	
LZ-405	PZL-104 Wilga 35A	18830761	
LZ-406	PZL-104 Wilga 35A	19840815	
LZ-407	PZL-104 Wilga 35A	19840816	
LZ-408	PZL-104 Wilga 35A	19840817	
LZ-409	PZL-104 Wilga 35A	19840818	
LZ-410	PZL-104 Wilga 35A	19840819	
LZ-411	PZL-104 Wilga 35A	19840820	
LZ-412	PZL-104 Wilga 35A	19860842	
LZ-413	PZL-104 Wilga 35A	19860843	
LZ-414	PZL-104 Wilga 35A	19860844	(Z3-DCJ) LZ-414
LZ-415	PZL-104 Wilga 35A	19860845	
LZ-416	PZL-104 Wilga 35A	19870859	
LZ-417	PZL-104 Wilga 35A	19880869	
LZ-418	PZL-104 Wilga 35A	85245	DOSAAF
LZ-419	PZL-104 Wilga 35A	85238	DOSAAF
LZ-521	Yakovlev Yak-18T	unkn	
LZ-522	Yakovlev Yak-18T	unkn	
LZ-523	Yakovlev Yak-18T (For sale)	22202034031	CCCP44487
LZ-524	Yakovlev Yak-18T	unkn	
LZ-526	Yakovlev Yak-18T	unkn	
LZ-527	Yakovlev Yak-18T	22202034090	
LZ-528	Yakovlev Yak-18T	unkn	(Z3-DCK) LZ-528
LZ-530	Yakovlev Yak-18T	unkn	
LZ-551	Zlin Z.50LS	unkn	
LZ-552	Zlin Z.50LS (For sale)	unkn	
LZ-554	Zlin Z.50LS	0049	
LZ-801	Zlin Z.42	0055	
LZ-802	Zlin Z.42MU	0058	
LZ-803	Zlin Z.42M	0057	OK-ELB
LZ-804	Zlin Z.42	0059	
LZ-805	Zlin Z.42	0056	
LZ-806	Zlin Z.42	0136	

LZ-807	Zlin Z.42 (For sale)	0137	
LZ-810	Zlin Z.42	0442	
LZ-811	Zlin Z.42	0466	
LZ-901	Antonov An-2	110406	
LZ-902	Antonov An-2	113616	
LZ-903	Antonov An-2M	500308	
LZ-904	Antonov An-2M	500304	
LZ-905	Antonov An-2	1G147-18	
LZ-906	Antonov An-2	115708	
LZ-907	Antonov An-2	117005	
LZ-908	Antonov An-2	1G55-17	
LZ-909	Antonov An-2	1G56-44	
LZ-911	Antonov An-2	1G181-60	
LZ-912	Antonov An-2	1G33-13	
LZ-914	Antonov An-2R	1G55-26	
LZ-915	Antonov An-2R	1G55-29	
LZ-917	Antonov An-2R	1G86-08	
LZ-918	Antonov An-2	1G55-11	(Z3-DCI) LZ-918 LZ-1018 LZ-1130
LZ-919	Antonov An-2R	1G155-09	
LZ-923	Antonov An-2	1G55-09	
LZ-1008	Antonov An-2	1G55-01	
LZ-1021	Antonov An-2	1G79-23	
LZ-1022	Antonov An-2	1G79-29	
LZ-1023	Antonov An-2	1G79-30	
LZ-1024	Antonov An-2	1G79-31	
LZ-1033	Antonov An-2	unkn	
LZ-1040	Antonov An-2	unkn	
LZ-1044	Antonov An-2R	unkn	
LZ-1057	Antonov An-2	1G92-05	
LZ-1081	Antonov An-2R	1G93-46	LZ-030
LZ-1084	Antonov An-2	1G93-49	
LZ-1088	Antonov An-2	1G79-28	
LZ-1089	Antonov An-2R (Museum)	1G82-46	
LZ-1090	Antonov An-2R	1G86-02	
LZ-1091	Antonov An-2R	1G86-04	
LZ-1092	Antonov An-2R	1G86-05	
LZ-1093	Antonov An-2R	1G86-06	
LZ-1095	Antonov An-2R	1G92-03	
LZ-1098	Antonov An-2T	117412	
LZ-1099	Antonov An-2R	1G135-51	
LZ-1100	Antonov An-2R	1G135-52	
LZ-1101	Antonov An-2R	1G135-53	
LZ-1103	Antonov An-2R	1G135-55	
LZ-1106	Antonov An-2R	1G135-58	
LZ-1107	Antonov An-2R	1G135-59	
LZ-1108	Antonov An-2R	1G135-60	
LZ-1109	Antonov An-2R	1G145-48	
LZ-1110	Antonov An-2R	1G145-49	
LZ-1111	Antonov An-2R	1G145-50	
LZ-1112	Antonov An-2R	1G145-51	
LZ-1113	Antonov An-2R (W/o 3.4.02)	1G145-52	
LZ-1114	Antonov An-2R	1G145-53	
LZ-1115	Antonov An-2R	1G145-54	
LZ-1116	Antonov An-2R	1G145-45	
LZ-1117	Antonov An-2R	1G145-46	
LZ-1118	Antonov An-2R	1G145-47	LZ-1097 ?
LZ-1119	Antonov An-2 (Awaiting rebuild 11.99)	17904	DM-SKF
LZ-1122	Antonov An-2R	1G155-01	
LZ-1123	Antonov An-2R	1G155-02	
LZ-1124	Antonov An-2R	1G155-03	
LZ-1125	Antonov An-2R	1G155-04	
LZ-1126	Antonov An-2R	1G155-05	
LZ-1127	Antonov An-2R	1G155-06	
LZ-1128	Antonov An-2R	1G155-07	
LZ-1131	Antonov An-2R	1G155-10	
LZ-1133	Antonov An-2	unkn	
LZ-1134	Antonov An-2	114616	DM-SKO
LZ-1135	Antonov An-2R	1G158-39	
LZ-1136	Antonov An-2R	1G158-40	
LZ-1138	Antonov An-2R	1G158-42	
LZ-1140	Antonov An-2R	1G158-44	
LZ-1141	Antonov An-2R	1G158-45	
LZ-1142	Antonov An-2R	1G158-46	
LZ-1144	Antonov An-2R	1G158-48	
LZ-1145	Antonov An-2R	1G160-04	
LZ-1146	Antonov An-2R	1G160-05	
LZ-1147	Antonov An-2R (Accident 18.4.02)	1G160-06	
LZ-1149	Antonov An-2R	1G161-01	
LZ-1150	Antonov An-2R	1G160-09	
LZ-1151	Antonov An-2R	1G160-10	
LZ-1152	Antonov An-2R	1G160-11	
LZ-1153	Antonov An-2R	1G160-12	
LZ-1154	Antonov An-2R	1G160-13	
LZ-1156	Antonov An-2R	1G163-57	
LZ-1157	Antonov An-2R	1G163-58	
LZ-1158	Antonov An-2R	1G163-59	
LZ-1159	Antonov An-2R	1G163-60	
LZ-1160	Antonov An-2R	1G166-11	
LZ-1161	Antonov An-2R	1G166-12	
LZ-1162	Antonov An-2R	1G166-13	
LZ-1163	Antonov An-2R	1G166-14	
LZ-1164	Antonov An-2R	1G166-15	
LZ-1166	Antonov An-2R	1G168-16	
LZ-1167	Antonov An-2R	1G168-17	
LZ-1168	Antonov An-2R	1G168-18	

LZ-1169	Antonov An-2R	1G169-10	
LZ-1171	Antonov An-2	116803	DM-SKR
LZ-1173	Antonov An-2	19506	DM-SKL
LZ-1175	Antonov An-2	19503	DM-SKQ(2) DM-SKJ(1)
LZ-1177	Antonov An-2	117316	DM-SKV
LZ-1178	Antonov An-2	117417	DM-SKX
LZ-1180	Antonov An-2R	1G181-47	
LZ-1185	Antonov An-2R	1G181-55	
LZ-1186	Antonov An-2R	1G181-56	
LZ-1187	Antonov An-2R	1G181-57	
LZ-1188	Antonov An-2R	1G181-58	
LZ-1189	Antonov An-2R	1G181-59	
LZ-1190	Antonov An-2R	1G182-01	
LZ-1191	Antonov An-2R	1G182-02	
LZ-1194	Antonov An-2R	1G182-05	
LZ-1195	Antonov An-2R	1G206-12	
LZ-1196	Antonov An-2R	1G206-13	
LZ-1197	Antonov An-2R	1G206-14	
LZ-1198	Antonov An-2R	1G206-15	
LZ-1199	Antonov An-2R	1G206-16	
LZ-1200	Antonov An-2R	1G206-17	
LZ-1201	Antonov An-2R	1G206-18	
LZ-1203	Antonov An-2R	1G206-20	
LZ-1204	Antonov An-2R	1G206-21	
LZ-1205	Antonov An-2R	1G206-22	
LZ-1206	Antonov An-2R	1G206-23	
LZ-1210	Antonov An-2TP	1G129-04	CCCP.....
LZ-1211	Antonov An-2TP	1G119-40	CCCP02497
LZ-1212	Antonov An-2TP	1G125-08	CCCP02730
LZ-1213	Antonov An-2TP	1G125-26	CCCP.....
LZ-1214	Antonov An-2TP	1G125-33	CCCP.....
LZ-1215	Antonov An-2	unkn	
LZ-1216	Antonov An-2TP	1G146-13	CCCP07184
LZ-1217	Antonov An-2R	1G213-08	
LZ-1218	Antonov An-2R	1G213-09	
LZ-1220	Antonov An-2R	1G213-11	
LZ-1221	Antonov An-2R	1G213-12	
LZ-1222	Antonov An-2R	1G213-13	
LZ-1223	Antonov An-2R	1G213-14	
LZ-1224	Antonov An-2R	1G213-15	
LZ-1225	Antonov An-2R	1G213-16	
LZ-1226	Antonov An-2R	1G213-17	
LZ-1228	Antonov An-2R	1G213-19	
LZ-1231	Antonov An-2R	1G216-18	
LZ-1236	Antonov An-2R	1G216-23	
LZ-1237	Antonov An-2R	1G216-24	
LZ-1238	Antonov An-2R	1G216-25	
LZ-1239	Antonov An-2R	1G216-26	
LZ-1240	Antonov An-2R	1G216-27	
LZ-1241	Antonov An-2R	1G216-28	
LZ-1242	Antonov An-2R	1G216-29	
LZ-1243	Antonov An-2R	1G216-30	
LZ-1244	Antonov An-2R	1G216-31	
LZ-1245	Antonov An-2R	1G216-32	
LZ-1246	Antonov An-2R	1G216-33	
LZ-1248	Antonov An-2R	1G216-35	
LZ-1251	Antonov An-2	unkn	
LZ-1262	Antonov An-2	unkn	
LZ-1401	Antonov An-2	unkn	
LZ-1402	Antonov An-2	unkn	
LZ-1403	Antonov An-2	unkn	
LZ-1404	Antonov An-2	1G164-15	CCCP16061
LZ-1405	Antonov An-2	1G165-07	CCCP16083
LZ-1406	Antonov An-2	unkn	
LZ-1407	Antonov An-2	unkn	
LZ-1408	Antonov An-2	1G187-17	EW-54924 CCCP54924
LZ-1409	Antonov An-2	unkn	
LZ-1410	Antonov An-2	unkn	
LZ-1411	Antonov An-2	unkn	
LZ-1502	Antonov An-2	1G166-04	RA-19750 CCCP19750
LZ-1503	Antonov An-2	1G148-33	RA-07272 CCCP07272
LZ-1504	Antonov An-2	1G199-12	Z3-BGO LZ-1504 CCCP31503
LZ-1505	Antonov An-2	1G189-22	Z3-BGP LZ-1505 RA-84555 CCCP84555
LZ-1601	Antonov An-2	unkn	
LZ-1602	Antonov An-2	unkn	
LZ-1604	Antonov An-2	unkn	
LZ-1605	Antonov An-2	unkn	
LZ-1606	Antonov An-2	unkn	
LZ-2002	Antonov An-2	unkn	
LZ-2006	Antonov An-2M	unkn	
LZ-2010	Antonov An-2M	801825	
LZ-3013	LET Z-37 Cmelák	14-26	
LZ-3040	LET Z-37 Cmelák	14-28	
LZ-3101	LET Z-37 Cmelák	unkn	
LZ-3102	LET Z-37 Cmelák	unkn	
LZ-3103	LET Z-37 Cmelák	unkn	
LZ-3104	LET Z-37 Cmelák	unkn	
LZ-3105	LET Z-37 Cmelák	unkn	

LZ-3107	LET Z-37 Cmelák	unkn	
LZ-3108	LET Z-37 Cmelák	unkn	
LZ-3110	LET Z-37 Cmelák	unkn	
LZ-....	LET Z-37A Cmelák	17-29	D-ENSK
			DDR-SSK
			DM-SSK
LZ-5021	Mil Mi-2	544721036	
LZ-5022	Mil Mi-2	544722036	
LZ-5023	Mil Mi-2	544723046	
LZ-5024	Mil Mi-2	525928128	
LZ-5025	Mil Mi-2	525929128	
LZ-5027	Mil Mi-2	526008039	
LZ-5028	Mil Mi-2	526014029	
LZ-5030	Mil Mi-2	526016029	
LZ-5031	Mil Mi-2	526017029	
LZ-5032	Mil Mi-2	526018029	
LZ-5033	Mil Mi-2	526019029	
LZ-5035	Mil Mi-2	526021029	
LZ-5036	Mil Mi-2	526022029	
LZ-5037	Mil Mi-2	526445010	
LZ-5038	Mil Mi-2	526446010	
LZ-5039	Mil Mi-2	526447010	
LZ-5040	Mil Mi-2	526448010	
LZ-5041	Mil Mi-2	526449010	
LZ-5042	Mil Mi-2	526450010	
LZ-5043	Mil Mi-2	526501010	
LZ-5044	Mil Mi-2	526502010	
LZ-5045	Mil Mi-2	526503010	
LZ-6003	Kamov Ka.26	7101703	
LZ-6012	Kamov Ka.26	unkn	
LZ-6013	Kamov Ka.26	7202407	
LZ-6015	Kamov Ka.26	unkn	
LZ-6017	Kamov Ka.26	unkn	
LZ-6019	Kamov Ka.26	unkn	
LZ-6024	Kamov Ka.26	unkn	
LZ-6025	Kamov Ka.26	unkn	
LZ-6027	Kamov Ka.26	7404310	
LZ-6030	Kamov Ka.26	7504808	
LZ-6031	Kamov Ka.26	7504809	
LZ-6032	Kamov Ka.26	7504810	
LZ-6033	Kamov Ka.26	7504811	
LZ-6036	Kamov Ka.26	7504819	
LZ-6040	Kamov Ka.26	unkn	
LZ-6042	Kamov Ka.26	7505314	
LZ-6044	Kamov Ka.26	unkn	
LZ-6045	Kamov Ka.26	7605502	
LZ-6047	Kamov Ka.26	unkn	
LZ-6048	Kamov Ka.26	unkn	
LZ-6049	Kamov Ka.26	unkn	
LZ-6050	Kamov Ka.26	unkn	
LZ-6052	Kamov Ka.26	unkn	
LZ-6053	Kamov Ka.26	unkn	
LZ-6056	Kamov Ka.26	7615807	
LZ-6059	Kamov Ka.26	unkn	
LZ-6061	Kamov Ka.26	unkn	
LZ-6063	Kamov Ka.26	7706002	
LZ-6067	Kamov Ka.26	unkn	
LZ-6069	Kamov Ka.26	7806407	Z3-HHC
			LZ-6069
LZ-6071	Kamov Ka.26	unkn	
LZ-6072	Kamov Ka.26	unkn	
LZ-6073	Kamov Ka.26	7102207	
LZ-6078	Kamov Ka.26	unkn	
LZ-6079	Kamov Ka.26	unkn	
LZ-6080	Kamov Ka.26	unkn	
LZ-8001	PZL M-18 Dromader (Museum)	1Z008-11	
LZ-8002	PZL M-18 Dromader	1Z008-12	
LZ-8003	PZL M-18 Dromader	1Z008-13	
LZ-8005	PZL M-18 Dromader	1Z009-07	
LZ-8006	PZL M-18 Dromader	1Z009-08	
LZ-8008	PZL M-18 Dromader	1Z009-12	Z3-BGL
			LZ-8008
LZ-8010	PZL M-18 Dromader	1Z009-22	
LZ-8012	PZL M-18 Dromader	1Z009-24	
LZ-8014	PZL M-18 Dromader	1Z009-26	
LZ-8017	PZL M-18 Dromader	1Z009-29	Z3-BGN
			LZ-8017
LZ-9001	Ayres S.2R-T34 Turbo Thrush	T34-058DC	
LZ-9002	Ayres S.2R-T34 Turbo Thrush	T34-059DC	
LZ-9003	Ayres S.2R-T34 Turbo Thrush	T34- 60	
LZ-9004	Ayres S.2R-T34 Turbo Thrush	T34-061DC	
LZ-9005	Ayres S.2R-T34 Turbo Thrush	T34-071DC	
LZ-9006	Ayres S.2R-T34 Turbo Thrush	T34-077DC	
LZ-...	Bell 206BJet Ranger II	4504	N82407
			C-GFNU
LZ-...	Bell 206BJet Ranger II	4506	N82401
			C-FOEP
LZ-...	Bell 206BJet Ranger II	4508	N8264U
			C-GFNQ
LZ-...	Bell 206BJet Ranger II	4510	N82744
			C-FOFB
LZ-...	Bell 206BJet Ranger II	4512	N8268J
			C-GBUP
LZ-...	Bell 206BJet Ranger II	4514	N8267W
			C-GAJN
LZ-...	Bell 430	49061	N23459
			C-GLZE
LZ-...	Cessna 150L	15075078	N10841
LZ-...	Cessna 152	15285201	N6223Q
LZ-...	Reims/Cessna F172K	F17200781	D-ECOI
LZ-...	Reims FR172H Rocket	FR17200330	D-EEXC
LZ-...	Enstrom 280FX Shark	2096	N280BR
LZ-...	MBB Bö.105S (To LZ-BAN or -BAP?)	S-570	D-HDPS(2)
LZ-...	MBB Bö.105S (To LZ-BAN or -BAP?)	S-872	D-HHIT
			N5096Y
			D-HMBN
			(D-HFND)
LZ-...	Mil Mi-8	93507	N507SL
			LZ-MOY
LZ-...	Piper PA-28-151 Cherokee Warrior	28-7415538	OO-JPR
			N9513N
LZ-...	Aviat Pitts S-2B	5224	N789JB
LZ-...	SOCATA TB-10 Tobago (To LZ-ACR?)	681	D-EACR(2)

BALLOONS

LZ-001	Cameron A-210 HAFB	1437
LZ-002	Cameron V-56 HAFB	1721
LZ-004	Tomi AX-7 HAFB	BAV067/1989
LZ-005	Tomi AX-7 HAFB	BAV068/1989
LZ-006	Tomi AX-7 HAFB	BAV069/1989
LZ-007	Tomi AX-7 HAFB	BAV076/1989
LZ-008	Cameron V-77 HAFB	3034

GLIDERS

LZ-02	LET L-13 Blanik	172530	
LZ-06	LET L-13 Blanik	173926	
LZ-07	LET L-13 Blanik	173826	
LZ-09	LET L-13 Blanik	174029	
LZ-10	LET L-13 Blanik	174030	
LZ-11	LET L-13 Blanik	174112	
LZ-12	LET L-13 Blanik	174113	
LZ-16	LET L-13 Blanik	174716	
LZ-22	LET L-13 Blanik	174727	
LZ-23	LET L-13 Blanik	026843	
LZ-25	LET L-13 Blanik	174726	
LZ-26	LET L-13 Blanik	026429	DOSAAF
LZ-200	SZD-36 Cobra 15	W-570	
LZ-201	SZD-36 Cobra 15	W-571	
LZ-304	SZD-32A Foka 5 (Museum)	W-421	
LZ-305	SZD-32A Foka 5 (Wfu)	W-422	
LZ-306	SZD-32A Foka 5 (Wfu)	W-423	
LZ-307	SZD-32A Foka 5	W-467	
LZ-308	SZD-32A Foka 5	W-468	
LZ-309	SZD-32A Foka 5	W-545	
LZ-602	SZD-38A Jantar 1	B-670	
LZ-603	SZD-41A Jantar Standard	B-794	
LZ-604	SZD-41A Jantar Standard	B-885	
LZ-606	SZD-42-2 Jantar 2B	B-964	
LZ-607	SZD-48-1 Jantar Standard 2	W-910	
LZ-608	SZD-48-1 Jantar Standard 2	W-923	
LZ-609	SZD-42-2 Jantar 2B	B-940	
LZ-612	SZD-42-2 Jantar 2B	B-1381	
LZ-613	Rolladen-Schneider LS4A	4659	
LZ-614	Rolladen-Schneider LS4A	4660	

Other marks known include Kometa 1 Standard LZ-901,Kometa 2 Standards LZ-902-911,and Kometa 3 Standards LZ-912-931 of which some of the latter may still be extant

MICROLIGHTS

A handful of examples with normal 3-letter regns are listed in the main register sequence

LZ-X01	Optimum-88 Microlight	unkn
LZ-....	Funk FK-9	71
LZ-....	Funk FK-9	79
LZ-281	Kosmos (Accident 15.7.02)	unkn
LZ-....	Mainair Sea Alpha 582	903-0492-W698
LZ-....	Mainair Gemini 462 Flash IIA	586-1087-W375

OE - AUSTRIA

Regn.	Type	C/n	Prev.Id.
OE-AAA	Diamond DA 20-A1 Katana	10064	N844DF
OE-AAB	Piper J-3C-65 Cub	11717	HB-OBK
			43-30426
OE-AAC(2)	Diamond DA 20-A1 Katana	10104	N530SS
OE-AAD(2)	Diamond DA 20-A1 Katana	10112	N538FD
			N538SS
OE-AAE(2)	Diamond DA 20-A1 Katana	10213	N687DA
OE-AAG	Piper J-3C-65 Cub	13120	HB-OUW
			44-80824
OE-AAH(2)	Diamond DA 20-A1 Katana	10312	C-GFTJ
			N642DA
OE-AAI (2)	Diamond DA 20-A1 Katana	10114	N540SS
OE-AAK(2)	Pottier P.50P	014	
OE-AAL(2)	Diamond DA 20-A1 Katana	10205	N675DA
OE-AAM(2)	Diamond DA 20-A1 Katana	10294	N33UV
			N594DA
OE-AAN(2)	Diamond DA 20-A1 Katana	10124	N552SS
OE-AAP(2)	Diamond DA 20-A1 Katana	10221	N221DA
OE-AAQ	Diamond DA 20-A1 Katana	10005	OE-VPZ
	(C/n confirmed but officially regd as 10006)		N847DF
			C-FTJH
OE-AAR(2)	HOAC DV-20 Katana	20114	
OE-AAS(2)	HOAC DV-20 Katana	20126	OE-AIW
OE-AAT	Auster Mk.5	845	G-ANGW
			MS980
OE-AAX	Jodel D.95 Bébé	189	
OE-AAZ(2)	Diamond DA 20-A1 Katana	10121	N548ND
			N548SS
OE-ABA	Meteor FL.54	1114	I-FELC
OE-ABB	Jodel D.112 Club	661/7	
OE-ABC(2)	HOAC DV-20 Katana	20151	G-BWLV
OE-ABE	Piper J-3C-90 Cub	11210	D-EKWU
			OE-ABE
			HB-ONN
			43-29919
OE-ABF(2)	Diamond DA 20-A1 Katana	10087	N86MF
OE-ABH(2)	Europa Aviation Europa	194	
OE-ABJ	Bücker T-131P Jungmann (from kit)	T-101	OE-VPI
OE-ABL	Jodel D.112 Club	672/8	
OE-ABV(2)	Christen A-1 Husky	1152	N9608B
OE-ABX	Piper PA-18-150 Super Cub	18-7694	N10F
OE-ABZ	Piper J-5A Cub Cruiser	5-814	N35926
			NC35926
OE-ACC	Piper PA-18-150 Super Cub	MDC-1042	HB-ORX
	(Crashed 29.3.03)		
OE-ACF	Piper PA-18 Super Cub 95	18-6112	AAF:2A-AW
			N10F
OE-ACG(2)	HOAC DV-20 Katana	20036	D-EZMM
			N35DV
OE-ACK	Meteor FL.53BM	1135	I-FELX
OE-ACO(2)	HOAC DV-20 Katana	20030	N30DV
OE-ACR	Piper J-3C-65 Cub	12863	HB-OSS
	(F/n 12693 quoted officially as c/n)		44-80567
OE-ADB	Tipsy T.66H Nipper	17	
OE-ADD(2)	Europa Aviation Europa	133	
OE-ADE	Champion 7GCB Challenger 180	53	
OE-ADF	Piper PA-18-150 Super Cub	18-7510	
OE-ADK	Piper PA-18-150 Super Cub	18-4291	(D-ELTE)
			N2416P
OE-AEJ	HOAC DV-20 Katana	20127	G-BWFD
OE-AEO(2)	Piper PA-18 Super Cub 95	18-6111	AAF:2A-AV
			N10F
OE-AEP(2)	HOAC DV-20 Katana	20113	
OE-AER	Piper PA-18 Super Cub 95	18-5587	AAF:2A-AP
			N10F
OE-AES(2)	Diamond DA 20-A1 Katana	10168	C-FAMM
OE-AEZ	Champion 7GCBC Citabria	097	D-ENBR
OE-AFB	PZL-101A Gawron	119325	
OE-AFC	Piper PA-18 Super Cub 95	18-5500	AAF:2A-AO
			N10F
OE-AFE	Piper PA-18-150 Super Cub	18-6336	AAF:2A-BJ
	(Built as PA-18 Super Cub 95, wears code 2A-AW)		N10F
OE-AFF	PZL-101A Gawron	52076	
OE-AFG(2)	HOAC DV-20 Katana	20071	
OE-AFK	Piper PA-18-105 Super Cub	18-2415	N301T
OE-AFP	PZL-101A Gawron	63090	
OE-AFT	PZL-101A Gawron	63102	
OE-AFU	Piper PA-18-150 Super Cub	18-5513	AAF:2A-AT
			N10F
OE-AGA(2)	HOAC DV-20 Katana	20009	
OE-AGB	Piper PA-18-150 Super Cub	18-7445	N10F
OE-AGC	Binder CP.301S Smaragd	106	D-EFIR
OE-AGE	Aviamilano P.19 Scricciolo	326	
OE-AGG(2)	HOAC DV-20 Katana	20054	N54DV
			C-FSRY
OE-AGH(2)	HOAC DV-20 Katana	20147	G-BWIO
OE-AGI	Piper PA-18-150 Super Cub	18-7609058	
OE-AGL	Aero C-104 Jungmann	166	(D-EEST)
			OE-AGL
			OK-AXL
			Czech AF
OE-AGO	Piper PA-18 Super Cub 95	18-156	F-BIRP
			F-DAAA
			HB-OOK
OE-AGP	Piper PA-38-112 Tomahawk	38-78A0176	N9700N
OE-AGS	HOAC DV-20 Katana	20032	
OE-AGT	HOAC DV-20 Katana	20109	
OE-AGU	Robin HR.200/120 Club	13	
OE-AGW	Piper PA-18-90 Super Cub	18-6882	OE-AGV
			(OE-AGF(2))
OE-AGX	HOAC DV-20 Katana	20047	
OE-AHB(2)	Brditschka HB-202 V1	202-001	
OE-AHC	Cessna 150M	15078589	N704GA
OE-AHE	Champion 7GCBC Citabria	227-70	N7566F
OE-AHG	Cessna 150A	15059176	N7076X
OE-AHI	Brändli BX-2 Cherry	103	
OE-AHK	Cessna A152 Aerobat	A1520989	N761VG
OE-AHL	SAN Jodel DR.1050 Ambassadeur (Cr. 5.8.93)	177	OE-AWG
OE-AHM(2)	HOAC DV-20 Katana	20080	D-ETMG
OE-AHR	Rand-Robinson KR-2	3317	
OE-AHT	HOAC DV-22 Speed Katana	22002	
OE-AIC	HOAC DV-20 Katana	20098	N98DV
OE-AIF	Piper PA-18-150 Super Cub	18-4401	OE-BIF
			N2772P
OE-AIL	Piper PA-18-180 Super Cub	18-7505	OE-BIL
			N3747Z
OE-AIN	Piper PA-18-180 Super Cub	18-7803	OE-BIN
	(Modified from PA-18-150, 1993)		N10F
OE-AIO	Piper PA-18-180 Super Cub	18-8115	OE-BIO
			N7273Y
OE-AIR(2)	HOAC DV-20 Katana	20007	
OE-AIS	Cessna 150B	15059433	N7333X
OE-AIZ	Piper PA-22-108 Colt	22-8475	OE-BIZ
			N10F
OE-AJK	Aero Designs Pulsar XP	469	
OE-AKA	Fieseler Fi.156C Storch S-14b	110202	Fv3814
OE-AKD(2)	Bücker T.131P Jungmann	116	OE-VKD
OE-AKE(2)	Europa Aviation Europa	250	OE-VPL
OE-AKF	Bücker Bü.133 Jungmeister	18	HB-MIR
			U-71
OE-AKG(2)	Diamond DA 20-A1 Katana	10153	N97ES
OE-AKH(2)	SG Aviation Europa Storm 320E	136	OE-VKH
OE-AKK	Bücker-Lerche R-180	96	HB-URT
	(Lycoming Bü 131 conversion)		A-83
OE-AKL	HOAC DV-20 Katana	20003	
OE-AKM(2)	HOAC DV-20 Katana	20087	N87DV
OE-AKN	Diamond DA 20-A1 Katana	10172	N152SE
OE-AKT	Bücker Bü.133C Jungmeister	43	HB-MKD
			U-96
OE-AKY	Diamond DA 20-A1 Katana	10059	N199DA
OE-ALA	Piper J-3C-65 Cub	8637	N62752
			42-36513
OE-ALB	Cessna F150H	F150-0343	(D-EGAA)
OE-ALD	Cessna F150J	F150-0470	
OE-ALE	Cessna F150J	F150-0403	
OE-ALG(2)	Brditschka HB-207V RG Alfa	207005	
OE-ALH	Reims/Cessna FA150K Aerobat	FA1500050	
OE-ALI	Aero Jodel D.11A Club	614	
OE-ALJ	HOAC DV-20 Katana	20089	
OE-ALN	Reims/Cessna F150K	F15000607	D-ECEY
OE-ALO	Reims/Cessna F150K	F15000642	F-BSIF
OE-ALP	Reims/Cessna F150K	F15000639	F-BRXI
OE-ALU	Reims/Cessna F150L	F15000732	
OE-ALZ	Reims/Cessna FRA150L Aerobat	FRA1500137	
OE-AMA	Beech 77 Skipper	WA-251	D-EFCQ
OE-AMB(2)	Diamond DA 20-A1 Katana	10235	(D-EVDA)
			N237DA
OE-AMC	Diamond DA 20-A1 Katana	10117	D-EAGH(3)
			N544SS
OE-AMH	HOAC DV-20 Katana	20063	
OE-AMI	Starlite SL-1	113	
OE-AML	Piel CP.301A Emeraude	02	
OE-AMM	Boeing Stearman E75	75-5032	N5379N
			42-16869
OE-AMN	Jodel D.95 Bébé	673	
OE-AMS	Europa Aviation Europa	183	
OE-AMW(2)	Christen Pitts S-2B Special	5158	
OE-ANB	Piper PA-18 Super Cub 95	18-1459	D-ENCB
			F-MAEA (ALAT)
			51-15459
OE-AND	Piper PA-18 Super Cub 95	18-1582	D-EETL
			ALAT
			51-15582
OE-ANF	Piper PA-18 Super Cub 95	18-2056	D-ENAW
			R-71
			52-2456
OE-ANX	Diamond DA 20-A1 Katana	10313	N313DA
OE-ANZ	Diamond DA 20-A1 Katana	10049	C-FWNK
OE-AOB	Bellanca 7GCBC Citabria	678-74	
OE-AOC	Bellanca 7GCBC Citabria	696-74	
OE-AOD	Bellanca 7GCBC Citab ia	697-74	
OE-AON	Bellanca 7GCBC Citabria	760-74	
OE-APA	Piper PA-18-150 Super Cub	18-8872	N8474Y
OE-APC(2)	Aero Designs Pulsar XP 100	433	OE-VPC
OE-APG	Piper PA-18-150 Super Cub	18-8691	N4369Z
OE-APK	Piper PA-18-150 Super Cub	18-8629	N4317Z
OE-APL	Christen A-1 Husky	1104	D-EBAD(5)

OE-APN	Piper PA-18-150 Super Cub	18-8119	N4112Z
OE-APW	Piper PA-18-150 Super Cub	18-8672	N4354Z
OE-ARD	Christen A-1 Husky	1112	D-EARD
OE-ARE	Aero Designs Pulsar XP	429	
OE-ARF	Piel CP.301A Emeraude	048	
OE-ARG	Piper PA-38-112 Tomahawk II	38-81A0102	(D-ECZW)
			YV-459CP
			N9653N
OE-ARK	Denney Kitfox II	471	
OE-ARU	Diamond DA 20-A1 Katana	10113	N539SS
OE-ARW(2)	Diamond DA 20-A1 Katana	10077	C-GDEC(3)
OE-ARY	Diamond DA 20-A1 Katana	10109	N535SS
OE-ASA	Bölkow BO.208C Junior	698	(D-EABL)
OE-ASK(2)	Cessna 150M	15075982	N66311
OE-ASP(2)	HOAC DV-22 Speed Katana	22001	
OE-ASW	Aero-Jodel D.11A Club	632	
OE-ATB	Reims/Cessna F150L	F15000867	
OE-ATD	Reims/Cessna F150L	F15000937	
OE-ATF	Reims/Cessna FRA150L Aerobat	FRA1500197	
OE-ATL	Reims/Cessna F150L	F15000936	
OE-ATM	Reims/Cessna F150L	F15001039	
OE-ATN	Reims/Cessna F150L	F15001079	
OE-ATO	Reims/Cessna F150L	F15001081	
OE-ATS(2)	Bellanca 7KCAB Citabria	486-74	N142TS
			OO-RJM
			OE-AOP
			N22KA
OE-ATV	Reims/Cessna F150L	F15001057	
OE-ATW	Reims/Cessna FRA150L Aerobat	FRA1500225	(G-BBTC)
OE-ATX	Reims/Cessna F150L	F15001047	(G-BBTD)
OE-AUA	Reims/Cessna F150L	F15000790	OE-BUA
			OE-ATA
OE-AUE(2)	Piper PA-18-150 Super Cub	18-8009053	OE-BUE
			(D-EFSC)
			N2351P
OE-AUL(2)	Piper PA-18-150 Super Cub	18-8826	OE-BUL
			N4491Z
			N9678N
OE-AUR	Reims/Cessna F152	F15201951	OE-BUR
OE-AUS	Pitts S-1S Special	K-101	
OE-AUW	CASA I-131E Jungmann	2059	D-EDFD
			(D-EOOL)
			E3B-510
OE-AVD	Cessna F150F	F150-0027/15063012	
OE-AVE	Cessna F150F	F150-0034/15063107	
OE-AVG	Cessna F150F	F150-0028/15063028	
OE-AVI	Cessna F150F	F150-0033/15063104	
OE-AVR	Cessna F150G	F150-0138	
OE-AVV	Cessna F150H	F150-0229	
OE-AXR	Westermayer WE.4 Gyrocopter	04	
OE-AXW	Bensen B.8M Austria Gyrocopter	01	
OE-AYE	Cessna 150C	15059841	N2041Z
OE-AYK	Cessna 150C	15060006	N7906Z
OE-AYX	Cessna 150E	15061494	N4094U
OE-BAX	Cessna 182P Skylane	18262985	OE-DGF
			N52982
OE-BBB	Beech 200 Super King Air	BB-526	
OE-BXA	Agusta-Bell 206B Jet Ranger III	8613	
OE-BXB(2)	Agusta-Bell 206B Jet Ranger III	8644	
OE-BXC(2)	Agusta-Bell 206B Jet Ranger III	8618	
OE-BXD(4)	Aérospatiale AS.355N Ecureuil 2	5581	OE-XEZ
			OE-BXD(4)
			F-WYMK
OE-BXE(2)	Agusta-Bell 206B Jet Ranger III	8666	
OE-BXI (2)	Aérospatiale AS.350B1 Ecureuil	1899	
OE-BXK(2)	Aérospatiale AS.350B1 Ecureuil	1900	
OE-BXL(2)	Aérospatiale AS.350B1 Ecureuil	2049	
OE-BXM(2)	Aérospatiale AS.350B1 Ecureuil	2113	
OE-BXN(2)	Aérospatiale AS.350B1 Ecureuil	2214	
OE-BXO(2)	Bell 206B3 Jet Ranger III	4440	
OE-BXP(2)	Bell 206B3 Jet Ranger III	4410	C-FYDD
OE-BXR(3)	Bell 206B3 Jet Ranger III	4413	C-FYDH
OE-BXT(2)	Bell 206B3 Jet Ranger III	4441	
OE-BXU(3)	Aérospatiale AS.355F2 Ecureuil 2	5485	F-WYMA
OE-BXW(2)	Aérospatiale AS.355F2 Ecureuil 2	5528	F-WYMA
OE-BXX(2)	Aérospatiale AS.355N Ecureuil 2	5558	OE-XEY
			OE-BXX(2)
			F-WYMF
OE-CAA(2)	Brditschka HB 207VRG Alpha	207-002	
OE-CBB	Diamond DA 20-A1 Katana	10303	N603DA
OE-CBE	Cessna F150J	F150-0396	(D-EWOR)
			HB-CBE
			OE-AVZ
OE-CBH	Brändli BX-2 Cherry	78	
OE-CBK	Brditschka HB-207V RG Alpha	207012	
OE-CBL	Cessna F150J	F150-0509	D-EBBL
OE-CBP	Diamond DA 20-A1 Katana	10190	N290DA
OE-CBR	HOAC DV-20 Katana	20010	
OE-CBS	Piper PA-18-150 Super Cub	18-8083	N4092Z
OE-CBW	HOAC DV-20 Katana	20160	
OE-CCC	HOAC DV-20 Katana	20095	N95DV
OE-CCH	Pitts S-1S Special	001	
OE-CCI(2)	Cessna L-19E Bird Dog (305C)	23936	AAF:3A-BI
			57-6022
OE-CCS	HOAC DV-20 Katana	20097	N197DV
OE-CDF	Viking Dragonfly	EDO-1	
OE-CDM(2)	Piper PA-18-150 Super Cub	1809019	N189PC
OE-CDP	Piper PA-18-150 Super Cub	18-5664	D-EADP
			OE-ADH
			(D-ECEQ)
			N7196D
OE-CDV(2)	HOAC DV-20 Katana	20081	OY-JAC
			OE-AII
OE-CEA	Cessna 152	15280019	D-EBKF
			N757US
OE-CEB	Cessna 152	15280994	D-EDLO
			N48838
OE-CEF	HOAC DV-20 Katana	20014	
OE-CEL	Denney Kitfox	PA470.001	
OE-CEM	HOAC DV-20 Katana	20099	N199DV
OE-CEO	Bellanca 7GCAA Citabria	362-78	VH-WEO
OE-CEP(2)	Brändli BX-2 Cherry	91	
OE-CET	Etrich-Taube F Replica	01	
OE-CEW(2)	Diamond DA 20-A1 Katana	10156	
OE-CEX	Piper J-3C-65 Cub	11030	D-EGIS
			HB-OHD
			43-29739
OE-CFB(2)	Europa Aviation Europa	174	
OE-CFC	Reims/Cessna F152	F15201596	
OE-CFE	Reims/Cessna F152	F15201639	
OE-CFF	Reims/Cessna F152	F15201719	
OE-CFK	Reims/Cessna F152	F15201760	
OE-CFN	Cessna 152	15284468	N6623L
OE-CFT	Cessna 150E	15061097	D-EDTD
			N2597J
OE-CFV	Extra EA 300/L	1181	
OE-CFY	Brditschka HB-207V-RG	207029	
OE-CGC	Cessna A152 Aerobat	A1520984	N761TA
OE-CGD	Cessna 152	15285793	N94817
OE-CGG	Reims/Cessna F150L	F15000736	D-ECGG
OE-CGO	Reims/Cessna F150L	F15000905	N9693N
			D-ECVV
OE-CGW(2)	Brditschka HB-202-V2	202-003	
	(Model change from V1 to V2, 1990)		
OE-CHA	Brditschka HB-207V-RG Alpha	207003	
OE-CHB(2)	Diamond DA 20-A1 Katana	10240	D-ETEB
OE-CHC	Brditschka HB-207V-RG Alpha	207001	
OE-CHE	Polliwagen Supernova PW235	0613	
OE-CHG	Brändli BX-2 Cherry	64	
OE-CHI	Brändli BX-2 Cherry	98	
OE-CHK	Piper PA-38-112 Tomahawk II	38-82A0047	HB-PHK
			N91535
OE-CHL	Europa Aviation Europa	227	
OE-CHM	Bede BD-5B	2537	
OE-CHR	Christen A-1 Husky	1240	D-EXAD
OE-CHS(2)	Aero Designs Pulsar XP-II	257	OE-VHS
OE-CHW	Denney Kitfox IV	HCU-078	
OE-CIC	HOAC DV-20 Katana	20073	
OE-CIF	Denney Kitfox III	642	
OE-CIG	Denney Kitfox II/IV	641	
OE-CIH	Piper PA-18-180 Super Cub	18-6765	OE-BIH
	(Modified from PA-18-150, 1994)		N10F
OE-CII	Cessna 150M	15077396	N211AR
			N211AF
			N63562
OE-CIK	Piper PA-18-180 Super Cub	18-7414	OE-BIK
OE-CIW	HOAC DV-20 Katana	20070	
OE-CKD	Europa Aviation Europa	134	
OE-CKH	Brändli BX-2 Cherry	106	
OE-CKL	HOAC DV-20 Katana	20125	OE-VPP
			TF-FTZ
			OY-JAK
OE-CKR	Rutan Long-Ez	1201/583	OE-VPG
OE-CLA	Cessna 152	15284007	N4898H
OE-CLB	Brändli BX-2 Cherry	126	
OE-CLG	Aero Designs Pulsar XP	427	OE-VPK
OE-CLM	Diamond DA 20-A1 Katana	10012	N604F
OE-CLT	Diamond DA 20-A1 Katana	10262	N25UV
OE-CLW	Lischak LW-02	01	
OE-CMB	Reims/Cessna F150M	F15001226	
OE-CMC(2)	Diamond DA 20-A1 Katana	10194	N694DA
OE-CMD	Reims/Cessna F150M	F15001283	
OE-CME	Reims/Cessna F150M	F15001227	
OE-CMG	Reims/Cessna F150M	F15001305	
OE-CMH	Reims/Cessna F150M	F15001271	(F-BXQJ)
OE-CMI	Reims/Cessna F150M	F15001397	
OE-CMK	Reims/Cessna F150M	F15001384	
OE-CML	Reims/Cessna F150M	F15001410	
OE-CMM	Reims/Cessna F150M	F15001409	
OE-CMN	Reims/Cessna F150M	F15001387	
OE-CMP	Reims/Cessna FA152 Aerobat	FA1520342	
OE-CMR	Reims/Cessna F152	F15201446	
OE-CMS	Reims/Cessna F152	F15201456	
OE-CMV(2)	Diamond DA 20-A1 Katana	10202	C-GDIM
			N673DA
OE-CMW(2)	Europa Aviation Europa	173	
OE-CMY	Reims/Cessna F152	F15201449	
OE-CNC	Reims/Cessna F152	F15201853	D-EANC(2)
OE-CNH	Europa Aviation Europa	132	
OE-COC	HOAC DV-20 Katana	20111	
OE-COG	HOAC DV-20 Katana	20100	
OE-CON	HOAC DV-20 Katana	20108	
OE-CPC	Piper PA-38-112 Tomahawk	38-80A0091	N9682N
OE-CPE	Reims/Cessna F150M	F15001374	F-GAQS

OE-CPR	Diamond DA 20-A1 Katana	10002	C-FTJB
OE-CPT	SG Aviation Europa Storm 320E	268A3	OE-VPT
OE-CPU	HOAC LF-2 (DV-20 Katana)	20002	
OE-CPW	Piper PA-18A-180 Super Cub (Modified from PA-18-150, 1991)	18-5859	N7572D
OE-CRK	Zlin Z.326 Trenér Master	646-08	HA-TRK
OE-CRN	Denney Kitfox-Mk IV Speedster	FCS118	
OE-CRS	Reims/Cessna F152	F15201954	
OE-CRW	Brändli BX-2 Cherry	93	
OE-CSA	Zlin Z.526F Trenér Master	1242	HA-SAR
OE-CSC	Diamond DA 20-A1 Katana	10123	N564SS
OE-CSK	Quickie Aircraft Corp Quickie Q.2	2284	
OE-CSM	Cessna 152	15284433	D-EKCU(2) PH-SCU N6555L
OE-CSP	Diamond DA 20-A1 Katana	10279	N579DA C-GBUV
OE-CST	Brändli BX-2 Cherry	125	
OE-CSZ	Bellanca 8KCAB Decathlon	349-77	
OE-CTA	Diamond DA 20-A1 Katana	10074	N519SS
OE-CTB	Diamond DA 20-A1 Katana	10085	N526SS
OE-CTO	Brändli BX-2 Cherry	115	
OE-CTR	HOAC DV-20 Katana	20096	N96DV
OE-CTW	Boeing Stearman E75	75-5439	N5180N 42-17276
OE-CUB	Piper J-3C-65 Cub	18282	N98128 NC98128
OE-CUC	Cessna F150H	F150-0304	OE-BUC OE-ALC
OE-CUG	Reims/Cessna FA152 Aerobat	FA1520381	OE-BUG OE-AIM
OE-CUM	Cessna 150M	15077165	D-EFJF N63191
OE-CUS	Cessna 152	15284488	N4889M
OE-CVB	Light Aero Avid Flyer Mk.IV	1050D	
OE-CVC	Reims/Cessna F150L	F15000719	HB-CVQ
OE-CWM	Diamond DA 20-A1 Katana	10136	N101EC
OE-CWR	Cessna 150M	15078222	N9272U
OE-CXG	Hughes 269C	71-1063	N1110K
OE-CXT	Robinson R-22	0126	D-HEMI SE-HOD
OE-CXX	Robinson R-22 Beta	1570	
OE-CYY	Aquila AT01	AT01-124	
OE-CYZ	Rutan Cozy	E-730	
OE-DAA(2)	Piper PA-32RT-300T Turbo Lance II	32R-7887053	D-ETAS OE-KRR D-EJHW PH-BRO N36552
OE-DAB(2)	Diamond DA 40D Star	D4.152	OE-VPW
OE-DAC(2)	Diamond DA 40D Star	D4.099	
OE-DAD	Cessna 170B	26920	HB-COV N2977D
OE-DAF(3)	Diamond DA 40D Star	D4.129	
OE-DAI	Cessna 172B Skyhawk	17247801	N6901X
OE-DAW(2)	Reims/Cessna F182Q Skylane	F18200065	OE-BAW OE-DOL
OE-DBR	Cessna 182B Skylane (Crashed 28.10.01)	51700	N2400G
OE-DBU(2)	Reims/Cessna FR172K Hawk XP	FR17200661	N988PK (D-EBKP) HB-CNU
OE-DBW	Cessna 170B	26490	D-EFYL N3447C
OE-DCC	Robin DR.400/180R Remorqueur	1030	D-EGPS
OE-DCD	SOCATA MS.893E Rallye 180GT Gaillard	12492	F-BVLK
OE-DCG	Cessna 175B Skylark	17556856	N8156T
OE-DCN	Cessna P172D Skyhawk Powermatic	P17257170	N8570X
OE-DCS	Cessna F172E	F172-0060	OE-DOS
OE-DCV	Cessna F172E	F172-0065	
OE-DCZ(2)	Diamond DA 40D Star	D4.120	OE-VPU
OE-DDK	Cessna 182G Skylane	18255195	N3795U
OE-DDN	Cessna 182H Skylane	18255998	N1898X
OE-DDT	Cessna 182K Skylane	18257779	N2579Q
OE-DDU	Cessna 182L Skylane	18258898	
OE-DDV	Cessna 182M Skylane	18259404	N70881
OE-DDW	Cessna 182K Skylane	18258365	N2665R
OE-DEC	Cessna 210	57259	D-EJAV N9459T
OE-DEF(2)	Diamond DA 40-V1 Star	40001	OE-VPC
OE-DEH	SOCATA MS.893A Rallye Commodore 180	12031	F-BTPQ
OE-DER	Cessna P206B Super Skylane	P206-0342	N4742F
OE-DET(2)	Diamond DA 40D Star	D4.097	OE-VPU
OE-DEX(2)	Piper PA-28R-201 Arrow	2844089	N989G N53598
OE-DFD(2)	Diamond DA 40-V2 Star	40002	OE-DED(2) OE-VPE
OE-DFL	Piper PA-28-180 Cherokee G	28-7205008	N2158T
OE-DFR	GEMS MS.893A Rallye Commodore 180	10601	(D-EHYN)
OE-DFS	Robin DR.400/180R Remorqueur	970	
OE-DFX	Piper PA-28-181 Cherokee Archer II	28-7790239	N8439F
OE-DGA	Cessna 182P Skylane	18260911	
OE-DGB	Cessna 182P Skylane	18261104	
OE-DGC	Cessna 182P Skylane	18261534	
OE-DGH	Cessna F172D	F172-0001/17249991	F-WLIK
OE-DGM	SOCATA MS.893A Rallye Commodore 180	10639	
OE-DGN	Cessna 182P Skylane	18263534	N5785J
OE-DGU	Cessna 182P Skylane	18263497	N5717J
OE-DGW(2)	Cessna TR182 Turbo Skylane RG	R18201391	N4705S
OE-DGZ	Piper PA-28-151 Cherokee Warrior	28-7415396	N9585N
OE-DHB	Reims/Cessna F172N Skyhawk II	F17201800	
OE-DHF	Reims/Cessna F172N	F17201861	
OE-DHG(2)	Cessna 172S	172S8540	N282ME
OE-DHH	Piper PA-28-161 Cherokee Warrior II	28-7816076	N9615N
OE-DHN	Robin DR.400/180R Remorqueur	1395	
OE-DHU	Piper PA-28-151 Cherokee Warrior	28-7415449	N9616N
OE-DHV	Reims/Cessna F172N	F17201950	
OE-DHW(2)	Diamond DA 40 Star	40234	N609DS C-GDMB
OE-DHX	Reims/Cessna FR172K Hawk XP	FR17200619	
OE-DIA(2)	Diamond DA 40 Star	D4.072	
OE-DID	Cessna 182P (Reims-assembled with "c/n" 0062)	18264446	N1789M
OE-DIG	Reims/Cessna F182Q Skylane	F18200035	
OE-DIH	SOCATA MS.893A Rallye Commodore 180	12030	F-BTJD
OE-DII	SOCATA MS.892E Rallye 150ST	2818	
OE-DIK	GEMS MS.892A Rallye Commodore 150	10526	D-EDNY
OE-DIM	SOCATA MS.893E Rallye 180GT Gaillard	12843	
OE-DIP(2)	Cessna 182P Skylane (Reims-assembled with "c/n" 0058)	18264384	OE-BIP OE-DGX N1594M
OE-DIR	Reims/Cessna F182Q Skylane	F18200046	(G-BENA)
OE-DIV	Reims/Cessna F182Q Skylane	F18200058	(F-GAQH) (D-EBXP)
OE-DJA	Cessna 172 R	17281230	
OE-DJB	Diamond DA 40D Star	D4.113	
OE-DKB	Robin DR.400/140 Major	885	
OE-DKD	Cessna 210M Centurion	21062358	(N761MF)
OE-DKF	Robin DR.400/180R Remorqueur	750	
OE-DKK(2)	Diamond DA 40D Star	D4.100	OE-VPW
OE-DKS(2)	SOCATA Rallye 235F	3390	F-OHDZ F-WNGX
OE-DKT	Piper PA-28-181 Cherokee Archer II	28-7890244	N9517N
OE-DKV	SOCATA Rallye 180T Galérien	3240	
OE-DKY	SOCATA Rallye 180T Galérien	3223	
OE-DLA	Cessna F172F	F172-0132	
OE-DLH	Cessna F172H	F172-0323	
OE-DLI	Cessna F172H	F172-0435	
OE-DLL	Cessna 177A Cardinal	17701285	
OE-DLP	Reims FR172G Rocket	FR17200179	
OE-DLR	Reims/Cessna F172K	F17200764	
OE-DLS	Reims FR172H Rocket	FR17200236	
OE-DLU(2)	Reims/Cessna F182Q Skylane	F18200120	OE-BIU (OE-DNF)
OE-DLW	Reims/Cessna F172K	F17200771	
OE-DLY	Reims/Cessna F172L	F17200821	
OE-DLZ	Reims FR172H Rocket	FR17200279	
OE-DMF	Beech B19 Musketeer Sport	MB-674	
OE-DMH	Beech C23 Sundowner	M-1549	
OE-DMP	Beech C23 Sundowner	M-1818	
OE-DMR	Reims FR172H Rocket	FR17200258	D-ELAL
OE-DMS	Cessna 175A Skylark	56288	N6788E
OE-DMW	Piper PA-28-151 Cherokee Warrior	28-7415364	N9581N
OE-DMZ	Robin DR.400/180R Remorqueur	979	
OE-DND	Reims/Cessna F182Q Skylane	F18200083	
OE-DNF	Reims/Cessna F182Q Skylane	F18200125	(D-EKEB)
OE-DNI	Cessna TR182 Turbo Skylane RG	R18200866	(N737PN)
OE-DNK	Piper PA-28-180 Cherokee Challenger	28-7305309	N11C
OE-DNL	Reims/Cessna F182Q Skylane	F18200117	
OE-DNM	Robin DR.400/180R Remorqueur	1219	
OE-DNN	Piper PA-28RT-201 Arrow IV	28R-7918261	N9631N
OE-DNP	Robin DR.400/180R Remorqueur	1200	
OE-DNR	Piper PA-28R-200 Cherokee Arrow II	28R-7435111	N54484
OE-DNS	Reims FR172H Rocket	FR17200273	D-ECNS
OE-DNW	Robin DR.400/180R Remorqueur	1158	
OE-DOC	Oberlerchner Job 15-150/2	071	(D-EKEP) OE-DOC
OE-DOE	Oberlerchner Job 15-150/2	073	
OE-DOI	Piper PA-28-236 Dakota	28-7911249	N2921F
OE-DOK	SIAI-Marchetti S.205-20/R	4-218	
OE-DON(2)	Cessna 182R Skylane	18267887	D-EDGN N2287U
OE-DOR(2)	Reims/Cessna F182Q Skylane	F18200042	OE-BIR
OE-DOS(3)	SOCATA TB-10 Tobago	102	HB-EZL
OE-DOT	Reims/Cessna F182Q Skylane	F18200143	
OE-DOU	Piper PA-28RT-201 Arrow IV	28R-8018038	N8153E
OE-DOX	Cessna T210M Turbo Centurion	21062757	N6394B
OE-DPA	Piper PA-28-140 Cherokee	28-21500	N11C
OE-DPB	Piper PA-28-180 Cherokee B	28-1664	N7759W
OE-DPD	Piper PA-28-140 Cherokee	28-22232	HB-OYR N11C
OE-DPF	Piper PA-28-140 Cherokee Fliteliner	28-7125242	N5078S
OE-DPL	Piper PA-28-180 Cherokee D	28-4500	N5312L N11C
OE-DPM	Piaggio P.149D	344	AAF:3E-AB
OE-DPW	Piper PA-28R-200 Cherokee Arrow	28R-35680	N4908S
OE-DPX	Piper PA-28-140 Cherokee E	28-7225427	N11C
OE-DRA	Piper PA-28RT-201 Arrow IV	28R-7918235	N2954S
OE-DRE	Robin HR.100/210 Safari	146	
OE-DRN	Piper PA-28RT-201 Arrow IV	28R-7918050	N2192P
OE-DRU	Piper PA-28-161 Warrior II	28-8116281	N2397U
OE-DSB	Robin DR.400/180R Remorqueur	734	

OE-DSC	Cessna 182C Skylane	52757	D-EBCE N8857T
OE-DSD	Cessna 210B	21057947	N9647X
OE-DSE	Robin DR.400/180R Remorqueur	1155	
OE-DSL	Piper PA-28-180 Cherokee Archer	28-7405009	N9564N
OE-DSN	Piper PA-28R-201 Arrow III	28R-7737118	N38774
OE-DSR(2)	Diamond DA 40 Star	40394	
OE-DSY	SOCATA MS.893A Rallye Commodore 180	12068	F-BTRV
OE-DSZ	SOCATA MS.893E Rallye 180GT Gaillard	12962	
OE-DTA	Reims/Cessna F172L	F17200857	
OE-DTB	Reims/Cessna F172M	F17200939	
OE-DTI	Robin DR.400/180R Remorqueur	757	
OE-DTJ	Diamond DA 40 Star	40030	D-EBIR(2) OE-VPI
OE-DTL	GEMS MS.892A Rallye Commodore 150	10506	
OE-DTN	Reims/Cessna F172M	F17201090	
OE-DTP	Reims/Cessna F172M	F17201102	
OE-DTS(2)	Diamond DA 40 Star	40352	
OE-DTT	Reims/Cessna F172M	F17201114	
OE-DTV	Reims/Cessna F172M	F17201429	
OE-DTX	Robin DR.400/180R Remorqueur	1095	
OE-DTY	Reims/Cessna F172N	F17201577	
OE-DTZ	Piper PA-28R-200 Cherokee Arrow II	28R-7335376	D-EAYE N56185
OE-DUF	Cessna T210N Turbo Centurion II	21063973	(N4665Y)
OE-DUI	Piper PA-28RT-201 Arrow IV	28R-8018076	N8217Z
OE-DUM	Cessna U206F Stationair	U20601806	
OE-DUR	Cessna T210N Turbo Centurion II	21063862	(N6317C)
OE-DUT	SOCATA TB-10 Tobago	23	F-ODKA
OE-DUW	SOCATA MS.893E Rallye 180GT Gaillard	12845	
OE-DUY	SOCATA TB-10 Tobago	198	
OE-DVD	Reims/Cessna F172N	F17201568	
OE-DVE	Reims/Cessna F172N	F17201578	
OE-DVF	Piper PA-28-180 Cherokee Challenger	28-7305399	N55616
OE-DVG	Reims/Cessna F172N	F17201623	(OE-DWC)
OE-DVH	Reims/Cessna F172N	F17201615	(SX- . . .)
OE-DVK	Reims/Cessna F172N	F17201761	
OE-DVL	Cessna U206E Stationair	U20601638	D-EDWJ OY-AKN
OE-DVM	Piper PA-28-160 Cherokee B	28-784	HB-OVM N5679W
OE-DVO	Reims/Cessna F182Q Skylane	F18200136	
OE-DVV	Reims/Cessna FR172K Hawk XP	FR17200670	
OE-DVW	Robin DR.400/180R Remorqueur	1069	
OE-DXM	Bell 206A Jet Ranger	42	D-HEAS N9B
OE-DYF	Rockwell Commander 112A	0216	
OE-DYI	Robin DR.400/180R Remorqueur	1233	D-EEPG
OE-DYK	Mooney M.20J Model 201	24-0889	D-ENMF(2) N4770H (N4822H)
OE-DYM	Piper PA-28R-201 Arrow III	28R-7837072	N2233M
OE-DYR	SOCATA MS.892E Rallye 150T	2777	
OE-DYU	Reims/Cessna F172N	F17201883	D-EOWW
OE-DYV	Robin DR.400/180R Remorqueur	1562	
OE-DYX	Robin DR.400/120D Petit Prince	1559	
OE-DZB(2)	Diamond DA 40D Star	D4.089	
OE-EAS	Chance-Vought F4U-4 Corsair	"96995"?	N4908M BuA96995
OE-EDM	Cessna 208 Caravan I	20800257	N666CS N5135A
OE-EKD	Pilatus PC-12/45	142	HB-FRD
OE-EMD	Pilatus PC-6/B2-H4 Turbo Porter	928	HB-FLT HC-CAC HB-FLT
OE-EMS	SOCATA TBM 700C2	315	
OE-EPC	Pilatus PC-12/45	536	HB-FPO
OE-ESA	North American T-28B	200-250	N3905H BuA138179
OE-ESK	SOCATA TBM 700	279	
OE-ESM	SOCATA TBM 700	001	D-FTBM F-GLBE N300PW F-OHBM
OE-EXE	Aérospatiale SA.315B Lama	2406	F-WXFS
OE-EXF	Aérospatiale SA.315B Lama	2278	F-BVUF F-WMHI LN-OQD
OE-EXS	Bell 205A-1	30265	N5002N
OE-EXU	Aérospatiale SA.315B Lama	2478	
OE-FAA(3)	Cessna 414A	414A0492	N111KR N36952
OE-FAB(3)	Diamond DA 42 Twin Star	42.008	OE-VPY
OE-FAN	Cessna 500 Citation I	500-0289	N939KS XA-KAH N5591A YV-50CP N5289J N289CC
OE-FAR(2)	Piper PA-34-200T Seneca II	34-8070053	D-GMOX N8134A
OE-FBF	Cessna 414A Chancellor	414A0415	(N26918)
OE-FBI (2)	Piper PA-34-220T Seneca III	34-8433062	N4361N
OE-FBR(2)	Piper PA-34-220T Seneca III	3448009	D-GCWO N9197Z
OE-FBS(2)	Cessna 551 Citation II /SP	551-0574	N60GF N60GL (N1299B)
OE-FCA(3)	Cessna 525 CitationJet	525-0354	N821P (D-IMMP) N821P N5225K
OE-FCD(2)	Diamond DA 42D Twin Star	42.007	
OE-FCI	Cessna 340A	340A0690	N6347X
OE-FCK	Cessna 310R	310R1837	N2739D
OE-FCM(2)	Cessna 500 Citation	5000294	OY-VIP SE-DVB N924AS (N501LG) HL7226 N5294J
OE-FCY(2)	Cessna 525A CitationJet CJ2	525A0204	
OE-FDA(2)	Diamond DA 42D Twin Star	42.005	
OE-FDE(2)	Short SC-7 Skyvan Series 3	SH.1886	C9-ASN G-BKMF A40-SO G-AYJO G-14-58
OE-FDK	Short SC-7 Skyvan Series 3A	SH.1901	OY-JRK N8117V 9M-AXT SE-GEX LN-NPA G-AZRY G-14-73
OE-FDM	Cessna 501 Citation I/SP	501-0140	N96CF N96TD (N99TD) (N2651R)
OE-FDO	Piper PA-34-220T Seneca III	3433158	N9176B
OE-FDS	Piper PA-31T Cheyenne	31T-7720056	(N82169)
OE-FEE	Piper PA-34-220T Seneca III	34-8133066	D-GILS D-IILS N8372B
OE-FEG	Cessna 421C Golden Eagle II	421C1078	D-IBMF(2) N6866X
OE-FEP	Piper Aerostar 601P	61P-0623-7963283	HB-LKZ N8222J
OE-FFE	Cessna 421C Golden Eagle II	421C0120	N811VQ N3853C
OE-FFF	Partenavia P.68C	221	SE-LBZ EC-FPZ N2200R (N13PK) N2200R D-GEME
OE-FFP	Cessna 340A	340A1503	D-IAEH OE-FFP D-IAMO N68696
OE-FFY	Piper PA-23-250 Aztec E	27-7405365	HB-LHY N54016
OE-FGA	Piper PA-34-200T Seneca II	34-7870207	N9661C
OE-FGD	Cessna 525 CitationJet	525-0020	N1329D "OO-LFU" N1329D
OE-FGI	Cessna 525 CitationJet	525-0254	N5183V
OE-FGN	Cessna 500 Citation I	500-0291	N291DS ZS-JOO N5291J
OE-FGT	Cessna T303 Crusader	T30300086	(N2277C)
OE-FGW	Partenavia P.68B	122	D-GERO
OE-FHD	Piper PA-44-180 Seminole	44-7995111	N61624 C-GUPJ N3017B
OE-FHH	Cessna 501 Citation I/SP	501-0246	N26LC N85RS N2627N
OE-FHL	Beech C90A King Air	LJ-1115	D-IBPE
OE-FHM(2)	Beech C90A King Air	LJ-1284	N25GA OY-GEM
OE-FHW	Cessna 501 Citation I/SP	501-0121	D-IANO HB-VID D-IANO N26506
OE-FIL	Partenavia P.68C	226	HB-LPW I-KDUE
OE-FJU	Cessna 525 CitationJet	525-0295	N295CM N5209E
OE-FKG	Piper PA-31T Cheyenne II	31T-8020036	N30DJ N2570W
OE-FKH(2)	Piper PA-31T1 Cheyenne I	31T-8104029	N803CA (N90WA) N2484X
OE-FKV	Piper PA-23-250 Aztec C	27-2743	D-IBIW N5660Y
OE-FLG(2)	Cessna 525 CitationJet	525-0103	D-IVHA (N203CJ) N5204D
OE-FLN	Cessna T303 Crusader	T30300080	OO-VJI N2266C

OE-FLT(2)	Rockwell Commander 685	12027	HB-GGN OO-JPP G-BBHA N9161N
OE-FLX	Cessna 421C Golden Eagle	421C0248	(D-IDEM) N5536G
OE-FLY(3)	Piper PA-34-200T Seneca II (Officially listed as PA-34-220T since 2001)	34-7770047	N300AZ N6857F
OE-FMA(2)	Cessna 525 CitationJet	525-0188	D-IVIN (D-IVID) N51342
OE-FME(2)	Beech 300LW Super King Air	FA-228	HB-GJC (D-CAIR(2)) N80806
OE-FMG(2)	Beech C90A King Air	LJ-1236	D-IPEL N5598L
OE-FMH	Cessna 340A	340A0289	D-IAAB N4117G
OE-FMS	Cessna 501 Citation I/SP	501-0239	N164CB LV-MYN LV-PDZ N26497
OE-FMU	Cessna 525 CitationJet	525-0040	N525AJ VP-CCC D-ISCH N1959E
OE-FOO	Beech 58 P Baron	TJ-300	D-IOOO(3) N3687X
OE-FOW	Swearingen SA-226T Merlin IIIB	T-318	D-IBBD N1006F
OE-FOX(2)	Cessna 340A	340A0963	PH-AMT D-ICMA N4621G N981JC N4621G
OE-FPA(2)	Cessna 551 Citation II /SP	551-0552	
OE-FPC	Piper PA-34-200T Seneca II	34-8070286	N8241Z
OE-FPS(3)	Cessna 525A CitationJet CJ2	525A-0142	N5207A
OE-FPT	Cessna 337D Super Skymaster	33701177	N86405
OE-FPU	Cessna 414A Chancellor	414A0505	D-IHAB(2) N36993
OE-FPY	Piper PA-44-180 Seminole	44-7995247	
OE-FRA(2)	Cessna 525A CitationJet CJ2	525A-0150	N525GM
OE-FRD(2)	Piper PA-34-220TSeneca III	34-8133069	D-GESN N8372R
OE-FRH	Cessna 414A Chancellor	414A0027	
OE-FRR(2)	Cessna 525	525-0124	VP-CWW (ZS-BSS) VP-CWW N525JH N5090A
OE-FRS(2)	Beech C90A King Air	LJ-1124	N90EP D-IALL N7246B
OE-FSL	Piper PA-31 Navajo C	31-7912058	N3519C
OE-FSM	Piper PA-34-200T Seneca II	34-7970359	D-GIAS D-IGAS N2918U
OE-FSO	Beech 300LW Super King Air	FA-215	N8017G
OE-FSS(2)	Cessna 525 CitationJet	525-0226	TC-LIM N1216N N5214J
OE-FST(2)	Piper PA-34-220T Seneca IV	34-48079	D-GANU N9255Q
OE-FSW(2)	Piper PA34-220T Seneca V	34-49135	N9508N N4146L G-SENV SP-KFL
OE-FTE	Piper PA-31.Turbo Navajo B	31-7400978	D-IHOY N7586L
OE-FTI	Piper PA-34-220T Seneca III	34-8533002	N4376N
OE-FTW	Piper PA-34-200T Seneca II	34-7570288	D-INIX N1566X
OE-FUJ	Cessna 525 CitationJet	525-0544	
OE-FWS	Grumman G.44A Widgeon (SCAN-30) (Damaged 29.3.05 Lake Garda)	30	N151SA N2814D
OE-FXA	Aérospatiale AS.355F1 Ecureuil 2	5056	
OE-FXB	Aérospatiale AS.355F1 Ecureuil 2	5252	D-HLTK
OE-FXH	Aérospatiale AS.355F2 Ecureuil 2	5429	
OE-GAA	Cessna 560 Citation V	560-0111	(N91AN) (N6802T)
OE-GBA	Cessna 550 Citation II	550-0085	N57AJ OY-GKC (N2663Y)
OE-GBB	Dornier 328-100	3078	D-CDXG
OE-GBC	Cessna 550 Citation II	550-0717	SE-RBM Fv.103002 TC-SES N600GH XA-TCM (N1205M)
OE-GBD	IAI-1125 Astra SPX	133	D-CGMA VP-CAR N65GX 4X-CGV
OE-GCB	Cessna 560 Citation Ultra	560-0517	N424HH G-OTGT N5145V
OE-GCC	Cessna 560 Citation V	560-0125	N6809V
OE-GCD	Cessna 560 Citation Ultra	560-0497	N497EA TC-MET N5161J
OE-GCF	Gates Learjet 55C	55C-136	N155PS N767NY N767AZ N3811G
OE-GCH(2)	Cessna 650 Citation VII	650-7006	TC-KOC(3) N966K (N706VP) N966K N966H (N1259Y)
OE-GCI	Cessna 550 Citation II	550-0041	N177HH N985BA N341AG N8418B N3279M
OE-GCN	Cessna 650 Citation III	650-0014	(N855DH) OE-GCN C-GHOO N650CJ (N664RB) (N1306B) N1305V
OE-GCO	Cessna 650 Citation III	650-0012	N15VF N1305V
OE-GCP(2)	Cessna 560 Citation V	560-0214	(N1285D)
OE-GDA	Cessna 560 Citation V	560-0200	
OE-GDI	Bombardier Learjet 45	45-037	N50145
OE-GDM	Cessna 550 Citation II	550-0707	(SE-DYY) N707EA RP-C4654 N1202T
OE-GEG	Cessna 560XL Citation XLS	560-5529	N5262X
OE-GEJ	Cessna 560 Citation V	560-0665	N5200R
OE-GEO	Hawker 800XP	258477	N44767
OE-GGB	Bombardier Learjet 40	45-2018	N5018G
OE-GHM	Beech 400A Beechjet	RK-148	N663AJ TC-SMB N1108T
OE-GHP(2)	Cessna 550 Citation Bravo	550-0998	N5165P
OE-GHU	Hawker 800 XP	258335	OY-RAC LN-AAA(3) N335XP
OE-GIF	SAAB-Scania SF.340A	340A-100	G-GNTD SE-ISK SE-E01
OE-GII	Bombardier Learjet 60	60-169	N5014F
OE-GIL	Cessna 550 Citation II	550-0060	N315CK N98BE N75KR (N550KR) N26610
OE-GKK	Cessna 550 Citation Bravo	550-0872	N5093L
OE-GKP(2)	Bombardier Learjet 60	60-280	
OE-GLL(2)	Cessna 550 Citation Bravo	550-1069	N5093Y
OE-GLS(2)	Cessna 650 Citation VII	650-7110	N657JW RP-C650 (N12909) N52235
OE-GME	Cessna 560XL Citation Excel	560-5113	N52178
OE-GMI	Cessna 560 Citation Ultra	560-0362	N5183U
OE-GNI	Bombardier Learjet 60	60-236	I -IINL N5015T
OE-GNL(2)	Bombardier Learjet 60	60-032	N5013D
OE-GNW	Cessna 560 XL Citation Excel	560-5339	N51143
OE-GPA(2)	Cessna 560 XL Citation Excel	560-5265	N5100J
OE-GPG	IAI-1125 Astra SPX	115	C-GRGE HB-VMR N526GA
OE-GPH	Cessna 560 Citation Ultra	560-0590	N5166T
OE-GPS(2)	Cessna 550 Citation Bravo	550-0837	N5185J
OE-GPZ	Cessna 560 XL Citation Excel	560-5067	HB-VMZ N42PA
OE-GRR	Gates Learjet 55	55-059	D-CAEP (N211BY)
OE-GTF	Bombardier Learjet 60	60-281	N5013U
OE-GTI	Cessna 560XL Citation Excel	560-5037	D-CIII N5214J
OE-GTM	Beech 400A Beechjet	RK-343	N106DD N806GG N4357H
OE-GTZ	Cessna 550 Citation Bravo	550-0864	N864CB
OE-GUK	Beech 400A Beechjet	RK-124	N124BG TC-MSA N1124Z
OE-GYG	Bombardier Learjet 60	60-197	P4-AVM N23PZ N5010U

OE-HAA	Dornier 328-300	3200	D-BDXN (G-CJAB) D-BDXN N328BC D-BDMO D-BDXN (V5-NMC) (D-BMAH)
OE-HET	Canadair CL.600-1A11 Challenger	1085	N600ST N20GX N20G C-GLXQ
OE-HGG	Cessna 750 Citation X	750-0214	N5154J
OE-HIT	Dassault Falcon 50	222	D-BELL F-WWHM
OE-HLE	Canadair CL.600-2A12 Challenger	3047	N602TJ N602HJ B-4006 C-GBZQ C-GLXM
OE-HMS	Dornier 328-300	3121	D-BDXI D-BMYD
OE-HPS	Dassault Falcon 50	0334	N335EX F-WWHP
OE-HRR	Bombardier BD.100-1A10 Challenger 300	20033	C-FCMG
OE-HTG	Dornier 328-300	3162	D-BDXG(2)
OE-HTI	IAI/Gulfstream 200	089	N289GA 4X-CVH
OE-HTJ	Dornier 328-300	3114	D-BDXA(1)
OE-IAS	Embraer EMB-135BJ	14500832	(N832SG) PT-SIL
OE-ICF	Dassault Falcon 900	22	N54DC N416FJ F-WWPD
OE-IDM	Dassault Falcon 900EX	51	F-GVDP F-WWFU
OE-IEL	Bombardier BD.700-1A10 Global Express	9099	C-GZKL N700CU (ZS-DFN) N700CU C-GIPJ
OE-IFA(2)	McDonnell-Douglas DC-9-83	49809	3B-AGC 9K-AGC KuwaitAF:26
OE-IGS	Bombardier BD.700-1A10 Global Express	9044	I-MOVE N700BP C-GFKX
OE-IIA	Gulfstream V	641	HB-IIZ N641GA
OE-IJA	Gulfstream IV	1157	N457GA 9K-AKA N17581
OE-IKP	Canadair CL 600-2B16 Challenger	5599	C-GLWX
OE-ILA	Lockheed 188C Electra	1145	LN-FOH LN-MOI N9746C N5767 CF-IJJ N9746C
OE-ILB(2)	Lockheed 188AF Electra	1039	N356Q N355WS N356Q VH-RMA
OE-ILF	Boeing 737-3Z9	23601	
OE-ILW	Fokker F.27 Friendship 500	10681	N505AW PH-EXN
OE-IMB	Canadair CL-600-2B16 Challenger	5585	N585BD C-GLXO
OE-INF	Canadair CL-600-2B16 Challenger	5303	OY-TNF N609BD N604BD HL7522 C-FXKE
OE-INI	Canadair CL.600-2B16 Challenger	5595	C-FCOE C-GLXB
OE-ISN	Embraer EMB-135BJ Legacy	14500851	PT-SIO
OE-ITA	Boeing 737-3L9	27924	N730PA OY-MAT
OE-IVK	Dassault Falcon 900EX	138	F-WWFP
OE-IVV	Gulfstream V-SP	5054	N954GA
OE-IVY	Gulfstream V	687	N687GA
OE-IWP	Embraer EMB-135BJ Legacy	14500841	PT-SIN
OE-IYA	Canadair CL.600-2B16 Challenger	5435	N604PN C-GLWZ
OE-KAA	Reims/Cessna F172P	F17202145	
OE-KAC	Piper PA-28RT-201 Arrow IV	28R-8218013	N8156L
OE-KAE	SIAI-Marchetti S.208	1-14	D-EATS(2) LX-FLY(1) OO-IAT I-SJAT
OE-KAH	SAAB S.91D Safir	91470	AAF: 3F-SL

OE-KAI	Diamond DA 40D Star	D4003	
OE-KAP	Piper PA-46-350P Malibu Mirage	46-36003	HB-PNH
OE-KAS(2)	Diamond DA 40 Star	40051	
OE-KAW	Cessna 182Q Skylane	18266383	N759ZF
OE-KAZ	Piper PA-32-301 Saratoga	3206044	N9150G
OE-KBS	Piper PA-28-181 Archer II	28-8390087	N43149
OE-KCA	Cessna 182N Skylane	18260411	HB-CGG G-AYIU N92885
OE-KCC	Reims/Cessna F172N	F17201942	D-EKCC
OE-KCD	SAAB S.91D Safir	91459	AAF: 3F-SU
OE-KCM	Piper PA-28R-201 Arrow	2837041	D-EBLH(2) N9191X
OE-KDC	Diamond DA 40D Star	D4.084	
OE-KDI	Diamond DA 40D Star	D4.020	
OE-KDS	Diamond DA 40 Star	40016	OE-KRW
OE-KDW	Prescott Pusher (Not yet officially regd as such, possibly OE-VPJ)	unkn	
OE-KEH	Cessna 182R Skylane	18268387	N8187E
OE-KEM	Piper PA-28-181 Cherokee Archer II	28-7890072	N47434
OE-KEP	Cessna P210N Pressurized Centurion II	P21000777	D-EAMP(2) N4563P C-GOPM (N6435W)
OE-KES	Piper PA-28R-201T Turbo Arrow	2803007	D-EALV N9182N
OE-KEU	Piper PA-46-350P Malibu Mirage	4636110	G-BXER
OE-KEX	Cessna 172P	17274957	D-EVIP N54323
OE-KEZ	Robin DR.400/180R Remorqueur	1665	D-EEWZ
OE-KFA(2)	SOCATA TB-20 Trinidad	442	D-EIPW
OE-KFE	SOCATA TB-20 Trinidad	481	
OE-KFG	Cessna 182J Skylane	18257234	D-EMCA N3134F
OE-KFK	Reims/Cessna F172M	F17201447	D-EECZ
OE-KFL(2)	Diamond DA 40D Star	D4.081	
OE-KFR	SOCATA TB-20 Trinidad	1340	
OE-KFS	Cessna TU206G Turbo Stationair 6	U20605232	N5351U
OE-KFT	Piper PA-28RT-201T Turbo Arrow IV	28R-8431030	D-ETUL N4372Z N9605N
OE-KFU	Robin DR.400/180R Remorqueur	1725	
OE-KFW	Cessna 172P	17275823	N65701
OE-KGB	Piper PA-46-500TP Malibu Meridian	4697035	N77Y
OE-KGF	Beech K35 Bonanza	D-5793	N5328E
OE-KGH	Cessna 177RG Cardinal RG	177RG1120	N45469
OE-KGK	SAAB S.91D Safir	91449	AAF: 3F-SN
OE-KGM	Cessna 182M Skylane	18259721	D-EAGM N71696
OE-KGN	Cessna 182J Skylane	18257199	D-ECGY(2) N3099F
OE-KGO	Cessna 182H Skylane	18256179	D-EEJM N2079X
OE-KGP	Zlin Z.143L	0009	OK-AGP
OE-KGW(2)	Diamond DA 40D Star	D4.053	
OE-KHK	Cessna F172H	F172-0615	D-EDMR PH-TGU
OE-KHO	SAAB S.91D Safir	91452	AAF: 3F-SQ
OE-KHR	Cessna R182 Skylane RG	R18201844	HB-CHR N5257T
OE-KHW	Robin DR.400/180R Remo 180	2269	
OE-KIK	Cessna P210N Pressurized Centurion	P21000445	N731DP
OE-KIM	Cessna P210N Pressurized Centurion II	P21000211	N4583K
OE-KIS	Piper PA-28RT-201T Turbo Arrow IV	28R-8531012	N2506V
OE-KIT	Cessna 182P Skylane (Reims-assembled with "c/n" 0005)	18263819	D-EGAS (SE-GKK) N6737M
OE-KJE	Reims FR172J Rocket	FR17200569	D-EKJE
OE-KKB	Diamond DA 40D Star	D4.095	OE-VPU
OE-KKK	SOCATA TB-9 Tampico	927	
OE-KKS	Diamond DA 40 Star	40348	
OE-KLA(2)	Diamond DA 40D Star	D4.008	
OE-KLB	Robin DR.400/180R Remo 180	2180	
OE-KLL	Diamond DA 40 Star	40074	
OE-KLM	Piper PA-24-250 Comanche	24-1184	D-EBEW N6299P
OE-KLP	Cessna 172 S	172S8814	N814LP
OE-KLR	Piper PA-28RT-201T Turbo Arrow IV	28R-8231018	D-EKCM N80225
OE-KLS	Piper PA-28R-201T Turbo Arrow	2803009	D-ENXH N9184D
OE-KMA	Piper PA-28-181 Archer II	28-8590001	N4377Z
OE-KMC	Piper PA-28-181 Cherokee Archer II	28-7790368	D-EBBI OE-DOW N1994H
OE-KME	SOCATA TB-9 Tampico	1273	
OE-KMG(2)	Commander Aircraft 114B	14578	D-EJDM
OE-KMH	Piper PA-32R-301T Turbo Saratoga SP	32R-8529007	N6912B N9529N
OE-KMI	Cessna P210N Pressurized Centurion II (Damaged 23.5.01 but not yet cancelled)	P21000685	N5411W
OE-KML	Mooney M.20J Model 205	24-3025	N205MG

OE-KMM	Piper PA-28RT-201T Turbo Arrow IV	28R-8531005	N4388F
			N9533N
OE-KMO(2)	Mooney M.20R Ovation	29-0094	
OE-KMS	Piper PA-32R-301T Turbo Saratoga SP	32R-8029090	D-EDET(3)
			N82009
OE-KMT	Cessna R172K Hawk XP	R1722434	D-EBGF
			N736DA
OE-KMU	Piper PA-32R-301T Turbo Saratoga SP	32R-8229046	HB-PHA
OE-KMV	Piper PA-28-181 Archer III	2843012	N9258L
OE-KMW	Piper PA-32R-301T Turbo Saratoga SP	32R-8329035	N4314B
OE-KMX	Beech F33A Bonanza	CE-1711	
OE-KND	Robin DR.400/180R Remorqueur	834	D-EIVU
OE-KNG	Cessna 172 R	17281169	D-ERRP
			N5358C
OE-KNI	Mooney M.20M Model 257 TLS	27-0194	
OE-KNN	Piper PA-28RT-201T Turbo Arrow IV	28R-8331017	D-EKBV
			OE-KBC
			D-ELUR(2)
			N4292P
OE-KOG	Mooney M.20K Model 252 TSE	25-1066	N252SS
OE-KOL	Piper PA-28-181 Archer II	2890182	D-ETCF
			N9169Z
OE-KOS	Piper PA-28-181 Cherokee Archer II	28-7790591	OY-BTL
OE-KPA	SOCATA MS.893E Rallye 180GT Gaillard	12989	D-EGYO
OE-KPC	Cessna TU206F Turbo Stationair	U20602898	N1451Q
OE-KPG	Reims/Cessna F182Q Skylane	F18200153	D-EBMW(3)
			(HB-CNY)
OE-KPP	Diamond DA 40-P10 Star	40010	OE-VPP
	(originally with Lycoming, converted as experimental with Thielert Centurion 1.7 diesel engine)		
OE-KPT(2)	Diamond DA 40 Star	40017	
OE-KPW	Diamond DA 40-P7 Star	40007	OE-VPW
OE-KRH	Beech F33A Bonanza	CE-1703	N55572
OE-KRM	Diamond DA 40D Star	D4.090	
OE-KRP	Cessna 172R	17280394	D-EKRP
			N9552B
OE-KRT	Piper PA-28R-201T Turbo Cherokee Arrow III		
		28R-7703150	D-EHRW
			N5691V
OE-KSB(2)	Cirrus SR20	1426	N514CD
OE-KSD	SAAB S.91D Safir	91466	AAF: 3F-SH
OE-KSF	Piper PA-28RT-201T Turbo Arrow IV	28R-8331016	N8346Y
OE-KSK	Diamond DA 40 Star	40021	
OE-KSL	Reims/Cessna FR172K Hawk XP	FR17200618	D-EGTC
OE-KSM	Piper PA-28-161 Cadet	2841012	D-EFXB
			N9140X
OE-KSP	Cessna 172S	172S9567	N20942
OE-KSR	Robin DR.400/180R Remorqueur	1786	G-BNRB
OE-KSS	SAAB S.91D Safir	91456	AAF: 3F-SS
OE-KST(2)	Mooney M.20M Model 257 TLS	27-0233	N10824
OE-KSV	SAAB S.91D Safir	91461	AAF: 3F-SV
OE-KTB	Diamond DA 40D Star	40084	OE-VTB
	(Originally with Lycoming, converted as experimental with Thielert Centurion 1.7 diesel engine)		
OE-KTC	Robin DR.400/180R Remorqueur	1655	
OE-KTP	SAAB S.91D Safir	91464	AAF: 3F-SX
OE-KTS	Mooney M.20M Model 257 TLS	27-0190	(OE-KID)
OE-KTT	Diamond DA 40 Star	40011	D-EETA(5)
OE-KUB	Robin DR.400/180R Remorqueur	1256	OE-BUB
OE-KUD	Robin DR.400/180R Remorqueur	1447	OE-BUD
OE-KUI	Robin DR.400/180R Remo 180	2059	OE-BUI
OE-KUM	Robin DR.400/180R Remorqueur	1671	D-EDQG(2)
OE-KUN	Reims/Cessna FR182 Skylane RG	FR18200026	OE-BUN
			(OE-DNI)
OE-KUS	Robin DR.400/180R Remorqueur	1892	F-GGXH
OE-KVG	Piper PA-46-350P Malibu Mirage	4636093	D-EMPK
			N92862
OE-KVT	Mooney M.20J Model 205	24-3395	
OE-KWL	Diamond DA 40D Star	D4.022	
OE-KWR	Diamond DA 40 Star	40335	
OE-KXE	Bell 206L Long Ranger	45028	D-HAVS
			C-GSHX
			N9945K
			(N87TA)
OE-KXH	Aérospatiale AS.350B Ecureuil	1761	D-HAFP
OE-KXM	Bell 206B Jet Ranger II	2997	D-HMHS(2)
			N904SD
			N1086D
OE-KXY(2)	Reims/Cessna F182Q Skylane	F18200111	OE-BIT
OE-KYH	SOCATA TB-21 Trinidad TC	555	D-EDED(2)
OE-KYV	Cessna 172N	17273693	YV-178E
			YV-623P
OE-LAE(2)	Boeing 767-3Z9ER	30383	
OE-LAG(2)	Airbus A340-211	075	F-WWJR
OE-LAH(2)	Airbus A340-211	081	F-WWJO
OE-LAK(2)	Airbus A340-313X	169	F-WWJC
OE-LAL(2)	Airbus A340-313X	263	F-WWJU
OE-LAM(2)	Airbus A330-223	223	F-WWKQ
OE-LAN(2)	Airbus A330-223	195	F-WWKJ
OE-LAO(2)	Airbus A330-223	181	F-WWKA
OE-LAP	Airbus A330-223	317	F-WWYQ
OE-LAT	Boeing 767-31AER	25273	PH-MCK
			I-LAUD
			OE-LAT
			PH-MCK
			N6046P
OE-LAW	Boeing 767-3Z9ER	26417	

OE-LAX	Boeing 767-3Z9ER	27095	
OE-LAY	Boeing 767-3Z9	29867/731	D-ABUV
			OE-LAY
			EC-HVG
			OE-LAY
OE-LAZ	Boeing 767-3Z9ER	30331	D-ABUW
			OE-LAZ
OE-LBA(2)	Airbus A321-111	552	D-AVZH
OE-LBB	Airbus A321-111	570	D-AVZQ
OE-LBC(2)	Airbus A321-111	581	D-AVZS
OE-LBD(2)	Airbus A321-211	920	D-AVZN
OE-LBE	Airbus A321-211	935	D-AVZR
OE-LBF	Airbus A321-211	1458	D-AVXE
OE-LBN(2)	Airbus A320-214	768	F-WWDH
OE-LBO	Airbus A320-214	776	F-WWDM
OE-LBP	Airbus A320-214	797	F-WWDV
OE-LBQ	Airbus A320-214	1137	F-WWDF
OE-LBR	Airbus A320-214	1150	F-WWBP
OE-LBS	Airbus A320-214	1189	F-WWDV
OE-LBT	Airbus A320-214	1387	F-WWIS
OE-LBU	Airbus A320-214	1478	F-WWDS
OE-LCF	Canadair CL.600-2B19 Regional Jet	7094	
OE-LCG	Canadair CL.600-2B19 Regional Jet	7103	C-FMNB
OE-LCH	Canadair CL.600-2B19 Regional Jet	7110	C-FMMB
OE-LCI (2)	Canadair CL.600-2B19 Regional Jet	7133	(OE-LCK)
			C-FMNB
OE-LCJ	Canadair CL.600-2B19 Regional Jet	7142	B-3017
			OE-LCJ
			(OE-LCL)
			C-FMMN
OE-LCK	Canadair CL.600-2B19 Regional Jet	7148	C-FMNB
OE-LCL	Canadair CL.600-2B19 Regional Jet	7167	B-3015
			OE-LCL
			C-FMLT
OE-LCM	Canadair CL.600-2B19 Regional Jet	7205	
OE-LCN	Canadair CL.600-2B19 Regional Jet	7365	C-FMOI
OE-LCO(2)	Canadair CL.600-2B19 Regional Jet	7371	"C-FMMY"
			C-FMMX
OE-LCP	Canadair CL.600-2B19 Regional Jet	7480	C-FMOW
OE-LCQ	Canadair CL.600-2B19 Regional Jet	7605	C-FMOI
OE-LCR	Canadair CL.600-2B19 Regional Jet 200R	7910	C-FMMW
OE-LDA(2)	Airbus A319-112	2131	D-AVWS
OE-LDB(2)	Airbus A319-112	2174	D-AVYP
OE-LDC(2)	Airbus A319-114	2262	D-AVWE
OE-LDD(2)	Airbus A319-114	2416	D-AVWN
OE-LFG	Fokker F.28-0070	11549	PH-EZW
OE-LFH	Fokker F.28-0070	11554	PH-EZN
OE-LFI	Fokker F.28-0070	11529	PH-WXF
			PK-JGI
			PH-EZL
OE-LFJ	Fokker F.28-0070	11532	PH-WXG
			PK-JGJ
			PH-EZR
OE-LFK	Fokker F.28-0070	11555	PH-EZP
OE-LFL	Fokker F.28-0070	11573	PH-WXE
			I-REJE
			PH-EZW
OE-LFO	Fokker F.28-0070	11559	PH-EZV
OE-LFP	Fokker F.28-0070	11560	PH-EZW
OE-LFQ	Fokker F.28-0070	11568	PH-EZC
OE-LFR	Fokker F.28-0070	11572	PH-EZD
OE-LGA	Bombardier DHC-8Q Series 402	4014	C-GDNG
OE-LGB	Bombardier DHC-8Q Series 402	4015	C-GDOE
OE-LGC	Bombardier DHC-8Q Series 402	4026	C-GEVP
OE-LGD	Bombardier DHC-8Q Series 402	4027	C-GEWI
OE-LGE	Bombardier DHC-8Q Series 402	4042	C-FNGB
OE-LGF	Bombardier DHC-8Q Series 402	4068	C-GERC
OE-LGG	Bombardier DHC-8Q Series 402	4074	C-GFCF
OE-LGH	Bombardier DHC-8Q Series 402	4075	C-GFCW
OE-LGI	Bombardier DHC-8Q Series 402	4100	C-FAQR
OE-LIR	Dornier 328-100	3115	D-CDXG(5)
OE-LJR	Dornier 328-300	3213	D-BDXJ
OE-LKA	Dornier 328-100	3110	D-CDXI
OE-LKB	Dornier 328-100	3036	HB-AEH
			D-CDXB(1)
			(D-CDHV)
OE-LKC	Dornier 328-100	3119	D-CDXK(4)
OE-LKD	Dornier 328-110	3072	HS-PBB
			D-CDXY(2)
OE-LKE	Dornier 328-100	3063	D-CALP
			F-GNPA
			D-CDXK(2)
OE-LKF	Dornier 328-100	3073	D-CHOC
			D-CDXG(4)
			F-GNPB
			D-CDXZ(2)
OE-LKG	Dornier 328-100	3089	D-CGEP
			D-CDX.
			F-GTJL
			D-CDXL
OE-LMD	McDonnell-Douglas DC-9-83	49933	
OE-LME	McDonnell-Douglas DC-9-83	53377	

OE-LNI	Boeing 737-4Z9	27094	
OE-LNJ	Boeing 737-8Z9	28177	N1768B (OE-LAY)
OE-LNK	Boeing 737-8Z9	28178	N1784B
OE-LNM	Boeing 737-6Z9	30138	N1795B
OE-LNN	Boeing 737-7Z9	30418	N1787B
OE-LNO	Boeing 737-7Z9	30419	N1786B
OE-LNP	Boeing 737-8Z9	30420	
OE-LNQ	Boeing 737-8Z9	30421	
OE-LOE	Airbus A320-232	659	D-ALAE F-WWIV
OE-LOF	Airbus A320-232	667	D-ALAF(2) F-WWBC
OE-LOR	Airbus A320-232	1459	D-ALAR(2) F-WWIR
OE-LOS	Airbus A321-231	1487	D-ALAS(2) D-AVZQ
OE-LPA	Boeing 777-2Z9 IGW	28698	N5022E
OE-LPB	Boeing 777-2Z9 IGW	28699	
OE-LPC	Boeing 777-2Z9 IGW	29313	
OE-LRE	Canadair CL.600-2B19 Regional Jet	7059	(JA02RJ) OE-LRE C-FMND
OE-LRF	Canadair CL.600-2B19 Regional Jet	7061	C-FMNQ
OE-LRG	Canadair CL.600-2B19 Regional Jet	7063	C-FMNY
OE-LRH	Canadair CL.600-2B19 Regional Jet	7125	C-FMMB
OE-LSB(2)	DHC-8 Series 314	525	C-FDHY
OE-LSC(2)	Canadair CL.600-2B19 Regional Jet	7299	N781BC G-MSKO C-FMOS
OE-LSD(2)	Canadair CL.600-2B19 Regional Jet	7329	N786BC G-MSKP C-FMOS
OE-LSE(2)	Canadair CL.600-2B19 Regional Jet	7990	C-FMOW
OE-LSS	Canadair CL.600-2B19 Regional Jet	7283	N785BC OY-MBS G-MSKN
OE-LTD	DHC-8 Series 314	400	VH-TQB OE-LTD C-GFQL
OE-LTF	DHC-8 Series 314	423	VH-TQC
OE-LTG	DHC-8 Series 314	438	C-GDFT
OE-LTH	DHC-8 Series 314Q	442	C-GFUM
OE-LTI	DHC-8 Series 314Q	466	C-GFQL
OE-LTJ	DHC-8 Series 314Q	481	C-GDOE
OE-LTK	DHC-8 Series 314Q	483	(YR-GPO) C-GDFT
OE-LTL	DHC-8 Series 314Q	485	C-GFYI
OE-LTM	DHC-8 Series 314Q	527	C-FGNP
OE-LTN	DHC-8 Series 314Q	531	C-GDNK
OE-LTO	DHC-8 Series 314Q	553	C-FWBB
OE-LTP	DHC-8 Series 314Q	554	C-GDLK
OE-LTU	Airbus A320-214	1504	D-ALTE F-WWBH
OE-LVA	Fokker F.28-0100	11490	PH-ZFB N1464A PH-EZU
OE-LVB	Fokker F.28-0100	11502	PH-ZFE N1469D PH-EZN
OE-LVC	Fokker F.28-0100	11446	PH-ZFF N1443A PH-EZN
OE-LVD	Fokker F.28-0100	11515	PH-ZFG N1473K PH-EZY
OE-LVE	Fokker F.28-0100	11499	PH-ZFH N1467A PH-EZL
OE-LVF	Fokker F.28-0100	11483	N1463A PH-JCD PH-EZF
OE-LVG	Fokker F.28-0100	11520	PH-ZFJ N1474D PH-EZV
OE-LVH	Fokker F.28-0100	11456	PH-ZFK N1447L PH-EZA
OE-OXR	Aérospatiale SA.315B Lama	1025	Fr.AF

OE-U . . series has been used for ferry registrations

OE-UDV Permanently assigned to Diamond Aircraft for ferry flights

OE-V . . series used as ferry/test/experimental registrations. Current users:

OE-VAI	Zenair CH-801 STOL	unkn	
OE-VAT	Bücker T-131PA Jungmann	unkn	
OE-VBC	Pischof Autoplan (Crashed Klagenfurt, possible rebuild?)	01	
OE-VCA	GS Aviation Storm 280 G	unkn	
OE-VCB	TEAM V-Max	unkn	
OE-VCD	Bücker T-131PA Jungmann	02	(SP-YPY) SP-FPY
OE-VCF	Bede BD-5 G	unkn	
OE-VDA	Diamond DA 42 V2 Twin Star	42002	
OE-VDB	Diamond DA 42 D4 Twin Star	42004	
OE-VDC	Diamond DA 42 Twin Star (Lycoming)	L001	
OE-VDG	Diamond DA 40D	D4.111	
OE-VHI	Brändli BX-2 Cherry	unkn	
OE-VHP	Brditschka HB-207 Blue Bird (Exhibited 4.03)	unkn	
OE-VPA	Viking Dragonfly	unkn	
OE-VPD	Rand-Robinson KR-2S	unkn	
OE-VPE	Brändli BX-2 Cherry	unkn	
OE-VPF	Rutan Long-Ez	unkn	
OE-VPG	Neico Lancair IV-P	unkn	
OE-VPH	Neico Lancair IV	unkn	
OE-VPI	Permanently assigned to Diamond Aircraft (used for DA 42D testing)		
OE-VPJ	Prescott Pusher (Intended OE-KDW?)	025	
OE-VPL	Europa Aviation Europa	250	
OE-VPN	T-131PA Jungmann	unkn	
OE-VPM	Diamond DA 40 - P4	40004	N218DS C-GJPK OE-KPM OE-VPM
OE-VPO	Brändli BX-2 Cherry	unkn	
OE-VPP	Brditschka HB-204 Tornado	unkn	
OE-VPR	Lischak LW 03	unkn	
OE-VPS	Diamond DA 42 V1 Twin Star (Believed shown as "D-GENI" statically in 2002)	42001	
OE-VPU	Permanently assigned to Diamond Aircraft (used for DA 40D testing)		
OE-VPV	Stoddard-Hamilton GlaStar	unkn	
OE-VPW	Permanently assigned to Diamond Aircraft (used for DA 40D testing)		
OE-VPX	Permanently assigned to Diamond Aircraft		
OE-VPY	Permanently assigned to Diamond Aircraft (used for DA 42D testing)		
OE-VPZ	Permanently assigned to Diamond Aircraft (used for DA 20A1 maintenance flights)		
OE-VRL	Europa Aviation Europa	unkn	
OE-VRV	Van's RV-8	unkn	
OE-VSH	One Design DR 107	unkn	
OE-VTA	Assigned to Diamond Aircraft, DA.40 test flights		
OE-VTB	Assigned to Diamond Aircraft, DA.40 test flights		
OE-VWP	Van's RV-8 (f/f 17.5.2004)	unkn	
OE-VXB	Rotary Air Force RAF 2000 GTX-SE	unkn	
OE-VXS	Camcopter 5.1	unkn	
OE-VXT	Camcopter 5.1	unkn	
OE-VXU	Camcopter 5.1	unkn	
OE-VXV	Camcopter 5.1	unkn	
OE-VXW	Camcopter 5.1	unkn	
OE-VXX	Camcopter 5.1	unkn	
OE-VXY	Camcopter 5.1	unkn	
OE-VZA	RCO 9.01	unkn	

OE-XAA(2)	Eurocopter EC-120B Colibri	1045	D-HEHM D-HEHH
OE-XAG	Aérospatiale AS.355 F2 Ecureuil 2	5478	C-FJUP RP-C1501 I-ALKE
OE-XAH	Eurocopter EC-135T1	0105	SE-JFP
OE-XAP	Aerospàtiale AS.355N Ecureuil 2	5598	OY-HOY HB-XJI
OE-XAR	MBB-Kawasaki BK.117B-2	7018	D-HDRG(3) PK-NZG D-HBKT
OE-XAS	MBB-Kawasaki BK.117B-2	7008	D-HDDD(5) PK-NZH (N39186) D-HBKJ
OE-XAW	WE-04 Gyrocopter	05	
OE-XBA	Agusta-Bell 206B Jet Ranger 3	8557	HB-XPW G-TKHM G-MKAN G-DOUG
OE-XBB(2)	Agusta-Bell 206B Jet Ranger 3	8604	OE-BXY
OE-XBP	Robinson R-22B2 Beta	2834	
OE-XBS	Agusta-Bell 206B Jet Ranger 2	8403	OE-BXS
OE-XCC	Bell 206B Jet Ranger II	4256	
OE-XCH	Aérospatiale AS.350B2 Ecureuil	2799	F-WYMU
OE-XCX	Robinson R-22 Beta	3290	D-HFCA(2)
OE-XDD	Agusta-Bell 206B Jet Ranger 2	8434	HA-LFA(2) OE-XDD G-OABY G-BCWM
OE-XDM	Aérospatiale AS.355N Ecureuil 2	5708	F-WWPR
OE-XDS	Robinson R 22 Beta	3322	
OE-XEA	Eurocopter EC-135T1	0025	
OE-XEB	Eurocopter EC-135T1	0050	
OE-XEC	Eurocopter EC-135T1	0053	
OE-XED	Eurocopter EC-135T1	0072	D-HECN
OE-XEE	Eurocopter EC-135T1	0097	
OE-XEF	Eurocopter EC-135T1	0127	
OE-XEG	Eurocopter EC-135T1	0128	
OE-XEH	Eurocopter EC-135T1	0160	D-HECA
OE-XEI	Eurocopter EC-135T1	0168	D-HECO
OE-XEJ	Eurocopter EC-135T1	0181	
OE-XEK	Eurocopter EC-135T1	0182	
OE-XEL	Eurocopter EC-135T1	0187	
OE-XEM	Eurocopter EC-135T1	0196	
OE-XEN	Eurocopter EC-135T1	0199	D-HECA
OE-XEO	Eurocopter EC-135T12	0205	D-HECF

OE-XEP	Eurocopter EC-135T1	0210	D-HECK
OE-XEQ	Eurocopter EC-135T1	0220	
OE-XER	Eurocopter EC-135T1	0221	
OE-XES	Eurocopter EC-135T1	0305	
OE-XET	Eurocopter EC-135T1	0308	
OE-XEU	Eurocopter EC-135T2	0325	
OE-XEV	Eurocopter EC-135T2	0359	
OE-XEW	Eurocopter EC-135T2	0368	
OE-XEX	Eurocopter EC-135T2	0387	
OE-XFH	Agusta A.109A-II	7318	VH-AUG ZK-HXI N109BL N109BA
OE-XFK	Klampfl K-236	01	
OE-XFS(2)	Aérospatiale AS.355F1 Ecureuil 2	5090	OH-HAQ N500HH N5788K
OE-XFZ	Robinson R-22 Beta	3640	
OE-XGE	Bell 206B Jet Ranger II (W/o 25.3.05)	4528	N876M N2352S C-GLZW
OE-XGG	McDonnell-Douglas MD.520N	LN-053	HB-XUL
OE-XGS	Aérospatiale AS.355F1 Ecureuil 2	5161	C-GTDF N5795M
OE-XHA	Hughes 369E	0336E	D-HABC F-GGCJ
OE-XHD	Agusta A.109E Power	11033	
OE-XHE	Hughes 369D	77-0166D	D-HHOP OO-VCH
OE-XHH	Robinson R-44 Astro	0518	
OE-XHM(2)	Aérospatiale AS.350B3 Ecureuil	3555	F-WQDN
OE-XHO	Aérospatiale AS.350B3 Ecureuil	3549	F-WQDO
OE-XHP	Aerospatiale AS.350B3 Ecureuil	3812	
OE-XHR	Robinson R-22 Beta	3624	
OE-XHS	Agusta-Bell 206B Jet Ranger 3I	8605	OE-BXZ
OE-XHT(2)	Robinson R-44 Astro	0979	
OE-XHX	Robinson R-44 Raven	1444	
OE-XIW	Robinson R-22 Beta	1483	G-DAMI
OE-XJG	Aérospatiale SA.315B Lama	2540	F-GHUF N9006S
OE-XJH	Aerospàtiale AS.355 N Ecureuil 2	5590	N81061 JA8754
OE-XKA	Robinson R-22 Beta	3767	
OE-XKH	Bell 206B Jet Ranger II	3814	(D-HHTC) OE-XKH N3189T
OE-XKI	McDonnell-Douglas MD.520N	LN-033	OO-MRI N52024
OE-XKK(2)	Eurocopter EC-120B Colibri	1026	D-HAPL
OE-XKP	Aérospatiale AS.350B3 Ecureuil	3295	VH-LUB
OE-XKT	Robinson R-44 Astro	0966	
OE-XLA	Robinson R-22B2 Beta	2966	
OE-XLH	Agusta A.109E Power	11110	
OE-XLM	Agusta-Bell 206B Jet Ranger 2	8046	G-COUR G-FSDG G-ROOT G-JETR G-BKBR OO-CDP
OE-XMF	Hughes 269C	114-0372	N9585F
OE-XMI	Schweizer 269C	S-1640	D-HMIE N69A
OE-XMM(2)	Robinson R-44 Raven	1449	
OE-XMU	Bell 407	55358	N407MB
OE-XNY	Robinson R-22B2 Beta	2985	
OE-XOF	RAF 2000 GTX SE	H2-01-12-498	
OE-XOO	Eurocopter EC-120B Colibri	1098	D-HHSR F-WQDJ
OE-XPB(2)	Robinson R-22B2 Beta	3123	
OE-XPC	Robinson R-22B2 Beta	3175	
OE-XPG	Robinson R-22 Beta	3553	N75355
OE-XPH	Robinson R-22 Beta	3639	
OE-XPK	Robinson R-22B2 Beta	2882	N7118Z
OE-XQQ	Robinson R-44 Astro	0245	
OE-XRB	Bell 206B Jet Ranger II	2311	D-HAUO EC-FBX EC-496 D-HEDO(2) HB-XLB D-HHPS
OE-XRD	Schweizer 269C	S-1380	D-HKHP OY-HDV D-HBIG N7508E
OE-XRE	Schweizer 269C	S-1582	D-HBSF N86G
OE-XRF	Agusta-Bell 206A Jet Ranger 2	8246	G-BNRE Oman-603
OE-XRG	Eurocopter EC-120B Colibri	1298	F-WQDQ
OE-XRH(2)	Bell 206B Jet Ranger II	2795	N4383X N113TV
OE-XSA	Agusta A.109E Power	11100	
OE-XSC	Agusta A.109E Power	11148	
OE-XSD	Bell 206B-3 Jet Ranger III	4289	
OE-XSH	Robinson R-44 Raven	1092	
OE-XSL	Agusta A.109C	7647	OO-WGW I-SEIG
OE-XSM	Robinson R-22 Beta	3664	N74317
OE-XSR	Eurocopter AS.355N Ecureuil 2	5562	JA6731
OE-XSS	Aérospatiale AS.355 F2 Ecureuil 2	5461	JA6645
OE-XST	Eurocopter EC-120BColibri	1215	
OE-XTR	RAF 2000 GTX SE	H2-97-8-311	
OE-XTS	Robinson R-22 Beta	3625	
OE-XTW	Aérospatiale AS.350B3 Ecureuil	3743	
OE-XWG	Bell 407	53062	D-HASI(4)
OE-XWS	Robinson R-44 Raven	1171	N100T
OE-XWW	Agusta-Bell 206B Jet Ranger II	8379	D-HBLK
OE-XXA	Rotorway Exec	3598	OE-VXA
OE-XXZ	Aérospatiale AS.355F1 Ecureuil 2	5214	N378E
OE-XYZ	Robinson R-22 Beta	2536	
OE-XZZ	Robinson R-22 Beta	2694	

BALLOONS AND AIRSHIPS

Austrian balloons belonging to the same owner may carry the same registration marks at the same time. This has led to duplications as will be evident below from the suffix letters which correspond to those used on the Certificates of Registration.

OE-AZC	Cameron V-31 HAFB	2147	
OE-AZM(b)	Cameron N-105 HAFB	3987	
OE-AZM(c)	Kubicek BB-45 HAFB	177	OE-ZPO(c) OK-0177
OE-AZW	Thunder AX6-56A HAFB	684	
OE-CZH	Colt 21A HAFB	689	G-BMBG
OE-CZS	Colt AX7-77A HAFB	538	
OE-DZD	Cameron O-77 HAFB	151	
OE-DZK	Cameron N-77 HAFB	293	G-BTOY
OE-DZL	Cameron V-77 HAFB	783	
OE-DZS	Cameron O-77 HAFB	65	G-BAMA
OE-DZU	Colt 77A HAFB	614	
OE-DZW	Thunder AX8-105 HAFB	372	
OE-DZY	Cameron O-105 HAFB	845	
OE-KZA	Cameron A-105 HAFB	1237	
OE-KZB	Thunder AX7-77S1 HAFB	803	
OE-KZE(c)	Kubicek BB-30 HAFB	89	
OE-KZP(a)	Cameron O-77 HAFB	1081	
OE-KZP(b)	Cameron O-120 HAFB	4681	
OE-KZT(a)	Thunder AX7-77S1 HAFB	872	
OE-KZT(b)	Ultramagic M-145 HAFB	145/14	
OE-KZU	Colt 105A HAFB	591	
OE-MZA	Venus 2600 HAFB (Shown as manufactured by Thunder & Colt)	100.187	
OE-MZD(b)	Balloon Works Firefly 8 HAFB	F8-431	
OE-MZE(b)	Cameron A-120 HAFB	4391	
OE-MZH(a)	Cameron A-105 HAFB	1591	
OE-MZH(b)	Cameron Mug-90 SS HAFB	2154	OE-CZG
OE-MZI	Cameron O-105 HAFB	1170	
OE-MZI(b)	Cameron Z-120 HAFB	10408	
OE-MZL(a)	Colt 105A HAFB	1127	
OE-MZM(b)	Colt 77A HAFB	1551	OE-ZCC(a) OE-SZY G-BRRV
OE-MZM(c)	Cameron A-140 HAFB	2698	OE-ZZB(c) OE-ZMZ
OE-MZR(a)	Cameron N-105 HAFB	1516	
OE-MZX	Thunder AX8-105S1 HAFB	1148	
OE-MZX(b)	Schön Neptun 2500 HAFB	S065/5/2003	
OE-MZY	Cameron N-90 HAFB	1544	
OE-PZA	Cameron A-105 HAFB	1728	
OE-PZD(b)	Cameron N-105 HAFB	4967	
OE-PZE	Cameron O-105 HAFB	1787	
OE-PZH	Cameron A-105 HAFB	1680	
OE-PZI	Cameron A-120 HAFB	1756	
OE-PZK	Cameron A-105 HAFB	1774	
OE-PZL	Cameron A-105 HAFB	1621	
OE-PZP	Cameron N-90 HAFB	1580	
OE-PZP(b)	Cameron N-90 HAFB	10494	
OE-PZR	Cameron A-105 HAFB	1909	
OE-PZS	AA-1050/1 Gas Balloon	1269	
OE-PZT(a)	Cameron O-105 HAFB	1624	
OE-PZT(b)	Sky 105-24 HAFB	066	
OE-PZT(d)	Kubicek BB-37 HAFB	111	
OE-PZV	Cameron A-105 HAFB	1883	
OE-PZY	Cameron O-120 HAFB	1722	
OE-RZA(b)	Cameron N-105 HAFB	2879	OE-ZZU(b)
OE-RZA(c)	Kubicek BB 30 HAFB	282	OK-0282
OE-RZD	Cameron N-105 HAFB	2062	
OE-RZE	Raven-Europe S-60A HAFB	E-143	
OE-RZF(a)	Cameron A-105 HAFB	1916	
OE-RZF(b)	Schön Saturn 3500 HAFB	S021/3/98	
OE-RZG	Cameron Bulb-120 SS HAFB	2219	
OE-RZI	Schön Saturn 3400 HAFB	S001/3/89	
OE-RZI(b)	Cameron N-105 HAFB	2636	D-OABC
OE-RZK	Cameron O-120 HAFB	1957	
OE-RZR	Cameron N-105 HAFB	2359	
OE-RZR(b)	Cameron A-120 HAFB	2015	OE-RZZ(b)
OE-RZR(c)	Cameron A-140 HAFB	3354	OE-ZZW(a)
OE-RZS(a)	Cameron N-90 HAFB	2090	
OE-RZS(b)	Cameron A-120 HAFB	2966	

OE-RZU(a)	Schröder Fire Balloons G HAFB	109	
OE-RZU(b)	Ultramagic M-77C HAFB	77209	
OE-RZV(b)	Cameron N-133 HAFB	3740	
OE-RZV(c)	Cameron O-105 HAFB	2111	OE-RZY(a)
OE-RZZ(c)	Cameron O-105 HAFB	10377	
OE-RZZ(d)	Cameron N-56 HAFB	3172	OE-ZCH(a)
OE-SZB(b)	Kubicek BB 30 HAFB	219	
OE-SZC	Cameron N-105 HAFB	2137	G-BRSB
OE-SZD	Schröder Fire Balloons G HAFB	143	
OE-SZE(a)	Schröder Fire Balloons G HAFB	163	
OE-SZE(b)	Cameron O-84 HAFB	1299	OE-CZA
OE-SZF(a)	Schön Saturn 2400 HAFB	S002/3/90	
OE-SZF(c)	Colt AA-1050 Gas Balloon	2151	OE-ZZI(b)
OE-SZH	Colt 77A HAFB	1688	
OE-SZK(a)	Schön Neptun 3000 HAFB	S002/5/90	
OE-SZK(b)	Cameron A-105 HAFB	4538	
OE-SZK(c)	Ultramagic M-77C HAFB	77/254	
OE-SZK(d)	Kubicek BB-37 HAFB	338	OK-0338
OE-SZM	Cameron A-105 HAFB	2285	
OE-SZN	Schröder Fire Balloons G HAFB	106	
OE-SZP(a)	Schön Saturn 3400 HAFB	S001/3/90	
OE-SZP(b)	Schön Saturn 3000 HAFB	S016/3/95	
OE-SZU	Cameron N-105 HAFB	2179	
OE-SZV	Cameron N-105 HAFB	2503	
OE-SZZ	Schön Neptun 3000 HAFB	S004/5/90	
OE-ZAA(a)	Schröder Fire Balloons G HAFB	449	
OE-ZAA(b)	Ultramagic S-105 HAFB	105/124	
OE-ZAB	Cameron O-105 HAFB	3355	
OE-ZAC	Schön Neptun 4000 HAFB	S035/5/98	
OE-ZAD(a)	Cameron A-120 HAFB	2567	
OE-ZAD(b)	Schön Neptun 2500 HAFB	S010/5/93	
OE-ZAG(b)	Kubicek BB-60 HAFB	223	
OE-ZAG(c)	Kubicek BB-37 HAFB	122	OE-PZO(b)
OE-ZAH	Colt 105A HAFB	1564	D-Telgate/1
OE-ZAI	Schön Saturn 3000 HAFB	S020/3/97	
OE-ZAK(2)(a)	Thunder AX7-77 HAFB	2386	OE-SZF(b) OE-ZAF OE-KZE(b) OE-ZAK(a)
OE-ZAM	Ultramagic S-105 HAFB	105/75	
OE-ZAO	Schön Neptun 3500 HAFB	S067/5/03	
OE-ZAR	Schön Saturn 3000 HAFB	S015/3/94	
OE-ZAS	Colt 105A HAFB	2340	
OE-ZAT	Schön Saturn 4000 HAFB	S017/3/95	
OE-ZAW(b)	Kubicek BB-60 HAFB	153	OK-0153
OE-ZAW(c)	Kubicek BB 70 Z HAFB	308	OK-0308
OE-ZAY	Sky 120-24 HAFB	074	
OE-ZAZ	Sky 220-24 HAFB	172	
OE-ZBA(b)	Schön Neptun 3000 HAFB	S026/5/97	
OE-ZBB(b)	Cameron N-90 HAFB	1547	OE-ZMK(a) OE-MZK
OE-ZBC	Ultramagic N-250 HAFB	250/27	
OE-ZBF	Colt 90A HAFB	2368	D-OCES
OE-ZBG	Raven FS-57 A HAFB	E-181	D-Azzuro
OE-ZBO	Ultramagic M-77C HAFB	77/258	
OE-ZBP	Kubicek BB 30 Z HAFB	259	OK-0259
OE-ZBR	Cameron N-105 HAFB	3046	
OE-ZBS(b)	Cameron N-120 HAFB	2663	OE-ZOP(a)
OE-ZBS(d)	Cameron A-140 HAFB	1782	OE-PZG
OE-ZBS(e)	Cameron O-65 HAFB	2577	OE-ZYY
OE-ZBT	Cameron N-105 HAFB	2587	G-BTMM
OE-ZBW	Schön Neptun 3000 HAFB	S024/5/97	
OE-ZCA	Kubicek BB 37 HAFB	264	OK-0264
OE-ZCA(b)	Lindstrand LBL-240A HAFB	867	
OE-ZCB(a)	Cameron N-90 HAFB	2760	G-BUHN
OE-ZCB(c)	Cameron N-145 HAFB	10116	
OE-ZCC(b)	Thunder AX8-90S2 HAFB	2401	
OE-ZCD	Schön Neptun 3000 HAFB	S008/5/92	
OE-ZCE(b)	Cameron O-77 HAFB	949	OE-ZCU(b) OE-KZX
OE-ZCF	Schön Neptun 3000 HAFB	S037/5/98	
OE-ZCK(a)	Cameron N-77 HAFB	1335	
OE-ZCK(b)	Cameron O-105 HAFB	4186	
OE-ZCK(c)	Thunder AX7-77S1 HAFB	2510	D-ODJL
OE-ZCM	Cameron A-105 HAFB	3043	
OE-ZCO(a)	Schröder Fire Balloons G 33/24 HAFB	638	
OE-ZCP(a)	Cameron A-105 HAFB	2018	OE-RZC
OE-ZCS(b)	Schröder Fire Balloons G 30/24 HAFB	1098	
OE-ZCU(a)	Cameron Can-100 SS HAFB	2178	OE-CZU
OE-ZCU(c)	Cameron N-105 HAFB	3738	
OE-ZDD	Schön Neptun 3000 HAFB	S056/5/01	
OE-ZDF(a)	Schön Saturn 3000 HAFB	S012/3/94	
OE-ZDF(b)	Schön Neptun 3000 HAFB	S016/5/95	
OE-ZDF(c)	Schön Neptun 3000 HAFB	S061/5/02	
OE-ZDS	Cameron C-90 HAFB	10482	
OE-ZDT	Cameron N-133 HAFB	4900	
OE-ZDV	Schön Neptun 3000 HAFB	S044/5/99	
OE-ZEB(a)	Balloon Works Firefly 7 HAFB	F7-130	
OE-ZEB(b)	Balloon Works Firefly 7-15 HAFB	F7-880	
OE-ZED	Aerostar RXS-8 HAFB	RXS8-3003	HB-BXD N3596P
OE-ZEG	Cameron N-145 HAFB	4107	
OE-ZEH	Schön Neptun 3000 HAFB	S053/5/00	
OE-ZEK	Kubicek BB-30 HAFB	158	OK-0158
OE-ZER	Schön Neptun 3000 HAFB	S048/5/00	
OE-ZES	Schröder Fire Balloons G HAFB	708	
OE-ZEW(b)	Kubicek BB-30 HAFB	59	
OE-ZFA(a)	Schön Saturn 3000 HAFB	S001/3/91	
OE-ZFA(b)	Cameron V-77 HAFB	1652	OE-ZZB(a) OE-ZZU(a) OE-MZU
OE-ZFE(a)	Schön Neptun 3000 HAFB	S047/5/99	
OE-ZFE(b)	Cameron O-90 HAFB	1824	OE-ZBS(a) OE-PZX
OE-ZFF	Schön Neptun 3000 HAFB	S030/5/97	
OE-ZFH	Schön Saturn 3000 HAFB	S011/3/93	
OE-ZFK	Lindstrand LBL-120A HAFB	599	OE-PZT(c)
OE-ZFR	Cameron A-105 HAFB	3117	
OE-ZFS	Schön Neptun 3000 HAFB	S054/5/01	
OE-ZFW	Schön Neptun 3000 HAFB	S045/5/99	
OE-ZGA	Schröder Fire Ballons G HAFB	1082	
OE-ZGB	Schön Neptun 3000 HAFB	S031/5/97	
OE-ZGE	Schön Neptun 3000 HAFB	S023/5/97	
OE-ZGG(c)	Cameron O-120 HAFB	4745	OE-ZZG(b)
OE-ZGI	Kubicek BB-30 HAFB	8664	
OE-ZGK	Schön Saturn 2500 HAFB	S022/3/99	
OE-ZGP	Schön Neptun 3500 HAFB	S025/5/97	
OE-ZGR	Schön Neptun 3500 HAFB	S055/5/01	
OE-ZGW(a)	Cameron N-105 HAFB	4422	
OE-ZGW(b)	Cameron O-90 HAFB	2982	OE-ZSH(b) OE-ZGG(b)
OE-ZGW(c)	Cameron Z-140 HAFB	10634	
OE-ZHA	Kubicek BB-37 HAFB	124	OE-ZHH(a) OK-0124
OE-ZHB(a)	Schön Neptun 3500 HAFB	S012/5/94	
OE-ZHB(b)	Cameron Z-140 HAFB	10486	
OE-ZHF	Cameron N-105 HAFB	4248	
OE-ZHH(b)	Kubicek BB-37 HAFB	129	
OE-ZHK	Cameron Z-150 HAFB	10509	
OE-ZHM	Kubicek BB-37 HAFB	271	
OE-ZHP	Schröder Fire Balloons G HAFB	695	
OE-ZHS(a)	Schön Saturn 3000 HAFB	S009/3/92	
OE-ZHS(b)	Schön Neptun 3400 HAFB	S009/5/93	OE-ZLW
OE-ZHT(b)	Cameron O-84 HAFB	929	OE-ZMM(a) OE-KZW
OE-ZHY	Colt AS-105 Hot Air Airship	886	ZK-ALE G-BNCP
OE-ZII	Cameron N-120 HAFB	4539	
OE-ZIN	Schön Neptun 3500 HAFB	S036/5/98	
OE-ZIW	Cameron N-90 HAFB	3189	OE-ZKW(b) G-BVGU
OE-ZJH(b)	Kubicek BB 26 HAFB	126	OK-0026
OE-ZJM	Cameron N-105SV HAFB	3371	
OE-ZJS	Kubicek BB-30 HAFB	72	
OE-ZKA	Cameron N-145SV HAFB	3938	
OE-ZKB(a)	Schön Neptun 3500 HAFB	S063/5/02	
OE-ZKE	Schön Neptun 3000 HAFB	S027/5/97	
OE-ZKF	Schön Neptun 3500 HAFB	S066/5/03	
OE-ZKG(a)(2)	Cameron/Colt Graz Box-110 HAFB	10324	
OE-ZKK(b)	Schön Neptun 3500 HAFB	S050/5/00	
OE-ZKM(a)	Schön Neptun 3000 HAFB	S015/5/95	
OE-ZKM(b)	Schön Neptun 3500 HAFB	S041/5/98	
OE-ZKW(c)	Cameron Z-120 HAFB	10633	
OE-ZLC	Cameron A-105 HAFB	2520	
OE-ZLI	Schön Neptun 3500 HAFB	S049/5/00	
OE-ZLM(b)	Sky 120-24 HAFB	107	
OE-ZLR	Ultramagic MV-65 HAFB	65/133	
OE-ZLZ	Cameron Newspaper SS HAFB	4679	
OE-ZMA	Ultramagic S-160 HAFB	160/30	
OE-ZMB(a)	Schön Neptun 3000 HAFB	S014/5/95	
OE-ZMB(c)	Thunder & Colt AX - 77A HAFB	984	OE-PZN OE-ZPN(b)
OE-ZMC	Lindstrand LBL-105A HAFB	529	D-ORIC
OE-ZME(a)	Kubicek BB60 HAFB	202	OK-0202
OE-ZMF(a)	Neptun 3000 HAFB	S001/5/91	
OE-ZMF(b)	Schön Neptun 3000 HAFB	S001/5/91	
OE-ZMG	Lindstrand LBL-120 A HAFB	970	
OE-ZMH	Schön Neptun 3000 HAFB	S019/5/96	
OE-ZMI (a)	Schön Saturn 3400 HAFB	S018/3/95	
OE-ZMI (b)	Cameron Mickey-90 HAFB	2671	OE-ZMM(b)
OE-ZMK(c)	Cameron N-120 HAFB	3452	
OE-ZMK(d)	Schön Neptun 3000 HAFB	S033/5/98	OE-AZK(b)
OE-ZML(a)	Cameron N-145 HAFB	3946	
OE-ZML(b)	Cameron N-120 HAFB	4333	
OE-ZML(c)	Cameron Z-160 HAFB	10350	
OE-ZMM(a)(2)	Schön Saturn 2500 HAFB	S023/3/01	
OE-ZMN	Cameron N-105 HAFB	10002	
OE-ZMP(b)	Cameron V-90 HAFB	2681	
OE-ZMP(c)	Cameron O-120 HAFB	2600	OE-ZUW
OE-ZMR(b)	Schön Neptun 3000 HAFB	S007/5/92	
OE-ZMR(c)	Sky 105-24 HAFB	132	
OE-ZMW	Cameron A-140 HAFB	2061	OE-ZSW(b) OE-RZX(a)
OE-ZMW(b)	Schön Neptun 3400 HAFB	S020/5/96	OE-ZHT(a)
OE-ZNA	Cameron V-77 HAFB	2639	
OE-ZNH	Cameron Z-120 HAFB	10581	
OE-ZNO	Tomi AX-7 HAFB	12/1993	
OE-ZNR	Schön Saturn 3000 HAFB	S002/3/89	OE-RZN
OE-ZNS	Schön Neptun 3500 HAFB	S040/5/98	
OE-ZNW	Cameron A-105 HAFB	3419	
OE-ZOE(a)	Kubicek BB-37 HAFB	134	
OE-ZOM	Schön Neptun 5000 HAFB	S059/5/01	

OE-ZOO(b)	Lindstrand LBL-48LHAFB	552	
OE-ZOO(c)	Sky 200-24 HAFB	146	OE-ZSG(e)
OE-ZOP(c)	Lindstrand LBL-48L HAFB	553	
OE-ZOR	Schröder Fire Balloons G HAFB	840	
OE-ZOS	Schröder Fire Balloons G HAFB	377	
OE-ZOX(a)	Kubicek BB Fox HAFB	207	OK-0207
OE-ZPA	Schön Neptun 3500 HAFB	S018/5/95	
OE-ZPC	Cameron N-105 HAFB	3113	D-ONKH
OE-ZPE	Kubicek BB-60 HAFB	127	OK-0127
OE-ZPF	Aerotechnik AB-8 HAFB	910.542	
OE-ZPG(a)	Cameron A-105 HAFB	3173	
OE-ZPG(b)	Cameron Z-120 HAFB	10508	
OE-ZPH(a)	Cameron A-120 HAFB	10344	
OE-ZPM	Cameron N-77 HAFB	3223	
OE-ZPN(a)	Schön Saturn 2550 HAFB	S013/3/94	
OE-ZPN(c)	Schön Neptun 3000 HAFB	S062/5/02	
OE-ZPO(b)	Cameron A-140SV HAFB	3813	
OE-ZPO(d)	Kubicek BB 45, N-Type HAFB	226	
OE-ZPP(a)	Cameron A-140 HAFB	2832	
OE-ZPP(b)	Schön Saturn 3000 HAFB	S014/3/94	OE-ZAQ
OE-ZPQ(b)	Kubicek BB-37 HAFB	173	OK-0173
OE-ZPR	Schön Neptun 3000 HAFB	S051/5/00	
OE-ZPS	Cameron Z-105 HAFB	4623	
OE-ZPT	Schön Neptun 4000 HAFB	S057/5/01	
OE-ZPW(b)	Raven Europe RX-8 HAFB	E-243	
OE-ZPX	Cameron A-140 HAFB	10171	OE-RZX(c)
OE-ZPZ	Kubicek BB-60 HAFB	142	
OE-ZRB(b)	Colt 21A Cloudhopper HAFB	BU307	
OE-ZRD	Schön Neptun 3000 HAFB	S034/5/98	
OE-ZRD(b)	Cameron Z-120 HAFB	10535	
OE-ZRE	Kubicek BB-37 HAFB	27	
OE-ZRG	Schön Neptun 3500 HAFB	S021/5/96	
OE-ZRI (a)	Schön Neptun 3000 HAFB	S022/5/97	
OE-ZRI (b)	Schön Neptun 2500 HAFB	S060/5/02	
OE-ZRW	Schön Neptun 3000 HAFB	S029/5/97	
OE-ZRX	Cameron O-105 HAFB	3000	
OE-ZSA(a)	Cameron V-77 HAFB	1080	OE-ZMP(a) OE-MZP
OE-ZSB	Schön Saturn 2400 HAFB	S008/3/92	
OE-ZSC	Cameron Z-120 HAFB	10272	
OE-ZSE(c)	UltraMagic N-250 HAFB	250/22	
OE-ZSF	Cameron A-140 HAFB	3814	
OE-ZSG(d)	Thunder AX-11-250S2 HAFB	4015	
OE-ZSG(f)	Lindstrand LBL-425A HAFB	838	
OE-ZSG(g)	Cameron A-180 HAFB	2786	OE-ZSG(a)
OE-ZSH(c)	Cameron N-105 HAFB	3654	OE-ZZU(c)
OE-ZSI(a)	Aerotechnik AB-2c N-30 HAFB	400.591	
OE-ZSI(b)	Aerotechnik AB-8 N-30 HAFB	410.591	
OE-ZSI(c)	Kubicek BB 37 HAFB	257	OK-0257
OE-ZSK	Cameron Z-120 HAFB	10652	
OE-ZSO	Schön Neptun 3000 HAFB	S038/5/98	
OE-ZSP	Kubicek BB-30 HAFB	6	
OE-ZSR	Cameron O-105 HAFB	2228	OE-SZA
OE-ZSS(a)	Schön Saturn 3000 HAFB	S019/3/96	OE-ZSA(b)
OE-ZSS(b)	Schön Neptun 3000 HAFB	S046/5/99	
OE-ZST	Schön Neptun 3000 HAFB	S052/5/00	
OE-ZSV	Cameron N-133 HAFB	2907	
OE-ZSW(a)	Schön Neptun 3400 HAFB	S011/5/93	
OE-ZSW(c)	Schön Neptun 3500 HAFB	S058/5/01	
OE-ZSZ	Cameron A-105 HAFB	4459	
OE-ZTA(a)	Schön Neptun 4500 HAFB	S064/5/3	
OE-ZTF	Schön Neptun 3500 HAFB	S042/5/99	
OE-ZTH(a)	Cameron N-133 HAFB	3454	OE-ZKG(b)
OE-ZTH(c)	Kubicek BB-30 HAFB	214	OK-0214
OE-ZTL(a)(2)	Schön Neptun 3000 HAFB	S013/5/95	
OE-ZTT	Cameron N-105 HAFB	4293	
OE-ZTZ	Aerotechnik AB.20 HAFB	230587	
OE-ZUA	Cameron N-105 HAFB	4387	
OE-ZUA(b)	Cameron Z-105 HAFB	10645	
OE-ZUS	Schön Neptun 4000 HAFB	S028/5/97	
OE-ZVA	Schön Neptun 3000 HAFB	S017/5/95	
OE-ZVM	Schön Neptun 3000 HAFB	S039/5/98	
OE-ZVP	Schön Neptun 3500 HAFB	S043/5/99	
OE-ZVS	Cameron N-145 HAFB	3965	
OE-ZZA(a)	Cameron A-160 HAFB	4331	
OE-ZZA(b)	Kubicek BB-45 HAFB	187	OK-0187
OE-ZZA(c)	Kubicek BB-30 HAFB	166	OE-ZZS OK-0166
OE-ZZG	Schön Neptun 3500 HAFB	S032/5/97	
OE-ZZK(a)	Kubicek BB-45 HAFB	117	
OE-ZZK(b)	Kubicek BB-45 HAFB	206	
OE-ZZP	Colt 105A HAFB	1552	OE-ZTL(a) OE-RZP
OE-ZZT	Cameron N-133 HAFB	3384	
OE-ZZU(d)	Cameron O-140 HAFB	4390	
OE-ZZW(b)	Cameron A-140 HAFB	10045	
OE-ZZX(a)	Schön Saturn 3400 HAFB	S003/3/90	OE-SZX
OE-ZZX(b)	Cameron V-77 HAFB	652	OE-DZX
OE-ZZY	Cameron A-105 HAFB	4688	OE-RZY(b)
OE-ZZZ(a)	Kubicek BB-60 HAFB	131	
OE-ZZZ(b)	Kubicek BB-37 HAFB	266	

MOTOR-GLIDERS

OE-9006	Scheibe SF-24B Motorspatz	4027	(D-KACY)
OE-9014	Scheibe SF-24B Motorspatz	4046	(D-KOBA)
OE-9021	Scheibe SF-25A Motorfalke	4554	(D-KOGO)
OE-9022	Raab Krähe V	024	
OE-9024	Schleicher Kaiser Ka.2 Rhönschwalbe	V-1	D-KAIS
OE-9026	Scheibe SF-25D Falke	4659	(D-KABK)
OE-9027	Scheibe SF-25B Falke	4665	(D-KACJ)
OE-9042	Scheibe SF-25B Falke	46218	(D-KAAT)
OE-9043	Scheibe SF-25B Falke	46216	(D-KASX)
OE-9046	Sportavia-Pützer RF-5B Sperber	51018	
OE-9047	Scheibe SF-25B Falke	46239	(D-KAIE)
OE-9052	Scheibe SF-25C Falke	46249	(D-KAVI)
OE-9054	Scheibe SF-25C Falke	46246	(D-KAVF)
OE-9059	Scheibe SF-25C Falke	4444	(D-KDAD)
OE-9061	Brditschka HB-3 BR	058	
OE-9062	Scheibe SF-25C Falke	4423	(D-KHOG)
OE-9065	Scheibe SF-28A Tandem-Falke	5729	(D-KOAR)
OE-9068	Scheibe SF-25C Falke	4466	(D-KOAY)
OE-9072	Scheibe SF-28A Tandem-Falke	5743	(D-KOEE(2))
OE-9073	Scheibe SF-28A Tandem-Falke	5701	D-KAFJ
OE-9074	Scheibe SF-28A Tandem-Falke	5723	(D-KAUN)
OE-9075	Scheibe SF-25C Falke	4481	(D-KEIA)
OE-9077	Scheibe SF-28A Tandem-Falke	5748	(D-KOEZ)
OE-9079	Brditschka HB-3AR	061	
OE-9082	Scheibe SF-25C Falke	4489	(D-KEII)
OE-9085	Sportavia/ Fournier RF-4D	4056	D-KAQU
OE-9086	Scheibe SF-25C Falke	4495	(D-KEIM)
OE-9087	Scheibe SF-25C Falke	4497	(D-KEIO)
OE-9090	Brditschka HB-3 BR	060	
OE-9091	Scheibe SF-25B Falke	4675	D-KATD
OE-9096	Scheibe SF-25D Falke	46169D	D-KBIO
OE-9098	Scheibe SF-28A Tandem-Falke	5778	D-KCLH
OE-9099	Scheibe SF-25C Falke	44126	D-KLDC
OE-9104	Alpla AVO 68v Samburo	003	
OE-9106	Alpla AVO 68v Samburo	002	
OE-9107	Scheibe SF-25C Falke	44135	(D-KDDJ)
OE-9109	Alpla AVO 68s Samburo	005	
OE-9111	Alpla AVO 68v Samburo	006	
OE-9112	Brditschka HB-21-V2	21005	
OE-9113	Brditschka HB-3BR	055	
OE-9116	Scheibe SF-25C Falke	44148	D-KLUG (D-KDEF)
OE-9125	Sportavia/ Scheibe SF-25B Falke	4831	D-KANF HB-2011 (D-KAHP)
OE-9126	Scheibe SF-25C Falke	44192	(D-KADO)
OE-9127	Scheibe SF-25E Super-Falke	4328	(D-KDFF)
OE-9129	Brditschka HB-21/2400	21009	
OE-9130	Scheibe SF-25B Falke	46258	D-KEAR
OE-9133	Scheibe SF-25C Falke	44204	(D-KDFJ)
OE-9136	Scheibe SF-25C Falke	44145	D-KDEC
OE-9141	Scheibe SF-25C Falke	44226	(D-KDFX)
OE-9143	Brditschka HB-21/2400	21011	
OE-9145	Scheibe SF-25C Falke	44125	D-KLDB
OE-9148	Scheibe SF-25C Falke	44230	(D-KDCC)
OE-9149	Sportavia/ Fournier RF-4D	4130	D-KALH
OE-9153	Brditschka HB-21/2400	21012	
OE-9157	Brditschka HB-21	21014	
OE-9160	Brditschka HB-21/2400 B	21023	
OE-9161	Scheibe SF-25D Falke	46137D	D-KCAD
OE-9162	Scheibe SF-25B Falke	46192	D-KASG
OE-9164	Scheibe SF-25C Falke	44275	(D-KDBX)
OE-9170	Scheibe SF-25D Falke	4844	D-KHFB
OE-9171	Scheibe SF-25C Falke	44233	D-KDCC
OE-9173	Scheibe SF-25B Falke	4626	D-KIMA (D-KIMG)
OE-9175	Sportavia/ Scheibe SF-25B Falke	4861	D-KAEH
OE-9180	Scheibe SF-25C Falke	44301	(D-KDGW)
OE-9181	Scheibe SF-25D Falke	AB46308D	(D-KDGG(3))
OE-9185	Scheibe SF-25D Falke	46164D	HB-2015 (D-KBII)
OE-9186	Scheibe SF-25C Falke	44309	D-KOOB
OE-9189	Scheibe SF-25D Falke	4679D	D-KBAE
OE-9191	Grob G.109	6014	(D-KISI)
OE-9194	Brditschka HB-21	21025	
OE-9196	Glaser-Dirks DG-400	4/13	
OE-9204	Hoffmann H-36 Dimona	3502	
OE-9205	Eiri PIK-20E	20277	D-KIDM
OE-9206	Hoffmann H-36 Dimona	3615	
OE-9208	Hoffmann H-36 Dimona	3621	
OE-9209	Hoffmann H-36 Dimona	3631	
OE-9214	Hoffmann H-36 Dimona	3652	
OE-9218	Hoffmann H-36 Dimona	3530	
OE-9220	Scheibe SF-25C Falke	44231	D-KDCF
OE-9221	Hoffmann H-36 Dimona	3675	
OE-9222	Scheibe SF-25D Falke	4858D	D-KAAH
OE-9223	Hoffmann H-36 Dimona	3637	
OE-9224	Sportavia/ Fournier RF-5	5048	OE-9101 D-KLUB
OE-9228	Brditschka HB-23-V2	23002	
OE-9233	Hoffmann H-36 Dimona	36138	
OE-9235	Grob G.109B	6272	
OE-9238	Hoffmann H-36 Dimona	3672	
OE-9242	Brditschka HB-23/24 Scanliner	23003	

OE-9247	Grob G.109B	6230	D-KGFN
OE-9252	Brditschka HB-23/2400	23007	
OE-9256	Grob G.109B	6386	
OE-9260	Scheibe SF-25C Falke	44191	HB-2037 D-KADI
OE-9261	Scheibe SF-25C Falke	44382	(D-KNIE)
OE-9262	Brditschka HB-23/2400	23009	
OE-9263	Brditschka HB-23/2400	23014	
OE-9265	Brditschka HB-23/2400	23015	
OE-9266	Brditschka HB-23/2400	23010	
OE-9271	Brditschka HB-23/2400	23016	
OE-9272	Brditschka HB-23/2400	23017	
OE-9275	AVO-68V Samburo	022	D-KAGM(2)
OE-9277	Brditschka HB-23/2400	23018	
OE-9278	Hoffmann H-36 Dimona	36221	
OE-9279	Brditschka HB-23/2400	23019	
OE-9280	Scheibe SF-25C Falke	44401	(D-KNIJ)
OE-9282	Hoffmann H-36 Dimona	36239	
OE-9283	Brditschka HB-23/2400	23020	
OE-9287	Brditschka HB-23/2400	23022	
OE-9296	Brditschka HB-23/2400	23027	
OE-9298	Brditschka HB-23/2400 Scanliner	23024-S-6	
OE-9299	Scheibe SF-28A Tandem-Falke	5708	D-KHOR
OE-9302	Brditschka HB-23/2400	23031	
OE-9303	Scheibe SF-25C Falke	44262	D-KDOX
OE-9309	Hoffmann H-36 Dimona	36266	
OE-9311	Brditschka HB-23/2400	23033	
OE-9312	Brditschka HB-23/2400 Scanliner	23028-S-7	
OE-9314	Brditschka HB-23/2400	23036	
OE-9315	Brditschka HB-23/2400	23035	
OE-9317	Brditschka HB-23/2400 Hobbyliner	23038	
OE-9320	Scheibe SF-25C Falke	44150	D-KDEH
OE-9321	Brditschka HB-23/2400SP	23041	
OE-9322	Brditschka HB-23/2400SP	23040	
OE-9326	Skyhopper	001	
OE-9331	Brditschka HB-23/2400SP	23045	
OE-9333	Aeronautica-Umbra AU-SF-25B Falke	AU-008D	D-KIAY I-AUAB
OE-9336	Brditschka HB-23/2400 Scanliner	23047-S-9	
OE-9338	Schleicher ASH 25E	25091	
OE-9339	Scheibe SF-25C Falke	44278	D-KDBT(3)
OE-9342	Scheibe SF-25C Falke	44274	D-KABL(2)
OE-9344	Hoffmann HK-36R Super Dimona	36302	
OE-9345	Schempp-Hirth Nimbus 3DT	4/15	OE-5445 D-0962
OE-9348	Brditschka HB-23/2400	23034	HB-2143
OE-9349	Hoffmann HK-36R Super Dimona	36308	
OE-9353	Schempp-Hirth Discus bT	53/371	
OE-9354	Hoffmann HK-36R Super Dimona	36307	
OE-9356	Schempp-Hirth Discus bT	52/369	
OE-9357	Schempp-Hirth Ventus cM	56/506	(D-KDHH)
OE-9358	Sportavia/ Scheibe SF-25C Falke	4202	D-KAOG
OE-9359	Schleicher ASH 25E	25114	
OE-9360	Hoffmann HK-36R Super Dimona	36324	
OE-9362	Hoffmann HK-36R Super Dimona	36326	
OE-9364	Schempp-Hirth Nimbus 3T (C/n correction)	5/55	D-KOWS
OE-9369	Grob G.103C Twin IIISL	35021	
OE-9370	Schempp-Hirth Ventus cM	83/559	
OE-9372	Scheibe SF-25C Falke	44459	D-KIAJ(2)
OE-9373	Technoflug Piccolo B	059	D-KIMV
OE-9377	Schempp-Hirth Ventus cM	87/569	
OE-9378	Schempp-Hirth Discus bT	89/426	
OE-9380	Valentin Kiwi	K3016	D-KEGX(4)
OE-9381	Scheibe SF-25C Falke	44283	D-KDGC(2)
OE-9382	Hoffmann HK-36R Super Dimona	36374	
OE-9385	Schempp-Hirth Discus bT	119/475	
OE-9386	Schempp-Hirth Discus bT	123/481	
OE-9387	Schempp-Hirth Ventus cT	80/321	D-KMMY
OE-9389	Scheibe SF-25C Falke	44433	D-KIAO (D-KNIY)
OE-9390	Eiri PIK-20E	20220	HB-2049
OE-9399	Schempp-Hirth Discus bT	129/491	
OE-9404	Scheibe SF-25C Rotax Falke	44601	D-KTIV(1)
OE-9405	Schempp-Hirth Discus bT	143/521	
OE-9408	HOAC HK-36TTC Super Dimona	36540	
OE-9410	HOAC HK-36TTC Super Dimona	36545	
OE-9411	Schempp-Hirth Ventus 2cM	78/161	
OE-9412	HOAC HK-36TTC Super Dimona	36542	
OE-9413	HOAC HK-36TTC Super Dimona	36620	
OE-9414	HOAC HK-36TTC Super Dimona	36561	
OE-9418	HOAC HK-36TTC Super Dimona	36606	
OE-9420	Scheibe SF-25C Falke	44339	D-KBCL
OE-9421	HOAC HK-36TTC Super Dimona	36590	
OE-9423	Schempp-Hirth Discus bT	28/324	D-KEBG(2)
OE-9424	HOAC HK-36TTS Super Dimona	36624	
OE-9425	HOAC HK-36TTC Super Dimona	36525	
OE-9426	Schleicher ASH 26E	26062	
OE-9428	Diamond HK-36 TC Super Dimona	36731	
OE-9429	Brditschka HB-23/2400 Scanliner	23048-S-10	OO-HBO PH-906
OE-9430	HOAC HK-36TTC Super Dimona	36682	
OE-9431	HOAC HK-36TTC Super Dimona	36531	
OE-9432	HOAC HK-36TTC Super Dimona	36532	
OE-9435	Scheibe SF-25C Falke	44415	D-KGAZ(2)
OE-9437	Diamond HK-36TTC Super Dimona	36645	N844WS
OE-9438	HOAC HK-36TTC Super Dimona	36538	
OE-9439	Diamond HK-36TC Super Dimona	36734	
OE-9441	HOAC HK-36TTC Super Dimona	36541	
OE-9442	Scheibe SF-25C Falke Rotax	44598	D-KTIU
OE-9445	HOAC HK-36TC Super Dimona	36650	
OE-9446	HOAC HK-36TTC Super Dimona	36546	
OE-9447	HOAC HK-36TC Super Dimona	36671	
OE-9449	Scheibe SF-25C Falke 1700	44344	D-KBCO
OE-9451	HOAC HK-36TTC Super Dimona	36698	
OE-9452	HOAC HK-36TTC Super Dimona	36552	
OE-9456	HOAC HK-36TTC Super Dimona	36656	
OE-9457	HOAC HK-36TTC Super Dimona	36557	
OE-9458	HOAC HK-36TTC Super Dimona	36658	PH-1183
OE-9459	HOAC HK-36TTC Super Dimona	36559	
OE-9460	HOAC HK-36TTC Super Dimona	36665	
OE-9461	Schleicher ASH 26E	26161	
OE-9462	HOAC HK-36TTC Super Dimona	36562	
OE-9464	HOAC HK-36TC Super Dimona	36640	OE-9999 N640TT
OE-9465	Scheibe SF-25C Falke	44677	D-KIEJ(2)
OE-9466	HOAC HK-36TTC Super Dimona	36659	
OE-9467	Technoflug Piccolo B	086	D-KIIA
OE-9470	Schempp-Hirth Ventus 2cM	69/141	
OE-9476	Scheibe SF-25C Rotax Falke	44600	D-KTIU(2)
OE-9477	HOAC HK-36TS Super Dimona	36502	PH-1081
OE-9480	Scheibe SF-25C Falke	44561	D-KWGB
OE-9482	HOAC HK-36TTC Super Dimona	36681	
OE-9484	Brditschka HB-23/2400 Scanliner	23012-S2	OE-9284
OE-9488	HOAC HK-36TTC Super Dimona	36683	
OE-9489	HOAC HK-36TTC Super Dimona	36589	
OE-9490	Schempp-Hirth Ventus cT	151/480	
OE-9494	Diamond HK-36TTC Super Dimona	36680	
OE-9495	HOAC HK-36TTC Super Dimona	36710	
OE-9499	HOAC HK-36TTC Super Dimona	36675	
OE-9500	HOAC HK-36TTC Super Dimona	36549	
OE-9505	HOAC HK-36TTC Super Dimona	36707	
OE-9512	HOAC HK-36 TTC Super Dimona	36564	D-KKCB HB-2296
OE-9666	Brditschka HB-23/2400 SP	23043	PH-910 OE-9329

OE-999# series used as test/experimental registrations. Current users:

OE-9990	CJW 20		
OE-9997	Taifun 17E)		
OE-9998	HK-36 series) Diamond Aircraft Industries		
OE-9999	HK-36 series)		
OE-9999	HK-36TTC Super Dimona (Observed 15.6.2002 at Wiener Neustadt)	36706	JA20BB

GLIDERS

OE-0001	Grunau Baby IIb	unkn
OE-0004	Grunau Baby IIb	30340
OE-0038	Grunau Baby IIb	004290
OE-0061	Grunau Baby IIb	005
OE-0097	SG-38 Schulgleiter	7
OE-0129	Grunau Baby IIb Edelweiss	007
OE-0135	Grunau Baby IIb	011
OE-0187	Scheibe Bergfalke II/55	04/261
OE-0227	Grunau Baby IIb	1
OE-0243	Schneider ESG.31 Grunau Baby IIB	1
OE-0248	Scheibe Spatz A	268
OE-0249	Scheibe Bergfalke II/55	4
OE-0254	Grunau Baby IIb	023
OE-0261	Grunau Baby IIb	024
OE-0266	Mü.13E Bergfalke	3
OE-0288	Musger Mg.19 Steinadler	09
OE-0298	Scheibe Bergfalke II	114/55
OE-0299	Scheibe L-Spatz 55	542
OE-0345	Musger Mg.19b	017
OE-0346	Grunau Baby IIb Edelweiss	031
OE-0362	Scheibe L-Spatz	03
OE-0363	Scheibe Bergfalke II	2
OE-0367	Scheibe L-Spatz	205
OE-0374	Grunau Baby IIb	032
OE-0387	Scheibe Mü-18 Spatz B (Museum, Wr Neustadt)	1
OE-0390	Musger Mg.19a	025
OE-0396	Musger Mg.19b	030
OE-0398	Musger Mg.19b	032
OE-0400	Musger Mg.19b	034
OE-0401	Musger Mg.19b	035
OE-0402	Super Futar R 22S	E-1147
OE-0407	Musger Mg.23	06
OE-0408	Musger Mg.23	008
OE-0409	Musger Mg.19a	040
OE-0412	Grunau Baby IIb	38
OE-0415	Musger Mg.19a	036
OE-0423	Grunau Baby IIb	01
OE-0425	Musger Mg.23	05
OE-0427	Scheibe Bergfalke II/55	047
OE-0428	Scheibe Bergfalke II/55	048
OE-0430	Scheibe L-Spatz 55	544
OE-0435	Schleicher Ka 6BR Rhönsegler	463
OE-0442	Grunau Baby IIb	42
OE-0448	Grunau Baby IIb	41

OE-0449	Grunau Baby IIb	44	
OE-0457	Scheibe L-Spatz 55	215/503	
OE-0460	Scheibe L-Spatz 55	R219/H234	
OE-0463	Scheibe L-Spatz 55	3	
OE-0465	Scheibe Zugvogel IV	1040	
OE-0472	Grunau Baby IIb	1	
OE-0475	Schleicher Ka 6CR Rhönsegler	569	
OE-0477	Olympia-Meise 51	17	
OE-0478	Scheibe L-Spatz 55	R56/H229	
OE-0479	Scheibe L-Spatz 55	R55/H227	
OE-0480	SZD-9 bis Bocian 1D	P-349	
OE-0485	Musger Mg.19a	20	
OE-0488	Schleicher K 8	666	
OE-0490	Schleicher K 7 Rhönadler	632	
OE-0498	Schleicher K 8B	830	
OE-0501	Grunau Baby IIb	47	
OE-0505	Scheibe L-Spatz 55	20	
OE-0506	Fauvel AV-36C	201	
OE-0508	Scheibe L-Spatz 55	R218/H232	
OE-0510	Scheibe L-Spatz 55	21	
OE-0511	Scheibe L-Spatz 55	22	
OE-0518	Scheibe L-Spatz 55	719	
OE-0520	Scheibe Bergfalke II/55	305	
OE-0529	Schleicher K 8B	910	
OE-0532	SZD-22C Mucha Standard	598	
OE-0534	SZD-22C Mucha Standard	600	
OE-0538	SZD-22C Mucha Standard	610	
OE-0540	SZD-9bis Bocian 1D	F-873	SP-2506
OE-0547	Scheibe L-Spatz	R232/H244	
OE-0548	Scheibe L-Spatz	R234/H254	
OE-0551	Schleicher Ka 6CR Rhönsegler	1077	
OE-0556	Schleicher K 7 Rhönadler	1007	
OE-0561	Schleicher K 8B	1017	
OE-0567	Schleicher K 8B	1098	
OE-0573	Musger Mg.23SL	09	
OE-0575	Lehrmeister FES.530/1	232	
OE-0578	Schleicher K 8B	1152	
OE-0579	Schleicher K 8B	1154	
OE-0583	Rhönlerche II	3018	
OE-0584	Schleicher K 8B	8153	
OE-0585	Schleicher K 7 Rhönadler	7002	
OE-0587	Schleicher K 7 Rhönadler	7060	
OE-0588	Schleicher Ka 6CR Rhönsegler	1130	
OE-0595	Schleicher K 7 Rhönadler	24	
OE-0596	Schleicher K 8B	25	
OE-0597	Schleicher K 8B	26	
OE-0600	Musger Mg.23SL	13	
OE-0602	Scheibe L-Spatz 55	R53/H240	
OE-0610	Grunau Baby IIb	45	
OE-0616-BB	Grunau Baby IIb	597	
OE-0617	Meise	196	
OE-0625	Scheibe SF-26 Standard	5006	
OE-0628	Schleicher K 8B	KR-1	
OE-0630	Schleicher Ka 6CR Rhönsegler	6147	
OE-0633	Schleicher K 8B	8160	
OE-0637	Schleicher K 8B	8158	
OE-0639	Schleicher Ka 6CR Rhönsegler	6134	
OE-0640	Schleicher Ka 6CR Rhönsegler	6204	
OE-0641	Schleicher K 8B	8179	
OE-0644	Schleicher Ka 6CR Rhönsegler	6164	
OE-0645	Schleicher K 8B	8251	
OE-0652	Schleicher K 7 Rhönadler	7085	
OE-0653	Schleicher K 8B	8804	
OE-0657	Schleicher K 7 Rhönadler	7097	
OE-0658	Schleicher K 8B	8322	
OE-0659	Schleicher Ka 6CR Rhönsegler	6275	
OE-0660	Schleicher Ka 6CR Rhönsegler	6232	
OE-0662	Standard Austria	13	
OE-0665	LG-125 Sohaj 2	519	
OE-0672	Schleicher K 8B	8315	
OE-0673	Schleicher K 8B	8325	
OE-0677	Schleicher K 7 Rhönadler	7140	
OE-0678	Schleicher K 8B	8363	
OE-0679	Schleicher Ka 6CR Rhönsegler	6405	
OE-0682	Scheibe L-Spatz-W	258	
OE-0683	Scheibe Zugvogel IIIB	1083	
OE-0687	Fauvel AV-36CR	216	
OE-0695	Bölkow Phoebus B-1	946	
OE-0699-PM	Scheibe L-Spatz W	259	
OE-0700	Scheibe Bergfalke III	5565	
OE-0702	Lehrmeister FES.530/II	214	
OE-0703	Schleicher K 8B	8232	
OE-0704	Glasflügel H.301 Libelle	16	
OE-0712	LET L-13 Blanik	174506	
OE-0714	FFA-Diamant 16.5	066	
OE-0715	Schleicher Ka 6CR Rhönsegler	6532/Si	
OE-0716	Rolladen-Schneider LS1A	15	
OE-0717	SZD-30 Pirat	B-336	
OE-0718	Bölkow Phoebus C	770	
OE-0719	Scheibe Spatz A	103/54	OE-0276
OE-0721	Schleicher K 8B	8413	
OE-0722	Schleicher Ka 6CR Rhönsegler	6351	
OE-0725	Schleicher Ka 6CR Rhönsegler (same c/n as OY-XMJ)	6420	
OE-0726	Schleicher Ka 6CR Rhönsegler	6440	
OE-0727	Schleicher Ka 6E	4016	
OE-0730	Schleicher K 8B	8476	
OE-0731	Schleicher K 8B	8231	
OE-0733-S3	Scheibe Bergfalke III	5523	
OE-0735	Grunau Baby IIb	03	
OE-0737(2)	LET L-13 Blanik	175019	D-1067
OE-0738	Schleicher Ka 6CR Rhönsegler	7	
OE-0739	LET L-13 Blanik	173219	
OE-0741	Schleicher Ka 6CR Rhönsegler	6364	
OE-0743	Schleicher K 8B	8463	
OE-0747	Schleicher Ka 6E	4017	
OE-0748	Schleicher K 8B	8546	
OE-0749	Schleicher K 8B	8545	
OE-0751	Standard Austria SH.1	66	
OE-0752	Musger Mg.23SL	24	
OE-0753	Schleicher K 8B	8434/ZW	
OE-0754	Schleicher K 8B	8233	
OE-0757	Scheibe SF-26 Standard	5053	
OE-0758	LET L-13 Blanik	173311	
OE-0763	SZD-9 bis Bocian 1D	875	
OE-0769	Scheibe L-Spatz 55	551	
OE-0772	Schleicher K 8B	8554	
OE-0773	Schleicher Ka 6CR Rhönsegler	6498	
OE-0777	Schleicher K 8B	8597	
OE-0778	Schleicher K 8B	8598	
OE-0779	Schleicher K 8B	8599	
OE-0781	Scheibe SF-27	6026	
OE-0782	Scheibe Bergfalke II/55	2	
OE-0783	Schleicher K 8B	8506/ZW	
OE-0784	Schleicher K 8B	8507/ZW	
OE-0789	Scheibe SF-27A	1702E	
OE-0791	Musger Mg.23SL	26	
OE-0793	Scheibe SF-27B	1701E	
OE-0794	Schleicher K 8B	8430a	
OE-0797	Schleicher Ka 6E	4064	
OE-0800	Schleicher K 8B	8731	
OE-0801	Schleicher Rhönlerche II	3070/BR	
OE-0802	Schleicher K 8B	8648	
OE-0803	Schleicher K 8B	8649	
OE-0804	Schleicher K 7 Rhönadler	7219A	
OE-0805	Scheibe SF-27A	6056	
OE-0806	Schleicher Ka 6E	4063	
OE-0810	Schleicher Rhönlerche	3075/BR	
OE-0811	Schleicher Ka 6E	4089	
OE-0814	Schleicher K 8B	8686	
OE-0820	Bölkow Phoebus C	924	
OE-0822	Scheibe SF-27A	1703E	
OE-0824	Schleicher Ka 6BR Rhönsegler	570	
OE-0826	Schleicher Ka 6E	4003	D-4401
OE-0828	Bölkow Phoebus B-1	780	
OE-0829	Scheibe Bergfalke III	5603	
OE-0830	Schleicher K 8B	8050A	
OE-0833	Scheibe L-Spatz 55	01	
OE-0834	Schleicher Rhönlerche II	3076/BR	
OE-0838-FB	Bölkow Phoebus C	799	
OE-0840	Bölkow Phoebus A-1	803	
OE-0844	Bölkow Phoebus B-1	761	
OE-0846	Bölkow Phoebus C	821	
OE-0847	SZD-22C Mucha Standard	753	OE-0601
OE-0848	Schempp-Hirth SHK.1	48	D-8187
OE-0851	Bölkow Phoebus B-1	757	
OE-0853	Glasflügel H401 Kestrel	55	
OE-0854	Bölkow Phoebus C	842	
OE-0855	Bölkow Phoebus C	832	
OE-0858	Schleicher Rhönlerche II	102/60	D-5058
OE-0859	Schleicher K 8B	8440	
OE-0860	Bölkow Phoebus C	848	
OE-0861	Schleicher K 8B	8830	
OE-0862	Schleicher ASW 15	15008	
OE-0864	Schleicher ASW 15	15067	
OE-0868	Bölkow Phoebus C	950	
OE-0873	Glasflügel H201B Standard Libelle	042	
OE-0875	Schempp-Hirth SH.2 Cirrus	35	
OE-0877	Schleicher Ka 6CR Rhönsegler	6325	OE-0737
OE-0881	Scheibe Bergfalke III	5624	
OE-0882	Glasflügel H201B Standard Libelle	15	
OE-0887	Glasflügel H201B Standard Libelle	53	
OE-0895	Scheibe Bergfalke III	5639	
OE-0898	SZD-22C Mucha Standard	609	OE-0541
OE-0899	Rolladen-Schneider LS1D	79	
OE-0900	Bölkow Phoebus C-1	804	
OE-0901	Schleicher K 8B	8083A	
OE-0905	Schleicher K 8B	8852	
OE-0907	LET L-13 Blanik	174810	
OE-0908	FFA-Diamant 18	78	
OE-0911	Schleicher ASK 13	13306	
OE-0912	Schleicher K 8B	8371	
OE-0914	Glasflügel H201B Standard Libelle	221	
OE-0917	FFA-Diamant 18	079	
OE-0918	Schleicher ASK 13	13320	
OE-0920	Schempp-Hirth Cirrus	57	D-0220
OE-0921	Schleicher ASW 15	15162	
OE-0922	Glasflügel H201B Standard Libelle	262	
OE-0923	Glasflügel H201B Standard Libelle	257	
OE-0924	Glasflügel H201B Standard Libelle	256	
OE-0925	Glasflügel H201B Standard Libelle	198	
OE-0926	Schleicher ASK 13	13376	
OE-0928	Bölkow Phoebus B-1	730	
OE-0932	LET L-13 Blanik	175120	

OE-0934	LET L-13 Blanik	175122	
OE-0935	LET L-13 Blanik	175117	
OE-0936	Glasflügel H201B Standard Libelle	307	
OE-0943	SZD-30 Pirat	B-493	
OE-0946	Schleicher ASW 15B	15224	
OE-0947	Schleicher K 8B	8905	
OE-0949	Glasflügel H401 Kestrel 17	71	
OE-0957	Schleicher K 8B	844	OE-0525
OE-0958	Glasflügel H401 Kestrel	76	
OE-0960	Schleicher Ka 6CR Rhönsegler	6286	D-4673
OE-0961	Schleicher ASW 15B	15259	
OE-0963	Schleicher ASW 15B	15256	
OE-0965	Pilatus B4-PC11	052	
OE-0967-BB	Glasflügel H401 Kestrel	53	
OE-0971	Pilatus B4-PC11	012	
OE-0975	Standard Austria	4	OE-0555
OE-0976	Schleicher ASW 15B	15283	
OE-0978-52	Schleicher ASW 15B	15289	
OE-0980	Pilatus B4-PC11	076	
OE-0985	Pilatus B4-PC11	099	
OE-0988	Glasflügel H401 Kestrel	102	
OE-0989	Glasflügel H201BStandard Libelle	514	
OE-0992	LET L-13 Blanik	025915	
OE-0993	LET L-13 Blanik	025929	
OE-5002	Schleicher ASW 15B	15366	
OE-5003	Schleicher K 7 Rhönadler	7248	
OE-5004	Glasflügel H401 Kestrel	111	
OE-5007	Rolladen-Schneider LS1C	140	
OE-5009	LET L-13A Blanik	026042	
OE-5013	Schleicher ASW 15B	15367	
OE-5014	Glasflügel H201B Standard Libelle	584	
OE-5015	Schleicher K 8B	W-18	
OE-5017	Glasflügel H401 Kestrel	117	
OE-5018	Glasflügel H201B Standard Libelle	583	
OE-5022	LET L-13 Blanik	026136	
OE-5023	Schleicher ASW 15B	15385	
OE-5024	Glasflügel H401 Kestrel	120	
OE-5025	Schleicher ASW 15B	15413	
OE-5026	Glasflügel H401 Kestrel	58	
OE-5031	Schleicher ASK 13	13496	
OE-5034	LET L-13 Blanik	026150	
OE-5036	LET L-13 Blanik	026225	
OE-5039	Schleicher ASK 18	18003	
OE-5040	Schleicher K 8C	81005	
OE-5042	LET L-13 Blanik	026248	
OE-5043	Scheibe Bergfalke III	5652	
OE-5045	Schleicher ASK 18	18011	
OE-5046	Grunau Baby IIb	3366	OE-0092
OE-5047	Schleicher ASK 18	18010	
OE-5050	SZD-9 bis Bocian 1E	P-712	
OE-5051	Schleicher ASW 15	15046	
OE-5053	Grob G.102 Astir CS	1049	
OE-5054	Grob G.102 Astir CS	1058	
OE-5055	Grob G.102 Astir CS	1060	
OE-5056	Schempp-Hirth Standard Cirrus	594	
OE-5059	Schleicher K 8B	8824AB	
OE-5064	Grob G.102 Astir CS	1152	
OE-5070	Schleicher ASW 19	19024	
OE-5073	Schleicher Ka 6E	4042	HB-853
OE-5076	Pilatus B4-PC11AF	191	
OE-5078-78	Grob G.102 Astir CS	1283	
OE-5079	Schempp-Hirth Standard Cirrus 75	670	
OE-5080	Grob G.102 Astir CS	1255	
OE-5083	Schleicher ASK 13	13553	
OE-5084	Grob G .102 Astir CS	1324	
OE-5087	Grob G.102 Astir CS	1357	
OE-5092	Grob G.102 Astir CS	1384	
OE-5094	Glaser-Dirks DG-100G	85G6	
OE-5096	LET L-13 Blanik	026647	
OE-5098	Eiri PIK-20D	20515	
OE-5099	Eiri PIK-20D	20516	
OE-5101	Eiri PIK-20D	20518	
OE-5102	Eiri PIK-20D	20519	
OE-5104	Schleicher ASW 15	15102	
OE-5105	Grob G.102 Astir CS	1466	
OE-5109	Pilatus B4-PC11AF	230	
OE-5112	Grob G.102 Astir CS	1496	
OE-5113	Grob G.102 Astir CS	1483	
OE-5119	Grob G.102 Astir CS 77	1627	
OE-5120	Grob G.102 Astir CS	1531	
OE-5121	Grob G.102 Astir CS 77	1621	
OE-5124	Glaser-Dirks DG-100G	95G-12	
OE-5126-26	Grob G.102 Astir CS 77	1659	
OE-5129-2Y	Grob G.102 Astir CS Jeans	2009	
OE-5131	Schleicher ASW 19	19147	
OE-5133	Eiri PIK-20D	20559	
OE-5137	Grob G.102 Astir CS Jeans	2038	
OE-5138	Grob G.102 Astir CS Jeans	2045	
OE-5139	Grob G.102 Astir CS Jeans	2046	
OE-5141-ET	Glaser-Dirks DG-200	2-15	
OE-5146	Valentin Mistral C	MC 009/77	
OE-5149	SZD-41A Jantar Standard	B-811	
OE-5150-W8	Grob G.103 Twin Astir	3022	
OE-5151	Grob G.102 Astir CS Jeans	2062	
OE-5158-M4	Schleicher ASW 19B	19162	
OE-5159	Schleicher ASW 15B	15310	OE-0986
OE-5160	Schempp-Hirth Mini-Nimbus HS-7	42	

OE-5161	LET L-13 Blanik	026927	
OE-5164	Schleicher ASK 13	13586	
OE-5165	Grob G.102 Astir CS Jeans	2060	
OE-5166	Schleicher ASW 19	19164	
OE-5169	Glaser-Dirks DG-100	46	
OE-5172	Glasflügel H206 Hornet	50	
OE-5174	Schleicher ASW 19	19168	
OE-5176-Z1	Lanaverre CS-11/75L St.Cirrus	33	
OE-5177	Grob G.103 Twin Astir	3176	
OE-5178	Scheibe L-Spatz III	822	
OE-5179	Schleicher Ka 6CR Rhönsegler	6279	
OE-5180	Schleicher ASW 19	19200	
OE-5182	Grob G.102 Astir CS Jeans	2153	
OE-5183	LET L-13 Blanik	027064	
OE-5184	Glasflügel H303 Mosquito B	129	
OE-5185	Grob G.102 Astir CS Jeans	2161	
OE-5186	Grob G.102 Astir CS 77	1742	
OE-5190	Grob G 103 Twi n Astir	3208	
OE-5191	Schleicher Rhönlerche II	3069/Br	
OE-5194	SZD-48 Jantar Standard 2	W-883	
OE-5195	SZD-48 Jantar Standard 2	W-888	
OE-5200	Glaser-Dirks DG-100 Elan	E-4	
OE-5202	Schleicher K 8B	AB 81002	
OE-5203	Glaser-Dirks DG-100G	E9-G3	
OE-5205	Schempp-Hirth Standard Cirrus	393	D-9225
OE-5207-21	SZD-48 Jantar Standard 2	W-894	
OE-5209	Grob G.102 Astir CS 77	1820	
OE-5211	Schleicher ASK 13	13569	
OE-5212	Grob G.102 Astir CS 77	1826	
OE-5213	Grob G.102 Astir CS Jeans	2241	
OE-5214	Schleicher ASW 17	17037	
OE-5215	Schleicher K 8B	8479/A	
	(Identity quoted as ex VH-GPA, VH-GMA but this has c/n 8479/GFA/HB/57 and has been concurrent with OE-5215))		
OE-5217	Schempp-Hirth Mini-Nimbus C	132	
OE-5218	Grob G.102 Speed Astir	4057	
OE-5219	Schleicher ASW 20	20223	
OE-5221	Scheibe Bergfalke III	5656	
OE-5225	Grob G.102 Astir CS 77	1838	
OE-5226	Grob G.102 Astir CS Jeans	2037	
OE-5228-28	Schleicher ASW 19B	19290	
OE-5235	Schleicher ASW 19B	19293	
OE-5236(2)-BF	PZL PW-5 Smyk	17.04.016	
OE-5240	Glaser-Dirks DG-200/17	2-105/1716	
OE-5244-44	Grob G.103 Twin Astir	3172	
OE-5246	Schleicher ASK 21	21022	
OE-5248-80	Glaser-Dirks DG-100G Elan	E30-G15	
OE-5249	SZD-48-1 Jantar Standard 2	B-1024	
OE-5253	SZD-42-2 Jantar 2B	B-947	
OE-5258	Grob G.103 Twin II	3522	
OE-5259	Grob G.103 Twin Astir	3074	D-4859
OE-5261-8R	Rolladen-Schneider LS1F	310	
OE-5262	Schleicher K 8B	8642/19	
OE-5263	Schleicher ASK 21	21041	
OE-5265	SZD-48-1 Jantar Standard 2	B-1135	
OE-5267	Grob G.103A Twin II Acro	3620-K-7	
OE-5270	Glaser-Dirks DG-100G Elan	E50-G28	
OE-5272	Rolladen-Schneider LS4	4048	
OE-5273	Glaser-Dirks DG-100G	E51-G29	
OE-5274	Grob G.103A Twin II Acro	3634-K-21	
OE-5278	Rolladen-Schneider LS3A	3076	
OE-5279	Grob G.103A Twin II Acro	3655-K-24	
OE-5280	Schleicher ASK 21	21070	
OE-5281	Schleicher ASK 21	21064	
OE-5286	SZD-48-1 Jantar Standard 2	B-1179	
OE-5287	Schleicher K 8B	222/61	
OE-5288	Rolladen-Schneider LS4	4145	
OE-5290	Glaser-Dirks DG-200/17	2-96/1711	
OE-5292-A2	Schleicher ASW 20	20484	
OE-5293	Schempp-Hirth Ventus b/16.6	93	
OE-5295	Schleicher K 8B	8081	
OE-5298	Glaser-Dirks DG-100G Elan	E109-G79	
OE-5300-53	Rolladen-Schneider LS4	4267	
OE-5305	Grob G.102 Club IIIB (Accident 3.5.95, still reg)	5585CB	
OE-5308	Rolladen-Schneider LS4	4295	
OE-5309	Grob G.102 Speed Astir IIB	4034	
OE-5310-KB	Schempp-Hirth Nimbus III	39	
OE-5312	Grob G.103 Twin II	3746	
OE-5313	Grob G.102 Club IIIB	5592CB	
OE-5314-W4	Rolladen-Schneider LS4	4175	
OE-5315	Schempp-Hirth Ventus b	135	
OE-5316	Schleicher K 7 Rhönadler	7198	
OE-5318	Rolladen-Schneider LS4	4298	
OE-5319	Valentin Mistral C	MC 022/79	PH-674
OE-5320	Schleicher Ka 6CR Rhönsegler	827	
OE-5321	Rolladen-Schneider LS4	4219	
OE-5324	Schempp-Hirth Ventus b (Cr 26.7.89, still regd)	87	D-3200
OE-5325	Rolladen-Schneider LS4	4308	
OE-5328	Scheibe Specht	64	
OE-5329	Scheibe L-Spatz	233	OE-0607
OE-5330	Valentin Mistral C	MC 054/83	
OE-5331	Schleicher ASW 15B	15347	OE-5001
OE-5332	Schempp-Hirth Ventus b/16.6	167	
OE-5333	LET L-13 Blanik	025508	D- . . . .
OE-5335	Grob G.102 Speed Astir IIB	4033	
OE-5336	Schempp-Hirth Ventus b/16.6	168	
OE-5337	Scheibe Spatz A	2	OE-5067

OE-5338	Rolladen-Schneider LS4	4377	
OE-5339	Schleicher ASW 20CL	20709	
OE-5340	Rolladen-Schneider LS4	4369	
OE-5344	Glasflügel H.401 Kestrel	81	
OE-5345	Schempp-Hirth Ventus b/16.6	188	
OE-5346	Grob G.103 Twin Astir Trainer	3110	PH-614
OE-5349	Scheibe Bergfalke III	5521	
OE-5354	Glaser-Dirks DG-300 Elan	3E-68	
OE-5357	Glaser-Dirks DG-300 Elan	3E-63	
OE-5358	Schleicher ASK 13	13639AB	
OE-5359	Rolladen-Schneider LS4	4456	
OE-5361	Glaser-Dirks DG-100G Elan	E175-G141	
OE-5362	Glaser-Dirks DG-100G Elan	E176-G142	
OE-5365	Glaser-Dirks DG-300 Elan	3E-85	
OE-5366	Schleicher ASK 21	21262	
OE-5367	Grob G.102 Astir Standard III	5631S	
OE-5370	Schleicher ASW 15B	15418	D-8663
OE-5374	Pilatus B4-PC11AF	122	HB-1134
OE-5375	Schleicher K 7 Rhönadler	7160	
OE-5376	Schempp-Hirth Ventus b	267	
OE-5377	Rolladen-Schneider LS6a	6058	
OE-5378	Schleicher ASK 21	21271	
OE-5382	Grob G.102 Club Astir II	5011C	D-6815
OE-5383	Rolladen-Schneider LS6	6078	
OE-5384	Grob G.103A Twin II Acro	34068-K-298	
OE-5385	Schleicher K 8B	8535	PH-347
OE-5387	Glaser-Dirks DG-100G Elan	E193-G159	
OE-5389	Schleicher K 7 Rhönadler	345	D-7075
OE-5390-7	Schempp-Hirth Discus b	107	
OE-5391	Rolladen-Schneider LS4	4545	
OE-5393	Glaser-Dirks DG-300 Elan	3E-195	
OE-5394	Glaser-Dirks DG-300 Elan	3E-194	
OE-5395	Schleicher ASK 23B	23075	
OE-5396	Schleicher K 8B	8872	D-3901
			PH-420
OE-5397	Scheibe SF-34B	5125	
OE-5398	Rolladen-Schneider LS4	4593	
OE-5400	Schleicher ASW 20L	20401	
OE-5401	Rolladen-Schneider LS4	4606	
OE-5402	Glaser-Dirks DG-100G Elan	E203-G169	
OE-5403	Glaser-Dirks DG-100G Elan	E204-G170	
OE-5406	Rolladen-Schneider LS4	4628	
OE-5407-XA	Glaser-Dirks DG-100G Elan	E198-G164	
OE-5410	SG-38 Schulgleiter	01	
OE-5411	Schempp-Hirth Ventus b	63	D-7711
OE-5414-C1	Rolladen-Schneider LS6A	6133	
OE-5415	Glasflügel H201B Standard Libelle	352	D-1112
OE-5416	Schleicher K 8B	FWB.20	
OE-5419	Grob G.102 Astir CS Jeans	2157	D-4553
OE-5422	Schleicher ASK 21	21354	
OE-5424-K3	SZD-50-3 Puchacz	B-1629	
OE-5425	Pilatus B4-PC11	071	HB-1888
			D-2200
OE-5426	Rolladen-Schneider LS4A	4672	
OE-5428-M7	Schleicher ASW 20CL	20861	
OE-5429	Schleicher Rhönlerche II	486	OE-0929
OE-5430	Schleicher ASW 24	24063	
OE-5432	Schleicher ASH 25	25036	
OE-5433	Grob G.102 Astir CS	1276	D-7370
OE-5434	Glaser-Dirks DG-100G Elan	E43-G24	
OE-5435	Schleicher K 8B	181/60	D-5797
OE-5437	Glaser-Dirks DG-300 Elan	3E-294	
OE-5438	LET L-13 Blanik	026026	D-9295
OE-5439	Scheibe SF-34B	5131	
OE-5440	Musger Mg.19a Steinadler	039	OE-0440
OE-5441	SZD-50-3 Puchacz	B-1721	
OE-5443-D2	SZD-50-3 Puchacz	B-1724	
OE-5446	Schleicher ASK 21	21400	
OE-5447-DG	Glaser-Dirks DG-300 Elan	3E-317	
OE-5448-JP	Glaser-Dirks DG-100G Elan	E7-G1	D-6488
OE-5449-MI	Rolladen-Schneider LS7	7035	D-1672
OE-5450	Glaser-Dirks DG-600	6-25	
OE-5452	SZD-51-1 Junior	B-1830	
OE-5453	Glaser-Dirks DG-300 Club Elan	3E-333/C30	
OE-5454	Schempp-Hirth Discus b	263	
OE-5455-ZL	Rolladen-Schneider LS7WL	7040	D-1689
OE-5456	Glaser-Dirks DG-100G Elan	E221-G187	
OE-5458	Glaser-Dirks DG-300 Club Elan	3E-332/C29	
OE-5461	Glaser-Dirks DG-300 Club Elan	3E-331/C28	
OE-5463	Glaser-Dirks DG-300 Elan	3E-334	
OE-5465	Schempp-Hirth Nimbus 2B	135	D-2202
OE-5466	SZD-36 Cobra 15A	W-670	OE-5005
OE-5469	Grob G.103C Twin III Acro	34134	
OE-5470-U1	Rolladen-Schneider LS4	4754	
OE-5471	Glaser-Dirks DG-300 Elan	3E-41	
OE-5473	Glaser-Dirks DG-300 Club Elan	3E-361/C46	
OE-5474-BL	Glaser-Dirks DG-600	6-47	
OE-5475	SZD-36A Cobra 15	W-658	D-2243
OE-5476	Grob G.102 Astir CS Jeans	2151	D-4892
OE-5479	Rolladen-Schneider LS4	4477	D-3457
OE-5481	Grob G.103A Twin II Acro	3688-K-39	D-8693
OE-5482	Rolladen-Schneider LS7WL	7117	BGA3672/GAE
OE-5483-U2	Rolladen-Schneider LS7	7100	
OE-5484	Schleicher ASK 21	21446	
OE-5486	Schleicher K 8B	8693	D-9171
OE-5487	Schleicher K 7 Rhönadler	7277	D-5222
OE-5488	Schleicher K 8B	843	D-5788

OE-5489	Rolladen-Schneider LS7WL	7113	
OE-5490	Schleicher ASK 13	13290	D-0661
OE-5491	Glaser-Dirks DG-300 Elan	3E-400	
OE-5492	Schleicher K 8B	610	HB-630
OE-5493	Rolladen-Schneider LS7	7105	
OE-5494-N5	Glaser-Dirks DG-300 Elan	3E-399	
OE-5495-HV	Grob G.102 Astir CS	1005	D-8942
OE-5496	Schleicher K 8B	8197	D-2064
			OE-0643
OE-5498	Glaser-Dirks DG-300 Elan	3E-393	
OE-5499	LET L-13A Blanik	027015	OE-5175
OE-5500	Schempp-Hirth Janus B	158	D-3146
OE-5501	LET L-23 Super Blanik	917812	
OE-5502	LET L-23 Super Blanik	917822	
OE-5503	Rolladen-Schneider LS7WL	7158	
OE-5504	Schempp-Hirth Standard Cirrus	550G	D-4754
OE-5505	Glaser-Dirks DG-300 Club Elan	3E-418/C69	
OE-5506	Rolladen-Schneider LS4B	4838	
OE-5508	LET L-23 Super Blanik	917902	
OE-5509	Glaser-Dirks DG-300 Elan	3E-219	D-7187
OE-5511	Schempp-Hirth Discus CS	048CS	
OE-5512	Schleicher Rhönlerche II	3044/Br	D-4108
OE-5515	Glaser-Dirks DG-300 Elan	3E-281	
OE-5516	Glaser-Dirks DG-300 Elan	3E-224	OY-XYZ
OE-5518	Schleicher ASW 24	24173	
OE-5520	Glaser-Dirks DG-300 Club Elan	3E-421/C70	
OE-5521	Schleicher ASH-25	25154	
OE-5523	Glaser-Dirks DG-300 Elan	3E-368	
	(Current but this c/n also regd as D-1199)		
OE-5524	Schleicher ASW 24	24162	
OE-5526	Schempp-Hirth Ventus c	570	
OE-5527	Grob G.102 Astir CS Jeans	2030	D-3877
OE-5528-U3	Rolladen-Schneider LS7	7045	D-5162
OE-5529	Schempp-Hirth Discus CS	115CS	
OE-5531	Grob G.102 Astir CS Jeans	2206	D-3823
OE-5533	Schleicher ASW 15B	15404	D-8651
OE-5534	Schempp-Hirth Discus CS	109CS	
OE-5535	Schleicher ASK 21	21560	
OE-5536	Schleicher ASK 21	21564	
OE-5541	Glasflügel H205 Club Libelle	105	HB-1261
OE-5544-55	Glaser-Dirks DG-300 Club Elan	3E-438/C74	
OE-5546	Rolladen-Schneider LS6B	6152	D-8090
OE-5547	Schempp-Hirth Discus CS	138CS	
OE-5548	Bölkow Phoebus C	852	D-0089
OE-5549	Schempp-Hirth Discus CS	146CS	
OE-5550	LET L-23 Super Blanik	917908	
OE-5553-D4	SZD-55-1	551192049	
OE-5554	Marganski Swift S-1	P-07/P-02	SP-3533
OE-5555	Standard Austria	14	OE-0669
OE-5556	Glasflügel H401 Kestrel	21	D-0518
OE-5557-41	Schempp-Hirth Discus CS	154CS	
OE-5558	Schleicher ASW 20CL	20855	D-4758
OE-5560	Rolladen-Schneider LS4B	4922	
OE-5562	Schleicher ASH 25	25085	D-2509
OE-5563	Rolladen-Schneider LS4B	4945	
OE-5564	Schempp-Hirth Discus b	503	
OE-5565	SZD-55-1	551193053	SP-3584
OE-5566(2)	Pilatus B4-PC11AF	307	
OE-5567	Schleicher ASW 15B	15361	D-2369
OE-5568	Schempp-Hirth Discus CS	038CS	
OE-5569	Rolladen-Schneider LS4B	4957	
OE-5570-A1	Schempp-Hirth Discus CS	158CS	
OE-5571	Rolladen-Schneider LS4B	4978	D-5544
OE-5572	Glaser-Dirks DG-303 Club Elan Acro	3E-447C77A10	
	(Believed w/o 1.8.98 but regd to new owner .00)		
OE-5574	Grob G.103C Twin III Acro	34200	
OE-5576	Grob G.103 Twin Astir	3057	OE-5347
			D-4847
OE-5577	Schleicher ASH 25	25007	D-4810
OE-5578	Grob G.103 Twin Astir	3199	D-5958
OE-5579-G8	PZL PW-5 Smyk	17.03.015	
OE-5580	Schleicher ASK 13	13426	D-2134
OE-5581-K1	Schempp-Hirth Discus CS	173CS	
OE-5582-S1	SZD-51-1 Junior	B-2136	SP-3609
OE-5583	Schempp-Hirth Duo Discus	188	
OE-5584	Schempp-Hirth Discus CS	202CS	
OE-5585	SZD-55-1	551195064	
OE-5586	SZD-59 Acro	B-2165	
OE-5588	Rolladen-Schneider LS8A	8044	D-3640
OE-5590-ST	SZD-55-1	551194063	
OE-5591-D9	Grob G.102 Astir CS	1253	HB-1310
OE-5592-A1	Schempp-Hirth Discus CS	088CS	D-1374
OE-5593	Schleicher K 8B	8200	HB-717
OE-5594	Glaser-Dirks DG-300 Club Elan	3E-458/C81	
OE-5598	Marganski MDM-1 Fox	206	
OE-5599	SZD-51-1 Junior	B-2145	
OE-5600	Schempp-Hirth Discus CS	194CS	
OE-5601	Marganski MDM-1 Fox	P15	SP-3604
OE-5603-I1	Schempp-Hirth Ventus 2b	24	
OE-5604	PZL PW-5 Smyk	17.03.007	
OE-5605	Glaser-Dirks DG-300 Club Elan Acro	3E-457C80A15	
OE-5607	Marganski Swift S-1	102	SP-3537
OE-5608	Marganski MDM-1 Fox	P14	SP-3598
			SP-P598
OE-5610	Marganski MDM-1 Fox	205	
OE-5611	Schempp-Hirth Duo Discus	59	
OE-5612	Glaser-Dirks DG-303 Elan	3E-467	

OE-5613	Schempp-Hirth Discus CS	212CS	
OE-5615-A3	Glaser-Dirks DG-500 Elan Orion	5E-160X16	
OE-5616	Rolladen-Schneider LS8A	8051	D-3702
OE-5617	Rolladen-Schneider LS8A	8054	D-3751
OE-5618	LET L-23 Super Blanik	948205	
OE-5619	Rolladen-Schneider LS4B	41002	
OE-5621	Rolladen-Schneider LS4B	41001	
OE-5622	Grob G.102 Astir CS	1240	D-7321
OE-5627	DG Flugzeugbau DG-300 Elan	3E-471	
OE-5630	SZD-55-1	551196090	
OE-5631-EY	Grob G.103C Twin III Acro	34201	D-8687
OE-5632	PZL PW-5 Smyk	17.04.013	
OE-5633	Grob G.102 Astir CS Jeans	2078	D-7591
OE-5634-3M	DG Flugzeugbau DG-300 Club Elan	3E-474C84	
OE-5635	Schleicher ASW 24B	24247	
OE-5637	Rolladen-Schneider LS4	4406	D-9144
OE-5638-LB	PZL PW-5 Smyk	17.05.010	
OE-5639	Schempp-Hirth Discus CS	084CS	D-2084
OE-5640	Grob G.102 Astir CS	1174	OE-5074
OE-5643	Glaser-Dirks DG-100	4	HB-1264
OE-5644-BF	SZD-59 Acro	B-2167	SP-3614
OE-5646	Rolladen-Schneider LS4B	4871	D-8103
OE-5647	PZL PW-5 Smyk	17.05.014	
OE-5648	Marganski MDM-1 Fox	211	
OE-5649-W1	PZL PW-5 Smyk	17.07.024	
OE-5650-W2	PZL PW-5 Smyk	17.07.025	
OE-5651	PZL PW.5 Smyk	17.08.010	
OE-5652	SZD-55-1	551197095	
OE-5653	Grob G.103A Twin II Acro	3635-K-16	D-3075
OE-5654	Schempp-Hirth Ventus 2b	65	
OE-5655	SZD-51-1 Junior	B-2155	
OE-5656	Glasflügel H201B Standard Libelle	283	D-0380
OE-5657	Schempp-Hirth Duo Discus	161	
OE-5658	Glaser-Dirks DG-100	15	D-3731
OE-5659	Schempp-Hirth Discus b	103	D-2952
OE-5660	Grob G.103 Twin Astir	3105	D-3962
OE-5661	Grob G.102 Club Astir II	5019C	D-6816
OE-5662	Schleicher ASK 21	21552	D-9331
OE-5663	Marganski MDM-1 Fox	222	
OE-5664	Rolladen-Schneider LS8A	8202	
OE-5665-W2	Grob G.102 Standard Astir III	5502	D-3080
OE-5666	Marganski MDM-1 Fox	225	
OE-5667	LET L-23 Super Blanik	988414	
OE-5668	Rolladen-Schneider LS4B	41032	
OE-5669	Rolladen-Schneider LS3	3037	D-2803
OE-5671	Schempp-Hirth Discus CS	060CS	D-7114
OE-5672	Schempp-Hirth Discus CS	256CS	
OE-5673	SZD-51-1 Junior	B-2193	
OE-5674	LET L-23 Super Blanik	998411	
OE-5676	LET L-13 Blanik	026529	I-BZEL
OE-5677	SZD-51-1 Junior	511199244	
OE-5678	Schleicher ASW 15	15089	D-1019
OE-5679	Rolladen-Schneider LS8-18	8273	D-8527
OE-5682	Marganski MDM-1 Fox	229	
OE-5683-A5	Glaser-Dirks DG-505 Elan Trainer	5E-107T43	D-8012
OE-5684	Schempp-Hirth Duo Discus	388	
OE-5685	Grob G.102 Astir CS Jeans	2183	D-7758
OE-5686-WO	Glaser-Dirks DG-505 Elan Orion	5E205X49	S5-7519
OE-5687	Glasflügel H401 Kestrel	114	D-3714
OE-5688	WA Silent	006	
OE-5689	Glasflügel H201BStandard Libelle	442	D-2170
OE-5690	Schleicher ASW 27B	27150	
OE-5691	Rolladen-Schneider LS8-18	8359	
OE-5692	Glasflügel Kestrel	63	HB-1057
OE-5694	Schleicher ASW 20BL	20646	OH-711
OE-5695	PZL PW-6U	78.02.05	
OE-5696	Rolladen-Schneider LS4A	4653	D-8024
OE-5697	Grob G.103C Twin III Acro	34175	D-8950 (OE-5697) D-8950
OE-5698	Schempp-Hirth Duo Discus	35	D-2153
OE-5699	Schleicher ASW 28	28055	
OE-5700	Caproni A21S Calif	253	I-GCCP
OE-5701	Schleicher ASK 21	21610	I-BZAS
OE-5702	Schleicher K 8B	8180	OE-0642
OE-5703	Schleicher K 8B	8341	HB-1092
OE-5704	PZL PW-6U	78.03.07	
OE-5705	Scheibe L-Spatz	773	D-1843
OE-5707	Marganski Swift-S1	123	
OE-5708-U4	Glaser-Dirks DG-300 Elan	3E-248	D-0502 HB-1914
OE-5709	Glasflügel H.201B Standard Libelle	595	OY-XCC
OE-5710	DG-Flugzeugbau DG 1000 S	10-43S42	
OE-5711	Glaser-Dirks DG 500 Elan Orion	5E29(T)X45	I-CNDA
OE-5712-JH	SZD-55-1	551A04001	
OE-5715	Schempp-Hirth Discus CS	132CS	
OE-5714	Allstar SZD-59 Acro	590.A.05.003	
OE-5716	Pilatus B4-PC11 AF	277	
OE-5717	DG-Flugzeugbau DG-300 Elan Acro	3E-505A39	
OE-5718	Schleicher ASW 20B	20397	

OE-699# series used as test/experimental registrations:

OE-6991	Test regn for Fa.Neura GmbH		

MICROLIGHTS

OE-6000 class (Powered Hang-gliders, not self-launching)

OE-6003	Sport 167/HHM 210/1	16090/109	
OE-6016	Super Sport 163/HHM 210/1	18906	OE-8116
OE-6065	Sport 167AT/HHM210/1	17205/101	OE-8065
OE-6075	Super Sport 163/HHM 210/1	18410	OE-8075
OE-6096	Sport 167/HHM 210/1	15424/118	OE-8096
OE-6105	Sport 167/HHM 210/1	15112	OE-8105

OE-7000 class (Three-axis Microlights)

OE-7000	Comco Ikarus C-42B	0305/6529	
OE-7003	Pioneer Flightstar	373	
OE-7007	Comco Ikarus Fox-C22	3063	
OE-7008	Albatros	111	
OE-7009	Sky-Walker II-300E	191	
OE-7010	Albatros	117	
OE-7012	Rotec Rally 2B	7012	
OE-7015	Thruster T.300	88-330	
OE-7016	Platzer Kiebitz-B	89	
OE-7019	Comco Ikarus Fox-C22	9206-3433	
OE-7021	Comco Ikarus Fox-C22	9303-3493	
OE-7022	Sunwheel R	011	
OE-7025	Comco Ikarus Fox-C22	9201-3383	
OE-7026	Comco Ikarus Fox-C22	9402-3568	
OE-7027	Comco Ikarus Fox-C22	9209-3406	
OE-7029	Comco Ikarus Fox-C22B	9502-3652	
OE-7031	Comco Ikarus Fox-C22B	9503-3674	
OE-7032	Comco Ikarus Fox-C22B	9505-3673	
OE-7033	Rodaro Storch	7IA16	
OE-7035	Comco Ikarus Fox-C22	9603-3705	
OE-7038	Comco Ikarus C-42 Cyclone	9702-6007	
OE-7039	Comco Ikarus C-42 Cyclone	9708-6051	
OE-7040	Comco Ikarus C-42 Cyclone (Cr. 15.5.98)	9704-6020	
OE-7041	Comco Ikarus C-42 Cyclone	9801-6079	
OE-7042	Flight Design CT	98-02-03-23	
OE-7043	Zenair CH-601OE Zodiac	6-3654	
OE-7044	Flight Design CT	00-03-04-90	
OE-7047	Air Light Wild Thing	039	
OE-7050	Comco Ikarus C-42 Cyclone	9801-6060	
OE-7055	Comco Ikarus C-42 Cyclone	9904-6153	
OE-7056	Pioneer Flightstar II	990402	
OE-7058	Comco Ikarus C-42B	0203-6433	
OE-7060	Flight Design CT 2K	01-08-05-25	
ÓE-7066	Flight Design CT-SW	unkn	
OE-7070	Zenair CH-601OE Zodiac	6-3655	
OE-7071	Comco Ikarus C-42B	0203-6434	
OE-7072	Comco Ikarus C-42B	0204-6435	
OE-7075	Comco Ikarus C-42B	0301-6510	
OE-7077	WT 9 Dynamic	DY-019	OH-U415
OE-7088	TL Ultralight TL-96 Star	04 ST 89	
OE-7102	WT 9 Dynamic	DY-061	
OE-7103	WT 9 Dynamic	DY-070	

OE-8000 class (Flex-wing types)

OE-8025	Austro Trike/Euro IIIM	1123	
OE-8035	Vega 16M/Steinbach	88/428	
OE-8038	Apollo CX/1500 Racer GT	MZEA 20/88	
OE-8041	Vega Duo Trike	89/510/DO02	
OE-8044	Apollo CX/1500 Racer GT	MZEA 21/88	
OE-8045	Apollo CX/1500 Racer GT	MZEA 13/90	
OE-8046	Apollo CX/1500 Racer GT	MZEA 22/89	
OE-8051	Vega Duo Trike	90/566D03	
OE-8053	Apollo CX/1500 Racer GT	MZEA 22/90	
OE-8057	Apollo CX/1500 Racer GT	MZEA 43/90	
OE-8059	Apollo CX/1500 Racer GT	A220494	
OE-8060	Apollo CX/1500 RacerGT	MZEA 13/91	
OE-8061	Hazard 15M/Racer GT	03/922015	
OE-8063	Apollo CX/1500 Racer GT	MZEA 85/91	
OE-8066	HP-AT158/HHM210/1	23112	
OE-8067	Apollo CX/1500 Racer GT	MZEA 15/91	
OE-8070	Saphir 17/Minimum	15265	
OE-8071	Sport 167/HHM 210/1	17525	
OE-8072	Apollo CX/1500 Racer GT	A290693	
OE-8073	Apollo CX/1500 Racer GT	A280693	
OE-8076	Apollo CX/1500 Racer GT	A021293	
OE-8077	Sport 167/HHM 210/1	16075	
OE-8078	Sport 167/HHM 210/1	14577	
OE-8080	Apollo CX/1500 Racer GT	MZ 06/91	
OE-8081	Apollo CXM/Racer GT/R	MZ/37/92	
OE-8084	Apollo CX/1500 Racer GT	A191093	
OE-8085	Royal/Hazard 15M	6751	
OE-8086	Apollo CXM Racer GT	A280494	
OE-8087	Royal Trike R503/Karat 13	04-9409	
OE-8090	Apollo CXM Racer GT (Seaplane)	A010894	
OE-8091	Apollo CXM Racer GT	A030295	
OE-8093	Apollo CXM Racer GT	A220395	
OE-8094	Spider/Hazard 13M	097/93/2707	
OE-8095	Apollo CXM/Racer GT	A020595	
OE-8100	Super Sport 163/HHM 210/1	18135/115	
OE-8101	Apollo C-15D Delta Jet/R	A081195	

OE-8102	Spider/Hazard 15M	048/95/1905	
OE-8103	Apollo CXM/Racer GT	A240795	
OE-8104	Apollo CX/1500 Racer GT	MZEA 82/91	
OE-8107	Royal/Hazard 13M	144/95	
OE-8108	Apollo CXM/Racer GT	A020295	
OE-8109	Apollo CXM/Racer GT	A00196	
OE-8110	Apollo CXM/Racer GT	A00296	
OE-8111	Laser 14/HHM 210/1	050-2/7123	
OE-8112	Apollo CXM/Racer GT	A071195	
OE-8113	Spider 6D/Hazard 15M	196	
OE-8114	Apollo CXMD/Delta Jet/R	A0396	
OE-8117	Super Sport 167/HHM 210/1	15613	
OE-8118	Apollo CXM/Racer GT	A0496	
OE-8119	Apollo C15/Racer GT/R	141194	
OE-8124	Sport 167/HHM 210/1	14538	
OE-8125	Apollo CXM/Racer GT/R	A0597	
OE-8126	Apollo CXM/Racer GT/R	A0697	
OE-8127	Apollo CXM/Racer GT/R	A0797	
OE-8128	Apollo CXM/Racer GT/R	A0198	
OE-8129	Apollo CX/1500 Racer GT	A11591	
OE-8130	Apollo CXMD Delta Jet/R	A0298/1998	
OE-8131	Apollo CXMD Delta Jet/R	A0200/2000	
OE-8132	Apollo-C-XM/Racer GT/R	A04/02	
OE-8134	Apollo Delta Jet	A-02/04	

OH - FINLAND

Regn.	Type	C/n	Prev.Id.
OH-ACN	Rockwell Commander 690A	11301	(N81405)
OH-ADA	Swearingen SA.226T Merlin III	T-248	N120TT
			F-GGGH
			N10WL
			N5338M
OH-AFI	Boeing 757-2K2	26330	PH-TKD
			XA-TMU
			PH-TKD
			C-GTSR
			PH-TKD
OH-AFJ	Boeing 757-28A	26269	N321LF
OH-AFK	Boeing 757-28A	25622	N364LF
			PH-AHS
			C-GTSV
			S7-AAX
OH-AKD	Lake LA-4-200 Buccaneer	592	N65660
OH-AKF	Lake LA-4-200 Buccaneer	710	N1205L
OH-ARI	Cessna T210N Turbo Centurion II	21064184	OY-CKV
			D-EHSD
			(N5368Y)
OH-AUA	Auster Mk.5	1556	G-AJFI
			TJ531
OH-AUE	Auster 6A Tugmaster	3734	SE-ELE
			WJ373
OH-AWA	Cessna 172P	17274155	N5489K
OH-AWB	Cessna 152	15283512	C-GMYM
			N49754
OH-AYA	American AA-1 Yankee	AA1-0402	(LN-KAZ)
			(N6202L)
OH-AYC	Grumman-American AA-1A Trainer	AA1A-0088	
OH-AYE	Grumman-American AA-1A Trainer	AA1A-0301	
OH-AYF	American AA-1 Yankee	AA1-0404	(LN-BFP)
			N6204L
OH-AYG	Grumman AA-1B Trainer 2	AA1B-0039	
OH-AYH	Grumman AA-5 Traveler	AA5-0196	
OH-AYK	Grumman AA-5 Traveler	AA5-0334	N5434L
OH-AYM	Grumman AA-5 Traveler	AA5-0431	N7131L
OH-AYO	Grumman AA-5 Traveler	AA5-0478	N7178L
OH-AYP	Grumman AA-5 Traveler	AA5-0765	
OH-AYR	Grumman AA-5 Traveler	AA5-0762	
OH-AYT	Grumman AA-5B Tiger	AA5B-0219	
OH-BAB	Beech 23-B19 Musketeer Sport	MB-822	
OH-BAR	Beech B60 Duke	P-477	N100CD
OH-BAX	Beech C90 King Air	LJ-984	LN-FOD
			N1823A
OH-BBK	Beech A36 Bonanza	E-2374	
OH-BBL	Beech A36 Bonanza	E-2375	
OH-BBM	Beech A36 Bonanza	E-2376	
OH-BBN	Beech A36 Bonanza	E-2497	
OH-BCA	Bellanca 7ECA Citabria	1198-77	N4212Y
OH-BCK	Stinson 108-2 Voyager	863	SE-BCK
			NC97863
OH-BCX	Beech C90 King Air	LJ-770	N88CG
			N4770M
OH-BDA	Beech 35-B33 Debonair	CD-789	
OH-BDX	Beech 60 Duke	P-194	N4AJ
			(N5AJ)
			N86TP
OH-BEX	Beech C90 King Air	LJ-978	N725KR
			ZS-LBF
			N3835Z
OH-BGE	Beagle B.121 Pup 100	098	G-35-098
OH-BJT	Bellanca 8KCAB Decathlon	26-72	N11716
OH-BKA	Beech 100 King Air	B-39	HB-GEN
OH-BMD	Beech A23-19 Musketeer Sport III	MB-163	
OH-BMK	Beech 19A Musketeer Sport	MB-298	
OH-BML	Beech 19A Musketeer Sport	MB-299	
OH-BSA	Beech 300 Super King Air	FA-205	N5672A
OH-BSB	Beech 300 Super King Air	FA-206	N5672J
OH-CAC	Cessna U206F Stationair	U20602364	SE-GGI
			N2387U
OH-CAD	Cessna 182F Skylane	18254999	SE-EHS
			N3599U
OH-CAE	Reims/Cessna F172H	F17200670	SE-FMB
			LN-LJP
OH-CAF	Reims/Cessna F172M	F17201184	SE-FMF
			D-EEIA
OH-CAH	Reims FR172F Rocket	FR17200065	SE-FEY
OH-CAK	Cessna 172N	17273208	C-GBGT
			(N6373F)
OH-CAL	Cessna 172H	17255695	9J-RFH
			ZS-ETE
			N2495L
OH-CAM	Cessna 172P	17274753	N53455
OH-CAN	Cessna 172N	17269701	N737VD
OH-CAO	Cessna 152	15281506	C-GYBK
			(N64973)
OH-CAP	Cessna 152	15279955	C-GVGD
			N757RY
OH-CAQ	Cessna 152-II	15284712	N6404M
OH-CAS	Cessna 152-II	15285573	N93919
OH-CAU	Cessna 172N	17272511	N53140
OH-CAV	Cessna 172N	17270621	N739LE
OH-CAW	Cessna 172N	17270218	N738TE
OH-CAY	Cessna 172P	17274597	N555RT
			N52744
OH-CAZ	Cessna 172N	17273806	N5476J
OH-CBA	Cessna A185E Skywagon	185-1458	N2297T
OH-CBI	Cessna F150J	F150-0448	
OH-CBL	Cessna F150J	F150-0468	
OH-CBP	Cessna F150J	F150-0478	
OH-CBR	Cessna 180H Skywagon	18052071	N91404
OH-CBU	Reims/Cessna FA150K Aerobat	FA1500012	
OH-CBW	Reims/Cessna FA150K Aerobat	FA1500025	
OH-CBX	Reims/Cessna FA150K Aerobat	FA1500026	
OH-CBZ	Reims/Cessna FA150K Aerobat	FA1500033	
OH-CCF	Cessna F172H	F172-0455	
OH-CCO	Cessna F150H	F150-0253	
OH-CCS	Cessna F150H	F150-0323	
OH-CCY	Cessna A185E Skywagon	185-1352	N2200T
OH-CCZ	Reims FR172E Rocket	FR17200017	(G-AVYJ)
			F-WLIS
OH-CDA	Reims/Cessna FA150K Aerobat	FA1500034	
OH-CDD	Reims/Cessna FA150K Aerobat	FA1500037	
OH-CDE	Reims/Cessna FA150K Aerobat	FA1500038	
OH-CDF	Reims FR172G Rocket	FR17200188	
OH-CDI	Cessna A185E Skywagon	185-1529	N2779J
OH-CDK	Cessna A185E Skywagon (Robertson STOL)	18501675	N1959U
OH-CDO	Cessna A185E Skywagon	18501773	N5804J
OH-CDW	Reims/Cessna F172H	F17200679	
OH-CEB	Cessna F172F	F172-0118	
OH-CEE	Cessna F150G (Taildragger mod.)	F150-0075	
OH-CEF	Cessna 150E	15061433	N4033U
OH-CEG	Cessna 185D Skywagon	185-0863	
OH-CEN	Cessna F150F	F150-0061/15063540	(G-ATNF)
OH-CER	Cessna 180H	18051823	N7920V
OH-CES	Cessna F150G	F150-0162	
OH-CET	Cessna F150G	F150-0142	
OH-CEV	Cessna A185E Skywagon	185-1180	N4726Q
OH-CEW	Cessna F172H	F172-0344	
OH-CEZ	Cessna F172H (Modified)	F172-0386	
OH-CFA	Reims FR172G Rocket	FR17200180	
OH-CFF	Reims/Cessna F172H	F17200753	
OH-CFJ	Reims/Cessna F172L	F17200834	
OH-CFO	Cessna 188A Agwagon B	18800789	N9989G
OH-CFQ	Reims/Cessna F172M	F17200962	
OH-CFS	Reims/Cessna F172M	F17200963	
OH-CGC	Reims/Cessna F150M	F15001147	
OH-CGD	Reims/Cessna F150M	F15001177	
OH-CGE	Cessna A188B Agwagon	18801229	N8092G
OH-CGH	Reims/Cessna F172M	F17201045	(SE-FZL)
OH-CGI	Cessna F172H (Modified)	F172-0595	SE-FME

			LN-AEF
OH-CGJ	Reims/Cessna F150L	F15000674	SE-FRH
OH-CGL	Reims/Cessna FA150L Aerobat	FA1500089	SE-FXA
OH-CGM	Cessna A188B Agtruck	18801506T	N9507G
OH-CGO	Cessna A185E Skywagon	18502010	SE-FXM N70130
OH-CGT	Cessna A188B Agtruck	18801959T	(OH-CGQ) N78763
OH-CGU	Cessna A188B Agtruck	18801502T	N9497G
OH-CGW	Cessna 401B	401B0009	G-AXVA N7909Q
OH-CGX	Reims/Cessna F172M	F17201449	
OH-CHD	Cessna 170B	26528	D-EFYT N3485C
OH-CHE	Cessna 175A Skylark	56727	SE-CTT N8927T
OH-CHM	Cessna 401A	401A0125	LN-TVN (LN-VYM) N3151K
OH-CHO	Cessna TU206G Turbo Stationair II	U20603634	N7364N
OH-CHQ	Reims/Cessna F182P Skylane	F18200024	
OH-CHS	Cessna 402B	402B1082	FinAF:CB-52 OH-CHS N1780G
OH-CHU	Cessna TU206G Turbo Stationair 6	U20604332	(N756SZ)
OH-CHV	Reims/Cessna F182Q Skylane	F18200071	
OH-CHY	Reims/Cessna F172N	F17201893	
OH-CHZ	Cessna TU206G Turbo Stationair 6	U20604970	(N735VJ)
OH-CIA	Champion 7ECA Citabria	279	
OH-CIC	Champion 7ECA Citabria	288	
OH-CID	Reims/Cessna F172N	F17201897	
OH-CII	Cessna TU206G Turbo Stationair 6	U20605466	N6385U
OH-CIL	Reims/Cessna F172P	F17202080	
OH-CIN	Reims/Cessna F152	F15201874	
OH-CIO	Cessna TU206G Turbo Stationair 6	U20606090	(N5269Z)
OH-CIP	Reims/Cessna F152	F15201857	
OH-CIR	Reims/Cessna FR172K Hawk XP	FR17200673	D-EANJ (D-EDMY)
OH-CIS	Reims/Cessna F152-II	F15201900	
OH-CIW	Cessna 172M	17265340	SE-GCZ N5097H
OH-CJJ	Cessna A185E Skywagon	185-1418	LN-VIX N2260T
OH-CJM	Cessna 152	15283317	N48277
OH-CKB	Reims/Cessna FA152 Aerobat	FA1520388	
OH-CKC	Reims/Cessna FA152 Aerobat	FA1520389	
OH-CKE	Reims/Cessna FA152 Aerobat	FA1520419	
OH-CKF	Reims/Cessna FA152 Aerobat	FA1520420	
OH-CKH	Cessna 172N	17270074	SE-KKG N738LZ
OH-CKI	Cessna 182R Skylane	18268278	N4855E
OH-CKK	Cessna 172N	17267772	N75512
OH-CKL	Cessna 172K	17259090	N7390G
OH-CKN	Cessna 177B Cardinal	17702264	N35204
OH-CKO	Cessna 152	15283579	C-GQQD N4687B
OH-CKQ	Cessna 172M	17267244	C-GDRP N73033
OH-CKR	Cessna A185F Skywagon	18503548	N4686Q
OH-CKU	Cessna 172N	17273892	C-FJIK N6567J
OH-CKV	Cessna 150M	15076935	C-GEDJ (N45461)
OH-CKW	Cessna 180K Skywagon	18053053	N2739K
OH-CKY	Cessna 150M	15076334	N2959V
OH-CLE	Cessna 152	15280803	(SE-IXM) OH-CLE N25828
OH-CLO	Cessna 172P	17274464	OY-CPO N15BH N52260
OH-CMD	Cessna 172N	17268649	N733YF
OH-CME	Cessna 172M	17266014	N9205H
OH-CMG	Cessna T210N Turbo Centurion II	21064546	N9550Y
OH-CMH	Cessna 172N	17268309	N733HP
OH-CMI	Cessna 172N	17271770	N5209E
OH-CMJ	Cessna 152-II	15285425	N93162
OH-CMK	Cessna 152	15280276	N24479
OH-CML	Cessna 152	15281594	N65507
OH-CMM	Cessna 152	15281774	N67356
OH-CMO	Cessna 172P	17274899	N54169
OH-CMP	Cessna 172P	17274422	N52141
OH-CMR	Cessna 182P Skylane	18264924	N1361S
OH-CMT	Cessna U206F Stationair	U20602702	LN-HAP (N33266)
OH-CMU	Cessna 152	15283464	C-GQOG (N49503)
OH-CMV	Cessna 152-II	15282281	N68355
OH-CMX	Cessna 150L	15073228	N5328Q
OH-CNB	Reims FR172E Rocket	FR17200042	
OH-CNJ	Reims FR172E Rocket	FR17200001	F-WLIK N20001
OH-CNM	Cessna 177A Cardinal	17701349	N30594
OH-CNN	Cessna 177A Cardinal	17701301	N30522
OH-CNO	Cessna 150J	15070066	N60099
OH-CNQ	Reims FR172F Rocket	FR17200077	
OH-CNR	Cessna 150J	15070065	N60092
OH-CNU	Reims FR172F Rocket	FR17200100	
OH-CNV	Cessna F150J	F150-0459	
OH-CNW	Cessna 180H Skywagon	18052002	N91215
OH-CNX	Cessna 150J	15070304	N60436
OH-COA	Cessna 152	15281987	N67737
OH-COD	Cessna 152	15282645	N89137
OH-COE	Cessna 152	15281990	N67744
OH-COF	Cessna 152	15281698	C-GLNJ N66973
OH-COG	Cessna 152	15283780	C-GULK N5156B
OH-COJ	Cessna A152 Aerobat	A1520773	N7581B
OH-COK	Cessna 172N	17267709	C-GYDH (N73835)
OH-CON	Cessna 172N	17273561	C-GDGY (N5542G)
OH-COO	Cessna 172C	17248855	SE-CYN N8355X
OH-COQ	Cessna 150L	15072425	N6925G
OH-COR	Reims/Cessna F172L	F17200833	SE-FXL
OH-COT	Cessna 172N	17269416	N737GW
OH-COU	Cessna F172H	F172-0624	SE-FEX
OH-COV	Cessna 172N	17270301	N738WU
OH-COX	Cessna A152 Aerobat	A1520897	N4809A
OH-COY	Cessna 152	15279480	C-GRDC N714WA
OH-CPA	Piper J-3C-65 Cub	12471	SE-ATF 44-80175
OH-CPE	Piper J-2 Cub (Modified)	1157	OH-LPA OH-SNB
OH-CPG	Piper J-3C-85 Cub	16879	D-EDIP N92415 NC92415
OH-CPO	Piper PA-22-108 Colt	22-9122	SE-CZB
OH-CPP(2)	Cessna 150G	15066344	C-FHCF CF-HCF N8444J
OH-CPT	Piper PA-18A-150 Super Cub	18-2632	SE-BXW N10F
OH-CPW	Piper PA-28-180 Cherokee B	28-1518	N7572W
OH-CRA	Cessna 152	15281374	N49873
OH-CRG	Cessna 177RG Cardinal RG	177RG0654	N333WE N2681V
OH-CRH	Cessna 170B	20918	C-GJZM N8066A
OH-CSA	Cessna 140	12679	SE-BFS
OH-CSC	Cessna 195B	16067	LN-BDR N4483C
OH-CSN	Cessna 180	30797	N2497C
OH-CSO	Cessna 170B	26766	N4422B
OH-CSP	Cessna 170B (Modified)	25167	N1111 N8315A
OH-CSU	Cessna U206A Super Skywagon	U206-0620	N4920F
OH-CSW	Cessna 150D	15060598	N4598U
OH-CSX	Cessna 140	8899	N89854
OH-CSY	Cessna 140	8292	N89268
OH-CTC	Cessna 152	15282266	C-GZZS N68339
OH-CTD	Cessna 172N	17268254	C-GWZQ N733FD
OH-CTE	Cessna TU206G Turbo Stationair 6	U20606883	OY-CGE N9534R
OH-CTH	Cessna 152	15283570	C-GDZL (N46628)
OH-CTL	Cessna 172M	17266211	N9537H
OH-CTM	Cessna 152	15279733	C-GPSS N757GR
OH-CTP	Cessna 172N	17273624	N9173G
OH-CTQ	Cessna 182P Skylane	18264729	C-GVPF N9184M
OH-CTU	Cessna 172M	17267525	C-GQNP N73517
OH-CTW	Cessna 150H	15067736	CF-WPW N7036S
OH-CTY	Cessna 182Q Skylane	18267492	N4971N
OH-CUB	Piper J-3C-65D Cub	12320	D-EFIL HB-OBT 44-80024
OH-CVA	Cessna 150F	15063334	N699LC N6734F
OH-CVB	Cessna 172P	17275246	N62286
OH-CVD	Cessna 172P	17275310	N62610
OH-CVE	Cessna 182P Skylane	18263510	N5741J
OH-CVK	Cessna 172N	17273786	N5418J
OH-CVL	Cessna 172M	17265792	C-GVOT N9848Q
OH-CVM	Cessna 172P	17274014	N5214K
OH-CVO	Cessna F150J	F150-0417	LN-NFR SE-FKP N13724
OH-CVP	Cessna 152	15283201	N47258
OH-CVQ	Cessna 172P	17274072	N5342K
OH-CVS	Cessna 172RG Cutlass RG	172RG0327	N5295U
OH-CVT	Cessna A185F Skywagon (W/o 25.6.03)	18502977	N500BW C-GJBI N102WC (N5012R)

OH-CVY	Cessna 152	15282185	C-GYRY (N68207)
OH-CVZ	Cessna 172P	17275663	C-FHXS N64979
OH-CWB	Cessna 172M	17262571	C-GCZC N13204
OH-CWE	Cessna 182H Skylane	18256418	D-EKWE N8318S
OH-CWH	Cessna 175C Skylark	17557108	SE-EAI N8508X
OH-CWM	Cessna 152	15280391	N204JA (N24808)
OH-CWO	Cessna 152	15282757	N89465
OH-CWQ	Cessna 170B	25798	C-GMJJ N3154A
OH-CWW	Cessna U206C Super Skywagon	U206-1076	LN-IKC N29106
OH-CYY	Cessna R172K Hawk XP	R1723121	N232JA N758HZ
OH-DAK	Cessna A185F Skywagon	18502880	LN-DAK (N3445Y)
OH-EKR	Cessna 421C Golden Eagle II	421C1235	N421MJ N421CF N396CC (N236MA) (N8BV) N2723C
OH-EBE	Embraer EMB.145LU	145351	HB-JAI PT-SNQ
OH-EBF	Embraer EMB.145LU	145387	HB-JAK PT-SQL
OH-EMA	Scintex Piel CP.301C2 Emeraude	574	
OH-ESM	Piper PA-32R-301T Turbo Saratoga SP	32R-8429026	N4377D N9630N
OH-EWA	Extra EA.300	020	D-EFCS
OH-FAE	SAAB-Scania SF.340A	139	SE-F39
OH-FAF	SAAB-Scania SF.340B	167	SE-F67
OH-FDA	Diamond DA 40D Star	D4.029	OE-VPU
OH-FEX	Dassault Falcon 2000EX	27	F-WWGZ
OH-FIX	Dassault Falcon 2000	179	F-WWMF
OH-FMA	Fouga CM-17D Magister	37	FinAF:FM-37
OH-FMM	Fouga CM-17D Magister	51	FinAF:FM-51
OH-FPC	Dassault Falcon 20F	345	N133AP F-GHMD N678BM N4463F F-WMKI
OH-HAF	Robinson R-22 Beta	0655	
OH-HAO	Robinson R-22 Beta	0988	D-HHAI G-HTRF
OH-HAP	Hughes 369HM	44-0247M	FinAF:HH-1
OH-HAT(2)	Agusta-Bell 206B Jet Ranger III	8720	
OH-HAV	Schweizer 269C	S-1277	SE-HUY OY-HED
OH-HAY	Hughes 269C	127-0662	SE-HNK N58210
OH-HBB	Robinson R-44 Raven II	10435	
OH-HCB	MBB Bö.105S	S-396	N10360
OH-HCC	MBB Bö.105CBS	S-546	AB-6 Dubai Pol:106 D-HDNU
OH-HCD	MBB Bö.105CBS	S-547	AB-7 Dubai Pol:107 D-HDNV
OH-HCF	DHC-1 Chipmunk (Lycoming 0-360-A3A)	C1/0016	OH-HCD G-AOSV WB564
OH-HCG	Aérospatiale AS.350B2 Ecureuil	2710	SE-JBX
OH-HCH	Eurocopter EC.135P1	0008	D-HPOZ D-HECH
OH-HCI	Sikorsky S-76C	760508	N7600P
OH-HCJ	Sikorsky S-76C	760510	
OH-HCK	Eurocopter EC.135P2	0378	
OH-HCL	Eurocopter EC.135P2	0379	
OH-HED	Robinson R-44 Clipper	0298	
OH-HEK	Robinson R-22 Beta	0742	
OH-HHC	Hiller UH-12B	732	RNethAF:O-4 54-2938
OH-HHT	Robinson R-44 Astro	0014	SE-JDG N144CH
OH-HIF	Agusta-Bell 206B Jet Ranger II	8372	
OH-HJJ	Eurocopter EC.120BColibri	1208	
OH-HJL	Bell 206L Long Ranger	45084	SE-HSO C-GISM N16628
OH-HJS	Schweizer 269C-1 (Reservation 2.05)	0202	N1565B
OH-HKC	Heinonen HK-1B	003	
OH-HKH	Bell 206B Jet Ranger II	4054	N206HM JA9817 C-GLZK
OH-HKI	MBB Bö.105S	S-731	D-HECB Fv.09415 D-HDRS
OH-HKP	Robinson R-22 Beta	0730	
OH-HKX	Heinonen HK-2 Valkuainen	1	
OH-HLA	Hughes 369D	50-0718D	SE-HLA OH-HLA OY-HSA SE-HLA
OH-HLK	Agusta-Bell 206B Jet Ranger II	8532	G-BEPP F-GAML
OH-HLL	Robinson R-44 Raven II (Res 3.12.04)	unkn	
OH-HLP	Bell 206B Jet Ranger II	1766	N49587
OH-HLT	Hughes 269C	128-0737	N58222
OH-HMA	MBB Bö.105C	S-88	D-HDCM HB-XEI D-HDCM
OH-HMB	MBB Bö.105S	S-891	D-HBIV D-HMB . (D-HFNW)
OH-HMC	MBB Bö.105CBS-4	S-341	SE-JFD D-HMVC
OH-HME	Robinson R-22 Beta	1357	LN-OBO N8081J
OH-HMH	Robinson R-22 Beta	2184	LN-OTV(3) G-BVLY SP-GSA
OH-HMP	Hughes 369D	51-0981D	N7102G N5012G
OH-HMS	MBB Bö.105S	S-703	D-HMBV(3) Fv09414 D-HNRK (D-HDRK)
OH-HMW	MBB Bö.105S	S-756	N724MB D-HDXR
OH-HMZ	Robinson R-22 Beta	1881	G-RZZB
OH-HNS	MBB Bö.105S	S-762	D-HNWI D-HDXX
OH-HOC	Robinson R-22 Beta	1339	
OH-HOE	Robinson R-22 Beta	1979	
OH-HOH	Bell 206L Long Ranger	45030	C-GIIP N221AM N66BH N66LJ N49770
OH-HOI	Aérospatiale AS.350B Ecureuil	1867	SE-HUO D-HHLL
OH-HOT	Bell 206B Jet Ranger II	3552	JA9321 N2230W
OH-HPF	Robinson R-44 (Reservation 1.05)	unkn	
OH-HPH	Robinson R-22 Beta	2115	OK-XIA
OH-HPJ	Robinson R-22 Beta	2411	LN-OBD N8152H
OH-HPK	Robinson R-22 Beta	1991	N2345P
OH-HPS	Schweizer 269C-1	0108	
OH-HPV	Robinson R-22 Beta	1735	
OH-HRG	Agusta-Bell 206A Jet Ranger II	8295	
OH-HRH	Agusta-Bell 206B Jet Ranger II	8380	
OH-HRI	Agusta-Bell 206B Jet Ranger III	8599	
OH-HRW	Robinson R-44 Astro	0364	OE-XSP
OH-HTE	Robinson R-22 Mariner	1771M	G-ISPL SE-JAL
OH-HTO	Robinson R-22 Beta	1270	LN-OBH SE-JGD OH-HWD HB-XVG
OH-HUG	Enstrom 280C Shark	1123	SE-HGN
OH-HUI	Bell 206BJet Ranger II	3128	OY-HHT G-BWBX D-HOLY N20WW N57521
OH-HVD	Agusta-Bell AB.412	25540	
OH-HVE	Agusta-Bell AB.412	25541	
OH-HVF	Aérospatiale AS.332L Super Puma	2218	F-WMHE F-WYMI
OH-HVG	Aérospatiale AS.332L Super Puma	2221	
OH-HVH	Agusta-Bell AB.412	25609	
OH-HVI	Aérospatiale AS.332L1 Super Puma	2341	
OH-HVJ	Agusta-Bell AB.412EP	25903	
OH-HVK	Bell 412EP	36242	N6390Z C-GAHJ
OH-HWC	Robinson R-22 Mariner (W/o 24.3.00)	2055M	OY-HFS
OH-HWF	Robinson R-22 Beta	1702	HB-XXX
OH-HWH	Hughes 369D	50-0702D	D-HSUR CS-HCU D-HSUR G-HEWT N808F N1095D
OH-HWI	Aérospatiale AS.350B2 Ecureuil	9044	
OH-HYY	Enstrom 280C Shark (Res 31.10.03)	1083	N280EC TG-WEY
OH-HZH	Robinson R-44 Astro	0254	D-HHEY
OH-H . .	Hughes 369E	0546E	N7027P
OH-H . .	Hughes 369E	0552E	N7032R
OH-ILI	Klemm Kl.25D.VIIR	1129	
OH-IPJ	Bombardier Learjet 45	45-104	N40012
OH-IRB	Pylväläinen/Tiira replica	02	

OH-JSR	Cessna 172R (Reservation 13.12.04)	17281239	
OH-JTM	Piper PA-28R-201 Cherokee Arrow III (Reservation .04)	28R-7737074	D-ENKW
			SE-GPV
OH-JUS	Maule M-4-210C Rocket	1047C	SE- IGF
			LN-VYD
OH-KJJ	SOCATA TBM-700C (Res as D-FTBM .03)	258	
OH-KLS	Cessna 152	15282409	SE-KLS
			N68940
OH-KNE	Mitsubishi MU-300 Diamond	A.014SA	N339DM
			N15TW
OH-KOG	DHC-6 Twin Otter 310	642	
OH-KRA	Aérospatiale/Alenia ATR-72-201	126	F-WWEM
OH-KRB	Aérospatiale/Alenia ATR-72-201	140	F-WWER
OH-KRC	Aérospatiale/Alenia ATR-72-201	145	F-WWES
OH-KRD	Aérospatiale/Alenia ATR-72-201	162	F-WWEM
OH-KRE	Aérospatiale/Alenia ATR-72-201	174	F-WWEE
OH-KRF	Aérospatiale/Alenia ATR-72-201	324	F-WWEU
OH-KRH	Aérospatiale/Alenia ATR-72-201	212	B-22705
			F-WWEB
OH-KRK	Aérospatiale/Alenia ATR-72-201	251	B-22706
			F-WWEV
OH-KRL	Aérospatiale/Alenia ATR-72-201	332	B-22710
			F-WWLN
OH-KST	Piper PA-28-151 Cherokee Warrior	28-7415281	SE-KST
			N41582
OH-KYC	Piper PA-31-350 Chieftain	31-8052186	SE-KYC
			N4502V
OH-KZE	S.A.I. KZ-VII Laerke	168	OY-ABC
OH-LBO	Boeing 757-2Q8	28172	N1789B
OH-LBR	Boeing 757-2Q8	28167	
OH-LBS	Boeing 757-2Q8	27623	N5573K
OH-LBT	Boeing 757-2Q8	28170	
OH-LBU	Boeing 757-2Q8	29377	
OH-LBV	Boeing 757-2Q8	30046	
OH-LBX	Boeing 757-2Q8	29382	
OH-LCH	Douglas DC-3C	6346	FinAF:DO-11
			OH-LCH
			42-2033
			(NC34953)
OH-LGA	McDonnell-Douglas MD-11	48449	
OH-LGB	McDonnell-Douglas MD-11	48450	
OH-LGC	McDonnell-Douglas MD-11	48512	
OH-LGD	McDonnell-Douglas MD-11	48513	
OH-LGE	McDonnell-Douglas MD-11	48780	P4-SWM
			P4-TKB
			OO-CTC
OH-LGF	McDonnell-Douglas MD-11	48766	P4-BDL
			OO-CTB
			N6203D
OH-LMG	McDonnell-Douglas DC-9-87	49625	
OH-LMH	McDonnell-Douglas DC-9-83	53245	
OH-LMX	McDonnell-Douglas DC-9-82	49906	
OH-LMY	McDonnell-Douglas DC-9-82	53244	
OH-LPA	McDonnell-Douglas DC-9-82	49900	EC-FJQ
			EC-893
			N64480
			N6202D
OH-LPB	McDonnell-Douglas DC-9-82	49966	SE-DLX
			N6204N
OH-LPC	McDonnell-Douglas DC-9-82	49965	SE-DLV
			N6204C
OH-LPD	McDonnell-Douglas DC-9-83	49710	EC-GFJ
			EC-159
			SX-BAQ
			HB-IUI
			XA-TOR
OH-LPG	McDonnell-Douglas DC-9-83	49708	EC-GKS
			EC-440
			EC-FVV
			EC-607
			TC-RTU
			XA-TUR
			N6203U
OH-LVA	Airbus A319-112	1073	F-WWID
			D-AVWG
OH-LVB	Airbus A319-112	1107	D-AVWS
OH-LVC	Airbus A319-112	1309	D-AVWY
OH-LVD	Airbus A319-112	1352	D-AVYW
OH-LVE	Airbus A319-112	1791	D-AVYS
OH-LVF	Airbus A319-112	1808	D-AVWG
OH-LVG	Airbus A319-112	1916	(OH-LVF)
			D-AVYG
OH-LVH	Airbus A319-112	1184	EI-CZE
			OO-SSH
			D-AVYR
OH-LVI	Airbus A319-112	1364	F-WQQZ
			(F-GYYY)
			OO-SSL
			D-AVWL
OH-LVK	Airbus A319-112	2124	D-AVWB
OH-LVL	Airbus A319-112	2266	D-AVWS
OH-LXA	Airbus A320-214	1405	F-WWDH
OH-LXB	Airbus A320-214	1470	F-WWDO
OH-LXC	Airbus A320-214	1544	F-WWIX
OH-LXD	Airbus A320-214	1588	F-WWBQ
OH-LXE	Airbus A320-214	1678	F-WWIF

OH-LXF	Airbus A320-214	1712	F-WWIY
OH-LXG	Airbus A320-214	1735	F-WWBM
OH-LXH	Airbus A320-214	1913	F-WWIZ
OH-LXI	Airbus A320-214	1989	F-WWDN
OH-LXJ	Airbus A320-214 (Reservation)	unkn	
OH-LXK	Airbus A320-214	2065	F-WWIQ
OH-LXL	Airbus A320-214	2146	F-WWDN
OH-LXM	Airbus A320-214	2154	F-WWDP
OH-LZA	Airbus A321-211	941	D-AVZT
OH-LZB	Airbus A321-211	961	D-AVZU
OH-LZC	Airbus A321-211	1185	D-AVZI
OH-LZD	Airbus A321-211	1241	D-AVZG
OH-LZE	Airbus A321-211	1978	D-AVZV
OH-LZF	Airbus A321-211	2208	D-AVZI
OH-MAB	Maule M-6-235C Super Rocket	7384C	N49846
OH-MAE	Maule M-7-235C Super Rocket	4097C	N9224T
OH-MAF	Cessna U206A Super Skywagon	U206-0639	N4939F
			5Y-ANK
			N4939F
OH-MAI	Maule M-5-235C Lunar Rocket	7314C	N5638M
OH-MAJ	Maule MX.7-180 Star Rocket	11064C	
OH-MAT	Maule M-7-235 Super Rocket	4030C	N56636
OH-MAU	Maule MX.7-235 Star Rocket	10068C	
OH-MIK	Maule M-6-235C Super Rocket	7392C	N5649D
OH-MIL	Maule M-6-235C Super Rocket	7427C	N56485
OH-MIV	Piper PA-32R-301 Saratoga SP	32R-8213035	SE-KRU
			N8146R
OH-MOI	Maule M-6-235C Super Rocket	7189C	N235LY
OH-MVN	Dornier 228-212	8233	D-CBDB(4)
			D-CATE(2)
OH-MVO	Dornier 228-212	8232	D-CATD(2)
OH-MXN	Lake LA-4-200 Buccaneer	934	G-BMXN
			EC-DHI
			N2872P
OH-NAD	Cessna 170A	19600	N5547C
OH-NBB	Cessna 172M	17263963	N21526
OH-NBE	Piper PA-34-200T Seneca II	34-8170050	OY-NBB
			(OY-CJN)
			N8306H
			C-GSVL
			N8306H
OH-NEU	Reims/Cessna FA152 Aerobat	FA1520422	
OH-NTE	FFA AS.202/18A4 Bravo	224	G-BNTE
OH-NTF	FFA AS.202/18A4 Bravo	225	G-BNTF
OH-NTH	FFA AS.202/18A4 Bravo	227	G-BNTH
OH-NTI	FFA AS.202/18A4 Bravo	228	G-BNTI
OH-NTJ	FFA AS.202/18A4 Bravo	229	G-BNTJ
OH-NTK	FFA AS.202/18A4 Bravo	230	G-BNTK
OH-NTL	FFA AS.202/18A4 Bravo	231	G-BNTL
OH-NTN	FFA AS.202/18A4 Bravo	233	G-BNTN
OH-NTO	FFA AS.202/18A4 Bravo	234	G-BNTO
OH-ONE	Cessna 560XL Citation Excel	560-5157	N40577
			N5163G
OH-OTL	Cessna 208 Caravan I (Res 20.12.04)	unkn	
OH-PAC	Piper PA-28-180 Cherokee Archer	28-7505109	
OH-PAD	Piper J-3C-65 Cub	12522	D-EJIB
			LN-SAG
			44-80226
OH-PAE	Piper J-3C-65 Cub	13137	D-EMYR
			OO-AVZ
			44-80841
OH-PAF	Piper PA-28RT-201 Arrow IV	28R-8018069	FinAF: PA-11
			OH-PAF
OH-PAI	Piper PA-28RT-201 Arrow IV	28R-8018093	FinAF: PA-14
			OH-PAI
OH-PAM	Piper PA-28R-200 Cherokee Arrow	28R-7635265	SE-GNK
OH-PAN	Piper PA-28-151 Cherokee Warrior	28-7615164	
OH-PAR	Piper PA-30 Twin Comanche B	30-1597	(G-BBYN)
			OH-PAR
			G-BBYN
			PH-ATS
			N8437Y
OH-PAW	Piper PA-28R-200 Cherokee Arrow II	28R-7335208	FinAF:PA-5
			SE-GDC
OH-PAX	Cessna T206H Turbo Stationair	T20608283	N35342
OH-PAY	Piper PA-42-1000 Cheyenne 400	42-5527040	JA8870
			N9219G
			N9524N
OH-PBA	Piper PA-28RT-201T Turbo Arrow IV	28R-8431007	N4332J
OH-PCB	Piper PA-28-140 Cherokee B	28-26116	
OH-PCE	Piper PA-28-140 Cherokee B	28-26276	N5552U
OH-PCH	Piper PA-28-160 Cherokee B	28-26296	
OH-PCI	Piper PA-28-160 Cherokee B	28-26297	
OH-PCJ	Piper PA-28-140 Cherokee B	28-26298	
OH-PCK	Piper PA-28-140 Cherokee B	28-26309	
OH-PCL	Piper PA-28-140 Cherokee C	28-26605	
OH-PCN	Piper PA-28-140 Cherokee C	28-26699	N5867U
OH-PCO	Piper PA-28-140 Cherokee C	28-26763	
OH-PCP	Piper PA-28-140 Cherokee C	28-26774	
OH-PCW	Piper PA-28-140 Cherokee C	28-26411	SE-FHI
OH-PDB	Piper PA-28-140 Cherokee C	28-26610	SE-FPD
OH-PDD	Piper PA-28R-200 Cherokee Arrow	28R-7135010	SE-FPP
OH-PDF	Piper PA-28-140 Cherokee E	28-7325150	
OH-PDG	Piper PA-28R-200 Cherokee Arrow II	28R-7335165	FinAF:PA-6
			OH-PDG
OH-PDH	Piper PA-28-140 Cherokee E	28-7325217	
OH-PDI	Piper PA-28-140 Cherokee E	28-7325337	

OH-PDJ	Piper PA-28-160E Cherokee	28-7325330	
OH-PDL	Piper PA-28-160F Cherokee	28-7425006	
OH-PDO	Piper PA-18-150 Super Cub	18-1446	D-EKQB
			ALAT
			51-15446
OH-PDP	Piper PA-28-160E Cherokee	28-7325323	SE-GAV
OH-PDQ	Piper PA-28-140 Cherokee (Modified)	28-20094	SE-EIT
OH-PDT	Piper PA-28-140 Cherokee Cruiser	28-7525077	
OH-PDU	Piper PA-28-160 Cherokee F	28-7425414	
OH-PDV	Piper PA-28-161 Warrior II	28-7916336	SE-ICI
OH-PDW	Piper PA-25-235 Pawnee B	25-3673	SE-EPX
OH-PDX	Piper J-3C-85 Cub	15179	D-EFIB
			N42857
			NC42857
OH-PDY	Piper PA-28R-200 Cherokee Arrow II	28R-7435013	FinAF:PA-2
OH-PDZ	Piper PA-25-235 Pawnee C	25-4163	SE-EZA
OH-PEA	Piper PA-28R-201 Cherokee Arrow III	28R-7737036	C-GQHD
OH-PEM	Piper PA-28R-180 Cherokee Arrow	28R-30406	SE-FDM
			N4545J
OH-PEN	Piper PA-28-181 Archer II	2890113	SE-KIC
OH-PEO	Piper PA-23-250 Aztec B	27-2104	SE-ECO
OH-PEP	Piper PA-18-135 Super Cub	18-3105	LN-LJL
			OL-L31
			53-4705
OH-PEU	Piper PA-28-161 Warrior II	28-8116165	N8345T
OH-PEV	Piper PA-28-180 Cherokee C	28-2133	SE-EMT
OH-PEW	Piper PA-25-235 Pawnee	25-2579	SE-IUR
			G-ATYA
			5B-CAA
			N6885Z
			N10F
OH-PGA	Piper PA-28RT-201T Turbo Arrow IV	28R-8331014	N8341F
OH-PHE	Piper PA-28-161 Cherokee Warrior II	28-7716103	SE-GPS
			N9622N
OH-PIA	Piper PA-28-140 Cherokee	28-21561	SE-EYF
OH-PIF	Piper PA-28-140 Cherokee	28-21864	SE-EYW
OH-PIG	Piper PA-25-235 Pawnee B	25-3959	N7766Z
OH-PIJ	Piper PA-28-140 Cherokee	28-23353	
OH-PIL	Piper PA-25-235 Pawnee C	25-4164	N10F
OH-PIO	Piper PA-28-140 Cherokee	28-22707	N4332J
OH-PIR	Piper PA-28-140 Cherokee	28-23580	
OH-PIT	Piper PA-18-150 Super Cub	18-8598	
OH-PIY	Piper PA-28-235 Cherokee B	28-10919	SE-EYK
OH-PJC	Piper PA-28-140 Cherokee	28-24341	
OH-PJD	Piper PA-28-140 Cherokee	28-24426	SE-FDK
OH-PJE	Piper PA-28-140 Cherokee	28-24196	N1774J
OH-PJF	Piper PA-28-140 Cherokee B	28-25482	
OH-PJH	Piper PA-28-140 Cherokee B	28-25590	
OH-PJJ	Piper PA-28-140 Cherokee B	28-25686	
OH-PJK	Piper PA-18-150 Super Cub	18-8787	
OH-PJO	Piper PA-28-140 Cherokee B	28-26050	
OH-PJR	Piper PA-28R-200 Cherokee Arrow	28R-35257	SE-FFX
OH-PJS	Piper PA-28-140 Cherokee B	28-25698	SE-FHF
OH-PJU	Piper PA-28R-200 Cherokee Arrow	28R-35286	
OH-PJV	Piper PA-28R-200 Cherokee Arrow	28R-35267	SE-FHK
OH-PJX	Piper PA-28R-200 Cherokee Arrow	28R-35383	
OH-PJY	Piper PA-28-140 Cherokee B	28-26009	
OH-PKO	Piper PA-34-220T Seneca V	3449173	SE-ITV
			N9524N
OH-PKT	Piper PA-28-181 Archer II	28-8490093	N4368M
OH-PLL	Piper PA-28-181 Archer II	28-43269	LN-TFR
			N9526N
OH-PMI	Piper PA-28R-180 Cherokee Arrow	28R-30225	LN-UXN
OH-PMJ(2)	Piper PA-18-150 Super Cub	18-7933	D-ENPO
OH-PMK	Piper PA-28R-200 Cherokee Arrow II	28R-7335030	N15161
OH-PMU	Piper PA-32R-301T Turbo Saratoga SP	32R-8129083	N8409B
OH-PNB	Piper PA-31 Turbo Navajo	31-609	N6714L
OH-PNJ	Piper PA-23-250 Aztec E	27-7304983	N14388
OH-PNL	Piper PA-31 Turbo Navajo	31-253	SE-FLE
			D-INKA
			(D-IDUL)
			N919OY
OH-PNU	Piper PA-31-350 Navajo Chieftain	31-7752027	N62993
OH-PNX	Piper PA-31-350 Chieftain	31-8052040	ES-PAG
			SE-IDC
OH-PNY	Piper PA-31-350 Navajo Chieftain	31-7652079	LN-SAB
			SE-GNX
			N9690N
OH-POK	Piper PA-18-150 Super Cub (Mod.)	18-8509	
OH-PPG	Piper PA-36-300 Pawnee Brave	36-7560005	SE-GIV
OH-PPI	Cessna 750 Citation X	750-0115	N5085E
OH-PPR	Dassault Falcon 900EX	118	F-WWFS
"OH-PPS"	Piper PA-23-250 Aztec D	27-4017	N612RS
	(Painted as such but not officially regd.)		N6744Y
OH-PRB	Piper PA-31 Navajo C	31-7812124	N27793
OH-PRK	Piper PA-28RT-201 Arrow IV	28R-8118064	N83730
OH-PRS	Piper PA-28-140 Cherokee	28-20305	LN-AEB
			N11C
OH-PRT	Piper PA-32RT-300 Lance II	32R-7885011	N3602M
OH-PSA	Piper PA-18-150 Super Cub	18-6900	(OH-XWZ)
			OH-PSA
			LN-BDL
			OY-AIM
			N9878D
OH-PTA	Piper PA-38-112 Tomahawk	38-78A0056	
OH-PTC	Piper PA-38-112 Tomahawk	38-78A0463	D-EXSN
			OE-ASN
			N9723N
OH-PTH	Piper PA-28-161 Warrior II	28-8016293	SE- IDL
OH-PTI	Piper PA-28-180 Cherokee B	28-1650	SE-EIL
OH-PTJ	Piper PA-28R-200 Cherokee Arrow II	28R-7235221	(SE-KLP)
			N5299T
OH-PUL	Piper PA-24-180 Comanche	24-3021	N7802P
OH-PUM	Piper PA-20 Pacer 125	20-341	SE-CTC
			N7431K
OH-PVD	Piper PA-34-200 Seneca	34-7250186	OY-MVD
			D-GHFC
			N4939T
OH-PVL	Piper PA-28-151 Cherokee Warrior	28-7415493	C-GCXZ
			N43442
OH-PVN	Piper PA-28R-180 Cherokee Arrow	28R-30484	SE-FCF
OH-PWB	Piper PA-28-161 Warrior II	28-8616030	N9258A
OH-PYM	Piper PA-28RT-201T Turbo Arrow IV	28R-8131139	N8392M
OH-PYW	Piper PA-28-181 Cherokee Archer II	28-7790557	N81AB
OH-PZL	Piper PA-34-200T Seneca II	34-7970047	SE-IZL
			N2120H
OH-RAB	Robin HR.200/120B	81	
OH-SAH	Avro 146-RJ85	E-2383	G-6-383
OH-SAI	Avro 146-RJ85	E-2385	G-6-385
OH-SAJ	Avro 146-RJ85	E-2388	G-6-388
OH-SAK	Avro 146-RJ85	E-2389	G-6-389
OH-SAL	Avro 146-RJ85	E-2392	G-6-390
OH-SAM	Avro 146-RJ100	E-3386	G-NBAA
OH-SAN	Avro 146-RJ100	E-3387	G-CBMF
OH-SAO	Avro 146-RJ85	E-2393	G-CBMG
OH-SAP	Avro 146-RJ85	E-2394	G-CBMH
OH-SAS	SAAB 2000	044	SE-LSC
			SE-044
OH-SAT	SAAB 2000	042	SE-LSA
			SE-042
OH-SAU	SAAB 2000	043	SE-LSB
			SE-043
OH-SAW	SAAB 2000	046	SE-LSE
			SE-046
OH-SAX	SAAB 2000	055	SE-LSG
			SE-055
OH-SBA	Short SC.7 Skyliner 3A-100	SH.1908	SE-GEY
			LN-NPC
			G-BAIT
			G-14-80
OH-SCC	SOCATA MS.893A Rallye Commodore 180	10697	
OH-SCF	SOCATA MS.893A Rallye Commodore 180	10720	
OH-SCK	SOCATA MS.880B Rallye-Club	1286	
OH-SCM	SOCATA MS.880B Rallye-Club	1320	
OH-SCN	SOCATA MS.880B Rallye-Club	1330	
OH-SCT	SOCATA MS.880B Rallye-Club	1343	
OH-SCU	SOCATA MS.893A Rallye Commodore 180	10994	
OH-SCV	SOCATA MS.883 Rallye 115	1367	
OH-SCX	SOCATA MS.880B Rallye-Club	1375	(G-AXHH)
OH-SCZ	SOCATA MS.894A Minerva 220	11069	
OH-SDA	SOCATA MS.893A Rallye Commodore 180	11447	
OH-SDC	SOCATA MS.892A Rallye Commodore 150	11444	
OH-SDE	SOCATA MS.883 Rallye 115 (Res 8.03)	1530	
OH-SDG	SOCATA MS.880B Rallye-Club	1563	
OH-SDI	SOCATA MS.880B Rallye-Club	1650	
OH-SDJ	SOCATA MS.892A Rallye Commodore 150	11490	
OH-SDL	SOCATA MS.892A Rallye Commodore 150	11429	
OH-SDM	SOCATA MS.893A Rallye Commodore 180	11449	
OH-SDN	SOCATA MS.892A Rallye Commodore 150	11640	F-BSFH
OH-SDO	SOCATA MS.892A Rallye Commodore 150	11717	
OH-SDR	SOCATA MS.880B Rallye-Club	1737	
OH-SDU	SOCATA MS.880B Rallye-Club	1962	
OH-SDV	SOCATA MS.893A Rallye Commodore 180	11925	
OH-SDW	SOCATA MS.894A Minerva 220	11974	
OH-SDX	SOCATA MS.894A Minerva 220	11942	
OH-SDZ	SOCATA MS.8808 Rallye-Club	1964	
OH-SEA	SOCATA MS.892A Rallye Commodore 150	11878	
OH-SEB	SOCATA MS.894A Minerva 220	11976	
OH-SED	SOCATA MS.893A Rallye Commodore 180	11867	F-BTHX
OH-SEE	SOCATA MS.893E Rallye 180GT Gaillard	12530	
OH-SEG	SOCATA MS.892E Rallye 150T	2652	
OH-SEH	SOCATA MS.880B Rallye Club	2557	
OH-SEI	SOCATA Rallye 235E Gabier	12800	
OH-SEW	SOCATA Rallye 235E-D Gabier	12799	D-EDRK
OH-SFF	SAAB S.91D Safir	91350	FinAF:SF-4
OH-SFH	SAAB S.91D Safir	91415	FinAF:SF-27
OH-SFJ	SAAB S.91D Safir	91412	FinAF:SF-24
OH-SFN	SAAB S.91D Safir	91362	FinAF:SF-16
OH-SFP	SAAB S.91D Safir	91410	FinAF:SF-22
OH-SIS	Cessna 208 Caravan I	20800105	LN-PBD
			OY-TCA
			(LN-PBA)
			OY-TCA
			(OY-CJL)
			N9604F
			N105YV
			N9604F
OH-SLK	DHC-6 Twin Otter 300	260	SE-GEG
			CF-JCH
OH-SPA	Gyroflug SC.01B-160 Speed Canard	S-30	SE- IVB
			(OH-SPA)
OH-SPP	Cessna T206HTurbo Stationair	T20608357	N5167D

OH-SUN	Cessna 182Q Skylane	18265392	SE-KUL
			N735FQ
OH-SZJ	Focke-Wulf FW.44J Stieglitz	2927	FinAF:SZ-24
OH-SZR	Focke-Wulf FW.44J Stieglitz	unkn	FinAF:SZ-10
OH-TBG	SOCATA TB-10 Tobago	631	SE-KBE
			F-GFDX
			N20EY
OH-TJS	SOCATA TB-21 Trinidad TC	744	F-GFQL
OH-TOW	Valmet PIK-23 Towmaster	001	
OH-TUG	Valmet PIK-23 Suhinu	002	N255H
	(W/o 11.6.91)		OH-TUG
OH-TZA	Zlin 126 (Lycoming, modified)	847	
OH-UDZ	Cessna T207A Turbo Skywagon (Soloy Pac)	20700388	D-EXWG
			HB-CLR
			N1788U
OH-USI	Cessna 208 Caravan I	20800275	
OH-UTI	Rockwell Commander 690A	11204	SE-GSR
			D- IGAA
OH-VAA	Valmet L-70	31	
OH-VFR	Cessna 180H	18052106	LN-UXY
			N9006M
OH-VJL	PZL-104 Wilga 35A	20890874	
OH-VKW	Cessna T188C Ag Husky	T18803674T	N3842J
OH-VTP	Valmet L-90TP Redigo	001	
OH-WAA	Wassmer CE-43 Guepard	440	
OH-WAC	Wassmer WA.54 Atlantic	138	
OH-WBA	Mitsubishi MU-2N (MU-2B-36A)	718SA	N150BA
			C-GJSD
			N715US
			VH-ENH
			N889MA
OH-WIC	Canadair CL.600-2B16 Challenger	5452	N452WU
			C-GLXM
OH-WIF	Dassault Falcon 20F	461	N353CP
			N747V
			N469F
			F-WMKG
OH-WIN	Dassault Falcon 20F	481	N250RA
			N502F
			F-WLCS
OH-WIP	Dassault Falcon 20F	359	N369CE
			N369CA
			(N508L)
			N50SL
			N35RZ
			N647JP
			N64769
			HZ-AO1
			HZ-TAG
			(N64769)
			F-WRQR
OH-XAB	Corby Starlet	492	
OH-XAL	Brügger MB-2 Colibri	04	
OH-XAP	Rand-Robinson KR-2	188	
OH-XAR	Pitts S-12 (Reservation 2.05)	31-62-04	
OH-XAS	Rand-Robinson KR-2	01	
OH-XAT	ATOL 575SF (Reservation 9.03)	0901	
OH-XCC	Fantasy Air Cora Arius F (Mod)	99-302	OH-U367
OH-XCG	Rutan Cozy Classic	1033	
OH-XCH	Denney Kitfox III	961	9H-ACH
OH-XCO	Brügger MB-2 Colibri	1	
OH-XCY	Kaipainen PK-3 Rallyette	01	
	(Built from MS.883 Rallye 115 c/n 1361 ex OH-SCY)		
OH-XBK	Bleriot XI Replica	410	
OH-XEA	Christen Eagle II	01	
OH-XEB	Nicollier HN.700 Ménestrel II	48	
OH-XEC	Fox Christen Eagle II	002	N444LF
OH-XEL	Aero Designs Pulsar XP (Reservn 5.03)	unkn	
OH-XES	Druine D.31 Turbulent (Modified)	01	
OH-XFA	Bowers Fly-Baby A-1	02	
OH-XFK	Rotorway Exec	226	
OH-XGA	Grob G.115 (Reservation 6.10.04)	8068	OO-NZD
			OO-XZD
			G-BPSY
			D-EAMH
OH-XGK	Stoddard-Hamilton Glasair ITD	355	
OH-XGT	Gloster Gauntlet II (Modified)	G5/35957	FinAF:GT-400
	(Painted as "GT-400")		K5271
OH-XHC	Revolution Mini 500	0110	
OH-XHI	Rotorway Exec	223	
OH-XHN	Christen Eagle II	2	
OH-XHO	Rotorway Exec	1059	
OH-XHU	Denney Kitfox	334	
OH-XHW	Rotorway Exec 162F	6232	
OH-XJA	Jodel D.92 Bébé (Reservation 1.05)	43	F-PEHO
OH-XJB	Pottier P.220S Koala	464	
OH-XJH	Bowers Fly Baby 1A	85-1	
OH-XJJ	Zenair CH-701 STOL (Reservation 6.03)	513	
OH-XJK	Acey Deucy P-70	01	
OH-XJP	Neico Lancair 320	169	
OH-XJO	Europa Aviation Europa XS (Res 17.10.03)	unkn	
OH-XJT	Van's RV-6 (Reservation 26.5.04)	unkn	
OH-XKD	Van's RV-4	3006	
OH-XKJ	Neico Lancair 320	1	

OH-XKK	Pereira Osprey 2	01	
OH-XKR	Denney Kitfox IV	1617	
OH-XKS	Rans S-10 Sakota	0291126	
OH-XKV	Rotorway Exec	855	
OH-XLA	de Havilland DH.82A Tiger Moth	85167	OH-ELA
	(Lycoming Mod)		G-AMJR
			T6958
OH-XLS	Cessna 150XL	0317	OH-CCT
	(Tailwheel conversion of Cessna F150H c/n F150-0317)		
OH-XLT	Taylor JT-1 Monoplane	01	
OH-XMA	Monnett Sonerai I	123	
OH-XMB	Monnett Sonerai I (Reservation 11.01)	unkn	
OH-XME	PIK-21 Super-Sytky	402	
OH-XMR	PIK-21 Super-Sytky	4/453	
OH-XMT	Van's RV-6	1	
OH-XOH	Rotorway Exec 162F	6119	
OH-XOT	Van's RV-6	20261	
OH-XPA	Pitts S-1 Special	01	
OH-XPC	Pitts S-1S Special	04	
OH-XPF	Pitts S-1 Special	541-H	N51DM
OH-XPH	Super Colibri PH1 (Reservation 11.02)	unkn	
OH-XPS	EAA Biplane B2	1-596	SE-XHF
			N3DB
OH-XPW	Monnett Sonerai IIL	936	
OH-XRK	Tervamaki JT-5	01	
OH-XRM	Monnett Sonerai II (Reservation 12.1.04)	unkn	
OH-XRS	Murphy Renegade Spirit (Mod.)	349	OH-U279
OH-XRV	Van's RV-6 (Reservation 10.2.04)	unkn	
OH-XRW	Van's RV-6	22452	
OH-XSF	Ultimate 10-300S	300-003	
OH-XSH	Aero Designs Pulsar XP	137	
OH-XSS	Smyth Sidewinder RG	01	
OH-XST	Light Aero Avid Flyer Speed Wing	344	
OH-XSW	Sorrell SNS-7 Hiperbipe	294	
OH-XTA	Taylor JT.1 Monoplane	01	
OH-XTI	PIK-18 Sytky	01	
OH-XTK	Van's RV-4	1945	
OH-XTM	PIK-21 Super-Sytky	01	
OH-XTR	Van's RV-6	22033	
OH-XVB	Evans VP-2	02	
OH-XVO	Rand-Robinson KR-2	01	
OH-XVP	Pober Pixie	352	(OH-XOV)
			(OH-XPV)
OH-XVX	Tervamaki JT-5	04	
OH-XVY	Taupila HAT-4 gyrocopter (Bensen B-8M mod.)	03	
OH-XWS	PIK-18 Sytky (Reservation 12.9.03)	394	
OH-XXS	Cessna F172G (Reservation 2.02)	F172-0254	ES-. . .
			OH-CEM
OH-XYA	PIK-27 (Reservation 4.03)	unkn	
OH-XYM	Tervamaki JT-5	02	
OH-XYQ	Tervamaki-Eerola ATE-3	02	
OH-YHB	PIK-15 Hinu	002	
OH-YHD	PIK-15 Hinu	006	
OH-YHE	PIK-15 Hinu	005	
OH-YHF	PIK-15 Hinu	004	
OH-YMC	PIK-11 Tumppu	3	

HOT-AIR BALLOONS AND AIRSHIPS

OH-AAH	Cameron Pack-130 SS HAFB	10101	
OH-APU	Cameron N-65 HAFB	4586	
OH-ARM	Ultramagic V-77 HAFB	77/31	
OH-BKK	Lindstrand LBL-120A HAFB	527	
OH-DBF	Ultramagic N-180 HAFB	180/12	
OH-DCF	Ultramagic M-65 HAFB	65/80	
OH-DEF	Lindstrand LBL-69A HAFB (Res 7.1.05)	unkn	
OH-DFA	Thunder AX7-65 HAFB	1176	
OH-DKK	Ultramagic H-77 HAFB	77/223	
OH-DUO	Lindstrand LBL-150A	590	
OH-ENV	Ultramagic V-90 HAFB	90/18	
OH-ERI	Lindstrand LBL-150A HAFB	449	
OH-ESA	Cameron A-300 HAFB	10310	
OH-ESO	Cameron N-90 HAFB	4030	
OH-FUN	Colt 105A HAFB	992	G-TALK
OH-GAS	Colt 69A HAFB	1800	
OH-GAZ	Lindstrand LBL-77A HAFB	567	
OH-GSM	Lindstrand LBL-120A HAFB	031	
OH-IDA	Cameron A-140 HAFB	4062	
OH-ISO	Lindstrand LBL-210A HAFB	522	
OH-JEP	Cameron Concept C-70 HAFB	4417	
OH-JOY	Colt 77A HAFB	1106	
OH-JTI	Cameron A-180 HAFB	2107	G-TIBC
OH-JUL	Cameron O-77 HAFB	1498	
OH-KFF	Lindstrand LBL-105A HAFB	872	
OH-KID	Thunder AX7-77 HAFB	1288	
OH-KUU	Ultramagic H-65 HAFB	65/53	
OH-KVT	Colt 69A HAFB	1949	
OH-KWH	Cameron Concept C-70 HAFB	4418	
OH-MAA	Ultramagic V-56 HAFB	56/07	
OH-MIN	Ultramagic M-145 HAFB	145/17	
OH-MMH	Cameron A-275 HAFB	4574	
OH-MPM	Lindstrand LBL-77A HAFB	610	
OH-MUS	Cameron N-90 HAFB	1791	
OH-NET	Cameron C-90 HAFB	10415	

OH-NMT	Lindstrand LBL-56A HAFB	030	
OH-OJP	Ultramagic S-160 HAFB	160/28	
OH-OLY	Cameron N-105 HAFB	10213	
OH-OOH	Cameron Concept C-70 HAFB	10318	
OH-OPE	Ultramagic H-65 HAFB	65/32	
OH-POP	Cameron O-77 HAFB	510	
OH-PRO	Kubicek BB-22 HAFB	281	OK-0281
OH-RBB	Lindstrand LBL-330A HAFB	1014	
OH-RJH	Cameron Concept C-80 HAFB	4968	
OH-SBS	Ultramagic M-145 HAFB	145/18	
OH-SKI	Kubicek BB-45 HAFB	258	OK-0258
OH-SMT	Cameron N-120 HAFB	4816	
OH-SOL	Ultramagic S-130 HAFB	130/09	
OH-SSK	Ultramagic H-65 HAFB	65/136	
OH-TKP	Lindstrand LBL-77B HAFB	206	
OH-TON	Colt 56A HAFB	1541	
OH-TSS	Thunder AX7-77 HAFB	692	
OH-TTR	Thunder AX7-77 HAFB	1221	
OH-TWW	Thunder AX7-77 HAFB (Res 20.4.04)	1142	
OH-TYA	Colt 56A HAFB	1816	
OH-VAL	Colt 77A HAFB	1285	
OH-VLK	Cameron N-65 HAFB	10040	
OH-XSK	Cameron O-56 HAFB	419	
OH-YIT	Ultramagic M-77 HAFB	77/157	
OH-ZDD	Viking 69A HAFB	SLB-007	SE-ZDD

GLIDERS AND MOTOR-GLIDERS

OH-031	PIK-7 Harakka III	2	H-31
OH-034	Harakka II	5	H-35
OH-151	PIK-5c Cumulus (Restored, formerly PIK-5b)	15	OH-PAP
OH-170	Schleicher Ka 2B Rhönschwalbe	23	OH-KKA
OH-171	Schleicher Ka 2B Rhönschwalbe	24	OH-KKB
OH-183	Scheibe Bergfalke II/55	250	OH-KBF
OH-207	Rhönlerche II	591	OH-KRB
OH-213X	Motorlerche	671	OH-KRE
OH-216	Schleicher Ka 6CR Rhönsegler	684	OH-RSD
OH-218	Schleicher Ka 6CR Rhönsegler	683	OH-RSC
OH-220	Schleicher Ka 6CR Rhönsegler	720	OH-RSF
OH-222	Schleicher Ka 6CR Rhönsegler	729	OH-RSH
OH-229	PIK-3c Kajava	9	OH-YKR
OH-230X	Schleicher Rhönlerche II	761	OH-KRL
OH-231	Schleicher Ka 6CR Rhönsegler	719	OH-RSG
OH-237	PIK-5c Cumulus	31	OH-PBI
OH-239	Schleicher Ka 6CR Rhönsegler	971	OH-RSK
OH-242	Schleicher Ka 6CR Rhönsegler	961	OH-RSI
OH-244	PIK-3c Kajava	6	OH-YKU
OH-245	PIK-3c Kajava	8	OH-YKS
OH-247	PIK-3c Kajava	14	OH-YKL
OH-249X	Schleicher Rhönlerche II Mod.	1/61	OH-KRJ
OH-250	PIK-3c Kajava	13	OH-YKM
OH-255	Schleicher K 8B	990	OH-RTD
OH-260-'6'	Schleicher Ka 6CR Rhönsegler	969	OH-RSJ
OH-265	Schleicher K 8B	8033	OH-RTF
OH-268X	Schleicher Ka 6CR Rhönsegler (Motorised)	6034	OH-RSL
OH-270	Schleicher K 8B	8058	OH-RTG
OH-277	PIK-3c Kajava	16	OH-YKJ
OH-280	PIK-16c Vasama	8	OH-VAH
OH-281	PIK-16c Vasama	9	OH-VAI
OH-287	Schleicher K 8B	8185	OH-RTH
OH-294	Schleicher K 8B	8299	OH-294X OH-294 OH-RTI
OH-296	Schleicher K 7 Rhönadler	7081	OH-KKI
OH-301	Schleicher Ka 6CR Rhönsegler	6269	OH-RSR
OH-303	PIK-16c Vasama	27	OH-VAM
OH-304	PIK-3c Kajava	17	OH-YKI
OH-310	Schleicher K 8B	8324	OH-RTJ
OH-312	Schleicher K 8B	02	OH-RTL
OH-313	Schleicher K 8B	01	OH-RTK
OH-314	Schleicher K 8B	03	OH-RTM
OH-324	Schleicher Ka 6CR Rhönsegler	6407	OH-RST
OH-325	Schleicher Ka 6CR Rhönsegler	6408	OH-RSU
OH-326	Schleicher K 8B	06	OH-RTO
OH-327X	LET L-13M Blanik	173318	OH-BLB
OH-332	Schleicher K 7 Rhönadler	7250	OH-KKN
OH-333X	IKVasama IKV-3 Kotka	1	OH-333 OH-XKO
OH-334	Schleicher K 7 Rhönadler	7262	OH-KKO
OH-339	SZD-9bis Bocian 1D	F-878	OH-KBO
OH-344	Schleicher K 8B	24	OH-RTV
OH-348	Schleicher K 8B	14	OH-RTU
OH-350	PIK-5C	24	OH-PBO OH-PBB
OH-352	Schleicher K 8B	23	OH-RTY
OH-353	PIK-16c Vasama	35	OH-VAO
OH-354	Schleicher Ka 6E	4102	OH-RSZ
OH-356	Schleicher Ka 6E	4146	OH-REA
OH-365	Schleicher K 8B	19	OH-RTZ
OH-367X	Sportavia/ Fournier RF-4D Mod.	4096	OH-FIA
OH-369	Schleicher Ka 6E	4190	OH-REB
OH-370	Sportavia/ Fournier RF-4D	4098	OH-FIB
OH-371	Sportavia/ Fournier RF-4D	4106	OH-FIC
OH-374	Sportavia/ Fournier RF-4D	4110	OH-FIF
OH-380	Sportavia/ Fournier RF-4D	4144	OH-FIH
OH-381X	Sportavia/ Fournier RF-4D	4143	OH-FIG
OH-382	Sportavia/ Fournier RF-4D	4145	OH-FII
OH-383	Sportavia/ Fournier RF-5	5023	OH-FKA
OH-386	Sportavia/ Fournier RF-5	5019	OH-FKC
OH-389	Sportavia/ Fournier RF-5	5035	OH-FKD
OH-390	Sportavia/ Fournier RF-4D	4142	OH-FIJ (SE-TGT)
OH-392	Sportavia/ Fournier RF-5	5043	OH-FKE
OH-393	SZD-30 Pirat	B-335	OH-FPB
OH-397	Schleicher K 8B	17	OH-RTQ
OH-401	Scheibe SF-25B Falke	46130	OH-FLA (D-KADG)
OH-405	Schleicher ASK 13	13301	OH-KKT
OH-406	Schleicher ASK 13	13328	OH-KKU
OH-411	Schempp-Hirth Standard Cirrus	352	
OH-414	LET L-13 Blanik	175109	
OH-415	Slingsby T-61C Falke	1754	
OH-417	Glasflügel H201 Standard Libelle	398	
OH-422	Glasflügel H20I Standard Libelle	331	
OH-426X	Pilatus B4-PC11 (Motorised)	49	
OH-428	LET L-13 Blanik	025417	
OH-436	LET L-13 Blanik	025515	
OH-438-WA	PIK-16c Vasama	53	
OH-440	Schleicher ASK 14	14011	D-KANK
OH-442	Eiri PIK-20	20022	
OH-454	Eiri PIK-20	20007	
OH-458	Scheibe SF-28A Tandem-Falke	5775	(D-KCLE)
OH-463	Schleicher ASW 15B	15406	
OH-465	Eiri PIK-20	20018	
OH-466-TM	Eiri PIK-20	20028	
OH-469	Eiri PIK-20	20035	
OH-470	Eiri PIK-20	20032	
OH-476	Eiri PIK-20D	20527	BGA2233
OH-477	Eiri PIK-20B	20106	
OH-480	Glaser-Dirks DG-100	2	D-7099
OH-482	Eiri PIK-20	20041	
OH-484	Eiri PIK-20B	20113	
OH-485	Eiri PIK-20B	20136C	SE-TVT OH-485
OH-486	Eiri PIK-20B	20137C	
OH-489-TS	Eiri PIK-20B	20133C	
OH-493	Eiri PIK-20	20066	
OH-496X	Motorlerche	417	D-0022
OH-497	Eiri PIK-20B	20118C	SE-TPY OH-497
OH-501	LET L-13 Blanik	026239	
OH-502	Eiri PIK-20D	20624	
OH-503	Schleicher Ka 6E	4394/AB	
OH-504	Glasflügel H206 Hornet	53	
OH-506	SZD-30 Pirat	S-06.46	
OH-507	Eiri PIK-20B	20142C	
OH-510X	Eiri PIK-20D	20501	
OH-511-MA	Schleicher ASW 20	20056	
OH-512	Eiri PIK-20D	20529	
OH-513	LET L-13 Blanik	026603	
OH-514	LET L-13 Blanik	026604	
OH-516	Eiri PIK-20D	20536	
OH-518	Schleicher K 8B	15	OY-DXF
OH-519	LET L-13 Blanik	026851	
OH-521-FL	Eiri PIK-20D	20547	
OH-522	Eiri PIK-20D	20554	
OH-532	Schleicher ASW 19B	19246	
OH-536	Eiri PIK-20D	20648	
OH-537	Grob G.102 Astir CS Jeans	2207	
OH-540	Grob G.102 Astir CS Jeans	2142	
OH-542	SZD-41A Jantar Standard	B-843	
OH-543-TIY	Schleicher ASK 21	21026	
OH-546	Schleicher ASK 21	21259	
OH-547	Schleicher ASK 21	21133	
OH-549	Eiri PIK-20D	20639	
OH-552	Grob G.102 Astir CS Jeans	2233	
OH-556	Schleicher ASW 19B	19328	
OH-557	Schleicher ASK 21	21115	
OH-561	Eiri PIK-20E	20270	
OH-562	Eiri PIK-20D	20603	
OH-565	Eiri PIK-20D	20533	BGA2236
OH-571	PIK-16c Vasama	38	
OH-572	Schleicher ASW 20	20212	
OH-573	Schleicher ASK 21	21038	
OH-582	Eiri PIK-20E	20272	
OH-583	Eiri PIK-20E	20290	
OH-586	SZD-48-1 Jantar Standard 2	B-1044	
OH-587	SZD-48-1 Jantar Standard 2	B-1097	
OH-591-EE	Grob G.102 Astir CS Jeans	2210	
OH-592	Schleicher ASW 19	19017	D-4529
OH-598	Scheibe SF-25C Falke	4487	D-KEIG
OH-599	Eiri PIK-20E	20263	
OH-602	Eiri PIK-20E	20279	
OH-604	Schleicher ASW 20	20379	
OH-605	Eiri PIK-20E	20213	G-OCPA
OH-607	Eiri PIK-20E	20292	
OH-608-PC	Glasflügel H304	217	
OH-610	Eiri PIK-20D	20665	
OH-614	SZD-48-1 Jantar Standard	B-1163	
OH-619	Rolladen-Schneider LS4A	4124	

OH-623	Scheibe SF-25C Falke	4432	OY-XLA D-KMSO
OH-625	Valentin Mistral C	MC 035/81	
OH-627	Scheibe SF-25C Falke	4462	OE-9064 (D-KOAV)
OH-628	Grob G.103 Twin Astir II	3660	
OH-631	LET L-13 Blanik	026640	
OH-632X	Schleicher Ka 6EM	1	
OH-636	Glaser-Dirks DG-100G Elan	E68-G43	
OH-637	Scheibe SF-25C Falke	4458	D-KOAE
OH-639	Grob G.102 Club Astir II	5569C	
OH-642	Glasflügel H304	260	
OH-643	Grob G.109	6088	
OH-646	Grob G.109	6092	
OH-647	Grob G.109	6094	
OH-648	Grob G.102 Club Astir II	5052C	
OH-649	Grob G.109	6073	
OH-650-FK	Grob G.102 Club Astir II	5574C	
OH-651X	Motorlerche (Rhönlerche II)	3043/Br	
OH-653	Grob G.109	6114	
OH-655	Rolladen-Schneider LS4A	4345	
OH-657-PV	Grob G.102 Club Astir IIIB	5590CB	
OH-658-ST	Grob G.102 Astir CS	1088	D-6988
OH-659	Grob G.109	6097	D-KENA
OH-661	Grob G.102 Club Astir II	5059C	
OH-664	Glaser-Dirks DG-300	3E-31	
OH-665	Grob G.109	6107	
OH-667	Grob G.102 Club Astir IIIB	5575CB	
OH-668-OW	Rolladen-Schneider LS4A	4346	
OH-669	Rolladen-Schneider LS4A	4344	
OH-670-T8	Grob G.102 Astir CS Jeans	2025	
OH-671	Grob G.109	6020	D-KETO
OH-675	SZD-50-3 Puchacz	B-973	
OH-676	Centrair 101 Pégase	101-062	
OH-677	Schleicher ASK 21	21189	
OH-678	Schleicher ASK 21	21190	
OH-679	Rolladen-Schneider LS4	4533	
OH-680-TO	Schleicher ASW 20	20208	
OH-681-TK	Centrair 101A Pégase	101A-0109	
OH-684-VW	Rolladen-Schneider LS4A	4343	
OH-685	Schempp-Hirth Janus B	186	
OH-687	Grob G.109	6111	
OH-688	Valentin Taifun 17E	1022	D-KIHL
OH-691	Rolladen-Schneider LS4A	4347	
OH-692	Glaser-Dirks DG-300	3E-30	
OH-693	Rolladen-Schneider LS4A	4396	
OH-694	Eiri PIK-20E	20288	PH-694
OH-696	Schleicher ASK 23	23029	
OH-697	Schleicher ASK 23	23026	
OH-701	SZD-51-1 Junior	W-960	
OH-703	Schleicher ASK 23B	23069	
OH-704	Schleicher ASK 23B	23070	
OH-705	Scheibe SF-25C Falke	4427	D-KHOK
OH-707	Glaser-Dirks DG-300	3E-25	
OH-710	Rolladen-Schneider LS4A	4393	
OH-712	Glasflügel H304B	347	
OH-713	Rolladen-Schneider LS4A	4462	
OH-715	Rolladen-Schneider LS6	6024	
OH-716	Grob G.109B	6339	
OH-717	Rolladen-Schneider LS4	4391	
OH-719	Schempp-Hirth Janus C	222	
OH-721	Grob G.109	6032	D-KELC
OH-723	Rolladen-Schneider LS4A	4578	
OH-724	SZD-50-3 Puchacz	B-1601	
OH-726	Rolladen-Schneider LS6B	6081	
OH-727	Grob G.109	6050	D-KLFM
OH-728	SZD-51-1 Junior	W-948	
OH-729	Schempp-Hirth Discus b	124	
OH-732-PD	Schempp-Hirth Ventus c	307	
OH-733-FQ	Grob G.103A Twin II Acro	34049-K-280	
OH-735	Rolladen-Schneider LS6	6047	
OH-737	Grob G.109B	6338	
OH-740	Grob G.109B	6413	
OH-742	SZD-51-1 Junior	W-958	
OH-743	SZD-51-1 Junior	B-1769	
OH-744	SZD-51-1 Junior	W-949	
OH-745	SZD-50-3 Puchacz	B-1608	
OH-746	Grob G.102 Astir CS Jeans	2156	OE-5373 HB-1441
OH-750	SZD-51-1 Junior	W-942	
OH-751	SZD-50-3 Puchacz	B-1618	
OH-752	SZD-51-1 Junior	B-1776	
OH-753	SZD-48-3 Jantar Standard 3	B-1661	
OH-754	Rolladen-Schneider LS6B	6134	
OH-755	Rolladen-Schneider LS4A	4600	
OH-756	SZD-50-3 Puchacz	B-1627	
OH-760-PH	Schleicher ASW 20BL	20952	
OH-765	Rolladen-Schneider LS6B	6162	
OH-767	Rolladen-Schneider LS6B	6132	
OH-768	Schleicher ASK 21	21362	
OH-769	Schempp-Hirth Discus b	226	
OH-770-PO	Schempp-Hirth Discus b	235	
OH-772	SZD-50-3 Puchacz	B-1720	
OH-773	SZD-51-1 Junior	B-1814	
OH-776	SZD-51-1 Junior	B-1815	
OH-778	Rolladen-Schneider LS4A	4691	
OH-779	SZD-50-3 Puchacz	B-1617	
OH-780	Schempp-Hirth Discus b	2	D-8111
OH-783	Schleicher ASK 21	21380	
OH-784	SZD-50-3 Puchacz	B-1723	
OH-785	SZD-48-3 Jantar Standard 3	B-1713	
OH-786	SZD-50-3 Puchacz	B-1722	
OH-787-FM	Rolladen-Schneider LS4A	4715	
OH-788	Rolladen-Schneider LS7	7003	D-1254
OH-790	Schleicher ASW 24	24020	
OH-791-PP	Schleicher ASW 24	24025	
OH-792-HB	Schleicher ASW 24	24057	
OH-794-TI	Schleicher ASW 24	24058	
OH-795	Hoffmann HK-36R Super Dimona	36312	
OH-798	SZD-51-1 Junior	B-1935	
OH-799	SZD-55-1	551190007	
OH-801	SZD-50-3 Puchacz	B-1875	
OH-802	SZD-51-1 Junior	B-1852	
OH-804	SZD-51-1 Junior	B-1853	
OH-805	Rolladen-Schneider LS7	7019	D-4635
OH-806	Rolladen-Schneider LS6B	6149	D-8077
OH-808	SZD-55-1	X-146	
OH-810	Grob G.103C Twin III Acro	34125	
OH-811	Schleicher ASW 24	24070	
OH-812	Rolladen-Schneider LS7	7056	
OH-813	Hoffmann H-36 Dimona	3661	SE-TUT
OH-814	Brditschka HB-21/2400B	21019	LN-GAK OE-9178
OH-815	Grob G.103C Twin III Acro	34120	
OH-816	SZD-50-3 Puchacz	B-1877	
OH-817	Schleicher ASK 21	21455	
OH-818	Grob G.102 Astir CS	1243	D-4212
OH-821	Schempp-Hirth Ventus c	470	
OH-822-IY	Rolladen-Schneider LS4A	4785	
OH-823	Rolladen-Schneider LS7	7092	
OH-824	SZD-55-1	551190005	
OH-827	Schempp-Hirth Discus A	331	
OH-828	SZD-50-3 Puchacz	B-2026	
OH-829	SZD-51-1 Junior	B-1929	
OH-832	SZD-50-3 Puchacz	B-2027	
OH-833	Schempp-Hirth Discus CS	018CS	SE-UPA (SE-ULX) BGA4028/HLL OH-833
OH-834	Rolladen-Schneider LS6C	6220	
OH-835	SZD-55-1	551191013	
OH-836	Schempp-Hirth Discus A	376	
OH-837	Rolladen-Schneider LS6C	6225	
OH-838	Grob G.109B	6227	D-KGFJ
OH-839	SZD-51-1 Junior	B-1992	
OH-842	SZD-51-1 Junior	B-1816	SE-UGO
OH-845	SZD-55-1	551191025	
OH-846	SZD-55-1	551191026	
OH-848	Schempp-Hirth Discus b	407	
OH-849	SZD-51-1 Junior	B-2004	
OH-850	LET L-23 Super Blanik	917918	
OH-851	LET L-13 Blanik	026611	
OH-852	Schempp-Hirth Janus CT	18/281	
OH-853	Schempp-Hirth Janus CT	19/282	
OH-855	SZD-55-1	551191022	
OH-856	SZD-55-1	551192040	
OH-858	Grob G.102 Club Astir IIIB	5627CB	D-7603
OH-859	SZD-50-3 Puchacz	B-2084	
OH-860	LET L-13 Blanik	174210	DOSAAF
OH-862	SZD-55-1	551192046	
OH-864	SZD-51-1 Junior	B-2128	
OH-865	Rolladen-Schneider LS6-18W	6315	
OH-866	Rolladen-Schneider LS6-18W	6316	D-4518
OH-867	LET L-23 Super Blanik	938108	
OH-868	LET L-23 Super Blanik	938109	
OH-869	Schleicher ASW 24	24226	
OH-870	LET L-33 Solo	940219	
OH-871	SZD-42-1 Jantar 2	B-777	SE-TPX
OH-872	PZL PW-5 Smyk	17.04.008	
OH-875	PZL PW-5 Smyk	17.03.016	
OH-876	PZL PW-5 Smyk	17.04.009	
OH-877	Schempp-Hirth Ventus 2c	3	
OH-878	Rolladen-Schneider LS7	7083	SE-UPP
OH-879	Rolladen-Schneider LS6-18W	6372	
OH-880	PZL PW-5 Smyk	17.04.015	
OH-881	Grob G.102 Astir CS77	1739	SE-UEB D-4898
OH-882	Rolladen-Schneider LS8A	8062	
OH-883	Rolladen-Schneider LS8A	8101	
OH-884	Rolladen Schneider LS-8A	8119	
OH-885	PZL PW-5 Smyk	17.05.007	
OH-886	Schleicher ASH 25	25165	BGA4026/HLJ (BGA4023)
OH-887	SZD-36A Cobra 15	W-731	LY-GIT DOSAAF
OH-889	Grob G.109A	6046	SE-UAG OY-XLW
OH-890	Rolladen-Schneider LS4B	41015	
OH-891	SZD-42-2 Jantar 2B	B-1376	LY-G . . DOSAAF
OH-892	Schleicher Ka 6E	4026	OY-XGH D-6475 D-9375
OH-893	Schleicher ASH 26E	26136	

OH-894	Rolladen-Schneider LS8A	8175	
OH-895	Rolladen-Schneider LS8A	8196	
OH-896	Rolladen-Schneider LS7WL	7016	SE-UGX D-4639
OH-897	Rolladen Schneider LS8A	8195	
OH-898	Rolladen Schneider LS8A	8134	D-3382
OH-899	Schempp-Hirth Nimbus 2	85	(D-....) OH-899 D-2784
OH-900	Schempp-Hirth Ventus 2b	68	
OH-901	DG Flugzeugbau DG-800B	8-90B26	D-KWDG(1)
OH-902	Schempp-Hirth Ventus 2c	42/122	
OH-903	Schempp-Hirth Discus 2B	30	D-7316
OH-904	Schempp-Hirth Ventus 2a	88	
OH-905	Eiri PIK-20B	20101	LN-GAZ
OH-907	Schempp-Hirth Discus 2B	67	
OH-908	Schempp-Hirth Ventus 2b	98	
OH-909	Rolladen Schneider LS8A	8322	
OH-910	Rolladen Schneider LS8A	8324	
OH-911	Schempp-Hirth Ventus 2a	97	
OH-912	Scheibe L-Spatz 55	620	D-5094
OH-915	Rolladen-Schneider LS3 (Reservation 9.01)	unkn	
OH-916	SZD-42-1 Jantar Standard 2	B-781	SE-TPI
OH-917	Rolladen Schneider LS8-18	8357	
OH-918	Rolladen Schneider LS8-18	8373	
OH-919	Stemme S-10VT	11-060	
OH-920	Schempp-Hirth Ventus 2a	120	
OH-921	Grob G.109	6112	D-KIWO(2) OE-9203
OH-922	Rolladen Schneider LS8A	8372	
OH-923	Rolladen Schneider LS8-18	8370	
OH-924	Schleicher ASK 21	21735	
OH-925	Rolladen Schneider LS8A	8023	PH-1048 D-2598
OH-926	Glaser-Dirks DG-300 Elan	3E-155	SE-UEC
OH-927	Schempp-Hirth Ventus 2c	70	
OH-928	Schempp-Hirth Discus 2a	111	
OH-929	Grob G.102 Astir CS	1082	D-3312
OH-930	Schempp-Hirth Discus 2b	133	
OH-931	Schempp-Hirth Ventus 2b	123	
OH-932	Schempp-Hirth Ventus 2cM	28/50	D-KGBS
OH-933	Schempp-Hirth Ventus 2BX	129	
OH-934	Grob G.103 Twin Astir	3080	OY-XIO
OH-935	Rolladen Schneider LS8-18	8037	D-8047 BGA4193/HTQ D-2993
OH-936	Schempp-Hirth Discus 2b	164	D-0444
OH-937	Grob G.102 Astir CS	1284	OY-XLV D-7376
OH-938	Rolladen Schneider LS3-17	3364	SE-TTP
OH-939	Schempp-Hirth Ventus 2BX	136	D-2734
OH-941	Bölkow Phoebus C	810	LN-GAR SE-TFP
OH-942	LAK-17A	144	
OH-943	LAK-19	011	LY-GER
OH-944	SZD-55-1	551194072	D-6464
OH-945	Rolladen-Schneider LS8T	8472	D-KOAR
OH-946	Rolladen-Schneider LS-7WL	7060	SE-UGY
OH-947	Schleicher K 7 Rhönadler	7104	OY-MNX D-3609
OH-948	Schempp-Hirth Nimbus 4DM	55	
OH-949	Glasflügel H401 Kestrel (Reservation 12.02)	unkn	
OH-950	Schempp-Hirth Nimbus 4D	001	D-1211
OH-951	Fauvel AV-36 (Reservation 18.11.03)	unkn	
OH-952	DG Flugzeugbau DG-500 Elan Orion	5E-195X39	D-5062 S5-7517
OH-953	Sportavia RF-5B Sperber	51001	D-KHEK
OH-954	Schempp-Hirth Janus B (Res 10.1.05)	66	F-CHVU D-7770
OH-955	Schempp-Hirth Ventus 2cX (Res 6.10.04)	unkn	
OH-956	LAK-17 (Reservation 2.05)	unkn	
OH-957	Schempp-Hirth Janus B	90	
OH-958	LET L-23 Super Blanik	917813	SE-UKC

MICROLIGHTS

OH-U017	Comco Ikarus Fox C-22	8808-3151	
OH-U029	La Mouette Cosmos Hermes 14-BID	unkn	
OH-U035	Air Création Safari GT-BI	unkn	
OH-U036	Southdown Puma Raven	unkn	
OH-U039	Southdown Puma Raven	unkn	
OH-U045	Hiway Trike	21T5	OH-U001
OH-U046	Southdown Puma Raven	ML-001	
OH-U047	Mainair Gemini/Flash	491-1086-4/W255	
OH-U048	Southdown Puma Raven X/Ghost Mod	"U048"	
OH-U053	Southdown Puma Raven X	unkn	
OH-U055	Comco Ikarus Fox C-22	8701-3057	
OH-U056	Comco Ikarus Fox C-22	8701-3058	
OH-U057	Southdown Raven Trike	001	
OH-U058	Southdown Raven X462LQ	P19351	
OH-U060	Southdown Raven X462	3585264	
OH-U063	Southdown Puma Raven X462	unkn	
OH-U065	Renegade Spirit	370	
OH-U070	Fisher FP-404 Classic	4053	
OH-U075	Sky-Walker II	172	
OH-U082	Raven 447	unkn	
OH-U084	Comco Ikarus Fox C-22	8804-3127	
OH-U087	La Mouette Cosmos Azur 19/Trike	unkn	
OH-U088	Mainair Gemini/Flash IIA	619-188-5/W408	
OH-U090	La Mouette Azur 17/Trike	LN1795	
OH-U092	Mainair Gemini/Flash IIA	644-588-6/W434	
OH-U094	Comco Ikarus Fox C-22	8810-3157	
OH-U096	Comco Ikarus Fox C-22	8805-3131	
OH-U100	Murphy Renegade Spirit	107	
OH-U101	Murphy Renegade Spirit	141	U101
OH-U103	Murphy Renegade Spirit	195	
OH-U105	Murphy Renegade II Mod.	140	
OH-U106	Kolb Twinstar Mark II	TX 2501 1188	
OH-U108	Southdown Raven	MV02	
OH-U110	Comco Ikarus Fox C-22	8808-3150	
OH-U119	Southdown Puma Sprint	T29	
OH-U120	Murphy Renegade II	175	
OH-U121	Firebird Sierra	unkn	
OH-U123	Firebird Sierra	364	
OH-U126	Medway Hybred R447/R503	MR . . ./54 ?	
OH-U127	Southdown Puma Sprint	unkn	
OH-U128	Kolb Twinstar	194	
OH-U130	Murphy Renegade II	377	
OH-U133	Southdown Puma Sprint	unkn	
OH-U135	Comco Ikarus Fox C-22	8902-3190	
OU-U136	Southdown Puma Sprint	U136/13	
OH-U138	Kolb Twinstar Mark II	193	
OH-U143	Beaver RX-550 Mod.	0014	
OH-U144	Murphy Renegade Spirit	225	
OH-U146	Southdown Puma Sprint	unkn	
OH-U150	Southdown Puma Sprint	44	
OH-U153	Kolb Twinstar Mark II	TX 255	
OH-U154	Murphy Renegade II	0142	
OH-U157	Southdown Puma Sprint	unkn	
OH-U158	Southdown Puma Sprint	1231-0052	
OH-U159	Murphy Renegade II	197	
OH-U166	Southdown Puma Sprint	unkn	
OH-U168	Beaver RX-550	0056	
OH-U169	Beaver RX-550	0053	
OH-U178	Beaver RX-550	0055	
OH-U179	La Mouette Cosmos Hermes Profil 19/Chronos 16	3549726	
OH-U180	Cosmos Profil 19/Chronos 16	unkn	
OH-U182	Southdown Puma Raven	SN 2232-0093	
OH-U183	Rans S-6 Coyote II	03890387	
OH-U184	Rans S-6 Coyote II	0689041	
OH-U186	Mainair Gemini/Flash IIA	396-186-4	
OH-U187	Southdown Puma Raven X	unkn	
OH-U188	Murphy Renegade Spirit	263	
OH-U189	Murphy Renegade Spirit	246	
OH-U190	Southdown Puma Raven	unkn	
OH-U192	Southdown Raven Sprint	T67	
OH-U196	Kolb Twinstar Mark II	196	
OH-U204	Murphy Renegade Spirit	226	
OH-U205	Murphy Renegade Spirit	205	
OH-U207	Comco Ikarus Fox C-22	8906-3205	
OH-U208	Comco Ikarus Fox C-22	8903-3206	
OH-U209	Comco Ikarus Fox C-22	8906-3208	
OH-U212	Rans S-6 Coyote II	0689035	
OH-U214	Rans S-6 Coyote IIES	1190147	
OH-U215	Azur 17/Trike	003-90	
OH-U216	Rans S-6 Coyote IIES	1190146	
OH-U218	Rans S-6 Coyote II (Mod)	1289103	
OH-U219	Rans S-6 Coyote II	1089096	
OH-U221	Murphy Renegade II	199	
OH-U222	Rans S-6 Coyote II	0489022	
OH-U224	Rans S-6 Coyote II	1089088	
OH-U226	Rans S-6 Coyote II	0989073	
OH-U228	Rans S-6 Coyote II	1089087	
OH-U232	Beaver RX-550	0108	
OH-U235	Mosler N3-2 Pup	0043LA-2	
OH-U236	Beaver RX-550	0103	
OH-U238	Sky Sports Yarrow Arrow 2	016	
OH-U240	Rans S-7 Courier	1189059	
OH-U243	Rans S-6 Coyote II	1289100	
OH-U244	Rans S-6 Coyote II Mod.	1289099	
OH-U245	Comco Ikarus Fox C-22	9007-3276	
OH-U247	Rans S-6 Coyote II	1289102	
OH-U248	Rans S-7L Courier (Accident 16.11.02)	0190065	
OH-U249	Rans S-6 Coyote II	1289105	
OH-U251	Murphy Renegade Spirit	0247	
OH-U254	Rans S-6 Coyote II	0690126	
OH-U255	Rans S-6 Coyote II	0490118	
OH-U256	Rans S-6 Coyote II	0190110	
OH-U258	Rans S-6 Coyote II Mod.	0490121	
OH-U262	Beaver RX-650	0002	
OH-U263	Beaver RX-650	0014	
OH-U264	Beaver RX-650 Mod.	0004	
OH-U269	Beaver RX-650	0010	
OH-U270	Beaver RX-650	0011	
OH-U271	Beaver RX-650	0012	
OH-U273	Rans S-9 Chaos	190083	
OH-U274	Beaver RX-650	0015	
OH-U275	Rans S-6 Coyote IIES	0890137	
OH-U277	Rans S-4 Coyote I	90138	

OH-U280	LAK-16AM	001	LY-GLU?
OH-U281	Rans S-6 Coyote II Mod.	0790130	
OH-U285	Aviasud Mistral 582	134	
OH-U291	Rans S-6 Coyote II ES	0291164	
OH-U292	Kolb Twinstar Mark III Mod.	M3-018	
OH-U293	Rans S-6 Coyote II	1289101	
OH-U297	Rans S-6 Coyote II ES	0491179	
OH-U298	Rans S-6 Coyote II ES	0491180	
OH-U299	Rans S-6 Coyote II ES	0491181	
OH-U303	Light Aero Avid Flyer STOL	923	
OH-U304	Kolb Twinstar Mark III Mod.	M3R5001	
OH-U305	Kolb Twinstar Mark II	TS-166	
OH-U306	Murphy Renegade Spirit	273	
OH-U311	Rans S-6 Coyote II ES	1190145	
OH-U312	S.M.A.N. Pétrel	031	
OH-U313	Rans S-12 Airaile Ultramarin	1090.033	
OH-U315	Fisher Super Koala	SK011	
OH-U320	Counts Wolfen Super Pup	85001	
OH-U321	Rans S-6 Coyote II ES	1190144	
OH-U323	Cirka Nieuport 11/16	266	
	(Officially regd as Nieuport 17)		
OH-U333	Murphy Renegade Spirit	381	
OH-U345	Zenair CH-701 STOL	7-1593	
OH-U346	Chronos ULM Cosmos	426	
OH-U347	Lamco Eurocub Mk.1	CAH-002	
OH-U348	Kolb Twinstar Mark III Mod.	M3-069	
OH-U349	Zenair CH-701 STOL	7-3049	
OH-U350	Aeronave ULM U1064 Modelo Nieuport II	198	OH-U1064
OH-U351	Beaver RX-650	BRX-016	
OH-U352	Lamco Eurocub 912Mk.1	CAH-001	
OH-U353	Lamco Eurocub 912 Mk.1	CAH-007	SE- . . . ?
OH-U354	Kolb Twinstar Mark II	unkn	
OH-U355	PIK-26 Mini-Sytky	387	
OH-U356	PIK-26 Mini-Sytky	392	
OH-U358	Denney Kitfox II	325	OH-XKF
OH-U361	Monnet Sonerai 1	11289	
OH-U362	Martenko ATOL 500	446	
OH-U365	Fantasy Air Cora 200	98-301	
OH-U366	FIB Polaris	98A4278/98A3709	
OH-U368	Fantasy Air Cora 200 Arius F	99-304	
OH-U369	Comco Ikarus C-42 Cyclone	9907-6203	
OH-U370	Fantasy Air Cora 200 Arius FT	99-303	
OH-U371	Comco Ikarus C-42 Cyclone	9912-6219	
OH-U372	Comco Ikarus C-42B	0006-6263	D-MSCO
OH-U374	Comco Ikarus C-42S Cyclone	0011-6293	
OH-U375	Amfi 10	401	
OH-U376	Nicollier HN-434 Super Ménestrel	83	
OH-U377	Comco Ikarus C-42 Cyclone	9905-6187	D-MREC
OH-U379	Druine D.31 Turbulent (Mod)	488	
OH-U381	Chronos II / Unknown trike	unkn	
OH-U382	Flight Design CT-2K	08.08.03.16	
OH-U383	Comco Ikarus C-42 Cyclone	0010-6294	
OH-U384	Evektor EV-97 Eurostar	2001-1001	
OH-U385	Evektor EV-97R Eurostar	2001-1005	
OH-U386	Evektor EV-97R Eurostar	2001-1203	
OH-U387	Comco Ikarus C-42 Cyclone (Cr.11.6.03)	9919-6217	SE-YVI
OH-U388	Fantasy Air Cora 200 Arius F	01-305	
OH-U389	Evektor EV-97R Eurostar	2001-1103	
OH-U390	Comco Ikarus C-42 Cyclone	0106-6364	
OH-U391	Flight Design CT-2K	01.01.05.02	
OH-U392	Lamco Eurocub 912UL Mk.1	CAH-020	
OH-U393	Fischer Classic II	88056	
OH-U394	Fantasy Air Cora 2000 Arius F	02-307	
OH-U395	Fantasy Air Cora 2000 Arius F	02-306	
OH-U396	Comco Ikarus C-42 Cyclone	0107-6366	
OH-U397	Comco Ikarus C-42 Cyclone	0003-6260	
OH-U398	Comco Ikarus C-42	0201-6430	
OH-U399	Comco Ikarus C-42B	0205-6465	
OH-U400	Evektor EV-97R Eurostar	2001-1201	
OH-U401	Rans S-10 Sakota	0709108	OH-XTJ
OH-U402	Evektor EV-97 Eurostar	2001-1210	
OH-U403	PIK-26 Mini-Sytky	456	
OH-U404	PIK-26 Mini-Sytky	1	
OH-U405	Comco Ikarus C-42	0206-6486	
OH-U406	Comco Ikarus C-42	0204-6439	
OH-U407	Rans S-10 Sakota	0790106	OH-XOO
OH-U408	Comco Ikarus C-42B	0208-6463	
OH-U409	Fantasy Air Cora 200 Arius F	02-308	
OH-U410	Evektor EV-97R Eurostar	2002-1509	
OH-U411	TLUltralight TL-96 Star	02S-121	
OH-U412	Evektor EV-97 Eurostar	99-0603	I-5981
OH-U413	Comco Ikarus C-42	0302-6526	
OH-U414	Comco Ikarus C-42B	0211-6503	
OH-U417	Comco Ikarus C-42 Cyclone	9902-6151	OE-7045
OH-U418	Comco Ikarus C-42	0212-6513	
OH-U419	Evektor EV-97R Eurostar	2003-1607	
OH-U420	Comco Ikarus C-42B	0301-6519	
OH-U421	FIB Polaris 582	0231020/02B4607	
OH-U422	FIB Polaris 582	0231026/02B4613	
OH-U423	Comco Ikarus C-42B	0304-6527	
OH-U424	Comco Ikarus C-42	0303-6539	
OH-U425	Evektor EV-97R Eurostar	2003-1707	
OH-U426	Comco Ikarus C-42 Cyclone (Res. 12.02)	unkn	
OH-U427	Rand Robinson KR-2	01-03	
	(C/n originally quoted as 159)		
OH-U428	Zenair CH-701D STOL	7-9331	
OH-U429	Comco Ikarus C-42B	0310-6575	
OH-U430	Evektor EV-97R Eurostar	2003-1716	
OH-U431	ICP MXP-740Savannah (Reservation 3.03)	536	
OH-U432	Evektor EV-97 Eurostar	98-0306	D-MOHD
OH-U433	Advanced Aviation Cobra (Res 3.03)	unkn	
OH-U434	Aerospool WT- 9 Dynamic	DY029/2003	
OH-U435	Comco Ikarus C-42B	9810-6137	D-MSHS
OH-U436	Air Création GTE 912/Kiss 450	T03052	
OH-U437	Evektor EV-97 Eurostar	99-0512	I-6278
OH-U438	Evektor EV-97R Eurostar	2002-1606	I-6933
OH-U439	Comco Ikarus C-42B	0001-6224	LN-YWC
OH-U440	Comco Ikarus C-42B	0308-6569	
OH-U441	Zenair CH-601HD (Reservation 12.03)	6-9454	
OH-U442	Comco Ikarus C-42B	0310-6576	
OH-U443	Comco Ikarus C-42B	0311-6580	
OH-U444	Evektor EV-97R Eurostar	2004-2004	
OH-U445	Evektor EV-97R Eurostar	1520-2002	I-7537
OH-U446	Evektor EV-97R Eurostar	1810-2003	
OH-U447	Light Aero Avid Flyer Mk IV	1162D	I-3413
OH-U448	Evektor EV-97R Eurostar	2002-1528	I-7119
OH-U449	Kappa 77 KP-2U Sova	2089108	
OH-U450	Evektor EV-97R Eurostar	2004-2105	
OH-U451	Evektor EV-97R Eurostar	2004-2108	
OH-U452	Evektor EV-97R Eurostar	2003-1804	I-7236
OH-U453	Rans S-7 Courier	unkn	I-5076
OH-U454	Comco Ikarus C-42 Cyclone	0104-6347	D-MRFD
OH-U455	Jabiru UL-2200	UL529	LN-YMY
OH-U456	Comco Ikarus C-42B	0403-6586	D-MDIF
OH-U457	Comco Ikarus C-42B	0405-6606	
OH-U458	Evektor EV-97R Eurostar	2004-2125	
OH-U459	Comco Ikarus C-42B	0407-6619	
OH-U460	Evektor EV-97R Eurostar	2004-2210	
OH-U461	Evektor EV-97R Eurostar	2004-1915	
OH-U462	ATEC Zephyr 2000C	Z190300A	
OH-U463	Kappa 77 KP-2U Sova	21-01-117J	
OH-U464	Kappa 77 KP-2U Sova	20-99-116J	
OH-U465	Funk FK-9 Mk 3 Utility	0903 U201	
OH-U466	Zenair CH-701 STOL SP RTF	7-9558	
OH-U467	Zenair CH-701 STOL SP	7-9571	
OH-U468	Comco Ikarus C-42B	0409-6636	
OH-U469	Comco Ikarus C-42B	0407-6618	
OH-U470	TL Ultralight TL-96 Star	04S139	
OH-U471	Comco Ikarus C-42B	0406-6605	
OH-U472	Martenko ATOL 500	0906	
OH-U473	Comco Ikarus C-42 Cyclone	9910-6216	PH-3G9
OH-U474	Aerospool WT-9 Dynamic	DY-0075	
OH-U475	Martenko ATOL 475 LT	0905	
OH-U476	Evektor EV-97 Eurostar	2005-2314	
OH-U477	Comco Ikarus C-42B	0503-6664	
OH-U478	Comco Ikarus C-42B floatplane	unkn	
OH-U481	Evektor EV-97 Eurostar R	2005-2414	
OH-U482	Funk FK-9 Mk.IV (Res 13.12.04)	unkn	
OH-U483	Funk FK-9 Mk 3 (Res 13.12.04)	unkn	
OH-U484	Funk FK-9 Mk 3 (Res 13.12.04)	unkn	
OH-U485	Jabiru UL 450 (Reservation 1.05)	unkn	
OH-U486	Fresh Breeze (Reservation 2.05)	044	D- . . . .

OK - CZECH REPUBLIC

Regn.	Type	C/n	Prev.Id.
OK-AAG	Cessna TU206G Turbo Stationair 6-II	U20604336	I-IPAP N756TD
OK-ABC	Reims/Cessna F172N	F17201833	D-ELPH
OK-ABS	Cessna 210D Centurion	21058385	N585CC D-EKFO N3885Y
OK-AFE	Aérospatiale/Alenia ATR-42-420	487	F-WWEF
OK-AFF	Aérospatiale/Alenia ATR-42-420	491	F-WWLC
OK-AGR	LET Z-37A Cmelák	25-38	
OK-AHA	Bell 427	56009	N427L C-GFQQ
OK-AHB	Bell 427	56002	N427FW C-GDSJ
OK-AIA	Aérospatiale AS.355F2 Ecureuil 2	5512	RP-C355 F-OHEM
OK-AIO	LET Z-37A Cmelák	14-10	
OK-AIP	LET Z-37A Cmelák (Stored)	14-09	
OK-AIX	LET Z-37A Cmelák	13-17	OM-AIX OK-AIX
OK-AIZ	LET Z-37A Cmelák (Dismantled)	14-12	
OK-AJE	LET Z-37 Cmelák (Stored)	13-19	HA-MCJ
OK-AJF	LET Z-37 Cmelák (Dismantled)	13-02	HA-MCA
OK-AJI	LET Z-37 Cmelák (Stored)	13-03	HA-MCB
OK-AJJ	LET Z-37 Cmelák	13-13	HA-MCF
OK-AJK	LET Z-37A Cmelák	13-15	HA-MCH
OK-AJP	LET Z-37 Cmelák	11-16	
OK-AJQ	LET Z-37 Cmelák (Dismantled)	11-17	
OK-AJR	LET Z-37 Cmelák	11-18	
OK-AJS	LET Z-37A-C3 Cmelák	11-24	
OK-AJX	LET Z-37 Cmelák	12-05	
OK-AKA	Piper PA-28-161 Warrior III	2842004	N9257B OK-AKA
OK-AKC	LET Z-37A Cmelák (Stored)	11-22	
OK-AKF	LET Z-37A Cmelák	13-26	
OK-AKI	LET Z-37 Cmelák	14-07	HA-MCS
OK-AKM	Cessna F172H	F172-0250	D-ECMZ
OK-AKO	LET Z-37A Cmelák (Stored)	12-16	
OK-AKP	LET Z-37 Cmelák	12-18	OM-AKP OK-AKP
OK-AKQ	LET Z-37 Cmelák (Stored)	12-23	
OK-AKR	LET Z-37 Cmelák (Dismantled)	12-24	
OK-AKS	LET Z-37A-C2 Cmelák	12-25	
OK-AKV	LET Z-37A Cmelák	12-28	
OK-AKZ	LET Z-37 Cmelák (Dismantled)	13-08	
OK-ALN	LET Z-37 Cmelák (Dismantled)	13-18	
OK-ANA	Zlin Z.242LA	0690	
OK-AXZ	Mil Mi-8T	2142	OM-AXZ UR-25526
OK-AYA	Letov L.11	960001	
OK-BEK	Zlin Z.526FTrenér Master	1253	SP-GOR SP-CTC
OK-BFG	Aérospatiale/Alenia ATR-42-320	409	F-OKMR F-WWEA
OK-BFH	Aérospatiale/Alenia ATR-42-320	412	F-OKMS F-WWEC
OK-BGQ	Boeing 737-43Q	28494	N462PR B-18677
OK-BIC	Aérospatiale AS.355F2 Ecureuil 2	5388	F-WQED GN-8884
OK-BIG	Robinson R-22B2 Beta	2611	
OK-BLB	Diamond DA 20-A1 Katana	10212	N812CH
OK-BLD	Diamond DA 20-A1 Katana	10160	N181DA
OK-BYA(3)	Eurocopter EC.135T2	0310	D-HECO
OK-BYB(3)	Eurocopter EC.135T2	0340	D-HECO
OK-BYC(3)	Eurocopter EC.135T2	0348	D-HECP
OK-BZF	Reims/Cessna F172M	F17201266	D-EBZF
OK-CEC	Airbus A321-211	674	C-GKOH D-AMTG F-GTAA D-AVZP
OK-CED	Airbus A321-211	684	C-GKOJ D-AMTE F-GTAC D-AVZQ
OK-CGH	Boeing 737-55S	28469	
OK-CGI	Boeing 737-49R	28882	N461PR N35050 N1786B
OK-CGJ	Boeing 737-55S	28470	
OK-CGK	Boeing 737-55S	28471	
OK-CGT	Boeing 737-46M	28549	OO-VEC VH-VGC OO-VEC C-GBIW OO-VEC C-GBIW OO-VEC C-GBIW OO-VEC (F-GMJO) OO-VEC
OK-CIA	Cessna 414	414-0505	OY-BSD (N505ML) D-IGOR OY-BSD G-BBYT (G-BBRK) N9092Q
OK-CIC(2)	Cessna T210N Turbo Centurion II	21063807	D-ECLL(2) OE-KKE N6113C
OK-CJA	LET Z-37A Cmelák (Stored)	16-16	
OK-CJB	LET Z-37A Cmelák (Stored)	16-17	
OK-CJD	LET Z-37A Cmelák	16-14	
OK-CJE	LET Z-37A Cmelák	16-21	
OK-CJG	LET Z-37A Cmelák (Stored)	16-23	
OK-CJH	LET Z-37A Cmelák	16-24	OK-CJH OM-CJH
OK-CJL	LET Z-37A Cmelák (Stored)	17-01	
OK-CJS	LET Z-37 Cmelák (Stored)	15-06	
OK-CJT	LET Z-37 Cmelák (Dismantled)	15-07	
OK-CJV	LET Z-37A Cmelák	15-09	
OK-CJW	LET Z-37 Cmelák (Dismantled)	15-10	
OK-CJZ	LET Z-37A Cmelák	15-28	
OK-CKP	LET Z-37 Cmelák (Dismantled)	16-15	
OK-CKR	LET Z-37A Cmelák (Stored)	16-26	
OK-CKU	LET Z-37 Cmelák	17-06	
OK-CKW	LET Z-37A Cmelák	17-08	
OK-CLO	Diamond DA 20-A1 Katana	10228	N228DA
OK-COA	Zlin Z.43	0001	
OK-COB	Zlin Z.43	0002	
OK-COC	Zlin Z.43	0004	
OK-COD	Zlin Z.43	0005	
OK-COE	Zlin Z.43	0007	
OK-COG	Zlin Z.43	0010	
OK-CRA	Zlin Z.526F Trenér Master	1251	
OK-CSR	Mraz M.1 Sokol	0142	
OK-CTA	Zlin Z.226MS Trenér	0104	
OK-CTB	Zlin Z.226MS Trenér	0105	
OK-CTD	Cessna F150H	F150-0296	HB-CTD
OK-CXA	Zlin Z.526AFS-V Akrobat	1218	
OK-CXB	Zlin Z.526AFS-V Akrobat	1219	
OK-CXC	Zlin Z.526AFS-V Akrobat	1220	
OK-CXF	Zlin Z.526AFS-V Akrobat	1224	
OK-CXQ	Z.37A-C2 Cmelák (Stored)	16-25	OK-CKQ
OK-CZD	LET L-610G	970301	
OK-DEV	Piper PA-28-181 Archer III	2843518	N376PA
OK-DGB	Boeing 737-5L9	28997	OY-APN
OK-DGC	Boeing 737-5L9	28935	OY-APR
OK-DGL	Boeing 737-55S	28472	
OK-DGM	Boeing 737-45S	28473	
OK-DGN	Boeing 737-45S	28474	
OK-DIB	Cessna 207 Skywagon 207	20700165	OE-DIB(2) OE-BIB OE-DEX N1565U
OK-DJO	LET Z-37A Cmelák	17-16	
OK-DJP	LET Z-37A Cmelák (Stored)	17-17	
OK-DJS	LET Z-37A Cmelák	17-20	
OK-DKJ	Cessna 172M	17262698	N13360
OK-DKK	Cessna 172M	17262539	N13161
OK-DKP	Piper PA-34-200 Seneca	34-7350288	D-GCZA N7130G D-GCZA N56133
OK-DKS	LET Z-37A Cmelák (Wfu, dismantled)	19-25	
OK-DKT	LET Z-37 Cmelák (Dismantled)	19-26	
OK-DKU	LET Z-37A Cmelák	19-27	
OK-DKV	LET Z-37A Cmelák	19-28	
OK-DKW	LET Z-37A Cmelák	19-29	
OK-DOA	Zlin Z.43	0011	
OK-DOB	Zlin Z.43	0013	
OK-DOC	Zlin Z.43	0014	
OK-DOD	Zlin Z.43	0016	
OK-DOE	Zlin Z.43	0028	
OK-DOF	Zlin Z.43	0029	
OK-DOG	Zlin Z.43	0032	
OK-DOH	Zlin Z.43	0033	
OK-DOI	Zlin Z.43	0035	
OK-DOJ	Zlin Z.43	0036	
OK-DOS(2)	Zlin Z.43MAF	0033	
OK-DRC	Zlin Z.726K Universal	1075	OK-078 OK-YRC
OK-DSA	Eurocopter EC.135T1	0083	D-HECK CC-CGL
OK-DSB	Eurocopter EC.135T2	0360	D-HECB
OK-DSC	Eurocopter EC.135T2	0363	D-HECF
OK-DSD	Eurocopter EC.135T2	0371	D-HECC
OK-DSN	Aérospatiale AS.355F Ecureil 2	5086	D-HHRR YV-05CP N5781P
OK-DVG	Zlin Z.126 Trenér 2	525	OK-EKA
OK-DVM	Reims FR172J Rocket	FR17200425	D-EGJI
OK-DZA	LET L-410MA Turbolet	730207	OK-158
OK-EGO	Boeing 737-55S	28475	
OK-EGP	Boeing 737-45S	28476	N1786B
OK-EHO	Zlin Z.526 Akrobat	1070	I-ZLIN OK-YRD

OK-EIH	MBB Bö.105C	S-175	D-HBOB (D-HDFM)
OK-EIN	Robinson R-44 Astro	0662	
OK-EJA	Z-137T Agro-Turbo	052	
OK-EKD	Reims/Cessna F172M	F17201125	D-EENM
OK-EKI	Reims/Cessna F150L	F15001053	D-EENV
OK-EKK	Cessna 172M	17261924	N12320
OK-EKM	Reims FR172J Rocket	FR17200471	D-EENS
OK-EKR	Cessna 172M	17263033	N13896
OK-EKS	Beech 95-B55 Baron	TC-1686	N4482W
OK-EKT	Cessna U206F Stationair	U20602276	D-EEVR (D-EAHP) N1906U
OK-EKU	Piper PA-23-250 Aztec E	27-7405402	G-JASP C-GREG N9669N
OK-ELM	Reims/Cessna F172M	F17201193	D-EOQI
OK-ELN	Cessna F172G	F172-0266	D-EBBO
OK-ELO	Cessna T303 Crusader	T30300205	D-ISEE N988PK G-BTLN N9688C
OK-EMI	Bell 427	56006	N7561A C-GFCK
OK-EOA	Zlin Z.43	0045	
OK-EOC	Zlin Z.43	0048	
OK-EOD	Zlin Z.43	0049	
OK-EOE	Zlin Z.43	0051	
OK-EOF	Zlin Z.43	0053	
OK-EOH	Zlin Z.43	0056	
OK-EOI	Zlin Z.43	0057	
OK-ERE	Zlin Z.526AFS-V Akrobat	1307	HA-SAW OK-DHB OK-ERE
OK-ESM	Maule M-5-210C Strata Rocket	6034C	N51596
OK-ESO	Zlin Z.42MU	0054	LZ-800
OK-EUR	Europa Aviation Europa XSTurbo	370	
OK-EVA	IBIS Aerospace Ae.270P	0007	
OK-EVE	Evektor VUT100 Cobra (F/f 16.11.04)	0001	
OK-FAI	Zlin Z.50LS	0052	OK-VZB OK-072
OK-FAL	Zlin Z.143L	0041	
OK-FAN	Boeing 737-33A	27469	
OK-FBI	Cessna 340	340-0114	OY-RPV OE-FKI N4576L
OK-FGR	Boeing 737-45S	28477	N1786B
OK-FGS	Boeing 737-45S	28478	
OK-FJO	LET Z-37A Cmelák	21-09	
OK-FJP	LET Z-37A Cmelák (Dismantled, stored)	21-10	
OK-FJT	LET Z-37A Cmelák	21-14	
OK-FJU	LET Z-37A Cmelák	21-15	
OK-FJW	LET Z-37A Cmelák	21-17	OM-FJW OK-FJW OM-FJW OK-FJW
OK-FJY	LET Z-37A Cmelák	21-19	
OK-FKD	Cessna 172N	17266144	N9403H
OK-FKL	Cessna 150M	15076965	N45540
OK-FKU	Cessna 172M	17265255	D-EXEL N64474
OK-FLY	Piper PA-28-181 Archer III	2843346	N41832 (OK-FLY)
OK-FOF	Zlin Z.43	0061	
OK-FOG	Zlin Z.43	0063	
OK-FOH	Zlin Z.43	0064	
OK-FOI	Zlin Z.43	0067	
OK-FOJ	Zlin Z.43	0068	
OK-FOK	Zlin Z.43	0069	
OK-FOL	Zlin Z.43	0070	
OK-FOM	Zlin Z.43	0072	
OK-FUN	Boeing 737-33A	27910	
OK-FZZ	Piper PA-34-220T Seneca V	3449254	N53523
OK-GEA	Airbus A320-214	1439	CS-TQA EI-CWU OO-SNI F-WWBM
OK-GEB	Airbus A320-214	1450	CS-TQB EI-CWV OO-SNJ F-WWBX
OK-GEO	Cessna 402B	402B0921	D-INAB (2) N87116
OK-GIB	Antonov An-2	1G168-01	
OK-GIC	Antonov An-2TD	1G168-03	
OK-GJC	LET Z-37A Cmelák	22-18	
OK-GJO	LET Z-37A Cmelák	22-07	OM-GJO OK-GJO
OK-GJS	LET Z-37A Cmelák	22-11	
OK-GJU	LET Z-37A Cmelák	22-13	
OK-GJV	LET Z-37A Cmelák (Stored)	22-14	
OK-GJW	LET Z-37A-C2 Cmelák	22-15	
OK-GKA	Cessna 172M	17266459	N80228
OK-GKG	Cessna 172M	17266111	N9354H
OK-GKH	Cessna 172M	17265979	D-ETRW N9154H
OK-GKO	Piper PA-28R-200 Cherokee Arrow II	28R-7635119	D-EFEI N7828C
OK-GOS	LET L.200DMorava	171414	SP-NEB CCCP02130
OK-GTJ	Beech 300LW Super King Air	FA-223	D-IHHB N80775
OK-HIR	Antonov An-2	1G176-39	UR-62570 CCCP62570
OK-HIT	Cessna P210NPressurized Centurion (Accident 10.11.03)	P21000797	N6564W
OK-HJB	LET Z-37A Cmelák (Stored)	23-02	
OK-HJC	LET Z-37 Cmelák (Dismantled)	23-03	
OK-HJD	LET Z-37A Cmelák (Stored)	23-04	
OK-HJF	LET Z-37A Cmelák	23-07	
OK-HJG	LET Z-37A Cmelák (Dismantled)	23-10	
OK-HJH	LET Z-37 Cmelák	23-11	
OK-HJI	LET Z-37A Cmelák (Stored)	23-14	
OK-HJJ	LET Z-37 Cmelák (Stored)	23-15	
OK-HJK	LET Z-37A Cmelák	23-17	
OK-HJM	LET Z-37A Cmelák	23-19	
OK-HJU	LET Z-37 Cmelák	23-23	
OK-HKC	Reims/Cessna F150M	F15001422	D-EBXD
OK-HKD	Cessna 172N	17268857	TF-IDA N734HB
OK-HKE	Cessna TU206G Turbo Stationair II	U20603877	I-IPAC (N7336C)
OK-HKS	Piper PA-23-250 Aztec F	27-7754134	N95EB N63811
OK-HLF	Zlin Z.126 Trenér 2	715	CzAF213
OK-HLH	Zlin Z.126 Trenér 2	718	CzAF216
OK-HLJ	Zlin Z.126 Trenér 2	721	CzAF219
OK-HLK	Zlin Z.126 Trenér 2	722	CzAF220
OK-HOP	Zlin Z.143L	0050	
OK-HYA	LET Z-37-2C Cmelák	23-08	
OK-HZL	Zlin Z-400	1	
OK-IAN	MBB Bö.105C	S-415	D-HBOE (D-HDMN)
OK-IFG	Zlin Z.126 Trenér 2	746	
OK-IFH	Zlin Z.126 Trenér 2	748	
OK-IHK	Zlin Z.126 Trenér 2	731	CzAF229
OK-IHQ	Zlin Z.126 Trenér 2	778	CzAF243
OK-IKA	Cessna 152	15282048	N67837
OK-IKC	Cessna 152	15281978	N67713
OK-IKF	Cessna 152	15281144	D-EYAP(1) OH-CKX C-GGTJ N49091
OK-IKH	Cessna 152	15282176	N68193
OK-IKQ	Cessna 172N	17271299	N2487E
OK-ILP	Zlin Z.42M	0158	
OK-ILQ	Zlin Z.42M	0159	
OK-IMG	Zlin Z.126 Trenér 2	776	CzAF241
OK-IMI	Zlin Z.126T Trenér 2	780	CzAF245
OK-INA	IBIS Aerospace Ae.270P	0006	
OK-IRJ	Zlin Z.50LA	0020	
OK-ITC	Cessna T182T Turbo Skylane	T18208067	D-EOPJ N35105
OK-IVA	Zlin Z.126 Trenér 2	737	CzAF
OK-JAR	Reims/Cessna F152	F15201696	D-EFDG
OK-JAS	Reims FR172G Rocket	FR17200222	D-ECKG
OK-JCA	Zlin Z.226MS Trenér	839	
OK-JET	Aero L-39C Albatros	131904	UKrAF:53yellow
OK-JFJ	Aérospatiale/Alenia ATR-42-512	623	F-WWLD
OK-JFK	Aérospatiale/Alenia ATR-42-512	625	F-WWLF
OK-JFL	Aérospatiale/Alenia ATR-42-512	629	F-WWLJ
OK-JGD	Zlin Z.126 Trenér 2	860	
OK-JGL	Zlin Z.126 Trenér 2	801	
OK-JGT	Zlin Z.226MS Trenér	804	
OK-JHA	Zlin Z.126 Trenér 2	811	
OK-JHC	Zlin Z.126 Trenér 2	816	DM-WAR OK-JHC
OK-JHE	Zlin Z.126 Trenér 2	818	
OK-JID	Antonov An-2R (Stored)	1G186-18	
OK-JIF	Antonov An-2T (Stored)	1G186-20	OM-JIF OK-JIF OM-JIF OK-JIF
OK-JIH	Antonov An-2R	1G186-22	OM-JIH OK-JIH
OK-JII	Antonov An-2R (Reserved as D-FPET)	1G186-23	
OK-JIJ	Antonov An-2R	1G186-24	
OK-JIL	Antonov An-2R (Derelict)	1G186-26	
OK-JIM	Antonov An-2R (Preserved)	1G186-27	
OK-JIP	Cessna 421C Golden Eagle	421C0156	N6VH N246RS N5283J
OK-JIQ	Antonov An-2R (Stored)	1G186-28	
OK-JIX	Mil Mi-2	536012029	OM-JIX OK-JIX
OK-JJA	LET Z-37A Cmelák (Stored)	24-08	
OK-JJB	LET Z-37A Cmelák	24-02	
OK-JJC	LET Z-37A Cmelák	24-09	
OK-JJD	LET Z-37A Cmelák (Stored)	24-05	
OK-JKA	LET Z-37A Cmelák (Stored) (C/n now quoted as 23-21, possibly a rebuild?)	24-01	

OK-JKF	Cessna 172N	17271045	D-EVOA N1556E
OK-JKS	Piper PA-34-200T Seneca II	34-7970494	D-GELD N8080Y
OK-JKV	Cessna 172N	17272765	D-ESBD N6379D
OK-JLA	Zlin Z.126 Trenér 2 (Stored)	781	CzAF246
OK-JLB	Zlin Z.126 Trenér 2	785	CzAF250
OK-JLE	Zlin Z.126 Trenér 2	827	CzAF259
OK-JLF	Zlin Z.126 Trenér 2	820	CzAF252
OK-JOA	Aero L-60S Brigadyr	03	
OK-JSB	Zlin Z.42M	0182	
OK-JSC	Zlin Z.42M	0183	
OK-JSD	Zlin Z.42M	0185	
OK-JSE	Zlin Z.42M	0186	
OK-JSF	Zlin Z.42M	0187	
OK-JST	Reims/Cessna F172N	F17201882	D-EIYQ
OK-JXA	SK.1 Trempik (Homebuilt)	01	OK-006
OK-JZE	Yakovlev Yak-C11	171511	OK-242 OK-JIL
OK-KFM	Aérospatiale/Alenia ATR-42-512 (Res .05)	unkn	
OK-KFN	Aérospatiale/Alenia ATR-42-512 (Res .05)	unkn	
OK-KFO	Aérospatiale/Alenia ATR-42-512 (Res .05)	unkn	
OK-KFQ	Aérospatiale/Alenia ATR-42-512 (Res .05)	unkn	
OK-KGB	Aero 45S	04-016	
OK-KIC	Antonov An-2R (Derelict)	1G186-34	
OK-KID	Antonov An-2RD	1G186-35	
OK-KIE(2)	Antonov An-2R	1G186-36	
OK-KII	Antonov An-2R	1G190-04	
OK-KIJ	Antonov An-2R	1G190-05	OM-KIJ OK-KIJ
OK-KIK	Antonov An-2R	1G190-06	
OK-KIL	Antonov An-2R (Derelict)	1G190-07	
OK-KIN	Antonov An-2R	1G190-09	OM-KIN OK-KIN
OK-KIP	Antonov An-2R (Derelict)	1G190-10	
OK-KIQ	Antonov An-2R	1G190-11	OK-KIR
OK-KIT	Antonov An-2R	1G190-14	OM-KIT OK-KIT
OK-KIV	Antonov An-2R (Derelict)	1G190-16	
OK-KIZ(2)	Mil Mi-2	526847100	RA-20208 CCCP20208
OK-KJA	Aero L-60SF Brigadyr	150205	CzAF 0205
OK-KJB	LET Z-37A Cmelák	23-28	
OK-KJT	LETZ-37ACmelák	24-16	
OK-KKA	Cessna 127RG Cutlass	0128	N6266R
OK-KKB	LET Z-37A Cmelák (Stored)	24-10	
OK-KKD	Cessna 172N Skyhawk II	17273712	N5138J
OK-KKK	Cessna 172S	172S8698	D-EIIR(2) N765SP
OK-KLN	LET Z.37A-2 Cmelák (C/n 11-11 OK-AJO rebuilt)	24-19	OM-KLN OK-KLN
OK-KMB	Zlin Z.226AS Akrobat Special	02-08	
OK-KMJ	Zlin Z.226MS Trenér	11-08	
OK-KMK	Zlin Z.226T Trenér 6	08-12	
OK-KMM	Zlin Z.126T Trenér 2	08-14	
OK-KMO	Zlin Z.226M Trenér	0016	
OK-KMP	Zlin Z.226MS Trenér (C/n formerly quoted as 08-07)	0017	
OK-KMR	Zlin Z.226MS Trenér	0019	
OK-KMS	Zlin Z.226M Trenér (C/n formerly quoted as 09-21; most likely 0021)	08-21	
OK-KMT	Zlin Z.226MS Trenér (W/o 14.7.04)	0022	
OK-KNA	Zlin Z.226M Trenér	0028	
OK-KNB	Zlin Z.226M Trenér	09-29	
OK-KNC(2)	Zlin Z.142	0206	
OK-KND	Zlin Z.226M Trenér	0031	
OK-KNF	Zlin Z.226MS Trenér	0033	
OK-KNG	Zlin Z.226 MS Trenér	0034	
OK-KNH	Zlin Z.142	0221	
OK-KNK	Zlin Z.142	0228	
OK-KNL	Zlin Z.142	0229	
OK-KNM	Zlin Z.226M Trenér	0040	
OK-KNN	Zlin Z.226MS Trenér	0041	
OK-KNR	Zlin Z.126T Trenér 2	103	
OK-KNX	Zlin Z.226MS Trenér	0047	
OK-KOS	Zlin Z.43	0083	
OK-LEA	Robinson R-22B2 Beta	2998	
OK-LES	Hughes 369E	0259E	D-HDHF(2) F-GOTM C-FYTZ N535JP N1603K
OK-LFA	Cessna 152	15284293	D-EOMV N5310L
OK-LHA	Zlin Z.326M Trenér Master	301	
OK-LIB	IBIS Aerospace Ae.270	0005	
OK-LIT	Cessna T303 Crusader	T30300226	D-ISLA(2) F-GFTP N510TF N9868C
OK-LJA	LET Z-37A Cmelák (Stored)	24-14	
OK-LJR	Mil Mi-2	537327091	OM-LJR OK-LJR
OK-LKA	LET Z-37A Cmelák	24-12	
OK-LKB	Cessna 152	15284784	N4620P
OK-LKF	Aero L-60S Brigadyr	150727	
OK-LKG	Aero L-60S Brigadyr	150728	
OK-LKH	Aero L-60S Brigadyr	150729	
OK-LKJ	Aero L-60S Brigadyr	150801	
OK-LKN	Aero L-60 Brigadyr	150507	
OK-LKP	Cessna 182R Skylane	18267924	D-EXAP SE- IHB (N9063H)
OK-LKR	Aero L-60S Brigadyr	150413	
OK-LLF	Zlin Z.226MS Trenér	121	
OK-LLH	Zlin Z.226T Trenér 6	123	
OK-LLK	Zlin Z.226MS Trenér	126	
OK-LMB	Zlin Z.226MS Trenér	124	OK-LLI
OK-LMD	Zlin Z.226M Trenér	120	OK-LLE
OK-LME	Zlin Z.226MS Trenér	119	OK-LLD
OK-LMF	Zlin Z.226MS Trenér	139	OK-LLW
OK-LMG	Zlin Z.226M Trenér	135	OK-LLS
OK-LMH	Zlin Z.226M Trenér	118	OK-LLC
OK-LMI	Zlin Z.226MS Trenér (Crash, 15.7.00)	128	OK-LLM
OK-LMJ	Zlin Z.226MS Trenér	137	OK-LLU
OK-LNA	Zlin Z .142	0231	
OK-LNB	Zlin Z .142	0232	
OK-LNC	Zlin Z .142	0235	
OK-LND	Zlin Z .142	0242	
OK-LNE	Zlin Z .142	0247	
OK-LNG	Zlin Z .142	0251	
OK-LNH	Zlin Z .142	0252	
OK-LNI	Zlin Z .142	0253	
OK-LNJ	Zlin Z .142	0254	
OK-LNK	Zlin Z .142	0258	
OK-LNL	Zlin Z .142	0259	
OK-LNN	Zlin Z.226MS Trenér	105	OK-KNU
OK-LRA	LET L-410UVP-E	882216	CCCP67605
OK-LSI	Zlin Z. 143L	0042	
OK-LSV	Maule MX-7-235 Star Rocket	10062C	D-EKMM(2) OE-KUW
OK-MAL	LET L.200D Morava	171402	SP-NXY SP-NAC
OK-MAP	Cessna 150M	15078155	PH-GUT N9204U
OK-MAT	Piper PA-44-180T Turbo Seminole	44-8207020	G-FRST N8236B N9615N
OK-MCP	Cessna 172S Skyhawk	172S9676	N6124A
OK-MFE	Zlin Z.226MS Trenér	149	
OK-MFK	Zlin Z.226M Trenér	155	
OK-MFO	Zlin Z.226M Trenér	159	
OK-MFP	Zlin Z.226T Trenér 6	160	
OK-MFQ	Zlin Z.226MS Trenér	161	
OK-MFV	Zlin Z.226MS Trenér	168	
OK-MFX	Zlin Z.226T Trenér 6	163	
OK-MFY	Zlin Z.226MS Trenér	170	
OK-MGD	Zlin Z.226MS Trenér	175	
OK-MGF	Zlin Z.226T Trenér 6	177	
OK-MGJ	Zlin Z.226MS Trenér	181	
OK-MGK	Zlin Z.226MS Trenér	182	
OK-MGM	Zlin Z.226MS Trenér	184	
OK-MGQ	Zlin Z.226M Trenér	188	
OK-MGR	Zlin Z.226MS Trenér	189	
OK-MGU	Zlin Z.226MS Trenér	193	
OK-MGV	Zlin Z.226MS Trenér	194	
OK-MGX	Zlin Z.226MS Trenér	190	
OK-MHC	Zlin Z.226AS Trenér	200	
OK-MIA	Aérospatiale AS.355F2 Ecureuil 2	5187	N5799W
OK-MIK	PZL Kania	900103	SP-SSA
OK-MJL	Aero L-60S Brigadyr	151011	
OK-MJM	Bell 206BJet Ranger II (Crashed 17.5.02)	3601	D-HANE N206PW N911SE N911SL N2262F
OK-MJN	Aero L-60 Brigadyr	150826	
OK-MJP	Aero L-60 Brigadyr	151128	
OK-MKD	Antonov An-2R	1G186-31	HA-MKD OM-JIT OK-JIT
OK-MLA	Cessna 172P Skyhawk II	17275132	G-BTGF N55195
OK-MLR	Piper PA-44-180 Seminole	44-8095018	SE-KZS 9Q-CJR OO-HLR N8147H
OK-MME	Orlican L-40 Meta-Sokol	150203	
OK-MML	Orlican L-40 Meta-Sokol	150607	
OK-MMM	Orlican L-40 Meta-Sokol	150608	
OK-MMQ	Orlican L-40 Meta-Sokol	150207	
OK-MMR	Orlican L-40 Meta-Sokol	150612	
OK-MMS	Cessna 182K	18257993	D-ELGS N2793Q
OK-MMT	Orlican L-40 Meta-Sokol	150307	
OK-MNA	Zlin Z.142	0266	
OK-MNB	Zlin Z.142	0267	
OK-MNC	Zlin Z.142	0279	
OK-MND	Zlin Z.142 (Accident 22.6.00)	0280	
OK-MNE	Zlin Z.142	0306	
OK-MNF	Zlin Z.142 (Stored)	0283	
OK-MNG	Zlin Z.142	0285	

OK-MNH	Zlin Z.142	0286	
OK-MNI	Zlin Z.142	0288	
OK-MNJ	Zlin Z.142	0289	
OK-MNL	Zlin Z.142	0295	
OK-MNM	Zlin Z.142	0302	
OK-MNU	Zlin Z.142	0301	
OK-MPA	Zlin Z.226MS Trenér	246	
OK-MPB	Zlin Z.226MS Trenér	247	
OK-MPG	Zlin Z.226MS Trenér	252	
OK-MPJ	Zlin Z.226B Trenér	255	
OK-MPK	Zlin Z.226MS Trenér	256	
OK-MPP	Zlin Z.226MS Trenér	261	
OK-MPT	Zlin Z.226MS Trenér	266	
OK-MPV	Zlin Z.226MS Trenér	268	
OK-MQB	Zlin Z.226MS Trenér	273	
OK-MQE	Zlin Z.226MS Trenér	276	
OK-MQG	Zlin Z.226B Trenér	278	
OK-MQH	Zlin Z.226MS Trenér	279	
OK-MQI	Zlin Z.226B-SL Trenér	280	
OK-MQJ	Zlin Z.226MS Trenér	281	
OK-MQL	Zlin Z.226B Trenér	283	
OK-MQM	Zlin Z.226MS Trenér	284	
OK-MQN	Zlin Z.226MS Trenér	285	
OK-MRA	Zlin Z.226MS Trenér	198	OK-MHA
OK-MRK	Cessna 150L	15073601	N17044
OK-MTA	Aero L-60S Brigadyr	150820	
OK-MTF	Aero L-60S Brigadyr	151202	
OK-MTG	Aero L-60S Brigadyr (Damaged)	151203	
OK-MTH	Aero L-60S Brigadyr	150813	
OK-MTI	Aero L-60S Brigadyr	150815	
OK-MTK	Aero L-60S Brigadyr (Stored)	150810	
OK-MTT	Piper PA-29-181 Archer III	2843566	N5352G
OK-MYA	Antonov An-2 (Scrapped)	19507	
OK-NAV	Reims/Cessna F152	F15201734	D-EKMT
OK-NEW	Piper PA-28-181 Archer III	2843271	N4147V
			N9507N
OK-NHE	Aero 145 Super Aero	19013	
OK-NJA	LET Z-37A Cmelák	25-01	
OK-NJB	LET Z-37A Cmelák	25-02	
OK-NJD	LET Z-37A Cmelák (Dismantled)	25-06	
OK-NJE	LET Z-37 Cmelák (Stored)	25-07	
OK-NJG	LET Z-37A Cmelák	25-09	
OK-NJH	LET Z-37A Cmelák	25-10	
OK-NJJ	LET Z-37A Cmelák	25-13	
OK-NJK	LET Z-37A Cmelák	25-14	
OK-NJL	LET Z-37A Cmelák	25-15	
OK-NJM	LET Z-37A Cmelák (Stored)	25-17	
OK-NJN	LET Z-37A Cmelák (Dismantled)	25-18	
OK-NJO	LET Z-37A Cmelák (Dismantled)	25-19	
OK-NJP	LET Z-37A Cmelák (Stored)	25-20	
OK-NJR	LETZ-37ACmelák	25-04	OM-NJR
			OK-NJR
OK-NMO	Orlican L-40 Meta-Sokol	150308	
OK-NNB	Aero L-60S Brigadyr	151207	
OK-NNG	Aero L-60S Brigadyr	151212	
OK-NNH	Aero L-60S Brigadyr	151213	
OK-NNJ	Aero L-60S Brigadyr	151215	
OK-NOA	Zlin Z.142	0309	
OK-NOB	Zlin Z.142	0310	
OK-NOC	Zlin Z.142	0312	
OK-NOD	Zlin Z.142	0327	
OK-NOE	Zlin Z.142	0328	
OK-NOF	Zlin Z .142	0330	
OK-NOG	Zlin Z..142	0320	
OK-NOH	Zlin Z .142	0331	
OK-NOJ	Zlin Z .142	0337	
OK-NOK	Zlin Z .142	0338	
OK-NOL	Zlin Z .142	0340	
OK-NOM	Zlin Z .142	0341	
OK-NON	Zlin Z .142	0349	
OK-NOO	Zlin Z .142	0350	
OK-NOP	Zlin Z .142	0352	
OK-NOR	Orlican L-40 Meta-Sokol	150905	G-AROF
OK-NPE	Orlican L-40 Meta-Sokol	150504	
OK-NPF	Orlican L-40 Meta-Sokol	150714	
OK-NPK	Orlican L-40 Meta-Sokol	150804	
OK-NPL	Orlican L-40 Meta-Sokol	150805	
OK-NPM	Orlican L-40 Meta-Sokol	150907	G-ARSP
OK-NPN	Orlican L-40 Meta-Sokol	150807	
OK-NPR	Orlican L-40 Meta-Sokol	150811	
OK-NPS	Orlican L-40 Meta-Sokol	150812	
OK-NPU	Orlican L-40 Meta-Sokol	150814	OM-NPU
			OK-NPU
OK-NPV	Orlican L-40 Meta-Sokol	150815	
OK-NPW	Orlican L-40 Meta-Sokol	150703	D-EGPO
OK-NXX	LET L.200D Morava	171206	SP-NXX(2)
			HA-LDA
OK-OFB	LET L.200A Morava	170606	OM-OFB
			OK-OFB
			OE-FSE
			OK-OFB
OK-OFI	LET L.200A Morava	170614	OE-FSC
			OK-OFI
OK-OFK	LET L.200A Morava	170620	
OK-OFL	LET L.200A Morava	170618	CzAF0618
OK-OGA	LET L.200D Morava	170317	OK-BYB
OK-OGB	LET L.200A Morava	170318	OK-BYC
OK-OHE	LET L.200A Morava	170102	
OK-OHF	LET L.200A Morava	170215	
OK-OHG	LET L.200A Morava	170617	
OK-OHH	LET L.200A Morava	170619	
OK-OJA	LET Z-37A Cmelák (Stored)	25-25	
OK-OJB	LET Z-37A Cmelák (Stored)	25-26	
OK-OJC	LET Z-37A Cmelák (Stored)	25-27	
OK-OJD	LET Z-37A Cmelák	25-29	
OK-OJE	LET Z-37A Cmelák (Stored)	25-30	
OK-OJF	LET Z-37A Cmelák (Dismantled)	25-31	
OK-OJG	LET Z-37A Cmelák (Stored)	25-33	
OK-OJH	LET Z-37A Cmelák (Stored)	25-34	
OK-OJI	LET Z-37A Cmelák (Stored)	25-35	
OK-OJJ	LET Z-37A Cmelák (Stored)	25-37	
OK-OJL	LET Z-37A Cmelák	25-39	
OK-OKD	Piper PA-34-220T Seneca V	3449218	N5325A
OK-OKR	Piper PA-34-220T Seneca V	3449163	N41770
			OK-OKR
			N9527N
OK-OKZ	LET L.200A Morava	170320	
OK-ONR	Zlin Z.142 (Wo 18-10-03)	0381	
OK-OPA	Zlin Z.142	0357	
OK-OPB	Zlin Z.142	0358	
OK-OPC	Zlin Z.142	0360	
OK-OPD	Zlin Z.142	0361	
OK-OPE	Zlin Z.142	0363	
OK-OPG	Zlin Z.142	0371	
OK-OPH	Zlin Z.142	0372	
OK-OPI	Zlin Z.142	0379	
OK-OPJ	Zlin Z.142	0380	
OK-OPK	Zlin Z.142	0382	
OK-OPL	Zlin Z.142	0383	
OK-OPM	Zlin Z.142	0385	
OK-OPN	Zlin Z.142	0386	
OK-OQF	Reims/Cessna F172M	F17201189	D-EOQF
OK-OTA	Zlin Z.326M Trenér Master	604	CzAF0604
OK-OTB	Zlin Z.326 Trenér Master	605	CzAF0605
OK-OTD	Zlin Z.326 Trenér Master	609	CzAF0609
OK-OTE	Zlin Z.326 Trenér Master	610	CzAF0610
OK-PDC	LET L-410FG	851524	CzAF1524
OK-PDO	LET L-410UVP (Stored)	851411	UR-67507
			CCCP67507
OK-PEK	SOCATA TB-10 Tobago	420	HB-KAG
OK-PFM	LET L.200A Morava	170710	
OK-PHG	LET L.200A Morava	170805	
OK-PHJ	LET L.200A Morava	170802	
OK-PHR	Beech 58P Pressurized Baron	TJ-237	D-IBEE
			OE-FKP
			N600PA
			4X-DZG
			N6680L
OK-PIM	Schweizer 269C	S-1185	SE-JAB
			N7503Q
OK-PJA	LET Z-37T Agro-Turbo	001	
OK-PJN	LET Z-37T Agro-Turbo (Dismantled)	002	OK-PXH
OK-PLA	LET L.200A Morava	170713	
OK-PLG	LET L.200A Morava	170720	
OK-PLH	LET L.200A Morava	170722	
OK-PLI	LET L.200D Morava	170723	
OK-PLJ	LET L.200D Morava	170724	
OK-PLL	LET L.200D Morava	170726	
OK-PLO	LET L.200A Morava	170729	
OK-PLR	LET L.200A Morava	170801	
OK-PLS	LET L.200A Morava	170803	
OK-PLV	LET L.200D Morava	170815	SP-NXX
			SP-GBA
			CCCP-34454
OK-PNB	Zlin Z.142	0393	
OK-PNC	Zlin Z.142	0395	
OK-PND	Zlin Z.142	0399	
OK-PNE	Zlin Z.142	0401	
OK-PNF	Zlin Z.142	0402	
OK-PNG	Zlin Z.142	0404	
OK-PNH	Zlin Z.142	0407	
OK-PNI	Zlin Z.142	0409	
OK-PNJ	Zlin Z.142	0410	
OK-PNK	Zlin Z.142	0412	
OK-PNL	Zlin Z.142	0418	
OK-PNM	Zlin Z.142	0415	
OK-PPA	Zlin Z.142	0416	
OK-PPM	Zlin Z.142	0413	
OK-PRA	Cessna 414	414-0040	D-ILOT
	(Damaged 1.7.01)		N414BT
			C-GCIC
			N414JB
			C-GCIC
			(N12DT)
			C-GCIC
			N8140Q
OK-PRO	LET L.200A Morava	170705	CubanAF
	(C/n confirmed, previously listed as 170105)		CzAF0705
OK-PYA	Antonov An-2	115718	
OK-RAV	Raven-257 Experimental	001	
OK-RAY	Cessna T210J Turbo Centurion	T2100408	D-ELRG
			(N2258R)
OK-RDA	LETL-410UVP-E5	871813	OM-RAY
			OM-RDA
			OK-RDA

OK-RFP	LET L.200D Morava	171114	
OK-RHH	LET L.200D Morava	171418	YU-BBI
OK-RID	Antonov An-2	117008	CzAF7008
OK-RIE	Antonov An-2 (Stored)	117413	CzAF7413
OK-RJJ	LET Z-37T Agro-Turbo (Stored)	016	
OK-RJL	LET Z-37T Agro-Turbo (Stored)	018	
OK-RJM	LET Z-37T Agro-Turbo (Stored)	019	
OK-RMA	LET L.200D Morava	171124	
OK-ROC	Cessna 150F	15062325	D-EYMR N3525L
OK-RRD	Zlin Z.50LS	0047	
OK-RTT	Reims FR172FRocket	FR17200141	D-EBTR
OK-RXE	Aero C-104S (Jungmann)	X001	OK-AXT
OK-SDK	Piper PA-28-180 Cherokee B	28-1710	D-ESDK D-ECKC(1) 5U-BAA (F-OCDX) N7749W
OK-SDS	LET L-410UVP-E	871928	RusAF:1928
OK-SEN	Zlin Z.326 Trenér Master	893	F-BMQR
OK-SHG	Zlin Z.50LX	0069	
OK-SIV	Piper PA-32-301FT 6x	3232027	N3095G
OK-SJB	Z-137T Agro-Turbo	023	HA-MGF OK-SJB
OK-SKY	LET L-410UVP Turbolet	851418	CCCP67514
OK-SLA	Cessna 525 CitationJet	525-0310	D-IIJS D-IVBG
OK-SLD	LET L-410UVP-E9 Turbolet	022634	
OK-SLI	Beech 58 Baron	TH-1757	N3257N
OK-SLN	Embraer EMB.135BJ Legacy	145796	PT-SIF
OK-SLS	Cessna 560 Citation V	560-0088	D-CMCM OE-GSW (N6783X)
OK-SNZ	Zlin Z.142	0441	HA-SGP
OK-SUR	Cessna 421C Golden Eagle	421C0861	D-IOAA OE-FBL (N26602)
OK-SWU	Boeing 737-522	26703	N955UA
OK-SWV	Boeing 737-522	26696	N951UA
OK-SWY	Boeing 737-530	24815	D-ABIA N3521N
OK-SYK	Cessna 152	15282182	N68203
OK-TEC	Reims/Cessna FR172KHawk XP	FR17200627	D-EOMS
OK-TEK	Reims/Cessna F150M	F15001380	D-EMKK(2)
OK-TGD	PZL M-18A Dromader	1Z018-13	
OK-TGG	PZL M-18A Dromader	1Z018-16	OM-TGG OK-TGG
OK-TGH	PZL M-18A Dromader	1Z018-17	HA-MVC OK-TGH
OK-TGL	PZL M-18A Dromader	1Z018-26	
OK-TGR	PZL M-18A Dromader (Stored)	1Z019-16	OM-TGR OK-TGR
OK-TKF	Cessna 421BGolden Eagle	421B0931	OE-FBY OE-BAY OE-FLK N5381J
OK-TLU	Piper PA-34-220T Seneca V	34-8170041	D-GOFY (3) N8297L
OK-TRM	Zlin Z.50M	0053	OM-TRM OK-080 OK-TRM
OK-TRO	Zlin Z.50LS	0055	(G-MATE)
OK-TRP	Zlin Z.50L	0059	
OK-TRQ	Zlin Z.50L	0060	
OK-TVA	Boeing 737-86N	32243	
OK-TVB	Boeing 737-8CX	32362	
OK-TVC	Boeing 737-86Q	30278	N289CD (OO-CYH)
OK-TVD	Boeing 737-86N	28595	CN-RNO N1784B (TC-IAK) N1795B
OK-TVF	Boeing 737-8FH	29669	
OK-TVR	Boeing 737-4YO	23870	G-OBMG N1791B
OK-TVS	Boeing 737-4YO	24011	HA-LKA OK-TVS SE-DTB EI-CIX OY-MBK PT-WBJ PP-SQJ (TC-ADA)
OK-UDS	LET L-410UVP-E13	892321	
OK-UIA	Antonov An-2	1G237-36	
OK-UIC	Mil Mi-2	548149053	OM-UIC OK-UIC LY-HBL YL-LHL Soviet Mil
OK-UJD	LET Z-37 Cmelák	005	
OK-UJK	Z-137T Agro-Turbo	027	
OK-UJL	Z-137T Agro-Turbo (Damaged 17.8.02)	028	
OK-UJO	Z-137T Agro-Turbo	031	OM-UJO OK-UJO
OK-UKB	PZL-104 Wilga 80	20890882	SP-FWS
OK-UKC	Cessna F172G	F172-0233	HB-CBO
OK-UKD	Piper PA-28-180 Cherokee C	28-2318	HB-OLN N819IW
OK-UKJ	Cessna 172F	17252606	N172DP N8702U
OK-UXE	Piper J-3C-65 Cub (L-4J) (C/n quoted as 001/89 after rebuild)	12254	OK-YIE 44-79958
OK-UZI	Beech 400 Beechjet	RJ-56	G-BSZP N1556W
OK-VDA	LET L-410UVP-E	902403	RA-44477 RA-67621 CCCP67621
OK-VFI	Aérospatiale/Alenia ATR-42-300	173	F-WQNE D-BHHH F-WWED
OK-VGB	PZL M-18A Dromader	1Z021-19	
OK-VGZ	Boeing 737-K5	24769	EC-HXT D-ABAB N11AB
OK-VHC	Antonov An-2TP	1G238-24	
OK-VHD	Antonov An-2TP (Stored)	1G238-25	
OK-VHJ	Antonov An-2TP	1G234-02	
OK-VII	Z-137T Agro-Turbo (Dismantled)	040	
OK-VIL	PZL Kania	900305	
OK-VJT	LET Z-37A Cmelák	01-12	
OK-VJV	LET Z-37C-3 Cmelák	01-14	
OK-VJX	LET Z-37 Cmelák	01-16	
OK-VKF	Cessna F172G	F172-0277	D-EKER(2)
OK-VLA	Evektor EV-97VLA Harmony	990001	
OK-VLK	Cessna 152	15284278	N5216L
OK-VNB	Zlin Z.142	0514	
OK-VNC	Zlin Z.142	0515	
OK-VNF	Zlin Z.142	0528	
OK-VNJ	Zlin Z.142	0517	HA-SHA
OK-VSZ	Cessna 550 Citation Bravo	550-1040	N12378 N52446
OK-WAA	Airbus A310-304	564	F-WWCB
OK-WAB	Airbus A310-304	567	F-WWCD
OK-WDC	LET L-410UVP-E8D	912531	
OK-WDT	LET L-410UVP-E20C	912615	CCCP67684
OK-WEL	Zlin Z.43	0089	
OK-WGD	Boeing 737-59D	25065	LX-LGN G-OBMX SE-DNE (SE-DND)
OK-WGF	Boeing 737-4Y0	24903	9M-MJN
OK-WGG	Boeing 737-4Y0	24693	9M-MJM
OK-WGX	Boeing 737-436	25349	G-DOCD
OK-WGY	Boeing 737-436	25839	G-DOCI
OK-WHB	Antonov An-2	1G85-55	
OK-WHN	LET L.200D Morava	171415	
OK-WIQ	Aérospatiale AS.355F2 Ecureuil 2	5483	OM-WIQ OK-WIQ SE-JET F-WYMA
OK-WJD	LET Z-37 Cmelák	02-04	
OK-WJQ	LET Z-37 Cmelák	03-11	
OK-WJT	LET Z-37 Cmelák	03-14	
OK-WJU	LET Z-37 Cmelák	03-17	HA-MGC
OK-WKF	Cessna 150G	15066672	C-FWBL CF-WBL (N2772S)
OK-WNL	Zlin Z.142C	0525	C-FKII OK-WNL
OK-WOA	Zlin Z.43	0090	
OK-WOB	Zlin Z.43	0085	
OK-WOC	Zlin Z.43	0086	
OK-WOD	Zlin Z.43	0087	
OK-WOE	Zlin Z.43	0088	
OK-WOF	Zlin Z.43	0091	
OK-WOH	Zlin Z.43	0101	
OK-WOI	Zlin Z.43	0102	
OK-WOJ	Zlin Z.43	0103	
OK-WOK	Zlin Z.43 (Damaged 26.6.03)	0095	
OK-WOL	Zlin Z.43	0104	
OK-WWW	Cessna 150M	15077681	N6398K
OK-WXA	Zlin Z.526ASM Akrobat	1026	
OK-WXE(2)	Extra EA.300	026	D-EIUE
OK-WYI	LET L-410UVP	912616	CCCP67685
OK-XFA	Aérospatiale/Alenia ATR-72-201	285	(F-GIGU) F-WWLO
OK-XFB	Aérospatiale/Alenia ATR-72-201	297	F-WWLW
OK-XFC	Aérospatiale/Alenia ATR-72-201	299	F-WWLX
OK-XFD	Aérospatiale/Alenia ATR-72-201	303	F-WWLB
OK-XGA	Boeing 737-55S	26539	(OO-SYL) N1790B
OK-XGB	Boeing 737-55S	26540	(OO-SYM)
OK-XGC	Boeing 737-55S	26541	(OO-SYN)
OK-XGD	Boeing 737-55S	26542	(OO-SYO)
OK-XGE	Boeing 737-55S	26543	(OO-SYP)
OK-XGV	Boeing 737-5H6	26445	F-GJNQ 9M-MFA
OK-XGW	Boeing 737-5H6	26446	F-GJNR 9M-MFB
OK-XIB	Robinson R-22 Beta (W/o 19.12.99)	2120	
OK-XIF	Robinson R-22M Mariner	2233M	N2352Y
OK-XIG	Antonov An-2T	1G98-70	
OK-XIS	Bell 206L-3 Long Ranger III	51602	N5129G

OK-XJA	Zlin Z.137T Agro-Turbo	046	
OK-XKB(2)	Cessna 150H	15069265	N91AV
OK-XKG	Cessna F172G	F172-0201	G-ATKS
OK-XKH	Cessna 150J	15069891	N51280
OK-XKJ	Cessna F150H (W/o 19.9.00)	F150-0325	HB-CTE F-BPEV HB-CTE
OK-XNB	Zlin Z.142C	0550	
OK-XOA	Zlin Z.43	0105	
OK-XOD	Zlin Z.43	0108	
OK-XOE	Zlin Z.43	0111	
OK-XOF	Zlin Z.43	0110	OM-LNL OK-XOF
OK-XOG	Zlin Z.43	0112	
OK-XOH	Zlin Z.43	0113	
OK-XRA	Zlin Z.50LX	0071	Not listed
OK-XRB	Zlin Z.50LX	0072	
OK-XRC	Zlin Z.50LX	0073	
OK-XRD	Zlin Z.50LX	0074	
OK-XRK	Zlin Z.50M	0078	
OK-XYC	Mil Mi-8T	99250952	RA-27004 CCCP27004
OK-XYJ	Zlin Z.143L	0093/04	OK-078
OK-XZA	LET L-610G (Originally reported as c/n 910101)	920102	OK-136
OK-YAC	Airbus A310-325ET	672	F-OHPX F-WIHP HB-IPN F-WWCD
OK-YAD	Airbus A310-325	674	F-OIHS N837AB F-WWCH
OK-YGA	Boeing 737-4Q8	26290	HA-LEZ TC-APB TC-JEE
OK-YGU	Boeing 737-4Q8	26289	G-BUHK
OK-YIJ	Robinson R-22 Beta	2366	N8029Q
OK-YIP	Bell 206L-4 Long Ranger IV	52068	N2137P
OK-YIT	Robinson R-22 Beta (W/o 11.8.04)	2322	OM-YIT OK-YIT N23627
OK-YJA	Boeing 737-4Q8	26290	HA-LEZ TC-APB TC-JEE
OK-YJF	LET Z-37 Cmelák	08-01	HA-SCA
OK-YJH	Z-137T Agro Turbo	047	
OK-YKD	LET Z-37A-2 Cmelák	07-19	
OK-YNB	Zlin Z.242L	0655	
OK-YXB	Mil Mi-8T	041032	CzAF1032
OK-YXC	Mil Mi-8T	051632	CzAF1632
OK-YXJ	Jodel/Falconar F-11	6268	
OK-ZIL	Robinson R-22 Beta	2400	N8101G
OK-ZIN	Robinson R-22 Beta (W/o 8.10.96)	2415	
OK-ZIO	Robinson R-44 Astro	0150	
OK-ZIU	Bell 206LT Twin Ranger	52032	N93LT
OK-ZJC	LET Z-37A Cmelák (Dismantled)	09-10	HA-MGP
OK-ZJD	LET Z-37A Cmelák (Stored)	09-17	HA-MGJ
OK-ZJF	LET Z-37 Cmelák	10-01	HA-MGM
OK-ZJG	LET Z-37A Cmelák (Actually wears c/n 21-15)	10-08	
OK-ZJH	LET Z-37A-C3 Cmelák (Stored)	10-27	HA-MGS
OK-ZJP	LET Z-37 Cmelák	09-12	
OK-ZJV	LET Z-37 Cmelák	10-11	
OK-ZKB	LET Z-37A Cmelák	09-02	
OK-ZKC	LET Z-37 Cmelák (Wfu, dismantled)	09-03	
OK-ZLA	Diamond DA 20-A1 Katana	10006	N106CM
OK-ZLI	Zlin Z.526F Akrobat	1153	D-EFHZ SP-CDO
OK-ZOE	Zlin Z.143L	0003	
OK-ZRA	Zlin Z.526AFS-V Akrobat	1118	
OK-ZRB	Zlin Z.526AFS-V Akrobat	1119	
OK-ZRD	Zlin Z.526F Trenér Master	1147	
OK-ZSC	Zlin Z.42MU	0003	OK-XSB
OK-ZSD	Zlin Z.42MU	0004	
OK-ZSE	Zlin Z.42MU	0006	
OK-ZSF	Zlin Z.42MU	0007	
OK-ZSG	Zlin Z.42MU	0009	
OK-ZSH	Zlin Z.42MU	0010	
OK-ZYV	Inteco VM-23 Variant	23 X 01	
OK-2617	LET L-410UVP-E20	912617	CCCP67686
OK- . . .	Beech C90 King Air	LJ-837	N364D
OK- . . .	Cessna 172P	17274664	D-EVAD N53020
OK- . . .	Cessna 172S	172S9744	N65692
OK- . . .	Cessna 182T	18281551	N716HP
OK- . . .	Cessna T210N	21063807	D-ECLL(2) OE-KKE N6113C
OK- . . .	Hughes 369D	38-0289D	D-HFOX ZK-HLP
OK- . . .	Maule M-7-235 Super Rocket	25098C	D-EEAQ
OK- . . .	SAAB-Scania SF-340A	104	N104CQ N344BE SE-F04
OK- . . .	Zlin Z.142	0524	4X-AIZ OK-VNE

PROTOTYPE SERIES

OK-016	Mikoyan Mig-21U	0816	CzAF
OK-020	Yakovlev Yak-40 (Preserved)	9431436	OK-EXB OK-EEA OK-020
OK-028	LET L-410UVP Turbolet (Preserved)	810625	
OK-042	VSO-10 Gradient	150001	
OK-044	VSO-10 Gradient	unkn	
OK-064	Aerotechnik L-13SW Vivat	920425	
OK-070	Zlin Z.50LS (Prototype)	0001	
OK-112	Zlin Z.142	unkn	
OK-120	LET L-33 Solo (Prototype)	unkn	
OK-126	LET L-23 Blanik T	unkn	
OK-130	LET L-610	880001/X-01	OK-TZB OK-038 OK-130
OK-164	LET L-410UVP	770103	OK-IYC OK-164
OK-182	Aero L-39MS Albatros (Preserved)	X-24	
OK-184	Aero L-39MS Albatros (Wfu)	X-22	
OK-188	Aero L-39ZA Albatros (InstAfm)	X-10	
OK-190	Aero L-39 Albatros (Preserved)	X-11	CzAF 3911 OK-HXA
OK-192	Aero L-39 Albatros	unkn	
OK-194	Aero L-39 Albatros	4853	
OK-198	Aero L-39 Albatros	unkn	
OK-208	Aero L-39 Albatros	unkn	
OK-230	Aero Designs Pulsar	001	
OK-230	Alpha Air J-1B Don Quixote	unkn	
OK-238	LET L-213A	unkn	

MICROLIGHTS

As is traditional with Czech registrations, the first letter indicates the year of construction (for example H=2002), most then contain a U (Ultralight) or H (Helicopter) followed by a letter and numbers for the individual identity. Marks are most frequently applied on the aircraft without the use of the second hyphen and we have now removed these from the entire list.

OK-004	SP-1 Spunt		
OK-006	ZA-01 Microlight		
OK-008	Letov LK-2 Sluka		
OK-066	Type unknown		
OK-122	ULM-1 Gryff		
OK-210	Type unknown		
OK-212	Type unknown		OK-21
OK-220	Letov LK-2 Sluka		
OK-AHA 01	Dragon Fly 333		
OK-AUA 01	Toresi Straton D8 Moby Dick		
OK-AUA 02	Fly Synthesis Storch		
OK-AUA 06	Straton		
OK-AUA 07	Pegass		
OK-AUA 09	Fantasy Air Cora Legato		
OK-AUA 12	Jura (Jora ?)		
OK-AUA 22	Toresi Straton D8 Moby Dick		
OK-AUB 01	Twist		
OK-AUB 02	Toresi Straton D8 Moby Dick		
OK-AUD 01	Rans S-6 Coyote II		
OK-AUD 04	Pegass 582		
OK-AUD 07	J-3 Kitten		
OK-AUD 09	Rans S-6 Coyote II	011	
OK-AUD 10	Pegass 582		
OK-AUD 12	Pegass		
OK-AUD 14	Willy		
OK-AUD 15	Lomcovak		
OK-AUD 19	Pegass		
OK-AUD 20	Pegass 582		
OK-AUD 22	Pegass		
OK-AUE 28	Letov LK-2 Sluka	01-03	
OK-AUH 01	Type unknown "26"		
OK-AUI 03	Toresi Straton D.8 Moby Dick		
OK-AUI 05	Type unknown		
OK-AUI 09	Toresi Straton D.8 Moby Dick		
OK-AUL 01	WK-94		
OK-AUL 05	Type unknown		
OK-AUL 08	Straton D.7 Mobil		
OK-AUL 11	TEAM Hi-MAX		
OK-AUO 02	Mis-5		
OK-AUO 03	KA-4 Sumak		
OK-AUO 05	Letov LK-2MSluka		
OK-AUO 11	CRO SPOL Swing		
OK-AUO 12	Straton		
OK-AUO 14	Rhönlerche		
OK-AUO 15	Rhönlerche		
OK-AUO 16	Rhonlerche II (Motorised)		
OK-AUO 16	Motor-glider, type unknown		
OK-AUO 19	TEAM Hi-MAX (or Mini-MAX?)		
OK-AUO 23	Highlander		
OK-AUP 06	Rans S-6 Coyote II		
OK-AUR 01	EV-95 Eurofox (Also reported as 'Ungo')		
OK-AUR 03	EV-95 Eurofox		
OK-AUR 04	LET-Mont Tulak		

OK-AUR 05	Aeropro Fox		
OK-AUR 06	Aeropro Fox		
OK-AUR 07	Type unknown		
OK-AUR 08	EV-95 Eurofox		
OK-AUR 09	L-60 Replica (?)		
OK-AUR 10	Aeropro Fox		
OK-AUR 11	Aeropro Fox (?)		
OK-AUR 12	EV-95 Eurofox (Also reported as Vektor)		
OK-AUR 17	EV-95 Eurofox	EV95 07	
OK-AUR 25	Letov LK-2 Sluka		
OK-AUT 02	Letov LK-2 Sluka		
OK-AUT 05	EV-95 Eurofox		
OK-AUU 03	TL Ultralight TL-132 Condor	95C03	
OK-AUU 04	TL Ultralight TL-132 Condor		
OK-AUU 05	TL Ultralight TL-132 Condor		
OK-AUU 06	Letov LK-2M Sluka	829409x16	OK-WXA-O
OK-AUU 07	Letov ST-4 Aztek		
OK-AUU 09	Fantasy Air Cora		
OK-AUU 12	TL Ultralight TL-132 Condor		
OK-AUU 14	Fantasy Air Cora		
OK-AUU 15	Rans S-6ES Coyote II		
OK-AUU 16	TEAM Mini-MAX		
OK-AUU 20	Fantasy Air Cora		
OK-AUU 24	Toresi Straton D.8 Moby Dick		
OK-AUU 25	TL Ultralight TL-132 Condor II	95C07	
OK-AUU 26	Rans S-6ES Coyote II		
OK-AUU 28	Racek		
OK-AUU 33	Type unknown		
OK-AUU 36	Schempp-Hirth HIM45 Ornis (Code M7)	062-1995	
OK-AUU 37	Letov LK-2M Sluka		
OK-AUU 39	TL Ultralight TL-132 Condor		
OK-AUU 41	Type unknown		
OK-AUU 43	TEAM Hi-MAX		
OK-AUU 44	TL Ultralight TL-132 Condor		
OK-AUX 01	Toresi Straton D.8 Moby Dick		
OK-AZG 08	Trike, type unknown		
OK-AZG 15	Mara Wing MW135		
OK-AZG 27	Type unknown (Flexwing)		
OK-AZL 01	TL Ultralight TL-22 Duo		
OK-AZU 08	Junkers Profly II	20	
OK-AZU 07	Junkers Profly II		
OK-AZU 09	Junkers Profly II		
OK-BGA 1	Powered Para-Glider (Type unknown)		
OK-BPM 02	Jet Pocket (Para-Glider)		
OK-BUA 01	Fantasy Air Cora		
OK-BUA 03	Fantasy Air Cora Legato		
OK-BUA 04	Fantasy Air Cora		
OK-BUA 07	Turkan (Tukan?)		
OK-BUA 10	Fantasy Air Cora		
OK-BUA 11	D-10 Tukan		
OK-BUA 14	Fantasy Air Cora		
OK-BUA 15	Fantasy Air Cora		
OK-BUA 16	Fantasy Air Cora		
OK-BUD 01	Fantasy Air Cora		
OK-BUD 04	LET-Mont Tulak		
OK-BUD 05	Piper UL		
OK-BUD 07	Icom		
OK-BUD 08	Schleicher Ka.4 Rhonlerche (Motorised)		HB-. . .
OK-BUD 10	Pottier P.200ULKoala		
OK-BUD 11	Pegass 912		
OK-BUD 14	TL Ultralight TL-232 Condor		
OK-BUD 15	LET-Mont Tulak		
OK-BUD 20	Maja (Fantasy Air Cora?)		
OK-BUE 29	Letov LK-2M Sluka		OK-XXAV
OK-BUH 01	TEAM Hi-MAX		
OK-BUI 05	Test-1 Alpin glider		
OK-BUI 06	TST-6 Duo		
OK-BUI 09	LET-Mont Tulak		
OK-BUI 11	Sedolet G-91		
OK-BUI 28	Type unknown		
OK-BUK 01	LET-Mont Tulak		
OK-BUK 04	L2000	01/1996	
OK-BUL 05	Srsen		
OK-BUL 06	Fantasy Air Cora Legato		
OK-BUL 08	Fantasy Air Cora		
OK-BUL 10	Fantasy Air Cora		
OK-BUL 17	Air Design Qualt 200L		
OK-BUL 46	LET-Mont Tulak		
OK-BUO 01	Mini Straton TR.1		
OK-BUO 08	Rhönlerche (Motor conversion)		HB-. . .
OK-BUO 09	Rhönlerche (Motor conversion)		
OK-BUO 10	Rhönlerche II (Motor conversion)		
OK-BUO 11	TL Ultralight TL-532 Fresh		
OK-BUO 12	Type unknown "Asterix"		
OK-BUP 01	Type unknown		
OK-BUP 02	HEC-601		
OK-BUP 05	Fantasy Air Cora Legato		
OK-BUP 08	TEAM Mini-MAX		
OK-BUQ 01	IIISky Arrow 450TCE		
OK-BUQ 02	Rans S-6XL Coyote II		
OK-BUQ 03	IIISky Arrow 450 TCE		
OK-BUQ 04	TEAM Hi-MAX		
OK-BUR 01	EV-95 Eurofox (C/n now quoted as EV9603, correct for year of regn)	EV95 08	
OK-BUR 02	EV-95 Eurofox		
OK-BUR 03	EV-95 Eurofox	EV96 09	
OK-BUR 04	EV-95 Eurofox	EV96 10	

OK-BUR 05	EV-95 Eurofox	
OK-BUR 08	Yetti 03 Skoda	
OK-BUR 09	Evektor EV-97 Eurostar	96007486
OK-BUR 14	Pottier P.200ULKoala	960002
OK-BUR 18	EV-95 Eurofox	
OK-BUR 20	Aerospool Compact	
OK-BUR 22	Yetti J-03	
OK-BUR 24	Type unknown	
OK-BUR 23	Yetti J-03	
OK-BUS 01	Falcon	
OK-BUS 02	CR-090P	
OK-BUS 03	Pony Max	
OK-BUS 10	Twin	
OK-BUT 03	Fantasy Air Cora	
OK-BUT 04	Fantasy Air Cora	
OK-BUT 05	Fantasy Air Cora	
OK-BUU 01	Letov LK-3 Nova	
OK-BUU 02	TL Ultralight TL-132 Condor	
OK-BUU 03	Schempp-Hirth HIM45 Ornis	
OK-BUU 07	EOL-2 Racek	
OK-BUU 08	Jora	
OK-BUU 10	TL Ultralight TL-232 Condor Plus	96C02
OK-BUU 14	Type unknown	
OK-BUU 15	Tecnam P.92 Echo	
OK-BUU 16	Letov LK-2 Sluka	819109004
OK-BUU 18	Jora	
OK-BUU 19	Fantasy Air Cora	
OK-BUU 20	Type unknown "Amos"	
OK-BUU 21	Urban Air UFM-13 Lambada	01/13
OK-BUU 22	Letov LK-2 Sluka	
OK-BUU 23	Kappa 77 KP-2U Sova	
OK-BUU 25	Zenair CH-701 STOL	
OK-BUU 26	EOL-2 Racek	
OK-BUU 29	TL Ultralight TL-232 Condor Plus	96C10
OK-BUU 30	Letov LK-2M Sluka	82960001
OK-BUU 31	Fisher FP-404 Classic	
OK-BUU 34	Straton D.8 Moby Dick	
OK-BUU 35	TEAM Hi-MAX	
OK-BUU 38	TL Ultralight TL-232 Condor Plus	96C22
OK-BUU 39	Fantasy Air Cora	
OK-BUU 40	TL Ultralight TL-32 Typhoon	9601
OK-BUU 42	TL Ultralight TL-132 Condor	
OK-BUU 43	TL Ultralight TL-232 Condor	
OK-BUU 45	Tecnam P.92 Echo	
OK-BUU 46	Pottier Super Koala	
OK-BUU 48	TL Ultralight TL-232 Condor Plus	
OK-BUU 51	Urban Air UFM-11 Lambada (Also quoted as UFM-13, c/n 13. Converted?)	04/11
OK-BUU 60	Letov LK-2 Sluka	
OK-BUX 14	TST-1 Alpin	
OK-BUY 02	Aeropro Fox	1501
OK-BUY 04	Aeropro Fox	
OK-BZC 02	TL Ultralight TL-1/E90	D17
OK-BZC 04	TL Ultralight TL-2/E90	
OK-BZC 05	TL Ultralight TL-22 Duo	
OK-BZF 02	Junkers Pro-Fly II	
OK-BZF 03	ESO-2 Trike	
OK-BZF 08	ESO-2 Trike	
OK-BZF 12	Unidentified trike	
OK-BZG 09	Trike	
OK-BZG 11	Super Wing MW-155	
OK-BZH 05	Trike	
OK-BZH 06	Trike	
OK-COR 97	Aerotecknik EV97 Eurostar	
OK-CUA 01	Atec Zephyr	BA-96
OK-CUA 02	Fantasy Air Cora Legato	
OK-CUA 04	Fantasy Air Cora Farm	
OK-CUA 05	Tukan D (Accident 10.1.01)	
OK-CUA 08	Fantasy Air Cora	
OK-CUA 22	Fantasy Air Cora Legato	
OK-CUB 01	Twist	
OK-CUD 02	LET-Mont Tulak	
OK-CUD 03	LET-Mont Tulak	
OK-CUD 05	Type unknown	
OK-CUD 08	Straton Moby Dick	
OK-CUD 11	TEAM Hi-MAX	
OK-CUD 12	Kolibrik	
OK-CUD 15	TEAM Hi-MAX	
OK-CUD 44	Mara Wing Piper L-4U Cub "329601"	203/9
OK-CUE 01	J-103 Tiger	
OK-CUE 34	Mates	
OK-CUE 35	Fantasy Air Cora	
OK-CUI 01	TST-5Variant	
OK-CUI 02	TST-3 Alpin	
OK-CUI 03	Fantasy Air Cora Allegro	
OK-CUI 04	TST-5Variant	
OK-CUI 05	Fantasy Air Cora Legato	
OK-CUI 09	TST-5Variant	
OK-CUI 10	TST-1 Alpin	
OK-CUK 01	LET-Mont Tulak	
OK-CUL 01	Air Design Qualt 200L	
OK-CUL 04	TL Ultralight TL-32 Typhoon	
OK-CUO 02	Vandrák	
OK-CUO 03	Vandrák	
OK-CUO 05	Raxis	
OK-CUO 07	CRO SPOL Swing	
OK-CUO 08	LET L-13M Blanik	

OK-CUO 10	Sumak K4	
OK-CUO 11	Schleicher K 8B/T motor glider	
OK-CUO 12	"Piper Twin" (Tulak?)	
OK-CUO 15	Fantasy Air Cora	
OK-CUO 17	Powered glider, type unknown	
OK-CUO 20	Ivana	
OK-CUP 01	Fantasy Air Cora Allegro	
OK-CUP 02	Denney Kitfox	
OK-CUP 03	Aeros SRO Flamingo	
OK-CUP 05	Rans S-10 Sakota	
OK-CUP 06	SD.7 Straton	
OK-CUP 07	Fantasy Air Cora Allegro	
OK-CUQ 10	Rainbow	
OK-CUQ 11	Corvus	
OK-CUQ 16	Brändli BX-2 Cherry	970102
OK-CUR 01	Pottier P.200ULKoala	970006
OK-CUR 02	Pottier P.200ULKoala	
OK-CUR 03	Pottier P.200ULRKoala	
OK-CUR 05	Pottier P.200ULKoala	
OK-CUR 07	Evektor EV-97 Eurostar	
OK-CUR 08	CRO Metallica LG 2	
OK-CUR 09	Pottier P.200ULKoala	
OK-CUR 11	Aerotecknik CZ	
OK-CUR 13	Skyboy	
OK-CUR 15	Evektor EV-97 Eurostar	
OK-CUR 16	Evektor EV-97 Eurostar	
OK-CUR 17	Aerotecknik P.220SKoala	9701-09
OK-CUR 19	Pottier P.200ULKoala	
OK-CUR 20	Pottier P.200ULRKoala	
OK-CUR 25	Evektor EV-97 Eurostar	9700X3
OK-CUR 99	Pottier P.200ULKoala	970104
OK-CUS 05	Sraen	
OK-CUT 01	Type unknown	
OK-CUT 04	Kolibrik (Accident 1.5.01)	
OK-CUU 01	TEAM Hi-MAX	
OK-CUU 02	TL Ultralight TL-232 Condor Plus	
OK-CUU 08	LET L-13M Blanik (Motorised)	
OK-CUU 09	Kappa 77 KP-2U Sova	
OK-CUU 11	TL Ultralight TL-232 Condor	
OK-CUU 12	Fantasy Air Cora Legato	
OK-CUU 14	TL Ultralight TL-232 Condor Plus	
OK-CUU 15	TL Ultralight TL-232 Condor Plus	
OK-CUU 18	Zenair CH-601 Zodiac	
OK-CUU 19	Tecnam P.92 Echo	235
OK-CUU 21	Tecnam P.92 Echo	
OK-CUU 22	Fantasy Air Cora	
OK-CUU 24	TL Ultralight TL-232 Condor	
OK-CUU 25	Avia BH-1 Replica	
OK-CUU 27	Lazava	
OK-CUU 32	TL Ultralight TL-232 Condor Plus	
OK-CUU 34	Tecnam P.92 Echo	
OK-CUU 35	Tecnam P.92 Echo	
OK-CUU 40	Zenair CH-601 Zodiac	
OK-CUU 41	Letov LK-2MSluka	
OK-CUU 43	Urban Air UFM-11Lambada	02/11
OK-CUU 44	Type unknown	
OK-CUU 45	Fantasy Air Cora Legato	
OK-CUX 18	TL Ultralight TL-232 Condor	
OK-CUX 19	TS-01	
OK-CUX 22	Letov LK-2 Sluka	8192090107/1993
	(Also reported as Yetti)	
OK-CUY 01	Fantasy Air Cora (Wo 18.10.03)	
OK-CUY 02	Type unknown	
OK-CVA 01	Banjo	
OK-CZF 03	Mara Wing MW155-W02	
OK-CZF 04	Junkers Profly	
OK-CZG 17	ESO-2	
OK-CZJ 04	MZK	
OK-CZL 03	Cosmos / ESO-3	
OK-CZU 07	ESO-	
OK-DUA 01	ATEC Zephyr	
OK-DUA 02	W1 Drevak	
OK-DUA 06	Toresi Straton Tukan	
OK-DUA 08	Fantasy Air Allegro	
OK-DUB 01	N-98	
OK-DUD 02	Aero L-60 Brigadyr (scale replica)	
OK-DUD 04	LET-Mont Tulak	
OK-DUD 05	EV-95 Eurofox	
OK-DUD 06	SGAvn Storm 280	
OK-DUD 07	Fokker DR.1 UL replica	425/17
OK-DUD 14	Aeropro Fox	
OK-DUD 15	Fantasy Air Cora Allegro	
OK-DUD 16	Maja	
OK-DUD 18	Type unknown	
OK-DUD 20	Fokker DR.1 UL replica	
OK-DUD 21	EV-95 Eurofox	
OK-DUE 01	SD.7 Straton D.4	
OK-DUI 02	Fantasy Air Allegro	
OK-DUI 03	TST-9 Junior	
OK-DUI 04	Kosak 2	
OK-DUI 05	Variant	
OK-DUI 11	Fantasy Air Allegro	
OK-DUI 12	TST-7 Junior	
OK-DUK 01	LET-Mont Tulak	
OK-DUK 02	TEAM Hi-MAX	
OK-DUK 11	Fantasy Air Allegro	
OK-DUL 01	Swing	
OK-DUL 02	TL Ultralight TL-132 Condor	
OK-DUL 05	LET-Mont Tulak	
OK-DUL 07	Fantasy Air Cora	
OK-DUL 08	Fantasy Air Cora Legato D	
OK-DUL 09	Air Design Qualt 200L	
OK-DUL 11	LET-Mont Tulak	
OK-DUL 14	DS-1 Twin	1998
OK-DUL 17	Air Design Qualt 200L	
OK-DUL 18	Air Design Qualt 200J	
OK-DUO 01	Swift	
OK-DUO 02	Pietenpol Aircamper	
OK-DUO 04	Mara Wing Piper L-4U Cub (Mikron engine)	
OK-DUO 05	Jora	
OK-DUO 06	Toresi Straton D.7 Mini	
OK-DUO 09	TL Ultralight TL-132 Condor	
OK-DUO 10	S Wing FX.60 Tango	
OK-DUP 01	Toresi Straton D.8 Moby Dick	
OK-DUP 02	SD.2 Straton	
OK-DUP 03	Aeropro Fox	
OK-DUP 05	Fantasy Air Cora Allegro	
OK-DUP 07	LET-Mont Tulak (Damaged)	
OK-DUP 12	Letov LK-2 Sluka	
OK-DUP 14	Mosquito	
OK-DUQ 02	Type unknown	
OK-DUQ 05	Eagle	
OK-DUQ 07	Brändli BX-2 Cherry	
OK-DUR 01	Pottier P.200ULRKoala	980114
OK-DUR 03	Fischer Koala	
OK-DUR 05	Evektor EV-97 Eurostar	
OK-DUR 08	Evektor EV-97 Eurostar	
OK-DUR 09	Evektor EV-97 Eurostar	980117
OK-DUR 10	Evektor EV-97 Eurostar	
OK-DUR 11	Evektor EV-97 Eurostar	980106
OK-DUR 12	Evektor EV-97 Eurostar	980307
OK-DUR 13	Type unknown	
OK-DUR 16	Bek B1	
OK-DUR 18	Evektor EV-97 Eurostar	980205
OK-DUR 20	Evektor EV-97 Eurostar	990601
OK-DUR 24	Yetti S-03	
OK-DUR 25	Evektor EV-97 Eurostar	
OK-DUR 26	Pottier P.200ULRKoala	980119
OK-DUR 29	Type unknown	086
OK-DUR 91	Type unknown	980114
OK-DUR 99	Zenair CH-601XL Zodiac	6-9078
OK-DUS 01	Fantasy Air Cora	07291
OK-DUS 03	JP-2	
OK-DUT 01	Kolibrik	
OK-DUT 05	Fantasy Air Cora	
OK-DUT 06	Fantasy Air Cora	
OK-DUT 07	Fantasy Air Cora	
OK-DUU 01	Maja	
OK-DUU 06	Letov	
OK-DUU 03	Fantasy Air 200 Arius F	
OK-DUU 07	Type unknown	
OK-DUU 09	Letov LK-2 Sluka	
OK-DUU 11	Fantasy Air Cora Allegro	
OK-DUU 12	Fantasy Air 200 Arius	
OK-DUU 14	TL Ultralight TL-96 Star	
OK-DUU 15	Urban Air UFM Moira Lambada	3/11
OK-DUU 16	Kappa 77 KP-2U Sova	
OK-DUU 18	TL ULtralight TL-32 Typhoon	
OK-DUU 21	EOPL-2 Racek	
OK-DUU 23	Urban Air UFM-13 Lambada	
OK-DUU 25	ATEC Zephyr	
OK-DUU 26	Kappa 77 KP-2U Sova	
OK-DUU 28	Fantasy Air Allegro SW	
OK-DUU 29	TL Ultralight TL-96 Star	
OK-DUU 30	Type unknown	
OK-DUU 32	Fantasy Air Cora	
OK-DUU 33	Evektor EV-97 Eurostar	2000-06-12
OK-DUU 34	Fantasy Air Cora	
OK-DUU 35	Fantasy Air Cora 200	
OK-DUU 37	Tecnam P.96 Golf	
OK-DUU 55	Moira Lambada	
OK-DUU 40	Letov ST-4 Aztek	
OK-DUU 41	Letov LK-2M Sluka	
OK-DUU 43	Kappa 77 Sova	
OK-DUU 46	TL Ultralight TL-96 Star	98S06
OK-DUU 51	TL Ultralight TL-96 Star	
OK-DUU 52	Urban Air UFM-13 Lambada	
OK-DUU 54	Kappa 77 KP-2U Sova	
OK-DUU 99	Zenair CH-601ULZodiac	(6-9131)
	(Noted 7.00, but regn used for testing/delivery by other examples)	
OK-DUX 25	Fischer Classic	
OK-DUX 27	Pietenpol Aircamper	
OK-DUY 02	Air Bike	
OK-DUY 03	Jora	
OK-DUY 31	LET-Mont Tulak	
OK-DZF 03	Fiti I / F128	
OK-DZF 04	TL Ultralight TL-32 Typhoon	
OK-DZG 03	Dolphin Tomi III	
OK-DZU 06	Super Wing MW-155	
OK-EUA 01	ATEC Zephyr	
OK-EUA 03	ATEC Zephyr	
OK-EUA 04	ATEC Zephyr	
OK-EUA 06	Fantasy Air Cora	
OK-EUA 07	Fantasy Air Cora	

OK-EUA 08	Vaclav Brandejs/Pro-fe Banjo		
OK-EUA 14	Toresi Straton Mini		
OK-EUC 01	Larus		
OK-EUC 03	Larus		
OK-EUD 06	Aeropro Fox		
OK-EUD 07	LET-Mont Tulak		
OK-EUD 08	SG Aviation Storm 280G		
OK-EUD 10	LET-Mont Tulak		
OK-EUD 12	TL Ultralight TL-232 Condor		
OK-EUD 16	Max (Modified TEAM Hi-MAX)		
OK-EUE 01	Straton D.7 Mini		
OK-EUE 03	Urban Air UFM Moira Lambada		
OK-EUE 05	Type unknown, Condor?		
OK-EUI 04	TST-9 Junior	07010399	
OK-EUI 06	LET-Mont Tulak EP-1		
OK-EUI 07	TST-3 Alpin TM (Accident 2.8.00)		
OK-EUI 08	TST-8 Alpin DM		
OK-EUI 09	Type unknown		
OK-EUJ 44	Mara Wing Piper L-4UCub		
	Previously reported as UL-2000 Flamingo		
OK-EUK 02	Prdola		
OK-EUL 03	Zenair CH-601 Zodiac		
OK-EUL 05	TL Ultralight TL-22 Duo		
OK-EUL 06	Straton D.8 Moby Dick		
OK-EUL 07	Air Design Qualt 235MX		
OK-EUL 10	Air Design Qualt 235MX		
OK-EUL 16	LET-Mont Tulak		
OK-EUL 18	Pegass 912		
OK-EUL 22	LET-Mont Tulak		
OK-EUO 02	Asso Aeri Asso V Champion		
OK-EUO 05	Asso Aeri Asso V Champion		
OK-EUO 06	Schleicher Rhönlerche II		OE-....
	(Also reported as Piper Cub UL)		
OK-EUO 07	Straton		
OK-EUO 08	Piper UL		
OK-EUO 11	Blue Bird 1 (Also reported as Evans VP-1)		
OK-EUO 13	Scheibe Bergfalke 55	298	
OK-EUO 14	Air Design Qualt 200L		
OK-EUO 16	Omega		
OK-EUO 19	Asso Aeri Asso V Champion		
OK-EUP 01	Zenair CH-601 Zodiac		
OK-EUP 02	Type unknown		
OK-EUP 08	Tulak Piper UL		
OK-EUP 09	Twin-A		
OK-EUP 12	Light Aero Avid Flyer		
OK-EUQ 03	Baccara		
OK-EUR 01	Pottier P.200ULRKoala	975007	
OK-EUR 03	Evektor EV-97 Eurostar		
OK-EUR 06	Skyfox		
OK-EUR 07	Evektor EV-97 Eurostar	990508	
OK-EUR 09	Evektor EV-97 Eurostar	990510	
OK-EUR 18	Evektor EV-97 Eurostar		
OK-EUS 01	Banjo STX		
OK-EUS 11	FOR-1		
OK-EUT 03	Denney Kitfox		
OK-EUU 01	TL Ultralight TL-96 Star		
OK-EUU 03	Tecnam P.96 Golf		
OK-EUU 04	Tecnam P.92 Echo		
OK-EUU 05	Kappa 77 KP-2U Sova		
OK-EUU 07	Fantasy Air Cora 2000		
OK-EUU 08	ATEC Zephyr 2000		
OK-EUU 10	Dyn'Aero MCR-01		
OK-EUU 12	TL Ultralight TL-96 Star		
OK-EUU 14	Tecnam P.92 Echo	353	
OK-EUU 15	Kappa 77 KP-2U Sova		D-MNOK
OK-EUU 16	Kappa 77 KP-2U Sova		
OK-EUU 18	TL Ultralight TL-96 Star		
OK-EUU 19	TL Ultralight TL-96 Star		
OK-EUU 21	Kappa 77 KP-2U Sova		
OK-EUU 22	TL Ultralight TL-96 Star		
OK-EUU 23	Letov LK-2MTSluka	829809	
OK-EUU 24	Urban Air UFM Moira Lambada		
OK-EUU 25	TL Ultralight TL-96 Star 99 Special		
OK-EUU 26	EOL-2 Racek	E-15	
OK-EUU 27	Kappa 77 KP-2U Sova		
OK-EUU 29	Fantasy Air Cora	023/1999	
OK-EUU 30	TL Ultralight TL-96 Star		
OK-EUU 31	TL Ultralight TL-232 Condor Plus		
OK-EUU 33	TL Ultralight TL-96 Star		
OK-EUU 34	Kappa 77 KP-2U Sova		
OK-EUU 36	Tecnam P.92 Echo	369	
OK-EUU 37	Tecnam P.92 Echo		
OK-EUU 38	Urban Air UFM-10 Samba	02/10	
OK-EUU 39	Urban Air UFM-10 Samba	10 3 001	
OK-EUU 40	Urban Air UFM-13 Lambada		
OK-EUU 41	Fenix		
OK-EUU 42	Kappa 77 KP-2U Sova		
OK-EUU 44	UL-2000 Flamingo		
OK-EUU 46	TL Ultralight TL-96 Star		
OK-EUU 47	Tecnam P.92 Echo		
OK-EUU 52	TL Ultralight TL-96 Star		
OK-EUU 55	Urban Air UFM Moira Lambada		
OK-EUU 56	Urban Air UFM Moira Lambada	12/11	
OK-EUU 57	Evektor EV-97 Eurostar		
OK-EUU 58	Zenair CH-601 Zodiac		
OK-EUU 59	Kappa 77 KP-2U Sova		
OK-EUU 61	EOL-2 Racek 99 (W/o 19.2.00)		
OK-EUU 62	TL Ultralight TL-96 Star		
OK-EUU 63	Fantasy Air Allegro 2020		
OK-EUU 66	TL Ultralight TL-232 Condor Plus (Accident 21.10.00)		
OK-EUU 68	TL Ultralight TL-96 Star		
OK-EUU 70	Let-Mont Tulak		
OK-EUU 71	TL Ultralight TL-96 Star		
OK-EUX 29	Type unknown		
OK-EUY 04	EV-95 Eurofox 912		
OK-EUY 05	ATEC Zephyr R582		
OK-EZG 11	Mara Wing MW155		
OK-EZR 01	Type unknown		
OK-EZW 03	Stranger		
OK-FGA 01	Elisport CH-7 Kompress		
OK-FGA 02	Elisport CH-7 Kompress		
OK-FHA 01	Elisport CH-7 Kompress		
OK-FUA 02	Zephyr (ATEC?)		
OK-FUA 03	Fantasy Air Cora		
OK-FUA 05	Urban Air UFM-10 Samba	13/11	OK-EUU 02
OK-FUA 10	Banjo MH		
OK-FUD 01	Fläming Air Trener Baby		
OK-FUU 04	Type unknown		
OK-FUD 05	Let Mont Tulak UL		
OK-FUD 08	Let Mont Tulak EP-1		
OK-FUD 14	Pirat		
OK-FUD 17	Fantasy Air Cora		
OK-FUD 19	Maja		
OK-FUD 20	Maja		
OK-FUD 24	Aeropro Fox		
OK-FUH 01	ATEC Zephyr Solo (Prototype)		
OK-FUI 01	TST-9 Junior	09010100	
OK-FUI 02	TST-9 Junior	03021500	
OK-FUI 03	TST Gradient		
OK-FUL 07	Air Design Qualt 288MT		
OK-FUL 15	Type unknown		
OK-FUL 21	Let Mont Tulak		
OK-FUL 24	Pegass		
OK-FUL 28	Curtiss Jenny replica "34135"		
OK-FUL 45	Type unknown		
OK-FUO 05	Lavel Busky		
OK-FUO 09	Asso Aeri Asso IV Whisky		
OK-FUO 11	Asso Aeri Asso IV Whisky		
OK-FUO 12	Piper UL		
OK-FUP 01	Mara Wing Vrabec		
OK-FUP 02	Zenair CH.701 STOL		
OK-FUP 08	UL-2000 Flamingo		
OK-FUQ 25	Shark Ultralight		
OK-FUR 01	Evektor EV-97 Eurostar		
OK-FUR 04	Evektor EV-97 Eurostar		
OK-FUR 05	Evektor EV-97 Eurostar		
OK-FUR 09	Evektor EV-97 Eurostar	20000803	
OK-FUR 10	Evektor EV-97 Eurostar		
OK-FUR 14	Evektor EV-97 Eurostar		
OK-FUR 19	Evektor EV-97 Eurostar	20000809	
OK-FUR 20	Evektor EV-97 Eurostar		
OK-FUR 25	Evektor EV-97 Eurostar		
OK-FUR 26	Evektor EV-97 Eurostar		
OK-FUR 51	P-51 Mustang replica (Painted as "414911/P")		
OK-FUR 88	Zenair CH-701 STOL	7-9137 and 7-9138	
	(Both noted 9.00, regn used for testing/delivery by multiple examples)		
OK-FUS 01	Fantasy Air Cora		
OK-FUT 04	Fantasy Air Cora		
OK-FUU 02	SF-45-SASpirit		
OK-FUU 06	TL Ultralight TL-96 Star		
OK-FUU 07	TL Ultralight TL-96 Star		
OK-FUU 08	TL Ultralight TL-96 Star		
OK-FUU 09	EV-97 Eurostar	07	
OK-FUU 11	TL Ultralight TL-96 Star		
OK-FUU 12	Fantasy Air Cora Allegro SW		
OK-FUU 13	TL Ultralight TL-96 Star		
OK-FUU 14	TL Ultralight TL-96 Star		
OK-FUU 18	TL Ultralight TL-96 Star		
OK-FUU 20	Fantasy Air Cora Allegro 2000		
OK-FUU 24	ATEC Zephyr		
OK-FUU 25	Toresi Straton		
OK-FUU 29	TL Ultralight TL-96 Star	00S63	
OK-FUU 31	Urban UFM-10 Samba	03/10	
OK-FUU 33	Tecnam P.92 Echo		
OK-FUU 34	Letov LK-2Msluka		
OK-FUU 35	TL Ultralight TL-96 Star		
OK-FUU 40	Aerotrade Racek 2		
OK-FUU 41	Kappa 77 KP-2U Sova		
OK-FUU 42	Tecnam P.96 Golf 100		
OK-FUU 43	Tecnam P.92 Echo		
OK-FUU 45	Kappa 77 KP-2U Sova		
OK-FUU 47	Letov ST-4M Sluka	800009	
OK-FUU 48	TL Ultralight TL-96 Star		
OK-FUU 50	Kappa 77 KP-2U Sova		
OK-FUU 51	Kappa 77 KP-2U Sova (also reported as TL-96 Star)		
OK-FUU 52	TL Ultralight TL-96 Star		
OK-FUU 54	Kappa 77 KP-2USova		
OK-FUU 56	Kappa 77 KP-2U Sova		
OK-FUU 59	Tecnam P.96 Golf		
OK-FUV 01	Tandem		
OK-FWA 01	RAF-2000 UL gyrocopter		
OK-FZC 03	Javrmil 10 / Fiti 1		
OK-FZF 04	Junkers Profly		
OK-FZU 01	Junkers Profly trike/Fiti F-128	2000/06-92	

OK-GHA 01	Elisport CH-7 Kompress	
OK-GHA 02	Elisport CH-7 Kompress	
OK-GHA 03	Elisport CH-7 Kompress	
OK-GHA 04	Elisport CH-7 Kompress	
OK-GHA 07	Elisport CH-7 Kompress	
OK-GUA 12	Urban Air UFMMoira Lambada	
OK-GUA 13	Adventurer	
OK-GUA 15	ATEC Zephyr 2000	
OK-GUA 16	Urban UFM-10 Samba	
OK-GUA 17	Fantasy Air Cora	
OK-GUA 18	Jora	
OK-GUA 19	Urban UFM-10 Samba	
OK-GUA 20	TEAM Hi-MAX	
OK-GUA 21	TEAM Hi-MAX	
OK-GUA 22	Faltynek Mojmir MF-01	01/2001
OK-GUA 28	Urban Air UFM-10 Samba	21/10
OK-GUD 05	Brouzdalik	
OK-GUD 10	Trener Baby Z126UL	
OK-GUE 01	Varia	
OK-GUE 02	Paja	
OK-GUI 04	Jora	
OK-GUL 02	TEAM Mini-MAX	
OK-GUI 05	Evektor EV-97 Eurostar	
OK-GUL 04	Pottier P.200ULKoala	
OK-GUL 05	TL Ultralight TL-22 Duo-2	
OK-GUL 09	ATEC Zephyr	
OK-GUL 11	Air Design Qualt 200	
OK-GUL 13	Straton D.7	
OK-GUL 15	Zenair CH-601UL	
OK-GUO 01	Asso Aeri Asso V Champion	
OK-GUO 03	Fantasy Air Cora (Also reported as ATEC Zephyr 2000)	
OK-GUO 04	Fly Synthesis Storch	
OK-GUO 07	Zephyr 2002LS	
OK-GUO 10	Fly Synthesis Storch	
OK-GUO 16	TEAM Hi-MAX	
OK-GUO 18	Piper UL	
OK-GUO 21	Type unknown	
OK-GUP 03	Flamingo UL2000	
OK-GUP 06	Flamingo UL2000	
OK-GUP 05	Tiger Moth replica	
OK-GUP 09	LK-3 Nova	
OK-GUR 11	Pottier P.220S Koala	
OK-GUR 15	Kadet	
OK-GUR 17	Evektor EV-97 Eurostar	
OK-GUR 19	Evektor EV-97 Eurostar	
OK-GUR 22	Evektor EV-97 Eurostar	
OK-GUR 26	Evektor EV-97 Eurostar	
OK-GUR 28	Zenair CH-701 STOL	
OK-GUR 29	Evektor EV-97 Eurostar	20011206
OK-GUR 30	Evektor EV-97 Eurostar	
OK-GUR 45	Evektor EV-97 Eurostar	
OK-GUS 04	ATEC Zephyr	
OK-GUS 06	TEAM Hi-MAX	
OK-GUT 05	Dallach D4B Fascination	
OK-GUT 07	Zenair CH-601 Zodiac	
OK-GUT 08	WDFLFascination	
OK-GUT 09	Bobcad	12002
OK-GUT 11	Sunwheel D8	
OK-GUU 01	Fantasy Air Allegro 2000	0132
OK-GUU 02	Kappa 77 KP-2U Sova	
OK-GUU 03	Tecnam P.96 Golf	
OK-GUU 04	Tecnam P.96 Golf	
OK-GUU 09	Let-Mont Tulak	
OK-GUU 10	TL Ultralight TL-2000 Sting	00S65
OK-GUU 11	Kappa 77 KP-2U Sova	
OK-GUU 12	Kappa 77 KP-2U Sova	
OK-GUU 13	Zephyr (ATEC?)	
OK-GUU 14	Kappa 77 KP-2U Sova	
OK-GUU 18	Zenair CH-601 Zodiac	
OK-GUU 19	TL Ultralight TL-96 Star	
OK-GUU 20	TL Ultralight TL-96 Star	
OK-GUU 21	Type unknown	
OK-GUU 24	Zenair CH-601 Zodiac	
OK-GUU 25	Avia BH-1 Replica	
OK-GUU 26	Tecnam P.96 Golf	
OK-GUU 28	Tecnam P.96 Golf	
OK-GUU 29	TL Ultralight TL-2000 Sting Cobra	
OK-GUU 31	Kappa 77 KP-2U Sova	
OK-GUU 34	TL Ultralight TL-2000 Sting	01ST04
OK-GUU 35	TL Ultralight TL-96 Star	
OK-GUU 36	Fantasy Air Allegro 2000	
OK-GUU 37	Fantasy Air Cora	
OK-GUU 38	TL Ultralight TL-2000 Sting	
OK-GUU 39	TL Ultralight TL-2000 Sting	
OK-GUZ 02	Ivanov B-612	
OK-GZC 08	MW-155	
OK-GZF 07	F128 Fitti 1	96020 225
OK-GZH 02	MZK	
OK-HHA 06	Elisport CH-7 Kompress	
OK-HHA 07	Elisport CH-7 Kompress	
OK-HUA 35	Zenair CH-601XL Zodiac	
OK-HUA 36	Banjo MH	
OK-HUA 38	Urban Air UFM-10 Samba	15/10
OK-HUA 40	TL Ultralight TL-2000 Sting	
OK-HUA 41	Falcon	
OK-HUA 43	TL Ultralight TL-2000 Sting	
OK-HUA 46	TL Ultralight TL-2000 Sting	

OK-HUD 02	Let Mont Tulak	
OK-HUD 03	Dewald Leonardo 2000	
OK-HUD 06	Flaming Air Trener Baby UL	
OK-HUD 09	Flaming Air Trener Baby UL	
OK-HUE 01	LET-Mont Tulak	
OK-HUE 02	Zenair CH-601XL Zodiac	
OK-HUG 02	TEAM Hi-MAX	
OK-HUG 05	Mara Wing Fokker E-III UL Replica "317/15"	
OK-HUG 06	ATEC Zephyr 2000	
OK-HUG 09	ATEC Zephyr 2000	
OK-HUI 04	Morane MS.230 replica	
OK-HUI 05	TST-9 Junior 2002	09020302
OK-HUJ 01	Zenair CH-601 Zodiac	
OK-HUL 01	CGM-13 motor glider	
OK-HUL 02	Bu.131 Jungmann replica	
OK-HUL 04	Kolrik 2	
OK-HUL 05	Air Design Qualt 200	
OK-HUO 01	ATEC Zephyr	
OK-HUO 04	TL Ultralight TL-232 Condor Plus	
OK-HUP 02	Replica Plans SE-5A	
OK-HUQ 28	P-51DMustang replica "413685"	
OK-HUR 01	Zenair CH-701 STOL	
OK-HUR 02	Zenair CH-701 STOL	7-9308
OK-HUR 07	Evektor EV-97 Eurostar	
OK-HUR 23	Evektor EV-97 Eurostar	
OK-HUR 88	Zenair CH-601XLZodiac	6-9303
OK-HUR 99	Zenair CH-601XLZodiac	6-9314
OK-HUS 09	Tecnam P.96 Golf 100	
OK-HUT 01	WDFL Fascination	
OK-HUT 04	Airbike	
OK-HUT 06	Dallach D4 Fascination	
OK-HUU 36	Tecnam P.92 Echo	
OK-HUU 40	TL Ultralight TL-2000 Sting	
OK-HUU 41	Kappa 77 KP-2U Sova	
OK-HUU 42	Kappa 77 KP-2U Sova	
OK-HUU 43	Kappa 77 KP-2U Sova	
OK-HUU 44	Tecnam P.92 Echo	
OK-HUU 50	Bleriot Replica	
OK-HUU 52	Straton Moby Dick	
OK-HUU 53	Type unknown	
OK-HUU 58	Fantasy Air Allegro 2000	
OK-HUU 59	Zenair CH-601 Zodiac	
OK-HUU 60	Kappa KP-2U Sova	
OK-HUU 65	Tecnam P.92 Echo	
OK-HUU 66	Tecnam P.92 Echo	
OK-HUU 67	Kappa 77 KP-2U Sova	
OK-HUU 71	Tecnam P.92 Echo Super	
OK-HUU 72	Tecnam P.96 Golf 100	230
OK-HUX 14	Falcon	
OK-HWA 07	Gyro Trainer	
OK-IHA 10	Ultrasport 496	
OK-IUA 51	Profe Banjo-M	
OK-IUA 52	TL Ultralight TL-96 Star	
OK-IUA 54	Urban Air Samba XXL	01/03/2003
OK-IUA 59	TL Ultralight TL-96 Star	
OK-IUA 60	TL Ultralight TL-96 Star	
OK-IUA 63	Zenair CH-601XL Zodiac	
OK-IUA 68	Urban Air UFM-11 Lambada (To EI-DGP)	15/11
OK-IUA 77	TL Ultralight TL-2000 Sting RG	
OK-IUD 06	Direct Fly ALTO	
OK-IUD 07	Aerospool WT-9 Dynamic	
OK-IUD 10	Mara Wing Malamut	
OK-IUE 01	Fantasy Air Cora Allegro	
OK-IUG 10	Mara Wing Malamut	
OK-IUG 12	Zenair CH-601 Zodiac	
OK-IUG 15	ATEC 321 Faeta	
OK-IUL 01	Falcon (Also reported as Interplane Skyboy 2000L)	
OK-IUL 03	Airsport Sonet	
OK-IUO 11	Cessna 182 Scale replica	
OK-IUR 03	Evektor EV-95 Eurofox	
OK-IUR 10	Evektor EV-97 Eurostar	
OK-IUR 22	Pottier P.220S Koala	
OK-IUS 01	Evektor EV-97 Eurostar	
OK-IUS 10	Letov LK-2M Sluka	
OK-IUS 11	ATEC Zephyr	
OK-IUT 02	Type unknown	
OK-IUT 03	Type unknown	
OK-IUT 07	Dallach D4 Fascination	
OK-IUU 04	Kappa KP-2UR Sova	
OK-IZF 07	Tomi Cross Skyglider	990.4.0324
OK-IZW 02	Kremen Sport	
OK-JUA 04	Urban Air Samba XXL	
OK-JUA 73	Cechna	
OK-JUA 77	TL Ultralight TL-2000 Sting extra	
OK-JUA 90	TL Ultralight TL-2000 Sting carbon (Also reported as TEAM Hi-MAX .04)	
OK-JUA 95	ATEC Zephyr	
OK-JUG 22	ATEC Zephyr 2000	
OK-JUO 21	Fly Synthesis Storch	
OK-JUR 01	TL Ultralight TL-32 Typhoon (Wrecked)	
OK-JUR 06	Flyitalia MD-3 Rider	
OK-JUR 11	Evektor EV-97 Eurostar	
OK-JUU 20	Tecnam P.2002 Sierra	034
OK-JUU 21	KLN VL-3	
OK-JUU 44	Qualt 201J	
OK-JUU 55	MFI-9 UL	

OK-JUV 14	Fantasy Air Allegro 2000		
OK-KUA 05	TL Ultralight TL-2000 Sting carbon		
OK-KUG 31	ATEC 321		
OK-KUG 32	ATEC 212		
OK-KUG 34	Mara Wing L1 Malamut STOL		
OK-KUR 07	Flyitalia MD-3 Rider		
OK-KWA 01	Pro-Air Skywalk GL 165		
OK-SXAA	WT-2S Chinook		
OK-WUA 06	Klokon		
OK-WUA 08	Quicksilver		
OK-WUA 12	Denney Kitfox		
OK-WUA 15	Toresi Straton		
OK-WUA 17	Vojacek 07 Stratton Mini	1991	
OK-WUC 01	LET ULM-01 Aspic		
OK-WUC 03	Ti 3		
OK-WUC 09	Type unknown		
OK-WUD 02	V-tail Homebuilt Glider (Trabant)		
OK-WUE 02	Bugic UL Sarancha	03	
OK-WUI 1	TST Klokon	02	
OK-WXAF	Letov LK-2 Sluka	81910900004	
OK-WXAJ	Letov LK-2 Sluka		
OK-WZA 01	Jan Bem Cosmos Wing		N901ME
OK-WZD 2	Type unknown		
OK-WZF 4	Type unknown		
OK-WZF 20	Horizont 11/F		
OK-WZF 28	Hirth ?		
OK-WZF 28	ESO-2 Trike		
OK-WZG 8	Type unknown		
OK-WZI 03	MZK		
OK-WZJ 15	Type unknown "Opel Decker"		
OK-WZL 2	Type unknown		
OK-WZL 06	MZK		
OK-WZL-9	Aerodelta		
OK-WZL 11	Type unknown		
OK-XUA 04	Aero C-104 ULReplica "K12"		
OK-XUA 11	Toresi Straton D.8 Moby Dick		
OK-XUA 12	Toresi Straton D.8 Moby Dick		
OK-XUA 13	TL Ultralight TL-32 Typhoon		
OK-XUA 17	Toresi Straton D.8 Moby Dick		
OK-XUA 18	K-91 Kosak		
OK-XUB 02	TEAM Mini-MAX		
OK-XUD 05	TEAM Mini-MAX (Cr 13.5.97)		
OK-XUE 05	Gryf T.I.B.	191	OK-WUC 02
OK-XUE 06	Type unknown		
OK-XUE 07	Masarka		
OK-XUE 10	Letov LK-2M Sluka		
OK-XUE 012	Letov LK-2 Sluka		
OK-XUE 15	TL Ultralight TL-32 Typhoon		
OK-XUI 07	Letov LK-2M Sluka		
OK-XUJ 20	TL Ultralight TL-32 Typhoon		
OK-XUO 02	Toresi Straton Mini		
OK-XUO 04	TEAM Hi-MAX (Mini-MAX?)		
OK-XUU 02	Letov LK-3 Nova		
OK-XUU 04	Letov LK-2M Sluka		
OK-XUU 05	Letov LK-2M Sluka		
OK-XUU 07	Letov LK-2M Sluka		
OK-XUU 08	Letov Sluka HC2	8192090102	
OK-XUU 10	TL Ultralight TL-32 Typhoon		
OK-XUU 17	Ultra Aero Storch		
OK-XUU 20	TL Ultralight TL-32 Typhoon		
OK-XUU 70	Letov LK-2 Sluka	8192090114	
OK-XXAB	Denney Kitfox II	1501	
OK-XXAC	Denney Kitfox II	1502	
OK-XXAE	Denney Kitfox II	1504	
OK-XXAS	Letov LK-2 Sluka		
OK-XZD 13	Type unknown		
OK-XZF 13	TL Ultralight TL-32 Typhoon		
OK-XZF 19	Type unknown		
OK-XZF 20	Type unknown		
OK-XZG 07	Mara Wing 155		
OK-XZU 02	ESO-2		
OK-YUA 02	Toresi Straton D.8 Moby Dick		
OK-YUA 03	Toresi Straton D.8 Moby Dick		
OK-YUA 04	Straton D.7 Mini	025	
OK-YUA 06	Type unknown		
OK-YUA 11	Broucek W-01 motor glider		OK-YXA
OK-YUD 10	Aeropro Fox		
OK-YUD 15	Lasotronic CS		
OK-YUD 16	TEAM Hi-MAX		
OK-YUD 17	Type unknown		
OK-YUD 19	Toresi Straton		
OK-YUD 20	Letov LK-2 Sluka		
OK-YUD 23	Motor Glider (Type unknown)		
OK-YUD 26	Toresi Straton D.8 Moby Dick		
OK-YUD 28	Letov LK-3 Nova		
OK-YUE 011	Type unknown		
OK-YUE 017	TEAM Hi-MAX (Mini-MAX?)		
OK-YUH 01	Straton D.7 Mini		
OK-YUK	Pelican	02	
OK-YUK 01	Straton D.7 Mini		
OK-YUK 02	Pelican Club	582	
OK-YUO 7	Twin DS-01		
OK-YUP 03	TEAM Hi-MAX		
OK-YUU 01	Straton		
OK-YUU 02	Letov LK-2M Sluka		
OK-YUU 03	Denney Kitfox		
OK-YUU 07	Letov LK-2S Sluka	819209010	

OK-YUU 11	TL Ultralight TL-32 Typhoon		
OK-YUU 12	TL Ultralight TL-32 Typhoon		
OK-YUU 15	Aeropro Fox		
OK-YUU 19	Denney Kitfox		
OK-YUU 22	TL Ultralight TL-32 Typhoon		
OK-YUU 23	TL Ultralight TL-32 Typhoon		
OK-YUU 26	Aeropro Fox		
OK-YUU 27	Interplane Skyboy		
OK-YUU 28	TL Ultralight TL-32 Typhoon		
OK-YUU 31	TL Ultralight TL-32 Typhoon		
OK-YUU 34	Letov LK-2M Sluka		
OK-YUU 36	TL Ultralight TL-32 Typhoon		
OK-YUU 37	TL Ultralight TL-32 Typhoon		
OK-YUU 38	Type unknown		
OK-YUU 39	TL Ultralight TL-32 Typhoon	A017/1993	
OK-YUU 41	TEAM Hi-MAX		
OK-YUU 43	TL Ultralight TL-32 Typhoon		
OK-YUU 52	Letov LK-2M Sluka		
OK-YUU 54	JORA Jora		
OK-YUU 57	Denney Kitfox III	637	
OK-YUU 59	Letov LK-3 Nova		
OK-YUU 60	TL Ultralight TL-32 Typhoon		
OK-YUU 65	Toresi Straton D.7 Mini		
OK-YUU 66	Rans S-12 Airaile		
OK-YUU 67	Rans S-6ES Coyote II	102	
OK-YUU 71	TL Ultralight TL-32 Typhoon Sprint	93A040	
OK-YZF 06	Trike, type unknown		
OK-YZF 16	Stronger WM02 1993 Madlo		
OK-YZG 08	MW167		
OK-YZG 10	Type unknown		
OK-YZG 15	Type unknown		
OK-YZG 39	Mara Wing MW155		
OK-YZP 13	Trike, type unknown		
OK-YZR 03	Vyrobce Vlastni		
OK-YZR-05	Type unknown		
OK-ZBF 08	Junkers		
OK-ZUA 01	Type unknown		
OK-ZUA 03	Type unknown		
OK-ZUA 05	Toresi Straton D.7 Mini		
OK-ZUA 07	Fantasy Air Cora		
OK-ZUA 08	TEAM Mini-MAX		
OK-ZUA 09	Toresi Straton D.7 Mini		
OK-ZUD 01	Toresi Straton D.7 Mini		
OK-ZUD 03	Straton		
OK-ZUD 08	Type unknown		
OK-ZUD 09	Type unknown		
OK-ZUD 11	LET-Mont Tulak	TUL-01	
OK-ZUD 15	Thomas Glaeser Nieuport IIreplica	63	N124TG
OK-ZUD 17	Aeropro Fox		
OK-ZUE 18	Toresi Straton D.8 Moby Dick		
OK-ZUE 21	Letov LK-2 Sluka		
OK-ZUH 03	TEAM Mini-MAX		
OK-ZUH 05	MAT-20		
OK-ZUI 01	Toresi Straton D.8 Moby Dick (Cr 8.6.97)		
OK-ZUK	Pelican VS		
OK-ZUK 03	Ultravia Pelican	004	
OK-ZUO 03	Pietenpol replica		
OK-ZUO 04	TEAM Mini-MAX		
OK-ZUO 07	TEAM Mini-MAX		
OK-ZUO 08	Schleicher Rhonlerche II (motorised)		
OK-ZUO 09	TEAM Mini-MAX		
OK-ZUO 15	Scheibe Spatz A (Wankel engine) (Damaged)	02	OE-0292
OK-ZUO 16	Rans S-6 Coyote II		
OK-ZUO 19	Greenhorn		
OK-ZUO 22	Berfalk		
OK-ZUO 25	Fantasy Air Cora		
OK-ZUO 26	Fantasy Air Cora		
OK-ZUP 02	TEAM Mini-MAX		
OK-ZUP 03	Rans S-6XL Supra	013	
OK-ZUR 03	J-03 Yetti		
OK-ZUR 04	Type unknown		
OK-ZUR 05	Evektor EV-96 Fox 582	9401/2	
OK-ZUR 07	Interplane Skyboy		
OK-ZUS 02	TEAM Mini-MAX	CR096P	
OK-ZUS 07	Toresi Straton D.7 Mini		
OK-ZUS 08	TEAM Mini-MAX		
OK-ZUT 01	Denney Kitfox		
OK-ZUT 02	Kolibrik		
OK-ZUU 01	VBS-2 Kunkadlo		
OK-ZUU 02	Toresi Straton D.7 Mini 98		
OK-ZUU 03	Type unknown		
OK-ZUU 04	TL Ultralight TL-132 Condor	94C02	
OK-ZUU 07	JORA 199		
OK-ZUU 08	TL Ultralight TL-32 Typhoon		
OK-ZUU 09	TL Ultralight TL-32 Typhoon Sprint		
OK-ZUU 10	Letov LK-3 Nova		
OK-ZUU 12	Zenair CH-701 STOL		
OK-ZUU 18	Aeropro Fox		
OK-ZUU 21	TL Ultralight TL-32 Typhoon		
OK-ZUU 24	TL Ultralight TL-132 Condor		
OK-ZUU 29	Rans S-6 Coyote II	004	
OK-ZUU 31	TL Ultralight TL-232 Condor Plus	94C04	
OK-ZUU 35	Letov LK-2M Sluka		
OK-ZUU 36	TEAM Mini-MAX		
OK-ZUU 37	Top Air Cobra	9491	
OK-ZUU 38	TL Ultralight TL-232 Condor Plus	94C05	
OK-ZUU 39	TL Ultralight TL-132 Condor		

OK-ZUU 41	Letov LK-2M Sluka	829409X04	
OK-ZUU 43	M7 Orlican		
OK-ZUU 45	TL Ultralight TL-132 Condor		
OK-ZUU 46	TL Ultralight TL-32 Typhoon		
OK-ZUU 47	Rans S-6XL Supra	005	
OK-ZUU 49	TL Ultralight TL-132 Condor		
OK-ZUU 50	TL Ultralight TL-132 Condor		
OK-ZUU 51	Toresi Straton D.8 Moby Dick		
OK-ZUU 52	TEAM Mini-MAX		
OK-ZUU 55	Ikarus C-22		
OK-ZUU 56	TL Ultralight TL-132 Condor	94C08	
OK-ZUU 58	Type unknown		
OK-ZUU 60	TL Ultralight TL-132 Condor		
OK-ZUU 61	TL Ultralight TL-132 Condor "Autoprim"	94C09	
OK-ZZB 01	Super Wing MW-155		
OK-ZZC 02	TL Ultralight TL-1/K21		
OK-ZZF 04	Laser Sprint 150M		
OK-ZZF 09	VM Brothers Triumph 142 Viper		
OK-ZZF 10	VM Brothers Triumph 142 Viper		
OK-ZZF 11	Justra Stratos	037.92	
OK-ZZG 03	MZK		
OK-ZZG 09	Type unknown		
OK-ZZG 11	Trike		
OK-ZZG 29	Super Wing MW-155		
OK-ZZI 76	Trike		
OK-ZZL 07	TL Ultralight TL-22 Duo	95C08	

BALLOONS AND AIRSHIPS

OK-0020	Schröder Fire Balloons G 26/24 HAFB		
OK-0037	Kubicek BB HAFB (Model unknown)	137	
OK-0039	Kubicek BB HAFB (Model unknown)	139	
OK-0040	Kubicek BB HAFB (Model unknown)	140	
OK-0043	Kubicek BB HAFB (Model unknown)	143	
OK-0048	Kubicek BB HAFB (Model unknown)	148	
OK-0050	Kubicek BB HAFB (Model unknown)	150	
OK-0051	Kubicek BB-37 HAFB	151	
OK-0052	Kubicek BB-22 HAFB	152	
OK-1012	Aerotechnik AB-8 HAFB	910534	
OK-1014	Aerotechnik N-22 HAFB	910535	
OK-1016	Aerotechnik AB-8 HAFB	910537	
OK-1017	Aerotechnik AB-2C HAFB	910538	
OK-1018	Aerotechnik AB-8 HAFB	910539	
OK-1021	Aerotechnik AB-2C HAFB	910543	
OK-1022	Aerotechnik AB-8 HAFB	910544	
OK-1024	Aerotechnik AB-2C HAFB	910546	
OK-1026	Aerotechnik AB-8 HAFB	910548	
OK-1027	Aerotechnik AB-8 HAFB	910422	
OK-1041	Kubicek BB SS Wine Bottle HAFB	161	
OK-1056	Kubicek BB-30 HAFB	176	
OK-1060	Kubicek BB-30 HAFB	180	
OK-1065	Kubicek BB SS Mug HAFB	185	
OK-1068	Kubicek BB-30N HAFB	188	
OK-2002	Kubicek BB-12 HAFB	01	
OK-2003	Kubicek Poppetje-SS HAFB	02	
OK-2004	Kubicek Beer Keg SS HAFB	03	
OK-2005	Kubicek BB-30 HAFB	04	
OK-2010	Aerotechnik AB-8 HAFB	920549	
OK-2017	Kubicek BB-30 HAFB	07	
OK-2018	Kubicek BB-20 HAFB	10	
OK-2020	Kubicek BB-30 HAFB	11	
OK-2021	Kubicek BB-30 HAFB	16	
OK-2058	Kubicek BB-30 HAFB	208	
OK-2063	Kubicek BB Suding (Pig) SS HAFB	203	
OK-2092	Kubicek BB-20GP HAFB	211	
OK-3000	Kubicek BB-30 HAFB	213	
OK-3007	Cameron HAFB (Type unknown)	10384	
OK-3025	Kubicek BB-20 HAFB	18	
OK-3027	Kubicek BB-12 HAFB	20	
OK-3028	Kubicek BB-30 HAFB	21	
OK-3029	Kubicek BB-22 HAFB	22	
OK-3030	Kubicek BB-20 HAFB	23	
OK-3031	Kubicek BB-20 HAFB	24	
OK-3032	Kubicek BB-30 HAFB	25	
OK-3035	Aerotechnik AB- HAFB	930552	
OK-3036	Kubicek BB-30 HAFB	26	
OK-3038	Kubicek BB-30 HAFB	28	
OK-3039	Kubicek BB-22 HAFB	29	
OK-3041	Kubicek BB-26 HAFB	31	
OK-3050	Kubicek BB-42Z HAFB	234	
OK-3053	Kubicek BB-26 HAFB	172	
OK-4000	Cameron DP-90 Hot Air Airship	3214	
OK-4003	Kubicek DHL Box SS HAFB	312	OK-0312
OK-4005	Kubicek BB-20GP HAFB	304	OK-0304
OK-4007	Kubicek BB-30Z HAFB	319	OK-0219
OK-4010	Kubicek BB-20GP HAFB	300	OK-0300
OK-4012	Aviatik AB-2 HAFB	02	
OK-4014(2)	Aviatik AB-2 HAFB	03	
OK-4016	Aviatik AB-2 HAFB	04	
OK-4018	Aviatik AB-2 HAFB	05	
OK-4020	Kubicek BB- HAFB	322	OK-0322
OK-4044	Kubicek BB-22 HAFB	34	
OK-4045	Kubicek BB-22 HAFB	35	
OK-4046	Kubicek BB-22 HAFB	36	
OK-4047	Kubicek BB-22 HAFB	37	
OK-4048	Kubicek BB-30 HAFB	38	
OK-4049	Kubicek BB-30 HAFB	39	
OK-4053	Aerotechnik AB- HAFB	940553	
OK-4054	Aerotechnik AB- HAFB	940554	
OK-4056	Aerotechnik AB- HAFB	940555	
OK-4057	Aerotechnik AB- HAFB	560594	
OK-5009	Cameron O-77 HAFB	3540	S5-OHB
OK-5052	Kubicek BB Kriglok SS HAFB	42	
OK-5054	Kubicek BB-22 HAFB	44	
OK-5055	Kubicek BB-30 HAFB	45	
OK-5056	Kubicek BB-22 HAFB	46	
OK-5057	Kubicek BB-20 HAFB	47	
OK-5058	Kubicek BB-22 HAFB	48	
OK-5059	Kubicek BB-30 HAFB	49	
OK-5060	Kubicek BB-30 HAFB	50	
OK-6050	Aerotechnik AB- HAFB	960550	
OK-6051	Aerotechnik AB-2 HAFB	960551	
OK-6056	Kubicek BB-22 HAFB	56	
OK-6057	Kubicek BB Vorwerk SS HAFB	57	
OK-6060	Kubicek BB-22 HAFB	60	
OK-6061	Kubicek BB-22 HAFB	61	
OK-6062	Kubicek BB-22 HAFB	62	
OK-6063	Kubicek BB-30 HAFB	63	
OK-6068	Kubicek BB-37 HAFB	68	
OK-7004	Aerotechnik AB-2a HAFB	02/87	
OK-7006	Aerotechnik AB-2a HAFB	870206	
OK-7071	Kubicek BB-22 HAFB	71	
OK-7075	Kubicek BBLIAZ HAFB	75	
OK-7079	Kubicek BB-22 HAFB	79	
OK-8006	Cameron 0-77 HAFB	387	
OK-8007	Aviatik AB-2A HAFB	880309	
OK-8018	Kubicek BB-37 HAFB	88	
OK-8020	Kubicek BB-22 HAFB	90	
OK-8024	Kubicek BB-30 HAFB	94	
OK-8025	Kubicek BB-26 HAFB	95	
OK-8036	Kubicek AV-2 Hot Air Airship	106	OM-ADS OK-8036
OK-8038	Kubicek BB-37 HAFB	108	
OK-9002	Aerotechnik AB-8 HAFB	890417	
OK-9004	Aerotechnik AB-2B HAFB	890415	
OK-9006	Colt 21A Cloudhopper HAFB	1446	G-LUGG
OK-9007	Thunder AX9-140 HAFB	1490	D-OHBH(1) D-Stadt-Calw(2)
OK-9039	Kubicek BB-26 HAFB	109	
OK-9045	Kubicek BB-30 HAFB	115	
OK-9046	Kubicek BB BEMB SS HAFB	116	
OK-9050	Kubicek BB Krigl SS HAFB	120	
OK-9053	Kubicek Jäger Bottle SS HAFB	123	
OK-	Cameron N-90 HAFB	3152	

GLIDERS AND MOTORGLIDERS

OK-0007-AX	Schempp-Hirth Ventus 2ax	unkn	
OK-0019-PUP	Schleicher ASW 19B	19398	HB-1724
OK-0101	Aerotechnik L-13SE Vivat	900328	
OK-0103-KY	Schempp-Hirth Standard Cirrus	102	OO-ZLT D-0735
OK-0105	Aerotechnik L-13SE Vivat	900402	
OK-0107	Aerotechnik L-13SE Vivat	900404	
OK-0108	Aerotechnik L-13SE Vivat	900405	
OK-0113	Aerotechnik L-13SE Vivat	900410	
OK-0115	Aerotechnik L-13SE Vivat	900412	
OK-0116	Aerotechnik L-13SW Vivat	900413	
OK-0117	Aerotechnik L-13SE Vivat	900414	
OK-0119	Aerotechnik L-13SE Vivat	900416	
OK-0201-X	LET L-23 Super Blanik	907601	
OK-0202	LET L-23 Super Blanik	907602	
OK-0205	LET L-23 Super Blanik	907605	
OK-0207	LET L-23 Super Blanik	907607	
OK-0208	LET L-23 Super Blanik	907608	
OK-0210-V	LET L-23 Super Blanik (Crashed)	907613	
OK-0211-N	LET L-23 Super Blanik	907614	
OK-0213	LET L-23 Super Blanik	907616	
OK-0214	LET L-23 Super Blanik	907617	
OK-0216-K4	LET L-23 Super Blanik	907619	
OK-0217-EH	LET L-23 Super Blanik	907709	
OK-0219-V1	LET L-23 Super Blanik	907711	
OK-0220	LET L-23 Super Blanik	907712	
OK-0222-T	LET L-23 Super Blanik	907714	
OK-0223	LET L-23 Super Blanik	907715	
OK-0225	LET L-23 Super Blanik	907722	
OK-0226-Y1	LET L-23 Super Blanik	907723	
OK-0228-FV	LET L-23 Super Blanik	907725	
OK-0229	LET L-23 Super Blanik	907726	
OK-0234	LET L-23 Super Blanik	907717	
OK-0237	LET L-23 Super Blanik	907718	
OK-0239	LET L-23 Super Blanik	907626	(BGA3668)
OK-0240-AM	LET L-23 Super Blanik (W/o 9.11.03)	907625	(BGA3667(1))
OK-0302	LET L-13 Blanik	174722	
OK-0304	LET L-13 Blanik	174723	
OK-0308	LET L-13 Blanik	174408	DOSAAF
OK-0365-65	Schempp-Hirth Discus CS	001CS	

OK-0370-CE	Schempp-Hirth Discus CS	006CS	
OK-0372-LH	Schempp-Hirth Discus CS	010CS	
OK-0453	Schempp-Hirth Standard Cirrus	13	D-0453
OK-0455-IF	Schempp-Hirth Standard Cirrus G	16	D-0455
OK-0501-CZ	Schempp-Hirth Ventus 2c	61/180	
OK-0507-JM	Schleicher ASW 15B	15047	D-0507
OK-0512-C2	VSO-10 Gradient	150014	
OK-0514-C3	VSO-10 Gradient	150016	
OK-0516-C4	VSO-10 Gradient	150018	
OK-0518	VSO-10 Gradient	150019	
OK-0520-C6	VSO-10 Gradient	150020	
OK-0522-C7	VSO-10 Gradient	150022	
OK-0524-C8	VSO-10C Gradient	150024	
OK-0526-C9	VSO-10C Gradient	150025	
OK-0528-D1	VSO-10 Gradient	150026	
OK-0530-D2	VSO-10 Gradient	150028	
OK-0569-AW	Schempp-Hirth Standard Cirrus	50	D-0569
OK-0600-99	VSO-10B Gradient	150224	
OK-0601-00	VSO-10 Gradient	150225	OM-0601
			OK-0601
OK-0603-U2	Schempp-Hirth Janus	31	OO-ZML
			LX-CPC
			OO-ZPY
OK-0688-C1	Schempp-Hirth Standard Cirrus	536	D-0688
OK-0690-90	Schempp-Hirth Standard Cirrus	89	D-0690
OK-0713-HV	Schleicher ASW 15	15112	D-0713
OK-0732	Schempp-Hirth Standard Cirrus	95	D-0732
			OK-0732
			D-0732
OK-0737-JR	Schempp-Hirth Standard Cirrus	105	D-0737
OK-0744	LG.125 Sohaj	544/139	
OK-0771	LG.125 Sohaj	572	
OK-0784-84	Schempp-Hirth Standard Cirrus	193	D-0784
OK-0817	Letov Lunak LF-107	26	
OK-0819	Letov Lunak LF-107	33	
OK-0822-TZ	Schleicher ASW 15	15159	D-0822
OK-0829	Letov Lunak LF-107	45	
OK-0838	Letov Lunak LF-107	54	
OK-0902	LET L-13 Blanik	170910	
OK-0904	LET L-13 Blanik	170912	
OK-0905	LET L-13 Blanik	170913	
OK-0906-L1	LET L-13 Blanik	170914	
OK-0908-JA	LET L-13 Blanik	170916	
OK-0910	LET L-13 Blanik	170918	
OK-0911	LET L-13 Blanik	170919	
OK-0914-O	LET L-13 Blanik	171106	
OK-0915	LET L-13 Blanik	171107	
OK-0916	LET L-13 Blanik	171108	
OK-0917-F	LET L-13 Blanik	171109	
OK-0918	Letov Lunak LF-107	27	
OK-0920	LET L-13 Blanik	171303	
OK-0921	LET L-13 Blanik	171304	
OK-0924	LG.125 Sohaj	191	
OK-0937	LG.125 Sohaj	537	
OK-1000-ET	Schempp-Hirth Nimbus 4M	16	D-KOZX(4)
OK-1001	Stemme S-10VT	11-077	D-KSTE
OK-1100-Y5	Schleicher ASW 20	20566	SE-TXS
OK-1111-ET	Glasflügel 304CZ	16	
OK-1122	Schempp-Hirth Standard Cirrus	250	F-CHBR(2)
			D-1122
OK-1193-63	Schempp-Hirth Standard Cirrus	418	HB-1193
OK-1212-12	LAK-12	6235	
OK-1213	Marganski MDM-1P Fox	233	
OK-1234-X3	Grob G.103 Twin Astir	3008	OY-XHV
OK-1242	LG.130 Kmotr	13	
OK-1260	LG.130 Kmotr	31	
OK-1272	Schleicher ASW 15B	15246	D-1272
			OE-0956
OK-1301-VP	Schempp-Hirth Discus CS	285CS	
OK-1302-CS	Schempp-Hirth Discus CS	291CS	
OK-1313-AT	Schleicher ASW 15	15165	D-0828
OK-1343-A1	Schempp-Hirth Standard Cirrus B	693	HB-1343
OK-1406	VSO-10 Gradient	150102	
OK-1411	VSO-10 Gradient (Cld ?)	150107	
OK-1500-E1	VSO-10 Gradient	150029	
OK-1504-E3	VSO-10 Gradient	150031	
OK-1506-E4	VSO-10 Gradient	150032	
OK-1507	LAK-17	141	
OK-1508-E5	VSO-10 Gradient	150035	
OK-1510-E6	VSO-10 Gradient	150036	
OK-1512-E7	VSO-10 Gradient	150037	
OK-1514-E8	VSO-10 Gradient	150038	
OK-1516-E9	VSO-10 Gradient	150041	
OK-1518-F	VSO-10 Gradient	150042	
OK-1520-F2	VSO-10 Gradient	150043	
OK-1522	VSO-10 Gradient	150045	
OK-1524-XL	VSO-10C Gradient	150046	
OK-1526-V3	VSO-10 Gradient	150047	
OK-1600-A1	Schleicher ASW 19B	19332	
OK-1700-M	LET L-13A Blanik	817401	
OK-1702-JJ	LET L-13A Blanik	817402	
OK-1717-LK	LAK-17	118	
OK-1777	Schleicher ASW 15	15255	D-2113
OK-1765	LG-125 Sohaj	602	
OK-1800	LET L-13 Blanik	171408	
OK-1803-L1	LET L-13 Blanik	171411	
OK-1804-5	LET L-13 Blanik	171412	

OK-1806	LET L-13 Blanik	171414	
OK-1807	LET L-13 Blanik	171415	
OK-1810	LET L-13 Blanik	171611	
OK-1812	LET L-13 Blanik	171613	
OK-1813	LET L-13 Blanik (Accident 18.10.03)	171614	
OK-1816	LET L-13 Blanik	171617	
OK-1817	LET L-13 Blanik	171618	
OK-1820	LET L-13 Blanik	171912	
OK-1822	LET L-13 Blanik	171914	
OK-1823	LET L-13 Blanik	171915	
OK-1824	LET L-13 Blanik	171930	
OK-1825	LET L-13 Blanik	172001	
OK-1827	LET L-13A Blanik	172003	
OK-1828	LET L-13 Blanik (Wreck noted 8.02)	172004	
OK-1829	LET L-13 Blanik	172005	
OK-1830-4	LET L-13 Blanik	172006	
OK-1831-IL	LET L-13 Blanik	172007	
OK-1840	LET L-13 Blanik	172016	
OK-1850	LET L-13 Blanik	175005	
OK-1852-H	LET L-13 Blanik	175025	
OK-1854	LET L-13 Blanik	175026	
OK-1856-V	LET L-13 Blanik	174927	
OK-1900	Schleicher ASW 19B	19239	OO-ZVH
OK-1911-ZP	Schleicher ASW 15B	15210	D-0907
OK-1948	Schempp-Hirth Janus C	unkn	
OK-1968	LG-125 Sohaj	605	OK-1768
OK-1991-ZS	Schempp-Hirth Standard Cirrus	286G	D-1991
OK-2000-LB	Glasflügel H304CZ	10	C-GHED
OK-2029-BH	Schleicher ASW 15	15399	D-2029
OK-2053-DI	Schempp-Hirth Standard Cirrus	292	D-2053
OK-2121-21	Schleicher ASK 21	21442	D-2516
OK-2210	LAK-17	140	
OK-2215	LF-109 Pionyr	23	
OK-2222-22	Glasflügel H304C	48	
OK-2276	LF-109 Pionyr	90	
OK-2287-MD	Schempp-Hirth Standard Cirrus B	664	D-2287
OK-2294	Schempp-Hirth Standard Cirrus	402G	D-2294
OK-2323	Schempp-Hirth Duo Discus C	350	
OK-2330-LZ	Schleicher ASW 15B	15335	D-2330
OK-2371-JK	Schleicher ASW 15B	15363	D-2371
OK-2403-36	M-35 (Converted from VT-116 c/n 151705)	02	
OK-2412	VT-16 Orlik	150304	
OK-2424-CK	Glaser-Dirks DG-202	unkn	
OK-2429-MB	VT-16 Orlik	150503	
OK-2431	VT-16 Orlik	150503	
OK-2433	VT-16 Orlik	150505	
OK-2487	Schempp-Hirth Ventus 2c	74	
OK-2500-F8	VSO-10 Gradient	150050	
OK-2502-F9	VSO-10A Gradient	150051	
OK-2504-G1	VSO-10 Gradient	150053	
OK-2506-G2	VSO-10 Gradient	150054	
OK-2508-G3	VSO-10 Gradient	150056	
OK-2510-G4	VSO-10 Gradient	150057	
OK-2514-G5	VSO-10C Gradient	150060	
OK-2516-G6	VSO-10 Gradient	150061	
OK-2530-LF	Schempp-Hirth Ventus c	574	
OK-2666	Lanaverre CS-11/75 Standard Cirrus	25	D-2666
OK-2700	LET L-13 Blanik	175215	
OK-2702	LET L-13 Blanik	175216	
OK-2704	LET L-13 Blanik	175217	
OK-2706	LET L-13A Blanik	827404	
OK-2708	LET L-13 Blanik	827405	
OK-2710-Z	LET L-13A Blanik	827407	
OK-2714-T1	LET L-13 Blanik	827410	
OK-2716	LET L-13 Blanik	827411	
OK-2718	LET L-13A Blanik	827413	
OK-2720-25	LET L-13A Blanik	827414	
OK-2722	LET L-13A Blanik	827416	
OK-2724-AF	LET L-13A Blanik	827417	
OK-2728-X	LET L-13 Blanik	827420	
OK-2781	Schempp-Hirth Standard Cirrus	500	D-2781
OK-2800	LET L-13 Blanik	172028	
OK-2803	LET L-13 Blanik	172101	
OK-2804	LET L-13 Blanik	172102	
OK-2805	LET L-13 Blanik	172103	
OK-2806	LET L-13 Blanik	172104	
OK-2807	LET L-13 Blanik	172105	
OK-2808	LET L-13 Blanik	172106	
OK-2809- I	LET L-13 Blanik	172107	
OK-2810	LET L-13 Blanik	172108	
OK-2811	LET L-13 Blanik	172109	
OK-2812	LET L-13 Blanik	172110	
OK-2813-OJ	LET L-13 Blanik	172111	
OK-2814-U	LET L-13 Blanik	172112	
OK-2815	LET L-13 Blanik	172113	
OK-2816	LET L-13 Blanik	172114	
OK-2817	LET L-13 Blanik	172115	
OK-2818	LET L-13 Blanik	172116	
OK-2819	LET L-13 Blanik	172117	
OK-2820	LET L-13 Blanik	172419	
OK-2822	LET L-13 Blanik	172420	
OK-2823	LET L-13 Blanik	172421	
OK-2824	LET L-13 Blanik	172422	
OK-2828	Schleicher ASW 20CL	20149	PH-828
			D-6860
			BGA2492/BYV

OK-2900	SZD-36A Cobra 15	W-574	OM-2900
			OK-2900
OK-2901	Universal M-35	1	
OK-2902	SZD-36A Cobra 15	W-575	
OK-2903	M-28	10.XI	
OK-2906	Slingsby T-59DKestrel 19	1788	
OK-2909	VT-16 Orlik	150301	
OK-2910	Schempp-Hirth Cirrus VTC	124	
OK-2912-XJ	Slingsby T-59DKestrel 19	1794	
OK-2916	M-25 Standard	8	
OK-2920	LET L-213A (Dismantled, stored)	213X01	
OK-2921	LET L-33 Solo (prototype)	X2	
OK-2923	VT-16 Orlik	150405	
OK-2924	VT-16 Orlik	150404	
OK-2947-TS	Schempp-Hirth Standard Cirrus	313	D-2947
OK-2954-LM	Schempp-Hirth Standard Cirrus	309G	D-2954
OK-2966-HC	Schempp-Hirth Standard Cirrus	323	
OK-3004	Schempp-Hirth Standard Cirrus	336	D-3004
OK-3005-K	Schempp-Hirth Standard Cirrus	315	I-LETJ
			(D-2035)
			I-LETJ
			D-2949
OK-3104	Aerotechnik L-13SEH Vivat	930512	
OK-3122-ZM	Schempp-Hirth Standard Cirrus	547	D-3122
OK-3137-LT	Rolladen-Schneider LS1F	379	D-3137
OK-3254-KA	Schempp-Hirth Standard Cirrus	444G	D-3254
OK-3265	Schempp-Hirth Standard Cirrus	527	D-3265
OK-3300-LL	Schleicher ASW 15B	15311	
OK-3301-S3	Rolladen-Schneider LS1D	151	D-2106
OK-3302	Schleicher ASW 15B	15312	
OK-3303	Schempp-Hirth Discus 2t	31/...	
OK-3304-17	Schleicher ASW 15B	15313	
OK-3305-SH	Schempp-Hirth Discus CS	304CS	
OK-3306-X	Schleicher ASW 15B	15314	
OK-3403	VT-16 Orlik	150604	
OK-3404-T1	LET L-33 Solo	930104	
OK-3405	VT-16 Orlik	150606	
OK-3411	VT-16 Orlik	150702	
OK-3414	VT-16 Orlik	150715	
OK-3422	VT-16 Orlik	150805	
OK-3424	VT-16 Orlik	150807	
OK-3500-H5	VSO-10 Gradient	150071	
OK-3502-H6	VSO-10 Gradient	150072	
OK-3504-H7	VSO-10 Gradient	150074	
OK-3506-H8	VSO-10 Gradient	150075	
OK-3508-H9	VSO-10 Gradient	150077	
OK-3510	VSO-10 Gradient	150078	
OK-3512-I2	VSO-10 Gradient	150080	
OK-3514-I3	VSO-10B Gradient	150081	
OK-3516-I4	VSO-10 Gradient	150083	
OK-3518-I5	VSO-10 Gradient	150084	
OK-3520-G8	VSO-10 Gradient	150063	
OK-3522-G9	VSO-10B Gradient	150064	
OK-3524-H1	VSO-10 Gradient	150066	
OK-3526-H2	VSO-10 Gradient	150067	
OK-3528-H3	VSO-10 Gradient	150069	
OK-3530	VSO-10 Gradient	150070	
OK-3600	Aerotechnik L-13SE Vivat	830001	
OK-3700	LET L-13 Blanik	025426	
OK-3702	LET L-13A Blanik	025806	
OK-3704-FH	LET L-13 Blanik	025808	
OK-3712	Schempp-Hirth CS-11/75 Standard Cirrus	643	F-CEMP
OK-3800-D	LET L-13 Blanik	172613	
OK-3801	LET L-13 Blanik	172602	
OK-3802	LET L-13 Blanik	172614	
OK-3803	LET L-13 Blanik	172615	
OK-3805	LET L-13 Blanik	172607	
OK-3806	LET L-13 Blanik	172616	
OK-3807	LET L-13 Blanik	172608	
OK-3808	LET L-13 Blanik	172609	
OK-3809-V	LET L-13 Blanik	172610	
OK-3811	LET L-13 Blanik	172612	
OK-3812	LET L-13 Blanik	172820	
OK-3813	LET L-13 Blanik	172821	
OK-3814-WT	LET L-13 Blanik	172822	
OK-3817	LET L-13 Blanik	172825	
OK-3819	LET L-13 Blanik	172827	
OK-3820	LET L-13 Blanik	172828	
OK-3821-V7	LET L-13 Blanik	172829	
OK-3822	LET L-13 Blanik	172830	
OK-3823	LET L-13 Blanik	172901	
OK-3824	LET L-13 Blanik	172902	
OK-3825	LET L-13 Blanik	172903	
OK-3826	LET L-13 Blanik	172904	
OK-3827-Y	LET L-13 Blanik	172905	
OK-3828	LET L-13 Blanik	172906	
OK-3829	LET L-13 Blanik	172907	
OK-3900	Universal M-17	02	
OK-3901	SZD-48-1 Jantar Standard	B-1269	DOSAAF
OK-3902	VT-16 Orlik	150603	
OK-3903	LF-109 Pionyr	120	
OK-3908	LF-109 Pionyr	115	
OK-3985	Schleicher ASW 15B	15433	D-3985
OK-4212	LET L-23 Super Blanik	948111	
OK-4214-L1	LET L-23 Super Blanik	948124	
OK-4215	LET L-23 Super Blanik	948125	
OK-4300-VL	Schempp-Hirth Discus CS	171CS	
OK-4301-CV	Schempp-Hirth Standard Cirrus	unkn	
OK-4307	VT-116 Orlik II ZK	151010	
OK-4314	VT-116 Orlik II ZK	151017	
OK-4321	VT-116 Orlik II	151024	
OK-4402	LET L-33 Solo	940212	
OK-4404-JW	LET L-33 Solo	940306	
OK-4406	LET L-33 Solo	940218	
OK-4407	LET L-33 Solo	940305	
OK-4408	LET L-33 Solo	940301	
OK-4444	Schempp-Hirth Standard Cirrus	295G	D-4167
			HB-1096
OK-4489-XZ	Schleicher ASW 19B	19088	D-4489
OK-4500-I6	VSO-10 Gradient	150086	
OK-4502-I7	VSO-10 Gradient	150087	
OK-4504-I8	VSO-10B Gradient	150089	
OK-4506-I9	VSO-10 Gradient (Dismantled, stored)	150090	
OK-4510	VSO-10 Gradient	150093	
OK-4512-J2	VSO-10B Gradient	150095	
OK-4516-J4	VSO-10 Gradient	150098	
OK-4518-J5	VSO-10 Gradient	150099	
OK-4520-J6	VSO-10B Gradient	150101	
OK-4522-J7	VSO-10 Gradient	150102	
OK-4524-J8	VSO-10 Gradient	150104	
OK-4526-J9	VSO-10 Gradient	150105	
OK-4528-JO	VSO-10B Gradient	150107	
OK-4530-L1	VSO-10B Gradient	150108	
OK-4581	Schempp-Hirth Standard Cirrus	282	PH-458
OK-4600	Aerotechnik L-13SE Vivat	840002	
OK-4602	Aerotechnik L-13SE Vivat	840004	
OK-4603	Aerotechnik L-13SE Vivat	840006	
OK-4604	Aerotechnik L-13SW Vivat	840005	
OK-4607	Aerotechnik L-13SW Vivat	840007	
OK-4608	Aerotechnik L-13SE Vivat	840008	
OK-4609	Schempp-Hirth Ventus b/16.6	195	OE-5343
OK-4612-VT	Schempp-Hirth Ventus bT	23/181	D-KFSU
			D-2928
OK-4700	LET L-13 Blanik	025924	
OK-4701	LET L-13 Blanik	026203	OM-4701
			OK-4701
OK-4702	LET L-13 Blanik	025926	
OK-4704	LET L-13 Blanik	025928	
OK-4706-0	LET L-13 Blanik	026030	OE-5010
OK-4708	LET L-13 Blanik	026229	
OK-4710	LET L-13 Blanik	026230	
OK-4712	LET L-13 Blanik	026231	
OK-4714	LET L-13 Blanik	026232	
OK-4716	LET L-13 Blanik	026233	
OK-4718	LET L-13 Blanik	026106	
OK-4720	LET L-13 Blanik	026107	
OK-4800	LET L-13 Blanik	173021	
OK-4801	LET L-13 Blanik	173023	
OK-4802	LET L-13 Blanik	173024	
OK-4803	LET L-13 Blanik	173025	
OK-4804-33	LET L-13 Blanik	173026	
OK-4805-FL	LET L-13 Blanik	173027	
OK-4806	LET L-13 Blanik	173028	
OK-4807	LET L-13 Blanik	173029	
OK-4808	LET L-13 Blanik	173030	
OK-4809-MT	LET L-13 Blanik	173035	
OK-4810-OL	LET L-13 Blanik	173036	
OK-4811	LET L-13 Blanik	173037	
OK-4812	LET L-13 Blanik	173038	
OK-4814-JK	LET L-13 Blanik	173040	
OK-4815-T5	LET L-13 Blanik	173048	
OK-4817	LET L-13 Blanik	173051	
OK-4818	LET L-13 Blanik	173053	
OK-4819-F	LET L-13 Blanik	173054	
OK-4821	LET L-13 Blanik	173056	
OK-4822	LET L-13 Blanik	173057	
OK-4829	LET L-13 Blanik	173104	
OK-4830	LET L-13 Blanik	173105	
OK-4831-H	LET L-13 Blanik	173106	
OK-4832	LET L-13 Blanik	173107	
OK-4833	LET L-13 Blanik	173108	
OK-4900	Matejcka M-17.3 Universal	03	OK-066
OK-4901-TS	Schempp-Hirth Standard Cirrus	463G	F-CEFT
OK-5100	Aerotechnik L-13SW Vivat	850101	
OK-5102	Aerotechnik L-13SW Vivat	850102	
OK-5104	Aerotechnik L-13SW Vivat	850104	
OK-5106	Aerotechnik L-13SE Vivat	850105	
OK-5108	Aerotechnik L-13SW Vivat	850107	
OK-5110	Aerotechnik L-13SW Vivat	850108	
OK-5112	Aerotechnik L-13SE Vivat	850110	
OK-5114	Aerotechnik L-13SW Vivat	850111	
OK-5116	Aerotechnik L-13SW Vivat	850113	
OK-5117	Schleicher ASW 19	19104	OE-5117
OK-5147-77	Schempp-Hirth Standard Cirrus	15	OE-5147
OK-5283-AE	Schleicher ASW 19B	19343	OE-5283
OK-5310-Y	Schleicher ASW 15B	15428	
OK-5320-HD	Schempp-Hirth Discus CS	200CS	
OK-5326-ZB	Schempp-Hirth Discus CS	206CS	
OK-5333	LG-425 Sohaj	0409	
OK-5372	LG-425 Sohaj 3	0419	
OK-5399	LG-425 Sohaj 3	0521	
OK-5423-P	LET L-33 Solo	950318	
OK-5509	VT-116 Orlik II ZK	151216	
OK-5510	VT-116 Orlik II ZK	151217	

OK-5512-ZV	Schempp-Hirth Ventus b/16.6	253	
OK-5524	VT-116 Orlik II ZK	151411	
OK-5600-L2	VSO-10 Gradient	150110	
OK-5602-L3	VSO-10 Gradient	150111	
OK-5604-L4	VSO-10 Gradient	150113	
OK-5606-L5	VSO-10B Gradient	150114	
OK-5612	VSO-10 Gradient	150119	
OK-5614-L9	VSO-10 Gradient	150120	
OK-5616-LO	VSO-10B Gradient	150122	
OK-5618-ML	VSO-10 Gradient	150123	
OK-5620	VSO-10 Gradient	150125	
OK-5622-MJ	VSO-10 Gradient	150126	
OK-5624-1	VSO-10 Gradient	150128	
OK-5626-2	VSO-10B Gradient	150129	
OK-5628-3	VSO-10 Gradient	150131	
OK-5630-4	VSO-10 Gradient	150132	
OK-5632	VSO-10 Gradient	150134	
OK-5634-6	VSO-10B Gradient	150135	
OK-5711	LET L-13 Blanik	026345	D-8999
OK-5712-02	Schleicher ASW 19B	19393	D-5712
OK-5977	LG.425 Sohaj 3	0424	
OK-5988	LG.425 Sohaj 3	0510	
OK-6100	Aerotechnik L-13SW Vivat	860114	
OK-6102	Aerotechnik L-13SE Vivat	860115	
OK-6104	Aerotechnik L-13SW Vivat	860117	
OK-6106	Aerotechnik L-13SW Vivat	860118	
OK-6108	Aerotechnik L-13SE Vivat	860120	
OK-6110	Aerotechnik L-13SE Vivat	860121	
OK-6112	Aerotechnik L-13SW Vivat	860123	
OK-6114	Aerotechnik L-13SW Vivat	860124	
OK-6116	Aerotechnik L-13SW Vivat	860126	
OK-6118	Aerotechnik L-13SW Vivat	860127	
OK-6200	SZD-48-3 Jantar Standard 3	B-1581	
OK-6203	VSM-40 Démant (Kbely Museum)	04	
OK-6301-YA	Schempp-Hirth Ventus 2bx	156	
OK-6304	LET L-13A Blanik	026643	OE-5304
OK-6306-MT	Schempp-Hirth Nimbus 2	130	
OK-6415	VT-116 Orlik II ZK	151515	
OK-6426	LET L-33 Solo	950402	
OK-6427-2	VT-116 Orlik II ZK	151607	
OK-6429	VT-116 Orlik II ZK	151609	
OK-6430	VT-116 Orlik II ZK	151610	
OK-6434	VT-116 Orlik II ZK	151614	
OK-6444	VT-116 Orlik II ZK	151624	
OK-6446	VT-116 Orlik II ZK	151626	
OK-6493	Schempp-Hirth Standard Cirrus	599	D-6493
OK-6500-7	VSO-10 Gradient	150136	
OK-6502-8	VSO-10B Gradient	150138	
OK-6504-9	VSO-10B Gradient	150139	
OK-6506	VSO-10B Gradient	150141	
OK-6508-21	VSO-10 Gradient	150142	
OK-6510-22	VSO-10B Gradient	150144	
OK-6512-23	VSO-10B Gradient	150145	
OK-6514-24	VSO-10B Gradient	150147	
OK-6516-25	VSO-10B Gradient	150148	
OK-6518-26	VSO-10B Gradient	150150	
OK-6520-27	VSO-10B Gradient	150151	
OK-6522-28	VSO-10 Gradient	150153	
OK-6524-29	VSO-10 Gradient	150154	
OK-6526	VSO-10B Gradient	150156	
OK-6528-31	VSO-10B Gradient	150157	
OK-6530-32	VSO-10B Gradient	150159	
OK-6532-33	VSO-10 Gradient	150162	
OK-6555-MI	Schempp-Hirth Standard Cirrus	448	PH-655
			D-7057
OK-6556-S1	Schempp-Hirth Standard Cirrus	591G	F-CEML
OK-6557	Schempp-Hirth Standard Cirrus	299G	D-2057
OK-6601-AH	Schleicher ASW 19B	19051	D-6724
OK-6608-SB	Schempp-Hirth Standard Cirrus	388G	D-6688
			D-9230
OK-6618	Schempp-Hirth Nimbus 2	62	D-3118
OK-6666	Glasflügel 304CZ	35C	
OK-6700	LET L-13 Blanik	026815	
OK-6704-BF	LET L-13 Blanik	026816	
OK-6705-W	LETL-13 Blanik	026818	OM-6705
			OK-6705
OK-6706	LET L-13 Blanik		
OK-6722-KL	Schleicher ASW20	20568	OH-672
OK-6804	LET L-13 Blanik	173424	
OK-6805-L	LET L-13A Blanik	173425	
OK-6806	LET L-13 Blanik	173426	
OK-6807	LET L-13 Blanik	173427	
OK-6808-L	LET L-13 Blanik	173428	
OK-6812	LET L-13 Blanik	173432	
OK-6813	LET L-13 Blanik	173433	
OK-6814-A1	LET L-13 Blanik	173434	
OK-6815	LET L-13 Blanik	173435	
OK-6816	LET L-13 Blanik	173436	
OK-6817	LET L-13 Blanik	173437	
OK-6818	LET L-13 Blanik	173438	
OK-6819-EE	LET L-13 Blanik	173439	
OK-6831-HD	LET L-13 Blanik	173408	
OK-6836	LET L-13 Blanik	173351	
OK-6838	LET L-13A Blanik	968501	
OK-6839	LET L-13A Blanik	968502	
OK-6840	LET L-13A Blanik	968505	
OK-6869-AI	Schleicher ASW 15B	15436	D-6869
OK-6880-FS	Schleicer ASW-15	15445	D-6880
OK-6901-VM	VSO-10 Gradient	150001	
OK-6902	SZD-45A Ogar	B-658	SP-0019
OK-6907-UO	VT-116 Orlik II ZK	151507	OK-6407
OK-6922	VT-116 Orlik II ZK	151602	
OK-6969-UP	Schleicher ASW 15	15029	F-CDRY
OK-7007-JB	Rolladen-Schneider LS8-18	8433	
OK-7077-CX	Schempp-Hirth Standard Cirrus	385	D-4739
OK-7104	Aerotechnik L-13SW Vivat	870202	
OK-7106	Aerotechnik L-13SW Vivat	870204	
OK-7108	Aerotechnik L-13SW Vivat	870205	
OK-7110	Aerotechnik L-13SW Vivat	870207	
OK-7111-T	Schleicher ASW 15	15119	HB-1020
OK-7112	Aerotechnik L-13SE Vivat	870208	
OK-7114	Aerotechnik L-13SW Vivat	870210	
OK-7118	Aerotechnik L-13SW Vivat	870213	
OK-7120	Aerotechnik L-13SW Vivat	870214	
OK-7171-ZZ	LAK-17	142	
OK-7241	Schempp-Hirth Standard Cirrus	629	D-7241
OK-7262	Schempp-Hirth Standard Cirrus	651	D-7262
OK-7272	Schleicher ASW 27	27214	
OK-7300-TB	Schempp-Hirth Janus	49	
OK-7304-IH	Glasflügel 304CZ	1	
OK-7402	VT-116 Orlik II ZK	151702	
OK-7403	VT-116 Orlik II ZK	151703	
OK-7404-14	VT-116 Orlik II ZK (Dismantled)	151704	
OK-7413-4	VT-116 Orlik II ZK	151713	
OK-7425	VT-116 Orlik II ZK	151805	
OK-7427-LS	LET L-33 Solo	970414	
OK-7438	VT-116 Orlik II ZK	151818	
OK-7445	VT-116 Orlik II ZK	151825	
OK-7501-OK	Schempp-Hirth Standard Cirrus	601	PH-519
OK-7502-34	VSO-10B Gradient	150163	
OK-7504-35	VSO-10 Gradient	150164	
OK-7506-36	VSO-10B Gradient	150166	
OK-7507	LET L-13 Blanik	026506	D-3675
OK-7512	VSO-10 Gradient	150170	
OK-7514	VSO-10 Gradient	150172	
OK-7516-51	VSO-10 Gradient	150173	
OK-7518-52	VSO-10 Gradient	150175	
OK-7520-53	VSO-10B Gradient	150176	
OK-7522-54	VSO-10 Gradient	150178	
OK-7524-55	VSO-10B Gradient	150179	
OK-7526-56	VSO-10B Gradient	150181	
OK-7528-57	VSO-10 Gradient	150182	
OK-7529-58	VSO-10B Gradient	150183	
OK-7530-59	VSO-10B Gradient	150184	
OK-7531-60	VSO-10B Gradient	150186	
OK-7542-Z	VSO-10 Gradient (W/o 29.5.02)	150003	OK-044
OK-7575-C30	Schempp-Hirth Standard Cirrus	551G	F-CEMB
OK-7700	LET L-13 Blanik	027069	
OK-7702	LET L-13 Blanik	027070	
OK-7704	LET L-13 Blanik (Damaged)	027101	
OK-7705	LET L-13 Blanik	027032	YL-DBR
			DOSAAF
OK-7706	LET L-13 Blanik	026852	
OK-7707	Schempp-Hirth Standard Cirrus	616	F-CEMN
OK-7711	LET L-13 Blanik	170711	OO-ZTH
			D-0138
			SP-1795
OK-7755-YU	Schempp-Hirth Standard Cirrus	653	OY-XYU
			D-7248
OK-7777-KN	Glasflügel 304CZ	2	
OK-7801	Marganski MDM-1 Fox	220	
OK-7900	VSB-62 Vega	150052	
OK-7906	Antonov A-15	0501	
OK-8101	Aerotechnik L-13SW Vivat	880217	
OK-8103	Aerotechnik L-13SW Vivat	880219	
OK-8104	Aerotechnik L-13SE Vivat	880220	
OK-8106	Aerotechnik L-13SE Vivat	880222	
OK-8107	Aerotechnik L-13SW Vivat	880223	
OK-8109	Aerotechnik L-13SW Vivat	880225	
OK-8110	Aerotechnik L-13SW Vivat	880226	
OK-8111-BS	Rolladen-Schneider LS8A	8111	D-4518
OK-8112	Aerotechnik L-13SW Vivat	880228	
OK-8113	Aerotechnik L-13SW Vivat	880229	
OK-8115	Aerotechnik L-13SW Vivat	880301	
OK-8116	Aerotechnik L-13SW Vivat	880302	
OK-8118	Aerotechnik L-13SE Vivat	880304	
OK-8119	Aerotechnik L-13SW Vivat	880305	
OK-8130	Aerotechnik L-13SEH Vivat	980621	
OK-8200	LET L-23 Super Blanik	X02	
OK-8205	LET L-23 Super Blanik	988312	
OK-8233	Z-24 Krajánek	225	
OK-8310-PD	Schempp-Hirth Duo Discus C	170CS	
OK-8320	Grob G.103 Twin Astir	3104	D-3961
OK-8401	VT-116 Orlik II ZK	151901	
OK-8405- I	VT-116 Orlik II ZK	151905	
OK-8406	VT-116 Orlik II ZK	151906	
OK-8408	VT-116 Orlik II ZK (Dismantled, stored)	151908	
OK-8412	VT-116 Orlik II ZK	150912	
OK-8413-4	VT-116 Orlik II ZK	151913	
OK-8416	VT-116 Orlik II ZK	151916	
OK-8424-5	VT-116 Orlik II ZK (Dismantled)	151924	
OK-8425	VT-116 Orlik II ZK	151925	
OK-8429	VT-116 Orlik II ZK	151929	
OK-8430	VT-116 Orlik II ZK	151930	

OK-8431	VT-116 Orlik II ZK	152001	
OK-8435	VT-116 Orlik II ZK	152005	
OK-8436	VT-116 Orlik II ZK	152006	
OK-8438-E	VT-116 Orlik II ZK	152008	
OK-8439	VT-116 Orlik II ZK	152009	
OK-8440-LB	LET L-33 Solo	980419	
OK-8441	LET L-33 Solo	980409	
OK-8501-61	VSO-10B Gradient	150187	
OK-8502-62	VSO-10B Gradient	150188	
OK-8504-63	VSO-10B Gradient	150190	
OK-8505-64	VSO-10B Gradient	150191	
OK-8507-65	VSO-10B Gradient	150193	
OK-8508-66	VSO-10B Gradient	150194	
OK-8510-67	VSO-10B Gradient	150196	
OK-8511-68	VSO-10B Gradient	150197	
OK-8514-70	VSO-10B Gradient	150200	
OK-8516-71	VSO-10B Gradient	150202	
OK-8520-AZ	Schempp-Hirth Ventus 2a	63	
OK-8540-B6	VSO-10B Gradient	150004	
OK-8565	Zlin 24 Krajanek	260	
OK-8600-AX	Schempp-Hirth Nimbus 2B	182	
OK-8602-AY	Schempp-Hirth Nimbus 2B	183	
OK-8641	Schleicher ASW 15	15397	D-8641
OK-8661-BC	Schleicher ASW 15B	15416	D-8661
OK-8700	LET L-13 Blanik	027226	
OK-8702	LET L-13 Blanik	027227	
OK-8704	LET L-13 Blanik	027228	
OK-8706-L	LET L-13 Blanik	027229	
OK-8708-KV	LET L-13 Blanik	027231	
OK-8710-U	LET L-13 Blanik	027233	
OK-8712	LET L-13 Blanik	027235	
OK-8801-F1	LET L-13 Blanik	170101	
OK-8802	LET L-13 Blanik	170102	
OK-8805	LET L-13 Blanik	170105	
OK-8812	LET L-13AC Blanik Acro	988604	
OK-8818-BS	Rolladen-Schneider LS8-18	8111	D-4518
OK-8824	LET L-13 Blanik	173820	
OK-8825	LET L-13 Blanik	173822	
OK-8826	LET L-13 Blanik	173823	
OK-8827	LET L-13 Blanik	173824	
OK-8828	LET L-13 Blanik	173825	
OK-8829	LET L-13 Blanik	173905	
OK-8830	LET L-13 Blanik	173907	
OK-8831-ZY	LET L-13 Blanik	173908	
OK-8833	Zlin Z-25 Sohaj	42	D-8857
			D-4029
			D-4000
OK-8888- CI	Schempp-Hirth Standard Cirrus	669	F-CEMX
OK-8902	LET L-13B Blanik	173725	
OK-8903	SZD-45A Ogar	B-773	SP-0022
OK-9100	Aerotechnik L-13SW Vivat	890307	
OK-9103	Aerotechnik L-13SW Vivat	890310	
OK-9104	Aerotechnik L-13SW Vivat	890311	
OK-9106	Aerotechnik L-13SW Vivat	890313	
OK-9107	Aerotechnik L-13SE Vivat	890314	
OK-9108	Aerotechnik L-13SW Vivat	890315	
OK-9110	Aerotechnik L-13SE Vivat	890319	
OK-9111	Aerotechnik L-13SE Vivat	890320	
OK-9113	Aerotechnik L-13SE Vivat	890322	
OK-9114	Aerotechnik L-13SE Vivat	890323	
OK-9117	Aerotechnik L-13SW Vivat	890316	
OK-9119	Aerotechnik L-13SE Vivat	890326	
OK-9120	Schleicher ASH 26E	26150	
OK-9200	LET L-23 Super Blanik	897501	
OK-9201	LET L-23 Super Blanik	897502	
OK-9202	LET L-23 Super Blanik	897503	
OK-9204	LET L-23 Super Blanik	897505	
OK-9245-LY	Schempp-Hirth Standard Cirrus	412	D-9245
OK-9252	LET L-13A Blanik	170211	
OK-9301-L3	Schempp-Hirth Discus b	305	
OK-9302	Schempp-Hirth Discus CS	253CS	
OK-9303-MD	Schempp-Hirth Discus CS	261CS	
OK-9304-DJ	Glasflügel 304CZ/17	26	
OK-9306-BW	Schempp-Hirth Discus CS	264CS	
OK-9307-SH	Schempp-Hirth Discus CS	263CS	
OK-9403	VT-116 Orlik II ZK	152013	
OK-9407-7	VT-116 Orlik II ZK	152017	
OK-9410	VT-116 Orlik II ZK	152020	
OK-9411	VT-116 Orlik II ZK	152021	
OK-9415	VT-116 Orlik II ZK	152025	
OK-9434	Schempp-Hirth Standard Cirrus	494G	D-9434
OK-9458-LY	Schempp-Hirth Standard Cirrus	534G	D-9458
OK-9500-B2	VSO-10C Gradient	150006	
OK-9502-B2	VSO-10C Gradient	150007	
OK-9504-B3	VSO-10C Gradient	150008	
OK-9506-B4	VSO-10C Gradient	150010	
OK-9510-VI	VSO-10C Gradient	150013	
OK-9600	VSO-10B Gradient	150204	
OK-9602-74	VSO-10B Gradient	150206	
OK-9603-75	VSO-10B Gradient	150207	
OK-9605-76	VSO-10B Gradient	150209	
OK-9606-77	VSO-10B Gradient	150210	
OK-9608-78	VSO-10B Gradient	150212	
OK-9609-79	VSO-10B Gradient	150213	
OK-9611-90	VSO-10B Gradient	150215	
OK-9612-91	VSO-10B Gradient	150216	
OK-9614-92	VSO-10B Gradient	150218	
OK-9615-93	VSO-10B Gradient	150219	
OK-9617-94	VSO-10B Gradient	150221	
OK-9618-95	VSO-10B Gradient	150222	
OK-9703	LET L-13 Blanik	173914	
OK-9704-LX	LET L-13 Blanik	173915	
OK-9705	LET L-13 Blanik	173916	
OK-9706-I	LET L-13 Blanik	173917	
OK-9707	LET L-13A Blanik	174003	
OK-9709-LT	LET L-13 Blanik	174005	
OK-9711	LET L-13 Blanik	174007	
OK-9712	LET L-13 Blanik	174008	
OK-9713	LET L-13 Blanik	174110	
OK-9716	LET L-13 Blanik	174012	
OK-9717	LET L-13 Blanik	174013	
OK-9718	LET L-13 Blanik	174014	
OK-9719-WE	LET L-13 Blanik	174015	
OK-9720	LET L-13 Blanik	174111	
OK-9722	LET L-13 Blanik	"6901ND"	
OK-9821	LET L-13J Blanik	170106	
OK-9822	LET L-13 Blanik	170107	
OK-9823	LET L-13 Blanik	170108	
OK-9824	LET L-13 Blanik	170109	
OK-9825-HE	LET L-13 Blanik	170201	
OK-9828	LET L-13 Blanik	170204	
OK-9829	LET L-13 Blanik	170205	
OK-9846-CF	LET L-13 Blanik	170715	
OK-9847	LET L-13 Blanik	170716	
OK-9848	LET L-13 Blanik	170717	
OK-9849	LET L-13 Blanik	170719	
OK-9850-A	LET L-13 Blanik	170720	
OK-9851	LET L-13 Blanik	170801	
OK-9902	VSM-40 Demant	08	
OK-9909	Schempp-Hirth Ventus b/16.6	175	PH-990
			D-5326
OK-9999-99	Glasflügel 304C Wasp	unkn	
OK-A001	TST-3 Alpin TM	03021000	
OK-A004	TST-3 Alpin TM		
OK-A102	TST-3 Alpin TM		
OK-A103	TST-3 Alpin TM		
OK-A104	TST-3 Alpin TM	03021901	
OK-A105	TST-3 Alpin T		
OK-A201	Schleicher Rhönlerche	3065A	D-8591
OK-A205	TST-8 Alpin D		
OK-A208	TST-10M	10010102	
OK-A313	Zlin Z-23 Honza	207	
OK-A415	Hol's der Teufel replica	EU-LKM-01	
OK-A701	Banjo		
OK-A707	Banjo		
OK-A801	TST-3 Alpin TM	01021196	
OK-A802	Banjo		
OK-A804	TST-8 Alpin TM	03010198	
OK-A908	TST-3 Alpin TM	0302699	
OK-A910	SG-38 Schulgleiter	1	
OK-	Grob G.103A Twin II Acro	34073-K-303	D-6458
OK-	Rolladen-Schneider LS1-f	285	D-5887
OK-	Schempp-Hirth Janus C	116	D-0056
OK-	Schempp-Hirth Standard Cirrus	392	PH-486
OK-	Schempp-Hirth Standard Cirrus	691	OY-LXP
			D-3087
OK-	Schempp-Hirth Ventus 2a	158	
OK-	Schleicher ASW 15	15149	PH-845
			D-0797
OK-	Schleicher ASW 15B	15335	D-2330
OK-	Schleicher ASW 15B	15408	D-8656
OK-	Schleicher ASW 19	19054	OO-ZWT

OM - SLOVAKIA

Regn.	Type	C/n	Prev.Id.
OM-AAD	Boeing 737-33A	23636	N509DC (G-TEAD) N509DC EC-EHJ EC-135 N1789B N3283G
OM-ABB	Cessna 172RG Cutlass RG	172RG0551	D-EIRJ N5519V
OM-ABC	WagAero CUBy	1909/07	
OM-AES	Cessna U206F Stationair	U20602718	OM-FCB HA-SKB SE-KUR LN-ASK (SE-KLY) LN-ASL (N33297)
OM-AFA	Orlican L-40 Meta-Sokol	150605	OK-MMJ
OM-AIT	LET Z-37 Cmelák (Dbr 6.4.00, to museum)	13-30	OK-AIT
OM-AIU	LET Z-37A Cmelák	14-14	OK-AIU
OM-AIV	LET Z-37A Cmelák	18-08	D-ESSR DDR-SSR DM-SSR
OM-AJB	LET Z-37A Cmelák	13-11	OK-AJB HA-MCD
OM-AJG	LET Z-37 Cmelák	13-04	OK-AJG OM-AJG OK-AJG HA-MCC
OM-AJY	LET Z-37 Cmelák	12-06	OK-AJY
OM-AKC	Cessna R182 Skylane RG II (Reims-assembled with "c/n" 0006)	R18201030	D-EDPH N756BG
OM-AKU	LET Z-37 Cmelák	12-27	OK-AKU
OM-ALQ	Zlin Z.42MU	0011	OK-ALQ OK-ASA
OM-ALR	Zlin Z.42MU	0027	OK-ALR
OM-AMA	Wassmer WA.81 Piranha	819	OE-CPL D-EERB
OM-ANA	Antonov An-2R	1G176-25	OK-MDC HA-MDC
OM-ARC	Cessna 150M	15078768	D-ERDL N704PP
OM-ARH	Zlin Z.50LS	0076	
OM-ARI	Bell 206B Jet Ranger II	3027	N163BH N57380
OM-ARU	Zlin Z.526ALS-V Akrobat	1213	OK-ARU
OM-ATA	Agusta A.109K2	10015	HB-XWO
OM-ATB	Agusta A.109K2	10009	HB-XWI
OM-ATC	Agusta A.109K2	10011	HB-XWK
OM-AYF	Aero Designs Pulsar	328-003	
OM-BMT	Dynamic BM-17	045	
OM-BYE	Yakovlev Yak-40	9440338	OK-BYE
OM-BYL	Yakovlev Yak-40	9940560	OK-BYL
OM-BYO	Tupolev TU-154M	89A-803	OK-BYO
OM-BYR	Tupolev TU-154M	98A-1012	
OM-CAA	Z-137T Agro-Turbo (Identity not confirmed)	P002/83	HA-MFE OK-NXH OK-PJH OK-PXH
OM-CAB	Z-137T Agro-Turbo	049	HA-MGX OK-YJI
OM-CAR	Cessna 172N	17268697	OK-HKI N734AF
OM-CAS	LET Z-37-2 Cmelák	12-20	HA-MFB D-EOZK DDR-SLK DM-SLK
OM-CAW	Zenair CH-2000	20-009	
OM-CJF	LET Z-37A Cmelák	16-30	OK-CJK
OM-CJH	LET Z-37 Cmelák	16-07	D-ESRN DDR-SRN DM-SRN
OM-CJI	LET Z-37 Cmelák	16-27	OK-CJI
OM-CJN	LET Z-37A Cmelák	18-18	OK-DJV
OM-CJP	LET Z-37 Cmelák	15-03	OK-CJP
OM-CJQ	LET Z-37 Cmelák	15-04	OK-CJQ
OM-CJX	LET Z-3A7 Cmelák	15-26	OK-CJX
OM-CKO	LET Z-37A Cmelák	15-30	OK-CKO
OM-CKT	LET Z-37 Cmelák	17-02	OK-CKT
OM-CKY	LET Z-37 Cmelák	17-10	OK-CKY
OM-COO	Zlin Z.43	0006	OK-COO
OM-COP	Zlin Z.43	0009	OK-COP
OM-CRN	Zlin Z.526F Trenér Master	1179	OK-CRN
OM-CRO	Zlin Z.526F Trenér Master	1180	OK-CRO
OM-CYL	Neico Lancair 320ES	046-08-96	
OM-CZA	PZL-104 Wilga 35A	62151	OK-CZA
OM-DAA	LET L-410T	820929	CzAF 0929
OM-DAY	Embraer EMB.120RT Brasilia	120244	F-GIYI LX-LGM (F-GHEZ) PT-STQ
OM-DGK	Boeing 757-236	24772	N88AM C-GTSJ C-GNXB I-BRJF G-BRJF (I-BRJF) G-BRJF EC-EVD EC-432 G-BRJF
OM-DJA	LET Z-37A Cmelák	18-30	D-ESUL DDR-SUL DM-SUL
OM-DJT	LET Z-37 Cmelák	18-04	OK-DJT
OM-DJU	LET Z-37 Cmelák	18-05	OK-DJU
OM-DJW	LET Z-37 Cmelák	18-19	OK-DJW
OM-DJX	LET Z-37 Cmelák (Noted 9.04 wearing c/n 18-10)	19-11	OK-DJX
OM-DKA	Cessna P210NPressurized Centurion	P21000322	OE-DHO(2) D-EDEN(3) N4794K
OM-DKB	Reims/Cessna F172M	F172-1030	F-BUEV
OM-DKN	LET Z-37 Cmelák	19-22	OK-DKN
OM-DKZ	LET Z-37A Cmelák	19-30	OK-DKZ
OM-DLS	Zlin Z.42MU	0048	OK-DLS OK-DZI
OM-DOQ	Zlin Z.143M	0031	OK-072
OM-DOR	Zlin Z.43	0015	OK-DOR
OM-DOS	Zlin Z.43	0030	OK-DOS(1)
OM-DOT	Zlin Z.43	0034	OK-DOT
OM-DOU	Zlin Z.43	0037	OK-DOU
OM-DYL	Neico Lancair 360 Mk.II	401/09/97	
OM-DYM	Neico Lancair	124/15	
OM-EIA	Antonov An-2T	1G157-03	OK-EIA
OM-EIB	Antonov An-2P	1G151-53	HA-YHA
OM-EJD	LET Z-37A Cmelák	19-19	D-ESUV DDR-SUV DM-SUV
OM-EJE	LET Z-37A Cmelák	20-16	D-ESVM DDR-SVM DM-SVM
OM-EJG	LET Z-37A Cmelák	19-10	D-ESUP DDR-SUP DM-SUP
OM-EJH	LET Z-37A Cmelák	17-26	D-ESSH DDR-SSH DM-SSH
OM-EOV	Zlin Z.43	0047	OK-EOV
OM-EOY	Zlin Z.43	0055	OK-EOY
OM-EOZ	Zlin Z.43	0058	OK-EOZ
OM-ERS	Zlin Z.526AFS Akrobat	1306	OK-ERS
OM-EVA	Mil Mi-8T	98417157	RA-22896
OM-FAB	Cessna 172S	172S8874	N35587
OM-FEH	Hughes 269C	65-0413	PH-HZH SE-HHD N7403F
OM-FIN	Mil Mi-2	514307095	OK-FIN
OM-FJA	LET Z-37A Cmelák	21-05	D-ESWF DDR-SWF DM-SWF
OM-FJB	LET Z-37A Cmelák	22-01	OK-FJB OM-FJB D-ESWJ DDR-SWJ DM-SWJ
OM-FJC	LET Z-37A Cmelák	20-19	D-ESVP DDR-SVP DM-SVP
OM-FJD	LET Z-37A Cmelák	20-09	D-ESVF DDR-SVF DM-SVF
OM-FJQ	LET Z-37 Cmelák	21-11	OK-FJQ
OM-FJR	LET Z-37 Cmelák	21-12	OK-FJR
OM-FJV	LET Z-37A Cmelák	21-16	OK-FJV
OM-FJX	LET Z-37 Cmelák	21-18	OK-FJX
OM-FJZ	LET Z-37A Cmelák	21-06	D-ESWG DDR-SWG DM-SWG
OM-FLY	Embraer EMB.120RT Brasilia	120239	F-GIYH LX-LGL PT-STL
OM-FOF	Cessna 172P	17275225	OM-FGF HB-CLC OK-064 HB-CLC N62179
OM-FON	Zlin Z.43	0062	OK-FON
OM-FOO	Zlin Z.43	0065	OK-FOO
OM-FOP	Zlin Z.43	0066	OK-FOP
OM-FOR	Zlin Z.43	0073	OK-FOR
OM-GHN	Antonov An-2T	1G168-02	OK-GHN
OM-GJA	LET Z-37 Cmelák	22-16	OK-GJA
OM-GJP	LET Z-37A Cmelák	22-08	OK-GJP
OM-GJQ	LET Z-37A Cmelák	22-09	OK-GJQ
OM-GJT	LET Z-37A Cmelák	22-12	OK-GJT
OM-GJX	LET Z-37A Cmelák	22-19	OK-GJX
OM-GJY	LET Z-37A Cmelák	22-20	OK-GJY

OM-HHB	Zlin Z.126 Trenér 2	774	OK-IHP
OM-HHC	Zlin Z.126 Trenér 2	726	OK-HHC
			CzAF 224
OM-HJH	LET Z-37 Cmelák	23-22	OK-HJT
			OM-HJT
			OK-HJT
OM-HJN	LET Z-37A Cmelák	23-20	OK-HJN
OM-HJO	LET Z-37A Cmelák	23-06	OK-HJO
OM-HJR	LET Z-37A Cmelák	23-16	OK-HJR
OM-HJS	LET Z-37A Cmelák	23-21	OK-HJS
OM-HJV	LET Z-37A Cmelák	23-24	OK-HJV
	(Now listed as c/n 23-26ND, ex ?)		
OM-HJX	LET Z-37 Cmelák	23-25	OK-HJX
OM-HLB	LET L-410UVP-E10A	871914	Russian AF
			1914/89 red
OM-HLH	Diamond DA 40D Star	D4.036	OE-DDC
OM-HLJ	Diamond DA 20-A1 Katana	10025	C-FUIT
OM-HLL	Diamond DA 40D Star	D4.087	D-EDAM
			OE-VPU
OM-HSI	Zlin Z.42M	0134	OK-HSI
OM-HYU	LET Z-37-2C Cmelák	23-09	OK-HYU
OM-IFE	Zlin Z.126 Trenér 2	741	OK-IFE
OM-IGO	Zlin Z.126 Trenér 2	708	OK-IGO
OM-ILR	Zlin Z.42M	0160	OK-ILR
OM-IZN	Cessna 172N	17273647	SE-IZN
			OY-CPT
			N2770J
OM-JET	Aero L-29 Delphin	691901	Slovak AF 6901
OM-JJX	LET Z-37A Cmelák	24-04	OK-JJX
OM-JLV	Zlin Z.42M	0190	OK-JLV
OM-JSN	Zlin Z.42M	0181	OK-JSN
OM-JSO	Zlin Z.42	0184	OK-JSO
OM-JSP	Zlin Z.42M (W/o 23.8.03)	0188	OK-JSP
OM-KAB	Reims/Cessna F172M	F17201008	OE-KSG
			D-EJXE
OM-KAT	Diamond DA 20-A1 Katana	10032	N332GH
			C-GDMQ
OM-KGB	Cessna 182Q	18265410	D-ESIG
			SE-KOF
			N735GJ
OM-KJP	Mil Mi-2	516641040	OK-KJP
OM-KJR	LET Z-37A Cmelák	24-06	OK-KJR
OM-KJS	LET Z-37A Cmelák	24-07	OK-KJS
OM-KMF	Zlin Z.226M Trenér	07	OK-KMF
OM-KMI	Zlin Z.226MS Trenér	10-08	OK-KMI
OM-KNI	Zlin Z.226MS Trenér	36-09	OK-KNI
OM-KNO	Zlin Z.142	0201	OK-KNO
OM-KNP	Zlin Z.142	0202	OK-KNP
OM-KNQ	Zlin Z.142	0204	OK-KNQ
OM-KNS	Zlin Z.142	0203	OK-KNS
OM-KNT	Zlin Z.226M Trenér	104	OK-KNT
OM-KNU	Zlin Z.142	0205	OK-KNU
OM-KNW	Zlin Z.226MS Trenér	107	OK-KNW
OM-KOZ	Zlin Z.43	0081	OK-KOZ
OM-KRN	Cessna T303 Crusader	T30300148	OM-AFB
			D-IKER(2)
			N6179C
OM-LHL	Rotorway Exec 90	5156/010/97	
OM-LIA	Antonov An-2R	1G194-30	HA-MEU
OM-LJQ	Mil Mi-2	537326101	OK-LJQ
OM-LKE	Aero L-60S Brigadyr	150726	OK-LKE
OM-LKL	Aero L-60S Brigadyr (Wfu, stored)	150803	OK-LKL
OM-LKO	Aero L-60S Brigadyr	150505	OK-LKO
OM-LLL	Zlin Z.226MS Trenér	127	OK-LLL
OM-LLO	Zlin Z.226MS Trenér (Wrecked)	130	OK-LLO
OM-LLP	Zlin Z.226MS Trenér	131	OK-LLP
OM-LLR	Zlin Z.226MS Trenér	133	OK-LLR
OM-LLV	Zlin Z.226MS Trenér	138	OK-LLV
OM-LLX	Zlin Z.226MS Trenér	134	OK-LLX
OM-LLY	Zlin Z.226MS Trenér	140	OK-LLY
OM-LMJ	Sukhoi SU-31M	01-01	(RA-01405)
OM-LNP	Zlin Z.142	0233	OK-LNP
OM-LNR	Zlin Z.142	0248	OK-LNR
OM-LNS	Zlin Z.142	0249	OK-LNS
OM-LNT	Zlin Z.142	0260	OK-LNT
OM-LNU	Zlin Z.142	0261	OK-LNU
OM-LNV	Zlin Z.142	0263	OK-LNV
OM-LNZ	Zlin Z.142	0265	OK-LNZ
OM-LOT	Cessna 172S	172S8084	N671SP
OM-LOW	Zlin Z.43L	0084	OK-LOW
OM-MFN	Zlin Z.226MS Trenér	158	OK-MFN
OM-MGL	Zlin Z.226MS Trenér	183	OK-MGL
OM-MGO	Zlin Z.226MS Trenér	186	OK-MGO
OM-MHE	Zlin Z.226MS Trenér	202	OK-MHE
OM-MHG	Zlin Z.226MS Trenér	204	OK-MHG
OM-MJR	Aero L-60 Brigadyr	151129	OK-MJR
OM-MJS	Aero L-60 Brigadyr	151127	OK-MJS
OM-MMK	Orlican L-40 Meta-Sokol	150606	OK-MMK
OM-MMS	Orlican L-40 Meta-Sokol	150305	OK-MMS
OM-MNP	Zlin Z.142	0281	OK-MNP
OM-MNQ	Zlin Z.142	0284	OK-MNQ
OM-MNR	Zlin Z.142	0287	OK-MNR
OM-MNS	Zlin Z.142	0290	OK-MNS
OM-MNT	Zlin Z.142	0296	OK-MNT
OM-MNV	Zlin Z.142	0304	OK-MNV
OM-MNW	Zlin Z.142	0307	OK-MNW
OM-MNX	Zlin Z.142	0308	OK-MNX
OM-MPE	Zlin Z .226MS Trenér	250	OK-MPE
OM-MPO	Zlin Z .226MS Trenér	260	OK-MPO
OM-MPS	Zlin Z .226MS Trenér	265	OK-MPS
OM-MPX	Zlin Z .226MS Trenér	264	OK-MPX
OM-MPY	Zlin Z .226MS Trenér	270	OK-MPY
OM-MQC	Zlin Z .226M Trenér	274	OK-MQC
OM-MQD	Zlin Z.226 Trenér	275	OK-MQD
OM-MQK	Zlin Z 226MS Trenér	282	OK-MQK
OM-MRK	Orlican L-40 Meta-Sokol	150302	OK-MRK
			HB-TAZ
			OK-MMG
OM-NHS	Aero 145 Super Aero	171422	OK-NHS
OM-NJI	LET Z-37A Cmelák	25-11	OK-NJI
OM-NJS	LET Z-37A Cmelák	25-12	OK-NJS
OM-NJT	LET Z-37A Cmelák	25-16	OK-NJT
OM-NNC	Aero L-60S Brigadyr	151208	OK-NNC
OM-NNE	Aero L-60S Brigadyr	151210	OK-NNE
OM-NNP	Zlin Z.142	0329	OK-NNP
OM-NNQ	Zlin Z.142	0334	OK-NNQ
OM-NNR	Zlin Z.142	0336	OK-NNR
OM-NNS	Zlin Z.142	0339	OK-NNS
OM-NNT	Zlin Z.142	0348	OK-NNT
OM-NNU	Zlin Z.142	0351	OK-NNU
OM-NPJ	Orlican L-40 Meta-Sokol	150803	OK-NPJ
OM-NRA	Reims/Cessna F172N	F172-1030	D-EFEW
OM-NRB	Cessna 152	15285384	D-ECCF(3)
			N93045
OM-NRC	Reims/Cessna F150M	F15001389	D-EOKU
OM-NRG	Cessna 172RG Cutlass RG	172RG1142	D-EDEM(3)
			ZS-LED
			N9376D
OM-NSH	Boeing 767-231	22569	N606TW
OM-ODQ	LET L-410UVP	841320	OK-ODQ
			CCCP67096
OM-OFH	LET L.200A Morava	170613	OK-OFH
			OE-FSF
			OK-OFH
OM-OFS	LET L.200D Morava	170213	OK-OFS
OM-OHJ	LET L.200A Morava	170321	OK-OHJ
			CzAF:0321
OM-OIU	Mil Mi-2	529012124	OK-OIU
			CCCP23417
OM-OIV	Mil Mi-2	528603034	OK-OIV
			CCCP20921
OM-OIW	Mil Mi-2	529013124	OK-OIW
			CCCP23418
OM-OJN	LET Z-37 Cmelák	25-21	OK-OJN
OM-OJP	LET Z-37 Cmelák	25-24	OK-OJP
OM-OJQ	LET Z-37 Cmelák	25-24	OK-OJQ
OM-OJR	LET Z-37 Cmelák	25-28	OK-OJR
OM-OJS	LET Z-37 Cmelák	25-32	OK-OJS
OM-OJU	LET Z-37 Cmelák	25-40	OK-OJU
OM-ONN	Zlin Z.142 (Accident 8.5.00, w/o)	0359	OK-ONN
OM-ONP	Zlin Z.142	0370	OK-ONP
OM-ONQ	Zlin Z.142	0373	OK-ONQ
OM-ONS	Zlin Z.142	0384	OK-ONS
OM-ONT	Zlin Z.142	0387	OK-ONT
OM-ORO	Mil Mi-8	10448	HA-. . .
			Hung.AF
OM-OTN	Zlin Z.326 Trenér-Master	606	OK-OTN
OM-OTP	Zlin Z.326 Trenér-Master	612	OK-OTP
OM-PIQ	Mil Mi-2	529310065	OK-PIQ
OM-PLF	LET L.200A Morava	170719	OK-PLF
OM-PLK	LET L.200A Morava (Accident 27.10.00)	170725	OK-PLK
OM-PLM	LET L.200A Morava	170727	OK-PLM
OM-PLO	LET L.200A Morava	170731	OK-PLQ
			OM-PLQ
			OK-PLQ
OM-PLP	LET L.200A Morava	170730	OK-PLP
OM-PMT	Diamond DA20 -A1 Katana	10043	N36HA
			C-FDVP
OM-PNN	Zlin Z.142	0394	OK-PNN
OM-PNO	Zlin Z.142	0400	OK-PNO
OM-PNQ	Zlin Z.142	0408	OK-PNQ
OM-PNS	Zlin Z.142	0414	OK-PNS
OM-PNU	Zlin Z.142	0406	OK-PNU
OM-PNV	Zlin Z.142	0417	OK-PNV
OM-PRL	Pritel D2-X	001-X/01/98	
OM-PST	Cessna TR182 Turbo Skylane RG	R18201030	D-EDPH
	(Reims-assembled with "c/n" 0006)		N756BG
OM-PYB	Antonov An-2	115720	OK-PYB
OM-RAN	Boeing 737-230	23156	N621AC
			D-ABMD
OM-RIP	Antonov An-2	117410	OK-RIP
			CzAF7410
OM-RIQ	Antonov An-2 (Wfu, stored)	117414	OK-RIQ
			CzAF7414
OM-RMS	Zlin Z.726 Universal	1360-24	S5-DBP
			SL-DBP
			YU-CDJ
OM-RNN	Zlin Z.142	0421	OK-RNN
OM-ROB	DIXI	02-KB-2003	
OM-SAB	LET L-410MA	750405	Slovak AF 0405
			CzAF0405

OM-SAY	Embraer EMB.120ER Brasilia	120235	F-GTSP
			LX-RCT
			(PH-BRI)
			OO-DTN
			PT-STH
OM-SDA	LET L-410UVP	872006	Sov.AF 2006
OM-SEA	Boeing 737-5Y0	25186	N186LS
			PT-SLU
			XA-RKP
OM-SEB	Boeing 737-5Y0	25191	N191LS
			PT-SSM
			N191AP
			VT-JAL
			N191G
			(B-)
			N191G
			XA-SAS
OM-SEC	Boeing 737-5Y0	25288	TC-JDU
			(EI-CFT)
OM-SED	Boeing 737-53C	24826	SP-LKH(2)
			F-GHUL
OM-SEE	Boeing 737-53C	24827	SP-LKI(2)
			F-INL
OM-SHY	Embraer EMB.120ER Brasilia	120253	F-GMMU
			PH-BRK
			(PH-BRJ)
			OO-DTO
			PT-STZ
OM-SIF	Aérospatiale AS.350B2 Ecureuil	3066	
OM-SKY	Embraer EMB.120RT Brasilia	120175	PH-BRP
			N286UE
			PT-SQN
OM-SNA	Boeing 757-27B	24135	N335FV
			PH-AHE
			OY-SHE
			PH-AHE
			OY-SHE
			PH-AHE
OM-SNY	Zlin Z .142	0444	OK-SNY
OM-SPP	Agusta-Bell 206B Jet Ranger 2	8255	D-HAFW
			OE-BXO
OM-SPY	Embraer EMB.120RTBrasilia	120092	N92GL
			N281UE
			PT-SMJ
OM-STC	Cessna 172S	172S9550	N2161J
OM-SVK	Cessna 152	15280131	HB-CQJ
			N757ZJ
OM-SYI	LET L-410UVP-E6	882019	OK-SYI
OM-TFA	PZL Kania	900202	SP-SSE
			B-3211
			SP-SSE
OM-TKB	Neico Lancair ES (W/o 28.10.01)	103/12	
OM-TNA	Cessna 172P	17274391	HB-CLW
			N51993
OM-TNB	Cessna 172L	17259772	OK-AKL
			CF-ZZO
			(N9872G)
OM-UHC	LET L.200D Morava	171403	SP-NXM
			SP-NAD
OM-UJG	LET Z-37 Kurier	009P	OK-UJG
OM-UKA	Piper PA-34-220T Seneca III	3433160	OK-UKA
			N9182B
OM-UNA	Zlin Z.142	0467	OK-UNA
OM-UNO	Zlin Z.142	0502	OK-UNO
OM-VHB	Antonov An-2	1G238-54	OK-VHB
OM-VIA	Z-137T Agro-Turbo	032	HA-MGM
			OM-VIA
			OK-VIA
OM-VIG	Z-137T Agro-Turbo	038	HA-MGK
			OM-VIG
			OK-VIG
OM-VIP	Piper PA-31T Cheyenne II	31T-7920002	D-IXXX(2)
			N141DT
			N400PB
			N431Y
			N431PC
			N6152A
OM-VKB	LET Z-37 Cmelák	01-20	OK-VKB
OM-VKE	Beech C90A King Air	LJ-1222	OK-VKE
			N15627
OM-VLC	Cessna 172R	17280195	D-EXEL(2)
			N9943F
OM-VLK	Reims/Cessna FR172K Hawk XP	FR17200602	D-EOHY(2)
OM-VOR	Zlin Z.526M Trenér Master (cvtd from Z.326)	909	F-BNMX
OM-WKD	LET Z-37-2 Cmelák	010	OK-VKD
OM-WMN	Zlin Z.226T Trenér 6	102	OK-WMN
			EAF-. . .
OM-WON	Zlin Z.43	0094	OK-WON
OM-XOM	Zlin Z.43	0114	OK-XOM
OM-XON	Zlin Z.43	0109	OK-XON
OM-XYP	Aero Designs Pulsar	235/001	OK-XYP
OM-YJE	LET Z-37 Cmelák	05-01	OK-YJE
			HA-MGD
OM-YJG	LET Z-37 Cmelák	08-07	OK-YJG
			HA-SCB
OM-YXO	LET Z-37A-3 Cmelák	08-22	OM-YJO
			OK-YJO
OM-ZJA	LET Z-37 Cmelák	10-02	OK-ZJA
			HA-MGN
OM-ZJE	LET Z-37 Cmelák	09-18	OK-ZJE
			HA-MGK
OM-ZJY	LET Z-37 Cmelák	10-14	OK-ZJY
OM-ZLO	Zlin Z.42MU	0005	OK-ZLO
OM-ZLP	Zlin Z.42MU	0008	OK-ZLP
OM-ZNP	LET Z-37 Cmelák	09-30	OK-ZNP
			HA-SCD
OM- . . .	Bell 222U	47549	D-HTEN
			JA9628
OM- . . .	Cessna 152	15283563	N4651B
OM- . . .	Cessna 152	15285188	N6186Q
OM- . . .	Cessna A152 Aerobat	A1520759	N555DU
OM- . . .	Cessna A152 Aerobat	A1520944	N761EH
OM- . . .	Cessna TR182 Turbo Skylane RG II	R18200871	D-EABX(3)
			(N737QD)
OM- . . .	Fokker F.28-0100	11372	N892US
			PH-EZE
OM- . . .	Robinson R-44 Astro	0587	D-HOCY(2)

MICROLIGHTS

The first microlight registration systems used either a four-letter identity or an alpha-numeric system similar to the Czechs. The later system, introduced in 2000, uses the OM-M prefix followed by a three digit number for 3-axis machines and the OM-H prefix for weight-shift types, but the extent of re-registration is at present unknown. The OM-P series is used for paramotors.

OM-AERO	Aerospool WT-9 Dynamic (Re-useable test reg)		
OM-AFCC	Aeropro Fox 912 2A	08700	
OM-AHOJ	Rans S-6E Super Coyote II	1193559	
OM-AKPD	Aerospool WT-9 Dynamic Club T	DY077-2005	
OM-ALBA	Excel WT-8/II	04/2000	
OM-ATIS	Zenair CH-601 Zodiac	6-2212	
OM-AUB-01	Sky Pup TP		
OM-AUD-01	Type unknown		
OM-AUOB	Straton D-8	K-03	
OM-AUQ-0	Aviatik JORA		
OM-AUQ-03	Toresi Straton D8 Moby Dick		
OM-AUQ-04	Type unknown		
OM-AUQ-06	Type unknown		
OM-AWKO	Aeropro Fox-S	011	
OM-AXAL	Aeropro Fox 912-2Z	014095	
OM-AXAO	Twin Type unknown	01	
OM-AXAZ	Storch	87	
OM-AXM	ICP MXP-741 Savannah	A8-03-95-50-026	
OM-BIRD	Aeropro Fox-S	01S03	
OM-BUU	TL Ultralight TL-232 Condor	97C01	
OM-CUU	TL Ultralight TL-232 Condor	96C24	
OM-COMP	Aerospool WT-9 Dynamic Club T	DY078-2005	
OM-CXAR	Pottier P.220 ULR Koala (W/o 24.6.03)	960003	
OM-CXBK	Zenair CH-601 Zodiac	002	
OM-CYRO	Aeropro Fox 912-2A	EV9505	
OM-CZQ-04	U-01		
OM-DARO	Aeropro Fox 582-3B	021095	
OM-DNPL	Type unknown		
OM-DNZL	Aeropro Fox 912	075099	
OM-DUCH	Aeropro Fox 912-3A	12802	
OM-DUP-07	Let Mont Tulak (Accident 30.9.00)		
OM-DXAP	Pottier P.200 ULR Koala	970106	
OM-DXBP	DSBS-01 Koma Twin	DSBS-1	
OM-DXCH	Aeropro Fox 912 SA		
OM-DYCH	Aeropro Fox 912-3A	15003	
OM-DYNA	Aerospool WT-9 Dynamic	DY027-2003	
OM-EMBT	Type unknown		
OM-EFOX	Aeropro Fox 582-3K	049098	
OM-ERIK	Aeropro Fox 3K	052098	
OM-FERO	Aeropro Fox-S	016/2001	
OM-GATS	Type unknown		
OM-IGOR	Aeropro Fox-S	001	
OM-INKA	Aeropro Fox 912-2Z	043098	
OM-JURO	Falko FA-95	001	
OM-LANE	Aeropro Eurofox	unkn	
OM-LANJ	Aeropro Eurofox	unkn	
OM-LINE	Aeropro Fox 3K	16004	
OM-LUBI	Aerospool WT-9 Dynamic	DY046-2004	
OM-MAJA	Aeropro Fox SF	F2	
OM-MILA	Aeropro Fox 503-2Z	05093	
OM-MISO	Letov LK-2M Sluka	829309X02	
OM-OWYD	Aeropro Fox 912	EV9506	
OM-SBCN	Aviatik JORA	002/2000	
OM-SGCT	Aerospool WT-9 Dynamic	DY047-2004	
OM-TIBI	Elisport CH-7 Kompress	4418030	
OM-VLAV	Pottier P.200 ULR Koala	965001	
OM-WZC-8	Type unknown		
OM-WZG-7	Type unknown		OK-WZG-7
OM-XUL-02	Toresi Straton D.8 Moby Dick		
OM-XZB-13	Type unknown		
OM-YUA-07	Toresi Straton D.8 Moby Dick		
OM-YUB-06	AeroPro Fox		OK-YUB-06
OM-YUB-14	Letov LK-21 Sluka	829309X02	
OM-YUF-01	Type unknown		

OM-YUL-01	Type unknown		
OM-YUU-50	TL Ultralight TL-32 Typhoon		OK-YUU-50
OM-YUU-53	TL Ultralight TL-32 Typhoon		
OM-YUU-59	TL Ultralight TL-32 Typhoon		OK-YUU-59
OM-YXR	Murphy Rebel	096	OK-YXR-002
OM-YZB-1	Type unknown		
OM-YZG-02	Type unknown		
OM-YZG-17	Type unknown		
OM-ZUB-01	Aeropro Fox		OK-ZUB-01
OM-ZUB-07	Rans S-6S Super Coyote II	1193559	
OM-ZUC-02	AgroLET Junior		OK-ZUC-02
OM-ZUC-04	AgroLET Junior		
OM-ZUQ-01	Type unknown		
OM-ZZB-2	MZK Skypala		
OM-ZZB-3	MZ Apollo		

OM-H01	Type unknown
OM-H001	Radoga 2
OM-H005	(Murova?) MW197
OM-H007	Type unknown
OM-H012	Murova MW 117
OM-H013	(Murova?) MW 155
OM-H020	Rogalo
OM-H022	Type unknown (Subaru EA-81)

OM-M001	Letov LK-21 Sluka
OM-M002	Aeropro Fox
OM-M003	Micro Mong
OM-M004	Sky Pup
OM-M005	Aeropro Fox-S (Accident 22.7.00)
OM-M006	TL Ultralight TL-32 Typhoon
OM-M007	Falko 95 Mk.1
OM-M008	Fantasy Air Cora
OM-M010	Zenair CH-601 Zodiac
OM-M011	Aeropro Fox 503
OM-M017	Toresi Straton D8 Moby Dick
OM-M020	Junior
OM-M107	TEAM Hi-MAX
OM-M111	Kolibrik
OM-M115	Toresi Straton D8 Moby Dick
OM-M117	Twix
OM-M123	Aeropro Fox
OM-M124	Letov LK-2 Sluka
OM-M231	Fantasy Air Allegro 2000
OM-M236	TL Ultralight TL-132 Condor
OM-M258	Toresi Straton D8 Moby Dick
OM-M333	Fantasy Air Cora
OM-M410	Falco FA-95
OM-M666	Tucniak
OM-M737	Fisher Classic
OM-M747	Toresi Straton D8 Moby Dick
OM-M757	Kacer
OM-M777	ST-4 Aztek
OM-M787	TEAM Mini-MAX
OM-M937	TL Ultralight TL-32
OM-M986	Fantasy Air Cora (W/o 26.8.01)
OM-M999	Aeropro Fox

OM-P701 to OM-P720 are paramotor registrations so far known to have been allocated.

BALLOONS AND AIRSHIPS

OM-0001	Kubicek BB-26 HAFB	146	OK-0146
OM-0011	Kubicek BB-26 HAFB	128	OK-0128
OM-1840	Ultramagic M-90 HAFB	90/63	
OM-2003	Kubicek BB-30 HAFB	220	OK-0220
OM-2345	Ultramagic M-77C HAFB	77/211	
OM-3033	Kubicek BB-26 HAFB	19	OK-3033
OM-6001	Kubicek BB-30 HAFB	55	
OM-6003	Kubicek BB Pneu-SS HAFB	54	
OM-6004	Kubicek BB-22 HAFB	65	
OM-6005	Kubicek BB-22 HAFB	66	
OM-6006	Kubicek BB-22 HAFB	67	
OM-7007	Kubicek VS SSHAFB	73	
OM-8001	Kubicek BB-37 HAFB	87	
OM-8002	Kubicek BB-37 HAFB (Accident 15.9.00)	97	
OM-8003	Kubicek BB-37 HAFB	98	
OM-8004	Kubicek BB-22 HAFB	103	
OM-8005	Kubicek BB-22 HAFB	104	
OM-9001	Aerotechnik AB-2B HAFB	890416	
OM-9003	Aerotechnik AB-8 HAFB	890312	
OM-9005	Aerotechnik AB-2 HAFB	890311	
OM-9007	Kubicek BB-26 HAFB	118	
OM-9008	Kubicek BB-26 HAFB	163	OK-0163
OM-9009	Kubicek BB-26 HAFB	121	

GLIDERS AND MOTORGLIDERS

OM-0102	Aerotechnik L-13SE Vivat	900329	OK-0102
OM-0112	Aerotechnik L-13SE Vivat (W/o 24.4.00)	900409	OK-0112
OM-0114	Aerotechnik L-13SW Vivat	900411	OK-0114
OM-0203	LET L-23 Super Blanik	907603	OK-0203
OM-0206-C9	LET L-23 Super Blanik	907606	OK-0206
OM-0209	LET L-23 Super Blanik	907612	OK-0209
OM-0212-I	LET L-23 Super Blanik	907615	OK-0212
OM-0215-23	LET L-23 Super Blanik (Crashed)	907618	OK-0215
OM-0218-NV	LET L-23 Super Blanik	907710	OK-0218
OM-0221	LET L-23 Super Blanik	907713	OK-0221
OM-0224	LET L-23 Super Blanik	907721	OK-0224
OM-0227-L1	LET L-23 Super Blanik	907724	OK-0227
OM-0230	LET L-23 Super Blanik	907727	OK-0230
OM-0233	LET L-23 Super Blanik	907707	OK-0233
OM-0300-NV	LET L-13 Blanik	174721	OK-0300
OM-0369-AR	Schempp-Hirth Discus CS	005CS	
OM-0371-LZ	Schempp-Hirth Discus CS	009CS	
OM-0501-D3	VSO-10 Gradient	150015	OK-0501
OM-0503-D4	VSO-10 Gradient	150017	OK-0503
OM-0505-D5	VSO-10 Gradient	150021	OK-0505
OM-0507-D6	VSO-10 Gradient	150023	OK-0507
OM-0509-D7	VSO-10 Gradient	150027	OK-0509
OM-0601(2)-75	Schempp-Hirth Standard Cirrus	699	OO-ZCI
OM-0818-FX	Rolladen-Schneider LS8-b	8470	
OM-0903-Z	LET L-13 Blanik	170911	OK-0903
OM-0907	LET LF-107 Lunak	23	OK-0814
OM-091-B22	LET L-13 Blanik	170920	OK-0912
OM-0913	LET L-13 Blanik	171105	OK-0913
OM-0922	LET L-13 Blanik	171305	OK-0922
OM-0972	Lunak LF-107	28	OK-0972
OM-1000-XXL	SchleicherASW-20	20500	D-0773
OM-1100-101	Centrair 101A Pégasse	101A-0150	F-CGBL
OM-1111-AA	Schleicher ASW-20	20104	D-1152
OM-1175-MP	Schempp-Hirth Standard Cirrus (Cr 30.5.04)	404G	F-CEFI
OM-1176	Schempp-Hirth Standard Cirrus	505	OY-XCH
OM-1501-F3	VSO-10 Gradient	150033	OK-1501
OM-1503-F4	VSO-10 Gradient	150034	OK-1503
OM-1505	VSO-10 Gradient	150039	OK-1505
OM-1507	VSO-10 Gradient	150040	OK-1507
OM-1509	VSO-10 Gradient	150044	OK-1509
OM-1515-A15	Schleicher ASW-15	15147	BGA4910 D-0791
OM-1528-F6	VSO-10 Gradient	150048	OK-1528
OM-1602-A4	Schleicher ASW 19 (W/o 30.10.99)	19333	
OM-1701-H	LET L-13 Blanik	175006	OK-1701
OM-1703-C	LET L-13 Blanik	175020	OK-1703
OM-1705	LET L-13 Blanik	175022	OK-1705
OM-1707	LET L-13 Blanik	175023	OK-1707
OM-1709-A	LET L-13 Blanik	175024	OK-1709
OM-1711	LET L-13 Blanik	175027	OK-1711
OM-1713	LET L-13 Blanik	817403	OK-1713
OM-1808	LET L-13 Blanik	171416	OK-1808
OM-1814-IJ	LET L-13 Blanik	171615	OK-1814
OM-1815-K2	LET L-13 Blanik	171616	OK-1815
OM-1833-Y	LET L-13 Blanik	172009	OK-1833
OM-1834	LET L-13 Blanik	172010	OK-1834
OM-1835	LET L-13 Blanik	172011	OK-1835
OM-1836-L	LET L-13 Blanik	172012	OK-1836
OM-1837	LET L-13 Blanik	172013	OK-1837
OM-1838-TL	LET L-13 Blanik	172014	OK-1838
OM-1839	LET L-13 Blanik	172015	OK-1839
OM-1841	LET L-13 Blanik	172017	OK-1841
OM-2000-AM	VTC-75 Standard Cirrus	371	HA-4294
OM-2001-MB	Schleicher ASW 15	15194	D-0880
OM-2002-LK	Glaser-Dirks DG-300 Elan	3E-501	
OM-2004	Schleicher ASW 15B	15158	S5- D-0804
OM-2005	SZD-22B Mucha Standard	614	HB-686
OM-2200-99	Schempp-Hirth Standard Cirrus	647	SE-TPS
OM-2400-AP	Schleicher ASW 15B	15250	OE-0954
OM-2501-H4	VSO-10 Gradient	150049	OK-2501
OM-2503	VSO-10 Gradient	150052	OK-2503
OM-2505-H6	VSO-10 Gradient	150055	OK-2505
OM-2507-H7	VSO-10 Gradient	150059	OK-2507
OM-2512-G7	VSO-10 Gradient	150058	OK-2512
OM-2701	LET L-13 Blanik	175218	OK-2701
OM-2703-V	LET L-13 Blanik	175219	OK-2703
OM-2705	LET L-13 Blanik	175330	OK-2705
OM-2707	LET L-13A Blanik	827406	OK-2707
OM-2709-Y	LET L-13 Blanik	827409	OK-2709
OM-2711	LET L-13A Blanik	827412	OK-2711
OM-2713-T1	LET L-13 Blanik	827415	OK-2713
OM-2715	LET L-13A Blanik	827418	OK-2715
OM-2801	LET L-13 Blanik	172029	OK-2801
OM-2802	LET L-13 Blanik	172030	OK-2802
OM-2904-MI	Slingsby T-59D Kestrel 19	1785	
OM-2908-V	Schempp-Hirth Cirrus VTC	123	OK-2908
OM-3501-K9	VSO-10 Gradient	150073	OK-3501
OM-3503-K5	VSO-10 Gradient	150076	OK-3503
OM-3505-K6	VSO-10 Gradient	150079	OK-3505
OM-3507	VSO-10 Gradient	150082	OK-3507
OM-3509-KZ	VSO-10 Gradient (Accident 6.7.00)	150085	OK-3509
OM-3511-K1	VSO-10 Gradient	150062	OK-3511
OM-3513-A	VSO-10 Gradient	150065	OK-3513
OM-3515-K3	VSO-10 Gradient	150068	OK-3515
OM-3535-LI	Schempp-Hirth Ventus c	586	OK-3535
OM-3596-EF	Centrair ASW 20FL	20183	BGA.2722/EJL
OM-3701	LET L-13 Blanik	025427	OK-3701
OM-3703	LET L-13 Blanik	025807	OK-3703
OM-3815	LET L-13 Blanik	172823	OK-3815

OM-3816-KZ	LET L-13 Blanik	172824	OK-3816
OM-3818	LET L-13 Blanik	172826	OK-3818
OM-4101	Aerotechnik L-13SEH Vivat	940523	OK-4603
OM-4400-MF	Schempp-Hirth Nimbus 2	78	OK-4400
OM-4503-K0	VSO-10 Gradient	150091	OK-4503
OM-4505-M1	VSO-10C Gradient	150094	OK-4505
OM-4507-M2	VSO-10 Gradient	150097	OK-4507
OM-4509-M3	VSO-10 Gradient	150100	OK-4509
OM-4511-M4	VSO-10 Gradient	150103	OK-4511
OM-4515-M9	VSO-10 Gradient	150109	OK-4515
OM-4605	Aerotechnik L-13SW Vivat	840009	OK-4605
OM-4607	Aerotechnik L-13SW Vivat	840010	OK-4607
OM-4608-TB2	Rolladen-Schneider LS6	6063	HB-1858
OM-4609-TB1	Schempp-Hirth Ventus b/16.6	195	OE-5343
OM-4610-7F	Schempp-Hirth Ventus b/16.6	220	OK-4610
OM-4668-PJ	Schempp-Hirth Nimbus 2	63	OE-0996
OM-4701-Q	LET L-13 Blanik	025925	OK-4701
OM-4703	LET L-13 Blanik	025927	OK-4703
OM-4705	LET L-13 Blanik	026001	OK-4705
OM-4707	LET L-13 Blanik	026002	OK-4707
OM-4709	LET L-13 Blanik	026009	OK-4709
OM-4826	LET L-13 Blanik	173101	OK-4826
OM-4827	LET L-13 Blanik	173102	OK-4827
OM-4828-Y	LET L-13 Blanik	173103	OK-4828
OM-4836	LET L-13 Blanik	173111	OK-4836
OM-4901-SA	Schempp-Hirth Standard Cirrus	423G	D-2239
OM-5101	Aerotechnik L-13SW Vivat	850103	OK-5101
OM-5103	Aerotechnik L-13SW Vivat	850106	OK-5103
OM-5105	Aerotechnik L-13SW Vivat	850109	OK-5105
OM-5107	Aerotechnik L-13SW Vivat	850112	OK-5107
OM-5401-BA1	Schempp-Hirth Nimbus 2	89	OK-5401
OM-5343	LG-425 Sohaj III	0314	OK-5343
OM-5601	VSO-10B Gradient	150112	OK-5601
OM-5603-M8	VSO-10B Gradient	150115	OK-5603
OM-5605-M6	VSO-10 Gradient	150118	OK-5605
OM-5607-M0	VSO-10 Gradient	150121	OK-5607
OM-5609-LK	VSO-10 Gradient	150124	OK-5609
OM-5611-LJ	VSO-10 Gradient	150127	
OM-5613-10	VSO-10 Gradient	150130	OK-5613
OM-5615-11	VSO-10 Gradient	150133	OK-5615
OM-5619	Zlin 23 Honza replica	01	
OM-5959-W	Schempp-Hirth Cirrus 75	363	HA-4286
OM-6103	Aerotechnik L-13SE Vivat	860119	OK-6103
OM-6105	Aerotechnik L-13SW Vivat	860122	OK-6105
OM-6107	Aerotechnik L-13SW Vivat	860125	OK-6107
OM-6300-L7	Schempp-Hirth Discus b	130	OK-6300
OM-6501-12	VSO-10 Gradient	150137	OK-6501
OM-6503-13	VSO-10 Gradient	150140	OK-6503
OM-6505-14	VSO-10 Gradient	150143	OK-6505
OM-6507-15	VSO-10 Gradient	150146	OK-6507
OM-6509-16	VSO-10 Gradient	150149	OK-6509
OM-6511-17	VSO-10B Gradient	150152	OK-6511
OM-6513-18	VSO-10C Gradient	150155	OK-6513
OM-6515-19	VSO-10C Gradient	150158	OK-6515
OM-6517-40	VSO-10 Gradient	150160	OK-6517
OM-6519-41	VSO-10 Gradient	150161	OK-6519
OM-6600-PIK	Eiri PIK-20	20110	
OM-6701	LET L-13 Blanik	026817	OK-6701
OM-6802	LET L-13 Blanik	173422	OK-6802
	(This c/n also quoted for YR-206, N7088K, probably 173442)		
OM-6803	LET L-13 Blanik	173423	OK-6803
OM-6809-K1	LET L-13 Blanik	173429	OK-6809
OM-6810	LET L-13 Blanik	173430	OK-6810
OM-6811-X1	LET L-13 Blanik	173431	OK-6811
OM-6820	LET L-13 Blanik	173440	OK-6820
OM-6832	LET L-13 Blanik	173409	OK-6832
OM-6833	LET L-13 Blanik	173410	OK-6833
OM-6834-B	LET L-13 Blanik	173411	OK-6834
OM-7101	Aerotechnik L-13SE Vivat	870203	OK-7101
OM-7103	Aerotechnik L-13SW Vivat	870206	OK-7103
OM-7107	Aerotechnik L-13SW Vivat	870212	OK-7107
OM-7109	Aerotechnik L-13SW Vivat	870215	OK-7109
OM-7301-I	Schempp-Hirth Janus	53	OK-7301
OM-7410	VT-116 Orlik II	151710	
OM-7501-42	VSO-10 Gradient	150165	OK-7501
OM-7503-43	VSO-10 Gradient	150168	OK-7503
OM-7505-44	VSO-10B Gradient	150171	OK-7505
OM-7507-45	VSO-10 Gradient	150174	OK-7507
OM-7509-46	VSO-10 Gradient	150177	OK-7509
OM-7511-47	VSO-10 Gradient	150180	OK-7511
OM-7513-48	VSO-10 Gradient	150185	OK-7513
OM-7777-PI	Schemp-Hirth Nimbus 4DM	52	
OM-8079	Grob G.103 Twin Astir Trainer	3245-T-27	OE-5201
OM-8102	Aerotechnik L-13SE Vivat	unkn	
OM-8108	Aerotechnik L-13SW Vivat	880224	OK-8108
OM-8111	Aerotechnik L-13SE Vivat	880227	OK-8111
OM-8114	Aerotechnik L-13SE Vivat	880230	OK-8114
OM-8117	Aerotechnik L-13SW Vivat	880303	OK-8117
OM-8120	Aerotechnik L-13SW Vivat	880306	OK-8120
OM-8409-1	VT-116 Orlik II	151909	OK-8409
OM-8410	VT-116 Orlik II ZK	151910	OK-8410
OM-8503-49	VSO-10 Gradient	150189	OK-8503
OM-8506-80	VSO-10 Gradient	150192	OK-8506
OM-8509-81	VSO-10 Gradient	150195	OK-8509
OM-8512-82	VSO-10 Gradient	150198	OK-8512
OM-8515-83	VSO-10 Gradient	150201	OK-8515
OM-8517-72	VSO-10 Gradient	unkn	

OM-8701	LET L-13 Blanik	027230	OK-8701
OM-8703	LET L-13 Blanik	027232	OK-8703
OM-8705	LET L-13A Blanik	027234	OK-8705
OM-8804-I	LET L-13 Blanik	170104	OK-8804
OM-8822	LET L-13 Blanik	173818	OK-8822
OM-8823	LET L-13 Blanik	173819	OK-8823
OM-8832	LET L-13 Blanik	173909	OK-8832
OM-8833	LET L-13A Blanik	173910	OK-8833
OM-9102	Aerotechnik L-13SW Vivat	890309	OK-9102
OM-9105	Aerotechnik L-13SW Vivat	890312	
OM-9109	Aerotechnik L-13SE Vivat	890318	
OM-9112	Aerotechnik L-13SE Vivat	890321	OK-9112
OM-9115	Aerotechnik L-13SE Vivat	890324	OK-9115
OM-9116	Aerotechnik L-13SE Vivat	890325	OK-9116
OM-9203	LET L-23 Super Blanik	897504	OK-9203
OM-9205	LET L-23 Super Blanik	897516	OK-9205
OM-9505-B7	VSO-10 Gradient	150005	OK-9505
OM-9507-B8	VSO-10 Gradient	150009	OK-9507
OM-9509-XV	VSO-10B Gradient	150011	
OM-9601-84	VSO-10 Gradient	150205	OK-9601
OM-9604-85	VSO-10B Gradient	150208	
OM-9607-86	VSO-10B Gradient	150211	OK-9607
OM-9610-87	VSO-10B Gradient	150214	OK-9610
OM-9613	VSO-10B Gradient	150217	OK-9613
OM-9616-89	VSO-10B Gradient	150220	OK-9616
OM-9619-96	VSO-10B Gradient	150223	OK-9619
OM-9700	LET L-13 Blanik	173911	OK-9700
OM-9701	LET L-13 Blanik	173912	OK-9701
OM-9702	LET L-13A Blanik	173913	OK-9702
OM-9708	LET L-13 Blanik	174004	OK-9708
OM-9710	LET L-13 Blanik	174006	OK-9710
OM-9715-B2	LET L-13 Blanik	174011	OK-9715
OM-9826	LET L-13 Blanik	170202	OK-9826
OM-9827	LET L-13 Blanik (Stored 10.03)	170203	
OM-9845	LET L-13 Blanik	170714	OK-9845
OM-	DG Flugzeugbau DG-800S	8-245S45	

OO - BELGIUM

Regn.	Type	C/n	Prev.Id.
OO-AAP	Piper PA-18 Super Cub 95	18-3214	(OO-ACF)
	(Dismantled and stored)		OL-L40
			L-140
			53-4814
OO-ABO	CEA Jodel DR.1051M1 Sicile Record	591	PH-ABC
	(CofA exp. 31.8.90, stored)		OO-JOZ
OO-ABS	Mooney M.20F Executive	22-1219	N7442V
OO-ABZ	Beech 35-C33 Debonair	CD-890	G-BABZ
			SE-EKI
OO-ACR	Agusta-Bell 206A Jet Ranger II	8177	OH-HIE
OO-ACS	Reims/Cessna F152	F15201758	D-EIYU
OO-ACT	Dassault Falcon 900C	194	F-WWFZ
OO-ADA	SOCATAMS.893A Rallye Commodore 180	10566	D-ENNC
			F-BNNC
OO-ADC	Piper PA-28-180 Cherokee B	28-1638	5N-ADC
	(Wfu, used as instructional airframe)		N7758W
OO-ADO	Reims FR172H Rocket	FR17200260	F-BSHF
OO-AED	Piper J-3C-90 Cub	12379	OO-LIL
	(CofA exp. 17.11.82, stored)		44-80083
OO-AEH	Bell 47G (Reservation 5.03)	23	N412SF
			N139SA
			OH-HTP
			N412SF
			N10191
			Arg.Navy: 4
			N169B
OO-AEM	SEEMS MS.892B Rallye Commodore 150	10281	F-BLBA
	(CofA exp. 29.9.94, stored)		F-WLBA
OO-AEP	Mooney M.20K Model 231	25-0537	N9871P
OO-AET	Grumman-American AA-5 Traveler	AA5-0083	G-KASH
			G-AZUG
OO-AFB	Piper PA-28-180 Cherokee Archer	28-7505184	(OO-AFP)
			N51JD
OO-AFD	Cessna 310H	310H-0057	N343AS
	(Damaged 18.3.04)		N350RX
			N1057Q
OO-AFJ	SNCAN/Stampe SV.4C (Damaged 20.1.02)	197	F-BCFJ
	(Dismantled)		
OO-AFK	Piper PA-28RT-201 Arrow IV	28R-7918249	OO-HLB
	(W/o 25.6.89)		N2969Y

OO-AGP	Cessna 172H (W/o 16.6.91)	17254976	EL-AGP 5N-AHJ N1481F
OO-AHH	Wassmer WA.40A Super IV	124	F-BNZR
OO-AHO	Scintex CP.1330 Super Emeraude (CofA exp. 9.1.98)	924	F-BJMY
OO-AHY	Cessna 182P Skylane	18261644	G-BAHY N21460
OO-AIF	Piper PA-28-140 Cherokee	28-24668	CS-AIF N11C
OO-AJK	Nord 1203 Norécrin (Restoration project)	261	F-BFJE
OO-ALC	Reims/Cessna F150L	F15000953	
OO-ALD	Reims/Cessna F150L	F15000951	
OO-ALE	Reims/Cessna F172M	F17201126	
OO-ALW	Reims/Cessna F177RG Cardinal RG	F177RG0097	D-EIQT
OO-ALZ	Piper PA-18 Super Cub 95 (Also using parts of 18-2116)	18-2083	ALAT: F-MAKA 52-2483
OO-AMD	Eurocopter EC.120BColibri	1342	
OO-AMZ	SNCAN/Stampe SV.4C (W/o 18.11.68, restoration project)	1137	F-BAMZ
OO-ANI	Piper PA-28-161 Warrior II	28-8016321	OO-HLW N8200Y
OO-ANM	Cessna 152 -II	15281455	N648CA N64871
OO-ANO	Reims/Cessna F152	F15201745	OO-HNQ
OO-ANR	Zlin Z.526F Trenér Master	1265	YR-ZAM
OO-API	SOCATA Rallye 110ST Galopin	3289	PH-AFI
OO-APV	Cessna 152	15279842	D-EAPV OH-CQC C-GQSW (N757ME)
OO-ARA	Grumman-American AA-5B Tiger	AA5B-1203	(OO-RTJ)
OO-ARD	SOCATA MS.880B Rallye Club	1659	F-BSKB
OO-ARM	SOCATA Rallye 110ST Galopin	3293	F-GBXP
OO-ASE	Beech 77 Skipper	WA-149	D-EBCS
OO-ASM	SNCASE SE.3130 Alouette II	1920	F-GNVB V-66
OO-ATN	SOCATA MS.880B Rallye Club (Stored)	2624	F-BXTN
OO-ATY	Piper PA-18 Super Cub 95	18-3221	OL-L47 L-147 53-4821
OO-AUW	Brändli BX-2 Cherry	117	OO-137
OO-AVA	Piper PA-34-200T Seneca II	34-7970301	N2872C
OO-AWC	Reims/Cessna F152-II	F15201614	PH-AXJ
OO-AWT	Reims/Cessna F172M	F17201236	N94723
OO-AWY	Cessna F172H	F172-0563	
OO-AYA	Reims/Cessna F150M	F15001290	F-BUDY (F-GAAR)
OO-AYL	Robin R.2160 Alpha Sport	150	F-GAXL
OO-AYZ	Beech A36 Bonanza	E-454	(OO-PYZ) D-EHWC
OO-AZM	Christen A-1 Husky	1123	SE-KNE
OO-BAK	Enstrom F.28A	168	
OO-BDV	Wassmer Jodel D.120 Paris-Nice	316	F-BNZE
OO-BET	Reims/Cessna F152-II	F15201716	LX-XYZ
OO-BFZ	Piper PA-28R-200 Cherokee Arrow II	28R-7335337	G-BBFZ N9516N
OO-BIR	Piper PA-28-181 Archer II	28-7990189	N2136F
OO-BLD	Robin HR.100/210 Royale	197	
OO-BLY	SEEMS MS.885 Super Rallye (Wfu)	5389	F-BLBY
OO-BNO	Bellanca 8KCAB Decathlon	610-80	
OO-BOM	SOCATA Rallye 150T	2775	
OO-BPL	Stampe & Renard/Stampe SV.4B	1194	(OO-GWC) OO-BPL V-52
OO-BPW	Piper PA-32-300 Cherokee Six B	32-40765	N8970N
OO-BTL	SOCATA Rallye 100ST	2424	F-BVZN
OO-BUC	Piper PA-32-260 Cherokee Six	32-833	(OO-MRA) LN-UXP N3887W
OO-BUK	CEA DR.315 Petit Prince	443	
OO-BYL	de Havilland DH.82A Tiger Moth	3882	G-ANBU W7952 G-AFNR
OO-CAR	CEA Jodel DR.1051M1 Sicile Record	605	
OO-CAT	Jodel D.112 Club	88	OO-HDD F-BHDD
OO-CCB	SOCATA MS.894A Minerva 220	11051	F-BRJY
OO-CCD	CEA DR.220A/2+2 (CofA exp. 21.8.1971, wfu and stored outside)	83	F-BPCF
OO-CEA	CEA DR.315 Petit Prince (Dbr 26.3.03)	409	
OO-CEK	Piper J-3C-65 Cub	"12760"	9Q-CEK 9O-CEK OO-CEK OO-GEK 44-80464
OO-CFD	Diamond DA 42 Twin Star (Reservn 3.05)	unkn	
OO-CGH	Beech 95-B55 Baron	TC-766	9Q-CXH
OO-CHA	Robinson R-22	0124	
OO-CHD	Cessna 150M	15076554	N3586V
OO-CIA	Grumman-American AA-5 Traveler	AA5-0705	
OO-CID	Cessna 172N	17270050	N738KZ
OO-CIN	Piper J-3C-85 Cub (f/n 11644 is officially quoted as c/n)	11818	D-ECIN HB-ODS 43-30527

OO-CIS	Cessna P210NPressurized Centurion	P21000706	N5531W
OO-CJD	Robin HR.200/120B	255	
OO-CJF	Piper PA-28RT-201 Arrow IV	28R-8018044	F-GCJF N8164D
OO-CJP	Cessna 414A Chancellor	414A0229	G-WITE G-LOVO G-KENT N8828K
OO-CKC	Cessna 182S	80787	D-ECKG N2467A
OO-CKD	Robin R.2112 Alpha	189	PH-SVB
OO-CLD	Robin DR.400/180RP Remorqueur	1922	F-GGXR
OO-CLF	Reims/Cessna F152 II	F15201977	G-BMTL
OO-CLK	Reims/Cessna F152	F15201603	(OO-WWE) G-BGSX
OO-CLM	Beech 35-C33 Debonair	CD-1021	D-ECLM
OO-CLP	Cessna 182P Skylane	18262694	G-BCBW N52593
OO-CLS	SOCATA MS.880B Rallye Club	1194	
OO-CNA	Reims/Cessna F150M	F15001198	HB-CNA
OO-CNC	Reims/Cessna F172M	F17201440	
OO-CNH	Reims/Cessna FR172K Hawk XP	FR17200596	N96098
OO-CNO	Reims/Cessna F152	F15201472	(OO-HNO)
OO-CNP	Reims/Cessna F152	F15201497	OO-HNP
OO-CNW	Reims/Cessna F172N	F17202032	PH-AYM(3)
OO-COA	Cessna 172N	17273978	N5133K
OO-COB	Bell 206B Jet Ranger II	385	G-AYTF N1453W
OO-COC	Piper PA-28-181 Cherokee Archer II	28-7890496	N36143
OO-COD	Agusta-Bell 206B Jet Ranger II	8378	D-HCAC(2) G-BBXM HP-635 G-BBXM
OO-COP	Agusta-Bell 206A Jet Ranger	8284	D-HAVA
OO-COV	Reims/Cessna FR182 Skylane RG (Damaged 12.5.02)	FR18200008	PH-LTN
OO-CPC	Reims/Cessna FRA150M Aerobat	FRA1500292	(OO-WAX)
OO-CPD	Robin DR.400/120 Dauphin 2+2	2215	
OO-CQD	Robin DR.400/120 Dauphin 2+2	2273	
OO-CRG	Reims/Cessna F152	F15201524	
OO-CRO	Robinson R-22 Beta	1745	F-GHKK
OO-CRZ	Piper PA-38-112 Tomahawk	38-78A0729	N9746N
OO-CSD	Robin DR.400/160 Major	2392	
OO-CTD	Robin DR.400/140B Major	2201	
OO-CUD	Cessna 172N	17270426	N739CA
OO-CVT	Cessna 150H	15067974	N7274S
OO-CYD	Cessna 150M	15077540	N6131K
OO-CZD	Robin DR.400/140B Dauphin 4	2401	
OO-DAF	Noorduyn/ N.American AT-16 Harvard IIB	14A-1494	MLD/KM:098, B-84, FT454, 43-13195
OO-DAJ	Mooney M.20J Model 201	24-0422	F-GJSB N201AY
OO-DAN	Wassmer Jodel D.112 Club	1305	F-BMYQ
OO-DAP	Mooney M.20K Model 231	25-0572	G-BJGT N10485
OO-DAR	Cessna 150L	15073982	N18607
OO-DAS	Piper PA-18 Super Cub 95	18-1558	OO-HMP ALAT 51-15558
OO-DAT	Piper PA-28-161 Warrior II	28-8016066	N8085D
OO-DAY	SOCATA MS.893A Rallye Commodore 180	11453	F-BSAZ
OO-DAZ	Cessna 182P Skylane	18264103	N6088F
OO-DBM	Boeing-Stearman A75N1	75-5714	G-BPMD N5084N 42-17551
OO-DBR	Grumman-American AA-5A Cheetah	AA5A-0634	(OO-HRH)
OO-DBW	Robinson R-22 Beta (W/o 24.4.02)	2539	
OO-DCJ	Grumman-American AA-5 Traveler	AA5-0591	N9591L
OO-DDF	Bell 206B Jet Ranger II	3179	3A-MTR N6TR N3895C
OO-DEC	Piper PA-28R-200 Cherokee Arrow	28R-35694	D-EEFQ N4974S
OO-DFB	Piper PA-28R-201T Turbo Arrow III	28R-7803280	F-GEPH N9819C
OO-DFJ	Mooney M.20J Model 201	24-0717	D-EDFN(2) HB-DFH (N4352H)
OO-DFK	Piper PA-38-112 Tomahawk	38-79A0004	N9657N
OO-DFL	Piper PA-38-112 Tomahawk	38-79A0084	N2486B
OO-DFP	Christen Pitts S-2B	5070	N260PJ N77JL
OO-DFS	Piper PA-18 Super Cub 95	18-1637	ALAT 51-15637
OO-DHS	Boeing 727-223F (Cancelled, Instructional airframe at Charleroi)	20189	N6836
OO-DIA	Beech 35-C33 Debonair	CD-886	D-EKVI
OO-DIB	Airbus A.300B4-203F	274	EI-DHL PH-SFM (N59274) N227KW N14977 N235EA F-GDVC

OO-DIC	Airbus A.300B4-203F	220	EI-SAF
			PH-SFL
			N860PA
			SE-DSF
			N74989
			(N989C)
			N231EA
			F-GBNY
OO-DJE	BAe.146 Series 200	E-2164	G-6-164
OO-DJF	BAe.146 Series 200	E-2167	G-6-167
OO-DJG	BAe.146 Series 200	E-2180	(G-BSZZ)
			G-6-180
OO-DJH	BAe.146 Series 200	E-2172	G-BSSG
			G-6-172
OO-DJJ	BAe 146 Series 200	E-2196	SE-DRM
			OO-DJJ
			G-6-196
OO-DJK	Avro 146-RJ85	E-2271	G-6-271
OO-DJL	Avro 146-RJ85	E-2273	G-6-273
OO-DJN	Avro 146-RJ85	E-2275	G-6-275
OO-DJO	Avro 146-RJ85	E-2279	G-6-279
OO-DJP	Avro 146-RJ85	E-2287	G-6-287
OO-DJQ	Avro 146-RJ85	E-2289	G-6-289
OO-DJR	Avro 146-RJ85	E-2290	G-6-290
OO-DJS	Avro 146-RJ85	E-2292	G-6-292
OO-DJT	Avro 146-RJ85	E-2294	G-6-294
OO-DJV	Avro 146-RJ85	E-2295	G-6-295
OO-DJW	Avro 146-RJ85	E-2296	G-6-296
OO-DJX	Avro 146-RJ85	E-2297	G-6-297
OO-DJY	Avro 146-RJ85	E-2302	G-6-302
OO-DJZ	Avro 146-RJ85	E-2305	G-6-305
OO-DKM	Piper PA-28-181 Cherokee Archer II	28-7690296	C-GXEE
			N75113
OO-DLC	Airbus A.300B4-203F	152	N221EA
			F-GBNP
OO-DLD	Airbus A.300B4-203F	259	N865PA
			TC-ALG
			OB-1634
			(AP-BFG)
			SE-DSG
			N72990
			(N990C)
			N232EA
			F-GBNZ
OO-DLE	Airbus A.300B4-203F	236	N222KW
			N207PA
			F-WZMI
OO-DLG	Airbus A.300B4-203F	208	N212PA
			F-OHPN
			F-WHPJ
			SX-BAY
			N212PA
			F-WZMQ
OO-DLH	Piper PA-22-160 Tri-Pacer	22-7419	G-ARAL
			N10F
OO-DLI	Airbus A.300B4-203F	234	N206PA
			F-OHPA
			F-WZMF
OO-DLJ	Boeing 757-23APF	24971	N573CA
			G-OBOZ
			N5002K
OO-DLM	Hughes 269C	64-0323	G-OSHC
			N8989F
OO-DLN	Boeing 757-236SF	22172	G-BIKA
OO-DLP	Boeing 757-236SF	22179	G-BIKH
			(G-BIKI)
OO-DLQ	Boeing 757-236SF	22175	G-BIKD
OO-DLR	Airbus A.300B4-203F	095	EI-EAE
			N226KW
			9M-MHC
			F-WZEM
OO-DLT	Airbus A.300B4-203F	250	EI-EAC
			N10970
			N970C
			F-WZMU
OO-DLU	Airbus A.300B4-203F	289	EI-EAD
			N13972
			N972C
			F-WZMM
OO-DLV	Airbus A.300B4-203F	150	EI-EAA
			F-WQGT
			SU-BCC
			F-WZMD
OO-DLW	Airbus A.300B4-203F	199	EI-EAB
			F-WQFO
			SU-BDF
			(SU-BCD)
			F-WZMF
OO-DLY	Airbus A.300B4-203F	116	EI-EAT
			F-WQFR
			D-ASAY
			SU-BCB
			F-WZES
OO-DMB	SOCATA TB-20 Trinidad (Damaged 28.5.01)	560	D-EPMT
			F-GJGL
			N43AS

OO-DMC	Beech F33A Bonanza	CE-1273	G-JBET
			N15574
OO-DMF	Reims/Cessna F172M	F17201015	D-EJXA
OO-DMS	Reims/Cessna FA150L Aerobat	FA1500087	(OO-WIJ)
OO-DMT	Robinson R-44 Astro	0413	D-HIFF
OO-DNB	SOCATA TB-9 Tampico	1541	F-GLFR
OO-DOC	Robin DR.300/125 Petit Prince	623	
OO-DOU	Agusta-Bell 206B Jet Ranger III	8718	G-RNGR
OO-DPB	Boeing 757-236SF	22183	G-BIKL
			(G-BIKM)
OO-DPF	Boeing 757-236SF	22173	G-BIKB
OO-DPG	Grumman-American AA-5 Traveler	AA5-0647	OO-HAE
			(OO-WAE)
OO-DPH	Schweizer 269C (W/o 8.2.92)	S-1467	D-HHOF
OO-DPI	Boeing 757-236SF	24102	G-BMRG
OO-DPJ	Boeing 757-236SF	23493	G-BIKX
OO-DPK	Boeing 757-236SF	23492	G-BIKW
OO-DPL	Boeing 757-236SF	24267	G-BMRI
OO-DPM	Boeing 757-236SF	22189	G-BIKR
OO-DPN	Boeing 757-236SF	23533	G-BIKY
OO-DPO	Boeing 757-236SF	23398	G-BIKT
OO-DRB	SOCATA TB-9 Tampico (W/o 23.8.02)	1631	D-EMIC(2)
OO-DRE	Cessna 152-II	15282930	N89962
	(Sold in France, not yet cancelled)		
OO-DRI	Cessna 152 II	15279850	D-EITF(2)
			N757MN
OO-DSA	Robin DR.400/180R Remorqueur	1703	(OO-FWC)
			F-WEIQ
			(D-EAFA)
			F-WEIQ
OO-DSB	SOCATA TB-20 Trinidad	1926	F-OILD
OO-DSD	Piper PA-28-181 Archer III	2843075	N92864
OO-DTT	Robinson R-44 Astro	0230	
OO-DWA	Avro 146-RJ100	E-3308	G-6-308
OO-DWB	Avro 146-RJ100	E-3315	G-6-315
OO-DWC	Avro 146-RJ100	E-3322	G-6-322
OO-DWD	Avro 146-RJ100	E-3324	G-6-324
OO-DWE	Avro 146-RJ100	E-3327	G-6-327
OO-DWF	Avro 146-RJ100	E3332	G-6-332
OO-DWG	Avro 146-RJ100	E-3336	G-6-336
OO-DWH	Avro 146-RJ100	E-3340	G-6-340
OO-DWI	Avro 146-RJ100	E-3342	G-6-342
OO-DWJ	Avro 146-RJ100	E-3355	G-6-355
OO-DWK	Avro 146-RJ100	E-3360	G-6-360
OO-DWL	Avro 146-RJ100	E-3361	G-6-361
OO-DXZ	Beech F33A Bonanza	CE-500	D-EDXZ
OO-DYD	Robinson R-44 Raven	0933	
OO-DYN	Gyroflug SC.01B-160 Speed Canard	S-24	D-ECES
OO-EAB	Piper J-3C-65 Cub (W/o 15.5.00)	12220	44-79924
OO-EAN	Bell 206B Jet Ranger II	1595	G-BORX
			C-GHYQ
OO-EBH	Robinson R-22	0064	D-HEXE
			N9033Y
OO-EBL	Valtion Vliima II	VI-3	G-BAAY
			OH-VIG
			VI-3
OO-EBT	Beech A24R Sierra	MC-745	N3711G
OO-EBU	Piper PA-28-161 Cadet	2841246	(OO-PRO)
OO-ECB	Eurocopter EC.120B Colibri	1096	F-WQDK
OO-ECF	SOCATA MS.883 Rallye 115	1549	F-BSAJ
OO-ECS	Cessna 172RG Cutlass RG	172RG1126	N9338D
OO-EDM	Gyroflug SC-01B-160 Speed Canard	S-31	D-EJDB
			(PH-AVO)
OO-EDY	SEEMS MS.892A Rallye Commodore 150	10459	F-BLSJ
OO-EEJ	SIAI-Marchetti SF.260	2-41	(OO-EEG)
OO-EET	Cessna F172H	F172-0602	D-EETB
OO-EFA	Tipsy T.66 Nipper II	75	
OO-EFN	SNCAN/Stampe SV.4C	625	(OY-EFN)
			D-EDFN(1)
			F-BDFU
OO-EGB	Robinson R-22 Beta	1840	
OO-EGC	Robinson R-22 Beta	1839	
OO-EGH	Robinson R-22 Beta	1360	
OO-EGJ	Robinson R-44 Astro	0284	G-BWWR
OO-EGM	Bell 206B Jet Ranger II	1097	G-BBBM
			N18090
OO-EII	Bücker B.133C Jungmeister	51	D-EIII (2)
			SpAF:E.1-. . .
OO-EIR	Stampe & Renard/Stampe SV.4B	1144	V-4
OO-ELV	Jodel D.112 Club	310	F-BHGD
OO-EMC	Gyroflug SC-01B-160 Speed Canard	S-32	D-EAND
OO-EMF	Beech V35B Bonanza	D-10076	D-EEMF(2)
OO-EMG	Tipsy T.66 Nipper II	60	(PH-EMG)
			OO-EMG
OO-EMS	McDonnell-Douglas MD.900 Explorer	00020	SE-JCG
OO-ENO	Beech A23 Musketeer II	M-790	D-EMNI
OO-EOD	Beech F33A Bonanza	CE-291	N3797A
OO-EOT	Tipsy B	18	G-AISB
	(Damaged 20.5.94)		
OO-EPM	Cessna 340A /RAM	340A0716	OY-RAV
			N98976
			F-GCSQ
			N98976
OO-EPV	Epervier (W/o 21.9.1991)	01	OO-964
OO-ERD	Beech 76 Duchess	ME-374	(OO-VHE)
			(OO-RDE)
			N3706L

OO-ERG	Hughes 269A	66-0602	G-FSDH
			N602CH
			66-18319
OO-ESV	Stampe & Renard/Stampe SV.4B	1165	V-23
OO-ESX	SOCATA TB-9 Tampico	299	D-EESX
	(Damaged in accident 30.1.05)		
OO-ETW	Beech F33A Bonanza	CE-1108	D-EBUM(3)
OO-EVE	de Havilland DH.82A Tiger Moth	85953	T-25
			ETA-25
			EM722
OO-EVZ	Morane-Saulnier MS.885 Super Rallye	233	F-BKUA
OO-EWL	Robin HR.100/200B Royale	125	D-EJYJ
			(OO-NDW)
			D-EJYJ
OO-EYP	Eurocopter EC.120BColibri	1285	F-WQQR
			F-WQDB
OO-FAC	Nord NC.858D	12	F-BFIA
OO-FAS	Nord NC.858D	104	F-BEZK
OO-FBI	Robin DR.400/120 Dauphin 2+2	2036	F-GJZZ
OO-FBL	Agusta-Bell 47G-2	111	F-BXXD
			(OO-FBL)
			F-BXXD
			ALAT
OO-FBV	Cessna F150F	F150-0023/15062918	OO-SIJ
			(N8818G)
OO-FCA	Reims/Cessna F177RG Cardinal RG	F177RG0040	
	(Reims-assembled 177RG c/n 177RG0204)		
OO-FCE	Reims/Cessna F172M	F17201470	
OO-FDQ	Wassmer Jodel D.120A Paris-Nice	270	
OO-FDS	Wassmer Jodel D.120A Paris-Nice	272	
OO-FDU	Wassmer Jodel D.120A Paris-Nice	276	
OO-FDV	Wassmer Jodel D.120A Paris-Nice	277	
OO-FEE	Schweizer 269C	S-1596	D-HHEX
			N41S
OO-FES	Beech 35-C33 Debonair	CD-1011	D-ECLC
OO-FFT	DHC-1 Chipmunk 22A	C1/0475	G-AOTZ
			WG401
OO-FGW	Beech F33A Bonanza	CE-982	N1849Z
			(F-GGBM)
			N1849Z
OO-FIC	Rockwell 114 Commander	14089	N4759W
OO-FIF	GEMS MS.892A Rallye Commodore 150	10534	F-BNBF
OO-FIR	Piper PA-18 Super Cub 95	18-1371	OO-HMZ
	(Frame stored)		ALAT
			51-15371
OO-FJL	Schweizer 269C	S-1636	D-HMAC(3)
	(Damaged 18.5.04)		N69A
OO-FJZ	Cessna 182P Skylane	18262728	F-BVJZ
			N52631
OO-FKV	Cessna R182 Skylane RG	R18201429	N4788S
OO-FLA	Piper PA-28-140 Cherokee Cruiser	28-7625105	OO-HAX
			N9509N
OO-FLC	Reims/Cessna F152	F15201624	OO-HNS
OO-FLE	Piper PA-34-200T Seneca II	34-7770135	OO-HCC
			N1693H
OO-FLM	Piper PA-28-181 Archer II	28-7990544	OO-HCE
			N2907T
OO-FLN	Cessna 525A CitationJet 2	525A-0179	N179FZ
OO-FLS	Piper PA-32-300 Cherokee Six	32-7940074	N2226W
OO-FLW	Piper PA-18 Super Cub 95	18-1562	OO-HMS
			ALAT
			51-15562
OO-FLZ	SOCATA Rallye 180T Galérien	3207	
OO-FMC	Cessna F172H (Dbr 14.3.03)	F172-0614	
OO-FMX	Reims/Cessna F172N	F17202031	D-EFMX
OO-FOI	Dassault Falcon 900EX EASy	121	F-GSEF
	(Reservation 27.1.05)		F-WWFW
OO-FPA	Cessna 560XL Citation Excel	560-5248	HB-VNR
			N5109R
OO-FSF	Cessna 150M	15077651	G-LFSF
			G-BSRC
			N6337K
OO-FSI	Reims/Cessna F150M	F15001399	F-GASN
OO-FST	Cessna F150H	F150-0350	
OO-FTL	SEEMS MS.885 Super Rallye	5395	F-BLSZ
OO-FTO	Cessna 172R	17280068	G-BXXD
			N9739F
OO-FUS	Cessna 208BGrand Caravan	208B0794	N13047
			N5263D
OO-FVR	Agusta-Bell 206B Jet Ranger III (Cr. 4.99)	8590	D-HORA(2)
			HB-XIV
OO-FWA	Robin R.3000/160	136	
OO-FWD	Robin DR.400RP Remorqueur	1872	F-GGQV
OO-FWP	Piaggio FWP.149D	059	D-EEHH
			90+45
			JD+390
			BF+702
			BC+702
			AS+486
OO-FXS	Robinson R-44 Raven	1369	
OO-FYG	Cessna 550 Citation Bravo	550-1027	N52691
OO-GAC	SOCATA MS.880B Rallye Club	2302	(F-BULT)
OO-GAM	Grumman-American AA-5A Cheetah	AA5A-0011	OO-HAZ
OO-GAQ	Cessna 172N	17268074	N75968
OO-GAS	SOCATA MS.880B Rallye Club	1700	F-BSZS
			F-BSKS
OO-GAZ	Grumman-American AA-5B Tiger	AA5B-0971	OO-HRD

OO-GCO	Grumman-American AA-5A Cheetah	AA5A-0526	OO-HGB
OO-GDE	Piper PA-18-100 Super Cub	18-3106	OL-L32
			53-4706
OO-GEL	Piper J-3C-85 Cub	12682	OO-AVP
	(Believed rebuilt using parts from OO-GEK)		44-80386
OO-GEM	Beech 35-C33 Debonair	CD-1090	G-AVHG
OO-GFC	SOCATA MS.880B Rallye Club	1796	
OO-GFD	Dassault Falcon 2000	101	F-WWVU
			N399FA
			N2093
OO-GHM	Piper PA-34-220T Seneca III	34-8133021	N8341U
	(Damaged 3.02)		
OO-GIN	Wassmer WA.52 Europa (Crashed)	71	F-BTLT
OO-GIO	Aeronca 7AC Champion	4458	
OO-GJM	Agusta A.109E Power	11128	
	(Damaged in accident 4.2.2004)		
OO-GJY	Reims/Cessna F150L	F15000975	D-EGJY
OO-GLB	Grob G.115C2	82045	D-EXGR
OO-GLO	Robin HR.100/210 Royale	172	
OO-GLR	Wassmer Jodel D.112 Club	1002	F-BIXO
OO-GMC	Piper PA-34-200T Seneca II	34-7970007	N2213B
OO-GMD	Piper PA-38-112 Tomahawk	38-79A0487	(OO-TLT)
			N9661N
OO-GMX	Maule MX.7-180 Star Rocket	11034C	F-GGMX
			F-WGMX
			N61071
OO-GPS	Cessna 404 Titan	404-0609	
OO-GSM	Reims/Cessna FR182 Skylane RG	FR18200013	OO-HNN
OO-GTR	SAN Jodel D.117 Grand Tourisme	694	F-BIDE
OO-GUY	CEA Jodel DR.1051 Sicile	308	F-BKIN
OO-GVA	SOCATA MS.883 Rallye 115	1391	F-BRRJ
OO-GVB	Piper PA-28-181 Archer III	2843423	OK-MFD
			N5319L
OO-GVE	Beech 77 Skipper	WA-293	HB-EJL
OO-GVF	Beech 77 Skipper	WA-173	D-EDLD
			N806Y
OO-GWA	SNCAN/Stampe SV.4C	478	N1024N
			F-BDBO
OO-GWB	Stampe & Renard/Stampe SV.4B	1171	(OO-GWR)
			V-29
OO-GWC	SNCAN/Stampe SV.4A	1	N9480A
			F-BFVA
			FrNavy
			FrAF
OO-GWD	Stampe & Renard/Stampe SV.4B	1160	G-BRMC
			SLN-03
			V-18
OO-GYS	SOCATA MS.880B Rallye Club	2857	
OO-GYT	SOCATA MS.880B Rallye Club	2260	
OO-GZM	Reims/Cessna FR182 Skylane	FR18200045	D-EIYO
OO-HBG	Piper PA-18 Super Cub 95	18-3228	OL-L18
			L-154
			53-4828
OO-HBI	Reims/Cessna F150L	F15000747	
OO-HBM	Schweizer 269C	S-1526	D-HSPH
OO-HBQ	Piper PA-18 Super Cub 95	18-3130	OL-L56
	(CofA exp. 18.1.90, stored)		53-4730
OO-HBR	Reims/Cessna F172M	F17201484	(D-EITA)
OO-HBT	Reims/Cessna F150M	F15001254	D-EIHF
			(F-BXQA)
OO-HBU	Reims/Cessna F172N	F17201916	(F-GCHN)
OO-HBW	Cessna F150G	F150-0144	D-EJRO
OO-HCT	Robinson R-44 Raven	1324	
OO-HDZ	Robinson R-22B2 Beta	3532	
OO-HEO	SIAI-Marchetti S.208 (Cvtd from 205-22/R)	4-231	
OO-HER	Cessna 172M	17263034	N13899
OO-HEY	Robinson R-44 Raven	10164	
	(Damaged in accident 29.1.05)		
OO-HFA	Reims/Cessna F152-II	F15201866	
OO-HFD	Hughes 269C	47-0585	G-BMGP
			ZS-HMK
			N7496F
OO-HFE	Reims/Cessna F152-II	F15201877	
OO-HFI	Cessna 172N	17272136	C-GLIV
			N8084E
OO-HFL	Robinson R-44 Raven	0973	
OO-HFS	Hughes 369D	120-0880D	LX-HLE
			OO-HFS
			G-BIOA
OO-HFZ	Hughes 269C	99-0823	(OO-DMG)
			G-BOVZ
			VH-TID
OO-HGZ	CEA Jodel DR.1051 Sicile	301	F-BKIG
OO-HNE	Robinson R-44 Raven II	10503	
OO-HOE	AIAA/Stampe SV.4C	1132	(OO-OEV)
	(Dbf 5.9.1984, restoration in progress)		F-BALH
OO-HPK	Cessna U206G Stationair 6 (Soloy conv)	U20605788	(OO-HSD)
			D-EATU
			HB-CJG
			N5474X
OO-HPP	Eurocopter EC.120BColibri	1354	
OO-HPS	Robinson R-22B2 Beta (Reservation .05)	3832	
OO-HSB	Aérospatiale AS.355F1 Ecureuil 2	5223	G-PLAX
			G-BPMT
			N380E
OO-HSG	Aérospatiale AS.355F1 Ecureuil 2	5116	N5791M

OO-HSH	Aérospatiale AS.355F1 Ecureuil 2	5157	G-OBIG
			G-SVJM
			G-BOPS
			I-MOST
OO-HSI	Robinson R-22B2 Beta	3188	
OO-HUS	Christen A-1 Husky	1128	N9603R
OO-HVB	Reims/Cessna 152	F15201795	D-EMSG
			PH-CBE
OO-HYW	SNCAN/Stampe SV.4C	552	F-BDCX
OO-IAL	Beech F90 King Air	LA-100	D-IWAL
			(OO-SAL)
			D-IWAL
			HB-GHP
			G-BIED
OO-IBL	HP.137 Jetstream 200	241	G-GLOS
			G-BCGU
			G-AXRI
OO-IBR	Piper PA-32R-301 Saratoga SP	32R-8213002	N8469A
			N8459A
OO-IFR	Piper PA-28-181 Archer II	28-8590056	N69135
OO-IKA	Grumman-American AA-5B Tiger	AA5B-0543	OO-HGA
OO-ILS	Piper PA-28-181 Archer III	2843432	N5160F
	(Reservation 2.05)		
OO-IPZ	CEA Jodel DR.1050-M1 Sicile Record	02	F-BIPZ
			F-WIPZ
OO-ISE	Cessna T303 Crusader	T30300160	LX-YNC
			N65NC
			G-BPZN
			G-RSUL
			(G-BPZN)
			N6610C
OO-IVB	Cessna T210L Turbo Centurion	21061063	D-ELSY(2)
			N2097S
OO-IXY	Wassmer Jodel D.120A Paris-Nice	145	F-BIXY
OO-JAC(5)	Beech V35A Bonanza	D-8745	
OO-JAE	Piper PA-28R-200 Cherokee Arrow	28R-35676	D-EJAE
			N4904S
OO-JAG	Piper PA-28-161 Cadet	2841247	N9192Z
OO-JAK(3)	Piper PA-22-150 Tri-Pacer	22-7640	F-BJAK
			ALAT
			N10F
OO-JBH	SAN Jodel D.150 Mascaret	51	
OO-JBO	Robin R.2160 Alpha Sport	348	F-GTZV
OO-JCJ	Piper PA-28-140 Cherokee	28-25242	(OO-NEW)
			N8001N
OO-JCM	Piper PA-28-181 Archer II	28-7990499	N2853D
OO-JCO	Wassmer WA.51 Pacific	03	F-BPTU
OO-JCS	Schweizer 269C	S-1749	D-HPIF
			SX-HMA
			N41S
OO-JDA	Robinson R-22 Beta	0840	G-JWSD
OO-JDC	Piper J-3C-65 Cub	12476	OO-AJK
			44-80180
OO-JDG	Robinson R-22 Beta	0821	F-GICD
	(crashed 12.5.04)		
OO-JDV	Pilatus PC-6/B2-H4 Turbo-Porter	911	
	(Sold in Indonesia, not yet cancelled)		
OO-JEE	Cessna 208B Grand Caravan	208B0879	N209AA
			(C-GIKG)
			N5267J
OO-JEH	Boeing-Stearman A75-N1	75-442	G-BPTB
			N55581
			40-1885
OO-JEN	SAAB S.91A Safir	91140	PH-UEF
			SE-BNU
OO-JEP	Piel CP.301A Emeraude	231	F-BIMF
OO-JGA	Piper PA-28-181 Archer II	28-8090313	N87GA
			CX-BNB-F
			N9558N
OO-JIM	Robinson R-22 Beta	1512	G-BUZW
			OH-HJA
			(N151NH)
OO-JIR	Wassmer WA.40 Super IV	3	F-BJIR
OO-JKM	Beech F33 Bonanza	CE-487	N4386W
OO-JLH	Extra EA.300/L	039	D-ETZX
	(Destroyed by fire at Wevelgem 15.10.03)		
OO-JLJ	Beech 95-A55 Baron	TC-450	D-ILDU
	(Damaged 11.5.85, stored)		
OO-JLM	Cessna 177RG Cardinal RG	177RG1295	PH-BRA
			N52874
OO-JMB	Piper PA-32R-300 Cherokee Lance	32R-7780226	N1226Q
OO-JMC	Piper PA-28-181 Archer II	28-7990550	N2910H
OO-JMF	Piper PA-28-140 Cherokee D	28-7125468	PH-SRB
			N11C
OO-JMI	Reims/Cessna F172M	F17201437	F-BXQR
OO-JMK	Mooney M.20K Model 231	25-0734	N5615G
	(W/o 7.12.03)		
OO-JMP	Cessna 208B Grand Caravan	208B0173	N4695B
OO-JMS	Robin DR.300/108 2+2	586	
OO-JNS	Beech A36 Bonanza	E-1108	C-GJLS
			N18380
OO-JOA	CEA Jodel DR.1051 Sicile (W/o 11.8.92)	220	
OO-JOB	Wassmer Jodel D.112F Club	1119	
OO-JOG	Piper PA-32R-301T Turbo Saratoga SP	32R-8329022	N42989
OO-JPD	Piper PA-28-140 Cherokee	28-7425107	N9593N
OO-JPF	Piper PA-28-140 Cherokee Cruiser	28-7625062	OO-HAV
			N9636N

OO-JPL	Boisavia B.601L Mercurey	115	(OO-UPL)
			F-BIGZ
OO-JPS	Piper PA-28-140 Cherokee E	28-7225575	N15460
OO-JPW	Piper PA-28R-200 Cherokee Arrow II	28R-7635397	N4209F
OO-JRB	Cessna F150J	F150-0510	(HB-CTX)
OO-JRD	Reims/Cessna F177RG Cardinal RG	F177RG0046	
OO-JSY	Robinson R-44 Astro	0463	D-HIBB
OO-JUL	Morane-Saulnier MS.317	6530/276	(OO-MIL)
	(Wears French Navy c/s as "3S2")		F-BFZO
OO-JUS	Naval Aircraft Factory N3N-3	2909	N45172
			BuA . . . . .
OO-JVE	Piper PA-28-235 Cherokee	28-10894	OO-HSL
			N9226W
OO-KAA	Beech A36 Bonanza	E-445	N808T
OO-KAC	Robin DR.400/180R Remorqueur	1404	OE-DKU
OO-KAJ	PZL-110 Koliber 150	03900039	(OO-CAJ)
			PH-BEE
OO-KAT	SNCAN/Stampe SV.4C (Lycoming 0-360)	416	F-BCQZ
OO-KAY	Mooney M.20K Model 231	25-0332	N231NV
OO-KBB	Schweizer S.269C	S-1680	D-HMOL(2)
OO-KBH	Robinson R-44 Raven I	1128	HB-ZDU
OO-KBM	Bell 206B Jet Ranger II	1788	G-BVWS
	(W/o 28.4.01)		C-GGXX
			N49610
OO-KBT	Bell 206L Long Ranger	45099	G-BZBK
			N765M
			SE-HSH
			PH-HLH
OO-KCH	Robinson R-22 Beta	2220	D-HOLO
OO-KDN	Robinson R-44 Astro	0532	D-HOME
OO-KER	de Havilland DH.115 Vampire T.55	22277	N4368F
			U-1237
OO-KES	Piper PA-28-140 Cherokee F	28-7325013	N15196
	(w/o 26.3.89)		
OO-KEY	Beech A36 Bonanza	E-1150	(OO-AZM)
			D-EFIT(4)
			OE-KMK
			D-EEHZ
			HB-EHZ
OO-KFC	Piper PA-18-135 Super Cub	18-1633	OO-HNH
	(W/o 16.10.87, wreck sold in the US)		ALAT
			51-15633
OO-KID	Grumman-American AA-5A Cheetah	AA5A-0661	(OO-HRI)
OO-KKA	Robinson R-44 Raven II	1462	
	(Reservation .05)		
OO-KKK	Piper PA-18 Super Cub 95	18-3155	D-EKKK
			OL-L77
			L-77
			53-4755
OO-KLO	Boisavia B.601L Mercurey	22	F-BHVH
OO-KMA	Robinson R-22 Beta	1501	N4033S
OO-KMB	Robin DR.400/180 Régent	1112	F-GABY
	(Damaged 2.8.04)		
OO-KMG	Grob G.115A	8066	D-ENFM
			G-BRUR
			D-EHTA
OO-KMP	Cessna 152	15283278	D-EMKF
			N48080
OO-KMS	Cessna 152	15282406	N68927
OO-KMT	American Champion 8GCBC Scout	383-97	
OO-KND	Robinson R-44 Raven	1054	D-HALI
OO-KNK	SOCATA TB-20 Trinidad	1013	SE-KNK
OO-KPA	Cessna 172R Skyhawk	17280521	D-EPRP
			N9573G
OO-KPW	Cessna 172R	17280065	N697SC
OO-KRC	Canadair CL.600-2B16 Challenger	5577	N577CJ
	(Reserved 12.03)		C-GLWX
OO-KTJ	Morane-Saulnier MS.880B Rallye Club	214	F-BKTJ
OO-KVU	Beech 35-C33 Debonair	CD-1036	D-EKVU
OO-KWP	Cessna 152	15285995	(OO-KWT)
			N95992
OO-KWS	Cessna 152	15285985	N95920
OO-KWT	Cessna 172N	17268274	N733GA
OO-LAA	Piper J-5A Cub Coupé	5-868	N38057
			NC38057
OO-LAC	Beech 200C Super King Air	BL-16	F-GLTX
			(OO-SKN)
			F-GLTX
			N57LM
			LN-TWI
			N62GA
			F-GFAA
			N200RG
			N621AW
OO-LAK	Grumman-American AA-5B Tiger	AA5B-0099	
OO-LCB	Jodel D.112 Club	669	F-BIGM
OO-LCM	Cessna 500 Citation	500-0036	N18HJ
			D-IEXC
			SE-DEU
			OY-DVL
			N536CC
OO-LDJ	Beech 77 Skipper	WA-117	(OO-DAL)
			N131DB
			N3725Z
OO-LDR	Robin R.3000/140	101	F-GDYI
OO-LEA	Robinson R-22HP	0207	F-GIVI
			HB-XMW

OO-LED	SNCAN/Stampe SV.4C	388	F-BBTR Fr.AF
OO-LEE	SNCAN/Stampe SV.4E (Lycoming 0-360)	99	F-BNDA F-BJCF F-BBAG
OO-LEL	Stampe & Renard/Stampe SV.4B (Restoration in progress)	1197	PH-BOZ OO-RLC V-55
OO-LEM	Aeronca 11AC Chief	1607	
OO-LEO	Tipsy T.66 Nipper II	62	
OO-LER	Bell 206B Jet Ranger II	2043	G-BVWT C-GUXC N9965K
OO-LES	Cessna F150G	F150-0072	PH-LES
OO-LET	Beech B200 Super King Air	BB-1473	N8210X PT-OXG N8064Q
OO-LEV	Schweizer 269C-300	S-1726	
OO-LEX	Robinson R-44 Astro	0367	D-HISS
OO-LFM	Piper PA-18-135 Super Cub	18-2543	(OO-VVQ) OO-HMC ALAT 52-6225
OO-LFN	Bombardier Learjet 45XR	45-250	N40050
OO-LFS	Bombardier Learjet 45	45-018	N418LJ
OO-LFV	Gates Learjet 35A	35A-481	N27NR N729HS HK-3122/X N729HS N728MP N666KK N6666K
OO-LGB	Piper PA-18 Super Cub 95 (Exchanged fuselages with c/n 18-1650 - see OO-SPG) (Painted in Belgian Army L-156 markings)	18-2060	OO-SPG R-53 52-2460
OO-LGD	Cessna F150H	F150-0351	
OO-LHM	Dornier Do.27A-3	417	57+00 CA+047 GB+384
OO-LIB	Wassmer WA.41 Baladou	96	F-BMYV
OO-LJR	Robinson R-22 Beta	1844	G-EDDI
OO-LKV	Aérospatiale AS.350BEcureuil	1805	G-OFHL EI-BPM G-BLSP
OO-LMC	Fokker S.11- 1 Instructor	6216	(PH-HOB) E-25
OO-LME	CEA Jodel DR.1051M1 Sicile Record	432	F-BLME
OO-LMI	Bell 206B Jet Ranger II	1231	G-BRMH N39AH G-BRMH G-BBUX N18091
OO-LMO	Reims/Cessna F406 Caravan II	F406-0034	D-ILIM OY-PAB PH-PHO AP-BFB N443AB G-BPSX F-WZDX
OO-LMZ	Piper PA-18 Super Cub 95	18-1474	ALAT 51-15474
OO-LNA	SOCATA MS.893E Rallye 180GT Gaillard	12270	F-BUJT
OO-LNC	Reims/Cessna F172M (Stored)	F17201510	F-BUDU
OO-LOP	Robin R.2112 Alpha	178	F-GCAC
OO-LOQ	Gyroflug SC-01 Speed Canard	S-12	
OO-LOT	Piper PA-18 Super Cub 95	18-3218	OL-L12 L-144 53-4818
OO-LOU	Piper PA-18 Super Cub 95	18-1617	OO-HNF ALAT 51-15617
OO-LOV	Beech V35A Bonanza	D-8799	F-GCME N8464N
OO-LPE	Grumman AA-5B Tiger	AA5B-0468	D-ELPE(2)
OO-LSY	SEEMS MS.892A Rallye Commodore 150	10448	F-BLSY
OO-LTH	Hughes 369E	0469E	OO-XTH
OO-LTM	Boeing 737-3M8	25070	F-GMTM OO-LTM F-GLTM OO-LTM
OO-LUC	Percival P.40 Prentice 1	5840/18	G-AOLM VS396
OO-LUK	Stampe & Renard/Stampe SV.4B	1183	V-41
OO-LUX	Alpavia Jodel D.117A Grand Tourisme	1060	F-BJEL
OO-LUY	Schweizer 269C	S-1780	(OO-LEC) N41S
OO-LVB	Cessna 152-II	15284883	N5124P
OO-LVI	Piper PA-25-235 Pawnee C	25-5115	N8665L
OO-LVJ	Reims/Cessna FA152 Aerobat	FA1520378	HB-CHL N96954 (D-EJDG) N96954
OO-LVL	Maule MX7-180 Star Rocket	11045C	
OO-LVN	Piper PA-25-235 Pawnee D	25-7656121	N82407
OO-LVP	Piper PA-18-135 Super Cub	18-3593	EI-202 I-EIYW MM542393 54-2393
OO-LVR	Mooney M.20J Model 205	24-3280	D-EBRW
OO-LVW	Mooney M.20J Model 205 (Dbr 1.01)	24-3250	D-ESEO
OO-LVZ	Piper PA-18 Super Cub 95 (Dismantled)	18-1405	ALAT 51-15405
OO-LWI	Piaggio FWP.149D (Displayed in garden at Zenst)	154	91+32 BF+701 KB+131
OO-LYR	SNCAN/Stampe SV.4C	109	F-BMME Fr.Mil
OO-MAF	Hispano HA.1112MIL	201	C4K-121
OO-MAH	Piper PA-28-161 Warrior III	2842167	N53554
OO-MAK	Piaggio FWP.149D	056	90+42 AS+407 AS+483
OO-MAM	Reims/Cessna F182Q Skylane	F18200144	OO-HNK(2)
OO-MAN	SOCATA MS.880B Rallye Club	2251	G-BAOI
OO-MAR	Grumman-American AA-5 Traveler	AA5-0424	N7124L
OO-MAY	SAN Jodel DR.105A Ambassadeur	98	LX-MAY
OO-MBS	Piper PA-18-150 Super Cub	18-4046	(OO-LVT) EI-297 I-EIZC MM542646 54-2646
OO-MCA	Piper PA-32-301 Saratoga	32-8006013	N81648
OO-MCH	Fokker S-11- I Instructor	6208	(PH-HOE) E-17
OO-MCL	Morane-Saulnier MS.733 Alcyon	186	Fr.Navy
OO-MDA	Cessna R182 Skylane RG	R18201057	N182MR (N756EX)
OO-MDF	Reims/Cessna F172N	F17201890	OO-HNV
OO-MDG	Cessna 172N	17273913	F-GJAA N7378J
OO-MDM	Aeronca 7AC Champion	3623	
OO-MDP	Schweizer 269C	S-1787	N69A
OO-MEA	SIAI-Marchetti S.205-18/R	4-164	OO-HEA
OO-MEV	Piaggio FWP.149D	053	90+39 BF+405 AS+480
OO-MFG	Zlin Z.526F Trenér Master	1266	YR-ZAN
OO-MHB	Piper PA-28-236 Dakota	28-8011143	G-BMHB D6-PAD N81321 N9593N
OO-MIL	SEEMS MS.885 Super Rallye	5390	F-BLSD
OO-MJE	BAe.146 Series 200	E-2192	(OO-DJI) G-6-192
OO-MJK	Beech A36 Bonanza	E-1319	D-EKIX(2)
OO-MKD	Reims/Cessna F150K	F15000546	
OO-MLB	Reims/Cessna F150M	F15001335	
OO-MLD	Tipsy T.66S Nipper III	2071	
OO-MLF	Piper PA-34-200T Seneca II	34-7970216	N2245Z
OO-MLG	Cessna 560XL Citation Excel	560-5028	CS-DDB N528XL N5203J
OO-MLS	Piper PA-28R-200 Cherokee Arrow II	28R-7335221	D-EORW N55358
OO-MMD	SNCAN/Stampe SV.4C	56	F-BMMD (OO-MMD) F-BMMD ALAT F-BAYR CEV
OO-MMJ	Cessna 172R (Conversion to Thielert diesel in progress)	17280361	D-ERPB F-WQLN 4X-CHY N567A 4X-AHY
OO-MMR	Robinson R-22B2 Beta	3134	
OO-MNM	Piper PA-18-150 Super Cub	18-8009035	N82675
OO-MOB	SOCATA TB-10 Tobago	786	D-EALL(2)
OO-MOG	Wassmer Jodel D.112 Club	1293	F-BMOG
OO-MOM	Commander Aircraft 114B	14615	N6031Y
OO-MON	Stampe & Renard/Stampe SV.4B	1172	V-30
OO-MOR	Morane-Saulnier MS.317	6533/279	N315MS F-BGIL Fr.AF
OO-MOU	SAN Jodel DR.1050 Ambassadeur	399	F-BLJC
OO-MPG	Beech A36 Bonanza	E-2461	G-BPHM N1558W
OO-MPJ	Holste MH.1521M Broussard	195	F-GDPY Fr.AF
OO-MPK	Cessna 172RG Cutlass RG	172RG0057	N5359R
OO-MPS	Robinson R-44 Raven	1003	D-HALC
OO-MQA	Cessna 150M	15077810	N7684U
OO-MQD	Cessna 172M	17261945	N12355
OO-MQH	Hughes 269C (Damaged 9.2001)	112-0168	N8952F G-BIRW
OO-MSA	Morane-Saulnier MS.733 Alcyon	178	Fr.Navy
OO-MSG	Piper PA-38-112 Tomahawk	38-79A1113	N24355
OO-MSH	Fokker S-11- I Instructor (Painted as "E-26")	6269	(PH-HOC) E-26 PH-NEK

OO-MSN	Cessna Turbo 310R	310R0562	LX- III (6)
			5B-CGN
			D-IFOP
			N87743
OO-MUA	Reims/Cessna F172N	F17201801	OO-HNT
OO-MVG	Reims/Cessna F172M	F17201130	
OO-MVH	Cessna 182P Skylane	18262473	G-BBSG
			N52234
OO-MWM	Piper PA-28-180 Cherokee E	28-5777	D-EMWM
			N3674R
OO-NAT	SOCATA MS.880B Rallye Club	2253	G-BAOK
OO-NEA	Hughes 369E	0419E	HB-XQG
			D-HJAA
			F-GMMC
			D-HJAA
OO-NEE	Schweizer 269C-1	0163	N86G
OO-NEN	SIAI-Marchetti S.208 (Cvtd 205-20/R)	4-250	OO-HEN
OO-NHF	McDonnell-Douglas MD.900	900-00015	N9015P
OO-NHU	Aérospatiale AS.365N3 Dauphin 2	6665	F-WWOS
OO-NHV	Aérospatiale AS.365N3 Dauphin 2	6510	F-WWOZ
OO-NHZ	Aérospatiale AS.365N2 Dauphin 2	6450	N4H
			ZS-RDL
			G-BUTR
			F-WYMM
OO-NIK	Reims/Cessna F172M	F17201018	PH-GUS
OO-NIQ	North American Navion 4	NAV-4-1259	HB-ESE
			N4259K
OO-NKM	Robinson R-44 Astro	0092	D-HINN
OO-NLG	Piper PA-18 Super Cub 95	18-2044	PH-NLG
			R-67
			52-2444
OO-NLW	Piper PA-28-140 Cherokee	28-25368	PH-NLW
			N8172N
OO-NNA	SOCATA MS.893A Rallye Commodore 180	10604	F-BNNA
OO-NPT	Beech A23-19 Musketeer Sport III	MB-31	(OO-NBS)
			F-BNOX
OO-NQD	Schweizer 269C	S-1745	
OO-NRJ	Cessna U206G Stationair II	U20603579	G-BNRJ
			N7242N
OO-NSA	SOCATA MS.893A Rallye Commodore 180	10612	F-BNSA
OO-NTB	Robin DR.400/180R Remorqueur	1441	PH-NTR
OO-NTF	Reims FR172H Rocket	FR17200244	
OO-NUE	Aerotek Pitts S-2A	2078	(OO-RUT)
			N5VC
			N4C
OO-NVM	SOCATA MS.894A Minerva 220	11008	
OO-NYL	Piper PA-28-180 Cherokee D	28-4654	N5351L
OO-NZA	Reims/Cessna FRA150M Aerobat	FRA1500336	
OO-NZD	Grob G.115A	8068	OO-XZD
	(Sold as OH-XGA but not yet cancelled.)		G-BPSY
			D-EAMH
OO-NZF	Piper PA-28-181 Archer II	28-8590043	G-BRLE
			OY-CGY
			N152AV
OO-NZG	Piper PA-28-161 Warrior II	28-8316050	G-LADN
			G-BOLK
			N4295C
OO-NZM	Mooney M.20K Model 231	25-0295	N231LD
OO-OAA	Piper PA-18-135 Super Cub	18-568	(OO-OOA)
	(Built as PA-18 Super Cub 125 / L-21A)		R-213
			51-15682
			N7197K
OO-OAC	Robin HR.200/120B Club	298	
OO-OAW	Piper PA-18-150 Super Cub	18-5346	D-EOAW
			ALAT
			N10F
OO-OCC	Grob G.115A	8040	D-ENDS
			I-GROD
			D-EGVV
OO-OEL	Robinson R-22B2 Beta	3690	
OO-OLD	Piper J-3C-65 Cub	3307	N24619
			NC24619
OO-OLE	CASA I-131E Jungmann	1078	EC-DKV
			E3B-379
OO-OLI	Grumman-American AA-5A Cheetah	AA5A-0010	OO-HAL
OO-OMA	Cessna 172N	17270037	C-GQPQ
			N738KL
OO-ONG	Cessna 207A Stationair 8	20700601	D-EEFB(2)
	(Damaged 11.5.01)		N73512
OO-OPA	Reims/Cessna F172N	F17201670	OO-HNK(1)
OO-OPS	Boeing-Stearman PT-13D Kaydet	75-5093	G-ERIX
			N5055V
			42-16930
OO-OTO	SOCATA MS.880B Rallye Club	1264	
OO-OUI	SOCATA MS.893A Rallye Commodore 180	11710	N4389
			F-BSTL
OO-PAJ	Schweizer 269C	S-1777	PH-MDE
			N69A
OO-PAM	Stampe & Renard/Stampe SV.4B	1190	V-48
OO-PAS	Grumman-American AA-5 Traveler	AA5-0507	
OO-PAW	Piper PA-25-235 Pawnee C	25-5396	N8932L
OO-PAX	Stampe & Renard/Stampe SV.4B	1147	V-5
	(Major restoration in progress at owners' home)		
OO-PBL	Beech 77 Skipper	WA-250	D-EFBV
OO-PCH	Fokker S-11- 1 Instructor	6199	(PH-HOA)
OO-PCL	Cessna U206G Stationair 6-II	U20604724	(OO-LPK)
	(Reims-assembled with "c/n" 0011)		N732UF

OO-PCV	Pilatus PC-6/B2-H4 Turbo Porter	882	D-FSPA
OO-PCZ	Cessna T207A Turbo Stationair 7 (Soloy)	20700520	HB-CJL
			VH-SUQ
			N6425H
OO-PDG	Robinson R-44 Astro	0609	D-HALN
OO-PDP	Schweizer 269D	0010	N6139U
OO-PEF	Gulfstream-American AA-5B Tiger	AA5B-1128	OO-HRG
OO-PEP	SOCATA MS.880B Rallye Club	1814	F-BSZK
OO-PET	Piper PA-32-260 Cherokee Six	32-708	N3785W
OO-PEV	Hughes 269B	128-0402	
OO-PFB	Robinson R-44 Clipper	1274	
OO-PHI	Cessna 525 CitationJet	525-0115	(OO-TAU)
			N52141
OO-PHR	SAN Jodel DR.1050 Ambassadeur	97	F-BJJB
OO-PIF	Piper PA-32-300 Cherokee Six	32-7440073	N552TW
OO-PJC	Piel CP.301A Emeraude	211	F BIJK
OO-PJG	CEA DR.221 Dauphin	89	F-BPCM
OO-PKP	Piper PA-34-200T Seneca II	34-7570055	N328VA
			OO-PKP
			(OO-PVW)
			N32800
OO-PLC	SIAI-Marchetti S.208	2-21	OO-HIK
OO-PLM	SIAI-Marchetti S.205-18/F	002	OO-HAG
			I-SIAA
OO-PLR	Wassmer WA.40 Super IV	47	PH-PUT
OO-PMA	Enstrom F-28A	263	(OO-BAN)
OO-PMB	Robin DR.400/180R Remorqueur	1366	
OO-PMH	Robinson R-22B2 Beta	2832	
OO-PMS	Grumman-American AA-1B Trainer	AA1B-0354	
OO-PMT	Robinson R-22B2 Beta	3447	N71980
OO-POO	Robinson R-44 Raven	1282	D-HALE
OO-POS	SAN Jodel D.117 Grand Tourisme	430	F-BHNO
OO-POU	Piper PA-18-150 Super Cub	18-7865	D-EHRY
OO-PPD	Schweizer 269C	S-1295	D-HLAB
OO-PPE	Cessna F172H	F172-0557	
OO-PRA	Piper PA-28-140 Cherokee D	28-7125218	PH-SRA
			N11C
OO-PRB	Robinson R-22B2 Beta	2937	N937JC
OO-PRF	Reims/Cessna F150L	F15000840	F-BTUA
OO-PRG	Reims/Cessna F150M	F15001185	F-BVXS
OO-PRH	Reims/Cessna F150M	F15001183	F-BVXP
OO-PRK	Cessna 150M (Wfu, sold as spares)	15077811	N7685U
OO-PRL	Reims/Cessna FA150K Aerobat	FA1500008	
OO-PRN	Reims/Cessna FA150K Aerobat	FA1500031	
OO-PRS	Reims/Cessna F172M	F17201044	N14498
OO-PRV	Enstrom F-28A	146	F-BUIL
OO-PRW	Enstrom F-28A	258	G-LERN
			G-BBRS
OO-PST	Robinson R-44 Astro	0693	D-HALU(2)
OO-PTC	Grumman-American AA-1B Trainer	AA1B-0466	D-EFDM
			(N9866L)
OO-PTF	Piper PA-30 Twin Comanche B	30-1586	I-UMBO
			N8429Y
OO-PTR	Robinson R-44 Raven II	10476	
	(Reservation .05)		
OO-PUS	Erco 415CD Ercoupe	4577	NC3876H
OO-PVA	Tipsy T.66 Nipper III	A-116	OO-79
	(Used wings of c/n 78 (OO-69) in construction)		
OO-PVI	Christen Pitts S-2B	5144	N260K
	(Damaged 7.8.04)		
OO-PWA	SNCAN/Stampe SV.4C	279	N4BH
			F-WCKQ
			F-BCKQ
OO-PWW	Cessna 182P	18261095	G-LSKW
			OO-PWW
			N7455Q
OO-PYT	Cirrus SR.20	1461	N504CD
OO-RAA	Piper PA-38-112 Tomahawk	38-79A0625	N2426K
OO-RAB	Piper PA-38-112 Tomahawk	38-79A0569	D-EKTS
			N2313K
OO-RAC	CEA DR.220 2+2	4	F-BNVF
OO-RAG	Piper PA-32R-301 Saratoga SP	3213004	G-WILI
			N9128N
			N9582N
OO-RAQ	Reims/Cessna F172K	F17200788	(D-ECKJ)
OO-RAV	Piper PA-32R-300 Cherokee Lance	32R-7680031	OO-HAQ
			N4578X
OO-RCY	Piper PA-28-161 Cadet	2841166	G-RCYI
			N9185F
OO-REL	Cessna 140	9067	OO-ACA
OO-RES	Rockwell Commander 112A	373	(OO-CWR)
			G-NELL
			OY-DLJ
			N1373J
OO-RFF	Robinson R-44 Raven II	10691	
	(Reservation .05)		
OO-RIK	Aeronca 11AC Chief	1598	
OO-RJA	Robinson R-22 Beta	1838	
OO-RJC	Robin DR.300/125 Petit Prince	646	
OO-RJL	Robinson R-22 Beta	2319	
OO-RJP	Robinson R-22 Beta	1867	N4063C
OO-RJR	Robinson R-22 Beta	1624	
OO-RLD	Miles M.65 Gemini 1A	6285	G-AISD
			OO-RLD
			(OO-PRD)
			VP-KDH
			G-AISD

OO-RMA	SOCATA TB-9 Tampico	80	G-BKPL SE-GFL
OO-RMB	Reims/Cessna FA150K Aerobat	FA1500079	
OO-RMF	SNCAN/Stampe SV.4C (CofA exp. 18.7.97; restoration in progress)	480	F-BDBQ
OO-RMU	Reims/Cessna F150M	F15001339	(N1646C) N96103
OO-ROB	Rockwell 690B Commander	11409	N81646
OO-ROC	Maule M-7-235C Super Rocket	4037C	(OO-NDA) N5671R
OO-ROD	Beech A36 Bonanza	E-316	N9488Q
OO-ROR	Stampe & Renard/Stampe SV.4B (Restoration project)	1161	V-19
OO-ROS	Mooney M.20J Model 201	24-0592	N6201S
OO-ROX	Cessna 150M (Damaged in accident 21.1.2004)	15076064	PH-ROX N66462
OO-RSJ	Reims/Cessna FA150L Aerobat	FA1500110	(OO-BSJ) PH-BSJ D-ECPN
OO-RTD	Gulfstream-American AA-5A Cheetah	AA5A-0826	OO-HRP
OO-RTE	Gulfstream-American AA-5B Tiger	AA5B-1135	(OO-HRV)
OO-RTF	Reims/Cessna F177RG Cardinal RG (Reims-assembled 177RG c/n 177RG0196)	F177RG0033	(N8296G)
OO-RTK	Gulfstream-American AA-5A Cheetah	AA5A-0766	(OO-HRO)
OO-RTN	Varga 2150A Kachina	VAC152-80	OO-HTA N8360J
OO-RTO	Gulfstream-American AA-5A Cheetah	AA5A-0726	OO-HRE
OO-RTP	Bellanca 8GCBC Scout	342-80	OO-HTF
OO-RUD	Robin HR.100/200B Royale	123	
OO-RWB	Robinson R-22 Beta	1868	N4076A
OO-RWC	Robinson R-22B2 Beta	3473	N75170
OO-RWF	Robinson R-44 Astro	0458	
OO-RWG	Cessna 401	401-0204	D-IAMG G-AWDM (N7836F)
OO-RYB	Dassault Falcon 20F-5 (Reservation 31.1.05)	262	(OO-MDN) D2-ESV F-GHVR C-GTLU N501AS VH-WLH N750ME N720ML N4427F F-WJMK
OO-RYP	Rockwell 112 Commander	167	D-EGHT LX-GHB N1167J
OO-RZA	Robinson R-44 Raven	0883	
OO-RZZ	Robinson R-22 Beta	1461	N4023K
OO-SAB	Piper PA-23-250 Aztec	27-152	OY-AFE N4633P
OO-SAN	Piper PA-32-260 Cherokee Six	32-646	G-AZYE 5Y-AEA N3732W
OO-SAR	Robinson R-44 Raven II (Reservation .05)	10666	
OO-SAT	Bell 407	53061	C-GFNQ
OO-SAV	Cessna 560XL Citation Excel	560-5189	OY-GKC N5073G
OO-SDU	Beech B300 Super King Air	FL-368	N6068V
OO-SEP	Cessna F172G	F172-0183	
OO-SER	Cessna 152 (Wfu and stored)	15279819	N757LF
OO-SEU	Cessna 172M	17261130	(OO-SEX) N20249
OO-SEV	Cessna 152	15281644	N65603
OO-SEY	Cessna F172G	F172-0214	
OO-SEZ	Cessna 150E	15061495	N4095U
OO-SFL	Rockwell Commander 114	14018	N10481 D-EFWH
OO-SFM	Airbus A.330-301	030	F-GMDA F-WWKD
OO-SFN	Airbus A.330-301	037	F-GMDB
OO-SFO	Airbus A.330-301	045	F-GMDC
OO-SGI	Cessna P210N Pressurized Centurion II (Written off 8.8.01)	00753	N6333W
OO-SHB	Reims/Cessna F152	F15201570	
OO-SHC	Reims/Cessna F172N	F17201770	
OO-SHD	Reims/Cessna F172N	F17201773	
OO-SHE	Reims/Cessna F182Q Skylane	F18200098	
OO-SHT	Robinson R-22B2 Beta (Written off 15.3.03)	3190	
OO-SII	Cessna 150F	15062208	N8908S
OO-SIL	Cessna F150F	F150-0022/15062890	(N8790G)
OO-SKB	Cessna F150J	F150-0423	
OO-SKI	Robin HR.100/250TR (CofA expired 22.3.96, stored)	540	F-GFBD F-OCAM F-GAEM
OO-SKL	Beech B200 Super King Air	BB-1348	D2-EST S9-NAO N2842B
OO-SKM	Beech B200 Super King Air	BB-1407	D2-ESQ N2763B
OO-SKP	Cessna S550 Citation SII	550-0007	CS-DCE N30CX TC-SAM N573CC N51JH (N1256P)
OO-SKV	Cessna 560 Citation V	560-0153	SE-DYZ N1SN (N153VP) N502F N502T N6804Y
OO-SLQ	Robinson R-44 Raven	10070	
OO-SML	SIAI-Marchetti SF.260	2-33	
OO-SMM	SIAI-Marchetti SF.260	2-47	
OO-SMO	SIAI-Marchetti SF.260	2-53	
OO-SOO	Hughes 369E	0447E	D-HGWM(2)
OO-SOT	Westland Lysander Mk.IIIA (Painted as RCAF2442-"D-MA") (Damaged 17.7.01, restoration in progress)	unkn	
OO-SPC	Cessna 150F	15062039	PH-ICA N8739S
OO-SPE	Cessna F150G	F150-0191	SE-FBB LN-BDO SE-FBB
OO-SPG	Piper PA-18 Super Cub 95 (Exchanged fuselage with c/n 18-2060 - see OO-LGB) (Painted in Belgian Army OL-L47 markings)	18-1650	(OO-VIC) OO-LGB OO-HMU ALAT 51-15650
OO-SPJ	Piper PA-18 Super Cub 95	18-1547	ALAT 51-15547
OO-SPM	SNCAN/Stampe SV.4C	349	F-BCOC
OO-SPP	Cessna 152	15285903	PH-PJM G-BRCB N95490
OO-SPQ	Piper PA-18 Super Cub 95 (Belgian Army L-44 markings)	18-3118	LN-LJI OL-L44 L-44 53-4718
OO-SPU	Cessna U206G Stationair 6-II	U20605375	F-GMSA N6189U
OO-SPY	Cessna F172H	F172-0569	
OO-SSG	Airbus A.319-112	1160	EI-CZF OO-SSG D-AVWL
OO-SSK	Airbus A.319-112	1336	F-WQRU G-CBTP OO-SSK D-AVYL
OO-SSM	Airbus A.319-112	1388	F-WQRV G-CBSY OO-SSM D-AVYG
OO-SST	Rockwell 114A Commander	14521	D-EDGT N5904N
OO-STG	Cessna 421C Golden Eagle	0879	D-IXXX N5638C (N80WD) N5638C
OO-STK	Slingsby T.67M Firefly Mk.II (Reservation .05)	2018	S5-DGS HB-NBC G-BMIT
OO-STL	Robinson R-22B2 Beta	3691	
OO-STP	Robinson R-44 Astro	0871	
OO-STY	Cessna 172N	17270980	N1381E
OO-SUN	Beech C23 Sundowner 180	M-1484	G-BBAT
OO-SUP	Schweizer 269C	S-1495	G-BSUP
OO-SVA	Stampe & Renard/Stampe SV.4B	1191	V-49
OO-SVB	Stampe & Renard/Stampe SV.4B	1185	PH-ZLS OO-SVB V-43
OO-SVG	Stampe & Renard/Stampe SV.4B (Preserved)	1163	V-21
OO-SVH	Stampe & Renard/Stampe SV.4B	1168	V-26
OO-SVK	Robin HR.200/120B	250	PH-SVK F-GMKA
OO-SVS	SNCAN/Stampe SV.4C	320	N2272K N320RL N10WN F-BCLT
OO-SVT	SNCAN/Stampe SV.4E	9	N9SV N15JJ N17810 F-BGGO Fr.Mil
OO-SVV	Stampe & Renard/Stampe SV.4B	1200	G-DANN OO-SVV V-58
OO-SWT	Robinson R-44 Raven II	10305	
OO-SXA	Embraer EMB.121 Xingu	121038	PT-MBF
OO-SXB	Embraer EMB.121 Xingu (CofA exp. 10.11.02, wfu and used for spares)	121040	PT-MBH
OO-SXC	Embraer EMB.121 Xingu	121042	PT-MBJ
OO-SXD	Embraer EMB.121 Xingu	121043	PT-MBK
OO-SXE	Embraer EMB.121 Xingu (CofA exp. 15.12.00, stored engineless)	121045	PT-MBM
OO-TAA	BAe. 146 Series 300QT	E-3151	G-TNTR SE-DIT G-BRGM
OO-TAB	SOCATA TB-9 Tampico	130	
OO-TAC	SEEMS MS.892A Rallye Commodore 150	10473	

OO-TAD	BAe. 146 Series 300QT	E-3166	G-TNTM RP-C480 G-TNTM G-BSLZ G-6-166
OO-TAE	BAe. 146 Series 300QT	E-3182	G-TNTG G-BSUY
OO-TAF	BAe. 146 Series 300QT	E-3186	G-TNTK G-BSXL G-6-186
OO-TAH	BAe. 146 Series 300QT	E-3168	G-TNTL RP-C479 G-TNTL G-BSGI (RP-C479) G-BSGI G-6-168
OO-TAJ	BAe. 146 Series 300QT	E-3153	G-TNTE G-BRPW
OO-TAK	BAe. 146 Series 300QT	E-3150	G-TJPM SE-DIM G-BRGK
OO-TAO	SEEMS MS.892A Rallye Commodore 150	10457	(OO-TAC)
OO-TAR	BAe. 146 Series 200QT	E-2067	G-TNTB G-5-067 (N145AC) (G-BNFG)
OO-TAS	BAe. 146 Series 300QT	E-3154	EC-FFY EC-712 G-TNTF G-BRXI G-6-154
OO-TAU	BAe. 146 Series 200QT	E-2100	EC-GQP D-ANTJ G-TNTJ G-BOHK G-5-100
OO-TAW	BAe. 146 Series 200QT	E-2089	EC-EPA EC-281 G-TNTH (F-GTNT) G-BNYC G-5-089
OO-TBB	SOCATA TB-10 Tobago	1449	
OO-TCI	Airbus A.320-214	1975	EI-DBD F-WWBI
OO-TCJ	Airbus A.320-214	1787	EI-DBC SE-RCB F-WWDT
OO-TCK	Airbus A.320-212	343	F-OHFT G-UKLK G-BWKO N485GX F-WWDC
OO-TCL	Airbus A320-212	436	F-GJVU G-BXAT F-GJVY (PH-GCL) F-WWDE
OO-TDA	Robin R.2160 Acrobin	310	
OO-TDF	SOCATA MS.894A Minerva 220	12136	F-BUGF
OO-TES	Cessna TR182 Skylane	R18201331	F-GHDQ N2330S
OO-TGM	de Havilland DH.82A Tiger Moth	3318	G-ADCG A2126 A728 BB731 G-ADCG
OO-THL	Schweizer 269C	S-1400	HB-XVJ
OO-THO	SOCATA MS.887 Rallye 125	2171	F-OCYR
OO-TIT	SOCATA Rallye 110ST Galopin	3212	
OO-TJK	Partenavia P.68B Observer	372-28-OB	
OO-TMC	Cessna 152	15282624	N89085
OO-TMD	Reims/Cessna F152	F15201513	D-EETK(2) F-GBJC
OO-TME	Bombardier Learjet 60	60-255	N5013U
OO-TMG	Piper PA-28-181 Archer II	28-8590022	D-EFMG(3) N4385C
OO-TML	Piper PA-34-220T Seneca V	3449089	N4137X
OO-TMM	Beech 35-C33 Debonair	CD-1050	F-BNTH
OO-TMT	Piper PA-28-161 Warrior II	28-7916112	N9538N
OO-TMW	de Havilland DH.82A Tiger Moth	84207	G-AMTF ZK-AVE G-AMTF T7842
OO-TNA	Boeing 737-3T0	23569	N13331
OO-TNB	Boeing 737-3T0	23578	N39340
OO-TNC	Boeing 737-301F	23513	N559AU N334US N323P
OO-TND	Boeing 737-301F	23515	N346US N325P
OO-TNE	Boeing 737-3Q8	23535	TF-ELQ TF-SUN N535GE TJ-CBF SP-LMB N102GU EC-EAK
OO-TNF	Boeing 737-3Q8F (Reservation 2.05)	24131	CS-TGP OO-LTX EC-FFC EC-592 EC-EII EC-159
OO-TOB	SOCATA TB-10 Tobago	26	
OO-TOR	Robinson R-44 Raven II	10639	
OO-TOT	SOCATA MS.880B Rallye Club	1226	
OO-TOW	Cessna 150K	15071603	N6103G
OO-TOX	SNCAN/Stampe SV.4C	150	F-BMMF Fr.Mil
OO-TOY	Robin DR.400/120 Petit Prince	1042	F-BXJJ
OO-TPA	Cessna T210N Turbo Centurion II	21064604	N9808Y
OO-TRB	Reims/Cessna F172P	F17202108	OO-HRB(2)
OO-TRD	Reims/Cessna F152	F15201950	
OO-TRJ	Reims/Cessna F172P	F17202140	(OO-XRJ)
OO-TRU	SOCATA Rallye 110ST Galopin	3209	F-GBKR
OO-TTB	SOCATA TB-200 Tobago XL	2082	F-OIUL
OO-TTD	Aérospatiale AS.350BA Ecureuil	9017	
OO-TUA	Boeing 737-4K5	24127	D-AHLL SP-KEK D-AHLL
OO-TUB	Boeing 737-4K5	27831	D-AHLU
OO-TUC	Boeing 767-341ER	24844	N484TC PP-VOL
OO-TUF	Fokker F.28-0100	11373	(OM-AAC) N893US PH-EZL
OO-TUG	Piper PA-25-235 Pawnee C	25-4088	N4447Y
OO-TUI	Boeing 737-4K5	24125	EC-IPF D-AHLJ SP-KEI D-AHLJ
OO-TUJ	Reims/Cessna F177RG Cardinal RG	F177RG0064	F-BTUJ
OO-TUT	SOCATA Rallye 100ST-D	2888	D-EDVO(2)
OO-TVB	Reims/Cessna F150L	F15001118	
OO-TVI	Robinson R-22 Beta	0824	G-OLIE G-BOUW
OO-TVK	Piper PA-32R-301 Saratoga IIHP	3246141	PH-AEH N41409
OO-TVO	Piper PA-28-140 Cherokee F	28-7325008	N15158
OO-TWA	Piper PA-28-180 Cherokee E	28-5608	(D-EHGC) N2394R
OO-TWJ	Aeronca 7AC Champion	3625	
OO-TWP	Aeronca 7AC Champion	3624	
OO-TYP	CEA DR.250/160 Capitaine	81	F-BNVV
OO-TZA	Airbus A.300B4-203F	155	G-TNTI N72987 TC-ALR N72987 (N987C) N224EA F-GBNS
OO-TZB	Airbus A.300B4-203F	261	N229KW TC-ALV N229KW N14975 N233EA F-GDVA
OO-TZC	Airbus A.300B4-203F	210	N210TN G-BYDH F-OHPO F-WHPK SX-BAZ N213PA F-WZMK
OO-TZD	Airbus A.300B4-203F	247	F-WWAO OO-TZD N247TN PK-JIE N247JM VR-BNK N205PA F-WZMP
OO-UAR	CEA Jodel DR.1051 Sicile	419	F-BLAR
OO-UBY	Reims FR172J Rocket	FR17200498	D-EDJV
OO-ULM	Robinson R-22B2 Beta	3692	
OO-UNY	Schweizer 269CB-300	0012	
OO-UOZ	Robin HR.100/210 Safari	165	F-BUOZ
OO-URS	Mooney M.20J Model 201	24-1138	N952AP
OO-USA	Piper PA-18-150 Super Cub	18-3824	R-134 54-2424
OO-USK	Christen A-1 Husky	1056	F-GGAQ F-WGAQ N9590C
OO-USN	Boeing-Stearman E75N1	75-4695	N17PT N37744 YS-272P N54280 42-16532
OO-VAB	SOCATA MS.880B Rallye Club	879	(TU-TDW)
OO-VAC	Boeing 737-8BK	33014	N334CT OO-VAC N5573L N1787B
OO-VAD	Slingsby T-67M Firefly	2010	G-BLER

OO-VAF	Nord 1101 Noralpha	119	F-BHER F-ZJDG
OO-VAK	Reims/Cessna FR182 Skylane RG	FR18200001	(F-GDPL) TR-LBF F-GBFH F-WZAU
OO-VAP	Eurocopter AS.355N Ecureuil (Stored)	5730	F-WQDN
OO-VAS	Boeing 767-86Q	30285	N712BA
OO-VBA	Bell 206B Jet Ranger II	4535	C-GGDQ (N2418P)
OO-VBR	Boeing 737-4YO	24314	F-GMBR HL7256
OO-VCB	Robinson R-22 Beta	0697	
OO-VCC	Bell 206B Jet Ranger II	4057	(OO-RJL) PH-VCK (PH-VCH) (PH-VCK) OO-VCC C-FFNM
OO-VCD	Robinson R-22 Beta	1063	N8046J
OO-VCE	Robinson R-22 Beta	0505	OO-XCE G-BMIZ N2270B
OO-VCG	Cessna 152 (Crashed 24.7.04)	15279528	C-GUSO
OO-VCJ	Robinson R-22 Beta	1817	
OO-VCL	Reims/Cessna FA152 Aerobat	FA1520423	SE-LBK OH-NEW
OO-VCM	Cessna 152	15281215	N49274
OO-VCR	Cessna 152-II	15283529	N53295
OO-VCT	Piper PA-28-140 Cherokee	28-22552	PH-VCT N11C
OO-VCU	Piper PA-28-161 Warrior II	2841245	
OO-VCY	MBB-Kawasaki BK.117A-3	7056	OO-XCY (OO-VCY) (N156BK) D-HBND
OO-VDB	Cessna 210F Centurion	21058726	N1826F
OO-VDG	Piper PA-28RT-201 Arrow IV	28R-7918228	N2936F (N999EA) N2936F
OO-VDJ	Piper PA32RT-300 Lance II	32R-7985102	PH-CBU N2113Z
OO-VDK	Enstrom F.28F	765	G-BSAU N5FX
OO-VDS	Jodel D.112 Club (Type "D.11-09") (Damaged 7.6.00)	1461	
OO-VEG	Boeing 737-36N	28568	EI-TVQ OO-VEG
OO-VEH	Boeing 737-36N	28571	EI-TVR OO-VEH
OO-VEJ	Boeing 737-405	24271	LN-BRB
OO-VEK	Boeing 737-405	24270	LN-BRA
OO-VEL	Robinson R-44 Astro	0538	D-HALD
OO-VEN	Boeing 737-36N	28586	EI-TVN N1786B
OO-VEP	Boeing 737-43Q	28489	VH-VGA EI-TVA B-18671
OO-VES	Boeing 737-43Q	28493	VH-VGE EI-TVB B-18676
OO-VEX	Boeing 737-36N	28670	EI-TVS OO-VEX
OO-VFB	Beech A36 Bonanza	E-1910	N1835P
OO-VFI	Beech A36 Bonanza	E-926	F-GJFY OO-CJA F-GCJA F-ODDL
OO-VFK	Piper PA-28-181 Archer II	28-8390004	N82674
OO-VFR	Piper PA-28-181 Archer II	2890200	LX-EDZ N9247Q
OO-VGV	Rockwell Commander 112	196	OO-HRF N1196J
OO-VHB	Piper PA-28RT-201 Arrow IV	28R-7918079	N2212W
OO-VHL	SOCATA MS.880B Rallye Club	2558	F-BXDI
OO-VHV	Beech E90 King Air	LW-316	N77WZ N57MS F-GJHM N38CR N46HM N70YC N70KC
OO-VIA	SOCATA TB-20 Trinidad	1031	F-GHZP
OO-VIC	Schweizer 269C	S-1493	G-JHAS
OO-VIK	Piper PA-18 Super Cub 95	18-5822	N7484D
OO-VIP	Piper PA-32RT-300 Lance II	32R-7985066	OO-HCU N3050K
OO-VIW	Piper PA-18 Super Cub 95	18-1544	OO-HMW ALAT 51-15544
OO-VKB	Beech A36 Bonanza	E-994	N17602
OO-VLE	Fokker F.27-050	20132	PH-ARG D-AFKD (LN-AKG) PH-EXF
OO-VLJ	Fokker F.27-050	20105	PH-ARE Z-WPH PH-ARE SX-BSF PH-ARE D-AFKB PH-EXE
OO-VLK	Fokker F.27-050	20122	PH-FZF OE-LFA PH-EXG
OO-VLL	Fokker F.27-050	20144	TF-JMG PH-DMD SE-LEM OE-LFD PH-EXS
OO-VLM	Fokker F.27-050	20135	PH-VLM OO-VLM LN-BBD (LN-AKH) PH-EXI
OO-VLN	Fokker F.27-050	20145	PH-VLN OO-VLN LN-BBE (LN-AKI) PH-EXT
OO-VLO	Fokker F.27-050	20127	ES-AFL OY-MMJ PH-EXL
OO-VLQ	Fokker F.27-050	20159	EC-GBH EC-869 D-AFKI PH-LBT (ST-ALP) PH-EXC
OO-VLR	Fokker F.27-050	20121	PH-ARF (OO-VLJ) PT-SLL PH-ARF D-AFKC PH-EXF
OO-VLS	Fokker F.27-050	20109	EC-GBG EC-868 D-AFKH (VH-FND) PH-EXR (PH-WDL) PH-EXR
OO-VLV	Fokker F.27-050	20160	EC-GDD EC-871 D-AFKJ PH-EXD (PH-LBV) (ST-ALR) PH-EXD
OO-VLX	Fokker F.27-050	20177	PH-ZFD OO-VLX EI-FKC PH-EXC
OO-VLY	Fokker F.27-050	20181	PH-ZFC OO-VLY EI-FKD PH-EXG
OO-VLZ	Fokker F.27-050	20264	TF-JMU T9-BBC TF-JMU PH-DMB OE-LFF PH-EXA
OO-VMB	Dassault Falcon 2000	74	F-GJSC HB-IUZ F-WWMH
OO-VMC	Piper PA-28-161 Warrior III	2842016	N9262L
OO-VMH	Piaggio FWP.149D	026	90+16 AC+402 DE+392
OO-VMS	Robin DR.400/160 Chevalier	1124	
OO-VMX	Piper PA-28-261 Warrior III	2842040	(LX- . . .) N9506N N41225
OO-VOP	Piel CP.301A Emeraude	238	OO-VOR(1) OO-ANA
OO-VOR	Fiat G.46-4A	199	I- AEKI MM53293
OO-VOS	SAAB S.91D Safir	91434	PH-RLW
OO-VOV	Piper PA-25-235 Pawnee C	25-4340	F-BVOV N4626Y
OO-VPA	Robin HR.200/100 Club	91	
OO-VPC	Cessna 182P (Reims-assembled with "c/n" 0019) (Damaged 26.7.1994, stored at Southampton, UK)	18263928	D-EHTW N9859E
OO-VPD	Piper PA-34-220T Seneca III	3433140	I-KIDE N91648
OO-VPH	Dornier Do.27A-3 (Wfu and stored)	411	56+95 SA+116 SB+734 GA+387
OO-VPI	Robin DR.400/180 Régent (Damaged 15.5.01)	1216	

OO-VPJ	Dornier Do.27A-4	446	57+18 PY+223 PD+101
OO-VRE	Reims/Cessna F172M	F17201287	(OO-WAO)
OO-VRM	Cessna 152	15281478	D-EBTF N64922
OO-VRV	Jodel D-11 Club	CD.02	
OO-VSA	Robin HR.200/100 Club	63	
OO-VSL	Robin DR.400/160 Chevalier	875	
OO-VSV	SNCAN/Stampe SV.4C	248	F-BEKI Fr. Navy F-BCKE
OO-VTM	American AG-5BTiger	10054	LX-AWD N11927
OO-VTS	Cessna 172L	17259253	N7553G
OO-VVA	Piper PA-18-150 Super Cub (Stored)	18-8281	
OO-VVB	Piper PA-18-150 Super Cub (Stored)	18-8282	
OO-VVC	Piper PA-18-150 Super Cub	18-8286	
OO-VVD	Piper PA-18-150 Super Cub	18-8304	
OO-VVF	Piper PA-18-150 Super Cub	18-8319	
OO-VVG	Piper PA-18-150 Super Cub	18-8332	
OO-VVH	Piper PA-18-150 Super Cub	18-8381	
OO-VVK	SAN Jodel D.140R Abeille	503	
OO-VWE	Agusta-Bell 206B Jet Ranger III	8563	G-NATO G-FLCH G-BGGX
OO-VWK	Piper PA-34-220T Seneca III	34-8133182	HB-LQL N2913L
OO-VZZ	Robin DR.400/180R Remorqueur	962	D-EEJA
OO-WAC	Reims/Cessna F150M	F15001250	
OO-WAD	Reims/Cessna F172M	F17201342	
OO-WAE	Reims/Cessna FRA150M Aerobat (W/o 14.9.02)	FRA1500274	
OO-WAF	Reims/Cessna FRA150L Aerobat	FRA1500148	PH-WAE
OO-WAL	Cessna 182R Skylane	18268083	N9870H
OO-WAN	Grumman-American AA-5 Traveler	AA5-0517	
OO-WAO	Reims/Cessna F172M	F17201324	
OO-WAR	Piper PA-28-161 Warrior III	2816112	N9252Q
OO-WBF	Robinson R-22B2 Beta	3446	N71970
OO-WBS	Robinson R-44 Raven II	10429	
OO-WDB	Robinson R-22 Beta	2081	N23272
OO-WEA	Beagle B.121 Pup 100	012	G-AWEA
OO-WEJ	Robin R.1180TD Aiglon	275	F-GCUJ
OO-WEO	Reims/Cessna FA150K Aerobat	FA1500002	D-EKKF
OO-WER	Eurocopter EC.120BColibri	1321	F-WQDI
OO-WIF	Grumman-American AA-1B Trainer	AA1B-0264	
OO-WIL	Stampe & Renard/Stampe SV.4B	1184	V-42
OO-WIM	SEEMS MS.880B Rallye Club	342	F-BKZH
OO-WIN	Reims/Cessna F172K	F17200760	F-WLIO
OO-WIQ	Reims/Cessna FRA150L Aerobat	FRA1500158	
OO-WIU	Reims/Cessna F172M	F17200912	
OO-WIW	Reims/Cessna F177RG Cardinal RG	F177RG0053	
OO-WIX	Reims/Cessna F150L	F15000890	
OO-WIY	Reims FR172J Rocket	FR17200353	
OO-WLA	Schweizer 269C	S-1815	
OO-WLF	Grob G.115A	8032	D-EOFT(2)
OO-WMB	Wassmer WA.41 Baladou	153	F-BOYN
OO-WOT	Tipsy T.66 Nipper II (Cr.7.7.84 - under rebuild using fuselage of kit c/n 71, ex OO-69 ntu)	49	PH-MEV (PH-MES) (PH-SUS) EL-AEV OO-MON (OY-AEU)
OO-WOU	SEEMS MS.880B Rallye Club	329	F-BKYX
OO-WPS	Piper PA-32-301T Turbo Saratoga	32-8024011	N8169Y
OO-WVS	Cessna 172N	17269394	C-GZJI (N737FY)
OO-WWE(2)	Cessna 152	15285576	D-ESBE N93952
OO-YAC	Piper PA-28-161 Warrior II	28-8316019	N83094
OO-YAK	Yakovlev Yak-11 (Reserved as F-AZYA 1.2004)	unkn	EAF-079
OO-YAO	Reims/Cessna F172H (Robertson STOL)	F17200695	G-AYAO
OO-YIO	Robin DR.400/120 Dauphin 2+2	2038	
OO-YOB	Robin DR.400/160 Chevalier	1943	
OO-YOL	Piper J-3C-65 Cub	12949	F-BCPD 44-80653
OO-YUG	Zlin Z.526F Trenér Master	1031	YU-DJX JRV41106
OO-YVO	SOCATA MS.880B Rallye Club	2848	
OO-. . .	Cessna 414A (Candidate 2003)	414A1008	(N414CC) (N1244V)
OO-. . .	SOCATA MS.880B Rallye Club	1252	F-BPYZ

BALLOONS AND AIRSHIPS

OO-ADL	Cameron V-56 HAFB	496	
OO-AFC	Cameron N-77 HAFB (CofA exp. 27.9.94, stored)	1077	G-JAFC
OO-BAA	Thunder/Colt 77A HAFB	653	(OO-BEM)
OO-BAD	Cameron O-77 HAFB	1103	
OO-BAF	Schröder Fire Balloons G 26/16 HAFB	414	
OO-BAG	Cameron V-56 HAFB	417	
OO-BAH	Cameron A-315 HAFB	4255	
OO-BAI	Duronadeau L-250 HAFB	21	
OO-BAJ	Cameron N-77 HAFB	1163	
OO-BAL	Van dem Bemden 460m3 Gas Balloon	VDB.86	
OO-BAO	Ultramagic S-90 HAFB	90/42	
OO-BAQ	Schröder Fire Balloons G 30/24 HAFB	954	
OO-BAU	Cameron N-77 HAFB	2354	
OO-BAX	Cameron N-56 HAFB (Wfu and stored)	385	G-BSUN
OO-BAY	Cameron N-65 HAFB (Wfu and stored)	1032	
OO-BAZ	Stuttgart 360m3 Gas Balloon	unkn	
OO-BBB	Raven S-60A HAFB	179	D-Ruttgers-Club
OO-BBD	Cameron N-90 HAFB	2607	
OO-BBF	Cameron V-77 HAFB	1715	
OO-BBG	Cameron A-210 HAFB	2846	G-BUGF
OO-BBH	Cameron A-180 HAFB	3243	G-BVIU
OO-BBI	Cameron N-77 HAFB	1483	(OO-BDS)
OO-BBJ	Durondeau L-250 HAFB	19	
OO-BBK	Raven Europe FS-57A HAFB	E-390	
OO-BBL	Cameron V-56 HAFB (CofA exp. 31.5.2000, wfu and stored)	1243	(OO-BOS)
OO-BBM	Colt 90A HAFB	2129	
OO-BBN	Cameron V-77 HAFB	1671	
OO-BBP	Cameron N-77 HAFB (Wfu and stored)	1513	
OO-BBS	Cameron O-90 HAFB	2054	
OO-BBU	Kubicek Orangina SS HAFB	43	
OO-BBV	Kubicek BB-37 HAFB	17	OK-3024
OO-BBW	Kubicek BB-60 HAFB	92	
OO-BBX	Aviatik B&B Ax8 HAFB	5	
OO-BBZ	Ultramagic M-160 HAFB (Reservn 1.05)	unkn	
OO-BCA	Cameron V-77 HAFB	596	
OO-BCD	Libert L.3000 HAFB	252-006	F-G . . . OO-BCD
OO-BCE	Ultramagic M-105 HAFB	105/03	EC-021
OO-BCF	Ultramagic H-77 HAFB	77/51	
OO-BCG	Raven-Europe S-60A HAFB	E-293	
OO-BCH	Lindstrand LBL-105A HAFB	158	
OO-BCI	Durondeau L.250 HAFB	006	
OO-BCJ	Cameron N-77 HAFB	2243	
OO-BCK	Schröder Fire Balloons G 36/24 HAFB	769	
OO-BCL	Cameron V-90 HAFB	2853	
OO-BCM	Durondeau L-220 HAFB (Wfu and stored)	003	
OO-BCN	Durondeau L.180 HAFB	001	
OO-BCO	Schröder Fire Balloons G 33/24 HAFB	748	
OO-BCP	Aerostar RX-7 HAFB	3233	
OO-BCQ	Schröder Fire Balloons G 40/24 HAFB	976	
OO-BCR	Ultramagic V-105 HAFB	105/17	
OO-BCS	Thunder AX10-150 S-II HAFB (Wfu and stored)	4906	
OO-BCT	Schröder Fire Balloons G 36/24 HAFB	742	
OO-BCU	Schröder Fire Balloons G 45/24 HAFB	900	
OO-BCV	Cameron N-105 HAFB (Wfu and stored)	1852	
OO-BCW	Kubicek BB-30 HAFB	101	
OO-BCX	Wörner NL-1000/STU Gas Balloon	1054	D-OCOX
OO-BCY	Libert L.3000 HAFB	286-011	
OO-BCZ	Kubicek BB-60 HAFB	168	
OO-BDA	Cameron N-105 HAFB (Wfu and stored)	3087	
OO-BDB	Cameron O-105 HAFB	3130	
OO-BDC	Lindstrand LBL-105A HAFB	530	
OO-BDD	Cameron O-77 HAFB	1734	(OO-BTJ)
OO-BDE	Cameron N-120 HAFB	3755	
OO-BDF	Aerostar S-60A HAFB	3263	
OO-BDG	Cameron A-210 HAFB	3728	
OO-BDH	Kubicek BB-45 HAFB	93	
OO-BDI	Lindstrand LBL-150A HAFB	616	
OO-BDJ	Lindstrand LBL-105A HAFB	571	
OO-BDK	Thunder/Colt AX8-90 S-II HAFB	1135	
OO-BDL	Raven-Europe S-55A HAFB	E-114	
OO-BDM	Ultramagic M-77 HAFB	77/48	
OO-BDN	Libert L.3000 HAFB	294-018	
OO-BDP	Lindstrand HS-110 Hot Air Airship	362	G-BWOO
OO-BDS	Raven-Europe S-55A HAFB	E-082	
OO-BDT	Thunder AX10-160 HAFB	1388	G-BPLU
OO-BDU	Cameron N-105 HAFB	3463	
OO-BDW	Ultramagic M-77 HAFB (Wfu and stored)	77/50	
OO-BDX	Cameron N-133 HAFB	4826	
OO-BDY	Cameron Z-180 HAFB	10218	
OO-BDZ	Cameron N-90 HAFB	1961	(LX-DLH)
OO-BEB	Raven-Europe FS-57A HAFB	E-O99	
OO-BEC	Libert L.3000 HAFB	292-016	
OO-BED	Cameron O-77 HAFB (Replaces envelope c/n 1262)	4487	
OO-BEF	Kubicek BB-26 HAFB	76	
OO-BEG	Cameron A-180 HAFB	10057	
OO-BEH	Cameron A-180 HAFB	10073	
OO-BEJ	Cameron N-120 HAFB (Wfu and stored)	4605	
OO-BEL	Cameron Waving Flag SSHAFB	10069	
OO-BEM(2)	Ultramagic M-105 HAFB	105/18	
OO-BEO	Cameron O-77 HAFB	1384	
OO-BEP	Schröder Fire Balloons G 30/24 HAFB	437	

OO-BEQ	Ultramagic M-145 SS HAFB	145/34	
OO-BER	Cameron N-77 HAFB	2279	
OO-BES	Thunder AX7-77 HAFB	950	PH-JVH
OO-BEU	Libert L.3000 HAFB	286-009	
OO-BEW	Cameron A-105 HAFB	2940	
OO-BEX	Cameron N-90 HAFB	2722	PH-BIH
OO-BEZ	Ultramagic S-90 HAFB	90/57	
OO-BFA	Cameron N-90 HAFB	4807	
OO-BFB	Cameron N-90 HAFB	2521	
OO-BFE	Cameron V-90 HAFB	3132	
OO-BFF	Cameron N-145 HAFB	2466	
OO-BFG(2)	HAFB, type unknown	unkn	
OO-BFH	Cameron N-90 HAFB	3543	
OO-BFO	Aerostar S-60A HAFB	3219	
OO-BFP	Colt 105A HAFB	1781	
OO-BFR	Colt 105A HAFB	711	PH-IFR
			G-BMHO
OO-BFT	Cameron N-90 HAFB	2594	
OO-BFU	Durondeau L.250 HAFB	007	
	(CofA exp. 14.7.1999, wfu and stored)		
OO-BFV	Cameron N-120 HAFB	4263	
OO-BGA	Cameron SS Montgolfiere HAFB	806	
	(Wfu and stored)		
OO-BGB	Schröder Fire Balloons G 26/24 HAFB	545	
OO-BGC	Cameron N-90 HAFB	2608	
OO-BGD	Cameron N-145 HAFB	3547	
OO-BGG	Cameron V-65 HAFB	2765	
OO-BGH	Cameron N-90 HAFB	3249	G-BVKI
	(Wfu and stored)		
OO-BGI	Cameron N-90 HAFB	2307	
OO-BHA	Kubicek BB-37 HAFB	112	
OO-BHB	Libert L.800 HAFB	140	
OO-BHC	Cameron Smurf SS HAFB	4266	
OO-BHD	Durondeau L-300 HAFB	20	
OO-BHF	Thunder AX6-56Z HAFB	355	G-DOLL
OO-BHH	Cameron V-65 HAFB	2766	
OO-BHI	Raven S-60A HAFB	244	F-GIBH
			HB-BDI
OO-BHJ	Cameron N-77 HAFB	1314	G-OOFI
OO-BHK(2)	Cameron A-160 HAFB	4929	
OO-BHL	Cameron O-90 HAFB	2865	
OO-BHM	Raven Europe S-60A HAFB	E-389	
OO-BHN	Libert L.1800 HAFB	296-020	
OO-BHO	Lindstrand LBL-90A HAFB	661	
OO-BHP	Raven Europe RX-7 HAFB	E-337	
OO-BHQ	Ultramagic N-250 HAFB	250/17	
OO-BHR	Raven Europe FS-57A HAFB	E-363	
OO-BHS	Lindstrand LBL-77B HAFB	444	
OO-BHT	Cameron Z-160 HAFB	10311	
OO-BHU	Cameron N-105 HAFB	3413	
OO-BHV	Lindstrand LBL-105A HAFB	764	
OO-BHW	Cameron Z-210 HAFB	10180	
OO-BIC	Durondeau L.220 HAFB	014	
	(Wfu and stored)		
OO-BID	Ultramagic N-180 HAFB	180/18	
OO-BIE (2)	Cameron A-180 HAFB	10075	
	(New envelope replacing c/n 2869, .01)		
OO-BIF	Libert L.3000 HAFB	290-014	(OO-BFI)
OO-BIG	Cameron N-77 HAFB	798	
	(Wfu and stored)		
OO-BIH	Cameron Hex Glass 84SS HAFB	2618	
OO-BII	Ultramagic M-65C HAFB	65/74	
OO-BIJ	Kubicek BB-30 HAFB	82	OK-7082
OO-BIK	Cameron A-210 HAFB	10300	
	(Formerly c/n 10021, W/o 23.3.02 and rebt with new envelope)		
OO-BIL	Cameron O-65 HAFB	265	
OO-BIM	Cameron Salami SS HAFB	1048	
OO-BIN	Cameron N-77 HAFB	1608	
OO-BIO	Cameron O-77 HAFB	1405	
	(Wfu and stored)		
OO-BIP	Schröder Fire Balloons G 26/24 HAFB	223	
OO-BIQ	Colt 180A HAFB	10065	
OO-BIS	Thunder AX8-90 SII HAFB	1129	
OO-BIT	Cameron O-160 HAFB	4119	
OO-BIU	Cameron A-120 HAFB	4241	G-BXNL
OO-BIV	Cameron N-90 HAFB	2584	
OO-BIW	Cameron N-160 HAFB	1967	
OO-BIX	Ultramagic M-56C HAFB	56/26	
OO-BIZ	Ultramagic N-300 HAFB	300/03	
OO-BJA	Raven Europe FS-57A HAFB	E-227	
OO-BJB	Cameron O-77 HAFB	2224	
OO-BJC	Cameron A-210 HAFB	10306	
OO-BJD	Schröder Fire Balloons S 40/24 HAFB	671	
OO-BJE	Libert L.12-2600 HAFB	291-015	
OO-BJF	Cameron N-105 HAFB	4615	
OO-BJG	Cameron A-140 HAFB	10241	
OO-BJH	Durondeau L.220 HAFB	011	
OO-BJI	Thunder AX7-77Z HAFB	1549	PH-JIM
OO-BJJ	Cameron N-90 HAFB	2094	
OO-BJK	Cameron A-140 HAFB	4087	
OO-BJL	Cameron N-77 HAFB	1128	
	(Wfu and stored)		
OO-BJM	Libert L.3000 HAFB	288-012	
OO-BJN	Libert L.3000 HAFB	249-004	
OO-BJO	Cameron O-105 HAFB	1239	
OO-BJP	Thunder AX7-65 HAFB	500	
OO-BJQ	Ultramagic N-180 HAFB	180/32	

OO-BJT	Raven Europe S-57A HAFB	E-219	
OO-BJU	Cameron Z-105 HAFB	10329	
OO-BJV	Durondeau E.220 HAFB	010	
OO-BJW	Cameron O-120 HAFB	4951	
OO-BJX	Cameron Z-160 HAFB	10372	
OO-BJY	Kubicek BB-60 HAFB	171	OK-0171
OO-BKA	Ultramagic H-77 HAFB	77/60	
	(Wfu and stored)		
OO-BKB	Cameron O-90 HAFB	3231	G-BVIJ
OO-BKC	Cameron A-120 HAFB	4637	
OO-BKD	Cameron N-90 HAFB	2430	
OO-BKE	Cameron A-105 HAFB	3745	
OO-BKF	Ultramagic M-130 HAFB	130/39	
OO-BKG	USSR Airship Works Association		
	DC-AT8.0000-0 Balloon	0791-02-008	
OO-BKH	Cameron N-90 HAFB	2193	(OO-BWB)
OO-BKI	Cameron A-160 HAFB	10051	
OO-BKJ	Lindstrand LBL-90A HAFB	073	
OO-BKK	Cameron A-120 HAFB	4777	
OO-BKL (2)	Colt 77A HAFB	4457	
	(New envelope replacing c/n 1477)		
OO-BKO	Cameron A-210 HAFB	4718	
OO-BKP	Cameron Z-120 HAFB	10418	
OO-BKQ	Ultramagic N-210 HAFB	210/19	
OO-BKR	Cameron A-210 HAFB	3316	
OO-BKS	Cameron N-90 HAFB	4964	
OO-BKT	Cameron N-160 HAFB	10279	
OO-BKV	Cameron N-145 HAFB	4789	
OO-BKW	Cameron V-77 HAFB	1905	G-BPVV
OO-BKY	Cameron N-105 HAFB	4716	
OO-BKZ	Kubicek Hart-SS HAFB	15	OK-3023
OO-BLA	Cameron N-77 HAFB	1267	
OO-BLB	Cameron N-90 HAFB	2346	
OO-BLC	Raven-Europe S-50A HAFB	E-017	
OO-BLE	Colt 77A HAFB	016	G-NILE
OO-BLF	Kubicek BB-30 HAFB	96	
OO-BLG	Libert L.5000 HAFB	293-017	
OO-BLJ	Cameron N-56 HAFB	518	
	(Wfu and stored)		
OO-BLK	Cameron N-105 HAFB	3048	
OO-BLL	Cameron O-90 HAFB	2297	
OO-BLN	Cameron N-65 HAFB	742	
OO-BLO	Kubichek BB-37 HAFB	119	
OO-BLP	Raven-Europe S-55A HAFB	E-081	
OO-BLQ	Lindstrand LBL-105A HAFB	035	G-BVAR
OO-BLS	Libert L-600 HAFB	200-002	
OO-BLT	Raven-Europe S-52A HAFB	E-146	
OO-BLU	Cameron A-210 HAFB	4760	
	(New envelope replacing c/n 4575, .99)		
OO-BLW	Ultramagic M-77 HAFB	77/25	
OO-BLX	Ultramagic M-145 HAFB	145/13	
OO-BLZ	Libert L-4800 HAFB	298-022	
OO-BMA	Cameron N-77 HAFB	841	(OO-BVR)
OO-BMB	Lindstrand Salami SS HAFB	033	G-BUYP
OO-BMC	Ultramagic SS HAFB	F7/01	
OO-BMD	Cameron N-105 HAFB	2283	
OO-BME	Cameron N-90 HAFB	2422	
OO-BMF	Sky 140-24 HAFB	122	
OO-BMG	Durondeau L.220 HAFB	005	
OO-BMH	Ultramagic V-105 HAFB	105/30	
OO-BMK	Schröder Fire Balloons SS HAFB	566	D-OKOP
			(OO-BMK)
OO-BML	Cameron O-56 HAFB	31	G-AZNR
OO-BMM	Cameron N-105 HAFB	3281	
OO-BMN	Cameron N-133 HAFB	3905	
OO-BMO	Cameron N-120 HAFB	4337	
OO-BMP	Cameron V-77 HAFB	478	
OO-BMR	Cameron O-77 HAFB	1253	
OO-BMS	Chaize CS.2200 F32 HAFB	22	
OO-BMU	Raven Europe S-60A HAFB	E-057	F-GEZH
OO-BMV	Cameron DP-70 Hot Air Airship	1612	
OO-BMX	Kubicek BB-30 HAFB	145	
OO-BMZ	Lindstrand LBL-210A HAFB	723	
OO-BNA	Cameron A-210 HAFB	4760	
OO-BNB	Raven-Europe S-60A HAFB	E-044	
OO-BNC	Thunder AX3-17 Sky Chariot HAFB	01	
OO-BND	Ultramagic M-105 HAFB	105/61	D-ONAP
OO-BNH	Ultramagic T-180 HAFB	180/29	
OO-BNI	Cameron N-180 HAFB	4651	
OO-BNJ	Cameron N-90 HAFB	1533	
OO-BNM	Cameron N-105 HAFB	3495	
OO-BNN	Ultramagic N-180 HAFB	180/15	
OO-BNP	Cameron N-77 HAFB	856	
OO-BNS	Schröder Fire Balloons G 30/24 HAFB	450	
OO-BNT	Cameron N-160 HAFB	4540	
OO-BNU	Cameron N-160 HAFB	4837	
OO-BNV	Cameron A-140 HAFB	10145	
OO-BNW	Cameron Z-225 HAFB	10670	
OO-BNY	Cameron A-160 HAFB	3025	G-BUVU
OO-BNZ	Ultramagic M-145 HAFB	145/29	
OO-BOA	Durondeau L.220 HAFB	009	
OO-BOE	Cameron Z-105 HAFB	4891	
OO-BOF	Cameron N-160 HAFB	10070	
OO-BOG	Cameron Z-160 HAFB	10569	
OO-BOI	Thunder AX10-210 SII HAFB	10146	G-CBDE
OO-BOJ	Cameron N-90 HAFB	2922	
OO-BOK	Ultramagic M-77 HAFB (Wfu and stored)	77/21	

OO-BOL	Cameron O-65 HAFB	189	
OO-BOO	Colt 21A Cloudhopper HAFB	480	
OO-BOP	Raven Europe RX-7 HAFB	E-403	
OO-BOT	Raven-Europe RX-7 HAFB	E-083	
OO-BOU	Cameron V-77 HAFB	727	G-BMOU
OO-BOW	Kubicek BB-26 HAFB	100	
OO-BOX	Ultramagic M-77 HAFB	77/30	
OO-BOZ	Cameron A-140 HAFB	4927	
OO-BPA	Cameron N-90 HAFB	3040	G-BUVV
OO-BPB	Cameron N-77 HAFB	379	
	(Wfu and stored)		
OO-BPD	Cameron N-105 HAFB	3005	
OO-BPE	Cameron O-65 HAFB	125	G-BCOA
	(Wfu and stored)		
OO-BPF	Raven Europe FS-57A HAFB	E-119	
OO-BPH	Libert L.3000 HAFB	251-005	
OO-BPI	Libert L.3000 HAFB	287-010	
OO-BPJ	Cameron V-77 HAFB	1195	
OO-BPK	Kubicek BB-37 HAFB	85	
OO-BPM	Durondeau L.220 HAFB	013	
OO-BPO	Cameron Orange-120 SS HAFB	4959	
OO-BPP	Cameron V-77 HAFB	964	
	(Wfu and stored)		
OO-BPQ	Cameron N-105 HAFB	4872	
OO-BPR	Ultramagic M-77 HAFB	77/28	
OO-BPS	Cameron A-105 HAFB	3656	
OO-BPT	Raven-Europe S-57A HAFB	E-189	
OO-BPU	Ultramagic M-105 HAFB	105/99	
OO-BPV	Raven-Europe S-55A HAFB	E-218	
OO-BPX	Schröder Fire Balloons S 40/24 HAFB	653	
OO-BPY	Thunder AX7-77 HAFB	1005	
OO-BPZ	Raven Europe S-57A HAFB	E-247	
OO-BQA	Libert L.3000 HAFB	299-023	
OO-BQB	Cameron Z-120 HAFB	10525	
OO-BQC	Ultramagic N-180 HAFB (Reservn .05)	unkn	
OO-BQE	Ultramagic N-300 HAFB	300/13	
	(Reervation 3.1.05)		
OO-BQF	Cameron Z-105 HAFB	10245	
OO-BQI	Kubicek BB-60 HAFB	212	OK-0212
OO-BQL	Lindstrand LBL-150A HAFB	986	
OO-BQM	Ultramagic M-130 HAFB	130/33	
OO-BQS	Cameron Z-120 HAFB	10445	
OO-BQT	Ultramagic M-160 HAFB	160/35	
OO-BQU	Lindstrand LBL-150A HAFB	631	
	(Wfu and stored)		
OO-BRA	Thunder AX8-90 HAFB	1376	
OO-BRB	Cameron V-77 HAFB	1804	G-BPBX (G-BPCU)
OO-BRC	Ultramagic M-65C HAFB	65/75	
OO-BRD	Lindstrand LBL-120A HAFB	255	
OO-BRE	Cameron N-145 HAFB	2812	
OO-BRG	Lindstrand LBL-105A HAFB	983	
OO-BRH	Cameron N-77 HAFB	2264	G-SKIL
OO-BRI	Cameron V-77 HAFB	1202	
OO-BRJ	Cameron V-90 HAFB	2699	
OO-BRL	Lindstrand LBL-105A HAFB	414	
OO-BRM	Thunder-Colt AX-7 Fiesta HAFB	1111	
	(Wfu and stored)		
OO-BRN	Cameron N-120 HAFB	4761	
OO-BRO	Cameron N-90 HAFB	2750	
OO-BRQ	Ultramagic M-180 HAFB	180/44	(OO-BQR)
OO-BRR	Thunder AX8-90 HAFB	1223	
OO-BRT	Cameron O-77 HAFB	1367	
OO-BRV	Colt 17A Cloudhopper HAFB	1245	G-DIPZ
OO-BRW	Cameron N-90 HAFB	2118	
	(Wfu and stored)		
OO-BRX	Lindstrand LBL-120A HAFB	454	
OO-BRY	Libert L.3000 HAFB	302-026	
OO-BSB	Schröder Fire Balloons G 60/24 HAFB	732	
OO-BSD	Raven-Europe FS-57A HAFB	E-120	
OO-BSE	Balloon Works Firefly F7 HAFB	F7-859	
OO-BSF	Raven-Europe FS-55A HAFB	E-151	
OO-BSG	Cameron N-90 HAFB	2866	G-BUPD
OO-BSH	Raven Europe RX-7 HAFB	E-306	
OO-BSI	Cameron V-77 HAFB	1783	
	(Wfu and stored)		
OO-BSJ	Thunder AX3-17A Sky Chariot HAFB	279	F-GCKP G-BHVW
OO-BSK	Cameron N-145 HAFB	4294	
OO-BSL	Cameron N-90 HAFB	1815	
OO-BSM	Adams LD.S HAFB	072	
OO-BSN	Cameron N-180 HAFB	2613	
OO-BSO	Aerostar S-60A HAFB	3244	
OO-BSP	Aviatik B&B Ax8 Replika SS HAFB	8	
OO-BSQ	Schröder Fire Balloons G42/24 HAFB	1089	
OO-BSR	Cameron A-105 HAFB	2695	
OO-BSS	Cameron O-42 HAFB	1072	
OO-BST	Cameron N-105 HAFB	3246	
OO-BSU	Cameron Marshmallow 105SS HAFB	2362	G-BSOP
OO-BSV	Raven Europe FS-57A HAFB	E-379	
OO-BSW	Cameron N-90 HAFB	2226	
OO-BSX	Schröder Fire Balloons G 36/24 HAFB	972	
OO-BSY	Durondeau L-250 HAFB	017	
OO-BSZ	Raven Europe Aurora 54K HAFB	E-387	
OO-BTB	Cameron O-77 HAFB	1001	
	(Wfu and stored)		
OO-BTC	Raven RX-65 HAFB	E-014	

OO-BTD	Kubicek BB-37 HAFB	78	
OO-BTE	Cameron N-90 HAFB	3556	
OO-BTF	Cameron N-90 HAFB	2551	
OO-BTG	Cameron N-120 HAFB	4759	
OO-BTI	Cameron V-77 HAFB	1892	
OO-BTJ	Cameron V-77 HAFB	1823	
OO-BTK	Cameron N-180 HAFB	2403	
OO-BTM	Cameron A-250 HAFB	3378	
OO-BTN	Thunder AX7-77 HAFB	976	G-BTWH
OO-BTO	Lindstrand LBL-9OA HAFB	177	
OO-BTP	Lindstrand LBL-150A HAFB	495	
OO-BTQ	Ultramagic N-210 HAFB	210/23	
OO-BTS	Cameron N-90 HAFB	2627	
OO-BTT	Cameron A-140 HAFB	4415	
OO-BTU	Cameron Z-120 HAFB	10339	
OO-BTV	Ultramagic V-90 HAFB	90/02	
OO-BTW	Cameron O-77 HAFB	1481	
OO-BTZ	Ultramagic M-145 HAFB	145/33	
OO-BUB(2)	Cameron A-105 HAFB	10001	
	(Replacement for A-105 c/n 2787, .01)		
OO-BUD	Libert L.4000 HAFB	289-013	
OO-BUE	Colt Orangina SS HAFB	1247	G-PULP
	(Wfu and stored)		
OO-BUF	Cameron O-90 HAFB	3385	
OO-BUG	Cameron V-77 HAFB	1812	
OO-BUH	Libert L.3000 HAFB	301-025	
OO-BUI	Cameron A-250 HAFB	4821	
OO-BUL	Raven S-55A HAFB	855	N4047G
OO-BUM	Ultramagic M-77 HAFB	77/20	
	(Wfu and stored)		
OO-BUN	Cameron N-90 HAFB	2175	
OO-BUR	Cameron V-77 HAFB	787	
	(Wfu and stored)		
OO-BUS	Cameron O-140 HAFB	2282	
	(Dbf 2004)		
OO-BUU	Kubicek BB-37 HAFB	81	OK-7081
OO-BUW	Ultramagic N-180 HAFB (Reservn .05)	unkn	
OO-BUY	Ultramagic S-160 HAFB	160/23	
OO-BVA(2)	Thunder AX8-90 HAFB	1576	(OO-BVT)
OO-BVB	Raven-Europe RX-7 HAFB	E-071	
OO-BVD	Cameron N-90 HAFB	3212	G-BVII
OO-BVE	Cameron N-90 HAFB	1873	
OO-BVF	Cameron Z-105 HAFB	10410	
OO-BVG	Cameron N-145 HAFB	4117	(OO-BVN)
	(Wfu and stored)		
OO-BVH	Ultramagic M-105 HAFB	105/20	
OO-BVI	Ultramagic M-77 HAFB	77/22	
	(Wfu and stored)		
OO-BVJ	Cameron A-210 HAFB	4915	
OO-BVK	Schröder Fire Balloons G 33/24 HAFB	770	
OO-BVL	Colt 90A HAFB	1698	
	(Wfu and stored)		
OO-BVN	Raven-Europe S-55A HAFB	E-182	
OO-BVO	Lindstrand LBL-150A HAFB	842	
OO-BVQ	Ultramagic H-42 HAFB	42/07	
OO-BVR	Durondeau L.180 HAFB	012	
OO-BVS	Cameron V-90 HAFB	3151	
OO-BVU	Libert L.3400 HAFB	297-021	
OO-BVV	Libert L.2200 HAFB	003	
OO-BVW	Cameron N-90 HAFB	1938	
OO-BVX	Cameron O-160 HAFB	10179	
OO-BVY	Libert L.3000 HAFB	304-028	
OO-BVZ	Lindstrand LBL-180A HAFB	829	
OO-BWA	Kubicek BB-45 HAFB	261	(OO-BWL) OK-0261
OO-BWB	Aerostar S-60A HAFB	3231	
OO-BWE	Schröder Fire Balloons G 36/24 HAFB	476	PH-SUS
OO-BWF	Cameron N-120 HAFB	10247	
OO-BWH	Ultramagic M-145 HAFB (Reservn 12.04)	unkn	
OO-BWJ	Cameron V-90 HAFB	2733	
OO-BWL(2)	Cameron N-90 HAFB	10068	
	(Replacement for N-90 c/n 2880, .01)		
OO-BWM	Cameron V-77 HAFB	872	
OO-BWN	Cameron N-145 HAFB	4770	
OO-BWO	Cameron N-160HAFB	4892	
OO-BWP	Cameron N-105 HAFB	1951	
OO-BWR	Cameron Z-160 HAFB	10168	
OO-BWS	Libert L.3000 HAFB	265-007	
OO-BWT	Kubicek BB-60 HAFB	91	OK-8021
OO-BWU	Ultramagic M-120 HAFB	120/07	
OO-BWV	Cameron N-90 HAFB	1714	
OO-BWW	Cameron O-105 HAFB	1059	G-BLIV
OO-BWY	Cameron N-160 HAFB	10621	
OO-BXA	Ultramagic M-145 HAFB	145/05	
OO-BXB	Ultramagic N-355 HAFB	355/03	
OO-BXC	Lindstrand LBL-210A HAFB	995	
OO-BXG	Libert L.3400 HAFB	305-029	
OO-BXI	Lindstrand LBL-105A HAFB	113	
OO-BXK	Schröder Fire Balloons G 34/24 HAFB	828	
OO-BXL	Cameron N-77 HAFB	662	LX-BIL
OO-BXP	Cameron Z-160 HAFB	10550	
OO-BXS	Ultramagic M-105 HAFB	105/109	
OO-BXT	Cameron N-160 HAFB	10552	(OO-BZT)
OO-BXU	Libert L.2000 HAFB	295-019	
OO-BXV	Cameron H-20 HAFB (Reservation .04)	2028	G-BRCJ
OO-BXX	Lindstrand LBL-31A HAFB	140	
OO-BXY	Lindstrand LBL Battery SS HAFB	621	G-MAXX

OO-BXW	Cameron A-210 HAFB (Damaged 15.2.03)	4083	G-BXWZ
OO-BXZ	Ultramagic M-160 HAFB	160/36	
OO-BYA	Raven-Europe S-67 HAFB	E-186	
OO-BYC	Libert L.2600 HAFB	300-024	
OO-BYD	Cameron Z-105 HAFB	10532	
OO-BYE	Cameron V-65 HAFB (Wfu and stored)	773	
OO-BYG	Ultramagic T-180 HAFB	180/34	
OO-BYK	Cameron N-145 HAFB	4259	
OO-BYM	Thunder AX10-210SII HAFB	4756	D-OABB
OO-BYP	Schröder Fire Balloons G 34/24 HAFB	888	D-OEMA
OO-BYR	Cameron Z-425LW HAFB	10566	
OO-BYS(2)	Libert L.3000 HAFB	303-027	
OO-BYT	Cameron Z-315 HAFB	10321	
OO-BYV	Cameron N-133 HAFB	4642	
OO-BYW	Cameron O-90 HAFB	3049	G-BUWB
OO-BYX	Cameron Z-160 HAFB	10263	
OO-BYZ	Raven Europe S-55A HAFB	E-118	
OO-BZA	UltraMagic M-42 HAFB	42/10	
OO-BZB	Cameron N-133 HAFB	4598	
OO-BZD	Cameron Z-160 HAFB	10370	
OO-BZE	Cameron Z-160 HAFB	10379	
OO-BZG	Cameron Z-225 HAFB	10537	
OO-BZH	Cameron Paint Can 115SS HAFB	10572	
OO-BZI	UltraMagic M-105 HAFB	105/123	
OO-BZL	Lindstrand LBL-180A HAFB (Res .05)	1025	
OO-BZM	Cameron A-400 HAFB	10164	
OO-BZN	Cameron A-250 HAFB	10448	
OO-BZO	Cameron N-160 HAFB	10449	
OO-BZP	Schröder Fire Balloons G 34/24 HAFB	1001	
OO-BZQ	UltraMagic T-180 HAFB	180/36	
OO-BZT	Cameron Z-160 HAFB	10575	
OO-BZW	Lindstrand LBL-120A HAFB	585	
OO-BZY	Colt 105A HAFB	10378	
OO-BZZ	Thunder AX7-77 HAFB	010	G-BBKO
OO-CBE	Cameron N-90 HAFB	1316	
OO-CGM	Raven S-55A HAFB	655	
OO-EOL	Cameron O-84 HAFB (Wfu and stored)	27	
OO-GDB	Cameron S-65 HAFB (Wfu and stored)	14	
OO-GDC	Cameron S-65 HAFB (Wfu and stored)	20	
OO-GDF	Cameron O-77 HAFB (Wfu and stored)	155	
OO-GKB	Raven S.55A HAFB (Wfu and stored)	686	
OO-JBC	Cameron N-56 HAFB	506	
OO-JOH	Thunder AX6-56 HAFB	264	
OO-LAM	Cameron N-77 HAFB	584	
OO-LAN	Cameron V-65 HAFB	646	
OO-LOM	Cameron V-77 HAFB	1273	
OO-LON	Cameron N-77 HAFB	381	
OO-MRA	Cameron O-77 HAFB	364	
OO-RUP	Cameron O-77 HAFB (Wfu and stored)	437	
OO-SAX	Cameron O-77 HAFB	244	
OO-SWF	Schaut 1500m3 Gas Balloon (Wfu 7.86)	1	
OO-WFS	Cameron O-77 HAFB	1328	
OO-WTM	Cameron V-56 HAFB	651	
OO-YAN	Cameron N-77 HAFB	374	
OO-B . .	Cameron Z-225 HAFB	10670	

GLIDERS AND MOTOR-GLIDERS

OO-CHM	Grob G.103 Twin Astir II	3750	(OO-ZKG)
OO-DAC	Schweizer SGU-2-22	19	
OO-DRS	Scheibe SF-24B Motorspatz	4043	D-KBWS D-KIDI
OO-ERA	Sportavia/ Fournier RF-5	5085	
OO-FPJ	Schempp-Hirth Nimbus 4 DM	37-52-868	
OO-FRA	Grob G.103 Twin Astir II	3701	
OO-FRI	Eiri PIK-20E	20262	D-KOSO
OO-GRS	Glaser-Dirks DG-600M	6-86M32	F-CGRS
OO-ICD	Schleicher ASK 14	14057	D-KICD
OO-JAZ	Alpavia/ Fournier RF-3	78	D-KILA
OO-JLB	Sportavia/ Fournier RF-4D	4088	
OO-JVM	Scheibe SF-24B Motorspatz (Stored, dismantled)	4020	D-KECI
OO-KDB-KB	Schempp-Hirth Janus CT	233/6	(OO-ZDK)
OO-KEI	Schleicher Rhönlerche II	unkn	OO-ZUA(1)
OO-KUL	Grob G.102 Astir Jeans	2066	
OO-LEI	Scheibe SF.27M-A	6307	D-KIML
OO-LGA-GA	Schempp-Hirth HS.7 Mini-Nimbus	54	
OO-LIT-IT	Schempp-Hirth Ventus b	132	D-3518
OO-LNO	Aerotechnik L-13SL Vivat	900415	OK-0118
OO-LUS	Sportavia/ Fournier RF-4D	4036	F-BOXE
OO-MFS	Sportavia/ Scheibe SF-25C Falke	4213	D-KAWB
OO-MIG-4	LET L-13 Blanik	026134	
OO-MJC	Schempp-Hirth Ventus cM	17/444	
OO-MLV	Scheibe SF-25B Falke	44281	D-KDGH
OO-MRM	Sportavia-Pützer RF-5B Sperber	51034	N55SH (D-KEAP)
OO-MTA	Alpavia/ Fournier RF-3	30	F-BMDJ
OO-MVA	Scheibe SF-25B Falke (Wfu, stored)	4650	D-KEBJ
OO-MVB	Scheibe SF-25B Falke	4654	D-KICG
OO-MVC	Scheibe SF-25C Falke	44287	D-KDGO
OO-MVF	Scheibe SF-25C Falke	46121	D-KABT
OO-NAM(2)	Schleicher ASW 20 (Code 'AM')	20139	
OO-NKD	Schempp-Hirth Nimbus 4 DM	35/50	
OO-NKL	Sportavia-Pützer RF-5B Sperber	51022	D-KCAW
OO-NMC	Scheibe SF-28A Tandem-Falke	5755	D-KMGE
OO-NSC	Alpavia/ Fournier RF-3	64	F-BMTI
OO-NZT-ZT	Schleicher ASW 20	20086	
OO-OSI	Stemme S-10	10-43	D-KGCU
OO-PAA-PS	Schempp-Hirth Nimbus 4DM	42/ . .	
OO-PDM	Glaser-Dirks DG-300 Elan	3E-330	
OO-PIK	Eiri PIK-20E	20235	
OO-PRJ	Stemme S-10VT	11-017	
OO-SZA	Scheibe Spatz A	515	
OO-SZB	Scheibe Spatz A	517	
OO-SZD	Schleicher Ka 2B Rhönschwalbe	196/56	
OO-SZE	SZD-9 bis Bocian 1C	P-311	
OO-SZP	Schleicher Ka 6CR Rhönsegler	196	
OO-SZW	Hoffmann H-36 Dimona	3609	(OO-LCL)
OO-ULB	Alpavia/ Fournier RF-3 (Dismantled)	71	OO-WAA
OO-VCN	Stemme S-10V	14-003	(OO-VCI) D-KGCI (4)
OO-WCA	Aerotechnik L-13SL Vivat (Crashed 18.7.99)	930515	(OO-ZFX)
OO-YAA	Rolladen-Schneider LS1C	43	D-0558
OO-YAB	Scheibe Bergfalke II/55	04	D-6259
OO-YAD	SZD-48-3 Jantar Standard 3	B-1971	F-CBZD
OO-YAE-AH	Schleicher K 8B	8885/AB	D-7297
OO-YAH	Schleicher K 8B	8212	D-5452
OO-YAJ-OP	Rolladen-Schneider LS6A	6084	F-CAJM F-WAJM OH-738
OO-YAL	Schleicher ASW 19B	19303	D-6526
OO-YAR-HF	Schleicher Ka 6E Rhönsegler	4317	F-CDRS
OO-YAS	Schleicher Ka 6E Rhönsegler	4011	D-9362
OO-YAW	Eiri PIK-20D	20636	PH-633
OO-YAZ-7M	Eiri PIK-20D	20632	D-6584
OO-YBA	Schleicher K 8B	8494	HB-825
OO-YBB	Scheibe L-Spatz 55	726	D-8592
OO-YBI	Valentin Mistral C	Mc 024/79	PH-672
OO-YBL-BL	Glaser-Dirks DG-200/17	2-175/1758	D-5892
OO-YBO	Schempp-Hirth Discus 2b	174	
OO-YBP-T16	Grob G.103 Twin Astir	3144	F-CFBF
OO-YBR-FU	Schempp-Hirth Ventus cT	78/317	D-KBRC
OO-YBV	Schleicher ASK 13	13556	Air Cadets PL-66
OO-YBW	Rolladen-Schneider LS1C	69	D-0672
OO-YCI-T41	Grob G.103 Twin Astir	3567	F-CFHP
OO-YCJ	Schleicher Ka 6CR Rhönsegler	6207	Air Cadets PL-51
OO-YCM	Carmam M.100S Mésange	48	F-CCXM
OO-YCN	Schleicher Ka 6E Rhönsegler	4058	Air Cadets PL-59
OO-YCR	Valentin Mistral C	MC 011/78	D-4911
OO-YCT	Schempp-Hirth Ventus 2cT	58/188	
OO-YCU	Schleicher ASK 13	13166	Air Cadets PL-62
OO-YDD -VY	Rolladen-Schneider LS1C	161	OE-5297
OO-YDF	Schleicher Ka 6CR Rhönsegler	60/03	D-1181
OO-YDK	Schleicher ASW 19B	19365	F-CBDK
OO-YDM	Schleicher ASK 13	13400	D-0988
OO-YDN	Schleicher ASK 13	13197	D-0346
OO-YDP	Schleicher K 8B	8346	Air Cadets PL-53
OO-YDR	Glaser-Dirks DG-300 Elan (Code K36)	3E-202	F-CFVQ F-WFVQ
OO-YDS	Schleicher ASH 26	26133	
OO-YDT	Schleicher K 8B	8367	Air Cadets PL-55
OO-YDV-ES	Schleicher ASW 19B	19237	PH-640
OO-YDW	Schleicher ASW 20L (Code DW)	20261	D-6540
OO-YEB	Eiri PIK-20D	20557	D-4768
OO-YEC	Glaser-Dirks DG-300	3E-260	LX-CDE
OO-YEH-NY	Schempp-Hirth Discus 2B	54	
OO-YEK -AG	Centrair 101A Pégase	101A-OI90	F-CGEK
OO-YEP	Schleicher ASK 21	21128	D-1487
OO-YER	Schleicher ASW 20L	20406	D-3297
OO-YEV-VP	Schempp-Hirth Ventus 2cT	51	
OO-YEZ	Eiri PIK-20D	20580	PH-590
OO-YFJ	Schleicher K 8B	8653	Air Cadets PL-57
OO-YFK	Grob G.103 Twin Astir	3102	SE-UFK D-3959
OO-YFM	Schempp-Hirth Discus 2B	101	
OO-YFR	Schleicher ASK 13	13579	AirCadets PL-67
OO-YGE	Glaser-Dirks DG-600	6-24	HB-1927
OO-YGF	Bölkow Phoebus A-1	713	D-9073
OO-YGG	Schempp-Hirth Ventus b	40	D-4060
OO-YGI	Schempp-Hirth Ventus cT	118/392	OY-PHX LX-CDT D-KHUM
OO-YGM	Wassmer WA.26P Squale	71	F-CDZF
OO-YGN	Schempp-Hirth Mini-Nimbus	37	BGA2353/DSW RNGSA.N33

OO-YHD	Caproni A.21S Calif	208	F-CCDI
			I-SERI
OO-YHH-38	Centrair 101D Pégase	101D-0511	F-CGHH
OO-YHI	Glasflügel H.206 Hornet	86	D-6599
			LX-CHF
			OO-ZAD
OO-YHJ	Schleicher ASW-19	19198	OY-XIP
OO-YHN-PJ	Rolladen-Schneider LS6	6040	D-6258
OO-YHP	Schempp-Hirth Standard Cirrus	460	D-3690
OO-YII-II	Schleicher K 7 Rhönadler	887	D-5014
OO-YIL-ED	Rolladen-Schneider LS8A	8093	
OO-YIN-IN	Rolladen-Schneider LS6C-18w	6381	
OO-YJH-JH	Rolladen-Schneider LS8A	8084	D-1617
OO-YJJ-66	Schleicher ASK 13	13478	D-2366
OO-YJP	Schempp-Hirth Janus C	168	N806JC
OO-YJR-52	Eiri PIK-20D	20543	D-7652
OO-YKA	Schleicher ASK 13	13094	D-2018
OO-YKB	Schleicher ASK 21	21392	HB-1964
OO-YKC	Schleicher K.8B	122	D-1670
OO-YKE	Schleicher K.8B	8245/A	D-5411
OO-YKH	Rolladen-Schneider LS4	4466	D-5164
OO-YKP	Schleicher ASK 13	13550	D-6717
OO-YKR	Schleicher ASK 13	13021	D-6063
OO-YKV	Schleicher K 8B	8652	Air Cadets
			PL-56
OO-YLA	SZD-48-1 Jantar Standard	B-1000	LX-CHO
			HB-1523
OO-YLE-JM	Centrair 201A Marianne	201A-037	F-CBLE(2)
OO-YLL	Schempp-Hirth Janus C	241	HB-1930
OO-YLM	Schempp-Hirth Ventus 2B	157	
OO-YLQ	Centrair 201A Marianne	201A-044	F-CBLQ
OO-YMA-MA	Schempp-Hirth Nimbus 3T	13/82	D-KCMA
			D-KHIA(4)
OO-YMB	Schleicher ASK 13	13128	D-9420
OO-YMC	Schleicher ASK 13	13060	D-4364
OO-YMF	Glaser-Dirks DG-100G Elan	E160-G127	D-1168
OO-YMN-MN	Grob G.102 Astir CS	1376	PH-549
OO-YMO	Rolladen-Schneider LS4	4188	D-9046
OO-YMP	Rolladen-Schneider LS4	4548	D-7871
OO-YMR-52	Schempp-Hirth Discus 2B	102	
OO-YNG	Valentin Mistral C	MC 066/85	D-4996
OO-YOD	Schleicher K 8B	203/61	Air Cadets
			PL-58(2)
			D-5053
OO-YOG-BG	Rolladen-Schneider LS7WL	7137	D-3673
OO-YOO	Glaser-Dirks DG-200/17	2-90/1707	D-6844
OO-YOU-42	Grob G.102 Astir CSJeans	2080	PH-600
OO-YPB	Schleicher ASK 13	13538	AirCadets
			PL-65
OO-YPC	Glasflügel H205 Club Libelle	108	PH-524
OO-YPF	Valentin Mistral C	MC 065/83	D-4965
OO-YPI	Schleicher ASK 13	13512	(OO-YPA)
	(C/n 13521 quoted but this is F-CEJW)		AirCadets
			PL-63
OO-YPJ	Schleicher Ka 6CR Rhönsegler	853	D-5540
OO-YPM	Schleicher ASH.25E	25083	D-KERB
OO-YPW-1C	PZL PW-5 Smyk	17.03.013	HB-3020
OO-YPX	PZL PW-6U	78.02.03	
OO-YRD	Rolladen-Schneider LS1D	138	D-0957
OO-YRG	SZD-50-3 Puchacz	B-1876	HB-3010
OO-YRJ	Schempp-Hirth Nimbus 3DT	62	F-CFUQ
OO-YRL	Centrair 101AP Pégase	101AP-0214	F-CGFA
OO-YRR	Wassmer WA.28F	99	F-CDZS
OO-YRS	Eiri PIK-20D	20529	OH-512
OO-YRV	Schleicher K 8B	182/60	D-4081
OO-YRZ	Schempp-Hirth Ventus cT	166/ 543	OY-XRZ
			D-KNMA
OO-YSM-PE	Schempp-Hirth Nimbus 2B	170	LX-CRC
			D-6442
OO-YSV	Scheibe L-Spatz 55	701	D-8894
OO-YTD	Schleicher K 8B	8366	Air Cadets
			PL-54
OO-YTM	Schempp-Hirth Duo Discus T	356/65	
OO-YTS-TS	Schempp-Hirth Ventus 2cX	unkn.	
	(Reserved 4.1.05)		
OO-YTW-ST	Grob G.103 Twin II	3763	D-1310
OO-YUE	Centrair 101A Pégase	101A-0151	F-CGBM
	(Code B151)		
OO-YUU	Schempp-Hirth Duo Discus T	91	
OO-YVA-VA	Grob G.103 Twin Astir	3051	D-4843
OO-YVB-ND	Eiri PIK-20D	20583	D6696
OO-YVG	Schleicher ASW 20C	20758	D-8123
OO-YVI	Centrair 101A Pégase	101A-329	F-CGOI
OO-YVM	Schleicher ASK 18	18013	D-6881
OO-YVN	Schempp-Hirth Duo Discus	228	OY-XVN
OO-YVS	Schleicher ASW 15A	15172	D-0851
OO-YVT-2C	Schempp-Hirth Ventus 2cxT (Res 4.03)	112/ . .	
OO-YWA	Schleicher ASW 15B	15355	D-2363
OO-YWB	Bölkow Phoebus B-1	855	BGA4901/JYZ
			OE-0872
OO-YWI-2C	PZL PW-5 Smyk	17.12.020	
OO-YWL	Slingsby T.45 Swallow	1566	BGA1339/BYK
OO-YWT-E1	Schleicher ASK 21	21086	D-6129
OO-YXL	Schempp-Hirth Nimbus 4M (Reservation)	12/34	OO-XXL
	(Built as Nimbus 4 c/n 14/34)		D-4789
OO-YYL	Schempp-Hirth Discus B	172	OY-XYK
OO-YYL	Schleicher ASW 20	20609	D-5151

OO-YYO	Glaser-Dirks DG-300 Elan	3E-339	I-HOPS
OO-YYP-YP	Rolladen-Schneider LS4	4119	D-5985
OO-YYV	Schleicher ASW 15	15108	OE-0909
OO-YYX	Schleicher ASW 27	27069	OE-5681
OO-YZA-4M	Schleicher ASK 13	13577	D-7557
OO-YZB	Schleicher K 8B	8353	D-1958
OO-YZC-77	Schleicher ASW 19B	19062	D-6777
OO-YZE	Centrair 201B Marianne	201B-077	F-CGTJ
OO-YZH	Rolladen-Schneider LS1f	377	F-CEKB
OO-YZI	Glaser-Dirks DG-100G Elan	E80-G55	D-2505
OO-YZT	Schleicher K 8B	8001	D-5190
OO-YZW	Scheibe SF-34	5105	D-1134
OO-YZY	Schempp-Hirth Nimbus 4DT	8/29	F-CFUY
OO-ZAB	Schleicher Ka 6B Rhönsegler	204	D-8352
OO-ZAC	Schleicher K 7 Rhönadler	7025	D-5231
OO-ZAE-MW	Schleicher K.7 Rhönadler	7168	
OO-ZAF	Schleicher K 7 Rhönadler	7169	
OO-ZAH	Schleicher K 7 Rhönadler	7221	
OO-ZAI	Grob G.102 Astir CS 77	1736	
OO-ZAK	Schleicher K 7 Rhönadler	7268	
OO-ZAL	Schleicher K 7 Rhönadler	7269	
OO-ZAM	Schleicher K 7 Rhönadler	631	D-5758
OO-ZAN	Schleicher K 7 Rhönadler	7270	
OO-ZAO	Schleicher K 8B	8628	
OO-ZAP	Schleicher K 8B	8629	
OO-ZAQ	Schleicher K 8B	8630	
OO-ZAR	Schleicher K 8B	8703	
OO-ZAS	Schleicher K 8B	8704	
OO-ZAT	Schleicher K 8B	8705	
OO-ZAU	Schleicher K 8B (Dbr 5.99)	8706	
OO-ZAV	Schleicher K 8B	8707	
OO-ZAW	Schleicher K 8B	8708	
OO-ZAX	Schleicher K 8B	143/59	D-5139
			D-KACH
OO-ZAY	Schleicher K 7 Rhönadler	700	D-4042
OO-ZAZ	Schleicher K 8B	unkn	D-6271
OO-ZBA-BA	Schleicher ASW 15	15025	
OO-ZBB	Schleicher K 7 Rhönadler	7273	
OO-ZBC	Schleicher Ka 6CR Rhönsegler	6103	D-5898
OO-ZBD	Schleicher Ka 6E Rhönsegler	4086	
OO-ZBE	Schleicher K 7 Rhönadler	447	D-6263
OO-ZBF	Schleicher Ka 6E Rhönsegler	4066	
OO-ZBH	Schleicher K 8B	8764	
OO-ZBJ	Schleicher Ka 6E Rhönsegler	4148	D-2038
			OO-ZBJ
OO-ZBK	Rolladen-Schneider LS1F	189	
OO-ZBL	Schleicher Ka 6CR Rhönsegler	854	D-5800
OO-ZBP-BP	Rolladen-Schneider LS1D	94	
OO-ZBQ-2G	Rolladen-Schneider LS3A	3128	D-6834
OO-ZBR	Glasflügel H.301 Libelle (C/n same as N301RP)	56	
OO-ZBS-7	Rolladen-Schneider LS1F	353	
OO-ZBU	Schleicher K 8B	8311	D-5390
OO-ZBW-BW	Schleicher Ka 6CR Rhönsegler	6331	D-4651
OO-ZBX-JB	Schempp-Hirth Standard Cirrus	223	D-0973
OO-ZBY-Y	Rolladen-Schneider LS1D	93	
OO-ZCB	SZD-9 bis Bocian 1C	P-274	F-CCDM
	(Believed w/o 16.8.82)		SP-1569
OO-ZCC-A6	Schempp-Hirth Standard Cirrus	451G	
OO-ZCD	SZD-24C Foka C	W-193	
OO-ZCF	Schleicher Ka 6CR Rhönsegler (or c/n 1013?)	101/43	D-8382
OO-ZCG-Z2	Rolladen-Schneider LS4	4413	
OO-ZCJ-CJ	Schempp-Hirth Standard Cirrus B	694	
OO-ZCK-CK	Schleicher K 8B	8608	D-4042
OO-ZCL	Avialsa-Scheibe A.60 Fauconnet	12	F-CCLH
OO-ZCN	Scheibe Specht	822	D-5588
OO-ZCP	Scheibe L-Spatz 55	02/658	D-7131
OO-ZCQ	Bölkow Phoebus C	882	F-CDOB
OO-ZCR	Avialsa-Scheibe A.60	113K	F-CDFP
OO-ZCS	LET L-13 Blanik	026111	
OO-ZCU-719	Glasflügel H201 Standard Libelle	319	F-CEBF
OO-ZCV	Schempp-Hirth Standard Cirrus	389G	
OO-ZCW	Scheibe L-Spatz B-13	600	D-5511
OO-ZDB	Schleicher Ka 6E Rhönsegler	265	HB-582
OO-ZDE	SZD-42-1 Jantar 2A	B-792	BGA3907/HFJ
			RAFGGA:100
			OO-ZDE
OO-ZDF	Schleicher K 7 Rhönadler	7173	
OO-ZDH	Caudron C.800	354/10314	F-CAPI
			Fr.Navy
OO-ZDK-AH	Glaser-Dirks DG-300 Elan	3E-17	D-4450
OO-ZDM	Siren C.30S Edelweiss	39	AirCadets
			PL-79
			F-CDAT
OO-ZDO-E7	Schleicher ASW 15	15043	D-0490
OO-ZDQ	Slingsby T.31B Cadet TX.3	904	XE791
OO-ZDR-11	Schleicher Ka 6E Rhönsegler	4316	F-CDRR
OO-ZDT-DT	Schleicher K 8B	8909	PH-452
OO-ZDU-DU	Grob G.102 Astir Jeans	2118	D-7643
OO-ZDW	Avialsa-Scheibe A.60 Fauconnet	102K	F-CDFE
OO-ZDX	Bölkow Phoebus C	782	D-9210
OO-ZDZ	Scheibe L-Spatz 55	570	(OO-JDL)
			D-5089
OO-ZEA	Schleicher Rhönlerche II	611/59	AirCadets PL-1
OO-ZEC	Schleicher Rhönlerche II	706/60	AirCadets PL-3
OO-ZED	Schleicher Rhönlerche II	707/60	AirCadets PL-4
OO-ZEE	Schleicher Ka 6CR Rhönsegler	6106	D-5253
OO-ZEF	LET L-13 Blanik	025413	

OO-ZEH	Schleicher Rhönlerche II	799/60	
OO-ZEI	Schleicher Rhönlerche II	872/60	
OO-ZEK	Schleicher Rhönlerche II (Dismantled)	874/60	
OO-ZEL	Schleicher Rhönlerche II	915/60	AirCadets PL-5
OO-ZEN-W	Schleicher K 8B	8929	
OO-ZEO	Siebert Sie 3 (W/o)	3020	
OO-ZEP-3D	Schleicher Ka 6CR Rhönsegler	901	D-7122
OO-ZEQ-EQ	Schleicher Ka 6CR Rhönsegler	6263	(OO-ZGI)
			(OO-ZXW)
			D-5093
OO-ZER-L1	PIK-16C Vasama	41	LX-CEH
OO-ZET	Schleicher K 7 Rhönadler	7079	
OO-ZEU	SZD-24C Foka C	W-174	
OO-ZEV-EV	Grob G.102 Astir Standard III	5614S	
OO-ZEW	Schleicher Rhönlerche II	3063/Br	D-5461
OO-ZEX-EX	Grob G.102 Astir Jeans	2175	
OO-ZEY-EY	Grob G.103 Twin Astir II	3618	
OO-ZEZ	Carmam M.100S Mésange	36	F-CCSZ
OO-ZFB-FB	Grob G.102 Astir Standard	1377	
OO-ZFC	SZD-22C Mucha Standard	F-526	OO-ZSM
	(Rebuilt using parts from OO-ZSU c/n 532 - q.v.)		
OO-ZFD-FD	Scheibe Zugvogel IIIB	1105	D-6364
OO-ZFG	Schleicher K 8	102/58	D-5719
OO-ZFH	Grunau Baby III	unkn	
OO-ZFI	Schempp-Hirth Standard Cirrus	85	BGA1633/CLS
OO-ZFK	Grob G.103 Twin Astir	3096	D-3952
OO-ZFM	Schleicher Ka 6CR Rhönsegler	6241	D-4101
OO-ZFN-FN	Rolladen-Schneider LS3A	3145	
OO-ZFO	Issoire E78 Silène	6	F-CFEC
OO-ZFP-70	Schleicher ASW 19	19065	D-4470
OO-ZFQ	Schempp-Hirth Janus C	122	D-6848
OO-ZFR	Schleicher Ka 6CR Rhönsegler	6097/Si	D-5280
OO-ZFS-717	Glasflügel H201B Standard Libelle	304	F-CEBD
OO-ZFT	Schempp-Hirth Standard Cirrus	341G	(OO-ZFC)
			(OO-EFC)
			F-CEFC
OO-ZFU	Grob G.103 Twin Astir	3072	D-4857
OO-ZFV-J3	Eiri PIK-20D	20651	
OO-ZFW	Schleicher ASK 21	21417	
OO-ZFX-520	Schempp-Hirth Discus b	256	BGA3405/FNY
OO-ZFZ	Grob G.103 Twin Astir	3069	D-4855
OO-ZGC-EP	Carmam M.200 Foehn	46	F-CDHY
OO-ZGD	Schleicher Ka 6E Rhönsegler	4151	LX-CBP
OO-ZGE-GE	Schleicher ASW 20L	20238	LX-CGE
OO-ZGG	Siren C.30S Edelweiss	53	F-CDGL
OO-ZGH-G	Schleicher ASW 20	20207	
OO-ZGI	Centrair ASW-20F (code X118)	20518	F-CERZ
OO-ZGJ	Schleicher Ka 6CR Rhönsegler	6228/Si	D-9104
OO-ZGK-CB	Rolladen-Schneider LS3-17	3250	D-3185
OO-ZGM	Glasflügel H201BStandard Libelle	596	OO-NAM(1)
OO-ZGO-L32	Rolladen-Schneider LS1D	221	F-CEHH
OO-ZGR-GR	SZD-48-3 Jantar Standard 3	B-1638	
OO-ZGS-PG	Schempp-Hirth Cirrus	60	D-0189
OO-ZGT-GT	Lanaverre CS11/75L Standard Cirrus	2	F-CEVC
OO-ZGU	Schempp-Hirth Cirrus	48	D-0179
OO-ZGV-GV	Schleicher K 8B	8911	D-0990
OO-ZGW-HE	Rolladen-Schneider LS7	7031	D-1301
OO-ZGX	Avialsa-Scheibe A.60	154	F-CDNG
OO-ZHA-HA	Schleicher Rhönlerche II (Stored)	549	D-4362
OO-ZHB	Schleicher ASW 20	20132	
OO-ZHC	Centrair 101A Pégase	101A-046	F-CFQI
OO-ZHD-17	Schempp-Hirth Standard Cirrus	568G	
OO-ZHE	Schleicher Rhönlerche II	216/57	AirCadets PL-7
OO-ZHH	Carmam M.200 Foehn	34	F-CDHH
OO-ZHJ-14	Schleicher Ka 6E	4375	D-0759
OO-ZHK	Schleicher ASW 15	15137	HB-1028
OO-ZHL	LET L-13 Blanik	175129	
OO-ZHO	Schleicher Ka 6E	4284	D-0231
OO-ZHQ	Nord 2000	63/10393	F-CAYP
OO-ZHR	Fauvel AV.36	1	D-5513
	(Stored, still marked D-5513)		
OO-ZHU-MR	Start & Flug H-101 Salto	39	D-9239
OO-ZHV	Neukom S4D Elfe 16	409AB	D-7700
OO-ZHX-HX	Rolladen-Schneider LS6	6032	PH-761
OO-ZHY	Schempp-Hirth Nimbus 2	115	OE-5075
OO-ZHZ-F1	Schempp-Hirth Discus CS	057CS	
OO-ZID	Karpf Baby II	unkn	
OO-ZIE	Scheibe L-Spatz 55	503B	
OO-ZIF	LET L-13 Blanik	026857	
OO-ZIG	Fauvel AV.36	1	D-5510
	(Stored)		
OO-ZIJ-IJ	Schleicher K 8B	8733	D-4416
OO-ZIK-26	Schleicher ASW 17	17039	
OO-ZIO	DFS Grunau Baby III	unkn	
OO-ZIT	EoN Olympia (Dismantled)	EON/0/052	
OO-ZIV	Schleicher ASW 20	20304	
OO-ZIW	Spalinger S-15	unkn	
OO-ZIX	Akaflieg München Mü.13E Bergfalke	unkn	D-6050
OO-ZIZ	Doppelraab VI	unkn	D-1206
OO-ZJA-JA	Eiri PIK-20D	20635	
OO-ZJC-19	Scheibe Zugvogel IIIB	1089	
OO-ZJD	Wassmer WA.30 Bijave	210	F-CDJD
OO-ZJG-45	Bölkow Phoebus C	894	F-CDOD
OO-ZJI-X89	Centrair ASW-20F	20189	F-CEUT
OO-ZJK-4V	Schempp-Hirth Janus C	218	HB-1829
OO-ZJN	Breguet 905S Fauvette	45	F-CCJO
OO-ZJP-JP	Schleicher Ka 6CR Rhönsegler	676	D-5737

OO-ZJQ	LET L-13 Blanik	026928	D-0935
			OE-5236
OO-ZJU	Rolladen-Schneider LS3-17	3405	D-7893
OO-ZJV	Scheibe L-Spatz 55	2	D-5608
OO-ZJW	Scheibe Spatz B	SF-01	D-1233
OO-ZJX-25	Glasflügel H201B Standard Libelle	362	F-CEBL
OO-ZJY	Schempp-Hirth Janus B	79	D-1153
			N177BC
OO-ZJZ	Rolladen-Schneider LS3-17	3269	D-2868
OO-ZKB	Schleicher K 8B	8822	
OO-ZKC	Schleicher ASK 23	23058	
OO-ZKD	LET L-13 Blanik	025707	D-2298
OO-ZKF-66	Schleicher K 8B	8449/SH	D-5807
OO-ZKG-KG	Schempp-Hirth Nimbus 3T	59/7	D-KHRG
			D-3111
OO-ZKI	Schleicher Rhönlerche II	01	D-8835
OO-ZKJ-111	Schleicher Ka 6BR Rhönsegler	408	D-5628
OO-ZKK	LET L-13 Blanik	026146	
OO-ZKL-KL	Grob G.103 Twin Astir II	3619	
OO-ZKM	Avialsa-Scheibe A.60 Fauconnet	36K	F-CCQN
OO-ZKN	Schleicher ASK 13	13254	
OO-ZKO	Schleicher ASK 13	13244	
OO-ZKP	Schleicher ASK 13	13261	
OO-ZKQ	Schleicher K 8B	8685/A	D-5158
OO-ZKR-11	Schleicher K 8B	8347	D-4635
OO-ZKS-KS	Schleicher ASK 13	13239	OH-396
			OH-KKS
OO-ZKU	Schleicher K 8B	8155	OY-XFF
			RDAF:Z-966
OO-ZKV-KV	Grob G.103 Twin Astir II	3644	
OO-ZKW-KW	Grob G.103 Twin Astir	3231	
OO-ZKX	Grob G.102 Astir CS	1426	PH-560
OO-ZKY	Schleicher ASK 23B	23091	
OO-ZKZ-KZ	Centrair 101A Pégase	101A-0273	
OO-ZLD	Schleicher K 8B	8055/A	D-5466
OO-ZLE-A7	VTC-75 Cirrus	114Y	D-0503
OO-ZLF	Carmam M.200	45	F-CDHV
OO-ZLG-LG	Schempp-Hirth Standard Cirrus	189	D-0704
OO-ZLH-30	SZD-36A Cobra 15	W-721	
OO-ZLI	Rolladen-Schneider LS4	4001	D-2628
OO-ZLJ-LJ	Glasflügel H.201B Standard Libelle	378	
OO-ZLK-BY	Schempp-Hirth Standard Cirrus	268	D-1981
OO-ZLL	Schempp-Hirth Standard Cirrus	62	
OO-ZLM	Akaflieg München Mü.13E Bergfalke	8	D-5236
OO-ZLN-G	Schleicher ASK 21	21007	
OO-ZLO	Schempp-Hirth Nimbus II	47	
OO-ZLP	Olympia Meise 52	unkn	D-6434
OO-ZLQ	Schempp-Hirth Ventus cT	152/487	
OO-ZLR	Schleicher Ka 6CR Rhönsegler	6186	D-5347
OO-ZLU	Schleicher Rhönlerche II (Dismantled)	90/55	D-5418
OO-ZLV	Schleicher K 8B	8709	
OO-ZLW	Schleicher K 7 Rhönadler	7196	
OO-ZLX-LX	Schempp-Hirth Standard Cirrus	416	D-4750
OO-ZLY	Carmam M.200 Foehn	28	F-CDDY
OO-ZLZ	Scheibe L-Spatz 55	534	D-1215
OO-ZMB	Schleicher ASW 15A	15166	D-0827
OO-ZMC	Scheibe L-Spatz 55	515	D-4018
OO-ZMD	Schleicher K 7 Rhönadler	1093	D-5072
	(Unmarked)		
OO-ZMG	Scheibe L-Spatz 55	1	D-5166
OO-ZMJ	Schleicher K 7 Rhönadler	2/59	D-5650
OO-ZMK	Schleicher Ka 6CR Rhönsegler	6114	D-1897
OO-ZMM	Glasflügel H.301 Libelle	11	D-8897
OO-ZMN	Scheibe SF-27A	6019	D-9374
	(Code JL)		
OO-ZMO-JY	Grob G.102 Astir Club Standard	1396	
OO-ZMP	Carmam M.200 Foehn	58	F-CDPO
OO-ZMQ	Slingsby T.31B Cadet TX.3	853	XA311
OO-ZMR-P	SZD-48-1 Jantar Standard 2	W-895	
OO-ZMS-52	Schempp-Hirth Mini-Nimbus B	74	
OO-ZMT-MT	Schleicher Ka 6CR Rhönsegler	6464	D-5104
OO-ZMV	Schleicher K 8B	175/60	D-6390
OO-ZMW	Grob G.102 Astir CS Jeans (Code MW)	2205	
OO-ZMX-MG	Schempp-Hirth Ventus A	92	D-1480
OO-ZMY-MY	Rolladen-Schneider LS1D	97	D-0436
OO-ZNB-729	Glasflügel H.201B Standard Libelle	258	
OO-ZNC	Schleicher K 7 Rhönadler	835	D-5787
OO-ZND-YT	ICA-Brasov IS.28B-2	271	
OO-ZNE	Scheibe/LCA.11 Topaze	23	F-CEEX
OO-ZNF-NF	Eiri PIK-20D	20544	OH-535
OO-ZNG-MG	Grob G.102 Speed Astir IIB	4103	D-6817
OO-ZNH-NH	Rolladen-Schneider LS1F	412	D-2753
OO-ZNK	Grob G.102 Standard Astir II	5033S	D-6265
OO-ZNM-JL	Schleicher Ka 6CR Rhönsegler	6001	(OO-ZMN)
			D-4091
OO-ZNO-3M	Grob G.102 Astir CS Jeans	2158	D-4554
OO-ZNP	Schleicher K 7 Rhönadler	284	D-5544
OO-ZNQ	LET L-23 Super Blanik	907624	OK-0238
			(BGA3666/FZY)
OO-ZNR- I	SZD-48-1 Jantar Standard 2	B-1025	OE-5250
OO-ZNS-BO	Schleicher ASW 19	19221	
OO-ZNT	Scheibe Bergfalke IV	5860	(OO-ZJT(2))
			D-5941
OO-ZNW-J	SZD-51-1 Junior	B-1993	
OO-ZNX	SZD-50-3 Puchacz	B-1391	SP-3284
OO-ZNY	Schempp-Hirth Standard Cirrus	425G	F-CEFL
OO-ZNZ-37	Schleicher ASW 20	20437	PH-703

OO-ZOB	Aeromere M.100S	054	
OO-ZOC	Scheibe L-Spatz 55	561	D-5441
OO-ZOD-21	Schleicher K 6E Rhönsegler	4032	
OO-ZOE	Schleicher K 8B	8734	D-5847
OO-ZOG-OG	Grob G.102 Speed Astir IIB	4049	D-8715
OO-ZOI	Schleicher K 8B	8953	PH-476
OO-ZOJ	Schleicher K 8B	586	D-5706
OO-ZOK	LET L-13 Blanik	175018	
OO-ZOL-AB	Schleicher K 8B	8891	
OO-ZOM	Schleicher K 8B	8654	AirCadets
			PL-58(1)
OO-ZON	Schleicher K 8B	8573	
OO-ZOP	Breguet 905S Fauvette	3	F-CCIG
OO-ZOQ-114	Schleicher Ka 6E Rhönsegler	4163	
OO-ZOT-HI	Schempp-Hirth Janus CM	5	D-KONI
			(D-KJMD)
OO-ZOV-AV	Schempp-Hirth Janus C	103	D-7997
OO-ZOW	Schleicher K 7 Rhönadler	2	D-5754
OO-ZOX	Schleicher K 8B	173/01AB	D-0131
OO-ZOY	Wassmer WA.30 Bijave	17	F-CCMN
OO-ZPC-PC	Schleicher ASW 20	20049	
OO-ZPE	Akaflieg München Mü.13E Bergfalke	186	D-6090
OO-ZPF-PF	Grob G.102 Speed Astir IIB (Restd as D-6818?)	4104	D-6818
OO-ZPH	Akaflieg München Mü.13E Bergfalke	131	LX-CBA
OO-ZPJ-17	Akaflieg Braunschweig SB-5B Sperber	5025	D-8617
OO-ZPK	Scheibe Zugvogel IIIB	1077	D-1975
OO-ZPM-PM	Rolladen-Schneider LS4	4049	
OO-ZPO	Zsebo-Bohn Z-03B Ifjusag	unkn	
OO-ZPP-PP	Schleicher ASW 15	15157	D-0807
OO-ZPQ-HB	SZD-48-3 Jantar Standard 3	B-1961	(OO-ZCY)
OO-ZPR	Grunau Baby III	unkn	
OO-ZPT	Schleicher K 8B	8075	PH-289
OO-ZPU	Schleicher ASW 15	15140	D-0790
OO-ZQA	Schleicher Ka 2B Rhönschwalbe	69/55	AirCadets
			PL-10
OO-ZQB	Schleicher Ka 2B Rhönschwalbe	71/55	AirCadets
			PL-11
OO-ZQE	VTC Cirrus	136Y	D-2968
OO-ZQF-L2	SZD-55-1	551193057	
OO-ZQG-GG	Neukom S4D Elfe 15	401	D-4599
OO-ZQH-QH	Eiri PIK-20D	20568	D-6703
OO-ZQI-QI	Schempp-Hirth Discus bT	81/414	
OO-ZQJ-GF	Schleicher ASW 15B	15270	F-CEGF
OO-ZQK-9	Glasflügel H303 Mosquito	46	D-8986
OO-ZQL-QL	SZD-59 Acro	B-2163	
OO-ZQM	Grob G.102 Astir CS Jeans	2070	D-7584
OO-ZQN-DS	Grob G.102 Standard Astir II	5007S	D-4884
OO-ZQO	Schleicher K 7 Rhönadler	7224	D-5819
OO-ZQP	Grob G.102 Astir CS 77	1818	D-6754
OO-ZQQ-76	Schleicher ASW 27	27016	
OO-ZQU	Schleicher K 7 Rhönadler	698	D-5753
OO-ZQV-704	Glasflügel H201B Standard Libelle	601	F-CELI
OO-ZQW	Wassmer WA.30 Bijave	78	F-CCTB
OO-ZQY	Schleicher K 7 Rhönadler	10	D-5667
OO-ZRB	Schleicher K 8B	12	D-1130
OO-ZRC-YT	Rolladen-Schneider LS6	6056	D-6522
OO-ZRD	Avialsa-Scheibe A.60	47K	F-CCQZ
OO-ZRE	Schleicher Ka 2B Rhönschwalbe	319	D-6216
OO-ZRG	Wassmer WA.22A Super Javelot	96	F-CCRG
OO-ZRK-23	Glasflügel H.201B Standard Libelle	16	D-0108
OO-ZRM	Schleicher K 7 Rhönadler	7135/A	D-5415
OO-ZRN	Schleicher ASH 25	25012	
OO-ZRO-57	Glasflügel H.201B Standard Libelle	8	
OO-ZRP	Carmam M.100S Mésange	13	F-CCSB
OO-ZRR-LV	Schempp-Hirth Standard Cirrus 75	614	
OO-ZRU	Schleicher K 8B	8438GV	D-8815
OO-ZRV	Briegleb BG.12-16	236	(OO-ZJK)
			(OO-51)
OO-ZRX-01	Rolladen-Schneider LS1C	88	D-0305
OO-ZRY-8	Rolladen-Schneider LS6	6035	
OO-ZRZ-70	Schleicher ASW 20	20299	
OO-ZSA	SZD-8ter-Z0 Jaskolka	247	
	(Displayed in AELR Museum Brussels)		
OO-ZSB	Akaflieg Braunschweig SB-5B Sperber	5009	
OO-ZSC	SZD-8ter-Z0 Jaskolka	254	
OO-ZSD	SZD-8ter-Z0 Jaskolka	255	
OO-ZSH	Slingsby T.30B Prefect	880	OO-SZH
OO-ZSI	SZD-22B Mucha Standard	518 ?	
OO-ZST	SZD-22C Mucha Standard (W/o in 1988)	531	
OO-ZSU	SZD-22C Mucha Standard	532	
	(Rebuilt using parts from OO-ZSM/OO-ZFC c/n		
	526 - which is still current as OO-ZFC)		
OO-ZSX	SZD-9 bis Bocian 1D	P-393	
OO-ZTA	Carmam M.200 Foehn	17	F-CDDI
OO-ZTB	Carmam M.100S Mésange	84	F-CDKY
OO-ZTD	Grob G.103 Twin Astir	3016	HB-1389
OO-ZTE	Schempp-Hirth SHK-1	V-2	OY-BXP
			D-6438
			D-9338
OO-ZTF-21	Glasflügel H.201B Standard Libelle	490	PH-475
OO-ZTG	Schleicher Ka 6CR Rhönsegler	6179	OY-XFO
			RDAF:Z-967
OO-ZTI	Schleicher Ka 6CR Rhönsegler	6132	D-4350
OO-ZTJ	Schleicher K 7 Rhönadler	7096	D-8884
OO-ZTK-C87	Jastreb Standard Cirrus G/81	244	F-CEBY
OO-ZTL -YL	Schempp-Hirth SH.1 Standard Austria	55	
OO-ZTM	Schleicher Ka 6CR Rhönsegler	492	D-4004
OO-ZTO	Schempp-Hirth Ventus cT	102/362	D-KFAH
OO-ZTQ-TQ	Rolladen-Schneider LS4	4113	PH-716
OO-ZTS	Schleicher Ka 6E Rhönsegler	4197	D-1100
OO-ZTV-T1	Valentin Mistral C	059/85	D-4959
OO-ZUA	Schleicher Rhönlerche II	unkn	
OO-ZUB	Schleicher Rhönlerche II	unkn	
OO-ZUD	SZD-22C Mucha Standard	F-776	
OO-ZUE	Schleicher Rhönlerche II	428/58	
OO-ZUH	Schleicher Rhönlerche II	431/58	
OO-ZUJ	Schleicher Rhönlerche II	594/59	
OO-ZUL	Schleicher Rhönlerche II	596/59	
OO-ZUM	Schleicher Rhönlerche II	425/58	
OO-ZUO	Schempp-Hirth SH-1 Standard Austria	78	D-4004
			LX-CWV
OO-ZUR	Scheibe L-Spatz 55	680	
OO-ZUS	Grob G.103 Twin Astir II	3645	
OO-ZUV	Wassmer WA.26CM	04	F-CDUV
OO-ZUW-UW	Neukom S-4A Elfe	45	HB-1224
OO-ZUX	SZD-8ter-Z0 Jaskolka	240	
OO-ZVC	Grob G.103 Twin Astir	3238	
OO-ZVF-VF	Grob G.103 Twin Astir II	3517	
OO-ZVG	Schleicher K 8B	8335/A	D-5451
OO-ZVI	Schempp-Hirth Standard Cirrus	296G	D-2055
OO-ZVJ	Grob G.103 Twin Astir	3260	
OO-ZVK-VK	Schempp-Hirth Janus C	205	
OO-ZVM-76	Schleicher ASW 20	20047	
OO-ZVN-VN	Schleicher Ka 6CR Rhönsegler	6336	PH-336
OO-ZVO	Schleicher Rhönbussard	unkn	(OO-ZJH)
			OO-ZVA(1)
OO-ZVP	Glasflügel H.201B Standard Libelle	17	OE-0880
OO-ZVQ	Grob G.104 Speed Astir IIB	4070	OO-YMG
			BGA4260/HWK
			OO-ZVQ
			LX-CRT
OO-ZVR	Grob G.102 Astir Club IIIB	5589	
OO-ZVT	Scheibe L-Spatz 55	667	
OO-ZVU	Scheibe L-Spatz 55	4	D-5505
OO-ZVX	Grob G.102 Astir Club Standard	1813	
OO-ZVY-ICI	Grob G.102 Astir Standard Jeans	2048	
OO-ZVZ	Grob G.102 Astir Standard Jeans	2047	
OO-ZWA	Schleicher Ka 6CR Rhönsegler	6591	D-3659
OO-ZWB	Grob G.102 Astir CS Jeans	2137	
OO-ZWD	Schleicher K 8B	8816	
	(W/o 19.7.2003)		
OO-ZWF-7	Avialsa-Scheibe A.60	8	F-CCLD
OO-ZWG	Grob G.102 Astir Club Standard Jeans	2182	
OO-ZWH	Schleicher Ka 6CR Rhönsegler	6224	D-1853
OO-ZWJ	SZD-48 Jantar Standard 2 (Dbr 9.5.99)	W-884	
OO-ZWK	Wassmer WA.30 Bijave	25	F-CCMV
OO-ZWL	Wassmer WA.30 Bijave	12	F-CCMJ
OO-ZWM	SZD-48-3 Jantar Standard 3 (code WM)	B-1419	
OO-ZWR	Schleicher K 7 Rhönadler	7042	D-5206
OO-ZWU-WU	Schleicher ASK 13	13485	OH-441
OO-ZWV	Schleicher K 7 Rhönadler	886	D-5003
OO-ZWX-49	Rolladen-Schneider LS3A	3403	
OO-ZWZ-WZ	Grob G.102 Astir Club Standard	1776	
OO-ZXC	Schleicher K 7 Rhönadler	7199	D-5567
	(Res. 12.4.88 but not registered, active as such)		
OO-ZXC	Schempp-Hirth Duo Discus	44	
OO-ZXD	Schleicher K 8B	8255	D-5387
OO-ZXE	SZD-24C Foka	W-158	SP-2376
OO-ZXG	Wassmer WA.28F	106	F-CEOA
OO-ZXH	Carmam M.100S Mésange	47	F-CCXL
OO-ZXI	Schleicher K 8B	8293	D-6032
OO-ZXJ	Schleicher K 7 Rhönadler	7103	D-3608
OO-ZXK-K	Schleicher ASK 21	21511	
OO-ZXM	Schleicher ASK 21	21535	
OO-ZXN	Slingsby T-31B Cadet	1179	XN240
OO-ZXO-XO	Glaser-Dirks DG-300 Elan	3E-128	D-2857
OO-ZXP-XP	Schempp-Hirth Discus bT	61/383	D-KHEI (2)
OO-ZXR-OB	Schempp-Hirth Discus b	217	
OO-ZXT-71	Schleicher ASW 20L	20243	D-3373
OO-ZXU-AL	Glaser-Dirks DG-200	2-184	PH-722
OO-ZXV	Schempp-Hirth Discus CS	122CS	
	(Res. 5.4.94 but not registered, active as such)		
OO-ZXW	Schleicher K 8B	8269	HB-763
OO-ZXX-JA	Rolladen-Schneider LS3A	3229	
OO-ZYA	Schleicher Ka 6CR Rhönsegler	6615	
OO-ZYB-HO	Glasflügel H.205 Libelle	145	(OO-ZQB)
			(OO-EQB)
			F-CEQB
OO-ZYC	Grob G.104 Speed Astir	4032	D-4504
OO-ZYE	Schleicher Ka 6BR Rhönsegler	527	D-8130
OO-ZYF	Schleicher K 7 Rhönadler	7013	D-1785
OO-ZYG	Schleicher Ka 6CR-PE Rhönsegler	6112	D-8457
OO-ZYH-64	Schempp-Hirth Janus	29	OY-XDH
OO-ZYJ	SZD-48-3 Jantar Standard 3	B-1968	LX-CEE
OO-ZYK-YK	Schleicher ASH 25	25008	D-4741
OO-ZYO	Rolladen-Schneider LS1D	5	D-0125
OO-ZYP	ICA-Brasov IS.28B2	311	
OO-ZYQ-CG	Rolladen-Schneider LS1F	352	D-2744
OO-ZYS-PT	Rolladen-Schneider LS1F	410	D-3144
OO-ZYV	Schleicher Ka 6CR Rhönsegler	6182	D-4679
OO-ZYX	Pilatus B4-PC11	155	HB-1147
OO-ZZA	Rolladen-Schneider LS3A	3150	
OO-ZZC	Grob G.102 Astir CS 77	1665	
OO-ZZD	Glaser-Dirks DG.100 Club Elan	E34-G18	

OO-ZZG	Glaser-Dirks DG-300 Elan	3E-179	D-5702
OO-ZZK-K3	Glasflügel H303 Mosquito	3	D-4321
OO-ZZN-L5	Rolladen-Schneider LS3A	3118	D-3899
OO-ZZO-51	Schleicher Ka 6CR Rhönsegler	60/2	D-5792
OO-ZZP-DM	Rolladen-Schneider LS3A	3301	D-6953
OO-ZZR-ZR	Glaser-Dirks DG-300 Elan	3E-133	D-9353
OO-ZZS-7	Rolladen-Schneider LS4	4126	
OO-ZZT-C52	Schempp-Hirth CS-11/75 Standard Cirrus	678	F-CEMY
OO-ZZU-D11	Schempp-Hirth Discus b	180	F-CGGJ
			F-WGGJ
OO-ZZV	Schleicher K 8B	8820	PH-417
OO-ZZW-ZW	Schleicher ASH 25E	25126	
OO-ZZX-ZX	Glaser-Dirks DG-300 Elan	3E-125	N301LA
OO-ZZY	Schleicher K 8B	8952	PH-478
OO-ZZZ-13	Schleicher Ka 6E Rhönsegler	192/56	
OO-Y . .	Centrair 101D Pégase (Bought 4.02)	101D-0511	F-CGHH
OO-Y . .	Centrair 201B Marianne	201B-049	F-CBLX(2)
	(Candidate .05)		
OO-Y . .	Glaser-Dirks DG-600M (Bought 4.02)	6-86M32	F-CGRS
OO-Y . .	Grob G.103 Twin Astir II	3611	D-6438
OO-Y . .	Grob G.104 Speed Astir IIB (Candidate .03)	4085	PH-1128
			D-2593
			N166SS
			D-2593
OO-Y . .	Schleicher K 8B	8245/A	D-4511
OO-Y . .	Slingsby T.38 Grasshopper TX.1	1263	BGA3439/FQJ
	(Flying unregistered, will not be registered)		XP464

HOMEBUILT AIRCRAFT

OO-11	Mignet HM.293 Pou-du-Ciel	unkn	
	(On display in Brussels Air Museum)		
OO-15	Jodel D.9 Bébé	unkn	
	(On display in Brussels Air Museum, incomplete)		
OO-19	Jodel D.92 Bébé	CD-03	
OO-22	Jodel D.9 Bébé (W/o 3.5.89)	386	
OO-29	Pottier P.80S	47	
OO-30	Druine D.31 Turbulent	378	
OO-31	Jodel D.9 Bébé	487	
	(Built using parts from OO-14 and OO-26)		
OO-32	Mignet HM.293 Pou-du-Ciel (Stored)	821	F-PKFK
OO-33	Mignet HM.293 Pou-du-Ciel	unkn	
	(On dismplay in the Brussels Air Museum)		
OO-43(2)	Breezy RLU-1	5537	
OO-45	Jodel D.9 Bébé	629	
OO-54	Pottier P.80S	54	PH-SOM
			(PH-NOK)
			(OO-89)
OO-66	Evans VP-1 Volksplane	V-2574	
	(CofA exp. 17.5.95)		
OO-69	Tipsy T.66 Nipper 1L	29	
	(Also regd as G-BWHR with c/n PFA/25-12843)		
OO-70	Monerai S	190	
OO-71	Monnet Monerai S	241	
OO-72	Monerai S	265	
OO-77	Heintz Zenith CH-200	A250	
	(Reserved, almost complete by 3.05)		
OO-80	EAA Super Acro Sport	864	(OO-RAG)
OO-83	Evans VP-2 (Stored at Overmere)	3730	
OO-88	Evans VP-2 (CofA exp 9.88)	V2-3274	
OO-93	Pober P-9 Pixie	unkn	
OO-96	Mignet HM.293A Pou-du-Ciel (W/o 8.99)	B-001	
OO-99	Monnet Sonerai IIL	919	
OO-100	Mass 302 (Stored)	001	
OO-102	Rutan VariEze	1434	
OO-103	Rutan VariEze (Stored)	1433	
OO-104	Rutan VariEze (CofA exp 11.88, to F-PZMM?)	1847	
OO-106	Colomban MC-15 Cri-Cri	163	
OO-107	SCWALL 101 ATL	001	
OO-108	Pcttier P.80S	052	
OO-111	Grinvalds G-802 Orion	80/014	(OO-ION)
	(Stored)		(N802JS)
OO-118	JP.II (Homebuilt)	01	OO-LJP
	(On display in Brussels Air Museum)		
OO-119	Marco J-5	05	(OO-GUN)
	(CofA exp. 17.1.1995, stored)		
OO-122	Murphy Renegade Spirit	0292	
	(W/o 12.8.91)		
OO-125	Rand-Robinson KR-2	001	
OO-126	Stoddard-Hamilton Glasair III	3143	
OO-129	CFM Streak Shadow	K156-SA	(OO-A62)
OO-130	Neico Lancair 320	363	
OO-132	Brandli BX.2 Cherry	157	
	(Sold in the Netherlands but not yet cancelled)		
OO-134	Rans S-10 Sakota	0892145	
	(CofA exp. 21.2.01, stored)		
OO-136	Neico Lancair 320	813	
OO-137	Brandli BX.2 Cherry	117	
	(Sold as PH-POS but not yet cancelled)		
OO-138	Rotorway Exec 162F	6045	
	(CofA exp. 31.5.00)		
OO-139	Europa Aviation Europa	172	
OO-140	Fisher Celebrity	Av1103	
OO-141	Stoddard-Hamilton Glasair IIRG	2078	
OO-142	Monnet Moni	81	
OO-143	Zenair CH-601 Zodiac	6-9111	
OO-144	Van's RV-6A	22605	
OO-145	Europa Aviation Europa	382	

MICROLIGHTS

OO-502	Weedhopper JC.24B	873	
OO-503	Grasshopper Model Mono 01	GH/01/81/001	
OO-504	Romibutter (Modified Butterfly)	0101	(OO-753)
OO-505	Microbel	unkn	
OO-506	Fulmar Trident I	unkn	
OO-507	Fulmar Trident I	unkn	
OO-508	Véliplane Mosquito	340	
OO-509	JC.24B Weedhopper B	972	
OO-510	Aero-Marcq Marcq 1	0001	
OO-511	Fulmar Tricycle	81-012	
OO-512	Franken FR-II	unkn	
OO-513(2)	Micronef BI Hi	0839	
OO-514	Microbel SC-330	unkn	
OO-515	Cosmos/La Mouette Dragster	90/2618	
OO-516	JC.31A Weedhopper Two	unkn	
OO-517	JC.24B Weedhopper B	1597	
OO-518	Fulmar Tyger II	82-8230051	
OO-519	Butterfly	03	
OO-520	JC.24C Weedhopper C	2210	
OO-523	Microbel/Hiway Trike	unkn	
OO-524	Fulmar Trident I	T1-81-005	
OO-525	Fulmar Trident I	82-006	
OO-526	JC.24C Weedhopper C	108	
OO-527	JC.24C Weedhopper C	unkn	
OO-528	Fulmar Trident I	82-013	
OO-529	Fulmar Trident I	82-012	
OO-530	Rotec Rally 3B	25037	
OO-531	Fulmar Trident I	82-015	
OO-532	B.Danis Aile Delta	001	
OO-533	Eipper Quicksilver MX-II	1101	
OO-534	Fulmar Standart	TS-8003	
OO-535	Danis-Sabre	1018	
OO-536	Mainair Triflyer 440/Lightning DS	105121182	
	(Registered as a Southdown Puma, above correct)		
OO-537	Fulmar Tyger I	82-017	
OO-538	Microbel SC-250	20-28	
OO-539	Microbel SC-250	8000085	
OO-540	Microbel Big Fun	83-00296	
OO-541	Weedhopper Moustique	001	
OO-542	Fulmar Tricycle KDA	1143	
OO-543	Microbel Super Costaud SC-250	82-00503	
OO-544	Eipper Quicksilver MX-II	1174	
OO-545	Microbel SC-250	923/651	
OO-546	Microbel SL-20CV	83-102	
OO-547	Butterfly	04	
OO-548	Microbel SC-250	MR-8290	
OO-549	Fulmar Tyger I	TT-83-023	
OO-550	Microbel SC-440	82-001	
OO-551	Microbel SC-250	unkn	
OO-552	Sofrec Mustang	unkn	
OO-553	Baroudeur	83-3004	
OO-554	Cosmos/La Mouette Dragster 25	83-4156	
OO-556	Fulmar Heron MP15	001	
OO-557	Fulmar Tyger I	unkn	
OO-558	Fulmar Trident I	unkn	
OO-559	Microbel SC-503	83-113	
OO-560	Southdown Puma MS	83-2696	
OO-561	Mainair 440 Triflyer	KR137-7383-2	
	(Correct type confirmed, not Southdown Puma MS)		
OO-562	Fulmar Trident	82-007	
OO-563	Fulmar Tyger I	TTB-83030	
OO-564	Hunter Pathfinder II	110	
OO-565	Fulmar Tyger I	TTB-82018	
OO-567	Eipper Quicksilver MX-L	unkn	
OO-568	Microbel SC-250	unkn	
OO-569	Butterfly	03-01	
OO-570	Hunter Pathfinder II	124	
OO-571	Eipper Quicksilver MX-II	unkn	
OO-572	Véliplane OQ	248/82	
OO-573	Dragon 150	043	
OO-574	Microbel Big Fun	unkn	
OO-576	Microbel SC-432	02783	
OO-577	Microbel SC-440	unkn	
OO-578	Rotec Rally 3B	25039	
OO-579	Rotec Rally 3B	25056	
OO-581	Dragon 150	049	
OO-582	Dragon 150	050	
OO-583	Fulmar Tricycle	unkn	
OO-584	Fulmar Trident II	82-1003	
OO-585	JC.24C Weedhopper C	2052	
OO-586	Southdown Puma MS	830076	
OO-587	Mainair Triflyer 440/Lightning DS	177-287-3	
OO-588	Southdown Puma MS	8300146	
OO-589	ULAC X99	187	
OO-590	Airion Lezart Volant	B-11	

OO-592	Fulmar Gold Tricycle	63M2135	
OO-593	Fulmar Tyger I	321	
OO-594	Fulmar Tyger I	TTB-83035	
OO-595	Eipper Quicksilver MX-II	1751	
OO-596	Southdown Puma MS	8300017	
OO-597	Butterfly	31-02	
OO-598	Microbel SC-250	unkn	
OO-599	Fulmar Tyger II	TTB-83039	
OO-600	Fulmar Tyger I	TTB-83032	
OO-601	Butterfly 04	001	
OO-602	Mitchell Wing P-38 Lightning	5602	
OO-603	Fulmar Tyger 1	TTB-83040	
OO-604	Microbel SC-250	82-00317	
OO-605	JC.31C Weedhopper	4010020	
OO-606	Phoenix SR44	0016	
OO-607	Eipper Quicksilver MX-II	1750	
OO-608	Eipper Quicksilver MX-II	1755	
OO-609	American Aircraft Falcon	500180	
OO-611	American Aircraft Falcon	500182	
OO-612	American Aircraft Falcon	500187	
OO-613	JC.31C Weedhopper	4010017	
OO-614	Microbel SC-250	83-121	
OO-615	Southdown Puma MS	8300022	
OO-616	Aériane Sirocco	048	
OO-617	Microbel SC-440	111	
OO-618	Microbel SC-440	83-00849	
OO-619	Fulmar Tyger II	84-3070	
OO-620	Southdown Puma MS	8200151	
OO-621	JC.31C Weedhopper	3486385	
OO-623	JC.31C Weedhopper	4040034	
OO-625	Huntair Pathfinder II	154	
OO-626	Huntair Pathfinder II	155	
OO-627	Southdown Puma MS	84-3249	
OO-628	Baroudeur	499C00-401-43	
OO-629	Chickinox 34	3478171	
OO-630	Weedhopper JC-24D	4040047	
OO-631	Microbel SC-330	83602	
OO-632	Southdown Puma Sprint MS	8300208	
OO-633	Eipper Quicksilver MX-II	1756	
OO-634	JC.31C Weedhopper	4040035	
OO-635	Weedhopper Gipsy	001	
OO-636	JC.24D Weedhopper	4040052	
OO-637	JC.31C Weedhopper	4050070	
OO-638	Phoenix SR44	unkn	
OO-639	Butterfly 03	04	
OO-640	Southdown Puma MS	unkn	
OO-641	Butterfly 03	20	
OO-642	Microbel SC	863753	
OO-643	American Aircraft Falcon	500192	(OO-ETA)
OO-644	JC.31C Weedhopper	4050057	
OO-645	Fulmar Trident	TT-84048	
OO-646	Fulmar Trident	TT-83	
OO-647	Fulmar Tyger I	TTB-084	
OO-648	Microbel Mono	unkn	
OO-649	Butterfly	02	
OO-650	Fulmar Standard	28183	
OO-651	Sofrec Baroudeur	56-2050955	
OO-653	Microbel SC-440	8402	
OO-654	Microbel SC-250	84315	
OO-656	JC.31C Weedhopper	4050068	
OO-657	Aériane Sirocco	unkn	
OO-659	Eipper Quicksilver MX-II	1816	
OO-660	Southdown Puma Sprint MS	8300142	
OO-662	Fulmar Tyger I	270-IA-03E	
OO-663	JC.31C Weedhopper	4072001	
OO-664	Microbel	RK-01-1984	
OO-665	Microbel	NP-70ZN2	
OO-666	Microbel	82-00457	
OO-667	Fulmar Tyger I	TTB83038	
OO-668	Microbel	82-00472	
OO-669	Microbel	863673	
OO-670	Cosmos/La Mouette Bidulum 44	83-00011	
OO-671	Zodiac Ultrastar	123	
OO-672	Microbel SC-250	unkn	
OO-673	Fulmar Tyger II	85-2608	
OO-674	Aériane Sirocco	123	
OO-675	Albatros 83/003 (Homebuilt) (w/o 30.6.85)	unkn	(OO-108)
OO-676	Dynali Chickinox	unkn	
OO-677	Dynali Chickinox	077	
OO-678	Dynali Chickinox	004	
OO-679	Microbel SC-337	8503	
OO-680	Solar Wings Pegasus XL-R	T1084-1224	
OO-681	JC.24D Weedhopper	4040048	
OO-682	Southdown Puma Sprint MS	T-519	
OO-683	Southdown Puma Sprint MS	P-554/T-516	
OO-684	Aériane Sirocco	99	
OO-686	Dynali Chickinox	AAB-40	
OO-687	Fulmar R	82-496	
OO-688	Microbel	unkn	
OO-689	Dynali Chickinox	AAA-00	
OO-690	Microbel SC-447	8561	
OO-691	Butterfly 03	018	
OO-692	Baroudeur	095	
OO-693	Microbel SC-493	864474	
OO-694	Dynali Chickinox Bi	31	
OO-695	Dynali Chickinox Tandem	035	
OO-696	Dynali Chickinox	032	
OO-697	JC.31D Weedhopper	5072150	
OO-698	Microbel Bi	26-12-84-861	
OO-699	Microbel	unkn	
OO-700	Fulmar Tyger I	83044	
OO-701	JC.24D Weedhopper	404-0051	
OO-703	Microbel Big Fun	86-5166	
OO-704	Fulmar Tyger II	865116	
OO-705	Fulmar Tyger III	T3-85101	
OO-707	Fulmar Tyger I	86-1244	
OO-708	Dynali Chickinox	061	
OO-709	Microbel SC-330	001	
OO-710	Microbel SC-330	002	
OO-711	Fulmar Trident I	TT-83-019	
OO-712	Lejong I	001	
OO-713	Microbel SC-447	8621	
OO-714	Dynali Chickinox Bi	0063	
OO-716	Aériane Sirocco	unkn	
OO-717	Microbel SC-440 Big Fun	8401	OO-652
OO-718	Microfun SC-330 Typhoon	MF-850501	
OO-719	JC.24D Weedhopper	4040053	
OO-720	Dragon 150	024	
OO-721	IPES 1	86-4019	
OO-722	Lux 1	001	
OO-723	Microbel SL-447	8651	
OO-724	Microbel SL-447	8509	
OO-725	Dynali Chickinox	070	
OO-726	Dynali Chickinox Kot Kot	084	
OO-727	Microbel SC-330	003	
OO-728	Solar Wings Pegasus Panther XL	86-6277	
OO-729	Dynali Chickinox	075	
OO-730	Eipper Quicksilver MX-II	1754	
OO-731	Cosmos Bidulum	005	
OO-732	Cosmos Bidulum	006	
OO-734	Dynali Chickinox Tandem	036	
OO-735	Fulmar Tyger III	T3-86106	
OO-736	Centrair Parafan	03	
OO-737	Dynali Chickinox Kot Kot	86-3231	
OO-738	Fulmar Tyger III	T3-86105	
OO-739	Eipper Quicksilver MX-II	1896	
OO-740	Dynali Chickinox Kot Kot	86-2832	
OO-743	Fulmar Tyger	unkn	
OO-744	Microbel SC-330	83601	
OO-745	Cabis II	001	
OO-747	Centrair Parafan 1	41045	
OO-748	Dynali Chickinox Tandem	AAD-00	
OO-749	Microbel Chaser 377	86121	
OO-750	Microbel Trident II	86107	
OO-751	Durondeau 377 Parafan	1	
OO-752	Southdown Raven X	2000/0143	
OO-753	Baroudeur Biplace	142	
OO-754	Dynali Chickinox Kot Kot	210187012	
OO-755	Micronef Sc.Bi.Fu	008	
OO-756	Micronef Cosmos Bidulum	007	
OO-757	Microlight Trident II	87-108	
OO-758	Southdown Raven X	unkn	
OO-759	Microbel Cosmos Dragster	333-66	
OO-760	Fulmar Tyger III	T3-86103	
OO-762	Dynali Chickinox Kot Kot	31016691	
OO-763	Aériane Sirocco	148	
OO-764	JC.24D Weedhopper	6081069	
OO-765	Microbel CH-447	87503	
OO-766	Dynali Chickinox	040	
OO-767	Microbel CH-447	87501	
OO-768	Microbel CH-447	87502	
OO-769	Micronef Cosmos SC BI-FU	009	
OO-770	Micronef Cosmos	011	
OO-771	Microbel SC-330	86121	
OO-772	Dynali Chickinox Kot Kot	31014948	
OO-773	Dynali Chickinox Kot Kot	087	
OO-774	Dynali Chickinox Kot Kot	3950823	
OO-776	Centrair Parafan 1	41039	
OO-777	Weedhopper Europa II	7032300	
OO-778	Southdown Puma MS	87-5929	
OO-779	J-3 Kitten	242861	
OO-781	Microbel SL-503	86101	
OO-782	Microbel CH-377	87801	
OO-783	JC.31C Weedhopper	4040030	
OO-784	American Aircraft Falcon	0019	
OO-785	Fulmar Trident I	unkn	
OO-786	Dynali Chickinox Kot Kot	3102109	
OO-787	Rotec Rally 3B	65176	
OO-788	Dynali Chickinox	21045876	
OO-789	Dynali Chickinox Kot Kot	AAC-00	
OO-790	Solar Wings Pegasus XL-R	T-1287/87	
OO-791	Aerokart 4320	B83	
OO-792	Dynali Chickinox Kot Kot	3982423	
OO-793	Dynali Chickinox Kot Kot	3965960	
OO-794	Dynali Chickinox	21033455	
OO-795	Centrair Parafan 1	41035	
OO-796	Durondeau 447	M37711	
OO-797	American Aircraft Falcon	SM-016	
OO-798	American Aircraft Falcon XP	SMB01-PX	
OO-799	Micronef SC BI-FU	013	
OO-800	Micronef Cosmos	012	
OO-801	Fulmar Trident I	TT-82014	
OO-802	Dynali Chickinox Kot Kot	31035487	

OO-803	Dynali Chickinox Tandem	unkn	
OO-804	Cosmos Micronef	014	
OO-805	Cosmos Micronef Racer SX12	016	
OO-806	Dynali Chickinox Kot Kot	3109596	
OO-807	Microbel TD 1+1	88101	
OO-808	JC.24D Weedhopper	7071079	
OO-809	Aviasud Mistral 532	46	83-CR
OO-810	Microbel SC-330	83-101	
OO-811	Microbel Tandem 1+1	88-301	
OO-812	Dynali Chickinox Tandem	21008533	
OO-813	Aeronautic 2000 Baroudeur	28	
OO-814	Cosmos Bidulum	015	
OO-815	Cosmos Bidulum	017	
OO-816	Zodiac Ultrastar	unkn	
OO-817	Microbel SC-330	unkn	
OO-818	Aériane Sirocco	069	83-BN
OO-819	Air Création Safari GT-BI 462	unkn	
OO-820	Air Création Racer	019	
OO-821	Microbel SL-503	88402	
OO-823	Pterodactyl Ascender II	unkn	
OO-824	Microbel SC-447	88601	
OO-825	Dynali Chickinox Tandem	21176133	
OO-826	Dynali Chickinox Kot Kot	31075538	
OO-827	Dynali Chickinox Kot Kot	3115062	
OO-828	Solar Wings Pegasus XL-Q	SW-WQ-0072/SW-TB-1353	
OO-829	Aermas 386	03	
OO-830	Cosmos Bidulum	020	
OO-833	Croses Airplume	23	
OO-834	Dynali Chickinox Kot Kot	31138394	
OO-835	Dynali Chickinox Kot Kot	31099441	
OO-836	Dynali Chickinox Kot Kot	31111730	
OO-837	Centrair Parafan B1	43006	
OO-838	Centrair Parafan	43008	
OO-839	Fulmar Trident II	TR2-88109	
OO-840	Aviasud Mistral 532	58	WAE-58
OO-842	Centrair Parafan B1	43009	
OO-843	Air Création GT RO 503	021	
OO-844	Fulmar Tyger I	F-01	OO-513
OO-845	Dynali Chickinox Kot Kot	31177480	
OO-846	Dynali Chickinox Tandem	21060765	
OO-847	Microbel TD 1+1	88901	
OO-848	Dynali Chickinox Kot Kot	31100392	
OO-849	Solar Wings Pegasus Quasar XL-Q	SW-WQ-0085/SW-TE-0081	
OO-850	JC-24D Weedhopper D	4072016	
OO-851	Air Création	022	
OO-852	Manta Fledge	unkn	
OO-853	Air Création Racer SX12	023	
OO-854	Eipper Quicksilver MX-II	2426	
OO-855	Dynali Chickinox	31139873	
OO-856	Dynali Chickinox	31178826	
OO-857	Dynali Chickinox	31073464	
OO-858	Dynali Chickinox	31073596	
OO-859	H.M.14	001	
OO-860	Cosmos Micronef	025	
OO-861	Microbel	88903	
OO-862	Microbel TD 1+1	88121	
OO-863	Microbel TD 1+1	88122	
OO-866	Air Création GT BI RO 462	026	
OO-867	Dynali Chickinox	31061478	
OO-868	Dynali Chickinox	31180952	
OO-870	Microbel TD 1+1	88111	
OO-871	Dynali Chickinox	31063736	
OO-872	Dynali Chickinox	21293226	
OO-873	Air Création GT BI RO 503-2	028	
OO-874	Air Création GT BI RO 503-2	027	
OO-875	Microbel TD 1+1	89031	
OO-876	Weedhopper Europa II	9022462	
OO-877	Dynali Chickinox	31227996	
OO-878	Weedhopper AX-2	9032466	
OO-879	Air Création GT BI 503-2	030	
OO-880	Micronef Cosmos BI RO 503-2	033	
OO-881	Air Création GT BI RO 503	029	
OO-882	Dynali Chickinox	31268256	
OO-883	Microbel	89041	
OO-884	Aviasud Mistral 532	02/89/73	
OO-885	Dynali Chickinox	31241592	
OO-886	Weedhopper Europa II	9022463	
OO-887	Microbel TD 1+1	89034	
OO-888	Dynali Chickinox	31089621	
OO-889	Dynali Chickinox	31063604	
OO-890	Zodiac Ultrastar (W/o 1.5.97)	118	
OO-891	JC.31C Weedhopper	5042102	
OO-892	Microbel Pendulaire	89090	
OO-893	Microbel	89091	
OO-894	Microbel TD 1+1	88801	
OO-895	Aviasud Mistral 532	079	
OO-896	Euronef ATTL-1	1	
OO-897	Fulmar	8200733	
OO-898	Dynali Chickinox	1601833	
OO-899	Microbel TD 1+1	89601	
OO-900	Dynali Chickinox	31203880	
OO-901	Air Création Racer SX12	031	
OO-902	Air Création Racer SX12	032	
OO-903	Air Création Racer SX12	034	
OO-904	Air Création GT BI RO 532	035	
OO-905	Microbel TD 1+1	89603	
OO-906	Microbel TD 1+1	89604	
OO-907	Weedhopper Europa II	99052501	
OO-908	Dynali Chickinox Kot Kot	31231072	
OO-910	Microbel TD 1+1	89602	
OO-911	Weedhopper AX-2	9062508	
OO-912	Fulmar Tyger 1	90-2684	
OO-913	Zodiac Ultrastar	106	
OO-914	J-3 Kitten	242868	
OO-915	Air Création GT BI AR 500	043	
OO-916	Air Création GT BI SX 16	036	
OO-917	Air Création GT BI SX 16	038	
OO-918	Dynali Chickinox Kot Kot	31111598	
OO-919	Microbel TD 1+1	89-101	
OO-920	Dynali Chickinox Kot Kot	31312014	
OO-921	Microbel SL-447	89-901	
OO-922	Solar Wings Pegasus Quasar XL-Q	SW-WQ-0236/SW-TE-0221	
OO-923	Dynali Chickinox Kot Kot	31193069	
OO-924	Aviasud Mistral 532	098	
OO-925	Cosmos Bidulum	039	
OO-926	Microbel TD 1+1	89-111	
OO-929	Weedhopper AX-3	9092547	
OO-930	Solar Wings Pegasus Quasar XL-Q	SW-WQ-0254/SW-TE-0231	
OO-931	Dynali Chickinox Kot Kot	31244404	
OO-932	Dynali Chickinox Kot Kot	3120552	
OO-933	JC.31 Weedhopper	9112562	
OO-934	Kaiman 462 Cosmos	982807	
OO-935	Air Création Racer 447	041	
OO-936	Air Création Racer 447	042	
OO-937	Dynali Chickinox Kot Kot	31296821	
OO-938	Dynali Chickinox Kot Kot	31231890	
OO-939	Microbel TD 1+1	89121	
OO-940	JC.31 Weedhopper	9122578	
OO-941	Air Création Racer 447	045	
OO-942	Air Création Racer 447	050	
OO-943	Air Création GT BI	041	
OO-944	Air Création Racer 447	048	
OO-945	Air Création Racer 447	049	
OO-946	Air Création Racer 447	047	
OO-947	Cosmos Bidulum 50	B0294	
OO-949	Dynali Chickinox Tandem	32112	
OO-950	Dynali Chickinox Tandem	37933	
OO-951	Dynali Chickinox	31245354	
OO-952	Weedhopper AX-3	0022604	
OO-953	Dynali Chickinox	3788844	
OO-954	Solar Wings Pegasus Quasar XL-Q	SW-WQ-0300	
	(C/n refers to wing only, trike unit type and c/n unidentified)		
OO-955	Dynali Chickinox	328776	
OO-956	Dynali Chickinox Kot-Kot	31296821	
OO-957	Microbel TD 1+1	90501	
OO-958	Solar Wings Pegasus Quasar	SW-WQQ-0310/SW-TQ-0003	
OO-959	Aériane Sirocco	B-90041	
OO-960	Microbel TD 1+1	90502	
OO-961	Weedhopper AX-3	0062662	
OO-962	Microbel TD 1+1	90601	
OO-963	Microbel TD 1+1	90602	
OO-965	Air Création GT BI	052	
OO-966	Eipper Quicksilver MX-II	2436	
OO-967	Eipper Quicksilver MX-II	2437	
OO-968	Dynali Chickinox	241712	
OO-969	Dynali Chickinox	369327	
OO-970	Mignet HM.14	02	OO-123 OO-970
OO-971	Microbel TD 1+1	90801	
OO-972	Dynali Chickinox	21205319	
OO-973	Dynali Chickinox	356826	
OO-974	Dynali Chickinox	3119342	
OO-975	Air Création GT BI 582-ES	055	
OO-976	Air Création Cosmos BI 503-2E	051	
OO-977	Air Création GT BI 502-2E	054	
OO-978	Weedhopper AX-2	0042643	
OO-979	Dynali Chickinox	344537	
OO-981	Dynali Chickinox	384282	
OO-982	Dynali Chickinox	370554	
OO-983	Eipper Quicksilver MX-II	2438	
OO-984	Solar Wings Pegasus XL-Q	SW-WQ-0010/SW-TE-0036	G-MTTV
OO-985	Microbel TD 1+1	90-1001	
OO-986	Microbel TD 1+1	90-1002	
OO-987	Weedhopper AX-2	9032465	
OO-988	Dynali Chickinox	345237	
OO-989	Microbel XL TD 1+1	90-1003	
OO-990	Dynali Chickinox	344405	
OO-991	Dynali Chickinox	3110168	
OO-992	Microbel TD 1+1	90-1101	
OO-993	Eipper Quicksilver MXL-II	178	
OO-994	Air Création GT BI 582-ES	053	
OO-995	Air Création GT BI 503-2	056	
OO-996	Weedhopper AX-2	0102821	
OO-997	Weedhopper Europa II	0112839	
OO-998	Aériane Sirocco	90-101	
	(Possibly sold as PH-1Z2 which is c/n 89-101 ?)		
OO-999	Weedhopper AX-2	0092801	

OO-A01	Solar Wings Pegasus XL-R	SW-WA-1343/SW-TB-1356	G-MVBX
OO-A02	CFM Shadow Series CD	155CD	
OO-A03	Eipper Quicksilver MX-IIHP	5004	
OO-A04	Micronef Cosmos BI RO	059	
OO-A05	Aviasud Mistral	0142	
OO-A06	Dynali Chickinox	319454	
OO-A07	Aériane Sirocco	87	
OO-A08	Dynali Chickinox	32521332	
OO-A09	Air Création Safari GT BI	unkn	
OO-A10	Aviasud Mistral	141	
OO-A11	Air Création GT BI 582-ES	060	
OO-A14	Mircobel	91/0502	
OO-A15	Micronef Cosmos	8579	
OO-A16	Air Création GT BI 582-ES	062	
OO-A17	Dynali Chickinox	912053738	
OO-A18	Rans S-12 Airaile	10090027	
OO-A19	Aviasud Mistral	148	
OO-A20	Dynali Chickinox	2391872	
OO-A21	Fulmar	341406	
OO-A22	Kolb Firestar	unkn	
OO-A23	CFM Shadow Series CD	K103	
OO-A24	Dynali Chickinox	3191874	
OO-A25	Cosmos Bidulum 447	8667	
OO-A26	Microbel TS 1+1	91/0901	
OO-A27	Micronef SC BI RO 503	603	
OO-A28	Dynali Chickinox	3391879	
OO-A30	Air Création GT BI 582-ES	064	
OO-A31	Air Création GT BI 582-ES	065	
OO-A32	Dynali Chickinox	21109064	
OO-A33	Dynali Chickinox	358001	
OO-A34	Air Création GT BI 503S	066	
OO-A35	Aviasud Mistral	0156	
OO-A36	Aviasud Mistral	0155	
OO-A37	Micronef Cosmos 503-1	068	
OO-A38	Air Création GT BI	070	
OO-A39	Microbel TD 1+1	910501	
OO-A40	Dynali Chickinox	0792889	
OO-A41	Dynali Chickinox	0792890	
OO-A43	Dynali Chickinox	3891B84	
OO-A44	Air Création GT BI 503S	069	
OO-A45	Micronef Cosmos BI 582-2S	071	
OO-A46	HM.1000 Balèrit	HM.1000/52	
OO-A47	Microbel TD 1+1	92/0401	
OO-A48	Dynali Chickinox	3591B78	
OO-A50	HM.1000 Balèrit	69	
OO-A51	Racer SX2-503S	072	
OO-A53	Rans S-6 Coyote II (Also flies as 59-QM)	1091222	
OO-A54	Rans S-12 Airaile	0991126	N61ME?
OO-A55	Merlin Stoll	A0006	
OO-A56	Weedhopper AX-3	B1032881	
OO-A57	Dynali Chickinox	1792892	
OO-A58	Dynali Chickinox	3980021	
OO-A59	Dynali Chickinox	393240	
OO-A60	Rans S-6 Coyote II (Now/also 59-NK)	0891214	
OO-A61	Dynali Chickinox Kot-Kot	0492885	
OO-A63	Eipper Quicksilver MX-II Sprint	323	
OO-A64	CFM Shadow Series CD	189CD	
OO-A65	Air Création GT BI 582ES	073	
OO-A66	Rans S-6 Coyote II ESD	0292271	
OO-A67	Cosmos Trike	0791241	
OO-A68	Air Création GT BI 582ES	074	
OO-A70	Air Création Safari GT BI 503	075	
OO-A71	Weedhopper AX-3	B2043009	
OO-A72	Dynali Chickinox	2592B98	
OO-A73	Air Création Racer 447	079	
OO-A74	Dynali Chickinox	2692B96	
OO-A75	Air Création Safari GT BI 503S	081	
OO-A76	Air Création Safari GT BI 582	078	
OO-A77	Air Création Safari GT BI 503S	076	
OO-A78	Air Création Racer 447	077	
OO-A79	Solar Wings Pegasus Quasar II.TC	SW-WQT-0548/SW-TQD-0109	
OO-A81	Mignet HM.1000 Balèrit	72	
OO-A82	Air Création Safari GT BI 503S	080	
OO-A84	Dynali Chickinox	4092B105	
OO-A85	Cosmos BI II	B971	
OO-A86	Cosmos BI II 582	B983	
OO-A87	Dynali Chickinox	5092B110	
OO-A88	Weedhopper AX2-503	B1032886	
OO-A89	Mignet HM.1000 Balèrit	75	
OO-A90	Air Création GT BI	082	
OO-A91	Dynali Chickinox (Also wears 59-CEI)	5092B109	
OO-A92	TEAM Mini-MAX 1500	610	
OO-A93	Dynali Chickinox	2491B71	
OO-A94	Air Création Racer SX 12	3909789	PH-2F9
OO-A95	CFM Shadow Series CD	200CD	
OO-A96	Dynali Chickinox	4192B106	
OO-A97	Air Création GT BI 503	084	
OO-A98	Rans S-6 Coyote II ESD (Also wears 59-TT) Co 93/0201		
OO-A99	Dynali Chickinox	4792B111	
OO-B01	Eipper Quicksilver GT-500	202	
OO-B02	Mignet HM.1000 Balèrit	76	
OO-B03	Dynali Chickinox	D3079B00114	
OO-B04	Dynali Chickinox Kot-Kot	4092B103	
OO-B05	Pendulaire Quasar QII 582	SW-WQT-0588/SW-TQD-0128	
OO-B06	Weedhopper AX-3	C3023096	
OO-B07	Murphy Renegade Spirit	unkn	68-EB
OO-B09	Dynali Chickinox	312131341	
OO-B12	Weedhopper JC-31	4010018	
OO-B14	Rans S-5 Coyote I	92191	
OO-B15	Microbel SC-447	921101	
OO-B16	Eipper Quicksilver MX-IIHP	5006	
OO-B17	Weedhopper AX-3	C3033098	
OO-B18	Rans S-6ESD Coyote II	1292413	
OO-B19	Rans S-6ESD Coyote II	1192394	
OO-B21	Cosmos Phase II	978	
OO-B22	Rans S-12 Airaile	1192321	
OO-B23	Air Création GT BI 503-2	085	
OO-B24	Quasar Q II	930601	
OO-B25	Microbel Q II	930401	
OO-B26	Microbel TD 1+1	920801	
OO-B27	Rans S-6 Coyote II	1092370	
OO-B28	Zenair CH-701 STOL	7-2012	
OO-B29	American Aircraft Falcon	018	
OO-B30	Weedhopper AX-3	C3063118	
OO-B31	Solar Wings Pegasus Q-462	93/0701	
OO-B32	Rans S-6ES Coyote II	1192382	
OO-B33	Rans S-6ES Coyote II	0393456	
OO-B34	Zenair CH-701 STOL	7-2014	
OO-B35	Rans S-6ES Coyote II	0393461	
OO-B36	Weedhopper AX-3	C3073127	
OO-B37	Rans S-6ES Coyote II	1192391	
OO-B38	Dynali Chickinox	1693B117	
OO-B39	CFM Shadow Series CD	K216	
OO-B40	Air Création GT BI 582S	087	
OO-B41	Air Création GT BI 582S	088	
OO-B43	Rans S-6ESD Coyote II	1192390	
OO-B44	Air Création SX2 Racer 503S	083	
OO-B45	Aviasud Albatros 522	008	
OO-B46	Dynali Chickinox Kot-Kot	3393B123	
OO-B48	Rans S-6ESD Coyote II	0793518	
OO-B49	Dynali Chickinox	3692B102	
OO-B50	Weedhopper JC.31D-BI	4072020	
OO-B51	Air Création GT BI 503-S	089	
OO-B52	Aviasud Mistral	194	
OO-B53	Air Création GT BI 582-S	092	
OO-B54	Weedhopper AX3/503	C3093150	
OO-B55	Air Création GT BI 582S	094	
OO-B56	Dynali Chickinox	3792B100	
OO-B57	Weedhopper AX-3	C3113172	
OO-B58	Weedhopper AX-3	C3113171	
OO-B59	UltraCraft Calypso	001	
OO-B60	Weedhopper AX3-503	C3113170	
OO-B61	Dynali Chickinox Kot Kot	4793B127	
OO-B62	Aviasud Mistral 582	199	
OO-B63	Weedhopper AX-3	C3113182	
OO-B64	Rans S-4 Coyote I	93204	
OO-B65	Air Création GT BI 582S	093	
OO-B66	Rans S-6ES Coyote II	0993534	
OO-B67	Zenair CH-701 STOL	003	
OO-B68	Pegasus Quantum	6782	
OO-B70	Aviasud Mistral 582	201	
OO-B71	Noble Hardman Snowbird Mk.IV	SB-008	G-MTXV
OO-B72	Air Création GT BI 503S	095	
OO-B73	Cosmos BI 503-2	096	
OO-B74	CFM Shadow Series CD	K219/1	
OO-B75	Air Création GT BI 582S XP	097	
OO-B76	TEAM Mini-MAX 1600	779	
OO-B77	CFM Shadow Series CD	K229/CD	
OO-B78	CFM Shadow Series CD	247/1	
OO-B79	Air Création 582S	098	
OO-B80	Air Création GT BI 503S	099	
OO-B81	Dynali Chickinox	2992P6	
OO-B82	Rans S-6 Coyote II	0294586	
OO-B83	Weedhopper AX-3	C3103164	
OO-B84	Rans S-6ES Coyote II	0594619	
OO-B86	Aviasud Mistral	0686/012	D-MTIF
OO-B87	Rans S-6ES Coyote II	0393468	
OO-B88	Dynali Chickinox (Crashed 8.99)	2391F73	
OO-B89	Solar Wings Pegasus Quantum 15	6794	
OO-B90	Rans S-5 Coyote I	93194	
OO-B91	Air Création GT BI 503S	100	
OO-B92	Air Création Racer 337 Fun 14	101	
OO-B93	Dynali Chickinox	3891B82	
OO-B94	CFM Shadow Series CD	K226/1	
OO-B95	Rans S-6ES Coyote II	0594621	
OO-B96	Weedhopper 55ES Europa II	8022383	
OO-B97	Cosmos Phase II	B913	
OO-B98	Rans S-6 Coyote II	0994673	
OO-B99	Rans S-6ES Coyote II	1194685	
OO-C01	Rans S-6ES Coyote II	0994674	
OO-C02	Rans S-6ES Coyote II	0195725	
OO-C03	Microbel Q TD 1+1	950101	
OO-C04	Microbel Bandit TD 1+1	950301	
OO-C05	Air Création GT BI 503-S	102	
OO-C06	Rans S-6ES Coyote II-582	0295732	59-QS OO-C06
OO-C07	Weedhopper AX-3	B3023097	
OO-C08	Rans S-6ES Coyote II-582	0295737	
OO-C09	Cosmos Phase II Chronos 16M	21078	
OO-C10	Aviasud Mistral	55	55-DC
OO-C11	Rans S-6ES Coyote II	0395780	

OO-C12	Rans S-6ES Coyote II	0595816	
OO-C13	Rans S-6ES Coyote II	0595822	
OO-C15	Eipper Quicksilver GT-500	0123	
OO-C17	Rans S-6ES Coyote II-582TD	0595821	
OO-C18	Weedhopper AX-3	0082792	28-EM
OO-C21	Rans S-6ES Coyote II	1195892	
OO-C22	Aviasud Mistral	195	D-MNAT
	(Also carries French marks 59-PN)		
OO-C23	Air Création Clipper 582-SXP 15	104	
OO-C24	Air Création Clipper 582-SXP 15	106	
OO-C25	Mainair Kolb Twinstar 3	Kit 0021	
OO-C26	Air Création GTE 582S Mild	109	
OO-C27	Aviasud Mistral	184	D-MBTH
OO-C29	Rans S-6ES Coyote II	46545051	
OO-C30	TEAM Mini-MAX 1500R	854	
OO-C31	Rans S-6ES Coyote II	0496976	
OO-C32	TEAM Mini-MAX 1100	1552P	
OO-C33	CFM Shadow Series CD	K267CD	
OO-C34	Cosmos Phase II 582	B-21165	
OO-C35	Rans S-6ESD Coyote IITD	0496981	
OO-C36	Air Création GTE-503S XP	108	
OO-C37	Air Création GTE-503S Mild	110	
OO-C38	Air Création GTE-582S Clipper	114	
OO-C39	Rans S-6ES Coyote IIXL	0396955	
OO-C40	Air Création GTE-503S	111	
OO-C41	Air Création GTE-503S Mild	112	
OO-C42	Rans S-6ES Coyote II	07961017	
OO-C43	Rans S-6 Coyote II	0596994	
OO-C44	Mainair Blade 582	1099-1096-7-W902	
OO-C45	Microbel TD 1+1	960301	
OO-C46	Rans S-6ES Coyote II	09961037	
OO-C48	Air Création GTE 582-S XP15	119	
OO-C50	Pegasus Quantum 582	7294	
OO-C51	CFM Shadow Series CD	K285/1	
OO-C52	Rans S-6 Coyote II	02971090	
OO-C54	Rans S-6ES Coyote II	08961029	
OO-C55	Rans S-6ES Coyote II	0696996	
OO-C56	UltraCraft Calypso	002	
OO-C57	Air Création GTE 503-S	122	
OO-C58	Air Création GTE 582-S	115	
OO-C60	Rans S-6ES Coyote II	01971087	
OO-C61	Air Création GTE 503-SL Mild	123	
OO-C62	Air Création GTE 503S	126	
OO-C63	Air Création GTE 582S Clipper	125	
OO-C64	Air Création GTE 582S XP-15	128	
OO-C65	Murphy Renegade Spirit	R583	
OO-C66	Dynali Chickinox Tandem	2692B962	
OO-C68	UltraCraft Calypso 1A	003	
OO-C69	Air Création GTE 503S	130	
OO-C70	Air Création Safari GT 1+1	unkn	
OO-C71	Rans S-6ES Coyote II	0295752ES	47-HY
OO-C72	Zenair CH-701 STOL	7-2886	59-SN
OO-C73	Air Création GTE 503S	132	
OO-C74	Paramotor Solo 210	unkn	
OO-C75	Pegasus Quantum 15	7089	
OO-C76	JC.24D Weedhopper D	10.1138	PH-1F9
OO-C77	UltraCraft Calypso	007	
OO-C79	Adventure F3	L1906	
OO-C80	Adventure Z4	8261	
OO-C81	Adventure F3	L1926	
OO-C82	Adventure F3	N2046	
OO-C83	Adventure F3	N2004	
OO-C84	Adventure F3	N2042	
OO-C85	Adventure F3	N2041	
OO-C86	Adventure F3	N2003	
OO-C87	Adventure F3	1641	
OO-C88	Adventure F3	1611	
OO-C89	Murphy Maverick	97	
OO-C90	TEAM Mini-MAX 1600	967	
OO-C91	Adventure F3	2018N	
OO-C92	Adventure F3	Q2193	
OO-C93	Adventure F3	02148	
OO-C94	Adventure F3	2168	
OO-C95	Adventure F3	1959	
OO-C96	Adventure F3	2017N	
OO-C97	Air Création GTE	135	
OO-C98	Air Création GTE	136	
OO-C99	Air Création GTE	133	
OO-D01	Air Création GT BI	137	
OO-D02	Weedhopper JC.31	3788844	59-XJ
OO-D03	Rans S-6ES Coyote II	07981250	
OO-D04	Rans S-6ES Coyote II	06991323	
OO-D05	Rans S-6ES Coyote II	06981238	59-YN
OO-D06	Rans S-6ES Coyote II	07971139	59-WA
OO-D07	Ultracraft Calypso 1	005	
OO-D08	Air Création GTE	138	
OO-D09	Air Création GTE	139	
OO-D10	Murphy Renegade Spirit	388	OO-128
OO-D11	Air Création GTE	140	
OO-D12	Air Création GTE	107	
OO-D13	Chapelet Big Bang Lazer	112EB04996E05	
OO-D15	Murphy Renegade IV	R602	
OO-D16	Dyn'Aero MCR-01	51	
OO-D17	Funk FK-9 Mk.3	148	
OO-D18	Ultracraft Calypso	004	
OO-D19	Air Création GTE	B 101510	
OO-D20	Rans S-6ES Coyote II	11991347	

OO-D21	Rans S-10 Sakota	0893164	OO-131
	(Still marked OO-131 under the wing)		
OO-D22	Zenair CH-701 STOL	7-9000	59-XS
OO-D23	Air Création GTE	142	
OO-D24	Aviasud Albatros	129	59-ZI
OO-D25	Funk FK-9 Mk.3	134	
OO-D26	EV-97 Eurostar	980203	OK-DUR-19
OO-D27	Pegasus Quantum	7623	59-ACC
OO-D28	Rans S-6ES Coyote II	0894667	59-NV
OO-D29	Murphy Renegade	628R	
OO-D31	Fly Synthesis Storch	243	59-ZV
OO-D33	Murphy Renegade Limair III	627	
OO-D34	Dyn'Aero MCR-01 UL	112	21-QP
OO-D35	Dyn'Aero MCR-01 UL	155	
OO-D36	Ultracraft Calypso 1A	006	
OO-D37	Aviasud AE209 Albatros	050	59-LZ
OO-D38	Microbel	990701	
OO-D39	Murphy Renegade Spirit	646	
OO-D40	AK-3 Kolibri	04	PH-3B3
OO-D41	Pegasus Quantum	7527	
OO-D42	Rans S-6 Coyote II	11001400	
OO-D43	Aviasud AE209 Albatros	126	
	(Call sign OQ-BKK)		
OO-D44	Funk FK-9 Mk.3	161	
OO-D45	Dyn'Aero MCR-01 UL	203	
OO-D46	Microbel	010701	
OO-D47	Zenair CH-601 Zodiac	6-9119	
OO-D48	Funk FK-9 Mk.3	178	
OO-D49	Microbel TD 1+1	000501	
OO-D50	Rans S-6 Coyote II	06971124	59-WE
OO-D51	Dyn'Aero MCR-01 UL	151	
OO-D53	Zenair CH-601 Zodiac	6-9071	
OO-D54	Ultracraft Calypso 2A	001	
OO-D55	Funk FK-9 Mk.3	150	
OO-D56	Jabiru UL-450	0403	
OO-D58	Air Création GTE	144	
OO-D59	Fly Synthesis Storch	155	59-TD
OO-D60	Zenair CH-601 Zodiac	6-9130	59-VX
OO-D61	Aeropro Eurofox	10001	PH-3M7
OO-D62	Aeropro Eurofox	081099	PH-3H5
OO-D63	Fly Synthesis Texan	2002/0012	
OO-D64	Pegasus Quantum	7882	
OO-D65	Aeropro Eurofox	050698	PH-3G5
OO-D66	Fly Synthesis Storch	250	59-AAJ
OO-D67	Dyn'Aero MCR-01 UL	188	
OO-D69	Fly Synthesis Texan	2002/0015	
OO-D70	Aeropro Eurofox	09400	PH-3K7
OO-D71	Funk FK-9 Mk.3	187	
OO-D72	Zenair CH-601 Zodiac	6-9123	
OO-D73	Rans S-6 Coyote II	11011425	
OO-D76	Air Création GTE	146	59-CBA
OO-D77	Fly Synthesis Texan	2002/0016A	
OO-D78	Fly Synthesis Storch	258	
OO-D80	Impulse 100	02	
OO-D81	Funk FK-9 Mk.3	189	
OO-D82	Zenair CH-701 STOL	7-9129	
OO-D83	Best Off Sky Ranger	0112153	
OO-D85	Air Création GTE	T02075	
OO-D86	TEAM Mini-MAX 1600R	837	
OO-D87	Funk FK-9 Mk.3	193	
OO-D88	Aeropro Eurofox	09700	
OO-D89	Microbel TD 1+1	990901	
OO-D90	Dynali Chickinox Kot Kot	0997B1	
OO-D91	Funk FK-14 Polaris	030	
OO-D92	Fly Synthesis Texan 912 ULS	2002/0021	
OO-D93	Funk FK-14 Polaris	031	
OO-D94	Funk FK-9 Mk.3	194	
OO-D95	Flight Design CT	02-03-03-12	
OO-D96	Air Création GT Clipper	103	59-RJ
OO-D97	Air Création GTE 582S Kiss	145	59-CDX
	(French c/n was quoted as AO1195-1208)		
OO-D98	ATEC Vos Zephyr 2000C	Z490102S	W59-CES
OO-D99	Fantasy Air Allegro SW582	02-1501	
OO-E01	Air Création GTE 582SKiss 450	T02076	
OO-E02	Funk FK-9 Mk.3	192	
OO-E03	Cosmos BI90/Micronef Bidulm	521	
OO-E04	Chapelet Big Bang Lazer	FT 2003-01	
OO-E05	Aviasud AE.209 Albatros	024	59-LH (OO-B91) 59-LH
OO-E06	Flight Design CT-2K	03-01-01-01	
OO-E07	Dyn'Aero MCR UL	248	
OO-E08	Dyn'Aero MCR UL	230	
OO-E09	Funk FK-14 Polaris	023	D-MABH
OO-E10	Fly Synthesis Wallaby	2002-005	
OO-E11	Aeropro Eurofox	13203	
OO-E12	Aeropro Eurofox	13803	
OO-E13	Asso Aeri AssoV Champion V	025	
OO-E14	Rans S-6 Coyote II	0593502	59-NJ
OO-E15	Fly Synthesis Wallaby	2002-002	
OO-E16	Zenair CH-601XL Zodiac	6-9415	
OO-E17	Air Creation GTE 582S	T 02107	
OO-E18	Chapelet Lazer XP15	FT 2003/02	
OO-E19	Murphy Renegade	664	
OO-E20	Murphy Maverick	098M	
OO-E21	Aeropro Eurofox	12402	
	(Call sign OQ-BKM)		

OO-E22	Ultracraft Calypso 2A	002	
OO-E23	Zenair CH-701 STOL	7-2103	59-MT
OO-E24	Flight Design CT-2K (Damaged .04)	03-03-06-13	
OO-E25	Fly Synthesis Storch HS	2003/331	
OO-E26	Jabiru UL-450	556	
OO-E27	Rans S-6ES Coyote II	unk.	
OO-E28	Fly Synthesis Texan 912 ULS	2003/029	
OO-E29	Air Creation GTE 582S iXess	T03077	
OO-E30	Alpi Aviation Pioneer 200WF	38	
OO-E31	DTA Feeling 912S Dynamic 450	00-64	58-FC
OO-E32	Dyn'Aero MCR-01 ULC	269	
OO-E33	Funk FK-9 Mk.3	09-04-216	
OO-E34	Rans S.10 Sakota (C/n quoted as 0892.145 which is ZK-SWJ, above believed correct)	0892143	OO-134
OO-E35	Dynali Chickinox BI (Was regd in Luxembourg as c/n 3192B91)	3987360	LX-XGH
OO-E36	Air Création GTE	T03096	
OO-E37	Dyn'Aero MCR UL	267	
OO-E38	Best Off Sky Ranger	0212303	
OO-E39	Halley Appolo Fox	B02/2002	59-CET
OO-E40	Rans S-6 Coyote II	08031512ES	
OO-E41	Aeropro Eurofox	14803	
OO-E42	DTA Dynamic	OO-65	58-FD
OO-E43	Air Création GTE	T03046	
OO-E44	Funk FK-9 Mk.3	217	
OO-E45	Pegasus Quik 912S Executive	8013	
OO-E46	Flight Design CT-2K	03-05-05-24	
OO-E47	Aeropro Eurofox	14904	
OO-E48	Best Off Sky Ranger	0311416	
OO-E49	Asso Aeri Asso V Champion V	032	
OO-E50	Rans Coyote II	12031539	
OO-E51	Alpi Aviation Pioneer 200WF	67	
OO-E52	Flight Design CT-2K	02-02-02-07	62-ACI W62-ACI
OO-E53	Rans S-6ES Coyote II	0895872ES	59-RB
OO-E54	Fly Synthesis Storch	2004-344	
OO-E55	Fly Synthesis Storch	2004-348	
OO-E56	Air Création GTE 582S-XP15	T 99052	54-QA
OO-E57	Funk FK-9 Mk.3 Paraplegic	232	
OO-E58	Rans S-6 Coyote II	0895866	59-RA
OO-E59	Air Création GTE 582S Ixess 15	T 03076	
OO-E60	Vol Mediterrani VM-1 Esqual	E-180030	
OO-E61	Funk FK-9 Mk.3	242	
OO-E62	Alisport Yuma	1970540	
OO-E63	Finale 24 Falco 95	07/04	
OO-E64	Dyn'Aero MCR UL	282	
OO-E65	Rans Coyote II	02041550	
OO-E66	SG Aviation Storm 280GS	S2-OIR-0025	
OO-E67	Aeropro Eurofox	16204	
OO-E68	DTA Feeling 912S Dynamic 450	191	
OO-E69	AMS-Flight Apis M (Powered glider with retractable engine)	A016M06	S5-AMS2
OO-E70	SG Aviation Rally 105C	R2-OOR-0001	
OO-E71	Fly Synthesis Storch	350	
OO-E72	Funk FK-14 Polaris	014-048	
OO-E73	Air Création GTE 582S XP15	117	59-WB
OO-E74	Rans S-6ES Coyote II	06041586	
OO-E75	Funk FK-14 Polaris	014-047	
OO-E76	Pipistrel Sinus	026S582 01 01	59-CBR
OO-E77	Funk FK-9 Mk.3	249	
OO-E78	Rans S-6ES Coyote II	05041576	
OO-E79	Ultracraft Calypso 1B	01	
OO-E80	Rans S-6ES Coyote II	06041583	
OO-E81	Fly Synthesis Wallaby	2004-022	
OO-E82	Funk FK-14 Polaris	014-050	
OO-E83	Aeropro Eurofox	16504	
OO-E84	Aeroprakt A22 Vision	92	
OO-E85	Air Création Racer 503-S XP11	147	59-WB

Parapentes (powered parachutes) are now being entered in a separate sequence although earlier examples remain in the ULM register above.

OO-P0001	Fly	70ZN2++MAHLE W2
OO-P0002	Adventure F4	2174
OO-P0003	Fly Castelluccio	SMA 1955
OO-P0004	Adventure F3	V 2346
OO-P0006	Adventure F4	V-2395
OO-P0007	Centrair Parafan Mono	41035

A number of French registered microlights based in Belgium have been noted using radio call-signs with a Belgian OQ- prefix. Known examples are as follows and, as usual, additions would be gratefully received.

OQ-AXH	Rans S-6 Coyote II	also 59-TN
OQ-AYW	Rans S-6 Coyote II	also 59-PV

OY - DENMARK

Regn.	Type	C/n	Prev.Id.
OY-AAC	S.A.I. KZ-III U-2	108	
OY-AAD	S.A.I. KZ-VII U-4 Laerke	157	
OY-AAM	Piper PA-22 Tri-Pacer 125	22-113	(LN-. . .) OY-AAM SE-CLU EI-AJU XB-NOU N811A
OY-AAU	S.A.I. KZ-VII U-4 Laerke	158	
OY-AAV	S.A.I. KZ-VII U-4 Laerke	160	D-EHED OY-AAV
OY-AAZ	S.A.I. KZ-VII U-4 Laerke	165	
OY-ABF	S.A.I. KZ-VII U-4 Laerke	164	
OY-ABG	S.A.I. KZ-VII U-4 Laerke *(Dismantled)*	167	
OY-ABJ	Piper PA-22-150 Caribbean	22-6918	N10F
OY-ABL	S.A.I. KZ-VII U-4 Laerke	171	D-EABE OY-ABL
OY-ABM	S.A.I. KZ-VII U-4 Laerke	172	D-EFIF(2) OY-ABM ZS-BXX OY-ABM
OY-ABT	Piper J-3F-50 Cub	2475	
OY-ACG	S.A.I. KZ-III U	51	RDAF:612 RDAF:51
OY-ACH	S.A.I. KZ-VII U-7 Laerke	200	
OY-ACO	S.A.I. KZ-VII U-4 Laerke	166	
OY-ACS(2)	Piper PA-22-108 Colt	22-9116	SE-CRY
OY-ACW	Piper PA-22-150 Caribbean	22-7538	G-ARHO N3643Z
OY-ADR	Mooney M.20A	1532	N8354E
OY-ADW	Cessna 172B	17248072	(N7572X)
OY-AEA	S.A.I. KZ-II Coupé	27	OH-KZT OH-SPJ SE-ANR (OY-DUY)
OY-AFD	Piper PA-22-108 Colt	22-9388	LN-IKM
OY-AFH	Morane-Saulnier MS.885 Super Rallye	11	
OY-AFP	Cessna 172B	17247957	SE-CXG N7457X
OY-AFT	Piper PA-22-108 Colt	22-8284	N10F
OY-AFV	Cessna 172C	17249168	N1468Y
OY-AFW	Taylor J-2 Cub	S.559	SE-AEW
OY-AGB	Cessna F172H	F172-0527	(G-. . . .) OY-AGB
OY-AGF	Cessna F172H	F172-0552	
OY-AGG	Cessna F172H	F172-0539	(SE-FMP)
OY-AGH	Cessna F172H	F172-0485	
OY-AGI	Cessna F150H	F150-0327	
OY-AGL	Cessna F172H	F172-0589	
OY-AGW	Reims/Cessna F172M	F17201131	
OY-AHD	Cessna F172H	F172-0473	
OY-AHF	Cessna F172H	F172-0434	
OY-AHM	Cessna F150H	F150-0316	
OY-AHY	Cessna F172H	F172-0494	
OY-AIE	Scintex Piel CP.301C-1 Emeraude	555	
OY-AIK	Piper PA-23-180 Apache	23-1759	OH-PNU OY-AIK N4260P
OY-AIN	Piper PA-20 Pacer 125	20-42	VP-KIR ZS-DDU
OY-AJI	Piper PA-34-200 Seneca	34-7250312	SE-FND N1413T
OY-AJJ	SOCATA MS.880B Rallye Club	3031	
OY-AJL	Cessna 172N Skyhawk II	17269173	N734WM
OY-AJM	Reims/Cessna F172N	F17201682	(D-EIIC)
OY-AJN	SOCATA MS.893E Rallye 180GT Gaillard *(Damaged 20.11.96)*	13087	
OY-AJU	Reims/Cessna F150L	F15000673	D-EKNC PH-GKG
OY-AKE	Reims/Cessna FA150L Aerobat	FA1500100	
OY-AKH	Reims/Cessna F172K	F17200775	
OY-AKM	Piper PA-16 Clipper	16-101	D-EKUW N9979F HB-OOE
OY-AKP	Cessna 337D Super Skymaster	33701076	(G-AWYD) N86095
OY-AKT	Cessna F172H	F172-0532	D-EMTG
OY-AKY	Reims/Cessna F172L	F17200819	
OY-ALA	Aeronca 7AC Champion	7AC-1024	N9120U G-TINE (OY-ALA) D-EBGF(2) N82391
OY-ALB	Piper PA-18 Super Cub 95	18-1355	D-EFCZ ALAT 51-15355
OY-ALC	Piper PA-12 Super Cruiser	12-2838	D-ELEB N3950M NC3950M
OY-ALD	DHC-1 Chipmunk 22	C1/0902	RDAF: P-147 RDAF: 12-147

OY-ALF	Piper J-3C-65 Cub	12591	D-EGAR HB-OBR 44-80295
OY-ALJ	Piper PA-18-150 Super Cub	18-8220	PH-NKF N10F
OY-ALL	DHC-1 Chipmunk 22	C1/0881	RDAF: P-142 RDAF: 12-142
OY-ALM	Piper J-3C-65 Cub	8766	D-EMOG OO-AAH 42-36642
OY-ALR	Piper J-3C-65 Cub	12987	D-EDMA D-ECYC HB-OCL 44-80691
OY-ALW	Miles M.28 Mercury 6	6268	D-EHAB G-AHAA
OY-ALZ	DHC-1 Chipmunk 22	C1/0067	RDAF: P-121 RDAF: 12-121
OY-AME	Jodel D.112 Club	1152	
OY-AMG	Druine D.31 Turbulent	274	
OY-AMJ	Druine D.31 Turbulent	1	
OY-AMO	Jodel D.112 Club	956	
OY-AMR	Druine D.31 Turbulent	282	
OY-AMS	Druine D.31 Turbulent	1	
OY-ANF	Piper J-3C-65 Cub	13052	D-EFPE (D-EGPI) OE-AAR (D-EDYR) 44-80756
OY-ANG	Reims/Cessna F172M	F17201232	
OY-ANH	Reims/Cessna F172M	F17201224	(OY-RYZ)
OY-AOL	S.A.I. KZ-X Mk II	205	OY-ACL
OY-AOZ	Beech 23 Musketeer	M-446	
OY-APB	Boeing 737-5L9	28084	G-MSKE OY-APB
OY-APH(2)	Boeing 737-5L9	28721	
OY-API (2)	Boeing 737-5L9	28722	
OY-APK(2)	Boeing 737-5L9	28995	
OY-APL(2)	Boeing 737-5L9	28996	SP-LKK OY-APL
OY-APN(2)	Boeing 737-5L9	28997	
OY-APP(2)	Boeing 737-5L9	29234	N1786B
OY-APR(2)	Boeing 737-5L9	29235	N1786B
OY-ARJ	Cessna 414	414-0614	D-IAWM N69397
OY-ARL	Cessna 182P (Reims-assembled with "c/n" 0028)	18263958	D-EATU N9938E
OY-ARY	Grumman AA-1A Trainer	AA1A-0420	SE-FTU (N6220L)
OY-ASJ	Beech D95A Travel Air	TD-541	SE-EEX OY-DCM
OY-ASM	Reims/Cessna F172M	F17201316	
OY-ASW	Piper PA-34-200T Seneca II	34-7670105	D-ILBI N7843C
OY-ASY	Embraer EMB.110P1 Bandeirante	110308	EI- BPI OY-ASY PT-SCO
OY-ATC	Reims/Cessna F172L	F17200853	D-ECSB
OY-ATD	DHC-1 Chipmunk 22	C1/0891	RDAF: P-145 RDAF: 12-145
OY-ATE	DHC-1 Chipmunk 22	C1/0885	RDAF: P-144 RDAF: 12-144
OY-ATF(2)	DHC-1 Chipmunk 22 *(Flies as WD319)* *(Replacement fuselage for OY-ATF(1) c/n C1/0787, damaged 29.7.97 and noted at Stauning 6.00. Still officially regd as C1/0787) (Permit 10.01)*	C1/0256	HB-TUE G-AOZJ EI-AHV WD319
OY-ATI	S.A.I. KZ-VII Laerke	178	RDAF: 0-616 RDAF: 63-616
OY-ATJ	S.A.I. KZ-VII Laerke	186	RDAF: 0-623 RDAF: 63-623
OY-ATL	DHC-1 Chipmunk 22	C1/0897	RDAF: P-146 RDAF: 12-146
OY-ATM	S.A.I. KZ-VII Laerke	181	RDAF: 0-619 RDAF: 63-619
OY-ATO	DHC-1 Chipmunk 22 *(Painted as P-129)*	C1/0108	RDAF: P-129 RDAF: 12-129
OY-ATR	DHC-1 Chipmunk 22	C1/0802	RDAF: P-140 RDAF: 12-140
OY-ATT	Piper PA-28-180 Cherokee Challenger	28-7305118	G-BASF N11C
OY-ATY	DHC-6 Twin Otter 300	561	C-GRZH-X
OY-AUN	Piper PA-28-181 Archer II	28-8090021	N2974L
OY-AUR	SOCATA Rallye 235C Gabier	13261	N354RA
OY-AUU	Cessna 172L	17259274	LN-BGF N7574G
OY-AUW	SOCATA MS.893E Rallye 180GT Gaillard	13085	F-GBCE
OY-AUY	Auster J/1 Autocrat	2241	D-EJSA OE-AAH(1) G-AJAI
OY-AVC	Piper J-3C-65 Cub	12833	D-EBES 44-80537
OY-AVF	DHC-1 Chipmunk 22	C1/0794	RDAF: P-139 RDAF: 12-139
OY-AVG	Piper J-4 Cub Coupé	4-441	D-EDED G-AFPP
OY-AVH(2)	S.A.I. KZ-VII U-8	183	RDAF: 0-621 RDAF: 63-621

OY-AVK	S.A.I. KZ-VII Laerke U-8	197	D-ENIM LX-AIT
OY-AVL	DHC-1 Chipmunk 22	C1/0107	RDAF: P-128 RDAF: 12-128
OY-AVM(2)	Yakovlev Yak-55	890709	ZU-BSL ES-FYL DOSAAF: 62blue
OY-AVN	Aeronca 11AC Chief	11AC-1601	D-EKUD HB-UPK D-ECAB N9953F LX-AID
OY-AVR	S.A.I. KZ-VII	176	RDAF: 0-615 RDAF: 63-615
OY-AVT	Piper PA-18 Super Cub 95	18-3202	D-ELFT OL-L05 L-128 53-4802
OY-AVU	Piper PA-12 Super Cruiser	12-1272	D-ELKE N2835M NC2835M
OY-AVV	Beagle A.61 Terrier 2	B.612	D-EBMU (D-ECKO) G-ASBT WE603
OY-AVY	Auster Mk.5	1400	D-EJON PH-NEG PH-NAD G-AJYH TJ352
OY-AVZ	Bücker Bü.181B Bestmann	25073	D-ELET Fv25073
OY-AYA	American AA-1 Yankee	AA1-0411	
OY-AYF	American AA-1 Yankee	AA1-0446	SE-INF OY-AYF (N6246L)
OY-AYL	Grumman-American AA-5 Traveler	AA5-0021	
OY-AYM	Grumman-American AA-5 Traveler	AA5-0020	
OY-AYN	Grumman-American AA-1B Trainer 2	AA1B-0311	
OY-AYP	Grumman-American AA-5 Traveler	AA5-0359	(N5459L)
OY-AYR	Grumman-American AA-5 Traveler	AA5-0360	(N5460L)
OY-AYS	Grumman-American AA-5 Traveler	AA5-0420	(N7120L)
OY-AYW	Grumman-American AA-5 Traveler	AA5-0264	
OY-AYY	Grumman-American AA-5 Traveler	AA5-0265	
OY-AYZ	Grumman-American AA-5 Traveler	AA5-0361	(N5461L)
OY-AZC	Reims/Cessna F150L	F15000683	PH-EHD
OY-AZD	Reims/Cessna F150L	F15001078	PH-GDR
OY-AZE	Reims/Cessna F172M	F17201021	PH-SMH
OY-AZH	Cessna F172E	F172-0058	PH-LZE D-ELZE
OY-AZK	Reims/Cessna F172M	F17201072	PH-ADF
OY-AZM	Reims/Cessna F172N	F17201718	PH-AXA(2)
OY-AZR(2)	Piper PA-18 Super Cub 95	18-3151	RDAF: Y-652 RDAF: 66-652 L-89 53-4751
OY-AZU	Robin DR.400/160 Chevalier	1144	LN-BEZ
OY-AZZ	Piper PA-18-135 Super Cub	18-3165	RDAF:Y-654 RDAF:66-654 OL-L91 53-4765
OY-BAB	Piper PA-28-235 Cherokee	28-10143	N8628W
OY-BAF	Piper PA-28-140 Cherokee	28-20680	
OY-BAG	Piper PA-28-235 Cherokee	28-10640	LN-BEC OY-BAG
OY-BAZ	Piper PA-28-180 Cherokee C	28-2497	
OY-BBA	Piper PA-28-140 Cherokee	28-21160	
OY-BBB	Piper PA-28-180 Cherokee C	28-2589	SE-EPH
OY-BBC	Piper PA-28-140 Cherokee	28-21145	
OY-BBD	Piper PA-28-140 Cherokee	28-20972	SE-EOF
OY-BBE	Piper PA-28-140 Cherokee	28-20987	SE-EPL
OY-BBI	Piper PA-28-140 Cherokee	28-21451	
OY-BBJ	Piper PA-28-180 Cherokee C	28-3205	SE-EYP
OY-BBK	Piper PA-28-140 Cherokee	28-21064	N11C
OY-BBM	Piper PA-28-140 Cherokee	28-22412	SE-EPP
OY-BBN	Piper PA-28-140 Cherokee	28-22502	SE-EPH
OY-BBP	Piper PA23-250 Aztec C	27-3038	(SE-...) OY-BBP N10F
OY-BBR	Piper PA-28-140 Cherokee *(Damaged 20.8.95)*	28-22877	
OY-BBS	Piper PA-28-180 Cherokee C	28-4209	
OY-BBT	Piper PA-28-180 Cherokee C	28-3487	SE-EZA
OY-BBV	Piper PA-28-140 Cherokee	28-22977	
OY-BBW	Piper PA-28-180 Cherokee C	28-2737	N11C
OY-BBY	Piper PA-28-180 Cherokee C	28-3663	
OY-BCA	Piper PA-28-180 Cherokee C	28-3971	
OY-BCB	Piper PA-28-140 Cherokee	28-22942	
OY-BCF	Piper PA-28-140 Cherokee	28-22842	SE-EZX
OY-BCG	Piper PA-28-180 Cherokee C	28-3966	SE-FAH
OY-BCK	Piper PA-28-140 Cherokee	28-22997	N560W OY-BCK N9560W
OY-BCL	Piper PA-28R-180 Cherokee Arrow	28R-30156	
OY-BCR	Piper PA-32-260 Cherokee Six	32-838	N3892W
OY-BCU	Piper PA-28-180 Cherokee D	28-4814	

OY-BCY	Piper PA-28-140 Cherokee	28-24406	
OY-BDC	Piper PA-28R-200 Cherokee Arrow	28R-35313	(OY-BDG)
OY-BDF	Piper PA-28-140 Cherokee B *(Dbr 1.8.98)*	28-26074	
OY-BDG	Piper PA-28-180 Cherokee D	28-5456	
OY-BDI	Piper PA-28R-180 Cherokee Arrow	28R-31079	
OY-BDU	Piper PA-28-140 Cherokee E	28-7225140	
OY-BDV	Piper PA-28R-200 Cherokee Arrow II	28R-7235068	
OY-BEF	Piper PA-23-250 Aztec F	27-7654185	LN-NAX
			N62734
OY-BEI	Reims/Cessna F177RG Cardinal RG	F177RG0125	LN-ASZ
			N94721
OY-BFE	Cessna 182P Skylane	18262478	SE-GXZ
			OY-BFE
			N52243
OY-BFI	Reims/Cessna F172M	F17201079	
OY-BFK	Reims/Cessna F172M	F17201094	
OY-BFL	Cessna 182P Skylane	18261610	N21399
OY-BFM	Reims/Cessna F172M	F17201096	
OY-BFP	Reims/Cessna F172M	F17201104	
OY-BFS	Piper PA-28-140 Cherokee	28-24371	SE-EYK
OY-BFV	Reims/Cessna F172M	F17200942	(OY-RYV)
OY-BFW	Reims/Cessna F172M	F17200997	
OY-BFY	Reims/Cessna F172M Skyhawk	F17201142	
OY-BGB	Piper PA-28-140 Cherokee E	28-7225285	SE-FYZ
OY-BGC	Piper PA-28-180 Cherokee Challenger	28-7305290	
OY-BGI	Piper PA-34-200 Seneca	34-7250260	SE-GAI
OY-BGN	Piper PA-28-140 Cherokee	28-7425151	
OY-BGP	Piper PA-28R-200 Cherokee Arrow II	28R-7335170	SE-GDF
OY-BGR	Piper PA-28-140 Cherokee Cruiser	28-7425257	
OY-BGS	Piper PA-28-151 Cherokee Warrior	28-7415258	
OY-BGW	Piper PA-28-140 Cherokee Cruiser	28-7425100	SE-GDZ
OY-BGZ	Piper PA-28-140 Cherokee Cruiser	28-7425104	
OY-BHF	Piper PA-31 Turbo Navajo	31-245	G-BXAZ
			G-AXAZ
			N9184Y
OY-BHI	Cessna 172N Skyhawk II	17273831	5H-OCG
			N5744J
OY-BHS	Viking Dragonfly	480	(OY-83X12)
OY-BHT	Embraer EMB.110-P2 Bandeirante	110161	(N891AC)
			N4942S
			G-CELT
OY-BHU	Piper PA-31T1 Cheyenne 1	31T-7904004	N131SW
			N6173A
OY-BHZ	de Havilland DH.104 Dove 8 *(Wfu)*	04270	G-BLPZ
			WB534
OY-BIE	Reims/Cessna F172M	F17201220	
OY-BIJ	Cessna 182P Skylane	18263703	N4704K
OY-BIK	Reims/Cessna F172M	F17201333	(SE-GKH)
OY-BIL	Reims/Cessna F177RG Cardinal RG	F177RG0122	SE-GKN
OY-BIU	Reims/Cessna F172M	F17201179	(F-BVSF)
OY-BIY	Cessna 182P	18263917	SE-GKI
	(Reims-assembled with "c/n" 0017)		N9810E
OY-BJC	Malmö MFI-9B Trainer *(Crashed 23.10.00)*	70	SE-EWG
OY-BJD	Cessna F150H	F150-0270	SE-IYA
			OY-BJD
			SE-FBX
OY-BJF	Reims/Cessna F150M	F15001421	
OY-BJL	Reims/Cessna F172N	F17201654	
OY-BJM	Reims/Cessna F150M	F15001427	
OY-BJO	Piper PA-28RT-201T Turbo Arrow IV	28R-7931051	G-BGNX
			N2191N
OY-BJP	Fairchild Swearingen SA.227AC Metro III	AC-499	F-GHVG
			SE-KHH
			LN-HPF
			OY-BJP
			N3106D
OY-BJW	Reims/Cessna F172N	F17201649	(D-EGQE)
OY-BKA	Piper PA-28-140 Cherokee	28-24436	
OY-BKC	Laverda F.8L Falco IV	414	
OY-BKD	Piper PA-28-180 Cherokee D	28-4774	
OY-BKG	Piper PA-28R-180 Cherokee Arrow	28R-30680	
OY-BKJ	Piper PA-28-180 Cherokee D	28-5132	
OY-BKK	Piper PA-28-140 Cherokee	28-25009	(N5573F)
OY-BKL	Piper PA-28R-180 Cherokee Arrow	28R-30869	
OY-BKM	Piper PA-28-140 Cherokee	28-24821	
OY-BKN	Piper PA-28-140 Cherokee B	28-25398	
OY-BKP	Piper PA-28-180 Cherokee D *(Wrecked)*	28-5255	
OY-BKS	Piper PA-28-140 Cherokee B	28-25680	
OY-BKU	Piper PA-28-140 Cherokee B *(Dam.12.5.95)*	28-25554	(N8738N)
OY-BKW	Piper PA-28-140 Cherokee B	28-25254	
OY-BKY	Piper PA-28-140 Cherokee B	28-25338	
OY-BLA	Piper PA-28-180 Cherokee Archer	28-7505234	
OY-BLB	Piper PA-28-151 Cherokee Warrior	28-7515420	
OY-BLH	Cessna 150L	15074145	SE-FMI
			N19074
OY-BLI	Cessna 150L	15073891	SE-FMH
			N18238
OY-BLL	Piper PA-28-181 Cherokee Archer II	28-7690145	
OY-BLN	Piper PA-28-151 Cherokee Warrior	28-7615120	
OY-BLO	Piper PA-28-151 Cherokee Warrior	28-7615217	
OY-BLP	Piper PA-28-151 Cherokee Warrior	28-7615218	
OY-BLS	Piper PA-28-181 Cherokee Archer II	28-7690269	
OY-BLU	Piper PA-28-181 Cherokee Archer II	28-7690457	
OY-BLY	Piper PA-28-181 Cherokee Archer II	28-7790121	
OY-BLZ	Piper PA-28-151 Cherokee Warrior	28-7715092	
OY-BMC	Druine D.31 Turbulent	334	
OY-BMH	Druine D.31 Turbulent	325	
OY-BMI	Druine D.31 Turbulent	328	
OY-BMR	Jodel D.112 Club (Modified)	1435	
OY-BMW	Jurca MJ.2 Tempête *(Reservation)*	25	
OY-BNF	Reims/Cessna F172N	F17201854	
OY-BNG	Reims/Cessna F182Q Skylane	F18200126	
OY-BNH	Reims/Cessna F172N Skyhawk II	F17201983	
OY-BNP	Rutan Cozy Mk IV *(Reservation 7.96)*	0688	
OY-BNR	Reims/Cessna FR172K Hawk XP	FR17200674	
OY-BNS	Dornier Do.228-212 *(Reservn 14.7.03)*	8181	9N-AFS
			RP-C2282
			D-CBDG
			YV-535C
			D-CIBA
			D-CBDP
OY-BNW(2)	Piper PA-28-236 Dakota	28-8111077	D-EVAP(2)
			G-BOUI
			N84017
OY-BPB	Douglas C-47A	20019	RDAF:K-682
			RDAF:682
			LN-IAT
			43-15553
OY-BPT	Grumman-American AA-5B Tiger	AA5B-1165	HB-UCP
OY-BRA	Piper PA-28-181 Cherokee Archer II	28-7890426	
OY-BRC	Piper PA-28R-201T Turbo Arrow III	28R-7803322	
OY-BRE	Piper PA-28-181 Cherokee Archer II	28-7890532	
OY-BRI	Piper PA-28-181 Cherokee Archer II	28-7890502	
OY-BRO	Piper PA-38-112 Tomahawk	38-79A0266	
OY-BRP	Piper PA-38-112 Tomahawk	38-78A0748	SE-KDL
			OY-BRP
OY-BRT	Piper PA-28-181 Archer II	28-7990266	
OY-BRY	Piper PA-28-181 Archer II	28-8090220	
OY-BSA	Champion 7GCBC Citabria	155	D-EGPB
OY-BSE	Partenavia P.68B	174	SE-GEU
OY-BSF	Piper PA-34-200 Seneca	34-7350073	SE-GAK
			OH-PND
			SE-GAK
OY-BSI	Piper PA-34-200 Seneca	34-7350334	OO-TNT
			N56458
OY-BSM	Rutan Long-Ez	8202/715	(OY-82X02)
			(OY-8202)
OY-BSO	Cessna 340A	340A0666	D-IGMN
			(LN-LFA)
			D-IGMN
			PH-LTR
			N1913E
OY-BSS(2)	Piper PA-11 Cub Special	11-914	D-EMIX
			N5034H
OY-BSV	Reims/Cessna F172M	F17201435	SE-GOF
OY-BSZ	Piper PA-28R-180 Cherokee Arrow	28R-30332	SE-FCU
OY-BTD	Piper PA-28-161 Cherokee Warrior II	28-7716118	
OY-BTE	Piper PA-28-161 Cherokee Warrior II	28-7716161	
OY-BTF	Piper PA-28-181 Cherokee Archer II	28-7790288	
OY-BTH	Piper PA-28-161 Cherokee Warrior II	28-7716117	
OY-BTI	Piper PA-28-161 Cherokee Warrior II	28-7816146	
OY-BTJ	Piper PA-28-181 Cherokee Archer II	28-7790371	
OY-BTM	Piper PA-28R-201T Turbo Cherokee Arrow III	28R-7703215	
OY-BTO	Piper PA-28-181 Cherokee Archer II	28-7790586	
OY-BTS	Piper PA-18-150 Super Cub	18-7709065	N9166T
OY-BTT	Piper PA-28-181 Cherokee Archer II	28-7890245	
OY-BTU	Piper PA-28-161 Cherokee Warrior II	28-7816374	
OY-BTV	Piper PA-28-161 Cherokee Warrior II	28-7816375	
OY-BTY	Piper PA-32RT-300 Lance II	32R-7885038	
OY-BTZ	Piper PA-31-350 Navajo Chieftain	31-7752031	SE-GPM
OY-BUA	Reims/Cessna F172M	F17201477	
OY-BUD	Cessna 210L Centurion II	21061351	N5421S
OY-BUE	Reims/Cessna F172M	F17201446	
OY-BUF	Reims/Cessna F172M	F17201453	
OY-BUG	Reims/Cessna F182P Skylane	F18200010	
OY-BUJ	Cessna 182P Skylane II	18264453	N1802M
	(Reims-assembled with "c/n" 0064)		
OY-BUK	Reims/Cessna F172M	F17201398	
OY-BUM	Reims/Cessna F172M	F17201468	
OY-BUR	Reims/Cessna F172N	F17201588	
OY-BUV	Reims/Cessna F172N	F17201536	
OY-BUY	Cessna U206G Stationair II	U20603631	N7359N
OY-BVA	Beech 65-90 King Air	LJ-68	D-IKAO
	(Cld but still In use as engine test vehicle .03)		*D-ILNE*
OY-BVB	Beech 200 Super King Air	BB-419	N256EN
			N555FP
OY-BVN	Beech F33A Bonanza	CE-1151	
OY-BVP(2)	Bölkow BO.208C Junior	588	D-EJNE
OY-BVR	Beech F33A Bonanza	CE-1200	
OY-BVS	Beech B90 King Air (Modified)	LJ-418	SE-LEN
			OK-XKN
			OY-BVS
			N49CM
			(N49CN)
			N715K
			N725K
OY-BVT	Beech F33A Bonanza	CE-1151	
OY-BVU	Beech F33A Bonanza	CE-1139	
OY-BVV	Beech E33A Bonanza	CE-1123	
OY-BVW	Beech 200 Super King Air	BB-705	D-IBAB
			G-GKNB
OY-BYA	Reims/Cessna F182Q Skylane	F18200114	SE-IBA
OY-BYC	Piper PA-28R-201T Turbo Arrow III	28R-7803246	SE-GVP

OY-BYD	Cessna F150G	F150-0168	D-EGEW
OY-BYE	Cessna 150L	15072775	LN-KAD N1475Q
OY-BYI	Piper PA-34-200T Seneca II	34-7570249	SE-ITG OY-BYI PH-PEM OO-HAM N1452X
OY-BYR	Reims/Cessna F337G Skymaster (Reims-assembled 337G with US c/n 33701584) *(Wfu 1990)*	F33700069	C5-CLD N1025A ST-AFM D-IKED
OY-BYT	Beech A23 Musketeer II *(Dbr 19.6.95, stored)*	M-677	D-EHWU
OY-BYV	Bölkow BO.208C Junior	706	D-ENYU
OY-BYW	Cessna 140A	15426	OO-BNV N5306C
OY-BYZ	Reims/Cessna F337F Super Skymaster (Reims-assembled 337F with US c/n 33701333)	F33700025	D-IHAW (N1733M)
OY-BZA	Cessna F150G	F150-0113	D-EGDA
OY-BZB	Cessna F150G	F150-0141	D-EFSE
OY-BZE	Reims/Cessna F172N	F17201600	D-EOTA
OY-BZT	Cessna 550 Citation II	550-0259	N810JT VH-KDP N68617
OY-BZZ	Reims/Cessna F172M	F17201475	D-EEPV
OY-CAA	Partenavia P.68B	48	
OY-CAB	Partenavia P.68B	72	
OY-CAC	Partenavia P.68B	179	
OY-CAF	Partenavia P.68B	196	(G-BHEE)
OY-CAG	Partenavia P.68 Observer	243-03-OB	
OY-CAH	SOCATA TB-10 Tobago	395	
OY-CAK	SOCATA TB-10 Tobago	185	
OY-CAL	SOCATA TB-9 Tampico *(W/o 28.7.91)*	175	
OY-CAM	SOCATA TB-9 Tampico	51	F-GCEC
OY-CAP	SOCATA TB-9 Tampico	52	
OY-CAR	SOCATA TB-10 Tobago	53	
OY-CAT	Britten-Norman BN.2A-26 Islander	2224	EC-FFZ EC-750 G-BRPD
OY-CAW	SOCATA MS.880B Rallye Club	3030	
OY-CBA	Mooney M.20J Model 201	24-0735	(N4449H)
OY-CBN	SOCATA MS.894A Minerva 220	12019	LN-BIQ
OY-CBP	Beech 200 Super King Air	BB-235	N9BK
OY-CBT	DHC-7 Series 103	10	C-GRQB-X
OY-CBU	DHC-7 Series 103	20	
OY-CCJ	Gates Learjet 35A	35A-468	N468LM VH-ANI
OY-CDB	SOCATA TB-20 Trinidad	553	
OY-CDC	Partenavia P.68C	211	D-GEMD
OY-CDD	SOCATA TB-9 Tampico	158	SE-GFM
OY-CDJ	SOCATA TB-9 Tampico Club	1271	
OY-CDL	SOCATA TB-9 Tampico Club	1272	
OY-CDN	SOCATA TB-21 Trinidad TC	969	F-GKVQ N25198
OY-CDO	SOCATA TB-9 Tampico	883	F-OIDM SE-KBD
OY-CDP	SOCATA TB-9 Tampico Club	1868	F-GSZL
OY-CDR	SOCATA TB-10 Tobago	2009	
OY-CDS	SOCATA TB-20 Trinidad	1912	F-OIGY
OY-CDT	SOCATA TB-20 Trinidad	2089	F-OIUD
OY-CEE	Piper PA-28-181 Archer II	2890053	
OY-CET	Piper PA-34-200T Seneca II	34-7570240	SE-LOD OY-CET D-IHGB N1415X
OY-CEV	Cessna 500 Citation	500-0329	N4999H XC-PPM XC-IPP N5329J ZS-JOK N5329J
OY-CFA	PZL-104 Wilga 35A	118403	HB-EZI
OY-CFB	Bellanca 8KCAB Decathlon	487-79	SE-GEZ
OY-CFH	PZL-104 Wilga 35A	18840811	SP-ZOD
OY-CFJ	Cessna 172P	17275198	N62023
OY-CFL	Grumman AA-5B Tiger	AA5B-0565	LN-NFY (N5479Y) D-EFZW N28333
OY-CFM	Maule M-5-235C Lunar Rocket	7369C	N56423
OY-CFN	Piaggio FWP.149D	172	D-EHLG 91+50 EB+390 DA+386 KB+148
OY-CFU	Mooney M.20J Model 201	24-0841	LN-MON (LN-RAN) SE-GXH
OY-CFW	Cessna 182B Skylane	52048	D-EGLT N2748G
OY-CFY	Reims/Cessna F172P	F17202239	
OY-CFZ	Piper PA-28-181 Archer II	2890004	N9090D
OY-CGB	Reims/Cessna F172M	F17201296	D-EEON
OY-CGD	WAR FW190 Replica *(Reservation 1.87)*	unkn	
OY-CGF	Maule M-5-235C Lunar Rocket *(W/o 14.3.93)*	7325C	SE-IEL
OY-CGL	Cessna 150B	15059395	D-EBIX OE-AYB N7295X
OY-CGP	Piper PA-23-250 Aztec E	27-4614	N1JX N1JG N13996
OY-CGS(4)	Brändli BX-2 Cherry *(Reservation 5.98)*	188	
OY-CGV	Piper PA-28-180 Cherokee Archer	28-7505088	LN-BGV
OY-CHD(2)	Cessna 172L	17259403	N1003M
OY-CHM	Cessna 172N	17269528	N737MT
OY-CHO	Piper PA-28R-200 Cherokee Arrow II	28R-7235076	SE-FYM
OY-CHR	Piper PA-28-151 Cherokee Warrior	28-7715089	SE-GNY
OY-CHT	Bede BD-5 *(Reservation 1.99)*	1386B	
OY-CIB	Aérospatiale/Alenia ATR-42-300	007	(F-GFLL) OY-CIB F-WWEC
OY-CID	Aérospatiale/Alenia ATR-42-300	079	D-BATA(2) F-WWEE
OY-CIE	Aérospatiale/Alenia ATR-42-300	082	D-BATB F-WWEH
OY-CIG	Aérospatiale/Alenia ATR-42-300	019	YU-ALL VH-AQD F-WWEF
OY-CIH	Aérospatiale/Alenia ATR-42-300	238	F-WWEC
OY-CIL	Aérospatiale/Alenia ATR-42-512	514	F-WWLO
OY-CIM	Aérospatiale/Alenia ATR-72-212A	468	F-WWLV
OY-CIN	Aérospatiale/Alenia ATR-72-212	568	F-WWEH
OY-CIO	Aérospatiale/Alenia ATR-72-212	595	F-WWEB
OY-CIP	Aérospatiale/Alenia ATR-72-201	147	EI-CBC PH-SCY EC-GQS EI-CBC (N974NA) F-WWET
OY-CIR	Aérospatiale/Alenia ATR-42-310	107	F-GHPX EI-BXR F-WWEE
OY-CIU	Aérospatiale/Alenia ATR-42-300	112	C-FIQB F-WWEI
OY-CIV	Aérospatiale/Alenia ATR-72-201	150	EI-CBD PH-SCZ EC-GUL EI-CBD (N975NA) F-WWEI
OY-CIW	Aérospatiale/Alenia ATR-72-212	422	F-WQNR HS-PGJ F-OHLB F-WWLZ
OY-CJB	Piper PA-28R-201 Arrow III	28R-7837285	N36586
OY-CJL(2)	Aero Designs Pulsar	0292/174	
OY-CJO	Polliwagen *(W/o 27.4.98)*	8501-1753N	
OY-CJP	Piper PA-28R-200 Cherokee Arrow	28R-35141	N9429N
OY-CKB	Piper PA-18-150 Super Cub	18-1463	D-ELTC ALAT 51-15463
OY-CKE	Cessna 650 Citation VII	650-7070	N654EJ (N770VP) N322RG N22RG N95CM N51176
OY-CKG	Piper PA-32R-300 Cherokee Lance	32R-7680134	SE-GNC
OY-CKH	Dassault Falcon 50 *(Reservation 11.01)*	134	N134FJ F-WQBN F-GUDP VP-BCD F-GOGL VP-CLD VR-CLD HB-IEC F-WPXK
OY-CKI	Dassault Falcon 2000	154	F-WWVL
OY-CKN	Dassault Falcon 2000	76	F-WWML
OY-CKO	Canadair CL.600-1A10 Challenger *(Reservation 3.01, not yet taken up)*	1025	(OY-VIA) N620SB N888LW HB-ILH N111J N111G N2636N C-GLXF
OY-CKU	Piper PA-32R-300 Lance	32R-7780491	N38966
OY-CKV	Cessna T210N Turbo Centurion II	21064184	D-EHSD (N5368Y)
OY-CLA	Cessna 172N	17269903	N738DU
OY-CLD	Canadair CL.600-2B16 Challenger 3A	5070	(D-AAFX) N305FX N780HC N980HC C-GLXO
OY-CLH	Grumman-American AA-1B Trainer	AA1B-0184	N9684L
OY-CLJ	Grumman-American AA-1B Trainer	AA1B-0106	N9606L
OY-CLM	Short SC-7 Skyvan *(Reservation)*	SH.1913	VH-WGG SAF-700 G-14-85
OY-CLN	Dassault Falcon 2000EX *(Reserved 2.9.03)*	unkn	
OY-CLW	Piper PA-30 Twin Comanche	30-1856	G-RNTV G-AXDL N8707Y

OY-CMB	Jodel D.112M Club (Mod.)	S52/1470	
OY-CMN	Jodel D.112M Club (Mod.) *(Temp reg 10.89, 10.96)*	9303/555/FR1501	
OY-CMO	Jodel D.112 Club *(W/o 27.6.97)*	0191-1445	
OY-CMP(2)	Ultimate 10/200 *(Temp reg 1.95)*	6710-200/040	
OY-CMR	Denney Kitfox IV 1200 *(Temp reg 6.97)*	1689-10/1992	
OY-CMS	Rans S-10 Sakota *(Reservation 8.93)*	unkn	
OY-CMV	Van's RV-6A *(Temp reg 4.96)* *(Badly damaged 5.5.01)*	0892-22342	
OY-CMY	Rand-Robinson KR-1 *(Reservation 11.90)*	0886	
OY-CMZ(2)	Rand-Robinson KR-2	8802-5275	
OY-CPB	Cessna 172N	17272960	N1115F
OY-CPC	Piper PA-28-181 Archer II	28-8090175	N8136T
OY-CPD	Beech A36 Bonanza	E-990	N17606
OY-CPH	Cessna 172E	17251334	N5434T
OY-CPI	Cessna 172F	17252887	N5357R
OY-CPP	Christen Eagle II	0001	N22JF
OY-CPR	Reims/Cessna F150M	F15001310	SE-GMR
OY-CPZ	Cessna F172F	F172-0158	D-EMGI
OY-CRA	Maule M-7-235 Super Rocket	4056C	N6122Q
OY-CRC	Cessna 177RG Cardinal RG	177RG0700	N1524H
OY-CRF	Grob G.115	8033	(LN-AES) OY-CRF (D-EGVV)
OY-CRG	BAe.146 Series 200	E.2075	N193US N369PS (G-5-075)
OY-CRP	HP.137 Jetstream 1 *(Wfu, scrapped)*	209	N2209 N5VH N5VP N74169 N5V G-AXEP G-8-7
OY-CRS	HP.137 Jetstream 1 *(Wfu, scrapped)*	225	N12225 N10AB G-AXON G-8-10
OY-CRW	Piper PA-32-300 Cherokee Six	32-7240118	SE-KRZ OY-CRW SE-FLF G-BAHV N1400T
OY-CSC	Piper PA-28RT-201 Arrow IV	28R-7918135	N29026
OY-CSE	Cessna 152 *(Dismantled)*	15282883	N89824
OY-CSF	Piper PA-28-140 Cherokee	28-25033	SE-FFN
OY-CSG	Piper PA-28-140 Cherokee D	28-7125294	SE-FYD
OY-CSK	Cessna 182A	34083	SE-CDY N6083B
OY-CSL	Cessna 152	15283210	N47295
OY-CSP	Cessna 172N	17270336	N738YF
OY-CSV	Piper PA-28R-201 Cherokee Arrow III	28R-7737107	N16DB N728P
OY-CTC	DHC-7 Series 102	101	G-BNDC ZK-NEW C-GFQL
OY-CTH(2)	Cessna R172K Hawk XP II	R1722236	SE-GOU N2998V
OY-CTI	Piper PA-28-181 Archer II	28-8090045	N2433U
OY-CTL	Pützer Elster B	018	D-ECAY 97+11 D-EDUF
OY-CTR	Piper PA-31 Navajo C	31-8012066	LN-SAY (SE-IDI)
OY-CTU	Cessna R172K Hawk XP II	R1723348	N758TM
OY-CTV	Cessna 172P	17274255	N51037
OY-CTZ	Cessna 172M	17267356	N73300
OY-CUA	Neico Lancair 320	01289-408	
OY-CUC	Christen Pitts S-2B	5220	
OY-CUD	Cessna 172N	17268483	N733RE
OY-CUE	Druine D.31 Turbulent *(Ditched 20.5.92)*	329	(OY-88X02)
OY-CYF	Piper PA-28-140 Cherokee Cruiser	28-7625122	N8523C
OY-CYL	Cessna 172N Skyhawk II	17273590	N6360G
OY-CYN	Grumman AA-5B Tiger	AA5B-1251	N4559Z
OY-CYP	Piper PA-25-235 Pawnee C	25-4760	G-BDCT CS-AIV N9653N
OY-CYR	Jodel D.18	73	(OY-86X03)
OY-CYU	Rand-Robinson KR-2	6513	
OY-CYV	Cessna 550 Citation II	550-0440	N120TC N31FT N31F (N1220D)
OY-CYY	Piper PA-25-235 Pawnee C *(W/o 26.7.90)*	25-4018	G-AXFD OH-PIK N4502Y
OY-CYZ	Christensen Opus 3	0188-001/92	
OY-DAB	S.A.I. KZ-III U-2	82	
OY-DBC	Stampe & Renard/ Stampe SV.4B	1204	RBAF:V-62
OY-DBK	Cessna 150L	15072077	XB-CXY XC-FUQ XB-NUA (N6577G)
OY-DBM	Champion 7FC Tri-Traveler	7FC-454	(OY-DBB) N9922Y
OY-DBT(2)	SAAB S-91D Safir	91441	(OY-IRN) SE-IOC OH-SFK SF-32
OY-DBZ	Cessna 170A	19758	D-ENQI D-EHON N1204D
OY-DCB	Piper PA-22-150 Tri-Pacer	22-5233	N7506D
OY-DCC	Piper PA-23-250 Aztec B	27-2473	N5398Y
OY-DCH	Cessna 172	28858	SE-CMN N6758A
OY-DCL	Piper PA-22-160 Tri-Pacer *(W/o 16.8.93)*	22-6874	N10F
OY-DCR	Piper PA-22-160 Tri-Pacer	22-7469	G-ARES N3558Z
OY-DCV	Piper PA-22-108 Colt	22-9133	SE-CZN
OY-DDF	Gardan GY-80 Horizon 180	186	
OY-DDJ	Champion 7GCAA Citabria	97	
OY-DDL	Mooney M.20C Mark 21	2920	N79805
OY-DDT	SOCATA MS.880B Rallye Club	845	
OY-DEB	S.A.I. KZ-III U-2	94	D-EJUM OY-DEB
OY-DEJ	S.A.I. KZ-III U-2	54	D-EDUD OY-DHI
OY-DEU	Scintex Piel CP.301C Emeraude	516	F-BJFD
OY-DEW	Cessna F172D	F172-0011/17250181	
OY-DEY	Scintex Piel CP.301C-2 Emeraude	587	OH-EMB
OY-DEZ	de Havilland DH.87B Hornet Moth	8040	G-AMZO SE-ALD OY-DEZ VR-RAI
OY-DFD	Mooney M.20F Executive	670327	N2968L
OY-DFP	Piper PA-28-140 Cherokee B	28-25422	LN-BNX (N8218N)
OY-DGD	CEA DR.250/160 Capitaine	83	
OY-DGH	de Havilland DH.82A Tiger Moth	85939/E-8	D-EDAS DF203
OY-DGP	Cessna F172G	F172-0226	
OY-DGT	Cessna 172 I *(Dbr 24.12.88)*	17257008	N46045
OY-DGV	S.A.I. KZ-III U	47	SE-APT
OY-DGY	Auster J/1 Autocrat	2025	
OY-DHC	Piper J-3C-65 Cub	13173	D-EBER HB-OSC 45-4433
OY-DHD	Piper PA-28-140 Cherokee	28-24829	LN-LMQ
OY-DHG	Cessna 150B	15059575	LN-IKT N1175Y
OY-DHK	S.A.I. KZ-II Coupé Series 3	23	SE-ANN (OY-DEY)
OY-DHM	Piper PA-28-140 Cherokee	28-20694	LN-BFH SE-EOI
OY-DHN	Piper J-3C-65 Cub	11065	SE-AWE 43-29774
OY-DHP	Polyt V *(C/n originally 17)*	70-1	
OY-DHY	S.A.I. KZ-III U-1	55	
OY-DIV	Piper PA-22-150 Tri-Pacer (Tailwheel conversion)	22-6639	LN-HAH N9727D
OY-DIZ	S.A.I. KZ-IV	43	
OY-DJD	SOCATA MS.880B Rallye Club	1284	
OY-DJG	SOCATA MS.892A Rallye Commodore 150	10952	
OY-DJK	Beagle A.61 Terrier 1	3741	SE-ELN WE554
OY-DJS	SOCATA MS.880B Rallye Club	1907	SE-FSI
OY-DJU	SOCATA MS.883 Rallye 115	1505	
OY-DJV	Partenavia P.68B	22	
OY-DJZ	Beech V35B Bonanza	D-9528	N115TW
OY-DKK	Piper PA-28-180 Cherokee C *(Wrecked)*	28-3671	LN-AEF N9542J
OY-DKM	Beech A23-19 Musketeer Sport III	MB-193	
OY-DKO	S.A.I. KZ-III U-2	61	
OY-DKU	S.A.I. KZ-III U-2	107	
OY-DKV	Cessna 150F	15061763	N8163S
OY-DLF	Mraz M.1C Sokol	270	D-ENOV OK-DHK
OY-DLY	Piper PA-31 Turbo Navajo	31-229	G-AWOW N9172Y
OY-DMD	SOCATA MS.892A Rallye Commodore I50	10541	
OY-DME	S.A.I. KZ-III	67	
OY-DMG	Piper PA-22-150 Tri-Pacer	22-5337	SE-CEI N10F
OY-DMJ	S.A.I. KZ-VII U-9 Laerke	174	D-ECOC HB-EPZ
OY-DMM	Piper PA-22-150 Tri-Pacer (Taildragger conversion 2.95)	22-5842	LN-AEF SE-CEL
OY-DMO	S.A.I. KZ-III U-2	105	
OY-DMY	Piper PA-22-150 Tri-Pacer	22-4295	LN-AEH TG-CIR
OY-DMZ	Piper PA-24-250 Comanche	24-759	SE-CKT N5687P
OY-DNK	Beech 35-C33A Debonair	CE-163	
OY-DNN	Cessna F172H	F172-0523	(OY-FKT) LN-FKT SE-FMV (LN-TST) OY-DNN LN-LMT
OY-DNO	Auster J/1 Autocrat	2110	
OY-DOJ	Piper PA-28-140 Cherokee	28-20373	

OY-DOZ	S.A.I. KZ-III	42	
OY-DPI	Auster J/1 Autocrat	2129	
OY-DPL	Beech A23 Musketeer II	M-637	
OY-DRG	SAAB-MFI-9B Junior	067	SE-FIE
			OY-DRG
OY-DRI	Piper PA-28-140 Cherokee	28-23815	LN-UXV
OY-DRR	S.A.I. KZ-VIII	203	D-EBIZ
OY-DRS	Reims/Cessna F172K	F17200786	LN-LJY
	(Res. as SE-LKY 2.02 but damaged and ntu)		
OY-DRZ	Piper PA-28-140 Cherokee B	28-25608	LN-BDX
OY-DSA	Beech A23-19A Musketeer Sport	MB-300	
OY-DSB	S.A.I. KZ-VII Laerke	191	HB-EPT
OY-DSF	Piper PA-28-140 Cherokee D	28-7125326	LN-MTK
OY-DSH	Taylorcraft Plus D	228	D-ECOD
			G-AHKO
			LB381
OY-DSI	S.A.I. KZ-III U-2 *(Damaged 12.7.94)*	64	D-EDEP
			OY-DSI
OY-DSN	Piper PA-28-140 Cherokee	28-23283	LN-UXL
OY-DSO	S.A.I. KZ-III U-2	65	
OY-DSS	Piper PA-28-180 Cherokee C	28-3655	LN-NPS
			SE-EZK
OY-DSV	Auster J/1 Autocrat	1824	D-ENUM
			G-AGTR
OY-DSZ	Taylorcraft Plus D	173	D-ELUV
			N .?.
			D-ELUS
			G-AHHX
			LB314
OY-DTP	Auster J/1 Autocrat	2332	D-EJYN
			G-AJIN
OY-DTS	SOCATA MS.880B Rallye Club	1180	
OY-DUI	S.A.I. KZ-III/U2	103	SE-AMF
			OY-DUI
			D-ECUF
			OY-DUI
OY-DUS	Piper PA-22-150 Caribbean	22-7588	LN-BDB
			SE-CUN
			N3717Z
OY-DVA	S.A.I. KZ-III U-2	74	D-ENYL
			OY-DVA
OY-DVB	Beagle B.121 Pup 150	107	SE-FOB
			G-35-107
OY-DVG	Piper PA-32-260 Cherokee Six	32-455	LN-HHU
			N11C
OY-DVI	S.A.I. KZ-III U-2 *(Dismantled)*	75	D-ECOT
			OY-DVI
OY-DVN(2)	Rockwell Commander 112TC	13090	D-EIXN
			N4585W
OY-DVZ	Transavia PL-12 Airtruk	1238	VH-ETZ
OY-DZA	S.A.I. KZ-III U-3 Ambulance	66	
OY-DZB	S.A.I. KZ-VII U-9 Laerke	198	OH-KZB
OY-DZD	Piper PA-28-140 Cherokee F	28-7325226	LN-DBJ
OY-DZF	Piper PA-28-140 Cherokee	28-21815	LN-NPL
			SE-EYX
OY-DZJ	Cessna 182M Skylane	18259434	N70954
OY-DZT	SOCATA MS.880B Rallye Club	2406	
OY-EAI	Cessna 150C	15059809	N2009Z
OY-EAM	Piper PA-18A-150 Super Cub	18-6796	N9694D
OY-EAT	Piper PA-22-108 Colt	22-9253	N10F
OY-EAY	Mooney M.20C Mark 21 Ranger	2144	SE-EDK
OY-EBU	EAA Acrosport II *(Reservation 12.00)*	9107	
OY-ECC	Piper PA-28-235 Cherokee	28-10435	LN-AEE
			SE-EMU
			N8919W
OY-ECD	Cessna 172M	17261536	N92007
OY-ECE	Cessna 172M	17262101	N12596
OY-ECF	Piper PA-28-235 Cherokee B	28-10964	LN-LMF
			N9293W
OY-ECG	Auster J/4	2071	D-EFYW
			D-ECYS
			LX-REX
			G-AIJO
OY-ECH	de Havilland DH.82A Tiger Moth	85234	OO-DLA
			G-ANCY
			DE164
OY-ECI	Piper PA-32-260 Cherokee Six E	32-7300024	LN-BNR
OY-ECJ	Cessna 421B Golden Eagle	421B0508	D-ICOA
	(Dbr 28.1.94, fuselage stored)		N69855
OY-ECN	Reims/Cessna F172M	F17201041	(D-EIQI)
OY-ECR	S.A.I. KZ-III U-2	106	
OY-ECS	Piper J-3C-65 Cub	13367	D-EGPL
			D-EGPI
			(D-EDUX)
			PH-UCO
			45-4627
OY-ECT	Piper J-3C-65 Cub Special	22617	D-EDAP
			N4492M
			NC4492M
			NC3401N
OY-ECU	Piper PA-28-140 Cherokee Fliteliner	28-7225541	N736FL
OY-ECV	Piper J-3C-65 Cub	8391	D-ECIZ
	(Painted as "215272")		NC49642
			42-15272
OY-ECY	Robin HR.100/210 Royale	189	
OY-ECZ	Piper PA-28-140 Cherokee Fliteliner	28-7225559	N738FL
OY-EDG	Cessna 182S Skylane	18280139	N9522J

OY-EEF	Beech B200 Super King Air	BB-1548	
OY-EEZ	Rutan Long-Ez	245	N245R
OY-EFA	Piper PA-18 Super Cub 95	18-1477	D-EKMM
			OO-SPE
			ALAT
			51-15477
OY-EFB	Cessna 140	9203	D-EGAN
			NC90142
OY-EFE	Piper J-3C-65 Cub	11578	D-EBIR
			HB-OAM
			43-30287
OY-EFF	SNCAN/ Stampe SV.4C	222	G-BUNA
	(Wfu and stored)		N10SV
			F-BCBG
OY-EFI	Auster 5	1815	D-ENIR
			G-AOSL
			TW477
OY-EFJ	Wassmer Jodel D.120A Paris-Nice	292	D-EMTL
			F-BMYZ
OY-EFL	Cessna 140	10220	D-EHEP
			N73015
OY-EFP	Stinson HW-75 Reliant	7249	D-EMUB
			SL-AAN
			F-BESY
			Fr.Navy
			5143
OY-EFU	Beagle-Auster A.61 Terrier 2	2296/B.630	D-EDTU
			(OH-BEA)
			G-ARRN
			VF527
OY-EFY	Piper PA-18 Super Cub 95	18-6039	D-EJEQ
			SE-CLH
			N7879D
OY-EGG	Cessna F172H	F172-0330	
OY-EGJ	Cessna F150G	F150-0087	
OY-EGK	Cessna F150G	F150-0163	
OY-EGM	Cessna F172H	F172-0391	
OY-EGP	Cessna F172H	F172-0356	
OY-EGU	Cessna F172H	F172-0396	
OY-EGV	Cessna F172H	F172-0410	
OY-EGZ	Cessna F172H	F172-0324	N17013
OY-EIG	Mooney M.20J Model 201	24-1674	N5274V
OY-EJJ	Epervier EX 252	001	OO-EPB
OY-EKA	Piper PA-28RT-201 Arrow IV	28R-8018075	N8212S
OY-EKC	Cessna 560XL Citation Excel	560-5217	(OY-LEG)
			N5079V
OY-EKU	Reims/Cessna F172H	F17200691	SE-FKU
OY-ELG	PA-18 Super Cub	18-1596	D-EXCO
			ALAT
			51-15596
OY-ELM	Bölkow BO.208CJunior	699	D-EABI(2)
			D-EABM(1)
OY-ELW	Mooney M.20R Ovation	29-0045	G-BVZY
OY-ELY	Cessna 550 Citation II	550-0139	PT-ORD
			(PT-WQG)
			PT-ORD
			N39FA
			PT-LJA
			N222MJ
			ZS-KOO
			N2646Y
OY-ELZ	Cessna 550 Citation II	550-0600	N415AJ
	(Res 11.99)		(N675DM)
			PT-LSR
			N1303H
OY-ENV	Reims/Cessna F172M	F17201055	G-BBPJ
OY-ERD	Van's RV-4 *(Reservation 7.98)*	9507	
OY-ERY	Cessna 550 Citation II	550-0469	N50N
	(Reserved 7.02, for rebuild)		N123SR
			HB-VIP
			VR-BIZ
			G-BKSR
			N1251V
OY-ESI	Europa Aviation Europa *(Reservation 12.97)*	300	
OY-ESK	Rans S-10E Sakota *(Reservation 3.95)*	1189069	
OY-EUR	Europa Aviation Europa *(Reservation 1.94)*	158	
OY-EYA	Stoddard-Hamilton Glasair II-S RG *(Res. 4.92)*	unkn	
OY-EYE	Cessna 525 CitationJet *(Reservn 8.9.03)*	unkn	
OY-FAA	Taylor J-2 Cub	964	LN-EAP
OY-FAK	S.A.I. KZ-II Trainer	115	RDAF:11-107
			RDAF:11-115
OY-FAT	S.A.I. KZ-II Trainer	109	RDAF:11-101
			RDAF:11-109
OY-FCE	Cessna 525 CitationJet *(Res 16.10.03)*	525-0165	D-IJYP
			N51488
OY-FCJ	Cessna T182R Turbo Skylane II	18267996	N9751H
OY-FCK	Maule MX-7-235 Star Rocket *(Res. 10.95)*	10012C	N15CK
			N56589
OY-FDS	Piper PA-28R-180 Cherokee Arrow	28R-30683	SE-FDS
OY-FEY	de Havilland DH.82A Tiger Moth	84197	N82MT
			ZS-FEY
			ZS-DEU
			SAAF 579
			T7814
OY-FFB	Cessna 500 Citation	500-0406	SE-DET
			(N67829)

OY-FGA	Fouga CM.170 Magfister	230	F-GLMO, Fr.AF
OY-FIN(2)	Rockwell Commander 114 *(Res 11.12.03)*	14397	G-CCDT, D-EKGD, OE-KGD, D-EIBC
OY-FKA	Aérospatiale/Alenia ATR-42-300 *(Res. 10.97)*	095	F-GKYN, F-ODUL
OY-FLC	Cessna 182 (Reserved 5.9.03)	unkn	
OY-FLI	Piper PA-38-112 Tomahawk	38-78A0138	G-BOEC, N9587T
OY-FLV	DHC-1 Chipmunk 22 *(Reservation 4.94)*	C1/0878	RDAF: P-143, RDAF: 12-143
OY-FRC	Piper PA-28-140 Cherokee	28-7325016	SE-GAP
OY-FRD	Grumman AA-1C Trainer 2	AA1C-0133	LN-KLA, (D-EGDB)
OY-FRE	Piper PA-31 Turbo Navajo	31-632	G-AXYA, N6731L
OY-FRG	Piper PA-28-140 Cherokee	28-7325407	D-ELLF, N11C
OY-FRK	Bölkow BO.208C Junior	691	D-ENVD
OY-FRO	Piper PA-28-151 Cherokee Warrior	28-7515428	SE-GLD
OY-FSA	Piper PA-44-180 Seminole *(Reservn 8.01)*	unkn	
OY-FTN	Piper PA-31-350 Navajo Chieftain	31-7852132	4X-CCX, N7HF, N27735
OY-FUN	Rans S-10 Sakota *(Reservation 10.92)*	unkn	
OY-FUR(2)	Cessna 172P	17275370	LN-MTL, N62969
OY-GAB	Grumman-American AA-5 Traveler	AA5-0421	N7121L
OY-GAC	Grumman-American AA-1 Yankee	AA1-0405	LN-UXQ, (N8955L)
OY-GAI	Grumman-American AA-5B Tiger	AA5B-0131	
OY-GAJ	Grumman-American AA-5A Cheetah	AA5A-0083	
OY-GAL	Grumman-American AA-5B Tiger	AA5B-0197	
OY-GAN	Grumman-American AA-5 Traveler	AA5-0199	SE-FTR, N6099L
OY-GAT	Grumman-American GA-7 Cougar	0048	
OY-GAV	Grumman-American GA-7 Cougar	0057	(OY-SVO(2)), LN-ALY, OY-GAV, N770GA
OY-GBH	SOCATA Rallye 110ST Galopin	3297	D-EGRH
OY-GBK	Reims/Cessna F337F Super Skymaster (Reims-assembled 337F with US c/n 33701349) *(Reservation, awaiting rebuild)*	F33700030	SE-GOK, D-ICEL, N1749M
OY-GCF	Cessna 340A	340A0224	D-ILMW, OE-FLV, N3894G
OY-GDS	Europa Aviation Europa Classic *(Kit No.151)*	9406	
OY-GEB	Beech 200C Super King Air	BL-40	VH-NSR, N44344, VH-OTH, N3837R
OY-GEG	Beech 1900C-1	UC-132	YemenAF:1180, OY-GEG, N55201
OY-GEO	Beech 58 Baron	TH-1647	
OY-GET	Beech F33A Bonanza	CE-1358	
OY-GEU	Beech B200 Super King Air	BB-1341	VT-SAD, N41AV, N341YV
OY-GEV	Beech F33A Bonanza	CE-1370	
OY-GEW	Beech B200 Super King Air	BB-1342	VT-SAE, N99DX, N250AF, N342YV
OY-GFL	Cessna TR182 Turbo Skylane RG	R18200659	D-EWYY, N9042R
OY-GGG	Cessna 650 Citation VII	650-7039	D-CACM, N12643
OY-GHC	Reims/Cessna FR182 Skylane RG	FR18200038	D-EIYI
OY-GIP(2)	Hawker 800XP	258367	N367DM, N3263E
OY-GJA	Rans S-10 Sakota *(Temp reg 10.92)*	0790109	D-MUHS
OY-GKC(2)	Cessna 560XLCitation Excel	560-5189	N5073G
OY-GKE	Piper PA-18-150 Super Cub	18-8109024	N4410E
OY-GKM	Piper PA-32R-301T Saratoga II TC	3257071	
OY-GLA	Bombardier BD.700-1A10 Global Express	9094	ZS-DLJ, (ZS-DAJ), C-GIOX
OY-GMA	Beech B200 Super King Air	BB-1340	N256AF, (N132AZ), N256AF, N340YV
OY-GMB	Cessna 550 Citation II *(Reservn 5.02)*	550-0071	CS-DCI, N404BF, (N404BV), N404BF, C-GDPD, N4308G
OY-GMC	Cessna 550 Citation II	550-0025	9H-ACR, N78PR, N78PH, N664J, N664JB, N9014S, EP-KIC, (EP-KID), N3239M

OY-GMJ	Cessna S550 Citation SII	S550-0134	SE-DYO, D-CFAI, N134QS, N1294M
OY-GMK	Cessna 550 Citation II	550-0071	CS-DCI, N404BF, (N404BV), N404BF, C-GDPD, N4308G
OY-GML	Beech 1900C	UC-69	F-GPYS, N69ZR, N520LX, N15466
OY-GNM	Beech 1900C	UC-172	F-GHSE
OY-GPC	Pereira GP-4 Osprey	0692	
OY-GRB	Beech 200 Super King Air	BB-845	N486DC, N38535
OY-GRD	DHC-7 Series 102	9	A6-ALM
OY-GRE	DHC-7 Series 103	106	N54026, (N53994), C-GFYI
OY-GRF	DHC-7 Series 102	113	OE-LLU, C-GFCF, (G-BOAZ)
OY-GRL	Boeing 757-236	25620	TF-GRL, G-CSVS, G-IEAC
OY-GRN	Airbus A330-222	230	OO-SFP, F-WWKT
OY-GSA	Pilatus PC-12/45	421	HB-FRN
OY-GSC	Rockwell 112 Commander	487	SE-GSC
OY-GTE	Grumman AA-5 Traveler *(Rebuild of AA5-0299 to AA-5A standard using parts of AA5--0197 G-BEFB)*	AA5-0299/0197	G-BAOV, N7299L
OY-GTM	Reims/Cessna F172P Skyhawk II	F17202026	SE-IFE
OY-GUM	Cessna 550 Citation II *(Reservation 8.98)*	unkn	
OY-GVD	Piper PA-32RT-300 Lance II	32R-7885130	D-EBRB, G-XMAS, N31793
OY-GZE	Reims/Cessna FRA150M Aerobat	FRA1500287	SE-GZE, (F-BOFD)
OY-HAF	Sikorsky S-61N	61267	N10045
OY-HAG	Sikorsky S-61N	61268	N10046
OY-HAJ	Bell 47G-5	25003	N8170J
OY-HBZ	Hughes 269C *(W/o 9.7.80, rebuilt)*	36-0480	
OY-HCY	Bell 212	31166	
OY-HDC	Agusta-Bell 206B Jet Ranger II	8499	SE-HGU
OY-HDD	Bell 206B Jet Ranger II	3649	N130S, C-GTXA, N3982M
OY-HDM	Bell 212	31142	N57545
OY-HDN	Bell 212	31136	N5752K
OY-HDT	Aérospatiale AS.332L Super Puma	2017	G-BWHN, C-GSLC, HC-BQJ, C-GSLC, HC-BNC, C-GSLC
OY-HEC	Aérospatiale AS.350B1 Ecureuil *(W/o 13.9.96)*	1999	
OY-HEG	Schweizer 269C *(Damaged 12.96, stored)*	S-1706	N41S
OY-HEO	Aérospatiale AS.332LSuper Puma	2007	G-CHCA, F-WQDZ, C-GSEM, HC-B . ., C-GSEM, HC-BPE, C-GSEM, HK-3197X, C-GSEM, N332CH, OE-GXB
OY-HEP(2)	McDonnell-Douglas MD-500N	LN-022	G-NOTA, VR-CPD, N520QP, N52113
OY-HFC	Robinson R-22 Beta	1251	
OY-HFE	Robinson R-22 Beta	1480	
OY-HFF	Robinson R-22M Mariner	1629M	
OY-HFI	Robinson R-22M Mariner *(W/o 23.9.00)*	1708M	
OY-HFJ	Robinson R-22M Mariner	1777M	
OY-HFK	Robinson R-22M Mariner	1948M	
OY-HFL	Robinson R-22M Mariner	1778M	
OY-HGA	Aérospatiale AS.350B2 Ecureuil	2600	
OY-HGK	Aérospatiale AS.350B2 Ecureuil	2570	C-FNJW
OY-HGL	Aérospatiale AS.350B2 Ecureuil	2950	N4074E
OY-HHA	Aérospatiale AS.332L Super Puma	2015	G-CHCB, F- . . . ., C-GQYX, HC-BRH, C-GQYX, HC-BOZ, C-GQYX, P2-PHY, C-GQYX, N5789M

OY-HHC	Aérospatiale AS.332L Super Puma	2179	G-BOZK F- WQED LN-OMQ G-BOZK G-GINN
OY-HHH	Robinson R-22 Beta	1080	SE-JCY D-HOLZ N8048W
OY-HIA	Bell 222U	47529	(N3188V) TC-HCS N3188V
OY-HIB	Bell 222U	47519	D-HCED C-FVUZ JA9961 N8154Q VH-LAJ
OY-HIC	Bell 222U	47522	PT-HXC N77UT
OY-HID	Bell 222U	46548	D-HCAN N222HW SE-HOU
OY-HIE	Bell 222U	47501	D-HUKM N222AD PH-HBP N3179U
OY-HIF	Bell 222UT	47512	N256SP N129SP N12SP
OY-HIS	Robinson R-44 Raven II *(Res 2.04)*	10257	
OY-HIW	Sikorsky S-76A +	760183	G-BVCX N951L N5450M
OY-HIZ	Aérospatiale AS.350B3 Ecureuil *(Res 2.04)*	3727	LN-ODM
OY-HJH	Eurocopter EC.135T1 *(Reservation 9.02)*	unkn	
OY-HJN	Eurocopter EC.120B Colibri	1072	
OY-HJP(2)	Eurocopter EC.155B1 Dauphin 2	6655	F-WWOI
OY-HJS	Rotorway Exec 90	9305-5128	
OY-HJT	Eurocopter EC.135T2	0252	D-HECA
OY-HJW	Schweizer 269C	S-1651	OO-HJW N69A
OY-HKE	Robinson R-44 Raven II *(Res 1.04)*	10241	
OY-HLK	Robinson R-22	0086	D-HHOI
OY-HLM	Enstrom F-28A *(Reservation 5.02)*	116	SE-HFX LN-OMZ(1) SE-HFX
OY-HLN	Robinson R-44 Clipper	1085	G-CBBE
OY-HLP	Robinson R-44 Raven II	10191	
OY-HMB	Bell 212	30686	LN-OSR
OY-HMD	Bell 212	31125	(LN-ORI)
OY-HOT	Aérospatiale AS.365N3 Dauphin 2 *(Res 1.03)*	6646	F-WWOA
OY-HOX	Hoffman H-36 Dimona	36271	D-KLUG(2)
OY-HOY	Aérospatiale AS.355F2 Ecureuil 2	5598	HB-XJI
OY-HPA	Schweizer 269C	S-1620	F-GMMM D-HCMF N41S
OY-HPH	Robinson R-22B2 Beta *(Res .04)*	3659	
OY-HPP	Robinson R-44 Raven II *(Res 1.04)*	10254	
OY-HRA	Sikorsky S-61N *(Reservation 1.99)*	unkn	
OY-HRB	Robinson R-44 Raven *(Reserved 19.6.03)*	unkn	
OY-HRH	Aérospatiale AS.365N2 Dauphin 2	6419	SE-JFH JA6675 F-WYMC
OY-HSL	Eurocopter EC.155B1 Dauphin	6658	
OY-HSR	Bell 412EP	36133	N62734
OY-HTK	Eurocopter EC.120BColibri	1220	
OY-HTL	Bell 427 *(Reservation 3.02)*	56030	N40598 C-GAEP
OY-HTO	Robinson R-44 Raven	1251	
OY-HTV	Rotorway Exec 162F *(Reservation 1.02)*	unkn	
OY-HVM	Rotorway Exec 162F *(Reservation 11.95)*	9409	
OY-IBM	Cessna 172RG Cutlass RG	172RG0567	PH-TWD D-EIZZ N5545V
OY-ICF	Cessna 182P	18261164	D-EEXT N20734
OY-IDB	Piper PA-28-236 Dakota	28-8011043	SE-IDB
OY-IHB	Rans S-10 Sakota *(Reservation 11.93)*	unkn	
OY-IIB	Noorduyn/ N.American AT-16 Harvard IIB	14A-966	31-309 FS826 43-12667
OY-III	Cessna F172H	F172-0377	SE-EXB OH-CSQ
OY-IKA	Mustang II *(Res 8.99)*	unkn	
OY-ILB	SAAB MFI-15-200A *(Reservn 11.03)*	15-808	SE-ILB
OY-IMR	SOCATA TB-9 Tampico	413	SE-IMR
OY-JAD	Piper PA-32R-301T Saratoga II TC	3257065	
OY-JAI	Cessna 500 Citation	500-0193	N293S XA-SQZ XC-GOW N193CC
OY-JAL	Piper PA-28-181 Archer III	2843046	
OY-JAN	Cessna 177B Cardinal	17701917	TF-RUN TF- ILO TF- IOO(2) N34640
OY-JAP	Piper PA-28-181 Cherokee Archer II *(Reservation 6.99)*	28-7690148	SE-GNE
OY-JAR	Beech 200C Super King Air	BL-13	PH-ILG
OY-JAS	Piper PA-28-181 Archer III	2843456	N9522N
OY-JAU	Piper PA-34-200T Seneca V	3449136	N9510N
OY-JAV	Piper PA-28-181 Archer III	2843093	
OY-JBB	Europa Aviation Europa	9405	
OY-JBC	Rutan Long-Ez *(Reservation 6.97)*	97-03	
OY-JBF	Piper PA-28-161 Cadet	2841319	D-EKSH N9213Q
OY-JBO	Brändli BX-2 Cherry *(Reservation 3.95)*	unkn	
OY-JCP	Neico Lancair 320 *(Permit 3.01)*	91/03	
OY-JEB	Piper PA-28-161 Cadet	2841098	SE-KLZ OY-JEB
OY-JEC	Piper PA-28-161 Cadet	2841099	
OY-JED	Piper PA-28-161 Cadet	2841177	
OY-JEE	Piper PA-28-161 Cadet	2841175	
OY-JEL(2)	AkroTech Giles G.202 *(Temp regd 8.99)*	31-05/1997	
OY-JES	Van's RV-6 *(Reservation 3.94)*	9401-2306	
OY-JET(3)	Cessna 525A CitationJet CJ2	525A-0089	
OY-JEV	Cessna 550 Citation II	550-0284	I-ARIB N6801R
OY-JHS	Piper PA-34-220T Seneca V	3449056	
OY-JHN	Hughes S.269C (HKP 5B)	S-1218	SwArmy: Fv.05237
OY-JIB	Dyn'Aéro MCR-01 ULC *(Permit 10.00)*	163	
OY-JKA	Cessna 172N	17273613	C-GDKJ (N7022G)
OY-JMC	Cessna 525 CitationJet	525-0277	N277CJ
OY-JMP	Cessna TP.206D Turbo Skywagon	0537	D-ECAJ N8737Z
OY-JPA	Piper PA-28RT-201 Arrow IV	28R-7918101	SE-IAY
OY-JPC	Cessna 172M	17267193	N70102
OY-JPD	Piper PA-44-180 Seminole	44-7995322	D-GGOD N4509L
OY-JPE	Piper PA-38-112 Tomahawk	38-79A0894	D-EJRK N9672N
OY-JPG	Piper PA-38-112 Tomahawk II	38-81A0029	F-GDMV N25635
OY-JPJ(2)	Cessna 650 Citation III	650-0060	N220TV N220TW N660TJ TC-CAO N848US HB-VHW (N1313J)
OY-JPL	Piper PA-32R-301T Saratoga II TC	3257226	N9516N
OY-JRF	Beech 1900C	UB-66	F-OJAS F-GTOT N823BE N3044C
OY-JRI	Beech 1900C-1	UC-44	SE-KXX N31261 (N144GP) N31261 JA8864 N31261
OY-JRJ	Aérospatiale/Alenia ATR-42-320	036	F-WQIS 9J-HFJ F-OHFJ F-GEGF F-WWER
OY-JRK	Short SC.7 Skyvan 3A-100	SH.1901	N8117V 9M-AXT SE-GEX LN-NPA G-AZRY G-14-73
OY-JRN	Beech 200 Super King Air	BB-364	(OY-JRB) F-GHYV N66171 XC-DIK N18450
OY-JRO	Beech 65-B90 King Air	LJ-327	N827K (N507M) N827K
OY-JRR	DHC-2 Turbo-Beaver III	1632/TB-18	N911CC C-FUKK CF-UKK
OY-JRU	Lockheed T-33A *(Rebuilding, reservn .97)*	580-697. ?	N49239 51-91 . .
OY-JRV	Beech 1900D	UE-338	N23381
OY-JRY	Aérospatiale/Alenia ATR-42-320	063	F-WQOC(2) F-GNPL F-ODUC(2)
OY-JSN	Piper J-3C-65 Cub	5368	N311PB N31154 NC31154
OY-JTG	Andreasson MFI-15-200A *(From spares)* *(Reservation 1.02)*	825-1041	SE-XUB
OY-JVL	Beech B350 Super King Air	FL-273	N4473E
OY-KBA	Airbus A340-313X	435	F-WWJU
OY-KBB	Airbus A321-232	1642	D-AVZR
OY-KBC	Airbus A340-313X	467	(SE-REE) F-WWJE
OY-KBD	Airbus A340-313X	470	(SE-REF) F-WWJF
OY-KBE	Airbus A321-232	1798	D-AVZG
OY-KBF	Airbus A321-232	1807	D-AVZH

OY-KBH	Airbus A321-232	1675	(OY-KBC) (SE-REL) F-WWBG D-AVZY
OY-KBI	Airbus A340-313X	430	(SE-REC) F-WWJR
OY-KBK	Airbus A321-232	1587	(SE-REI) D-AVZK
OY-KBL	Airbus A321-232	1619	(SE-REK) D-AVZB
OY-KBM	Airbus A340-313X	450	(SE-RED) F-WWJD
OY-KBN	Airbus A330-343	496	F-WWKK
OY-KCD(2)	Bombardier DHC-8Q Series 402	4054	(LN-RDY) C-GFRP
OY-KCE(2)	Bombardier DHC-8Q Series 402	4057	(LN-RDZ) C-GHRI
OY-KCF(2)	Bombardier DHC-8Q Series 402	4062	(LN-RDI) C-GDNG
OY-KCG	Bombardier DHC-8Q Series 402	4063	(LN-RDK) C-GDSG
OY-KCH	Bombardier DHC-8Q Series 402	4064	(LN-RDL) C-GELZ
OY-KEJ	Van's RV-8 *(Reservation 5.99)*	unkn	
OY-KGT	McDonnell-Douglas DC-9-82	49380	N845RA OY-KGT N19B
OY-KGY	McDonnell-Douglas DC-9-81	49420	
OY-KGZ	McDonnell-Douglas DC-9-82	49381	
OY-KHC	McDonnell-Douglas DC-9-81	49436	
OY-KHE	McDonnell-Douglas DC-9-82	49604	N842RA OY-KHE N6200N
OY-KHF	McDonnell-Douglas DC-9-87	49609	
OY-KHG	McDonnell-Douglas DC-9-81	49613	
OY-KHI	McDonnell-Douglas DC-9-87	49614	
OY-KHK	McDonnell-Douglas DC-9-82 (formerly -81)	49910	
OY-KHM	McDonnell-Douglas DC-9-82 (formerly -81)	49914	
OY-KHN	McDonnell-Douglas DC-9-81	53000	
OY-KHP	McDonnell-Douglas DC-9-81	53007	
OY-KHR	McDonnell-Douglas DC-9-81	53275	
OY-KHT	McDonnell-Douglas DC-9-82	53296	
OY-KHU	McDonnell-Douglas DC-9-87	53336	
OY-KHW	McDonnell-Douglas DC-9-87	53348	
OY-KIL	McDonnell-Douglas MD-90-30	53458	
OY-KIM	McDonnell-Douglas MD-90-30	53460	
OY-KIN	McDonnell-Douglas MD-90-30	53544	
OY-KIS	Yakovlev Yak-52 *(Temp regd 4.01)*	867304	SE-LCS ES-FYI DOSAAF
OY-KKG(2)	Boeing 737-683	28300	(LN-RPC) N1786B
OY-KKH(2)	Boeing 737-683	28301	(LN-RPD) N1795B
OY-KKI (2)	Boeing 737-783	28315	N1796B
OY-KKK(2)	Boeing 737-783 *(Reservation)*	28314	
OY-KKL(2)	Boeing 737-783 *(Reservation)*	28319	
OY-KKR	Boeing 737-783	28316	(OY-KKK) N1786B
OY-KKS	Boeing 737-683	28322	LN-RPC SE-DTZ N1782B N1795B N1786B (LN-RPL) (SE-DTN) (LN-RPL)
OY-KZI	S.A.I. KZ-I Replica *(Temporary regn for exhibition flying each summer season)*	8605/2	(OY-CMZ)
OY-KZS	S.A.I. KZ-VIII (Mod.) *(Replica, built 1996, c/n formerly KZ8R-001)*	8703	
OY-LAE	Extra EA.300/LX	113	
OY-LAF	Piper PA-34-220T Seneca V	3449183	N9523N
OY-LAG	Piper PA-28-161 Warrior III	2843464	N9530N
OY-LAI	Piper PA-28-161 Warrior III	2843431	N9520N
OY-LAJ	SOCATA TB-9 Tampico	1090	F-GLAJ
OY-LAK	Piper PA-34-220T Seneca V	3449251	N53489
OY-LAL	Piper PA-28-181 Archer III	2890210	D-EOYC PH-AEB
OY-LAN	Neico Lancair 360 *(Reservation 11.93)*	473	
OY-LAO	Piper PA-32R-301T Saratoga IITC *(Res 1.02)*	3257266	N113AF
OY-LAS	Piper PA-46-350P Malibu Mirage	4636330	N53517
OY-LAT	Piper PA-32R-301T Saratoga IITC	3257250	N9514N
OY-LAW(2)	Piper PA-46-500TP Malibu Meridian	4697138	
OY-LCF	Cessna F150H *(Reservation 6.02)*	F150-0234	G-AVUG
OY-LDA	Piper PA-46-500TP Malibu Meridian	4697147	
OY-LEK	Van's RV-8 *(Reservation 5.98)*	1197	
OY-LEN	AkroTech Giles G-200 *(Reservation 12.96)*	9	
OY-LGI	Bombardier Learjet 60	60-243	N50287
OY-LHM	Neico Lancair ES *(Reservation 3.00)*	unkn	
OY-LJF	Bombardier Learjet 60	60-173	
OY-LJG	Bombardier Learjet 45	45-083	N5013Y
OY-LJH	Bombardier Learjet 60	60-051	N63BL N5051X
OY-LJJ	Bombardier Learjet 45	45-116	N50111
OY-LJK(2)	Bombardier Learjet 60	60-256	N5013K
OY-LJN	Gates Learjet 31A *(Reservation 7.02)*	31A-170	ZS-OLW ZS-OML (ZS-DHL) N31NR
OY-LKA	Zenair CH-601HD Zodiac *(Reservation 9.96)*	unkn	
OY-LLE	Aero Designs Pulsar XP *(Permit 11.00)*	96/03/474	
OY-LLL	Beech B200 Super King Air *(Res 11.03)*	BB-1861	
OY-LMM	Piper PA-46-500TP Malibu Meridian	4697108	N480M
OY-LPJ	Fairchild F.24W-41A Argus II *(Reservation 3.94)*	834	(OY-ANO) D-EHIB HB-EAK HB597 43-14870
OY-LRI	Pilatus PC-12/45 *(Reservation 5.02)*	unkn	
OY-LSA	Beech C90B King Air	LJ-1610	N44406
OY-LSD	Aero L-29 Delfin *(Reservation 10.01)*	394952	LY-XAK
OY-LTT	Piper PA-46-350P Malibu Mirage	4636319	N5347A
OY-LUI	Van's RV-6 *(Reservation 1.93)*	unkn	
OY-LYN	Rans S-10 Sakota *(Temp regn 7.93)*	0189038	
OY-MAE	Boeing 737-5L9	25066	G-MSKC OY-MAE
OY-MAV	Canadair CL.600-2B19 Regional Jet	7386	G-MSKS C-FMNW
OY-MBI	Canadair CL.600-2B19 Regional Jet	7436	G-MSKT C-FMKZ
OY-MBJ	Canadair CL.600-2B19 Regional Jet	7442	G-MSKU C-GHTK C-FMLU
OY-MBT	Canadair CL.600-2B19 Regional Jet	7617	C-GKDI C-FMLB
OY-MBU	Canadair CL.600-2B19 Regional Jet	7373	G-MSKR C-FMNB
OY-MCF	Piper PA-34-200 Seneca	34-7350110	D-GLAN N15932
OY-MDC	Bede BD-5B *(Reservation 3.95)*	2235D	
OY-MED	Zenair CH-701 STOL *(Reservation 3.98)*	unkn	
OY-MEI	Piper PA-28-181 Archer III	2843036	
OY-MEN	Beech B300 Super King Air	FL-229	N9WV
OY-MIG	MiG-15UTI *(Res 10.99)*	unkn	
OY-MKA	Piper PA-22-108 Colt *(Reservation 10.97)*	22-9069	LN-IKE N10F
OY-MLW	Boeing 737-75B *(Reservn 4.04)*	28106	PR-GOE D-AGEW
OY-MMM(2)	Canadair CL.600-2B16 Challenger	5430	C-GFOE N604MA C-GLXF
OY-MRC	Boeing 737-7L9	28006	N5573K
OY-MRD	Boeing 737-7L9	28007	N1786B
OY-MRE	Boeing 737-7L9	28008	N1786B
OY-MRF	Boeing 737-7L9	28009	N1780B N1787B
OY-MRG	Boeing 737-7L9	28010	N1786B
OY-MRH	Boeing 737-7L9	28013	
OY-MRI	Boeing 737-7L9	28014	N1786B
OY-MRJ	Boeing 737-7L9	28015	
OY-MRK	Boeing 737-7L9	28012	
OY-MRL	Boeing 737-7L9	28011	
OY-MSI	Bombardier BD.700-1A10 Global Express	9032	G-CBNP G-52-26 (N2T) N700HE C-GFAK
OY-MST	Piper PA-31 Turbo Navajo B	31-7300967	G-BNDD G-BBMK N7571L
OY-MUD	Short SD.3-60	SH.3692	N693PC G-BMNH G-14-3692
OY-MUE	BAe.Jetstream Series 3102	758	G-BTAI (OM-SKY) G-BTAI I-ALKD G-BTAI I- BLUI G-31-758
OY-MUH	Aérospatiale/Alenia ATR-42-300	125	N425TE F-WWEV
OY-NAJ	Mooney M.20J Model 201	24-1545	SX-AEM N3KN N2KN
OY-NET	Reims FR172J Rocket	FR17200384	D-ECWG
OY-NEW	Piper PA-46-400TP Malibu Meridian *(Res.6.99)*	4697014	
OY-NFK	Cessna TU206G Stationair 6 (Soloy conv)	U20604287	HB-CLG VH-SUL N756RC
OY-NHF	Piper PA-28-161 Warrior II	28-8316072	N4306W
OY-NIF	Aero Designs Pulsar 582 *(Temp regn 5.98)*	0591-220	
OY-NIW	Canard NX-77C *(Reservation 5.96)*	8709	
OY-NJH	Cessna 182T Skylane	18281040	N3539Q
OY-NJK	Europa Aviation Europa *(Reservation 2.02)*	9606	
OY-NLA	Cessna 650 Citation III	650-0070	LN-NLD N370TG N370QS N149C (N1315A)

OY-NMH	GAF N-24A Nomad	N24A-74	ZK-NMH N870US PH-HAG (PH-DHL) N5579K VH-PNF
OY-NPA	Swearingen SA.226TC Metro II	TC-258	C-GBDF 4X-CSA N5463M
OY-NPB(2)	Fairchild Swearingen SA.227AC Metro III	AC-420	N67TC (N568G) N67TC N1014D
OY-NPD(2)	Fairchild SA.227DC Metro 23	DC-865B	9M-BCH N30289
OY-NPE	Fairchild SA.227DC Metro 23	DC-867B	N23VJ 9M-APA (VH-MYE) 9M-APA N3029R
OY-NPF	Fairchild SA.227DC Metro 23	DC-880B	TF-JME N3002K
OY-OBC	Cessna 421A	421A0013	OH-CBC N2213Q
OY-OBP	Aero Designs Pulsar XP (Permit 1.02)	97/12	
OY-OCM	Partenavia P.68B (Damaged 23.10.96)	180	PH-SPB D-GEKA
OY-ODA	Europa Aviation Europa Classic	9408	
OY-ODB	Helio H.295 Super Courier (Reservn 8.97)	1466	N6DB
OY-OFW	Gates Learjet 31 (Res 4.99)	31-031	ZS-OFW N31HA N9132Z N5000E
OY-OIV	Jurca MJ.52 Sirocco (Temp regn 4.97)	101	(OY-CGS)
OY-OKC	Cessna 177B Cardinal II	17702663	N20373
OY-OKK	Dassault Falcon 900EX	128	F-WWFE
OY-OLE	Piper PA-31-350 Navajo Chieftain	31-7752061	SE-KCY OY-OLE PH-DAE N353AC N63748
OY-PBA	Pilatus PC-6/B2-H4 Turbo Porter	678	LN-VIT HB-FEY I-ALPJ HB-FEY
OY-PBG(2)	Reims/Cessna F406 Caravan II	F406-0015	G-TINI PH-FWE EC-FOH EC-177 PH-FWE F-WZDX
OY-PBH(2)	LET L-410UVP-E20	972736	OK-DDC
OY-PBI (2)	LET L-410UVP-E20	871936	OK-SDM Sov.AF:1936
OY-PBT	SOCATA TB-9 Tampico	738	LN-KLR
OY-PCA	Piper PA-32RT-300 Lance II	32R-7885087	SE-GXA N1822C
OY-PCC	Reims/Cessna F172M	F17201486	SE-GMV
OY-PCH	DHC-1 Chipmunk (Reservation 7.02)	unkn	
OY-PCL	Beech B200 Super King Air	BB-1675	N2355Z
OY-PCW	Cessna 500 Citation	500-0278	N103PL (SE-RDA) VP-BBE N103PL XB-UAG XB-FQO N278SP ZS-LYB (N278SR) N278SP N278CC (N5278J)
OY-PDN	Cessna 551 Citation II/SP	551-0412	N413VP G-OMCL N12160
OY-PEB	Beech 200 Super King Air	BB-309	5Y-NUR OY-PEB D-ILNY G-BEUZ
OY-PEL	Piper PA-28RT-201 Arrow IV	28R-8018024	SE-IDE
OY-PEM	Piper PA-44-180 Seminole	44-8195020	N333X N8383A
OY-PEN	Cessna 172M	17264743	N61702
OY-PEV	Cessna 172P	17274367	LN-MTA N51872
OY-PEW	Reims/Cessna F172N Skyhawk II	F17201599	LN-MTZ SE-GOV
OY-PEY	LET L-410UVP-E (Temp regd 3.99)	912604	N42484 OK-WDU CCCP67674
OY-PHA	Piper PA-32R-301T Saratoga IITC	3257292	
OY-PHB	Piper PA-34-220T Seneca V	3449293	N53681 OY-PHB N9510N
OY-PHD	Piper PA-46-500TP Malibu Meridian	4697193	N3096D
OY-PHE	Piper PA-32-301XTC 6xt (Res 2.04)	3255020	
OY-PHG	Piper Pa-32R-301T Saratoga IITC	3257364	
OY-PHH	Piper PA-28-181 Archer III (Res 6.04)	2843599	N399MA
OY-PHN	Dassault Falcon 100	209	HB-VKR N312AT (N312AR) N312AT N272FJ F-WZGP
OY-PIF	Cessna 182M	18259566	D-ELWL N71294
OY-PIL	Cessna 177RG Cardinal RG	177RG0422	SE-KRP N2022Q
OY-PIN	Rutan Long-Ez	103-116	SE-XFG
OY-PJA	Maule M-7-235 Super Rocket (Dismantled)	4004C	N56562
OY-PJJ	Piper J-3C-65 Cub	12417	G-BKGO CN-TVO F-DACK CN-TUK F-BDTK 44-80121
OY-PJP	SOCATA MS.894A Minerva 220	12077	SE-FSV
OY-PMA	Piper PA-34-220T Seneca V	3449222	
OY-PMT	Cessna R172K Hawk XP	R1722688	YN-CEK N736PU
OY-PND	Neico Lancair 235 (Reserved 17.7.03)	unkn	
OY-POE	Cessna 182P Skylane	18261335	N20977 (G-BAFJ)
OY-POF	DHC-6 Twin Otter 300	235	N6868
OY-POS	SOCATA MS.893E Rallye 180GT Gaillard	12674	
OY-POT	Piaggio FWP.149D (Built from Piaggio airframe c/n 340)	016	D-EOPG 90+08 BD+392
OY-POW	Piper PA-28R-200 Cherokee Arrow II	28R-7435267	G-BCKR N9633N
OY-POZ	Piper PA-28-151 Cherokee Warrior	28-7415248	D-EOEP N9547N
OY-PPL	Reims/Cessna F172M	F17201348	D-EOGO
OY-PPS	Piper PA-34-220T Seneca III	3433021	OE-FKL D-GOAT N9091N
OY-PRA	Piper PA-28R-180 Cherokee Arrow	28R-30464	SE-FCE
OY-PRB	Piper PA-28-140 Cherokee Cruiser	28-7425394	N44199
OY-PRE	Rockwell Commander 112A (Cr 22.9.04)	480	(N1480J)
OY-PRF	SOCATA MS.893A Rallye Commodore 180	11924	SE-FSK
OY-PRG	SOCATA MS.880B Rallye Club	2779	
OY-PRI	SOCATA MS.892E Rallye 150ST	2687	
OY-PRJ	SOCATA MS.893E Rallye 180GT Gaillard	12727	
OY-PRK	SOCATA MS.880B Rallye Club	2925	
OY-PRL	SOCATA Rallye 100ST-D	2744	D-EBWN F-ODDH
OY-PRM	SOCATA MS.893E Rallye 180GT Gaillard	12736	F-ODEZ
OY-PRS	SOCATA MS.880B Rallye Club (Reserved for PA-34 8.02, but Rallye still current?)	2948	
OY-PRU	SOCATA MS.893E Rallye 180GT Gaillard	12959	
OY-PRZ	SOCATA MS.893E Rallye 180GT Gaillard	12754	
OY-PUP	Beagle B.121 Pup 150 (Reservation 10.95)	105	LN-HHC G-AXNO
OY-PZL	PZL-104 Wilga 80	CF14800560	SP-KEB
OY-RAA	BAe. 125-800B	258235	D-CWOL (PH-WOL) D-CWOL N258SA OY-RAA G-BWVA D-CBVW(3) G-5-774
OY-RAF	Europa Aviation Europa (Reservation 1.97)	313	
OY-RAM	Boeing Stearman A75N1 Kaydet	75-2186	N51771 41-8627
OY-RAS	Piper PA-34-220T Seneca III	34-8233058	I-CGAJ S5-CAA SL-CAA YU-BPI N8042M
OY-RCA	BAe.146-200	E-2045	G-CLHE OY-RCA G-DEBH N185US N362PS
OY-RCB	BAe.146-200	E-2094	SE-DRD G-CSJH G-5-094
OY-RCF	Piper PA-28RT-201T Turbo Arrow IV (Reservation 8.04)	28R-8231046	D-EHBF N8196U
OY-RCM	Auster J/1 Autocrat (Reservation 3.01)	1980	G-AHCN
OY-RCW	BAe.146 Series 200	E-2115	SE-DRA G-BRXT C-GRNY G-5-115 G-11-115
OY-RGG	Cessna 525 CiatationJet	525-0495	N5246Z
OY-RPE	Aeronca 11AC Chief	11AC-1603	D-EJUN OO-GUS OO-USG
OY-RPH	Cessna 150L	15073011	N1711Q
OY-RPJ	Reims/Cessna F172M	F17201206	
OY-RPO	Piper PA-23-250 Aztec E	27-7554144	N54845

OY-RPR	SOCATA MS.880B Rallye Club	1283	SE-CIU
OY-RPT	Beech E33 Bonanza	CD-1213	D-EKXI
OY-RPY	Piper PA-18-150 Super Cub	18-8092	PH-NKE N4078Z
OY-RRG	Cessna 177RG Cardinal RG	177RG1214	LN-LGP N52609
OY-RSC	Cessna TR182 Turbo Skylane RG	R18201575	N5455S
OY-RTA	Aérospatiale/Alenia ATR-72-202	260	F-WQNF EC-FIV EC-873 F-WWEH
OY-RTB	Aérospatiale/Alenia ATR-72-201	267	F-WQNI EC-FJX EC-874 F-WWEM
OY-RTC	Aérospatiale/Alenia ATR-72-202	508	F-WQNK (T9-. . .) F-WQNK G-UKTM F-WWLU
OY-RTD	Aérospatiale/Alenia ATR-72-202	509	F-OHFQ F-WQNH G-UKTJ VN-B242 G-UKTJ F-WWLC
OY-RTE	Aérospatiale/Alenia ATR-72-202	154	F-WQNF EC-ESS EC-383 F-WWEK
OY-RTF	Aérospatiale/Alenia ATR-72-202	496	F-WQNL G-UKTN F-WWLT
OY-RTG	Aérospatiale/Alenia ATR-72-202	157	F-WQNH EC-EUJ EC-384 F-WWEL
OY-RUB	Aérospatiale/Alenia ATR-72-201	301	F-WQNS G-BXXA F-WQGJ F-OHAG F-WWLY
OY-RUC	Aérospatiale/Alenia ATR-72-201	227	F-GHPU (F-GHPH)
OY-RUK	Cessna 195	7358	N117DH N3888V
OY-RUM	Aérospatiale/Alenia ATR-42-300	010	N110VV F-GLIA F-GDXL F-WDXL
OY-RUT	Lockheed T-33A-5-LO Shooting Star (Temp regd 8.00)	536091GNB89	N32GB 53-6091
OY-RVA	Van's RV-6A	9707-25032	
OY-RVI	Van's RV-6A (Permit 5.02)	94/12	
OY-RVS	Van's RV-8 (Reservation 10.01)	81624	
OY-RVY	CEA DR.220A-B 2+2	136	F-BRVY
OY-RVZ	Van's RV-7 (Reservation 10.02)	unkn	
OY-RYB	Reims/Cessna F172L	F17200862	
OY-RYE	Reims/Cessna F172M	F17200927	
OY-RYI	Cessna 182P Skylane	18261811	N79309
OY-RYJ	Cessna 182P Skylane	18262271	
OY-RYN	Cessna 182P Skylane	18262267	N58738
OY-RYO	Reims/Cessna F172M	F17201053	
OY-RYP	Reims/Cessna F172M	F17200944	
OY-RYU	Reims/Cessna F172M	F17201140	
OY-RYW	Cessna U206F Stationair	U20601776	
OY-RYY	Reims/Cessna F172M	F17201116	
OY-SAV	Cessna 402B	402B0201	N7873Q
OY-SBR	Aérospatiale SN.601 Corvette	23	F-BVPF
OY-SBU	Beech C90 King Air	LJ-768	LN-KCG(3) OY-SBU
OY-SCI	Pilatus PC-12/45	496	N496DT HB-FRD
OY-SEA	Boeing 737-8Q8	28213	N3521N
OY-SEB	Boeing 737-8Q8	28214	N1786B
OY-SEC	Boeing 737-8Q8	28221	N1787B
OY-SED	Boeing 737-8Q8	28237	N1786B
OY-SEH	Boeing 737-85H	29444	N1787B
OY-SEI	Boeing 737-85H	29445	N1786B
OY-SEJ	Boeing 737-86Q	30289	
OY-SEK	Boeing 737-86Q	30292	
OY-SEL	Boeing 737-8BK	33018	
OY-SEM	Boeing 737-8BK	33019	
OY-SFU	Cessna TR182 Turbo Skylane RG	R18201113	G-BOYE N756MK
OY-SIG	Cessna 180H	18052565	LN-BGJ N9910N
OY-SMD	Piper PA-34-220T Seneca V	3449234	N371C N53436
OY-SMI	Yakovlev Yak-52 (Reservation 1.97)	unkn	
OY-SML	Cessna 525 CitationJet	525-0258	N108CR N5203J
OY-SPL	Piper PA-28-181 Archer III	2843164	N9502N
OY-SRF	Boeing 767-219ER	23327	N327MR ZK-NBB N6055X
OY-SRG	Boeing 767-219ER	23328	N328MT ZK-NBC N6009F
OY-STJ	S.A.I. KZ-VII U-8 Laerke	199	D-EKID HB-EPA OH-KZG
OY-SUA	Mooney M.20K Model 231 (LN-ACR reserved 7.04)	25-0875	SE-KZU OY-SUA N5809Y
OY-SUC	Cessna 207A Stationair 8	20700781	N9999M
OY-SUK	Cessna 152	15282543	TF-FTG N69194
OY-SUN	Cessna 402C	402C0461	ZS-KUU N6837C
OY-SUP	Reims/Cessna FRA150M Aerobat	FRA1500323	PH-KDI PH-AXQ
OY-SUR	Partenavia P.68C Observer	246-04-OB	D-GEMG
OY-SUW	Piper PA-34-200 Seneca	34-7250257	G-BADF N5446T
OY-SVB	BAe. Jetstream Series 3217	985	JA8591 G-31-985
OY-SVC	Piper PA-31 Turbo Navajo B (Wfu in Sweden)	31-722	LN-RAZ SE-FYV
OY-SVD	Piper PA-28-180 Cherokee G	28-7305490	SE-GDK
OY-SVF	BAe. Jetstream Series 3102	686	G-BSFG PH-KJF G-31-686
OY-SVI	BAe. ATP	2061	G-BUYW HL5227 G-BUYW G-11-061
OY-SVJ	BAe. Jetstream Series 3102	711	G-BTYG N415MX G-31-711
OY-SVM	Cessna 172P	17274818	N53796
OY-SVR(2)	BAe. Jetstream Series 3217	925	JA8877 G-31-925
OY-SVT(2)	BAe. ATP	2062	G-11-062
OY-SVU	BAe. ATP	2063	G-BWYT HL5228 G-11-063
OY-SVV(2)	Piper PA-28-181 Archer III	2843494	N282PA
OY-SVW	BAe. Jetstream Series 4102	41047	(OY-SVT) G-BVZC G-4-047
OY-SVY(2)	BAe Jetstream Series 3217	981	JA8865 G-31-981
OY-SVZ(2)	BAe. Jetstream Series 3102	641	(SE-LGC) OY-SVZ G-MACX OY-SVZ SE-IPD G-REGB SE-IPD G-31-641
OY-TAC	Cessna U206C Super Skywagon	U206-1178	LN-VIY (N29226)
OY-TAO	Rutan Cozy Mk IV (Reservation 2.95)	9410-0349	
OY-TAW	Aviat A-1 Husky	1279	D-EJHU(2)
OY-TBB	Lockheed T-33 (Reserved 14.11.03)	580-6668	RDAF DT-884 51-8884
OY-TBI	Piper PA-28-161 Warrior II	28-8016014	N45094
OY-TBJ	Piper PA-28R-201 Arrow III	28R-7837005	N47804
OY-TBL	Piper PA-28-140 Cherokee B	28-25583	N8761N
OY-TBS	Rutan Long-Ez (Reservation 8.95)	9503	
OY-TCP	Cessna 500 Citation (Reservation 10.97)	500-0315	SE-DRZ N55SH N55SK N5315J
OY-TDI	Diamond DA 40D Star	D4.010	
OY-TEA	Piper PA-28-181 Archer III	2843313	N9520N
OY-TEI	Piper PA-28-181 Archer III	2843040	
OY-TEK	SOCATA TB-9 Tampico	1289	SX-AEK F-GRBE EC-FFM F-GKVJ
OY-TFB	Beech A36 Bonanza	E-3003	N821SA
OY-TFC	Beech A36 Bonanza	E-3009	N1109Q
OY-TFD	Beech A36 Bonanza	E-3013	N1113J
OY-TFE	Beech A36 Bonanza	E-3034	N1096Y
OY-TFK	Piper PA-28-151 Cherokee Warrior	28-7415339	SE-GBM
OY-TFL	Piper PA-28-151 Cherokee Warrior	28-7415650	SE-GBV
OY-TFM	Piper PA-28-151 Cherokee Warrior (Reservation 8.02)	28-7515107	SE-GIE
OY-TFT	Piper PA-32-301T Turbo Saratoga II TC	3257050	
OY-TIM	Neico Lancair 360 (Reservation 12.02)	226	
OY-TIN	Erco 415 Ercoupe (Reservation 11.94)	unkn	
OY-TLC	Partenavia P.68B	147	G-CNIS G-BJOF EI-BKH G-PAUL
OY-TLE	Cessna 172RG Cutlass RG (Res 8.04)	172RG0254	SE-KPK LN-AFA N5138U
OY-TLL	Yakovlev Yak-55	901104	SE-LOO RA-07777
OY-TLS	Mooney M.20M TLS Model 257	27-0096	HS-ATA

OY-TMA	Cessna 550 Citation II	550-0457	N63TM
			N457CF
			N220CC
			N1250L
OY-TOE	Piper PA-28-151 Cherokee Warrior	28-7415656	
OY-TOF	Piper PA-28-140 Cherokee Cruiser	28-7425324	(D-ESAW)
			OY-TOF
			N9597N
OY-TOG	Piper PA-28-180 Cherokee Archer	28-7505142	
OY-TOH	Piper PA-28-151 Cherokee Warrior	28-7515329	
OY-TOI	Piper PA-28-140 Cherokee Cruiser	28-7525045	
OY-TOM	Piper PA-18 Super Cub 105	18-1639	OO-SPN
			ALAT
			51-15639
OY-TON	Piper PA-31 Turbo Navajo	31-414	D- ILTD
			N6458L
OY-TOS	Piper PA-28-180 Cherokee Archer	28-7505177	
OY-TOT	Piper PA-28-151 Cherokee Warrior	28-7515096	(OY-TOL)
OY-TOU	Piper PA-28R-200 Cherokee Arrow II	28R-7535262	
OY-TPC	Cessna 208B Grand Caravan	208B0805	D-FPUL
			N87258
			N52682
OY-TRD	Cessna 150C	15059770	N1970Z
OY-TRE	Cessna F172E	F172-0044	
OY-TRP	Piper J-3C-65 Cub (L-4H)	11964	OO-MCG
			44-79668
OY-TRR	Reims/Cessna F172M	F17200991	LN-BFD
OY-TRY	Piper PA-28R-200 Cherokee Arrow	28R-35167	OO-ISF
			N9452N
OY-TRZ	Cessna P206E Super Skylane	P20600621	D-EDEV
			OE-DEY
			N5721J
OY-TVA	Reims/Cessna F152	F15201525	D-EACY
OY-UAK	Lake LA-4-200 Buccaneer	778	(OY-CJM)
			SE-GRN
			N6125V
OY-UCA	Cessna 525A CitationJet 2	525A-0209	N5085A
OY-USD	Boeing 757-24APF	25465	N434UP
OY-VAF	Cessna TR182 Turbo Skylane RG	R18201458	N4919S
OY-VAM	de Havilland DH.100 Vampire FB.6 (Res. 3.94)	693	SE-DXY
			J-1184
OY-VIA	BAe.125-700A (Reservation 4.01)	257105	N560SB
			HB-VLL
			N700DE
			N44BB
			N125TA
			N125BA
			G-5-11
OY-VIB	Stoddart-Hamilton Glastar (Reservation 5.98)	unkn	
OY-VIM	Cessna 340A	340A1543	D-IXXI
			N1228K
OY-VIS	Cessna 550 Citation II	550-0672	G-OTIS
			N550PF
			PT-OMB
			N6763C
OY-VKA	Airbus A321-211	1881	D-AVZO
OY-VKB	Airbus A321-211	1921	F-WWIX
			D-AVZQ
OY-VKC	Airbus A321-211	1932	D-AVXB
OY-VKE	Airbus A321-211	1887	G-CTLA
			D-AVZC
OY-VKF	Airbus A330-243	309	G-CSJS
			F-WWYM
OY-VKG	Airbus A330-343X	349	F-WWYG
OY-VKH	Airbus A330-343X	356	F-WWYJ
OY-VKI	Airbus A330-343X	357	F-WWKA
OY-VKM	Airbus A320-214	1889	F-WWBV
OY-VKP	Airbus A320-214	2183	F-WWIQ
OY-VKR	Airbus A320-214	1942	G-DHRG
			F-WWIY
OY-VKS	Airbus A320-214	1954	G-YLBM
			F-WWIL
OY-VRV	Van's RV-4 (Temp Reg 9.5.03)	9505/4017	
OY-VSG	Hummelbird (Temp regn 1.99)	SR3019P-06/1995	
OY-YAC	Yakovlev Yak-52	9511904	LY-AOD
OY-YAK	Yakovlev Yak-52	899408	RA-01364
			DOSAAF-20
OY-YYY	Cessna P210N Pressurized Centurion II	P21000438	SE-KGT
			N3RS
			N731CG

BALLOONS

OY-BOD(2)	Cameron V-77 HAFB	2288	
OY-BOE	Thunder AX7-65 HAFB	062	
OY-BOH	Cameron V-77 HAFB	757	
OY-BOL	Cameron N-77 HAFB	1891	
OY-BOM(2)	Cameron O-105 HAFB	4156	
OY-BOO	Cameron N-56 HAFB	393	
OY-BOR	Cameron Tuborg Bottle SS 52 HAFB	809	
OY-BOT	Cameron N-77 HAFB	569	
OY-BOW	Colt 77A HAFB	014	SE-ZVB
OY-BOZ	Colt 77A HAFB	1359	
OY-COA	Balloon Works Firefly F7 HAFB	F7-601	
OY-COB	Galaxy 7 HAFB	GLX-1197	VH-HGX
OY-COC	Cameron N-90 HAFB	2006	
OY-COD	Cameron N-77 HAFB	2320	
OY-COE(2)	Lindstrand LBL-60A HAFB	210	G-BWDK
OY-COG	Cameron V-77 Viva HAFB	3232	
OY-COH	Colt 77A HAFB	1325	
OY-COI	Thunder AX7-77 HAFB	2081	
OY-COJ	Lindstrand LBL-21A HAFB	083	
OY-COK	Colt 77A HAFB	1914	
OY-COM	Cameron N-77 HAFB	2801	
OY-CON	Cameron N-77 HAFB	3904	
OY-COO	Colt 56A HAFB	1379	
OY-COP	Thunder AX7-77SI HAFB	1889	
OY-COR	Lindstrand LBL-21A HAFB	080	
OY-COS	Sky 77-24 HAFB	037	
OY-COT	Cameron O-77 HAFB	2620	
OY-COU	Cameron V-90 HAFB	3583	G-BWBN
OY-COV	Lindstrand LBL-60A HAFB	638	
OY-COW	Colt 77A HAFB	1980	
OY-COY	Colt 77A HAFB	757	
OY-COZ	Cameron V-77 HAFB	3009	
OY-EOA	Cameron N-105 HAFB	1082	SE-ZCK
	(Severely damaged 15.2.04)		G-BLOZ
OY-EOB	Cameron A-250 HAFB	3822	SE-ZGO
OY-EOC	Cameron A-210 HAFB (Res 2.03)	1912	SE-ZCZ
OY-EOD	Cameron A-210 HAFB (Res 2.03)	unkn	
OY-FOR	Colt 56A HAFB (Res 2.03)	038	G-BGIP
OY-GOA	Balloon Works Firefly C8	FC8-001	HB-BRX
OY-GOB	Cameron V-77 HAFB	3699	
OY-GOC	Ultramagic 77 HAFB (Res .04)	unkn	
OY-GOD(2)	Lindstrand LBL-90 HAFB	729	
OY-GOE	Lindstrand LBL-60A	210	G-BWDK
OY-GOF	Cameron V-77 HAFB	3248	
OY-GOG	Sky 77-24 HAFB	024	
OY-GOK	Cameron N-77 HAFB	3286	
OY-GOM	Cameron V-77 HAFB	3701	
OY-GON	Cameron N-77 HAFB	4836	
OY-GOO	Cameron N-90 HAFB	4811	
OY-GOP	Lindstrand LBL-77A HAFB	366	
OY-GOS	Cameron V-77 HAFB	2963	
OY-GOT	Cameron V-77 HAFB	4874	
OY-GOV	Lindstrand LBL-90A HAFB	045	
OY-GOZ	Cameron N-77 HAFB	2855	F-GMAA
OY-LOA	Cameron C-60 Concept HAFB	10242	
OY-LOR	Cameron O-84 HAFB (Res 4.03)	unkn	
OY-LOT	Lindstrand LBL-310A HAFB	911	
OY-MOR	Cameron O-84 HAFB	1465	D-OLBI
			G-GWIT
OY-NOA	'Model 77' HAFB (Reservation 1.02)	unkn	
OY-SOL	Cameron N-77 HAFB	10211	
OY-SON	Lindstrand LBL-77A HAFB	456	
OY-SSK	Ultramagic 65 HAFB (Reservn 5.04)	65/136	

GLIDERS AND MOTOR-GLIDERS

OY-AEX-19	Schleicher Ka 6 Rhönsegler	279	
OY-AIX	Hogslund/Traugott-Olsen 2G	1	OY-123
OY-AJX-38	Schleicher Ka 6BR Rhönsegler	339	D-5812
			D-3561
OY-AVX	Hogslund/Traugott-Olsen 2G	DA-7	OY-121
OY-AXE	Grunau Baby IIb	3	
OY-AXN	Grunau Baby IIb	12	
OY-AXO	Grunau Baby IIb	3	OY-93
OY-AXV	Scheibe L-Spatz 55	525	
OY-AXY-101	Scheibe L-Spatz 55	527	
OY-AXZ-M5	Schleicher K 8B	8106	
OY-AYX	Schleicher K 8B	1104	
OY-BAX-R9	VEB FES.530/1 Lehrmeister	0178	
OY-BCX	Grunau Baby IIb (Dismantled)	2	OY-120
OY-BJX-63	Scheibe SF-26A Standard	5022	
OY-BNX-D8	Scheibe Bergfalke II	188	D-4617
OY-BOX	Scheibe Bergfalke II	249	
OY-BXA-06	PIK-16C Vasama	34	
OY-BXD	Schleicher K 8B	5	
OY-BXJ-XJ	Schleicher K 8B	8647	
OY-BXK-K8	Schleicher K 8B	839	D-1675
OY-BXL-D7	Schleicher K 7 Rhönadler	7261	
OY-BXN	Scheibe Bergfalke II	102	D-5394
			D-9338
OY-BXT-47	Schleicher K 8B	8714	
OY-BXV-J7	Schleicher K 8B	8	
OY-BYX-98	Schleicher Ka 6CR Rhönsegler	6059	
OY-CBX-BX	Schempp-Hirth Ventus b/16.6	51	OH-606
OY-CCX	Schempp-Hirth Ventus c	510	
OY-CLX	Rolladen-Schneider LS1C	45	D-0442
OY-CPX	Schempp-Hirth Standard Cirrus 75	695	OO-ZAA
OY-CRX	Schempp-Hirth Mini-Nimbus HS-7	59	SE-TSP
OY-CXC	Schleicher ASW 27	27008	D-6642
OY-CZX	Aerotechnik L-13SW Vivat	870201	OK-7102
OY-DBX-35	SZD-22C Mucha Standard	672	
OY-DCX-65	SZD-24C Foka	W-146	
OY-DDX-36	Schleicher Ka 6CR Rhönsegler	6120	
OY-DGXGX	Scheibe Bergfalke II/55	392	
OY-DJX-34	Schleicher Ka 6CR Rhönsegler	6177	

OY-DKX	Schleicher K 8B	8368	
OY-DMX-26	Schleicher Ka 6CR Rhönsegler	6358	
OY-DNX	Schleicher Rhönlerche II	139	D-4340
OY-DSX-A2	SZD-9 bis Bocian 1D	861	
OY-DTX	Burgfalke Lo 150B	27	D-8279
OY-DVX-40	SZD-25A Lis	762	
OY-DXC-86	Glasflügel H201B Standard Libelle	422	
OY-DXG-M2	Schleicher Ka 6E	4168	
OY-DXK-H7	FES.530/1 Lehrmeister	0223	
OY-DXX-XX	SZD-25A Lis	757	
OY-EDX-43	Schleicher Ka 6CR Rhönsegler	6309	
OY-EEX	Schleicher K 8B	8471	D-4062
OY-EHX-W2	SZD-22C Mucha Standard	589	SP-2167
OY-EIX-30	Schleicher Ka 6CR Rhönsegler	6413	
OY-EMX	SZD-9 bis Bocian 1D	870	
OY-EOX-L6	SZD-22C Mucha Standard	539	SP-2121
OY-EPX-05	SZD-24 Foka	200	
OY-ETX-W1	SZD-25A Lis	759	
OY-EUX-S8	Schleicher K 8	742	
OY-EXC	Rolladen-Schneider LS8A	8122	
OY-EXE	Glaser-Dirks DG-600	6-41	D-2224
			BGA3554/FVG
OY-EXM	Schleicher ASW 27	27226	
OY-EZX-08	Schleicher Ka 6CR Rhönsegler	6513	
OY-EXZ	DG-Flugzeugbau DG-1000S	10-9S9	D-5374
OY-FAX	Schleicher K 8B	658	
OY-FBX-F3	Scheibe Bergfalke III	5517	D-3201
OY-FEX-105	Aeromere M-100S Series V	052	
OY-FFX-71	SZD-9bis Bocian 1E	P-440	
OY-FHX-H3	Scheibe Bergfalke III	5630	
OY-FIX-IX	EoN Olympia 2	EON/056	RDAF: Z-963
			RDAF: 96-963
OY-FJX-D2	Schleicher Ka 6CR Rhönsegler	6146	D-6034
OY-FMX-62	Schempp-Hirth SHK-1	41	OO-ZLJ
OY-FPX-13	Schempp-Hirth SHK-1	23	D-8807
OY-FTX-41	Scheibe Zugvogel IIIB	1068	D-1888
OY-FXF	Rolladen-Schneider LS8A	8242	
OY-FXS-XS	Glasflügel H.201B Standard Libelle	103	SE-TIN
OY-FYX-60	Schleicher Ka 6E	4158	
OY-FZX-11	Schleicher Ka 6CR Rhönsegler	6575	D-1019
OY-HCX	DG Flugzeugbau DG-800S	8-38S9	BGA4103/HPU
			(BGA4704)
OY-HBX-49	Schempp-Hirth Standard Cirrus	30	
OY-HFX-A3	SZD-9 bis Bocian 1E	P-462	
OY-HIX	Schleicher ASW 15A	15138	D-0843
OY-HOX	Hoffman H-36 Dimona	36271	D-KLUG(2)
OY-HSX	Schempp-Hirth Ventus b/16.6	206	D-8422
OY-HXB-HB	Schempp-Hirth Ventus b/16.6	72	D-6720
OY-HXX	Schempp-Hirth Ventus bT	22/178	D-KEVV
OY-IBX	Schempp-Hirth Ventus 2cT	22/86	
OY-IKX	Schempp-Hirth Duo Discus T	68/. . .	
OY-IXI	Schempp-Hirth Ventus c	374	OH-748
OY-JBX	Rolladen-Schneider LS8A	8408	D-5830
OY-JIX	Eiri PIK-20D	20622	SE-TVO
			OH-531
OY-JNX	Schempp-Hirth Ventus bT (Res 10.04)	1/96	D-KBBT
OY-JOX	Rolladen-Schneider LS8-18	8323	
OY-JXF	Schempp-Hirth Janus C	256	D-5062
OY-JXM	Schempp-Hirth Discus 2b	103	
OY-KFX	Schleicher K 8B	8758	SE-TFW
OY-KHX-3T	Schempp-Hirth Nimbus 3T	06/57	D-KHXB
OY-KRX	Kranich II (Reservation 10.03)	077	SE-SPK
			Fv8216
OY-LAX	Centrair 101APégase	101A-0250	F-CGNU
OY-LEX	Schempp-Hirth Janus CE	302	SE-UKZ
OY-LFX	Grob G.103 Twin II	3511	D-3064
OY-LHX	Schleicher ASK 15 (Reservation 6.03)	unkn	
OY-LMX	Schleicher K 8B	8574/A	D-5299
OY-LPX	Rolladen-Schneider LS6-18W	6285	D-7390
OY-LSX	Glaser-Dirks DG-400	4-224	G-DGCD
			D-KEIT
OY-LUX	Schleicher ASW 20	20324	SE-UIT
			OH-539
OY-LVX	Schleicher ASK 21	21326	D-5421
OY-LXT	Schleicher K 8B	8482	SE-TCL
OY-MBX-T9	Aeromere M-100S Series V	060	D-1095
OY-MEX	Scheibe Spatz A	01	(D-7263)
			D-1263
			D-3206
OY-MIX-48	Glasflügel H201 Standard Libelle	209	
OY-MKX-B6	Rolladen-Schneider LS1-c	83	
OY-MLX-S9	Scheibe Bergfalke II	185	D-3655
			D-3209
OY-MMX-28	Rolladen-Schneider LS1-0	2	D-4734
OY-MRX-67	Glasflügel H201 Standard Libelle	251	
OY-MSX-57	Schleicher Ka 6E	4277	D-0204
OY-MTX-73	Glasflügel H201 Standard Libelle	261	
OY-MXE	Rolladen-Schneider LS4-a	4158	HB-1594
OY-MXH	Schleicher ASW 15	15163	OO-ZWP
			D-0808
OY-MXL	Schleicher ASH 25E	25195	N234RH
OY-MXM	DG-Flugzeugbau DG-1000S (Reservn 2.02)	10-7S7	
OY-MXS	Rolladen-Schneider LS4	4444	D-3438
OY-MYX-89	Schleicher Ka 6CR Rhönsegler	6386	SE-TCO
OY-NAX	Sportavia/ Scheibe SF-25C Falke 1700	4237	D-KAOW
OY-NIX	LET L-13 Blanik	173004	OE-0697
OY-NVX	Schleicher ASK 23	23031	OH-695

OY-NXS	Schleicher K 8B (Res 1.04)	36	
OY-NYX	Start &Flug H-101 Salto	32	D-2194
OY-OXL	Schleicher ASW 17	17015	D-2131
OY-OXO	Scheibe SF-25E4 Super Falke	4312	D-KDDB
OY-PAX	Rolladen-Schneider LS3-a	3191	D-5894
OY-PCX	Rolladen-Schneider LS4-b	4925	D-4156
OY-PEX	Schempp-Hirth Ventus bT	15/152	D-KAUY
			N3YC
OY-PFX	Schempp-Hirth Discus CS	139CS	
OY-PJX-A3	Schleicher ASK 13	13607	D-6969
OY-PKX	SZD-51-1 Junior	B-2187	
OY-PNX	Rolladen-Schneider LS4-b	4859	D-3955
OY-PXF	Schempp-Hirth Duo Discus T	22/282	
OY-PXJ	Rolladen-Schneider LS1-f	335	D-9483
OY-PXW	DG Flugzeugbau DG-800S	8-79S22	D-3899
OY-RAX	Schempp-Hirth Duo Discus T	28/294	
OY-RBX	Rolladen-Schneider LS8-a	8176	
OY-RCX	Schleicher ASW 28	28029	BGA4900/JYY
OY-RDX	Glaser-Dirks DG-400	4-181	F-CGRA
OY-RFX	Aerotechnik L-13SDM Vivat	950609	D-KLIH
OY-RGX	Centrair 101A Pégase	101A-077	HB-1710
OY-RIX-2W	Rolladen-Schneider LS10T (Res 3.03)	unkn	
OY-RKX	Schleicher ASK 23B	23149	
OY-RLX-LX	Schleicher ASW 24	24083	SE-UIC
OY-RMX-MX	Schempp-Hirth Duo Discus	208	
OY-RRX	Schempp-Hirth Duo Discus T	98	
OY-RTX	Schempp-Hirth Duo Discus T	118	
OY-RXR-4R	Schleicher ASW 24	24014	BGA3380/FMX
OY-SBX	LET L-23 Super Blanik	917910	OE-5540
OY-SEX	Rolladen-Schneider LS8A	8201	
OY-SHX	Schempp-Hirth Ventus 2b	96	
OY-SLX	Glaser-Dirks DG-300 Elan	3E-335	D-6077
OY-SPX	Schleicher ASW 27	27153	D-3127
OY-SSX	Jastreb Standard Cirrus G/81	258	SE-TYV
OY-SXD	Hoffman HK-36R Super Dimona	36322	D-KMPC
OY-SXG	Schempp-Hirth Discus b	487	D7302
OY-SXP	Schleicher ASW 20CL (Res 2.04)	unkn	
OY-TDX	Hoffman H-36 Dimona	3638	D-KHUK(2)
OY-TFX	Grob G.102 Club Astir IIIB (Reservn 5.02)	unkn	
OY-TMX	Hoffman H-36 Dimona	3646	D-KBES
OY-TNX	Rolladen-Schneider LS8A	8075	D-3751
OY-TTX	Hoffmann H-36 Dimona	36243	D-KEWG
OY-TVX	Schempp-Hirth Janus CE	286	D-9202
OY-TXK	Schempp-Hirth Standard Cirrus	641	PH-533
OY-TXY	Diamond HK-36R Super Dimona TC100	36716	
OY-VAX	Grunau Baby IIB	"1944/2002"	OY-68
OY-VBX-R8	Schleicher K 8B	8238	
OY-VCX-B3	Schleicher Ka 6CR Rhönsegler	6465-Si	D-4404
OY-VEX	Scheibe Specht	401	
OY-VFX-W8	Scheibe Bergfalke III	5571	
OY-VHX-33	Schleicher Ka 6E	4169	
OY-VLX-B5	Schleicher Ka 6BR Rhönsegler	617	D-6144
OY-VMX-24	Schleicher Ka 6E	4077	
OY-VRX-K9	Schleicher ASK 13	13342	
OY-VSX	Grob G.103 Twin Astir	3770-K-56	D-1311
OY-VXB-94	Schleicher Ka 6CR Rhönsegler	986	D-5046
OY-VXC-B8	Schleicher ASK 13	13448	
OY-VXD	Slingsby T-61A Falke	1741	G-AYZV
OY-VXG-25	Rolladen-Schneider LS1F	183	
OY-VXJ	Scheibe Bergfalke II	101	D-5349
OY-VXK-74	Glasflügel H201B Standard Libelle	439	
OY-VXS-407	Glasflügel H201 Standard Libelle	276	(BGA1520)
OY-VXT-D4	Pilatus B4-PC11	105	
OY-VXX-109	Glasflügel H201 Standard Libelle	268	BGA1710
OY-VXZ-A5	Rolladen-Schneider LS1F	171	
OY-VYX	Schleicher Ka 6CR Rhönsegler	6121	
OY-XAB	Schleicher Rhönlerche II	709	
OY-XAI	SZD-22B Mucha Standard	512	
OY-XAO-39	Schleicher K 8B	749	
OY-XAR-R3	FES.530/1 Lehrmeister	0222	
OY-XAU-W5	FES.530/1 Lehrmeister	0219	
OY-XAY	FES.530/1 Lehrmeister	0220	
OY-XAZ	Schleicher K 8B	8063	
OY-XBB-BB	Carman M-200 Foehn	01	F-CCXG
			F-WCXG
OY-XBE	Scheibe Bergfalke II/55	351	OH-KBE
OY-XBF-72	Glasflügel H201B Standard Libelle	406	
OY-XBH-C6	Pilatus B4-PC11	058	
OY-XBI-C7	Pilatus B4-PC11	059	
OY-XBM-85	Glasflügel H201B Standard Libelle	423	
OY-XBP-90	Pilatus B4-PC11	054	
OY-XBR-92	Pilatus B4-PC11	055	
OY-XBS-104	Scheibe L-Spatz 55	66	D-1506
OY-XBT-103	Scheibe Bergfalke II/55	308	D-1615
OY-XBX-100	Pilatus B4-PC11	082	
OY-XBY-106	Rolladen-Schneider LS1C	187	
OY-XBZ-99	Glasflügel H201B Standard Libelle	405	
OY-XCD-C1	Glasflügel H205 Club Libelle (Cr 12.5.01)	62	
OY-XCE-E2	Glasflügel H201B Standard Libelle	567	
OY-XCG-C5	Schempp-Hirth Standard Cirrus	565G	
OY-XCL-N1	SZD-36A Cobra 15	W-683	
OY-XCM	SZD-36A Cobra 15	W-690	
OY-XCN	SZD-8ter ZO Jaskolka	248	OH-211
			OH-JAD
OY-XCT-L1	Schempp-Hirth Standard Cirrus	569G	
OY-XCV-H6	Scheibe SF-28A Tandem-Falke	5742	D-KOED
OY-XCW-N4	Glasflügel H205 Club Libelle	106	

OY-XCX-C2	Pilatus B4-PC11	142	
OY-XCY-M8	Schleicher K 7 Rhönadler	7194	D-4074
OY-XDC-P1	Schempp-Hirth Standard Cirrus 75	637	
OY-XDF-B7	Eiri PIK-20B	20090	
OY-XDJ-E7	Grob G.102 Asti r CS	1079	
OY-XDK-37	Grob G.102 Astir CS	1129	
OY-XDL-V2	Grob G.102 Astir CS	1095	
OY-XDM-Y2	Grob G.102 Astir CS	1406	
OY-XDN-V3	Grob G.102 Astir CS	1096	
OY-XDO-79	Grob G.102 Astir CS	1080	
OY-XDP-V5	Grob G.102 Astir CS	1097	
OY-XDS-V6	Grob G.102 Astir CS	1131	
OY-XDU-P7	Schempp-Hirth Standard Cirrus B	634	
OY-XDV-E9	Glaser-Dirks DG-100	44	
OY-XDX	Scheibe SF-25B Falke	46141	D-KCAH
OY-XDY-K2	Grob G.102 Astir CS	1361	
OY-XEA-17	Schleicher Ka 6CR Rhönsegler	6237	
OY-XEC-40	SZD-22C Mucha Standard	528	OO-ZSQ
OY-XED-ED	Scheibe L-Spatz 55	794	D-1530
OY-XEF	EoN Olympia Series 2	EON/059	RDAF: Z-962
			OY-BKX
			RDAF: Z-962
			RDAF: 96-962
OY-XEG-N3	Schleicher ASK 13	13313	
OY-XEH-88	Schleicher ASW 15	15016	
OY-XEI -12	Scheibe Zugvogel IIIB	1069	SE-TCI
OY-XEJ-20	SZD-24C Foka	W-196	
OY-XEN	Grunau Baby IIb	1	D-3673
			D-5333
OY-XES	Mü.13E Bergfalke	107	D-6312
OY-XET-A4	Siebert SIE-3	3011	
OY-XEW-81	Scheibe Bergfalke IV	5819	
OY-XEZ-31	Schempp-Hirth Standard Cirrus	40	
OY-XFA	Polyt III	1	RDAF: Z-931
			RDAF: 98-931
OY-XFC-FC	Schleicher K 7 Rhönadler	476	RDAF: Z-982
			RDAF: 98-982
OY-XFD-G8	Schleicher K 7 Rhönadler	477	RDAF: Z-983
			RDAF: 98-983
OY-XFE-42	Schleicher K 8B	973	RDAF: Z-965
OY-XFH-66	Schleicher K 8B	8370	RDAF: Z-969
OY-XFI -22	Schleicher K 8B	8495	RDAF: Z-970
OY-XFK-F8	Schleicher K 8B	8496	RDAF: Z-971
OY-XFM-54	Schleicher K 8B	8498	RDAF: Z-972
OY-XFN-E1	Schleicher Ka 6CR Rhönsegler	779	RDAF: Z-964
			OY-XAD
			RDAF: Z-964
			OY-XAD
			RDAF: Z-964
OY-XGA-H5	Schleicher ASK 14	14021	D-KOMI
OY-XGF-G5	Grob G.102 Astir CS	1427	
OY-XGG-G6	Grob G.102 Astir CS	1476	
OY-XGI	Sportavia/ Scheibe SF-25B Falke	4829	D-KHEI
OY-XGJ-P8	Scheibe SF-25B Falke	46120	D-KABS
OY-XGK-K4	Schempp-Hirth Cirrus (W/o 21.4.01)	86	SE-TIR
OY-XGL-H1	Grob G.102 Astir CS	1472	
OY-XGM-F6	Schleicher Ka 6CR Rhönsegler	6640-Si	D-8581
OY-XGN-GN	Schleicher Ka 6CR Rhönsegler	1111	D-5012
OY-XGO-Z4	Schempp-Hirth Standard Cirrus B	666	
OY-XGP-K6	Scheibe SF-25B Falke	4689	D-KOSC
OY-XGT-Z9	Grob G.102 Astir CS	1185	
OY-XGY-M6	Grob G.102 Astir CS	1471	
OY-XHA-W7	Grob G.102 Astir CS	1474	
OY-XHC-21	Schempp-Hirth Standard Cirrus	198	D-0882
OY-XHE-69	Grob G.102 Astir CS	1344	
OY-XHI -H9	Scheibe SF-25C Falke	4493	D-KAUV
OY-XHK-03	Schempp-Hirth Standard Cirrus	537	D-3097
OY-XHN-K7	Eiri PIK-20D	20545	
OY-XHP-F4	Grob G.102 Astir CS	1418	
OY-XHR-Z3	Grob G.102 Astir CS	1484	
OY-XHS-G9	Schempp-Hirth Standard Cirrus	43	SE-TIZ
OY-XHW-P3	Schempp-Hirth Standard Cirrus	142	SE-TKV
OY-XHX-P9	Eiri PIK-20D	20552	
OY-XHY-T1	Eiri PIK-20B	20083	
OY-XHZ	Schempp-Hirth Duo Discus T	40/315	D-KOAV(2)
OY-XIA-L5	Grob G.102 Astir CS 77	1650	
OY-XID	Scheibe SF-25A Motorfalke	4541	D-KALU
OY-XIG-N8	Glasflügel H303 Mosquito	59	
OY-XIJ-A1	Schempp-Hirth Standard Cirrus	258	D-1137
OY-XIK	Grob G.102 Astir CS	2107	
OY-XIL -IL	Schleicher ASW 19	19192	
OY-XIM-T8	Schleicher ASW 20	20091	
OY-XIN-Z2	Schleicher ASK 13	13594	
OY-XIU	Scheibe SF-25B Falke	46252	D-KEAS
OY-XIV-R6	Eiri PIK-20B	20021	OH-461
OY-XIW-R7	Grob G.102 Astir CS 77	1710	
OY-XIZ-G7	Eiri PIK-20D	20616	
OY-XJA-E4	Grob G.103 Twin Astir	3126	
OY-XJD-52	Grob G.103 Twin Astir	3192	
OY-XJE-JE	Schleicher ASW 20	20215	
OY-XJJ-59	Grob G.103 Twin Astir	3191	
OY-XJK-L4	Glasflügel H201B Standard Libelle	509	D-2409
OY-XJL-P5	Schleicher ASW 19B	19234	
OY-XJP-00	Rolladen-Schneider LS3A	3380	
OY-XJR-K3	Rolladen-Schneider LS1C	175	D-2950
OY-XJV	Hogslund/Traugott-Olsen 2G	unkn	RDAF: Z-923
			RDAF: 92-923

OY-XJY-X2	Rolladen-Schneider LS3A	3345	
OY-XJZ-Y4	Schleicher ASW 19B	19271	
OY-XKB-A8	Glasflügel H201B Standard Libelle	566	SE-TNT
OY-XKD-N7	Centrair ASW-20F	20130	
OY-XKF-W4	Centrair ASW 20F	20131	
OY-XKH-70	Rolladen-Schneider LS3A	3412	
OY-XKI	Schleicher ASK 21	21023	
OY-XKK-KK	Rolladen-Schneider LS1C	117	D-0698
OY-XKL-KL	Rolladen-Schneider LS1F	309	D-2761
OY-XKM-KM	Schleicher ASW 20	20441	
OY-XKO-R2	Schleicher ASK 21	21056	
OY-XKP-X5	Rolladen-Schneider LS3A	3414	
OY-XKS-CC	Schleicher ASW 20 (Conv to ASW 20L, 6.88)	20415	
OY-XKT-KT	Schleicher ASW 20	20301	
OY-XKV -X7	Rolladen-Schneider LS4	4108	
OY-XKW-KW	Schleicher ASW 20 (Conv to ASW 20L, 6.88)	20278	
OY-XKX-KX	Rolladen-Schneider LS4	4011	
OY-XKZ-KZ	Grob G.103 Twin II	3575	D-6436
OY-XLD-LD	Rolladen-Schneider LS4	4216	
OY-XLH-LH	Centrair ASW-20F	20504	
OY-XLI U1	Rolladen-Schneider LS4	4215	D-0510
OY-XLK-LK	Rolladen-Schneider LS4	4217	
OY-XLL -LL	Centrair ASW-20F	20199	
OY-XLM-N9	Rolladen-Schneider LS4	4159	D-0296
OY-XLN-LN	Centrair ASW-20F	20514	
OY-XLP-W3	Rolladen-Schneider LS4	4296	D-2897
OY-XLS-LS	Grob G.102 Astir CS	1220	D-7284
OY-XLT-LT	Schleicher ASK 13	13484	D-2381
OY XLY-LY	Schleicher ASK 21	21094	D-7760
OY-XLZ-LZ	Grob G.103 Twin Astir II	3697	
OY-XMA	IAR IS.28M2	54	YR-1982
OY-XMC-X8	Scheibe SF-34	5114	
OY-XMD-MD	Rolladen-Schneider LS4	4392	D-4582
OY-XMF-X1	Schleicher ASK 21	21205	
OY-XMH-MH	Schleicher ASW 19B	19400	
OY-XMJ-MJ	Schleicher Ka 6CR Rhönsegler	6420	OH-306
	(Same c/n as OE-0725)		OH-RSS
OY-XMK-MK	Schleicher K 7 Rhönadler	AB 7282	D-8673
OY-XML-ML	Rolladen-Schneider LS4	4307	D-8503
OY-XMM-MM	Centrair 101AP Pégase	101-041	
OY-XMN(2)	Schleicher ASK 23B	23098	OE-5423
OY-XMO-L7	Rolladen-Schneider LS4	4375	D-9101
OY-XMS-MS	Schleicher ASW 19B	19401	
OY-XMT-MT	Schempp-Hirth Nimbus 2	29	OO-ZGB
			D-2942
OY-XMU-MU	Grob G.109B	6225	
OY-XMW-MW	Grob G.109	6149	
OY-XMY-MY	Grob G.103A Twin II Acro	3743-K-49	D-0820
OY-XNB	Grob G.109B	6232	
OY-XNC	Grob G.109	6033	D-KAZE
OY-XND-ND	Grob G.109B	6286	
OY-XNE-NE	Rolladen-Schneider LS4	4404	
OY-XNF-NF	Schleicher ASW 20L	20284	D-6553
OY-XNG	Scheibe SF-25B Falke	46135	D-KADM
OY-XNH-U7	Glaser-Dirks DG-200/17C	2-163/CL-14	D-9428
OY-XNL-T6	Glaser-Dirks DG-300 Elan	3E-91	
OY-XNO	Hoffmann H-36 Dimcna	3691	
OY-XNP-NP	Grob G.102 Astir CS	1400	D-7432
OY-XNR-X4	Rolladen-Schneider LS6	6016	
OY-XNT-NT	Jastreb Standard Cirrus G/81	307	
OY-XNU-NU	Centrair 101A Pégase	101A-0208	
OY-XNV-V8	Rolladen-Schneider LS4	4470	D-5172
OY-XNX-NX	Schleicher ASK 21	21240	
OY-XNY-NY	Glaser-Dirks DG-400	4-136	
OY-XNZ-NZ	Grob G.103 Twin Astir	3643	D-6157
OY-XOA	Scheibe SF-25E Super Falke	4336	D-KDCG
OY-XOB-75	SZD-50-3 Puchacz	B-1483	
OY-XOD	Schleicher ASK 23	23050	
OY-XOF-R4	Glaser-Dirks DG-100G	E60-G36	D-6846
OY-XOH-E5	Schempp-Hirth Nimbus II	96	D-8930
OY-XOJ-J2	Grob G.103A Twin II Acro	34057-K-287	
OY-XOK-X9	Schempp-Hirth Discus b	32	
OY-XOL-OL	Schempp-Hirth Discus b	95	
OY-XOM-Y3	Schempp-Hirth Nimbus 2B	147	D-3366
OY-XOS-U3	Glaser-Dirks DG-300 Elan	3E-176	
OY-XOT-93	Scheibe SF-25E Super Falke	4327	D-KEBS
OY-XOV	Scheibe SF-25E Super Falke	4339	D-KIEL
OY-XOZ-OZ	Glaser-Dirks DG-200/17C	2-165/CL-15	HB-1627
OY-XPA-PA	SZD-51-1 Junior	W-951	
OY-XPB-PB	Glaser-Dirks DG-600	6-36	
OY-XPC	Schleicher ASK 21	21316	
OY-XPD-PD	Glaser-Dirks DG-400	4-183	
OY-XPE-PE	Schleicher ASW 20CL	20853	
OY-XPF-PF	Schleicher ASW 20CL	20862	
OY-XPG	Sportavia-Pützer RF-5B Sperber	1005	D-KLLI
			EAF-. . .
OY-XPK-PK	Schleicher ASW 20CL	20852	
OY-XPL-PL	Schleicher ASK 21	21356	
OY-XPM-PM	Schempp-Hirth Discus b	112	
OY-XPN	Scheibe SF-25C Falke	44176	D-KDEI
OY-XPO-PO	Glaser-Dirks DG-300 Elan	3E-278	
OY-XPP-PP	Glaser-Dirks DG-300 Elan	3E-165	D-7213
OY-XPS-PS	Glaser-Dirks DG-400	4-230	(D-KIDG)
OY-XPT-PT	Glasflügel H201B Standard Libelle	65	LN-GIE
			SE-TIE
OY-XPU-PU	Rolladen-Schneider LS6A	6160	
OY-XPV	Sportavia/ Scheibe SF-25B Falke	4837	D-KHET

OY-XPW-PW	Rolladen-Schneider LS1F	180	LN-GAF
OY-XPX-PX	Rolladen-Schneider LS4A	4654	D-8028
OY-XPY-Z5	Schleicher ASW 19B	19372	D-1488
OY-XPZ-PZ	Glaser-Dirks DG-300 Elan	3E-301	
OY-XRA-RA	SZD-50-3 Puchacz	B-1725	
OY-XRB	Rolladen-Schneider LS6B (Reservation)	unkn	
OY-XRE-55	Schempp-Hirth Ventus c	419	
OY-XRF-RF	Rolladen-Schneider LS4A	4788	
OY-XRG-G2	Rolladen-Schneider LS6C	6217	D-4057
OY-XRI	Sportavia/ Scheibe SF-25C Falke	4238	D-KAJA(2)
OY-XRM-RM	Schempp-Hirth Ventus cM	41/479	
OY-XRN-RN	Schempp-Hirth Discus CS	026CS	
OY-XRO-D1	Schleicher ASW 24	24022	
OY-XRP-RP	SZD-50-3 Puchacz	B-1991	
OY-XRS-27	Schempp-Hirth Discus b	270	
OY-XRU-RU	Glaser-Dirks DG-300 Elan	3E-403	
OY-XRY-RY	Eiri PIK-20	20060	SE-TOO
OY-XSA-SA	Schempp-Hirth Janus CT	10/268	
	(Built as Janus C c/n 268, modified to Janus CE, 3.94; then CT, 4.98)		
OY-XSC-SC	Schempp-Hirth Discus CS	160CS	
OY-XSD	Grob G.102 Astir CS	1173	D-7294
OY-XSE	Stamer-Lippisch	01-92	
OY-XSF-SF	Schempp-Hirth Janus C	260	
OY-XSG	Scheibe SF-25B Falke	4666	D-KAPB
OY-XSH-H8	Rolladen-Schneider LS7	7139	
OY-XSI	Slingsby T.21B Sedbergh	MHL.012	SE-SMA
			WB985
OY-XSK	Schempp-Hirth Ventus bT	32/211	PH-747
OY-XSL-SL	Scheibe SF-25E Super Falke	4355	D-KDGO
OY-XSN	SZD-51-1 Junior	B-2014	SP-3576
			SP-P576
OY-XSO	Schempp-Hirth Ventus 2cT	7/15	
OY-XSP	SZD-50-3 Puchacz	B-2094	
OY-XSR	Rolladen-Schneider LS8A	8120	
OY-XST-ST	Schempp-Hirth Discus b	478	
OY-XSU	Schempp-Hirth Discus CS	183CS	
OY-XSV-SV	PZL PW-5 Smyk	17.03.017	
OY-XSW-SW	Schempp-Hirth Ventus 2cT	12/45	
	(Conv from Ventus 2c c/n 18/45, 4.98)		
OY-XSX-SX	Schempp-Hirth Nimbus 4DT	2/2	D-KKFM
OY-XSY	Schempp-Hirth Discus 2T	14/127	D-KKAH
OY-XSZ	Rolladen-Schneider LS4B	41011	D-1180
OY-XTA-TA	Schempp-Hirth Nimbus 3T	2/44	N45U
			N806MD
			D-KHIA
OY-XTB-TB	Schempp-Hirth Ventus c	542	
OY-XTF-T5	Rolladen-Schneider LS4B	4857	
OY-XTG-TG	Grob G.103C Twin III	34180	
OY-XTH-TH	Schempp-Hirth Standard Cirrus	363	D-2153
OY-XTI -TI	Schempp-Hirth Ventus cT	176/577	
OY-XTK-T4	SZD-51-1 Junior	B-2011	
OY-XTL-TL	Rolladen-Schneider LS4A	4815	D-3448
OY-XTM(2)	Rolladen-Schnieder LS-3A	3147	SE-TTK
OY-XTN	Rolladen-Schneider LS7	7138	(D-3674)
OY-XTO-TO	Scheibe SF-25E Super Falke	4354	G-BHAG
			(D-KDGO)
OY-XTS-TS	Glaser-Dirks DG-500-22 Elan	5E-118S17	
OY-XTT-77	Scheibe SF-34	5103	SE-UEA
			D-3337
OY-XTV	Hoffmann H-36 Dimona	36220	SE-UBO
OY-XTX-TX	Schempp-Hirth Ventus c	469	
OY-XTY-TY	Rolladen-Schneider LS4A	4812	D-3398
OY-XTZ	Schleicher ASK 23B	23125	
OY-XUA	Schleicher ASK 21	21666	
OY-XUB	Schempp-Hirth Discus CS	046C	D-2172
OY-XUC	PZL PW-5 Smyk	17.04.011	
OY-XUD	Schleicher ASK 23B	23065	OH-699
OY-XUE	Schempp-Hirth Discus b	452	D-7955
OY-XUF	Schempp-Hirth Discus b	169	OH-739
OY-XUG-G3	Schempp-Hirth Discus CS	181CS	
OY-XUH	Hoffmann H-36 Dimona	36208	G-LIDR
			G-BMSK
OY-XUI	Schleicher ASW 20CL (Res 4.04)	unkn	
OY-XUM	Schempp-Hirth Discus 2T	28/. . .	
OY-XUN-UN	Schempp-Hirth Discus CS	209CS	
OY-XUP	Schempp-Hirth Discus 2T	18/139	
OY-XUR	Scheibe SF-25C Falke (Res 4.04)	unkn	
OY-XUS	Glaser-Dirks DG-800B	8-84B21	D-KCHD
OY-XUT-UT	SZD-50-3 Puchacz	B-1729	SE-UGS
OY-XUU-51	Schempp-Hirth Ventus cT	184/604	
OY-XUW	Schempp-Hirth Nimbus 4T	10	D-KJAA
OY-XVA	Grob G.103C Twin III SL	35006	D-KLMA
OY-XVB	Schleicher ASK 23B	23140	D-5523
OY-XVC	Schleicher ASK 21	21415	D-6254
OY-XVD	Schempp-Hirth Discus 2b	95	
OY-XVE	Schleicher ASW 24	24212	D-6962
OY-XVF	Schempp-Hirth Duo Discus T	66	
OY-XVG	Grob G.103 Twin Astir IIISL	35014	OE-9374
OY-XVH	Scheibe SF-25C Falke	44342	D-KNAF
OY-XVI	Schleicher ASW 24	24061	D-7724
OY-XVJ	Schempp-Hirth Ventus 2cT	38/128	
OY-XVK	Schempp-Hirth Duo Discus	057	
OY-XVL-VL	Schleicher ASH 25E	25033	D-KKSR
OY-XVM	SZD-55-1	551196082	D-9551
OY-XVN(2)	Schempp-Hirth Duo Discus T	101	
OY-XVP	Schempp-Hirth Ventus 2cM	86/182	PH-1242
			OY-XVP
OY-XVR	Scheibe SF-25C Falke	44703	D-KBCO(2)
OY-XVS-VS	Schleicher ASW 24B	24245	
OY-XVT	Rolladen-Schneider LS3-17	3146	D-2848
OY-XVX-VX	Schempp-Hirth Discus CS	162CS	
OY-XVZ	Schleicher ASK 21	21670	
OY-XXA	Schempp-Hirth Ventus 2a	70	
OY-XXC	Rolladen-Schneider LS8-18	8423	
OY-XXD	PZL PW-5 Smyk	17.06.022	
OY-XXE	Schempp-Hirth Ventus cxT (Res 9.04)	unkn	
OY-XXL	Schempp-Hirth Nimbus 4M	12	D-KHXL
OY-XXM	Rolladen-Schneider LS8A	8114	D-4604
OY-XXN-2A	Schempp-Hirth Discus 2a	167	
OY-XXR	Glasflügel H101 Salto	58	D-6637
OY-XYB	Hoffmann H-36 Dimona	36217	
OY-XYD-YD	Glaser-Dirks DG-300 Elan	3E-192	
OY-XYF(2)-YF	Rolladen-Schneider LS6	6258	D-2571
OY-XYH-Y6	Schempp-Hirth Ventus b/16.6	228	D-5237
OY-XYL-YL	Rolladen-Schneider LS4	4568	
OY-XYM-YM	Schempp-Hirth Standard Cirrus	493G	D-9443
OY-XYN-YN	Rolladen-Schneider LS6A	6129	
OY-XYO	Grob G.102 Astir CS	1191	D-7308
OY-XYP	Scheibe SF-25C Falke	44164	D-KEFP
OY-XYS	Scheibe SF-25C Falke	44696	(SE-UNR)
			(SE-UDK)
			D-KBCJ
OY-XYT	Scheibe SF-25E Super Falke	4316	D-KEFL
OY-XYV-YV	Schleicher ASK 21	21310	
OY-XZA	Schempp-Hirth Ventus 2cT	02/03	BGA4667/JPG
			D-KLYC
OY-XZB(2)	SZD-48-3 Jantar Standard 3	B-1737	SE-UGM
OY-XZC	Schempp-Hirth Ventus 2cT	106/...	
OY-XZD	Hoffman HK-36TTC Super Dimona	36733	
OY-XZF	Schempp-Hirth Janus cT	11/270	D-KDOA(2)
OY-XZG	Scheibe SF-25C Falke	44509	D-KIOJ(3)
OY-XZH	Schempp-Hirth Discus bT	114/467	OE-9384
OY-XZI	Rolladen-Schneider LS4	4290	D-8189
OY-XZK	Schleicher ASK 21	21726	
OY-XZL	Scheibe SF-25C Falke	44684	
OY-XZM	HOAC HK-36TTC Super Dimona	36618	
OY-XZO-ZO	Hoffmann H-36 Dimona	3514	SE-UCK
			N408DH
OY-XZP	HOAC HK-36TTC Super Dimona	36536	
OY-XZT-ZT	Schempp-Hirth Discus CS	191CS	
OY-XZW	Glaser-Dirks DG-800	unkn	
OY-ZLX-ZL	Rolladen-Schneider LS4	4255	OE-5306
OY-ZWX	SZD-51-1 Junior	B-1850	HB-3014
OY- . . .	Glaser-Dirks DG-400	4-181	F-CGRA
OY- . . .	Schempp-Hirth Ventus 2cM	86/182	PH-1242
			OY-XVP

MICROLIGHTS

KLASSE A (Weightshift control)

8-1	Demon Hiway
8-2	Solar Wing/Ultra Sport Trike
	(Noted as TriFun 330DL, 6.00)
8-3	Fledgewing
8-4	Airwave Gliders UP Comet
8-5	Solar Wing/Mainair Trike
8-6	Demon Hiway/Hiway Trike
8-7	Flexiform Striker/Mainair Trike
8-8	Southdown Puma Sprint
8-9	Azur/Trifun
8-10	Airwave Gliders UP Comet
8-11	Solar Wing/Hiway Trike
8-12	Typhoon/Trifun
8-13	Southdown Puma Sprint
8-14	Typhoon/Trifun
8-15	Typhoon/Trifun
8-16	Azur/Trifun
8-17	Demon Hiway/Monopole Trike
8-18	Demon Hiway/Hiway Trike
8-19	Firebird Sierra/Monopole Trike
8-20	Flexiform Striker/Air Play Trike
8-21	Lightning 2
8-22	Typhoon Solar Wing/Hiway Trike
8-23	Lightning/Air Play Trike
8-24	Firebird Sierra
8-25	Typhoon Trifun
8-26	Typhoon XL
8-27	Southdown Puma Sprint
8-28	Southdown Puma DS
8-29	Moyes Missiles GT
8-30	Firebird Sierra
8-31	Flexiform Striker/Mainair Trike
8-32	Gold Marque Sports/Hiway Skymaster
8-33	Solar Wings/Trifun 330
8-34	Southdown Puma Sprint
8-35	Firebird Sierra/Air Play Trike
8-36	Airplay Magic 3
8-37	Dual Strike

8-38 Southdown Puma Sprint
8-39 Flexiform Striker/Mainair Sport Trike
8-40 Flexiform Striker
8-41 Southdown Puma Sprint
8-42 Mainair Gemini/Flash (Cancelled?)
8-43 Southdown Puma Sprint/Air Play Trike
8-44 Typhoon S Medium
8-45 Firebird Sierra
8-46 Typhoon S Medium/Kopi Air Play Trike
8-47 Lite Air/Air Play Trike
8-48 Southdown Puma Sprint/Air Play Trike (Damaged 24.8.03)
8-49 Striker/Air Play Trike
8-50 Striker/Air Play Trike
8-51 Typhoon 180/Hiway Trike
8-52 Striker/Air Play Trike
8-53 Southdown Puma Sprint
8-54 Striker/Air Play Trike
8-55 Southdown Puma Sprint
8-56 Raven T15/Air Play Trike
8-57 Raven/Air Play Trike
8-58 Raven/Air Play Trike
8-59 Raven 25 Two-seater
8-60 Demon-JTM
8-61 Firebird Sierra
8-62 Fledgwing
8-63 La Mouette Tri Fun
8-64 Pegasus/Air Play Trike
8-65 Chaser JTM
8-66 Alpha JTM A130XL
8-68 Mistral GTR/Taifun
8-69 Typhoon Trifun
8-70 Solar Wings Pegasus XL
8-71 Striker/Air Play Trike
8-72 Solar Wings Pegasus XL
8-73 Firebird Sierra/Air Play Trike
8-74 Southdown Puma Sport
8-75 Solar Wings Pegasus XL
8-77 Steinbach Delta
8-79 Mainair Gemini/Flash II
8-80 Aerial Arts 130SX
8-81 Aerial Arts 130SX
8-82 Aerial Arts Winder JTM
8-83 Raven/Air Play Trike
8-84 Aerial Arts 110LX JTM
8-85 Bicla OSS
8-86 Solar Wings Pegasus XL-Q
8-87 Aerial Arts 130SX
8-88 Aerial Arts 110SX JTM
8-89 Solar Wings Pegasus XL-Q
8-90 Aerial Arts Chaser 110
8-91 Solar Wings Pegasus XL
8-92 Solar Wings Pegasus XL-Q
8-93 Typhoon TH
8-94 Aerial Arts Power W
8-95 Solar Wings Pegasus XL
8-96 Tyhoon S4
8-97 Demon Trifun
8-98 Solar Wings Pegasus XL
8-99 Aerial Arts 130SX
8-100 Aerial Arts Chaser 110SX JTM
8-101 Aerial Arts Chaser 110SX JTM
8-102 Bicla Spider
8-103 C-S Prototype 1
8-105 Solar Wings Pegasus XL
8-106 Solar Wings Pegasus XL (Crashed)
8-107 Solar Wings Pegasus XL
8-108 Airwave Magic III
8-109 Lotni Polen
8-110 Magic 165
8-111 Solar Wings Pegasus XL
8-112 Magic III 166
8-113 Solar Wings Pegasus XL (W/o 20.7.03)
8-114 Hiway Demon
8-115 JTM llOSX
8-116 JTM llOSX
8-117 Solar Wings Pegasus XL
8-118 Solar Wings Typhoon 180B
8-119 Solar Wings Pegasus XL
8-120 Solar Wings Pegasus XL
8-121 Solar Wings Pegasus XL
8-122 Solar Wings Pegasus XL
8-123 Solar Wings Pegasus XL
8-124 Solar Wings Pegasus XL/JTM
8-125 JTM 110
8-126 Solar Wings Pegasus XL
8-127 JTM Spar 2
8-128 Southdown Puma Sprint
8-129 Southdown Puma Sprint
8-130 Aerial Arts JTM
8-131 Aerial Arts
8-132 JTM Spar 2
8-133 Solar Wings Pegasus XL
8-134 JTM Spar 2
8-135 Southdown Raven/Airplay Trike
8-136 Solar Wings Pegasus XL
8-137 Solar Wings Pegasus XL/Airplay Trike
8-138 JTM
8-139 Southdown Raven
8-140 JTM 130SX
8-141 JTM 115SX
8-142 Solar Wings Pegasus XL-Q
8-143 Solar Wings Pegasus XL-Q
8-144 Southdown Puma Sprint 2 seat
8-145 Aerial Arts Chaser 2
8-146 Solar Wings Pegasus XL-Q
8-147 JTM 110SX
8-148 Solar Wings Pegasus XL
8-149 Magic 4 Christian
8-150 Aerial Arts Chaser 110SX
8-151 Solar Wings Pegasus Quasar
8-152 Solar Wings Pegasus XL
8-153 Southdown Raven
8-154 Solar Wings Pegasus XL-Q
8-156 Chaser S
8-157 Pegasus Quasar
8-158 Deltalet Record MD-20
8-159 La Mouette Chronos 16
8-160 La Mouette
8-161 Pai Aero
8-162 JTM Spar 2
8-163 Solar Wings Pegasus XL-Q Mk2
8-164 La Mouette
8-165 Aerial Arts JTM
8-166 Solar Wings Pegasus XL-Q Mk2 (W/o 16.6.03)
8-167 Lotni Polen Airo
8-168 Southdown Puma Sprint
8-169 PZL ML 1
8-172 La Mouette Chronos 16
8-173 PZL ML 1 (Dbr 6.8.03)
8-174 Mainair Gemini/ Flash II Alfa
8-175 Solar Wings Pegasus XL-Q
8-176 PZL ML 1
8-178 Solar Wings Pegasus XL
8-179 TL-22 Duo
8-180 JTM Puma Sprint
8-182 La Mouette
8-183 PZL ML 1
8-184 Air Création XP 15
8-185 ESO 14
8-187 Air Création Fun 14
8-189 Jazz trike (Damaged 6.6.03)
8-190 Pegasus Flash II
8-192 Polaris FIB

KLASSE B (Conventional 3-axis control)

9-1 Eipper Quicksilver MX-II
9-2 Huntair Pathfinder 2 (Crashed)
9-3 Huntair Pathfinder 2 (Crashed)
9-4 Dragon 150
9-5 Sirocco
9-6 Dragon 150
9-7 Dragon 150
9-8 Eipper Quicksilver MX-II
9-9 Scout
9-10 Dragon 150
9-11 Sirocco
9-12 Eipper Quicksilver MX
9-13 Dragon 150 (Crashed) 064
9-14 Rotec Rally 3
9-15 Rotec Rally Sport
9-16 Eipper Quicksilver MX
9-17 Dragon 150 (Believed c/n 068, now G-MNJF)
9-18 Dragon 150
9-19 Eipper Quicksilver MX-II
9-20 Eipper Quicksilver MX-II
9-21 Eipper Quicksilver MX-II
9-22 Sirocco (Sold?)
9-24 Dragon 150-M1
9-25 Pioneer Flightstar
9-26 Robertson B1-RD (Single seat) (Crashed)
9-27 Robertson B1-RD (Two-seat)
9-28 Rotec Rally 2B (Wfu)
9-29 Rotec Rally 3
9-30 Pioneer Flightstar
9-31 Eipper Quicksilver MX-II
9-32 Sherpa II
9-33 Sherpa II
9-34 Sherpa Fox I
9-35 BUF-1 (Crashed)
9-36 Eipper Quicksilver MX-II
9-37 Comco Ikarus Fox-C22
9-38 Midlt FS
9-39 Eipper Quicksilver MX-II
9-40 Comco Ikarus Fox C-22
9-41 Comco Ikarus Fox-C22
9-42 Comco Ikarus Fox-C22
9-43 Comco Ikarus Fox-C22
9-44 Pioneer Flightstar
9-45 Challenger Two-seater
9-46 Pioneer Flightstar
9-47 Skywalker II
9-49 Comco Ikarus Fox-C22

9-50	J-3 Kitten		
9-51	J-3 Kitten (Crashed)		
9-52	Comco Ikarus Fox-C22		
9-53	Comco Ikarus Fox-C22		
9-54	Helff Albatros	107	
9-55	Helff Albatros		
9-56	Eipper Quicksilver GT-400		
9-57	Comco Ikarus Fox-C22		
9-58	Comco Ikarus Fox-C22		
9-59	Rotec Rally 3		
9-60	SE5A Replica (Wfu)		
9-61	Comco Ikarus Fox-C22		
9-62	Eipper Quicksilver MX-II		
9-64	Pioneer Flightstar		
9-65	Spectrum RX-550		
9-66	Comco Ikarus Fox-C22		
9-67	Eipper Quicksilver 1		
9-68	Comco Ikarus Fox-C22		
9-70	Quad City Challenger II		
9-71	Quad City Challenger II		
9-72	Quad City Challenger II (Damaged 14.9.03)		
9-73	Comco Ikarus Fox-C22		
9-74	Comco Ikarus Fox-C22		
9-75	Albatros		
9-76	Comco Ikarus Fox-C22		
9-77	Quad City Challenger II (Crashed)		
9-78	Sky Walker II		
9-79	Rans S-6E Coyote II (Crashed)		
9-80	Rans S-6E Coyote II		
9-81	Rans S-6E Coyote II		
9-82	Skywalker II		
9-83	Rans S-6E Coyote II		
9-84	Quad City Challenger II		
9-85	Kolb Twinstar II		
9-86	HFL Stratos 300	300-017K	
9-88	Rans S-6E Coyote II (Crashed)		
9-90	Spectrum Beaver RX-550E		
9-91	Rans S-6E Coyote II		
9-92	Fisher FP-303		
9-93	Rans S-10E Sakota		
9-94	CZ-ULF 1		
9-95	Rans S-6E Coyote II		
9-96	Rans S-6E Coyote II		
9-97	Sky Walker II (Crashed)		
9-98	Rans S-10E Sakota		
9-99	Rans S-6E Coyote II		
9-100	HFL Stratos 300	300-023K	
9-101	Rans S-6E Coyote II		
9-102	Rans S-6E Coyote II		
9-103	Aviasud Mistral (Sold?)		
9-104	Rans S-6E Coyote II (Damaged 15.10.03)		
9-105B	Rotec Panther 2 Plus		
9-106	Sky Walker II		
9-107	Rans S-7E		
9-108	Rans S-9 Chaos (or S-10E Sakota ?)		
9-109	Sky Walker II		
9-110	Pioneer Flightstar		
9-111	Rans S-10E Sakota (Intended OY-LEO ?)		
9-112	TEAM Mini-MAX		
9-113	Rans S-12E Airaile		
9-114	Rans S-12E Airaile		
9-115	Rans S-6ES Coyote II		
9-116	Rans S-7E Courier		
9-117	Rans S-10E Sakota		
9-118	Rans S-12E Airaile		
9-119	Bobcat Special		
9-120	Rans S-12E Airaile		
9-121	Rans S-12E Airaile		
9-122	Rans S-5 Coyote I		
9-123	Rans S-10E Sakota		
9-124	Rans S-12ES Airaile		
9-125	Comco Ikarus Fox-C22		
9-126	Rans S-12E Airaile		
9-127	Rans S-6E Coyote II		
9-128	TEAM Mini-MAX (Crashed)		
9-129	Rans S-12E Airaile		
9-130	Rans S-12E Airaile (mod.)		
9-131	Rans S-6ES Coyote II		
9-132	Mosler N3-2 Pup		
9-133	Rans S-12ES Airaile		
9-134	Rans S-12ES Airaile		
9-135	Comco Ikarus Fox-C22		
9-136	Rans S-12ES Airaile (Crashed)		
9-137	Rans S-6ES Coyote II (Crashed)		
9-139	Rans S-12ES Airaile		
9-140	Explorer Airaile		
9-142	Rans S-12ES Airaile		
9-143	Rans S-12E Airaile (Cr 20.6.00)	691095	
9-146	WAGAero CUBy 2		
9-148	Tandem Air Sunny Sport		
9-149	Comco Ikarus Fox C-22	9204-3378	
9-150	Rans S-12E Airaile		
9-152	Rans S-12E Airaile		
9-153	Quad City Challenger II		
9-154	Comco Ikarus Fox C-22		
9-155	Quad City Challenger II		
9-156	TEAM Mini-MAX (Damaged 20.9.03)		
9-157	Rans S-12E Airaile		
9-158	Rans S-12E Airaile		
9-159	WAG Aero CUBy 2		
9-160	Comco Ikarus Fox C-22		
9-162	TEAM Z-Max		
9-163	Comco Ikarus Fox C-22		
9-164	Rans S-6ES Coyote II		
9-165	TEAM Z-Max 1300		
9-166	CFM Shadow CD	225	
9-167	Quad City Challenger II		
9-168	Rans S-12ES Airaile		
9-171	Comco Ikarus Fox C-22		
9-172	Rans S-12ES Airaile		
9-173	Rans S-6ES Coyote II		
9-174	TEAM Mini-MAX		
9-175	Mosler N3 Pup		
9-176	Kolb Twinstar Mk.3		
9-177	CFM Shadow CD	K.234	
9-178	Quad City Challenger II		
9-179	Kolb Twinstar Mk 3		
9-180	Comco Ikarus Fox C-22		
9-181	Rans S-12ES Airaile		
9-183	Rans S-12ES Airaile		
9-184	TEAM Mini-MAX (W/o 24.5.98)	1646P	
9-185	TEAM Mini-MAX		
9-186	Aviasud Mistral		
9-187	JORA Jora		
9-189	Wendell WAP 200		
9-190	Murphy Renegade 2		
9-191	Rans S-6ES Coyote II		
9-192	Rans S-6ES Coyote II XL		
9-193	Rans S-6ES Coyote II		
9-194	Interplane Skyboy		
9-195	Quad City Challenger II		
9-196	Quad City Challenger II		
9-198	Rans S-6ES Coyote II		
9-199	TEAM Hi-MAX		
9-201	Rans S-6ES Coyote II		
9-202	Denney Kitfox		
9-203	Airbike		
9-204	Fisher Horizon		
9-205	Pioneer Flightstar		
9-206	Rans S-6 Coyote II		
9-207	Rans S-6 Coyote II		
9-209	Interplane Skyboy		
9-210	Micro-Mong		
9-211	JORA Jora		
9-212	Rans S-6 Coyote II		
9-214	JORA Jora		
9-216	Murphy Renegade Spirit		
9-218	JORA Jora SRO	C-92	
9-219	JORA Jora		
9-220	Rans S-6ES Coyote II		
9-221	Pioneer Flightstar II (Damaged 14.6.03)		
9-222	JORA Jora		
9-224	Quad City Challenger		
9-225	Rans S-6ES Coyote II		
9-226	JORA Jora		
9-228	JORA Jora (Damaged 13.1.01)	5306654-2000	
9-229	Rans S-6ES Coyote II		
9-230	WAP 2.01		
9-231	Quad City Challenger II		
9-232	Rufax		
9-235	JORA Jora		
9-236	Fantasy Air Allegro 2000		
9-237	JORA Jora		
9-238	Comco Ikarus C-42		
9-239	Fisher Super Koala		
9-240	Fantasy Air Allegro 2000		
9-241	JORA Jora		
9-242	Fantasy Air Allegro 2000		
9-243	Comco Ikarus C-42	0207-6479	D-MTRV
9-244	JORA Jora		
9-245	Fantasy Air Allegro 2000		
9-246	Fantasy Air Allegro 2000		
9-247	Fantasy Air Allegro 2000		
9-248	Jabiru UL450	0481	
9-249	Evektor EV-97 Eurostar		
9-250	Remos G.3 Mirage		D-M . . .
9-251	Evektor EV-97 Eurostar 2000		
9-252	Evektor EV-97 Eurostar 2000		
9-253	Evektor EV-97 Eurostar 2000 (Damaged 17.9.03)		
9-255	Comco Ikarus C-42B	0304-6522	
9-256	Pioneer Flightstar IISC		
9-258	ICP MXP-740 Savannah		
9-259	Fantasy Air Allegro 2000		
9-260	Langeland Lodel-1	LM-1	
9-261	Ragwing Special		
9-262	ICP MXP-740 Savannah		
9-263	Evektor EV-97 Eurostar 2000		
9-264	Zenair CH-601 Zodiac	6-9460	
9-265	Zenair CH-701 STOL	7-9403	
9-266	Evektor EV-97 Eurostar		
9-267	Zenair CH-601 Zodiac		
9-268	Zenair CH-601UL Zodiac	6-9490-1898	
9-269	JORA Jora UL-2		
9-270	Aerospool WT-9 Dynamic		

9-271	Aerospool WT-9 Dynamic	
9-272	Titan Tornado	
9-274	ICP MXP-740 Savannah	
9-275	JORA Jora	
9-276	Evektor EV-97 Eurostar	
9-277	Fantasy Air Allegro 2000	
9-279	Zenair CH-601 Zodiac	
9-280	Zenair CH-701 STOL	
9-281	ICP MXP-740 Savannah	
9-283	ICP MXP-740 Savannah	04-06-51-298

GYROCOPTERS

10-1	Air Command 532
10-2	Air Command 532 (Crashed)
10-3	Air Command 532
10-4	Humlan
10-5	Air Command 532
10-6	Campbell Cricket (Crashed)
10-7	Air Command 532 (Crashed)
10-8	PL Air Command
10-9	Campbell-Bensen B.8
10-10	Parson Trainer
10-11	Humlan
10-12	Air Command 532
10-14	Tornado 2
10-15	Air Command 532 (W/o 15.6.04)
10-16	PL Air Command 2
10-17	PL Air Command 2
10-18	PL Air Command 2

NON-CURRENT AIRCRAFT

The following non-active aircraft are known to exist in Denmark - most are held by members of the KZ-Club for storage or rebuild and some may aspire to full airworthiness in due course but purely museum specimens have been excluded. Incomplete homebuilt projects have now also been removed from this list.

OY-AAN	S.A.I. KZ-VII U-4 Laerke	148	F-BFXA G-AJHM OY-AAN
OY-AAP	S.A.I. KZ-VII U-4 Laerke	152	
OY-AAS	S.A.I. KZ-VII U-4 Laerke	155	D-EMES OY-AAS
OY-AAT	S.A.I. KZ-III U-2	91	OO-MAT
OY-ACC	S.A.I. KZ-VII U-4 Laerke	177	D-EDOP OY-ACC
OY-ACE	S.A.I. KZ-IX Ellehammer (Replica)	204	
OY-ACT	S.A.I. KZ-III U	50	RDAF:611 RDAF:50
OY-AEZ	Orlican L-40 Meta-Sokol	150613	D-ENZY OY-AEZ
OY-AFF	S.A.I. KZ-III U-2	77	D-EGIR OY-DZE
OY-AFG	Piper J-3C-65 Cub	10858	SE-CEW LN-MAP 43-29567
OY-ALT	de Havilland DH.82A Tiger Moth	85621	D-ELYG (HB-UBG) (SL-AAF) G-ANBZ DE680
OY-ALV	Auster Mk.4	906	D-ELIT G-ANHP MT170
OY-ANK	Piper J-3C-65 Cub (Frame no. 8351, dismantled)	9059	D-ELSU OE-ABF HB-OWX N46448 NC46448 43-2914
OY-ANY	S.A.I. KZ-III U	52	SE-ASH
OY-ATK	S.A.I. KZ-VII U-4 Laerke	182	RDAF: O-620 RDAF: 63-620
OY-AVH(1)	Piper J-4 Cub Coupé	4-449	D-EBYP N22765 NC22765
OY-AVJ	Rearwin 9000	567D	SE-AGB
OY-AVM	Auster J/1N Alpha	1980	G-AHCN
OY-AVW	Piper PA-17 Vagabond	17-70	D-EEMM N4665H
OY-DAA	S.A.I. KZ-III U-2	89	
OY-DBA	Corben Junior Ace (Unofficial reservation)	2	SE-AGC LN-NJS (LN-LJS) SE-AGC
OY-DBL	Auster J/5PAutocar (Unofficial reservation)	2912	D-EGHG D-EMYD (D-EKEL) HB-EOU
OY-DGI	Auster J/1 Autocrat	2010	G-AHHG
OY-DGU	Auster J/1 Autocrat	2031	D-ENIT OY-DGU
OY-DHJ	DHC-1 Chipmunt Mk.21	C1/0470	G-AMMA
OY-DIA	S.A.I. KZ-III U-2	79	
OY-DMB	S.A.I. KZ-III U-2	90	9M-AMF (VR-RCW) VR-OAD VR-RBK VR-SCH
OY-DRA	Auster J/1 Autocrat	2142	
OY-DTA	S.A.I. KZ-III U-2	73	
OY-DTE	S.A.I. KZ-III U-2	71	
OY-DVP	de Havilland DH.82ATiger Moth	85506	N38013 D-EDIS DE526
OY-DYZ	S.A.I. KZ-III U-1	56	D-EFID OY-DYZ
OY-DZU	S.A.I. KZ-IV U-1	70	(SE-EGX) OY-DZU
OY-EFG	Globe GC-1B Swift (Intended marks unconfirmed) (Including parts from D-EAWS c/n 1469)	1325	D-ECEZ N3323K
OY-EFL	Cessna 140	10220	D-EHEP N73015
OY-EFM	Piper TG-8 Cub	G1	D-EMUG N46490 NC46490 43-3009
OY-EFW	Piper PA-18 Super Cub 95	18-1375	(OY-AJY) (D-EAUI) (D-EAUT) ALAT 51-15375
OY-FAE	S.A.I. KZ-II Trainer	119	RDAF: 11-111 RDAF: 11-119
OY-FAN	S.A.I. KZ-II Trainer	110	RDAF: 11-102 RDAF: 11-110
OY-POL	Piper J-3C-65 Cub	12818	44-80522

PH - NETHERLANDS

Regn.	Type	C/n	Prev.Id.
PH-ABB	Piper PA-38-112 Tomahawk II	38-82A0005	N91340 (PH-ABB) N91340
PH-ABV	Cessna 172P Skyhawk	17274260	N51054
PH-ACG	Fokker S.11.1 Instructor	6279	MLD:179/K E-36
PH-ACH	Reims/Cessna F152-II (Rebuilt 1985-6 using fuselage of F.152 D-EOWT c/n 1883)	F15201838	OO-HRD(2) (OO-JDH) (OO-HDO) OO-HRD(2)
PH-ACI	Cessna T303 Crusader	T30300236	N9914C JA5295 N9914C
PH-ACM	Cessna 172P Skyhawk	17275454	N63602
PH-ACV	Dyn'Aero MCR Club	76	PH-3D1
PH-ACW	Velocity 173FG	DMO066	
PH-ACX	Diamond DA-20-A1 Katana	10008	N50ZR C-FTKX
PH-ADE	Reims/Cessna F172M Skyhawk	F17201118	D-EENJ
PH-ADJ	Murphy Elite (Reservation, not official)	NVAV-400	
PH-ADP	Piper PA-32RT-300 Lance II	32R-7885061	N9619C
PH-ADQ	Pander D replica (Reservation 07.02)	Unk	
PH-ADW	Reims/Cessna F172L	F17200841	OK-CKB PH-ADW
PH-AEC	Piper PA-28-181 Archer III	2843039	(PH-AEG)
PH-AED	Piper PA-28-181 Archer III	2843089	N92883
PH-AEE	Piper PA-28-181 Archer III	2843076	OY-JAZ
PH-AEQ	Pander D replica (Reservation 07.02)	Unk	
PH-AFA	SOCATA Rallye 180T Galérien	2685	
PH-AFG	SOCATA Rallye 150ST	3174	
PH-AFK	SOCATA TB-9 Tampico	182	F-BNGX
PH-AFP	Pottier P.170S	020	
PH-AFS	Fokker S.11.1 Instructor	6205	(PH-HOO) E-14
PH-AFT	SOCATA TB-20 Trinidad GT	2204	F-OIMO
PH-AGR	DHC-8 Series 315	601	(PH-VOO), C-FDHD
PH-AHQ	Boeing 767-383ER	24477	OY-KDL (SE-DKR)
PH-AHX	Boeing 767-383ER	24847	LN-RCD

PH-AHY	Boeing 767-383ER	24848	(LN-RLY) OY-KDN SE-DKS
PH-AIJ	Piper PA-34-200T Seneca II	34-7870029	LN-AKP N9030K
PH-AIL	SIAI-Marchetti S.208 (Built as S.205-22/R)	4-232K	OO-HEP
PH-AIP	Robin DR.400/120 Dauphin 80	1797	
PH-AJA	Brändli BX-2 Cherry	71/NVAV-101	
PH-AJB	Piper PA-36-285 Pawnee Brave	36-7560040	N9929P
PH-AJC	Brändli BX-2 Cherry	67/NVAV-103	
PH-AJD	Piper PA-34-220T Seneca IV	3448044	N9246N
PH-AJK	Robinson R-22 Beta	1738	G-MISR
PH-AJM	Dyn'Aero MCR-01S ULC	141	PH-3K2
PH-AJR	Robinson R-44 Raven	1192	
PH-AJU	Douglas DC-2 (Reservation 2.87 for Dutch Dakota Assn BV, stored)	1288	VH-CRH/ A30-14 NC13738
"PH-AJU"	Douglas DC-2-142 (Based at Lelystad as N39165, painted as PH-AJU)	1404	N39165 NC39165 9993
PH-AKJ	Cessna 177RG Cardinal RG	177RG1019	N34907 (PH-RAP) N34907
PH-ALI	Reims/Cessna F150M Commuter	F15001161	
PH-ALT	Piper PA-38-112 Tomahawk	38-79A0801	OO-TLT N9651N
PH-ALW	Reims/Cessna F172M Skyhawk II	F17201226	
PH-AMA	Piper PA-18-150 Super Cub	18-8009042	N82678
PH-AMB	Reims/Cessna F172N Skyhawk II	F17201921	PH-AXM(3)
PH-AMD	Europa Aviation Europa	322	
PH-AMI	Cirrus SR20	1341	N8134D
PH-AMR	Piper PA-28-161 Warrior II	28-8416077	N4353B
PH-ANA	Aquila A210	AT01-103	(D-EAQA) D-EANW
PH-ANF	Piper PA-28RT-201 Arrow IV	28R-8018004	N8099H
PH-ANG	Cessna 172M Skyhawk	17267384	N73336
PH-ANH	Reims/Cessna F172P Skyhawk II	F17202244	PH-AXP(5)
PH-ANJ	Cessna 150M	15077028	N45706
PH-ANR	Rans S-6S Coyote II (Reservn .02)	unkn	
PH-AOA	Airbus A330-201 (CoA appl. 1.05)	0682	
PH-AOB	Airbus A330-201 (CoA appl. 1.05)	0686	
PH-AOC	Airbus A330-201 (CoA appl. 1.05)	0703	
PH-APA	Piper PA-18-135 Super Cub	18-3814	R-124 54-2414
PH-APE	Reims/Cessna FRA150L Aerobat	FRA1500247	D-EDJJ
PH-APR	Grumman G.164B Agcat	204B	G-BFTN N6687Q
PH-APV	Dassault Falcon 200 (Reservation 2.05)	490	N917JG N917JC (N280RT) N200RT N35JT N2TF N806F N14EN N204FJ F-WPUY
PH-APZ	SSVB Lambach HL.II	20002	
PH-ARC	SOCATA TB-10 Tobago	12	F-ODKB
PH-ARJ	Cessna 150M	15078911	N704VQ
PH-ARK	Fuji FA-200-160 Aero Subaru	174	
PH-ARV	ARV Super 2	015	G-BMWH
PH-ASE	SAN Jodel DR.1050 Ambassadeur	142	
PH-ASY	Cessna 172P Skyhawk	17275551	N64375
PH-ATM	Beech 200 Super King Air	BB-123	N120DA N123YV N911LR N711AR N9123S
PH-AVB	Reims/Cessna F172P Skyhawk II	F17202185	PH-AXM(4)
PH-AVF	Reims/Cessna F172P Skyhawk II	F17202212	PH-AXR(4)
PH-AVG	Fokker F.27-050	20278	(PH-LXS)
PH-AVH	Fokker F.27-050	20281	
PH-AVJ	Fokker F.27-050	20285	
PH-AVN	Fokker F.27-050	20296	
PH-AVO	Fokker F.27-050	20297	
PH-AVT	Piper PA-28-181 Archer II	28-7990075	N22324
PH-AWI	Reims/Cessna F172M Skyhawk II	F17201343	D-EDHZ (F-BXZU) (D-EDQJ)
PH-BAD	Reims/Cessna F172M Skyhawk II	F17201284	
PH-BAI	Cessna 172P Skyhawk	17274695	(PH-BIS) N53167
PH-BAW	SOCATA TB-9 Tampico Club	1470	OE-KMN
PH-BBQ	Piper PA-32-260 Cherokee Six (Res. 5.04)	32-833	OO-BUC (OO-MRA) LN-UXP N3887W
PH-BDA	Boeing 737-306	23537	
PH-BDC	Boeing 737-306	23539	
PH-BDD	Boeing 737-306	23540	
PH-BDE	Boeing 737-306	23541	
PH-BDG	Boeing 737-306	23542	
PH-BDI	Boeing 737-306	23544	
PH-BDK	Boeing 737-306	23545	
PH-BDN	Boeing 737-306	24261	
PH-BDO	Boeing 737-306	24262	
PH-BDP	Boeing 737-306	24404	
PH-BDR	Boeing 737-406	24514	
PH-BDS	Boeing 737-406	24529	
PH-BDT	Boeing 737-406	24530	
PH-BDU	Boeing 737-406	24857	
PH-BDW	Boeing 737-406	24858	
PH-BDY	Boeing 737-406	24959	
PH-BDZ	Boeing 737-406	25355	
PH-BEA	SOCATA TB-9 Tampico	1130	
PH-BEC	Piper PA-28RT-201T Turbo Arrow IV	28R-8131041	D-EIJK N8308H
PH-BEG	Piper PA-28-181 Cherokee Archer II	28-7890419	G-BTGE N9514C
PH-BFA	Boeing 747-406	23999	N6018N
PH-BFB	Boeing 747-406	24000	
PH-BFC	Boeing 747-406M Combi	23982	N6038E
PH-BFD	Boeing 747-406M Combi	24001	
PH-BFE	Boeing 747-406M Combi	24201	N6046P
PH-BFF	Boeing 747-406M Combi	24202	N6046P
PH-BFG	Boeing 747-406	24517	(PH-BFH)
PH-BFH	Boeing 747-406M Combi	24518	(PH-BFG) N60668
PH-BFI	Boeing 747-406M Combi	25086	
PH-BFK	Boeing 747-406M Combi	25087	
PH-BFL	Boeing 747-406	25356	
PH-BFM	Boeing 747-406M Combi	26373	
PH-BFN	Boeing 747-406	26372	
PH-BFO	Boeing 747-406M Combi	25413	
PH-BFP	Boeing 747-406M Combi	26374	
PH-BFQ	Boeing 747-406 (Reservation 3.87)	unkn	
PH-BFR	Boeing 747-406M Combi	27202	
PH-BFS	Boeing 747-406M Combi	28195	
PH-BFT	Boeing 747-406M Combi	28459	
PH-BFU	Boeing 747-406M Combi	28196	(PH-BFT)
PH-BFV	Boeing 747-406M Combi	28460	
PH-BFW	Boeing 747-406M Combi	30454	
PH-BFX	Boeing 747-406 (Reservation 3.87)	unkn	
PH-BFY	Boeing 747-406	30455	N6005C
PH-BFZ	Boeing 747-406 (Reservation 3.87)	unkn	
PH-BGB to BGI, BGK to BGO, BGR to BGT	Reserved for Boeing 747-406s for KLM		
PH-BGV	Europa Aviation Europa	264	
PH-BIK	Reims/Cessna F150M Commuter	F15001256	D-EIHC (F-BJDK)
PH-BIT	Reims/Cessna F172N Skyhawk II	F17201863	
PH-BLE	Blériot XI replica	NVAV-78	
PH-BMD	Airbus A.320-214	1370	D-ABLB F-WQQI OO-SNG F-WWIT
PH-BNK	Beech F33C Bonanza	CJ-140	
PH-BOA	Mitsubishi MU-2B-60 Marquise	1507SA	N888FS (N415HH) N888FS N976MA N612CC N413MA
PH-BON	Aviat A-1 Husky	1212	D-EXON
PH-BOS	Piper PA-28-151 Cherokee Warrior	28-7615375	OO-HAZ N9605N
PH-BPB	Boeing 737-4Y0	24344	G-UKLB VT-MGF G-UKLB 9M-MLI G-UKLB 9M-MJL G-UKLB C-GATJ C-FVNC G-UKLB
PH-BPC	Boeing 737-4Y0	24468	G-UKLE VT-MGG G-UKLE
PH-BPM	Neico Lancair 360	747	
PH-BPS	Dassault Falcon 20F	321	N104SB (PH-BPS) N20FM N244CA N702SC N2525 N4454F F-WJMJ
PH-BQA	Boeing 777-206ER	33711	N5014K
PH-BQB	Boeing 777-206ER	33712	
PH-BQC	Boeing 777-206ER	29397	
PH-BQD	Boeing 777-206ER	33713	(PH-BQB)
PH-BQE	Boeing 777-206ER	28691	
PH-BQF	Boeing 777-206ER	29398	
PH-BQG	Boeing 777-206ER	32704	
PH-BQH	Boeing 777-206ER	32705	(PH-BQI) N5016R
PH-BQI	Boeing 777-206ER	33714	(PH-BQH)
PH-BQK	Boeing 777-206ER	29399	
PH-BQL	Boeing 777-206 (CoA appl. 1.05)	34711	
PH-BQM	Boeing 777-206 (CoA appl. 1.05)	34712	
BQL to BQP, BQR to BQZ	Reserved for KLM		
PH-BRL	Embraer EMB.120RT Brasilia	120083	N278UE PT-SMA

PH-BRT	SOCATA TB-9 Tampico	125	F-GCOC
PH-BSA	Cessna 172S Skyhawk	172S8387	N23842
PH-BSF	Cessna 172N	17272710	N6309D
PH-BSM	Cessna 182Q Skylane	18266773	N96596
PH-BSV	Cessna 152	15281403	N521DG
			N49932
PH-BSX	Reims/Cessna F177RG Cardinal RG	F177RG0095	
PH-BTA	Boeing 737-406	25412	
PH-BTB	Boeing 737-406	25423	
PH-BTC	Boeing 737-406	25424	
PH-BTD	Boeing 737-306	27420	
PH-BTE	Boeing 737-306	27421	
PH-BTF	Boeing 737-406	27232	
PH-BTG	Boeing 737-406	27233	
PH-BTH	Boeing 737-306	28719	
PH-BTI	Boeing 737-306	28720	N1786B
PH-BTH to BTR, BTT to BTZ Reserved for Boeing 737s for KLM			
PH-BUH	Boeing 747-206B Combi (EUD)	21110	
PH-BVE	Cessna 172R Skyhawk	17280188	N9941F
PH-BVL	Reims/Cessna F172N Skyhawk	F17201868	PH-AXE
			(PH-AXC)
PH-BVT	Piper PA-28-181 Archer II	2890086	N9149R
PH-BWA	Beech A36AT Bonanza	E-2581	
PH-BWE	Beech A36AT Bonanza	E-2615	N1568
			PH-BWE
PH-BWG	Beech A36AT Bonanza	E-2619	
PH-BWR	Cessna F150H Commuter	F150-0365	D-ELND
PH-BXA	Boeing 737-8K2	29131	(PH-EBA)
			N1786B
PH-BXB	Boeing 737-8K2	29132	(PH-EBB)
			N1786B
PH-BXC	Boeing 737-8K2	29133	(PH-EBC)
PH-BXD	Boeing 737-8K2	29134	(PH-EBD)
			N1784B
			N1786B
PH-BXE	Boeing 737-8K2	29595	N1787B
PH-BXF	Boeing 737-8K2	29596	N1787B
PH-BXG	Boeing 737-8K2	30357	N1787B
PH-BXH	Boeing 737-8K2	29597	N1786B
PH-BXI	Boeing 737-8K2	30358	N1787B
PH-BXK	Boeing 737-8K2	29598	N1015G
PH-BXL	Boeing 737-8K2	30359	
PH-BXM	Boeing 737-8K2	30355	
PH-BXN	Boeing 737-8K2	30356	
PH-BXO	Boeing 737-9K2	29599	
PH-BXP	Boeing 737-9K2	29600	N1786B
PH-BXR	Boeing 737-9K2	29601	N1796B
PH-BXS	Boeing 737-9K2	29602	N1786B
PH-BXT	Boeing 737-9K2	32944	(PH-HZO)
PH-BXW, Y, Z Reserved for Boeing 737s for KLM			
PH-BYA	Beech 58 Baron	TH-1609	F-GKZC
			(F-GIIC)
PH-BYB	Beech 58 Baron	TH-1613	F-GKZD
			(F-GJED)
PH-BYC	Beech 58 Baron	TH-1922	G-WHIS
			N31622
PH-BZA	Boeing 767-306ER	27957	
PH-BZB	Boeing 767-306ER	27958	
PH-BZC	Boeing 767-306ER	26263	
PH-BZD	Boeing 767-306ER	27610	
PH-BZE	Boeing 767-306ER	28098	
PH-BZF	Boeing 767-306ER	27959	(PH-BZE)
PH-BZG	Boeing 767-306ER	27960	N6009F
			(PH-BZF)
PH-BZH	Boeing 767-306ER	27611	(PH-BZG)
PH-BZI	Boeing 767-306ER	27612	
PH-BZK	Boeing 767-306ER	27614	
PH-BZM	Boeing 767-306ER	28884	
PH-BZN	Fuji FA-200-180AO Aero Subaru	278	D-EFSH
PH-BZO	Boeing 767-306ER	30393	
PH-BZP, BZR to BZZ Reserved for Boeing 767-306ERs for KLM			
PH-CAE	Diamond DA-40D Star	D4.145	OE-VPU
PH-CAN	Cessna 150M	15076686	C-GDQX
			N4053V
PH-CAQ	Ultravia Pélican PL	686	
PH-CAR	Fuji FA-200-160 Aero Subaru (Dismantled)	210	
PH-CBB	Reims/Cessna F152-II	F15201782	
PH-CBD	Reims/Cessna F152-II	F15201791	
PH-CBF	Reims/Cessna F152-II	F15201799	
PH-CBG	Reims/Cessna F152-II	F15201803	
PH-CBN	Reims/Cessna F172N Skyhawk	F17201985	PH-AYA(3)
PH-CBO	Ultravia Pélican PL	689/NVAV-196	
PH-CBX	Brändli BX-2 Cherry (Res. 12.02)	NVAV-142	
PH-CDD	Dijkhastar IV	001	
PH-CDL	Piper PA-34-220T Seneca III	32-8233053	D-GFKI
			N8011Q
PH-CDS	Cessna 152	15279972	D-EADZ
			N757SR
PH-CHC	Robinson R44 Raven II	0342	OO-CHC
PH-CIO	Reims/Cessna F172N	F17201556	PH-AXU(1)
PH-CJC	Piper PA-28-181 Archer III	2843595	N3102Z
PH-CJI	Cessna 560XLCitation Excel	5128	N5228Z
PH-CKA	Boeing 747-406ERF	33694	
PH-CKB	Boeing 747-406ERF	33695	
PH-CKC	Boeing 747-406ERF	33696	(PH-CKB)
PH-CKD to CKN, CKP to CKZ Reserved for KLM			
PH-CLA	Airbus A.300B4-103	44	N204EA
			F-WUAX
PH-CLE	Reims/Cessna F406 Caravan II	F406-0032	LN-TWH
			PH-CLE
			AP-BFA
			N442AB
			G-BPSW
			F-WZDU
PH-CLZ	SOCATA TBM-700	299	F-OIKL
PH-CMC	Beech F33A Bonanza	CE-1598	
PH-COA	Cessna 140	14737	HB-COA
			N2469V
PH-COL	Neico Lancair 320	399	
PH-COM	Piper PA-30 Twin Comanche	30-279	G-MAAG
			G-ASOB
			N10F
PH-COP	SOCATA TB-10 Tobago	2113	F-OIUQ
PH-COU	Cessna 172M	17267385	(PH-MUG)
			N73337
PH-COW	Ultravia Pélican PL	649	
PH-CPM	AEA P-51 Mustang X (Reservation 6.03)	AEA1	N21770
PH-CRI	Colomban MC-15 Cri-Cri	2 / NVAV-130	
PH-CRJ	Van's RV-6A	23773	
PH-CRL	Piper PA-31P Pressurized Navajo	31P-7300136	OY-CKA
			N150TT
			N666BC
			(N444PM)
			N666BC
			N36PC
			N7657L
PH-CSE	Cessna U206G Stationair 6- II	U20605952	OO-CAD
	(Robertson STOL conversion)		N6570X
PH-CSL	de Havilland DH.82A Tiger Moth	86609	OO-DJU
			A-2
			PG712
PH-CVH	Bowers Fly-Baby 1B	3	
PH-CVT	Cessna 172P Skyhawk	17275333	N62766
PH-CVW	Robinson R-22 Beta II	3758	
PH-CYB	SOCATA TB-9 Tampico	106	D-EFOE
PH-DAC	DAC RangeR (CoA appl. 10.04)	001	
PH-DAI	Diamond DA-40D Star (Res. 1.05)	D4.135	OE-VPW
PH-DAY	Ultravia Pélican PL	637	
	(9.00 type changed from PL-914 to PL)		
PH-DBO	Neico Lancair 360	245	
PH-DDB	Beech 200 Super King Air	BB-221	SE-KYL
			F-GJEB
			N711FD
			N711UE
			N20004
			N200PB
PH-DDD	Piper PA-28R-201T Turbo Cherokee Arrow III		
		28R-7703348	N40F
			N9608N
PH-DDZ	Douglas DC-3C	19754	(EI-BSJ)
			SU-BFY
			N920
			6O-SAA
			6OS-AAA
			N161
			43-15288
PH-DES	Cessna 182P Skylane	18263920	N9816E
	(Reims-assembled with "c/n" 0016)		
PH-DFC	SOCATA TB-10 Tobago	1586	G-BZRK
			VH-YHD
PH-DFJ	SOCATA TB-10 Tobago	1588	G-BZRL
			VH-YHF
PH-DFW	SOCATA TB-10 Tobago	1585	G-BZWA
			VH-YHC
PH-DGY	Mooney M.20K Model 252 TSE	25-1145	HB-DGY
PH-DHC	DHC-2 Beaver 1	965	G-BUVF
			S-9
			55-4585
PH-DIB	Schweizer 269C	S-1612	N86G
PH-DIX	Pilatus PC-12/45	309	HB-FRG(2)
PH-DKE	Reims/Cessna F152	F15201832	OO-TRH
PH-DKF	Reims/Cessna F172P Skyhawk	F17202124	G-BJCE
PH-DKG	Cessna 172P Skyhawk	17275386	N63052
PH-DKH	Cessna 172P Skyhawk	17275655	N64933
PH-DKI	Partenavia P.68C	297	F-GEGT
			G-BKTD
PH-DKJ	Reims/Cessna F150M	F15001347	HB-CXM
PH-DKS	Cessna 182P Skylane	18262475	D-EDZP
			(G-BBUN)
			N52238
PH-DLA	Reims/Cessna FR172K Hawk XP	FR17200608	PH-AXR(1)
PH-DMO	Fokker F.27-050	20103	SX-BTI
			PH-DMO
			OY-MBM
			PH-DMO
			OO-VLC
			PH-DMO
PH-DMQ	DHC-8 Series 315	567	C-GDOE
PH-DMR	DHC-8 Series 315	569	C-GETI
PH-DMS	Fokker F.27-050	20209	EI-FKF
			PH-EXE
PH-DMT	Fokker F.27-050	20208	EI-FKE
			PH-EXA

PH-DMU	DHC-8 Series 315	568	C-GERL
PH-DMV	DHC-8 Series 315	570	C-GEVP
PH-DMW	DHC-8 Series 315	573	(PH-DMY) C-GFCF
PH-DON	Cessna 172P Skyhawk	17274985	N54484
PH-DPC	Cessna 172RG Cutlass RG	172RG0369	PH-AYH(3) N4717V
PH-DOO	Ultravia Pélican PL	692	
PH-DRI	Fokker DR.1 (Replica)	152/17	
PH-DRL	Beech A36 Bonanza (Res. 7.03)	E-1784	OO-CMD N8308Y
PH-DRN	SOCATA TB-10 Tobago	1135	D-ENFG
PH-DRT	Piper PA-28-181 Archer II	28-8490055	(D-EXUL) N4347Y
PH-DTR	Neico Lancair 320	603-320-349	(PH-TDR)
PH-DUB	Piper PA-28R-200 Cherokee Arrow II	28R-7435139	D-EBFF N40898
PH-DUC	Stoddard-Hamilton Glasair IIRG-S	2069	N51DA
PH-DUK	Cessna 185 Skywagon (amphibian)	185-0046	(PH-DUC) LN-TSM N9846X
PH-DVT	SOCATA TB-10 Trinidad	2062	D-EFFJ
PH-DVW	Reims FR172H Rocket	FR17200342	
PH-DWH	SOCATA TB-9 Tampico	1438	D-EVHN
PH-DYB	Swearingen SA.226T(B) Merlin IIIB	T-294	N15KR XA-JSC N802ME N800TA
PH-DYE	Cessna 550 Citation Bravo	550-0927	(PH-CTU) N5061P
PH-DYM	Fairchild-Swearingen SA.227AC Metro III	AC-523	D-CABE(2) N3109C
PH-DYN	Cessna 550 Citation Bravo	550-0928	(PH-CTV) N5000R
PH-EAG	Euro-ENAER EE-10 Eaglet	04	
PH-EAH	Piper PA-28-181 Archer II	28-7990445	N29517
PH-EAL	Grumman AA-5B Tiger	AA5B-0703	G-MURF G-JOAN G-BFML
PH-EAM	Reims/Cessna F172N Skyhawk	F17201602	PH-AXP(1)
PH-EAN	Airbus A300B4-103	041	N201EA F-WUAZ
PH-EBF	Fokker DR.1 (Replica) (Carries c/n 1867 but believed by builder to be 102)	155/17	N6178N N5505V
PH-ECC	Pilatus PC-12	107	N62JT HB-FQD
PH-ECD	Eurocopter EC.120B Colibri	1169	(PH-ECP)
PH-ECE	Eurocopter EC.120B Colibri (CoA appl. 3.05)	1005	ZK-HKE (N62HC) JA120B F-WWPL (?)
PH-ECI	Cessna 525 CitationJet	525-0321	D-IAAS
PH-ECJ	Eurocopter EC.130B4 Ecureuil	3604	F-WQDP
PH-ECK	Eurocopter EC.120B Colibri (CoA appl. 3.05)	1209	ZK-HJK ZK-HVQ
PH-ECL	Cessna 525A CitationJet 2	525A-0054	(PH-EDL) D-IAAS (EI-OPM) N5161J
PH-ECN	Robin R.1180TD Aiglon	228	F-GBVD
PH-ECZ	Eurocopter EC.130B4 Ecureuil	3624	F-WQDI
PH-EDD	Piper PA-28-161 Warrior II	28-8116202	N83726
PH-EDH	Piper PA-24-250 Comanche	24-3361	N8111P
PH-EDM	Dassault Falcon 900C	188	F-WWFZ
PH-EEE	Piper PA-28-161 Warrior II	28-8316088	N4310M
PH-EGC	Piper PA-34-220T Seneca III	34-8133115	N83658 (N986N) (N888PC) N83658 N9542N
PH-EHN	Reims/Cessna F172M Skyhawk	F17201186	D-EEIB
PH-EHO	Cessna 172M Skyhawk	17267148	N1481U
PH-EHV	Cessna 172M Skyhawk	17264973	N64027
PH-EIJ	SOCATA Rallye 150ST	3141	
PH-EIN	III Sky Arrow 1450L	053/01	
PH-ELA	Dyn'Aero MCR Club	213	F-PKRE
PH-ELI	Robinson R-44 Astro	0656	
PH-ELP	Eurocopter EC.135 T2	370	
PH-ELT	Christen A-1 Husky	1131	G-BSVA N9604X
PH-EMG	Skystar Kitfox V Vixen	V9411-0021	
PH-EMS	Eurocopter EC.135 T2	374	
PH-END	Bölkow BO.208 Junior	515	D-ENDA VH-UES D-ENDA
PH-ENG	Bölkow BO.208 Junior	510	D-ENCE
PH-ENJ	Piper PA-18-150 Super Cub	18-2540	D-ELKG ALAT 182540 52-6222
PH-EPO	Piper PA-28-181 Archer II	28-7990557	N2919N
PH-ERH	Utravia Pelican PL	688	
PH-ERO	Cessna 182R Skylane	18267960	(PH-HBP) N9530H
PH-ESA	Cessna TU206F Turbo Stationair	U20602001	D-EEYU(2) N51404
PH-ESB	SOCATA TB-10 Tobago	2117	F-OIUP
PH-ESE	SOCATA TB-20 Trinidad GT	2202	
PH-ESF	SOCATA TB-10 Tobago GT	2200	F-GOIH
PH-EVF	Reims/Cessna F152	F15201770	PH-AYI (3)
PH-EVR	Eurocopter EC.120B Colibri	1293	D-HMFR F-WQDA
PH-EWK	Tecnam P.92J Echo	011	
PH-FAC	Piper PA-34-220T Seneca V	3449004	N9282V
PH-FAM	Piper PA-28RT-201T Turbo Arrow IV	28R-8031123	(PH-VAM) N222SQ (PH-ELL) N222SQ N82283
PH-FAS	WDFL Fascination D4 E	051	PH-3E5
PH-FBP	Fokker F.27 Friendship 100 (Reservation 5.02)	10150	KLu: C-3 PH-FBP
PH-FCH	SOCATA TB-9 Tampico	1300	(PH-ECH) D-ETAY SE-KBK
PH-FEA	SOCATA TB-20 Trinidad	1920	F-OIGZ
PH-FHC	Robinson R-22B2 Beta	3010	N9081U
PH-FHG	Piper PA-46-350P Malibu Mirage	4636022	
PH-FIS	Cessna 525 CitationJet CJ	525-0514	N514RV N52136
PH-FLE	Reims/Cessna F172N Skyhawk	F17201553	D-ENTE
PH-FLF	Cessna 337B Super Skymaster	337-0669	N2369S
PH-FLK	Diamond DA-20-A1 Katana (built by Diamond Aircraft Industries Ltd., Canada)	10280	(PH-DFK) D-EPOS N925JS
PH-FMA	Aérospatiale AS.365N Dauphin 2	6526	CX-BTE/090 F-WQDK
PH-FTO	Cessna 172RG Cutlass RG	172RG0546	D-EIKZ N5491V
PH-FUT	Velocity 173RG	F02RG-001	(PH-FAE)
PH-FVZ	Robinson R-44 Raven	1111	D-HALG
PH-FZG	Fokker F.27-050	20202	EC-HZA PH-FZG PT-MLC PH-FZG HB-IAP PH-EXL
PH-FZH	Fokker F.27-050	20210	EC-IAD PH-FZH PT-MLD PH-FZH HB-IAR PH-EXB
PH-GAU	Piper PA-18-135 Super Cub	18-3871	R-181 54-2471
PH-GAW	Cessna F172E	F172-0083	OO-PAT
PH-GAZ	Piper PA-18-135 Super Cub	18-3537	R-109 54-2337
PH-GBA	Piper PA-18-150 Super Cub	18-7909047	(PH-UBA) G-BUBA N6BL N83522
PH-GCT	Mudry CAP.10B	12	F-GMCT Fr.AF: 12
PH-GEN	Piper J-3C-90 Cub	12893	(PH-CUB) PH-GEN OO-SKY D-EGUH HB-OWN 44-80597
PH-GEO	Reims/Cessna F172N Skyhawk	F17201837	
PH-GGG	Piper PA-28RT-201T Turbo Arrow IV	28R-8131186	N8442N N9562N N84207
PH-GGT	Denney Kitfox III	1079	
PH-GIN	Fuji FA-200-180 Aero Subaru	255	
PH-GLG	SOCATA TB-20 Trinidad	1907	F-OIGX
PH-GOM	RAF 2000 GTX-SE	H2-97-8-300	
PH-GOZ	Aviat A-1 Husky	1211	D-EVII
PH-GRA	Reims/Cessna F150L Commuter	F15001006	F-BUMZ
PH-GRB	Fokker S 11-I Instructor	6211	(PH-GRA) E-20
PH-GRC	Piper PA-18-135 Super Cub (Still officially regd as c/n 18-3828)	18-3829	R-139 54-2429
PH-GRG	American AG-5B Tiger	10174	D-ELYN N1198Z
PH-GRH	Cessna 172P Skyhawk	17274269	N51114
PH-GRY	Fokker S.11.1 Instructor	6280	MLD 197/K E-37
PH-GSY	Diamond DA-40-180 Star	40060	
PH-GSZ	Dyn'Aero MCR-01	161	
PH-GVB	Cessna 172S Skyhawk	172S8231	N282SP
PH-GVN	Piper PA-32-260 Cherokee Six	32-582	(PH-GEM) (PH-GRD) (PH-SET) N3673W
PH-GWW	Ruschmeyer R.90-230RG	014	D-EECJ(2)
PH-GYS	Reims/Cessna F172N Skyhawk	F17201871	D-EFOU
PH-GZC	Bellanca 8GCBC Scout	344-80	OO-VVX
PH-HAN	Neico Lancair 360 (Same c/n quoted for F-PRKZ)	248	
PH-HBB	SOCATA TB-20 Trinidad	1079	D-EAGT(2)
PH-HBH	Hughes 269C	110-0986	SE-HNC PH-HBH C-GDLW N1108T

PH-HBR	Viking Dragonfly II	124/ NVAV-48	
PH-HBW	Cessna 172S Skyhawk	172S8113	N810SP (PH-HBW) N810SP
PH-HCG	Reims FR172J Rocket	FR1720400	(PH-HGC) D-ECXH
PH-HCW	Reims/Cessna F172M	F17201011	D-EJXF
PH-HDE	Cessna P210N Pressurized Centurion II (Soloy Silver Eagle conversion)	P21000709	N210MN JA4019 N5537W
PH-HDW	Ken Brock KB-2	NVAV-76	(PH-JDW)
PH-HED	Eurocopter EC-120B Colibri	1068	G-YSON
PH-HEW	Robinson R-44 Astro	0785	
PH-HGL	Sequoia F.8L Falco	001	N360SF
PH-HGO	Reims/Cessna F152-II	F15201701	(PH-AXI (3))
PH-HHA	Schweizer 269D	S-0014	N86G
PH-HHB	Schweizer 269D	S-0016	N69A
PH-HHC	Aérospatiale AS.355F1 Ecureuil 2	5049	I-VIEY N357E
PH-HHE	Reims/Cessna F172N Skyhawk	F17201617	PH-AXW(1)
PH-HHF	Schweizer 269D	S-0022	N41S
PH-HHJ	Aérospatiale AS.355F2 Ecureuil 2	5356	RP-C1556 N300LG N79D
PH-HIL	Cessna 150L	15075161	(PH-SKN) N19050
PH-HJG	SOCATA TB-20 Trinidad	1922	F-OILG
PH-HLD	Cessna 172M	17265860	D-EMBY N9916Q
PH-HLE	Cessna 152	15283822	D-EALO N5270B
PH-HLF	Cessna 182P Skylane II (Reims-assembled with "c/n" 0034))	18264085	N6069F
PH-HLM	Piper PA-34-200T Seneca II	34-7770393	OO-HCJ N47405
PH-HMA	Cessna 550 Citation Bravo	550-0972	N52462
PH-HMK	Reims/Cessna F172N Skyhawk	F17201836	
PH-HNK	Cessna 340A	340A0546	OO-DKE D-IHAF N4554N
PH-HOG	Fokker S.11.1 Instructor	6275	(PH-HOH) MLD:199/K E-39 PH-NFA (E-32)
PH-HOI	Fokker S.11.1 Instructor	6282	(PH-DHF) PH-HOI MLD:175/K E-32
PH-HOK	Fokker S.11.1 Instructor	6272	E-29
PH-HOL	Fokker S.11.1 Instructor	6270	E-27
PH-HOY	SkyStar Denney Kitfox IV Speedster	GBS029	
PH-HPH	Hughes 269B	128-0400	D-HARA (D-HCRB)
PH-HTA	Robinson R-22 Beta	1670	G-BTDI
PH-HTC	Fokker S.11.1 Instructor	6209	E-18
PH-HTM	Reims/Cessna F182P Skylane II	F18200008	D-EJCH
PH-HUB	SOCATA TBM-700	127	F-OHBV F-WWRL
PH-HVD	Bölkow BO.208C Junior	616	(D-EHET)
PH-HVH	Aérospatiale AS.355F1 Ecureuil 2	5215	ZS-HMF
PH-HVP	Reims/Cessna F150M Commuter	F15001194	
PH-HWH	Agusta-Bell 206B Jet Ranger II	8076	(PH-HXH) G-AWLL
PH-HXH	Bell 206L Long Ranger	45103	SE-HSA N16773
PH-HZA	Boeing 737-8K2	28373	
PH-HZB	Boeing 737-8K2	28374	
PH-HZC	Boeing 737-8K2	28375	N1786B
PH-HZD	Boeing 737-8K2	28376	N1786B
PH-HZE	Boeing 737-8K2	28377	N1786B
PH-HZF	Boeing 737-8K2	28378	N1796B
PH-HZG	Boeing 737-8K2	28379	N1786B
PH-HZI	Boeing 737-8K2	28380	
PH-HZJ	Boeing 737-8K2	30389	N1796B
PH-HZK	Boeing 737-8K2	30390	N1786B
PH-HZL	Boeing 737-8K2	30391	N1786B
PH-HZM	Boeing 737-8K2	30392	N1786B
PH-HZN	Boeing 737-8K2 (Reservation 7.01)	32943	
PH-HZU	Boeing 737-8BG (Reservation 2.05)	32358	ZS-SJP PH-HZU ZS-SJP
PH-HZV	Boeing 737-8K2	30650	
PH-HZW	Boeing 737-8K2	29245	
PH-HZX	Boeing 737-8K2	28248	
PH-HZY	Boeing 737-8K2	30646	
PH-HZZ	Boeing 737-8S3 (Reservation 2.05)	32356	ZS-SJL PH-HZZ (ZS-SJL) N1786B
PH-IBI	North American AT-16-ND Harvard IIB (Reservation 5.02)	14-543	B-181 FE809 42-12296
PH-IBL	Pottier P.220S Koala	467	(PH-MAY)
PH-IBU	SOCATA Rallye 235E Gabier	13125	
PH-IBY	North American AT-16-ND Harvard IIB (Reservation 5.02)	14-1100	B-184 FS960 43-12903
PH-ICN	Piper PA-32R-301 Saratoga SP	32R-8013004	D-ERUM N8112A N9639N
PH-IDA	Piper PA-31-350 Navajo Chieftain	31-7852160	N27806
PH-IEN	Europa Aviation Europa XS TG	305	(PH-IEE)
PH-IIB	Noorduyn/ N.American AT-16ND Harvard IIB	14A-1467	B-118 FT427 43-13168
PH-ILC	Dassault Falcon 900B	161	G-GSEB VP-CTT F-GSAA F-WWFF
PH-IMR	Mooney M.20K Model 231	25-0817	(PH-INR) N231VH
PH-INE	Cvjetkovic CA-65	NL-001/ NVAV-117	
PH-INS	Aerosport Scamp	001/ NVAV-25	
PH-IRO	Reims/Cessna F172M Skyhawk	F17201088	D-EIQX
PH-JAC	Piper PA-28-161 Warrior II	28-8416130	(PH-JAN) N122AV N9631N
PH-JAI	Europa Aviation Europa XS TG	460	
PH-JAN	Piper PA-28-161 Warrior II	28-8416049	N646AS PH-JAN D-EZUL N4341B
PH-JAP	Piper PA-25-260 Pawnee C (Built as PA-25-235 B, modified on rebuild .83)	25-3811	SE-EZI N7666Z
PH-JAS	Cessna 208 Caravan I	20800226	(N9823F)
PH-JBB	Reims/Cessna F172M	F17200971	
PH-JBF	Reims/Cessna F172N Skyhawk	F17201757	
PH-JBG	Reims/Cessna F172P Skyhawk II	F17202072	PH-AYE(4)
PH-JBH	Reims/Cessna F172M Skyhawk II	F17201182	D-EDJS
PH-JBI	Cessna R172K Hawk XP	R1722969	N758BR
PH-JBJ	Piper PA-34-220T Seneca III	3433157	
PH-JBY	Cessna U206F Stationair	U20603230	OO-CNF N8369Q
PH-JCH	Fokker F.28-0070	11528	OE-LFS PH-JCH N528YV PH-JCH PH-EZS
PH-JCT	Fokker F.28-0070	11537	OE-LFT PH-JCT N537YV PH-JCT PH-EZV
PH-JDG	Reims/Cessna F152	F15201558	D-EEJP
PH-JDL	Ruschmeyer R.90-230G	010	D-EEAU(2)
PH-JDM	Reims/Cessna F150M Commuter	F15001391	PH-AXM(2)
PH-JDP	Viking Dragonfly (Res., not official)	NVAV-57	
PH-JEI	Robinson R-44 Astro	0811	
PH-JEJ	Fuji FA.200-180 AO Aero Subaru	253	(PH-BOG)
PH-JEN	Rutan LongEz (Res., not official)	NVAV-51	
PH-JEU	Europa Aviation Europa (Res. 5.01)	NVAV-223	
PH-JFB	Sequoia F.8L Falco	1228	(PH-JBF/ -ALC/ -SFJ/ -JSF/) -SEB)
PH-JFC	Robinson R44 Raven II	10127	OO-JFC (PH-XFC)
PH-JFD	Pilatus PC-6/B2-H4 Turbo Porter	909	(PH-JRK/-KST/ -YRK) OO-PKZ
PH-JFH	Cessna P210N Pressurized Centurion II Soloy	00726	HB-CQK N6185W
PH-JFS	Pilatus PC-12/45	477	HB-FPD (PH-JKS) HB-FQH
PH-JGB	Robin DR.400/160 Chevalier	2302	F-GORX
PH-JGN	ICP MXP-740 Savannah	01-03-51-055	
PH-JGR	Robinson R-22B2 Beta	2920	
PH-JGT	Robinson R-22 Beta	3403	(PH-JRT)
PH-JGW	Europa Aviation Europa XS	206	
PH-JJM	Reims/Cessna F152-II	F15201673	PH-AXC(3) (D-EIVR)
PH-JKG	Diamond DA-40 Star	40073	
PH-JLM	Ultravia Pélican PL	580	
PH-JMB	Piper PA-28RT-201T Turbo Arrow IV	28R-7931061	N3061N
PH-JML	Pottier P.80S	NVAV-34	
PH-JMP	Cessna 208B Grand Caravan	208B0583	(PH-JLP) N1115P N52645
PH-JMS	Reims/Cessna F182Q Skylane	F18200168	SX-AJR F-WZIZ
PH-JNA	Cessna 172P	17275773	N65524 LN-NFK N65524
PH-JNP	Cessna 172N Skyhawk	17267803	N75554
PH-JOE	Cessna 425 Corsair	425-0168	G-BJYC (N6872T)
PH-JOP	Viking Dragonfly II	210	
PH-JOS	Reims/Cessna F150L Commuter	F15001016	
PH-JPO	Reims/Cessna F172N Skyhawk	F17202010	
PH-JPR	Neico Lancair 360	SFB2001-442	
PH-JRM	Piper PA-32R-301T Saratoga IITC	3257164	N41850
PH-JSA	Cessna 182N Skylane	18260367	N92809

PH-JSP	Mooney M.20J Model 201	24-1269	N1159N
PH-JTH	Piper PA-18-135 Super Cub (Res. 5.04)	18-3606	(PH-GAM)(?) R-116 54-2406
PH-JUR	Piper PA-32R-301T Turbo Saratoga SP	32R-8229033	N8107T
PH-JVB	Cessna 152	15280786	D-EADX N25789
PH-JVD	SOCATA TB-20 Trinidad	2052	F-OILT
PH-JVG	Piper PA-28-161 Warrior II	28-7916008	N28VG N39769
PH-JVO	Reims/Cessna FA150K Aerobat	FA1500041	
PH-JWF	Pilatus PC-7 Turbo Trainer	520	HB-HDF(5) F-GMEB HB-HMB
PH-JXJ	Fokker F.27-050	20232	PT-SLJ (PT-OQB) PH-JXJ
PH-JXK	Fokker F.27-050	20233	PT-SLK (PT-OQA) PH-JXK
PH-JXM	Fokker F.27-050	20237	PK-PFH PH-JXM PT-SLZ PH-JXM D-AFKV PH-JXM
PH-JXN	Fokker F.27-050	20239	EC-GFP EC-152 PH-JXN (PH-JXW) (PH-JYB) D-AFKW PH-JXN
PH-JXW	Fokker F.28-0100	11390	XA-SGS PH-JXW
PH-KAC	Cessna 172M Skyhawk	17262999	N13758
PH-KAD	Reims/Cessna F172N Skyhawk	F17201532	PH-AXD(1)
PH-KAI	Slingsby T.67M Firefly	2038	G-7-116
PH-KAJ	Slingsby T.67M Firefly	2039	G-7-117
PH-KAO	Robin R.3140	112	
PH-KAU	Slingsby T.67M Firefly	2040	G-7-118
PH-KAX	Piper PA-28-181 Archer II	2890001	N9087U
PH-KBA	Cessna 172P Skyhawk	17275109	N55106
PH-KBX	Fokker F.28-0070	11547	(PH-PCL) (PH-PBY) (PH-PWA)
PH-KBY	Cessna 172R Skyhawk	17280482	N9537F
PH-KCA	McDonnell-Douglas MD-11P	48555	N6202D
PH-KCB	McDonnell-Douglas MD-11P	48556	
PH-KCC	McDonnell-Douglas MD-11P	48557	
PH-KCD	McDonnell-Douglas MD-11P	48558	
PH-KCE	McDonnell-Douglas MD-11P	48559	N91566
PH-KCF	McDonnell-Douglas MD-11P	48560	
PH-KCG	McDonnell-Douglas MD-11P	48561	
PH-KCH	McDonnell-Douglas MD-11P	48562	
PH-KCI	McDonnell-Douglas MD-11P	48563	PP-SPM PH-KCI
PH-KCK	McDonnell-Douglas MD-11P	48564	
PH-KDF	Reims/Cessna F150L Commuter	F15001111	D-EDJF (F-BSGP)
PH-KDL	Reims/Cessna F152-II	F15201489	PH-AXH(1)
PH-KDN	Reims/Cessna F172N Skyhawk II	F17201735	D-EFEA
PH-KED	Piper PA-23-250 Aztec E	27-7305116	(PH-KNP) N40357
PH-KGJ	Eurocopter EC.120BColibri	1265	
PH-KHD	MBB BO.105CBS-4	S-324	HB-XGM D-HDJD (D-HDJB)
PH-KHE	MBB BO.105CBS-4	S-329	HB-XGT D-HDJG
PH-KHV	Beech 3NM (D-18S)	A-904 / CA-254	(PH-DDB) (PH-BBA) (PH-BBJ) N5369X C-FAID N7820 CF-AID RCAF2375
PH-KIK	Piper PA-28-181 Archer II	2890155	D-ETAN N92117
PH-KIS	Christen A-1 Husky	1109	
PH-KLA	Piper PA-18-150 Super Cub (Officially quoted with f/n 18-1582)	18-1595	ALAT 51-15595
PH-KLD	Fokker F.28-0100	11269	G-UKFM PH-KLD F-GIDQ F-OGQL F-GIDQ PH-KLD
PH-KLE	Fokker F.28-0100	11270	G-UKFN PH-KLE F-GIDP PH-KLE
PH-KLG	Fokker F.28-0100	11271	G-UKFO PH-KLG F-GIDO F-OGQM F-GIDO
PH-KLI	Fokker F.28-0100	11273	G-UKFR PH-KLI F-GIDM F-OGQB PH-KLI
PH-KLJ	Brändli BX-2 Cherry	182/NVAV-168	
PH-KLU	Noorduyn/ N.American AT-16ND Harvard IIB (Officially regd.with incorrect c/n 14-664)	14A-1184	B-59 FT144 43-12885
PH-KMS	Cessna P210N Pressurized Centurion (Soloy Silver Eagle conversion)	0626	N322KD N232W N255TJ XC-FUV (N4785W)
PH-KNE	Piper PA-18-135 Super Cub	18-3825	(PH-KNF) (OO-TAN) R-135 54-2425
PH-KNF	Piper PA-18-135 Super Cub	18-3826	(PH-KNG) R-136 54-2426
PH-KNG	Piper PA-18-135 Super Cub	18-3816	(PH-KND) R-126 54-2416
PH-KNL	Piper PA-18-135 Super Cub	18-3849	(PH-KNN) R-159 54-2449
PH-KNR	Piper PA-18-135 Super Cub	18-3867	(PH-KNT) R-177 54-2467
PH-KOR	Dijkhastar III	001/ NVAV-100	
PH-KPD	Piper PA-32RT-300T Turbo Lance II	32R-7887236	N21880
PH-KRC	Cessna 180K	18052799	SE-KRC N61790
PH-KRI	Cessna F172G	F172-0218	
PH-KRN	Cessna 182Q Skylane	18265228	D-ELAP N7579S
PH-KST	Zenair CH-601 Zodiac (Reservation 11.02)	6-9159	
PH-KVA	Fokker F.27-050	20189	PH-EXC
PH-KVB	Fokker F.27-050	20190	PH-EXD
PH-KVC	Fokker F.27-050	20191	PH-EXF
PH-KVD	Fokker F.27-050	20197	
PH-KVE	Fokker F.27-050	20206	
PH-KVF	Fokker F.27-050	20207	
PH-KVG	Fokker F.27-050	20211	
PH-KVH	Fokker F.27-050	20217	
PH-KVI	Fokker F.27-050	20218	
PH-KVK	Fokker F.27-050	20219	
PH-KXH	Fokker F.27-050	20249	G-UKTC PH-KXH
PH-KXJ	Fokker F.28-0100	11400	XA-SGT PH-KXJ
PH-KXM	Fokker F.27-050	20252	PT-SLO (PT-OQC) PH-KXM
PH-KYK	Bellanca 8KCAB-180CS Super Decathlon	606-80	N5069K
PH-KZA	Fokker F.28-0070	11567	(PK-JGM)
PH-KZB	Fokker F.28-0070	11562	(PK-JGK)
PH-KZC	Fokker F.28-0070	11566	(PK-JGL)
PH-KZD	Fokker F.28-0070	11582	(PK-JGN)
PH-KZE	Fokker F.28-0070	11576	(PH-EZF)
PH-KZF	Fokker F.28-0070	11577	(G-BVTH) (PH-EZG)
PH-KZG	Fokker F.28-0070	11578	(G-BWKI) (PH-EZI)
PH-KZH	Fokker F.28-0070	11583	
PH-KZI	Fokker F.28-0070	11579	(I-REJC) (PH-EZK)
PH-KZK	Fokker F.28-0070	11581	(I-REJD) (PH-EZM)
PH-KZL	Fokker F.28-0070	11536	9V-SLK PH-EZH
PH-KZM	Fokker F.28-0070	11561	9V-SLL PH-EZR
PH-KZN	Fokker F.28-0070	11553	PK-PFE PH-MXN PH-EZZ
PH-KZO	Fokker F.28-0070	11538	G-BVTE PH-EZX
PH-KZP	Fokker F.28-0070	11539	G-BVTF PH-EZZ (PH-EZA)
PH-KZR	Fokker F.28-0070	11551	G-BVTG PH-EZK
PH-LAB	Cessna 550 Citation II	550-0712	(PH-LNR/-NLY/ -SLV) N12030
PH-LAG	Piper PA-28-181 Archer II	28-8090296	OO-HLY N82001
PH-LAW	Cessna T310R	310R0096	D-IARW N5449X
PH-LBR	Cessna 208 Caravan I	20800101	N99U N9555F
PH-LDF	Lockheed 749A Constellation (Res. 2.04)	2604	(PH-FLE) (PH-LEL) N749NL, N749VR, C-GXKR, N9465, 48-612

PH-LEF	Cessna 182Q Skylane	18267283	N4645N
PH-LEN	Reims/Cessna F172N Skyhawk	F17201619	
PH-LFA	Cessna 172P Skyhawk	17274058	N5309K
PH-LFB	Cessna 172P Skyhawk	17275363	N62943
PH-LFC	Fuji FA-200-160 Aero Subaru	181	D-EIDD
PH-LFX	Cessna R182 Skylane RG	R18201823	N5149T
PH-LGW	Piper PA-34-220T Seneca V	3449107	C-FFAX N9528N
PH-LIK	Piper J-3C-65 Cub	12162	D-EJAO G-AJAO OO-RAM ALAT 44-79866
PH-LIN	Cessna 172H Skyhawk	17256239	N8039L
PH-LJM	Piper PA-28-181 Archer III	2843235	N4126V
PH-LMA	Fokker F.27-050	20118	(PH-LCA) OY-EBB EI-FKA PH-LMA (VH-FNM) PH-EXB
PH-LMB	Fokker F.27-050	20119	(PH-LCD) EI-FKB OY-EBD PH-LMB (VH-FNN) PH-EXC
PH-LMJ	Reims/Cessna FA150L Aerobat	FA1500112	D-ECGJ
PH-LMR	Piper PA-32-260 Cherokee Six	32-7700021	(PH-TES) N38982
PH-LMT	Fokker F.27-050	20192	EC-HYJ PH-LMT PT-MLB PH-LMT HB-IAO PH-LMT PH-EXC
PH-LNC	Neico Lancair 360	677	OO-133
PH-LPH	Eurocopter EC.120B Colibri	1256	
PH-LPO	Reims/Cessna F172M Skyhawk	F17201500	
PH-LRM	Piper PA-18-135 Super Cub	18-3131	OO-GDH OL-L57 53-4731
PH-LSK	Noorduyn/ N.American AT-16-ND Harvard IIB	14-641	B-64 12-6 B-64 FE907 42-12394
PH-LUU	Reims/Cessna F172L	F17200861	
PH-LVS	Jabiru SK	121	
PH-LXJ	Fokker F.27-050	20270	G-UKTE PH-LXJ
PH-LXK	Fokker F.27-050	20271	G-UKTF PH-LXK
PH-LXP	Fokker F.27-050	20276	G-UKTG PH-LXP
PH-LXR	Fokker F.27-050	20277	G-UKTH PH-LXR
PH-LXT	Fokker F.27-050	20279	G-UKTI PH-LXT
PH-LXW	Fokker F.27-050	20266	
PH-LYM	American AG-5B Tiger	10026	D-EYWM N1192G
PH-LYT	Robinson R44 Astro	0634	OO-LYT
PH-MBK	Fuji FA-200-160 Aero Subaru	226	
PH-MBL	Piper PA-31-350 Navajo Chieftain	31-7405428	G-BTLE D-IBPL N54288
PH-MBM	Fuji FA-200-160 Aero Subaru	260	(PH-NAM)
PH-MBR	Beech C23 Sundowner 180	M-1977	
PH-MBS	Beech C23 Sundowner 180	M-1968	
PH-MBU	Reims/Cessna F172N	F17201785	PH-AYK (F-GBJS)
PH-MBV	Reims/Cessna F172N Skyhawk	F17201849	PH-AYO(2)
PH-MBW	Fuji FA-200-160 Aero Subaru	286	G-BEYU
PH-MCE	Boeing 747-21AC Combi	23652	N6038E
PH-MCF	Boeing 747-21AC Combi	24134	N6009F
PH-MCG	Boeing 767-31AER	24428	
PH-MCH	Boeing 767-31AER	24429	
PH-MCI	Boeing 767-31AER	25312	
PH-MCL	Boeing 767-31AER	26469	
PH-MCM	Boeing 767-31AER	26470	
PH-MCN	Boeing 747-228F	25266	(F-GCBN)
PH-MCP	McDonnell-Douglas MD-11F	48616	N90187
PH-MCR	McDonnell-Douglas MD-11F	48617	
PH-MCS	McDonnell-Douglas MD-11F	48618	
PH-MCT	McDonnell-Douglas MD-11F	48629	
PH-MCU	McDonnell-Douglas MD-11F	48757	
PH-MCV	Boeing 767-31AER	27619	5Y-QQQ PH-MCV
PH-MCW	McDonnell-Douglas MD-11F	48788	
PH-MCY	McDonnell-Douglas MD-11F	48445	N626FE HB-IWC
PH-MDB	Cessna 172K Skyhawk	17258604	N84758
PH-MDF	Reims/Cessna F172N	F17201842	(PH-MFD)
PH-MDW	Piper PA-32RT-300 Lance II	32R-7885186	N36388
PH-MDY	Mudry CAP.21	17	F-GDTS

PH-MEC	Piper PA-38-112 Tomahawk	38-79A0764	(PH-MEG) (PH-MGF) G-BVFD N2551L
PH-MEG	American AG-5B Tiger	10171	N1001A
PH-MEX	Cessna 650 Citation VI	650-0217	N217CM (N6828S)
PH-MGA	Jodel DR.1050	868	
	(contains parts of c/n 557 OO-MGA ex F-BMGA)		
PH-MGJ	Piper PA-28RT-201T Turbo Arrow IV	28R-7931139	N2077Y
PH-MGT	Cessna 525 CitationJet	525-0042	N96GD (N3230M)
PH-MHE	Piper PA-32R-301 Saratoga SP	32R-8013089	D-EGIF(2) N8188S
PH-MIJ	Rand-Robinson KR-2S	6898	
PH-MJB	Piper PA-28R-201 Arrow III	28R-7837227	N30028
PH-MJF	BAe ATP (Res 7.04)	2033	G-BTTO EC-HNA G-BTTO EC-GJU G-BTTO G-OEDE G-BTTO TC-THV G-BTTO S2-ACZ G-11-033
PH-MJG	BAe ATP (Res 7.04)	2038	G-BTNI EC-GSE EC-GKJ G-OEDI (N238JX) G-BTNI TC-THU G-BTNI (G-SLAM)
PH-MJK	BAe ATP (Res 7.04)	2038	G-BTPL EC-HES G-BTPL EC-GLH G-BTPL G-11-042
PH-MJL	BAe ATP (Res 7.04)	2038	G-BUKJ EC-HCO G-BUKJ EC-GLD G-OEDF G-BUKJ TC-THZ G-BUKJ
PH-MJM	Reims/Cessna F406 Caravan II	F406-0037	5Y-BIS D-ICAS F-WZDT
PH-MJS	Beech A23A Musketeer Custom III	M-1077	VH-MJS N2824B
PH-MJW	Europa Aviation Europa XS	182	
PH-MLA	American AG-5B Tiger	10140	
PH-MLB	American AG-5B Tiger	10141	
PH-MLF	Cessna R172K Hawk XP	R1722578	N736KB
PH-MLK	SOCATA TB-20 Trinidad	2036	F-OILQ
PH-MLL	SOCATA TB-20 Trinidad	2038	F-OILR
PH-MLM	Noorduyn/N.American AT-16ND Harvard IIB	14A-1444	B-71 FT404 43-13145
PH-MLN	Piper PA-44-180 Seminole	4496166	N53658
PH-MLO	Socata TB-10 Tobago GT	2087	F-GSZT
PH-MLQ	Socata TB-10 Tobago GT	2155	F-GOIA
PH-MLR	Socata TB-10 Tobago GT	2184	F-GOIB
PH-MLS	Socata TB-10 Tobago GT	2188	F-GOIC
PH-MMM	Cessna 177B Cardinal	17702528	N18114
PH-MNZ	Dornier 228-212	8206	D-CDIV D-CDOQ
PH-MOM	Cirrus SR20	1090	N196CD
PH-MOP	Beech F33A Bonanza	CE-1169	(PH-MPO) N3084A
PH-MPD	Airbus A.320-232	1944	F-WWDC
PH-MPE	Airbus A.320-232	1945	F-WWDE
PH-MPF	Airbus A.320-232	2167	F-WWIY
PH-MRA	Cessna 172M Skyhawk	17266964	C-GASV (N1269U)
PH-MRB	General Avia F.22B Pinguino	014	
PH-MRC	General Avia F.22C Pinguino Sprint	008	
PH-MRD	Cessna P210N Pressurized Centurion II	P21000388	G-HRIS N4972K
PH-MRE	Piper PA-31-350 Navajo Chieftain	31-7652083	SE-GNI N9663N
PH-MRG	General Avia F-22C Pinguino Sprint	023	G-RAJS
PH-MRM	Piper PA-34-200T Seneca II	34-8070086	D-GIGF N99GN C-FJRN N35717
PH-MRO	Cessna 421C Golden Eagle	421C0478	(PH-MRF) D-IHOS N6845C
PH-MSE	Mooney M.20J Model 205	24-3359	
PH-MSI	Cessna 172P Skyhawk	17275726	D-EGRP(2) N65309

PH-MVR	Robinson R-44 Raven	1057	
PH-MVT	Cessna U206F Stationair	U20601705	N9505G
PH-MXF	Fokker F.27-050	20283	PK-PFK PH-MXF PT-SLX PH-MXF
PH-MXJ	Fokker F.27-050	20288	
PH-MXS	Fokker F.27-050	20299	(PH-MXT)
PH-MXT	Fokker F.27-050	20300	
PH-MXZ	Fokker F.27-050	20301	
PH-MYF	Neico Lancair 360	244	
PH-NCE	Erco 415D Ercoupe	4765	
PH-NDA(2)	Piper PA-12 Super Cruiser	12-2918	D-ECON N4034M NC4034M
PH-NDD	SOCATA TB-20 Trinidad GT	2207	F-GOIJ
PH-NDJ	Robin HR.100/210 Safari	210	P4-NDJ (PH-MMS) OO-PRO F-ODDK
PH-NDL	Fairchild F.24R-46A Argus III (Reservation)	961	HB723 43-14997
PH-NEH	Auster J/5B Autocar	2932	
PH-NEN	Cessna 195	7496	D-EVLA N9817A
PH-NET	Auster 5	1416	G-AIPE TJ347
PH-NGK	Auster III	344	8A-11 R-18 MZ231
PH-NIC	Cessna P210N Pressurized Centurion	P21000440	N210MJ D-EDPW HB-CCU N213CC (N731CR)
PH-NIE	Brady Nieuport 28 C1	1	N6256
PH-NLB	Piper PA-34-220T Seneca V	3449020	N997SV SU-BMY N9286L
PH-NLZ	Swearingen SA.226TC Metro II	TC-277	(PH-TST) N5651M
PH-NOD	Reims/Cessna F150M Commuter	F15001165	
PH-NPT	Reims/Cessna F172N Skyhawk	F17201641	PH-AXF(1)
PH-NRA	Piper PA-38-112 Tomahawk	38-80A0092	(PH-ARN) (PH-GEC) OO-HKH N9684N
PH-NVF	Fokker F.27 Friendship 100 (on display at Aviodrome Lelystad)	10102	D-BAKI PH-NVF
PH-NVK	Cessna 340A	340A1018	N24CP N340GB (N4614N)
PH-NWG	Gyroflug SC-01B-160 Speed Canard	S-40	D-ENWG
PH-NZD	Sikorsky S-61N Mk.II	61489	EI-CTK PH-NZD
PH-NZG	Sikorsky S-61N Mk.II	61753	
PH-NZK	Sikorsky S-61N Mk.II	61773	LN-OMO PH-NZK
PH-NZS	Sikorsky S-76B	760325	G-UKLS PH-NZS
PH-NZT	Sikorsky S-76B	760326	G-UKLT PH-NZT
PH-NZU	Sikorsky S-76B	760329	G-UKLU PH-NZU
PH-NZV	Sikorsky S-76B	760336	G-UKLM PH-NZV
PH-NZW	Sikorsky S-76B	760381	G-OKLE PH-NZW
PH-NZZ	Sikorsky S-76B	760316	N373G N363G N34RP N5AZ
PH-OAL	Piper PA-31 Navajo C	31-7812037	D-ICAT N27595 N27495
PH-OEI	Piper J-3C-65 Cub	17360	N4210W N21922 CF-JVX N70376 NC70376
PH-OFA	Fokker F.28-0100	11246	G-UKFA N602RP C-FICY PH-EZB
PH-OFB	Fokker F.28-0100	11247	G-UKFB N602TR C-FICW PH-EZC
PH-OFC	Fokker F.28-0100	11263	G-UKFC N602DG C-FICL PH-EZF
PH-OFD	Fokker F.28-0100	11259	G-UKFD (F-GIOY) C-FICP PH-EZJ
PH-OFE	Fokker F.28-0100	11260	G-UKFE (F-GIOZ) C-FICQ PH-EZK
PH-OFF	Fokker F.28-0100	11274	G-UKFF (G-FIOB) PH-ZCK PH-EZB (PH-KLK)
PH-OFG	Fokker F.28-0100	11275	G-UKFG (G-FIOC) PH-ZCL PH-EZV (PH-KLL)
PH-OFH	Fokker F.28-0100	11277	G-UKFH (G-FIOD) PH-ZCM PH-EZW (PH-KLN)
PH-OFI	Fokker F.28-0100	11279	G-UKFI (G-FIOE) PH-ZCN PH-EZX (PH-KLO)
PH-OFJ	Fokker F.28-0100	11248	G-UKFJ F-GIOV C-FICB PH-INC PH-EZD
PH-OFK	Fokker F.28-0100	11249	G-UKFK F-GIOX C-FICO PH-INA PH-EZE
PH-OHN	DHC.6 series 300 (Reservation 8.03)	700	TJ-OHN LN-WFD
PH-OII	Cessna 182P Skylane	18262722	D-EJXU N52625
PH-OKE	Hughes 269C	93-0241	D-HNAH F-GALG G-BCHI
PH-OLI	Dassault Falcon 900	035	F-GNDK PP-PAA F-GLMU HB-IAD F-WWFC
PH-OLL	SOCATA TB-20 Trinidad	1244	F-GKVD
PH-OMI	Rand-Robinson KR-2S	7318/NVAV-93	
PH-ONE	Asso Champion V (Res. 11.03)	Unk	
PH-OOY	Brändli BX-2 Cherry	15/ NVAV-92	
PH-OPA	Stampe & Renard/ Stampe SV.4B	1202	(PH-PTB) (PH-SLZ) OO-SVC V-60
PH-OPC	Piper PA-28RT-201T Turbo Arrow IV	28R-8331031	N42978 (PH-MMM) (PH-JJJ) N42978
PH-OSD	Beech 76 Duchess	ME-341	D-GBTF
PH-OTH	Piper PA-31-350 Navajo Chieftain	31-7552075	G-BXUV PH-OTH G-BXUV PH-OTH N59979
PH-OTJ	Cessna T207A Turbo Stationair 8 II	20700590	N37443 OE-DNU (N73432)
PH-OTK	Reims/Cessna F172N Skyhawk	F17201963	PH-AXY(3)
PH-OUQ	Supermarine VS.361 Spitfire LF.IXc	CBAF.IX.1732	G-HVDM 8633M 3W-17 H-25 MK732
PH-OXY	Ultravia Pélican PL	683	
PH-PAB	Neico Lancair 360	766	
PH-PAC	Reims/Cessna F182Q Skylane	F18200118	
PH-PAD	Piper PA-28-181 Archer II	28-8090316	N8218Q
PH-PAL	Dyn'Aero MCR-4S	04/NVAV-232	
PH-PAU	Stoddard-Hamilton Glasair IIRG	1065	(PH-IPA)
PH-PAW	Piper PA-25-260 Pawnee	25-2203	N6695Z N10F
PH-PBA	Douglas DC-3C (wings, tail and engines of c/n 9836, G-BVOL, ZS-NJE, 6867, FD938, 42-23974)	19434	(PH-TCB) PH-PBA (PH-RLD) PH-PBA 42-100971
PH-PBB	Stinson L-5B-VW Sentinel	76-3401	OO-PBB PH-PBB 44-17113
PH-PBY	Consolidated PBY-5A Catalina	300	N27311 C-FHHR CF-HHR N18446 NC18446 11022 (RCAF) BuNo.2459
PH-PBL	Cessna 172M Skyhawk	17267417	N73384

PH-PCF	Cessna U206G Stationair 6 (Soloy)	U20605691	HB-CKM
			N5375X
PH-PCT	Cessna U206F Stationair	U20602337	N2092U
PH-PCV	Fuji FA-200-180AO Aero Subaru	271	
PH-PDL	Piper PA-18-150 Super Cub (amphibian floats)	18-8276	N5509Y
PH-PDZ	Fuji FA-200-180AO Aero Subaru	249	
PH-PEB	Cessna 210J Centurion	21059085	D-EAST(2)
			OE-DRW
			N6185F
PH-PEJ	Cessna 172P Skyhawk	17275401	LN-SJK
			OY-JRG
			N63187
PH-PEP	Aviat Pitts S-2B	5251	G-CDEE
			N17IJH
PH-PET	Brändli BX-2 Cherry (Reservation 8.03)	NVAV-237	
PH-PGH	Zenair CH-601HDS Zodiac	6-3459	(PH-PGW/
			-PGO/ -PCM/
			-PCG/ -KIS)
PH-PGP	Aerotek Pitts S.2A	2186	
PH-PHE	Piper PA-28RT-201T Turbo Arrow IV	28R-8331022	N42921
PH-PHY	Schweizer 269C	S-1668	N69A
PH-PHZ	Schweizer 269C	S-1384	OO-COM
			D-HGUS
PH-PIE	Piper PA-28RT-201T Turbo Arrow IV	28R-8031165	D-EBHN
			N8253Y
PH-PIG	SOCATA TB-20 Trinidad	1053	(PH-PGI)
			SE-KBM
PH-PIM	Cessna R172K Hawk XP	R1722376	N736AQ
PH-PJB	Piper PA-28-235 Cherokee E	28-7110004	D-EHBW
			N8583N
PH-PJL	Cessna 172P Skyhawk	17275586	N64578
PH-PJT	SOCATA TB-10 Tobago	1462	
PH-PLC	Ultravia Pélican PL	690	
PH-PLF	SOCATA TB-20 Trinidad	971	(PH-PPK)
			F-GGPK
PH-PLG	Piper PA-28-181 Archer II	28-8190138	G-HUKT
			N8321P
PH-PLI	North American P-51 Mustang (Res. 10.04)	Unk	
PH-PLK	Gardan GY-80 Horizon 180	239	
PH-PMA	SOCATA TB-20 Trinidad	2160	F-OIUZ
PH-PME	SOCATA TB-10 Tobago	188	F-GHXO
			OO-TBT
			(OO-AJD)
PH-PNA	Partenavia P.68B	038	N777EW
			9Q-CMQ
			N777EW
PH-POP	Europa Aviation Europa	157	
PH-POS	Brändli BX-2 Cherry	117	OO-137
PH-PPP	Piper PA-28RT-201T Turbo Arrow IV	28R-7931020	N2101J
PH-PPS	Cessna 208B Super Cargomaster	208B0773	N599BA
PH-PPW	Piper PA-18-135 Super Cub	18-3812	(PH-JZM)
			(PH-GAP)
			R-122
			54-2412
PH-PRH	Fokker F.27-050	20200	
PH-PRJ	Fokker F.27-050	20212	
PH-PRM	Piper PA-44-180 Seminole	44-7995279	OO-HCV
			N2203X
PH-PRO	Reims/Cessna F172M Skyhawk II	F17201039	
PH-PSC	Piper PA-18-135 Super Cub	18-3827	R-137
			54-2427
PH-PSI	North American P51D Mustang	122-40965	N11T
			N6522D
			N51HB
			N6522D
			RCAF 9591
			44-74425
PH-PTC	Piper PA-31-350 Navajo Chieftain	31-7852052	G-CLAN
			N27549
PH-PUL	Aero Designs Pulsar XP	252/NVAV-111	
PH-PVG	Reims/Cessna F172M Skyhawk	F17201473	
PH-PWA	Van's RV-8	80836	
PH-PXL	Curtiss P-40 (Res. 10.04)	unkn	
PH-PYL	Neico Lancair 360	609	
PH-RAA	Piper PA-28-161 Cadet	2841145	D-EDCC
			N9509N
PH-RAB	Diamond DA-40D Star (Res. 2.05)	unkn	
PH-RAC	Diamond DA-40D Star (Res. 2.05)	unkn	
PH-RAD	Diamond DA-40D Star (Res. 2.05)	unkn	
PH-RAH	Beech 1900D	UE-31	OY-GEP
			N31YV
PH-RAJ	Cessna 421C Golden Eagle	421C0457	D-INAT
			N6774C
			D-INAT
			N6774C
PH-RAK	Aérospatiale/Alenia ATR-42-300	032	ZS-OUY
			I-ATRD
			F-WWEN
PH-RAP	Neico Lancair 360 (CoA appl. 4.2004)	266	N420BA
PH-RAQ	Aérospatiale/Alenia ATR-42-300	139	ZS-OSN
			C-GXCP
			F-WWEL
PH-RAR	Beech 1900D	UE-372	ZS-ONS
			N30287
PH-RAY	Denney Kitfox IV	1411	

PH-RAZ	Swearingen SA.226TC Metro II	TC-252	OY-AZW
			D-IBCF
			OY-AZW
			N5456M
PH-RBC	Eurocopter EC.120B Colibri	1069	F-WQDY
PH-RCF	Reims/Cessna F172N Skyhawk	F17202034	PH-AYO(3)
PH-RCM	SOCATA TB-20 Trinidad	1451	F-GLFO
PH-RCV	SOCATA TB-10 Tobago	1318	
PH-REK	Brändli BX-2 Cherry	157/NVAV-227	
PH-RER	Piper PA-28-181 Archer III	2843255	N41478
PH-RES	Reims/Cessna F172N Skyhawk II	F17201597	PH-AXN(1)
PH-RIC	Mudry CAP.10B	02	(PH-RIK)
			D-EQVA
			F-GNVA
			Fr.AF F-TFVA
			F-TFVQ
			F-ZWRM
PH-RIN	Reims/Cessna F150M	F15001365	PH-AYD(1)
PH-RJB	SAAB S.91B Safir	91309	D-EBUC
			SE-XAU
PH-RJH	Brändli BX-2 Cherry	NVAV-127	
PH-RLA	SAAB S.91D Safir	91367	
PH-RLB	SAAB S.91D Safir	91368	
PH-RLD	SAAB S.91D Safir	91370	
PH-RMD	Piper PA-32R-301T Saratoga IITC	3257281	N53557
PH-RNC	SOCATA Rallye 150ST	3177	
PH-ROB	Piper PA-18-150 Super Cub	18-7910	N3974Z
PH-RPB	Cessna F172H	F172-0568	
PH-RPH	Cessna 182R Skylane	18267808	(PH-HCP)
			N6243N
PH-RPI	Cessna 182R Skylane	18267809	(PH-HDP)
			N6245N
PH-RPJ	Cessna 182R Skylane	18267833	N6390N
			(PH-AXQ (4))
			N6390N
PH-RPR	MBB BO.105C	S-356	D-HDGS
PH-RPS	MBB BO.105C	S-355	D-HDGR
PH-RPV	MBB BO.105CB	S-249	D-HDHI
PH-RPW	MBB BO.105CB	S-250	D-HDHJ
PH-RPX	MBB BO.105CBS-4	S-425	D-HARU
			D-HDMX
PH-RPY	MBB BO.105CBS-4	S-544	D-HADO
			(D-HDNS)
PH-RRF	Fokker F.27-050	20220	EC-HNS
			PH-RRF
			PT-MLE
			PH-RRF
			HB-IAS
			PH-RRF
			PH-EXS
PH-RRR	Piper PA-28-181 Archer II	28-8290156	N8244X
PH-RSA	Cessna 560XLCitation Excel	560-5110	N5200Z
PH-RTR	Robinson R-22B2 Beta	3177	
PH-RUB	Beech A36AT Bonanza	E-2719	D-EGBS(2)
PH-RUD	Reims/Cessna F150M Commuter	F15001163	
PH-RVA	Bensen B-8MRR	RVA001	
PH-RVB	Air Command 536 Elite 2-seater	RVA002	
PH-RVC	Parsons II Tandem	RVA003	
PH-RVG	Piper PA-28-181 Archer II	28-8390024	N8316W
PH-RVH	Piel CP.328A Super Emeraude	NVAV-75	
PH-RVS	Partenavia P.68B	98	
PH-RWL	SOCATA TB-9 Tampico	1268	F-GKVC
PH-RXA	Embraer EMB.145MP	145216	
PH-RXB	Embraer EMB.145MP	145320	PT-SML
PH-RXC	Embraer EMB.145LR	145106	EC-GZU
PH-RYF	Hughes 269C	105-0444	(PH-HAH)
			PH-RYF
			OY-HCE
			D-HKEP
PH-SAV	Piper PA-31-350 Navajo Chieftain	31-7652056	N59818
PH-SBK	Beech 200 Super King Air	BB-180	G-BHVX
			PH-SBK
			G-BHVX
			5N-AKR
PH-SBM	Reims/Cessna F172N	F17201637	D-EECW
			(SU- . . .)
PH-SBR	Europa Aviation Europa XS TG	A168	N303AU
PH-SBY	Piper PA-28-161 Warrior II	28-7916006	N39746
PH-SBZ	Piper PA-28-161 Warrior II	28-7916007	N39768
PH-SCP	Van's RV-7A (Reservation 8.04)	70359	(PH-SJP)
PH-SCX	Cessna 152	15282148	N68146
			(PH-SCX)
			N68146
PH-SDB	Piper PA-28-161 Warrior II	28-8016322	OO-HLX
			N82000
PH-SDH	DHC-8 Series 102	222	C-GFUM
PH-SDK	DHC-8 Series 311	254	C-GFYI
PH-SDN	Piper PA-28R-200 Cherokee Arrow II	28R-7535192	N33773
			PH-SDN
			N33773
PH-SEL	Cessna 172P Skyhawk	17274194	(PH-SCW)
			N6409K
PH-SEN	Stinson L-5B Sentinel (CoA appl. 3.05)	76-489	N57797
			42-98248
PH-SGB	Slingsby T-67C-3 Firefly	2077	(PH-SBB)
			G-7-136

PH-SGE	Slingsby T-67C-3 Firefly	2083	G-7-146 PH-SGE G-7-140
PH-SGF	Slingsby T-67C-3 Firefly	2087	OO-SGF PH-SGF G-7-141
PH-SGG	Slingsby T-67C-3 Firefly	2099	G-7-142
PH-SGH	Slingsby T-67C-3 Firefly	2100	G-7-143
PH-SHF	McDonnell-Douglas MD.900	900-00080	N7008Q
PH-SHI	Eurocopter EC.155B Dauphin	6657	F-WWOB
PH-SIG	Cessna 182P Skylane	18263129	D-EDJX N7345N
PH-SII	Fokker S.11.1 Instructor (Reservn 5.02)	6215	KLu: E-24
PH-SIL	Piper PA-28RT-201T Turbo Arrow IV	28R-8231053	(PH-STI) N8392A "HB-PGY"
PH-SIR	Reims/Cessna F172M Skyhawk	F17201263	D-ELEX
PH-SIY	Fokker S.14.1 Mach Trainer (Reservn 5.02)	7362	KLu: L-17
PH-SKB	Reims/Cessna F172N Skyhawk	F17201549	PH-AXM(1)
PH-SKC	Reims/Cessna F172N Skyhawk II	F17201673	PH-AXH(2) F-BNGR (SX-. . .)
PH-SKE	Cessna 172P Skyhawk	17274730	N53364
PH-SKF	Cessna 150M	15078927	N704WG
PH-SKG	Cessna 152	15285168	N6145Q
PH-SKJ	Cessna 172M Skyhawk	17266607	N80474 C-GXBB N80474
PH-SKN	Cessna 172M Skyhawk	17265655	N6939H
PH-SLA	Cessna 180J Skywagon	18052637	G-BDSI N9982N
PH-SLO	Fokker S.11.1 Instructor	6281	(PH-HOH) MLD:198 E-38
PH-SLR	Cessna 172N Skyhawk	17271965	N5930E (N5830E)
PH-SMA	Cessna F172H	F172-0506	D-EDDF
PH-SMT	SOCATA TB-20 Trinidad GT	2076	N209GT F-WWRB
PH-SNB	Piper PA-34-220T Seneca III	34-8133131	N8399D
PH-SNE	Piper PA-28-180 Cherokee Archer	28-7505181	N33794
PH-SNJ	Piper PA-34-220T Seneca III	34-8233119	N82115 (TG-BUH) N9649N
PH-SOK	Partenavia P.68C	218	G-BJCR OO-EEC
PH-SOL	Cessna 525 CitationJet	525-0417	(PH-SLD) D-IEAI N5203B
PH-SPC	Grob G.115A	8044	(D-EGVV)
PH-SPD	Grob G.115A	8078	(D-EGVV)
PH-SPE	Robin R.3000/140	137	
PH-SPF	Piper PA-28RT-201T Turbo Arrow IV	28R-8531006	N4388U
PH-SPH	Grob G.115	8024	G-BOCD
PH-SPI	Cessna 182S Skylane	18280065	N9882F
PH-SRN	Piper PA-28-151 Cherokee Warrior	28-7615053	(PH-GMA) N9644N
PH-SRP	Piper PA-28-151 Cherokee Warrior	28-7715209	(PH-SRO) OO-HCA N9539N
PH-SRU	Piper PA-28-161 Cherokee Warrior II	28-7816485	OO-HCN N9500C
PH-SSW	Aérospatiale SA.365N Dauphin 2 (CoA appl. 1.05)	6103	PP-MCA PH-SSW V8-UDW
PH-SSX	Aérospatiale SA.365N Dauphin 2	6030	5N-BAR F-GCPH
PH-STL	Cessna U206G Stationair 6 II (Soloy)	U20604266	HB-CKZ N756QF
PH-STM	Ryan STM-S2 (Reservation 9.02)	458	N9761 LN-TVF (LN-TAF) VR-HDL (VH-AGY) (A50-19) MLD: S-16
PH-STV	Mudry CAP.10B	89	F-BXHW
PH-SVE	Robin DR.400/120 Dauphin 80	1499	
PH-SVG	Piper PA-28-161 Warrior II	28-8616055	(F-GHLY) N9085V
PH-SVH	Piper PA-28-161 Cadet	2841300	(PH-VCR) N9528N
PH-SVI	Piper PA-28-161 Warrior II	28-8416075	N4352P
PH-SVL	Robin DR.400/120 Dauphin 2+2	2379	
PH-SVM	Robin DR.400/120 Dauphin 2+2	2388	
PH-SVN	Robin R.2160	343	F-GTZF
PH-SVP	Piper PA-28-181 Archer III	2843102	N181TA VH-MGA
PH-SVQ	Robin DR.400/160 Major	2555	
PH-SVW	Stoddard-Hamilton Glasair IIS RG	2037	
PH-SVY	Piper PA-31T Cheyenne II	31T-8020041	N198CC N198AA PT-OHS N2312V
PH-SWN	Cessna 414A Chancellor II	414A0420	D-IAAQ (N2692Y)
PH-SXA	SOCATA TB-20 Trinidad	1856	F-OIGH
PH-SXB	SOCATA TB-20 Trinidad	1857	F-OIGI
PH-SXD	SOCATA TB-20 Trinidad	1859	F-OIGK
PH-SYD	Piper PA-28RT-201 Arrow IV	28R-8018094	N8246S
PH-SXI	Fokker F.28-0100	11335	3D-ALM PH-EZR (PH-EZL)
PH-SZW	Cessna 172S Skyhawk	172S8056	N649SP
PH-TAJ	Pottier P.220S Koala	166	
PH-TAT	Slepcev Storch Mk.4	0049	
PH-TBR	Noorduyn/ N.American AT-16ND Harvard IIB	14A-808	B-182 FS668 43-12509
PH-TBT	SOCATA TB-9 Tampico	56	
PH-TCN	Piaggio P-180 Avanti	1089	
PH-TDI	Diamond DA-40D Star	D4.146	
PH-TDR	Tecnam P.92J Echo	012	
PH-TEB	SOCATA TB-10 Tobago	393	D-EJPF
PH-TEC	Tecnam P.92-JS Echo	017	
PH-TEJ	Pottier P.180S	107/NVAV-80	(PH-TEI) (PH-JET)
PH-TES	Tecnam P.92JS Echo	031	
PH-TEX	Reims/Cessna F172M	F17201010	F-BUMX
PH-TEY	Gyroflug SC-01B-160 Speed Canard	S-25	D-EOSC
PH-TEZ	Cessna T182 Turbo Skylane	T18208059	N35017
PH-TFS	SOCATA TB-200 Tobago XL	1445	LX-FAR
PH-TGA	Reims/Cessna F150M Commuter	F15001394	PH-AYH(1)
PH-TGB	Reims/Cessna F152-II	F15201742	PH-AYC(3)
PH-TGC	Cessna 182R Skylane	18268401	PH-AXS(4) N9352E
PH-TGD	Cessna 152-II	15285960	(PH-TDG) N95705
PH-TGF	Piper PA-28-181 Archer II	28-8590011	(PH-TGV) N147AV
PH-TGH	Cessna 172P Skyhawk	17275457	OY-CPA N63625
PH-TGK	Piper PA-28-181 Archer II	2890012	N9107Z
PH-TGM	Reims/Cessna F172N Skyhawk	F17201887	PH-AXV(3) (D-EEOR)
PH-TGV	Reims/Cessna F172N Skyhawk	F17201640	
PH-THB	Robinson R-22 Beta	2333	OO-MCT PH-THB (N82246) N2352Y
PH-THE	Colomban MC-15 Cri-Cri	2/ NVAV-131	
PH-THS	Cessna 172N Skyhawk	17272193	N8374E
PH-TIM	Robin DR.400/180 Régent	2311	
PH-TLC	Neico Lancair 360 (Built as 320)	001	N360LA
PH-TMH	Piper PA-38-112 Tomahawk	38-79A0261	N2314D
PH-TML	Zenair CH-601HD Zodiac	6-9044	
PH-TOF	Piper PA-25-260 Pawnee D	25-7405573	N54000
PH-TOG	Ayres S.2R Turbo Thrush Commander (Marsh conversion)	2441R	EC-DES N8923Q
PH-TOK	Piper PA-18-135 Super Cub	18-3604	R-114 54-2404
PH-TOL	Cessna 172M Skyhawk	17263133	N4383R
PH-TOO	Cessna U206G Stationair 6 II	U20606258	N6376Z
PH-TOP	Piper PA-18-150 Super Cub	18-8257	
PH-TOR	Piper PA-25-260 Pawnee C	25-4960	N8539L
PH-TOW	Morane-Saulnier MS.885 Super Rallye	5254	(PH-FOW) D-EHQA OH-MRD
PH-TOY	Ayres S.2R Turbo Thrush Commander (Marsh conversion)	2410R	N5632X
PH-TSN	Diamond DA-42 Twin Star (Res. 6.04)	42.017	OE-VPI
PH-TTY	Ultravia Pélican PL	687	
PH-TVB	Piper PA-31-300 Navajo (built as PA-31 Turbo Navajo)	31-408	N6453L
PH-TWB	Reims/Cessna F172N Skyhawk	F17201572	D-EBJG
PH-TWM	Cessna 172P Skyhawk	17275859	N73ER N6575S
PH-TWP	Piper PA-28RT-201 Arrow IV	28R-7918215	N2910W (PH-TWP) N2910W (PH-NDE) N2910W
PH-TWR	Ken Brock KB-2 Gyroplane	1006	
PH-TWT	SOCATA TB-20 Trinidad	459	D-EDEJ
PH-TWY	Reims/Cessna F172M Skyhawk	F17201513	
PH-TWZ	Christen A-1 Husky	1110	
PH-TXD	Cessna 150M (Res. as D-EUUH .05)	15079342	(PH-USB) N714QC
PH-TXL	Cessna 172P Skyhawk	17275067	N54850
PH-TZC	Piper PA-18-135 Super Cub	18-3839	(PH-KNK) R-149 54-2439
PH-UCI	Piper J-3C-65 Cub	13351	45-4611
PH-UCS	Piper J-3C-65 Cub	13228/ NVAV-50	45-4488
PH-UGS	Piper PA-28-161 Warrior II	28-7916340	(PH-WVG) N2133X N9629N
PH-ULH	Revolution Mini-500	246	
PH-ULN	Tecnam P.92J Echo	006	
PH-ULP	Eurocopter EC.135 T2	0376	
PH-UNN	Eurocopter EC.120B Colibri	1310	
PH-URK	Piper PA-31 Turbo Navajo	31-478	N8504G N686DC N904AR N6562L

PH-USA	Cessna 172P Skyhawk II	17274718	N53297
PH-USC	Cessna 172P Skyhawk	17273517	N4970G
PH-USH	HOAC DV-20 Katana	20024	
PH-USI	HOAC DV-20 Katana	20072	
PH-USJ	HOAC DV-20 Katana	20139	
PH-USK	Diamond DA-40-180 Star	40057	
PH-USL	Diamond DA-40-180 Star	40078	
PH-UUB	Robinson R-44 Astro	0739	
PH-UUU	SOCATA TB-9 Tampico Club	919	D-ENDU
PH-UWL	Cessna 421C Golden Eagle	421C1234	(PH-UWG) N2722U
PH-VBC	Piper PA-25-260 Pawnee (Built as PA-25-235, re-engined)	25-2264	(PH-VCW) G-ASLJ ST-ADS G-ASLJ ST-ACH G-ASLJ N6694Z
PH-VBG	Dassault Falcon 2000EX	005	F-GUDN LX-DKC F-WWGE
PH-VCF	SOCATA TB-10 Tobago	784	F-GFQZ
PH-VCM	Cessna 421C Golden Eagle II	421C1212	OE-FEM PH-VCM (PH-ASA) N26610
PH-VCX	Piper PA-18 Super Cub 125 (Officially regd. with f/n 18-939)	18-851	(PH-VCH) R-205 51-15686
PH-VCY	Piper PA-18 Super Cub 95 (Built as -135hp) (Officially regd. with f/n 18-3785)	18-3601	R-111 54-2401
PH-VDC	Cessna T210M Turbo Centurion (Reims-assembled with "c/n" 0008)	21062368	(PH-AXZ(2)) N761MR
PH-VDM	Cessna 172R Skyhawk	17280187	N9939F
PH-VDS	Mooney M.20K Model 252 TSE	25-1001	N252JS (N251JS)
PH-VES	Reims/Cessna F172P Skyhawk	F17202063	D-ECCA
PH-VFA	Piper PA-28-161 Cadet	2841360	D-ETPZ N9248Z (N137ND)
PH-VFB	Piper PA-28-161 Cadet	2841361	D-ETPV N92482 (N9233Z)
PH-VFC	Piper PA-28-161 Cadet	2841314	D-EJTS N9271N N9210P
PH-VGA	Cessna T303 Crusader	T30300157	N6503C
PH-VGB	Piper PA-28-161 Warrior II	28-8616003	N2427Q
PH-VGC	Cessna 172N Skyhawk	17271277	N2426E
PH-VGH	Dyn'Aero MCR-4S	24	
PH-VII	Light Aero Avid Flyer (Res 4.04)	unkn	
PH-VIN	Brändli BX-2 Cherry	039/NVAV-121	
PH-VIS	Eurocopter EC.120B Colibri	1326	F-WQDL
PH-VKA	Piper PA-44-180 Seminole	44-8095027	N8230Z
PH-VKB	Cessna F150J	F150-0451	D-EEBA
PH-VKL	Ultravia Pélican PL	685	
PH-VLH	Revolution Mini-500	0145	
PH-VLK	Piper PA-28-181 Cherokee Archer II	28-7890268	N2803M
PH-VLS	Reims/Cessna F172N Skyhawk	F17201631	PH-AXZ(1)
PH-VMA	Piper PA-32R-301T Turbo Saratoga SP	32R-8129098	N8430F
PH-VMV	SOCATA TB-20 Trinidad	1923	F-OILH
PH-VOS	Reims/Cessna F150L Commuter	F15001092	(PH-WAC)
PH-VPA	Piper PA-34-200 Seneca	34-7250182	D-GKZW N2873T
PH-VPI	Evans VP-1 Volksplane (NVAV No. 27)	V2567	(PH-VDK)
PH-VRW	Reims/Cessna F150K Commuter (Rebuild of FA150K Aerobat c/n FA1500071)	FA1500071	
PH-VSF	Reims/Cessna F172L	F17200877	(PH-WAH)
PH-VSN	Reims/Cessna F152-II	F15201714	PH-AXW(3)
PH-VSP	Reims/Cessna F172N Skyhawk	F17201951	(PH-AXN(3))
PH-VSR	Reims/Cessna F172P Skyhawk II	F17202041	F-GCYG
PH-VSS	Reims/Cessna F172P Skyhawk II	F17202199	D-EBDA
PH-VSU	Robin DR.400/100	1932	
PH-VSX	Piper PA-28-181 Archer II	2890231	LX-ABZ
PH-VSY	Piper PA-28-161 Warrior III	2842018	N9273N
PH-VSZ	Reims/Cessna F172P Skyhawk II	F17202101	D-EOFR
PH-VTW	Piper PA-32RT-301T Turbo Saratoga SP	32R-8129089	N8415J (PH-VTW) N8415J
PH-VVB	Commander Aircraft 114B	14622	N77HQ N77HK N500JR
PH-VVD	Reims/Cessna F150M	F15001372	PH-AYE(1)
PH-VXM	Impuls (Reservation 4.02)	Unk	
PH-WAA	Reims/Cessna F172L	F17200818	
PH-WAI	Reims/Cessna F172M	F17200961	(OO-WAP)
PH-WBR	Cessna 175C Skylark	17557033	D-EHZE N8333T
PH-WBW	Robinson R-44 Astro	0359	G-OPHA CS-HDW G-OPHA
PH-WCK	Ultravia Pélican PL	677	
PH-WCU	Piper PA-28R-201T Turbo Cherokee Arrow III	28R-7703094	N3156Q
PH-WDR	Piper PA-18-135 Super Cub	18-3852	R-162 54-2452

PH-WDY	Brandt/Aerotek Pitts S-1S	WELL4Q2	N44R
PH-WEE	Cessna 152	15280083	G-BMNN
PH-WEN	Hughes 269C	47-0591	
PH-WFW	Robinson R-44 Astro	0106	G-KYDD N2123E D-HDLW
PH-WGL	Cirrus SR20	1211	N270CD
PH-WIM	Piper PA-38-112 Tomahawk	38-78A0592	C-GHPH
PH-WKA	SOCATA TB-10 Tobago	1027	D-EABE
PH-WMA	Reims/Cessna F172P Skyhawk II	F17202064	D-EODP (D-EJIM)
PH-WRF	Robinson R-44 Astro	0816	
PH-WRW	Eurocopter EC.120B Colibri	1277	
PH-WSF	Piper PA-28-140 Cherokee Cruiser	28-7325019	HB-OKM N11C
PH-WVL	Rans S-10 Sakota	1192150	
PH-WVS	Revolution Mini-500	339	
PH-WXA	Fokker F.28-0070	11570	(PH-WWA) I- REJO PH-EZZ
PH-WXC	Fokker F.28-0070	11574	I-REJI PH-EZY
PH-WXD	Fokker F.28-0070	11563	HA-LMD PH-WXD I-REJA PH-EZT
PH-WYN	Cessna 177B Cardinal	17702310	N35291
PH-XII	Pilatus PC-12/45	550	(PH-XXI)
PH-XLB	Embraer EMB.120RT Brasilia	120091	F-GFTB (F-GFTC) PT-SMI
PH-XOC	Bede BD-5A (Reservation 8.03)	HJC.4523	G-BCOX
PH-XPI	Piper PA-31-350 Navajo Chieftain	31-7752187	G-BFFR N27388
PH-XRA	Boeing 737-7K2	30784	N1786B
PH-XRB	Boeing 737-7K2	28256	
PH-XRC	Boeing 737-7K2	29347	
PH-XRD	Boeing 737-7K2	30659	
PH-XRE	Boeing 737-7K2	30668	
PH-XRV	Boeing 737-7K2 (CoA appl. 10.04)	34170	
PH-XRW	Boeing 737-7K2	33465	
PH-XRX	Boeing 737-7K2	33464	
PH-XRY	Boeing 737-7K2	33463	
PH-XRZ	Boeing 737-7K2	33462	
PH-XXV	North American B-25N Mitchell (Re-reservation 1.02)	-	
PH-YAK	IAV/Bacau YAK-52 (Reservation 7.03)	877401	RA-3326K LY-AQC
PH-YCM	Brändli BX-2 Cherry	164	
PH-ZCR	Piper PA-18-135 Super Cub	18-3865	(PH-KNS) R-175 54-2465
PH-ZCT	Piper PA-18-135 Super Cub (Dismantled at Eindhoven)	18-3859	R-169 54-2459
PH-ZFL	Fokker F.28-0100	11456	N1456D PH-EZM
PH-ZLA	Reims/Cessna FA150K Aerobat	FA1500007	OO-SKD
PH-ZOD	Zenair CH-601HDZodiac	6-9024	PH-3C7
PH-ZSM	Skystar Kitfox V Speedster	S9411-0064	
PH-ZSS	Reims/Cessna F172M Skyhawk	F17201377	D-EMAO
PH-ZVC	Piper PA-18-135 Super Cub	18-3855	(PH-KNP) R-165 54-2455
PH-ZWA	DHC-1 Chipmunk 22	C1/0736	(PH-DET) G-BDET (PH-RTH) G-BDET WP851
PH-ZZF	Cessna T207A Turbo Stationair 8 (Soloy)	20700747	(PH-GEA/ -HOO/ -MMB/ -SEX) HB-CLM N9896M
PH-ZZY	Morane Saulnier M.S. 893 E Rallye 180GT	12704	OO-AON F-GACN

BALLOONS AND AIRSHIPS

PH-AAN	Cameron Cockerel-130 SS HAFB	4650	
PH-ABH	Cameron N-120 HAFB	4088	
PH-ABP	Lindstrand LBL-77A HAFB	087	VH-SPB G-BVNZ
PH-ABS	Colt 90A HAFB	2383	
PH-ACK	Lindstrand LBL-260A HAFB	496	
PH-ADV	Schröder Fire Balloons G HAFB	405	
PH-ADR	Lindstrand LBL-210A HAFB	603	D-OGRE
PH-AFB	Cameron A-210	10635	
PH-AFN	Cameron A-180 HAFB	4344	
PH-AGP	Lindstrand LBL-120A HAFB	924	
PH-AGT	Cameron A-415 HAFB	4726	
PH-AHA	Cameron O-105 HAFB	3362	PH-AHA
PH-AHW	Colt 90A HAFB	1494	
PH-AIR	Thunder AX7-65 Bolt HAFB	236	
PH-AIX	Thunder AX10-180 SII HAFB	3909	

PH-AMM	Cameron Z-140 HAFB	10499	
PH-AMS	Lindstrand LBL-105A HAFB	328	
PH-AMV	Colt 69A HAFB	1332	G-BPGI
PH-ASK	Ultramagic M-130 HAFB	130/22	
PH-ATH	Lindstrand LBL-69A HAFB	351	
PH-ATN	Cameron Z-350 HAFB	10354	
PH-AUW	Cameron Peacock-90 SS HAFB	3054	
PH-AWS	Lindstrand LBL-310A HAFB	686	
PH-AXO	Cameron N-133 HAFB	4112	
PH-AYA	Schröder Fire Balloons G HAFB	1051	
PH-AYF	Ultramagic M-145 HAFB	145/02	
PH-AYS	Cameron O-105 HAFB	4996	
PH-BAF	Schröder Fire Balloons G HAFB	1042	
PH-BAL	Cameron Bunch-100 SS HAFB	2898	
PH-BAM	Schröder Fire Balloons G HAFB	129	
PH-BAV	Colt Beer Glass SS HAFB	2007	
PH-BBR	Colt 120A HAFB	2206	OO-BBR
PH-BBW	Cameron N-105 HAFB	3612	
PH-BCJ	Raven Europe RX-8 HAFB	E-209	
PH-BEL	Colt 77A HAFB	1502	
PH-BEN	Cameron O-56 HAFB	15	
PH-BEO	Colt 90A HAFB	2038	
PH-BEV	Cameron N-77 HAFB	2186	OO-BEV G-BRWH
PH-BHB	Schröder Fire Balloons G HAFB	837	(PH-BMB)
PH-BHK	Cameron N-105 HAFB	2691	
PH-BIB	Thunder AX10-150 SII HAFB	4684	
PH-BIO	Cameron A-180 HAFB	3274	
PH-BJA	Lindstrand LBL-180A HAFB	579	
PH-BJB	Lindstrand LBL-120A HAFB	804	
PH-BKB	Colt 21A Cloudhopper HAFB	1251	(PH-HAS) G-TPII
PH-BKN	Colt 90A HAFB	613	
PH-BLN	Lindstrand LBL-105A HAFB	114	G-BXSO HB-BBJ
PH-BMK	Cameron Z-160 HAFB	10545	
PH-BOE	Thunder AX7-77SI HAFB	1969	
PH-BRB	Cameron Z-105 HAFB	10427	
PH-BSD	Schröder Fire Balloons G	1118	(PH-BVD)
PH-BSL	Cameron A-180 HAFB	2332	G-BSLG
PH-BSY	Cameron N-105 HAFB	3001	
PH-BVM	Cameron A-300 HAFB	10341	
PH-BYN	Cameron N-133 HAFB	10403	(PH-WVZ/ PH-ZOT)
PH-BYR	Cameron A-400 HAFB	4762	
PH-CAP	Cameron N-133 HAFB	4018	
PH-CCC	Colt 90A HAFB	982	
PH-CDJ	Cameron N-133 HAFB	3596	
PH-CHH	Cameron N-133 HAFB	10353	
PH-CLC	Cameron A-140 HAFB	4322	
PH-CMB	Cameron A-120 HAFB	4017	
PH-CML	Colt 120A HAFB	2277	
PH-CMP	Thunder AX8-105 SII HAFB	2298	G-BURA
PH-CMV	Cameron N-90 HAFB	2488	
PH-CUY	Schröder Fire Balloons G HAFB	919	
PH-CWT	Lindstrand LBL-150A HAFB	974	
PH-CZN	Cameron Z-210 HAFB	4971	
PH-DAJ	Cameron N-133 HAFB	10082	(PH-DAY)
PH-DBV	Thunder AX9-120 SII HAFB	2209	
PH-DCX	Cameron N-133 HAFB	4649	(PH-IDC)
PH-DDM	Cameron N-90 Nail SS HAFB	2233	
PH-DDL	Cameron Z-120 HAFB	10636	
PH-DHM	Cameron N-133 HAFB	3892	
PH-DHT	Sky 120-24 HAFB	155	
PH-DIA	Cameron A-140 HAFB	4796	(PH-OKI)
PH-DID	Ultramagic M-145 HAFB	145/19	
PH-DJB	Schröder Fire Balloons G HAFB	819	
PH-DJO	Thunder AX6-56Z HAFB	398	
PH-DLY	Cameron N-120 HAFB	4603	
PH-DOS	Thunder AX7-77Z HAFB	449	
PH-DOT	Lindstrand LBL-150A HAFB	773	
PH-DPV	Raven Europe S-71A HAFB	E-213	(PN-DPV)
PH-DRP	Lindstrand LBL-150A HAFB	580	
PH-DTZ	Cameron A-210 HAFB	2993	
PH-DVA	Lindstrand LBL-105A HAFB	343	
PH-DVB	Cameron A-140 HAFB	4354	
PH-DWB	Cameron A-105 HAFB	2134	
PH-DZB	Kubicek BB-60 HAFB	323	
PH-EAR	Cameron C-80 HAFB	3600	
PH-ECU	Colt 120A HAFB	2055	
PH-EDE	Cameron Z-160 HAFB	10584	
PH-EEL	Cameron O-90 HAFB	10048	D-OLEX(2)
	(Formerly envelope c/n 3356, officially still regd as such)		
PH-EGO	Cameron A-140 HAFB	4325	
PH-EJM	Cameron O-105 HAFB	3723	
PH-EKM	Cameron A-105 HAFB	4687	
PH-ELD	Schröder AX9-205G HAFB	358	
PH-ELS	Cameron V-77 HAFB	3085	
	(New envelope, formerly c/n 538 and officially still regd as such)		
PH-EMR	Cameron A-105 HAFB	4784	
PH-ENH	Lindstrand LBL-105A HAFB	844	
PH-ENR	Cameron Z-69 HAFB	10588	
PH-ENS	Colt 105A HAFB	1435	
PH-EPY	Lindstrand LBL-150A HAFB	722	
PH-ESG	Lindstrand LBL-210A HAFB	963	
PH-ESH	Lindstrand LBL-120A HAFB	745	
PH-ESV	Cameron O-140 HAFB	10062	
PH-EVA	Cameron O-140 HAFB	2927	D-OEVA
PH-EVE	Cameron N-120SV HAFB	3903	
PH-EVH	Cameron N-90 HAFB	1385	
PH-EWS	Kubicek BB-37 HAFB	155	(PH-GRM) D-OBKT OK-0155
PH-FDT	Cameron A-300 HAFB	10556	
PH-FRJ	Schröder Fire Balloons G HAFB	396	(PH-FRL) (PH-FRY)
PH-FUK	Cameron Z-105 HAFB	10385	
PH-FWJ	Lindstrand LBL-150A HAFB	896	
PH-FYN	Cameron N-120SP HAFB	3721	
PH-GBF	Cameron Grolsch 105SS HAFB	3977	
PH-GBN	Cameron Z-133 HAFB	2988	
PH-GBT	Lindstrand LBL-150A HAFB	687	
PH-GGN	Cameron N-133 HAFB	4976	
PH-GHJ	Cameron O-105 HAFB	3777	
PH-GJA	Lindstrand LBL 25A HAFB	342	
PH-GMZ	Cameron Z-140 HAFB	10231	
PH-GOG	Cameron Van Gogh-110SS HAFB	10269	
PH-GPI	Lindstrand LBL-120A HAFB	664	
PH-GPJ	Lindstrand LBL-240A HAFB	324	G-BXMK
PH-GPP	Lindstrand LBL-210A HAFB	653	
PH-GPR	Cameron A-140 HAFB	3698	
PH-GPS	Kubicek BB-45 HAFB	279	OK-0279
PH-GPU	Cameron N-90 HAFB	3934	
PH-GPW	Ultramagic N-250 HAFB	250/18	
PH-GRF	Lindstrand LBL-105A HAFB	639	
PH-GSP	Cameron A-210 HAFB	10138	
PH-GWJ	Colt 105A HAFB	2210	G-NIMO
PH-GWK	Cameron N-105 HAFB	3652	
PH-HAR	Colt 56B HAFB	2573	
PH-HBA	Cameron A-275 HAFB	4988	
PH-HBC	Augsburg K630/1-RI Gas Balloon	9886	(PH-BAL)
PH-HBE	Cameron A-250 HAFB	4010	
PH-HCB	Colt 120A HAFB	2531	
PH-HCV	Lindstrand LBL-120A HAFB	507	
PH-HDB	Cameron N-105 HAFB	4610	
PH-HDV	Ultramagic N-355 HAFB	355/04	
PH-HHI	Cameron Inverted Balloon-78 SS HAFB	4454	
PH-HIO	Cameron N-133 HAFB	4456	
	(New envelope 1998, formerly c/n 3484, still regd as such)		
PH-HKC	Schröder Fire Balloons G HAFB	134	D-OCOE D-Fuchs
PH-HOJ	Schröder Fire Balloons G HAFB	1049	
PH-HOO	Cameron N-105 HAFB	10064	
PH-HOR	Thunder AX6-56Z HAFB	444	G-BKGP
PH-HOS	Cameron Nissan Micra SS HAFB	2883	
PH-HOV	Thunder AX7-77 SI HAFB	1768	
PH-HPC	Colt 69A HAFB	2567	
PH-HPY	Schröder Fire Balloons G HAFB	1107	
PH-HSL	Cameron V-77 HAFB	2495	
PH-HTD	Cameron A-140 HAFB	3190	
PH-HUS	Schröder Fire Balloons G HAFB	1023	
PH-HYM	Cameron N-105 HAFB	4341	
PH-IAB	Cameron N-180 HAFB	3981	
PH-IAC	Cameron N-145 HAFB	3979	
PH-IAD	Cameron N-210 HAFB	4059	
PH-IAE	Cameron C-80 HAFB	4032	
PH-ICR	Colt 120A HAFB	2309	
PH-IDR	Lindstrand LBL-150A HAFB	652	
PH-IEJ	Kubicek BB-42Z HAFB	268	OK-0268
PH-IGH	Schröder Fire Balloons G HAFB	654	D-OOEG
PH-IHI	Cameron N-133 HAFB (formerly c/n 4233, .01)	4977	
PH-IHO	Cameron N-133 HAFB (formerly c/n 4080, .01)	10056	
PH-IIH	Cameron HAFB (Reservation 7.02)	unkn	
PH-IJF	Monica Calafiore Hassa u Wolf MW77 HAFB	01	D-OGGI
PH-IKE	Lindstrand LBL-105A HAFB	675	
PH-IMA	Cameron N-133 HAFB	10088	
PH-IMN	Ultramagic M-130 HAFB	130/13	
PH-INT	Cameron N-77 HAFB	1386	
PH-IOI	Cameron HAFB (Reservation 7.02)	unkn	
PH-IRE	Cameron O-120 HAFB	4336	
PH-ISS	Schröder Fire Balloons G HAFB	1131	
PH-ISU	Colt 90A HAFB	932	
PH-ITR	Lindstrand LBL-150A HAFB	497	
PH-ITS*	Colt 69A	1317	SE-ZDH
PH-IVO	Schröder Fire Balloons G HAFB	73	
PH-IZA	Lindstrand LBL-105A HAFB	660	
PH-JAB	Cameron N-133 HAFB	4079	
PH-JAG	Raven Europe S-60A HAFB	E-130	
PH-JEF	Cameron N-56 HAFB	397	D-Bruijn (2) SE-ZYH
PH-JEL	Cameron N-77 HAFB	2199	
PH-JEM	Raven S-49A HAFB	3064	
PH-JGG	Cameron N-105 HAFB	1949	
PH-JHS	Rans S-6S Super Coyote II	06981239	PH-3H1
PH-JJH	Cameron N-133 HAFB	4548	
PH-JKJ	Cameron O-105 HAFB	4397	
PH-JLA	Cameron A-180 HAFB	10666	
PH-JLG	Cameron N-133 HAFB	4987	
PH-JLW	Cameron N-105 HAFB	2252	(PH-ABB)
PH-JNJ	Lindstrand LBL-180A HAFB	128	G-BVPG
PH-JOL	Cameron Z-210 HAFB	10367	
	(type corrected from Z-120 to Z-210 6.03)		
PH-JON	Lindstrand LBL-240AHAFB	691	
PH-JOU	Colt 77A HAFB	1089	

PH-JOY	Thunder AX7-77 HAFB	922	
PH-JPH	Raven Europe RX-8 HAFB	E-401	
PH-JRZ	Lindstrand LBL-105B HAFB	341	
PH-JSH	Cameron N-105 HAFB	4383	
PH-JVJ	Cameron A-105 HAFB	3396	
PH-JVK	Colt 120A HAFB	1618	D-OBPZ HB-BPZ
PH-JVR	Cameron N-133 HAFB	2989	
PH-JWM	Thunder AX8-105 SII HAFB	4179	
PH-KBE	Cameron N-105 HAFB	4066	
PH-KEI	Thunder AX8-90 HAFB	2500	
PH-KIP	Cameron Chicken-105 SS HAFB	2796	
PH-KIT	Colt 90A HAFB	2283	
PH-KMB	Cameron O-105 HAFB	2640	D-OCHS D-Ochsenfrosch
PH-KMK	Cameron A-375 HAFB	3481	
PH-KNP	Thunder AX8-90 SII HAFB	1234	
PH-KNY	Lindstrand LBL-150A HAFB	479	
PH-KOA	Cameron A-315SP HAFB	4970	
PH-KON	Ultramagic S-160 HAFB	160/33	
PH-KRE	Colt 120A HAFB	3746	G-BWJS
PH-KRH	Cameron A-180 HAFB	4388	
PH-KTS	Wörner NL-1000/STU Gas Balloon	1046	
PH-KUB	Kubicek BB-85 (Res. 12.04)	unkn	
PH-KUS	Schröder Fire Balloons G HAFB	723	
PH-KWB	Cameron A-140 HAFB	3687	
PH-KWC	Lindstrand LBL-150AHAFB	625	
PH-KWW	Cameron Z-150 HAFB	10264	
PH-LAK	Lindstrand LBL-180A HAFB	611	
PH-LBL	Lindstrand LBL-69A HAFB	315	G-BWMT
PH-LCT	Cameron A-140 HAFB	4732	
PH-LFF	Lindstrand LBL-180A HAFB	319	
PH-LIV	Lindstrand LBL-150A HAFB	607	
PH-LJP	Colt 105A HAFB	1866	(PH-BDH)
PH-LKA	Cameron A-275 HAFB	10553	
PH-LKM	Schröder Fire Balloons G HAFB	1133	
PH-LLP	Cameron N-120 HAFB	4902	
PH-LOR	Cameron A-300 HAFB	3862	
PH-LOX	Colt 105A HAFB	2341	
PH-LPT	Cameron Can 120 SS HAFB	10086	
PH-LUK	Schröder Fire Balloons G HAFB	993	
PH-LUV	Cameron Heart 120 SS HAFB	4639	
PH-LYS	Kavanagh B105 HAFB	B105-286	
PH-LZN	Cameron A-415 HAFB (Res. 9.04)	unkn	
PH-MAJ	Colt Flying Windmill SS HAFB	1625	
PH-MDR	Cameron N-105 HAFB	2868	
PH-MEB	Cameron N-77 HAFB	865	
PH-MEE	Cameron A-140 HAFB	10630	
PH-MGZ	Lindstrand LBL-105A HAFB	591	
PH-MJV	Lindstrand LBL-120A HAFB	435	
PH-MMB	Schröder Fire Balloons G HAFB	1003	
PH-MMF	Schröder Fire Balloons G HAFB	514	
PH-MMG	Schröder Fire Balloons G HAFB	780	
PH-MMH	Schröder Fire Balloons G HAFB	805	
PH-MNM	Cameron Z-150 HAFB	10381	
PH-MOI	Cameron Concept C-80 HAFB	4469	
PH-MPB	Sky 120-24 HAFB	139	
PH-MTD	Cameron N-133 HAFB	3837	
PH-MVV	Cameron Z-210 HAFB	10424	
PH-NAJ	Ultramagic N-180 HAFB	180/25	
PH-NGN	Cameron A-530 HAFB	10170	G-CBLC
PH-NHN	Lindstrand LBL-210AHAFB	763	
PH-NIJ	Cameron A-160 HAFB	4819	
PH-NLM	Cameron A-160 HAFB	4652	
PH-NMD	Cameron Z-160 HAFB	10511	
PH-NON	Cameron O-105 HAFB	3435	(PH-NOO)
PH-NYK	Lindstrand LBL-150A HAFB	897	
PH-NYM	Cameron N-133 HAFB	3581	
PH-NYN	Colt 77A HAFB	4674	
PH-OAG	Cameron A-105 HAFB	3624	
PH-OBE	Schröder Fire Balloons G HAFB	1009	
PH-OBF	Cameron A-210 HAFB	10063	
PH-OCE	Cameron A-105 HAFB	2862	G-BVIY PH-OCE
PH-OEF	Cameron Concept C-80 HAFB	4182	
PH-OEK	Cameron N-100 HAFB	4339	
PH-OHE	Cameron A-210 HAFB	4425	
PH-OHI	Cameron Inverted 78 SS HAFB (Rebuild of c/n 4078, .01)	10055	
PH-OIH	Cameron Inverted 78 SS HAFB (New envelope 1999, originally c/n 3485)	4455	
PH-OIL	Cameron O-105 HAFB	3177	
PH-OIN	Cameron N-100 HAFB	4261	
PH-OJO	Cameron C-80 HAFB	3921	
PH-OLE	Schröder Fire Balloons G HAFB	1059	
PH-OME	Colt 77A HAFB	1354	
PH-ONG	Colt 105A HAFB	1858	G-BTAV
PH-OOK	Thunder AX7-77Z HAFB	463	
PH-OOR	Cameron N-105 HAFB	2972	
PH-OPP	Cameron N-42 HAFB	3256	G-BVLC
PH-OUN	Cameron A-140 HAFB	10117	
PH-OVU	Cameron N-145 HAFB	2159	
PH-OWA	Lindstrand LBL-180A HAFB	569	
PH-PAM	Cameron N-133 HAFB	4291	
PH-PBJ	Schröder Fire Balloons G HAFB	1021	
PH-PBN	Cameron A-180 HAFB	4234	
PH-PCI	Cameron N-120 HAFB	3606	

PH-PER	Schröder Fire Balloons G HAFB	144	
PH-PGL	Cameron N-77 HAFB	1369	G-LOSS
PH-PGU	Lindstrand LBL-105A HAFB	774	
PH-PIN	Colt 120A	2326	
PH-PJH	Raven Europe FS-83A HAFB	E-198B	HB-BRR
PH-PJW	Cameron Z-140 HAFB	10386	
PH-PKB	Cameron A-140 HAFB	4775	
PH-PMS	Cameron N-105 HAFB	3168	
PH-PNK	Colt 105A HAFB	1934	D-Telekom
PH-POM	Colt 90A HAFB	1932	
PH-PON	Ultramagic N-180 HAFB	180/24	
PH-PPJ	Kubicek BB-42Z	251	(PH-IHV) D-OOCC OK-0251
PH-PPL	Kubicek BB-30 HAFB	184	OK-0184
PH-PPM	Cameron N-120 HAFB	4636	
PH-PRS	Cameron N-160 HAFB	2260	
PH-PRT	Cameron N-133 HAFB	3978	
PH-PRX	Cameron A-105 HAFB	4321	
PH-PUC	Cameron N-133 Face SS HAFB	4602	
PH-PUK	Colt 31A HAFB	1254	
PH-PVH	Cameron A-250 HAFB	10155	
PH-PVL	Thunder AX7-77 SI HAFB	892	
PH-PVO	Cameron N-120 HAFB	3883	(PH-AJV)
PH-RAF	Colt 90A HAFB	2554	
PH-RAI	Cameron N-145 HAFB type formerly N-105	2338	
PH-RBG	Ultramagic M-145 HAFB	145/40	
PH-RBN	Cameron N-105 HAFB	1950	
PH-RDD	Cameron A-300 HAFB	3710	D-ORED(1)
PH-RDE	Colt 77A HAFB	1076	G-BNNM
PH-RDF	Cameron N-120 HAFB	3567	
PH-RDJ	Lindstrand LBL-210A HAFB	828	
PH-RDR	Cameron N-105 HAFB	4060	
PH-REE	Cameron N-133 HAFB	4353	
PH-REM	Cameron N-105 HAFB	4758	
PH-REY	Cameron A-140 HAFB	4992	D-OBAY
PH-RFA	Cameron A-105 HAFB	3382	
PH-RGM	Cameron A-210 HAFB	3150	
PH-RIJ	Schröder Fire Balloons G 34/24 HAFB	911	
PH-RJC	Schröder Fire Balloons G HAFB	869	(PH-RYC)
PH-RKG	Cameron A-180 HAFB	4997	
PH-RMC	Schröder Fire Balloons G HAFB	507	D-OLHM
PH-ROC	Cameron Frog 90 SS HAFB	4101	
PH-ROF	Kubicek BB-37 HAFB	289	OK-0289
PH-ROK	Cameron A-120 HAFB	4113	
PH-ROM	Cameron A-140 HAFB	3645	
PH-ROY	Cameron A-180 HAFB	3980	
PH-ROZ	Thunder AX7-77 HAFB	2509	
PH-RTD	Lindstrand LBL-150A HAFB	840	
PH-RTF	Cameron Z-140 HAFB	10363	
PH-RTK	Lindstrand LBL-90B HAFB	750	
PH-RTT	Cameron Z-140 HAFB	10275	(PH-RIT)
PH-RTV	Schröder Fire Balloons G HAFB	591	
PH-RUN	Sky 160-24 HAFB	119	
PH-RUT	Lindstrand LBL-150A HAFB	344	
PH-RWB	Cameron N-90 HAFB	920	
PH-RWW	Cameron O-105 HAFB	1447	
PH-RYM	Cameron A-140 HAFB	3705	
PH-SBL	Schröder Fire Balloons G HAFB	982	
PH-SIB	Cameron N-105 HAFB (formerly c/n 2939, .01)	4982	
PH-SIM	Thunder AX7-77Z HAFB	884	
PH-SMF	Schröder Fire Balloons G HAFB	452	(PH-SUS)
PH-SMR	Cameron A-300 HAFB	10507	
PH-SND	Cameron Z-160 HAFB	10578	
PH-SOD	Thunder AX7-77Z HAFB	1112	
PH-SPK	Cameron Z-120 HAFB	10307	
PH-STO	Cameron V-77 HAFB	3029	
PH-SUP	Lindstrand Stove SS HAFB	302	
PH-SUU	Schröder Fire Balloons G HAFB	924	
PH-SWI	Cameron N-120 HAFB	3039	
PH-SYS	Cameron A-105 HAFB	2432	(PH-PWO)
PH-TBI	Cameron Z-105 HAFB	19582	
PH-TEE	Thunder Ax7-77A Golfball SS HAFB	384	G-BJUY EI-BDE
PH-TIB	Colt 105A HAFB	2223	
PH-TIG	Lindstrand LBL-310A HAFB	769	
PH-TIJ	Cameron N-105 HAFB	3206	
PH-TIR	Ultramagic M-65C HAFB	65/97	
PH-TJB	Cameron N-133 HAFB	3771	
PH-TNC	Colt 120A HAFB	1523	
PH-TSL	Schröder Fire Balloons G HAFB	1064	
PH-TYN	Cameron N-210 HAFB	10027	
PH-TYR	Cameron N-77 HAFB	2267	
PH-UII	Cameron Onion 105 SS HAFB	10265	
PH-UNX	Cameron Unox Hat 110 SS HAFB	4323	(PH-NOX)
PH-USG	Cameron N-145 HAFB	10003	
PH-UVO	Cameron Spaceship 110 SS HAFB	4041	(PH-IDF) G-BWZO
PH-VBH	Lindstrand LBL-240A HAFB	525	
PH-VBN	Lindstrand LBL-310A HAFB	807	
PH-VBO	Cameron O-105 HAFB	4310	
PH-VBV	Cameron V-90 HAFB	3028	
PH-VBW	Cameron A-140A HAFB (original A-140)	4396	
PH-VCB	Cameron A-105 HAFB	2968	
PH-VCS	Schröder Fire Balloons G HAFB	1083	

PH-VDB	Schröder Fire Balloons G HAFB	72	
PH-VDV	Schröder Fire Balloons G HAFB	93	
PH-VEN	Cameron A-105 HAFB	3639	
PH-VGN	Cameron Z-140 HAFB	10371	
PH-VGO	Cameron A-140 HAFB	4525	
PH-VHG	Cameron Z-105 HAFB	4752	
PH-VIP	Cameron C-100 HAFB (Res. 8.04)	unkn	
PH-VLT	Cameron Z-315 HAFB	10266	
PH-VNK	Cameron Z-120 HAFB	10585	
PH-VOC	Cameron N-105 HAFB	4800	
PH-VRI	Cameron N-133 HAFB	10172	
PH-VTF	Cameron N-105 HAFB	4314	
PH-VUT	Thunder AX10-180 SI HAFB	3646	G-BWUY
PH-VYF	Cameron C-100 HAFB	4357	
PH-VZS	Colt 105A HAFB	1888	
PH-WAU	Ultramagic N-250 HAFB	250/26	
PH-WBA	Cameron A-250 HAFB	2932	
PH-WBB	Cameron N-105 HAFB	2004	
PH-WBC	Cameron N-120 HAFB	2783	
PH-WBF	Cameron N-120 HAFB	3820	
PH-WBG	Cameron A-300 HAFB	3437	
PH-WBK	Cameron N-105 HAFB	3218	
PH-WBL	Ultramagic N-355 HAFB	355/02	
PH-WBM	Ultramagic N-250 HAFB	250/08	
PH-WBN	Cameron N-120 HAFB	4604	
PH-WBT	Ultramagic M-130 HAFB	130/11	
PH-WBX	Ultramagic N-425 HAFB	425/01	
PH-WCJ	Lindstrand LBL-180A HAFB	150	G-BWCL
PH-WEB	Cameron Z-140 HAFB	10574	
PH-WEO	Cameron O-77 HAFB	3093	
PH-WFG	Cameron N-90 HAFB	2389	D-ORIT D-WESTFALEN
PH-WGN	Cameron N-105 HAFB	4492	
PH-WIE	Cameron C-80 HAFB	3265	
PH-WIJ	Cameron Z-133 HAFB	4817	(PH-VHC)
PH-WIN	Cameron N-77 HAFB	2885	
PH-WJB	Ultramagic M-105 HAFB	105/29	
PH-WJH	Cameron Z-160 HAFB	10546	
PH-WLC	Cameron A-120 HAFB	3722	
PH-WLD	Cameron A-105 HAFB	4776	(PH-WDL)
PH-WLE	Cameron O-105 HAFB	10166	
PH-WLF	Cameron O-105 HAFB	10229	
PH-WMV	Schröder Fire Balloons G HAFB	1105	
PH-WPV	Colt 77A HAFB	2273	
PH-WRS	Cameron N-90 HAFB	4394	
PH-WSI	Schröder Fire Balloons G HAFB	511	D-OWSI
PH-WVM	Colt 105A HAFB	1516	
PH-WWF	Lindstrand LBL-77A HAFB	595	G-XWWF
PH-WWT	Cameron N-133 HAFB	3623	
PH-WWW	Cameron A-210 HAFB	4472	
PH-XXL	Cameron O-105 HAFB	2187	
PH-YRD	Schröder Fire Balloons G HAFB	967	
PH-YTS	Raven Europe S-55A HAFB	E-124	
PH-YYY	Cameron N-105 HAFB	2838	
PH-YZR	Lindstrand LBL-310A HAFB	570	
PH-ZES	Cameron N-133 HAFB	4402	
PH-ZOT	Sky 140-24 HAFB	154	
PH-ZOZ	Thunder AX7-77Z HAFB	794	
PH-ZSC	Cameron Z-105 HAFB	10294	

GLIDERS AND MOTOR-GLIDERS

PH-58	Grunau Baby IIA (restoration will be finished soon)	5 serie I	PH-58
PH-102	Grunau Baby IIA	8 serie III	
PH-103	Kranich II	49	D-9019 EC-OBN
PH-104	Schleicher Rhönlerche II	706	(PH-1003) D-5433
PH-105	Schleicher Ka 2B Rhönschwalbe	44	BGA2909/ESF I-BGMR HB-570 D-5350
PH-106	Breguet 904S Nymphale	13	F-CCFX
PH-107	Scheibe Bergfalke II/55	363	D-7102
PH-108	Schleicher K 7 Rhönadler	7048	D-1923
PH-109	Bölkow Phoebus A-1	703	D-1180
PH-118	Schneider ESG	6006	
PH-167	Grunau Baby IIb	6049	BGA3972/HJB PH-167
PH-176	DFS Meise Olympia	6058	OO-ZJB PH-176
PH-192	Slingsby T-30A Prefect	735	
PH-194	Slingsby T-30A Prefect	737	
PH-196	Slingsby T-30A Prefect	739	
PH-198	Slingsby T-30A Prefect	741	
PH-206	Wolf Hirth Govier 4 III	416	
PH-207	Wolf Hirth Govier 4 III	417	
PH-210	Wolf Hirth Govier 4 III	420	
PH-212	Schleicher Grunau Baby IIb	91	
PH-213	Schleicher Grunau Baby IIb	92	
PH-214	Schleicher Grunau Baby IIb	93	
PH-222	Slingsby T-41 Skylark II	1000	
PH-226	Slingsby T-41 Skylark II	1004	
PH-234	Schleicher Rhönlerche II	152	
PH-236	Schleicher Rhönlerche II	154	
PH-239	Schleicher Rhönlerche II	157	
PH-240	Schleicher Rhönlerche II	158	
PH-246	Schleicher Rhönlerche II	164	
PH-247	Schleicher Rhönlerche II	165	
PH-260	Schleicher Ka 6CR Rhönsegler	663	
PH-262-MD	Schleicher Ka 6CR Rhönsegler	661	
PH-264	Schleicher K 7 Rhönadler	868	
PH-268	Schleicher K 7 Rhönadler	870	
PH-270	Schleicher K 7 Rhönadler	1078	
PH-271	Schleicher K 7 Rhönadler	1079	
PH-272	Schleicher K 7 Rhönadler	1080	
PH-273	Schleicher K 7 Rhönadler	1081	
PH-274-ZM	Schleicher K 7 Rhönadler	1082	
PH-275	Schleicher K 7 Rhönadler	1083	
PH-276-54	Schleicher K 7 Rhönadler	7006	
PH-278-VP	Schleicher K 7 Rhönadler	7008	
PH-279	Schleicher Rhönlerche II	1023	
PH-283	Schleicher K 7 Rhönadler	7055	
PH-284	Schleicher K 7 Rhönadler	7058	
PH-285	Schleicher K 8B	8073	
PH-286	Schleicher K 8B	8078	
PH-288-49	Schleicher K 8B	8074	
PH-291	Schleicher K 8B	8118	
PH-294	Schleicher K 8B	8121	
PH-295	Schleicher K 8B	8122	
PH-300	Schleicher K 8B	8127	
PH-303	Schleicher K 8B	8128	
PH-311	Schleicher K 8B	8143	
PH-312-A2	Schleicher K 8B	8264	
PH-314-AD	Schleicher K 7 Rhönadler	7094	
PH-315	Schleicher K 7 Rhönadler	7095	
PH-316-50	Schleicher Ka 6CR Rhönsegler	6214	
PH-318-HI	Schleicher Ka 6CR Rhönsegler	6216	
PH-321-V3	Schleicher Ka 6CR Rhönsegler	6332	
PH-322-6	Schleicher Ka 6CR Rhönsegler	6333	
PH-324-89	Schleicher Ka 6CR Rhönsegler	6334	
PH-327-RH	Schleicher Ka 6CR Rhönsegler	6223	D-5093
PH-334	Schleicher K 8B	8405	
PH-335-63	Schleicher Ka 6CR Rhönsegler	6335	
PH-337	Schleicher K 8B	6337	
PH-338-T1	Schleicher Ka 6CR Rhönsegler	6342	
PH-339-VM	Schleicher Ka 6CR Rhönsegler	6354	
PH-340-5	Schleicher Ka 6CR Rhönsegler	6471	
PH-342-10	Schleicher Ka 6CR Rhönsegler	6473	
PH-343	Schleicher Ka 6CR Rhönsegler	6474	
PH-345	Schleicher K 8B	8533	
PH-348-17	Schleicher K 8B	8536	
PH-351	Schleicher K 7 Rhönadler	7245	
PH-353	Schleicher K 8B	8552	
PH-354	Brockmeier/Schleicher Rhönlerche II	3061/Br	
PH-355	Brockmeier/Schleicher Rhönlerche II	3068/Br	
PH-356	Schleicher K 8B	8553	
PH-357-4	Schleicher Ka 6CR Rhönsegler	6455	
PH-360	Schleicher K 8B	8657	
PH-361	Schleicher K 8B	8658	
PH-364	Schleicher Ka 6E Rhönsegler	4171	
PH-365-SE	Schleicher Ka 6E Rhönsegler	4172	
PH-367	Schleicher ASK 13	13063	
PH-370	Schleicher K 8B	8678	
PH-372-3	Schleicher K 8B	8680	
PH-374-PA	Schleicher Ka 6CR Rhönsegler	6568	
PH-375	Brockmeier/Schleicher Rhönlerche II	3078/Br	
PH-378-61	Schleicher Ka 6E Rhönsegler	4067	
PH-379-SL	Schleicher Ka 6CR Rhönsegler	6569	
PH-380-KB	Schleicher K 8B	8600/A	
PH-381-KZ	Schleicher Ka 6CR Rhönsegler	6511/A	
PH-382	Schleicher K 8B	8752	
PH-384-C1	NV Vliegtuigbouw Sagitta 013	005	
PH-385-22	Schleicher Ka 6E Rhönsegler	4242	
PH-386-ND	Schleicher ASK 13	13137	
PH-388	Schleicher K 7 Rhönadler	171/60	
PH-389	Schleicher K 8B	8767	
PH-394	Schleicher K 8B	8769	
PH-395-83	Schleicher Ka 6E Rhönsegler	4241	
PH-396-MN	Schleicher Ka 6E Rhönsegler	4251	
PH-397-NE	Schleicher Ka 6E Rhönsegler	4234	
PH-399	SZD-24 Foka 4A	W-349	
PH-401	Schleicher Ka 6E Rhönsegler	4179	
PH-403	NV Vliegtuigbouw Sagitta 013	21	
PH-404-30	Schleicher Ka 6E Rhönsegler	4236	
PH-405	Schleicher ASK 13	13199	
PH-406	Schleicher ASK 13	13414	
PH-407-79	Glasflügel H.205 Club Libelle	143	
PH-408-JV	Schleicher K 8B	8943	
PH-409	Schleicher ASK 13	13200	
PH-411	Schleicher ASK 13	13202	
PH-412-16	Schleicher Ka 6E Rhönsegler	4315	
PH-413-VE	Schleicher K 8B	8808	
PH-414	Schleicher K 8B	8809	
PH-415-V9	Schleicher K 8B	8810	
PH-416	Schleicher K 8B	8818	
PH-419	Schleicher ASK 13	13283	
PH-421	Schleicher K 8B	8838	
PH-423	Schleicher ASK 13	13284	
PH-425	Grob G.102 Astir CS Jeans	1154	

PH-429	Schleicher K 8B	8947	
PH-430-WP	SZD-30 Pirat	B-455	
PH-431	Schleicher ASK 13	13529	(PH-511)
PH-434-FE	Schleicher Ka 6E Rhönsegler	4387	
PH-435	Schleicher K 8B	8888	OO-ZNJ PH-435
PH-436	Schleicher ASK 13	13378	
PH-439-A7	Glasflügel H.206 Hornet	62	(PH-511)
PH-440-15	Glasflügel H.201B Standard Libelle	335	D-1089
PH-442-CEO	Schempp-Hirth CS.II Standard Cirrus	190	
PH-443	SZD-36A Cobra 15	W-568	
PH-444	Schleicher K 8B	8894	
PH-447	SZD-30 Pirat	B-466	
PH-448-92	Pilatus B4-PC11	025	
PH-449	Schleicher ASK 13	13413	
PH-450	SZD-36A Cobra 15	W-567	
PH-453	Schleicher ASK 13	13530	
PH-454-L4	Schleicher ASK 13	13442	
PH-455	Schleicher K 8B	8948	
PH-457	Schleicher ASK 13	13439	
PH-462	Schleicher ASK 13	13441	
PH-465-E1	Grob/Schempp-Hirth CS.II Standard Cirrus	156G	D-1100
PH-466-E2	Schleicher ASK 13	13460	
PH-468-31	Glasflügel H.201B Standard Libelle	522	
PH-473	Schempp-Hirth CS.II Standard Cirrus	524	
PH-474-43	Schleicher K 8B	8942	
PH-480-80	Schempp-Hirth CS.II Standard Cirrus	391	
PH-482-34	Glasflügel H.201B Standard Libelle	504	
PH-483-VT	Glasflügel H.201B Standard Libelle	526	
PH-485-00	Glasflügel H.201B Standard Libelle	366	
PH-490	Pilatus B4-PC11AF	124	PH-490
PH-492-55	Schleicher ASK 13	13467	
PH-493-66	Glasflügel H.201B Standard Libelle	503	
PH-494-S2	Schempp-Hirth CS.II Standard Cirrus	199	D-0883
PH-495-88	Schempp-Hirth CS.II Standard Cirrus	394	
PH-497	Schleicher ASK 13	13474	
PH-498-36	Siebert SIE 3	3025	
PH-499-13	Schempp-Hirth CS.II Standard Cirrus	430	
PH-501-T5	Schempp-Hirth CS.II Standard Cirrus	458	
PH-502-WW	Grob/Schempp-Hirth CS.II Standard Cirrus	424G	
PH-503-72	Glasflügel H.201B Standard Libelle	560	
PH-510-AG	Schleicher ASW 15B	15371	
PH-513-B2	Schleicher K 8B	8975	
PH-514-TX	Pilatus B4-PC11AF	178	
PH-515	Schleicher ASW 15B	15391	
PH-516	Schleicher ASK 13	13499	
PH-517	Schleicher K 8C	81003	
PH-521	Schleicher ASK 13	13498	
PH-522-52	Siebert SIE 3	3027	
PH-523	Pilatus B4-PC11AF	126	
PH-526-ME	Glasflügel H.205 Club Libelle	110	
PH-527-RA	Glasflügel H.205 Club Libelle	109	
PH-528-68	Schleicher ASW 15B	15442	
PH-530-12	Schleicher ASW 15B	15443	
PH-531	Pilatus B4-PC11AF	207	
PH-536-A1	Schempp-Hirth CS.II Standard Cirrus	655	
PH-538-JA	Schleicher ASW 19	19089	(PH-567)
PH-539-DL	Glaser-Dirks DG-100 Elan	58	
PH-544	Grob G.102 Astir CS	1192	
PH-547	Grob G.102 Astir CS	1267	
PH-548	Grob G.102 Astir CS	1354	
PH-550-LS	Rolladen-Schneider LS3	3023	(PH-600) D-7913
PH-554-MK	Grob G.102 Astir CS	1442	
PH-556-E5	Grob G.102 Astir CS	1386	
PH-557-R1	Grob G.102 Astir CS	1431	
PH-558-R2	Schleicher ASK 18	18045	(PH-533)
PH-561-FB	Grob G.102 Astir CS	1451	
PH-563-KK	Grob G.102 Astir CS	1407	
PH-564-KP	Rolladen-Schneider LS3	3139	
PH-565-KN	Schleicher ASW 19	19094	
PH-567-TP	Grob G.102 Astir CS	1462	
PH-568-K1	Grob G.102 Astir CS	1491	
PH-577-NC	Rolladen-Schneider LS3	3138	
PH-580-D1	Schleicher ASW 19	19129	
PH-582-78	Schleicher ASW 19B	19135	
PH-583-WB	Schleicher ASW 19B	19142	
PH-585-BS	Rolladen-Schneider LS3	3159	
PH-586-MA	Rolladen-Schneider LS3	3141	
PH-588-BU	Schempp-Hirth HS.7 Mini-Nimbus	39	(PH-585)
PH-592-BL	Grob G.102 Astir CS Jeans	2051	
PH-594	Schempp-Hirth HS.7 Mini-Nimbus	49	
PH-595-HV	Schempp-Hirth Janus B	60	D-7352
PH-598	Rolladen-Schneider LS3	3231	
PH-607-38	Schempp-Hirth HS.7 Mini-Nimbus B	63	(PH-606)
PH-609-VC	Grob G.102 Astir CS Jeans	2131	
PH-611-BR	Rolladen-Schneider LS3A	3177	
PH-615-BY	Rolladen-Schneider LS3	3085	(PH-605) D-2823
PH-618-E3	Grob G.102 Astir CS 77	1728	
PH-619-56	Grob G.102 Astir CS Jeans	2138	
PH-620	Eiri PIK-20D	20625	
PH-621-V4	Eiri PIK-20D	20626	
PH-626	Sportavia-Pützer RF-5B Sperber	51072	(D-KMPH)
PH-628-R6	Glasflügel H.303 Mosquito B	130	
PH-630-LB	Eiri PIK-20E	20211	
PH-631-RS	Rolladen-Schneider LS3A	3180	D-6944
PH-632-PF	Grob G.102 Astir CS 77	1749	
PH-636-AL	Schleicher ASW 20	20111	
PH-637-KL	Schleicher ASW 20	20122	
PH-641	Scheibe SF-25C Falke	44122	PH-ART D-KACJ
PH-642	Eiri PIK-20D	20642	
PH-643-B6	Glasflügel H.303 Mosquito B	146	
PH-644	Valentin Mistral C	MC 018/79	(PH-616)
PH-647-A9	Glasflügel H.303 Mosquito B	150	
PH-649-VA	Rolladen-Schneider LS3A	3235	D-2483
PH-650-HM	Rolladen-Schneider LS3A	3234	D-3919
PH-652-DE	Rolladen-Schneider LS3A	3167	D-5902
PH-653	Eiri PIK-20D	20656	
PH-654-CM	Rolladen-Schneider LS3A	3140	D-2842
PH-656-KT	Eiri PIK-20D	20658	
PH-661-SV	Eiri PIK-20D	20655	
PH-662	Sportavia-Pützer RF-5B Sperber	51059	(D-KKOB) EC-CUQ D-KKOB
PH-664	Schleicher ASK 13 (Rebuiltd of PH-376 with fuselage no.1582)	1582	
PH-666-PK	Eiri PIK-20D	20659	(PH-656)
PH-668-PG	Rolladen-Schneider LS3A	3310	D-4285
PH-669	Grob G.102 Astir CS Jeans	2198	
PH-673-GP	Rolladen-Schneider LS3A	3382	D-3188
PH-676	Scheibe SF-25E Super Falke	4352	(D-KDGQ)
PH-678	Scheibe SF-25C Falke	44291	D-KDGT
PH-681-R7	Schleicher ASW 20L	20251	
PH-682	Schleicher ASK 21	21003	
PH-683	Sportavia-Pützer RF-5B Sperber	51054	D-KITT
PH-685-VB	Rolladen-Schneider LS3-17	3387	
PH-686	Schleicher ASK 21	21019	
PH-687	Schleicher ASK 21	21052	
PH-688-VL	Schleicher ASK 21	21020	
PH-690-W9	Rolladen-Schneider LS3-17	3388	D-3546
PH-691	Rolladen-Schneider LS3A	3389	D-6940
PH-692-ML	Schleicher ASW 20L	20328	
PH-693-DR	Eiri PIK-20E	20271	(PH-694)
PH-697	Grob G.103 Twin Astir II	3577	
PH-698-HA	Rolladen-Schneider LS4	4004	D-6577
PH-699-DK	Glaser-Dirks DG-200/17C	2-138/CL10	D-7267
PH-701-ZT	Glaser-Dirks DG-100G Elan	E46-G25	
PH-708-MB	Grob G.103 Twin Astir II	3646	
PH-710	Grob G.109	6045	D-KGRO
PH-712-T4	Schleicher ASK 21	21087	
PH-713	Schleicher ASK 21	21075	
PH-714-YY	Schleicher ASK 21	21093	
PH-715-KM	Rolladen-Schneider LS4	4114	D-0245
PH-718	Grob G.103 Twin Astir II	3696	
PH-721-E4	Schleicher ASK 21	21109	
PH-723-NV	Glaser-Dirks DG-400	4-33	
PH-725	Scheibe SF-25C Club Falke	44334	D-KOOZ
PH-726	Grob G.102 Club Astir IIIb	5588 CB	D-6192
PH-727-SA	Centrair 101A Pégase	101-061	
PH-728	Sportavia-Pützer RF-5B Sperber	51014	OO-PIL D-KCIM
PH-730	Grob G.102 Club Astir IIIb	5609 CB	BGA3226/FFM PH-730
PH-731-WY	Centrair 101A Pégase	101-074	
PH-733-NF	Schleicher ASK 21	21185	
PH-734	Olympia Meise	16	D-5444 OE-0455
PH-735-TH	Schleicher ASW 19B	19314	D-7615
PH-737-FF	Schleicher ASW 20CL	20741	
PH-739-RR	Schempp-Hirth Ventus b/16.6	186	
PH-740	Rolladen-Schneider LS4	4380	D-6924
PH-742-FJ	Glaser-Dirks DG-400	4-84	(D-KLRS)
PH-743-FT	Glaser-Dirks DG-300 Elan	3E-35	
PH-745	Grob G.109B	6299	
PH-746	Grob G.109B	6315	
PH-751-FK	Grob G.103 Twin II Acro	33941K-K-174	
PH-752-MT	Glaser-Dirks DG-300 Elan	3E-80	
PH-753	Schleicher ASK 21	21255	
PH-754-YX	Schleicher ASW 19B	19118	D-7556
PH-755-RC	Schleicher ASK 23B	23024	
PH-756-DT	Schempp-Hirth Discus b	29	
PH-757-JH	Rolladen-Schneider LS3A	3249	D-2850
PH-758-AM	Rolladen-Schneider LS6	6017	D-3466
PH-759-V5	Schleicher ASK 21	21261	
PH-760-CF	Schleicher ASK 23B	23032	
PH-762	Schelicher K.8B	547	D-1590
PH-764-T7	Schleicher ASK 23B	23035	
PH-765-HS	Schleicher ASK 23B	23039	
PH-766-ZE	Schleicher ASK 23B	23030	
PH-767-EA	Schleicher ASK 23B	23043	
PH-768-PW	Glaser-Dirks DG-300 Elan	3E-110	
PH-769	Schleicher ASK 23B	23041	
PH-770-E7	Schleicher ASK 23B	23042	
PH-774-74	Schleicher ASK 23B	23048	
PH-775-75	Schleicher ASK 23B	23049	
PH-776-AH	Glaser-Dirks DG-300 Elan	3E-130	
PH-777	Schempp-Hirth Discus b	146	D-3906 PH-777
PH-778-YD	Rolladen-Schneider LS4	4532	D-3483
PH-781	Scheibe SFS-31 Milan	6609	OE-9041 (D-KAGT)
PH-782-NK	Schleicher ASK 23B	23052	

PH-784	Glaser-Dirks DG-300 Elan	3E-160	
PH-785-WF	Rolladen-Schneider LS6	6068	D-1505
PH-786-AV	Rolladen-Schneider LS4	4569	D-3539
PH-790-HG	Rolladen-Schneider LS4	4579	(PH-786)
			D-3613
PH-791	Schleicher ASK 13	13238	OH-395
			OH-KKR
PH-794	Rolladen-Schneider LS4	4177	D-3503
PH-795-SP	Centrair 101A Pégase	101A-0260	
PH-798	Schleicher ASK 23B	23077	
PH-799	Slingsby T-21B Sedbergh	613	WB946
PH-800-LL	Schempp-Hirth Ventus c	304	
PH-802	Rolladen-Schneider LS4	4599	D-5265
PH-803	Schleicher ASW 20L	20392	D-8833
PH-806-AX	Schempp-Hirth Discus b	86	D-5242
PH-807	Caudron C.800	10008/348	F-CAAK
PH-808	Grob G.103A Twin II Acro	34043-K-274	D-6405
PH-809-E8	Schleicher ASK 23B	23094	
PH-810-DH	Schleicher ASK 23B	23093	
PH-812	Grob G.103 Twin Astir	3003	D-7476
PH-813	Schleicher ASK 23B	23095	
PH-814	Raab Doppelraab V	1	D-1177
PH-817	Schleicher ASK 23B	23096	
PH-818	Scheibe SF-25B Falke	4629	D-KIMO
			(D-KIMG)
			(D-KIMA)
PH-819	Grob G.103T Twin Astir Trainer	3190-T-21	F-CFBY
PH-820	Grob G.102 Astir CS	1518	D-7454
PH-821	Schleicher K 7 Rhönadler	864	D-5804
PH-822	Schleicher K 7 Rhönadler	7150	D-5397
PH-823	Schempp-Hirth Ventus b/16.6	70	D-3048
PH-824	Glaser-Dirks DG-300 Elan	3E-258	
PH-825	Scheibe L-Spatz 55	688	D-1690
PH-826	Scheibe SF-25B Falke	4812	D-KBAU
PH-827	Slingsby T-43 Skylark 3B	1027	BGA739/AXH
PH-829	Schleicher ASK 23B	23103	
PH-830	Glaser-Dirks DG-300 Elan	3E-275	
PH-831	Glaser-Dirks DG-400	4-222	(D-KIDG)
PH-834-DG	Glaser-Dirks DG-600/18	6-15	
PH-835	Grob G.109	6035	OO-PRZ
			D-KGRO
PH-837	Glaser-Dirks DG-600/18	6-19	
PH-838	Scheibe L-Spatz 55	763	D-5922
PH-842	Schleicher K 7 Rhönadler	1085	D-5133
PH-843	Schleicher ASK 23B	23107	
PH-844-HY	Schleicher ASK 21	21382	
PH-846-TU	Schempp-Hirth Janus C	138	N19WK
PH-847	Rolladen-Schneider LS4a	4161	D-3571
PH-849	Rolladen-Schneider LS3	3040	D-2806
PH-850-AM	Rolladen-Schneider LS7 WL	7005	D-1257
PH-852	Schleicher ASW 19B	19226	D-2690
PH-853	Scheibe SF-25C Falke	44229	D-KDCA
PH-856	Schleicher Ka 6CR Rhönsegler	6130/Si	D-1899
PH-857	Glasflügel H303 Mosquito B	186	D-2558
PH-858	Schempp-Hirth Ventus cM	44/484	
PH-859	Rolladen-Schneider LS4	4736	D-1361
PH-860	Schleicher ASK 23B	23112	
PH-861	Rolladen-Schneider LS7.WL	7007	D-1264
PH-865	Schleicher ASK 21	21419	
PH-867-TE	Schleicher ASK 21	21420	
PH-868	Rolladen-Schneider LS6a	6066	D-1497
PH-869	Glaser-Dirks DG-100G Elan	E70G45	OO-ZZE
PH-870	Schleicher Ka 6CR Rhönsegler	6172	D-7041
PH-871	Rolladen-Schneider LS3A	3379	D-5899
PH-872-SW	Schempp-Hirth Ventus cT	140/430	
PH-874-SH	Schleicher Ka 6BR-PE Rhönsegler	341	D-3226
PH-875	Schempp-Hirth Discus bT	13/296	
PH-876	SZD-51-1 Junior	B-1845	(PH-874)
PH-878	Rolladen-Schneider LS4	4769	D-9031
PH-879	Rolladen-Schneider LS3-17	3402	D-6775
PH-880	Schleicher Ka 2B Rhönschwalbe	171	D-5457
PH-881-MH	Schleicher ASK 21	21436	
PH-882	Schleicher ASK 23B	23113	
PH-884	Glaser-Dirks DG-200/17	2-132/1731	D-6544
PH-885	Slingsby T-38 Grasshopper T.Mk.1	754	WZ758
PH-888	Rolladen-Schneider LS4A	4771	D-9033
PH-889	Rolladen-Schneider LS6B	6105	D-1179
PH-890	Hoffmann H-36 Dimona	3517	TF-SKI
PH-891	Schempp-Hirth Ventus cM	23/454	
PH-892	Glaser-Dirks DG-300 Elan	3E-371	
PH-893	Glaser-Dirks DG-300 Elan	3E-370	
PH-894	Schempp-Hirth Mini-Nimbus	60	D-6444
			(PH-606)
PH-895	Technoflug Piccolo	045	D-KGTA
PH-897	Scheibe SF-25C Falke	4405	D-KAAN
PH-898	Glaser-Dirks DG-600	6-46	
PH-899	Schleicher Ka 2B Rhönschwalbe	242	(PH-900)
			D-8562
PH-901	Rolladen-Schneider LS4A	4801	D-0579
PH-902-FI	Rolladen-Schneider LS7.WL	7110	D-1509
PH-903	Grob G.102 Astir CS Jeans	2074	D-7587
PH-904	Grob G.103 Twin III Acro	34155	
PH-905	Rolladen-Schneider LS4A	4795	D-0564
PH-907	Schleicher ASW 20CL	20806	D-3547
PH-908	Schleicher ASK 18	18037	D-4539
PH-909	Rolladen-Schneider LS6C	6203	
PH-911	Slingsby T-21B Sedbergh	1207	BGA1705/CPT
			RAFGSA251
			BGA878
PH-912	Sportavia RF-5B Sperber	51078	D-KECE(2)
PH-914-BY	Rolladen-Schneider LS6C	6210	(PH-838)
			(PH-913)
PH-915	Rolladen-Schneider LS7 WL	7123	
PH-916	SZD-48-3 Jantar Standard 3	B-1958	
PH-919	Schleicher Ka 2B Rhönschwalbe	186	OO-ZWO
			D-5460
PH-920	SZD-51-1 Junior	B-1934	
PH-921	Eiri PIK-20D	20582	D-6694
PH-922	Schleicher Ka 6CR Rhönsegler	6558Si	D-5830
PH-923-R9	Glaser-Dirks DG-300 Elan	3E-392	
PH-924	Rolladen-Schneider LS6C/17.5	6211	
PH-928	Rolladen-Schneider LS4A	4827	D-3529
PH-929-V7	Schleicher ASK 23B	23127	
PH-931-NR	Rolladen-Schneider LS6C/18W	6231	
PH-932-AY	Rolladen-Schneider LS6C/17.5	6212	D-6420
PH-934	SZD-51-1 Junior	B-1994	
PH-935	Grob G.103 Twin Astir	3087	D-3948
PH-936	Rolladen-Schneider LS4A	4843	D-3587
PH-937	Glaser-Dirks DG-400	4-200	D-KCDG
PH-940	Slingsby T-61F Venture	1872	XZ552
PH-942	Schempp-Hirth Discus bT	73/401	N43573
PH-944	Scheibe SF-25C Falke	44520	D-KIOJ(4)
PH-945	Sportavia-Pützer RF-5B Sperber	51038	D-KFAG
			(D-KEAU)
PH-946-XX	Rolladen-Schneider LS6C	6247	D-2527
PH-949	Bölkow Phönix T	403	(PH-900)
			OO-ZQD
			D-0738
			HB-746
			D-8354
PH-951	Rolladen-Schneider LS4B	4861	
PH-952-HZ	Schleicher ASK 21	21529	
PH-953	Schleicher ASH 25E	25037	D-4904
PH-954	Grob G.103C Twin IIISL	35009	D-KOIC(2)
PH-955	Rolladen-Schneider LS6A	6053	D-8991
PH-956	Schleicher ASW 20BL	20643	D-5342
			OE-5342
PH-957	SZD-51-1 Junior	B-2005	(PH-953)
PH-958	Schleicher K 7 Rhönadler	499	D-8309
PH-959	Schempp-Hirth Ventus cT	167/545	
PH-961	Schempp-Hirth Discus CS	074CS	
PH-962	Rolladen-Schneider LS6C	6259	D-2572
PH-963	Glasflügel H303 Mosquito B	160	D-6463
PH-964-3F	Glaser-Dirks DG-600/18	6-102S57	D-3120
PH-966	Schleicher K 7 Rhönadler	7190	D-3626
PH-967	Schleicher Ka 6E	4175/A37	D-4735
PH-968	Glaser-Dirks DG-300 Elan	3E-215	D-4594
PH-970	Grob G.109	6021	OO-GRB
			F-CFOA
			D-KGRO
PH-973-T6	Glaser-Dirks DG-500 Elan Trainer	5E-75T31	
PH-974	Rolladen-Schneider LS4B	4894	
PH-975	Schleicher ASK 21	21565	
PH-976	SZD-51-1 Junior	B-2015	
PH-977	Rolladen-Schneider LS4B	4897	
PH-980	SZD-51-1 Junior	B-2017	
PH-982-KE	Rolladen-Schneider LS4A	4529	D-3486
PH-983-BD	Glaser-Dirks DG-500M	5E-85M36	
PH-984	Schempp-Hirth Janus C	242	BGA3333/FKY
PH-985	Scheibe SF-25D Falke	4649D	(PH-984)
			D-KDVL
			(D-KEBH)
PH-987-KN	Rolladen-Schneider LS4A	4612	D-0205
PH-988	Rolladen-Schneider LS6C/18	6223	D-4199
PH-989	Rolladen-Schneider LS4B	4919	
PH-992	SZD-36A Cobra 15	W-660	OY-VXL
PH-994	Glaser-Dirks DG-400	4-16	D-KAIC(2)
PH-995	Scheibe SF-25D Falke	4640D	D-KOHH
			(D-KEDC)
PH-997	Schleicher ASW 24	24019	BGA3966/HHV
			RAFGSA-R19
PH-998	Schleicher ASW 19B	19390	(PH-1001)
			(PH-998)
			D-8710
PH-999	Bölkow FS.24 Phönix T	408	D-8411
PH-1001	Grob G.103C Twin III Acro	34187	
PH-1002	Schleicher Ka 2B Rhönschwalbe	79/55	OO-ZQC
			PL-12
PH-1003	Glaser-Dirks DG-400	4-11	D-KLAA
PH-1004	Grob G.103 Twin Astir I	3067	D-4853
PH-1005	Schleicher K 7 Rhönadler	5	D-1942
PH-1006	SZD-51-1 Junior	B-2129	
PH-1007	Schleicher K 7 Rhönadler	7037A	D-6029
PH-1009	Rolladen-Schneider LS4B	4923	
PH-1010	Glaser-Dirks DG-500M	5E-105M48	
PH-1011-FR	Schempp-Hirth Discus bT	133/506	
PH-1013-TV	Schleicher ASK 13	13636	BGA3987/HJS
			RAFGGA 502
PH-1014	Schempp-Hirth HS.4 Standard Cirrus	269	OO-ZVW
			D-1982
PH-1015	SZD-51-1 Junior	B-2131	
PH-1016	Rolladen-Schneider LS4B	4927	
PH-1017	Rolladen-Schneider LS3	3094	HB-1360

PH-1018	Schleicher ASK 21	21605	
PH-1019	Schleicher ASW 24	24206	D-7217
PH-1020	Rolladen-Schneider LS6C	6215	D-5458
			OH-793
PH-1021	Schleicher K 7 Rhönadler	648	OO-ZYI
			D-5730
PH-1022	Scheibe Bergfalke II/55	355	D-9066
PH-1023	SZD-51-1 Junior	B-2134	
PH-1024	SZD-50-3 Puchacz	B-2089	(SP-4147)
PH-1025	Schempp-Hirth Discus CS	165CS	
PH-1027-LY	Rolladen-Schneider LS4	4575	D-3604
PH-1028	Rolladen-Schneider LS4B	4939	
PH-1029	Schempp-Hirth Discus bT	145/523	
PH-1031	Rolladen-Schneider LS6C	6242	(PH-1013)
			BGA3813/HBN
			D-6116
PH-1032	Brditschka HB-23/2400SP Hobbyliner	23046	OE-9332
			D-KSCV
PH-1033	Glaser-Dirks DG-300 Elan	3E-38	HB-1734
PH-1034	Hoffmann H-36 Dimona	3684	D-KERI
PH-1035-SAL	Schempp-Hirth Duo Discus	023	
PH-1037	Glaser-Dirks DG-800S	8-44S13	D-0037
PH-1038	Grob G.102 Astir CS Jeans	2193	D-3816
PH-1039	Schleicher K 7 Rhönadler	503	D-6247
PH-1040	LET L-13SEH Vivat	900401	D-KIIP
			OK-0104
			D-KPPP
			OK-0104
PH-1041	PZL PW-5 Smyk	17.02.005	
PH-1042-CU	PZL PW-5 Smyk	17.02.003	
PH-1043	Schempp-Hirth Discus CS	186CS	
PH-1045	Slingsby T.21B Sedbergh	1214	BGA884/BDK
PH-1046	Glaser-Dirks DG-500M	5E-141M55	(PH-1045)
PH-1047-SM	Rolladen-Schneider LS8A	8022	D-2285
PH-1050-JE	Schleicher ASW 24	24041	D-6252
PH-1051	SZD-51-1 Junior	B-2146	
PH-1052-ZB	SZD-51-1 Junior	B-2147	
PH-1053	Rolladen-Schneider LS4B	4984	
PH-1056	Schleicher ASW 19B	19105	D-3859
PH-1057-DX	Schempp-Hirth Duo-Discus	47	
PH-1058	Schempp-Hirth Discus CS	061CS	D-4111
PH-1059	Schleicher Ka 6CR Rhönsegler	328	D-8951
			HB-801
PH-1060	Schleicher ASH 26E	26064	(PH-1111)
			D-KBEB(2)
PH-1064	Grob G.102 Astir CS	1307	D-7349
PH-1066	Grob G.102 Astir CS	1439	D-7429
PH-1067-EH	Schempp-Hirth Duo Discus	60	
PH-1068	Grob G.103 Twin Astir I	3028	D-2555
PH-1070	Schleicher K 7 Rhönadler	7156	D-5492
PH-1071-XB	Schempp-Hirth Janus CM	12/177	XB-EJP
PH-1072	Glaser-Dirks DG-500 Elan Orion	5E-153X10	D-1491
PH-1073	Scheibe SF-25C Falke	44602	D-KTIW
PH-1074	Rolladen-Schneider LS8A	8050	D-3693
PH-1075	Schempp-Hirth Ventus 2a	28	
PH-1076	Schempp-Hirth Discus CS	141CS	D-4295
PH-1078-HJ	Schempp-Hirth Janus C	188	D-7719
PH-1079	Rolladen-Schneider LS4A	4426	D-4542
PH-1080	Rolladen-Schneider LS8A	8065	
PH-1082	Glaser-Dirks DG-500/22	5E-35S7	D-5219
PH-1083	Rolladen-Schneider LS4A	4291	D-8190
PH-1084	Schleicher ASK 13	13363	D-0857
PH-1085	Schleicher Ka 6CR Rhönsegler	1038	OO-ZFJ
			D-9151
PH-1086	Grob G.102 Astir CS Jeans	2173	D-7755
PH-1091	Marganski MDM-1 Fox	213	
PH-1092	Grob G.103 Twin II	3547	D-2921
PH-1093	Schempp-Hirth Discus CS	230CS	
PH-1094	Schleicher ASW 27	27032	
PH-1095	Grob G.103 Twin Astir	3056	D-4846
PH-1096	Rolladen-Schneider LS8A	8105	
PH-1097-KIM	Schleicher ASK 21	21648	
PH-1098	Glaser-Dirks DG-400	4-29	D-KDAU
PH-1099	Schempp-Hirth Duo Discus	119	
PH-1100	Glaser-Dirks DG-800B	8-81B18	(PH-1097)
			D-KDIL
PH-1101	HOAC HK-36TC Super Dimona	36520	
PH-1103	Schempp-Hirth Ventus cT	134/414	D-KCMB
PH-1105	SZD-50-3 Puchacz	B-2107	
PH-1106	Grob G.109B	6429	D-KHGJ
PH-1107	Schempp-Hirth Ventus 2cM	30/53	D-KTLL
PH-1108	Glaser-Dirks DG-505/20 Elan	5E-170W8	
PH-1109	Glaser-Dirks DG-800B	8-97B32	D-KMAF
PH-1111-CC	Schempp-Hirth Ventus 2cT	17/66	
PH-1112	Schempp-Hirth Janus CT	9/264	D-KEAR(3)
PH-1113	Schleicher ASW 24	24079	D-9021
PH-1114	HOAC HK-36TC Super Dimona	36527	
PH-1115	Grob G.103 Twin Astir	3006	D-7479
PH-1116	SZD-50-3 Puchacz	B-2113	
PH-1117	Rolladen-Schneider LS3A	3295	D-4583
PH-1118	Schempp-Hirth Ventus cT	180/596	LX-CCC
PH-1119	Schempp-Hirth Duo Discus	157	
PH-1120	Schempp-Hirth Nimbus 4 DM	28/42	
PH-1121	Slingsby T.31B Cadet III	PFA/42-11827/ 712	(PH-1120)
	(Converted to Motor Cadet)		G-BSHM
			BGA3289/FJC
			WT917
PH-1122	Schleicher ASK 13	13445	D-2991
PH-1123	Rolladen-Schneider LS8A	8179	
PH-1124	Schleicher ASK 23B	23148	
PH-1125	Scheibe Bergfalke II/55	342	D-8870
PH-1126	Caproni-Vizzola A.21s Calif	250	I- IVCA
PH-1130	Schleicher Ka 6E	4014	D-5204
PH-1131-LR	Schleicher ASW 27	27081	
PH-1133	HOAC HK-36TC Super Dimona	36528	
PH-1134	Grob G.103C Twin III Acro	34146	D-5531
PH-1135	Hoffman HK-36R Super Dimona	36394	HB-2259
PH-1136	Rolladen-Schneider LS6C-18	6252	D-6436
			SE-UKO
PH-1137	Schempp-Hirth Janus CM	4	D-KKDR
			(D-KJMC)
PH-1138	HOAC HK-36TTC Super Dimona	36592	
PH-1139	Siren C.30S Edelweiss	36	F-CDAQ
PH-1140	Schleicher ASW 15	15136	D-0763
PH-1142	Glasflügel H303 Mosquito	38	D-4452
PH-1143	Glasflügel H303B Mosquito	149	HB-1454
PH-1144	HOAC HK-36TC Super Dimona	36530	
PH-1145	Schleicher ASW 20	20495	D-6393
PH-1147	PZL PW-5 Smyk	17.12.001	
PH-1148	Schempp-Hirth Discus b	167	D-5579
PH-1149	Schempp-Hirth Janus CM	11	D-KHID
PH-1150	Rolladen-Schneider LS8-18	8233	D-4569
PH-1151	Grob G.103C Twin III Acro	34157	D-0659
PH-1152	Schempp-Hirth Ventus 2cM	62/123	
PH-1153	Schempp-Hirth Nimbus 4 DM	11/19	D-KWMA
PH-1154	Schempp-Hirth Ventus 2b	85	
PH-1156	Schleicher ASH 26	26146	
PH-1157	HOAC HK-36TC Super Dimona	36647	
PH-1159	Grob G.102 Club Astir IIIB	5646CB	D-3625
PH-1160	Schempp-Hirth Discus 2b	23	
PH-1161	Grob G.102 Club Astir IIIB	5591CB	D-4726
			D-6306
			ZK-GNF
PH-1162	Schempp-Hirth Discus CS	090CS	D-0279
PH-1163	Slingsby T.31B Cadet TX.III	678	WT868
	(Converted to Motor Cadet, c/n quoted as FF1383)		
PH-1165	Glaser-Dirks DG-300 Elan	3E-157	D-4718
PH-1166	Schempp-Hirth Ventus 2cM	83/ . . .	
PH-1167	Schempp-Hirth Discus bT WL	67/393	D-KSKI
PH-1168	SZD-50-3 Puchacz	B-2207	
PH-1169	Glaser-Dirks DG-800B	8-163B87	
PH-1170	Schempp-Hirth SHK-1	3	BGA1592/CJZ
			D-9349
PH-1171	Schempp-Hirth Duo Discus	219	
PH-1172	Rolladen-Schneider LS8-18	8261	D-0189
PH-1173	Rolladen-Schneider LS8A-18	8266	D-0207
PH-1174	Rolladen-Schneider LS4B	4892	D-2398
PH-1175-YA	Schempp-Hirth Ventus 2cM	74/155	
PH-1176	Glasflügel H401 Kestrel	77	D-1047
			HB-1047
PH-1177	SZD-9 bis Bocian 1E (Reservation 5.99)	P-463	OY-FVX
PH-1178-3W	Schleicher ASW 27B	27110	
PH-1179	Glaser-Dirks DG-400	4-177	I-KILF
			D-KILF
PH-1180	Schempp-Hirth Ventus 2cM	84/ . . .	
PH-1181	Grob G.103C Twin III Acro	34103	D-6868
PH-1184	Schempp-Hirth Discus bT	68/395	D-KKAX
PH-1185	Scheibe Sperber (Reservation 12.99)	820	D-1365
PH-1186	Scheibe SF-25C Falke	44181	D-KDEM
PH-1187	Schempp-Hirth Ventus c	531	D-3117
PH-1188	Neukom Elfe S4	67	HB-1164
PH-1189-4A	Rolladen-Schneider LS4B	4987	HB-3184
PH-1190	Grob G.103A Twin II Acro	3558-K-4	D-8749
PH-1192	Rolladen-Schneider LS3	3122	D-7747
PH-1193	HOAC HK-36TTC Super Dimona	36669	
PH-1194	Schempp-Hirth Discus bT	161/567	D-KBBK
PH-1195	Grob G.103 Twin II	3526	D-8751
PH-1196	Valentin Mistral C	MC015/78	D-4915
PH-1197	Rolladen-Schneider LS6C	6303	BGA3984/HJP
PH-1198	Schempp-Hirth Duo Discus T	12/258	D-KODX
PH-1199	Schempp-Hirth Duo Discus T	27/292	D-KHRC
PH-1201	Schempp-Hirth Janus A	06	OO-ZPI
			D-6496
PH-1202	Schleicher ASK 13	13209	D-3558
			RAFGGA.554
PH-1203	Slingsby T.59F Kestrel 19	1786	OO-ZDG
			BGA1682/CNU
PH-1205	HOAC HK-36TTC Super Dimona	36676	
PH-1206	Schleicher K 8B	8176	D-5292
PH-1207	Glaser-Dirks DG-505MB	5E-191MB6	
PH-1208	Scheibe Bergfalke III	5643	D-0577
PH-1209	HOAC HK-36TC Super Dimona	36679	
PH-1210	Schempp-Hirth Discus 2b	89	
PH-1211	Schempp-Hirth Duo Discus T	19/273	D-KMAF(3)
	(Converted from Duo Discus c/n 273, .01)		PH-1211
PH-1212	Grob G.103 Twin Astir Trainer	3139	D-7790
PH-1213	Schempp-Hirth Duo Discus	280	
PH-1214	Schleicher Ka 2 Rhönschwalbe	48	OY-XRD
			D-8757
PH-1215	Glaser-Dirks DG-505MB	5E-206MB10	
PH-1216-28	Schleicher ASW 28	28020	D-5829
PH-1217	Schleicher ASW 27	27157	
PH-1218-VV	Schempp-Hirth Ventus 2cT	69/...	
PH-1219	Rolladen-Schneider LS4B	41017	D-2830

PH-1220	Schleicher ASK 23B	23099	D-1547
PH-1221	HOAC HK-36TTC Super Dimona	36654	G-BYRL
PH-1222-3T	Schempp-Hirth Nimbus 3T	26/92	OO-ZTN
			(OO-ZJT)
PH-1223	Schleicher Ka 6E	4262	D-0160
PH-1224	HOAC HK-36TTC Super Dimona	36543	G-BXGI
			OE-UHK
PH-1225	Rolladen-Schneider LS4	4103	D-0477
PH-1226	SZD-51-1 Junior	B-1843	HB-1997
PH-1228	Grob G.103C Twin III SL	35020	D-KGHH
PH-1229	Glaser-Dirks DG-300 Elan	3E-263	D-0061
PH-1231	DGFlugzeugbau DG-800B	8-237B151	
PH-1232-FUN	Schempp-Hirth Discus 2T	7/106	D-KBDW(2)
PH-1233	Glasflügel H304	255	D-3032
PH-1234-CT	Schempp-Hirth Ventus 2cT	74/ . .	
PH-1235	Glaser-Dirks DG-200	2-32	D-6785
PH-1236	Grob G.102 Astir CS Jeans	2166	D-4562
PH-1237	Schleicher K 8B	8362	D-5424
PH-1238	LET L-13SEH Vivat	940520	D-KXYA
PH-1239	Schleicher K 7 Rhönadler	7109	D-1875
PH-1240	DGFlugzeugbau DG-800S	8-77S20	D-4568
PH-1241	Schempp-Hirth Ventus 2a	124	D-2908
PH-1243	Scheibe SF-25C Falke	44285	D-KDGE
PH-1244	Schleicher ASK 23B	23005	BGA4662/JPB
			AGA.18
PH-1245	DGFlugzeugbau DG-505 Elan Orion	5E-188X37	D-5058
PH-1247	Valentin Kiwi	3004	D-KBGH
PH-1248	Schempp-Hirth Discus 2T	16/131	D-KGBC
PH-1249	DG Flugzeugbau DG-800B	8-259B167	
PH-1250	Schleicher ASK 21	21058	D-2497
PH-1251	Schempp-Hirth Discus CS	015CS	D-8229
PH-1252-VZ	Schempp-Hirth Janus B	64	D-2727
PH-1253	Rolladen-Schneider LS4	4268	D-3501
PH-1254	Schempp-Hirth Ventus bT	284/69	BGA3204/FEP
PH-1255	Schleicher ASK 24E	24839	D-KAXO
PH-1256	Schempp-Hirth Duo Discus T	52/336	
PH-1257	Hoffman H-36 Dimona	3603	D-KENI
PH-1258	DGFlugzeugbau DG-505 Elan Orion	5E-234X72	
PH-1259	Glasflügel H304C	57C	
PH-1260	Schempp-Hirth Duo Discus T	63/352	
PH-1261	Glasflügel H205 Club Libelle	66	D-8205
			F-CEQA
PH-1262	Schempp-Hirth Nimbus 4 DM	49	
PH-1263	HOAC HK-36TTC Super Dimona	36711	
PH-1264-F8	Rolladen-Schneider LS8A	8450	
PH-1265-HS	Rolladen-Schneider LS4B	4758	D-1389
PH-1266	Schleicher K 8B	8039	D-0050
PH-1267	DG Flugzeugbau DG-500MB	5E-236B16	
PH-1268-BVO	Schempp-Hirth Discus CS	199CS	D-2887
PH-1269	Rolladen-Schneider LS3	3049	D-6657
PH-1270	Schleicher K 8B	8588/Gö	D-8623
PH-1271	Scheibe SF-25C Rotax-Falke	44542	D-KBFM
PH-1272	Schempp-Hirth Duo Discus T	62/351	
PH-1273	Rolladen-Schneider LS7WL	7147	D-3875
PH-1274	Rolladen-Schneider LS4B	4888	D-2293
PH-1275	Schempp-Hirth Nimbus 2	83	D-9666
			OE-5019
PH-1276-SAR	DG Flugzeugbau DG-1000S	10-18S18	
PH-1277	Rolladen-Schneider LS3A	3123	D-7749
PH-1278	Schempp-Hirth Discus bT	51/368	OE-9573
			OE-5573
			D-5404
PH-1280	Schleicher ASK 23B	23067	D-8385
PH-1282-HS	Rolladen-Schneider LS4B	4964	D-6375
PH-1283-4G	Schleicher ASK 21	21757	
PH-1284	Schleicher ASK 21	21206	D-5714
PH-1285	Grob/Schempp-Hirth CS.II Standard Cirrus	442G	D-3107
PH-1286	Schleicher ASW-24E	24802	D-KLTS
PH-1287	Schempp-Hirth Duo Discus T	86/400	
PH-1288	Schleicher ASK 13	13111	D-0078
PH-1289	Schempp-Hirth Discus CS	068CS	D-1546
PH-1290-KG	Schleicher ASK 21	21291	D-5422
PH-1291	Schempp-Hirth Nimbus 2B	134	D-7396
PH-1292-E6	Schleicher ASK 21	21768	
PH-1293	SZD-51-1 Junior	511.A.03.002	
PH-1294	DG Flugzeugbau DG-1000S	10-36S35	
PH-1295-7L	Schempp-Hirth Nimbus 3 DT	45	N567L
PH-1296-KY	Schleicher ASK 23B	23082	D-5350
PH-1297	Schleicher ASH 26E	26221	
PH-1298	Schleicher ASW 24	24021	D-3473
PH-1299-F1	Schempp-Hirth Ventus cT	137/421	BGA3472/FRT
PH-1300	Schempp-Hirth Duo Discus T	89/404	
PH-1301	DG Flugzeugbau DG-1000S	10-52S51	
PH-1302	Schempp-Hirth Ventus 2cT	16/63	D-KKRH
PH-1303	Rolladen-Schneider LS6C/18W	6371	BGA4760/JTD
			D-2571
PH-1304	Glaser-Dirks DG-400	4-27	G-DGDG
PH-1305	Glaser-Dirks DG-500M	5E82M34	F-CHJL
			D-KJRB
PH-1306	Schleicher ASK 21	21365	D-4732
PH-1307	Schleicher ASK 21	21458	D-3794
PH-1308	Schempp-Hirth Ventus 2cT	44/143	OY-NSX
			D-KISK
PH-1309	SZD-51-1 Junior	B-2019	D-8586
			SP-3583
PH-1310	Schempp-Hirth Ventus bT	45/237	D-KGEB
PH-1311	Schleicher ASK 21	21585	CX-COE
PH-1312	Rutan Solitair (Res. 5.04)	unkn	
PH-1313	Centrair 101B Pégase	101B0280	F-CGNY
PH-1314	Scheibe SF-25C Falke 1700	44195	D-KDAF
PH-1315	Eiri PIK-20B	20128C	SE-TVF
			OH-487
PH-1316	Schleicher ASW 20L	20415	OO-YYY
			OY-XKS
PH-1317	Schempp-Hirth Discus CS	311CS	
PH-1318	Schleicher Ka 2B Rhönschwalbe (CoA appl. 9.04)	01-62	OO-ZFA
			D-6143
PH-1319	Schempp-Hirth Discus CS	292CS	N431WA
PH-1320	Rolladen-Schneider LS4A	4675	D-0134
PH-1321	Schempp-Hirth Duo Discus T	39/314	D-KKFU
PH-1322	Schempp-Hirth Duo Discus T	117	
PH-1323	Schleicher ASW 28 (CoA appl. 11.04)	unkn	
PH-1324	Scheibe SF-25C Falke	44707	
PH-1325	Schempp-Hirth Discus b	214	OH-763
PH-1326	Glaser-Dirks DG-300 Elan	3E250	D-5290
PH-1327	Alpha AVO 68R Samburo	020	D-KLVS
PH-1328	Schempp-Hirth Discus-2 cT(CoA appl. 12.04)	unkn	
PH-1329	Grob G.102 Astir CS (CoA appl. 12.04)	1168	D-7293
PH-1330	Schempp-Hirth Nimbus 2 M	28	N21WK
			N80PR
PH-1331	Scheibe SF-25C Falke	4465	(PH-9067)
			OE-9067
			(D-KOAX)
PH-1332	Rolladen-Schneider LS8A	8092	D-4828
PH-1333	Schleicher ASH 25E	25129	D-KMKK
PH-1334	Schleicher ASK 21	21789	
PH-1335	Schleicher ASK 21	21790	
PH-1336	Glasflügel H.303 Mosquito	61	OY-XIF
PH-1337	Schleicher ASK 21	21629	PL40
PH-1338	SZD-51-1 Junior (CoA appl. 3.05)	unkn	
PH-1339	Schempp-Hirth Ventus cT (CoA appl. 3.05)	166/543	OO-YRZ
			OY-XRZ
			D-KNMA
PH-1343	Schleicher K 7 Rhönadler	7202	D-5698

MICROLIGHTS

PH-1G9	Eipper Quicksilver MXQ-II	1090	G-MMOS
			PH-1G9
			G-MMOS
PH-1J2	American Aerolights Eagle XL	E5444	
PH-1J8	Behlen Lloyd Ladas	RFD-8301	
PH-1K1	Continental Aerolights Eagle XL	300357	
PH-1K8	Skyin Sherpa II	141282/1036	
PH-1M1	Skyin Sherpa II	8311/1049	
PH-1M4	Firebird Sierra	333	
PH-1M5	Continental Aerolights Eagle CA	831102	
PH-1M8	Comco Ikarus Fox-D	84/0010	
PH-1M9	Skyin Sherpa II	8403/1053	
PH-1N5	Behlen Vampir IIM 14.2	RFD-84102	
PH-1P2	Continental Aerolights Eagle XL	84083102	
PH-1P5	Comco Ikarus Sherpa II	84 . .-1065	
PH-1P6	Comco Ikarus Sherpa II	8412-1086	
PH-1R1	Ultrasport Panther XL	870117	
PH-1R3	Continental Aerolights Eagle XL	85081015	
PH-1R4	Behlen Vampir IIM 14.2	1161951	
PH-1R7	Comco Ikarus Sherpa II	8602-1113	
PH-1S7	Aériane Sirocco	129	
PH-1S9	UPM Funplane 1	860013	
PH-1T1	Sky-Walker 1+1	26152	
PH-1T2	Comco Ikarus Fox-C22	8703-3061	
PH-1T4	Comco Ikarus Fox-D	8710-FD42	
PH-1T5	Comco Ikarus Fox-C22	8802-3118	
PH-1T6	Sky-Walker 1+1	038-153	
PH-1T7	NST Minimum Saphir 17M	M207/102355	
PH-1T9	UPM Funplane 1	870022	
PH-1U2	Sky Walker II	177	
PH-1U3	Aviasud Mistral	143	
PH-1U7	Sky Walker II	183	
PH-1U9	Sky Walker II	188	
PH-1V1	Fisher FP.202 Koala	NVAV-97	
PH-1V2	Comco Ikarus Fox-C22	8803-3123	
PH-1V4	Sky Walker II	204	
PH-1V5	Sky Walker II	206	
PH-1V6	UPM Omega/Lotus 18	880052	
PH-1V9	Comco Ikarus Fox-D	8811-FD45	
PH-1W3	HFL Stratos 300	008	
PH-1W4	Sky-Walker II	217	
PH-1W5	Comco Ikarus Fox-C22	8903-3192	
PH-1W6	Comco Sherpa II	8403-1057	D-MSKG
PH-1W7	Behlen Vampir II 14.2	89017	
PH-1W8	Behlen Vampir II 14.2	EA 89-02	
PH-1X2	Behlen Vampir II 14.2	EA 89-04	
PH-1X5	Behlen Vampir II 14.2	EA 89-07	
PH-1X6	Sky-Walker II	239	
PH-1Y2	Comco Ikarus Fox-C22	8908-3214	
PH-1Y3	Behlen Vampir IIM 14.2	S-88	
PH-1Y5	Behlen Vampir IIM 14.2	10/071/88/06	
PH-1Y6	Air Création Racer SX-12	952911	
PH-1Y9	Comco Ikarus Fox-C22	9002-3255	
PH-1Z1	Aériane Sirocco	89-103	

PH-1Z2	Aériane Sirocco	89-101	
PH-1Z3	Aériane Sirocco	89-102	
PH-1Z4	UPM Omega Lotus 18	900086	
PH-1Z5	Murphy Renegade Spirit	214/PFA/188-11423	G-MVSF
PH-1Z7	Sky-Walker II	273	
PH-2A1	Solar Wings Pegasus Quasar [MAT"4"]	SW-WQQ-0373/SW-TQ-0036	
PH-2A2	Solar Wings Pegasus Quasar [MAT"2"]	SW-WQQ-0376/SW-TQ-0039	
PH-2A3	Solar Wings Pegasus Quasar [MAT"3"]	SW-WQQ-0375/SW-TQ-0038	
PH-2A8	Solar Wings Pegasus Quasar	SW-WQQ-0380/SW-TQ-0041	
	(c/n officially quoted as 0034)		
PH-2B3	Comco Ikarus Fox-C22	9007-3273	
PH-2B4	Comco Ikarus Fox-C22	9007-3274	
PH-2B6	Air Création Racer SX-12	262561	
PH-2C1	Behlen Vampir IIM 14.2	90029	
PH-2C2	Konsuprod Moskito 1b	90008	
PH-2C3	Air Création Racer SX 12	262562	
PH-2C5	NST Minimum Magic IV-177	LF90-01	
PH-2C6	NST Minimum Magic IV-177	LF90-02	
PH-2C7	NST Minimum Saphir 17M	LF90-03	D-MHOF
PH-2D1	Sky-Walker II	320	
PH-2D2	Comco Ikarus Fox C-22	9009-3286	
PH-2D7	Platzer Kiebitz B	58	D-MHRM
PH-2D8	Cosmos BI 90	576	
PH-2E2	Solar Wings Pegasus XL-Q	SW-WQ-0417/SW-TE-0311	
PH-2E5	Cosmos BI 90	604	
PH-2E6	Light Aero Avid Flyer	442	D-MIPS
PH-2E8	Light Aero Avid Flyer (CoA appl. 9.04)	942	
PH-2E9	Solar Wings Pegasus XL-Q	SW-WQ-0441/SW-TE-0320	
PH-2F2	Cosmos BI 90	638	
PH-2F4	Comco Ikarus Fox-C22	9108-3367	
PH-2F5	Comco Ikarus Fox-C22	9109-3368	
PH-2F6	Aviasud Mistral	152	
PH-2F7	Aviasud Mistral	154	
PH-2F8	Cosmos BI 90	669	
PH-2G1	Comco Ikarus Fox-C22	9110-3371	
PH-2G3	Solar Wings Pegasus Quasar II	SW-WQT-0466/SW-TQC-0072	
PH-2G4	Tandem Air Sunny	28-92	
PH-2G5	Sky-Walker II	324	
PH-2G7	NST Minimum Magic IV-177	LF39-28	
PH-2H1	Comco Ikarus Fox-C22	9207-3439	
PH-2H6	UPM-Cobra/Raven 15	920118	
PH-2H7	Light Aero Avid Flyer	1137D	
PH-2J2	Rans S-12 Airaile	0692234	
PH-2J3	Rans S-12 Airaile (CoA appl. 12.04)	0692231	
PH-2J6	Solar Wings Pegasus XL-Q /Quasar	SW-WQT-0555/SW-TE-0412	
PH-2J7	Solar Wings Pegasus XL-Q /Quasar	SW-WQT-0559/SW-TE-0424	
PH-2J9	Solar Wings Pegasus XL-Q /Quasar	SW-WQT-0561/SW-TE-0426	
PH-2K1	Solar Wings Pegasus XL-Q /Quasar	SW-WQT-0562/SW-TE-0427	
PH-2K2	Comco Ikarus Fox-C22	9302-3490	
PH-2K3	Comco Ikarus Fox-C22	9303-3502	
PH-2K4	Cosmos BI 90	0380	
PH-2K5	Solar Wings Pegasus Quasar IITC	SW-WX-0019/SW-TQ-0061	G-65-7
	(Rotax 582/40) prototype [MAT"5"]		
PH-2K6	Comco Ikarus Fox-C22	9303-3503	
PH-2K7	Sky-Walker II	201	D-MOBO
PH-2K8	Fisher FP.202 Koala	400	
PH-2K9	Light Aero Avid Flyer	1275D	
PH-2L1	Solar Wings Pegasus XL-Q / Quasar	SW-WQT-0578/SW-TE-0435	
PH-2L5	Aviasud AE-209 Albatros	30	
PH-2L6	Aviasud AE-209 Albatros	34	
PH-2L7	Comco Ikarus Fox-C22	9306-3527	
PH-2L8	Rodaro Storch	ST11004304	
PH-2L9	Aviasud AE-209 Albatros	03	83-EV
PH-2M1	Solar Wings Pegasus Q-462	6563	
PH-2M2	Pioneer Flightstar	680	D-MAUR
PH-2M3	Aviasud Mistral	153	
PH-2M9	Take Off Merlin	G20793	
PH-2N1	Cosmos BI 90	1000	
PH-2N2	Cosmos BI 90	959	
PH-2N3	Solar Wings Pegasus Quantum 15	6609	G-65-10
	(This c/n quoted for G-MYLE, reference also made to c/n 6669 and to SW WX 0021. The pi was allocated to a Chaser export) G-65-10 is connected to G-MYLE !)		
PH-2N4	UPM-Cobra/Raven 15	930125	
PH-2N7	Air Création Mild GT-582ES	N4171753	
PH-2N9	Comco Ikarus Fox-C22	9406-3570	
PH-2P3	Aviasud AE-209 Albatros	62	
PH-2P4	Aviasud AE-209 Albatros	65	
PH-2P5	Aviasud AE-209 Albatros	63	
PH-2P6	Cosmos Chronos BI 90	21034	
PH-2P7	Comco Ikarus Fox-C22	9404-3580	
PH-2R1	Light Aero Avid Flyer IV	1428D	
PH-2R3	Sky Star XL (Reservation 2.94, ntu?)	LCX 015	
PH-2R4	Aviasud Mistral	144	
PH-2R5	TL Ultralight TL-32 Typhoon	"M503945"	
	(C/n incorrect, possibly could be 94.05)		
PH-2R6	TL Ultralight TL-2 Eso	E494H2735	
PH-2R8	Aviasud Mistral BRD	181	D-MNOS
PH-2R9	Bison Klüver 2 (Reservation, ntu?)	unkn	
PH-2S1	TEAM Minimax 1600R	868	
PH-2S2	Comco Ikarus Fox-C22B	9501-3641	
PH-2S3	Fisher FP-202 Koala	0253	
PH-2S5	CFM Shadow Series CD	K232	
PH-2S6	Aviasud Mistral BRD	179	D-MONF
PH-2S7	III Sky Arrow 450TH	19	
PH-2S8	Pegasus Quantum 15	6723	G-MYNM
PH-2T1	Rans S-6S Super Coyote II	0194.717	
PH-2T2	SMAN Pétrel	0-55	
PH-2T6	TL UltralightTL-132 Condor	95C15	
PH-2T8	Take Off Merlin	23545	
PH-2U1	Ultralair Weedhopper AX-3	C3123183	
PH-2U2	Pegasus Quasar II.TC [MAT"1"]	SW-QT-7071	
PH-2U4	Funk FK-9TG	048	D-MRTB
PH-2U5	Toresi Mini Straton D-7	033	
PH-2U7	Aviasud Mistral BRD	086	D-MACS
PH-2U9	Tecnam P.92 Echo	136	
	(to become PH-MUG)		
PH-2V1	TL Ultralight TL-232 Condor	95C18	
	(type changed from TL-131 to -232 08.01)		
PH-2V3	Interplane Griffon	1195B	
PH-2V4	TL Ultralight TL-132 Condor	96C03	
PH-2V5	Tecnam P.92 Echo	154	
PH-2V6	Tecnam P.92 Echo	153	
PH-2V7	Kolb Twinstar III	003	
PH-2V8	Take Off Merlin Trike	25926	
PH-2V9	Comco-Ikarus Fox C-22	9210-3446	D-MKRO
PH-2W1	Aviasud Mistral BRD	126	D-MJJJ
PH-2W2	TL Ultralight TL-232 Condor II	96C05	
PH-2W3	Comco Ikarus Fox-C22	9603-3706	
PH-2W5	Aviasud Mistral BRD	176	D-MMOO
PH-2W8	Comco Ikarus Fox-C22	9606-3709	
PH-2X1	Rans S-6 Super Coyote II	1095885	
PH-2X2	Microlight AK-4 Kolibri	005	
PH-2X3	TLUltralight TL-232 Condor II	96C12	
PH-2X4	NST Minimum Saphir 17M	04589-01NST	
PH-2X5	NST Minimum Magic IV-177	04589	
PH-2X6	Letov ST-4 Aztek	402	
PH-2X8	Air Création Mild GT 582ES	0113	
PH-2X9	Tecnam P.92 Echo	196	
PH-2Y1	Tecnam P.92 Echo	195	
PH-2Y2	Tecnam P.92J Echo	206	
PH-2Y3	Comco Ikarus Fox-C22C	9612-3721	
	(type changed from C22 to C22C 12.97)		
PH-2Y4	Take Off Merlin	26508	
PH-2Y5	Comco Ikarus C-42 Cyclone	9701-6022	
PH-2Y6	JORA Jora	4795776	
PH-2Y7	Tecnam P.92 Echo	219	
PH-2Y8	Solar Wings Pegasus Quantum 15	7314	
PH-2Y9	Aviasud AE-209 Albatros	123	OE-7014
PH-2Z1	Air Création Mild GTE-503S	118	
PH-2Z2	JORA Jora	4837805	
PH-2Z7	Tecnam P.92 Echo	249	
PH-2Z9	Rans S-6S Super Coyote II	02971098	
PH-3A1	Air Light Wild Thing	98011	
PH-3A2	Aviasud Mistral BRD	113	D-MBGK
PH-3A3	Comco Ikarus C-42 Cyclone	9710-6076	
PH-3A5	Flight Design CT	97-11-03-15	D-MPIW
PH-3A7	Air Création Mild 582XP	T98005/4890750	
	('4890750' is the c/n of the engine, type changed from GT-582ES to 582XP 6.00)		
PH-3A8	TL Ultralight TL-132 Condor	98C02	
PH-3A9	Flight Design CT	98-01-01-18	
PH-3B2	TL Ultralight TL-232 Condor	98C06	
PH-3B4	Air Création Clipper GT582XP	E101510	
	(type changed from Mild GT582ES to Clipper GT582XP 6.00)		
PH-3B6	Tecnam P.92 Echo	302	
PH-3B7	Tecnam P.96 Golf	014	
PH-3B8	Air Création Clipper 582XP	4559554	59-SP
PH-3B9	Remos G-3 Mirage	043	
PH-3C4	Cosmos BI Phase II	21271	
PH-3C8	Kappa 77 KP-2UR Sova	05/98	
PH-3C9	TL Ultralight TL-96 Star	98S20	
PH-3D4	Solar Wings Pegasus Quantum 15-912	74.77	G-69-41
PH-3D5	Kappa 77 KP-2UR Sova	06/98	
PH-3D7	Kappa 77 KP-2UR Sova	01039802	
PH-3D8	Kappa 77 KP-2UR Sova	08/98	
PH-3E1	Rans S-6S Super Coyote II	01981200	
PH-3E2	Mitchell Wing B10 (Reservation 12.98)	P.1444	
	(Also recorded as NVAV-77 / RLD No.A84-0045)		
PH-3E6	Cosmos BI Phase II	21325	
PH-3E7	Zenair CH-601UL Zodiac	6-9051	
PH-3E8	Tecnam P.96 Golf	55	
PH-3E9	Kappa 77 KP-2UR Sova	0103/98	OK-DUU-31
PH-3F1	Fantasy Air Allegro 2000	01-1002	
PH-3F2	Remos G-3 Mirage	056	
PH-3F3	Comco Ikarus C-42 Cyclone	9904-6147	
PH-3F4	Zenair CH-601UL Zodiac	6-9050	
PH-3F5	Zenair CH-601UL Zodiac	6-9045	
PH-3F6	Comco Ikarus C-42 Cyclone	9907-6192	
PH-3F7	Pioneer Flightstar	385	
PH-3F8	Comco Ikarus C-42 Cyclone	9907-6200	

PH-3F9	Comco Ikarus C-42 Cyclone	9908-6201	
PH-3G1	ATECZephyr	Z 100699 A	
PH-3G2	TL Ultralight TL-96 Star	99-S-29	
PH-3G3	TL Ultralight TL-96 Star	99-S-34	
PH-3G4	Air Création Clipper 582XP	5305983	
PH-3G7	Cosmos Samba	90	
PH-3H2	Behlen Focus 20	85029	
	(Reg 6.00 but also res as Behlen Power Trike 064/87-5 ex D-MUMY 5.00)		
PH-3H3	Zenair CH-701 STOL	7-9074	
PH-3H4	Urban Air UMF13 Lambada	5/15	
PH-3H6	Comco Ikarus C-42 Cyclone	9912-6234	
PH-3H7	Comco Ikarus C-42 Cyclone	0001-6238	
PH-3H8	TLUltralight TL-232 Condor	02700	
PH-3H9	Aeropro Fox	08500	
PH-3J1	WDFL Fascination D4 BK	065	
PH-3J2	WDFL Fascination D4 BK	066	
PH-3J4	ASO Viper Hazard 15	V111 12065408	D-MHAF
PH-3J5	Comco Ikarus Fox-C22C	9304-3467	
PH-3J6	Tecnam P.92 Echo	451	
PH-3J7	Euro Jet Fox 91-D	D 0017	D-MNCE
PH-3J9	Flight Design CT	99-12-0579	
PH-3K3	Air Création Mild GT582ES	T00026	
PH-3K4	Zenair CH-701 STOL	7-9058	
PH-3K5	Comco Ikarus Fox-C22C	0007-3745	
PH-3K6	Aeropro Fox	09300	
PH-3K8	Urban Air UFM-10 Samba	6/10	
PH-3L1	ASO Viper Hazard 15	V111 12070503	
PH-3L2	Comco Ikarus Fox-C22C	0011-3746	
PH-3L3	Comco Ikarus C-42 Cyclone	0101-6298	
PH-3L4	Aeropro Fox	10201	
PH-3L5	ATEC Zephyr	Z410601A	
PH-3L6	Fantasy Air Allegro 2000	01-1001	
PH-3L7	Comco Ikarus C-42 Cyclone	0106-6332	
PH-3L8	Comco Ikarus Fox-C22	9306-3460	D-MKRA
PH-3L9	Tecnam P.92 Echo	545	
PH-3M1	Kappa 77 KP-2UR Sova	4347G	
PH-3M2	Tecnam P.92-2000 RG Echo	450	
PH-3M4	Aeropro Fox	10701	
PH-3M5	Comco Ikarus C-42 Cyclone	0106-6349	
PH-3M6	Aeropro Fox	10501	
PH-3M8	Evektor EV-97 Eurostar 2000	2000 0804	
PH-3M9	Take Off Merlin	22744	
PH-3N1	Rans S-6S Super Coyote II	02001359S	
PH-3N2	ATEC Zephyr	Z420801A	
PH-3N3	Aerospool Dynamic WT9	DY 00301	
PH-3N4	ATEC Zephyr	Z150199V	
PH-3N5	Aeropro Fox	10901	
PH-3N6	Zenair CH.601UL Zodiac	6-9096	
PH-3N7	Comco Ikarus Fox-C22C	0109-3747	
PH-3N8	Aeropro Fox	11501	
PH-3N9	TLUltralight TL-2000 Sting	1.02s108	
PH-3P1	Aeropro Fox	11702	
PH-3P2	Aeropro Fox	11002	
PH-3P3	WDFL D4/BK Fascination	106	
PH-3P4	TL Ultralight TL-2000 Sting	02ST14	
PH-3P5	ATEC Zephyr	Z230402TU	
PH-3P6	Tecnam P.92 Echo 2000RG	029	
PH-3P7	Aeros Skyranger	SKR 01 03 096	
PH-3P8	Comco Ikarus C-42B	0208-6481	
PH-3P9	Rans S-6S Super Coyote II	11001397	
PH-3R1	Evektor EV-97 Eurostar 2000	2000 1143	
PH-3R3	Aeropro Fox	12502	
PH-3R4	Evektor EV-97 Eurostar 2000	2000 0812	
PH-3R5	Kappa 77 KP-2UR Sova	6677H	
PH-3R6	Alpi Avn Pioneer 300N	0072	
PH-3R7	Air Création Clipper 582XP	5381041	
PH-3R8	Aeropro Fox	08800	(PH-DRM)
PH-3R9	Cosmos Phase III	21532	
PH-3S1	Aeropro Fox	12902	
PH-3S2	Aerospool WT9 Dynamic	DY022/2002	
PH-3S3	Evektor EV-97 Eurostar 2000	2002 01530	
PH-3S4	Comco Ikarus C-42B	0212-6517	
PH-3S6	Zenair CH-701 STOL	7-9161	
PH-3S7	Kappa 77 KP-2UR Sova	7B961	
PH-3S8	Air Création XP15 GTE582S	T03047	
PH-3T1	Aerospool WT9 Dynamic	DY028/2003	
PH-3T2	Cosmos BI Phase II	21255	
PH-3T3	Evektor EV-97 Eurostar 2000	1144	
PH-3T4	Aerospool WT9 Dynamic	DY032/2003	
PH-3T5	Take Off Merlin	273100	
PH-3T6	Remos G-3 Mirage	083	D-MSCI
PH-3T7	Tecnam P.92 Echo	773	
PH-3T8	Comco-Ikarus C-42B	0309-6564	
PH-3T9	Aerospool WT9 Dynamic	DY012/2002	
PH-3U1	Zenair CH-701 STOL	7-9067	
PH-3U2	Funk FK-9 Mark 3	09-03-209	
PH-3U3	Aeropro Eurofox	14603	
PH-3U4	Comco-Ikarus C-42B (Res. 11.03)	0309-6520	9-254
PH-3U5	Take Off Merlin 1100	1000104	
PH-3U7	Klüver Twin Racer Quartz SX 16	407112	D-MSGV
PH-3U8	Aeropro Eurofox	054098	D-MTWD
PH-3U9	Kappa KP-2UR Sova	8398I/2003	OK-IUU04
PH-3V1	Aeropro Eurofox	15304	
PH-3V2	Kappa KP-2UR Sova	6879H/2002	OK-HUU62
PH-3V4	Flight Design CT SW	04-07-04	
PH-3V3	Kappa KP-2UR Sova	61G	
PH-3V5	Tecnam P.92S Echo 80	577	

PH-3V6	Evektor EV 97 Eurostar Model 2000	2004-2118	
PH-3V7	Zenair CH-601UL Zodiac	6-9572	
PH-3V8	Zenair CH601XL Zodiac	6-9524	
	(built by Czech Aircraft Works)		
PH-3V9	Aeropro Fox	16304	
PH-3W1	Platzer Kiebitz B	220	
PH-3W2	Platzer Kiebitz B	247	
PH-3W4	Zenair CH601UL Zodiac	6-9374	
PH-3W6	Zenair CH601XL Zodiac	6-9666	
	(built by Czech Aircraft Works)		
PH-9P1	Adventure A4	AP 3394	
PH-9P4	Fresh Breeez Simo 122	339	
PH-9P9	Adventure A4	3377	
PH-9Q2	G. Büttner Crazyplane III	126	
PH-9Q4	Adventure A3	2132	
PH-9Q9	Adventure A4	3399	
PH-9R5	Adventure R3 (Res. 3.05)	DR103	
PH-9R3	Fresh Breezee 122 AL 2F	2526	
PH-9R6	Fresh Breeez Simo 122	308	
PH-9R9	Sky Service Pagojet M4	262	
PH-9S2	Fresh Breezee Simo 122	228	
PH-9S3	Aircraft Sales and Parts (Res. 11.04)	3145	
PH-9S5	Adventure S4	KM 22683	
PH-9S6	Fresh Breezee Monster	245	
PH-9S7	Adventure A4	AO 3291	
PH-9S8	Adventure A3	AL 3009	
PH-9T2	Fly Product Power 115	70ZN2	
PH-9T6	Adventure A4	3269	
PH-9T8	Pap Team PAP 1300 TDL	3615	
PH-9T9	Fresh Breezee Monster	271	
PH-9U1	Fresh Breezee 122 AL 2F	1570	
PH-9U4	Walkerjet Sky	06004	
PH-9U6	Parasport Fun-Alu 125	AT12092004	
PH-9U7	Fresh Breezee Monster	199	
PH-9U8	Adventure A4	3077	
PH-9U9	Fresh Breeze 122 AL 2F	825	
PH-9V1	Fresh Breeze A4	2939	
PH-9V2	Fresh Breeze Simo 122	M22335	
PH-9V3	Adventure A3	3051726	
PH-9V4	Adventure A4	AP 3376	
PH-9V5	Adventure A4	AO3305	
PH-9V6	Walkerjet RR	M022504	
PH-9V7	Adventure F3	2133	
PH-9V9	Fresh Breeze 122 AL 2F	2360	
PH-9W1	G. Büttner Crazyplane III	70ZN2	
PH-9W2	Fresh Breeze Simo 122	85	
PH-9W5	TimetoFly Scooter	M22208	
PH-9W6	Fresh Breeze 110 AL 2F	1407	
PH-9W7	Fresh Breeze 110 AL 2F	1481	
PH-9W8	Fresh Breeze 122 AL 2F	842	
PH-9X1	Fresh Breeze Simo 122	149	
PH-9X2	Fresh Breeze 122 AL 2F	931	
PH-9X3	Fresh Breeze 122 AL 2F	951	
PH-9X4	MS Parafly Skyward III	MS0401336	
PH-9X5	Parasport Fun-Alu 125	IS10082004So-NL	
PH-9X7	Fresh Breeze 122 AL 2F	2376	
PH-9X8	Fresh Breeze Monster	222	
PH-9X9	Fresh Breeze Simo 122	135	
PH-9Y1	Fresh Breeze 122 AL 2F	1416	
PH-9Y2	Adventure S3	HM21418	
PH-9Y3	Adventure A3	2018N	
PH-9Y4	FlyProduct Power 115	70Z55	
PH-9Y5	Fresh Breeze Simo 122	147	
PH-9Y6	Adventure A4	A0-3341	
PH-9Y7	Adventure A4	A0-3211	
PH-9Y8	Fresh Breeze Simo 122	M21458	
PH-9Y9	Fresh Breeze 122 AL 2F	2070	
PH-9Z1	FlyProduct Power 130	70Z02	
PH-9Z2	Adventure R3	ER115	
PH-9Z3	Walkerjet RR	M022081	
PH-9Z5	Fresh Breeze 122 AL 2F	2223	
PH-9Z6	Hirth 310 (Res. 4.04)	F33	D-MEZA
PH-9Z7	Fresh Breeze 122 AL 2F	1249	
PH-9Z8	Adventure A4	A4-3148	
PH-9Z9	Adventure A4	A4-3183	

SE - SWEDEN

Many aircraft are still officially listed although long since destroyed or unairworthy.

Regn.	Type	C/n	Prev.Id.
SE-ADF	de Havilland DH.82A Tiger Moth	3113	SE-ATI Fv568 Fv5568 SE-ADF
SE-AGC	Corben Junior Ace (Build Permit EAA1125 8.01)	164	(OY-DBA) LN-NJS (LN-LJS) SE-AGC
SE-AGE	de Havilland DH.87B Hornet Moth	8136	
SE-AGO	Piper J-2 Cub (W/o 1.5.66)	993	
SE-AHG	Götaverken GV-38	8	
SE-AIC	Piper J-3C-65 Cub	2486	
SE-ALM	de Havilland DH.82A Tiger Moth	172	RNoAF:163
SE-AMA	S.A.I. KZ-III U-2 (EAA No.111)	81	OY-DVU
SE-AMB	Piper J-3C-65 Cub (Dbf 5-6.2.88)	12802	D-ENAC SL-AAX F-BFQB 44-80506
SE-AMC	Auster Mk.5	1159	D-EGAT I-METE HB-EON G-AKSI RT497
SE-AMD	CASA I.131E Jungmann	2141	G-OBLE E3B-541
SE-AME	S.A.I. KZ-III U-2	93	OY-DEA
SE-AMG	de Havilland DH.82A Tiger Moth	84589	OY-DET D-EKUR G-ANTV T6122
SE-AMH	de Havilland DH.82A Tiger Moth (W/o 4.8.99)	84959	G-AIIZ T6645
SE-AMI	de Havilland DH.82A Tiger Moth	86526	G-AYVY F-BGCZ Fr.AF PG617
SE-AML	Cessna C-34 Airmaster (Reserved 5.92)	302	NC15463
SE-AMM	de Havilland DH.82A Tiger Moth (W/o 7.9.99)	83226	G-ANEF T5493
SE-AMN	Auster J/2 Arrow	2387	OY-ALY D-EMYG OO-AXG OO-AXC
SE-AMO	de Havilland DH.60 Moth replica (Under construction using wings of Fox Moth SE-AFL and Hermes engine)	unkn	(SE-BBT)
SE-AMR	de Havilland DH.82A Tiger Moth	ASJA.49	Fv517
SE-AMW	Boeing Stearman A75-N1 (Res 10.99)	75-3129	N68494 41-25622
SE-AMY	de Havilland DH.82A Tiger Moth	82720	N81DH G-ASSC R4776
SE-AMZ	Bleriot XI /Thulin A	EAA-1184-SE	
SE-ANX	Skandinaviska Aero BHT-1 Beauty	1	LN-JHC SE-ANX
SE-ARG	Auster J/I Autocrat	1882	
SE-ARK	Auster J/I Autocrat	1953	
SE-ARR	Auster J/2 Arrow (Permit 7.02)	2358	
SE-ASP	Piper J-3C-65 Cub (Permit 7.04)	11928	44-79632
SE-ASR	Piper J-3C-65 Cub	10486	D-EDOZ SE-ASR 43-29195
SE-ASS	Piper J-3C-65 Cub	11994	44-79698
SE-ASU	Piper J-3C-65 Cub	11708	43-30417
SE-ASX	Piper J-3C-65 Cub	11711	43-30420
SE-ATE	Piper J-3C-65 Cub	11965	44-79669
SE-ATG	Piper J-3C-65 Cub	12043	OH-CPH SE-ATG 44-79747
SE-ATL	Piper J-3C-65 Cub	11243	43-29952
SE-ATO	Piper J-3C-65 Cub (Rebuilding 12.02)	12517	44-80221
SE-ATT	Piper J-3C-65 Cub	11979	44-79683
SE-ATU	Piper J-3C-65 Cub	12146	44-79850
SE-ATZ	Piper J-3C-65 Cub (Rebuilding 2.04)	12319	44-80023
SE-AUE	Piper J-3C-65 Cub	9460	43-599 (42-59409)
SE-AUF	Piper J-3C-65 Cub (Permit)	12387	44-80091
SE-AUH	Piper J-3C-65 Cub	12685	44-80389
SE-AUK	Piper J-3C-65 Cub (Permit 7.04)	11697	43-30406
SE-AUL	Piper J-3C-65 Cub	12066	(LN-BDB) SE-AUL 44-79770
SE-AUM	Piper J-3C-65 Cub	10875	D-ELOL SE-AUM 43-29584
SE-AUR	SAAB S.91A Safir	91103	
SE-AUU	Piper J-3C-65 Cub (W/o 7.7.82)	11661	43-30370
SE-AUW	Piper J-3C-65 Cub	11686	43-30395
SE-AWK	Piper J-3C-65 Cub	12418	44-80122
SE-AWL	Piper J-3C-65 Cub	12044	44-79748
SE-AWW	Piper J-3C-65 Cub	16352	
SE-AXB	Republic RC-3 Seabee	268	
SE-AXF	Republic RC-3 Seabee (Permit 6.04)	592	D-ELPO N6363K
SE-AXG	Republic RC-3 Seabee (Rebuilding 2.04)	399	
SE-AXM	Republic RC-3 Seabee	467	
SE-AXR	Republic RC-3 Seabee	270	LN-IKK SE-AXR (PP-. . .)
SE-AXX	Republic RC-3 Seabee	829	LN-TVV SE-AXX
SE-AXY	Republic RC-3 Seabee	830	(NC6560K)
SE-AYI	Fairchild F.24W Argus 2	572	43-14608
SE-AYM	Miles M.65 Gemini 1A (Permit 10.02)	6296	G-AKDA
SE-AYZ	Piper J-3C-65 Cub	13264	45-4524
SE-AZU	Luscombe 8A Silvaire	4865	(NC2138K)
SE-AZY	S.A.I. KZ-III U-2	102	OY-DYB
SE-BCC	Stinson 108 Voyager	108-543	(NC97543)
SE-BCD	Globe GC-1B Swift	1065	OY-ADP SE-BCD (NC80660)
SE-BCL	Stinson 108-1 Voyager	2103	LN-BEJ SE-BCL N9103K NC9103K
SE-BCM	Stinson 108-1 Voyager	2113	N9113K NC9113K
SE-BCS	Piper PA-12 Super Cruiser	12-1257	
SE-BCW	Piper J-3C-85 Cub	16354	
SE-BCX	Piper J-3C-65 Cub	12672	LN-RAT 44-80659(2) 44-80376
SE-BCZ	Piper PA-18 Super Cub 95	18-370	
SE-BEA	Stinson 108-3 Voyager	4874	OY-AVE D-EKES N8674M
SE-BEB	Jodel D.112 Club	02	OY-ALE PH-VRG F-BBBG F-WBBG
SE-BEC	Piper J-3C-65 Cub	12904	OY-AVP LN-RAL (LN-RAK) 44-80608
SE-BED	Piper PA-14 Family Cruiser (Rebuilding 2.03)	14-497	OH-CPI N5179H
SE-BEE	Erco 415C Ercoupe	2614	N99991 NC99991
SE-BEG	Piper J-3C-65 Cub (Officially quoted with f/n 13214)	13384	D-EDYR (D-EDET) 45-4644
SE-BEH	Piper J-3C-65 Cub (Officially quoted with f/n 8644 - repaired using c/n 12281 in 6.50)	8535	D-ELAT HB-OWD 44-79985
SE-BEI	Piper J-3C-65 Cub	15500	N87882 NC87882
SE-BEK	Piper PA-12 Super Cruiser	12-558	HB-OOD OO-SCD
SE-BEL	Piper J-3C-65 Cub	10951	G-AITP OO-AAO 43-29660
SE-BEM	SNCAN/ Stampe SV.4C	33	D-EEMQ F-BCUU
SE-BEN	Piper J-3C-65 Cub	11968	OY-ALI D-EMAC OO-AAF 44-79672
SE-BEO	Piper J-3C-65 Cub	13707	N68199 NC68199 45-4967
SE-BEP	Beech 35 Bonanza	D-718	N3270V NC3270V
SE-BER	Erco 415C Ercoupe	3283	(SE-XNL) N2658H NC2658H
SE-BES	Piper J-3C-65 Cub (Rebuilt using fuselage from SE-AST c/n12007)	12025	LN-HOL LN-HHF 44-79729
SE-BET	Piper J-3C-65 Cub	17017	LN-AET D-EGEF N92648 NC92648
SE-BEU	Boeing Stearman A75-N1 (Res 11.02)	75-3189	N56188 41-25682
SE-BEV	Piper J-3C-65 Cub	18658	9Q-CET 5Y-KIM VP-KIM VR-TAL ZS-AZX
SE-BEZ	de Havilland DH.82A Tiger Moth (Reservation 3.02, EAA No.1146)	86072	G-AHMM EM870
SE-BFD	Piper J-3C-65 Cub (Permit)	12535	44-80239
SE-BFK	Piper J-3C-65 Cub	11821	43-30530
SE-BFM	Cessna 140	12503	NC2111V
SE-BFX	Erco 415D Ercoupe	4413	(NC3788H)
SE-BFY	Erco 415D Ercoupe	4409	(NC3784H)
SE-BIS	S.A.I. KZ-III U-2 (C/n 84-962 now quoted)	84	OY-DVE

SE-BIT	Stinson 108-1 Voyager	108-1793	LN-BNE N8793K NC8793K
SE-BKA	Aeronca 7AC Champion	6340	(SE-KSR) C-FDVT CF-DVT
SE-BKB	Aeronca 65C-A	CA14141	N33886 NC33886
SE-BKH	Percival P.66 Pembroke (Regd with c/n "K66/045")	P66/82	G-BNPG XK884
SE-BMC	Piper J-3C-65 Cub	12847	LN-KLT(2) OY-ALP (D-EFPB) LX-ABO OE-ABO HB-OAB 44-80551
SE-BMH	Holste MH.1521MBroussard	78	LN-WNA (G-. . . .) (LN-WNA) F-GHUG ALAT
SE-BNI	Piper J-3C-65 Cub	12608	LN-IKH SE-BNI 44-80312
SE-BNK	Bücker Bu.181 Bestmann	108/"Lfs-1-1949"	CR+YU
SE-BNN	SAAB S.91A Safir	91130	OY-DBT OO-MUG OO-HUG PH-UEB SE-BNN
SE-BOA	Boeing Stearman E75	75-1410	N59732 N4988G BuA03633
SE-BOE	Boeing Stearman A75N1 (Painted as '498')	75-294	N4988G N56402 40-1737
SE-BOG	Boeing Stearman B75N1	75-7128	N59085 BuA07524
SE-BOZ	Boeing Stearman 75 (Permit 10.04)	75-294	
SE-BPT	Klemm Kl.35D (Painted as Fv5033)	1922	Fv5033
SE-BPU	Klemm Kl.35D (Permit 10.04)	2009	(SE-BPO) Fv5060
SE-BRY	Beech D-17S	4920	G-BDGK HB-UIH SE-BRY OO-VIT FZ430 43-10872
SE-BSZ	Focke-Wulf FW.44J Stieglitz (Officially quoted with incorrect c/n 2778)	2775	SZ-12
SE-BUU	Lockheed 18-56 Lodestar (Scrapped in 1966)	2076	VP-KFA G-AGBT
SE-BWM	Focke-Wulf FW.44J Stieglitz	655	Fv.655
SE-BWU	Focke-Wulf FW.44J Stieglitz	39	OY-DVW D-ENYF SE-BWU Fv.657
SE-BXB	Republic RC-3 Seabee	953	LN-MAL
SE-BXC	Republic RC-3 Seabee	203	CS-AHA
SE-BXX	Andreasson BA-6	1	
SE-BYH	SAAB B17A	139	Fv.17239
SE-BYL	de Havilland DH.82A Tiger Moth (Major damage 14.9.97, rebuilding)	ASJA.73	Fv.553
SE-BYR	Piper PA-18-150 Super Cub	18-2928	N10F
SE-BYT	Auster J/5G Autocar (W/o 26.8.64)	3083	
SE-BYU	Auster J/1 Autocrat	1886	G-AHAO
SE-BZM	de Havilland DH.85 Leopard Moth	7061	LN-TVT G-ACRW AX783 G-ACRW
SE-BZP	Stinson V-77 Reliant	6375	OO-NUT FB536
SE-BZT	Piper PA-20-150 Pacer	20-1078	N10F
SE-CAB	SAAB S.91B-2 Safir	91334	RNo.AF:334 57334/'UA-O'
SE-CAE	SAAB S.91B Safir	91306	SE-XAR
SE-CAL	Piper J-3C-65 Cub	9994	LN-SAT 43-1133 (42-59943)
SE-CAN	Piper J-3C-65 Cub (Officially quoted with f/n 12475 as c/n)	12645	44-80349
SE-CBL	Piper PA-23 Apache	23-549	
SE-CBN	Piper PA-18-150 Super Cub	18-4846	LN-NAT N10F
SE-CBS	Auster J/5G Autocar (W/o 12.4.63)	3082	LN-BDA
SE-CDA	Piper PA-22-135 Tri-Pacer	22-1556	N8977C
SE-CDF	Stinson 108-1 Voyager (W/o 16.6.95)	1846	OY-EFK LN-BEK SE-CDF N8846K
SE-CDG	Cessna 170B (W/o 27.5.88)	26988	N3445D
SE-CDW	Beech A-35 Bonanza	D-1866	ET-P-12 N8448A
SE-CEB	Piper PA-18A-150 Super Cub	18-5533	N10F
SE-CEE	Piper PA-18-150 Super Cub	18-5700	
SE-CEF	Piper J-3C-65 Cub	19580	N6402H (NC6402H)
SE-CEH	Piper PA-18-150 Super Cub	18-5821	N10F
SE-CER	Piper PA-22-135 Tri-Pacer	22-1089	LN-AEK SE-CER N1847A
SE-CES	Piper PA-22-135 Tri-Pacer	22-1163	N1406C
SE-CET	Piper J-3C-65 Cub	11304	LN-MAE 43-30013
SE-CEZ	Piper PA-18A-150 Super Cub (W/o 24.11.68)	18-4748	N3988P
SE-CFP	Douglas C-47A	13883	Fv79006 SE-CFP LN-IAF 43-30732
SE-CFZ	SAAB S.91D Safir	91308	G-AVGS SE-CFZ SE-XAT
SE-CGM	Noorduyn UC-64A/S Norseman IV	780	LN-TSN R.NoAF:'RA-F' 44-70515
SE-CHF	Republic RC-3 Seabee	646	LN-PAF
SE-CHG	de Havilland DH.82A Tiger Moth	85867	G-APOU DF118
SE-CHP	North American AT-6A Texan (Sk.16B)	77-4524	Fv16269 41-16443
SE-CIA	Jodel D.126	861	
SE-CIB	Jodel D.113	789	
SE-CIC	Jodel D.126	787	
SE-CID	Jodel D.119	958	
SE-CIE	Jodel D.119	784	
SE-CIF	Jodel D.126	527	
SE-CIH	Jodel D.112 Club	785	OY-TRL SE-CIH
SE-CII	Jodel D.112 Club	783	
SE-CIK	Jodel D.112/113 (Reservatrion)	71	
SE-CIM	Jodel D.119	959	
SE-CIN	Bowers Fly Baby 1A	SE-01	
SE-CIO	Jodel D.113 (Reservation 10.00)	1535	
SE-CIS	SOCATA MS.880B Rallye Club	1211	OY-DTU
SE-CKB	Piper PA-18A-150 Super Cub	18-6455	Army:51260 SE-CKB N10F
SE-CKC	Piper PA-18A-150 Super Cub	18-6458	Army:51261 SE-CKC N10F
SE-CKD	Piper PA-18A-150 Super Cub	18-6521	Army:51258 SE-CKD N10F
SE-CKE	Piper PA-18A-150 Super Cub	18-6520	Army:51257 SE-CKE N10F
SE-CKO	Piper PA-22-160 Tri-Pacer (W/o 14.5.61)	22-5976	N7180D
SE-CKR	Piper PA-22S-150 Caribbean	22-6611	N10F
SE-CKU	Piper PA-22-150 Tri-Pacer (CofA exp 6.75)	22-6346	N10F
SE-CKY	Piper PA-18 Super Cub 95 (W/o 28.7.95)	18-7149	N10F
SE-CKZ	Piper PA-22S-150 Tri-Pacer (W/o 5.9.71)	22-6250	N8103D
SE-CLA	Piper PA-22-150 Tri-Pacer (Permit)	22-3064	N2757P
SE-CLD	Piper PA-20-150 Pacer (Originally a PA-22 Tri-Pacer 125 converted to PA-20 standard)	22-100	N697A
SE-CLF	Piper PA-18S-95 Super Cub	18-3109	LN-BEE OL-L35 L-35 53-4709
SE-CLI	Piper PA-18 Super Cub 95	18-5725	D-EJAQ SE-CLI N7363D
SE-CLK	Piper PA-22-150 Tri-Pacer	22-4710	N6057D
SE-CLM	Aeronca 7AC Champion	392	N81769 NC81769
SE-CLN	Stinson SR-10J Reliant	5-5820	N21101
SE-CLP	Cessna 172	46518	N6418E
SE-CLR	Piper J-3C-65 Cub	11794	LN-BWN SE-CLR 43-30503
SE-CLT	Cessna 172	36840	N3940F
SE-CLY	Cessna 150	17030	(EI-AKH) N5530E
SE-CLZ	Noorduyn UC-64A/S Norseman IV (Tp 78) (Displayed at Flygvapenmuseum at Linkoping painted as Fv78001)	492	Fv78001 SE-ASC 43-35418
SE-CMC	Auster 5	1603	D-EERK D-ELIR D-EFIR G-AMNU TJ587
SE-CME	Auster 5 Alpha	3410	G-APNN
SE-CMF	Auster 5D	1376	OY-ADY VR-RCC TJ295
SE-CMO	Cessna 175A (CofA exp 4.87)	56367	N6867E
SE-CMP	Cessna 150	17777	OY-AEG
SE-CMR	Morane-Saulnier MS.885 Super Rallye	14	LN-BWV
SE-CMU	Mooney M.20B Mark 21 (CofA exp 2.81)	1860	

SE-CMY	Cessna 140	11721	OY-BAI SE-CMY LN-TSK N77259
SE-CMZ	Cessna 185 Skywagon	185-0053	LN-TSR N9853X
SE-CNA	Champion 7EC Traveler (Rebuilding .01)	7EC-704	
SE-CNB	Champion 7EC Traveler	7EC-705	
SE-CND	Champion 7EC Traveler	7EC-719	
SE-CNR	Cessna 210 (W/o 27.11.96)	57331	N9531T
SE-CNS	Cessna 180B (W/o 4.8.82)	50658	N9158T
SE-CNW	Cessna 172A	47137	N7537T
SE-CNY	Cessna 180B	50629	N9129T
SE-COG	de Havilland DH.82A Tiger Moth	85593	G-APLI DE639
SE-COO	de Havilland DH.82A Tiger Moth (W/o 26.9.81)	86372	G-ANKJ NL929
SE-CPB	Noorduyn UC-64 Norseman IV (Preserved in Arlanda Museum)	89	(LN-AEN) R.NoAF:'RA-Y' 42-5050 RCAF 3538
SE-CPG	Malmö MFI-9 Junior	02	
SE-CPI	Malmö MFI-10B Vipan (Displayed at Flygvapenmuseum painted as Fv.54382)	03	Fv.54382 Fv.54002 SE-CPI
SE-CPL	Ryan Navion A	NAV-4-1786	(D-ELMI) N9828F N4786K
SE-CPT	Piper PA-18 Super Cub 95	18-6749	N9497D
SE-CPZ	Piper PA-18 Super Cub 95	18-5883	N7587D
SE-CRC	Piper PA-18 Super Cub 95	18-6998	N9942D
SE-CRE	Piper PA-22-108 Colt	22-8743	
SE-CRF	Piper PA-22-108 Colt (Cr 13.8.00)	22-8795	
SE-CRI	Piper PA-22-108 Colt	22-9120	
SE-CRK	Piper PA-22-V6 STOL Colt Magnum 2000 (Highly-modified PA-22-108) (Res 8.03)	22-9081	
SE-CRU	Piper PA-22-108 Colt (W/o 12.10.70)	22-9113	
SE-CRW	Piper PA-22-108/150 Colt	22-9114	
SE-CSB	Piper PA-18-150 Super Cub	18-7280	
SE-CSD	Piper PA-18-150 Super Cub	18-7287	
SE-CSF	Piper PA-22-150 Caribbean (W/o 26.9.61)	22-7133	
SE-CSG	Piper PA-22-150 Caribbean (W/o 6.1.70)	22-7136	
SE-CSH	Piper PA-22-150 Caribbean (W/o 4.3.73)	22-7137	
SE-CSM	Piper PA-22-150 Caribbean	22-7380	
SE-CSN	Piper PA-22S-150 Caribbean	22-7375	
SE-CSO	Piper PA-22-150 Caribbean (Sold to Norway in 1975)	22-7245	
SE-CSP	Piper PA-22-150 Caribbean	22-7306	
SE-CSR	Piper PA-22-150 Caribbean	22-6942	N10F
SE-CST	Piper PA-20-150 Pacer	20-616	N7789K
SE-CSU	Piper PA-20 Pacer 125	20-489	N7668K
SE-CSW	Piper PA-28-160 Cherokee B (W/o 7.11.85)	28-1260	
SE-CSZ	Piper PA-22-150 Caribbean	22-7350	N3435Z
SE-CTD	Piper PA-24-180 Comanche	24-976	N5891P
SE-CTE	Piper J-4A Cub	4-612	OH-CPB G-AFWS ES923 G-AFWS NC23491
SE-CTG	Piper PA-18A-150 Super Cub (Rebuilding .04)	18-6832	N9472D
SE-CTM	Cessna 185A Skywagon	185-0381	N4181Y
SE-CTO	Cessna 175A	56767	N8067T
SE-CUR	Piper PA-22-150 Caribbean (Permit 5.02 with c/n 22-7453-1076)	22-7453	OH-CPR SE-CUR N3544Z
SE-CUT	Piper PA-22-108 Colt (W/o 19.4.75)	22-8455	
SE-CUZ	Piper PA-22-108 Colt	22-8628	
SE-CVT	Beech G35 Bonanza (Permit 8.03)	D-4856	N4671D
SE-CWF	Binder CP.301S Smaragd	120	D-EDRI
SE-CWG	de Havilland DH.82A Tiger Moth	3364	G-AORA BB750 G-ADLV
SE-CWL	Maule M-4-210 Rocket (W/o 26.6.77)	1034	LN-HHI N15B
SE-CWS	Cessna 177 Cardinal	17700504	OY-DLB N3204T
SE-CXB	Cessna 172A (W/o 25.2.68)	47518	N9718T
SE-CXD	Cessna 172A	47193	N7593T
SE-CXE	Cessna 172A (Modified)	47500	N9700T
SE-CXF	Cessna 180C (W/o 27.6.65)	50895	N9395T
SE-CXI	Cessna 150C	15059871	N2071Z
SE-CXK	Cessna 175B	17556888	N8188T
SE-CXL	Cessna 172B	17248199	N7699X
SE-CXM	Cessna 180D	18050968	LN-AEM SE-CXM N6468X
SE-CXN	Cessna 180D	18050969	LN-TVW (LN-AEL) SE-CXN N6469X
SE-CXW	Cessna 172B	17248223	N7723X
SE-CYA	Cessna 182D	18253322	N8922X

SE-CYH	Cessna 150B	15059461	LN-DBK SE-CYH N7361X
SE-CYI	Cessna 172C (CofA exp 2.80)	17248883	N8383X
SE-CYL	Cessna 182E	18253680	N9280X
SE-CYO	Cessna 150	15059166	OY-DGB SE-CXR N7066X
SE-CYZ	Cessna 210B (W/o 19.1.72)	21058078	OY-EGC SE-CYZ N9778X
SE-CZA	Piper PA-22-108 Colt	22-9121	
SE-CZC	Piper PA-22-108 Colt	22-9123	
SE-CZE	Piper PA-22-108/150 Colt	22-9125	
SE-CZF	Piper PA-22-108 Colt	22-9126	
SE-CZG	Piper PA-22-108/150 Colt (W/o 23.8.75)	22-9127	
SE-CZH	Piper PA-28-150 Cherokee B (Instructional airframe at FTC Vasteras)	28-1188	
SE-CZI	Piper PA-22-108 Colt	22-9129	
SE-CZK	Piper PA-22-108/150 Colt	22-9130	
SE-CZL	Piper PA-22-108 Colt	22-9131	
SE-CZM	Piper PA-22-108/150 Colt	22-9132	
SE-CZN	Piper PA-28-180 Cherokee B (W/o 2.9.67)	28-1356	N7227W
SE-CZO	Piper PA-22-108/150 Colt	22-8953	LN-BDB LV-PQX N10F
SE-CZT	Piper PA-22-108 Colt	22-9109	
SE-CZU	Piper PA-22-108 Colt	22-9110	
SE-CZZ	Piper PA-18-150 Super Cub (W/o 12.7.90)	18-7046	OY-ACL
SE-DDY	Cessna 550 Citation II	550-0115	OY-CCU SE-DDY N127SC N2745L
SE-DEB	SE.210 Caravelle 10R	247	EC-CIZ D-ANYL F-WJAM
SE-DEC	SE.210 Caravelle 10R (W/o at Arlanda 6.1.87 - used for fire practice)	263	(LN-TEC) EC-CYI F-WJAK F-OCKH D-ABAF F-WJAN OY-SAZ F-WJAN
SE-DEG	Cessna 500 Citation	500-0276	N29EB (N340TB) SE-DEG N473LR N473LP N100CM N276CC (N5276J)
SE-DEY	Cessna 500 Citation	500-0370	N36897
SE-DEZ	Cessna 501 Citation I/SP	501-0279	N66HD SE-DEZ N43BG N371GP (N371GA) (N371GP) SE-DEZ N36919
SE-DGE	Fokker F.28 Fellowship 4000	11112	PH-EXK
SE-DGI	Fokker F.28 Fellowship 4000	11122	PH-EXP
SE-DHO	Gates Learjet 35A	35A-195	N555JE D-CONY N1471B
SE-DHP	Gates Learjet 35A	35A-075	N30FN N48RW (N117DA) N3503F JY-AFE HB-VEV N3503F
SE-DIB	McDonnell-Douglas DC-9-87	49605	N19B
SE-DIC	McDonnell-Douglas DC-9-87	49607	
SE-DIF	McDonnell-Douglas DC-9-87	49606	
SE-DIK	McDonnell-Douglas DC-9-82	49728	(SE-DIE)
SE-DIL	McDonnell-Douglas DC-9-81	49913	
SE-DIN	McDonnell-Douglas DC-9-81	49999	
SE-DIP	McDonnell-Douglas DC-9-87	53010	
SE-DIR	McDonnell-Douglas DC-9-81	53004	
SE-DIS	McDonnell-Douglas DC-9-81	53006	
SE-DIU	McDonnell-Douglas DC-9-87	53011	
SE-DLB	Dassault Falcon 100	183	N183SR N82CR N249FJ F-WZGO
SE-DLZ	Cessna 500 Citation	500-0411	G-NCMT G-BIZZ N6784Y
SE-DMA	McDonnell-Douglas DC-9-87 (W/o 8.10.01)	53009	
SE-DMB	McDonnell-Douglas DC-9-81	53314	
SE-DMF	McDonnell-Douglas MD-90-30	53457	
SE-DMG	McDonnell-Douglas MD-90-30	53461	
SE-DMH	McDonnell-Douglas MD-90-30	53543	

SE-DMT	McDonnell-Douglas DC-9-81	48003	N480LP
			(N312TT)
			N480LP
			SE--DMT
			TF-MDA
			SE-DMT
			HB-IND
SE-DNX	Boeing 737-683	28304	EC-INT
			SE-DNX
			N1787B
SE-DOR	Boeing 737-683	28305	EC-IND
			OY-KKE
			N1787B
SE-DOT	Boeing 737-683	28306	EC-ING
			OY-KKY
			LN-RPE
			N1795B
SE-DPB	Boeing 737-33A	25402	N33AW
SE-DPC	Boeing 737-33A	25426	N34AW
SE-DRS	Beech 400A Beechjet	RK-37	N8014Q
			(F-GLOR)
			N8014Q
			(F-GLPD)
SE-DRZ	Cessna 500 Citation	500-0315	N55SH
	(Reserved as OY-TCP 10.97, ntu)		N55SK
			N5315J
SE-DSB	Lockheed 1011-385-1 Tristar	1059	N31015
SE-DSO	Avro 146-RJ100A	E-3221	N504MM
			G-OIII
SE-DSP	Avro 146-RJ100A	E-3242	N505MM
			G-6-242
SE-DSR	Avro 146-RJ100A	E-3244	N506MM
			G-6-244
SE-DSS	Avro 146-RJ100A	E-3245	N507MM
			G-6-245
SE-DST	Avro 146-RJ100A	E-3247	N508MM
			G-6-247
SE-DSU	Avro 146-RJ100A	E-3248	N509MM
			G-6-248
SE-DSV	Avro 146-RJ100A	E-3250	N510MM
			G-6-250
SE-DSX	Avro 146-RJ100A	E-3255	N511MM
			G-6-255
SE-DSY	Avro 146-RJ100A	E-3263	N512MM
			G-6-263
SE-DTH	Boeing 737-683	28313	(OY-KKI)
			(SE-DTH)
SE-DUP	Boeing 757-236	24793	G-CDUP
			SE-DUP
			G-OOOT
			G-BRJJ
			EC-490
			G-BRJJ
SE-DUZ	Cessna 500 Citation	500-0143	N787BA
			N14T
			N14JZ
			N3W
			XB-CXF
			XC-GUQ
			N143CC
SE-DVD	Hawker 800XP	258339	N23395
SE-DVE	Dassault Falcon 900EX	23	F-WWFS
SE-DVH	Airbus A320-212	190	PH-DVR
			G-UKLJ
			G-BWKN
			N484GX
			F-WWDD
SE-DVN	Lockheed 1101-385-3 Tristar	1196	N596AH
			JY-AGF
			D-AERL
SE-DVP	Dassault Falcon 100	224	N135FJ
			C-FREE
			N128FJ
			F-WZGM
SE-DVT	Cessna 550 Citation II	550-0634	N550SB
			PH-MDX
			(N1258B)
SE-DVU	Boeing 737-85F	28825	N501GX
			N1784B
			N1787B
SE-DVY	Cessna 650 Citation VII	650-7011	N700VP
			(N6111)
			N5111
			N1260N
SE-DXA	Hawker Hunter F.Mk.58	41H-697456	(OY-SKB)
			J-4089
SE-DXB	SAAB J-29F	29670	Fv29670
SE-DXH	Hawker Hunter T. Mk 7A	41H-695448	G-BWIE
	(Previously given as 41H-695336)		9223M
			XL616
SE-DXI	Hawker Hunter F.Mk.58 (Res 3.04)	41H-697440	G-RUUD
			J-4073
SE-DXL	SAAB J32B Lansen	unkn	Fv.32605/ 26
SE-DXM	Hawker Hunter F.Mk.58	41H697449	J-4082
SE-DXS	de Havilland DH.100 Vampire FB.6	705	J-1196
SE-DXT	de Havilland DH.115 Vampire T.55	972	U-1212

SE-DXU	de Havilland DH.115 Vampire T.55	40279	U-1238
			XD440
SE-DXV	de Havilland DH.115 Vampire T.55	981	U-1221
SE-DXX	de Havilland DH.115 Vampire T.55	40303	U-1236
SE-DXY	de Havilland DH.100 Vampire FB.6	693	J-1184
SE-DXZ	de Havilland DH.100 Vampire FB.6	630	HB-RVD
	(W/o 6.7.93)		J-1121
SE-DYB	Dassault Falcon 100	216	N999WJ
			9M-ATM
			VH-JDW
			N100H
			N276FJ
			F-WZGZ
SE-DYC	Boeing 737-883 (Reservation .01)	32276	
SE-DYD	Boeing 737-883 (Reservation .01)	30471	(SE-DTR)
SE-DYE	Hawker 800XP	258382	N23451
SE-DYF	Reserved for Boeing 737 for Novair		
SE-DYL	Boeing 737-36E (Reservation)	25264	EC-FLG
			EC-706
SE-DYR	Cessna 551 Citation II/SP	551-0132	N78GA
			C-GTBR
			(C-FCFP)
			N2663J
SE-DYU	Reserved for Boeing 737 for SAS		
SE-DYV	Hawker 800XP	258385	N23466
SE-DYX	Cessna 560XL Citation Excel	560-5029	N5203S
SE-DZB	Embraer EMB.145	145113	PT-SCP
SE-DZE	Reserved for Embraer EMB.145 for West Air Sweden		
SE-DZH	Boeing 737-804	28227	N1786B
SE-DZI	Boeing 737-804	28229	
SE-DZK	Boeing 737-804	28231	N1786B
			(G-BYNC)
SE-DZL	Boeing 737-804	30465	PH-AAV
	(Reserved as D-ATUA .05)		G-BYNC
			N1786B
			(SE-DZK)
SE-DZM	Boeing 737-804	30466	PH-ABE
	(Reserved as D-ATUB .05)		G-BYNB
			N1786B
SE-DZP/R/S/T/U	Reserved for Embraer EMB-145s for Skyways AB		
SE-DZV	Boeing 737-804	32904	
SE-DZZ	Gates Learjet 35A	35A-415	D-COSY(2)
			N415DJ
			N19GL
			N125AX
SE-EAC	Cessna 172C	17249209	N1509Y
SE-EAE	Cessna 172C	17249354	N1654Y
SE-EAF	Cessna 172C	17249259	N1559Y
SE-EAL	Cessna 172F	17252008	N8108U
SE-EAN	Cessna 150B	15059581	N1181Y
SE-EAP	Cessna 172D	17249678	N2178Y
SE-EAR	Cessna 205	205-0101	N8101Z
SE-EAS	Cessna F172F	F172-0157	
SE-EAT	Cessna 172F	17252107	N8207U
SE-EAU	Cessna F172F	F172-0163	
SE-EAW	Cessna F172F	F172-0150	
SE-EBS	SAAB MFI-9 Junior	07	LN-BFA
			SE-EBS
SE-ECC	Piper PA-25-235/260 Pawnee (Permit 5.02)	25-2166	N6613Z
			N10F
SE-ECD	Piper PA-28-180 Cherokee B (W/o 18.8.68)	28-995	
SE-ECE	Piper PA-23-235 Apache (W/o 26.9.75)	27-505	N4915P
SE-ECG	Piper PA-25-235 Pawnee	25-2230	
SE-ECM	Piper PA-23-250 Aztec B (W/o 4.3.75)	27-2281	(G-ASDX)
			N10F
SE-ECN	Piper PA-18-150 Super Cub	18-7902	
SE-ECR	Piper PA-28-180 Cherokee B (W/o 11.7.73)	28-1351	
SE-ECS	Piper PA-30 Twin Comanche (CofA exp 6.87)	30-57	N10F
SE-ECT	Piper PA-28-180 Cherokee B	28-1320	N11C
			N7432W
SE-ECZ	Piper PA-18-150 Super Cub	18-8076	
SE-EDD	SAAB S.91C Safir	91318	OE-DSA
			(EI-AGY)
			SE-XBE
SE-EDO	Piper PA-22-108 Colt	22-8689	OH-CPL
			(G-AROM)
SE-EDY	Aero Commander 680E	335-28	N6828S
	(Scrapped after CofA expiry 4.88)		
SE-EEC	Cessna 180D (W/o 12.8.65)	18051029	OY-AEP
			LN-DBA
			N8629X
SE-EEE	Binder CP.301S Smaragd	119	(D-EDFO)
SE-EES	Beech D95A Travel Air	TD-539	
	(Scrapped after wheels-up landing in 1984)		
SE-EET	Piper PA-18 Super Cub 95	18-6331	OH-CPK
	(W/o 21.11.91)		SE-CEP
			N10F
SE-EEU	Beech D95A Travel Air	TD-540	OY-DPV
			SE-EEU
SE-EFC	SAAB MFI-9 Junior (W/o 29.12.88)	16	
SE-EFF	SAAB MFI-9 Junior	19	OH-MFC
			SE-EFF
SE-EFH	SAAB MFI-9 Junior	21	
SE-EFM	SAAB MFI-9B Trainer	025	SE-202
SE-EFO	SAAB MFI-9B Trainer	027	LN-DAA
			SE-EFO
SE-EFR	SAAB MFI-9B Trainer	029	

SE-EFS	SAAB MFI-9B Trainer	030	
SE-EFW	SAAB MFI-9B Trainer	033	
SE-EGD	Morane-Saulnier MS.880B Rallye Club	73	EL-ADM
SE-EGE	Lake LA-4 Skimmer (W/o 24.7.84)	303	N1141L
SE-EGK	Gardan GY-80 Horizon 160 (CofA expired 4.79)	52	
SE-EGL	Gardan GY-80 Horizon 160	26	OY-ATH
			SE-EGL
			F-BLVA
SE-EGN	Gardan GY-80 Horizon 160 (W/o 8.9.76)	106	(F-WLSE)
SE-EGO	Gardan GY-80 Horizon 160	113	
SE-EGT	Focke-Wulf FW.44J Stieglitz	081	D-EOIL
			OH-SZS
			SE-EGT
			Fv629
SE-EGU	Gardan GY-80 Horizon 180	143	F-BNQE
SE-EGY	Aero Commander 680FL	1410-61	(D-IBEZ)
	(Scrapped after CofA expiry 4.89)		N6374U
SE-EHA	Cessna 185B Skywagon	185-0559	N2559Z
SE-EHD	Cessna 185C Skywagon	185-0702	N5802T
SE-EHF	Cessna F172E	F172-0030/17250606	
SE-EHI	Cessna F172E	F172-0039/17250769	
SE-EHK	Cessna F172F	F172-0091	OY-TRM
SE-EHO	Cessna 206 Super Skywagon	206-0114	N5114U
SE-EHT	Cessna 172E	17251653	N5753T
SE-EHU	Cessna F172F (W/o 8.3.65)	F172-0096	
SE-EHW	Cessna F172F	F172-0106	
SE-EHX	Cessna F172F	F172-0102	OY-BAH
SE-EIH	Piper PA-18A-150 Super Cub	18-6875	OY-AIO
			N9798D
SE-EIM	Piper PA-28-180 Cherokee B (W/o 24.6.86)	28-1610	
SE-EIN	Piper PA-30 Twin Comanche	30-348	N10F
SE-EIO	Piper PA-28-180 Cherokee B	28-1368	N7465W
SE-EIX	Piper PA-28-180 Cherokee B	28-1684	
SE-EKG	Beech A23 Musketeer II (W/o 5.6.71)	M-638	
SE-EKL	Beech A23 Musketeer II (W/o 22.6.66)	M-721	
SE-EKR	Beech 95-B55 Baron (Instructional airframe)	TC-944	
SE-EKW	Beech D-95A Travel Air	TD-648	
SE-ELA	Beagle-Auster 6A Tugmaster	3724	G-ASHY
	(W/o 21.8.71)		VX110
SE-ELB	Beagle-Auster 6A Tugmaster (Rebuilding 12.02)	3732	TW538
SE-ELD	Beagle A.61 Terrier 1 (W/o 6.2.82)	3733	WE553
SE-ELF	Beagle-Auster 6A Tugmaster	3735	TW571
SE-ELG	Beagle-Auster 6A Tugmaster	3736	VF600
SE-ELK	Beagle A.61 Terrier 1 (W/o 16.7.76)	3739	VX935
SE-ELS	Cessna 182K Skylane	18258259	OY-AHA
			N2559R
SE-ELY	Cessna F172H	F172-0490	OH-CNE
SE-ELZ	Cessna 185B Skywagon	185-0578	LN-MAE
			SE-ELZ
			LN-DBH
			N2578Z
SE-EMB	Piper PA-28-140 Cherokee	28-20064	
SE-EMD	Piper PA-28-140 Cherokee	28-20053	
SE-EMH	Piper PA-28-180 Cherokee B	28-1746	N7738W
SE-EMI	Piper PA-18-150 Super Cub (W/o 30.6.72)	18-8149	
SE-EML	Piper PA-18-150 Super Cub	18-8294	OH-PDK
	(W/o 14.2.82)		SE-EML
SE-EMN	Piper PA-28-140 Cherokee	28-20361	
SE-EMR	Piper PA-28-150 Cherokee C	28-2081	
SE-EMW	Piper PA-28-180 Cherokee C	28-2192	
SE-EMX	Piper PA-25-235 Pawnee B	25-3125	
SE-END	SAAB MFI-9B Trainer	039	
SE-ENE	SAAB MFI-9B Trainer	040	
SE-ENG	SAAB MFI-9B Trainer	054	LN-LJA
			SE-ENG
SE-EOB	Piper PA-28-150 Cherokee C	28-2234	
	(CofA expired 9.85)		
SE-EOC	Piper PA-28-150 Cherokee C	28-2220	
SE-EOD	Piper PA-28-180 Cherokee C	28-2481	
	(W/o 8.7.73, remains sold to Norway)		
SE-EOE	Piper PA-28-180 Cherokee C	28-3086	
SE-EOF	Piper PA-28-140 Cherokee (W/o 11.11.67)	28-21151	N11C
SE-EOH	Piper PA-25-235 Pawnee B	25-3199	
SE-EOK	Piper PA-30 Twin Comanche	30-157	N7135Y
SE-EOM	Piper PA-28-150 Cherokee C	28-2384	
	(Cr.8.10.72 - wreck sold to Norway)		
SE-EOO	Piper PA-28-180 Cherokee C	28-2185	
SE-EOP	Piper PA-28-140 Cherokee	28-20814	
SE-EOR	Piper PA-28-180 Cherokee C	28-2416	
SE-EOS	Piper PA-28-180 Cherokee C	28-2533	
SE-EOT	Piper PA-28-180 Cherokee C	28-2461	
SE-EOU	Piper PA-24-250 Comanche (W/o 27.10.99)	24-3506	OH-CPV
			N8202P
SE-EOZ	Piper PA-28-150 Cherokee C	28-2477	
SE-EPB	Piper PA-25-235 Pawnee B (Permit)	25-3264	
SE-EPF	Piper PA-18-150 Super Cub	18-8249	
SE-EPG	Piper PA-22-160 Tri-Pacer	22-7629	LN-BWS
SE-EPI	Piper PA-28-140 Cherokee	28-20976	
SE-EPK	Piper PA-28-140 Cherokee	28-20981	
SE-EPL	Piper PA-28-140 Cherokee	28-22422	
SE-EPM	Piper PA-18-150 Super Cub	18-8297	
SE-EPO	Piper PA-28-235 Cherokee	28-10614	N9038W
SE-EPR	Piper PA-23-250 Aztec C	27-3126	
SE-ERT	Republic RC-3 Seabee	846	N6573K
SE-ERU	SOCATA MS.880B Rallye Club	1267	
	(Converted to Rallye 150ST)		
SE-ERW	SOCATA MS.892A Rallye Commodore 150	11407	

SE-ERZ	SOCATA MS.892A Rallye Commodore 150	11442	OY-DJR
SE-ESA	Cessna 337 Super Skymaster (W/o 2.1.72)	33700097	N2197X
SE-ESB	Cessna 150E	15061007	OH-CEC
			N2507J
SE-ESC	Cessna 140	13284	OH-CSZ
			N3036N
SE-ESD	Cessna F172F	F172-0125	OH-CED
			SE-ESD
SE-ESF	Cessna 182H Skylane (W/o 4.5.67)	18256211	N2311X
SE-ESG	Cessna P206 Super Skylane (Dbf 27.4.67)	P206-0138	N2638X
SE-ESO	Cessna 150F	15062142	N8842S
SE-ESS	Cessna F172H	F172-0341	
SE-EST	Cessna 205	205-0364	N8364Z
SE-ESU	Cessna F172G	F172-0248	
SE-ESX	Cessna F172G (W/o 14.7.74)	F172-0280	
SE-ETA	Cessna 150F	15061882	N8282S
SE-ETB	Cessna F172G (W/o 20.1.81)	F172-0228	
SE-ETC	Cessna F172G	F172-0242	
SE-ETD	Cessna F150F	F150-0021/15062874	
SE-ETE	Cessna 182J Skylane	18257122	N3022F
SE-ETF	Cessna F172H (W/o 16.6.75)	F172-0374	
SE-ETL	Cessna 180H	18051468	LN-BIG(1)
			N4768U
SE-ETN	Cessna F150G	F150-0193	
SE-ETO	Cessna F150G	F150-0196	
SE-ETP	Cessna 172H	17255282	N3787F
SE-ETR	Cessna 150F	15062718	N11B
			N8618G
SE-ETX	Cessna 150D (Rebuilding 2.03)	15060105	LN-BFS
			N4105U
SE-ETZ	Cessna 336 Skymaster	336-0063	OY-TRH
	(CofA exp 12.81)		(HB-LCZ)
			N1763Z
SE-EUC	SAAB MFI-9B Trainer (W/o 27.4.75)	057	
SE-EUF	SAAB MFI-9B Trainer	060	
SE-EUM	SAAB MFI-9B Trainer	043	Fv:801-43
			(SE-ENH)
SE-EUO	SAAB MFI-9B Trainer (Rebuiling 12.01)	045	Fv:801-45
			(SE-EUC)
SE-EUR	de Havilland DH.104 Dove 6A	04496	G-ATAP
			HB-LAP
SE-EUX	Beech A23-24 Musketeer Super III	MA-131	
	(Sold to Germany after CofA expiry 12.74)		
SE-EWC	SAAB MFI-9B Trainer	048	Fv:801-48
			(SE-EUF)
SE-EWD	SAAB MFI-9B Trainer	049	Fv:801-49
			(SE-EUG)
SE-EWN	Beech A23-24 Musketeer Super III (W/o 3.6.95)	MA-174	
SE-EWP	Beech 95-C55 Baron (W/o 9.93)	TE-403	
SE-EWW	Beech A23-24 Musketeer Super III (W/o 11.10.84)	MA-191	
SE-EWY	Beech A23-19 Musketeer Sport III	MB-192	
SE-EXA	Cessna 182K Skylane	18257739	(OY-EGR)
			N2539Q
SE-EXC	Cessna F150H	F150-0254	LN-FAI
SE-EXD	Cessna F150J	F150-0463	
SE-EXF	Cessna 185D Skywagon	185-0902	N1544F
SE-EXW	Beech 95-B55 Baron	TC-1073	
SE-EYA	Piper PA-25-235 Pawnee B (Damaged 1.5.00)	25-3676	
SE-EYB	Piper PA-25-235 Pawnee B	25-3680	
SE-EYC	Piper PA-28-180 Cherokee C	28-3114	
SE-EYI	Piper PA-28-180 Cherokee C	28-3163	
SE-EYL	Piper PA-18-150 Super Cub	18-8347	N4166Z
SE-EYO	Piper PA-28-180 Cherokee C (Dbr 4.9.02)	28-3198	
SE-EYT	Piper PA-25-235 Pawnee B (W/o 6.7.70)	25-4076	
SE-EYU	Piper PA-28-140 Cherokee (W/o 7.10.89)	28-21794	
SE-EYX	Piper PA-25-235 Pawnee B	25-3898	
SE-EYY	Piper PA-28-140 Cherokee	28-21843	
SE-EZC	Piper PA-28-180 Cherokee C	28-3543	
SE-EZD	Piper PA-28-180 Cherokee C	28-3583	
SE-EZE	Piper PA-18S-150 Super Cub	18-8444	
SE-EZF	Piper PA-32-260 Cherokee Six	32-768	
SE-EZO	Piper PA-28-140 Cherokee	28-24361	
SE-EZT	Piper PA-28-140 Cherokee	28-22967	SE-EPW
SE-EZU	Piper PA-28-180 Cherokee C	28-3679	
SE-EZX	Piper PA-18-150 Super Cub	18-8610	
SE-EZY	Piper PA-31 Turbo Navajo (W/o 26.11.79)	31-22	N9016Y
SE-EZZ	Piper PA-18-150 Super Cub	18-8484	
SE-FAA	Piper PA-28-140 Cherokee	28-23338	
SE-FAC	Piper PA-28-180 Cherokee C (Stored)	28-4287	
SE-FAD	Piper PA-28-180 Cherokee C	28-4319	
SE-FAG	Piper PA-28-140 Cherokee (W/o 16.10.89)	28-23173	N9700W
SE-FAH	Piper PA-18-150 Super Cub (Rebuilding 3.02)	18-8618	
SE-FAI	Piper PA-28-140 Cherokee	28-22647	
SE-FAL	Piper PA-28-180 Cherokee D	28-4383	
SE-FAO	Piper PA-28-140 Cherokee	28-23298	
SE-FAX	Piper PA-28-140 Cherokee	28-22687	
SE-FAZ	Piper PA-18-150 Super Cub (W/o 2.7.95)	18-8495	N4281Z
SE-FBE	Cessna F172H	F172-0478	
SE-FBF	Cessna F150H	F150-0262	
SE-FBG	Cessna F150H (W/o 10.5.80)	F150-0272	
SE-FBL	Cessna F150H	F150-0260	
SE-FBM	Reims FR172E Rocket	FR17200012	F-WLIL
	(W/o 10.7.87)		
SE-FBP	Reims FR172E Rocket	FR17200029	
SE-FBT	Reims FR172E Rocket	FR17200034	
SE-FCD	Piper PA-28-140 Cherokee	28-23455	N9931W
SE-FCG	Piper PA-28R-180 Cherokee Arrow	28R-30504	

SE-FCH	Piper PA-28-140 Cherokee	28-23905	
SE-FCI	Piper PA-28-140 Cherokee	28-23920	
SE-FCK	Piper PA-32-260 Cherokee Six	32-943	
SE-FCM	Piper PA-28-180 Cherokee D	28-4766	
SE-FCN	Piper PA-28-140 Cherokee	28-23556	N11C N3437K
SE-FCO	Piper PA-28-140 Cherokee	28-23504	N11C N9957W
SE-FCP	Piper PA-28-140 Cherokee (W/o 8.8.89)	28-23533	N11C N9985W
SE-FDA	Piper PA-28-140 Cherokee	28-24386	
SE-FDC	Piper PA-28-140 Cherokee	28-24451	
SE-FDD	Piper PA-28-140 Cherokee	28-24422	
SE-FDE	Piper PA-28-140 Cherokee	28-24433	
SE-FDH	Piper PA-28R-180 Cherokee Arrow (W/o 22.2.75)	28R-30664	
SE-FDI	Piper PA-28-140 Cherokee	28-24391	
SE-FDL	Piper PA-28-180 Cherokee D	28-4758	
SE-FDP	Piper PA-28R-180 Cherokee Arrow (W/o 5.9.71)	28R-30837	
SE-FDT	Piper PA-28R-180 Cherokee Arrow (Accident 6.5.95)	28R-30687	
SE-FDV	Piper PA-28R-180 Cherokee Arrow	28R-30729	
SE-FEL	Cessna F150J	F150-0412	
SE-FEP	Cessna 182M Skylane	18259395	N70854
SE-FER	Cessna 207 Skywagon 207	20700042	LN-BIP SE-FER N91055
SE-FES	Cessna 177A Cardinal (W/o 2.10.79)	17701315	N30543
SE-FFC	Piper PA-28-140 Cherokee B	28-25013	
SE-FFD	Piper PA-28-140 Cherokee B	28-25017	
SE-FFF	Piper PA-28-180 Cherokee D	28-4524	N5230L
SE-FFG	Piper PA-24-250 Comanche	24-2748	G-ARXI N7542P
SE-FFH	Piper PA-28-180 Cherokee D	28-5080	
SE-FFI	Piper PA-28-180 Cherokee D	28-5096	
SE-FFM	Piper PA-28-140 Cherokee B (W/o 14.8.70)	28-25092	
SE-FFR	Piper PA-28-140 Cherokee B	28-25446	
SE-FFU	Piper PA-28R-200 Cherokee Arrow (CofA exp 9.86. Instructional airframe at Nykoping)	28R-35242	
SE-FFV	Piper PA-28-140 Cherokee B (W/o 4.7.82)	28-26152	
SE-FFX	Piper PA-28-140 Cherokee C	28-26842	
SE-FFY	Piper PA-22-135 Tri-Pacer	22-656	ZS-DHB
SE-FFZ	Piper PA-28-140 Cherokee B	28-25440	
SE-FGD	Maule M-4-220C Strata Rocket	2054C	N2061U
SE-FGI	Bellanca 7GCBC Citabria	309-71	
SE-FGK	Maule M-4-220C Strata Rocket	2063C	N2075U
SE-FGM	Champion 7GCAA Citabria	200	
SE-FGN	Fuji FA-200-180 Aero Subaru	3	JA3336
SE-FGO	Mitsubishi MU.2B-20	102	HB-LED
SE-FGR	Beagle B.121 Pup 100	047	G-35-047
SE-FGU	Beagle B.121 Pup 150	068	G-35-068
SE-FGV	Beagle B.121 Pup 100	079	G-35-079
SE-FGY	Beagle B.121 Pup 100 (Rebuilding 12.02)	100	G-35-100
SE-FGZ	Beagle B.121 Pup 100	102	G-35-102
SE-FHG	Piper PA-28-140 Cherokee B	28-25716	N8861N
SE-FHH	Piper PA-28-140 Cherokee B (W/o 9.5.71)	28-26140	OH-PCD
SE-FHI	Piper PA-28-140 Cherokee C	28-26844	
SE-FHN	Piper PA-28-140 Cherokee C	28-26721	
SE-FHO	Piper PA-28-180 Cherokee E	28-5614	
SE-FHT	Piper PA-31 Turbo Navajo (Instructional airframe at Linkoping)	31-488	N6566L
SE-FHU	Piper PA-28-140 Cherokee B (Cr.9.8.80 - instructional airframe at Vasteras)	28-26068	
SE-FHV	Piper PA-32S-300 Cherokee Six C	32-40919	
SE-FHY	Piper PA-28-140 Cherokee B (W/o 15.3.72)	28-26255	N5534U
SE-FHZ	Piper PA-28-140 Cherokee B	28-26250	N5533U
SE-FIA	SAAB MFI-9B Trainer	063	
SE-FIB	SAAB MFI-9B Trainer	064	
SE-FID	SAAB MFI-9B Trainer	066	OY-DRF
SE-FIG	SAAB MFI-9B-130 Trainer	069	
SE-FIM	SAAB MFI-15-200 Safari	006	
SE-FIO	SAAB MFI-15-200 Safari	15-901	ET-AGC SE-FIO
SE-FIP	SAAB MFI-15-200 Safari	15-902	ET-AGD SE-FIP
SE-FIS	Bölkow BO.208C Junior	617	OY-POK G-ATYP (D-EHUW)
SE-FIT	SAAB MFI-15-200A Safari	15-832	N24AF SE-FIT
SE-FKA	Reims FR172F Rocket	FR17200110	
SE-FKD	Cessna F150J	F150-0453	
SE-FKH	Reims FR172F Rocket (W/o 30.10.70)	FR17200114	
SE-FKL	Reims FR172F Rocket	FR17200132	
SE-FKO	Cessna 177A Cardinal (Damaged 30.4.00)	17701340	(LN-FAK) (OY-AGM) N30579
SE-FKS	Cessna 182M Skylane	18259572	N71310
SE-FKX	Reims/Cessna F150K	F15000595	
SE-FKY	Cessna A185ESkywagon (W/o 22.11.79)	18501672	N1958U
SE-FLA	Piper PA-25-260 Pawnee C (Permit 2.02)	25-4487	LN-VYM
SE-FLG	Piper PA-31 Turbo Navajo (Instructional airframe at Vasteras)	31-361	LN-LMU
SE-FLI	Piper PA-31 Turbo Navajo (Instructional airframe at Nykoping)	31-343	(OY-BKE)
SE-FLR	Rockwell Commander 112A	328	(N1328J)
SE-FLS	Rockwell Commander 112A	350	(N1350J)
SE-FLY	Rockwell Commander 114	14010	
SE-FMA	Cessna 172K (W/o 5.8.87)	17258872	(LN-VYC) N7172G
SE-FMK	Reims/Cessna F172M	F17201237	D-EORE N94724
SE-FML	Reims FR172F Rocket	FR17200136	
SE-FMO	Cessna 150H	15068537	N22816
SE-FMU	Cessna U206E Skywagon 206	U20601478	N1478M
SE-FMX	Cessna A185E Skywagon	18501740	N1986U
SE-FMY	Reims/Cessna F172M (W/o 28.6.94)	F17200907	
SE-FMZ	Cessna 182P Skylane	18261431	N21126
SE-FNA	de Havilland DH.82A Tiger Moth	82003	D-EMWT D-EMWE N6730
SE-FNB	Beech A24R Sierra	MC-86	
SE-FNC	Robin HR.100-210 Safari	180	LN-BIW SE-FNC (G-BAYM)
SE-FNE	Piper PA-31-350 Navajo Chieftain	31-7405434	N54306
SE-FNK	Beech 95-B55 Baron (W/o 15.6.84)	TC-1373	
SE-FNN	DHC-1 Chipmunk 22 (Dbf 13.4.76)	C1/0252	G-BCBF WD309
SE-FNO	Cessna U206A Super Skywagon	U206-0561	LN-DBS N4861F
SE-FNP	DHC-1 Chipmunk 22	C1/0756	G-BCYA WP867
SE-FNZ	Beech 95-B55 Baron	TC-933	OH-BBZ SE-FNZ N354RJ
SE-FOG	Beagle B.121 Pup 150 (W/o 13.12.79)	045	G-AXCW G-35-045
SE-FOK	Beagle B.121 Pup 150	086	G-AXID
SE-FOO	DHC-1 Chipmunk 22	C1/0676	G-BBWI WP785
SE-FPC	Piper PA-28-140 Cherokee C	28-26723	OY-ANR SE-FPC
SE-FPD	Piper PA-28-140 Cherokee C	28-26511	
SE-FPI	Piper PA-28-140 Cherokee C	28-26838	
SE-FPK	Piper PA-25-260 Pawnee C (W/o 3.7.77)	25-5199	N8753L N9736N
SE-FPL	Piper PA-23-250 Aztec D	27-4552	
SE-FPM	Piper PA-28-140 Cherokee D (W/o 10.2.79)	28-7125046	
SE-FPO	Piper PA-28R-180 Cherokee Arrow	28R-31263	N3292R
SE-FPP	Piper PA-28-140 Cherokee F (W/o 2.1.79)	28-7325017	
SE-FPR	Piper PA-25-260 Pawnee C (W/o 26.10.71)	25-5280	(CC-PGM) N8793L
SE-FPS	Piper PA-18-150 Super Cub (W/o 31.7.95)	18-8733	LN-LMS
SE-FPT	Piper PA-28-140 Cherokee D	28-7125172	
SE-FPV	Piper PA-28-140 Cherokee D	28-7125156	
SE-FRC	Cessna 310Q (Instructional airframe)	310Q0119	OY-BFG SE-FRC N7619Q
SE-FRD	Cessna 414	414-0085	N8185Q
SE-FRE	Reims/Cessna FA150K Aerobat	FA1500067	
SE-FRF	Cessna 185D Skywagon	185-0909	LN-HHS N1548F
SE-FRM	Cessna U206E Skywagon 206 (W/o 1.8.81)	U20601453	LN-BEV N1453M
SE-FRN	Cessna F150J	F150-0414	LN-AEC
SE-FRP	Cessna U206F Stationair	U20601970	(N51012)
SE-FRR	Cessna A185F Skywagon (W/o 9.8.97)	18502160	(N70416)
SE-FRV	Cessna F172F	F172-0101	OY-TRN
SE-FRY	Cessna 185C Skywagon (Damaged 4.9.98)	185-0661	OH-CSS N2661Z
SE-FRZ	Cessna A185E Skywagon (W/o 23.876)	18501772	LN-AED (LN-BEA) N5803J
SE-FSA	SOCATA MS.893A Rallye Commodore 180	10719	OY-DKR
SE-FSD	SOCATA MS.880B Rallye Club (Permit 3.00)	1698	
SE-FSE	SOCATA MS.880B Rallye Club	1732	
SE-FSG	SOCATA MS.880B Rallye Club	1864	
SE-FSM	SOCATA MS.880B Rallye Club	1916	
SE-FSN	SOCATA MS.893A Rallye Commodore 180	11926	
SE-FSO	SOCATA MS.892A Rallye Commodore 150	11944	
SE-FSP	SOCATA MS.892A Rallye Commodore 150	11945	
SE-FSR	SOCATA MS.892A Rallye Commodore 150	12035	
SE-FSU	SOCATA MS.894A Minerva 220	12076	
SE-FSY	SOCATA MS.893A Rallye Commodore 180	12103	
SE-FSZ	SOCATA MS.880B Rallye Club	2409	F-BUZJ
SE-FTP	Aero Commander 680E (W/o 25.7.90)	623-1	HB-GOR D-IBUC N6235B
SE-FTT	American-Aviation AA-1A Trainer	AA1A-0195	OY-AYJ N9295L
SE-FTV	American-Aviation AA-5 Traveler	AA5-0422	N7122L
SE-FTY	Aerotek Pitts S-2A (W/o 20.5.95)	2049	G-BAPU
SE-FTZ	Gardan GY-80 Horizon 180	173	OY-DDG
SE-FUO	Maule M-4-210C Rocket (W/o 4.10.82)	1086C	
SE-FUR	Ryan Navion 4	4-1818	HB-ESF N4818K
SE-FUT	Tipsy T.66 Nipper II	53	HB-SVI
SE-FUU	Bellanca 7ECA Citabria	809-71	
SE-FUV	Maule M-4-220C Strata Rocket	2122C	
SE-FUX	Mooney M.20B Mark 21	1780	D-ELER

SE-FUZ	Noorduyn AT-16 Harvard IIB	14-526	Fv16144
			FE792
			42-12279
SE-FVR	HOAC DV-20 Katana	20021	G-KATA
SE-FVV	SAAB S.91B-2 Safir	91252	LN-HHW(2)
			(SE-LBG)
			LN-HHW(2)
			RNoAF: 040
			Fv50040
SE-FXB	Cessna 182N Skylane	18260529	N8989G
SE-FXC	Cessna F172F	F172-0103	OH-CSJ
SE-FXP	Cessna U206F Stationair	U20601779	N9579G
SE-FXR	Reims/Cessna F172L	F17200830	
SE-FXT	Reims/Cessna F172L	F17200856	
SE-FXV	Cessna 182P Skylane	18261259	N20853
SE-FYC	Piper PA-28-140 Cherokee D	28-7125167	
SE-FYF	Piper PA-28-140 Cherokee E	28-7225144	
	(W/o 11.10.78)		
SE-FYG	Piper PA-25-260 Pawnee C	25-5328	N8907L
			N9688N
SE-FYH	Piper PA-25-260 Pawnee C (W/o 8.6.72)	25-5351	N8840L
SE-FYK	Piper PA-18-150 Super Cub	18-8777	LN-BNY
SE-FYL	Piper PA-28-140 Cherokee E	28-7225145	
SE-FYN	Piper PA-28-180 Cherokee F	28-7105152	
SE-FYO	Piper PA-28-140 Cherokee E	28-7225196	
SE-FYS	Piper PA-28-180 Cherokee Challenger	28-7305009	N11C
SE-FYZ	Piper PA-28-140 Cherokee F (W/o 18.2.79)	28-7325006	
SE-FZE	Cessna 182P Skylane (W/o 21.11.89)	18261597	N21379
SE-FZK	Cessna 402A (W/o 8.5.82)	402A0057	OY-AGN
			N4557Q
SE-FZL	Cessna 414	414-0382	G-BARE
			N1602T
SE-FZO	Reims/Cessna F172M	F17201145	
SE-FZS	Reims/Cessna F172M	F17201132	
SE-FZU	Reims/Cessna F172M	F17201036	
SE-FZY	Reims/Cessna F172M	F17201024	(D-EJXU)
SE-FZZ	Reims/Cessna F177RG Cardinal RG	F177RG0099	
SE-GAD	Piper PA-34-200 Seneca	34-7350211	(SE-LCA)
			OH-PNE
			SE-GAD
SE-GAF	Piper PA-28-140 Cherokee E (W/o 30.7.82)	28-7225292	
SE-GAL	Piper PA-28-180 Cherokee G	28-7205256	
SE-GAN	Piper PA-28-180 Cherokee G	28-7205251	
SE-GAO	Piper PA-34-200 Seneca	34-7250224	LN-AED
			SE-GAO
SE-GAT	Piper PA-28-180 Cherokee Challenger	28-7305420	
SE-GAV	Piper PA-28-180 Cherokee Archer	28-7405203	
SE-GAZ	Piper PA-28-140 Cherokee F	28-7325216	
SE-GBE	Piper PA-28-151 Cherokee Warrior	28-7415071	
SE-GBF	Piper PA-25-235D/260 Pawnee	25-7305529	N8925L
	(Permit 1.05)		N9688N
SE-GBG	Piper PA-31 Turbo Navajo B	31-7401234	
SE-GBH	Piper PA-28-151 Cherokee Warrior	28-7415307	
SE-GBL	Piper PA-34-200 Seneca	34-7450147	
SE-GBO	Piper PA-31 Turbo Navajo B	31-7400983	
SE-GBP	Piper PA-28-151 Cherokee Warrior	28-7415582	
SE-GBS	Piper PA-31 Turbo Navajo B	31-7400984	OH-MRS
			SE-GBS
SE-GBY	Piper PA-28-151 Cherokee Warrior	28-7515027	
SE-GBZ	Piper PA-32-260 Cherokee Six D	32-7200006	N8668N
SE-GCB	Piper PA-18-150 Super Cub	18-8542	Army:51235
	(Damaged 9.4.00)		N10F
SE-GCC	Piper PA-18-150 Super Cub	18-8544	Army:51236
			N10F
SE-GCD	Piper PA-18-150 Super Cub	18-8545	Army:51237
			N10F
SE-GCF	Piper PA-18-150 Super Cub	18-8600	Army:51239
			N10F
SE-GCG	Piper PA-18-150 Super Cub	18-8441	Army:51241
			N10F
SE-GCH	Piper PA-18-150 Super Cub	18-8361	Army:51242
			N10F
SE-GCI	Piper PA-18-150 Super Cub	18-8363	Army:51244
			N10F
SE-GCK	Piper PA-18-150 Super Cub	18-7918	Army:51245
			N10F
SE-GCL	Piper PA-18-150 Super Cub	18-7919	Army:51246
			N10F
SE-GCM	Piper PA-18-150 Super Cub	18-7920	Army:51247
			N10F
SE-GCN	Piper PA-18-150 Super Cub (W/o 16.3.75)	18-7921	Army:51248
			N10F
SE-GCR	Piper PA-18-150 Super Cub	18-6806	Army:51254
			SE-CKL
			N10F
SE-GCV	Reims/Cessna F337G Skymaster	F33700068	OH-CGN
	(Reims-assembled 337G with US c/n 33701583)		
SE-GCY	Cessna 150M	15076410	N3179V
SE-GDB	Piper PA-28-180 Cherokee Challenger	28-7305304	
SE-GDD	Piper PA-28-140 Cherokee Cruiser	28-7425411	
	(W/o 29.8.82)		
SE-GDE	Piper PA-28R-200 Cherokee Arrow II (W/o)	28R-7335160	
SE-GDG	Piper PA-28-140 Cherokee F	28-7325205	
SE-GDL	Piper PA-28-151 Cherokee Warrior	28-7415303	
SE-GDM	Piper PA-28-180 Cherokee Challenger	28-7305529	
SE-GDN	Piper PA-31 Turbo Navajo B (W/o 12.99)	31-7300947	
SE-GDV	Piper PA-32-260 Cherokee Six	32-7400029	

SE-GEE	DHC-6 Twin Otter 300	364	F-GFAH
			SE-GEE
			D-IDOT
SE-GEH	Cessna 402B (W/o 28.11.88)	402B1351	N6388X
SE-GEL	Cessna R172K Hawk XP	R1722879	N736XW
	(W/o 5.95, sold to Norway)		
SE-GEM	Cessna 185D Skywagon (W/o 26.5.79)	185-0827	LN-BIE
			N11B
			N4087F
SE-GEN	Cessna 180B	50510	LN-TSH
			N5210E
SE-GES	Cessna A185E Skywagon (W/o 21.5.98)	185-1467	LN-RTN
			N2717J
SE-GET	Cessna U206F Stationair	U20601959	LN-BFI
			N50950
SE-GEV	Bellanca 8GCBC Scout (W/o 25.6.83)	199-76	LN-HOA
SE-GFA	SOCATA MS.894A Minerva 220	12004	(D-ENML)
SE-GFB	SOCATA MS.893A Rallye Commodore 180	10944	OY-DJH
			SE-CIY
SE-GFE	SOCATA Rallye 180T Galérien	3243	
SE-GFF	SOCATA Rallye 180T Galérien	3244	
SE-GFH	SOCATA TB-10 Tobago	45	F-ODMH
SE-GFI	SOCATA TB-9 Tampico	81	OH-TBB
			SE-GFI
SE-GFN	Partenavia P.68B (W/o 20.4.87)	56	
SE-GFP	SOCATA TB-10 Tobago (W/o 1.7.95)	159	
SE-GFR	SOCATA TB-10 Tobago (W/o 8.7.91)	160	
SE-GFT	SOCATA TB-9 Tampico	180	
SE-GFX	SOCATA TB-10 Tobago (Under rebuild)	264	F-OGLR
SE-GGB	Reims/Cessna F172M	F17201046	
SE-GGK	Cessna A185F Skywagon	18502456	N1736R
SE-GGO	Reims/Cessna F172M	F17201171	OY-BFT
SE-GGX	Reims/Cessna F172M	F17201326	
SE-GHA	Mitsubishi MU.2B-20	283	N327MA
SE-GHB	Mitsubishi MU.2B-20	287	N331MA
SE-GHC	Mitsubishi MU.2B-20	289	N334MA
SE-GHD	Mitsubishi MU.2B-20	293	N453MA
SE-GHE	Mitsubishi MU.2B-20	294	N454MA
SE-GHF	Mitsubishi MU.2B-20	299	N459MA
SE-GHH	Mitsubishi MU.2B-20	222	N5PN
			N4PN
			N188MA
SE-GHI	Bellanca 8KCAB Decathlon (W/o 18.2.80)	486-79	
SE-GHL	Robin R.2100A	172	
SE-GHO	Cessna R182 Skylane RG (W/o 27.8.87)	R18200287	N3630C
SE-GHR	Maule M-5-235C Lunar Rocket (W/o 24.6.83)	7257C	
SE-GIC	Piper PA-34-200T Seneca II	34-7570028	LN-KLK
			(LN-KLS)
			SE-GIC
SE-GII	Piper PA-28-151 Cherokee Warrior	28-7515216	
SE-GIK	Piper PA-28-180 Cherokee Archer	28-7505095	(N.....)
			SE-GIK
SE-GIL	Piper PA-28-140 Cherokee Cruiser	28-7525116	
SE-GIN	Piper PA-31 Navajo C	31-7512039	
SE-GIO	Piper PA-28-180 Cherokee Archer	28-7505131	
SE-GIP	Piper PA-34-200T Seneca II	34-7570210	
SE-GIR	Piper PA-28R-200 Cherokee Arrow	28R-7535140	
SE-GIS	Piper PA-31 Navajo C (W/o 30.6.83)	31-7512028	
SE-GIT	Piper PA-31 Navajo C	31-7512041	
SE-GIX	Piper PA-28R-200 Cherokee Arrow II	28R-7435106	N54448
	(W/o 25.7.96)		
SE-GIZ	Piper PA-28-180 Cherokee Archer	28-7505015	N32009
SE-GKC	Reims/Cessna F150M	F15001216	
SE-GKD	Reims/Cessna F172M	F17201228	
SE-GKE	Reims/Cessna F172M	F17201230	
SE-GKF	Reims/Cessna F172M	F17201231	
SE-GKR	Cessna 337A Super Skymaster	33700365	D-GIPY
			(N6365F)
SE-GKT	Reims/Cessna F172M	F17201329	
SE-GKY	Reims/Cessna F172M	F17201215	OY-BID
SE-GKZ	Reims/Cessna F172M	F17201332	OY-BIF
SE-GLC	Piper PA-28-180 Cherokee Archer	28-7505241	
SE-GLE	Piper PA-31 Navajo C	31-7512056	
SE-GLH	Piper PA-28-181 Cherokee Archer II	28-7790159	
SE-GLR	Piper PA-28-181 Cherokee Archer II	28-7690040	
	(W/o 12.7.84)		
SE-GLS	Piper PA-28-181 Cherokee Archer II	28-7690076	
	(W/o 11.2.93)		
SE-GLU	Piper PA-28-151 Cherokee Warrior	28-7615031	
SE-GMA	Reims/Cessna F172M	F17201463	
SE-GMC	Reims/Cessna F172M	F17201456	
SE-GMD	Reims/Cessna F172M	F17201430	
SE-GME	Reims/Cessna F177RG Cardinal RG	F177RG0143	
SE-GMF	Reims/Cessna F150M (W/o 25.9.87)	F15001288	
SE-GMI	Cessna A185F Skywagon	18502583	N4638C
SE-GMK	Cessna U206F Stationair	U20603256	(N8395Q)
SE-GMM	Reims/Cessna F337G Skymaster	F33700077	
	(Reims-assembled 337G with US c/n 33701676)		
SE-GMN	Reims/Cessna FRA150M Aerobat	FRA1500286	
SE-GMO	Cessna 402B	402B0809	LN-AED
	(Current status unknown)		N3817C
SE-GMS	Reims/Cessna F150M	F15001315	
SE-GMT	Reims/Cessna F150M	F15001320	
SE-GMU	Reims/Cessna F172M	F17201481	
SE-GNA	Piper PA-31 Navajo C	31-7612034	N9721N
SE-GNF	Piper PA-28-181 Cherokee Archer II	28-7690149	
SE-GNG	Piper PA-28-151 Cherokee Warrior	28-7615216	

SE-GNH	Piper PA-28-181 Cherokee Archer II	28-7690226	
	(W/o 22.5.79)		
SE-GNL	Piper PA-28-151 Cherokee Warrior	28-7615280	
SE-GNN	Piper PA-28-181 Cherokee Archer II	28-7690347	
	(W/o 1.2.96)		
SE-GNR	Piper PA-32R-300 Cherokee Lance	32R-7680252	N75053
SE-GNS	Piper PA-28-151 Cherokee Warrior	28-7615340	
SE-GNU	Piper PA-28-181 Cherokee Archer II	28-7690466	
	(W/o 28.1.95)		
SE-GNV	Piper PA-32R-300 Cherokee Lance	32R-7680221	N9430K
SE-GOA	Cessna A185F Skywagon	18502603	N4853C
SE-GOB	Reims/Cessna F172M	F17201175	D-EDJQ
SE-GOH	Cessna A185F Skywagon	18503079	N29070
SE-GOL	Cessna A185F Skywagon (W/o 19.9.83)	18502900	N8712Z
SE-GON	Cessna 172M	17267511	N73501
SE-GOP	Cessna U206G Stationair II (W/o 6.8.04)	U20603528	(N8776Q)
SE-GOR	Reims/Cessna F172M	F17201050	G-BBKH
SE-GOY	Cessna A185F Skywagon	18503170	N93040
SE-GOZ	Cessna A185F Skywagon	18502994	N5065R
SE-GPD	Piper PA-28-151 Cherokee Warrior	28-7715242	
SE-GPE	Piper PA-28-181 Cherokee Archer II	28-7790232	
SE-GPF	Piper PA-18-150 Super Cub (W/o 16.7.00)	18-7709057	
SE-GPG	Piper PA-18-150 Super Cub	18-7709068	
SE-GPH	Piper PA-28-161 Cherokee Warrior II	28-7716116	
SE-GPL	Piper PA-28-181 Cherokee Archer II	28-7790291	
SE-GPN	Piper PA-28-161 Cherokee Warrior II	28-7716051	
SE-GPO	Piper PA-28-181 Cherokee Archer II	28-7790373	
SE-GPR	Piper PA-28-161 Cherokee Warrior II	28-7716120	N9630N
	(Badly damaged 2.9.00)		
SE-GPT	Piper PA-28R-201 Cherokee Arrow III	28R-7737014	
SE-GPU	Piper PA-28-161 Cherokee Warrior II	28-7716200	
SE-GPX	Piper PA-34-200T Seneca II	34-7770290	N9538N
SE-GRA	de Havilland DH.104 Dove 6	04437	G-AMZN
SE-GRD	Lake LA-4-200 Buccaneer	499	OH-AKA
			N5042L
SE-GRE	Beech A23-24 Musketeer Super III	MA-164	OH-BMF
SE-GRG	Maule M-5-210C Strata Rocket	6166C	
SE-GRK	DHC-1 Chipmunk 22	C1/0104	RDAF: P-125
SE-GRO	Maule M-5-235C Lunar Rocket	7069C	
	(Damaged 16.8.97)		
SE-GRS	Lake LA-4-200 Buccaneer	826	TF-GRS
			(SE-GRS)
			N6173V
SE-GRV	Maule M-5-235C Lunar Rocket	7080C	
SE-GRZ	Piper PA-32R-300 Cherokee Lance	32R-7680231	N9586K
SE-GSE	Rockwell Commander 112B	508	
SE-GSF	Rockwell Commander 112B	537	
SE-GST	Thrush Commander S2R-T34	1723R	OH-VKY
	(W/o 3.6.82)		N5523X
SE-GSV	Robin R.2100A	157	
SE-GSY	Robin HR.200/100 Club	107	
SE-GTC	SOCATA Rallye 235EGabier	12798	
SE-GTD	SOCATA Rallye 100ST	2908	
SE-GTG	SOCATA MS.892E Rallye 150T	2969	
SE-GTI	SOCATA MS.893E Rallye 180GT Gaillard	12846	
SE-GTL	Cessna 172N	17269254	N734ZW
SE-GTM	Cessna U206G Stationair II	U20603731	N9930N
SE-GTN	SOCATA MS.892E Rallye 180T	3133	
SE-GTO	Thurston TSC-1A2 Teal II	31	N2031T
SE-GTP	SOCATA MS.892E Rallye 180T	3092	
SE-GTZ	Piper PA-18-150 Super Cub	18-559	PH-LUD
	(F/n 18-494 quoted officially as c/n - rebuilt		PH-GAV(1)
	using parts of PH-NGU c/n 18-5538)		R-208
			51-15673
			N7188K
SE-GUA	Piper PA-23-250 Turbo Aztec D	27-4523	D-IETT
			N13887
SE-GUD	Cessna F172H	F172-0491	OY-AGE
SE-GUF	Cessna U206G Stationair II	U20603596	N7272N
SE-GUN	Cessna A185E Skywagon (W/o 28.8.83)	185-1461	LN-BFU
			(N2711J)
SE-GUO	Aero Commander 680	535-204	C-FFAC
	(W/o 7.7.94)		CF-FAC
			N1333
SE-GUP	Reims/Cessna F172H	F17200672	OH-CBS
SE-GUS	Bellanca 7GCBC Citabria (Cr 21.3.98)	1029-78	
SE-GUT	Reims FR172J Rocket	FR17200373	OH-CFR
SE-GUV	Bellanca 8KCAB Decathlon	409-78	
SE-GUY	Bellanca 8GCBC Scout	228-76	N7833S
SE-GUZ	Grumman-American AA-5B Tiger	AA5B-0831	
SE-GVA	Piper PA-28R-201 Arrow III	28R-7837027	
SE-GVB	Piper PA-28-161 Cherokee Warrior II	28-7816195	
	(Damaged 11.4.00)		
SE-GVE	Piper PA-28-161 Cherokee Warrior II	28-7816164	
SE-GVH	Piper PA-38-112 Tomahawk	38-78A0053	
	(CofA exp 5.81 - parts to G-BLNN/38-78A0505)		
SE-GVI	Piper PA-32RT-300 Lance II	32R-7885129	
SE-GVR	Piper PA-28R-200 Cherokee Arrow II	28R-7535014	OH-PAA
SE-GVS	Piper PA-28-161 Cherokee Warrior II	28-7816436	
SE-GVT	Piper PA-28-161 Cherokee Warrior II	28-7816435	
SE-GVU	Piper PA-28-181 Cherokee Archer II	28-7890467	
	(W/o 8.5.02)		
SE-GVV	Piper PA-28R-201 Arrow III	28R-7837213	
SE-GVX	Piper PA-28-181 Cherokee Archer II	28-7890524	
SE-GVY	Piper PA-28-181 Cherokee Archer II	28-7890427	
SE-GVZ	Piper PA-31 Turbo Navajo C	31-7812079	
SE-GXB	Cessna U206G Stationair 6- II	U20604497	N756ZX
SE-GXI	Mooney M.20J Model 201	24-0844	
SE-GXU	Maule M-5-235C Lunar Rocket	7324C	
SE-GXY	Cessna 182P Skylane	18263554	OY-ANT
			N5820J
SE-GYB	Reims/Cessna F172N	F17201552	
SE-GYE	Reims/Cessna F172N	F17201687	
SE-GYH	Reims/Cessna F172N	F17201700	
SE-GYO	Reims/Cessna F172N	F17201740	
SE-GYT	Reims/Cessna F172N	F17201780	
SE-GYV	Reims/Cessna F152	F15201586	(OE-CFC)
SE-GYX	Reims/Cessna F172N	F17201794	
SE-GYY	Reims/Cessna F172N	F17201820	
SE-GYZ	Reims/Cessna F172N	F17201791	
SE-GZM	Reims/Cessna FR172K Hawk XP	FR17200600	
SE-GZO	Cessna 210M Centurion (W/o 18.4.86)	21061767	N732TS
SE-GZP	Reims/Cessna F150M	F15001287	(F-BXQY)
			(F-BXQO)
SE-GZR	Reims/Cessna F182P Skylane	F18200018	
SE-GZS	Cessna 150J	15070373	OH-CBD
			N60523
SE-GZT	Reims/Cessna FA150K Aerobat	FA1500027	OH-CBT
SE-GZU	Reims FR172G Rocket	FR17200178	OH-CDZ
SE-GZV	Reims FR172E Rocket (W/o 2.7.99)	FR17200005	OH-CCM
			F-WLIO
SE-HAL	Agusta-Bell 47G-2	016	(LN-OTS)
			OH-HIG
			SE-HAL
SE-HBP	Bell 47G-5 (W/o 30.9.74)	7954	
SE-HCA	Bell 47G-2	1492	N2819B
SE-HCB	Agusta-Bell 47J-2	1026	(LN-OQF)
			(LN-OPL)
			SE-HCB
SE-HCM	Hughes 269B	98-0388	
SE-HCW	Hughes 269B (W/o 25.7.75)	116-0276	N9480F
SE-HDD	SNCASE SE.3130 Alouette II (HKP-2)	1177	Fv84002
SE-HEE	Agusta-Bell 206A Jet Ranger II	8285	
SE-HEH	Bell 206B JetRanger II (Dbr 14.11.98)	734	N2915W
SE-HEI	Agusta-Bell 206B Jet Ranger II	8348	
SE-HEL	Agusta-Bell 206B Jet Ranger II	8332	
SE-HEM	Agusta-Bell 206B Jet Ranger II	8329	
SE-HEO	Bell 47G-2 (H-13E)	600	LN-OQE
			D-HIFI
			51-13959
SE-HEV	Enstrom F-28A	085	
SE-HEX	Enstrom F-28A	084	
SE-HFF	Hughes 269C	83-0229	LN-OPW
			SE-HFF
SE-HFL	Hughes 369HS (W/o 15.9.82)	74-0618S	
SE-HFN	Hughes 269C (Dbr 13.8.79)	75-0420	
SE-HFT	Hughes 369HS	15-0692S	LN-OTT
			SE-HFT
SE-HFU	Enstrom F-28A	310	OY-HBO
SE-HFV	Enstrom F-28A (W/o 8.8.81)	296	OY-HBN
SE-HFX	Enstrom F-28A (W/o 17.7.02)	116	LN-OMZ(1)
			SE-HFX
SE-HFZ	Enstrom F-28A (W/o 17.8.00)	108	
SE-HGC	Bell 47G-4	3346	OH-HIZ
			SE-HGC
			OH-HIZ
			SE-HGC
			G-BCCM
			N1193W
SE-HGY	Aérospatiale SA.315B Lama	2443	
SE-HGZ	Sikorsky S-55T	55-1252	N62540
			MM575981
			57-5981
SE-HHF	Hughes 369D (W/o 24.8.91)	116-0049D	
SE-HHN	Enstrom F-28A (W/o 17.8.78)	295	OY-HBL
SE-HHO	Enstrom F-28A	379	
SE-HHT	Enstrom F-28C (W/o 23.7.79)	429	
SE-HIA	AS350BA Ecureil	1017	LN-OMY
			SE-HIA
SE-HIC	Air & Space 18A (W/o 1.7.87)	18-73	N6161S
SE-HII	Agusta-Bell 206B Jet Ranger II	8290	D-HEPY
SE-HIN	Hughes 269C	128-0749	
SE-HIO	Enstrom F-28C (W/o 23.3.02)	425	N51754
SE-HIU	Agusta-Bell 206B Jet Ranger II (W/o 25.6.86)	8537	G-BFGT
SE-HIZ	Enstrom F-28A	225	N9250
SE-HKA	Enstrom 280C Shark	1184	
SE-HKC	Bell 206L-1 Long Ranger II	45321	
SE-HKF	Hughes 269C	89-0821	
SE-HKI	Hiller UH-12B (W/o 11.6.90)	743	OH-HHD
			N8507
			Neth: O-15
			54-2949
SE-HKK	Agusta-Bell 206B Jet Ranger III (HKP-6A)	8603	Army:
			06283/ 804
			SE-HKK
SE-HKL	Enstrom 280C Shark	1134	OH-HLK
SE-HKP	Bell 206B Jet Ranger II	2987	LN-OSM
			SE-HKP
SE-HKR	Bell 206L-1 Long Ranger II	45444	
SE-HLI	Hughes 369D	120-0879D	
SE-HLK	Agusta-Bell 206A Jet Ranger	8047	LN-ORY
SE-HLP	Hughes 369D	61-0986D	
SE-HLS	Aérospatiale SA.360C Dauphin	1016	F-BZAQ
			F-WZAQ
			F-WXFB

SE-HMK	Hughes 269C (Damaged 21.11.99)	46-0490	D-HHEI C-GLJQ
SE-HMM	Aérospatiale AS.350B Ecureuil	1693	
SE-HMO	Bell 206L-1 Long Ranger II	46605	TC-HHC SE-HMO G-JAMI N18090
SE-HMY	Hughes 269C (W/o 16.12.88)	1154	
SE-HNB	Hughes 269C (W/o 29.5.02)	80-0036	PH-HEH D-HKIS OO-JJS
SE-HNL	Hughes 369D (W/o 5.12.86)	89-0557D	EC-DIX
SE-HNO	Hughes 369D (Reservation 4.04)	79-0543D	D-HERD SE-HNO N779FA
SE-HNR	Enstrom F-28F	739	
SE-HNU	Hiller UH-12B	510	G-ASVH XB474 BuA134724
SE-HNZ	Hughes 369E (W/o 8.7.91)	0157E	LN-OMV
SE-HOK	Bell 206B Jet Ranger II	1693	N73DH N13SG
SE-HOM	Bell 206B Jet Ranger II	2394	N48EA N119AL
SE-HON	Bell 206B Jet Ranger II	1593	Fv06593 SE-HON N90132
SE-HOO	Enstrom 280C Shark	1056	G-MEAD N581H
SE-HOT	Agusta-Bell 206B Jet Ranger II	8094	LN-OQA SE-HEP G-AWOY
SE-HOY	Enstrom 280C Shark	1064	G-HOVA G-BEYR
SE-HOZ	Bell 206B Jet Ranger II	1827	A40-AR N49644
SE-HPA	Agusta-Bell 47G-4	2511	
SE-HPG	Bell 47G-5A	25081	
SE-HPH	Bell 206B Jet Ranger II (Destroyed 6/7.2.02)	1005	
SE-HPK	Bell 206B Jet Ranger II	1091	
SE-HPL	Bell 206L-1 Long Ranger II (Crashed 21.2.01)	45212	
SE-HPM	Bell 206L-1 Long Ranger II	45425	
SE-HPN	Bell 206L-1 Long Ranger II	45320	
SE-HPO	Bell 206L-1 Long Ranger II	45533	
SE-HPS	Eurocopter EC.135P2	0203	
SE-HPT	Eurocopter EC.135P2	0207	
SE-HPU	Eurocopter EC.135P2	0225	
SE-HPV	Eurocopter EC.135P2	0237	
SE-HPX	Eurocopter EC.135P2	0240	
SE-HPY	Eurocopter EC.135P2	0265	D-HECF
SE-HPZ	Eurocopter EC.135P2	0282	
SE-HRE	Bell 206B Jet Ranger II	642	N7905J
SE-HRF	Hughes 269C	36-0479	N7438F
SE-HRH	Schweizer 269C	S-1227	LN-OTW SE-HRH (SE-HRN) N41S
SE-HRK	Hughes 369D	1187D	LN-OPM SE-HRK LN-OMT SE-HMN
SE-HRM	Bell 206B Jet Ranger II	2323	N21CK N16936
SE-HRP	Schweizer 269C (Ditched 13.8.00)	S-1237	N41S
SE-HSB	Schweizer 269C (Damaged 8.6.97)	S-1262	N69A
SE-HSG	MBB Bö.105C (HKP-9A)	S-439	Army-09077 D-HDMM
SE-HSI	Hughes 369D	81-1041D	D-HAFE(2) SE-HSI N50867
SE-HSP	Aérospatiale SA.315B Lama	2604	LN-OTB
SE-HST	Schweizer 269C	S-1290	N41S
SE-HSY	Enstrom 280FX Shark	2020	
SE-HSZ	Enstrom 280C Shark	1217	OH-HSK N5698M
SE-HTC	Bell 206B Jet Ranger II	3153	D-HBAD N5759Q
SE-HTH	Sud Avn SA.316BAlouette III	1836	F-GIQL EC-FEM F-GEPF HC-BOB F-GEPF F-ODTE FAP:9380
SE-HTP	Bell 206B Jet Ranger II	1717	N49592
SE-HTR	Bell 206L Long Ranger	45395	C-GLMO
SE-HTU	Schweizer 269C	S-1353	N69A
SE-HTV	Bell 206B Jet Ranger II	4049	
SE-HUB	Bell 206L-3 Long Ranger III	51304	C-FGDY
SE-HUC	Bell 206L-3 Long Ranger III	51310	
SE-HUE	Bell 206L Long Ranger	45009	OH-HKR SE-HUE D-HAFV F-BXPH N49682
SE-HUF	Bell 206L-3 Long Ranger III	51348	N80EA G-BVIB SE-HUF C-FHZY
SE-HUI	Enstrom 280C Shark	1033	N999NJ
SE-HUK	Enstrom F-28C	459	N4953M C-GAIK N5687J
SE-HUM	Sud Avn SA.318C Alouette Astazou	2189	N8264
SE-HUN	Aérospatiale SA.342JGazelle	1057	EC-EQU C-GEJE N341NA N9042U C-FGCE CF-GCE
SE-HUP	Schweizer 269C	S-1356	N69A
SE-HUU	Hughes 369D (W/o 11.4.94)	109-0594D	OY-HCJ
SE-HVA	Hughes 369HS (W/o 27.8.96)	61-0323S	OY-HSE N1040Z RP-C1146 PI-C1146
SE-HVE	Bell 206B Jet Ranger II	2949	G-OFAB N22AB N5734X
SE-HVI	Bell 206L-3 Long Ranger III	51407	
SE-HVM	Agusta-Bell AB.204B (Cr 7.9.01)	3211	OH-HAK LN-ORZ
SE-HVN	Aérospatiale AS.350B1 Ecureuil	2157	HB-XSA
SE-HVS	Schweizer 269C (Damaged 27.8.00)	S-1418	N426MS
SE-HVU	Schweizer 269C	S-1446	N41S
SE-HVY	Hughes 369D	97-0188D	VR-HPC VR-HHM(2) N9550F
SE-HVZ	Robinson R-22 Mariner (W/o 17.8.00)	0436M	N85351
SE-HXA	Humlan Autogyro	001	
SE-HXB	Humlan Autogyro (Reservation)	unkn	
SE-HXE	Humlan Autogyro	003	
SE-HXF	Schramm/Rotorway Scorpion	SE-1	
SE-HXH	Humlan Autogyro	05	
SE-HXI	Humlan Autogyro	12	
SE-HXK	Hollmann HA-2M Sportster	65	
SE-HXL	Humlan Autogyro	31	
SE-HXN	Hollmann HA-2M Sportster	121	
SE-HXO	Humlan Autogyro	14-56	
SE-HXP	Tervamaki JT-5 (Permit)	unkn	
SE-HXR	Humlan Autogyro (Reservation)	37	
SE-HXT	Humlan Autogyro (Reservation)	unkn	
SE-HXU	Humlan Autogyro (Reservation)	unkn	
SE-HXV	Humlan Autogyro (Reservation)	24	
SE-HXX	Humlan Autogyro (Permit)	48	
SE-HXY	Humlan Autogyro (Reservation)	26	
SE-HXZ	Humlan Autogyro (Reservation)	unkn	
SE-HYA	Humlan Autogyro (Reservation)	unkn	
SE-HYB	Humlan Autogyro	112-419	
SE-HYC	Humlan Autogyro (Permit)	110	
SE-HYD	Humlan Autogyro (Reservation, dbr 14.7.01?)	unkn	
SE-HYE	Humlan Autogyro (Reservation)	unkn	
SE-HYF	Humlan Autogyro (Reservation)	unkn	
SE-HYG	Humlan Autogyro (Permit)	123	
SE-HYH	McCullogh J-2 (W/o 2.7.95)	012	N4302G
SE-HYI	Humlan Autogyro	104	
SE-HYK	Humlan Autogyro (Permit)	202	
SE-HYL	Barnett J-4B Gyroplane	2-830	N7818
SE-HYM	Humlan Autogyro	55	
SE-HYN	Canadian Home Rotors Safari	172	
SE-HYO	Rotorway Exec 90 (Permit)	5021	N4258S
SE-HYP	Hollmann HA-2MSportster (Reservation 9.00)	159	
SE-HYR	Chayair Sycamore Mk.1	SYCA 0020	ZU-CJI
SE-HYT	Hiller UH-12B	612	N90403 51-16364
SE-HYU	Humlan Autogyro (Res 11.04)	79-365	
SE-IAA	Piper PA-31-350 Navajo Chieftain (W/o 23.1.90)	31-7952113	LN-PAA (SE-ICP)
SE-IAE	Piper PA-32RT-300T Turbo Lance II (W/o 20.5.91)	32R-7887183	
SE-IAM	Piper PA-28-161 Cherokee Warrior II	28-7816651	
SE-IAN	Piper PA-38-112 Tomahawk	38-78A0400	
SE-IAP	Piper PA-28-181 Archer II	28-7990094	
SE-IAR	Piper PA-38-112 Tomahawk	38-79A0265	
SE-IAS	Piper PA-31 Turbo Navajo (Originally built as PA-31-325 Navajo C/R)	31-7912028	
SE-IAU	Piper PA-28R-201T Turbo Arrow IV	28R-7931046	
SE-IAX	Piper PA-28-161 Warrior II	28-7916290	
SE-IBC	Reims/Cessna FR182 Skylane RG	FR18200039	(LN-. . .) SE-IBC
SE-IBD	Reims/Cessna F172N	F17201695	(LN-ALI)
SE-IBG	Reims/Cessna F172N	F17201862	(OY-BNJ)
SE-IBK	Reims/Cessna F182Q Skylane (W/o 28.12.81)	F18200147	
SE-IBO	Cessna 340A	340A0613	N8674K
SE-IBT	Reims/Cessna F152 (W/o 29.7.84)	F15201761	
SE-IBU	Reims/Cessna F172N	F17201923	
SE-IBV	Reims/Cessna F172N (Accident 22.7.97)	F17201948	
SE-IBX	Reims/Cessna F172N	F17201964	
SE-ICA	Piper PA-18-150 Super Cub	18-7909083	
SE-ICE	Piper PA-38-112 Tomahawk	38-79A0744	
SE-ICF	Piper PA-38-112 Tomahawk	38-79A0745	

SE-ICL	Piper PA-28-181 Archer II	28-7990371	
SE-ICM	Piper PA-28-181 Archer II	28-7990372	
SE-ICT	Piper PA-28-161 Warrior II	28-7916470	
SE-ICV	Piper PA-28-181 Archer II	28-7990482	
SE-ICZ	Piper PA-18-150 Super Cub	18-8009016	
SE-IDA	Piper PA-18-150 Super Cub	18-8009015	
SE-IDF	Piper PA-28-151 Cherokee Warrior	28-7415243	OH-PDR
SE-IDG	Piper PA-28-161 Warrior II	28-8016259	
SE-IDK	Piper PA-28-181 Archer II	28-8190161	
SE-IDR	Piper PA-31 Turbo Navajo	31-7712085	LN-DAB
	(Originally built as PA-31-325 Navajo C/R)		SE-IDR
			LN-RAO
			(LN-RAG)
			LN-PAG
SE-IDS	Piper PA-28-181 Archer II	28-8190090	
	(W/o 28.4.89 in mid-air collision with OY-XOR)		
SE-IDT	Piper PA-32R-301T Turbo Saratoga SP	32R-8129026	
SE-IDY	Piper PA-28-161 Warrior II	28-8116220	
SE-IEC	Cessna 172N	17270709	LN-HHE
			N739PZ
SE-IED	Cessna A185F Skywagon Amphibian	18503320	OH-COW
			(SE-IED)
			N124JD
			(N5075H)
SE-IEE	Gulfstream American AA-5B Tiger	AA5B-1140	LN-KLJ
	(W/o 27.9.81)		
SE-IER	Piper J-3C-65 Cub	19861	OY-DRJ
			D-EHEC
			N6657H
			NC6657H
SE-IEU	Bellanca 8KCAB Decathlon	563-79	
SE-IEV	Maule M-5-235C Lunar Rocket (W/o 20.2.83)	7330C	
SE-IEX	Maule M-5-235C Lunar Rocket (W/o 7.8.81)	7332C	
SE-IFB	Reims/Cessna F172N	F17202005	
SE-IFC	Cessna 172RG Cutlass RG	172RG0397	N4837V
SE-IFD	Reims/Cessna F172N	F17201864	(LX-SOS)
SE-IFF	Reims/Cessna F172N	F17201969	
SE-IFL	Reims/Cessna F172P	F17202074	
SE-IFR	Reims/Cessna FR182 Skylane RG	FR18200047	
SE-IFX	Reims/Cessna F152	F15201802	
SE-IFZ	Reims/Cessna F152	F15201805	
SE-IGE	Reims FR172F Rocket (W/o in 1986)	FR17200098	OH-CNT
SE-IGG	Bellanca 8KCAB Decathlon (W/o 15.5.82)	605-80	
SE-IGK	SAAB S.91B Safir	91227	Fv50025
SE-IGM	SAAB S.91B Safir	91256	Fv50044
SE-IGO	SAAB S.91B Safir	91228	Fv50026
SE-IGR	SAAB S.91B Safir (Damaged 29.6.02)	91208	Fv50008
SE-IGT	Cessna TU206G Turbo Stationair 6- II	U20605593	N5204X
	(W/o 1.8.89)		
SE-IGU	Cessna F150H (Damaged 5.8.98)	F150-0294	OH-CND
SE-IHC	Cessna 172RG Cutlass RG	172RG0802	(N9352B)
SE-IHF	Cessna 172RG Cutlass RG	172RG0413	LN-HOU
	(Accident 11.7.95)		(N4899V)
SE-IHI	Reims/Cessna F172P	F17202167	
SE-IHR	Piper PA-23-250 Aztec E	27-7554033	LN-VIL
			SE-IHR
			HB-LIU
			N54239
SE-IHV	Cessna R182 Skylane RG	R18201867	N5446T
SE-IIA	Britten-Norman BN-2A-26 Islander	48	G-AWVY
			N48BN
			G-AWVY
SE-IIB	Beech C90 King Air	LJ-723	OY-ASI
SE-IID	Piper J-3C-65 Cub	23175	OY-AVS
			D-EGOZ
			N78434
			NC78434
SE-IIK	Aerotek Pitts S-2A (W/o 15.8.86)	2118	N39CB
SE-IIL	SAAB S.91B Safir	91211	Fv50011
SE-IIN	Cessna 172N	17270712	N739QC
SE-IIO	Republic RC-3 Seabee	120	N14R
	(Under restoration)		N87558
SE-IIP	Beech 77 Skipper	WA-263	N3833L
SE-IIR	Beech 77 Skipper	WA-264	N3833P
SE-IIT	Cessna 172M (W/o 7.6.83)	17267175	N1583U
SE-IIX	Cessna U206A Super Skywagon	U206-0591	LN-NPD
			LN-HHE
			N4891F
SE-IKB	Cessna 140	9624	OY-EFT
			D-EBAP
			N72459
SE-IKE	SAAB S.91B-2 Safir	91339	LN-SAV
			57339
			339/'UA-T'
SE-IKF	Piper PA-24-250 Comanche	24-3591	OY-BAW
			N8399P
			N10F
SE-IKI	SAAB S.91D Safir (W/o 2.6.85)	91359	SF-13
SE-IKK	SAAB S.91D Safir	91363	SF-17
SE-IKN	Robin R.2160D	161	D-EFSJ
			F-ODIL
SE-IKO	Piper PA-18 Super Cub 95	18-2038	LN-KCP
			R-46
			52-2438
SE-IKR	SAAB S.91D Safir	91417	OH-SFG
			SF-29

SE-IKV	Piper PA-31-350 Navajo Chieftain	31-7405148	G-BDFN
			EI-BKI
			G-BDFN
			5Y-ASI
			N9675N
SE-IKX	Cessna A185E Skywagon	185-1530	LN-BDQ
			(N2780J)
SE-ILD	Piper PA-28-161 Warrior II	28-8116293	
SE-ILE	Piper PA-28-181 Archer II	28-8190294	
SE-ILG	Piper PA-28-161 Warrior II	28-8216224	N9619N
SE-ILL	Piper PA-31-350 Navajo Chieftain	31-7305117	4X-CCH
			N676GL
			N676LL
			N6767L
SE-ILN	Piper PA-38-112 Tomahawk II	38-82A0100	
	(W/o 27.6.88)		
SE-ILO	Piper PA-28-140 Cherokee	28-21703	OY-BBF
SE-ILP	Piper PA46-350P Malibu Mirage	4636258	
SE-ILV	Piper PA-28-181 Archer III	2843426	
SE-ILY	Piper PA-31-350 Navajo Chieftain	31-7852051	G-FTTA
			N27535
SE-IMA	Reims/Cessna F152	F15201720	OY-BNO
SE-IMB	Reims/Cessna F150M	F15001425	OY-AZS
			D-EOKY
SE-IME	SAAB MFI-9B Trainer	038	OY-DUJ
			SE-ENC
SE-IMF	Piper PA-18 Super Cub 95	18-1994	OY-ANW
			I- EIBA
			MM522394
			52-2394
SE-IMH	Piper J-3C-65 Cub	12308	OY-AVD
			D-EFQK
			F-BFQK
			OO-ZOU
			44-80012
SE-IMP	SOCATA TB-10 Tobago (W/o 28.9.97)	368	F-BNGQ
SE-IMT	SOCATA TB-20 Trinidad	522	
SE-IMX	SOCATA MS.893A Rallye Commodore 180	10638	F-BODB
SE-IMY	SOCATA TB-10 Tobago	656	N20HN
SE-INL	Cessna T210N Turbo Centurion II	21064692	N1403U
	(W/o 26.12.92)		
SE-INM	Britten-Norman BN-2A Islander	84	D-IAWD
SE-INN	Cessna F172H	F172-0556	PH-KAR
SE-INT	Cessna U206D Skywagon 206	U206-1333	LN-LJR
			(LN-LJP)
			LN-LJR
			N95411
SE-INY	Cessna A185E Skywagon	18502030	LN-BNF
			(N70164)
SE-IOD	Cessna F150H	F150-0238	G-AVTM
SE-IOI	SAAB S.91B-2 Safir (W/o 5.7.85)	91331	LN-BEE
			57331
			331/'UA-L'
SE-IOV	Mitsubishi MU-2B-26	337	N522MA
SE-IOZ	Mitsubishi MU-2B-26	320	N641KE
			N30EM
			N641KE
			N14645
			N508MA
SE-IPG	Reims/Cessna F172P (W/o 7.11.90)	F17202234	
SE-IPI	Reims/Cessna F172P	F17202240	
SE-IPR	Cessna R182 Skylane RG	R18200704	N9410R
SE-IPS	Cessna 172P	17275462	OY-CPY
			N63658
SE-IPT	Cessna 340A	340A1816	N202MM
			PH-PSM
			N6603Q
			C-GJAV
			N1232P
SE-IPZ	Cessna 210R Centurion II (W/o 20.4.90)	21064956	N6490U
SE-IRC	Reims/Cessna F172P (Damaged 16.12.01)	F17202173	LN-NFP
			D-EAPY
SE-IRD	Reims/Cessna F172N	F17201976	LN-NFJ
			D-EOOY
SE-IRI	Cessna A185F Skywagon	18503177	N93094
SE-IRK	Piper PA-28R-200 Cherokee Arrow II	28R-7535091	LN-NFK
			D-EFFL
			N32795
SE-IRN	SAAB S.91D Safir	91369	PH-RLC
SE-IRS	Cessna A185F Skywagon	18502409	LN-BGN
			(N1686R)
SE-IRT	American AA-1 Yankee	AA1-0416	OY-AYE
SE-IRV	Cessna A185E Skywagon	185-1161	LN-KAL
			N4707Q
SE-IRX	Christen Pitts S-2B	5039	N53234
SE-IRY	SAAB S.91D Safir	91360	OH-SFS
			SF-14
SE-IRZ	Piper PA-23-250 Aztec D	27-4257	LN-AEZ
SE-ISD	SAAB-Scania SF.340A	145	ZK-FXQ
			SE-ISD
			SE-F45
SE-ISE	SAAB-Scania SF.340A	156	YL-BAP
			ZK-NLF
			SE-ISE
			SE-F56
SE-ISG	SAAB-Scania SF.340A	162	SE-F62

SE-ISL	SAAB-Scania SF.340A	130	LN-SAA
			(SE-ISL)
			SE-F30
SE-ISP	SAAB-Scania SF.340A	015	SE-E15
SE-ISR	SAAB-Scania SF.340A	017	SE-E17
SE-IST	SAAB-Scania SF.340A	035	SE-E35
SE-ISV	SAAB-Scania SF.340A	045	SE-E45
SE-ISY	SAAB-Scania SF.340A	080	SE-E80
SE-ITA	Piper PA-31 Navajo C	31-8012028	D-ICAS
			N3552U
SE-ITB	Piper PA-31 Navajo C	31-8012059	N3585G
SE-ITC	Piper PA-31 Navajo C	31-8012048	C-GBJE
	(Originally built as PA-31-325 Navajo C/R)		
SE-ITD	Piper PA-31 Navajo C	31-8012035	N3553E
SE-ITE	Piper PA-31 Navajo C	31-8012010	N3545C
SE-ITK	SAAB S.91D Safir (Reservation 2.00)	91413	SF-25
SE-ITR	Beech E55 Baron	TE-1021	N7253R
SE-ITS	Piper PA-31 Navajo C	31-8212018	N4097P
SE-ITT	Piper PA-31 Navajo C	31-8112065	N40943
SE-ITU	Piper PA-31 Navajo C	31-8012085	N325EC
			N35910
SE-ITY	Piper PA-25-235 Pawnee	25-2657	G-ASOV
			N10F
SE-ITZ	Reims/Cessna F172M	F17201197	LN-ASG
SE-IUA	Mitsubishi MU-2B-26	345	N730MP
			N730MA
SE-IUC	Piper PA-34-220T Seneca IV	3447013	N9260P
	(Damaged 14.12.99)		
SE-IUD	Piper PA-28-181 Archer II	2890065	
SE-IUF	Piper PA-28-181 Archer II	2890069	
SE-IUH	Piper PA-34-220TSeneca III	3433102	
SE-IUO	Beech 95-B55 Baron	TC-1716	OY-POC
	(Crashed in 1990, to instructional airframe)		N35BW
SE-IUS	Cessna A185E Skywagon	185-1471	LN-VIQ
			(N2721J)
SE-IUU	PZL-104 Wilga 35 (Rebuilding 3.04)	62165	OE-DRS
			SP-WDC
SE-IUX	Beech 200 Super King Air	BB-675	N26AD
	('004' of SOS Flygambulans, c/s SAG004)		N26SD
			N6747T
SE-IVE	CASA C.212CE Aviocar	343	
SE-IVF	CASA C.212CE Aviocar	346	
SE-IVK	Taylorcraft F21B (Damaged 18.8.01)	1512	N4417R
SE-IVL	Taylorcraft F21B	1513	N44177
SE-IVM	Piper PA-25-235 Pawnee B	25-3577	N7533Z
SE-IVO	Piper PA-18-150 Super Cub	18-2054	LN-KCV
			R-69
			52-2454
SE-IVY	Vickers V.815 Viscount	375	G-AVJB
	(Scrapped at Malmö -Sturup in 1992)		(LX-LGD)
			G-AVJB
			AP-AJF
SE-IXC	Beech B200 Super King Air	BB-1210	N7213J
	('005' of SOS Flygambulans, c/s SAG005)		
SE-IXD	Piper PA-28RT-201T Turbo Arrow IV	28R-7931179	N20950
SE-IXH	Maule M-6-235CSuper Rocket	7473C	N5662T
SE-IXI	Piper PA-25-235 Pawnee	25-2900	G-ASWG
			ST-ADM
			G-ASWG
			N7113Z
SE-IXK	Cessna U206F Stationair	U20603341	LN-ALM
			OY-BUT
			N8483Q
SE-IXN	Reims FR172G Rocket	FR17200196	OH-CDG
SE-IXP	Cessna A185F Skywagon	18503727	LN-ALI
	(W/o 13.7.88)		N8533Q
SE-IXR	SAAB S.91D Safir	91-352	OH-SFI
			SF-6
SE-IXS	Piper PA-34-220T Seneca III	34-8133008	N8329L
	(W/o 3.8.93)		
SE-IXT	Reims/Cessna F150M	F15001199	OY-AZJ
			PH-VST
SE-IXV	Cessna 172P	17274575	N52646
SE-IYD	Cessna 172P (Accident 2.3.95)	17275052	N54788
SE-IYE	Piper PA-25-235 Pawnee D	25-7756005	G-BEXL
			N82428
SE-IYF	Cessna 172M (W/o 4.7.04)	17262765	OY-CPJ
			N13455
SE-IYG	Cessna P210N Pressurized Centurion II	00527	(SE-IPN)
	(W/o 29.7.89)		N99WA
SE-IYI	Cessna 172P	17274976	N54451
SE-IYN	Cessna 172N	17273424	N4877G
SE-IYT	PZL-104 Wilga 35A	18840776	SP-WDD
SE-IZG	Piper PA-28-161 Warrior II	28-7916103	N3003A
SE-IZH	Piper PA-28-161 Warrior II	28-8216075	N80021
SE-IZI	Piper PA-28-161 Warrior II	28-8016081	N8092D
SE-IZO	Beech 99 (W/o 8.5.89)	U-48	N299ME
			N7699N
SE-IZP	Piper PA-25-235 Pawnee	25-2235	N6640Z
SE-IZS	Piper PA-22-108 Colt	22-8548	LN-AEW
			SE-CUX
SE-IZT	Piper PA-32R-300 Cherokee Lance	32R-7780538	N701JB
			N44850
SE-IZY	Rockwell Commander 112TC	13100	LN-RAF
	(W/o 23.6.03)		N4610W
SE-IZZ	Piper PA-28-161 Warrior II	28-8416058	OY-CEB
			SE-ILP

SE-JAH	Schweizer 269C	S-1528	OY-HEB
			SE-JAH
SE-JAI	Schweizer 269C (Damaged 30.1.03)	S-1529	LN-OMF
			SE-JAI
			N69A
SE-JAN	Aérospatiale AS.350B2 Ecureuil	2348	N502AL
	(W/o 10.2.92)		
SE-JAP	Schweizer 269C	S-1333	HB-XSZ
SE-JAU	Hughes 369E (Reservation)	unkn	
SE-JAV	Schweizer 269C	S-1579	N41S
SE-JBB	Schweizer 269C	S-1463	G-WISK
			N41S
SE-JBD	Schweizer 269C	S-1580	N69A
SE-JBJ	Schweizer 269D	0005	
SE-JBU	Hughes 369D	48-0294D	OY-HGD
SE-JBZ	MBB-Kawasaki BK.117A-4 (Reservation)	1023	B-77008
			ZK-HKA
			JA9921
SE-JCI	Hughes 269C (W/o 6.7.99)	96-0537	OY-HBW
SE-JCK	Aérospatiale SA.365N Dauphin 2	6090	G-BKXE
SE-JDA	Enstrom 480	5016	
SE-JDB	Agusta A.109A	7287	TC-HMK
			D-HOOB
			N109BH
SE-JDC	Hughes 269C	1077	LN-OTF
			(SE-HMG)
SE-JDH	Robinson R-44 Astro	0273	
SE-JDM	Aérospatiale AS.355F1 Ecureuil 2	5172	N302PS
			N57973
SE-JDP	Eurocopter EC.120B Colibri	1019	
SE-JDS	Eurocopter EC.120B Colibri	1025	
SE-JDT	Eurocopter EC.120B Colibri	1062	F-WWPT
SE-JDX	Aérospatiale AS.350B3 Ecureuil	3063	F-WQDX
SE-JDY	Eurocopter EC.120B Colibri	1114	F-WQDE
SE-JEB	Bell 407	53006	(N62828)
			C-FXDK
SE-JEC	Eurocopter EC-135T1 (Reservation)	unkn	
SE-JEH	SNCASE SE.3160 Alouette III	1542	NethAF: A-542
SE-JEK	SNCASE SE.3160 Alouette III	1494	NethAF: A-494
SE-JEL	SNCASE SE.3160 Alouette III	1500	NethAF: A-500
SE-JEO	Aérospatiale AS.350B3	3225	
SE-JEP	Eurocopter EC.120B Colibri	1018	
SE-JER	Bell 206B Jet Ranger II	2491	LN-OHR
			(LN-OFF)
			OY-HDJ
			HB-XBE
			D-HEPE
			(YV-O-PTJ-4)
SE-JEU	Eurocopter EC-135T1 (Reservation)	unkn	
SE-JEX	Bell 407	53145	N72243
SE-JEZ	Sikorsky S-76A	760215	N72WW
			N5423V
SE-JFG	IRMA/SNCASE SE.316B Alouette III	5377	F-GJGS
			F-OHGS
			CS-HBH
			F-GBDU
SE-JFJ	Bell 407	53418	N2416G
			C-GFNL
SE-JFK	Aérospatiale AS.350B1 Ecureuil	1983	F-GPAT
SE-JFM	Robinson R-22 Beta (Damaged 25.4.99)	2009	OY-HFT
SE-JFN	Eurocopter EC.135T1	0214	D-HEC .
SE-JFO	Aérospatiale AS.350B Ecureuil	3374	
SE-JFT	Aérospatiale AS.350B3 Ecureuil	3312	F-WQDH
SE-JFV	Robinson R-22 Mariner	2008M	OY-HFO
SE-JFY	Eurocopter EC.120B Colibri (Damaged 28.8.00)	1137	
SE-JGA	Robinson R-44 Clipper	0673	
SE-JGB	Hughes 369E	0252E	LN-OCC
			(SE-HSM)
SE-JGC	Robinson R-22 Beta	0692	OE-CXY
SE-JGE	Hughes 369D (Reservation 12.01)	47-0112D	OY-HGE
			D-HOLG
			CS-HCD
			D-HOLG
			C-GYXP
SE-JGF	Hughes 369D	116-0037D	VH-AKT
			RP-C257
			(F-GAMZ)
SE-JGG	Robinson R-44 Astro	0084	D-HIBB
SE-JGK	Aérospatiale AS.350B2 Ecureuil (W/o 6.1.01)	2930	RP-C8888
			F-OHNQ
SE-JGL	Eurocopter EC.120B Colibri	1309	
SE-JGP	Eurocopter EC.120B Colibri	1056	F-WWPF
SE-JGR	Aérospatiale AS.350B3 Ecureuil	3563	
SE-JGS	Schweizer 269D	0019	N61456
SE-JGU	Aérospatiale AS.365N2 Dauphin 2 (Res 12.02)	6420	(OY-HLL)
			JA6677
SE-JGV	Aerospatiale AS.350BA Ecureil	1130	N930M
			JA9235
SE-JGX	Robinson R44 Astro	0113	LN-OTG(2)
			D-HLAX
SE-JGZ	Aérospatiale AS.350B2 Ecureuil	9014	
SE-JHA	Eurocopter EC.120B Colibri	1174	
SE-JHB	Eurocopter EC.120B Colibri	1214	F-WWXS
SE-JHD	Aérospatiale AS.350B3 Ecureuil	3612	
SE-JHE	Aérospatiale AS.350B3 Ecureuil	3623	
SE-JHH	Eurocopter EC.120B Colibri	1200	

SE-JHI	Aérospatiale AS.350B2 Ecureuil	3650	
SE-JHJ	Robinson R-44 Raven (W/o 11.9.04)	1382	
SE-JHK	Aérospatiale AS.350B3 Ecureuil	3445	
SE-JHL	Aérospatiale AS.350B2 Ecureuil	2878	PH-PLA
			F-WQDL
			F-WQDC
SE-JHM	Hughes 269C	970634	N8666F
SE-JHN	Schweizer 269C	S-1218	Fv.05237
SE-JHO	Robinson R-44 (Res 6.04)	unkn	
SE-JHP	Westland-Bell 47G-3B-1	WA/340	G-BGID
			XT181
SE-JHR	MBB Bö.105CBS-4	S-433	LN-OTD
			D-HDMG
SE-JHS	Robinson R-44 Astro	0792	
SE-JHT	Eurocopter EC.120B Colibri	1349	
SE-JHZ	Eurocopter EC.120B Colibri (Dam. 24.9.03)	1109	F-WQDS
SE-JIA	Aérospatiale AS.365N3 Dauphin 2	6415	XA-RWZ
			N886TW
			XA-RWZ
			F-WYMF
SE-JIF	Bell 206B Jet Ranger II	4260	N251SN
			N317HK
			N9SN
			N72EA
			A2-HAI
			C-GLZS
SE-JIK	Robinson R-44 Raven II	10395	
SE-JIL	Eurocopter EC.120B Colibri	1284	N750PG
			(N120QP)
			N750PG
			(N120JJ)
			N750PG
SE-JIM	Aérospatiale AS.350B2 Ecureuil	3697	
SE-JIR	Schweizer 269C	S-1269	Fv05245
SE-JIS	Schweizer 269C (Res 11.03)	S-1270	Fv05246
SE-JIT	Robinson R-44 Raven II	10581	
SE-JJA	Bell 206L-3 Long Ranger III (Reservation 11.04)	51368	N368M
			JA6744
			N100TH
			N7156H
SE-JJB	Bell 206L-4 Long Ranger IV (Reservation 11.04)	52110	HP-8881EIS
			HP-1289
			N2102J
SE-JJM	Eurocopter EC.120B Colibri	1388	
SE-JLB	Eurocopter EC.120B Colibri	1225	
SE-JLD	Eurocopter EC.120B Colibri	1318	
SE-JLE	Robinson R-44 Raven	1359	
SE-JLF	Aérospatiale AS.350B2 Ecureuil	9041	F-GTRR
SE-JLZ	Eurocopter EC.120B Colibri	1213	
SE-JMB	Aérospatiale AS.355F2 Ecureuil 2 (Res 3.01)	unkn	
SE-JMC	Robinson R-44 Raven II (Res 11.04)	10529	
SE-JME	Eurocopter EC.120B Colibri	1184	
SE-JMK	Fuji-Bell 204B	CH-34	JA9142
SE-JML	Bell 206B Jet Ranger II	2843	N1068C
SE-JMM	Robinson R-44 Astro	0868	
SE-JMN	Schweizer 269C	S-1573	N103WP
			N107LU
SE-JMP	Eurocopter EC.120B Colibri	1008	
SE-JMR	Hughes 369D	126-0066D	N163D
			HL9148
			VH-MHM
			N8352F
SE-JMS	Robinson R-44 Raven	1196	
SE-JMT	Robinson R-22B2 Beta	3620	
SE-JMX	Robinson R-22 Beta	3680	
SE-JMY	Robinson R-44 Raven	1313	D-HALI (3)
SE-JMZ	Eurocopter EC.120B Colibri	1036	(LN-OCQ)
			SE-JMZ
			3A-MYO
SE-JNA	Aérospatiale SA.315B Lama	2643	LN-OMU
			(LN-OLL)
			F-WXFC
SE-JNH	Robinson R-22 Beta	3660	
SE-JNN	Robinson R-22 Beta	3523	
SE-JUA	Robinson R-44 Clipper	0728	N728PK
SE-JUC	Sikorsky S-76A +	760219	N18KH
			G-OAUS
			N3122M
SE-JUJ	Sikorsky S-76C	760424	N523KH
			VH-EKQ
SE-JUL	MBB-Kawasaki BK.117B-1	7186	D-HIMC
			JY-ACD
			D-HIMC
SE-JUM	Robinson R-44 Raven II	1417	
SE-JUR	Aérospatiale AS.350B Ecureuil (Res 6.01)	3426	
SE-JUS	Sikorsky S-76A	760172	PT-YBG
			N770AM
SE-JUU	Robinson R-22 Beta	2176	OH-HWG
			G-BVCI
SE-JUY	Sikorsky S-76C	760407	N154AE
SE-JUZ	Sikorsky S-76A +	760282	N92RR
			N92RP
			N63WW
SE-J . .	Agusta A.109C	7622	N67SH
			9M-SJI
			M38-03
			9M-TMJ

SE-J . .	Hughes 369D (Reservation 1.04)	116-0037D	VH-AKT
			RP-C257
			(F-GAMZ)
SE-J . .	Sikorsky S-76C (Res 3.05)	760377	N50KH
			VP-CHC
			G-BXGR
			I-PRLT
			N62375
			JA6692
SE-J . .	SNCASE SE.3160 Alouette III (Res 3.05)	1539	N316HP
			JA9031
			F-WMHC
SE-KBA	SOCATA TB-20 Trinidad	789	
SE-KBF	SOCATA TB-10 Tobago	662	F-GFEK
			N20JU
SE-KBH	SOCATA TB-9 Tampico	887	
SE-KBL	SOCATA TB-9 Tampico	1048	
SE-KBN	Piper PA-28RT-201 Arrow IV	28R-7918113	N2161Z
SE-KBO	Piper PA-18-150 Super Cub (W/o 10.8.02)	18-7338	LN-BEB
			SE-EIK
			OY-ADD
SE-KBS	Piper PA-25-235 Pawnee D	28-7856033	OY-BRF
SE-KBT	Christen A-1 Husky	1036	
SE-KBU	Christen A-1 Husky	038	
SE-KBX	Mitsubishi MU-2B-35 (W/o 3.1.89)	247	N5TQ
			N5TC
SE-KBZ	Cessna R172K Hawk XP	R1722637	N736MQ
SE-KCB	Cessna 172P	17274854	N54040
SE-KCC	Cessna 172P	17276631	N9839L
SE-KCE	Antonov An-2	1G189-59	ES-CAE
			CCCP84592
SE-KCF	SAAB 2000	028	F-GNEI
			EI-CPM
			SE-KCF
			F-GMVR
			(V7-9509)
			SE-028
SE-KCK	DHC-2 Beaver	119	C-FGQQ
			CF-GQQ
SE-KCL	Cessna U206G Stationair6- II	U20604270	LN-ALJ
			(N756QK)
SE-KCM	Cessna 150L	15075261	OH-CTV
			C-FGWA
SE-KCN	Piper PA-46-350P Malibu Mirage	4636028	LN-ENE
			N350PM
			N92646
SE-KCO	Maule M-4-210C Rocket	1035C	LN-VYB
			N15B
SE-KCP	Swearingen SA.226TC Metro II	TC-330	N7217N
			ZS-LJC
			N30TR
			(F-GEJX)
			N30TR
			ZS-LJC
			HB-LLC
			N1007Y
SE-KCR	SAAB-Scania 340A	065	OH-FAA
			SE-E65
SE-KCS	SAAB-Scania 340A	066	OH-FAB
			SE-E66
SE-KCT	SAAB-Scania 340A	070	OH-FAC
			SE-E70
SE-KCU	SAAB-Scania 340A	135	OH-FAD
			SE-F35
SE-KCX	SAAB-Scania SF.340B (Reservation)	163	OM-UGU
			OK-UGU
			OO-RXL
			(F-GGZM)
			HB-AXZ
			(OO-RXL)
			SE-F63
SE-KDC	Yakovlev Yak-52	801002	(OY-SMI)
			OY-EMC
			SE-KDC
			UR-BNQ
			SE-KDC
			DOSAAF
SE-KDD	Yakovlev Yak-52	801003	UR-BNP
			DOSAAF-21
SE-KDE	Cessna 177RG Cardinal RG	177RG1166	N836CW
			(N52090)
SE-KDF	Reims/Cessna F182P Skylane	F18200014	OH-CGY
SE-KDH	Piper PA-25-235 Pawnee D	25-7856030	G-BGFN
			N9176T
SE-KDK	Beech B200 Super King Air	BB-909	N171M
			N36784
SE-KDM	Grob G.115A	8034	(D-EGVV)
SE-KDN	Piper PA-38-112 Tomahawk (Reservn, ntu)	38-79A0758	N2545L
SE-KDO	Piper PA-38-112 Tomahawk	38-78A0273	N9988T
SE-KDP	Cessna 172N	17269731	N737WL
SE-KDS	Cessna 180H Skywagon	18052175	N123BD
			N9075M
SE-KDT	Piper PA-38-112 Tomahawk	38-79A0985	N2416P
SE-KDU	Piper PA-38-112 Tomahawk	38-79A0965	N2367P
SE-KDV	Cessna T210N Turbo Centurion II	21063855	N6288C
SE-KDX	Piper PA-38-112 Tomahawk	38-79A0945	N2321P

SE-KDZ	Piper PA-28-161 Warrior II	28-8416056	N4345A
SE-KEC	Piper PA-31-350 Navajo Chieftain	31-7952098	LN-FAM G-TROT N35176
SE-KEE	Beech B36TC Bonanza	EA-484	
SE-KEG	Piper PA-18-150 Super Cub	18-1415	D-ELWK ALAT 51-15415
SE-KEI	Piper PA-28-161 Warrior II	2816072	
SE-KEK	Piper PA-28-161 Cadet (Badly damaged 18.3.00)	2841309	N9266N N9208Q
SE-KEN	Piper PA-28-161 Cadet	2841310	N9267N N9208Z
SE-KEO	Piper PA-28-161 Cadet	2841311	D-ERAP SE-KEO N9268N N9209B
SE-KET	Cessna R172K Hawk XP	R1722838	(SE-KDS) N736WD
SE-KEV	Cessna 172N (Damaged 15.8.99)	17270165	N738QX
SE-KEZ	Piper PA-25-235 Pawnee B	25-3701	N6955Z
SE-KFB	Cessna 172P	17274993	N54506
SE-KFD	SAAB S.91D Safir	91442	OH-SFM SF-33
SE-KFE	Piper PA-34-220T Seneca III (Sold to Norway 6.97, operated as SE-KFE)	34-8133015	N100LA N9519N
SE-KFF	Cessna U206F Stationair	U20601942	LN-HAO OH-CKA LN-HOM (LN-RTA) N50590
SE-KFH	Maule M-6-235C Super Rocket	7496C	
SE-KFK	Cessna 210L Centurion (Reservation)	unkn	
SE-KFL	Piper PA-28-151 Cherokee Warrior	28-7715160	N5962F
SE-KFM	Piper PA-28-181 Archer II	28-8190196	N8361P
SE-KFN	Mooney M.20J Model 201	24-1082	N8651M
SE-KFP	Beech B200C Super King Air ('006' of SOS Flygambulans, c/s SAG006)	BL-132	
SE-KFR	Piper PA-34-200T Seneca II (Accident 18.8.95)	34-7870170	N9224C
SE-KFT	Boeing Stearman E75 (Damaged 13.6.99)	75-5844	N1723B 41-17681
SE-KFU	Cessna 180F	18051258	LN-BDR N2158Z
SE-KFV	FFV Aerotec MFI-BA14	unkn	
SE-KFX	Cessna 172M	17263417	N5200R
SE-KFY	Cessna 172N	17273654	OY-CPF N6412J
SE-KFZ	Piper PA-28-181 Archer II	28-8090183	N3561A
SE-KGD	Christen A-1 Husky (Cr 23.7.98)	1075	
SE-KGE	Christen A-1 Husky	1076	
SE-KGG	SOCATA MS.893A Rallye Commodore 180	10699	OY-DTI
SE-KGH	Piper PA-31-350 Navajo Chieftain	31-7305007	OY-BYF LN-MTK N7677L
SE-KGM	Bölkow BO.208C Junior	531	D-EGPU
SE-KGN	Piper PA-28-161 Cherokee Warrior II	28-7816521	N9716C
SE-KGP	Reims/Cessna F172M	F17200957	OY-RYR
SE-KGS	Piper PA-28-161 Cherokee Warrior II	28-7816666	N789DT N9624N
SE-KGU	Maule M-7-235 Super Rocket	4067C	
SE-KGZ	SAAB S.91B Safir	91259	FV50047
SE-KHD	Yakovlev Yak-55	870209	RA-02183
SE-KHF	Piper PA-25-235 Pawnee D	25-7756019	G-BFBW N82452
SE-KHI	Piper PA-28-151 Cherokee Warrior	28-7615165	LN-NAJ
SE-KHK	Piper PA-25-235 Pawnee	25-8056007	D-EIAG N2383Q
SE-KHN	Cessna F172E	F172-0034/17250659	LN-BIN
SE-KHP	Piper PA-28-181 Archer II	28-8390029	N8332T
SE-KHS	Piper PA-28RT-201T Turbo Arrow IV	28R-7931065	N2193P
SE-KHT	Beech B24R Sierra	MC-253	N2546W
SE-KHU	Piper PA-28-181 Archer II	28-7990285	D-EFSB N3020Q N9589N
SE-KHX	Cessna 172N	17272604	N6109D
SE-KHY	Cessna 172N	17269989	N738HL
SE-KIB	Piper PA-28-161 Cadet	2841089	
SE-KIE	Piper PA-28-181 Archer II (Cr 6.5.98)	2890110	
SE-KIF	Piper PA-28-181 Archer II (W/o 8.1.91)	2890111	
SE-KII	Piper PA-28-161 Cadet	2841155	(F-GHBA)
SE-KIK	Piper PA-28-161 Cadet	2841139	N9241G
SE-KIL	Piper PA-28-161 Cadet (Damaged 14.12.99)	2841138	N9240 F
SE-KIM	Piper PA-28-161 Cadet	2841088	
SE-KIT	Piper PA-28-181 Archer II	2890106	
SE-KIU	Piper PA-28-181 Archer II	2890133	
SE-KIX	Piper PA-28-181 Archer II (Destroyed)	2890135	
SE-KKA	Gyroflug SC-01B Speed Canard (Reservation)	unkn	
SE-KKB	Gyroflug SC-01B Speed Canard (Reservation)	unkn	
SE-KKC	Piper PA-25-235 Pawnee D	25-7756014	G-BEOT N82481
SE-KKD	DHC-2 Turbo Beaver	1629/TB-17	N4482 CF-YOD TI-407L
SE-KKE	Cessna 140	13250	OY-EFH D-ENAM NC2992M

SE-KKF	Cessna TU206G Turbo Stationair 6- II (Accident 30.7.95)	U20606386	N9315Z
SE-KKI	Cessna 172P	17276017	N89929
SE-KKK	Beech B60 Duke	P-330	N6033S
SE-KKM	Beech B200 Super King Air	BB-932	Fv101004 SE-KKM OY-CCE D-IBCI
SE-KKU	Piper PA-34-220T Seneca III	34-8133018	N8340V
SE-KKV	Piper PA-28RT-201T Turbo Arrow IV	28R-8131208	N410FC N8441P
SE-KKY	Beech 60 Duke	P-94	G-DOOK D-ICAV G-AXEN
SE-KLA	Piper PA-28-140 Cherokee D (W/o 3.1.91)	28-7125043	OY-BDJ SE-FPK
SE-KLB	Piper PA-25-235 Pawnee D	25-7656089	G-BFKV N82343
SE-KLD	Beech B24R Sierra 200	MC-275	D-EEGA
SE-KLG	Bellanca 8KCAB Decathlon (Damaged 10.9.99)	393-78	LN-HOB
SE-KLI	Piper PA-28-181 Archer II	28-8390026	N83222
SE-KLR	Cessna 172N	17271522	N3373E
SE-KLU	SOCATA MS.880B Rallye Club	1557	OY-DJN
SE-KLV	Piper PA-28-181 Archer II	28-8190139	OY-CEK G-BMKL ZS-KWL N8323L
SE-KMA	Piper PA-28-181 Archer II	2890142	
SE-KMB	Piper PA-18-150 Super Cub (On rebuild)	1809055	
SE-KMD	Piper PA-28-181 Archer II	28-8490020	N4329K
SE-KMF	Cessna 337D Super Skymaster	33701014	D-GALA N85894
SE-KMG	Piper PA-28-161 Cadet	2841276	
SE-KMH	Piper PA-28-161 Cadet	2841277	
SE-KMI	Piper PA-28-161 Cadet	2841278	
SE-KML	Piper PA-28-161 Cadet	2841279	
SE-KMM(2)	Piper PA-28R-201T Turbo Cherokee Arrow II	28R-7703102	N3337Q
SE-KMO	Piper PA-28-181 Archer II	2890147	
SE-KMR	Piper PA-28-181 Archer II	28-8490023	N4329V
SE-KMU	Piper PA-28-181 Archer II (Dbr 27.6.01)	2890160	
SE-KMZ	Piper PA-28R-201 Arrow	2837056	N9235Q
SE-KNA	Robin HR.200/160	106	OY-AJP
SE-KNB	Cessna 172P	17274112	LN-MTD N5445K
SE-KNC	Piper PA-28-140 Cherokee B	28-25302	LN-BNC
SE-KNF	Christen A-1 Husky	1125	
SE-KNG(2)	Mooney M.20K Model 231	25-0169	OY-CBC LN-DBW OY-CBC
SE-KNH	Piper PA-28-181 Archer II	28-8390071	TF-GBG N4309M
SE-KNL	SOCATA Rallye 235C	13074	
SE-KNR	SOCATA TB-200 Tobago XL	1382	
SE-KNS	SOCATA Rallye 235F	12105	F-GAFE F-ZWRT
SE-KNY	SOCATA Rallye 235F	13395	
SE-KNZ	SOCATA TB-10 Tobago	1049	F-GRBC EC-FMM EC-962 F-GHZZ
SE-KOA	Piper PA-28-181 Archer II	28-8490085	N4365V
SE-KOE	Piper PA-28-181 Archer II	28-8490104	OH-PKR N135AV
SE-KOL	Beech 300LW Super King Air	FA-189	N2808B N7241V
SE-KOO	Cessna 172M	17261981	OY-DLG N12436
SE-KOR	Piper PA-28-181 Archer II	28-8090043	N2417U
SE-KOY	Piper PA-34-200T Seneca II	34-7870423	N39949
SE-KOZ	Cessna 207A Stationair 8	20700784	N1721Q
SE-KPD	SAAB-Scania SF.340A	037	PH-KJL LN-NVD SE-E37
SE-KPE	SAAB-Scania SF.340A	055	PH-KJH LN-NVE SE-E55
SE-KPF	Cessna 337G Skymaster	33701806	N701AD
SE-KPM	Cessna 185B Skywagon	185-0558	LN-DBO (N2558Z)
SE-KPN	SAAB S.91D Safir	91435	LN-MAA (LN-MAY) G-BCFT PH-RLX
SE-KPP	Cessna A185F Skywagon	18503661	OH-CKS N8339Q
SE-KPR	Cessna TU206D Turbo-Skywagon 206	U206-1287	LN-BEU N93411
SE-KPS	Piper PA-18 Super Cub 95	18-1423	LN-TEI D-EOCB ALAT 51-15423
SE-KPU	Piper PA-22-150 Tri-Pacer	22-3017	OY-DDD N2711P
SE-KPV	Piper PA-28R-201 Arrow III	28R-7837120	N3535M

SE-KPX	Maule M-5-235C Lunar Rocket	7138C	N9228E
SE-KPY	Bellanca 7ECA Citabria (On rebuild)	1344-80	N5069R
SE-KPZ	Cessna TU206G Turbo Stationair 6- II	U20606818	D-EDES(4) F-GEDS N6382R
SE-KRD	Cessna U206G Stationair 6- II	U20605771	N5457X
SE-KRE	SAAB S.91B Safir	91257	Fv.50045
SE-KRF	SAAB S.91B Safir	91283	Fv.50073
SE-KRG	Piper PA-28-181 Archer II	28-8090060	N8074N
SE-KRH	Piper PA-28-140 Cherokee	28-24351	LN-DAD SE-FCZ
SE-KRI	Bellanca 7ECA Citabria	1349-80	
SE-KRK	Robin R.2160 Acrobin	159	LN-RAC
SE-KRL	Piper PA-23-250 Aztec E	27-7305173	OY-DZZ N40457
SE-KRR	Republic RC-3 Seabee (On rebuild)	653	N1CD N6409K
SE-KSC	SOCATA TB-9 Tampico	191	LN-KLJ
SE-KSD	Piper PA-28RT-201T Turbo Arrow IV	28R-7931027	N2166K
SE-KSF	Piper PA-28-181 Archer II	28-7990534	N2894A
SE-KSL	Piper PA-25-235 Pawnee C	25-4557	N4786Y
SE-KSM	Piper PA-28-181 Cherokee Archer II	28-7790421	OY-BTG
SE-KSN	SOCATA MS.880B Rallye Club	860	OY-DGG
SE-KSO	Cessna 172B	17248484	N444CY N444CW N7984X
SE-KSP	Mooney M.20E Super 21	1199	OY-DDS G-BHPC OY-DDS N9250M
SE-KSS	Beech A23-19 Musketeer Sport III	MB-250	OY-DKS
SE-KSZ	American AG-5B Tiger (Accident 6.7.95)	10086	N1194Y
SE-KTB	Reims/Cessna F172K	F17200755	OH-CFD
SE-KTC	Fokker F.27-050	20124	OY-MMG PH-EXI
SE-KTD	Fokker F.27-050	20125	OY-MMH PH-EXJ
SE-KTE	SAAB-Scania SF.340B	230	XA-TQY SE-KTE F-GHVS SE-G30
SE-KTF	Piper PA-31-350 Navajo Chieftain	31-7852119	LN-TSC(2) N27720
SE-KTG	Piper PA-18-150 Super Cub	18-8336	9Q-CEL N4168Z
SE-KTH	Cessna 208 Caravan	20800245	N622JW N1006K N51872
SE-KTI	Cessna 172N	17272593	OH-CAJ N5529D
SE-KTK	SAAB-Scania SF.340B	276	F-GHVT SE-G76
SE-KTP	SOCATA TB-21 Trinidad TC	715	HB-KDE F-GLAD D-EIBP
SE-KTR	Piper PA-28R-200 Cherokee Arrow	28R-7435046	N56812
SE-KTS	Piper PA-28-181 Archer II (Reservation)	unkn	
SE-KTT	Piper PA-28-161 Warrior II	28-8216097	N8064Z
SE-KTU	Piper PA-28-181 Archer II	28-8290066	N84698
SE-KTY	Bellanca 7ECA Citabria	1261-78	N5503M
SE-KTZ	Cessna 172N	17272290	N9927E
SE-KUA	SAAB S.91B Safir	91254	Fv50042
SE-KUB	SAAB S.91B Safir	91275	Fv50066
SE-KUC	SAAB S.91C Safir	91408	Fv50093
SE-KUD	Cessna 172P	17274397	OH-CMQ N52024
SE-KUF	Robin DR.400/180R Remo 180	2118	
SE-KUS	Cessna 414 / RAM conversion	414-0482	OY-CYB N7812Q
SE-KUT	SAAB-Scania SF.340A	087	LN-NVF OK-SGY SE-KUT N110TA LN-NVF SE-E87
SE-KUV	Piper PA-28-181 Cherokee Archer II	28-7790183	N7111F
SE-KUY	Piper PA-28-235 Cherokee C	28-11135	N9410W
SE-KUZ	Cessna 150M	15077694	N6419K
SE-KVB	SAAB S.91B Safir	91215	Fv50015
SE-KVD	SAAB S.91B Safir	91248	Fv50050
SE-KVE	Piper PA-32R-301 Saratoga SP	32R-8613004	N9289Y
SE-KVG	CASA C.212-CE	229	EC-502 T-534 CX-BPK FAU-534
SE-KVI	Piper PA-18 Super Cub 95	18-1448	LN-RTF ALAT 51-15448
SE-KVK	Piper PA-28-161 Cherokee Warrior II	28-7816384	N3895M
SE-KVM	Reims/Cessna F177RG Cardinal RG	F177RG0115	LN-NFV D-EFST
SE-KVP	Piper PA-28-161 Cherokee Warrior II	28-7816650	OH-PMM N36685
SE-KVR	Cessna U206D Skywagon 206	U206-1277	LN-RTP N72084
SE-KVS	SAAB S.91B Safir	91221	Fv50019
SE-KVT	Piper PA-28-161 Warrior II	28-8116137	OH-PWA N83291
SE-KVU	SAAB S.91B Safir	91218	Fv50018
SE-KVX	SAAB S.91B Safir	91269	Fv50060
SE-KVY	SAAB S.91C Safir	91397	Fv50082
SE-KVZ	SAAB S.91C Safir	91403	Fv50088
SE-KXM	Beech 200 Super King Air	BB-459	Fv101002 OY-BVC N75X
SE-KXN	Beech 200 Super King Air (Reservation 11.04)	BB-619	Fv101003 OY-CTJ LN-MOD N10PC N4255E YV-350P
SE-KXO	BAe. ATP (Reservation 12.04)	2054	G-MANC G-LOGF G-11-54
SE-KXP	BAe. ATP (Reservation 12.04)	2056	G-MANA G-LOGO G-11-52
SE-KXR	Grumman G.164A Agcat	1120	N5085
SE-KXS	Piper PA-28-140 Cherokee	28-22792	LN-SAS G-AVGF N11C
SE-KXT	Cessna 152	15281671	N66935
SE-KYA	SAAB S.91C Safir	91395	Fv50080
SE-KYD	SAAB S.91D Safir	91280	Fv50070
SE-KYF	SAAB S.91D Safir	91249	Fv50037
SE-KYG	SAAB S.91D Safir	91396	Fv50081
SE-KYH(2)	Cessna 208B Grand Caravan (W/o 31.1.05)	208B0817	N5262W
SE-KYI	Cessna 208B Grand Caravan	208B0629	
SE-KYM	Robin R.3000/160	163	
SE-KYN	Robin HR.200/120B	282	
SE-KYP(2)	ARV Super 2 (ASL Opus 280)	033	G-73-1 G-BNVJ
SE-KYR	Yakovlev Yak-52	888412	RA-44495 DOSAAF
SE-KYU	Antonov An-2	1G138-50	ES-CAI CCCP70232
SE-KYV	Antonov An-2	1G77-12	ES-CAL CCCP29329
SE-KYX	Cessna 172 (Rebuilt with Volvo B5254 engine)	28379	G-AYOD F-OARV N5779A
SE-KYZ	Antonov An-2	1G233-23	SP-FAI
SE-KZB	SAAB S.91B Safir	91255	Fv50043
SE-KZC	SAAB S.91B Safir	91399	Fv50084
SE-KZD	Fokker F.27 Friendship 100	10245	LN-SUE PH-FFL
SE-KZE	Fokker F.27 Friendship 100	10248	LN-SUL PH-SAF LN-SUL PH-FFO
SE-KZL	Piper PA-28-140 Cherokee	28-22852	LN-NPU
SE-KZM	SAAB S.91B Safir	91237	Fv50035
SE-KZN	SAAB S.91B Safir	91 . . .	Fv500 . .
SE-KZO	SAAB S.91B Safir	91 . . .	Fv500 . .
SE-KZP	Reims/Cessna F172P	F17202238	LN-AFE G-BLZO
SE-KZR	PZL-150 Koliber	0389048	OY-CRY SP-WGE
SE-KZT	Piper PA-32R-301 Saratoga SP	32R-8213012	G-ROYI G-BMEY N8005Y ZS-LCN N8005Y
SE-KZV	Antonov An-2	1G233-20	SP-FAG
SE-KZX	Antonov An-2	1G233-24	SP-FAK
SE-KZY	Antonov An-2	1G234-01	SP-FAN
SE-KZZ	SAAB S.91C Safir (W/o 1.3.97)	91406	Fv50091
SE-LAA	Piper PA-28-181 Archer II	28-8490112	(SE-KDD) N134AV N9638N
SE-LAF	Piper PA-32R-300 Cherokee Lance	32R-7680509	N9830F
SE-LAG	LET L-200 Morava	171404	SP-TNB
SE-LAH	PZL-104 Wilga 35 (W/o 29.7.91)	62172	SP-FVA SP-WDA
SE-LAI	Piper PA-28RT-201 Arrow IV	28R-7918021	N3022K
SE-LAK	SAAB S.91B Safir	91271	Fv50062
SE-LAL	SAAB S.91B-2 Safir	91335	OO-NOR RNoAF57335/ 'UA-P'
SE-LAM	Rockwell Commander 114A	14512	N5899N
SE-LAO	SAAB S.91B Safir (Reservn 7.92, stored)	91253	Fv50041
SE-LAP	SAAB S.91C Safir	91400	Fv50085
SE-LAR	SAAB S.91B Safir	91270	Fv50061
SE-LAS	SAAB S.91B Safir	91285	Fv50075
SE-LAT	Cessna U206G Stationair 6- II	U20604466	LN-FAZ N756YQ
SE-LAU	Sukhoi SU-26M	011	RA-02166
SE-LAY	SAAB S.91B Safir (Reservation)	912 . .	Fv500 . .
SE-LAZ	SAAB S.91C Safir	91407	Fv50092
SE-LBD	Slingsby T-67M Firefly	2049	LN-TFD G-7-124
SE-LBG	Yakovlev Yak-55	901007	4L-GFA DOSAAF:90blue

SE-LBI	Maule M-7-235 Super Rocket	4029C	OY-JRM N5664M
SE-LBL	Mooney M.20R Ovation	29-0044	
SE-LBM	Mooney M.20R Ovation	29-0057	
SE-LBN	Piper PA-28-140 Cherokee B	28-25668	LN-BNZ
SE-LBO	Mooney M.20M Model 257 TLS	27-0057	N50LD
SE-LBP	SAAB-Scania SF.340A	340A-007	OY-SCF (OY-GMS) SE-LBP OH-SAG YL-BAG SE-LBP HB-AHB SE-E07
SE-LBS	Yakovlev Yak-52	800504	DOSAAF
SE-LBT	Piper PA-28R-200 Cherokee Arrow II	28R-7535006	9H-ABK G-BCSZ N9584N
SE-LBU	Piper PA-38-112 Tomahawk	38-79A0606	N2382K
SE-LBV	Mooney M.20J Model 205	24-3365	
SE-LBY	Robin R.2160 Acrobin	287	
SE-LCA	Piper PA-34-220T Seneca III	3448007	OY-SMP G-BSMP N9196W
SE-LCD	SAAB S.91C Safir	91401	Fv50086
SE-LCF	ASL Opus 280	040	(G-BNVR)
SE-LCG	Antonov An-2	1G238-11	SP-FBG
SE-LCH	Antonov An-2	1G238-12	SP-FBH
SE-LCI	Antonov An-2	1G238-13	SP-FBI
SE-LCK	Piper PA-28-180 Cherokee D	28-5241	OH-PCG SE-FFV
SE-LCL	Mooney M.20J Model 201	24-1522	N5785X
SE-LCN	Rockwell 500S Shrike Commander	3177	CS-APZ N57078
SE-LCO	Cessna A185E Skywagon	185-1466	LN-BFZ (N2716J)
SE-LCR	Cessna 152	15280685	OH-NAA N25481
SE-LCU	American Champion 8KCAB	832-99	
SE-LCV	Sukhoi SU-29 (Reservation)	81-02	RA-01606
SE-LCX	Beech 1900D	UE-275	N11189
SE-LCY	Piper PA-46-310P Malibu	4608016	N9101V
SE-LCZ	Cessna A185F Skywagon	18502444	LN-ASE N1723R
SE-LDB	CASA C.212-CB	154	N125JM
SE-LDD	SAAB S-91B Safir	91250	Fv50038
SE-LDK	Short SC.7 Skyvan Mk.III	SH.1870	SX-BBO G-AXLC G-14-42
SE-LDL	Beech A100 King Air (Reserved as LN-AWA 7.04)	B-213	F-GFEV N660CB N7243R
SE-LDN	Reims/Cessna F182Q Skylane	F18200141	D-EFNQ
SE-LDT(2)	Robin R.2160 Acrobin	271	F-GMXT
SE-LDU	Piper PA-28-181 Archer III	2843237	OY-JAF N41352 OK-NEW N9516N
SE-LDY	Piper PA-28RT-201T Turbo Arrow IV (Reservation 2.00)	28R-7931198	OY-CSA N29333
SE-LDZ	Piper PA-18-150 Super Cub (Officially quoted as c/n 18-1984)	18-7686	LN-HHQ D-EDPA
SE-LEA	Fokker F.27-050	20116	PH-GHK D-AFKX PH-GHK OE-LFY (VH-FNK) PH-EXJ
SE-LEB	Fokker F.27-050	20120	PH-JHD D-AFKZ PH-JHD (VH-FNO) PH-EXE
SE-LEC	Fokker F.27-050	20112	VH-FNG OE-LFX VH-FNG PH-EXW
SE-LED	Fokker F.27-050	20111	VH-FNF VT-RAB VH-FNF PH-EXV
SE-LEF	Fairchild Swearingen SA.227AC Metro III	AC-451B	VH-NEM N211CA
SE-LEG	HS.748 Series 2A	1723	D-AFSF
SE-LEH	Fokker F.27-050	20108	VH-FNC PH-EXP
SE-LEI	Cessna A185E Skywagon	185-1176	(SE-LEM) LN-NPF N4722Q
SE-LEK	HS.748 Series 2A	1725	D-AFSH
SE-LEL	Fokker F.27-050	20110	VH-FNE VT-RAA VH-FNE PH-EXL
SE-LEP	SAAB-Scania SF.340A	127	B-12200 SE-F27
SE-LES	SAAB-Scania SF.340A	129	B-12299 SE-F29
SE-LEU	Fokker F.27-050	20115	9M-MGZ VH-FNJ OE-LFW VH-FNJ PH-EXD
SE-LEX	HS.748 Series 2A	1727	D-AFSJ
SE-LEZ	Fokker F.27-050	20128	PH-PRA
SE-LFS	Fokker F.27-050	20216	PH-EXO
SE-LGB	BAe. Jetstream Series 3101	639	N639JX N409MX G-31-639
SE-LGC	BAe. Jetstream Series 3108	645	G-BXLM N645JD PH-KJA G-31-645
SE-LGD	Cessna 172R	17280359	
SE-LGF	Reims/Cessna F172L	F17200828	LN-BWC
SE-LGG	Piper PA-34-200T Seneca II	34-8070021	N8111H
SE-LGH	BAe. Jetstream Series 3112	773	OY-SVO C-FAMK G-31-773
SE-LGI	Cessna 172R	17280381	LN-PWE N9519P
SE-LGK	Cessna F172H	F172-0647	OY-AGM
SE-LGL	Cessna 172R	17280059	LN-PWB N376ES
SE-LGO	Grumman AA-5A Cheetah	AA5A-0462	OY-GAO
SE-LGP	Piper PA-28-161 Warrior II	28-8016372	HB-PFH N82469 N8244V
SE-LGR	Piper PA-28-161 Warrior II	28-8216137	HB-PGW
SE-LGS	SAAB-Scania 340A	071	OK-REK SE-E71 D-CDIA SE-E71
SE-LGT	Piper PA-32-260 Cherokee Six	32-7600017	N6155J
SE-LGU	BAe. ATP	2022	N853AW G-11-022
SE-LGV	BAe. ATP	2034	N857AW G-11-034
SE-LGX	BAe. ATP	2036	N859AW G-11-036
SE-LGY	BAe. ATP	2035	N858AW G-11-035
SP-LGZ	BAe. ATP	2021	N852AW (G-BRKM) G-11-021 G-11-21
SE-LHB	BAe. Jetstream Series 3201	844	N844JX N844AE G-31-844
SE-LHC	BAe. Jetstream Series 3201	846	N846JX N846AE G-31-846
SE-LHE	BAe. Jetstream Series 3201	854	N854JX N854AE G-31-854
SE-LHF	BAe. Jetstream Series 3201	855	N855JX N855AE G-31-855
SE-LHG	BAe. Jetstream Series 3201	857	N857JX N857AE G-BREV G-31-857
SE-LHH	BAe. Jetstream Series 3201	848	N848JX N848AE N332QP G-31-848
SE-LHI	BAe. Jetstream Series 3201	841	N841JX N841AE G-BPZL N338AE G-31-841
SE-LHK	BAe. Jetstream Series 3201	864	N864AE Z3-ASA N864AE G-31-864
SE-LHR	Reims/Cessna F177RG Cardinal RG	F177RG0168	HB-CXU
SE-LHS	SOCATATB-9 Tampico	692	LN-KLO
SE-LHT	Piper PA-28-161 Cherokee Warrior II	28-7816147	OY-BTN
SE-LIA	HS.748 Series 2A (Wfu 4.04)	1717	F-GFYM ZS-JAY F-BUTR G-BASZ G-11-9
SE-LIB	HS.748 Series 2B	1776	FAC-1108 G-11-14
SE-LIC	HS.748 Series 2B	1778	C-FKTL 5U-BAS G-11-20
SE-LID	HS.748 Series 2A (Wfu 9.04)	1760	J5-GAT G-BFVR G-11-9
SE-LIE	HS.748 Series 2A	1595	A10-595
SE-LIF	HS.748 Series 2	1596	A10-596

SE-LIH	Maule M-5-210C Strata Rocket (Reservn 1.01)	6055C	D-EFKE(2)
SE-LII	Yakovlev Yak-52	867015	ES-FYD DOSAAF-106
SE-LIL	Fairchild Swearingen SA.227AC Metro III	AC-432B	F-GLPE N33042 TC-FAB N1014T
SE-LIN	Fokker F.27-050	20138	PH-PRB
SE-LIO	Fokker F.27-050	20146	PH-PRC
SE-LIP	Fokker F.27-050	20147	PH-PRD SE-LIP PH-PRD
SE-LIR	Fokker F.27-050	20151	PH-PRE
SE-LIS	Fokker F.27-050	20152	PH-PRF
SE-LIT	Fokker F.27-050	20194	PH-ZDF OY-KAI PH-EXS
SE-LIY	SOCATATB-10 Tobago	547	OY-PLL LN-KLL
SE-LIZ	Opus 280	041	(PH-. . .) SE-V01
SE-LJA	BAe. Jetstream 3212 (Reservation 1.05)	978	G-BZYP F-GMVL G-31-978
SE-LJB	BAe. Jetstream 3212 (Reservation 1.05)	980	G-CBEP F-GMVN G-31-980
SE-LJC	BAe. Jetstream 3212 (Reservation 1.05)	982	G-CBER F-GMVO G-31-982
SE-LJD	BAe. Jetstream 4101 (Reservation 1.05)	41052	ZK-JSM C-FTVN G-4-052
SE-LJE	BAe. Jetstream 4101 (Reservation 1.05)	41053	ZK-JSN C-FTVP G-4-053
SE-LJF	BAe. Jetstream 4101 (Reservation 1.05)	41056	ZK-JSO C-FTVQ G-4-056
SE-LJG	Fokker F.27-050 (Res 2.05)	20168	LX-LGC PH-EXH
SE-LJH	Fokker F.27-050	20171	LX-LGD PH-EXJ
SE-LJI	Fokker F.27-050 (Res 2.05)	20180	LX-LGE PH-EXF
SE-LKA	Beech 76 Duchess	ME-295	(SE-LLL) F-GESU N6705Y
SE-LKC	EMB.120RBrasilia	120-046	N273UE PT-SJP
SE-LKD	EMB.120RBrasilia (Reservation)	unkn	
SE-LKE	EMB.120RBrasilia (Reservation)	unkn	
SE-LKF	EMB.120RBrasilia (Reservation)	unkn	
SE-LKG	Piper PA-34-200TSeneca II	34-7770258	ZS-MXX A2-AGQ N5670V
SE-LKH	SAAB S.91 Safir (Reservation 6.00)	91247	(SE-KYH(1)) Fv50048
SE-LKI	Partenavia P.68C	366	G-JACT G-NVIA
SE-LKK	Piper PA-22-108 Colt	22-9064	LN-BDK LV-PQV N10F
SE-LKL	Piper PA-34-200TSeneca II	34-7870260	G-SKYZ N31712
SE-LKM	Cessna 182R Skylane	18267785	OY-CKM OH-CIU N5551N
SE-LKN	Cessna 172RG Cutlass RG	172RG0532	N5438V
SE-LKO	Cessna 172RG Cutlass RG	172RG0682	N6421V
SE-LKP	Cessna 172RG Cutlass RG	172RG0055	N5353R
SE-LKR	Cessna 172RG Cutlass RG	172RG0718	N6466V
SE-LKS	Cessna 172RG Cutlass RG	172RG0135	N6273R
SE-LKT	Cessna 172RG Cutlass RG	172RG0491	N5263V
SE-LKU	Cessna 172RG Cutlass RG	172RG0915	N9605B
SE-LKV	Piper PA-28-181 Archer II	2890083	D-EOXC N9148N
SE-LKY	Beech B200C Super King Air	BL-127	D2-ESO
SE-LKZ	Reims FR172E Rocket	FR17200039	OH-CNF (SE-FBU)
SE-LLA	Scottish Avn SAL-100 Bulldog (SK-61D)	BH100-138	Fv.61031 G-AZJP
SE-LLM	Scottish Avn SAL-101 Bulldog (SK-61D)	BH100-111	Fv.61011 G-AZAP
SE-LLN	Fokker F.27-050	20260	PH-KXV D-AFKT PH-KXV PT-SLY PH-KXV PK-PFJ PH-KXV
SE-LLO	Fokker F.27-050 (Reservation 12.04)	20237	PH-JXM D-AFKV PH-JXM PT-SLZ PH-JXM PK-PFH PH-JXM
SE-LLP	Piper PA-28R-201 Arrow III	28R-7837022	D-EAVD N47986
SE-LLU	Beech B300 Super King Air	FL-175	N1071S RP-C7000 N1071S
SE-LLV	Piper PA-28-181 Archer III	2890215	OY-MNA G-PIPA N92516
SE-LLX	Cessna U206F Stationair 6	U20603199	LN-NAA(2) N11KB (N8338Q)
SE-LLY	Yakovlev Yak-52	844105	ES-XYN UR-B . . . DOSAAF
SE-LLZ	Diamond DA 40 Star	40061	
SE-LMA	Mooney M.20J Model 201	24-3202	D-EMON
SE-LMD	SOCATA TB-20 Trinidad	2098	F-OJBN
SE-LMR	SAAB-Scania 340A	141	OK-UFO ZK-NSL SE-KRS D-CHBA SE-F41
SE-LMS	Piper PA-28-140 Cherokee	28-23885	OY-JAZ LN-VYO
SE-LMU	Cessna 172S	172S9069	N969FA
SE-LMV	SAAB-Scania 340A	018	OK-PEP HB-AHD SE-E18
SE-LMX	SAAB-Scania 340A	056	9N-AGK N456EA N361CA SE-E56
SE-LMY	Cessna P210NPressurized Centurion II (Reservation 6.01)	P21000394	OY-LCK LN-LOK N6181K
SE-LMZ	Piper PA-28-181 Archer III	2843241	OY-JAY N9520N
SE-LNA	Scottish Avn SAL-101 Bulldog (SK-61E)	BH100-119	Fv.61017 G-AZEP
SE-LNB	Scottish Avn SAL-100 Bulldog (SK-61E)	BH100-124	Fv.61020 G-AZHV
SE-LNC	Scottish Avn SAL-100 Bulldog (SK-61E)	BH100-125	Fv.61021 G-AZHW
SE-LND	Scottish Avn SAL-100 Bulldog (SK-61E)	BH100-165	Fv.61050 G-AZPS
SE-LNE	Scottish Avn SAL-100 Bulldog (SK-61E)	BH100-171	Fv.61053 G-AZTZ
SE-LNF	Scottish Avn SAL-100 Bulldog (SK-61E)	BH100-121	Fv.61018 G-AZES
SE-LNG	Scottish Avn SAL-100 Bulldog (SK-61E)	BH100-128	Fv.61023 G-AZHY
SE-LNH	Scottish Avn SAL-100 Bulldog (SK-61E)	BH100-157	Fv.61045 G-AZPM
SE-LNI	Scottish Avn SAL-100 Bulldog (SK-61E)	BH100-163	Fv.61048 G-AZPP
SE-LNK	Mooney M.20K Model 252 TSE	25-1016	OY-BHB
SE-LNL	Scottish Avn SAL-100 Bulldog (SK-61E)	BH100-164	Fv.61049 G-AZPR
SE-LNM	Scottish Avn SAL-100 Bulldog (SK-61E)	BH100-166	Fv.61051 G-AZTX
SE-LNO	Scottish Avn SAL-100 Bulldog (SK-61E)	BH100-126	Fv.61022 G-AZHX
SE-LNP	Scottish Avn SAL-100 Bulldog (SK-61E)	BH100-167	Fv.61052 G-AZTY
SE-LNR	Scottish Avn SAL-100 Bulldog (SK-61E)	BH100-162	Fv.61047 G-AZPO
SE-LNS	Scottish Avn SAL-100 Bulldog (SK-61E)	BH100-158	Fv.61046 G-AZPN
SE-LNU	BAe. Jetstream Series 3201	949	VH-XFC N949AE G-31-949
SE-LNV	BAe. Jetstream Series 3201	951	VH-XFD N951AE G-31-951
SE-LNX	BAe. ATP (Reservation 4.02)	2057	G-OBWL G-11-057
SE-LOA	Cessna 172N (Reservation 8.01)	17271640	N4775E
SE-LOB	Cessna 182N	18260163	OY-AKG N92342
SE-LOC	Yakovlev Yak-52	855708	ES-XYC DOSAAF
SE-LOE	Piper PA-28-181 Archer III	2843383	N9511N
SE-LOF	Diamond DA 20 Katana	10132	N562SS
SE-LOG	SAAB 2000	031	HB-IZP SE-031
SE-LOH	Piper PA-28-181 Archer III	2890210	OY-LAL D-EOYC PH-AEB
SE-LOI	SOCATA MS.893E Rallye 180GT Gaillard	12214	D-EEWT F-BUCU
SE-LOK	Cessna R172K Hawk XP	R1722423	LN-MTR N736CP
SE-LOL	HOAC DV-20 Katana	20035	OE-CES C-FSBS
SE-LOM	SAAB 2000	035	HB-IZS SE-035
SE-LOP	Diamond DA 40-180 Star (Temp reg 12.01)	40070	

SE-LOR	Yakovlev Yak-52 (Reservation 7.02)	855707	ES-XYA DOSAAF
SE-LOT	SAAB 2000	013	F-GTSI EI-CPQ F-GTSA D-ADSA SE-013
SE-LOU	Lake LA-4-200 Buccaneer	764	OH-AKI SE-GRM N6009V
SE-LOY	Diamond DA 40-180 Star	40069	OY-LBA
SE-LOZ	Tecnam P.92JS Echo	021	
SE-LPA	Cessna 172R	17280907	
SE-LPB	Cessna 172R	17280928	
SE-LPC	Cessna 172R	17280929	
SE-LPD	Cessna 172R	17280957	N24527
SE-LPE	Cessna 172R	17280958	N72703
SE-LPF	Cessna 172R	17280959	N2463A
SE-LPG	Cessna 172R	17281086	N35532
SE-LPH	Cessna 172R	17281123	N52580
SE-LPI	Cessna 172R	17281197	N21614
SE-LPK	Cessna 172R	17281201	N2093S
SE-LPL	Cessna 172R	17281202	N2014T
SE-LPR	BAe. ATP	2057	G-OBWL G-11-57
SE-LPT	BAe. ATP	2058	(SE-LNX) G-OBWM G-11-058
SE-LPV	BAe. ATP	2041	G-BTPK EC-GSG EC-GLC G-BTPK G-11-041
SE-LPY	Cessna 172S	172S8632	N655SP
SE-LRA to LRZ Reserved for DHC-8-400s for SAS			
SE-LSH	SAAB 2000	052	SE-052
SE-LSI	SAAB 2000	050	OM-DGA SE-050
SE-LSK	Cessna 208BGrand Caravan	208B1012	N5236L
SE-LSL	Cessna 208BGrand Caravan	208B0810	OY-TPG D-FROG(2) S5-CAN N1223A
SE-LSP	SAAB-Scania SF.340A	340A-126	G-GNTG HB-AHR SE-F26
SE-LSR	SAAB-Scania SF.340B	340B-078	N407BH SE-E78
SE-LSS	Reims/Cessna F337FSuper Skymaster (Reims-assembled 337F with US c/n 33701333) (Reservation 10.02)	F33700025	OY-BYZ D-IHAW (N1733M)
SE-LTA	Beech 76 Duchess	ME-196	N6046R
SE-LTB	Beech 76 Duchess	ME-230	N66319
SE-LTC	Rockwell Commander 112TCA	13150	PH-RWM (PH-PPP) N4619W
SE-LTE	Cessna P337H Pressurized Skymaster	P337-0352	N73S N6MQ
SE-LTF	Diamond DA 40DStar	D4.007	
SE-LTG	Reims FR172J Rocket	FR17200540	(LN-ABU) D-EDZG PH-RPF F-BJDY
SE-LTH	Piper PA-28-181 Archer III	2843274	LN-TFT
SE-LTI	SAAB-Scania SF.340A (Reservn 10.03)	340A-010	N107PX N370CA SE-E10
SE-LTK	Cessna 172R	17280103	N385ES
SE-LTL	Beech 200 Super King Air	BB-582	LN-MOA(3) N47PA N78LB N82LB
SE-LTM	Piper PA-46-500TP Malibu Meridian	4697090	N189DB N46WK N46WE N5343C
SE-LTN	Piper PA-28R-201 Arrow III	28R-7837229	OY-ELL D-EJRG N30489
SE-LTO	SAAB-Scania SF-340A	340A-074	SE-E74 N406BH SE-E74
SE-LTP	Diamond DA 40D Star	D4.086	
SE-LTR	Fokker F.27-050	20226	LN-KKE PT-SLQ PH-JXC PH-EXC
SE-LTS	Fokker F.27-050	20230	PH-JXF LN-KKD PT-SLR PH-JXF
SE-LTT	Piper PA-31-325 Navajo C/R	31-8012041	N125TT OO-DFC C-GZVV N69XX N3584X
SE-LTU	SAAB 2000	062	HB-IYG SE-062
SE-LTV	SAAB 2000	063	HB-IYH SE-063
SE-LTX	SAAB 2000	024	HB-IZM SE-024
SE-LTY	Cessna 172S	172S8601	N783SA
SE-LTZ	Rockwell 114B	14563	N144CA
SE-LUA	Mooney M.20F Executive	680130	D-ELOI N3849N
SE-LUB	Piper PA-31T Cheyenne II	38T-7820051	OE-FBO D-IGAK LN-AET OY-BRL N9739N
SE-LUC	Cirrus SR20	1479	N53329
SE-LUD	Cirrus SR20	1480	N53330
SE-LUE	Cirrus SR20	1481	N53335
SE-LUF	Cirrus SR20	1482	N53345
SE-LUG	Cirrus SR20	1483	N53353
SE-LUS	Cessna TU206G Turbo Stationair	U20603601	D-EXAB(2) I-IPAA N7383N
SE-LUV	Yakovlev Yak-52	844707	ES-XYP DOSAAF 112 red
SE-LUX	Beech B55 Baron	TC-1269	(SE-KXE) N555BG OH-BBT
SE-LVA	Diamond DA 40D Star	D4.093	
SE-LVD	Piper PA-28R-200 Cherokee Arrow II	28R-7435131	OY-BGT
SE-LVF	Piper PA-31-350 Navajo Chieftain (Reservation 2.05)	31-7405418	N545SW PH-BKE G-OLLY G-BCES N66916
SE-LVH	Yakovlev Yak-52	9111412	ES-PAE CCCP05050 DOSAAF 47
SE-LVS	Cessna 172SP	172S8706	(SE-LUT) N776SP
SE-LVT	Cessna 172S	172S8438	N158ME
SE-LXB	Yakovlev Yak-52	833205	ES-XYL DOSAAF 44
SE-LYA	Diamond DA 40D Star	D4.104	
SE-LYB	Diamond DA 20-A1 Katana	10016	OE-VPZ N125MF N516WA
SE-LYC	Diamond DA 40D Star (Reservn 4.04)	unkn	
SE-L . .	BAe Jetstream 3101 (Res 02.04)	806	N428UE N331QV C-FBII N331QV G-31-806
SE-L . .	Cessna 172SP	172S9069	N969FA
SE-L . .	SAAB 2000	007	G-CCTJ SE-007 HB-IZD (D-ADIA) SE-007
SE-L . .	SAAB 2000	016	F-GNEH EI-CPW F-GTSC D-ADSC SE-016
SE-L . .	Maule M-7-235 Super Rocket	4102C	N9209F
SE-RAA	Embraer EMB.135ER	145210	
SE-RAB	Embraer EMB.135ER	145453	
SE-RAC	Embraer EMB.135LR	145098	N285CD (F-OJKH) (F-OIKH) (F-GNZI) N285CD EC-GZI PT-SBU
SE-RAG to -RAZ Reserved for Airbuses for SAS, 7.00			
SE-RBA(2)	McDonnell-Douglas DC-9-87	49403	EC-HMI OH-LMA
SE-RBE	McDonnell-Douglas DC-9-82	49152	OH-LMP
SE-RBF	Airbus A330-200 (Reservation 5.00)	353	F-WWYN (SE-DYI)
SE-RBG	Airbus A330-200 (Reservation 5.00)	362	F-WWKD (SE-DYK)
SE-RBK	Cessna 550 Citation II	550-0315	N59GU N618DB N90JD N6889Z
SE-RBO	Beech 400ABeechjet	RK-303	N400HD N400HS N695TA

SE-RBV(3)	Boeing 767-2Q8ER	24150	PH-AAL N339LF OB-1766-P OB-1766 CC-CJP N141LF PH-TAG ZK-NBE N6038E
SE-RBX	Cessna 560XL Citation Excel	560-5056	N688AG EC-IRU D-CVHB N51993
SE-RBY	Cessna 550 Citation Bravo	550-1038	N551VB (N551VP) N551VB
SE-RBZ	Cessna 501 Citation I/SP	501-0061	N202CF N1401L N34DL N436CC N2757A
SE-RCA	Gates Learjet 35A	35A-175	D-CDWN
SE-RCH	Airbus A320-214 (Reservation 4.02)	764	G-VTAN G-BXTA F-WWDF
SE-RCO	Boeing 737-33A	23635	F-GFUA G-OUTA N6069D N3282Y
SE-RCP	Boeing 737-33A	24025	F-GHVO G-MONU F-GFUB
SE-RCR	Boeing 737-33A	24026	F-GHVM G-MONT F-GFUC
SE-RCS	Boeing 737-3Q8	24299	N299NY S7-RGM N611LF PP-SFM N956WP EC-FER (G-BWJA) EC-FER EC-594 EC-ELJ EC-189
SE-RCX	Cessna 550 Citation II (Res 6.04)	550-0302	N792MA N33BC N133BC N441T N329CC N6888T
SE-RDB	HS.125 (Reservation 3.01)	unkn	
SE-RDC	Dassault Falcon 900 (Reservation 3.01)	unkn	
SE-RDE	McDonnell-Douglas DC-9-83	49857	HB-IUO D-ALLN (9Q-C . .)
SE-RDF	McDonnell-Douglas DC-9-83	49769	HB-IUN D-ALLK
SE-RDG	McDonnell-Douglas DC-9-83	49856	HB-IUP D-ALLM
SE-RDK	McDonnell-Douglas DC-9-83 (Reservn 4.03)	49449	TF-MDB D-ALLE
SE-RDM	McDonnell-Douglas DC-9-83	49662	N766BC F-GHEC G-PATC N1005W (N940MC)
SE-RDN	Airbus A321-200	2211	D-AVZK
SE-RDO	Airbus A321-200	2216	D-AVZN
SE-RDP	Airbus A321-200 (Reservn 7.03)		
SE-RDR	McDonnell-Douglas DC-9-82	49151	N619DB OH-LMO (XA-AMQ)
SE-RDS	McDonnell-Douglas DC-9-83	49401	OH-LPE EC-FZQ EC-749 N902PJ EI-CBN EC-FEQ EC-714 EI-CBN EC-ECN N6200N
SE-RDT	McDonnell-Douglas DC-9-82	49278	OE-LMA
SE-RDU	McDonnell-Douglas DC-9-82	49372	OE-LMC
SE-RDV	McDonnell-Douglas DC-9-83	49574	OH-LPF EC-FVR EC-591 N594PJ EC-EFU EC-348
SE-RDX	Gulfstream 550	5019	N919GA
SE-REE(2)	Airbus A330-343 (Originally res for c/n 467 now OY-KBC)	515	F-WWYY
SE-REF	Airbus A330-343X	568	(OY-KBS) F-WWYS
SE-REG	Airbus A321-232	1848	(SE-REN) D-AVZU
SE-RFA	McDonnell-Douglas DC-9-83	49623	OH-LPH SE-DHN
SE-RFB	McDonnell-Douglas DC-9-82	53246	OH-LMZ
SE-RGA	Canadair CL.600-2B19 Regional Jet (Reservation 5.04)	7958	

EXPERIMENTAL AND HOMEBUILT AIRCRAFT

The c/n suffix quoted for many examples in ABN is the EAAChapter 222 allocation, these have been omitted from the listing below.

SE-XCA	Andreasson BA-4B	2	
SE-XCC	Andreasson BA-4B	3	
SE-XCD	Andreasson BA-4B	4	
SE-XCE	Andreasson BA-4B	5	
SE-XCF	SAAB MFI-15 (W/o 17.12.88)	02	
SE-XCG	Bede BD-4	SE-01	
SE-XCH	Druine D.31 Turbulent	352	OY-CMA
SE-XCI	Jodel D.119-100	786	
SE-XCK	Andreasson Stil BA-11	1	
SE-XCL	Cassutt Racer IIIM	SE-75-01	
SE-XCO	Bede BD-4	unkn	
SE-XCP	Brügger MB-2 Colibri	05	
SE-XCR	Brügger MB-2 Colibri	09	
SE-XCS	Brügger MB-2 Colibri	10	
SE-XCT	Wittman Tailwind	206	SE-XFI
SE-XCV	Brügger MB-2 Colibri	SE-03	
SE-XCX	Evans VP-2	V2 1269-15	
SE-XCY	Stewart Headwind	unkn	
SE-XCZ	Coot-A	001	
SE-XDA	Jodel D.113	526	
SE-XDB	Brügger MB-2 Colibri	19	
SE-XDC	Brügger MB-2 Colibri	11	
SE-XDD	Zenith CH-200	A.242/1979	
SE-XDE	Jodel D.113-3	1431	OY-BMF
SE-XDF	CEA Jodel DR.1050 Ambassadeur	222	OY-DHF F-BKGD
SE-XDG	Jodel D.113-3	030	
SE-XDH	Jodel D.112 Club	1420	OY-BMV
SE-XDI	JC-24A Weedhopper	0291	
SE-XDK	MFI-9HB Trainer (MFI-11 standard, built from MFI-9 c/n 08)	P1-827	
SE-XDL	Cassutt IIIM	589	
SE-XDM	MFI-9HB Trainer	07	
SE-XDN	Brügger MB-2 Colibri	unkn	
SE-XDO	Jodel D.113-3	36	
SE-XDP	Christen Eagle II	0020	
SE-XDR	Jungster 1	7207	
SE-XDS	Aerosport Scamp-A	01	
SE-XDT	Druine D.31 Turbulent (CofA exp 8.89)	266	OY-AMC
SE-XDU	Brügger MB-2 Colibri	158	
SE-XDV	Druine D.31 Turbulent	232	OY-AMZ
SE-XDX	Jodel D.113	1460	OY-BMZ
SE-XDY	Jodel D.112 Club	830	OY-BMD
SE-XDZ	Jodel D.113	1151	OY-BMA
SE-XEA	Brügger MB-2 Colibri	12	
SE-XEB	Wassmer Jodel D.120 Paris-Nice	160	D-EDAW
SE-XEC	Rutan VariEze	1707	
SE-XED	Jodel D.119	1400	OY-AMT
SE-XEE	Stolp Starduster	1840	
SE-XEG	Druine D.31 Turbulent	298	OY-AMK
SE-XEH	Jodel D.113-3	S-64	
SE-XEI	Piel CP.301A Emeraude	102-53	D-EFKO
SE-XEK	Jodel D.119	1483	OY-CMC
SE-XEL	Evans VP-1 Volksplane	01	
SE-XEN	Druine D.31 Turbulent (W/o 20.8.88)	327	OY-BME
SE-XEO	Pitts S-1S-E	7-0419	SE-XEM
SE-XEP	Rutan VariEze	2091	
SE-XER	Piaggio P.149D-A4	317	D-EBQP 96+20 AC+468 AS+468
SE-XES	Brügger MB-2 Colibri	173	
SE-XET	Andreasson MFI-9HB	031	LN-BFL
SE-XEU	SAN Jodel D.117 Grand Tourisme (W/o 25.12.94)	910	D-EMBI HB-SVY OE-AFA
SE-XEV	Jodel D.112 Club	1153	OY-AMU
SE-XEX	Jodel D.112/108	1395	OY-AMD
SE-XEY	Rand-Robinson KR-2	034	
SE-XEZ	Rutan Long-Ez	360	
SE-XFB	Fike-D	219	
SE-XFC	Janowski J-1B Don Quixote	085	
SE-XFD	Piel CP.301A Emeraude	181	OY-AOU F-BHMN
SE-XFF	Jurca MJ.2D Tempête	81	OY-AMV
SE-XFH	Jodel D.113-3	1436	OY-BMK
SE-XFK	Stoddard-Hamilton SH-2 Glasair	404	
SE-XFL	SAN Jodel DR.100 Ambassadeur	83	OY-DIJ OE-ADA(1)
SE-XFM	Rutan Long-Ez (Bt 1981, see SE-XRS)	746	
SE-XFO	DHC-1 Chipmunk T.20	C1/0695	RDAF P-131

SE-XFP	Zlin Z.226T Trenér 6	365	LN-MAX
			D-EDEW
			OH-TZD
			OK-M . .
SE-XFR	Viking Dragonfly Mk.II	517	
SE-XFS	Rand-Robinson KR-2	AWV-28	
SE-XFT	Binder CP.301S Smaragd	114	OY-EAG
SE-XFU	Stoddard-Hamilton SH-2 Glasair	158	
SE-XFV	Rutan Vari-Viggen	517	
SE-XFX	Brügger MB-2 Colibri	189	
SE-XFY	Nilz-1/Zlin Z.326 Trenér Master	839	D-ENGA
			OK-SNB
SE-XFZ	Wassmer Jodel D.120L Paris-Nice	153L	D-EKIK
SE-XGA	Thorp T-18	1308	
SE-XGB	Rand-Robinson KR-2	4065	
SE-XGC	CEA Jodel DR.1050 Ambassadeur	36	D-EJRB
			F-BJRB
SE-XGD	Mraz M.1D Sokol	339	(OY-DNV)
			D-EMUP
			OE-AAY
			OK-D . .
SE-XGF	Stoddard-Hamilton SH-2 Glasair RG	476R	
SE-XGG	SAN Jodel DR.1050 Ambassadeur	286	D-EFJR
SE-XGH	Jodel D.113-3	1448	OY-CME
SE-XGI	Van's RV-3A	726	
SE-XGK	Wassmer Jodel D.120 Paris-Nice	49	D-EAFD
			F-BHYS
SE-XGL	Super Baby Great Lakes	8410K	
SE-XGM	Tipsy T.66 Nipper Mk.II	23	(D-EJAB)
	(Restoration project)		OY-ABO
SE-XGN	EAA Biplane	101	G-BJNW
			N67279
SE-XGO	SAN Jodel DR.1050 Ambassadeur	272	D-ELME
SE-XGP	Monnet Sonerai IILT	1180	
SE-XGS	Le Gare Sea Hawker	70	
SE-XGT	Rutan Long-Ez	607	
SE-XGU	Pitts S-1S Special	370-H/ PFA/1526	G-AYLU
	(C/n officially quoted as K-064)		
SE-XGV	Extra EA.230 Ultimate (W/o 1.8.91, rebuilding)	011	D-EMIN(3)
SE-XGX	Bölkow BO.207	250	D-EJFY
SE-XGZ	Rutan Cozy	unkn	
SE-XHB	Laser 200	01	
SE-XHC	Scintex Piel CP.301C Emeraude	524	OY-AAW
SE-XHD	Andreasson MFI-9HB	43	
SE-XHE	Light Aero Avid Flyer	208	
SE-XHG	Andreasson MFI-9HB	50	
SE-XHI	Aviamilano P.19 Scricciolo	337	I-PIND
SE-XHK	Beagle A.61 Tugmaster 6A	3744	LN-AEV
SE-XHM	Wassmer Jodel D.120A Paris-Nice	178	F-BJIV
SE-XHN	Rand-Robinson KR-2	3405	
SE-XHO	Stolp SA.700 Acroduster 1	151	
SE-XHP	Andreasson BA-6B	3	
SE-XHR	Aerotek Pitts S-2A (W/o 21.6.91)	2163	N84PS
SE-XHS	Viking Dragonfly Mk.II	588	
SE-XHU	Wassmer WA.41 Baladou	112	F-BNHR
SE-XHV	Evans VP-1 Volksplane	V-2302	
SE-XHX	Pitts S-1C Special	JC-1	
SE-XHY	Monnet Sonerai IIL	01626L	
SE-XIA	Piper PA-18-150 Super Cub	18-5990	OY-AZI
			D-EMUC
SE-XIC	Neico Lancair 235	101	
SE-XID	Bölkow BO.208C Junior	700	PH-CEP
			D-EABN
SE-XIE	Light Aero Avid Amphibian	11	
SE-XIF	Light Aero Avid Flyer	325	
SE-XIH	Stoll Starlite	206	
SE-XII	Quickie	unkn	
SE-XIK	Pitts S-1C Special (Permit 9.04)	1021	N2900V
SE-XIL	CVM 01 Tummelisa	362	
SE-XIM	WagAero Super CUBy	1465	
SE-XIN	Stoddard-Hamilton Glasair SH-2	159	
SE-XIO	Van's RV-4	432	
SE-XIP	Thorp T.18	548	
SE-XIR	Wassmer WA.40A Super IV	65	HB-DCC
SE-XIS	Andreasson MFI-9HB	062	
SE-XIT	CEA Jodel DR.1050-M1 Sicile Record	593	F-BMPD
SE-XIV	Zlin Z.526F Trenér Master	1318	
SE-XIX	Rutan Long-Ez	2031L	
SE-XIY	Orlican L-40 Meta-Sokol	150406	OH-SMA
SE-XIZ	Extra EA.300	006	
SE-XKA	Druine D.31 Turbulent	330	OY-CMF
SE-XKB	Piper PA-22-160 Tri-Pacer	22-6521	LN-TVL
			N9611D
SE-XKC	Binder CP.301S Smaragd	111	OY-EAF
SE-XKD	Light Aero Avid Flyer	390	
SE-XKE	Janowski J-1 Don Quixote	unkn	
SE-XKF	Neico Lancair 235	188	
SE-XKG	Rand-Robinson KR-2 Turbo (W/o 5.8.98)	84	
SE-XKH	Rutan Long-Ez	1939L	
SE-XKI	Spezio DAL-1	7	N1334
SE-XKK	Kukulka	T-026382	SP-PHN
SE-XKL	Pottier P.180S	147	
SE-XKM	Piaggio FWP.149D	133	OY-CPV
			D-EFRB(2)
			91+12
			D-EBDO
			KB+110
SE-XKN	Viking Dragonfly	127	
SE-XKO	Pottier P.180S	190	
SE-XKP	Light Aero Avid Amphibian	28	SE-YSP
SE-XKR	Druine D.31 Turbulent	363	OY-CMG
SE-XKT	Pottier P.180S	189	
SE-XKU	DHC-1 Chipmunk	C1/0102	OY-ATG
			P-123
			12-123
SE-XKV	Pitts S-1C Special (W/o 2.7.94)	203H	N139
SE-XKX	Denney Kitfox II	524	
SE-XKY	Neico Lancair 235	102	
SE-XKZ	Aero Designs Pulsar	166	
SE-XLA	Zlin Z.526F Trenér Master (Damaged 16.5.99)	1150	SP-CDL
SE-XLB	Zlin Z.526F Trenér Master	1114	SP-CDH
SE-XLC	Zlin Z.526F Trenér Master	1248	SP-CPG
SE-XLD	Van's RV-6 (Damaged 17.7.03)	20273	
SE-XLE	Rutan Long-Ez	9753	
SE-XLH	Binder CP.301S Smaragd	110	HB-SEM
			D-EGAZ
SE-XLI	Light Aero Avid Amphibian	22	
SE-XLK	Rans S-10 Sakota	0989061	
SE-XLL	Stoddard-Hamilton SH-2 Glasair RG	358	N100DE
SE-XLM	WagAero Super CUBy	562	
SE-XLN	Neico Lancair 235	165	
SE-XLO	Murphy Renegade Spirit EXP	0342	
SE-XLP	CEA Jodel DR.1050 Ambassadeur	569	PH-XAN
SE-XLR	Andreasson BA-4B	unkn	
SE-XLU	Light Aero Avid Amphibian	35	
SE-XLV	Corby CJ-1 Starlet	181	
SE-XLX	Stoddard-Hamilton SH-2 Glasair RG	1142	
SE-XLY	Light Aero Avid Amphibian	34	
SE-XLZ	Rutan Long-Ez	1868	
SE-XMA	Light Aero Avid Flyer Aerobat	781	
SE-XMB	Light Aero Avid Flyer Aerobat	737	
SE-XMC	Blériot XI (painted as 'A14')	82	
SE-XMD	Piper PA-18 Super Cub 95	18-1576	LN-TSO
			OO-HMR
			ALAT
			51-15576
SE-XME	Light Aero Avid Flyer (Permit 9.02)	391	
SE-XMF	Jodel D.18 (Same c/n quoted as F-PPJJ)	274	
SE-XMG	Light Aero Avid Flyer	322	
SE-XMH	SAAB MFI-15-200A	847	
SE-XMI	Van's RV-6	20285	
SE-XMK	Light Aero Avid Flyer	549	
SE-XML	Light Aero Avid Flyer (Permit 5.02)	326	
SE-XMM	Light Aero Avid Amphibian	043	
SE-XMN	Light Aero Avid Amphibian	83A	
SE-XM0	Light Aero Avid Amphibian	92A	
SE-XMP	Bushby Mustang II	1259	
SE-XMR	Brügger MB-2 Colibri	03	
SE-XMS	Nord 3400	39	ALAT
SE-XMV	Jodel D.113	523	
SE-XMX	Light Aero Avid Flyer	1035	
SE-XMY	SAN Jodel DR.1050 Ambassadeur	363A	D-ENJE
			D-EAHW
SE-XNA	Schweizer TSC-1A1 Teal	21	LN-BNO
			G-BAUL
			N202IT
SE-XNB	SAN Jodel D.140C Mousquetaire III	90	F-BKSI
			F-BKSE
SE-XNC	Neico Lancair 320	457	
SE-XND	Piel CP.301A Emeraude	003	D-EBUW
SE-XNE	Light Aero Avid Amphibian (W/o 24.9.95)	82A	
SE-XNF	Nord 3400	68	ALAT
SE-XNG	Steen Skybolt	JSG-1	N101JG
SE-XNH	Murphy Renegade Spirit 912	0338	
SE-XNI	SOCATA ST-10 Diplomate	138	F-BJCT
SE-XNK	Smith Miniplane DSA-1	7337	N5093D
SE-XNM	Van's RV-6	20934	
SE-XNN	Denney Kitfox IV	1519	
SE-XNO	Denney Kitfox III	1067	
SE-XNP	SAAB MFI-15-200A	15-848	
SE-XNR	Hummelbirg Wandwagon	625	
SE-XNS	Steen Skybolt	1	OH-XTS
SE-XNT	Steen Skybolt	SE-1	
SE-XNU	Midget Mustang VJ-1	VJ129	N3151
SE-XNV(2)	Nord 3400	121	ALAT
SE-XNX	Rans S-10 Sakota	0989062	(SE-XNV)
			(SE-XNX)
SE-XNY	Stoddard-Hamilton Glasair II-FT	1108	
SE-XNZ	Pober Pixie	PP001	
SE-XOA	Pottier P.180S	193	
SE-XOB	CASA I-131E Jungmann	2075	EC-332
	(Painted as "781-60")		E3B-475
SE-XOC	Rand-Robinson KR-2	19	N1352A
SE-XOD	Smith Sidewinder	17	
SE-XOG	Yakovlev Yak-50	760806	LY-AKZ
			DOSAAF-08
SE-XOH	Kaminski Jungster 1 Super 150	8509	
SE-XOI	Van's RV-6	20898	
SE-XOK	Light Aero Avid Amphibian	84A	
SE-XOL	Van's RV-4 (Permit)	420	
SE-XOM	Van's RV-6	21717	
SE-XON	Jodel D.18	2731	
	(Believed to incorporate parts of SE-XMT c/n 273, w/o 3.5.95)		
SE-XOO	Steen Skybolt	001	N619JS

SE-XOP	Neico Lancair 320	493	
SE-XOR	Murphy Renegade Spirit	327	
SE-XOT	Neico Lancair 320	53	
SE-XOU	Rand-Robinson KR-2	8493	
SE-XOV	Light Aero Avid Amphibian	12	
SE-XOX	Pereira GP3 Osprey II (Permit 3.02)	1228	
SE-XOY	Jodel D.18	262	
SE-XOZ	Periera GP3 Osprey II	87	
SE-XPA	Jodel D.112 Club (Permit 5.02)	62	
SE-XPB	Piper PA-22-108 Colt	22-9134	LN-IKW SE-CZO
SE-XPC	Jodel D.18	384	
SE-XPD	WagAero Super CUBy Sport Trainer	600	
SE-XPE	Pitts S-1S Special	03	OH-XPE
SE-XPF	Tipsy T.66H Nipper II	26	OO-HAL (OY-AEL)
SE-XPG	Light Aero Avid Mk IV	1432A	
SE-XPH	Ultravia Aero Pelican PL	TP101-41	
SE-XPI	Van's RV-6	21371	
SE-XPK	Van's RV-4	3610	
SE-XPL	T-131P Jungmann	01	SP-FPF
SE-XPN	Light Aero Avid Catalina EXP 912	128A	
SE-XPO	Murphy Rebel (W/o 8.9.00, rebuilding .04)	468	(N797R)
SE-XPP	CSS-13	0430	SP-FZP
SE-XPR	Murphy Rebel	238	
SE-XPS	T-131P Jungmann	04	SP-FBF
SE-XPT	SAN Jodel D.117 Grand Tourisme	647	D-EJDO F-BIBX
SE-XPU	Reynolds Wildcat Special	001	N7XS
SE-XPV	Aeronca 11AC Chief	1773	G-RONC G-BULV N3493E NC3493E
SE-XPX	Neico Lancair 360	635	
SE-XPY	Piper PA-18-135 Super Cub (F/n 18-2416 was quoted as c/n but aircraft is now designated as replica with c/n 1 due to lack of paperwork)	18-2588	Turkish AF/ 52-6270
SE-XPZ	Ridder Silent Two	1	
SE-XRA	SAN Jodel DR.1050 Ambassadeur	460	D-ELFB
SE-XRC	Christensen OPUS-3	002	
SE-XRD	Rutan Cozy III	124	
SE-XRE	Jodel D.112 Club	1408	
SE-XRF	Europa Aviation Europa (Permit)	304	
SE-XRG	Rans S-7 Courier (Permit)	0297212	
SE-XRH	Neico Lancair 360 (Permit)	921	
SE-XRI	Piaggio FWP.149D	122	D-EIOH 91+02 SB+216 SB+422 D-ELHY AS+413
SE-XRK	Van's RV-4 (Reservation)	2572	
SE-XRL	Andreasson MFI-9HB	105	
SE-XRM	Jodel D.18 (Reservation)	324	
SE-XRN	Piper PA-18-150 Super Cub	18-5330	D-EEKL ALAT N10F
SE-XRO	Rans S-6SCoyote II	11971187	
SE-XRP	Neico Lancair 320 (Dbr 19.3.00)	536-320-283	N3073Q
SE-XRR	Seawind Europe Seawind 3000 (Permit)	136	
SE-XRS	Rutan Long-Ez (Bt 1986 with same c/n as SE-XFM. Same set of plans?)	746	
SE-XRT	Europa Aviation Europa (Reservation)	318	
SE-XRU	Neico Lancair IVP (Permit, accident 6.5.00)	LIV-284	N205AF
SE-XRV	Van's RV-6	23793	
SE-XRX	Europa Aviation Europa	300	
SE-XRY	Fisher Celebrity	AV1086	
SE-XRZ	Rutan VariEze (Permit)	140-10665	N529SK
SE-XSA	Monnet Monerai	unkn	
SE-XSB	Monnet Monerai	unkn	
SE-XSC	Monnet Monerai	unkn	
SE-XSD	Windex 1100	001	
SE-XSE	Schleicher Rhönlerche II	321	D-8234
SE-XSF	Monnet Monerai	335	
SE-XSH	Windex 1200	001	
SE-XSI	Monnet Monerai	309	
SE-XSK	Sportavia/ Fournier RF-4D	4104	SE-TGX
SE-XSL	Fauvel AV-222	11	
SE-XSM	Windex 1200	unkn	
SE-XSN	Windex 1200	016	
SE-XSO	Windex 1200C	005	
SE-XSP	Windex 1200C	006	
SE-XSR	Monnet Monerai Max	378	LN-GHM(2)
SE-XST	Sportavia/Fournier RF-4D (Res 6.04)	4026	G-AVNX
SE-XUA	Van's RV-6A	23563	
SE-XUC	Stoddard-Hamilton SH-1 Glastar (Reservn 2.02)	5194	
SE-XUD	Van's RV-6A (Permit 6.03)	23413	
SE-XUE	EAA Acro Sport II (Ntu ?)	2047	
	Europa Aviation Europa (Permit 10.04)	436	
SE-XUF	Piper PA-22-160 TriPacer (Reservn 10.02)	22-7608	LN-BWR
SE-XUG	Stoddard-Hamilton SH-1 Glastar (Reservn 1.03)	5454	
SE-XUH	SAAB MFI-15-200A	15849	
SE-XUI	SAAB MFI-15-200A (Reservation 2.02)	unkn	
SE-XUK	Stoddard-Hamil;ton SH-2 Glasair IIRG	2025	OE-CGH
SE-XUL	SAAB MFI-15-200A (Reservation 4.03)	851	
SE-XUM	Jodel DR.105A (Reservation 6.04)	63	HB-EMS F-BIVN

SE-XUN	Piper PA-18 Super Cub (Reservation 9.04)	18-430	TC-EAV TAF:50-1774
SE-XUP	Piper PA-18-150 Super Cub	18-8874	9XR-TR 9Q-CTP N439EA 5Y-ANH G-AYDN N9736N
SE-XUT	Europa Aviation Europa XS	324	
SE-XUV	Van's RV-6A (Res 7.04)	25191	N12WN
SE-XUY	SAAB MFI-15-200 (Reservation 4.04)	852	
SE-XVA	Van's RV-3A (Permit 12.01)	663-90	
SE-XVB	Extra EA.230	12A	G-XTRA D-EDLF
SE-XVD	Stoddard-Hamil;ton SH-2 Glasair III	3182	
SE-XVE	Van's RV-6A	24814	
SE-XVF	Stoddard-Hamilton SH-1 Glastar (Permit 10.02)	5519	
SE-XVG	Stoddard-Hamilton SH-1 Glastar	5303	
SE-XVH	Brändli BX-2 Cherry (Permit 4.03)	37	
SE-XVI	Stoddard-Hamilton SH-2 Glasair III	3156	
SE-XVK	Pottier P.180S (Reservation 8.00)	166	
SE-XVL	Piper PA-22-108 Colt (Build Permit 12.01)	22-8987	LN-BNW N10F
SE-XVM	Van's RV-6A (Reservation 3.01)	60380	
SE-XVN	Piper PA-22-108 Colt (Permit 7.03)	22-9391	(SE-KYI) LN-IKN
SE-XVO	Fokker D.VII replica (Reservation 4.01)	10400/18	
SE-XVP	Rans S-6SCoyote II (Reservation 1.02)	10981275	(SE-YVG)
SE-XVR	Europa Aviation Europa (Reservn 6.02)	238	
SE-XVS	Europa Aviation Europa XS (Res 02.04)	476-1120	
SE-XVT	Europa Aviation Europa XS	416	(SE-XVH)
SE-XVV	Rans S-7 Courier	1297235	
SE-XVX	Van's RV-6A (Res 5.03)	21007	
SE-XVY	Europa Aviation Europa XS (Res 11.03)	472	
SE-XVZ	Aero Designs Pulsar XP	515	
SE-XXU	Van's RV-8 (Res 12.04)	80018	
SE-XXX	Neico Lancair IV (Res 1.04)	LIV-440	
SE-XYR	Akrotech Giles G-202	038	N202BR
SE-XYT	Extra EA.230	001	N230X
SE-XYY	Stoddard-Hamilton SH-1 Glastar (Reservation 11.04)	5099	(OY-ZRF) C-FZRV
SE-XYZ	Zenith CH-300 (Res 8.03)	3-2321	
SE-X . .	Brügger MB-2 Colibri	246	
SE-X . .	Fitzgerald Skybolt (Res 3.04)	JEF-1	N931JF
SE-X . .	Piper PA-22-108 Colt	22-9131	SE-CZL
SE-X . .	Taylor JT-1 Monoplane (Res 9.03)	PFA/055-10569	G-BNAR
SE-X . .	Van's RV-7A	71683	

BALLOONS ANDAIRSHIPS

SE-ZAA	Cameron DS-140 Hot Air Airship	200	G-BEHI
SE-ZAE	Colt AS-56 Hot Air Airship	624	G-BLVJ
SE-ZAG	Colt AS-105 Hot Air Airship	815	
SE-ZAM	Colt AS-56 Hot Air Airship	687	OH-AIR
SE-ZBB	Colt 69A HAFB	552	
SE-ZBD	Colt 69A HAFB	638	
SE-ZBF	Cameron N-77 HAFB	1142	
SE-ZBH	Thunder/Colt AX6-56A HAFB	685	
SE-ZBI	Colt 105A HAFB	467	G-BKLX
SE-ZBK	Colt 160A HAFB	681	
SE-ZBM	Colt 77A HAFB	713	
SE-ZBN	Colt 77A HAFB	706	
SE-ZBP	Cameron N-77 HAFB	1236	
SE-ZBR	Colt 69A HAFB	785	
SE-ZBS	Balloon Works Firefly 6 HAFB	F6-008	
SE-ZBT	Colt 56A HAFB	807	
SE-ZBU	Colt 105A HAFB	828	
SE-ZBV	Colt 77A HAFB	798	
SE-ZBZ	Colt 14A Cloudhopper HAFB	340	G-BKDS
SE-ZCA	Cameron N-77 HAFB	1338	
SE-ZCB	SLB 56A HAFB	SLB-001	
SE-ZCC	Colt 105A HAFB	861	
SE-ZCD	Colt 120A HAFB	854	
SE-ZCE	Colt 69A HAFB	885	
SE-ZCF	Colt 17A HAFB	697	G-BMDA
SE-ZCG	Colt 90A HAFB	911	
SE-ZCH	Balloon Works Firefly 8-24 HAFB	F8-097	
SE-ZCI	Colt 77A HAFB	978	
SE-ZCL	Colt 69A HAFB	1062	
SE-ZCM	Colt 180A HAFB	1048	
SE-ZCP	Cameron A-210 HAFB	1479	
SE-ZCR	Cameron A-105 HAFB	1522	
SE-ZCT	Colt 105A HAFB	1155	
SE-ZCU	Cameron N-77 HAFB	1617	
SE-ZCV	Colt 240A HAFB	1160	
SE-ZCX	Thunder AX9-140 HAFB	1177	
SE-ZCY	Cameron A-210 HAFB	1687	
SE-ZCZ	Cameron A-210 HAFB	1912	
SE-ZDA	SLB Viking 77A SL HAFB	SLB-003	
SE-ZDB	SLB Viking 77A SL HAFB	SLB-004	
SE-ZDC	SLB Viking 180A HAFB	SLB-006	
SE-ZDE	Colt 77A HAFB	1225	
SE-ZDF	SLB Viking 120A HAFB	SLB-008	

SE-ZDG	SLB Viking 77A SL HAFB	SLB-OO9	
SE-ZDI	Colt 90A HAFB	1347	
SE-ZDK	Cameron V-77 HAFB	1381	
SE-ZDL	Colt 77A HAFB	1410	
SE-ZDM	Cameron A-120 HAFB	1860	
SE-ZDN	Colt 105A HAFB	1216	
SE-ZDO	Cameron N-90 HAFB	1927	
SE-ZDP	Colt 120A HAFB	1390	
SE-ZDR	Cameron A-210 HAFB	1942	
SE-ZDS	Cameron N-77 HAFB	1136	G-BLWO
SE-ZDU	Cameron A-120 HAFB	1943	
SE-ZDV	Colt 240A HAFB	1408	
SE-ZDX	SLB Viking 77A HAFB	SLB-015	
SE-ZDZ	SLB Viking 120A HAFB	SLB-011	
SE-ZEC	Colt 77A HAFB	1566	
SE-ZED	SLB Viking 105A HAFB	SLB-017	
SE-ZEE	Colt 180A HAFB	1666	
SE-ZEF	SLB Viking 180A HAFB	SLB-016	
SE-ZEG	Colt 105A HAFB	1619	
SE-ZEH	Colt 90A HAFB	1406	
SE-ZEI	Colt 105A HAFB	1684	
SE-ZEK	Cameron N-105 HAFB	2204	
SE-ZEL	Cameron N-105 HAFB	2203	
SE-ZEM	Cameron N-77 HAFB	2152	
SE-ZEN	Cameron A-180 HAFB	2250	
SE-ZEO	Cameron A-180 HAFB	2251	
SE-ZEP	Cameron A-105 HAFB	1859	
SE-ZER	Thunder AX-77Z HAFB	1612	G-BRDK
SE-ZES	Colt 180A HAFB	1636	
SE-ZET	Cameron N-180 HAFB	2257	
SE-ZEU	SLB Viking 120A HAFB	SLB-018	
SE-ZEV	SLB Viking 77A HAFB	SLB-019	
SE-ZEX	Cameron N-105 HAFB	2386	
SE-ZEY	SLB Viking 56A HAFB	SLB-023	
SE-ZEZ	SLB Viking 105A HAFB	SLB-025	
SE-ZFB	Cameron A-105 HAFB	2494	
SE-ZFC	Thunder AX10-160 SII HAFB	1921	
SE-ZFD	Colt 240A HAFB	1887	
SE-ZFE	Cameron V-90 HAFB	2582	
SE-ZFF	Thunder AX7-77 HAFB	1499	
SE-ZFG	SLB Viking 84A HAFB	SLB-028	
SE-ZFH	Colt 240A HAFB	2079	
SE-ZFI	Cameron V-90 HAFB	2701	
SE-ZFM	Cameron A-210 HAFB	2633	
SE-ZFN	SLB Viking 105A HAFB	SLB-029	
SE-ZFO	SLB Viking 84A HAFB	031	
SE-ZFP	Colt 240A HAFB	2175	
SE-ZFR	Colt 240A HAFB	2180	
SE-ZFS	SLB Viking 105A HAFB	032	
SE-ZFT	SLB Viking 120A HAFB	SLB-033	
SE-ZFU	Colt 120A HAFB	2114	
SE-ZFX	SLB Viking 120A HAFB	034	
SE-ZFY	Cameron A-210 HAFB	3220	
SE-ZFZ	SLB Viking 69A HAFB	SLB-030	
SE-ZGA	Lindstrand LBL-77A HAFB	107	
SE-ZGB	Lindstrand LBL-310A HAFB	100	
SE-ZGC	Lindstrand LBL-77A HAFB	084	
SE-ZGD	Lindstrand LBL-77A HAFB	166	
SE-ZGE	Lindstrand LBL-310A HAFB	086	
SE-ZGF	Colt 105A HAFB	944	G-BNEU
SE-ZGG	Lindstrand LBL-400A HAFB	200	
SE-ZGH	Lindstrand LBL-240A HAFB	199	
SE-ZGK	Lindstrand LBL-240A HAFB	197	
SE-ZGL	Lindstrand LBL-9OA HAFB	201	
SE-ZGM	Lindstrand LBL-240A HAFB	258	
SE-ZGN	Lindstrand LBL-77A HAFB	284	
SE-ZGS	Lindstrand LBL-180A HAFB	350	
SE-ZGT	Cameron A-250 HAFB	3877	
SE-ZGU	Cameron Clown SS HAFB	2857	
SE-ZGV	Lindstrand LBL-9OA HAFB	426	
SE-ZGY	Cameron Flying Beer Can 77SS HAFB	3239	G-BVLB
SE-ZGZ	Colt 90A HAFB	863	G-IZMO
SE-ZHA	Ultramagic N-250 HAFB	250/06	
SE-ZHC	Lindstrand LBL Flying Newspaper SS HAFB	059	G-BVGK
SE-ZHD	Lindstrand LBL-240A HAFB	018	
SE-ZHE	Colt 56SS Flying Head HAFB	309	G-HEAD
SE-ZHF	Brita Balloon	001	
SE-ZHG	Lindstrand LBL-400A HAFB	300	
SE-ZHH	Lindstrand LBL-240A HAFB	377	
SE-ZHI	Lindstrand LBL-240A HAFB	378	
SE-ZHK	Lindstrand LBL-105A HAFB	461	
SE-ZHL	Lindstrand LBL-500C HAFB	820	
SE-ZHM	ZHM Kubicek BB-PNEU HAFB	053	OM-6002
SE-ZHN	Sky 400-28 HAFB	121	
SE-ZHO	Cameron SS Cabin HAFB	2820	G-ODIS
SE-ZHP	Lindstrand LBL-77A HAFB	209	
SE-ZHR	Lindstrand LBL-77A HAFB	034	G-BUYA
SE-ZHS	Colt Jeans SS HAFB	1747	G-JCJC
SE-ZHT	Ultramagic M-77 HAFB	77/151	
SE-ZHU	Sky 500-28 HAFB	151	
SE-ZHV	Ultramagic M-65C HAFB	65/79	
SE-ZHX	Sky 500-28 HAFB	157	
SE-ZHY	Sky 77-24 HAFB	176	
SE-ZHZ	Cameron A-415 HAFB	10277	
SE-ZIA	Ultramagic N-355 HAFB	355/01	
SE-ZIC	Lindstrand LBL-9OA HAFB	786	
SE-ZID	Kubicek BB-30Z HAFB	198	OK-0198
SE-ZIE	Ultramagic N-300 HAFB	300/05	
SE-ZIF	Lindstrand LBL-600C HAFB	900	
SE-ZIH	Colt 90A HAFB	4496	
SE-ZII	Ultramagic M-130 HAFB	130/14	
SE-ZIK	Lindstrand LBL-105A HAFB	880	
SE-ZIM	Lindstrand LBL-310A HAFB (Res 6.03)	930	
SE-ZIN	Lindstrand LBL-310A HAFB (Res 6.03)	919	
SE-ZIO	Lindstrand LBL-310A HAFB	989	
SE-ZIP	Lindstrand LBL-210A HAFB	613	
SE-ZIR	Colt 250 S II HAFB (Res10.04)	10647	
SE-ZIS	Kubicek BB-37 HAFB	303	OK-0303
SE-ZIT	Ultramagic N-300 HAFB	300/07	
SE-ZIZ	Lindstrand LBL-310A HAFB	909	
SE-ZKB	Ultramagic M-160 HAFB (Res 3.02)	160/29	
SE-ZKF	Lindstrand LBL Drinks Can SS HAFB	642	
SE-ZKG	Cameron A-340HL HAFB	4377	
SE-ZKK	Lindstrand LBL-310A HAFB	901	
SE-ZKS	Ultramagic M-120 HAFB	120/4	
SE-ZKZ	Lindstrand LBL-310A HAFB	910	
SE-ZLI	Ultramagic N-425 HAFB	425/3	
SE-ZMP	Colt A260 HAFB	10423	
SE-ZSB	Larsson SLB Balloon	unkn	
SE-ZVA	Colt 56A HAFB	008	
SE-ZVD	Colt 77A HAFB	018	
SE-ZVE	Colt 56A HAFB	029	
SE-ZVF	Colt 56A HAFB	031	
SE-ZVG	Colt 77A HAFB	036	
SE-ZVH	Colt 56A HAFB	042	
SE-ZVI	Thunder AX6-56Z HAFB	198	
SE-ZVK	Colt 56A HAFB	046	
SE-ZVL	Colt 56A HAFB	044	
SE-ZVM	Colt 56A HAFB	051	
SE-ZVO	Colt 77A HAFB	052	
SE-ZVT	Colt 56A HAFB	058	
SE-ZVU	Colt 56A HAFB	059	
SE-ZVV	Colt 56A HAFB	083	
SE-ZVZ	Cameron O-84 HAFB	174	N65BB
SE-ZXB	Colt 56A HAFB	090	
SE-ZXC	Colt 56A HAFB	092	
SE-ZXE	Colt 21A Cloudhopper HAFB	096	
SE-ZXK	Colt 77B HAFB	084	G-BHRZ
SE-ZXL	Colt 77B HAFB	362	
SE-ZXM	Colt 56B HAFB	400	
SE-ZXN	Colt 69A HAFB	412	
SE-ZXR	Colt 77A HAFB	482	
SE-ZXS	Colt 77A HAFB	015	G-BHBD
SE-ZXT(2)	Cameron N-77 HAFB	893	
SE-ZXU	Colt 56A HAFB	500	
SE-ZXV	Colt 56A HAFB	511	
SE-ZXX	Colt 77A HAFB	515	
SE-ZXZ	SLB Viking 84A HAFB	SLB-026	
SE-ZYB	Thunder AX7-77A HAFB	090	
SE-ZYC	Thunder AX8-90 HAFB	092	
SE-ZYD	Cameron V-56 HAFB	368	
SE-ZYF	Colt 56A HAFB	004	
SE-ZYG	Colt 77A HAFB	006	G-BFRG EI-BDJ
SE-ZYI	Colt 56A HAFB	006	
SE-ZYL	Colt 56A HAFB	005	
SE-ZYN	Colt 56A HAFB (ex c/n "001")	321	
SE-ZYO	Colt 56A HAFB	002	
SE-ZYP	Colt 77A HAFB	009	
SE-ZYR	Colt 77A HAFB	001	
SE-ZYU	Colt 77A HAFB	005	
SE-ZYX	Colt 77A HAFB	002	
SE-ZZA	Piccard AX6-56 HAFB	102	
SE-ZZB	Piccard AX6-56 HAFB	114	
SE-ZZD	Cameron O-56 HAFB	103	
SE-ZZF	Thunder AX7-77A HAFB	040	
SE-ZZG	Cameron V-56 HAFB	214	
SE-ZZH	Thunder AX7-77A HAFB	066	
SE-ZZL	Thunder AX7-77A HAFB	072	
SE-ZZM	Cameron O-84 HAFB	160	
SE-ZZN	Thunder AX7-77A HAFB	034	
SE-ZZO	Thunder AX8-105A HAFB (C/n still officially quoted as 026 - now G-THOR)	129	
SE-ZZP	Cameron 0-84 HAFB	112	
SE-ZZR	Cameron 0-84 HAFB	122	
SE-ZZS	Cameron 0-84 HAFB	99	
SE-ZZT	Cameron 0-84 HAFB	22	G-AZAA
SE-ZZU	Cameron 0-56 HAFB	78	
SE-ZZV	Cameron 0-84 HAFB	77	
SE-ZZY	Cameron 0-84 HAFB	44	
SE-ZZZ(2)	Cameron 0-84 HAFB (Formerly c/n 53 ex G-BAGH)	363	
SE-Z . .	Colt 180A HAFB	1172	
SE-Z . .	Colt Chips Bag SS HAFB	1430	G-BREC

GLIDERS AND MOTOR-GLIDERS

SE-SFE	Grunau Baby IIB-2	113	
SE-SHG	DFS Olympia	1	
SE-SMB	Slingsby T-31B Cadet	699	WT904

SE-SMD	Slingsby T-21B Sedbergh	609	WB942
SE-SME	Slingsby T-21B Sedbergh	663	BGA3309/FJY
			BGA3242/FGD
			WG496
SE-SMF	Schulgleiter SG-38	162	
SE-SMG	Anfanger I	20	
SE-SMH	EoN Olympia 2B	EON/0/147	BGA1422/CBX
SE-SMI	Anfanger II	1	
SE-SMK	Slingsby T-21B Sedbergh	621	WB960
SE-SML	Grunau Baby IIb	8/125	OY-ADX
			OY-50
SE-SMM	Schweizer SGU-2-22E	194	C-FWTY
			CF-WTY
			N2745Z
SE-SMN	MHL/Slingsby T.21B Sedbergh	nil	WB979
SE-SOL	SZD-36A Cobra	W-796	LN-GGB(3)
			LY-. . .
			DOSAAF
SE-SUI	Scheibe Bergfalke II/55	217	
SE-SUM	Scheibe Bergfalke II/55	219	
SE-SUR	Scheibe Bergfalke II/55	223	
SE-SUT	Scheibe Bergfalke II/55	231	
SE-SUU	Scheibe Bergfalke II/55	232	
SE-SUX	Scheibe Bergfalke II/55	234	
SE-SUY	Scheibe Bergfalke II/55	236	
SE-SVS	Scheibe Specht	808	D-6680
SE-SWA	Scheibe L-Spatz 55	576	
SE-SWB	Scheibe L-Spatz 55	577	
SE-SWF	Scheibe L-Spatz 55	643	
SE-SWT	Schleicher K 8B	845	
SE-SWU	Schleicher Ka 6CR Rhönsegler	962	
SE-SWX	Schleicher K 8B	917	
SE-SXA	Scheibe Bergfalke II/55	235	
SE-SXB	Scheibe Bergfalke II/55	261	
SE-SXD	Scheibe Bergfalke II/55	263	
SE-SXF	Scheibe Bergfalke II/55	265	
SE-SXI	Scheibe Bergfalke II/55	267	
SE-SXK	Scheibe Bergfalke II/55	269	
SE-SXL	Scheibe Bergfalke II/55	270	
SE-SXO	Scheibe Bergfalke II/55	282	
SE-SXP	Scheibe Bergfalke II/55	283	
SE-SXU	Scheibe Bergfalke II/55	286	
SE-SXW	Scheibe Bergfalke II/55	287	
SE-SXY	Scheibe Bergfalke II/55	289	
SE-SXZ	Scheibe Bergfalke II/55	291	
SE-SYC	Scheibe Zugvogel IV	1030	
SE-SYG	Scheibe Zugvogel IVA	1514	
SE-SYH	Schleicher Ka 6CR Rhönsegler	6231	
SE-SYI	Schleicher Ka 6CR Rhönsegler	6246	
SE-SYK	Schelicher K.8B	8304	
SE-SYL	Schleicher K 8B	8305	
SE-SYN	Scheibe Bergfalke II/55	292	
SE-SYO	Scheibe Bergfalke II/55	293	
SE-SYR	Scheibe Bergfalke II/55	295	
SE-SYT	Scheibe Bergfalke II/55	296	
SE-SYW	Scheibe Bergfalke II/55	298	
SE-SYX	Scheibe Bergfalke II/55	299	
SE-SYY	Scheibe Bergfalke II/55	300	
SE-SZC	Schelicher Ka.6CR Rhönsegler	963	
SE-SZE	Schleicher K 8B	8005	
SE-SZH	SZD-25A Lis	F-764	
SE-SZI	SZD-22C Mucha Standard	768	SP-2235
SE-SZK	SZD-24C Foka	W-165	SP-2234
SE-SZ0	Schleicher Ka 6CR Rhönsegler	6140	
SE-SZP	Schleicher K 8B	8202	
SE-SZR	Schleicher K 8B	8156	
SE-SZT	Schleicher K 8B	8157	
SE-SZU	Schleicher K 8B	8201	
SE-SZY	PIK-16C Vasama	14	
SE-SZZ	PIK-16C Vasama	20	
SE-TAA	Scheibe Bergfalke II/55	311	
SE-TAB	Scheibe Bergfalke II/55	312	
SE-TAC	Scheibe Bergfalke II/55	313	
SE-TAE	Scheibe Bergfalke II/55	316	
SE-TAF	Scheibe Bergfalke II/55	317	
SE-TAG	Scheibe Bergfalke II/55	318	
SE-TAI	Scheibe Bergfalke II/55	325	
SE-TAK	Scheibe Bergfalke II/55	327	
SE-TAM	Scheibe Bergfalke II/55	329	
SE-TAN	Scheibe Bergfalke II/55	331	
SE-TAO	Scheibe Bergfalke II/55	334	
SE-TAR	Scheibe Bergfalke II/55	336	
SE-TAU	Scheibe Bergfalke II/55	345	
SE-TAX	Scheibe Bergfalke II/55	354	
SE-TAY	Scheibe Bergfalke II/55	356	
SE-TAZ	Scheibe Bergfalke II/55	360	
SE-TBA	Scheibe Bergfalke II/55	361	
SE-TBB	Scheibe Bergfalke II/55	365	
SE-TBD	Scheibe Bergfalke II/55	367	
SE-TBE	Scheibe Bergfalke II/55	368	
SE-TBG	Scheibe Bergfalke II/55	377	
SE-TBI	Scheibe Bergfalke II/55	381	
SE-TBL	Scheibe Bergfalke II/55	384	
SE-TBP	Scheibe Bergfalke III	5504	
SE-TBR	Scheibe Bergfalke III	5505	
SE-TBS	Scheibe Bergfalke III	5506	
SE-TBT	Scheibe Bergfalke III	5512	
SE-TBU	Scheibe Bergfalke III	5513	
SE-TBW	Scheibe Bergfalke III	5514	
SE-TBX	Scheibe Bergfalke III	5518	
SE-TBZ	Scheibe Bergfalke III	5532	
SE-TCA	PIK-16C Vasama	15	
SE-TCF	Scheibe L-Spatz 55	513	OY-DXU
SE-TCG	Scheibe Zugvogel IIIB	1091	
SE-TCK	Schleicher K 8B	8579	
SE-TCM	Schleicher K 8B	8462	LN-GLT
			SE-TCM
SE-TCR	Schleicher Ka 6CR Rhönsegler	6388	
SE-TCX	Schleicher K 8B	8441	
SE-TCY	Schleicher K 8B	8442	
SE-TCZ	Schleicher K 8B	8330	
SE-TDA	SZD-22C Mucha Standard	602	OH-MSC
SE-TDC	SZD-22C Mucha Standard	590	SP-2168
SE-TDF	SZD-22C Mucha Standard	591	SP-2169
SE-TDG	SZD-22C Mucha Standard	638	SP-2253
SE-TDM	SZD-22C Mucha Standard	568	SP-2148
SE-TDP	Scheibe SF-27A	6044	
SE-TDU	Scheibe SF-27	6014	D-1771
SE-TDX	Scheibe SF-26 Standard	5041	
SE-TEB	Scheibe Bergfalke III	5536	
SE-TEE	Scheibe Bergfalke III	5551	
SE-TEF	Scheibe Bergfalke III	5552	
SE-TEG	Scheibe Bergfalke III	5572	
SE-TEH	Scheibe Bergfalke III	5573	
SE-TEI	Scheibe Bergfalke III	5574	
SE-TEK	Scheibe Bergfalke III	5576	
SE-TEN	Scheibe Bergfalke III	5579	
SE-TEO	Scheibe Bergfalke III	5589	
SE-TEP	Scheibe Bergfalke III	5590	
SE-TEW	Scheibe Bergfalke III	5600	
SE-TEX	Scheibe Bergfalke III	5602	
SE-TEY	Scheibe Bergfalke III	5604	
SE-TFD	Schleicher Ka 6CR Rhönsegler	6463/Si	
SE-TFG	Schleicher K 8B	20	
SE-TFL	Bölkow Phoebus A-1	798	
SE-TF0	Schleicher K 8B	8738	
SE-TFX	Schleicher Ka 6CR Rhönsegler	6647	
SE-TGA	Bölkow Phoebus C	828	
SE-TGD	Schleicher Ka 6CR Rhönsegler	6501	D-8903
SE-TGF	Schleicher K 8B	18	
SE-TGL	Schleicher Ka 6CR Rhönsegler	6653	
SE-THA	Scheibe Bergfalke III	5613	
SE-THB	Scheibe Bergfalke III	5616	
SE-THC	Scheibe Bergfalke III	5621	
SE-THD	Scheibe Bergfalke III	5622	
SE-THE	Scheibe Bergfalke III	5623	
SE-THG	Scheibe Bergfalke III	5633	
SE-THH	Scheibe Bergfalke III	5636	
SE-THI	Scheibe Bergfalke III	5638	
SE-THK	Scheibe Bergfalke III	5637	
SE-THL	Scheibe Bergfalke III	5642	
SE-THN	Scheibe Bergfalke III	5645	
SE-THO	Scheibe Bergfalke III	5646	
SE-THP	Grob G.102 Astir CS	1090	
SE-THR	Grob G.102 Astir CS	1141	
SE-THS-U3	Grob G.102 Astir CS	1165	
SE-THT	Grob G.102 Astir CS	1475	
SE-THU	Grob G.102 Astir CS	1227	
SE-THV	Grob G.102 Astir CS	1308	
SE-THX	Grob G.102 Astir CS	1247	
SE-THY	Grob G.102 Astir CS	1408	
SE-THZ	Grob G.102 Astir CS	1416	
SE-TIB	Glasflügel H301B Libelle	111	
SE-TIF	Glasflügel H201B Standard Libelle	66	
SE-TIL	Schleicher K 8B	25	
SE-TIV	Schleicher ASW 15	15011	
SE-TIX	Schempp-Hirth Standard Cirrus	31	D-0528
SE-TKD	SZD-30 Pirat	B-537	
SE-TKE	SZD-30 Pirat	B-536	
SE-TKH	Scheibe L-Spatz	528	D-1185
SE-TKM	Schleicher K 8B	609	D-5693
SE-TKN	Schleicher K 8B	8866	
SE-TKP	Schleicher Ka 6CR Rhönsegler	6616	D-7609
SE-TKT	Schempp-Hirth Standard Cirrus	215	
SE-TKZ	SZD-36A Cobra 15	W-622	SP-2658
SE-TLA	Scheibe Bergfalke IV	5808	
SE-TLB	Scheibe Bergfalke IV	5809	
SE-TLC	Scheibe Bergfalke IV	5810	
SE-TLD	Scheibe Bergfalke IV	5801	
SE-TLG	Scheibe Bergfalke IV	5821	
SE-TLH	Scheibe Bergfalke IV (W/o 24.6.03)	5830	
SE-TLI	Scheibe Bergfalke IV (Damaged 14.5.00)	5833	
SE-TLM	Scheibe Bergfalke IV	5848	
SE-TLO	Scheibe Bergfalke IV	5849	
SE-TLP	Scheibe Bergfalke IV	5850	
SE-TLT	Scheibe Bergfalke IV	5859	
SE-TLZ	Scheibe SF-25B Falke	4643	D-KHEO
SE-TMA	Scheibe SF-25A Motorfalke	4519	D-KAJA
SE-TMB	Scheibe SF-25B Falke	46102	D-KECP
SE-TMC	Scheibe SF-25A Motorfalke	4532	D-KAMY
SE-TMD	Slingsby T-61A Falke (For restoration)	1733	G-AYYJ
SE-TMF	Scheibe SF-26A	5046	OE-0734
SE-TMK	SZD-30 Pirat	S-02.05	
SE-TML	SZD-30 Pirat	S-02.04	

SE-TMN	SZD-30 Pirat	S-02.22	
SE-TMR	Scheibe L-Spatz 55	5	D-1425
SE-TMS	SZD-30 Pirat	B-553	SP-2657
SE-TMV	Schempp-Hirth Standard Cirrus	340	
SE-TNB	Glasflügel H401 Kestrel 17	103	
SE-TND	Schempp-Hirth Standard Cirrus	439G	
SE-TNE	SZD-30 Pirat	S-02.19	
SE-TNM	Schleicher Ka 6CR Rhönsegler	6151	
SE-TNN	SZD-41A Jantar Standard	X-123	
SE-TNO	SZD-30 Pirat	S-02.26	
SE-TNP	SZD-30 Pirat	S-02.23	
SE-TNR	SZD-22C Mucha	797	OH-308
			OH-MSG
SE-TNU	Pilatus B4/PC-11	160	
SE-TNV	SZD-41A Jantar Standard	X-124	
SE-TNX	Eiri PIK-20	20009	
SE-TNY	Scheibe L-Spatz 55 (W/o 12.7.97)	768	D-8472
SE-TNZ	Scheibe L-Spatz 55	774	OY-MJX
			D-5354
SE-TOA	SZD-24 Foka 4A	W-226	D-9391
SE-TOC	SZD-41A Jantar Standard	B-633	
SE-TOE	SZD-36A Cobra	W-716	
SE-TOF	SZD-41A Jantar Standard	B-632	
SE-TOI	SZD-41A Jantar Standard	B.631	
SE-TOK	SZD-30 Pirat	S-05.11	
SE-TOL	Eiri PIK-20	20048	
SE-TOM	Eiri PIK-20	20049	
SE-TOP	Glasflügel H101 Salto	53	
SE-TOR	SZD-36A Cobra 15	W-724	SP-2895
SE-TOV	Scheibe SF-25C Falke	44138	D-KDAL
			(D-KDDM)
SE-TOZ	Glasflügel H205 Club Libelle	88	
SE-TPA	SZD-41A Jantar Standard	B-695	
SE-TPC	SZD-30 Pirat	S-07.10	
SE-TPD	SZD-30 Pirat	S-08.06	
SE-TPG	SZD-41A Jantar Standard	B-705	LN-GHJ
			SE-TPG
SE-TPH	SZD-41A Jantar Standard	B-711	
SE-TPK	SZD-30 Pirat	S-06.44	
SE-TPL	Glasflügel H206 Hornet	39	
SE-TPN	Schleicher K 8B	95	D-5683
SE-TPP	Rolladen-Schneider LS1F	382	
SE-TPU	Schleicher ASW 19B	19016	
SE-TPV	Pilatus B4-PC11	192	
SE-TPZ	Schempp-Hirth Standard Cirrus	690	
SE-TRA	Rolladen-Schneider LS3	3055	
SE-TRB	Rolladen-Schneider LS3	3062	
SE-TRD	Rolladen-Schneider LS3A	3071	
SE-TRE	Rolladen-Schneider LS3	3009	
SE-TRF	Rolladen-Schneider LS1F	385	
SE-TRG	Rolladen-Schneider LS1F	464	
SE-TRH	Rolladen-Schneider LS1F	465	
SE-TRI	Rolladen-Schneider LS1F	466	
SE-TRK	Rolladen-Schneider LS1F	467	
SE-TRM	Rolladen-Schneider LS3	3129	
SE-TRN-T5	SZD-41A Jantar Standard	B-804	
SE-TRP	SZD-30 Pirat	S-09.30	
SE-TRS	SZD-41A Jantar Standard	B-844	
SE-TRU	SZD-48 Jantar Standard 2	W-882	
SE-TRV	SZD-48 Jantar Standard 2	W-898	
SE-TRY	SZD-48 Jantar Standard 2	W-865	
SE-TRZ	Schleicher K 8B	667	LN-GGM
			OY-XAV
SE-TSA	Schempp-Hirth Standard Cirrus B	683	
SE-TSB	Scheibe SF-25C Falke	4407	D-KAAX
SE-TSC	Scheibe SF-25B Falke (Permit 12.04)	4624	D-KIMF
SE-TSF	Scheibe SF-25B Falke	46138	D-KCAE
SE-TSG	SZD-24C Foka	W-203	OY-BXM
SE-TSH	Scheibe SF-25B Falke	4610	D-KOGU
SE-TSL	Pilatus B4-PC11	100	OY-XBV
SE-TSM	Eiri PIK-20B	20006	OH-451
SE-TSO	Grob G.102 Speed Astir IIB	4041	
SE-TSP	Schempp-Hirth Mini-Nimbus HS.7	59	
SE-TSS	Grob G.102 Astir CS	1440	
SE-TSU	Grob G.102 Astir CS 77	1607	
SE-TSX	Grob G.102 Astir CS 77	1709	
SE-TSY	Grob G.102 Astir CS 77 (W/o 4.9.00)	1712	
SE-TSZ	Grob G.102 Astir CS Jeans	2117	
SE-TTB	Eiri PIK-20D	20594	
SE-TTC	Grob G.102 Standard Astir III	5527S	
SE-TTH	Valentin Mistral C	MC 013/78	
SE-TTI	Eiri PIK-20	20019	OH-449
SE-TTL	Rolladen-Schneider LS3A	3360	
SE-TTM	Rolladen-Schneider LS3-17	3362	
SE-TTN	Rolladen-Schneider LS3A	3361	
SE-TTO	IAR IS-28.M2	034	
SE-TTR	Rolladen-Schneider LS4	4063	
SE-TTS	Rolladen-Schneider LS4	4065	
SE-TTX	Schleicher ASW 19B	19120	
SE-TTZ	Schleicher ASW 20	20323	
SE-TUA	Scheibe SF-25C Falke	44152	D-KEFB
SE-TUB	Eiri PIK-20E	20273	
SE-TUC	IAR IS-28.M2	035	
SE-TUD	Sportavia/ Fournier RF-5	5055	D-KINC
SE-TUE	Sportavia/ Scheibe SF-25C Falke	4223	D-KORK
SE-TUF	Scheibe SF-25B Falke	46201	D-KASP
SE-TUG	Scheibe SF-25B Falke	4627	D-KIMM
SE-TUH	Sportavia/ Scheibe SF-25C Falke	4224	OY-XKY
			D-KEAE
SE-TUI	Hoffmann H-36 Dimona	3611	
SE-TUK	Scheibe SF-25B Falke	46256C	D-KLAP
SE-TUL	Scheibe SF-25D Falke (W/o 31.8.00)	"4670-D"	
	(C/n 4670D is also quoted for OE-9103)		
SE-TUN	Scheibe SF-24B Motorspatz	4039	D-KICO
SE-TUO	Hoffmann H-36 Dimona	3505	
SE-TUP	Scheibe SF-25B Falke	46119	D-KABR
SE-TUR	Scheibe SF-28A Tandem-Falke	5728	OY-XEE
			D-KAUN
			(D-KOAQ)
SE-TUU	Scheibe SF-25C Falke	44238	D-KDCL
SE-TUX	Scheibe SF-25B Falke	4603	D-K . . .
			SE-TUX
			D-KODA
SE-TUY	Hoffmann H-36 Dimona	3685	
SE-TVA	Schempp-Hirth Mini-Nimbus C	121	
SE-TVC	Schempp-Hirth Mini-Nimbus C	124	
SE-TVE	Pilatus B4-PC11	128	OH-544
SE-TVG	Grob G.102 Astir CS	1189	D-7306
SE-TVH	Schleicher ASK 21	21024	
SE-TVI	Scheibe Bergfalke II/55	355	D-1417
SE-TVK	Scheibe SF-30A Club-Spatz	6804	
SE-TVL	Pilatus B4-PC11AF	116	LN-GGX
			HB-1145
SE-TVM	Scheibe Bergfalke II/55	369	D-1817
SE-TVP	Schempp-Hirth Ventus A	20	
SE-TVR	Pilatus B4-PC11AF	312	
SE-TVS	Schleicher ASW 19B	19329	
SE-TVV	Glaser-Dirks DG-100G Elan	E54-G31	
SE-TVX	Schleicher ASW 20	20436	
SE-TVY	Scheibe Bergfalke III	5659	
SE-TVZ	Scheibe Bergfalke III	5658	
SE-TXC	Rolladen-Schneider LS4	4181	
SE-TXD	Rolladen-Schneider LS4	4182	
SE-TXE	Rolladen-Schneider LS4	4410	
SE-TXH	Rolladen-Schneider LS4 (Damaged 4.7.03)	4467	
SE-TXM	Scheibe Bergfalke II/55	290	LN-GBA
SE-TXO	Eiri PIK-20B	20138	OH-483
SE-TXP	SZD-50-3 Puchacz	B-968	SP-3237
SE-TXR	Grob G.103A Twin II Acro	3692-K-43	
SE-TXT	Pilatus B4-PC11	010	OH-424
SE-TXU	Grob G.102 Astir CS	1054	OH-553
			D-7238
SE-TXV	Glaser-Dirks DG-100G Elan	E97-G67	
SE-TXX	Eiri PIK-20	20015	OH-457
SE-TXY	Pilatus B4-PC11AF	246	D-7843
SE-TXZ	Schleicher K 8B	756	LN-GAQ
			OY-VUX
SE-TYA-YA	Rolladen-Schneider LS6	6069	
SE-TYB	Rolladen-Schneider LS6	6013	
SE-TYC	Rolladen-Schneider LS6	6086	
SE-TYD	Rolladen-Schneider LS6	6136	
SE-TYL	Glaser-Dirks DG-100G Elan	E103-G73	
SE-TYM	Scheibe Bergfalke III	5526	
SE-TYN	Schleicher ASW 15B	15196	OH-409
SE-TYP	Schempp-Hirth Ventus b	114	
SE-TYR	Jastreb Standard Cirrus G/81	251	
SE-TYS	Scheibe Bergfalke IV	5868	D-6930
SE-TYT	Scheibe Bergfalke III	5511	
SE-TYU	Schempp-Hirth Janus B	172	
SE-TYZ	Grob G.102 Astir CS	1225	D-4199
SE-TZA	Grob G.103 Twin Astir Trainer	3169-T-16	D-7806
SE-TZE	Centrair 101AP Pégase	101AP-100	
SE-TZG	Jastreb Standard Cirrus G/81	306	
SE-TZI	Glaser-Dirks DG-300 Elan	3E-27	LN-GHZ
			SE-TZI
SE-TZL	Grob G.103 Twin Astir	3173	D-7809
SE-TZN	Grob G.103A Twin II Acro	34048-K-279	
SE-TZO	Schempp-Hirth Discus b	93	
SE-TZP	Grob G.103 Twin II	3612	OH-725
SE-TZR	Eiri PIK-20	20020	OH-467
SE-TZV	Glaser-Dirks DG-300 Elan	3E-101	
SE-TZX	Schempp-Hirth Discus b	28	
SE-TZY	Schleicher ASK 21	21251	
SE-TZZ	Schleicher ASW 20C	20739	
SE-UAB	Grob G.109B	6290	
SE-UAC	Scheibe SF-25B Falke	46238	OY-XEY
			(D-KAID)
SE-UAD	Scheibe SF-25B Falke	4620	D-KEGE
SE-UAE	Grob G.109B	6293	
SE-UAH	Scheibe SF-28A Tandem-Falke	5745	OY-XNI
			D-KOEW
SE-UAK	Scheibe SF-25B Falke	46152	D-KCAR
SE-UAL	Grob G.109B	6348	
SE-UAN	Sportavia/ Scheibe SF-25C Falke	4247	D-KMPB
SE-UAO	Grob G.109B	6349	
SE-UAP	Scheibe SF-25B Falke	46122	D-KABV
SE-UAR	Scheibe SF-25B Falke (Permit 12.04)	4678	D-KBAD
SE-UAS	Scheibe SF-25C Falke	44212	D-KDFH
SE-UAT	Scheibe SF-25C Falke	44112	D-KIPB
SE-UAU	Scheibe SF-25D Falke	46193D	D-KASH
SE-UAV	Scheibe SF-25C Falke	44392	(D-KNIG(1))
SE-UAX	Sportavia/ Fournier RF-5	5005	D-KIGO
SE-UAY	Sportavia/ Scheibe SF-25C Falke	4201	D-KAOF
SE-UAZ	Scheibe SF-25C Falke	44198	D-KDEX

SE-UBG	Scheibe SF-25C Falke	4430	D-KHON
SE-UBH	Scheibe SF-25B Falke	46154	D-KCAT
SE-UBI	Scheibe SF-25C Falke	44155	D-KEFE
SE-UBK	Scheibe SF-25C Falke	44227	OE-9150 (D-KDFY(2))
SE-UBL	Scheibe SF-25C Falke	44414	D-KNIO(1)
SE-UBN	Scheibe SF-25B Falke	46235	OY-MVX (D-KAEO(1))
SE-UBP	Scheibe SF-25C Falke	44160	D-KEFM
SE-UBT	Sportavia/ Scheibe SF-25C Falke	4214	D-KAWC
SE-UBU	Scheibe SF-25C Falke	44203	D-KDFK
SE-UBV	Scheibe SF-25C Falke	44325	D-KOON
SE-UBX	Scheibe SF-25C Falke	44173	D-KEFV
SE-UBZ	Scheibe SF-25C Falke	4482	D-KEIB
SE-UCA	Valentin Taifun 17E-II	1131	(D-KHVA)
SE-UCB	Valentin Taifun 17E-II	1133	(D-KHVA)
SE-UCC	Scheibe SF-25C Falke	44241	D-KDCQ
SE-UCD	Grob G.109B	6248	D-KBGO
SE-UCF	Slingsby T.61F Venture	1983	ZA664
SE-UCG	Eiri PIK-20E	20282	OH-620
SE-UCI	Aerotechnik L-13SW Vivat	880216	OH-803
SE-UCL	Scheibe SF-25B Falke	4636	OY-XNA D-KETI
SE-UCM	Sportavia/ Scheibe SF-25C Falke	4233	D-KAOT
SE-UCO	Scheibe SF-25CFalke	4452	OH-581 D-KDAE
SE-UCP	Scheibe SF-25C Falke	44393	D-KNIE(3)
SE-UCR	HOAC HK-36TTC Super Dimona	36653	OE-9453
SE-UCS	AVO-68-R100 Samburo	004	D-KACP
SE-UCT	IAR IS.28M2/GR	77	
SE-UCY	HOAC H-36 Dimona	36262	(SE-UCX) D-KCCC OE-9305
SE-UCZ	HOAC HK-36R Super Dimona	36309	D-KKAA
SE-UDA	HOAC HK-36R Super Dimona	36353	OE-9376
SE-UDB	Scheibe SF-25C Falke 2000	44362	D-KNAX
SE-UDC	HOAC HK-36TTC Super Dimona	36701	OY-STX
SE-UDE	HOAC HK-36TTC Super Dimona	36655	OE-9419
SE-UDF	Scheibe SF-25B Falke	46211	D-KASJ
SE-UDG	HOAC HK-36TC Super Dimona	36720	OE-9448
SE-UDH	HOAC HK-36TTS Super Dimona	36587	D-KHPR
SE-UDI	Sportavia/ Fournier RF-5B Sperber	51007	D-KCIH
SE-UDK	Scheibe SF-25C Falke	44696	OY-XYS (SE-UNR) (SE-UDK)
SE-UDL	HOAC HK-36TTC Super Dimona	36684	
SE-UDM	Grob G.109	6044	D-KGIB
SE-UDO	Grob G.109B	6342	PH-996 F-CAQK F-WAQK
SE-UDT	Grob G.109	6031	OH-674 OE-9192
SE-UDU	Scheibe SF-25C Falke 2000	44282	D-KDGL
SE-UDX	Grob G.109 (Res 5.03)	6110	LN-GPF OH-782 D-KBGF(2)
SE-UED	Glaser-Dirks DG-300 Elan	3E-156	
SE-UEE	Schleicher ASW 20C	20845	
SE-UEF-EF	Schempp-Hirth Discus b	98	
SE-UEG	Grob G.103 Twin Astir Trainer	3089	D-3950
SE-UEH	Grob G.103 Twin Astir	3127	D-7789
SE-UEK	Scheibe Bergfalke IV	5802	LN-GBP D-0374
SE-UEL	Grob G.102 Astir CS Jeans	2034	D-3880
SE-UEM	Pilatus B4-PC11AF	23	D-1185 HB-1115
SE-UEN	Molino PIK-16C	25	OH-297 OH-VAL
SE-UEO	Scheibe Bergfalke III	5519	D-8625
SE-UEP	Rolladen-Schneider LS4A	4398	OH-714
SE-UER-ER	Schleicher ASK 21	21307	
SE-UES	Grob G.103 Twin Astir Trainer	3284-T-44	OH-673 (SE- . . .) OH-673 F-CFHL
SE-UET	Glasflügel H304	227	OH-613
SE-UEU	Rolladen-Schneider LS4	4601	
SE-UEV	Rolladen-Schneider LS4A	4613	
SE-UEY	Schempp-Hirth Discus b	157	
SE-UFA-G8	Rolladen-Schneider LS4A	4615	
SE-UFC-FC	Schempp-Hirth Ventus c	335	
SE-UFD	Grob G.103 Twin Astir	3157	BGA2409/DVF
SE-UFG	Schempp-Hirth Discus b	170	
SE-UFH-FH	Schempp-Hirth Discus b	171	
SE-UFI	Rolladen-Schneider LS6B	6139	
SE-UFL	Eiri PIK-20D	20530	OH-555 PH-555
SE-UFM	Scheibe SF-34	5111	BGA2786/EMC
SE-UFN	Grob G.102 Astir CS	1467	OY-XLR D-7438
SE-UFR-FR	Schleicher ASK 21	21357	
SE-UFS	Glaser-Dirks DG-300 Elan	3E-187	D-3343
SE-UFT	Glasflügel H304	226	OH-616
SE-UFU	Grob G.103 Twin Astir	3079	D-3943
SE-UFV	Schempp-Hirth Discus b	221	
SE-UFY	Schleicher ASK 21	21375	

SE-UFZ	Grob G.103 Twin II	3833	OH-682
SE-UGA	Grob G.103 Twin II Acro	3802-K-69	OE-5326
SE-UGB	Glasflügel H304	205	OH-564
SE-UGC-GC	Schleicher ASH 25	25043	
SE-UGD	Grob G.102 Speed Astir IIB	4031	OH-656 F-WFKA(1)
SE-UGE	Grob G.102 Astir CSJeans	2026	HB-1572
SE-UGF	Schleicher ASK 21	21373	
SE-UGG	Glaser-Dirks DG-600	6-20	
SE-UGI -Z8	Schempp-Hirth Discus b	230	
SE-UGK	Centrair 201B Marianne	201B-072	
SE-UGL	Schempp-Hirth Ventus c	383	
SE-UGN	Glasflügel H304B	325	OH-722
SE-UGP	Centrair 201B Marianne	201B-074	
SE-UGR	Glasflügel H304B	348	OH-718
SE-UGT	Grob G.103 Twin Astir	3189-T-20	D-7814
SE-UGU	Schleicher ASW 20C	20745	F-CBDJ F-WBDJ
SE-UGV	Rolladen-Schneider LS7	7013	D-4680
SE-UHA-HA	Schleicher ASW 24	24037	
SE-UHB	Schempp-Hirth Janus C	254	
SE-UHD	Rolladen-Schneider LS7	7052	D-1714
SE-UHE	Rolladen-Schneider LS7	7017	D-4638
SE-UHF	Schempp-Hirth HS-7 Mini-Nimbus C (Damaged 25.6.03)	158	D-2797
SE-UHG	Grob G.103 Twin Astir Trainer (Quoted as c/n 3265-T-32 ex D-2394 but above is correct)	3264-T-32	BGA2561/EBT
SE-UHI -T	Scheibe SF-34 (Damaged 18.7.03)	5121	D-7746
SE-UHL	Grob G.102 Astir CS	1122	D-1100
SE-UHM-6V	Rolladen-Schneider LS6B	6174	D-0299
SE-UHN	Rolladen-Schneider LS6B (Cr 2.8.01)	6122	D-3711
SE-UHP	SZD-48-3 Jantar Standard 3	B-1896	
SE-UHR	SZD-24-4A Foka 4A	W-385	SP-2522
SE-UHS	SZD-50-3 Puchacz	B-1879	
SE-UHT	Grob G.103C Twin III	34135	
SE-UHU	SZD-50-3 Puchacz	B-1880	
SE-UHV	Grob G.103 Twin Astir	3113	OH-809
SE-UHX	Schleicher ASK 21	21434	
SE-UHY	Grob G.103 Twin Astir	3118	D-7785
SE-UIA	Rolladen-Schneider LS4A	4780	
SE-UIB-IB	SZD-41A Jantar Standard	B-701	SP-3049
SE-UID-ID	Schleicher ASW 19B	19392	LN-GAN
SE-UIE	Schleicher ASW 24	24092	
SE-UIF	Glaser-Dirks DG-500 Elan Trainer	5E-38T12	
SE-UIH	Schleicher Ka 6CR Rhönsegler	6041	OH-274 OH-RSN
SE-UIL	Glaser-Dirks DG-500 Elan Trainer	5E-28-T8	
SE-UIO	SZD-48-4 Jantar Standard 4	X-143	SP-3378 SP-P378
SE-UIP	Schempp-Hirth Janus C	266	
SE-UIR	SZD-24C Foka	W-159	SP-2377
SE-UIS	Eiri PIK-20D	20540	OH-517
SE-UIV	Schempp-Hirth Discus b	361	
SE-UIX	SZD-48-3 Jantar Standard 3	W-903	SP-3171
SE-UIY	Pilatus B4-PC11	141	OY-VXO
SE-UIZ	Rolladen-Schneider LS6C	6245	
SE-UKA	Schleicher ASW 24	24090	
SE-UKB	Schempp-Hirth Discus CS	021CS	
SE-UKC	LET L-23 Super Blanik	917813	
SE-UKD	Scheibe SF-34B	5134	
SE-UKE	Rolladen-Schneider LS4B	4856	D-3812
SE-UKF	SZD-24C Foka	W-138	SP-2366
SE-UKG	Schempp-Hirth Discus b	413	
SE-UKH-KH	Schleicher ASK 21	21545	
SE-UKN	Rolladen-Schneider LS6C	6253	
SE-UKR	SZD-55-1	551191014	SP-3521
SE-UKS	SZD-48-1 Jantar Standard	B-1015	OH-633
SE-UKT	LET L-13 Blanik	172127	DOSAAF
SE-UKU	Glaser-Dirks DG-300 Elan Acro	3E-433A3	
SE-UKV	Schempp-Hirth Discus b	496	
SE-UKY	Eiri PIK-20	20040	OH-481
SE-ULB-B	Rolladen-Schneider LS6C	6332	
SE-ULC	Grob G.103 Twin Astir Trainer	3253-T-30	OH-541
SE-ULD	SZD-48-1 Jantar Standard	B-1014	LN-GIQ OH-617
SE-ULF	Schleicher Ka 6CR Rhönsegler	6030/Si	D-5209
SE-ULG	ICA-Brasov IS.28B2	359	
SE-ULH	Glaser-Dirks DG-100G Elan	E137-G105	OH-690
SE-ULI	Glaser-Dirks DG-500 Elan Trainer	5E-133T58	D-9050
SE-ULL	SZD-55-1	551190001	
SE-ULM	SZD-50-3 Puchacz	B-2101	
SE-ULN	Schempp-Hirth Standard Cirrus B	574	LN-GAW
SE-ULO	Schleicher ASK 21	21644	
SE-ULP	Schempp-Hirth Duo Discus	116	
SE-ULR	SZD-50-3 Puchacz	B-2105	
SE-ULU-LU	PZL PW-5 Smyk	17.07.010	
SE-ULY	Grob G.103 Twin Astir	3538	D-8731
SE-ULZ	Rolladen-Schneider LS7	7055	D-1490
SE-UMA	Glaser-Dirks DG-500 Elan Trainer	5E-66T27	
SE-UMB	DG Flugzeugbau DG-800B	8-144B68	
SE-UMD	Grob G.103C Twin III	36005	OH-841
SE-UME	Pilatus B4-PC11	174	D-7400
SE-UMF	Schempp-Hirth Discus b	68	OH-826
SE-UMG	Glasflügel H303 Mosquito	26	OH-567
SE-UMH	Grob G.102 Astir CS77	1753	LN-GHW OY-XNW LN-GLC D-4566

SE-UMI	Schempp-Hirth Duo Discus	241	
SE-UMK	Grob G.103 Twin Astir	3021	LN-GLY OY-XLJ OE-5154
SE-UML	Schempp-Hirth Ventus cM	105/602	HB-2246
SE-UMM-MM	Genesis 2	2018	
SE-UMN	Schleicher ASK 21	21129	OY-XMN
SE-UMO	Grob G.103C Twin IIISL Acro	35042	D-KGRP
SE-UMP	Schleicher ASK 21	21718	
SE-UMT	LET L-13 Blanik	026702	YL-DBO DOSAAF
SE-UMU	DG Flugzeugbau DG-300 Elan Acro	3E-483A25	S5-3335
SE-UMV	Schempp-Hirth Ventus cM	49/492	D-KICC(2)
SE-UMX	Schleicher ASW 19 (Res 10.04)	19013	OY-CAX D-3767
SE-UMY	DGFlugzeugbau DG-1000S	10-5S5	
SE-UMZ	Schleicher ASK 21	21660	
SE-UNA	Schempp-Hirth Discus bT	108/455	F-CGGX
SE-UNB	SZD-48-1 Jantar Standard (Res 4.02)	B-1191	Latv.Nat.Guard YL-DCR DOSAAF
SE-UNC	Schleicher ASK 21	21746	
SE-UND	Glaser-Dirks DG-500 Elan Trainer	5E-100T40	D-0839
SE-UNE	Rolladen-Schneider LS7WL	70215	D-1326
SE-UNF	Schempp-Hirth Duo Discus T	38/313	D-KMAE(2)
SE-UNG	Rolladen-Schneider LS8A	8248	
SE-UNH	Schleicher ASK 21	21769	
SE-UNI	Schempp-Hirth Ventus 2cM	6/23	D-KRKR D-2945
SE-UNK	Schleicher ASK 21	21758	
SE-UNL	Schleicher ASK 21	21755	
SE-UNM	Rolladen-Schneider LS4	4428	D-5696
SE-UNN	Centrair 101A Pégase	101A-0276	OY-XYR
SE-UNO	Rolladen-Schneider LS8A	8145	
SE-UNP	DG Flugzeugbau DG-1000S	10-39S38	
SE-UNS	Schleicher ASW-22	22003	D-2203
SE-UNT	Rolladen-Schneider LS8-18	8061	F-CGZN
SE-UNU	Schleicher ASH 25Mi (Res 9.04)	25253	
SE-UNV	Schempp-Hirth Duo Discus T	109	
SE-UNX	Rolladen-Schneider LS8B	8426	D-3230
SE-UNZ	Schempp-Hirth Discus 2b	21	
SE-UOA	Schempp-Hirth Discus 2T	9/109	
SE-UOB-BB	Schempp-Hirth Janus Ce	291	D-8288
SE-UOC	Schempp-Hirth Ventus 2ax	154	
SE-UOD	Rolladen-Schneider LS6	6048	D-9292
SE-UOE	Rolladen-Schneider LS8-a (Res 2.05)	8380	D-6389
SE-UOF	Schleicher Ka 6CR Rhönsegler	6510-Si	OY-MXX D-3642
SE-UOK	Glaser-Dirks DG-500 Elan Trainer	5E-55T22	D-5033
SE-UOL	Schempp-Hirth Ventus a	24	D-6766
SE-UOM	Schempp-Hirth Ventus 2b	163	
SE-UOO	Schleicher ASW 20	20048	F-CERQ
SE-UOX	Schempp-Hirth Ventus bx (Res 8.04)	unkn	
SE-UPC	Schempp-Hirth Ventus 2b	42	
SE-UPD	Schleicher ASW 24	24089	
SE-UPE	Rolladen-Schneider LS6A	6012	D-8866
SE-UPF	Rolladen-Schneider LS8A	8166	
SE-UPG	PIK-20E (Res 9.04)	20291	G-OFJC OH-641
SE-UPI-PI	Glaser-Dirks DG-600M	6-45M3	D-KJPJ
SE-UPK	Schempp-Hirth Ventus c	558	
SE-UPM	Rolladen-Schneider LS8-18	8116	D-4920
SE-UPN-PN	Glaser-Dirks DG-505	5E-181X32	
SE-UPR	SZD-48-3 Jantar Standard 3	B-1662	OH-761
SE-UPS	Schleicher ASK 21	21738	
SE-UPT	Grob G.103 Twin III SL	35030	LN-GCL D-KHEE (D-KSOL)
SE-UPV	PZL PW-5 Smyk	17.04.021	
SE-UPX	Schempp-Hirth Ventus 2ax	164	
SE-UPY	Schleicher ASH-25E (Res 4.04)	25111	D-KNBY
SE-UPZ	DG Flugzeugbau DG-1000S	10-48S47	
SE-URB	Rolladen-Schneider LS4	4415	D-1676
SE-URC	Grob G.103CTwin III	34173	D-2941
SE-URE	HPH/Glasflügel 304C (Incorrectly quoted as c/n 49C)		
SE-URF	DG Flugzeugbau DG-1000S	10-62S57	
SE-URH	Marganski MDM-1 Fox	226	
SE-URI	Schempp-Hirth Duo Discus	16	
SE-URK	Schleicher ASW 24	24166	
SE-URL	Schempp-Hirth Ventus 2cM	126/. . .	(SE-UDS) (D-KNNM)
SE-URO	Rolladen-Schneider LS8-18	8452	
SE-URX	Schempp-Hirth Janus B	80	D-1216
SE-URY	Schempp-Hirth Ventus 2cM	156	
SE-URZ	Schleicher ASW 20	20147	BGA3499/FSW ZS-GRF D-3329
SE-USA	Rolladen-Schneider LS8A	8102	
SE-USB	Schleicher ASW 27	27204	
SE-USD	Rolladen-Schneider LS8A	8243	
SE-USE	Rolladen-Schneider LS8A	8128	
SE-USF	Rolladen-Schneider LS8A	8131	
SE-USG	Schleicher ASK 21	21788	
SE-USI	Rolladen-Schneider LS4	4553	D-7903
SE-USK	Rolladen-Schneider LS8-18	8238	D-3361
SE-USO	Schleicher ASW 27B (Res 5.00)	unkn	
SE-USP	Rolladen-Schneider LS8T	8478	
SE-USR	Rolladen-Schneider LS8A (Res 3.00)	8034	D-2940
SE-USZ	Schempp-Hirth Ventus b /16.6	223	LN-GCW D-5236
SE-UTA	Schempp-Hirth Discus 2T	8/107	
SE-UTC	Schleicher ASW 27	27003	
SE-UTD	Schempp-Hirth Nimbus 2b	159	D-7929
SE-UTE	Schempp-Hirth Ventus 2a	15	
SE-UTF	Slingsby T-59F Kestrel 19	1762	BGA1515/CFU
SE-UTG	Schempp-Hirth Duo Discus T	30/301	D-KIBF
SE-UTI	Glasflügel H303 Mosquito	25	OY-XHF
SE-UTK	Schleicher ASH-26E	26188	D-KSAG(2)
SE-UTL	Schleicher ASK 21	216553	
SE-UTN	Schempp-Hirth Ventus 2b	33	BGA4353/JAF (BGA4306)
SE-UTO	Schleicher ASW 27	27020	
SE-UTR	Schempp-Hirth Ventus 2cM (Res 6.03)	unkn	
SE-UTT	Schempp-Hirth Discus 2b	40	
SE-UTV	Glaser-Dirks DG-500 Elan Trainer	5E-54T21	D4520
SE-UTX	Schempp-Hirth Duo Discus T	29/297	
SE-UTZ	Schempp-Hirth Ventus cT	77/314	(SE-UTY) D-KAMH
SE-U . .	Rolladen-Schneider LS8-a	8380	D-6839

MICROLIGHTS

The SE-Yxx block was allocated, but not completed, before the SE-Vxx block came into use.

SE-VAA	Fisher FP-202 Super Koala	SK-081-842	
SE-VAB	TL Ultralight TL-32 Typhoon	93A028	
SE-VAC	Denney Kitfox III	PFA/172-11921	G-BTRA
SE-VAD	Denney Kitfox III	1064	
SE-VAE	TL Ultralight TL-32 Typhoon (Permit 9.04)	93A030	
SE-VAF	TL Ultralight TL-132 Condor	98C01	
SE-VAG	MCP Allegro 2000	04-1701	
SE-VAH	Denney Kitfox IV (Reservation 2.02)	1518	SE-XOF
SE-VAI	Brügger MB-2 Colibri (Reservation 1.00)	211	
SE-VAK	Comco Ikarus C-42 Cyclone	0103-6313	
SE-VAL	Comco Ikarus C-42 Cyclone	0003-6257	
SE-VAM	Evektor EV-97 Eurostar 2000	20031711	
SE-VAN	Evektor EV-97 Eurostar	20010907	
SE-VAP	ATEC Zephyr 2000C	Z430801A	
SE-VAR	Evektor EV-97 Eurostar 2000	20031710	
SE-VAS	Jabiru ST3 UL	0287/UL0075	LN-YMP
SE-VAT	Jabiru ST3 UL	0171/UL0018	
SE-VAU	Comco Ikarus C-42 Cyclone (Reservn 2.01)	0101-6300	
SE-VAV	Rans S-6ES Coyote II	0393455	9-161
SE-VAX	Flight Design CT-2K	03-05-03-22	
SE-VAY	Lamco EuroCUB MkIV	DAH-002	
SE-VAZ	Light Aero Avid Flyer (Res 11.03)	466	I-2591
SE-VBA	TL Ultralight TL-22 Duo ESO 2	96G10	
SE-VBB	Mainair Gemini/Flash IIA	897-0492-7-W692	G-MWYX
SE-VBC	TL Ultralight TL-22 Duo ESO-2	95C09	
SE-VBD	TL Ultralight TL-2 ESO-2	95C10	
SE-VBE	TL Ultralight TL-22 Duo ESO-2	96G11	
SE-VBF	TL Ultralight TL-2 ESO-2	96G13	
SE-VBG	TL Ultralight TL-2 ESO-2	96G14	
SE-VBH	Solar Wings Pegasus XL-R/Se	SW-WA-1176/SW-TB-1175	G-MTHL
SE-VBI	GTE Clipper/XP GTE	0396048	
SE-VBK	Mainair Gemini/Flash IIA	891-0392-7-W686	G-MWYK
SE-VBL	FIB Polaris 582	96A4189/963631	
SE-VBM	Air Création GTE XP-15	1G026	
SE-VBN	FIB Polaris 582	96A-4187/963632	
SE-VBO	Mayes Mosquito XS-155	1566/A10-207	
SE-VBP	TL Ultralight TL-2 ESO-2	97T001	
SE-VBR	Pegasus Quantum	7283	
SE-VBS	Pegasus Quantum	7282	
SE-VBT	FIB Polaris	96A4193/963636	
SE-VBU	FIB Polaris	96A4188/963630	
SE-VBX	TL Ultralight TL-2 ESO-2	97T002	
SE-VCA	FIB Polaris	99A4353/993779	
SE-VCB	FIB Polaris	99A4360/993789	
SE-VCC	FIB Polaris	99A4354/993780	
SE-VCD	FIB Polaris	99A4355/993781	
SE-VCE	FIB Polaris	99A4359/993788	
SE-VCF	Polaris/ESO-2	993782/990501	
SE-VCG	FIB Polaris	00A4420/003845	
SE-VCH	FIB Polaris	00A4421/003846	
SE-VCI	FIB Polaris	00A4422/003847	
SE-VCK	FIB Polaris	00A4423/003848	
SE-VCL	FIB Polaris	00A4424/003849	
SE-VCM	Tomi Cross 5.1/MW155	5/212	
SE-VCN	FIB Polaris	00A4432/003857	
SE-VCO	Mainair Blade 912S (Res 5.04)	1365-05047-W1160	
SE-VCR	Air Création XP-Clipper 912	T99028	
SE-VCS	Pegasus Quasar	SW-WQQ-0452/SW-TQC-0068	ES-KZO ES-YZO
SE-VCT	Pegasus Quantum 15	7608	
SE-VCV	Mosquito A10/Hermes 15 Minimum	89029/A10598	
SE-VCX	FIB Polaris	00A4448/003867	
SE-VCY	Mainair Blade 912	1253-0600-7-W1047	
SE-VCZ	FIB Polaris	00A4433/003858	

SE-VDA	Take Off Merlin 1100 (Reservation 9.00)	35700	
SE-VDB	TL Ultralight TL-2 ESO-2	TL2-920212	OK-WZL-14
SE-VDC	FIB Polaris	01A4485/013903	
SE-VDD	FIB Polaris	01A4486/013904	
SE-VDE	FIB Polaris	01A4487/013905	
SE-VDF	Pegasus Quantum 15	7726	
SE-VDG	Apollo C15TNJetstar	S-01/2001	
SE-VDH	FIB Polaris	01B4495/013907	
SE-VDI	FIB Polaris	01B4500/013915	
SE-VDK	Pegasus Quantum 15	7725	
SE-VDL	FIB Polaris	01B4499/013913	
SE-VDM	FIB Polaris	01B4509/013924	
SE-VDN	FIB Polaris	01B4507/013922	
SE-VDO	FIB Polaris	01B4523/013940	
SE-VDP	FIB Polaris	01B4520/013939	
SE-VDR	Pegasus Quantum 15	7832	
SE-VDS	FIB Polaris	01B4540/013957	
SE-VDU	Apollo Racer CT/R (Reservation 11.01)	150598	
SE-VDV	Apollo Jetstar CT/R	S-03/2001	
SE-VDX	FIB Polaris	04B4716/0431117	
SE-VDY	Tomi Cross 5.1/MW155	unkn	OK-EZG 01
SE-VDZ	Apollo Jetstar/R	310102	
SE-VEA	Apollo PPC (Reservation 6.01)	PPC01/01	
SE-VEB	Pegasus Quantum 15	7877	
SE-VEC	FIB Polaris	02B4572/023986	
SE-VED	FIB Polaris	02B4574/023988	
SE-VEE	FIB Polaris	02B4573/023987	
SE-VEF	FIB Polaris	02B4579/023991	
SE-VEG	FIB Polaris	02B4578/023990	
SE-VEH	Pegasus Quantum 15	7880	
SE-VEI	Pegasus Quantum 15	7881	
SE-VEK	FIB Polaris	02B4608/0231019	
SE-VEL	Apollo Racer GT/R	S-05/2002	
SE-VEM	Take Off Merlin 1100	43101	
SE-VEN	Apollo Jetstar/R	S-02/2002	
SE-VEO	FIB Polaris	02B4617/0231027	
SE-VEP	Apollo Racer GT/R	S-01/2003	
SE-VER	FIB Polaris	03B4639/0331051	
SE-VES	FIB Polaris	03B4626/0331040	
SE-VET	FIB Polaris	03B4641/0331053	
SE-VEU	FIB Polaris	03B4640/0331052	
SE-VEV	Mosquito NRG	NRG001206/069	
SE-VEX	FIB Polaris	03B4642/0331054	
SE-VEY	FIB Polaris	03B4655/0331055	
SE-VEZ	FIB Polaris	03B4634/0331056	
SE-VFA	FIB Polaris	02B4589/0231002	OH-U416
SE-VFB	FIB Polaris	03B4658/0331066	
SE-VFC	Apollo Jet Star /R	S-03/03	
SE-VFD	FIB Polaris	03B4679/0331086	
SE-VFE	FIB Polaris 582	04B4691/0431095	
SE-VFF	FIB Polaris 582	04B4690/0431094	
SE-VFG	FIB Polaris	04B4692/0431096	
SE-VFH	FIB Polaris	04B4693/0431097	
SE-VFI	Airborne Windsports Edge X	582-889-5741-949	
SE-VFK	FIB Polaris	97A4262/983695	OH-U364
SE-VFL	FIB Polaris (Res 3.04)	04B4694/0431098	
SE-VFM	Apollo Jet Star /R	S-01/04	
SE-VFN	Apollo Racer GT/R (Res 3.04)	S-02/04	
SE-VFO	FIB Polaris	03B4764/0532276	
SE-VFP	FIB Polaris	04B4717/0431118	
SE-VFR	DTA Voyageur II (Permit 10.04)	197	
SE-VFS	FIB Polaris	04B4729/0331055	
SE-VFT	Mainair Pegasus Quik (Permit 10.04)	8011	G-CCRM
SE-VFU	Apollo Jet Star (Res 1.05)	S-03/04	
SE-VGA	Brügger MB-2 Colibri (Res 11.03)	246	
SE-VGB	Lamco EuroCUB MkIV (Permit 12.04)	DAH-003	
SE-VGC	Comcolkarus C-42 Cyclone	9903-6164	D-MRKJ
SE-VGD	Comco Ikarus Fox-C22	9108-3366	PH-2F3
SE-VGF	Comcolkarus C-42 Cyclone	9902-6167	D-MWFF
SE-VGG	Quicksilver MX-III (Res 4.04)	398	I-3169
SE-VGH	Quicksilver MX-III (Res 5.04)	1810	(OY) 9-23
SE-VGI	JORA Jora (Res 6.04)	C-127	(OY) 9-237
SE-VGK	Evektor EV-97 Eurostar	2004-2202	
SE-VGL	TEAM Hi-MAX (Res 7.04)	171	
SE-VGM	Flight Design CTSW (Permit 10.04)	04.07.05	
SE-VGN	Comco Ikarus C-42B	0412-6645	
SE-VGO	Rans S-10 Sakota (Res 1.05)	0588016	SE-XIU
SE-VGP	Flight Design CTSW (Res 2.05)	05.03.04	
SE-VGR	Evektor EV-97 Eurostar	2003-1720	
SE-VGS	Flight Design CTSW (Res 2.05)	05.05.01	
SE-VGT	Evektor EV-97 Eurostar	2003-1713	
SE-VGU	Flight Design CTSW (Res 2.05)	05.05.08	
SE-VIK	Evektor EV-97 Eurostar R	2004-2105	OH-U450
SE-VIL	Evektor EV-97 Eurostar (Res 1.05)	2004-2219	
SE-VIM	Evektor EV-97 Eurostar	2003-1719	
SE-VIP	ATEC Zephyr 2000C	Z970404A	
SE-VIT	Storch CLJ Amphibian	274A330	
SE-VIX	Jabiru 450UL	429	LN-YMW
SE-VIZ	Zenair CH-701 STOL	7-9675	
SE-VPE	Best Off Sky Ranger (Res 8.04)	SKR0403464	
SE-VPH	Rans S-7 Courier (Reservation 4.99)	889056	(SE-YUS)
SE-VPM	Denney Kitfox II (Res 10.04)	678	SE-XPM
SE-VPN	Zenair CH-701 STOL	7-9409	
SE-V . .	Avid Amphibian	103A	N9233N
SE-V . .	Evektor EV-97 Eurostar (Res 12.04)	2004-2214	
SE-V . .	Evektor EV-97 Eurostar (Res 1.05)	2004-2305	

SE-V . .	Zenair CH-701 STOL (Res 1.05)	7-9467
SE-V . .	MCP Allegro 2000 (Res 4.04)	03-1701
SE-YAD	Eipper Quicksilver MX	3017
SE-YAI	Eipper Quicksilver MX	3019
SE-YAK	Eipper Quicksilver MX	3020
SE-YAL	Eipper Quicksilver MX	3022
SE-YAM	Eipper Quicksilver MX	3023
SE-YAN	Eipper Quicksilver MX	3024
SE-YAO	Eipper Quicksilver MX	3025
SE-YAS	Weedhopper JC-24B	1417
SE-YAU	Weedhopper JC-24B	1348
SE-YAV	Eipper Quicksilver MX	3080
SE-YAX	Eipper Quicksilver MX-II	3099
SE-YAY	Eipper Quicksilver MX-II	3098
SE-YAZ	Eipper Quicksilver MX-I	3093
SE-YBA	Weedhopper JC-24B	1414
SE-YBB	Weedhopper JC-24B	1511
SE-YBC	Weedhopper JC-24B	1513
SE-YBD	Weedhopper JC-24B	1506
SE-YBE	Mitchell P-38 Lightning	unkn
SE-YBG	Weedhopper JC-24B	1507
SE-YBI	Weedhopper JC-24C	1940
SE-YBK	Weedhopper JC-24B	1508
SE-YBL	Mitchell U-2 Super Wing	unkn
SE-YBM	Weedhopper JC-24C	1942
SE-YBN	Weedhopper JC-24B	1505
SE-YBO	Weedhopper JC-24C	1941
SE-YBU	Weedhopper JC-24C	1939
SE-YBZ	Eipper Quicksilver MX	2082
SE-YCC	Weedhopper JC-24C	2077
SE-YCD	Weedhopper JC-24C	2075
SE-YCG	Mitchell Wing B10	B-1140
SE-YCH	Mitchell P-38 Lightning	unkn
SE-YCI	Wizard J-3	S-01
SE-YCR	Eipper Quicksilver MX	1216
SE-YCS	Eipper Quicksilver MX-I	3087
SE-YCT	Weedhopper JC-24C	2079
SE-YCU	Weedhopper JC-24C	2081
SE-YCV	Weedhopper JC-24C	2186
SE-YCX	Weedhopper JC-24C	2187
SE-YCY	Weedhopper JC-24C	2188
SE-YCZ	Weedhopper JC-24C	2189
SE-YDA	Weedhopper JC-24C	2190
SE-YDB	Weedhopper JC-24C	2080
SE-YDC	Weedhopper JC-24C	2083
SE-YDD	Weedhopper JC-24C	2082
SE-YDE	Weedhopper JC-24B	1515
SE-YDF	Eipper Quicksilver MX	3086
SE-YDG	Eipper Quicksilver MX	3097
SE-YDH	Eipper Quicksilver MX-II	3702
SE-YDI	Eipper Quicksilver MX-I	3089
SE-YDK	Eipper Quicksilver MX	3081
SE-YDM	Eipper Quicksilver MX	3739
SE-YDP	Eipper Quicksilver MX	3189
SE-YDT	Weedhopper JC-24C	2193
SE-YDU	Weedhopper JC-24C	2194
SE-YDY	Weedhopper JC-24C	2197
SE-YEA	Weedhopper JC-24C	2199
SE-YEC	Eipper Quicksilver MX-II	unkn
SE-YED	Lazair	A-477
SE-YEG	Eipper Quicksilver MX-II	3986
SE-YEK	Eipper Quicksilver	3974
SE-YEL	Eipper Quicksilver MX-II	3983
SE-YEM	Eipper Quicksilver MX	3737
SE-YEO	Eipper Quicksilver MX-II	3976
SE-YEP	Eipper Quicksilver MX-I	3738
SE-YER	Eipper Quicksilver MX-II	3977
SE-YES	Aerodyne Vector 610	1291
SE-YEU	Eipper Quicksilver MX	3991
SE-YEY	Eipper Quicksilver MX-II	3987
SE-YEZ	Eipper Quicksil ver MX-II	3979
SE-YFB	Eipper Quicksilver MX-II	3972
SE-YFC	Eipper Quicksilver MX-I	3095
SE-YFE	Lazair	A-479
SE-YFF	Lazair	A-481
SE-YFH	Eipper Quicksilver MX-II	3984
SE-YFK	Eipper Quicksilver MX-II	3987
SE-YFL	Lazair	unkn
SE-YFM	Dragon 150	0012
SE-YFN	Teman Monofly	unkn
SE-YFP	Aerodyne Vector 610	1388
SE-YFR	Eipper Quicksilver MX	3995
SE-YFT	Lazair	A-478
SE-YFX	Dragon 150	0052
SE-YFY	Akka (Tierra 2)	unkn
SE-YFZ	BJ Enduro	215
SE-YGA	Dragon 150	0053
SE-YGB	Eurowing Goldwing	unkn
SE-YGC	Tiger Cub 440	unkn
SE-YGF	Aériane Sirocco/KFM	37
SE-YGG	MFI BA-12	BA12.01
SE-YGI	Dragon 150	0060
SE-YGL	Teratorn Tierra II (Crashed 27.3.00)	40002
SE-YGN	Aériane Sirocco	64
SE-YGS	Mitchell B-10 Mitchell Wing	unkn
SE-YGU	Dragon 150	0075

SE-YGV	Mitchell P-38 Lightning	317	
SE-YGX	Mitchell P-38 Lightning	unkn	
SE-YGY	Lazair II	B027	
SE-YGZ	Dragon 150	0061	G-MMDL
SE-YHA	Aériane Sirocco	78	
SE-YHB	Aériane Sirocco	76	
SE-YHC	Eipper Quicksilver MX-II	1753	
SE-YHD	Mitchell P-38 Lightning	06	
SE-YHF	Fisher FP-212 Koala	unkn	
SE-YHG	Teratorn Tierra II	40007	
SE-YHH	Teratorn Tierra II	40006	
SE-YHK	Teratorn Tierra II	40017	
SE-YHL	Teratorn Tierra II	40003	
SE-YHM	Teratorn Tierra II	40013	
SE-YHN	Teratorn Tierra II	40008	
SE-YHO	Teratorn Tierra II	40004	
SE-YHP	Teratorn Tierra II	40015	
SE-YHR	Teratorn Tierra II	40016	
SE-YHS	Teratorn Tierra II	40011	
SE-YHT	Teratorn Tierra II	40014	
SE-YHV	Teratorn Tierra II	40018	
SE-YHX	Teratorn Tierra II	40021	
SE-YHY	Teratorn Tierra II	40019	
SE-YHZ	Teratorn Tierra II	40010	
SE-YIA	Teratorn Tierra II	40025	
SE-YIB	Teratorn Tierra II	40024	
SE-YIC	Teratorn Tierra II	40022	
SE-YID(2)	Filcoa J-6 Karatoo	529/9/267	
SE-YIE	Sonaca-Falcon	SM-OO9	
SE-YIF	Mitchell P-38 Lightning	JS-07	
SE-YIH	Fisher FP-202 Koala	2195	
SE-YII	Fisher Super Koala	unkn	
SE-YIK	J-3 Kitten	24861	
SE-YIL	MFI BA-12	002	
SE-YIM	Fisher Super Koala	SK012	
SE-YIN	Birdman Chinook WT-IIS	752	
SE-YIO	Mitchell U-2 Super Wing	unkn	
SE-YIP	Akka Flyg Akka	40027	
SE-YIR	Sonaca Falcon	SM-005	
SE-YIS	Baker Bobcat	218	
SE-YIT	Mitchell P-38 Lightning	40	
SE-YIU	Birdman Chinook WT-IIS	01082	
SE-YIV	Akka Flyg Akka	40023	
SE-YIZ	MFI-BA12 Rotax	3-509-688	
SE-YKA	MFI-BA12 Rotax	004	
SE-YKB	MFI-BA12 Rotax	005	
SE-YKD	TEAM Hi-Max	617	
SE-YKE	Mitchell B-10 Mitchell Wing	P1313-6	
SE-YKF	Rans S-7 Courier	1087.022	
SE-YKG	Rans S-9 Chaos	1187.032	
SE-YKI	Filcoa J-3 Kitten	2901858	
SE-YKK	Fisher FP-202 Super Koala	SK-40	
SE-YKL	Rans S-9 Chaos	1187.029	
SE-YKN	Fisher FP.202 Super Koala	0001	N4549B
SE-YKO	Comco Ikarus Fox-C22	8905-3199	
SE-YKP	Lazair	A-524	
SE-YKS	Rans S-6 Coyote II	0789.043	
SE-YKU	Murphy Renegade Spirit 532	249	
SE-YKV	Fisher Super Koala	SK039	
SE-YKX	Fisher FP-202 Super Koala	SK026	
SE-YKY	J-6 Karatoo	1881-5101	
SE-YLA	Lazair II	A526	
SE-YLB	First Strike Bobcat	513	
SE-YLC	Murphy Renegade Spirit	0272	
SE-YLD	Lidholm WLC-2	2	
SE-YLE	Rans S-6 Coyote II	1289.104	
SE-YLF	Murphy Renegade Spirit UL	248	
SE-YLG	Fisher FP-202 Super Koala	SKO-15-554	
SE-YLH	Murphy Renegade Spirit 532UL	273	
SE-YLI	Mitchell B-10 Mitchell Wing	P1276	
SE-YLK	Fisher FP-202 Super Koala	SKO-25	
SE-YLL	Fisher FP-202 Super Koala	73	
SE-YLM	Aces High Cuby II	LC 2091012 L1	
SE-YLN	ELAN Cuby II	AAH002	
SE-YLO	ELAN Cuby II	AAH003	
SE-YLP	ELAN Cuby II	AAH004	
SE-YLR	ELAN Cuby II	AAH005	
SE-YLS	ELAN Cuby II	AAH006	
SE-YLU	ELAN Cuby II 912	AAH010	
SE-YLX	Fischer FP-202 Koala	2197	
SE-YLZ	Eipper Quicksilver MX-II	339	
SE-YMT	Fisher FP-404 Classic	4045	
SE-YMU	Filcoa J-6 Karatoo	264	
SE-YMV	Aviasud Mistral 532	114/90	
SE-YMX	Rans S-7 Courier	0290067	
SE-YMY	Fisher Super Koala	SKO-45	
SE-YNA	Solar Wings Pegasus XL-Q	SW-WQ-0234/SW-TE-0219	
SE-YNB	Solar Wings Pegasus XL-Q	SW-WQ-0235/SW-TE-0220	
SE-YNC	Solar Wings Pegasus XL-Q	SW-WQ-0259/SW-TE-0235	
SE-YND	Solar Wings Pegasus XL-Q	SW-WQ-0277/SW-TE-0253	
SE-YNF	Air Création Safari GT B1 16SX	S-100-028	
SE-YNH	Air Ceation Racer ESO2	S-101-030	
SE-YNI	Slater Skytrike/Chronos 14	S-103	
SE-YNK	Air Création Safari GT B1	S-102	
SE-YNN	Mosquito	A10	
SE-YNO	Solar Wings Pegasus Quasar	SW-WQQ-0356/SW-TQ-0027	
SE-YNP	Solar Wings Pegasus Quasar	SW-WQQ-0359/SW-TQ-0028	
SE-YNR	Solar Wings Pegasus Quasar	SW-WQQ-0355/SW-TQ-0026	
SE-YNS	Solar Wings Pegasus Quasar	SW-WQQ-0354/SW-TQ-0025	
SE-YNU	Mosquito/Bauter Zephir	A10-106/1470	
SE-YNV	Solar Wings Pegasus XL-Q	SW-WQ-0237/SW-TE-0222	
SE-YNX	Mosquito/Rumour 14.5	A10-215/008	
SE-YNY	Cosmos Bidulum/Chronos 14	652	
SE-YNZ	Cosmos Bidulum/Chronos 14	655	
SE-YOA	Bautek/NST Saphir	47565/M	
SE-YOB	Behlen Trike Vampir II	2702R03/571	
SE-YOC	Behlen Trike/La Mouette PR.19	369	
SE-YOD	Solar Wings Pegasus XL-R	SW-WA-1251/SW-TB-1246	
SE-YOE	Behlen Trike/La Mouette PR	895	
SE-YOF	Behlen Trike/Hermes 16M LA M	601	
SE-YOG	Behlen Trike/La Mouette PR.19	493	
SE-YOH	Mainair TriFlyer 440/Flexiform Dual Striker	176-0783-1	
SE-YOI	Behlen Trike/La Mouette	612	
SE-YOK	Solar Wings Pegasus XL-R	SW-WA-1330/SW-TB-1318	G-MTWB(1)
SE-YOL	Behlen Trike/Hermes 16M LA	633	
SE-YOM	Magic 177 Minimum	M-315	
SE-YON	Solar Wings Pegasus XL-R	SW-WA-1376/SW-TB-1368	
SE-YOO	Solar Wings Pegasus XL-Q	SW-WQ-0139/SW-TE-0130	
SE-YOP	Solar Wings Pegasus XL-Q	SW-WQ-0115/SW-TE-0102	
SE-YOR(2)	Mainair Gemini/Flash II A	712-1188-6-W502	
SE-YOV	Solar Wings Pegasus XL-Q	SW-WQ-0160/SW-TE-1	
SE-YOX	Mainair Scorcher 503	769-989-2-W562	
SE-YOY	Behlen Trike/Hermes 16M	2120-021	
SE-YOZ	Solar Wings Pegasus XL-Q	SW-WQ-0223/SW-WQ-0256	(SE-YOV) (SE-YOR)
SE-YPA	Cosmos Bidulum/Chronos 14	617	
SE-YPC	Cosmos Bidulum/Chronos 14	722	
SE-YPD	Cosmos Bidulum/La Mouette PR19	N-286	
SE-YPF	Cosmos Bidulum/Chronos 14	T-798/V92-39-05	
SE-YPG	Cosmos Bidulum/Chronos 14	777-68	
SE-YPH	Solar Wings Pegasus XL-R	SW-WA-1151/SW-TB-1153	
SE-YPI	Solar Wings Pegasus Quasar II.TC	SW-WQT-0549/SW-TQD-0110	
SE-YPK	Mainair Gemini/Flash IIA (Cr 4.7.00)	919-0992-/-W717	
SE-YPP	Mainair Gemini/Flash IIA	898-0492-7-W693	G-MWYW
SE-YPR	Pegasus Quasar 2TL	SW-TQD-0107/SW-WQT-0545	
SE-YPS	Mainair Mercury	9261192-7-W725	
SE-YPT	Mainair Gemini/Flash IIA	949-0693-7-W744	
SE-YPU	Mainair Gemini/Flash IIA	956-0793-7-W751	
SE-YPV	Solar Wings Pegasus XL-R	6597	
SE-YPY	Mainair Gemini/Flash IIA	965-0993-7-W760	
SE-YPZ	Cosmos Chronos 16	938	
SE-YRA	Solar Wings Pegasus Quasar 2TC	6653	
SE-YRB	Pegasus Quantum 15	6670	
SE-YRC	Solar Wings Pegasus XL-Q (Correct c/n may be SW-WQ-0023/SW-TE-0044)	SW-TB-0023/SW-WQ-24	LN-YKR
SE-YRD	Pegasus Quantum 15	6696	
SE-YRE	NST Pamir Minimum	M595/020511	
SE-YRF	Chronos 9 Bidulum	0030/3786881	LN-YJH
SE-YRG	Mainair Mercury	992-0694-7-W789-0694-5	
SE-YRH	TL Ultralight TL-2 ESO-2	94E018	
SE-YRI	Solar Wings TSR-85 Typhoon	T585-1403-SW-TC-1002	
SE-YRK	Air Création XP-GTE Clipper (W/o 12.6.99)	0595084	
SE-YRL	TL Ultralight TL-2 ESO-2	95T22	
SE-YRM	TL Ultralight TL-2 ESO-2	95T23	
SE-YRN	Mainair Blade	1023-0295-7-W821	
SE-YRO	Air Création XP-GTE Clipper	0695097	
SE-YRP	TL Ultralight TL-22 Duo ESO-2	95E034	
SE-YRR	Mainair Blade	1113-0297-7-W916	
SE-YRS	Mainair Blade	1038-0595-7-W836	
SE-YRT	Mainair Blade	1026-0295-7-W824	
SE-YRU	Mainair Blade	1032-0495-7-W830	
SE-YRV	FIB Polaris	0411	
SE-YRX	Solar Wings Pegasus XL-Q-LC	SW-WQ-0017/SW-TB-1302	G-MTUO
SE-YRY	Solar Wings Pegasus XL-Q-LC	SW-WQ-0192/SW-TE-0183	G-MVSA
SE-YRZ	Solar Wings Pegasus XL-R	SW-WA-1180/SW-TE-0018	G-MTHP
SE-YSA	TL Ultralight TL-32 Typhoon (Correct c/n may be 95A036)	93A036	
SE-YSB	Rans S-12 Airaile	0291057	
SE-YSC	Fisher FP-202 Super Koala	723	
SE-YSD	Light Aero Avid Catalina UL-582	138AB	
SE-YSE	Lamco EuroCUB 912UL	BAH001-1015	
SE-YSH	Jodel D.18 (Crashed 22.9.00)	404	
SE-YSI	Kolb Twin Star Mk II	78811891	OH-U149

SE-YSK	Light Aero Avid Flyer	B.324	SE-XHT
SE-YSL	Lamco EuroCUB Mk 1	CAH-006	
SE-YSM	Light Aero Avid Flyer	389	SE-XLF
SE-YSN	Fisher FP.202 Super Koala	SK-074	
SE-YSO	TL Ultralight TL-32 Typhoon	9501	
SE-YSR	TL Ultralight TL-132 Condor	95C06	
SE-YSS	Denney Kitfox III	PFA/172-11918	G-RMGW
SE-YST	CFM Streak Shadow	K261SA	
SE-YSU	Fisher FP-303	3028	
SE-YSV	Comco Ikarus Fox-C22	8809-3156	OH-U102
SE-YSX	Jodel D.9 Bébé	834	
SE-YSY	Rans S-6E Coyote II	0689034	9-89
SE-YSZ	Light Aero Avid Catalina UL912	136AB	
SE-YTC	Fisher FP-202 Super Koala	SK0-61	
SE-YTD	Lidholm WLC-2	1	
SE-YTE	Comco Ikarus Fox-C22	8903-3195	
SE-YTF	Light Aero Avid Amphibian	127	(SE-XOE)
SE-YTG	TEAM Mini-Max (Permit)	1250-P	
SE-YTH	EuroCUB Mk I (W/o 9.99?)	CAH-012	
SE-YTI	Fisher FP.202 Super Koala (Permit 7.02)	SKO-14	
SE-YTK	Tomi 3 Delphin	3/2127	
SE-YTL	Rans S-6S Coyote II	0196927	
SE-YTM	Rans S-6S Coyote II	0195896	
SE-YTN	Light Aero Avid Amphibian	83A	SE-XMN
SE-YTO	Pelican Club GS	PFA/165-11214	G-PELI
SE-YTR	Denney Kitfox IV	172	N53PA
SE-YTS	EuroCUB Mk I	CAH-14	
SE-YTT	Jodel D.18UL	427	
SE-YTV	Diehl XTC	445	
SE-YTY	Fisher FP.202 Super Koala	SKO-84	
SE-YTZ	Denney Kitfox Classic IV	C174	
SE-YUA	Rans S-6S Coyote II	1193562	N5290H
SE-YUC	Light Aero Avid Amphibian	119A	SE-XMZ
SE-YUD	Light Aero Avid Amphibian	33	SE-XKS
SE-YUE	Comco Ikarus Fox C22	8804-3128	OH-U085
SE-YUF	Rans S-12XL Airaile	04970795	
SE-YUH	Rans S-6S Coyote II	10961056	
SE-YUI	Light Aero Avid Amphibian	21	SE-XIB
SE-YUK	Comco Ikarus C-42 Cyclone	9806/6102	
SE-YUL	Lamco EuroCUB Mk.1 912UL (Reservation)	CAH-015	
SE-YUM	Comco Ikarus C-42 Cyclone	9807/6108	
SE-YUN	Rans S-12X2 Airaile	04970796	
SE-YUO	CFM Shadow CD	K.146	G-MYCD
SE-YUP	TL Ultralight TL-232 Condor II	99C01	
SE-YUR	Rans S-6 Coyote II (W/o 10.6.00)	07981251	
	(Appears to have been re-regd SE-YYB)		
SE-YUS	Lamco EuroCUB Mk.1 912UL	CAH-016	
	(Reserved earlier for Rans S-7 Courier a/n 0889056)		
SE-YUT	Rans S-6S Coyote II (Permit)	10971170S	
SE-YUU	Jabiru ST-3 UL	0178	LN-YNN(1)
SE-YUV	Ultraflight Lazair III (Reservation)	A523	
SE-YUX	Anglin J-6 Karatoo UL	573196-025	
SE-YUY	Rans S-7L Courier (Reservation)	1189061	
SE-YUZ	Jodel D.18UL	408	SE-XUZ
SE-YVA	Rans S-6S Coyote II	10971176	
SE-YVB	Jodel D.18UL (Permit)	438	
SE-YVC	Jabiru 2000UL (Reservation 7.01)	174	
SE-YVD	Filcoa J-6 Karatoo (Reservation)	529/9/269	
SE-YVE	Filcoa J-6 Karatoo (Reservation)	529/9/267	
SE-YVF	Rans S-6 Coyote II	0795853XL	9-197
SE-YVH	Jodel D.18UL (Reservation)	224	
SE-YVK	Anglin J-6 Karatoo UL	573198	
SE-YVL	Comco Ikarus C-42 Cyclone	0003-6226	
SE-YVN	Jabiru ST-3 UL	286	LN-YNN(2)
SE-YVO	Comco Ikarus C-42 Cyclone	0005-6261	
SE-YVP	Zenair CH-701 STOL	7-9121	OK-FUR-88
SE-YVR	Filcoa J-6 Karatoo (Reservation 3.00)	573096	
SE-YVS	Comco Ikarus C-42 Cyclone	0008-6277	
SE-YVT	TEAM Hi-Max 1400Z (Permit 10.03)	1714 P	
SE-YVU	Rans S-12 Airaile (Reservation 8.02)	0193370	LN-YIW
SE-YVV	EuroCUB 912 Mk IV	DAH-001	
SE-YVX	Fisher Super Koala (Permit 9.02)	SKO-80	
SE-YVY	Comco Ikarus C-42 Cyclone	0111-6346	
SE-YVZ	Rans S-6S Coyote II	01981275bS	
SE-YXA	Medway Raven X	MRB-139-120	
SE-YXB	Medway Raven X	MRB-141-123	
SE-YXC	FIB Polaris	97A4214/973655	
SE-YXD	Medway Raven X	MRB140/122	
SE-YXE	Medway Raven X	MRB142/124	
SE-YXF	TL Ultralight TL-2 ESO-2	MRB141/123	
SE-YXG	Medway Puma Sprint	"M515/126"	
	(Corrupt c/n. If 126 is the wing this could be Raven X c/n MRB126/108		
	previously G-MYVU cancelled 10.95, or an engine serial)		
SE-YXH	TL Ultralight TL-2 ESO-2 (Cr 1.8.00)	TL2G23/97E077	
SE-YXI	Solar Wings Pegasus Flash	SW-WF-0005	G-MNJI
SE-YXK	FIB Polaris	95A5162/954038	
SE-YXL	TL Ultralight TL-2 ESO-2	97TL020	
SE-YXM	TL Ultralight TL-2 ESO-2	97TL021	
SE-YXN	FIB Polaris	96A4207/963628	
SE-YXO	Tomi 3 Delfin	31239/1124	OK-BZG-06
SE-YXP	FIB Polaris	98A4264/973690	
SE-YXT	Airborne Edge X	E304/E317	
SE-YXU	Airborne Edge X	E293/E321	
SE-YXV	FIB Polaris	98A4277/983708	
SE-YXX	FIB Polaris	98A4276/983707	
SE-YXY	FIB Polaris	98A4282/983714	
SE-YXZ	FIB Polaris	98A4286/983721	
SE-YYA	Flight Design CT-2K (W/o 12.5.02)	01.03.01.08	
SE-YYB	Rans S-6SCoyote II	07981251-100S	SE-YUR
	(Appears to be SE-YUR re-regd after rebuild)		
SE-YYC	Jabiru UL 2200	174	
SE-YYD	Flight Design CT-2K	01.07.05.21	
SE-YYE	Rans S-6ESCoyote II	0490117	LN-YKE
SE-YYF	Mitchell Wing U2 (Reservation 9.01)	U625	
SE-YYH	Fisher Youngster (Reservn 10.01)	01B4540-013957	
SE-YYI	Rans S-9 Chaos (Permit 9.02)	1199165	
SE-YYK	Comco Ikarus C-42 Cyclone	0002/6240	D-MOSE
SE-YYL	Murphy Renegade Spirit 912	0290	SE-XLG
SE-YYM	Flight Design CT-2K	03.01.02.02	
SE-YYN	Light Aero Avid Flyer IV (Permit 9.03)	1116D	
SE-YYO	Tecnam P.92-EM Echo (Permit 10.04)	668JAB	
SE-YYR	Comco Ikarus C-42B	0307-6552	
SE-YYT	Comco Ikarus Fox C-22B	9503-3661	(OY) 9-188
SE-YYU	Jodel D.18UL (Permit 5.03)	458	
SE-YYV	Comco Ikarus C-42B	0308-6568	
SE-YYX	Jodel D.18UL (Permit 11.04)	221	
SE-YYY	Lamco EuroCUB Mk 1 912UL	CAH-OO9	
SE-YYZ	Zenair CH-601UL Zodiac	6-9445	OK-DUR 99
SE-YZA	FIB Polaris ESO-2	98A4279/97G21	
SE-YZB	Mainair Blade 912	1159-0698-7-W962	
SE-YZC	Mosquito A10/Zephir	25070	
SE-YZD	Medway Raven X	MRB 154/133	
SE-YZE	Raven X	MRB153/132	
SE-YZF	TL Ultralight TL-2 ESO-2	TL-2/98-06	
SE-YZG	TL Ultralight TL-2 ESO-2	TL-2/98-07	
SE-YZH	Mainair Blade 912	1181-1098-7-W984	
SE-YZI	Tomi Cross 5.1/MW155 (Destroyed 10.11.99)	S/2107	OK-DZG-8
SE-YZK	Pegasus Quantum 15	7485	
SE-YZL	TL Ultralight TL-2 ESO-2	940201/TL-2-01	SP-FNN?
SE-YZM	FIB Polaris	99A4336/993746	
SE-YZN	TL Ultralight TL-2 ESO-2	980902/990202	
SE-YZO	Pegasus Quantum 15	7542	
SE-YZP	TL Ultralight TL-2 ESO-2	TL-2/980901	
SE-YZR	FIB Polaris	92A4498/890003709	
SE-YZS	FIB Polaris (Reservation)	99A4376/99A3802	
SE-YZT	FIB Polaris (Reservation)	99A4373/99A3801	
SE-YZU	NST Minimum/Pamir	M735	
SE-YZV	Cosmos Bidulm/La Mouette	KSAKT0001-V001	
	(Reservation 10.99)		
SE-YZX	TL Ultralight TL-2/ESO-2	99T03	
SE-YZZ	Pegasus Quantum 15	7581	
SE-Y . .	Mainair Blade 912	1253-0800-7/W1047	
SE-Y . .	Jabiru UL 450	488	
SE-Y . .	Raj Hamsa X'Air F	unkn	

NON-CURRENT AIRCRAFT (For possible Restoration)

SE-ACR	Albatros B.II	unkn	SE-94
			SwNavy 5
SE-AHC	Götaverken GV-38	4	
SE-AHP	Piper J-3C-50S Cub	2371	NC21517
SE-AHU	Götaverken GV-38	12	
SE-ARB	Auster J/1 Autocrat	1847	
SE-ARD	Auster J/1 Autocrat	1867	
SE-ATH	Piper J-3C-65 Cub	12444	44-80148
SE-ATP	Piper J-3C-65 Cub	12057	44-79761
SE-AWR	Fairchild F.24W-41A Argus II	805	HB578
			43-14841
SE-AWS	Fairchild F.24W-41A Argus II	804	HB577
			43-14840
SE-BFH	de Havilland DH.60T Moth Trainer	1720	Fv.560
	(C/n quoted incorrectly after rebuild as 1718		Fv.5110
	which was the former SE-BFI, Fv.5108)		
SE-BGA	Klemm Kl.35D	1983	Fv.5054
SE-BXI	Focke-Wulf FW.44J Stieglitz	34	Fv.652
SE-CAP	Auster 5	922	MT277
			G-ANHV
SE-CEM	Piper PA-22-150 Tri-Pacer	22-5935	
SE-CFN	Auster V Alpha	3409	G-APNM
SE-CHY	Stinson 108-2 Voyager	1792	N8792K
SE-CIG	Jodel D.11	788	
SE-CNC	Champion 7EC Traveler	7EC-718	
SE-CRK	Piper PA-22 V-6 STOL	22-9081	
SE-EBP	MFI-9 Junior	05	OH-MFA
SE-EGC	Tipsy T.66 Nipper	22	OY-ABP
SE-EUH	SAAB MFI-9B/S Trainer	50	
SE-FXK	Reims/Cessna FRA150L Aerobat	FRA1500133	
	(Taildragger)		
SE-IET	Piper PA-22-150 Caribbean	22-6947	LN-HAI (2)
			N2973Z
SE-SAH	Grunau Baby II A	1752	
SE-STH	Grunau Baby II B	026	OY-BMX
			SE-STH
			Fv.8113
SE- . . .	de Havilland DH.82A Tiger Moth	85427	G-APMM
			DE419
SE- . . .	North American Harvard IIB	14-566	Fv.16106
			FE832
SE- . . .	Piper PA-14 Family Cruiser	14-201	OO-JAK
SE- . . .	Piper PA-18 Super Cub	18-2506	CF-NIO
			N1294C

SP - POLAND

Regn.	Type	C/n	Prev.Id.
SP-AAB(3)	Yakovlev Yak-12M	112602	PLW-602 ?
SP-AAC(3)	Yakovlev Yak-12M	112604	PLW-604 ?
SP-AAF(3)	Yakovlev Yak-12M	03531	PLW-...
SP-AAG(3)	Yakovlev Yak-12M	312626	PLW-626 ?
			SP-CAA
SP-AAI (3)	Yakovlev Yak-12M	7127147	PLW-...
SP-AAK(3)	Yakovlev Yak-12M	7127148	PLW-...
SP-AAL(3)	Yakovlev Yak-12M	158569	PLW-569 ?
SP-AAM(3)	Yakovlev Yak-12M	189774	PLW-774 ?
SP-AAN(3)	Yakovlev Yak-12M	169664	PLW-664 ?
SP-AAO(3)	Yakovlev Yak-12A	30113	PLW-113 ?
SP-AAP(3)	Yakovlev Yak-12M	200972	PLW-972 ?
SP-AAU(2)	Yakovlev Yak-12M	169661	PLW-661 ?
SP-AAY(2)	Antonov An-2T	1G26-15	SP-FAY
			PLW-2615
SP-ABA(3)	Yakovlev Yak-12A	30125	PLW-125 ?
SP-ABB(3)	Yakovlev Yak-12A	30114	PLW-114 ?
SP-ABC(3)	Yakovlev Yak-12A	30115	PLW-115 ?
SP-ABD(3)	Yakovlev Yak-12A	30132	PLW-132 ?
SP-ABE(3)	Yakovlev Yak-12M	200971	PLW-971 ?
SP-ABM	Antonov An-2R	1G144-46	SP-WLF
SP-ABT(3)	Yakovlev Yak-12M	169662	PLW-...
SP-ABX(3)	Yakovlev Yak-12A	30121	PLW-121 ?
SP-ACB(3)	Yakovlev Yak-12M	2101000	PLW-...
SP-ACC(3)	Yakovlev Yak-12M	169655	PLW-...
			SP-RAF
			PLW-...
SP-ACD(3)	Yakovlev Yak-12M	200991	PLW-...
SP-ACE(3)	Yakovlev Yak-12A	19007	SP-FKE
			SP-CXO
			PLW-...
SP-ACM(3)	Extra EA.300/L	048	D-ETQ .?
SP-ADA(2)	Zlin Z.42M	0070	
SP-ADB(3)	Zlin Z.42M	0071	
SP-ADC(3)	Zlin Z.42M	0072	
SP-ADD(3)	Zlin Z.42M	0073	
SP-ADE(3)	Zlin Z.42M	0074	
SP-ADF(4)	Zlin Z.42M	0075	
SP-ADG(3)	Zlin Z.42M	0076	
SP-ADH(3)	Zlin Z.42M	0077	
SP-ADM(3)	Zlin Z.42M	0081	
SP-ADO(3)	Zlin Z.42M	0091	
SP-ADP(3)	Zlin Z.42M	0092	
SP-ADR(3)	Zlin Z.42M	0093	
SP-ADS(3)	Zlin Z.42M	0094	
SP-ADU(3)	Zlin Z.42M	0096	
SP-ADW(3)	Zlin Z.42M	0097	
SP-ADY(3)	Zlin Z.42M	0098	
SP-ADZ(3)	Zlin Z.42M	0099	
SP-AEA(3)	Zlin Z.42M	0101	
SP-AEC(3)	Zlin Z.42M	0103	
SP-AED(3)	Zlin Z.42M	0104	
SP-AEF(3)	Zlin Z.42M	0106	
SP-AEG(3)	Zlin Z.42M	0107	
SP-AEH(3)	Zlin Z.42M	0108	
SP-AEI (2)	Zlin Z.42M	0109	
SP-AEM(3)	Zlin Z.42M	0117	
SP-AEN(3)	Zlin Z.42M	0118	
SP-AEO(4)	Zlin Z.42M	0122	
SP-AER(3)	Zlin Z.42M	0121	
SP-AES(3)	Zlin Z.42M	0124	
SP-AET(4)	Zlin Z.42M	0125	
SP-AEU(3)	Zlin Z.42M	0126	
SP-AEX(3)	Zlin Z.42M	0129	
SP-AEZ(3)	Zlin Z.42M	0128	
SP-AFA(3)	PZL-104 Wilga 35A	140538	
SP-AFB(3)	PZL-104 Wilga 35A	140539	
SP-AFC(3)	PZL-104 Wilga 35A	140540	
SP-AFE(3)	PZL-104 Wilga 35A	96318	SP-WFH
			SP-WHM
SP-AFK(3)	PZL-104 Wilga 80	CF15810602	
SP-AFL(3)	PZL-104 Wilga 35A	16820629	
SP-AFM(3)	PZL-104 Wilga 35A	16820630	
SP-AFR(2)	PZL-104 Wilga 35A	16820641	
SP-AFT(2)	PZL-104 Wilga 35A	16820643	
SP-AFV	PZL-104 Wilga 35A	17830704	
SP-AFW(3)	PZL-104 Wilga 35A	17820686	
SP-AFY	Piper L-4H Cub	12185	SP-FPA (1)
			SP-AMH(2)
			SP-AFY (1)
			44-79889
SP-AFZ(3)	PZL-104 Wilga 35A	17830691	
SP-AGA(3)	PZL-104 Wilga 35A	17830711	
SP-AGC(3)	PZL-104 Wilga 35A	17830713	
SP-AGD(2)	PZL-104 Wilga 35A	17830714	
SP-AGE(3)	PZL-104 Wilga 35A	17830715	
SP-AGF(3)	PZL-104 Wilga 35A	17830733	
SP-AGG(3)	PZL-104 Wilga 35A	18840762	
SP-AGH(3)	PZL-104 Wilga 35A	18840763	
SP-AGI (3)	PZL-104 Wilga 35A	18840764	
SP-AGK(3)	PZL-104 Wilga 35A	18840765	
SP-AGN(3)	PZL-104 Wilga 35A	18840768	
SP-AG0(3)	PZL-104 Wilga 35A	18840769	
SP-AGP(3)	PZL-104 Wilga 35A	18840770	
SP-AGR(3)	PZL-104 Wilga 35A	18840771	
SP-AGS(3)	PZL-104 Wilga 35A	18840777	
SP-AGT(3)	PZL-104 Wilga 35A	18840814	
SP-AGU(3)	PZL-104 Wilga 35A	19850822	
SP-AGV	PZL-104 Wilga 35A	19860849	
SP-AGW(3)	PZL-104 Wilga 35A	19850823	
SP-AGX(3)	PZL-104 Wilga 35A	19860848	
SP-AGY(2)	PZL-104 Wilga 35A	19860847	
SP-AGZ(3)	PZL-104 Wilga 35A	19850824	
SP-AHC(3)	PZL-104 Wilga 35A	118405	
SP-AHD(4)	PZL-104 Wilga 35A	19870854	
SP-AHG(3)	PZL-104 Wilga 35A	19870855	
SP-AHH(3)	PZL-104 Wilga 35A	19870856	
SP-AHI (3)	PZL-104 Wilga 35A	19870857	
SP-AHK(3)	PZL-104 Wilga 35A	129452	D-EDDU
SP-AHL(3)	PZL-104 Wilga 35A (Crashed 8.8.03)	19880871	
SP-AHM(3)	PZL-104 Wilga 35A	19880872	
SP-AHR(3)	PZL-104 Wilga 35A	129443	SP-TW0
SP-AHS(3)	PZL-104 Wilga 35A	74206	PLW-206
SP-AHU(4)	PZL-104 Wilga 35A	74200	PLW-200
SP-AHV	PZL-104M Wilga 2000	00970002	
SP-AHW(3)	PZL-104 Wilga 35A	74204	PLW-204
SP-AHY(3)	PZL-104 Wilga 35A	20890877	SP-FWF
SP-AHZ(3)	PZL-104 Wilga 35A	74201	PLW-201
SP-AKC(2)	Zlin Z.42M	0163	
SP-AKD(3)	Zlin Z.42M	0164	
SP-AKE(3)	Zlin Z.42M	0170	
SP-AKF(3)	Zlin Z.42M	0171	
SP-AKG(3)	Zlin Z.42M	0172	
SP-AKH(3)	Zlin Z.42M	0173	
SP-AKP(3)	Cessna 152	15284473	SP-KDM
			N4648M
SP-AKS(3)	LET L.200D Morava	171203	SP-NXZ
			SP-NAB
SP-AKT(2)	Cessna F172H	F17200738	OH-CLT
			D-ECIT
SP-AKU(3)	Cessna F172H	F172-0408	D-EGCE
SP-AKW(3)	Cessna 152	15283490	SE-IPP
			N49653
SP-AKZ	Cessna 185A Skywagon (Reservn 06.04)	185-0449	SP-FBD
			SP-FKA
			N1649Z
SP-ALB(4)	Reims/Cessna F150L	F15001016	PH-JOS
SP-ALD(2)	Zlin Z.42M	0145	
SP-ALF(3)	Zlin Z.42M	0147	
SP-ALH(3)	Zlin Z.42M	0149	
SP-ALI (3)	Antonov An-2T	1G157-07	PWL-5707
SP-ALK(3)	Zlin Z.42M	0151	
SP-ALL(3)	Zlin Z.42M	0152	
SP-ALN(3)	Zlin Z.42M	0154	
SP-ALO(3)	Zlin Z.42M	0155	
SP-ALP(3)	Zlin Z.42M	0156	
SP-ALS(2)	Robinson R-44 Raven II	10053	SP-GWW(1)
SP-AML(3)	Antonov An-2TD	1G168-05	
SP-AMM(3)	Antonov An-2P	1G151-65	SP-KNE
SP-AMN(2)	Antonov An-2P	1G174-41	SP-DRA
SP-AMO(3)	Antonov An-2T	1G52-17	PLW-5217
SP-AMS(2)	SOCATA MS.893A Rallye Commodore 180	11497	SP-FRX
			D-ECCX
SP-AMX(2)	Cessna F172H	F172-0548	SP-FMX(3)
			D-EILE
SP-ANA(3)	Antonov An-2T	1G29-21	PLW-2921
SP-ANC(3)	Antonov An-2TD	1G52-14	PLW-5214
SP-AND(3)	Antonov An-2TD (Dismantled .03)	1G15-26	PLW-1526
SP-ANH(4)	Antonov An-2TD	1G29-20	PLW-2920
SP-ANI (3)	Antonov An-2TD	1G85-56	
SP-ANK(3)	Antonov An-2TD	1G52-13	PLW-5213
SP-ANL(5)	Antonov An-2TD	1G147-16	
SP-ANM(3)	Antonov An-2P	1G149-08	
SP-ANN(3)	Antonov An-2TD	1G142-31	
SP-ANO(4)	Antonov An-2TD	1G25-01	PLW-2501
SP-ANR(4)	Antonov An-2TD	1G15-27	PLW-1527
SP-ANS(3)	Antonov An-2TD	1G157-10	
SP-ANT(5)	Antonov An-2TD	1G98-64	PLW-9864
SP-ANU(4)	Antonov An-2TD	1G119-66	PLW-1966
SP-ANV	Antonov An-2TD	1G137-60	PLW-3760
SP-AOA(3)	Antonov An-2TP	1G233-21	
SP-AOB(3)	Antonov An-2TD	1G73-51	PLW-7351
SP-AOC(3)	Antonov An-2TP	1G108-66	PLW-0866
SP-AOD(3)	Antonov An-2T	1G108-64	PLW-0864
SP-AOF(3)	Antonov An-2T	1G98-67	PLW-9867
SP-AOH(3)	Antonov An-2T	1G73-57	PLW-7357
SP-AOI (3)	Antonov An-2P	1G141-83	PLW-4183
SP-AOL(2)	CSS-13	0342	PLW-...
SP-AOM(3)	Antonov An-2P	1G159-27	PLW-5927
SP-AOO(3)	Antonov An-2T	1G108-65	PLW-0865
SP-AOP(3)	Antonov An-2P	1G159-26	PLW-5926
SP-AOR(3)	Antonov An-2T	1G157-09	PLW-5709
SP-AOU(3)	Antonov An-2P	1G159-47	SP-TBF
SP-AOW(2)	Antonov An-2S	1G211-01	SP-UXE
SP-AOY	Antonov An-2(Reservation 10.04)	1G118-51	PLW-1851
SP-AOZ(3)	Antonov An-2P	1G117-70	PLW-1770
SP-APD(2)	CSS-13	42085	PLW-...
SP-APL(2)	Reims/Cessna F152	F15201608	SP-KOY
			D-EHNH

SP-ARI (2)	PZL-110 Koliber	24021	
SP-ARL(3)	PZL-110 Koliber	25026	
SP-ARM(2)	PZL-110 Koliber	25027	
SP-ARN(2)	PZL-110 Koliber	25028	
SP-ARO(2)	PZL-110 Koliber	038529	
	(Ex c/n 25029 and still referred to as such in a/c documents)		
SP-ARP(3)	PZL-110 Koliber	25030	
SP-ARR(2)	PZL-110 Koliber	038531	
SP-ARS(2)	PZL-110 Koliber	038532	
SP-ASA(2)	Zlin Z.142	0347	
SP-ASC(4)	Zlin Z.142	0354	
SP-ASE(2)	Zlin Z.142	0356	
SP-ASF(3)	Zlin Z.142	0364	
SP-ASG(2)	Zlin Z.142	0365	
SP-ASH(2)	Zlin Z.142	0366	
SP-ASK(2)	Zlin Z.142	0369	
SP-ASL(3)	Zlin Z.142	0491	
SP-ASM(2)	Zlin Z.142	0492	
SP-ASN(2)	Zlin Z.142	0493	
SP-ASO(2)	Zlin Z.142	0494	
SP-ASW(2)	Mil Mi-2	5311106040	SP-FSG
			SP-FSE
SP-ATA(2)	Zlin Z.142	0268	
SP-ATC	Zlin Z.142	0270	
SP-ATE	Zlin Z.142	0276	
SP-ATF	Zlin Z.142	0277	
SP-ATG	Zlin Z.142	0278	
SP-ATH	Zlin Z.142	0292	
SP-ATI	Zlin Z.142	0293	
SP-ATK	Zlin Z.142	0294	
SP-ATL	Zlin Z.142	0297	
SP-ATM	Zlin Z.142	0298	
SP-ATP	Zlin Z.142	0316	
SP-ATU	Zlin Z.142	0322	
SP-ATV	Zlin Z.142	0333	
SP-ATW	Zlin Z.142	0323	
SP-ATX	Zlin Z.142	0332	
SP-ATZ	Zlin Z.142	0326	
SP-AUA	Zlin Z.50L	0008	OK-090
SP-AUB	Zlin Z.50L	0009	OK-092
SP-AUC	Zlin Z.50LS	0032	
SP-AUD	Zlin Z.50LS	0035	
SP-AWA	Yakovlev Yak-12A	30128	PLW- . . .
SP-AWB	Yakovlev Yak-12M	138488	PLW- . . .
SP-AWC	Yakovlev Yak-12M	189776	PLW- . . .
SP-AWD	Yakovlev Yak-12M	179728	PLW- . . .
SP-AWF	Yakovlev Yak-12M	179727	PLW- . . .
SP-AWG	Yakovlev Yak-12M	169663	PLW- . . .
SP-AWI	Yakovlev Yak-12M	158568	PLW- . . .
SP-AWK	Yakovlev Yak-12M	169665	PLW- . . .
SP-AWL	Yakovlev Yak-12M	179729	PLW- . . .
SP-AWM	Yakovlev Yak-12M	2101003	PLW-003 ?
SP-AWO	Funk FK-9	027	
SP-AWP	Piper J-3C-65 Cub	10123	SE-AWD
	(Regd officially as c/n 1-1948)		43-1262
			(42-60072)
SP-AWR	Antonov An-28	1AJ007-03	RA-28718
			CCCP28718
SP-AWZ	Yakovlev Yak-12A	30123	PLW-123 ?
SP-AZB	Zlin Z.142	0208	
SP-AZC(2)	Zlin Z.142	0209	
SP-AZE(2)	Zlin Z.142	0211	
SP-AZF(2)	Zlin Z.142	0212	
SP-AZG(2)	Zlin Z.142 (Stored)	0213	
SP-AZH(2)	Zlin Z.142	0214	
SP-AZI	Zlin Z.142	0215	
SP-AZK	Zlin Z.142	0216	
SP-AZL	Zlin Z.142	0227	
SP-AZM	Zlin Z.142	0230	
SP-AZN	Zlin Z.142	0244	
SP-AZO	Zlin Z.142	0245	
SP-AZR	Zlin Z.142	0257	
SP-AZT	Zlin Z.142	0458	
SP-CAG	Yakovlev Yak-12A	30133	SP-CXG
SP-CDF	Zlin Z.526F Trenér Master	1108	
SP-CDN	Zlin Z.526F Trenér Master	1152	
SP-CDS	Zlin Z.526F Trenér Master	1165	
SP-CDW	Zlin Z.526F Trenér Master	1168	
SP-CEA(2)	PZL-101A Gawron	119301	SP-RXI
SP-CEE(3)	PZL-101A Gawron	107219	SP-RXE
SP-CER	PZL-101A Gawron	96176	
SP-CEY	PZL-101A Gawron	96179	
SP-CFC(2)	PZL-101A Gawron	96180	
SP-CFK(2)	PZL-101A Gawron	96181	
SP-CFR	PZL-101 Gawron	63079	
SP-CFZ	PZL-101A Gawron	96183	
SP-CGC(2)	PZL-101A Gawron	96184	
SP-CGE	PZL-101A Gawron	96185	
SP-CGF	PZL-101A Gawron	96186	
SP-CGK	PZL-101A Gawron (W/o 10.5.97)	96190	
	(Status unknown)		
SP-CHC	PZL-101A Gawron	63118	
SP-CHF	PZL-101A Gawron	74136	
SP-CHG	PZL-101 Gawron	63111	
SP-CHO	PZL-101A Gawron	85165	
SP-CKC	PZL-101A Gawron	107203	
SP-CKD	PZL-101A Gawron	107204	

SP-CKF	PZL-101A Gawron	107206	
SP-CKG	PZL-101A Gawron	107207	
SP-CKH	PZL-101A Gawron	107208	
SP-CKK	PZL-101A Gawron	107210	
SP-CKL	PZL-101A Gawron	107211	
SP-CKM	PZL-101A Gawron	107212	
SP-CKN	PZL-101A Gawron	107213	
SP-CKO	PZL-101A Gawron	107214	
SP-CKR	PZL-101A Gawron (Crashed 25.8.03)	119300	
SP-CPH	Zlin Z.526F Trenér Master	1247	
SP-CRL	PZL-104 Wilga 35A	59060	
SP-CRP	PZL-104 Wilga 35A	59084	
SP-CRX	PZL-104 Wilga 35A	59059	
SP-CSA	Zlin Z.526AFS Akrobat	1201	
SP-CSB	Zlin Z.526AFS Akrobat	1202	
SP-CSE	PZL-104 Wilga 35A	61098	
SP-CSU	Zlin Z.526AFS Akrobat	1226	
SP-CSW	Zlin Z.526AFS Akrobat	1227	
SP-CSY	Zlin Z.526AFS Akrobat	1228	
SP-CTA	Zlin Z.526F Trenér Master	1250	
SP-CTB	Zlin Z.526F Trenér Master	1252	
SP-CUB	Piper J-3C-65 Cub	16842	D-EMOT
			N92380
			NC92380
SP-CUH	Pottier P.220S AT-3 Koala	001	SP-GUH
			SP-PUH
SP-CUU	Yakovlev Yak-12A (Reservation 12.00)	30118	SP-CXU
			PLW- . . .
SP-CZG	PZL-104 Wilga 35A	16820635	SP-FZG
			SP-TWY
SP-DDA	PZL M-28 Skytruck	AJE001-01	SP-FYV
SP-DIF	PZL M-26-01 Iskierka	1AP002-07	
SP-DLA(2)	Antonov An-2P	1G178-08	
SP-DMA(3)	PZL M-20 Mewa	1AHP01-01	SP-PKA(1)
SP-DNH	Antonov An-2R	1G86-10	
SP-DNL	Antonov An-2TD	1G86-47	
SP-DWA(2)	PZL-104 Wilga 35A	19850829	
SP-EAA	PZL-104 Wilga 35A	48031	
SP-EAB	PZL-104 Wilga 35A	48032	
SP-EAF	PZL-104 Wilga 35A	48036	
SP-EAG	PZL-104 Wilga 35A	48037	
SP-EAH	PZL-104 Wilga 35A	48038	
SP-EAN	PZL-104 Wilga 35A	59069	
SP-EAO	PZL-104 Wilga 35A	59070	
SP-EAP	PZL-104 Wilga 35A	59071	
SP-EAU	PZL-104 Wilga 35A	59075	
SP-EAZ	PZL-104 Wilga 35A	59078	
SP-EBA	PZL-104 Wilga 35A	59080	
SP-EBE	Cessna 150D	15060455	SP-FBE
			N4455U
SP-EBF	PZL-104 Wilga 35A	59085	
SP-EBI	PZL-104 Wilga 35A	61122	
SP-EBK	PZL-104 Wilga 35A	61123	
SP-EBT	PZL-104 Wilga 80	CF1480558	
SP-ECB	PZL-104 Wilga 35A	62155	
SP-ECC	PZL-104 Wilga 35A	62156	
SP-ECF	PZL-104 Wilga 35A	62159	
SP-ECH	PZL-104 Wilga 35A	62160	(DM-WBV)
SP-ECL	PZL-104 Wilga 35A	61126	PLW-126
SP-ECN	PZL-104 Wilga 35A	61136	
SP-ECO	PZL-104 Wilga 35A	61137	
SP-ECU	PZL-104 Wilga 35A	62173	
SP-EDA	Aérospatiale/Alenia ATR-42-512	516	F-GPYG
			F-WWLU
SP-EDB	Aérospatiale/Alenia ATR-42-512	522	F-GPYH
			F-WWLC
SP-EDC	Aérospatiale/Alenia ATR-42-512	526	F-GPYI
			F-WWLM
SP-EDD	Aérospatiale/Alenia ATR-42-512	530	F-GPYJ
			F-WWLH
SP-EDE	Aérospatiale/Alenia ATR-42-512	443	F-WWEZ
SP-EFA	PZL-102B Kos (Wfu .91, stored .03)	209	SP-GLO
			(VH-CGC)
			SP-GLO
SP-EGA	Antonov An-2TD	1G168-06	
SP-EGB	Antonov An-2TD	1G168-07	
SP-EGC	Antonov An-2TD	1G168-08	
SP-EGR	Cessna F150G	F150-0161	SP-FGR
			D-EBZE
SP-EGZ	Cessna 152-II	15282477	SP-FGZ
			N69082
SP-EHA	Zlin Z.526F Trenér Master	1317	
SP-EHD	Zlin Z.526F Trenér Master	1320	
SP-EHE	Zlin Z.526F Trenér Master	1321	
SP-EHF	Zlin Z.526F Trenér Master	1322	
SP-EHG	Zlin Z.526F Trenér Master	1323	
SP-ELB	Zlin Z.526AFS Akrobat	1327	
SP-ELD	Zlin Z.526AFS Akrobat	1310	
SP-ELE	Zlin Z.526AFS Akrobat	1329	
SP-EMB	Zlin Z.526F Trenér Master	1269	
SP-EME	Zlin Z.526F Trenér Master	1272	
SP-EMF	Zlin Z.526F Trenér Master	1273	
SP-EMG	Zlin Z.526F Trenér Master	1274	
SP-EML	Zlin Z.526F Trenér Master	1279	
SP-EMN	Zlin Z.526F Trenér Master	1281	
SP-EMR	Zlin Z.526F Trenér Master	1284	
SP-EMS	Zlin Z.526F Trenér Master	1285	

SP-EMT	Zlin Z.526ML Trenér Master	921	OK-WRR
			F-BORR
SP-ENA	Zlin Z.526AFS Akrobat	1301	
SP-ENS	Cessna 172N	17273602	D-ENSP
			N6506G
SP-ERH	PZL-110 Koliber	23015	SP-FRH
			SP-ARE(2)
SP-ERP	PZL-110 Koliber	24019	SP-FRP
			SP-ARG(3)
SP-ERS	PZL-110 Koliber	038637	SP-FRS
			SP-WGD
			SP-ARZ(3)
SP-ETA	Cessna 150J	15070776	OH-CTT
			C-GASR
			N61065
SP-EZB	PZL-104 Wilga 35A	59065	SP-FZB
			SP-CRT
SP-EZH	Reims/Cessna F150M	F15001411	SP-FZH
			D-EOVO
SP-FAH	Antonov An-2TP	1G233-22	
SP-FAR	Antonov An-2T	1G187-06	SP-TCF
			SP-TTA
			SP-DTA
SP-FAS	PZL-104 Wilga 35A	19860846	
SP-FAV	Antonov An-2TP	1G214-06	SP-UXH
SP-FBC	Christen A-1 Husky	1193	
SP-FBD	Cessna 185A Skywagon	185-0449	SP-FKA
			N1649Z
SP-FBI (2)	Cessna 310Q	310Q1032	C-GTIL
			N69941
			C-GGDR
			N69941
SP-FBU	PZL M-18A Dromader	1Z023-11	
SP-FBX	PZL M-18B Dromader	1Z023-15	
SP-FBY	PZL M-18B Dromader	1Z023-14	
SP-FCD(2)	Reims/Cessna F172P	F17202247	D-EFCD(2)
SP-FCE(2)	Reims/Cessna F150K	F15000613	D-ECEP(2)
SP-FCN(2)	CSS-13	420-102	SP-BHB
SP-FCT	Cessna 525 Citationjet CJ (Reservn .03)	525-0466	N119CS
SP-FCU	Zlin Z.142 (Crashed 22.6.02)	0518	
SP-FCV	SOCATA TB-20 Trinidad	1899	F-OIGU
SP-FCW	Zlin Z.142	0519	
SP-FCX	Zlin Z.142	0522	
SP-FCY	Zlin Z.142	0521	
SP-FCZ	Zlin Z.142	0520	
SP-FDA	PZL-104 Wilga 35A	62161	(DM-WBW)
SP-FDB	Cessna 172C	17248744	D-EMLO
			N8244X
SP-FDK	Bell 206B Jet Ranger III	2972	N209AA
			VT-ETH
			G-BOZL
			N701BG
			(N48EA)
			N70ED
			N1084H
SP-FDN(2)	Bell 407	53051	N1119J
SP-FDO	Antonov An-26B	10503	RA-26031
			CCCP26031
SP-FDP	Antonov An-26B	11903	RA-26098
			CCCP26098
SP-FDR	Antonov An-26B	11305	RA-26067
			CCCP26067
SP-FDS(2)	Antonov An-26B	12205	RA-26116
			CCCP26116
SP-FDT	Antonov An-26B	12102	RA-26110
			CCCP26110
SP-FDU	Antonov An-2T	1G195-01	SP-TWN
SP-FDV	Antonov An-2TP	1G237-35	
SP-FDW	Antonov An-2P	1G114-62	PWL-1462
SP-FDZ	Antonov An-2T	1G74-43	PWL-7443
SP-FEE	Antonov An-2R	1G173-01	SP-TCB
SP-FEM	Schweizer 269C	S-1678	D-HUFR
			N69A
SP-FEN	Reims/Cessna F172M	F17201138	D-EENN
SP-FEO	Reims/Cessna F150M	F15001148	SP-FEU
	(Crashed 9.10.01 but still regd)		D-EOQB
SP-FEP	Reims/Cessna F172N	F17201658	D-EFNM
SP-FES	Mil Mi-8	99150472	UR-25603
			CCCP25603
SP-FET	Reims/Cessna FA150K Aerobat	FA1500059	OO-WIB
SP-FEV	Cessna 421B Golden Eagle	421B0273	OY-BNY
			N4032L
SP-FEW	Reims FR172F Rocket	FR17200125	D-EJZA
SP-FEX	Piper PA-28-181 Archer II	2890183	D-ETCG
			N9172N
SP-FEY	Reims/Cessna F172L	F17200845	(SP-FLR)
			D-ECSV
SP-FEZ	Cessna 150M	15077212	D-EWAC
			N63261
SP-FFB	Antonov An-2T (Reservation 12.00)	1G108-63	PWL-0863
SP-FFC	PZL M-18B Dromader	1Z023-25	
SP-FFD	PZL M-18B Dromader	1Z023-26	
SP-FFH	PZL M-18B Dromader	1Z023-30	SP-DDO
			SP-PDM
SP-FFN	Antonov An-28	1AJ006-08	TC-FEB
			SP-DDD

SP-FFR	Piper PA-28-181 Archer III	2843231	D-ETAS
			N4129P
			(XS-OJP)
			N4129P
SP-FFS	PZL M-18B Dromader	1Z023-19	
SP-FFT	PZL M-18B Dromader	1Z023-17	
SP-FFV	PZL M-18B Dromader	1Z023-24	
SP-FFW	PZL M-18B Dromader	1Z023-20	(SP-FWW)
			SP-PBE(2)
SP-FFX	PZL M-18B Dromader	1Z023-23	
SP-FFY	PZL M-18B Dromader	1Z023-21	
SP-FFZ	PZL M-18B Dromader	1Z023-22	
SP-FGC	CSS-13	0431	SP-AIA(2)
SP-FGD	PZL-101A Gawron	107220	SP-RXF
SP-FGF	Cessna 172M	17262625	C-GAXX
			N13267
SP-FGG(2)	Piper PA-28-181 Archer II	28-8190239	D-EGFL
			N8389X
SP-FGL(2)	Reims/Cessna F150L	F15000988	D-EJXI
SP-FGN	Grumman-American AA-1B Trainer	AA1B-0618	SP-WGN
SP-FGO	PZL-101A Gawron	107215	SP-RXA
SP-FGP	PZL-101A Gawron	63119	SP-KZG
			SP-KXG
SP-FGS	Maule M-7-235C Super Rocket	25011C	
SP-FGV	Cessna 152-II	15283584	N1368F
SP-FGW	Beech A23-19 Musketeer Sport III	MB-32	HB-ENO
SP-FGX	Cessna 152-II	15284441	N6571L
SP-FGY	Cessna 152-II	15282746	N89437
SP-FHK	Mil Mi-2	525933019	SP-SBU
SP-FHL	Mil Mi-2	568826104	PLW-8826
SP-FHM	Mil Mi-2	514520115	SP-SPE
SP-FHS	Antonov An-28	1AJ007-10	RA-28725
			CCCP28725
SP-FIA	Antonov An-2R	1G161-02	SP-WOM
SP-FIE	Antonov An-2TP	1G185-02	SP-TWH
SP-FIF	Antonov An-2R	1G153-25	EW-05712
			CCCP05712
SP-FIG	PZL-106BR Kruk	09870204	(D-FODA)
			DDR-TDA
SP-FII	PZL-106BR Kruk	10890234	D-FOEP
			DDR-TEP
SP-FIN	Antonov An-2T	1G98-57	PLW-9857
SP-FIT	Antonov An-2P	1G159-45	PLW-5945
SP-FIX	Antonov An-2TPS	1G185-05	SP-FIW
			SP-UXC
SP-FIY	Antonov An-2P	1G159-56	SP-TBE
SP-FIZ	Antonov An-2T	1G73-53	PLW-7353
SP-FKP	Yakovlev Yak-12A	19003	SP-CXM
			PLW- . . .
SP-FKR	Yakovlev Yak-12M	7127123	PLW- . . .
			SP-CFN (1)
			PLW- . . .
SP-FKT	Radwan / Rand-Robinson KR-2PM3	YL-002-SVL	
	(SP-YKT reserved but not yet taken up)		
SP-FKX	Yakovlev Yak-12A	19001	SP-CXP(2)
			PLW-001
SP-FKY	Yakovlev Yak-12A	30127	SP-CXS(2)
			PLW-127
SP-FLA(2)	TL Ultralight TL-32 Typhoon	9502	
SP-FLF	Cessna 177RG Cardinal RG	177RG0522	N2122Q
SP-FLG	Reims/Cessna F177RG Cardinal RG	F177RG0014	OH-CFX
	(Reims-assembled 177RG c/n 177RG0128)		SE-FXH
SP-FLI	Reims FR172J Rocket	FR17200493	D-EECD
SP-FLK	Cessna 172P	17275030	N546CF
			N54664
SP-FLL	Reims/Cessna F152	F15201975	D-EIFD(3)
SP-FLM	Reims FR172J Rocket	FR17200479	OY-BFO
SP-FLN	Cessna 172P	17275314	D-EDGJ
			N62626
SP-FLO	Reims/Cessna F152	F15201711	D-EDND(3)
			HB-CNR
SP-FLP	Reims/Cessna F172P	F17202170	D-EOWD
SP-FLR	Reims FR172H Rocket	FR17200307	D-ECSP
SP-FLS	Cessna 172M	17261292	D-EHHH
			N20444
SP-FLT	Cessna F172H	F172-0322	D-EGMI (2)
SP-FLY	Antonov An-2R	1G170-45	SP-UXA
SP-FLZ	Antonov An-2R	1G204-47	EW-17846
			CCCP17846
SP-FMA	Antonov An-2P	1G163-35	
SP-FMC	AT- 1	001	SP-PMC
SP-FMD	PZL M-20 Mewa	1AH001-03	SP-KMA
			SP-PKC
SP-FME	PZL M-20 Mewa	1AH002-07	SL-BPK
			(YU-BPK)
SP-FMF	PZL M-20 Mewa	1AH002-10	SP-DMC
SP-FMH	Antonov An-2T	1G98-61	PLW-9861
SP-FML	Antonov An-2R	1G187-07	SP-TCE
			SP-TTB
			SP-DTB
SP-FMM	Antonov An-2R	1G173-02	SP-TCC
SP-FMN	Antonov An-2P	1G177-21	SP-TWE
			SP-DFN
SP-FMO(2)	Cessna 150K	15071529	SE-FMC
			LN-VYL
			(LN-VYS)
			(N6029G)

SP-FMP	Antonov An-2T	1G147-23	PWL-4723
SP-FMR	Antonov An-2P	1G163-34	SP-KOZ SP-FMR SP-GFA
SP-FMT	Antonov An-2	1G85-51	PWL-8551
SP-FMV	Cessna 150J	15070996	N1016M
SP-FMW	LET L-200D Morava	171001	SP-FAU SP-MNK CCCP34500
SP-FMY	Cessna 150M	15076386	N3109V
SP-FMZ	Cessna 150L (Reservation 3.99)	15074312	N19294
SP-FND	SOCATA TB-20 Trinidad	1381	SE-KNP
SP-FNE	SOCATA TB-9 Tampico	1089	SE-KNM
SP-FNH	Beech 300LW Super King Air (Reservation since .97)	FA-227	D-ICBC N81418
SP-FNI	TL Ultralight TL-32 Typhoon	9601	OK-BUU-40
SP-FNK(2)	Beech A36 Bonanza	E-3014	N3263W
SP-FNL	SOCATA TB-9 Tampico	469	D-EGUF(2)
SP-FNN	TL Ultralight TL-32 Typhoon	9402	
SP-FNS	Beech B300 Super King Air	FL-134	N3252V
SP-FNU	Reims/Cessna F172L	F17200835	OY-RYM
SP-FNV	Cessna 421C Golden Eagle	421C0805	D-INAS(2) N1206N JRV . . . . OE-FBI (1) N26565
SP-FOB	Cessna F172E	F172-0076	D-EFVE
SP-FOF	PZL M-18B Dromader	1Z024-05	
SP-FOG(2)	PZL M-18B Dromader	1Z024-06	
SP-FOH	PZL M-18B Dromader	1Z024-07	
SP-FOI	PZL M-18B Dromader	1Z024-08	
SP-FOK	PZL M-18B Dromader	1Z024-09	
SP-FOL	PZL M-18B Dromader	1Z025-13	
SP-FOM	PZL M-18B Dromader	1Z025-14	
SP-FON	PZL M-18B Dromader	1Z025-15	
SP-FOO	PZL M-18B Dromader	1Z025-16	
SP-FOR	Cessna 172M	17262639	D-EOFD C-FCFD LHR-11 CF-CFD N1528S
SP-FOS	Cessna 182N	18260235	HB-CUX N92503
SP-FOT	Piper PA-28R-200 Cherokee Arrow II	28R-7635273	N75181
SP-FOV	Reims/Cessna F150K	F15000535	D-EMTM
SP-FOY	Reims/Cessna F150L	F15000806	D-EEYF
SP-FPA(2)	Reims FR172J Rocket	FR17200395	D-ECZT
SP-FPC	Piper PA-28-140 Cherokee	28-24606	N7261J
SP-FPD	Piper PA-28R-200 Cherokee Arrow II	28R-7235180	N5033T
SP-FPK	Piper PA-31 Turbo Navajo	31-273	OH-PNO SE-FDR
SP-FPN	Reims/Cessna F182Q Skylane	F18200084	G-BPPN (G-BFFN) (G-BLHN)
SP-FPO	SOCATA Rallye 100T	2890	F-GAKF
SP-FPS	Piper Aerostar 601P	61P-0710-7963342	N6075U (N311DS) N6075U
SP-FPT	Cessna 172M	17264137	N30373
SP-FPU	Cessna 172P	17273151	N6118F
SP-FPW	Cessna 172N	17271715	D-EHMG(2) N5109E
SP-FRA	SOCATA Rallye 150T	2661	D-EBWK F-ODDG
SP-FRC	SOCATA Rallye 110ST Galopin	2743	SP-WGA F-ODDF
SP-FRE	PZL-110 Koliber 150	23011	SP-ARA(2)
SP-FRG	SOCATA Rallye 110ST Galopin	2854	SP-WGB F-ODER
SP-FRI	PZL-110 Koliber	24020	SP-ARH(3)
SP-FRK	PZL-110 Koliber 150	24022	SP-ARK(2)
SP-FRL	PZL-110 Koliber 150	19003	SP-ZKA
SP-FRM	PZL-110 Koliber 150	19006	SP-ZKD
SP-FRN	PZL-110 Koliber	23013	SP-ARC(2)
SP-FRO	PZL-110 Koliber	23014	SP-ARD(2)
SP-FRR	PZL-110 Koliber	24018	SP-ARF(2)
SP-FRT	PZL-110A Koliber 150A	04940061	(D-ESDP)
SP-FRU	PZL-110A Koliber 150A	04950075	SP-WCF (N150AX)
SP-FRW	SOCATA MS.893E Rallye 180GT Gaillard	12753	OO-MIP
SP-FRY	SOCATA MS.880B Rallye Club	2504	F-BVHE
SP-FRZ	SOCATA MS.893E Rallye 180GTGaillard	12535	D-EKLI F-BVZR
SP-FSK	Mil Mi-2	510549127	PLW-0549
SP-FST	Mil Mi-2 (Reservation 7.02)	529942106	SP-SOB
SP-FSV	Mil Mi-2	5210539038	SP-STC
SP-FSW	Mil Mi-2	532816023	PLW-2816
SP-FSX	Mil Mi-2	535401107	SP-SKM
SP-FTA	Cessna 172N	17268002	G-BGIC N75854
SP-FTB	Cessna 172N	17270230	N738TS
SP-FTC	Cessna 172M	17263858	N160SH N20861
SP-FTD	Cessna 402B	402B0417	N678AC N69295
SP-FTN(2)	LET L-410UVP-E10	902515	SP-FGI (SP-TAE)

SP-FTT(2)	SOCATA Rallye 235E-D Gabier	12795	D-EIHH(2) OO-ADN F-GACT
SP-FTV	LET L-410UVP-E10	882038	SP-TAA
SP-FTW	SOCATA MS.892A Rallye Commodore 150	11874	D-EESW F-BTJA
SP-FTX	LET L-410UVP-E10	892301	SP-TAB
SP-FTY	LET L-410UVP-E10	892317	SP-TAC
SP-FUP	Cessna 182P	18263561	OY-BII N5833J
SP-FVB	Antonov An-2TP	1G214-07	SP-UXI
SP-FVC	PZL-104 Wilga 35A (Crashed 9.7.95)	74193	PLW-193
SP-FVH	SOCATA MS.893A Rallye Commodore 180	11667	D-EFHH(2)
SP-FVM	Antonov An-2T	1G188-35	SP-TWM
SP-FVN	Antonov An-2TD	1G187-27	SP-OSA
SP-FVO	Boeing 737-36N	28590	OK-FIT N1787B
SP-FVT	Reims/Cessna F182P Skylane	F18200016	D-EATF
SP-FVV	Cessna 421B Golden Eagle	421B0525	D-ILPD N421YS N69889
SP-FVW	Reims/Cessna F150L	F15000672	D-EIGN SE-FXD
SP-FVY	Cessna 150L	15074774	N10078
SP-FVZ	Cessna 150M	15078143	N9192U
SP-FWD	PZL-104 Wilga 32 (Reservation 5.01)	25021	SP-PBN
SP-FWH	PZL-104 Wilga 35A	20890887	
SP-FWK(2)	Cessna T210L Turbo Centurion	21061152	(N103AG) D-EAWO N2191S
SP-FWL	Cessna 182P	18261803	D-ECYB
SP-FWU	PZL-104 Wilga 35A	18840773	SP-ZOG
SP-FWW	PZL-104 Wilga 35A	19840812	SP-ZOE
SP-FWY	PZL-104 Wilga 35A	19850827	SP-ZOH
SP-FYB	Aviat Pitts S-2S (No CofR issued)	3018	
SP-FYE	Reims/Cessna F172M	F17201502	D-EBXC
SP-FYF	Antonov An-2P	1G181-53	SP-TWK
SP-FYL	Antonov An-2P	1G185-57	SP-TBL
SP-FYM	Antonov An-2TP	1G137-58	SP-TBM G-BTOV N2AN SP-KNA
SP-FYN	Bell 206B Jet Ranger III	4208	C-FNSV N206BF
SP-FYO	Antonov An-2P	1G185-56	SP-TBK
SP-FYR	Antonov An-2T	1G174-43	SP-TWB
SP-FYW	Beech 58 Baron	TH-1625	D-IAKM
SP-FYX	Antonov An-2	1G215-05	LY-AVC CCCP40870
SP-FYZ	Cessna 175C	17557099	SE-CXO
SP-FZC	PZL-104 Wilga 80	CF21930940	SP-WDH
SP-FZD	PZL-104 Wilga 35A	74203	SP-FWX PLW-203
SP-FZE	PZL-104 Wilga 80	CF21950961	
SP-FZF	PZL-104 Wilga 35A	20890889	SP-FWK(1)
SP-FZK	Cessna 152	15281272	D-EAPN(2) N49444
SP-FZL	PZL-104 Wilga 80	CF15810601	(SP-FWB) SP-AFI (2)
SP-FZO	Maule MT-7-235 Super Rocket	18042C	
SP-FZT	Zlin Z.142	0311	OK-NNN
SP-FZU	SOCATA TB-10 Tobago	64	D-EGRV
SP-FZV	Cessna 152	15280052	D-ESBB N532CA N757WB
SP-FZW	Cessna 152	15285617	N94187
SP-FZX	Cessna 172N	17273731	C-FFOZ N5206J
SP-FZY	Cessna 152	15285240	D-EKCO(2) N6386Q
SP-FZZ	Zlin Z.42M	0165	SP-WIA
SP-GAB	Robinson R-44 Raven II	10291	
SP-GAG	Enstrom 280C Shark	1114	D-HENS N51687
SP-GAH	Enstrom 280C Shark	1043	G-MHCH
SP-GAI	Enstrom 280C-UK Turbo Shark (Reservn 2.02)	1060	G-SHSS
SP-GAZ	Agusta-Bell 206BJet Ranger II	8405	D-HOCH(3) G-BHSM EI-BHE OO-MHS F-BVEM
SP-GBG	Robinson R-44 Raven	0962	
SP-GBW	Cessna 182S	18280194	(SP-FWB) F-GSCJ N2638A
SP-GHD	Zlin Z.42M	0119	
SP-GHE	Zlin Z.42M	0123	
SP-GHF	Zlin Z.42M	0140	
SP-GIL(2)	PZL I-23 Manager	002	SP-PIL
SP-GIT	Reims/Cessna F172N	F17201722	D-EICP
SP-GKA	Piper PA-34-200T Seneca II	34-7670279	(HB-L . . .) N6299J
SP-GKS	Cessna 152	15280891	D-EGKS N25978
SP-GLS	Robinson R-44 Astro	0346	SP-GSE

SP-GOS	T-131PA Jungmann	107	(SP-FUS)
SP-GRA	Eurocopter EC.120B Colibri	1053	G-ECZZ
SP-GRV	Enstrom F28F Falcon (Reservation 9.03)	761	G-SNAZ G-BRCP
SP-GRY	Eurocopter EC.120B Colibri	1353	
SP-GSC	Robinson R-44 Astro	0272	
SP-GSD	Robinson R-44 Astro	0322	
SP-GSF	Robinson R-44 Astro	0355	
SP-GSH	Robinson R-22B2 Beta	2983	
SP-GSI	Robinson R-44 Astro	0706	
SP-GSK	Robinson R-44 Raven	0781	
SP-GSL	Robinson R-44 Raven	0840	
SP-GSN	Robinson R-44 Raven	0787	D-HXYZ
SP-GSP	Robinson R-44 Raven (Cr. 1.8.03)	0977	N7195U
SP-GSS	Robinson R-44 Raven II	10398	
SP-GST	Robinson R-44 Raven II	10258	
SP-GSW	Robinson R-44 Raven	0801	
SP-GTF	Robinson R-44 Raven II	10211	SP-GWW(2) N123PZ
SP-GWB	PZL-104 Wilga 35A	19870858	
SP-GWW(3)	Robinson R-44 Raven II	10647	
SP-GZZ	Enstrom 280FX Shark	2025	N344JS JA7747
SP-HII	Eurocopter EC.120B Colibri	1381	F-WQVA
SP-HIT	Eurocopter EC.120B Colibri	1368	SP-HIL
SP-HKL	Yakovlev Yak-12M	179714	SP-FKL SP-RAB
SP-HKM	PZL-104 Wilga 35A	74191	SP-FKM PLW-191
SP-HKN	PZL-104 Wilga 35A	74199	SP-FKN PLW-199
SP-ITC(2)	Piper PA-31-350 Navajo Chieftain	31-7405491	PH-ITC N61479
SP-KAA	Antonov An-2P	1G117-69	
SP-KAB	Piper PA-34-200 Seneca	34-7350223	D-GAGI N55496
SP-KAD	Cessna 152	15279512	N714XK
SP-KAE	Reims/Cessna 152(Reservation 09.04)	F15201696	D-EFDG
SP-KAF	Cessna 172S	172S8971	N5087Q
SP-KAG	Cessna 421	421-0075	YL-KAG N40JL N4075L
SP-KAH	Cessna 152	15281482	N64932
SP-KAI	Cessna 152	15283561	N4644B
SP-KAK	Cessna 152	15284258	N5092L
SP-KAL	Cessna 152	15284911	N5317P
SP-KAP	Cessna 172S	172S9652	N2169J
SP-KAR	Cessna 150M	15078490	(SP-FMX(1)) N7048V
SP-KAS	PZL M-20 Mewa	AH002-16	
SP-KAT	Reims/Cessna F172N	F17201977	SP-FTE G-BHNU
SP-KAZ	Yakovlev Yak-12A	30130	SP-CAZ SP-CXZ PLW-130
SP-KBA	Antonov An-2P	1G185-06	
SP-KBB	SOCATATB-10 Tobago	117	D-EEEB
SP-KBC	Maule MXT-7-180 Starcraft	14106C	
SP-KBE	SOCATAMS.894A Minerva 220	12195	G-VAJT EI-BAB (S9-NAF) EI-BAB (G-BLPN) EI-BAB
SP-KBF	SOCATA MS.892A Rallye Commodore 150	10528	D-EASR(2) D-EGGI(1)
SP-KBG	Piper PA-34-220T Seneca V	3449162	N41812 (SP-KBG) N9524N
SP-KBK	Maule MXT-7-180A Starcraft	21071C	
SP-KBM	Cessna 500 Citation	500-0269	D-ICCC (PH-CTW) D-ICCC (D-IKUC) N5269J
SP-KBR	Antonov An-2T	1G78-12	Polish Navy: 7812
SP-KBT(2)	Antonov An-2P	1G151-55	SP-KTK(1) SP-AON(3) PLW-5155
SP-KCA	Aérospatiale/Alenia ATR-42	085	F-WQNY C-FLCP F-WWEK
SP-KCB	Cessna 402B (Reservation 7.01)	402B1082	OH-CHS FinAF:CB-52 OH-CHS N1780G
SP-KCC	Cessna 152	15285773	N94722
SP-KCD	Cessna 152	15284341	N5534L
SP-KCE	Cessna 152	15285288	N65481
SP-KCF	Cessna 150K	15071266	N5766G
SP-KCG	Reims/Cessna F150M	F15001274	PH-UWA LX-AVI LX-AIN
SP-KCL	Cessna 525 CitationJet	525-0526	N526LC
SP-KCM	Cessna 152	15282637	N89113
SP-KCP	Cessna 150M	15076099	N66523

SP-KCR	Cessna A152 Aerobat	A1520838	N4597A
SP-KCT	Reims/Cessna F172H	F172-0437	D-ECTI
SP-KCU	Cessna A152 Aerobat	A1521021	N758YW
SP-KCW	Cessna 172P	17275595	D-EFOT(2) N64622
SP-KCZ	Cessna R172KHawk XP	R1723005	OH-CMY N7580D
SP-KDR	Cessna F150J	F150-0515	D-EHMD
SP-KDS	Cessna 150L	15074167	N19097
SP-KDT	Cessna 150J	15070339	N60476
SP-KEA	PZL-104 Wilga 35A	59048	
SP-KFA	Zlin Z.43	0080	
SP-KFC	PZL-110 Koliber	19002	
SP-KFE	PZL M-20 Mewa	1AH002-13	
SP-KFK	Piper PA-22-160 Tripacer	22-5933	PH-TRT D-ELPE N8750D
SP-KFT	Cessna 402B	402B1003	N87147
SP-KGA	Cessna 172S (Reservation 9.03)	172S9129	N929MC
SP-KGB	Cessna 172S	172S8266	N343SP
SP-KGC	Piper PA-34-220TSeneca V	3449194	N41842
SP-KGE	PZL M-18 Dromader (Reservation 8.02)	1Z009-11	LZ-8007 Z3-BGK LZ-8007
SP- KGH	Cessna F150J	F150-0464	OO-HBD (D-EBUA)
SP- KGI	Cessna 172N	17270074	OH-CKH SE-KKG N738LZ
SP-KGT	Cessna 172S	172S8811	S5-DGK N2456V
SP-KHA	Bell 427	56014	(SP-FZS) (SP-FJS) N427AG C-GGDR
SP-KHO	Reims/Cessna F182Q	F18200156	HB-CJK D-EFQN
SP-KIA	Reims/Cessna F152	F15201949	SE-IPA
SP-KIB	Cessna F150J	F150-0450	SE-FET
SP-KIC	Cessna 150J	15069630	N50903
SP-KID	Reims FR172JRocket	FR17200416	OH-CFW
SP-KIE	Reims/Cessna F172N	F17201554	D-EHGN
SP-KIG	Reims/Cessna F150L	F15000705	D-ECHG
SP-KIH	Reims/Cessna F152	F15201723	D-EIFY(2)
SP-KII	Reims/Cessna F150M	F15001180	D-EEVG
SP-KIK	Reims/Cessna FA150L Aerobat	FA1500088	D-ECBU(2)
SP-KIL	Cessna 150M	15077114	D-ESBA N63116
SP-KIM	Reims/Cessna F150L	F15000779	D-ECSH
SP-KIN	Cessna T207A Stationair 7	20700455	C-FBAM N98DF ZK-FQA N6260H
SP-KIO	Cessna 152	15285077	N5115Q
SP-KIP	Cessna 172S (Reservation 10.03)	172S9469	N245SP
SP-KIR	TS-11 Iskra	1H0806	PLW-806
SP-KIS	Cessna 152	15284836	N4877P
SP-KIW	Cessna 152	15280964	N48781
SP-KIR	Cessna F150L	F1500851	F-BUBR
SP-KIT	Cessna 152	15285554	N93802
SP-KIV	SOCATA TB-9 Tampico	1540	SX-AED F-GLFQ
SP-KIY	Cessna 152	15281774	OH-CMM N67356
SP- KIZ	Reims/Cessna F150L	F15001127	D-ELOS(2) (D-EOQB)
SP-KKB	Mil Mi-8 (Reservation 8.02)	95659	RA-25511
SP-KKC	Mil Mi-8 (Reservation 8.02)	95523	RA-25184
SP-KKF	Beech B55 Baron (Reservation 07.04)	TC-1279	OH-BBX
SP-KKG	HOAC DV-20 Katanna	20120	OE-AEA(2) D-ESIM
SP-KKH	Piper PA-31T Cheyenne II	31T-8120041	N220SC N8361T (N79CA) N8361T N816SW (N818SW) N2604X
SP-KKI	Piper PA-31 Turbo Navajo	31-540	N282SA D-IABS N6610L
SP-KKK	Piper PA-32-300 Six	32-7940142	I-VOLP N2821X
SP-KKL	Piper PA-32R-301T Saratoga	32-8224007	N363PZ HB-PKJ N824MC N9503N N8177C
SP-KKM	Zlin Z.326 Trenér Master	777	SP-FZA SP-CDC
SP-KKP	Enstrom 280FX Shark (Reservation 10.04	2047	C-GZZG H-183
SP-KKT	Cessna T303 Crusader	T30300024	D-IKMA(2) N9545tT
SP-KKU	Bell 427	56032	N10248 C-GZKH

SP-KKW	Cessna T206H Turbo Stationair	T20608378	N403PW
			C-GUSA
			N52092
SP-KLA	Yakovlev Yak-12A	30126	PLW-. . .
SP-KLE	Piper PA-28-161 Warrior II	28-7916396	D-ETLK
			HB-PDY
			N3016Z
SP-KLP	Cessna 172S	172S9469	N245SP
SP-KMB	Cessna F172G	F172-0236	D-EDOZ(2)
SP-KMC	Cessna 182Q Skylane	18266424	D-EVER
			N94393
SP-KMD	Cessna 182P Skylane	18262781	D-EDJT
			N52700
SP-KMI	LET L.200D Morava	171408	SP-NXA(4)
			HA-LDF
SP-KMK	Reims/Cessna F337G Skymaster	F33700064	OY-BIV
	(Reims-assembled 337G with US c/n 33701552)		LN-NPE(4)
			OY-BIV
			N14500
SP-KMM	Cessna 182S	18280504	N7278J
SP-KMR	Piper PA-28R-201T Turbo Cherokee Arrow III		N25ML
		28R-7803259	D-EHWW
			N9441C
SP-KMS	Piper PA-34-200T Seneca II	34-7570245	OY-CJK
			N854WM
			N34PT
			C-GNWX
SP- KMT	Piper PA-28R-201 Arrow	2837031	N177NB
			N177ND
SP-KNG	Antonov An-2T (Reservation 1.01)	1G26-17	SP-ANG(3)
			PLW-2617
SP-KOI	Cessna 152	15284909	N5294P
SP-KOS	Aero AT-3 R100	AT-3 010	
SP-KOW	Cessna T182T Turbo Skylane	T18208205	SE-LUU
			N2125G
SP-KPA	PZL-104MN Wilga 2000	00010011	
SP-KPB	PZL-104MN Wilga 2000	00010012	
SP-KPC	Van's RV-6A	25281	
SP-KPD	Maule MX-7-180 Star Rocket (Cr. 4.10.03)	11038C	D-EACS(5)
SP-KPM	SOCATA TB-21 Trinidad TC	690	D-ESHG
			HB-KBG
SP-KPS	LET L.410UVP-E2	831138	OK-NDG
			OK-NZG
			OK-OZG
			OK-178(2)
SP-KPW	SOCATA MS.887 Rallye 125	2163	SP-FPV
			F-BUJA
SP-KPY	LET L-410UVP-E	902439	OK-VDF
			RA-67646
			CCCP67646
SP-KPZ	LET L-410UVP-E	902431	OK-VDE
			RA-67638
			CCCP67638
SP-KRC	Yakovlev Yak-12M	169653	PLW-. . .
			SP-RAE
			PLW-. . .
SP-KRD	Yakovlev Yak-12M	2101001	PLW-. . .
SP-KRM	Cessna T182T	T18208189	N53296
SP-KRS	Zlin Z.526F Trenér Master	1107	SP-CDE
SP-KRZ	Reims FR172K Rocket XP	FR17200640	D-EDEA(2)
			I-BZEA
SP-KSA	Antonov An-2TP	1G214-10	
SP-KSB	Gardan GY-80 Horizon 160	69	D-EBVT
			F-BLVN
SP-KSE	Beech 23 Musketeer	M-15	G-ASBB
SP-KSG	Piper PA-28-235 Cherokee Pathfinder	28-7510016	D-EBSH
			N32281
SP-KSL	Cessna 172S	172S9691	N65326
SP-KST	SOCATA TB-9 Tampico	882	OH-TBC
			SE-KBC
SP-KSW	Zlin Z.142	0527	OK-VNH
SP-KTD	SOCATA TB-10 Tobago	1642	D-EDDR
SP-KTK	Antonov An-2T	1G15-28	SP-AAZ(3)
			SP-FAZ
			PLW-1528
SP-KTL	LET L-410UVP-E16A Turbolet	902414	SP-TXB
SP-KTR	Aérospatiale/Alenia ATR-42-300	092	D-BAAA
			N92BN
			9J-AFC
			F-WWER
SP-KTS	Antonov An-2TD	1G167-13	SP-MMT
SP-KTT	Piper PA-28-181 Archer III	2843597	N3098H
SP-KTZ	Cessna 182N	18260465	D-ECIR(3)
			N8925G
SP-KUB	Piper J-3C-90 Cub	11295	D-EGZG(2)
			N9829F
			"N9830F"
			G-AIYV
			43-30004
SP-KUW	Reims FR172H Rocket	FR17200307	D-EEYM
SP-KWB	Partenavia P.68B	124	VH-IYE
SP-KWM	Yakovlev Yak-12A	39108	SP-FKH
			SP-CXR(2)
			PLW-108
SP-KWR	Piper PA-28-181 Archer III	2843395	N4185B
			N9522N

SP-KYK	Extra EA.300/S	029	(SP-FEM)
			D-ETYU
SP-KYM	Cessna 175B Skylark	17556898	(SP-HKO)
			SP-KYM
			D-EFWH(2)
			N8198T
SP-KYP	Cessna 182S	18280827	N2459M
SP-KZB	PZL-101A Gawron	96173	SP-KXZ
SP-KZD	PZL-101A Gawron	52073	SP-KXD
SP-KZE(2)	SOCATA TB-10 Tobago	103	HB-EZM
SP-KZF	PZL-101A Gawron	96167	SP-KXF
SP-KZH(2)	Cessna F172G	F172-0302	D-EJPA
SP-KZI	PZL-104 Wilga 35A	74209	
SP-KZO	PZL-101A Gawron	96168	SP-KXO
SP-KZS	PZL-101A Gawron	63117	SP-KXS
SP-KZU	PZL-101A Gawron	85164	SP-KXU
SP-KZY	Cessna F172H	F172-0439	(SP-FOU)
			D-ELBG
			(PH-MIB)
SP-LDA(3)	Embraer EMB-170ST	17000023	"SP-LGA"
	(Mispainted in error)		PT-SKQ
SP-LDB(2)	Embraer EMB-170ST	17000024	PT-SKR
SP-LDC(2)	Embraer EMB-170ST	17000025	PT-SKS
SP-LDD	Embraer EMB-170ST	17000027	PT-SK .
SP-LDE	Embraer EMB-170LR	17000029	PT-SK .
SP-LDF	Embraer EMB-170LR	17000035	PT-SK .
SP-LDG	Embraer EMB-170LR	17000065	PT-SVQ.
SP-LDH	Embraer EMB-170LR	17000069	PT-SVU
SP-LDI	Embraer EMB-170LR	17000073	PT-SVY
SP-LDK	Embraer EMB-170LR	17000074	PT-SVZ
SP-LFA(2)	Aérospatiale/Alenia ATR-72-201	246	F-WWEM
SP-LFB(2)	Aérospatiale/Alenia ATR-72-201	265	F-WWEJ
SP-LFC(2)	Aérospatiale/Alenia ATR-72-201	272	F-WWEN
SP-LFD(2)	Aérospatiale/Alenia ATR-72-201	279	F-WWLD
SP-LFE(2)	Aérospatiale/Alenia ATR-72-201	328	F-WWLJ
SP-LFF(2)	Aérospatiale/Alenia ATR-72-201	402	F-WWLM
SP-LFG	Aérospatiale/Alenia ATR-72-201	411	F-WWEO
SP-LFH	Aérospatiale/Alenia ATR-72-202	478	F-WWEK
SP-LGA(2)	Embraer EMB-145EU	145155	PT-SEJ
SP-LGB(2)	Embraer EMB-145EU	145165	PT-SEK
SP-LGC	Embraer EMB.145EU	145227	PT-SHM
SP-LGD	Embraer EMB.145MP	145244	PT-SII
SP-LGE	Embraer EMB.145MP	145285	PT-SKC
SP-LGF	Embraer EMB.145EP	145308	PT-SKZ
SP-LGG	Embraer EMB.145EP	145319	PT-SMK
SP-LGH	Embraer EMB.145EP	145329	PT-SMV
SP-LGI	Embraer EMB.145EP	145336	PT-SNC
SP-LGK	Embraer EMB.145EP	145339	PT-SNF
SP-LGL	Embraer EMB.145MP	145406	PT-STD
SP-LGM	Embraer EMB.145MP	145408	PT-STF
SP-LGN	Embraer EMB.145MP	145441	PT-SUM
SP-LGO	Embraer EMB.145LR	145560	PT-SZV
SP-LKA(2)	Boeing 737-55D	27416	
SP-LKB(2)	Boeing 737-55D	27417	
SP-LKC(2)	Boeing 737-55D	27418	
SP-LKD(2)	Boeing 737-55D	27419	
SP-LKE(2)	Boeing 737-55D	27130	
SP-LKF(2)	Boeing 737-55D	27368	
SP-LKG(2)	Boeing 737-53C	24825	F-GHOL
SP-LLA(2)	Boeing 737-45D	27131	
SP-LLB	Boeing 737-45D	27156	UR-VVH
			SP-LLB
SP-LLC(2)	Boeing 737-45D	27157	
SP-LLD	Boeing 737-45D	27256	
SP-LLE	Boeing 737-45D	27914	
SP-LLF	Boeing 737-45D	28752	
SP-LMC	Boeing 737-36N	28668	
SP-LMD	Boeing 737-36N	28669	
SP-LOA	Boeing 767-25DER	24733	N6046P
SP-LOB	Boeing 767-25DER	24734	
SP-LOT	RWD-5R replica	01	
SP-LPA(2)	Boeing 767-35DER	24865	
SP-LPB(2)	Boeing 767-35DER	27902	
SP-LPC(2)	Boeing 767-35DER	28656	
SP-LPE(2)	Boeing 767-341ER	24843	PP-VOK
SP-MAK	SOCATA MS.880B Rallye Club	2893	SP-FPR
			F-GAKN
SP-MAM	Piper L-4H Cub	11806	SP-BAL(2)
			SP-ALD(1)
			43-30515
SP-MAX	Antonov An-2TP	1G233-54	SP-ZFU
			SP-FAM
SP-MBA	LET L.410UVP-E2	861803	
SP-MRA	PZL M-20 Mewa	1AH002-03	SP-PRA
			SP-MRA
SP-MXA(2)	PZL M-20 Mewa	1AH002-08	SP-DMB(2)
SP-MXB(2)	PZL M-20 Mewa	1AH002-12	
SP-MXC(2)	PZL M-20 Mewa	1AH002-14	
SP-MXH	Piaggio P.180 Avanti	1079	
SP-MXK	Antonov An-2TP	1G177-37	SP-TWC
SP-NEA(2)	PZL M-20 Mewa	1AH002-05	SP-PUE
SP-NEB	Beech C90A King Air	LJ-1285	N900BT
			HP-1264
			N191SP
SP-NEH	Antonov An-2TD	1G188-34	
SP-NSK	Antonov An-2TD	1G167-12	

SP-OAK	Cessna 150M	15077716	SP-FMG
			D-EMSR
			N6464K
SP-OBK	Reims/Cessna F150L	F15001102	SP-FOX
			D-EDJB
SP-OMS	Cessna 172N	17273670	D-EQQQ
			N4725J
SP-ORL	PZL-104M Wilga 2000	00970003	SP-GSM
SP-ORT	Piper PA-28R-180 Cherokee Arrow	28R-30156	OY-BCL
SP-PAV	Akro-Viper (Res as SP-YBV)	001	
SP-PCG	PZL-130TC-II Turbo Orlik	04990047	PLW-047
SP-PCM	DEKO-9 / Kaiser Magic	DK9.00.01	
	(Never formally regd.)		
SP-PDC	Airtech 01 (Reservation 3.01)	01012000	
SP-PEE	Aircab K-01 (Reservation .95 ntu)	unkn	
SP-PEF	HM.293 Pou du Ciel (Never formally regd.)	unkn	
SP-PEG	E &K SBM-03 (Never formally regd.wfu)	unkn	
SP-PGU	Taifun TL-32 TOP	unkn	
	(Reservation 1.00 believed, res as SP-YAK)		
SP-PHN	Kukulka	"T-026382"	SP-YKU
	(C/n quoted may be engine number)		SP-FKU
			SE-XKK
			SP-PHN
SP-PMB	PZL-126P Mrowka	00000002	
	(Originally reserved 2.98 as c/n 00980001)		
SP-PRG	PZL-112 Junior	00000001	
SP-SSL	PZL W-3A2 Sokol	370508	(SP-SYO)
SP-PSW	PZL SW-4	600103	
SP-PSZ	PZL SW-4	600104	
SP-PUV	Bü.233P Jungmeister (Reservation)	101	
SP-PVX	RAF-2000 GTX-SE (Reservation 12.99)	"616521"	
SP-RAC(2)	PZL-101A Gawron	107217	SP-RXC
SP-RCL	PZL-101A Gawron	119303	SP-RXL
SP-RCM	PZL-101A Gawron	119304	SP-RXM
SP-SAS	Mil Mi-2	525612048	
SP-SBC	Mil Mi-2plus	524740046	
SP-SBL	Mil Mi-2	525147037	
SP-SBN	Mil Mi-2	525149037	SU-BHY
			SP-SBN
SP-SCU	Mil Mi-2	529631026	
SP-SDC	Mil Mi-2	543908124	
SP-SDH	Mil Mi-2	524004025	
SP-SDM	Mil Mi-2	530322047	SP-PSC(1)
SP-SEN	Mil Mi-2 (Stored)	534537125	
SP-SEP	Mil Mi-2	525518028	
SP-SER	Mil Mi-2	544535125	
SP-SES(2)	Mil Mi-2	5210018116	
SP-SET	Mil Mi-2	5210019116	
SP-SEV	Mil Mi-2	5410217047	YL-LHV
			RA-15735
			Sov.mil
SP-SFD	Mil Mi-2	526507010	
SP-SFF	Mil Mi-2	5210008106	
SP-SFG	Mil Mi-2	5210009106	
SP-SFW	Mil Mi-2	5311149 . . .	
SP-SGI	Mil Mi-2	5210432029	
SP-SGL	Mil Mi-2	5210434049	
SP-SGN	Mil Mi-2	5210436069	
SP-SGR	Mil Mi-2	5210439069	
SP-SGS	Mil Mi-2	5210440099	
SP-SGZ	Mil Mi-2	510621028	SP-ASZ(2)
			SP-FDD
			PLW-0621
SP-SHO	Mil Mi-2	515039017	
SP-SLI	Mil Mi-2	525645068	
SP-SLM	Mil Mi-2	525837108	
SP-SPR	Mil Mi-2	535744098	
SP-SPU	Mil Mi-2	535747098	
SP-SSH	Schweizer 269D	0018	HB-XJT
			N69A
SP-SSL	PZL W-3A2 Sokol	370508	SP-PSL
			(SP-SYO)
SP-STD	Mil Mi-2	5311230 . . .	
SP-SUA	PZL W-3 Sokol	310208	
SP-SUB	PZL W-3 Sokol	310412	
SP-SUC	PZL W-3 Sokol	300201	SP-PSF
SP-SUF	PZL W-3AS Sokol	310308	CCCP04111
SP-SUG	PZL W-3 Sokol	310313	CCCP04116
SP-SUH	PZL W-3AS Sokol	310205	CCCP04103
			SP-PSI
SP-SUI	PZL W-3AS Sokol	310301	SP-PUI
SP-SUL	PZL W-3 Sokol	310303	CCCP04107
SP-SUM	PZL W-3AS Sokol	310305	CCCP04108
SP-SUN	PZL W-3AS Sokol	310306	CCCP04109
SP-SUR	PZL W-3 Sokol	310320	CCCP04396
SP-SUS	PZL W-3 Sokol	310321	CCCP04397
SP-SUT	PZL W-3 Sokol	310307	CCCP04110
SP-SUW	PZL W-3W Sokol	360318	ZU-AGU
			SP-SUW
SP-SUY	PZL W-3 Sokol	310206	CCCP04104
SP-SUZ	PZL W-3AS Sokol	310207	RA-04105
			CCCP04105
SP-SWM	Mil Mi-2	526510010	
SP-SXA(2)	Mil Mi-2	517002011	
SP-SXB(2)	Mil Mi-2	517301081	
SP-SXF	Mil Mi-2	519845076	

SP-SXG	Mil Mi-2	519943106	
SP-SXH	Mil Mi-2	5110007106	
SP-SXW	PZL W-3 Sokol	370908	SP-SYE
SP-SYA	PZL W-3AS Sokol	310204	CCCP04102
SP-SYB	PZL W-3 Sokol	310310	CCCP04113
SP-SYC	PZL W-3 Sokol	310311	CCCP04114
SP-SYD	PZL W-3 Sokol	310312	CCCP04115
SP-SYG	PZL W-3RM Sokol	390411	PLW-0411
SP-SYR	PZL W-3AS Sokol	310314	SP-SUO
			RA-04117
			CCCP04117
SP-TAK	Reims/Cessna F150L	F15000776	D-ECRP(2)
			(OY-BYY)
			D-ECRF(1)
SP-TFC	Cessna 172M (Reservation 10.04)	172.....	
SP-TKA	PZL-110 Koliber	19007	
SP-TKB	PZL-110 Koliber	19008	
SP-TKC	PZL-110 Koliber	19009	
SP-TKD	PZL-110 Koliber	19010	
SP-TKE	PZL-110 Koliber	24016	
SP-TKF	PZL-110 Koliber	24017	
SP-TKG	PZL-110 Koliber	24023	
SP-TKH	PZL-110 Koliber	24024	
SP-TKI	PZL-110 Koliber	25025	
SP-TKK	PZL-110 Koliber	038633	
SP-TKL	PZL-110 Koliber	038634	
SP-TKM	Aérospatiale AS355N Ecureuil 2	5113	OM-OTO
			F-WQDP(5)
			N5786D
SP-TPA	LET L-410UVP-E15 Turbolet	892318	
SP-TPB	LET L-410UVP-E15 Turbolet	892329	
SP-TPC	Aero AT-3-R100	001	
SP-TPD	Aero AT-3-L100	002	
SP-TPE	Aero AT-3-L100	003	
SP-TPF	Aero AT-3-L100 (Reservation)	004	
SP-TPG	Aero AT-3-R100	005	
SP-TUA	PZL M-20 Mewa	1AHP01-02	SP-PKB
SP-TUB	PZL M-20 Mewa	1AHP01-04	SP-PKD
SP-TUC	PZL M-20 Mewa	1AH002-02	SP-PKE
SP-TUD	PZL M-20 Mewa	1AH002-04	
SP-TUK	SOCATA TB-9 Tampico Club	1635	F-OHDO
SP-TUL	SOCATA TB-9 Tampico Club	1722	F-OHDS
SP-TUM	SOCATA TB-9 Tampico Club	1787	F-OHTZ
SP-TWI	Antonov An-2TP	1G185-03	
SP-TWL	Antonov An-2P	1G181-54	
SP-TXA	LET L-410UVP-16 Turbolet	892319	
SP-TZB	PZL-104 Wilga 35A	18830759	
SP-WDB	PZL-104 Wilga 35A	62164	
SP-WEB	PZL-101A Gawron	119324	
SP-WEC	PZL-104 Wilga 35A	61134	
SP-WEE(2)	PZL-104 Wilga 35A (W/o 20.4.01 not cld)	21960958	
SP-WEF(2)	PZL-104 Wilga 35A	21960962	(TC-ECZ)
SP-WEW	PZL-104 Wilga 35A	62169	DOSAAF
			SP-WER
SP-WGP	PZL-111 Koliber 160A	04020089	
SP-WHG(2)	PZL-104M Wilga 2000	00960001	SP-PHG
SP-WHI	PZL-111 Koliber 235A Senior	00950001	SP-PHI
SP-WIB	Zlin Z.42M	0166	
SP-WID	Zlin Z.42M	0168	
SP-WKA	Antonov An-2TD (Reservation 11.04)	1G108-62	PLW-0862
SP-WKB	Antonov An-2TD	1G135-47	
SP-WKF(2)	Antonov An-2R	1G148-03	SP-WLN
SP-WKH	Antonov An-2R	1G144-26	
SP-WKP	Antonov An-2R	1G144-33	
SP-WKR	Antonov An-2R	1G144-34	
SP-WKS	Antonov An-2R	1G144-35	
SP-WKT	Antonov An-2R	1G144-36	
SP-WLA	Antonov An-2R	1G144-41	
SP-WLB	Antonov An-2R	1G144-42	
SP-WLC	Antonov An-2TD	1G144-43	
SP-WLD	Antonov An-2R	1G144-44	
SP-WLI	Antonov An-2R (Crashed 5.99)	1G144-49	
SP-WLR	Antonov An-2R	1G148-06	
SP-WMA	Antonov An-2R	1G156-16	
SP-WME	Antonov An-2R	1G156-20	
SP-WMH	Antonov An-2R	1G156-23	
SP-WMI	Antonov An-2R	1G156-24	
SP-WMK	Antonov An-2R	1G156-25	
SP-WMM	Antonov An-2R	1G156-27	
SP-WMO	Antonov An-2R	1G156-29	
SP-WMW	Antonov An-2R	1G156-35	
SP-WMX	Antonov An-2R	1G156-38	
SP-WND	Antonov An-2R	1G156-41	
SP-WNF	Antonov An-2R (Crashed 6.98)	1G156-43	
SP-WNI	Antonov An-2R	1G155-16	
SP-WNM	Antonov An-2R	1G155-19	
SP-WNN	Antonov An-2R	1G155-20	
SP-WNS	Antonov An-2R	1G155-24	
SP-WNW	Antonov An-2R	1G155-27	
SP-WOA	Antonov An-2R	1G160-14	
SP-WOC	Antonov An-2R	1G160-16	
SP-WOG	Antonov An-2R	1G161-14	
SP-WOH	Antonov An-2R	1G160-21	
SP-WOP	Antonov An-2R	1G161-05	
SP-WPA	Antonov An-2R	1G163-07	

SP-WPC	Antonov An-2R	1G163-09	
SP-WPD	Antonov An-2R	1G163-10	
SP-WPG	Antonov An-2R	1G163-13	
SP-WPL	Antonov An-2R	1G163-17	
SP-WPN	Antonov An-2R	1G167-22	
SP-WPZ	Antonov An-2R	1G167-31	
SP-WSA	Antonov An-2R	1G167-33	
SP-WSC	Antonov An-2R	1G167-35	
SP-WSG	Antonov An-2R	1G167-39	
SP-WSI	Antonov An-2R	1G167-41	
SP-WSK	Antonov An-2R	1G167-42	
SP-WSL	Antonov An-2R	1G167-43	
SP-WSN	Antonov An-2R	1G167-45	
SP-WSU	Antonov An-2R	1G168-37	
SP-WSX	Antonov An-2R	1G168-20	
SP-WWB	Antonov An-2R	1G173-53	
SP-WWC	Antonov An-2R	1G173-54	
SP-WWL	Antonov An-2R	1G177-02	
SP-WWZ	Antonov An-2R	1G180-03	
SP-WXG	Mil Mi-2 (Stored)	513306123	
SP-WXK	Mil Mi-2	513407044	
SP-WXL	Mil Mi-2	513901124	
SP-WXM	Mil Mi-2	513904015	
SP-WXN	Mil Mi-2	513902015	
SP-WXO	Mil Mi-2 Plus	5111301054	
SP-WXT	Mil Mi-2	513925015	
SP-WXU	Mil Mi-2	514045035	
SP-WZG	Antonov An-2R	1G182-27	
SP-WZM	Antonov An-2R	1G187-08	(SP-FML) SP-WZM
SP-ZCI	PZL-106BR Kruk	08850166	
SP-ZCK	PZL-106BR Kruk	08850167	
SP-ZCN	PZL-106BR Kruk	08850170	
SP-ZCP	PZL-106BR Kruk	08850172	
SP-ZCR	PZL-106BR Kruk	08850173	
SP-ZCV	PZL-106BR Kruk	09870201	
SP-ZCY	PZL-106BR Kruk	08860177	DDR-TDA
SP-ZEG	Antonov An-2R	1G187-42	
SP-ZES	Antonov An-2R	1G174-59	PLW-7459
SP-ZOI	PZL-104 Wilga 35A	19850826	
SP-ZOM	PZL-104 Wilga 35A	20890886	(SP-FWL?)
SP-ZOO	PZL-104 Wilga 35A	20900900	
SP-ZPB	PZL-106B T-601 Turbo Kruk	10880218	
SP-ZPD	PZL-106B T-601 Turbo Kruk	10880220	
SP-ZUA	PZL M-18B Dromader	1Z002-05	
SP-ZUB	PZL M-18B Dromader	1Z003-01	
SP-ZUC	PZL M-18B Dromader	1Z004-06	SP-DIC
SP-ZUD	PZL M-18 Dromader	1Z012-34	SP-DAV
SP-ZUE	PZL M-18B Dromader	1Z013-36	SP-DBA(2)
SP-ZUF	PZL M-18B Dromader	1Z013-37	SP-DBB(2)
SP-ZUG	PZL M-18B Dromader	1Z003-08	SP-DWA(I)
SP-ZUL	PZL M-18B Dromader	1Z014-11	
SP-ZUM	PZL M-18B Dromader	1Z012-16	SP-DAY
SP-ZUN	PZL M-18B Dromader (Cr. 7.8.00 not cld)	1Z013-49	SP-DBF
SP-ZUO	PZL M-18B Dromader	1Z012-40	SP-DAA(3)
SP-ZUP	PZL M-18B Dromader	1Z013-01	SP-DAT(2)
SP-ZUS	PZL M-18B Dromader	1Z016-28	
SP-ZUT	PZL M-18B Dromader (Cr. 25.7.02 not cld)	1Z016-29	
SP-ZUU	PZL M-18B Dromader	1Z016-30	
SP-ZUV	PZL M-18B Dromader	1Z017-06	
SP-ZUW	PZL M-18BS Dromader	1Z017-02	
SP-ZUZ	PZL M-18B Dromader (W/o 10.10.02)	1Z017-03	
SP-ZWA	PZL M-18B Dromader	1Z010-12	HA-MUO
SP-ZWB	PZL M-18B Dromader	1Z010-13	HA-MUP
SP-ZWC	PZL M-18B Dromader	1Z011-11	HA-MUS
SP-ZWE	PZL M-18B Dromader	1Z006-02	HA-MTH
SP-ZWG	PZL M-18B Dromader	1Z009-14	HA-MTY
SP-ZWI	PZL M-18B Dromader	1Z018-23	
SP-ZWK	PZL M-18B Dromader	1Z018-24	
SP-ZWL	PZL M-18B Dromader	1Z020-13	
SP-ZWM	PZL M-18B Dromader	1Z020-14	
SP-ZWN	PZL M-18B Dromader	1Z020-15	
SP-ZWO	PZL M-18B Dromader	1Z005-10	HA-MTF
SP-ZWP	PZL M-18B Dromader (Cr. 14.7.02 not cld)	1Z006-04	HA-MTJ
SP-ZWR	PZL M-18B Dromader	1Z009-16	HA-MUB
SP-ZWS	PZL M-18B Dromader	1Z010-21	SP-TDA
SP-ZWT	PZL M-18B Dromader (Cr. 25.7.02 not cld)	1Z011-20	SP-TDB SP-DAH
SP-ZWU	PZL M-18B Dromader	1Z001-01	SP-BBU(2) SP-PBU
SP-ZWW	PZL M-18B Dromader	1Z001-05	SP-BBT(2)
SP-ZWX	PZL M-18B Dromader	1Z015-07	SP-DDN D-FOHR DDR-TKR
SP-ZWY	PZL M-18B Dromader	1Z014-17	SP-DBC
SP-ZWZ	PZL M-18B Dromader	1Z012-15	SP-DAZ
SP-ZXC	Mil Mi-2	514408105	
SP-ZXE	Mil Mi-2	544304085	
SP-ZXT	Mil Mi-2	515301087	
SP-ZXU	Mil Mi-2plus	515832108	
SP-ZXY	Mil Mi-2	516531030	
SP-ZXZ	Mil Mi-2	535643068	
SP-ZZB	PZL M-18 Dromader	1Z008-14	LZ-8004
SP-ZZD	PZL M-18 Dromader	1Z009-25	LZ-8013
SP-ZZE	PZL M-18 Dromader	1Z009-27	LZ-8015
SP-ZZF	PZL M-18 Dromader	1Z009-30	LZ-8018
SP-ZZH(2)	PZL M-18 Dromader	1Z009-28	LZ-8016

SP-...	Beech A36 Bonanza	E-2169	N7214Y
SP-...	Bell 206L-1 Long Ranger	45456	F-GCVU HB-XLO (D-HIFA) (D-HIVA) HB-XLO
SP-...	Cessna 150M	15075785	N66027
SP-...	Cessna 152	15283866	N5413B
SP-...	Cessna 152	15284305	N5376L
SP-...	Cessna 152	15284665	N6306M
SP-...	Cessna 152	15284805	N4725P
SP-...	Cessna 152	15285009	N6378P
SP-...	Cessna 152	15285012	N6409P
SP-...	Cessna 152	15285432	N93180
SP-...	Cessna 172S	172S8510	N583SP
SP-...	Piper PA-38-112 Tomahawk	38-78A0594	N4405E
SP-...	Piper PA-38-112 Tomahawk	38-79A0186	G-BNDF EI-BUS G-BNDF N2439C

BALLOONS AND AIRSHIPS

SP-BAA(2)	Cameron V-77 HAFB	2679	D-OREG
SP-BAC(2)	Kubicek BB-22 HAFB	167	OK-0167
SP-BAD(2)	Cameron O-160 HAFB	1595	OO-BYY PH-YUP G-BOBE
SP-BAE(2)	Kubicek BB-22 HAFB	170	OK-0170
SP-BAF(2)	Cameron A-120 HAFB	2673	D-Biberach
SP-BAG(2)	Firefly Balloons Firefly F-7B-15 HAFB	F7B-2004	
SP-BAI (2)	Cameron C-80 Concept HAFB	10255	
SP-BAK(2)	Cameron C-60 Concept HAFB	4185	C-GBBN
SP-BAM(2)	Colt 240A HAFB	2320	D-ONUT
SP-BAN(2)	Ultramagic M-145 HAFB	145/11	D-OREA
SP-BAO(2)	Cameron C-80 Concept HAFB	10335	
SP-BAP(2)	Cameron V-77 HAFB	5756	N7501Y
SP-BAR(2)	Ultramagic M-77 HAFB	77/219	
SP-BAS(2)	Sekpol N-22 HAFB	04/01/03	
SP-BAT	Schröder Fire Balloons G HAFB	"1.128-1"	D-Alexander
SP-BAU	Cameron O-120 HAFB (Reservation .03)	unkn	
SP-BAV	Cameron N-105 HAFB (Reservation .03)	2429	D-OOLG D-Colgate(2)
SP-BAW(2)	Schröder Fire Balloons G Ax-8 HAFB	192	D-Feuerball
SP-BAX(2)	Cameron N-77 HAFB	10457	
SP-BAY	Cameron N-105 HAFB	5809	N75076
SP-BAZ	Cameron V-77 HAFB	10374	
SP-BBA(2)	Cameron O-90 HAFB	2304	D-Urlaub
SP-BBB(2)	Firefly Balloons Firefly F-8 HAFB	F8-393	D-OKSA N9066D
SP-BBC	Cameron N-77 HAFB	10533	
SP-BBE	Lindstrand LBL-105A HAFB	379	D-OUTA
SP-BBF(2)	Cameron V-90 HAFB	5698	N3991G
SP-BBG	Thunder & Colt AX8-90 S2 HAFB	2011USA	N208TC
SP-BBH	Kubicek BB-22 HAFB	305	OK-0305
SP-BBI	Stuttgart K-1000/3-TU Gas Balloon	0306	D-OICO
SP-BBK	Schröder Fire Balloons G AX-8 HAFB (Res 10.04)	unkn	
SP-BBL	Colt 120A HAFB (Reservation 10.04)	unkn	
SP-BBO	Cameron N-120 HAFB	10623	
SP-BBS	Thunder AX9 HAFB	2594	
SP-BIA(2)	Kubicek BB-30 HAFB	77	
SP-BIB(2)	Sekpol N-22 HAFB	00198	
SP-BIC	Kubicek BB-22 HAFB	86	
SP-BID	Cameron N-77 HAFB	4309	
SP-BIE	Cameron EB-90 SS HAFB	4120	
SP-BIF	Balloon Works Firefly F-7B-15 HAFB	381	
SP-BIG	Cameron Coldrex Mug 90SS HAFB	4405	
SP-BIH	Balloon Works Firefly F7-15 HAFB	F7-1043	
SP-BII	Ultramagic M-65 HAFB	65/83	
SP-BIK	Schröder Fire Balloons G HAFB	706	
SP-BIL	Balloon Works Firefly F-7B-15 HAFB	382	
SP-BIM	Kubicek BB-30 HAFB (W/o 16.11.99 Repaired?)	110	
SP-BIN	Aerotechnik AB-2 HAFB	910545	"SP-BVN" (SP-BTA) OK-1023
SP-BIO	Cameron C-70 Concept HAFB	4632	
SP-BIP	Cameron C-70 Concept HAFB	4614	
SP-BIR	Colt 69A HAFB	2447	D-OPUY N712TC
SP-BIS	Sekpol N-22 HAFB	02/1/99	
SP-BIU	Cameron V-77 HAFB	1541	D-Taubertal HB-BKO
SP-BIV	Kubicek AX-7 HAFB	133	
SP-BIX	Ultramagic M-105 HAFB	105/66	
SP-BIY	Sekpol N-22 HAFB	03100	
SP-BIZ	Schröder Fire Balloons GHAFB	866	
SP-BSC	Colt AS.105 Mk.II Hot Air Airship	4619	
SP-BVA	Cirkon Moskwa ATP-2401 HAFB	6240119304C	SP-PVA
SP-BVB	Interavia Moskwa AX-8 Balloon	0650393	
SP-BVC	Kubicek BB-22 HAFB	51	
SP-BVD	Cameron N-90 HAFB	3628	
SP-BVG	Aerotechnik AB-8 HAFB	910530	OK-1010
SP-BVH	Cameron N-90 HAFB	3906	

SP-BVI	Kubicek BB-30 HAFB	58	
SP-BVL	Kubicek BB-22 HAFB	069	
SP-BVM	Balloon Works Firefly F-8B HAFB	F8B-528	
SP-BVO(2)	Sky 105-24 HAFB	087	G-BXFO
SP-BVP	Cameron V-65 HAFB	4116	
SP-BVR	Cameron C-80 HAFB	4138	
SP-BVS	Cameron O-65 HAFB	4780	
SP-BVT	Cameron V-65 HAFB	4184	
SP-BVU	MOS-1 1050m Gas Balloon (Reservation ntu?)	4/90	
SP-BVV	Cameron C-80 HAFB	4139	
SP-BVW	Cameron C-80 HAFB	4155	
SP-BVZ	Balloon Works Firefly F7B-15 HAFB	376	
SP-BWB	Tomi AX-8 HAFB	BAV061/1988	
SP-BWC	Tomi AX-7 HAFB	BAV075/1989	
SP-BWD	RSZ-05 HAFB	1990/04	
SP-BWE	Tomi AX-7 HAFB	BAV074/1989	
SP-BWF	RSZ-03/1 HAFB	1989/002	
SP-BWG	Aerotechnik AB-8 HAFB	920550	
SP-BWI	Interavia Moskwa Ax-8 HAFB	0670793	
SP-BWK	Dirizablestroj AT-8 Balloon	059204012	
SP-BWL	Cameron N-65 HAFB	4374	
SP-BWM	Aerotechnik AB-2C HAFB	890418	
SP-BWN	Cameron C-60 HAFB	3847	
SP-BWO	Cameron V-77 HAFB	3466	
SP-BWP	Cameron O-65 HAFB	3004	
SP-BWR	Cameron V-65 HAFB	2709	
SP-BWS	Interavia Moskwa ZSRR AX-8 HAFB	037/442920457	
SP-BWT	Cameron C-80 HAFB	3334	
SP-BWU	Cameron N-77 HAFB	2457	G-BTBO
SP-BWV	Cirkon Moskwa ATP-2401 HAFB	70GA	
SP-BWW	Raven-Europe S-55A HAFB	E-248	
SP-BWX	Thunder AX8-90 HAFB	1709	D-Kitekat
SP-BWY	Thunder AX8-90 HAFB	1714	D-Cesar
SP-BWZ	Thunder AX8-90 HAFB	1717	D-Chappi
SP-BYA	ZSTiT BC-1 HAFB	001	
SP-BYB	Tomi AX-7 HAFB	029/1986	
SP-BYE	Tomi AX-7 HAFB	027/1986	
SP-BYF	Tomi AX-7 HAFB	025/1986	
SP-BYH	Tomi AX-7 HAFB	BAV038/1987	
SP-BYI	Tomi AX-7 HAFB	BAV036/1987	
SP-BYK	Tomi AX-7 HAFB	BAV037/1987	
SP-BYL	Tomi AX-7 HAFB	BAV035/1987	
SP-BYM	Tomi AX-7 HAFB	BAV033/1987	
SP-BYN	Tomi AX-7 HAFB	BAV040/1987	
SP-BYO	Tomi AX-7 HAFB	BAV043/1988	
SP-BYP	Tomi AX-7 HAFB	BAV042/1988	
SP-BYR	Tomi AX-7 HAFB	BAV041/1988	
SP-BYS	Tomi AX-7 HAFB	BAV046/1988	
SP-BYT	Tomi AX-7 HAFB	BAV044/1988	
SP-BYU	Tomi AX-7 HAFB	BAV045/1988	
SP-BYV	Tomi AX-7 HAFB	BAV053/1988	
SP-BYW	Tomi AX-7 HAFB	BAV055/1988	
SP-BYX	Tomi AX-7 HAFB	BAV054/1988	
SP-BZI	Cameron N-90 HAFB	1106	
SP-BZO	ZSTiT 1200m3 Gas Balloon	1	
SP-BZU	RSZ-05 HAFB	1985/B/01	
SP-BZV	Tomi AX-7 HAFB	017/1986	
SP-BZX	Tomi AX-7 HAFB	015/1986	
SP-BZY	Tomi AX-7 HAFB	016/1986	
SP-B . .	Cameron A-105 HAFB	2616	D-Rechenstein
SP-B..	Thunder AX10-150SIIHAFB	4588	D-OPDS

HOMEBUILTS AND MICROLIGHTS

In 2001 Poland introduced a new series for non JAR/FAR certified and homebuilt/kit aircraft commencing SP-YAA and numbers in this section are now growing. Existing aircraft in the SP-F and SP-P series are now being re-registered in this block. Another series introduced around 2000/1 uses the prefix AP- with four letters following, commencing with A for three-axis types and M for flexwings and it was expected that together the two new groups would replace the earlier PL- allocations but most recent information indicates that AP- registrations will be abandoned.
For ease of reference all the groups are listed together below.

SP-YAA	Kappa KP-2UR Sova	4242G	
SP-YAB	E&K SMB-03 Kos (Not offically registered)	unkn	
SP-YAC	J-5 Marco	10S	SP-FAC
SP-YAD	Birdman Chinook 2 Plus	02123	SP-FNP
SP-YAE	Birdman Chinook 2 Plus (Reservation)	unkn	
SP-YAF	KO-9 Max	001	SP-PFL
SP-YAG	Kappa KP-2U Sova (Reservation)	unkn	
SP-YAH	Zenair CH-601 Zodiac	004/BW/00	
SP-YAI	Ekolot JK-05 Junior	05-01-01	
SP-YAK	TL Ultralight TL-32 Typhoon	unkn	SP-PFL
SP-YAL	Zenair CH.701 STOL (Reservation)	K-1	
SP-YAN	TL Ultralight TL-32 Typhoon	94C08	OK-ZUU 56
	(C/n is for OK-ZUU 56 but SP-YAN is quoted as		
	ex OK-ZUU 20 and may be c/n 94C03)		
SP-YAO	Let-Mont Tulak (Reservation)	TUL-08	
SP-YAP	Zenair CH.601 Zodiac (Reservation)	unkn	
SP-YAR	Super Pulsar 100	602	
SP-YAS	Tecnam P.96 Golf 100	190	
SP-YAU	Ekolot JK-05 Junior	05-01-05	
SP-YAV	Funk FK-14 Polaris	032	
SP-YAW	Ekolot JK-05 Junior	05-01-06	
SP-YAY	EOL Special UL-04	E-35	
SP-YAZ	Tecnam P.92 Echo S100	625	
SP-YBA	TS-8 Bies	1E04-26	SP-FBA(2)
			SP-EFM
			PLW-0426
SP-YBB	Ekolot JK-05 Junior	05-01-04	
SP-YBC	Evektor EV-97 Eurostar	001	
SP-YBD	TS-8 Bies	1E-1009	SP-FFA
			PWL-1009
SP-YBE	TS-8 Bies (Cr. 27.5.04)	1E-0401	SP-EFG
			PWL-0401
SP-YBF	EOL Special UL-06	E-38	
SP-YBG	Sky-Walker II (Reservation)	159	D-MSWV
SP-YBH	Zenair CH.601 Zodiac (Reservation)	unkn	
SP-YBI	Zenair CH.601 Zodiac	SG-02	
SP-YBK	Let-Mont Tulak (Reservation 8.02)	unkn	
SP-YBL	Let-Mont Tulak	TUL-01	
SP-YBM	Let-Mont Tulak	TUL-05	SP-KAM
			SP-PAM
SP-YBN	YALO GM-01 Gniady	YL-003SH	SP-PBN(2)
SP-YBO	Pipistrel Sinus 912	068S9120402	
SP-YBP	Ekolot JK-05 Junior	05-01-08	
SP-YBR	Ekolot JK-05 Junior (Reservation)	05-02-07	
SP-YBS	3xtrim 550 Trener Special 02	E-42	
SP-YBT	GM-1SM Gniady (Reservation)	YL-032SH	
SP-YBU	Zenair CH.601 Zodiac	011/BW/02	
SP-YBV	Akro-Viper (Reservation)	001	SP-PAV
SP-YBW	Zenair CH.601 Zodiac	ZZ120308S	
SP-YBY	Zenair CH.701 STOL	020/BW/04	
SP-YBZ	Zenair CH.601 Zodiac	ZS010418P	
SP-YCA	Cessna 150H	15067857	N7157S
SP-YCB	3xtrim 550 Trener Special 02	E-43	
SP-YCC	3xtrim 550 Trener Special 09	E-46	
SP-YCM	3xtrim 550 Trener Special 09	E-48	
SP-YCS	T-131PA Jungmann	120	
SP-YDA	Airtech 01R503 (Reservation 9.02)	01.02.2002	
SP-YDB	Zenair CH.701 STOL	7-9472	
SP-YDK	T-131PA Jungmann (Damaged 12.5.01)	112	(SP-KDK)
SP-YDR	Kappa KP-2U Sova	2095112J	
SP-YDS	Let-Mont Tulak	TUL-06	SP-FUZ
SP-YDW	T-131PA Jungmann	111	(SP-KDW)
SP-YEA	Funk FK-9 Mk.3	127	SP-FEA
SP-YEC	KO-8 For You	001	SP-FEC
			SP-PEC
SP-YED	KO-9 Los	01	SP-FED
SP-YEK	Aerotrophy TT2000 Trophy	11	
SP-YEM	Marganski EM-10 Bielek	P-21	
SP-YEN	Marganski EM-11 Orka	P-22	
SP-YEO	J-3 Kitten (Reservation)	unkn	SP-FEO
			SP-PEO
SP-YES	T-131PA Jungmann	107	(SP-YOS)
			SP-GOS
			(SP-FUS)
SP-YET	Let-Mont Tulak	TUL-09	
SP-YEX	3xtrim Special 06	E-44	
SP-YGA	Croses EC-3 Pouplume	SAK-01	SP-FGA
			(SP-AMA(3))
			SP-0023
SP-YGB	Kappa KP-2U Sova	01/98	
SP-YGH	T-131PA Jungmann	118	
SP-YGM	T-131PA Jungmann	105	(SP-YLM)
			(SP-YDL)
			SP-KLM
			(SP-FUP(2))
SP-YGT	Air Design Qualt 200L	18/2001	OK-GUD 08
SP-YGW	T-131PA Jungmann	122	
SP-YHF	Aerospool WT-9 Dynamic	DY065/2004	
SP-YHK	T-131PA Jungmann	123	
SP-YHL	T-131PA Jungmann	110	(SP-KHL)
SP-YHS	T-131PA Jungmann	114	(SP-KHS)
SP-YKA	EuroCub Mk.IV (Reservation)	unkn	
SP-YKB	KO-5 Pelikan	01	SP-FKB
SP-YKC	3xtrim 550 Trener Special 03	E-39	
SP-YKH	EOL-VL-X (Also reported as 3xtrim 550 Trener)	E10	SP-FUE
			SP-PUS
SP-YKN	Zenair CH.701 STOL (Reservation 11.04)		
SP-YKO	KO-11 Goska	001	SP-FKO
			SP-PKO
SP-YKP	Tecnam P.96 Golf	044	
SP-YKR	Tecnam P.96 Golf	127	
SP-YKT	Radwan/Rand Robinson KR-2PM3	YL-002-SVL	SP-FKT
	(Reservation 9.02 stored as SP-FKT 5.03)		SP-PKT
SP-YKZ	Zenair CH.601 Zodiac	008/BW/01	
SP-YLT	Zenair CH.601 Zodiac (Reservation)	unkn	
SP-YLZ	KO-10 Sea Witch	01	(SP-KLZ)
			(SP-PLZ)
SP-YMA	Remos G-3 Mirage	124	
SP-YMH	Evektor EV-97 Eurostar	20042112	
SP-YMK	Evektor EV-97 Eurostar	980104	OK-DUR 07
SP-YMU	J-3 Kitten	01	
SP-YNA	Zenair CH.601HDS Zodiac	009/BW/02	
SP-YND	Zenair CH.601XL Zodiac	6-9520	
SP-YOA	Funk FK-12 Comet	061	
SP-YOD	Zenair CH-701 STOL	7-9521	
SP-YOK	Zenair CH.601HD Zodiac (Reservation 10.04)	6-9387	

SP-YOO	Aerospool WT-9 Dynamic	DY056/2004	
SP-YOR	Orlinski RO-7 Orlik	0001	
SP-YOW	Let-Mont Tulak	03	SP-FOW
SP-YOY	3xtrim 450 Ultra-09	E-50	
SP-YPA	Zenair CH.601 Zodiac (Reservation)	unkn	
SP-YPB	CSS-13	420-76	SP-APA(2) SP-AIM(2) PLW-. . .
SP-YPE	TL Ultralight TL-232 Condor	97C02	SP-FPE
SP-YPM	CASA C-1-131E Jungmann	2138	D-EOUT E3B-523
SP-YPN	T-131PA Jungmann	117	
SP-YPX	T-131PA Jungmann	102	SP-FPX
SP-YPY	T-131PA Jungmann	103	SP-FUY
SP-YPZ	T-131P Jungmann	03	SP-FPZ
SP-YRA	Ekolot JK-05 Junior	05-01-11	
SP-YRD	Zenair CH-701 STOL	7-9559	
SP-YRK	T-131PA Jungmann	115	(SP-KRK)
SP-YRS	T-131PA Jungmann	113	(SP-KRS)
SP-YRW	Zenair CH-701 STOL	006/8W/00	
SP-YSA	Rotorway Exec 162F	6502	
SP-YSB	Rotorway Exec 162F	6592	
SP-YSG	Aeroprakt A-22 Vision	22-005	
SP-YSW	Sky Cruiser (Reservation 10.04)	1/JS/1433/2004	
SP-YSO	3xtrim 450 Ultra-08	E-41	
SP-YSS	TS-8 Bies	1E-0921	SP-CNS PLW-0921
SP-YTA	TL Ultralight TL-32 Typhoon	93A-006	OK-YUU 20
SP-YTK	EOL-Special UL-05	E-36	
SP-YTL	Let-Mont Tulak	TUL-04	SP-FOZ
SP-YTS	T-131PA Jungmann	109	SP-KTS
SP-YUA	Ech-1 Kraska	01-Ech	
SP-YUC	EOL-2BMW	E01.1	SP-FUC SP-PUC
SP-YUD	EOL-Special UL-02	E-37	
SP-YUF	EOL-2R	E04.5	SP-FUF SP-PUF
SP-YUH	EOL-2M	EK.01..2	SP-FUH
SP-YUK	Fly Synthesis Storch	39R	SP-FUK
SP-YUL	Pottier P.220S-AT2 Koala	001	SP-FUL SP-PUL
SP-YUM	EOL-2R2 (Reservation 8.04)	E16-17	SP-YUZ AP-AAAD SP-PUM
SP-YUN	BU-133P Jungmann (Reservation) (Locally-built at Jungmann factory)	101	
SP-YUO	EOL-2	EK.04.05	SP-FUO SP-PUO
SP-YUP	EOL-VLA Special	E19	SP-PUP
SP-YUR	EOL-Special	E18	
SP-YUT	EOL-2	EK.05.6	SP-FUT
SP-YUU	EOL-2 R912	EK.03.4	SP-FUU
SP-YUX	T-131PA Jungmann	104	SP-FUX
SP-YUZ	TL Ultralight TL-32 Typhoon (Res 10.04)	92A018	OK-YUU 10
SP-YVD	Cessna 177 Cardinal (Cr. 15.6.04)	17700180	(SP-FVD) N2380Y
SP-YWA	Ekolot JK-05 Junior (Cr. 22.6.03)	05-02-03	
SP-YWB	Ekolot JK-05 Junior	05-01-11	
SP-YWS	3xtrim Special-07	E-45	
SP-YYP	Rotorway Exec 162F	6152	SP-FYP
SP-YYY	Yakovlev Yak-18	EM-005	SP-FYY SP-AOP(2)
SP-YZK	3xtrim 450 Ultra-07	E-40	
SP-YZN	CSS-13 Jungmann	420-37	SP-FZN SP-AHT(2) PLW-. . .
SP-YZR	Funk FK-9 TG	080	SP-FZR
SP-Y . .	LAMCO EuroCub 912UL (This appears to be a different aircraft to OH-U347 which is c/n CAH002-1016)	BAH002-1016	SE-YSF

Three-axis microlights:

AP-AAAA	Aeroprakt A-22 Vision	002	
AP-AAAB	Aeroprakt A-22 Vision	012	
AP-AAAC	Aeroprakt A-22 Vision	003	
AP-AAAD	EOL 2.R2	E16.17	SP-FUM SP-PUM
AP-AAAE	Zenair CH-701 STOL "Granit"	unkn	

Weight-shift microlights:

"Type" in this group is defined as the wing type. This group post-dates the PL- series with very few duplications of the 'last three'.

AP-MAAA	Libre II
AP-MAAB	Libre II
AP-MAAC	Hazard 1511
AP-MAAD	Alek
AP-MAAE	Alek
AP-MAAF	Alek
AP-MAAG	Alek
AP-MAAH	Alek
AP-MAAI	Stranger 15
AP-MAAJ	Alek
AP-MAAK	Alek
AP-MAAL	Alek
AP-MAAM	Alek
AP-MAAN	Alek
AP-MAAO	Alek
AP-MAAP	Alek
AP-MAAR	Alek
AP-MAAS	Alek
AP-MAAT	Alek
AP-MAAU	Alek
AP-MAAV	Alek
AP-MAAW	Alek
AP-MAAX	Alek
AP-MAAY	Alek
AP-MAAZ	Alek
AP-MABA	Nowakowski
AP-MABB	Nowakowski
AP-MABC	Nowakowski
AP-MABD	Alek
AP-MABE	Alek
AP-MABF	Alek
AP-MABG	Alek
AP-MABH	Alek
AP-MABR	Stream
AP-MABS	Nowakowski
AP-MABT	Nowakowski
AP-MABU	Stratus
AP-MABW	Moyes Extralite 137
AP-MABY	Orwat
AP-MABZ	Kanion Bravo
AP-MACA	Alek
AP-MACB	Alek
AP-MACC	Alek
AP-MACD	Alek
AP-MACE	Alek
AP-MACF	Hazard 15
AP-MACZ	Libre 3
AP-MAEE	Dobrzanski
AP-MBAA	Perkoz-1
AP-MBAB	XP-1 Kliper
AP-MBAC	XP
AP-MBAD	Wiraz II
AP-MBGK	Libre 3
AP-MBAE	Perkoz-2
AP-MBAF	Perkoz-2
AP-MBAG	Perkoz-2
AP-MBAH	XP-15
AP-MBAI	Perkoz-2
AP-MBAK	Wiraz
AP-MBAL	Perkoz-3
AP-MBAM	Buran-Perkoz-3
AP-MBAN	Tango
AP-MBAO	Stratus P-2
AP-MBAP	Libre II
AP-MBAU	Stratus P-2
AP-MBAV	Stranger
AP-MBAW	ESO / TL-22 Duo
AP-MBAX	Stream
AP-MBAY	Stranger
AP-MBAZ	Tango
AP-MBGK	Libre 3
AP-MBIA	Stratus P-2
AP-MBIB	Stranger
AP-MCAB	XP
AP-MCAC	Cosmos Chronos
AP-MCAD	Czibis
AP-MCAE	Stranger
AP-MCAF	Libre 3
AP-MGDA	Stream
AP-MGDB	Stranger
AP-MGDC	Stratus P-2L
AP-MGDD	Libre 3
AP-MGDK	Stranger
AP-MGDU	Stranger
AP-MGKT	Stranger
AP-MIAA	Type unknown
AP-MIAB	Type unknown
AP-MIAC	Type unknown
AP-MIAD	Type unknown
AP-MIAE	Type unknown
AP-MKAD	Stratus P.2S
AP-MKAI	Pipistrel / Hazard
AP-MKAR	XP-17
AP-MKEA	Libre III
AP-MKIA	Stratus P-2
AP-MKIB	La Mouette
AP-MKIF	Stratus P-2S
AP-MKII	Stratus P-2
AP-MKIK	Stratus P-2
AP-MKOT	Libre
AP-MKVH	Libre 2
AP-MKVR	Libre 3
AP-MLAA	Orwat
AP-MLAB	Stranger
AP-MLAC	Libre 2M2
AP-MLAD	Libre 3
AP-MLAE	Libre 2
AP-MLAF	Orwat
AP-MLAG	Orwat
AP-MLAH	Stranger 15

AP-MLDA	XP-14	
AP-MLDC	Ohar/1966	
AP-MLDE	Libre 3	
AP-MLDF	Z-80B	
AP-MLDG	Libre 2	
AP-MLDL	Ania	
AP-MLDN	Libre II	
AP-MLDO	Vega	
AP-MLDP	Libre 2	
AP-MLDR	Libre 3	
AP-MLDT	Libre 2	
AP-MLDU	Stratus P2-S	
AP-MLDW	Ohar	
AP-MLEA	Atlas	
AP-MLEB	Stratus	
AP-MLEC	Libre 3	
AP-MLED	Libre 3	
AP-MLEE	Libre 2	
AP-MLEF	Stranger	
AP-MLEG	Stranger	
AP-MLEI	Stranger	
AP-MLEH	Delta Wing	
AP-MLEK	Libre 2	
AP-MLEL	Type unknown	
AP-MLEM	Type unknown	
AP-MLEN	Libre 2	
AP-MLEO	XP-15	
AP-MLEP	Libre 3	
AP-MLER	Libre 3	
AP-MLES	Libre 3	
AP-MLEU	Libre 2	
AP-MLEV	Libre 2	
AP-MLEW	Ohar	
AP-MLEX	Zefir 2	
AP-MLEY	XP-17	
AP-MLEZ	Magic 177	
AP-MLFA	Orwat	
AP-MLFB	Orwat	
AP-MLUA	Stranger	
AP-MLUB	Stranger	
AP-MLUC	Stranger	
AP-MLUE	Stratus P-2	
AP-MLUF	Stranger	
AP-MLUG	Stranger	
AP-MLZA	Libre 3	
AP-MLZB	Libre 3	
AP-MLZC	Cosmos Chronos	
AP-MLZD	Libre 2	
AP-MLZE	ESO 14	
AP-MLZG	Libre III	
AP-MLZI	Stranger 14.8m	
AP-MLZJ	Libre II	
AP-MMIG	MG-3 Shaman 2	
AP-MNSC	Aeros-Stream	
AP-MPLM	Libre	
AP-MPZM	Type unknown	
AP-MPZR	Air Création XP 15	A99048-9051
AP-MRWG	Libre II	
AP-MRWL	Libre IIM	
AP-MRWM	Libre I	
AP-MSAO	Echo trike/Libre wing	
AP-MSUC	Libre II	
AP-MSUD	Stranger-Aeros	
AP-MSUF	Stranger-Aeros	
AP-MSWH	Libre II	
AP-MSWK	Type unknown	
AP-MSWS	Cosmos	
AP-MTRC	Air Création XP 17	A00142-0132
AP-MWAD	Stratus P-2	
AP-MWBL	Stratus P-2	
AP-MWST	Stratus P-2S	
AP-MZAA	Stratus P-2	
AP-MZAP	Stranger	
AP-MZGA	Atlas	
AP-MZGB	Stranger	
AP-MZGC	Stranger	
AP-MZGD	Atlas-21	
AP-MZGE	Atlas-21	
AP-MZGF	Atlas-21	
AP-MZGG	Stratus R3	
AP-MZGH	Libre II	
AP-MZGI	Atlas-21	
AP-MZGK	Z-84	
AP-MZGL	Atlas-21	
AP-MZGM	Hermes 17	
AP-MZGN	Stranger	
AP-MZGO	Lusus	

AP-LLEA ?	Moyes GTR-162
APL-WAB	Type unknown
APL-WSE	Type unknown

(The last two entries appear to have been simply re-painted from PL-WAB, -WSE and should possibly have become AP-MWAB, -MWSE)

PL-AAW	Libre II
PL-APB	Type unknown
PL-APG	Aero APT
PL-APH	Aero APT
PL-BAA	Plywajac
PL-BAE	Plywajac
PL-BAF	Plywajac
PL-BAG	Plywajac
PL-BAI	Plywajac
PL-BAK	Plywajac
PL-BAL	Plywajac
PL-BAM	Plywajac
PL-BAN	Plywajac
PL-BAO	Plywajac
PL-BAP	Libre II M2
PL-BAR	Libre II M2
PL-BAS	Stratus 2
PL-BAT	Plywajac
PL-BAU	Plywajac
PL-BAW	Plywajac
PL-BAZ	Plywajac
PL-BBA	Libre II
PL-BBB	Balans
PL-BBC	Stratus E-2
PL-BBD	Demon
PL-BBE	Kanion-G
PL-BBH	Kanion-K
PL-BBI	Express
PL-BBJ	'UP'
PL-BBK	Kanion-G
PL-BBL	Vega MX
PL-BBN	Type unknown
PL-BBO	Kanion-B
PL-BBP	Demon
PL-BBR	Balans
PL-BBS	Aero
PL-BBT	Libre I
PL-BBU	Kanion-H
PL-BBV	Kanion-K
PL-BBW	Demon
PL-BBX	Balans
PL-BBY	Weekend
PL-BBZ	Sensor
PL-BCA	Kanion-B
PL-BCB(1)	Kanion-I (Built 1985. Still in use?)
PL-BCB(2)	Air Création Racer SX-II (Rotax 462) (Also noted as AC Apollo SX-II)
PL-BCB(3)	Racer (Rotax 447)
	(Note: All three a/c have different CofR nos, but (2) and (3) , both of 1994, may be the same aircraft re-engined)
PL-BCC	Demon
PL-BCD	Kanion-H
PL-BCE	Libre II
PL-BCF	Stratus R-15
PL-BCG	Balans
PL-BCH	Kanion-K
PL-BCI	Demon
PL-BCJ	R-Z
PL-BCK	Demon
PL-BCL(1)	Demon (Out of use?)
PL-BCL(2)	Horizont
PL-BCM	Demon
PL-BCN	Kanion-B
PL-BCO	Kanion-H
PL-BCP	Demon
PL-BCR	Kanion-B
PL-BCS	Kanion-B
PL-BCT	Magic
PL-BCU	Magic
PL-BCV	Magic Kiss
PL-BCX	Magic Kiss
PL-BCY	Moyes GTR
PL-BCZ	Moyes GTR
PL-BXD	Libre II
PL-BXH	Kanion-B
PL-BXU	Libre II
PL-BYJ	Libre II
PL-BYS	Stratus P-2
PL-BYW	XP-15
PL-GDC	Type unknown
PL-GDG	Type unknown
PL-GDL	Stratus P2 (Cancelled?)
PL-GDP	"Aska" (Cancelled?)
PL-GDW	"Goosia" (Cancelled?)
PL-GWG ?	Aero 21 (Reported as SP-GWG in 7.94)
PL-INA	Libre II
PL-INO	Kannion-BM
PL-INZ	Libre II
PL-KIA	Type unknown
PL-KIC	Moyes XS142
PL-KID	Fecske
PL-KIE	Moyes XS155
PL-KIG	Moyes XS155
PL-KIL	Moyes GTR162
PL-KIR	Vega MX-2
PL-KRW	E-2 Minim
PL-KVA	Type unknown
PL-LDA	Anla
PL-LDB	Cross Rush
PL-LDD	Libre II
PL-LDF	Z-80B

PL-LDH	Libre II	
PL-LDI	Libre II	
PL-LDN	Libre II (Regn possibly used by another a/c 1996?)	
PL-LDR	Vega	
PL-LDS	Sokol	
PL-LDT	Vega	
PL-LDW	Ohar	
PL-LDX	Ohar	
PL-LDY	Ohar	
PL-LEG	Libre II M	
PL-LEL	Sierra	
PL-LEM	Kanion-B	
PL-LER	Libre IIM2	
PL-LET	Libre IIM2	
PL-LEW	Ohar	
PL-MIA	Libre IIPL (Szaman trike noted 8.97)	
PL-MIC	Type unknown	
PL-MID	Libre II	
PL-MIE	Stratus R-IIc	
PL-MIF	Stratus R-IIc	
PL-MII	Stratus R-IIc	
PL-MIK	Stratus E-2	
PL-MIL	Libre IIM2	
PL-MIM	Libre	
PL-MIP	FL-33	
PL-MIT	Stratus E-3	
PL-NSA	Libre IIPL	
PL-NSC	Stranger	
PL-NSJ	Horyzont M2	
PL-OLA	Libre II	
PL-OLL	Demon	
PL-OPA	Balans	
PL-OPB	Libre II	
PL-OPC	Moyes	
PL-OPD	Vega	
PL-OPE	Kanion-B	
PL-OPF	Libre II	
PL-OPG	Sawa	
PL-OPH	Kanion-B	
PL-OPI	Kanion-B	
PL-OPJ	Kanion-B	
PL-OPK	Libre II	
PL-OPL	Z-80	
PL-OPM	LibreII	
PL-OPN	Kanion-B	
PL-OPO	Kosmos	
PL-OPP	Kanion-B	
PL-OPR	Kanion	
PL-OPS	Aero	
PL-OPT	Z-80	
PL-OPU	Kanion-B	
PL-OPV	Horyzont M-2	
PL-OPW	Balans	
PL-OPX	Kanion-B	
PL-OPY	Kanion-B	
PL-OPZ	Balans	
PL-OVE	Demon	
PL-PIE	Stranger	
PL-PIG	Lilienthal	
PL-PIJ	Libre II M	
PL-PIK	La Moet	
PL-PIS	Racer	
PL-PIT	Magic IV	
PL-PKA	Kanion-B	
PL-PKB	Libre II	
PL-PKC	Libre II	
PL-PKD	Libre II	
PL-PKI	Libre II	
PL-PKJ	Kanion-B	
PL-PKL	Libre II	
PL-PNX	Type unknown	
PL-PTE	Ohar	
PL-PZU	Type unknown	
PL-RAB	Libre II	
PL-RAC	Kanion	
PL-RAD	Super	
PL-RAE	Libre II	
PL-RAF	Super	
PL-RAG	Atlas 21	
PL-RAH	Libre II	
PL-RAI	Hazard	
PL-RAJ	Racer SX-II	
PL-RAK	Atlas 21	
PL-RAL	Hazard	
PL-ROL	Kanion-B	
PL-ROW	Kanion-B	
PL-ROZ	Kanion-B	
PL-RWA	Libre II (Second trike noted with this regn 1996)	
PL-RWB	Libre I	
PL-RWC	Kanion-G	
PL-RWD	Magic IV	
PL-RWE	Demon	
PL-RWF	Kanion-K 160M	
PL-RWG	Libre II	
PL-RWH	Flaming	
PL-RWI	Libre II	
PL-RWJ	Kanion-G	
PL-RWK	Stratus E-2s	
PL-SAA	Kanion-K 160	
PL-SAB	Libre II	
PL-SAD	C 14 Radziecka	
PL-SAE	Demon	
PL-SAF	Demon	
PL-SAG(1)	Libre II	
PL-SAG(2)	Stranger	
PL-SAG(3)	LAK-16M (Motorised LAK-16 glider)	296
PL-SAH	Demon	
PL-SAI	Kanion-K 120	
PL-SAK	Expres	
PL-SAO	Libre II	
PL-SAP	Demon	
PL-SAR	Libre II	
PL-SIA	Aero	
PL-SID	Echo	
PL-SII	Kanion Tornado	
PL-SIJ	Demon	
PL-SIK	Kanion-B	
PL-SIL	Demon	
PL-SIP	Libre II	
PL-SIS	Demon	
PL-SIT	Magic	
PL-SIU	Libre II	
PL-SIV	Libre II	
PL-SIX	Stratus R150	
PL-SIY	JKanion-K 160	
PL-SIZ	Kanion-B	
PL-SUA	Slawuticz	
PL-SUB	Type unknown	
PL-SUC(1)	Libre II (VW-engined, re-engined as -SUC(3) or later AP-MSUC?)	
PL-SUC(2)	Plywajac	
PL-SUC(3)	Libre II (Buran-engined, ex -SUC(1) ?)	
PL-SUD	Stranger	
PL-SUE	Stranger	
PL-SWA	Vega	
PL-SWB	Magic	
PL-SWC	Magic	
PL-SWD	Balans (Also reported as type 'ML-1')	
PL-SWE	Stratus R-16	
PL-SWF	Slawuticz	
PL-SWG	Kanion-B	
PL-SWH	Stranger	
PL-SWI	Slawuticz	
PL-SZA	Libre II	
PL-SZB	Balans	
PL-SZC	Kanion-B	
PL-SZD	Stranger	
PL-SZE	Un-named type, WSK engine	
PL-SZF	Slawuticz	
PL-SZG	Stranger	
PL-SZI	Stranger	
PL-SZJ	Libre IIM	
PL-SZK	Stranger	
PL-SZL	Stranger	
PL-TAI	Magic	
PL-TAW	Libre II	
PL-TOA	UFO	
PL-TOC	UFO	
PL-TOF	UFO	
PL-TOG	UFO	
PL-TOH	Stratus P-2	
PL-TOJ	Libre II	
PL-TOK	UFO	
PL-TOL	Antonow (Reported as Chibis KHDZ-29 c/n 0105 - same a/c?)	
PL-TOM	UFO	
PL-TON	UFO	
PL-TOO	Antonow	
PL-TOR	Libre II	
PL-TOU	Stranger	
PL-TOW	UFO	
PL-TOZ	Libre II	
PL-TRG	Libre II	
PL-TRJ	Stratus P-2	
PL-TRK	Libre II	
PL-WAE	Hazard 15	
PL-WAF	Hazard 15	
PL-WAJ	Stratus E-3	
PL-WAO	Type unknown	
PL-WAR	Stratus E-3	
PL-WBH	Stratus P-2	
PL-WBI	Stratus P-2	
PL-WBL	Stratus P-2	
PL-WBO	Hazard 13	
PL-WBS	Hazard	
PL-WBT	Hazard	
PL-WBU	Stratus P-2	
PL-WBV	Stratus P-2 (Two photos show different trike type 1996, 1997)	
PL-WBW	Type unknown	
PL-WBY	Stratus P-2	
PL-WBZ	Z-80/96 (Zem-03)	
PL-WDF	Moyes GTR	
PL-WDG	Moyes GTR	
PL-WDI	Eros 175	
PL-WRA	Libre II	
PL-WRB	Zefir	

PL-WRC	Libre II
PL-WRD	Libre II
PL-WRE	Libre II
PL-WRF	Un-named type, Trabant engine
PL-WRH	Libre II
PL-WRI	Libre II
PL-WRJ	Libre II
PL-WRK	Un-named type, Trabant engine
PL-WRM	Libre II
PL-WRO	Libre II
PL-WRR	Libre II
PL-WRS	Racher
PL-WRT	Racher
PL-WSK	Type unknown
PL-ZOA	Stratus P-2

Finally, in a new experimental microlight series we have:

H5B14	Buccaneer II amphibian (Noted 5.04)	unkn

MOTOR-GLIDERS

SP-0001	SZD-45 Ogar	X-107	
SP-0003	SZD-45A Ogar	B-598	
SP-0005	SZD-45A Ogar (Dismantled .03)	B-599	
SP-0006	SZD-45A Ogar	B-602	
SP-0008	SZD-45A Ogar	B-603	
SP-0010	SZD-45A Ogar	B-605	
SP-0012	SZD-45A Ogar	B-643	
SP-0015	SZD-45A Ogar	B-646	
SP-0017	SZD-45A Ogar	B-651	
SP-0021	SZD-45A Ogar	B-654	SE-TLY SP-0018
SP-0024	SZD-45A Ogar	B-757	
SP-0025	SZD-45A Ogar	B-770	
SP-0026	SZD-45A Ogar	B-756	
SP-0028	SZD-45A Ogar	B-822	
SP-0029	SZD-45A Ogar	B-759	
SP-0031	SZD-45A Ogar	B-821	SP-0020
SP-0032	SZD-45A Ogar	B-823	SP-0030
SP-P044	Janowski J-2a Polonez (Status unknown)	unkn	
SP-0046	Janowski J-6 Fregate	001	SP-P046
SP-0047	SZD-45A Ogar	B-644	SP-0013
SP-P048	Janowski J-2B Polonez (Status unknown)	unkn	
SP-0049	Janowski J-6 Fregate	002	SP-P049
SP-0052	Aerotechnik L-13SDM Vivat	950608	D-KULT
SP-0053	Malgosia (Motorized Marganski MDM-1 Fox)	P-17	SP-P053 (SP-3607)
SP-8006	Bocian M2000 (Built from SZD-9bis Bocian c/n 809)	YL-005	SP-P054 SP-2398
SP-0055	Aerotechnik L-13SW Vivat	870209	OM-7105 OK-7105
SP-0057	Schempp-Hirth Ventus 2cT	73/227	
SP-0059	Schempp-Hirth Ventus 2cT	81/247	
SP-0060	Aerotechnik L-13SE Vivat	910420	OM-1303
SP-0061	Aerotechnik L-13SE Vivat	01/78	OM-8900
SP-0062	Aerotechnik L-13SDM Vivat	930509	D-KSDM OK-3905
SP-0063	Stemme S-10 (Reservation 10.03)	10-48	HB-2235

GLIDERS

SP-1433	SZD-12 Mucha 100	59	
SP-1492(2)	SZD-42-2 Jantar 2B (Code "HA")	B-873	HB-1492
SP-1493(2)	SZD-42-2 Jantar 2B (Code "RS")	B-874	(SP-3664) HB-1493
SP-1745	SZD-12 Mucha 100	W-13	
SP-1790	SZD-12A Mucha 100A	340	
SP-1797	SZD-12A Mucha 100A	347	
SP-1801	SZD-12A Mucha 100A	351	
SP-1813	SZD-12A Mucha 100A	363	
SP-1819	SZD-12A Mucha 100A	369	
SP-1823	SZD-12A Mucha 100A	373	
SP-1833	SZD-12A Mucha 100A	383	
SP-1844	SZD-12 Mucha 100	W-16	
SP-1847	SZD-10bis Czapla	W-21	
SP-1858	SZD-10bis Czapla	W-34	
SP-1937	SZD-12A Mucha 100A	398	
SP-1942	SZD-12A Mucha 100A	403	
SP-1960	SZD-12A Mucha 100A (Reservation 7.02)	F-421	
SP-1962	SZD-12A Mucha 100A	F-423	
SP-1975	SZD-12A Mucha 100A	F-436	
SP-1979	Fauvel AV-36C (Stored 5.02)	200/04	OE-0414
SP-1992	SZD-12A Mucha 100A	F-453	
SP-1999	SZD-12A Mucha 100A	F-460	
SP-2003	SZD-12A Mucha 100A	F-464	
SP-2007	SZD-12A Mucha 100A	F-468	
SP-2017	SZD-12A Mucha 100A	F-483	
SP-2021	SZD-12A Mucha 100A (Reservation 9.02)	F-482	
SP-2026	SZD-12A Mucha 100A	F-488	
SP-2033	SZD-9bis Bocian 1D	P-390	
SP-2105	SZD-22C Mucha Standard	271	
SP-2106	SZD-22C Mucha Standard	272	
SP-2107	SZD-22B Mucha Standard (Mod. to SZD-22C)	F-497	
SP-2124	SZD-22C Mucha Standard	F-542	
SP-2136	SZD-22C Mucha Standard	F-554	
SP-2139	SZD-22C Mucha Standard	F-559	
SP-2151	SZD-22C Mucha Standard	F-572	
SP-2160	SZD-22C Mucha Standard	F-582	
SP-2173	SZD-22C Mucha Standard	F-595	
SP-2239	SZD-22A Mucha Standard	269	
SP-2258	SZD-22C Mucha Standard	F-642	
SP-2259	SZD-22C Mucha Standard	F-643	
SP-2261	SZD-22C Mucha Standard	F-645	
SP-2263	SZD-22C Mucha Standard	F-647	
SP-2268	SZD-22C Mucha Standard	F-652	
SP-2278	SZD-22C Mucha Standard	F-664	
SP-2279	SZD-22C Mucha Standard (Dismantled .03)	F-665	
SP-2284	SZD-22C Mucha Standard (Cr. 2.5.02)	F-670	
SP-2287	SZD-22C Mucha Standard	F-662	
SP-2288	SZD-22C Mucha Standard	F-603	
SP-2291	SZD-22C Mucha Standard (Reservation)	F-606	
SP-2295-J	SZD-22C Mucha Standard	F-681	
SP-2296	SZD-22C Mucha Standard	F-682	
SP-2304	SZD-22C Mucha Standard	F-690	
SP-2312	SZD-22C Mucha Standard	F-698	
SP-2314	SZD-22C Mucha Standard	F-615	
SP-2315	SZD-22C Mucha Standard	F-701	
SP-2326	SZD-22C Mucha Standard	F-713	
SP-2328	SZD-22C Mucha Standard	F-715	
SP-2331	SZD-22C Mucha Standard	F-718	
SP-2334	SZD-22C Mucha Standard	F-721	
SP-2336	SZD-22C Mucha Standard	F-723	
SP-2339	SZD-22C Mucha Standard	F-746	
SP-2361	SZD-25A Lis	F-745	
SP-2375	SZD-24C Foka	W-157	
SP-2379	SZD-24C Foka	W-161	
SP-2380	SZD-24C Foka	W-162	
SP-2381	SZD-24C Foka	W-163	
SP-2383	SZD-24C Foka	W-168	
SP-2384(2)	SZD-24C Foka	W-179	
SP-2386	SZD-24C Foka	W-171	
SP-2390	SZD-24C Foka	W-185	
SP-2395	SZD-24C Foka	W-186	
SP-2396	SZD-24C Foka	W-187	
SP-2406	SZD-22C Mucha Standard	F-793	
SP-2409	SZD-30 Pirat	B-369	
SP-2410	SZD-30 Pirat	B-370	
SP-2415	SZD-24 Foka 4A (Reservation .03)	W-236	
SP-2416	SZD-24 Foka 4A	W-245	
SP-2417	SZD-24 Foka 4A	W-229	
SP-2419	SZD-24 Foka 4A	W-238	
SP-2423	SZD-24 Foka 4A (Mod. to 4M?)	W-247	
SP-2440	SZD-9bis Bocian 1D	F-849	
SP-2444	SZD-9bis Bocian 1D	F-853	
SP-2449	SZD-9bis Bocian 1D	F-858	
SP-2451	SZD-24 Foka 4A	W-234	
SP-2452(2)	SZD-30 Pirat	B-372	
SP-2454	SZD-24C Foka	W-217	
SP-2455	SZD-24C Foka	W-218	
SP-2456	SZD-24C Foka	W-219	
SP-2457	SZD-24C Foka	W-220	
SP-2458	SZD-24C Foka (Dismantled .03)	W-221	
SP-2459	SZD-24C Foka	W-222	
SP-2460	SZD-24C Foka	W-223	
SP-2480	SZD-21-2B Kobuz 3	W-268	
SP-2482	SZD-21-2B Kobuz 3	W-270	
SP-2500	SZD-21-2B Kobuz 3	W-287	
SP-2503	SZD-30 Pirat	W-290	
SP-2504	SZD-32A Foka 5	W-291	
SP-2509	SZD-30 Pirat	W-317	
SP-2512	SZD-24C Foka	W-210	
SP-2513	SZD-24C Foka (Reservation .03)	W-211	
SP-2514	SZD-30 Pirat	B-374	
SP-2516(2)	SZD-30 Pirat	B-376	
SP-2527	SZD-32A Foka 5	W-431	
SP-2530	SZD-32A Foka 5	W-434	
SP-2536	SZD-22C Mucha Standard	F-657	(SP-3654) SP-2536 SP-2272
SP-2537	SZD-36 Cobra	W-474	
SP-2540	SZD-39 Cobra 17	W-477	
SP-2541	SZD-22C Mucha Standard	F-565	SP-2145
SP-2542	SZD-9bis Bocian 1E	P-504	
SP-2543	SZD-9bis Bocian 1E	P-505	
SP-2545	SZD-30 Pirat	B-346	
SP-2548	SZD-30 Pirat	B-349	
SP-2549	SZD-30 Pirat	B-350	
SP-2551-Y	SZD-30 Pirat	B-377	
SP-2553	SZD-35 Bekas	X-100	
SP-2554	SZD-30 Pirat	B-378	
SP-2555-EI	SZD-30 Pirat (Dismantled .03)	B-379	
SP-2556-T	SZD-30 Pirat	B-380	
SP-2557	SZD-35 Bekas	X-101	
SP-2558	SZD-30 Pirat	B-355	
SP-2565	SZD-30 Pirat	B-387	
SP-2566	SZD-30 Pirat	B-388	
SP-2568	SZD-30 Pirat	B-390	
SP-2569-MR	SZD-30 Pirat	B-391	

SP-2570	SZD-30 Pirat	B-392	
SP-2572	SZD-30 Pirat	B-416	
SP-2573-C	SZD-30 Pirat	B-417	
SP-2574-AL	SZD-30 Pirat	B-418	
SP-2575-M	SZD-30 Pirat	B-419	
SP-2578	SZD-30 Pirat	B-422	
SP-2579	SZD-36 Cobra 15	W-556	
SP-2582	SZD-36 Cobra 15	W-560	
SP-2583-PW	SZD-48 Jantar Standard 2	X-134	
SP-2585	SZD-42-2 Jantar 2B	B-858	
SP-2586	SZD-42-2 Jantar 2B	B-859	
SP-2587	SZD-9bis Bocian 1E	P-555	
SP-2588	SZD-9bis Bocian 1E	P-556	
SP-2589	SZD-9bis Bocian 1E	P-557	
SP-2590	SZD-9bis Bocian 1E	P-586	
SP-2593	SZD-30 Pirat	B-450	
SP-2594-JB	SZD-30 Pirat	B-451	
SP-2595	SZD-30 Pirat	B-452	
SP-2596	SZD-30 Pirat	B-453	
SP-2598	SZD-30 Pirat	B-456	
SP-2601	SZD-30 Pirat	B-423	(SP-2581)
SP-2602-M	SZD-30 Pirat	B-482	
SP-2605-PS	SZD-30 Pirat	B-487	
SP-2606	SZD-30 Pirat	B-488	
SP-2608-OO	SZD-30 Pirat	B-484	
SP-2610	SZD-30 Pirat	B-511	
SP-2611	SZD-30 Pirat	B-521	
SP-2612-A	SZD-30 Pirat	B-522	
SP-2615	SZD-30 Pirat	B-525	
SP-2616	SZD-30 Pirat	B-526	
SP-2617-T	SZD-32A Foka 5	W-531	
SP-2621	SZD-32A Foka 5	W-536	
SP-2622	SZD-32A Foka 5	W-537	
SP-2623-X4	SZD-32A Foka 5	W-538	
SP-2624	SZD-32A Foka 5	W-539	
SP-2626-M	SZD-32A Foka 5	W-541	
SP-2627-7	SZD-32A Foka 5	W-542	
SP-2628	SZD-32A Foka 5	W-543	
SP-2630-H	SZD-30 Pirat	B-426	
SP-2631-Y	SZD-30 Pirat	B-448	
SP-2633	SZD-32A Foka 5	W-544	
SP-2639	SZD-9bis Bocian 1E	P-592	
SP-2640	SZD-9bis Bocian 1E	P-593	
SP-2641	SZD-9bis Bocian 1E	P-594	
SP-2643	SZD-22C Mucha Standard	F-576	SP-2155
SP-2645	SZD-40X Halny	X-106	
SP-2646	SZD-30 Pirat	B-554	
SP-2647-T	SZD-30 Pirat	B-555	
SP-2648-M	SZD-30 Pirat	B-556	
SP-2655	SZD-30 Pirat	B-589	
SP-2662	SZD-9bis Bocian 1E	P-621	
SP-2663	SZD-9bis Bocian 1E	P-622	
SP-2664	SZD-9bis Bocian 1E	P-623	
SP-2666	SZD-9bis Bocian 1E	P-630	
SP-2667	SZD-9bis Bocian 1E	P-631	
SP-2668	SZD-9bis Bocian 1E	P-632	
SP-2672-7	SZD-36A Cobra 15	W-653	
SP-2673	SZD-36A Cobra 15	W-654	
SP-2676	SZD-30 Pirat	B-592	
SP-2677	SZD-30 Pirat	B-593	
SP-2680	SZD-30 Pirat	B-571	
SP-2684-2K	SZD-36A Cobra 15	W-606	
SP-2685-PK	SZD-41 Jantar Standard	X-110	
SP-2686-W	SZD-41 Jantar Standard	X-111	
SP-2687	SZD-9bis Bocian 1E	P-643	
SP-2689	SZD-36ACobra 15	W-663	
SP-2692-IL	SZD-36A Cobra 15	W-675	
SP-2693	SZD-36A Cobra 15	W-676	
SP-2694-69	SZD-36A Cobra 15	W-679	
SP-2695	SZD-36A Cobra 15	W-681	
SP-2697	SZD-36A Cobra 15	W-706	
SP-2698	SZD-36A Cobra 15	W-707	
SP-2704	SZD-30 Pirat	S-03.03	
SP-2705	SZD-30 Pirat	S-03.17	
SP-2708	SZD-30 Pirat	S-02.24	
SP-2711-ET	SZD-30 Pirat	S-01.37	
SP-2714	SZD-30 Pirat	S-02.10	
SP-2715	SZD-30 Pirat	S-02.11	
SP-2716	SZD-30 Pirat (Dismantled .03)	S-02.12	
SP-2717-KW	SZD-30 Pirat	S-02.13	
SP-2719	SZD-30 Pirat	S-02.16	
SP-2720	SZD-30 Pirat	S-02.29	
SP-2721	SZD-30 Pirat	S-02.30	
SP-2723	SZD-30 Pirat	S-02.32	
SP-2724-JS	SZD-30 Pirat	S-02.35	
SP-2725-S	SZD-30 Pirat	S-03.50	
SP-2727-9	SZD-30 Pirat	S-03.31	
SP-2728	SZD-30 Pirat	S-03.35	
SP-2730	SZD-30 Pirat (Reservation 03)	S-03.37	
SP-2732-J	SZD-30 Pirat	S-02.45	
SP-2734	SZD-30 Pirat	S-04.06	
SP-2735-K	SZD-30 Pirat	S-04.13	
SP-2736	SZD-30 Pirat	S-04.14	
SP-2737	SZD-30 Pirat	S-04.15	
SP-2738	SZD-30 Pirat	S-04.16	
SP-2741	SZD-30 Pirat (Dismantled .03)	S-04.22	
SP-2743	SZD-9bis Bocian 1E	P-710	

SP-2744	SZD-9bis Bocian 1E	P-711
SP-2746	SZD-9bis Bocian 1E (Dismantled .03)	P-772
SP-2747	SZD-9bis Bocian 1E	P-773
SP-2751	SZD-9bis Bocian 1E	P-645
SP-2753	SZD-9bis Bocian 1E	P-647
SP-2754	SZD-9bis Bocian 1E	P-648
SP-2755	SZD-9bis Bocian 1E	P-649
SP-2758	SZD-9bis Bocian 1E	P-652
SP-2759	SZD-9bis Bocian 1E	P-653
SP-2760	SZD-9bis Bocian 1E	P-654
SP-2762	SZD-9bis Bocian 1E	P-656
SP-2763	SZD-9bis Bocian 1E	P-657
SP-2765	SZD-9bis Bocian 1E (Dismantled .03)	P-659
SP-2766	SZD-9bis Bocian 1E	P-660
SP-2767	SZD-9bis Bocian 1E	P-661
SP-2768	SZD-9bis Bocian 1E	P-662
SP-2769	SZD-9bis Bocian 1E	P-663
SP-2772	SZD-9bis Bocian 1E	P-666
SP-2774-IW	SZD-38A Jantar 1	B-621
SP-2776	SZD-9bis Bocian 1E	P-667
SP-2778	SZD-9bis Bocian 1E	P-669
SP-2779	SZD-9bis Bocian 1E	P-672
SP-2780	SZD-9bis Bocian 1E (Dismantled .03)	P-673
SP-2781	SZD-9bis Bocian 1E	P-674
SP-2784-DS	SZD-38A Jantar 1	B-619
SP-2789	SZD-38A Jantar 1	B-626
SP-2790	SZD-38A Jantar 1	B-627
SP-2792	SZD-38A Jantar 1	B-636
SP-2793-WA	SZD-38A Jantar 1	B-637
SP-2796	SZD-9bis Bocian 1E	P-677
SP-2797	SZD-9bis Bocian 1E	P-678
SP-2798	SZD-9bis Bocian 1E	P-679
SP-2799	SZD-9bis Bocian 1E	P-680
SP-2800	SZD-9bis Bocian 1E	P-681
SP-2801	SZD-9bis Bocian 1E	P-682
SP-2803	SZD-9bis Bocian 1E	P-684
SP-2804	SZD-9bis Bocian 1E	P-685
SP-2805	SZD-9bis Bocian 1E	P-686
SP-2806	SZD-9bis Bocian 1E	P-688
SP-2808	SZD-9bis Bocian 1E	P-690
SP-2809	SZD-9bis Bocian 1E	P-691
SP-2810	SZD-9bis Bocian 1E	P-692
SP-2811	SZD-9bis Bocian 1E	P-693
SP-2812	SZD-9bis Bocian 1E	P-695
SP-2813	SZD-9bis Bocian 1E	P-671
SP-2815	SZD-9bis Bocian 1E	P-697
SP-2816	SZD-9bis Bocian 1E	P-698
SP-2817	SZD-9bis Bocian 1E	P-699
SP-2818	SZD-9bis Bocian 1E	P-700
SP-2820	SZD-9bis Bocian 1E	P-702
SP-2821	SZD-9bis Bocian 1E	P-703
SP-2822	SZD-9bis Bocian 1E (Dismantled .03)	P-704
SP-2823	SZD-9bis Bocian 1E	P-707
SP-2824	SZD-9bis Bocian 1E	P-708
SP-2825	SZD-9bis Bocian 1E	P-709
SP-2827	SZD-30 Pirat	S-04.09
SP-2830	SZD-30 Pirat	S-04.29
SP-2831	SZD-30 Pirat	S-04.30
SP-2835	SZD-30 Pirat	S-04.39
SP-2837	SZD-30 Pirat	S-04.41
SP-2838	SZD-30 Pirat	S-04.42
SP-2839-T	SZD-30 Pirat	S-04.43
SP-2841	SZD-30 Pirat	S-04.45
SP-2842-01	SZD-30 Pirat	S-04.46
SP-2843	SZD-30 Pirat	S-04.47
SP-2844-M	SZD-30 Pirat	S-04.48
SP-2845-ES	SZD-30 Pirat	S-05.27
SP-2846	SZD-30 Pirat	S-05.28
SP-2848	SZD-30 Pirat	S-05.02
SP-2849	SZD-30 Pirat	S-05.03
SP-2850	SZD-30 Pirat	S-05.04
SP-2851-11	SZD-30 Pirat	S-05.05
SP-2852	SZD-30 Pirat	S-05.06
SP-2853	SZD-30 Pirat	S-05.07
SP-2854	SZD-30 Pirat	S-05.08
SP-2855	SZD-30 Pirat	S-05.09
SP-2856-V	SZD-30 Pirat	S-05.10
SP-2858	SZD-30 Pirat	S-05.12
SP-2859	SZD-30 Pirat	S-05.13
SP-2860	SZD-30 Pirat	S-05.14
SP-2861	SZD-30 Pirat	S-05.15
SP-2863	SZD-30 Pirat	S-05.24
SP-2866	SZD-30 Pirat	S-05.25
SP-2867	SZD-30 Pirat	S-04.36
SP-2869	SZD-30 Pirat	S-05.21
SP-2871	SZD-30 Pirat	S-05.32
SP-2872	SZD-30 Pirat	S-05.33
SP-2874	SZD-30 Pirat	S-05.35
SP-2875	SZD-30 Pirat	S-05.36
SP-2876	SZD-30 Pirat	S-05.47
SP-2877	SZD-30 Pirat	S-05.48
SP-2878-Z	SZD-30 Pirat	S-05.49
SP-2879	SZD-30 Pirat	S-05.50
SP-2880-NB	SZD-30 Pirat	S-06.01
SP-2881	SZD-30 Pirat	S-06.02
SP-2882	SZD-30 Pirat	S-06.03
SP-2883-K	SZD-30 Pirat	S-06.04

SP-2886	SZD-30 Pirat	S-06.50	
SP-2887	SZD-30 Pirat	S-07.17	
SP-2890	SZD-30 Pirat	S-07.37	
SP-2891	SZD-38A Jantar 1	B-616	
SP-2892	SZD-38A Jantar 1	B-671	
SP-2893	SZD-38A Jantar 1	B-675	
SP-2894	SZD-38A Jantar 1	B-666	
SP-2900-SM	SZD-38A Jantar 1	B-678	
SP-2903	SZD-36A Cobra 15 (Dismantled .03)	W-736	
SP-2904	SZD-36A Cobra 15	W-741	
SP-2905	SZD-36A Cobra 15	W-742	
SP-2906	SZD-36A Cobra 15	W-743	
SP-2907-X	SZD-36A Cobra 15	W-744	
SP-2908	SZD-36A Cobra 15	W-745	
SP-2909	SZD-36A Cobra 15	W-746	
SP-2911	SZD-36A Cobra 15 (Reservation 10.04)	W-748	
SP-2912	SZD-36A Cobra 15	W-749	
SP-2913-AG	SZD-38A Jantar 1	B-683	
SP-2918-L4	SZD-36A Cobra 15	W-751	
SP-2919-VV	SZD-36A Cobra 15 (Dismantled .03)	W-752	
SP-2920	SZD-36A Cobra 15	W-753	
SP-2921-Q	SZD-36A Cobra 15	W-754	
SP-2922-I	SZD-36A Cobra 15	W-755	
SP-2923-L4	SZD-36A Cobra 15 (Dismantled .03)	W-756	
SP-2924	SZD-36A Cobra 15	W-757	
SP-2925-X	SZD-36A Cobra 15	W-758	
SP-2931-X	SZD-30 Pirat	S-06.07	
SP-2932-H	SZD-30 Pirat	S-06.08	
SP-2933-V	SZD-30 Pirat	S-06.09	
SP-2935	SZD-30 Pirat	S-06.11	
SP-2936	SZD-30 Pirat	S-06.12	
SP-2938	SZD-30 Pirat	S-06.14	
SP-2939	SZD-30 Pirat	S-06.15	
SP-2941-TR	SZD-30 Pirat	S-06.17	
SP-2942	SZD-30 Pirat	S-06.18	
SP-2943-AC	SZD-30 Pirat	S-06.19	
SP-2944-T	SZD-30 Pirat	S-06.20	
SP-2946	SZD-30 Pirat	S-06.22	
SP-2947	SZD-30 Pirat	S-06.23	
SP-2948	SZD-30 Pirat	S-06.24	
SP-2949	SZD-30 Pirat	S-06.25	
SP-2950-71	SZD-30 Pirat	S-06.26	
SP-2951	SZD-30 Pirat	S-06.27	
SP-2954	SZD-30 Pirat	S-07.38	
SP-2955	SZD-30 Pirat	S-06.31	
SP-2959-MA	SZD-41-1 Jantar Standard	B-700	
SP-2962	SZD-36A Cobra 15	W-762	
SP-2963	SZD-36A Cobra 15	W-763	
SP-2964	SZD-36A Cobra 15	W-764	
SP-2966	SZD-36A Cobra 15	W-789	
SP-2967	SZD-36A Cobra 15	W-801	
SP-2968	SZD-36A Cobra 15	W-802	
SP-2969-W	SZD-36A Cobra 15	W-803	
SP-2970	SZD-36A Cobra 15	W-804	
SP-2971	SZD-36A Cobra 15	W-805	
SP-2972	SZD-30 Pirat	S-07.42	
SP-2973	SZD-30 Pirat	S-07.43	
SP-2974	SZD-30 Pirat	S-07.44	
SP-2975	SZD-30 Pirat	S-07.45	
SP-2976	SZD-30 Pirat (Dismantled .03)	S-07.46	
SP-2978	SZD-30 Pirat	S-07.34	
SP-2983	SZD-30 Pirat	S-07.49	
SP-2985	SZD-30 Pirat	S-08.01	
SP-2986	SZD-30 Pirat	S-08.02	
SP-2987	SZD-30 Pirat	S-08.03	
SP-2989-V	SZD-30 Pirat	S-08.05	
SP-2990	SZD-30 Pirat	S-08.11	
SP-2991	SZD-30 Pirat	S-08.12	
SP-2992-TP	SZD-30 Pirat	S-08.08	
SP-2997	SZD-30 Pirat	S-08.15	
SP-3001	SZD-30 Pirat	S-08.49	
SP-3004	SZD-30 Pirat	S-09.02	
SP-3006	SZD-30 Pirat	S-09.04	
SP-3007	SZD-30 Pirat	S-09.05	
SP-3008	SZD-30 Pirat	S-09.06	
SP-3009	SZD-30 Pirat	S-09.07	
SP-3011	SZD-30 Pirat	S-09.09	
SP-3012	SZD-30 Pirat	S-09.10	
SP-3014	SZD-30 Pirat	S-09.12	
SP-3015	SZD-30 Pirat	S-09.13	
SP-3016	SZD-30 Pirat	S-09.14	
SP-3020-3K	SZD-30 Pirat	S-09.18	
SP-3021	SZD-30 Pirat	S-09.19	
SP-3022	SZD-30 Pirat	S-09.21	
SP-3023	SZD-30 Pirat	S-09.22	
SP-3024-J	SZD-30 Pirat	S-09.23	
SP-3025	SZD-30 Pirat	S-09.24	
SP-3026-EB	SZD-30 Pirat (Dismantled .03)	S-09.25	
SP-3029	SZD-9bis Bocian 1E	P-729	
SP-3030	SZD-9bis Bocian 1E	P-730	
SP-3031	SZD-9bis Bocian 1E	P-731	
SP-3032	SZD-9bis Bocian 1E	P-732	
SP-3033	SZD-9bis Bocian 1E	P-735	
SP-3034	SZD-9bis Bocian 1E	P-736	
SP-3035	SZD-9bis Bocian 1E	P-737	
SP-3036	SZD-9bis Bocian 1E (Dismantled .03)	P-738	
SP-3037	SZD-9bis Bocian 1E	P-743	
SP-3038	SZD-9bis Bocian 1E	P-742	
SP-3039	SZD-9bis Bocian 1E	P-741	
SP-3040	SZD-9bis Bocian 1E	P-744	
SP-3042	SZD-9bis Bocian 1E	P-749	
SP-3043	SZD-9bis Bocian 1E	P-751	
SP-3044	SZD-9bis Bocian 1E	P-752	
SP-3046	SZD-9bis Bocian 1E	P-759	
SP-3047	SZD-9bis Bocian 1E	P-760	
SP-3048	SZD-9bis Bocian 1E	P-761	
SP-3050	SZD-41-1 Jantar Standard	B-702	
SP-3051-LZ	SZD-41-1 Jantar Standard	B-703	
SP-3052	SZD-41A Jantar Standard	B-728	
SP-3053	SZD-41A Jantar Standard	B-730	
SP-3054	SZD-41A Jantar Standard	B-731	
SP-3056-ZS	SZD-41A Jantar Standard (Dismantled .03)	B-729	
SP-3059-MF	SZD-41B Jantar Standard	X-125	
SP-3061-AO	SZD-42-2 Jantar 2B	B-869	
SP-3062-AW	SZD-42-2 Jantar 2B	B-864	
SP-3063	SZD-9bis Bocian 1E	P-745	
SP-3065	SZD-36A Cobra 15	W-806	
SP-3066-AJ	SZD-41A Jantar Standard	B-723	
SP-3067-A	SZD-41A Jantar Standard	B-725	
SP-3068	SZD-36A Cobra 15 (Dismantled .03)	W-580	(F-CCHM)
SP-3069	SZD-50-1M	X-127	SP-P069 SP-3069
SP-3070-ZM	SZD-41A Jantar Standard	B-732	
SP-3071-AP	SZD-41A Jantar Standard	B-733	
SP-3074-MR	SZD-41A Jantar Standard	B-736	
SP-3075	SZD-36A Cobra 15	W-775	
SP-3076-T	SZD-36A Cobra 15	W-794	
SP-3078	SZD-36A Cobra 15	W-808	
SP-3079	SZD-41A Jantar Standard	B-738	
SP-3080-M	SZD-48 Jantar Standard 2	W-848	
SP-3085-JM	SZD-36A Cobra 15 (Dismantled .03)	W-814	
SP-3087-V	SZD-36A Cobra 15	W-818	
SP-3088	SZD-36A Cobra 15	W-819	
SP-3090	SZD-36A Cobra 15	W-823	
SP-3093	SZD-36A Cobra 15	W-827	
SP-3094	SZD-36A Cobra 15	W-828	
SP-3095	SZD-36A Cobra 15	W-829	
SP-3096	SZD-36A Cobra 15	W-830	
SP-3097	SZD-36A Cobra 15	W-831	
SP-3098	SZD-36A Cobra 15	W-832	
SP-3099	SZD-9bis Bocian 1E	P-767	
SP-3100	SZD-9bis Bocian 1E	P-768	
SP-3101	SZD-9bis Bocian 1E	P-769	
SP-3102	SZD-9bis Bocian 1E	P-770	
SP-3103	SZD-9bis Bocian 1E	P-771	
SP-3104-TM	SZD-42-1 Jantar 2A	B-782	
SP-3105	SZD-9bis Bocian 1E	P-777	
SP-3106	SZD-9bis Bocian 1E	P-778	
SP-3107	SZD-9bis Bocian 1E	P-779	
SP-3109	SZD-9bis Bocian 1E	P-781	
SP-3110	SZD-9bis Bocian 1E	P-782	
SP-3111	SZD-38A Jantar 1	B-677	
SP-3112	SZD-30 Pirat	S-09.27	
SP-3113	SZD-30 Pirat	S-09.28	
SP-3115	SZD-50-2 Puchacz	X-129	
SP-3116-TK	SZD-42-2 Jantar 2B	X-131	
SP-3117-KA	SZD-48 Jantar Standard 2	W-846	
SP-3121-A	SZD-30C Pirat (Dismantled .03)	P-791	
SP-3123	SZD-30C Pirat	P-793	
SP-3125	SZD-30C Pirat	P-795	
SP-3129	SZD-30C Pirat	P-799	
SP-3131	SZD-30C Pirat	P-822	
SP-3134	SZD-30C Pirat	P-805	
SP-3135	SZD-30C Pirat	P-806	
SP-3136-21	SZD-30C Pirat	P-807	
SP-3137-22	SZD-30C Pirat	P-810	
SP-3138	SZD-30C Pirat	P-811	
SP-3140	SZD-30C Pirat	P-813	
SP-3141	SZD-30C Pirat	P-814	
SP-3145	SZD-30C Pirat	P-818	
SP-3146	SZD-30C Pirat	P-819	
SP-3147	SZD-30C Pirat	P-820	
SP-3149	SZD-30C Pirat	P-823	
SP-3150-VT	SZD-48 Jantar Standard 2	W-852	
SP-3151	SZD-48 Jantar Standard 2	W-849	
SP-3152-DG	SZD-48 Jantar Standard 2	W-878	
SP-3154	SZD-50-3 Puchacz	B-903	(SP-3081)
SP-3155	SZD-50-3 Puchacz	B-904	
SP-3157	SZD-50-3 Puchacz	B-906	
SP-3160	SZD-30C Pirat	P-825	
SP-3161	SZD-30C Pirat	P-826	
SP-3162	SZD-30C Pirat	P-827	
SP-3163	SZD-30C Pirat	P-828	
SP-3167	SZD-48-1 Jantar Standard 2	B-1102	
SP-3168-S	SZD-42-2 Jantar 2B	B-944	
SP-3170-MB	SZD-48-1 Jantar Standard 2	W-912	
SP-3172-LZ	SZD-48-1 Jantar Standard 2	B-999	
SP-3173-IF	SZD-48-1 Jantar Standard 2	B-1001	
SP-3174	SZD-48-1 Jantar Standard 2	B-1002	
SP-3177-HV	SZD-48-1 Jantar Standard 2	B-1005	
SP-3178-TT	SZD-48-1 Jantar Standard 2	B-1006	
SP-3179	SZD-48-1 Jantar Standard 2	B-1007	
SP-3181	SZD-50-3 Puchacz	B-959	
SP-3182-T	SZD-48-1 Jantar Standard 2	B-1103	

SP-3183	SZD-48-1 Jantar Standard 2	B-1106	
SP-3184-UT	SZD-48-1 Jantar Standard 2	B-1113	
SP-3185	SZD-48-1 Jantar Standard 2	B-1116	
SP-3186-HY	SZD-48-1 Jantar Standard 2	B-1117	
SP-3187-O	SZD-48-1 Jantar Standard 2	B-1121	
SP-3189-AB	SZD-48-1 Jantar Standard 2	B-1123	
SP-3190-MC	SZD-48-1 Jantar Standard 2	B-1124	
SP-3191-T	SZD-48-1 Jantar Standard 2	B-1146	
SP-3193	SZD-48-1 Jantar Standard 2	B-1148	
SP-3194-KL	SZD-48-1 Jantar Standard 2	B-1149	
SP-3195	SZD-48-1 Jantar Standard 2	B-1150	
SP-3196-MK	SZD-42-2 Jantar 2B	B-948	
SP-3197-RS	SZD-42-2 Jantar 2B	B-1069	
SP-3198-KS	SZD-42-2 Jantar 2B	B-1071	
SP-3199-AL	SZD-42-2 Jantar 2B	B-1072	
SP-3201	SZD-50-3 Puchacz	B-957	
SP-3202	SZD-50-3 Puchacz	B-965	
SP-3203	SZD-50-3 Puchacz	B-960	
SP-3204	SZD-50-3 Puchacz	B-961	
SP-3205	SZD-50-3 Puchacz (Dismantled .03)	B-962	
SP-3208	SZD-50-3 Puchacz	B-1080	
SP-3209	SZD-50-3 Puchacz	B-966	
SP-3210	SZD-50-3 Puchacz	B-969	
SP-3211-PJ	SZD-51-1 Junior	X-115	
SP-3212	SZD-48-1 Jantar Standard 2	B-1157	
SP-3213-ER	SZD-48-1 Jantar Standard 2	B-1158	
SP-3214-YY	SZD-52-0 Jantar 15	X-136	
SP-3215-VI	SZD-52-0 Jantar 15	X-137	SP-3294(1)
SP-3216-YY	SZD-42-2 Jantar 2B	B-1311	
SP-3218	SZD-48-1 Jantar Standard 2	B-1199	
SP-3219	SZD-48-1 Jantar Standard 2	B-1200	
SP-3220-I	SZD-48-1 Jantar Standard 2	B-1201	
SP-3221-LX	SZD-48-1 Jantar Standard 2	B-1202	
SP-3223-FL	SZD-48-1 Jantar Standard 2	B-1204	
SP-3224-ZJ	SZD-48-1 Jantar Standard 2 (Dismantled .03)	B-1260	
SP-3225-TT	SZD-48-3 Jantar Standard 3	B-1298	
SP-3226	SZD-48-3 Jantar Standard 3	B-1300	
SP-3227-BK	SZD-48-3 Jantar Standard 3	B-1301	
SP-3228-BC	SZD-48-3 Jantar Standard 3	B-1302	
SP-3231	SZD-48-3 Jantar Standard 3	B-1345	
SP-3233	SZD-50-3 Puchacz	B-981	
SP-3234-NI	SZD-50-3 Puchacz	B-982	
SP-3235	SZD-50-3 Puchacz	B-983	
SP-3236	SZD-50-3 Puchacz	B-984	
SP-3238-FK	SZD-52-1 Jantar 15S	X-135	
SP-3240	SZD-52-3 Krokus S	X-138	
SP-3241	SZD-52-4 Krokus S	X-140	
SP-3244	SZD-52-3 Krokus S	X-139	
SP-3245-KM	SZD-52-4 Krokus	X-142	
SP-3246-TE	SZD-51-1 Junior	X-116	
SP-3248-17	SZD-48-3 Jantar Standard 3	B-1348	
SP-3251-IM	SZD-48-3 Jantar Standard 3	B-1351	
SP-3252-LK	SZD-48-3 Jantar Standard 3	B-1352	
SP-3253-BM	SZD-48-3 Jantar Standard 3	B-1353	
SP-3254-I	SZD-42-2 Jantar 2B	B-1320	
SP-3255-SZ	SZD-42-2 Jantar 2B	B-1321	
SP-3256	SZD-50-3 Puchacz	B-1338	
SP-3257	SZD-50-3 Puchacz	B-1339	
SP-3258	SZD-48-1 Jantar Standard 2	B-1178	
SP-3260-MI	SZD-48-3 Jantar Standard 3	B-1355	
SP-3261-KG	SZD-48-3 Jantar Standard 3	B-1356	
SP-3262-D	SZD-48-3 Jantar Standard 3	B-1357	
SP-3263-TC	SZD-48-3 Jantar Standard 3	B-1359	
SP-3264	SZD-48-3 Jantar Standard 3	B-1360	
SP-3265-T7	SZD-48-3 Jantar Standard 3	B-1361	
SP-3267-A1	SZD-48-3 Jantar Standard 3	B-1365	
SP-3268	SZD-48-3 Jantar Standard 3	B-1366	
SP-3269-DW	SZD-48-3 Jantar Standard 3	B-1367	
SP-3270-JR	SZD-48-3 Jantar Standard 3	B-1358	
SP-3271-RA	SZD-48-3 Jantar Standard 3	B-1362	
SP-3272-KA	SZD-48-3 Jantar Standard 3	B-1368	
SP-3274	SZD-48-3 Jantar Standard 3	B-1370	
SP-3275	SZD-48-3 Jantar Standard 3	B-1371	
SP-3276	SZD-48-3 Jantar Standard 3	B-1374	
SP-3277-C1	SZD-42-2 Jantar 2B	B-1323	
SP-3278-HR	SZD-42-2 Jantar 2B	B-1375	
SP-3279-C3	SZD-42-2 Jantar 2B	B-1380	
SP-3280-C2	SZD-42-2 Jantar 2B	B-1382	
SP-3281	SZD-42-2 Jantar 2B	B-1485	
SP-3282	SZD-50-3 Puchacz	B-1385	
SP-3286	SZD-50-3 Puchacz	B-1393	
SP-3287	SZD-50-3 Puchacz	B-1468	
SP-3288	SZD-50-3 Puchacz	B-1469	
SP-3289	SZD-50-3 Puchacz	B-1476	
SP-3290	SZD-50-3 Puchacz	B-1477	
SP-3291	SZD-50-3 Puchacz	B-1484	
SP-3292-AA	SZD-48-3 Jantar Standard 3	B-1373	
SP-3293-ZK	SZD-48-3 Jantar Standard 3	B-1418	
SP-3295	SZD-48-3 Jantar Standard 3	B-1415	
SP-3296-AF	SZD-48-3 Jantar Standard 3	B-1431	
SP-3297-ET	SZD-48-3 Jantar Standard 3	B-1432	
SP-3298-LN	SZD-51-1 Junior	B-1495	(SP-3289)
SP-3300	SZD-51-1 Junior	B-1497	(SP-3291)
SP-3301	SZD-51-1 Junior	B-1498	
SP-3302-J	SZD-51-1 Junior	B-1499	
SP-3303-LK	SZD-51-1 Junior	B-1501	
SP-3304-1	SZD-51-1 Junior	B-1502	

SP-3305-BA	SZD-51-1 Junior	B-1615	
SP-3306-L	SZD-51-1 Junior	W-927	
SP-3307	SZD-51-1 Junior	W-928	
SP-3308	SZD-51-1 Junior	W-929	
SP-3309-YY	SZD-51-1 Junior	W-931	
SP-3310-DC	SZD-51-1 Junior	W-932	
SP-3311	SZD-51-1 Junior	W-933	
SP-3312-E	SZD-51-1 Junior	W-934	
SP-3313-P	SZD-51-1 Junior	W-935	
SP-3314	SZD-51-1 Junior	W-936	
SP-3315	SZD-51-1 Junior	W-937	
SP-3316	SZD-51-1 Junior	W-941	
SP-3317	SZD-51-1 Junior	W-943	
SP-3318	SZD-50-3 Puchacz	B-1544	
SP-3319	SZD-50-3 Puchacz	B-1545	
SP-3320	SZD-50-3 Puchacz	B-1546	
SP-3321	SZD-50-3 Puchacz	B-1547	
SP-3322	SZD-50-3 Puchacz	B-1548	
SP-3323	SZD-50-3 Puchacz	B-1549	
SP-3324	SZD-50-3 Puchacz	B-1550	
SP-3327-BB	SZD-42-2 Jantar 2B	B-1493	
SP-3328-HC	SZD-42-2 Jantar 2B	B-1556	
SP-3329	SZD-48-3 Jantar Standard 3	B-1504	
SP-3330-VI	SZD-48-3 Jantar Standard 3	B-1505	
SP-3331	SZD-48-3 Jantar Standard 3	B-1512	
SP-3332-CU	SZD-48-3 Jantar Standard 3	B-1507	
SP-3333-BZ	SZD-48-3M Brawo	B-1508	
SP-3335	SZD-48-3M Brawo	B-1510	
SP-3339	PW-2 Gapa	U-02	SP-P339
SP-3342	SZD-51-1 Junior	W-944	
SP-3343-P	SZD-51-1 Junior	W-945	
SP-3344-Y7	SZD-51-1 Junior	W-946	
SP-3345-SU	SZD-51-1 Junior	W-947	
SP-3346	SZD-51-1 Junior	W-953	
SP-3347-IH	SZD-51-1 Junior	W-954	
SP-3348-Cx	SZD-51-1 Junior	W-955	
SP-3349-ZG	SZD-51-1 Junior	W-956	
SP-3350	SZD-50-3 Puchacz	B-1553	
SP-3351	SZD-50-3 Puchacz	B-1594	
SP-3352	SZD-50-3 Puchacz	B-1595	
SP-3353	SZD-50-3 Puchacz	B-1596	
SP-3354	SZD-50-3 Puchacz	B-1597	
SP-3355	SZD-50-3 Puchacz	B-1598	
SP-3356	SZD-50-3 Puchacz	B-1599	
SP-3357	SZD-50-3 Puchacz	B-1600	
SP-3358	SZD-50-3 Puchacz	B-1602	
SP-3359	SZD-50-3 Puchacz	B-1603	
SP-3360	SZD-50-3 Puchacz	B-1611	
SP-3361	SZD-50-3 Puchacz	B-1612	
SP-3363	SZD-50-3 Puchacz	B-1604	
SP-3364	SZD-50-3 Puchacz	B-1605	
SP-3365	SZD-50-3 Puchacz	B-1606	
SP-3366	SZD-50-3 Puchacz	B-1609	
SP-3367	SZD-50-3 Puchacz	B-1610	
SP-3368-SW	SZD-42-2 Jantar 2B	B-1557	
SP-3369-JJ	SZD-42-2 Jantar 2B	B-1558	
SP-3370-C4	SZD-42-2 Jantar 2B	B-1559	
SP-3371-C5	SZD-42-2 Jantar 2B	B-1560	
SP-3372-ZO	SZD-42-2 Jantar 2B	B-1562	
SP-3373	SZD-48-3 Jantar Standard 3	B-1589	
SP-3374-FK	SZD-48-3 Jantar Standard 3	B-1590	
SP-3375-H2O	SZD-48-3 Jantar Standard 3	B-1591	
SP-3377	SZD-48-3 Jantar Standard 3	B-1640	
SP-3379-FY	SZD-51-1 Junior	W-964	
SP-3382-DH	SZD-48-3 Jantar Standard 3	B-1687	
SP-3383	SZD-48-3 Jantar Standard 3	B-1688	
SP-3384-Y3	SZD-48-3 Jantar Standard 3	B-1690	
SP-3387-EI	SZD-48-3 Jantar Standard 3	B-1705	
SP-3388-XT	SZD-42-2 Jantar 2B	B-1670	
SP-3389-ST	SZD-42-2 Jantar 2B	B-1671	
SP-3390-IV	SZD-42-2 Jantar 2B	B-1672	
SP-3391-C7	SZD-42-2 Jantar 2B	B-1673	
SP-3392	SZD-50-3 Puchacz	B-1621	
SP-3395	SZD-50-3 Puchacz	B-1624	
SP-3396	SZD-50-3 Puchacz	B-1625	
SP-3397-T	SZD-50-3 Puchacz	B-1628	
SP-3398	SZD-50-3 Puchacz (Crashed 29.2.00)	B-1630	
SP-3399	SZD-50-3 Puchacz	B-1631	
SP-3400	SZD-50-3 Puchacz	B-1632	
SP-3403	SZD-50-3 Puchacz	B-1635	
SP-3404	SZD-50-3 Puchacz	B-1636	
SP-3405	SZD-50-3 Puchacz	B-1717	
SP-3406	SZD-50-3 Puchacz	B-1718	
SP-3407	SZD-50-3 Puchacz	B-1719	
SP-3408	SZD-50-3 Puchacz	B-1728	
SP-3409	SZD-50-3 Puchacz	B-1730	
SP-3410	SZD-50-3 Puchacz	B-1731	
SP-3411	SZD-50-3 Puchacz	B-1732	
SP-3412-V	SZD-51-1 Junior	B-1767	
SP-3413-PN	SZD-51-1 Junior	B-1771	
SP-3414-Y	SZD-51-1 Junior	B-1772	
SP-3415-M	SZD-51-1 Junior	B-1773	
SP-3416	SZD-51-1 Junior	B-1774	
SP-3417-RF	SZD-51-1 Junior	B-1777	
SP-3419	SZD-51-1 Junior	B-1779	
SP-3420-K	SZD-51-1 Junior	B-1780	
SP-3421-KVolt	SZD-51-1 Junior	B-1782	

SP-3422	SZD-51-1 Junior	B-1783	
SP-3423-EZ	SZD-51-1 Junior	B-1784	
SP-3424	SZD-51-1 Junior	B-1786	
SP-3425-V2	SZD-51-1 Junior	B-1787	
SP-3426- i	SZD-51-1 Junior	B-1789	
SP-3427-AB	SZD-51-1 Junior	B-1792	
SP-3428-JA	SZD-51-1 Junior	B-1793	
SP-3429-P	SZD-51-1 Junior	B-1794	
SP-3430-AC	SZD-51-1 Junior	B-1795	
SP-3431-R	SZD-51-1 Junior	B-1796	
SP-3432	SZD-51-1 Junior	B-1797	
SP-3433-FI	SZD-51-1 Junior	B-1798	
SP-3435	SZD-51-1 Junior	B-1800	
SP-3436-X	SZD-51-1 Junior	B-1801	
SP-3437-ME	SZD-51-1 Junior	B-1802	
SP-3438-A	SZD-51-1 Junior	B-1803	
SP-3439-R	SZD-51-1 Junior	B-1804	
SP-3440	SZD-51-1 Junior	B-1805	
SP-3441	SZD-51-1 Junior	B-1806	
SP-3443-TY	SZD-51-1 Junior	B-1808	
SP-3444-TH	SZD-48-3 Jantar Standard 3	B-1708	
SP-3445-HI	SZD-48-3 Jantar Standard 3	B-1709	
SP-3446-GT	SZD-48-3 Jantar Standard 3	B-1710	
SP-3447-LC	SZD-48-3 Jantar Standard 3	B-1711	
SP-3448-JW	SZD-48-3 Jantar Standard 3	B-1712	
SP-3449	SZD-48-3 Jantar Standard 3	B-1714	
SP-3451	SZD-48-3 Jantar Standard 3	B-1739	
SP-3452-DL	SZD-48-3 Jantar Standard 3	B-1885	
SP-3453	SZD-48-3 Jantar Standard 3	B-1886	
SP-3454-ZT	SZD-42-2 Jantar 2B	B-1675	
SP-3455-PC	SZD-42-2 Jantar 2B	B-1676	
SP-3456	SZD-42-2 Jantar 2B	B-1678	
SP-3457-P7	SZD-42-2 Jantar 2B	B-1679	
SP-3458	SZD-51-1 Junior	B-1809	
SP-3459-SJ	SZD-51-1 Junior	B-1810	
SP-3460-RS	SZD-51-1 Junior (Dismantled .03)	B-1811	
SP-3461	SZD-51-1 Junior	B-1812	
SP-3462	SZD-51-1 Junior	B-1813	
SP-3463	SZD-51-1 Junior	B-1837	
SP-3464-E	SZD-51-1 Junior	B-1838	
SP-3465-QM	SZD-51-1 Junior	B-1817	
SP-3466-AG	SZD-51-1 Junior	B-1820	
SP-3467-AP	SZD-51-1 Junior	B-1823	
SP-3468	SZD-51-1 Junior	B-1824	
SP-3469	SZD-51-1 Junior	B-1825	
SP-3470	SZD-51-1 Junior	B-1826	
SP-3471-4TH	SZD-51-1 Junior	B-1828	
SP-3472	SZD-51-1 Junior	B-1829	
SP-3473-TJ	SZD-51-1 Junior	B-1832	
SP-3474	SZD-51-1 Junior	B-1833	
SP-3476-H	SZD-51-1 Junior	B-1835	
SP-3477	SZD-51-1 Junior	B-1836	
SP-3478-SC	SZD-51-1 Junior	B-1839	
SP-3479	SZD-51-1 Junior	B-1842	
SP-3480	SZD-50-3 Puchacz	B-1734	
SP-3481-F	SZD-50-3 Puchacz	B-1736	
SP-3482	SZD-50-3 Puchacz	B-1862	
SP-3483	SZD-50-3 Puchacz	B-1863	
SP-3484	SZD-50-3 Puchacz	B-1864	
SP-3485	SZD-50-3 Puchacz	B-1865	
SP-3486	SZD-50-3 Puchacz	B-1866	
SP-3487	SZD-50-3 Puchacz	B-1867	
SP-3488	SZD-50-3 Puchacz	B-1868	
SP-3489	SZD-50-3 Puchacz	B-1871	
SP-3490	SZD-50-3 Puchacz	B-1872	
SP-3491	SZD-50-3 Puchacz	B-1873	
SP-3492	SZD-50-3 Puchacz	B-1874	
SP-3493	KR-03A Puchatek	01-01	
SP-3494	KR-03A Puchatek	01-02	
SP-3495	KR-03A Puchatek	01-03	SP-P495
SP-3496	KR-03A Puchatek	01-04	
SP-3497	KR-03A Puchatek	01-05	
SP-3498	KR-03A Puchatek	01-06	
SP-3500	PW-3 Bakcyl	L-01	SP-P500
SP-3503	SZD-51-1 Junior	B-1847	
SP-3504-EI	SZD-51-1 Junior	B-1848	
SP-3505-I	SZD-51-1 Junior	B-1855	
SP-3506-H	SZD-51-1 Junior	B-1856	
SP-3507	SZD-51-1 Junior	B-1857	
SP-3508-MM	SZD-51-1 Junior	B-1854	
SP-3509	SZD-51-1 Junior	B-1858	
SP-3510-AN	SZD-51-1 Junior	B-1914	
SP-3517	SZD-12A Mucha 100A	435	SP-1974
SP-3523	SZD-50-3 Puchacz	B-1973	
SP-3524	SZD-50-3 Puchacz	B-1980	
SP-3525	SZD-9bis Bocian 1D	F-812	SP-2401
SP-3527-AC	SZD-55-1	551191017	
SP-3529	Swift S1 (Dismantled .03)	P-05/P2	SP-P601
SP-3530	PW-2D Gapa	U-08	
SP-3531	PW-2D Gapa	U-09	
SP-3532	Swift S1	P-08/P-03	
SP-3534	SZD-25A Lis	F-730	SP-2346
SP-3538	SZD-48-3 Jantar Standard 3	B-1887	
SP-3539-SO2	SZD-48-3 Jantar Standard 3	B-1888	
SP-3540-VL	SZD-48-3 Jantar Standard 3	B-1889	
SP-3542-X1	SZD-48-3 Jantar Standard 3	B-1894	
SP-3543	SZD-48-3 Jantar Standard 3	B-1897	

SP-3544	KR-03A Puchatek	02-01	
SP-3545	KR-03A Puchatek	02-02	
SP-3546	KR-03A Puchatek	02-03	
SP-3547-S	KR-03A Puchatek	02-04	
SP-3548	KR-03A Puchatek	02-05	
SP-3549	SZD-12 Mucha 100A	F-463	SP-2002
SP-3550	KR-03A Puchatek	02-06	
SP-3551	KR-03A Puchatek	02-07	
SP-3552	KR-03A Puchatek	02-08	
SP-3553	KR-03A Puchatek	02-09	
SP-3554	KR-03A Puchatek	02-10	
SP-3555	KR-03A Puchatek	02-11	
SP-3556	KR-03A Puchatek	02-12	
SP-3557	KR-03A Puchatek	02-13	
SP-3558	KR-03A Puchatek	02-14	
SP-3559	KR-03A Puchatek	02-15	
SP-3562	SZD-38A Jantar 1	B-622	SP-2775
SP-3564-PV	SZD-56 Diana (Prototype)	X-147	SP-P564
SP-3572-J	SZD-50-3 Puchacz	B-1622	SP-3393
SP-3575	PW-5 Smyk (Reservation as SP-8005)	K-01	SP-P575
SP-3578-LOT	Schleicher ASH 25	25081	
SP-3588	LAK-12 Lietuva	6204	
SP-3589	PW-5 Smyk	17.02.001	SP-P589
SP-3590-F	PW-5 Smyk	17.02.002	SP-P590
SP-3595-A	Schleicher ASW 22	22063	D-4651
SP-3596	PW-2Dbis Gapa	U-19	
SP-3601	PW-2D Gapa	U-18	SP-P601
SP-3603-TS	PW-5 Smyk	17.03.003	(ZK-GWW)
SP-3605	SZD-12A Mucha 100A	344	SP-1794
SP-3611	SZD-9bis Bocian 1D	P-371	SP-2061
SP-3616	SZD-9bis Bocian 1D	F-835	SP-2425
SP-3617-BC	SZD-55-1	551196084	
SP-3618-E	PW-5 Smyk	17.04.006	
SP-3620	SZD-24C Foka (Reservation)	W-183	SP-2388
SP-3621-LOT	PW-5 Smyk	17.07.014	
SP-3622-F1	PW-5 Smyk	17.07.015	
SP-3623	Marganski MDM-1 Fox	215	SP-P619
SP-3626	SZD-9bis Bocian 1D	F-846	(SP-0051)
			SP-2437
SP-3627	SZD-24 Foka 4A	W-388	SP-2525
SP-3628	SZD-22C Mucha	F-506	SP-2116
SP-3630	SZD-24C Foka	W-137	SP-2365
SP-3631	PZL PW-6	78.00.00	SP-P631
SP-3633	PZL PW-5 Smyk	17.12.002	
SP-3634	SZD-24C Foka	W-188	SP-2092
SP-3635-V&P	Schleicher ASW 27	27104	
SP-3636	SZD-48-1 Jantar Standard 2	B-1056	DOSAAF
SP-3637	SZD-55-1	551198107	
SP-3638	SZD-48-1 Jantar Standard 2	B-1210	DOSAAF
SP-3645	SZD-32A Foka 5	W-546	BGA1690/CPC
SP-3648	SZD-48-3 Jantar Standard 3	B-1967	D-4401
SP-3650	PZL PW-5 Smyk	17.12.008	SP-3644
SP-3651	PZL PW-5 Smyk	17.12.007	SP-3643
SP-3652	SZD-30 Pirat	B-363	D-3759
			DDR-1759
			DM-1759
SP-3654	SZD-22C Mucha Standard (Reservation)	F-657	SP-2536
			SP-2272
SP-3657	PZL PW-6U	78.02.02	
SP-3659-JB	SZD-55-1	551194073	SP-3608
SP-3660	PZL PW-6U	78.01.01	
SP-3661	Bielsko 1 PW-5 Smyk	05.001.01	"N205PS"
SP-3662	Bielsko 1 PW-5 Smyk	05.001.03	
SP-3665	Rolladen-Schneider LS8-18	8384	
SP-3666	Bielskol 1 PW-5 Smyk	05.001.06	
SP-3667-AH	SZD-48-3 Jantar Standard 3	B-1449	HB-1781
SP-3670	Bielskol 1 PW-5 Smyk	05.001.07	
SP-3671	SZD-48-3 Jantar Standard 3	B-1694	DOSAAF
SP-3672	SZD-48-2 Jantar Standard 2B (Reservation)	B-1210	DOSAAF:
			95 blue
SP-3673	SZD-48-3 Jantar Standard 3	B-1660	DOSAAF
SP-3674	SZD-48-3 Jantar Standard 3	B-1517	DOSAAF
SP-3675	SZD-8ter-Z0 Jaskolka	256	OO-ZSE
SP-3676	PZL PW-6U	78.03.04	
SP-3677	PZL PW-6U	78.03.05	
SP-3678	SZD-48-3 Jantar Standard 3	B-1578	DOSAAF
SP-3679	SZD-48-3 Jantar Standard 3	B-1514	DOSAAF
SP-3680	SZD-48-3 Jantar Standard 3	B-1456	DOSAAF
			CCCP-1456
SP-3681	SZD-22C Mucha Standard	F-551	SP-2133
SP-3682	SZD-48-3 Jantar Standard 2	B-1663	D-2060
			DOSAAF
SP-3686	SZD-48-3 Jantar Standard 2	B-1236	DOSAAF
SP-3688	SZD-48-3 Jantar Standard 3	B-1522	DOSAAF
SP-3689	LAK-12 Lietuva	6144	
SP-3692	SZD-48-3 Jantar Standard 2B	B-949	LZ-610
SP-3693	SZD-55-1	551191018	SP-3526
SP-3694	SZD-48-1 Jantar Standard 2	B-1198	HA-4487
	(Reservation 10.04)		HB-1644
SP-3695	SZD-41 Jantar Standard	B-809	D-1958
	(Reservation 10.04)		HB-1396
SP-3696	SZD-51-1 Junior (Reservation 10.04)	B-1925	BGA3665/FZX
SP-3697	SZD-56-2 Diana	XB-01	
SP-....	SZD-48-1 Jantar Standard 2	W-880	SE-TRT

Gliders and motor-gliders with SP-80** registrations are on the "special" register- the equivalent of SP-Y** for powered aircraft

SP-8000	Marganski MDM-1 Solo-Fox	P-11	SP-3587
			SP-P587
SP-8002	MB-01 Jantar MB	Z-01	
SP-8003	SZD-9bis Bocian M	YL-001/P-344	SP-0045
			SP-P045
			SP-2048
SP-8004	SZD-39 Cobra 17	W-476	SP-2539
SP-8005	PW-5 Smyk	K-01	SP-3575
			SP-P575
SP-8007	HBV Diamant S4 16.5	020	N1144G
SP-8009	SZD-10bis Czapla	W-30	SP-1854
SP-8050	PW-4	S-02	SP-0050
			SP-P050
SP-8056	Janowski J-6 Fregata	003	SP-P056

SX - GREECE

Regn.	Type	C/n	Prev.Id.
SX-AAL(2)	Piper PA-32-301T Turbo Saratoga	32-8124004	HB-PFY
			N83166
SX-AAO	Air Tractor AT-301	301-0362	N2316T
SX-AAP	Air Tractor AT-301	301-0339	N653JC
SX-AAT	Cessna F172M	F17201313	D-EFAU(2)
			PH-JAK
			G-BCUI
SX-AAV	Piper PA-18-150 Super Cub	18-8271	N55WF
			N7155Z
SX-AAW	Cessna 172N	17271024	N1497E
SX-AAX	Cessna A188B Agtruck	18801851T	C-GYDL
			N70150
SX-AAY	Cessna A188B Agtruck	18802559T	C-GDTO
			N4822Q
SX-AAZ	Piper PA-31 Turbo Navajo	31-604	OY-BDK
			N6718L
			N6726L
SX-ABH	Glaser-Dirks DG-400	4-155	G-WRMN
SX-ABI	Reims/Cessna F182Q Skylane	F18200028	G-BEZM
			G-WALK
			G-BEZM
			F-WZDX
SX-ABJ	Piper PA-34-200T Seneca II	34-7670012	C-GGJA
SX-ABK	Piper PA-28R-180 Cherokee Arrow	28R-30319	N3971T
SX-ABL	Piper PA-46-350P Malibu Mirage	4636020	N9264X
SX-ABN	Grumman-American AA-5A Cheetah	AA5A-0142	N9742U
SX-ABR	Cessna 320E Executive Skyknight	320E0004	N6ER
SX-ABS	Piper PA-28-181 Cherokee Archer II	28-7890456	N30682
SX-ABW	Mooney M.20	1155A	C-GJBD
SX-ABZ	Piper PA-28-151 Cherokee Warrior	28-7615333	N211SA
			N6215J
SX-ACK	Cessna TP.206D Super Skylane	0522	D-EETG
			N8722Z
SX-ACL	Cessna 150H	15068330	N22516
SX-ACM	Beech B24R Sierra	MC-426	OO-EBS
			N1984L
SX-ACT	Piper PA-28R-200 Cherokee Arrow II	28R-7435103	N54425
SX-ACV	Piper PA-32R-301T Saratoga II TC	3257257	N5346S
SX-ADA	Auster Mk.5 (CofA expired)	1453	G-ANIP
			TJ394
SX-ADC	Beech 35 Bonanza (CofA expired)	D-1049	SX-EAC
			HB-ECO
SX-ADD	Piper PA-11 Cub Special (CofA expired)	11-1313	Turkey?
			49-2838
SX-ADE	SOCATA TB-9 Tampico Club	1424	F-GLFE
SX-ADF	Piper PA-11 Cub Special (CofA expired)	11-1298	Turkey?
	(Also quoted as 18-3744 and as 11-1638)		49-2823
SX-ADL	SOCATA MS.892A Rallye Commodore 150	10928	
SX-ADN	Cessna 180H	18051672	N2472F
SX-ADQ	Piper PA-18 Super Cub 95 (CofA expired)	18-1012	RHAF115315
	(Officially quoted with f/n 18-1084)		51-15315
SX-ADW	Piper PA-18-135 Super Cub	18-458	RHAF
			50-1802
SX-ADX	Piper PA-18-135 Super Cub	18-451	RHAF
	(Officially quoted with f/n 18-460)		50-1795
SX-AEC	SOCATA TB-9 Tampico	1435	F-GLFH
SX-AEL	Cessna 172N	17272266	C-GLGR
			N9446E
SX-AEP	Cessna F172N	F17201815	N9059H
			OY-CBZ
			(D-EOSS)
SX-AER	SOCATA TB-9 Tampico Club	1443	F-GIRN
			F-OGSZ
SX-AEV	SOCATA TB-9 Tampico	1016	F-GLAM
SX-AFD	SOCATA MS.892A Rallye Commodore 150	11443	
SX-AFG	Cessna F150G (CofA expired)	F150-0147	
SX-AFH	Piper PA-18 Super Cub (ex.PA-11)	18-3743	
	(CofA expired)		
SX-AFL	SOCATA MS.893A Rallye Commodore 180	11774	
SX-AFM	SOCATA MS.880B Rallye Club	1860	
SX-AFN	SOCATA MS.880B Rallye Club (CofA expired)	1861	
SX-AFO	SOCATA MS.894A Minerva 220 (CofA expired)	11830	F-BSML
SX-AFQ	Bölkow BO.209 Monsun	165	D-EAAE
SX-AFS	North American Navion 4 (CofA expired)	4-658	CS-ACP
			N8658H
SX-AFT	SOCATA MS.893E Rallye 180GT Gaillard	12181	
SX-AFU	Fuji FA-200-180 Aero Subaru	187	
SX-AFV	SOCATA MS.880B Rallye Club	2245	
SX-AFW	SOCATA MS.880B Rallye Club	2225	
SX-AFZ	Cessna A1888 Agtruck	18801085T	G-BBCV
			N21865
SX-AGA	Piper PA-28-140 Cherokee	28-23768	N3895K
SX-AGC	Piper PA-36-285 Pawnee Brave	36-7360040	N56349
SX-AGD	Piper PA-28-140 Cherokee	28-7425131	N54434
SX-AGE	SOCATA TB-9 Tampico	1434	F-GRBF
			EC-FLV
			EC-952
			F-GLFG
SX-AGH	SOCATA MS.880B Rallye Club	2478	
SX-AGI	Boeing Stearman PT-17 (N2S-5)	75-8499	SX-EAZ
			BuA43405
SX-AGJ	SOCATA MS.880B Rallye Club	2517	
SX-AGK	Piper PA-34-200 Seneca	34-7350113	G-BATO
			N15964
SX-AGM	SOCATA Rallye 150ST	2615	
SX-AGN	Piper PA-18-135 Super Cub	unkn	SX-ADY
	(Officially quoted with spare f/n 18-5000)		RHAF
SX-AGO	SOCATA MS.893E Rallye 180GT Gaillard	12637	
SX-AGR	SOCATA MS.892E Rallye 150ST (Wfu)	2694	
SX-AGT	SOCATA MS.892E Rallye 150ST	2665	
SX-AGU	Piper PA-18-135 Super Cub	unkn	SX-ADS
	(Officially quoted with spare f/n 18-5066)		RHAF
SX-AGV	Piper PA-25-235 Pawnee	25-2635	SE-FPZ
			OY-DDB
			SE-EIF
SX-AGX	SOCATA MS.892E Rallye 150ST	2749	(SX-AGS)
SX-AHA	Piper PA-18-135 Super Cub	18-3585	EI-195
			I-EIYO
			MM542385
			54-2385
SX-AHH	Brantly B-2	112	N5970X
SX-AHZ	Grumman-American AA-5A Cheetah	AA5A-0481	N26374
SX-AIA	Cessna F150J	F150-0475	HB-CTT
SX-AIB	Reims/Cessna F152-II	F15201505	F-BRQH
SX-AIJ	Piper PA-25-235 Pawnee	25-2039	4X-APW
			N6511Z
SX-AIK	Piper PA-25-235 Pawnee	25-4210	(SU- . . .)
			4X-APO
SX-AIR	Cessna A188B Agtruck	18803301T	N1957J
	(Reims-assembled with "c/n" 0021)		
SX-AJP	Pitts S-1S Special	IF-1	ZS-UHZ
SX-AJQ	Cessna 310Q	310Q0533	N7565Q
SX-AJT	Reims/Cessna FR172K Hawk XP	FR17200617	D-EJDP
			(F-GAQK)
SX-AJV	SOCATA TB-20 Trinidad	1665	F-OHDP
SX-AJW	Cessna 210	57007	G-ARDC
			N7307E
SX-AJX	Cessna 172L	17259874	N2874Q
SX-AJY	Piper PA-18-150 Super Cub	18-7609116	PH-NKI
			N83392
SX-AKH	Reims/Cessna F150L	F15000749	D-EKOD
			PH-LUO
SX-AKJ	Piper PA-28-161 Warrior II	28-7916367	5B-CEF
			N2228Y
SX-AKK	Reims/Cessna F172N (Ditched 8.8.01)	F17201844	
SX-AKL	Reims/Cessna F152-II	F15201631	
SX-AKP	Reims/Cessna F172M	F17201400	5B-CCU
			(SX- . . .)
			F-BSGY
SX-AKR	Reims/Cessna F172N	F17201876	F-WZIB
SX-AKU	Cessna F150H	F150-0295	D-ECXE
SX-AKV	Reims/Cessna F152-II (Ditched 2.9.01)	F15201689	N1661C
			F-WZIF
SX-AKW	Reims/Cessna F172N II	F17202025	(D-EHPP)
			F-WZIT
SX-AKX	Pitts S-1S Special	100	
SX-AKY	Cessna 172RG Cutlass RG	172RG0462	D-EIRF
			(N5189V)
SX-ALB	Reims/Cessna F172N	F17201936	F-WZIN
SX-ALD	Cessna 152-II	15282672	D-EOWL
			N89203
SX-ALE	Piper PA-38-112 Tomahawk	38-80A0117	G-BHZD
			N25381
SX-ALF	SOCATA MS.892E Rallye 150ST	2666	
SX-ALI	Piper PA-25-235 Pawnee	25-2040	5B-CDZ
			4X-APG
SX-ALM	Reims/Cessna F150M	F15001205	D-EEVI
SX-ALO	Piper PA-18-135 Super Cub (L-21B)	18-3544	RHAF
			54-2344
SX-ALQ	Piper PA-18-135 Super Cub (L-21B)	unkn	RHAF
	(Officially quoted with spare f/n 18-4924)		

SX-ALT	Piper PA-18-135 Super Cub (L-21B)	unkn	RHAF
	(Officially quoted with f/n 18-5096. Greek records also give the identity RHAF 53-4869 which should be L-21B c/n 18-2969)		
SX-ALV	Gardan GY-80 Horizon 180	214	F-BNYZ
SX-ALY	Reims/Cessna F152	F15201964	F-WZIB
SX-ALZ	SOCATA TB-9 Tampico	178	F-GCOT
SX-AMF	Reims/Cessna F152	F15201962	F-WZIA
SX-AMG	Piper PA-28-181 Cherokee Archer II	28-7790517	HB-PCL
			N5963V
SX-AMI	SOCATA TB-9 Tampico	356	F-GDBQ
SX-AML	Beech F33A Bonanza	CE-1106	N3021U
SX-AMM	Cessna 152-II	15280216	C-GZKY
			(N24325)
SX-AMO	Mooney M.20K Model 231 (Marks not carried)	25-0335	
SX-AMR	Snow Commander S.2D-600	1332D	4X-ASY
			SE-ENK
			(N1732S)
SX-AMS	Snow Commander S.2D-600	1375D	4X-AWI
			F-OGDE
			N1775S
SX-AMT	Snow Commander S.2D-600	1319D	4X-AWU
			ZK-CPK
			(N1719S)
SX-AMU	Snow Commander S.2D-600 (Wfu)	" 9702"	4X-AUM
SX-AMV	Snow Commander S.2D-600	1402D	4X-ASB
			N1787S
SX-AMX	Cessna 172M	17261361	N20523
SX-ANB	Cessna A188B Agtruck (Robertson mods)	18802548T	N4810Q
SX-ANE	SOCATA TB-10 Tobago	935	F-ODVB
SX-ANF	Piper PA-32 Cherokee Six	32-7740060	N3162Q
			(D-EIRF)
			N3162Q
SX-ANG	Cessna 150L	15074838	N10315
SX-ANL	SOCATA TB-20 Trinidad	984	F-ODVX
SX-ANM	Cessna A188B Agtruck	18802705T	N4971Q
SX-ANR	Cessna 150E	15060801	N6101T
SX-ANS	Cessna 150H	15067984	N7284S
SX-ANT	Cessna 172M	17264001	N21746
SX-ANU	Piper PA-32-300 Cherokee Six	32-7840022	N47989
SX-ANV	Cessna 172N	17267702	C-GDGW
			N73824
SX-ANW	Cessna 172N	17269164	C-GIXY
			N734WC
SX-ANY	SOCATA TB-9 Tampico	1075	F-ODTH(2)
SX-ANZ	Rockwell S.2D Snow Commander	1382D	4X-AWE
			C-GMAD
			N1766S
SX-AOA	Rockwell S.2D Snow Commander (Wfu)	1318D	4X-AWK
			(4X-AWF)
			N1720S
			YS-. . .
			N1720S
SX-AOB	Rockwell S.2D Snow Commander	1358D	4X-AWW
			ZK-CPQ
			(ZK-CTK)
			(N1758S)
SX-AOC	Rockwell S.2D Snow Commander (Wfu)	1354D	4X-AWC
			CF-UNR
SX-AOD	Rockwell Commander 112A	427	N1427J
SX-AOG	Cessna A188B Agtruck	18802608T	N6500L
			C-GWWX
			(N4872Q)
SX-AOI	Piper PA-18-150 Super Cub	18-7964	N4014Z
SX-AOL	Cessna A188B Agtruck	18802907T	SU-BHZ
			SX-AMA
			5B-CDE
			N731HK
SX-AOM	Cessna A188B Agtruck	18803312T	SU-IAB
			SX-AJC
			N1975J
SX-AOS	Cessna 421B Golden Eagle	421B0570	N224DR
	(Wfu, Hellenikon)		N80F
			N41033
SX-AOT	Piper PA-23 Apache	23-585	9J-RGC
			ZS-CRD
			VP -YOO
			N2013P
SX-AOU	Piper PA-32-260 Cherokee Six	32-1294	N4853S
SX-AOV	Cessna 172N	17271185	
SX-AOY	Piper PA-28-161 Cherokee Warrior II	28-7716228	N38156
SX-AOZ	SOCATA TB-9 Tampico	1026	F-ODRV
			SX-. . .
			F-ODTO
SX-APA	Cessna 172M	17261849	N12154
SX-APB	Cessna 150H	15068580	N22873
SX-APC	Piper PA-23-250 Aztec B	27-2310	N5251Y
SX-APD	Cessna 402	402-0055	N3255Q
SX-APE	Cessna 172P	17275547	F-GJCE
			N64338
SX-APG	Cessna A188B Agtruck	18801313T	N8812G
SX-APH	Cessna A188B Agtruck	18802750T	N731AT
SX-API	Beech 58 Baron	TH-970	N2034K
SX-APJ	Beech 200 Super King Air	BB-401	OY-JAO
			F-GBLG
SX-APK	Cessna 182E	18253630	N371VU
			N9230X
SX-APL	Cessna 172M	17265367	C-GSJL
			N5190H
SX-APM	Rand-Robinson KR.2	273	
SX-APO	Piper PA-28-140 Cherokee E	28-7225584	N15078
SX-APP	Piper PA-31-350 Chieftain	31-8152171	TF-ORF
			N4093G
SX-APQ	Cessna 182P	18261087	N7447Q
SX-APS	Cessna 152	15282810	G-BXUZ
			N89638
SX-APT	Piper PA-28-140 Cherokee E	28-7225257	N2865T
SX-APU	Cessna 411	411-0159	N4959T
SX-APV	Cessna 172N	17268819	D-ENEI (2)
			N734FK
SX-APW	Cessna 182E	18254349	D-EMBE
			N3349Y
SX-APZ	Cessna 172M	17266299	N9662H
SX-ARA	Piper PA-28-161 Warrior II	28-8316053	N4294Y
SX-ARB	Piper PA-28-161 Warrior II	28-8316078	N8238Q
SX-ARC	Piper PA-28-181 Archer III	2843188	N4130Q
			N41300
			(SX-ARC)
			N9508N
SX-ARD	Piper PA-28-161 Warrior III	2842158	N53453
SX-ARF	Cessna 172P	17276383	D-EBTH
			N98940
SX-ARG	Cessna T210L Turbo Centurion II	21060610	N37TF
			N31DF
			N1TF
			N8118L
SX-ARK	Piper PA-32R-301 Saratoga SP	3213012	G-HIHI
SX-ARL	Reims/Cessna F150L	F1500769	PH-LFE
			D-ECRC
SX-ARP	Piper PA-32R-301FT 6x	3232017	N3064J
SX-ART	Cessna 182F	18254663	F-BKQX
			N3263U
SX-ARV	Van's RV-6A (Officially c/n 20874)	20844	
SX-ASI	Cessna P210NPressurized Centurion	P21000190	D-EWOS
			N6571P
SX-ASP	SOCATA TB-9 Tampico	1262	I-IAEV
SX-ASZ	SOCATA TB-20 Trinidad	2088	F-OJBO
SX-ATB	SOCATA TB-20 Trinidad	1209	F-GNHC
			F-ODSQ
SX-ATC	Reims/Cessna F172M	F17201491	G-BEUR
			EI-BGE
			G-BEUR
SX-ATG	SOCATA TB-20 Trinidad	1799	F-OHUR
SX-ATH	Cessna 182S Skylane	182S80426	N2357D
SX-ATI	SOCATA TB-9 Tampico	925	F-GHZD
SX-ATK	SOCATA TB-20 Trinidad	1800	F-OHUS
			F-WWRB
SX-ATL	SOCATA TB-9 Tampico Club	1269	F-GKVG
SX-ATN	Cessna 172M	17265290	C-GNRL
			N64534
SX-ATS	SOCATA TB-20 Trinidad	1014	F-OHUV
			EC-FCE
			F-GHZN
SX-AVA	Piper PA-31T Cheyenne II	31T-8020026	N155DS
			N89CA
			N2473W
SX-AVB	Piper PA-31T Cheyenne II	31T-8020027	N2483W
			(N248WW)
			N2483W
SX-AVC	Piper PA-31T Cheyenne II	31T-8020038	N300HP
			N804CM
SX-AVD	Light Aero Avid Flyer IV	unkn	
SX-AVL	Diamond DA 20-A1 Katana	10182	N282DA
SX-AXD	Reims/Cessna F172N	F17201914	G-BZKB
			CS-AQW
SX-	Beech A24R	MC-426	OO-EBS
			N1984L
SX-. . .	Beech 58 Baron	TH-1341	N6342U
SX-. . .	Beech B200 Super King Air	BB-1493	N3015Q
SX-. . .	Cessna 152	15285705	N94528
SX-. . .	Reims/Cessna F172M	F17201091	OO-SKG
SX-. . .	Normand Dubé Aerocruiser	AND912-62	C-FQZR
SX-. . .	Piper PA-28-140 Cherokee Cruiser	28-7625029	N4420X
SX-. . .	Piper PA-28-140 Cherokee Cruiser	28-7725063	N5593F
SX-. . .	Piper PA-28-140 Cherokee Cruiser	28-7725065	N5766F
SX-. . .	Piper PA-44-180T Turbo Seminole	44-8107010	OY-BHN
			N8244T
SX-. . .	SOCATA TB-20 Trinidad	1315	F-GNHF
			F-OGSE
SX-BAO	Aérospatiale/Alenia ATR-72-202	326	F-GKOG
			F-WWLI
SX-BAR	BAC One-Eleven 215AU	096	N1130J
	(Wfu, stored)		N11181
SX-BBU	Boeing 737-33A	25743	EC-FMP
			EC-970
			N3519L
SX-BBX(2)	Fairchild Swearingen SA.227AC Metro III	AC-657	N26902
SX-BCA	Boeing 737-284 (Stored)	21224	
SX-BCB	Boeing 737-284 (Stored)	21225	
SX-BCC	Boeing 737-284 (Stored)	21301	
SX-BCD	Boeing 737-284 (Stored)	21302	N40112
SX-BCI	Boeing 737-284 (Stored)	22343	

SX-BCL	Boeing 737-284 (Stored)	22401	
SX-BDI	Piper PA-28-140 Cherokee E	28-7225175	N4608T N4502T
SX-BDK	Piper PA-28-140 Cherokee E	28-7325010	N15466
SX-BDL	Piper PA-23-250 Aztec E (Wfu)	27-7305081	N40268
SX-BDM	Piper PA-28-140 Cherokee F	28-7325007	N15149
SX-BDP	Reims/Cessna F152 (Wfu)	F15201634	F-WZID N1646Q
SX-BDQ	Reims/Cessna FA152 Aerobat	FA1520360	
SX-BDR	Reims/Cessna F152	F15201747	F-WZIH
SX-BDZ	Piper PA-44-180 Seminole	4496024	N4134R (SX-BDZ) N9526N
SX-BEM	Airbus A300B4-605R	603	B-2310 N166PL VH-YMB F-WWAV
SX-BFL	Piper PA-31-350 Navajo Chieftain	31-7952171	N64TT (N701RM) N64TT PH-SHA (PH-DAH) (N300SF) N300SM N27909
SX-BFU	Piper PA-31P Pressurized Navajo	31P-7530002	G-EHJM N54934 OE-FHT N54934 N54940
SX-BFW	Short SD.3-60	SH.3769	EI-COR G-ZAPG G-CPTL G-BOFI G-14-3739
SX-BFY	Boeing 737-35B	24238	D-AGEE
SX-BGH	Boeing 737-4Y0	23866	N4360W B-2969 EI-CMO VT-EWL TC-ADA
SX-BGJ	Boeing 737-4S3	25595	N280CD TC-APA 9M-MLG
SX-BGK	Boeing 737-3Y0	24679	9V-TRA
SX-BGN	Boeing 737-45D	28753	SP-LLG
SX-BGR	Boeing 737-408	25063	TF-FID
SX-BGS	Boeing 737-4Q8	26279	TC-AFM
SX-BGU	Fairchild Swearingen SA.227AC Metro III	AC-615B	EC-HJO N972GA VH-NEK N615AV
SX-BGV	Boeing 737-4Q8	26308	HL7235
SX-BGW	Boeing 737-31S	29264	D-ADBT N1795B
SX-BGY	Boeing 737-31S	29100	D-ADBR
SX-BGZ	Boeing 737-31S	29265	D-ADBU N1787B
SX-BHC	Dornier 228-200	8030	D-IDBB
SX-BHD	Dornier 228-200	8034	D-IDBE
SX-BHE	Dornier 228-201	8050	D-IDBR(1)
SX-BHF	Dornier 228-201	8057	D-CAPO(1)
SX-BHH	Dornier 228-201	8079	D-CLEC
SX-BHI	Dornier 228-201	8080	D-COLE
SX-BIA	Aérospatiale/Alenia ATR-42-300	169	F-WWEW
SX-BIB	Aérospatiale/Alenia ATR-42-300	182	F-WWER
SX-BIC	Aérospatiale/Alenia ATR-42-300	197	F-WWEE
SX-BID	Aérospatiale/Alenia ATR-42-300	219	F-WWEG
SX-BIE	Aérospatiale/Alenia ATR-72-202	239	F-WWED
SX-BIF	Aérospatiale/Alenia ATR-72-202	241	F-WWEA
SX-BIG	Aérospatiale/Alenia ATR-72-202	290	F-WWLQ
SX-BIH	Aérospatiale/Alenia ATR-72-202	305	F-WWLC
SX-BII	Aérospatiale/Alenia ATR-72-202	353	F-WWEK
SX-BIK	Aérospatiale/Alenia ATR-72-202	350	F-WWEG
SX-BIL	Aérospatiale/Alenia ATR-72-202	437	F-WWLC
SX-BIM	Aérospatiale/Alenia ATR-42-320	337	F-WQNQ TR-LFD F-OGXO F-WQHC N984MA F-WWLB
SX-BIN	Aérospatiale/Alenia ATR-42-320	291	F-WQNZ EP-ATR F-WWLZ
SX-BIO	DHC-8 Series 102	330	C-GZQZ LV-ZOD LV-POD N826MA C-GFHZ
SX-BIP	DHC-8 Series 102	347	C-GZRA LV-ZPM LV-PIB N849MA C-GEVP
SX-BIQ	DHC-8 Series 102	361	C-GZRD LV-ZIZ N859MA
SX-BIR	DHC-8 Series 102	364	C-GZRF LV-ZGB N865MA C-GFQL
SX-BIS	DHC-8 Series 106	355	OE-LLE C-GFEN
SX-BKA	Boeing 737-484	25313	
SX-BKB	Boeing 737-484	25314	
SX-BKC	Boeing 737-484	25361	
SX-BKD	Boeing 737-484	25362	
SX-BKE	Boeing 737-484	25417	
SX-BKF	Boeing 737-484	25430	
SX-BKG	Boeing 737-484	27149	
SX-BKH	Boeing 737-4Q8	24703	N407KW LN-BUB 9M-MJA
SX-BKI	Boeing 737-4Q8	24704	N405KW 9M-MJB
SX-BKK	Boeing 737-4Q8	25371	N404KW VR-CAA
SX-BKL	Boeing 737-4Y0	24915	9M-MJT OO-VDO 9M-MJP
SX-BKM	Boeing 737-4Q8	24709	N406KW 9M-MJG
SX-BKN	Boeing 737-4Q8	26281	N401KW
SX-BKY	Beech C90B King Air	LJ-1334	D-IIKY N22VK N5VN N5VK N8148N
SX-BLA	Boeing 737-33R	28869	N964WP
SX-BLM	Boeing 737-42C	24813	(D-ABDD) PH-BPF G-UKLF
SX-BLO	Embraer EMB-145LU	145426	
SX-BLP	Embraer EMB-145LU	145440	PT-. . .
SX-BLW	Boeing 757-236	24397	G-OOOS F-BRJD EC-ESC EC-349 G-BRJD
SX-BMC	Boeing 737-42J	27143	N734AB TC-JEA
SX-BMG	DHC-6 Twin Otter 300 floatplane	375	C-GHAZ F-GJDS TR-LDH C-FKDN F-GFAE SE-GEC
SX-BMK	Cessna 550 Citation Bravo	550-0907	HB-VMM N316MA N5155G
SX-BMM	Fairchild SA.227BC Metro III	BC-774B	N774MW XA-RXH N27617
SX-BMO	Fairchild SA.227AC Metro III	AC-430B	N788C N344AE N1014S XB-AEE N1014S
SX-BMP	McDonnell-Douglas DC-9-82	49279	OE-LMB
SX-BMS	Piper PA-31-350 Navajo Chieftain	31-7752122	HP-1049PS HP-1049P HP-1049 N27246
SX-BMT	Fairchild SA.227AC Metro III	AC-699	EC-GYB N458AM
SX-BNA	DHC-7 Series 102	90	C-GELW S5-ACA SL-ACA YU-AIE C-GFRP
SX-BNB	Piper PA-31P Pressurized Navajo	31P-48	N91884 OO-WNG (OO-RBR) (OO-UTP) F-BUTP HB-LGG N6844L
SX-BNE	Piper PA-44-180T Turbo Seminole (W/o 19.8.01)	44-8107012	OY-BHN N8244T
SX-BNI	Piper PA-31P Pressurized Navajo	31P-7400209	N7330L
SX-BNJ	BAe. Jetstream Series 3112	829	C-GMDJ G-BSIW G-OEDL G-OAKK G-BSIW HB-AED G-31-829 C-FCPG G-31-829
SX-BNK	Piper PA-32-301 Saratoga	32-8306005	N8301J
SX-BNL	Embraer EMB.110P2 Bandeirante	110224	N614KC PT-GMQ
SX-BNM	Cessna 421C Golden Eagle	421C0117	N3848C

SX-BNN	Fairchild SA.227BC Metro III	BC-771B	N771MW
			XA-RVR
			N71NE
SX-BOA	Boeing 717-2K9	55056	
SX-BOB	Boeing 717-2K9	55053	
SX-BOC	Boeing 717-23S	55065	
SX-BOG	Reims/Cessna FA150K Aerobat	FA1500063	SX-BDG
SX-BSA	Piper PA-34-200T Seneca II	34-7870044	N5151S
			C-GQYF
SX-BSB	Piper PA-34-200T Seneca II	34-7970282	N2851A
SX-BSI	SOCATA TB-10 Tobago (Wrecked)	101	G-EWBJ
SX-BSK	Piper PA-23-250 Aztec C	27-3473	C-FUSD
			CF-USD
SX-BSM	SOCATA TB-200 Tobago XL	1425	F-GLFF
SX-BSP	Piper PA-18-150 Super Cub	18-7667	N3899Z
SX-BSR	BAe. Jetstream Series 3102	718	G-OAKI
			N417MX
			G-31-718
SX-BSS	HS. 125-3A	25116	N726CC
			N345CT
			(N90SR)
			N345DA
			N136LK
			N93TC
			G-ATZN
SX-BST	Beech 1900D	UE-236	SE-KXY
SX-BSZ	SOCATA TB-20 Trinidad	466	F-OHDM
			F-GENE
SX-BTI	Fokker F.27-050	20103	PH-DMO
			OY-MBM
			PH-DMO
			OO-VLC
			PH-DMO
SX-BTK(2)	BAe. ATP	2005	G-MANM
			G-OATP
			G-BZWW
			(N375AE)
SX-BTV	Gates Learjet 55	55-124	N58CQ
			N58CG
			N39391
SX-BVA	Airbus A320-232	425	N340LA
			HC-BUH
			N340LA
			F-WWIX
SX-BVB	Airbus A320-231	1992	F-WWBJ
SX-BVC	Airbus A320-232	2016	F-WWBS
SX-BVL	Boeing 757-2G5	26278	G-JMCG
			D-AMUQ
SX-CVA	Lockheed 1011-385-3 Tristar	1246	C-FTSW
			V2-LEJ
			CS-TEF
			JY-AGI
			N48354
SX-CVB	Lockheed 1011-385-3 Tristar	1239	C-GTSR
			CS-TEA
			(CS-TTA)
SX-CVD	Lockheed 1011-385-3 Tristar	1236	C-GATM
			4R-ULA
			G-BLUT
			4R-ULA
SX-C . .	Lockheed 1011-385-1-15 Tristar	193N-1198	N102CK
			G-BHBM
SX-CVP	McDonnell-Douglas DC-10-15	48294	(SX-CPH)
			N9053N
			V2-LER
			OO-HPN
			V2-LER
			N1004A
			XA-MEW
			N1004A
SX-DCA	Dassault Falcon 2000EX/EASy	29	F-WWGD
SX-DCE	Cessna 560XL Citation Excel	560-5288	N5117U
SX-DCI	Cessna 560 Citation Ultra	560-0366	N52352
SX-DCM	Cessna 560XL Citation Excel	560-5051	N1324B
			N5226B
SX-DFA	Airbus A340-313X	235	F-WWJN
SX-DFB	Airbus A340-313X	239	F-WWJC
SX-DFC	Airbus A340-313X	280	F-WWJJ
SX-DFD	Airbus A340-313X	292	F-WWJB
SX-DKB	Britten-Norman BN-2A-36 Islander	2004	G-BESO
SX-DVA	Avro 146-RJ100	E-3341	(TC-RJA)
			G-6-341
SX-DVB	Avro 146-RJ100	E-3343	G-6-343
SX-DVC	Avro 146-RJ100	E-3358	G-6-358
SX-DVD	Avro 146-RJ100	E-3362	G-6-362
SX-DVE	Avro 146-RJ100	E-3374	G-6-374
SX-DVF	Avro 146-RJ100	E-3375	G-6-375
SX-ECG	Beech 200 Super King Air	BB-372	N4937M
SX-GEB	Sportavia-Pützer RF-5B Sperber	51070	D-KMPD
SX-GEO	Technoflug Piccolo B	065	D-KIMY
SX-HAQ	Bell 47G-4	3165	N1145W
SX-HAS	Enstrom 280C Shark	1044	
SX-HAY	MBB Bö.105S	S-389	D-HDLY

SX-HBA	Bell 47G-4	2861	SX-HAU
			G-BDRA
			N73944
SX-HBB	Hughes 369E	0427E	D-HFAZ
SX-HBF	Bell 206B Jet Ranger II	3003	
SX-HBR	Hiller UH-12E	5128	5B-CEH
SX-HBT	Aérospatiale AS.355F Ecureuil 2	5296	F-WZFL
SX-HBU	Bell 47G-4A	7682	G-AYAE
			N1489W
SX-HBW	Bell 47G-4A	7543	N1385X
SX-HBZ	Bell 47G-5	7930	N710KC
			N1452W
SX-HCC	Westland-Bell 47G3B1	WA/713	G-BHKW
			XW193
SX-HCD	Hiller UH-12E	2292	G-BDYY
			EI-BCA
			G-BDYY
			XS705
SX-HCE	Hiller UH-12E	2025	G-BFLR
			N706WA
			XB-NOS
			XA-TUF
			XB-XIU
			XC-CEC
SX-HCF	Agusta A.109A-II	7207	N71PT
			N4263A
SX-HCH	Bell 47G-4	3330	N1157W
SX-HCI	Hiller UH-12E	2007	N5339V
SX-HCJ	Hiller UH-12E	5150	N4030C
SX-HCK	MBB Bö.105S	S-593	D-HDQP(2)
			Sweden " 73"
			D-HDQP(2)
SX-HCL	Hiller UH-12E	HA-3021	N121HA
SX-HCM	Hughes 369HS	109-0204S	5B-CGY
			SU-BKJ
			JA9041
SX-HCP	Robinson R-22 Mariner	1620M	
SX-HCQ	Robinson R-22 Beta	1761	N40761
SX-HCR	Bell 206L-3 Long Ranger III	51559	SX-HOR ?
			N4048G
			C-FMTE
SX-HCS	Bell 47G-4	3145	JA . . . .
			VH-KHR
			C-FPVV
			CF-PVV
SX-HCT	Hiller UH-12E	5142	N32062
			JA7669
SX-HCU	Hiller UH-12E	5121	N32064
			JA7667
SX-HCW	Robinson R-22 Beta	1875	
SX-HCX	Bell 47G-5A	25079	N14808
SX-HCY	Bell 206B Jet Ranger II	3943	N3209V
SX-HCZ	Bell 206B Jet Ranger II	4233	C-FNYU
SX-HDA	Agusta A.109A-II	7422	
SX-HDC	Aérospatiale SA.341G Gazelle	1205	YU-HBG
SX-HDD	Agusta A.109A-II +	7431	D-HPLE
			JA9948
SX-HDI	Bell 206B Jet Ranger II	976	N823C
			N823H
			N83130
SX-HDL	Aérospatiale SA.341G Gazelle	1566	N7448Y
			9Y-TGU
SX-HDM	Bell 47J-2	2837	N73949
SX-HDP	Robinson R-22M2 Mariner	2724M	
SX-HDR	Agusta A.109E Power (W/o 17.6.02)	11060	
SX-HDT	Agusta A.109E Power	11066	
SX-HDV	Agusta A.109E Power	11096	
SX-HED	Hiller UH-12E	2164	G-BBLC
			N31702
			CAF112275
			RCAF10275
SX-HEE	Hiller UH-12E	2177	G-BBLE
			N31705
			(N31706)
			CAF112280
			RCAF10280
SX-HEG	Hiller UH-12E	5030	N530HA
SX-HEH	Bell 47G-5	25021	(SX-HBX)
			SU-BGS
			5B-CET
			SX-HAV
			OY-HAZ
			SE-HEC
SX-HEK	Bell 47G-4	3331	N1158W
SX-HEM	Aérospatiale AS.350B Ecureuil	1911	F-GIAN
			3A-MMD
			HB-XPZ
SX-HEO	Aérospatiale AS.355N Ecureuil 2	5646	
SX-HEP	Aérospatiale AS.355F2 Ecureuil 2	5110	(C- . . . .)
			N355DS
			N117SB
			N5081S
SX-HER	MBB Bö.105S	S-879	D-HTKH
			D-HMBV
			D-HFNK
SX-HES	Bell 430	49016	VP-BGS
			B-55532
			N6845C

SX-HET	MBB Bö.105CBS-4	S-864	D-HFHV
SX-HEV	Bell 206B Jet Ranger II	1468	OY-HBF
SX-HEW	Robinson R-22 Mariner	2516M	N83291
SX-HEX	Aérospatiale AS.355F2 Ecureuil 2	5394	F-WQIG
SX-HEZ	Bell 430	49007	N6283T
SX-HFA	Aérospatiale AS.355F2 Ecureuil 2	5563	F-WYMO
SX-HFB	Aérospatiale AS.355F2 Ecureuil 2	5565	F-WY . .
SX-HFC	Bell 407	53337	N8070Q
SX-HFD	MBB-Kawasaki BK.117C-2	7535	
SX-HFE	MBB-Kawasaki BK.117C-2	7536	
SX-HFF(2)	Aérospatiale AS.332L-1 Super Puma	2593	
SX-HIA	Aérospatiale AS.355F1 Ecureuil 2	5141	F-GOUT
			N5793Y
SX-HIB	Aérospatiale AS.355N Ecureuil 2	5258	(N . . . .)
			RP-C426
SX-HIG	Aérospatiale AS.355N Ecureuil 2	5586	RP-C8838
			RP-C8888
			F-OHND
SX-HIK	Bell 206B Jet Ranger II	4384	N9199C
SX-HIN	Aérospatiale AS.355F2 Ecureuil 2	5406	F-WQEE
SX-HJB	Robinson R-44 Clipper	0556	
SX-HJS	Aérospatiale AS.355F2 Ecureuil 2	5484	N909GS
			N838M
			9M-TAS
SX-HKA	Robinson R-44 Clipper	0550	
SX-HMJ	Hiller UH-12E	OH-23D	N96168
			55-4129
SX-HMK	MBB Bö.105	S-579	5B-CBE
			D-HDQB(2)
SX-HNA	Schweizer 269C-1	S-1691	N61460
			(N61376)
			(VT- . . .)
			N61376
SX-HNB	Schweizer 269C	S-1728	N41S
SX-HNM	Aérospatiale AS.355N Ecureuil 2	5547	F-GMRZ
SX-HNT	Robinson R-22 Beta	0517	N2297X
SX-HOB	Robinson R-22 Beta	0608	N2549C
SX-HOR	Robinson R-22M2 Mariner II	3414M	
SX-HPA	MBB Bö.105CBS-5	S-897	D-HSMA
SX-HPB	MBB Bö.105CBS-5	S-899	D-HSMB
SX-HPC	MBB Bö.105CBS-5	S-909	D-HSTR
SX-HPD	Eurocopter EC.135T1	0156	D-HECC
SX-HPE	Eurocopter EC.135T1	0158	D-HECF
SX-HPR	Schweizer 269C	S-1203	D-HOLL
SX-HPS	Eurocopter EC.135T1	0011	9M-TMP
			D-HTMP
SX-HRA	Robinson R-44 Astro	0494	
SX-HRB	Robinson R-22M2 Mariner II	2848M	
SX-HRC	Robinson R-22B2 Beta	3051	
SX-HRK	Robinson R-44 Clipper	0633	
SX-HRL	Hughes 269B	68-0371	N9532F
SX-HTG	Bell 230	23005	(N60856)
			9M-BCN
			N230E
			D-HHEH
			C-FPOI
SX-HTJ	Bell 206B Jet Ranger II	unkn	
SX-HTN	Robinson R-44 Astro	0742	
SX-HTO	Agusta A.109C	7671	D-HPMA
			N1TV
SX-HTR	Agusta A.109C	7656	I-CFBU
SX-HVA	Eurocopter EC.120B Colibri	1099	F-WQLO
SX-HVB	Eurocopter EC.120B Colibri	1101	F-WQLP
SX-HVC	Eurocopter EC.120B Colibri	1126	F-WQLY
SX-HVD	Eurocopter EC.135T1	0034	D-HECU
			UAE AF
SX-HVE	Eurocopter EC.120B Colibri	1143	F-WQOF
			F-WQDF
			F-WQOF
SX-HVF	Eurocopter EC.120B Colibri	1147	F-WQOG
			F-WQDL
			F-WQOG
SX-HVP	Robinson R-44 Raven II	10389	
SX-H . .	Aérospatiale SA.330J Puma	1611	ZS-HIZ
			VN-8606
			ZS-HIZ
SX-H . .	Agusta A.109C	7617	D-HAAP
			JA9989
SX-H . .	Bell 206BJet Ranger II	2433	D-HONY(2)
			N5002U
SX-H . .	Bell 206B Jet Ranger II	4320	N317CA
SX-H..	Enstrom 280-UK		G-MHCD
SX-H . .	Hiller UH-12E	2270	G-BEFY
			XS169
SX-H . .	MBB-Kawasaki BK.117C-1	7541	D-HSTP(2)
			D-HHTT(3)
SX-H . .	Robinson R-44 Raven II	10498	
SX-H . .	Sikorsky S-76	760136	N1548U
SX-KOS	Cessna 150M	15075897	G-BPMO
			N66177
SX-NAI	ERCO Ercoupe 415C	1477	N94154
			NC94154
SX-NGA	Piper PA-34-200T Seneca 11	34-8070213	N440GA
			D-GEMY
			D-IEMY
			N81993
SX-ROB	Robin R.3000/160	156	F-WWZE
			F-WWZU?

BALLOONS AND AIRSHIPS

SX-MAA	Cameron O-77 HAFB	145	
SX-MAB	Cameron D-50 Hot Air Airship	756	
SX-MAC	Reservation for Balloon		
SX-MAE	Aerotechnik AB8 (c/n as officially quoted but uncertain)	"90 05 28"	
SX-MAG	Lindstrand LBL-77A HAFB	624	
SX-MAL	Cameron C-80 HAFB	4335	
SX-MAN	Cameron N-77 HAFB	3295	G-BVOF
SX-MAW	Lindstrand LBL-77A HAFB	623	
SX-MOA	Sky 120-24 HAFB	60	
SX-M . .	Cameron Demestica SS HAFB	836	G-BLMO

GLIDERS AND MOTOR-GLIDERS

SX-106	Roda	unkn	YU-5180
SX-107	Chavka	unkn	YU-2149
SX-108	Roda	unkn	
SX-109	Focke Wulf Weihe	unkn	YU-4082
SX-110	Roda	unkn	YU-5219
SX-111	Chavka	unkn	YU-2235
SX-112	Chavka	unkn	
SX-113	Chavka	unkn	
SX-114	Chavka	unkn	
SX-116	Chavka	unkn	
SX-117	SZD-9bis Bocian 1D	P-378	
SX-118	SZD-9bis Bocian 1D	P-367	
SX-120	Schleicher ASK 13	13451	
SX-123	Glasflügel H303 Mosquito	95	
SX-125	Glaser-Dirks DG-100	100	N64790
SX-127	SZD-48-1 Jantar Standard 2	B-1114	
SX-128	SZD-48-1 Jantar Standard 2	B-1115	
SX-130	Schleicher ASK 21	21231	
SX-132	Schleicher K 7 Rhönadler	AB-02	D-8571
SX-133	ICA-Brasov IS-28M2A	60	G-BLWS
SX-134	Scheibe Bergfalke II/55	228	D-9085
SX-135	Schleicher Ka 6CR Rhönsegler	6516	D-0045
SX-136	Scheibe SF-25A Motorfalke	4510	D-KLOU
			(D-KAGO)
SX-137	LET L-13 Blanik	173448	YR-211
SX-138	LET L-13 Blanik	173419	YR-203
SX-140	LET L-23 Super Blanik	958220	
SX-141	Schleicher Ka 6CR Rhönsegler	6252A	D-4629
SX-142	Schleicher Ka 6CR Rhönsegler	6469	D-6372
SX-143	Schleicher Ka 6CR Rhönsegler	7188	D-6357
SX-144	Schleicher K.7 Rhönadler	7214	D-4634
SX- . . .	Scheibe SF-25A Motorfalke	4526	D-KAKA
SX- . . .	Scheibe SF-25B Falke	4695	D-KOSI

(See also SX-ABH)

MICROLIGHTS

SX- . . .	Aerial Arts 130SX	130SX-319	G-MNWH
SX- . . .	Mainair 503 Gemini Flash 2A	768-1289-W569	
SX- . . .	Mainair 462 Gemini Flash 2A	786-0590-W579	
SX- . . .	Mainair 582 Gemini Flash 2A	915-0792-W714	
SX- . . .	Solar Wings 462 Pegasus XL-Q	SW-WQ-0566/SW-TE-0428	
SX- . . .	Solar Wings 447 Pegasus XL-R	SW-WA-1177/SW-TB-1176	G-MTHM
SX- . . .	Solar Wings 462 Pegasus XL-R	SW-WA-1583/SW-TE-0440	
SX- . . .	Solar Wings 582 Quasar IITC	SW-WQT-0563/SW-TQD-0115	
SX- . . .	Solar Wings 582 Quasar IITC	SW-WQT-0587/SW-TQD-0127	
SX- . . .	Solar Wings 582 Quasar IITC	SW-WQT-0589/SW-TQD-0129	
SX-LS2	Hellenic Aeronautical Technologies LS2	unkn	

A new sequence for microlights was adopted with effect from August 1997 but so far only these examples have been reported:

HE-U100	Comco Ikarus Fox-C22	unkn
HE-U150 ?	Pegasus 582 Quantum 15 (Quoted as HE-VISO)	unkn
HE-U160	Fly Synthesis Storch	unkn

S5 - SLOVENIA

Regn.	Type	C/n	Prev.Id.
S5-AAA	Airbus A320-231	043	SX-BAS S5-AAA SL-AAA YU-AOA F-WWDO
S5-AAB	Airbus A320-231	113	SX-BAT S5-AAB SL-AAB YU-AOD F-WWIH
S5-AAC	Airbus A320-231	114	SX-BAU SL-AAC YU-AOE F-WWII
S5-AAD	Canadair CL.600-2B19 Regional Jet	7166	C-FZWS
S5-AAE	Canadair CL.600-2B19 Regional Jet	7170	C-GAIK
S5-AAF	Canadair CL.600-2B19 Regional Jet	7272	C-FMND
S5-AAG	Canadair CL.600-2B19 Regional Jet	7384	C-FMMT
S5-AAH	Canadair CL.600-2B19 Regional Jet	7032	HA-LNX OE-LRA C-FRKQ C-FMNW
S5-AAI	Canadair CL.600-2B19 Regional Jet	7248	G-DUOH G-MSKM OY-MBR G-MSKM C-FMMN
S5-AAJ	Canadair CL.600-2B19 Regional Jet	8010	C-FMMX
S5-BAA	Gates Learjet 35A	35A-618	SL-BAA YU-BOL N10871
S5-BAE	LET L-410UVP-E	902503	UR-67650 RA-67650 CCCP67650
S5-BAF	LET L-410UVP-E8C	912540	OM-WDA OK-WDA
S5-BAG	LET L-410AB Turbolet (Wrecked)	750409	OK-FDE
S5-BAX	Cessna S550 Citation S II	S550-0028	HB-VHH (N1260L)
S5-BAY	Cessna 525 CitationJet	525-0315	D-IAME D-IIRR
S5-BAZ	Cessna 560XL Citation Excel	560-5236	N236LD N51072
S5-BBB	Cessna 525A CitationJet 2	525A-0019	N67GH N57GH N51942
S5-CAE	Cessna 441 Conquest II	441-0150	SL-CAE YU-BMG (N2628B)
S5-CAF	Cessna 310F	310-0149	SL-CAF YU-BAJ (HB-LBN) (N5849X)
S5-CAG	Piper PA-34-200 Seneca	34-7250356	N15052
S5-CAL	Antonov An-2	1G178-53	CCCP62661
S5-CAN	Cessna 208B Grand Caravan	208B0810	N1223A N5262W
S5-CAO	Antonov An-2P	1G238-53	OK-VHA
S5-CAP	Antonov An-2P	1G132-54	HA-ANH
S5-CAR	Antonov An-2	1G186-51	CCCP54903
S5-CBW	Piper PA-34-200 Seneca	unkn	
S5-CER	Partenavia P.68C	231	G-BJRZ G-OAKP G-BJRZ
S5-CGB	Cessna 421A	421A0157	S5-CAB SL-CAB YU-BGE N3357Q
S5-CGC	Piper PA-31-350 Navajo Chieftain	31-7952153	S5-CAC SL-CAC YU-BMC (D-ILEE) N3529B
S5-CGS	Piper PA-46-350P Malibu Mirage	4636141	N146GS
S5-CMO	Beech C90A King Air	LJ-1360	N1560U
S5-DAA	Piper PA-38-112 Tomahawk	38-78A0476	SL-DAA YU-DEO D-EHSU N9702N
S5-DAB	Piper PA-28R-201T Turbo Arrow	2803011	SL-DAB YU-BPN N9198R
S5-DAC	Piper PA-28R-201T Turbo Arrow	2803012	SL-DAC YU-BPM N91782
S5-DAD	Maule MX.7-180 Star Rocket	11017C	SL-DAD N5658T
S5-DAE	Cessna U206B Super Skywagon	U206-0851	SL-DAE YU-BDL (N3851G)
S5-DAF	Reims/Cessna F172N	F17201781	SL-DAF YU-DDE
S5-DAG	Reims/Cessna F152	F15201529	SL-DAG YU-DFI N4996U
S5-DAH	Champion 7GCBC Citabria	289-70	SL-DAH YU-CAO
S5-DAI	Piper PA-18-150 Super Cub (C/n quoted as -7809103, current as N62639)	18-7909103	SL-DAI YU-DDV N9754N
S5-DAJ	Super Aero 145	19-11	SL-DAJ YU-BBL
S5-DAK	Piper PA-28-161 Cherokee Warrior II	28-7816379	SL-DAK YU-DEV D-ELAO N9538N
S5-DAN	Reims/Cessna F172M	F17200985	SL-DAN YU-DBF (D-EGBT)
S5-DAO	Piper PA-38-112 Tomahawk	38-78A0615	SL-DAO YU-DDP N9674N
S5-DAP	Champion 7GCBC Citabria	288-70	SL-DAP YU-CAN
S5-DAR	Piper PA-18-150 Super Cub	18-7809173	SL-DAR YU-DCG N84222
S5-DAS	Piper PA-38-112 Tomahawk	38-79A0446	SL-DAS YU-DDR N9683N
S5-DAT	Reims/Cessna F172H	F17200678	SL-DAT YU-BHI
S5-DAU	Piper PA-18-150 Super Cub	18-7909093	SL-DAU YU-DDU N9753N
S5-DAV	Piper PA-18-150 Super Cub	18-8475	SL-DAV YU-DBG OE-APT N4246Z
S5-DAW	Reims/Cessna F150L	F15000940	SL-DAW YU-DBE OE-ATK
S5-DAX	Cessna F172G	F172-0264	SL-DAX YU-BDS(2) OE-DLF(1)
S5-DAY	Piper PA-18-150 Super Cub	18-611	SL-DAY YU-DMG D-EFGE XB-PEF N1039A
S5-DAZ	Piper PA-38-112 Tomahawk	38-79A0258	SL-DAZ SL-DDM YU-DDM N9712N
S5-DBA	Cessna U206G Stationair (Identity unconfirmed)	U20603821	N9672G
S5-DBB	Bellanca 7KCAB Scout	507-75	SL-DBB YU-DME OE-AOR
S5-DBC	Champion 7GCBC Citabria	291-70	SL-DBC YU-CAT
S5-DBD	SOCATA MS.893A Rallye Commodore 180	11773	SL-DBD YU-DLB D-EAHI
S5-DBF	Piper PA-18-150 Super Cub	unkn	
S5-DBG	Piper PA-18-150 Super Cub	18-8493	SL-DBG YU-CXH N4263Z
S5-DBH	Piper PA-38-112 Tomahawk	38-78A0423	SL-DBH G-KING N9672N
S5-DBI	Piper PA-18-150 Super Cub	18-7809160	SL-DBI YU-DCE N82091
S5-DBJ	Cessna 172N	17272625	SL-DBJ YU-DEJ N6193D
S5-DBK	Piper PA-28-161 Warrior II	28-7916174	SL-DBK YU-DDS N9557N
S5-DBL	Piper PA-38-112 Tomahawk	38-78A0618	SL-DBL YU-DDI N9675N
S5-DBM	Piper PA-38-112 Tomahawk	38-79A0742	SL-DBM YU-DDN N9677N
S5-DBN	Piper PA-18-150 Super Cub	18-7909104	SL-DBN YU-DDW N9759N
S5-DBO	Zlin Z.526F Trenér Master	1316	SL-DBO YU-CDK OK-GRH
S5-DBR	Piper PA-25-235 Pawnee	25-2424	SL-DBR YU-BBB N6815Z
S5-DBS	Cessna TU206G Turbo Stationair 6- II (Reims-assembled with "c/n" 0009)	U20604717	SL-DBS YU-DIJ OE-DVT N732TB

S5-DBT	Piper PA-38-112 Tomahawk	38-78A0482	SL-DBT YU-DDL N9701N
S5-DBU	Piper PA-38-112 Tomahawk	38-79A0743	SL-DBU YU-DDK N9678N
S5-DBV	Piper PA-18-150 Super Cub	18-7809161	SL-DBV YU-DCD N82096
S5-DBW	Piper PA-32-300 Cherokee Six D	32-7140066	SL-DBW YU-BHM N4897S
S5-DBX	Reims/Cessna F172N	F17202021	SL-DBX YU-DFV
S5-DBY	Reims/Cessna F172N	F17201782	SL-DBY YU-DDG
S5-DBZ	Reims/Cessna F172H	F17200710	SL-DBZ YU-BHA OE-DLN
S5-DCA	Utva -75	unkn	SL-DCA YU-DEE JRV53108
S5-DCB	Utva -75	unkn	SL-DCB YU-DFA JRV53117
S5-DCC	Utva -75	unkn	SL-DCC YU-DLV JRV53207
S5-DCE	Utva -75	unkn	SL-DCE YU-DHM RV53198
S5-DCG	Utva -75	unkn	SL-DCG YU-DFS JRV53165
S5-DCH	Utva -75	unkn	SL-DCH YU-DIU JRV53210
S5-DCI	Utva-75	unkn	SL-DCI YU-DGF JRV53171
S5-DCJ	Utva -75	unkn	SL-DCJ YU-DHC JRV53188
S5-DCK	Utva -75	unkn	SL-DCK YU-DHE JRV53
S5-DCM	Utva -75	unkn	SL-DCM YU-DHP JRV53201
S5-DCN	Utva -75	unkn	SL-DCN YU-DJH JRV53223
S5-DCO	Utva -66	0806	YU-CDP JRV51103
S5-DCP	Utva -66	unkn	SL-DCP YU-DLK JRV51114
S5-DCR	SOCATA MS.893A Rallye Commodore 180	11670	D-EAHE
S5-DCS	Piper PA-28-140 Cherokee D	28-7125203	YU-DAZ N1821T
S5-DCT	Piper PA-38-112 Tomahawk	38-78A0479	YU-DDO N9732N
S5-DCU	Piper PA-18-150 Super Cub	18-7809167	YU-DCF N82188
S5-DCV	Piper PA-18-150 Super Cub	18-7909094	YU-DDT N9756N
S5-DCW	Piper PA-28-161 Warrior II	28-7916052	SL-DCW YU-DCW N21796
S5-DCZ	Piper PA-32-300 Cherokee Six	32-7540038	9H-AAI N32406
S5-DDA	Piper PA-18-150 Super Cub	18-8637	SL-DDA SL -CYV YU-CYV N4334Z
S5-DDC	Cessna 172N	17272614	SL-DDC YU-DEI N6151D
S5-DDD	Christen Pitts S-2B	5268	
S5-DDE	Piper PA-18-150 Super Cub	18-7809174	YU-DCH N82448
S5-DDF	Cessna 150L	15073255	SE-IRA OY-RPI N5355Q
S5-DDG	Cessna 172N	17272582	N5480D
S5-DDH	Cessna 150M	15076204	N66678
S5-DDI	Cessna 172N	17272307	N9982E
S5-DDJ	Piper PA-38-112 Tomahawk	38-78A0611	SL-DDJ YU-DDJ N9677N
S5-DDK	Maule MX.7-180 Star Rocket	11035C	D-ECQM(2) N61076
S5-DDM	Cessna 150M	15076219	N66701
S5-DDN	Beech C23 Sundowner	M-1797	N923JS F-OGNA N923JS F-OGHJ
S5-DDO	Maule MX-7-180 Star Rocket	11020C	D-ESHH PH-TZK (PH-ZCT) N56633
S5-DDP	Cessna F172E (Wrecked)	F172-0042	OE-DCP
S5-DDR	Cessna 172N	17268943	
S5-DDS	Bellanca 8GCBC Citabria	658-74	D-EBER(2)
S5-DDU	Cessna 172N	17270516	N739FV
S5-DDX	Cessna 172N	17271918	N5683E
S5-DDY	Cessna 172N	17270664	N739NB
S5-DDZ	Piper PA-38-112 Tomahawk	38-78A0382	N2137A C-GIYI
S5-DEA	Champion 7GCBC Citabria	290-70	YU-CAP(2)
S5-DEG	Reims/Cessna F172N	F17202014	SE-IFA
S5-DEH	Cessna 152	15284451	N6589L
S5-DEI	Cessna 172N	17270322	N738XR
S5-DEJ	Zlin Z.242L	0665	
S5-DEK	Zlin Z.242L	0666	
S5-DEL	Zlin Z.242L	0667	
S5-DEM	Piper PA-25-235 Pawnee C	25-7305526	9A-BIS RC-BIS YU-BIS N6784L
S5-DEN	Cessna 150M	15075919	N66207
S5-DEO	Piper PA-25-235 Pawnee C	25-7305547	9A-BIU RC-BIU YU-BIU N6826L N9657N
S5-DER	Zlin Z.142	0529	OK-WNI
S5-DES	Piper PA-28-161 Cherokee Warrior II	28-7816048	C-GQXS
S5-DET	Zlin Z.50M	0079	OK-. . . ZS-NEJ OK-WRP
S5-DEW	Robin DR.400/180R Remorqueur	1695	HB-KAV
S5-DEX	Cessna 172P	17275550	N64366
S5-DEY	Cessna 150M	15078573	C-GRXM N704FH
S5-DEZ	Cessna 172P	17275803	N65657
S5-DGA	Rockwell Commander 112A	256	C-GNUY
S5-DGB	SOCATA MS.893E Rallye 180GTGaillard	12129	I- SUDT
S5-DGC	Zlin Z.242L	704	
S5-DGD	Zlin Z.242L	705	
S5-DGE	Zlin Z.242L	706	
S5-DGF	Zlin Z.242L	707	
S5-DGG	Zlin Z.242L	708	
S5-DGH	Zlin Z.143	8	
S5-DGI	Zlin Z.143	10	
S5-DGK	Cessna 172SP	unkn	
S5-DGM	Yakovlev Yak-55M	920510	
S5-DGN	Piper PA-46-350PMalibu Mirage	4622148	D-EMVF N1221K N9235X
S5-DGS	Slingsby T-67M Mk.II Firefly	2018	HB-NBC G-BMIT
S5-DGW	Cessna 182T	18280987	N24630
S5-DGY	SOCATA Rallye 150ST	3140	S5-DCY 9H-AAY F-GBKP
S5-DHD	Cessna 172P	17275414	N63289
S5-DHH	Cessna 150L	15072668	N814DA N1368Q
S5-DHI	Cessna 150M	15077375	
S5-DHL	Cessna 172N	17271491	C-FJHA N3280E
S5-DHO	Reims/Cessna F172N	F17202013	D-EGOI
S5-DHP	Cessna 172N	71544	D-EADK N3428E
S5-DHT	Cessna 172N	17273706	N5112J
S5-DIC	Reims/Cessna F172N	F17201767	D-EFUH(2)
S5-DIO	Piper PA-28-181 Cherokee Archer II	28-7790024	C-GDIO N4382F
S5-DKB	Cessna P206 Super Skylane	P206-0113	C-GJMQ N2613X
S5-DKK	Cessna 182P	18261659	D-ECWW N21480
S5-DKL	Robin DR.400/180S Régent	1889	D-EKPT(2)
S5-DKR	SOCATA TB-9 Tampico	1834	F-GOIE 5N-CAP
S5-DKS	Robin DR.400/180R Remo 180	2198	OE-KLW
S5-DMA	Cessna 182S	18280001	N182NU
S5-DMC	Reims/Cessna F150L	F15000983	D-EJXG
S5-DMD	Zlin Z.242L	0657	
S5-DMG	Reims/Cessna F152	F15201920	SE-IHG
S5-DMI	Reims/Cessna F152	unkn	
S5-DML	Reims/Cessna F172N	F17201533	G-BEIB
S5-DMM	Cessna 172N	17270502	S5-DEE
S5-DMR	Piper PA-28-140 Cherokee E	28-7225071	C-GMMC N2398T
S5-DMS	Cessna 182G	18255279	D-EFQY N2079R
S5-DMT	Piper PA-28-140 Cherokee Cruiser	28-7725191	D-EAYZ N9620N
S5-DMV	Piper PA-36-300 Brave	36-7860087	9A-BLS RC-BLS YU-BLS N9697N

S5-DMY	Piper PA-23-250 Aztec	unkn	
S5-DNU	Cessna 182S	18280369	
S5-DOI	Cessna 172	unkn	
S5-DON	Yakovlev Yak-52	9010612	HA-JAN
			DOSAAF-54
S5-DPM	Utva -75	unkn	YU-DJE
			JRV53216
S5-DPP	Extra EA.300/L	140	G-IILI
			D-EXLB
S5-DSA	Cessna 172R	17280505	
S5-DSP	Piper PA-28R-200 Cherokee Arrow II	28R-7535092	YU-DMW
			OE-DSK
			N32809
S5-DSS	Cessna 152	15280199	9A-DAA
			SE-KEB
			LN-MTG
			N24293
S5-DST	Cessna 210	57472	N9672T
S5-DTA	Tecnam P.92JS Echo	unkn	
S5-DTT	Cessna 150G	15064767	N4717X
S5-D . .	Reims/Cessna F150L	F15001031	PH-VSG
S5-D . .	Cessna 150M	15076275	D-ETKO
			N6678Z
S5-D . .	Reims/Cessna F150M	F15001298	D-EMFL
S5-D . .	Reims/Cessna F152 (To S5-DMI?)	F15201756	SE-IBR
S5-D . .	Reims/Cessna F172M	F17201008	D-EWSG
			OE-KSG
			S-EJXE
S5-D . .	Reims/Cessna F172N	F17201710	D-EFEW(3)
S5-D . .	Cessna 172P	17276339	N98723
S5-D . .	Cessna 172RG Cutlass RG II	172RG1142	D-EDEM(3)
			ZS-LED
			N9376D
S5-D . .	Cirrus SR20	1203	N274CD
S5-D . .	Extra EA.300/L	140	G-IILI
			D-EXLB
S5-D . .	Piper PA-28-140 Cherokee	28-23548	SE-FCA
			N3419K
S5-D . .	Piper PA-34-220T Seneca III	34-8633014	N6788W
	(To S5-CBW?)		D-GAPA
			N9297Y
S5-D . .	SOCATA TB-9 Tampico	1834	F-GOIE
			5N-CAP
S5-D . .	Soko Galeb G-2	unkn	YU-YAD
			JRV23187
S5-D . .	Utva-66	unkn	YU-DLE
			JRV51108
S5-D . .	Cessna 172M	17266598	PH-WSD
			N80459
S5-HCA	Robinson R-22 Beta	0626	
S5-HCC	Bell 206B Jet Ranger III	2739	YU-HBW
			N2770H
S5-HCD	Schweizer S.269C	unkn	
S5-HCE (2)	Eurocopter EC.120B Colibri	1271	
S5-HCF	Enstrom F-28C	385	N663H
S5-HCH	Soko/Aérospatiale SA.341GGazelle	009	YU-HEF
			JRV12617
S5-HCM	Enstrom F-28C (Crashed, 1999?)	516-2	
S5-HCN	Agusta A.109E Power	11179	D-HARY(2)
S5-HCO	Enstrom F-28C	448	N51775
S5-HCR	Soko/Aérospatiale SA.341HGazelle	027	YU-HDP
			JRV12659
S5-HCW	Robinson R-22 Beta	1933	OE-XYY
			G-BTUP
S5-HCZ	Aérospatiale AS.350BAEcureuil	3053	RA-04101
			F-WQDR
S5-HGC	Bell 412EP	36093	N22909
S5-HKM	Bell 206B Jet Ranger II	4311	N2292E
S5-HMP	Canadian Home Rotors Safari	unkn	
S5-HPA	Agusta-Bell AB.412	25546	SL-HPA
			YU-HCX
S5-HPB	Agusta-Bell AB.212	5714	SL-HPB
			YU-HCJ
S5-HPD	Agusta-Bell 206B Jet Ranger III	8646	SL-HPD
			YU-HCV
			(G-BIZD)
S5-HPE	Agusta-Bell 206B Jet Ranger III	8643	SL-HPE
			YU-HCW
			(G-BIZC)
S5-HPG	Agusta A.109E Power	11224	
S5-HPK	Bell 206B Jet Ranger II	4403	N6276G
S5-HZJ	Bell 206B Jet Ranger II	4313	N2292J
S5-H . .	Agusta-Bell 206B Jet Ranger	8255	D-HAFW(3)
			OE-BXO(1)
S5-H . .	Enstrom 280FX	2005	N941SA
			C-FHOG
			N8626Z
S5-JAA	RAF-2000GTX	H2-94-5-151	C-FWIU
S5-KAM-SI	Schleicher ASH 25M	25209	
S5-KAY	DG Flugzeugbau DG-800B	unkn	
S5-KJJ	DG Flugzeugbau DG-505 Elan Orion	unkn	
	(Also marked S5-AMS01)		
S5-KKA	HOAC HK-36TTCSuper Dimona	36677	
S5-KKI	LET L-13M Motor-Blanik	unkn	
S5-KKJ	DG Flugzeugbau DG-800B	8-161B85	
S5-KKM	Glaser-Dirks DG-400/17	unkn	
S5-AMS01	DG Flugzeugbau DG-505 Elan Orion (see S5-KJJ above)		
S5-AMS02	Albastar Apis M	unkn	

HOMEBUILT AND KIT AIRCRAFT

S5-MAA	K1-Pajo	1	YU-ZAB
S5-MAB	Rand-Robinson KR-2	7531	YU-ZAM
S5-MAJ	Albastar Apis WR (ultralight glider)	A 004	
S5-MAK	Rand-Robinson KR-2	unkn	
S5-MAM	Zenair CH-701 STOL	7-1280	
S5-MAZ	Light Aero Avid Flyer STOL	1360	
S5-MBA	LIBIS/LET L.200 Morava	170717	YU-BAM
S5-MBB	Aero-3	unkn	YU-CPX
			JRV40199
S5-MBC	LET L-13M Blanik	026235	YU-5354
S5-MBF	Murphy Renegade Spirit	unkn	
S5-MBG	WagAero Sport Trainer	unkn	
S5-MBL	Piper PA-18 Super Cub	18-2034	OE-COR
			D-EMOR
			R-37
			52-2434
S5-MHE	Rotorway Exec 90	unkn	
S5-MJT	Cijan Kurier	unkn	YU-DAM
			JRV50174
S5-NAA	Light Aero Avid Flyer	592	YU-ZAL
S5-NAC	Light Aero Avid Flyer	598	YU-ZAK
S5-NAD	Light Aero Avid Flyer	891	
S5-NAE	Light Aero Avid Flyer	786	
S5-NAG	Light Aero Avid Flyer	319	
S5-NAH	Light Aero Avid Flyer	890	
S5-NAI	Light Aero Avid Flyer	882	YU-ZAR
S5-NAJ	Light Aero Avid Flyer	788	
S5-NAK	Light Aero Avid Flyer	595	YU-ZAJ
S5-NAL	Light Aero Avid Flyer	784	
S5-NAM	Light Aero Avid Flyer	669	
S5-NAO	Light Aero Avid Flyer	unkn	
S5-NAP	Light Aero Avid Flyer	unkn	
S5-NAT	Light Aero Avid Flyer	unkn	
S5-NAU	Light Aero Avid Flyer STOL	unkn	
S5-NAV	Light Aero Avid Flyer	791	
S5-NAX	Light Aero Avid Flyer STOL	unkn	
S5-NAZ	Light Aero Avid Mk IV STOL	unkn	
S5-NBA	Murphy Renegade Spirit	434	
S5-NBB	F.Works FW2C65 Capella	1105791	
S5-NBE	Kolb Twinstar Mk III	unkn	
S5-NBF	Fisher FP.404 Classic	unkn	
S5-NBG	Bagalini 0	unkn	
S5-NBH	EDA-V replica	unkn	
S5-NBI	Bagalini	unkn	
S5-NBJ	Funk FK-9	95	
S5-NBK	Eurofly Flash Light	unkn	
S5-NBP	Flight Team Sinus	unkn	
S5-NGF	Eurofly Flash Light	001	
S5-NHA	Rotorway Exec-90	unkn	
S5-NHB	Rotorway Exec-90	unkn	
S5-NHC	Rotorway Exec-90	unkn	
	(Two of these 3 Rotorway Execs sold to Italy .02)		
S5-NKA	Albastar Apis	unkn	
S5-NKB	Lastovka P01	unkn	
S5-NKC	Albastar Apis	unkn	
S5-NKD	Albastar Apis	TRA-003	
S5-NKR	Albastar/AMS Apis Future e-e	A015KE01	

BALLOONS AND AIRSHIPS

S5-OAA	Cameron 0-105 HAFB	2847	SL-OAA
S5-OAB	Cameron V-77 HAFB	2827	SL-OAB
S5-OAE	Cameron N-90 HAFB	1109	G-BPZT
S5-OAF	Cameron V-77 HAFB	2325	SL-OAF
			YU-OAF
S5-OAI	Cameron V-77 HAFB	2943	SL-OAI
S5-OAJ	Cameron N-90 HAFB	3152	
S5-OAK	Tomi AX8 HAFB	14/1994	
S5-OAL	Cameron V-77 HAFB	3319	
S5-OAM	Cameron C-80 HAFB	3417	
S5-OAN	Cameron V-77 HAFB	3469	
S5-OAQ	Tomi AX-8 HAFB	34/1966	
S5-OAR	Cameron O-77 HAFB	3538	
S5-OAS	Cameron V-77 HAFB	3539	
S5-OAT	Cameron 0-77 HAFB	3599	
S5-OAU	Tomi AX-7 HAFB	21/1995	
S5-OAV	Cameron N-77 HAFB	1222	LX-INT
S5-OAW	Cameron V-77 HAFB	1524	9A-OAE(1)
S5-OAY	Cameron N-77 HAFB	1726	LX-BUL
S5-OAZ	Cameron N-90 HAFB	3874	
S5-OBA	Cameron C-80 HAFB	3967	

S5-OBB	Head Balloons AX9-118 HAFB	252	
S5-OBC	Kubicek BB-22 HAFB	102	
S5-OBD	Kubicek BB-45 HAFB	114	
S5-OBE	Kubicek BB-22 HAFB	99	
S5-OBF	Tomi AX-7 HAFB	44/99	
S5-OBH	Kubicek BB-22 HAFB	125	OK-0125
S5-OBI	Kubicek BB-22 HAFB	132	OK-0132
S5-OBJ	Balloon Works Firefly 7-15 HAFB	F7-720	HB-BRY
S5-OBK	Kubicek BB-26 HAFB	154	OK-0154
S5-OBL	Kubicek BB-22 HAFB	164	OK-0164
S5-OBM	Cameron O-77 HAFB	4893	
S5-OBO	Kubicek BB-22 HAFB	113	(OO-BHK)
S5-OBP	Sky 80-16 HAFB	153	
S5-OBR	Cameron A-105 HAFB	4671	
S5-OBT	Balloon Works Firefly F-9B HAFB	F9-068	
S5-OCA	Kubicek BB-30Z HAFB	263	OK-0263
S5-OHA	Cameron N-90 HAFB	3115	
S5-OHB(2)	Cameron 0-77 HAFB	3540	
S5-OHC	Galaxy 9B HAFB	GLX-1059B	
S5-OHE	Type unknown		
S5-OHG	Firefly 8-Cube HAFB	FC8-01	
S5-OHH	Galaxy 11 HAFB	GLX-11012	
S5-OHL	Type unknown		
S5-OHO	Type unknown		
S5-OHT	Galaxy 11 HAFB	GLX-10511	
S5-OHY	Galaxy 8 HAFB	GLX-1098	
S5-OJD	Kubicek BB Jupol HAFB	130	OK-0130
S5-OLZ	Cameron DP-70 Hot Air Airship	1703	G-BOPZ
S5-OPA	Balloon Works Firefly 7-15 HAFB	F7-112	
S5-OPJ	Kubicek Jägermeister SS HAFB	107	OK-8037
S5-OPP	Mecsek AX-10 HAFB	46/1999	
S5-OPQ	Kubicek BB-30 HAFB	136	OK-0136
S5-OPR	SCB AX-7 SS HAFB	SCB 108/94	
S5-OPS	Kubicek BB-30 HAFB	178	OK-0178
S5-OSA	Balloon Works Firefly F8B-15 HAFB	F8B-536	
S5-OSG	Type unknown		
S5-OSL	Cameron N-90 HAFB	2946	SL-OSL
S5-OSP	Balloon Works Firefly 7-15 HAFB	F7-1010	
S5-OST	Balloon Works Firefly 7-15 HAFB	F7-782	N25621
S5-OSW	Balloon Works Firefly 8B-15	F8B-573	
S5-O . .	Balloon Works Firefly F8B-15 HAFB	F8B-2063	N21880
S5-O . .	Cameron O-77 HAFB	3541	
S5-O . .	Cameron O-77 HAFB	3542	
S5-O . .	Cameron C-80 Concept HAFB	3418	
S5-O . .	Colt Bullet 56 HAFB	3550	
S5-O . .	Colt 56A HAFB	484	G-BKND

MICROLIGHTS

S5-PAA	Rodaro Storch	110	
S5-PAB	Rodaro Storch	13	
S5-PAC	Ferrari Tucano S	5	
S5-PAD	Eurofly Fire Fox	unkn	
S5-PAE	Rodaro Storch II	unkn	
S5-PAF	Rodaro Kangaroo	unkn	
S5-PAH	Bagalini	unkn	
S5-PAI	Bagalini	unkn	
S5-PAJ	Rodaro Storch II	36	
S5-PAK	Ikarus-Comco Fox-C22	9005-3265	
S5-PAL	Pipistrel (?)	unkn	
S5-PAM	Rodaro Storch	57	
S5-PAN	Rodaro Storch II	unkn	
S5-PAP	Fisher FP.404 Classic	C069	
S5-PAR	Type unknown		
S5-PAS	Euro Fly Fire Fox	1090	
S5-PAV	Ferrari Tucano S	unkn	
S5-PAW	Rodaro Storch	34	
S5-PAX	Type unknown		
S5-PAZ	Type unknown		
S5-PBA	Ferrari Tucano	unkn	
S5-PBB	Ferrari Tucano	003	
S5-PBC	Rodaro Wallaby	unkn	
S5-PBE	Eurofly Fire Fox 22000	unkn	
S5-PBF	Pipistrel Sinus 503	004S5030699	
S5-PBG	Pipistrel Virus 912	002V0799SLO	
S5-PBI	Rodaro Storch	unkn	
S5-PBJ	Rodaro Storch I	unkn	
S5-PBM	Ultralight Challenger II	unkn	
S5-PBN	Tecnam P.92 Echo	unkn	
S5-PBO	Tecnam P.96 Golf	unkn	
S5-PBP	Fly Synthesis Storch HS 582	050798	
S5-PBS	Pipistrel Sinus 503	007S5031299	
S5-PBT	Tecnam P.92 Echo Super	unkn	
S5-PBU	Pipistrel Virus 912	003V9120799	
S5-PBV	Pipistrel Sinus	unkn	
S5-PBW	Pipistrel Sinus 503	006S5030300	
S5-PBX	III Sky Arrow 450TS	091	
S5-PBZ	Bagalini	unkn	
S5-PCA	Pipistrel Virus	unkn	
S5-PCB	Pipistrel	unkn	
S5-PCC	Zenair CH-701 STOL	unkn	
S5-PCD	Eurofly Fire Fox	unkn	
S5-PCF	Eurofly Fire Fox 22000	4173357	
S5-PCJ	Evektor EV.97 Eurostar	unkn	
S5-PCK	Pipistrel	unkn	
S5-PCO	Tecnam P.96 Golf 100	unkn	
S5-PCP	Pipistrel Virus	unkn	
S5-PCS	Eurofly Fire Fox 22000	630/4173357	
S5-PCT	Pipistrel Sinus	unkn	
S5-PCV	Pipistrel Sinus	unkn	
S5-PCX	Evektor EV.97 Eurostar	unkn	
S5-PCZ	Zenair CH-601 Zodiac	unkn	
S5-PDM	Pipistrel	unkn	
S5-PDS	Pipistrel Virus	unkn	
S5-PHA	Lisport CH-7 Angel	unkn	
S5-PIR	Tecnam P.92 Echo Super	unkn	
S5-PIS	Tecnam P.2002 Sierra	unkn	
S5-PIT	Albastar Apis-M (Code 'RC')	unkn	
S5-PKA	Type unknown	unkn	YU-8040
S5-PKB	MZ Pipistrel	unkn	YU-8039
S5-PKC	Type unknown		
S5-PKD	Type unknown		
S5-PKE	Type unknown		
S5-PKF	Type unknown		
S5-PKG	MZ Pipistrel Hazard	unkn	
S5-PKH	Type unknown		
S5-PKI	Type unknown		
S5-PKJ	Type unknown		
S5-PKK	Type unknown		
S5-PKL	Type unknown		
S5-PKM	Type unknown		
S5-PKN	Cosmos Chronos 14	unkn	
S5-PKO	MZ Pipistrel Hazard	unkn	
S5-PKP	MZ Pipistrel	unkn	
S5-PLC	MZ Pipistrel Hazard	unkn	
S5-PLM	Type unknown		
S5-PLS	MZ Pipistrel Hazard	unkn	
S5-PMH	MZ Pipistrel Hazard	unkn	
S5-PMR	MZ Pipistrel Hazard 15	unkn	
S5-PMX	Type unknown		
S5-PNA	MZ Pipistrel	unkn	
S5-POB	MZ Pipistrel Hazard	unkn	
S5-POL	MZ Pipistrel Hazard	unkn	
S5-POP	Firefly	unkn	
S5-PPR	MZ Pipistrel Hazard	unkn	
S5-PRC	Type unknown		
S5-P1102	Pipistrel Taurus 503 (Prototype)	unkn	

GLIDERS

S5-1000	SZD-12 Mucha	unkn	YU-4147
S5-1003	Vaja (Weihe)	unkn	YU-4 . . .
S5-1008	Vaja (Weihe)	unkn	YU-4115 ?
S5-1053	Libis Jastreb-54 (Preserved, Ljubliana Airport)	248	YU-3053
S5-1111	VTC Trener	100	YU-4190 ?
S5-1112	Libis KBI-14	252	YU-4112
S5-1124	Utva Grunau Baby III	unkn	YU-2124
S5-1135	VTC Delfin 3 (C/n officially '8/2')	F.BR.042	YU-4135
S5-1183	Utva Cavka	unkn	YU-2183
S5-2000	L-Spatz 55	537/2	D-5634
S5-3000-MT	Glaser-Dirks DG-600	6-23	SL-3000 YU-4458
S5-3001-AT	Glaser-Dirks DG-300 Elan (C/n incorrectly quoted as 3E-56)	3E-65	SL-3001 YU-4387
S5-3002-UK	SZD-48-3 Jantar Standard 3	B-1957	SL-3002 YU-4461
S5-3004-PW	Glaser-Dirks DG-300 Elan	3E-204	SL-3004 YU-4424
S5-3005	Glaser-Dirks DG-100G Elan	E57-G33	SL-3005 YU-4289
S5-3006	SZD-41A Jantar Standard	B-849	SL-3006 YU-4271
S5-3007-PM	SZD-41A Jantar Standard	B-799	SL-3007 YU-4240
S5-3009-B8	Glaser-Dirks DG-100G Elan	E105-G74	SL-3009 YU-4338
S5-3010-10	SZD-41A Jantar Standard	B-800	SL-3010 YU-4241
S5-3011-AJ	Glaser-Dirks DG-100G Elan	E210-G176	SL-3011 YU-4440
S5-3012	Glaser-Dirks DG-100G Elan	E207-G173	SL-3012 YU-4439
S5-3013-G1	Glaser-Dirks DG-100G Elan	E153-G120	SL-3013 YU-4350
S5-3014	Pilatus B4-PC11AF	299	SL-3014 YU-4259
S5-3016	VTC-75 Standard Cirrus	201	SL-3016 YU-4297
S5-3017	Glaser-Dirks DG-300 Elan	3E-89	SL-3017 YU-4410
S5-3018-PH	Bölkow Phoebus A	847	SL-3018 YU-4197
S5-3019	Glaser-Dirks DG-100G Elan	E27-G14	SL-3019 YU-4314
S5-3020-B5	Glaser-Dirks DG-100G Elan	E214-G180	SL-3020 YU-4441
S5-3021-A9	Glaser-Dirks DG-300 Elan	3E-40	SL-3021 YU-4369

S5-3022-L3	Glaser-Dirks DG-100G Elan	E127-G95	SL-3022 YU-4343
S5-3023-E2	Glaser-Dirks DG-100G Elan	E59-G35	SL-3023 YU-4290
S5-3026-E1	Glaser-Dirks DG-100 Elan	E-1	SL-3026 YU-4298
S5-3027-27	Pilatus B4-PC11AF	112	SL-3027 YU-4217
S5-3028	Glaser-Dirks DG-100G Elan	E140-G108	SL-3028 YU-4348
S5-3029-PJ	Glaser-Dirks DG-300 Elan (Same c/n given for N98WX)	3E-13	SL-3029 YU-4456
S5-3030	Glaser-Dirks DG-100G Elan	E107-G76	SL-3030 YU-4339
S5-3031	VTC-75 Standard Cirrus	223	SL-3031 YU-4315
S5-3032-VI	Glaser-Dirks DG-101G Elan	E112-G81	SL-3032 YU-4341
S5-3033	Glasflügel H303 Mosquito	108	SL-3033 YU-4275
S5-3034	Pilatus B4-PC11AF	186	SL-3034 YU-42 . .
S5-3035	Pilatus B4-PC11AF	301	SL-3035 YU-4261
S5-3036	Glaser-Dirks DG-300 Elan	3E-266	SL-3036 YU-4444
S5-3037	Glaser-Dirks DG-101G Elan	E155-G122	SL-3037 YU-4362
S5-3038-M7	Glaser-Dirks DG-101G Elan	E77-G52	SL-3038 YU-4337
S5-3039-M9	Glaser-Dirks DG-101G Elan	E154-G121	SL-3039 YU-4349
S5-3041-M1	VTC-75 Standard Cirrus	202	SL-3041 YU-4294
S5-3042-MC	VTC-75 Standard Cirrus	206	SL-3042 YU-4296
S5-3043-38	SZD-41A Jantar Standard	B-741	SL-3043 YU-4238
S5-3046	Glaser-Dirks DG-300 Elan	3E-291	SL-3046 YU-4450
S5-3047-11	Glaser-Dirks DG-100 Elan	E-18	SL-3047 YU-4311
S5-3048	Grob G.102 Astir CS	1266	SL-3048 YU-4235
S5-3049	SZD-41A Jantar Standard	B-850	SL-3049 YU-4272
S5-3051	Glaser-Dirks DG-101G Elan	E129-G97	SL-3051 YU-4344
S5-3052	Glaser-Dirks DG-100G Elan	E157-G124	SL-3052 YU-4385
S5-3053-31	Glasflugel H205 Libelle	134	SL-3053 YU-4231
S5-3054	Glasflugel H205 Libelle	171	SL-3054 YU-4237
S5-3056-09	Schempp-Hirth Standard Cirrus	222	SL-3056 YU-4209
S5-3057-CB	VTC-75 Standard Cirrus	199	SL-3057 YU-4293
S5-3060	Glaser-Dirks DG-101G Elan	E76-G51	SL-3060 YU-4336
S5-3061	Glaser-Dirks DG-100 Elan	E-49	SL-3061 YU-4286
S5-3062-56	Pilatus B4-PC11AF	296	SL-3062 YU-4256
S5-3063	VTC-75 Cirrus 17A	141	SL-3063 YU-4211
S5-3064-57	Pilatus B4-PC11AF	297	SL-3064 YU-4257
S5-3065	Pilatus B4-PC11AF	298	SL-3065 YU-4258
S5-3067	Glaser-Dirks DG-300 Elan	3E-434	
S5-3068	Schempp-Hirth Nimbus 3	2	BGA2759/EKZ D-2148
S5-3069	Glaser-Dirks DG-303 Elan	3E-443	
S5-3070-LV	VTC-76 Vuk-T	291	YU-4378
S5-3071-PS	VTC-76 Vuk-T	302	YU-4373
S5-3072	VTC-76 Vuk-T	287	YU-4366
S5-3073-MV	VTC-76 Vuk-T	317	YU-4395
S5-3074	VTC-76 Vuk-T	384	YU-4438
S5-3075	VTC-76 Vuk-T	338	YU-4414
S5-3076	VTC-76 Vuk-T	263	YU-4352
S5-3077	VTC-76 Vuk-T	344	YU-4420
S5-3085	Glaser-Dirks DG-303 Elan	3E-449	
S5-3086-VS	Glaser-Dirks DG-303 Elan Acro	3E-456A14	
S5-3087	Glaser-Dirks DG-303 Elan	3E-459	
S5-3088-JP	Glaser-Dirks DG-303 Club Elan	3E-442C76	
S5-3089-GS	LET L-33 Solo	960407	
S5-3090	SZD-49-3 Jantar Standard 3	B-1902	DOSAAF
S5-3093-CF	Glaser-Dirks DG-100 Elan	E-41	YU-4320
S5-3095-CX	Glaser-Dirks DG-300 Elan (Reservation)	3E-203	YU-4423
S5-3099	Glasflügel H303 Mosquito	97	D-6797
S5-3100	SZD-48 Jantar Standard 2	W-887	OE-5196
S5-3101	Glaser-Dirks DG-101G Elan	E-221R	SL-3101 YU-4454
S5-3102	Glaser-Dirks DG-100GElan	E8-G2	D-2594
S5-3105	VTC-75 Standard Cirrus	238	YU-4329
S5-3106-PI	Rolladen-Schneider LS6	6318	D-4790

S5-3107-BP	Glaser-Dirks DG-600	6-26	SL-3107 YU-4459
S5-3111	LAK-17A	107	
S5-3112	LAK-12 Lietuva	6149	CCCP6149
S5-3117-MZ	LAK-17A	103	
S5-3120	LAK-12 Lietuva	6232	
S5-3122	LAK-12 Lietuva	6183	
S5-3125	Pilatus B4-PC11	182	YU-4223
S5-3131	LAK-12 Lietuva	6233	
S5-3133	LET L-35 Solo	950320	
S5-3300-E3	Glaser-Dirks DG-300 Elan	3E-34	SL-3300 YU-4363
S5-3303-CD	Glaser-Dirks DG-303 Elan	3E-448	
S5-7100	LET L-23 Super Blanik	907704	SL-7100 OK- . . . .
S5-7101	LET L-13 Blanik	026922	SL-7101 YU-5374
S5-7102	LET L-13 Blanik	174902	SL-7102 YU-5330
S5-7103	LET L-23 Super Blanik	917920	SL-7103
S5-7104	LET L-23 Super Blanik	917919	SL-7104
S5-7105	LET L-13 Blanik	174822	SL-7105 YU-5325
S5-7106	LET L-13A Blanik	026238	SL-7106 YU-5353
S5-7107	LET L-13A Blanik	026237	SL-7107 YU-5352
S5-7109	LET L-13 Blanik	174424	SL-7109 YU-5313
S5-7110	LET L-13 Blanik	026923	SL-7110 YU-5376
S5-7111	LET L-13 N-10 Blanik	174101	SL-7111 YU-5314
S5-7112	LET L-13 N-10 Blanik	174414	SL-7112 YU-5312
S5-7114	LET L-13 N-10 Blanik	027046	SL-7114 YU-5381
S5-7115	LET L-13A Blanik	026241	SL-7115 YU-5357
S5-7116	LET L-13 Blanik	174103	SL-7116 YU-5310
S5-7117	LET L-13 Blanik	174901	SL-7117 YU-5329
S5-7118	LET L-13 Blanik	025309	SL-7118 YU-5386 I-PUFF
S5-7119	LET L-13 Blanik	175004	SL-7119 YU-5338
S5-7120	LET L-13 Blanik	027014	SL-7120 YU-5379
S5-7122	LET L-13 Blanik	174425	SL-7122 YU-5311
S5-7123	LET L-13 Blanik	174829	SL-7123 YU-5323
S5-7124-24	LET L-13 Blanik	027045	SL-7124 YU-5380
S5-7125-25	LET L-13 Blanik	026801	SL-7125 YU-5370
S5-7126-26	LET L-13 Blanik	174929	SL-7126 YU-5337
S5-7127	LET L-23 Super Blanik	917820	SL-7127
S5-7128	LET L-23 Super Blanik	917821	SL-7128
S5-7129	LET L-13 Blanik	026637	SL-7129 YU-5362
S5-7130	LET L-13 Blanik	026252	SL-7130 YU-5363
S5-7131	LET L-13 Blanik	027023	SL-7131 YU-5383
S5-7132	LET L-13 Blanik	026850	SL-7132 YU-5373
S5-7133	LET L-23 Super Blanik	917925	
S5-7134	LET L-13 Blanik	026236	YU-5355
S5-7135	LET L-13 Blanik	027024	YU-5385
S5-7136	LET L-13 Blanik	174532	S5-7121 YU-5316
S5-7137	LET L-13 Blanik	026540	CCCP6540
S5-7138	LET L-13A Blanik	827419	OK-2726
S5-7139	LET L-13 Blanik	172606	OK-3804
S5-7140	LAK-12 Lietuva 2R (2-seater)	620	CCCP-620
S5-7141-CG	Schempp-Hirth Duo Discus	unkn	
S5-7515	DG-Flugzeugbau DG-500 Elan Orion	5E-177X29	
S5-7516	DG-Flugzeugbau DG-500M Elan	5E-194X38	
S5-7520-E6	Glaser-Dirks DG-500/20 Elan	5E-132W4	
S5-7777	Marganski MDM-1 Fox	203	OE-5575
S5-9050	Glaser-Dirks DG-500 Elan Orion	5E-133T58	SE-ULI D-9050
S5-	DG Flugzeugbau DG-800B (To S5-KAY?)	8-251B164	
S5-	Rolladen-Schneider LS3	3100	OO-ZUQ D-1151 D-2859 OO-ZOZ
S5-	Schempp-Hirth Nimbus 4DM	52/ . . .	
S5-	SZD-22C Mucha Standard	525	OO-ZSO

The following YU- registered aircraft are thought to be in Slovenia, either in store or awaiting registry:-

YU-BBF	LIBIS/ LET L-200D Morava	302-02	
YU-BCY	Macchi AL.60B-2	49/6229	
YU-CMY	Polikarpov Po-2 (Under restoration)	unkn	JRV0076
YU-CZC	Aero 3 (Stored)	unkn	JRV40126
YU-DLE	Utva-66 (Stored)	unkn	JRV51108
YU-4260	Pilatus B4-PC11	300 ?	
YU-4310	Glaser-Dirks DG-100 Elan	E-. . .	
YU-4391	VTC-76 Vuk-T	313 ?	
YU-4406	VTC-76 Vuk-T	333	
YU-4421	VTC-76 Vuk-T	345 ?	
YU-5043	DFS-108-30 Kranich II	211	

TC - TURKEY

Regn.	Type	C/n	Prev.Id.
TC-AAB	Boeing 737-86N	28620	TC-SUD
			N17886B
TC-AAC	Piper PA-18-150 Super Cub	18-2598	Turkish AF
	(Officially quoted with f/n 18-2422)		52-6280
	(NB: All the Turkish AF L-21B Super Cubs would originally be PA-18-135 but are now quoted as -150 or other engines)		
TC-ABI	Cessna 172N	17267601	N73665
TC-ABK	Airbus A300B4-203F	101	N59101
			EC-HND
			N59101
			I-BUSB
			F-WZEA
TC- ABS	Aerotek Pitts S-2S	2002	N26MW
			N13AS
TC-ACS	Antonov An-26	9709	UR-. . . . .
TC-ACT	Airbus A300C4-203F	083	TC-ORH
			TC-MNG
			EI-BZB
			RP-C3007
			EI-BZB
			D-AHLB
			F-WZES
TC-ADD	Yakovlev Yak-18T	unkn	
	(Marks not confirmed maybe TC-ADO)		
TC-ADI	Cessna 172N	17267601	N73665
TC-AEA	Boeing 737-268	21275	HZ-AGH
TC-AEB	Boeing 737-268	21276	HZ-AGI
TC-AEC	Boeing 737-268C	20575	HZ-AGB
TC-AEZ	Cessna 172N	17273362	PH-DBR
			N4814G
TC-AFZ	Boeing 737-4Y0	23981	EI-CEW
			F-GNFS
			SU-BLL
			EI-CEW
			EC-EMY
			EC-251
TC-AHS	Hawker 800XP	258504	N50048
TC-AHU(2)	Cessna 172R	17280027	N9719F
TC-AIO	Robinson Starduster Too	124	
TC-AIR	SOCATA TB-9 Tampico	1022	F-GHZT
TC-AKK	Dassault Falcon 900B	171	F-WWFW
TC-AKL	McDonnell-Douglas DC-9-83	53184	TC-FBG
			N878RA
TC-AKP	Airbus A310-203	352	N441LF
			5B-DAS
			F-WZEO
TC-AKV	Airbus A310-203	309	N431LF
			5B-DAR
			F-WZEM
TC-ALN	Airbus A300B4-2C	065	OO-MKO
			V2-LDY
			(OO-MKO)
			HS-TAY
			N404UA
			N205EA
			F-GBNA
			F-WZEN
TC-ALS	Airbus A300B4-103	066	OO-ING
			HS-TAZ
			N405UA
			N206EA
			F-GBNB
			F-WZEO
TC-ANC	BAe.125 Series 800B	258208	G-BUID
			(TC-ANC)
			G-5-700
			G-BUID
TC-ANI	Airbus A300B4-203	046	EI-TLM
			RP-C8882
			SX-BEB
			F-WZER
			F-WZEK
			F-WLGB
TC-ANT	Cessna 650 Citation VI	650-0229	N1302X
TC-APD	Boeing 737-42R	29107	
TC-APF	Boeing 737-86N	28642	N1787B
TC-APG	Boeing 737-82R	29329	N1786B
TC-APH	Boeing 737-8S3	29250	N1787B
TC-API	Boeing 737-86N	32732	
TC-APJ	Boeing 737-86N	32735	
TC-APK	Boeing 737-86N (Reservation .01)	28643	
TC-APM	Boeing 737-809	28403	B-18602
			N1786B
TC-APN	Boeing 737-86N	28628	N5573L
			N1786B
TC-APR	Boeing 737-4YO	24685	EC-GXR
			PT-TDB
			EC-EVE
			EC-402
TC-APS	Cessna 340A	340A0247	N3964G
TC-APU	Boeing 737-82R	29344	
TC-APV	Boeing 737-86N	28639	
TC-APY	Boeing 737-86N	28591	TC-IAH
TC-APZ	Boeing 737-809	29103	B-18603
			N1784B
			N1786B
TC-ARC	Bombardier Learjet 60	60-094	N93BA
			A6-SMS
			N60LR
TC-ARE	Fletcher FU-24-950	247	ZK-EGY
TC-ART(2)	Cessna 340A	340A0478	N340LM
			N340BS
			(N340HL)
			N340BS
			N6307X
TC-ARZ(2)	Beech A36 Bonanza	E-2722	TC-ARI (2)
			N80225
TC-ATA(3)	Gulfstream IV	1043	TC-ANA(2)
			N1761B
TC-AUB	Antonov An-2R	1G234-11	
TC-AUC	SOCATA TB-20 Trinidad	958	F-ODXS
TC-AUD	SOCATA TB-20 Trinidad	964	F-ODXT
TC-AUE	SOCATA TB-20 Trinidad	1223	F-ODXU
TC-AUF	SOCATA TB-20 Trinidad	1224	F-ODXV
TC-AUG	SOCATA TB-20 Trinidad	1225	F-ODXX
TC-AUH	SOCATA TB-20 Trinidad	1226	F-ODXY
TC-AUI	Piper PA-18-150 Super Cub	18-4227	Turkish AF
			54-2827
TC-AUJ	SOCATA TB-9 Tampico	unkn	
TC-AUL	SOCATA TB-9 Tampico	unkn	
	(Two of c/ns 1851, 1852, 1853 - see unknown regns)		
TC-AUM	American AG-5B Tiger	10098	N1195Z
TC-AUN	American AG-5B Tiger	10129	
TC-AUO	American AG-5B Tiger	10130	
TC-AUR	Beech 76 Duchess	ME-192	G-BXSK
			EI-CMX
			N60450
TC-AUT	Beech C90 King Air	LJ-622	N104TT
			F-BUYS
TC-AUV	Beech C90 King Air	LJ-587	N61KA
			(N110PS)
			N61KA
TC-AUY	Beech 200 Super King Air	BB-333	F-GHLH
			C-FANG
			N3207
			N308F
TC-AYH	Cessna R172K Hawk XP	R1723203	TC-ASH ?
			N758MK
TC-AYL	Auster Mk.5	1375	TC-AYLA
			G-AKWK
			TJ299
TC-AZE	Cessna 172N	17271875	PH-DBC
			N5471E
TC-AZK	Mooney M.20J Model 205	24-3314	N1082Z
TC-BAF	Bellanca 7GCBC Citabria	"10121"	
TC-BAS	Cessna 421B Golden Eagle	421B0331	N77MH
			(N5991M)
TC-BBJ	Mil Mi-2	5210231057	RA-23230
			CCCP23230
TC-BBS	Beech B24R Sierra	MC-266	N2179W
TC-BIL	Piper PA-34-220T Seneca III	3448005	
TC-BLL	Piper PA-28-140 Cherokee	28-23704	N3726K
TC-BNT	Dassault Falcon 50EX	305	F-WWHG
TC-CAC(2)	Piper PA-31P Pressurized Navajo	31P-57	F-BTQB
	(Wfu)		F-BTDV
			N7304L
TC-CAE	Cessna U206B Super Skywagon	U206-0884	N11B
TC-CAF	Cessna U206B Super Skywagon	U206-0885	N11B
TC-CAN	Cessna U206G Stationair 6- II	U20606181	N6185Z
TC-CAP	Cessna U206G Stationair 6- II	U20606074	N5163Z

TC-CAR	Cessna U206G Stationair 6- II	U20606128	N5517Z
TC-CAT	Cessna U206G Stationair 6- II	U20606230	N6314Z
TC-CAU	Cessna 208 Caravan I	20800248	N1123X
TC-CAV	Cessna 208 Caravan I	20800256	N1249T
TC-CAY	Cessna 402B Utililiner	402B1073	T.Army:10007 N1552G
TC-CAZ	Cessna 421C Golden Eagle	421C0089	T.Army:10006 N98783
TC-CBC	Slingsby T-67M-200 Firefly	2032	G-BMBL
TC-CBD	Slingsby T-67M-200 Firefly	2033	G-BMBM
TC-CBF	Slingsby T-67M-200 Firefly	2055	G-BOFP
TC-CBG	Slingsby T-67M-200 Firefly	2056	G-BOFR
TC-CBH	Slingsby T-67M-200 Firefly	2057	G-BOFS
TC-CBK	Slingsby T-67M-200 Firefly	2059	G-BOFU
TC-CBL	Slingsby T-67M-200 Firefly	2066	G-BOXL
TC-CBM	Slingsby T-67M-200 Firefly	2067	G-BOXM
TC-CBN	Slingsby T-67M-200 Firefly	2068	G-BPET
TC-CBP	Slingsby T-67M-200 Firefly	2069	G-BPEU
TC-CBR	Slingsby T-67M-200 Firefly	2075	G-BPEV
TC-CBT	Slingsby T-67M-200 Firefly	2078	G-BPMZ
TC-CCA	CCF/Beech T-34A Mentor	34-9	TAF: OK-06/ 54-5206 (RCAF24206)
TC-CCB	CCF/Beech T-34A Mentor	34-10	TAF: OK-07/ 54-5207 (RCAF24207)
TC-CCC	CCF/Beech T-34A Mentor	34-14	TAF: OK-11/ 54-5211 (RCAF24211)
TC-CCD	CCF/Beech T-34A Mentor	34-15	TAF: OK-12/ 54-5212 (RCAF24212)
TC-CCE	CCF/Beech T-34A Mentor	34-17	TAF: OK-14/ 54-5214 (RCAF24214)
TC-CCF	CCF/Beech T-34A Mentor	34-27	TAF: OK-23/ 54-5223 (RCAF24223)
TC-CCG	CCF/Beech T-34A Mentor	34-18	TAF: OK-15/ 54-5215 (RCAF24215)
TC-CCH	CCF/Beech T-34A Mentor	34-19	TAF: OK-16/ 54-5216 (RCAF24216)
TC-CCI	CCF/Beech T-34A Mentor	34-20	TAF: OK-17/ 54-5217 (RCAF24217)
TC-CCO	Piper PA-18 Super Cub	18-426	Turkish AF 50-1770
TC-CDA	Cessna 185D Skywagon/U-17A	185-0838	T.Army:13154 64-17927
TC-CDB	Cessna 185D Skywagon/U-17A	185-0840	T.Army: 64-17928
TC-CDC	Cessna 185D Skywagon/U-17A	185-0841	T.Army:14050 64-17929
TC-CDD	Cessna 185D Skywagon/U-17A	185-0843	T.Army:11059 64-17931
TC-CDE	Cessna 185D Skywagon/U-17A	185-0845	T.Army:12251 64-17932
TC-CDF	Cessna 185D Skywagon/U-17A	185-0846	T Army:11061 64-17933
TC-CDG	Cessna 185D Skywagon/U-17A	185-0847	T.Army:13155 64-17934
TC-CDH	Cessna 185D Skywagon/U-17A	185-0851	T.Army:14055 64-17937
TC-CDI	Cessna 185D Skywagon/U-17A	185-0853	T.Army:11158 64-17939
TC-CDJ	Cessna 185D Skywagon/U-17A	185-0855	T.Army: 64-17940
TC-CDK	Cessna 185D Skywagon/U-17A	185-0856	T.Army:13052 64-17941
TC-CDL	Cessna 185D Skywagon/U-17A	185-0860	T.Army:11164 64-17944
TC-CEN	Dassault Falcon 20E (Reportedly resvd as TC-GGG .04)	326/521	PH- ILY F-WRQQ
TC-CHA	Piper PA-18 Super Cub (L-21)	" 7203-L-21"	
TC-COA	Airbus A300B4-120	128	OY-CNL SE-DFL F-WZEE
TC-COG	Piper PA-18-150 Super Cub	18-7585	TC-KPC
TC-CSS	Piper PA-18-150 Super Cub (Officially quoted with f/n 18-7813 - identity not confirmed)	18-7626	TC-KPI
TC-CUP	Piper PA-18-150 Super Cub	18-7909145	N2402S
TC-CYA	Piper PA-18-135 Super Cub (Officially quoted with f/n 18-3905)	18-3884	Turkish AF 54-2484
TC-CYC	Piper PA-18-135 Super Cub (Owners now quote c/n 18-7626, possibly rebuilt with parts of TC-CSS above?)	18-3969	Turkish AF 54-2569
TC-DAN	Cessna 172N	17272691	N6284D
TC-DAT	Rockwell Commander 112B	538	N1475J
TC-DAZ	Beech C90 King Air (Identity given as LJ-587 which is TC-AUV)		
TC-DBA	Cessna 172RG Cutlass RG	172RG1070	D-EGLC(2) N9889B
TC-DBB	Cessna 340 / RAM	340-0018	D-IFJB N340HP N5064Q
TC-DBC	Cessna 172N	17272286	D-EFZL(2) N9907E
TC-DBD	Cessna F150H	F150-0310	D-ENBX
TC-DBE	Reims/Cessna F150K	F15000578	D-ECBI
TC-DBF	Cessna 172N	17274103	D-EFZD N5420K
TC-DBJ	Cessna 172N	17273773	(D-EUCD) N5383J
TC-DBK	Cessna 172N	17271413	N3042E
TC-DBM	Cessna 172N	17272170	(D-EUCC) N8284E
TC-DBN	Cessna 172N	17272731	(D-EUCE) N6345D
TC-DBO	Cessna 172P	17275288	N62509
TC-DBS	Cessna 172P	17275167	N55356
TC-DBT	Cessna 172N	17273107	N4950F
TC-DBU	Cessna 172P	17275887	G-BRNL N5017J C-GRNU N65787
TC-DBV	Cessna R172K Hawk XP	R1723327	N758SQ
TC-DBZ	Beech C90 King Air	LJ-703	N793MA N300CK
TC-DCK	Piper PA-28-140 Cherokee Cruiser	28-7725273	N38278
TC-DEL	Boeing 727-225	22439	N808EA
TC-DGC	Dassault Falcon 2000	166	F-WWVD
TC-DHH	Canadair CL.600-2B16 Challenger	5448	N604CB C-GLXD
TC-DKU	Reims/Cessna F172M	F17200957	SE-KGP OY-RYR
TC-DLA	SOCATA TB-10 Tobago	7	F-GBHC
TC-DME	Cessna 150K (Tailwheel convn)	15071718	N6218G
TC-DPT(2)	Piper PA-31P Pressurized Navajo (Wfu)	31P-35	PT-DSP PT-CCY N6830L
TC-DYC	Rockwell Commander 114	14013	N514CA
TC-EAN	SIAT-223K-1 Flamingo (Seen on pole at Selcuk Airfield near Ephesus)	034	
TC-EAP	Piper PA-18-150 Super Cub	18- ?	Turkish AF 50-1715 ?
TC-EAY	Piper PA-18 Super Cub	18-431	Turkish AF 50-1775
TC-EAZ	Piper PA-18-150 Super Cub	18-433	Turkish AF 50-1777
TC-EBD	Piper PA-18 Super Cub	18-981	Turkish AF 51-15284
TC-EBH	Piper PA-18-95 Super Cub	18-977	51-12580
TC-EBR	Piper PA-18-150 Super Cub	18-3072	Turkish AF 53-4672
TC-EBT(2)	Piper PA-18-150 Super Cub	18-4228	Turkish AF 54-2828
TC-EBV	Piper PA-18A-135 Super Cub (Officially quoted with f/n 18-2414)	18- ?	Turkish AF
TC-ECB	Piper PA-18-135 Super Cub (Officially quoted with f/n 18-3908)	18-3895	Turkish AF 52-2495
TC-ECH	Piper PA-18-150 Super Cub	18-4232	Turkish AF 54-2832
TC-ECI	Piper PA-18A Super Cub (Officially quoted with f/n 18-4551)	18-3973	Turkish AF 54-2573
TC-ECJ	Piper PA-18A Super Cub (Officially quoted with f/n 18-4560)	18-3979	Turkish AF 54-2579
TC-ECK	Piper PA-18-135 Super Cub	18-5481	Turkish AF 55-4581
TC-ECL	PZL-104 Wilga 35A (Museum, Istanbul)	140545	SP-WAA(1)
TC-ECM	PZL-104 Wilga 35A	140546	SP-WAB(1)
TC-ECS(2)	PZL-104 Wilga 80	CF21950952	
TC-ECU	PZL-104 Wilga 35A	19870851	
TC-ECY	PZL-104 Wilga 35A	19870861	
TC-ECZ(2)	PZL-104 Wilga 80	CF21950959	
TC-EDA	Piper PA-18-135 Super Cub	18-3996	TC-ECF Turkish AF 54-2596
TC-EDB	Piper PA-18-150 Super Cub (Officially quoted with f/n 18-469)	18-465	TC-EBI Turkish AF 50-1809
TC-EDR	Siray 1-TX Experimental	1	
TC-EEZ	Cessna 172	unkn	
TC-EGE(2)	Mil Mi-2	5210725098	RA-14106 CCCP14106
TC-EHA	Light Aero Avid Amphibian	A-46	
TC-ELL	Bombardier Learjet 60	60-030	N164PA N4030W
TC-EMR	Cessna 340A	340A0269	N340AD EC-EVR N4075G
TC-EMS	Cessna R172KHawk XP	unkn	
TC-EST	SOCATA TB-21 Trinidad TC	2077	F-OJBG
TC-ETO	SOCATA TB-20 Trinidad	unkn	
TC-FAD	Piper PA-31P-425 Pressurized Navajo	31P-7400225	N7341L
TC-FAE	Cessna U206G Stationair 6- II	U20606614	N9701Z
TC-FAF	Robin DR.400/180 Régent	1698	
TC-FAH	Piper PA-42 Cheyenne III	42-5501033	
TC-FAI	Maule MX.7-235 Star Rocket	10059C	
TC-FAJ	Cessna U206G Stationair 6- II	U20605368	N6182U
TC-FAM	Robin DR.400/180 Régent	1719	
TC-FAN	Piper PA-30-160 Twin Comanche B	30-1521	I-TJTJ N8449Y

TC-FAO	Cessna 172R	17280287	N9524P
TC-FAP	Cessna 421C Golden Eagle	421C0513	N67Q N88536
TC-FAV	Piper PA-34-200T Seneca II	34-7970113	N3979S (4X-CAS) SE-ILZ N2211N
TC-FAY	Maule MX.7-235 Star Rocket	10052C	
TC-FBB	McDonnell-Douglas DC-9-83	53185	N879RA
TC-FBD	McDonnell-Douglas DC-9-83	53186	N880RA
TC-FBE	Airbus A320-211	132	SE-RCG F-WKCI F-GKCI C-GVXH F-GLGN N482GX F-WWIY
TC-FBF	Airbus A320-212	288	9H-AED SE-RCC VH-HYX N491GX TC-ONA F-WWBV
TC-FBT	McDonnell-Douglas DC-9-83	49949	N882RA G-RJER
TC-FCA	Maule MX.7-235 Star Rocket	10061C	N6109C
TC-FCK	Cessna 172RG Cutlass RG	172RG0408	N4879V
TC-FET	SOCATA TB-20 Trinidad	1052	F-GHZY
TC-FHA	Reims/Cessna FR172K Hawk XP	FR17200625	G-KERR PH-AXB
TC-FIR	Beech 200 Super King Air	BB-1082	N801BC N971BE N6354X
TC-FLA	Airbus A300B4-203	127	TC-GTB 6Y-JMJ G-BIMA F-WZED
TC-FLE	Airbus A300B2K-3C	163	JA8472 F-WZMJ
TC-FLF	Airbus A300B4-203	194	JA8293 PP-VNE F-WZER
TC-FLG	Airbus A300B4-203	110	JA8292 PP-CLB F-WZEB
TC-FLH	Boeing 737-3Q8	24300	EI-PAR F-OMAI N737FA XA-AMH N737FA B-2980 G-OBML SE-DLA G-KKUH
TC-FLJ	Airbus A300B2K-3C	082	JA8464 F-WZEQ
TC-FLK	Airbus A300B4-203	151	JA8263 VH-TAB D-AITB VH-TAB F-WZME
TC-FLL	Airbus A300C4-203	256	JA8237 F-WZMA
TC-FLM	Airbus A300B2K-3C	176	JA8473 F-WZMU
TC-FLY	Piper PA-18-150 Super Cub	18-2608	Turkish AF 52-6300
TC-FSA	Cessna 172RG Cutlass RG	172RG0350	N4658V
TC-FSM	Cessna 172N	17273532	N5083G
TC-FYT	Piper PA-31P-425 Pressurized Navajo (Wfu)	31P-7400200	N38353 D-IHWT LN-MTF N7316L
TC-GAP(2)	Grumman G-1159B Gulfstream IV	1027	N416GA
TC-GHC	Boeing 737-7L9	28004	OY-MRA N35153
TC-GIZ	Piper PA-32R-301 Saratoga	32R-8013064	N8160X
TC-GTA	Airbus A300B4-103	054	HS-THL HS-TGL F-WZED
TC-GTC	Airbus A300B2-202	048	F-BUAO F-ODRF D-AIAD F-WNDB
TC-HAA	Aérospatiale AS.355F2 Ecureuil 2	5362	
TC-HAB	Aérospatiale AS.355F2 Ecureuil 2	5363	
TC-HAC	Bell 206L-3 Long Ranger III	51598	N5130B C-FOKJ
TC-HAF	Rotorway Executive	F73415	
TC-HAG	Mil Mi-8MTV-1	95588	
TC-HAK(2)	Mil Mi-8P	8027	TC-HER
TC-HAL	Mil Mi-8P	5966	UR-25583 CCCP25583
TC-HAT(2)	Agusta A.109A	7191	D-HXXH N605FM N4210T I-CVMO

TC-HBE	Bell 206B Jet Ranger III	3827	
TC-HBF	Agusta-Bell 206B Jet Ranger III	8702	
TC-HBH(2)	Bell 222UT	47525	C-FVVA JA9962 N8171P VH-HIA
TC-HBK	Bell 206B Jet Ranger III	3950	
TC-HBL	Bell 206B Jet Ranger III	3948	
TC-HBM	Bell 206B Jet Ranger III (Crashed 22.06.1998)	3083	N30DM N5747V
TC-HBS	Hughes 369D	41-0943D	N1106U
TC-HCA	Agusta A.109C	7632	N61453 (N109AP) N61453 JA6611
TC-HCD	Aérospatiale SA.365N1 Dauphin 2	6303	F-WYMQ
TC-HCF	Aérospatiale SA.365N1 Dauphin 2	6302	F-WYMP
TC-HCG	Aérospatiale AS.355F2 Ecureuil 2	5354	F-WYML
TC-HCH	Aérospatiale AS.355F2 Ecureuil 2	5369	F-WYMN
TC-HCJ	Aérospatiale AS.355F2 Ecureuil 2	5357	F-WYMM
TC-HCK	Aérospatiale AS.365N2 Dauphin 2	6434	F-WYMN
TC-HCM(2)	Bell 430	49032	N5254W
TC-HDA	Mil Mi-8PS	8561	TC-HEM UR-..... CCCP.....
TC-HDB	Mil Mi-8MTV-1	95479	UR-25170 CCCP25170
TC-HDC	Mil Mi-8	98730615	UR-24231 CCCP24231
TC-HDD	Mil Mi-8MTV-1	95528	CCCP25418
TC-HDE	Mil Mi-8MTV-1	95529	CCCP25419
TC-HDF	Mil Mi-8MTV-1	95740	RA-25124 CCCP25124
TC-HDG	Mil Mi-8MTV-1	95866	RA-27032 CCCP27032
TC-HDH	Mil Mi-8MTV-1	95895	RA-27061 CCCP27061
TC-HDK	Mil Mi-8PS	8562	CCCP.....
TC-HDO	Aérospatiale AS.365N2 Dauphin 2	6497	F-WWOF F-WQDC(3)
TC-HGA	Bell UH-1 (205)	4205	
TC-HIS	Mil Mi-8MTV-1	95486	CCCP.....
TC-HIU	Bell 407	unkn	
TC-HKJ(2)	Aérospatiale SA.365 Dauphin 2 (Reservation)	unkn	
TC-HKN	Sikorsky S-76B	760339	N22QP N22CP
TC-HKR	Sikorsky S-76C	760512	
TC-HKS	Robinson R-22 Beta	1233	G-OJAK
TC-HLK	Robinson R-22 Beta	1705	
TC-HMC(2)	Hughes 369D	50-0696D	EI-BYV G-ITUP G-KSBF G-BMJH
TC-HMD	Bell 430	49010	N62839
TC-HMM	Bell 407	53573	C-GZMP (N8067Z)
TC-HMS	Mil Mi-8	22400	
TC-HMZ	Bell 430	49097	N7085Y C-FEXW
TC-HNA	Mil Mi-8	8702	RA-.....
TC-HNH(2)	Bell 430	49033	N8060J
TC-HNL	Mil Mi-2	562817043	D-HZPN (DDR-VGJ) LSK:420
TC-HNS	Bell 206B Jet Ranger II	1965	N922DR N9522K
TC-HRH	Bell 206L3 Long Ranger III	unkn	
TC-HRS	Robinson R-44	unkn	
TC-HRT	Sikorsky S-76C	760506	N728TP
TC-HSA	Mil Mi-8	24299	CCCP24299
TC-HTS	Bell 230	23021	N5292L
TC-HUS	Mil Mi-8	5806	EZ-25960 CCCP25960
TC-HYS	Bell 206L-1 Long Ranger II (W/o 8.7.02)	45296	N77AR N71BH N71BR
TC-IEA	Boeing 737-8CX	32361	
TC-IEB	Boeing 737-8CX	32363	
TC-IEC	Fokker F28-0100	11410	PH-KXR XA-SHG PH-KXR
TC-IED	Fokker F28-0100	11420	PH-LXG XA-SHH PH-LXG
TC-IEE	Fokker F28-0100	11326	F-OLLB PT-MQV SE-DUE PH-CFD PH-EZJ (G-FIOW) PH-EZJ
TC-IHK	CCF/Beech T-34A Mentor	34-24	TAF: OK-21/ 54-5221 (RCAF24221)
TC-IHL	CCF/Beech T-34A Mentor	34-25	TAF: OK-22/ 54-5222 (RCAF24222)

TC-IHM	Cessna 152	unkn	
TC-ILC	Piper PA-18A-150 Super Cub (Rebuilt 1966 using spare fuselage 18-8620)	18-4737	TC-IL3
TC-ILS	Cessna 172N	17269863	N738CC
TC-IYA	Boeing 727-2F2	22999	TC-JCE
TC-IYB	Boeing 727-243	21664	TC-JCK (N581PE) I-DIRL
TC-JBF	Boeing 727-2F2	20980	
TC-JBG	Boeing 727-2F2	20981	
TC-JBJ	Boeing 727-2F2	20983	
TC-JCA	Boeing 727-2F2 Cargo	22992	
TC-JCO	Airbus A310-203	386	F-WWBC
TC-JCR	Airbus A310-203	370	F-WZLH
TC-JCS	Airbus A310-203	389	F-WWBG
TC-JCT	Airbus A310-304	502	TF-ELE N502AN F-GEMN F-WWCD
TC-JCV	Airbus A310-304	476	F-WWCT
TC-JCY	Airbus A310-304	478	F-WWCX
TC-JCZ	Airbus A310-304	480	F-WWCZ
TC-JDA	Airbus A310-304	496	F-WWCV
TC-JDB	Airbus A310-304	497	F-WWCH
TC-JDC	Airbus A310-304	537	F-WWCO
TC-JDD	Airbus A310-304	586	F-WWCK
TC-JDF	Boeing 737-4Y0	24917	
TC-JDG	Boeing 737-4Y0	25181	
TC-JDH	Boeing 737-4Y0	25184	
TC-JDJ	Airbus A340-311	023	F-WWJN
TC-JDK	Airbus A340-311	025	F-WWJP
TC-JDL	Airbus A340-311	057	F-WWJF
TC-JDM	Airbus A340-311	115	F-WWJN
TC-JDN	Airbus A340-313X	180	F-WWJU
TC-JDT	Boeing 737-4Y0	25261	
TC-JDY	Boeing 737-4Y0	26065	(EI-CFS)
TC-JEC	Boeing 727-228	22287	F-GCDF
TC-JEM	Boeing 737-4Q8	26302	
TC-JEN	Boeing 737-4Q8	25376	
TC-JEO	Boeing 737-4Q8	25377	
TC-JER	Boeing 737-4Y0	26073	
TC-JET	Boeing 737-4Y0	26077	
TC-JEU	Boeing 737-4Y0	26078	
TC-JEV	Boeing 737-4Y0	26085	
TC-JEY	Boeing 737-4Y0	26086	
TC-JEZ	Boeing 737-4Y0	26088	
TC-JFC	Boeing 737-8F2	29765	N1786B
TC-JFD	Boeing 737-8F2	29766	
TC-JFE	Boeing 737-8F2	29767	
TC-JFF	Boeing 737-8F2	29768	
TC-JFG	Boeing 737-8F2	29769	
TC-JFH	Boeing 737-8F2	29770	
TC-JFI	Boeing 737-8F2	29771	
TC-JFJ	Boeing 737-8F2	29772	
TC-JFK	Boeing 737-8F2	29773	N1786B
TC-JFL	Boeing 737-8F2	29774	
TC-JFM	Boeing 737-8F2	29775	
TC-JFN	Boeing 737-8F2	29776	
TC-JFO(2)	Boeing 737-8F2	29777	
TC-JFP	Boeing 737-8F2	29778	
TC-JFR	Boeing 737-8F2	29779	
TC-JFT	Boeing 737-8F2	29780	N1787B
TC-JFU	Boeing 737-8F2	29781	N1795B
TC-JFV	Boeing 737-8F2	29782	
TC-JFY	Boeing 737-8F2	29783	N1785B
TC-JFZ	Boeing 737-8F2	29784	
TC-JGA	Boeing 737-8F2	29785	N1786B
TC-JGB	Boeing 737-8F2	29786	
TC-JGC	Boeing 737-8F2	29787	
TC-JGD	Boeing 737-8F2	29788	
TC-JGE	Boeing 737-8F2	29789	
TC-JGF	Boeing 737-8F2	29790	
TC-JGG	Boeing 737-8F2 (Reservation)	29791	
TC-JIH	Airbus A340-311	270	F-WWJF
TC-JKA	Boeing 737-4Q8	26300	SX-BFA TC-JEL
TC-JKB	Boeing 737-4Y0	23981	CS-TGW TC-AFS EI-CEW F-GNFS SU-BLL EI-CEW EC-EMY EC-251
TC-JKC	Boeing 737-4Y0	24469	HL7257
TC-JKD	Boeing 737-4Y0	24493	HL7258
TC-JLA	Airbus A320-214	545	HB-IJB F-WWII
TC-JLB	Airbus A320-214	562	HB-IJF F-WWDQ
TC-JLC	Airbus A320-214	566	HB-IJG F-WWIN
TC-JLD	Airbus A320-214	574	HB-IJH F-WWDN
TC-JLE	Airbus A320-214	992	EC-HAD F-WWBS

TC-JLF	Airbus A320-214	1413	SU-LBE EI-CWT OO-SNH F-WWBS
TC-JLG	Airbus A320-214	1054	F-OHJZ F-WIHD OO-SNE F-WWIN
TC-JLH	Airbus A320-214	553	EI-CZV HB-IJD F-WWIE
TC-JLI	Airbus A320-214	559	EI-CZW HB-IJE F-WWIP
TC-JLJ	Airbus A320-232	1856	EI-DIV I-PEKS F-WQSK F-WWDI
TC-JLK	Airbus A320-232	1909	EI-DIW I-PEKT F-WQSL F-WWDS
TC-JLL	Airbus A320-232	1956	EI-DIX I-PEKV N996SE D-ALAT F-WWIM
TC-JMA	Airbus A321-111	522	HB-IOD D-AVZX
TC-JMC	Airbus A321-231	806	G-MIDA D-AVZQ
TC-JMG	Airbus A321-211	2060	N118CH G-JOEE D-AVZH
TC-JYK	Airbus A310-203	172	F-GEMF F-WZLI
TC-KAR(2)	Antonov An-24 (Wfu, stored)	47309603	RA-46671 ? CCCP46671 ?
TC-KBN	Delta Kanat	386	
TC-KET(2)	Antonov AN-12BP (Wfu, stored)	402808	RA-11366 CCCP11366
TC-KEU	Cessna 208 Caravan	20800317	N52234
TC-KIM	Cessna 150M	unkn	
TC-KON(2)	Cessna 650 Citation VII	650-7084	N1127G TC-KON(2) N5094D
TC-KPE	Piper PA-18-150 Super Cub	18-7558	N3819Z
TC-KPS	Piper PA-18-150 Super Cub	18-8538	
TC-KTC	Airbus A321-211	1451	EI-DDS I-PEKM D-AVXC
TC-KTD	Airbus A321-211	2117	(G-OMYA) D-AVZB
TC-KTY	Airbus A321-211	1012	D-ABLC F-WQRS G-CBOI OO-SUC D-AVZH
TC-KUR	Britten-Norman BN-2A-3 Islander	290	G-51-290 (N20JL)
TC-KZU	Airbus A300C4-203F	173	(TC-ORJ) N511TA C-FICI N68173 I-BUSL F-WZMS
TC-KZV	Airbus A300B4-103F	041	PH-EAN N201EA F-WUAZ
TC-KZY	Airbus A300B4-103F	044	PH-CLA N204EA F-WUAX
TC-LAA	Cessna 560 Citation V	560-0212	N1284X
TC-LAB	Cessna 560 Citation V	560-0216	N1285N
TC-LEY(2)	HFB-320 Hansa (Reserved as D-CHFB(2) .04)	1043	TC-KHE 16+03 D-CIRI
TC-LMK	Beech C90A King Air	LJ-1080	N6931W
TC-MAE	Dornier Do.27Q-5	2141	
TC-MAO	Boeing 737-86N	28645	N1795B
TC-MBA	Fokker F.27 Friendship 500	10654	G-CEXE SU-GAF PH-EXJ
TC-MBB	Fokker F.27 Friendship 500	10660	G-CEXF SU-GAE PH-EXC
TC-MBC	Fokker F.27 Friendship 500CRF	10530	OK-ABA N737A PH-EXK
TC-MBD	Fokker F.27 Friendship 500CRF	10531	OK-ABB N739A PH-EXM
TC-MBE	Fokker F.27 Friendship 500	10639	D-ACCT G-JEAG D-ADAP G-JEAG VH-EWX PH-EXG

TC-MDG	Canadair CL.600-2B16 Challenger	5110	N308BX N308FX N392PT C-GLXU
TC-MED	Mil Mi-2	5210126027	RA-23205 CCCP23205
TC-MEK(3)	Bombardier Learjet 60	60-016	N50163
TC-MEL	Cessna R172K Hawk XP	R1722577	N736KA
TC-MGM	Beech F33A Bonanza	CE-562	TC-MVK N4125S
TC-MHK	Cessna 152	15284971	N5538P
TC-MHS	Beech 390 Premier	RB-77	N6177A
TC-MIA	Cessna R172K Hawk XP	R1722818	N736VH
TC-MKA	Cessna 550B Citation Bravo	550-0960	N52229 N960CB
TC-MNA	Airbus A300C4-203F	019	N742SC F-BVGG
TC-MNE	Airbus A300B4-203	222	ZS-SDH RP-C3006 ZS-SDH RP-C3006 ZS-SDH 9V-STF F-WZMA
TC-MNF	Boeing 737-4K5	24126	D-AHLK(2)
TC-MNH	Boeing 737-448	24773	EI-BXC
TC-MNI	Boeing 737-4K5	24128	D-AHLO(2)
TC-MNJ	Airbus A300B4-203	123	N59123 PH-JLH N59123 I-BUSF F-WZEJ
TC-MNL	Boeing 737-4Q8	25374	TC-ANL TC-JEG
TC-MNM	Boeing 737-4Q8	25375	TC-ANH TC-JEJ
TC-MNN	Airbus A300B4-203	126	N13974 N968C F-OGTA RP-C3006 9V-STC F-WZEC
TC-MNO	McDonnell-Douglas DC-9-82	49138	N821US N945PS
TC-MNP	McDonnell-Douglas DC-9-82	49142	N823US N947PS N1005G
TC-MNR	McDonnell-Douglas DC-9-82	48097	N817US N942PS
TC-MNS	McDonnell-Douglas DC-9-82	48098	N818US N943PS
TC-MNT	McDonnell-Douglas DC-9-82	48096	N816US N941PS
TC-MNU	Airbus A300C4-203F	047	N740SC G-HLAA EI-TLN G-HLAA N740SC D-BVGJ F-WUAX
TC-MNY	Airbus A300B4-203	299	G-TTMC OH-LAA (LX-LGP) F-WZMX
TC-MNZ	Airbus A300B4-203	302	G-SWJW OH-LAB F-WZMY
TC-MSB(2)	Beech 400A Beechjet	RK-170	TC-MCX N2289B
TC-MSO	Boeing 737-8S3	29246	
TC-MSS	Beech C90A King Air	LJ-1276	N8065R
TC-MTR	Cessna 182R Skylane II	18267968	G-BKKP N9600H
TC-MZZ	Boeing 737-8S3	29247	N1786B
TC-NAG	Callair B-1A	10021	N7274V N29A
TC-NAK	Rockwell A-9B Quail Commander	1450	
TC-NEO	Beech 400A Beechjet	RK-130	N1130B
TC-NOA	Lockheed L1329 Jetstar 2	unkn	
TC-NSK	Cessna R172K Hawk XP	R1722790	N736UC
TC-NUR	Cessna 172N	17269384	N737FM
TC-OAB	Airbus A300B4-605R	749	TU-TAI F-WWAN
TC-OAE	Airbus A321-231	0663	F-OHMP D-AVZK
TC-OAF	Airbus A321-231	0668	F-OHMQ D-AVZN
TC-OAG	Airbus A300B4-605R	747	F-OHLN A6-EKO F-WWAT
TC-OAH	Airbus A300B4-605R	584	S7-RGO B-2309 N165PL VH-YMA F-WWAU
TC-OAI	Airbus A321-231	787	D-ALAG D-AVZL
TC-OAK	Airbus A321-231	954	D-ALAI D-AVZD
TC-OAL	Airbus A321-231	1004	D-ALAK D-AVZI
TC-OAN	Airbus A321-231	1421	D-ALAP D-AVZH
TC-OAO	Airbus A300B4-605R	764	D-AIAW F-WWAJ
TC-OGD	Boeing 757-2G5	24176	N500GX SE-RCE D-AMUY
TC-OGE	Airbus A320-214	764	G-VTAN G-BXTA F-WWDF
TC-OGF	Airbus A320-214	978	G-VMED SE-RCF PH-ABI G-VMED F-WWDC
TC-OGG	Boeing 757-225	23983	HS-OGB TC-OGC D-AMUX
TC-OGH	Boeing 757-225	22688	HS-OGA TC-OGA D-AMUU EC-FIY EC-896 D-AMUU N542EA
TC-OGI	Airbus A320-232	640	N381LF F-OHMO F-WWDF
TC-OGJ	Airbus A320-232	676	N391LF F-OHMR F-WWBG
TC-OGK	Airbus A320-233	460	N951LF F-WWDN
TC-OGL	Airbus A320-233	461	N941LF F-WWDP
TC-OIM	Airbus A300B4-120	094	OY-CNK SE-DFK F-WZEJ
TC-ONJ	Airbus A321-131	385	D-AVZG F-WWIB
TC-ONK	Airbus A300B4-103	086	TC-TKA N14980 (N980C) N209EA F-GBNE
TC-ONL	Airbus A300B4-103	087	TC-TKB N29981 (N981C) N210EA F-GBNF
TC-ONM	McDonnell-Douglas DC-9-88	53546	
TC-ONN	McDonnell-Douglas DC-9-88	53547	
TC-ONO	McDonnell-Douglas DC-9-88	53548	
TC-ONP	McDonnell-Douglas DC-9 88	53549	
TC-ONR	McDonnell-Douglas DC-9-88	53550	
TC-ONS	Airbus A321-131	364	D-AVZD F-WWIA
TC-ONT	Airbus A300B4-203	138	ZS-SDE F-WWAG C-GIZJ ZS-SDE F-WZEQ
TC-ONU	Airbus A300B4-203	192	ZS-SDF G-BSZE SU-DAN ZS-SDF C-GIZL ZS-SDF F-WZML
TC-ONV	Airbus A300B4-2C	057	F-BUAQ D-AIBB F-WZEG (D-AIAF)
TC-ONY	Airbus A300B2K-3C	037	ZS-SDB F-WUAU
TC-ORJ	Airbus A300B4-203F	173	N511TA C-FICI N68173 I-BUSL F-WZMS
TC-OYC	Airbus A300B4-120	079	OY-CNA LN-RCA F-WZEN
TC-OZD	Beech B200 Super King Air	BB-1496	N3047L
TC-OZT	Boeing Stearman PT-17 (Identity unconfirmed)	75-5989	N5325N 42-17826 ?
TC-OZY	Beech B200 Super King Air	BB-1545	N1070E
TC-PRK	Dassault Falcon 2000	191	F-GUYM F-WWVB
TC-RMK	Dassault Falcon 2000	157	F-WWVQ
TC-RTO	Mooney M.20J Model 205	24-3311	N1081W
TC-RXS	Bombardier Learjet 60	60-282	N5013Y

TC-SAN(2)	Canadair CL.600-2B16 Challenger	5114	VP-BOA VR-BOA C-FOSK C-GLYA
TC-SAT	Piper PA-18-135 Super Cub (Officially quoted with f/n 18-395)	18-413	TC-EAS Turkish AF 50-1757
TC-SGA	Airbus A300B2K-3C	090	JA8466 F-WZEG
TC-SGB	Airbus A310-304	562	N351LF CP-2232 F-GKTE F-WWCA
TC-SGD(2)	Piper PA-18-135 Super Cub (Officially quoted with f/n 18-2440)	18-2597	Turkish AF 52-6279
TC-SHF	Cessna T207A Turbo Stationair 8	20700658	D-EDDJ N75954
TC-SHK	Piper PA-18-150 Super Cub (Officially quoted with f/n 18-3011)	18-3074	Turkish AF 53-4674
TC-SKA	Boeing 737-4YO	23865	PH-BPA G-UKLA VT-MGE G-UKLA 9M-MLC G-UKLA
TC-SKB	Boeing 737-430	27004	EI-CPU SX-BFV EI-CPU D-ABKF (D-ABKK) (D-ABKE)
TC-SKC	Boeing 737-85F	30478	
TC-SKD	Boeing 737-4Q8	25372	TC-JDI
TC-SKE	Boeing 737-4Q8	25163	VH-TJV H4-SOL
TC-SKY	Piper PA-18-150 Super Cub (Officially quoted with f/n 18-5506)	18-4055	Turkish AF 54-2655
TC-SMA	Grumman G.159 Gulfstream 1 (Wfu, stored Geneva)	172	N172ED N11Y N44MC N700DB
TC-SMS	Beech A36 Bonanza	E-2731	N80287
TC-SSS	Lockheed 1329 Jetstar 2	5226	N308SG N815RC N2MK N4026M
TC-STR	Hawker 800XP	258415	TC-BHD N31016
TC-SUC	Boeing 737-86N	28616	N1786B
TC-SUG	Boeing 737-8CX	32365	
TC-SUH	Boeing 737-8CX	32366	
TC-SUI	Boeing 737-8CX	32367	
TC-SUL	Boeing 737-85F	28222	SE-DVO
TC-SUM	Boeing 737-85F	28826	SE-DVR
TC-SUO	Boeing 737-86Q	30272	VH-VOE N90CD OO-CYN N1787B
TC-SUU	Boeing 737-86Q	30274	VH-VOF N91CD OO-CYI N1786B
TC-TAC	HOAC DV-20 Katana	20082	OE-CEC
TC-TAD	HOAC DV-20 Katana (Dismantled)	20093	D-ECET
TC-TAE	HOAC DV-20 Katana	20101	
TC-TAF	HOAC DV-20 Katana	20107	
TC-TAN	Canadair CL.600-2B16 Challenger	5459	N459MT C-GLYA
TC-TAR	Cessna 150M	unkn	
TC-TAY(2)	Piper PA-28-236 Dakota	2811032	
TC-TBA	Cessna 210M Centurion	21062303	N761JX
TC-TCB	Airbus A319-115X	1002	MM62173 D-AJWF D-AVYJ
TC-TEK(3)	BAe.125 Series 800A	258229	N229RY PT-OTH N683BA G-5-748
TC-THA	Avro 146-RJ100	E-3232	G-6-232
TC-THD	Avro 146-RJ100	E-3237	G-6-237
TC-THE	Avro 146-RJ100	E-3238	G-6-238
TC-THH	Avro 146-RJ100	E-3243	G-6-243
TC-THI	Avro 146-RJ70	E-1229	G-BUFI
TC-THJ	Avro 146-RJ70	E-1230	G-6-230 (N835BE)
TC-THK	Piper PA-42 Cheyenne III	42-5501031	TC-FAG
TC-THL	Avro 146-RJ70	E-1249	G-6-249
TC-THM	Avro 146-RJ100	E-3264	G-6-264 (N836BE)
TC-THN	Avro 146-RJ70	E-1252	G-6-252 (N837BE)
TC-THO	Avro 146-RJ100	E-3265	G-6-265
TC-TIP	Mil Mi-2	5210624058	RA-14080 CCCP14080
TC-TJA	Boeing 737-3Q8	24699	G-IGOZ G-OBWZ N699PU PK-GWG

TC-TKG	Pilatus Britten-Norman BN-2T Turbine Islander	2231	G-BSAD
TC-TLS	Beech 60 Duke (Wfu)	P-117	YU-BGF HB-GDX
TC-TOI	Boeing 737-4Q8	25375	TC-JEJ
TC-TOM	Piper PA-38-112 Tomahawk	38-78A0683	N2427A
TC-TOR	Antonov An-24 (Wfu, stored)	67310507	
TC-TPK	SOCATA TB-20 Trinidad	unkn	
TC- TPS	Aviat Pitts S-2B (Either c/n 5190 N6068U or c/n 5322 N1585P)		
TC-TRI	Dornier Do.28D Skyservant	4003	Turkish Army D-IBYL
TC-TRK	Dornier Do.28D Skyservant	4002	Turkish Army D-IBYK
TC-TRL	Dornier Do.28D-2 Skyservant	4119	T.Army:10024 58+44
TC-TRM	Dornier Do.28D-2 Skyservant	4122	T.Army:10031 58+47
TC-TRO	Dornier Do.28D-2 Skyservant	4035	Turkish Army D-IEHB(1)
TC-TRP	Thorp T.211	007	N89DB
TC-UPS	Swearingen SA.226AT Merlin IV	AT-044	TC-BPS C-GGPT N544F N5441F
TC-VBV	Piper PA-28-140 Cherokee Cruiser	28-7425044	N56818
TC-VOR	Cessna 172N	17269704	N737VG (D-EUSW) N737VG
TC-YBB	Grumman AA-5B Tiger (See TC-YSF)	AA5B-0654	N28613
TC-YBD	Grumman AA-5BTiger	AA5B-0632	N80JL N28609
TC-YBE	Grumman AA-5B Tiger	AA5B-1288	N4537L
TC-YSB	Piper PA-18 Super Cub 95	"10-10371"	TC-. . .
TC-YSF	Grumman AA-5B Tiger (C/n quoted is same as TC-YBB, error or re-regd?)	AA5A-0654	N28613
TC-YUZ	Cessna 172	unkn	
TC-YYB	Piper PA-18 Super Cub 95	18-449	TC-EAR 50-1793
TC-ZAA	PZL M-18A Dromader	1Z-015-28	
TC-ZAB	PZL M-18A Dromader	1Z-015-29	
TC-ZAF	PZL M-18A Dromader	1Z-017-08	
TC-ZAG	Antonov An-2R	1G230-23	SP-ZZG
TC-ZAH	Antonov An-2R	1G230-24	SP-ZZH
TC-ZAJ	Antonov An-2R	1G230-25	SP-ZZI
TC-ZAK	Antonov An-2R	1G230-26	SP-ZZK
TC-ZAN	PZL M-18A Dromader (W/o 1998)	1Z-020-18	SP-DBT
TC-ZAP	PZL M-18A Dromader	1Z-020-19	SP-DBU
TC-ZAR	PZL M-18B Dromader	1Z-025-27	SP-DDR
TC-ZAT	PZL M-18B Dromader	1Z-025-29	SP-DDT
TC-ZAU	PZL M-18B Dromader	1Z-025-30	SP-DDU
TC-ZAV	PZL M-18B Dromader (W/o 2003)	1Z-026-11	SP-DEK
TC-ZAY	PZL M-18B Dromader	1Z-026-12	SP-DEL
TC-ZBC	Norman NAC-6 Fieldmaster 34	6002	G-NACM
TC-ZBD	Norman NAC-6 Firemaster 65	6003	G-NACN Z-NACN G-NACN
TC-ZBE	PZL M-18A Dromader	1Z018-08	CS-ASC
TC-ZBF	PZL M-18A Dromader	1Z018-09	CS-ASD
TC-ZBG	PZL M-18A Dromader	1Z019-04	CS-AVP SP-FCG
TC-ZBH	PZL M-18A Dromader	1Z019-28	CS-AVQ SP-FCA
TC-ZBI	PZL M-18A Dromader	1Z019-29	CS-AVR SP-FCB
TC-ZKE	Ayres S.2R-T34 Turbo Thrush	2449R	N8941Q
TC-ZPD	Piper PA-25-235 Pawnee C	25-4250	N4664Y
TC-ZPE	Piper PA-25-235 Pawnee C	25-4257	N4666Y
TC-ZPH	Piper PA-25-235 Pawnee C	25-4319	N4638Y
TC-ZPK	Piper PA-25-260 Pawnee C	25-4658	N4945Y
TC-ZPL	Piper PA-25-260 Pawnee C	25-4638	N4948Y
TC-ZPM	Piper PA-25-260 Pawnee C	25-4513	N4755Y
TC-ZPP	Piper PA-25-260 Pawnee C	25-4420	N4689Y
TC-ZPV	Piper PA-25-235 Pawnee C	25-4876	N4373Y
TC-ZPY	Piper PA-25-235 Pawnee C	25-4882	N4380Y
TC-ZRC	Piper PA-25-260 Pawnee C	25-4812	N4355Y N9723N
TC-ZRD	Piper PA-25-260 Pawnee C	25-4963	N8542L
TC-ZRH	Piper PA-25-260 Pawnee C	25-4942	N4380Y
TC-ZRR	Piper PA-25-260 Pawnee C	25-5045	N8616L
TC-ZRV	Piper PA-25-235 Pawnee C	25-5146	N8694L
TC-ZSA	Piper PA-25-260 Pawnee C	25-5193	N8751L N9704N
TC-ZSB	Piper PA-25-235 Pawnee C	25-5085	N8646L
TC-ZSC	Piper PA-25-260 Pawnee C	25-5322	N8817L
TC-ZSF	Cessna A188B Agwagon C	18800929	N21643
TC-ZSJ	Cessna A188B Agwagon C	18800959	TC-ZTI TC-ZSJ N21668
TC-ZSK	Cessna A188B Agwagon C	18800961	N21690
TC-ZSL	Cessna A188B Agwagon C	18800966	N21699
TC-ZSM	Cessna A188B Agwagon C	18800857	N4457Q
TC-ZSP	Piper PA-25-260 Pawnee C	25-5437	N8743L
TC-ZSR	Piper PA-25-260 Pawnee C	25-5438	N8744L
TC-ZSV	Piper PA-25-260 Pawnee C	25-5435	N8712L
TC-ZSZ	Piper PA-25-260 Pawnee C	25-5443	N8746L

TC-ZTA	Rockwell S.2R Thrush Commander	1660R	
TC-ZTD	Cessna A188B Agtruck	18801126T	N5637G
TC-ZTE	Cessna A188B Agwagon	18801141	
TC-ZTG	Cessna A188B Agwagon	18801146	N5755G
TC-ZTH	Cessna A188B Agtruck	18801151T	N5838G
TC-ZTK	Cessna A188B Agwagon	18801104	N1697C
			N21893
TC-ZTL	Cessna A188B Agwagon	18801160	N5886G
TC-ZTN	Cessna A188B Agtruck	18801250T	N1668C
TC-ZTP	Cessna 402B	402B0412	N69289
TC-ZTS	Ayres S.2R-T34 Turbo Thrush	1717R	TC-TZS
			TC-ZTS
			N5517X
TC-ZTT	Piper PA-36-285 Pawnee Brave	36-7360012	N55858
TC-ZUA	Piper PA-36-285 Pawnee Brave	36-7360008	N55350
TC-ZUB	Piper PA-36-285 Pawnee Brave	36-7360006	N15690
TC-ZUC	Grumman G.164A Agcat	1067	N4760
TC-ZUD	Grumman G.164A Agcat	1024	N5411
TC-ZUF	Rockwell S.2R Thrush Commander	1685R	N5585X
TC-ZUG	Piper PA-36-285 Pawnee Brave	36-7360024	N9526N
TC-ZUH	Piper PA-36-285 Pawnee Brave	36-7360026	N9527N
TC-ZUJ	Piper PA-36-285 Pawnee Brave	36-7360030	N9532N
TC-ZUK	Piper PA-36-285 Pawnee Brave	36-7360034	N9533N
TC-ZUN	Piper PA-25-235 Pawnee D	25-7405566	N6833L
			N9676N
TC-ZUP	Piper PA-25-235 Pawnee D	25-7405567	N6834L
			N9688N
TC-ZUR	Piper PA-25-260 Pawnee D	25-7405568	N6832L
			N9678N
TC-ZUS	Piper PA-36-285 Pawnee Brave	36-7360064	N56643
TC-ZUT	Piper PA-25-235 Pawnee D	25-7405562	N6830L
			N9652N
TC-ZUU	Piper PA-36-285 Pawnee Brave	36-7360042	N56369
TC-ZUY	Rockwell S.2R Thrush Commander	2001R	N4233X
TC-ZVA	Rockwell S.2R Thrush Commander	1899R	N4898X
TC-ZVE	Piper PA-25-260 Pawnee D	25-7556131	N9832P
TC-ZVG	Piper PA-25-235 Pawnee D	25-7556124	N9825P
TC-ZVH	Bellanca 8GCBC Scout	106-74	OE-AOW
TC-ZVJ	Cessna 402B	402B1073	N1552G
TC-ZVK	Piper PA-25-260 Pawnee D	25-7405612	N9527P
TC-ZVL	Piper PA-25-260 Pawnee D	25-7656118	N82402
TC-ZVM	Piper PA-25-235 Pawnee D	25-7756006	N82430
TC-ZVR	Ayres S.2R Thrush Commander	2487R	
TC-ZVT	Ayres S.2R Thrush Commander	2495R	
TC-ZVU	Piper PA-25-235 Pawnee D	25-7756008	N82437
TC-ZVV	Piper PA-25-235 Pawnee D	25-7756007	N82432
TC-ZVY	Piper PA-25-235 Pawnee D	25-7756031	N82488
TC-ZVZ	Piper PA-25-260 Pawnee D	25-7656061	N82306
TC-ZYA	Piper PA-25-260 Pawnee D	25-7656071	N82307
TC-ZYC	Piper PA-25-235 Pawnee D	25-7856017	N9165T
TC-ZYE	Piper PA-25-235 Pawnee D	25-7756028	N82461
TC-ZYF	Antonov An-2R	1G-18558/1	SP-DMA(2)
TC-ZYG	Antonov An-2R	1G185-59	TC-ZIG ?
			TC-ZYG
			SP-DMB(1)
TC-ZYH	Antonov An-2R	1G191-01	(YV-382A)
			SP-DBA(1)
TC-ZYI	Antonov An-2R	1G19-102	(YV-384A)
			SP-DBB(1)
TC-ZYJ	PZL M-18 Dromader	1Z-006-07	SP-DAA(2)
TC-ZYN	Cessna A188B Agtruck	18803910T	(N9981J)
TC-ZYP	Cessna A188B Agtruck	18803864T	(N9925J)
TC-ZYR	Cessna A188B Agtruck	18803890T	(N9961J)
TC-ZYS	Antonov An-2T	1G-20635	SP-ZYS
TC-ZYT	Antonov An-2T	1G-20803	SP-ZYT
TC-ZYU	Antonov An-2T	1G-20804	SP-ZYU
TC-ZYV	Antonov An-2R	1G-20801	SP-ZYV
TC-ZYY	Antonov An-2R	1G-20802	SP-ZYY
TC-ZYZ	Antonov An-2R	1G-19904	SP-ZYZ

Aircraft sold to Turkey for which new registrations are not yet known:

TC-H . .	Aérospatiale AS.350B3 Ecureuil	3804	SE-JHV
TC-H . .	Agusta A.109A-II	7414	N250SC
			ZP-HMD
			N88FA
			JA9919
TC- . . .	Aviat Pitts S-2B Special	5190	N6068U
TC- . . .	Aviat Pitts S-2B Special	5322	N1585P
TC- . . .	Ayres S.2R-600 Thrush Commander	2502R	N40055
TC- . . .	Beech 400A Beechjet	RK-211	N3028U
	(Believed to TC-NNK, unconfirmed)		
TC-H . .	Bell 206L-3 Long Ranger III	51398	N206XP
			PT-YBE
			N33GH
			JA6029
TC-H . .	Bell 206L-3 Long Ranger III	51547	D-HMKB(2)
			F-GHYO
			C-FMEI
TC-H . . .	Bell 222U	47572	N32GH
			(N326H)
			JA9935
			N3209D
TC-H . .	Bell 230	23036	N67354
TC-H . .	Bell 407	53085	
TC-H . .	Bell 407	53263	N407BE
TC-H . .	Bell 407	53468	N9138L
			C-GLZA
TC- . . .	Cessna 150M	15078330	N9381U
TC- . . .	Cessna 152	15281589	N65499
TC- . . .	Cessna 152	15281854	N67475
TC- . . .	Cessna 152	15285300	N67513
TC- . . .	Cessna 152	15285384	D-ECCF(3)
			N93045
TC- . . .	Cessna 172G	17254812	N1317F
TC- . . .	Cessna 172M	17264020	N21790
TC- . . .	Cessna 172R	17280368	N9505V
TC- . . .	Cessna 172R	17281236	N66162
TC- . . .	Cessna 172RG	172RG0853	N9505V
TC- . . .	Cessna 182A Skylane	51400	N2100G
TC- . . .	Cessna 182T	18281511	N69545
TC- . . .	Cessna A188B Agwagon C	18800998	N21744
TC- . . .	Cessna A188B Agtruck	18801755T	N53314
TC- . . .	Cessna A188B Agwagon	18801984	N84470
TC- . . .	Cessna A188B Agtruck	18802137T	N9169R
TC- . . .	Cessna A188B Agtruck	18802789T	N731CK
TC- . . .	Cessna A188B Agtruck	18803017T	N731ND
TC- . . .	Cessna A188BAgtruck	18803027T	N731NP
TC- . . .	Fisher Super Koala	SK002	N200SK
TC- . . .	Fokker F.27 Friendship 600	10405	G-BNIZ
			OY-SRA
			G-BNIZ
			9Q-CLQ
			PH-FOD
TC- . . .	Fokker F.27 Friendship 500	10459	G-CEXG
			G-JEAP
			9Q-CBI
			OY-APF
			9Q-CBI
			PH-RUA
			VH-EWR
			F-BYAH
			OY-APF
			PH-EXD
TC- . . .	Grumman G.164A Agcat	1033	N5418
TC- . . .	Grumman G.164A Agcat	534	N5254
TC- . . .	Grumman G.164B Agcat	665B	N8367K
TC- . . .	Gulfstream AG-5B Tiger	10157	PH-MLE
			N1198B
TC-H . .	Hughes 369HS	54-0595S	N9191F
TC- . . .	Maule M-5-235C Lunar Rocket	7329C	D-EJYY
			N5639Y
			N30MD
			N5639Y
TC- . . .	Maule M-7-235 Super Rocket	4121C	N360FS
TC- . . .	Piper PA-25-260 Pawnee C	25-4678	N4875Y
TC- . . .	Piper PA-25-260 Pawnee D	25-7556205	N9895P
TC- . . .	Piper PA-25-235 Pawnee D	25-7405687	N9547P
TC- . . .	Piper PA-28-140 Cherokee	28-7425044	N56818
TC- . . .	Piper PA-28R-200 Cherokee Arrow II	28R-7335006	D-EJES(3)
			HB-OIY
			N15056
TC- . . .	Piper PA-36-285 Pawnee Brave	36-7560060	N9949P
			XB-FGS
			N9949P
TC- . . .	Piper PA-36-285 Pawnee Brave	36-7760023	N59696
TC- . . .	Piper PA-36-300 Pawnee Brave	36-7760068	N59657
TC- . . .	Piper PA-36-375 Pawnee Brave	36-8202022	N2401X
TC- . . .	Pitts S-1 Special	J-B-1	N240PS
TC- . . .	PZL M-18A Dromader	IZ-021-13	D-FOMG
			DDR-TMG
TC- . . .	PZL M-18A Dromader	IZ-021-15	D-FOMI
			DDR-TMI
TC- . . .	Robin ATL	102	F-GFSV
TC- . . .	Rockwell S.2R Thrush Commander	1913R	N4062X
TC- . . .	Rockwell S.2R Thrush Commander	2341R	N8854Q
TC- . . .	Rockwell S.2R Thrush Commander	2392R	N5691X
TC-H . .	Rotorway Executive 90	5075	G-BUIS
TC-H . .	Schweizer 269C	S-1291	
TC-H . .	Schweizer 269C	S-1292	
TC-H . .	Sikorsky S-70A	701882	N50056
TC- . . .	SOCATA TB-9 Tampico)	1851	F-OIDP
TC- . . .	SOCATA TB-9 Tampico) see TC-AUJ/L	1852	F-OIDQ
TC- . . .	SOCATA TB-9 Tampico)	1853	F-OIDR
TC- . . .	SOCATA TB-10 Tobago	750	PH-GDH
			D-EJHF
TC- . . .	SOCATA TB-10 Tobago	1307	N5555N
TC- . . .	SOCATA TB-20 Trinidad	1712	F-OHIT
TC- . . .	SOCATA TB-20 Trinidad	1713	F-OHIU
TC- . . .	SOCATA TB-20 Trinidad	1714	F-OHIV
TC- . . .	SOCATA TB-20 Trinidad	2129	F-GYQE
TC- . . .	SOCATA TB-20 Trinidad	2131	F-OIUI
TC- . . .	SOCATA TB-20 Trinidad	2133	F-OIUK

BALLOONS AND AIRSHIPS

TC-AVK	American Blimp Corporation A150 Airship	3	N153LG
TC-BAA	Cameron V-77 HAFB	935	
TC-BAB	Raven S-55A HAFB	1026	
TC-BAC(2)	Colt 69A HAFB	528	
TC-BAD	Cameron V-77 HAFB	2078	
TC-BAE	Colt 105A HAFB	1267	

TC-BAL	Cameron N-77 HAFB	2384	
TC-BAT(2)	Colt 105A HAFB	4941	
TC-BBD	Ultramagic M-90 HAFB	unkn	
TC-BBH(2)	Ultramagic N-250 HAFB	unkn	
TC-BBJ	Thunder AX10-210 SII HAFB	4979	
TC-BBP	Cameron O-120 HAFB	3678	
TC-BDG	Cameron N-105 HAFB	3017	
TC-BIG	Ultramagic N-355	355/...	
TC-BIK	Cameron V-77 HAFB	3676	
TC-BIS	Colt 105A HAFB (Reservation)	4644	
TC-BRO	Colt 105A HAFB	1898	
TC-BRP(2)	Ultramagic N-250 HAFB	unkn	
TC-B . .	Cameron A-210	4245	G-BXNM
TC-B . .	Cameron N-105 HAFB	5936	N1602T
TC-B . .	Colt 180A	1851	G-BSUU
TC-B . .	Colt 210A HAFB	2272	G-ZEBR
TC-B . .	Colt 240A HAFB	2682	G-BVVT
TC-B . .	Colt 300A HAFB	2096	G-RAVI
TC-B . .	Head AX7-77B HAFB	250	N8303F

GLIDERS

TC-PCU	SZD-22C Mucha Standard	F-755	
TC-PCV	SZD-22CMucha Standard	F-601	
TC-PCY	SZD-10bis Czapla	W-134	
TC-PCZ	SZD-10bis Czapla	W-135	
TC-PDA	SZD-9bis Bocian 1D	P-398	
TC-PDD	SZD-10bis Czapla	W-131	
TC-PDI	Scheibe Bergfalke II/55	5823	
TC-PDJ	Scheibe Bergfalke II/55	5824	
TC-PDK	Sportavia-Pützer RF-5BSperber	51049	D-KATM(1)
TC-PDL	Sportavia-Pützer RF-5BSperber	51052	D-KILO
TC-PDO	SZD-48-1 Jantar Standard 2	B-1154	
TC-PDP	SZD-48-1 Jantar Standard 2	B-1156	
TC-PDR	SZD-48-1 Jantar Standard 2	B-1167	
TC-PDS	SZD-48-1 Jantar Standard 2	B-1073	
TC-PDT	SZD-48-1 Jantar Standard 2	B-1180	
TC-PDU	SZD-48-1 Jantar Standard 2	B-1181	
TC-PDV	SZD-48-1 Jantar Standard 2	B-1125	
TC-PDY	SZD-42-2 Jantar 2B	B-1126	
TC-PDZ	SZD-50-3 Puchacz	B-967	
TC-PEA	SZD-50-3 Puchacz	B-971	
TC-PEF	SZD-50-3 Puchacz	B-974	
TC-PEG	SZD-50-3 Puchacz	B-977	
TC-PEH	SZD-50-3 Puchacz	B-978	
TC-PEI	SZD-50-3 Puchacz	B-979	
TC-PEJ	SZD-50-3 Puchacz	B-1398	
TC-PEK	SZD-50-3 Puchacz	B-1399	
TC-PEL	ICA Brasov IS.29D2	185	
TC-PEM	ICA Brasov IS.29D2	186	
TC-PEN	ICA Brasov IS.29D2	187	
TC-PEP	ICA Brasov IS.29D2	191	
TC-PER(2)	SZD-50-3 Puchacz	B-1466	
TC-PET	SZD-50-3 Puchacz	B-1467	
TC-PFA	SZD-50-3 Puchacz	B-1727	
TC-PFB	SZD-50-3 Puchacz	B-1726	
TC-PFC	SZD-50-3 Puchacz	B-1733	
TC-PFD	SZD-50-3 Puchacz	B-1735	
TC-PFE	SZD-50-3 Puchacz	B-1869	
TC-PFF	SZD-50-3 Puchacz	B-1870	
TC-PFG	PZL PW-5 Smyk	17.08.008	
TC-PFH	PZL PW-5 Smyk	17.08.009	
TC-PFM	Schempp-Hirth Discus b	276	
TC-PFN	Schempp-Hirth Discus b	277	
TC-PFP	Schempp-Hirth Ventus c	428	
TC-PFR	Schempp-Hirth Ventus c	429	

MICROLIGHTS

TC-UAB	Phantom MCHU Microlight	2071	
TC-UAC	Type unknown (Phantom?)	2010	
TC-UAD	Comco Ikarus Fox II	8604-1118	
TC-UAF	Comco Ikarus Fox II	8601-1114	
TC-UAH	Type unknown (Phantom?)	2003	
TC-UAI	Type unknown (Phantom?)	2022	
TC-UAJ	Type unknown (Phantom?)	2017	
TC-UAK	Rotec Panther 2 Plus	3563247	
TC-UAL	Rotec Panther 2 Plus	unkn	
TC-UAM	Rotec Panther 2 Plus	unkn	
TC-UAN	Rotec Panther 2 Plus	2538676	
TC-UAP	Type unknown	unkn	
TC-UAR	Type unknown (Phantom?)	2019 ?	
TC-UAS	Type unknown (Phantom?)	2019 ?	
TC-UAT	Comco Ikarus Fox II	8604-1121	
TC-UAU	Comco Ikarus Fox II	8604-1117	
TC-UAY	Type unknown	11110	
TC-UCA	SMAN Pétrel UL	034	
TC-UCB	Air Command 532	unkn	
TC-UFO	Type unknown (This is presumably the Powerchute Kestrel 00431, see below)	431	
TC-UYK	YUKA Ultralight	1	
TC-U . .	Powerchute Kestrel	00431	G-MYFC
TC-U . .	Solar Wings 462 Pegasus XL-Q	SW-WQ-0038/SW-TE-0048	G-MTYB
TC-U . .	Solar Wings 447 Pegasus XL-R	SW-WA-1184/SW-TB-1181	G-MTIF
TC-U . .	Solar Wings 582 Quasar IITC	7226	

TF - ICELAND

Icelandic civil aircraft all carry their unique CofR Number externally. This stays with the airframe even if the registration changes. As a potential aid to identification we now include this number below in the second column.

Regn.		Type	C/n	Prev.Id.
TF-ABA	780	Boeing 747-267B	22530	B-HID VR-HID
TF-ABB	426	Cessna 172N	17269176	TF-USA(3) N734WQ
TF-ABC(2)	168	Zlin Z.326 Trenér Master	908	
TF-ABD	837	Arctic Raven 2XS	1	
TF-ABJ(3)	737	Groves/ Pitts S-1J Special (Damaged 2.7.02)	02	C-GSMP
TF-ABP(2)	781	Boeing 747-267B	22429	B-HIC VR-HIC
TF-ADA	930	Piper PA-31-350 Navajo Chieftain	31-7305038	PH-KID N78CF PJ-PLA PH-KID PJ-PLA PH-KID G-BBEJ N74905
TF-ADB	702	Dornier 228-202K	8046	TF-ELF LN-NVC D-IDBN
TF-ADC	932	Dornier 228-202K	8065	G-BUXT D-CBOL TC-FBM D-CBOL
TF-ADD	732	Dornier 228-20K	8070	TF-ELH G-RGDT TF-ELH SE-KVV TF-ELH SE-KVV LN-NVG D-CLIC
TF-AFI	99	Piper PA-18A-150 Super Cub	18-6968	TF-KAZ N10F
TF-AIB	113	Cessna 140	13825	N1653V (NC1653V)
TF-AIG	125	Cessna 140 (Restoration)	9421	N72247 (NC72247)
TF-AIR	852	SOCATA TB-10 Tobago	1901	N363DG G-GINS F-OILN
TF-AKK	540	Piper PA-12 Super Cruiser	12-3340	N4400M NC4400M
TF-ALK	437	Piper PA-18 Super Cub 105 (Also quoted with f/n 18-419)	18-468	OY-ALK D-EGLG (D-EHFV) Greek AF 50-1812
TF-ALP	438	Piper PA-12 Super Cruiser	12-2223	D-EJEZ N3374M NC3374M
TF-AMA	908	Boeing 747-412	24063	9V-SMC 3B-SMC 9V-SMC
TF-AMB	909	Boeing 747-412	24065	9V-SME
TF-AMC	927	Boeing 747-2B3F	21835	F-GBOX
TF-AMD	928	Boeing 747-243B	23476	N518MC I-DEMW
TF-AME	933	Boeing 747-312	24063	F-GSEA N121KG (9V-SKG) (9V-SQZ)

TF-AMF	935	Boeing 747-230B	23286	D-ABYZ I-DEMX D-ABYZ N6055X
TF-AMH	937	Boeing 747-230B	23393	D-ABZC N6046C
TF-AMI	938	Boeing 747-412	24065	9V-SMO
TF-API	548	Cessna 152 (No current CofA)	15280923	N48637
TF-ARC	587	Alon A-2 Aircoupe	A-164	N5664F
TF-ARD	870	Boeing 757-225	22211	G-OOOV N521EA
TF-ARE	861	Boeing 757-225	22611	G-OOOW N522EA
TF-ARF	862	Boeing 747-236B	22305	G-BDXL N8280V (G-BDXM)
TF-ARG	863	Boeing 747-236B	22303	G-BDXK
TF-ARH	873	Boeing 747-230F	22669	N742SA D-ABYW
TF-ARI	875	Boeing 757-2Y0ER	25240	G-OOOU
TF-ARJ	864	Boeing 747-236B	23735	G-BDXN N6046P
TF-ARK	890	Boeing 757-225	22612	G-OOOM SE-DUN G-OOOM N523EA
TF-ARL	872	Boeing 747-230F	22671	N743SA D-ABYY
TF-ARM	874	Boeing 747-230F	22363	N744SA D-ABYT
TF-ARN	871	Boeing 747-2F6B	22382	N745SA N623FF N744PR
TF-ARO	886	Boeing 747-243B	23301	N73718 I-DEMV N6018N
TF-ARP	888	Boeing 747-230B	23348	D-ABZB N747MC D-ABXB N6005F
TF-ARR	889	Boeing 747-230B (W/o 7.11.04)	23621	D-ABZF N6046P
TF-ARS	887	Boeing 747-357	22996	ZS-SKA HB-IGF N221GF HB-IGF
TF-ART	856	Van's RV-6	21289	
TF-ARU	892	Boeing 747-344	22970	ZS-SAT N8279V
TF-ARV	907	Boeing 747-230B	24138	D-ABZI N6005C
TF-ARW	906	Boeing 747-256B	24071	N528UP EC-EEK EC-136 N6005C
TF-ARY	905	Boeing 747-329	24837	N24837 OO-SGD
TF-AST	116	Cessna 140	9359	TF-JET N72186 (NC72186)
TF-ATD	798	Boeing 747-267B	21966	B-HIA VR-HIA
TF-ATI	803	Boeing 747-341	24107	N824DS PP-VOB N6018N
TF-ATJ	804	Boeing 747-341	24108	N420DS PP-VOC N6005C
TF-ATT	854	Boeing 767-383ER	24358	OY-KDH I-AEJB
TF-ATU	829	Boeing 767-3YOER	26204	N204GE CC-CEL XA-RKJ
TF-ATX	842	Boeing 747-236B	23711	G-BDXM
TF-ATZ	835	Boeing 747-236B	24088	G-BDXP
TF-AVA(2)	371	Cessna 152-II (CofA exp 31.8.01)	15281871	TF-KGL N67501
TF-BAA	108	Piper PA-23 Apache	23-606	N2031P
TF-BAY	814	Buddy Baby Great Lakes	AS1	
TF-BBC	858	Boeing 737-3Q4	24209	N209PK PT-TEG
TF-BBD	818	Boeing 737-3YO	24463	OY-SEE N955WP EI-BZR YV-99C EI-BZR EC-ENT EC-245 N1779B
TF-BBE	899	Boeing 737-36EF	25256	N314FL EC-FHR EC-704
TF-BBF	900	Boeing 737-36EF	25264	N316FL EC-FLG EC-706
TF-BBE	901	Boeing 737-36EF	25263	N317FL EC-FLF EC-705
TF-BCX	851	Yakovlev Yak-52	822414	UR-BCX DOSAAF
TF-BCZ	811	Yakovlev Yak-52	855710	UR-BCZ DOSAAF
TF-BEB	473	Beech 77 Skipper (CofA exp 31.8.02)	WA-237	TF-BED OY-BEV N3833R
TF-BEZ	474	Beech 77 Skipper (CofA exp 31.7.00)	WA-238	OY-BEZ N3833U
TF-BGH	165	Piper PA-22-160 Tri-Pacer (CofA expired 31.7.97)	22-6306	N9246D
TF-BKB	329	Cessna 177 Cardinal	17701163	OY-AHU N30268
TF-BMC	584	Beech C23 Sundowner	M-1083	N6937Q
TF-BMW	720	Partenavia P.68 Observer	389-02-OB2	N8082Y I-DOLF
TF-BMX	593	Cessna 337G Skymaster (CofA expired 30.4.02)	33701701	N53559
TF-BOJ	519	Cessna 152 (CofA exp 31.5.96)	15279935	TF-FTK N757RC
TF-BON	375	Beech C23 Sundowner (CofA expired 30.9.94)	M-1784	TF-ISL(2) TF-OLI N9171S
TF-BOR	637	Piper PA-22-160 Tri-Pacer	22-6578	N9662D
TF-BOY	533	Piper PA-28-161 Cherokee Warrior II	28-7816404	N6282C
TF-BTH	480	Pitts S-2S Special	BTH-1	
TF-CCB	749	Yakovlev Yak-55	870309	HA-JAI DOSAAF-177 DOSAAF-22
TF-CSA	931	Dornier 328	3091	D-CPRU
TF-CUB(2)	176	Piper J-3C-65 Cub (L-4H) (Akureyri museum, airworthy)	10606	TF-JMF(1) N51550 43-29315
TF-CUP	432	Piper J-3C-65 Cub (Officially quoted as c/n 12990 but f/n is 11663 which results in c/n above)	11837	TF-GEV G-BCYS F-BFYH HB-ZAH 43-30546
TF-DAB	787	Piper PA-16 Clipper (CofA expired 30.6.02)	16-238	(TF-DUF) (TF-SPO) N5627H
TF-DGA(2)	351	Cessna 182P Skylane	18263610	N6033J
TF-DGB	156	Cessna 150F (CofA exp 31.3.93)	15063171	N6571F
TF-DHC	479	DHC-1 Chipmunk 22 (CofA expired 31.8.93)	C1/0744	OY-AVI RDAF: P-137 RDAF: 12-137
TF-DUA	153	Cessna 172C (CofA exp 31.5.90)	17248915	TF-DGA(1) N8415X
TF-DUF	-	Piper PA-16 Clipper (Reservation)	16-238	(TF-SPO) N5627H
TF-DUO	576	Cessna 152	15282146	N68143
TF-DYR	111	Piper J-3C-65 Cub	14578	TF-JMA(1) N42328 NC42328
TF-EFF(2)	277	Cessna 150M	15075896	TF-FTC N66176
TF-EGD	632	Piper PA-38-112 Tomahawk	38-79A0059	N2433B
TF-EGG	189	Piper PA-23-160 Apache G	23-2044	TF-TOC TF-EGG G-ASDG N10F
TF-EGO	727	SOCATA TB-20 Trinidad	1463	
TF-EHA	81	Erco 415C Ercoupe	2105	N99482 (NC99482)
TF-EJG	537	Cessna R172K Hawk XP	R1723035	N758EK
TF-ELA	904	Boeing 737-33A	25401	SE-DPA N1787B
TF-ELD	878	Boeing 737-46B	24124	EC-IFN EI-CRC PT-TDH EC-HME EI-CRC (EC-HCP) EI-CRC EC-GNC SU-SAB EC-GHF EC-309 SU-SAA EC-FYG EC-655 N689MA G-BOPK
TF-ELG	882	Airbus A300C4-605	758	OO-CTU F-WWAR
TF-ELJ	913	Boeing 737-46B	24124	OO-SBJ G-BROC
TF-ELK	934	Airbus A300B4-622RF	557	EI-DGU F-WQTL SU-GAR F-WWAQ
TF-ELL(2)	765	Boeing 737-210C	20138	N41026 F-GGFI N4906

TF-ELM(2)	896	Boeing 737-3M8	24021	F-GIXP, 9V-SQZ, N40495, OO-LTB, (F-GKTE), OO-ITB, (F-ODSU), (OO-BTB)
TF-ELN	786	Boeing 737-3Q8	23766	OO-ILK, VH-NJE, N101GU, N188LF, EC-EHM, EC-153, N315SC, G-BNCT, N1716B
TF-ELO	865	Boeing 737-33A	24028	F-GIXK, G-MONP
TF-ELP	914	Boeing 737-429	25729	OO-SBM
TF-ELR	915	Airbus A.310-325	624	OE-LAD(2), EC-HIF, OE-LAD(2), F-WWCE
TF-ELS	841	Airbus A.310-304	552	N283TR, PP-SFH, F-GKTD, F-WWCZ
TF-ELU	847	Airbus A.300B4-622R	657	N622RG, TF-ELU, TU-TAG, N622RG, HL7521, PK-GAP, F-WWAJ
TF-ELV	853	Boeing 737-4S3	24796	G-TREN
TF-ELW	866	Airbus A.300C4-605R	755	D-ABFH(2), OO-CTT, F-WWAX
TF-ELX	555	Cessna A185F Skywagon	18503214	N93296
TF-ELY	903	Boeing 737-4Q8	25168	F-GNAO, F-WNAO, N725SK, G-BSNV
TF-ELZ	916	Boeing 737-4Y0	23980	N239CT, OO-VJO, VH-VGD, OO-VJO, F-GMJO, HL7255
TF-EMM	191	Cessna 150K (CofA exp 31.12.00)	15071523	N6023G
TF-EOS	349	Piper PA-28-151 Cherokee Warrior	28-7715027	N4377F
TF-ESI	348	Cessna 150M	15077405	(SE-KPG), TF-ESI, N63576
TF-ETT	205	Piper PA-23-250 Aztec D	27-4445	N13797
TF-EXI	793	Rotorway Exec 162F	6373	
TF-EXP	427	Cessna R172K Hawk XP (CofA expired 31.8.95)	R1722189	N1426V
TF-FAA	870	Piper PA-28-161 Warrior II	28-8016299	OY-BNL, D-EICI
TF-FAB	312	Piper PA.38-112 Tomahawk	38-78A0361	TF-JMB(4), TF-SKA
TF-FAD	311	Piper PA-38-112 Tomahawk	38-78A0370	TF-SIM, TF-JMF(2)
TF-FAL	816	Falconar F-11 (No current CofA)	F6119	N9620
TF-FAR	181	Aero Commander 100	243	(TF-AFI), TF-JEG(1)
TF-FBA	279	Piper PA-28R-200 Cherokee Arrow	28R-35666	TF-FHA, SE-FPA, N3097R
TF-FBI	606	Cessna R172K Hawk XP (No current CofA)	R1722664	N736NT
TF-FET	249	Piper PA-28-180 Cherokee Challenger	28-7305182	N15907
TF-FFB	488	Beech 77 Skipper (CofA exp 31.8.90)	WA-83	N6720Z
TF-FFC	604	Beech 77 Skipper	WA-10	TF-TOX, TF-FFC, C-GJPL
TF-FFD(2)	547	Cessna 172N (No current C0fA)	17270582	TF-FTS(1), N739JP
TF-FFE	605	Beech 77 Skipper (CofA exp 30.11.03)	WA-50	C-GTJR
TF-FFH(3)	498	Piper PA-28R-201T Turbo Arrow III	28R-7803202	N3929M
TF-FFL	624	Cessna 172N (CofA exp 30.6.03)	17272816	N6465D
TF-FHB	173	Cessna 150G	15063872	N4822X
TF-FHE(2)	499	Cessna 152-II	15283998	TF-BMW, N4887H
TF-FHI (2)	454	Cessna 152-II (CofA exp 31.8.03)	15283911	N6443B
TF-FHR	589	Cessna R172K Hawk XP	R1722054	TF-SJS, N7317K
TF-FIA(4)	881	Boeing 767-3Y0ER	24953	N632TW, EI-CAM, XA-RWX, (EI-CAM)
TF-FIB(2)	895	Boeing 767-383ER	25365	N365SR, LN-RCL, SE-DKX
TF-FIC(2)	924	Boeing 767-383ER	24846	N2484B, LN-RCE, SE-DKR, N60697
TF-FIF	350	Cessna 172N	17267963	TF-GOD, N75804
TF-FIG	796	Boeing 757-23APF	24456	N571CA
TF-FIH	671	Boeing 757-208	24739	
TF-FII	670	Boeing 757-208	24760	
TF-FIJ(2)	674	Boeing 757-208	25085	G-BTEJ, (TF-FIJ)
TF-FIK	736	Boeing 757-28A	26276	
TF-FIM(4)	687	Piper PA-18-150 Super Cub	18-5621	SE-CEC, N10F
TF-FIN(2)	770	Boeing 757-208	28989	N1790B
TF-FIO(2)	773	Boeing 757-208	29436	
TF-FIP(2)	789	Boeing 757-208	30423	N1006K
TF-FIR(2)	859	Boeing 757-256	26242	EC-FYJ, EC-608, N35030
TF-FIS	876	Boeing 757-256	26245	N542NA, EC-FYM, EC-611
TF-FIT(2)	940	Boeing 757-256	26244	N262SR, HS-KAK, N262SR, TC-FLD, N508NA, EC-FYL, EC-610
TF-FIU	910	Boeing 757-256	26243	PH-ITA, EC-FYK, EC-609
TF-FIV	817	Boeing 757-208	30424	
TF-FIW	806	Boeing 757-2J4	24838	D-ABNX, PH-AHL
TF-FIX	836	Boeing 757-308	29434	N60659
TF-FKR	612	Cessna P206C Super Skylane	P206-0481	N8681Z
TF-FLY(2)	651	Light Aero Avid Flyer	225	
TF-FMS	747	Beech B200 Super King Air	BB-1221	(TF-UUU), D-IUUU, F-GKGH, N7230U
TF-FOX(2)	408	Cessna 177RG Cardinal RG (CofA expired 30.9.03)	177RG0751	N177CB, (N1577H)
TF-FRK	354	Cessna 172N (STOL)	17270553	N739HJ
TF-FRM	538	Stinson 108-2 Voyager	108-2-2156	TF-SRM, (TF-SUL), TF-SRM, N9156K, NC9156K
TF-FRU(6)	326	Cessna 172M	17264679	TF-FTU, TF-FRI, TF-FRU(2), N61617
TF-FTB	267	Cessna 150L	15072885	N1585Q
TF-FTD	278	Cessna 150M (CofA exp 30.11.96)	15076466	N3340V
TF-FTE	594	Cessna 152-II	15283646	N4805B
TF-FTF	324	Cessna 152-II (CofA exp 28.2.87)	15280838	N25893
TF-FTG(2)	513	Cessna A152 Aerobat	A1520890	TF-TPB(1), N4781A
TF-FTI	531	Cessna 172N	17269376	TF-HUS, N737FC
TF-FTJ	468	Cessna 152 (CofA exp 30.6.97)	15280591	TF-OFS, N25318
TF-FTL(2)	621	Cessna 152 (Damaged 11.5.02, no current CofA)	15279824	N757LL
TF-FTN	783	Piper PA-44-180 Seminole	44-7995239	N2288C, OO-SEM, (OO-TIM), N66515, YV-1507P, N9600N
TF-FTP(2)	549	Cessna 172N	17270823	TF-UGL, N739UT
TF-FTS(2)	557	Cessna 152	15285540	TF-FFD(1), N93707
TF-FTT	583	Cessna 152	15281326	TF-PEP, TF-SKM, N49803
TF-FTU	929	Piper PA-44-180 Seminole	44-7995179	G-SOIF, G-HSFT, EI-CCB, N2093K
TF-FUN	898	American Champion 7ECA Citabria	1356-95	N608AC
TF-GAG	490	Piper PA-22-150 Tri-Pacer	22-4093	D-EFOT, N10F
TF GEM	923	Miles M.65 Gemini 3A (Rebuild, CofA not yet issued)	6483	G-AKEK
TF-GIN	57	Piper PA-12 Super Cruiser (CofA expired 30.9.92)	12-1098	TF-CAB, TF-CUB(1)
TF-GJA	553	Cessna 172N	17272240	C-GJPS, N9364E
TF-GMG	921	Cessna 170B	26715	N4371B
TF-HAL	352	Cessna 172N	17267906	N75727
TF-HER	251	Piper PA-28-140 Cherokee	28-20682	N6593W
TF-HFN	623	Cessna R172K Hawk XP	R1722515	N736GL

TF-HHG	634	Bell 206L-1 Long Ranger II	45677	F-GHHH N87BF N2088V
TF-HHK	897	Agusta Bell 206B Jet Ranger II	8190	D-HAUF(2) OE-BXN(1)
TF-HHX	774	Hughes 269C (No current CofA)	S-1587	D-HSSB (D-HINS(2)) N41S
TF-HIS	77	Cessna 180	30310	N1610C
TF-HOF	175	Piper PA-23-160 Apache (CofA expired 30.6.87)	23-1487	N4012P
TF-HRB	575	Aeronca 7AC Champion (CofA expired 31.8.95)	5208	N1643E NC1643E
TF-IBK	508	Cessna 182Q Skylane (CofA expired 31.8.91)	18265988	N759GS
TF-IBM	521	Piper PA-20 Pacer (CofA exp 30.4.87) (Built as Pacer 125 but reported as PA-20-150)	20-148	N7040K
TF-ICE	327	Cessna 150M	15076111	N66542
TF-ICI	590	Cessna 152-II	15283438	N49222
TF-ICY	509	Cessna 152	15283677	N4858B
TF-IOI	212	Reims/Cessna F172L (CofA expired 31.12.91)	F17200815	TF-IOO (1)
TF-IOO(5)	98	Cessna 180	31603	TF-GVG TF-DVD N4705B
TF-ISC(3)	565	Cessna 172N (CofA exp 30.10.99)	17270782	N739TA
TF-ISE(2)	424	Cessna 172N	17270142	N738PY
TF-IVR	430	Aeronca 7DC Champion (CofA exp 31.7.96)	109	N4492E NC4492E
TF-JEC	412	Cessna 150M (CofA exp 31.120.91)	15075901	TF-JEG(2) N803AA
TF-JEG(3)	534	Cessna 172N	17272954	N1088F
TF-JFA	183	Beech C-45H (CofA exp 31.8.97)	AF-602	TF-JMP TF-JME(1) 52-10672
"TF-JFP"	-	Arnason JFP-2s-8 (Jet-powered homebuilt, not officially regd or resvd)	unkn	
TF-JMC(2)	570	DHC-6 Twin Otter 300	413	C-GIZR SE-GRX D-IDLT
TF-JMD(3)	627	DHC-6 Twin Otter 300	475	C-GDAA
TF-JMH	100	Piper PA-23 Apache	23-1027	N3107P
TF-JMK	662	Fairchild Swearingen SA.227AC Metro III	AC-467	N3046L
TF-JML	760	Fairchild SA.227DC Metro 23	DC-881B	N3004D
TF-JMM	917	Fokker F.27-050	20214	D-AFKM PH-EXD
TF-JMN	918	Fokker F.27-050	20223	D-AFKN PH-EXX
TF-JMO	919	Fokker F.27-050	20205	D-AFKK PH-EXN
TF-JMR	675	Fokker F.27-050	20243	TF-FIR PH-EXM
TF-JMS	676	Fokker F.27-050	20244	TF-FIS(2) PH-EXN
TF-JMT	677	Fokker F.27-050	20250	TF-FIT PH-EXT
TF-JON	270	S.A.I. KZ-VII-U4 Laerke	156	OY-AIR
TF-JPP	568	Cessna 172M (No current C0fA)	17264798	TF-FTK(2) TF-VIV (SE-KRB) TF-VIV N61784
TF-JSO	529	Cessna 172M	17264972	N64026
TF-JVB	711	Cessna 402B (CofA expired 31.5.02)	402B0875	TF-SUD OY-BIR SE-GKV OY-BIR N5788J
TF-JVD	215	Piper PA-23-250 Aztec D	27-4146	TF-JMA(2) N6808Y
TF-JVE	788	Macchi AL.60B2 (C0fA expired)	57/6237	I-GROS
TF-JVF	751	Piper PA-31 Turbo Navajo	31-779	TF-MYF 9H-ACF SE-KFG N7402L
TF-JXA	911	McDonnell-Douglas DC-9-82	49555	LN-RMD (OY-KHD)
TF-JXB	912	McDonnell-Douglas DC-9-82	49909	SE-DII
TF-KAD(2)	134	Cessna 150D (CofA expired 31.5.99)	15060518	TF-BAD (TF-BAC) N4518U
TF-KAF(2)	668	Cessna 170B	20525	N2373D
TF-KAH(2)	647	Cessna 180	31997	N370G N3199D
TF-KAI	182	Piper PA-22-108 Colt (CofA exp 30.9.99)	22-8663	TF-KAX (G-AROL)
TF-KAJ(2)	650	Piper PA-18-150 Super Cub	18-7609019	N9669P
TF-KAK	29	Piper J-3C-65 Cub (CofA exp 30.9.91)	15271	
TF-KAN	48	Fleet 16B Finch II (CofA exp 31.10.95)	651	RCAF4772
TF-KAO(2)	415	Piper J-3C-65 Cub	19694	TF-GUL N6507H NC6507H
TF-KAP	72	Piper J-3C-65 Cub (L-4H) (Officially regd as c/n 15328; CofA expired 31.1.01)	12328	G-ALGH 44-80545(2) 44-80032
TF-KAS	52	Piper J-3C-65 Cub Special (CofA expired 31.5.97)	22596	NC3401N

TF-KAT(2)	417	Piper J-3C-85 Cub	16863	(N103CT) N92401 NC92401
TF-KAU	27	Boeing Stearman A75N1 (PT-17) (No current CofA)	75-1556	41-7997
TF-KEA	407	Evans VP-1 Volksplane (CofA expired 31.5.86)	2341	
TF-KEM	370	Cessna 152-II (CofA expired 30.4.96)	15281898	(SE-KPH) TF-KEM TF-KLM(1) N67536
TF-KFX	611	Denney Kitfox (CofA exp 30.9.92)	155	
TF-KGK	256	Cessna F150H (CofA exp 30.6.89)	F150-0277	TF-TOB TF-FHI OY-AHJ
TF-KIK	216	Piper PA-22-108 Colt (CofA exp 31.8.90)	22-8098	N4589Z
TF-KJO	768	Piper PA-20 Pacer 125 (CofA exp 31.5.99)	20-764	N1561A
TF-KLM(2)	422	Cessna 172N	17273004	N1464F
TF-KLO	431	Cessna 172N	17271646	TF-MUS N4781E
TF-KNM	577	Piper PA-22-160 Tri-Pacer	22-6363	N9341D
TF-KOK	293	Cessna 172N	17269422	N737HD
TF-KOT(3)	657	HS.44 Aerokot	101	
TF-KOZ	300	Bellanca 7GCBC Citabria	1021-78	N2949Z
TF-KRA(2)	526	Cessna 172N	17268349	N733KH
TF-KZA	44	S.A.I. KZ-III U-2 (CofA exp 30.9.88)	86	
TF-LBP	-	Auster 5 (Reservation, on rebuild)	1577	TJ592
TF-LDS	782	Dornier Do.27A-4 (C/n given as 27-1003-433 incorrectly)	443	OO-LVH D-ENAT 57+15 PX+222 PP+108
TF-LEO	411	Piper PA-18-150 Super Cub	18-7509074	N7479L
TF-LIF	733	Aérospatiale AS.332L Super Puma	2210	F-WQDA F-WKAZ F-WYMX
TF-LIZ	598	Piper PA-22-150 Tri-Pacer (CofA expired 31.7.02)	22-5168	N7407D
TF-LMB	880	SOCATA TB-10 Tobago	1826	(TF-WOW) SE-LMB F-OILC
TF-LOA	762	Aeronca 11AC Chief	1283	N9642E NC9642E
TF-LOW	648	Dornier Do.28B-1	3091	TF-DOW TF-DOV(2) TF-CWE SE-CWP
TF-LRL	294	Cessna 150M (CofA exp 30.11.82)	15076216	TF-FLY(1) N66694
TF-MAX	832	SOCATA TB-200 Tobago XL	1813	F-GRBY
TF-MAY	306	Cessna 172N	17267700	TF-LAX N73821
TF-MBF	425	Bellanca 7KCAB Citabria	505-75	TF-MBL N8623V
TF-MBL	813	Kolb Twinstar Mk.III	1086	
TF-MED(2)	566	Piper PA-28-161 Cherokee Warrior II	28-7816194	N9781K
TF-MEL	685	Piper PA-25-235 Pawnee B	25-3271	N4238C C-GIBA N7323Z
TF-MEY	250	Piper PA-28-180 Cherokee C (CofA expired 31.12.88)	28-3355	TF-MEN TF-MED(1) TF-MEY N9276J
TF-MID	386	Cessna 152-II	15282328	N68712
TF-MIN	284	Piper PA-28-161 Cherokee Warrior II	28-7716275	
TF-MLP	235	Cessna 172M (CofA exp 30.6.81)	17261109	N20224
TF-MOS	610	Bellanca 7GCAA	225-70	TF-TWA N9048L
TF-MRS	524	Cessna 140	10553	N76156 NC76156
TF-MYA	574	Cessna 152 (Accident 11.3.02; CofA exp 30.4.02)	15283296	N48178
TF-MYV	619	Piper PA-31-350 Navajo Chieftain	31-7852139	TF-OOJ N355SB N355SS
TF-MYY(2)	525	Cessna U206F Stationair	U20602831	N35960
TF-NDB	543	Piper PA-22-135 Tri-Pacer (CofA expired 28.2.91)	22-2165	N3360B
TF-NES	400	Cessna 172M	17266122	N9371H
TF-NEW	535	Cessna 172M	17264560	N124JV N9927V
TF-NPK	34	Douglas C-47A-60-DL (Also quoted as c/n 13861/23506 ex.TF-ISH, KG762, 43-48045)	13861	TF-ISH 43-30710
TF-ODO	542	Piper PA-22-150 Tri-Pacer (No current CofA)	22-4561	N5900D
TF-OIA	254	Cessna A185F Skywagon (CofA expired 31.3.89)	18502508	N1792R
TF-OII	230	Reims/Cessna F150L	F15000945	
TF-OIL	625	Cessna A185E Skywagon (No current CofA)	18501815	N42LS
TF-OLA	366	Piper PA-28-151 Cherokee Warrior	28-7615061	N7706C
TF-OLB	413	SEEMS MS.892A Rallye Commodore 150 (CofA expired 31,7,88)	10487	(TF-OBL) F-BMVQ
TF-OMI	578	Piper PA-38-112 Tomahawk (CofA expired 30.6.03)	38-79A0128	N2573B
TF-OND	362	Cessna 152-II	15279862	N757NA

TF-ONE	316	Cessna 172M	17262726	N13395
TF-ORD	920	Reims/Cessna F406 Caravan II	F406-0047	D-IAAD(2) N6589A (PH-ALN) F-WZDV
TF-ORF(3)	883	Cessna 441 Conquest II	4410057	N441AK N56MS N441AK N88796
TF-ORN	545	Cessna A185F Skywagon	18502355	TF-IOD N53068
TF-OSK(3)	409	SOCATA MS.894A Minerva 220	12088	G-BBAB
TF-OWL	735	Denney Kitfox III (CofA exp 31.5.01)	1115	
TF-OXO	541	Piper PA-22-150 Tri-Pacer	22-4656	N6005D
TF-PAC	683	Piper PA-18 Super Cub 95 (Composite rebuilt aircraft)	18-3442	D-EDCM 96+19 QW+901 QZ+001 AC+507 AS+506 54-742
TF-PAM	586	Piper PA-28-161 Cherokee Warrior II (No current CofA)	28-7716134	N3072Q
TF-PIA	384	Piper PA-28-161 Warrior II	28-8016294	SE-IDI
TF-PJE	297	Cessna 172M	17264323	N8967V
TF-POL	491	Reims FR172J Rocket	FR17200454	TF-PQL F-BURG
TF-POU	448	Piper PA-28-140 Cherokee Cruiser (Accident 8.6.02, CofA exp 31.7.02)	28-7425038	OY-POU N56797
TF-REF(2)	445	SAN Jodel D.140C Mousquetaire III	16	TF-JDL F-BJQR F-OBLF
TF-REK	562	Rockwell Lark Commander 100/180	5188	N4088X
TF-REX(2)	922	Alpavia Jodel D.117A Grande Tourisme	1061	D-ECUP(2)
TF-RJC	483	Piper PA-28-181 Archer II	28-7990231	N3069H
TF-RJR	433	CEA DR.250/160 Capitaine	94	F-BOCD
TF-RLR	626	Cessna R172K Hawk XP	R1723156	N758KL
TF-RPM(2)	286	Cessna 150H	15068273	N22428
TF-RUT	585	Cessna 172N	17272066	C-GCJH N6788E
TF-RVM(2)	592	Piper PA-28-181 Cherokee Archer II	28-7890367	N6380C
TF-SEX	346	Cessna 172M	17265398	N5303H
TF-SGA	263	SOCATA MS.893E Rallye 180GT Gaillard	12679	TF-SOE TF-SGA
TF-SIF(3)	496	Aérospatiale SA.365N Dauphin 2	6136	F-WYMM
TF-SIR	261	Piper PA-28-140 Cherokee (CofA exp 31.3.88; dismantled)	28-22799	TF-ROM(1) N4405J
TF-SJM	224	Reims/Cessna F172L (CofA expired 30.11.97)	F17200809	N5196
TF-SJO	622	Lake LA-4-200 Buccaneer (No current CofA)	550	N39786
TF-SKA(2)	503	Cessna 150J (CofA expired 31.1.94; dismantled)	15070966	LX-MVE N61326
TF-SKN	363	Cessna 172N	17269445	TF-LUX N737JD
TF-SKO	367	Cessna 172N	17267822	N75578
TF-SKY	273	Cessna 337A Super Skymaster	33700397	G-ATPU F-OCLP (G-ATPU) N6397F
TF-SMA	705	Quickie Quickie 2 (CofA exp 30.9.99)	74	
TF-SMS	688	Rans S-10 Sakota (Possibly c/n 0490.100)	"100-SMS"	
TF-SNF	728	Denney Kitfox III (No current CofA)	1198	
TF-SPA	364	Piper PA-28-151 Cherokee Warrior	28-7615257	TF-KRA N75135
TF-SPY	377	Cessna 172N (No current CofA)	17269581	TF ONO N737QA
TF-STR	333	Cessna 172M	17264692	TF-HFL(1) N61638
TF-SUE	745	Piper PA-22-150 Tri-Pacer	22-5571	N8046D
TF-SUX	-	Klemm L.25E (Preserved at Vestmannaeyjar)	847	D-ESUX
TF-SVO(2)	839	SOCATA TB-10 Tobago	922	D-EAFV
TF-SVQ	467	SOCATA TB-10 Tobago (CofA expired 31.12.98)	44	TF-SVO(1) F-GBHP
TF-SWP	597	Piper PA-22-160 Tri-Pacer	22-6442	N9526D
TF-SYN	274	Fokker F.27 Friendship 200	10545	(PH-EXC)
TF-TAL	802	Cessna P206 Super Skylane	P206-0141	PH-KFF OO-DRJ PH-KFF N2641X
TF-TBX	801	SOCATA TB-10 Tobago	723	HB-KIX D-ENGU(2)
TF-TOB	313	Piper PA-28-180 Cherokee C	28-2830	TF-HRE TF-HRL N8866J
TF-TOD	203	Piper PA-28-140 Cherokee B (CofA expired 31.12.03)	28-25647	TF-ENN N8802N
TF-TOE	140	Piper PA-28-140 Cherokee	28-20257	TF-AIT N6299W
TF-TOF	460	CEA DR.220 2+2	5	TF-DUK TF-LAK G-BLAK F-BNVH
TF-TOG	291	Cessna 305A Bird Dog (L-19)	22615	N5270G 51-12301
TF-TOH	233	Piper PA-28-180 Cherokee B	28-1566	TF-RSH TF-NFJ TF-SPG TF-FFH TF-FHE OY-DTH LN-HAF N7607W
TF-TOI	867	Piper PA-28-140 Cherokee (No current CofA)	28-24087	N1685J
TF-TOK	868	Cessna 150J (No current CofA)	15070997	TF-TOJ N1047M
TF-TOY	833	Aviat Pitts S-2B	5247	N93WS
TF-TPB(2)	335	Cessna 172M	17264839	TF-MYY(1) TF-FRU(3) N61847
TF-TUG	161	Piper PA-25-235 Pawnee B	25-4037	TF-TUN(1) N4418Y
TF-TWO	314	Cessna 150L	15073801	TF-KAB TF-TWO N18122
TF-UFO(2)	296	Mudry CAP.10B	86	
TF-ULF(2)	410	SAN Jodel D.140C Mousquetaire III	132	F-BMBO
TF-ULV	588	SAN Jodel DR.1050 Ambassadeur	119	OY-ACJ
TF-UNA(2)	330	Cessna 172M	17265801	N9857Q
TF-UPS	378	Piper PA-28-161 Cherokee Warrior II (No current CofA)	28-7816056	N47234
TF-UTA	523	Cessna 172M	17265561	TF-MWL N6742H
TF-VEB	746	Partenavia P.68B	79	TF-JVI TF-GTM(2) OY-PRW
TF-VEL(3)	734	Partenavia P.68C	219	TF-FTP G-WTBC G-SITU G-NEWU G-BHJX
TF-VEV	665	Piper PA-31-350 Chieftain	31-8152007	N4051Q
TF-VEY	738	Partenavia P.68B	109	G-JVMR G-JCTI G-OJOE SE-GUI
TF-VHH	539	Cessna A185F Skywagon	18502092	N70283
TF-VIP	532	Cessna T337H Turbo Skymaster (CofA expired 31.8.00)	33701928	N1496S
TF-VOT	779	Gislason Aventura II	AP2A0036	N8199G
TF-YRD	778	Jodel D.9 Bébé	PFA/928A/940 / SAS/001/	G-AXKI
TF-ZZZ	658	Erco 415C Ercoupe	82	N37115
			NC37115	
TF-. . .		Bellanca 8KCAB	419-78	N5503Z
TF-. . .		Cessna 180F	18051267	N2167N
TF-. . .		Mainair 503 Gemini Flash 2A	489-1086-W283	G-MNWJ

GLIDERS AND MOTOR-GLIDERS

Gliders had their own CofR Number sequence until the mid-1970s, since then they have been incorporated into the powered aircraft sequence.

TF-SAA(3)	879	HOAC HK-36TTC Super Dimona	36615	
TF-SAB(2)	395	Schleicher K 7 Rhönadler	7052/A	D-5309
TF-SAC	719	Schleicher ASK 21	21617	
TF-SAE(2)	303	Schleicher Ka 6E	4264	D-0152
TF-SAF	3	Schweizer TG-3A (CofA exp 31.7.99)	unkn	42-53117
TF-SAG(2)	616	Schleicher ASW 19	19034	N19EM
TF-SAJ	13	Grunau Baby II (CofA exp 31.12.94)	37/54	
TF-SAL	790	Rolladen-Schneider LS4	4498	HB-1761
TF-SAP	22	LET L-13 Blanik	173323	
TF-SAR	23	Schleicher K 8B	8701	
TF-SAT	25	Schleicher Rhönlerche II (CofA expired 31.12.94)	524	OY-BZX D-5051 D-6188
TF-SAV	379	Schleicher K 8B	159/59	D-5286
TF-SBA	9	Schweizer TG-3A (CofA expired 31.12.93; to Akureyri museum)	unkn	42-53120
TF-SBE	17	Schleicher Rhönlerche II (CofA expired 31.12.96; to Akureyri museum)	3006	
TF-SBF	21	Schleicher K 8B	8592	
TF-SBK	459	Schleicher K 7 Rhönadler	1	D-0202
TF-SBN	758	PZL PW-5 Smyk	17.07.011	
TF-SBS	815	LAK-12 Lietuva	6184	(TF-SBJ) LY-GLA DOSAAF
TF-SDA	15	Grunau Baby IIb	43/54	
TF-SDF	718	LAK-12 Lietuva	6207	LY-GJO
TF-SIA	5	Schreder HP-16 (Kit) (CofA exp 31.12.92)	1341	
TF-SIG	510	Schleicher K 8B (No current CofA)	8044	TF-SAM(2) D-6332
TF-SIK	305	Eiri PIK-16C Vasama	42	OY-XCO OO-ZAD
TF-SIP	338	Grob G.102 Speed Astir IIB	4087	
TF-SIS(2)	730	LAK-12 Lietuva	6189	DOSAAF
TF-SKG	742	LAK-12 Lietuva	6141	LY-GKG
TF-SLS	361	Rolladen-Schneider LS3-17	3428	

TF-SOL(2)	328	Grob G.102 Standard Astir CS 77	1829	
TF-SON	402	Breglieb BG-12/16 (Kit) (CofA exp31.12.94)	HÞ-01	
TF-SPO	556	Eiri PIK-20B	20132C	OH-490
TF-STE	682	Centrair 101A Pégase	101A-0132	N40KG
TF-STK	824	Rolladen-Schneider LS4A	4775	OH-913 D-1594
TF-SWK	939	Schleicher ASH 25	25004	N80WK
TF-SZD	743	SZD-36A Cobra	W-697	DOSAAF
TF-UTU	580	Fibera KK 1e Utu (CofA exp 31.12.96)	14	(TF-SBJ) OY-FKX

T7 - SAN MARINO

The following are believed current

Regn.	Type	C/n	Prev.Id.
T7-001	Type unknown		
T7-035	Tecnam P.92 Echo	unkn	
T7-036	Tecnam P.92 Echo	unkn	
T7-037	Tecnam P.92 Echo	unkn	
T7-038	SG Aviation Storm 280	51	
T7-040	Light Aero Avid Flyer (or Kitfox ?)	unkn	
T7-041	Eurofly Flash 912	unkn	
T7-042	Tecnam P.92S Echo	unkn	
T7-043	Tecnam P.96 Golf	unkn	
T7-044	Evektor EV-97 Eurostar	unkn	
T7-045	SGAviation Storm 400 Century	unkn	
T7-046	Evektor EV-97 Eurostar	unkn	
T7-047	Tecnam P.92 Echo 2000RG	unkn	
T7-048	Tecnam P.92 Echo	unkn	
T7-049	Tecnam P.92 Echo Super	unkn	
T7-050	Alpi Avn Pioneer 300S	61	
T7-052	Flight Design CT-2SW	unkn	
T7-. . .	Cessna 208B Grand Caravan	208B0988	LN-PBL N52655

T9 - BOSNIA-HERZEGOVINA & REPUBLIKA SRPSKA

Regn.	Type	C/n	Prev.Id.
T9-AAB	Soko/Aérospatiale SA.341 Gazelle	unkn	
T9-AAC	McDonnell-Douglas DC-9-81	48093	N813US N937PS
T9-ABA	CASA C.212-CD	302	F-GHOX TT-LAL F-ODTT
T9-ABB	Ilyushin IL-18D	184007405	EL-ADY LZ-AZO RA-75553 D-AOAO DDR-STF DM-STF CCCP75553
T9-ABC(1)	Douglas C-47B (Cancelled, but still extant in Malta)	16187/32935	3C-JJN N48ME F-GILV F-ODQL (D-CDST) F-ODQL ZS-EYO 7Q-YKM VP-YKM G-AMPT KN462 44-76603
T9-ABE	Antonov An-74	36547097932	ES-NOE UR-74042 CCCP74042
T9-AHA	Bell 206B Jet Ranger II	3435	(T9-HBI) 9A-HAF TC-HNO N411SB N20879
T9-BSA	Piper PA-34-200T Seneca II	34-7970340	TC-SER F-GCJJ OO-HLK N2908U
T9-CAB	Ilyushin IL-76TD	1023408265	T9-QAB EP-ALD 9L-LBO RA-76355
T9-CAC	Ilyushin IL-76TD	0023437076	T9-CAA T9-QAA EP-ALB EP-TQC 9L-LBK RA-76383 CCCP86909
T9-CDG	Zlin Z.526F Trenér Master	1296	YU-CDG
T9-CLM	Utva-75	unkn	YU-DHB JRV53187
T9-CLO	Piper PA-18-150 Super Cub	18-7809162	YU-DCB N82168
T9-DBZ	Piper PA-18-150 Super Cub	18-7809158	YU-DBZ N82084
T9-DCA	Piper PA-18-150 Super Cub	18-7809159	YU-DCA N82086
T9-DDY	SEEMS MS.880B Rallye Club	314	D-EKYN(3) F-BKYN
T9-DEE	SOCATA MS.894A Minerva 220	12016	OE-DRY F-BTRY
T9-DGI	Utva-75	unkn	YU-DGI JRV53173
T9-DJB	Utva-75	unkn	YU-DJB JRV53221
T9-DKI	Utva-75	unkn	YU-DKI JRV53161
T9-DKY	Utva-75	unkn	YU-DKY JRV53161
T9-DQI	SEEMS MS.885 Super Rallye	5426	D-EBQI
T9-EDO	SOCATA MS.893A Rallye Commodore 180	11890	D-EODL
T9-HAA	Mil Mi-8	unkn	
T9-HAB	Mil Mi-8	unkn	
T9-HAF	Mil Mi-8	unkn	
T9-HAI	Mil Mi-8	unkn	
T9-HAL	Mil Mi-8	unkn	
T9-HIB	Bell 206BJet Ranger II	3435	9A-HAF TC-HNO N411SB N20879
T9-PCG	Reims/Cessna FRA150L Aerobat	FRA1500166	YU-CBK
T9-PDA	Utva-75	unkn	RSrp 50105 YU-DIZ JRV53219
T9-PDB	Utva-75	unkn	YU-DGV JRV53182
T9-PDC	Utva-75	unkn	YU-DLY JRV53238
T9-PDD	Reims/Cessna FR172J	FR1720436	RSrp 51103 YU-DBJ

T9-PDG	Piper PA-18-150	18-7809157	RSrp 51102
			YU-DBY
T9-PDI	Utva-66	unkn	YU-CDW
			JRV51138
T9-RCA	Piper PA-25-235 Pawnee	25-2437	(T9-BBC)
			9A-BBC
			RC-BBC
			YU-BBC
			N6830Z
			N10F
T9-RDA	Utva-75	unkn	RSrp AF
T9-RDB	Utva-75	unkn	YU-DIW
			JRV53212
T9-RDC	Utva-66	unkn	RSrp 5 . . . .
			JRV51 . . .
T9-SBA	Cessna 500 Citation	500-0399	YU-BML
			N2069A
T9-SHA	Soko/Aérospatiale SA.341H Gazelle	046	RSrpska/
			JRV12663
T9- . . .	Antonov An-2	1G158-14	9A-DBZ
			CCCP07694
T9- . . .	Aviasud Mistral	112	PH-2T5

GLIDERS

T9-4102	VTC VUK-T	373	YU-4427
T9-4103	VTC-75 Standard Cirrus	234	YU-4324
T9-4104	Spatz 5S	03 L-105	
T9-4106	Schleicher K 8B	8667	D-0247
T9-4432	Schleicher K 8B	186/60	D-5809
T9-4582	VTC-75 Standard Cirrus (Id unconfirmed)	224	YU-4317
T9-4583	Glaser-Dirks DG-101G Elan (Id unconfirmed)	E128G96	YU-4345
T9-4584	VTC VUK-T	290	YU-4377
T9-4585	VTC VUK-T	330	YU-4403
T9-5101	LET L-13 Blanik	026926	YU-5377
T9-5105	Sportavia/ Scheibe SF-25B Falke	4867	D-KAOB
T9-5220	Aerotechnik L-13SW Vivat	980610	
T9-5221	Aerotechnik L-13SW Vivat	980611	
T9-5341	LET L-13 Blanik	173344	OK-6835
T9-5350	LET L-13 Blanik (C/n unconfirmed)	0262 . .	YU-5350
T9-5461	LET L-13 Blanik	174010	OK-9714
T9-5581	LET L-13 Blanik (Identity unconfirmed)	026254	YU-5361

MICROLIGHTS

T9-D111	Rodaro Storch	46	
T9-D444	Apollo CX Racer GT/R	MZ74/91	HA-YNAI
T9-D555	Apollo Fox 912	220201	
T9-M003	Apollo CX 18	T-M003	
T9-M004	Apollo CX 19	MZE 03589	
T9-M005	Pipistrel C-15TN	191	
T9-M006	Apollo CX 18 Racer GT	MZEY 71/90	
T9-M007	Apollo CX 19	MZE 05589	
T9-SU001	Fire Fix	001/2001	
T9-V001	Light Aero Avid Flyer	T-V001	
T9-V002	Light Aero Avid Flyer STOL	596	

The following aircraft are confirmed as active in Bosnia-Herzogovina or Republika Srpska and may be expected to take up T9- marks in due course.

YU-DEP	Utva-75	unkn	JRV53109
YU-DMV	Cessna 150	unkn	
YU-4269	Pilatus B4-PC11	306	
YU-4288	VTC-75 Standard Cirrus	unkn	
YU-4291	VTC-75 Standard Cirrus	unkn	
YU-4309-C9	VTC-75 Standard Cirrus	unkn	
YU-4326	VTC-75 Standard Cirrus	unkn	
YU-4435	VTC-76 VUK-T	381	
YU-4442-BL	Glaser-Dirks DG-300 Elan	3E-242	
YU-5335	LET L-13 Blanik	174914	
JRV51143	Utva-66	unkn	
JRV53194	Utva-75	unkn	YU-DHI
RSrp:50201	Utva-75	unkn	YU-DKS
			JRV53121
RSrp:50202	Utva-75	unkn	YU-DIW
			JRV53212
RSrp:50203	PZL-104 Wilga 80 (But w/o 1.6.03)	CF15810607	YU-DHV
RSrp:50204	Piper PA-18-150 Super Cub	18-7809032	YU-CDN
			D-ELRI
			N82949
RSrp:50205	Zlin 526F Trenér Master	1262	YU-DEU
			JRV41114
RSrp:50209	Reims FR172J Rocket	FR17200436	YU-DBK
			(D-EJXW)

UR - UKRAINE

Regn.	Type	C/n	Prev.Id.
UR-AAJ	Mil Mi-2	unkn	
UR-AAM	Mil Mi-2	unkn	
UR-BAJ	Mil Mi-2	548630044	
UR-BAW	Mil Mi-2	unkn	
UR-BBI	Yakovlev Yak-52	9010310	107
			07yellow
UR-BBJ	Yakovlev Yak-52	832912	07
			06yellow
UR-BBM	Yakovlev Yak-52	9010315	12
			12yellow
UR-BBN	Yakovlev Yak-52	833808	37
			137
UR-BBO	Yakovlev Yak-52	9010404	116
			16yellow
UR-BBS	Yakovlev Yak-52	9010309	106
			06yellow
UR-BBT	Yakovlev Yak-52	9011110	27
			127
UR-BBU	Yakovlev Yak-52	9010313	10yellow
UR-BBV	Antonov An-2	1G160-29	
UR-BBW	Antonov An-2	1G236-22	
UR-BCD	Aero L-29 Delfin	unkn	
UR-BCV	Yakovlev Yak-52	9010406	118
			18yellow
UR-BDS	Mil Mi-2	547145061	
UR-BDT	Mil Mi-2	546113049	
UR-BDU	Mil Mi-2	546225079	
UR-BDV	Mil Mi-2	545619048	
UR-BDW	Antonov An-2	1G159-55	
UR-BEG	Aeroprakt A-20	unkn	
UR-BEI	Antonov An-2R	1G153-44	CCCP05731
UR-BEJ	Antonov An-2R	1G172-46	CCCP40774
UR-BEL	Antonov An-2R	1G165-15	CCCP19701
UR-BEN	Yakovlev Yak-18T	22202044541	
UR-BEO	Yakovlev Yak-18T	22202044261	
UR-BEQ	Antonov An-2	1G236-21	
UR-BEY	Antonov An-2	1G238-01	SovAF 51white
UR-BGV	PZL-104 Wilga 35A	21910915	02
UR-BJD	Antonov An-2	1G160-20	
UR-BJE	Antonov An-2	113047315	
UR-BJV	Antonov An-2T	1G160-60	
UR-BKU	Antonov An-2	1G236-28	
UR-BLA	Yakovlev Yak-52	899913	100
UR-BLD	Yakovlev Yak-52	899914	101
UR-BLH	Yakovlev Yak-52	9010708	
UR-BLI	Yakovlev Yak-52	9010705	62yellow
UR-BLJ	Yakovlev Yak-52	9010501	
UR-BLL	Yakovlev Yak-55	911206	
UR-BLR	Yakovlev Yak-52	856113	143
UR-BLS	Yakovlev Yak-52	867206	
UR-BLT	Yakovlev Yak-52	867209	
UR-BLU	Yakovlev Yak-52	877712	
UR-BLV	Yakovlev Yak-52	878115	
UR-BLX	Yakovlev Yak-52	899415	
UR-BOM	Aero L-39C Albatros	unkn	37
UR-BOO	Aero L-39C Albatros	unkn	
UR-BOP	Aero L-39C Albatros	unkn	52
UR-BOQ	Aero L-39C Albatros	unkn	54
UR-BOR	Aero L-39C Albatros	unkn	56
UR-BOT	Aero L-39C Albatros	unkn	10
UR-BOW	Aero L-39C Albatros	430302	
UR-BPI	Antonov An-2	1G63-08	
UR-BRT	Antonov An-2	14847320	
UR-BSK	Antonov An-2	1G195-60	
UR-BSL	Antonov An-2	1G136-14	CCCP70088
UR-BSM	Antonov An-2	1G237-47	
UR-BVH	Mil Mi-2	548028023	
UR-BVI	Mil Mi-2	548029023	
UR-BVL	Yakovlev Yak-18T	6200911	
UR-BVY	Boeing 737-2Q8	22760	F-GEXJ
			N861L
UR-BWA	Mil Mi-2	548537024	
UR-BWC	Yakovlev Yak-18T	22202030003	
UR-BWE	Yakovlev Yak-40	9530943	RA-87241
			CCCP87241
UR-BWF	Yakovlev Yak-40	9711352	RA-88258
			CCCP88258
UR-BWH	Yakovlev Yak-40	9640951	RA-88238
			CCCP88238
UR-BWM	Antonov An-12BK	00347004	UkrAF 20blue
UR-BWY	Antonov An-26	97308205	UR-26670
			RA-26670
			CCCP26670
UR-BWZ	Antonov An-26	27312208	UR-26119
			RA-26119
			CCCP26119
UR-BXA	Antonov An-24B	99902107	RusAF 01blue
UR-BXB	Antonov An-26	6207	UR-26
			RusNavy 45 blue

UR-BXC	Antonov An-24RV	37308902	UR-46636 TC-MOC TC-JUZ RA-46636 CCCP46636
UR-BXD	Ilyushin IL-18D	unkn	SovAF ?
	(C/ns 172011401 and 175011701 quoted. both IL-20s?)		
UR-BXU	Antonov An-26B	11703	RA-26081 CCCP26081
UR-BXV	Antonov An-26B	27312110	UR-26113 CCCP26113
UR-BYH	Antonov An-74	36547098946	LZ-MNM UR-74053
UR-BYL	McDonnell Douglas DC-9-51	47657	N2248F I-SMEJ OY-CTB SE-DFN HB-ISN
UR-BYY	Tupolev Tu-134B-3	62820	UR-65720 RA-65720 CCCP65720
UR-BZY	Tupolev Tu-134A-3	48565	ER-TCH OM-GAT ES-AAF CCCP65034
UR-CAC	Antonov An-74	36547136013	UN-74011 RA-74011
UR-CAO	Antonov An-24B	unkn	
UR-CAT	Ilyushin IL-76TD	0053464922	UR-76663 CCCP76663
UR-CAP	Ilyushin IL-76TD	0063466989	UR-76394 CCCP76394
UR-CAR	Yakovlev Yak-40	unkn	
UR-CAU	Kamov Ka-26	6900403	
UR-CBG	Antonov An-12BP	6343705	RA-..... SovAF
UR-CBH	Antonov An-12BP	8345710	RA-..... SovAF
UR-CBR	Ilyushin IL-76TD	unkn	
UR-CBU	Antonov An-12BP	9346308	4K-AZ18 RA-12108 LZ-BFE RA-12108 CCCP12108
UR-CBV	McDonnell Douglas DC-9-51	47772	OH-LYV N8713Q
UR-CBY	McDonnell Douglas DC-9-51	47773	OH-LYW N8714Q
UR-CBZ	Antonov An-12BP	402707	RA-11117 RA-11652
UR-CCB	Dassault Falcon 20C-5	141	(UR-BCA) F-BIHY F-BPIO F-WMKF
UR-CCC	Dassault Falcon 50	235	(UR-ACA) F-GKRU F-WWHM
UR-CCK	McDonnell Douglas DC-9-51	48134	OH-LYX
UR-CCR	McDonnell Douglas DC-9-51	47736	OH-LYR
UR-CCS	McDonnell Douglas DC-9-51	47737	OH-LYS 9Y-TFF (OH-LYS)
UR-CCY	Antonov An-12	unkn	
UR-CDB	Antonov An-12	401605	RA-11766 CCCP11766
UR-CEL	McDonnell-Douglas DC-9-83	49390	N390LS EI-CMZ 9Y-THN
UR-DWA	Antonov An-26B	13905	UR-26598(2?)
UR-DWB	Antonov An-26B	unkn	
UR-ECL	Yakovlev Yak-40K	9932059	RA-87219 CCCP87219
UR-ELA	Antonov An-26B	57313505	UR-26583
UR-ELB	Antonov An-26B	58314005	UR-26201
UR-ELC	Antonov An-24RV	57310410	UR-47313 CCCP47313
UR-ELD	Antonov An-26B	14010	UR-26203 CCCP26203
UR-ELE	Antonov An-26B	27312108	UR-26111 CCCP26111
UR-ELF	Antonov An-26B	27312204	UR-26115 CCCP26115
UR-ELG	Antonov An-26B	37312902	UR-26140 CCCP26140
UR-ELH	Antonov An-26B	12908	UR-26143 CCCP26143
UR-ELI	Antonov An-26B	57314009	UR-26202 CCCP26202
UR-ELL	Antonov An-24RV	67310503	UR-47316 CCCP47316
UR-ELM	Antonov An-24RV	67310506	UR-47319 CCCP47319
UR-ELN	Antonov An-24B	89901607	UR-47155 CCCP47155
UR-ELR	Antonov An-26B	07309807	UR-26004 CCCP26004
UR-ETG	Yakovlev Yak-40	9531143	RA-87243 87243 CCCP87243
UR-FRU	Yakovlev Yak-40	9440737	RA-87211 CCCP87211 OK-EEC
UR-GAC	Boeing 737-247	23188	B-2509 N240WA
UR-GAH	Boeing 737-32Q	29130	N1779B
UR-GAJ	Boeing 737-5Y0	25192	PT-SSA XA-SAC
UR-GAK	Boeing 737-5Y0	26075	PT-SLN
UR-GAL	Boeing 737-341	24275	PP-VOD
UR-GAM	Boeing 737-4Y0	25190	HA-LEU TC-SUT OY-MBL EC-FMJ EC-991
UR-GAN	Boeing 737-36N	28569	F-GRFC
UR-GAO	Boeing 737-4Z9	25147	OE-LNH (OE-ILH)
UR-GAP	Boeing 737-529	25419	N419CT OO-SYI
UR-GLS	Antonov An-26B	07310109	UR-26017 RA-26017 CCCP26017
UR-HLC	Mil Mi-8	unkn	
UR-ISD	Yakovlev Yak-40	9530541	RA-88291
UR-KIV	Boeing 737-4YO	24686	F-GQQJ F-WQQJ EC-FZZ EC-772 9M-MJH
UR-KMA	LET L-410 UVP	851420	RA-67516 CCCP67516
UR-KRB	Antonov An-26	07309510	
UR-LAI	Antonov An-12V	8345505	RA-12954 CCCP12954
UR-LEV	Yakovlev Yak-40	9720154	LY-AAA CCCP88279
UR-LMI	Antonov An-12BK	6344605	UkrAF 73blue
UR-LTG	Antonov An-12V	00347201	RA-12986 CCCP12986
UR-LUX	Yakovlev Yak-40	9541542	UR-87230 HA-LJF ER-87230 UR-87230 87230 CCCP87230
UR-MIG	Yakovlev Yak-40	9641250	EP-LBA RA-88225 CCCP88225
UR-MIR	Antonov An-2R	1G154-38	CCCP05798
UR-MLD	LET L-410 UVP	820830	UR-67330 RA-67330 CCCP67330
UR-MLR	Antonov An-2R	1G154-60	CCCP07559
UR-MSI	Antonov An-24RV	27307608	UR-47699 RA-47699 TC-MOB CCCP47699
UR-NIK	Dassault Falcon 20C	112	UR-CCD CS-ATF N200CX N830MF N2989 N991F F-WJMJ
UR-NPO	LET L-410UVP-E3	871932	FLARF-01833 SovAF:1932
UR-NTD	Antonov An-140	0101	
UR-NTK	Antonov An-70	unkn	
UR-NTO	Antonov An-140	unkn	
UR-NTP	Antonov An-140	unkn	
UR-ORG	Yakovlev Yak-40	9741056	UR-87591(1) OK-HEQ
UR-ORO	Yakovlev Yak-40	9740656	RA-98106 CCCP98106
UR-PAS	Antonov An-12	2401105	
UR-PLV	Antonov An-12	4342308	UkrAF 61red
UR-PVI	Mil Mi-8T	99150873	
UR-PWA	Antonov An-24B	67302608	RA-46820 CCCP46820
UR-PWO	Antonov An-140	36525301003	
UR-RPC	Yakovlev Yak-40	9721353	YL-TRB RA-88275 CCCP88275
UR-SKD	LET L-410 UVP	810721	UR-67084 CCCP67084
UR-SMA	Antonov An-12BP	7345208	UR-11348 UkrAF 21blue SovAF 84
UR-SVG	Antonov An-12BK	4342409	TN-AGE RA-11320
UR-TMD	Ilyushin IL-18D	187009903	ER-ICL YR-IML
UR-TSI	Antonov An-12BP	6344701	UR-UAA

UR-UAF	Antonov An-12BP	3341108	
UR-UCA	Ilyushin IL-76	0073479394	UR-76715 CCCP76715
UR-UCB	Ilyushin IL-76MD	0063467003	UR-76676 CCCP76676
UR-UCC	Ilyushin IL-76MD	0083489647	UR-78775 CCCP78775
UR-UCD	Ilyushin IL-76MD	0083488643	UR-78774 CCCP78774
UR-UCE	Ilyushin IL-76MD	0083484522	UR-76398 CCCP76398
UR-UCF	Ilyushin IL-76MD	0083488638	UR-76412 CCCP76412
UR-UCG	Ilyushin IL-76	0083482478	UR-76414 CCCP76414
UR-UCH	Ilyushin IL-76MD	0083484536	UR-78756 CCCP78756
UR-UCJ	Ilyushin IL-76MD	0083484531	UR-78755 CCCP78755
UR-UCK	Antonov An-12BK	9346905	UR-11304 11304
UR-UCL	Ilyushin IL-76MD	0043456692	UR-76620
UR-UCN	Antonov An-12BP	00347604	UR-11303 RA-11303
UR-UCO	Ilyushin IL-7 MD	0053458749	CCCP76630
UR-UCP	Antonov An-26	4407	HA-TCM UR-26602 CCCP26602
UR-UCQ	Ilyushin IL-76MD	0063465963	UR-76671 4K-76671 UR-76671
UR-UCR	Ilyushin IL-76MD	0073475270	UR-76728 CCCP76728
UR-UCS	Ilyushin IL-76MD	0063470113	RA-76444 UR-76444 CCCP76444
UR-UCT	Ilyushin IL-76MD	0063470089	UR-76691 CCCP76691
UR-UCU	Ilyushin IL-76MD	0073476275	UR-76729 CCCP76729
UR-UCV	Ilyushin IL-76MD	0043451517	UR-76397 CCCP76587
UR-UCW	Ilyushin IL-76MD	0053458733	UR-76317 RA-76317 CCCP76627
UR-UCX	Ilyushin IL-76MD	0063470112	UR-76695
UR-UCY	Ilyushin IL-76MD	0083485566	UR-76399 CCCP78760
UR-UCZ	Tupolev Tu-154B2	82A-561	UR-85561 85561 P85561
UR-UDB	Ilyushin IL-76MD	0043455686	UR-76320 CCCP76619
UR-UDC	Ilyushin IL-76MD	0063467011	CCCP76678
UR-UDD	Antonov An-12	unkn	
UR-UFB	Airbus A.320-211	0027	N270SE UR-UFB N270SE VH-HYF F-WWDD
UR-UKA	Sukhoi Su-31	03-04	
UR-UKB	Sukhoi Su-29	80-04	
UR-UKC	Aeroprakt A-20	unkn	
UR-UKD	Aeroprakt A-22 Vision	003	
UR-UTN	LET L-410UVP-E	912614	UR-67716 OK-WDN CCCP67683
UR-UZE	Bell 430	49094	N51335 C-FZSS
UR-VIK	Antonov An-24RV	37308706	RA-46619
UR-VVA	Boeing 737-3Q8	24492	N492GD XA-TMB N492KR PK-GWE
UR-VVB	Boeing 737-529	26537	OO-SYJ
UR-VVD	Boeing 737-529	25419	N419CT OO-SYI
UR-VVE	Boeing 737-448	24521	EI-BXB
UR-VVF	Boeing 767-383ER	24476	N4476F LN-RCI SE-DOB OY-KDK
UR-VVG	Boeing 767-383ER	24729	N102AB LN-RCK SE-DKU (LN-RCD)
UR-VVI	Boeing 737-33A	24461	N446CT VH-CZQ G-OBMJ (G-OBMI)
UR-VVJ	Boeing 737-448	24474	OO-SLW SU-HMD EI-BXA
UR-VVK	Boeing 737-4Q8	26280	EC-HNB G-OBMO
UR-VVL	Boeing 737-448	25052	EI-BXI
UR-XYZ	Yakovlev Yak-40	9610946	RA-88155 CCCP88155
UR-YMR	Antonov An-12BK	9346302	UR-11349(2)
UR-ZVA	Ilyushin IL-76TD *(W/o 4.3.04)*	0063468036	UR-76684 CCCP76684
UR-ZVB	Ilyushin IL-76TD	0053463902	UR-76658 CCCP76658
UR-ZVC	Ilyushin IL-76	unkn	
UR-. . .	A-28 Victor	SA-28-001	N61450
UR-. . .	Antonov An-26	13-08	PLW-1308
UR-. . .	Antonov An-124	159305	
UR-. . .	Bell 407	53219	N219WB
UR-	BAe. Jetstream 3201	953	VH-XFE N953LM G-31-953
UR-. . .	Ilyushin IL-76MD	0033442238	CCCP76540
UR-. . .	Kamov Ka-26	7404009	YR-FLY YR-19484 YR-UKA CCCP19484
UR-. . .	LET L-200D Morava	170212	OK-OHD OK-BYA
UR-. . .	McDonnell-Douglas DC-9-82	49634	N34838
UR-. . .	Mil Mi-2	525741088	UR-20646 HA-BCZ CCCP20646
UR-. . .	Mil Mi-2	529120035	OK-PIB CCCP23299
UR-. . .	Mil Mi-8T	9743714	OK-EXC
UR-. . .	Robinson R-44 Raven II	1437	
UR-. . .	Schweizer 269C	S.1399	G-SAND
UR-. . .	Yakovlev Yak-52	811515	
UR-01725	Antonov An-2P	1G106-22	CCCP01725
UR-01765	Antonov An-2P	1G107-12	CCCP01765
UR-02233	Antonov An-2	1G235-04	
UR-02239	Antonov An-2	1G235-10	CCCP02239
UR-02257	Antonov An-2R	1G238-34	
UR-02410	Antonov An-2P	1G117-21	
UR-02422	Antonov An-2	1G117-33	CCCP02422
UR-02428	Antonov An-2	1G117-39	
UR-02438	Antonov An-2P	1G117-49	CCCP02438
UR-02507	Antonov An-2	1G119-50	
UR-02810	Antonov An-2R	1G54-15	
UR-05788	Antonov An-2R	1G154-28	CCCP05788
UR-05794	Antonov An-2R	1G154-34	CCCP05794
UR-06130	Mil Mi-8T	22686	
UR-06131	Mil Mi-8T	22688	
UR-07194	Antonov An-2TP	1G146-23	CCCP07194
UR-07250	Antonov An-2	1G148-11	CCCP07250
UR-07273	Antonov An-2R	1G148-34	CCCP07273
UR-07275	Antonov An-2R	1G148-36	CCCP07275
UR-07357	Antonov An-2P	1G149-61	
UR-07450	Antonov An-2P	1G151-25	
UR-07463	Antonov An-2	1G151-38	CCCP07463
UR-07466	Antonov An-2P	1G139-46	
UR-07522	Antonov An-2	1G152-50	CCCP07522
UR-07571	Antonov An-2	1G156-11	CCCP07571
UR-07582	Antonov An-2R	1G155-37	CCCP07582
UR-07604	Antonov An-2R	1G155-59	CCCP07604
UR-07605	Antonov An-2R	1G155-60	
UR-07684	Antonov An-2	1G158-04	CCCP07684
UR-07695	Antonov An-2	1G158-15	CCCP07695
UR-07725	Antonov An-2R	1G158-55	CCCP07725
UR-07830	Antonov An-2R	1G169-45	CCCP07830
UR-07888	Antonov An-2P	1G170-50	
UR-07899	Antonov An-2	1G170-64	CCCP07899
UR-09307	Antonov An-22A	043481244	UR-ADB UR-09307 CCCP09307
UR-11300	Antonov An-12BP	402211	
UR-11305	Antonov An-12	01347803	
UR-11306	Antonov An-12	9346205	
UR-11314	Antonov An-12BK	8345604	RA-13357 SovAF 87
UR-11315	Antonov An-12BP	4342307	CCCP11315
UR-11316	Antonov An-12BP	9346810	RA-11316 CCCP11316
UR-11319	Antonov An-12BP	4342510	
UR-11326	Antonov An-12BP	2400802	RA-11326 UR-11326 11326
UR-11332	Antonov An-12BP	4342202	T9-CAD UR-11332 SovAF 84blue
UR-11346	Antonov An-12BP	8345702	UkrAF 54red
UR-11528	Antonov An-12BP	3341005	CCCP11528
UR-11765	Antonov An-12BP	401705	LZ-SFM
UR-11819	Antonov An-12BP	6344009	
UR-11833	Antonov An-12BP	3341008	CCCP11833
UR-13332	Antonov An-12BP	4341707	SovAF 82red
UR-13395	Antonov An-26	2605	CCCP13395
UR-14001	Antonov An-140	36525301003	UR-PWO
UR-14002	Antonov An-140	36525302006	
UR-14004	Antonov An-140	unkn	
UR-14005	Antonov An-140	unkn	

UR-14006	Antonov An-140	unkn	
UR-14090	Mil Mi-2	5210649078	
UR-14091	Mil Mi-2	5210650078	
UR-14117	Mil Mi-2	5210828019	SovAF 22yellow
UR-14137	Mil Mi-2	5210909049	
UR-14248	Mil Mi-2	5211135050	OK-VIK CCCP14248
UR-14302	Mil Mi-2	546042039	HA-BFI SovAF 45yellow
UR-14304	Mil Mi-2	546133049	
UR-14305	Mil Mi-2	546041039	SovAF 21yellow
UR-14312	Mil Mi-2	546214069	
UR-14337	Mil Mi-2	546044039	
UR-14338	Mil Mi-2	546134049	
UR-14340	Mil Mi-2	546111049	
UR-14341	Mil Mi-2	546215069	
UR-14362	Mil Mi-2	535110027	
UR-14383	Mil Mi-2	525241077	
UR-15605	Mil Mi-2	529938096	CCCP15605
UR-15610	Mil Mi-2	529945106	CCCP15610
UR-15611	Mil Mi-2	529946106	
UR-15614	Mil Mi-2	529949106	CCCP15614
UR-15969	Kamov Ka-26	7504816	CCCP15969
UR-16002	Antonov An-2TP	1G162-52	CCCP16002
UR-16003	Antonov An-2TP	1G162-53	CCCP16003
UR-16022	Antonov An-2R	1G163-26	CCCP16022 7O-ABD CCCP16022
UR-16060	Antonov An-2R	1G164-13	CCCP16060
UR-17718	Antonov An-2R	1G202-38	CCCP17718
UR-17719	Antonov An-2	1G202-39	CCCP17719
UR-17720	Antonov An-2	1G202-40	CCCP17720
UR-17735	Antonov An-2	1G202-55	CCCP17735
UR-17749	Antonov An-2R	1G203-10	CCCP17749
UR-17764	Antonov An-2R	1G203-25	CCCP17764
UR-17765	Antonov An-2R	1G203-26	CCCP17765
UR-17769	Antonov An-2R	1G203-30	
UR-17770	Antonov An-2R	1G203-31	
UR-17772	Antonov An-2	1G203-33	CCCP17772
UR-17862	Antonov An-2R	1G205-03	
UR-17915	Antonov An-2R	1G205-56	CCCP17915
UR-17916	Antonov An-2R	1G205-57	CCCP17916
UR-17918	Antonov An-2	1G205-59	CCCP17918
UR-17919	Antonov An-2R	1G205-60	CCCP17919
UR-17928	Antonov An-2R	1G206-09	
UR-17929	Antonov An-2R	1G206-10	
UR-17960	Antonov An-2R	1G209-44	CCCP17960
UR-17961	Antonov An-2R	1G209-45	CCCP17961
UR-17962	Antonov An-2R	1G209-46	SP-ZFK CCCP17962
UR-17997	Antonov An-2	1G210-21	CCCP17997
UR-17998	Antonov An-2	1G210-22	CCCP17998
UR-17999	Antonov An-2R	1G210-23	17999 CCCP17999
UR-19104	Kamov Ka-26	7102202	CCCP19104
UR-19326	Kamov Ka-26	7303209	HA-MMH
UR-19333	Kamov Ka-26	7303409	YR-UKG CCCP19333
UR-19379	Kamov Ka-26	7202703	YR-CXL CCCP19379
UR-19383	Kamov Ka-26	7202707	YR-CXT CCCP19383
UR-19391	Kamov Ka-26	7202805	
UR-19393	Kamov Ka-26	7202901	CCCP19393
UR-19411	Kamov Ka-26	7404505	CCCP19411
UR-19463	Kamov Ka-26	7303709	
UR-19471	Kamov Ka-26	7303810	CCCP19471
UR-19474	Kamov Ka-26	7303903	
UR-19495	Kamov Ka-26	7404201	CCCP19495
UR-19510	Kamov Ka-26	7404501	CCCP19510
UR-19563	Kamov Ka-26	7404802	
UR-19568	Kamov Ka-26	7504815	
UR-19600	Kamov Ka-26	7504917	CCCP19600
UR-19606	Kamov Ka-26	7505007	CCCP19606
UR-19608	Kamov Ka-26	7505009	
UR-19668	Kamov Ka-26	7605508	CCCP19668
UR-19677	Kamov Ka-26	7706304	
UR-19722	Antonov An-2R	1G165-36	CCCP19722
UR-19732	Antonov An-2	1G165-46	CCCP19732
UR-20125	Mil Mi-2	543026063	
UR-20202	Mil Mi-2	Unknown	
UR-20202	Mil Mi-2	526841100	
UR-20203	Mil Mi-2	526842100	OK-KJJ HA-BFH CCCP20203
UR-20216	Mil Mi-2	537005011	
UR-20216	Mil Mi-2	547005011	
UR-20217	Mil Mi-2	547006011	
UR-20217	Mil Mi-2	537006011	
UR-20219	Mil Mi-2	537008011	
UR-20221	Mil Mi-2	537010011	
UR-20222	Mil Mi-2	537011011	
UR-20222	Mil Mi-2	547011011	
UR-20261	Mil Mi-2	547219071	
UR-20276	Mil Mi-2	547316091	
UR-20360	Mil Mi-2	529805056	
UR-20396	Mil Mi-2	5298443076	
UR-20581	Mil Mi-2	524705036	
UR-20640	Mil Mi-2	525707068	
UR-20641	Mil Mi-2	525708068	
UR-20643	Mil Mi-2	525710068	
UR-20644	Mil Mi-2	525711068	
UR-20647	Mil Mi-2	525742088	
UR-20652	Mil Mi-2	unkn	
UR-20655	Mil Mi-2	526444010	OK-KIM CCCP20655
UR-20676	Mil Mi-2	526639050	
UR-20677	Mil Mi-2	526640050	OM-KIH CCCP20677
UR-20750	Mil Mi-2	547705062	
UR-20769	Mil Mi-2	517806082	
UR-20800	Mil Mi-2	527922112	
UR-20801	Mil Mi-2	527923112	HA-BFE CCCP20801
UR-20822	Mil Mi-2	528026013	CCCP20822
UR-20838	Mil Mi-2	548119033	
UR-20839	Mil Mi-2	548120043	
UR-20841	Mil Mi-2	548122043	
UR-20920	Mil Mi-2	568602024	
UR-21510	Antonov An-12BP	0901404	SovAF 88red
UR-22230	Mil Mi-8	6360	
UR-22234	Mil Mi-8T	6365	
UR-22283	Mil Mi-8T	6967	
UR-22404	Mil Mi-8T	7447	CCCP22404
UR-22406	Mil Mi-8T	7451	
UR-22415	Mil Mi-8T	5107	
UR-22525	Mil Mi-8T	0723	
UR-22622	Mil Mi-8T	7969	
UR-22715	Mil Mi-8T	98308422	
UR-22886	Mil Mi-8T	98415987	SP-FSZ CCCP22886
UR-22887	Mil Mi-8T	98415999	
UR-22897	Mil Mi-8T	98417135	CCCP22897
UR-23273	Mil Mi-2	529042015	
UR-23277	Mil Mi-2	529046025	
UR-23336	Mil Mi-2	549244065	HA-BFL CCCP23336
UR-23350	Mil Mi-2	528722054	CCCP23350
UR-23357	Mil Mi-2	548729064	
UR-23358	Mil Mi-2	528730064	
UR-23483	Mil Mi-2	526242089	
UR-23492	Mil Mi-2	526309089	HA-BCW CCCP23492
UR-23511	Mil Mi-2	525914118	
UR-23512	Mil Mi-2	525915118	
UR-23514	Mil Mi-2	525917118	
UR-23517	Mil Mi-2	unkn	
UR-23535	Mil Mi-2	546027029	
UR-23539	Mil Mi-2	526031029	
UR-23540	Mil Mi-2	526032029	
UR-23595	Mil Mi-2	534616016	
UR-23646	Mil Mi-2	546321099	SovAF 25yellow
UR-23648	Mil Mi-2	547324091	
UR-23869	Mil Mi-2	521317010	
UR-23943	Mil Mi-2	531925061	CCCP23943
UR-24165	Mil Mi-8T	98941935	CCCP24165
UR-24218	Mil Mi-8T	98730395	CCCP24218
UR-24229	Mil Mi-8	98730591	
UR-24275	Mil Mi-8T	98734295	CCCP24275
UR-24355	Kamov Ka-26	7605619	CCCP24355
UR-24444	Mil Mi-8T	98628099	
UR-24447	Mil Mi-8T	2704	SovAF 81white
UR-24558	Mil Mi-8T	98522979	
UR-24604	Mil Mi-8T	8230	
UR-24635	Mil Mi-8PS	8561	
UR-24636	Mil Mi-8PS	8562	
UR-25170	Mil Mi-8MTV-1	95479	
UR-25301	Mil Mi-8T	98203673	CCCP25301
UR-25444	Mil Mi-8MTV-1	95583	CCCP25444
UR-25514	Mil Mi-8MTV-1	95662	CCCP25514
UR-25852	Mil Mi-8T	5110	
UR-25855	Mil Mi-8T	5120	
UR-25899	Mil Mi-8T	5174	
UR-26015	Antonov An-26B	10103	
UR-26016	Antonov An-26B	10105	
UR-26033	Antonov An-26	unkn	UN-26033 CCCP26033
UR-26042	Antonov An-26B	10710	CCCP26042
UR-26059	Antonov An-26B	11104	ER-26059 CCCP26059
UR-26070	Antonov An-26	11404	26070 RA-26070 CCCP26070
UR-26072	Antonov An-26B	11409	RA-26072 CCCP26072
UR-26073	Antonov An-26B	17311410	
UR-26077	Antonov An-26	11603	RA-26077 CCCP26077
UR-26094	Antonov An-26B	12706	CCCP26094
UR-26097	Antonov An-26B	11902	
UR-26129	Antonov An-26B	12703	CCCP26129
UR-26175	Antonov An-24RV	77310810A	26175 CCCP26175
UR-26178	Antonov An-26B	13303	

UR-26194	Antonov An-26	0202	CCCP26194 CCCP26184(1)
UR-26197	Antonov An-26B	12609	CCCP26197
UR-26198	Antonov An-26	5209	
UR-26199	Antonov An-26	5806	CCCP58645 S3-ABC
UR-26204	Antonov An-26B	14103	ER-26204
UR-26214	Antonov An-26B	14403	CCCP26214
UR-26215	Antonov An-26	4707	LZ-NHB CCCP26215 CCCP78734
UR-26244	Antonov An-26	97307705	CCCP26244
UR-26407	Antonov An-26	unkn	
UR-26514	Antonov An-26	6907	CCCP26514
UR-26519	Antonov An-26	7010	CCCP26519
UR-26526	Antonov An-26	7208	
UR-26531	Antonov An-26	7403	CCCP26531
UR-26555	Antonov An-26	3203	CCCP26555
UR-26578	Antonov An-26B	13404	CCCP26578
UR-26580	Antonov An-26B	13408	TC-GZT UR-26580 RA-26580
UR-26581	Antonov An-26B	57313503	RA-26581
UR-26596	Antonov An-26	unkn	
UR-26598	Antonov An-26	4102	CCCP26598(1)
UR-26599	Antonov An-26	4206	CCCP26599
UR-26604	Antonov An-26	4606	CCCP26604
UR-26650	Antonov An-26B	7507	UN-26650 CCCP26650
UR-26651	Antonov An-26	7508	CCCP26651
UR-26676	Antonov An-26B	8602	RA-26676
UR-26680	Antonov An-26	8609	
UR-26689	Antonov An-26B	9005	CCCP26689
UR-26911	Antonov An-26	unkn	
UR-27126	Mil Mi-8MTV-1	95953	CCCP27126
UR-28710	PZL-Mielec/Antonov An-28	1AJ006-20	RA-28710 CCCP28710
UR-28712	PZL-Mielec/Antonov An-28	1AJ006-22	RA-28712 CCCP28712
UR-28721	PZL-Mielec/Antonov An-28	1AJ007-08	RA-28721
UR-28731	PZL-Mielec/Antonov An-28	1AJ007-16	ES-DAA RA-28731 CCCP28731
UR-28737	PZL-Mielec/Antonov An-28	1AJ007-25	RA-28737 CCCP28737
UR-28739	PZL-Mielec/Antonov An-28	1AJ008-02	RA-28739 CCCP28739
UR-28754	PZL-Mielec/Antonov An-28	1AJ004-03	CCCP28754
UR-28764	PZL-Mielec/Antonov An-28	1AJ004-13	CCCP28764
UR-28765	PZL-Mielec/Antonov An-28	1AJ004-14	CCCP28765
UR-28766	PZL-Mielec/Antonov An-28	1AJ004-15	RA-28766 CCCP28766
UR-28768	PZL-Mielec/Antonov An-28	1AJ004-17	RA-28768 CCCP28768
UR-28772	PZL-Mielec/Antonov An-28	1AJ005-04	RA-28772 CCCP28772
UR-28773	PZL-Mielec/Antonov An-28	1AJ005-05	RA-28773 CCCP28773
UR-28787	PZL-Mielec/Antonov An-28	1AJ005-20	RA-28787 CCCP28787
UR-28799	PZL-Mielec/Antonov An-28	1AJ006-10	RA-28799 CCCP28799
UR-28800	PZL-Mielec/Antonov An-28	1AJ001-01	CCCP28800
UR-28802	PZL-Mielec/Antonov An-28	1AJ001-04	CCCP28802
UR-30000	Antonov An-30A	1401	CCCP30000
UR-30005	Antonov An-30	1406	RA-30005 CCCP30005
UR-30022	Antonov An-30	0404	CCCP30022
UR-30025	Antonov An-30	0503	CCCP30025
UR-30026	Antonov An-30	0505	CCCP30026
UR-30030	Antonov An-30	0605	CCCP30030
UR-30036	Antonov An-30	0703	CCCP30036
UR-30044	Antonov An-30	0906	CCCP30044
UR-31413	Antonov An-2R	1G197-36	CCCP31413
UR-31497	Antonov An-2	1G199-06	CCCP31497
UR-31504	Antonov An-2	1G199-13	CCCP31504
UR-32295	Antonov An-2TP	1G97-07	
UR-32327	Antonov An-2TP	1G97-39	
UR-32364	Antonov An-2	1G100-15	CCCP32364
UR-32379	Antonov An-2TP	1G100-30	
UR-32501	Antonov An-2T	1G103-28	CCCP32501
UR-32637	Antonov An-2R	1G219-36	CCCP32637
UR-32654	Antonov An-2	1G118-03	
UR-32746	Antonov An-2R	1G212-51	SP-ZFS SP-ZFL CCCP32746
UR-32747	Antonov An-2R	1G212-52	
UR-32749	Antonov An-2R	1G212-54	CCCP32749
UR-33000	Antonov An-2R	1G217-40	
UR-33001	Antonov An-2R	1G217-41	CCCP33001
UR-33003	Antonov An-2	1G217-43	CCCP33003
UR-33004	Antonov An-2R	1G217-44	
UR-33005	Antonov An-2R	1G217-45	CCCP33005
UR-33006	Antonov An-2R	1G217-46	CCCP33006
UR-33377	Antonov An-2	1G226-36	
UR-33388	Antonov An-2R	1G226-47	CCCP33388
UR-33473	Antonov An-2R	1G228-23	

UR-33488	Antonov An-2	1G228-39	
UR-33516	Antonov An-2R	1G229-08	CCCP33516
UR-33570	Antonov An-2R	1G230-07	CCCP33570
UR-33571	Antonov An-2R	1G230-08	CCCP33571
UR-33587	Antonov An-2R	1G230-29	CCCP33587
UR-33590	Antonov An-2R	1G230-32	CCCP33590
UR-33639	Antonov An-2R	1G233-29	CCCP33639
UR-33640	Antonov An-2R	1G233-30	CCCP33640
UR-33641	Antonov An-2R	1G233-31	CCCP33641
UR-33644	Antonov An-2	1G233-34	
UR-35019	Antonov An-2TP	1G109-25	CCCP35019
UR-35072	Antonov An-2TP	1G110-38	CCCP35072
UR-35189	Antonov An-2P	1G114-13	CCCP35189
UR-35327	Antonov An-2R	1G134-20	CCCP35327
UR-35521	Antonov An-2P	1G114-33	CCCP35521
UR-35535	Antonov An-2P	1G114-47	CCCP35535
UR-35544	Antonov An-2P	1G114-56	
UR-40218	Antonov An-2R	1G220-08	CCCP40218
UR-40219	Antonov An-2R	1G220-09	
UR-40221	Antonov An-2R	1G220-11	
UR-40289	Antonov An-2R	1G221-19	CCCP40289
UR-40293	Antonov An-2R	1G221-23	CCCP40293
UR-40307	Antonov An-2R	1G221-37	CCCP40307
UR-40329	Antonov An-2R	1G222-06	
UR-40350	Antonov An-2R	1G222-27	CCCP40350
UR-40361	Antonov An-2R	1G222-40	
UR-40365	Antonov An-2R	1G222-44	CCCP40365
UR-40374	Antonov An-2R	1G222-53	CCCP40374
UR-40375	Antonov An-2R	1G222-54	
UR-40416	Antonov An-2R	1G223-40	CCCP40416
UR-40419	Antonov An-2R	1G223-45	
UR-40422	Antonov An-2R	1G223-48	
UR-40423	Antonov An-2R	1G223-49	
UR-40432	Antonov An-2R	1G223-58	CCCP40432
UR-40435	Antonov An-2R	1G224-04	CCCP40435
UR-40483	Antonov An-2R	1G224-60	
UR-40486	Antonov An-2R	1G225-03	
UR-40522	Antonov An-2TP	1G83-25	CCCP40522
UR-40600	Antonov An-2R	1G212-55	
UR-40613	Antonov An-2R	1G213-20	CCCP40613
UR-40631	Antonov An-2R	1G213-38	
UR-40737	Antonov An-2R	1G172-09	
UR-40780	Antonov An-2	1G173-07	CCCP40780
UR-40783	Antonov An-2R	1G173-10	CCCP40783
UR-40798	Antonov An-2R	1G173-25	
UR-40811	Antonov An-2	1G173-38	CCCP40811
UR-40814	Antonov An-2R	1G173-41	CCCP40814
UR-40820	Antonov An-2R	1G173-47	
UR-40831	Antonov An-2R	1G174-09	CCCP40831
UR-40853	Antonov An-2R	1G174-49	CCCP40853
UR-40883	Antonov An-2R	1G215-18	
UR-40885	Antonov An-2R	1G215-20	CCCP40885
UR-40892	Antonov An-2	1G215-29	CCCP40892
UR-40949	Antonov An-2R	1G216-49	CCCP40949
UR-40951	Antonov An-2R	1G216-51	CCCP40951
UR-40952	Antonov An-2R	1G216-52	CCCP40952
UR-40956	Antonov An-2	1G216-56	CCCP40956
UR-40984	Antonov An-2R	1G217-24	
UR-40989	Antonov An-2R	1G217-29	
UR-40999	Antonov An-2R	1G217-39	CCCP40999
UR-42308	Yakovlev Yak-42	11040303	CCCP42308
UR-42310	Yakovlev Yak-42	11040403	CCCP42310
UR-42317	Yakovlev Yak-42	4520422202039	42317 CCCP42317
UR-42318	Yakovlev Yak-42	4520423402051	RA-42318 CCCP42318
UR-42319	Yakovlev Yak-42	4520423402062	42319 CCCP42319
UR-42327	Yakovlev Yak-42	4520424402161	T9-ABF UR-42327 CCCP42327
UR-42337	Yakovlev Yak-42	4520423606235	UN-42337 RA-42337 LY-AAM CCCP42337
UR-42342	Yakovlev Yak-42	4520421706302	EX-42342 UN-42342 LY-AAP CCCP42342
UR-42348	Yakovlev Yak-42	4520423711342	CCCP42348
UR-42352	Yakovlev Yak-42	4520421811395	RA-42352 LY-AAS CCCP42352
UR-42358	Yakovlev Yak-42	4520422811413	CCCP42358
UR-42366	Yakovlev Yak-42	4520424814047	T9-ABH EP-SAG CCCP42366
UR-42369	Yakovlev Yak-42D	4520422914190	CCCP42369
UR-42372	Yakovlev Yak-42D	4520423914266	CCCP42372
UR-42376	Yakovlev Yak-42D	4520424914477	EP-CPK UR-42376 CCCP42376
UR-42377	Yakovlev Yak-42D	4520421014479	CCCP42377
UR-42381	Yakovlev Yak-42D	4520422014576	EP-SAF UR-42381 CCCP42381

UR-42383	Yakovlev Yak-42D	4520422016201	T9-ABD UR-42383 CCCP42383
UR-42403	Yakovlev Yak-42D	4520422116588	CCCP42403
UR-42405	Yakovlev Yak-42D	4520423116624	CCCP42405
UR-42409	Yakovlev Yak-42D	4520421216707	ER-42409 RA-42409 CCCP42409
UR-42410	Yakovlev Yak-42D	4520421219029	EP-CPB UR-42410 CCCP42410
UR-42416	Yakovlev Yak-42D	4520423219102	EP-CPE UR-42416 EP-CPA CCCP42416
UR-42419	Yakovlev Yak-42D	4520423201016	
UR-42426	Yakovlev Yak-42D	4520423304016	TC-IYI EP-LAM EP-LAE RA-42426
UR-42449	Yakovlev Yak-42D	4520421401018	EP-CPC UR-42449
UR-42527	Yakovlev Yak-42	11040903	CCCP42527
UR-42530	Yakovlev Yak-42	11120204	CCCP42530
UR-42540	Yakovlev Yak-42	11140604	T9-ABC(2)? CCCP42540
UR-42544	Yakovlev Yak-42	11151004	T9-ABC(1) UR-42544 CCCP42544
UR-43950	Antonov An-2R	1G210-27	CCCP43950
UR-43954	Antonov An-2R	1G210-31	CCCP43954
UR-43968	Antonov An-2R	1G210-45	SP-ZFT SP-ZFN CCCP43968
UR-43983	Antonov An-2	1G210-60	CCCP43983
UR-43986	Antonov An-2R	1G211-05	CCCP43986
UR-43993	Antonov An-2R	1G211-12	CCCP43993
UR-43994	Antonov An-2R	1G211-13	
UR-46015	Antonov An-32	unkn	IndianAF K2729
UR-46017	Antonov An-32	unkn	
UR-46205	Antonov An-24B	67302803	RA-46205
UR-46249	Antonov An-24B	77303207	UR-46569(1) CCCP46569
UR-46251	Antonov An-24B	77303303	CCCP46251
UR-46254	Antonov An-24B	77303402	RA-46254 CCCP46254
UR-46278	Antonov An-24B	77303701	CCCP46278
UR-46279	Antonov An-24B	77303702	CCCP46279
UR-46293	Antonov An-24B	77303805	CCCP46293
UR-46301	Antonov An-24B	97305201	CCCP46301
UR-46302	Antonov An-24B	97305202	CCCP46302
UR-46305	Antonov An-24B	97305205	CCCP46305
UR-46311	Antonov An-24B	97305307	LZ-MND UR-46311 CCCP46311
UR-46312	Antonov An-24B	97305308	CCCP46312
UR-46326	Antonov An-24B	97305503	CCCP46326
UR-46330	Antonov An-24B	97305507	CCCP46330
UR-46336	Antonov An-24T	8910709	RA-46336 CCCP46336
UR-46338	Antonov An-24B	97305606	RA-46338 CCCP46338
UR-46343	Antonov An-24B	97305703	CCCP46343
UR-46372	Antonov An-24B	07306003	CCCP46372
UR-46383	Antonov An-24B	07306106	CCCP46383
UR-46397	Antonov An-24B	07306301	RA-46397 CCCP46397
UR-46403	Antonov An-24B	77303906	CCCP46403
UR-46416	Antonov An-24B	87304101	CCCP46416
UR-46434	Antonov An-24B	87304304	CCCP46434
UR-46440	Antonov An-24B	87304401	CCCP 46440
UR-46441	Antonov An-24B	87304402	CCCP46441
UR-46464	Antonov An-24RV	27307810	ER-46464 UR-46464 CCCP46464
UR-46469	Antonov An-24RV	27307907	CCCP46469
UR-46475	Antonov An-24RV	27308003	CCCP46475
UR-46477	Antonov An-24RV	27308005	CCCP46477
UR-46514	Antonov An-24RV	37308410	RA-46514 CCCP46514
UR-46517	Antonov An-24RV	37308503	CCCP46517
UR-46521	Antonov An-24B *(Noted carrying c/n 67302309)*	67302308	LZ-SFP CCCP46521
UR-46527	Antonov An-24RV	47310006	CCCP
UR-46536	Antonov An-24RV	57310110	CCCP
UR-46547	Antonov An-24	unkn	CCCP
UR-46558	Antonov An-24B	87304605	CCCP
UR-46569	Antonov An-24B	87304710	CCCP
UR-46577	Antonov An-24B	87304902	CCCP
UR-46585	Antonov An-24B	97305004	CCCP
UR-46586	Antonov An-24B	97305006	CCCP
UR-46596	Antonov An-24B	97305106	CCCP
UR-46622	Antonov An-24RV	37308709	CCCP
UR-46633	Antonov An-30	0202	CCCP46633
UR-46647	Antonov An-24RV	37309107	CCCP46647
UR-46661	Antonov An-24RV	47309305	CCCP46661
UR-46666	Antonov An-24RV	47309507	YL-LCG CCCP46666
UR-46675	Antonov An-24RV	47309607	CCCP46675
UR-46677	Antonov An-24RV	47309609	CCCP46677
UR-46688	Antonov An-24RV	47309805	CCCP46688
UR-46742	Antonov An-24B	47300804	
UR-46777	Antonov An-24B	77301504	CCCP46777
UR-46783	Antonov An-24B	57301701	CCCP46783
UR-46796	Antonov An-24B	57301905	UN-46796 CCCP46796
UR-46813	Antonov An-24B *(C/n quoted as 67302204)*	67302402	CCCP46813
UR-46833	Antonov An-24	17306710	CCCP46833
UR-46838	Antonov An-24RV	17306805	CCCP46838
UR-47179	Antonov An-24B	99901904	CCCP47179
UR-47256	Antonov An-24RV	27307708	TC-MOB CCCP47256
UR-47257	Antonov An-24RV	27307709	CCCP47257
UR-47258	Antonov An-24RV	27307609	RA-47258 CCCP47258
UR-47265	Antonov An-24RV	27307807	CCCP47265
UR-47266	Antonov An-24B	07306304	CCCP47266
UR-47278	Antonov An-24B	07306408	CCCP47378
UR-47281	Antonov An-24B	07306501	CCCP47281
UR-47287	Antonov An-24B	07306507	CCCP47287
UR-47294	Antonov An-24RV	07306604	
UR-47296	Antonov An-24RV	07306609	CCCP47296
UR-47297	Antonov An-24RV	07306610	CCCP47297
UR-47300	Antonov An-24RV	57310203	CCCP47300
UR-47308	Antonov An-24RV	57310308	CCCP47308
UR-47311	Antonov An-24RV	57310402	CCCP47311
UR-47312	Antonov An-24RV	57310403	RA-47312 CCCP47312
UR-47401	Antonov An-26	unkn	CCCP47401
UR-47702	Antonov An-24B	59900203	CCCP47702
UR-47705	Antonov An-24B	59900303	CCCP47705
UR-47711	Antonov An-24B	69900501	CCCP47711
UR-47743	Antonov An-24B	79901106	CCCP47743
UR-47783	Antonov An-24B	89901508	CCCP47783
UR-47791	Antonov An-24B	67303004	LZ-MNF TG-MNF TG-RVS LZ-MNF UR-47791
UR-47801	Antonov An-24RV	17306810	CCCP47801
UR-47824	Antonov An-24RV	17307205	CCCP47824
UR-47836	Antonov An-24B	17307308	CCCP47836
UR-47837	Antonov An-24B	17307309	CCCP47837
UR-47846	Antonov An-24B	17307408	CCCP47846
UR-48004	Antonov An-32P	1306	CCCP48004
UR-48005	Antonov An-32	unkn	
UR-48008	Antonov An-32B	3405	
UR-48012	Antonov An-32B	unkn	
UR-48016	Antonov An-32	3206	
UR-48017	Antonov An-32B	3302	
UR-48023	Antonov An-32B	3409	HK-4006X UR-48023
UR-48053	Antonov An-32	2803	
UR-48054	Antonov An-32	2804	CCCP48054
UR-48055	Antonov An-32B	2805	
UR-48078	Antonov An-32B	unkn	CCCP48078
UR-48079	Antonov An-32B	unkn	CCCP48079
UR-48081	Antonov An-32B	3106	CCCP48081
UR-48083	Antonov An-32B	3001	CCCP48083
UR-48084	Antonov An-32	2602	CCCP48084
UR-48086	Antonov An-32P	2901	CCCP48086
UR-48087	Antonov An-32B	2904	CCCP48087
UR-48093	Antonov An-32	0703	CCCP48093
UR-48097	Antonov An-24RV	57310409	CCCP48097
UR-48131	Antonov An-32B	3204	
UR-49248	Antonov An-24B	67302205	49248 SP-LTB
UR-49249	Antonov An-24B	67302504	49249 SP-LTG
UR-49250	Antonov An-24B	67302505	49250 SP-LTH
UR-49251	Antonov An-24B	67302506	49251 SP-LTI
UR-49252	Antonov An-24B	67302507	49252 SP-LTK
UR-49253	Antonov An-24B	67302801	49253 SP-LTO PLW: 011 (1)
UR-49254	Antonov An-24B	67302802	49254 SP-LTP PLW: 012 (1)
UR-49255	Antonov An-24B	97305701	49255 SP-LTT PLW: 011 (2)
UR-49256	Antonov An-24T	9911104	
UR-49260	Antonov An-26	unkn	RA-49260
UR-50583	Antonov An-2M	1G131-25	CCCP50583
UR-54812	Antonov An-2R	1G184-19	CCCP54812
UR-54815	Antonov An-2	1G184-22	CCCP54815
UR-54819	Antonov An-2R	1G184-26	
UR-54839	Antonov An-2R	1G185-12	
UR-54840	Antonov An-2	1G185-13	CCCP54840
UR-54843	Antonov An-2R	1G184-50	CCCP54843

UR-54856	Antonov An-2R	1G185-16	SP-ZEW CCCP54856
UR-54861	Antonov An-2R	1G185-21	CCCP54861
UR-54862	Antonov An-2R	1G185-22	CCCP54862
UR-54863	Antonov An-2R	1G185-23	CCCP54863
UR-54869	Antonov An-2R	1G185-29	CCCP54869
UR-54870	Antonov An-2R	1G185-30	CCCP54870
UR-54870	Antonov An-2	1G185-31	
UR-54872	Antonov An-2R	1G185-32	
UR-54873	Antonov An-2R	1G185-33	CCCP54873
UR-54886	Antonov An-2R	1G185-54	
UR-54888	Antonov An-2R	1G186-01	CCCP54888
UR-54897	Antonov An-2	1G186-45	CCCP54897
UR-54920	Antonov An-2R	1G187-13	CCCP54920
UR-54927	Antonov An-2R	1G187-20	CCCP54927
UR-54928	Antonov An-2R	1G187-21	CCCP54928
UR-56390	Antonov An-2R	1G180-20	CCCP56390
UR-56393	Antonov An-2R	1G180-23	CCCP56393
UR-56394	Antonov An-2R	1G180-24	CCCP56394
UR-56442	Antonov An-2	1G181-26	CCCP56442
UR-56446	Antonov An-2T	1G181-30	CCCP56446
UR-56447	Antonov An-2	1G181-31	CCCP56447
UR-56466	Antonov An-2R	1G182-23	CCCP56466
UR-56469	Antonov An-2R	1G182-26	
UR-56483	Antonov An-2R	1G182-40	CCCP40810
UR-56506	Antonov An-2R	1G183-04	
UR-56512	Antonov An-2	1G183-10	CCCP56512
UR-62478	Antonov An-2	1G42-26	
UR-62511	Antonov An-2	1G175-34	CCCP62511
UR-62528	Antonov An-2R	1G175-51	CCCP62528
UR-62529	Antonov An-2R	1G175-52	CCCP62529
UR-62534	Antonov An-2R	1G175-57	CCCP62534 SP-ZEU CCCP62534
UR-62542	Antonov An-2R	1G176-05	CCCP62542
UR-62548	Antonov An-2	1G176-11	CCCP62548
UR-62569	Antonov An-2	1G176-38	
UR-62615	Antonov An-2	1G177-60	CCCP62515
UR-62664	Antonov An-2R	1G178-56	CCCP62664
UR-62665	Antonov An-2R	1G178-57	
UR-62676	Antonov An-2R	1G179-04	CCCP62676
UR-62677	Antonov An-2R	1G179-05	CCCP62677
UR-62679	Antonov An-2	1G179-09	CCCP62679
UR-62682	Antonov An-2	1G179-12	CCCP62682
UR-64459	Antonov An-22	0101	CCCP64459 CCCP46191
UR-64460	Antonov An-22	0103	LZ-SFD LZ-SGB CCCP64460 CCCP67691
UR-65023	Tupolev Tu-134A	48415	LY-ABB CCCP65023
UR-65037	Tupolev Tu-134A-3	48850	CCCP65037
UR-65048	Tupolev Tu-134A-3	49750	CCCP65048
UR-65073	Tupolev Tu-134A	49980	CCCP65073
UR-65076	Tupolev Tu-134A-3	60001	CCCP65076
UR-65077	Tupolev Tu-134A-3	60028	65077 CCCP65077
UR-65081	Tupolev Tu-134A-3	60076	LY-ABE CCCP65081
UR-65089	Tupolev Tu-134A	60180	CCCP65089
UR-65107	Tupolev Tu-134A	60328	CCCP65107
UR-65114	Tupolev Tu-134A-3	60395	CCCP65114
UR-65135	Tupolev Tu-134A-3	60648	CCCP65135
UR-65556	Tupolev Tu-134A-3	66372	CCCP65556
UR-65718	Tupolev Tu-134A-3	63668	65718 UR-65718 CCCP65718
UR-65746	Tupolev Tu-134A-3	2351608	CCCP65746
UR-65752	Tupolev Tu-134A-3	61079	CCCP65752
UR-65757	Tupolev Tu-134A	62215	CCCP65757
UR-65761	Tupolev Tu-134A-3	62244	CCCP65761
UR-65765	Tupolev Tu-134A	62315	CCCP65765
UR-65773	Tupolev Tu-134A-3	62495	CCCP65773
UR-65782	Tupolev Tu-134A-3	62672	CCCP65782
UR-65790	Tupolev Tu-134A-3	63100	CCCP65790
UR-65826	Tupolev Tu-134A-3	12083	CCCP65826
UR-65841	Tupolev Tu-134A	18120	CCCP65841
UR-65852	Tupolev Tu-134A	23244	CCCP65852
UR-65864	Tupolev Tu-134A	28284	CCCP65864
UR-65877	Tupolev Tu-134A-3	31250	CCCP65877
UR-65888	Tupolev Tu-134A-3	36175	CCCP65888
UR-65917	Tupolev Tu-134A-3M	63991	RA-65917 CCCP65917
UR-67000	LET L-410UVP	810601	CCCP67000
UR-67001	LET L-410UVP	810602	CCCP67001
UR-67004	LET L-410UVP	810605	CCCP67004
UR-67020	LET L-410UVP	810621	CCCP67020
UR-67023	LET L-410UVP	810624	RA-67023 CCCP67023
UR-67024	LET L-410UVP	810626	RA-67024 CCCP67024
UR-67030	LET L-410UVP	800501	
UR-67059	LET L-410UVP	810635	CCCP67059
UR-67068	LET L-410UVP	810704	CCCP67068
UR-67069	LET L-410UVP	810705	RA-67069 CCCP67069

UR-67082	LET L-410UVP	810719	CCCP67082
UR-67083	LET L-410UVP	810720	CCCP67083
UR-67085	LET L-410UVP	810722	CCCP67085
UR-67102	LET L-410UVP	841328	HA-LAP CCCP67102
UR-67122	LET L-410UVP	790318	CCCP67122
UR-67128	LET L-410UVP	790324	CCCP67128
UR-67129	LET L-410UVP	790325	CCCP67129
UR-67141	LET L-410UVP	800407	RA-67141 CCCP67141
UR-67161	LET L-410UVP	800427	
UR-67169	LET L-410UVP	790205	CCCP67169
UR-67195	LET L-410UVP	790301	RA-67195 CCCP67195
UR-67197	LET L-410UVP	790303	CCCP67197
UR-67198	LET L-410UVP	790304	CCCP67198
UR-67199	LET L-410UVP	790305	CCCP67199
UR-67254	LET L-410AS	720106	RA-67254 CCCP67254
UR-67332	LET L-410UVP	820832	CCCP67332
UR-67340	LET L-410UVP	820840	HA-LAC CCCP67340
UR-67356	LET L-410UVP	820916	CCCP67356
UR-67357	LET L-410UVP	820917	CCCP67357
UR-67366	LET L-410UVP	820922	RA-67366 CCCP67366
UR-67368	LET L-410UVP	830936	RA-67368 CCCP67368
UR-67372	LET L-410UVP	830940	CCCP67372
UR-67389	LET L-410UVP	831017	CCCP67389
UR-67392	LET L-410UVP	831020	CCCP67392
UR-67393	LET L-410UVP	831021	CCCP67393
UR-67395	LET L-410UVP	831023	CCCP67395
UR-67409	LET L-410UVP	831037	CCCP67409
UR-67411	LET L-410UVP	831039	CCCP67411
UR-67417	LET L-410UVP	831108	CCCP67417
UR-67419	LET L-410UVP	831110	CCCP67419
UR-67439	LET L-410UVP	841204	YL-KAH ? HA-LAU
UR-67449	LET L-410UVP	841214	CCCP67449
UR-67472	LET L-410UVP	841237	CCCP67472
UR-67477	LET L-410UVP	841302	CCCP67477
UR-67479	LET L-410UVP	841304	RA-67479 CCCP67479
UR-67481	LET L-410UVP	841306	RA-67481 CCCP67481 OK-OZB
UR-67492	LET L-410UVP	841317	ES-LLD HA-LAL CCCP67492
UR-67504	LET L-410UVP	851408	HA-LAN CCCP67504
UR-67506	LET L-410UVP	851410	CCCP67506
UR-67520	LET L-410UVP	851424	RA-67520 CCCP67520
UR-67524	LET L-410UVP	851431	CCCP67524
UR-67526	LET L-410UVP	851433	CCCP67526
UR-67527	LET L-410UVP	851434	CCCP67527
UR-67528	LET L-410UVP	851435	RA-67528 CCCP67528
UR-67536	LET L-410UVP	851503	RA-67536 CCCP67536
UR-67543	LET L-410UVP	851510	LZ-MNB CCCP67543
UR-67555	LET L-410UVP	851519	LZ-MNC CCCP67555
UR-67556	LET L-410UVP	851520	CCCP67556
UR-67601	LET L-410UVP	810637	9L-LBL UR-67061 CCCP67061
UR-67658	LET L-410UVP-E	902512	CCCP67658
UR-67659	LET L-410UVP-E	902513	CCCP67659
UR-67663	LET L-410UVP-E	902525	CCCP67663
UR-67715	LET L-410UVP-E	912613	OK-WDM CCCP67682
UR-68022	Antonov An-2R	1G192-54	CCCP68022
UR-68023	Antonov An-2R	1G192-55	CCCP68023
UR-68051	Antonov An-2R	1G193-23	
UR-68074	Antonov An-2R	1G193-44	CCCP68074
UR-68075	Antonov An-2R	1G193-45	
UR-68084	Antonov An-2R	unkn	CCCP68084
UR-68097	Antonov An-2R	1G195-02	
UR-68100	Antonov An-2	1G195-05	CCCP68100
UR-68104	Antonov An-2R	1G195-09	CCCP68104
UR-68110	Antonov An-2	1G195-15	CCCP68110
UR-69312	Antonov An-26	29-06	CCCP69312
UR-70202	Antonov An-2R	1G138-20	
UR-70278	Antonov An-2P	1G139-37	CCCP70278
UR-70281	Antonov An-2P	1G139-40	
UR-70289	Antonov An-2	1G139-48	CCCP70289
UR-70290	Antonov An-2	1G139-39	CCCP70290
UR-70342	Antonov An-2	1G140-46	CCCP70342
UR-70355	Antonov An-2P	1G141-09	
UR-70391	Antonov An-2	1G141-45	CCCP70391
UR-70393	Antonov An-2P	1G141-47	
UR-70447	Antonov An-2	1G143-26	CCCP70447
UR-71188	Antonov An-2	1G200-31	CCCP71188

UR-71191	Antonov An-2R	1G200-34	CCCP71191
UR-71206	Antonov An-2	1G200-49	CCCP71206
UR-71207	Antonov An-2	1G200-50	CCCP71207
UR-71216	Antonov An-2	1G200-59	CCCP71216
UR-72003	Antonov An-74	unkn	CCCP72003
			CCCP72200
			CCCP780334
			CCCP19795
UR-74007	Antonov An-74	36547095903	RA-74007
			HK-3809X
			CCCP74007
UR-74010	Antonov An-74T	36547030450	CCCP74010
UR-74026	Antonov An-74-200	36547096919	HK-3810X
			CCCP74026
UR-74028	Antonov An-74	unkn	CCCP58642
UR-74038	Antonov An-74TK-200	36547097933	RA-74038
			UR-74038
UR-74057	Antonov An-74-200	36547098960	
UR-74300	Antonov An-74TK-300	36547098984	RA-74300
UR-76316	Ilyushin IL-76MD	0043454633	CCCP76606
UR-76318	Ilyushin IL-76MD	0023437127	CCCP86918
UR-76321	Ilyushin IL-76MD	0053457713	76321
			UR-76321
			CCCP76625
UR-76322	Ilyushin IL-76MD	0053462873	76322
			UR-76322
			CCCP76652
UR-76323	Ilyushin IL-76MD	0063466988	76323
			UR-76323
			CCCP76673
UR-76390	Ilyushin IL-76MD	0043453562	
UR-76391	Ilyushin IL-76MD	0043453568	CCCP76594
UR-76392	Ilyushin IL-76MD	0043454602	CCCP76600
UR-76393	Ilyushin IL-76MD	0043455653	CCCP76611
UR-76395	Ilyushin IL-76MD	0033443255	CCCP76543
UR-76423	Ilyushin IL-76MD	0053457720	RA-76423
			CCCP76423
			CCCP76626
UR-76431	Ilyushin IL-76	unkn	
UR-76441	Ilyushin IL-76MD	unkn	CCCP76441
UR-76443	Ilyushin IL-76MD	0043452534	CCCP76443
			CCCP76589
UR-76532	Ilyushin IL-76MD	0023441201	CCCP76532
UR-76541	Ilyushin IL-76MD	0033442241	CCCP76541
UR-76563	Ilyushin IL-76MD	0033447372	
UR-76568	Ilyushin IL-76MD	0033448420	CCCP76568
UR-76570	Ilyushin IL-76MD	0033448427	CCCP76570
UR-76571	Ilyushin IL-76MD	0033448429	CCCP76571
UR-76573	Ilyushin IL-76MD	0043449437	CCCP76573
UR-76574	Ilyushin IL-76MD	0033449441	CCCP76574
UR-76576	Ilyushin IL-76MD	0043449449	CCCP76576
UR-76579	Ilyushin IL-76MD	0043449471	CCCP76579
UR-76581	Ilyushin IL-76MD	0043450484	CCCP76581
UR-76582	Ilyushin IL-76MD	0043450487	CCCP76582
UR-76583	Ilyushin IL-76MD	0043450491	CCCP76583
UR-76584	Ilyushin IL-76TD	0043450493	CCCP76584
UR-76590	Ilyushin IL-76MD	0043452544	CCCP76590
UR-76595	Ilyushin IL-76MD	0043453571	CCCP76595
UR-76603	Ilyushin IL-76MD	0043454623	CCCP76603
UR-76609	Ilyushin IL-78	0043453597	CCCP76609
UR-76610	Ilyushin IL-78	0043454640	CCCP76610
UR-76614	Ilyushin IL-76MD	0043455665	CCCP76614
UR-76624	Ilyushin IL-76MD	0053457710	CCCP76624
UR-76628	Ilyushin IL-76TD	0053458741	CCCP76628
UR-76629	Ilyushin IL-76MD	0053458745	CCCP76629
UR-76631	Ilyushin IL-76MD	0053458756	CCCP76631
UR-76636	Ilyushin IL-76MD	0053459781	CCCP76636
UR-76637	Ilyushin IL-76MD	0053460797	CCCP76637
UR-76656	Ilyushin IL-76MD	0053463891	CCCP76656
UR-76662	Ilyushin IL-76MD	0053464919	CCCP76662
UR-76670	Ilyushin IL-78	0063465958	CCCP76670
UR-76680	Ilyushin IL-76MD	0063467020	76680
			CCCP76680
UR-76681	Ilyushin IL-76MD	0063467021	CCCP76681
UR-76682	Ilyushin IL-78	0063467027	
UR-76687	Ilyushin IL-76MD	0063469051	CCCP76687
UR-76688	Ilyushin IL-76MD	0063469062	CCCP76688
UR-76689	Ilyushin IL-78	0063469066	76689
			CCCP76689
UR-76690	Ilyushin IL-78	0063469080	CCCP76690
UR-76700	Ilyushin IL-76MD	0063471134	CCCP76700
UR-76704	Ilyushin IL-76TD	0063471150	CCCP76704
UR-76705	Ilyushin IL-76MD	0063472158	RA76705
			76705
			CCCP76705
UR-76706	Ilyushin IL-76MD	0063472163	CCCP76706
UR-76716	Ilyushin IL-76MD	0073474211	
UR-76717	Ilyushin IL-76MD *(Damaged 27.7.02)*	0073474216	4K-76717
			UR-76717
			CCCP76617
UR-76727	Ilyushin IL-76MD	0073475268	CCCP76727
UR-76744	Ilyushin IL-76	0073478359	CCCP76744
UR-76749	Ilyushin IL-76MD	0073479392	76749
			CCCP 76749
UR-76777	Ilyushin IL-76MD	0083482490	
UR-76778	Ilyushin IL-76MD	0083482502	CCCP76778
UR-78734	Ilyushin IL-76TD	1013409303	HA-TCA
			CCCP78734
UR-78752	Ilyushin IL-76MD	0083483519	CCCP78752
UR-78758	Ilyushin IL-76MD	0083484551	CCCP78758
UR-78759	Ilyushin IL-78	0083485558	CCCP78759
UR-78772	Ilyushin IL-76MD	0083487627	CCCP78772
UR-78785	Ilyushin IL-76MD	0083489691	CCCP78785
UR-78786	Ilyushin IL-76MD	0083490694	CCCP78786
UR-79165	Antonov An-26	54-09	CCCP26219
UR-79169	Antonov An-26	99-03	CCCP79169
UR-81515	Antonov An-2	1G208-15	CCCP81515
UR-81525	Antonov An-2	1G208-25	CCCP81525
UR-81528	Antonov An-2R	1G208-28	CCCP81528
UR-81530	Antonov An-2R	1G208-30	
UR-81542	Antonov An-2	1G208-42	CCCP81542
UR-81626	Antonov An-2R	1G209-20	
UR-81628	Antonov An-2R	1G209-22	CCCP81628
UR-81629	Antonov An-2R	1G209-23	CCCP81629
UR-81630	Antonov An-2R	1G209-24	CCCP81630
UR-81632	Antonov An-2R	1G209-26	CCCP81632
UR-81642	Antonov An-2R	1G209-36	CCCP81642
UR-81649	Antonov An-2R	1G209-43	CCCP81649
UR-82007	Antonov An-124	19530501005	CCCP82007
UR-82008	Antonov An-124	19530501006	CCCP82008
UR-82009	Antonov An-124	19530501007	CCCP82009
UR-82027	Antonov An-124	19530502288	CCCP82027
UR-82029	Antonov An-124	19530502630	CCCP82029
UR-82060	Antonov An-225 *(Wfu, stored)*	unkn	UR-480182
	(Space shuttle carrier, sole prototype)		UR-82060
			CCCP82060
			CCCP480182
UR-82070	Antonov An-124	9773051359127	RA-82070
UR-82072	Antonov An-124	9773053359136	RA-82072
UR-82073	Antonov An-124	9773054359139	RA-82073
UR-82808	Antonov An-2R	1G166-40	
UR-82816	Antonov An-2	1G166-48	CCCP82816
UR-82826	Antonov An-2R	1G166-58	CCCP82826
UR-82893	Antonov An-2R	1G169-09	CCCP82893
UR-82895	Antonov An-2R	1G169-12	CCCP82895
UR-82899	Antonov An-2R	1G169-16	
UR-82907	Antonov An-2R	1G169-24	CCCP82907
UR-82910	Antonov An-2T	1G167-16	
UR-84526	Antonov An-2R	1G188-51	CCCP84526
UR-84559	Antonov An-2R	1G189-26	CCCP84559
UR-84560	Antonov An-2R	1G189-27	
UR-84573	Antonov An-2R	1G189-40	CCCP84573
UR-84574	Antonov An-2R	1G189-41	CCCP84574
UR-84577	Antonov An-2R	1G189-44	CCCP84577
UR-84587	Antonov An-2R	1G189-54	CCCP84587
UR-84588	Antonov An-2R	1G189-55	
UR-84593	Antonov An-2R	1G189-60	CCCP84593
			SP-ZFO
			CCCP84593
			SP-ZFH
			CCCP84593
UR-84598	Antonov An-2	1G190-30	CCCP84598
UR-84605	Antonov An-2R	1G190-37	CCCP84605
UR-84608	Antonov An-2R	1G190-40	SP-ZFB
			CCCP84608
UR-84609	Antonov An-2	1G190-41	CCCP84609
UR-84612	Antonov An-2	1G190-44	CCCP84612
UR-84623	Antonov An-2R	1G190-55	CCCP84623
UR-84624	Antonov An-2R	1G190-56	CCCP84624
UR-84627	Antonov An-2R	1G190-59	CCCP84627
UR-84635	Antonov An-2	1G191-13	CCCP84635
UR-84645	Antonov An-2R	1G191-23	CCCP84645
UR-84773	Antonov An-2	1G202-35	CCCP84773
UR-84774	Antonov An-2R	1G202-36	CCCP84774
UR-85009	Tupolev Tu-154	7-09	CCCP85009
UR-85068	Tupolev Tu-154B	74A-068	CCCP85068
UR-85074	Tupolev Tu-154A	74A-074	CCCP85074
UR-85093	Tupolev Tu-154B	75A-093	CCCP85093
UR-85116	Tupolev Tu-154A	75A-116	CCCP85116
UR-85118	Tupolev Tu-154B	75A-118	CCCP85118
UR-85132	Tupolev Tu-154B	76A-132	CCCP85132
UR-85137	Tupolev Tu-154B	76A-137	CCCP85137
UR-85148	Tupolev Tu-154B	76A-148	CCCP85148
UR-85152	Tupolev Tu-154B	76A-152	CCCP85152
UR-85154	Tupolev Tu-154B	76A-154	CCCP85154
UR-85179	Tupolev Tu-154B1	76A-179	CCCP85179
UR-85218	Tupolev Tu-154B	77A-218	CCCP85218
UR-85232	Tupolev Tu-154B1	77A-232	CCCP85232
UR-85288	Tupolev Tu-154B1	78A-288	RA-85288
			CCCP85288
UR-85316	Tupolev Tu-154B2	78A-316	CCCP85316
UR-85350	Tupolev Tu-154B2	79A-350	CCCP85350
UR-85362	Tupolev Tu-154B2	79A-362	4K-85362
			UR-85362
			CCCP85362
UR-85368	Tupolev Tu-154B2	79A-368	CCCP85368
UR-85379	Tupolev Tu-154B2	79A-379	CCCP85379
UR-85399	Tupolev Tu-154B2	80A-399	CCCP85399
UR-85407	Tupolev Tu-154B2	80A-407	CCCP85407
UR-85424	Tupolev Tu-154B2	80A-424	CCCP85424
UR-85445	Tupolev Tu-154B2	80A-445	CCCP85445
UR-85460	Tupolev Tu-154B2	81A-460	CCCP85460
UR-85476	Tupolev Tu-154B2	81A-476	CCCP85476

UR-85482	Tupolev Tu-154B2	81A-482	CCCP85482
UR-85490	Tupolev Tu-154B2	81A-490	CCCP85490
UR-85499	Tupolev Tu-154B2	81A-499	CCCP85499
UR-85513	Tupolev Tu-154B2	81A-513	CCCP85513
UR-85526	Tupolev Tu-154B2	82A-526	CCCP85526
UR-85535	Tupolev Tu-154B2	82A-535	CCCP85535
UR-85701	Tupolev Tu-154M	91A-876	85701 CCCP85701
UR-85707	Tupolev Tu-154M	91A-882	CCCP85707
UR-85710	Tupolev Tu-154M	91A-885	RA-85710 UR-85710 CCCP85710
UR-86132	Ilyushin IL62M *(Wfu)*	1034152	SP-LBB
UR-86133	Ilyushin IL62M	1138234	CCCP86133 SP-LBD
UR-86134	Ilyushin IL62M *(Wfu)*	1138546	CCCP86134 SP-LBE
UR-86135	Ilyushin IL62M	1748445	CCCP86135 SP-LBH
UR-86451	Ilyushin IL62	4521152	86451 CCCP86451
UR-86527	Ilyushin IL62M	4037758	86527 CCCP86527
UR-86528	Ilyushin IL62M	4038111	86528 CCCP86528
UR-86529	Ilyushin IL62M	4038625	86529 CCCP86529
UR-86580	Ilyushin IL62M *(Wfu)*	2343554	CCCP86580 SP-LBF
UR-86581	Ilyushin IL62M *(Wfu)*	2932526	CCCP86581 SP-LBA
UR-86582	Ilyushin IL62M *(Wfu)*	3036253	CCCP86582 SP-LBC
UR-86920	Ilyushin IL-76MD	0023440152	86920 CCCP86920
UR-86924	Ilyushin IL-76MD	0023441174	CCCP86924
UR-87215	Yakovlev Yak-40	9510540	OK-FEJ
UR-87237	Yakovlev Yak-40	9530343	CCCP87237 87237 CCCP87237
UR-87245	Yakovlev Yak-40	9531343	RA-87245 UR-87245 CCCP87245
UR-87266	Yakovlev Yak-40	9310227	RA-87266 UR-87266 CCCP87266
UR-87276	Yakovlev Yak-40	9311227	CCCP87276
UR-87296	Yakovlev Yak-40	9321328	UK-87296 CCCP87296
UR-87298	Yakovlev Yak-40	9241325	CCCP87298
UR-87308	Yakovlev Yak-40	9320429	CCCP87308
UR-87327	Yakovlev Yak-40	9330630	CCCP87327
UR-87345	Yakovlev Yak-40	9511439	CCCP87345
UR-87389	Yakovlev Yak-40	9410133	CCCP87389
UR-87405	Yakovlev Yak-40	9421733	RA-87405 CCCP87405
UR-87421	Yakovlev Yak-40	9421734	CCCP87421
UR-87432	Yakovlev Yak-40	9420835	CCCP 87432
UR-87435	Yakovlev Yak-40 *(Stored)*	9431135	CCCP87435
UR-87463	Yakovlev Yak-40	9430237	CCCP87463
UR-87469	Yakovlev Yak-40	9441437	CCCP87469
UR-87479	Yakovlev Yak-40	9441838	CCCP87479
UR-87508	Yakovlev Yak-40	9521040	CCCP87508
UR-87512	Yakovlev Yak-40	9521440	CCCP87512
UR-87528	Yakovlev Yak-40	9521041	CCCP87528 ?
UR-87547	Yakovlev Yak-40	9531242	CCCP87547
UR-87562	Yakovlev Yak-40	9211321	CCCP87562
UR-87566	Yakovlev Yak-40	9211821	SP-FYU UR-87566 CCCP87566
UR-87574	Yakovlev Yak-40	9220622	CCCP87574
UR-87590	Yakovlev Yak-40K	9741156	OK-HER
UR-87592	Yakovlev Yak-40K	9730555	OK-HEP
UR-87624	Yakovlev Yak-40	9140519	CCCP87624
UR-87642	Yakovlev Yak-40	9140320	CCCP87642
UR-87649	Yakovlev Yak-40	9141020	CCCP87649
UR-87660	Yakovlev Yak-40	9240425	CCCP87660
UR-87806	Yakovlev Yak-40	9231223	CCCP87806
UR-87814	Yakovlev Yak-40	9230524	RA-87814 CCCP87814
UR-87818	Yakovlev Yak-40	9230924	CCCP87818
UR-87832	Yakovlev Yak-40	9241825	CCCP87832
UR-87841	Yakovlev Yak-40	9330930	CCCP87841
UR-87918	Yakovlev Yak-40 *(Dbr 28.4.03 ?)*	9830855	87918 CCCP87918
UR-87951	Yakovlev Yak-40K	9810957	CCCP87951
UR-87961	Yakovlev Yak-40	9820458	CCCP87961
UR-87964	Yakovlev Yak-40	9820758	87964 CCCP87964
UR-87965	Yakovlev Yak-40	9820858	RA-87965 CCCP87965
UR-87987	Yakovlev Yak-40	9541144	CCCP87987
UR-87998	Yakovlev Yak-40	9540245	CCCP87998
UR-88151	Yakovlev Yak-40	9610546	CCCP88151
UR-88203	Yakovlev Yak-40	9630549	88203 CCCP88203
UR-88219	Yakovlev Yak-40	9630550	CCCP88219
UR-88237	Yakovlev Yak-40	9640751	88237 CCCP88237
UR-88290	Yakovlev Yak-40K	9840459	88290 CCCP88290
UR-88299	Yakovlev Yak-40	9321028	RA-88299 OK-BYI
UR-88309	Yakovlev Yak-40	9840859	5R-MUA
UR-88310	Yakovlev Yak-40	9940760	5R-MUB
UR-91777	Antonov An-2	1G38-24	
UR-98104	Antonov An-24B	67302310	CCCP98104

GLIDERS

UR-UKL	Schempp-Hirth Ventus 2b	73
UR-USD-SD	Schempp-Hirth Nimbus 4DM	57/77

BALLOONS

UR-BWI	unidentified type	
UR-BWJ	Interavia HAFB	unkn
UR-BWK	AUS HAFB	unkn
UR-BWT	Interavia AS-075 HAFB	unkn
UR-BWV	AUS HAFB	76
UR-KDK	AUS HAFB	81
UR-THK	unidentified type	
UR-TNK	unidentified type	
UR-UMC	AUS HAFB	83
UR- . . .	Cameron O-77 HAFB	3541
UR- . . .	Cameron O-77 HAFB	3542

Λ **A-** Privately-owned aircraft may be registered in a sequence prefixed LA- which is written on the aircraft in Cyrillic characters. Recently-reported examples include:

LA0433	Aviaklub Ikar AI-10	unkn	
LA-0461	Krukowsky VK Gyrocopter	01	F-WTYD
LA0511	Gemini	unkn	
LA-2026	Aeroprakt A-20	026	
LA-2027	Aeroprakt A-20	027	
LA-2207	Aeroprakt A-22 Vision	unkn	
LA2246	Aeroprakt A-22 Vision	046	
LA-2777	Aeroprakt A-22 Vision	009	
LA-3002	Aeroprakt A-20	unkn	

YL - LATVIA

Regn.	Type	C/n	Prev.Id.
YL-APN	Antonov An-26B	12010	LY-APN UR-BXF YL-LDC CCCP26109
YL-BAK	BAe.146 Series RJ70	E-1223	EI-CUO G-BZFA VH-NJW YL-BAK VH-NJW YL-BAK N832BE G-6-223
YL-BAL	BAe.146 Series RJ70	E-1224	N833BE G-6-224
YL-BAN	BAe.146 Series RJ70	E-1225	N834BE G-6-225
YL-BAR	Fokker F.27-050	20149	PH-LVL OY-MMT PH-EXV
YL-BAS	Fokker F.27-050	20162	OY-KAE PH-EXE
YL-BAT	Fokker F.27-050	20163	OY-KAF PH-EXF
YL-BAU	Fokker F.27-050	20126	PH-AAO ES-AFK OY-MMI PH-EXK
YL-BAW	Fokker F.27-050	20148	OY-MMS PH-EXU
YL-BAZ	Fokker F.27-050	20153	ES-AFM OY-MMU PH-EXN
YL-BBA	Boeing 737-505	24646	N646LS LN-BRN
YL-BBB	Boeing 737-505	24273	LN-BRJ D-ACBC
YL-BBC	Airbus A.320-211	142	D-AKFX (EK-32009) D-AKFX VH-HYJ F-WWDI
YL-BBD	Boeing 737-53S	29075	F-GJNU N1786B
YL-BBE	Boeing 737-53S	29073	EI-DDT F-GJNS N1786B
YL-BBF	Boeing 737-548	24878	EI-CDA YR-BGZ EI-CDA EI-BXE
YL-BBG	Boeing 737-548	24919	EI-CDB
YL-BBH	Boeing 737-548	24968	EI0CDC
YL-CAB	Sport Nika (Homebuilt)	0001	
YL-CAC	Antonov An-2T	1G85-22	DOSAAF
YL-CAF	American AG-5B Tiger	10153	
YL-CAJ	American AG-5B Tiger	10109	N1196F
YL-CAK	PZL-104 Wilga 35A	107340	DOSAAF
YL-CAL	PZL-104 Wilga 35A	96303	DOSAAF
YL-CAM	PZL-104 Wilga 35A	16820652	DOSAAF
YL-CAN	PZL-104 Wilga 35A	17830701	DOSAAF
YL-CAO	Antonov An-2T	1G98-48	DOSAAF
YL-CAS	PZL-104 Wilga 35A	15800569	DOSAAF
YL-CAT	PZL-104 Wilga 35A	128421	DOSAAF
YL-CAV	PZL-104 Wilga 35A (W/o 28.12.04)	139479	DOSAAF
YL-CBA	PZL-104 Wilga 35A	15800575	DOSAAF
YL-CBB	PZL-104 Wilga 35A	15800571	DOSAAF
YL-CBL	Yakovlev Yak-18T	17-33	
YL-CBN	Cessna 150L (Identity unconfirmed)	15072614	N1314Q
YL-CBR	Grumman AA-5ACheetah	AA5A-0466	C-GXSJ
YL-CBZ	Cessna 152	15281070	N48955
YL-CCA	Jodel D.18	422	
YL-CCB	Piper PA-34-200 Seneca	34-7250121	F-BTMG F-BTDX N4516T
YL-CCC	Antonov An-2R	1G185-18	LY-AEP CCCP54858
YL-CCD	Cessna 172N	17269293	N737BP
YL-CCE	Cessna 182H	18256392	D-EDZY N2492X
YL-CCF	Antonov An-2T	1G96-22	LY-LEA CCCP32260
YL-CCG	Antonov An-2R	1G225-39	LY-AVG RA-33320 CCCP33320
YL-CCH	Aeroprakt-22	021	
YL-CCI	Zenair CH-701 STOL	7-9240	
YL-CCJ	Piper PA-38-112 Tomahawk	38-78A0640	D-ETAZ HB-PCR N9695N
YL-CCK	Piper PA-28-235 Cherokee	28-10473	N8906W
YL-CCL	Yakovlev Yak-18T	22202034089	
YL-CCM	Rotary Air Force RAF-2000	H2-013-525	
YL-CCN	Antonov An-2M	1G197-45	Latvian Army 257 YL-LEE CCCP31422I
YL-CCO	Reims FR172E Rocket	FR1720049	D-EEES D-EBXO
YL-CCP	Mooney M.20J Model 201	24-0345	S5-DEC OO-NEC N29784 C-GXUH
YL-CCU	Christen Pitts S-2B Special	5083	N776TA N5341U
YL-CCW	Cessna 172F	17252009	OH-CKT SE-EAO N8109U
YL-CCX	Piper PA-31 Turbo Navajo	31-647	OY-AUS LN-KCM N6741L
YL-CCZ	Cessna 172N	17267697	N73817 N5341U
YL-CDA	Cessna 172N	17268704	D-EKRL N734AN
YL-CHD	Piper PA-46-350P Malibu Mirage	4636330	OY-LAS N53517
YL-DCU	Yakovlev Yak-52	unkn	DOSAAF- 46grey
YL-DIA	Diamond DA 20-A1 Katana	10011	N85MF
YL-HMA	Mil Mi-8T	4886	CCCP25948
YL-HMB	Mil Mi-8T	4887	CCCP25949
YL-HMC	Hughes 369E	0473E	D-HHMC (F-GHTX)
YL-HMD	Bell 206BJet Ranger II	4549	C-GIZJ (N91755)
YL-HMF	Agusta-Bell 206B Jet Ranger	unkn	
YL-KAA	LET L-410UVP	851425	CCCP67521
YL-KAB	Antonov An-28	1AJ009-15	CCCP28949
YL-KAD	Antonov An-28	1AJ004-02	CCCP47747
YL-KAE	LET L-410UVP	790209	RA-67173 CCCP67173
YL-KAF	Antonov An-28	1AJ009-09	RA-28943 CCCP28943
YL-KAJ	LET L-410UVP	851507	RA-67540 CCCP67540
YL-KSA	Antonov An-74-200	36547098957	RA-74030
YL-KSB	Antonov An-74 200	36547136013	UR-CAC UN-74011 RA-74011
YL-LAB	Tupolev TU-154B-1	81A-515	CCCP-85515
YL-LAK	Ilyushin IL-76	0003424707	RA-76522 CCCP76522
YL-LAL	Ilyushin IL-76T	0013433984	RA-76755 CCCP76755 YI-ALL IAF-4600
YL-LBT	Yakovlev Yak-42D	4520424404018	B-2758
YL-LBU	Yakovlev Yak-42D	4520423403018	B-2757
YL-LCK	Antonov An-24V	79901110	YL-LCN CCCP47747
YL-LEB	Antonov An-2	1G41-16	CCCP62446
YL-LEO	Antonov An-2R	1G178-41	CCCP62649
YL-LEV(2)	Antonov An-2P	1G140-41	LY-AFG RA-70337 CCCP40337
YL-LHC	Mil Mi-2	527541032	CCCP20724
YL-LHH	Mil Mi-2	549329075	CCCP23349
YL-LHJ	Mil Mi-2	534637026	CCCP20566
YL-LHO(2)	Mil Mi-2	5311119020	RA-14232 OK-VIT CCCP14232
YL-MAR	Hawker 800XP	258389	YR-VPA I-DDVA N23493
YL-NST	Hawker 800XP	258424	N1899K
YL-RAA(2)	Antonov An-26B	11206	CCCP26064
YL-RAB(2)	Antonov An-26B	10508	CCCP26032
YL-RAC	Antonov An-26	09903	CCCP79169
YL-RAD	Antonov An-26B	13909	RA-26589 CCCP26589
YL-RAE	Antonov An-26	14004	CCCP26200
YL-RAF	Antonov An-74TK-100	36547095905	RA-74025 UR-74025 RA-74025 CCCP74025
YL-VIP(2)	BAe.125-800B	258078	OE-GHS ZS-FSI G-BNEH G-5-713 G-BHEH G-5-544
YL-WBD	Canadair CL.600-2B16 Challenger	5442	G-POAJ N604PS C-GLWR
YL-. . .	Agusta-Bell 206A Jet Ranger II (Probably YL-HMF above)	8286	OH-HRF
YL-. . .	Cessna 152	15282942	N45905

YL-. . .	Comco Ikarus Fox-C22	9007-3275	PH-2B5
YL-. . .	Robinson R-44 Raven	1356	N75339

GLIDERS

YL-DAA	LAK-12 Lietuva	692	DOSAAF
YL-DAB	LAK-12 Lietuva	6146	DOSAAF
YL-DAD	SZD-41A Jantar Standard	B-887	DOSAAF
YL-DAE	SZD-41A Jantar Standard	B-745	CCCP6745
			DOSAAF
YL-DAF	SZD-48-1 Jantar Standard 2	B-1258	DOSAAF
YL-DAG	SZD-48-1 Jantar Standard 2	B-1055	DOSAAF
YL-DAH	SZD-48-1 Jantar Standard 2	B-1270	DOSAAF
YL-DAI - 91	SZD-48-3 Jantar Standard 3	B-1511	DOSAAF
YL-DAJ	LET L-13 Blanik	172223	DOSAAF
YL-DAK	LET L-13 Blanik	172227	DOSAAF
YL-DAL	LET L-13 Blanik	174636	DOSAAF
YL-DAO	LET L-13 Blanik	027030	DOSAAF
YL-DBA	LET L-13 Blanik	027154	DOSAAF
YL-DBD	LET L-13 Blanik (C/n not possible)	"027263"	DOSAAF
YL-DBE	LET L-13 Blanik	172414	DOSAAF
YL-DBF	LET L-13 Blanik	027322	DOSAAF
YL-DBG	LET L-13 Blanik	173001	DOSAAF
YL-DBH	LET L-13 Blanik	173474	DOSAAF
YL-DBI	LET L-13 Blanik	174515	DOSAAF
YL-DBJ	LET L-13 Blanik	174315	DOSAAF
YL-DBL	LET L-13 Blanik	026432	DOSAAF
YL-DBN	LET L-13 Blanik	026701	DOSAAF
YL-DBP	LET L-13 Blanik	027160	DOSAAF
YL-DBS	LET L-13 Blanik	027027	DOSAAF
YL-DBT	SZD-48-1 Jantar Standard 2	B-1047	DOSAAF
YL-DBU	SZD-48-3 Jantar Standard 3	B-1586	DOSAAF
YL-DBV	SZD-48-3 Jantar Standard 3	B-1281	DOSAAF
YL-DBZ	LAK-12 Lietuva	6124	DOSAAF
YL-DCA	LAK-12 Lietuva	676	DOSAAF
YL-DCB	Sigma 4P	6	
YL-DDL	LET L-13MBlanik	172299	
YL-655	LAK-12 Lietuva	unkn	
YL-670	LAK-12 Lietuva	unkn	

MICROLIGHTS

YL-MIG	Aviatika MAI-890 Baby MIG	037	

BALLOONS

YL-001	Interavia 80TA Balloon	231291	
YL-002	DC-AT8 Dirigible Moscow Balloon	0792-04-014	
YL-003	Interavia 70TA Balloon	0640393	
YL-004	Interavia 80TA Balloon	841293	
YL-005	Interavia 80TA Balloon	860291	
YL-006	Cameron V-77 HAFB	2276	G-BSGM
YL-007	Colt 90A HAFB	4479	
YL-008	Cameron Z-90 HAFB	4863	
YL-009	Cameron Concept C-80 HAFB	4877	
YL-010	Ultramagic M-77 HAFB	77/253	

YL - LATVIA

Regn.	Type	C/n	Prev.Id.
YR-AAP	Antonov An-2	1G199-34	HA-MAP
			RA-31525
			CCCP31525
YR-ABB	Boeing 707-3K1C	20804	
YR-ADR(2)	PZL-104 Wilga 35A	17830700	LY-AKT
			DOSAAF
YR-AER	Antonov An-2	1G154-45	UR-05805 ?
			CCCP05805
YR-ANT	Antonov An-2R (CofA expired)	1G108-67	
YR-AOA	Antonov An-2	1G197-38	UR-31415
			CCCP31415
YR-AOB	Antonov An-2R	1G176-09	UR-62546?
			CCCP62546
YR-AOZ	Antonov An-2R	1G155-08	LZ-1129
YR-APB	Antonov An-2R (CofA expired)	1G116-43	
YR-APD	Antonov An-2R (CofA expired)	1G116-45	
YR-APG	Antonov An-2R	1G124-27	
YR-API	Antonov An-2R	1G124-29	
YR-APL	Antonov An-2R (CofA expired)	1G124-33	
YR-APO	Antonov An-2R	1G124-36	Rom.AF 36
			YR-APO
YR-APR	Antonov An-2	1G124-37	Rom.AF 37
			YR-APR
YR-APX	Antonov An-2R (CofA expired)	1G124-44	
YR-APY	Antonov An-2R	1G124-45	
YR-ATA	Aérospatiale/Alenia ATR-42-512	566	F-WWLF
YR-ATB	Aérospatiale/Alenia ATR-42-512	569	F-WWLH
YR-ATC	Aérospatiale/Alenia ATR-42-512	589	F-WWLR
YR-ATD	Aérospatiale/Alenia ATR-42-512	591	F-WWLS
YR-ATE	Aérospatiale/Alenia ATR-42-512	596	F-WWLY
YR-ATF	Aérospatiale/Alenia ATR-42-512	599	F-WWEB
YR-ATG	Aérospatiale/Alenia ATR-42-512	605	F-WWLG
YR-BAA	Boeing 737-33A	27267	ZK-CZU
			VH-CZU
YR-BEA	Bell 206B Jet Ranger II	unkn	
YR-BEL	Bell 206L-1 Long Ranger II	45375	N573W
			N5735P
YR-BGA	Boeing 737-38J	27179	
YR-BGB	Boeing 737-38J	27180	
YR-BGC	Boeing 737-38J	27181	
YR-BGD	Boeing 737-38J	27182	
YR-BGE	Boeing 737-38J	27395	
YR-BGF	Boeing 737-78J	28440	
YR-BGG	Boeing 737-78J	28442	
YR-BGH	Boeing 737-78J	28438	
YR-BGI	Boeing 737-78J	28439	
YR-BMB	Antonov An-24RV (CofA expired)	57310106	
YR-BME	Antonov An-24RV (CofA expired)	57310310	
YR-BMH	Antonov An-24RV (CofA expired)	57310407	
YR-BMI	Antonov An-24RV	57310408	
YR-BMM	Antonov An-24RV	77310807	
YR-BMN	Antonov An-24RV	77310808	
YR-BNH	Britten-Norman BN-2A-27 Islander (Wfu)	775	G-BDMX
			YR-BNH
			G-BDMX
YR-BNK	Britten-Norman BN-2A-27 Islander (Wfu)	778	G-BDNA
			YR-BNK
			G-BDNA
YR-BNL	Britten-Norman BN-2A-27 Islander (Wfu)	790	G-BDRX
			YR-BNL
			G-BDRX
YR-BNM	Britten-Norman BN-2A-27 Islander (Wfu)	808	G-BDYV
YR-BNN	Britten-Norman BN-2A-27 Islander (Wfu)	804	G-BDYR
YR-BNP	Britten-Norman BN-2A-27 Islander (Wfu)	822	G-BELE
YR-BNR	Britten-Norman BN-2A-27 Islander (Wfu)	824	G-BELG
YR-BNV	Britten-Norman BN-2A-27 Islander (Wfu)	840	G-BEMS
YR-BOR	Antonov An-2	1G192-13	HA-MAN
			CCCP84695
YR-BRC	ROMBAC One-Eleven 561RC (Stored)	403	YU-ANS
			YR-BRC
YR-BRE	ROMBAC One-Eleven 561RC	405	
YR-BRH	ROMBAC One-Eleven 561RC	408	
YR-BRI	ROMBAC One-Eleven 561RC	409	
YR-BVC	IAR-46	02	
YR-BVD	IAR-46S	03	
YR-BVE	IAR-46S	04	
YR-BVF	IAR-46S	05	
YR-BVG	IAR-46S (Reservation .02)	06	
YR-BVH	IAR-46S	07	
YR-BVI	IAR-46S	08	
YR-BVJ	IAR-46S	09	
YR-BVK	IAR-46S	10	
YR-CAA	Beech B300 Super King Air	FL-73	N8270R
			(G-CCCB)
			N8270R
YR-CCF	Antonov An-2	1G141-15	UR-70361
			CCCP-70361
YR-CLB	Bell 222SP	47051	N60MJ
			N729P
YR-COR	Antonov An-2R	1G225-14	HA-MAK
			UR-40497?
			CCCP40497
YR-COS	Aérospatiale AS.350B2 Ecureuil	2616	LN-OPI
			OY-HEL

YR-CSA	Kamov Ka-26	7101807	ER-19294 YR-CTE YR-CXE YR-19294 19294 CCCP19294
YR-CSB	Kamov Ka-26	7303309	ER-19327 YR-CYM ER-19327 YR-CZD CCCP19327 YR-19327 CCCP19327
YR-CSC	Kamov Ka-26	7303402	ER-19330 YR-CZG YR-19330 CCCP19330
YR-CSD	Kamov Ka-26	7404706	ER-19547 YR-19547 CCCP19547
YR-CSH	Kamov Ka-26	7102004	ER-19262 CCCP19262
YR-CTA	Kamov Ka-26	7303509	ER-129343 YR-CZH 19343 CCCP19343
YR-CTG	Kamov Ka-26	7404202	ER-19496 YR-CYR ER-19496 YR-CZB YR-19496 ER-19496 CCCP19496
YR-CXW	Kamov Ka.26	7605705	UR ? YR-CXN CCCP24360
YR-CXX	Kamov Ka.26	7504805	UR-19564 YR-19564 CCCP19564
YR-CYA	Kamov Ka.26	7404419	UR-19424 YR-19424 CCCP19424
YR-CYB	Kamov Ka.26	7504914	UR- ? YR-CXO CCCP19587
YR-DAN	Antonov An-2R	1G208-48	UR-81544 CCCP81544
YR-DAR	Antonov An-2R	1G208-46	UR-81542 CCCP81542
YR-DAV	Antonov An-2	1G183-17	UR-56519 ? CCCP56519
YR-DOG	Kamov Ka.26	6900404	
YR-DON	Kamov Ka.26	7806320	HA-MPW
YR-EAD	Kamov Ka.26	7806412	
YR-EAF	Kamov Ka.26	7806414	
YR-EAJ	Kamov Ka.26	7806418	
YR-EAM	Kamov Ka.26	7806501	
YR-EAN	Kamov Ka.26	7303505	CCCP19339
YR-EAO	Kamov Ka.26	7705912	CCCP24395
YR-EKE	Kamov Ka.26	7000803	
YR-EKL	Kamov Ka.26	7202806	
YR-EKN	Kamov Ka.26	7202808	
YR-EKO	Kamov Ka.26	7202809	
YR-EKT	Kamov Ka.26	7706102	
YR-EKV	Kamov Ka.26	7706202	
YR-EKY	Kamov Ka.26	7706103	
YR-ELC	Sud Avn SA.316B Alouette III	1909	
YR-ELR	IAR/Sud Avn SA.316B Alouette III	50	
YR-ELS	IAR/Sud Avn SA.316B Alouette III	93	
YR-ELT	IAR/Sud Avn SA.316B Alouette III (Wfu)	94	
YR-EWA	Extra EA.300/L	096	
YR-EWB	Extra EA.300/L	097	
YR-EWD	Extra EA.300/L	102	D-EXIH
YR-EWE	Extra EA.300/L	106	
YR-EWF	Extra EA.300/L	107	
YR-EWH	Extra EA.300/L	151	
YR-FLA	Antonov An-2	1G238-37	UR-02260 CCCP02260
YR-FLB	Antonov An-2	1G190-57	UR-84625 CCCP84625
YR-FLC	Antonov An-2	1G238-36	UR-02259 CCCP02259
YR-FWT	PZL-104 Wilga 35A	61104	SP-FWT SP-WHE PLW-104
YR-IMM	Ilyushin IL-18D	187009904	
YR-ION	Antonov An-2	1G210-04	HA-MAO RA-17980 CCCP17980
YR-ISG	IAR-824	06	
YR-ISH	IAR-824	07	
YR-ITA	Antonov An-26	6407	LZ-MNH UR-26504 CCCP-26504
YR-IVA	Antonov An-2R (CofA expired)	1G190-01	OK-KIG
YR-JBA	BAC One-Eleven 528FL	234	G-BJRT D-ALFA
YR-JBB	BAC One-Eleven 528FL (CofA expired, stored)	238	G-BJRU D-ANUE
YR-JCA	Boeing 707-327C (CofA expired, stored)	19530	CC-CYA N707ME B-2424 N707ME 9V-BDC N7103
YR-KLA	Robinson R-44 Astro	0085	YR-RAG
YR-KLB	Robinson R-22 Beta	2549	YR-COB
YR-LAR	Antonov An-2R	1G221-45	UR-40240 CCCP40240
YR-LCA	Airbus A.310-325	636	F-WWCG
YR-LCB	Airbus A.310-325	644	F-WWCO
YR-LGT	Kamov Ka.26	7404409	YR-CYS ER-19415 CCCP19415
YR-LMC	Kamov Ka.26	7101702	HA-MRT HAF-702
YR-MAC	Antonov An-2	1G209-53	HA-MAI RA-17969 CCCP17969
YR-MAR	Kamov Ka-26	7202706	ER- ? YR-CXD EW-19382 CCCP19382
YR-MCR	Kamov Ka-26	7203007	UR-19311 CCCP19311
YR-MDA(2)	Cessna 172S	172S8114	N856SP
YR-MDB	Cessna 172S	172S8354	N428SP
YR-MDC	Cessna 172S	172S8356	N439SP
YR-MDD	Cessna 172S	172S8517	N72773
YR-MDE(2)	Piper PA-34-220TSeneca V	3449197	N4185T (YR-MDE) N9516N
YR-MDF(2)	Piper PA-34-220TSeneca V	3449202	N5119N (YR-MDF) N50758
YR-MDG	Eurocopter EC.120B Colibri	1369	
YR-MDH	Eurocopter EC.155B Dauphin	6637	
YR-MEG	IAR-823	29	
YR-MEH	IAR-823	37	
YR-MLA	Mil Mi-8PS (CofA expired)	10731	
YR-MLB	Mil Mi-8PS	10735	
YR-NCV	Kamov Ka.26	7202309	ER-19358 YR-19358 CCCP19358
YR-NDT	Kamov Ka-26	7202606	ER- ? YR-CXC EW-19373 CCCP19373
YR-PAA	Antonov An-2R (CofA expired)	1G124-46	
YR-PAB	Antonov An-2R	1G124-47	
YR-PAD	Antonov An-2R	1G164-32	
YR-PAE	Antonov An-2R (CofA expired)	1G164-33	
YR-PAF	Antonov An-2R	1G137-06	
YR-PAH	Antonov An-2R	1G164-35	
YR-PAJ	Antonov An-2R (CofA expired)	1G164-37	
YR-PAK	Antonov An-2R	1G164-38	
YR-PAM	Antonov An-2R	1G164-40	
YR-PAO	Antonov An-2R	1G164-51	
YR-PAP	Antonov An-2R (CofA expired)	1G164-52	
YR-PAS	Antonov An-2R	1G164-53	
YR-PAT	Antonov An-2R	1G164-54	
YR-PAU	Antonov An-2R	1G164-55	
YR-PAW	Antonov An-2R	1G164-57	
YR-PAX	Antonov An-2R	1G164-58	
YR-PAY	Antonov An-2R (CofA expired)	1G164-59	
YR-PAZ	Antonov An-2R (CofA expired)	1G164-60	
YR-PBA	Antonov An-2R	1G166-36	
YR-PBC	Antonov An-2R	1G177-26	
YR-PBD	Antonov An-2R	1G177-27	
YR-PBF	Antonov An-2R	1G177-29	
YR-PBG	Antonov An-2R	1G180-43	
YR-PBI	Antonov An-2R	1G185-41	
YR-PBJ	Antonov An-2R	1G185-42	
YR-PBK	Antonov An-2R (CofA expired)	1G196-35	
YR-PBL	Antonov An-2R	1G196-36	
YR-PBM	Antonov An-2R	1G196-51	
YR-PBO	Antonov An-2R	1G202-21	
YR-PBP	Antonov An-2R	1G202-22	
YR-PBR	Antonov An-2R	1G202-23	
YR-PBT	Antonov An-2R	1G215-21	
YR-PBV	Antonov An-2R	1G224-06	
YR-PBW	Antonov An-2R	1G224-07	
YR-PBX	Antonov An-2R (CofA expired)	1G224-08	
YR-PEP	Zlin Z.142	0222	OK-KNE
YR-PMA	Antonov An-2R (CofA expired)	1G227-11	
YR-PMB	Antonov An-2R	1G227-12	
YR-PMC	Antonov An-2R	1G227-13	
YR-PMD	Antonov An-2R	1G227-14	
YR-PME	Antonov An-2R	1G227-15	
YR-PMI	Antonov An-2R	1G231-35	
YR-PMJ	Antonov An-2R (CofA expired)	1G231-36	
YR-PMK	Antonov An-2R	1G231-37	
YR-PML	Antonov An-2R	1G231-38	
YR-PMM	Antonov An-2R	1G231-39	
YR-PMN	Antonov An-2R	1G231-40	
YR-PMR	Antonov An-2R	1G233-03	
YR-PMS	Antonov An-2R	1G233-04	
YR-PMT	Antonov An-2R	1G233-05	
YR-PMU	Antonov An-2R	1G233-06	
YR-PMV	Antonov An-2R	1G233-07	

YR-PMX	Antonov An-2R	1G233-09	
YR-PRA	IAR/Sud Avn SA.316B Alouette III	201	
YR-PSA	Antonov An-2R	1G177-22	
YR-PSB	Antonov An-2R (CofA expired)	1G177-23	
YR-PSD	Antonov An-2R	1G177-25	
YR-PVA	Antonov An-2R (CofA expired)	1G175-01	
YR-PVB	Antonov An-2R	1G175-02	
YR-PVC	Antonov An-2R	1G175-03	
YR-PVD	Antonov An-2R	1G175-04	
YR-PVG	Antonov An-2R	1G175-06	
YR-PVH	Antonov An-2R	1G175-07	
YR-PVI	Antonov An-2R	1G175-08	
YR-PVL	Antonov An-2R (CofA expired)	1G175-10	
YR-PVM	Antonov An-2R	1G175-12	
YR-PVN	Antonov An-2R	1G175-13	
YR-PVO	Antonov An-2R	1G175-14	
YR-PVP	Antonov An-2R	1G175-15	
YR-PVR	Antonov An-2R	1G175-16	
YR-PVU(2)	Antonov An-2R	870901	
YR-RAP	Bell 206LT Twin Ranger	52170	N6275S
YR-RCO	Robinson R-44 Astro	0181	D-HGPT
YR-RCP	Robinson R-44 Astro	0181	
YR-RDA	Robinson R-22 Beta (CofA expired)	2549	
YR-RDV	Robinson R-44 Astro (CofA expired)	0164	
YR-REA(2)	Robinson R-44 Raven	0852	
YR-REE	Robinson R-22 Beta	2356	OE-XPB(1) N8013Q
YR-RGN	Kamov Ka.26	7706203	YR-EAA
YR-RRA	Antonov An-2	1G216-16	LZ-1229
YR-SAF	Antonov An-2	unkn	
YR-SAN	Antonov An-2	1G182-24	UR-56467 CCCP56467
YR-SBA	SAAB 2000	038	HB-IZV SE-038
YR-SBB	SAAB 2000	026	HB-IZN SE-026
YR-SBC	SAAB 2000	039	HB-IZW SE-039
YR-SBD	SAAB 2000	004	HB-IZA SE-004
YR-SBE	SAAB 2000	041	HB-IZX SE-041
YR-SNG	IAR/Sud Avn SA.316B Alouette III	26	YR-ELL
YR-SRJ	Antonov An-2R	1G233-33	ER-33643 YR-SRF ER-33643 YR-SRA(2) ER-33643 YR-33643 CCCP33643
YR-STA	Antonov An-2	1G159-43	UR-07765 CCCP07765
YR-STF	Gemini Ultra	unkn	
YR-TRG	BAe. Jetstream Series 3202	835	G-BUIO OH-JAB G-BUIO C-GZRT G-31-835
YR-VAL	Kamov Ka-26	7303206	ER-19323 YR-CYK ER-19323 YR-CXG YR-19323 CCCP19323
YR-VGM	SAAB-Scania SF. 340B	208	HB-AKI VR-VGM HB-AKI SE-G08
YR-VGN	SAAB-Scania SF. 340B	200	HB-AKH SE-E02
YR-VGO	SAAB-Scania SF. 340B	215	HB-AKL SE-G15
YR-VGP	SAAB-Scania SF. 340B	228	HB-AKO SE-G28
YR-VGR	SAAB-Scania SF. 340B	225	HB-AKN SE-G25
YR-VGS	SAAB-Scania SF. 340B	168	HB-AKP ER-SGA ER-ASA HB-AKP F-GKLA SE-F68
YR-VGT	SAAB-Scania SF. 340B	185	F-GPKG HB-AKG SE-F85
YR-VIB	PZL-104 Wilga 35 (Wfu)	25026	
YR-VIC	PZL-104 Wilga 35 (Inactive)	25020	SP-CRK
YR-VIF	PZL-104 Wilga 35 (Inactive)	25022	
YR-VIG	PZL-104 Wilga 35 (Wfu)	48044	
YR-VIJ	PZL-104 Wilga 35 (Inactive)	59053	
YR-VIK	PZL-104 Wilga 35 (Wfu)	59054	
YR-VIM	PZL-104 Wilga 35 (Inactive)	59056	
YR-VIN	PZL-104 Wilga 35 (Inactive)	59057	
YR-VIO	PZL-104 Wilga 35A (Wfu)	118379	
YR-VIP	PZL-104 Wilga 35A (Wfu)	118380	
YR-VIR	PZL-104 Wilga 35A	118381	
YR-VIS	PZL-104 Wilga 35A	118382	
YR-VIT	PZL-104 Wilga 35A	118383	
YR-VIU	PZL-104 Wilga 35A	118384	
YR-VIV	PZL-104 Wilga 35A	118385	
YR-VIW	PZL-104 Wilga 35A (CofA expired)	118386	
YR-VIX	PZL-104 Wilga 35A	118387	
YR-VIY	PZL-104 Wilga 35A	118390	
YR-VIZ	PZL-104 Wilga 3 A	118388	
YR-VLA	PZL-104 Wilga 35A	118389	
YR-VLB	PZL-104 Wilga 35A	129445	
YR-VLC	PZL-104 Wilga 35A	129446	
YR-VLD	PZL-104 Wilga 35A (CofA expired)	129447	
YR-VLE	PZL-104 Wilga 35A	139502	
YR-VLF	PZL-104 Wilga 35A	139503	
YR-VLG	PZL-104 Wilga 35A	139504	
YR-VLH	PZL-104 Wilga 35A	139509	
YR-VLI	PZL-104 Wilga 35A (Wfu)	149514	
YR-VLK	PZL-104 Wilga 35A (Wfu)	149516	
YR-VLL	PZL-104 Wilga 35A	149517	
YR-VLN	PZL-104 Wilga 35A	149519	
YR-YAV	Antonov An-2	1G124-47	RusAF:47 YR-PAB
YR-ZAV	Zlin Z.50LA (Inactive)	0015	
YR-ZAX	Zlin Z.50LS (Inactive)	0034	
YR-ZAY	Zlin Z.50LS (CofA expired)	0036	
YR-ZBA	Zlin Z.726 Universal	1336	
YR-ZBB	Zlin Z.726 Universal	1337	
YR-ZBC	Zlin Z.726 Universal	1338	
YR-ZBD	Zlin Z.726 Universal	1339	
YR-ZBF	Zlin Z.726 Universal	1341	
YR-ZBG	Zlin Z.726 Universal	1342	
YR-ZBH	Zlin Z.726 Universal	1343	
YR-ZBI	Zlin Z.726 Universal	1344	
YR-ZBJ	Zlin Z.726 Universal	1345	
YR-ZBK	Zlin Z.726 Universal	1346	
YR-ZBL	Zlin Z.726 Universal	1347	
YR-ZBM	Zlin Z.726 Universal	1348	
YR-ZBN	Zlin Z.726 Universal	1349	
YR-ZBP	Zlin Z.726 Universal	1351	
YR-ZBR	Zlin Z.726 Universal	1352	
YR-ZCA	Zlin Z.142	0396	
YR-ZCB	Zlin Z.142	0397	
YR-ZCD	Zlin Z.142 (CofA expired)	0391	
YR-ZCF	Zlin Z.142	0423	
YR-ZCG	Zlin Z.142 (Wfu)	0424	
YR-ZCI	Zlin Z.142	0461	
YR-ZCJ	Zlin Z.142 (Wfu)	0462	
YR-ZCK	Zlin Z.142 (Wfu)	0463	
YR-ZCL	Zlin Z.142	0464	
YR-ZCM	Zlin Z.142	0465	
YR-ZCN	Zlin Z.142 (Wfu)	0468	
YR-ZCO	Zlin Z.142	0469	
YR-ZCP	Zlin Z.142 (CofA expired)	0470	
YR-ZLJ	Zlin 526F Trenér Master	1092	
YR-ZNA	Zlin Z.50LS (CofA expired)	0039	
YR-ZNB	Zlin Z.50LS (Inactive)	0043	
YR- . . .	Aérospatiale SA.330J Puma	1268	N372MH PK-PEM
YR- . . .	IPTN/Aérospatiale SA.330J Puma	1661/NP-1	N383MH PK-PIA PK-XPA
YR- . . .	IPTN/Aérospatiale SA.330J Puma	1664/NP-2	N380MH PK-PIC PK-XPB
YR- . . .	IPTN/Aérospatiale SA.330J Puma	1668/NP-3	N382MH PK-PID PK-XPC
YR- . . .	IPTN/Aérospatiale SA.330J Puma	1670/NP-4	N381MH PK-PIE PK-XPD
YR- . . .	Bell 206B Jet Ranger	2757	D-HHFS(2) G-SHJJ N220PJ N27676
YR- . . .	Bell 206L-1 Long Ranger	45456	F-GCVU HB-XLO (D-HIFA) (D-HIVA) HB-XLO
YR- . . .	Bell 412EP	36154	N7233Z C-GFNM
YR- . . .	BAe.146 Series 200	E-2227	G-BVMS I-FLRO G-BVMS G-6-227
YR- . . .	Boeing 737-201	22354	C-FNAJ N239US N784N
YR- . . .	Cessna F150G	F150-0185	D-EBZO
YR- . . .	Eurocopter EC.135P2	0290	
YR- . . .	Eurocopter EC.135T2	0334	
YR- . . .	Extra EA.300/L	1189	
YR- . . .	Piper PA-32-300 Cherokee Six	32-40038	(USA) G-AVFS
YR- . . .	Robinson R-22B2 Beta	3287	N83658

GLIDERS AND MOTOR-GLIDERS

YR-101(2)	SZD-48 Jantar Standard 2 (Dismantled)	W-859	
YR-102(2)	SZD-48 Jantar Standard 2 ((Dismantled)	W-867	
YR-103	SZD-41A Jantar Standard	B-909	
YR-105	SZD-48 Jantar Standard 2 (Dismantled)	W-873	SP-3153

YR-106	SZD-48-1 Jantar Standard 2 (Dismantled)	B-987
YR-107-RF	SZD-48-1 Jantar Standard 2 (Dismantled)	B-1099
YR-108	SZD-48-1 Jantar Standard 2	B-1100
YR-109-RT	SZD-48-1 Jantar Standard 2	B-1250
YR-110-RC	SZD-48-1 Jantar Standard 2	B-1252
YR-131-VT	SZD-42-2 Jantar 2B	B-863
YR-132	SZD-42-2 Jantar 2B	B-870
YR-133-RN	SZD-42-2 Jantar 2B	B-908
YR-134	SZD-42-2 Jantar 2B	B-1065
YR-135-RL	SZD-42-2 Jantar 2B	B-1313
YR-156	SZD-24-4A Foka	W-303
YR-157	SZD-24-4A Foka (Dismantled)	W-309
YR-158	SZD-24-4A Foka	W-339
YR-159	SZD-24-4A Foka	W-362
YR-160	SZD-24-4A Foka	W-363
YR-162	SZD-24-4A Foka	W-333
YR-163	SZD-24-4A Foka	W-331
YR-164	SZD-24-4A Foka (Dismantled)	W-355
YR-165	SZD-24-4A Foka (Dismantled)	W-356
YR-166	SZD-24-4A Foka (Dismantled)	W-357
YR-167	SZD-24-4A Foka	W-358
YR-168	SZD-24-4A Foka	W-369
YR-169	SZD-24-4A Foka	W-375
YR-170	SZD-24-4A Foka	W-376
YR-171	SZD-24-4A Foka	W-377
YR-172	SZD-24-4A Foka	W-381
YR-173	SZD-24-4A Foka	W-382
YR-174	SZD-32A Foka 5	W-435
YR-175	SZD-32A Foka 5	W-436
YR-176	SZD-32A Foka 5	W-437
YR-178	SZD-32A Foka 5	W-439
YR-179	SZD-32A Foka 5 (Dismantled)	W-446
YR-180	SZD-32A Foka 5	W-447
YR-181	SZD-32A Foka 5	W-463
YR-184	SZD-32A Foka 5	W-466
YR-188	IAR IS.29D	26
YR-192	IAR IS.29D	45
YR-193	IAR IS.29D	48
YR-194	IAR IS.29D2 (Dismantled)	55
YR-196	IAR IS.29D2	57
YR-205	LET L-13 Blanik (Dismantled)	173421 ?
YR-212	LET L-13 Blanik (Dismantled)	173449 ?
YR-213	LET L-13 Blanik (Dismantled)	173458 ?
YR-281	IAR IS.28B2	06
YR-282	IAR IS.28B2	07
YR-283	IAR IS.28B2	141
YR-284	IAR IS.28B2	21
YR-286	IAR IS.28B2	30
YR-287	IAR IS.28B2	50
YR-291	IAR IS.29B2	65
YR-292	IAR IS.29D2 (Dismantled)	75
YR-294	IAR IS.28B2	104
YR-295	IAR IS.28B2	107
YR-296	IAR IS.28B2	131
YR-298	IAR IS.28B2	133
YR-300	IAR IS.28B2	135
YR-301	IAR IS.28B2	136
YR-302	IAR IS.28B2	137
YR-304	IAR IS.28B2	139
YR-305	IAR IS.28B2	149
YR-307	IAR IS.28B2	162
YR-310	IAR IS.28M2	140
YR-311	IAR IS.28M2	161
YR-312	IAR IS.28B2 (Dismantled)	165
YR-313	IAR IS.28B2 (C/n now given as 107)	166
YR-315	IAR IS.28B2	168
YR-317	IAR IS.28B2 (Dismantled)	142
YR-319	IAR IS.28B2	150
YR-323	IAR IS.28B2 (Derelict)	unkn
YR-325	IAR IS.28B2	180
YR-326	IAR IS.28B2	181
YR-327	IAR IS.28B2 (Dismantled)	unkn
YR-328	IAR IS.28B2 (Dismantled)	183
YR-329	IAR IS.28B2	184
YR-331	IAR IS.28B2	186
YR-332	IAR IS.28B2	187
YR-333	IAR IS.28B2	188
YR-334	IAR IS.28B2	144
YR-336	IAR IS.28B2	205
YR-337	IAR IS.28B2	210
YR-340	IAR IS.28B2	220
YR-343	IAR IS.28B2	223
YR-345	IAR IS.28B2	225
YR-346	IAR IS.28B2	unkn
YR-347	IAR IS.28B2	155
YR-348	IAR IS.28B2	158
YR-350	IAR IS.28B2	157
YR-351	IAR IS.28B2	226
YR-353	IAR IS.28B2	255
YR-354	IAR IS.28B2	230
YR-356	IAR IS.28B2	146
YR-357	IAR IS.28B2 (Dismantled)	256
YR-358	IAR IS.28B2	261
YR-360	IAR IS.28B2	231
YR-361	IAR IS.28B2	239
YR-362	IAR IS.28B2	251
YR-363	IAR IS.28B2	253
YR-364	IAR IS.28B2	257
YR-366	IAR IS.28B2	259
YR-367	IAR IS.28B2	262
YR-368	IAR IS.28B2	263

YR-369	IAR IS.28B2 (Dismantled)	264	
YR-370	IAR IS.28B2 (Now quoted as c/n 281)	284	
YR-371	IAR IS.28B2	282	
YR-372	IAR IS.28B2	283	
YR-373	IAR IS.28B2	233	
YR-374	IAR IS.28B2	234	
YR-375	IAR IS.28B2	265	
YR-376	IAR IS.28B2	266	
YR-377	IAR IS.28B2	267	
YR-378	IAR IS.28B2	unkn	
YR-380	IAR IS.28B2	285	
YR-381	IAR IS.28B2	287	
YR-383	IAR IS.28B2 (Dismantled)	268	
YR-384	IAR IS.28B2	unkn	
YR-385	IAR IS.28B2	276	
YR-388	IAR IS.28B2	307	
YR-390	IAR IS.28B2 (Dismantled)	305	
YR-391	IAR IS.28B2	316	
YR-392	IAR IS.28B2	317	
YR-393	IAR IS.28B2	313	
YR-394	IAR IS.28B2	314	
YR-395	IAR IS.28B2	325	
YR-502	IAR IS.29D2 (Dismantled)	89	
YR-503-E	IAR IS.29D2 (Dismantled)	74	
YR-504	IAR IS.28B2	unkn	
YR-508	IAR IS.29D2 (Dismantled)	unkn	
YR-511-C	IAR IS.29D2 (Dismantled)	101	
YR-512	IAR IS.29D2	102	
YR-513	IAR IS.29D2 (Dismantled)	103	
YR-514-J	IAR IS.29B1 (Dismantled)	108	
YR-516	IAR IS.29D2	111	
YR-517	IAR IS.29D2	113	
YR-518	IAR IS.29D2 (Now quoted as c/n 67)	114	
YR-520	IAR IS.28B2 (Dismantled)	unkn	
YR-524	IAR IS.29D2	120	
YR-526	IAR IS.29D2	124	
YR-524	IAR IS.29D2	120	
YR-528	IAR IS.29D2	126	
YR-531	IAR IS.28D2	122	
YR-532	IAR IS.29D2 (Dismantled)	123	
YR-534	IAR IS.29D2	137	
YR-535	IAR IS.29D2	138	
YR-537	IAR IS.28D2	140	
YR-538	IAR IS.29D2	141	
YR-539	IAR IS.29D2	134	
YR-540	IAR IS.29D2	135	
YR-541	IAR IS.28D2	136	
YR-543	IAR IS.28D2	143	
YR-545	IAR IS.29D2	145	
YR-546	IAR IS.29D2	146	
YR-548	IAR IS.29D2	148	
YR-550	IAR IS.28D2	152	
YR-551	IAR IS.28B2	unkn	
YR-555	IAR IS.29D2	195	
YR-557-W	IAR IS.29D2	198	
YR-558	IAR IS.29D2 (Now quoted as c/n 135)	162	
YR-559	IAR IS.28D2	188A	
YR-560	IAR IS.29D2 (Dismantled)	204	
YR-561	IAR IS.29D2	205	
YR-600	IAR IS.32A	07A	
YR-602	IAR IS.28D2 (?)	12	
YR-603	IAR IS.32A	14	
YR-604	IAR IS.32A	15	
YR-801	IAR IS.28M2	unkn	
YR-802	IAR IS.28M2	24	
YR-803	IAR IS.28M2	06	
YR-806	IAR IS.29M2	41	
YR-809	IAR IS.29M2	47	
YR-811	IAR IS.29M2	49	
YR-812	IAR IS.29M2 (Dismantled)	66	
YR-904	IAR IS.3D (Stored)	unkn	
YR-905	IAR IS.3D (Dismantled)	unkn	
YR-909	IAR IS.3D (Dismantled)	unkn	
YR-910	IAR IS.3D (Dismantled)	unkn	
YR-911	IAR IS.3D (Stored)	unkn	
YR-994	IAR IS.28M2	67	
YR-1003	IAR-35 Acro	02	YR-1033
YR-1004	IAR-35 Acro	04	
YR-1005	IAR-35 Acro	03	
YR-1006	IAR IS.29C	unkn	
YR-1007	IAR IS.28B	01	
YR-1012	IAR IS.29D 2	unkn	
YR-1013	IAR IS.28B - M2	01	
YR-1015	IAR IS.28M (Dismantled)	02	
YR-1017	IAR IS.32	01	
YR-1018	IAR IS.28M-1	01	
YR-1020	IAR IS.30 Metallique	01	
YR-1023	IAR IS.34	02	
YR-1026	IAR IS.28M-A	01	
YR-1028	IAR IS.29D2	93	
YR-1030-YA	Schempp-HirthDiscus 2a	194	
YR-1031-YB	Schempp-HirthDiscus 2a	195	
YR-1036	IAR-35 Acro	01	
YR-1037	IAR-46	01	
YR-1926	IAR IS.28M2	unkn	
YR-1976	IAR IS.28M2	56	
YR-	Schempp-Hirth Discus 2a	194	
YR-	Schempp-Hirth Discus 2a	195	

MICROLIGHTS

YR-1500	Quicksilver GT-500	unkn	
YR-5000	AK-22	unkn	
YR-5005	FIB Polaris	unkn	
YR-5053	Jurca MJ-52 Zephir	unkn	
YR-6100	Comco Ikarus Fox-C22	unkn	
YR-6103	Apollo 50	unkn	
YR-6104	Blue Angel	unkn	
YR-6106 ?	Servoplant Aerocraft	unkn	
YR-6117	Servoplant Aerocraft	02	
YR-6118	Girex	unkn	
YR-6119	Apollo	unkn	
YR-6120	Servoplant Aerocraft	03	
YR-6121	Eipper Quicksilver GT-500	unkn	
YR-6123	Girex	unkn	
YR-6125	Wankel-16	unkn	
YR-6126	Zenair CH-601HDS Super Zodiac (Cr 10.2.99)	unkn	
YR-6130	Pietenpol GN-1 Aircamper	unkn	
YR-6131	Condor (TL-132 ?)	unkn	
YR-6138	Aerostar 01	unkn	
YR-. . . .	Mainair Gemini/Flash II	486-1086-4-W278	G-MTAC

BALLOONS ANDAIRSHIPS

YR-003	Tomi AX-8 HAFB	47	
YR-9000	Thunder & Colt AS-56 Hot Air Airship	663	OE-AZU
YR-9001	Tomi AX-9 HAFB	41	
YR-9002	Tomi AX-9 HAFB	unkn	
YR-9003	Tomi AX-8 HAFB	unkn	
YR-9004	Kubicek BB-22 HAFB	150	OK-0050
YR-9005	Cameron Concept C-80 HAFB	10153	
YR-9006	Firefly Galaxy II HAFB	GLX-10811	
YR-9007	Firefly Galaxy II HAFB	GLX-10911	
YR-	Cameron/Colt 120A HAFB	4197	SE-ZHB(2)

The Tomi company name was changed to Northeisz recently.

YU - SERBIA & MONTENEGRO

The status of many aircraft on the Register is still unknown.

Regn.	Type	C/n	Prev.Id.
YU-AHN	McDonnell-Douglas DC-9-32 (Wfu, stored)	47470	
YU-AHU	McDonnell-Douglas DC-9-32 (Wfu, stored)	47532	
YU-AHV	McDonnell-Douglas DC-9-32 (Wfu, stored)	47460	
YU-AJI	McDonnell-Douglas DC-9-32	47563	N1346U
YU-AJJ	McDonnell-Douglas DC-9-32	47567	Z3-ARE, YU-AJJ, N1347U
YU-AJK	McDonnell-Douglas DC-9-32	47568	Z3-ARD, YU-AJK
YU-AJL	McDonnell-Douglas DC-9-32	47571	Z3-AAB, YU-AJL
YU-AJM	McDonnell-Douglas DC-9-32	47582	
YU-AKB	Boeing 727-2H9 (Wfu, stored)	20931	
YU-AKD	Boeing 727-2L8	21040	OY-SBJ, YU-AKD, JRV74302, JRV14302, YU-AKD
YU-AKE	Boeing 727-2H9 (Wfu, stored)	21037	
YU-AKF	Boeing 727-2H9 (Wfu, stored)	21038	
YU-AKG	Boeing 727-2H9 (Wfu, stored)	21039	
YU-AKH	Boeing 727-2L8	21080	OY-SBP, YU-AKH, JRV74301, JRV14301, (YU-AKH)
YU-AKI	Boeing 727-2H9	22393	
YU-AKJ	Boeing 727-2H9 (Wfu, stored)	22394	N8281V
YU-AKK	Boeing 727-2H9	22665	TS-JEA, YU-AKK, N1780B
YU-AKL	Boeing 727-2H9	22666	TS-JEB, YU-AKL
YU-AKM	Boeing 727-243	22702	PK-EPV, YU-AKM, HK-3618X, YU-AKM, I-DIRT
YU-AKP	Yakovlev Yak-40 (Also op by Serbian AF?)	9120707	JRV71501
YU-AKT	Yakovlev Yak-40 (Also op by Serbian AF?)	9222020	JRV71503
YU-AKV	Yakovlev Yak-40 (Also op by Serbian AF?)	9630849	JRV71505
YU-ALN	Aérospatiale/Alenia ATR-72-201	180	F-WWEP
YU-ALO	Aérospatiale/Alenia ATR-72-201	186	F-WWEW
YU-ALP	Aérospatiale/Alenia ATR-72-201	189	F-WWED
YU-ALR	Aérospatiale/Alenia ATR-72-202	357	G-BVTK, F-WWEW, F-GKOJ
YU-AMB	McDonnell-Douglas DC-10-30	46988	
YU-AMI	Ilyushin Il-76MD	00934 99982	RA-76822, CCCP76822
YU-AND	Boeing 737-3H9	23329	
YU-ANF	Boeing 737-3H9	23330	
YU-ANH	Boeing 737-3H9	23415	TC-CYO, YU-ANH, PP-SNY, YU-ANH
YU-ANK	Boeing 737-3H9	23715	
YU-ANP	Boeing 737-2K3	23912	
YU-ANV	Boeing 737-3H9	24140	
YU-ANW	Boeing 737-3H9	24141	TS-IED, YU-ANW
YU-AOJ	Fokker F.28 Fellowship 4000	11187	F-WQPL, (5A-DTI), F-WQPL, G-BXRE, 5A-DTI, G-BXRE, N102EW, 9G-ADA, PH-EXW
YU-AOK	Fokker F.28-0100	11272	G-UKFP, PH-KLH, F-GIDN, F-OGQA, PH-KLH
YU-AOL	Fokker F.28-0100	11268	G-UKFL, PH-KLC, F-GIDT, F-OGQI, F-GIDT, F-OGQI, PH-KLC
YU-AOM	Fokker F.28-0100	11321	G-BYDP, F-WQJA, N132ML, SE-DUA, PH-RRC, G-FIOS, PH-EZA

YU-AON	Boeing 737-3Q4	24208	N181LF
			S7-RGL
			PT-TEF
YU-AOO	Boeing 737-4Q8	24070	N240LF
			EI-CXH
			N112TR
			G-BNNL
YU-AOQ	Boeing 747-4S3	24165	N7588C
			VT-SIH
			VT-JAI
			N690MA
			G-BPKC
YU-AOS	Boeing 737-4B7	24551	N429US
YU-AOT	Fokker F.28-0100	11350	F-WLLE
			F-OLLE
			F-GLLS
			PT-MQB
			PH-LNN
			SE-DUH
			PH-LNN
YU-BCB	Piper PA-25-235 Pawnee B (C/n incorrect)	"253065"	
YU-BCC	Antonov An-2M	600310	
YU-BCJ	Antonov An-2M	600407	
YU-BCL	Antonov An-2M	600406	
YU-BCM	Antonov An-2M	600408	
YU-BCW	Piper PA-25-235 Pawnee B	25-3848	N7691Z
YU-BCZ	Macchi AL.60B-2 (Wfu)	73/6253	
YU-BDW	LET Z-37 Cmelák	02-06	
YU-BEI	Antonov An-2M	701725	
YU-BEK	Antonov An-2M (Cld ?)	701726	
YU-BEM	Piper PA-25-235 Pawnee B	25-3872	
YU-BEV	Grumman G.164 Agcat (Cld ?)	499	
YU-BEY	Piper PA-25-235 Pawnee C	25-4173	
YU-BFX	Piper PA-25-235 Pawnee	25-2590	SE-EIB
YU-BGB	Piper PA-30 Turbo Twin Comanche C	30-1903	N8750Y
YU-BGW(3)	PZL-104 Wilga 35A	140547	(SP-WDD)
	(Possible error for YU-DGW ?)		
YU-BHK(2)	Beech A60 Duke	P-164	N4232A
YU-BHL	Beech A60 Duke	P-176	N9325Q
YU-BIB	Utva-66	0841	
YU-BIC	Piper PA-25-235 Pawnee	unkn	
YU-BII	Cessna 402B	402B0352	N5088Q
YU-BIW	Cessna 340	340-0345	N69508
YU-BIX	Cessna 402B	402B0593	N3735C
YU-BJF	Antonov An-2R	1G160-03	
YU-BJI	Grumman G.164A Agcat	1422	
YU-BJK	Grumman G.164A Agcat (Cld ?)	1466	
YU-BJN	Grumman G.164A Agcat (Cld ?)	1420	
YU-BJT	Grumman G.164A Agcat (Cld ?)	1484	
YU-BJX	Piper PA-25-235 Pawnee	25-2592	YU-BFY
			SE-EID
YU-BJZ	Antonov An-2R (To Z3- ?)	1G167-04	
YU-BKG	Antonov An-2T (To T9- ?)	1G167-28	
YU-BKK	Antonov An-2R	1G167-08	
YU-BKL	Antonov An-2R	1G167-11	
YU-BKM	Antonov An-2R	1G172-49	
YU-BKO	Antonov An-2R	1G172-51	
YU-BKV	Grumman G.164B Agcat	228B	N6712Q
YU-BKW	Grumman G.164B Agcat	235B	N6724Q
YU-BKX	Grumman G.164B Agcat	246B	N6732Q
YU-BLB	Antonov An-2	1G179-07	
YU-BLE	PA-25-235 Pawnee B	25-3756	YU-BDI
			N7789Z
			N10F
YU-BLG	Grumman G.164B Agcat (Cld ?)	329B	N6871Q
YU-BLH	Grumman G.164B Agcat	330B	N6872Q
YU-BLJ	Piper PA-25-260 Pawnee D	25-7856035	N9180T
YU-BLK	Cessna Turbo 310R	310R1431	D-IBEK(2)
			YU-BLK
			N5287C
YU-BLM	Cessna Turbo 310R	310R1433	N5290C
YU-BLX	PZL M-18 Dromader	1Z001-03	SP-PBY
YU-BLZ	PZL M-18 Dromader	1Z001-04	SP-PBX
YU-BMH	Transavia PL-12 Airtruck	G995	
YU-BMI	PZL M-18 Dromader (Noted .03)	unkn	
YU-BMJ	Grumman G.164B Agcat (Wfu)	379B	N6583K
YU-BMM	Piper PA-31T Cheyenne II	31T-8020021	"YU-IIQO"
			(D- IIOO)
			N2382W
YU-BMY	PZL M-18A Dromader	1Z010-02	
YU-BMZ	PZL M-18A Dromader	1Z010-03	
YU-BNA	Dassault Falcon 50	43	JRV72102
			F-WZHO
YU-BNB	PZL M-18A Dromader	1Z010-04	
YU-BNC	PZL M-18A Dromader	1Z010-05	
YU-BND	PZL M-18A Dromader	1Z010-06	
YU-BNG	PZL M-18A Dromader	1Z010-14	
YU-BNH	PZL M-18A Dromader	1Z010-15	
YU-BNJ	Cessna 310	unkn	
YU-BNK	PZL M-18A Dromader	1Z010-18	
YU-BNL	PZL M-18A Dromader	1Z010-19	
YU-BNM	PZL M-18A Dromader	1Z010-20	
YU-BNO	PZL M-18 Dromader (Noted .03)	unkn	
YU-BNT	PZL M-18A Dromader	1Z013-11	
YU-BNU	PZL M-18A Dromader	1Z013-12	
YU-BNV	PZL M-18A Dromader	1Z013-13	
YU-BNW	PZL M-18A Dromader	1Z013-38	
YU-BNY	PZL M-18A Dromader	1Z013-41	
YU-BOA	Antonov An-2R	1G216-02	
YU-BOB	Antonov An-2R	1G216-01	
YU-BON	Antonov An-2R	1G221-60	
YU-BOS	PZL M-18A Dromader	1Z016-12	
YU-BOT	Antonov An-2R	1G223-11	
YU-BOU	Antonov An-2R	1G223-12	
YU-BOV	PZL M-18A Dromader	1Z016-13	
YU-BOX	Antonov An-2R	1G223-39	
YU-BPA	Antonov An-2R	1G225-31	
YU-BPB	PZL M-18A Dromader	1Z016-11	SP-DBO
YU-BPC	Antonov An-2R	1G228-45	SP-BPC
YU-BPD	PZL M-18A Dromader	1Z017-01	SP-DBN
YU-BPE	Antonov An-2R	1G228-25	
YU-BPF	Piper PA-31T Cheyenne II	31T-8020006	N801CM
			N2516R
YU-BPG	Piper PA-31T Cheyenne II	31T-8020012	N2328W
YU-BPH	Piper PA-31T Cheyenne II	31T-8020063	N2389V
YU-BPO	Antonov An-2R	1G231-56	SP-DNC
YU-BPP	Robin DR.400/180 Régent	1984	
YU-BRC	Cessna 210 Centurion	unkn	
YU-BRD	Piper PA-32-300 Cherokee Six	32-40209	N4141W
YU-BRI	Cessna 172	unkn	
YU-BRK	Antonov An-2R	1G230-18	CCCP33581
YU-BRL	Antonov An-2R	1G218-52	SP-FLD
			RA-33065
			CCCP33065
YU-BRM	Cessna 421C (Identity unconfirmed)	421C0893	N282PT
YU-BRN	Antonov An-2R	1G229-06	SP-FLE
			RA-33514
			CCCP33514
YU-BRO	Cessna 421C Golden Eagle	unkn	
YU-BRP(2)	Antonov An-2R	unkn	Z3-. . .
YU-BRR	PZL M-18B Dromader	1Z028-11	SP-DET
YU-BRS	PZL M-18A Dromader	1Z028-04	SP-DES
YU-BRV	Aero Commander 680FP	1290-133	D-IHAS
YU-BRZ	Gates Learjet 31A	31A-045	N67SB
			N50159
YU-BSM	Cessna 550 Citation II	550-0808	SE-DVZ
			N1299B
			N5216A
YU-BSS	Cessna 172	unkn	
YU-BTT	Cessna 551 Citation II/SP	551-0038	N551BB
			N103M
			N550DA
			D-IBPF
			N6801Z
YU-BVV	Cessna 550 Citation II	550-0272	SE-DVV
			Fv.103001
			SE-DVV
			VP-BVV
			VR-BVV
			HB-VKZ
			VH-JPK
			9M-WAN
			N68633
YU-BXX	LET L-410UVP	902422	RA-67629
			CCCP67629
YU-BZI	Piper PA-34-200T Seneca	unkn	
YU-CAB	Champion 7GCBC Citabria	2. .-70	
YU-CAK	Champion 7GCBC Citabria (To T9- ?)	282-70	
YU-CAS	Champion 7GCBC Citabria (Damaged)	294-70	
YU-CAW	Champion 7GCBC Citabria	unkn	
YU-CCI	Reims/Cessna F150L	F15001056	(I-NOLQ)
YU-CCK	Reims/Cessna F172M	F17201148	
YU-CCM	Reims/Cessna F172M	F17201073	
YU-CCN	Reims/Cessna F172M	F17201074	
YU-CCO	Reims/Cessna F172M	F17201077	
YU-CCP	Reims/Cessna F172M	F17201078	
YU-CCS	Reims/Cessna F172M	F17201154	
YU-CCT	Reims/Cessna F172M	F17201155	
YU-CCU	Reims/Cessna F172M	F17201160	
YU-CCV	Reims/Cessna F172M	F17201167	
YU-CCW	Reims/Cessna F172M	F17201172	
YU-CCX	Reims/Cessna F172M	F17201173	
YU-CCY	Reims/Cessna F172M	F17201177	
YU-CCZ	Reims/Cessna F172M	F17201183	
YU-CDL	Zlin Z.526F Trenér Master	1325	OK-GRI
YU-CES	Cessna 170B	25928	HB-COF
			N3284A
YU-DAY	Piper PA-28-140 Cherokee D	28-7125609	N11C
YU-DBL	Reims FR172J Rocket	FR17200439	
YU-DBW	Piper PA-18-150 Super Cub	18-7809055	N4077E
YU-DBX	Piper PA-18-150 Super Cub	18-7809156	N82096
YU-DCC	Piper PA-18-150 Super Cub (To T9- ?)	18-7809163	N82169
YU-DCJ	Piper PA-18-150 Super Cub	18-7809164	N82172
YU-DCK	Piper PA-18-150 Super Cub	18-7809165	N82177
YU-DCL	Piper PA-18-150 Super Cub	18-7809166	N82182
YU-DCM	Piper PA-18-150 Super Cub	18-7809154	N82071
YU-DCN	Reims/Cessna F172N	F17201738	
YU-DCO	Reims/Cessna F172N	F17201741	
YU-DCP	Reims/Cessna F172N	F17201742	
YU-DCR	Reims/Cessna F172N	F17201745	
YU-DCS	Reims/Cessna F172N	F17201746	
YU-DCT	Reims/Cessna F172N	F17201747	
YU-DCU	Reims/Cessna F172N	F17201748	
YU-DCV	Piper PA-28-161 Warrior II	28-7916051	N21714

YU-DCX	Piper PA-28-161 Warrior II	28-7916053	N21797
YU-DCZ	Piper PA-28-161 Warrior II	28-7916055	N21865
YU-DDB	Piper PA-28-161 Warrior II	28-7916057	N21963
YU-DDF	Champion 7GCBC Citabria (To T9- ?)	unkn	
YU-DEK	PZL-104 Wilga 35A	118378	
YU-DEL	PZL-104 Wilga 35A (Noted .03)	118401	
YU-DEP	Utva-75 (To T9- ?)	unkn	JRV53109
YU-DER	Utva-75	unkn	JRV53110
YU-DET	Utva-75	unkn	JRV53 . . .
YU-DEW	Utva-75	unkn	JRV53113
YU-DEZ	Utva-75	unkn	JRV53116
YU-DFC	PZL-104 Wilga 35A	139505	
YU-DFD	PZL-104 Wilga 35A	139506	
YU-DFE	PZL-104 Wilga 35A (Wrecked)	139507	
YU-DFF	PZL-104 Wilga 35A	139508	
YU-DFG	Utva-75	unkn	JRV53002
YU-DFL	Utva-75 (W/o 11.10.03)	unkn	JRV53119
YU-DFP	Utva-75	unkn	JRV53163
YU-DFY	Zlin Z.526F Trenér Master	unkn	JRV41116
YU-DGC	Utva-75	unkn	JRV53170
YU-DGG	Utva-75	unkn	JRV53172
YU-DGM	Utva-75	unkn	JRV53178
YU-DGR	Zlin Z.526F Trenér Master	unkn	JRV . . . . .
YU-DGT	Utva-75	unkn	JRV53180
YU-DGU	Utva-75	unkn	JRV53181
YU-DHA	Utva-75	unkn	JRV53186
YU-DHD	Utva-75	unkn	Z3-DCG YU-DHD JRV53189
YU-DHH	Utva-75	unkn	JRV53193
YU-DHJ	Utva-75	unkn	JRV53195
YU-DHK	Utva-75	unkn	JRV53196
YU-DHO	Utva-75	unkn	JRV53200
YU-DHR	PZL-104 Wilga 35	15810603	
YU-DHS	PZL-104 Wilga 80	CF15810604	
YU-DHY	PZL-104 Wilga 80	CF15810612	
YU-DIA	Reims/Cessna F172P	F17202157	
YU-DIB	Reims/Cessna F172P	F17202158	
YU-DIC	Reims/Cessna F172P	F17202159	
YU-DID	Utva-75	unkn	JRV53202
YU-DIE	Utva-75	unkn	JRV53 . . .
YU-DIL	Utva-75	unkn	JRV53208
YU-DIR	Zlin Z.526F Akrobat (W/o 31.8.03)	unkn	JRV41111
YU-DIS	Reims/Cessna F172P	F17202192	F-WZNE
YU-DIT	Reims/Cessna F172P	F17202193	F-WZNF
YU-DIV	Utva-75	unkn	JRV53211
YU-DIX	Utva-75	unkn	JRV53 . . .
YU-DIY	Utva-75	unkn	JRV53 . . .
YU-DJF	Utva-75 (W/o .93)	unkn	JRV53217
YU-DJJ	Utva-75	unkn	JRV53225
YU-DJK	Utva-75	unkn	JRV53226
YU-DJU	Utva-75	unkn	JRV53234
YU-DJW	Utva-75	unkn	JRV53236
YU-DJY	Reims/Cessna FA152 Aerobat	FA1520383	F-WZNG
YU-DJZ	Reims/Cessna FA152 Aerobat	FA1520386	F-WZNH
YU-DKA	Reims/Cessna FA152 Aerobat	FA1520387	F-WZNI
YU-DKB	Utva-75	unkn	JRV53240
YU-DKC	Utva-75	unkn	JRV53241
YU-DKI	Utva-75	unkn	JRV53158
YU-DKL	Utva-75	unkn	JRV53124
YU-DKM	Utva-75	unkn	JRV53250
YU-DKO	Utva-75	unkn	JRV53136
YU-DLG	Utva-66	unkn	JRV51109
YU-DLH	Utva-66 (Derelict .04)	unkn	JRV51 . . .
YU-DLG	Utva-66 (Same serial quoted for 9A-DAZ, to Canada 7.99)	unkn	JRV51109
YU-DLL	Utva-66	unkn	JRV51102
YU-DMH	Zlin Z.142 (Wfu ?)	0531	
YU-DMI (2)	Cessna 172	unkn	
YU-DML(2)	Piper PA-28-161 Warrior II (W/o 2.4.05)	28-8116319	N8436H
YU-DMM(2)	Utva-75	unkn	JRV53247
YU-DMN	Utva-66	unkn	JRV51182
YU-DMO	Cessna 152	unkn	
YU-DMP	Piper PA-28-181 Archer II	unkn	
YU-DMR	Utva-66	unkn	JRV51 . . .
YU-DMT	Utva-66	unkn	JRV51 . . .
YU-DMV	Cessna 150/152	unkn	
YU-DMX	Cessna 152	unkn	
YU-DMY	Piper PA-28-140 Cherokee (Unconfirmed)	28-20970	D-EKZA N6830W
YU-DNA	Cessna 172N	17268503	
YU-DNB	Piper PA-38-112 Tomahawk	unkn	
YU-DNC	Cessna 150	unkn	
YU-DND	Piper PA-32-260 Cherokee Six (Unconfirmed)	32-388	N3507W
YU-DNE	Cessna 172	unkn	
YU-DNF	Cessna 172	unkn	
YU-DNG	Cessna 152	unkn	
YU-DNI	Reims/Cessna F172N	F17201546	D-EKBS
YU-DNJ	Grumman-American AA-5	unkn	
YU-DNK	Cessna 172	unkn	
YU-HAS	Agusta-Bell 206A Jet Ranger II	8311	
YU-HAT	Agusta-Bell 206A Jet Ranger II	8317	
YU-HAU	Agusta-Bell 206A Jet Ranger II	8316	
YU-HAW	Agusta-Bell 206A Jet Ranger II	8314	
YU-HAY	Agusta-Bell 206A Jet Ranger II	8318	
YU-HAZ	Agusta-Bell 206A Jet Ranger II	8319	
YU-HBB	Aérospatiale SA.341G Gazelle (Cld ?)	1020	
YU-HBH	Aérospatiale SA.341G Gazelle	1292	
YU-HBJ	Aérospatiale SA.341G Gazelle	1304	
YU-HBK	Aérospatiale SA.341G Gazelle	1348	
YU-HBS	Bell 206L-1 Long Ranger II	45274	N2769C
YU-HBU	Bell 206B Jet Ranger II	2731	N2769P
YU-HBV	Bell 206B Jet Ranger II	2735	N2770D
YU-HBX	Bell 206B Jet Ranger II	2747	N2770N
YU-HBY	Bell 206B Jet Ranger II	2749	N2769X
YU-HCA	Agusta-Bell 212	5709	
YU-HCB	Agusta-Bell 212	5710	
YU-HCC	Agusta-Bell 212	5712	
YU-HCD	Agusta-Bell 212	5711	
YU-HCE	Agusta-Bell 212	5713	
YU-HCL	Bell 206B Jet Ranger II	2897	
YU-HCN	Bell 206L-1 Long Ranger II	45399	N1082A
YU-HCO	Bell 206B Jet Ranger II	2978	N1086S
YU-HCS	Soko/Aérospatiale SA.341HGazelle	066	
YU-HCT	Soko/Aérospatiale SA.341H Gazelle (noted .03)	unkn	
YU-HCY	Soko/Aérospatiale SA.341G Gazelle	024	JRV12656
YU-HDD	Mil Mi-2 (Stored, France)	541108069	
YU-HDE(1)	Mil Mi-2 (Stored, France)	541129069	
YU-HDE(2)	Soko/Aérospatiale SA.341H Gazelle	unkn	
YU-HDI	Soko/Aérospatiale SA.341G Gazelle	unkn	JRV126 . .
YU-HDL	Soko/Aérospatiale SA.341G Gazelle	unkn	JRV126 . .
YU-HDN	Soko/Aérospatiale SA.341G Gazelle	unkn	JRV126 . .
YU-HDR	Mil Mi-2 (W/o .00?)	unkn	
YU-HDU	Bell 206B Jet Ranger II	unkn	
YU-HDY	Soko/Aérospatiale SA.341G Gazelle	055	JRV126 . .
YU-HEB	Aérospatiale SA.342 Gazelle	unkn	JRV12 . . .
YU-HEG	Sikorsky S-76B	760444	
YU-HEE	Soko/Aérospatiale SA.341G Gazelle	unkn	JRV12622
YU-HEH	Soko/Aérospatiale SA.341G Gazelle	011	JRV12619
YU-HEI	Soko/Aérospatiale SA.341G Gazelle	012	JRV12620
YU-HEJ	Mil Mi-2	unkn	
YU-HEK	Soko/Aérospatiale SA.341G Gazelle	012 ?	JRV12620
YU-HEL	Mil Mi-2	511109059	JRV12511
YU-HEM	Soko/Aérospatiale SA.341H Gazelle	092	JRV12713
YU-HEN	Soko/Aérospatiale SA.341H Gazelle	unkn	JRV12611
YU-HEO	Aérospatiale SA.341H Gazelle	1140	JRV126 . . "JRV12011"
YU-HER	Mil Mi-2 (W/o 28.12.02)	unkn	JRV125 . .
YU-HES	Aérospatiale SA.342J Gazelle	1057	F-GOSO EC-EQU C-GEJE N341NA N9042U C-FGCE CF-GCE
YU-HEV	Aérospatiale SA.342J Gazelle	1393	F-GCCZ (KAF-401)
YU-H . .	Aérospatiale SA.342J Gazelle	1204	F-GFDG TG-KOV
YU-H . .	Robinson R-22 Beta	0643	N24VH D-HESI
YU-YAA	Soko J-20 Kraguj	unkn	JRV30136
YU-YAC	Soko Galeb G-2A	unkn	JRV23196
YU-YAD	Soko Galeb G-2A	unkn	JRV23187
YU-YAE	Soko Galeb G-2A	unkn	JRV23177
YU-YAF	Soko Galeb G-2A	unkn	JRV23180
YU-YAG	Soko Galeb G-2A (Based Germany)	unkn	JRV23194
YU-ZBG	RAF-2000GTX-SE	unkn	
YU-ZBI	Zrno (Destroyed in crash)	unkn	
YU-ZBJ	Aero Poni V (Destroyed in crash)	unkn	
YU-ZBK	Rans S-6 Coyote II (Kojot)	unkn	
YU-ZBM	Rans S-6 Coyote II (Kojot)	unkn	
YU-ZBP	Zenair CH-701	unkn	OK-FUR 88
YU- . . .	Reims/Cessna F152	F15201572	D-EABN(2)
YU- . . .	Cessna 172N	17270770	D-ETER N739SN
YU- . . .	Cessna 172N	17272428	D-ETIC N5121D
YU- . . .	Cessna 172N	17273933	N9847J
YU- . . .	Sukhoi SU-29	unkn	HA-YAO
YU- . . .	Piper PA-34-200T Seneca (To YU-BZI ?)	34-7970286	D-GAMI C-GMDJ N2850N

BALLOONS AND AIRSHIPS

YU-O........	Colt 69A HAFB	916	
YU-O........	Colt 77A HAFB	917	
YU-O........	Colt 69A HAFB	918	
YU-O........	Colt AS-56 Hot Air Airship	919	
YU-OAE	Cameron V-77 HAFB (Correct c/n possibly 1909, not connected with S5-OAE)	8909	
YU-OAH(2)	Kubicek BB- HAFB	291	OK-0291
YU-OAJ	Type unknown		

GLIDERS

The following gliders include those known to have been active in Serbia in 1990/1 prior to hostilities, together with recent reports of current aircraft. The current status of many cannot be confirmed.

YU-4207-VS	VTC Cirrus	unkn
YU-4208-08	Schempp-Hirth Standard Cirrus	unkn
YU-4215-15	VTC-75 Standard Cirrus	unkn
YU-4220-ET	VTC-75 Standard Cirrus	unkn
YU-4221-21	VTC Cirrus 17	unkn
YU-4227-27	VTC-75 Standard Cirrus	unkn
YU-4229-29	VTC Cirrus 17	unkn
YU-4256-6	VTC-75 Standard Cirrus	unkn
YU-4265	VTC-75 Standard Cirrus	unkn
YU-4268	Pilatus B4-PC11 (To T9- ?)	unkn
YU-4276	VTC-75 Standard Cirrus	186
YU-4277-77	VTC-75 Standard Cirrus	unkn
YU-4284	VTC-75 Standard Cirrus	unkn
YU-4299	VTC-75 Standard Cirrus	unkn
YU-4303-03	VTC-75 Standard Cirrus	unkn
YU-4305-05	VTC-75 Standard Cirrus	unkn
YU-4310	Glaser-Dirks DG-100 Elan (To S5- ?)	unkn
YU-4313	VTC-75 Standard Cirrus	unkn
YU-4327-HL	VTC-75 Standard Cirrus	unkn
YU-4330-30	Glaser-Dirks DG-100E Elan	E-53
YU-4332-32	VTC-75 Standard Cirrus	unkn
YU-4333	VTC Cirrus 17A	181
YU-4334	VTC Cirrus 17A	unkn
YU-4335	VTC-76 VUK-T	unkn
YU-4342-VA	Glaser-Dirks DG-100 Elan	unkn
YU-4345-NJ	Glaser-Dirks DG-100G Elan	unkn
YU-4347-NS	Glaser-Dirks DG-100G Elan	unkn
YU-4355	VTC-76 VUK-T	266
YU-4356	VTC-76 VUK-T	267
YU-4357	VTC-76 VUK-T	268
YU-4359	VTC-76 VUK-T	270
YU-4360	VTC-76 VUK-T (W/o ?)	271
YU-4361	VTC-76 VUK-T	272
YU-4364	VTC-76 VUK-T	285
YU-4371	VTC-76 VUK-T	unkn
YU-4375	VTC-76 VUK-T	298
YU-4376	VTC-76 VUK-T	305
YU-4380	VTC-76 VUK-T	301
YU-4381	VTC-76 VUK-T	304
YU-4383	VTC-76 VUK-T	308
YU-4386-ZR	Glaser-Dirks DG-101G Elan	3E-60
YU-4389	VTC-76 VUK-T	311
YU-4392	VTC-76 VUK-T	314
YU-4394	VTC-76 VUK-T	316
YU-4400	VTC-76 VUK-T	327
YU-4401	VTC-76 VUK-T	328
YU-4402	VTC-76 VUK-T	329
YU-4415	VTC-76 VUK-T	339
YU-4422	VTC-76 VUK-T (Belgrade Museum)	346
YU-4425-AM	Glaser-Dirks DG-300 Elan	3E-240
YU-4426	VTC-76 VUK-T	372
YU-4428	VTC-76 VUK-T	374
YU-4429	VTC-76 VUK-T	375
YU-4430	VTC-76 VUK-T	376
YU-4431	VTC-76 VUK-T	377
YU-4432	VTC-76 VUK-T	378 ?
YU-4434	VTC-76 VUK-T	380
YU-4436	VTC-76 VUK-T	382
YU-4457	Glaser-Dirks DG-300 Elan	unkn
YU-5322	LET L-13 Blanik	unkn
YU-5326	LET L-13 Blanik	174830
YU-5331	LET L-13 Blanik	174915 ?
YU-5332	LET L-13 Blanik	174905
YU-5333	LET L-13 Blanik	174916
YU-5346-7	LET L-13 Blanik	unkn
YU-5356	LET L-13 Blanik	026240
YU-5364	LET L-13 Blanik	unkn
YU-5366	LET L-13 Blanik	unkn
YU-5367	LET L-13 Blanik	unkn
YU-5371	LET L-13 Blanik	026721
YU-5375	LET L-13 Blanik	026921
YU-5377	LET L-13 Blanik	unkn
YU-5387	LET L-13 Blanik	unkn
YU-5392	LET L-23 Super Blanik	897514
YU-5393	KR-03A Puchatek	03-02
YU-5394	LET L-23 Super Blanik	907630
YU-5395	LET L-13 Blanik	unkn
YU-5396	LET L-23 Super Blanik	917806
YU-6012	Grob G.109	unkn

MICROLIGHTS

YU-8022	Apollo CX-19 (Crashed 13.7.99)	unkn	
YU-8054	Unknown weightshift type	unkn	
YU-8064	Unknown weightshift type	unkn	
YU-8071	Unknown weightshift type	unkn	
YU-8089	Type unknown		
YU-WAA	Type unknown		
YU-XAD(2)	Utva Vila (Fairy)	unkn	
YU- . . .	Maja	unkn	OK-DUD 15

ZA - ALBANIA

Regn.	Type	C/n	Prev.Id.
ZA-ADA	Embraer EMB.110P1 Bandeirante	110303	F-GCMQ
			PT-SCK
ZA-HOV	Bell 222UT	47555	AL-HOV
			SE-HOV
ZA-HTB	Aérospatiale AS.350B Ecureuil	1851	
ZA-HTD	Aérospatiale AS.350B Ecureuil	1852	
ZA-H . .	Aérospatiale AS.350B Ecureuil	1853	
ZA-MAK	BAe.146 Series 100	E-1085	G-CCLN
			B-635L
			B-2710
			G-5-085
ZA-MAL	BAe.146 Series 200	E-2054	G-BZWP
			SE-DRG
			N696AA
			N144AC
			G-5-054
			N144AC
			G-5-054
ZA-MAN	Piper PA-31-350 Chieftain	31-8152195	N444TS
			(N716MA)
			N444TS
			N4097T
ZA-MEV	BAe.146 Series 300	E-3197	VH-EWS
			G-6-197

The following quasi-civil 'registrations' are used by the Albanian forces:

ZA-XFM	Sud Avn SA.319B Alouette III	2299	HB-XFM
ZA-XHP	Sud Avn SA.319B Alouette III	1995	HB-XHP
			N17414
ZA-XHZ	Sud Avn SA.319B Alouette III	2378	HB-XHZ
ZA-XRJ	Sud Avn SA.319B Alouette III	2139	HB-XRJ
			F-BVEQ

Z3 - MACEDONIA

Regn.	Type	C/n	Prev.Id.
Z3-AAA	Boeing 737-3H9	23416	YU-ANI
Z3-AAE	Fokker F.28-0100	11268	YU-AOL
			G-UKFL
			PH-KLC
			F-GIDT
			F-OGQI
			F-GIDT
			F-OGQI
			PH-KLC
Z3-AAF	Boeing 737-3B7	23858	N532AU
			N392AU
Z3-ARF	Boeing 737-3H9	23716	YU-ANL
			TS-IEC
			YU-ANL
Z3-BAA	Gates Learjet 25B	25B-205	YU-BKJ
			N1468B
Z3-BGA	Antonov An-2R	1G167-01	YU-BJV
Z3-BGB	Antonov An-2R	1G160-15	YU-BLD
			SP-WOB
Z3-BGC	Antonov An-2R	1G167-03	YU-BJY
Z3-BGD	Antonov An-2R	1G111-15	YU-BGK
Z3-BGF	Antonov An-2R	1G231-55	YU-BPJ
Z3-BGG	Antonov An-2R	1G115-15	YU-BGZ
Z3-BGH	Antonov An-2R	1G111-12	YU-BGH
Z3-BGJ	Antonov An-2	1G166-04	LZ-1502
			RA-19750
			CCCP19750
Z3-BGK	Antonov An-2	1G197-35	LZ-1504
			CCCP31412
Z3-BGL(2)	Antonov An-2R	1G206-19	LZ-1202
Z3-CGP	CASA CN.235	unkn	
Z3-DCA	Antonov An-2	unkn	
Z3-DCB	UTVA-66	unkn	YU-DLN
			JRV51117
Z3-DCC	UTVA-75	unkn	YU-DFB
			JRV53118
Z3-DCD	UTVA-75	unkn	YU-DKR
			JRV53159
Z3-DCF	UTVA-75	unkn	YU-DGX
			JRV53183
Z3-DCH	UTVA-75	unkn	YU-DLX
			JRV53 . . .
Z3-DCL	Reims/Cessna F172M	F17201062	D-ELON(3)
Z3-DCM	Zlin Z.242L	0700	OK-BNE
Z3-DCN	Zlin Z.242L (Code: "VAM-102")	0701	OK-BNF
Z3-DCO	Zlin Z.242L (Code: "VAM-103")	0702	OK-BNG
Z3-DCP	Zlin Z.242L (Code: "VAM-104")	0703	OK-BNH
Z3-DCR	Antonov An-2	unkn	LZ- ?
Z3-DCS	Zlin Z.143L	0054	OK-DCS
Z3-DCT	Zlin Z.242L	unkn	
Z3-HAA	Agusta-Bell 206B Jet Ranger II	8365	YU-HBD
Z3-HAB	Agusta-Bell 212	5626	YU-HBP
Z3-HHA	Agusta-Bell 206A Jet Ranger II	8365	YU-HBD
Z3-HHC(2)	Bell 412EP	36260	N9026S
			C-GLZM
Z3-HHD	Mil Mi-17 (Reservation)	unkn	
Z3-HHE	Mil Mi-17 (Reservation)	unkn	
Z3-HHF	Mil Mi-17 (Reservation)	unkn	
Z3-MKD	Bombardier Learjet 60	60-279	N50145
Z3- . . .	Antonov An-2R	1G167-04	YU-BJZ
Z3- . . .	Cessna 172N	72864	LN-HOH
			N6556D
Z3- . . .	Cessna 210K Centurion	21059422	D-EOCV
			N8122G
Z3- . . .	Piper PA-28-181 Archer II	28-8490030	N4332B
Z3- . . .	SOCATA TB-9 Tampico	90	LN-KAZ
Z3- . . .	Zlin Z.143L	unkn	

BALLOONS

Z3-OOA	Cameron V-65 HAFB	657	G-BHOU

GLIDERS

Z3-4001	Pilatus B4-PC11AF	303	YU-4266
Z3-4002	Pilatus B4-PC11AF	304	YU-4267
Z3-4003	VTC-75 Standard Cirrus	193 ?	YU-4279 ?
Z3-4004	Glaser-Dirks DG-100 Elan	E-37	YU-4318
Z3-4005	VTC-76 VUK-T	343	YU-4419
Z3-4006	VTC-76 VUK-T	297	YU-4382
Z3-4007	VTC-76 VUK-T	319	YU-4397
Z3-4008	VTC-76 VUK-T	379	YU-4433
Z3-4009	VTC-76 VUK-T	269	YU-4358
Z3-4010	VTC-76 VUK-T	303	YU-4374
Z3-4011	VTC-76 VUK-T	337	YU-4413
Z3-4012	VTC-76 VUK-T	286	YU-4365
Z3-4013	VTC-76 VUK-T	334	YU-4407
Z3-5001	LET L-13 Blanik	174903	YU-5327
Z3-5002	LET L-13 Blanik	174904	YU-5328
Z3-5003	LET L-23 Super Blanik	897515	YU- . . . .
Z3-5004	LET L-23 Super Blanik	968301	
Z3-5005	LET L-23 Super Blanik	968302	
Z3-5006	LET L-23 Super Blanik	988318	

3A - MONACO

Regn.	Type	C/n	Prev.Id.
3A-MAC(2)	Aérospatiale AS.350B Ecureuil	1673	HB-XBC
			F-WZKS
3A-MAR	Robinson R-44 Raven	1263	
3A-MBF	SIAI-Marchetti SF.260D	789	
3A-MBG	Cessna R182 Skylane RG	R18201979	N6322T
3A-MBR	Eurocopter EC.120B Colibri	1179	SE-JLA
3A-MCH	Cessna 310R	310R0128	F-BFOD
			N5004J
3A-MCM	Aérospatiale AS.365N Dauphin 2	6076	F-WQEE
			N9UW
			N1UW
			N365AH
3A-MCO	Robinson R-44 Raven	1109	
3A-MCR	Eurocopter EC.120B Colibri	1358	
3A-MFC	Eurocopter EC.130B4 Ecureuil	3768	
3A-MGR(2)	Dassault Falcon 2000	167	F-WWVG
3A-MIK	Aérospatiale AS.350BA Ecureuil	1091	I-ELIL
	(W/o 8.6.04)		3A-MMB
			HB-XGW
3A-MIO	Piper PA-31T Cheyenne II	31T-7920001	I- NANE
			N123HK
			N333P
			N6150A
3A-MJP	Aérospatiale SA.365C3 Dauphin 2	5015	F-WYMC
			N90049
3A-MKB	Beech C90 King Air	LJ-867	D-IEKG
			HB-GIH
			D-IIIS
			(D-IFOM)
3A-MLC	Aérospatiale AS.350B1 Ecureuil	2271	EC-ERR
3A-MLM	SOCATA TB-20 Trinidad	720	F-GHGA
			D-EKHC
3A-MMB(2)	Robinson R-22 Mariner	2432M	I-MALC
	(Ditched 27.10.04)		N8254Z
			I-MALC
			N8254Z
3A-MOI	Partenavia P.68B	19	F-GDRY
			I-VICV
			G-BCFM
3A-MON(4)	Beech F90 King Air	LA-129	F-GKKK
			OY-BEL
3A-MPJ	Eurocopter EC.130B4 Ecureuil	3662	
3A-MRB	Cessna 551 Citation II/SP	551-0421	D-IAWA(2)
			N550RD
			OE-GES
			SE-DEF
			OO-RJE
			(N421CJ)
			N1217V
			(N64735)
3A-MRC	Cessna 172R	17280808	N72656
3A-MSI	Piper PA-31T1 Cheyenne I	31T-7904026	EC-EIM
			N458SC
			XC-CUA
			(TG- . . .)
			N23447
			N9746N
3A-MST	Mooney M.20M Model 257 TLS	27-0135	I-TLST
			N9159D
3A-MTP	Aérospatiale AS.350B2 Ecureuil	1996	I-LOLO
3A-MTT	Aérospatiale AS.350B2 Ecureuil	1967	I-LUPJ
3A-MVB	Cessna 152	15280070	F-GHKC
			N757WV
3A-MXL	Aérospatiale AS.355NEcureuil 2	5713	
3A-UAD	Raj Hamsa X'Air	unkn	
3A-M . .	Piper PA-31T Cheyenne II	31T7920049	F-GFVO
			N500FE
			(N500FC)
			N500FE
			N23310

BALLOONS

3A-MCB	Lindstrand LBL-77A HAFB	964	

GLIDERS

3A-MCD(2)	Rolladen-Schneider LS7	7135	
3A-MPV	Caproni Vizzola A.21S Calif	202	F-CGPV
			I- CCPV
3A-MTO	Siren C.30S Edelweiss	22	F-CCUT

4K - AZERBAIJAN

Regn.	Type	C/n	Prev.Id.
4K-325	Tupolev Tu-154 B2	79A-325	HA-LCM
4K-473	Tupolev Tu-154 B2	81A-473	HA-LCO
4K-474	Tupolev Tu-154 B2	81A-474	HA-LCP
4K-AZ1	Boeing 727 235	19460	N4740
			4K-4201
			N4740
4K-AZ5	Mil Mi-14	74121	
4K-AZ6	Mil Mi-8MTV-1	96109	
4K-AZ7	Mil Mi-8MTV-1	96122	
4K-AZ10	Tupolev Tu-154 M	98A-1013	
4K-AZ14	Ilyushin IL-76 TD	1023412389	UK-76447
			76447
			CCCP76447
4K-AZ15	Ilyushin IL-76 TD	1033417569	RA-76379
			17569
4K-AZ16	Ilyushin IL-76 TD	1023412411	UK-76410
4K-AZ17	Tupolev Tu-154 M	85A-718	B-2603
4K-AZ19	Ilyushin IL-76 MD	0053460820	UR-76408
			CCCP76642
4K-AZ20	Antonov An-26B	11404	ER-AWE
			UR-26070
			26070
			RA-26070
			CCCP26070
4K-AZ23	Antonov An-12BK	8345605	11715
			CCCP11715
4K-AZ24	Aérospatiale AS.332L2 Super Puma	2625	F-WWOM
4K-AZ25	Douglas DC-8 62F	45920	LX-TLC
	(Wfu. Stored Ostend without marks)		N924BV
			C-GMXY
			N923CL
			HB-IDF
4K-AZ26	Ilyushin IL-76 TD	1033416525	UK-76844
			YL-LAR
			UK-76844
			CCCP76844
4K-AZ27	Ilyushin IL-76 TD	0053460827	ER-IBS
			UR-76433
			RA-76433
			CCCP766644
4K-AZ30	Antonov An-12BP	5343410	CCCP11404
4K-AZ31	Ilyushin IL-76 TD	1013405184	ER-ACG
			RA-76426
			CCCP76426
4K-AZ32	Antonov An-12B	5343006	CCCP 11430
4K-AZ33	Antonov An-12BK	8346201	RA-11267
			CCCP11267
4K-AZ34	MBB Bö.105LSA-3	2016	N204LF
			N7035P
			C-FCRM
			C-GERG
			(D-HLSP)
4K-AZ36	Antonov An-12BK	8345807	CCCP 11846
4K-AZ37	Antonov An-12BK	00347506	CCCP 11938
4K-AZ38	Boeing 757-256	26246	N262CT
			EC-FYN
			EC-612
4K-AZ39	Antonov An-26	97307805	45 blue
			CCCP 49272
4K-AZ40	Ilyushin Il-76TD	1043419632	
4K-AZ41	Ilyushin Il-76TD	1093420673	
4K-AZ42	Boeing 727 230	20525	4K-AZ8
			OM-AHK
			N877UM
			OB-1572
			N877UM
			XA-SJK
			N877UM
			XA-RJV
			N877UM
			D-ABFI
			N1779B
4K-AZ43	Boeing 757-2M6	23453	V8-RBB
4K-AZ48	Antonov An-140	36525307036	
4K-AZ54	Airbus A320-211	331	9H-ADZ
			VH-HYY
			N490GX
			TC-ONB
			F-WWII
4K-AZ56	Antonov An-12TB	3341209	RA-11408(2)
			CCCP11408
4K-AZ58	Antonov An-12	unkn	
4K-AZ59	Antonov An-12TA	2340801	RA-11098
			CCCP11098
4K-AZ . .	Eurocopter EC.155B1 Dauphin	6683	F-WWOF
4K-07247	Antonov An-2 R	1G147-38	CCCP07247
4K-07575	Antonov An-2 R	1G156-15	CCCP07575
4K-07706	Antonov An-2 R	1G158-26	CCCP07706
4K-07845	Antonov An-2 R	1G169-60	CCCP07845
4K-12425	Antonov An-12BP	2401103	SovAF
4K-14071	Mil Mi-2	5210550048	CCCP14071

4K-14072	Mil Mi-2	5210616058	CCCP14072
4K-14073	Mil Mi-2	5210617058	CCCP14073
4K-15113	Mil Mi-8 MTV	341M13	CCCP 151
4K-15315	Mil Mi-8 MTV	341M15	CCCP 153
4K-16046	Antonov An-2 R	1G163-54	CCCP16046
4K-16047	Antonov An-2 R	1G163-55	CCCP16047
4K-17762	Antonov An-2 R	1G203-23	CCCP17762
4K-17763	Antonov An-2 R	1G203-24	CCCP17763
4K-17814	Antonov An-2 R	1G204-15	CCCP17814
4K-17815	Antonov An-2 R	1G204-16	CCCP17815
4K-17826	Antonov An-2 R	1G204-27	CCCP17826
4K-17827	Antonov An-2 R	1G204-28	CCCP17827
4K-19719	Antonov An-2 R	1G165-33	CCCP19714
4K-20366	Mil Mi-2	529813066	CCCP20366
4K-20367	Mil Mi-2	529814066	20367
			CCCP20367
4K-20368	Mil Mi-2	529815066	CCCP20368
4K-20874	Mil Mi-2	528235073	CCCP20874
4K-20876	Mil Mi-2	528237073	CCCP20876
4K-20985	Mil Mi-2	549720046	20985
			CCCP20985
4K-20986	Mil Mi-2	549721046	CCCP20986
4K-22652	Mil Mi-8 T	8099	CCCP22652
4K-23253	Mil Mi-2	5210327087	CCCP23253
4K-23254	Mil Mi-2	5210328087	CCCP23254
4K-23255	Mil Mi-2	5210329087	CCCP23255
4K-24168	Mil Mi-8 T	98941998	CCCP24168
4K-24173	Mil Mi-8 T	98943127	CCCP24173
4K-24572	Mil Mi-8 T	98839157	CCCP24572
4K-24573	Mil Mi-8 T	98839212	CCCP24573
4K-24590	Mil Mi-8 T	98839403	CCCP24590
4K-24596	Mil Mi-8 T	98839439	24596
			CCCP24596
4K-25110	Mil Mi-8 MTV1	95726	
4K-25115	Mil Mi-8 MTV1	95731	
4K-25140	Mil Mi-8 T	99047511	CCCP25140
4K-25152	Mil Mi-8 T	99047749	CCCP25152
4K-25157	Mil Mi-8 T	99047863	CCCP25157
4K-25193	Mil Mi-8 T	98943859	25193
			CCCP25193
4K-25482	Mil Mi-8 MTV1	95627	
4K-25494	Mil Mi-8 MTV1	95639	
4K-25925	Mil Mi-8 T	5560	25925
			CCCP25925
4K-26584	Antonov An-26 B	135-09	26584
			CCCP26584
4K-26585	Antonov An-26 B	138-0226585	26585
			CCCP26585
4K-27026	Mil Mi-8 PS	8699	
4K-27036	Mil Mi-8 MTV1	95870	
4K-27037	Mil Mi-8 MTV1	95871	
4K-27038	Mil Mi-8 MTV1	95872	
4K-31436	Antonov An-2 R	1G197-59	CCCP31436
4K-31442	Antonov An-2	1G198-07	CCCP31442
4K-31447	Antonov An-2	1G198-12	CCCP31447
4K-31448	Antonov An-2	1G198-13	CCCP31448
4K-31461	Antonov An-2	1G198-26	CCCP31461
4K-32619	Antonov An-2 R	1G219-18	CCCP32619
4K-32677	Antonov An-2 R	1G211-36	CCCP32677
4K-33050	Antonov An-2 R	1G218-37	CCCP33050
4K-33053	Antonov An-2 R	1G218-40	CCCP33053
4K-33327	Antonov An-2 R	1G225-46	CCCP33327
4K-33328	Antonov An-2 R	1G225-47	CCCP33328
4K-33367	Antonov An-2 R	1G226-26	CCCP33367
4K-33497	Antonov An-2 R	1G228-49	CCCP33497
4K-33498	Antonov An-2 R	1G228-50	CCCP33498
4K-33517	Antonov An-2 R	1G229-09	CCCP33517
4K-33518	Antonov An-2 R	1G229-10	CCCP33518
4K-33519	Antonov An-2 R	1G229-11	CCCP33519
4K-40222	Antonov An-2 R	1G220-12	CCCP40222
4K-40229	Antonov An-2 R	1G220-19	CCCP40229
4K-40267	Antonov An-2 R	1G220-57	CCCP40267
4K-40414	Antonov An-2 R	1G223-38	CCCP40414
4K-40474	Antonov An-2 R	1G224-51	CCCP40474
4K-40475	Antonov An-2 R	1G224-52	CCCP40475
4K-40638	Antonov An-2 R	1G213-45	CCCP40638
4K-40639	Antonov An-2 R	1G213-46	CCCP40639
4K-40703	Antonov An-2 R	1G215-01	CCCP40703
4K-40704	Antonov An-2 R	1G215-02	CCCP40704
4K-40750	Antonov An-2 R	1G172-22	CCCP40750
4K-40754	Antonov An-2 R	1G172-26	CCCP40754
4K-40756	Antonov An-2 R	1G172-28	CCCP40756
4K-40759	Antonov An-2 R	1G172-31	CCCP40759
4K-40761	Antonov An-2 R	1G172-33	CCCP40761
4K-40803	Antonov An-2 R	1G173-30	CCCP40803
4K-40805	Antonov An-2 R	1G173-50	CCCP40805
4K-40823	Antonov An-2 R	1G174-01	CCCP40823
4K-40866	Antonov An-2 R	1G175-20	CCCP40866
4K-40868	Antonov An-2 R	1G215-03	CCCP40868
4K-40936	Antonov An-2 R	1G216-36	CCCP40936
4K-40937	Antonov An-2 R	1G216-37	CCCP40937
4K-43958	Antonov An-2 R	1G210-35	CCCP43958
4K-43959	Antonov An-2 R	1G210-36	CCCP43959
4K-43961	Antonov An-2 R	1G210-38	CCCP43961
4K-43962	Antonov An-2 R	1G210-39	CCCP43962
4K-43963	Antonov An-2 R	1G210-40	CCCP43963
4K-48136	Antonov An-32 B	31-03	48136
4K-48137	Antonov An-32 B	31-05	48137
4K-56358	Antonov An-2 R	1G179-48	CCCP56358
4K-56359	Antonov An-2 R	1G179-49	CCCP56359
4K-56361	Antonov An-2 R	1G179-53	CCCP56361
4K-62499	Antonov An-2 R	1G175-22	CCCP62499
4K-62508	Antonov An-2 R	1G175-31	CCCP62508
4K-62522	Antonov An-2 R	1G175-45	CCCP62522
4K-62540	Antonov An-2	1G176-03	CCCP62540
4K-62551	Antonov An-2	1G176-14	CCCP62551
4K-62666	Antonov An-2 R	1G178-58	CCCP62666
4K-62672	Antonov An-2	1G177-57	CCCP62672
4K-65496	Tupolev Tu-134/135 conversion	63468	4K-65985
			65985
			CCCP65985
4K-65702	Tupolev Tu-134 B-3	63375	65702
			CCCP65702
4K-65704	Tupolev Tu-134 B-3	63410	YL-LBJ
			CCCP65704
4K-65705	Tupolev Tu-134 B-3	63415	65705
			CCCP65705
4K-65708	Tupolev Tu-134 B-3	63447	65708
			AL-65708
			CCCP65708
4K-65709	Tupolev Tu-134 B-3 *(Wfu ?)*	63484	65709
			CCCP65709
4K-65711	Tupolev Tu-134 B-3	63498	AL-65711
			65711
			AL-65711
			CCCP65711
4K-65713	Tupolev Tu-134 B-3	63520	65713
			CCCP65713
4K-65714	Tupolev Tu-134 B-3	63527	65714
			CCCP65714
4K-70760	Antonov An-2	1G132-15	RA-70760
			CCCP70760
4K-78130	Ilyushin IL-76 MD	0043454611	CCCP76602
4K-81548	Antonov An-2 R	1G208-52	CCCP81548
4K-81549	Antonov An-2 R	1G208-53	CCCP81549
4K-82896	Antonov An-2 R	1G169-13	CCCP82896
4K-82900	Antonov An-2 R	1G169-17	CCCP82900
4K-82901	Antonov An-2 R	1G169-18	CCCP82901
4K-85192	Tupolev Tu-154 B1	77A-192	85192
			CCCP85192
4K-85364	Tupolev Tu-154 B2	79A-364	CCCP85364
4K-85391	Tupolev Tu-154 B2	80A-391	85391
			CCCP85391
4K-85524	Tupolev Tu-154 B2	82A-524	YL-LAG
			CCCP85524
4K-85548	Tupolev Tu-154 B2	82A-548	85548
			CCCP85548
4K-85698	Tupolev Tu-154M	91A-871	85698
			CCCP85698
4K-85729	Tupolev Tu-154 M	92A-911	
4K-85732	Tupolev Tu-154 M	92A-914	
4K-85738	Tupolev Tu-154 M	92A-921	
4K-85734	Tupolev Tu-154 M	92A-916	85734
4K-86810	Ilyushin IL-76 M	053404094	RA-86810
			CCCP86810
4K-87218	Yakovlev Yak-40	9440937	HA-LJC
			87218
			HA-LJC
			CCCP87218
			OK-EEF
4K-87257	Yakovlev Yak-40	9311426	87257
			CCCP87257 ?
4K-87278	Yakovlev Yak-40	9311427	87278
			CCCP87278
4K-87415	Yakovlev Yak-40	9420734	CCCP87415
4K-87478	Yakovlev Yak-40	9440638	87478
			CCCP87478
4K-87812	Yakovlev Yak-40	9230424	87812
			CCCP87812
4K-87817	Yakovlev Yak-40	9230824	87817
			CCCP87817
4K-88211	Yakovlev Yak-40	9631749	88211
			CCCP88211
4K-92961	Antonov An-2 R	1G171-18	CCCP92961
4K-92963	Antonov An-2 R	1G171-20	CCCP92963

4L - GEORGIA

Regn.	Type	C/n	Prev.Id.
4L-AAA	Eurocopter EC.155B Dauphin	6630	F-WQDH F-WWOV
4L-AAB	Tupolev Tu-134 B3	63340	YL-LBH CCCP65700
4L-AAD	Tupolev Tu-134 B3	63295	YL-LBF CCCP65696
4L-AAE	Tupolev Tu-134 A	60282	OK-IFN
4L-AAG	Tupolev Tu-154 B2	82A-547	4L-85547 GR-85547 CCCP85547
4L-AAH	Tupolev Tu-154 B2	82A-558	4L-85558 YL-LAH CCCP85558
4L-AAJ	Tupolev Tu-134 A	63860	4L-65993 CCCP65993 SovAF:993 CCCP65993
4L-AAK	Yakovlev Yak-40	9531043	4L-87242 RA-87242 ? CCCP87242
4L-AAL	Antonov An-72	unkn	
4L-AAR	Yakovlev Yak-42 D	4520423116650	B-2751
4L-AIR	Antonov An-12BK	00347102	4K-AZ35 ER-ACA CCCP ?
4L-ASA	X-32 Snipe (Cr 30.6.04)	unkn	
4L-AVC	Yakovlev Yak-40	9342031	4L-87370 CCCP87370 ?
4L-AVD	Yakovlev Yak-40	9430537	4L-87466 87466
4L-AVK	Yakovlev Yak-40	9311526	4L-87258 CCC87258P
4L-CAA	Antonov An-12BP	402102	4L-11241 RA-11241 CCCP11241
4L-MGC	Yakovlev Yak-40	9320129	4L-87305 CCCP87305
4L-TAS	Antonov An-12BP	00347408	
4L-TGA	Boeing 737-529	25218	N218CT UR-GAI OO-SYE
4L-TGG	Yakovlev Yak-42 D	4520423116579	4L-AAM B-2754
4L-TGL	Boeing 737-3B7	23859	N524AU N393AU
4L-TGT	Boeing 737-4Q8	26306	N411LF SP-KPK TC-AFA
4L-XLA	Embraer EMB.120RT Brasilia	120081	PH-XLA G-BRAZ F-GFTC G-BRAZ PT-SKY
4L-XLF	Embraer EMB.120RT Brasilia	120082	PH-XLF (PH-XLS) OO-DTF PT-SKZ
4L-ZIL	Ilyushin IL-76 MD	0053464926	4K-AZ22 UR-76664 CCCP76664
4L-. . .	Aérospatiale AS.350B3 Ecureuil	9079	F-GTED
4L-. . .	Cessna 182J	18257276	N3176F
4L-14065	Mil Mi-2	5410544038	CCCP14065 ?
4L-14179	Mil Mi-2	5410544038	CCCP14179 ?
4L-20290	Mil Mi-2	5410544038	CCCP20290
4L-20372	Mil Mi-2	5410544038	CCCP20372 ?
4L-20403	Mil Mi-2	5410544038	CCCP20403
4L-20745	Mil Mi-2	5410544038	CCCP20745
4L-20755	Mil Mi-2	5410544038	CCCP20755
4L-20863	Mil Mi-2	5410544038	RA-20863 CCCP20863 ?
4L-20866	Mil Mi-2	5410544038	CCCP20866
4L-20956	Mil Mi-2	5410544038	CCCP20956 ?
4L-23338	Mil Mi-2	5410544038	CCCP23338 ?
4L-23501	Mil Mi-2	5410544038	CCCP23501 ?
4L-24202	Mi1 Mi-8	98730117	24202 CCCP24202
4L-24204	Mi1 Mi-8	98730131	
4L-24630	Mi1 Mi-8T	8298	
4L-24667	Mi1 Mi-8T	9815727	
4L-25174	Mi1 Mi-8 MTV-1	95484	
4L-25176	Mi1 Mi-8 MTV-1	95486	TC-HIS 4L-25176
4L-25448	Mi1 Mi-8 MTV-1	95587	
4L-25449	Mi1 Mi-8 MTV-1	95588	TC-HAG 4L-25449
4L-26087	Antonov An-26 B	126-01	GR-26087 CCCP26087
4L-27012	Mil Mi-8 T	99254357	LithAF:02blue
4L-65053	Tupolev Tu-134 A	49838	CCCP65053
4L-65061	Tupolev Tu-134 A-3	49874	RA-65061 CCCP65061
4L-65774	Tupolev Tu-134 A-3	62519	65774 CCCP65774
4L-65798	Tupolev Tu-134 A	63179	65798 CCCP65798
4L-65808	Tupolev Tu-134 A	3352109	CCCP65808
4L-65817	Tupolev Tu-134 A	4352301	CCCP65817
4L-65857	Tupolev Tu-134 A-3	23255	CCCP65857
4L-65865	Tupolev Tu-134 A	28286	CCCP65865
4L-65879	Tupolev Tu-134 A-3	31265	CCCP65879
4L-85168	Tupolev Tu-154 B	76A-168	85168 CCCP85168
4L-85430	Tupolev Tu-154 B2	80A-430	85430 CCCP85430
4L-85496	Tupolev Tu-154 B2	81A-496	85496 CCCP85496
4L-85518	Tupolev Tu-154 B2	81A-518	85518 CCCP85518
4L-85713	Tupolev Tu-154 M	91A-889	RA-85713 CCCP-85713
4L-86558	Ilyushin IL62 M	4952928	RA-86558 CCCP-86558
4L-87358	Yakovlev Yak-40	9340731	RA-87358
4L-87374	Yakovlev Yak-40	9410832	RA-87374
4L-88158	Yakovlev Yak-40	9611246	CCCP88158 ?
4L-88183	Yakovlev Yak-40	9620348	CCCP88183 ?

5B - CYPRUS

Regn.	Type	C/n	Prev.Id.
5B-CAR	Cessna F172H	F172-0461	
5B-CAS	Piper PA-25-235 Pawnee C	25-4247	N4579Y
5B-CBP	Reims/Cessna F150L	F15000744	N4798
5B-CBW(2)	Reims/Cessna F172M	F17200999	(D-EGBX)
5B-CDM	Piper PA-31 Turbo Navajo (Wfu)	31-263	5B-CHO N9196Y
5B-CDP	Piper PA-28-140 Cherokee B (Wfu)	28-25790	G-AXIP N11C
5B-CDR	Cessna 152	15282172	G-BGIA G-SACC G-BGIA N68187
5B-CDU	Cessna 182P Skylane	18260868	G-AZLD N9328G
5B-CDV	Piper PA-38-112 Tomahawk	38-78A0523	HB-PCT N4413E
5B-CDW	Piper PA-25-260 Pawnee C	25-5377	5B-CBM N8914L
5B-CEK	Reims/Cessna F152-II	F15201643	N1662Q N8812L
5B-CEM	Reims/Cessna F172P	F17201445	G-BEMC
5B-CEN	Cessna 172M	17261918	N8064H OD-PAI (N12296)
5B-CFC	Bell 47G-5	7868	4X-BBB
5B-CFM	Piper PA-23-250 Aztec B (Wfu)	27-2311	G-ASFG N10F
5B-CFO	Piper PA-28-140 Cherokee B	28-26253	G-AXTG N11C
5B-CFR	Agusta-Bell 47G-3B1 (CofA exp 8.6.89)	1590	G-BFFV XT124
5B-CFU	Agusta-Bell 47G-3B1 (CofA exp 8.6.89)	1577	G-BIEB HB-XHS XT111
5B-CFV	Bell 47G-2A1	3173	G-BJFI TF-HUG 63-13673
5B-CFX	Bell 47G-5A	25084	G-AZVW N14811
5B-CFY	Bell 47G-5A	25085	G-AZVX N14812
5B-CFZ	Piper PA-28-140 Cherokee D Fliteliner	28-7125287	N481FL
5B-CGA	Piper PA-28-140 Cherokee E Fliteliner	28-7225317	N709FL
5B-CGE	Piper PA-23-250 Aztec C	27-2546	G-BAJU N5459Y
5B-CGI	Westland-Bell 47G-3B1	WA/566	G-BDVJ 8430M XV312 G-17-14
5B-CGL	Cessna 310K (Wfu 1996)	310K0068	G-ATLD N6968L
5B-CGS	Cessna 340A	340A0076	C-GAWM N1377G
5B-CGU	Piper PA-31 Turbo Navajo	31-681	G-TISH G-BFKJ N506V N9730N
5B-CHC	Cessna 150F	15062319	N3519L
5B-CHD	Britten-Norman BN-2A-26 Islander	166	(OD-. . .) G-BJWL 4X-AYC G-51-166
5B-CHJ	Cessna 150M (Wfu)	15077421	N63603
5B-CHM	Piper PA-28-181 Cherokee Archer II	28-7790178	N7050F
5B-CHP	Cessna 172N	17272480	N5263D
5B-CHQ	Cessna 150M (Wfu)	15079143	N714FN
5B-CHS	Cessna 150K	15071827	N6327G
5B-CHU	Piper PA-44-180 Seminole (Wfu)	44-7995028	N39726
5B-CHW	Grob G.115A	8101	
5B-CHY	Grob G.115A	8097	D-EGVV F-GGOK (A6-. . .)
5B-CIA	Piper PA-28R-201 Arrow III	28R-7837131	N3705M
5B-CIB	Reims/Cessna F152 (Wrecked)	F15201611	G-BGVI
5B-CIC	Reims/Cessna FA152 Aerobat	FA1520362	G-STAP EI-BIE
5B-CIH	Helio H-700 Courier Amphibian (Wfu)	H-7	N961RD N40353
5B-CII	Piper PA-38-112 Tomahawk II	38-82A0082	N91591
5B-CIK	Piper PA-31-350 Navajo Chieftain (Wfu)	31-7305111	N66549 C-GNIR N74962
5B-CIR	Cessna F172H	F172-0482	5B-CCC G-AWGW
5B-CIT	Cessna 152	15285310	N67794
5B-CIV	Rockwell Commander 112B	500	N1162J
5B-CIW	Cessna 150E	15061383	G-ATEG N3983U
5B-CIX	Piper PA-34-200 Seneca	34-7350250	OH-PNH (SE-IRO) OH-PNH SE-GDF
5B-CIY	Cessna F172H	F172-0448	G-AVUL
5B-CIZ	Slingsby T-61D Falke	1723	NEJSGSA-9 G-AYPY
5B-CJA	Piper PA-38-112 Tomahawk II	38-82A0018	N91373
5B-CJB	Cessna 150M	15078205	G-BRLW N9255U
5B-CJF	Republic RC-3 Seabee	894	N6621K
5B-CJH	Hughes 269C	100-0050	N9633F
5B-CJI	Piper PA-34-220T Seneca III	34-8233134	G-MRPP N8202P
5B-CJJ	Republic RC-3 Seabee	441	C-GGXD N6238K
5B-CJK	Cessna 310R	310R0252	SX-CRY (SX-AAT) N44HB
5B-CJL(2)	Beech C90 King Air	LJ-979	N777VH N777NQ N777NG N12LA
5B-CJN	Cirrus SR20 (Reservation .02)	unkn	
5B-CJO	Robinson R-44 Clipper	0632	
5B-CJP	Cessna T337GP Pressurized Skymaster	P3370185	D-ICSK HB-LHX N87S
5B-CJQ	Cessna A150L Aerobat	A1500344	4X-CEN N6044J
5B-CJR	Cessna 150G (Reservation 2.00)	15066854	4X-ALZ N9454S
5B-CJS	Agusta A.109E Power	11071	
5B-CJT	Robinson R-44 Astro	0580	LN-OAL
5B-CJV	Beech 58 Baron	TH-1341	N6342U
5B-CJW	Bell 206L3 Long Ranger III	51300	G-BXIB EC-EQQ
5B-CJX	Piper PA-34-220T Seneca III	34-8133023	D-GOBN N8344M
5B-CJY	Cessna 421B Golden Eagle	421B0026	C-FTGB N710MS N18SH N1WP N8026Q
5B-CJZ	Beech 65-80 Queen Air (Reservn 5.02)	LD-80	(5B-CJL) N99BA N33NY N178L N2120 N212Q
5B-CKA	Bell 206L4 Long Ranger IV	52043	VP-BSR VR-BSR
5B-CKB	Bell 427	56024	N4036Q C-GIIT
5B-CKC	Beagle B.121 Pup	B121-166	G-AZCY HB-NAW G-AZCY
5B-CKD	Cessna 150 (Reservation .02)	unkn	
5B-CKE	Cessna P172D Skyhawk Powermatic	P17257154	SX-APN HB-CMF N7454E
5B-CKF	Mooney M.20J Model 201	24-1589	D-EFEM(3)
5B-CKG(2)	SOCATA TB-20 Trinidad	2093	N85GT
5B-CKH	Beech A24R Sierra	MC-11	D-EKXY N8014R
5B-CKI	SOCATA TB-10 Tobago	1296	GBTHR
5B-CKK	Canadair CL.600-2B16 Challenger	5094	VP-BZT N675CF TC-DHB TC-OVA C-FKNN C-GLWT
5B-CKL	Hawker 800XP	258495	C-GGCH N51495
5B-C . .	Cessna 150L	15072490	4X-CEG N6990G
5B-C . .	Cessna 525 CitationJet CJ	525-0466	N119CS
5B-C . .	Dassault MD.312 Flamant	250	F-AZEN Fr.AF
5B-C . .	Piper PA-28-140 Cherokee Cruiser	28-7425268	N41656
5B-C . .	Piper PA-28R-200 Cherokee Arrow II	28R7435266	D-EEDM[2] N43391
5B-DAU	Airbus A320-231	035	F-WWDX
5B-DAV	Airbus A320-231	037	F-WWDN
5B-DAW	Airbus A320-231	038	F-WWDZ
5B-DBA	Airbus A320-231	180	F-WWIT
5B-DBB	Airbus A320-231	256	F-WWBH
5B-DBC	Airbus A320-231	295	F-WWIE
5B-DBD	Airbus A320-231	316	F-WWBC
5B-DBH	Boeing 737-86N	30806	
5B-DBI	Boeing 737-86N	30807	
5B-DBO	Airbus A319-132	1729	D-AVWR
5B-DBP	Airbus A319-132	1768	D-AVWB
5B-DBQ	ROMBAC One-Eleven 561RC (Reservn .02)	408	YR-BRH
5B-DBR	ROMBAC One-Eleven 561RC (Reservn .02)	409	YR-BRI
5B-DBS	Airbus A330-243	505	F-WWKO
5B-DBT	Airbus A330-243	526	F-WWKY
5B-DBU	Boeing 737-8Q8	32796	N6055X N1786B
5B-DBV	Boeing 737-8Q8	30654	

5B-DBW	Boeing 737-8Q8	30671	
5B-DBX	Boeing 737-8Q8	33699	
5B-DBY	Boeing 737-31S	29099	D-ADBQ
5B-PBY	Canadian Vickers PBY-5A Catalina	CV-333	C-FPQF CF-PQF RCAF11042

ULTRALIGHTS

5B-HAA	Bensen B-80 Gyrocopter	2513	
5B-HAD	Quicksilver MXL-II	249	
5B-HAE	Reservation for Homebuilt for D.Charalantas	-	
5B-HAF	Murphy Rebel (Not a Murphy c/n, possibly PFA232-12174 ?)	"12174"	
5B-HAG	Bede BD-5B (Reservation)	5156	(5B-CBR(2))
5B-HAH	FIB Polaris	unkn	
5B-HAI	FIB Polaris	unkn	
5B-HAJ	Mainair Gemini/Flash 2A (Reservation) (Possibly Mainair 462 Gemini/Flash 2A c/n 794-0690-W587)	unkn	
5B-HAK	Mainair 503 Gemini/Flash 2A	818-0191-7-W612	G-MWRA
5B-HAL	Bill Parsons Gyrocopter (Reservation)	unkn	
5B-HAM	Dominator Gyroplane (Reservation .00)	unkn	
5B-HAN	Six Chuter SR7XL Powered Parachute	99-2374	
5B-HAO	Ultrasport 596 (Reservation 5.01)	2043	ZU-BUB
5B-HAP	Mainair Rapier	1288-0601-7-W1083	
5B-HAQ	Rans S-12XL Airaile (Reservation .01)	unkn	
5B-HAR	Mainair Blade 912	1307-1201-7-W1102	
5B-HAS	Murphy Renegade Spirit	PFA-188-11771	G-MWGF
5B-HAT	Pegasus Quantum 15	7520	
5B-HAU	QAC Quickie Q235	2583	G-BPUC N250CE

9A - CROATIA

Regn.	Type	C/n	Prev.Id.
9A-BAA(2)	Antonov An-2	1G110-36	(9A-BTT) UR-35070 CCCP35070
9A-BAD	Antonov An-2	1G170-42	HA-ABT CCCP07883
9A-BAL	LET L-410UVP-E4	871924	HA-LAS HAF: 924
9A-BAN	LET L-410UVP	851407	UR-67503 CCCP67503
9A-BDJ	Piper PA-25-235 Pawnee B	25-3260	RC-BDJ YU-BDJ N7314Z
9A-BDM	Cessna F172H	F172-0351	YU-BDM
9A-BDR	Cessna F172H (New fuselage c/n 2062 fitted?)	F172-0412	RC-BDR YU-BDR
9A-BFT	Antonov An-2R	1G99-16	YU-BFT
9A-BHT	Antonov An-2R	1G135-43	Croatia AF YU-BHT
9A-BHV	Antonov An-2R	1G135-45	YU-BHV
9A-BIE	Cessna A188B Agwagon	18801073	RC-BIE YU-BIE N21847
9A-BKA	Antonov An-2	1G167-05	Croatia AF YU-BKA
9A-BKC	Antonov An-2R	1G167-07	YU-BKC
9A-BKK	Antonov An-2	1G185-28	UR-54868 CCCP54868
9A-BKP	Cessna A188B Agtruck	18802875T	YU-BKP N731GB
9A-BKS	Cessna A185F Skywagon	18503325	RC-BKS YU-BKS N5152H
9A-BLA	Cessna A188B Agwagon	18802943	RC-BLA YU-BLA N731KA
9A-BLF	Piper PA-25-235 Pawnee C	25-7305527	RC-BLF YU-BLF YU-BIT N6785L
9A-BMH	Piper PA-28R-201T Turbo Arrow III	28R-7803313	N36192
9A-BNA	LET L-410UVP	851518	CCCP67554
9A-BOF	Antonov An-2R	1G223-56	RC-BOF YU-BOF
9A-BOG	Antonov An-2	1G214-08	CroatiaAF YU-BOG
9A-BOL	Cessna 172N	17269410	N174LG N737GQ
9A-BOW	Antonov An-2R	1G223-57	RC-BOW CroatAF"BOW" YU-BOW
9A-BPR	Reims FR172J Rocket	FR17200578	RC-BPR YU-BPR PH-DIK D-EDBF
9A-BTA	LET L-410UVP-E	912538	OK-WDO J2-KBE OK-WDD CCCP67670
9A-BTB	LET L-410UVP-E	902506	LZ-KLA CCCP67653
9A-BTC	LET L-410UVP-E3	902507	LZ-KLB CCCP67654
9A-BTD	Fokker F.28-0100	11407	N1424M PH-EZS
9A-BTE	Fokker F.28-0100	11416	N1431B PH-EZY
9A-BTT	Reims/Cessna F172M	F17200972	(9A-BAF) D-EDEI F-WLIL
9A-BUG	Yakovlev Yak-52	822708	LY-NXE DOSAAF
9A-BZB	Antonov An-2	1G225-40	RA-33321 CCCP33321
9A-CAF	Champion 7GCBC Citabria	255-70	YU-CAF
9A-CBC	McDonnell-Douglas DC-9-82	49143	N824US N948PS N1005J
9A-CBD	McDonnell-Douglas DC-9-82	48095	N815US N940PS
9A-CBF	McDonnell-Douglas DC-9-82	49221	I-DAVH
9A-CBG	McDonnell-Douglas DC-9-82	49430	I-DAVI
9A-CBH	McDonnell-Douglas DC-9-82	49 . . .	I-DA . .
9A-CCE	Cessna 207 Skywagon 207	20700232	RC-CCE YU-CCE N1632U
9A-CCG	Reims/Cessna F150L	F15001044	RC-CCG YU-CCG
9A-CCH	Reims/Cessna F150L	F15001040	RC-CCH YU-CCH
9A-CDA	McDonnell-Douglas DC-9-83	49602	N491GX TF-MDD D-ALLF

9A-CDH	Reims/Cessna F150M	F15001368	RC-CDH YU-CDH
9A-CDZ	Cessna F172H	F172-0427	YU-CDZ D-EBUF
9A-CGZ	SOCATA MS.893E Rallye 180GT Gaillard	12269	OE-KTL D-EEOG F-BUJG
9A-CRO(2)	Canadair CL.600-2B16 Challenger	5322	N604CL C-GLXY
9A-CTF	Airbus A320-211	258	F-OKAI F-GMAI (F-GHQN) F-WWBJ
9A-CTG	Airbus A319-112	767	F-WWDF D-AVYA
9A-CTH	Airbus A319-112	833	D-AVYJ
9A-CTI	Airbus A319-112	1029	D-AVYC
9A-CTJ	Airbus A320-214	1009	F-WWDN
9A-CTK	Airbus A320-214	1237	F-WWIK
9A-CTL	Airbus A319-112	1252	D-AVYS
9A-CTM	Airbus A320-212	671	C-GJUQ C-GVXF F-WWDE F-WWBE F-WWEB
9A-CTS	Aérospatiale/Alenia ATR-42-300	312	F-WWEK
9A-CTT	Aérospatiale/Alenia ATR-42-300	317	F-WWEO
9A-CTU	Aérospatiale/Alenia ATR-42-300	394	F-WWLJ
9A-DAB	Cessna T210N Turbo Centurion II	21064104	(9A-CBA) SL-CBA (YU-BPT) N5168Y
9A-DAD	Cessna 172R	17280174	N9362F
9A-DAE	Aero Commander 560F	1279-55	D-IACT (SE-EDX)
9A-DAF	Reims FR172J Rocket	FR17200390	D-ECZP
9A-DAG	Scheibe SF-25B Falke	4542	D-KALY
9A-DAH	Reims/Cessna F150K	F15000631	RC-DAH YU-DAH F-BRXV
9A-DAI	Diamond DA 20-A1	10035	C-FUJE
9A-DAJ	Reims/Cessna F150L	F15000814	D-EEYS
9A-DAL	Cessna 175A/Horton STOL conversion	56586	C-FCZV CF-CZV N7086E
9A-DAM	Antonov An-2	1G212-53	CCCP32748
9A-DAN	Cessna 172N	17268595	D-ETCO N733VZ
9A-DAO	Reims/Cessna F172M	F17200917	D-EEDR
9A-DAP	Cessna 172R	17280690	N2285P
9A-DAS	Cessna 172N	17269567	N737PL
9A-DAT	Piper PA-23-250 Aztec E	27-7554060	OY-BLK
9A-DAV	Antonov An-2	1G199-09	CCCP31500
9A-DAX	Piper PA-23-250 Aztec F	27-7854135	N606RW N6532A
9A-DAZ	Utva-66	unkn	JRV51109
9A-DBD	Piper PA-31-325 Navajo C/R	31-7512008	D-INJA N61508
9A-DBG	Valentin Taifun 17E-II (Diesel engine)	1094	D-KTAE OE-9292 D-KEWI (1)
9A-DBK	Reims FR172J Rocket	FR17200463	D-EIQR
9A-DBM	Piper PA-18-150 Super Cub	18-7509013	CroatiaAF YU-DBM N9677P
9A-DBN	Cessna 172N	17268327	S5-DDT N733JJ
9A-DBR	Piper PA-18-150 Super Cub	18-7809172	RC-DBR YU-DBR N82405
9A-DBS	Piper PA-18-150 Super Cub	18-7809170	RC-DBS YU-DBS N82370
9A-DBU	Piper PA-18-150 Super Cub	18-7809169	RC-DBU YU-DBU N82196
9A-DBV	Scheibe SF-25C Falke 1700	44161	D-KEFN
9A-DCA	Cessna 411	unkn	
9A-DCB	Piper PA-28RT-201 Arrow IV	28R-7918214	SE-IYY N2910P
9A-DCC	Cessna 152	15283429	N49133
9A-DCI	Piper PA-18-150 Super Cub	18-7809155	YU-DCI N82073
9A-DDA	Piper PA-28-161 Warrior II	28-7916056	RC-DDA YU-DDA N21952
9A-DDD	Cessna 172N	17273541	N5092G
9A-DDH	Reims/Cessna F172N	F17201783	RC-DDH YU-DDH
9A-DDM	Cessna T310Q	310Q0929	D-IBIS(4) OE-FEX D-IKPW N69702
9A-DDO	Cessna 182	unkn	
9A-DEF	Cessna 172N	17272636	RC-DEF YU-DEF N6209D
9A-DEG	Cessna 172N	17272640	RC-DEG YU-DEG N6216D
9A-DEL	Piper PA-34-200TSeneca II	34-7870076	D-GFLD OE-FLD N2271M
9A-DEM	Reims/Cessna F182Q Skylane	F18200095	RC-DEM YU-DEM N90114
9A-DFH	Reims/Cessna F172N	F17201880	RC-DFH YU-DFH N1661Q
9A-DFK	Reims/Cessna F172N	F17201978	RC-DFK YU-DFK
9A-DFO	Cessna 310R-II	310R1537	RC-DFO YU-DFO N5296C
9A-DGV	Cessna T303 Crusader	T30300186	D-IHDM N303CE (N9558C)
9A-DGZ	Sportavia/ Scheibe SF-25B Falke	4815	D-KBAX
9A-DHL	Cessna 172N	17271491	S5-DHL C-FJHA N3280E
9A-DIP	Beech A36TC Bonanza	EA-104	N36787
9A-DIT	Cessna A150K Aerobat (Texas Taildragger conversion)	A1500046	N8346M
9A-DJZ	Piper PA-28-140 Cherokee Cruiser	28-7425212	N4998C N170SU N41259
9A-DKB	Piper PA-46-350P Malibu Mirage	4636352	N3088X
9A-DKG	Air Tractor AT-400	400-0353	OE-ERP
9A-DKH	Piper PA-28-161 Warrior II	28-8216100	N8268D
9A-DKJ	Air Tractor AT-400	400-0372	YU-DLR OE-ETP N10126
9A-DLA	Lake LA-4-200 Buccaneer	974	C-GFZP N3067P
9A-DLC	Cessna TU206G Turbo Stationair 6- II	U20607001	YU-DLC N9960R
9A-DLH	Piper PA-28RT-201T Turbo Arrow IV	28R-8531008	D-EJFG N43846
9A-DLR	Beech A60 Duke (Stored, for sale)	P-233	N71DG N711MP (N510NE) N710DL N711AA
9A-DMA	Reims/Cessna F172N	F17201515	YU-DMA D-EMFM
9A-DMB	Cessna 172N	17269959	YV-1919P N738GD
9A-DMI	Cessna 150M	15076522	RC-DMI YU-DMI (1)
9A-DMJ	Reims FR172F Rocket	FR17200078	RC-DMJ YU-DMJ D-EBMJ
9A-DML	Cessna 150M	15076479	RC-DML YU-DML(1) N3373V
9A-DMM	Cessna 150M	15079061	RC-DMM YU-DMM N714BY
9A-DMT	Cessna R172K Hawk XP	R1722991	N758CP
9A-DMZ	Piper PA-28-201T Turbo Dakota	28-7921087	N2890G
9A-DNA	Cessna 177B Cardinal (W/o 26.5.03)	17701713	N34220
9A-DNB	Reims/Cessna F172M	F17201272	D-EDPT
9A-DNC	Cvjetkovic CA-65B	001	
9A-DON	Cessna 172S	172S8811	S5-D . .
9A-DOR	Piper PA-34-200T Seneca II	34-7870037	D-GAMM D-IDMM N9777K
9A-DRT	Reims/Cessna F150L	F1500880	OH-CFY
9A-DSB	Piper PA-25-235 Pawnee B	25-3876	Croatia AF YU-BDH N7713Z
9A-DSG	Piper PA-31 Navajo C	31-7912098	G-IKPS D-IKPS (N444BK) D-IKPS N3539G
9A-DVS	Cessna TU206G Turbo Stationair 6- II (Reims-assembled with "c/n" 0010) (Crashed 10.11.02)	U20604656	9A-DEN RC-DEN YU-DEN N732BZ
9A-DVJ	Cessna 172K	17258601	N87452
9A-DVT	Cessna 172M	17263632	(D-E . . .) OH-CMB C-GWMO N1503V
9A-DZB	Piper PA-23-250 Aztec E	27-7305143	OE-FKM D-IBRM N40379
9A-DZD	Reims/Cessna F172M	F17201143	S5-DDB SL-DDB YU-CCJ (D-EIQW)

9A-DZF	Reims/Cessna F172P	F17202156	D-EDIH(2)
9A-DZP	Cessna 210L Centurion	21060163	N127S
			N59212
9A-EMZ	Robin R.1180TD Aiglon	271	D-EOUP
			F-GCUP
9A-HAC	Mil Mi-8MTV-1	95978	RA-27155
	(Sold as LY- .03?)		CCCP-27155
9A-HAD	Mil Mi-8MTV-1	95988	RA-27138
			CCCP-27138
9A-HAG	Robinson R-22 Beta	2541	N595HS
9A-HAS	Robinson R-44 Raven	1105	
9A-HAT	SNCASE SE.313B Alouette II	1841	I-DSLP
			F-GNEA
			FAP9208
			76+96
			PY+211
			PO+139
			F-WJDD
9A-HBC	Agusta-Bell 206A Jet Ranger II	8333	RC-HBC
			YU-HBC
9A-HBD	Rotorway Exec 90	5184	
9A-HBM	Agusta-Bell AB.212	5569	RC-HBM
			YU-HBM
9A-HBZ	Bell 206B Jet Ranger II	2762	RC-HBZ
			YU-HBZ
			N27697
9A-HCG	Bell 206B Jet Ranger II	2754	RC-HCG
			YU-HCG
			N27731
9A-HDB	Bell 206B Jet Ranger II	4152	RC-HDB
			YU-HDB
9A-HIT	Bell 407	53013	N4075F
9A-HMF	Bell 206B Jet Ranger II	4290	N289CA
9A-HRH	Mil Mi-8MTV-1	95876	RA-27042
			CCCP27042
9A-ISC	Dornier Do.28D-2 Skyservant	4178	D-IDRP
	(Unofficial regn, used by Croatian AF)		59+03

The following aircraft are known to be currently in Croatia - either in storage or awaiting registry:-

OO-DEM	Cessna 182P	0042/18264142	N6259F
D-ELGP	Cessna F172F	F172-0111	
D-EDIH(2)	Reims/Cessna F172P	F17202156	
D-EEIR	Beech V35B Bonanza	D-9602	
D-ETOG	Cessna 172N	12773228	SE-KGL
			N6473F
HA-ABT	Antonov An-2	1G170-42	CCCP-07883
N32CC	Pereira Osprey II	1146	
N2838G	Piper PA-28-161 Warrior II	28-7916465	
N3644Q	Beech A23 Musketeer II	M-1046	
YU-BIR	Piper PA-25-235 Pawnee C	25-7305525	N6766L
YU-CAR	Champion 7GCBC Citabria	2 . . -70	
YU-CES(2)	Cessna 170	19045	YU-CDO
YU-CNI	Polikarpov Po-2	unkn	JRV0027
YU-CPE	Aero-3	unkn	JRV40173
YU-CWE	Aero-3	unkn	JRV40105

GLIDERS

9A-GAA	VTC-76 Vuk-T	310	YU-4388
9A-GAB	VTC-76 Vuk-T	383	YU-4437
9A-GAJ	SZD-51-1 Junior	B-1932	YU-4460
9A-GBA	LET L-13 Blanik	027048	(9A-GAA)
			9A-5378
			RC-5378
			YU-5378
9A-GBB	LET L-13 Blanik (Wfu ?)	174102	(9A-GAB)
			9A-5309
			RC-5309
			YU-5309
9A-GBC	LET L-13 Blanik	174918	(9A-GAF)
			9A-5339
			RC-5339
			YU-5339
9A-GBD	LET L-13 Blanik	026720	(9A-GAG)
			9A-5368
			RC-5368
			YU-5368
9A-GBE	LET L-13 Blanik	026641	(9A-GAM)
			9A-5365
			RC-5365
			YU-5365
9A-GBF	LET L-13 Blanik	174809	(9A-GAO)
			9A-5321
			RC-5321
			YU-5321
9A-GBG	LET L-13 Blanik	173059	OK-4824
9A-GBH	LET L-13 Blanik	026149	YU-5349
9A-GBK	LET L-13 Blanik	174530	(9A-GAU)
			9A-5318
			RC-5318
			YU-5318
9A-GBM	LET L-13 Blanik	174529	YU-5317
9A-GBN	SZD-48-3 Jantar Standard 3	B-1901	DOSAAF
9A-GBR	Glaser-Dirks DG-100 Elan	E-45	YU-4325
9A-GBS	VTC-75 Standard Cirrus	213	YU-4304
9A-GCA	VTC-75 Standard Cirrus (Crashed 9.99)	198	(9A-GAE)
			9A-4285
			RC-4285
			YU-4285
9A-GCB	VTC-75 Standard Cirrus	214	(9A-GAH)
			9A-4308
			RC-4308
			YU-4308
9A-GCD	VTC-75 Standard Cirrus	212	(9A-GAT)
			9A-4306
			RC-4306
			YU-4306
9A-GCK	VTC-76 Vuk-T	315	RC-9343
			YU-4393
9A-GCN	VTC-76 Vuk-T	320	YU-4398
9A-GHS	VTC-3 Delfin	012	9A-XHS
			YU-4125
9A-GJA	SZD-41A Jantar Standard	B-801	(9A-GAJ)
			9A-4263
			RC-4263
			YU-4263
9A-GKC	LET L-13 Blanik	174928	OK-1858
9A-GLM	Pilatus B4-PC11AF	288	S5-3008
			SL-3008
			YU-4248
9A-GMF	TST Alpin-8 DM	8011102	
9A-GPA	Pilatus B4-PC11AF	291	(9A-GAC)
			9A-4251
			RC-4251
			YU-4251
9A-GPB	Pilatus B4-PC11AF	293	(9A-GAL)
			9A-4253
			RC-4253
			YU-4253
9A-GPC	Pilatus B4-PC11AF	285	(9A-GAN)
			9A-4245
			RC-4245
			YU-4245
9A-GPD	Pilatus B4-PC11AF	287	(9A-GAP)
			9A-4247
			RC-4247
			YU-4247
9A-GPE	Pilatus B4-PC11AF	295	(9A-GAR)
			9A-4255
			RC-4255
			YU-4255
9A-GPF-54	Pilatus B4-PC11AF	294	(9A-GAV)
			9A-4254
			RC-4254
			YU-4254
9A-GPI	Pilatus B4-PC11AF	292	YU-4252
9A-GP .	Pilatus B4-PC11AF	283	YU-4243
9A-GPL	Pilatus B4-PC11AF	unkn	
9A-GPO	Pilatus B4-PC11AF	unkn	
9A-GRA	SZD-30 Pirat	B-393	(9A-GAD)
			9A-4199
			RC-4199
			YU-4199
9A-GSB	LET L-13 Blanik	174821	YU-5324
9A-GSO	Meteor 57	unkn	RC-4111
			YU-4111
9A-GVG-VG	VTC-76 Vuk-T (W/o 1.6.02)	336	YU-4409

The following gliders are in Croatia awaiting registration or restoration:

9A-G . .	Libis-18	279-03	YU-5057
9A-G . .	Libis-18	unkn	YU-50 . .
9A-G . .	Utva Vrabac	unkn	YU-2 . . .
9A-G . .	VTC-76 Vuk-T	262	YU-4351
9A-G . .	VTC-76 Vuk-T	265	YU-4354
9A-G . .	VTC-76 Vuk-T	unkn	YU-4368
9A-G . .	VTC-76 Vuk-T	unkn	YU-4372
9A-G . .	VTC-76 Vuk-T	292	YU-4379
9A-G . .	VTC-76 Vuk-T	unkn	YU-4403
9A-G . .	VTC-76 Vuk-T	unkn	YU-4404
9A-G . .	VTC-76 Vuk-T	335	YU-4405
9A-G . .	VTC-76 Vuk-T	unkn	YU-4418
BGA1382?CAF	EoN Olympia 2B	EoN/O/131	
BGA3299	Slingsby T-31B Cadet TX.3	698	WT903

BALLOONS

9A-OAA	Thunder AX7-77 HAFB	1372	"YU-Zagreb 01"
			YU-OAA
9A-OAB	Cameron O-56 HAFB	1739	YU-OAB
9A-OAC	Colt 77B HAFB	4296	
9A-OAD	Thunder AX7-77 HAFB	1632	RC-OAD
			YU-OAD
9A-OAE(2)	Tomi AX-6 HAFB	35/1997	
9A-OAF	Tomi AX-7 HAFB	38/1997	HA- . . .
9A-OAG	Kubicek BB-26 HAFB	195	OK-0195

9A-OAH	Kubicek BB-26 HAFB	144	OK-0144
9A-OAI	HAFB, type unknown		
9A-OAR	Thunder AX8-90 HAFB	2634	
9A-OAS	Kubicek BB-33 HAFB	84	
9A-OA .	Colt 77A HAFB	1864	G-BTEH
9A-ONY	Ultramagic H-77 HAFB	77/214	
9A-OOO	Colt 56 Bullet HAFB	3550	
9A-OZG	Ultramagic S-90 HAFB	90/65	

MICROLIGHTS

9A-UAA	Apollo CX-19	unkn	
9A-UAB	Apollo CX-19	09/90	RC-UAB
9A-UAC	Apollo CX-19	51/90	RC-UAC
9A-UAE	Apollo CX-19	43/89	
9A-UAG	Lomac Trick	I P 0495	
9A-UAH	Polaris Lomac	unkn	
9A-UAI	HFL Stratos IIE UL	001	D-M . . .
9A-UAJ	Spider	212	
9A-UAL	Polaris Lomac	unkn	
9A-UAN	Polaris Lomac	unkn	
9A-UAP	Pipistrel-15	unkn	
9A-UAR	Apollo CX Tandem	unkn	
9A-UAS	Apollo CX RGT	47/89	
9A-UAT	Struc TR 600	unkn	
9A-UAU	Rodaro Storch (Damaged 16.8.98)	67	
9A-UAV	Apollo CXM Racer GT	MZ 40/92	
9A-UAZ	Apollo CX-M	091997	
9A-UBA	Apollo CX	0165-94	
9A-UBC	Apollo C4M	74/90	
9A-UBE	Apollo CX	MZE 049/89	
9A-UBF	Cross Country 503	0079-95	
9A-UBG	Apollo CX 19	01014390	
9A-UBH	Euro III Eurotrike	unkn	
9A-UBI	Apollo CX	67/90	
9A-UBJ	Pipistrel 15	15560150291	
9A-UBK	Apollo CX-M	51/89	
9A-UBL	Apollo CX GYEV	02-017	
9A-UBM	Apollo C15	220	
9A-UBO	Lomac Trick 582	271/01	
9A-UBR	Pipistrel-15	01045	
9A-UBS	Kangaroo	unkn	
9A-UBT	Lomac Trick	983716	
9A-UCB	Type unknown	0331/90	
9A-UCC	Type unknown	0328/92	
9A-UCE	Steinbach	025/89	
9A-UCF	Apollo CX18	181989	
9A-UCG	Type unknown	0330/93	
9A-UCH	Pipistrel Basic	0325/90	
9A-UCI	Type unknown	0329/94	
9A-UCJ	Apollo	unkn	
9A-UCL	Apollo CX	MZEY 71/90	
9A-UCN	Wallaby	0212/01	
9A-UCO	Rand-Robinson KR-2	0308/98	
9A-UCV	Rodaro Storch	020	9A-UVC
9A-UDA	Light Aero Avid Flyer STOL	879	
9A-UDB	Apollo CX	MZE 047/89	
9A-UDD	Tucanov	104	RC-UDD
9A-UDI	Pipistrel/Zen Sinus 912	118S9120903	
9A-UDK	Weedhopper JC31 Europe II	B11 2984	
9A-UDM	Avid Amphibian	unkn	
9A-UDN	Cosmos 50	unkn	
9A-UDT	Apollo CXM Racer GT/R	100394	HA-YCAC
9A-UDZ	Rodaro Wallaby	unkn	
9A-UEI	Apollo CX	890605	
9A-UEM	Alpi Avn Pioneer 200	064	
9A-UER	Hazzard-15	090/90-8	
9A-UEZ	Apollo CX	MZ 09/91	
9A-UFG	Moto Delta	3682554	
9A-UFM	Apollo CX-M	960226	
9A-UFO	Rodaro Storch HS	190	
9A-UFS	Genesis	065	
9A-UGV	Apollo CX-M	960220	
9A-UHC	Pipistrel Spider	191	
9A-UHM	Zenair CH-701 STOL	7-3697	
9A-UHS	Apollo C4M	125/90	
9A-UIB	Type unknown	unkn	
9A-UIT	TL Ultralight TL-2000 Sting carbon	02ST27	
9A-UIV	Rodaro Storch	unkn	
9A-UJB	ZSLS Mucha 100 A(M)	459	
9A-UJI	Eurofly Fire Fox	unkn	
9A-UJN	Evektor EV-97R Eurostar	2004-2119	
9A-UJT	Zenair CH-701RTF STOL	7-9235	
9A-UJZ	Apollo C4M 1500	73/90	
9A-UKB	Firefly	unkn	
9A-UKC	Apollo CX-19	02368	
9A-UKZ	Apollo C4M	9017	
9A-ULI	Apollo CX-19	unkn	
9A-UMA	UL Plus 7	1511190494	
9A-UMN	Pipistrel 15	370070990	
9A-UMS	Stiglec	001/2001	
9A-UMT	Zenair CH-601 Zodiac	unkn	
9A-UNG	Light Aero Avid STOL	596	S5-NAB YU-ZAI
9A-UNK	Apollo CX-14	unkn	
9A-UNM	Apollo CX Hazar	unkn	
9A-UPZ	Rand-Robinson KR-1	nil	RC-ZAD YU-ZAD
9A-URI	Rand-Robinson KR-2 (Ditched, 1.6.98)	nil	RC-ZAA YU-Z . .
9A-URK	Pipistrel 15+4	1461140294	
9A-USB	Apollo CX	960248	
9A-USD	Pipistrel Basic	606-90	
9A-USM	Soko 2	002	
9A-UTE	Pipistrel 5	unkn	
9A-UTM	Teenie Two	15/2029	(YU-XAE)
9A-UTS	Apollo Jet Star	040400	
9A-UTZ	Pipistrel 15	560240191	
9A-UUM	Ferrari Hazard 15 Sirio	0351/02	
9A-UVC(2)	Pipistrel Basic	0231/96	
9A-UVG	Apollo CX-14	unkn	
9A-UVI	Pipistrel 15	unkn	
9A-UVJ	Polaris Lomac Trick	4890380	
9A-UVL	Pipistrel 15	unkn	
9A-UVM	Alpi Avn Pioneer 300	96S	
9A-UVS	Pipistrel Plus 7	MZ150061190	
9A-UZD	Light Aero Avid Amphibian	AA-066	9A-XZD
9A-UZG	Rand-Robinson KR-1	002	9A-XZG

EXPERIMENTAL REGISTER

9A-XAC	Light Aero Avid Amphibian Catalina	140AB	
9A-XGB	Soko N-60 Galeb	unkn	JRV23122
9A-XNC	Cvjetkovic CA-64	unkn	
9A-XPC	Utva Aero-3	unkn	YU-CPC JRV 40154
9A-XSS	Europa Aviation Europa XS	unkn	
9A-XZV	Homebuilt	0001	RC-XZV

9H - MALTA

Regn.	Type	C/n	Prev.Id.
9H-AAP	CASA C.212-100 Aviocar	009	EC-CRV
9H-AAR	CASA C.212-200 Aviocar	161	
9H-AAS	CASA C.212-200 Aviocar	162	
9H-ABR	Boeing 737-3Y5	25613	
9H-ABS	Boeing 737-3Y5	25614	
9H-ABT	Boeing 737-3Y5	25615	
9H-ABW	Piper PA-28-160 Cherokee	28-586	HB-OVK N5500W
9H-ACL	Cessna 172M	17260955	N20042
9H-ADH	Boeing 737-33A	27459	
9H-ADI	Boeing 737-33A	27460	N1787B
9H-ADU	Tecnam P.92JEcho	003	HB-KEM
9H-ADW	Cessna U206B Super Skywagon	U206-0779	LN-DBF N3479L
9H-ADX	RP Kestrel	001/PFA-262-12665	
9H-ADY	Airbus A320-214	1769	F-WWDK
9H-AEA	Piper PA-34-200T Seneca II	34-7970193	HB-LKT N2135Y
9H-AEB	Piper PA-34-200T Seneca II	34-7870066	D-GCVP SP-FPP D-GARA(2) D-IARA N2127M
9H-AEC	Tecnam P.92J Echo	008	
9H-AEE	Bombardier Learjet 60	60-170	D-COWS N50154
9H-AEF	Airbus A320-214	2142	F-WWBZ
9H-AEG	Airbus A319-112	2113	D-AVWQ
9H-AEH	Airbus A319-111	2122	D-AVWA
9H-AEI	Airbus A320-214	2189	F-WWDL
9H-AEJ	Airbus A319-111	2186	D-AVWJ
9H-AEK	Airbus A320-214	2291	F-WWBT
9H-AEL	Airbus A319-111	2332	D-AVYC
9H-AER	Airbus A320-214	2178	(SU-LBF) F-WWIP
9H-AES	Cessna 152	15283455	N49412
9H-AET	Dornier 328-110	3117	D-COMM D-CDXL (D-CGAC) D-CDXV
9H- . . .	Piper PA-28-140 Cherokee F	28-7325009	D-EEGV OO-TGB N15167
9H- . . .	PZL-104 Wilga 35A	74205	D-ETVS SP-FWV PLW-205

MICROLIGHTS

9H-UMA	Polaris Cross Microlight	4159717	
9H-UMB	Polaris FIB Amphibian	429713	
9H-UMC	Thruster T600N (To Malta Aviation Museum .05)	9099-T600N-038	
9H-UMD	Thruster T600N-450JAB Sprint	0031-T600N-051	
9H-UME	Ferrari Tucano	0122	I-3060
9H-UMF	Flylab Tucano SRL	0022	
9H-UMG	Euroala Jet Fox	003/92	
9H-UMH	Skystar Kitfox III	unkn	I-3982
9H-UMI	JORA Jora	unkn	
9H-UMJ	ICP MX-740 Savannah	unkn	
9H-UMK	Fly Synthesis Storch CL	unkn	I-
9H-U . .	Solar Wings Panther XL-S	SW-WA-1004	G-MNAJ

AIR-BRITAIN SALES